DEBRETT'S

Peerage
and Baronetage

Photograph by Tim Graham

*HM The Queen and HRH The Duke of Edinburgh at a
Thanksgiving Service at Westminster Abbey to mark their
Golden Wedding Anniversary, 20 November 1997*

DEBRETT'S

Peerage
and Baronetage

Founded in 1769
Renamed Debrett in 1802

COMPRISES INFORMATION CONCERNING
THE ROYAL FAMILY, THE PEERAGE AND BARONETAGE

Edited by
Charles Kidd and David Williamson
Assistant Editor
Lydia Collins

DEBRETT'S PEERAGE LIMITED
LONDON
MACMILLAN

First published 2000 jointly by
DEBRETT'S PEERAGE LIMITED
86–88 Edgware Road
London W2 2YW
and Macmillan Publishers Ltd
25 Eccleston Place London SW1W 9NF
Basingstoke and Oxford
Associated companies throughout the world
www.macmillan.co.uk

and in the United States of America by
ST MARTINS PRESS, INC.
175 Fifth Avenue, New York, NY 10010

ISBN 0 333 54577 X
0 333 78025 6 (Leather)

9 8 7 6 5 4 3 2 1

A CIP catalogue record for this book is available from
the British Library.

Printed and bound in Great Britain by
M.P.G. Books Ltd, Cornwall

CONTENTS

PREFACE

The conferment of an earldom rather than a dukedom upon Prince Edward on the occasion of his marriage is a return to the custom of the middle ages when Earl was the highest title existing in England. Before the time of Edward III the younger sons of our sovereigns received earldoms while still at a tender age. Wessex, of course, was never a county, being the telescoped name for the kingdom of the West Saxons, and has never been an earldom in the modern sense.

Earl Godwin, the powerful councillor of King Canute and later of King Edward the Confessor, was styled Earl of Wessex, the title being derived from the old Anglo-Saxon title of Ealdorman. He was succeeded in that title by his son Harold, who was crowned King after the death of his brother-in-law Edward the Confessor in January 1066, and fell at Hastings later that year.

We have been told that the Earl of Wessex will eventually succeed to his father's dukedom of Edinburgh after the deaths of both Prince Philip and the Queen. This statement has been widely misunderstood and needs some explanation. In the event of Prince Philip's death his hereditary titles of Duke of Edinburgh, Earl of Merioneth and Baron Greenwich will pass automatically to his eldest son the Prince of Wales. When Prince Charles succeeds his mother as King, all his peerage honours will "merge in the crown", and only then will it be possible for any of them to be re-created.

One of the happiest events of 1999 was the celebration on 4th August of Her Majesty Queen Elizabeth the Queen Mother's ninety-ninth birthday. It is our fervent hope that this greatly-loved lady will celebrate her hundredth birthday in 2000. She already holds the record for longevity of any European Queen, her nearest competitor being the Empress Zita of Austria, who died in 1989 aged 96.

Our royal family has not been remarkable in the longevity stakes, only two sovereigns (George III and Victoria) and three Queen Consorts (Eleanor of Aquitaine, Queen Alexandra and Queen Mary) passing the age of eighty. However, HRH Princess Alice, Countess of Athlone, a granddaughter of Queen Victoria, was a little over a month short of her 98th birthday when she died in January 1981.

In the past years devolution has brought the establishment of the Welsh Assembly and the Scottish Parliament, both of which were opened by Her Majesty the Queen. The opening of the Scottish Parliament was a particularly pleasing event. The Queen wore a very well-chosen outfit and hat inspired by the colours of the thistle, and drove in state in an open carriage accompanied by Prince Philip and the Prince of Wales, Duke of Rothesay. The crown of Scotland was carried into Parliament by the Duke of Hamilton and reposed on its cushion beside Her Majesty throughout the ceremony guarded by the members of the Lyon Court in their resplendent tabards.

The proposed reform of the House of Lords is another subject which has caused much misunderstanding. Some people seem to be under the impression that titles will be abolished altogether. This is not so. The hereditary peers will lose their seats in the Lords, but will continue to use and succeed to their titles and courtesy titles as before (this subject is discussed in more detail by Patric Dickinson, Richmond Herald, in his special article). The hereditary peers will gain the right to vote in general elections from which they were previously barred, and there is no reason why an hereditary peer who has shown some particular interest in a matter of national importance, or has distinguished himself in some way, should not be created a life peer to sit in the Lords for life.

Life Peers will continue to be created at regular intervals, and if the present trend continues, many of them will opt to apply for grants of arms and supporters, to which their rank entitles them, and our heraldic artists will be kept busier than ever.

Various statistics we have collated over the past ten years reveal that the hereditary peerage is remarkably consistent in its survival ratings. During the five years that

4

elapsed between the 1990 and 1995 editions the deaths of 129 hereditary peers and peeresses were recorded, thirteen titles becoming dormant or extinct. The following five year interval recorded the deaths of 109 hereditaries, thirteen titles again becoming dormant or extinct.

The big discrepancy between the 1995 and 2000 editions of *Debrett* lies in the number of Life Peerages created by the Labour government: 210 compared to 116 under the Conservatives.

Since the 1995 edition two hereditary peerages have gone into abeyance, the barony of Audley and the barony of Howard de Walden (the latter peerage since we went to press), but these abeyances have been compensated by three other peerages re-emerging, namely the barony of Berners (after an abeyance of only three years), the barony of Arlington (which had been in abeyance for sixty-three years), and the barony of Seaford, which had merged with the older title of Howard de Walden in 1845, and was released by that barony going into abeyance in 1999.

Of the baronetage 148 deaths were recorded between the 1990 and 1995 editions (not including peers who also hold baronetcies), compared to 140 deaths between 1995 and 2000. Sir Denis Thatcher remains the sole baronet to be created since 1964, although we have also noted that the baronetcy of St John-Mildmay has been successfully claimed and added to the Official Roll of the Baronetage, having been dormant since 1955.

Each edition of *Debrett* draws upon the specialist knowledge of a great many individuals, and it is impossible to list everyone by name. However, the editorial team would like to give particular thanks to Patric Dickinson, Richmond Herald, who has given valuable advice (and moral support) on all manner of peerage and heraldic questions, and has also contributed a special article for this edition. Warm thanks are also due to our heraldic artists, Jenny Bush Kurzin and Sister Maximilian Marnau, who together have accomplished over 150 new arms drawings, often at the drop of a helmet.

We are also most grateful to Robert Hardman for his special article for this edition.

Sir Malcolm Innes of Edingight, Lord Lyon King of Arms, Mrs Christopher Roads, Carrick Pursuivant and Lyon Clerk, and Peter Drummond-Murray of Mastrick, Slains Pursuivant to the Earl of Erroll, have all contributed most generously to this edition. John Hope of the Lord Chamberlain's Office, and Lt-Col Robert Cartwright, Secretary of the Central Chancery of the Orders of Knighthood, have kindly updated their respective pages in the preliminary chapters. Mr C. I. P. Denyer of the Crown Office, House of Lords, has kept us apprised of the new life peers, and Mrs F. G. Bright, Assistant Registrar of the Baronetage, has continued to keep us informed on the present state of the Roll of the Baronetage.

Peter and Les Morton have taken great pains with the production and design of the book, and we are very glad to have had their expertise for the fourth consecutive edition.

Marlene Eilers has again been kind enough to make her inimitable contribution to the Royal Family section.

The staff both past and present of Debrett's *People of Today* have all been of great support. Michael Bedford, Michael Rhodes, Alwyn Arkle and Frances Johnston have all helped in various ways, and special thanks must go to Matthew Green, who stepped in at a moment of clerical crisis and saved the day.

CHARLES KIDD DAVID WILLIAMSON AND

LYDIA COLLINS

THE MONARCHY IN THE 21ST CENTURY

The hereditary principle, without which this book would not exist, enters the new millennium in poor condition. The desire to bequeath one's birthright and assets to one's offspring is a natural human emotion. But the idea that one should inherit a public position by dint of birth is now deemed obsolete and is regarded, by some, as repugnant. With the hereditary element expunged from the democratic process, there are, therefore, some profound questions for the future of the institution around which the entire framework of the state is constructed.

Since heredity has become a dirty word in Parliament, the omens would not seem good for a hereditary monarchy which is recovering from a damaging period of turbulence magnified by a media which has seldom been more powerful, more trivial or less forgiving.

Against such a backdrop, the 21st Century would seem a bleak, possibly terminal, period of decline for the British monarchy.

That gloomy prognosis, though, neglects two factors which lead me to believe that the monarchy should be in a healthy state 100 years from now: the inherent attractions of a monarchical system and the enduring popularity of the institution itself. The task that lies ahead for the Palace of tomorrow is to promote the former and consolidate the latter.

Throughout the highs and lows of the last 25 years, the Silver Jubilee, the weddings, the marital splits, the public debates about royal finances and the death of Diana, Princess of Wales, the opinion polls have remained surprisingly steady with between 70 and 80 per cent of people believing that a monarchy is preferable to a republic.

These are the findings of thorough, dispassionate market research organisations, not knee-jerk telephone polls. Their figures may fluctuate on particular questions pertaining to individuals but the consistency of responses to the central question is very clear.

We start, then, from the premise that the monarchy is not "in crisis" or even "under threat" but actually quite secure as it enters the 21st Century. So before examining what may threaten the institution, it is necessary to look at its strengths.

The monarchy's greatest asset, to my mind, is its role as a force for stability and continuity. It represents the nation to itself, a living embodiment of the foundations of the state. Serial flag-flying is not a British trait. Britain has no desperate urge to cling to constitutional tablets of stone as a means of proclaiming a national identity. They are there in the flesh, encapsulated by a human institution standing above the political melee of the moment.

The monarchy also stands for service and duty. Whatever the prevailing trends of the day, the Sovereign and her family represent, in the most prominent way, those whose lives are dedicated to the service of the state.

In this, the hereditary principle is not an anachronism but an essential. It is not only tamper-proof but it provides the institution with principals of all ages who can identify and be identified with the different generations of the general public. Thus, it can redefine and regenerate itself with time. It is not determined by a textbook but by people.

It is also a powerful focal point for the nation in times of danger and celebration. Whether in the dark depths of war, or celebrating 50 years of peace, it is a potent symbol of the national mindset. In short, it is unifying, benign, efficient – a benchmark of a civilised society.

But these are no grounds for complacency There are factors which, in time, could threaten the security of the institution and they should be recognised sooner rather than later. The same opinion polls which show robust support for the institution of the monarchy also show similar support for a vague, unspecified idea that it should "modernise" and be "more in touch".

At present, the issue of monarchy versus republic is not a political one. None of the main political parties has manifested a desire to alter this particular status quo. On the Labour benches there are a large number of MPs, possibly more than half, whose fundamental leanings are towards a republican model of government but who have little appetite for an upheaval which would be both extremely unpopular and fraught with legislative difficulties.

In a free society, there should be nothing to prevent open debate on alternatives to the monarchical system and yet only a handful of politicians are prepared to voice their desire for reform of the monarchy. However, that could change if there is political capital to be made.

Palace officials believe that one of the most serious threats to the monarchy is ignorance of the monarchy's role among young people. If youthful perceptions that the Crown is nothing more than a publicly-funded soap opera go unchallenged and are taken into middle age by future generations, then future politicians may become less reticent about expressing republican sentiments.

Indifference towards the monarchy, increasingly discernible among those in their twenties and below, needs only so much prompting before it can descend to doubt, then displeasure and, ultimately, contempt.

In this, it is not just the educational system but the media which has a powerful role to play. A media which concentrates almost entirely on the personal lives of the component parts rather than the whole is inevitably, in time, going to perpetuate misconceptions about the monarchy to the point where they become accepted as fact. And the more intrusive that media becomes, the more it will have a corrosive effect on the performance of the individuals it is scrutinising so closely.

At the core of all these strengths and weaknesses, of course, are the principal players. Any forecast of the royal fortunes in the 21st century must be based around these known quantities.

The first substantial royal event of the new century is likely to be the 100th birthday of Queen Elizabeth the Queen Mother. It will be a colourful, upbeat event marked by informal pageantry rather than the full pomp of a state occasion. It will be an occasion for reflection on a life devoted to duty.

At the extremes, there will be, on one side, sugary adulation and, on the other, the carping ennui of a few commentators who will demand to know what all the fuss is about. Certainly, some of the recent -- surprisingly sharp -- barbs cast at the Queen Mother following reports about her overdraft showed that old age and a steadfast application to royal duty are no shield against an increasingly vitriolic media.

Overall, though, the vast majority will be pleased to see, if not join in the celebrations for a national figure whose life has touched directly on most of the momentous events of the preceding century.

For the Queen Mother herself, however, one suspects that the event she is really looking forward to is the one that follows two years later. Turning 100 is not so unusual but no one has seen their own daughter clock up 50 years on a throne.

The Queen's golden jubilee in 2002 represents both the greatest challenge and the greatest opportunity for the monarchy in the immediate future. The silver jubilee of 1977 started quietly. The monarchy, during the Seventies, had been in a state of gentle stagnation. There had been none of the euphoria of the early Eighties nor the anguish of the Nineties. Princess Anne had married, Princess Margaret had divorced, the economy declined and the Royal Family had simply gone about its business with little in the way of media interest by today's standards.

At the start of 1977, a few jubilee events were announced to polite interest. But as the summer progressed, the nation gradually entered the party spirit which culminated in a climax of street parties, pageants and marathon walkabouts. Suddenly, the monarchy had achieved a new resonance with the public, particularly the young.

The problem with major set-piece royal milestones, however, is that they can lead to an excess of retrospection which, in turn, can throw up doubts rather than confidence about the future.

This did not happen in 1977. The Prince of Wales was still unmarried, the Queen had only just turned 50 and, to most people, the Royal Family had its best yet to come. In 2002, however, the Queen will be 76 and the atmosphere will be somewhat different. For the first time, many of that majority which has never known another head of state may wake up to the fact that the Queen cannot go on forever.

Marking a faultless half century of the constitutional rule is something worthy of a very substantial celebration. But royal aides must not allow the occasion to become a backward-looking festival of nostalgia without playing up the monarchy's strength through continuity. It is unquestionably the Queen's show, with a major supporting role for Prince Philip, but the Prince of Wales and, to an extent, Prince William will have to play a prominent part.

As golden as the jubilee is the opportunity to show what the monarchy does and represents here and abroad. While the Queen's role as head of the Commonwealth is well-known, it is often forgotten that she is the head of state of 15 independent countries quite apart from Britain – Antigua and Barbuda, Australia, the Bahamas, Barbados, Belize, Canada, Grenada, Jamaica, New Zealand, Papua New Guinea, St Christopher and Nevis, St Lucia, St Vincent and the Grenadines, the Solomon Islands and Tuvalu.

With several of these countries expressing an interest in Australian-style constitutional reviews, there is a danger that the jubilee may look like a last hurrah for the vanishing remnants of imperial influence. That need not be the case. 2002 would certainly be incomplete without a clear recognition of the Queen's responsibilities, past and present, to these nations.

But the jubilee must focus on the fact that these realms are not governed by the British Crown but their own. When the Queen is in New Zealand, she is Queen of New Zealand and answerable to her ministers in Wellington. The British Prime Minister has no more influence over what she does or says than the French president. It is a point well worth underlining.

Considering that the Queen will be turning 76, it may be unreasonable to expect a full tour of these realms, let along the remaining 38 Commonwealth countries. And yet, the Palace must enable these realms to mark her jubilee in their own way, without making them feel like minor adjuncts to a British celebration. There could be individual broadcasts to each country if not visits to each one. Those that the Queen cannot visit should receive a visit from the Prince of Wales or even Prince William.

In Britain, the committee of Palace officials and civil servants which is organising the jubilee has a further goal, however. The jubilee, they believe, must be a two-way process. The Palace acknowledges that it must not simply be an occasion for the monarch to receive the acclamation of her subjects. "The public will not want an event which is just a case of take, take, take. There must be a sense of the monarch 'giving something back' to her subjects," as one senior royal official put it.

This might, perhaps, involve an announcement that Kensington Palace is to be emptied of royal cousins and thrown open to the public or that Buckingham Palace is to be opened to the public on a regular basis rather than simply during August and September, ideas both previously advocated by the media as ways of "modernising the monarchy". Such gestures run the risk of being labelled, by a few, as reluctant concessions but they would generally be broadly welcomed.

Once the jubilee is over, the monarchy will, very slowly, move towards a period of gentle transition. Although the Queen's workload has been impressively steady over the last 20 years, no one expects an octogenarian Queen to follow the same schedules which applied when she was 60. In the last few years, there has been a slight reduction in the number of her public engagements – 585 in 1996, 495 in 1998 – and that is a trend which, quite naturally, will continue.

Thus, the Prince of Wales will need to become a quasi-monarch long before he is a real one. In the next few years, he will need to take on many of the duties presently performed by his mother. Some, such as investitures and state visits, will be automatic. Others, though, will depend on his own personal priorities.

One area which will require extra attention will be the Commonwealth, something which has been very much the preserve of the Queen. The Prince will have to decide sooner rather than later whether he intends to maintain his mother's level of interest in the organisation. If not, it might be better to prepare for a loosening of the link between the Commonwealth and the Crown. The same goes for the 15 countries, other than Britain, of which he will be King.

For here, I believe, lie the seeds of a problem which might otherwise bedevil the start of his reign.

At present, no one is prepared to discuss what might happen to the Commonwealth or the realms after the Queen's death. There is a tendency to regard any such "forward planning" as impertinent. But some politicians in these countries will voice, in private, a sense that a change of reign would be the appropriate moment for a change in those countries' relationship with the Crown.

Even the old Sixties firebrands who led their colonial states to independence on a wave of Marxist rhetoric have come to respect and admire the Queen. There remains a deep personal affection for her throughout her realms and across the wider Commonwealth. While some realms may follow Australia's moves towards constitutional reform, most will see little reason to part company with a head of state who has served them well.

Come the succession, though, that could change in a number of cases. It will be nothing to do with the Prince of Wales but a reflection of the changing nature of national identities and regional affiliations. "When she goes," one elder statesman of a hitherto loyal realm told me, "it will be time to move on. It is nothing to do with Charles, nothing personal. But it will be the logical next step."

While Britain has no say in the affairs of these countries, the Crown is inevitably seen as a British symbol. And whereas Britain was once seen as a reassuring economic and military protector, it is now regarded as part of a European economic bloc which is in direct competition with these countries, even if they do retain the Queen on the banknotes.

If the first months and years of the next reign are to be dominated by stories of countries arguing about their royal heritage, it will do little for confidence in the new King at home and abroad. It will not be his fault but it will be ammunition for those who would capitalise on a change of monarch to attack the monarchy itself.

Far better, surely, to instigate some quiet and reasoned discussions in advance rather than allow a run on the Crown in a period of great sensitivity. As he showed in 1994 in his historic – though, thanks to a would-be assasin, upstaged – speech to the Australian people, the Prince has a pragmatic and constitutionally correct position on such matters: they are entirely a matter for the democracies concerned. He will not become involved in a talent contest and it would be improper if he did.

However, through the network of politicians, governor-generals and private secretaries, there should be some sort of predetermined position on where the Prince stands in these countries once he becomes King.

At home, if one issue tends to cloud popular discussion about the monarchy's future more than any other, it is the Prince of Wales's domestic arrangements. Speculation about his relationship with Camilla Parker Bowles and the distant question of remarriage has created, among many observers, a sense of a constitutional crisis waiting to happen.

For the moment, the position remains the same as it has been for several years. The Prince has "no intention" of remarrying and, from what can be divined of what is an entirely private matter, neither party wishes to give the friendship any official, let alone royal status.

There has been a tendency to regard every tentative step towards a more "normal" relationship – a joint appearance at a private event, a holiday – as a preparatory signal of some impending change in the nature of the friendship. In fact, it seems that the nature of the friendship has changed very little whereas its public profile is gradually increasing.

While some will always be opposed to the Prince's friendship with Mrs Parker Bowles – or, for that matter, any other woman – public opinion has been moving in the opposite direction. A slender but increasing majority now believe that such a relationship is acceptable. Those whose views are held as paramount – the children involved – have given every indication that they are happy with the arrangement. How much longer before yesteryear's tabloid protests at the friendship turn into demands for the Prince to "make an honest woman" of his friend?

Where there is general public agreement is on the question of whether Mrs Parker Bowles should be crowned Queen. A substantial majority have repeatedly expressed opposition to this scenario, although they appear to be pushing at an open door. By all accounts, she would not want to be.

None the less, the Prince's future role as Supreme Governor of the Church of England does legitimise the relationship as a matter of public interest. Of further importance are the wishes of the Queen who, thus far, has shown an indifference to the friendship which is not hard to translate as opposition.

There are numerous outcomes to this and too many unknowns to make any firm predictions. It is highly likely that the status quo will persist until there is a good reason to change it.

Some general trends, however, can be projected. The Government, which has a constitutional obligation to consider the matter, will take its cue from public opinion. It is probable that, in time, the public will grow not only to accept but expect Mrs Parker Bowles at the Prince's side in private while objecting to any future role as Queen. Such acceptance will come in tandem with increasing public demands for a more clearly-stated arrangement.

The indications are that an increasingly "inclusive" Church would broadly tolerate the prospect of a divorced and remarried Supreme Governor, although there would be vocal opposition and some resignations. Moreover, the Church would be reluctant to undertake such a marriage without the approval of the Queen, suggesting that an event might have to wait until the Prince succeeds to the throne.

It is possible that succession may be followed by some sort of reinterpretation of the Sovereign's relationship with the Church. The Prince's oft-quoted desire to be a "defender of faith" rather than "Defender of the Faith" was not a call for disestablishment but could presage a move towards an arrangement such as exists with the Church of Scotland, an "established" but self-governing church outside parliamentary control.

As with the Church of Scotland, the Sovereign would no longer be Supreme Governor of the Church of England but would be obliged to protect it. At a time when Parliament is prepared to contemplate changes to the Act of Settlement – both in terms of male primogeniture and the ban on royal marriages to Catholics – cautious examination of some of the links between Church, Crown and State is conceivable. It must be conducted very carefully, however. Opening up this delicate and complicated historical organ runs the risk of killing the patient.

The task of establishing a title and, with it, some sort of *modus operandi* for a King consort is not as difficult as some have suggested. The changes planned for the Dukedom of Edinburgh, as discussed in the preface, are an indication of the flexibility available to the monarchy when required.

As for his public role, the Prince of Wales's major challenge is in securing a smooth succession and gradually crafting the sort of monarchy which he – and his ministers – feel is appropriate for the 21st Century.

Few monarchs will have come to the throne with more training or a better understanding of their nation and its people. As the creator of the largest charitable network in Britain, the Prince's Trust, the Prince is also particularly attuned to the problems of the young.

As King, he will increasingly be supported by his sons, just as he is now taking on some of the Queen's duties. Prince William and Prince Harry have, so far, had little public exposure but will be the subjects of intense interest when they have finished their education. The hysteria which accompanied their brief, half-day appearance in Vancouver, Canada in 1998 is a mere foretaste of what lies ahead.

Contrary to popular belief, they have suffered less media intrusion than their father. In his teens, the Prince of Wales was chased down streets by the press and had to endure the embarrassment of seeing the contents of a stolen school essay book reprinted all over the world. His sons have had a more sheltered preparation, albeit marred by great personal loss.

One can only hazard a guess as to what sort of royal careers lie ahead for the Princes, let alone what the standing and direction of the monarchy will be during the reign of King William V. For any other profession, it would be ludicrous to start predicting the middle-aged outlook and abilities of someone who is now a teenager.

At present, the main problem for Prince William is a surfeit of expectation. Having endured the most public of personal tragedies with remarkable poise, the Prince, as well as his brother, may play a key role in reuniting the Windsor-sceptic element of the public with the House of Windsor. They are the link with the Princess and Prince William's striking resemblance to his mother will not, in the medium term, be lost on a significant portion of the population.

There will inevitably, be changes to the Royal Family itself, not least in terms of its size. A repeated criticism of the monarchy is that it props up an extravagant network of underperforming cousins at the public's expense. This is to neglect the extensive and unsung work of the Queen's cousins and the fact that they actually cost very little.

Each year, the so-called "minor royals" – by which I mean Princess Margaret, the Duke and Duchess of Gloucester, the Duke and Duchess of Kent and Princess Alexandra – perform around 1,500 engagements on behalf of many of the thousands of good causes with which they are actively involved.

It may not make the papers, let alone permeate the national consciousness, when Princess Alexandra has visited a hospice, a lifeboat station or a charity reception in the regions. For the organisations concerned and all those present, however, it leaves a lifelong memory and a sense of recognition by the state in human form. There is also an important fund-raising dimension. Around 40 per cent of all "minor royal" engagements are charity-related.

These members of the Royal Family, however, will disappear from public life in the early part of the 21st Century and they will not be replaced. The next generations of Kents and Gloucesters are already private citizens who know that there will be no role and no grace-and-favour residence for them. The same will go for many of those further up the line of succession.

The Princess Royal will continue to devote most of her time to public duties – her annual workload of nearly 700 engagements makes here the busiest member of the family in public – but her children will have no royal positions. Indeed, her refusal to accept any titles for them and her fierce insistence on their leading "normal" lives is an indication of her support for a streamlined Royal Family.

The Duke of York is likely to retain a Services-related royal role after his eventual departure from the Royal Navy but his daughters will have no royal duties. At present, they enjoy the style of Royal Highness although this may disappear, given that any children of the Earl and Countess of Wessex will not be Royal Highnesses. The Earl and Countess of Wessex themselves, both pursuing their own careers outside the royal machine, will move further out on the royal fringe.

Thus, we will end up with an active Royal Family consisting of just King Charles and his two sons plus, in a supporting role, his sister and one of his brothers. It will be a far cry from the extended, empire-trotting family model beloved of George V a century before.

In the short-term, it is expected that the Queen will come to some sort of "pension" arrangement with her cousins. If Kensington Palace remains a prominent, high-maintenance residence for an increasingly elderly and inactive collection of royal relations, then the semblance of extravagance will increase.

Alternative accommodation is likely to be found for the cousins while much of Kensington Palace is opened up to the public. Given the problems of conveying the monarchy's role to young people, it would be the perfect site for a museum of royal history. It could, on the other hand, be used to house a large number of the administrative personnel currently based in Buckingham Palace, thus allowing Buckingham Palace itself to be opened up on a more permanent basis.

The Prince of Wales has no deep attachment to the symbolic seat of monarchical power – preferring the symbolic seat of family power, namely Windsor Castle – and a small Royal Family unit will not require a base the size of Buckingham Palace. St James's Palace and Kensington Palace could house the officials and the machinery of monarchy while Buckingham Palace took on the role of museum-cum-state entertainment centre.

All of which will have a positive impact on another aspect of the monarchy which is the subject of serious misunderstanding: cost. It is commonly believed that the Royal Family not only owns assets worth billions but consumes billions without restraint.

The Crown Estate, the Crown Jewels and the occupied royal palaces are routinely lumped together as personal possessions of the Queen creating a portfolio which, if accurate, would indeed make her "the richest woman in the world", as she is often described. These things, though, belong to the state and the Queen could not more sell these than Hyde Park or the Tower of London.

In fact, her personal wealth is valued at somewhere between £50 and £100 million, making her a rich woman but nothing remarkable in the spectrum of modern business leaders whose personal wealth is often considerably more.

The total public cost of running the monarchy, on 1999 figures, is £38 million per year, not including security. Of that, £15.9 million is spent on the grant-in-aid which covers the maintenance of the royal palaces, £12.8 million is spent on official travel, £7.9 million is spent on the Civil List, which covers the Queen's costs as head of state and head of the Commonwealth and £1 million is spent on the public duties of the Queen Mother and Prince Philip.

The other members of the Royal Family receive parliamentary annuities (public funds) worth a total of £1.5 million to carry out their public duties each year but all of these payments are repaid to the Treasury by the Queen.

The Prince of Wales is self-financing thanks to the Duchy of Cornwall. He receives its surplus of around £6 million, before tax, as income and uses it to pay for all his staff and outgoings, public and private. Responsibility for its accounts lie, ultimately, with the Treasury and no Prince of Wales can touch the capital.

In recent years, the cost of the monarchy has dropped substantially from £53 million in 1996 to £38 million, largely through increased efficiency and the decommissioning of the Royal Yacht. Deduct the fixed costs which would still have to be paid if Britain had a president instead of a monarch and I calculate that the annual cost of the monarchy to each Briton is less than the cost of a postage stamp.

That calculation, however, neglects the cost of a presidential election every few years which might cost rather more, quite apart from the tourist benefits and the spectacle which the Royal Family provides.

Thus, in response to the class warrior's cry of "why can't the royals pay their own way?", the answer is: they could but only for a year. Then, we would be left with a bankrupt monarchy. Despite all the economies of recent years, the media and Parliament will continue to demand further savings and transparent accounting.

One reform which should be made as soon as possible is an end to the system of parliamentary annuities for most members of the Royal Family. If the Queen is going to repay the cost anyway, then it would surely be better not to receive the money from Parliament in the first place. The present system simply reinforces the perception that the taxpayer is paying the wages of the Queen's cousins when it is the Queen who is footing the bill.

It would be alarming and counter-productive, though, if the monarchy were to be forced to go beyond reasonable and sensible economies and to embark on petty penny-pinching for the sake of it. A monarchy cannot be subjected to the sort of scrutiny which applies in a widget factory. A Sovereign must have a regal bearing and a certain majesty. That costs money.

The public, while disliking what it sees as profligacy, expects its Royal Family to travel and appear in a certain style and with a certain dignity. Expensive tastes did nothing to undermine the popularity of the late Diana, Princess of Wales. But when the Princess Royal was seen wearing a 27-year-old dress at a 1999 engagement, there was a degree of sneering in the media.

As has been pointed out, a smaller "active" Royal Family is bound to cost less, and therefore, attract less criticism. What may provoke more opposition is its stance on various social issues. For example, an abiding royal passion for field sports may cause constitutional difficulties if a major political party adopts manifesto pledge to ban (rather than hold a free vote on) a particular royal recreation.

Similarly, there will be increasing political and media criticism if advisers and staff at the Palace fail to reflect a "correct" social mix. Despite the fact that all the Prince of Wales's main officials were state-educated, there remains a perception that senior royal positions are determined by background rather than merit. In time, a Prime Minister may feel obliged to advise the Royal Family that the next generation should be sent to the local comprehensive and not to public schools.

12

The sensitivity of these issues, as with so much which will affect the monarchy of tomorrow, are determined by the two principal external factors outlined at the start of this essay: education and the media.

If much of this article leads readers towards a gloomy conclusion that the monarchy's future is determined more by perception than by substance, I am afraid there is a considerable degree of truth in this. The same applies to so much else in a mediacentric age.

In the past, it was assumed that the Royal Family were doing good deeds and performing a service to the nation without those good deeds being chronicled every day. Now, perceptions are based on what the family is seen to be doing. If a week's diligent work is ignored by the press but an hour's shopping at the weekend is splashed across the front pages, then many people will draw the conclusion that the Royal Family's main preoccupation is shopping.

The Palace has gone some way to countering these misconceptions, embracing the Internet revolution and establishing an excellent web site which is one of the most popular in the world.

The huge abiding interest in the Royal Family also ensures that the principal events in the royal calendar continue to receive substantial media coverage. Public affection is strongest for those members of the Royal Family who are the closest to the throne and are the busiest. It is those who are closest to the throne who tend to be the busiest.

It is also those on the fringes who, sometimes unfairly, attract most of the adverse publicity and they are the ones who will fade and then vanish from the royal scene.

Royalists can enter the 21st Century with some concerns but considerable confidence. As long as the monarchy continues to adapt in its own way and at its own pace – prompted by common sense but not by fashion – and as long as Britons retain a sense of history and national identity, I believe that the constitutional system which has served us well for nine centuries will be serving us well right through the tenth.

©ROBERT HARDMAN of *The Daily Telegraph*

THE REFORM OF THE HOUSE OF LORDS AND ITS EFFECT ON PEERAGE SUCCESSIONS

The year 2000 is upon us, and amidst the plethora of millennial predictions and expectations, the end of the 20th century has turned out to be a fateful time for the old aristocracy. It seems only yesterday that Mrs. Thatcher re-introduced the creation of hereditary peerages. Who would have guessed a decade ago that before the century was out a Government would have succeeded in depriving hereditary peers of their parliamentary seats? Who would have suspected that for the first time in the history of *Debrett* most of the hereditary peers listed in its pages would have lost their ancient role in the nation's political life?

Outlined in the Labour Party's 1997 election manifesto, and announced in The Queen's Speech in November 1998, the House of Lords Bill was introduced in the House of Commons on 19 January 1999. In a White Paper published at the same time, the Government quoted with approval the words of Tom Paine, written in *The Rights of Man* in 1791: "The idea of hereditary legislators is as inconsistent as that of hereditary judges, as hereditary juries; and as absurd as an hereditary mathematician, or an hereditary wise man; as absurd as an hereditary Poet Laureate." And it may indeed seem astonishing to future generations that in a democratic state members of its legislature could have continued for so long to be selected on the basis of birth.

In the White Paper, which was entitled *Modernising Parliament: Reforming the House of Lords*, the Government's intentions were spelt out. The purpose of the Bill was to deprive hereditary peers of all the privileges they enjoy as members of Parliament. They would also cease to be automatically excusable from jury service – but they would be able to vote in parliamentary elections and to stand as candidates for the House of Commons.

The White Paper also indicated that the much-reduced House of Lords envisaged in the Bill would be a transitional House only. A Royal Commission would be set up to consider the future role and composition of the Second Chamber with a view to producing its report by 31 December 1999. Its recommendations would then be referred to a Joint Committee of both Houses, and the Government's hope was that a second stage of reform would follow within the life of the 1997 Parliament.

During the course of 1999, as so often with parliamentary bills, amendments were made, and compromises effected. By the time the present article was written (August 1999), the Government's plans had been thrown into mild confusion. At the end of July, the House of Lords voted to delay the Third Reading of the Bill by sending it to the Committee for Privileges for adjudication on two legal points – first, as to whether the Bill mistakenly assumed that the right of hereditary peers to sit derived from their titles rather than from their writs of summons. If this were the case, it was suggested, the Bill as presently worded would allow existing hereditary peers to retain their seats until the next General Election.

The Lords also asked the Committee to consider whether the Bill violated the provisions of the 1707 Treaty of Union guaranteeing the right of a number of Scottish hereditary peers to sit in the House.

Some commentators saw the referring of these points as a mere delaying tactic. If the Bill failed to become law by the end of the parliamentary session in October 1999, hereditary peers could win a year's reprieve. But it seemed equally likely that, even if the Committee did rule against the Bill on legal grounds, the Government could get the Bill amended in time to enact it before the end of the parliamentary session. Whatever the outcome of these antics, it is safe to assume that by some time in 2000 the House of Lords will find itself in an oddly transitional state.

Even before the Bill had been published, a classic British compromise had secured the temporary retention of parliamentary seats for 92 hereditary peers. These included (*ex officio*) the Earl Marshal and the Lord Great Chamberlain. In the summer of 1999 a complicated (some would say bizarre) voting system for the election of the remaining 90 peers was agreed in accordance with recommendations from the Lords' procedure committee, whose report on the subject was described by the political correspondent of *The Times* as "beyond even the comic genius of W.S. Gilbert when writing *Iolanthe*".

What seemed to him particularly nonsensical were the procedures for filling vacancies after any of the chosen hereditary peers die. The plan is that, for the remainder of the 1997 Parliament and until the end of the first session of the following one, their places will be taken by the runners-up in the first elections. Thereafter, it is intended that gaps should be filled by by-elections for which the electorate will be not the whole body of hereditary peers but merely those still sitting in the House.

Nevertheless, these curious arrangements do have one practical consequence for the hereditary peerage as a whole. Unless the Government proceeds to the second stage of Lords reform by the end of the first session of the next Parliament, it will in theory be possible for any hereditary peer (other, of course, than the deprived Irish peers) to be 'elected' to the House of Lords. A residual right therefore exists, and while this is so, the question of peerage succession will continue to be a matter of parliamentary concern. It is therefore reasonable to suppose that the current procedures for proving a succession will remain in place.

But some modifications will have to be made from the outset. Up until now, the succession to any peerage carrying with it the right to sit in Parliament has been officially recognised by the issuing of a writ of summons. But in the new arrangements writs will of course be issued only to those hereditaries lucky enough to be elected or (in the case of the Earl Marshal and the Lord Great Chamberlain) excepted. The question therefore arises how the majority of peerage successions will be dealt with. In the short term, at least, it seems that all the existing processes, other than the issuing of a writ, will remain unchanged.

Thus, in the case of straightforward successions, evidence in support of a claim will continue to be submitted to the Crown Office, which forms part of the Lord Chancellor's Department of the House of Lords. Up until now, if the Lord Chancellor has been satisfied that the claim is made out, he has gone ahead and authorised the issuing of a writ of summons. Now and for the foreseeable future, it seems likely that his satisfaction will be signified by a simple letter to the peer concerned, recognising that the succession has been established. This is a procedure that already exists in the case of peers who succeed to titles while still in their minority.

In doubtful cases, it has long been the Lord Chancellor's practice to refer a claim to the Committee for Privileges, which includes four Law Lords and can only sit if three of them are present; its sittings are therefore in the nature of judicial hearings. (An interesting use of the procedure occurred in 1997, when the Committee had to consider whether the colourful 3rd Baron Moynihan had left any legitimate male offspring; the Committee's negative finding had the effect of allowing the former MP Colin Moynihan to be summoned as the 4th Baron.) This practice is also expected to continue for the time being.

Where a peerage has fallen into abeyance and one of the co-heirs wishes to have the abeyance terminated in his favour, a formal petition, addressed to The Queen, has to be submitted, together with evidence supporting the claim, through the Home Office. The matter is then referred to the Attorney General, the evidence in the case being examined by the Treasury Solicitor. If the claimant comes within certain exceptions, and if the Attorney General is satisfied that no question of law or pedigree is at issue and that no improper arrangement has been made between the co-heirs, he may make a direct recommendation that the royal discretion be exercised. If he has any doubts on these scores, then the claim will be referred to the Committee for Privileges.

In the case of Scottish peerages, or peerages with a strong Scottish connection, the Lord Advocate is asked to report upon it. In practice, he has usually relied on the opinion of Lyon King of Arms, who has his own procedures for determining such claims and who is also consulted by the Crown Office in doubtful cases other than those that involve the termination of an abeyance. But whether it is the Lord Advocate or the Attorney General or the Committee for Privileges that decides on the propriety of a claim, the termination of an abeyance remains an act of grace on the part of the Sovereign. If the royal discretion is thus exercised, it has been usual for a writ of summons to be issued.

This arcane procedure, described in detail in the last edition of *Debrett* (in an article concerning the Barony of Grey of Codnor), continues to be invoked. As recently as May 1999 the Barony of Arlington, created in 1672 and in abeyance since the death of the 9th Duke of Grafton in 1936, was terminated in favour of his niece Mrs. Jennifer Forwood, who will almost certainly enjoy the distinction of being the last person to achieve a seat in parliament by such means. (In passing, it is worth noting that she also has a claim to the Earldom of Arlington, created at the same time as the Barony. Although this Earldom is subject to the same remainder as the Barony, there has always been some doubt as to whether the doctrine of abeyance can be applied to Earldoms. It seems likely that the point will now be tested in the Arlington case, and if so, its resolution will be keenly observed by those interested in abstruse legal questions of this kind.)

With no parliamentary seat and therefore no writ of summons available, the likely conclusion to abeyance cases in future will be the issuing of Letters Patent by the Sovereign allowing the claim. This would mirror the procedure that was in force for women in the days when they could neither sit not vote in the House of Lords. It now seems quite remarkable that in the century when universal suffrage was finally achieved it was not until 1963 that hereditary peeresses in their own right could sit in the House of Lords; up until then they were in much the same position as hereditary peers will be after the present reforms.

On the face of it, the continuance of the old procedures makes sense while a number of hereditary peers are still allowed to sit in the House and while it remains possible for a newly succeeding peer to become eligible to fill a vacancy in their ranks. How long this situation lasts will depend on the nature of the permanent reforms that follow the Wakeham Commission's report and the timing of their implementation.

If, however, the Government manages to achieve its declared aim of an entirely reformed House of Lords, completely devoid of the hereditary element, the position will clearly be different. At that point, it is surely arguable that the time of parliamentary officials – or at any rate the energies of the Lord Chancellor's Department – should not be spent on matters that have no parliamentary aspect or no connection with the other work of that Department. Similarly, would a Committee of the Upper House still be a suitable tribunal for the resolution of complicated abeyance cases?

One answer to this is that, for historical and administrative reasons, it would be desirable to keep the present procedures in place, but to make sure that the public purse does not suffer. At the present time, no fee is payable by a peer proving a straightforward succession if the claim proceeds through the Crown Office and is not referred to the Committee for Privileges. Similarly, in abeyance cases, no charge is made for the initial stages of the claim and the Treasury Solicitor's work. Fees are, however, payable to Counsel for the Attorney General, and claimants do of course have to bear the costs of preparing the evidence and employing solicitors and their own counsel, which can mount up considerably when a claim goes before the Committee for Privileges.

If there is no parliamentary seat at stake, there might be an argument for making claimants to hereditary titles contribute to the official costs of dealing with the claims. However, this might produce a situation where people needed substantial means in order to prove their claim to ancient titles. It would be a shame if the official recognition of hereditary peerages became available only to the very rich.

Moreover, no official charge is presently made for the equivalent procedure involved in settling a baronetcy claim. And it is baronets that provide the most obvious parallel to the exiled peers. After the second stage of Lords reform, their titles will be in much the same category – hereditary honours without parliamentary seats attached. It is therefore worth keeping in mind the arrangements that exist for proving a succession to a baronetcy.

When a newly succeeding baronet wishes to establish his right to the title, he submits evidence in support of the claim to the Home Office (two of the officials there hold the positions of Registrar and Assistant Registrar of the Baronetage). Whether the claim is straightforward or complicated, it is referred, together with the evidence, to Garter King of Arms, who then reports on the matter. Novia Scotia baronetcies, and those with a Scottish territorial designation, are referred to Lyon King of Arms. If the appropriate King of Arms is satisfied with the claim, then the Home Secretary recognises it, and the individual concerned is placed on the Official Roll of the Baronetage. Although the Home Office makes no charge, the newly succeeding baronet must bear the cost of preparing the evidence.

There has been at least one notable invocation of this procedure since the last edition of *Debrett*, and that concerned the succession to the baronetcy of St. John-Mildmay, which had been dormant since the death of the 10th Baronet in 1955. In 1997, his second cousin twice removed, Walter John Hugh St. John-Mildmay, who had been regarded as the likely heir since the death of his father in 1993, was recognised as the *de facto* 11th holder of the title. The Mildmays are a striking example of a family whose male line has dramatically shrunk in a short space of time. When the present baronet's father was born in 1901, he was twenty-fifth in line of succession, a greater distance from the title than Louis Mazzini was from the Dukedom of Chalfont in that inexhaustibly delightful film *Kind Hearts and Coronets*. Happily, no skullduggery has been necessary in the devolution of the Mildmay baronetcy.

The arrangements for establishing a right to a baronetcy were instituted in 1910 by a Royal Warrant of Edward VII, slightly amended by George V in 1922. In difficult cases, provision is made for the Attorney General (or, for Scottish baronetcies, the Lord Advocate) to be consulted. Acting on their advice, the Home Secretary is empowered to refer the matter to the Privy Council. Indeed, until the 1970s there was a designated Baronetage Committee of the Privy Council (analogous to the Committee for Privileges in peerage matters), although it rarely if ever sat.

On the whole, baronetage successions do not involve complicated questions of law, nor are they likely to generate the huge quantity of documents and arguments that have sometimes been necessary in abeyance cases. In recent years, the more interesting cases have tended to arise north of the border; these have been resolved less by the procedures laid down in the 1910 Royal Warrant than by the decisions of Lyon King of Arms acting in his judicial and heraldic capacity.

Thus, it was Lyon's decision in 1965 that the Nova Scotia Baronetcy of Dunbar of Hempriggs, having been conferred with remainder to 'heirs whatsoever', could descend to a woman, with the consequence that Dame Maureen Dunbar of Hempriggs became the first ever baronetess. There seems a good chance, in the case of this family, that history will repeat itself: her son, the present baronet, has two daughters and no sons.

Another Dunbar baronetcy was the subject of Lyon's scrutiny in 1984 when Lt Colonel William Dunbar of Kilconzie unsuccessfully petitioned Lyon to succeed to the baronetcy of Dunbar of Mochrum. Colonel Dunbar had been born in 1893, nearly twenty years before his parents' marriage, but he was legitimated in terms of the Legitimation (Scotland) Act 1968 and was thus brought within the remainder of the baronetcy. In the meantime, on the death of the 11th baronet in 1953, the title had passed to a branch of the family junior to Colonel Dunbar. Lyon ruled that the successions of the 12th and 13th baronets could not be undone and the baronetcy must continue to descend in that junior branch.

This digression into baronetage successions may seem of dubious relevance, but it does demonstrate the existence of official procedures to deal with claims to titles that carry no parliamentary privileges. If, in the course of time, it is considered inappropriate for peerage matters to be dealt with by the Lord Chancellor and the Committee for Privileges, the machinery for baronetage successions might prove a useful model. An Official Roll of the Peerage could be instituted, with claims referred in the first instance to the Kings of Arms and then (if necessary) to the Law Officers. A Privy Council Committee (rather than the Committee for Privileges) might then be a suitable body to deal with contested successions and abeyance cases. This would, after all, allow for the possibility of the Committee's hearings being quasi-judicial. Not only Law Lords but Lord Justices of Appeal are members of the Privy Council, which therefore contains a large pool of judicial personnel.

On the other hand, considerations of history and tradition and sheer practical convenience may argue in favour of continuity, in which case it is conceivable that peerage successions will go on being established through the same channels as before. Certainly this is likely to happen until such time as hereditary peers are deprived of the last vestiges of their legislative function.

Over and above these possible procedural changes, there is the more general question of how the holders of hereditary titles will in future be regarded. According to the explanatory notes issued in January 1999, the House of Lords Bill "does not affect the rights of holders of a hereditary peerage to keep all the other titles, rights, offices, privileges and precedents attaching to the peerage which are unconnected with membership of the House of Lords."

On this basis one might reasonably expect to see the serried ranks of coroneted figures playing their part at the next Coronation. But how will the removal of its parliamentary role affect the general repute and standing of the British aristocracy? Will titled individuals still find it easier to get tables in restaurants? More seriously, will the loss of their constitutional position diminish the respect paid to those whose names happen to include titles?

On the face of it, one might expect some decline in prestige, but the tugging of forelocks is not an entirely rational activity, and one has a shrewd suspicion that things will go on much as before. Why should this be so? One possible reason is that a significant quantity of hereditary peers (albeit a tiny minority of their total number) continue to own large houses and vast estates, and as long as that remains the case, the old aristocracy will go on being associated in the public mind with stately homes and superior economic status.

Even were this not so, endangered species do tend to be viewed with affection. Ironic though it may seem, the petty snobberies that go with title-worship are often more apparent when the titles concerned have a purely social significance, devoid of a political character. This certainly seems to be the experience of the continental aristocracy. Even in countries where titles have been officially abolished, there is no shortage of people willing to acknowledge the time-honoured handlebars attached to the names of old families.

All in all, a curious business. One of Oscar Wilde's characters reckoned that the peerage was 'the best thing in fiction the English ever did'. It seems highly improbable that such a long-running novel is anywhere near its final chapter.

©P.L. Dickinson

ABBREVIATIONS

AA Anti Aircraft, Architectural Association, and Automobile Association
AAA Amateur Athletic Association
AA & QMG Assistant Adjutant and Quartermaster-General
AACCA Associate of Association of Certified Corporate Accountants
AAG Assistant Adjutant-General
AAI Associate of Chartered Auctioneers' and Estate Agents' Institute
AAIM Associate of Australian Institute of Management
AAMC Australian Army Medical Corps
AASA Associate of Australian Society of Accountants
A & SH Argyll and Sutherland Highlanders
A/asia Australasia
ABCA Army Bureau of Current Affairs
ABCM Associate British College of Music
AC Companion of Order of Australia
ACA Associate of Institute of Chartered Accountants
ACAA Associate of Australian Institute of Cost Accountants
Acad Academy
ACCA Associate of the Association of Certified Accountants
ACCM Advisory Council for the Church's Ministry
ACCS Associate of Corporation of Secretaries
A/Cdre Air Commodore
ACGI Associate of City and Guilds of London Institute
ACIB Associate of the Corporation of Insurance Brokers
ACII Associate of Chartered Insurance Institution
ACIS Associate of Chartered Institute of Secretaries and Administrators
ACIT Associate of Chartered Institute of Transport
ACM Air Chief Marshal
ACMA Associate of Institute of Cost and Management Accountants
ACT Australian Capital Territory
ACWA Associate of Institute of Cost and Works Accountants
AD Dame of Order of Australia
ADC Aide-de-Camp
ADEME Assistant Director of Electrical and Mechanical Engineering
Adjt Adjutant
Adm Admiral
ADME Assistant Director of Mechanical Engineering
Admin Administrative, Administration, Administrator
ADMS Assistant Director of Medical Services
ADOS Assistant Director of Ordnance Services
AE Air Efficiency Award
AEGIS Aid for the Elderly in Government Institutions
AER Army Emergency Reserve
AEU Amalgamated Engineering Union
AFAIM Associate Fellow of Australian Institute of Management
AFC Air Force Cross
AFCIA Associate Fellow of Canadian Aeronautical Institute
AFGI Associate Fellow of Grocers' Institute
AFM Air Force Medal
AFRAeS Associate Fellow of Royal Aeronautical Society
A-G Adjutant-General
AGI Associate Member of Grocers' Institute
Agric Agriculture and Agricultural
AGSM Associate of Guildhall School of Music; Australian Graduate School of Management
AIAA Associate Architect Member of Incorporated Association of Architects and Surveyors
AIB Associate of Institute of Bankers
AICE Associate of Institution of Civil Engineers
AICS Associate of Institute of Chartered Shipbrokers
AIF Australian Imperial Forces
AIM Associate of Institute of Metallurgists (*now see* MIM)
AIMM Associate of Institute of Mining and Metallurgy
AInstP Associate of Institute of Physics
AIOB Associate of Institute of Building
AIWSP Associate of Institute of Work Study Practitioners
AK Knight of Order of Australia
AKC Associate of King's College, London
Ala Alabama (USA)
ALAS Associate of Land Agents Society
ALCM Associate of London College of Music
ALI Associate of the Landscape Institute
AM Albert Medal (now GM), Member of Order of Australia; Alpes Maritimes (France); Master of Arts (USA); Member of the Welsh Assembly
AMA Australian Medical Association
AMBIM Associate Member of the British Institute of Management
AMCT Associate of Manchester College of Science and Technology
AMet Associate of Metallurgy (Sheffield University)
AMF Australian Military Forces
AMICE Associate Member of Institution of Civil Engineers
AMIEA Associate Member of Institute of Engineers, Australia
AMIEE Associate Member of Institution of Electrical Engineers (*now see* MIEE)
AMIERE Associate Member of Institution of Electronic and Radio Engineers
AMI Ex Associate Member of Institute of Export
AMI Gas E Associate Member of Institution of Gas Engineers
AMIMechE Associate Member of Institution of Mechanical Engineers (*now see* MIMechE)
AMIMunE Associate Member of Institution of Municipal Engineers
AMInstPet Associate Member of Institute of Petroleum
AMInstW Associate Member of Institute of Welding
AMINucE Associate Member of Institution of Nuclear Engineers
AMIPM Associate Member of Institute of Personnel Management
AMIRSE Associate Member of Institution of Railway Signal Engineers
AMIStructE Associate Member of Institution of Structural Engineers
AMRAeS Associate Member of Royal Aeronautical Society
AMREF , African Medical and Research Foundation
AMRINA Associate Member of Royal Institution of Naval Architects
AMRTS Associate Member Royal Television Society
AMS Assistant Military Secretary
AMSE Associate Member of Society of Engineers
AMTPI Associate of Town Planning Institute
ante before
ANZAAS Australian and New Zealand Association for the Advancement of Science
AO Officer of Order of Australia
AOA Air Officer in Charge of Administration
AOC Air Officer Commanding
AOC-in-C Air Officer Commander in Chief
APEA Affiliate Physical Education Association
APM Assistant Provost Marshal
Apt Apartment
APTC Army Physical Training Corps
AQMG Assistant Quartermaster-General
ARA Associate of Royal Academy
ARAeS Associate of Royal Aeronautical So
ARAIA Associate of Royal Australian Institute of Architects
ARAM Associate of Royal Academy of Music
ARCA Associate Royal College of Art
ARCM Associate of Royal College of Music
ARCO Associate of Royal College of Organists
ARCS Associate of Royal College of Science
ARCST Associate of Royal College of Science and Technology (Glasgow)

ARCVS Associate of Royal College of Veterinary Surgeons
ARIBA Associate of Royal Institute of British Architects
ARIC Associate of Royal Institute of Chemistry
ARICS Professional Associate of Royal Institution of Chartered Surveyors
Ariz Arizona (USA)
Ark Arkansas (USA)
Armd Armoured
ARPS Associate Royal Photographic Society
ARRC Associate Royal Red Cross
ARSA Associate of the Royal Scottish Academy
ARSM Associate of Royal School of Mines
ARTC Associate of Royal Technical College (Glasgow)
ARTS Associate of Royal Television Society
ASDA Associate Speech and Drama Australia
AS For Associate of the Royal Society of Foresters of Great Britain
ASH Anti-Smoking and Health
ASIA Associate of Society of Industrial Artists and Designers
Assist Assistant
Asso Association, Associate
AssocICE Associate of Institution of Civil Engineers
Assocn Association
ATAF Allied Tactical Air Force
ATC Air Training Corps
ATII Associate Member of Institute of Taxation
ATS Auxiliary Territorial Service
Aust Australia
Austn Australian
Av Avenue
AV-M Air Vice-Marshal
aws Graduate of RAF College of Air Warfare

B Baron
b born
BA Bachelor of Arts
BAC British Aircraft Corporation
BAFTA British Academy of Film and Television Arts
BAgr Bachelor of Agriculture
BAI Bachelor of Engineering
BAO Bachelor of Obstetrics
BAOR British Army of the Rhine
Bar Barrister
BArch Bachelor of Architecture
BASC British Association of Shooting and Conservation
Batn Battalion
BBC British Broadcasting Corporation
BBS Bachelor of Business Studies
BC British Columbia
BCE Bachelor of Civil Engineering
BCh Bachelor of Surgery
BChir Bachelor of Surgery
BCL Bachelor of Civil Law
BCom Bachelor of Commerce
BComSc Bachelor of Commercial Science
BD Bachelor of Divinity
Bde Brigade
BDS Bachelor of Dental Surgery
BE Bachelor of Engineering (Australia)
BEA British European Airways
BEc Bachelor of Economics (Australia)
BEcon Bachelor of Economics
BEd Bachelor of Education
BEF British Expeditionary Force
BEM British Empire Medal
BEng Bachelor of Engineering
Berks Berkshire
BFI British Film Institute
BFWG British Federation of Women Graduates
BGS Brigadier General Staff
BL Bachelor of Law
BLitt Bachelor of Letters
BM Bachelor of Medicine
BMA British Medical Association
BME Bachelor of Mining Engineering
Bn Battalion
BNEC British National Export Council
BNFL British Nuclear Fuels (Limited)
BOAC British Overseas Airways Corporation
BPharm Bachelor of Pharmacy
BRCS British Red Cross Society
Brig Brigadier, Brigade

BS Bachelor of Surgery
Bs Baroness
BSc Bachelor of Science
Bt Baronet
Btss Baronetess
Bty Battery
Bucks Buckinghamshire
BVSc Bachelor of Veterinary Science
By Barony

C Conservative, *c*, crowned
CA Member of Institute of Chartered Accountants of Scotland, and County Alderman
CAA Civil Aviation Authority
CAAV Central Association of Agricultural Valuers
Cal California (USA)
Camb Cambridge
Cambs Cambridgeshire
Capt Captain
Cav Cavalry
CB Companion of the Bath
CBE Commander of British Empire
CBI Confederation of British Industry
CBIM Companion of British Institute of Marketing
CC Companion of Order of Canada and County Councillor
CCRA Commander Corps Royal Artillery
C Chem Chartered Chemist
CD Canadian Forces Decoration
CDA College Diploma of Agriculture
Cdr Commander
CE Civil Engineer
CEI Council of Engineering Institutions
CEng Chartered Engineer
CENTO Central Treaty Organisation
CEO Chief Education Officer
CFMS Canadian Forces Medical Services
CFR Commander of Order of Federal Republic of Nigeria
cfs Qualified Central Flying School
CGeol Chartered Geologist
CGIA Insignia Award of City and Guilds of London Institute
CGM Conspicuous Gallantry Medal
CGS Chief of General Staff
CH Companion of Honour
Ch Chief
Chap Chaplain
Chap St J Chaplain of St John of Jerusalem
ChB Bachelor of Surgery
Ch Ch Christ Church
Ches Cheshire
Chm Chairman
ChM Master in Surgery
CI Lady of Imperial Order of the Crown of India, and Channel Islands
CIA Chemical Industries Association
CIE Companion of the Indian Empire
CIEE Companion of Institution of Electrical Engineers
CI Gas E Companion of Institution of Gas Engineers
CIGS Chief of Imperial General Staff
CIMarE Companion of Institute of Marine Engineers
CIMechE Companion of Institution of Mechanical Engineers
C in C Commander in Chief
CInstMC Companion Inst of Measurement and Control
CIOS International Committee for Scientific Management
CLA Country Landowners' Association
CLit Companion of Royal Society of Literature
Cllr Councillor
CM Master in Surgery and Member of Order of Canada
CMF Central Mediterranean Force and Commonwealth Military Forces
CMG Companion of St Michael and St George
CMM Commander of Order of Military Merit
CMS Church Missionary Society
CMZS Corresponding Member Zoological Society
CNAA Council for National Academic Awards
Co County, Company
COI Central Office of Information
Col Colonel
Coldm Gds Coldstream Guards

Coll College
Colls Collateral Branches
Colo Colorado (USA)
Com Commander
Comd Commander (Mil)
Comdg Commanding
Comdt Commandant
Com-in-Ch Commander-in-Chief
Commn Commission
commn'd commissioned
Commr Commissioner
Comp IEE Companion of Institution of Electrical Engineers
CompIERE Companion of Institution of Electronic and Radio Engineers
CON Commander of Order of the Niger (Nigeria)
Confedn Confederation
Conn Connecticut (USA)
Cos Counties, Companies
CP Cape Province (S Africa)
CPA Commonwealth Parliamentary Association; Chartered Patent Agent
CPM Colonial Police Medal for Gallantry and Colonial Police Medal for Meritorious Service
CQSW Certificate of Qualification in Social Work
cr creation
CRA Commander Royal Artillery
CRAC Commander Royal Armoured Corps
CRAeS Companion Royal Aeronautical Society
CRASC Commander Royal Army Service Corps
CRE Commander Royal Engineers
CREME Commander Royal Electrical and Mechanical Engineering
CSC Conspicuous Service Cross
CSI Companion of the Star of India
CSIRO Commonwealth Scientific and Industrial Research Organisation
CSO Chief Signal Officer
CStJ Commander of St John of Jerusalem
Cttee Committee
CV Cross of Valour
CVO Commander of Royal Victorian Order

d died
D Duke
da, dau daughter
DA Deputy Advocate, and Diploma in Anaesthesia
DA (Dundee) Diploma of Associate, Duncan of Jordanstone College of Art, Dundee
DA (Edin) Diploma of Associate, Edinburgh College of Art
DAA & QMG Deputy Assistant Adjutant and Quartermaster General
DAAG Deputy Assistant Adjutant-General
DA & QMG Deputy Adjutant and Quartermaster-General
DABR Diploma of American Board of Radiology
DACG Deputy Assistant Chaplain-General
DADMS Deputy Assistant Director of Medical Services
DADOS Deputy Assistant Director of Ordnance Services
DADST Deputy Assistant Director of Supplies and Transport
DAG Deputy Adjutant-General
DAMS Deputy Assistant Military Secretary
DAPM Deputy Assistant Provost Marshal
DAQMG Deputy Assistant Quartermaster-General
DAv Med Diploma in Aviation Medicine
DBE Dame Commander of Order of British Empire
DC District of Columbia (USA)
DCAe Diploma of College of Aeronautics
DCB Dame Commander of Order of the Bath
DCH Diploma in Child Health
DCL Doctor of Civil Law
DCLI Duke of Cornwall's Light Infantry
DCM Distinguished Conduct Medal
DCMG Dame Commander of Order of St Michael and St George
DCP Diploma in Clinical Pathology
DCSc Doctor of Commercial Science
DCVO Dame Commander of Royal Victorian Order
DD Doctor of Divinity
DDEME Deputy Director of Electrical and Mechanical Engineering
DDME Deputy Director of Mechanical Engineering
DDMS Deputy Director of Medical Services
DDOS Deputy Director of Ordnance Services

DDS Doctor of Dental Surgery
DDSc Doctor of Dental Science
DDST Deputy Director of Supplies and Transport
Del Delaware (USA)
DEME Director of Electrical and Mechanical Engineering
DEng Doctor of Engineering
Dep Deputy
Derbys Derbyshire
DES Department of Education and Science
DesRCA Designer of the Royal College of Art
DFC Distinguished Flying Cross
DFH Diploma of Faraday House Engineering College
DGO Diploma in Gynaecology and Obstetrics
DHL Doctor of Hebrew Literature
DIC Diploma of Imperial College of Science
DIH Diploma in Industrial Health
DipAD Diploma in Art and Design
DipEd Diploma in Education
DipINSEAD Diploma in European Institute of Business Administration (L'Institut European d'administration des affaires)
Diplo Diplomatic
DipTP Diploma of Town Planning
Dir Director
Dist District
Div Division
DL Deputy Lieutenant
DLC Diploma Loughborough College
DLI Durham Light Infantry
DLit Doctor of Letters
DLitt Doctor of Letters
DLO Diploma in Laryngology and Otology
DM Doctor of Medicine
DME Director of Mechanical Engineering
DMilSc Doctor of Military Science
DMJ Diploma in Medical Jurisprudence
DMRD Diploma in Medical Radiological Diagnosis
DMS Director of Medical Services
DMus Doctor of Music
DoE Department of the Environment
DObstRCOG Diploma Royal College of Obstetricians and Gynaecologists
DO Diploma in Opthalmology
DOMS Diploma in Ophthalmic Medicine and Surgery
DOS Director of Ordnance Services
DPA Diploma in Public Administration
DPH Diploma in Public Health
DPhil Doctor of Philosophy
DPM Deputy Provost Marshal, Diploma of Psychological Medicine
DPRM Diploma in Physical and Rehabilitation Medicine
DQMG Deputy Quartermaster-General
DRA Director of Royal Artillery
Drag Dragoon (Guards)
DRCOG Doctor of the Royal College of Obstetricians and Gynaecologists
DrUniv Doctor of University
DSAO Diplomatic Service Administration Office
DSC Distinguished Service Cross
DSc Doctor of Science
DSIR Department of Scientific and Industrial Research
DSM Distinguished Service Medal
DSO Companion of Distinguished Service Order
dsp decessit sine prole (died without issue)
dspl decessit sine prole legitima (died without legitimate issue)
dspm decessit sine prole mascula (died without male issue)
dspms decessit sine prole mascula superstite (died without surviving male issue)
dsps decessit sine prole superstite (died without surviving issue)
dunm died unmarried
dvp decessit vita patris (died in the lifetime of the father)
dvm decessit vita matris (died in the lifetime of the mother)
DST Director of Supplies and Transport
DStJ Dame of St John of Jerusalem
DTD Dekoratie voor Trouwe Dienst (Decoration for Devoted Service)
DTech Doctor of Technology
DTM & H Diploma in Tropical Medicine and Hygiene

DVSM Diploma in Veterinary State Medicine
DVSc Doctor of Veterinary Science

E Earl or East
ECU English Church Union
ED Efficiency Decoration
ed educated
EDC Economic Development Committee
EEC European Economic Community
el eldest
EFTA European Free Trade Association
Eng Engineering
ERD Army Emergency Reserve Decoration
Estab Establishment
ext extinct
Extraor Extraordinary

FAA Fellow of Australian Academy of Science
FAAH Fellow of Australian Academy of the Humanities
FAAV Fellow of Central Association of Agricultural Valuers
FACCA Fellow of Association of Certified and Corporate Accountants
FACD Fellow of American College of Dentistry
FACE Fellow of Australian College of Education
FACMA Fellow of Australian College of Medical Administrators
FACOG Fellow American College of Obstetricians and Gynaecologists
FACP Fellow of American College of Physicians
FACS Fellow of American College of Surgeons
FACST Fellow of Australian College of Speech Therapists
FAHA Fellow of Australian Academy of the Humanities
FAI Fellow of Chartered Auctioneers and Estate Agents Institute
FAIAA Fellow of American Institute of Aeronautics and Astronautics
FAIAS Fellow of Australian Institute of Agricultural Science
FAIB Fellow of Australian Institute of Building
FAIM Fellow of Australian Institute of Management
FANY First Aid Nursing Yeomanry
FANZCA Fellow Australian and New Zealand College of Anaesthetists
FANZCP Fellow Australian and New Zealand College of Psychiatrists
FAO Food and Agricultural Organisation
FAPHA Fellow of American Public Health Association
FAPI Fellow of Australian Planning Institute
FARELF Far East Land Forces
FASA Fellow of Australian Society of Accountants
FBA Fellow of British Academy
FBCS Fellow of British Computer Society
FBHI Fellow of British Horological Institute
FBI Federation of British Industries
FBIM Fellow of British Institute of Management
FBIS Fellow British Interplanetary Society
FBOA Fellow of British Optical Association
FBPsS Fellow of British Psychological Society
FBS Fellow Building Societies Institute
FCA Fellow of Institute of Chartered Accountants
FCAA Fellow of Australasian Institute of Cost Accountants
FCANZ Fellow of Institute of Chartered Accountants in New Zealand
FCASI Fellow of Canadian Aeronautics and Space Institute
FCBA Fellow of Canadian Bankers Association
FCCA Fellow Association of Certified Accountants
FCCP Fellow of American College of Chest Physicians
FCCS Fellow of Corporation of Secretaries
FCGI Fellow of City and Guilds of London Institute
FCIB Fellow of Corporation of Insurance Brokers
FCII Fellow of Chartered Insurance Institute
FCIT Fellow of Chartered Institute of Transport
FCIV Fellow of Commonwealth Institute of Valuers (Australia)
FCMA Fellow of Institute of Cost and Management Accountants
FCO Foreign and Commonwealth Office
FCOG Fellow of College of Gynaecologists
FCP Fellow of College of Preceptors

FCRA Fellow of College of Radiologists of Australia
FCS Fellow of Chemical Society and Fellow College of Surgeons
FDS Fellow in Dental Surgery
FDS, RCPS Fellow in Dental Surgery, Royal College of Physicians and Surgeons (Glasgow)
Fedn Federation
FEng Fellow Royal Academy (formerly Fellowship) of Engineering
FEIS Fellow of Educational Institute of Scotland
FFA, RACS Fellow of Faculty of Anaesthetists, Royal Australasian College of Surgeons
FFA, RCS Fellow of Faculty of Anaesthetists, Royal College of Surgeons
FFA, RCSI Fellow of Faculty of Anaesthetists, Royal College of Surgeons in Ireland
FFAS Fellow, Faculty of Architects and Surveyors, London
FFA (SA) Fellow of Faculty of Anaesthetists, South Africa
FFB Fellow of Faculty of Building
FFCM Fellow of Faculty of Community Medicine
FFD, RCS Fellow of Faculty of Dentistry, Royal College or Surgeons
FFD, RCSIreland Fellow of Faculty of Dentistry, Royal College of Surgeons, Ireland
FFR Fellow of Faculty of Radiologists
FGI Fellow of Grocers' Institute
FGS Fellow of Geological Society
FGSM Fellow of Guildhall School of Music and Drama
FHA Fellow of Institute of Hospital Administrators
FHCIMA Fellow of Hotel Catering and Institutional Management Association
FIA Fellow of Institute of Actuaries
FIAA Fellow of Institute of Administrative Accountants
FIAL Fellow of International Institute of Arts and Letters
FIAM Fellow of International Academy of Management
FIArb Fellow of Institute of Arbitrators
FIAS Fellow of Institute of Aeronautical Sciences (US)
FIB Fellow of Institute of Bankers
FIBiol Fellow of Institute of Biology
FICD Fellow of Institute of Civil Defence
FICE Fellow of Institute of Civil Engineers
FICeram Fellow of Institute of Ceramics
FICM Fellow of Institute of Credit Management
FICS Fellow of Institute of Chartered Shipbrokers
FICSA Fellow of the Institute of Chartered Secretaries and Administrators
FIEA Fellow of Institution of Engineers, Australia
FIEE Fellow of Institute of Electrical Engineers
FIEEE Fellow of Institute of Electrical and Electronics Engineers, USA
FIEI Fellow of Institution of Engineering Inspection
FIERE Fellow of Institution of Electronic and Radio Engineers
FIFST Fellow of Institute of Food Science and Technology
FIHE Fellow of Institute of Health Education
FIHM Fellow of Institute of Housing Managers
FIHVE Fellow of Institution of Heating and Ventilation Engineers
FIIP Fellow of Institute of Incorporated Photographers
FIL Fellow of Institute of Linguists
FIM Fellow of Institution of Metallurgists
FIMA Fellow of Institute of Mathematics and its Applications
FIMC Fellow of Institute of Measurement and Control (New Zealand), *formerly* Automatic Control and Instrumentation Society (New Zealand)
FIMechE Fellow of Institute of Mechanical Engineers
FIMgt Fellow of Institute of Management
FIMI Fellow of Institute of Motor Industry
FIMinE Fellow of Institution of Mining Engineers
FIMM Fellow of Institute of Mining and Metallurgy
FIMTA Fellow of Institute of Municipal Treasurers and Accountants
FIMunE Fellow of Institution of Municipal Engineers
FInstAM Fellow of Institute of Administrative Management
FInstD Fellow of Institute of Directors
FInstF Fellow of Institute of Fuel

FInstHE Fellow of Institute of Highways Engineers
FInstLEx Fellow of Institute of Legal Executives
FInstM Fellow of Institute of Marketing
FInstMet Fellow of Institute of Metals
FInst, Nav Fellow of Institute of Navigation
FInstP Fellow of Institute of Physics and Physical Society
FInstPet Fellow of Institute of Petroleum
FInstPS Fellow of Institute of Purchasing and Supply
FInstMSM Fellow of Institute of Marketing and Sales Management
FInstW Fellow of Institute of Welding
FIO Fellow of Institute of Ophthalmology
FIOB Fellow of Institute of Building
FIPA Fellow of Institute of Public Administration
FIPlantE Fellow of Institution of Plant Engineers
FIPM Fellow of Institute of Personnel Management
FIPR Fellow of Institute of Public Relations
FIProdE Fellow of Institution of Production Engineers
FIQ Fellow of Institute of Quarrying
FIQA Fellow of Institute of Quality Insurance
FIREE (Aust) Fellow of Institution of Radio and Electronics Engineers (Australia)
FIStructE Fellow of Institution of Structural Engineers
FITD Fellow of Institute of Training and Development
FIWE Fellow of Institute of Water Engineers
FIWM Fellow of Institution of Works Managers
FIWSP Fellow of Institution of Work Study Practitioners
Fla Florida (USA)
FLAS Fellow of Chartered Land Agents Society
FLCM Fellow of London Coll of Music
Flints Flintshire (now Clwyd)
Fl Lt Flight Lieutenant
FLS Fellow of Linnean Society
FMA Fellow of Museums Association
FNI Fellow of the Nautical Institute
FNZIE Fellow of New Zealand Institution of Engineers
FNZIM Fellow of New Zealand Institute of Management
FNZSA Fellow of New Zealand Society of Accountants
F/O Flying Officer
FOIC Flag Officer in Charge
FPANZ Fellow Public Accountant of New Zealand
FPEA Fellow Physical Education Association
FPhysS Fellow of Physical Society
FPI Fellow of Plastics Institute
FPS Fellow of Pharmaceutical Society
FRACDS Fellow of Royal Australian College of Dental Surgeons
FRACGP Fellow of Royal Australian College of General Practitioners
FRACI Fellow of Royal Australian Chemical Institute
FRACMA Fellow of Royal Australian College of Medical Administrators
FRACP Fellow of Royal Australasian College of Physicians
FRACR Fellow of Royal Australasian College of Radiologists
FRACS Fellow of Royal Australasian College of Surgeons
FRAeS Fellow of Royal Aeronautical Society
FRAgS Fellow of Royal Agricultural Societies of Great Britain
FRAI Fellow of Royal Anthropological Institute
FRAIA Fellow of Royal Australian Institute of Architects
FRAM Fellow of Royal Academy of Music
FRANZCP Fellow of Royal Australian and New Zealand College of Psychiatrists
FRAPI Fellow of Royal Australian Planning Institute
FRAS Fellow of Royal Astronomical Society
FRASE Fellow of the Royal Agricultural Society of England
FRCGP Fellow of Royal College of General Practitioners
FRCA Fellow Royal College of Anaesthetists
FRCM Fellow of Royal College of Music
FRCO Fellow of Royal College of Organists
FRCOG Fellow of Royal College of Obstetricians and Gynaecologists

FRCOphth Fellow of Royal College of Ophthalmologists (formerly FCOphth)
FRCP Fellow of Royal College of Physicians
FRCPC Fellow of Royal College of Physicians and Surgeons of Canada (formerly FRCSCan)
FRCPsych Fellow Royal College of Psychiatrists
FRCR Fellow of Royal College of Radiologists
FRCSEngland, FRCSEd, and FRCSI Fellow of Royal College of Surgeons of England, Edinburgh and Ireland respectively
FRCPS Fellow of Royal College of Physicians and Surgeons (of Glasgow)
FRCVS Fellow of Royal College of Veterinary Surgeons
FREconS Fellow of Royal Economical Society
FRES Fellow of Royal Entomological Society of London
FRFPS Fellow of Royal Faculty of Physicians and Surgeons
FRGS Fellow of Royal Geographical Society
FRHistS Fellow of Royal Historical Society
FRHS Fellow of Royal Horticultural Society
FRIAS Fellow of Royal Incorporation of Architects in Scotland
FRIBA Fellow of Royal Institute of British Architects
FRIC Fellow of Royal Institute of Chemistry
FRICS Fellow of Royal Institute of Chartered Surveyors
FRIH Fellow of Royal Institute of Horticulture (NZ)
FRIN Fellow of Royal Institute of Navigation
FRINA Fellow of Royal Institute of Naval Architects
FRIPHH Fellow of Royal Institute of Public Health and Hygiene
FRMCM Fellow of Royal Manchester College of Music
FRMetS Fellow of Royal Meteorological Society
FRPS Fellow of Royal Photographic Society
FRS Fellow of Royal Society
FRSA Fellow of Royal Society of Arts
FRSAMD Fellow of Royal Scottish Academy of Music and Drama
FRSC Fellow of Royal Society of Canada
FRSCM Fellow of Royal School of Church Music
FRSE Fellow of Royal Society of Edinburgh
FRSGS Fellow of Royal Scottish Geographical Society
FRSH Fellow of Royal Society for Promotion of Health
FRSL Fellow of Royal Society of Literature
FRSM Fellow of Royal Society of Medicine
FRSNZ Fellow of Royal Society of New Zealand
FRSSA Fellow of Royal Society of South Africa
FRTPI Fellow Royal Town Planning Institute
FRTS Fellow Royal Television Society
FRVCM Fellow of Royal Victorian Coll of Music
FRZS (Scot) Fellow of Royal Zoological Society of Scotland
FSA Fellow of Society of Antiquaries
FSAA Fellow of Society of Incorporated Accountants and Auditors
FSAE Fellow of National Society for Art Education
FSE Fellow of Society of Engineers
FSFor Fellow of Society of Foresters of Great Britain
FSIA Fellow of Society of Industrial Artists and Designers
FSS Fellow of Royal Statistical Society
FSVA Fellow of Incorporated Society of Valuers and Auctioneers
FTCL Fellow of Trinity College of Music, London
FTIA Fellow of Taxation Institute of Australia
FWAAS Fellow of World Academy of Arts and Sciences
FWAG Farming and Wildlife Advisory Group
FZS Fellow of Zoological Society

Ga Georgia (USA)
GATT General Agreement of Tariffs and Trade
GBE Knight or Dame Grand Cross of British Empire
GC George Cross
GC and CS Government Code and Cypher School
GCB Knight or Dame Grand Cross of the Bath
GCFR Grand Commander of Order of Federal Republic of Nigeria
GCIE Knight Grand Commander of Indian Empire
GCMG Knight or Dame Grand Cross of St Michael

and St George
GCON Grand Commander of the Order of Niger (Nigeria)
GCSI Knight Grand Commander of Star of India
GCStJ Bailiff or Dame Grand Cross of St John of Jerusalem
GCVO Knight or Dame Grand Cross of Royal Victorian Order
Gen General
GGSM Graduate in Music, Guildhall School of Music and Drama
GHQ General Headquarters
Glam Glamorgan
GLC Greater London Council
Glos Gloucestershire
GM George Medal
GMMG Grand Master of St Michael and St George
GOC General Officer Commanding
Gov Governor
Govt Government
GP General Practitioner
GPMU Graphical, Paper and Media Union
GPO General Post Office
Gram Sch Grammar School
Gren Gds Grenadier Guards
GRNCM Graduate Royal Northern Coll of Music
GRO General Register Office
GRSM Graduate of Royal School of Music
GSO General Staff Officer
GTCL Graduate Trinity Coll of Music

ha heir apparent
HAA Heavy Anti Aircraft
HAC Honourable Artillery Company
Hants Hampshire
HCF Honorary Chaplain to the Forces
HDD Higher Dental Diploma
HEICS Honourable East India Company's Service
Herefords Herefordshire
Herts Hertfordshire
HG Home Guard
HGDH His or Her Grand Ducal Highness
HGV Heavy Goods Vehicles
HH His or Her Highness, His Holiness
HI&RH His or Her Imperial and Royal Highness
HIH His or Her Imperial Highness
HIllH His or Her Illustrious Highness
HLI Highland Light Infantry
HM His or Her Majesty
HMS His or Her Majesty's Ship
HMSO Her Majesty's Stationery Office
Hon Honourable, Honorary
HonGSM Honorary Guildhall School of Music
hp heir presumptive
HQ Headquarters
HRH His or Her Royal Highness
HSH His or Her Serene Highness
Hunts Huntingdonshire

IBA Independent Broadcasting Authority
IBERLANT Iberia Atlantic Area
ICI Imperial Chemical Industries, Ltd
ICS Indian Civil Service
idc Imperial Defence College
IDS Institute of Development Studies
IG Irish Guards
ILEA Inner London Education Authority
Ill Illinois (USA)
ILO International Labour Organisation
IMS Indian Medical Service
Inc Incorporated
Ind Independent or Indiana (USA)
Inf Infantry
Infra below
INSEAD **(Insead)** Institut Européen d'Administration des Affaires
Inst Institute
Instn Institution
IOM Isle of Man
IOW Isle of Wight
IPU Inter-Parliamentary Union
ISC Indian Staff Corps
ISO Companion of Imperial Service Order
ITN Independent Television News

JAG Judge Advocate-General

JD Doctor of Jurisprudence
JDipMA Joint Diploma in Management Accounting Services
Jnr Junior
JP Justice of the Peace
JSD Doctor of Juristic Science
jssc Joint Services Staff College

ka Killed in action; Killed on active service
Kan Kansas (USA)
KB Knight of the Bath (to 1814)
KBE Knight Commander of British Empire
KC King's Counsel
KCB Knight Commander of the Bath
KCH Knight Commander of the Hanoverian Order
KCIE Knight Commander of Indian Empire
KCMG Knight Commander of St Michael and St George
KCSG Knight Commander of St Gregory
KCSI Knight Commander of the Star of India
KCSS Knight Commander of the Order of St Silvester
KCVO Knight Commander of Royal Victorian Order
KG Knight of the Garter
KGFS King George's Fund for Sailors
KGStJ Knight of Grace of St John of Jerusalem
KIAD Kent Institute of Art and Design
KJStJ Knight of Justice of St John of Jerusalem
Knt Knight
KOSB King's Own Scottish Borderers
KOYLI King's Own Yorkshire Light Infantry
KP Knight of St Patrick
KPFSM King's Police and Fire Service Medal
KPM King's Police Medal
KRRC King's Royal Rifle Corps
KSLI King's Shropshire Light Infantry
KSS Knight of the Order of St Silvester
KStJ Knight of St John of Jerusalem
KT Knight of the Thistle
Ky Kentucky (USA)

L Lord, and Lancers
L Liberal
La Louisiana (USA)
LAA Light Anti Aircraft
Lab Labour
LAB Licentiate of the Associated Board (Board being the combined Roy Coll of Music and Roy Acad of Music)
LAC Leading Aircraftman
Lancs Lancashire
LCC London County Council
LCST Licentiate of College of Speech Therapists
LDS Licentiate of Dental Surgery
Leics Leicestershire
LG Life Guards; Lady of the Garter
LHD Literarum Humaniorum Doctor
LI Light Infantry
Lib Liberal; *Lib Dem* Liberal Democrat
Lieut Lieutenant
Lieut-Col Lieutenant-Colonel
Lincs Lincolnshire
LitHum Literae Humaniores
LittD Doctor of Letters
LKQCP Licentiate of the King and Queen's College of Physicians, Ireland
LLB Bachelor of Laws
LLCM Licentiate London College of Music
LLCM (TD) Licentiate London College of Music (Teachers Diploma)
LLD Doctor of Laws
LLM Master of Laws
LM Licentiate in Midwifery
LMCC Licentiate, Medical Council of Canada
LMRTPI Legal Member Royal Town Planning Institute
LMSSA Licenciate in Medicine and Surgery of the Society of Apothecaries
Lp Lordship
LPEA Licentiate Physical Education Association
LRAM Licentiate of Royal Academy of Music
LRCP Licentiate of Royal College of Physicians
LRCPS Licentiate of Royal College of Physicians and Surgeons
LRCS Licentiate of Royal College of Surgeons
LRFPS Licentiate of Royal Faculty of Physicians and Surgeons, Glasgow

LRIBA Licentiate of Royal Institute of British Architects
LRPS Licentiate of Royal Photographic Society
LSA Licentiate of Society of Apothecaries
LSE London School of Economics
LSIA Licentiate of Society of Industrial Artists and Designers
Lt Lieutenant
Lt-Cdr Lieutenant Commander
LTCL Licentiate of Trin Coll of Music, London
Lt-Col Lieutenant-Colonel
Lt-Gen Lieutenant-General
LU Liberal Unionist
LVCM Licentiate of the Victoria College of Music
LVO Lieutenant of Royal Victorian Order, *formerly* MVO (Fourth Class)
Ly Lady

M Marquess
m married or marriage
MA Master of Arts
MACE Member of Australian College of Education
MACR Member of American College of Radiology
MAgr Master of Agriculture
MAI Master of Engineering
MAIME Member of American Institute of Mining and Metallurgical Engineers
Maj Major
Maj-Gen Major-General
MANZCP Member Australian and New Zealand College of Psychiatrists
MAO Master of Obstetric Art
MAP Ministry of Aircraft Production
MAPsS Member of Australian Psychological Society
MASME Member of American Society of Mechanical Engineers
Mass Massachusetts (USA)
MAusIMM Member of Australian Institute of Mining and Metallurgy
MB Bachelor of Medicine and Medal of Bravery
MBA Master of Business Administration
MBAOT Member of British Association of Occupational Therapists
MBCS Member British Computer Society
MBE Member of Order of British Empire
MBIM Member of British Institute of Management
MBOU Member British Ornithologists' Union
MC Military Cross
MCC Marylebone Cricket Club
MCE Master of Civil Engineering
MCh Master in Surgery
MChOrth Master of Orthopaedic Surgery
MCIP Member Canadian Institute of Planners
MCIPS Member of Chartered Institute of Purchasing and Supply
MCIT Member of Chartered Institute of Transport
MCL Master in Civil Law
MCom Master of Commerce (Scotland)
MCPA Member of College of Pathologists of Australia
MCPS Member of College of Physicians and Surgeons
MCSP Member of Chartered Society of Physiotherapists
Md Maryland (USA)
MD Doctor of Medicine
m diss marriage dissolved
MDS Master of Dental Surgery
Me Maine (USA)
ME Master of Engineering
MEC Member of Executive Council
MEcon Master of Economics
Med Medical
MEd Master of Education
MEIC Member of Engineering Institute of Canada
MELF Middle East Land Forces
MEng Master of Engineering
Met Metropolitan
MFCM Member of Faculty of Community Medicine
mfg manufacturing
MFH Master of Foxhounds
MGI Member of Grocers' Institute
Mgmnt Management
MHA Member of House of Assembly
MHR Member of House of Representatives
MIABTI Member International Association of Bomb Technicians and Investigators
MICAS Member of Institute of Chartered Accountants of Scotland
MICE Member of Institution of Civil Engineers
MICFor Member Institute of Chartered Foresters
Mich Michigan
MIChemE Member of Institution of Chemical Engineers
Middx Middlesex
MIEA Member of Institution of Engineers, Australia
MIEE Member of Institution of Electrical Engineers
MIEI Member of Institution of Engineering Inspection
MIEIndia Member of Institution of Engineers in India
MIERE Member of Institution of Electronic and Radio Engineers
MIES Member of Institution of Engineers and Shipbuilders in Scotland
MIEx Member of Institute of Export
MIExpE Member Institute of Explosive Engineers
MI Gas E Member of Institution of Gas Engineers
MIHT Member of Institute of Highways and Transportation
MIIM Member of Institute of Industrial Management
Mil Military, Militia
MIM Member of Institute of Metallurgists
MIMarE Member of Institute of Marine Engineers
MIMC Member of Institute of Management Consultants
MIMechE Member of Institution of Mechanical Engineers
MIMI Member of Institute of Motor Industry
MIMinE Member of Institution of Mining Engineers
MIMM Member of Institute of Mining and Metallurgy
MIMTA Member of Institute of Municipal Treasurers and Accountants
MIMunE Member of Institution of Municipal Engineers
Min Minister or Ministry
MIN Member of Institute of Navigation
Minn Minnesota (USA)
MInstAM Member of Institute of Administrative Management
MInstF Member of Institution of Fuel
MInstHE Member of Institute of Highway Engineers
MInstM Member of Institute of Marketing
MInstMC Member of Institute of Measurement and Control
MInstMet Member of Institute of Metals
MInstNav Member of the Institute of Navigation
MInstPet Member of Institute of Petroleum
MInstPI Member of Institute of Patentees and Inventors
MInstPS Member of Institute of Purchasing and Supply
MInstW Member of Institute of Welding
MINucE Member of Institution of Nuclear Engineers
MIOB Member of the Institute of Building
MIPA Member of Institute of Public Administration
MIPlantE Member of Institution of Plant Engineers
MIPM Member of Institute of Personnel Management
MIPR Member of Institute of Public Relations
MIProdE Member of Institution of Production Engineers
MIQ Member of Institute of Quarrying
MIRSE Member of Institution of Railway Signal Engineers
MISM Member of Institute of Supervisory Management
Miss Mississippi
MIStructE Member of Institution of Structural Engineers
MITO Member Institution of Training Officers
MIWE Member of Institution of Water Engineers
MIWM Member of Institution of Works Managers
MIWSP Member of Institution of Work Study Practitioners
MLA Member of Legislative Assembly
MLC Member of Legislative Council
MLitt Master of Letters
MLitt Stud Master of Literary Studies (Australia)
MLS Master of Library Science
MM Military Medal
MME Master of Mining Engineering
MMGI Master Member of Grocers' Institute

MMM Member of Order of Military Merit
MMSA Master of Midwifery of Society of Apothecaries
MNI Member of Nautical Institute
MNIMH Member of National Institute of Medical Herbalists
Mo Missouri (USA)
MO Medical Officer
MOD Ministry of Defence
Mon Monmouthshire (now Gwent)
Mont Montana (USA)
MP Member of Parliament
MPEA Member Physical Education Association
MPS Member of Pharmaceutical Society
MRAC Member of Royal Agricultural Society
MRAeS Member of Royal Aeronautical Society
MRCGP Member of Royal College of General Practitioners
MRCOG Member of Royal College of Obstetricians and Gynaecologists
MRCP Member of Royal College of Physicians
MRCPA Member of Royal College of Pathologists of Australia
MRCPEd Member of Royal College of Physicians, Edinburgh
MRCPI Member of Royal College of Physicians, Ireland
MRCPsych Member of Royal College of Psychiatry
MRCS Member of Royal College of Surgeons
MRCVS Member of Royal College of Veterinary Surgeons
MRIA Member of Royal Irish Academy
MRICS Member of Royal Institution of Chartered Surveyors
MRIN Member of Royal Institute of Navigation
MRINA Member of the Royal Institution of Naval Architects
MRSC Member of Royal Society of Chemistry
MRSH Member of Royal Society for Promotion of Health
MRTPI Member Royal Town Planning Institute
MRTS Member Royal Television Society
MS Master of Surgery
MSAutE Member of Society of Automobile Engineers
MSc Master of Science
MSE Member of Society of Engineers
MSFor Member of the Society of Foresters of Great Britain
MSI Member of Securities Institute
MSIAD Member of Society of Industrial Artists and Designers
MSIT Member Society of Instrument Technology
MSM Meritorious Service Medal
MSP Member of the Scottish Parliament
MStJ Member of St John of Jerusalem
MSW Master of Social Work (Canada)
Mt Mount
MusB Bachelor of Music
MusD Doctor of Music
MVO Member of Royal Victorian Order

N Nationalist
N North
NAAFI Navy, Army and Air Forces Institutes
NADFAS National Association of Decorative and Fine Arts Societies
nat natural
NATO North Atlantic Treaty Organisation
NC North Carolina (USA)
NDA National Diploma of Agriculture
NDak North Dakota
NDH National Diploma of Horticulture
Nebr Nebraska (USA)
NEDC National Economic Development Council
NEDO National Economic Development Office
Nev Nevada (USA)
New Mex New Mexico (USA)
NFU National Farmers' Union
NH New Hampshire (USA)
NI Northern Ireland
NJ New Jersey (USA)
NL National Liberal
NOIC Naval Officer in Charge
Northants Northamptonshire
Notts Nottinghamshire
NSPCC National Society for the Prevention of Cruelty to Children

NSW New South Wales
NUJ National Union of Journalists
NUR National Union of Railwaymen
NUT National Union of Teachers
NY New York
NZ New Zealand
NZEF New Zealand Expeditionary Force

OAM Medal of Order of Australia
OBE Officer of Order of British Empire
OC Officer Commanding and Officer of Order of Canada
ODA Overseas Development Administration
OECD Organisation for Economic Co-operation and Development
OEEC Organisation for European Economic Co-operation
OFS Orange Free State
OJ Order of Jamaica
Okla Oklahoma (USA)
OM Member of Order of Merit
OMM Officer of Order of Military Merit
Ont Ontario
Oreg Oregon (USA)
OSB Order of St Benedict
OStJ Officer of St John of Jerusalem
OTC Officers' Training Corps
Oxon Oxfordshire

Pa Pennsylvania (USA)
Parl Parliamentary
PC Privy Counsellor
PEI Prince Edward Island
PGCE Postgraduate Certificate in Education
PhC Pharmaceutical Chemist
PhD Doctor of Philosophy
PHAB Physically Handicapped and Able Bodied
Pl Place
Plen Plenipotentiary
PMRAFNS Princess Mary's Royal Air Force Nursing Service
P/O Pilot Officer
PPS Parliamentary Private Secretary
PQ Province of Quebec
PRA President of the Royal Academy
Preb Prebendary
Pres President
Presb Presbyterian
Prin Principal
PRO Public Records Office
Prof Professor
psc Passed staff college
Pt Point
ptr partner
Pty Proprietary
PWD Public Works Department

QAIMNS Queen Alexandra's Imperial Military Nursing Service
QALAS Qualified Associate of Land Agents' Society
QARANC Queen Alexandra's Royal Army Nursing Corps
QARNNS Queen Alexandra's Royal Naval Nursing Service
QC Queen's Counsel
QFSM Queen's Fire Service Medal
QGM Queen's Gallantry Medal
QHDS Queen's Honorary Dental Surgeon
QHNS Queen's Honorary Nursing Sister
QHP Queen's Honorary Physician
QHS Queen's Honorary Surgeon
QHVS Queen's Honorary Veterinary Surgeon
Qld Queensland
QMG Quartermaster-General
QOY Queen's Own Yeomanry
QPM Queen's Police Medal
QSM Queen's Service Medal, NZ
QSO Queen's Service Order, NZ

R Rector; Royal
RA Royal Artillery, Royal Academician
RAAF Royal Australian Air Force
RAAMC Royal Australian Army Medical Corps
RAAOC Royal Australian Army Ordnance Corps
RAASC Royal Australian Army Service Corps

RAC Royal Armoured Corps and Royal Automobile Club
RAC Royal Agricultural College (Cirencester)
RAChD Royal Army Chaplain's Dept
RACT Royal Australian Corps of Transport
RADA Royal Academy of Dramatic Art
RADC Royal Army Dental Corps
RAEC Royal Army Educational Corps
RAF Royal Air Force
RAFRO Reserve of Air Force Officers
RAFVR Royal Air Force Volunteer Reserve
RAM Member of Royal Academy of Music
RAMC Royal Army Medical Corps
RAN Royal Australian Navy
RANR Royal Australian Naval Reserve
RANVR Royal Australian Naval Volunteer Reserve
RAOC Royal Army Ordnance Corps
RAPC Royal Army Pay Corps
RARO Regular Army Reserve of Officers
RASC Royal Army Service Corps
RASE Royal Agricultural Society of England
RAuxAF Royal Auxiliary Air Force
RAVC Royal Army Veterinary Corps
RC Roman Catholic
RCAF Royal Canadian Air Force
rcds Royal College of Defence Studies
RCN Royal Canadian Navy
RCNC Royal Corps of Naval Architects
RCNVR Royal Canadian Naval Voluntary Reserve
RCS Royal College of Surgeons
RCT Royal Corps of Transport
Rd Road
RD Royal Naval Reserve Officer's Decoration
RDC Rural District Council
RDI Royal Designer for Industry
RE Royal Engineers
Regt Regiment
REME Royal Electrical and Mechanical Engineers
Ret Retired
Rev Reverend
RF Royal Fusiliers
RFA Royal Field Artillery, and Royal Fleet Auxiliary
RFC Royal Flying Corps
RFD Reserve Forces Decoration (Australia)
RFN Registered Fever Nurse
RFus Royal Fusiliers
RGA Royal Garrison Artillery
RGJ Royal Green Jackets
RGN Registered General Nurse
RHA Royal Horse Artillery; Royal Hibernian Academy
RHF Royal Highland Fusiliers
RHG Royal Horse Guards
RH G/D The Blues and Royals (Royal Horse Guards and 1st Dragoons)
RHR Royal Highland Regiment
RI Member of Royal Institute of Painters in Water Colour on Rhode Island (USA)
RIAC Royal Irish Automobile Club
RIAS Royal Incorporation of Architects in Scotland
RIBA Royal Institute of British Architects
RIIA Royal Institute of International Affairs
RIR Royal Irish Rangers
RLC Royal Logistic Corps
Rly Railway
RM Royal Marines; Registered Midwife
RMA Royal Marine Artillery; Royal Military Academy
RMC Royal Military College
RMCS Royal Military College of Science
RMLI Royal Marine Light Infantry
RMP Royal Military Police
RMR Royal Marine Reserve
RMS Royal Mail Steamer
RN Royal Navy
RNAS Royal Naval Air Service
RNC Royal Naval College
RNEC Royal Naval Engineering College
RNLI Royal National Lifeboat Institution
RNR Royal Naval Reserve
RNT Registered Nurse Tutor
RNVR Royal Naval Volunteer Reserve
RNZAC Royal New Zealand Armoured Corps
RNZAF Royal New Zealand Air Force
RNZAMC Royal New Zealand Army Medical Corps
RNZN Royal New Zealand Navy
ROI Royal Institute of Oil Painters
RoSPA Royal Society for the Prevention of Accidents
Roy Royal
Roy Signals Royal Corps of Signals
RP Member of Royal Society of Portrait Painters
RQMS Regimental Quartermaster Sergeant
RRC Lady of the Royal Red Cross
RRF Royal Regiment of Fusiliers
RRW Royal Regiment of Wales
RSA Royal Scottish Academician
RSAC Royal Scottish Automobile Club
RSCN Registered Sick Children's Nurse
RSF Royal Scots Fusiliers
R Signals Royal Signals
RSPCA Royal Society for the Prevention of Cruelty to Animals
RSSPCC Royal Scottish Society for Prevention of Cruelty to Children
RSW Member of Scottish Royal Society of Painters in Water Colours
Rt Right
Rt Hon Right Honourable
RTPI Royal Town Planning Institute
RTR Royal Tank Regiment
RWF Royal Welch Fusiliers
RWS Member of Royal Society of Painters in Water Colours

s succeeded
S South
Salop Shropshire
Sask Saskatchewan
SAS Special Air Service Regiment
SASO Senior Air Staff Officer
SBStJ Serving Brother of Order of St John of Jerusalem
SC Senior Counsel, Star of Courage, or South Carolina (USA)
ScD Doctor of Science
SCF Senior Chaplain to the Forces
Sch School
SCLI Somerset and Cornwall Light Infantry
SCM State Certified Midwife, and Student Christian Movement
SD Scientiae Doctor (Doctor of Science)
SEAC South East Asia Command
SEATO South East Asia Treaty Organisation
Sec Secretary
Ser Service
SG Scots Guards
SGM Sea Gallantry Medal
SHAEF Supreme Headquarters Allied Expeditionary Force
SHAPE Supreme Headquarters Allied Powers in Europe
SJ Society of Jesus
SJD Scientiae Juridicea Doctor (Doctor of Juridical Science)
SLI Somerset Light Infantry
SM Medal of Service, and Master of Science
Snr Senior
So Society
Soc Society
SOE Special Operations Executive
SOGAT Society of Graphical and Allied Trades
Som Somerset
SomLI Somerset Light Infantry
SOS Stars Organisation for Spastics
SPCK Society for Promoting Christian Knowledge
Sqdn Squadron
Sqdn-Ldr Squadron Leader
SR Supplementary Reserve
SRC Science Research Council
SRN State Registered Nurse
SSAFA Soldiers', Sailors' and Airmen's Families' Association
SSC Solicitor, Supreme Court (Scotland)
SSStJ Serving Sister of Order of St John of Jerusalem
St Street, Staffs, Staffordshire
STSO Senior Technical Staff Officer
Sup Superintendent and Supplementary
Supt Superintendent
Surg Surgeon
SWOAC Scottish Woodland Owners Association (Commercial)

TA Territorial Army

TA & VR Assocn Territorial Auxiliary and Volunteer Reserve Association
T & AF Assocn Territorial and Auxiliary Forces Association
T & AVR Territorial & Army Volunteer Reserve
TARO Territorial Army Reserve of Officers
Tas Tasmania
TD Efficiency (Territorial) Decoration
TEng (CEI) Technician Engineer (Council of Engineering Institutions)
Tenn Tennessee (USA)
Tex Texas (USA)
TF Territorial Force
Trin Trinity
TUC Trades Union Congress
Tvl Transvaal

U Unionist
UCLA University of California at Los Angeles (USA)
UDC Urban District Council
UEA University of East Anglia
UK United Kingdom
UKAEA United Kingdom Atomic Energy Authority
UKLF United Kingdom Land Forces
UMIST University of Manchester Institute of Science and Technology
UN United Nations
UNA United Nations Association
UNESCO United Nations Educational, Scientific and Cultural Organisation
UNICEF United Nations Children's Fund
UNIDO United Nations Industrial Development Organisation
Univ University
UNO United Nations Organisation
UNRRA United Nations Relief and Rehabilitation Administration
UPNI Unionist Party of N Ireland
USAF United States Air Force
USPG United Society for the Propagation of the Gospel
USSR Union of Soviet Socialist Republics
UUUC United Ulster Unionist Coalition

V Vicar, Viscount, Volunteer
VA Lady of the Royal Order of Victoria and Albert
VAD Voluntary Aid Detachment
Va Virginia (USA)
Vt Vermont (USA)
VC Victoria Cross
VD Volunteer and Colonial Auxiliary Forces Officers' Decorations
Ven Venerable
Vet Veterinary
Vic Victoria
VMH Victoria Medal of Honour (Royal Horticultural Society)
Vol Volunteer(s)
VP Vice-President
VRD Royal Naval Volunteer Reserve Officer's Decoration
VUP Vanguard Unionist Party
Vy Viscountcy
W West
WAAF Women's Auxiliary Air Force
WAC(I) Womens' Army Corps, India
Wash Washington (State, USA)
WEU Western European Union
WG Welsh Guards
WHO World Health Organisation
Wing Cdr Wing Commander
Wis Wisconsin (USA)
WOI Warrant Officer Class I
WOII Warrant Officer Class 2
Worcs Worcestershire
WOSB War Office Selection Board
WRAC Women's Royal Army Corps
WRAF Women's Royal Air Force
WRNS Women's Royal Naval Service
WRVS Women's Royal Voluntary Service (formerly WVS)
WS Writer to the Signet
WVa West Virginia (USA)
WVS Women's Voluntary Services
Wyo Wyoming (USA)

Yeo Yeomanry
YMCA Young Men's Christian Association
Yorks Yorkshire
Yr Younger
Yst Youngest
YWCA Young Women's Christian Association

CLUBS REFERRED TO IN THE WORK

with addresses

Ladies' Clubs are marked *

All England Lawn Tennis Church Rd, Wimbledon SW19.
Alpine 55 Charlotte Rd, EC2A 3QT.
American 95 Piccadilly, W1.
Army and Navy 36 Pall Mall, SW1Y 5JN.
Arts 40 Dover St, W1X 3RB.
Arts Theatre 50 Frith St, W1V 5TE.
Athenæum 107 Pall Mall, SW1Y 5ER.
Authors' 40 Dover St, W1X 3RB.

Beefsteak 9 Irving St, WC2 7AT.
Boodle's 28 St James's St, SW1A 1HJ.
Brooks's St James's St, SW1A 1LN.
Buck's 18 Clifford St, W1X 1RG.

Caledonian 9 Halkin St, SW1X 7DR.
Caledonian 32 Abercromby Pl, Edinburgh.
Canning 4 St James's Sq. SW1Y 4JU.
Carlton 69 St James's St, SW1A 1PJ.
Cavalry and Guards' 127 Piccadilly, W1V 0PX.
Chelsea Arts 143 Old Church St, SW3 6EB.
City Livery 20 Aldermanbury, EC2V 7HP.
City of London 19 Old Broad St, EC2N 1DS.
City University 50 Cornhill, EC3V 3PD.
Constitutional c/o The Navy & Military Club, 4 St James's Sq, SW1Y 4JU.

East India, Devonshire, Sports and Public Schools 16 St James's Square, SW1Y 4LH.
English Speaking Union 37 Charles St, W1.

Farmers' 3 Whitehall Court, SW1A 2EL.
Flyfishers' 69 Brook St, W1Y 2ER.

Garrick 15 Garrick St, WC2E 9AY.
Green Room 9 Adam St, WC2N 6AA.
Groucho 45 Dean St, W1V 5AP.

Hibernian United Service 8 St Stephen's Green North, Dublin.
Highland 39 High St, Inverness.
Hurlingham Ranelagh Gdns, SW6 3PR.

Jockey High Street, Newmarket.

Kennel 1-5 Clarges St, W1Y 8AB.
Kildare Street and University 17 St Stephen Green, Dublin 2.

*Ladies' Caledonian 29 Queensferry St, Edinburgh 2.
*Ladies' VAD 44 Great Cumberland Place, W1.
Lansdowne 9 Fitzmaurice Place, Berkeley Sq, W1X 6JD.
Leander Henley-on-Thames, and Putney, SW.

Manchester 50 Spring Gardens, Manchester.
Marylebone Cricket Club (MCC) St John's Wood, NW8 8QN.

National Liberal Whitehall Place, SW1A 2HE.
Naval 38 Hill St, W1X 8DP.
Naval and Military 4 St James's Sq, SW1Y 4JU.
New 86 Princes Street, Edinburgh.
New Cavendish 44 Great Cumberland Pl, W1H 8BS.

Oriental Stratford House, Stratford Place, W1N 0ES.

Portland 42 Half Moon St, W1Y 7RD.
Pratt's 14 Park Place, St James's, SW1A 1LP.
Press 76 Shoe Lane, EC4.

Puffin's c/o The Edinburgh Wine Bar, 110 Hanover St, Edinburgh.

Queen's Palliser Road, W Kensington, W14 9EQ.

Reform 104-105 Pall Mall, SW1 5EW.
Roehampton Roehampton Lane, SW15 5LR.
Royal Air Force 128 Piccadilly, W1V 0PY.
Royal Air Force Reserve 38 Hill St, W1.
Royal Air Force Yacht Hamble, Southampton.
Royal and Ancient St Andrews.
Royal Automobile 89-91 Pall Mall, SW1Y 5HS.
Royal Burnham Yacht Burnham-on-Crouch.
Royal Channel Islands Yacht Jersey.
Royal Cinque Ports Yacht Waterloo Cres, Dover.
Royal Commonwealth Society 18 Northumberland Avenue, WC2.
Royal Corinthian Yacht Burnham-on-Crouch, Essex.
Royal Dorset Yacht 6 Charlotte Row, Weymouth.
Royal Irish Automobile 55 South Mall, Dublin.
Royal Lymington Yacht Bath Rd, Lymington, Hants.
Royal Munster Yacht Crosshaven, co Cork.
Royal Naval and Royal Albert Yacht Pembroke Road, Portsmouth.
RNVR Now the Naval Club.
Royal Ocean Racing 20 St James's Place, SW1A 1NN.
Royal Over-Seas League Over-Seas House, Park Place, St James's, SW1A 1LR.
Royal Scottish Automobile 11 Blythswood Sq, Glasgow.
Royal Southern Yacht Hamble, Southampton.
Royal Thames Yacht 60 Knightsbridge, SW1X 7LF.
Royal Torbay Yacht Torquay.
Royal Ulster Yacht Bangor, co Down.
Royal Victoria Yacht 91 Fishbourne Lane, Fishbourne, Isle of Wight.
Royal Western Yacht The Hoe, Plymouth.
Royal Yacht Squadron Cowes, Isle of Wight.

St James's 7 Charlotte St, Manchester.
St John House 50 Eaton Place, SW1.
St Stephen's Constitutional 34 Queen Anne's Gate, SW1H 9AB.
Savage 1 Whitehall Place, SW1A 2HD.
Savile 69 Brook Street, W1Y 2ER.
Ski Club of Great Britain The White House, 57-63 Church Rd, Wimbledon, SW19 5DQ.
Special Forces 8 Herbert Cres, SW1.
Stephen's Green 9 St Stephen's Green North, Dublin.

Thames Rowing Embankment, Putney SW15 1LB.
Travellers' 106 Pall Mall, SW1Y 5EP.
Turf 5 Carlton House Terr, SW1Y 5AQ.

Ulster 48 High St, Belfast.
Ulster Reform 4 Royal Avenue, Belfast BT1 1DA.
*United Nursing Services 40 South Street, W1.
United Oxford and Cambridge University 71 Pall Mall, SW1Y 5HD.
United Service and Royal Aero 116 Pall Mall, SW1.
United Sports 4 Whitehall Court, SW1.
*University Women's 2 Audley Sq, South Audley St, W1Y 6DB.

Victoria 1 North Court, Great Peter St, SW1P 3LL.
Victory Services 63-79 Seymour St, W2 2HF.

West Indian 4 Whitehall Court, SW1.
Western 32 Royal Exch Sq, Glasgow 1.
White's 37 St James's Street, SW1.
Wig and Pen 229-230 Strand, WC2R 1BA.

Yorkshire 17 Museum St, York.

HER MAJESTY'S OFFICERS OF ARMS

ENGLAND
College of Arms, Queen Victoria Street, London EC4V 4BT

EARL MARSHAL
His Grace the Duke of Norfolk, KG, GCVO, CB, CBE, MC

KINGS OF ARMS
Garter Peter Llewellyn Gwynn-Jones, CVO, FSA
Clarenceux (and Registrar) David Hubert Boothby Chesshyre, LVO, FSA
Norroy and Ulster Thomas Woodcock, LVO, FSA

HERALDS
Richmond (and Earl Marshal's Secretary) Patric Laurence Dickinson
York Henry Edgar Paston-Bedingfeld
Chester Timothy Hugh Stewart Duke
Lancaster Robert John Baptist Noel
Windsor William George Hunt, TD

PURSUIVANTS
Rouge Croix David Vines White
Rouge Dragon Clive Edwin Alexander Cheesman

HERALDS EXTRAORDINARY
New Zealand Phillippe Patrick O'Shea
Surrey (and Earl Marshal's Secretary) Sir Walter John George Verco, KCVO
Beaumont Francis Sedley Andrus, LVO
Maltravers John Martin Robinson, DPhil, FSA
Norfolk David Rankin Hunt
Wales Michael Powell Siddons, FSA
Arundel Alan Roger Dickins

PURSUIVANT EXTRAORDINARY
Fitzalan Alastair Andrew Bernard Reibey Bruce of Crionaich

SCOTLAND
Court of the Lord Lyon, HM New Register House, Edinburgh

THE RT HON THE LORD LYON KING OF ARMS
Sir Malcolm Rognvald Innes of Edingight, KCVO, WS, FSA Scot

HERALDS
Albany John Alexander Spens, RD, WS
Rothesay Sir Crispin Agnew of Lochnaw, Bt
Ross Charles John Burnett, FSA Scot

PURSUIVANTS
Kintyre John Charles Grossmith George, FSA Scot
Unicorn Alastair Lorne Campbell of Airds, yr, FSA Scot
Carrick Mrs Christopher Roads, MVO, FSA Scot

PURSUIVANTS OF EARLS
(Not forming part of Her Majesty's Household and not under the control of the Lord Lyon)
Pursuivants to the Earl of Erroll, the Countess of Mar and the Earl of Crawford

Slains Peter Drummond-Murray of Mastrick (Pursuivant to the Earl of Erroll)
Garioch David Gordon Allen d'Aldecamb Lumsden of Cushnie
(Pursuivant to the Countess of Mar)
Endure Hon Alexander Walter Lindsay (Pursuivant to the Earl of Crawford)

TABLE OF GENERAL PRECEDENCE

PEERS AND PEERESSES (in each degree) rank among themselves in the following order: those created (1) of England, (2) of Scotland, (3) of Great Britain, (4) of Ireland, and (5) of the United Kingdom and of Ireland created since the Union, according to the dates of their respective patents. BARONETS rank among themselves according to the dates of their respective patents *only*. PRECEDENCE OF LADIES is always derived from the father, or husband, except in the case of a Peeress in her own right.

Official precedence, such as that of the Great Officers of State, confers no corresponding precedence on their wives or daughters. The wives and issue of Archbishops and Bishops at present have no special precedence as such.

A Dowager Peeress, or widow of a Baronet, takes precedence of the wife of the incumbent of the title only while remaining a widow.

The children of a living Peer, or Baronet, have precedence above the children of the previous possessor, or possessors, of the title. If the daughter of a Peer marries a Peer she takes her husband's rank, but if she marries the eldest or younger son of a Peer she ranks either according to her own inherent precedence (*i.e.*, as the daughter of her father), or according to that of her husband (*i.e.*, as the wife of the eldest or younger son of a Duke, Marquess, Earl, etc), whichever happens to be the higher, no matter what the courtesy title may be.

Foreign titles of nobility borne by British subjects afford their holders no precedence in the United Kingdom.

PRECEDENCE IN ENGLAND

GENTLEMEN

The Duke of Edinburgh*
The Heir Apparent
The Sovereign's Younger Sons
The Sovereign's Grandsons
The Sovereign's Cousins
Archbishop of Canterbury
Lord High Chancellor
Archbishop of York
Prime Minister
Lord High Treasurer (when existing)
Lord President of the Council
Speaker of the House of Commons
Lord Privy Seal
Ambassadors and High Commissioners
Lord Great Chamberlain† ⎫
Lord High Constable (when existing) ⎪ Above all
Earl Marshal ⎬ Peers of
Lord Chamberlain of the Household ⎪ their own
Lord Steward of the Household ⎭ degree
Master of the Horse
Dukes of England
Dukes of Scotland
Dukes of Great Britain
Dukes of Ireland
Dukes of UK and Ireland since the Union
Eldest Sons of Dukes of the Blood Royal
Marquesses of England
Marquesses of Scotland
Marquesses of Great Britain
Marquesses of Ireland
Marquesses of UK and Ireland since the Union
Eldest Sons of Dukes
Earls of England
Earls of Scotland
Earls of Great Britain
Earls of Ireland
Earls of UK and Ireland since the Union
Younger Sons of Dukes of the Blood Royal
Marquesses' Eldest Sons
Dukes' Younger Sons
Viscounts of England

*By Royal Warrant dated 18 September, 1952, it was declared that HRH the Duke of Edinburgh henceforth to have Precedence next to HM the Queen, thus having place before the Heir Apparent.
†When in actual performance of official duty.

Viscounts of Scotland
Viscounts of Great Britain
Viscounts of Ireland
Viscounts of UK and Ireland since the Union
Earls' Eldest Sons
Marquesses' Younger Sons
Bishop of London
Bishop of Durham
Bishop of Winchester
Other English Diocesan Bishops according to seniority of consecration
Suffragan Bishops according to seniority of consecration
Secretaries of State, if of Baronial rank
Barons of England
Lords of Parliament, Scotland
Barons of Great Britain
Barons of Ireland
Barons of UK and Ireland since the Union, including Life Barons
Lords Commissioners of the Great Seal (when existing)
Treasurer of the Household
Comptroller of the Household
Vice-Chamberlain of the Household
Secretaries of State, being under Baronial rank
Viscounts' Eldest Sons
Earls' Younger Sons
Barons' Eldest Sons
Knights of the Garter
Privy Counsellors
Chancellor of the Exchequer
Chancellor of the Duchy of Lancaster
Lord Chief Justice of England
Master of the Rolls
President of the Family Division
Vice-Chancellor
Lord Justices of Appeal according to seniority of appointment
Judges of High Court of Justice, according to seniority of appointment
Viscounts' Younger Sons
Barons' Younger Sons
Sons of Life Peers and Lords of Appeal in Ordinary
Baronets, according to date of Patent
Knights of the Thistle*
Knights Grand Cross of the Bath
Knights Grand Commanders of the Star of India
Knights Grand Cross of St Michael and St George
Knights Grand Commanders of the Indian Empire
Knights Grand Cross of the Royal Victorian Order
Knights Grand Cross of the British Empire
Knights Commanders of the Bath
Knights Commanders of the Star of India
Knights Commanders of St Michael and St George
Knights Commanders of the Indian Empire
Knights Commanders of the Royal Victorian Order
Knights Commanders of the British Empire
Knights Bachelor
Circuit Judges in England and Wales, as follows:
(a) Vice-Chancellor of Co Palatine of Lancaster. (b) Circuit Judges who immediately before Jan 1st 1972, held office as Official Referees to Supreme Court (c) Recorder of London. (d) Recorders of Liverpool and Manchester, according to priority of appointment. (e) Common Serjeant. (f) Circuit Judges who immediately before Jan 1st, 1972 held office as Additional Judge of Central Criminal Court, Assistant Judge of the Mayor's and City of London Court, County Court judge, whole time Chm or whole time Dep Chm of courts of quarter sessions for Gtr London, Cheshire, Durham, Kent, and Lancs, according to priority of appointment. (g) Other Circuit Judges according to priority or order of their respective appointments
Companions of the Bath
Companions of the Star of India
Companions of St Michael and St George
Companions of the Indian Empire
Commanders of the Royal Victorian Order

*Knights of the Thistle have no relative precedence accorded to them by statute, but are customarily placed here. In Scotland they follow Knights of the Garter.

Commanders of the British Empire
Companions of the Distinguished Service Order
Lieutenants of the Royal Victorian Order
    Officers of the British Empire
Companions of the Imperial Service Order
Eldest Sons of the Younger Sons of Peers
Eldest Sons of Baronets
Eldest Sons of Knights of the Garter
Eldest Sons of Knights of the Thistle*
Eldest Sons of Knights of the Bath§
Eldest Sons of Knights of the Star of India§
Eldest Sons of Knights of St Michael and St George§
Eldest Sons of Knights of the Indian Empire§
Eldest Sons of Knights of the Royal Victorian Order§
Eldest Sons of Knights of the British Empire§
Eldest Sons of Knights Bachelor
Members of the Royal Victorian Order
Members of the British Empire
Younger Sons of Baronets
Younger Sons of Knights
Esquires
Gentlemen

*⁎ Lord-Lieutenants and High Sheriffs of Counties
have the first places in their own Counties during
office, the Lord-Lieutenant taking precedence of the
High Sheriff, but neither is assigned any place on
the Official Scale of General Precedence. The Lord-
Lieutenant has precedence within his jurisdiction
over a Mayor, even within his own Borough, when
present officially as the representative of the Crown.
On all Municipal occasions, however, whether of
business or entertainment, the Mayor should
preside, or act as host._

*⁎ Clergy (other than those mentioned above), Naval,
Military and Air Force Officers, Members of the
Legal and Medical Professions, Graduates of
Universities, and Citizens and Burgesses have no
precedence assigned to them, either by statute or by
any fixed principle._

LADIES

THE QUEEN
The Queen Mother
The Wife of the Heir Apparent
Wives of younger Sons of the Sovereign
The Sovereign's Daughter
The Sovereign's Sister
Wives of the Sovereign's Uncles
Wives of Dukes of the Blood Royal
Wives of Princes of the Blood Royal
The Sovereign's Cousin
Duchesses of England
Duchesses of Scotland
Duchesses of Great Britain
Duchesses of Ireland
Duchesses of UK and Ireland since the Union
Wives of the Eldest Sons of Dukes of the Blood Royal
Marchionesses of England
Marchionesses of Scotland
Marchionesses of Great Britain
Marchionesses of Ireland
Marchionesses of UK and Ireland since the Union
Wives of the Eldest Sons of Dukes
Daughters of Dukes
Countesses of England
Countesses of Scotland
Countesses of Great Britain
Countesses of Ireland
Countesses of UK and Ireland since the Union
Wives of the Younger Sons of Dukes of the Blood
    Royal
Wives of the Eldest Sons of Marquesses
Daughters of Marquesses
Wives of the Younger Sons of Dukes
Viscountesses of England
Viscountesses of Scotland
Viscountesses of Great Britain
Viscountesses of Ireland
Viscountesses of UK and Ireland since the Union
Wives of the Eldest Sons of Earls
Daughters of Earls
Wives of the Younger Sons of Marquesses
Baronesses of England

Ladies of Parliament, Scotland
Baronesses of Great Britain
Baronesses of Ireland
Baronesses of UK and Ireland since the Union,
    including Life Baronesses and Wives of Life Barons
Wives of the Eldest Sons of Viscounts
Daughters of Viscounts
Wives of the Younger Sons of Earls
Wives of the Eldest Sons of Barons
Daughters of Barons
Wives of Knights of the Garter
Privy Counsellors (Women)
Wives of the Younger Sons of Viscounts
Wives of the Younger Sons of Barons
Wives of Sons of Life Peers
Wives of Baronets, according to their husband's
    Patents
Wives of Knights of the Thistle
Dames Grand Cross of the Order of the Bath
Dames Grand Cross of the Order of St Michael and
    St George
Dames Grand Cross of the Royal Victorian Order
Dames Grand Cross of the British Empire
Wives of Knights Grand Cross of the Bath
Wives of Knights Grand Commanders of the Star of
    India
Wives of Knights Grand Cross of St Michael and St
    George
Wives of Knights Grand Commanders of the Indian
    Empire
Wives of Knights Grand Cross of the Royal Victorian
    Order
Wives of Knights Grand Cross of the British Empire
Dames Commanders of the Order of the Bath
Dames Commanders of the Order of St Michael and
    St George
Dames Commanders of the Royal Victorian Order
Dames Commanders of the British Empire
Wives of Knights Commanders of the Bath
Wives of Knights Commanders of the Star of India
Wives of Knights Commanders of St Michael and St
    George
Wives of Knights Commanders of the Indian Empire
Wives of Knights Commanders of the Royal Victorian
    Order
Wives of Knights Commanders of the British Empire
Wives of Knights Bachelor
Companions of the Order of the Bath
Companions of the Order of St Michael and St
    George
Commanders of the Royal Victorian Order
Commanders of the British Empire
Wives of Companions of the Bath
Wives of Companions of the Star of India
Wives of Companions of the St Michael and St
    George
Wives of Companions of the Indian Empire
Wives of Commanders of the Royal Victorian Order
Wives of Commanders of the British Empire
Wives of Companions of the Distinguished Service
    Order
Members of the Royal Victorian Order (4th class)
Officers of the British Empire
Wives of Members of the Royal Victorian Order (4th
    class)
Wives of Officers of the British Empire
Companions of the Imperial Service Order
Wives of Companions of the Imperial Service Order
Wives of the eldest sons of the Younger Sons of Peers
Daughters of the Younger Sons of Peers
Wives of the Eldest Sons of Baronets
Daughters of Baronets
Wives of the Eldest Sons of Knights of the Garter
Wives of the Eldest Sons of Knights
Daughters of Knights
Members of the Royal Victorian Order (5th class)
Members of the British Empire
Wives of Members of the Royal Victorian Order (5th
    class)
Wives of Members of the British Empire
Wives of the Younger Sons of Baronets
Wives of the Younger Sons of Knights
Wives of Esquires
Wives of Gentlemen

*⁎ Wives of the Clergy, Naval, Military and Air Force
Officers, Members of the Legal and Medical
Professions, Graduates of Universities, and Citizens
and Burgesses have no precedence assigned to them,
either by statute or by any fixed principle_

§Eldest sons of Knights Grand Cross take precedence
    of eldest sons of Knights of the 2nd degree

PRECEDENCE IN SCOTLAND

GENTLEMEN

The Duke of Edinburgh*
Lord High Commissioner to the General Assembly of the Church of Scotland (during sitting of General Assembly)
Duke of Rothesay (The Prince of Wales)
Sovereign's Younger Sons
Grandsons of the Sovereign
Sovereign's Cousins
Lord-Lieutenants of Counties†
Lord Provosts of Cities being *ex-officio* Lord-Lieutenants of those Cities†
Sheriffs Principal††
Lord Chancellor of Great Britain
Moderator of General Assembly of Church of Scotland (during office)
Keeper of the Great Seal of Scotland (the First Minister)
Presiding Officer
Secretary of State for Scotland
Hereditary High Constable of Scotland
Hereditary Master of the Household in Scotland
Dukes (as in English Table)
Eldest sons of Dukes of the Blood Royal
Marquesses (as in English Table)
Eldest Sons of Dukes
Earls (as in English Table)
Younger Sons of Dukes of the Blood Royal
Eldest sons of Marquesses
Younger Sons of Dukes
Lord Justice-General
Lord Clerk Register
Lord Advocate
Advocate-General
Lord Justice-Clerk
Viscounts (as in English Table)
Eldest Sons of Earls
Younger Sons of Marquesses
Barons or Lords of Parliament (Scotland) (as in English Table)
Eldest Sons of Viscounts
Younger Sons of Earls
Eldest Sons of Barons or Lords of Parliament
Knights of the Garter
Knights of the Thistle
Privy Counsellors
Senators of the College of Justice (Lords of Session), including Chairman of Scottish Land Court
Younger Sons of Viscounts
Younger Sons of Barons or Lords of Parliament
Baronets
Knights Grand Cross and Knights Grand Commanders of Orders (as in English Table)
Knights Commanders of Orders (as in English Table)
Solicitor-General for Scotland
Lyon King of Arms
Sheriffs Principal (when not within own county)
Knights Bachelor
Sheriffs
Companions of the Bath
Thence as in English Table

*By Royal Warrant dated 18 September 1952, it was declared that HRH the Duke of Edinburgh was henceforth to have Precedence next to HM the Queen, thus having place before the Lord High Commissioner.
†Lord-Lieutenants of a County and of a City during their term of office and within the limits of their jurisdiction have precedence before the Sheriffs Principal having concurrent jurisdiction.
††During term of office, and within their respective Sheriffdoms.

LADIES

The QUEEN
The Queen Mother
Duchess of Rothesay (The Princess of Wales)
Wives of Sovereign's younger Sons
Sovereign's Daughter
Sovereign's Sister
Wives of Sovereign's Uncles
Wives of Dukes of the Blood Royal
Wives of Princes of the Blood Royal
Sovereign's Cousin
Duchesses (as in English Table)
Wives of the Eldest Sons of Dukes of the Blood Royal
Marchionesses (as in English Table)
Wives of Eldest Sons of Dukes
Daughters of Dukes
Wives of Younger Sons of Dukes of the Blood Royal
Wives of Eldest Sons of Marquesses
Daughters of Marquesses
Wives of Younger Sons of Dukes
Countesses (as in English Table)
Viscountesses (as in English Table)
Wives of Eldest Sons of Earls
Daughters of Earls
Wives of Younger Sons of Marquesses
Baronesses, or Ladies of Parliament (Scotland) (as in English Table)
Wives of Eldest Sons of Viscounts
Daughters of Viscounts
Wives of Younger Sons of Earls
Wives of Eldest Sons of Barons or Lords of Parliament
Daughters of Barons or Lords of Parliament
Wives of Knights of the Garter
Wives of Knights of the Thistle
Privy Counsellors (women)
Wives of Younger Sons of Viscounts
Wives of Younger Sons of Barons
Wives of Baronets
Dames Grand Cross of Orders (as in English Table)
Wives of Knights Grand Cross and Knights Grand Commanders of Orders (as in English Table)
Dames Commanders of Orders (as in English Tables)
Wives of Knights Commanders of Orders (as in English Tables)
Wives of Knights Bachelor and Wives of Senators of the College of Justice (Lords of Session) including the wife of the Chairman of the Scottish Land Court§
Companions of the Order of the Bath
Thence as in English Tables

§Taking precedence among themselves according to the dates of their husbands' creation as Knights or appointment as Senators of the College of Justice, respectively.

A GUIDE TO THE WEARING OF
ORDERS, DECORATIONS, MINIATURES AND MEDALS
WITH DRESS OTHER THAN UNIFORM

(By courtesy of The Secretary, Central Chancery of Orders of Knighthood, 1971)

1 Introduction

Members of the various Orders of Chivalry and all persons who have been awarded Decorations and Medals may, should they wish to do so, wear their Insignia on those occasions when the person responsible for a function deems it fitting for Decorations to be worn. This Memorandum gives guidance on the wearing of Orders, Decorations, Miniatures and Medals with Full Evening Dress, Dinner Jacket, Morning Dress, Lounge Suit and Overcoats and supersedes all previous instructions on this subject.

2 Full Evening Dress

(a) The occasions when Decorations may be worn can be divided into two categories:

(i) **When The Queen, The Queen Mother or a Member of the Royal Family who is a Royal Highness is present.** The host should ascertain from the Member of the appropriate Household whether it is desired that Decorations should be worn.

(ii) **On all other occasions.** The host should decide whether the nature or importance of the occasion makes it appropriate for Decorations to be worn and then issue instructions on the Invitation Cards.

On occasions when it is desired that Decorations be worn, Invitations should state "Evening Dress—Decorations".

(b) The method of wearing Orders, Decorations and Miniatures when "Decorations" are prescribed is as follows:

(i) **Knights of the Garter and Knights of the Thistle; Knights and Dames Grand Cross, Knights Grand Commanders.**

Broad Riband and Badge of the senior British Order, unless it is more appropriate on certain occasions to wear the Riband and Badge of a junior British or Foreign Order.

Up to four Stars may be worn on the left side of the coat or dress.

When wearing more than one Star the precedence of the position of each Star is (looking at the wearer):

Four Stars	Three Stars	Two Stars
1	1	1
2 3	2 3	2
4		

One neck Badge suspended on a ribbon (miniature width) of the Order is worn under the collar and hanging close up below the tie. Miniature Badges of all Orders and Medals are worn on a medal bar. (The Garter, Thistle, Order of Merit, Crown of India, Companion of Honour and Baronet's Badge are not worn in Miniature.)

Collars are not worn.

(ii) **Knights and Dames Commanders.** Up to four Stars may be worn on the left side of the coat or dress as in (i) above. One neck Badge suspended on a ribbon (miniature width) of the Order is worn under the collar and hanging close up below the tie. Miniature Badges of all Orders, Decorations and Medals are worn on a medal bar. (The Order of Merit, Crown of India, Companion of Honour and Baronet's Badge are not worn in Miniature.) The Ladies' Badge is worn on a bow, below the Miniatures, on the left side.

(iii) **Companions and Commanders.** One neck Badge suspended on a ribbon (miniature width) of the Order is worn under the collar and hanging close up below the tie. Miniature Badges of all Orders, Decorations and Medals are worn on a medal bar. (The Order of Merit and Companion of Honour Badge are not worn in Miniature.) The Badges of a Companion of the Distinguished Service Order or Imperial Service Order are worn in Miniature on a medal bar and not as a neck Badge. The Ladies' Badge is worn on a bow, below the Miniatures, on the left side.

(iv) **Officers and Members.** Miniature Badges are worn on a medal bar.

(v) **Order of Merit, Companion of Honour.** These are neck Badges suspended on a ribbon (miniature width) of the Order worn under the collar and hanging close up below the tie. Only one neck Badge may be worn. Miniature Badges of all other Orders, Decorations and Medals are worn on a medal bar. (The Order of Merit and Companions of Honour Badges are not worn in Miniature). The Ladies' Badge is worn on a bow, below the Miniatures, on the left side.

(vi) **Baronet.** This Badge is worn as a neck Badge suspended on a ribbon (miniature width) worn under the collar and hanging close up below the tie. Miniature Badges of all other Orders, Decorations and Medals are worn on a medal bar. (The Baronet's Badge is not worn in Miniature.)

(vii) **Knight Bachelor.** This Badge is worn as an Order Star. Alternatively, in smaller dimensions as a neck Badge suspended on a ribbon (miniature width) worn under the collar and hanging close up below the tie. The Badge is also worn in Miniature on a medal bar in the same manner as Miniature Badges or Orders, Decorations and Medals.

(viii) **The Royal Victorian Chain.** This Chain is worn round the neck by men in place of a neck Badge and is adapted for wear by Ladies on a bow of the ribbon of the Order and worn on the left side above Miniatures.

At all times when "Evening Dress—Decorations" is prescribed, those not in possession of Full Evening Dress may wear a Dinner Jacket with Decorations as described in the next paragraph.

3 Dinner Jacket

(a) On occasions when it is desired that Dinner Jackets (and not Full Evening Dress) with Decorations are to be worn, Invitations should state "Dinner Jacket—Decorations".

In addition to Miniatures, only one Star (or the Badge of a Knight Bachelor) and one neck Badge may be worn.

(b) The method of wearing Orders, Decorations, Miniatures and Medals with a Dinner Jacket is as follows:

(i) **Knights of the Garter, Knights of the Thistle; Knights Grand Cross, Knights Grand Commanders.** One Star is worn on the left breast. Miniature Badges of all Orders, Decorations and Medals are worn on a medal bar. (The Garter, Thistle, Order of Merit, Crown of India, Companion of Honour and Baronet's Badge are not worn in Miniature.) Neither Collar nor Broad Riband and Badge will be worn.

(ii) **Knights Commanders.** One Star is worn on the left breast and one neck Badge suspended on a ribbon (miniature width) of the Order is worn under the collar and hanging close up below the tie. Miniature Badges of all Orders, Decorations and Medals are worn on the medal bar. (The Order of Merit, Crown of India, Companion of Honour and Baronet's Badge are not worn in Miniature.)

(iii) **Companions and Commanders.** One neck Badge suspended on a ribbon (miniature width) of the Order is worn under the collar and hanging close up below the tie. Miniature Badges of all Orders, Decorations and Medals are worn on a medal bar. (The Order of Merit and Companion of Honour Badge are not worn in Miniature.) The Badges of a Companion of the Distinguished Service Order or Imperial Service Order are worn in Miniature on a medal bar and not as a neck Badge.

(iv) **Officers and Members.** Miniature Badges are worn on a medal bar.

(v) **Order of Merit, Companion of Honour.** These are neck Badges suspended on a ribbon (miniature width) of the Order worn under the collar and hanging close up below the tie. Only one neck Badge may be worn. These Badges are not worn in Miniature.

(vi) **Baronet** This Badge is worn as a neck Badge suspended on a ribbon (miniature width) worn under the collar and hanging close up below the tie. This Badge is not worn in Miniature.

(vii) **Knight Bachelor.** This Badge is worn as an Order Star. Alternatively, in smaller dimensions as a neck Badge suspended on a ribbon (miniature width) worn under the collar and hanging close up below the tie. The Badge is also worn in Miniature on a medal bar in the same manner as Miniature Badges or Orders, Decorations and Medals.

(viii) **The Royal Victorian Chain.** The Chain may be worn round the neck in place of a neck Badge.

(c) **Ladies.** The regulations for the wearing of Orders, Decorations and Medals by Ladies are the same as in paragraph 2 (b) (ii) above.

4 Morning Dress

(a) The occasions when Orders, Decorations and Medals are worn with Morning Dress are comparatively rare. Such occasions may include special official public functions, religious Services connected with the Orders of Chivalry or Memorial Services. In each case the sponsor of the function or service should indicate whether the wearing of Decoratons would be appropriate. When Decorations are prescribed with Morning Dress not more than four Stars, one neck Badge and full size Medals should be worn. If a Star and neck Badge are worn they must be of different Orders.

Even so, on all such occasions the wearing of Insignia will be at the discretion of the holder.

(b) The method of wearing Orders, Decorations and Medals, when Decorations with Morning Dress are prescribed, is as follows:

(i) **Knights of the Garter, Knights of the Thistle; Knights and Dames Grand Cross, Knights Grand Commanders.** One Star only is worn on the left breast or, for Ladies, in a corresponding place on the dress. The Broad Riband and Badge is not worn. Collars are only worn with Morning Dress if ordered for a special occasion.

(ii) **Knights and Dames Commanders.** One Star only is worn on the left breast or, for Ladies, in a corresponding place on the dress. The neck Badge of a Knight Commander or the corresponding Badge of a Dame Commander may only be worn if belonging to a second Order. If worn with full-size Medals the Ladies' Badge, on a bow, is worn below the medal bar.

(iii) **Companions and Commanders.** One neck Badge suspended on a ribbon (miniature width) of the Order is worn under the collar. The Badge should hang three quarters of an inch below the tie knot in front of the tie. The Ladies' Badge is worn on a bow on the left side. If worn with full-size Medals the Badge is worn below the medal bar.

(iv) **Officers and Members.** The full-size Badge, whether worn singly or mounted on a medal bar, is worn on the left side in the same manner with civilian dress as with uniform. Companions of the Distinguished Service Order or Imperial Service Order wear their Insignia in this manner and not as a neck decoration. The Ladies' Badge, if worn separately, is worn on a bow on the left side of the dress. If worn with other Medals it is normally mounted on a medal bar and worn in the same manner with civilian dress as with uniform.

(v) **Order of Merit, Companion of Honour.** One neck Badge suspended on a ribbon (miniature width) of the Order is worn under the collar. The Badge should hang three quarters of an inch below the tie knot in front of the tie. The Ladies' Badge is worn on a bow on the left side. If worn with full-size Medals the Badge is worn below the medal bar.

(vi) **Baronet.** This Badge is worn as a neck Badge, suspended on a ribbon (miniature width) under the collar. The Badge should hang three quarters of an inch below the tie knot in front of the tie.

(vii) **Knight Bachelor.** This Badge is worn on the left breast as an Order Star. Alternatively, in smaller dimensions as a neck Badge suspended on a ribbon (miniature width) under the collar. The Badge should hang three quarters of an inch below the tie knot in front of the tie.

(viii) **The Royal Victorian Chain.** The Chain may be worn round the neck in place of a neck Badge.

5 Lounge Suit
(a) There are some occasions, such as Remembrance Sunday Services or Regimental gatherings, at which those attending are requested to wear Medals with lounge suits. On such occasions it is not customary to wear either Broad Ribands with Badges, Stars or the Royal Victorian Chain. One neck badge, suspended on a ribbon (miniature width) of the Order, worn under the collar and hanging close up below the tie knot in front of the tie; full-size Insignia mounted on a medal bar and worn on the left side as with uniform. On all such occasions the wearing of Insignia will be at the discretion of the holder.

(b) Appropriate strips of Ribbon, unattached to any Insiginia, of Orders, Decorations and Medals may be worn on all occasions with all forms of civilian dress at the discretion of the holder. If worn they should be sewn on the coat or dress or on to a medal bar and worn on the left hand side.

6 Overcoats
Full-size Medals may be worn on an overcoat, on the left hand side. No other insignia should be worn.

THE ROYAL FAMILY

THE SOVEREIGN'S OFFICIAL NAME

On succession, sovereigns choose the name under which they reign. This is a relatively recent development because until the end of the 17th century very few had more than one christian name. Although the Hanoverian kings all had more than one name they always chose the first as king, but when Queen Victoria, who had been christened Alexandrina Victoria, came to the throne, she chose the second of these. Her eldest son, Prince Albert Edward, also chose the second as Edward VII, because this was popular in English history, there having been three pre-Conquest and six subsequent kings of this name. Although Queen Victoria expressed her wish that all her male descendants should be christened Albert, this was disregarded after the Queen's death. George V and Edward VIII took their first names as kings; but after the Abdication of Edward VIII, he was succeeded by his brother Prince Albert, Duke of York, who chose his last name, reigning as George VI. It is possible, after the Abdication, that he wished to establish continuity with his father, and Albert, a foreign name, had strong associations with the Prince Consort. When the Queen succeeded it was a foregone conclusion that she would select her first name by which she has always been known.

NUMBERING OUR SOVEREIGNS

The first King of England to adopt enumeration on documents was Edward II, but "Henricus III" had appeared on the coins of Henry III, his grandfather. It is strange that, as Henry III particularly venerated Edward the Confessor and rebuilt Westminster Abbey, the three pre-Conquest Kings Edward were not included in the subsequent numbering, especially as William the Conqueror claimed the throne as the legitimate successor to Edward the Confessor.

In Scotland the first king to use numbering was Robert II who, in a preamble of a statute dated 1371-2, is described as "Secundus". The original does not exist but there is a contemporary text in *The Black Book*. He was also so described on 4 April 1373 in the Declaration of the Succession to the Scottish Throne, of which the original document survives. James IV introduced his numbering on coins, and James VI on Royal seals.

There was some difficulty with numbering when the thrones of England and Scotland were united in 1603. As this union did not unite the parliaments, which event did not take place until 1707, the Stuart kings continued the use of individual numbers for each country, such as James VI and VII in Scotland and James I and II in England. William III appeared as William II on the Scottish Royal seals. When Edward VII came to the throne a petition was sent from Scotland, which resulted in their letter boxes bearing ER instead of EVIIR. When the present Queen succeeded there was more intense feeling in Scotland on the matter, and it was announced that any subsequent sovereign whose number was different in England and Scotland would take the higher number, eg if we had another King James he would be known as James VIII instead of James III. The letter boxes in Scotland in the present reign now only bear a representation of the Scottish crown without any initials or numbers.

THE ROYAL SURNAME

The Queen declared in Council on 9 April 1952 that she and her children shall be styled and known as the House and Family of Windsor, as was her father King George VI. In this she followed the example, among others, of the Imperial Houses of Habsburg and Romanov and the Royal House of Orange. All these reigning Houses had passed through the female line to scions of the Houses of Lorraine, Holstein-Gottorp and Mecklenburg-Schwerin respectively. But, although the descendants belonged paternally to these Houses, in each case they continued the original House names of their predecessors in the female line. Despite the Queen's surname having been Mountbatten since her marriage in 1947 as Princess Elizabeth, this was then abandoned two months after her accession on the advice of Sir Winston Churchill.

On 8 February 1960 there was a declaration in Council that descendants of the Queen shall bear the surname of Mountbatten-Windsor, other than those bearing Royal attributes and female descendants who marry into other families. This followed a sermon by the Bishop of Carlisle (the Rt Rev Thomas Bloomer) delivered shortly before Prince Andrew's birth. The Bishop said that he did not like to think that any child born in wedlock should be deprived of his father's family name, a right and privilege that every other legitimate child possessed.

At the same time as the Queen's Declaration, the Press Secretary at Buckingham Palace issued a statement saying that "The Queen has always wanted, without changing the name of the Royal House established by her grandfather, to associate the name of her husband with her own and his descendants. The Queen has had this in mind for a long time and it is close to her heart".

The late Mr E. F. Iwi, an eminent constitutional lawyer, expressed the view that there was a distinction between the House and Family of Windsor collectively and members of the Royal Family as individuals. Consequently when, in 1973, Princess Anne married Captain Mark Phillips, her surname on her marriage certificate was shown as Mountbatten-Windsor. Thus the intention was to give a wider interpretation than that precisely stated in the 1960 Declaration.

A revised Declaration in Council to show that the family name is Mountbatten-Windsor would clarify the matter, because at present it is virtually impossible to be sure whether the Royal name is Windsor or Mountbatten-Windsor. That is, if the double name of Mountbatten-Windsor be adopted for both eventualities, (a) the Queen's descendants in the future who do not have royal styles and who are specially mentioned in the 1960 Declaration, and (b) a "hidden" surname for present members of the Royal Family, now occasionally used in certain official documents, there would no longer be such uncertainty as occurs at the present time. The first clause, which is already covered, will not come into effect until the birth of a great-grandchild to the Queen. The second clause, which is not covered, already occurs. A new Declaration would place the matter beyond all doubt.

It is unnecessary to add Mountbatten as the House name for the present Queen, for the reasons stated below (see Royal Houses).

The House and Family name of Windsor was adopted by King George V in 1917 on the suggestion of his Private Secretary, Lord Stamfordham, after many proposals had been rejected. This was a happy choice, for this Royal Castle has been a seat of the Royal Family since William the Conqueror. The Norman and early Plantagenet kings usually were known by nicknames or names bearing allusions to their parentage, such as William Rufus, Henry Beauclerc and Henry FitzEmpress. From the early 14th century it became customary to style members of the Royal Family by their birthplaces, such as Edward II, who was known as Edward of Caernarvon, Edward III and Henry VI who were known by their birthplace at Windsor and John of Gaunt who was born in Ghent.

It was only with the father of Edward IV that the name of Plantagenet as a surname came into being. The first recorded use of this name was in 1448. The origin goes back to Geoffrey, Count of Anjou, the father of Henry II, who was nicknamed Plantagenet from his adoption of a sprig of flowering broom or "Planta genista" as his badge.

The Tudors take their name from Henry VII's great-grandfather, Maredudd (Meredith) ap Tudur (Tudor). The Welsh did not have surnames at this time, sons bearing the qualification "ap" (meaning 'son of'), followed by their father's christian name. Henry VII's grandfather, Owen Tudor, son of Meredith, was also known sometimes as Owen Meredith. It is interesting to speculate that if the House had been known as Meredith instead of Tudor we would have a collection of "Ye Olde Meredith Tea Rooms".

Both the Bruces and Stewarts had these surnames before their succession to the Scottish throne. The Stewarts were so called from their hereditary office of High Steward of Scotland. In the time of Mary, Queen of Scots the French form of Stuart was first used, but her husband and kinsman, Henry, Lord Darnley, belonged to the Lennox branch of the Stewarts. Their son, James VI and I, also adopted the French spelling.

There has been controversy as to the surname of members of the Houses of Hanover and Saxe-Coburg and Gotha, but since both families were of ruling status before surnames came into being, they did not possess one. Nevertheless dynastic names, as distinct from surnames, came to be used. The House of Hanover is sometimes held to have the dynastic name of Guelph and sometimes that of Este. Their ancestors were lords of Este, a small feudal principality in Lombardy, from the 9th century. On marriage to a Bavarian heiress of the House of Guelph, they moved from Italy to Germany. The children of Queen Victoria's uncle, the Duke of Sussex, by a private marriage, used the name of d'Este, but another uncle, later William IV, was sometimes known as Guelph when he joined the Royal Navy. A former Clarenceux King of Arms dismissed as absurd the idea that the name was Guelph, and Queen Victoria sent a memo to dispute that this name should be used for an exhibition of treasures of the House of Hanover. Perhaps it would be more correct to term them Este-Guelph.

The family of Saxe-Coburg and Gotha has been traced to Thierry (Dietrich) of Buzici, a Thuringian noble living in 950, who founded the line of the Counts of Wettin, a small town on the banks of the river Saale in Saxony. The dynastic name of this family as Wettin thus cannot be regarded as a surname.

The Duke of Edinburgh belongs paternally to the House of Schleswig-Holstein-Sonderburg-Glücksburg which, in turn, is a branch of the House of Oldenburg. When the Duke of Edinburgh became a British subject in 1947, since he possessed no surname, one had to be selected. Oldcastle from Oldenburg was suggested, but rejected. Eventually he chose Mountbatten, the anglicised form of his mother's name of Battenberg. The Battenbergs were descended from the Grand Ducal Family of Hesse from a morganatic marriage of Prince Alexander of Hesse and the Rhine to Countess Julie von Hauke, who was created Princess of Battenberg. The Grand Ducal Family of Hesse descends in the male line from Regnier, Count of Hainault, who died in 915. The Percys, Earls of Northumberland belonged to the same male stock until 1670, and the present Duke of Northumberland shares this lineage with Prince Philip in the female line.

ROYAL HOUSES

In common with other monarchies the British Royal Family may be divided into houses or dynasties. Normally the male stock of one dynasty is given an all-embracing house name, such as the House of Stuart and House of Hanover. A difficulty arises with the Plantagenets, of which the first English sovereign was Henry II. The early monarchs were known as Angevins, belonging to the House of Anjou. However, when Henry of Bolingbroke seized the crown from Richard II, he is often considered as the first of the House of Lancaster, although he was Richard's first cousin of the same male line. Similarly, when Edward IV gained the crown from Henry VI, he is often considered to have founded the House of York. This situation also occurred in France with the House of Capet, descended from Hugh Capet who became king in 987. The Capets continued as kings of France, with some interruptions, until Louis Philippe was dethroned in 1848. Even so, for convenience, the monarchs were divided into Houses such as Valois, Bourbon and Orleans.

It is customary for the name of a Royal House to continue until the death of a Queen Regnant born into that Royal House. Thus Queen Mary I, after her marriage to Philip of Spain, remained a member of the House of Tudor, Mary II and Queen Anne belonged to the House of Stuart, and Queen Victoria was the last of the House of Hanover.

TITLES AND PEERAGES OF THE PRINCE OF WALES

The Prince of Wales has inherited other honours in addition to his main title. He is also Earl of Chester and Duke of Cornwall in the Peerage of England, and Duke of Rothesay and Earl of Carrick in the Peerage of Scotland. His other Scottish titles are Baron of Renfrew, Lord of the Isles and Prince and Great Steward of Scotland.

Only two of these dignities have to be specially created for the heir apparent, that of Prince of Wales and Earl of Chester. Prince Charles received these in 1958 when he automatically became a Knight Companion of the Garter as a constituent part of the Order, but he was not invested and installed as Prince and Earl at Caernarvon Castle until 1968. The remainder of the titles passed to him, as heir apparent, the moment his mother succeeded as Queen. The first Duke of Cornwall (and the first instance of the creation of a duke in England) was Edward the Black Prince, son and heir of King Edward III. The dukedom was created "with remainder to his heirs being Kings of England" and Henry VI expressly stated that his first begotten son at the time of his birth was Duke of Cornwall. Thereafter, heirs apparent who are also the Sovereign's sons become Duke of Cornwall either at birth or immediately their parent succeeds to the Crown. The only heir apparent not to become Duke of Cornwall was George III, who was not "filius regis", being a grandson of his predecessor, George II.

The first Duke of Rothesay was David, eldest son of Robert III, King of Scots, who received this peerage in 1398. Rothesay, and Albany (which was given to his uncle), were the first dukes to be created in Scotland. Although the charter conferring the dukedom of Rothesay is not extant, Winton, a contemporary, stated that the Duke of Rothesay was to

> "haif yat Tityl ay.-
> And efter hym (as yet was done
> All tym) ye Kingis eldeste sone
> and his air suld be alway,
> Be titil, Duke cald of Rothesay."

It was confirmed by Act of Parliament in 1469 that the heir apparent and he alone, holds the title of Duke of Rothesay. When the Prince of Wales is in Scotland he is termed Duke of Rothesay. Since the union in 1603 of the Crowns of England and Scotland, the limitation of the Dukedom of Rothesay being identical to that of Cornwall, they descend together, as do the other Scottish honours.

The Earldom of Carrick was already in existence in about 1186 when Duncan, descendant of the Lords of Galloway, obtained from King William the Lion the district of Carrick. His granddaughter, who was Countess of Carrick in her own right, married Robert Bruce, and their son Robert Bruce, in 1306, became King of Scots as Robert I. Some of the later Earls of Carrick were heirs apparent, and by Act of Parliament in 1469 it was declared that the Earldom should be annexed forever to the first born prince of the King of Scots. Under the same Act of Parliament, the Barony of Renfrew was also settled upon him. The heir apparent is also Lord of the Isles. The Macdonalds were Lords of the Isles (the Irish annalists styled them kings), but after forfeitures, James IV, King of Scots annexed the Lordship of the Isles to the Crown, and from that time onwards the heirs to the Scottish throne and their successors have always held the title.

Walter Fitz Alan, forebear of the Stewarts, was High Steward of Scotland in the reigns of David I and Malcolm IV. In 1371 Robert, 7th High Steward of Scotland, succeeded his half-uncle, David II, as Robert II, the first Stewart king. The hereditary office of High Steward was confirmed by Act of Parliament in 1469 on the first born prince of the King of Scots forever.

PEERAGES OF OTHER MEMBERS OF THE ROYAL FAMILY

Once a peerage is conferred upon a member of the Royal Family and becomes extinct, it is then reserved for a later prince and is not available to a subject. The Dukedom of Edinburgh, conferred in 1947 upon Prince Philip, was first bestowed (spelt "Edenburgh" in the patent) on Frederick Lewis, grandson of George I, but a year later, after his father succeeded as George II,he was created Prince of Wales. This peerage passed to his son, the future King George III, on his death before being merged into the Crown. George III conferred the title, together with the Dukedom of Gloucester, upon his brother Prince William Henry, but as Gloucester was the senior title, this was normally used. Both became extinct in 1834 on the death of his son, nicknamed "Silly Billy". Queen Victoria made her son, Prince Alfred, Duke of Edinburgh, who like Prince Philip, was a "Sailor Prince". His Dukedom became extinct in 1900, and was not conferred again until it was given to the present Duke.

The Dukedom of York has usually been conferred upon the second son of our sovereigns since Edward IV in 1474 bestowed the title on his younger son, Richard. This was the younger of the Princes in the Tower, whose fate has exercised the credulity of historians ever since. Before this, in 1385, Edmund of Langley, a son of Edward III, became Duke of York and was ancestor of the House of York, who warred with Lancaster in the Wars of the Roses. The victor, Edward, Duke of York, who had only succeeded for two months, seized the Crown at the age of eighteen, becoming Edward IV.

Three second sons who became Duke of York, and ultimately kings, were Henry VIII (son of Henry VII), Charles I (son of James I), and James II (son of Charles I). With George I a slight difference in this pattern occurred when he gave it in 1716 to his youngest brother Ernest Augustus, in conjunction with the Dukedom of Albany; and the next two Hanoverian dukes likewise received both creations. The first was Prince Edward Augustus, brother of George III, who received the title in 1760, but he died unmarried two years later. George III later returned to the traditional style by giving it to his second son, Prince Frederick, later Commander-in-Chief. He was involved in the scandal over the selling of commissions, a racket organised by his mistress, Mary Anne Clarke, but in 1811, two years after his resignation, he was restored to the office which he held for the rest of his life. He is best known from the nursery rhyme "The Grand Old Duke of York". Bonnie Prince Charlie's younger brother, Henry, held the Jacobite Dukedom of York, and was generally known as Cardinal York.

Queen Victoria did not approve of her Hanoverian uncles' reputation, and departed from tradition by creating her second son Prince Alfred, Duke of Edinburgh. As she reached such a great age, she had two grandsons in the direct line who were adults. She reluctantly agreed to bestow the title of Duke of York on the younger of these, the future King George V, mainly under pressure from his father the Prince of Wales. In 1920, Prince Albert, second son of George V, became Duke of York, and the tradition was perpetuated when the Queen bestowed the title upon her second son, Prince Andrew, in 1986.

Like York, Gloucester has always been a Royal Dukedom. In 1385 the same day that the Dukedom of York was first created, Thomas of Woodstock, the youngest son of Edward III, was created Duke of Gloucester by his nephew Richard II. Subsequent Dukes were the Lancastrian Humphrey, "the Good Duke", brother of Henry V, and the Yorkist Richard, later Richard III. Charles I's youngest son, Henry, had the title, but he died unmarried of smallpox very shortly after the Restoration. The last Stuart creation was the pathetic little son of Anne, her only child to survive infancy. Although declared Duke of Gloucester, he was never formally so created, and died at the age of eleven before his mother became Queen.

After George III's brother, Prince William, became Duke of Gloucester and Albany, which died out with his son, the title was not re-created until 1928, when George V bestowed it upon his third son, Prince Henry. The Dukedom is now possessed by his son, Prince Richard.

Unlike these other Dukedoms, Kent was originally non-Royal, borne by the Greys, until this became extinct in 1797. Two years later, George III then gave it to his fourth son, Prince Edward, father of Queen Victoria, but it became extinct in 1820 on his death. The Dukedom was next conferred by George V in 1934 upon Prince George, his fourth son. His son, the present Duke, succeeded in 1942 following his father's death on active service.

Other titles reserved for members of the Royal Family include the Dukedom of Clarence, derived from the Honour of Clare in Suffolk. The first was Lionel of Antwerp, third son of Edward III, from whom the Yorkists eventually derived their claim to the throne. Some of the Dukes of Clarence have been unfortunate. George, brother of Edward IV and Richard III, was murdered after being found guilty of high treason. The method used, according to popular tradition, was drowning after being pushed headfirst into a butt of malmsey. The last Duke of Clarence, elder son of the future Edward VII, died unmarried of pneumonia at the age of twenty-eight, a few weeks after his engagement to Princess Mary of Teck, who later married his brother.

Both the Dukedoms of Cumberland and Albany were attainted as a result of their holders, being Germans, taking up arms against Britain in the First World War. Ernest, Duke of Cumberland, the most unpopular of Queen Victoria's uncles, succeeded William IV as King of Hanover, where Salic law operated. The Dukedom of Albany, bestowed on Queen Victoria's youngest son, passed to his son, who, as a boy, succeeded as Duke of Saxe-Coburg and Gotha. Since both peerages were merely suspended, they cannot be re-conferred, because theoretically they could be restored by an Act of Parliament. The most notorious Duke of Cumberland was William Augustus, second son of George II, who was in command of the Royal troops at the battle of Culloden, and earned the name of "Butcher Cumberland" as a result of his severe repression in the Highlands.

The Dukedom of Kendal was twice conferred upon sons of James II who died in infancy, and the Dukedoms of Sussex and Connaught were each conferred once: Sussex on Queen Victoria's uncle, and Connaught upon her third son. The former died out on the Duke's death, and Connaught on the death of the second Duke in 1943 in Canada. The Dukedom of Cambridge was occasionally brought into use at previous times, the last creation in 1801 was to a son of George III. This died out with his son, formerly the Commander-in-Chief, at his death in 1904, but was re-conferred as a Marquessate, to his maternal nephew the Duke of Teck upon relinquishing his German title, and became extinct on the death of the 2nd Marquess in 1981.

Another Royal Dukedom was that of Lancaster. The second Duke, but the best known, was John of Gaunt, made more famous by Shakespeare as "Time-honoured Lancaster" than as the hated uncle of the King against whom the fury of the Peasants' Revolt was directed. When Henry Duke of Lancaster dethroned, and later murdered, Richard II, thereby becoming the first Lancastrian king, the Dukedom merged in the Crown and has never been re-created, although the sovereign always succeeds to the Duchy of Lancaster. The loyal toast in the North remains "The Queen, Duke of Lancaster".

It has long been the custom for Royal scions to receive more than one peerage. The "Butcher" Duke of Cumberland, for example, was also Marquess of Berkhamsted, Earl of Kensington, Viscount Trematon and Baron of the Isle of Alderney.

Prince Edward's creation as Earl of Wessex has been a break with precedent. Of the other Royal Dukedoms, Connaught is a province of the Republic of Ireland and therefore unlikely to be revived. Kendal has somewhat unfortunate connotations, as the last time the Dukedom was conferred it was upon an unpopular mistress of George I, vulgarly called "the Maypole" from her extremely emaciated figure; and Clarence has an unfortunate history.

Some peerages were selected conjointly from England, Scotland and Ireland, such as the lesser peerages of the Duke of Kent, which are the Earldom of St Andrews and Barony of Downpatrick. The second senior peerage is thus available for use as a courtesy title for the eldest son and heir when the holder ceases to use Royal styles and titles. Otherwise heirs to Royal peerages have not used courtesy peerages; thus the late Prince William of Gloucester was never known as Earl of Ulster, but this was not always so, Edward IV being known as Earl of March when his father was Duke of York.

THE TITLES AND STYLES OF MEMBERS OF THE ROYAL FAMILY

King George V, by Letters Patent issued on 30 October 1917, declared that henceforward only the children, the children of sons of the Sovereign, and the eldest living son of the eldest son of the Prince of Wales, would be entitled to the style of Royal Highness and the titles of Prince and Princess. This meant that more distant descendants of the Royal Family had to give up Royal styles, thus HH Prince Alastair of Connaught (later the 2nd Duke of Connaught), who was a great-grandson of Queen Victoria, then became known as the Earl of Macduff, a courtesy title belonging to his mother, who was Duchess of Fife in her own right.

On the day before the Duke of Edinburgh's marriage to the present Queen, he was created Royal Highness, but the children of the Dukes of Gloucester and Kent, as great-grandchildren of a sovereign, do not have Royal attributes. The sons and heirs of the Dukes of Gloucester and Kent therefore bear respectively the courtesy titles of Earl of Ulster and Earl of St Andrews, in the same way as the heirs of other dukes. The younger son and the daughter of the Duke of Kent are known as Lord Nicholas Windsor and Lady Helen Taylor, and the son and daughter of Prince Michael of Kent are known as Lord Frederick and Lady Gabriella Windsor, following the styles for younger sons and daughters of dukes as prescribed by further Letters Patent of 11 Dec 1917.

There has only been one example of children of a Princess and her non-Royal British husband receiving royal titles. When King Edward VII declared his eldest daughter to be Princess Royal, he instructed his Garter King of Arms to declare her two daughters Princesses. Garter is alleged to have told the King that this was impossible as there was no precedent. The King merely told him, "Do it." Accordingly, the two daughters, subsequently Princess Arthur of Connaught and the Countess of Southesk, were gazetted Princesses with the style of Highness and precedence immediately after all members of the Royal Family bearing the style of Royal Highness. The elder sister attained the style of Royal Highness on her marriage, but the younger ceased to use the style and title on her marriage without any specific declaration being made. It is believed this was to comply with the wishes of King George V, who had not approved of his father's action.

The case has never previously arisen when a grandson of a Sovereign has been untitled. Peter Phillips, the Queen's first grandchild, has no title, since neither of his parents has received a peerage, and there is no title to be passed on to their children. If a warrant of precedence could be given raising him to the rank of a son of a duke or marquess, Peter Phillips would at least be in the same position as the son of Prince and Princess Michael of Kent, by having the courtesy style of "Lord" before his name. There have been examples of such precedence being granted by previous sovereigns, such as Lady Katherine Brandram, previously Princess of Greece and Denmark, and Lady Valda Machell, formerly Countess Victoria Gleichen, daughter of Prince Victor of Hohenlohe-Langenburg and granddaughter of Admiral of the Fleet the Hon Sir George Francis Seymour. Brothers and sisters of peers, whose fathers never succeeded, may be given precedence as if their fathers had been peers.

THE ACT OF SETTLEMENT

The Act of Settlement, under which the Queen reigns, was passed in 1701 in the reign of William III. The Act was designed to ensure a Protestant succession to the throne. As the King was childless, the throne was to pass on his death to Queen Anne, whose only child to survive infancy had recently died. Then, in default of any issue, to the next Protestant descendant of the Royal House, the Electress Sophia of Hanover, niece of Charles I, and her descendants, being Protestants. This cut out the Roman Catholic descendants of James II. As Sophia predeceased Queen Anne, the Crown passed in 1714 to Sophia's son George I, first of the House of Hanover to ascend to the Throne.

The Act provides for a perpetual Protestant succession by debarring any person in line to the throne from reigning if he or she be a Roman Catholic or has married one. This question arose on the marriage of Prince Michael of Kent when he lost his right of succession through his marriage to a Roman Catholic, but according to the announcement from Buckingham Palace, their children and descendants remain in succession, provided that they are in communion with the Church of England.

THE ROYAL MARRIAGES ACT

The Royal Marriages Act was passed in 1772 following the marriages of the Dukes of Cumberland and Gloucester, which were considered unsuitable by their brother King George III. The Act provides that any descendant of George II, both male and female, is required to obtain the consent of the Sovereign, signified under the Great Seal and declared in Council, before any marriage is contracted. This does not apply to princesses, and their descendants, who marry into foreign families.

The Act also contains a proviso that princes and princesses, over the age of 25, are permitted to give notice to the Privy Council twelve calendar months before contracting such a marriage without the consent of the Sovereign. So far, this clause has never been utilised.

There have been marriages contracted by members of the Royal Family, for which the Sovereign's permission was not obtained, such as those of the Prince of Wales (later George IV) to Mrs Fitzherbert, and the marriages of his brother the Duke of Sussex and his nephew the Duke of Cambridge. These marriages, though presumably canonically valid, are legally null and void. There has been more than one attempt to repeal the Royal Marriages Act, and in 1967 a young constitutional lawyer, the late Mr Charles Farran, detected a flaw in it. He held that those descendants of princesses who married into foreign families who were therefore covered by the exemption clause, sometimes came to Britain to marry descendants of George II, who needed to seek permission to marry under the Act. It therefore followed that descendants of these marriages are also exempted, which was not foreseen when the Act was drawn up in 1772. Thus Princess Anne and Princess Alexandra, for example, are descended from Queen Alexandra who was herself descended from George II in the female line. Nearly all the Members of the Royal Family now fall into the category of being exempted.

THE SOVEREIGN, ROYAL FAMILY, PEERAGE, BARONETAGE AND OTHER DIGNITIES AND RANKS

Royal Crown as heraldically depicted

THE SOVEREIGN

THE SOVEREIGN is first in honour, dignity, and in power—and the seat and fountain of all three, possessing, according to Camden,

"Many rights and privileges peculiar to majesty termed by the learned lawyer, *sacra sacrorum*, that is, sacred and individual, or inseparable because they cannot be severed; and the ordinary royal prerogatives, termed the flowers of his crown, in which respect they affirm that the regal material crown is adorned with flowers. Some of these are held by positive or written law, others which, by right of custom, by a silent consent of all men without law, prescription of time has allowed, the king justly enjoys."

The Crown is held under the Act of Settlement (12 and 13 William III, cap. 2), the wording of which, with reference to succession is:—
"For default of issue of the said Princess Ann and of His Majesty respectively the crown and regall government of the said kingdoms of England France and Ireland and of the dominions thereunto belonging with the royall state and dignity of the said realms and all honours stiles and regalties prerogatives powers jurisdictions and authorities to the same belonging and appertaining shall be remain and continue to the said most excellent Princess Sophia (of Hanover) and the heirs of her body being Protestants."

Under the Statute of Westminster, 1931, any alteration in the law touching the Succession to the Throne or the Royal Style and Titles shall require the assent of the Parliaments of all the Dominions as well as of the Parliament of the United Kingdom. At present The Queen is Head of State of thirteen member countries of the Commonwealth. All member nations of the Commonwealth acknowledge The Queen as Head of the Commonwealth. Membership of the Commonwealth is subject to the approval of existing members.

Among the more clearly defined prerogatives of the British monarch are those of convoking, adjourning, removing, and dissolving Parliament, refusing assent to Bills, without which assent they cannot become law, increasing the number of Peers, declaring war at pleasure, choosing and appointing all commanders and officers by land, sea, and air, and all judges, councillors, officers of state, magistrates, Archbishops, Bishops, and high ecclesiastical dignitaries, bestowing all public honours, and pardoning criminals, besides exercising many other powers, by the advice of the Cabinet Ministers, who, however, alone are responsible, the theory of English law being that the Sovereign cannot commit wrong.

Another theory of our law is that the King (or Queen) never dies—substantially, that the throne is never vacant, the succession of the heir being instantaneous. A meeting of the Privy Council is held immediately after the Demise of the Crown (usually the next day) to give directions for proclaiming the new Sovereign. The proclamation takes place in London at St James's Palace, at Charing Cross, within the City Boundary at Temple Bar, and at the Royal Exchange, two or three days later. To this first meeting of the Privy Council of the new Reign, the Lord Mayor and Aldermen, etc, of London, although not themselves Privy Councillors, are invited. Since the Reform Act of 1867 Parliament does not dissolve at the Demise of the Crown, and, if at the time adjourned or prorogued, meets immediately, or, if dissolved, the old Parliament must meet at once and may serve for six months. The ceremony of a coronation, although essential, is a solemn recognition and confirmation of the royal descent and consequent right of accession, and is not necessary for the security of the title to the crown.

Before Edward I our Kings began to reign only after their coronations, being styled Duke of Normandy until that time.

Some of the styles of pre-Conquest kings were elaborate, such as King Edgar (957-975) call *Rex Anglorum* and *Basileus Anglorum*, and Edward the Martyr as *Gratia Dei Rex totius Albionis*. For styles since 1066, see "SOVEREIGNS."

It was not until Henry IV adopted the title of "Grace," that prefixes came into use. These prefixes were successively changed to "Excellent Grace," "High and Mighty Prince," and "Highness", until Henry VIII adopted those of "Majesty" and "Dread Sovereign."

The Sovereign's banner, commonly called the Royal Standard, is the personal flag of the Sovereign, and can only properly be flown over buildings or ships with Her Majesty's permission, which permission is only granted when the Queen is actually present in person, and not when Her Majesty is passing in processions.

THE QUEEN MOTHER

takes precedence amongst ladies immediately after the Queen, and has her own Household.

THE HEIR APPARENT TO THE CROWN

is next below the Sovereign in all honour and dignity—not as participating or comparing with the latter, who stands alone and supreme, but as enjoying the largest share of the honour which flows from the Crown; though in the present reign HRH the Duke of Edinburgh has ranked next to HM the Queen under the terms of a Royal Warrant dated 18 Sept 1952.

Plume of the
Eldest Son of The
Sovereign*

No person can hold this position save the son of the Sovereign, or, if the former be dead, his direct male descendant. A female can only hold the position if the eldest or only daughter of a male heir apparent who has died in the life time of the reigning sovereign leaving no male issue.

The Heir Apparent has, since the institution of the title by Edward I (who, in 1301, conferred it on his son, Edward, born at Caernarvon in 1284), usually but not invariably been *created* Prince of Wales. Since 1399, the Earldom of Chester has always been conferred, together with the Principality of Wales. There is no succession to this title, which, at every vacancy, becomes merged in the Crown, and is only renewed by the Sovereign's pleasure. Thus, had George IV died whilst Prince of Wales, his next brother, though heir apparent, would not have become the Prince of Wales without being so created.

The Sovereign's eldest son is Duke of Cornwall (peerage of England) and Duke of Rothesay (peerage of Scotland) from the moment of his birth or the Sovereign's accession, and becomes immediately entitled to the revenues of the Duchy of Cornwall. When there is no Duke of Cornwall, the Duchy is in the custody of, and the revenues are paid to, the Crown. The titles of Duke of Cornwall and Duke Rothesay, unlike that of Prince of Wales, do not become merged in the Crown on succession to the Monarchy or at death (unless the Sovereign has no son), but pass at once to the next heir apparent being the eldest living *son* of the Sovereign, to whom it is strictly limited.

Coronet of
Eldest Son of
The Sovereign

By course of the civil law the heir apparent sits at the right hand of the Sovereign in all solemn assemblies of state and honour; but he has no kingly prerogatives, and acknowledges reverence to his sovereign. He comes of age automatically on becoming Duke of Cornwall, however tender his years†. Thus he may take his seat in Parliament at the Sovereign's will.

A statute of Edward III enacts "that to compass or imagine the death of the King's eldest son and heir is *crimen læsæ majestatis*" (high treason).

In 1898 Letters Patent under the Great Seal were granted, declaring that the children of the eldest son of any Prince of Wales shall at all times have the title of "Royal Highness," but by further letters patent December 1917, this privilege was confined to the eldest living son only of the eldest son of the Prince of Wales.

The Prince of Wales was invested at Caernarvon Castle on 1 July 1969, as the 21st Prince of Wales, and was introduced to the House of Lords on 11 Feb 1970.

MEMBERS OF THE ROYAL FAMILY

*The rank and position of these are defined in the general
"Tables of Precedence"*

The Latin *Princeps* signified "the first." Before the reign of Henry VIII the only prince was the Prince of Wales. As a courtesy title the style of Prince and Princess gradually superseded Lord and Lady—though the latter styles were in use as late as the reign of Charles II for his nieces and Frederick, Prince of Wales, in the reign of George II, expressed a wish that his sons and

---

*This plume of feathers, generally spoken of as "The Prince of Wales's feathers," is not in reality such, but is the badge of the Heir Apparent, in whom it is vested whether created Prince of Wales or not.
†Princes (The) Case 1606, 8 Co Rep 1a, 13b, and note to Blackstone's Commentaries Vol 1, 15th ed p 242.

daughters should be so styled, though they do not appear to have been. In Scotland the style of Prince of Scotland is borne by the eldest son of the Sovereign. The first charter is one granted by Robert III on 10 Dec 1404, in favour of his son James. Until the Reform Act, 1832, tenancy of 40s freehold from the Prince of Scotland was a qualification for a vote in Scottish counties.

The Royal Marriages Act prohibits the marriage of personages (descendants of George II) connected with the Blood Royal (except issue of Princesses who have married into Foreign Families) without the sanction of the Sovereign, but this is considerably modified by a conditional proviso, by which marriage contracted after the age of twenty-five is valid if a year's notice has been given to the Privy Council and both Houses of Parliament, and they have not interfered during that period expressing their disapprobation. Private marriages do not give the rank of the husband to the wife or issue of the marriage, and although duly solemnized and the issue legitimate, do not confer upon the children any right of succession to hereditary honours.

| Coronet of the younger children of the Heir Apparent and of the daughters of the Sovereign's son | Coronet of the younger sons, daughters, brothers, and sisters of the Sovereign | Coronet of the grandsons (through younger sons) of the Sovereign | Coronet of the grandchildren (through daughters) of the Sovereign |

Up to 1917 the Sovereign's sons, daughters, grandsons and granddaughters (being issue of sons), brothers, sisters, and uncles and aunts (on the Sovereign's side), the children of the eldest son of any Prince of Wales were all styled "Royal Highness." Grandchildren who were issue of daughters were sometimes granted by Royal Warrant the title of "Highness". Since that date the style of "Royal Highness" has been confined to the issue of any Sovereign and to issue of the sons of any Sovereign. The titles of "Prince" and "Princess" are similarly confined to *all* children of any Sovereign and to the children of the sons of any Sovereign. (See also under Heir Apparent.) The style of "Princess Royal," which is held for life, is customarily granted by declaration to the eldest daughter of the Sovereign after a vacancy has occurred. The first Princess so styled was the eldest daughter of Charles I.

ROYAL CORONETS

Members of the royal family use above their arms an heraldic representation of the coronets which they actually wear at coronations. Since the Restoration in 1660 the design of royal coronets has gradually become standardised into five types and these are worn with royal robes of purple velvet by ladies and with scarlet robes with capes semee of ermine by men. Ladies' coronets are a smaller version of those worn by men.

The five types of royal coronet are as follows:—

(1) The coronet of the heir apparent composed of alternate crosses patees and fleurs-de-lys, surmounted by a single arch topped with an orb and cross. The original coronet of this design forms part of the crown jewels exhibited at the Tower of London and was made for Frederick Louis, Prince of Wales, the son and heir of King George II. It is often referred to incorrectly as the Prince of Wales's crown or coronet. However, as that title is only bestowed at the sovereign's pleasure, it would be better described as the Duke of Cornwall's coronet. Another coronet of similar design and also exhibited with the crown jewels was made for the future King George V to wear at his father's coronation in 1902. It was also used by the future King Edward VIII at the coronation of 1911*.

(2) The coronet of the younger sons, brothers, daughters and sisters of a sovereign is the same as the heir apparent's coronet with the omission of the arch. The eldest son of the heir apparent is also entitled to this coronet, but no other grandchildren of the sovereign use it. Originally exclusive to the sons and brothers of the sovereign, this type was extended by King Edward VII to his daughters, and King George VI approved its use by the Duke of Edinburgh.

(3) The coronet of younger children of the heir apparent and, since the time of Queen Victoria, of daughters of younger sons of the sovereign (oddly, the sons of younger sons use the next type) consists of two crosses patees, two strawberry leaves and four fleurs-de-lys. This type of coronet was also used by the daughters of sovereigns until King Edward VII allowed the use of the previous type to his daughters. Lady Patricia Ramsay continued to use her royal coronet even though she had renounced the title of Princess and style of Royal Highness on her marriage.

(4) The coronet of the sons of younger sons of a sovereign consists of alternate crosses patees and strawberry leaves. Until the reign of Queen Victoria all descendants in the male line with the style of Royal Highness bore this coronet, hence in 1902 the Duke of Cumberland and, it is presumed, his sister Princess Frederica, wore it at the coronation of King Edward VII. Queen Victoria promoted the daughters of younger sons to the preceding type, and King George V's exclusion of the German branches of the royal family after the first World War restricted its use to the present category.

*Two other coronets exist and are exhibited in the National Museum of Wales at Cardiff. They are the circlet of simple design made for the investiture of Edward, Prince of Wales in 1911, and the more elaborate interpretation in modern idiom of the single-arched crown or coronet made for the investiture of Prince Charles in 1969.

(5) A coronet composed of alternate fleurs-de-lys and strawberry leaves is generally stated to belong to the grandchildren of a sovereign through daughters. As Princesses generally married into other royal houses, this coronet first came into use for the daughters of the Princess Royal, Duchess of Fife. The Marquess of Carisbrooke was granted this type of coronet after renouncing his German titles and actually wore it at the 1937 coronation, lending it in 1953 to Lord Harewood, whose wife however wore the ordinary Countess's coronet since Lady Carisbrooke attended the coronation and there was only one lady's coronet of this type available. Since other grandchildren of sovereigns such as Princess Marie Louise (who, however, used it heraldically) and the Hon Gerald Lascelles did not wear robes or coronets, it might be concluded that this type of coronet appertains to the sovereign's grandchildren through daughters provided such persons are peers or peeresses.

THE PEERAGE

LORDS SPIRITUAL

Lords Spiritual consist of the Archbishops of Canterbury and York and twenty-four Bishops (by rotation, but including always the Bishops of London, Durham, and Winchester). The sixteen Junior Bishops do not have seats in the House of Lords. The Bishop of Sodor and Man is unable to vote in the House of Lords, as he is a legislator in the Isle of Man. It has been the custom to bestow a barony on a retired Archbishop. A bishop on resigning his see ceases to be a peer of Parliament.

The Archbishop of Canterbury is the first peer of England next to the Royal Family, preceding not only all Dukes, but all the great officers of the Crown. The Bishop of London is his provincial Dean, the Bishop of Winchester his Chancellor, and the Bishop of Worcester his Chaplain. "It belongs to him to crown the King"; and the Sovereign and his or her Consort, wherever they may be located, are *speciales domestici parochiani Arch Cant* (parishioners of the Lord Archbishop of Canterbury).

The Archbishop of Canterbury is Primate of *all* England, is entitled to the prefix of "Your Grace," and styles himself "By Divine Providence, Lord Archbishop of Canterbury."

The Archbishop of York is the third peer in the United Kingdom, and precedes all secular peers, except the Lord High Chancellor. He is "Primate of England," and is perpetual chaplain of the Queen Consort. He is entitled to the prefix of "Your Grace," styles himself "By Divine Providence, Lord Archbishop of York," and possesses within his own province powers nearly equivalent to those exercised by the Archbishop of Canterbury within his. His precedence rests on an Act of Parliament in 31st year of Henry VIII.

An Archbishop's mitre is the same as that of a Bishop.

Diocesan Bishops of England, with the exceptions noted, are also peers of the kingdom and of Parliament, and take precedence of the temporal barons.

The Bishops of London, Durham, and Winchester have precedence over all the other bishops who rank according to the seniority of their consecration.

A Diocesan bishop is entitled to the prefix of Lord, and styles himself "Right Reverend Father in God, by Divine Permission, Lord Bishop of —."

The mitre, placed over the arms of a bishop, is a round cap, pointed and cleft at the top, from which hang two pendants, fringed at the ends, it is surmounted by a fillet of gold, set with precious stones. The mitre of the Bishop of Durham (as nominally Count Palatine of Durham) is represented as issuing out of a ducal crest coronet.

Archbishops and Bishops who are entitled to a seat in the House of Lords possess all the faculties and privileges of Peers of Parliament during the time they hold office.

A bishop impales his arms with those of the See, but he does not bear crest, supporters, or motto. The wives and children of bishops do not have any precedence as such.

PEERS

The degrees of the Peerage of England, Scotland, Ireland, Great Britain and the United Kingdom are five—viz, *Dukes, Marquesses, Earls, Viscounts*, and *Barons* (including Life Barons).

Scottish peers take precedence of British peers of the same rank created since the Union with Scotland. *Irish peers* created before the Union with Ireland, in like manner, take place of British peers created since. Irish peers of later creation than the Union, rank according to the dates of their patents, among the peers of Great Britain and Ireland. Peers holding only Scottish titles have been enabled to sit in the House of Lords since the passing of The Peerage Act 1963. By that Act, the enactments relating to the election of Scottish Representative Peers, by which they were elected by their fellow-Peers for one Parliament only, ceased to have effect.

Peers holding only Irish titles are not eligible to sit in the House of Lords. Representative Peers were (before establishment of the Irish Free State) elected by their fellow peers for life.

Irish peers are not disqualified from being elected as members in the House of Commons for any constituency in the United Kingdom, and to vote at elections for the House of Commons whether or not they be members of that House.

Peers of England, Scotland, Great Britain, and the United Kingdom are not entitled to sit in the House of Commons.

Since 1958 women have been admitted to the Upper House as Life Peeresses, and also since 1963, hereditary Peeresses of England, Great Britain, the United Kingdom, and Scotland.

Peers may not take their seats in the House of Lords until they are of age. If they then desire to do so they are required to prove their right of succession, after which a writ of summons is issued. Peerage patents are on parchment, and bear no signature, only the Great Seal.

The ceremony of admitting a peer into the House of Lords. He is introduced by two peers of his own degree, who conduct him to the Lord Chancellor. His patent is carried by Garter King of Arms. The new peer presents it together with his writ of summons to the Lord Chancellor, who directs the same to be read. The oaths are administered, the peer takes his seat, and then, rising, returns to the Chancellor, who congratulates him upon his elevation.

PRIVILEGES OF PEERS

The privileges enjoyed by peers were formerly numerous. Amongst those abolished is the privilege in cases of treason and felony of being tried by their peers only, who gave their verdict simply *upon their honour*, in a court specially fitted up at the expense of the Crown. This was discontinued under the Criminal Justice Act of 1948.

The privileges which continue are:—

Exemption from Jury Service.

Immunity from attachment, *ie* freedom from arrest in civil cases for a period of 40 days before and after a meeting of Parliament (a privilege shared with Members of Parliament, but it is wider for a Peer, since under Common Law "the person of a peer is forever sacred and inviolable.")

A peer (but not a peer by courtesy, with the following exception) is entitled to have Supporters granted to be borne with his arms, and to the use of the coronet of his rank. Heirs apparent of peers of Scotland are enabled to bear the peer's supporters, debruised with a three point label.

CLAIMS TO PEERAGES

Claims to dormant or abeyant Peerages or to Peerages whose succession is in dispute, are dealt with by the Committee for Privileges of the House of Lords on petition to the Crown, presented through the Home Secretary, who first refers the accompanying documents to the Attorney-General in order that he may report upon them to the Sovereign and advise in the matter.

These the Attorney-General passes to the Counsel for the Crown in Peerage claims, and he reports to the Attorney-General, who then, to obtain further particulars and elucidate any further details necessary, hears the petitioner and his counsel, after which the Attorney-General himself reports to the Home Secretary. If his report is unfavourable to the petitioner he advises that the petition shall not be referred to the Committee for Privileges. If on the contrary, he considers that the proofs and documents submitted at the hearing made out a *prima facie* case, he advises the House of Lords to refer it to their Committee for Privileges, which goes into the case in detail, the petitioner and any opposing claimant being represented by counsel, while the Crown is represented by the Attorney-General and the counsel for Peerage claims. The Committee for Privileges reports to the Sovereign the conclusions at which it arrives. Since 1977, claims to Scottish Peerages, and, in certain cases where there is a sufficient Scottish connection, claims to Peerages of Great Britain and of the United Kingdom, should be lodged with the Secretary of State for Scotland.

The Select Committee on Peerages in Abeyance 1926 made the general recommendations that, in the absence of special circumstances or special reasons to the contrary, no abeyance should be terminated, the first commencement of which occurred more than 100 years before the presentation of the committee, and no petition should be allowed to proceed where the petition represents less than one-third of the entire dignity.

ACCELERATED PROMOTION TO HOUSE OF LORDS

On occasions the eldest son of a peer has been summoned to the House of Lords during his father's lifetime in one of his father's minor titles, and in such cases if he predeceased his father the title and seat passed to his son (if any). The last instance of this practice occurred in 1992 when the eldest son of the 6th Marquess of Salisbury was called to the House of Lords in his father's Barony of Cecil.

SELECTION OF PEERAGE TITLES

The Sovereign, as the fountain of all honour, can bestow any title He or She may please, but in practice the following rules are usually observed.

Titles once conferred upon any member of the Royal Family are not again bestowed outside the Royal Circle. A title once extinct but subsequently revived, is rarely re-created in a lower rank than before, but this rule is not an invariable one.

Every peer below the rank of Earl must be described in his patent as "of—" (somewhere), usually the seat of the recipient, or some place with which he has a connection. Some peers are *created* with a territorial designation as actually *part of the title*, such as *Baron Ritchie of Dundee*, of Welders, Chalfont St Giles, *Baron Brassey of Apethorpe*, of Apethorpe, and *Baron Ponsonby of Shulbrede*, of Shulbrede. It will be noted that in such cases there is a double territorial designation.

Any semblance of duplication of titles is avoided as far as ever possible.

A surname, if desired, may *always* be adopted as a title, although another dignity of the same style be at the time in existence. In that case the recipients of all such similar (surname) titles of the same rank, except the first (then existing one) to be created, *must* add the territorial designation as an affix to the title by which they are commonly known. For instance, Baron Stanley (creation 1455); Baron Stanley (creation 1832) known as "Lord Stanley of Bickerstaff"; Baron Stanley (creation 1828) as "Lord Stanley of Alderley"; Baron Stanley (creation 1886) as "Lord Stanley of Preston." Again, Baron Curzon (creation 1794), and Baron Curzon (creation 1898) as "Lord Curzon of Kedleston."

In the case of Life Peers the surname is usually adopted.

The name of a county or county town is not as a rule permissible as a peerage title below the rank of earl (although exception may be made in favour of anyone particularly eminent either as a statesman or in some other walk of life). Important towns are usually reserved for the higher steps in the peerage.

SIGNATURES

Peers sign by their titles only, as also do the eldest sons of peers bearing as a courtesy title one of their father's minor honours, but a peeress by marriage signs with her Christian name or initial prefixed to the title. A peeress in her own right, however, signs with the title only. Archbishops and Bishops sign with their Christian name, followed by province or see (in the cases of diocesan bishops the see is sometimes in Latin).

REMAINDERS TO PEERAGES

A peerage created by patent descends according to the limitation mentioned in the patent of creation, usually to the heir male of the body of the first peer, but special remainders are sometimes granted to others of the family (eg to daughters, brothers or sisters, etc, and the heirs male of their bodies). War leaders such as Nelson, Kitchener, Allenby, Mountbatten and Portal, if there was no male issue to inherit, were given special remainders for the peerages to have an extra chance of survival.

The complicated succession to Baronies which are held to have been created by a writ of summons to Parliament and the doctrine of abeyance have been discussed in detail in the Complete Peerage, Vol IV, Appendix H.

In the Peerage of Scotland remainders vary according to the limitation. The destination may be to heirs male whatsoever (ie to the senior male heir, despite the extinction of the male line descending from the first peer), heirs male of the body, heirs male of tailzie (entailed estates), heirs whatsoever (ie whether male or female), or a succession according to a series of named individuals. Some Scottish peerages were granted with "shifting remainders." An example is the Earldom of Selkirk. When a line of Earls became extinct, the next son of the Duke of Hamilton inherited. This occurred in 1885 and again in 1940 and 1997. Until the Act of Union 1707, Scottish Peerages were capable of being surrendered to the Crown, who re-conferred them with different remainders.

In the Peerage of Ireland succession descends according to the limitation. Though the origin of the more ancient peerages is not always known, it is held that there are now only two which could pass in the female line. These are the Viscountcy of Massereene and the Barony of Loughneagh, created in the 16th century, with remainder, in default of issue male, to the heirs general. Both of these are held by Viscount Massereene and Ferrard.

Legitimated children are included in the Peerage articles, but are not normally in remainder to the peerage concerned, a possible exception being that persons of Scottish domicile may be in remainder to a Peerage of Scotland.

LIFE PEERS AND PEERESSES

Prior to the passing of the Life Peerages Act of 1958 the only Life Peers were the Lords of Appeal in Ordinary and no women sat in the House of Lords. Since then, however, men and women have been appointed peers or peeresses and rank as Barons or Baronesses for life. Each is entitled to a writ of summons to attend, and to sit and vote in the House of Lords.

The Life Barons' wives rank as Baronesses, and are entitled to the prefix of "Lady," while their children, and those of Life Baronesses, are styled "Hon" for life and hold special precedence.

Lords of Appeal in Ordinary hold office during good behaviour, notwithstanding the demise of the Crown, but may be removed from such office, on the address of both Houses or Parliament.

DISCLAIMING OF PEERAGES

The Peerage Act 1963, which received Royal Assent on 31 July 1963, authorised the disclaimer for life of certain hereditary peerages. The principal provisions are summarized below.

(1) *Disclaimer of certain hereditary Peerages*
A person subsequent to this Act who is already a peer or who succeeds to a peerage of England, Scotland, Great Britain or the United Kingdom may, by an instrument of disclaimer delivered to the Lord Chancellor, disclaim that peerage for life.

The instrument for one who succeeds to a peerage shall be delivered within the period of 12 months beginning with the day of succession to the peerage. If the person is under 21 on succession, the period of 12 months begins with the day he attains that age. No instrument shall be delivered in respect of a peerage by one who has applied for a writ of summons to attend the House of Lords.

The period for one who succeeded before the commencement of this Act is 12 months beginning with the commencement of the Act, or if under 21, 12 months beginning with the day he attains that age. An instrument of disclaimer may be delivered notwithstanding that he has applied before commencement of this Act, for a writ of summons to attend the House of Lords.

In either case, in reckoning the period for delivery of the instrument, no account shall be taken of time during which, to the satisfaction of the Lord Chancellor, the person is rendered by infirmity incapable of exercising or determining whether to exercise his rights.

(2) *Disclaimer by MPs and Parliamentary Candidates*
The period for an MP who succeeds to a peerage is one month beginning with the date of succession. Until that period expires he shall not, by virtue of that peerage, be disqualified from membership of the House of Commons, whether or not he has delivered an instrument of

disclaimer, provided he does not sit or vote in the House of Commons whilst exempt from disqualification, or that he has not applied for a writ of summons to attend the House of Lords.

Where a person who succeeds to a peerage has been or is nominated at a Parliamentary election, held in pursuance of a writ issued before his succession, he shall not be disqualified by virtue of that peerage for election to the House of Commons at that election, unless he has applied for a writ of summons to the House of Lords. If he is elected, the above time limit will apply to him as if he had succeeded to the peerage immediately after the declaration of the result of the election.

Where an instrument of disclaimer is delivered by a person to whom this section applies, a copy shall be delivered by the Speaker.

In reckoning the period, no account shall be taken of any time during which (a) proceedings are pending on any parliamentary election petition in which the right to be elected or returned to the House of Commons is in issue (b) the person is shown to the satisfaction of the Speaker to have any infirmity as in Section 1 (c) Parliament is prorogued, or both Houses are adjourned for more than 4 days. If Parliament is dissolved during the period for delivery of disclaimer, the provisions of this section shall cease to apply to him in respect of the peerage in question.

(3) *Effects of Disclaimer*

The disclaimer of a peerage shall be irrevocable, and shall operate from the date by which the instrument is delivered to divest him, and his wife, of all right and interest to or in the peerage, and all titles, rights, offices, and privileges and precedence attaching thereto, and to relieve him of all obligations and disabilities (including any disqualification in respect of membership of the House of Commons and elections to that House) arising therefrom, but shall not accelerate the succession to that peerage nor affect its devolution on his death.

Where a peerage is disclaimed, no other hereditary peerage shall be conferred, and no writ of acceleration shall be issued in respect of that peerage to the person so entitled on his death.

STYLES AND PRECEDENCE OF THE CHILDREN OF PEERS WHO DISCLAIM THEIR PEERAGES
Statement issued by Garter King of Arms

Paragraph 4(b) of the Report of the Joint Committee on House of Lords Reform recommended that "the wife and descendants of a Peer who surrenders should not use the courtesy titles or enjoy the social precedence derived from such a Peer." The Peerage Act 1963, however, while dealing in terms with the effect of disclaimer on a disclaiming Peer himself and his wife, does not so deal with the effect on his children. This has, therefore, to be inferred and it might be argued on the one hand that the children of a Peer who disclaims are no longer the children of a Peer and so no longer enjoy the style and precedence which they would have enjoyed as such. Or it might be argued on the other hand that the Act does not deprive them of the styles and precedence they have enjoyed prior to their father's disclaimer and they may, therefore, still enjoy these just as the daughters of a peer continue to do so even if their father has died leaving no heir to his peerage."

The Home Office, which is concerned with precedence through the Home Secretary's responsibility for advising the Sovereign on Petitions for special precedence, has so far been unwilling to express a view on the point of law or to deal with the matter by recommending the issue of a Royal Warrant.

It is, therefore, necessary for the Earl Marshal, as the principal authority under The Crown for matters connected with style and precedence, to decide on a policy in the situation as it at present stands.

The Earl Marshal has been advised by Mr G. D. Squibb, QC, Norfolk Herald Extraordinary, that in his view the children of a disclaiming Peer retain their precedence as the children of a Peer and the same view has been expressed by the Lord Lyon King of Arms.

While, therefore, it is open to any child of a disclaiming Peer to say that he or she no longer wishes to be known by the courtesy title hitherto accorded him or her, in those cases where such children wish still to be accorded their courtesy titles the Earl Marshal and his Officers will so accord them.

PARLIAMENTARY QUALIFICATIONS OF SCOTTISH PEERS, IRISH PEERS, AND PEERESSES IN OWN RIGHT

The holder of a peerage in the peerage of Scotland shall have the same right to receive writs of summons to attend the House of Lords, and to sit and vote in that House, as the holder of a peerage in the peerage of the United Kingdom; and the enactments relating to the election of Scottish representative peers shall cease to have effect.

The holder of a peerage in the peerage of Ireland shall not by virtue of that peerage be disqualified—

(a) for being or being elected as a member of the House of Commons for any constituency in the United Kingdom, or

(b) for voting at elections for that House whether or not he is a Member of that House.

A woman who is the holder of an hereditary peerage in the peerage of England, Scotland, Great Britain or the United Kingdom shall (whatever the terms of the letters patent or other instrument, if any, creating that peerage) have the same right to receive writs of summons to attend the House of Lords, and to sit and vote in that House, and shall be subject to the same disqualifications in respect of membership of the House of Commons and elections to that House as a man holding that peerage.

DUKE This title (from Latin *Dux*, a leader) is the highest in our Peerage. As we have no "princes" outside the blood-royal, so pre-eminent in dignity is the ducal title that each royal prince, shortly after attaining his majority is usually created a Duke; the titular style of Prince, apart from the Prince of Wales, being one of courtesy. Thus, Prince Henry, son of King George V, was created *Duke* of Gloucester.

Since the title Duke signified Sovereign status, *eg* William the Conqueror was Duke of Normandy—it was not adopted until 1337, when Edward III conferred the Dukedom of Cornwall on his eldest son, the Black Prince. This was followed by Henry Duke of Lancaster in 1351. Both were created, in Parliament by the girding of the sword. Ceremonial attaching to the creation of this dignity was discontinued in 1615, and it now takes place by patent under the Great Seal.

Duke's coronet

The first subject to receive a dukedom who was not a member of the royal family, nor one nearly connected, was Sir William de la Pole, Marquess of Suffolk, who was created Duke of Suffolk in 1448.

There were no Dukedoms in existence during the reign of Elizabeth I, after the attainder of the Duke of Norfolk 1572, when the whole order according to Judge Blackstone "became utterly extinct." The Ducal order was revived in England by James I in the person of his favourite, George Villiers, Duke of Buckingham.

A Duke is styled *Most Noble* (or less formally *His Grace*), and by the Sovereign in public instruments, *Our right trusty and right entirely beloved cousin*, with the addition of *and counsellor* when a member of the Privy Council.

MARQUESS   The term *Marchio* was applied in the Norman period to the Earl or Baron guarding the Welsh or Scottish Marches, or border territories. Similarly in Germany the Count or Graf became known as the Markgraf, anglicised to Margrave. By the twelfth century it had lost its territorial significance. It was introduced to England by Richard II, brother-in-law of the Margrave of Brandenburg, the honour being conferred upon Robert de Vere, Earl of Oxford, who became Marquess of Dublin in 1385. The precedence between Dukes and Earls caused great offence to the latter, and the patent was revoked in 1386 in favour of the Dukedom of Ireland. The next recipient did not appreciate the degree. When John Beaufort, Marquess of Dorset, was attainted and the House of Commons appealed to Richard II for its restoration, Beaufort begged the king not to restore this particular title "as the name of Marquess is a strange name in this realm."

Marquess's coronet

The creation to this dignity was formerly attended with nearly the same ceremony as that of a duke.

The style of a marquess is *Most Honourable*. He is formally styled by the Sovereign, *Our right trusty and entirely beloved cousin* (*and counsellor* when of the Privy Council).

EARL   Before Canute an ealdorman administered a shire or province for the King. In Latin documents he was styled *Dux* or *Comes*, taking a place between the royal Atheling and the thegn. Under Canute the Danish equivalent of Earl was introduced.

Under the Normans the government of an earl was normally restricted to one county and became hereditary, though losing the functions of the King's representation in the county to the sheriff. An earl was usually invested with the third penny out of the sheriff's court of the county, of Anglo-Saxon origin.

The dignity was created by the girding on of the sword as a symbol of temporal authority, but this lost some of its significance when in 1328 Roger Mortimer was created Earl of March, derived neither from a county nor a city. The ceremony continued after earls were created by patent, and in the reign of Edward VI a cape of dignity and a golden circlet were added to the ceremony, but in 1615 such ceremonies ceased.

Earl's coronet

Earldoms were originally created in fee, but from the reign of Richard II they were either created for life or in tail male.

An Earl is styled *Right Honourable*, and is formally addressed by the Sovereign as *Our right trusty and entirely beloved cousin* (*and counsellor* when of the Privy Council.)

VISCOUNT   This title had its origin in the office of the deputy or the lieutenant (*Vice-Comes*) of a Count, which had become hereditary in the Empire by the beginning of the tenth century. It was also used as the Sheriff of a county. Henry VI, crowned King of England and France, created John Lord Beaumont in 1440 Viscount Beaumont in England and Viscount Beaumont in France (a title forfeited by the Duke of Alençon in 1415, and vacant on the death of the Duke of Bedford 1435), in order to integrate the titles of the two countries. The peerage title received precedence above all Barons, but it did not become popular until the seventeenth century. Viscounts were always created by patent.

Viscount's coronet

A Viscount's style is *Right Honourable*. He is addressed by the King or Queen as *Our right trusty and well-beloved cousin* (*and counsellor* when of the Privy Council).

BARON   Barons were introduced into England by the Normans, most of whom held that rank in Normandy before the Conquest. Baron meant literally a man, being the King's tenant in chief, ie holding his land directly from him. The burgesses and leading citizens of London were also known collectively as Barons, and this style was allowed them by clerks who wrote the writs of William II and Henry I. The barons of the Cinque Ports are a parallel to the barons of

London (see "Norman London" by Sir Frank Stenton, and "Social Life in Early England" edited by Geoffrey Barraclough, 1960). In the thirteenth century they were summoned to the Counsel or Parliament, but at first this did not imply that a successor would necessarily also be summoned to subsequent Parliaments. The more important would probably be summoned, but by the reign of Edward III it became usual for successors to receive writs as a matter of course. Thus the Baronage emerged into an hereditary dignity of the Peerage.

Baron's coronet

The first baron created BY PATENT was John Beauchamp de Holt, created Baron Kidderminster, by Richard II in 1387 with remainder to his heirs male, but baronies by writ also continued to be created long after this date.

The succession to baronies by writ is not limited to heirs male, but is vested in heirs-general. In the event of the death without male issue of a baron by writ the title will fall into abeyance should he leave two or more daughters, and so will continue until only one daughter or the sole heir of one of the daughters survives. The Crown can, however, at any time terminate the abeyance in favour of any one of the co-heiresses, but it cannot alienate the barony from the representatives of the first baron.

When a baron is called to the House of Peers by writ of summons, the writ is in the Sovereign's name.

A baron is styled *Right Honourable* and formally by the Sovereign *Right trusty and well-beloved* (*and counsellor* when a Member of the Privy Council).

In Scotland, Sir George Mackenzie, Lord Advocate to Charles II, made it clear that the equivalent of Barons in England are Lords of Parliament in Scotland, as the word "Baron" in Scots law relates to Feudal Barons. This claim was immediately and correctly put forward by several Scottish Lords when they received summons as Barons to the House of Lords. Their protests were accepted and they were sent fresh summonses as Lords.

LORDS OF SESSION IN SCOTLAND

AND CHAIRMAN OF SCOTTISH LAND COURT

are the Senators of the College of Justice in Scotland, and on appointment to the Bench take the judicial title of Lord——, with the prefix of "The Hon", by which they are known and addressed (though they subscribe by their initials and surname), with the exception of the Lord Justice-General and Lord Justice-Clerk. Both of these are not usually described by the judicial title by which they take their seats but by their official designations, being primarily Officers of State.

By Royal Warrant granted in February 1905, Scottish Lords of Session who have retired are permitted to retain the title of "The Honourable Lord," while their wives are also granted the title of "Lady," to be retained after the decease of the husband, but during widowhood only.

Since 1912, a chairman of Scottish Land Court receives a Judicial title, by which he is always known both in office and retirement. He is treated as a Lord of Session.

BARONETS

The term baronet was first applied to the nobility who lost the right of individual summons to Parliament; and in this sense was used in a statute of Richard II. It is said that Sir Robert Cotton's discovery of William de la Pole's patent in the 13th year of Edward III, conferring upon him the dignity of a Baronet in return for a sum of money, suggested the revival of the Order.

The hereditary Order of Baronets in England was erected by Letters Patent by King James I on 22 May 1611, for the settlement of Ireland. He offered the dignity to 200 gentlemen of good birth, with a clear estate of £1,000 a year, on condition that each one should pay into the King's Exchequer in three equal instalments a sum equivalent to three years' pay to 30 soldiers at 8d per day per man. The first instalment was to be paid on the delivery of the patent. The Baronets form the sixth division of *Nobiles Majores*, following the five degrees of the Peerage.

The *Baronetage of Ireland* was erected on 30 September 1611; the *Baronetage of Scotland* or *Nova Scotia* on 28 May 1625, for the establishment of the plantation of Nova Scotia. After the union of England and Scotland in 1707 no further Baronets of England or Scotland were created, the style being changed to Baronet of Great Britain. With the union of Great Britain and Ireland in 1801, all Baronets subsequently created were under the style of the United Kingdom.

The Official Roll of Baronets was first gazetted 23 February 1914. By a further Royal Warrant dated 10 March 1922, anyone who considers he is entitled to be enrolled therein is at liberty to petition the Crown through the Home Secretary. Every person succeeding to a Baronetcy must exhibit his proofs of succession to the Secretary of State. Should the Secretary of State find any difficulty in advising the Crown as to any claim, he refers the matter to the Law Officers for their opinion, and further, may, on consideration of that opinion, direct that the matter be referred to the specially appointed Committee of the Privy Council for examination and advice to the Crown. The Roll is kept at the Home Office by the Registrar of the Baronetage.

The Standing Council of the Baronetage, was founded in 1898 to maintain the ancient rights and privileges of the Degree.

A baronet's wife is entitled to the prefix of either "Dame" (followed by christian name) or "Lady" without christian name, but the former style is now only used in legal and formal documents.

A baronet's helmet is depicted as for a knight.

Privileges Under the first Letters Patent it was ordained that only two hundred Baronets of England were to exist at any one time. This limitation was soon withdrawn. No degree or dignity, etc, was ever to be created which would be superior or equal to the degree and dignity of Baronet.

Under the second Letters Patent it was stated that no person or persons should have place between Baronets and the younger sons of Viscounts and Barons. Privileges included the right of knighthood for Baronets and their eldest sons, and the addition of the Arms of Ulster as a canton or inescutcheon in armorial bearings, argent a sinister hand couped at the wrist and erect gules, known as the Badge of Ulster. A third Letters Patent, ratified and confirmed the above, and included the precedence of the eldest sons of Baronets before eldest sons of knights whatever the order, and with similar provisions respecting other sons. *Baronets of Ireland* have similar privileges except that in some cases the Baronets of Ireland have used a dexter hand for the Badge of Ulster. *Baronets of Scotland* or *Nova Scotia* were to enjoy the same privileges except the Ulster augmentation, and in addition grants of land in Nova Scotia, with plenary baronial rights and jurisdiction, and legislative powers in that plantation, but such grants ceased in 1683. They were given precedence above lesser Barons in Scotland, the addition of the Arms of Nova Scotia in armorial bearings, power to sit and vote by deputy in the Scottish Parliament when absent from the Kingdom, and the right to wear about the neck the badge of Nova Scotia, suspended by an orange-tawny ribbon. This consists of an escutcheon argent with a saltire azure thereon, an inescutcheon of the arms of Scotland, with an Imperial Crown above the escutcheon, and encircled with the motto *Fax mentis Honestae Gloria*. This Badge may be shown suspended by the ribbon below the shield of arms.

Badge of Ulster

Badge of Nova Scotia

Baronets of England and Ireland applied to Charles I for permission to wear a badge. Although a badge was worn in the 17th century, of which specimens still exist, it was not until 1929 that King George V granted permission to all baronets other than those of Scotland to wear round their necks a Badge. This was composed of the Arms of Ulster, on a silver field, a left hand gules, surmounted by an Imperial Crown, enamelled in proper colours, the whole enclosed by an oval border embossed with scroll work of (4) roses for baronets of England, (2) shamrocks for baronets of Ireland, (3) roses and thistles for baronets of Great Britain, and (4) roses, thistles and shamrocks combined for baronets of UK. The

Badge of Baronets of the United Kingdom

badge to be suspended from an orange riband with a narrow edge of dark blue on both sides, the total breadth to be 1¾ inches, and the breadth of each to be ¼ inch. The Badge may be shown suspended by its riband below the shield of arms. Baronets wishing to wear this badge may purchase it at their own expense. Application should be made to the Registrar of the Baronetage or the Standing Council of the Baronetage, if a Member of that body.

Baronets were accorded the courtesy title of Honourable from the erection of the degree, but this fell into disuse at the beginning of the 19th century. Despite petitions, this privilege has not been conceded by the Crown.

George IV revoked the privilege of demanding knighthoods for the eldest sons or heirs apparent of Baronets upon attaining their majority, but without prejudicing Letters Patent granted before 19 December 1827.

In 1874, Ludlow Cotter, son of Sir James Lawrence Cotter, 4th baronet of Rockforest, when 21 years of age, received the honour of knighthood. This is the latest instance of the privilege being exercised. Since then few claims have been made and they have all been refused, presumably on the ground that it was unconstitutional for a Sovereign to bind his successors to confer titles in the future on persons unborn.

REMAINDERS TO BARONETCIES

The destination of a baronetcy is in accordance with the limitation mentioned in the patent of creation. Though this is usually to the heirs male of the body of the first baronet, special remainders were sometimes granted (eg North of Southwell, 1920, failing heirs male of the body, to the male issue of daughters of the first baronet).

Baronetcies of Nova Scotia, or Scotland, were sometimes created with remainder to heirs male (ie the heir male of the first baronet, despite the extinction of his own descendants in the male line) and "heirs male and of tailzie". There are four existing Scottish baronets with the last remainder, whose descent, together with entail of estates, may pass to the heir general, viz Dalyell of the Binns, Dunbar of Hempriggs, Hope-Dunbar of Baldoon, and Stirling-Maxwell of Pollok, of whom the holder of the Dunbar of Hempriggs creation is a Baronetess.

Legitimated children are included in the Baronetage articles but are not normally in remainder to the baronetcy concerned. A possible exception is that a person of Scottish domicile may be in remainder to a Nova Scotia baronetcy.

KNIGHTS

Knighthood was a medieval institution of chivalry of both a religious and military character. Its

birth and growth in Europe is obscure. It was conferred upon sovereigns, princes and others of
noble rank, but not on ecclesiastics. The word has an affinity with horsemanship, a Roman knight,
eques, a horseman, had held rank next below the Senatorial. The name thus indicates its original
occupation as a military equestrian, hence the German Ritter and the French Chevalier. In old
English *cnight* meant at first a youth or military follower, and later a trusted servant.

Knighthood was introduced to England at least as early as the reign of Alfred the Great, who
made his grandson, Athelstan, a knight, and gave him a scarlet mantle set with precious stones
and a sword with a golden scabbard.

With the arrival of the Normans, knights formed an integral part of the feudal system.
In the Conqueror's time there were about 5,000 knights who served as fighting men under

the command of the King's Barons. The Barons granted them some of their lands in
return for military service when required, *ie*, by knight-service, theoretically for
periods not exceeding forty days. The knights in turn granted lands to sub-tenants,
and by 1100 there was a system of commuting military service by payment of money
known as scutage or shield money. Henceforward those in possession of knights fees
did not necessarily take up knighthood. Those eligible received knighthood on
coming of age. As a result of this system, landless knights for service in the field

Knight's
helmet

came into existence, from whom evolved the knights bachelor.

In early times a knight was dubbed by his lord, his father or another knight.
William Rufus was knighted by Archbishop Lanfranc. Matthew Paris recorded that the Earl of
Gloucester invested his brother William with a military girdle, and Gilbert de Clare was knighted
by Simon de Montfort. Kings used to send their sons to neighbouring courts to receive the honour
of knighthood; thus Henry II sent to David I, King of Scots, and Malcolm IV, King of Scots to
Henry II and Edward I to the King of Castile.

By the reign of Henry III reluctance for taking up knighthood became apparent, and in 1244
that King introduced distraints of knighthood and summons to those who qualified, with a fine for
those who declined. Elaborate ceremonial and pageantry were then introduced, accompanied by
feasting and jousting to make knighthood more attractive. From those who did not take up
knighthood arose the esquire class.

Two main methods of conferring knighthood were used in the Middle Ages. The simpler form
used on the battle-field was for the knight elect to kneel before the commander of the army who
struck him with the sword on his back and shoulder with words such as "Avancez chevalier au
nom de Dieu". The more elaborate method of knighting for which the dubbing became restricted to
the King took place on special occasions. This included presentation of robes, arms and spurs, and
was accompanied by vigil and bathing before being dubbed. This later evolved into the Knighthood
of the Bath, of whom knights were created at coronations, royal marriages, etc. The first record of
these knights is at the coronation of Henry IV, but they were not banded into any Society or Order
such as the Garter, founded by Edward III about 1348, until the reign of George I.

Knights Banneret were created from personal distinction in battle rather than on feudal tenure,
and were conferred on the field. All the greater nobility were entitled to bear banners, and on the
creation of a banneret the points of his pennon were ceremoniously cut by the commander of the
army. The last three Knights Banneret are believed to have been conferred by the Protector
Somerset after the Battle of Pinkie, 1547, upon Sir Ralph Fane, Sir Francis Bryan and Sir Ralph
Sadler.

See Orders of Knighthood for information concerning the various Orders of Chivalry.

The use of prefix "Sir" is not borne by honorary knights of these orders when, as is usually the
case, the accolade has not been conferred and no special warrant has been granted permitting use
of this appellation. This also applies to clerics of the Established Church, who likewise do not
receive the accolade (their wives being entitled to precedence, but not to style of "Lady").

The Imperial Society of Knights Bachelor has its Registry at 21 Old Buildings, Lincoln's Inn,
WC2.

The wife of a knight is entitled to the prefix of either "Dame" (followed by christian name), or
"Lady" (without christian name), but the former style is now only used in legal documents.

A knight's helmet is depicted with visor up and without bars. The seventeenth century English
rule that the helmet must be full faced may now be disregarded if inconvenient for the design of
the crest.

In 1926 a Badge was granted for the use of Knights Bachelor. (See Orders of Knighthood.)

ESQUIRES

Esquire (Latin, *scutarius*, shield-bearer) was a personal attendant on a knight, which evolved into
an apprentice knight, and later into a lord of a manor. The numbers were swelled by those of the
knightly class who did not take up knighthood. By the 14th century an esquire (armiger)
practically attained equality with a knight, both in function and privileges. With the rise of the
use of the term gentleman as a rank, it became increasingly difficult to know where the lower limit
should be drawn. Sir John Fearn, in his "Glory of Generositie" 1586, referred to four sorts of
esquires; by creation, birth, dignity, and office. He commented that this title "is no less abused and
profaned" than that of gentleman, and that "the degree of esquire is through custom tolerated to
many other sorts of gentlemen, but they all, or most of them, are. . .in function of some offices of
justice or government in the King's palace, as. . .annexed to the dignities of judges and barons of
the benches and courts of justice; to the advocates and procurators of the sovereign; to the degree
of sergeants at the coif; to the office of sheriff, escheator, and serjeant at arms; to the eldest born of
a baron and peer of the realm or of a knight, besides many others. But that the same should

descend from the father to the son, as the state of gentry doth, is mere fabulous. For the title of esquire of common right doth appertain to none, except that by creation he receives the same at the sovereign's hand, or else through the bearing of such an office as a dignity anent to the same, or else by right of birth as in cases aforesaid, and that through custom".

In 1580 Robert Glover, Somerset Herald drew up a list of those entitled and in 1681 an officer of arms, probably Dugdale, in a similar list, stated that heralds should only allow the title of esquire to 1, the heir male of the younger son of a nobleman; 2, the heir male of a knight; 3, those who by long prescription can show their lineal ancestors so styled; 4, sheriff of a county, a JP or those so styled in the King's commission (who cease to hold the title when the office ceases); 5, certain of the king's servants by reason of the office they bear, such as officers of arms, sergeants at arms, etc.

Esquire's helmet

To these should now be added Royal Academicians (included by George III), Companions, Commanders, Officers and Members of Orders of Knighthood and Chivalry, Sergeants at law, Queen's Counsel, Deputy Lieutenants and Commissioners of Lieutenancy, Commissioners of the Court of Bankruptcy, Masters of the Supreme Court; also persons to whom the Sovereign grants arms with the title of Esquire, persons who are styled Esquires by the Sovereign in their patents, commissions or appointments, and officers of and above the rank of Lieutenant RN, Captain in the Army and Flight Lieutenant.

An esquire's helmet is depicted with visor closed. The seventeenth century English rule that the helmet must be depicted in profile to the dexter may now be disregarded if inconvenient for the design of the crest. In Scotland the visor is garnished with gold.

Scottish Titles   Scottish law recognizes a number of special titles which fall under the jurisdiction of the Lord Lyon King of Arms, and are recognized by the Crown. Such recognized chiefly styles and territorial designations of chieftains (branch chiefs) and lairds are legally recorded as a part of the surname under Statute 1672, cap 47. A Scottish feudal baron is allowed the cap of dignity. Supporters are granted to chiefs of clans and ancient families, and feudal barons older than 1592.

GENTLEMEN

Originally gentlemen (Latin *gentilis*, Norman-French *gentil* and *gentilhomme*) meant no specific class but included barons, esquires and even franklins (free-tenants), ie all who were not ignoble. By the early 15th century it came to have a specific meaning. Sir George Sitwell contended that this arose from an Act of Parliament, 1413 (Statute I, Henry V, cap 5) that with all writs of action, personal appeals and indictments which involved processes of outlawry, the estate, degree or mystery of the defendant was to be stated. Thus in 1431, as printed in Feudal Aids, land-owners were classed as knights, esquires, gentlemen, yeomen, etc.

When gentlemen became regarded as a distinct order, they were associated with armigers, bearers of coats of arms. As late as the 15th century most of these were not granted in effect by the King, for the greater nobles maintained their own heralds and bestowed arms on their tenants. Sir George Sitwell asserted that heralds "were never authorised to make a gentleman", but Sir Anthony Wagner, Garter King of Arms (in *Heralds and Heraldry in the Middle Ages*, 1939) points out that there are many references as early as the reign of Henry VIII to grants containing an ennobling clause. Though a right to arms became decisive evidence of gentility, it is apparent from the records of the High Court of Chivalry that there were those who were non-armigerous who were allowed the status for other reasons, such as military rank held, the fact that the father held a certain office, or that the individual had influential relations. It is also clear that the manner of living had some effect, for a yeoman could be more wealthy than a gentleman, though he lived in rougher style. In one family various members were frequently accorded the rank of gentlemen, yeomen and husbandmen. Fearn in 1586 included a student of common law, a groom of the Sovereign's Palace, a churl's son made priest or canon, those brought up in the service of a Bishop or Baron, governors of cities, etc. Commissioned officers below the rank stated under esquire are given the rank of gentleman. The helmet is as for an esquire, though in Scotland there is a distinction in that a gentleman's helmet is ungarnished. Prior to 1672, Scots gentlemen were allowed shields only.

FOREIGN TITLES

Foreign titles cannot be valued in comparison with British ones, according to their nominal rank. Their devolution is different from and often much wider than the British peerage. Titles of the Holy Roman Empire descend to all male descendants in the male line *ad infinitum*, and certain of those of the old Italian States can be given or left by will at the pleasure of the holder. It was the practice for the Crown, on the advice of the Secretary of State for the Home Department, to grant licences for the use of foreign titles by those domiciled in this country. In 1930 King George V decided that no more licences for the use of foreign titles in this country should be granted. In 1932 a Royal Warrant was issued revoking all licences then in force, with the exception of those issued for the life of the holder and his heir apparent. At that time there were 31 dignities which were allowed under the exception clause.

ORDERS OF
KNIGHTHOOD AND CHIVALRY

CENTRAL CHANCERY OF THE ORDERS OF KNIGHTHOOD

St James's Palace, SW1A 1BH

Secretary   Lt-Col Robert Guy Cartwright.

The Central Chancery of the Orders of Knighthood is responsible for the provision and issue of insignia in connection with appointments to the Orders of Chivalry and other honours conferred by the Sovereign.

Collars are worn by KNIGHTS AND LADIES of the GARTER, THISTLE, and KNIGHTS AND DAMES GRAND CROSS OR GRAND COMMANDERS of the various Orders only on "Collar Days" and other special occasions, or when commanded by the Sovereign.

Collar Days are Easter Sunday, Ascension Day, Whit Sunday, Trinity Sunday, New Year's Day, Epiphany, Feb 6th (Accession Day), St. David, St. Patrick, Lady Day, April 21st (The Queen's Birthday), St George, St Philip and St. James, May 29th (Restoration of Royal Family), June 2nd (Coronation Day), 10th June (Duke of Edinburgh's Birthday), St John the Baptist, St. Peter, 4th Aug (Queen Elizabeth The Queen Mother's Birthday), St Michael and All Angels, All Saints, St. Andrew, and Christmas Day, and such other occasions of which due notification is given. Collars are also worn when attending the opening or prorogation of Parliament by the Sovereign, or when taking part in the Ceremony of an introduction of a Peer in the House of Lords, but not after sunset, nor when mounted on Ceremonial Parades, unless directions to that effect are specially given. With Uniform the Collar is placed under the shoulder board and is held in position by the pressure of the board. With Morning Dress the Collar is held in position by black cotton thread on a small gilt safety pin, the Collar hanging at equal distance back and front.

Only one Collar should be worn at a time.

When the Collar (from which the Badge is suspended) is worn, the Riband with its Badge should not be worn, but it may be replaced where appropriate by the Riband of another Order.

Collars are returnable to the Central Chancery upon the death of the holder.

KNIGHTS AND LADIES of the GARTER, THISTLE, and KNIGHTS AND DAMES GRAND CROSS of the various Orders are entitled to bear Supporters to their Arms.

On promotion to a higher class of an Order of Chivalry, the recipient should return the insignia of the lower class of that order to the Central Chancery, unless he or she has been honoured in both the Military and Civil Divisions of the same Order in which case the insignia of both Divisions may be worn and the post nominal letters of the senior class only may be used. The Orders of the Bath, Merit and the British Empire have a Military and Civil Division.

Instructions for the Wearing of Orders, Decorations, Miniatures with dress other than uniform will be found in the Preliminary Section. Instructions for wearing them with uniform is as laid down by the Service to which the recipient belongs or belonged. Ladies in uniform conform to the regulations for male holders.

THE MOST NOBLE ORDER OF THE GARTER

The Order of the Garter, constituted by King Edward III about August 1348, has, since June 28th, 1831, consisted of the Sovereign and twenty-four Knights Companions, such lineal descendants of King George I, as may have been elected, and of Sovereigns and extra Knights who have been admitted by special statutes. The Prince of Wales is a constituent part of the original institution.

The Habit and Ensigns of the Order are (*i*) A GARTER of dark blue velvet, edged with gold, bearing the motto, *Honi soit qui mal y pense,* in gold letters, with a buckle and pendant of gold, richly chased. (It is worn on the left, below the knee) (*ii*) A MANTLE of dark blue velvet lined with white taffeta, with a representation of the Garter encircling the Cross of St George on an escutcheon argent embroidered on the left shoulder, the Sovereign having the star. (*iii*) A HOOD of crimson velvet. (*iv*) A SURCOAT of crimson velvet, lined with white taffeta. (*v*) A HAT of black velvet, lined with white taffeta, and fastened thereto by a band of diamonds, a plume of white ostrich feathers. (*vi*) A COLLAR of gold (weighing thirty ounces, troy) consisting of twenty-four pieces, each in the form of a Garter surrounding the Tudor Rose, connected by twenty-four knots of chased gold, and pendent thereto (*vii*) the GEORGE, an enamelled figure of St. George on horseback, encountering the dragon. (*viii*) The LESSER GEORGE or BADGE of gold is worn pendent from a four-inch blue ribbon over the left shoulder. (*ix*) The STAR of eight points of silver, in the centre the Cross of St. George gules, encircled with the Garter. At death the Badge and Star are delivered up to Her Majesty

Insignia of the Order of the Garter.

by the Knight's male heir, the collar (with pendant Badge) and Garter being returned to the Central Chancery. The Queen's Royal Free Chapel of St George, Windsor Castle, is the chapel of the Order.

SOVEREIGN   HM The Queen

LADIES OF THE ORDER   HM Queen Elizabeth The Queen Mother, HRH The Princess Royal

ROYAL KNIGHTS COMPANIONS   HRH The Duke of Edinburgh, HRH The Prince of Wales, HRH The Duke of Kent, HRH The Duke of Gloucester.

EXTRA KNIGHTS COMPANIONS AND LADIES OF THE ORDER   Princess Juliana of the Netherlands, Grand Duke of Luxembourg, Queen of Denmark, King of Sweden, King of Spain, Queen of the Netherlands, Emperor of Japan

KNIGHTS COMPANIONS AND LADY OF THE ORDER   Earl of Longford, Marquess of Abergavenny, Duke of Grafton, Duke of Norfolk, Baron Richardson of Duntisbourne, Baron Carrington, Baron Callaghan of Cardiff, Baron Hailsham of St Marylebone, Viscount Leverhulme, The Duke of Wellington, Baron Bramall, Sir Edward Heath, Baron Sainsbury of Preston Candover, Viscount Ridley, Sir Ninian Stephen, Baron Kingsdown, Baron Ashburton, Baroness Thatcher, Sir Edmund Hillary, Duke of Devonshire, Sir Timothy Colman, Duke of Abercorn, Sir William Gladstone, Bt.

Prelate   The Bishop of Winchester

Chancellor   The Rt Hon Lord Carrington, KG, GCMG, CH, MC

Register   The Dean of Windsor

Garter Principal King of Arms   Peter Llewellyn Gwynn-Jones, CVO, FSA.

Usher of the Black Rod   General Sir Edward Jones, KCB, CBE

Secretary   David Hubert Boothby Chesshyre, LVO, FSA, Clarenceux King of Arms

THE MOST ANCIENT AND MOST NOBLE ORDER OF THE THISTLE

The date of the foundation of the Order of the Thistle is not known. When the Order was revived by King James VII and II in 1687 and by Queen Anne in 1703 it was narrated in the Royal Warrants that the Order had been instituted by "Achaius, King of Scots (of glorious memory)". This is now regarded as legendary. What seems more probable is that King Achaius instituted the veneration of St. Andrew who became the natural Patron Saint of

BADGE

STAR

THE COLLAR   AND BADGE.

Insignia of the Order of the Thistle.

the Order when in due time it was created. In "Les Souverains du Monde" (1722: Vol LV: P. 318) James II of Scotland is credited with "reviving" an Order of St Andrew in 1452 but it is to his eldest son and successor James III (1460-1488) that historical evidence now points as being the true founder of the Most Ancient and Most Noble Order of the Thistle. The order consists of the Sovereign and sixteen Knights.   Royal Knights and Extra Knights are admitted by special statutes in addition to the number of sixteen.

The insignia are (*i*) the STAR, consisting of a St. Andrew's cross of silver embroidery with rays emanating between the points of the cross; in the centre upon a field of gold, a Thistle of green heightened with gold, and surrounded by a circle of green, having thereon the motto in letters of gold, *Nemo me impune lacessit.* (It is worn affixed to the left breast.) (*ii*) The COLLAR of gold consists of thistles intermingled with sprigs of rue, pendant from the centre the St. Andrew of gold enamelled, with the gown green and the surcoat purple, bearing before him the cross enamelled white, and having round the image rays of gold going out from it in the form of a glory. (*iii*) The MANTLE is of green velvet bound with taffeta and tied with cords and tassels of green and gold; on the left shoulder is a representation of the Star of the Order. (*iv*) The BADGE (of gold enamelled) has on one side the image of St. Andrew with the cross before, enamelled as above described or cut in stone, and on the back enamelled a Thistle, gold and green, the flower reddish, with the before-mentioned motto round it, the Thistle on an enamelled green ground. (It is worn attached to a dark green ribbon passing over the left shoulder and resting on the right hip.) (*v*) The HAT is of black velvet, ornamented with white osprey plumes. At death the Badge and Star are delivered up to Her Majesty by the Knight's nearest male relative, the Collar (with pendant Badge) being returned to the Central Chancery. The Chapel of the Order is in St Giles's Cathedral, Edinburgh, and the Chancery at the Court of the Lord Lyon, HM New Register House, Edinburgh.

SOVEREIGN   HM The Queen

LADY OF THE ORDER   HM Queen Elizabeth The Queen Mother

ROYAL KNIGHTS   HRH The Duke of Edinburgh, HRH The Duke of Rothesay (The Prince of Wales)
KNIGHTS AND LADY OF THE ORDER   Earl of Wemyss and March, Sir Donald Cameron of Lochiel, Duke of Buccleuch, Earl of Elgin and Kincardine, Baron Thomson of Monifieth, Baron MacLehose of Beoch, Earl of Airlie, Capt Sir Iain Tennant, Viscount Younger of Leckie, Viscount of Arbuthnott, Earl of Crawford and Balcarres, Baron Macfarlane of Bearsden, Lady Marion Fraser, Baron Mackay of Clashfern.

Chancellor   The Duke of Buccleuch and Queensberry, KT, VRD.

Dean   The Very Rev Gilleasbuig Iain MacMillan, CVO.

Secretary   Sir Malcolm R. Innes of Edingight, KCVO, Lord Lyon King of Arms.

Usher of the Green Rod   Rear Adm C. H. Laymar, CB, DSC, LVO.

THE MOST HONOURABLE ORDER OF THE BATH

From Saxon times until the Coronation of King Charles II on great Royal occasions it was customary to confer "a degree of Knighthood" which, from the ceremonies associated with it, became known as the Knighthood of the Bath. Drawing on this ancient tradition, in 1725 King George I created a new military Order and called it the Order of the Bath. The Order was enlarged in 1815 and further extended in 1847, when new statutes regarding appointments were promulgated and the Civil branch established; the statutes were subsequently modified in 1905 and 1912. Under date of July 1925, all former statutes were repealed, and revised and consolidated statutes and ordinances were promulgated; these were further revised in 1930, 1936, 1939, 1969 and 1973. The Order now consists of three classes, each comprising two divisions (military and civil): (*i*) KNIGHTS AND DAMES GRAND CROSS. These Knights and Dames are entitled to receive a grant of supporters to their armorial bearings. (*ii*) KNIGHTS AND DAMES COMMANDERS. Each Knight of the Order is entitled to the distinctive appellation of knighthood. (*iii*) COMPANIONS. The Military division is open to Officers of the Navy, Army, and Air Force, and Naval, Military and Air Forces of the Commonwealth Countries. The Order consists of not more than 120 Knights and Dames Grand Cross (of whom the Great Master is the First and Principal), 355 Knights Commanders and Dames Commanders, and 1,870 Companions exclusive of Honorary Members and any Additional Members who may have been or may be appointed.

The Insignia are (*i*) the COLLAR of gold (weighing thirty ounces troy), composed of nine Imperial Crowns or and eight roses, thistles, and shamrocks, issuing from a gold sceptre, and

K.C.B. MILITARY. (STAR)

G.C.B. MILITARY. (STAR)

G.C.B. MILITARY. (COLLAR & BADGE)

K.C.B. MILITARY. (BADGE)

enamelled in their proper colours, linked together with seventeen knots enamelled argent, and having therefrom the Badge of the Order. (*ii*) The MILITARY KNIGHT AND DAME GRAND CROSS STAR is formed of rays of silver, charged with a Maltese cross or, in the centre whereof on the ground argent three Imperial Crowns, one and two or, the said three Imperial Crowns within a circle gules inscribed with the motto of the Order, *Tria juncta in uno*, in letters of gold, and the said circle encompassed by two branches of laurel proper, issuing from an escrol azure inscribed *Ich dien* in letters of gold. (*iii*) CIVIL KNIGHT AND DAME GRAND CROSS STAR is of rays of silver issuing from a centre and charged with three Imperial Crowns, one and two within a circle gules whereon is inscribed the motto of the Order in gold. The Collar and Badge are returned at death to the Central Chancery, but not so the investment Badge and Star. (*iv*) MILITARY KNIGHT AND DAME COMMANDER'S STAR is composed of four rays of silver, between each of which issues a smaller ray, also of silver, and has the same centre as the Knights Grand Cross, but without a gold Maltese cross thereon. (*v*) CIVIL KNIGHTS AND DAME COMMANDER'S STAR is of the same form and size, but without a laurel wreath round the circle containing the motto and the escrol, and without the words *Ich dien*

O.C.B. CIVIL (STAR)

O.C.B CIVIL (COLLAR & BADGE)

K.C.B. CIVIL (STAR)

K.C.B. CIVIL (BADGE)

underneath. (The Crowns in the Stars, which formerly were of different designs for the Civil and Military Divisions, are now all of the same pattern.) (*vi*) MILITARY BADGE is a gold Maltese cross of eight points, enamelled argent, edged gold, and terminating with small gold balls having in each of the four angles a lion passant guardant or and in the centre on a ground argent, the rose, thistle, and shamrock, issuing from a sceptre between three Imperial Crowns, all or,

C.B. MILITARY. (BADGE)

within a circle gules, thereon the motto of the Order, *Tria juncta in uno*, in gold letters and encompassed by two branches of laurel proper, issuant from an escrol azure inscribed *Ich dien* in letters of gold. (*vii*) CIVIL BADGE is of an oval shape, comprised of a rose, thistle, and shamrock, issuing from a sceptre between three Imperial Crowns, the whole pierced and encircled by the motto of the Order, all gold. The Badge is worn by Knights Grand Cross pendent from a four inch crimson riband, and by Dames Grand Cross pendent from a two and a quarter inch crimson riband passing from the

C.B. CIVIL (BADGE)

right shoulder obliquely to the left side. Knights Commanders wear the Badge of a smaller size suspended from the neck by a crimson ribbon of miniature width and wear on their left side a Star. Dames Commanders wear the Badge on a Bow except with coats of military pattern, when the Badge is worn in the same manner as a Knight Commander. The Bow and Star are both worn on the left side. Gentlemen Companions wear the Badge of a smaller size, on a crimson ribbon of miniature width suspended from the neck. Lady Companions wear this Badge on a Bow except with a coat of military pattern when the Badge is worn suspended on a ribbon from the neck. The Badge and Star of a KCB and a DCB and the Badge of a CB are not returned after death, but the Collar and Badge of a GCB should be returned to the Central Chancery of the Orders of Knighthood. The MANTLE of a Knight and Dame Grand Cross is of crimson satin lined with white taffeta and tied with a cordon of white silk with two tassels of crimson silk and gold attached thereto, on the left side of the mantle below a white silk lace is embroidered a representation of the Star of a Knight Grand Cross. The HAT is of black velvet, high crowned and with an upright plume of white feathers in the front. Henry VII's Chapel in Westminster Abbey has been the Chapel of the Order since 1725.

SOVEREIGN   HM The Queen

Great Master and First or Principal Knight Grand Cross   HRH The Prince of Wales.

Dean   The Dean of Westminster.

Bath King of Arms   General Sir Brian Kenny, GCB, CBE.

Secretary and Registrar   Rear Admiral D. E. Macey, CB.

Genealogist   Peter Llewellyn Gwynn-Jones, CVO, FSA, Garter Principal King of Arms.

Gentleman Usher of the Scarlet Rod   Air Vice-Marshal Sir Richard Peirse, KCVO, CB.

Deputy Secretary   The Secretary of the Central Chancery of the Orders of Knighthood.

THE ORDER OF MERIT

This is a very exclusive Order (the Ordinary Members of which do not exceed 24 in number), instituted by King Edward VII on 23 June 1902, by letters patent, but carries with it no special title or personal precedence.

The BADGE of the Order consists of a cross of red and blue enamel of eight points, having the words "For Merit" (the motto of the Order) in gold letters within a laurel wreath on a blue enamel centre. The reverse of the badge shows the Royal and Imperial cipher in gold (two silver swords with gold hilts, placed saltirewise between the angles of the cross, being added in the case of members chosen for naval or military distinction) also within a laurel wreath, on a blue enamel centre; and the whole is surmounted by the Imperial Crown enamelled in colour, and suspended by a parti-coloured ribbon of Garter blue and crimson, two inches broad. The Sovereign's insignia, except, of course for the modifications necessary to distinguish the Royal dignity of the wearer, is similar to the insignia worn by the ordinary members of the Order. The Badge of the Order is always worn round the neck by gentlemen, and may be suspended from Armorial Bearings, is never worn in miniature, and is not returnable at death. Ladies wear the Badge on a bow on the left side except with coats of military pattern when the Badge is worn in the same manner as by a gentleman. The ceremony of investiture is from time to time conducted by the Sovereign as in the case of any other Order. Members of the Order are entitled to attach a facsimile of its badge and ribbon to their arms, and add the letters OM after their names, after GCB. The Seal of the Order is a facsimile of the badge, impaled with the Royal Arms, on a white ground, with the legend, "The Seal of the Order of Merit." June 23rd is the anniversary of the Order. The Secretary and Registrar, who wears, as his badge of office, a decoration similar to that worn by the members of the Order, with the addition of two silver pens placed saltirewise between the angles of the cross. The Chancery of the Order is in the Central Chancery of the Orders of Knighthood.

SOVEREIGN   HM The Queen.

Secretary and Registrar   Sir Edward Ford, GCVO, KCB, DL.

Members   HRH The Duke of Edinburgh, Sir George Edwards, Rev Prof Owen Chadwick, Sir Andrew Huxley, Frederick Sanger, Prof Sir Ernst Gombrich, Dr Max Perutz, Dame Cicely Saunders, Baron Porter of Luddenham, Baroness Thatcher, Dame Joan Sutherland, Prof Francis Crick, Dame Ninette de Valois, Sir Michael Atiyah, Baron Jenkins of Hillhead, Lucien Freud, Mother Teresa (*d* 1997), Sir Aaron Klug, Sir John Gielgud, Baron Denning (*d* 1999), Baron Foster of Thames Bank, Sir Denis Rooke, Ted Hughes (*d* 1998), Cardinal Basil Hume (*d* 1999).

Honorary Member   Nelson Rohlilahla Mandela.

THE MOST EXALTED ORDER OF THE STAR OF INDIA

The Order of the Star of India was instituted by Queen Victoria in 1861, and enlarged 1866, 1875, 1897, 1902, 1911, 1915, 1920, 1927, and 1939, and the dignity of Knight Grand Commander was conferred on Princes or Chiefs of India, or upon British subjects for important and loyal service rendered to the Indian Empire; the second and third classes were for services in the Indian Empire of not less than thirty years in the department of the Secretary of State for India. It consists of the Sovereign, the first class of Knights Grand Commanders, the second class of Knights Commanders, and the third class of Companions. No appointments to this Order have been made since 14 August, 1947.

The Insignia are (i) the COLLAR of gold, composed of the lotus flower of India, of palm branches tied together in saltire, of the united red and white rose, and in the centre an Imperial Crown; all enamelled in their proper colours and linked together by gold chains.

THE COLLAR AND BADGE.

Insignia of the Order of the Star of India.

(ii) The STAR OF A KNIGHT GRAND COMMANDER is composed of rays of gold issuing from a centre, having thereon a star of five points in diamonds resting upon a light blue enamelled circular riband, tied at the ends and inscribed with the motto of the Order, *Heaven's Light our Guide,* also in diamonds. That of a Knight Commander is somewhat different, and is described below. (iii) The BADGE, on onyx cameo having Her Majesty Queen Victoria's Royal effigy thereon, set in a perforated and ornamented oval, containing the motto of the Order in diamonds ensigned with a star of five points, composed of silver. (iv) The MANTLE of light blue satin lined with white, and fastened with a cordon of white silk with two blue and silver tassels. On the left side a representation of the star of the Order. The Ribbon of the Order (four inches wide for Knights Grand Commanders) is light blue, having a narrow white stripe towards either edge, and is worn from the right shoulder to the left side. A KNIGHT COMMANDER wears (a) around his neck a ribbon two inches in width, of the same colours and pattern as a Knight Grand Commander, and pendent therefrom a badge of a smaller size, (b) on his left breast a STAR composed of rays of silver issuing from a gold centre, having thereon a silver star of five points resting upon a light blue enamelled circular ribbon, tied at the ends, inscribed with the motto of the Order in diamonds. A Companion wears suspended from the neck a badge of the same form as appointed for a Knight Commander, but of a smaller size pendent to a like ribbon of the breadth of one and a half inches. Only the GCSI Collar and Badge appendant are returnable at death to the Central Chancery.

Secretary and Registrar   The Secretary of the Central Chancery of Orders of Knighthood.

THE MOST DISTINGUISHED ORDER OF ST MICHAEL AND ST GEORGE

Ordinary Membership of the Order of St Michael and St George, which was instituted in 1818, and enlarged and extended in 1868, 1879, 1887, 1901, 1911, 1915, 1927, 1935, 1937, 1939, 1948, 1953, 1954, 1960, 1965, 1969 and 1974 is conferred on

THE COLLAR AND BADGE.

Insignia of the Order of St. Michael and St. George.

subjects of the Crown of the United Kingdom and certain classes of British protected persons, who may hold, or have held high and confidential offices, or may render or have rendered extraordinary and important services (other than military) within or in relation to any part of the British Dominions or Territories under British Protection or Administration, and in reward for important and loyal services in relation to foreign affairs. The Order consists of not more than one hundred and twenty Knights Grand Cross and Dames Grand Cross (of whom the Grand Master is the First and Principal), three hundred and ninety Knights Commanders and Dames Commanders, and one thousand seven hundred and seventy five Companions, exclusive of Honorary members, and any Additional members who have been or may be appointed. The Knights Grand Cross and Dames Grand Cross are entitled to bear supporters, and to surround their coats of arms with the Collar, circle, and Motto of the Order, and to suspend therefrom the Badge of the Order. The Knights Commanders, Dames Commanders and Companions are permitted to surround their arms with the circle and motto, from which is suspended the ribbon and Badge of the Order.

The Insignia are: (i) the STAR of the Knight Grand Cross and Dame Grand Cross which is composed of seven rays of silver having a small ray of gold between each of them, and over all the Cross of St. George gules; in the centre is the representation of the Archangel St. Michael holding in his dexter hand a flaming sword and trampling upon Satan, within a blue circle, inscribed with the motto, *Auspicium melioris aevi*, in letters of gold. The STAR for Dames being somewhat smaller than that for Knights. (ii) The COLLAR of gold, which is formed alternately of lions of England royally crowned, of Maltese crosses of white enamel, and of the cyphers S.M. and S. G. (also alternately), having in the centre the Imperial Crown over two winged lions, passant guardant, each holding in his fore paw a book and seven arrows; at the opposite end of the Collar are two similar lions, the whole linked together by small gold chains. The Chain for Dames is slightly smaller than that for Knights. (iii) The BADGE, which is a cross of fourteen points enamelled argent, edged gold, having in the centre on one side the Archangel St. Michael holding in his dexter hand a flaming Sword and trampling upon Satan, and on the other St. George on horseback and in armour with a spear encountering a dragon, each within a blue circle, on which is inscribed the motto of the Order in letters of gold; the Badge is ensigned by an Imperial Crown gold, and it is worn by the Knights Grand Cross and Dames Grand Cross (the Badge for Dames to be the same size as that for Knights Commanders) either attached to the Collar or to a four inch Saxon blue ribbon (for Knights Grand Cross) or to a two and one quarter inches ribbon (for Dames Grand Cross) with a scarlet central stripe, from the right shoulder to the left side. (iv) The MANTLE is of Saxon blue satin, lined with scarlet silk, tied with a cordon of blue and scarlet silk and gold, with two tassels of the same colours, and having on the left side an embroidered representation of the Star of the Order. Knight Commanders wear the Badge—one size smaller than the GCMG Badge—suspended on an Order ribbon of miniature width from the neck, and wear on their left side a STAR composed of four rays, thereon a small cross of eight points in saltire argent, surmounted by the Cross of St. George gules, and having the same centre as the Star of the Grand Crosses, while Dames Commanders wear a similar but slightly smaller Badge than Knights Commanders but tied in a bow and worn on the left shoulder, and they wear a slightly smaller Star. Companions wear the Badge or small Cross of the Order—smaller than the KCMG Badge—on an Order ribbon of miniature width, suspended from the neck; a Lady Companion wears the Badge on a bow one and three quarter inches wide and with an additional fitting on a ribbon suspended from the neck. The Chapel of the Order is in St. Paul's Cathedral, London. The Insignia of all classes of this Order are not returned at death, except in the case of the Collar of a Knight or Dame Grand Cross, provided it was awarded after 1948.

SOVEREIGN   HM The Queen

Grand Master   HRH The Duke of Kent, KG, GCMG, GCVO, ADC.

Prelate   The Rt Rev Simon Barrington-Ward, MA, Bishop of Coventry.

Chancellor   The Rt Hon Lord Carrington, KG, GCMG, CH, MC.

Secretary   The Permanent Under-Sec of State for the Foreign and Commonwealth Office.

Deputy Secretary   The Secretary of the Central Chancery of the Orders of Knighthood.

King of Arms   Sir Ewen Alastair John Fergusson, GCMG, GCVO.

Registrar   Sir John Alexander Noble Graham, Bt, GCMG.

Gentleman Usher of the Blue Rod   Sir John Oscar Moreton, KCMG, KCVO, MC.

Dean   The Dean of St. Paul's.

Honorary Genealogist   Peter Llewellyn Gwynn-Jones, CVO, FSA.

Chancery   Central Chancery of the Orders of Knighthood, St. James's Palace, SW1A 1BG.

THE MOST EMINENT ORDER OF THE INDIAN EMPIRE

This Order, instituted by HM Queen Victoria, Empress of India, 31 Dec 1877, and enlarged in 1886, 1887, 1892, 1897, 1902, 1911, 1915, 1920, 1927, and 1939, was conferred for services rendered to the Indian Empire, and consists of the Sovereign, Grand Commanders, Knights Commanders, and Companions. No appointments to this Order have been made since 14 August 1947.

The Insignia are: (*i*) The COLLAR of gold, formed of elephants, lotus flowers, peacocks in their pride, and Indian roses, in the centre the Imperial Crown, the whole linked together with chains; (*ii*) The STAR of the Knight Grand Commander, comprised of five rays of silver, having a smaller ray of gold between each of them, the whole alternately plain and scaled, issuing from a gold centre, having thereon Her Majesty Queen Victoria's Royal Effigy, within a purple circle, inscribed *Imperatricis Auspiciis*, in letters of gold, the circle ensigned by an Imperial Crown, also gold; (*iii*) The BADGE, consisting of a rose enamelled gules, barbed vert, and having in the centre Her Majesty Queen Victoria's Royal Effigy, within a purple circle, inscribed *Imperatricis Auspiciis*, in letters of gold ensigned with an Imperial Crown, also gold; (*iv*) The MANTLE is of purple satin, lined with and fastened by a cordon of white silk, with purple silk and gold tassels attached. On the left side a representation of the Star of the Order.

The ribbon of a KNIGHT GRAND COMMANDER is of Imperial purple and four inches in width. A Knight Commander wears: (*a*) around his neck a riband two inches in width, of the same colour

Insignia of the Order of the Indian Empire.

(Imperial purple) and pattern as a Knight Grand Commander, pendent therefrom a badge of smaller size: (b) on his left breast a star, similar to that of the first class, but the rays of which are alternately bright and chipped.

Only the GCIE Collar is returnable at death to the Central Chancery.

A Companion wears suspended from the neck a badge (not returnable at death) of the same form as appointed for a Knight Commander, but of smaller size, pendent from a like ribbon of the breadth of one and a half inches.

Secretary and Registrar   The Secretary of the Central Chancery of the Orders of Knighthood.

THE IMPERIAL ORDER OF THE CROWN OF INDIA

Instituted by Queen Victoria on 1 January 1878, to commemorate the assumption of the Imperial Title of Empress of India, and revised 14 May 1927, and 18 March 1939, this Order consists of the Sovereign, and of such of the Princesses of Her Majesty's Royal House, the wives or other female relatives of Indian Princes, and other Indian ladies, and of the wives or other female relatives of any of the persons who held the office of Viceroy and Governor-General of India, Governors of Madras, Bombay, or Bengal, or of Principal Secretary of State for India, or Commander-in-Chief in India. No appointments to this Order have been made since 14 August 1947.

The Order carries with it no title or precedence, but recipients are permitted to put the initials "CI" after their names, these being placed immediately before "GCVO".

The Badge of the Order consists of the Royal and Imperial Cypher of Queen Victoria, composed of the letters, V, R and I in diamonds, pearls, and turquoises, encircled by a border set with pearls, ensigned with the Imperial Crown jewelled and enamelled in proper colours, and is worn attached to a light blue watered riband, edged white, of an inch and a half in width, tied in a bow, on the left shoulder. The insignia is returnable at death to the Secretary of the Central Chancery of Orders of Knighthood, by whom the Register of the Order is kept.

SOVEREIGN   HM The Queen

LADIES OF THE ORDER   HM Queen Elizabeth The Queen Mother, HRH The Princess Margaret, Countess of Snowdon, HRH Princess Alice, Duchess of Gloucester.

THE ROYAL VICTORIAN ORDER

This Order, instituted by HM Queen Victoria, Empress of India, 21 April 1896, consists of the Sovereign, a Grand Master, Ordinary Members, and such Honorary Members as the

THE COLLAR   AND BADGE

Royal Victorian Order.

Sovereign shall from time to time appoint, the Members being divided into five classes, and designated respectively: (1) Knights and Dames Grand Cross, (2) Knights and Dames Commanders, (3) Commanders, (4) Members of the Fourth Class (now styled Lieutenants), and (5) Members of the Fifth Class. Under date of 29 May 1936, a Warrant was issued consolidating the Statutes of the Order so as to permit of its bestowal upon women.

The persons to be admitted as Ordinary Members of this Order shall be such persons, being male or female subjects of the British Crown, who, having rendered extraordinary, or important, or personal service to the Sovereign, merit Royal favour; and the Honorary Members of the several classes consist of those Foreign Princes and persons upon whom the Sovereign may think fit to confer the honour of being received into the Order.

The Members of the several grades in the Order are to have place and precedence as follows:—Knights Grand Cross immediately after Knights Grand Commanders of the Order of the Indian Empire, Dames Grand Cross immediately before Dames Grand Cross of the Order of the British Empire, Knights Commanders immediately after Knights Commanders of the Order of the Indian Empire, Dames Commanders immediately before Dames Commanders of the Order of the British Empire, men who are Commanders immediately after Companions of the Order of the Indian

Empire, women who are Commanders immediately before women who are Commanders of the Order of the British Empire, men who are Members of the Fourth Class (now Lieutenants) immediately after Companions of the Distinguished Service Order, women who are Members of the Fourth Class (now Lieutenants) immediately before women who are Officers of the Order of the British Empire, men who are Members (formerly of the Fifth Class) immediately after Companions of the Imperial Service Order, and women who are Members (formerly of the Fifth Class) immediately before women who are Members of the Order of the British Empire.

The number of the Members is unlimited, and the anniversary of the Order is the Twentieth day of June every year, being the day of Her late Majesty Queen Victoria's Accession to the Throne of these Realms.

The MANTLE of a Knight or Dame Grand Cross is of dark blue satin, edged with red satin two inches in width, the edging of the collar being half an inch wide, lined with white silk, the mantle being fastened by a cordon of dark blue silk and gold, having two dark blue silk and gold tassels attached thereto; on the left side of the mantle is embroidered a representation of the Star of a Knight or Dame Grand Cross of the Order. The COLLAR is of gold, composed of octagonal pieces and oblong perforated and ornamental frames alternately, linked together with gold; the said pieces edged and ornamented with gold, each containing upon a blue enamelled ground a gold rose jewelled with a carbuncle, and the said frames are of gold each containing a portion of the inscription "Victoria . . . Brit. Reg . . . Def Fid . . . Ind Imp" in letters of white enamel; in the centre of the collar, within a perforated and ornamental frame of gold, is an octagonal piece, enamelled blue, edged with red, and charged with a white saltire, thereon a gold medallion of Her late Majesty Queen Victoria's effigy, from which hangs the Cross of the Order (detachable).

The BADGE of Knights and Dames Grand Cross consists of white enamelled Maltese cross of eight points; on an oval centre of crimson enamel the Royal and Imperial cypher of Queen

Victoria (VRI) in gold, within a blue enamelled circle, thereon the motto of the Order, namely, "Victoria" in letters of gold, the circle being surmounted by an Imperial Crown enamelled in proper colours; and is worn over the right shoulder, suspended from a dark blue ribbon with a narrow edge either side of three stripes—red, white, and red—of the breadth of three inches and three-quarters in the case of Knights Grand Cross and of two inches and one quarter in the case of Dames Grand Cross, passing from the right shoulder to the left side.

G.C.V.O. and D.C.V.O. Badge.

The STAR of Knights and Dames Grand Cross consists of a silver chipped star of eight points; in the centre a representation of the Badge of the First Class of the Order.

The Knights Commanders wear around their necks a ribbon of miniature width of the same colours as that of the Knights Grand Cross, of the breadth of one inch and three-quarters, and pendent therefrom the badge, which is of the same pattern as, but of smaller size than, that of a Knight Grand Cross, whilst the Dames Commanders wear their badges attached to a Riband tied in a bow and worn on the left shoulder. The Star is composed of a Maltese cross in silver, with smaller rays issuing from the centre between the angles of the cross; in the centre the badge of the Order as before described, with the cross in frosted silver instead of white enamel.

Men who are Commanders wear around their necks the like riband and badge as that appointed for the Knights Commanders and women wear the bow and badge as appointed for Dames Commanders, but neither is entitled to wear the Star.

The Lieutenants (formerly Members of the Fourth Class) wear a badge of the same form and appearance as that appointed for the Commanders, but of smaller size, pendent from a ribbon of the same colours, of the breadth of an inch and a quarter, attached from the left breast in the case of men and tied in a bow and worn on the left shoulder in the case of women.

The Members wear, from their left breast or shoulder, the same riband and badge as that appointed for the Lieutenants, with the exception that the cross is of frosted silver instead of white enamel.

In uniform ladies wear their insignia in the same way as that adopted for male holders.

The collar is returnable at death or upon receipt of a Collar of an Order of Higher rank, but not the other Insignia.

The Queen's Chapel of the Savoy has been the Chapel of the Order since 1938.

("The Royal Victorian Medal" (silver-gilt, silver, or bronze, having on the obverse the Royal effigy, and on the reverse the Royal and Imperial cypher upon an ornamental shield within a wreath of laurel, in base a scroll, thereon the words "Royal Victorian Medal") was also instituted by Queen Victoria. This Medal is worn by men on the left breast of the coat or outer garment pendent from a ribbon of the breadth of one inch and a quarter of the same colour and pattern as that appointed for the members of the Royal Victorian Order, and by women from a ribbon tied in a bow on the left shoulder.)

SOVEREIGN   HM The Queen

Grand Master   HM Queen Elizabeth The Queen Mother.

Chancellor   The Lord Chamberlain.

Secretary   The Keeper of the Privy Purse.

Registrar   The Secretary of the Central Chancery of the Orders of Knighthood.

Chaplain Rev John Robson, LVO, AKC.

Hon Genealogist David Hubert Boothby Chesshyre, LVO, FSA, Clarenceux King of Arms.

ROYAL VICTORIAN CHAIN

King Edward VII founded in Aug 1902 the "Royal Victorian Chain", which is only bestowed on special occasions, and, although forming no part of the Royal Victorian Order, may be worn on all occasions when other insignia of British Orders of Chivalry are worn; it is of a different and much lighter design than the Collar.

HOLDERS OF ROYAL VICTORIAN CHAIN

HM The Queen, HM Queen Elizabeth The Queen Mother, Princess Juliana of the Netherlands, King of Thailand, Crown Prince Asfa Wossen of Ethiopia, King Mohamed Zahir Shah of Afghanistan, Queen of Denmark, King of Nepal, King of Sweden, Queen of the Netherlands, General Antonio Eanes, Dr Freiherr von Weizsäcker, Baron Coggan, King Fahd of Saudi Arabia, King of Spain, HRH The Princess Margaret, Countess of Snowdon, Baron Runcie, Baron Charteris of Amisfield, King of Norway, Earl of Airlie.

THE MOST EXCELLENT ORDER OF THE BRITISH EMPIRE

This Order, instituted by HM King George V in June 1917, extended Dec 1918, and altered March 1919, Dec 1922, June 1929, Nov 1933, March 1937, and Oct 1939, is conferred for important services rendered to the Empire, and is awarded to both men and women. It consists of the Sovereign and five classes:—(I) Knights Grand Cross and Dames Grand Cross, (II) Knights Commanders and Dames Commanders, (III) Commanders, (IV) Officers, (V) Members. Foreign persons upon whom the Order is conferred are "Honorary."

Further alterations to the Statutes of the Order were made in September 1959, May 1962, July 1964 and September 1969, limiting the numbers to be admitted to the Order in future, as follows:—

Knights and Dames Grand Cross (not to exceed Military 27, Civil 73),   Knights and Dames Commanders (not to exceed Military 215, Civil 630), and Commanders (not to exceed Military 1,660, Civil 7,300), specifying the numbers of each of these Classes that may be appointed in a given period;

also Officers (Military not more than 713 in any year, Civil not more than 745 in any year); and Members (Military not more than 228 in any year, Civil not more than 1,256 in any year).

The above-mentioned limitation does not affect those already admitted to the Order prior to 29 December 1922, who are not to be included within the foregoing numbers allotted to each Class of the Order, nor additional appointments made by special statute in commemoration of special occasions.

Appointments are made on the recommendation of the Minister of Defence, the Secretary of State for Foreign and Commonwealth Affairs, and the appropriate Minister of State for Commonwealth Countries other than the United Kingdom, as regards the Military Division, and the Secretary of State for Foreign and Commonwealth Affairs as regards the Civil Division.

COLLAR OF THE ORDER.

This Order ranks next to and immediately after the Royal Victorian Order; Knights Grand Cross have place and precedence next to and immediately after the Knights Grand Cross of the Royal Victorian Order; Dames Grand Cross next to and immediately after the Dames Grand Cross of the Royal Victorian Order, and may use the appellation and style of Dame before their Christian or first names; the Knights Commanders have place and precedence next to and immediately after the Knights Commanders of the Royal Victorian Order; Dames Commanders next to and immediately after the Dame Commanders of the Royal Victorian Order, and may use the appellation and style of Dame before their Christian or first names; men who are Commanders have place and precedence next to and immediately after the Commanders of the Royal Victorian Order and women who are commanders next to and immediately after women who are members of the Third Class of the Royal Victorian Order; Men who are Officers have place and precedence next to and immediately after Lieutenants of the Royal Victorian Order and women who are Officers next to and immediately after women who are Lieutenants of the Royal Victorian Order; Men who are Members have place and precedence next to and immediately after the Members of the Royal Victorian Order, and women who are Members next to and immediately after women who are Members of the Royal Victorian Order.

There are both Military and Civil Divisions of this Order; the Insignia for both is the same, but the Ribbon of the Military Division is distinguished by the narrow vertical pearl grey (formerly red) stripe in the centre which varies in width according to Class.

The COLLAR for Knights Grand Cross and Dames Grand Cross is of silver gilt composed of six medallions of the Royal Arms and six medallions of the Royal and Imperial Cypher of King George V alternately linked together with cables thereon the Imperial Crown between two sea-lions, from which hangs the Badge of the First Class of the Order. These Collars are returnable at death or upon receipt of a Collar of an Order of higher rank. The Mantle is of rose pink satin with pearl grey silk (originally purple satin lined with white silk) having the Grand Cross Star embroidered on the left side.

The Badge of the First Class of the Order consists of a cross patonce, enamelled pearl, fimbriated or, surmounted by a gold medallion bearing the crowned effigies of King George V, and Queen Mary combined with a circle gules inscribed with the motto, "For God and the Empire," in letters of gold ensigned with the Imperial Crown or, and on the reverse an engraving of the Royal and Imperial Cypher of King George V, the whole suspended from a rose pink riband edged with a pearl grey stripe (originally a purple riband) of the breadth of four inches for Knights Grand Cross, (with the addition, for Military Knights Grand Cross, of a vertical pearl grey stripe in the centre of a width of about one quarter of an inch), and two inches and one quarter for Dames Grand Cross, passing from the right shoulder to the left side, and on the left side of their coats or outer garments a Star (that for Dames being somewhat smaller than that worn by Knights), composed of chipped silver rays of eight points and charged with a medallion as above.

Knights Commanders wear around their necks a riband of miniature width of the same colour and pattern as that of Knights Grand Cross (the pearl grey stripe of Military Knights Commanders being about one sixteenth of an inch in width) and pendent therefrom the badge of the Knights Commanders of the Order, which shall be of a similar form and pattern to that appointed for Knights Grand Cross, but of smaller size, and also wear on the left side of their coats or outer garments a chipped silver Star composed of four greater and four lesser points, charged with a medallion as before, while Dames Commanders wear a badge of similar form and pattern as that appointed for Knights Commanders, attached to a riband, also similar to that worn by Knights Commanders, but tied in a bow and worn on the left shoulder, and they wear a like Star.

Commanders in the same manner wear the like riband and badge as that appointed for Knights or Dames Commanders, but are not entitled to wear the Star.

Officers wear a badge of similar form and pattern as that appointed for Commanders, but of a smaller size and of silver gilt, attached to a riband of the same colour and pattern of the breadth of one inch and a half (the vertical pearl grey stripe in the case of the Military Officers to be one sixteenth of an inch in width), attached to the left breast of their coats or outer garments by men, and tied in a bow on the left shoulder by women.

Members wear in like manner the same riband and badge as that appointed to Officers except that it is in silver.

The Insignia of all classes are, on promotion from a lower to a higher class in the same division, to be returned to the Registrar, but not at death except by Officials of the Order.

(There is a Military and Civil medal in connection with the Order which may be awarded to persons not Members of, or eligible for, any of its five classes, who render meritorious service. It is known as the BRITISH EMPIRE MEDAL, and entitles the recipients to place the letters "BEM" after their names.).

In 1957 it was decreed that appointments to and promotions in the Order of the British Empire and awards of the British Empire Medal, when granted for gallantry, should be distinguished by the wearing of an Emblem on the riband in crossed oak leaves, and in the announcement by an additional description "for gallantry." Gallantry awards in the Order continued until 19 June 1974, when The Queen's Gallantry Medal (QGM) was instituted.

SOVEREIGN   HM The Queen

Grand Master   HRH The Duke of Edinburgh, KG, KT, OM, GBE, AC, QSO, FRS.

Prelate   The Bishop of London.

King of Arms   Air Chief Marshal Sir Patrick Hine, GCB, GBE.

Registrar   The Secretary of the Central Chancery of the Orders of Knighthood.

Secretary   The Permanent Secretary to the Civil Service Department.

Dean   The Dean of St Paul's.

Gentleman Usher of the Purple Rod   Sir Robin Gillett, Bt, GBE, RD.

ORDER OF THE COMPANIONS OF HONOUR

Instituted on 4 June 1917 and altered 15 Oct 1919, consists of the Sovereign and not more than 65 Members (exclusive of Hon Members, and certain additional members appointed by special statute in commemoration of special occasions); it may be conferred on persons (women being eligible equally with men) for having done conspicuous national service, and for whom the distinction is deemed the most appropriate form of recognition, constituting as it does an honour dissociated either from acceptance of title or the classification of merit, and carrying with it no title or precedence, but recipients are permitted to put the initials "CH" after their names, these being placed subsequent to the initials "GBE." The Badge of the Order is oval, and consists of a gold medallion with representation of an oak tree and pendant from a branch a shield of the

Royal Arms; on the dexter a representation of a knight armed and in armour, mounted on a horse, the whole within a circle inscribed with the motto "In action faithful and in honour clear" in letters of gold ensigned with the Imperial Crown proper. Men suspend it around their necks from a carmine riband 1½ inches wide with a bordure interlaced gold; women wear it attached to a similar riband tied in a bow on the left shoulder. It is never worn in miniature, and is not returnable at death. A representation of the Badge may be suspended from an escutcheon of armorial bearings.

SOVEREIGN   HM The Queen

Secretary and Registrar   The Secretary of the Central Chancery of the Orders of Knighthood.

Members of the Order   Sir John Gorton, Baron Hailsham of St Marylebone, Baron Ashley of Stoke, Prof Max Perutz, Baron Glenamara, Baron Cledwyn of Penrhos, Malcolm Fraser, Sir John Gielgud, James Jones, Michael Somare, Baron Healey, Frederick Sanger, Brian Talboys, John Anthony, Dame Ninette de Valois, Baron Carrington, Lucian Freud, Hon Sir Steven Runciman, Pierre Trudeau, Sir Philip Powell, Sydney Brenner, Baron Tebbit, Anthony Powell, Professor Stephen Hawking, David Lange, Hon Peter Brooke, Baron Baker of Dorking, Thomas King, Charles Sisson, Dr Elsie Widdowson, Hon David Astor, Dame Janet Baker, Sir John Smith, Sir Alec Guinness, Prof Reginald Jones (d 1997), Baron Owen, César Milstein, Prof Carel Weight (d 1997), Sir Denys Lasdun, Sir David Attenborough, Sir Richard Doll, Baron Hurd of Westwell, Most Rev Derek Worlock (d 1996), Baron Howe of Aberavon, Dr A. L. Rowse (d 1997), David Hockney, Michael Heseltine, Prof Eric Hobsbawm, Christopher Patten, Peter Brook, John Major, Bridget Riley, Gen Alfred John Gardyne Drummond de Chastelain.

Honorary Members   Lee Kuan Yew, Dr. Joseph Luns.

KNIGHTS BACHELOR

The Word Knight is derived from the Saxon Cnyht, which signified a servant or attendant; and Knighthood is the most ancient title of honour known in this country, its origin dating back to Saxon times. The designation Knight Bachelor was in existence as long ago as the reign of King Henry III. Although for many centuries none but the Sovereign, or some person specially designated by him, has been able to create a Knight, originally both ecclesiastical and lay persons could confer the honour. Until 1926 Knights Bachelor had no insignia which they could wear, but in that year HM the King issued a Warrant authorising the wearing of a badge on all appropriate occasions. The Imperial Society of Knights Bachelor was founded for the maintenance and consolidation of the Dignity of Knights Bachelor in 1908, and obtained official recognition from the Sovereign in 1912. The Society keeps records of all Knights Bachelor, the interests of which its purpose is to maintain. The Knights Bachelor badge, which was approved in 1926, is worn on all appropriate occasions upon the left side of the coat or outer garment of those upon whom the degree of Knight Bachelor has been conferred. It measures 2⅜ inches in length and 1⅝ in width, is described as follows:—

"Upon an oval medallion of vermilion, enclosed by a scroll a cross-hilted sword belted and sheathed, pommel upwards, between two spurs, rowels upwards, the whole set about with the sword belt, all gilt".

In 1974 HM The Queen issued a further warrant authorising the wearing on appropriate occasions of a neck badge, slightly smaller in size, and in miniature. In 1988 a new certificate of authentication, a knight's only personal documentation, was designed by the College of Arms.

PATRON   HM The Queen

Knight Principal   Sir Conrad Swan, KCVO.
Hon Deputy Knight Principal   Sir Colin Cole, KCB, KCVO, TD.
Prelate   The Bishop of London.
Registrar   Sir Robert Balchin.
Treasurer   Sir Paul Judge.
Clerk to the Council
Registry and Library   21 Old Buildings, Lincolns Inn, WC2A 3UJ.

LIFE PEERS AND LAW LORDS

*LAW LORDS
‡ title gazetted too late for inclusion in main text

*Baron Ackner
Baron Ahmed
Baron Alderdice
Baron Alexander of Weedon
Baron Allen of Abbeydale
Baron Alli
Baron Alton of Liverpool
Baron Annan
Baron Archer of Sandwell
Baron Archer of Weston-super-Mare
Baron Armstrong of Ilminster
Baron Ashley of Stoke
Baron Attenborough
Baron Bach
Baron Bagri
Baron Baker of Dorking
Baron Balniel (Earl of Crawford)
Baron Barber
Baron Barber of Tewkesbury
Baron Barnett
Baron Bassam of Brighton
Baron Bauer
Baron Beaumont of Whitley
Baron Bell
Baron Bellwin
Baron Biffen
Baron Bingham of Cornhill
Baron Blackwell
Baron Blake
Baron Blaker
Baron Blease
Baron Blyth of Rowington
Baron Boardman
Baron Borrie
Baron Boston of Faversham
Baron Bowden
Baron Bowness
‡Baron Bradshaw
Baron Bragg
Baron Braine of Wheatley
Baron Bramall
‡Baron Brett
*Baron Bridge of Harwich
Baron Briggs
*Baron Brightman
Baron Brooke of Alverthorpe
Baron Brookes
Baron Brookman
Baron Brooks of Tremorfa
*Baron Browne-Wilkinson
Baron Bruce of Donington
Baron Bullock
Baron Burlison
Baron Burns
Baron Butler of Brockwell
Baron Butterfield
Baron Butterworth
Baron Buxton of Alsa
Baron Callaghan of Cardiff
Baron Cameron of Lochbroom
Baron Campbell of Alloway
Baron Campbell of Croy
‡Baron Carlile of Berriew
Baron Carlisle of Bucklow
Baron Carmichael of Kelvingrove
Baron Carr of Hadley
Baron Carter
Baron Carver
Baron Cavendish of Furness
Baron Chadlington
Baron Chalfont
Baron Chapple
Baron Charteris of Amisfield
Baron Chilver
Baron Chitnis
Baron Christopher
Baron Clark of Kempston
Baron Clarke of Hampstead
Baron Cledwyn of Penrhos
Baron Clement-Jones
Baron Clinton-Davis
*Baron Clyde
Baron Cockfield
Baron Cocks of Hartcliffe
Baron Coggan
Baron Constantine of Stanmore
Baron Cope of Berkeley
Baron Cooke of Islandreagh

Baron Cooke of Thorndon
Baron Cowdrey of Tonbridge
Baron Craig of Radley
Baron Crickhowell
Baron Crohan
Baron Cuckney
Baron Currie of Marylebone
Baron Dacre of Glanton
Baron Dahrendorf
Baron Davies of Coity
Baron Davies of Oldham
Baron Dean of Harptree
Baron Dearing
Baron Deedes
Baron Desai
Baron Dholakia
Baron Diamond
Baron Dixon
Baron Dixon Smith
Baron Donaldson of Lymington
Baron Donoghue
Baron Dormand of Easington
Baron Dubs
Baron Eames
Baron Eatwell
Baron Eden of Winton
‡Baron Elder
Baron Elis-Thomas
Baron Elliott of Morpeth
*Baron Elwyn-Jones
Baron Elystan Morgan
Baron Emslie
Baron Evans of Parkside
Baron Evans of Watford
Baron Ewing of Kirkford
Baron Ezra
Baron Falconer of Thoroton
Baron Fanshawe of Richmond
‡Baron Faulkner of Worcester
Baron Feldman
‡Baron Fellowes
Baron Fieldhouse
‡Baron Filkin
Baron Fitt
Baron Flowers
Baron Foot
‡Baron Forsyth of Drumlean
Baron Forte
‡Baron Foster of Thames Bank
Baron Fraser of Carmyllie
Baron Freeman
Baron Gallacher
Baron Garel-Jones
‡Baron Gavron
Baron Geraint
Baron Gibson
Baron Gibson-Watt
Baron Gilbert
Baron Gilmour of Craigmillar
Baron Gladwin of Clee
Baron Glenamara
*Baron Goff of Chieveley
‡Baron Goldsmith
Baron Goodhart
Baron Gordon of Strathblane
Baron Gormley
‡Baron Grabiner
Baron Graham of Edmonton
Baron Gray of Contin
Baron Greene of Harrow Weald
Baron Greenhill of Harrow
Baron Gregson
Baron Grey of Naunton
*Baron Griffiths
Baron Griffiths of Fforestfach
Baron Grimond
Baron Habgood
Baron Hailsham of St Marylebone
Baron Hambro
Baron Hamlyn
Baron Hanningfield
Baron Hanson
Baron Hardie
Baron Hardy of Wath
Baron Harmar-Nicholls
Baron Harris of Greenwich
Baron Harris of Haringey
Baron Harris of High Cross

Baron Harris of Peckham
‡Baron Harrison
Baron Hartwell
Baron Haskel
Baron Haskins
Baron Haslam
Baron Hattersley
Baron Hayhoe
Baron Healey
Baron Henderson of Brompton
Baron Higgins
Baron Hill-Norton
*Baron Hobhouse of Woodborough
*Baron Hoffmann
Baron Hogg of Cumbernauld
Baron Holderness
Baron Hollick
Baron Holme of Cheltenham
Baron Hooson
*Baron Hope of Craighead
Baron Howe of Aberavon
Baron Howell of Guildford
Baron Howie of Troon
Baron Hoyle
Baron Hughes
Baron Hughes of Woodside
Baron Hunt of Kings Heath
Baron Hunt of Tanworth
Baron Hunt of Wirral
Baron Hurd of Westwell
Baron Hussey of North Bradley
Baron Hutchinson of Lullington
*Baron Hutton
Baron Imbert
Baron Inge
Baron Ingrow
Baron Irvine of Lairg
Baron Islwyn
Baron Jacobs
Baron Jakobovits
*Baron Janner of Braunstone
*Baron Jauncey of Tullichettle
Baron Jenkin of Roding
Baron Jenkins of Hillhead
Baron Jenkins of Putney
Baron John-Mackie
Baron Johnston of Rockport
Baron Jopling
Baron Judd
Baron Keith of Castleacre
*Baron Keith of Kinkel
Baron Kelvedon
Baron Kilpatrick of Kincraig
Baron Kimball
Baron King of Wartnaby
‡Baron King of West Bromwich
Baron Kingsdown
Baron Kingsland
‡Baron Kirkham
Baron Kirkhill
Baron Knights
Baron Laing of Dunphail
‡Baron Laird
Baron Laming
Baron Lamont of Lerwick
*Baron Lane
Baron Lane of Horsell
Baron Lang of Monkton
Baron Lawson of Blaby
‡Baron Lea of Crondall
Baron Leonard
Baron Lester of Herne Hill
Baron Levene of Portsoken
Baron Levy
Baron Lewis of Newnham
‡Baron Lipsey
*Baron Lloyd of Berwick
Baron Lloyd of Kilgerran
Baron Lloyd-Webber
Baron Lofthouse
Baron Lovell-Davis
Baron Macaulay of Bragar
Baron Macdonald of Tradeston
Baron Macfarlane of Bearsden
Baron Mackay of Ardbrecknish
Baron MacKay of Clashfern
Baron MacKay of Drumadoon
‡Baron MacKenzie of Culkein

Baron Mackenzie of Framwellgate
Baron MacLaurin of Knebworth
Baron Mackenzie-Stuart
Baron Mackie of Benshie
Baron MacLehose of Beoch
Baron Marlesford
Baron Marsh
Baron Marshall of Knightsbridge
Baron Mason of Barnsley
Baron Mayhew of Twysden
Baron McAlpine of West Green
Baron McCarthy
Baron McCluskey
Baron McColl of Dulwich
Baron McConnell
Baron McIntosh of Haringey
Baron McNally
Baron Merlyn-Rees
*Baron Millett
Baron Mishcon
Baron Molloy
Baron Molyneaux of Killead
Baron Monro of Langholm
Baron Montague of Oxford
Baron Moore of Lower Marsh
Baron Moore of Wolvercote
Baron Morris of Castle Morris
Baron Morris of Manchester
Baron Moyola
Baron Murray of Epping Forest
Baron Murton of Lindisfarne
*Baron Mustill
Baron Naseby
Baron Neill of Bladen
Baron Newby
Baron Newton of Braintree
*Baron Nicholls of Birkenhead
Baron Nickson
*Baron Nolan
Baron Normand
Baron Northfield
Baron Norton of Louth
*Baron Oliver of Aylmerton
Baron Onslow of Woking
Baron Oram
Baron Orme
Baron Orr-Ewing
Baron Owen
‡Baron Oxburgh
Baron Paget of Northampton
Baron Palumbo
Baron Parkinson
Baron Parry
Baron Patel
Baron Patten
Baron Paul
Baron Pearson of Rannoch
Baron Pennock
Baron Perry of Walton
Baron Peston
Baron Peyton of Yeovil
Baron Phillips of Sudbury
*Baron Phillips of Worth Matravers
Baron Pilkington of Oxenford
Baron Plant of Highfield
Baron Plowden
Baron Plumb

Baron Plummer of St Marylebone
Baron Porter of Luddenham
Baron Prentice
Baron Prior
Baron Prys-Davies
Baron Puttnam
Baron Pym
Baron Quinton
Baron Quirk
Baron Randall of St Budeaux
Baron Rawlinson of Ewell
Baron Rayne
Baron Razzall
Baron Rees
Baron Rees-Mogg
Baron Renfrew of Kaimsthorn
‡Baron Rennard
Baron Renton
Baron Renton of Mount Harry
Baron Renwick of Clifton
Baron Rhodes
Baron Richard
Baron Richardson
Baron Richardson of Duntisbourne
Baron Rix
Baron Roberts of Conwy
‡Baron Robertson of Port Ellen
Baron Rodger of Earlsferry
Baron Rodgers of Quarry Bank
‡Baron Rogan
Baron Rogers of Riverside
Baron Roll of Ipsden
Baron Ross of Marnock
Baron Ross of Newport
Baron Runcie of Cuddesdon
Baron Russell-Johnston
Baron Ryder of Eaton Hastings
Baron Ryder of Wensum
Baron Saatchi
Baron Sainsbury of Preston Candover
Baron Sainsbury of Turville
Baron St John of Fawsley
Baron Sandberg
Baron Sanderson of Bowden
*Baron Saville of Newdigate
Baron Sawyer
Baron Scanlon
Baron Scarman
Baron Selkirk of Douglas
*Baron Sewel
‡Baron Sharman
Baron Shaw of Northstead
Baron Shawcross
Baron Sheppard of Didgemere
Baron Sheppard of Liverpool
Baron Shore of Stepney
Baron Sieff of Brimpton
Baron Simon of Glaisdale
Baron Simon of Highbury
Baron Simpson of Dunkeld
Baron Skidelsky
*Baron Slynn of Hadley
Baron Smith of Clifton
‡Baron Smith of Leigh
Baron Soulsby of Swaffham Prior
Baron Stallard
Baron Steel of Aikwood

Baron Sterling of Plaistow
Baron Stevens of Ludgate
‡Baron Stevenson of Coddenham
Baron Stewartby
*Baron Steyn
Baron Stodart of Leaston
Baron Stoddart of Swindon
Baron Stokes
Baron Stone of Blackheath
Baron Stonham
Baron Strauss
Baron Tanlaw
Baron Taverne
Baron Taylor of Blackburn
Baron Taylor of Gosforth
Baron Taylor of Gryfe
Baron Taylor of Warwick
Baron Tebbit
*Baron Templeman
Baron Thomas of Gresford
Baron Thomas of Gwydir
Baron Thomas of Macclesfield
Baron Thomas of Swynnerton
Baron Thomson of Monifieth
Baron Tombs
Baron Tomlinson
Baron Tope
Baron Tordoff
Baron Trotman
Baron Tugendhat
Baron Varley
Baron Vincent of Coleshill
Baron Vinson
Baron Waddington
Baron Wade of Chorlton
Baron Wakeham
‡Baron Waldegrave of North Hill
Baron Walker of Doncaster
Baron Walker of Worcester
Baron Wallace of Coslany
Baron Wallace of Saltaire
Baron Walton of Detchant
Baron Warner
Baron Watson of Invergowrie
‡Baron Watson of Richmond
Baron Weatherill
Baron Wedderburn of Charlton
Baron Weidenfeld
Baron Weinstock
Baron Whaddon
Baron Whitty
Baron Wigoder
*Baron Wilberforce
Baron Williams of Elvel
Baron Williams of Mostyn
Baron Williamson of Horton
Baron Willis
Baron Wilson of Tillyorn
Baron Winston
Baron Wolfson
Baron Wolfson of Sunningdale
*Baron Woolf
‡Baron Woolmer of Leeds
Baron Wright of Richmond
Baron Young of Dartington
Baron Young of Graffham
Baron Younger of Prestwick

LIFE PEERESSES

‡ *title gazetted too late for inclusion in main text*

Baroness Amos
Baroness Anelay
‡Baroness Ashton of Upholland
‡Baroness Barker
Baroness Blackstone
Baroness Blatch
‡Baroness Blood
Baroness Brigstocke
Baroness Brooke of Ystradfellte
Baroness Buscombe
Baroness Byford
Baroness Carnegy of Lour
Baroness Castle of Blackburn
Baroness Chalker of Wallasey
Baroness Cox
Baroness Crawley
Baroness Cumberlege
Baroness David
Baroness Dean of Thornton-le-Fylde

Baroness Delacourt-Smith of Alteryn
Baroness Denton of Wakefield
Baroness Dunn
Baroness Eccles of Moulton
Baroness Elles
Baroness Emerton
Baroness Falkender
Baroness Farrington of Ribbleton
Baroness Fisher of Rednal
Baroness Flather
Baroness Fookes
‡Baroness Gale
Baroness Gardner of Parkes
Baroness Goudie
Baroness Gould of Potternewton
Baroness Hamwee
‡Baroness Hanham
‡Baroness Harris of Richmond
Baroness Hayman

Baroness Hilton of Eggardon
Baroness Hogg
Baroness Hollis of Heigham
Baroness Hooper
‡Baroness Howells of St Davids
Baroness Hylton-Foster
Baroness James of Holland Park
Baroness Jay of Paddington
Baroness Jeger
Baroness Kennedy of the Shaws
Baroness Knight of Collingtree
Baroness Linklater of Butterstone
Baroness Lloyd of Highbury
Baroness Ludford
Baroness McFarlane of Llandaff
‡Baroness McIntosh of Hudnall
Baroness Macleod of Borve
Baroness Maddock
Baroness Mallalieu

Baroness Masham of Ilton
‡Baroness Massey of Darwen
Baroness Miller of Chilthorne Domer
Baroness Miller of Hendon
Baroness Nicholson of Winterbourne
Baroness Nicol
Baroness O'Cathain
Baroness O'Neill of Bengarve
Baroness Oppenheim-Barnes
Baroness Park of Monmouth
Baroness Perry of Southwark
Baroness Pike
Baroness Pitkeathley
Baroness Platt of Writtle
‡Baroness Prashar

Baroness Ramsay of Cartvale
Baroness Rawlings
Baroness Rendell of Babergh
Baroness Richardson of Calow
Baroness Ryder of Warsaw
Baroness Scotland of Asthal
Baroness Seccombe
Baroness Seear
Baroness Serota
Baroness Sharp of Guildford
Baroness Sharples
Baroness Smith of Gilmorehill
‡Baroness Stern
Baroness Symons of Vernham Dean

Baroness Thatcher
Baroness Thomas of Walliswood
Baroness Thornton
Baroness Trumpington
Baroness Turner of Camden
Baroness Warnock
Baroness Uddin
‡Baroness Warwick of Undercliffe
‡Baroness Whitaker
Baroness White
Baroness Wilcox
‡Baroness Wilkins
Baroness Williams of Crosby
Baroness Young

HEREDITARY PEERESSES IN THEIR OWN RIGHT

*of England   †of Scotland   ‡of The United Kingdom

*ARLINGTON, Baroness
*BERNERS, Baroness
*DACRE, Baroness
*DARCY DE KNAYTH, Baroness
*DUDLEY, Baroness
†DYSART, Countess of
†HERRIES OF TERREGLES, Lady
†KINLOSS, Lady

†LOUDOUN, Countess of
†MAR, Countess of
‡MOUNTBATTEN OF BURMA, Countess
†SALTOUN, Lady
*STRANGE, Baroness
†SUTHERLAND, Countess of
*WHARTON, Baroness
*WILLOUGHBY DE ERESBY, Baroness

PEERS WHO ARE MINORS

*and the dates when they are eligible to
sit in the House of Lords¶*

CRAVEN, Earl of. 12 June 2010.   ELPHINSTONE, Lord. 14 April 2001.

¶*Legally persons are deemed to obtain their majority, so far as sitting in the House of Lords is concerned, on completion of their twenty-first year (i.e. on the day prior to the twenty-first anniversary of their birth)*

THE ORDER OF SUCCESSION

1 HRH The Prince of Wales.
2 HRH Prince William of Wales.
3 HRH Prince Henry of Wales.
4 HRH The Duke of York.
5 HRH Princess Beatrice of York.
6 HRH Princess Eugenie of York.
7 HRH The Earl of Wessex.
8 HRH The Princess Royal.
9 Peter Phillips.
10 Zara Phillips.
11 HRH The Princess Margaret, Countess of Snowdon.
12 Viscount Linley.
13 Hon Charles Armstrong-Jones.
14 Lady Sarah Chatto.
15 Samuel Chatto.
16 Arthur Chatto.
17 HRH The Duke of Gloucester.
18 Earl of Ulster.
19 Lady Davina Windsor.
20 Lady Rose Windsor.
21 HRH The Duke of Kent.
22 Baron Downpatrick.
23 Lady Amelia Windsor.
24 Lady Marina-Charlotte Windsor.
25 Lord Nicholas Windsor.
26 Lady Helen Taylor.
27 Columbus Taylor.
28 Cassius Taylor.
29 Lord Frederick Windsor.
30 Lady Gabriella Windsor.

REIGNING SOVEREIGN

ELIZABETH II, BY THE GRACE OF GOD, OF THE UNITED KINGDOM OF GREAT BRITAIN AND NORTHERN IRELAND, AND OF HER OTHER REALMS AND TERRITORIES QUEEN, HEAD OF THE COMMONWEALTH, DEFENDER OF THE FAITH*.

Her Majesty ELIZABETH ALEXANDRA MARY, elder da of His late Majesty King George VI and of Lady Elizabeth Angela Marguerite Bowes-Lyon (*HM Queen Elizabeth The Queen Mother*) (*see page 92*), da of 14th Earl of Strathmore and Kinghorne; *b* at 17 Bruton Street W1, 21 April 1926: ascended the throne 6 February 1952, proclaimed Queen 8 February 1952, and crowned at Westminster Abbey 2 June 1953; declared in Council 9 April 1952, that she and her children shall be styled and known as the House and Family of Windsor; and further 8 Feb 1960, that her descendants, other than descendants enjoying the style, title, or attribute of HRH and the titular dignity of Prince or Princess, and female descendants who marry, and their descendants shall bear the name of Mountbatten-Windsor; attended the Thanksgiving Service for her Silver Jubilee in St Paul's Cathedral with the Duke of Edinburgh, 7 June 1977; Hon BMus, London 1946; FRS 1947; Hon DCL,

*The Queen's style and titles used in the United Kingdom. Different forms are used by each Commonwealth Country of which the Queen is Sovereign.

Oxford 1948; Hon LLD, Edinburgh; Hon MusD, Wales 1949; Hon LLD, London 1951; Hon FRCS and FRCOG 1951; Lord High Adm of the United Kingdom, Col-in-Ch of Life Guards, Blues and Royals (R Horse Guards and 1st Dragoons), R Scots Dragoon Guards (Carabiniers and Greys), The Queen's R Lancers, R Tank Regt, RE, Grenadier Guards, Coldstream Guards, Scots Guards, Irish Guards, Welsh Guards, R Welch Fusiliers, Queen's Lancashire Regt, Argyll and Sutherland Highlanders (Princess Louise's), R Green Jackets, Adjutant Gen Corps, The Royal Mercian and Lancastrian Yeo, Corps of Roy Mil Police, Calgary Highlanders, Canadian Forces Mil Engineers Branch, King's Own Calgary Regt, R. 22e Regt, Gov-Gen's Foot Guards, Canadian Grenadier Guards, Le Régiment de la Chaudière, R New Brunswick Regt, 48th Highlanders of Canada, Argyll and Sutherland Highlanders of Canada (Princess Louise's), Royal Aust Engineers, Royal Aust Inf Corps, R Aust Army Ordnance Corps, R Aust Army Nursing Corps, RNZ Engineers, RNZ Inf Regt, RNZ Army Ordnance Corps, Malawi Rifles, R Malta Artillery, Capt-Gen RA, Hon Artillery Co, Combined Cadet Force, R Canadian Artillery, R Regt of Aust Artillery, RNZ Artillery, RNZ Armoured Corps, Air-Commodore-in-Chief, R Aux AF, RAF Regt, R Observer Corps, R Canadian Air Force Aux, Aust Citizen Air Force, Territorial Air Force of NZ, Hon Air Commodore RAF Marham, Comdt-in-Chief, RAF Coll, Cranwell, Hon Commr, R Canadian Mounted Police, Master of the Merchant Navy and Fishing Fleets. Head of the Civil Defence Corps; Sovereign of all British Orders of Knighthood, Order of Merit, R Order of Victoria and Albert, Order of Crown of India, Order of Companions of Honour, Distinguished Ser Order, Imperial Ser Order, and Order of Canada, Sovereign Head of the Order of the Hospital of St John of Jerusalem, Order of Australia, and The Queen's Ser Order of NZ§; received Freedom of Drapers' Co, and of R Borough of Windsor 1947, Burgess of R Burgh of Stirling, and Cities of London and Cardiff 1948, and Cities of Edinburgh and Belfast 1949; Order of the Elephant of Denmark 1947, Grand Cordon of Order of El Kemal of Egypt 1948, Grand Cross (or Cordon) of Legion of Honour of France 1948, Order of Ojaswi Rajanya of Nepal 1949, Grand Cross of Order of the Netherlands Lion 1950, Order of the Seraphim of Sweden 1953, Gold Collar of Order of Manuel Amador Guerrero of Panama 1953, Chain of Order of El-Hussein Ibn Ali of Jordan 1953, Grand Collar of Order of Idris I of Libya 1954, Chain and Collar of Order of the Seal of Solomon of Ethiopia 1954, Grand Cross, with Chain, of Order of St Olav of Norway 1955, Grand Sash and Cross of the Three Orders of Christ, Aviz and Santiago of Portugal 1955, Grand Order of the Hashimi, with Chain, of Iraq 1956, Chevalier, with Grand Cross and Grand Cordon, of Order of Merit of the Republic of Italy 1958, Special Grand Cross with Star of Order of Merit of Federal Republic of Germany 1958, Grand Cross with diamonds of Order of the Peruvian Sun 1960, Nishan-i-Pakistan 1960, Grand Collar of Order of the Liberator General San Martin of Argentina 1960, Order of Royal House of Chakri of Thailand 1960, Mahendra Chain of Nepal 1961, Grand Collar of Order of Independence of Tunisia 1961, Collar of Order of the White Rose of Finland 1961, Grand Cross of National Order of Senegal 1961, Grand Cordon of Order of Knighthood of the Pioneers of the Republic of Liberia 1961, Grand Cross of National Order of Ivory Coast 1961, Collar and Grand Cordon of Order of the Chrysanthemum of Japan 1962, Grand Band of Order of the Star of Africa of Liberia 1962, Grand Cross of Ordre de la Valeur Camerounaise 1963, Grand Cordon of the Order of Leopold of Belgium, 1963, Grand Cross of the Order of the Redeemer of Greece 1963, Grand Cross, with Chain, of Order of the Falcon of Iceland 1963, the Chain of Honour of Sudan 1964, Grand Collar of Order of Merit of Chile 1965, Grand Cordon of Austrian Order of Merit 1966, Grand Collar of Order of the Southern Cross of Brazil 1968, Grand Commander of National Order of The Niger (Nigeria) 1969, and Order of Al Nahayyan (First Class) of Abu Dhabi 1969, Grand Cross of The Equatorial Star of Gabon, Order of Supreme Sun of Afghanistan 1971, Order of Golden Lion of House of Nassau of Luxembourg 1972, Order of the Great Yugoslav Star 1972, Darjah Utama Seri Mahkota Negara of Malaysia 1972, Order of Temasek of Singapore 1972, Most Esteemed Family Order 1st Class (Darjah Kerabat Yan Amat Di-Homali Darjah Pertama) of Brunei 1972, Distinguished Order of Ghaazi of the Maldive Islands 1972, Order of the Golden Heart of Kenya 1972, Grand Collar of National Order of Aztec Eagle of Mexico 1973, Grand Cordon of National Order of the Leopard of Zaire 1973, Star of Indonesia (First Class) 1974, Grand Commander of Order of the Republic of the Gambia 1974, Chain of Order of Seraphim of Sweden 1975, Collar of the Order of the Nile of Egypt 1975, Order of the Star of the Socialist Republic of Romania 1st Class 1978, Great Collar of the Order of S Tiago da Espada of Portugal 1978, Collar of Mubarak Al Kabir of Kuwait 1979, Order of the Khalifa Collar of Bahrain 1979, Collar of the Order of King Abdul Aziz of Saudi Arabia 1979, Collar of Independence of Qatar 1979, Order of Oman 1st Class 1979, Order of the Lion of Malawi 1st Class 1979, Presidential Order of Botswana 1979, Collar of the Grand Cordon of the Most Venerable Order of Knighthood of the Pioneers of the Republic of Liberia 1979, Grand Cordon of the Order of the Republic of

§As Princess Elizabeth, Her Majesty was appointed a Member of Imperial Order of the Crown of India, a Lady of the Most Noble Order of the Garter, and a Dame Grand Cross of Order of St John of Jerusalem 1947.

Tunisia 1980, Collier de la Classe Exceptionelle of the Order of El Mohammedi of
Morocco 1980, Order of Al Said of Oman 1982, Order of the Solomon Islands 1st
Class 1982, and additional insignia (Sash and Badge) of the Order of Qeladet El-
Hussein Ibn Ali (Jordan) 1984, Dominica Award of Honour 1985, The Trinity Cross
Medal of the Order of Trinity (TC) (Gold) of Trinidad and Tobago 1985, Collar of the
Order of Carlos III of Spain 1986, Grand Order of Mungunghwa of the Republic of
Korea 1986, Order of the Golden Fleece of Spain 1988, Grand Star of the Federal
Republic of Nigeria 1989, Chain of the Federation of the United Arab Emirates
1989, Grand Ribbon of the Order of Merit of the Republic of Poland 1991, Grand
Cross of the Order of Merit (Hungary) 1991, Royal Family Order of the Sultan of
Brunei 1992, Brunei Silver Jubilee Medal 1992, Grand Collar of the Order of Boyaca
(Colombia) 1993, Grand Cross of the Order of Good Hope (S Africa) 1995, Order of
the White Lion First Class (Czech Republic) 1996, Order of Merit of the Most
Excellent Order of the Grand Cross (Peru) 1998. HM *m* at Westminster Abbey 20
Nov 1947, HRH The Prince Philip, Duke of Edinburgh, KG, KT, OM, GBE, AC,
QSO, PC [see page 93], and has issue.

Residences—Buckingham Palace, SW1; Windsor Castle, Berkshire; Balmoral
Castle, Aberdeenshire; Sandringham House, Norfolk.

𝕮𝖗𝖔𝖜𝖓—A circle of gold, issuing therefrom four crosses patées and four fleurs-de-lis
arranged alternately; from the crosses patées arise two golden arches ornamented
with pearls, crossing at the top under a mound also gold, the whole enriched with
precious stones. The cap is of crimson velvet, turned up ermine. 𝕽𝖔𝖞𝖆𝖑 𝕬𝖗𝖒𝖘*—
Quarterly: 1st and 4th, gules, three lions passant guardant in pale or, *England*; 2nd,
or, a lion rampant within a double tressure flory counterflory gules, *Scotland*; 3rd,
azure, a harp or, stringed argent, *Ireland*, the whole encircled with the Garter.
𝕮𝖗𝖊𝖘𝖙𝖘—*England*, upon the royal helmet the Royal crown proper, thereon statant
guardant or, a lion imperially crowned also proper; *Scotland*, on the Crown proper a
lion sejant affrontée gules crowned or, holding in the dexter paw a sword, and in the
sinister a sceptre erect also proper; *Ireland*, on a wreath or and azure, a tower
triple-towered of the first, from the portal a hart springing argent, attired and
hoofed gold. 𝕾𝖚𝖕𝖕𝖔𝖗𝖙𝖊𝖗𝖘—*Dexter*, a lion rampant guardant or, crowned as the crest;
sinister, a unicorn argent, armed, crined, and unguled, or, gorged with a coronet
composed of crosses patées and fleurs-de-lis, a chain affixed thereto, passing
between the fore-legs, and reflexed over the back, of the last. 𝕭𝖆𝖉𝖌𝖊𝖘—*England*, the
red and white rose united, slipped and leaved proper; *Scotland*, a thistle, slipped
and leaved proper; *Ireland*, a shamrock leaf slipped vert; also a harp or stringed
argent; *United Kingdom*, the Rose of England, the Thistle of Scotland, and the
Shamrock of Ireland engrafted on the same stem proper, and an escutcheon charged
as the Union Flag (all the foregoing ensigned with the Royal Crown); *Wales*, upon a
mount vert a dragon passant wings elevated gules, and (Augmented Badge) within a
circular riband argent fimbriated or, bearing the motto "Y Ddraig goch Ddyry
Cychwyn" in letters vert, and ensigned with a representation of the Crown proper,
an escutcheon per fesse argent and vert and thereon the Red Dragon passant; *The
Royal House of Windsor*, on a mount vert the Round Tower of Windsor Castle argent
mason Sable, flying thereon the Royal Standard, the whole within two branches of
oak fructed or and ensigned with the Royal Crown.

*The Arms of HRH The Princess Royal, and
HRH The Princess Margaret, Countess of
Snowdon, are differenced by the following
Labels*—

SONS LIVING

HRH *PRINCE* CHARLES PHILIP
ARTHUR GEORGE, KG, GCB, AK, PC,
ADC (*Prince of Wales*), *b* at Buckingham
Palace 14 Nov 1948. (See page 95).

HRH *Prince* Andrew Albert Christian
Edward (*Duke of York*), CVO, ADC, *b* at
Buckingham Palace 19 Feb 1960. (See
page 97).

HRH *Prince* Edward Antony Richard
Louis (*Earl of Wessex*), CVO, *b* at
Buckingham Palace 10 March 1964. (See
page 98).

DAUGHTER LIVING

HRH *Princess* Anne Elizabeth Alice
Louise (*The Princess Royal*), LG, GCVO,
FRS, *b* at Clarence House 15 Aug 1950; ed
at Benenden Sch; Chancellor of
London Univ since 1981; Lord High Commissioner to the General Assembly of the
Church of Scotland 1996; Gold Stick and Col-in-Ch The Blues and Royals since

---

*Scottish usage shows the Royal Arms with the Lion of Scotland in the 1st and 4th quarters, in
conformity with the pattern prescribed for the Great Seal of Scotland, and appearing on Scottish
official publications and on the tabards of the Scottish Officers of Arms.

1998; Col-in-Ch 14th/20th King's Royal Hussars, The Royal Scots (The Royal Regiment) Worcs and Sherwood Foresters Regt (29th/45th Foot) and 8th Canadian Hussars (Princess Louise's), R Corps of Signals, Canadian Forces Communications and Electronics Branch, Royal Aust Corps of Signals, RNZ Corps of Signals, RNZ Nursing Corps, Grey and Simcoe Foresters Militia, The Royal Regina Rifles, Royal Newfoundland Regt, Hon Col Univ of London Contingent, OTC; Ch Comdt WRNS; Comdt in Chief Women's Transport Service (FANY), St John Ambulance and Nursing Cadets; Hon Air Commodore RAF Lyneham; Hon Air Commodore Univ of London Air Sqdn; Pres WRNS Benevolent Trust, British Academy of Film and Television Arts, Save the Children Fund, Windsor Horse Trials, Roy Sch for Daughters of Officers of Royal Navy and Royal Marines (Haslemere), Missions to Seamen, Nat Agricultural Centre Rural Trust, Council for National Academic Awards; Hon Pres Chartered Institute of Transport, Royal Caledonian Hunt; Joint Pres Lowland Brigade Club; Vice-Pres Royal Bath and West and Southern Counties Show; Patron All England Women's Lacrosse Association, Royal Lymington Yacht Club, Butler Trust, Association of WRNS, Riding for the Disabled Association (Australia), Home Farm Trust, Jersey Wildlife Preservation Trust, The Royal Corps of Signals Institution, The Royal Signals Association, The Canadian Communications and Electronic Branch Institution, The British School of Osteopathy, The Royal Tournament, Spinal Injuries Association, The Army and Royal Artillery Hunter Trials, Glos and N Avon Federation of Young Farmers' Clubs, Royal Port Moresby Society for Prevention of Cruelty to Animals, Horse of the Year Ball, Benenden Anniversary Ball 1999, National Union of Townswomen's Guilds, Canadian Therapeutic Riding Association, College of Occupational Therapists, Association of Combined Youth Clubs, Scottish Rugby Union, British Executive Service Overseas, Australian Veterinary Association, Intensive Care Society, British Olympic Medical Trust, The Royal Scots Club and The Flying Scot Club, World Student Debating Championships 1990, The Cranfield Trust, Ulster Sports and Recreation Trust, British Racing Schools Race Day, Home Farm Trust Development Trust, World Junior Cycling Championships, National Association of Prison Visitors, Gateshead National Garden Festival, Save the Children Fund Corporate Fund Raising Cttee, Hong Kong, Univ of West Indies Relief and Development Fund, Glos Rugby Union, British Nutrition Foundation, and International Literacy Year 1990 (run under ALBSU); Vice-Patron, British Show Jumping Assocn; Pres British Horse Soc; Commdt-in-Ch St John Ambulance and Nursing Cadets; Life Member of R British Legion Women's Section; Memb Internat Olympic Ctee since 1988; Member of Lloyd's 1989; received Freedom of City of London 1976; Royal Bencher Inner Temple 1990; Hon Liveryman Farriers' Co; Freeman of Fishmongers' Co; Hon Freeman, Farmers' Co, Loriners' Co, Yeoman Saddlers' Co; Master of Carmen's Co; Hon Life Member, RNVR Officers' Assocn; Hon Member, British Equine Veterinary Assocn; Visitor, Felixstowe Coll; Variety Club's Internat Humanitarian Award (1987); FRS (1987); FRCVS (1986), Hon FRCS (1986), Hon FIEE (1987), Hon FRCP (1990), cr GCVO 1974, Declared The Princess Royal 13 June 1987, LG 1994; m 1st, at Westminster Abbey 14 Nov 1973 (m diss 1992), Capt Mark Anthony Peter Phillips, CVO, ADC(P) (b at Tetbury, Glos 22 Sept 1948), only son of Maj Peter William Garside Phillips, MC, late 1st King's Drag Guards; 2ndly, at Crathie Church 12 Dec 1992, Cdre Timothy James Hamilton Laurence, MVO, RN (b at Camberwell 1 March 1955), yr son of late Cmdr Guy Stewart Laurence, RN, and has issue living (by 1st m): Peter Mark Andrew, b at St Mary's Hosp, Paddington 15 Nov 1977; ed Gordonstoun, and Exeter Univ,—Zara Anne Elizabeth, b at St Mary's Hosp, Paddington, 15 May 1981.

SISTER LIVING

HRH Princess Margaret Rose (*The Princess Margaret, Countess of Snowdon*), CI, GCVO, b at Glamis Castle, Angus, 21 Aug 1930; Hon DMus London 1957; Hon LLD Camb 1958; Hon DLitt Keele 1962; Hon LLD, Univ of BC 1958; Hon FRIBA 1953; Hon FRSM 1957, Hon FRCS, England 1963, and Hon FRCOG 1966; Hon Life FZS; Royal Master of the Bench of Lincoln's Inn and Treasurer 1967; Col-in-Ch of R Highland Fusiliers (Princess Margaret's Own Glasgow and Ayrshire Regt), The Light Dragoons, Princess Louise Fusiliers, Royal Canadian Infantry Corps (Militia), Highland Fusiliers of Canada, QARANC, and Dep Col-in-Ch of R Anglian Regt Hon Air Commodore RAF Coningsby; Pres of Scottish Children's League, Victoria League, R National Institute for the Blind, R Ballet, Birmingham Royal Ballet, National Soc for the Prevention of Cruelty to Children, R Scottish Soc for Prevention of Cruelty to Children, Friends of the Elderly, Invalid Children's Aid Nationwide (also Chm of Council), English Folk Dance and Song Soc, Horder Centre for Arthritics, and of The Guide Assocn; Hon Pres British Museum Development Trust; Joint-Pres of Lowland Bde Club; Pres R Agricultural Soc of England 1966; Patron-in-Ch of English Harbour Repair Fund; Patron of Light Infantry Club, QARANC Assocn, Barristers' Benevolent Assocn, Bristol R Workshops for the Blind, British and Internat Sailors' Soc, Friends of Southwark Cathedral, of St John's, Smith Sq Charitable Trust, Mary Hare Gram Sch, for the Deaf, National Pony Soc, Princess Margaret Rose Hosp, Edinburgh, Services Sound and Vision Corporation, of R Coll

of Nursing and National Council of Nurses of UK, of Princess Margaret Hosp,
Toronto, of The Mathilda and Terence Kennedy Inst of Rheumatology, St
Margaret's Chapel Guild, Edinburgh Castle, Scottish Community Drama Assocn,
Suffolk Regimental Assocn, of W Indies Olympic Assocn, of Architects' Benevolent
Soc, of Tenovus (Inst of Cancer Research) and Tenovus Scotland, of Migraine Trust,
of Zebra Trust, Purine Research Laboratory, London Lighthouse, and of St Pancras
Housing Assocn in Camden; Visitor, King George and Queen Elizabeth Foundation
of St Catharine; Patron (temporary) of R Caledonian Ball since 1956; a CStJ; Grand
President of St John Ambulance; Life Member of British Legion Women's Section,
Hon Member of Automobile Assocn, Order of the Road, R Automobile Club, Hallé
Concerts Soc, Heart Disease and Diabetes Research Trut, Northern Ballet Theatre,
Pottery and Glass Trades Benevolent Inst, R Anglian Regimental Assoc, and
Sealyham Terrier Breeders' Assocn; Hon Member and Patron of Grand Antiquity
Soc of Glasgow; Member of Haberdashers' Co 1966; received Freedom of City of
London 1966 and of R Burgh of Queensferry 1972; Hon Life Mem of Century House
Assoc (British Columbia); has Grand Cross of Order of Lion of the Netherlands
1948, Order of Brilliant Star of Zanzibar, first class 1956, Grand Cross of Order of
Crown of Belgium 1960, Order of the Crown, Lion and Spear of Toro Kingdom,
Uganda 1965, Order of Precious Crown of Japan first class 1971, and Grand Cross
(1st class), Order of Merit of Federal Republic of Germany; cr CI 1947, GCVO 1953,
Royal Victorian Chain 1990; m at Westminster Abbey 6 May 1960 (m diss 5 July
1978), 1st Earl of Snowdon, GCVO, and has issue:—

SON LIVING,—David Albert Charles (Viscount Linley), b at Clarence House 3 Nov
1961; ed Bedales, and John Makepeace Sch of Woodcraft, Beaminster, Dorset;
furniture designer: m at St Margaret's, Westminster 8 Oct 1993, Hon Serena
Alleyne Stanhope, only da of Charles Henry Leicester, Viscount Petersham (see E
Harrington), and has issue living, Hon Charles Patrick Inigo Armstrong-Jones, b 1
July 1999.

DAUGHTER LIVING,—Lady Sarah Frances Elizabeth, b at Kensington Palace 1 May
1964; ed Bedales; principal bridesmaid to HRH The Princess of Wales: m at St
Stephen's, Walbrook 14 July 1994, Daniel Chatto, yr son of late Thomas Chatto, and
has issue living, Samuel David Benedict, b 28 July 1996,—Arthur Robert Nathaniel,
b 5 Feb 1999.

MOTHER LIVING (Widow of King George VI)
Her Majesty QUEEN ELIZABETH THE QUEEN MOTHER. See page 92
WIDOW LIVING OF SON OF KING GEORGE V
See Princess Alice, Duchess of Gloucester, page 99.
OTHER LIVING DESCENDANTS OF KING GEORGE V

Issue of Field Marshal HRH the late Prince Henry William Frederick Albert,
KG, KT, KP, GCB, GCMG, GCVO, PC, 1st Duke of Gloucester, 3rd son of HM
the late King George V, b 31 March 1900, d 10 June 1974; m 6 Nov 1935,
Lady Alice Christabel Montagu-Douglas-Scott, GCB, CI, GCVO, GBE
(GCStJ), 3rd da of 7th Duke of Buccleuch and Queensberry:—
See D Gloucester, page 99.

Issue of Air-Commodore HRH the late Prince George Edward Alexander
Edmund, KG, KT, GCMG, GCVO, PC, RAF, 1st Duke of Kent, 4th son of HM
the late King George V, b 20 Dec 1902, d (on active ser during European War)
25 Aug 1942; m 29 Nov 1934, HRH Princess Marina, CI, GCVO, GBE, who d
27 Aug 1968, da of HRH the late Prince Nicholas of Greece and Denmark,
GCB, GCVO:—
See D Kent, page 100.

Issue of HRH the late Princess (Victoria Alexandra Alice) Mary (The Princess
Royal), CI, GCVO, CBE, RRC, TD, CD, only da of HM the late King George V,
b 25 April 1897, d 28 March 1965; declared Princess Royal 1 Jan 1932; m 28
Feb 1922, 6th Earl of Harewood, KG, GCVO, DSO, who d 24 May 1947:—
See E Harewood.

OTHER LIVING DESCENDANTS OF KING EDWARD VII

Grandson of HRH the late Princess Louise Victoria Alexandra
Dagmar (The Princess Royal, Duchess of Fife), el da of King Edward
VII, b 20 Feb 1867, d 4 Jan 1931; declared Princess Royal 28 Nov
1905: m 27 July 1889, 1st Duke of Fife, KG, KT, GCVO, who d 29 Jan
1912:—

Issue of HH the late Princess Maud Alexandra Victoria Georgina Bertha
(Countess of Southesk), b 3 April 1893, d 14 Dec 1945; granted title of
Princess, with style and attribute of "Highness" and precedence immediately
after all members of Royal Family enjoying style of "Royal Highness", 1905;
reverted to style of "Lady" after her marriage: m 12 Nov 1923, the 11th Earl
of Southesk, KCVO, who d 16 Feb 1992:—
See D Fife.

Grandchildren of HM the late Maud Charlotte Mary Victoria (Queen

of Norway), VA, CI, GCVO, youngest da of King Edward VII, *b* 26 Nov
1869, *d* 20 Nov 1938: *m* 22 July 1896, HRH Prince (Christian
Frederik) Carl Georg Valdemar Axel of Denmark, KG, GCB, GCVO
[elected King of Norway under style of HM Haakon VII 18 Nov 1905],
who *d* 21 Sept 1957, second son of HM the late King Frederik VIII of
Denmark, KG, GCB, GCVO:—
Issue of HM the late Olav V (Alexander Edward Christian Frederik) (*King of
Norway*), KG, KT, GCB, GCVO, *b* 2 July 1903, *d* 17 Jan 1991: *m* 21 March
1929, HRH Princess Märtha Sophie Louise Dagmar Thyra of Sweden, who *d*
5 April 1954, da of HRH the late Duke (Oscar Carl Wilhelm) of
Västergötland, GCVO:—

HM King Harald V (*King of Norway*), GCVO, *b* 21 Feb 1937; *ed* at Balliol Coll, **Norway**
Oxford; Sovereign of Order of St Olav of Norway and Norwegian Order of Merit; Hon
Gen British Army; has Grand Cross of Orders Elephant and Daunebrog of
Denmark, Seraphim of Sweden, Leopold of Belgium, Southern Cross of Brazil,
White Rose of Finland, the Redeemer of Greece, Falcon of Iceland, Merit of Republic
of Italy, Merit of Austria, Southern Cross of Brazil, Cross of Terra Mariana of
Estonia, Legion of Honour of France, Three Stars of Latvia, Vytautas the Great of
Lithuania, Chula Chom Klao of Thailand, Grand Star of Yugoslavia, Order of Merit
of Federal Republic of Germany, Merit of Adolph of Nassau of Luxembourg, White
Eagle of Poland, Order of Aviz of Portugal, Cape of Good Hope of S Africa, Charles
III of Spain, Crown Order of Family Order of Orange and Order of the Golden Ark of
The Netherlands, and Chrysanthemum of Japan; GCVO (Hon) 1955, Royal
Victorian Chain 1994: *m* 29 Aug 1968, Sonja, Grand Cross of St Olav of Norway, of
Elephant of Denmark, of White Rose of Finland, Icelandic Order of the Falcon,
Isabella the Catholic of Spain and other orders, da of late Carl August Haraldsen,
and has issue living, *HRH Prince* Haakon Magnus (*Crown Prince of Norway*), *b* 20
July 1973,— *HRH Princess* Märtha Louise, *b* 22 Sept 1971. — *Princess* Ragnhild
Alexandra, *b* 9 June 1930; bears the name of Princess Ragnhild, Mrs Lorentzen: *m*
15 May 1953, Erling Sven Lorentzen, of Av Visc de Albuquerque 333, Bl B, apt 403,
Rio de Janeiro, Brazil, and has issue living, Haakon, *b* 23 Aug 1954: *m* 14 April
1982, Martha Carvalho de Freitas, da of José Maria Gomes de Freitas, and has issue
living, Olav Alexander *b* 11 July 1985, Christian Frederik *b* 23 May 1988, Sophia
Anne *b* 28 June 1994, — Ingeborg, *b* 27 Feb 1957: *m* 4 June 1982, Paulo César
Pereira Ribeiro, son of Paulo César Ribeiro, and has issue living, Victoria Ragna *b*
19 Dec 1988, — Ragnhild Alexandra, *b* 8 May 1968. — *Princess* Astrid Maud
Ingeborg, *b* 12 Feb 1932; bears the name of Princess Astrid, Mrs Ferner; *ed* at Lady
Margaret Hall, Oxford; Grand Cross of Orders of St Olav of Norway and White Rose
of Finland: *m* 12 Jan 1961, Johan Martin Ferner, of Oslo, Norway, and has issue
living, Alexander, *b* 15 March 1965: *m* 27 July 1996, Margrét Gudmundsdóttir, da of
Gudmundur Jonsson, of Iceland, and has issue living, Edward *b* 28 March 1996,
Stella *b* 23 April 1998, — Carl-Christian, *b* 22 Oct 1972, — Cathrine, *b* 22 July 1962:
m 9 Dec 1989, Arild Johansen, and has issue living, Sebastian *b* 9 May 1990,
Madeleine *b* 7 March 1993, — Benedikte, *b* 27 Sept 1963: *m* 30 April 1994 (*m diss*
1998), Rolf Woods, — Elisabeth, *b* 30 March 1969: *m* 3 Oct 1992, Tom Folke
Beckmann, son of Jann Beckmann.

OTHER LIVING DESCENDANTS OF QUEEN VICTORIA

Descendants of HRH the Duke of Edinburgh (Duke of Saxe-Coburg and Gotha), 2nd son of Queen Victoria

Grandchildren of HRH late Princess Marie Alexandra Victoria (*Queen
of Roumania*), VA, CI, RRC (infra):—
Issue of HM the late King Carol II, KG, GCVO, *b* 16 Oct 1893, *d* 4 April 1953;
renounced succession to the throne of Roumania 8 Dec 1925, subsequently
proclaimed King as Carol II 8 June 1930; left Roumania 6 Sept 1940: *m* 1st,
in Russia, 31 Aug 1918 (*m* declared null and void in Roumania 8 Jan 1919),
Joana Maria Valentina (Zizi), who *d* 11 March 1953, da of Col Constantin
Lambrino; 2ndly, 10 March 1921 (*m diss* 21 June 1928), HRH Princess
Helen, who *d* 28 Nov 1982, eldest da of HM King Constantine I of the
Hellenes (infra); 3rdly, 3 July 1947, Elena (Magda), who assumed the style of
HRH Princess Elena of Hohenzollern, who *d* 29 June 1977, da of Nicolas
Lupescu (formerly Wolff), and formerly wife of Ion Tampeanu:—
(By 1st *m*) (Mircea Grigore) Carol (36 Doria Rd, SW6), *b* 8 Jan 1920; recognized as **Roumania**
legitimate by French Courts at Paris 17 Dec 1955, when he assumed the name and
style of HRH Prince Carol of Roumania: *m* 1st, 22 March 1944 (*m diss* 1960), Hélène
Henriette, da of Paul Nagavitzine; 2ndly, 20 Dec 1960 (*m diss* 1977), (Thelma)
Jeanne, who *d* 5 June 1988, da of Richard Williams, of Nashville, Tennessee, USA;
3rdly, 27 June 1984, Antonia, yr da of late Maj-Gen Edward Charles Colville, CB,
DSO (*see* V Colville of Culross, colls), and formerly wife of Garry Lacon Jock Ropner
(*see* Ropner Bt (cr 1904), colls), and has issue living, (by 1st *m*) Paul Philippe, *b* 13
Aug 1948; *ed* Gordonstoun, and Millfield: *m* 15 Sept 1996, Lia Georgia, da of Thomas

Triff, — (by 2nd *m*) (Ion George Nicholas) Alexander, *b* 1 Sept 1961; *ed* Ampleforth.
— (By 2nd *m*) *HM King* Mihai (Michael), GCVO, *b* 25 Oct 1921; reigned as King of Roumania (under regency) 20 July 1927-8 June 1930; re-ascended the throne on departure of his father 6 Sept 1940; deprived of the throne 30 Dec 1947; is Hon Air Ch Marshal, Roy Hellenic Air Force; a Ch Com of American Legion of Merit; Collar and Grand Master of the Order of Carol I of Roumania, Order of Michael the Brave, Grand Master of the Orders of Faithful Service, the Crown of Roumania and the Star of Roumania, Bailiff Grand Cross of Honour and Devotion, Sov Military Order of Malta, Marshal of the Roumanian Armed Forces, has Grand Cross of Order of the Redeemer of Greece, Grand Cross of the Order of Leopold of Belgium, Orders of Victory of Russia, and of Annunciation of Italy, and French Legion of Honour; GCVO (Hon) 1938: *m* 10 June 1948, HRH Princess Anne Antoinette Françoise Charlotte, has Grand Cross of Order of Carol I of Roumania, St Olga and St Sofia of Greece, Dame Grand Cross of Honour and Devotion, Sov Military Order of Malta, French Croix de Guerre, only da of HRH the late Prince René Charles Marie Joseph of Bourbon-Parma, and has issue living, *HRH Princess* Margarita, nominated Crown Princess of Roumania by her father 30 Dec 1997, has Grand Cross of the Order of Carol I of Roumania, *b* 26 March 1949: *m* 24 July (civ) and 21 Sept (relig) 1996, Radu Duda, named HSH Prince of Hohenzollern-Veringen by HSH the Prince of Hohenzollern 1 Jan 1999, son of René Duda, — *HRH Princess* Helen, *b* 15 Nov 1950: *m* 1st, 20 July (civ) and 24 Sept (relig) 1983 (*m diss* 1991), Dr (Leslie) Robin Medforth-Mills, son of Cyril Mills; 2ndly, 14 Aug 1998, Alexander Philips Nixon McAteer, son of Alexander McAteer, and has issue living (by 1st *m*), Nicholas Michael DE ROUMANIE-MEDFORTH-MILLS *b* 1 April 1985, Elisabetta Karina DE ROUMANIE-MEDFORTH-MILLS *b* 4 Jan 1989, — *HRH Princess* Irina, *b* 28 Feb 1953: *m* 4 Oct 1983 (civ) and 11 Feb 1984 (relig), John Kreuger, son of Torsten Kreuger, and has issue living, Michael Torsten *b* 25 Feb 1985, Angelica Margareta Bianca *b* 29 Dec 1986, — *HRH Princess* Sophie, *b* 29 Oct 1957: *m* 29 Aug 1998 (civ), Alain Michel Biarneix dit de Laufenbourg, son of Robert Alfred Biarneix, and has issue living, Elisabeta Maria Bianca Elena DE LAUFENBOURG *b* 15 Aug 1999, — *HRH Princess* Maria, *b* 13 July 1964: *m* 16 Sept 1995, Kazimierz Wieslaw Mystkowski, son of Eugeniusz Mystkowski. *Residence* - Villa Serena, 77 chemin Louis Degallier, CH-1290 Versoix, Geneva, Switzerland.

Granddaughter of Adm of the Fleet HRH late Prince Alfred Ernest Albert, KG, KT, KP, GCB, GCSI, GCMG, GCIE, GCVO, PC, Duke of Edinburgh (*cr* 1866), and reigning Duke of Saxe-Coburg and Gotha 1893-1900, 2nd son of Queen Victoria:—
Issue of HRH late Princess Marie Alexandra Victoria (*Queen of Roumania*), VA, CI, RRC, *b* 29 Oct 1875, *d* 18 July 1938: *m* 11 Jan 1893, HM King Ferdinand I of Roumania, KG, GCB, who *d* 20 July 1927:—

Austria †*HRH Princess* Ileana (*Mother Alexandra*), *b* 5 Jan 1909; an Orthodox nun: *m* 1st, 26 July 1931 (*m diss* 1954), HI & RH Archduke Anton Maria Franz Leopold Blanka Karl Joseph Ignaz Raphael Michael Margareta Nicetas of Austria, Prince of Tuscany, who *d* 22 Oct 1987; 2ndly, 19 June 1954 (*m diss* 1965), Dr Stefan Virgil Issarescu, and *d* 21 Jan 1991, having had issue, (by 1st *m*) †*HI & RH Archduke* Stefan; later known as Mr Stefan Habsburg-Lothringen, *b* 15 Aug 1932; US citizen: *m* 26 Aug 1954, (Mary) Jerrine, da of Charles B. Soper, of Boston, USA, and *d* 12 Nov 1998, leaving issue, Christopher *b* 26 Jan 1957: *m* 1st, 1 May 1987 (*m diss* 1991), Elisabeth Ann Blanchette, da of Larry Lee Popejoy; 2ndly, 15 Oct 1994, Catherine Q., da of Anthony Ripley (and has issue living (by 1st *m*), Stefan Christopher *b* 19 Jan 1990, Saygan Genevieve *b* 31 Oct 1987, (by 2nd *m*) Maria Antonia *b* 1 Oct 1997), Peter *b* 19 Feb 1959: *m* 1st, 27 June 1981 (*m diss* 1985 and annulled 1988), Shari Suzanne, da of William Marshall Reid; 2ndly, 17 June 1989, Lauren Ann, da of Martin John Klaus, Anton *b* 7 Nov 1964: *m* 5 Oct 1991, Ashley Byrd, da of Rev Dr William Douglas Carrell, Ileana *b* 4 Jan 1958: *m* 23 June 1979, David Scott Snyder (and has issue living, Nicholas David *b* 27 Feb 1987, Alexandra Marie *b* 18 Aug 1984, Constanza Ileana *b* 23 June 1994), Constanza *b* 2 Oct 1960: *m* 1st, 16 Jan 1987 (*m diss* 1995), Mark Lee Matheson, son of Robert Kenneth Matheson; 2ndly, 8 Nov 1997, Michael Dale Bain, son of Robert Eugene Bain, — *HI & RH Archduke* Dominic (San Stin 2368, I-30125 Venice, Italy), *b* 4 July 1937: *m* 11 June 1960, Virginia Engel, da of Friedrich Ditlev von Voss, of Houston, Texas, USA, and has issue living, Sandor *b* 13 Feb 1965, Gregor *b* 20 Nov 1968, — †*HI & RH Archduchess* Maria Ileana, *b* 18 Dec 1933: *m* 7 Dec 1957, Count Jaroslav Franz Josef Ignaz Maria Kottulinsky, and *d* (*k* in an air crash with her husband) 11 Jan 1959, leaving issue, *Countess* (Maria) Ileana *b* 25 Aug 1958: *m* 10 Oct 1997, Baron Noël van Innis, of Villa Odescalchi, Via Anzani 12, I-22040 Alzate Brianza, Italy, — *HI & RH Archduchess* Alexandra, *b* 21 May 1935: *m* 1st, 31 Aug 1962 (*m diss* 1972 and annulled 1973), HRH Duke Eugen Eberhard Albrecht Maria Joseph Joan Rylski Robert Ulrich Philipp Odo Carl Hubert of Württemberg; 2ndly, 29 Dec 1973, Baron Victor Franz Clemens Raoul Emil Wilhelm von Baillou, of Mönchsberg 33, A5020 Salzburg, Austria. — *HI & RH Archduchess* Maria Magdalena, *b* 2 Oct 1939: *m* 29 Aug 1959, Baron Hans Ulrich von Holzhausen, of Johann-Wolf-Strasse 6, Salzburg, Austria, and has issue living, *Baron* Johann Friedrich Anton *b* 29 July 1960, *Baron*

Georg-Ferdinand *b* 16 Feb 1962: *m* 30 April (civ) and 22 May (relig) 1993, Countess Elena Maria Victoria Ingeborg, da of Count Reinhart Heinrich Hubertus Maria von und zu Hoensbroech (and has issue living, *Baron* Alexander Justinian Victor Christoph *b* 28 Nov 1994, *Baron* Tassilo Christoph Johannes Donatus *b* 4 May 1997), *Baroness* Alexandra Maria *b* 22 Jan 1963, *m* 2 July (civ) and 7 July (relig) 1985, Christoph Alexander Rudolf Michael Ferch, son of Rudolf Maria Ferch (and has issue living, Ferdinand Georg Botho *b* 17 Oct 1986, Leopold Anton David *b* 18 Aug 1988, Benedikt Peter *b* 2 March 1993, Elisabeth Patricia Katherina *b* 23 Feb 1995), — *HI & RH Archduchess* Elisabeth, *b* 15 Jan 1942: *m* 31 July (civ) and 3 Aug (relig) 1964, Friedrich Josef Sandhofer, MD, of Gärtnerstrasse 2, Salzburg, Austria, and has issue living, Anton Dominic Friedrich *b* 26 Oct 1966: *m* 28 May (civ) and 29 May (relig) 1993, Katarzyna Marta, da of Wlodzimierz Wojkowski (and has issue living, Dominik Alexander *b* 7 Jan 1994), Margareta Elisabeth *b* 10 Sept 1968: *m* 20 June 1992, Ernst Helmut Klaus Lux, son of Ernst Johann Karl Lux (and has issue living, Mauritio Maria Ernst *b* 29 April 1999), Andrea Alexandra *b* 13 Dec 1969: *m* 30 Aug 1996 (civ) and 14 June 1997 (relig), Jörg Michael Zarbl, son of Horst Josef Zarbl (and has issue living Ferdinand Hans Friedrich Konstantin Maria *b* 8 Dec 1996, Benedikt Bonifatius Manfred Rainer Maria *b* 19 Feb 1999), Elisabeth Victoria Magdalena *b* 16 Nov 1971.

Grandson of HRH late Princess Marie (*Queen Marie of Yugoslavia*) (infra):—
Issue of HM late King Peter II of Yugoslavia (reigned 1934-45), *b* 6 Sept 1923, *d* 3 Nov 1970: *m* 20 March 1944, HRH Princess Alexandra, who *d* 30 Jan 1993, only da of HM late King Alexander I of the Hellenes (infra):—
HRH Crown Prince Alexander of Yugoslavia (Chancellery, 36 Park Lane, W1Y 3LE), *b* 17 July 1945; A/Capt 16th/5th The Queen's R Lancers: *m* 1st, 1 July 1972 (*m diss* 1985), HRH Princess Maria da Glória Dolores Lucia Micaela Rafaela Gabriela Gonzaga), elder da of HRH Prince Dom Pedro Gastão of Orleans and Bragança; 2ndly, 21 Sept 1985, Katherine Clairy, da of Robert Batis, of Athens, and has issue living (by 1st *m*), *HRH Prince* Peter, *b* 5 Feb 1980, — *HRH Prince* Alexander, *b* 15 Jan 1982, — *HRH Prince* Philip, *b* (twin) 15 Jan 1982.   **Yugoslavia**

Grandsons of HRH late Princess Marie Alexandra Victoria (*Queen of Roumania*), VA, CI, RRC (ante):—
Issue of HRH late Princess Marie (*Queen Marie of Yugoslavia*), *b* 9 Jan 1900, *d* 22 June 1961: *m* 8 June 1922, HM King Alexander I of Yugoslavia, who *d* (assassinated) 9 Oct 1934:—
HRH Prince Tomislav, *b* 19 Jan 1928; *ed* Oundle, and Clare Coll, Camb: *m* 1st, 6 June 1957 (*m diss* 1982), HGDH Princess Margarita Alice Thyra Viktoria Marie Louise Scholastica, only da of HRH late Margrave Berthold of Baden (infra); 2ndly, 17 Oct 1982, Linda Mary, da of late Holbrook Bonney, and has issue living, (by 1st *m*) *HRH Prince* Nikola, *b* 15 March 1958: *m* 30 Aug (civ) and 22 Nov (relig) 1992, Ljiljana, da of Lazar Licánin, and has issue living, *HRH Princess* Maria *b* 4 Aug 1993, — *HRH Princess* Katarina, *b* 28 Nov 1959: *m* 5 Dec 1987, (George) Desmond Lorenz de Silva, QC, KStJ, of 28 Sydney St, SW3, son of Edmund Frederick Lorenz de Silva, and has issue living, Victoria Marie Esme Margarita *b* 6 Sept 1991, — (by 2nd *m*) *HRH Prince* George, *b* 25 May 1984, — *HRH Prince* Michael *b* 15 Dec 1985. — †*HRH Prince* Andrej, *b* 28 June 1929; *ed* Oundle, and Clare Coll, Camb (BA 1950): *m* 1st, 1 Aug (civ) and 2 Aug (relig) 1956 (*m diss* 1962), HH Princess Christina Margarete, da of HH late Prince Christoph Ernst August of Hesse (infra); 2ndly, 18 Sept (civ) and 12 Oct (relig) 1963 (*m diss* 1972), HSH Princess Kira-Melita Feodora Maria Viktoria Alexandra, da of HSH the 6th Prince of Leiningen (infra); 3rdly, 30 March 1974, Eva Maria, da of Milan T. Andjelković, and formerly wife of Dr Frank Lowe, and *d* 7 May 1990, leaving issue (by 1st *m*) †*HRH Prince* Christopher, *b* 4 Feb 1960, *d* 14 May 1994 as the result of a motor accident, — *HRH Princess* (Maria) Tatiana, *b* 18 July 1957: *m* 30 June 1990, Gregory Per Edward Anthony Michael Thune-Larsen, son of Knut Thune Larsen, and has issue living, Sonia Tatiana *b* 29 Oct 1992, Olga Kristin *b* 26 Oct 1995, — (by 2nd *m*) *HRH Prince* Karl Vladimir Cyril Andrej, *b* 11 March 1964, — *HRH Prince* Dimitri Ivan Mihailo, *b* 21 April 1965. Prince Andrej and his second wife also formally adopted (15 Nov 1965) their natural da, *HRH Princess* (so recognised by King Petar II of Yugoslavia 1965) Lavinia Marie, *b* 18 Oct 1961: *m* 1st, 20 May 1989 (*m diss* 1993), Erastos Dimitrious Sidiropoulos, son of Aristotle Sidiropoulos; 2ndly, 4 Oct 1998, Austin Prichard-Levy, son of Hermann Martin Heinrich Levy, and has issue living (by 1st *m*), Andrej Aristotle *b* 22 Feb 1990, (by Roy Rexford Finnimore) Nadya-Marie SIDIROPOULOS *b* 11 Dec 1987.

Grandson of HRH Prince Alfred Ernest Albert, Duke of Edinburgh (ante):—
Issue of HRH late Princess Victoria Melita (Victoria Feodorovna) (*Grand Duchess Kirill (Cyril) of Russia*), VA, CI, *b* 25 Nov 1876, *d* 2 March 1936: *m*

1st, 19 April 1894 (*m diss* 21 Dec 1901), HRH Grand Duke Ernst Ludwig (Karl Albert Wilhelm) of Hesse and by Rhine, who *d* 9 Oct 1937 (infra); 2ndly, 8 Oct 1905, HIH Grand Duke Kirill (Cyril) Vladimirovitch of Russia (first cousin of late Emperor Nicholas II), who *d* 13 Oct 1938:—

Russia   (By 2nd *m*) †*HIH Grand Duke* Vladimir Kirillovitch, *b* 30 Aug 1917; *ed* London Univ; *s* his father as head of the Imperial House of Romanoff: *m* 13 Aug 1948, Princess Leonida, da of late Prince George Alexandrovitch Bagration-Mukhransky, and formerly wife of late Sumner Moore Kirby, and *d* 21 April 1992, leaving issue, *HIH Grand Duchess* Maria Vladimirovna, *b* 23 Dec 1953: *m* 22 Sept 1976 (*m diss* 1986), HRH Prince Franz-Wilhelm (Viktor Christof Stefan) of Prussia (infra), and has issue living, *HRH Prince* Georg, *b* 13 March 1981.

Grandchildren of HRH late Princess Victoria Melita (*Grand Duchess Kirill of Russia*), VA, CI (ante):—

Issue of HIH late Grand Duchess Marie Kirillovna, *b* 2 Feb 1907, *d* 27 Oct 1951: *m* 24 Nov 1925, HSH the 6th Prince (Friedrich Karl Eduard Erwin) of Leiningen, who *d* 2 Aug 1946:—

Leiningen †*HSH Prince* Emich Kirill Ferdinand Hermann (*7th Prince of Leiningen*), *b* 18 Oct 1926: *m* 10 Aug 1950, HH Duchess Eilika Stephanie Elisabeth Thekla Juliana, da of HRH Hereditary Grand Duke Nikolaus Friedrich Wilhelm of Oldenburg, and *d* 30 Oct 1991, leaving issue, *HSH Prince* Karl-Emich Nikolaus Friedrich Hermann (*8th Prince of Leiningen*), *b* 12 June 1952: *m* 1st, 8 June (civ) and 16 June (relig) 1984, *HSH Princess* Margarita Katharina Elisabeth, who *d* 27 Feb 1989, el da of HSH Kraft Hans Konrad, 8th Prince of Hohenlohe-Öhringen, 5th Duke of Ujest; 2ndly, 24 May (civ) and 15 June (relig) 1991 (*m diss* 1998), Gabriele Renate Thyssen, da of Helmut-Friedhelm Homey, and has issue living, (by 1st *m*) *HSH Princess* Cecilia Maria Stephanie *b* 10 June 1988, (by 2nd *m*) *HSH Princess* Theresa Anna Elisabeth *b* 26 April 1992, — *HSH Prince* Andreas, *b* 27 Nov 1955: *m* 5 Oct (civ) and 11 Oct (relig) 1981, HRH Princess Alexandra Irene Margaretha Bathildis, da of HRH Ernst August, Prince of Hanover (infra), and has issue living, *HSH Prince* Ferdinand Heinrich Emich Christian Karl *b* 12 Aug 1982, *HSH Prince* Hermann Ernst Johann Albrecht Paul *b* 13 Sept 1987, *HSH Princess* Olga Margarita Valerie Elisabeth Stephanie Alexandra *b* 23 Oct 1984, — *HSH Princess* Melita Elisabeth Bathildis Helene Margarita, *b* 10 June 1951: *m* 14 April 1978, Horst Legrum, who *d* 19 Sept 1994, son of Jakob Legrum, — *HSH Princess* Stephanie Margarita, *b* 1 Oct 1958. *Residence* - Odenwald 8762, Amorbach, Bavaria, Germany. — †*HSH Prince* Karl Vladimir Ernst Heinrich, *b* 2 Jan 1928: *m* 14 Feb (civ) and 20 Feb (relig) 1957 (*m diss* 1968), HRH Princess Marie-Louise, only da of HM late King Boris III of Bulgaria, and *d* 28 Sept 1990, leaving issue, *HSH Prince* Karl Boris (Frank Markwart), *b* 17 April 1960, *m* 1st, 14 Feb 1987 (*m diss* 1996), Millena Eileen, da of Wladimir Manov; 2ndly, 11 Sept (Protestant) and 6 Dec (Orthodox) 1998, Cheryl Ann, da of Henry Riegler, and has issue living (by 1st *m*), *HSH Prince* Nicholas Alexander Karel Friedrich *b* 25 Oct 1991, — *HSH Prince* Hermann Friedrich Roland Fernando, *b* 16 April 1963, *m* 16 May 1987, Deborah, da of Robert Cully, and has issue living, *HSH Princess* Tatiana Victoria Maureen *b* 27 Aug 1989, *HSH Princess* Nadia Christianne Ruth *b* 16 Dec 1991, *HSH Princess* Alexandra Sophia Maria *b* 18 Dec 1997. — †*HSH Prince* Friedrich Wilhelm Berthold, *b* 18 June 1938: *m* 1st, 9 July 1960 (*m diss* 1962), Karin Evelyne Goss; 2ndly, 23 Aug 1971, Helga, da of Hans Eschenbacher, and *d* 29 Aug 1998. — *HSH Princess* Kira-Melita Feodora Marie Viktoria Alexandra Petra Sofie, *b* 18 July 1930: *m* 18 Sept (civ) and 12 Oct (relig) 1963 (*m diss* 1972), HRH Prince Andrej of Yugoslavia, and has issue living (ante). — *HSH Princess* Margarita Ileana Viktoria Alexandra,

Hohen-   *b* 9 May 1932: *m* 3 Feb 1951, HH Prince Friedrich Wilhelm Ferdinand Josef Maria
zollern   Manuel Georg Meinrad Fidelis Benedikt Michael Hubertus of Hohenzollern, and has issue living, *HSH Hereditary Prince* Karl Friedrich (Emich Meinrad Benedikt Fidelis Maria Michael Gerold), *b* 20 April 1952: *m* 15 June 1985, Alexandra Petra Sofie, da of Clemens, Count Schenk von Stauffenberg, and has issue living, *HSH Prince* Alexander Friedrich *b* 16 March 1987, *HSH Princess* Philippa *b* 2 Nov 1988, *HSH Princess* Flaminia *b* 9 Jan 1992, *HSH Princess* Antonia Elisabeth Georgina Tatiana *b* 22 June 1995, — *HSH Prince* Albrecht Johannes Hermann Meinrad Stephan, *b* 3 Aug 1954, — *HSH Prince* Ferdinand Maria Fidelis Leopold Meinrad Valentin, *b* 14 Feb 1960: *m* 10 May (civ) and 3 Aug (relig) 1996, Countess Ilona Marie-Therese Renée Franziska, da of Count Alois Hugo Alexander Georg Guntram Maria Kálnoky de Köröspatak. *Residence* - Landhaus Josefslust, Sigmaringen, Hohenzollern, Germany. — *HSH Princess* Mechtilde Alexandra, *b* 2 Jan 1936: *m* 25 Nov 1961, Karl Anton Bauscher, of 8600 Bamberg, Ohmstrasse 6, Germany, and has issue living, Ulf Karl Heinz Stephan Kraft, *b* 20 Feb 1963, — Berthold Alexander Eric, *b* 31 Oct 1965: *m* 29 March (civ) and 30 March (relig) 1996, Anett Christin, da of Erich Gotthilf Kühfuss, and has issue living, Franka Silke Stephanie *b* 12 Sept 1996, — Johann Karl Joachim Fritz, *b* 2 Feb 1968.

Issue of HIH late Grand Duchess Kira Kirillovna, *b* 9 May 1909, *d* 8 Sept 1967: *m* 2 May 1938, HI & RH Prince Louis Ferdinand Viktor Eduard Adalbert Michael Hubertus of Prussia (infra):—
HRH Prince (Louis Ferdinand) Friedrich Wilhelm (Hubertus Michael Kirill) (Del-   **Prussia** iusweg 20, D-28359 Bremen, Germany), *b* 9 Feb 1939; renounced rights of succession for himself and his descendants 18 Sept 1967: *m* 1st, 22 Aug 1967 (*m diss* 1975), Waltraud, da of late Dr Alois Freydag, of Plön; 2ndly, 24 April 1976, Ehrengard Insea Elisabeth, da of Lt-Col Günther Ludwig Jobst Johann von Reden, and has issue living, (by 1st *m*) (*Prince*) Philipp Kirill Friedrich Wilhelm Moritz Boris Zdenko, *b* 23 April 1968: *m* 28 June (civ) and 2 July (relig) 1994, Anna Christine, da of Eggert Soltau, and has issue living, (*Prince*) Paul Wilhelm (Philipp Friedrich Aloysius Johannes Mose *b* 4 Oct 1995, (*Princess*) Maria Luise (Anna Helene Julie Margarethe Elisabeth) *b* 12 March 1997, — (by 2nd *m*) (*Prince*) Friedrich Wilhelm (Louis Ferdinand Kirill), *b* 16 Aug 1979, — (*Prince*) Joachim Albert Bernhard Christian Ernst, *b* 26 June 1984, — (*Princess*) Viktoria-Luise Kira Ehrengard, *b* 2 May 1982. — *HRH Prince* (Wilhelm Heinrich) Michael (Louis Ferdinand Friedrich Franz Wladimir) (Im Altenspohl 14, D-72406 Bisingen-Thanheim, Germany), *b* 22 March 1940; renounced rights of succession for himself and his descendants 29 Aug 1966: *m* 1st 23 Sept 1966 (*m diss* 1982), Jutta, da of Otto Jörn; 2ndly, 23 June 1982, Brigitte, da of Hans Viktor von Dallwitz, and has issue living, (by 1st *m*) (*Princess*) Micaela Maria, *b* 5 March 1967, — (*Princess*) Nataly Alexandra Caroline, *b* 13 Jan 1970. — *HRH Prince* Christian Sigismund (Louis Ferdinand Kilian) (Wümmehof, D-28357 Bremen, Germany), *b* 14 March 1946: *m* 29 Sept 1984, Countess Nina Helene Lydia Alexandra, da of Count (Carl) Ludwig Erich Ernst Victor Christian Detlev Alexander zu Reventlow, and has issue living, *HRH Prince* Christian Ludwig (Michael Friedrich Ferdinand), *b* 16 May 1986, — *HRH Princess* Irina Maria Vera Kira *b* 4 July 1988: Prince Christian Sigismund has recognized (17 Dec 1969) his da by Christiane Grandmontagne, Isabella Alexandra VON PREUSSEN, *b* 18 Sept 1969. — *HRH Princess* Marie Cécile (Kira Viktoria Luise), *b* 28 May 1942: *m* 3 Dec 1965 (*m diss* 1989), HH Duke Friedrich August Wilhelm Christian Ernst of Oldenburg, and has issue living, *HH Duke* Paul Wladimir (Nikolaus Louis Ferdinand Peter Max Karl Emich), *b* 16 Aug 1969, — *HH Duchess* Rixa (Marie-Alix Kira Altburg), *b* 17 Sept 1970, —   **Oldenburg** *Duchess* Bibiane (Maria Alexandra Gertrud), *b* 24 June 1974. — *HRH Princess* Kira (Auguste Viktoria Friederike), *b* 27 June 1943: *m* 10 Sept 1973 (*m diss* 1984), Thomas Frank Liepsner, and has issue living, Kira Marina, *b* 22 Jan 1977. — †*HRH Princess* Xenia (Sophie Charlotte Cecilie), *b* 9 Dec 1949: *m* 26 (civ) and 27 (relig) Jan 1973 (*m diss* 1978), Per-Edvard Lithander, and *d* 18 Jan 1992, leaving issue, Patrick Edvard Christian, *b* 25 June 1973, — Wilhelm Sebastian, *b* 21 Nov 1974.

Grandchildren of HIH late Grand Duchess Kira Kirillovna (*Princess Louis Ferdinand of Prussia*) (ante):—
Issue of HRH late Prince Louis Ferdinand (Oskar Christian), *b* 25 Aug 1944, *d* 11 July 1977: *m* 24 May 1975, H Ill H Countess Donata Emma (who *m* 2ndly, 9 Feb 1991, HH Duke Friedrich August Wilhelm Christian Ernst of Oldenburg (ante)), only da of HSH Siegfried (Casimir Friedrich), 4th Prince zu Castell-Rüdenhausen:—
HRH Prince Georg Friedrich (Ferdinand), *b* 10 June 1976; Head of the Royal House of Prussia since 25 Sept 1994. — *HRH Princess* Cornelie-Cécile (Viktoria Irene), *b* (*posthumous*) 30 Jan 1978.

Grandchildren of HRH late Princess Alexandra Louise Olga Victoria (*Princess of Hohenlohe-Langenburg*) (infra):—
Issue of HSH late Prince Gottfried Viktor Hermann Alfred Paul Maximilian (*8th Prince of Hohenlohe-Langenburg*), *b* 24 March 1897, *d* 11 May 1960: *m* 20 April 1931, HRH Princess Margarita, who *d* 24 April 1981, da of HRH late Prince Andrew of Greece and Denmark, GCVO (infra):—
HSH Prince Kraft Alexander Ernst Ludwig Georg Emich (*9th Prince of Hohenlohe-*   **Hohenlohe-** *Langenburg*), *b* 25 June 1935: *m* 1st, 5 June (civ) and 16 July (relig) 1965 (*m diss*   **Langen-** 1990), HSH Princess Charlotte Alexandra Maria Clothilde, da of HSH Prince   **burg** Alexander Georg Maria Josef Ignatius of Croy; 2ndly, 22 May 1992, Irma Gisela Christine, da of Eugen Pospesch, and has issue living (by 1st *m*), *HSH Hereditary Prince* Philipp Gottfried Alexander, *b* 20 Jan 1970, — *HSH Princess* Cecile Marita Dorothea, *b* 16 Dec 1967: *m* 6 June 1998, Comte Cyril Amédéo de Commarque, yr son of Raymond Godefroy Leonard, Marquis de Commarque, — *HSH Princess* Xenia Margarita Anne, *b* 8 July 1972. *Residence* - D-74595 Schloss Langenburg, Württemberg, Germany. — *HSH Prince* (Georg) Andreas Heinrich (Tristanstrasse 18a, D-80804 Munich, Germany), *b* 24 Nov 1938: *m* 14 Aug (civ) and 9 Sept (relig) 1968, HSH Princess Luise Pauline Amelie Vibeke Emma, da of HSH Prince Georg Ulrich of Schönburg-Waldenburg, and has issue living, *HSH Princess* Katharina Clementine Beatrix, *b* 21 Nov 1972, — *HSH Princess* Tatiana Louise, *b* 10 Feb 1975. — †*HSH Prince* Albrecht Wolfgang Christoph, *b* 7 April 1944: *m* 23 Jan 1976,

Maria Hildegard, da of Max Willy Fischer, and *d* 23 April 1992, leaving issue, (*Prince*) Ludwig (Altensteinstrasse 38a, D-14195 Berlin, Germany), *b* 21 April 1976.
— †*HSH Princess* Beatrix Alice Marie Melita Margarita, *b* 10 July 1936; *d* 15 Nov 1997.

Issue of HSH late Princess Marie Melita Leopoldine Victoria Feodora Alexandra Sophie, *b* 18 Jan 1899, *d* 8 Nov 1967: *m* 15 Feb 1916, HH (Wilhelm) Friedrich Christian Günther Albert Adolf Georg, Duke of Schleswig-Holstein-Sonderburg-Glücksburg, who *d* 10 Feb 1965:—
HH Princess Marie Alexandra Caroline Mathilde Viktoria Irene, *b* 9 July 1927: *m* 22 July 1970, Douglas Barton Miller, of Schloss-strasse l, D-88045 Friedrichschafen, Germany.

Grandchildren of HSH late Princess Marie Melita Leopoldine Victoria Feodora Alexandra Sophie (*Duchess of Schleswig-Holstein-Sonderburg-Glücksburg*):—
Issue of HH late Prince (Friedrich Ernst) Peter, Duke of Schleswig-Holstein-Sonderburg-Glücksburg, *b* 30 April 1922, *d* 30 Sept 1980: *m* 9 Oct 1947, HSH Princess Marie-Alix (Gut Bienebeck, Post Damp über Eckernförde, Germany), only da of HSH Prince Stephan Alexander Viktor of Schaumburg-Lippe:—

Schleswig- *HH Prince* Christoph (*Duke of Schleswig-Holstein-Sonderburg-Glücksburg*), *b* 22
Holstein Aug 1949: *m* 4 Oct 1981, HSH Princess Elisabeth, da of HSH Prince Alfred Karl of Lippe-Weissenfeld, and has issue living, *HH Prince* Friedrich-Ferdinand, *b* 19 July 1985, — *HH Prince* Constantin, *b* 14 July 1986, — *HH Prince* Leopold, *b* 5 Sept 1991, — *HH Princess* Sophie, *b* 9 Oct 1983. — *HH Prince* Alexander, *b* 9 July 1953: *m* 29 Aug (civ) and 3 Sept (relig) 1994, Barbara Beate, da of Fritz-Wilhelm Fertsch, and has issue living, *HH Prince* Julian Nicholas, *b* 20 Oct 1997, *HH Princess* Elena, *b* 25 Jan 1995. — *HH Princess* Marita, *b* 5 Sept 1948: *m* 23 May 1975, Baron Wilfrid von Plotho, of Sonnenweg 14, CH-4313 Möhlin bei Basel, Switzerland, and has issue living, *Baron* Christoph, *b* 14 March 1976, — *Baroness* Irina, *b* 28 Jan 1978. — *HH Princess* Ingeborg, *b* 9 July 1956: *m* 31 May (civ) and 1 June (relig) 1991, (Kurt) Nikolaus Albert Broschek, son of Curt Rudolph Broschek, and has issue living, Alexis Nikolaus Peter Johannes, *b* 12 Dec 1995.

Grandson of HRH Prince Alfred Ernest Albert, Duke of Edinburgh (ante):—
Issue of HRH late Princess Beatrice Leopoldine Victoria, VA, *b* 20 April 1884, *d* 13 July 1966: *m* 15 July 1909, HRH Prince Alfonso Maria Francisco Antonio Diego of Orleans, Infante of Spain, 5th Duke of Galliera, who *d* 10 Aug 1975:—

Bourbon- †*HRH Prince* Alvaro Antonio Fernando Carlos Felipe (*6th Duke of Galliera*), *b* 20
Orleans April 1910; *ed* Winchester; AFRAeS and AMIMechE: *m* 10 July 1937, Carla, who *d* 1999, el da of late Senator Leopoldo Girolamo Parodi-Delfino, and *d* 22 Aug 1997, having had issue, *Don* Alvaro Jaime de Orléans, *b* 1 March 1947: *m* 24 May 1974, Donna Giovanna, yst da of Don Casimiro San Martino d'Aglie di San Germano, Marchese di San Germano, and has issue living, *Don* Andrés *b* 7 July 1976, *Don* Alois *b* 24 March 1979, *Doña* Pilar *b* 27 May 1975, — *Doña* Gerarda (*Marquesa de Marchelina*), *b* 25 Aug 1939: *m* 1st, 26 July 1963 (*m diss* 1977 and annulled 1990), Harry Freeman Saint, son of Ellis Chandler Saint; 2ndly, 17 Nov 1990, Don Ignacio Eurique Romero y de Solis, Marqués de Marchelina, and has issue living (by 1st *m*), Marc *b* 20 March 1969: *m* 10 Dec 1990 (civ) and 6 July 1991 (relig) (*m diss* 1995 and annulled 1996), Dorothée Sophie, da of Michel André Horps, Carla *b* 22 May 1967: *m* 19 Sept 1992, John Stephen Lilly, son of Terence Lilly, — *Doña* Beatriz (*Marquesa de Torre Breva*), *b* 27 April 1943: *m* 25 April 1964 (*m diss* 1989), Dr Tomaso dei Conti Farini, Patrician of Ravenna, and has issue living, *Don* Gerardo Alfonso *b* 23 Nov 1967, Donna Elena *b* 27 Oct 1969: *m* 19 June 1998, Don Joaquin de Haro y Fernandez de Cordoba, son of Don Joaquin de Haro y Rodas and Doña Consuelo Fernandez de Cordoba y Ybarra.

Grandsons of HRH Prince Alvaro Antonio Fernando Carlos Felipe of Orleans (*6th Duke of Galliera*) (ante):—
Issue of late Don Alonso of Orleans, *b* 23 Aug 1941, *d* 6 Sept 1975; was Spanish Consul at Houston, Texas, USA: *m* 12 Jan 1966, Donna Emilia, da of Don Vincenzo Ferrara-Pignatelli, 12th Principe di Strongoli:—
Don Alfonso (*7th Duke of Galliera*), *b* 2 Jan 1968: *m* 28 March 1994, Veronique, da of Jean-Marie Goeders, and has issue living, Don Alonso Juan, *b* 15 July 1994. — *Don* Alvaro, *b* 4 Oct 1969.

Descendants of Field Marshal HRH the Duke of Connaught and Strathearn, 3rd son of Queen Victoria.

Grandchildren of HRH late Princess Margaret Victoria Augusta Charlotte Norah (*Crown Princess of Sweden, Duchess of Skåne*) (infra):—
Issue of HRH late Prince Gustaf Adolf (Oscar Fredrik Arthur Edmund) (*Duke of Västerbotten*), GCVO, *b* 22 April 1906, *d* 26 Jan 1947: *m* 20 Oct 1932, HH Princess Sibylla Calma Marie Alice Bathildis Feodora, who *d* 28 Nov 1972, da of HRH Prince (Leopold) Charles Edward George Albert, 2nd Duke of Albany (Duke of Saxe-Coburg and Gotha) (infra):—
HM King Carl XVI Gustaf (Folke Hubertus) (*King of Sweden*), KG (Royal Palace, S-11130 Stockholm, Sweden; Solliden Öland, Drottningholm), *b* 30 April 1946; *s* his **Sweden** grandfather King Gustaf VI Adolf 15 Sept 1973; Hon Adm RN 1975; has Orders of Seraphim of Sweden, Elephant of Denmark, Falcon of Iceland, Saint Olav of Norway, White Rose of Finland, Chrysanthemum of Japan; Roy Victorian Chain 1975, KG 1983: *m* 19 June 1976, Silvia Renate, da of Walther Sommerlath, of Heidelberg, and has issue living, *HRH Prince* Carl Philip (Edmund Bertil) (*Duke of Värmland*), *b* 13 May 1979, — *HRH Princess* Victoria Ingrid Alice Désirée (*Crown Princess of Sweden, Duchess of Västergötland*), *b* 14 July 1977; Crown Princess of Sweden since 1 Jan 1980, — *HRH Princess* Madeleine Thérèse Amelie Josephine (*Duchess of Hälsingland and Gästrikland*), *b* 10 June 1982. — *Princess* Margaretha Désirée Victoria (*Princess Margaretha, Mrs Ambler*), *b* 31 Oct 1934; has Order of Seraphim of Sweden: *m* 30 June 1964, John Kenneth Ambler (Knt Cdr Roy Order of Vasa), of Chippinghurst Manor, Cuddesdon, Oxon, and has issue living, (Charles) Edward, *b* 14 July 1966, — James Patrick, *b* 10 June 1969, — Sybilla Louise, *b* 14 April 1965: *m* 19 June 1998, Baron Henning Cornelius von Dincklage, son of Baron Hans Henning von Dincklage, and has issue living, *Baroness* Madeleine Charlotte Margaretha *b* 15 March 1999, — *HRH Princess* Birgitta Ingeborg Alice, *b* 19 Jan 1937; has Order of Seraphim of Sweden: *m* 30 May 1961, HSH Prince Johann Georg (Carl Leopold Eitel Friedrich Meinrad Maria Hubertus Michael) of Hohenzollern, and has issue living, *HSH Prince* Carl Christian (Friedrich Johannes Meinrad Maria Hubertus Edmund), *b* 5 April 1962: *m* 10 July 1999, Nicole Neschitsch, — *HSH Prince* Hubertus Gustav-Adolf Veit Georg Meinrad Maria Alexander, *b* 10 June 1966, — *HSH Princess* Désirée Margarethe Victoria Louise Sibylla Catharina Maria, *b* 27 Nov 1963: *m* 21 Sept (civ) and 6 Oct (relig) 1990, H Ill H Hereditary Count Heinrich Franz Josef Georg Maria of Ortenberg, eldest son of H Ill H Alram Karl Gottfried Hans Ladislaus, Count of Ortenberg, and has issue living, *H Ill H Count* Carl Theodor Georg Philipp Maria *b* 21 Feb 1992, *H Ill H Count* Frederik Hubertus Ferdinand Maria *b* 7 Feb 1995, *H Ill H Countess* Carolina Maria Franziska Christina Stephanie *b* 23 March 1997.
Residence - Dr Maxstrasse 70, D-8022 Grünwald, Germany. — *Princess* Désirée Elisabeth Sibylla (*Princess Désirée, Baroness Silfverschiöld*), *b* 2 June 1938; has Order of Seraphim of Sweden: *m* 5 June 1964, (Nils-August Otto Carl) Niclas, Baron Silfverschiöld, of Koberg, Sollebrunn, Sweden, and has issue living, *Baron* Carl Otto Edmund, *b* 22 March 1965, — *Baroness* Christina Louise (Ewa Madelaine), *b* 29 Sept 1966, — *Baroness* Hélène Ingeborg Sibylla, *b* 20 Sept 1968. — *Princess* Christina Louise Helena (*Princess Christina, Mrs Magnuson*), *b* 3 Aug 1943; has Order of Seraphim of Sweden: *m* 15 June 1974, Tord Gösta Magnuson, of Beylon, Ulriksdal, S-171 71 Solna, Sweden, and has issue living, (Carl) Gustaf Victor, *b* 8 Aug 1975, — (Tord) Oscar Fredrik, *b* 20 June 1977, — Victor Edmund Lennart, *b* 10 Sept 1980.

Grandchildren of FM HRH Prince Arthur William Patrick Albert, 1st Duke of Connaught and Strathearn, 3rd son of Queen Victoria:—
Issue of HRH late Princess Margaret Victoria Augusta Charlotte Norah (*Crown Princess of Sweden, Duchess of Skåne*), *b* 15 Jan 1882, *d* 1 May 1920: *m* 15 June 1905, HRH Crown Prince (Oscar Fredrik Wilhelm Olaf) Gustaf Adolf of Sweden, Duke of Skåne, GCB, GCVO, later HM King Gustaf VI Adolf, who *d* 15 Sept 1973:—
Count Sigvard Oscar Fredrik BERNADOTTE (af Wisborg) (Villagatan 10, S114 32 Stockholm, Sweden), *b* 7 June 1907; renounced right of succession, titles of Prince of Sweden and Duke of Uppland and style of HRH and assumed surname of Bernadotte 7 March 1934; *cr* Count Bernadotte af Wisborg by Grand Duchess of Luxembourg 2 July 1951, has Orders of North Star of Sweden and Elephant of Denmark: *m* 1st, 8 March 1934 (*m diss* 1943), Erika Maria Regina Rosalie, da of Anton Patzek; 2ndly, 26 Oct 1943 (*m diss* 1961), Sonja Helene, da of Robert Alexander Robbert, of Copenhagen, Denmark, shipowner; 3rdly, 30 July 1961, (Gullan) Marianne, only da of (Nils Gustaf) Helge Lindberg, of Helsingborg, and formerly wife of Gabriel Tchang, and has issue living, (by 2nd *m*) *Count* Michael Alexander Sigvard, *b* 21 Aug 1944: *m* 6 Feb 1976, Christine Diotima Elisabeth, da of Erwin Wellhöfer, and has issue living, *Countess* Kajsa Michaela Sophia, *b* 12 Oct 1980. — †*HRH Prince* Bertil Gustaf Oscar Carl Eugen (*Duke of Halland*), GCB, *b* 28 Feb 1912; Gen and Adm Roy Swedish Forces; was Assist Naval Attaché in London 1942-45; had Orders of Seraphim of Sweden and Elephant of Denmark; GCB (Hon Civil) 1956: *m* 7 Dec 1976, Lilian May, has Orders of Seraphim and of

North Star of Sweden, da of William John Davies, of Swansea, and formerly wife of William Ian (Ivan) Sackville Craig, and *dsp* 5 Jan 1997. — *Count* Carl Johan (Arthur) BERNADOTTE (af Wisborg) *b* 31 Oct 1916; renounced right of succession, titles of Prince of Sweden and Duke of Dalecarlia and style of HRH and assumed surname of Bernadotte 22 Feb 1946; *cr* Count Bernadotte af Wisborg by Grand Duchess of Luxembourg 2 July 1951; has Order of North Star of Sweden: *m* 1st, 19 Feb 1946, (Elin) Kerstin Margareta, who *d* 11 Sept 1987, 3rd da of Dr (Oscar) Henning Wilhelm Wijkmark, and formerly wife of Axel Johnson; 2ndly, 29 Sept 1988, Countess Gunilla Märta Louise, da of Count Nils Claës Ludvig Wachtmeister, and widow of Carl-Herman Albert Gerhard Bussler. *Residence* - Kungsberga, Båstad,

Denmark   Sweden. — *HRH Princess* Ingrid Victoria Sofia Louise Margareta (*HM Queen Ingrid, Queen Mother of Denmark*), *b* 28 March 1910: has Orders of the Elephant of Denmark, Seraphim of Sweden, etc: *m* 24 May 1935, HM King Frederik IX of Denmark, KG, GCB, GCVO, who *d* 14 Jan 1972, and has issue living, *HM Queen* Margrethe II (Alexandrine Thorhildur Ingrid) (*Queen of Denmark*), LG, *b* 16 April 1940; *ed* Girton Coll, Camb; Roy Victorian Chain 1974, Lady of Order of the Garter 1979: *m* 10 June 1967, Henri Marie Jean André de Laborde de Monpezat (*HRH Prince Henrik of Denmark* from 10 June 1967), Knt Order of the Elephant, Chancellor Roy Danish Orders, Adm Roy Danish Navy and Gen de Brigade Roy Danish Army, and has issue living, *HRH Crown Prince* Frederik André Henrik Christian *b* 26 May 1968, *HRH Prince* Joachim Holger Waldemar Christian *b* 7 June 1969: *m* 18 Nov 1995, Alexandra Christina, da of Richard Nigel Manley, of Hong Kong (and has issue living, a son *b* 1999), — *HRH Princess* Benedikte Astrid Ingeborg Ingrid, *b* 29 April 1944: *m* 3 Feb 1968, HSH Richard Casimir Karl August Konstantin, 6th Prince of Sayn-Wittgenstein-Berleburg (5920 Bad Berleburg, Westfalen, Germany), and has issue living, *HSH Prince* Gustav Frederik Philip Richard (*Hereditary Prince of Sayn-Wittgenstein-Berleburg*) *b* 12 Jan 1969, *HSH Princess* Alexandra Rosemarie Ingrid Benedikte *b* 20 Nov 1970: *m* 6 June 1998, Count Jefferson-Friedrich Volker Benjamin von Pfeil und Klein-Ellguth, *HSH Princess* Nathalie Xenia Margareta Benedikte *b* 2 May 1975, — *HRH Princess*

Greece   Anne-Marie Dagmar Ingrid (*HM Queen of the Hellenes*), *b* 30 Aug 1946: has Grand Cross of Order of the Redeemer of Greece: *m* 18 Sept 1964, HM King Constantine II of the Hellenes (infra), and has issue living, *HRH Crown Prince* Paul *b* 20 May 1967: *m* 1 July (relig) and 2 Aug (civ) 1995, Marie-Chantal Claire, da of Robert Warren Miller (and has issue living, *HRH Prince* Constantine Alexios *b* 29 Oct 1998, *HRH Princess* Maria Olympia *b* 25 July 1996), *HRH Prince* Nicholas *b* 1 Oct 1969, *HRH Prince* Philip *b* 26 April 1986, *HRH Princess* Alexia *b* 10 July 1965: *m* 9 July 1999, Carlos Morales Quintana, son of Luis Miguel Morales Armas, *HRH Princess* Theodora *b* 9 June 1983.

Issue of late Lady (Victoria) Patricia Helena Elizabeth Ramsay, VA, CI, CD, *b* 17 March 1886, *d* 12 Jan 1974; renounced on her marriage by Roy permission the style and title of HRH and Princess and assumed that of Lady with precedence before Marchionesses of England: *m* 27 Feb 1919, Adm Hon Sir Alexander Robert Maule Ramsay, GCVO, KCB, DSO, who *d* 8 Oct 1972:—

See E Dalhousie, colls.

Descendants of HRH the Duke of Albany, 4th son of Queen Victoria.

Saxe-   Grandchildren of HRH late Prince (Leopold) Charles Edward George
Coburg   Albert, 2nd Duke of Albany and reigning Duke of Saxe-Coburg and
and Gotha   Gotha (infra):—

Issue of HH late Hereditary Prince Johann Leopold (Wilhelm Albert Ferdinand Viktor):—
See Dukedom of Albany (infra).

Issue of HH late Princess Caroline Mathilde (Calma) Helene Ludwiga Auguste Beatrice, *b* 22 June 1912, *d* 5 Sept 1983: *m* 1st, 14 Dec 1931 (*m diss* 1938), H Ill H Count Friedrich Wolfgang (Otto) zu Castell-Rüdenhausen, who *d* (presumed killed in action) 11 June 1940; 2ndly, 22 June 1938, Capt Max Schnirring, German Air Force, who was *ka* 7 July 1944; 3rdly, 21 Dec 1946 (*m diss* 1949), Karl Otto (Jim) Andrée:—

(By 1st *m*) H Ill H Count Bertram Friedrich Wolfgang (Nibelungengasse 3/2/16, A-1110 Vienna, Austria), *b* 12 July 1932: *m* 10 Oct 1964, Countess Felizitas Anna Maria Elisabeth, only da of Count Hanno Herward Maria Josef Leo von Auersperg, and has issue living, *H Ill H Count* Dominik Dimitrij Johannes Friedrich, *b* 20 July 1965, — *H Ill H Count* Michael Alexej Wolfgang Friedrich, *b* 4 Nov 1967. — *H Ill H Count* Konradin Friedrich, *b* 10 Oct 1933: *m* 6 July 1961, Märta Catharina, da of Bjarne Lönegren, of Finland, and has issue living, *H Ill H Count* Carl-Eduard (Friedrich Hubertus) (Theklavej 9, 2tv, DK-2400 København NV, Denmark), *b* 15 March 1964: *m* 6 March 1999, Lisbeth, da of Leif Rauning, — *H Ill H Countess* Anne Charlotte (Catharina Victoria), *b* 7 April 1962: *m* 4 July 1986, Martti Kalevi Rappu, and has issue living, Patrick Martin Conradin *b* 3 Sept 1987, Richard Valdemar *b* 1 May 1989, Fredrik Carl Anton *b* 7 Nov 1990; Countess Anne Charlotte also has natural issue, Henrik Mikael Frederik ZU CASTELL-RÜDENHAUSEN *b* 23 Dec 1982.

— *H Ill H Countess* Victoria Adelheid Clementine Louise, *b* 26 Feb 1935: *m* 20 June 1960, (John) Miles Huntington-Whiteley, and has issue living (*see* Huntington-Whiteley, Bt). — (By 2nd *m*) Calma Barbara, *b* 18 Nov 1938: *m* 1st, 5 July 1961 (*m diss* 1973), Richard Darrell Berger; 2ndly, 15 May 1976, S. F. C. James Cook (132 Burnsdowne Road, Columbia, South Carolina 29210, USA), and has issue living, (by 1st *m*) Sascha Nikolaus Hubertus, *b* 22 Sept 1961: *m* 19 Nov 1982, Bonita Isabelle, da of James Olin Oden, and has issue living, Tristan Lee *b* 20 Nov 1984, Nicole Calma, *b* (twin) 20 Nov 1984, — Richard Darrel, *b* 3 July 1962: *m* 1st, 9 Aug 1982 (*m diss* 1988), Gypsy Dianna, da of Donald Eugene Wheeler; 2ndly, 9 July 1990, Ronda Rae, da of (Roland) Roger Ross, and has issue living (by 1st *m*), Richard Jonathan Ross, *b* 31 Aug 1984, — Victor Dean, *b* 28 Sept 1963: *m* 15 Aug 1986, Sylvia Diane, da of LeRoy McKinney, and has issue living, Mary Katherine, *b* 11 June 1985, — Samuel Clinton, *b* 28 May 1965, — Wesley Martha, *b* 11 Oct 1967: *m* 14 Feb 1994, Kristine Alicia, da of Isao Okamoto, — David Charles COOK (name changed from Berger 1988), *b* 25 Sept 1968: *m* 29 Sept 1990, Constance Marie, da of Donald Albert Mueller. — Dagmar Sibylla, *b* 22 Nov 1940: *m* 26 Feb 1964, Heinrich Walz, and has issue living, (Maria) Valesca, *b* 14 Aug 1965, — Larissa, *b* 16 Sept 1967: *m* 23 July 1991 (*m diss* 1995), Takys Panajotakulos.

Grandchildren of HRH late Princess Alice Mary Victoria Augusta Pauline, VA, GCVO, GBE, *b* 25 Feb 1883, *d* 3 Jan 1981: *m* 10 Feb 1934, Maj-Gen 1st Earl of Athlone, KG, GCB, GCMG, GCVO, DSO, PC, who *d* 16 Jan 1957, 3rd son of HH Prince Francis, Duke of Teck, GCB, by his wife HRH Princess Mary Adelaide Wilhelmina Elizabeth, yr da of HRH the 1st Duke of Cambridge, son of King George III:—
Issue of late Lady May Helen Emma Cambridge (formerly HSH Princess May Helen Emma of Teck), *b* 23 Jan 1906, *d* 29 May 1994: *m* 24 Oct 1931, Col Sir Henry Abel Smith, KCMG, KCVO, DSO, late RHG, who *d* 24 Jan 1993 (*see* D Somerset, colls, 1951 Edn):—

Abel Smith Richard Francis Abel (Blidworth Dale, Ravenshead, Notts NG15 9AL), *b* 11 Oct 1933; *ed* Eton; High Sheriff Notts 1978, Vice Lord Lieut 1991; late Capt RHG, cmd Sherwood Rangers Sqdn, Royal Yeo Regt 1967-69 (Hon Col 1979-89): *m* 28 April 1960, Marcia, High Sheriff Notts 1990, DL 1993, only da of late Maj-Gen Sir Douglas Anthony Kendrew, KCMG, CB, CBE, DSO, and has issue living, Katharine Emma, *b* 11 March 1961: *m* 16 Oct 1980 (*m diss* 1998), Hon Hubert Wentworth Beaumont, eldest son of Baron Baumont of Whitley (Life Baron), and has issue living (*see that title*), — Anne Mary Sibylla Abel, *b* 28 June 1932: *m* 14 Dec 1957 (*m diss* 1982), David Ian Liddell-Grainger (*see* E Lindsey, 1976 Edn), and has issue living, Ian Richard Peregrine *b* 23 Feb 1959: *m* 31 Oct 1985, Jill, only da of (Ralph) Nicol Nesbit, of Greenlaw, Berwickshire, and has issue living, Peter Richard *b* 6 May 1987, Sophie Victoria *b* 27 Dec 1988, May Alexandra *b* 9 Sept 1992, — Charles Montagu, *b* 23 July 1960: *m* 23 Jan 1992 (*m diss* 1999), Karen Peta, only da of Peter Humphryes, of St Luke's St, SW3, — Simon Rupert, *b* 28 Dec 1962: *m* 26 Jan 1984 (*m diss* 1999), Romana Maria, only da of late Roman Emmanuel Anton Rogoshewski, of Montreal, Canada, and formerly wife of Philippe Guillaume Perrot, — Malcolm Henry, *b* 14 Dec 1967: *m* 1 Aug 1994, Helen Jane, elder da of Jeremy Cecil Bright, and has issue living, Cameron Henry *b* 14 April 1997, — Alice Mary, *b* 3 March 1965: *m* 13 Aug 1990, Pietro Panaggio, eldest son of Giuseppe Panaggio, of Castelvetere in Valfortore, nr Naples, Italy, and has issue living, Danico Pietro *b* 19 March 1996, Jessica Alice *b* 24 June 1998, — Elizabeth Alice Abel, *b* 5 Sept 1936: *m* 29 April 1965 (*m diss* 1974), Peter Ronald Wise, son of Capt Anthony Forster Wise, and has had issue, Emma Charlotte Abel, *b* 2 Sept 1973, *d* 6 June 1974.

Descendants of HRH Princess Victoria Adelaide Mary Louisa (Princess Royal), German Empress and Queen of Prussia, eldest da of Queen Victoria.

Grandson of HIM late (Friedrich) Wilhelm II (Viktor Albert), German Emperor and King of Prussia, eldest son of HIM Victoria Adelaide Mary Louisa, VA, CI, RRC (*The Princess Royal*), German Empress and Queen of Prussia, eldest da of Queen Victoria:—
Issue of HIH late Crown Prince (Friedrich) Wilhelm Viktor August Ernst of Prussia, *b* 6 May 1882, *d* 20 July 1951; renounced rights of succession to the thrones of the German Empire and of Prussia 1 Dec 1918; head of the Royal House of Prussia 1941-51: *m* 6 June 1905, HH Duchess Cecilie Auguste Marie, who *d* 6 May 1954, da of HRH Grand Duke Friedrich Franz III of Mecklenburg-Schwerin:—

Prussia †*HIH Prince* Louis Ferdinand (Viktor Eduard Adalbert Michael Hubertus), *b* 9 Nov 1907; Dr Phil 1931, formerly Lieut German Air Force: *m* 2 May 1938, HIH Grand Duchess Kira Kirillovna, who *d* 8 Sept 1967, da of HIH late Grand Duke Kirill Vladimirovitch of Russia, and *d* 25 Sept 1994, having had issue (ante).

Grandchildren of late Crown Prince (Friedrich) Wilhelm Viktor

August Ernst of Prussia (ante):—
Issue of HRH late Prince Wilhelm Friedrich Franz Joseph Christian Olaf of
Prussia, Lieut German Inf, *b* 4 July 1906, *ka* 26 May 1940; renounced his
rights as first born son 1933: *m* 3 June 1933, Dorothea, who *d* 7 May 1972,
only da of Alexander von Salviati:—
HRH Princess Felicitas Cecilie Alexandrine Helene Dorothea, *b* 7 June 1934: *m* 1st,
12 Sept 1958 (*m diss* 1972), Dinnies Friedrich Karl von der Osten; 2ndly, 27 Oct
1972, Jörg Hartwig von Nostitz-Wallwitz, and has had issue, (by 1st *m*) †Hartwig
Dinnies Wilhelm Karl Alexander, *b* 15 Feb 1962, *d* 28 June 1989, — Hubertus
Christoph Joachim Friedrich, *b* 5 May 1964, — Friederike Thyra Marion
Wilhelmine Dorothea, *b* 14 July 1959: *m* 17 Aug 1984, Bernhard Ernst Dieter von
Reiche, and has issue living, Felicitas Catharini Malina Johanna *b* 28 Oct 1986,
Victoria Cecilie Alexandra Josephine *b* 19 Jan 1989, Donata Friederike Diana
Sophie *b* 28 Jan 1992, — Cecilie Felicitas Katharina Sophie, *b* 12 March 1967, — (by
2nd *m*) Diana Renata Friederike, *b* 7 Oct 1974. *Residence* - 21521 Wohltorf,
Lauenburg, Am Sachsenwald 3, Germany. — *HRH Princess* Christa Friederike
Alexandrine Viktoria, *b* 31 Oct 1936: *m* 24 March 1960, Peter Paul Eduard Maria
Clemens Maximilian Franz von Assisi Liebes, who *d* 5 May 1967. *Residence* -
Bürkleinstrasse 14, 80538 Munich, Germany.

Issue of HRH late Prince Hubertus Karl Wilhelm of Prussia, *b* 30 Sept 1909,
d 8 April 1950: *m* 1st, 29 Dec 1941 (*m diss* 1943), Baroness Maria-Anna
Sybilla Margarete, da of Baron Alexander Wilhelm Bernhard Ernst von
Humboldt-Dachroeden; 2ndly, 5 June 1943, HSH Princess Magdalene
Pauline (647 Büdingen, OHessen, Oberhof, Germany), el da of HSH Prince
Heinrich XXXVI Reuss:—
(By 2nd *m*) *HRH Princess* Anastasia Viktoria Cecilie Hermine, *b* 14 Feb 1944: *m* 8
Oct (civ) and 8 Nov (relig) 1965, HSH Prince Aloys-Konstantin (Karl Eduard Joseph
Johann Konrad Antonius Gerhard Georg Benediktus Pius Eusebius Maria), 9th
Prince of Löwenstein-Wertheim-Rosenberg, of 63924 Schloss Kleinheubach bei
Miltenberg, Germany, and has issue living, *HSH Hereditary Prince* Carl Friedrich
(Hubertus Georg Eduardo Paolo Nickolo Franz Alois Ignatius Hieronymus Maria), *b*
30 Sept 1966: *m* 16 May (civ) and 8 Aug (relig) 1998, Baroness Stephanie Sophie
Maria Coletta, da of Count Georg Ferdinand Servatius Michael Maria Droste zu
Vischering, Baron von und zu Brenken, — *HSH Prince* Hubertus Maximilian
Gabriel Louis Franz Konstantin Dominik Wunibald Maria, *b* 18 Dec 1968, — *HSH
Prince* Dominik-Wilhelm (Christian Nikolaus Sturmius Antonius Charles Benedikt
Felix Maria), *b* 7 March 1983, — *HSH Princess* Christina-Maria (Johanna Caroline
Magdalene Osy Cecilie Hermine Isidora Victoria Anastasia), *b* 4 April 1974.

Issue of HRH late Prince Friedrich Georg Wilhelm Christoph of Prussia, *b* 19
Dec 1911, *d* 20 April 1966; naturalised a British subject 1947 and acquired
dual nationality by re-admission as a German subject 1953; assumed by deed
poll 1951 the surname of von Preussen: *m* 30 July 1945, Lady Brigid
Katharine Rachel Guinness (who *d* 8 March 1995, having *m* 2ndly, 3 June
1967, Maj Anthony Patrick Ness, who *d* 20 Aug 1993), yst da of 2nd Earl of
Iveagh, KG, CB, CMG, FRS:—
(*HRH Prince*) (Frederick) Nicholas, *b* 3 May 1946: *m* 27 Feb 1980, Hon Victoria
Lucinda Mancroft, elder da of 2nd Baron Mancroft, and has issue living, (*Prince*)
Frederick Nicholas Stormont, *b* 11 June 1990, — (*Princess*) Beatrice Victoria, *b* 10
Feb 1981, — (*Princess*) Florence Jessica, *b* 28 July 1983 , — (*Princess*) Augusta Lily,
b 15 Dec 1986. — (*HRH Prince*) (William) Andrew, *b* 14 Nov 1947: *m* 2 Jan 1979,
Alexandra BLAHOVA (formerly BLAHOVA-ALSBITT), da of Frantisek Blaha, and has issue
living, (*Prince*) Frederick Alexander, *b* 15 Nov 1984, — (*Princess*) Tatiana Brigid
Honor, *b* 16 Oct 1980. — (*HRH Prince*) Rupert Alexander Frederick, *b* 28 April
1955: *m* 5 Jan 1982, Ziba, yst da of late Morteza Rastegar Javaheri, of Tehran, Iran,
and has issue living, (*Princess*) Brigid Elizabeth Soraya, *b* 24 Dec 1983, — (*Princess*)
Astrid Katherine Rabeéh, *b* 16 April 1985. — (*HRH Princess*) Victoria Marina
Cecilie, *b* 22 Feb 1952: *m* 3 May 1976, Philippe Alphonse Achache, and has issue
living, George Jean, *b* 8 June 1980, — Francis Maximilian Frederick, *b* 30 April
1982. — (*HRH Princess*) Antonia Brigid Elizabeth Louise (*Marchioness of Douro*),
b (twin) 28 April 1955: *m* 3 Feb 1977, Arthur Charles Valerian Wellesley, Marquess
of Douro, el son of 8th Duke of Wellington, MVO, OBE, MC, and has issue living (*see*
D Wellington).

Issue of HRH late Princess Cecilie Viktoria Anastasia Zita Thyra Adelheid of
Prussia, *b* 5 Sept 1917, *d* 21 April 1975: *m* 21 June 1949, Capt Clyde Kenneth
Harris, US Army, who *d* 2 March 1958:—
Kira Alexandrine Brigid Cecilie Ingrid, *b* 20 Oct 1954: *m* 22 May 1982 (*m diss* 1993),
John Mitchell Johnson, and has issue living, Philip Louis, *b* 18 Oct 1985.

Grandchildren of HRH late Prince Adalbert Berengar Ferdinand
Viktor of Prussia, 3rd son of HIM late Emperor Wilhelm II (ante):—

Issue of HRH late Prince Wilhelm Victor (Freund Ernst Friedrich Georg
Adalbert) of Prussia, *b* 15 Feb 1919, *d* 7 Feb 1989: *m* 20 July 1944, Countess
Maria Antoinette (Franziska Ladislaja Josepha Paula Bernhardine Agnes),
eldest da of Count Friedrich Heinrich Joseph Maria Gregor Kolumbus
Hoyos-Sprinzenstein, Baron zu Stichsenstein:—
HRH Prince Adalbert-Adelhart (Alexander Friedrich Joachim Christian), *b* 4 March
1948: *m* 14 June 1981, Eva-Marie, da of Dr Günther Claus Werner Kudicke, and has
issue living, *(Prince)* Alexander Markus Wilhelm-Victor, *b* 3 Oct 1984, — *(Prince)*
Christian Friedrich Wilhelm Johannes, *b* 3 July 1986, — *(Prince)* Philipp Heinrich
Adalbert Günther, *b* (twin) 3 July 1986. — *HRH Princess* Marie-Louise (Marina
Franziska), *b* 18 Sept 1945: *m* 19 May (civ) 22 May (relig) 1971, H Ill H Count Rudolf
Maria Emil Franz Friedrich Hubertus Joseph Wenzel Michael von Schönburg-
Glauchau, of Quinta Maria Luisa, Marbella, Malaga, Spain, and has issue living, *H
Ill H Count* Friedrich Wilhelm (Simeon Heinrich Dionysius Joachim Rudolf Maria
Adalbert), *b* 27 April 1985, — *H Ill H Countess* Sophie Anastasia Wilhelmine Marie
Antoinette, *b* 17 May 1979.

Issue of HRH late Princess Victoria Marina, *b* 11 Sept 1917, *d* 21 Jan 1981;
used the name of Countess Lingen: *m* 26 Sept 1947, Kirby William Patterson,
of Springfield, Missouri, USA, who *d* 4 June 1984:—
Berengar Orin Bernhard Kirby, *b* 21 Aug 1948; BS: *m* 31 Dec 1994, Pamela Lois, da
of James Ross Knight. — Marina Adelaide Emily, *b* (twin) 21 Aug 1948: *m* 24 Sept
1982, John William Engel, of 11520 Potter St, Norwalk, Cal 90650, USA, and has
issue living, William John, *b* 17 Feb 1983. — Dohna-Maria, *b* 7 Aug 1954: *m* 28
July 1974, Stephen Leroy Pearl.

Grandson of HRH late Prince August Wilhelm (Heinrich Günther
Viktor) of Prussia, 4th son of HIM late Emperor Wilhelm II (ante):—
Issue of HRH late Prince Alexander Ferdinand (Albrecht Achilles Wilhelm
Joseph Viktor Karl Feodor) of Prussia, *b* 26 Dec 1912, *d* 12 June 1985: *m* 19
Dec 1938, Irmgard, da of late Maj Friedrich Emil Georg Hermann Weygand,
German Art, and formerly wife of Werner Rosendorff:—
†*(Prince)* Stephan Alexander (Dieter Friedrich), *b* 30 Sept 1939: *m* 1st, 28 Feb 1964
(*m diss* 1976), Heide, da of Dr Ernst Arthur Julius Schmidt; 2ndly, 19 June 1981,
Hannelore-Maria, da of Leo Kerscher, and *d* 12 Feb 1993, leaving issue (by 1st *m*),
(Princess) Stephanie Viktoria-Luise Irmgard Gertrud, *b* 21 Sept 1966: *m* 19 April
1991, Amadi Mbaraka Bao, son of Mbaraka Saidi Bao, and has issue living, Aaron
Emanuel *b* 8 Oct 1994, Shoshana Twahia Sophie *b* 28 Aug 1996.

Issue of HRH late Prince Oskar Karl Gustav Adolf, 5th son of HIM late
Emperor Wilhelm II (ante), *b* 27 July 1888, *d* 27 Jan 1958; Gd Master of
Bailliage of Brandenburg of the Order of St John: *m* 31 July 1914, Countess
Ina Marie (Helene Adele Elise) (*cr* Countess von Ruppin 27 July 1914,
recognized as Princess of Prussia and HRH 26 Aug 1940), who *d* 17 Sept
1973, yr da of Count Karl Heinrich Ludwig von Bassewitz-Levetzow:—
HRH Prince Wilhelm-Karl (Adalbert Erich Detloff) (Einbeckerstrasse 21, 37603
Holzminden, Germany), *b* 30 Jan 1922; Gd Master of Bailliage of Brandenburg of
the Order of St John: *m* 1 March 1952, Armgard Else Helene, only da of Friedrich
(Fritz) von Veltheim, and has issue living, *HRH Prince* Wilhelm-Karl (Oskar
Friedrich), *b* 26 Aug 1955, — *HRH Prince* Oskar Hans Karl Michael, *b* 6 May 1959:
m 17 July (civ) and 3 Oct (relig) 1992, Auguste Therese Alexandra Hendrikje, da of
Ralf Emil Eberhard Julek Hennig Zimmermann von Siefart, and has issue living,
HRH Prince Oskar Julius Alvo Carlos *b* 29 Nov 1993, *HRH Prince* Albert Burchard
Carl Marcus Nicolaus *b* 13 July 1998, *HRH Princess* Wilhelmine Auguste Donata
Maria Armgard *b* 7 July 1995. — *HRH Princess* Donata-Victoria (Ina-Marie
Ottonie), *b* 24 Dec 1952.

Grandchildren of HRH late Prince Oskar Karl Gustav Adolf of
Prussia (ante):—
Issue of HRH late Princess Herzeleide-Ina-Marie (Sophie Charlotte Else) of
Prussia, *b* 25 Dec 1918, *d* 22 March 1989: *m* 16 Aug 1938, HSH Karl Peter
Franz Andreas Alexander, Prince Biron von Curland, who *d* 28 Feb 1982:—
HSH Prince Ernst-Johann (Karl Oskar Franz Eitel-Friedrich Peter Burchard), *b* 6
Aug 1940; is a physicist: *m* 14 Aug (civ) and 15 Aug (relig) 1967, Countess Elisabeth
Victoria Raimonda, yr da of Ludwig Joseph Albert Franz Heinrich Dieter, Count
von Ysenburg-Philippseich, and has two adopted das, Anja, *b* 5 Jan 1975, —
Christiana, *b* 28 May 1977. — *HSH Prince* Michael Karl August Wilhelm
(Rabenkopfstrasse 27, 8 Munich 90, Germany), *b* 20 Jan 1944; lawyer: *m* 1 July (civ)
and 2 July (relig) 1969, Kristin, 2nd da of Joachim Leo Jürgen Karl Martin von
Oertzen, and has issue living, *HSH Prince* Alexander, *b* 18 Sept 1972, — *HSH
Princess* Veronika, *b* 23 Jan 1970, — *HSH Princess* Stephanie, *b* 24 Sept 1975.
— *HSH Princess* (Viktoria) Benigna Ina-Marie Cecilie Friederike-Luise Helene, *b*

2 July 1939: *m* 3 May (civ) and 6 May (relig) 1968 (*m diss* 1993), Baron John Christopher Robert von Twickel, and has issue living (*see* Throckmorton Bt).

Grandchildren of late Prince Joachim Franz Humbert of Prussia, 6th son of HIM Wilhelm II (ante):—
Issue of HRH late Prince (Karl) Franz Josef (Wilhelm Friedrich Eduard Paul), *b* 15 Dec 1916, *d* 23 Jan 1975: *m* 1st, 1 Oct 1940 (*m diss* 1946), Princess Henriette Hermine Wanda Ida Luise, who *d* 16 March 1972, yr da of Prince Johann Georg (Ludwig Ferdinand August) von Schoenaich-Carolath; 2ndly, 9 Nov 1946 (*m diss* 1959), Luise Dora, who *d* 23 April 1961, da of Max Emil Theodor Hartmann, and formerly wife of Fritz Simon; 3rdly, 20 July 1959, Eva Maria, who *d* 6 March 1987, da of Norberto Herrera, of Lima, Peru:—
(By 1st *m*) *HRH Prince* Franz Wilhelm (Victor Christoph Stephan) (Apartado 6097, E-28080 Madrid, Spain), *b* 3 Sept 1943: *m* 4 Sept 1976 (*m diss* 1986), HIH Grand Duchess Maria, only da of HIH late Grand Duke Vladimir Kirillovitch of Russia, and has issue living (ante). — *HRH Prince* Franz Friedrich (Christian) (PO Box 1211, 21707 Himmelpforten, Germany), *b* 17 Oct 1944: *m* 23 Oct 1970 (*m diss* 1996), Gudrun Edith, da of Horst Winkler, and has issue living, (*Princess*) Christine, *b* 22 Feb 1968: *m* 6 Aug (civ) and 7 Aug (relig) 1993, Milos Kovacevic. — (By 3rd *m*) (*Princess*) Alexandra Marie Auguste Juana Consuelo Eva, *b* 29 April 1960: *m* 1st, 28 April 1989 (*m diss* 1992), Juan Diego Martinez Lercari, son of Juan Martinez Garay; 2ndly, 21 June (civ) and 7 Oct (relig) 1995, Juan Alberto Pedro Reboa Devoto, son of Alberto Francisco Reboa Rébora, and has issue living, Alberto Joaquin, *b* 8 April 1994, — Alexandra Augusta Victoria, *b* 8 July 1995. — (*Princess*) Désirée Anastasia Maria Benedicta, *b* 13 July 1961: *m* 25 May 1983, Juan Carlos Gamarra y Skeels, of Peruvian Embassy, Bucharest, Romania, son of Carlos Gamarra y Vargas, and has issue living, Juan Francisco, *b* 1 March 1987, — Inés Désirée, *b* 28 April 1989.

Grandchildren of HIM Wilhelm II, (ante):—
Issue of HRH late Princess Viktoria Luise (Adelheid Mathilde Charlotte), *b* 13 Sept 1892, *d* 11 Dec 1980: *m* 24 May 1913, HRH Ernst August (Christian), Duke of Brunswick and Lüneburg (1913-18), who *d* 30 Jan 1953, having assumed the title of Prince of Hanover 29 Aug 1931:—
See Dukedom of Cumberland and Teviotdale (infra.)

Grandchildren of HRH late Princess Viktoria Luise (Adelheid Mathilde Charlotte) of Prussia (*Duchess of Brunswick and Lüneburg*) (ante):—
Issue of HRH late Princess Friederike (Frederika) Luise Thyra Viktoria Margarete Sophie Olga Cecile Isabelle Christa (*Queen of the Hellenes*), *b* 18 April 1917, *d* 6 Feb 1981: *m* 9 Jan 1938, HM King Paul I of the Hellenes, who *d* 6 March 1964 (infra):—

Greece *HM King* Constantine II (4 Linnell Drive, Hampstead Way, NW11), *b* 2 June 1940; reigned as King of the Hellenes 6 March 1964-1 June 1973 (and nominally until 8 Dec 1974); Sovereign of Orders of the Redeemer, St George and St Constantine, George I, and the Phoenix of Greece, has Grand Cross of Order of the Elephant of Denmark, St Olav of Norway, of House of Orange of the Netherlands, and Grand Cordons of Legion of Honour of France and of King Idris I of Libya and Orders of Merit of Republic of Italy, of Golden Fleece of Spain, and of Annunciation of the House of Savoy; is Grand Officer of Order of St Charles of Monaco and Cdr of Legion of Merit of USA, Grand Cdr of Order of Dannebrog of Denmark, Collar of Order of the Nile of United Arab Republic, of Aztec Eagle of Mexico, and of Roy Order of Chakri of Thailand, and Grand Cross of Roy Order of Leopold of Belgium, of Seraphim of Sweden, of Al Nadha of Jordan, and Order of the Republic of Senegal: *m* 18 Sept 1964, HRH Princess Anne-Marie (Dagmar Ingrid), yst da of HM late King Frederik IX of Denmark, and has issue living (ante). — *HRH*

Spain Princess Sophie (Sofia) (*Queen of Spain*), *b* 2 Nov 1938; Hon LLD Cantab 1988, Hon Fellow Exeter Coll, Oxford 1988: *m* 14 May 1962, HM King Juan Carlos I of Spain, KG (*infra*), and has issue living, *HRH Infante* Felipe Juan Pablo Alfonso y Todos los Santos (*Prince of the Asturias*), GCVO, *b* 30 Jan 1968; GCVO 1988, — *HRH Infanta* Elena Maria Isabel Dominga (*Duchess of Lugo*), *b* 20 Dec 1963: *m* 18 March 1995, Don Jaime de Marichalar y Sáenz de Tejada, and has issue living, Don Felipe Juan Frolián y Todos los Santos *b* 17 July 1998, — *HRH Infanta* Cristina Federica Victoria Antonia (*Duchess of Palma de Mallorca*), *b* 13 June 1965: *m* 4 Oct 1997, Don Iñaki Urdangarin Liebaart. — *HRH Princess* Irene, *b* 11 May 1942; has Grand Cross of Roy Order of St Olga and St Sophia of Greece.

Grandchildren of HRH late Grand Adm Prince (Albert Wilhelm) Heinrich of Prussia, 2nd son of HIM Victoria Adelaide Mary Louisa, VA, CI, RRC (*Princess Royal*), German Empress and Queen of Prussia (ante):—
Issue of HRH late Prince (Wilhelm Viktor Karl August Heinrich) Sigismund of Prussia, *b* 27 Nov 1896, *d* 14 Nov 1978: *m* 11 July 1919, HH Princess

Charlotte Agnes (Ernestine Auguste Bathildis Marie Therese Adolfine), who *d* 16 Feb 1989, elder da of HH Duke Ernst II of Saxe-Altenburg:—

HRH Prince Alfred Friedrich Ernst Heinrich Konrad, of Apartado 856 Centro-Colon, 1007 San José de Costa Rica, *b* 17 Aug 1924: *m* 15 Dec 1984, Maritza, who *d* 1 Nov 1996, da of Julius Farkas de Zaladörgicse et Kiskapornok, and formerly wife of Dirke van Wilpe. — †*HRH Princess* Barbara Irene Adelheid Viktoria Elisabeth Bathildis, *b* 2 Aug 1920: *m* 11 July 1954, HRH Duke Christian Ludwig (Ernst August Maximilian Johann Albrecht Adolf Friedrich) of Mecklenburg, who *d* 18 July 1996, and *d* 31 May 1994, leaving issue, *HH Duchess* Donata, *b* 11 March 1956: *m* 14 Aug (civil) and 19 Sept (relig) 1987, Alexander von Solodkoff, son of George von Solodkoff and has issue living, Niklot Alexis *b* 8 Dec 1994, Thyra *b* 12 Oct 1989, Alix *b* 17 March 1992, — *HH Duchess* Edwina, *b* 25 Sept 1960: *m* 20 Sept (civ) and 14 Oct (relig) 1995, Konrad Egon Franz Maria von Posern, son of Hubertus Franz Hanscarl Fabian von Posern, and has issue living, (Ludwig) Leopold Bernhard Georg Maria *b* 27 Feb 1996, (Paul) Friedrich Christian Fabian Maria *b* 14 June 1997.

Prussia

Grandchildren of HRH late Princess Sophie Dorothea Ulrika Alice of Prussia, VA (*Queen of the Hellenes*) (infra):—

Issue of HM late King Alexander I of the Hellenes, *b* 1 Aug 1893, *d* 25 Oct 1920; reigned as King of the Hellenes 1917-20: *m* 4 Nov 1919, Aspasia, who *d* 7 Aug 1972 (having been recognized as Princess by Roy Decree 10 Sept 1922), da of Col Petros Mano:—

†*HRH Princess* Alexandra (*Queen of Yugoslavia*), *b* (*posthumous*) 25 March 1921; had Grand Cross of Order of Star of Karadjordje of Yugoslavia and Orders of White Eagle and Crown of Yugoslavia: *m* 20 March 1944, HM King Peter II of Yugoslavia, who *d* 3 Nov 1970, and *d* 30 Jan 1993, leaving issue (ante).

Greece

Issue of HM late King Paul I of the Hellenes, KG, GCVO, *b* 14 Dec 1901, *d* 6 March 1964; reigned as King of the Hellenes 1947-64: *m* 9 Jan 1938, HRH Princess Friederike (Frederika) Luise Thyra Viktoria Margarete Sophie Olga Cecilie Isabelle Christa, who *d* 6 Feb 1981, only da of HRH late Prince Ernst August (Christian Georg) of Hanover, Duke of Brunswick and Lüneburg (ante).

Issue of HRH late Princess Helen of Greece and Denmark (*Queen Helen the Queen Mother of Roumania*), *b* 3 May 1896, *d* 28 Nov 1982: *m* 27 Oct 1921 (*m diss* 21 June 1928), HM King Carol II of Roumania, KG, GCVO, who *d* 4 April 1955 (ante).

Issue of HRH late Princess Irene of Greece and Denmark (*Duchess of Aosta*), *b* 13 Feb 1904, *d* 15 April 1974: *m* 1 July 1939, Adm HRH Prince Aimone Roberto Margherita Maria Giuseppe Torino of Savoy, Duke of Spoleto, later 4th Duke of Aosta, who *d* 30 Jan 1948:—

HRH Prince Amedeo Umberto Costantino Giorgio Paolo Elena Maria Fiorenzo Zvonimir, 5th Duke of Aosta, Principe della Cisterna e di Belriguardo, Marchese di Voghera, Conte di Ponderano (Il Borro, San Giustino Valdarno, Prov d'Arezzo, Italy), *b* 27 Sept 1943: *m* 1st, 22 July 1964 (*m diss* 1982 and annulled 1987), HRH Princess Claude Marie Agnès Catherine of France, 5th da of HRH Prince Henri Robert Ferdinand Marie Louis Philippe of France, Comte de Paris, head of the Roy House of France; 2ndly, 30 March 1987, Donna Silvia Ottavia Costanza Maria, da of Don Vincenzo Paterno, Marchese di Regiovanni, Conte de Prades, Barone de Spedalotto, and has issue living (by 1st *m*), *HRH Prince* Aimone Umberto Emanuele Filiberto Luigi Amedeo Elena Maria Fiorenzo (*Duke of Apulia*), *b* 13 Oct 1967, — *HRH Princess* Bianca Irene Olga Elena Isabella Fiorenza Maria, *b* 2 April 1966: *m* 11 Sept 1988, Count Giberto Carbonello Tiberto Maria Arrivabene Valenti Gonzaga, son of Count Leonardo Arrivabene Valenti Gonzaga and has issue living, Viola Moreschina Nushi Adec Nicoletta Maria *b* 31 May 1991, Vera Clementina Verde Aimone Elena Maria *b* 18 Aug 1993, Mafalda Violante Giovanna Olga Maria *b* 27 Dec 1997, — *HRH Princess* Mafalda Giovanna Jolanda Shams Maria Fiorenza Isabella, *b* 20 Sept 1969: *m* 18 Sept 1994, Don Alessandro Francesco Ruffo di Calabria, son of Don Fabrizio Beniamino, Prince Ruffo di Calabric-Santapau, 13th Prince de Palazzolo, 14th Prince di Scilla, 13th Marquis di Licoda, 7th Duke di Guarda Lombarda. Princess Mafalda has Issue (by Francesco Ferrante Carlo Napoleone Lombardo di San Chirico), Anna Egizia Maria Carla Chiara Benedetta LOMBARDO DI SAN CHIRICO, *b* 11 April 1999.

Savoy Aosta

Grandchildren of HIM late Victoria Adelaide Mary Louisa, VA, CI, RRC (*Princess Royal*), German Empress and Queen of Prussia (ante):—

Issue of HRH late Princess Sophie Dorothea Ulrika Alice, VA (*Queen of the Hellenes*), *b* 14 June 1870, *d* 13 Jan 1932: *m* 27 Oct 1889, HM King Constantine I of the Hellenes, who *d* 11 Jan 1923 (having reigned as King of the Hellenes 1913-17 and 1920-23):—

HRH Princess Katherine (*Lady Katherine Brandram*), *b* 4 May 1913; granted by Roy Warrant the rank of a Duke's daughter 25 Aug 1947; has Grand Cross of Order of St Olga and St Sophia of Greece: *m* 21 April 1947, Maj Richard Campbell Andrew Brandram, MC, TD, RA, who *d* 28 March 1994, and has issue living, (Richard) Paul George Andrew, *b* 1 April 1948: *m* 12 Feb 1975 (*m diss* 1993), Jennifer Diane, da of Lt-Col Robert Steele, of St Leonard's Grange, Beaulieu, Hants, and has issue living, Nicholas George *b* 23 April 1982, Sophie Eila *b* 23 Jan 1981, Alexia Katherine *b* 6 Dec 1985. *Residence* - Croft Cottage, Pound Lane, Marlow, Bucks.

Issue of HRH late Princess Margarethe Beatrice Feodora of Prussia (*Landgravine of Hesse*), *b* 22 April 1872, *d* 22 Jan 1954: *m* 25 Jan 1893, HRH Friedrich Karl (Ludwig Konstantin), who *d* 28 May 1940 (elected King of Finland Oct 1918, but withdrew acceptance Nov 1918):—

†*HH Prince* Wolfgang Moritz, *b* (twin) 6 Nov 1896: *m* 1st, 17 Sept 1924, HGDH Princess Marie Alexandra (Thyra Viktoria Louise Carola Hilda), who *d* (killed in an air raid) 29 Jan 1944, only da of HGDH Prince Maximilian Alexander Friedrich Wilhelm of Baden; 2ndly, 7 Sept 1948, Ottilie, da of Ludwig Möller, and *dsp* 12 July 1989.

Grandchildren of HRH late Princess Margarethe Beatrice Feodora of Prussia (*Landgravine of Hesse*) (ante):—

Issue of HRH late Landgrave Philipp of Hesse, head of all the House of Hesse 1968-80, *b* 6 Nov 1896, *d* 25 Oct 1980: *m* 23 Sept 1925, HRH Princess Mafalda Maria Elisabetta Anna Romana of Savoy, who *d* (in Buchenwald Concentration Camp) 27 Aug 1944, 2nd da of HM King Victor Emmanuel III of Italy: —

Hesse   *HRH Landgrave* Moritz Friedrich Karl Emanuel Humbert (*Landgrave of Hesse*), head of all the House of Hesse since 1980 (Schloss Friedrichshof, 61476 Kronberg i. Taunus, Germany), *b* 6 Aug 1926; adopted by his kinsman late Prince Ludwig of Hesse and by Rhine, head of the Grand Ducal House of Hesse (who *d* 30 May 1968): *m* 3 June 1964 (*m diss* 1974), HSH Princess Tatiana Louise Ursula Therese Elsa, 2nd da of HSH Gustav Albrecht, 5th Prince of Sayn-Wittgenstein-Berleburg, and has issue living, *HRH Hereditary Prince* Heinrich Donatus Philipp Umberto, *b* 17 Oct 1966, — *HH Prince* Philipp Robin, *b* 17 Sept 1970, — *HH Princess* Mafalda Margarethe, *b* 6 July 1965: *m* 1st, 6 July (civ) and 8 July (relig) 1989 (*m diss* 1991), Don Enrico Giovanni Maria Consolata dei Conti Marone Cinzano, 2nd son of Alberto Marone Cinzano, 2nd Count Marone; 2ndly, 19 Dec 1991 (*m diss* 1998), Carlo Galdo, son of Luigi Galdo, and has issue (by 2nd *m*), Tatiana Maria, *b* 20 Jan 1992, — Polissena, *b* 30 Sept 1993. — *HH Princess* Elena Elisabeth Madeleine, *b* 8 Nov 1967. — *HH Prince* Heinrich Wilhelm Konstantin Victor Franz (Villa Polissena, Via San Filippo Martire 6, Rome, Italy; Villa la Falconara, Forio d'Ischia, Italy), *b* 30 Oct 1927; artist. — †*HH Prince* Otto Adolf, *b* 3 June 1937; prehistorian: *m* 1st, 5 April (civ) and 6 April (relig) 1965 (*m diss* 1969), Angela Mathilde Agathe, da of Maj-Gen (Wilhelm Konrad Rodrigo) Bernd von Doering, and formerly wife of Hans Peter Schmeidler; 2ndly, 28 Dec 1988, Elisabeth Marga Dorothea, da of Wilhelm Bönker, and *dsp* 3 Jan 1998. — *HH Princess* Elisabeth Margarethe Elena Johanna Maria Jolanda Polyxene (Fasanenstrasse 24, 63263 Neu-Isenburg (Gravensbruch), Germany), *b* 8 Oct 1940: *m* 28 Feb 1962, Count Friedrich Carl (Eduard Wilhelm Hans Franz Eusebius Michael Hubert Maria) von Oppersdorff, who *d* 11 Jan 1985, and has issue living, *Count* Friedrich Karl (Philipp Wilhelm Hans Moritz Maria), *b* 1 Dec 1962, — *Count* Alexander Wolfgang (Johannes Georg Victor Emanuel Maria), *b* 3 Aug 1965.

Issue of HH late Prince Christoph Ernst August of Hesse, *b* (twin) 14 May 1901, *d* 7 Oct 1943: *m* 15 Dec 1930, HRH Princess Sophie (who *m* 2ndly, 24 April 1946, HRH Prince Georg Wilhelm (Ernst August Friedrich Axel) of Hanover (ante)), da of HRH late Prince Andrew of Greece and Denmark (infra):—

HH Prince Karl Adolf Andreas, *b* 26 March 1937: *m* 18 April 1966, Countess Yvonne Margit Valerie, da of Count Béla Szapáry de Muraszombath, Széchysziget et Szapár, and has issue living, *HH Prince* Christoph, *b* 18 June 1969, — *HH Princess* Irina Verena, *b* 1 April 1971: *m* 30 April (civ) and 29 May (relig) 1999, H Ill H Alexander Georg Maria Ernst Heinrich István Ludwig Kisito Hubertus, Count and Lord of Schönburg-Glauchau. — *HH Prince* Rainer Christoph Friedrich, *b* 18 Nov 1939; author. — *HH Princess* Christina Margarete, *b* 10 Jan 1933: *m* 1st, 1 Aug (civ) and 2 Aug (relig) 1956 (*m diss* 1962), HRH Prince Andrej of Yugoslavia (ante); 2ndly, 3 Dec 1962 (*m diss* 1986), Robert Floris van Eyck, who *d* 19 Dec 1991, son of Pieter Nicolaus van Eyck, and has had issue, (by 1st *m*) (ante), (by 2nd *m*), Mark Nicholas, *b* 16 Feb 1966: *m* 12 June 1992 (*m diss* 199—), Joanne Marea, da of Michael John Green, — Helen Sophie, *b* 25 Oct 1963: *m* 24 Jan 1986, Roderick Alan Harman, son of Douglas John Harman, and has issue living, Sascha Alexandra Sophia *b* 26 July 1986, Pascale Olivia *b* 19 March 1989. — *HH Princess* Dorothea Charlotte Karin, *b* 24 July 1934: *m* 31 March (civ) and 1 April (relig) 1959, HSH Prince Friedrich Karl Hugo Maximilian Maria Cyrillus Felix Hubertus zu Windisch-Graetz, and has issue living, *HSH Princess* Marina Margherita Sophia Leontina Christina, *b* 3 Dec 1960: *m* 28 May 1988, Gyula Lajos Jakabffy, son of Tamás Jakabffy, and has issue living, Réka Dorothea Sita *b* 17 Sept 1988, Sophia Magdolna *b* 27 Aug 1989, — *HSH Princess* Clarissa Elisabetha Fiore, *b* 5 Aug 1966:

m 16 Nov 1985, Eric Michel Jacques de Waele, son of Jean August de Waele, and has issue living, Michel Jean Henri *b* 18 May 1986, Alexander Federico Mark *b* 3 July 1987, Mathieu Paul Philippe *b* 16 Dec 1988, Ruby Jade *b* 26 Jan 1994. — *HH Princess* Clarissa Alice (Clarisse de Hesse), *b* (posthumous) 6 Feb 1944: *m* 20 July 1971 (*m diss* 1976), Claude Jean Derrien, and has a natural da, Johanna Sophia VON HESSEN, *b* 25 Aug 1980. *Residence* - 108 rue Lepic, F-75118 Paris, France.

Descendants of HRH Princess Alice Maud Mary (Grand Duchess of Hesse and by Rhine), 2nd da of Queen Victoria.

Descendants of late George Louis Victor Henry Serge Mountbatten, 2nd Marquess of Milford Haven, GCVO, elder son of late Victoria Alberta Elizabeth Mathilde Marie, Marchioness of Milford Haven, VA (infra), eldest da of HRH late Princess Alice Maud Mary.

See M Milford Haven.

Descendants of late Louis Francis Albert Victor Nicholas Mountbatten, 1st Earl Mountbatten of Burma, KG, GCB, OM, GCSI, GCIE, GCVO, DSO, PC, FRS, yr son of late Victoria Alberta Elizabeth Mathilde Marie, Marchioness of Milford Haven, VA (infra), eldest da of HRH late Princess Alice Maud Mary.

See Cs Mountbatten.

Grandchildren of late Victoria Alberta Elizabeth Mathilde Marie, Marchioness of Milford Haven, VA (ante):—
Issue of HRH late Princess (Victoria) Alice Elizabeth Julia Marie, RRC, *b* 25 Feb 1885, *d* 5 Dec 1969: *m* 7 Oct 1903, HRH Prince Andrew of Greece and Denmark, GCVO, who *d* 3 Dec 1944:—
HRH The Prince Philip, KG, KT, OM, GBE, AC, QSO, PC (*Duke of Edinburgh*), *b* 10 **Greece** June 1921; *cr* Duke of Edinburgh 1947 (*see page* 93). — *HRH Princess* Sophie, *b* 26 June 1914: *m* 1st, 15 Dec 1930, HH Prince Christoph Ernst August of Hesse, who *d* 7 Oct 1943 (ante); 2ndly, 24 April 1946, HRH Prince Georg Wilhelm (Ernst August Friedrich Wilhelm Axel) of Hanover (ante).

Grandchildren of HRH late Princess (Victoria) Alice Elizabeth Julia Marie, RRC (*Princess Andrew of Greece and Denmark*) (ante):—
Issue of HRH late Princess Margarita of Greece and Denmark, *b* 18 April 1905, *d* 24 April 1981: *m* 20 April 1931, HSH Prince Gottfried Viktor Hermann Alfred Paul Maximilian, 8th Prince of Hohenlohe-Langenburg, who *d* 11 May 1960 (ante).

Issue of HRH late Princess Theodora of Greece and Denmark, *b* 30 May 1906, *d* 16 Oct 1969: *m* 17 Aug 1931, HRH Prince Berthold Friedrich Wilhelm Ernst August Heinrich Karl (*Margrave of Baden*), head of the Grand Ducal House of Baden 1929-63, who *d* 27 Oct 1963:—
HRH Prince Maximilian (Max) Andrew Friedrich Gustav Ernst August Bernhard **Baden** (*Margrave of Baden*) (Schloss Salem, D88682 Salem, Baden, Germany), *b* 3 July 1933; *ed* Gordonstoun; head of the Grand Ducal House of Baden since 1963: *m* 23 Sept (civ) and 30 Sept (relig) 1966, HI & RH Archduchess Valeric Isabelle Marie Anna Alfonsa Desideria Brigitte Sophia Thomasia Huberta Josepha Ignatia, 7th da of HI & RH late Archduke Hubert Salvator (Rainer Maria Joseph Ignatius) of Austria, and has issue living, *HRH Hereditary Prince* Bernhard Max Friedrich August Louis Kraft, *b* 27 May 1970, — *HGDH Prince* Leopold Max Christian Ludwig Clemens Hubert, *b* 1 Oct 1971, — *HGDH Prince* Michael Max Andreas, *b* 11 March 1976, — *HGDH Princess* Marie-Louise (Elisabeth Mathilde Theodora Cecilie Sarah Charlotte), *b* 3 July 1969. — *HGDH Prince* Ludwig Wilhelm Georg Ernst Christoph (Schloss Zwingenberg/N, D69439, Germany), *b* 16 March 1937: *m* 21 Sept 1967, HSH Princess Maria Anna (Marianne) Henriette Eleonore Gobertina, yst da of HSH Prince Karl Alain Maria Gobertus von Auersperg-Breunner, and has issue living, *HGDH Prince* Berthold Ernst-August Emich Rainer, *b* 8 Oct 1976, — *HGDH Princess* Sophie Thyra Josephine Georgine Henriette, *b* 8 July 1975, — *HGDH Princess* Aglaë Margareta Tatiana Mary, *b* 3 March 1981. — *HGDH Princess* Margarita Alice Thyra Viktoria Marie Louise Scholastica, *b* 14 July 1932: *m* 6 June 1957 (*m diss* 1982), as his 1st wife, HRH Prince Tomislav of Yugoslavia (ante).

Descendants of HRH Princess Beatrice Mary Victoria Feodore, 5th and yst da of Queen Victoria.

Grandson of late Alexander Albert Mountbatten, 1st Marquess of Carisbrooke, GCB, GCVO, el son of HRH late Princess Beatrice Mary Victoria Feodore, VA, CI, GCVO, GBE, RRC:—
Issue of late Lady Iris Victoria Beatrice Grace Mountbatten, *b* 13 Jan 1920, *d* 1 Sept 1982: *m* 1st, 15 Feb 1941 (*m diss* 1946), Maj Hamilton Joseph Keyes O'Malley, IG; 2ndly, 5 May 1957 (*m diss* 1957), Michael Neely Bryan, who *d*

20 Aug 1972; 3rdly, 11 Dec 1965, William Alexander Kemp, Canadian tv announcer, who *d* 12 Dec 1991:—
(By 2nd *m*) Robin Alexander, *b* 20 Dec 1957: has issue, (by Louise Houle) Edward Curtis HOULE, *b* 1979, (by Arizona ......) Faith *b* 1979, (by Pamela Jean Foster), Elijah Alexander BRYAN, *b* 14 May 1995.

Grandson of HRH late Infante Jaime Luitpoldo Isabelino Enrique Alejandro Alberto Alfonso Victor Acacio Pedro Pablo Maria of Spain (*Duke of Segovia*) (infra):—
Issue of HRH late Don Alfonso Jaime Marcelino Manuel Victor Maria (*Duke of Cadiz*), *b* 20 April 1936; granted style of HRH 22 Nov 1972; *d* 30 Jan 1989: *m* 8 March 1972 (*m diss* 1983), Doña Maria del Carmen (Esperanza Alejandra de la Santisima Trinidad y de Todos los Santos) Martinez-Bordiu y Franco, da of Don Cristobal Martinez-Bordiu, 10th Marqués de Villaverde, by his wife Doña Maria del Carmen Franco, 1st Duchess of Franco, only da of Generalisimo Francisco Franco, Spanish Head of State (*Caudillo*) 1936-75:—
Don Luis Alfonso (Gonzalo Victor Manuel Marco), *b* 25 April 1974.

Grandson of HRH late Princess Victoria Eugenie Julia Ena (*Queen of Spain*) (infra):—
Issue of HRH late Infante Jaime Luitpoldo Isabelino Enrique Alejandro Alberto Alfonso Victor Acacio Pedro Pablo Maria of Spain (*Duke of Segovia*), *b* 23 June 1908; renounced all rights of succession to the throne of Spain for himself and his descendants 21 June 1933; *d* 20 March 1975: *m* 1st, 4 March 1935 (*m diss* in Roumania 6 May 1947; confirmed at Turin 3 June 1949), Donna (Victoria Jeanne Josephine Pierre Marie) Emanuela de Dampierre, da of late Vicomte Roger Richard Charles Henri Etienne de Dampierre, 2nd Duke of San Lorenzo; 2ndly, 3 Aug 1949, Charlotte Louise Auguste, who *d* 3 July 1979, da of Otto Eugen Tiedemann, of Königsberg, E Prussia, and formerly wife of (1) — Buchler, and (2) — Hippler:—

Spain

(By 1st *m*) *Don* Gonzalo Victor Alfonso José Bonifacio Antonio Maria y Todos los Santos (Paseo de la Habana 15, 28036 Madrid, Spain), *b* 5 June 1937: *m* 1st, in Mexico 28 Jan 1983 (*m* not recognized in Spain), Maria del Carmen Harto Montealegre, da of Rafael Harto; 2ndly, 25 June (civil) and 30 June (religious) 1984 (*m diss* 1989), Maria de las Mercedes, er da of Don Luis Licer; 3rdly, 12 Dec 1992, Emmanuela Maria Lina, da of Vincenzo Pratolongo; has recognized a natural da (by Sandra Lee Landry), Stephanie Michelle DE BORBÓN, *b* 19 June 1968.

Grandchildren of HRH late Princess Beatrice Mary Victoria Feodore, VA, CI, GCVO, GBE, RRC, *b* 4 April 1857, *d* 26 Oct 1944: *m* 23 July 1885, HRH Prince Henry Maurice of Battenberg, KG, PC, who *d* 20 Jan 1896:—
Issue of HRH late Princess Victoria Eugenie Julia Ena (*Queen of Spain*), VA, *b* 24 Oct 1887; granted style of HRH 3 April 1906; *d* 15 April 1969: *m* 31 May 1906, HM King Alfonso XIII of Spain, who *d* 28 Feb 1941 (having reigned as King of Spain from his birth 17 May 1886 until 14 April 1931, when he left the country):—
†*HRH Infante Don* Juan Carlos Teresa Silverio Alfonso (*Count of Barcelona*), *b* 20 June 1913; Midshipman RN 1933-35; appointed Hon Lieut 1936 and Hon Adm 1987; formally renounced his rights of succession to the Spanish throne in favour of his son the reigning King 14 May 1977: *m* 12 Oct 1935, HRH Princess Maria de las Mercedes Cristina Januaria Isabel Luisa Carolina Victoria, da of HRH late Prince Carlos Maria Francisco de Asis Pascual Ferdinando Antonio de Padua Francisco de Paula Alfonso Andres Avelino Tancredo of Bourbon-Two Sicilies, Infante of Spain, and *d* 1 April 1993, leaving issue, *HM King* Juan Carlos I (Alfonso Victor Maria) of Spain, KG (Palacio de la Zarzuela, Madrid, Spain), *b* 5 Jan 1938; Hon LLD Cantab 1988; *s* as King of Spain 22 Nov 1975: *m* 14 May 1962, HRH Princess Sophie (Sofia) of Greece and Denmark, el da of HM late King Paul I of the Hellenes, and has issue living (ante), — *HRH Infanta* Maria del Pilar (Alfonsa Juana Victoria Luisa Ignacia y Todos los Santos) (*Duchess of Badajoz*), *b* 30 July 1936: *m* 5 May 1967, Don Luís Gómez-Acebo y Duque de Estrada, Vizconde de la Torre, who *d* 9 March 1991, and has issue living, *Don* Juan Filiberto (Nicolas) *b* 6 Dec 1969, *Don* Bruno Alejandro *b* 15 June 1971, *Don* (Luís) Beltrán Ataulfo, *b* 20 May 1973, *Don* Fernando Umberto *b* 13 Sept 1974, *Doña* (Maria de Fátima) Simoneta Luisa *b* 28 Oct 1968: *m* 12 Sept 1990, José Miguel Fernandez y Sastron, son of Jorge Fernandez y Menendez (and has issue living, *Don* Luís Juan *b* 23 Sept 1991, *Don* Pablo *b* 4 May 1995), — *HRH Infanta* Margarita Maria de la Victoria Esperanza Jacoba Felicidad Perpetua y Todos los Santos (*Duchess of Soria*), *b* 6 March 1939: *m* 12 Oct 1972, Don Carlos Emilio Juan Zurita y Delgado, of Castellana 63, Madrid 4, Spain, and has issue living, *Don* Alfonso Juan Carlos *b* 9 Aug 1973, *Doña* Maria Sofia Emilia Carmen *b* 16 Sept 1975. — *HRH Infanta* Beatriz Isabel Federica Alfonsa Eugenia Cristina Maria Teresa Bienvenida Ladislàa, *b* 22 June 1909: *m* 14 Jan 1935, Don Alessandro Torlonia, 5th Principe di Civitella-Cesi, who *d* 12 May 1986, and has issue living,

Don Marco Alfonso, 6th Principe di Civitella-Cesi (Palazzo Torlonia, 78 Via Bocca di Leone, Rome, Italy), *b* 2 July 1937: *m* 1st, 15 Sept 1960, Donna Orsetta, who *d* 10 March 1968, 2nd da of Don Adolfo Caracciolo dei Principi di Castagneto e Duchi di Melito; 2ndly, 9 Nov 1968 (*m diss* 1985), Philippa Catherine Blanche, da of John Linden McDonald, and formerly wife of Luc, Comte de Nanteuil; 3rdly, 11 Nov 1985, Blazena Anna Helena, da of Václav Jan Svitak, and has issue living, (by 1st *m*) *Don* Giovanni *b* 17 April 1962, (by 2nd *m*) *Donna* Victoria Eugenia Carolina Honor Paola Alexandra Maria *b* 8 May 1971: *m* 20 Dec 1997, Kenneth Lindsay, son of Angus Malcolm Lindsay (and has issue living, Josephine Honor *b* 11 July 1998), (by 3rd *m*) *Donna* Catarina Agnese *b* 14 June 1974, — †*Don* Marino Ricardo Francesco Maria Giuseppe, *b* 13 Dec 1939 *d* unm 28 Dec 1995, — *Donna* Sandra Vittoria, *b* 14 Feb 1936: *m* 20 June 1958, Conte Clemente Lequio di Assaba, who *d* 28 June 1971, and has issue living, *Conte* Alessandro Vittorio Eugenio Enrico *b* 20 June 1960: *m* 12 Oct 1987 (*m diss* 1997), Antonia Feodora, da of Donato Dell'Atte (and has issue living, Clemente Lorenzo *b* 2 April 1988; Conte Alessandro also has issue by Ana Garcia y Obregón, Alessandro Alfonso Lequio di Assaba y Obregón *b* 23 June 1992), *Contessa* Desideria Beatrice Elyse Francesca *b* 19 Sept 1962: *m* 11 Sept 1986, Count Oddone Paulo Tournon, son of Count Giovanni Felice Tournon (and has issue living, *Count* Giovanni Carlo Alberto Adriano Alessandro Costantino Demetrio Maria *b* 3 Sept 1991, *Count* Giorgio Brancaleone Ugo Ippolito Maria, *b* —Feb 1994), — *Donna* Olimpia, *b* 27 Dec 1943: *m* 26 June 1965, Paul-Annik Weiller, who *d* 2 Nov 1998, son of late Paul-Louis Weiller, and has issue living, (Aliki) Beatrice Victoria *b* 23 March 1967: *m* 23 June 1990, André Aranha Corrêa do Lago, son of Antonio Corrêa do Lago, Amb of Brazil, Sibilla Sandra *b* 12 June 1968: *m* 8 Sept (civ) and 24 Sept (relig) 1994, *HRH Prince* Guillaume Marie Louis Christian of Luxembourg, yst son of HRH Grand Duke Jean of Luxembourg (and has issue living, *HRH Prince* Paul-Louis Jean Marie Guillaume *b* 4 March 1998), Cosima Marie Elisabeth Edmee *b* 18 Jan 1984, Domitilla Luise Marie *b* 14 June 1985. — †*HRH Infanta* Doña Maria Cristina (Teresa Alejandra Guadalupe Maria de la Concepción Ildefonsa Victoria Eugenia), *b* 12 Dec 1911: *m* 10 June 1940, Enrico Eugenio Francesco Antonio Marone-Cinzano, 1st Count Marone, who *d* 23 Oct 1968, and *d* 23 Dec 1996, leaving issue, *Donna* Vittoria Alfonsa Alberta Pilar Enrica Paola (Jésus Aprendiz 10, Madrid 28007, Spain), *b* 5 March 1941: *m* 9 Jan (civ) and 12 Jan (relig) 1961, Don José Carlos Alvarez de Toledo y Gross, 8th Count of Villapaterna, and has issue living, *Don* Francisco de Borja, *b* 25 March 1964: *m* 25 July 1993, Jill Debra, da of Eugene Joseph Schlanger (and has issue living, *Don* Daniel *b* 1 June 1995, *Don* Jacobo *b* 20 March 1997), *Don* Marco Alfonso *b* 23 Jan 1965, *Don* Gonzalo *b* 1 Oct 1973, *Donna* Victoria Eugenia *b* 8 Oct 1961: *m* 29 Sept 1982, Don Alfonso Condorniu y Aguilar (and has issue living, *Don* Jaime, *b* 16 Feb 1985, *Doña* Ana *b* 24 Jan 1987, *Doña* Carla *b* 5 July 1991), — *Donna* Giovanna Paola Gabriella (Julio Palacios 3, Madrid 28002, Spain), *b* 31 Jan 1943: *m* 1st, 24 July 1967 (*m diss* 1980, Don Jaime Galobert y Satrústegui; 2ndly, 4 Aug 1989, Don Luis Angel Sánchez Merlo y Ruiz, and has issue living (by 1st *m*), *Don* Alfonso Alberto *b* 12 April 1969: *m* 26 June 1998, Alexandra Kindelan y Oteyza, da of Ultrano Kindelan y Everett, of Venezuela, — Donna Maria Teresa (Beatrice) (Sor Angela de la Cruz 12, Madrid 28020, Spain), *b* 4 Jan 1945: *m* 21 April (civ) and 22 April (relig) 1967 (*m diss* 1989), Don José Maria Ruiz de Arana y Montalvo, 5th Marqués de Brenes, 13th Marqués de Castromonte, Grandee of Spain, and has issue living, *Doña* Cristina Carmen Margarita *b* 24 March 1968, *Doña* Isabel Alfonsa *b* 17 May 1970, *Doña* Inés Carla *b* 27 Dec 1973, — *Donna* Anna Alessandra (Anna Sandra) Paola Maria Tommasa, *b* 21 Dec 1948: *m* 1st, 21 June 1969 (*m diss* 1985), Gian Carlo Stavro Santarosa, son of Guido Stavro Santarosa; 2ndly, 24 July 1986, Don Fernando Schwartz y Girón, of Joaquìn Costa 15, Madrid 28006, Spain, and has issue living, (by 1st *m*), Astrid Cristina Antonia *b* 24 April 1972, Yara Paola *b* 29 June 1974.

HER MAJESTY QUEEN ELIZABETH
THE QUEEN MOTHER

Her Majesty ELIZABETH ANGELA MAR-GUERITE, LG, LT, CI, GCVO, GBE (*Queen Elizabeth The Queen Mother*), da of 14th Earl of Strathmore and Kinghorne; *b* in London 4 Aug 1900; Hon LLD, Queen's Univ, Belfast 1924, St Andrews 1929, Glasgow 1932, Edinburgh 1937, Cape Town 1947, Camb 1948, Manchester 1951, Leeds and Columbia Univ, NY 1954, Melbourne and Liverpool 1958, Auckland 1966, Halifax (Nova Scotia) and Dundee 1967; Hon DCL, Oxford 1931; HonDLitt London 1937 and W Indies 1965; HonLittD Keele 1965; HonDMus, Sheffield 1966; Hon FRCOG 1949; Hon FRCS England 1950; Hon FRCP Edinburgh 1953; FRCP 1962; Bencher Middle Temple 1944 (Treasurer 1949); FRS; Col-in-Ch 1st The Queen's Dragoon Guards, The Queen's Royal Hussars (The Queen's Own and Royal Irish), 9th/12th R Lancers (Prince of Wales's), King's Regt, R Anglian Regt, Light Inf, The Black Watch (R Highland Regt), The RAMC; Hon Col R Yeo, The London Scottish (The London Regt) (TA), Col-in-Ch The Black Watch (R Highland Regt) of Canada, The Toronto Scottish Regt, CFMS, RAAMC, and RNZAMC; Comdt-in-Ch Women in The Royal Navy, Patron Women's Royal Army Corps Association, Comdt-in-Ch RAF Central Flying Sch and Women in the RAF; Comdt-in-Ch Nursing Corps and Divs, St John Ambulance Bde'; Hon Freeman of Grocers' Co, Butchers' Co, Merchant Taylors' Co, Shipwrights' Co, Musicians Co, and Barbers' Co; Hon Member of Lloyds; Pres of British Red Cross Soc 1937-52, since when Dept Pres; a GCStJ; has Grand Cross of Legion of Honour, and of Orders of the Lion of the Netherlands, of the Crown of Roumania, of St Olga and St Sophia of Greece, of St Sava of Serbia, of Lernor Ala of Afghanistan, of Sun of Peru, of Independence of Republic of Tunisia, and of Ojaswi Rajanya of Nepal; has French Red Cross Medal and Norwegian War Cross; received Freedom of City of Glasgow 1927, of Burghs of Stirling and Dunfermline 1928, of City of Perth 1935, of City of Edinburgh 1936, of Burgh of Inverness and of City of London 1953, of City of Dundee and of Borough of King's Lynn 1954, of Burghs of Forfar, Musselburgh, and Wick 1956, of City of Aberdeen 1959, and of City of St Albans 1961; Pres of R Highland and Agricultural Soc 1963-64; awarded gold Albert Medal of R Soc of Arts 1952; appointed Grand Master of R Victorian Order 1937; Pres of Univ Coll of Rhodesia and Nyasaland 1957-70; Chancellor of London Univ 1955-81, and first Chancellor of Dundee Univ 1967; Hon Fellow, Univ of London 1977, and of King's Coll London 1978; appointed Lord Warden and Admiral of the Cinque Ports and Constable of Dover Castle Sept 1978; received R Victorian Chain 1937; GBE (Civil) 1927, CI 1931, Lady of the Order of the Garter 1936, GCVO and Lady of the Order of the Thistle 1937: *m* at Westminster Abbey 26 April 1923, HM King George VI, who *d* 6 Feb 1952.

Arms—The Royal Arms, impaling quarterly 1st and 4th the arms of Bowes-Lyon; i.e. 1st and 4th argent, a lion rampant azure, armed and langued gules, within a double tressure flory-counterflory of the second, *Lyon*; 2nd and 3rd ermine, three bows, strings palewise proper, *Bowes*. **Supporters**—*Dexter*, that of the Sovereign; *sinister*, a lion per fesse or and gules, being one of the supporters of the Earls of Strathmore and Kinghorne.

Residences,—Clarence House, SW1A 1BA; Royal Lodge, Windsor Great Park, Berks; Castle of Mey, Caithness.

DUKE OF EDINBURGH

GOD IS MY HELP

His Royal Highness The Prince PHILIP, KG, KT, OM, GBE, AC, QSO, PC, 1st Duke, only son of HRH the late Prince Andrew of Greece and Denmark, GCVO, by HRH the late Princess (Victoria) Alice Elizabeth Julia Marie, RRC, da of 1st Marquess of Milford Haven; *b* at Mon Repos, Corfu 10 June 1921; ed at Cheam Sch, at Salem, Baden, at Gordonstoun, and at R Naval Coll, Dartmouth; 1939-45 War, with Mediterranean Fleet, in Home Waters, and with British Pacific Fleet in SE Asia and the Pacific [despatches, Greek War Cross, 1939-45, Atlantic, Africa, Burma (with Pacific rosette), and Italy Stars, War medal 1939-45 (with oak leaf) and French Croix de Guerre (with Palm)]; Hon LLD Wales 1949, London 1951, Edinburgh and Camb 1952, Karachi 1959, Malta 1964, and California 1966; Hon DCL Durham 1951, and Oxford 1964; Hon DSc Delhi 1959, Reading 1957, Salford (Lancs) and Southampton 1967; Hon DSc Univ of Victoria, BC, Canada 1969; Hon LLD Univ of Western Ontario 1983; Hon Degree, Univ of Jordan 1984; Hon Degree in Engineering, Lima 1962; Hon FRCP London 1952; Hon FRCSE, and Hon FRCS England; Hon Fellow Univ Coll, Oxford 1953; a Personal ADC to HM King George VI 1948; Adm of the Fleet, Field Marshal, Marshal of the RAF, Adm of the Fleet RAN, Field Marshal Aust Mil Forces, Field Marshal New Zealand Army, Marshal of the RAAF, Marshal of the RNZAF, Adm of the Fleet RNZ Navy, Capt Gen, R Marines, Dep Col-in-Ch Queen's Royal Hussars (The Queen's Own and Royal Irish), Col-in-Ch The Royal Gloucestershire, Berkshire and Wiltshire Regt Col-in-Ch The Highlanders (Seaforth, Gordons and Camerons), Intelligence Corps, Army Cadet Force, R Canadian Regt, Seaforth Highlanders of Canada, R Canadian Army Cadets, R Aust Electrical and Mechanical Engineers, Aust Cadet Corps, Col of Grenadier Guards, Hon Col Edinburgh and Heriot-Watt Univs Officers' Training Corps, Trinidad and Tobago Regt; Air Commodore-in-Chief Air Training Corps, Air Commodore of the Air Sqdn since 1983, R Canadian Air Cadets, Hon Air Commodore RAF Kinloss, Cmdt-in-Ch and Extra Master, Merchant Navy; Ranger of Windsor Great Park since 1952, and Lord High Steward of Plymouth since 1960; Chancellor of Univs of Edinburgh since 1952, Camb since 1976, Wales 1948-76, and Salford 1967-90; Visitor of Upper Canada Coll since 1955, Manchester Coll of Science and Technology since 1957, and Churchill Coll, Camb since 1959; Life Gov of King's Coll, London since 1954, Master of the Bench of Inner Temple since 1954; Elder Brother of Trin House since 1952 (Master since 1969) and Hon Brother of Hull Trin House since 1956; R Gov of Charterhouse since 1953; Pres Nat Playing Fields Assoc since 1948; Pres in Ch of British Racing Drivers' Club 1952-92 and Pres of British Amateur Athletic Board since 1952, Commonwealth Games Fedn 1955-90, British Sportsman's Club since 1958, Central Council of Physical Recreation since 1951, City and Guilds of London Inst since 1951, English-Speaking Union of the Commonwealth since 1952, Guinea Pig Club since 1960, Guards' Polo Club since 1955, R Agric Society of the Commonwealth since 1958, R Commn for Exhibition of 1851 since 1965, R Household Cricket Club since 1953, R Merchant Navy Sch since 1952, R Mint Advisory Cttee on design of seals, coins and medals since 1952, R Society of Arts since 1952, World Wild Life Fund 1961-82; Pres World Wild Life International (now World Wide Fund for Nature-International) 1981-96; Pres Federation Equestre International 1964-84; Pres Maritime Trust since 1969; Grand Pres British Commonwealth Ex-Services League since 1974; Pres R Bath and West and Southern Counties Soc 1981; Pres Royal Windsor Horse Show 1991-94; Pres Windsor Park Equestrian Club since 1982; Vice-Pres Soc of the Friends of St George's and the Descendants of Knights of the Garter since 1948; FRS 1951; Permanent Fellow of Inst of Petroleum since 1963; Hon Fellow of R Soc of Canada since 1957, Australian Acad of Science since 1962, and R Zoological Soc of Scotland since 1963; Trustee of Nat Maritime Museum, Greenwich since 1948, and R Agric Soc of England since 1957; Patron and first Hon Fellow of Ghana Acad of Sciences since 1961 (Hon Pres 1959-61); Patron of R Inst of Navigation and Lord's Taverners (Pres of Council 1960-61, since when Twelfth Man), of Charities Aid Foundation, and Inst of Chemical Engineers; Patron and Trustee of The Duke of Edinburgh's Award; a Liveryman and Assist of Shipwrights' Co (Prime Warden 1954, Permanent Master since 1955), a Freeman and Liveryman of Fishmongers' Co (Prime Warden 1961, 4th Warden 1962-63), a Freeman and Liveryman of Mercers' Co, Adm of the Master Mariners' Co, Grand Master of Guild of Air Pilots and Air Navigators, a Guild Brother of Glasgow, of Craft Rank Qua Hammermen, Trades House of Glasgow, Adm of Roy Yacht Squadron since 1953; Adm of House of Lords Yacht Club, of R Motor Yacht Club, of RN Sailing Assocn, of R Southern Yacht Club, of Bar Yacht Club, of Roy Dart Yacht Club, of R Gibraltar Yacht Club, of R Yacht Club of Victoria, Australia; Commodore-in-Chief, Sandringham Yacht Club, Victoria, since 1980, and of Great Navy of State of Nebraska, USA; received Freedom of City of London, Greenwich and City of Edinburgh 1948, City of Belfast 1949, City of Cardiff 1954, City of Glasgow 1955, City of Melbourne 1956, City of Dar-es-Salaam 1961, Hon Citizen of Montevideo 1962, City of Nairobi 1963, and Cities of Guadalajara and Acapulco, Mexico, and Bridgetown, Barbados 1964 and City of Los Angeles and Hon Citizen of Chicago 1966; Grand Cross Order of Redeemer of Greece, Order of Phoenix of Greece,

---

*By warrant dated 18 Sept 1952, the Duke was granted precedence next to HM The Queen except where otherwise provided by Act of Parliament.

Grand Cross Order of George I (with swords) of Greece, Order of St George and St Constantine (with swords) of Greece (4th Class), Knight of Order of the Elephant of Denmark 1947, Grand Cross of Order of St Charles of Monaco 1951, of Order of St Olav of Norway 1952, and of Manuel Amador Guerrero of Panama 1953, Order of the Seraphim of Sweden, and Chain of Most Exalted Order of the Queen of Sheba of Ethiopia 1954, Grand Cross of Order of the Tower and the Sword (Civil) of Portugal 1955, of Order of King Faisal I of Iraq 1956, and of the Legion of Honour of France 1957, Knight Grand Cross of Order of Merit of the Italian Republic, Grand Cross of Order of the Lion of the Netherlands, and of Order of Merit of Federal German Republic (1st Class) 1958, Order of Ojaswi Rajanya of Nepal 1960, Knight Grand Band of Star of Africa of Liberia 1961, Grand Cross of Order of San Martin of Argentina, of Order of the Condor of Bolivia, and of National Order of Southern Cross of Brazil, Chain of Chilean Order of Merit, Grand Cross Extraordinary of Order of Boyacá of Colombia, Grand Cross of National Order of Merit of Ecuador, National Order of Merit of Paraguay, and Great Cross of Order of the Sun, with Brilliants, of Peru, 1962, Grand Cordon of Order of Leopold of Belgium and Order of the Brilliant Star of Zanzibar (1st Class) 1963, and Decoration of Republic of Sudan (1st Class) and Grand Cross of Order of the Icelandic Falcon 1964, and Collar of the Aztec Eagle of Mexico 1964, Star and Riband of Order of Nahdah, Jordan 1966, Decoration of Honour for Services to Republic of Austria, Grand Cordon 1966, Grand Commander Order of Maritime Merit, San Francisco Port Authority 1968, Order of White Rose of Finland 1969, Order of Superior Sun of Afghanistan 1971, Grand Cordon of Supreme Order of Chrysanthemum of Japan 1971, Most Esteemed Family Order of Brunei 1972, Chevalier Grand Cross Order of Golden Lion of Luxembourg 1972, a Member of Distinguished Order of Izzuddin, of Republic of Maldives 1972, Hon Member of Darjah Utama Temasek of Singapore 1972, Grand Cross Yugoslav Star of Yugoslavia 1972, Grand Cordon of National Order of the Leopard (Mil) of Zaire 1973, Grand Collar of National Order of Infante Dom Henrique of Portugal 1973, Commander of Order of the Golden Ark of the Netherlands 1979, First Class (military) Order of Oman 1979, Collar of Order of Independence of Qatar 1979, 1st class Order of Muhammadi of Morocco 1980, Companion of the Queen's Service Order of New Zealand 1981, Canadian Forces Decoration 1982, Grand Cross of Order of Carlos III of Spain 1986, Companion of the Order of Australia 1988, Grand Ribbon of the Order of Merit of Poland 1991; King George VI Coronation Medal (1937), and Queen Elizabeth II Coronation Medal (1953), Commemoration Medal of New Zealand 1990, Sultan of Brunei Silver Jubilee Medal 1992, George Cross 50th Anniversary Medal of Malta 1992; appointed Grand Master and First or Principal Knt of Order of British Empire 1953; *cr.* KG, *Baron Greenwich*, of Greenwich co London, *Earl of Merioneth*, and *Duke of Edinburgh* (peerage of United Kingdom) 1947, KT 1952, GBE (Mil) 1953, and OM 1968; naturalized a British subject and adopted the surname of Mountbatten 28 Feb 1947; granted title, style and attribute of Royal Highness 1947; introduced to PC 1951, and to PC Canada 1957; granted style and titular dignity of a Prince of UK 1957: **m* 20 Nov 1947, HM Queen Elizabeth II, and has issue.

𝕬rms—Quarterly; 1st, or, semee of hearts gules, three lions passant in pale azure ducally crowned of the first; 2nd, azure, a cross argent; 3rd, argent, two pallets sable; 4th argent, upon a rock proper a castle triple towered sable, masoned argent, windows, port, turret caps, and vanes gules. 𝕮rest—A plume of five ostrich feathers alternately sable and argent issuant from a ducal coronet or. 𝕾upporters—Dexter, a representation of Heracles girt about the loins with a lion skin, crowned with a chaplet of oak leaves and holding in the dexter hand a club proper; sinister, a lion queue fourchee ducally crowned or and gorged with a naval coronet azure. 𝕮oronet A coronet composed of crosses-patées and fleurs-de-lis alternately or.

Residences—Buckingham Palace, SW1; Windsor Castle, Berkshire; Balmoral Castle, Aberdeenshire; Sandringham House, Norfolk.

*It was declared by Letters Patent of Oct 22nd, 1948, that the children of this marriage shall enjoy the style of "HRH" and the titular dignity of Prince or Princess.

PRINCE OF WALES

His Royal Highness Prince CHARLES PHILIP ARTHUR GEORGE, KG, KT, GCB, AK, PC, *Prince of Wales and Earl of Chester, Duke of Cornwall and Rothesay, Earl of Carrick, Baron of Renfrew, Lord of the Isles and Great Steward of Scotland*, eldest son of HM Queen Elizabeth II; *b* at Buckingham Palace 14 November 1948, ed at Cheam School, at Gordonstoun, at Geelong Grammar School, Trinity College, Cambridge (MA, Hon Fellow 1988), and University College of Wales, Aberystwyth; Bar Gray's Inn 1974, Hon Bencher 1975; Hon DCL Oxford Univ 1983, and Durham Univ 1998; Personal ADC to HM since 1973; Rear Adm RN since 1998; Maj-Gen in the Army since 1998; AV-M RAF since 1998; Colonel-in-Chief The Royal Regiment of Wales (24th/41st Foot) since 1969; Colonel Welsh Guards since 1975; Colonel-in-Chief The Cheshire Regiment since 1977; Dep Colonel-in-Chief The Highlanders since 1994; Colonel-in-Chief Lord Strathcona's Horse (Royal Canadian) Regiment since 1977; Colonel-in-Chief The Parachute Regiment since 1977; Colonel-in-Chief The Royal Australian Armoured Corps since 1977; Colonel-in-Chief The Royal Regiment of Canada since 1977; Colonel-in-Chief Royal Gurkha Rifles since 1977; Colonel-in-Chief The Royal Winnipeg Rifles since 1977; Colonel-in-Chief Papua New Guinea The Royal Pacific Islands Regt since 1984; Colonel-in-Chief Royal Canadian Dragoons since 1985; Colonel-in-Chief Army Air Corps since 1992; Colonel-in-Chief Royal Dragoon Gds since 1992; AV-M RAF since 1998; Hon Air Commodore Royal Air Force Brawdy 1977-92; Hon Air Commodore RAF Valley since 1993; Air Commodore in Chief Royal New Zealand Air Force since 1977; Colonel-in-Chief Air Reserve Group of Air Command in Canada since 1977; President Society of Friends of St George's and Descendants of Knights of the Garter since 1975; Admiral Royal Thames Yacht Club since 1986; High Steward Royal Borough of Windsor and Maidenhead since 1975; President of The Prince's Trust since 1976; President of United World Colleges 1978-93; President of The Royal Agricultural Society of England 1990-91; Chancellor of The University of Wales since 1976; Patron of the National Gallery Trust since 1993; Patron Royal Television Soc since 1997; Pres of Business in the Community since 1985, Scottish Business in the Community since 1985, Pres of The Disability Partnership since 1983, Pres of The Wildfowl and Wetlands Trust since 1979; Pres Prince of Wales Business Leaders Forum since 1990; Patron Royal Society for Nature Conservation since 1977; Patron of Ancient Monuments Society since 1990; Vice Patron British Council since 1984; Pres Royal Shakespeare Co since 1991; Pres The Prince of Wales's Foundation for Architecture and the Urban Environment since 1992; Chm Royal Collection Trust since 1993; Pres King's Fund since 1986; Pres Royal Coll of General Practitioners 1991-92; Patron of Royal Hospital for Sick Children, Bristol, since 1996; Patron Breakthrough since 1998; represented HM at Memorial Service for Prime Minister of Australia 1967; at Independence Celebrations in Fiji 1970, at Requiem Mass for General Charles de Gaulle 1970, at Bahamas Independence Celebrations 1973, at Papua New Guinea Independence Celebrations 1975, at Coronation of King of Nepal 1975, at funeral of Sir Robert Menzies 1978, and at funeral of President of Kenya, Jomo Kenyatta 1978; Coronation Medal 1953; the Queen's Silver Jubilee Medal 1977; Grand Cross of the White Rose of Finland 1969; Grand Cordon of the Supreme Order of the Chrysanthemum of Japan 1971; Grand Cross of the House of Orange of the Netherlands 1972; Grand Cross of the Order of Oak Crown of Luxembourg 1972; Knight of the Order of Elephant of Denmark 1974; Grand Cross of the Order of Ojasvi Rajanya of Nepal 1975; Kt of the Order of the Seraphim of Sweden 1975; Grand Cross of the Order of the Southern Cross of Brazil 1978; Grand Cross with Collar of the Republic of Egypt 1981; Gd Cross of the Order of Orange Nassau of the Netherlands 1982; Gd Cross Order of St Olav of Norway 1978; Offr Order of the Star of Ghana 1977; Grand Cross of the Legion of Honour of France 1984; Grand Cross of Order of Carlos III of Spain; Nepal Coronation Medal 1975; Grand Cross of Khalifiyyeh Order of Bahrain; Grand Cross of Order of the Lion of Malawi; Grand Cross of Order of Merit of Saudi Arabia; Papua New Guinea Independence Medal 1975; Fijian Independence Medal 1970; New Zealand Commemorative Medal 1990; Order of Merit of Qatar 1986; Order of Mubarak the Great of Kuwait 1993; created *Prince of Wales* and *Earl of Chester* 26 July 1958 (invested July 1st, 1969); KG 1958 (invested and installed 1968); KT 1977; Privy Counsellor 1977; GCB and Great Master of Order of the Bath 1975; Kt of the Order of Australia 1981; Extra Companion of Queen's Service Order of New Zealand 1983; received Freedom of City of Cardiff 1969, of Royal Borough of New Windsor 1970, of City of London 1971, of City of Chester 1973, of City of Canterbury 1978, of City of Portsmouth 1979, of City of Lancaster 1993, and of City of Swansea 1994; Liveryman of Fishmongers' Company 1971; a Freeman of Drapers' Company 1971, a Freeman Shipwrights' Company 1978; Honorary Member of the Honourable Company of Master Mariners 1977 (Master 1988-90), Liveryman of Gardeners' Company 1987; a Freeman of Goldsmiths' Company;

Liveryman of Farmers' Company 1980; Liveryman of Pewterers' Company 1982; Liveryman of the Fruiterers' Company 1989; Liveryman of the Carpenters' Company 1992; Bencher Middle Temple 1988: *m* at St Paul's Cathedral, London 29 July 1981 (*m diss* 28 Aug 1996), Lady Diana Frances Spencer, who *d* 31 Aug 1997, following a motor accident in Paris, yst da of 8th Earl Spencer, and has issue.

𝕬rms—The Royal Arms, differenced by a label of three points argent, and in the centre an escutcheon of the arms of the Principality of Wales, viz, quarterly or and gules, four lions passant guardant counterchanged, ensigned by the coronet of the Heir Apparent. 𝕮rest—The Royal Crest, differenced with a label of three points argent, but with the coronets of the Heir Apparent. 𝕾upporters—Same as the Royal Arms differenced by a label of three points argent, the *dexter* crowned with the Heir Apparent's coronet, and the *sinister* gorged with a coronet of fleurs-de-lis and crosses-pattées, a chain affixed thereto passing between the fore-legs and reflexed over the back, or. 𝕭adges—*Dexter*, a plume of three ostrich feathers argent, enfiled by a coronet, composed of fleurs-de-lis, and crosses-pattées or alternately with motto *Ich Dien*; *sinister*, a representation of the Royal Badge of Wales, namely on a mount vert, a dragon passant gules, differenced as in the Crest with a label of three points argent. Between the badges is the shield of the arms of the Duchy of Cornwall, viz, sable fifteen bezants or, ensigned by the coronet of the Heir Apparent. *Scottish Banner*, Quarterly, 1st and 4th, or a fess chequy azure and argent (for The Great Steward of Scotland), 2nd and 3rd, argent a lymphard sable flagged gules (for The Lord ofd the Isles), on an inescutcheon or a lion rampant gules armed and langued azure within a royal tressure gules and charged overall at the honour point with a label of three points azure (for the Duke of Rothesay). *Personal Flag in Wales*, Quarterly or and gules, four lions passant guardant counterchanged, over all an inescutcheon vert charged with the coronet of the Heir Apparent.

Residences—Highgrove House, nr Tetbury, Glos GL8 8TG; St James's Palace, SW1A 1BS.

SONS LIVING

HRH *Prince* William Arthur Philip Louis OF WALES, *b* at St Mary's Hosp, Paddington 21 June 1982; *ed* Eton.

HRH *Prince* Henry (Harry) Charles Albert David OF WALES, *b* at St Mary's Hosp, Paddington 15 Sept 1984; *ed* Eton.

DUKE OF YORK

His Royal Highness The Prince Andrew Albert Christian Edward, CVO, 2nd son of HM The Queen and HRH The Duke of Edinburgh; *b* at Buckingham Palace 19 February 1960; *ed* at Gordonstoun, Lakefield Coll, Ontario, Canada, and RNC Dartmouth; Cmdr RN 1999; served S Atlantic Campaign (1982) as helicopter pilot HMS *Invincible*; personal ADC to HM The Queen since 1984; Col-in-Ch Staffs Regt since 1989; Col-in-Ch The Royal New Zealand Army Logistic Regt since 1997; Col-in-Ch The Royal Irish Regt since 1992; Adm Sea Cadet Corps since 1992; visited St Helena to mark 150th anniversary of island becoming a Crown Colony 1984; visited Australia in HMS *Edinburgh* to be Reviewing Officer at Australian Bicentennial International Review 1988; visited Papua New Guinea to open 9th South Pacific Games 1991; assumed command of HMS *Cottesmore* 1993; received Freedom of City of York 1987; CVO 1979; *cr Baron Killyleagh, Earl of Inverness, and Duke of York* (UK) 1986: *m* at Westminster Abbey, 23 July 1986 (*m diss* 30 May 1996), Sarah Margaret (Pres Motor Neurone Disease Assocn since 1993, Patron Tommy's, Patron Teenage Cancer Trust, Founder and Chm Children in Crisis 1993), 2nd da of Maj Ronald Ivor Ferguson (*see* V Hampden, colls), and has issue.

DAUGHTERS LIVING

HRH Princess Beatrice Elizabeth Mary OF YORK, *b* at the Portland Hosp, London, 8 Aug 1988.

HRH Princess Eugenie Victoria Helena OF YORK, *b* at the Portland Hosp, London, 23 March 1990.

Residences - Buckingham Palace, London SW1; Sunninghill Park, Windsor, Berks.

𝕬rms—The Royal Arms, differenced by a label of three points argent, charged on the centre point with an anchor azure. 𝕮rest—On a coronet of crosses and fleurs-de-lys a lion statant guardant or, crowned with a like coronet and differenced by a label as in the Arms. 𝕾upporters—Same as the Royal Arms differenced by a like coronet and label.

EARL OF WESSEX

His Royal Highness The Prince Edward Antony Richard Louis, CVO, 3rd and yst son of HM The Queen and HRH The Duke of Edinburgh; *b* at Buckingham Palace 10 March 1964; *ed* at Gordonstoun, and Jesus Coll, Cambridge; former house tutor and junior master, Wanganui Collegiate Sch, NZ; 2nd Lieut RM 1983 (resigned 1987); Patron Classworks Theatre Cambridge since 1984; Patron Haddo House Hall Arts Trust since 1987; President National Youth Music Theatre since 1987; Patron National Youth Theatre of Great Britain since 1987; Patron The National Youth Orchestra of Scotland since 1987; Trustee The Duke of Edinburgh's Award International Foundation since 1987; Trustee The Duke of Edinburgh's Award since 1988; Patron Ocean Youth Trust since 1990; Patron Scottish Badminton Union since 1990; President Commonwealth games Federation since 1990; Patron London Mozart Players since 1990; Patron City of Birmingham Symphony Orchestra since 1991; President The Children's Film Unit since 1992; Patron Globe Theatre, Saskatchewan, Canada since 1992; CVO 1989; *cr Viscount Severn and Earl of Wessex* (UK) 19 June 1999: *m* at St George's Chapel, Windsor, 19 June 1999, Sophie Helen, only da of Christopher Bournes Rhys-Jones, of Church Cottage, Brenchley, Kent (*see* V Molesworth, colls).

Arms—The royal arms differenced by a label of three points argent charged on the centre point with a Tudor rose. **Crest**—On a coronet of crosses and fleurs-de-lys a lion statant guardant or crowned with a like coronet and differenced by a label as in the arms. **Supporters**—Same as the royal arms differenced by a like coronet and label.

Residences - Buckingham Palace, SW1; Bagshot Part, Surrey.

DUKE OF GLOUCESTER

His Royal Highness Prince RICHARD ALEXANDER WALTER GEORGE, KG, GCVO; 2nd Duke; *b* at Northampton 26 Aug 1944; *s* 1974; ed at Eton, and Magdalene Coll, Camb (MA, Dip of Arch); RIBA; FSA; KStJ; Pres Inst of Advanced Motorists since 1971, of Cancer Research Campaign since 1973, of Nat Assocn of Boys' Clubs since 1974, of St Bartholomew's Hosp since 1975, and of British Consultants Bureau since 1978; Vice-Pres of British Leprosy Relief Assocn since 1971; Patron of ASH since 1974, of Society of Engineers since 1974, of Richard III Society since 1980, of Silver Jubilee Walkway Trust since 1978, and of Victorian Society since 1976; Ranger of Epping Forest since 1975; Queen's Trustee of British Museum since 1973; FRSA, 1976; Dep Col-in-Ch The Royal Gloucestershire, Berkshire and Wiltshire Regt since 1994, and The Royal Logistic Corps since 1993; Hon Col R Monmouthshire Royal Engineers (Militia) since 1977; Commodore of Royal Ulster Yacht Club since 1974, Gov Building Centre Trust since 1991, Hon Life Memb Friends of All Saints, Brixworth since 1991, Pres Public Monuments and Sculpture Assocn since 1998, Patron Samsung British Legion Korean Scholarship Scheme since 1998; Grand Prior, Order of St John of Jerusalem since 1975; Liveryman of Vintners' Co and Hon Freeman of Grocers' Co; Hon Freeman and Liveryman of Goldsmiths' Co; has Grand Cross Order of St Olav of Norway; GCVO 1974, KG 1997: *m* at Barnwell Parish Church, 8 July 1972, Birgitte Eva, GCVO (1989), DStJ (Dep Col-in-Ch The Adjutant General's Corps, Col-in-Ch Royal Australian Army Educational Corps since 1977, and Royal NZ Army Educational Corps since 1985, Pres of London Regions WRVS, of Roy Alexander and Albert Sch, of Royal Sch of Needlework, of Civil Service Sports Council, and of Royal School of Bath; Patron of Federation of Army Wives, Nat Asthma Campaign, Assoc for Spina Bifida and Hydrocephalus, Scottish Opera, Cheltenham International Music Festival, Bobath Centre and Foundation for the Study of Infant Deaths; Vice Patron The Queen's Club), yr da of late Asger Preben Wissing Henriksen, lawyer, of Odense, Denmark (by his 1st wife, Vivian, da of the late Waldemar Oswald van Deurs, whose name she assumed), and has issue.

Arms—The Royal Arms, differenced by a label of five points argent, the centre and two outer points charged with a cross gules, and the inner points with a lion passant guardant. **Crest**—On a coronet composed of four crosses-pattées alternated with four strawberry leaves, a lion statant guardant or, crowned with the like coronet, and differenced with the label as in the Arms. **Supporters**—The Royal Supporters, differenced with the like coronet and label. (By Royal Warrant dated 24 Feb, 1975, the arms which were assigned to a grandchild of a Sovereign became hereditary.)

Residence—Kensington Palace, W8 4PU.

SON LIVING

ALEXANDER PATRICK GREGERS RICHARD *(Earl of Ulster)*, *b* at St Mary's Hosp, Paddington, 24 Oct 1974; *ed* Eton, and RMA Sandhurst; commn'd The King's Royal Hussars 1998.

DAUGHTERS LIVING

Lady Davina Elizabeth Alice Benedikte WINDSOR, *b* at St Mary's Hosp, Paddington, 19 Nov 1977
Lady Rose Victoria Birgitte Louise WINDSOR, *b* at St Mary's Hosp, Paddington 1 March 1980

WIDOW LIVING OF FIRST DUKE

Lady Alice Christabel Montagu-Douglas-Scott, GCB, CI, GCVO, GBE *(HRH Princess Alice, Duchess of Gloucester)*, 3rd da of 7th Duke of Buccleuch and Queensberry; *b* in London, 25 Dec 1901; ed at St James's Sch, W Malvern and in Paris; Air Chief Marshal, Col-in-Ch KO3D, RACT; Dep Col-in-Ch R Anglian Regt, and The King's Royal Hussars; a Member of Council British Red Cross Soc; Dep Comdt-in-Ch of Nursing Corps and Dive St John Ambulance Bde, since 1937; GCStJ; patron BFWG Charitable Foundation; received Freedom of Cities of Edinburgh 1937, Gloucester 1939, and Belfast 1952; GBE (Civil) and CI 1937, GCVO 1948, GCB (Civil) 1975; *m* at Buckingham Palace, 6 Nov 1935, HRH The Prince Henry William Frederick Albert, KG, KT, KP, GCB, GCMG, GCVO, PC, 1st Duke of Gloucester, who *d* at Barnwell Manor, Northants, 10 June 1974, 3rd son of HM King George V.

Residence—Kensington Palace, W8 4PU.

PREDECESSOR

[1] *HRH The Prince* HENRY WILLIAM FREDERICK ALBERT, KG, KT, KP, GCB, GCMG, GCVO,

PC, 3rd son of his late Majesty King George V; *b* at York Cottage, Sandringham 31 March 1900; Field Marshal, and Marshal of RAF; Gov-Gen and C-in-C, Commonwealth of Australia 1944-47; received Roy Victorian Chain 1932; cr *Baron Culloden, Earl of Ulster,*and *Duke of Gloucester* (peerage of UK) 1928: *m* 6 Nov 1935, Lady Alice Christabel Montagu-Douglas-Scott, GCB, CI, GCVO, GBE, 3rd da of 7th Duke of Buccleuch and Queensberry, *d* 10 June 1974; *s* by his yr son [2] RICHARD ALEXANDER WALTER GEORGE, 2nd Duke, and present peer; also Earl of Ulster, and Baron Culloden.

DUKE OF KENT

Field Marshal His Royal Highness Prince EDWARD GEORGE NICHOLAS PAUL PATRICK, KG, GCMG, GCVO, ADC, 2nd Duke; *b* at 3 Belgrave Square, W1, 9 Oct 1935; *s* 1942; ed at Eton, in Switzerland, and at RMA, Sandhurst; Hon DCL Durham 1961; Maj-Gen (ret) R Scots Dragoon Gds (Carabiniers and Greys), and Dep Col-in-Chief since 1993; Col-in-Ch R Regt of Fusiliers, Devonshire and Dorset Regt, and Lorne Scots Regt (Canada); Col Scots Gds; acted as Special Representative of HM The Queen at Independence Celebrations in Sierra Leone 1961, Uganda 1962, The Gambia 1965, and Guyana and Barbados 1966, and at Coronation of King of Tonga 1967; personal ADC to HM since 1966; GSO II E Command 1967-68, and a Co Instructor, RMA, Sandhurst 1968-70, and in command C Sqdn R Scots Greys 1970-71; ret as Lt-Col 1976, promoted Maj-Gen 1983, Field Marshal 1993; Hon Air Chief Marshal, RAF 1998; Hon Air Cdre to RAF Leuchars 1993; Grand Master of United Grand Lodge of Freemasons of England and Grand Master of Order of St Michael and St George since 1967; Pres of Wellington Coll since 1969, of Commonwealth War Graves Commn since 1970, and of Scout Assocn since 1975; Vice-Chm of British Overseas Trade Board 1976-99, since when Vice-Chm of successor body, British Trade International, Chm Duke of Edinburgh's Commonwealth Study Conference (UK Fund); Pres Royal Masonic Benevolent Inst, Royal Choral Soc, Imperial War Museum, Chest, Heart and Stroke Assocn, All England Lawn Tennis and Croquet Club, Wimbledon, Automobile Assocn since 1974, British Invisibles since 1999, and Engrg Council; Royal Patron Anglo-German Assoc since 1994, and The Help Poland Fund (Northern) since 1994; Patron, London Philharmonic Orchestra 1980, Hanover Band 1992, Trinity Coll of Music 1985, and the ME Assocn 1996; Pres Henley Soc since 1994; Chancellor of Univ of Surrey since 1977; Hon Fell of Royal Aeronautical Society 1993; Hon Freeman of Clothworkers' Co, Freeman Mercers' Co, and Hon Liveryman of Salters' Co and of Engineers' Co; received Hon Freedom of City of Georgetown, Guyana, 1966; has Orders of St George and St Constantine of Greece (1st Class), of Tri Shakti Patta of Nepal (1st Class), Grand Band of Order of the Star of Africa of Liberia, and Grand Cross of Order of Al-Nahda of Jordan; GCVO 1960, GCMG 1967, KG 1985: *m* at York Minster 8 June 1961, Katharine Lucy Mary, GCVO (Dep Col-in-Ch the Adjutant General's Corps since 1992, The Royal Dragoon Guards, and The Royal Logistic Corps; Pres Action Research since 1993, Royal Patron of Age Concern England since 1993, Patron ENABLE (formerly The Distressed Gentlefolks Association) and SCOPE (formerly The Spastics Society), Patron British Arts Festival Year 1995 since 1993, Patron Dyson Perrins Museum Appeal since 1993, of Nat Federation of Music Societies since 1993, of Ripon College, Cuddesdon since 1993, Pres Marie Curie Foundation since 1995; Hon Member of Royal Philharmonic Soc 1992, and Worshipful Company of Musicians 1993), only da of late Sir William Arthington Worsley, 4th Bt, and has issue.

Arms—The Royal Arms, differenced by a label of five points argent, the points charged with an anchor azure and a cross gules alternately. **Crests**—On a coronet of four crosses-pattées alternated with four strawberry leaves, a lion statant guardant or, crowned with the like coronet, and differenced with a label as in the Arms. **Supporters**—The Royal Supporters, differenced with the like coronet and label. (By Royal Warrant dated 24 Feb, 1975, the labels assigned to a grandchild of a Sovereign, except the eldest son of a Prince of Wales, became hereditary and are borne as part of the arms together with ordinary marks of difference when appropriate).

Residence—Wren Cottage, Kensington Palace, W8.

SONS LIVING

GEORGE PHILIP NICHOLAS (*Earl of St Andrews*), *b* at Coppins, Iver, Bucks 26 June 1962; ed at Eton, and Downing Coll, Camb: *m* at Leith 9 Jan 1988, Sylvana Palma, da of Maximilian Karl Tomaselli, and formerly wife of John Paul Jones, and has issue:—
　　SON LIVING— Edward Edmund Maximilian George (*Baron Downpatrick*), *b* at St Mary's Hosp, Paddington, 2 Dec 1988.
　　DAUGHTERS LIVING— *Lady* Marina-Charlotte Alexandra Katharine Helen WINDSOR, *b* at The Rosie Hospital, Cambridge 30 Sept 1992,—*Lady* Amelia Sophia Theodora Mary Margaret WINDSOR, *b* at The Rosie Hospital, Cambridge 24 Aug 1995.
Lord Nicholas Charles Edward Jonathan WINDSOR, *b* at King's College Hospital, London 25 July 1970.

DAUGHTER LIVING

Lady Helen Marina Lucy WINDSOR, *b* at Coppins, Iver, Bucks 28 April 1964: *m* at St George's Chapel, Windsor Castle 18 July 1992, Timothy Verner Taylor, eldest son of Cmdr Michael Verner Taylor, RN, and has issue living, Columbus George Donald, *b* 6 Aug 1994,—Cassius Edward, *b* 26 Dec 1996.

BROTHER LIVING

HRH Prince Michael George Charles Franklin OF KENT, KCVO, *b* at Coppins, Iver, Bucks 4 July 1942; ed at Eton, and at RMA Sandhurst; commn'd into 11th Hussars (PAO), later The Royal Hussars (PWO); Commodore RNR, member of HAC, Grand Master of the Lodge of Mark Master Masons, Hon Liveryman of the Clothworkers' Co, Leathersellers' Co, Scientific Instrument Makers' Co, Coachmakers' and Coach Harness Makers' Co; represented HM The Queen at the Funeral of President Ahmed of India 1977, and the Funeral of President Makarios of Cyprus 1977, the Independence Celebrations in Belize 1981, the Funeral of King Sobhuza II of Swaziland 1982, and the Coronation of King Mswati III of Swaziland 1986; Commonwealth Pres of the Royal Life Saving Soc, Pres of the Royal Automobile Club, the Inst of the Motor Industry, SSAFA, Medical Commn on Accident Prevention, the Dogs' Home Battersea, the Royal Patriotic Fund Corporation, Nat Eye Research Centre, the Kennel Club, the Institute of Road Safety Officers, and the Society of Genealogists; Patron of the Museum of Army Flying, the Veteran Car Club of Great Britain, Thames Rowing Club, the Popular Flying Association, the David Shepherd Conservation Fund, the Carriage Foundation, the Brooklands Museum Trust Appeal, and the Bermuda Maritime Museum; Founder of the Prince Michael Road Safety Award Scheme; Fell of the Institute of the Motor Industry and the Royal Aeronautical Society; Trustee of the National Motor Museum; Chm of Advisory Board of House of Windsor; *m* at Vienna, 30 June 1978, Baroness Marie Christine (Agnes Hedwig Ida) (Patron Society of Women Artists; Lady of the Constantinian Order of St George 1996), da of late Baron Günther Hubertus von Reibnitz, and formerly wife of Thomas Troubridge [*see* Troubridge, Bt] and has issue:—

SON LIVING,—*Lord* Frederick Michael David Louis WINDSOR, *b* at St Mary's Hosp, Paddington, 6 April 1979; *ed* Eton.

DAUGHTER LIVING,—*Lady* Gabriella (Ella) Marina Alexandra Ophelia WINDSOR, *b* at St Mary's Hosp, Paddington, 23 April 1981.

Residences—Kensington Palace, W8 4PU; Nether Lypiatt Manor, Stroud, Glos GL6 7LS.

SISTER LIVING

HRH Princess Alexandra Helen Elizabeth Olga Christabel OF KENT (*HRH Princess Alexandra, the Hon Lady Ogilvy, GCVO*), *b* at 3 Belgrave Square, SW1 25 Dec 1936; Hon LLD Queensland Univ, Australia 1959, Hong Kong 1961, and Mauritius 1974; Chancellor of Lancaster Univ 1964, Hon Fellow of R Faculty of Physicians and Surgs of Glasgow 1960 (known as Royal Coll since 1962), Faculty of Anaesthetists (known as Royal Coll since 1992), Royal Coll of Physicians since 1992, and of Royal Coll of Obstetricians and Gynaecologists since 1969; Col-in-Ch 17th/21st Lancers 1969-93, Queen's Own Rifles of Canada since 1960, The King's Own Border Regt since 1977, and The Canadian Scottish Regt (Princess Mary's) since 1977; Dep Col-in-Ch the LI since 1968, Dep Col-in-Ch The Queen's Royal Lancers since 1993, Dep Hon Col of Royal Yeo since 1975; Patron and Air Ch Comdt of Princess Mary's RAF Nursing Ser since 1966, Hon Comdt General Royal Hong Kong Police Force, and Royal Hong Kong Aux Police Force 1969-79; acted as Special Representative of HM the Queen at Independence Celebrations in Nigeria 1960, at 150th Anniversary Celebrations of founding of Modern Singapore 1969, and at Independence Celebrations of St Lucia 1979; Patron of QARNNS, and People's Dispensary for Sick Animals; Pres Sight Savers International — Roy Commonwealth Soc for the Blind, Children's Country Holidays Fund, Queen Alexandra's House Assocn, Royal Star and Garter Home for Disabled Sailors, Soldiers and Airmen, Alexandra Rose Day, British Sch at Rome, Royal Humane Soc, and World Wide Fund for Nature UK, Dep Pres British Red Cross Soc; received Hon Freedom of City of Lancaster 1987; GCVO 1960: *m* at Westminster Abbey, 24 April 1963, Rt Hon Sir Angus James Bruce Ogilvy, KCVO, PC, 2nd son of 12th Earl of Airlie, and has issue living, James Robert Bruce, *b* at Thatched House Lodge, Richmond, Surrey, 29 Feb 1964: *m* 30 July 1988, Julia, eldest da of Charles Frederick Melville Rawlinson, of Arkesden, Essex, and has issue living, Alexander Charles *b* 12 Nov 1996, Flora Alexandra *b* 15 Dec 1994,—Marina Victoria Alexandra, *b* at Thatched House Lodge, Richmond, Surrey, 31 July 1966: *m* 2 Feb 1990 (*m diss* 4 Dec 1997), Paul Julian Mowatt, son of David Mowatt, and has issue living, Christian Alexander *b* 4 June 1993, Zenouska May *b* 26 May 1990.

Residence—Thatched House Lodge, Richmond Park, Surrey. *Office*—Buckingham Palace, SW1A 1AA.

PREDECESSOR

[1] *HRH The Prince* GEORGE EDWARD ALEXANDER EDMUND, KG, KT, GCMG, GCVO, PC, 4th son of His late Majesty King George V; *b* at Sandringham House, Norfolk, 20 Dec 1902; Rear-Adm, Maj-Gen in the Army, and Air Commodore RAF, received Roy Victorian Chain 1936; *cr Baron Downpatrick, Earl of St Andrews, and Duke of Kent* (peerage of United

Kingdom) 1934: *m* at Westminster Abbey, 29 Nov 1934, HRH Princess Marina, CI, GCVO, GBE, who *d* at Kensington Palace, 27 Aug 1968, youngest da of HRH late Prince Nicholas of Greece and Denmark GCB, GCVO; *d* (killed on active ser during European War) 25 Aug 1942; *s* by his el son [2] EDWARD GEORGE NICHOLAS PAUL PATRICK, 2nd Duke and present peer; also Earl of St Andrews and Baron Downpatrick.

DUKEDOM OF ALBANY (Duke UK 1881, suspended 1917)

Prince HUBERTUS RICHARD ERNST LEOPOLD OF SAXE-COBURG AND GOTHA, in whom is vested the right to petition for restoration of the Dukedom of Albany; *b* 8 Dec 1961; *s* his father, *Prince* ERNST-LEOPOLD (EDUARD WILHELM JOSIAS) as lineal representative of HRH the 1st Duke of Albany, 1996: *m* 9 March 1993, Barbara, da of Eugen Weissmann, and has issue.

Residence - Scheefstrasse 24, 72074 Tübingen, Germany.

SON LIVING

Prince SEBASTIAN HUBERTUS, *b* 16 Jan 1994.

HALF-BROTHERS LIVING

Prince Ernst-Josias (Carl Eduard Hermann Leopold), *b* 13 May 1965: *m* 5 July (civ) and 13 July (relig) 1996, Birgit Michaela Marion, da of Elmar Bodo Archibald Meissner.————— *Prince* Carl-Eduard (Wilhelm Josias), *b* 27 July 1966: *m* 31 July (civ) and 25 Sept (relig) 1998, Stephanie, da of Hans Kolo, and has issue living, *Princess* Emilia, *b* 24 March 1999.—————*Prince* Friedrich-Ferdinand (Christian Georg Ernst Albert), *b* 13 Dec 1968.

HALF-SISTERS LIVING

Princess Victoria Feodora Monika, *b* 7 Sept 1963: *m* 28 Nov 1986, Peter Jakob Schmidt, who has taken the name Prince of Coburg (Prinz von Coburg), son of Ludwig Jakob Schmidt, and has issue living, Falk William Philip Albert Jakob, *b* 28 June 1990.————— *Princess* Alice-Sibylla (Calma Beatrice), *b* 6 Aug 1974.

UNCLE LIVING

Prince Peter Albert Friedrich Josias (Steinhauer Strasse 8, 59590 Geseke-Eringerfeld, Germany), *b* 12 June 1939: *m* 11 May 1964, Roswitha Henriette, da of Robert Breuer, and has issue living, *Prince* Peter Karl Eduard Alexander, *b* 4 Oct 1964: *m* 28 June (civ) and 30 June (relig) 1991, Kathrin, da of Dr Jan Hermann Kempin, and has issue living, *Prince* Malte Alexander Maximilian, *b* 20 Dec 1990, — *Prince* Malte Georg Albert, *b* 6 Oct 1966: *m* 11 July (civ) and 19 July (relig) 1997, Nicola Friederike, da of Klaus-Jürgen Friedrich Wilhelm von Seydlitz-Kurzbach.

AUNT LIVING

Princess (Caroline Mathilde Adelheid Sibylla) Marianne (Erica), *b* 5 April 1933: *m* 5 Dec 1953, Michael Adalbert Wilfried Nielsen, who *d* 20 Sept 1975, son of Friedrich Nielsen, and has issue living, Margarete Brigitte, *b* 31 Aug 1954: *m* 13 Dec 1991, Sascha Manuel Güttler, son of Horst Güttler, and has issue living, Grischa-Alexander *b* 25 July 1994, Diana-Kyra *b* 30 Jan 1992, — Renate Christine, *b* 1 April 1957: *m* 1st, 26 July 1978 (*m diss* 1981), (Wolfgang Willi) Reinhard Blechert, son of Willi August Blechert; 2ndly, 30 Sept 1986, Jörg Bracker, son of Erwin Günther Bracker.

MOTHER LIVING

Ingeborg, da of Richard Henig, of Herrenberg, Württemberg: *m* 1st, 3 Feb (civ) and 4 Feb (relig) 1961 (*m diss* 1963), as his 1st wife, Prince Ernst Leopold (Eduard Wilhelm Josias) of Saxe-Coburg and Gotha, who *d* 27 June 1996; 2ndly, ... 19—, ...

COLLATERAL BRANCH LIVING

Grandchildren of HRH Prince (Leopold) Charles Edward (George Albert), 2nd Duke of Albany, reigning Duke of Saxe-Coburg and Gotha 1900-18: *b* 1884, *d* 1954:— Issue of HH Prince Friedrich Josias (Carl Eduard Ernst Kyrill Harald), *b* 29 Nov 1918; *d* 23 Jan 1998; *s* as Head of the Ducal House of Saxe-Coburg and Gotha by virtue of the renunciation of his brother, HH Hereditary Prince Johann Leopold: *m* 1st, 25 Jan 1942 (*m diss* 1946), H Ill H Countess Victoria-Luise Friederike Caroline Mathilde, only da of H Ill H Count Hans Georg Eduard of Solms-Baruth; 2ndly, 14 Feb 1948 (*m diss* 1964), Denyse Henriette, da of Gaston Robert de Muralt, of Berne, Switzerland; 3rdly, 30 Oct 1964, Katrin Anna Dorothea, da of Dietrich Karl Bremme, of Berlin:—

(By 1st *m*) HH Prince Andreas Michael Armin Siegfried Friedrich Hans Hubertus (Elsasser Strasse 8, 96450 Coburg, Germany; Greinburg 3, 4360 Grein an der Donau, Upper Austria, Austria), *b* 21 March 1943; *s* his father as Head of the Ducal House of Saxe-Coburg and Gotha 1998: *m* 18 June 1971, Carin, da of Adolf Wilhelm Martin Dabelstein, and has issue living, HH Hereditary Prince Hubertus Michael, *b* 16 Sept 1975, — HH Prince Alexander Philipp, *b* 4 May 1977, — HH Princess Stephanie Sibylla, *b* 31 Jan 1972.————(by 2nd *m*) HH Prince Adrian Vincenz Edward (Luternau Weg 19, 3000 Bern, Switzerland), *b* 18 Oct 1955; musician as "Adrian Coburg": *m* 19 Oct 1984, Lea, da of Marcel Rinderknecht, and has issue living, Simon COBURG, *b* 10 March 1985, — Daniel COBURG, *b* 26 Jan

1988.————*HH Princess* (Maria) Claudia Sibylla, *b* 22 May 1949: *m* 17 March 1971, Gion Schäfer, son of Gézu Johann Robert Schäfer, and has issue living, (Maria) Christina Sibylla, *b* 23 June 1972, — Gianetta Antonia, *b* 18 Feb 1975.————HH Princess Beatrice Charlotte, *b* 15 July 1951: *m* 11 June (civ) and 12 June (relig) 1977, *HH Prince* Friedrich-Ernst George Bernhard of Saxe-Meiningen, of Sonnen Weg 5, 4313 Möhlin, Switzerland, and has issue living, *HH Prince* (Friedrich) Constantin, *b* 3 June 1980, — *HH Princess* Maria Alexandra (Marie-Alix) Elisabeth Beatrice, *b* 5 July 1978.

PREDECESSORS

[1] *HRH Prince* LEOPOLD GEORGE DUNCAN ALBERT, KG, KT, GCSI, GCMG, PC, 4th son of Queen Victoria, *b* 7 April 1853; *cr* Baron Arklow, Earl of Clarence and Duke of Albany, in the peerage of the United Kingdom, 24 May 1881: *m* 27 April 1882, Helena Frederica Augusta, VA, CI, RRC, who *d* 1 Sept 1922, 3rd da of Georg Viktor, Prince of Waldeck and Pyrmont; *d* 28 March 1884; *s* by his only son [2] (LEOPOLD) CHARLES EDWARD (GEORGE ALBERT), 2nd Duke, KG (1902-15, when struck off the Roll), *b* (posthumously) 19 July 1884; *s* his uncle as reigning Duke of Saxe-Coburg and Gotha 30 July 1900; abdicated 14 Nov 1918; deprived of his peerages by the Titles Deprivation Act 8 Nov 1917 and removed from the Roll of Peers by Order in Council 28 March 1919: *m* 11 Oct 1905, Victoria Adelheid (Helene Luise Marie Friederike), who *d* 3 Oct 1970, eldest da of Friedrich Ferdinand, Duke of Schleswig-Holstein-Sonderburg-Glücksburg; *d* 6 March 1954; *s* by his eldest son [3] JOHANN LEOPOLD (WILHELM ALBERT FERDINAND VIKTOR), Hereditary Prince of Saxe-Coburg and Gotha, *b* 2 Aug 1906; renounced his rights to the Duchy of Saxe-Coburg and Gotha but retained the right to petition for the restoration of the Dukedom of Albany: *m* 1st, 14 March 1932 (*m diss* 1962), Feodora Maria Alma Margarete, who *d* 23 Oct 1991, da of Baron (Alfred Hermann) Bernhard von der Horst, and formerly wife of Baron Wolf Sigismund Pergler von Perglas; 2ndly, 3 May 1962, Maria Theresia Elisabeth, who *d* 7 April 1996, da of Max Reindl, and formerly wife of Werner Müller; *d* 4 May 1972; *s* by his eldest son [4] ERNST-LEOPOLD (EDUARD WILHELM JOSIAS), *b* 14 Jan 1935: *m* 1st, 3 Feb (civ) and 4 Feb (relig) 1961 (*m diss* 1963), Ingeborg, da of Richard Henig, of Herrenberg, Wurttemberg; 2ndly, 29 May 1963 (*m diss* 1985), (Gertraude Maria) Monika, da of Hermann Horst Pfeiffer; 3rdly, 20 Jan 1986, Sabine Margarete, who *d* 27 June 1996, da of Alfred Carl Biller; *d* 27 June 1996; *s* by his eldest son [5] HUBERTUS RICHARD ERNST LEOPOLD, in whom is vested the right to petition for restoration of the British peerages.

DUKEDOM OF CUMBERLAND AND TEVIOTDALE
(Duke GB 1799, suspended 1917)

His Royal Highness Prince ERNST AUGUST (ALBERT PAUL OTTO RUPPRECHT OSKAR BERTHOLD FRIEDRICH-FERDINAND CHRISTIAN-LUDWIG) (*HRH The Prince of Hanover*), Duke of Brunswick and Lüneburg, Prince of Great Britain and Ireland, head of the Royal House of Hanover and Ducal House of Brunswick and Lüneburg since 1987; in whom is vested the right to petition for restoration of the Dukedom of Cumberland and Teviotdale; has Grand Cross Orders of St George, Guelph, and Ernst August of Hanover, and Order of Henry the Lion of Brunswick; *b* 26 Feb 1954; *s* his father, *HRH Prince* ERNST AUGUST (GEORG WILHELM CHRISTIAN LUDWIG FRANZ JOSEF NIKOLAUS), 1987: *ed* Salem, RAC Cirencester, and Univ of Guelph, Canada: *m* 1st 28 Aug (civ) and 30 Aug (relig) 1981 (*m diss* 1997), Chantal, da of Johann Gustav Hochuli, of Zürich, Switzerland; 2ndly, 23 Jan 1999, *HSH Princess* Caroline Louise Marguerite, elder da of HSH Prince Rainier III of Monaco and widow of Stefano Casiraghi, and has issue by 1st and 2nd *m*.

Residence - Schloss Marienburg, D-30978 Nordstemmen, Germany; Calenberg, D-30978 Pattensen, Germany; Königinvilla, A-4810 Gmunden, Austria; Hurlingham Lodge, SW6.

SONS LIVING (By 1st marriage)

HRH Prince ERNST AUGUST (ANDREAS PHILIPP KONSTANTIN MAXIMILIAN ROLF STEPHAN LUDWIG RUDOLF), *b* 19 July 1983.

HRH Prince Christian Heinrich Clemens Paul Frank Peter Welf Wilhelm-Ernst Friedrich Franz, *b* 1 June 1985.

DAUGHER LIVING (By 2nd marriage)

HRH Princess Alexandra, *b* 20 July 1999.

BROTHER LIVING

HRH Prince Heinrich Julius (Christian Otto Friedrich Franz Anton Gunther), *b* 29 April 1961: *m* 19 June 1999, Thyra Donata Sixtina, da of Burkhard von Westernhagen. Prince Heinrich has acknowledged issue (by Désirée Gerda Saskia Pamela Amneris Aida, da of Paul Nick), Oscar Julius Heinrich Ferdinand NICK, *b* 29 Sept 1996.

SISTERS LIVING

HRH Princess Marie Viktoria Luise Hertha Friederike, *b* 26 Nov 1952: *m* 5 June 1982, Count Michael Georg Botho von Hochberg, Baron zu Fürstenstein, only son of Count Konrad Eberhard Georg Botho von Hochberg, Baron zu Fürstenstein, and has issue living, *Count* Conrad Hans-Heinrich Ernst-August, *b* 17 June 1985, — *Count* Georg Karl Albert, *b* 8 Oct 1987.

HRH Princess Olga Sophie Charlotte Anna, *b* 17 Feb 1958.

HRH Princess Alexandra Irene Margaretha Elisabeth Bathildis, *b* 18 Feb 1959: *m* 5 Oct (civ) and 11 Oct (relig) 1981, HSH Prince Andreas of Leiningen, 2nd son of HSH Emich Cyril Ferdinand Hermann, 7th Prince of Leiningen, and has issue (*see* Leiningen ante).

UNCLES LIVING AND DECEASED

HRH Prince Georg Wilhelm Ernst August Friedrich Axel (Breitenstein Strassel, 83727 Neuhaus, nr Schliersee, Germany), *b* 25 March 1915; *ed* Marlborough, Vienna Univ, and Göttingen Univ (Dr jur 1948); late Maj 10th Cavalry Regt; late Headmaster of Salem Sch; Grand Cross of Order of the Redeemer of Greece: *m* 24 April 1946, HRH Princess Sophie, yst da of HRH late Prince Andrew of Greece and Denmark, and widow of HH Prince Christoph Ernst August of Hesse, and has issue living, *HRH Prince* Georg Paul Christian, *b* 9 Dec 1949: *m* 15 Sept 1973, Victoria Anne, yr da of Robert Bee, and has issue living, *HRH Princess* Vera Alice *b* 5 Nov 1976, *HRH Princess* Nora Sophie *b* 15 Jane 1979, — *HRH Princess* Friederike Elisabeth Victoria Luise Alice Olga Theodora Helene, *b* 15 Oct 1954: *m* 17 Aug 1979, Jerry William Cyr, son of Gordon Paul Cyr, and has issue living, Jean-Paul Welf *b* 6 March 1985, Julia Emma *b* 17 Sept 1982.

†*HRH Prince* Welf Heinrich Ernst August Georg Christian, *b* 11 March 1923; *ed* Univs of Munich, Vienna and Göttingen (Dr jur 1953); Grand Cross of Order of the Redeemer of Greece: *m* 21 Sept 1960, HSH Princess Alexandra Sophie Cecilie Anna Maria Friederike Benigna Dorothea, only da of HSH Otto Friedrich Viktor Ferdinand Maximilian Gustav Richard Bogislav, 3rd Prince of Ysenburg and Büdingen, and *dsp* 12 July 1997.

STEPMOTHER LIVING

HRH Princess MONIKA (*HRH The Dowager Princess of Hanover*), da of H Ill H Count Georg Friedrich of Solms-Laubach: *m* 17 July 1981, as his 2nd wife, HRH Prince Ernst August, Prince of Hanover, Duke of Brunswick and Lüneburg, who *d* 9 Dec 1987.

COLLATERAL BRANCHES LIVING

Grandson of HRH the late Prince Ernst August of Hanover (*d* 1987):—
Issue of HRH the late Prince Ludwig Rudolph Georg Wilhelm Philipp Friedrich Wolrad Maximilian, *b* 21 Nov 1955, *d* 28 Nov 1988: *m* 27 Aug (civ) and 4 Oct (relig) 1987, Countess Isabella Maria, who *d* 28 Nov 1988, da of Count Ariprand Raimund Georg Alexander Maria Josef Fortunatus von Thurn und Valsassina-Como-Vercelli:—
HRH Prince Otto Heinrich Ariprand Georg Johannes Ernst August Vincenz Egmont Franz, *b* 13 Feb 1988.

Granddaughter of HRH Prince Georg Wilhelm (ante):—
Issue of HRH the late Prince Welf Ernst August Andreas Philipp Georg Wilhelm Ludwig Berthold, *b* 25 Jan 1947, *d* 10 Jan 1981: *m* 23 May (civ) and 25 May (relig) 1969, Wibeke, da of Harry van Gunsteren:—
HRH Princess (Tania) Saskia Viktoria-Luise, *b* 24 July 1970: *m* 5 July 1990, as his 2nd wife, Michael Alexander Robert Naylor-Leyland (*see* Naylor-Leyland, Bt), and has issue living, Jake John, *b* 22 Sept 1993, — Gabriel George, *b* 26 March 1996.

Granddaughters of HRH the late Duke of Brunswick (*d* 1953):—
Issue of HRH the late Prince Christian Oskar Ernst August Wilhelm Viktor Georg Heinrich, *b* 1 Sept 1919, *d* 10 Dec 1981: *m* 25 Nov 1963 (*m diss* 1976), Mireille, da of Armand Dutry:—
    HRH Princess Caroline-Luise Mireille Irene Sophie, *b* 3 May 1965————
    HRH Princess Mireille Viktoria Luise Sophie Friederike Danielle, *b* 3 June 1971.

PREDECESSORS

[1] *HRH Prince* ERNEST AUGUSTUS, KG, KT, GCB, GCH, 5th son of King George III, *b* 5 June 1771; *cr* Earl of Armagh, and Duke of Cumberland and Teviotdale, in the peerage of Great Britain, 24 April 1799; Field Marshal 1813; *s* his brother King William IV as King of Hanover 20 June 1837: *m* 29 May 1815, Friederike Caroline Sophie Alexandrine, who *d* 29 June 1841, 5th da of Karl, Grand Duke of Mecklenburg-Strelitz, and widow of Prince Friedrich Wilhelm of Solms-Braunfels and previously of Prince Ludwig of Prussia; *d* 18 Nov 1851; *s* by his only son [2] GEORG V (FRIEDRICH ALEXANDER KARL ERNST AUGUST), KING OF HANOVER (until that Kingdom was annexed by the Kingdom of Prussia 20 Sept 1866), 2nd Duke, KG, *b* 27 May 1819: *m* 18 Feb 1843, (Alexandrine) Marie Wilhelmine Katharina Charlotte Therese Henriette Louise Pauline Elisabeth Friederike Georgine, VA, who *d* 9 Jan 1907, eldest da of Joseph, Duke of Saxe-Altenburg; *d* 12 June 1878; *s* by his only son [3] ERNST AUGUST (WILHELM ADOLF GEORG FRIEDRICH), 3rd Duke, KG, GCH, *b* 21 Sept 1845; deprived of his peerages by the Titles Deprivation Act 8 Nov 1917 and removed from the Roll of Peers by Order in Council 28 March 1919: *m* 21 Dec 1878, Thyra Amelia Caroline Charlotte Anne, CI, who *d* 26 Feb 1933, yst da of Christian IX, King of Denmark; *d* 14 Nov 1923; *s* by his only surviving son [4] ERNST AUGUST (CHRISTIAN GEORG), Reigning Duke of Brunswick 1913-18, *b* 17 Nov 1887: *m* 24 May 1913, Viktoria Luise (Adelheid Mathilde Charlotte), who *d* 11 Dec 1980, only da of Wilhelm II, German Emperor and King of Prussia; *d* 30 Jan 1953; *s* by his eldest son [5] ERNST AUGUST (GEORG WILHELM CHRISTIAN LUDWIG FRANZ JOSEF NIKOLAUS), Prince of Hanover, *b* 18 March 1914; re-established his legal right to be a British subject 1955/6: *m* 1st, 4 Sept 1951, Ortrud Bertha Adelheid Hedwig, who *d* 6 Feb 1980, 2nd da of Prince Albert of Schleswig-Holstein-Sonderburg-

Glücksburg; 2ndly, 17 July 1981, Monika, da of Count Georg Friedrich of Solms-Laubach; *d* 9 Dec 1987; *s* by his eldest son [6] ERNST AUGUST (ALBERT PAUL OTTO RUPPRECHT OSKAR BERTHOLD FRIEDRICH-FERDINAND CHRISTIAN-LUDWIG), in whom is vested the right to petition for restoration of the British peerages.

THE PEERAGE

THE PEERAGE

THE PEERAGE

The scope of EACH ARTICLE IN THE PEERAGE is designed to include information concerning every *living* male descended in the male line from the first Peer and of all *living* females being issue of males so descended. Legitimated children are included, but are not normally in remainder, except for the Peerage of Scotland.

DECEASED FEMALE COLLATERALS and their issue are not generally included.

ISSUE, where both parents are mentioned in the work, will usually be found under the father's name.

CHRISTIAN NAMES OF THE HEIR apparent or heir presumptive are given in capital letters.

CREATIONS:—   E.= England (prior to 1 May 1707).
                 S.= Scotland (prior to 1 May 1707).
                 I.= Ireland.
                 G.B.= Great Britain (1 May 1707 to 31 Dec. 1800).
                 U.K.= United Kingdom (since 1 Jan. 1801).

ABERCONWAY, BARON (McLaren) (Baron UK 1911, Bt UK 1902)

I am a son of the Church

CHARLES MELVILLE MCLAREN, 3rd Baron, and 3rd Baronet; *b* 16 April 1913; *s* 1953; *ed* Eton, and New Coll, Oxford (BA); Bar Middle Temple 1937; late RA; Chm of John Brown & Co Ltd 1953-78 (Pres 1978-85), of Sheepbridge Engineering Ltd 1961-79, and English China Clays Ltd 1963-84 (since when Pres); Dir National Westminster Bank (formerly National Provincial Bank) 1953-83; Dep Chm Sun Alliance & London Insurance Co Ltd 1976-85, and Westland Aircraft 1979-85; High Sheriff for Denbighshire 1950; Pres of Roy Horticultural Soc 1961-84 (since when Pres Emeritus); Commr Gen Internat Garden Festival Liverpool 1984: *m* 1st, 1941 (*m diss* 1949), Deirdre, da of John Knewstub; 2ndly, 1949, Ann Lindsay, only da of late Mrs Alexander Lindsay Aymer, of New York City, USA, and formerly wife of Maj Robert Lee Bullard III, and has issue living by 1st and 2nd marriages.

Arms – Or, two chevronels invected gules between two shepherds crooks in chief and in base a castle triple towered and with flags flying sable. Crest – A representation of the Virgin Mary with the dexter arm uplifted vested azure, holding in the sinister arm the child Jesus. Supporters – On either side a wyvern argent, wings erect gules, each supporting a banner or charged with a horse-shoe sable.
Seat – Bodnant, Tal-y-Cafn, Colwyn Bay, N Wales LL28 5RE. *Town Residence* – 25 Egerton Terrace, SW3.

SONS LIVING (*By 1st marriage*)

Hon (HENRY) CHARLES, *b* 26 May 1948; *ed* Eton, and Sussex Univ (BA): *m* 1981, Sally Ann, yr da of late Capt Charles Nugent Lentaigne, RN, of Hawkley Place, Hawkley, Liss, Hants, and formerly wife of Philip Charles Bidwell, and has issue living, Charles Stephen, *b* 27 Dec 1984, — Emily, *b* 1982.

(*By 2nd marriage*)

Hon Michael Duncan (27 Phillimore Gdns, W8), *b* 1958; *ed* Eton, and Christ's Coll, Camb (MA); Barrister-at-law (Middle Temple 1981): *m* 1985, Caroline Jane, elder da of late Air Chief Marshal Sir John Stacey, KCB, CBE, of Winchester, and has issue living, Angus John Melville, *b* 1987, — Hamish Charles Duncan, *b* 1993, — Iona Ann Mariel, *b* 1991.

DAUGHTERS LIVING (*By 1st marriage*)

Hon Julia Harriet, *b* 1942: *m* 1969, Capt Charles Walter Hays Ridley, MC, and has issue living, Casper Charles, *b* 1977, — Emma Jane, *b* 1970, — Harriet Deirdre, *b* 1971.

Hon Caroline Mary, *b* 1944; *ed* Imperial Coll, London (BSc, PhD, DIC, FLS); resumed surname of Sargent until remarriage: *m* 1st, 1962, Raimund Guernsey Sargent, of Massachusetts, USA; 2ndly, 1978, Graham Charles Steele, BSc, PhD; 3rdly, 1995, Dr William John Howard, yr son of John Howard, of Meonstoke, Hants, and has issue living (by 1st *m*), Dominic Fitzwilliam, *b* 1963; *ed* Blundell's Sch, Trin Hall, Camb (organ scholar), and Peabody Conservatory, USA, — Orlando Gorham, *b* 1964; *ed* Blundell's Sch, and Sussex Univ. *Residence* – Forest House, Barbadoes Hill, Tintern, Gwent NP6 6SX.

BROTHER LIVING

Hon Christopher Melville (31 Upper Addison Gdns, W14 8AJ; *Club* – Boodle's), *b* 1934; *ed* Eton, and King's Coll, Camb (MA); Bar Inner Temple 1961; Chm of Govs and Chancellor South Bank Univ since 1992 (previously Chm of Govs South Bank Polytechnic): *m* 1973, Jane Elizabeth, da of James Barrie, and has issue living, Robert Melville, *b* 1974, — Lara Jane Christabel, *b* 1976.

SISTER LIVING

(*Hon*) Anne Laura Dorinthea McLAREN, DBE, *b* 1927; *ed* Lady Margaret Hall, Oxford (MA, DPhil); FRS 1975, FRCOG 1986; does not use courtesy title, or the style of Dame; Vice-Pres and Foreign Sec Royal Soc 1991-96, Prin Research Associate Wellcome/Cancer Research Campaign Inst, and Research Fellow King's Coll, Camb since 1992, Pres British Assocn for the Advancement of Science 1993-94; *cr* DBE 1993: *m* 1952 (*m diss* 1959), Donald Michie, DPhil, and has issue living, Jonathan Mark (4 Health Villas, Savile Park, Halifax HX3 0BB), *b* 1957: *m* 1st, 19— (*m diss* 19—), Ann Logan; 2ndly, 19—, Carolyn Downs, and has issue living, — Susan Fiona Dorinthea, *b* 1955: *m* 1981 (*m diss* 1997), Andrew Philip Drummond-Murray, and has issue (*see* B Rankeillour), — Caroline Ruth, *b* 1959; has issue. *Residence* – Flat 1, 40 Ainger Rd, Primrose Hill, NW3 3AT.

WIDOW LIVING OF SON OF SECOND BARON

Lady Rose Mary Primrose Paget, da of 6th Marquess of Anglesey: *m* 1940, S/Ldr Hon John Francis McLaren, RAF, who *d* 1953, and has issue (see colls, infra). *Residence* – Old Bodnod, Eglwysbach, Colwyn Bay, N Wales LL28 5RF.

COLLATERAL BRANCHES LIVING

Issue of late S/Ldr Hon John Francis McLaren, RAF, 2nd son of 2nd Baron, *b* 1919, *d* 1953: *m* 1940, Lady Rose Mary Primrose Paget (ante) da of 6th Marquess of Anglesey:—
Victoria Mary Caroline, *b* 1945: *m* 1966, Jonathan Jeremy Kirwan Taylor, of 42 Addison Rd, W14, yst son of Sir Charles Stuart Taylor, TD, DL, and has issue living, Arabella Lucy Kirwan, *b* 1969, — Lucinda Sophia Kirwan, *b* 1972, — Caroline Samantha Kirwan, *b* 1976, — Katharine Polly Kirwan, *b* 1979. —— Harriet Diana Christabel, *b* 1949: *m* 1972, Hugh John Reay Geddes, of 20 Gatcombe Rd, N19, and has issue (*see* B Geddes).

Grandchildren of Hon Francis Walter Stafford McLaren, yr son of 1st Baron:—
Issue of late Maj Martin John McLaren, *b* 1914, *d* 1979, Gren Gds, Bar Middle Temple, MP for NW Div of Bristol (*C*) 1959-66, and 1970-74: *m* 1943, Nancy (Inkpen, Newbury, Berks; 30 Smith Sq, SW1), da of late Gordon Ralston, and of late Mrs Philip Cator:—
Richard Francis, *b* 1946; *ed* Eton, and Mansfield Coll, Oxford. —— †Francis Andrew, *b* 1949; *d* as the result of an accident 1960. —— †Patrick Andrew, *b* 1963; *ed* Eton, and Harvard Univ; *d* 1991.

Issue of late Guy Lewis Ian McLaren, *b* 1915, *d* 1978: *m* 1946, Maryse, who *d* 1987, da of late Alfred Jubin, of Lausanne, Switzerland:—
Michael (1 bis Rue du Printemps, 78 230 Le Pecq, France), *b* 1947; *ed* Eton, and St Andrew's Univ: *m* 1993, Sally, da of late James Reid, of Wellington, NZ, and has issue living, James Alexander Michael, *b* 1994, — Sophie Annabel Mary, *b* 1997. —— Mary Caroline, *b* 1951: *m* 1971, Nicholas John Durlacher, CBE, of Archendines, Chapel Rd, Fordham, Colchester, Essex, and has issue living, David Michael, *b* 1976.

PREDECESSORS – **(1)** *Rt Hon* CHARLES BENJAMIN BRIGHT McLaren, KC, 3rd son of late Duncan McLaren, of Newington House, Edinburgh (sometime MP for and Lord Provost of Edinburgh); *b* 1850; MP for Stafford (*L*) 1880-86, and for W, or Bosworth, Div of Leicestershire 1892-1910; cr a *Baronet* 1902, PC 1908, and *Baron Aberconway*, of Bodnant, co Denbigh (peerage of United Kingdom) 1911: *m* 1877, Laura, CBE, who *d* 1933, da of late Henry Davis Pochin, of Bodnant, Denbighshire; *d* 1934; *s* by his el son **(2)** HENRY DUNCAN, CBE, 2nd Baron; *b* 1879; was Parliamentary Private Sec to Pres of Board of Trade (Rt Hon D Lloyd George, MP) 1906-08, and Parliamentary Private Sec to Chancellor of the Exchequer (Rt Hon D Lloyd George, MP) 1908-10; sat as MP for Staffordshire, W Div (*L*) 1906-10, for Leicestershire, W, or Bosworth, Div 1910-18, and Bosworth Div 1918-22; Pres of Roy Horticultural Society 1931-53: *m* 1910, Christabel Mary Melville, who *d* 1974, da of late Sir Melville Leslie Macnaghten, CB (*see* Macnaghten, Bt, colls, 1972/73 Edn); *d* 1953; *s* by his eldest son **(3)** CHARLES MELVILLE, 3rd Baron and present peer.

ABERCORN, DUKE OF (Hamilton) Sits as MARQUESS OF ABERCORN (GB 1790) (Duke I 1868, Bt I 1660)

Virtue is the only nobility

JAMES HAMILTON, KG, 5th Duke, and 15th Baronet; *b* 4 July 1934; *s* 1979; *ed* Eton, and RAC Cirencester; late Lt Gren Gds; MP for Fermanagh and S Tyrone (UU) 1964-70; DL co Tyrone (High Sheriff 1970), and Lord Lieut since 1987; Pres Building Societies Assocn 1986-92; KG 1999: *m* 1966, Alexandra Anastasia, eldest da of late Lt-Col Harold Pedro Joseph Phillips, FRGS, Coldstream Gds (*see* Wernher, Bt, ext), and has issue.

Arms – Quarterly: 1st and 4th gules, three cinquefoils pierced ermine, *Hamilton;* 2nd and 3rd argent, an ancient ship or lymphad, with one mast, the sail furled and oars out sable, *Arran.* (Also claims, – over all an escutcheon azure, charged with three fleurs-de-lis or, surmounted by a French ducal coronet, *Chatelherault.*) **Crest** – Out of a ducal coronet or, an oak tree proper, fructed and penetrated through the stem transversely by a frame-saw proper, frame gold, the blade inscribed with the word "Through." **Supporters** – Two antelopes argent, horned, unguled, ducally gorged, hoofed, and the chains reflexed over their backs or.
Seat – Barons Court, Omagh, co Tyrone. *Town Residence* – 10 Little Chester St, SW1.

SONS LIVING

JAMES HAROLD CHARLES (*Marquess of Hamilton*), *b* 19 Aug 1969; a Page of Honour to HM The Queen 1982-84.
Lord Nicholas Edward Claud, *b* 1979.

DAUGHTER LIVING

Lady Sophia Alexandra, *b* 1973.

BROTHER LIVING

Lord (Claud) Anthony, *b* 1939; *ed* Eton; Lieut IG; DL co Fermanagh 1978, High Sheriff 1990, JP 1991: *m* 1982, Catherine Janet, eldest da of Dennis Faulkner, CBE, of Ringhaddy House, Killinchy, co Down, and has issue living, Alexander James, *b* 1987, — Anna Kathleen, *b* 1983. *Residence* – Killyreagh, Tamlaght, Enniskillen, co Fermanagh.

SISTER LIVING

Lady Moyra Kathleen, CVO, *b* 1930; a Maid of Honour to HM The Queen at Coronation 1953; appointed Lady-in-Waiting (temporary) to HRH Princess Alexandra of Kent 1954-64, a Lady-in-Waiting 1964-66 and an Extra Lady-in-Waiting 1966-69; CVO 1963: *m* 1966, Cdr Peter Colin Drummond Campbell, LVO, OBE, RN, of Hollybrook House, Randalstown, co Antrim, son of late Maj-Gen Sir (Alexander) Douglas Campbell, KBE, CB, DSO, MC, and has issue living, Rory Gerald Peter, *b* 1967, — Michael James Douglas, *b* 1970.

COLLATERAL BRANCHES LIVING

(Not in remainder to the Dukedom)

Grandchildren of late Col Douglas James PROBY, who assumed by Royal Licence 1904, the surname of Proby in lieu of his patronymic, only son of Rt Hon Lord Claud Hamilton, MP, brother of 1st Duke:—
See Proby, Bt.

Descendants of late John Hamilton (son of late John Hamilton, son of late William Hamilton, brother of 6th Earl of Abercorn), who was cr a *Baronet* 1776:—

See Hamilton, Bt, cr 1776.

PREDECESSORS – **(1)** CLAUD Hamilton, *b* 1543, 4th son of James, 1st Duke of Chatelherault in kingdom of France, and 2nd Earl of Arran, in peerage of Scotland, was cr *Lord Paisley* 1578; *d* 1621; his son JAMES, cr *Lord Abercorn* (peerage of Scotland) 1603, and *Earl of Abercorn*, and *Lord Paisley, Hamilton, Mountcastell*, and *Kilpatrick* (peerage of Scotland) 1606; *d* March 1617, leaving with other issue **(2)** JAMES, 2nd Earl, and CLAUD, cr *Baron of Strabane* (peerage of Ireland) 1634, an honour that had been conferred in 1617 upon the 2nd Earl who, however, petitioned King Charles I to transfer the dignity to his next brother; JAMES was *s* by his 3rd son **(3)** GEORGE, 3rd Earl, who *d unm*, when the earldom devolved upon **(4)** CLAUD, PC, 4th Earl, who had previously *s* as 4th Baron Strabane; in 1691 he was outlawed and the estates and Barony of Strabane were forfeited; he was *s* in the Earldom by his brother **(5)** CHARLES, 5th Earl, who obtained a reversal of the attainder and restoration of the estates; *dsp* 1701, when the honours devolved upon **(6)** JAMES, 6th Earl, grandson of Hon Sir George Hamilton (cr a *Baronet* 1660), 4th son of 1st Earl; cr *Baron Mountcastle* and *Viscount Strabane* (peerage of Ireland) 1701; *d* 1734; *s* by his eldest son **(7)** JAMES, PC, FRS, 7th Earl; *d* 1744; *s* by his eldest son **(8)** JAMES, 8th Earl, cr *Viscount Hamilton* (peerage of Great Britain) 1785, with remainder to the son of his next brother John; *d unm* 1789; *s* by his nephew **(9)** JOHN JAMES, KG, 9th Earl, cr *Marquess of Abercorn* (peerage of Great Britain) 1790; *d* 1818; *s* by his grandson **(10)** JAMES KG, PC, DCL, LLD, 2nd Marquess; *b* 1811; was Groom of the Stole to late Prince Consort 1846-59, Viceroy of Ireland 1866-8 and 1874-6 Envoy Extraor upon a special mission to King of Italy 1878, Lord-Lieut of Donegal, Grand Master of Masonic Order in Ireland, Lieut-Gen of Royal Co of Archers, and Chancellor of Royal Univ of Ireland; in 1864 established his claim to the French Dukedom of Chatelherault (cr 1548), and assumed the title of *Duke of Châtelherault* which had been abeyant since 1651, and his right was not contested before the French tribunals, but Napoleon III granted a new creation of the same title to the 12th Duke of Hamilton; cr *Marquess of Hamilton* and *Duke of Abercorn* (peerage of Ireland) 1868: *m* 1832, Lady Louisa Jane Russell, VA, who *d* 1905, da of 6th Duke of Bedford; *d* 31 Oct 1885; *s* by his son **(11)** JAMES, KG, PC, CB, 2nd Duke; *b* 1838; a Lord of the Bedchamber to the Prince of Wales 1866-86, Groom of the Stole 1886-1910, and Lieut of co Donegal; MP for co Donegal (C) 1860-80; acted as High Constable of Ireland at Coronation of King George V 1911: *m* 1869, Lady Mary Anna Curzon, who *d* 1929, da of 1st Earl Howe; *d* 1913; *s* by his eldest son **(12)** JAMES ALBERT EDWARD, KG, KP, 3rd Duke; *b* 1869; was MP for Londonderry City (C) 1900-13, Treasurer of the Household 1903-5, and first Gov of N Ireland 1922-45; appointed a PC (Great Britain) 1945, and (N Ireland) 1946; bore Canopy at Coronation of King George VI: *m* 1894, Lady Rosalind Cecilia Caroline Bingham, DBE, LLD, who *d* 1958, da of 4th Earl of Lucan; *d* 1953; *s* by his eldest son **(13)** JAMES EDWARD, 4th Duke; *b* 1904; a Senator of N Ireland 1949-62; Lord-Lieut for co Tyrone 1950-79 and High Sheriff 1946; Co Councillor for Tyrone 1946-79; Chancellor of New Univ of Ulster 1970-70: *m* 1928, Lady Mary Kathleen Crichton, GCVO, who *d* 1990, sister of 5th Earl of Erne; *d* 1979; *s* by eldest son **(14)** JAMES, 5th Duke and present peer; also Marquess of Hamilton, Viscount Strabane, Baron of Strabane, Baron of Mountcastle, Marquess of Abercorn, Earl of Abercorn, Viscount Hamilton, Lord Paisley, Lord Abercorn, and Lord Paisley, Hamilton, Mountcastell, and Kilpatrick.

ABERDARE, BARON (Bruce) (Baron UK 1873)

MORYS GEORGE LYNDHURST BRUCE, KBE, PC, 4th Baron; *b* 16 June 1919; *s* 1957; *ed* Winchester, and New Coll, Oxford; Hon LLD (Wales); DL Dyfed 1985; late Major Welsh Gds; J. Arthur Rank Organisation 1947-49, BBC 1949-56, Vice-Pres Commonwealth Games Cardiff 1958, Pres London Welsh Assocn 1959-63, and 1969-70; Min of State, Health and Social Security 1970-74, and Min without Portfolio 1974; Chm of Cttees, House of Lords 1976-92, and Chm House of Lords Broadcasting Cttee 1978-92; Chm The Football Trust 1979-98, Metlife (UK) Ltd 1986-92, and Albany Life Assurance Co Ltd 1975-92; Pres Nat Council of YMCAs of Wales, Kidney Research Unit for Wales Foundation, Tennis and Rackets Assocn, The Queen's Club 1994-97; *cr* PC 1974, and KBE (Civil) 1984; Prior for Wales, OStJ 1958-88; GCStJ: *m* 1946, Maud Helen Sarah, only da of Sir John Lindsay Dashwood, 10th Bt (*cr* 1707), and has issue.

꒰rms – Or, a saltire gules, on a chief of the last a martlet of the field. ꒰rest – A cubit arm in armour in bend, the hand holding a sceptre in bend sinister proper. ꒰upporters – *Dexter*, a lion argent collared or, pendant therefrom an escutcheon of the arms of *Knight*, viz, paly of six argent and azure, on a canton of the last a spur rowel downwards leathered or; *sinister*, a lion azure, collared or, pendant therefrom an escutcheon charged with the arms. *Residence* – 32 Elthiron Rd, SW6 4BW. *Clubs* – All England, Queen's, MCC, Boodle's.

SONS LIVING

Hon ALASTAIR JOHN LYNDHURST, *b* 2 May 1947; *ed* Eton, and Ch Ch Oxford: *m* 1971, Elizabeth Mary Culbert, da of John Foulkes, and has issue living, Hector Morys Napier, *b* 1974, — Sarah Katherine Mary, *b* 1976. *Residence* – 16 Beverley Rd, SW13 0LX.

Hon James Henry Morys, *b* 1948; *ed* Eton: *m* 1st, 1977, Grace, da of late Allen Jao Wu; 2ndly, 1991, Lucinda J., only da of Richard Temple West, and has issue living (by 1st *m*), Antonia Katherine Sarah, *b* 1979, — (by 2nd *m*) Robert Algernon Copley, *b* 1994, — Algernon Morys Lyndhurst, *b* 1997, — Augusta Jane Sophia, *b* 1992.

Hon (Henry) Adam Francis, *b* 1962; *ed* Eton, and Trin Coll, Oxford: *m* 1992, Victoria Gillian, yr da of Maj Ivor Basil Ramsden, MBE, of Cosheston Hall, Pembroke (*see* V St Davids, colls, 1976 Edn), and has issue living, Angus Ifor, *b* 1997.

Hon Charles Benjamin, *b* 1965; *ed* Eton: *m* 1990, Anna, da of late Bo Brannerydh, of Gävle, Sweden.

BROTHER LIVING

Hon Nigel Henry Clarence (Maitland Lodge, 21 The Causeway, Edinburgh EH15 3QA; Lansdowne Club), *b* 1921; *ed* Winchester, and New Coll, Oxford (MA); MSc, Dip SS; late Capt Welsh Gds and HM Diplomatic Service: *m* 1964, Catherine Marion, da of late Thomas Wolfe, and has issue living, Thomas, *b* 1965, — Sarah, *b* 1967.

SISTERS LIVING

Hon Rosalind Louise Balfour, *b* 1923; was in WRNS: *m* 1956, Benjamin Coote Heywood, and has issue living, Annabel Jane Louise, *b* 1958, — Olivia Sarah Rosalind, *b* 1961. *Residence* - 1 Elm Park Rd, SW3 6BD.

Hon Gwyneth Margaret, *b* 1928: *m* 1952, Robert McCheyne Andrew, of Hams Barton, Chudleigh, Newton Abbot TQ13 0DL, and has had issue, Robert Hugh Clarence, *b* 1954, — Caroline Margaret, *b* 1956, — Jennifer Anne Louise, *b* 1960; *d* 1984.

WIDOW LIVING OF SON OF SECOND BARON

Margaret Charlotte, da of Ernest Alfred Beechey, of The Old Vicarage, Hilgay, nr Downham Market, Norfolk: *m* 1941, as his 2nd wife, Hon Victor Austin Bruce, 4th son of 2nd Baron, who *d* 1978, and has issue (see colls infra). *Residence* - Cranmore, 1 Frog Grove Lane, Woodstreet Village, Guildford, Surrey GU3 3EY.

COLLATERAL BRANCHES LIVING

Issue of late Hon John Hamilton Bruce, CBE, 3rd son of 2nd Baron, *b* 1889, *d* 1964: *m* 1923, Cynthia Juliet Grant Duff, who *d* 1977, da of late Julian Grant Duff Ainslie (who assumed the surname of Grant Duff) (*see* V Molesworth, colls, 1925 Edn):—
David Hamilton Grant Duff (9 Woodley House, 11 Tern Walk, Blackbird Leys, Oxford OX4 5ZF), *b* 1933; *ed* Winchester, and New Coll, Oxford; late Coldstream Gds: *m* 1960 (*m diss* 1965), Diana Rosemary, da of Douglas Sinclair Miller. —— Daphne Juliet, *b* 1928: *m* 1953, Baron Carlo Giuseppe Ando, and has issue living, Alexander Francis Carlo *b* 1955: *m* 1982, Lorenza Raponi, and has issue living, Edward Carlo George *b* 1986, Nicholas Peter Ilario *b* 1992, Victoria Emanuela Eleanora *b* 1988, — Roderic David Clarence, *b* 1960. *Residences* - Casa Papale, Piazza San Sebastiano, Gallodoro, Messina, Sicily 98030; The New Villas, Sopworth, nr Chippenham, Wilts.

Issue of late Hon Victor Austin Bruce, 4th son of 2nd Baron, *b* 1897, *d* 1978; racing and rally driver, first Briton to win Monte Carlo Rally (1926): *m* 1st, 1926 (*m diss* 1941), Mildred Mary, the aviatrix, racing driver, and speed-boat pilot, who *d* 1990, da of late Lawrence Joseph Petre (*see* B Petre, colls, 1990 Edn); 2ndly, 1941, Margaret Charlotte (ante), da of Ernest Alfred Beechey, artist, of The Old Vicarage, Hilgay, nr Downham Market, Norfolk:—
(By 2nd *m*) Colin Michael Lyndhurst (Cranmore, 1 Frog Grove Lane, Woodstreet Village, Guildford, Surrey GU3 3EY), *b* 1944. —— Margaret Jill, *b* 1943: *m* 1970, Thomas Richardson Hope, of Browes Close, Mickleton, nr Barnard Castle, co Durham, and has issue living, Christopher Victor John, *b* 1977, — Louise Margaret, *b* 1971, — Karen Anne, *b* 1972. —— Wendy Elizabeth, *b* 1948: *m* 1966, Richard Keith Grimmond, of Inholms Farm, Woodstreet Green, Guildford, Surrey, and has issue living, Michael Richard, *b* 1971, — David Matthew, *b* 1984, — Nicola Jane, *b* 1966, — Caroline Anne, *b* 1967.

PREDECESSORS - **(1)** HENRY AUSTIN Bruce, GCB, PC, DCL, 2nd son of late John Bruce Pryce, of Duffryn, Glamorgan; *b* 1815; MP for Merthyr Tydfil (*L*) 1852-68, and Renfrewshire 1869-73; was Under-Sec for Home Depart 1862-4, Vice-Pres Education Board 1864-6, Second Church Estates Commr 1865-6, Sec of State for Home Depart 1868-73, and Lord Pres. of Council 1873-4; cr *Baron Aberdare*, of Duffryn, co Glamorgan (peerage of United Kingdom) 1873: *m* 1st, 1846, Annabella, who *d* 1852, da of late Richard Beadon, of Clifton; 2ndly, 1854, Norah Creina Blanche, who *d* 1897, da of late Gen Sir William Francis Patrick Napier, KCB; *s* by his eldest son **(2)** HENRY CAMPBELL, 2nd Baron, *b* 1851; Vice-Lieut for Glamorgan: *m* 1880, Constance Mary, who *d* 1932, only da of late Hamilton Beckett; *d* 1929; *s* by his son **(3)** CLARENCE NAPIER, GBE, 3rd Baron; *b* 1885; Hon LLD Wales 1953; Bar Inner Temple 1911; Hon. Col 282nd (Welsh) Regt RA (TA) 1930-52; Chm of National Fitness Council 1937-9, and Pres of National Children's Playground Asso 1942-52; Prior of Priory for Wales of Order of St John of Jerusalem, Chm of National Asso of Boys' Clubs, and of Queen's Institute of Dist Nursing: *m* 1st, 1912, Margaret Bethune, who *d* 1950, da of Adam Black; 2ndly, 1957, Griselda Harriet Violet Finetta Georgiana, who *d* 1980, da of late Dudley Francis Amelius Hervey, CMG (*see* M Bristol, colls); *d* 1957; *s* by his eldest son **(4)** MORYS GEORGE LYNDHURST, 4th Baron and present peer.

ABERDEEN AND TEMAIR, MARQUESS OF (Gordon) (Marquess UK 1916 Earl S 1682, Bt S 1642)

Let fortune follow

ALASTAIR NINIAN JOHN GORDON, 6th Marquess, 12th Earl, and 14th Baronet; *b* 20 July 1920; *s* 1984; *ed* Harrow; a Member of British Section, Assocn Internationale des Critiques d'Art; Memb Bach Choir 1939-82; Chm Arts Club 1966-76; 1939-45 War as Capt Scots Gds: *m* 1950, Anne, da of late Lt-Col Gerald Barry, MC (*see* Barry, Bt, colls), and has issue.

Arms – Azure, three boars' heads couped or armed proper and langued gules within a double tressure flowered and counterflowered interchangeably with thistles, roses, and fleurs-de-lys of the second. Crest – Two arms holding a bow and arrow straight upwards in a shooting posture and at full draught all proper. Supporters – *Dexter*, an Earl, and *sinister*, a Doctor of Laws, both habited in their robes proper.
Residence – Quicks Green, Ashampstead, Berks RG8 8SN. *Clubs* – Arts, Puffins, and MCC

SON LIVING

ALEXANDER GEORGE (*Earl of Haddo*) (The Estate Office, Mains of Haddo, Aberdeen; House of Formartine, Methlick, Ellon, Aberdeenshire, AB41 0EQ), *b* 31 March 1955; *ed* Harrow; DL Aberdeenshire 1998: *m* 1981, Joanna Clodagh, da of late Maj Ian George Henry Houldsworth, TD (*see* E Morton, colls, 1963 Edn), and has issue:—

SONS LIVING — George Ian Alastair (*Viscount Formartine*), *b* 4 May 1983, — *Hon* Sam Dudley, *b* 1985, — *Hon* Charles David, *b* 1990.
DAUGHTER LIVING — *Lady* Anna Katharine, *b* 1988.

DAUGHTERS LIVING

Lady Emma Cecile, *b* 1953: *m* 1980, Dr Rodney Foale, eldest son of Maurice Spencer Foale, of Melbourne, Australia, and has issue living, Archie Alexander, *b* 1984, — Jamie, *b* 1986. *Residence* – 25 Bristol Gdns, W9 2JQ.
Lady Sophia Catherine, *b* 1960.

ADOPTED CHILDREN OF FOURTH MARQUESS

Andrew David, *b* 1950; *ed* Harrow: *m* 1982, Lucy Mary Frances, eldest da of Canon William John Milligan, of 29 Stirling Rd, SW9 9EF, and has issue living, William David, *b* 1988, — Rosie Kate Jessamine, *b* 1986, — Rachel Mary Ishbel, *b* 1991. *Residence* – Laverockbrae, Oldmeldrum, Aberdeenshire AB51 0DA.
James Drummond, *b* 1953; *ed* Harrow: *m* 1985, Marilyn, yr da of A. F. Sim, of Sompting, Lancing, Sussex. *Residence* – 22 Normandy Drive, E Preston, Sussex BN16 1LU.
Mary Katharine, *b* 1946: *m* 1968, Simon Piers Welfare, 2nd son of late Kenneth William Welfare, of The Old Doctor's House, Stradbroke, Peasmarsh, Suffolk, and has issue living, Toby William David, *b* 1973, — Hannah Mary, *b* 1969, — Alice Emily Ishbel, *b* 1971. *Residence* – Den of Keithfield, Tarves, Ellon, Aberdeenshire.
Sarah Caroline, *b* 1948: *m* 1st, 1969 (*m diss* 1993), Patrick John Raleigh Scott, elder son of late R. S. G. Scott, of The Hermitage, Peasmarsh, Sussex; 2ndly, 1993, Eric Norman Money, only son of G. E. Money, of N Mimms, Herts, and has issue living (by 1st *m*), Edward Gilbert Raleigh, *b* 1971, — Oliver Dickon Robert, *b* 1972, — Simon Gordon Thomas, *b* 1977, — Sasha Adam Quintus, *b* 1979, — Jody Timothy Fingal, *b* 1981, — Silas Gabriel Uther, *b* 1982 (adopted son), — Georgiana Morag June, *b* 1974. *Residence* – Scot's Float, Star Lock, Playden, nr Rye, Sussex.

WIDOW LIVING OF FOURTH MARQUESS

BEATRICE MARY JUNE, CBE (*June, Marchioness of Aberdeen and Temair*) (Haddo House, Aberdeen); Hon LLD Aberdeen, DStJ, FRCM, FRSE, DL of Aberdeenshire, CBE (Civil) 1989, da of late Arthur Paul Boissier, of Moretons, Harrow-on-Hill: *m* 1939, the 4th Marquess, who *d* 1974.

COLLATERAL BRANCHES LIVING

(*In remainder to Earldom of Aberdeen*)

Grandson of late Gen Hon Sir Alexander Hamilton Gordon, KCB, 2nd son of 4th Earl of Aberdeen:—
Issue of late Lt-Gen Sir Alexander Hamilton Gordon, KCB, *b* 1859, *d* 1939: *m* 1888, Isabel, who *d* 1947, da of Maj-Gen George Newmarch, RE:—
Alan Herschel (Caixa Postal 499, Porto Allegre, Brazil), *b* 1898; *ed* Winchester; formerly Lieut RFA; entered Diplo Ser 1921; HM's Consul at Porto Alegre, Brazil, 1948-56; sometime Major and a GSO (Joint Intelligence Staff) War Cabinet Office: *m* 1933, Deenya Kovachevska, of Sofia, Bulgaria.

Descendants of late William Gordon (2nd son of late Hon Alexander Gordon, 4th son of 2nd Earl), who *s* his maternal uncle, Sir James Duff, 1st Bt, 1815, and assumed the additional surname of Duff. *See* Duff Gordon, Bt.

PREDECESSORS – **(1)** *Sir* GEORGE Gordon, of Haddo, 3rd *Baronet* of Nova Scotia (cr 1642), successively a Senator of the College of Justice, Pres of Court of Session, and Lord High Chancellor of Scotland, was *cr Lord Haddo, Methlic, Tarves,* and *Kellie, Viscount Formartine,* and *Earl of Aberdeen* (peerage of Scotland) 1682; *d* 1720; *s* by his only surviving son **(2)** WILLIAM, 2nd Earl, a Representative Peer for Scotland; *d* 1745; *s* by his eldest son **(3)** GEORGE, 3rd Earl, a Representative Peer for Scotland; *d* 1801; *s* by his grandson **(4)** GEORGE, KG, KT, PC, FRS, 4th Earl, eldest son of George, Lord Haddo; *b* 1784; was Lord-Lieut of Aberdeenshire, and a distinguished statesman who filled various high diplomatic and ministerial offices, and was First Lord of the Treasury and Prime Minister 1852-5; *cr Viscount Gordon* (peerage of United Kingdom) 1814; assumed by R licence 1818, the additional surname, arms, and supporters of Hamilton; *d* 1860; *s* by his eldest son **(5)** GEORGE JOHN JAMES, 5th Earl, *b* 1816; *m* 1840, Mary, who *d* 1900, da of late George Baillie, and sister of 10th Earl of Haddington; *d* 1864; *s* by his eldest son **(6)** GEORGE, 6th Earl, *b* 1841; having pursued a life of romantic adventure was accidentally drowned on 27 Jan 1870, off the coast of America when serving on board the *Hera*; *s* by his brother **(7)** *Rt Hon* JOHN CAMPBELL, KT, GCMG, GCVO, 7th Earl, *b* 1847; Lord-Lieut of Aberdeenshire 1880-1934, Lord High Commr to General Assembly of Church of Scotland 1881-5, and again 1915, Lord Lieut of Ireland, Jan to July 1886; Gov-Gen of Canada 1893-8, and again Lord-Lieut of Ireland 1905-15; *cr Earl of Haddo,* in co of Aberdeen, and *Marquess of Aberdeen and Temair,* in co of Aberdeen, in co of Meath, and in co of Argyll (peerage of United Kingdom) 1916; *m* 1877, Hon Ishbel Maria Marjoribanks, GBE, LLD, who *d* 1939, da of 1st Baron Tweedmouth; *d* 1934; *s* by his el son **(8)** GEORGE, OBE, 2nd Marquess, *b* 1879; Lord Lieut of Aberdeenshire 1934-59 *m* 1st, 1906, Mary Florence, who *d* 1937, da of late Joseph Clixby, of Owmby Cliff, Lincs, and widow of Edward Shepherd Cockayne, of Sheffield; 2ndly, 1940, Sheila, who *d* 1949, da of late Lt-Col John Foster Forbes, JP, DL, of Rothiemay Castle, Banffshire, and widow of Capt James William Guy Innes, CBE, DL, JP, RN (Innes, Bt colls); *d* 1965; *s* by his brother **(9)** DUDLEY GLADSTONE, DSO, 3rd Marquess, *b* 1883; Lt-Col Comdg 8th/10th and 5th Bns Gordon Highlanders; *m* 1st, 1907, Cecile Elizabeth, who *d* 1948, da of late George James Drummond (E Perth, colls); 2ndly, 1949, Margaret Gladys, ARRC, JP, who *d* 1990, only da of late Lt-Col Reginald George Munn, CMG; *d* 1972; *s* by his eldest son **(10)** DAVID GEORGE IAN ALEXANDER, CBE, TD, 4th Marquess, *b* 1908; Lord-Lieut for Aberdeenshire 1973-74; Prior of Order of St John of Jerusalem and KStJ; *m* 1939, Beatrice Mary June, CBE, da of late Arthur Paul Boissier, of Moretons, Harrow-on-the-Hill; *d* 1974; *s* by his brother **(11)** ARCHIBALD VICTOR DUDLEY, 5th Marquess, *b* 1913; writer and broadcaster; *d* 1984; *s* by his brother **(12)** ALASTAIR NINIAN JOHN, 6th Marquess and present peer; also Earl of Aberdeen, Earl of Haddo, Viscount Formartine, Viscount Gordon, and Lord Haddo, Methlic, Tarves, and Kellie.

Aberdour, Lord; son of Earl of Morton.

ABERGAVENNY, MARQUESS OF (Nevill) (Marquess UK 1876)

JOHN HENRY GUY NEVILL, KG, OBE, 5th Marquess; *b* 8 Nov 1914; *s* 1954; *ed* Eton and Trin Coll, Camb; Lt-Col late Life Gds; 1939-45 War in France (despatches), N-W Europe (OBE); Hon Col Kent and Co of London Yeo. 1948-62; a JP and DL for Sussex (Vice Lieut 1970-74; Lord-Lieut of E Sussex since 1974); KStJ; a Dir of Lloyds Bank plc (Chm SE Reg Board), and other Directorships; Member E Sussex Co Council 1947-54 (Alderman 1954-62); a Member of Nat Hunt Cttee since 1942 (Sen Steward 1955 and 63); Pres British Horse Soc 1970-71; a Trustee of Ascot Authority 1952-82; HM's Representative at Ascot 1972-82; Chancellor of The Order of the Garter 1977-95; Hon LLD Sussex 1986; OBE (Mil) 1945, KG 1974: *m* 1938, (Mary) Patricia, DCVO, da of Maj John Fenwick Harrison, JP (*see* B Burnham, 1969 Edn), and has had issue.

Arms – Gules, a saltire argent, charged with a rose of the field. **Crest** – Out of a ducal coronet, or a bull's head proper, charged with a rose gules. **Supporters** – On either side a bull argent, pied sable, armed, unguled, collared, and chained or, the latter terminating in a staple. **Badges** – *Dexter*, a rose gules, barbed and seeded proper; *sinister*, a portcullis or.
Seat – Eridge Park, Tunbridge Wells TN3 9JT. *Club* – White's.

Form no mean wish

SON DECEASED

†Henry John Montague (*Earl of Lewes*), *b* 2 Feb 1948; *ed* Eton; Page of Honour to HM 1962-64; *d* 2 April 1965.

DAUGHTERS LIVING

Lady Anne Patricia, *b* 1938: *m* 1971, Martin Frank Whiteley, who *d* 1984, and has issue living, Camilla Mary, *b* 1972, — Davina Marian Beatrice, *b* 1973, — Lucinda Jane, *b* 1978. *Residence* – Dalmar House, Culworth, nr Banbury, Oxon.

Lady Vivienne Margaret, *b* 1941: *m* 1962, Alan Lillingston, and has issue living, Luke, *b* 1963, — Andrew Harry, *b* 1972, — Georgina Patricia, *b* 1965: *m* 1988, Michael L. W. Bell, of Fitzroy House, Black Bear Lane, Newmarket, Suffolk, yr son of Capt Brian Bell, of Todenham Manor, Moreton-in-Marsh, Glos, and has issue living, Alexander Luke Wentworth *b* 1990, Nicholas Stewart Wentworth *b* 1997, Amy Kitty Wentworth *b* 1991, — Sophie Susan, *b* 1967. *Residence* – Mount Coote, Kilmallock, co Limerick.

Lady Rose, *b* 1950: *m* 1990, George Mark Somerset Clowes, son of Archibald Somerset Clowes, of Ashlands, Billesdon, Leics, and has issue living, Toby Harry Somerset, *b* 1990, — Lucy Elizabeth, *b* 1992. *Residence* –

WIDOW LIVING OF SON OF FOURTH MARQUESS

Lady Anne Camilla Eveline Wallop (*Lady Rupert Nevill*) (Old House Farm, Glynde, Lewes, Sussex; 35 Upper Addison Gdns, W14), da of 9th Earl of Portsmouth: *m* 1944, Lord Rupert Charles Montacute Nevill, CVO, who *d* 1982, and has had issue (see colls infra).

COLLATERAL BRANCHES LIVING

Issue of late Lord Rupert Charles Montacute Nevill, CVO, yr son of 4th Marquess, *b* 1923, *d* 1982: *m* 1944, Lady Anne Camilla Eveline Wallop (ante), da of 9th Earl of Portsmouth:—

†Guy Rupert Gerard, *b* 1945; *ed* Eton; a Page of Honour to HM 1958-61: *m* 1982, Lady Beatrix Mary Lambton (39 Basuto Rd, SW6; 251A Fulham Rd, SW3), 2nd da of Antony Claud Lambton (6th Earl of Durham until he disclaimed his title 1970), and *d* 1993. — Christopher George Charles (Sham Farm, Eridge Green, Kent), *b* 23 April 1955; *ed* Harrow: *m* 1985, Venetia J., elder da of late Frederick Gerard Maynard, of 43 Bury Walk, SW3, and has had issue, †George Rupert Gerard, *b* and *d* 1990, — Sophie Alice Augusta, *b* (twin) 1990. —— Angela Isabel Mary (2 Durham House, Durham Place, SW3), *b* 1948: *m* 1994, William Keating, who *d* 1998. —— Henrietta Emily Charlotte (35 Upper Addison Gdns, W14), *b* 1964: *m* 1991, Capt Timothy J. Purbrick, 17/21st Lancers, son of William Purbrick, and has issue living, Rose, *b* 1997, — Lily, *b* (twin) 1997.

(In remainder to Earldom and Barony of Abergavenny, and Viscountcy of Nevill only)

Grandsons of late Percy Llewelyn Nevill (infra):—
Issue of late Michael George Ralph Nevill, Lieut Scots Gds, *b* 1917, *ka* 1943: *m* 1940, Maureen Ethné David, JP (who *m* 2ndly, 1947, John Valentine Balfour, DSC, of Walnut Tree Farm, Birling, Maidstone, Kent (*see* Price, Bt, colls, 1950 Edn)), da of late Capt (Arthur) Tahu (Gravenor) Rhodes, MVO (*see* B Plunket, 1968 Edn):—
David Michael Ralph (Birling Place, Birling, Maidstone, Kent), *b* 1941; *ed* Bryanston: *m* 1972, Katherine Mary, da of Rossmore Derrick Westenra, of Halswell, Christchurch, NZ, and has issue living, Guy Michael Rossmore, *b* 1973, — Anna Louise, *b* 1976, — Georgina Rose, *b* 1981. —— Michael George Rathmore (*posthumous*), *b* 1943; *ed* Eton.

Granddaughter of Hon Ralph Pelham Nevill, 2nd son of 4th Earl:—
Issue of late Percy Llewelyn Nevill, *b* 1877, *d* 1927: *m* 1905, Marjorie, who *d* 1945, da of late Lord George Montacute Nevill (3rd son of 1st Marquess of Abergavenny):—
Cicely Rose, *b* 1915: *m* 1947, Peter Richard Nickols, who *d* 1990, and has issue living, two sons and one da. *Residence* – Pinewood Lodge, Spofforth, Harrogate, N Yorks.

PREDECESSORS – (1) *Sir* Ralph Nevill, KG, 6th son of 1st Earl of Westmorland, and 4th Baron Nevill, of Raby (cr 1294) (titles forfeited 13th Elizabeth I), a confidant of Edward IV, was summoned to the English Parliament as *Baron Bergavenny* 1450-72; *d* 1476; *s* by his son (2) *Sir* George, KB, 2nd Baron; was knighted at the battle of Tewkesbury; he *d* 1492, and was *s* by his eldest son (3) *Sir* George, KG, KB, 3rd Baron; was companion in arms of Henry VIII in his French wars, and held high and important commands; *d* 1536; *s* by his eldest son (4) Henry, 4th Baron; was committed to ward for striking the Earl of Oxford in the chamber of presence, but received special pardon within a month; was one of the peers who sat in judgement upon Mary, Queen of Scots; *d* 1586; at his decease the Barony was unsuccessfully claimed by his da Mary, wife of Sir Thomas Fane, who however, was subsequently granted the Barony of Le Despencer (cr by writ 1264), to which she was a co-heir; *s* by his cousin (5) Edward, 5th Baron, eldest son of Sir Edward Nevill, 2nd son of 2nd Baron; *d* 1589; *s* by his eldest son (6) Edward, 6th Baron; unsuccessfully claimed the Earldom of Westmorland; *d* 1622; *s* by his eldest son (7) Henry, 7th Baron; *d* 1641; *s* by his eldest son (8) John, 8th Baron; *d* 1660; *s* by his brother (9) George, 9th Baron; *d* 1666; *s* by his only son (10) George, 10th Baron, *dsp* 1694, when the barony reverted to his kinsman (11) George, 11th Baron, eldest son of Sir Christopher Nevill, 2nd son of 6th Baron; *d* 1720; *s* by his eldest son (12) George, 12th Baron; *dsp* 1723; *s* by his brother (13) Edward, 13th Baron; *d* 1724; *s* by his cousin (14) William, 14th Baron, son of Edward Nevill, brother of 11th Baron; the first to be styled *Lord Abergavenny* (in lieu of Bergavenny); *d* 1745; *s* by his eldest son (15) George, 15th Baron; cr *Viscount Nevill* and *Earl of Abergavenny* (peerage of Great Britain) 1784; *d* 1785; *s* by his son (16) Henry, KT, 2nd Earl; *d* 1843; *s* by his son (17) *Rev* John, 3rd Earl; *d* 1845; *s* by his brother (18) *Rev* William, 4th Earl, *b* 1792; *m* 1824, Caroline, who *d* 1873, da of Ralph Leeke, of Longford Hall, Salop; *d* 17 Aug 1868; *s* by his eldest son (19) William, KG, 5th Earl, *b* 1826; Lord-Lieut of Sussex 1892-1905; cr *Earl of Lewes* and *Marquess of Abergavenny* (peerage of United Kingdom) 1876: *m* 1848, Caroline, who *d* 1892, sister of 1st Baron Derwent; *d* 1915; *s* by his eldest son (20) Reginald William Bransby, 2nd Marquess, *b* 1853; *d* 1927; *s* by his brother (21) Henry Gilbert Ralph, 3rd Marquess, *b* 1854: *m* 1st, 1876, Violet, who *d* 1880, da of late Lieut-Col Henry Dorrien Streatfeild, of Chiddingstone Park, Kent; 2ndly, 1886, Maud Augusta, who *d* 1927, da of late William Beckett, MP (*see* B Grimthorpe, 1927 Edn); 3rdly, 1928, Mary Frances, who *d* 1954, da of late Hon Ralph Pelham Nevill, and widow of 3rd Viscount Hardinge; *d* 1938; *s* by his nephew (22) Guy Temple Montacute Larnach-Nevill (eldest son of late Lord George Montacute Nevill, 3rd son of 1st Marquess), 4th Marquess; *b* 1883; Capt Scots Guards; assumed by deed poll 1919 the additional surname of Larnach for himself and his wife only: *m* 1909, Isabel Nellie, who *d* 1953, only child of late James Walker Larnach: *d* 1954; *s* by his eldest son (23) John Henry Guy, 5th Marquess and present peer; also Earl of Abergavenny, Earl of Lewes, Viscount Nevill, and Baron Abergavenny (formerly Bergavenny).

ABERTAY, BARONY OF (Barrie) (Extinct 1940)

DAUGHTERS LIVING OF FIRST BARON

Hon June Jane Coupar, *b* 1928: *m* 1st, 1952 (*m diss* 1977), Col Alan Norman Breitmeyer, DL, High Sheriff of Cambs (1984), late Gren Gds; 2ndly 1977, Christopher Jeremy King Fordham, MA, FRICS, and has issue living (by 1st *m*), Timothy Hugh, *b* 1959; late Maj Gren Gds: *m* 1985, Henrietta Beatrice Jane, yst da of Maj Jonathan Michael Henry Balcon, TD (*see* Hillingdon, By), and has issue living, Sophie Rebecca *b* 1987, Georgina Louise *b* 1990, — Patricia Anne, *b* 1954: *m* 1979, Rupert Edward Hanbury, and has issue living, James Antony *b* 1983, Charlotte Emma *b* 1981, Araminta Laura Elizabeth *b* 1992. *Residence* – Odsey Park, Ashwell, Herts.

Hon Rosemary Ethel Coupar, *b* 1931; JP Glos 1973: *m* 1952, John Stuart Maitland, and has issue living, John Andrew Charles, *b* 1954; TD, ARICS, FAAV: *m* 1997, Susanna Helm, da of Lt-Col David Barker, of Up Nately, Hants, — Robin Neil, *b* 1958: *m* 1988, Deborah, yr da of Watson Stuart, of Lower Grantsfield, Kimbolton, Herefords, and has issue living, Thomas Stuart *b* 1992, Bruce Patrick *b* 1994, — Angus Kenneth, *b* 1963: *m* 1994, Helen C., elder da of Charles Gunther, of Fulham, SW6, — Fiona Romaire, *b* 1961: *m* 1990, Peter James Dunkerley Leathart, yr son of Scott Leathart, of Overmead, Lower Heyford, Bicester. *Residence* – The Grange, Stancombe, Dursley, Glos.

Abingdon, Earl of; see Earl of Lindsey and Abingdon.

ABINGER, BARON (Scarlett) (Baron UK 1835)

He stands by his own strength

JAMES RICHARD SCARLETT, 8th Baron; *b* 28 Sept 1914; *s* 1943; *ed* Eton, and Magdalene Coll, Camb (BA); Lt-Col late RA; DL Essex 1968; Vice-Pres Byron Soc; KStJ: *m* 1957, Isla Carolyn, only da of late Vice-Adm James William Rivett-Carnac, CB, CBE, DSC (*see* Rivett-Carnac, Bt), and has issue.

Arms – Checky or and gules, a lion rampant ermine; on a canton azure, a castle, triple towered argent. Crest – A Tuscan column, checky, or and gules, supported on either side by a lion's jamb ermines, erased gules. Supporters – on either side an angel vested argent, tunic azure, wings or; in the exterior hand of each a sword in bend proper, pommel and hilt or.
Residences – 7 Cumberland St, SW1V 4LS; Sheepcote House, Queen St, Castle Hedingham, Halstead, Essex CO9 3HA. *Clubs* – Carlton, Royal Automobile.

SONS LIVING

Hon JAMES HARRY, *b* 28 May 1959: *m* 1995, Tracy Lee, 2nd da of Normand Cloutier, of Ottawa, Canada.
Hon Peter Richard, *b* 1961: *m* 1992, Sharon Elizabeth, da of Derek Turl, of Exeter, Devon, and has issue living, Harry Alexander, *b* 1997.

WIDOW LIVING OF SON OF SEVENTH BARON

Bridget, da of late H. B. Crook, of 102 Stafford Court, W8: *m* 1947, Hon John Leopold Campbell Scarlett, CBE, who *d* 1994, and has issue (see colls, infra).

COLLATERAL BRANCH LIVING

Issue of late Hon John Leopold Campbell Scarlett, CBE, yr son of 7th Baron, *b* 1916, *d* 1994: *m* 1947, Bridget (ante), da of late H. B. Crook, of 102 Stafford Court, W8:—
Hugh Lawrence (Rock Hill, RMB 591, Maimuru, via Young, NSW 2594), *b* 1953: *m* 1985, Dinah, da of Richard Pinsent, of Thora, NSW, Australia, and has issue living, Skye Michelle, *b* 1995. — Felix James (Two Beeches, Meadow Lane, S Heath, Bucks HP16 9SH), *b* 1958: *m* 1991, Laura Stewart, only da of Edward Petrie, of Dundee, and has issue living, Robert Campbell, *b* 1992, — Rory Maclaren, *b* 1993, — Fraser Stewart, *b* 1995, — Honor Katherine, *b* 1996. — Sarah Elizabeth, *b* 1954: *m* 1996, Dr Alistair J. Cairns, PhD, of 104 Wodeland Av, Guildford, Surrey GU2 5LD, eldest son of late Ian Cairns, of Kinghorn, Fife.

PREDECESSORS – (1) *Sir* JAMES Scarlett, PC, KB, DCL; called to the Bar 1791; sat successively as MP for Cockermouth, Peterborough, and Norwich, and was sometime Attorney-Gen; appointed Lord Chief Baron of the Exchequer 1834, and *cr Baron Abinger*, of Abinger, co Surrey (peerage of United Kingdom) 1835; *d* 1844; *s* by his eldest son (2)

ROBERT CAMPBELL, 2nd Baron, *b* 1794; was a Barrister-at-Law: *m* 1824, Sarah, who *d* 1878, da of late George Smith, Chief Justice of Mauritius; *d* 24 June 1861; *s* by his eldest son (3) WILLIAM FREDERICK, CB, 3rd Baron, *b* 1826; Lieut-Gen in the Army: *m* 1863, Helen, who *d* 1915, da of Commodore George Allan Magruder, of the US Navy; *d* 1892; *s* by his son (4) JAMES YORK MACGREGOR, 4th Baron, *b* 1871; *d* 1903; *s* by his cousin (5) SHELLEY LEOPOLD LAURENCE (son of late Lieut-Col Leopold James Yorke Campbell Scarlett), son of late Hon Peter Campbell Scarlett, CB (3rd son of 1st Baron), 5th Baron, *b* 1872; Hon Com Roy Naval Vol Reserve; served during European War 1915-16: *m* 1899, Lila Lucy Catherine Mary, who *d* 1941 (having *m* 3rdly, 1921, Jean de Belot), da of late Rt Hon Sir William Arthur White, PC, GCB, GCMG, British Ambassador at Constantinople, and widow of Kammerherr Carl E de Geijer, Swedish Diplo Ser; *d* 1917; *s* by his brother (6) ROBERT BROOKE CAMPBELL, 6th Baron: *m* 1917, Jean Marguerite (Madame de Serignac), who *d* 1954, da of late Edouard Japy, and widow of Adolphe Steinheil, of Paris; *d* 1927; *s* by his brother (7) HUGH RICHARD, DSO, 7th Baron, *b* 1878; Lieut-Col RA (retired); S Africa 1900-1902; European War 1914-18 (DSO): *m* 1913, Marjorie Ursula, who *d* 1965, da of John MacPhillamy, of Blair Athol, Bathurst, NSW; *d* 1943; *s* by his eldest son (8) JAMES RICHARD, 8th Baron and present peer.

Aboyne, Earl of; son of Marquess of Huntly.

Acheson, family name of Earl of Gosford.

ACKNER, BARON (Ackner) (Life Baron 1986)

DESMOND JAMES CONRAD ACKNER, PC, son of Dr Conrad Ackner; *b* 18 Sept 1920; *ed* Highgate Sch, and Clare Coll, Camb (MA) Hon Fellow; Bar Middle Temple 1945, QC 1961, Bencher 1965; Chm Gen Council of Bar, and Vice-Pres Senate of Four Inns of Court 1968-70 (Pres 1980-82); Recorder of Swindon 1962-71, and Judge of Court of Appeal of Jersey and Guernsey 1967-71, Judge of High Court of Justice (Queen's Bench Div) 1971-80, Lord Justice of Appeal 1980-86; Treas Middle Temple 1984; a Lord of Appeal in Ordinary since 1986; *cr* Kt 1970, PC 1980, and *Baron Ackner*, of Sutton, W Sussex (Life Baron) 1986: *m* 1946, Joan, da of late John Evans, JP, and widow of K. B. Spence, and has issue.

𝔄rms – Sable in fess issuant from a barrulet wavy azure fimbriated argent a representation of the bridge at Clare College Cambridge proper the whole between two whales spouting naiant counter naiant gold. ℭrest – Upon a helm with a wreath or and sable a short-eared owl proper crowned or supporting with the dexter claw a clarion azure. 𝔖upporters – Two otters each holding in the mouth a trout gold the compartment comprising a river bank with bulrushes growing therefrom proper. 𝔐otto – Non servimus justitiae silendo.
Residences – Browns House, Sutton, nr Pulborough, W Sussex; 7 Rivermill, 151 Grosvenor Rd, SW1.

SON LIVING

Hon Martin Stewart, *b* 1951; *ed* Oundle, and Birmingham Univ (BSc): *m* 1983, Janet, da of late C. W. Williamson.

DAUGHTER LIVING

Hon Claudia Madeleine, *b* 1954; *ed* Roedean, and Girton Coll, Camb (BA); Barrister-at-law: *m* 1978, Iain Hughes.

ADOPTED STEPDAUGHTER LIVING

Moelwyn Ulva (da of late K. B. Spence), b 1943; ed St Michael's, Petworth, and Switzerland: m 1st, 19— (m diss 19—), J. K. Bouckley; 2ndly, 1980, Michael Healy, of Sylvan House, Goose Green, Gullane, E Lothian EH31 2AT, and has issue living (by 1st m), Joanna Helen Sarah Brooke, b 1969: m 1993, Simon William Young, twin son of Stephen Young, of Elgin.

A'Court, Holmes, Family name of Baron Heytesbury.

ACTON, BARON (Lyon-Dalberg-Acton) (Baron UK 1869, Bt E 1644)

RICHARD GERALD LYON-DALBERG-ACTON, 4th Baron, and 11th Baronet; b 30 July 1941; s 1989; ed St George's Coll, Salisbury, Rhodesia, and Trin Coll, Oxford (BA 1963, MA 1988); Bar Inner Temple 1976; a Dir Coutts & Co 1971-74; Sr Law Officer, Zimbabwe Ministry of Justice, Legal and Parliamentary Affairs, 1981-85; writer; a Patrician of Naples, patron of one living (but, being a Roman Catholic, cannot present): m 1st, 1965, Hilary Juliet Sarah, who d 1973, da of Dr Osmond Laurence Charles Cookson, MB BS, MRCS, LRCP, of Perth, W Australia; 2ndly, 1974 (m diss 1987), Judith Garfield, writer, da of Hon Sir Garfield Todd, sometime PM of Southern Rhodesia, of Hokonui Ranch, PO Dadaya, Zimbabwe; 3rdly, 1988, Patricia, only da of late M. Morey Nassif, of Cedar Rapids, Iowa, USA, and has issue by 1st m.

Arms – Quarterly: 1st and 4th gules semée of cross-crosslets fitché or, two lions passant in pale argent, Acton; 2nd quarterly, 1st and 4th azure, six fleurs-de-lis, three, two, and one argent, a chief dancettée of the last, 2nd and 3rd or, a cross patonce gules, over all an escutcheon of the first, thereon a tower argent, a chief dancettée of the last, Dalberg; 3rd azure, a lion passant or between three plates each charged with a griffin's head erased sable, Lyon. Crest – A human leg in armour flexed at the knee and couped at the thigh disgorging five drops of blood, Acton. Supporters – On either side a lion guardant proper, gorged with a chain or, and charged with a cross patonce gules.
Residences – Marcham Priory, Abingdon, Oxon; 100 Red Oak Lane SE, Cedar Rapids, Iowa 52403, USA.

SON LIVING (By 1st marriage)

Hon JOHN CHARLES FERDINAND HAROLD, b 19 Aug 1966; ed Winchester, and Balliol Coll, Oxford: m 1998, Lucinda A. F., da of Brig James Percival, of Marnhull, Dorset.

BROTHERS LIVING

Rev Hon (John) Charles (Westminster Diocesan Seminary, 28 Beaufort Street, SW3), b 1943; ed Gregorian Univ, Rome; Prof of Dogmatic Theology, Westminster Diocesan Seminary.
Hon Robert Peter (Rutland House, Saxon St, Newmarket, Suffolk), b 1946; stud mgr for Sheik Mohamed bin Rashid al Maktoum, Newmarket: m 1974, Michele, da of Henri Laigle, of 61 rue du Commerce, 92 Colombes, France, and has issue living, Christopher Richard Henri, b 1977, — Patrick John Pascal, b 1979, — William Benjamin, b 1986.
Hon Edward David Joseph (365 Unthank Rd, Norwich NR4 7QG); b 1949; ed York Univ, and St Edmund's Coll, Camb; Prof of Modern European History, E Anglia Univ; author of Alexander Herzen and the Role of the Intellectual Revolutionary (1979), Rethinking the Russian Revolution (1990), Russia: The Tsarist and Soviet Legacy (1995) etc: m 1972, Stella Marie, da of late Henry Conroy, of 8 Stirling Rd, Bolton, and has issue living, Helen Marie, b 1974, — Natalie Elizabeth b 1977.
Hon Peter Hedley (Dancing Dicks, Blunts Hall Rd, Witham, Essex); b 1950; ed RAC Cirencester; Trainee Manager,

Waterman & Ross: *m* 1981, Anne, da of James Sinclair, of Sanday, Orkney Is, and has issue living, Simon Richard, *b* 1981, — Emily, *b* 1989.

SISTERS LIVING

Hon Pelline Margot, *b* 1932: *m* 1953, Laszlo de Marffy von Versegh, of Ealing Farm, PO Box 29, Mvurwi, Zimbabwe, and has had issue, Denes, *b* 1954: *m* 1986, Rachel, da of Martin Lampard, of Tiverton, Devon, and has issue living, Edmond *b* 1988, Harry *b* 1991, George *b* 1994, Hannah *b* 1989, — Miklos, *b* 1986, Vibeke Jane, only da of Christopher Culley, of Moyard, co Galway, and has issue living, Benjamin *b* 1992, Hugh *b* 1997, Lucinda *b* 1988, Alice *b* 1990, — Joseph, *b* 1957: *m* 1987, Anne Margaret Elizabeth, da of Col Alexander W. D. Lewis, of Salcombe, S Devon, and Canberra, Australia and has issue living, Charles Alexander *b* 1989, Alexander *b* 1991, — Paul, *b* 1958: *m* 1987, Lesley-Anne, da of Douglas Hall, of Bournemouth, and has issue living, Tamas *b* 1987, James *b* 1989, William *b* 1992, — Robert, *b* 1962: *m* 1989, Katherine, da of Martin Graham, of Harare, Zimbabwe, and has issue living, Christopher *b* 1994, Peter *b* 1996, Philippa *b* 1992, — Stephen, *b* 1965: *m* 1995, Dymphna, da of Réné Straatman, and has issue living, Nicholas *b* 1996, Elizabeth *b* 1998, and Mika (adopted) *b* 1988, — Gabriella Mary, *b* 1960, *d* 1984.

Hon Catherine, *b* 1939: *m* 1960, Hon Joseph Mervyn Corbett (*see* B Rowallan). *Residence* – The Old Rectory, Coates, nr Cirencester, Glos.

Hon Jill Mary Joan, *b* 1947: *m* 1969, Nicholas Lampert (*see* V Ridley, colls, 1976 Edn), of 46 Clarence Rd, Moseley, Birmingham B13 9UH, and has issue living, Katherine, *b* 1969, — Frances, *b* 1971.

Hon Mary-Ann, *b* 1951: *m* 1972, Timothy John Sheehy, of 8 St Margaret's Rd, Oxford, and has issue living, Jane Elizabeth, *b* 1973, — Clare Anne, *b* 1975.

Hon Jane, *b* 1954: *m* 1st, 1975 (*m diss* 1982), Charles Thomas Pugh, who *d* 1989; 2ndly, 1983, Xan de Crespigny Smiley (*see* Smiley, Bt, colls), and has issue living (by 1st *m*), Charlotte, *b* 1978, — Rebecca, *b* 1979, — (by 2nd *m*) (*see* Smiley, Bt, colls). *Residence* – 68 Lonsdale Rd, Oxford OX2 7EP.

AUNT LIVING (*daughter of 2nd Baron*)

Hon Helen Mary Grace (602 Park West, W2), *b* 1910: *m* 1933 (*m diss* 1958), Prince Guglielmo Camillo Carlo Rospigliosi, who *d* 1990, and has issue (*see* E Newburgh, colls)

WIDOW LIVING OF THIRD BARON

Hon DAPHNE STRUTT (*Dowager Baroness Acton*), da of 4th Baron Rayleigh: *m* 1931, the 3rd Baron Acton, CMG, MBE, TD, who *d* 1989. *Residence* – 46 Clarence Rd, Moseley, Birmingham B13 9UH.

COLLATERAL BRANCHES LIVING   (*Male line of which is in remainder to Baronetcy only*)

Grandchildren of late Adm Baron Alfredo Acton (Hon KCB) (infra):—
Issue of late late Baron Ferdinando Amadeo Maria Acton, LLD, a Patrician of Naples, a 1st class Grandee of Spain, and 12th Prince of Leporano, *b* 1908, *d* 1979: *m* 1946, Emilia (a Dame Grand Cross of Constantinian Order of St George) (Palazzo Cellamare a Chiaja, Naples, Italy), only da of late Count Gioacchino del Balzo di Presenzano:—
Baron Giovanni Alfredo Maria (*Prince of Leporano*), *b* 1948; a Patrician of Naples, 13th Prince of Leporano, and a Knt of Justice of Constantinian Order of St George. *Residence* – Palazzo Cellamare a Chiaja, Naples. ——— Maria Eleanora Carlotta, *b* 1949; a Dame of Justice of Constantinian Order of St George: *m* 1972, Pier Luigi Taccone di Sitizano, a Patrician of Tropea, and a Knt of Justice of Constantinian Order of St George. *Residences* – Palazzo Cellences, Naples; Pizzo di Calabria, Italy.

Grandson of late Vice-Adm Ferdinando Acton, 6th son of late Commodore Charles Acton, eldest son of late Lt-Gen Joseph Edward Acton, brother of 6th baronet:—
Issue of late Adm Baron Alfredo Acton (Hon KCB; cr a Baron in Kingdom of Italy 1925), *b* 1867, *d* 1934: *m* 1907, Livia, who *d* 1963 (a Dame of Honour and Devotion of the Sovereign Order of Malta, and Dame Grand Cross of Constantinian Order of St George; Cross Pro Ecclesia et Pontifice), da of Giuseppe Giudice Caracciolo, 9th Prince of Villa and Cellamare, of Naples:—
Baron Francesco Eduardo Maria, *b* 1910; a Patrician of Naples Capt Italian Navy, a Knight of Sovereign Order of Malta, and a Knight Grand Cross of Constantinian Order of St George; cr a Baron of Kingdom of Italy 1940: *m* 1941, Marida (Dame of Justice of Constantinian Order of St George), only da of Baron Ameglio, and has had issue, †Alfred, *b* 1942; *d* as a result of an accident 1946. *Residence* – Palazzo Cellamare a Chiaja, Naples, Italy.

Grandsons of late Paul Reginald Acton, only son of late Capt Richard George Acton, only son of late Maj Henry Acton, son of late Capt Henry Acton, 2nd son of late Lt-Gen Joseph Edward Acton (ante):—
Issue of late Richard Le Duc Acton, *b* 1913, *d* 1989: *m* 1933, Alberta Althea (27211-A Via Capote, San Juan Capistrano, Calif 92675, USA), da of late Francis Joseph Budwiser, of Dubuque, Iowa:—
Dennis Richard, *b* 1938: *m* 1st, 1961 (*m diss* 1971), Susan Caroline, da of Hartvige Rudolph Miklethum, of Minneapolis, Minn; 2ndly, 1973, Frances Lee, da of Harold Stark, of Huntington Beach, Calif, and has issue living (by 1st *m*), Christopher Michael, *b* 1962, — Paul Reginald, *b* 1968, — Julia Ann, *b* 1964. ——— Paul Reginald *b* 1943: *m* 1983, Suzzanne, da of Eugene Erickson, of Minneapolis, Minn.

PREDECESSORS – (1) *Sir* EDWARD Acton, of Aldenham Hall (10th in lineal descent from William de Acton Burnel, temp Edward III), cr a *Baronet*, for his fidelity to Charles I 1644; *d* 1659; *s* by his eldest son **(2)** *Sir* WALTER, MP; *d* 1665; *s* by his eldest son **(3)** *Sir* EDWARD, MP; *d* 1716; *s* by his eldest son **(4)** *Sir* WHITMORE; *d* 1731; *s* by his son **(5)** *Sir* RICHARD; *d* 1791; *s* by his kinsman **(6)** *Sir* JOHN FRANCIS EDWARD, great-grandson of Walter, 2nd son of 2nd Bt; was successively Com-in-Ch of the land and Sea forces in Naples, and Neapolitan Prime Minister; *d* 1811; *s* by his son **(7)** *Sir* FERDINAND RICHARD EDWARD, *b* 1801; assumed by R licence in 1833 the additional surname of Dalberg: *m* 1832, Marie

Louise Pellina (who *m* 2ndly, 1840, 2nd Earl Granville, and *d* 1860), only child and heir of Emeric Joseph, Duke of Dalberg; *d* 1837; *s* by his son **(8)** *Sir* JOHN EMERICH EDWARD, KCVO, *b* 1834; MP for Carlow (*L*) 1859-65 and for Bridgnorth 1865-6; a Lord-in-Waiting to HM Queen Victoria 1892-5; Regius Professor of Modern History in Camb Univ 1895-1902; cr *Baron Acton* (peerage of United Kingdom) 1869: *m* 1865, Countess Marie, who *d* 1923, eldest da of Count Arco-Valley, of Munich; *d* 1902; *s* by his son **(9)** RICHARD MAXIMILIAN, KCVO, 2nd Baron, *b* 1870; a Lord-in-Waiting to King Edward VII. 1905-10, and to King George V 1910-15, and Envoy Extraor and Min Plen to Finland 1919-20; assumed by R licence the additional surname and arms of Lyon 1919: *m* 1904, Dorothy, who *d* 1923, only child of late Thomas Henry Lyon, JP, DL, of Appleton Hall, Cheshire, and Rutland Lodge, Rutland Gardens, SW; *d* 1924; *s* by his son **(10)** JOHN EMERICH HENRY, CMG, MBE, TD, 3rd Baron, *b* 1907; 1939-45 War as Maj Shropshire Yeo; Pres Rhodesian Royal Agric Soc 1960-64, Chm Gwebi Agric Coll 1958-62, and Chibero Agric Coll 1960-65, founding Chm Tattersalls Swaziland 1969: *m* 1931, Hon Daphne Strutt, da of 4th Baron Rayleigh; *d* 1989; *s* by his eldest son **(11)** RICHARD GERALD, 4th Baron and present peer.

Adderley, family name of Baron Norton.

ADDINGTON, BARON (Hubbard) (Baron UK 1887)

DOMINIC BRYCE HUBBARD, 6th Baron; *b* 24 Aug 1963; *s* 1982; *ed* Hewett Comprehensive Sch, Norwich, and Aberdeen Univ (MA 1988): *m* 1999, Elizabeth Ann, only da of Michael J. Morris, of Duxbury Park, Chorley, Lancs.

𝔄rms – Vert, a chevron engrailed, plain cotised argent, between three eagles' heads erased of the second, each gorged with a collar fleurettée gules. 𝔠rest – In front of a fasces fessewise proper an eagle's head as in the arms. 𝔖upporters – On either side an eagle argent, wings addorsed, gorged with a collar fleurettée gules, and pendent therefrom an escutcheon ermine charged with a rose gules.

Seeking things above

BROTHER LIVING

Hon MICHAEL WALTER LESLIE, *b* 7 July 1965; *ed* Hewett Comprehensive Sch, Manchester Univ (BA), and Leicester Polytechnic (MA).

SISTERS LIVING

Hon Frances Linden, *b* 1962; *ed* Southampton Univ (BA); Journalist: *m* 1996, Nicholas Hamilton Craven, and has issue living, Henry Benedict John, *b* 1997, — Toby Dominic, *b* 1998.
Hon Sally Anne, *b* 1966; *ed* Sch of Oriental and African Studies, London Univ (BA), and UCLA (MA, Fellow).

UNCLE LIVING (*brother of 5th Baron*)

Peter, *b* 1932; *ed* Eastbourne Coll.

HALF-AUNT LIVING (*half-sister of 5th Baron*)

Nicolette, *b* 1926: *m* 1953, Richard Joseph Pike, of Little Rising, Queen Catherine Rd, Steeple Claydon, Buckingham MK10 3PY, and has issue living, James Eben, *b* 1955, — William Joseph Fitzgerald, *b* 1960.

MOTHER LIVING

Alexandra Patricia, da of late Norman Ford Millar, formerly of Glasgow and of Burma: *m* 1961 (*m diss* 1974), the 5th Baron Addington, who *d* 1982. *Residence* – Thorpe Hamlet, Norwich.

COLLATERAL BRANCHES LIVING

Grandchildren of late Capt Gerald Napier Hubbard (infra):—

Issue of late Ralph Arthur Hubbard, *b* 1908, *d* 1981: *m* 1st, 1940 (*m diss* 1954), Hon Marion Woodruff, who *d* 1992, eldest da of 1st Baron Ashfield, and formerly wife of (i) James Hart Rutland, and (ii) James Henry Royds; 2ndly 1954, Elizabeth Gertrude, who *d* 1988, yr da of late Stephen Cozens, and formerly wife of (i) late Henry Reginald Gambier Colclough (ii) late Capt Michael Norton-Griffiths, RE (*see* Norton-Griffiths, Bt, colls), and (iii) George Paul Minchin Woodward:—
(By 1st *m*) Rosemary Jane, *b* 1942: *m* 1962, Andrew Peter Harold Parsons, Scots Gds, and has had issue, James Alastair Thomas, *b* 1964: *m* 1993, Sally Elizabeth Cunynghame, and has issue living, William Thomas Michael *b* 1996, George Louis James *b* 1999, — Edward Charles William, *b* 1968; *d* 1999, — Annabel Jane, *b* 1969. ——— Angela Mary (9 Napier Av, SW6 3PS), *b* 1945: *m* 1st, 1965, (Luke Edward) Timothy Hue Williams; 2ndly, 1972 (*m diss* 1997), Peter Anthony Charles Mordaunt, and has issue (*see* Mordaunt, Bt).

Issue of late S/Ldr Thomas Edward Hubbard, AuxAF 1939-43, *b* 1911, *d* 1985: *m* 1939 (*m diss* 1974), Bridget, da of late Charles Churchill Branch, OBE:—
Gerald Thomas Guy (19 Felden St, SW6), *b* 1947; *ed* Gordonstoun. ——— Charles Benjamin (89 St Mark's Rd, W10 6JS), *b* 1950; *ed* Gordonstoun. ——— Harriet Anne, *b* 1943: *m* 1972, Michael Frederick Bailey, of Great Dorweeke, Silverton, Exeter EX5 4BZ, and has issue living, Simon Douglas, *b* 1975, — Jessica Mary, *b* 1973.

Grandchildren of late Hon Arthur Gellibrand Hubbard, 4th son of 1st Baron:—
Issue of late Capt Gerald Napier Hubbard, *b* 1882, *d* 1939: *m* (Jan) 1908, Bertha Caroline, who *d* 1969, da of late Rev Edward Southwell Garnier, R of Quidenham, Attleborough:—
Derek, *b* 1920: *ed* Eton; 1939-45 Wars as Capt Sussex Yeo: *m* 1951, Joanne, who *d* 1998, da of late Donald D. Maclean, and has issue living, Rowan, *b* 1954: *m* 1978, Charles E. H. Collier-Wright, of 2 Burcote Rd, SW18 3LQ, and has issue living, Robert Edward *b* 1983, Emma *b* 1981, Frances Alexandra *b* 1986, — (Joanne) Candida, *b* 1957. *Residence* – Vine Cottage, The Street, Effingham, Surrey KT24 5LQ. ——— Susan d'Esterre (12A The Hollies, Peter St, Shepton Mallet, Som), *b* 1914: *m* 1st, 1936 (*m diss* 1951), Edward Ernest Harrison; 2ndly, 1952, Capt Herbert John Tindall Carter, late RHG, who *d* 1980, and has issue living (by 1st *m*) Martin Edward (The Chestnuts, Maugersbury, Glos; Brooks's Club), *b* 1937; *ed* Harrow, and Oriel Coll, Oxford: *m* 1965, Reziya Ahmad, Bar-at-law, and has issue living, Thomas Edward Henry *b* 1969; *ed* Westminster (Queen's Scholar), and Wadham Coll, Oxford (DPhil), Frances Catherine Saida *b* 1966; *ed* Trin Hall, Camb, and at Sch of Oriental and African Studies, Lond: *m* 1992, Kasra Naji, — (by 2nd *m*) Carolyn Rachel, *b* 1955: *m* 1st, 1982 (*m diss* 1986), Alan Laurence Kelly; 2ndly, 1991, John Richard House, of 16 Town St, Shepton Mallet, Som BA4 5BJ, and has issue living (by 1st *m*), John Laurence *b* 1983.

Grandchildren of late Eric Wyndham Hubbard (infra):—
Issue of late Evelyn Raymond WHEATLEY-HUBBARD, OBE, *b* 1921; assumed by deed poll 1949 the additional surname of Wheatley before his patronymic; *d* 1993: *m* 1949, Ann Christobel, OBE (The Dower House, Boyton, Warminster, Wilts), only child of late Col Charles Joshua Hirst Wheatley, of Berkswell Hall, Coventry:—
Thomas Henry, *b* 1952; *ed* Eton: *m* 1979, Caroline M. O., da of Col Hilary Lewis, of Reigny House, Newton Reigny, Penrith, Cumbria, and has issue living, Christopher Raymond, *b* 1982, — Andrew David, *b* 1984. ——— Caroline Sophia, *b* 1950.

Grandson of late Hon Evelyn Hubbard, 5th son of 1st Baron:—
Issue of late Eric Wyndham Hubbard, *b* 1885, *d* 1946: *m* 1918, Edith Sylvia, who *d* 1977, da of Herbert Picton Morris, of 61 Pont St, SW:—
Jasper Picton, *b* 1923; *ed* Eton, and Ch Ch, Oxford: *m* 1951, Ethne Mary, only da of late Henry Charles Frederick Pelham-Clinton (*see* D Newcastle, colls), and has had issue, †John Louis Pelham, *b* 1954; *d* 1996, — Charlotte Anne, *b* 1952, — Rose Mary, *b* 1957. *Residence* – Hammonds, Lewes Heath, Horsmonden, Tonbridge, Kent TN12 8EE.

PREDECESSORS – **(1)** JOHN GELLIBRAND Hubbard, PC, son of late John Hubbard, of Stratford Grove, *b* 1805; sat as MP for Buckingham (*C*) 1859-68, and for City of London 1874-87; cr *Baron Addington*, of Addington, Bucks (peerage of United Kingdom) 1887: *m* 1837, Hon Maria Margaret, who *d* 1896, da of 9th Baron Napier; *d* 1889; *s* by his eldest son **(2)** EGERTON, 2nd Baron; *b* 1842; partner in firms of John Hubbard and Co, Russian Merchants, of London, and Egerton Hubbard and Co, of Petrograd; MP for Buckingham (*C*) 1874-80, and for N, or Buckingham, Div of Buckinghamshire 1886-9: *m* 1880, Mary Adelaide, who *d* 1933, da of Sir Wyndham Spencer Portal, 1st Bt; *d* 1915; *s* by his son **(3)** JOHN GELLIBRAND, OBE, 3rd Baron; *b* 1883; British Custodian of Enemy Property in China 1923-28; *d* 1966; *s* by his brother **(4)** RAYMOND EGERTON, 4th Baron; *b* 1884; *d* 1971; *s* by his kinsman **(5)** JAMES (eldest son of Lt-Col John Francis Hubbard, OBE, eldest son of Hon Cecil John Hubbard, 3rd son of 1st Baron), 5th Baron; *b* 1930: *m* 1961 (*m diss* 1974), Alexandra Patricia, da of late Norman Ford Millar; *d* 1982; *s* by his elder son **(6)** DOMINIC BRYCE, 6th Baron and present peer.

Addington, family name of Viscount Sidmouth.

ADDISON, VISCOUNT (Addison) (Viscount UK 1945)

To serve is to live

WILLIAM MATTHEW WAND ADDISON, 4th Viscount; *b* 13 June 1945; *s* 1992; *ed* King's Sch, Bruton, and Essex Inst of Agric: *m* 1st, 1970 (*m diss* 19—), Joanna Mary, eldest da of late John Ivor Charles Dickinson, of Blyborough Grange, Gainsborough; 2ndly, 1991, Lesley Ann, da of George Colin Mawer, of Sudbeck Lane, Welton, Lincs, and has issue by 1st *m*.

𝕬rms – Per chevron vert and or, in chief a snake embowed head debruised between two garbs of the last and in base an anchor sable. 𝕮rest – In front of two keys in saltire, wards upwards, a sword point downwards or. 𝕾upporters – On either side a Lincolnshire red bull proper, the headstall also proper charged with a sun in splendour or. *Residence* – Stallingborough, Cotterstock, Peterborough PE8 5HH.

SON LIVING (*By 1st marriage*)

Hon PAUL WAND, *b* 18 March 1973; *ed* Rannoch Sch, Perthshire.

DAUGHTERS LIVING (*By 1st marriage*)

Hon Sarah Louise, *b* 1971.
Hon Caroline Amy, *b* 1979.

SISTERS LIVING

Hon Eleanor Brigit, *b* 1938: *m* 1972, Michael Girling. *Residence* – 16 Heatherwood, Midhurst, W Sussex GU29 9LII.
Hon Caroline Ruth, *b* 1942: *m* 1965, John Hollis Wearing, and has issue living, Patrick John, *b* 1969, — Jacalyn Ruth, *b* 1966. *Residence* – 12 Hill St North, Richmond, Nelson, NZ.

DAUGHTERS LIVING OF SECOND VISCOUNT

Hon Jacqueline Faith ADDISON, *b* 1944; has resumed her maiden name: *m* 1966 (*m diss* 1985), Jeremy Warren Payne, PhD, and has issue living, Katy Josephine, *b* 1972, — Christina Meriel, *b* 1975, — Anna Isabella, *b* 1978. *Residence* – 9A Kirk Park, Liberton, Edinburgh EH16 6HZ.
Hon Christine Gray, *b* 1946: *m* 1966, Terry Frederick Tidborough, of 2 Silver St, Willand, Cullompton, Devon.

WIDOW LIVING OF THIRD VISCOUNT

KATHLEEN (*Dowager Viscountess Addison*), only da of late Rt Rev and Rt Hon Bishop John William Charles Wand, KCVO, DD, formerly 110th Bishop of London: *m* 1936, the 3rd Viscount Addison, who *d* 1992. *Residence* – Old Stables, Maplehurst, Horsham, Sussex.

PREDECESSORS – (1) *Rt Hon* Christopher Addison, KG, PC, MD, FRCS, son of late Robert Addison, of Hogsthorpe, Lincolnshire; *b* 1869; appointed Hunterian Professor and Examiner in Anatomy in Camb and London Univs 1901, Parliamentary Sec to Board of Education 1914, Sec to Min of Munitions 1915, Min of Munitions in National Ministry 1916, Min of Reconstruction 1917, Pres of Local Govt Board 1919, first Min of Health 1919 (with seat in the Cabinet from 1919), Min without Portfolio (with a seat in the Cabinet) April 1921 (resigned in July 1921), Parliamentary Sec to Min of Agriculture 1929, Min of Agriculture and Fisheries 1930 (resigned 1931), and Sec of State for Dominion Affairs (afterwards Commonwealth Relations) and Leader of House of Lords 1945; was Lord Privy Seal 1947-51 (also Paymaster-Gen 1948-49) and Lord Pres of the Council March to Oct 1951; elected Leader of Labour Party in House of Lords 1940; Chm of Med Research Council 1948-51; author of *Politics from Within*, etc, and numerous medical works; sat as MP for Hoxton Div of Shoreditch (*L*) 1910-18, for Shoreditch 1918-22, and for Swindon Div of Wilts 1929-31 and 1934-35; cr *Baron Addison*, of Stallingborough, co Lincoln (peerage of United Kingdom) 1937, and *Viscount Addison*, of Stallingborough, co Lincoln (peerage of UK) 1945: *m* 1st, 1902, Isobel, who *d* 1934, da of late Archibald Gray; 2ndly, 1937, Beatrice Dorothy, who *d* 1982, da of late F. Percy Low, of Thames View House, Staines, Middlesex; *d* 1951; *s* by his son (2) CHRISTOPHER, 2nd Viscount; *b* 1904: *m* 1928, Brigit Helen Christine, who *d* 1980, da of Ernest Edwin George Williams, Bar-at-law, of Wimbledon, SW; *d* 1976; *s* by his brother (3) MICHAEL, 3rd Viscount, *b* 1914; Chm Fulham (later Hammersmith) Borough Youth Cttee 1961-68, and Snr Lecturer Polytechnic of Central London Sch of Management Studies 1966-76; 1939-45 War as F/O (Intelligence) RAFVR: *m* 1936, Kathleen, only da of late Rt Rev and Rt Hon Bishop John William Charles Wand, KCVO, DD, late 110th Bishop of London; *d* 1992; *s* by his only son (4) WILLIAM MATTHEW WAND, 4th Viscount and present peer.

ADEANE, BARONY OF (Adeane) (Extinct 1984)

SON LIVING OF LIFE BARON

Hon George Edward, CVO (B4 Albany, Piccadilly, W1), *b* 1939; *ed* Eton and Magdalene Coll, Camb (BA); Bar Middle Temple 1962; a Page of Honour to HM 1954-56; Private Sec to HRH The Prince of Wales 1979-85, and to HRH The Princess of Wales 1984-85; CVO (1985).

Adler, family name of Baroness Jay of Paddington.

ADRIAN, BARONY OF (Adrian) (Extinct 1995)

DAUGHTERS LIVING OF FIRST BARON

Hon Anne Pinsent, *b* 1924: *m* 1945, Prof Richard Darwin Keynes, CBE, FRS, and has had issue, Adrian Maynard, *b* 1946; *ed* Marlborough, and Merton Coll, Oxford: *m* 1971, Rosemary Anne McKinley (who *m* 2ndly, 1976, W. A. Longworth, of Colebrooke, Chelford, Cheshire), da of Dr Robert Young, and *d* 1974, leaving issue, Robert Geoffrey *b* 1974, — Randal Hume, OBE, *b* 1948; *ed* Marlborough, and New Coll, Oxford: *m* 1988, Zelfa, da of Cecil Amin Hourani, and has issue living, Alexander Amin Caspar *b* 1991, Soumaya Anne *b* 1989, — Roger John, *b* 1951; *ed* The Leys Sch, and Trin Coll, Camb: *m* 1st, 1975 (*m diss* 1983), Hilary Jane Ruth, only da of Lt-Col A. J. Lister, of Gooden Court, Harrow-on-the-Hill, Middx; 2ndly, 1993, Yasmina, da of Adel Kamal, of Worcester Rd, Sutton, Surrey, and has issue living (by 1st *m*), Oliver Adrian *b* 1978, Laura Margaret *b* 1979, (by 2nd *m*), Sophie Olivia Leila *b* 1997, — Simon Douglas, *b* 1952; *ed* The Leys Sch, and Trin Coll, Camb; has issue living (by Tethys Carpenter), Henry Francis Neville *b* 1992. *Residences* – 4 Herschel Rd, Cambridge; Primrose Farm, Wiveton, nr Holt, Norfolk.

Hon Jennet Parker, *b* 1927: *m* 1953, Peter Watson Campbell, and has issue living, Richard John, *b* 1956; *ed* Marlborough, Peterhouse, and Magdalene Coll, Camb: *m* 1987, Henrietta, da of John Wayne, and has issue living, Jocelyn Diggory *b* 1990, — Sally Anne, *b* 1958; has issue living, Agnes Jennet *b* 1990, Poppea May *b* 1991, — Emma Jane, *b* 1960. *Residence* – St Anthony in Roseland, Truro TR2 5EY, Cornwall.

WIDOW LIVING OF SECOND BARON

LUCY (*Baroness Adrian*), elder da of Alban Douglas Rendall Caroe, of 15 Campden Hill Sq, W8: *m* 1967, the 2nd Baron Adrian, MD, FRCP, FRS, who *d* 1995, when the title became extinct. *Residence* – Frostlake Cottage, Malting Lane, Cambridge.

Agar, family name of Earl of Normanton.

AHMED, BARON (Ahmed) (Life Baron 1998)

NAZIR AHMED, son of late Haji Sain Mohammed, of Mirpur, Azad Kashmir, Pakistan; *b* 24 April 1957; *ed* Spurley Hey Secondary Sch, Thomas Rotherham Coll, and Sheffield Hallam Univ (BA

1991); Business Development Manager since 1987; Councillor, Metropolitan Borough of Rotherham since 1990; JP Rotherham 1992; *cr Baron Ahmed*, of Rotherham, co S Yorks (Life Baron) 1998; *m* 1974, Sakina Bibi, da of Chaudhary Manga Khan, of Mirpur and Kashmir, and has issue.
Residence – 152 East Bawtry Rd, Rotherham, S Yorks, S60 4LG.

SONS LIVING

Hon Ahmar Nazir, *b* 1979; *ed* Wickersley Sch, and Huddersfield Univ: *m* 1996, Aysha, da of Mohammed Tariq, of 84 Gerard Rd, Rotherham.
Hon Babar Nazir, *b* 1982, *ed* Wickersley Comprehensive Sch.

DAUGHTER LIVING

Hon Maryam Nazir, *b* 1977; *ed* Wickersley Sch, and Sheffield Hallam Univ: *m* 1996, Nabil Tariq, son of Mohammed Tariq, of 84 Gerard Rd, Rotherham.

AILESBURY, MARQUESS OF (Brudenell-Bruce) (Marquess UK 1821, Bt E 1611)

MICHAEL SYDNEY CEDRIC BRUDENELL-BRUCE, 8th Marquess and 14th Baronet; *b* 31 March 1926; *s* 1974; *ed* Eton; late Lt RHG (Res); a Member of London Stock Exchange: *m* 1st, 1952 (*m diss* 1961), Edwina Sylvia, da of Lt-Col Sir (Ernest) Edward de Winton Wills, 4th Bt (*cr* 1904); 2ndly, 1963 (*m diss* 1974), Juliet Adrienne Lethbridge, da of late Hilary Lethbridge Kingsford; 3rdly, 1974 (*m diss* 1992), Caroline Elizabeth, da of Cdr Owen Francis MacTier Wethered, RN (ret), and formerly wife of Simon Romilly, and has issue by 1st and 2nd *m*.

Arms – Quarterly: 1st and 4th or, a saltire and chief gules; on a canton argent, a lion rampant azure, *Bruce*; 2nd and 3rd argent, a chevron gules, between three caps of maintenance, their fronts turned towards the sinister, *Brudenell*. Crest – 1st, a lion statant, tail extended azure; 2nd a seahorse naiant proper. Supporters – Two savages proper wreathed about the temples and loins vert, each holding in his exterior hand a lance, thereon a banner of the arms of Bruce.
Residence – Luton Lye, Savernake Forest, nr Marlborough, Wilts.

SON LIVING (By 1st marriage)

DAVID MICHAEL JAMES (*Earl of Cardigan*) (Savernake Lodge, Savernake Forest, nr Marlborough, Wilts), *b* 12 Nov 1952; *ed* Eton, Rannoch, and RAC Cirencester; 31st Hereditary Warden of Savernake Forest (since 1987): *m* 1980, Rosamond Jane, eldest da of Capt W. R. M. Winkley, of Wyke Champflower Manor, Bruton, Somerset, and has issue:—

SON LIVING— Thomas James (*Viscount Savernake*), *b* 11 Feb 1982; *ed* Radley.
DAUGHTER LIVING— *Lady* Catherine Anna, *b* 1984; *ed* Marlborough.

DAUGHTERS LIVING (By 1st marriage)

Lady Sylvia Davina, *b* 1954: *m* 1987, Peter M. Gould, yst son of late R. C. L. Gould, of Grouville, Jersey. *Residence* – La Pulente, St Brelade, Jersey, CI.
Lady Carina Doune BRUDENELL-BRUCE, *b* 1956; has resumed her maiden name: *m* 1982 (*m diss* 1988), Anthony Le Brun, only son of Basil Le Brun, of Beauchamp, Sion, Jersey. *Residence* – Le Perchoir, rue du Carrefour, Trinity, Jersey, CI.

(By 2nd marriage)

Lady Louise, *b* 1964: *m* 1995, Timothy A. Wilkinson, yst son of John E. Wilkinson, of Beaufort House, Dinnington, Yorks.
Lady Kathryn Juliet, *b* 1965.

HALF-BROTHER LIVING

Lord Charles Adam, *b* 1951; *ed* Eton; late Lieut Royal Hus: *m* 1996, Teresa P. H.-M. CHRIS, only da of G. T. Simons, of Collingbourne Ducis, Wilts.

WIDOW LIVING OF SON OF SEVENTH MARQUESS

Nelida Garcia Otero (*Lady Piers Brudenell-Bruce*) (Cortijo de la Plata, Zahara de los Atunes, Cadiz, Spain), da of Mariano Garcia Villalba, of Madrid: *m* 1958, as his 2nd wife, Lord Chandos Gerald Piers Brudenell-Bruce, who *d* 1980, and has issue (infra).

COLLATERAL BRANCHES LIVING

Issue of late Lord Chandos Gerald Piers Brudenell-Bruce, 2nd son of 7th Marquess, *b* 1929, *d* 1980: *m* 1st, 1951 (*m diss* 1957), Annie, only da of Henry Angelé, of Yamaa-el-Mokra, Tangier; 2ndly, 1958, Nelida Garcia Otero (ante), da of Mariano Garcia Villalba, of Madrid, Spain:—
(By 2nd *m*) Tamara Angela, *b* 1966. ——— Sandra Teresa, *b* 1969.

Grandchildren of late Lord Robert Thomas Brudenell-Bruce, 4th son of 3rd Marquess:—
Issue of late George Lionel Thomas BRUDENELL, *b* 1880, *d* 1962, who assumed by Royal licence 1917, the surname and arms of Brudenell only: *m* 1923, Mary Julia, who *d* 1972, da of Stephen Schilizzi (*see* Ralli Bt, 1952 Edn):—
Edmund Crispin Stephen James George, *b* 1928; *ed* Harrow, and RAC Cirencester; DL Northants 1977: *m* 1955, Hon Marian Cynthia Manningham-Buller, eldest da of 1st Viscount Dilhorne, and has issue living, Robert Edmund (Rose Cottage, Deene, Corby, Northants NN17 3EJ), *b* 1956; *ed* Stanbridge Earls Sch: *m* 1998, Charlotte Louise, only da of Robert Alexander Farquharson, CMG, of Tollard Royal, Salisbury, — Thomas Mervyn (twin) (70 Alderney St, SW1), *b* 1956; *ed* Eton: *m* 1st, 1984, Venetia Jane, who *d* 1993, da of Maj Robert Patricius Chaworth-Musters, of Felley Priory, Jacksdale, Notts; 2ndly, 1996, Mrs Amanda Jane Skiffington, only da of late (Alick) David Yorke Naylor-Leyland, LVO (*see* Naylor-Leyland, Bt, colls), and has issue living (by 1st *m*), Sophia *b* 1985, Victoria *b* 1987, — Anna Maria, *b* 1960; *ed* Benenden. *Seat* – Deene Park, Corby, Northants. *Town Residence* – 10 Lochmore House, Ebury St, SW1.

Issue of late Col Robert Hanbury Brudenell-Bruce, DSO, Norfolk Regt, *b* 1881, *d* 1955: *m* 1st, 1913, Olive Vera, who *d* 1920, da of Charles H. Richardson, of Cedar Hurst, co Down; 2ndly, 1922, Judith Iris, who *d* 1981, da of late Maj Bertram William Arnold Keppel (*see* E Albemarle colls, 1980 Edn):—
(By 2nd *m*) †Chandos Robert Henry, *b* 1923: *m* 1949, Dana Moira Angela (Busted House, Snailwell Stud, Snailwell, New-market, Suffolk), da of Stanhope Joel, of Perots Island, Bermuda, and *d* 1993, leaving issue, Andrew Robert Joel (26 Napier Av, SW6), *b* 1951; *ed* Eton: *m* 1974, Sophie, da of Robert Stuart Malcolm Douglas Inch, of 32 Harmont House, 20 Harley St, W1, and has issue living, Henry Robert Woolf *b* 1976, Alice Marie Antoinette *b* 1974, Christabel Marie-Jeanne *b* 1981, Florence Anne-Marie *b* 1985, — Joanna Dana, *b* 1954: *m* 1st, 1975, Charles FitzRoy, who *d* 1975, eldest son of Hon Charles James FitzRoy (later 6th Baron Southampton); 2ndly, 1977, Paul Farrant, of The Chestnuts, Dunsfold, Surrey, and has issue living (by 2nd *m*), Thomas Robert Jack *b* 1986, Rebecca Dana *b* 1979, Francesca Joanna *b* 1981, — Sara Vivien, *b* 1960: *m* 1985, Walter Hood, of Flint Barn, Snailwell, Newmarket, Suffolk, and has issue living, Talia Joelle *b* 1996.

Issue of late John Charles Brudenell-Bruce, MBE, *b* 1885, *d* 1960: *m* 1st, 1913 (*m diss* 1925), Else, da of Capt C. F. Dreschel, of Copenhagen; 2ndly, 1928, Sigrid Ellen, who *d* 1980, da of Anders Ammentorp, of Copenhagen:—
(By 2nd wife) David John, *b* 1927. ——— Simon Robert (47 Kings Rd, Paihia, NZ), *b* 1928: *m* 1st, 1964, Christine Muriel Heald, of Pokeno; 2ndly, 1986, Nina, da of Andreas Skjoth, of Kolding, Denmark, and has issue living (by 1st *m*), Peter Gregory (25 Alberta St, Pt Chevalier, Auckland, NZ), *b* 1965: *m* 1997, Lynley Smith, and has issue living, Daniel Wallace *b* 1996, Hayden Robert *b* 1998, — Barbara Ann, *b* 1967: *m* 1997, Thomas Charles Combrinck, of 15 Dudley House, West-moreland St, London W1M 7HJ, — Penelope Jane, *b* 1970. ——— Barbara Karen *b* (twin) 1928: *m* 1953, Charles Zeese, of 60-64 69th Av, Ridgewood, NY 11385, USA; 1211 N Miller Rd, Scottsdale, Arizona; and Rt 9N, Springmeyer Hills, Silver Bay, NY, USA, and has issue living, Kevin Bruce (3619 Tallwood Terrace, Fallschurch, Virginia; Rt 9N, Springmeyer Hills, Silver Bay, NY, USA), *b* 1955: *m* 1st, 1976 (*m diss* 1994), Dina Smith; 2ndly, 1995, Kendra, da of Richard Wright, and has issue living (by 1st *m*), Alexander Bruce *b* 1983, Daniel Alfred *b* 1988, — Mark Charles (13313 85th St, Ozone Park, NY, USA), *b* 1957: *m* 1989, Tatiana Taskova, and has issue living, Philip Taskova *b* 1994, Stefan Taskova *b* 1996, Kristina Taskova *b* 1990, — Eve Ellen, *b* 1962: *m* 1988, Todd Stevens, of 1165 Old White Plains Rd, Mamaroneck, NY, USA, and Rt 9N, Springmeyer Hills, Silver Bay, NY, USA, and has issue living, Jeremy Haris *b* 1994, Sara Evelyn *b* 1991. ——— Diana Mary (Little Denmark, Tortola, BVI, W Indies), *b* 1936; has issue living, John Adam, *b* 1963. ——— Arabella Anne (4316 W Oklahoma Av, Tampa, Florida 33616, USA), *b* 1941: *m* 1st, 1962 (*m diss* 1969), Jack Ball, of Ohio; 2ndly, 1972, Morgan J. Gatten, and has had issue (by 1st *m*), Robert Jack, *b* 1968: *m* 1992, Jennifer Lisa French, and *d* 1996, leaving issue, Anthony *b* 1992, — Lesley Anne, *b* 1963: *m* 1990, David L. Smith, and has issue living, Jonathan Matthew David *b* 1993, Robyn Arabella Anne *b* 1996, Suzanne Lesley *b* 1999, — Beth Sigrid, *b* 1965: *m* 1994, Robert Schwartzberg, and has issue living, Ian Gabriel *b* 1997, Alexandra Diana *b* 1995, — (by 2nd *m*), Michael J., *b* 1972; has issue living, Bianca Michelle *b* 1993, Jasmin Rose *b* 1995.

Grandchildren of late John Charles Brudenell-Bruce, MBE (ante):—
Issue of late Marc Hadrian Brudenell-Bruce, *b* 1930, *d* 1965: *m* 1st, 1953 (*m diss* 1957); 2ndly, 1957, Rayna Ellen, da of Ernest Herbert Nicholas Howell, of Tayforth Rd, Westmere, Wanganui, NZ:—
(By 2nd *m*) Marc Raymond Christopher (38 Intrepid Drive, Mermaid Waters, Gold Coast, Qld, Australia), *b* 1962. ——— Keren Suzanne (1 Wainwright Av, Mt Roskill, Auckland, NZ), *b* 1958: *m* 1983, — Kempster, and has issue living, Fiona Rochelle, *b* 1981, — Jade Michelle, *b* 1984.

PREDECESSORS – (1) CHARLES Bruce, 4th Earl of Elgin, 3rd Earl of Ailesbury, and 6th Lord Kinloss; was the last male descendant of that branch of the Bruce family which settled in England circa 1603. He selected as his heir his nephew, Hon Thomas Brudenell, 4th son of 3rd Earl of Cardigan by Elizabeth Bruce; cr *Baron Bruce*, of Tottenham (peerage of Great Britain) 1746, with remainder to Hon Thomas Brudenell (ante); *d* 1747 without surviving male issue, when the Earldom of Ailesbury became ext, the Earldom of Elgin reverted to the 9th Earl of Kincardine, the Lordship of Kinloss became abeyant, and the Barony of Bruce devolved upon his nephew (ante) (2) THOMAS, 2nd Baron; inherited also the Wardenship of Savernake Forest in Wilts (an ancient office which became hereditary in the Esturmy family (1066-1427), passed thence into the Seymour family (see D Somerset)) and so in 1676 to the Bruces; he assumed the additional name and arms of Bruce; cr *Earl of Ailesbury* (peerage of Great Britain) 1776; *d* 1814; *s* by his son (3) CHARLES, KT, 2nd Earl; cr *Viscount Savernake, Earl Bruce*, and *Marquess of Ailesbury* (peerage of United Kingdom) 1821: *m* 1st, 1793, Hon Henrietta Maria Hill, who *d* 1831, da of 1st Baron Berwick; 2ndly, 1833, Maria Elizabeth, who *d* 1893, da of Hon Charles Tollemache; *d* 1856; *s* by his elder son (4) GEORGE WILLIAM FREDERICK, KG, 2nd Marquess, *b* 1804; summoned to House of Lords in his father's Barony of Bruce 1839; was Lord-Lieut of Wilts and Master of the Horse 1868-74; *s* his kinsman, the 7th Earl of Cardigan, 1868 (see infra*): *m* 1837, Lady Mary Caroline Herbert, who *d* 1892, da of 11th Earl of Pembroke; *d* 6 Jan 1878; *s* by his brother (5) ERNEST AUGUSTUS CHARLES, PC, 3rd Marquess; was Lord-Lieut of Berks, MP for Marlborough (C) 1832-78, and Vice-Chamberlain to HM 1841-6, and 1852-8: *m* 1834, Hon Louisa Elizabeth Horsley-Beresford, who *d* 1891, da of 2nd Baron Decies; *d* 1886; *s* by his grandson (6) GEORGE WILLIAM THOMAS (son of George John Brudenell-Bruce, who *d* 1868, eldest son of 3rd Marquess), 4th Marquess, *b* 1863: *m* 1884, Dorothy Julia, who *d* 1917, da of Thomas Haseley, of Brighton; *d* 1894; *s* by his uncle (7) HENRY AUGUSTUS, 5th Marquess, *b* 1842; MP for N W, or Chippenham, Div of Wiltshire (C) 1886-92: *m* 1870, Georgiana Sophia Maria, who *d* 1902, da of George Henry Pinckney, formerly of Tawstock Court, Barnstaple: *d* 1911: *s* by his son (8) GEORGE WILLIAM JAMES CHANDOS, DSO, TD, 6th Marquess; *b* 1873; late 3rd Batn Argyll and Sutherland Highlanders, R Wilts Yeo, Middlesex Yeo, Wilts. Regt, RASC and RFA (TA); S Africa 1899-1900 with Army Transports as DAAG (DSO), European War 1915-19 with Guards Div Train: *m* 1st 1903, Caroline Sydney Anne, who *d* 1941, da of late John Madden; 2ndly, 1945, Mabel Irene, who *d* 1954, da of late John Samuel Lindsay, of Wrexham; 3rdly, 1955, Alice Maude Emily, who *d* 1960, da of late Capt John Forbes Pinhey, and widow of (1) Col John Henry Arthur Boyce, (2) Col Francis Byrne Johnson, and (3) Col Rowland Money, OBE; *d* 1961; *s* by his son (9) CHANDOS SYDNEY CEDRIC, 7th Marquess; *b* 1904: *m* 1st, 1924, Joan Houlton, who *d* 1937, da of Stephen Salter, of Pondwell, Ryde, I of Wight; 2ndly, 1944 (*m diss* 1948) Joyce Frances, da of Charles Warwick-Evans, and formerly wife of Peter Quennell; 3rdly, 1950, Jean Frances Margaret, who *d* 1999, da of late John Addison Wilson, of Bodlicote, Oxon, and widow of Richard Williamson, MBE; *d* 1974; *s* by his elder son (10) MICHAEL SYDNEY CEDRIC, 8th Marquess and present peer; also Earl of Cardigan, Earl Bruce, Viscount Savernake, Baron Brudenell, and Baron Bruce.

*(1) *Sir* THOMAS Brudenell, a zealous supporter of the royal cause during the Civil War, suffered long imprisonment in the Tower; cr a *Baronet* 1611, *Baron Brudenell* (peerage of England) 1628, and *Earl of Cardigan* (peerage of England) 1661; *d* 1663; *s* by his eldest son (2) ROBERT, 2nd Earl; *d* 1703: *s* by his grandson (3) GEORGE, 3rd Earl; Master of the Buckhounds to Queen Anne; *d* 1732; *s* by his elder son (4) GEORGE, KG, 4th Earl; Gov to the Prince of Wales and Prince Frederick; cr *Marquess of Monthermer* and *Duke of Montagu* (peerage of Great Britain) 1776, and *Baron Montagu*, of Boughton (peerage of Great Britain) 1786, with remainder to his grandson Henry James, 2nd son of 3rd Duke of Buccleuch; *d* 1790 without surviving male issue, when the Marquessate and Dukedom became extinct, the Barony passed to his grandson (ante), and the Earldom devolved upon his brother (5) JAMES, 5th Earl; *dsp* 1811; *s* by his nephew (6) ROBERT, 6th Earl, son of Hon Robert, 3rd son of 3rd Earl; *d* 1837, *s* by his son (7) JAMES THOMAS, KCB, a Lieut-Gen in the Army and Col 11th Hussars; served with distinction in the Crimea; *dsp* 1868; *s* by his cousin (8) GEORGE WILLIAM FREDERICK, 2nd Marquess of Ailesbury (ante).

AILSA, MARQUESS OF (Kennedy) (Marquess UK 1831)

Consider the end

ARCHIBALD ANGUS CHARLES KENNEDY, 8th Marquess; *b* 13 Sept 1956; *s* 1994: *m* 1979 (*m diss* 1989), Dawn Leslie Anne, only da of David A. Keen, of 64 Rue Emeriau, Paris, and has issue.

Arms – Argent, a chevron gules, between three cross crosslets fitchée sable, the whole within a double tressure flory counterflory of the second. **Crest** – A dolphin naiant, proper. **Supporters** – Two swans, wings inverted proper, beaked and membered gules.
Seat – Cassillis, Maybole, Ayrshire. *Club* – New (Edinburgh).

DAUGHTERS LIVING

Lady Rosemary Margaret, *b* 1980.
Lady Alicia-Jane Lesley, *b* 1981.

BROTHER LIVING

Lord DAVID THOMAS, *b* 3 July 1958; *ed* Strathallan Sch, and Berks Agric Coll: *m* 1991, Anne, da of Bernard Kelly, of Warwick, and has issue living, Archibald David, *b* 7 Sept 1995, — Katherine Jean, *b* 1993. *Residence* – Morriston Farm, Maidens, Maybole, Ayrshire KA19 8LB.

SISTER LIVING

Lady Elizabeth Helen, *b* 1955: *m* 1976, Rev Norman Walker Drummond, MA, BD, Chap to HM in Scotland, formerly Headmaster Loretto Sch and BBC Nat Governor for Scotland, and has issue living, Andrew, *b* 1977, — Christian, *b* 1986, — Ruaraidh, *b* 1993, — Margaret, *b* 1980, — Marie Clare, *b* 1981. *Residence* – Ach Nan Eun, Ellishader, Staffin, Isle of Skye.

WIDOW LIVING OF SEVENTH MARQUESS

MARY (*Marchioness of Ailsa*), da of late John Burn, of Amble, Northumberland: *m* 1954, Lt-Col the 7th Marquess, OBE, who *d* 1994. *Residence* – Cassillis, Maybole, Ayrshire.

COLLATERAL BRANCHES LIVING

Grandchildren of late John Gilbert Kennedy, eldest son of late Lord Gilbert Kennedy, 5th son of late Archibald, Earl of Cassillis, elder son of 12th Earl of Cassillis (afterwards 1st Marquess):—
Issue of late Capt Nigel Augustus Kennedy, *b* 1886, *d* 1957: *m* 1st, 1917 (*m diss* 1944), Gertrude Vera, who *d* 1990, da of late Brig-Gen Lionel Godolphin Brooke, CB (V Brookeborough, colls); 2ndly, 1946, Dorothy Mary, who *d* 1962, da of William Henry Langley, of 1358 Victoria Av, Victoria, BC, Canada, and widow of Lt-Col Richard Clive Cooper, Canadian Inf:—
(By 1st *m*) Ian Michael Godfrey, *b* 1921; European War 1941 as Pilot Officer RAF (invalided): *m* 1960, Josephine Helen, da of John Leslie Price, of Warham Court, Breinton, Hereford, and has issue living, Angus Michael David, *b* 1962; *ed* Malvern, and Charing Cross Hosp Med Sch; MRCP, MD 1995: *m* 1996, Fiona, MB, BS, da of James R. Alexander, of Leigh-on-Sea, Essex, and has issue living, Louis Michael James *b* 1998, — Virginia Anne Nicola, *b* 1964. *Residence* – The Camp Farm, Caynham, nr Ludlow, Shropshire. —— Lonia Hersey Joy, *b* 1924: *m* 1944 (*m diss* 1966), Donald MacLean, late Lt RCN, and has issue living, John Kennedy, *b* 1946: *m* 1983, Rosemary, yr da of F. P. Hillier, of Godalming, Surrey, — Alan Michael, *b* 1948: *m* 1971, Sandra, da of E. McDonald, of Vancouver, BC, and has issue living, Sarah Kennedy *b* 1978: *m* 1998, Gregory Spronken (and has issue living, Abigail Robin Kennedy *b* 1998), Gillian Anne *b* 1983, — Brian William, *b* 1950. *Residence* – 11371 Trumpeter Drive, Richmond, BC, Canada V7E 3X2.

Granddaughters of late Sir John Gordon Kennedy, KCMG, eldest son of late John Kennedy (infra):—
Issue of late Capt Aubrey Leo Kennedy, MC, *b* 1885, *d* 1965: *m* 1921, Sylvia Dorothy, who *d* 1968, da of late Arthur Herbert Meysey-Thompson (*see* Meysey-Thompson, Bt, colls, 1968 Edn):—
Elizabeth Dorothy (4 Gordon Place, W8), *b* 1922: *m* 1st, 1945 (*m diss* 1958), Charles Russell Scarr; 2ndly, 1960, her cousin, Jeremy John Le Mesurier (*see* Meysey-Thompson, Bt colls, 1972-73 Edn), and has had issue (by 1st *m*) Aubrey Mark Kennedy MEYSEY-THOMPSON (Spellow Hill, Knaresborough, Yorks), *b* 1949; assumed by deed poll 1978 the surname of Meysey-Thompson; Capt RGJ; TV prod: *m* 1975, Catharine Diana Jane Herdman-Newton, and *d* 1987, leaving issue, James Leo Charles *b* 1979, Emma Catherine *b* 1978, — Caroline Sarah (64 Hatfield Rd, Chiswick, W4), *b* 1951. —— Horatia Clare, *b* 1926: *m* 1969, Brian Huleatt Heddy, HM Dip Ser (ret), of Wynyards, Winsham, Chard, Somerset. —— Diana Helen Marjorie, *b* 1929.

(In remainder to Earldom of Cassillis)

Grandchildren of Edward Briggs Kennedy, 3rd son of John Kennedy (infra):—
Issue of late Capt Edward Coverley Kennedy, RN; *b* 1879, *ka* 1939: *m* 1918, Rosalind Margaret Innes, who *d* 1977, da of Sir Ludovic James Grant, 11th Bt:—
Sir Ludovic Henry Coverley, *b* 1919; *ed* Eton, and at Oxford Univ; is a broadcaster, writer, and lecturer; author of *On My Way to The Club* (1989); European War 1939-45 as Lieut RNVR; Ktd 1994: *m* 1950, Moira Shearer, the writer and former ballerina, da of late Harold Charles King, and has issue living, Alastair Charles Coverley, *b* 1963, — Ailsa Margaret, *b* 1952, — Rachel Katherine, *b* 1956: *m* 1988, William D'Arcy Hall, son of Prof Edward Thomas Hall, CBE, of Oxford, and has issue living, India Rose *b* 1989, Eleanor Louise *b* 1991, — Fiona Jane, *b* 1961. —— Morar Margaret, *b* 1926: *m* 1st, 1948 (*m diss* 1954), John Hamish Orr-Ewing; 2ndly, 1954, Royce Thomas Carlisle Ryton, of 10 Talbot Lodge, West End Lane, Esher, Surrey KT10 8NE, and has had issue (by 1st *m*), Roderick Coverley Hugh, *b* 1951: *m* 1984, Elisabeth Claire, only da of late Torolf Lyth, of 74 Princes House, Kensington Park Rd, W11, — Margaret, *b* 1950; *d* 1961, — (by 2nd *m*) Charlotte Susan, *b* 1955. —— Katherine, *b* 1927: *m* 1947, Ion Melville Calvocoressi, MBE, MC, late Maj Scots Gds (High Sheriff of Kent 1978), and has issue living, James Melville Ion, *b* 1948: *m* 1971, Richenda Victoria Hanson, eldest da of late Peter Blandy, and has issue living, Matthew James *b* 1973, Rupert Benedict *b* 1976, Christopher John *b* 1988, — Richard Edward Ion, *b* 1951: *m* 1976, Francesca, only da of late David Temple Roberts, and has issue living, Thomas David *b* 1977, Natalia Katherine *b* 1980, Hermione Beatrice *b* 1984, — Andrew Matthew Ion, *b* 1953, — Iona Rosalind, *b* 1957: *m* 1980, Richard James Priestley, and has issue (*see* Pollock, Bt, colls). *Residence* – Court Lodge, Westerham, Kent.

Granddaughter of Gilbert George Kennedy, 4th and yst son of John Kennedy, only son of Hon Robert Kennedy, 3rd son of 11th Earl of Cassillis:—
Issue of late Judge John de Navarre Kennedy, OBE, *b* 1888, *d* 1979: *m* 1st, 1914, Elsie Margaret, who *d* 1969, da of late Edwin Charles Pinks, of Lindsell, Essex; 2ndly, 1970, Marjorie Helen Troop (707 Weller St, Peterborough, Ontario, Canada K9J 4X2), da of late Albert Morton, of Dudley, Worcs:—
(By 1st *m*) Anne Macomb, *b* 1930: *m* 1953, Frank Edward Dudas, and has issue living, Edward Tibor, *b* 1959, — Linda Julianna Kennedy, *b* 1956, — Yone Anne Pinks, *b* 1962.

PREDECESSORS – (1) Sir GILBERT Kennedy, KB, cr *Lord Kennedy* (peerage of Scotland) 1452: was one of the six Regents of the Kingdom during the minority of James III; *s* by his son (2) JOHN, 2nd Lord; *d* 1508; *s* by his son (3) DAVID, PC, 3rd Lord; cr *Earl of Cassillis* 1509; *k* at Battle of Flodden 1513; *s* by his son (4) GILBERT, 2nd Earl; assassinated 1527 by Sir Hugh Campbell, of Loudon, Sheriff of Ayr, and a supporter of the Angus faction, from whom he had unsuccessfully attempted to rescue James V the previous year; *s* by his son (5) GILBERT, 3rd Earl, Lord High Treasurer of Scotland; *d* 1558; *s* by his son (6) GILBERT, 4th Earl; *d* 1576; *s* by his son (7) GILBERT, 5th Earl, Lord Treasurer of Scotland; *d* 1615; *s* by his nephew (8) JOHN, 6th Earl; *s* by his son (9) JOHN, 7th Earl; *d* 1701; *s* by his grandson (10) JOHN, 8th Earl; *dsp*, 1759, and in 1762 was by a resolution of House of Lords *s* by his kinsman (11) Sir THOMAS Kennedy, 4th Bt (cr 1682), of Culzean, 9th Earl; *d* unmarried 1775; *s* by his brother (12) DAVID, 10th Earl; *dsp*, 1792, when the Baronetcy became ext, and the peerage titles descended to the great-great-grandson of Hon Thomas, 2nd son of 3rd Earl (13) ARCHIBALD, 11th Earl, Capt RN; *d* 1794; *s* by his son (14) ARCHIBALD, KT, FRS, 12th Earl; cr *Baron Ailsa* (peerage of United Kingdom) 1806, and *Marquess of Ailsa* (peerage of United Kingdom) 1831; *d* 1846; *s* by his grandson (15) ARCHIBALD, KT, 2nd Marquess, *b* 1816; Lord-Lieut of Ayrshire: *m* 1846, Julia, who *d* 1899, da of Sir Richard Mounteney Jephson, 1st Bt; *d* 1870; *s* by his son (16) ARCHIBALD, 3rd Marquess, *b* 1847; Lord-Lieut of Ayrshire: *m* 1st, 1871, Hon Evelyn Stuart, who *d* 1888, 3rd da of 12th Baron Blantyre; 2ndly, 1891, Isabella, who *d* 1945, da of late

Hugh McMaster, of Kausani, N-W Provinces, India; *d* 1938; *s* by his son **(17)** ARCHIBALD, 4th Marquess, *b* 1872: *m* 1903, Frances Emily, who *d* 1949, da of Sir Mark John MacTaggart-Stewart, 1st Bt; *d* 1943; *s* by his brother **(18)** CHARLES, 5th Marquess, *b* 1875; Capt Ayrshire Yeo, and Lieut 3rd Batn, RSF: *m* 1st, 1925, Constance Barbara, who *d* 1931, da of late Edward Clark of Avishays, Chard, and widow of Adm Sir John Kennedy Erskine Baird, KCB; 2ndly, 1933, Helen Ethel, MBE, who *d* 1959, only da of late James McDouall, JP, DL, of Logan, and widow of Major Richard John Cunninghame, MC, of Hensol, Kirkcudbrightshire, *d* 1956; *s* by his brother **(19)** ANGUS, 6th Marquess; *b* 1882; formerly Capt RAF: *m* 1922; (Gertrude) Millicent, who *d* 1957, da of Gervas Weir Cooper, of Wordwell Hall, Bury St Edmunds; *d* 1957; *s* by his son **(20)** ARCHIBALD DAVID, OBE, 7th Marquess, *b* 1925; Lieut Scots Guards, Lt-Col RSF (TA), DL Ayrshire; Chm Anglo-Somali Soc: *m* 1954, Mary, da of late John Burn, of Amble, Northumberland; *d* 1994; *s* by his elder son **(21)** ARCHIBALD ANGUS CHARLES, 8th Marquess and present peer; also Earl of Cassillis, Lord Kennedy, and Baron Ailsa.

AILWYN, BARONY OF (Fellowes) (Extinct 1988)

ADOPTED STEPDAUGHTER LIVING OF FOURTH BARON

Joan, da of Charles William Cudemore; *b* 1921; legally assumed surname of Fellowes in lieu of her patronymic upon adoption 1938: *m* 1942, Geoffrey Homer, FRCS, and has issue living, Garth, *b* 1944: *m* 1974, Penelope Saunders, and has issue, one son and one da, — Keith, *b* 1947: *m* 1981, Dean Garrison, and has issue, two sons, — Bruce, *b* 1951. *Residence* – 3710 Cadboro Bay Rd, Victoria, BC V8P 5E1, Canada.

AIREDALE, BARONY OF (Kitson) (Extinct 1996)

DAUGHTER LIVING OF THIRD BARON

Hon Verona Vandeleur, OBE, TD, *b* 1920; Maj WRAC (TA); formerly Chm, Riding for the Disable Assocn, OBE (Civil) 1982, MBE (Mil) 1960. *Residence* – Pasture House, North Luffenham, Oakham, Leicestershire.

AIREY OF ABINGDON, BARONY OF (Airey) (Extinct 1992)

SONS AND DAUGHTER OF LIFE BARONESS (see Neave, Bt, colls)

AIRLIE, EARL OF (Ogilvy) (Earl S 1639)

To the end

DAVID GEORGE COKE PATRICK OGILVY, KT, GCVO, PC, 13th Earl, *b* 17 May 1926; *s* 1968; *ed* Eton; Capt Scots Gds (Res); DL Angus 1964, Lord Lieut Tayside Region, District of Angus, since 1989, JP; Lord Chamberlain HM's Household, and Chancellor Royal Victorian Order, 1984-97, since when a Permanent Lord in Waiting to HM; 2nd Bn Germany 1945, ADC to C-in-C, and High Commr Austria 1947-48; Chm, Schröders Ltd, Ashdown Investment Trust Ltd, Dep Chm, Gen Accident Fire and Life Assurance Corpn, Dir J Henry Schröder Wagg & Co Ltd, and other cos; Pres The Scout Assocn of Scotland; Hon LLD Dundee 1990; CStJ 1981; 1939-45 War; Malaya 1948-50; *cr* PC 1984, GCVO 1984, KT 1985; received Royal Victorian Chain 1997: *m* 1952, Virginia Fortune, DCVO, da of John Barry Ryan, of Moorland Farm, Newport, Rhode Island, USA, and has issue.

Arms – Argent, a lion passant guardant gules crowned with an imperial crown and collared with an open one proper. **Crest** – A lady from the waist upwards affrontée azure holding a portcullis gules. **Supporters** – Two bulls sable, armed and unguled vert, and gored with a garland of flowers.
Seats – Cortachy Castle, and Airlie Castle, Kirriemuir, Angus. *Town Residence* – 5 Swan Walk, SW3.

SONS LIVING

DAVID JOHN (*Lord Ogilvy*), *b* 9 March 1958; *ed* Eton, and Ch Ch, Oxford (MA); a Page of Honour to HM 1971-72: *m* 1st, 1981 (*m diss* 1990), Hon Geraldine Theodora Mary Gabriel Harmsworth, eldest da of 3rd Viscount Rothermere; 2ndly, 1991, Tarka, da of John Kings, of Austin, Texas, USA, and has issue by 1st and 2nd *m*:—

> SONS LIVING (by 2nd m) — *Hon* David Huxley (*Master of Ogilvy*), *b* 11 Dec 1991, — *Hon* Joseph Skene, *b* 1995, — *Hon* Michael Moir, *b* 1997.
> DAUGHTER LIVING (by 1st m) — *Hon* Augusta, *b* 1981.

Residence – Airlie Castle, Kirriemuir, Angus.

Hon Bruce Patrick Mark, *b* 1959.

Hon Patrick Alexander, *b* 1971.

DAUGHTERS LIVING

Lady Doune Mabell, *b* 1953: *m* 1977 (*m diss* 1995), Hereward Charles Wake, only son of Maj Sir Hereward Wake, 14th Bt, and has had issue (see that family).

Lady Jane Fortune Margaret, *b* 1955: *m* 1980, Francois Nairac, son of Paul Nairac, of Vacoas, Mauritius, and has issue living, Jessica Doune, *b* 1985, — Annabel Lydia, *b* 1988.

Lady Elizabeth Clementine, *b* 1965: *m* 1994, Jonathan Patrick Fortune Baring, and has issue (see B Northbrook, colls).

BROTHERS LIVING

Rt Hon Sir Angus James Bruce, KCVO, *b* 1928; *ed* Eton, and at Trin Coll, Oxford; Scots Gds 1946-48, Member HM Body Guard for Scotland (Royal Company of Archers); Pres Imperial Cancer Research Fund since 1964, The Carr-Gomm Soc since 1983, and Youth Clubs UK (formerly Nat Assocn of Youth Clubs) 1969-89 (Chm 1964-69), Chm of Council Prince's Youth Business Trust since 1986; Patron Arthritis Care (formerly British Rheumatism & Arthritis Assocn) since 1978 (Chm 1963-69, Pres 1969-78), and Scottish Wildlife Trust since 1974 (Pres 1969-74); Vice Pres Friends of the Elderly & Gentlefolks' Help since 1969 (Treas 1952-63, Chm 1963-69), Vice Patron Nat Children's Homes since 1986; Member Gov Council of SPCK since 1984, and of Council of Business in the Community since 1984; Trustee Leeds Castle Foundn since 1975, and GB-Sasakawa Foundation since 1985, etc; Dir various public cos; Grand Officer of Order of the Lion of Finland, and of Order of the Oak Crown of Luxembourg, KCVO 1989, PC 1997: *m* 1963, HRH Princess Alexandra Helen Elizabeth Olga Christabel, GCVO, da of HRH 1st Duke of Kent (see ROYAL FAMILY), and has issue living, James Robert Bruce, *b* 1964: *m* 1988, Julia, eldest da of Charles Frederick Melville Rawlinson, of Arkesden, Essex, and has issue living, Alexander Charles *b* 1996, Flora Alexandra *b* 1994, — Marina Victoria Alexandra, *b* 1966: *m* 1990 (*m diss* 1997), Paul Julian Mowatt, and has issue living, Christian Alexander *b* 1993, Zenouska May *b* 1990. *Residence* – Thatched House Lodge, Richmond Park, Surrey. *Club* – White's.

Hon James Donald Diarmid, *b* 1934; *ed* Eton; Scots Gds 1952-54, Member HM Body Guard for Scotland (Royal Company of Archers); a Partner, Rowe & Pitman 1964-86, Chm Rowan Investment Managers 1972-86, Chm Mercury Rowan Mullens, Vice-Chm Mercury Asset Management Ltd, Chief Exec Foreign & Colonial, and Dir of other Investment Cos; a Page of Honour to HM 1947-51: *m* 1st, 1959, Magdalen June Ruth, da of late Robert Ducas (see B Mowbray, colls); 2ndly, 1980, Lady Caroline Child-Villiers, da of 9th Earl of Jersey, formerly wife of (i) Viscount Melgund (later 6th Earl of Minto), and (ii) Hon John Douglas Stuart, son of 1st Viscount Stuart of Findhorn, and has issue living (by 1st *m*), Shamus Diarmid Ducas, *b* 1966, — Diarmid James Ducas, *b* 1970, — Laura Jane, *b* 1960: *m* 1990, Philippe G. Goffin, yr son of Jean Goffin, of Brussels, and has issue living, Sebastian *b* 1992, Orlando Benjamin Alberic *b* 1998, Charlotte *b* 1994, — Emma Louise, *b* 1962: *m* 1999, Jonathan Guy Cubitt (see B Ashcombe, colls). *Residence* – Sedgebrook Manor, Sedgebrook, Grantham, Lincs NG32 2EU. *Club* – White's.

SISTERS LIVING

Lady Victoria Jean Marjorie Mabell (*Baroness Lloyd*), *b* 1918: *m* 1942, 2nd Baron Lloyd, MBE, who *d* 1985. *Residence* – Clouds Hill, Offley, Hitchin, Herts.

Lady Margaret Isla Marion, *b* 1920; formerly in WRNS: *m* 1946, Capt Sir Iain Mark Tennant, KT, DL, Scots Gds (*see* B Glenconner, colls). *Residence* – Lochnabo House, Elgin, Morayshire.

PREDECESSORS – (1) *Sir* JAMES Ogilvy, KB; Ambassador from Scotland to Denmark 1491, was in that year cr *Lord Ogilvy of Airlie* (peerage of Scotland); *d* 1504; *s* by his eldest son (2) JOHN, 2nd Lord; he was *s* by his eldest son (3) JAMES, 3rd Lord; *s* by his eldest son (4) JAMES, 4th Lord, an Extraor Lord of Session; *d* 1554; *s* by his grandson (5) JAMES, 5th Lord; *d* 1606; *s* by his eldest son (6) JAMES, 6th Lord; *d* 1617; *s* by his son (7) JAMES, 7th Lord, a zealous partisan of Charles I; cr *Lord Ogilvy of Alyth and Lintrathen*, and *Earl of Airlie* (peerage of Scotland) 1639; *s* by his eldest son (8) JAMES, PC, 2nd Earl; being taken prisoner at the battle of Philiphaugh 1644, he was sentenced to death by the Parliament at St Andrew's, 26 Nov 1645, but escaped in his sister's clothes the night before his intended execution; pardoned by Act of Parliament 1649, and at the Restoration was sworn of the Privy Council; *s* by his son (9) DAVID, 3rd Earl; *d* 1717; his eldest son (10) JAMES, 4th Earl, assisted in the Earl of Mar's rising 1715, was attainted by Act of Parliament during his father's life, and afterwards pardoned; *d* 1731; *s* by his brother (11) JOHN, 5th Earl; *d* 1761; *s* by his son (12) DAVID, 6th Earl; he joined the Chevalier at Edinburgh 1745 at the head of 600 men, and was attainted by Act of Parliament; after the battle of Culloden he escaped to France where he commanded a Regiment of Foot, and attained the rank of Lt-Gen; in 1778 he received a pardon under the Great Seal; *d* 1803; *s* by his son (13) DAVID, 7th Earl; *d* unmarried; *s* by his uncle (14) WALTER, 8th Earl; *d* 1819; *s* by his eldest son (15) DAVID, 9th Earl, who had his honours confirmed by Act of Parliament 1826; was Lord-Lieut of Forfarshire and a Scottish Representative Peer; *d* 1849; *s* by his son (16) DAVID GRAHAM DRUMMOND, KT, 10th Earl, *b* 1826; a Representative Peer for Scotland, and Lord High Commr to Church of Scotland 1872-3: *m* 1851, Hon Henrietta Blanche Stanley, who *d* 1921, da of 2nd Baron Stanley of Alderley; *d* 25 Sept 1881; *s* by his eldest son (17) DAVID STANLEY WILLIAM, 11th Earl; *b* 1856: *m* 1886, Lady Mabell Frances Elizabeth Gore, GCVO, OBE, who *d* 1956, da of 5th Earl of Arran; *k* during S African War 1900; *s* by his son (18) DAVID LYULPH GORE WOLSELEY, KT, GCVO, MC, 12th Earl; *b* 1893; Col Scots Guards; Repres Peer for Scotland 1922-63; Lord-in-Waiting to HM 1926-29; Lord Chamberlain to HM Queen Elizabeth the Queen Mother 1937-65: *m* 1917, Lady Alexandra Marie Bridget Coke, who *d* 1984, da of 3rd Earl of Leicester; *d* 1968; *s* by his eldest son (19) DAVID GEORGE COKE PATRICK, 13th Earl and present peer; also Lord Ogilvy of Airlie, and Lord Ogilvy of Alyth and Lintrathen.

ALANBROOKE, VISCOUNT (Brooke) (Viscount UK 1946)

Glory the end

ALAN VICTOR HAROLD BROOKE, 3rd Viscount; *b* 24 Nov 1932; *s* 1972; *ed* Harrow; Capt (ret) RA.

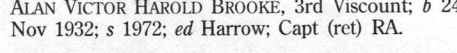

Arms – Or, a cross engrailed per pale gules and sable, in the first quarter a crescent of the second. **Crest** – A brock, proper. **Supporters** – On either side an officer of the Royal Horse Artillery in full dress proper supporting with the exterior hand an escutcheon azure charged with seven barrulets wavy argent surmounted by a salmon rising gules. *Residence* – Ferney Close, Hartley Wintney, Hants.

HALF-SISTER LIVING

Hon Rosemary, *b* 1918: *m* 1945, Capt Ronald Alastair Macdonald, RA, of Bottom Farm, Berkhamsted, Herts, and has issue living, Alastair Alan Graham, *b* 1947, — Ian Ronald, *b* 1952, — Janey Rosemary, *b* 1949.

PREDECESSORS – (1) *Field Marshal Sir* ALAN FRANCIS Brooke, KG, GCB, OM, GCVO, DSO, 6th son of Sir Victor Alexander Brooke, 3rd Bt (cr 1822) (*see* V Brookeborough); *b* 1883; late RA; Inspector of RA 1935-6, Dir of Mil Training War Office 1936-7, GOC, Mobile Div 1937-8, C-in-C, AA Command (TA) 1938-9, GOC-in-C, S Command 1939, GOC 2nd Corps 1939-40, C-in-C Home Forces 1940-41, CIGS 1941-6; Col Comdt RA 1939-57, RHA 1940-57, and Hon Artillery Co 1946-54, Master Gunner, St James's Park 1946-56, and Constable of Tower of London 1950-55; Lord High Constable of England at Coronation of HM Queen Elizabeth II: *m* 1st, 1914, Jane Mary, who *d* 1925, da of late Col John Mervyn Carleton Richardson; 2ndly, 1929, Benita Blanche, who *d* 1968, da of Sir Harold Pelly, 3rd Bt, and widow of Sir Thomas Evan Keith Lees, 2nd Bt (cr 1897); *d* 1963; *s* by his eldest son (2) THOMAS, 2nd Viscount; *b* 1920: *d* 1972; *s* by his half-brother (3) ALAN VICTOR HAROLD, 3rd Viscount and present peer.

ALBEMARLE, EARL OF (Keppel) (Earl E 1696)

Do not yield to evil

RUFUS ARNOLD ALEXIS KEPPEL, 10th Earl; *b* 16 July 1965; *s* 1979; *ed* St Christopher Sch, Letchworth, Chelsea Sch of Art, and Central Sch of Art (BA).

Arms – Gules, three escallops argent. **Crest** – Out of a ducal coronet or, a swan's head and neck argent. **Supporters** – Two lions ducally crowned or. *Residence* – 20A Pembroke Sq, W8 6PA.

HALF SISTERS LIVING (*Raised to the rank of an Earl's daughters,* 1980)

(*Daughters of late Lt-Col Viscount Bury, by his 1st wife Lady Mairi Elizabeth Vane-Tempest-Stewart, da of 7th Marquess of Londonderry*)

Lady Elizabeth Mairi (27 St Olaf's Rd, SW6 7DL), *b* 1941: *m* 1st, 1962 (*m diss* 1976), Alastair Michael Hyde Villiers (*see* D Roxburghe, 1968 Edn); 2ndly, 1980 (*m diss* 1988), 7th Baron Sudeley, and has issue living (by 1st *m*), Charles Alastair Hyde (Milton House, Milton, by Dumbarton G82 2TU), *b* 1963: *m* 1994, Emma M. J., da of J. B. W. Goodall, and has issue living, Clarissa Elizabeth Mairi *b* 1995, — Charlotte Mairi, *b* 1965: *m* 1995, Rupert E. Gather, son of late Antony Gather, of Sandybrook Hall, Ashbourne, Derbys, and of Mrs Andrew Rodger, of Stanton Old Hall, Matlock, Derbys, and has issue living, Felix Edinmore *b* 1997, Jessamy Elizabeth *b* 1999.

Lady Rose Deirdre Margaret, *b* 1943: *m* 1975, Peter Lathrop Lauritzen, of Palazzo da Silva, Cannaregio 1468, Venice, Italy, and has issue living, Frederick Alexander Mark, *b* 1977.

AUNTS LIVING (*Daughters of 9th Earl by 1st marriage*)

Lady Cecilia Elizabeth, *b* 1910: *m* 1934, David McKenna, CBE, late Lt-Col RE (Cdr Order of Merit, France, Member of Br Rlys Board 1968, Past Chm Sadlers Wells Foundation and Bach Choir), son of late Rt Hon Reginald McKenna, and has issue living, Myee Miranda, *b* 1935: *m* 1958, John Francis Hyde Villiers (*see* E Clarendon, colls), — Pamela Primrose, *b* 1937: *m* 1961, Christopher James Folke Arnander (*see* E Crawford, 1995 Edn), and has issue living, Conrad David Folke *b* 1963, Michael Theodore Per *b* 1964, Magnus William Thomas *b* 1970, Katharine Louise *b* 1967, — Sophia Mary (Ty-Mawr, Nant-y-Gwreiddyn, Brecon, Powys), *b* 1944: *m* 1965 (*m diss* 1971), John Boyd Wilson. *Residences* – Rosteague, Portscatho, Truro, Cornwall; 21 Kylestrome House, Cundy St, SW1W 9JT.

Lady Cynthia Rosalie, *b* 1918: *m* 1944, Prof Sir Michael Moissey Postan, FBA, who *d* 1981, Fellow of Peterhouse, Cambridge, and has issue living, Basil David, *b* 1946: *m* 1968, Maria, da of Samuel Carr, of Paultons Sq, SW3, — Alexander Henry Keppel, *b* 1948: *m* 1991, Jane, da of Dr J. Dillon, of Dublin.

HALF AUNT LIVING (*Daughter of 9th Earl by 2nd marriage*)

Lady Anne-Louise Mary, *b* 1932: *m* 1954, Maj Sir Hew Fleetwood Hamilton-Dalrymple, 10th Bt, KCVO. *Residence* – Leuchie, North Berwick, East Lothian EH39 5NT.

WIDOW LIVING OF SON OF NINTH EARL

Aline Lucy, da of late Brig-Gen John Harington, CB, CMG, DSO (*see* Harington, Bt, colls): *m* 1941, Lt-Cdr Hon Walter Arnold Crispian Keppel, DSC, RN, who *d* 1986, 2nd son of 9th Earl (by 1st *m*), and has issue (*see* colls, infra). *Residence* – Little Barton, Meonstoke, Southampton SO32 3NT.

MOTHER LIVING

MARINA (*Viscountess Bury*); ARIBA, AA Dip (Hurst Barns Farm, E Chiltington, Lewes, E Sussex), da of late Lt-Cdr Count Serge Orloff-Davidoff, RNVR (*see* B Howard de Walden, colls): *m* 1964, as his 2nd wife, Lt-Col Derek William Charles, Viscount Bury, 13th/18th Hussars, who *d* 1968.

WIDOW LIVING OF NINTH EARL

Dame DIANA CICELY, DBE, DLitt, DCL, LLD (*Countess of Albemarle*) (Seymours, Melton, Woodbridge, Suffolk), da of late Maj John A. Grove: *m* 1931, as his 2nd wife, the 9th Earl of Albemarle, MC, who *d* 1979.

COLLATERAL BRANCHES LIVING

Issue of late Lt-Cdr Hon Walter Arnold Crispian Keppel, DSC, RN, 2nd son of 9th Earl (by 1st *m*), *b* 1914, *d* 1986: *m* 1941, Aline Lucy (ante), da of late Brig-Gen John Harington, CB, CMG, DSO (*see* Harington, Bt, colls):—
CRISPIAN WALTER JOHN, *b* 29 Oct 1948; *ed* Eton: *m* 1990, Tina, elder da of Claus Ammann, of Stuttgart, Germany, and has issue living, Christin Alexa, *b* 1991. —— Colin Rupert Harington, *b* 1951; *ed* Eton: *m* 1981, Frances May, da of late Cdr Francis Montagu Maxwell Ommanney, DSC, RN, of Droxford, Hants, and has issue living, Oliver George Rupert, *b* 1982, — William Richard Crispian, *b* 1986, — Isabel Frances Bridget, *b* 1984. —— Judith Cynthia Aline KEPPEL, *b* 1942; has resumed her maiden name: *m* 1st, 1964 (*m diss* 1980), Desmond Leon Corcoran; 2ndly, 1985, Neil H. Shand, and has

issue living (by 1st *m*), Alexander Martin Desmond, *b* 1968: *m* 1995, Candida Caroline, da of David Brown, of Flayosc, France, and of Nobile Camilla de Martino di Monte Giordano, of St Petersburg, Russia, and has issue living, Milo William Teddy *b* 1995, — Sibylla Monacella, *b* 1966: *m* 1992, David J. Whitmore, yr son of John Whitmore, of Hartfield, Sussex, and has issue living, Atticus Jack *b* 1996, — Aline Rose, *b* 1972.

Granddaughters of late Col Edward George Keppel, MVO, son of late Rev William Arnold Walpole Keppel, son of late Rt Rev Hon Frederick Keppel, DD, Bishop of Exeter, 4th son of 2nd Earl:—
Issue of late Lt-Col Arnold Ramsay Keppel, *b* 1879, *d* 1930: *m* 1922, Launa Margaret, who *d* 1983 (having *m* 2ndly, 1961, Sir Richard Arthur Pease, 2nd Bt (*cr* 1920), who *d* 1969), da of Hughes Martin, formerly of Tullaghreine, co Cork:—
June Cecilia, *b* 1924: *m* 1st, 1946, Capt Edward Percy Canning Loyd, Coldstream Gds (*see* B Brabourne, 1967 Edn), who *d* 1977; 2ndly, 1990, Alexander K. H. Fletcher, of The Old Vicarage, Wighill, Tadcaster, N Yorks, and has issue living (by 1st *m*), David William Arnold (17 Larkhall Rise, SW4 6JB), *b* 1949; *ed* Eton: *m* 1985, Mrs Anabel Laura Dorothy Stapleton, only da of Hon Sir Charles Andrew Morrison (*see* B Margadale), and has issue living, James Canning *b* 1988, Rupert Charles Percy *b* 1990, Tabitha Launa Mary *b* 1992, — Caroline Evelyn, *b* 1947: *m* 1968, Anthony Havelock Hudson, of Flat 3, Whittingstall Mansions, Whittingstall Rd, SW6, elder son of late Sir Havelock Henry Trevor Hudson, of The Old Rectory, Stanford Dingley, Berks, and ot Mrs Roger Houssemayne du Boulay, of Anstey House, nr Buntingford, Herts. —— Bridget Anne (*Lady Martin Fitzalan Howard*), *b* 1925: *m* 1948, Capt Lord Martin Fitzalan Howard, late Gren Gds, of Brockfield Hall, York (*see* D Norfolk). —— Lavinia Mary (*Hon Mrs Richard Beaumont*), *b* 1928: *m* 1971, Hon Richard Blackett Beaumont, CVO (*see* V Allendale), of Flat 1, 13-16 Embankment Gdns, SW3 4LW.

PREDECESSORS – (1) ARNOLD JOOST Van Keppel, KG, a Member of the Nobles in Holland, accompanied the Prince of Orange in his expedition 1688, and on the establishment of the Prince on the throne of England was cr *Baron Ashford, Viscount Bury*, and *Earl of Albemarle* (peerage of England) 1696; *d* 1718; *s* by his son (2) WILLIAM ANNE, KG, 2nd Earl, a distinguished Gen and sometime Ambassador at the Court of Versailles; *d* 1754; *s* by his eldest son (3) GEORGE, KG, 3rd Earl, a Lt-Gen in the Army; Com-in-C Land Forces, engaged in combined expdn, with his brothers, Commodore Hon Augustus Keppel, First Lord of Admiralty (*cr* Viscount Keppel 1782, *ext* 1786), and Lt-Gen Hon William Keppel, which ended in the capture of Havanna, 1762; *d* 1772; *s* by his son (4) WILLIAM CHARLES, 4th Earl; *b* 1772: *m* 1792, Hon Elizabeth Southwell, who *d* 1817, da of 17th Baron Clifford; 2ndly, 1822, Charlotte Susannah, who *d* 1862, da of Sir Henry Hunloke, Bt; *d* 1849; *s* by his eldest son (5) AUGUSTUS FREDERICK, 5th Earl; *dsp* 1851, *s* by his brother (6) GEORGE THOMAS, 6th Earl, *b* 1799: served at Battle of Waterloo; MP for E Norfolk 1832-5, and for Lymington (*L*) 1847-50: *m* 1831, Susan, who *d* 1885, da of Sir Coutts Trotter, 1st Bt; *d* 1891; *s* by his eldest son (7) WILLIAM COUTTS, KCMG, PC, 7th Earl, *b* 1832; MP for Norwich (*L*) 1857-9, for Wick 1860-65, and for Berwick 1868-74; Treasurer of Queen Victoria's Household 1859 and Under-Sec of State for War 1878-80 and 1885-6; a Vol ADC to Queen Victoria; called to House of Lords during his father's lifetime as Baron Ashford 1876: *m* 1855, Sophia, who *d* 1917, da of Hon Sir Allan Napier Macnab, 1st Bt (*ext*), Prime Min of Canada; *d* 1894; *s* by his eldest son (8) ARNOLD ALLAN CECIL, GCVO, CB, VD, TD, 8th Earl, *b* 1858; Col in the Army; Vice-Lieut for Norfolk; S Africa 1900 (despatches, medal with four clasps, CB); an ADC to HM King Edward VII 1903-10 and King George V 1910-25, and a Lord-in-Waiting to HM Nov 1922-4; MP for Birkenhead (*C*) 1892-94: *m* 1881, Lady Gertrude Lucia Egerton, who *d* 1943, only child of 1st Earl Egerton of Tatton; *d* 1942; *s* by his eldest son (9) WALTER EGERTON GEORGE LUCIAN, MC, 9th Earl, *b* 1882; 1914-18 War as Lt-Cdr RN Div, and Maj Scots Gds (Machine Gun Co Cmdr) (despatches twice); ADC to Govs-Gen of Canada 1904-05 and India 1907-08, and to Gov of Orange River Colony 1907-08: *m* 1st, 1909, Lady Judith Sydney Myee Carrington, who *d* 1928, da of 1st Marquess of Lincolnshire (ext); 2ndly, 1931, Dame Diana Cicely, DBE, DLitt, DCL, LLD, da of late Maj John A. Grove; *d* 1979; *s* by his grandson (10) RUFUS ARNOLD ALEXIS (only son of late Derek William Charles, Viscount Bury, eldest son of 9th Earl), 10th Earl and present peer; also Viscount Bury, and Baron Ashford.

ALDENHAM, AND HUNSDON OF HUNSDON, BARON (Gibbs) (Baron UK 1896 and 1923)

VICARY TYSER GIBBS, 6th Baron Aldenham and 4th Baron Hunsdon of Hunsdon, *b* 9 June 1948; *s* 1986; *ed* Eton, Oriel Coll, Oxford, and RAC Cirencester; Liveryman Merchant Taylors' Co; Dir Montclare Shipping Co Ltd since 1986, Chm Herts and Middx CLA 1985-98, and Watling Chase Community Forest 1997-99: *m* 1980, Josephine Nicola, elder da of John Fell, of Lower Bourne, Farnham, Surrey, and has issue.

Arms – Argent, three battle-axes erect within a bordure nebuly sable. **Crest** – In front of a rock a dexter arm embowed in armour, the hand gauntleted proper, bearing a battle-axe in bend sinister sable. **Supporters** – On either side a man habited in buff leather jerkin, gloves, and boots, armed with a three-barred helmet, long gorget, and sword, all proper, and holding in the exterior hand a battle-axe over the shoulder sable.
Residence – Holwell Manor, nr Sherborne, Dorset DT9 5LE.

Tenacious of purpose

SONS LIVING

Hon HUMPHREY WILLIAM FELL, *b* 31 Jan 1989.
Hon Thomas Antony John, *b* 1992.

DAUGHTER LIVING

Hon Jessica Juliet Mary, *b* 1984.

BROTHER LIVING

Hon George Henry Paul (The Old Manor Farmhouse, Hempton Rd, Deddington, Banbury, Oxon OX15 0QG), *b* 1950: *m* 1st, 1973 (*m diss* 1989), Janet Elizabeth, da of Harold Leonard Scott; 2ndly, 1992, Elizabeth, da of late Prof Geoffrey Wingfield Harris, CBE, FRS, and has issue living (by 1st *m*), Piers Antony Scott, *b* 1973, — Corin William Tyser, *b* 1976.

SISTER LIVING

Hon Antonia Mary, *b* 1958: *m* 1989, Simon H. Johnson, son of E. A. Johnson, of Walmer, Kent, and has issue living, Edmund Antony Gibbs, *b* 1992, — Maud Eleanor Gibbs, *b* 1990, — Isabel Beatrice Gibbs, *b* 1995. —— Manor Farm, Middle Chinnock, Som.

WIDOW LIVING OF SON OF FOURTH BARON ALDENHAM

Jean Frances, CVO, da of late Capt Angus Valdimar Hambro, MP; appointed a Lady-in-Waiting to HM when Princess Elizabeth 1945, and an Extra Woman of the Bedchamber to HM 1953; CVO 1953: *m* 1st, 1942, Capt Hon Vicary Paul Gibbs, Gren Gds, who was *ka* 1944; 2ndly, 1946, Rev Hon Andrew Charles Victor Elphinstone, who *d* 1975 (*see* L Elphinstone); 3rdly, 1980, Lt-Col John William Richard Woodroffe, who *d* 1990 (*see* E Ducie, colls, 1968 Edn), and has issue (by 1st *m*) (see colls infra) (by 2nd *m*) (*see* L Elphinstone). *Residence* – Maryland, Worplesdon, Guildford, Surrey.

WIDOW LIVING OF FIFTH BARON

MARY ELIZABETH (*Mary, Baroness Aldenham*), only da of late Walter Parkyns Tyser, of Gordonbush, Brora, Sutherland: *m* 1947, the 5th Baron Aldenham, who *d* 1986. *Residence* – Rathgar, The Avenue, Sherborne, Dorset DT9 3AH.

COLLATERAL BRANCHES LIVING

Issue of late Capt Hon Vicary Paul Gibbs, Gren Gds, eldest son of 4th Baron Aldenham, *b* 1921, *ka* 1944: *m* 1942, Jean Frances, CVO (ante) (who *m* 2ndly, 1946, Rev Hon Andrew Charles Victor Elphinstone, who *d* 1975 (*see* L Elphinstone); and 3rdly, 1980, Lt-Col John William Richard Woodroffe, who *d* 1990 (*see* E Ducie, colls, 1968 Edn)), da of late Capt Angus Valdimar Hambro, MP:—
Jennifer Susan, *b* 1944; Lady-in-Waiting to HM Queen Elizabeth The Queen Mother since 1993: *m* 1974, Capt Michael Charles Gordon Lennox, RN, of Fishers Hill, Iping, Midhurst, W Sussex (*see* D Richmond and Gordon, colls).

Issue of late Hon Sir Geoffrey Cokayne Gibbs, KCMG, 2nd son of 1st Baron Hunsdon of Hunsdon, *b* 1901, *d* 1975: *m* 1926, Helen Margaret, CBE, who *d* 1979, da of late Charles Frederick Henry Leslie, of Epcombs, Hertford:—
David Charles Leslie, AM (Apt 181, St James, 350 St Kilda Rd, Melbourne, Victoria 3004, Australia; Toolang, Coleraine, Victoria 3315, Australia), *b* 1927; *ed* Eton, and Ch Ch, Oxford; a Dir Australia and New Zealand Banking Group, and other cos: *m* 1965, Charmian Fleur, only da of Dalzell Pulteney Mein, of Toolang, Coleraine, Victoria, Australia, and has issue living, Hugo Dalzell, *b* 1967, — Justin Geoffrey, *b* 1969, — Emma Victoria, *b* 1966, — Arabella Sarah, *b* 1970. —— Stephen Cokayne (Dougarie, Isle of Arran, KA27 8EB), *b* 1929; *ed* Eton; late 2nd Lt KRRC; a Dir Vaux Group plc, and of other Cos: *m* 1972, Lavinia Winifred, da of Sir Edmund Castell Bacon, 13th Bt, KG, KBE, TD, and has issue living, James Edmund Geoffrey, *b* 1975, — William Stephen, *b* 1978, — Emily Anna Maria, *b* 1973. —— Julian Herbert, *b* 1932; *ed* Eton. —— *Sir* Roger Geoffrey (23 Tregunter Rd, SW10), *b* 1934; *ed* Eton, and Millfield; Dir Arsenal Football Club 1980, Chm Howard de Walden Estates 1993, Chm Gerrard and Nat Discount Co plc 1975-89, Gov The Wellcome Trust since 1983, and Chm since 1989; Ktd 1994. —— Christopher Henry (Manor House, Clifton Hampden, Abingdon, Oxon; L6 Albany, W1), *b* 1938; *ed* Eton, Stanbridge, and Univ of Poitiers; Trustee J. Paul Getty Jr Charitable Trust since 1985. —— Elizabeth Helen (twin), *b* 1938: *m* 1963, Valentine Patrick Fleming, of Stonewall Park, Chiddingstone Hoath, Edenbridge, Kent (*see* Borthwick, Bt, colls), and has issue living, Matthew Valentine, *b* 1964, — Harry Geoffrey, *b* 1966, — Rupert Michael, *b* 1969, — Thomas Mungo, *b* 1971.

Issue of late Rt Hon Sir Humphrey Vicary Gibbs, GCVO, KCMG, OBE, 3rd son of 1st Baron Hunsdon of Hunsdon, *b* 1902, *d* 1990; Gov of S Rhodesia 1959-69: *m* 1934, *Dame* Molly Peel, DBE, CStJ, who *d* 1997, da of late John Peel Nelson, of Bulawayo:—
Jeremy Herbert (Upper Kennards, Leigh, Kent TN11 8RE), *b* 1935; *ed* Diocesan Coll, S Africa, and Ch Ch, Oxford (MA): *m* 1958, Alison Douglas, da of Col Douglas McCrone Martin, of Dunchattan, Troon, Ayrshire, and has issue living, Elizabeth Belinda, *b* 1959: *m* 1988, Ferrill D. Roll, yst son of M. W. Roll, of New Mexico, USA, and has issue living, James Herbert *b* 1992, Helen Mary *b* 1990, Alice Elizabeth *b* 1993, — Barbara Anne Camilla, *b* 1961, — Lucinda Jane, *b* 1965, — Arabella Sophie, *b* 1967: *m* 1995, Benedict J. A. Padovan, eldest son of John Padovan, of Westminster, and has issue living, Oliver Humphrey Umberto *b* 1997, Daisy Amelia *b* 1999. —— Nigel Henry Vicary (Cyrene, Horcott, Fairford, Glos), *b* 1937; *ed* Ruzawi Sch, Marandellas, Diocesan Coll, Rondebosch, Prince Edward Sch, Salisbury, and RAC Cirencester: *m* 1967, Barbara Boitumelo, 2nd da of Rev Canon Edward George Paterson, and has issue living, Paul Humphrey Paterson, *b* 1968: *m* 1992, Claire Diane, only da of Peter Freeman, of Johannesburg, S Africa, — Douglas Robert Nigel, *b* 1972, — Mairi Rosalind Diana, *b* 1970. —— Timothy Durant (Silver Street House, S Cerney, Cirencester, Glos GL7 5TP), *b* 1938; *ed* Ruzawi Sch, Marandellas, and Diocesan Coll, Rondebosch: *m* 1978, Susan Heather, da of Graham Melville Rankine, and widow of Robert Duncan Bothwell Fleming, and has issue living, James Rankine Fleming, *b* 1979, — Caroline Rose, *b* 1981, — and two adopted children, David Alexander FLEMING-GIBBS, *b* 1974, — Sarah Victoria FLEMING-GIBBS, *b* 1977. —— Kenneth Richard (The Old Vicarage, Appledore, Kent), *b* 1941; *ed*

Ruzawi Sch, Marandellas, Diocesan Coll, Rondebosch, and Cape Town Univ: *m* 1966, Mary Elizabeth Frances, only da of Francis Beamish, of E London, S Africa, and has issue living, Vicary James, *b* 1973, — Sara Jane, *b* 1970. —— Simon Humphrey (Brunswick Cottage, Church St, Kelvedon, Essex), *b* 1947; *ed* Peterhouse, Rhodesia, and Reading Univ: *m* 1974, Philippa Mary, da of Terence Astley Brand, and has issue living, Nicholas Geoffrey, *b* 1979, — Thomas Humphrey, *b* 1982, — Susannah Kate, *b* 1985.

(Male line in remainder to the Barony of Aldenham only)

Issue of late Ven Hon Kenneth Francis Gibbs, DD, 5th son of 1st Baron Aldenham, *b* 1856, *d* 1935: *m* 1894, Mabel Alice, who *d* 1953, da of Charles Edward Barnett (*see* B Ormathwaite, 1923 Edn):—
Andrew Antony, MBE, TD, *b* 1914; *ed* Winchester, and Ch Ch, Oxford (BA 1937, MA 1946); Maj Herts Regt (TA Res), a Dir of Barclays Bank 1962-84; 1939-45 War (despatches, MBE); MBE (Mil), 1945: *m* 1947, Elizabeth Joan, who *d* 1993, da of Major Eric Charles Montagu Flint, DSO, and widow of Capt Peter George William Savile Foljambe, Herts Regt (*see* E Liverpool), and has issue living, John Kenneth Andrew (The White Cottage, Old Heathfield, E Sussex), *b* 1948; *ed* Winchester; FCA, a Dir Balfour, Williamson & Co Ltd since 1988: *m* 1978, Julia Margaret, only da of Maurice Edwards, of Mullets, Piddletrenthide, Dorset, and has issue living, Simon Andrew Maurice *b* 1985, Emma Elizabeth *b* 1979, Louisa Mary *b* 1981, — Alan Francis (Midgham Park Farm, Midgham, nr Reading, Berks RG7 5VG), *b* 1953; *ed* Winchester, and Ch Ch, Oxford: *m* 1982, Francine Nicola, eldest da of Nicholas Preston, of Park Farm, Beverston, Tetbury, Glos, and has issue living, Alfred Andrew Vicary *b* 1997, Fleur Elizabeth *b* 1990, and a son, Leo Antony Francis *b* 1988. *Residence* – Kilvington Hall, Thirsk, Yorks. *Clubs* – Travellers', Pratt's.

Granddaughter of late Hon Henry Lloyd Gibbs, yst son of 1st Baron Aldenham:—
Issue of late Maurice Antony Crutchley Gibbs, *b* 1888, *d* 1974: *m* 1st, 1912 (*m diss* 1924), Elma, who *d* 1973, da of Sir William Gordon Gordon-Cumming, 4th Bt; 2ndly, 1933, Margaret Falkiner, who *d* 1964, only da of late Daniel Grant McBean, of Fairley Grange, NSW, and formerly wife of Reginald Francis Egerton, RN:—
(By 1st *m*) Daphne Marion, *b* 1912: *m* 1934, Percy Kirwan Agar, of La Haut, Dominica, and has issue living, Antony Edward (La Haut, Dominica), *b* 1936: *m* 1967, Madeleine Carmel, da of late Stephen Morrison, of Nova Scotia, and has issue living, Stephen Kirwan *b* 1968, Maurice Ashton *b* 1970: *m* 1998, Elise Rachel, da of Robert Johnston, of Montreal, Canada, Madeleine Daphne *b* 1972: *m* 1993, Michael Byron, son of Judge Denis Byron, of St Kitts-Nevis, W Indies (and has issue living, Danielle Monica Carmel *b* 1994, Chantelle Theresa *b* 1995), Francillia *b* 1975, — Elizabeth Anne *b* 1938: *m* 1958, Mark Varvill, of Lane End House, Ellanore Lane, W Wittering, W Sussex, and has issue living, Richard Antony *b* 1961: *m* 1998, Julie Mary Elizabeth, da of William Gerard O'Brien, of Ealing (and has issue living, Benedict Mark *b* 1999), Katherine Mary *b* 1963: *m* 1998, Henry Howard Cook, son of late Harry Bennett Cook, of Wilpshire, Lancs.

PREDECESSORS – (1) HENRY HUCKS Gibbs, FSA, son of late George Henry Gibbs, of Aldenham House, Herts, and of Clifton Hampden, Oxon, *b* 1819; senior partner in the firm of Antony Gibbs and Sons, bankers and merchants, of 15 Bishopsgate Street Within, EC; a Director of the Bank of England 1853-1901 (Gov 1875-7); MP for City of London (*C*) 1891-2; cr *Baron Aldenham*, of Aldenham, co Hertford (peerage of United Kingdom) 1896: *m* 1845, Louisa Anne, who *d* 1897, da of William Adams, LLD, formerly of Thorpe, Chertsey, Surrey; *d* 1907; *s* by his eldest son (2) ALBAN GEORGE HENRY, 2nd Baron, *b* 1846; MP for City of London (*C*) 1892-1906: *m* 1873, Bridget, who *d* 1896, da of late Rt Hon Alexander James Beresford Beresford Hope, PC, of Bedgebury Park, Kent; *d* 1936; *s* by his only son (3) GERALD HENRY BERESFORD, 3rd Baron, *b* 1879, a partner in the firm of Antony Gibbs & Sons, merchants and bankers, of 22 Bishopsgate, EC: *m* 1905, Lillie Caroline, who *d* 1950, eldest da of late Rev William Thomas Houldsworth, of 44 Lennox Gardens, SW; *d* 1939; *s* by his cousin (4) WALTER DURANT, 4th Baron, 2nd Baron Hunsdon of Hunsdon (see infra *), *b* 1888; Chm of Antony Gibbs & Sons, 1939-65, and Westminster Bank 1950-61: *m* 1919, Beatrix Elinor, who *d* 1978, da of Herbert Woodfield Paul (*see* Mackworth, Bt, colls, 1924 Edn), and widow of Algernon Hyde Villiers (*see* E Clarendon, colls): *d* 1969; *s* by his yr son (5) ANTONY DURANT, 5th Baron, *b* 1922, 1939-45 War as Lt RNVR; Dir Antony Gibbs & Sons Ltd: *m* 1947, Mary Elizabeth, only da of late Walter Parkyns Tyser; *d* 1986, *s* by his eldest son (6) VICARY TYSER, 6th Baron and present peer; also 4th Baron Hunsdon of Hunsdon.

(1) Hon HERBERT COKAYNE Gibbs, 4th son of 1st Baron Aldenham, *b* 1854; a partner in the firm of Antony Gibbs & Sons, bankers and merchants, of 22 Bishopsgate, EC; High Sheriff of Herts 1913; cr *Baron Hunsdon of Hunsdon*, of Briggens, co Hertford (peerage of United Kingdom) 1923: *m* 1885, Anna Maria, who *d* 1938, da of late Richard Durant, of High Canons, Herts, and Sharpham, Devon; *d* 1935; *s* by his eldest son (2) WALTER DURANT, 2nd Baron, who *s* as 4th Baron Aldenham 1939 (ante).

ALDERDICE, BARON (Alderdice) (Life Baron 1996)

JOHN THOMAS ALDERDICE, son of Rev David Alderdice, of Glenariff, Ballymena, NI; *b* 28 March 1955; *ed* Ballymena Acad, and Queen's Univ, Belfast (MB BCh, BAO 1978), MRCPsych 1983; FRCPsych 1997; FRCPI (Hon) 1997; Consultant Psychotherapist, E Health and Social Services Board since 1988, Hon Lecturer in Psychotherapy, Queen's Univ, Belfast 1990-99, Exec Medical Dir S & E Belfast Health & Social Services Trust 1994-97; Memb Alliance Party of NI since 1978, Leader 1987-98; Parliamentary Candidate 1987 and 1992; European Parliamentary Candidate 1989; Councillor, Belfast City Council 1989-97; leader of sundry Alliance Party delegations; Memb Forum for Peace and Reconciliation, Dublin 1994-96; Vice-Pres of Liberal International 1992-99, Bureau Memb of LI since 1996; Chm Human Rights Cttee of LI since 1999; Treasurer of Euro Liberal Democrat and Reform Party since 1995; elected Memb NI Forum 1996-98; elected Memb NI Assembly 1998 and First Speaker NI Assembly since 1998; *cr Baron Alderdice*, of Knock in the City of Belfast (Life Baron) 1996: *m* 1977, Joan Margaret, da of late James Hill, of Ballymena, NI, and has issue.

Arms – Or a fess wavy between two cotises wavy set on the outer edge with alder leaves all between three estoiles azure. **Crest** – In front of a boar salient to the sinister azure armed and unguled or a boar salient or armed and unguled azure. **Supporters** – On either side a Pegasus reguardant argent maned tailed unguled and winged or in the mouth a flax flower azure slipped and leaved or.
Address – c/o House of Lords, SW1A 0PW. *Clubs* – Ulster Reform (Belfast), National Liberal.

SONS LIVING

Hon STEPHEN DAVID, *b* 1980; *ed* Campbell Coll, Belfast.
Hon Peter James, *b* 1983; *ed* Campbell Coll, Belfast.

DAUGHTER LIVING

Hon Joanna Margaret (Anna), *b* 1988.

ALDINGTON, BARON (Low) (Baron UK, 1962)

Hope

TOBY (AUSTIN RICHARD WILLIAM) LOW, KCMG, CBE, DSO, TD, PC, 1st Baron, son of late Col Stuart Low, DSO (*see* B Atkin, 1957 Edn); *b* 25 May 1914; *ed* Winchester, and New Coll, Oxford (MA); Bar Middle Temple 1939; DL; Brig late The Rangers, KRRC (TA); Parl Sec to Min of Supply 1951-54, Min of State, Board of Trade 1954-57, and Dep Chm of Conservative Party Organization 1959-63; Chm GEC plc 1964-68 (Dep Chm 1968-84) Grindlays Bank Ltd 1964-76, Port of London Authority 1971-77, Gen Advisory Council BBC 1971-78, Cttee of Management, Inst of Neurology 1961-78, Sun Alliance and London Insurance plc 1971-85, Westland plc 1977-85, Nat Nuclear Corpn 1973-80; Dir Lloyds Bank plc 1967-85, Citicorp (USA) 1969-83; Chm Brain Research Trust 1971-86 (Pres 1986), and Leeds Castle Foundation 1984-94; Warden Winchester Coll 1979-87; Pres British Standards Instn 1986-89; 1939-45 War as Brig BGS 5 Corps Italy 1944-45, served Greece, Crete, Egypt, Libya, Tunisia, Sicily, Italy and Austria (despatches, DSO, MBE, CBE, French Croix de Guerre, Com of American Legion of Merit); MP for N Div of Blackpool (*C*) 1945-62; *cr* DSO 1941, MBE (Mil) 1944, CBE (Mil) 1945, PC 1954, KCMG 1957, and *Baron Aldington*, of Bispham, in Co Borough of Blackpool (peerage of UK) 1962: *m* 1947, Felicité Ann Araminta, da of late Sir Harold Alfred MacMichael, GCMG, DSO (*see* V Scarsdale, 1929 Edn, and E Leven and Melville, colls, 1946 Edn), and formerly wife of Capt Paul Humphrey Armytage Bowman, Coldstream Gds (*see* Bowman, Bt, colls), and has issue.

Arms – Gules a pale ermine on a chief argent masoned sable three saffrons stalked and leafed proper. Crest – Out of the battlements of a tower or a cubit arm proper, the hand grasping a hurt. Supporters – *Dexter*, a stag proper; *sinister* a black Labrador dog proper; pendant from the neck of each by its own chains a portcullis or.
Residence – Knoll Farm, Aldington, Kent. *Clubs* – Carlton, Royal St George's Golf, Royal and Ancient.

SON LIVING

Hon CHARLES HAROLD STUART, *b* 22 June 1948; *ed* Winchester, New Coll, Oxford, and INSEAD (Fontainebleau); Man Dir Deutsche Bank AG, London Branch since 1988: *m* 1989, Regine, da of late Erwin von Csongrady-Schopf, of Bielefeld, Germany, and has issue living, Philip Toby Augustus, *b* 1 Sept 1990, — Louisa Charlotte Patience, *b* 1992, — Marie-Therese Sophie Araminta, *b* (twin) 1992. *Residence* – 59 Warwick Sq, SW1. *Club* – Brooks's.

DAUGHTERS LIVING

Hon (Priscilla) Jane Stephanie, LVO, *b* 1949; *ed* Cranborne Chase Sch, Westfield Coll, London Univ, and Courtauld Inst of Art; Curator of Print Room, R Library, Windsor Castle since 1975; MVO 1985, LVO 1995: *m* 1975, Hugh Ashley Roberts, CVO, Dir of the Royal Collection and Surveyor of The Queen's Works of Art since 1996, son of Rt Rev Edward Roberts, sometime Bishop of Ely, and has issue living, Sophie Jane Cecilia, *b* 1978, — Amelia Frances Albinia, *b* 1982. *Residence* – Adelaide Cottage, Home Park, Windsor, Berks SL4 2JQ.

Hon (Lucy) Ann Anthea, *b* 1956; *ed* Cranborne Chase Sch, and Camberwell Sch of Arts and Crafts: *m* 1979, Alasdair North Grant Laing, and has issue (*see* E Stair, colls). *Residence* – Logie House, Forres, Morayshire IV36 0QN.

Alexander, family name of Earl of Caledon.

Alexander, Viscount; son of Earl of Caledon.

ALEXANDER OF HILLSBOROUGH, EARLDOM OF (Alexander) (Extinct 1965)

DAUGHTER LIVING OF FIRST EARL

Lady Beatrix Dora, *b* 1909; *ed* London Univ (BSc Econ 1932); a JP of Middlesex: *m* 1936, William Bernard Evison, BCom, and has issue living, Alexander Bernard, *b* 1948: *m* 1969, Joan Susan Hepworth, of Slaley, Northumberland, and has issue living, Deborah Claire *b* 1974, Carina Louise *b* 1976, Tanya Joan *b* 1978, — Jennifer Anne, *b* 1940; *ed* King's Coll, London (BSc and AKC 1962): *m* 1963, Wing Cdr Barry Charles Hunt, BSc, RAF, of 14 New Rd, Walters Ash, High Wycombe, Bucks, and has issue living, Geoffrey Alexander Waters *b* 1964; BEng: *m* 1990, Kelly Ann Vallee, of Seattle, Washington, USA, Toby Barry *b* 1966; BA (1966), Simon Charles *b* 1968; BSc (1968), Christopher Bernard *b* 1970. *Residence* – 101 Old Park Av, Enfield, Middx.

ALEXANDER OF POTTERHILL, BARONY OF (Alexander) (Extinct 1993)

SON LIVING OF LIFE BARON (*By 2nd marriage*)

Hon (Thomas) Bruce, *b* 1951; *ed* Oundle, and Clare Coll, Camb (MA): *m* 2ndly, 1984 (*m diss* 1993), Susan Joyce Allard, and has issue living, Thomas, *b* 1985. *Residence* – Suffolk House, Lidgate, nr Newmarket, Suffolk.

WIDOW LIVING OF LIFE BARON

Joan Mary (*Baroness Alexander of Potterhill*), da of Robert Baxter Williamson, of Sheffield: *m* 1949, as his 2nd wife, Baron Alexander of Potterhill (Life Baron), who *d* 1993. *Residence* – 3 Moor Park Gdns, Pembroke Rd, Moor Park, Middlesex HA6 2LF.

ALEXANDER OF TUNIS, EARL (Alexander) (Earl UK 1952)

By land, by sea, by the stars

Shane William Desmond Alexander, 2nd Earl; *b* 30 June 1935; *s* 1969; *ed* Harrow, and Ashbury Coll, Ottawa; Lt Irish Gds (Res); Liveryman Mercers' Co; a Lord-in-Waiting to HM Jan to March 1974; awarded Order of the Republic of Tunisia 1997: *m* 1st, 1971 (*m diss* 1976), Hilary, only da of John van Geest; 2ndly, 1981, Hon Davina Mary Woodhouse, LVO (a Lady-in-Waiting to HRH Princess Margaret, Countess of Snowdon), yst da of 4th Baron Terrington, and has issue by 2nd *m*.

𝕬rms – Per pale argent and sable, a chevron, and in base a crescent, all counterchanged; on a canton azure a harp or, stringed argent. 𝕮rest – An arm in armour, embowed, the hand holding a sword proper, hilt and pommel or. 𝕾upporters – *Dexter*, a piper of the Irish Guards holding under the interior arm a bagpipe; *sinister*, a sepoy of the 3rd/2nd Punjabi Regiment supporting with the exterior hand a rifle proper, each charged on the shoulder with an escutcheon barry nebuly of six argent and azure. *Residence* – 59 Wandsworth Common, West Side, SW18 2ED.

DAUGHTERS LIVING (*By 2nd marriage*)

Lady Rose Margaret, *b* 1982.
Lady Lucy Caroline, *b* 1984.

BROTHER LIVING

Hon BRIAN JAMES, *b* 31 July 1939; *ed* Harrow; Lieut Irish Gds (Res). *Residence* – 11 The Little Boltons, SW10 9LJ.

SISTER LIVING

Lady Rose Maureen, *b* 1932; Vice-Chm Berwick-upon-Tweed Preservation Trust since 1989: *m* 1956, Lt-Col Humphrey Crossman, JP, DL, High Sheriff Berwick-on-Tweed 1990, and has had issue, David Lindisfarne Alexander, *b* (Nov) 1956; *ed* Wellington Coll: *m* 1985, Mrs Jane Lusk, da of S. J. Hamp-Adams, of Harare, Zimbabwe, and *d* 1997, in a flying accident in Zambia, leaving issue, Alice Patricia *b* 1986, Sophia Rose *b* 1988, — Emma Margaret, *b* 1959: *m* 1984, Christopher William Kennard Baldwin, of Twyssenden Manor, Goudhurst, Kent, son of late Peter Godfrey Kennard Baldwin, of Lindsay Hill, Parham, Antigua, WI, and has issue living, John Lindsay Alexander *b* 1989, Isabelle Rose *b* 1992. *Residence* – West Hall, Cheswick House, Berwick-on-Tweed, Northumberland TD15 2RL.

ADOPTIVE SISTER LIVING

Susan Mary, *b* 1948: *m* 1970, Andrew Paulet Hamilton, son of Capt Hubert Charles Paulet Hamilton, R Irish Fus (*see* Williams-Wynne, Bt, 1980 Edn), and has issue living, Alexander Caspar Paulet, *b* 1974, — Romany Celia Margaret, *b* 1971, — Imogen Laetitia Alice, *b* 1981. *Residence* – Bank Farm, Egerton, Malpas, Cheshire SY14 8AF

PREDECESSORS – (1) FM Sir HAROLD RUPERT LEOFRIC GEORGE ALEXANDER, KG, GCB, OM, GCMG, CSI, DSO, MC, PC, 3rd son of 4th Earl of Caledon; *b* 1891; C-in-C British Forces in Burma 1942 and Middle East 1942-43, Dep C-in-C N Africa 1943, C-in-C 18th Army Group, N Africa 1943, C-in-C Allied Forces in Italy 1943-44 and Supreme Allied Comd Med 1944-45, Gov-Gen of Canada 1946-52, and Min of Defence 1952-54; Col Irish Gds 1947-69; *cr Viscount Alexander of Tunis*, of Errigal, co Donegal (peerage of UK) 1946, *Baron Rideau*, of Ottawa, and of Castle Derg, co Tyrone, and *Earl Alexander of Tunis* (peerage of UK) 1952: *m* 1931, Lady Margaret Diana Bingham, GBE, JP, who *d* 1977, da of 5th Earl of Lucan; *d* 1969; *s* by his eldest son (2) SHANE WILLIAM DESMOND, 2nd Earl and present peer; also Viscount Alexander of Tunis and Baron Rideau.

ALEXANDER OF WEEDON, BARON (Alexander) (Life Baron 1988)

ROBERT SCOTT ALEXANDER, QC, son of late Samuel James Alexander, of Newcastle, Staffs; *b* 5 Sept 1936; *ed* Brighton Coll, and King's Coll, Camb (BA 1959, MA 1963); Bar Middle Temple 1961, QC 1973, Bencher 1979, QC (NSW) 1983; Vice-Chm Bar Council 1984-85, Chm 1985-86; a Judge of Courts of Appeal of Jersey and Guernsey 1985-88; Chm Panel on Takeovers and Mergers 1987-89; Trustee Nat Gallery 1987-93; Non-Exec Dir RTZ Corpn plc 1991-96, The London Stock Exchange 1991-93, Dep-Chm Securities and Investments Board 1994-96, Member UK Panel on Sustainable Development, Chm House of Lords Delegated Powers Scrutiny Cttee; Chm Nat Westminster Bank plc 1989-99; Chancellor Exeter Univ since 1998; Chm RSC Foundation Board; Chm JUSTICE; Vice-Pres CRISIS; Non-exec Dir TOTAL; *cr Baron Alexander of Weedon*, of Newcastle-under-Lyme, co Staffs (Life Baron) 1988. *m* 1st, 1960 (*m diss* 1975), Frances Rosemary (*née* Pughe); 2ndly, 1978, Elizabeth (*née* Norman); 3rdly, 1985, Marie (*née* Sugrue), and has issue by 1st *m*.

Arms – Per fess azure and gules between two swords in pale points upward argent hilts pommels and quillons or a tower argent pierced of a cross gules masoned proper and with a portcullis or infess with two towers each issuant in the flanks masoned and with a portal gold. **Crests** – Upon a chapeau gules encircled by a coronet rayonny or and turned up ermine a lion sejant or head and mane gules collared ermine supporting by its staff or spearheaded also or a banner of the arms fringed argent and gules. **Supporters** – *Dexter*, a lamb statant erect in trian aspect collared ermine unguled or; *Sinister*, a lion statant erect or head and mane in trian aspect gules collared ermine.
Residence – House of Lords, SW1A 0PW. *Club* – Garrick.

SONS LIVING (*By 1st marriage*)

Hon David Robert James, *b* 1964: *m* 1993, Belinda A., da of Graeme Stormont, of Auckland, NZ, and has issue living, Clementine, *b* 1997, — Matilda, *b* (twin) 1997.
Hon William Richard Scott, *b* 1969.

DAUGHTER LIVING (*By 1st marriage*)

Hon Mary Frances Anne, *b* 1966: *m* 1994, Jonathan Charles David Sandelson, and has issue living, Jacob Alexander David, *b* 1996, — Florence Bella Hannah, *b* 1998.

ALINGTON, BARONY OF (Sturt) (Extinct 1940)

DAUGHTER LIVING OF THIRD BARON

Hon Mary Anna Sibell Elizabeth, OBE, *b* 1929; OBE (1980); High Sheriff Dorset 1989, DL 1989: *m* 1949, George Gosselin Marten, LVO, DSC, Lt-Com RN, who *d* 1997, son of late Vice-Adm Sir Francis Arthur Marten, KBE, CB, CMG, CVO, and has issue living, Napier Anthony Sturt, *b* 1959; a Page of Honour to HM 1973-75: *m* 1986 (*m diss* 1998), Virginie Charlotte, da of Alain R. E. Camu (*see* Crossley, Bt, colls), and has issue living, Maximillian Augustus *b* 1988, Tobias *b* 1991, Frederic *b* 1995, Constance Dorothea *b* 1987, — Victoria Mary, *b* 1950: *m* 1978, Ruaidhri McDonaugh, of 29 Regent's Park Rd, NW1 7TL, and has issue living, James Anthony *b* 1979, George Ruaidhri *b* 1981, Robert Francis *b* 1986, Hugo Napier *b* 1992, — Charlotte Diana, *b* 1952: *m* 1975, (Oswald) Alexander Mosley, and has issue (*see* B Ravensdale), — Georgina Elizabeth, *b* 1953: *m* 1st, 1973 (*m diss* 1980), Presley Francis Norton, of Ecuador; 2ndly, 1981, Augusto de Cruz, of The Galapagos Islands, and Quito, Ecuador, and has issue living (by 2nd *m*), Sebastian *b* 1982, Thomas *b* 1985, — Amabel Catherine, *b* 1954: *m* 1991, Ciaran Clarke, of Ardnamona House, Donegal, and has issue living, Theodore *b* 1995, Mary Anna *b* 1997, — Sophia Harriet, *b* 1962: *m* 1986, John Alexander, son of Peter Alexander, of 31 Rhenwyllan, Port St Mary, Isle of Man, and has issue living, George *b* 1999, Esmé Rose *b* 1992. *Residence* – Crichel, Wimborne, Dorset.

ALLAN OF KILMAHEW, BARONY OF (Allan) (Extinct 1979)

SON LIVING OF LIFE BARON

Hon Alexander Claud Stuart, *b* 1951: *m* 1978, Katie, da of Keith Clemson, NSW, Australia. *Residence* – Copse Hill Farm, Lower Froyle, Alton, Hants.

DAUGHTER LIVING OF LIFE BARON

Hon Jane Maureen, *b* 1952.

WIDOW LIVING OF LIFE BARON

MAUREEN (*Baroness Allan of Kilmahew*), da of late Harold Stuart Clark, of Singapore: *m* 1947, Baron Allan of Kilmahew (Life Baron), DSO, OBE, who *d* 1979.

ALLEN OF ABBEYDALE, BARON (Allen) (Life Baron 1976)

PHILIP ALLEN, GCB, yr son of late Arthur Allen, of Sheffield; *b* 8 July, 1912; *ed* King Edward VII Sch, Sheffield, and Queens' Coll, Camb (MA, Hon Fellow); Dep Chm Prison Commn 1950-52, Assist Under-Sec of State Home Office 1952-55, Dep Sec Min of Housing and Local Govt 1955-60, Dep Under-Sec of State Home Office 1960-62, Second Sec HM Treasury 1963-66, and Perm Under-Sec of State Home Office 1966-72; a Member of Security Commn 1973-91, and Chm of Gaming Board for Gt Britain 1977-85; cr CB (Civil) 1954, KCB (Civil) 1964, GCB (Civil) 1970, and *Baron Allen of Abbeydale*, of the City of Sheffield (Life Baron) 1976: *m* 1938, Marjorie Brenda, da of late Thomas John Colton Coe, of Sheffield.

Arms – Barry of twelve azure and argent two swords in saltire points in base proper hilts pommels and quillons or surmounted by a representation of the tower of Beauchief Abbey proper. **Crest** – Within a wreath of holly proper a boar's head erased behind the ears argent holding in the jaws a dice gold. **Supporters** – On either side a tricolour cavalier King Charles spaniel the compartment comprising a grassy mount growing therefrom sprigs of holly all proper. **Motto** – Ad recta tende.

Residence – Holly Lodge, Englefield Green, Surrey, TW20 0JP.

ALLEN OF FALLOWFIELD, BARONY OF (Allen) (Extinct 1985)

SON LIVING OF LIFE BARON

Hon Lionel Paul (Raeburn Farm, Penton, Carlisle, Cumbria), *b* 1943: *m* 1981, Irene Lynwen (*neé* Morris).

DAUGHTER LIVING OF LIFE BARON

Hon Judith Felicity, *b* 1946: *m* 1973, Graham Tonge, of Orchard House, Innhams Wood, Crowborough, E Sussex TN6 1TE, and has issue living, Daniel Allen, *b* 1974, — Lucy Clare, *b* 1977.

WIDOW LIVING OF LIFE BARON

RUBY MILLICENT (*Baroness Allen of Fallowfield*) (Pinewood Manor, Old Lane, St Johns, Crowborough, E Sussex TN6 1RX), da of Albert Hounsell: *m* 1940, Baron Allen of Fallowfield, CBE (Life Baron), who *d* 1985.

Allen, family name of Baron Croham.

ALLEN OF HURTWOOD, BARONY OF (Allen) (Extinct 1939)

DAUGHTER LIVING OF FIRST BARON

Hon Joan Colette (Polly) Clifford, *b* 1922. *Residence* – 10 Selwood Terrace, SW7.

ALLENBY, VISCOUNT (Allenby) (Viscount UK 1919)

MICHAEL JAFFRAY HYNMAN ALLENBY, 3rd Viscount; *b* 20 April 1931; *ed* Eton; *s* 1984; Lt-Col R Hus; CO R Yeo 1974-77; Dep Speaker House of Lords since 1993: *m* 1965, Sara Margaret, only da of Lt-Col Peter Milner Wiggin (*see* Wiggin, Bt, colls), and has issue.

With faith and work

Arms – Per bend argent and gules, in the sinister three crescents, two and one of the second, and in the dexter, three horses' heads erased, one and two, of the first, all within a bordure azure. **Crest** – Issuant out of a crescent gules, a demi-lion proper. **Supporters** – *Dexter*, a horse reguardant or; *sinister*, a camel reguardant argent.
Residence – Newnham Lodge, Newnham, Basingstoke, Hants. *Club* – Army and Navy.

SON LIVING

Hon HENRY JAFFRAY HYNMAN, *b* 29 July 1968: *m* 1996, Louise V., yr da of Michael Green, of Sands Farm, Faringdon, Oxon.

WIDOW LIVING OF BROTHER OF SECOND VISCOUNT

Barbara Marion (29 Hovedene, Cromwell Rd, Hove, Sussex BN3 3EH), da of John Hall, of Felpham, Sussex: *m* 1951, as his 2nd wife, Lt-Col Hon Claude William Hynman Allenby, who *d* 1975, having been raised to the rank of a Viscount's son 1939.

PREDECESSORS – (1) FM Sir EDMUND HENRY HYNMAN Allenby, GCB, GCMG, GCVO, son of late Hynman Allenby, of Felixstowe House, Felixstowe; *b* 1861; Bechuanaland Expedition 1884-5, Zululand 1888, S Africa 1899-1902, in command of a column (despatches, Brevets Lieut-Col and Col, CB), European War 1914-19, Comdg Cav Corps, and subsequently 5th Army Corps, 3rd Army, and Egyptian Expeditionary Force (despatches, KCB, Promoted Gen and Field-Marshal, Grand Cordons of the Nile, White Eagle of Serbia, Redeemer of Greece, Crown of Roumania, Wen Hu of China, Rising Sun of Japan (with flowers of Paulownia), El Nahda of the Hedjaz, and Michael the Brave of Roumania, Grand Officer of Legion of Honour, and Orders of Leopold of Belgium and Savoy of Italy, GCMG, American DSM, GCB, French and Belgian Croix de Guerre, thanked by Parliament, cr Viscount, granted £50,000); High Commr in Egypt 1919-25 (Arabic title— *Mandub es sami* (Very High Delegate)); received Grand Cordon of the Order of Mohamet Ali 1925, 1st class of Order of Al Rafidain of Iraq 1933, and Grand Cross (Mil) of Order of Leopold of Belgium 1935; Capt of Deal Castle 1925-7; elected Lord Rector of Edinburgh Univ 1935; cr *Viscount Allenby*, of Megiddo, and of Felixstowe. co Suffolk (peerage of United Kingdom) 1919, with remainder, in default of male issue, to his brother, Capt Frederick Claude Hynman Allenby, CBE, RN, and his male issue: *m* 1896, Adelaide Mabel, who *d* 1942, da of late Horace Edward Chapman, of Donhead House, Salisbury; *d* 1936; *s* by his nephew (2) DUDLEY JAFFRAY HYNMAN, son of late Capt Frederick Claude Hynman Allenby, CBE, RN (ante), 2nd Viscount, Lt-Col 11th Hus: *m* 1st, 1930 (*m diss* 1949), (Gertrude) Mary (Lethbridge), who *d* 1988, da of Edward Champneys, of Otterpool Manor, Sellindge, Kent; 2ndly, 1949, Daisy (CStJ), who *d* 1985, da of late Charles Francis Hancox, and formerly wife of (1) Carl Bendix, and (2) Capt Lionel George Cotterill Neame, Coldm Gds; *d* 1984; *s* by his only son (3) MICHAEL JAFFRAY HYNMAN, 3rd Viscount and present peer.

ALLENDALE, VISCOUNT (Beaumont) (Viscount UK 1911)

Trust, but see whom you trust

WENTWORTH HUBERT CHARLES BEAUMONT, 3rd Viscount; *b* 12 Sept 1922; *s* 1956; *ed* Eton; Flight-Lieut RAF Vol Reserve, Hon Air Commodore 3508 (co of Northumberland) Fighter Control Unit, Pres of Northumberland and Durham Asso of Building Sos, a DL for Northumberland, and an OStJ; Steward of Jockey Club 1963-65; ADC to Viceroy of India 1946; 1939-42 War (wounded, prisoner): *m* 1948 (*m diss* 198—), Hon Sarah Field Ismay, da of 1st Baron Ismay, and has issue.

Arms – Gules, a lion rampant or, armed and langued azure, between eight crescents in orle of the second. **Crest** – A bull's head erased quarterly argent and gules, charged with a mullet sable. **Supporters** – *Dexter*, a lion argent, semée of crescents gules; *sinister*, a bull quarterly argent and gules, the horns of the first tipped or.
Residences – Bywell Hall, Stocksfield-on-Tyne, Northumberland; Allenheads Hall, Allenheads, Northumberland.

SONS LIVING

Hon WENTWORTH PETER ISMAY (Bywell Castle, Stocksfield-on-Tyne, Northumberland; Flat 7, 8 Draycott Place, SW3 2SB), *b* 14 Nov 1948; *ed* Harrow: *m* 1975, Theresa Mary Magdalene, 2nd da of late Francis Ambrose More O'Ferrall (*see* Jackson, Bt, *cr* 1869), and has issue living, Wentworth Ambrose Ismay, *b* 11 June 1979, — Lucy Harriet, *b* 1981, — Alice Theresa, *b* 1983, — Martha Rose, *b* 1986.

Hon Mark Henry, *b* 1950; *ed* Eton: *m* 1982, Diana Elizabeth, yst da of Lt-Col John Elliott Benson, of Chesters, Humshaugh, Northumberland, and has issue living, George Richard Benson, *b* 1987, — John Wentworth, *b* 1989.

Hon Charles Richard (Swallowship House, Hexham, Northumberland, NE41 1RJ), *b* 1954; *ed* Eton, and RAC Cirencester: *m* 1979, Charlotte Sybil, yst da of Lt-Col Richard Ian Griffith Taylor, DSO, MC, JP, DL (*see* B Buckland, 1973-74 Edn), and has issue living, Edward, *b* 1983, — Harry, *b* 1987, — Laura, *b* 1985.

BROTHERS LIVING

Hon Richard Blackett, CVO, *b* 1926; *ed* Eton; RNVR 1944, Sub-Lt 1946; Personal Assist to Sir Walter Monckton (later Viscount Monckton of Brenchley) Hyderabad 1947-48, ADC to Sir Donald MacGillivray, Malaya 1954-55; James Purdey & Sons 1949, Dir 1952, Chm 1971, and Pres 1994; Master Gunmakers' Co 1969 and 1985; author *Purdey's, The Guns and the Family* 1984; CVO 1995: *m* 1971, Lavinia Mary, yst da of late Lt-Col Arnold Ramsay Keppel (*see* E Albemarle, colls). *Residence* – Flat 1, 13-16 Embankment Gdns, SW3 4LW.

Hon Sir (Edward) Nicholas Canning, KCVO, *b* 1929; *ed* Eton; Capt (ret) Life Gds; DL Berks 1982, Vice Lord Lieut 1989-94; Pres Baillie St John Ambulance Bde 1988-94, since when Dir High Gosforth Park; LVO 1976, CVO 1986, KCVO 1994: *m* 1953, Jane Caroline Falconer, da of Alexander Lewis Paget Falconer Wallace, JP, of Candacraig, Strathdon, Aberdeen, and has issue living, Thomas Wentworth, *b* 1962: *m* 1999, Mrs Pauline M. Murray, eldest da of Thomas Johnston, of Newcastle upon Tyne, — Henry Alexander Nicholas, *b* 1966; a Page of Honour to HM Queen Elizabeth the Queen Mother 1979-82. *Residence* – Low Shield House, Sparty Lea, Allendale, Northumberland NE47 9UW.

Hon Matthew Henry, *b* 1933; *ed* Bradfield: *m* 1st, 1959 (*m diss* 1972), Anne Christina Margaret, eldest da of Gerald John Hamilton (*see* M Bute, 1954 Edn); 2ndly, 1973, Belinda Jane Elizabeth, eldest da of late Harold David Cuthbert, of Beaufront Castle, Hexham, Northumberland (*see* Milnes Coates, Bt), and has issue living (by 1st *m*), Justin George Gerald, *b* 1960: *m* 1999, Jacqueline S., da of S. Baines, of Guisborough, N Yorks, — Charlotte Catherine Lucinda (*Lady Cardross*), *b* 1962: *m* 1987, Henry Thomas Alexander, Lord Cardross, elder son of 17th Earl of Buchan. *Residence* – Bearl House, Stocksfield, Northumberland NE43 7AJ.

SISTER LIVING

Hon Ela Hilda Aline (*Countess of Carlisle*), *b* 1925; an OStJ: *m* 1945, 12th Earl of Carlisle, who *d* 1994. *Residence* – St Mary's Vale, Lanercost, Brampton, Cumbria.

COLLATERAL BRANCHES LIVING

Grandchildren of late Lt-Col Hon Ralph Edward Blackett Beaumont, CBE, TD (infra):—
Issue of late John Ralph Beaumont, *b* 1927, *d* 1992: *m* 1951, Audrey Lilian Christie (Bron-y-Wennol, Llwyngwern, Machynlleth, Mon SY20 9RB), yr da of late Edward Thomas Hickling, of York:—
Ralph Wentworth Christopher (Llwyngwern Farm, Machynlleth, Mon SY20 9RB), *b* 1952; *ed* Peterhouse, Rhodesia: *m* 1979, Nicole Marie Blanche, da of R. J. Dubreuil, of Niort, France, and has issue living, Christopher Henry Louis, *b* 1982, — Aline Mary Helena, *b* 1985. —— Nigel Canning Vane (11 The Avenue, Chiswick, W4 1HA), *b* 1954; *ed* Shrewsbury: *m* 1991, Nicola Carron Toy, da of late R. T. West, of Brighton, Sussex, and has issue living, Francesca Daisy, *b* 1992, Georgia Lilly *b* 1996. —— Andrew John Blackett (12 Bishop's Mead, Laverstock, Salisbury, Wilts SP1 1PU), *b* 1956; *ed* Shrewsbury; Maj RWF: *m* 1988, Jane Margaret, only da of Colin Weedon, of Bournemouth, Hants, and has issue living, Henry George Canning, *b* 1993, — Lucinda Eleanor Christine, *b* 1991. —— Hugh Edward Stewart (Rock Cottage, Dunham Hill, Helsby, Cheshire WA6 0LT), *b* 1959; *ed* Shrewsbury: *m* 1988, Susan Elizabeth, da of Elfed Jones, of Wellington, Shropshire, and has issue living, Edward James, *b* 1994, — Charlotte Louise Margaret, *b* 1991. —— Peter-John Tempest (Llwyngwern Farm, Machynlleth, Mon SY20 9RB), *b* 1964; *ed* Wrekin: *m* 1993, Jill Nicola, only da of B. R. Rodgers, of Keighley, Yorks, and has issue living, Harry-John Tempest, *b* 1993. —— Louise Christine Winsmore, *b* (twin) 1956: *m* 1987, Allan N. Markham, of Felin Geri, Cym Con, New Castle, Emlyn, Dyfed SA38 9PA, only son of A. Markham, of Zambia, and has issue living, Lyon Frederick, *b* 1991, — Lily-Anne Winsmore, *b* 1988.

Issue of late Lt-Col Hon Ralph Edward Blackett Beaumont, CBE, TD, yr son of 1st Viscount, *b* 1901, *d* 1977: *m* 1926, Helena Mary Christine, who *d* 1962, da of Brig-Gen John Cecil Wray, CB, CMG, CVO, TD:—

David Christopher (Poolspringe, Much Birch, Herefordshire), *b* 1929: *m* 1st, 1954 (*m diss* 1974), Marion Edith, da of late H. J. Mallard, of 14 Stanbury Rd, Victoria Park, Bristol, and formerly wife of Thomas Harkness Davison; 2ndly, 1977, Valerie Margaret, da of late Talbot Wrigley Roberts, and has issue living (by 1st *m*), Timothy David, *b* 1955, — Sally Aline Christine, *b* 1956: *m* 1981, Peter Snell, of 41 Quennevaise Park, St Brelade, Jersey, CI, and has issue living, David Peter *b* 1984, Christine Iriene *b* 1982. —— Diana, *b* 1934: *m* 1954, Capt Brian Robert Outhwaite, RN, of Roseberry House, Westbourne, Emsworth, Hants, and has issue living, Mark Robert Canning, *b* 1957; *ed* Sherborne; Maj RTR (ret): *m* 1988, Sarah Elizabeth, only da of Michael Hipwell, of Affpuddle, Dorset, and has issue living, Catherine Rossana *b* 1992, Rosemary Charlotte *b* 1995, — James Edward, *b* 1961; *ed* Stowe: *m* 1997, Polly, da of King C. Yee, of Woodside, NY, USA, — Charles Cedric, *b* 1965; *ed* Sherborne.

In remainder to the Barony only

Grandson of late Hon Hubert George Beaumont, 3rd son of 1st Baron:—
Issue of late Major Michael Wentworth Beaumont, TD, *b* 1903, *d* 1958: *m* 1st, 1924, Hon Faith Muriel Pease, who *d* 1935, da of 1st Baron Gainford; 2ndly, 1935, Doreen Christian (Harristown House, Brannockstown, co Kildare), da of Sir Herbert William Goff Davis-Goff, 2nd Bt:—
(By 1st *m*) *Rev* Timothy Wentworth, *b* 1928; cr *Baron Beaumont of Whitley* (Life Baron) 1967 (see that title).

PREDECESSORS – (1) WENTWORTH BLACKETT Beaumont, son of late Thomas Wentworth Beaumont; *b* 1829; MP for S Northumberland (*L*) July 1852 to Nov 1885, and for Tyneside Div of Northumberland July 1886 to July 1892; cr *Baron Allendale*, of Allendale and Hexham, co Northumberland (peerage of United Kingdom) 1906: *m* 1st, 1856, Lady Margaret Anne, who *d* 1888, da of 1st Marquess of Clanricarde; 2ndly, 1891, Edith Althea, who *d* 1927, da of late Maj-Gen Henry Meade Hamilton, CB, and widow of Maj-Gen Sir George Pomeroy Pomeroy-Colley, KCSI, CB, CMG; *d* 1907; *s* by his eldest son (2) WENTWORTH CANNING BLACKETT, 2nd Baron, 1st Viscount, *b* 1860; Vice-Chamberlain to HM's Household Dec 1905 to Feb 1907, Capt of the Yeomen of the Guard 1907-11, and a Lord-in-Waiting to HM 1911-16; sat as MP for Hexham Div of Northumberland (*L*) 1895-1907; cr *Viscount Allendale*, of Allendale and Hexham, Northumberland (peerage of United Kingdom), 1911: *m* 1889, Lady Alexandrina Louisa Maud Vane-Tempest, who *d* 1945, da of 5th Marquess of Londonderry; *d* 1923; *s* by his eldest son (3) WENTWORTH HENRY CANNING, KG, CB, CBE, MC, 2nd Viscount; *b* 1890; Lieut-Col and Brevet Col Northumberland Yeo, and Lord Lieut for Northumberland; a Lord-in-Waiting to HM 1931-2, 1937-51, and 1952-4, and a Permanent Lord-in-Waiting 1954-6: *m* 1921, Violet Lucy Emily, who *d* 1979, da of Sir Charles Hilton Seely, 2nd Bt; *d* 1956; *s* by his eldest son (4) WENTWORTH HUBERT CHARLES, 3rd Viscount, and present peer; also Baron Allendale.

ALLERTON, BARONY OF (Jackson) (Extinct 1991)

GRANDDAUGHTERS LIVING OF THIRD BARON

Issue of late Capt Hon Edward Lawies Jackson, RHG, only son of 3rd Baron; *b* 1928, *d* 1982: *m* 1st, 1953 (*m diss* 1971), Sally Moore, only da of Ian Moore Hezlett, of Cranbourne Corner, Ascot, Berks; 2ndly, 1971, Susannah Albinia (infra) (who *m* 2ndly, 1997, John Walter Douglas Ewart, CBE, DL), da of late (Alfred) Drewett Chaytor (*see* Chaytor, Bt, colls):—
(By 1st *m*) Susan Caroline Lawies, *b* 1954: *m* 1st, 1974 (*m diss* 1978), J. Nicholas H. Purvis; 2ndly, 1978, (Charles) Simon Treadwell, eldest son of Charles James Treadwell, CMG, CVO, Midhurst, W Sussex, and has issue living (by 2nd *m*), (Charles) Timothy, *b* 1980, — James Edward, *b* 1983, — Katharine Claire, *b* 1986. —— Lavinia Jane Lawies, *b* 1957: *m* 1980, Robert James Hyde, of Copplestones, Sparry Bottom, Carharrack, nr Redruth, Cornwall TR16 5SH, son of J. Hyde, of The Dell, Woking, and has issue living, Nicholas John Edward, *b* 1986, — Christopher Allen James, *b* 1988, — Andrew Phillip Charles, *b* 1990, — Abigail Charlotte Grace, *b* 1994. —— (By 2nd *m*) Olivia Susannah, *b* 1975. —— Katharine Elizabeth, *b* 1978.

WIDOW LIVING OF SON OF THIRD BARON

Susannah Albinia (ante), da of late (Alfred) Drewett Chaytor (*see* Chaytor, Bt, colls): *m* 1st, 1971, as his 2nd wife, Capt Hon Edward Lawies Jackson, RHG (ante), who *d* 1982; 2ndly, 1997, John Walter Douglas Ewart, CBE, DL. *Residence* – Astrop Park, Banbury, Oxon OX17 3QN.

COLLATERAL BRANCH LIVING

Granddaughter of late Rt Hon Sir (Francis) Stanley Jackson, GCSI, GCIE, 2nd son of 1st Baron:—
Issue of late Maj Henry Stanley Lawies Jackson, *b* 1903, *d* 1963: *m* 1927, Grace Diana, who *d* 1974, da of Arthur Philip Beddard, MD:—
(Frances Harriet) Philippa (80 Melton Court, SW7), *b* 1947.

ALLI, BARON (Alli) (Life Baron 1998)

WAHEED ALLI, son of ...... Alli, of .....; b 1964; ed Norbury Manor Sch; Joint Man Dir Planet 24 Productions; Dir Teacher Training Agency 1997; Memb Creative Industry Taskforce 1997, and Panel 2000 1998; cr Baron Alli, of Norbury in the London Borough of Croydon (Life Baron) 1998. Address – c/o House of Lords, Westminster, SW1A 0PW.

Allsopp, family name of Baron Hindlip.

ALPORT, BARONY OF (Alport) (Extinct 1998)

SON LIVING OF LIFE BARON

Hon (Arthur) Edward Bingham, b 1954, ed Haileybury, and Exeter Univ (BSc); ACII (1979): m 1979, Anne Vivian, elder da of Patrick Alexander Grove-White, of Crown Piece, Wormingford, Colchester, and has issue living, Robert Michael Bingham, b 23 Aug 1983, — James Richard McCall, b 1989, — Catherine Rachel, b 1985. Residence – Huckleberry, Church St, Boxted, Colchester, Essex CO4 5SX.

DAUGHTER LIVING OF LIFE BARON

Hon Lavender Lilias Carole, b 1950: m 1974, Ian Colin Taylor, MBE, MP, of 7 The Cooperage, Regents Bridge Gdns, SW8 1JR, and has issue living, Arthur Lawrence Alport, b 1977, — Ralph George Alport, b 1980.

Althorp, Viscount; son of Earl Spencer.

ALTON OF LIVERPOOL, BARON (Alton) (Life Baron 1997)

DAVID PATRICK ALTON, son of late Frederick Alton, of Bow, London; *b* 15 March 1951; *ed* Edmund Campion Sch, Hornchurch, and Christ's Coll of Education, Liverpool; Teacher of children with special needs 1972-79; Councillor, Liverpool City Council 1972-80 (Dep Leader 1978-79, Chm Housing Cttee 1978-79); Nat Pres Nat League of Young Liberals 1979; MP (Lib and Lib-Dem) for Liverpool Edge Hill 1979-83, and for Liverpool Mossley Hill 1983-97; Crossbench peer since 1997; Chm Lib Party Standing Cttee (Policy) 1980-81; Memb Select Cttee on the Environment 1981-85; Lib Chief Whip 1985-87; Lib and Alliance Spokesman on NI 1986-87; Memb House of Commons Privileges Cttee 1994-96; Chm All-Party Mersey Barrage Group since 1990; Vice-Chm All-Party Drug Abuse Group 1992-96, and All-Party Mental Health Group 1995-97; Treasurer All Party Pro-Life Group since 1994, and All Party Mines Group since 1995; Prof of Citizenship, John Moore's Univ, Liverpool; Founder of Movement for Christian Democracy 1990; Patron of several charitable trusts and institutions; Patron of Jubilee Campaign for Release of Prisoners of Conscience since 1986; journalist and author; FRSA; *cr Baron Alton of Liverpool*, of Mossley Hill, Co Merseyside (Life Baron) 1997: *m* 1988, (Dilys) Elizabeth, yr da of Rev Philip Bell, of Melksham, Wilts, and has issue.

Arms – Gules a dove descending argent a bordure engrailed of twelve points terminating alternately in trefoils and Maltese crosses. **Crest** – An ankh gules pendant from the crossbar two bells or. **Supporters** – On either side a Liverbird wings elevated and addorsed gules legged and in the beak or a lily argent slipped and leaved or.
Residence – Jacob's Ladder, Lower Rd, Knowle Green, Lancs PR3 2YN.

SONS LIVING

Hon PADRAIG, *b* 1990.
Hon Philip, *b* 1992.
Hon James, *b* 1997.

DAUGHTER LIVING

Hon Marianne, *b* 1989.

ALTRINCHAM, BARONY OF (Grigg) (Baron UK 1945, disclaimed 1963)

JOHN EDWARD POYNDER GRIGG, *b* 15 April 1924; *s* as 2nd Baron 1 Dec 1955; disclaimed his Peerage for life 31 July 1963; a writer; Editor of *National and English Review* 1954-60, Columnist for *The Guardian* 1960-70, with *The Times* 1986-93; Chm The London Library 1985-91, Pres since 1996; publications include: *The Young Lloyd George, Lloyd George: The People's Champion, Lloyd George: From Peace to War, Nancy Astor: Portrait of a Pioneer, 1943: The Victory that Never Was, The Thomson Years* (vol VI in the History of The Times); FRSL; 1943-45 War as Lieut Gren Gds: *m* 1958, (Marion) Patricia, da of H. E. Campbell, of Newcastle, co Down.

𝕬rms – Sable, three owls argent, a chief azure, issuant from the base thereof a sun in splendour or. 𝕮rest – A grenade sable fired proper, between two roses argent barbed and seeded also proper. 𝕾upporters – (borne by Barons Altrincham), — On either side a lion gules gorged with a chain collar pendent therefrom a portcullis or, and supporting a date palm fructed proper. *Residence* – 32 Dartmouth Row, SE10 8AW. *Clubs* – Garrick, Beefsteak.

BROTHER LIVING

Hon ANTHONY ULICK DAVID DUNDAS, *b* 12 Jan 1934; *ed* Eton, and New Coll, Oxford; late 2nd Lieut Gren Gds: *m* 1965, Eliane de Cassagne de Beaufort, da of the late Marquis de Miramon, of Paris, and has issue living, (Edward) Sebastian, *b* 1965: *m* 1993, Rachel Sophia, yr da of Laurence Kelly (*see* V Camrose, 1995 Edn), and has issue living, Edward, *b* 11 Feb 1995, George *b* 1997, — Steven Thomas, *b* 1969, — Anne Casilda, *b* 1967.

To serve and to preserve

PREDECESSORS – (1) *Rt Hon Sir* EDWARD WILLIAM MACLEAY GRIGG, KCMG, KCVO, DSO, MC, PC, son of late Henry Bidewell Grigg, CIE, ICS; *b* 1879; was Mil Sec to HRH Prince of Wales during visits to Canada 1919 and Australia and New Zealand 1920, Private Sec to Prime Min (Rt Hon D Lloyd George) 1921-2, Gov and Com-in-Ch, Kenya 1925-30, Parliamentary Sec to Min of Information 1939-40, Financial Sec to War Office April to May, 1940, Joint Under-Sec of State for War 1940-2, and Min Resident in Middle East 1944-5; MP for Oldham (NL) 1922-5, and for Altrincham Div of Cheshire (C) 1933-45; cr *Baron Altrincham,* of Tormarton, co Gloucester (peerage of UK) 1945: *m* 1923, Hon Joan Alice Katherine Dickson-Poynder, who *d* 1987, da of 1st Baron Islington; *d* 1955; *s* by his eldest son (2) JOHN EDWARD POYNDER, 2nd Baron, until he disclaimed his Peerage 1963.

ALVINGHAM, BARON (Yerburgh) (Baron UK 1929)
(Name pronounced "Yarborough")

ROBERT GUY EARDLEY YERBURGH, CBE, 2nd Baron; *b* 16 Dec 1926; *s* 1955; *ed* Eton; DL Oxon 1996; Maj-Gen late Coldm Gds; Dir of Army Quartering, Min of Defence 1978; OBE (Mil) 1972, CBE (Mil) 1977: *m* 1952, Beryl Elliott, da of late William D. Williams, of Hindhead, Surrey, and has issue.

𝕬rms – Per pale argent and azure, on a chevron between three chaplets of roses counterchanged. 𝕮rest – A falcon close, belled or, preying on a mallard proper. 𝕾upporters – On either side a falcon, wings expanded, belled or, gorged with a chaplet of roses azure. *Residence* – Bix Hall, Henley-on-Thames, Oxon.

SON LIVING

Hon ROBERT RICHARD GUY (Valley Farm House, Bix Bottom, Henley-on-Thames, Oxon), *b* 10 Dec 1956; *ed* Eton; late Capt 17th/21st Lancers; attached to Army Air Corps as Pilot 1979-83: *m* 1st, 1981 (*m diss* 1993), Vanessa Kelty, yr da of Capt Duncan Kinloch Kirk; 2ndly, 1994, Karen L., elder da of Antony Baldwin, of Gt Missenden, Bucks, and has issue living (by 1st *m*), Robert William Guy, *b* 16 Sept 1983, — Edward Alexander Henry, *b* 1986, — (by 2nd *m*), Charles Antony George, *b* 1995, — Amelia Maisie Florence, *b* 1998.

DAUGHTER LIVING

Hon Susannah Elizabeth, *b* 1953: *m* 1979, Edward I. J. G. Moss, 2nd son of late E. F. Moss, of The Gardens, Sprotbrough, Yorks, and has issue living, Alice Elinor, *b* 1983, — Victoria Elizabeth, *b* 1986, — Theodora Katherine Rose, *b* 1992. *Residence* – 24 Rusham Rd, SW12 8TH.

SISTERS LIVING

Hon Dorothy Joan, *b* 1913: *m* 1934, Lt-Col William Aspinall Turner, late The Queen's Bays, who *d* 1994, and has issue living, Adrian Vernon Aspinall (The Old Rectory, Cheselbourne, Dorchester, Dorset) *b* 1946: *m* 1975, Jacquelyn Ann, eldest da of Wallace A. Seymour, of Summerfold, Child Okeford, Dorset, and has issue living, William Aspinall *b* 1980, Charles James Aspinall *b* 1982, Nicholas John Aspinall *b* 1988, — Caroline Sarah, *b* 1943: *m* 1965, Robin Gilman Arculus, of The Warren, Warren Row, Wargrave, Berks, and has issue living, James Edward Gilman *b* 1970, Henry William *b* 1974, Sophie Louise *b* 1972. *Residence* – Rectory Cottage, Cheselbourne, Dorchester, Dorset.

Hon Marjorie Elizabeth, *b* 1916: *m* 1st, 1938 (at Alexandria, Egypt), Abdul Hamid Mustafa Risk; 2ndly, 1952, Leon Setchim, and has issue living (by 2nd *m*) David Maurice (392 Sound Beach Av, Old Greenwich, CT 06870, USA), *b* 1952: *m* 1977, Marion Helena Grundy, of Dublin, and has issue living, James Ashley Yerburgh *b* 1983, Alexander William Yerburgh *b* 1986, Edward Jonathan Yerburgh *b* 1988, — Richard Victor (11 Albion Close, Hyde Park, W2 2AT), *b* 1954: *m* 1989, Elizabeth Mary, only da of H. F. Andrews, of Tilehurst, Reading, — (by 1st *m*) Diana Yerburgh, *b* 1940: *m* 1958, Andrew Robak, who *d* 1997, of 33 Murray Rd, Northwood, Middx, and has issue living, Michael Andrew *b* 1960, David Antony *b* 1961, Peter Howard *b* 1965. *Residence* – 22 Betjeman Close, Pinner, Middx HA5 5SP.

PREDECESSORS – **(1)** ROBERT DANIEL THWAITES Yerburgh, son of late Robert Armstrong Yerburgh, JP, DL (27 years MP for Chester), of Caythorpe Court, Lincolnshire (the Royal approval of a Peerage to whom had been signified in 1916, but who died before the patent was issued); *b* 1889; sat as MP for S Div of Dorset (*C*) 1922-9; cr *Baron Alvingham*, of Woodfold, co Lancaster (peerage of United Kingdom) 1929: *m* 1st, 1911, his cousin, Dorothea Gertrude, who *d* 1927, da of late John Eardley Yerburgh, of Wavendon Lodge, Bucks; 2ndly, 1936, Maud Lytton Grey, who *d* 1992, aged 99, da of late Charles Morgan, of Fairlight, Sussex, and formerly wife of R. E. Bright; *d* 1955; *s* by his son **(2)** ROBERT GUY EARDLEY, 2nd Baron and present peer.

Aman, family name of Barony of Marley.

Amberley, Viscount; son of Earl Russell.

AMERY OF LUSTLEIGH, BARONY OF (Amery) (Extinct 1996)

SON LIVING OF LIFE BARON

Hon Leopold Harold Hamar John, *b* 1956; *ed* Eton, and Balliol Coll, Oxford.

DAUGHTERS LIVING OF LIFE BARON

Hon (Caroline) Louise Michelle, *b* 1951. *Residence* – Cahamuckee, Kealkil, Bantry, co Cork.

Hon Theresa Catherine Roxanne, *b* 1954: *m* 1984, John Harvey Boteler, yr son of late Lt-Cdr John Harvey Trevor Boteler, RN, of Frinton-on-Sea, Essex, and 68 Park St, W1, and has issue living, Jack Francis Clair, *b* 1987, — Catherine Audrey Roxanne, *b* 1989. *Residence* – 17 Colnbrook St, SE1.

Hon (Alexandra) Elizabeth Charmian, *b* (twin) 1956: *m* 1988, (Alan Simon) Mercury Hare, and has issue (*see* E Listowel). *Residence* – 11 Denbigh St, SW1.

AMHERST OF HACKNEY, BARON (Cecil) (Baron UK 1892)

One heart, one way

(WILLIAM) HUGH AMHERST CECIL, 4th Baron; *b* 28 Dec 1940; *s* 1980; *ed* Eton; Dir E. A. Gibson Shipbrokers Ltd 1975-90, Seascope Sale and Purchase Ltd 1994-97, and Short Sea Europe Ltd since 1994; Younger Brother Trinity House; Memb Baltic Exchange since 1970: *m* 1965, Elisabeth, da of Hugh Humphrey Merriman, DSO, MC, TD, of Hazel Hall, Peaslake, Surrey, and has issue.

Arms – Quarterly: 1st and 4th, barry of ten argent and azure, six escutcheons, three, two and one sable, each charged with a lion rampant argent, a mullet for difference, *Cecil*; 2nd and 3rd, gules, three tilting spears, two and one or, headed argent, *Amherst* (also quartering Daniel, Tyssen, Auchmuty, Evering, Wayland, Sidnor, Morris, Earde, Babisford, and Leach). **Crest** – On a chapeau gules, turned up with ermine, a garb or, supported by two lions rampant, the dexter argent, the sinister azure. **Supporters** – Two herons proper, collared or.
Residence – Hillside House, Hyde, nr Fordingbridge, Hants SP6 2HD. *Clubs* – Royal Yacht Sqdn (Vice Commodore 1993-98), Royal Ocean Racing, Royal Cruising.

SON LIVING

Hon (HUGH) WILLIAM AMHERST, *b* 17 July 1968; *ed* Eton, and Bristol Univ; Maritime Lawyer: *m* 1996, Nicola J., elder da of Maj Timothy Michels, of Alderbury, Wilts.

DAUGHTER LIVING

Hon Aurelia Margaret Amherst CECIL, *b* 1966; has resumed her maiden name; Man Dir Aurelia Public Relations Ltd: *m* 1990 (*m diss* 1993), Giles Wilson Mervyn Crewdson (*see* B Grimthorpe).

BROTHER LIVING

Hon Anthony Henry Amherst, *b* 1947; *ed* Eton: *m* 1st, 1969 (*m diss* 1974), Fenella Jane, da of late David George Crichton, MVO (*see* E Erne, colls); 2ndly, 1974, Jane Elizabeth, da of late Philip Norman Elston Holbrook, and has issue living (by 2nd *m*), Henry Edward Amherst, *b* 1976, — Thomas Anthony Amherst, *b* 1981, — Georgiana Helen Amherst, *b* 1979. *Residence* – Incombe Farm, Compton Abbas, Shaftesbury, Dorset SP7 0LZ.

SISTER LIVING

Hon Angela Margaret Amherst, *b* 1955: *m* 1980, (Gavin) Ian Reid, son of Col (Percy Fergus) Ivo Reid, OBE, DL, of The Glebe House, Marston St Lawrence, Banbury, Oxford, and has had issue, Nicholas Andrew, *b* 1985, — Susanna Claire, *b* and *d* 1987, — Jessica Mary, *b* 1988. *Residence* – Queensford Farm, Dorchester-on-Thames, Wallingford, Oxon OX10 7PH.

WIDOW LIVING OF THIRD BARON

MARGARET EIRENE CLIFTON (*Margaret, Baroness Amherst of Hackney*), yst da of late Brig-Gen Howard Clifton Brown, MP (*see* Brown, Bt, *cr* 1863, colls): *m* 1939, Maj the 3rd Baron Amherst of Hackney, CBE, who *d* 1980.

COLLATERAL BRANCHES LIVING

Issue of late Hon Henry Kerr Auchmuty Cecil, Lieut Gordon Highlanders and Army Air Corps, brother of 3rd Baron, *b* 1914, *ka* 1942: *m* 1938, Elizabeth Rohays Mary (who *d* 1993, having *m* 2ndly, 1944, Capt Sir Cecil Boyd-Rochfort, KCVO, who *d* 1983), only da of Maj-Gen Sir James Lauderdale Gilbert Burnett of Leys, 13th Bt (cr 1626), CB, CMG, DSO:—
John Strongbow Amherst (The Old Rectory, Monk's Sherborne, nr Basingstoke, Hants), *b* 1939; *ed* Eton; Lt Scots Gds (Res): *m* 1966, Elizabeth Clare, da of C. Michael Hughes, of Penton Grafton, Andover, and has issue living, Richard Strongbow Amherst, *b* 1973, — Michael John Amherst, *b* 1977, — Miranda Elizabeth Rohays *b* 1974. —— James Comyn Amherst BURNETT OF LEYS (House of Crathes, Banchory, Kincardineshire), *b* 1941; *ed* Eton; recognized in the surname of Burnett of Leys by decree of Lyon Court 1966: *m* 1971, Fiona Mercedes, 2nd da of late Lt-Col Harold Pedro Joseph Phillips (*see* Wernher, Bt, ext), and has issue living, Alexander James Amherst, *b* 1973, — Victor Cecil Tobias, *b* 1982, — Eliza Amelia, *b* 1977. —— Henry Richard Amherst (*posthumous*) (Warren Place, Newmarket, Suffolk CB8 8QQ), *b* 1943; *ed* Canford; racehorse trainer: *m* 1st, 1966 (*m diss* 1990), Julia, da of late Sir (Charles Francis) Noel Murless; 2ndly, 1992, Natalie Payne, and has issue living (by 1st *m*), (Arthur) Noel Amherst, *b* 1973, — Katrina Henrietta Amherst, *b* 1971: *m* 1999, Craig Mackenzie, eldest son of Brian Mackenzie of Johannesburg. —— David Henry Amherst (*posthumous*) (twin) (Cornbaggers, Back St, E Garston, Hungerford, Berks), *b* 1943; *ed* Canford; restaurateur: *m* 1st, 1966 (*m diss* 1972), Hon Fiona Elizabeth Cameron Corbett, da of 2nd Baron Rowallan; 2ndly, 1973 (*m diss* 1995), Vanessa Josephine Bronislawna, da of late Wladyslaw Gallica; 3rdly, 1998, Joanna Christian, da of late David Cecil Howes, and has issue living (by 1st *m*), Rupert Lawrence Amherst, *b* 1967, — Benjamin David Amherst, *b* 1968: *m* 1998, Jenine, da of Fred Sahadi, of Calif, USA, — (by 2nd *m*) Anoushka Henrietta Amherst, *b* 1975, — Sapphire Rose, *b* 1981.

Grandsons of late Hon Thomas James Amherst Cecil, 2nd son of Mary Rothes Margaret, Baroness Amherst of Hackney:—
Issue of late Barclay James Amherst Cecil, *b* 1913, *d* 1987: *m* 1st, 1941 (*m diss* 1950), Suzanne, da of Frederick Dennett, of Melbourne, Australia; 2ndly, 1972, Jessica Iliffe Lane (Upcross Hotel, Berkeley Av, Reading, Berks RG1 6HY), da of Rev Thomas Ernest Matthews, of Grantham, Lincs:—
(By 1st *m*) Timothy Dennett Amherst, *b* 1942. —— Jonathan Peter Hedworth, *b* 1944.

Issue of late Hon John Francis Amherst Cecil, 3rd son of Mary Rothes Margaret, Baroness Amherst of Hackney, *b* 1890, *d* 1954: *m* 1924 (*m diss* 1934), Cornelia, who *d* 1976, da of late George W. Vanderbilt, of USA:—
George Henry Vanderbilt (2 Arboretum Rd, Biltmore, N Carolina 28803, USA), *b* 1925: *m* 1955, Nancy, da of Charles Dexter Owen, of Biltmore, North Carolina, USA, and has issue living, John Francis Amherst Vanderbilt, *b* 1956: *m* 1993, Sarah, da of Thomas M. Mettler, of Palm Beach, Florida, and has issue living, Thomas Amherst Vanderbilt *b* 1994, Hugh Brownlow Amherst *b* 1995, John Francis Amherst *b* 1997, — Christopher Henry Amherst, *b* 1965: *m* 1992, Ruth, da of William H. Taft, Jr, of Greenville, N Carolina, and has issue living, George Henry Vanderbilt II *b* 1994, Rachel Taft Amherst *b* 1996, — Edith Ann Cecil, *b* 1957; has resumed her maiden name: *m* 1983 (*m diss* 1991), Nicholas M. C. Stancioff, son of John Stancioff, and has issue living, Charlotte Eloïse *b* 1988, — Catherine Amherst Cecil, *b* 1959; resumed her maiden name: *m* 1982 (*m diss* 19—), William M. Whitehouse, and has issue living, Timothy Amherst *b* 1984, Henry Meredith *b* 1986, Brooks Cecil *b* 1989, — Margaret Elizabeth, *b* 1961: *m* 1987, John B. Sinnott, of Pittsburgh, PA, and has issue living, Peter Cecil *b* 1991, David Stuyvesant *b* 1993, Mollie Amherst *b* 1989, — Louisa Owen (twin), *b* 1965: *m* 1994, W. W. Rodes Harrison, of New York, NY. —— William Amherst Vanderbilt (Biltmore Estate, Biltmore, N Carolina, USA), *b* 1928: *m* 1957, Mary Lee, da of late John J. Ryan, of New York, and has issue living, William Amherst Vanderbilt, *b* 1958: *m* 1983, Virginia Lee, da of late Robert A. Rott, of Asheville, N Carolina, and has issue living, Ryan Jordan Vanderbilt *b* 1987, Aubrey Lea Amherst *b* 1990, William Robert Vanderbilt *b* 1994, — and an adopted da, Diana Marshall Ryan, *b* 1957 (adopted 1972): *m* 1985, George Wiley Pickering, son of George Wiley Pickering, of Black Mountain, N Carolina, USA, and has issue living, Chase Kennedy Cecil *b* 1987, Devon Lee Cecil *b* 1991.

Issue of late Hon Henry Mitford Amherst Cecil, OBE, RN, 4th son of Mary Rothes Margaret, Baroness Amherst of Hackney *b* 1893, *d* 1962: *m* 1923, Hon Yvonne Cornwallis, who *d* 1983, da of 1st Baron Cornwallis:—
Sir (Oswald) Nigel Amherst, KBE, CB (The Old Rectory, Shorewell, I of Wight PO30 3JL), *b* 1925; *ed* RNC Dartmouth; Rear-Adm (ret); 1939-45 War; Naval ADC to HM The Queen 1975, Senior British Naval Officer, S Africa, and Naval Attaché, Cape Town 1971-73 (as Commodore), NATO Commander SE Mediterranean 1975-77, Commander British Forces, Malta, and Flag Officer, Malta 1975-79; Lieut-Gov of Isle of Man and Pres of Tynwald 1980-85; CB (Mil) 1977, KBE (Mil) 1979; OStJ (1973), KStJ (1980): *m* 1961, Annette (CStJ 1980), da of late Maj Robert Edward Barclay, TD, and has issue living, Robert Barclay Amherst, *b* 1965. —— Rachel Mary, *b* 1924: *m* 1954, Brig Mortimer Cecil Lanyon, MBE, MC, of Woodman's Farm House, W Meon, Hants GU32 1JJ, and has issue living, Robert Henry Mortimer, *b* 1962: *m* 1994, Harriet Mary, elder da of Rev Antony Ansell (*see* B Ravensworth, colls) and has issue living, Jessica Mary *b* 1997, Isabel Sophia *b* 1998, — Charlotte Yvonne, *b* 1955: *m* 1977, Maj Paul Alistair Strutt (*see* B Rayleigh, colls), — Victoria Clare, *b* 1956: *m* 1987, Maj-Gen Angus Iain Ramsay, CBE, DSO (c/o Woodman's Farm, W Meon, Hants GU32 1JJ), son of late Col A.I. Ramsay, of Dalry, Kirkcudbright, and has issue living, James Ivor Iain *b* 1990, Alexandra Rachel Iona *b* 1988.

PREDECESSORS – (1) WILLIAM AMHERST Tyssen-Amherst, son of late William George Tyssen Tyssen-Amhurst, of Didlington, Norfolk; *b* 1835; assumed by Roy licence the surnames of Tyssen-Amherst in lieu of Tyssen-Amhurst 1877; MP for W Norfolk (*C*) 1880-85, and for S-W Div of Norfolk 1885-92; cr *Baron Amherst of Hackney*, in co London (peerage of United Kingdom) 1892, with remainder, in default of issue male, to his eldest da and her issue male: *m* 1856, Margaret Susan, who *d* 1919, only child and heiress of late Adm Robert Mitford, of Mitford, Northumberland, and Hunmanby Hall, York; *d* 1909, when the Barony devolved upon his eldest da (2) MARY ROTHES MARGARET, OBE, *b* 1857: *m* 1885, Lord William Cecil, CVO, who *d* 1943, 3rd son of 3rd Marquess of Exeter; *d* 1919; *s* by her grandson (3) WILLIAM ALEXANDER EVERING, CBE, eldest son of her eldest son, late Capt Hon William Amherst Cecil, MC, who was *ka* 1914, having *m* in 1910, Gladys (granted style and title of Baroness Amherst of Hackney 1920), da of Col Henry Charles Baggallay, 3rd Baron, *b* 1912; 1939-45 War as Maj R Horse Guards: *m* 1939, Margaret Eirene Clifton, yst da of late Brig-Gen Howard Clifton Brown, MP (*see* Brown, Bt, cr 1863, colls); *d* 1980; *s* by his son, (4) WILLIAM HUGH AMHERST, 4th Baron and present peer.

AMOS, BARONESS (Amos) (Life Baroness 1997)

VALERIE ANN AMOS, da of Edward Michael and Eunice Amos, of Wekenaam, Guyana, and Crayford, Kent; *b* 13 March 1954; *ed* Warwick Univ (BA 1976), Birmingham Univ (MA 1977), and Univ of East Anglia; Race Relations Adviser, Lambeth Borough Council 1981-82; Women's Adviser, London Borough of Camden 1983-85; head of training, London Borough of Hackney 1985-87; head of management services, London Borough of Hackney 1987-89; Chief Executive, Equal Opportunities Commn 1989-94; Man Dir Quality and Equality 1994-95; since when Dir Amos Fraser Bernard; non-exec Dir UCLH; Baroness-in-Waiting (Govt Whip) since 1998; author and presenter of numerous papers at National and Internat Conferences; Hon Prof Thames Valley Univ; Memb Cncl Institute of Employment Studies and Cncl King's Fund; Dep Chm Runnymede Trust; Chm Board of Govrs RCN; Tstee, Windsor Leadership Trust; Chm AFIYA Trust; Dir Hampstead Theatre; Tstee, Inst of

Public Policy Research; Tstee, Project Hope; Tstee, VSO; FRSA; *cr Baroness Amos*, of Brondesbury in the London Borough of Brent (Life Baroness) 1997.
Address – c/o House of Lords, Westminster, SW1A 0PW.

AMPTHILL, BARON (Russell) (Baron UK 1881)

What will be, will be

GEOFFREY DENIS ERSKINE RUSSELL, 4th Baron, CBE, PC; *b* 15 Oct 1921; *s* 1973; *ed* Stowe; 1939-45 War as Capt Irish Gds; Gen Manager Fortnum and Mason 1947-51, Chm New Providence Hotel Co Ltd 1951-64, Man Dir of Theatre Owning and Producing Cos 1953-81; Dep Speaker House of Lords since 1983, Chm of Cttees House of Lords 1992-94 (Dep Chm 1980-92); Chm Select Cttee on Channel Tunnel Bill 1987, Chm Channel Tunnel Rail Link Bill 1996, Dep Chm Express Newspapers 1989-98 (Dir 1985-98), and United Newspapers 1991-96 (Dir since 1981); he petitioned HM The Queen for a Writ of Summons as Baron Ampthill on the death of the 3rd Baron, and Cttee for Privileges, House of Lords, decided in his favour 1976; *cr* CBE (Civil) 1986, and PC 1995: *m* 1st, 1946 (*m diss* 1971), Susan Mary Sheila, da of late Hon Charles John Frederic Winn (*see* B St Oswald, colls); 2ndly, 1972 (*m diss* 1987), Elisabeth Anne Marie, da of late Claude Henri Mallon, of Paris, and has had issue by 1st *m*.

Arms – Argent, a lion rampant gules, on a chief sable three escallops argent, a mullet or for difference. Crest – A goat statant, armed and unguled or, charged on the body with a mulletsable for difference. Supporters – *Dexter*, a lion gules, ducally gorged and charged on the shoulder with a mullet or; *sinister*, an heraldic antelope gules, armed, crined and tufted or, ducally gorged, and charged on the shoulder with a mullet also or.
Residence – 6 North Court, Great Peter St, SW1P 3LL.

SONS LIVING AND DECEASED (*By 1st marriage*)

Hon DAVID WHITNEY ERSKINE (Sackville College, E Grinstead, W Sussex; *Club* – White's), *b* 27 May 1947; *ed* Stowe: *m* 1980, April McKenzie, yst da of Paul Arbon, of New York, and has issue living, Christabel Joan Susan, *b* 1981, — (Pauline Alexandra) Daisy, *b* 1983.

†James Nicholas Geoffrey, *b* 1948; *d* 1969, in a motor accident.

Hon Anthony John Mark (1681 Summitridge Drive, Beverly Hills, Calif 90210, USA), *b* 1952; *ed* Stowe: *m* 1985 (*m diss* 19—), Christine L., elder da of John O'Dell, and has issue living, William Odo Alexander, *b* 1986.

DAUGHTER LIVING (*By 1st marriage*)

Hon Vanessa Mary Linda, *b* 1960: *m* 1st, 1983 (*m diss* 1995), Charles Ivor Angus Burt; 2ndly, 1998, Jonathan Andrew Scott Bowles, of 6 Netherton Grove, SW10 9TQ, and has issue living (by 1st *m*), James Ivor Geoffrey, *b* 1984, — Emma Louise Victoria, *b* 1986.

HALF BROTHER LIVING

Hon John Hugo Trenchard (49 Limerston St, SW10 0BL; Ringstead Farm, Dorchester, Dorset DT2 8NF; *Club* – Turf), *b* 1950; *ed* Eton: *m* 1976, Susanna Helen, yr da of Peter Hugh Kennedy Merriam (*see* M Ailsa, 1985 Edn), and has issue living, Henry John Trenchard, *b* 1977; *ed* Eton, — James Peter Faber, *b* 1980; *ed* Eton, — Rose Susanna, *b* 1992.

HALF SISTER LIVING

Hon Georgiana Adeline Villiers, *b* 1953: *m* 1981, Charles Francis Hoare, who *d* 1991, son of Col Charles Edward Hoare.

WIDOW LIVING OF SON OF SECOND BARON

Barbara (Tall Pines, 308 Hearthstone Ridge, Landrum, South Carolina 29356, USA; Pony's Point, Iona, CBI, Nova Scotia, Canada B0A 1L0), da of late Baron Serge Alexandrovich Korff, of Russia: *m* 1st, 1941, Wing-Cdr Hon Edward Wriothesley Curzon Russell, OBE, RAFVR, who *d* 1982; 2ndly, 1988, Arthur Farwell, and has issue (by 1st *m*) (see colls infra).

WIDOW LIVING OF THIRD BARON

ADELINE MARY CONSTANCE (*Adeline, Baroness Ampthill*), eldest da of Rev Canon Henry Evelyn Hone, late V of Godalming: *m* 1948, as his 3rd wife, the 3rd Baron Ampthill, CBE, Capt RN, who *d* 1973.

COLLATERAL BRANCHES LIVING

Issue of late Adm Hon Sir Guy Herbrand Edward Russell, GBE, KCB, DSO, 2nd son of 2nd Baron, *b* 1898, *d* 1977: *m* 1939, Hon (Helen) Elizabeth Blades, who *d* 1995, da of 1st Baron Ebbisham:—
James Rowland (Sheepcote, Harrow Court, Stockbury, nr Sittingbourne, Kent ME9 7UQ), *b* 1940; *ed* Radley, and Clare Coll, Camb (MA, MB, BChir, DObst RCOG); Surg-Lt RN: *m* 1965, Glenys Pearl, da of Herbert George Lofting, of Nairobi, and has issue living, Robert James, *b* 1966; *ed* Radley, and Middlesex Hosp; MB BS, MRCP (UK); Maj RAMC: *m* 1994, Melanie Alexandra, da of late Bruce Cumming, of Chilham, Kent, and has issue living, Angus George Skeoch *b* 1995, Rory Douglas Skeoch *b* 1999, Esme Jane Skeoch *b* 1997, — Katherine May, *b* 1968; *ed* Royal Ballet Sch; choreologist at Ballet Rambert: *m* 1998, Raphael Friere, son of C. Friere, of Eastbourne, — Elizabeth Sarah, *b* 1970; *ed* Gordonstoun, and Exeter Univ, — Mary Glenys, *b* 1973; *ed* St Andrews Univ. ⸻ Oliver Henry (Ballindalloch Castle, Banffshire), *b* 1942; *ed* Radley, and Magdalene Coll, Camb; a Page of Honour to HM 1957-59, Member Queen's Body Guard for Scotland (Royal Company of Archers): *m* 1967, Clare Nancy, DL, da of Maj Sir Ewan George Macpherson-Grant, 6th Bt (ext), and has issue living, Guy Ewan, *b* 1968; a Page of Honour to HM 1981-83, — Edward Oliver, *b* 1970, — Lucy Clare Nancy, *b* 1972. ⸻ Margaret Elizabeth, *b* 1945: *m* 1975, James Anthony Fowell Buxton, of Galhampton Manor, Yeovil, and has issue (*see* Buxton, Bt, colls).

Issue of late Wing-Cdr Hon Edward Wriothesley Curzon Russell, OBE, RAFVR, 3rd son of 2nd Baron, *b* 1901, *d* 1982: *m* 1941, Barbara (who *m* 2ndly, 1988, Arthur Farwell) (ante), da of late Baron Serge Alexandrovich Korff, of Russia:—
Diana, *b* 1943. ⸻ Margaret Angela, *b* 1946: *m* 1992, Stephen Howell.

Issue of late Hon Sir Odo William Theophilus Villiers Russell, KCMG, KCVO, CB, 2nd son of 1st Baron, *b* 1870, *d* 1951: *m* 1910, Countess Marie Louise Ernestine, who *d* 1966, da of Count Rudolf Karl Caspar von Rex:—
Cosmo Rex Ivor (Parapet House, Lenham, Kent), *b* 1911; *ed* Eton, and Trin Coll, Oxford (MA); Dep Dir of Information, Council of Europe 1949-56, and Head, Political Studies Div, Secretariat-General of Council of Europe, 1956-63; a Public Relations Consultant 1963-71, since when a Reviser and Translator, European Commn; Maj Queen's Westminsters, KRRC (TA); sometime a Councillor of New Windsor, and a Co Councillor of Berks; Council of Europe Commemoration Medal; 1939-45 War (despatches, American Bronze Star Medal, Officer of Order of Orange Nassau of the Netherlands with swords): *m* 1941, Agnes Mary, da of late Rev Canon Richard Edward Parsons (*see* E Rosse, colls), and has issue living, Nicholas Odo Richard Desmond, *b* 1946; *ed* Strasbourg, Brickwall Sch, Northiam, and Munich Univ, overseas relief and development consultant: *m* 1982, Rashida Joan Anwar, — John Drummond Athelstan (The Hermitage, Peasmarsh, Rye, Sussex) *b* 1948; *ed* Strasbourg, and Brickwall Sch, Northiam; Lieut Irish Gds Res; Co Dir since 1979: *m* 1968, Toril, da of late Finn Tennfjord, of Norway, and has issue living, Rory Finn Cosmo *b* 1984, Maikki Natacha *b* 1969, Natacha Ann *b* 1971, Tatiana Agnes *b* 1973, — Cecilia Hester Marie Louise Constance, *b* 1942: *m* 1965, Peter Robert Nutting, of North Breache Manor, Ewhurst, Surrey (*see* Nutting, Bt, colls), — Jennifer Rose Ann, *b* 1945: *m* 1966, Julian Goldsmid, of 7 Phillimore Place, W8, and has issue living, Tara Alexandra *b* 1970, — Theodosia Mary, *b* 1952: *m* 1976, Christopher Gouldstone, late Lieut Queen's Lancashire Regt, of Thorndene, Pluckley, Ashford, Kent, and has issue living, Edward Oliver *b* 1981, Emma Charlotte Elizabeth *b* 1979, — Katharine Agnes, *b* 1955. ⸻ †Alaric Charles William, *b* 1912; *ed* Eton; formerly a Member of the London Stock Exchange, and Maj Queen's Westminsters KRRC (TA): *m* 1940, Iris Charmian (44 Linver Rd, SW6 3RD), da of Noel Van Raalte (*see* Graham, Bt, *cr* 1783, colls, 1976 Edn), and *d* 1986, leaving issue, Michael Noel (10A Highbury New Park, Islington, N5 2DB; *Clubs* – City of London, Pratt's) *b* 1941; *ed* Eton, — Amanda Charmian, *b* 1946: *m* 1966, Martyn Anthony Hedley, of 67 Dovehouse St, SW3 6JY, elder son of Anthony Martyn Hedley, and has issue living, Simon Martyn *b* 1972, Sophie Amanda *b* 1969: *m* 1998, David James Christian Faber (*see* E Stockton). ⸻ David Hastings Gerald (The Old House, School Hill, Burwash, E Sussex TN19 7EA), *b* 1915; late Lt RNVR: *m* 1940, Hester Clere, da of late Rev Canon Richard Edward Parsons (*see* E Rosse, colls), and has issue living, Wriothesley David Xavier (*Clubs* - Queen's, and Ski Club of Gt Britain), *b* 1941; *ed* Eton, and Trin Coll, Dublin: *m* 1992, Melissa Tan Hui Chui, — Rupert Edward Odo (Highleaze House, Oare, Marlborough, Wilts SN8 4JE; *Club* – Buck's), *b* 1944; *ed* Selwyn House Sch, Montreal, and Rannoch Sch, Perths; Solicitor 1973; a Member of Law Soc; Chm Cities of London and Westminster Conservative Assocn 1979-83 (Vice-Pres 1984); Chm Buck's since 1995: *m* 1981, Catherine Jill, da of William Gulliver, and formerly wife of 5th Baron Brougham and Vaux.

Grandchildren of late Brig-Gen Hon Alexander Victor Frederick Villiers Russell, CMG, MVO, 4th son of 1st Baron:—
Issue of late Lt-Col William Rodney Villiers Russell, MC, *b* 1914, *d* 1994: *m* 1950, Diana Marigold (43 Upper Headland Park Rd, Preston, Paignton, S Devon), da of Arthur Trafford, of Paignton:—
Rupert Alick Villiers (18 Romford Rd, Pembury, Kent TN2 4JA), *b* 1951: *m* 1974, Laura Suzanne Golds, and has issue living, Christopher John, *b* 1983, — Elinor Kate, *b* 1981. ⸻ Sarah Caroline Villiers, *b* 1956: *m* 1996, Brian Roy Wort, of 40 Tartar Rd, Cobham, Surrey KT11 2AR.

Issue of late Capt Stephen Alexander Villiers Russell, Black Watch, *b* 1916, *d* 1985: *m* 1945, Ailsa Mary (Godford Land, Honiton, Devon), 2nd da of William Hope Pilcher, of The Gows, Invergowrie, Dundee:—
John Alick Stephen Villiers (Godford Land Farm, Awliscombe, nr Honiton, Devon), *b* 1946; *ed* Wellington: *m* 1975 (*m* diss 1986), Verity Elizabeth Anne Murray, and has issue living, Alick Robin, *b* 1976, — Guy James Villiers, *b* 1983, — Rosie Alice Swallow, *b* 1978. ⸻ Camilla Mary Louise, *b* 1949: *m* 1978, Robin Geoffrey Murray, of Pulmans, Beacon, Luppitt, nr Honiton, Devon, and has issue living, Charles Tobias Heatley, *b* 1978, — William Barnaby Robin, *b* 1980. ⸻ Lucy Marjorie Eileen, *b* 1954: *m* 1974, Christopher Nigel Gordon Smith, of Tuck Mill Cottage, Payhembury, nr Honiton, Devon EX14 0HF, and has issue living, Ben Christopher Gordon, *b* 1979, — Flora Eileen Ailsa, *b* 1981.

PREDECESSORS – (1) *Lord* ODO WILLIAM LEOPOLD Russell, GCB, GCMG, PC, brother of 9th Duke of Bedford, *b* 1829; the eminent diplomatist; was Sec at Constantinople Washington, and Florence, and afterwards for twelve years HM's Representative at Rome; went on Special Mission to Versailles during Franco-Prussian War 1870; joint Plenipotentiary (with Earl of Beaconsfield and Marquess of Salisbury) at Berlin Congress 1878; was Ambassador to the German Empire 1871-84; cr *Baron Ampthill*, of Ampthill, co Bedford (peerage of United Kingdom) 1881: *m* 1868, Lady Emily Theresa Villiers, who *d* 1927, da of 4th Earl of Clarendon; *d* 1884; *s* by his son (2) OLIVER ARTHUR VILLIERS, GCSI, GCIE, 2nd Baron, *b* 1869; was Gov of Madras 1899-1906 (Viceroy and Gov-Gen of India *ad interim* 1904); European War 1914-19 (despatches thrice, Brevet Col): *m* 1894, Lady Margaret Lygon, CI, GCVO, GBE, who *d* 1957, da of 6th Earl Beauchamp; *d* 1935; *s* by his eldest son (3) JOHN HUGO, CBE, 3rd Baron, *b* 1896; Capt RN: *m* 1st, 1918 (*m diss* 1937), Christabel Hulme, who *d* 1976, da of Lt-Col John Hart, of Broadhurst, Heathfield, Sussex (Erskine, Bt, colls); 2ndly, 1937, Sibell Faithfull, who *d* 1947, da of Thomas Wilkinson Lumley; 3rdly, 1948, Adeline Mary Constance, eldest da of Rev Canon Henry Evelyn Hone, V of Godalming; *d* 1973; *s* by his eldest son (4) GEOFFREY DENIS ERSKINE, 4th Baron and present peer.

AMWELL, BARON (Montague) (Baron UK 1947)

KEITH NORMAN MONTAGUE, 3rd Baron, *b* 1 April 1943; *s* 1990; *ed* Ealing Gram Sch, and Nottingham Univ (BSc); CEng, CGeol, FICE, FGS, MIHT: *m* 1970, Mary, only da of Frank Palfreyman, of Potters Bar, Herts, and has issue.

SONS LIVING

Hon IAN, *b* 1973.
Hon Christopher, *b* 1977.

SISTER LIVING

Hon Sheila Elizabeth, *b* 1949.

AUNTS LIVING (*Daughters of 1st Baron*)

Hon Constance, *b* 1915: *m* 1938, Albert Henry Cecil Slade, who *d* 1991, and has issue living, David *b* 1943, — Lesley, *b* 1946, — Stephanie, *b* 1956. *Residence* – 24 Kershaw Rd, Swindon, Wilts.
Hon Betty, *b* 1920: *m* 1941, John Forbes Dudley, who *d* 1995, and has issue living, Lysbeth, *b* 1947: *m* 1972, Kenneth John Hall, of The Anchorage, The Chalks, Chew Magna, Bristol BS18 8SN. *Residence* – 76 Eastcourt Rd, Burbage, Wilts, SN8 3AG.

WIDOW LIVING OF SECOND BARON

KATHLEEN ELIZABETH (*Kathleen, Baroness Amwell*), da of Arthur Percival Fountain: *m* 1939, the 2nd Baron Amwell, who *d* 1990.

PREDECESSORS – (1) FREDERICK Montague, CBE, son of John Montague, of Clerkenwell, EC, *b* 1876; Under-Sec of State for Air 1929-31, Parl Sec Min of Transport 1940-41, and Min of Aircraft Production 1941-42; MP for W Islington (*Lab*) 1923-31, and 1935-47; cr *Baron Amwell*, of Islington, co London (peerage of UK) 1947: *m* 1911, Constance, who *d* 1964, da of James Craig, of Runcorn; *d* 1966; *s* by his only son (2) FREDERICK NORMAN, 2nd Baron, *b* 1912; ARAeS: *m* 1939, Kathleen Elizabeth, da of Arthur Percival Fountain; *d* 1990; *s* by his only son (3) KEITH NORMAN, 3rd Baron and present peer.

ANCASTER, EARLDOM OF (Heathcote-Drummond-Willoughby) (Earl UK 1892) (Extinct 1983) (see Bs Willoughby de Eresby)

Ancram, Earl of; son of Marquess of Lothian.

Anderson, family name of Viscount Waverley.

Andover, Viscount; son of Earl of Suffolk and Berkshire.

ANELAY OF ST JOHNS, BARONESS (Anelay) (Life Baroness 1996)

JOYCE ANNE ANELAY, DBE, da of late Stanley Charles Clarke, of Enfield, Middlesex; *b* 17 July 1947; *ed* Enfield County Sch, Bristol Univ (BA 1968), London Univ Inst of Education (Cert Ed 1969), and Brunel Univ (MA 1982); Teacher, St David's Sch, Ashford, Middx 1969-74; Voluntary Adviser, Woking CAB 1976-85 (Chm 1988-93); Memb Social Security Appeal Tribunal 1983-96 and Social Security Advisory Cttee for GB and NI 1989-96; Chm Conservative Women's National Cttee 1993-96 (Chm SE Area Women's Cttee 1987-90; Vice-Chm SE Area Exec Cttee 1990-93); Memb Nat Union of Conservative Party since 1987 (Vice-Pres 1996-97) and Women's National Commn 1990-93; Pres Woking Citizens Advice Bureau since 1996; JP NW Surrey since 1985; Opposition Whip since June 1997; Chm Govrs, Hermitage First and Middle Schs 1981-88; FRSA 1991; Hon Dr of Social Sciences Brunel Univ 1997; *cr* OBE 1990, DBE 1995, and *Baroness Anelay of St Johns*, of St Johns, co Surrey (Life Baroness) 1996: *m* 1970, Richard Alfred Anelay, QC, son of late Maurice Alfred Anelay, of Darlington, co Durham.

Arms – Barry of four azure and or five acorns in cross counterchanged. **Supporters** – On either side an angel ppr vested argent winged sashed and blowing a trumpet supported by the exterior hand or.
Address – House of Lords, Westminster, SW1A 0PW; *Clubs* – Carlton, Woking Golf.

ANGLESEY, MARQUESS OF (Paget) (Marquess UK 1815, Bt I 1730, Earl GB 1714, Baron E 1549)

By means of its own opposite

GEORGE CHARLES HENRY VICTOR PAGET, 7th Marquess, and 10th Baronet; *b* 8 Oct 1922; *s* 1947; *ed* Eton; Maj RHG; FSA 1952, FRSL 1969, Hon FRIBA 1971, FRHistS 1975, Hon DLitt Wales 1984; CC Anglesey 1951-67, JP 1959-68 and 1983-89, DL 1960, Vice Lieut 1960, Lord Lieut of Gwynedd 1983-89; patron of four livings, and Lord of the Manor of Burton-on-Trent; Pres Anglesey Conservative Assocn 1948-83, Nat Museum of Wales 1962-68; Member Friends of Friendless Churches 1966-84, Ancient Monuments Soc 1979-84, Historic Buildings Council for Wales 1953 (Chm 1977-90), Royal Fine Art Comm 1965-71, Redundant Churches Fund 1969-78, and Royal Commn on Historical Manuscripts 1984-90; Trustee Nat Portrait Gallery 1979-90, and Nat Heritage Memorial Fund 1980-92; Hon Fellow Royal Cambrian Acad and Free-man City of London; CStJ 1984; Military Historian: *m* 1948, Elizabeth Shirley Vaughan, DBE, LVO, da of late Charles Morgan, LLD, and has issue.

Arms – Sable, on a cross engrailed between four eagles displayed argent, five lions passant guardant, of the field. **Crest** – A demi heraldic tiger sable, maned, tufted, and ducally gorged argent. **Supporters** – Two heraldic tigers sable, maned, tufted, and ducally gorged argent.
Seat – Plas Newydd, Llanfair PG, Anglesey.

SONS LIVING

CHARLES ALEXANDER VAUGHAN (*Earl of Uxbridge*) *b* 13 Nov 1950; *ed* Eton, Exeter Coll, Oxford, and Sussex Univ (MA, DPhil): *m* 1986, Georganne Elizabeth Elliott, da of late Col John Alfred Downes, MBE, MC, of Tudor Cottage, Whittlesford, Cambs, and has issue:—

> SON LIVING — Benedict Dashiel Thomas (*Lord Paget de Beaudesert*), *b* 11 April 1986.
> DAUGHTER LIVING — *Lady* Clara Elizabeth Isis, *b* 1988.

Lord Rupert Edward Llewellyn, *b* 1957; *ed* Westminster, and Oxford Air Training Sch: *m* 1st, 1982 (*m diss* 1996), Louise Victoria, yst da of Peter Hugh Youngman, of Charsfield Hall, Woodbridge, Suffolk; 2ndly, 1997, Meryl, yst da of late Donald Stewart Williams, of Llangoed, Anglesey, and has issue living (by 1st *m*), Jack William Kyffin, *b* 1989, — Lily Florence Angharad, *b* 1992. *Residence* – 58 Castle St, Beaumaris, Anglesey LL58 8BB.

DAUGHTERS LIVING

Lady Henrietta Charlotte Eiluned, *b* 1949: *m* 1979, Timothy Megarry

Lady (Elizabeth) Sophia Rhiannon, *b* 1954: *m* 1983, Robert D. Keir, son of James Dewar Keir, QC, of Crossways, High St, Dormansland, Surrey, and has issue living, (Owen) Samuel, *b* 1986, — (James) Oliver Dewar, *b* 1987. *Residence* – Lakelands Farm, Plaistow Rd, Kirdford, W Sussex RH14 0JR.

Lady Amelia Myfanwy Polly, *b* 1963: *m* 1984, Andrew M. Singleton, 2nd son of late Sir Edward Singleton, of 62 Queen's Gate, SW7 (*see* Scott, Bt, *cr* 1806, 1970 Edn), and has issue living, Henry Edward, *b* 1993, — Isobella Polly, *b* 1990.

SISTERS LIVING

Lady Rose Mary Primrose, *b* 1919: *m* 1940, Hon John Francis McLaren, Squadron-Leader RAF (ret), who *d* 1953 (*see* B Aberconway). *Residence* – Old Bodnod, Eglwysbach, Colwyn Bay, N Wales LL28 5RF.

Lady Katharine Mary Veronica (twin), *b* 1922: *m* 1st, 1941 (*m diss* 1948), Lt-Col Jocelyn Eustace Gurney, DSO, MC, Welsh Gds, who *d* 1973, son of late Sir Eustace Gurney; 2ndly, 1949, Charles Farrell, MC, late Major Scots Gds, and HM Foreign Ser, and has issue living (by 1st *m*), Judith Marjorie Katherine, *b* 1942: *m* 1964, James Bowen, of Rishworth Hall, Sowerby Bridge, W Yorks, and has issue living, Rachel Katherine *b* 1964, Eleanor Elizabeth *b* 1967, — (by 2nd *m*) Gerald Charles William, *b* 1956: *m* 1981, Joanna Rosemary, yr da of Col Philip Turner van Straubenzee, DSO, of Spennithorne House, Leyburn, N Yorks, and has issue living, Frederick Desmond Casimir *b* 1987, William *b* 1992, — Louisa Caroline Mary, *b* 1949: *m* 1970 (*m diss* 1993), Robin James Lane-Fox, 3rd son of late James Henry Lane-Fox, FRICS, of Middleton House, Middleton Cheney, Banbury, Oxon, and has issue living, Henry *b* 1975, Martha *b* 1973, — Diana (Dido) Eileen Mary, *b* 1958, — Marjorie Elizabeth Mary, *b* 1962. *Residence* – Cuttmill House, Watlington, Oxon.

COLLATERAL BRANCHES LIVING

Granddaughter of late Capt Lord Victor William Paget, MC (infra):—
Issue of late Henry Alexander Reginald Paget, *b* 1914, *d* 1995: *m* 1938, Sonia, da of late Count Paul Chatoulenco:—

Tessa Ann, *b* 1947: *m* 1967, Alexander Ramsay Hardman, and has issue living, Cameron Ramsay, *b* 1971, — Chouka Sonia, *b* 1968: *m* 1993, Adrian Price, and has issue living, Tom *b* 1998, Alexandra *b* 1994, Jessica *b* 1995. *Residence* – The Grange, West Street, Banwell, nr Bristol BS29 6DB.

Issue of late Capt Lord Victor William Paget, MC, brother of 6th Marquess, b 1889, d 1952: m 1st, 1913 (m diss 1921), Olive Mary (the actress, Miss Olive May), who d 1947, da of George Meatyard; 2ndly, 1922 (m diss 1932), Hon Bridget Colebrooke, who d 1975, da of 1st Baron Colebrooke (ext; see 1973-74 Edn); 3rdly, 1935, May Beatrice (Mavis), who d 1977, da of William Crockford, and widow of Maj Herbert Dawson, MC:—
(By 1st m) Peggy Hester Pauline (10 Southwick Close, Longfield Rd, E Grinstead, W Sussex RH19 2EF), b 1913: m 1st, 1935, Nigel Arthur St George Gibbes, Lieut 8th Hus, who d of wounds received in action in the Middle East, 1942; 2ndly, 1944 (m diss 1950), Maj (Samuel) Peter Barrow, MC, RA, who d 1990; 3rdly, 1954, Ian Coward, who d 1988, in Malta, and has issue living (by 1st m), Michael Henry Arthur, b 1936; ed Eton, and Camb Univ: m 1961, Veronica Lillian, da of John Hamilton Mackenzie Ward, of SW15, and has issue living, Nigel Hamilton b 1967, Marina Jane b 1962, — (by 2nd m) Bryan Hugh Samuel (Weidweg 19, 8405 Winterthur, Switzerland), b 1946; ed Wellington Coll, and Newcastle Univ: m 1972, Vreni, da of Rudolf Kramer, of Winterthur, Switzerland, and has issue living, Janet Clare b 1973, Nadia Jane b 1975. —— (By 2nd m) Nicholas David (23 The Limes, 34-36 Linden Gdns, W2 4ET), b 1924: m 1st, 1952 (m diss 1956), Mrs Heather Betty Bevis, da of late Charles Smetham; 2ndly, 1956, Mrs Moya Lillian Hayim, who d 1962, da of Capt William John Enright, OBE, RD, RNR; 3rdly, 1962, Ellen Bridget O'Neill, who d 1963, and has had issue (by 3rd m), †John David, b 1962; d 1994, — Jane Bridget, b 1963: m 19—, Paul Andrews, and has issue living, Leo b 19—. — Ann, b 1923.

Grandchildren of late Gen Rt Hon Sir Arthur Henry Fitzroy Paget, GCB, KCVO, eldest son of late Gen Lord Alfred Henry Paget, CB (infra):—
Issue of late Capt Arthur Wyndham Louis Paget, MC, b 1888, d 1966: m 1928, Rosemary Victoria, who d 1970, da of late Brig-Gen Noel Armar Lowry-Corry, DSO (see E Belmore, colls, 1970 Edn):—
David Arthur Fitzroy (East Kennett Manor, Marlborough, Wilts), b 1929; ed Eton, and Ch Ch, Oxford. —— Rosalind Louise (East Kennett Manor, Marlborough, Wilts), b 1931: m 1958, Dr Clive Bremner Cameron, and has issue living, James Paget, (15 Sistova Rd, SW12 9QR), b 1961: m 1993, Margaret Adela Francis, da of Ian Douglas George Cox, of Sheep Shaw Farm, Brightling, Robertsbridge, Sussex, and has issue living, Benjamin Paget b 1994, Oliver Bremner Ian b 1996, — Andrew Wyndham Armar, b 1965, — Sarah Louise, b 1959.

Grandchildren of late Gen Lord Alfred Henry Paget, CB, 5th son of 1st Marquess:—
Issue of late Sir Almeric Hugh Paget, GBE, who was cr Baron Queenborough 1918 (see that title) (ext).

(In remainder to Earldom of Uxbridge and Barony of Paget de Beaudesert only)

Granddaughter of late Francis Edward Howard Paget, eldest son of late Howard Francis Paget, only son of Rev Francis Edward Paget, only son (by 1st m) of Gen Hon Sir Edward Paget (infra):—
Issue of late Capt Edward Francis Howard Paget, Gren Gds, b 1910, d 1985: m 1948 (m diss 1972), Bridget, who d 1979, da of late Charles Harold Ellis, of Willington House, nr Maidestone:—
Caroline Charlotte, b 1950; BSc: m 1974, Hensel John Peters, of Jamestown, St Helena, S Atlantic Ocean, and has issue living, Howard Hensel, b 1974, — Nicole Maria, b 1982.

Granddaughters of late Salisbury Howard Paget, 2nd son of late Howard Francis Paget (ante):—
Issue of late late John Henry Howard Paget, b 1925, d 1983: m 1948, Grace, da of E. Tunnicliffe, of Austrey, Warwicks:—
Deborah Ann, b 1952: m 1972, Norman Edward Sanford, and has issue living, Stephen Andrew, b 1980, — Michael Benjamin, b 1982. Residence – 69 Child Drive, Aurora, Ontario L4G 1Y8, Canada. —— Kathryn Mary, b 1956: m 1979, William John Scrafton. Residence – 98 Connaught Av, Willowdale, Ontario M2M 1H2.

Grandchildren of late Hugh Arthur Paget, 2nd son of late Rev Edward Heneage Paget (infra):—
Issue of late Clarence Arthur Edward Paget, b 1909, d 1991: m 1942, Cynthia Mary, who d 1977, da of late Herbert Hutchings:—
Hugh Charles Edward (27 Highbury Hill, N5 1SU), b 1946; ed Eton, and Merton Coll, Oxford: m 1977, Eleanor Mary, only da of late Rev Canon William Wallis, and has issue living, Francis Andrew Edward, b 1984, — Lucy Caroline Eleanor, b 1981. —— Caroline Hermione, b 1942: m 1966, Dr Theodore Bennett Robbins, of Box 257, North Pomfret, Vermont 05053, USA. —— Frances Catherine (Stark House Farm, Headley, Newbury, Berks RG19 8AR), b 1947. —— Selina Mary (64 Longlands Rd, Slaithwaite, W Yorks HD7 5DR), b 1950.

Granddaughter of late Rev Edward Heneage Paget, yst son (by 2nd m) of late Gen Hon Sir Edward Paget, GCB, 4th son of 1st Earl of Uxbridge:—
Issue of late Eric Morton Paget, b 1867, d 1929: m 1904, Georgina Byng, who d 1916, da of late Herbert Byng Paget, of Darley House, Darley Dale, Derbyshire:—
Celia Mary (twin), b 1916: m 1st, 1942 (m diss 1946), Charles Cecil Patrick Kirwan; 2ndly, 1954, Arthur John Goodman, who d 1964, and has issue living (by 2nd m), Mark, b 1957, — Ariane, b 1955: m 1984, Andrew Dykes Scott Bankes, who d 1987 (see Spicer, Bt). Residence – 49 Grantchester St, Cambridge CB3 9HZ.

Grandchildren of late Leopold Cecil Paget, 2nd son of late Berkeley Paget, eldest son of late Capt Catesby Paget, 2nd son of late Hon Berkeley Thomas Paget (infra):—
Issue of late Edward Catesby Paget, b 1903, d 1963: m 1940, Sibyl Gladys Rodney (L'Amunia, Apartado 20, Gaucín, Malaga, Spain) (who m 3rdly, 1963, Col Thomas Cromwell Williamson, DSO, who d 1987), da of late Col Charles Edward Duff, CB, and formerly wife of Col Robert Albert Glanville Bingley, CVO, DSO, OBE, 11th Hus, of Pegglesworth, Andoversford, Glos:—
(Anthony) Berkeley (Poco Poco, Avila 45, Sotogrande, Cadiz, Spain), b 1946: m 1st, 1976 (m diss 1979), Judith Mary Parry; 2ndly, 1981, Gabriele Mathilde Langer, of Munich, and has issue living (by 1st m), William Berkeley, b 1976, — (by 2nd m), Catesby Langer, b 1982, — Rodney Langer, b 1984. —— Diana Jenefer (L'Amunia, Apartado 20, Gaucín, Malaga Spain), b 1943.

Grandchildren of late Lt-Col Cyril Nevil Paget, VD (infra):—

Issue of late Richard Berkeley Paget, *b* 1928, *d* 1991: *m* 1965 (*m diss* 1986), Nicola Mary, eldest da of late Archibald Baird-Murray, of Old Park, Warninglid, Sussex:—
Edward Berkeley (1 Hart Hill, St John's Hill Rd, Woking, Surrey GU21 1RG), *b* 1977. ——Henrietta Elizabeth (5 Coleridge House, Churchill Gdns, Pimlico, SW1V 3HU), *b* 1966. ——Annabelle Mary (1 Hart Hill, St John's Hill Rd, Woking, Surrey GU21 1RG), *b* 1968. ——Charlotte Patricia, *b* 1971: *m* 1996, Javier Philipps, of 34 Edinburgh Rd, Chatham, Kent ME4 5BY.

Granddaughters of late Com Claude Paget, RN, 2nd son of late Col Leopold Grimston Paget, 3rd son of Hon Berkeley Thomas Paget, 6th son of 1st Earl of Uxbridge:—
Issue of late Lt-Col Cyril Nevil Paget, VD, *b* 1891, *d* 1980: *m* 1928, Eveleen Mary, who *d* 1983, da of late Barnaby Lanktree, of Cork:—
Mary Patricia, *b* 1931: *m* 1969, Lawrence Butterfield, TD, FRIBA, of Shepherds Wood, Sheffield Park, E Sussex. ——Caroline Eve Mary (20 Hampstead Gdns, NW11), *b* 1935: *m* 1st, 1956 (*m diss* 1984), Anthony Aljoe; 2ndly, 1984, Francis J. B. Smith, and has issue living (by 1st *m*), Mark Coade, *b* 1959: *m* 1988, Sally Hancock.

Granddaughters of late Bernard Leopold Paget, 2nd son of late Rev Cecil George Paget (infra):—
Issue of late Michael Robertson Paget, *b* 1936, *d* 1994: *m* 1960, Mrs Betty May Hobden (Chansons, 23 Ellesmere Rd, Uphill Village, Weston-super-Mare, Avon, BS23 4UT), da of Edwin Hobbs Browning, of Weston-super-Mare, and formerly wife of Ernest Ralph Hobden:—
Gérardine Carol-Louise, *b* 1961; BA, BPhil: *m* 1996, Dominic Francis Stockford, of Blandford, Dorset, and has issue living, Anna Clare, *b* 1998. ——Sarah Catherine, *b* 1963; BA.

Granddaughters of late Rev Cecil George Paget, 3rd son of Col Leopold Grimston Paget (ante):—
Issue of late Felix Barnaby Paget, *b* 1904, *d* 1985: *m* 1st, 1932, Marjorie Therese, who *d* 1962, da of late Lt-Col Charles Seaver-Smith, RAMC; 2ndly, 1964, Dora Josephine Adams Clark, MRCS, LRCP, who *d* 1990:—
(By 1st *m*) Susan Jane Seaver (Barn End, 54A Ruff Lane, Ormskirk, Lancs L39 4UL), *b* 1933; dental surgeon: *m* 1957 (*m diss* 1984), J. Keith Wood, MSc, PhD, AMIEE, and has issue living, Jonathan Piers Martin, *b* 1962, — Carolyn Jane, *b* 1965, — Elizabeth Anne, *b* 1967. ——Carolyn Elizabeth, *b* 1935: *m* 1st, 1962, Arthur James Sanderson, ACII, who *d* 1986; 2ndly, 1991, John Aston, of 125 Hardhorn Rd, Poulton-le-Fylde, Lancs FY6 7ES, and has issue living (by 1st *m*), Helen Louise, *b* 1965, — Wendy Elizabeth, *b* 1967, — Clare Marjorie, *b* 1970.

Granddaughter of late Lieut-Col Arthur Leopold Paget, 5th son of late Col Leopold Grimston Paget (ante):—
Issue of late Oswald Leopold Paget, Durham LI, *b* 1898, *d* 1955: *m* 1931, Barbara Mackintosh, who *d* 1968, da of Arthur Forman Balfour Paul, MC, FRIBA, of Peffermill, Craigmillar:—
Susan Blanche, *b* 1933: *m* 1956, Capt William Mitchell Miller, MVO, late Gren Gds, of Craighill, Kinellan Rd, Edinburgh EH12 6ES, and has issue living, Richard Neville (63 Grannes Terrase, 4044 Hafrasfjord, Norway), *b* 1964: *m* 1990, Eli Sondenaa, of Bryne, Norway, and has issue living, William Sebastian *b* 1996, Hanna Victoria *b* (triplet) 1996, Lotte Emilia *b* (triplet) 1996, — Anna Caroline (The Old Manse, 4 Claremont Park, Edinburgh), *b* 1959: *m* 1989 (*m diss* 1996), Jack Cummins, — Victoria Jane, *b* 1961: *m* 1987, Dr William Russell Alexander, of Veltheimer Strasse 18, 5105 Auenstein, Switzerland, and has issue living, Wilhelm Lachlan *b* 1990, Douglas Mitchell *b* 1992, Islay Barbara *b* 1994, Holly Alison *b* (twin) 1994.

Grandchildren of late Mark John Paget, 9th and yst son of late Col Leopold Grimston Paget (ante):—
Issue of late John Francis Paget, *b* 1903, *d* 1989: *m* 1932, Ann Millicent, who *d* 1981, da of Peter Arthur Blundell, formerly of Ridgelands, Cooparoo, Brisbane, Australia:—
Peter Jeremy Valentine, RD (West House, Stein, Waternish, I of Skye IV55 8GA), *b* 1933; *ed* Malvern; Lt-Cdr RNR, and Master Mariner: *m* 1st, 1963, Helene Boye Hansen, who *d* 1978, of Ormoy, Stavangar, Norway; 2ndly, 19—, Mrs Sara Veronica Mills, only da of late Mrs Joycella Colbourne, of 44 Gold St, Saffron Walden, Essex, and has issue living (by 1st *m*), Mark Sebastian Boye, *b* 1967, — Charles John Leopold, *b* 1974, — Caroline Elizabeth Astrid, *b* 1964; has issue living, Jake Aidan PAGET *b* 1993. ——Sarah Ann Victoria, *b* 1945: *m* 1968, James Lewis, RIBA, of 101 High St, Marshfield, Chippenham, Wilts, and has issue living, Brett, *b* 1970: *m* 1992, John Benjamin Gardner, of Nailey Farm, St Catherine's, Bath, and has issue living, Benjamin James *b* 1993, Joshua George *b* 1996, — Kim, *b* 1973. ——Jane Melanie, *b* 1947: *m* 1967, Lt-Col Richard Seymour Corkran, Gren Gds, of Crockfords, Waltham St Lawrence, Berks, and has issue living, Claire Melanie, *b* 1973, — Alexandra Frances Louise, *b* 1976.

(In remainder to Baronetcy only)

Grandchildren of late Col Edward Richard Bayly, grandson of late Rev Edward Bayly, R of Killurin, son of late Lambert Bayly, 3rd son of 1st Bt:—
Issue of late Maj Edward Archibald Theodore Bayly, DSO, *b* 1877, *d* 1959: *m* 1921, Ileene Caroline Ethel Otway, who *d* 1960, da of late Major Arthur Augustus Hamlet Inglefield, of Old Church House, Beckington, Bath:—
Edward Archibald Richard (Ballyarthur, Arklow, co Wicklow), *b* 1922; *ed* St Columba's Coll, Trin Coll, Dublin, and Trin Coll, Oxford: *m* 1964, Rosemarie Evelyn Gisela Steins, only da of late Paul Heinrich Johann Minkley, of Frankfurt-on-Main, and has issue living, Edward Alexander Christian Lambart, *b* 1967, — Selina Ileene Suzanne Rosemarie, *b* 1965: *m* 1986, Robert J. Kavanagh, of Raheen, Beech Rd, Arklow, co Wicklow, and has issue living, Emma-Sarah Rosemarie Isabelle *b* 1988, — Catriona Louise Alicia Lucinda, *b* 1977. ——Adelaide Elizabeth Mary, *b* 1923: *m* 1955, Patrick Mullen, of Rathquage, Bonmahon, co Waterford, and has issue living, Anthony Patrick Theodore (3 Dundela Av, Sandycove, co Dublin), *b* 1956; *ed* De La Salle Coll, and Univ Coll, Dublin: *m* 1980, Aideen Mary, yst da of Frederick Shackleton, of 3 Kenure Lawns, Rush, co Dublin, and has issue living, Benjamin Anthony *b* 1983, Patrick William *b* 1984, Constance Elizabeth Joy *b* 1989, India Margaret Eileen *b* 1993, — Annabelle Sandra (Boatstrand, Annestown, co Waterford), *b* 1957. ——Rosabelle Ileene Zahra, *b* 1931: *m* 1957, Donald Brian Robinson, Gp Capt RAF (ret), of Green Acres, nr Chepstow, Mon, and has issue living, Colan Denis (Trelowth Farm Cottage, Trelowth, St Austell, Cornwall PL26 7DZ), *b* 1958: *m* 1988, Jane Hilary Shrimpton, and has issue living, Matthew Conor *b* 1988, Tobias Ryan Edward *b* 1997, Anna Kirsten *b* 1990, — Timothy Rupert (Blue Tiles, Parkway Drive, Sonning, Berks RG4 6HG), *b* 1965: *m* 1994, Sally Anne, da of A. R. Manning, of Earley, Reading, Berks, and has issue living, Samuel Harvey *b* 1996, — Judith Sarah, *b* 1962.

PREDECESSORS – (1) Sir WILLIAM Paget, KG, PC, was summoned to Parliament of England as *Lord Paget de Beaudesert* 1549; *d* 1563; *s* by his eldest son (2) Sir HENRY, KB, 2nd Baron, *d* 1568; *s* by his brother (3) THOMAS, 3rd Baron, who was attainted and his property confiscated; *d* 1589; *s* by his only son (4) WILLIAM, 4th Baron, who was restored to his rank and honours by Parliament; *d* 1629; *s* by his eldest son (5) WILLIAM, 5th Baron, Lord-Lieut of Bucks; *d* 1678; *s* by his son (6) WILLIAM, 6th Baron, Ambassador to the Sublime Porte; *d* 1713; *s* by his son (7) HENRY, 7th Baron, cr *Baron Burton* 1712, and *Earl of Uxbridge* (peerage of Great Britain) 1714; *d* 1743; *s* by his grandson (8) HENRY, 2nd Earl; *d* unmarried 1769, when the Barony of Burton and Earldom of Uxbridge became extinct, and the Barony of Paget devolved upon the son of Caroline, Lady Bayly, wife of Sir Nicholas Bayly, 2nd Bt, and da of Brig-Gen Thomas Paget, son of Henry, 2nd son of 5th Baron (9) HENRY, 9th Baron, assumed the surname and arms of Paget only; cr *Earl of Uxbridge* (peerage of Great Britain), 1784 *d* 1812; *s* by his son (10) Field Marshal HENRY WILLIAM, KG, GCB, GCH, 2nd Earl, a distinguished Cavalry officer in the Peninsular war, who at the head of the United British, Hanoverian and Belgian Horse, rendered exceptionally substantial aid at the battle of Waterloo, where he lost a leg; was Col of Royal Horse Guards, Lord-Lieut of cos Anglesey and Stafford, twice Lord-Lieut of Ireland, and Master-Gen of Ordnance, etc; cr *Marquess of Anglesey* (peerage of United Kingdom) 1815; *d* 1854; *s* by his eldest son (11) HENRY, PC, 2nd Marquess, *b* 1797; a Col in the Army and Lord-Lieut of Anglesey; summoned to House of Lords 1832 in his father's barony of Paget: *m* 1st, 1819, Eleanora, who *d* 1828, da of John Campbell, of Shawfield; 2ndly, Henrietta Maria, who *d* 1844, da of Rt Hon Sir Charles Bagot, GCB; 3rdly, 1860, Ellen Jane, who *d* 1874, da of George Burnand; *d* 1869; *s* by eldest son (12) HENRY WILLIAM GEORGE, 3rd Marquess; *dsp* 1880; *s* by his half-brother (13) HENRY, 4th Marquess, *b* 1835; *m* 1st, 1858, Elizabeth, who *d* 1873, da of Joseph Norman; 2ndly, 1874, Blanche Mary, who *d* 1877, da of Curwen Boyd, of Merton Hall, co Wigton; 3rdly, 1880, Mary Livingstone, who *d* 1931, da of J. P. King, of Sandhills, Georgia, USA, and widow of Hon Henry Wodehouse (E Kimberley); *d* 1898; *s* by his son (14) HENRY CYRIL, 5th Marquess, *b* 1875; *m* 1898, Lilian Florence Maud (who *d* 1962, having *m* 2ndly, 1909, Capt John Francis Grey Gilliat), da of Sir George Chetwynd, 4th Bt; *d* 1905; *s* by his cousin (15) CHARLES HENRY ALEXANDER, GCVO (son of late Lord Alexander Victor Paget, 3rd son of 2nd Marquess), 6th Marquess, *b* 1885; Lord-Lieut of Anglesey; Lord Chamberlain to HM Queen Mary 1922-47: *m* 1912, Lady Victoria Marjorie Harriet Manners, who *d* 1946, da of 8th Duke of Rutland; *d* 1947; *s* by his only son (16) GEORGE CHARLES HENRY VICTOR, 7th Marquess and present peer; also Earl of Uxbridge and Lord Paget of Beaudesert.

ANNALY, BARON (White) (Baron UK 1863)

My strength and valour

LUKE RICHARD WHITE, 6th Baron; *b* 29 June 1954; *s* 1990; *ed* Eton, RMA Sandhurst, and RAC Cirencester; Royal Hussars 1974-78, RAC Res 1978-86: *m* 1983, Caroline Nina, yr da of late Lt-Col Robert Hugh Garnett, MBE, of Hope Bowdler Court, nr Church Stretton, Shropshire, and has issue.

Arms – Argent, on a chevron engrailed gules, between three roses of the last, a cross crosslet or. **Crest** – A cubit arm, proper, charged with a chevron engrailed gules, thereon a cross crosslet or; in the hand three roses gules, slipped proper. **Supporters** – *Dexter*, a horse argent, caparisoned with the trappings of 14th regiment of Light Dragoons, proper; *sinister,* an Irish wolf-hound proper, gorged with an antique crown, and chained or.
Residence – Heath Farm, Fritwell, nr Bicester, Oxon OX6 9QS. *Club* – Cavalry and Guards'.

SON LIVING

Hon LUKE HENRY, *b* 20 Sept 1990.

DAUGHTERS LIVING

Hon Lavinia Marye, *b* 1987.
Hon Iona Elizabeth, *b* 1989.

HALF-SISTERS LIVING (*daughters of 5th Baron by 2nd marriage*)

Hon Doone Patricia, *b* 1961: *m* 1995, Julian Gervase Smith, only son of Antony Gervase Smith, of Cozen's House, Orcheston, Wilts.
Hon Caroline Davina, *b* 1963.

AUNT LIVING (*daughter of 4th Baron*)

Hon Elizabeth Patricia, *b* 1923; European War 1942-45 in WAAF: *m* 1945, Lt-Cmdr (James) Osborne King, DSC, RNVR, and has issue living, James (Rademon, Crossgar, co Down), *b* 1952; *ed* Eton: *m* 1981, Sally Louisa, da of Alan Walker-Gray, of Nicholas Way Cottage, Northwood, Middx, and has issue living, James Charles Osborne *b* 1984, Dillon Alexander Jolyon *b* 1987, Justin Sheridan Vere *b* 1990, — Elizabeth Lavinia Sara (74 Castleward Rd, Strangford, co Down BT30 7JU), *b* 1946: *m* 1969 (*m diss* 1992), David Hugh Montgomery, son of late Maj Hugh Edward Montgomery, of Rosemount, Greyabbey, co Down (*see* E Carlisle, colls, 1940 Edn), and has issue living, Matthew Hugh *b* 1970,

Alexander James *b* 1974, — (Patricia) Rose (85 York Mansions, Prince of Wales Drive, SW11), *b* 1947: *m* 1970, Antony Douglas George North (PO Box 781336, Sandton 2146, S Africa), son of late William Douglas Herbert North, of North-dene, Rathfelder Av, Constantia, Cape Town, and has issue living, Christopher Douglas Antony *b* 1976, Richard James Patrick *b* 1978, Georgina Chloë Shallcross *b* 1972: *m* 1997, Richard W. Goldsbrough, son of Bill Goldsbrough, of W Lavington, Wilts. *Residence* – 20 The Craig Rd, Downpatrick, co Down.

WIDOW LIVING OF FIFTH BARON

BEVERLEY ELISABETH (*Beverley, Baroness Annaly*), da of late William Maxwell, of Essex, and formerly wife of Michael Healy; Founder Anastasia Trust 'Sign' Campaign for Deaf People: *m* 1984, as his 3rd wife, the 5th Baron Annaly, who *d* 1990. *Residence* – 33 Chipstead St, SW6 3SR.

PREDECESSORS – (1) HENRY, son of late Luke White, MP for Leitrim, *b* 1790; Lord-Lieut of co Longford, and MP for Dublin (*L*) 1823-32, and for co Longford 1837-47 and 1857-63; cr *Baron Annaly* (peerage of United Kingdom) 1863: *m* 1828, Ellen, who *d* 1868, da of William S Dempster, of Skibo Castle, Sutherlandshire; *d* 1873; *s* by his eldest son (2) LUKE, KP, 2nd Baron, *b* 1829; sat as MP for Longford (*L*) 1861-2, and for Kidderminster 1862-6; was Lord-Lieut of co Longford 1873-4: *m* 1853, Emily, who *d* 1915, da of James Stuart; *d* 1888; *s* by his eldest son (3) LUKE, GCVO, 3rd Baron, *b* 1857; a Lord of the Bedchamber to Prince of Wales 1908-10, and Permanent Lord-in-Waiting to King George V 1910-21: *m* 1884, Hon Lilah Georgina Augusta Constance Agar-Ellis, who *d* 1944, da of 3rd Viscount Clifden; *d* 1922; *s* by his son (4) LUKE HENRY, MC, 4th Baron, *b* 1885; Maj 11th Hussars: *m* 1919, Lady Lavinia Emily Spencer, who *d* 1955, da of 6th Earl Spencer; *d* 1970; *s* by his son (5) LUKE ROBERT, 5th Baron, *b* 1927, F/O RAF 1944-48, Ptnr W. Greenwell & Co, and Member of London Stock Exchange, Freeman City of London: *m* 1st, 1953 (*m diss* 1957), Lady Marye Isabel Pepys, who *d* 1958, da of 7th Earl of Cottenham; 2ndly, 1960 (*m diss* 1967), Jennifer Margaret, only da of late Rupert Saumarez Carey, OBE, of East Hoe Manor, Hambledon, Hants; 3rdly, 1984, Mrs Beverley Elisabeth Healy, da of late William Maxwell; *d* 1990; *s* by his only son (6) LUKE RICHARD, 6th Baron and present peer.

ANNAN, BARON (Annan) (Life Baron 1965)

NOEL GILROY ANNAN, OBE, son of late James Gilroy Annan, of Bryanston Court, W1; *b* 25 Dec 1916; *ed* Stowe, and at King's Coll, Camb (Fellow 1944-56, Provost 1956-66); a Member of Academic Planning Board of Univ of E Anglia, and Chm of Academic Planning Board of Univ of Essex; Senior Fellow of Eton Coll 1956-66; a Gov of Stowe Sch 1945-66, and of Queen Mary Coll, London 1956-60; Univ Lecturer in Politics 1948-66, a Trustee of Churchill Coll, Camb since 1958, of British Museum 1963-78, Trustee Nat Gallery 1978-85, Pres London Library 1984; Provost of Univ Coll, London 1966-78, Vice-Chancellor of Univ of London 1978-81; 1939-45 War as Lt-Col with Mil Intelligence in War Cabinet Office in London, and in France and Germany; Cdr of Roy Order of King George I of the Hellenes; *cr* OBE (Mil) 1946, and *Baron Annan*, of Royal Burgh of Annan, co Dumfries (Life Peerage) 1965: *m* 1950, Gabriele, da of Louis Ferdinand Ullstein, of Berlin, and has issue.
Residence – 45 Ranelagh Grove, SW1W 8PB.

DAUGHTERS LIVING

Hon Amanda Lucy, *b* 1952: *m* 1977, Spencer Thomas de Grey, CBE, and has issue (*see* B Walsingham, colls).
Hon Juliet Louise, *b* 1955: *m* 1987, Dr James Richard Le Fanu, of 24 Grafton Sq, SW4 0DB, 2nd son of Richard Le Fanu, of 8 Malvern Terr, N1, and has issue living, Frederick James, *b* 1989, — Allegra Frances, *b* 1992.

ANNANDALE AND HARTFELL, EARL OF (Johnstone of Annandale and that Ilk) (Earl S by Charter 1662 with precedence 1643)

PATRICK ANDREW WENTWORTH HOPE JOHNSTONE OF ANNAN-DALE AND THAT ILK, 11th Earl; *b* 19 April 1941; *s* 1983 (claim to Earldom admitted by Committee for Privileges of House of Lords, and a writ issued summoning him to Parliament in the Upper House 1985); *ed* Stowe, and RAC Cirencester; Hereditary Steward of Annandale, Hereditary Keeper of Lochmaben Castle, Chief of Clan Johnstone; DL Nithsdale and Annandale and Eskdale Districts 1987; Vice Lord Lieut 1992; Chm Royal Jubilee and Prince's Trusts for Dumfries and Galloway 1984-88, Dir Murray Lawrence Members Agency, London, 1988-92, an Underwriting Memb of Lloyds since 1976: *m* 1969, Susan, only da of Col Walter John Macdonald Ross, CB, OBE, TD, JP, DL, of Netherhall, Castle Douglas, Kirkcudbrightshire, and has issue.

Arms – Argent, a saltire sable, on a chief gules three cushions or. Crest – a winged spur or. Supporters – Dexter, a lion rampant argent armed and langued azure crowned with an imperial crown or. Sinister, a horse argent furnished gules. Motto – Nunquam non paratus (never unprepared).
Seat – Lochwood Castle, Dumfries-shire.

SON LIVING

Hon DAVID PATRICK WENTWORTH (*Master of Annandale and Hartfell; Lord Johnstone*), *b* 13 Oct 1971; *ed* Stowe, and St Andrews Univ.

DAUGHTER LIVING

Lady Julia Claire, *b* 1974; *ed* St Ann's Sch, Windermere, and West of England Univ, Bristol (BA).

SISTER LIVING

Lady Eileen Elizabeth, *b* 1948: *m* 1969, Andrew Walter Bryce Duncan, of Newlands, Kirkmahoe, Dumfries-shire, son of Sir Arthur Bryce Duncan, and has issue living, John Walter Bryce, *b* 1971, — Edward James Bryce, *b* 1974, — Henry Andrew Bryce, *b* 1975.

HALF-AUNT LIVING *(Daughter of de jure 9th Earl by 2nd marriage)*

Lady Jean Evelyn, *b* 1917: *m* 1950, Maj Robert Philip Henry Elwes, MBE, MC, who *d* 1976, and has issue living, Sarah Jane, *b* 1951: *m* 1975, (Arthur) Guy Galbraith, of Newbold Revel, Haddington, E Lothian EH41 4HE, and has issue (*see* V Hampden, colls). *Residence* – Meadbank, 12 Parkgate Rd, SW1 4NN.

COLLATERAL BRANCHES LIVING *(also in remainder, in male line, to Earldom of Hopetoun)*

Grandchildren of late Violet Constance, *b* 1881, *d* 1965, elder da of late Capt Percy Alexander Hope Johnstone, yr brother of John James Hope Johnstone (*de jure* 8th Earl of Annandale and Hartfell): *m* 1908, Capt Llewellyn Heywood Jones, late 5th Lancers, who *d* 19—:—

Issue of late Hugh HEYWOOD JONES, 10th Royal Hus and RAF, *b* 1909, *d* 1969: *m* 1937, Perena Grace, who *d* 1985, eldest da of late Sir Edward Ernest Pearson, JP (*see* Crofton, Bt, 1671, colls, 1971 Edn), and formerly wife of Capt Marcus George Roddick, 10th R Hus:—

Llewellyn HEYWOOD JONES (29 Flag Walk, Eastcote High Rd, Pinner, Middx), *b* 1937; *ed* Gordonstoun; Master Mariner, served Merchant Navy 1955-70, since when a civil servant with US Navy Mil Sealift Cmnd Office UK: *m* 1976, Irene Dorothy, SRN, da of late John Maurice Mark Andrews, of 18 Winchester Rd, Bexleyheath, Kent, and has issue living, Benjamin John, *b* 1980, — Perena, *b* 1978. —— Imogen Iris Heywood, *b* 1944: *m* 1965, Christopher Bowly, and has issue living, Hamish, *b* 1966, — Samantha, *b* 1970.

Issue of late Olwen Heywood Jones, *b* 1911, *d* 1980: *m* 1940, Anthony Abel Smith, 10th R Hus (*see* B Sudeley, 1926 Edn), who *d* 1979:—

Timothy Bertram ABEL SMITH, *b* 1941; *ed* Eton: *m* 1965, Susanna Mary, who *d* 1997, eldest da of Douglas Collins (*see* Backhouse, Bt, 1980 Edn), and has issue living, Lucy, *b* 1969, — Julia, *b* 1971. *Residence* – 30 Dawson Place, W2.

Grandson of late George Wentworth Hope Johnstone, eldest son of late Charles Cecil Gordon Hope Johnstone, elder son of George Gordon Hope Johnstone, 2nd son of John James Hope Johnstone (*de jure* 7th Earl):—

Issue of late George Ernest Gordon Hope Johnstone, *b* 1901, *d* 1994: *m* 1st, 1926, Anna Dorothea Florence, who *d* 1959, only da of late Hon (Edward) Grenville Gore-Langton (*see* E Temple of Stowe, colls, 1959 Edn); 2ndly, 1940, Aileen Stephen, who *d* 1987, da of late Alfred Ewing:—
(By 2nd *m*) John Wentworth Gordon, *b* 1944: *m* 1st, 1969 (*m diss* 1975), Trudy, da of Dennis Delmar Dalquist; 2ndly, 1979, Patricia, da of Phillip Fisher, and has isue living (by 1st *m*), Jared Jay, *b* 1972, — Jodi Marie, *b* 1974.

Grandsons of late George Granville Hope Johnstone, eldest son of late William James Hope Johnstone, yr son of George Gordon Hope Johnstone (ante):—
Issue of late Col William August Ludwig Vernon Alexander Hope Johnstone, *b* 1914, *d* 1993: *m* 1943 (*m diss* 1951), Pamela Maud, who *d* (6 Sept) 1994, elder da of late Lt-Col John Murray Cobbold, of Glemham Hall, Suffolk (*see* D Devonshire, 1985 Edn):—
Philip William HOPE-COBBOLD (Glemham Hall, Woodbridge, Suffolk), *b* 1943; *ed* Radley, and RMA Sandhurst; late Maj 13th/18th Royal Hus; assumed the surname of Hope-Cobbold in lieu of his patronymic by deed poll 1995, following his succession to the Glemham Hall estate: *m* 1968 (*m diss* 1984), Antonia Jay, da of late Jack Yuan Hutton-Potts, and has issue living, Thomas William, *b* 1974; *ed* Stowe,—Timothy Mark, *b* 1976; *ed* Stowe. —— †Charles John Victor, *b* 1948; *ed* Radley, and Grenoble and Madrid Univs; *d* (10 Sept) 1994.

Granddaughter (by 1st *m*) of late Charles Henry Edmund Hope Johnstone, son of late Capt William George Hope Johnstone, RN, son of Capt George James Hope Johnstone, RN, yr brother of John James Hope Johnstone (*de jure* 7th Earl) (ante):—
Issue of late George William Hope Johnstone, *b* 1902, *d* 1985: *m* 1st, 1925 (*m diss* 1932), Dorothy Charity, da of Frederic Beasley-Hartley, of Birkhead, NZ; 2ndly, 1933 (*m diss* 1946), Amelia Daphne, da of Thomas Henry de Auvergne de Thierry, of Puniho, Taranaki, NZ; 3rdly, 1946, Helen Louisa, who *d* 1964, da of late William Taylor, of Howick, Scotland:—
(By 2nd *m*) Carolyn Ann, *b* 1938: *m* 1960, Gordon John Bracher, of 14 Reiman St, New Lynn, Auckland, NZ, and has issue living, Jonathan Charles, *b* 1963: *m* 1989, Sonia Claudette Mary, da of Edward John Galea Phipps, — Louise Jane, *b* 1961: *m* 1983, Geoffrey Stuart David Cooke, of 8 Grandison Crescent, New Lynn, Auckland, NZ, and has issue living, Nathaniel David John *b* 1986, Sophia Jane *b* 1988, Elizabeth Ann *b* 1990, Juliette Rose *b* 1992.

Grandchildren of late George William Hope Johnstone (ante):—
Issue of late Graeme William Hope Johnstone, *b* 1934, *d* 1979: *m* 1961, Robin, da of late Edward Herbert, of Sydney, NSW:—
Gregory William, *b* 1963. —— Bruce Edward, *b* 1968. —— Trudy Anne (twin), *b* 1963: *m* 1989, Paul John Neave, RNZAF, and has issue living, Ryan Matthew, *b* 1993. —— Nerida Mae, *b* 1972.

Granddaughter of late Charles Henry Edmund Hope Johnstone (ante):—
Issue of late Charles James Hope Johnstone, *b* 1907, *d* 1964: *m* 1933, Ellen Sarah, da of Henry John Bennett Gason, of Temuka, S Canterbury, NZ:—
Robyn HOPE JOHNSTONE, *b* 1945; has resumed her maiden name: *m* 1954 (*m diss* 1992), Glen Douglas Ireland, of Kaiwaka, NZ, and has issue living, Kim Joanne, *b* 1967, — Gina Dianna, *b* 1969: *m* 1990, Matthew Harrison, — Jodi Hope, *b* 1971. *Address* – PO Box 101330, N Shore Mail Centre, NZ.

PREDECESSORS – JAMES JOHNSTONE, *b* 1602, cr *Lord Johnstone of Lochwood* 1633 (with limitation to his heirs male), and *Lord Johnstone of Lochwood, Moffatdale and Evandale*, and *Earl of Hartfell* 1643 (to him and his heirs male); *d* 1653; *s* by his elder son (1) JAMES, PC, 2nd Earl, *b* 1625, who by Letters Patent 1661 was also cr *Earl of Annandale* etc (with a direction that the titles should forever thereafter be named *Earl of Annandale and Hartfell*) with destination in the first instance to heirs male general; was further cr by Charter of 1662 *Earl of Annandale and Hartfell* (peerage of Scotland) with remainder to the heirs male of his body, whom failing to the eldest heirs female without division of his body and the heirs male of the body of such heirs female bearing the name and arms of Johnstone, whom all failing to his nearest heirs and assignees whomsoever; Hereditary Keeper of Lochmaben Castle and Hereditary Steward of Annandale: *m* (contract dated 1645), Henrietta, who *d* 1673, da of 1st Marquess of Douglas; *d* 1672; *s* by his eldest surv son (2) WILLIAM, KT, PC, 2nd Earl of Annandale and Hartfell, *b* 1664; thrice Lord Commr to Gen Assembly of Church of Scotland, Lord Privy Seal for Scotland May-Dec 1702 and 1715-21 (Great Seal for Scotland 1714-16), a Representative Peer for Scotland 1708-13 and 1715-21; cr *Lord Johnstone of Lochwood, Lochmaben, Moffatdale and Evandale, Viscount of Annand, Earl of Hartfell*, and *Marquess of Annandale* (Peerage of Scotland), with a destination to his heirs male whatsoever succeeding to his lands and estates, 1701: *m* 1st, 1682, Sophia, who *d* 1716, only da and heiress of John Fairholm, of Craigiehall, co Linlithgow; 2ndly, 1718, Charlotte Van Lore (who *m* 2ndly, Col John Johnstone (*see* B Derwent), who was *k* at Carthagena 1741), only da and heiress of John Vanden Bempde, of Hackness Hall, co York; *d* 1721; *s* by his eldest son (by 1st *m*) (3) JAMES, 2nd Marquess, who *dunm* 1730; *s* by his half-brother (4) GEORGE, 3rd Marquess, *b* 1720; declared to have been a lunatic by 1744 by an inquest in Chancery 1748; took the name of Vanden Bempde in accordance with the will of John Vanden Bempde by Act of Parliament 1744; *dunm* 1792, when the Marquessate and all the other honours became dormant; *s* (as 5th Earl according to the decision of the Committee for Privileges of House of Lords 1985*) by his kinsman (5) JAMES (son of 2nd Earl) of Hopetoun, who took the addl surname of Johnstone as stated in Charter of 1662, and grandson of 1st Earl of Hopetoun (by his wife, Lady Henrietta Johnstone, only surv da of 2nd Earl of Annandale and Hartfell), *de jure* 5th Earl of Annandale and Hartfell and 3rd Earl of Hopetoun (*see* M Linlithgow); *d* 1816; *s* by his eldest da (6) ANNE, *de jure* Countess of Annandale and Hartfell in her own right: *m* 1792, her 2nd cousin, Adm Sir William Hope, GCB (who took the addl surname of Johnstone before that of Hope); *d* 1818; *s* by her eldest son (7) JOHN JAMES, *de jure* 7th Earl, *b* 1796, MP for Dumfries-shire: *m* 1816, Alicia Anne, who *d* 1868, da of George Gordon, of Hallhead; *d* 1876; *s* by his grandson (8) JOHN JAMES, *de jure* 8th Earl, *b* 1843, MP for Dumfries-shire; *dunm* 1912; *s* by his nephew (9) EVELYN WENTWORTH, *de jure* 9th Earl, *b* 1879: *m* 1st, 1905, Eileen, who *d* 1909, da of Gustavus Villiers Briscoe, of Bellinter, co Meath; 2ndly, 1916 (*m diss* 1925), Marie Eleanor, who *d* 1969, da of Compton Charles Domvile; 3rdly, 1926, Mary Evelyn, who *d* 1962, da of late John Locke, of Kilbeggan, co Westmeath, and formerly wife of John Beardmore Batten; *d* 1964; *s* by his only son (by 1st *m*) (10) PERCY WENTWORTH, *de jure* 10th Earl, *b* 1909, 16th/5th Queen's Royal Lancers, Maj RA (TA) Lanarkshire Yeo, served World War II 1939-42 (prisoner): *m* 1st, 1932, Phyllis Athena, only child of late Edgar Errol Napier MacDonell, CMG; 2ndly, 1940, Margaret Jane, who *d* 1998, da of Herbert William Francis Hunter-Arundell, of Barjarg, Auldgirth, Dumfries-shire; *d* 1983; *s* by his only son (by 2nd *m*) (11) PATRICK ANDREW WENTWORTH, 11th Earl and present peer; also Lord Johnstone.

*The many previous claimants to the Earldoms (between 1792-1879) founded their claims upon the Letters Patent of 1661 and were all rejected by the Committee for Privileges. The claimant of 1985 founded his claim not upon the Letters

Patent but upon a Signature under the sign manual of King Charles II dated 23 April 1662 and the subsequent Charter. His contention that this Charter brought about the new creation of a separate Earldom in favour of the 1st Earl of Annandale and Hartfell, independent of the creation by Letters Patent, was accepted by the Committee for Privileges.

ANNESLEY, EARL (Annesley) (Earl I 1789)
(Name and Title pronounced Annsli)

From the love of valour

PATRICK ANNESLEY, 10th Earl; *b* 12 Aug 1924; *s* 1979; *ed* Strode's Gram Sch, Egham; late RN: *m* 1947, Catherine, only da of John Burgess, of Edinburgh, and has issue.

𝔄rms – Paly of six argent and azure, a bend gules. 𝔠rest – A Moor's head, couped at the shoulders, proper, wreathed round the temples argent and azure. Supporters – *Dexter*, a Roman soldier in armour or, tunic azure, helm of first, thereon three feathers argent and azure, resting his right hand on an antique shield or buckler proper; *sinister*, a Moorish prince in armour or, wreathed round the temples argent and azure, a quiver of arrows pendant from a belt over his left shoulder, and his left hand resting on a bow proper.

DAUGHTERS LIVING

Lady Jane Margaret, *b* 1948: *m* 1966, Vernon Hugh Gamester, of The Retreat, 23 Wendover Rd, Staines, Middlesex TW18 3DE, and has issue living, Carl Vernon, *b* 1970, — Colette Louise, *b* 1967, — Juliet Dawn, *b* 1969.

Lady Nora Kathleen, *b* 1950: *m* 1969, John Bathurst Shaw Binning, of 6 Barons Way, Egham, Surrey, and has issue living, Gareth, *b* 1971, — Gavin Douglas, *b* 1977, — Madeleine Rachel, *b* 1969, — Carina Lorraine, *b* 1975.

Lady Patricia Catherine, *b* 1952: *m* 1974, David Sidney Morehead, of 133 Oriental Rd, Woking, Surrey, has had issue, Duncan Patrick David, *b* 1977; *d* 1996, — George Sidney, *b* 1984, — Danielle Simone, *b* 1975.

Lady Frances Elizabeth, *b* 1957; has issue living, Peter Chamberlain, *b* 1995.

BROTHERS LIVING

Hon PHILIP HARRISON, *b* 29 March 1927; *ed* Strode's Gram Sch, Egham; late REME; Test and Calibration Engr Rediffusion Flight Simulation Ltd 1957, Systems Design Engr 1963, Systems Training Manager Hughes Rediffusion Simulation Ltd 1991: *m* 1951, Florence Eileen, who *d* 1995, only da of late John Arthur Johnston, of Gillingham, Kent. *Residence* – 17 Folly Mill Gdns, Bridport, Dorset DT6 3RN.

Hon Michael Robert, *b* 1933; *ed* Strode's Gram Sch, Egham; Warrant Officer RAF (ret); Fellow Int Assocn of Bookkeepers; Asso Member Soc of Licenced Aircraft Eng and Technologists: *m* 1956, Audrey Mary, only da of Ernest Goodwright, of Dartford, Kent, and has issue living, Michael Stephen, *b* 1957: *m* 1983, Angela, 2nd da of David Matthews, of Chipping Norton, Oxon, and has issue living, Michael David *b* 28 Jan 1984, Zara Jane *b* (twin) 1984, — Robert Francis, *b* 1962: *m* 1992, Sharon Anne, 5th da of John Fraser, of Stevenage, Herts, — Sheila Marie, *b* 1961. *Residence* – 16 Coltash Rd, Furnace Green, Crawley, W Sussex.

COLLATERAL BRANCHES LIVING

Grandchildren of late Richard Arthur Grove Annesley, eldest son of late Richard Grove Annesley, eldest son of late Lt-Gen Hon Arthur Grove Annesley, 3rd son of 2nd Earl:—

Issue of late (Richard Francis) Michael Grove Annesley, *b* 1908, *d* 1979: *m* 1st, 1931 (*m diss* 1939), Elizabeth, who *d* 1981, da of J. Anderson, of Edinburgh; 2ndly, 1939, Elsie Susannah, da of Jacob Daniel Krige, of Stellenbosch, CP, and formerly wife of Reginald de Beer, of Johannesburg:—
(By 1st *m*) Diana Elizabeth Doreen, *b* 1932: *m* 1954, Robin Keitley Duff, of Box 67419, Bryanston, Transvaal, and has issue living, Hugh Robert Keitley, *b* 1958; BA, LLB, Chamber of Mines, Johannesburg, — Margaret Jean Keitley, *b* 1955: *m* 1982, Nikola Vujovic, of 112 Buckingham Av, Craighall Park, 2196 Gauteng, S Africa, and has issue living, Jessica Olivia Saja *b* 1988. —— (By 2nd *m*) Richard David Fergus Robert Grove (3/64 Maesbury St, Kensington, Adelaide, Australia), *b* 1940: *m* 1st, 1966 (*m diss* 1978), Marina Soares, of Salisbury, Rhodesia; 2ndly, 1979 (*m diss* 1996), Mary Hurley, of Durban, Natal, and has issue living (by 1st *m*), Michael Richard Edward Grove, *b* 1970, — Robert Patrick Sean, *b* 1971, — (by 2nd *m*) James Richard, *b* 1980, — Paul Daniel, *b* 1982. —— Rozanne Mary, *b* 1942: *m* 1967, David Worsley, of 123 Maxwell Av, Bluff 4052, Durban, Natal, and has issue living, Nicolette Grace, *b* 1971, — Justine Elizabeth Mary, *b* 1975.

Issue of late (Edmund) Patrick Grove Annesley, OBE; *b* 1911; *d* 1975: *m* 1939, Ruth (Annes Grove, Castletownroche, co Cork), da of late Arthur Norman Rushforth, of Bouley Bay, Jersey:—
(Arthur) Noël Grove (Marlowe House, Dulwich Village, SE21; Brooks's Club), *b* 1941; *ed* Harrow, and Worcester Coll, Oxford; Dep Chm Christie's Internat plc since 1992; Trustee Dulwich Picture Gallery: *m* 1968, Caroline Susan Aurea, da of late Thomas Henry Waldore Lumley, and has issue living, Marcus Robert Grove (55 Barrington Rd, SW9), *b* 1972, —

James Alexander Grove, *b* 1974. —— (Francis) Patrick Grove (Annes Grove, Castletownroche, co Cork), *b* 1943; *ed* Harrow, and Univ Coll, Oxford: *m* 1968, Jane Frances, da of late Egbert James Neville Holder, and has issue living, Melanie Jane Ruth, *b* 1969: *m* 1994, Paul Muende, — Cressida Mary Siobhan, *b* 1971.

Granddaughter of late Henry Robert Grove Annesley, 5th son of late Lt-Gen Hon Arthur Grove Annesley (ante):—
Issue of late Arthur Geoffrey Grove Annesley, *b* 1867, *d* 1954: *m* 1898, Mary Edith, who *d* 1972, da of late William J. Roe, of Landscape, Celbridge, co Kildare:—
Phyllis Kathleen Rhona, *b* 1907: *m* 1934, Brig Averell John Daniell, CBE, DSO, Col Comdt RA, and has issue living, Patrick John, CBE (Abbey Cottage, Itchen Abbas, Winchester, Hants), *b* 1939; Col RA (ret); CBE (Mil) 1987, — Michael Hugh, *b* 1946: *m* 1983, Susan Jane Winsor, and has issue living, Timothy Edward Winsor *b* 1988, Helena Rose Winsor *b* 1986, Esther Marianna Winsor *b* 1992, — Susan Mary, *b* 1937: *m* 1973, Guy Vivian Fennell Robinson, of 46 Carson Rd, W Dulwich, SE21, and has issue living, Thomas James Daniell *b* 1977, Philip Henry Guy *b* 1979. *Residence* – Oak Lodge, 21 Hillside St, Hythe, Kent CT21 5EJ.

Grandchildren of late Capt William Robert Ewart Annesley, yr son of late Capt Hon William Henry Annesley, RN, 5th son of 2nd Earl:—
Issue of late Maj William Alan Cecil Annesley, RASC, *b* 1907, *d* 1976: *m* 1935, Dorothy Vaughan, who *d* 1971, da of late Frank Yewdall, ICS:—
David Robert Ewart (77 Park Av North, N8), *b* 1936; F/O RAF; sculptor: *m* 1st, 1960 (*m diss* 1968), Patricia, da of V. I. Jones, of London; 2ndly, 1992, Jane Victoria McLeod, elder da of Sir John Robert Whyte Ackroyd, 2nd Bt, and has issue living (by 1st *m*), Benjamin (Flat C, 77 Kingsgate Rd, NW6 4JY), *b* 1961, — (by 2nd *m*) William Harry McLeod, *b* 1992. —— William Gerald (33 Gypsy Lane, Frostenden, Beccles, Suffolk NR34 7HU), *b* 1937: *m* 19— (*m diss* 19—), Mary Edwards, and has issue living, Elizabeth Mary, *b* 1979, — Susanna Jane, *b* 1982. —— Simon Richard (154 Havelock Rd, SW19 8HB), *b* 1939: *m* 1st, 1961 (*m diss* 1974), Janine, da of late William Thomas Callum, and has issue living, (by 1st *m*) Emmanuel, *b* 1961: *m* 1982, Nadine ?? and has issue living, Adrien *b* 1982, Maxime *b* 1986, — (by 2nd *m*), Luke, *b* 1969: *m* 1999, Emma Louise, da of David Brech, of Chalford, Glos, and has issue living, Eve Maia *b* 1997, — Christian, *b* 1972. —— Sarah Elizabeth, *b* 1943: *m* 1962, Henry William Peter Thompson, who *d* 1997, of 34 Southam Rd, Greystone Park, Harare, Zimbabwe, and has issue living, Howard Luke, *b* 1964, — Paul David, *b* 1966.

PREDECESSORS – (1) WILLIAM, 6th son of Francis Annesley, 4th son of 1st Viscount Valentia, was cr *Baron Annesley*, of Castlewellan, co Down (peerage of Ireland) 1758, and *Viscount Glerawly*, of co Fermanagh (peerage of Ireland) 1766; *d* 1770; *s* by his eldest son (2) FRANCIS CHARLES, 2nd Viscount; cr *Earl Annesley*, of Castelwellan, co Down (peerage of Ireland) 1789; *d* 1802; under a special remainder was *s* by his brother (3) RICHARD, 2nd Earl; *d* 1824; *s* by his son (4) WILLIAM RICHARD, 3rd Earl, *b* 1772: *m* 1st, 1803 (*m diss* 1821), Lady Isabella St Lawrance, who *d* 1827, da of 2nd Earl of Howth; 2ndly, 1828, Priscilla Cecilia, da of Hugh Moore, of Eglantine, co Down; *d* 1838; *s* by his eldest son (5) WILLIAM RICHARD, 4th Earl, MP for Great Grimsby (*C*) 1852-7, and sometime a Representative Peer; *dsp* 1874; *s* by his brother (6) HUGH, 5th Earl, *b* 1831; a Representative Peer; Lieut-Col Scots Guards; MP for co Cavan (*C*) 1851-4: *m* 1st, 1877, Mabel Wilhelmina Frances, who *d* 1891, da of Col William Thomas Markham; 2ndly, 1892, Priscilla Cecilia, who *d* 1941, da of late William Armitage Moore, of Arnmore, co Cavan; *d* 1908; *s* by his son (7) FRANCIS, 6th Earl, *b* 1884; was a Sub-Lieut Roy Naval Reserve: *m* 1909, Evelyn Hester (Harrison), who *d* 1947, da of Alfred Edward Miller Mundy, of Shipley Hall, Derby; *ka* 1914, while serving with Royal Flying Corps; *s* by his cousin (8) WALTER BERESFORD (son of late Hon William Octavius Beresford Annesley, 6th son of 3rd Earl), 7th Earl, *b* 1861: *m* 1st, 1893, Maud Fleming, who *d* 1923, da of Haynes Bingham Higginson, of Glebe House, Walmer, Kent; 2ndly, 1924, Mabel Frances Aganoor, who *d* 1931, eldest da of late John Burnet; *d* 1934; *s* by his son (9) BERESFORD CECIL BINGHAM, 8th Earl; *b* 1894; sometime Lieut Roy Fusiliers: *m* 1st, 1921 (*m diss* 1941), Edith Constance, who *d* 1950, da of Major Alexander Albemarle Rawlinson, formerly of 4 Aldford Street, Park Lane, W1; 2ndly, 1945, Mrs Josephine Mary Repton, who *d* 1977; *d* 1957; *s* by his kinsman (10) ROBERT (son of late Arthur Albert O'Donel Valentia Annesley, grandson of late James Annesley, son of late Hon Robert Annesley, 2nd son of 2nd Earl), 9th Earl, *b* 1900; European Wars 1915-18 with RN and 1939-44 in France and W Africa with R Corps of Signals: *m* 1922, Nora, who *d* 1992, yst da of Walter Harrison, of Sapperton, Cirencester, Glos; *d* 1979; *s* by his eldest son (11) PATRICK, 10th Earl and present peer; also Viscount Glerawly, and Baron Annesley of Castlewellan.

Annesley, family name of Viscount Valentia.

Anson, family name of Earl of Lichfield.

Anson, Viscount; son of Earl of Lichfield.

ANTRIM, EARL OF (McDonnell) (Earl I 1785)

Always ready

ALEXANDER RANDAL MARK McDONNELL, 9th Earl; *b* 3 Feb 1935; *s* 1977, but continued to be known as Viscount Dunluce until 1995; *ed* Downside, Ch Ch Oxford, and Ruskin Sch of Art; Keeper of Conservation, Tate Gallery since 1975, Head of Collection Sers 1990-93, since when Dir; Member Exec Cttee City and Guilds of London Art Sch, and of Court of R Coll of Art; Dir Ulster TV; FRSA: *m* 1st, 1963 (*m diss* 1974), Sarah Elizabeth Anne, 2nd da late of St John Bernard Vyvyan Harmsworth (*see* Boothby, Bt, colls, 1980 Edn); 2ndly, 1977, Elizabeth, da of late Michael Moses Sacher, and has issue by 1st and 2nd *m*.

Arms – Quarterly, 1st and 4th grand quarters, quarterly 1st or, a lion rampant gules; 2nd, or a dexter arm, issuant from the sinister fesse point, out of a cloud, proper, in the hand a cross crosslet fitchée, erect azure; 3rd argent, a ship, with sails furled sable; 4th per fesse azure and vert, a dolphin naiant in fesse proper, *McDonnell*; 2nd and 3rd grand quarters, quarterly, 1st and 4th, azure, a sun in splendour or, 2nd, gules on a chevron argent three mullets of the field, 3rd, sable on a chevron between three unicorns' heads, argent, as many mullets of the field, *Kerr*. *Crests* – First, A dexter arm embowed in fesse, coupled at the shoulder, vested or, cuffs argent, holding in the hand a cross crosslet fitchée erect azure *McDonnell*; 2nd, a sun in splendour or, *Kerr*. *Supporters* – *Dexter* a wild man wreathed about the temple and loins with ivy, all proper; *sinister*, a falcon, wings inverted, proper, beaked, membered and belled or. *Seat* – Glenarm Castle, Glenarm, co Antrim. *Residence* – Deer Park Cottage, Glenarm, co Antrim BT44 0BQ.

SON LIVING (*By 1st marriage*)

RANDAL ALEXANDER ST JOHN (*Viscount Dunluce*), *b* 2 July 1967; *ed* Gresham's Sch, Holt, and Worcester Coll, Oxford (BA); Investment Manager. *Residence* – Glenarm Castle, Glenarm, co Antrim. *Clubs* – Savile, Beefsteak.

DAUGHTERS LIVING (*By 1st marriage*)

Lady Flora Mary, *b* 1963.
Lady Alice Angela Jane, *b* 1964: *m* 1991, Christian Gwinn, son of Richard Gwinn, of Philadelphia, USA, and has issue living, Louis, *b* 1991.

(*By 2nd marriage*)

Lady Rachel Frances, *b* 1978.

BROTHER LIVING

Hon Hector John (The Old Rectory, Glenarm, co Antrim), *b* 1947: *m* 1969 (*m diss* 1974), Catherine Elizabeth, da of Ronald Chapman, of Buttermilk Hall, Brill, Bucks, and has issue living, Colquitto Angus, *b* 1972, — Hannah Margaretta, *b* 1971.

UNCLE LIVING (*Son of 7th Earl*)

Hon James Angus Grey, *b* 1917; *ed* Eton; 2nd Lieut 7th Batn Roy Norfolk Regt (TA); European War 1939-40 (prisoner): *m* 1939, Jeanne Irene, da of late Col Stanley Leonard Barry, CMG, CBE, DSO (*see* Barry, Bt, colls), and has issue living, Sorley James, *b* 1940; *ed* Eton, — Louisa, *b* 1946. *Residence* – 36 Farley Court, Melbury Rd, W14.

PREDECESSORS – (1) *Sir* RANDAL MacSORLEY MacDonnell, KB; cr *Viscount Dunluce* (peerage of Ireland) 1618 and *Earl of Antrim* (peerage of Ireland) 1620; *d* 1636, *s* by his eldest son (2) RANDAL, 2nd Earl, cr *Marquess of Antrim* (peerage of Ireland) 1644; *dsp* 1682, when the Marquessate became extinct, and the inferior dignities devolved upon his brother (3) ALEXANDER, PC, Col-proprietor of Antrim Regt 1688-91 in King James II's Irish Army; agent for Irish Catholic landowners 1692-99, and supporter of Confederation of Kilkenny; his titles were twice attainted and twice restored; *d* 1699; *s* by his son (4) RANDAL, 4th Earl; *d* 1721; *s* by his only son (5) ALEXANDER, 5th Earl; *d* 1775; *s* by his son (6) RANDAL WILLIAM, 6th Earl; cr *Viscount Dunluce* and *Earl of Antrim* (peerage of Ireland) 1785 with remainder to his daughters primogeniturely and their male issue, and *Marquess of Antrim* (peerage of Ireland) 1789; *d* (without male issue) 1791, when the Viscountcy of Dunluce (cr 1618), the Earldom of Antrim (cr 1620), and the Marquessate of Antrim (cr 1789) became extinct, while the Viscountcy of Dunluce and Earldom of Antrim (cr 1785) devolved upon his da **(7)** ANNE CATHERINE, 2nd holder of 2nd creation; *d* 1834; *s* by her sister **(8)** CHARLOTTE, 3rd holder of 2nd creation, wife of Adm Lord Mark Robert Kerr (M Lothian); *d* 1835; *s* by her son **(9)** HUGH SEYMOUR, 4th Earl of 2nd creation; assumed in 1836 the surname of McDonnell by R licence; *d* 1855; *s* by his brother **(10)** MARK, 5th Earl of 2nd creation; *b* 1814: *m* 1849, Jane Emma Harriet, da of Major Macan, of Cariff, co Armagh; *d* 10 Dec 1869; *s* by his eldest son **(11)** WILLIAM RANDAL, 6th Earl, *b* 1851: *m* 1875, Louisa Jane, VA, who *d* 1949, 3rd da of late Gen Hon Charles Grey; *d* 1918; *s* by his eldest son **(12)** RANDAL MARK KERR, 7th Earl, *b* 1878: *m* 1904, Margaret Isabel, who *d* 1974, da of late Rt Hon John Gilbert Talbot, DCI (E Shrewsbury, colls); *d* 1932; *s* by his son **(13)** RANDAL JOHN SOMERLED, KBE 8th Earl, *b* 1911; Clerk in House of Lords 1933-35 and Chm National Trust 1965-77: *m* 1934, Angela Christina, who *d* 1984, da of Col Sir (Tatton Benvenuto) Mark Sykes (Bt cr 1783); *d* 1977; *s* by his son **(14)** ALEXANDER RANDAL MARK, 9th Earl of 2nd creation, and present peer; also Viscount Dunluce.

Apsley, Lord; son of Earl Bathurst.

ARBUTHNOTT, VISCOUNT OF (Arbuthnott) (Viscount S 1641)

Praise be to God

JOHN CAMPBELL ARBUTHNOTT, KT, CBE, DSC, FRSE, 16th Viscount; *b* 26 Oct 1924; *s* 1966; *ed* Fettes, and Gonville and Caius Coll, Camb (MA); FRICS; Lord-Lieut Grampian Region (Kincardineshire) since 1977; Far East and Pacific 1944-45 with Fleet Air Arm (DSC) FRSA, FRICS, FRSE; Dir of the Aberdeen and N Marts 1973-91 (Chm 1986-91); Dir Britoil 1988-90, BP Scot Advisory Board 1990-94, Clydesdale Bank 1985-92, Scottish Widows and Life Assur 1978-94 (Chm 1984-87), and Scottish Northern Investment Trust 1979-85; Pres of British Assoc for Shooting and Conservation 1973-92 and of RZS Scotland 1976-96; Pres of Royal Scottish Geographic Soc 1982-85, Deputy Chm of Nature Conservancy Council 1980-85; Pres Highland Territorial and Volunteer Assocn 1984-89; HM Lord High Commr to Gen Assembly of Church of Scotland 1986 and 1987, a Member Royal Commn on Historical Manuscripts 1987-94; *cr* CBE (civil) 1986, and KT 1996; KStJ 1982, Bailiff Grand Cross 1994, Prior of the OStJ in Scot 1984-96: *m* 1949, Mary Elizabeth Darley, eldest da of late Cdr Christopher Bernard Oxley, DSC, RN, and has issue.

Arms – Azure, a crescent between three mullets argent. **Crest** – A peacock's head, couped at the neck, proper. **Supporters** – Two wyverns, wings elevated, tails nowed vert, and vomiting flames proper.
Seat – Arbuthnott House, by Laurencekirk, Kincardineshire AB30 1PA.

SON LIVING

Hon (JOHN) KEITH OXLEY (*Master of Arbuthnott*) (Kilternan, Arbuthnott, Laurencekirk, Kincardineshire, AB3 1NA), *b* 18 July 1950; *ed* Fettes, and North Scotland Coll of Agric, Aberdeen (Higher Nat Diploma, and Diploma in Farm Business, Organisation and Management): *m* 1974, Jill Mary, eldest da of Capt Colin Farquharson, of Whitehouse, Alford, Aberdeenshire, and has issue living, Christopher Keith, *b* 20 July 1977, — Clare Anne, *b* 1974, — Rachel Sarah, *b* 1979.

DAUGHTER LIVING

Hon Susanna Mary (Warren Farm House, Finmere, Bucks MK18 4AJ), *b* 1954; *ed* Overstone, Northants; Dorset House Sch of Occupational Therapy, Oxford: *m* 1978, Hugh Turnbull Bradbridge Smith, yr son of Lewis Smith, of Darnlee, Melrose, Roxburghshire, and has issue living, Andrew Keith Turnbull, *b* 1981, — Emma Charlotte, *b* 1983.

BROTHERS LIVING

Hon (William) David, MBE, *b* 1927; *ed* Fettes; Col (ret) late Black Watch; Korea 1952-53, Kenya 1953-55, N Ireland 1974 (despatches); MBE (Mil) 1964: *m* 1955, Sonja Mary, eldest da of late Col Charles Newbigging Thomson, CBE, DSO,

TD, of The Garden House, Panmure, Carnoustie, Angus, and has issue living, Charles Robert (Harviestoun Farmhouse, Dollar, Falkirk FK14 7PX), *b* 1956; *ed* Fettes, and Silsoe Coll, Carnfield Inst of Technology (BSc (Engr)), *m* 1987, Patricia Diane, da of late Barrington Brooke, of Mukoko, Glendale, Zimbabwe, and has issue living, David Barrington *b* 1989, James Brooke *b* 1990, — Georgina Margaret, *b* 1964; *ed* Fettes, and St Andrew's Univ (MA), — Elizabeth Christian, *b* 1967: *m* 1996, José Luis Gomez, yr son of Raphael Gomez, of Castellon, Spain. *Residence* – The Old Manse, Trochry, Dunkeld, Perthshire PH8 0DY.

Hon Hugh Sinclair, *b* 1929; *ed* Fettes, Gonville and Caius Coll, Camb (MA 1952), and Edinburgh Univ (LLB 1954); FCIS; late 2nd Lt 4th/5th Batn Black Watch; with Shell International Petroleum Co 1953-83: *m* 1963, Anne Rosamond, only da of late Charles Bentley Terdre, of Appledore, Cherry Walk, High Salvington, Worthing, and has issue living, Hugh James Hamilton, *b* 1967: *m* 1996, Sally M., yr da of Geoffrey Davies, of Hatch End, Middx, — Katherine Anne, *b* 1970. *Residence* – Cairnhill, Forfar, Angus DD8 3TQ.

SISTER LIVING

Hon Christian Keith, *b* 1933; *ed* Edinburgh Univ (MA 1954): *m* 1954, Cdr Peter John Bing, OBE, CEng, FIMechE, FCIS, RN, of The Lodge, Church St, Edzell, Brechin, Angus DD9 7TQ, and has issue living, *Rev* Alan Charles (The Rectory, 15 Ford Park Crescent, Ulverston, Cumbria LA12 7JR), *b* 1956; *ed* Christ's Hospital, St Edmund Hall, Oxford (MA 1978), and Exeter Univ (MA 1996); ordained priest 1992: *m* 1985, Wendy Margaret, eldest da of late Dennis Capstick, of Simonstone, Lancs, and has issue living, Alison Ursula *b* 1988, Emma Florence *b* 1990, Julia Margaret *b* 1993, — Robert Adrian, *b* 1958; *ed* Christ's Hospital, and Magdalene Coll, Camb (MA 1980); ARICS 1982: *m* 1991, Sarah Frances, yst da of Laurence Greenwood, of Ticehurst, Sussex, and has issue living, Henry Jarvis *b* 1992, Adam Laurence *b* 1997, Eleanor Mary *b* 1994, — Andrew John Collingwood (Auldbar Station House, Belgavies, Forfar, Angus DD8 2TH), *b* 1960; *ed* Christ's Hospital, and Edinburgh Univ (MA 1984); Dip in Marketing 1985: *m* 1993, Isobel Donald (Zoë), da of John Wilson Muir, of Woodburn Gdns, Aberdeen, and has issue living, John Donald *b* 1997, Katherine Isobel Collingwood *b* 1996, — Sarah Lucy (11c Westbourne Rd, N7 8AR), *b* 1969; *ed* Marlborough, Edinburgh Univ (MA 1992), and Coll of Law, London; Solicitor 1997.

COLLATERAL BRANCHES LIVING

Grandchildren of late Hugh Corsar Arbuthnott, yr son of late Lt-Col Hon Hugh Arbuthnott, 3rd son of 8th Viscount:—
Issue of late Lt-Col Hugh Arbuthnott, *b* 1896, *d* 1961: *m* 1923, Jess Agnes, who *d* 1978, da of Robert Henderson:—
Hugh John, *b* 1924; *ed* Sedbergh, and Camb Univ (BA hon 1950, MA 1955); late Capt RE; European War 1945 (wounded, despatches): *m* 1954, Dorothy Ferguson, who *d* 1991, only da of Sir William Lang Denholm, TD, of Glenmill, Kilmalcolm, Renfrewshire, and has issue living, Carolyn Ann, *b* 1955; *ed* St Andrew's Univ (BSc): *m* 1981, Hugh Alexander Normand, of Garden Cottage, Ardoch, Cardross, Dunbartonshire, and has issue living, William Alexander *b* 1984, Andrew John Charles *b* 1989, Margaret Catherine *b* 1986, — Sarah Jean, *b* 1957: *m* 1978, Jeremy Spencer James MacLehose, of Hop Garden Cottage, Westergate, nr Chichester, W Sussex, son of (Norman) Donald MacLehose, DSO (and nephew of Baron MacLehose of Beoch) and has issue living, Benjamin Donald Robert *b* 1981, Fergus Donald Hugh *b* 1988, Anna Margaret *b* 1983, — Susan Mary, *b* 1962: *m* 1983, Roger James Clegg, of Braeside, 257 Bangor Rd, Newtownards, co Down, and has issue living, James Hugh *b* 1988, Victoria Rebecca *b* 1986, — Christine Elizabeth, *b* 1966. *Residence* – Ardmoy, Rhu, Dunbartonshire. —— Mary, *b* 1926; BSc hons 1946: *m* 1949, Col Laurence MacLellan Young, MBE, MC, late RE, of Plovers, East Boldre, Brockenhurst, Hants, and has issue living, Alice Mary, *b* 1951: *m* 1972, Peter James Summerhayes, of The Paddock, Borthwood Lane, Sandown, Isle of Wight, and has issue living, Catherine Elizabeth *b* 1976, Christina Mary (twin) *b* 1976, Kirsty Alice *b* 1979, — Christina Jess, *b* 1954; *ed* Imp Coll, London, London Sch of Hygiene & Tropical Medicine (PhD): *m* 1978, David Peter Turner, of White Hart Cottage, Brinkley, Newmarket, Suffolk, and has issue living, James Peter *b* 1984, Catriona Jane *b* 1982. —— Marianne Jean Elspeth, *b* 1937: *m* 1967, William Richard Woods Ballard, of Oliver's Cottage, Capel St Mary, Ipswich (*see* V Molesworth, colls).

Issue of late Archibald Arbuthnott, MBE, ED, *b* 1898, *d* 1977: *m* 1931, Barbara Joan, who *d* 1988, yr da of late John Hughman Worters, of The White House, Chipstead:—
John (Palmerhayes Farm, Wick, Honiton, Devon), *b* 1933; *ed* Sedburgh, and Emmanuel Coll, Camb (MA), CEng, FRAeS: *m* 1956, Ann, yr da of late Arthur Garton, of Gwynn House, Lower Sloane St, SW1, and has issue living, Ian (4 Broadleaze, Hook, Hants), *b* 1958; BSc, MBA: *m* 1986, Jane, da of Gary Redshaw, of Penllan, Stoney Lane, Llanbedr, Ruthin, Clwyd, and has issue living, Hannah *b* 1994, — David (Crenny, 15 Acorn Way, Shawbirch, Telford), *b* 1961; *ed* Aberdeen Univ (MA): *m* 1987, Dawn Grace, da of John Frederick Kirby, of Birmingham, and has issue living, Christopher John *b* 1991, Jennifer Ann *b* 1989, — Fiona, *b* 1957; MCSP: *m* 1984, Andrew Graham Sneddon, of Ty-Draw, Efenechtyd, Ruthin, Clwyd, and has issue living, John Andrew *b* 1986, Emily Fiona *b* 1988, Laura Alice *b* 1990, — Jane, *b* 1966; BA: *m* 1991, Robert Nicholas Shannon, of School Lodge, Cranbrook, Kent, son of Robert Henry Shannon, of Belfast, and has issue living, Jack Robert *b* 1997, Kate Ruth *b* 1994. —— Robert, CBE (Glazeley Old Rectory, nr Bridgnorth, Shropshire WV16 6AB), *b* 1936; *ed* Sedbergh, and Emmanuel Coll, Camb (MA); British Council 1960-93; late Lt The Black Watch; CBE (Civil) 1991: *m* 1962, Robina, el da of Robin Arthur Axford, of Burlington Gdns, London, and of Mrs Sophie Maud Axford, of Benacre, Plummers Plain, Horsham, and has issue living, Robert Keith, *b* 1968; BA Cantab: *m* 1997, Susan, da of Terence Scales, of Worsbrough, Yorks, and has issue living, Sophie Ellen *b* 1996, Charlotte Rose *b* 1998. — Alison Mary, *b* 1963; BSc Aberdeen, MA Sheffield: *m* 1998, David William Morley, of Parkhall, Balfron, nr Glasgow, — Catherine Anne, *b* 1965; MA St Andrews: *m* 1991 (*m diss* 1999), Owen A. Wheatley, elder son of Dr Garth Wheatley, of Lyddington, Rutland.

Grandsons of late Cdr James Gordon Arbuthnott, RN (infra):—
Issue of late John Hyde Arbuthnott, *b* 1932; *d* 1981: *m* 1955, Patience Sarah (who *m* 2ndly, 1990, David W. J. Hillier) (Hausse Cambe, 46700 Mauroux, France), da of Charles Wainman, of Hinton St George, Som:—
Anthony St John Gordon (Windward, Totland Bay, I of Wight), *b* 1956: *m* 1980, Susan A., yr da of late George Humphreys, of Herts. —— Nicholas Charles (The Ridings, Wilcote, nr Finstock, Chipping Norton, Oxon OX7 3DX), *b* 1958; *ed* Ampleforth, and CCC: *m* 1st, 1989 (*m diss* 1991), Tracey, yr da of Lesley Brett, of Eltham Park, Kent; 2ndly, 1994, Susan Fenella (Fanny), da of Maj Angus Dubes, of Suffolk, and has issue living, Carlos Nicholas Mark, *b* 1994, — Aldo Gerard Luke, *b* 1997, — Sendy Nina Ophelia, *b* 1994.

Grandchildren of late Donald Stuart Arbuthnott, CE, 4th and yst son of late Hon David Arbuthnott, CSI, 4th son of 8th Viscount:—

Issue of late Cdr James Gordon Arbuthnott, RN, *b* 1894, *d* 1985: *m* 1931, Margaret Georgiana, who *d* 1993, da of John Woolley Hyde, of Seaview, Instow, N Devon:—
Hugh James, CMG (c/o Foreign & Commonwealth Office, King Charles St, SW1), *b* 1936; *ed* Ampleforth, and New Coll, Oxford; late 2nd Lt Black Watch; with Foreign Office since 1960, HM Ambassador to Romania 1986-89, to Portugal 1989-93, since when to Denmark; CMG (Civil) 1984: *m* 1964, Vanessa Rose, only da of Edward Dyer, and has had issue, Dominic Hugh, *b* 1965, — †Justin Edward James, *b* 1967; *ed* Edinburgh Univ; drowned in a boating accident 1989, — Giles Sebastian, *b* 1970. —— Georgina Mary *b* 1940: *m* 1st, 1966 (*m diss* 1982), William Robert Sparling; 2ndly, 1988, Christian Toulet, of Les Boulevards, 46800 Montcuq, France, and has issue living (by 2nd husband), Christophe Jean James Alexandre, *b* 1979, — Claire Margaret Suzanne, *b* 1984. —— Elizabeth Grace, *b* 1945: *m* 1967, Rupert Arthur Rees Evans, Barrister-at-law, of St Jacques, St Peter Port, Guernsey, CI, and has issue living, Marcus James Julius, *b* 1972, — Frances Imogen, *b* 1975, — Adelaide Grace, *b* 1978.

Issue of late Hugh Forbes Arbuthnott, *b* 1906, *d* 1982: *m* 1937, Janet Elizabeth, who *d* 1990, da of late Vice-Adm Herbert John Temple Marshall, of Gayton Hall, Ross, Herefordshire:—
Robert Marshall, *b* 1938. —— James Francis (Stone House Cottage, Kidderminster, Worcs), *b* 1940; Maj Black Watch: *m* 1974, Hon Louisa Nina Hughes-Young, yst da of 1st Baron St Helens, and has issue living, John Patrick, *b* 1977; *ed* Ampleforth, and Jesus Coll, Oxford, — Albert Michael, *b* 1988, — Walter Francis, *b* 1991, — Elizabeth Nina, *b* 1980, — Florence Mary, *b* 1981. —— Simon David (Winterfold House, Chaddesley Corbett, Worcs), *b* 1942; *ed* Downside, and Ch Ch Oxford: *m* 1970, Suzanne Ruth, el da of Allen Mainwaring Parker, of Osmonds, Droitwich, and has issue living, Thomas James, *b* 1974, — Edward Alexander Hugh, *b* 1980, — Lucy Margaret, *b* 1972, — Katherine Anne, *b* 1976. —— Charles Philip (The Old Manse, Caputh, by Murthly, Perthshire), *b* 1946; *ed* Downside, and RMA Sandhurst: *m* 1983, Lindsay C., da of Angus Sillars, of Stuckenduff, Shandon, Dunbartonshire, and has issue living, Magnus Malcolm James, *b* 1989, — a son, *b* 1994, — Molly Victoria, *b* 1987. —— Hugh Andrew (La Almuna, Apt 20, 29480 Gaucín, Prov Malaga, Spain), *b* 1948; *ed* Downside: *m* 1974, Elizabeth Jane, da of late Col Lionel James Showers, DSO, of The Old Rectory, Kington St Michael, Wilts, and has issue living, Hugh Frederick Archibald, *b* 1982, — Arabella Elizabeth, *b* 1979. —— Nicholas Octavius (The Tallet, Calmsden, Cirencester, Glos GL7 5ET), *b* 1952; *ed* Downside: *m* 1984, Vanessa Julie, da of Richard Mather, of The Ghyll, Kendal, Cumbria, and has issue living, George Arthur Harben, *b* 1986, — Edmund, *b* 1992, — Rose Elizabeth Marshall, *b* 1987, — Florence (Flora) Lily Nott, *b* 1990. —— Margaret Mary (*Hon Mrs Hugh D. Donovan*), *b* 1943: *m* 1968, Hon Hugh Desmond Donovan, of 40 Felden St, SW6, eldest son of Baron Donovan (Life Baron), and has issue (*see* By Donovan). —— Janet Felicity, *b* 1950: *m* 1980, William George McMorran, of The Line House, Tedstone Delamere, nr Bromyard, Herefordshire, and has issue living, Donald Hugh, *b* 1983, — Roland Francis, *b* 1985, — Hugo Edmond, *b* 1988.

Descendants of Maj Hon Charles James Donald Arbuthnott, 6th son of 8th Viscount:—
Grandchildren of late David Arbuthnott, *b* 18—, *d* 19—: *m* 18—:—

PREDECESSORS – (1) *Sir* ROBERT Arbuthnott, was cr *Lord Inverbervie* and *Viscount of Arbuthnott*, with remainder to his heirs male (peerage of Scotland) 1641; *d* 1655; *s* by his eldest son (2) ROBERT, 2nd Viscount; *d* 1682, *s* by his eldest son (3) ROBERT, 3rd Viscount; *d* 1694; *s* by his eldest son (4) ROBERT, 4th Viscount; *dsp* 1710; *s* by his brother (5) JOHN, 5th Viscount; *dsp* 1756; *s* by his kinsman (6) JOHN, 6th Viscount, son of Hon John Arbuthnott, 2nd son of 2nd Viscount; *d* 1791; *s* by his eldest son (7) JOHN, 7th Viscount; *d* 1800; *s* by his eldest son (8) JOHN, 8th Viscount, *b* 1778; was Lord Lieut of Kincardineshire: *m* 1805, Margaret, who *d* 1870, da of Hon Walter Ogilvy (E Airlie); *d* Jan 10 1860; *s* by his eldest son (9) JOHN, 9th Viscount, *b* 1806: *m* 1837, Lady Jean Graham Drummond Ogilvy, da of 8th Earl of Airlie; *d* 1891; *s* by his eldest son (10) JOHN, 10th Viscount, *b* 1843: *m* 1871, Anna Harriet, who *d* 1892, da of late Edmund Allen: *d* 1895; *s* by his brother (11) DAVID, 11th Viscount; *d* 1845; *d* 1914; *s* by his brother (12) WILLIAM, 12th Viscount, *b* 1849; *d* 1917; *s* by his cousin (13) WALTER CHARLES WARNER (son of late Capt the Hon Walter Arbuthnott, 2nd son of 8th Viscount), 13th Viscount, *b* 1847: *m* 1878, Emma Marion, who *d* 1930, da of late Rev John Hall Parlby, JP, of Manadon, near Plymouth; *d* 1920; *s* by his eldest son (14) JOHN OGILVY, 14th Viscount; *b* 1882; HM Licut for Kincardineshire 1926-60; Convenor of Kincardineshire Co Council 1933; a Representative Peer for Scotland 1945-55: *m* 1914, Dorothy, OBE, who *d* 1990, yst da of late Adm Charles Lister Oxley, of The Hall, Ripon, Yorkshire; *d* 1960; *s* by his kinsman (15) ROBERT KEITH, CB, CBE, DSO, MC (son of John Campbell Arbuthnott, eldest son of late Lt-Col Hon Hugh Arbuthnott, 3rd son of 8th Viscount) 15th Viscount; *b* 1897; Maj-Gen late Black Watch (Col 1960-64); Lord Lt of Kincardineshire 1960-66: *m* 1924, Ursula, who *d* 1989, da of late Sir William Collingwood, KBE; *d* 1966; *s* by his eldest son (16) JOHN CAMPBELL, DSC, 16th Viscount and present peer; also Lord Inverbervie.

ARCHER OF SANDWELL, BARON (Archer) (Life Baron 1992)

PETER KINGSLEY ARCHER, PC, son of late Cyril Kingsley Archer, MM; *b* 20 Nov 1926; *ed* Wednesbury Boys' High Sch, Univ Coll, London (BA, LLB, Fellow 1978), and LSE (LLM); Bar Gray's Inn 1952, QC 1971, Bencher 1974, Recorder SE Circuit 1982-98; Chm Council on Tribunals since 1992; PPS to Attorney Gen 1967-70, UK Delegation to UN Gen Assembly (Third Cttee) 1969, Chm Amnesty Internat (British Section) 1971-74, Chm Soc of Labour Lawyers 1971-74 and 1980-92, since when Joint Pres; Pres Fabian Soc since 1993; Solicitor-Gen 1974-79; Opposition Frontbench Spokesman on Legal Affairs 1981-82, Trade 1982-83, and Shadow Sec NI 1983-87; author; MP Rowley Regis and Tipton (*Lab*) 1966-74, and Warley W 1974-92; *cr* PC 1977, and *Baron Archer of Sandwell*, of Sandwell, co W Midlands (Life Baron) 1992: *m* 1954, Margaret Irene, da of late Sydney John Smith, of London, Ontario, Canada, and has issue.
Residence – Highcroft, Hill View Rd, Wraysbury, nr Staines, Middx.

SON LIVING

Hon John Kingsley, *b* 1962; *ed* Watford Gram Sch, and Corpus Christi, Camb.

ARCHER OF WESTON-SUPER-MARE, BARON (Archer) (Life Baron 1992)

JEFFREY HOWARD ARCHER, son of late William Archer; *b* 15 April 1940; *ed* Wellington Sch, Som, and Brasenose Coll, Oxford; Member GLC for Havering 1966-70, Dep Chm Conservative Party 1985-86; Pres World Snooker Assoc since 1997; Pres Som Amateur Athletic Assocn 1973-99, Trustee RWS since 1989; FRSA 1973; author and playwright; MP Louth (*C*) 1969-74; *cr Baron Archer of Weston-super-Mare*, of Mark, co Somerset (Life Baron) 1992: *m* 1966, Mary Doreen, PhD, da of late Harold Norman Weeden, and has issue.

Residence – The Old Vicarage, Grantchester, Cambridge CB3 9ND. *Club* – MCC.

SONS LIVING

Hon William Harold, *b* 1972.
Hon James Howard, *b* 1974; *ed* Eton, and Brasenose Coll, Oxford.

ARCHIBALD, BARONY OF (Archibald) (Extinct 1996)

WIDOW LIVING OF LIFE BARON

DAPHNE MAY VINCENT, da of George Henry Henham: *m* 1971, Prof (George) Christopher Archibald, FRSC, 2nd Baron Archibald (until he disclaimed his peerage for life 1975), who *d* 1996.

Ardee, Lord; son of Earl of Meath.

ARDWICK, BARONY OF (Beavan) (Extinct 1994)

WIDOW LIVING OF LIFE BARON

GLADYS (*Baroness Ardwick*), da of late William Jones: *m* 1934, Baron Ardwick, who *d* 1994. *Residence* – Galsworthy House, 177 Kingston Hill, Surrey KT2 7LX.

ARGYLL, DUKE OF (Campbell) (Duke S 1701 and UK 1892, Bt (NS) 1627)

Forget not

IAN CAMPBELL, 12th Duke, and 14th Baronet; *b* 28 Aug 1937; *s* 1973; *ed* Le Rosey, Trin Coll, Glenalmond, and McGill Univ, Canada; late Capt Argyll and Sutherland Highlanders, Member Queen's Body Guard for Scotland (Royal Company of Archers); Lord Lieut Argyll and Bute 1996; KStJ 1975; Hereditary Master of HM's Household in Scotland, Keeper of The Great Seal of Scotland, Keeper of Dunoon, Carrick, Dunstaffnage and Tarbert Castles, Adm of the Western Isles, and Hereditary Sheriff of Argyll: *m* 1964, Iona Mary, only da of Capt Sir Ivar Iain Colquhoun of Luss, 8th Bt, and has issue.

𝔄rms – Quarterly: 1st and 4th gyronny of eight or and sable, *Campbell*; 2nd and 3rd argent a lymphad or ancient galley, sails furled, flags and pennants flying gules, and oars in action sable, *Lorne*; behind the shield are placed saltirewise a baton gules powdered with thistles or, ensigned with an Imperial crown proper thereon the Crest of Scotland (*Hereditary Great Master of Household in Scotland*), and a sword proper, pommel and hilt or (*High Justiciar of Scotland*). 𝔠rest – A boar's head fessewise, erased or, armed argent, langued gules. 𝔖upporters – Two lions guardant gules.
Seat – Inveraray Castle, Argyll. *Clubs* – White's, New (Edinburgh).

SON LIVING

TORQUHIL IAN (*Marquess of Lorne*), *b* 29 May 1968; a Page of Honour to HM 1981-83; *ed* Glenalmond, and RAC Cirencester.

DAUGHTER LIVING

Lady Louise Iona, *b* 1972: *m* 1998, Anthony Merrik Burrell (*see* Burrell, Bt).

BROTHER LIVING

Lord Colin Ivar, *b* 1946: *m* 1974 (*m diss* 1975), Georgia Ariana, da of Michael Ziadie. *Address* – 250 E 74th Street, New York City, NY 10021, USA.

HALF-SISTER LIVING

Lady Jeanne Louise CAMPBELL, *b* 1928; has resumed her maiden name: *m* 1st, 1962 (*m diss* 1963), Norman Mailer, the writer; 2ndly, 1963, John Sergeant Cram, and has issue living (by 1st *m*), Kate, *b* 1962: *m* 1993, Guy Nicholas Lancaster, of 242 West 11th Street, New York City, NY 10014, USA, — (by 2nd *m*), Cusi Charlotte Campbell Sergeant, *b* 1967. *Residences* – 244 West 11th Street, New York City, NY 10014, USA; Sifnos, Cyclades, Greece 84003.

COLLATERAL BRANCHES LIVING (*All in male line in remainder to Dukedom, Earldom and other titles in the Peerage of Scotland*)

Grandchildren of late Alexander Andrew Lochnell Campbell, 15th of Lochnell, son of late Archibald Argyll Lochnell Campbell, 13th of Lochnell, eldest son of Rev Colin Campbell, 4th son of Archibald Campbell, 11th of Lochnell, 8th in descent from John (Gorm) Campbell, 2nd son of 3rd Earl:—
Issue of late Alexander (Alasdair) Duncan Lochnell Campbell, 16th of Lochnell, *b* 1921, *d* 1993: *m* 1958, Rosemary Georgiana (who *m* 2ndly, 1995, Capt Christopher Stuart Rawlins, of Great House, Chipping Sodbury, Bristol BS37 6PX), only da of Cdr Hugh Hope-Grant Begbie, RN:—
Alexander (Alick) Hugh Edward, *b* 1961; 17th of Lochnell; *ed* Radley, York Univ, and RMA Sandhurst; late Capt 16th/5th The Queen's Royal Lancers; MBA (London Business Sch). —— Iain Charles Lochnell, *b* 1962: *m* 1999, Katharine Susanna, da of Peter Humphrey Alexander Van Oss (*see* Bazley, Bt, colls). —— Caroline Irene Lochnell, *b* 1965: *m* 1993, Paul David Watkinson, of Hall Farm, Swardeston, Norwich, 2nd son of David Watkinson, of Gowthorpe Manor, Swardeston, Norfolk, and has issue living, William Henry, *b* 1995, — George Nicholas, *b* 1997, — Alexander David, *b* 1999.

Granddaughter of late Brig-Surg Alexander Dugald Campbell, MD, IMS, son of late Rear-Adm Donald Campbell, 5th of Achanduin, and 3rd of Barbreck, gt-grandson of Archibald Campbell, 1st of Achanduin, 3rd son of Colin Campbell, 5th of Lochnell, 4th in descent from John (Gorm) Campbell (ante):—
Issue of late Col James Donald Campbell, DSO, 10th of Achanduin and 8th of Barbreck, *b* 1884, *d* 1974: *m* 1911, Hazel, who *d* 1950, da of late Col Benjamin W. Marlow, CSI, CIE:—

Margaret Mary (87 Bedford Gdns, W8 7EQ), b 1915.

Grandchildren of late Lt-Col Geordie Osmond Lorne Mackie-Campbell, MC (infra):—
Issue of late Capt Peter Lorne Campbell, Rifle Bde, b 1925, d 1993: m 1954, Ann Gillian (Stonefield, Tarbert, Argyll), da of Ian Pountney Coats:—
†George Logan, b 1956; d 1986. —— Ileene, b 1958: m 1987, Dr Neil Duncan, and has issue living, Iain Campbell Duncan, b 1988, — Cara, b 1990.

Granddaughter of late Lt-Col Colin George Pelham Campbell, 6th of Stonefield, 8th in descent from Archibald Campbell, 4th son of Archibald Campbell, 2nd of Lochnell, son of John (Gorm) Campbell (ante):—
Issue of late Lt-Col Geordie Osmond Lorne Mackie-Campbell, MC, b 1896, d 1956: m 1921, Jessie Isobel, who d 1971, da of Sir Peter Jeffrey Mackie, 1st and last Bt (cr 1920):—
Patricia Isobel (Barleythorpe, Belton House Mews, Belton in Rutland, Oakham, Rutland), b 1923: m 1946, Niall Campbell Macdiarmid, who d 1978, son of late Sir Allan Macdiarmid, and has had issue, Maunagh Elizabeth, b 1947; d 1973, — Fiona Jane, b 1949: m 1969, Roger Montague Prichard, son of Sir Montague Illtyd Prichard, CBE, MC, and has issue living, Duncan Montague b 1973, Cara Mae b 1971, — Glenda Ileene, b 1954: m 1987, Lt-Col Gilbert Peter Kerruish, of Barnhaven, Apethorpe, Peterborough, Lincs PE8 5DP, son of Albert William Kerruish, and has issue living, Emma Campbell Rosalind b 1987, Holly Campbell Louise b 1989.

Descendants of Sir John (Ian) Campbell, 3rd son of 2nd Earl:—
Campbells of Cawdor (see E Cawdor), Ardchattan, Aros, and Clunes, and their cadets.

Descendants of Donald Campbell, 4th son of 2nd Earl:—
Campbells of Keithock, and their cadets.

Descendants of Thomas Campbell, 2nd son of 1st Earl:—
Campbells of Lundy, and their cadets.

Descendants of Colin Campbell, 1st son (by 2nd m) of 1st Lord Campbell:—
Campbells of Glenorchy (see E Breadalbane) and their cadets, including Campbell of Aberuchill Bt (cr 1668).

Descendants of Colin Campbell, 2nd son (by 2nd m) of 1st Lord Campbell:—
Campbells of Auchinbreck (see Campbell, Bt, cr 1628), Glencardel, Glensaddel, Kilduskland, Kilmorie Wester Kames, Kilberry, Dana, and their cadets.

Descendants of Neil Campbell, 4th son (by 2nd m) of 1st Lord Campbell:—
Campbells of Ormidale, Ellengreig, and their cadets.

PREDECESSORS – (1) Sir DUNCAN Campbell, of Lochow, assumed the designation of Argyll, and was cr Lord Campbell (peerage of Scotland) 1445; d 1453; s by his grandson (2) COLIN, 2nd Lord, Lord High Chancellor of Scotland, cr Earl of Argyll (peerage of Scotland) 1457, and Lord Lorne 1470; d 1493; s by his son (3) ARCHIBALD, 2nd Earl, killed at Flodden 1513; s by his son (4) COLIN, 3rd Earl, Hereditary High Sheriff of Argyllshire and Justice Gen of Scotland; d 1533; s by his son (5) ARCHIBALD, 4th Earl, the first important personage in Scotland who embraced the Protestant religion; d 1558; s by his eldest son (6) ARCHIBALD, 5th Earl, he espoused the cause of Queen Mary, and commanded HM's Forces at battle of Langside 1568; was subsequently Lord High Chancellor of Scotland; d 1575; s by his halfbrother (7) Sir COLIN, PC, 6th Earl, Lord High Chancellor of Scotland; d 1584; s by his son (8) ARCHIBALD, 7th Earl, a distinguished military officer; d 1638; s by his eldest son (9) ARCHIBALD, 8th Earl, cr Marquess of Argyll (peerage of Scotland) 1641; was the first Commr from Scotland to the Parliament of England, and at the Coronation at Scone placed the crown upon Charles II's head; subsequently recognised Cromwell as Protector; upon the restoration of monarchy the Marquess repaired to London, but HM refused to see him and ordered his committal to the Tower; on 25 May 1661, he was tried for high treason and condemned to death, and on 27 May, he was beheaded at Edinburgh; s by his eldest son (10) ARCHIBALD, 9th Earl, who was restored to the Earldom; for refusing to subscribe to the Test Act was found guilty of high treason and condemned to death; he escaped, but was subsequently taken in an abortive attempt to invade Scotland, temp James II, and was beheaded 30 Jan 1685; s by his eldest son (11) ARCHIBALD, 10th Earl, in whom the Baronetcy, cr (NS) 1627, of Lundy (conferred upon Colin Campbell, grandson of 6th Earl of Argyll, with remainder to heirs male whatsoever), became vested in 1696 after the death of the 2nd Bt; cr in 1701 Lord Inverary, Mull, Morvern, and Tiry, Viscount Lochow and Glenilla, Earl of Campbell and Cowal, Marquess of Kintyre and Lorne, and Duke of Argyll (peerage of Scotland), with remainder to heirs male whomsoever; d 1703; s by his eldest son (12) JOHN, 2nd Duke, a Field Marshal in the Army, and a celebrated military commander; cr Baron Chatham and Earl of Greenwich, Kent (peerage of England) 1707, and Duke of Greenwich (peerage of Great Britain) 1719; d 1743 without male issue when the peerages of 1707 and 1719 became ext; s in Scottish titles by his brother (13) ARCHIBALD, 3rd Duke who in 1706 had been cr Lord Oronsay, Dunoon and Arase, Viscount Ilay, and Earl of Ilay (peerage of Scotland), which honours became extinct at his death 1761; s by his cousin (14) JOHN, 4th Duke, son of the Hon John Campbell, MP, 2nd son of 9th Earl; d 1770, s by his eldest son (15) JOHN, 5th Duke, cr Baron Sundridge (peerage of Great Britain) 1766, whose wife was cr Baroness Hamilton (peerage of Great Britain) 1776; d 1806; s by his eldest son (16) GEORGE WILLIAM, 6th Duke, who in 1790 had s to his mother's Barony of Hamilton; d 1839; s by his brother (17) JOHN DOUGLAS EDWARD HENRY, 7th Duke, b 1777: m 1st, 1802, Elizabeth, who d 1818, da of W. Campbell, of Fairfield; 2ndly, 1820, Joan, who d 1828, da of John Glassel, of Long Niddry; 3rdly, 1831, Anne Colquhoun, da of John Cunningham; d 26 April 1847; s by his son (18) GEORGE DOUGLAS, KG, PC, KT, 8th Duke; b 1823; Lord Privy Seal 1853-5, 1859-66, and 1880-81; Postmaster-Gen 1855-8, and Sec of State for India 1868-74; Lord-Lieut of Argyllshire; cr Duke of Argyll (peerage of United Kingdom) 1892: m 1st, 1844, Lady Elizabeth Georgiana Sutherland-Leveson-Gower, who d 1878, eldest da of 2nd Duke of Sutherland, KG; 2ndly 1881, Amelia Maria, who d 1894, da of Right Rev Thomas Legh Claughton, DD (formerly Bishop of St Albans), of Danbury Palace, Essex, and widow of Col Hon Augustus Henry Archibald Anson, VC (see E Lichfield); 3rdly, 1895, Ina Erskine, VA, who d 1925, da of Archibald McNeil, of Colonsay; d 1900; s by his eldest son (19) JOHN DOUGLAS SUTHERLAND, KT, GCMG, GCVO, PC, 9th Duke; b 1845; MP for Argyllshire (L) 1868-78 and for Manchester, S Div (LU) 1898-

1900; Private Sec to his father at India Office 1868-71, Gov-Gen of Canada and Com-in-Ch of Prince Edward Island 1878-83, and Gov and Constable of Windsor Castle 1892-1914; was Gov of Knights of Windsor, Lord-Lieut of Argyllshire, Hereditary Master of HM's Household in Scotland, Adm of the Western Isles, Chancellor of Order of St Michael and St George, Keeper of the Great Seal of Scotland, and Keeper of Dunoon, Carrick, and Dunstaffnage Castles: *m* 21 March 1871, HRH Princess Louise Caroline Alberta, VA, CI, GCVO, GBE, RRC, who *d* 1939, 4th da of HM Queen Victoria; *d* 1914; *s* by his nephew **(20)** NIALL DIARMID (only son of late Lord Archibald Campbell, 2nd son of 8th Duke), 10th Duke: *b* 1872; was Lord-Lieut of Argyllshire; *d* 1949; *s* by his kinsman **(21)** IAN DOUGLAS, TD (only son of late Douglas Walter Campbell, son of late Lord Walter Campbell, 3rd son of 8th Duke), 11th Duke; *b* 1903: *m* 1st, 1927 (*m diss* 1934), Hon Janet Gladys Aitken, who *d* 1988, da of 1st Baron Beaverbrook; 2ndly, 1935 (*m diss* 1951), Louise, who *d* 1970, da of late Henry Clews, of The Chateau of La Napoule, Alpes Maritimes, France, and formerly wife of late Hon Andrew Nicolas Armstrong Vanneck, MC (B Huntingfield); 3rdly, 1951 (*m diss* 1963), Margaret, who *d* 1993, da of late George Hay Whigham, and formerly wife of Charles Sweeny; 4thly, 1963, Mathilda Coster MORTIMER, who *d* 1997, da of Stanley Mortimer, of Lichfield, Conn, USA, and formerly wife of Prof Clemens Heller, of Paris; *d* 1973; *s* by his son **(22)** IAN, 12th Duke and present peer; also Marquess of Kintyre and Lorne, Earl of Argyll, Earl of Campbell and Cowal, Viscount Lochow and Glenilla, Lord Campbell, Lord Lorne, Lord Inverary, Mull, Morvern and Tiry, Baron Sundridge, and Baron Hamilton.

ARLINGTON, BARONESS (Forwood) (Baron E 1672)

JENNIFER JANE FORWOOD, *Baroness Arlington*, *b* 7 May 1939; *s* (on termination of abeyance) 1999: *m* 1964, Rodney Simon Dudley Forwood, late Capt Irish Guards, adopted stepson of Maj Sir Dudley Richard Forwood, 3rd Bt, and has issue.

Arms – not exemplified at time of going to press
Residence – The New House, Rectory Gardens, Salisbury St, Shaftesbury, Dorset SP7 8EJ.

SONS LIVING

Hon PATRICK JOHN DUDLEY, *b* 23 April 1967; *ed* Eton.
Hon James Roland Nelson, *b* 1969; *ed* Milton Abbey.

SISTER LIVING

(Juliet Auriol) Sally (*Sal, Lady Cholmeley*), *b* 1940: *m* 1960, Sir Montague John Cholmeley, 6th Bt, who *d* 1998, and has issue (see that title). *Residence* – Church Farm, Burton le Coggles, Grantham, Lincs.

AUNT LIVING (*Sister of 9th Duke of Grafton*) (*Raised to the rank of a Duke's daughter* 1961)

Lady Mary Rose, *b* (*posthumous*) 1918: *m* 1945 (*m diss* 1951), Francis Trelawny Williams, late Lieut KRRC, who *d* 1977 (*see* Salusbury-Trelawny, Bt, 1959 Edn), and has issue living, Linda Jane Auriol, *b* 1947. *Residence* – The Green, Oddington, Moreton-in-Marsh, Glos.

COLLATERAL BRANCHES LIVING

Issue of late Lady Cecilia Blanche Genevieve FitzRoy, yst da of 8th Duke of Grafton, *b* 1922, *d* 1974: *m* 1949, George Anthony Geoffrey Howard (later *Baron Howard of Henderskelfe*) (Life Baron), who *d* 1984:—
See E Carlisle, colls.

Descendants of 1st Duke of Grafton:—
See D Grafton.

Descendants of Lieut-Gen Charles FitzRoy (2nd son of Lord Augustus FitzRoy, 2nd son of 2nd Duke of Grafton), who was *cr* Baron Southampton 1780:—
See B Southampton.

Descendants of Sir John Bennet, KB (elder brother of 1st Earl of Arlington), who was *cr* Baron Ossulston 1682:—
See E Tankerville.

PREDECESSORS – **(1)** HENRY Bennet, KG, yr son of Sir John Bennet, of Dawley; *cr Baron Arlington* of Arlington, Middlesex (peerage of England) 1665, with special remainder, failing issue male, to the heirs of his body, and *Baron Arlington*, of Arlington, co Middlesex, *Viscount Thetford*, and *Earl of Arlington* (peerage of England) 1672, with like special remainder, and in default of heirs of his body, with a further remainder to his elder brother, Sir John Bennet, KB (*see* E Tankerville), and the heirs male of his body; Postmaster Gen 1665 until his death, likewise Lord Chamberlain from 1674 and Grand Master of the Freemasons from 1679: *m* 1665, Isabella, who *d* 1718, da of Louis de Nassau, Baron of Leck and Beverwaet; *dspm* 1685, when he was *s* (under the terms of the special remainder) by his only da **(2)** ISABELLA, 2nd holder of the title: *m* 1st, 1679, 1st Duke of Grafton, KG, 2nd natural son of King Charles II, who *d* 1690; 2ndly, 1698, Sir Thomas Hanmer, 3rd Bt, who *d* 1746; *d* 1723, when the peerages and the two Baronies of Arlington, and the Viscountcy of Thetford, merged into the Dukedom of Grafton, and so continued **(3-10)** until JOHN CHARLES WILLIAM FitzRoy, 9th Duke of Grafton and 10th Earl of Arlington, who *dunm* 1936, when the peerages fell into abeyance between his two sisters, Lady (Margaret) Jane Nelson and Lady Mary Rose Williams, and so continued until 1999, when the abeyance of the Barony of Arlington (1672) was terminated (after petition to HM The Queen) in favour of **(11)** JENNIFER JANE Forwood (elder da of late Lady (Margaret) Jane Nelson, *b* 1916, *d* 1995: *m* 1936, Maj-Gen Sir (Eustace) John Blois Nelson, KCVO, CBE, DSO, OBE, MC (*see* Blois, Bt, 1955 Edn), who *d* 1993), Baroness Arlington, the present peeress.

ARMSTRONG, BARONY OF (Watson-Armstrong) (Extinct 1987)

ADOPTED CHILDREN OF THIRD BARON

Francis William Paul, *b* 1965: *m* 1988, Sarah, elder da of Dr B. Gray, of Twyning, Glos. *Residence* – Bamburgh Castle, Northumberland.

Isabella Juliana Theresa, *b* 1970: *m* 1992, Charles Rutter, son of C. N. Rutter, of Kasama, Hillside Rd, Rothbury, North-umberland. *Residence* – Trewhitt Steads Farm, Thropton, Morpeth, Northumberland.

ARMSTRONG OF ILMINSTER, BARON (Armstrong) (Life Baron 1988)

ROBERT TEMPLE ARMSTRONG, GCB, CVO, only son of late Sir Thomas Henry Wait Armstrong, of 1 East Street, Olney, Bucks; *b* 30 March 1927; *ed* Eton (Fellow 1979-94), and Ch Ch Oxford (Hon Student 1985); Hon Bencher Inner Temple 1986; entered Treasury 1950 (Assist Prin 1950-55, Prin 1955-64); Assist Sec Cabinet Office 1964-66; Assist Sec Treasury 1967-68, jt Prin Private Sec to Chancellor of the Exchequer 1968, Under Sec Treasury (Home Finance, 1968-70); Prin Private Sec to PM 1970-75; Home Office 1975-79 (Dep Under Sec of State 1975-77, Permanent Under Sec of State 1977-79); Sec of the Cabinet 1979-87, Head of Home Civil Ser 1981-87; Dir Royal Opera House 1988-93 (Sec to Dirs 1968-87), Dir RAM since 1975 (Hon Fellow 1985), Council of Management Royal Philharmonic Society, Rhodes Trust since 1975, Pilgrim Trust since 1987, D'Oyly Carte Opera Trust 1988-93, and Leeds Castle Foundn since 1988; Chm of Trustees Victoria and Albert Museum since 1988; Chm Biotechnology Investments Ltd since 1989, Chm Bristol and West Building Soc since 1993 (Dir since 1988) non-exec Dir Shell Transport and Trading plc, NM Rothschild & Sons Ltd, and other Cos since 1988; *cr* CB 1974, CVO 1975, KCB 1978, GCB 1983, and *Baron Armstrong of Ilminster*, of Ashill, co Somerset (Life Baron) 1988; *m* 1st, 1953 (*m diss* 1985), Serena Mary Benedicta, who *d* 1994, elder da of Sir Roger James Ferguson Chance, 3rd Bt, MC; 2ndly, 1985, (Mary) Patricia, only da of late Charles Cyril Carlow, and has issue by 1st *m*.
Address – House of Lords, SW1. *Clubs* – Athenaeum, Brooks's.

DAUGHTERS LIVING (*By 1st marriage*)

Hon Jane Orlanda, *b* 1954.
Hon Teresa Brigid, *b* 1957.

ARMSTRONG OF SANDERSTEAD, BARONY OF (Armstrong) (Extinct 1980)

SON LIVING OF LIFE BARON

Hon Peter William (20 Ravensbourne Gdns, W13), *b* 1943: *m* 1967 (*m diss* 1984), Kathleen Frances Widdicombe.

DAUGHTER LIVING OF LIFE BARON

Hon Janet Elizabeth, *b* 1947: *m* 1968, Malcolm Turnbull, of 62 Queens Rd, Swanage, Dorset.

WIDOW LIVING OF LIFE BARON

GWENDOLINE ENID (*Baroness Armstrong of Sanderstead*) (Pinewood House, Pleasure Pit Rd, Ashtead, Surrey), da of John Bennett, of Putney, SW15: *m* 1942, Baron Armstrong of Sanderstead, GCB, MVO, PC (Life Baron), who *d* 1980.

ARRAN, EARL OF (Gore) Sits as BARON SUDLEY (UK 1884) (Earl I 1762, Bt I 1662)

Under this sign thou shalt conquer

ARTHUR DESMOND COLQUHOUN GORE, 9th Earl and 11th Baronet; *b* 14 July 1938; *s* 1983; *ed* Eton, and Balliol Coll, Oxford; late 2nd Lieut Gren Gds; Co-Chm Children's Country Holidays Fund; Govt Whip, House of Lords 1987-89; Under Sec of State, Ministry of Defence 1989-92, N Ireland Office, 1992-94, since when Under Sec of State, Dept of Environment; Capt Queen's Body Guard of Yeomen of The Guard (Dep Ch Whip) July 1994-Jan 1995: *m* 1974, Eleanor, elder da of Bernard van Cutsem (*see* E Fortescue), and has issue.

ᴁrms – Gules, a fesse between three cross crosslets fitchée or. ᴄrest – A wolf rampant argent collared gules. ᴤupporters – Two horses argent.
Residence – Castle Hill, Filleigh, Barnstaple, N Devon EX32 0RQ.
Clubs – Turf, Beefsteak, Pratt's, White's.

DAUGHTERS LIVING

Lady Laura Melissa, *b* 1975.
Lady Lucy Katherine, *b* 1976.

WIDOW LIVING OF EIGHTH EARL

FIONA BRYDE (*Fiona, Countess of Arran*), da of Sir Iain Colquhoun, 7th Bt, KT, DSO; first person to average 100 mph in an offshore boat (1980), awarded Segrave Trophy (1981): *m* 1937, the 8th Earl of Arran, who *d* 1983. *Residence* – Pimlico House, Hemel Hempstead, Herts.

COLLATERAL BRANCHES LIVING

Grandchildren of late Sir Francis Charles Gore, KCB, eldest son of Hon Charles Alexander Gore, brother of 4th Earl:—
Issue of late Charles Henry Gore, OBE, *b* 1881, *d* 1941: *m* 1st, 1911, Marguerite, who *d* 1918, da of Walter Langley; 2ndly, 1920, Hon Violet Kathleen Annesley, who *d* 1963, da of 11th Viscount Valentia:—
(By 2nd *m*) PAUL ANNESLEY, CMG, CVO (1 Burkitt Rd, Woodbridge, Suffolk), *b* 28 Feb 1921; *ed* Winchester, and Ch Ch, Oxford (MA); Capt late 16th/5th Lancers; Colonial Admin Ser 1948-65; cr CVO 1962, CMG 1964: *m* 1946, Gillian Mary, da of late Capt Tom Allen-Stevens, Dep Gov The Gambia 1962-65, and has had issue, †Charles Alexander, *b* 1947; *ed* Radley, and Southampton Univ: *m* 1st, 1970 (*m diss* 1973), Penelope, yr da of R. C. Caunce, of Maidenhead; 2ndly, 1984, Susan Diana, da of M. J. Hardy, and *d* 1985, — William Henry (106 Simpsons Rd, Bardon, Qld, Australia 4064), *b* 1950; *ed* Radley, and Lincoln Coll, Oxford: *m* 1st, 1980, Mrs Cecilia Nell McBean, who *d* 1990, da of R. Cox, of Brisbane, Australia; 2ndly 1993, Mrs Rosemary Lindholm, da of R. Payne, of Brisbane, Qld, and has issue living (by 1st *m*), Charles David *b* 1985, Letitia Sarah *b* 1982, — Nicholas David, *b* 1952; *ed* Radley: *m* 1983, Christine Mary, da of H. W. Clothier, of Evercreech, Som, and formerly wife of C. B. Tilley, and has issue living, Alastair Mark *b* 1984, Robert William *b* 1986. ——Ursula Mary, *b* 1922: *m* 1947, Com Edward Graham Ducat-Hamersley, RN, who *d* 1987, and has issue living, Penelope Tara, *b* 1948: *m* 1973, Stephen Hayes, of 11 Ashley Rise, Walton-on-Thames, Surrey, and has issue living, Timothy *b* 1975, Kirsty *b* 1977, Rosemary *b* 1980, — Priscilla Rosemary, *b* 1951: *m* 1st, 1982, David Henderson, of Qld, Australia, who *d* 1989; 2ndly, 1994, Keith Nobes, of Qld, Australia, and has issue living (by 1st *m*), Nathan Edward Vivien *b* 1982, Kelly Letitia *b* 1984, Tara Gae *b* 1988, (by 2nd *m*), Samantha Emily *b* 1996, — Felicity, *b* 1954: *m* 1978, Gerald Brian O'Brien, of 55 Hyde Abbey Rd, Winchester, Hants, and has issue living, Katherine *b* 1983, Eleanor *b* 1987, — Joanna, *b* 1957: *m* 1st, 1980 (*m diss* 1983), Charles Robert Sindell; 2ndly, 1983 (*m diss* 1988), George Bentham Walk-

er; 3rdly, 1990, Stephen Lockwood, and has issue living (by 2nd *m*), Hugh Simon *b* 1985, (by 3rd *m*) Thomas Edward *b* 1990, Alice Sophie *b* 1992. *Residence* – 1 Brookside, Watlington, Oxon. —— Rosemary Kathleen, *b* 1924; formerly in WRNS: *m* 1945, Arthur Emerson Mabin, Lt (A) RNZNVR, who *d* 1986, and has issue living, Richard Peter (Pratts Rd, RD3, Ramarama, Auckland, NZ), *b* 1965: *m* 1990, Elizabeth Katurah, yr da of James Doble, of Stony Stratton, Som, and has issue living, Angus Emerson *b* 1995, Emma Keturah *b* 1997, — Susan Kathleen, *b* 1946: *m* 1968, Leslie Howard Cook, of 9 Valhalla Lane, Richmond, Nelson, NZ, and has issue living, Timothy Peter *b* 1972, Sarah Kathleen *b* 1974, Helen Ruth *b* 1976, — Caroline Ruth, *b* 1947, — Helen Rosemary, *b* 1950: *m* 1973, Alan Archibald Winwood, of 19 Richmond Av, Nelson, NZ, and has issue living, Derek Emerson *b* 1978, Christopher Alan *b* 1982, Thomas Willem *b* 1984, Joanna Rosemary *b* 1980, — Victoria Jane, *b* 1953; PhD: *m* 1st, 1983, Willem Louis Frits van den Broek, who *d* 1984; 2ndly 1987, Christopher Mannings Sutton, PhD, of 8 Crofton Rd, Ngaio, Wellington, NZ, and has issue living (by 2nd *m*), Rebecca Jane *b* 1989, Emily Claire Mabin *b* 1991. *Residence* – 7 Manuka St, Nelson, NZ.

Issue of late John Francis Gore, CVO, TD, *b* 1885, *d* 1983: *m* 1926, Lady Janet Helena Campbell, who *d* 1982, da of 4th Earl Cawdor:—
Charles John (Port na Mine, Taynuilt, Argyll PA35 1HU), *b* 1932; *ed* Eton: *m* 1961, Jean, yr da of late Col Charles Ian Fraser, CBE, TD, of Reelig, Kirkhill, Inverness-shire, and has issue living, (Ian) Simon Francis (Marchfield House, Binfield, Berks RG42 4EB), *b* 1965: *m* 1993, Sarah E., yr da of Colin Frazer Frizzell, of Smewins Barn, Smewins Rd, White Waltham, Berks SL6 3SR, and has issue living, Samuel Charles Fraser *b* 1994, Milo Thomas Spencer *b* 1995, Marnie Rose *b* 1997, — John Alexander Charles, *b* 1971, — Helena Mary, *b* 1962: *m* 1992, Michael J. Bayler, and has issue living, Amelia Jane *b* 1993. —— Moyra, *b* 1927. —— (Mary) Elizabeth (*Elizabeth, Lady Cave*), *b* 1929: *m* 1957, Sir Charles Edward Coleridge Cave, 4th Bt, who *d* 1997, and has issue (see that title). *Residence* – Court Hall, Sidbury, Sidmouth, Devon EX10 0RS.

Grandchildren of late Spencer William Gore, 2nd son of Hon Charles Alexander Gore (ante):—
Issue of late George Pym Gore, *b* 1875, *d* 1959: *m* 1914, Alexandra Leila, who *d* 1970, da of late Rev Canon Frederick Alfred John Hervey, CVO (M Bristol, colls), and widow of Lt Sir Walter Clervaux Chaytor, RN, 5th Bt:—
Victoria Maud Lavinia Mary, *b* 1915: *m* 1944 (*m diss* 1955), Ian Alexander Kennedy, 16th/5th Lancers, and has issue living, Lavinia Susan, *b* 1948: *m* 1st, 1970 (*m diss* 1983), Timothy Scott Bigland, elder son of late Lt-Col Thomas Scott Bigland, DSO, MBE, TD; 2ndly, 1984, as his 2nd wife, Richard Hugh Chaytor Vaux, late Maj RAPC (*see* Chaytor, Bt, 1973-74 Edn), of The Moors, Boynes Wood Rd, Medstead, Alton, Hants GU34 5EA, and has issue living (by 1st *m*), Alexandra Rosalind *b* 1977, (by 2nd *m*) Philippa Clare Marisa *b* 1986, Lucinda Mary Diana *b* 1987.

Issue of late Spencer Frederick Gore, *b* 1878, *d* 1914: *m* 1912, Mary Joanna, who *d* 1968, da of Capt John Kerr:—
Frederick John Pym, CBE (Flat 3, 35 Elm Park Gdns, SW10 9QF), *b* 1913; *ed* Lancing Coll, and Trin Coll, Oxford; RA 1964; a Trustee of Imperial War Museum 1967-84; Head of Painting Dept, St Martin's Sch of Art, 1951-79, and Vice-Prin 1961-79; 1940-45 War as Maj RA; CBE (Civil) 1987: *m* 1st, 1945, Lili Reneé, da of L. Gaber; 2ndly, 1953, Constance Irene, da of W. H. Smith, of Brentford, Middx, and has issue living, (by 1st *m*) Georgiana Sarah, *b* 1950; PhD: *m* 1990, Laurent Christophe Michel Wierre, and has issue living, Natasha Anouk Eva *b* 1991, — (by 2nd *m*) Charles David (Flat 1, 2A Coleherne Mews, SW10), *b* 1954; PhD (SOAS): *m* 1993, Harriet Nkechi, da of late Abel O. Adimora, of Uga, Aguata, Anambra State, Nigeria, and has issue living, William Frederick Ebubechukwu Pym *b* 1998 (also has issue, James Spencer *b* 1988), — Geraldine Lucy, *b* 1957; BA.

Grandson of late Arthur Saunders Gore, 3rd son of Ven John Ribton Gore, 4th son of Very Rev Hon George Gore, LLD, Dean of Killala, 3rd son of 2nd Earl:—
Issue of late Arthur Henry Baldwin Gore, *b* 1883, *d* 1953: *m* 1913, Jane Browne, who *d* 1975:—
Arthur Francis, MD, *b* 1914: *m* 1939, Helen Claire Mullen, of Omaha, Nebraska, USA, and has issue living, James Arthur, *b* 1950, — Judith Ann, *b* 1940: *m* 1964, Fernando Joseph Ramirez, of 8719 La Roca, Fountain Valley, Calif, USA, and has issue living, Jane Ellen *b* 1965, Anne Marie *b* 1969, — Nancy Jane, *b* 1942, — Margaret Francis, *b* 1946, — Pamela Elizabeth, *b* 1948: *m* 1969, Paul Everett Adkins, and has issue living, Jennifer Claire *b* 1975, — Jill Marie, *b* 1957, — Martha Jane, *b* 1959.

Grandchildren of late Arthur Henry Baldwin Gore (ante):—
Issue of late John Douglas Gore, *b* 1916, *d* 1976: *m* 1946, Evelyn Mae (Lyn) Wagner (who *m* 2ndly, 1978, Gerald Louis Artaud, who *d* 1979):—
John Douglas, *b* 1947. —— Theresa Ann, *b* 1951: *m* 1973, Jon Patrick Ferguson, and has issue living, Stacy Ann, *b* 1975, — Dana Marie, *b* 1978. —— Margaret Jane, *b* 1957: *m* 1978, John Fisher.

Grandson of late Major James Arthur Charles Gore, eldest son of late Gen Hon Sir Charles Gore, KH, GCB, 6th son of 2nd Earl:—
Issue of late Col Edward John Mounsey Gore, *b* 1863, *d* 1949: *m* 1899, Hon Emilia Herbert Fullerton Napier, who *d* 1932, da of 1st Baron Napier of Magdala:—
Humphry Gerard Napier, *b* 1916; *ed* Sherborne; Major (ret) late Roy Ulster Rifles: *m* 1948, Leslie Marshal Peabody, of New York, USA, and has issue living, Mark Staveley (571 Glendale Av, Bridgeport, CT 06606, USA), *b* 1952; BA, MLS, — Brendon Bostwick (181 Amyand Park Rd, St Margarets, Twickenham, Middx TW1 3HN), *b* 1955; BSc: *m* 1990, Helen Elizabeth, yst da of P. A. Merker, of Wilts, and has issue living, Charles James Napier *b* 1995, Lucy Charlotte Geddes *b* 1998, — Timothy Francis (Longfield, Seal Hollow Rd, Sevenoaks, Kent), *b* 1957; BA, BSc, ARICS: *m* 1989, Amanda S., twin da of P. F. Kingsley, of Sussex, and has issue living, Edward Charles Theodore *b* 1994, Frederick Humphry William *b* 1999, Emma Philippa *b* 1991, Celia Frances *b* 1992. *Residence* – The Red Cottage, South Park, Sevenoaks, Kent.

Grandchildren of late William Stuart Gore, 5th son of late Maj James Arthur Charles Gore (ante):—
Issue of late Erroll Napier Gore, *b* 1897, *d* 1968: *m* 1926, Alma Maude, who *d* 1978, da of William Edward Kessell:—
†William Erroll, *b* 1926: *m* 1951, Joan Hetherington, and *d* 1969, leaving issue, William Arran (1 Newcastle St, Stockton, NSW, Australia), *b* 1965, — Jennifer Louise, *b* 1957: *m* 1977, Jonathon Smith, and has issue living, Justin William *b* 1987, Jacqueline Louise *b* 1984, Jessica Ashleigh *b* 1991, — Susan Michelle, *b* 1959: *m* 1979, Steven Cole, and has had issue, Christopher Steven *b* 1980; *d* 1983, Mathew Dean *b* 1984, — Alyson Maree, *b* 1961: *m* 1991, Christopher John Gearing,

and has issue living, Jack Ernest *b* 1993, — Catherine Anne, *b* 1968. —— Stuart Maxwell, *b* 1929: *m* 1988, Leovegilda Marcos, and has issue living, Benjamin Laurence Stuart, *b* 1990, — Kylie-Anne Shirley, *b* 1989. —— Ian Winn Bazalgette, *b* 1932; Maj Australian Staff Corps (ret): *m* 1961, Evelyne Phyllis, da of late Maj Charles William Sayers, of Melbourne, and has issue living, Robert Ian Charles, *b* 1966: *m* 1991, Tina Marie Kelly, and has issue living, Thomas Ian *b* 1992, — Belinda Jane, *b* 1967: *m* 1992, William Anthony Trewartha, and has issue living, William Ian Alexander *b* 1993. —— Laurence James, *b* 1935. —— Pamela Mary, *b* 1939: *m* 1961 (*m diss* 1967), Graham Richard Westwood, and has issue living, Nicholas Ian Richard, *b* 1964, — Jo-Anne Louise, *b* 1963.

Granddaughter of late William John Gore, son of late Capt Ralph Gore, RN, 2nd son of late Hon Paul Gore, 3rd son of 1st Earl:—
Issue of late Charles Arthur Gore, *b* 1845, *d* 1926: *m* 1st, 1883, Mary Goacher, who *d* 1894; 2ndly, 1907, Constance Gertrude (who *d* 1971, having *m* 3rdly, 1928, John James Sayers, who *d* 1955), da of John Burch, of 148 Ebury Street, SW1, and widow of Henry William Willis:—
(By 2nd *m*) Constance Joyce Gwendolen, *b* 1911; is a SRN: *m* 1937, Ernest Killingback, BSc, ARCS, who *d* 1939, and has issue living, Peter Gore (58 Highfields Dr, Loughborough, Leics LE11 3JT) *b* 1939: *ed* King Edward VI Gram Sch, Aston, London Sch of Pharmacy (BPharm), and Manchester Univ (MSc): *m* 1968, Janet Mary Reason, BSc, and has issue living, David Gore *b* 1971, Christopher Michael *b* 1975. *Residence* – 5 Orchard Cres, Enfield, Middx.

(In remainder to baronetcy only)

Descendants of late John Ralph ORMSBY-GORE (fourth in descent from late William Gore, MP, 3rd son of 1st Baronet), who was cr *Baron Harlech* 1876 (see that title).

PREDECESSORS – **(1)** *Sir* ARTHUR Gore, second son of Sir Paul Gore (who was cr a Baronet of Ireland 1621); cr a *Baronet* of Ireland 1662; *s* by his grandson **(2)** ARTHUR, 2nd Bt; MP for co Longford; *d* 1741; *s* by his eldest son **(3)** ARTHUR, 3rd Bt; cr *Baron Saunders* and *Viscount Sudley* (peerage of Ireland) 1758, and *Earl of Arran Islands* (peerage of Ireland) 1762; *d* 1773; *s* by his eldest son **(4)** ARTHUR SAUNDERS, KP, 2nd Earl; *d* 1809; *s* by his eldest son **(5)** ARTHUR SAUNDERS, 3rd Earl; *d* 1837; *s* by his nephew **(6)** PHILIP YORKE, KP, 4th Earl, *b* 1801: *m* 1838, Elizabeth Marianne, who *d* 1899, da of late Gen Sir William Francis Patrick Napier, KCB; *d* 25 June 1884; *s* by his son **(7)** ARTHUR SAUNDERS WILLIAM CHARLES FOX, KP, 5th Earl; *b* 1839; cr *Baron Sudley*, of Castle Gore, co Mayo (peerage of United Kingdom), 1884: *m* 1st, 1865, Hon Edith Jocelyn, who *d* 1871, da of Robert, Viscount Jocelyn, MP, and sister of 4th Earl of Roden; 2ndly, 1889, Winifred Ellen, who *d* 1921, da of late John Reilly, and widow of Hon John Montagu Stopford (*see* E Courtown, 1920 Edn), *d* 1901; *s* by his son **(8)** ARTHUR JOCELYN CHARLES, KP, PC, 6th Earl; *b* 1868: Brevet Major Roy Horse Guards; was HM Lieut and Custos Rotulorum for co Donegal 1917-20 and a KGStJ: *m* 1st, 1902, Mathilde Jacqueline Marie Beauclerk (a DGStJ), who *d* 1927, only da of Baron Huyssen van Kattendyke, of Kattendyke, Zeeland, Netherlands; 2ndly, 1929, Lillian Constance, who *d* 1961, da of late John Quick, of Crossdeep Place, Twickenham, and widow of Frank Browne, of Pyecroft Place, Chertsey; *d* 19 Dec 1958; *s* by his eldest son **(9)** ARTHUR PAUL JOHN CHARLES JAMES, *b* 1903; ADC to Gov-Gen of S Africa 1931; *d* 28 Dec 1958; *s* by his brother, **(10)** ARTHUR STRANGE KATTENDYKE DAVID ARCHIBALD, 8th Earl, *b* 1910; Attaché British Legation, Berne 1941-41, and British Embassy, Lisbon 1941-42, in Min of Information 1942-45 (Dir of Overseas Gen Div 1945), and in Central Office of Information 1945-49 (Dir of Secretariat); introduced in House of Lords, Sexual Offences Bill (now Act) (three times), and Badger Protection Bill (now Act); a Dir of *Daily Mail* and General Trust Ltd; Chm Children's Country Holidays Fund, and Hon Treas Moorfields Eye Hospital: *m* 1937, Fiona Bryde, eldest da of Sir Iain Colquhoun, 7th Bt, KT, DSO; *d* 1983; *s* by his only surv son **(11)** ARTHUR DESMOND COLQUHOUN, 9th Earl and present peer; also Viscount Sudley, Baron Saunders, and Baron Sudley.

Arthur, family name of Lord Glenarthur.

Arundel and Surrey, Earl of; son of Duke of Norfolk.

Arundel, Monckton-, family name of Viscount Galway.

Arundell, family name of Baron Talbot of Malahide.

ARUNDELL OF WARDOUR, BARONY OF (Arundell) (Extinct 1944)

DAUGHTER LIVING OF FIFTEENTH BARON

Hon Mary Isabella, *b* 1913: *m* 1935 (*m diss* 1955), Air Commodore Thomas Patrick Feltrim Fagan, RAF, who *d* 1985, and has issue living, Patrick Feltrim, CB, MBE (DG Mil Svy, Elmwood Av, Feltham, Middx TW13 7AH), *b* 1935; MBE (Mil) 1966, CB (Mil) 1990; Maj-Gen late RE: *m* 1967, Veronica, da of J. J. Lorant, and widow of Capt C. J. C. Thompson, RE, and has issue living, Daragh Patrick Feltrim *b* 1969, Rory Michael Feltrim *b* 1972, — Michael John, *b* 1940, — Deirdre Mairi, *b* 1937.

ARWYN, BARONY OF (Arwyn) (Extinct 1978)

SON LIVING OF LIFE BARON (*By 2nd marriage*)

Hon Arwyn Hugh Davies (Ewart, Ashley Rd, Bathford, Avon), *b* 1949; Bar Gray's Inn 1972: *m* 1977, Mary Elizabeth Gibson.

DAUGHTERS LIVING OF LIFE BARON (*By 1st marriage*)

Hon Mary Gwynne (28 Bloomfield Rd, Bath), *b* 1932: *m* 1954, Geoffrey James Webb, who *d* 1975, and has issue.
Hon Elisabeth Jocelyn, *b* 1938: *m* 1962, John Robb Macnab, of 186 Sedlescombe Road North, St Leonards-on-Sea, and has issue.

WIDOW LIVING OF LIFE BARON

BEATRIX EMILY (*Baroness Arwyn*) (Ormonde, Lostwithiel, Cornwall), da of Capt F. H. Organ of St Austell, Cornwall: *m* 1946, as his 2nd wife, Baron Arwyn (Life Baron), who *d* 1978.

ASHBOURNE, BARON (Gibson) (Baron UK 1885)

Open, oh, ye heavenly gates

(EDWARD) BARRY GREYNVILLE GIBSON, 4th Baron; *b* 28 Jan 1933; *s* 1983; *ed* Rugby; Lt-Cdr RN (ret); Stockbroker 1972-79; Chm Joshua Christian Trust, and Lords' and Commons' Family and Child Protection Group: *m* 1967, Yvonne Georgina, da of Mrs Flora Ham, and has issue.

Arms – Ermine, three keys fesswise in pale azure, and in chief as many trefoils slipped vert. **Crest** – A pelican in her piety on a bank of reeds proper. **Supporters** – *Dexter*, a female figure representing Mercy standing upon a fasces proper, habited argent, charged on the breast with a trefoil slipped vert, and resting her right hand on a sword point downwards proper, pommel or; *sinister*, a like figure representing Justice habited, charged and standing as the dexter, holding in her right hand a balance and in the left a sword erect proper.
Residence – Colebrook Barn, East Harting Farm, Petersfield, Hants GU31 5LU.

SONS LIVING

Hon (EDWARD) CHARLES D'OLIER, *b* 31 Dec 1967.
Hon (William) Rodney Colles, *b* 1970.
Hon Patrick Mayne, *b* 1977.

AUNT LIVING (*Raised to the rank of a Baron's daughter* 1943)

Hon Kathleen Mary, *b* 1908: *m* 1930, James Hamilton Russell, who *d* 1981, and has issue living, *Prof* Michael Anthony Hamilton (14 Courtlane Gdns, Dulwich Village, SE21), *b* 1932: MA Oxon; BM BCh, FRCPLond, FRCPsych, Emeritus Prof of Addiction, Inst of Psychiatry, London: *m* 1962, Audrey Anne Timms, and has issue living, James Hamilton *b* 1974, Nicholas Hamilton *b* 1977, — Timothy Patrick HAMILTON-RUSSELL (Hamilton Russell Vineyards, PO Box 158, Hermanus 7200, Western Cape, S Africa), *b* 1934: *m* 1958, Athene Wendy Isobel, da of late William Aubrey Bindon, and has issue living, Anthony James *b* 1962: *m* 1990, Arabella Sabina Lilian, only da of late Hon David Anthony Lawrence Caccia (*see* By Caccia) (and has issue living, Olivia Sabina *b* 1992, Ella Maria *b* (twin) 1992), Patrick David *b* 1969, Bridgid Mary *b* 1960: *m* 1986, Scipion Vernede, Julia Kathleen *b* 1965: *m* 1992, Robert David Marshall (*see* Montagu-Pollock, Bt, colls), — *Rt Rev* David Patrick Hamilton (Bishopsbourne, 17 Durban St, Grahamstown 6140, S Africa), *b* 1938; Bishop of Grahamstown: *m* 1980, Dorothea Martha Madden, and has issue living, Sipho Matthew *b* 1981, Thabo Andrew *b* 1983, — Robin James (Brooke Hall, Flodden Rd, SE5 9LH), *b* 1947: *m* 1977 (*m diss* 1989), Imogene Veronica King, and has issue living, George *b* 1982, Thomas Richard Henry *b* 1984, Frances *b* 1977, Virginia *b* 1979, — Jill Mary, *b* 1935: *m* 1965, Anthony Ronald Hall, who *d* 19—, of 20 Unthank Rd, Norwich, Norfolk NR2, and has issue living, Catherine Sian *b* 1967, Marion Ruth *b* 1970, — Diana Elizabeth Hamilton (2432 Grant St, Berkeley, Calif 94703, USA), *b* (twin) 1938; *ed* Cape Town Univ (BA), LSE, and Harvard (MA, PhD); Prof Emerita of Sociology, Mills Coll. *Residence* – Fairmead Court, 6 College Rd, Rondebosch, Cape Town, S Africa.

WIDOW LIVING OF BROTHER OF THIRD BARON

Sabina (formerly Sabine), da of late Dr Ernest Landsberg, of Cape Town, S Africa: *m* 1947, Lt-Col Hon (William) David Gibson, OBE, TD (raised to the rank of a Baron's son 1943), who *d* 1993, and has issue (see colls, infra). *Residence* – 43 Hunters Moon, Dartington, Totnes, Devon TQ9 6JT.

COLLATERAL BRANCHES LIVING

Issue of late Lt-Col Hon (William) David Gibson, OBE, TD (raised to the rank of a Baron's son 1943), yr brother of 3rd Baron, *b* 1914, *d* 1993: *m* 1947, Sabina (formerly Sabine) (ante), da of late Dr Ernest Landsberg, of Cape Town, S Africa:—
Celia Mary, *b* 1948: *m* 1977 (*m diss* 1993), Robert Sommers, and has issue living, Dominic Alexander, *b* 1977, — Abigail Jane, *b* 1980, — Jessica Sarah, *b* 1982. —— Monica Anne (2 Ley Crescent, Liverton, Newton Abbot, Devon TQ12 6JH), *b* 1951: *m* 1973, Andrew Vaughan Harding, and has issue living, James, *b* 1977, — Louise, *b* 1975. —— Philippa Constance (Maes-y-Morfa, Llangrannog, Llandysul, Dyfed SA44 6RU), *b* 1953.

Issue of late Hon (Ernest) Victor Gibson, yst son of 1st Baron, *b* 1875, *d* 1922: *m* 1st, 1905, Mary Wood Salisbury, who *d* 1905, da of Joseph L. R. Wood, of New York; 2ndly, 1909, Caroline, who *d* 1952, da of Frederic de Billier, of New York:—
(By 2nd *m*) John Frederic, DSC, *b* 1919; is Lt RNVR; 1939-45 War (DSC): *m* 1st, 1941 (*m diss* 1946), Margaret A. Booth; 2ndly, 1947, Lorna M. Pickering, and has issue living (by 1st *m*), Victor Russell (Barn Hill House, 16 Parsonage Lane, Market Lavington nr Devizes, Wilts), *b* 1949, *ed* Nautical Coll, Pangbourne: *m* 1968, Pamela Cherry, da of late Edward Cupitt-Eggleshaw, and has issue living, Geoffrey Andrew *b* 1971, Neil Henry *b* 1975, — (by 2nd *m*) Simon John (31844 Conrad Av, Clearbrook, BC, Canada V2T 2K3), *b* 1952: *m* 1976, Joy Beatrice, da of Walter Sidney Ridgway, of Vancouver, BC, and has issue living, Shari-Anne Joy *b* 1980, Alisa Julie *b* 1982, — Julia de Billier, *b* 1959: *m* 1985, Evert Van der Zee, and has issue living, Matthew James *b* 1988. *Residence* – 687 Erickson Rd, Campbell River, BC, Canada V9W 1S9.

PREDECESSORS – (1) *Rt Hon* EDWARD Gibson, LLD, son of late William Gibson, JP, of Merrion Square, Dublin; *b* 1837; Attorney-Gen for Ireland 1877-80, and Lord Chancellor of Ireland with a seat in the Cabinet 1885 to Jan 1886, July 1886 to Aug 1892, and June 1895 to Dec 1905 (many times acted as a Lord Justice of Ireland during absence of Lord-Lieut); MP for Dublin Univ (C) 1875-85; *cr Baron Ashbourne*, of Ashbourne, co Meath (peerage of United Kingdom) 1885: *m* 1868, Frances Maria Adelaide, who *d* 1926, da of late Henry Cope Colles; *d* 1913; *s* by his eldest son (2)

WILLIAM, 2nd Baron; *b* 1868: *m* 1896, Marianne, who *d* 1953, da of Henri Roger de Monbrison, of Avenue de Jena, Paris; *d* 1942; *s* by his nephew (3) EDWARD RUSSELL, CB, DSO (eldest son of late Hon Edward Graves Mayne Gibson, 3rd son of 1st Baron), 3rd Baron, *b* 1901; Vice-Adm; served 1914-18 War in HMS *Superb*, *Dreadnought* and *Monarch*: *m* 1929, Reta Frances Manning, who *d* 1996, elder da of Ernest Manning Hazeland, of Hong Kong; *d* 1983; *s* by his only son (4) (EDWARD) BARRY GREYNVILLE, 4th Baron and present peer.

ASHBROOK, VISCOUNT (Flower) (Viscount I 1751)

A mind conscious of rectitude

MICHAEL LLOWARCH WARBURTON FLOWER, 11th Viscount; *b* 9 Dec 1935; *s* 1995; *ed* Eton, and Worcester Coll, Oxford (MA); 2nd Lieut Gren Gds 1955; Solicitor 1963, Ptnr Farrer & Co 1966-76, March Pearson & Skelton, Manchester 1986-91, and Pannone March Pearson 1991-92, Consultant Pannone & Ptnrs 1992-96; DL Cheshire 1982, JP 1983, Vice Lord Lieut since 1990: *m* 1971, Zoë Mary, yst da of late Francis Henry Arnold Engleheart, of The Priory, Stoke-by-Nayland, Suffolk, and has issue.

Arms – Quarterly: 1st and 4th argent, two chevronels between three ravens, each having an ermine spot in its beak, sable, and between the chevronels, three pellets; 2nd and 3rd gules, three towers argent. **Crest** – A raven, having an ermine spot in its beak. **Supporters** – Two tigers reguardant proper, ducally collared and chained or.
Residence – The Old Parsonage, Arley Green, Northwich, Cheshire CW9 6LZ.
Club – Brooks's.

SONS LIVING

Hon ROWLAND FRANCIS WARBURTON, *b* 16 Jan 1975; *ed* Eton, and Newcastle Univ.
Hon Harry William Warburton, *b* 1977; *ed* Cokethorpe Sch.

DAUGHTER LIVING

Hon Eleanor Filumena, *b* 1973; *ed* St Mary's, Ascot, and Edinburgh Univ.

SISTER LIVING

Hon Jane Mary Elizabeth, *b* 1943; *ed* Lady Margaret Hall, Oxford (BA), and LSE (MSc): *m* 1967, Charles Francis Foster, and has issue living, Rupert Rowland, *b* 1970, — Antonia Elizabeth, *b* 1969: *m* 1995, Robert John Candlish Howatson, of 16 Dartmouth Park Av, NW5 1JN, yr son of Dr Alastair Howatson, of Oxford, and has issue living, Lucy Elizabeth *b* 1998, — Cordelia Rose, *b* 1974. *Residences* – East Wing, Arley Hall, Northwich, Cheshire; 18 Stanley Gardens, W11.

WIDOW LIVING OF SON OF TENTH VISCOUNT

Bridget Karen, yr da of John Duncan: *m* 1970, Hon Anthony John Warburton Flower, who *d* 1991, and has issue (see colls, infra). *Residence* – Prouts Farm, Hawkley, Liss, Hants.

WIDOW LIVING OF TENTH VISCOUNT

ELIZABETH (*Elizabeth, Viscountess Ashbrook*), elder da of late Capt John Egerton-Warburton (*see* Grey-Egerton, Bt, colls): *m* 1934, the 10th Viscount Ashbrook, KCVO, MBE, who *d* 1995. *Residence* – Woodlands, Arley, Northwich, Cheshire.

COLLATERAL BRANCHES LIVING

Issue of late Hon Anthony John Warburton Flower, yr son of 10th Viscount, *b* 1938, *d* 1991: *m* 1970, Bridget Karen (ante), yr da of John Duncan:—
Alexandra Jane, *b* 1972.

Issue of late Hon Reginald Henry Flower, yr son of 8th Viscount, *b* 1871, *d* 1938: *m* 1901, Katherine Ella (Kate), who *d* 1957, da of Col Edward William Cuming, of Crovar, co Cavan:—

Mollie Frances, *b* 1902: *m* 1st, 1929 (*m diss* 1945), John Albert Peacey; 2ndly, 1947, Maj Wilfrid Vincent Townshend Allen, of Duncan, BC, Canada.

PREDECESSORS – (1) WILLIAM Flower, MP for co Kilkenny; cr *Baron Castle Durrow* (peerage of Ireland) 1733; *d* 1746; *s* by his son (2) HENRY, 2nd Baron; cr *Viscount Ashbrook* (peerage of Ireland) 1751; *d* 1752; *s* by his son (3) WILLIAM, 2nd Viscount; *d* 1780; *s* by his eldest son (4) WILLIAM, 3rd Viscount; *d* 1802; *s* by his brother (5) HENRY JEFFREY, 4th Viscount; *d* 1847; *s* by his son (6) HENRY JEFFREY, 5th Viscount, *b* 1806: *m* 1828, Frances, who *d* 1886, da of Sir John Robinson, 1st Bt; *d* 1871; *s* by his eldest son (7) HENRY JEFFREY, 6th Viscount; *d* 1882; *s* by his brother (8) WILLIAM SPENCER, 7th Viscount, *b* 1830: *m* 1861, Augusta Madeline Henriette, who *d* 1906, da of late George Marton, of Capernwray Hall, Lancaster; *d* 1906; *s* by his brother (9) ROBERT THOMAS, 8th Viscount, *b* 1836: *m* 1866, Gertrude Sophia, who *d* 1911, da of late Rev Sewell Hamilton, of Bath; *d* 1919; *s* by his eldest son (10) LLOWARCH ROBERT, 9th Viscount, *b* 1870: *m* 1899, Gladys Lucille, who *d* 1968, da of late Gen Sir George Wentworth Alexander Higginson, GCB, GCVO; *d* 1936; *s* by his son (11) DESMOND LLOWARCH EDWARD, KCVO, MBE, 10th Viscount, *b* 1905; Member of Council of Duchy of Lancaster 1957-77, Chm Country Gentleman's Assocn 1955-62; served 1939-45 War as Maj RA (TA): *m* 1934, Elizabeth, elder da of late Capt John Egerton-Warburton (*see* Grey-Egerton, Bt, colls); *d* 1995; *s* by his elder (and only surv) son (12) MICHAEL LLOWARCH WARBURTON, 11th Viscount and present peer; also Baron Castle Durrow.

ASHBURTON, BARON (Baring) (Baron UK 1835)

Fortitude under difficulties

JOHN FRANCIS HARCOURT BARING, KG, KCVO, 7th Baron; *b* 2 Nov 1928; *s* 1991; *ed* Eton (Fellow 1982), and Trin Coll, Oxford (MA, Hon Fellow 1989), Hon Fellow Hertford Coll, Oxford 1976; DL Hants 1994; Chm Baring Bros & Co Ltd 1974-89, Barings plc 1985-89 (non-exec Dir 1989-94), and Accepting Houses Cttee 1977-81; Chm British Petroleum Co plc 1992-95 (Dir 1982 95); Chm of Council Baring Foundation 1987-98 (Memb of Council 1971-98); Dir Pye Holdings Ltd 1967-79, Royal Insurance Co Ltd 1964-82 (Dep-Chm 1975-82), Trafford Park Estates Ltd 1964-77, Dunlop Holdings 1981-84, Bank of England 1983-91, and Jaguar plc 1989-91; Chm Outwich Investment Trust 1965-86, and Baring Stratton Investment Trust plc 1986-97; Memb of President's Cttee CBI 1976-79, and a Vice-Pres Gen Council of British Bankers' Assocn 1977-81; Pres Overseas Bankers' Club 1977-78; Receiver-Gen Duchy of Cornwall 1974-90, Lord Warden of the Stannaries and Keeper of the Privy Seal of the Duchy 1990-94; a Rhodes Trustee 1970-99 (Chm 1987-99), Trustee Royal Jubilee Trusts 1979-95, National Gallery 1981-87, The Police Foundation (Hon Treas) since 1989, and Winchester Cathedral Trust since 1989 (Chm since 1993); Member Exec Cttee Nat Art-Collections Fund 1989-99; High Steward Winchester Cathedral since 1991; *cr* CVO 1980, Knt 1983, KCVO 1990, KG 1994: *m* 1st, 1955 (*m diss* 1984), Hon Susan Mary Renwick, eldest da of 1st Baron Renwick; 2ndly, 1987, Mrs Sarah Crewe, da of late John George Spencer-Churchill (*see* D Marlborough, colls), and has issue by 1st *m*.

Arms – Azure, a fesse or, in chief a bear's head proper, muzzled and ringed of the second, differenced by a cross formy fitchy azure. **Crest** – A mullet erminois, between two wings, argent. **Supporters** – On either side a bear proper, muzzled, collared, and chained, or, charged on the shoulder with a cross patée fitchée of the last.
Residence – Lake House, Northington, Alresford, Hants SO24 9TG. *Clubs* – Flyfishers', Pratt's, Beefsteak.

SONS LIVING (*By 1st marriage*)

Hon MARK FRANCIS ROBERT, *b* 17 Aug 1958; *ed* Eton, and Ch Ch, Oxford: *m* 1983, Miranda Caroline, 2nd da of Capt Charles St John Graham Moncrieff, of Easter Elcho, Rhynd, Perth (*see* Peto, Bt, *cr* 1927, colls), and has issue living, Frederick Charles Francis, *b* 25 June 1990, — Patrick John Robin, *b* 1995, — Aurea Rose, *b* 1988, — Flora May, *b* 1997. *Residence* – Abbotstone Farm House, nr Alresford, Hants SO24 9TE.
Hon Alexander Nicholas John, *b* 1964; *ed* Eton, and Oriel Coll, Oxford: *m* 1992, Lucy Caroline, yr da of Gen Sir David William Fraser, GCB, OBE (*see* Ly Saltoun), and has issue living, William John, *b* 1996, — Olive Rose, *b* 1994. *Residence* – 109 Portobello Rd, W11.

DAUGHTERS LIVING (*By 1st marriage*)

Hon Lucinda Mary Louise, *b* 1956: *m* 1978, Hon Michael John Wilmot Malet Vaughan, 2nd son of 8th Earl of Lisburne, and has issue (see that title). *Residence* – Itchen Stoke House, Alresford, Hants SO24 0QU.
Hon Rose Theresa, *b* 1961: *m* 1994, Barnaby Hugh Rogerson, and has issue living, Molly Frances Tripoli, *b* 1995, — Hannah Ruby Primrose, *b* 1998. *Residence* – 3 Inglebert St, EC1R 1XR.

BROTHER LIVING

Hon Robin Alexander, *b* 1931; *ed* Eton; late Sub-Lieut RNVR: *m* 1960, Ann Caroline Thalia, elder da of Maj Edward Fitzhardinge Peyton Gage (*see* V Gage, colls), and has issue living, Francesca Rhiannon, *b* 1963: *m* 1990, Stuart Douglas, and has issue living, Hamish Cameron, *b* 1995.

COLLATERAL BRANCHES LIVING

Grandchildren of late Lt-Col Hon Guy Victor Baring, MP, Coldstream Guards, 4th son of 4th Baron:—
Issue of late Simon Alexander Vivian Baring, *b* 1905, *d* 1962: *m* 1st, 1935 (*m diss* 1946), Jeanne, da of Felix Salmond, of London and New York; 2ndly, 1946, Pamela Rachel, who *d* 1985, da of late Sir Mark Beresford Russell Grant-Sturgis, KCB (*see* E Wharncliffe, 1968 Edn), and formerly wife of Allan Alexander Cameron:—
(By 1st *m*) Julian Guy Alexander (Manor Farm, Bradley, Alresford, Hants), *b* 1935: *m* 1971, Isla, da of late Sir Frank Samuel Tait, of Toorak, Melbourne, Victoria, Australia, and has issue living, Justin Frank Alexander, *b* 1971, — Rebecca Alexandra Viola, *b* 1973. —— (By 2nd *m*) Francis Esmond (Hill House, Monkwood, Alresford, Hants), *b* 1948: *m* 1978, Nicolette Mary Irving, yst da of late (Frederic) Alan (Irving) Muntz, of Les Hauts de Claires, Montauroux 83770, France, and has issue living, Simon Esmond Charles, *b* 1983, — Sophie Edwina, *b* 1980. —— Camilla Jane (Hamilton House, Bruton, Som BA10 0AH), *b* 1952; *ed* City and Guilds Coll of Art: *m* 1986, John Nicholas Robbins, and has issue living, Daniel John, *b* 1986, — William Francis, *b* 1987.

Issue of late Amyas Evelyn Giles Baring, *b* 1910, *d* 1986: *m* 1st, 1935 (*m diss* 1949), Mona Montgomerie, who *d* 1988, da of Lt-Col Willoughby Brooking Mullins, of Ambersham House, Midhurst, Sussex, and formerly wife of Maj William Frederick Husband; 2ndly, 1949, Peggy Michell, da of late Surg Vice-Adm Sir Arthur Gaskell, KCB, OBE, FRCS, and formerly wife of George Clive Reeves:—
(By 1st *m*) Claire Leonora (7 Callow St, SW3; Villa Cetinale, Sovicille, Siena, Italy), *b* 1936: *m* 1956 (*m diss* 1974), Hon Peter Alastair Ward, and has issue (*see* E Dudley).

Issue of late Sqd Ldr Aubrey George Adeane Baring, DFC, RAFVR, late Chm Twickenham Film Studios, *b* 1912, *d* 1987: *m* 1952, Marina (22 Farley Court, Melbury Rd, W14 8LJ), eldest da of Basil Bessel, and formerly wife of Sir Charles Richard Andrew Oakeley, 6th Bt:—
Alexander Esmond (32 Stanbridge Rd, SW15), *b* 1953: *m* 1986, Zane El Guindi, and has issue living, Adam Alexander Aubrey, *b* 1988, — Lara Louise, *b* 1987. —— Adrian Hugh Vasili, *b* 1962. —— Louise Olivia, *b* 1955: *m* 1997, Eric Franck, only son of late Louis Franck, of Gstaad, Switzerland, and has issue living, Misha Edward, *b* 1998.

Issue of late Lt-Col Esmond Charles Baring, OBE, *b* 1914, *d* 1963: *m* 1st, 1936 (*m diss* 1951), Zalia, who *d* 1986, da of late Sir Harold Edward Snagge, KBE (*see* B Avebury, colls, 1955 Edn); 2ndly, 1960, Judith (who *d* 1991, having *m* 3rdly, 1965, 3rd Marquess of Linlithgow, who *d* 1987), da of late Stanley Mathew Lawson, of Cincinnati, USA, and formerly wife of John Symonds Radway:—
(By 1st *m*) Oliver Alexander Guy (Deane House, Overton, Hants), *b* 1944: *m* 1967, Veronica, da of late Capt Ian Alexander Henderson (*see* B Faringdon, colls), and has issue living, Rupert Esmond Ian, *b* 1968, — Esmond Oliver Mark, *b* 1978, — Thomas Edward Joseph, *b* 1979, — Emma Rose, *b* 1970. —— Guy Esmond (126 Williams Rd, Prahran, Victoria 3181, Australia), *b* 1945: *m* 1970, Raina, who *d* 1979, da of David Campbell, of Palerang, Bungendore, NSW, and has issue living, Ben, *b* 1970, — Ned, *b* 1975, — Samantha Jane, *b* 1969: *m* 1996, Brent Thomson, eldest son of Kevin Thomson, of Timaru, NZ. —— Caroline Venetia, *b* 1937: *m* 1957, Henry Giles Francis Lascelles, who *d* 1998, of 119 Hambalt Rd, SW4, and has issue — Patricia (*Hon Mrs Mark H. Wyndham*), *b* 1938: *m* 1st, 1965, Maj Henry Claude Lyon Garnett, CBE, who *d* 1990; 2ndly, 1986, as his 2nd wife, Hon Mark Hugh Wyndham (*see* B Egremont), of Newmans Cottage, Froxfield Green, Petersfield, Hants, and has issue living (by 1st *m*), Charles Henry Esmond, *b* 1966, — Henrietta Patricia, *b* 1968: *m* 1995, Patrick J. J. W. Wallace, eldest son of Dr John Mansergh-Wallace, of Tipperary, and has issue living, John Henry Patrick *b* 1998.

Issue of late Hon Caryl Digby Baring, yst son of 4th Baron, *b* 1880, *d* 1956: *m* 1907, Ivy, who *d* 1971, da of late Humphrey Brooke Firman (formerly 16th Lancers), JP, of Stone Court, St Leonards-on-Sea:—
Leonora Jacqueline, *b* 1912.

PREDECESSORS – (1) The *Right Hon* ALEXANDER Baring, PC, DCL, 2nd son of Sir Francis Baring, 1st Baronet (B Northbrook), and cousin of Richard Dunning, 2nd Baron Ashburton (cr 1782, extinct 1823); cr *Baron Ashburton* (peerage of United Kingdom) 1835, was sometime Pres of Board of Trade and Master of the Mint; *d* 1848; *s* by his eldest son **(2)** WILLIAM BINGHAM, PC, 2nd Baron; was Sec of Board of Control 1841-5, Paymaster of the Forces and Treasurer of the Navy 1845-6, and seventeen years MP for various constituencies: *d* 1864; *s* by his brother **(3)** FRANCIS, 3rd Baron, *b* 24 May 1800; sat as MP for Thetford (*L*) 1832-41 and 1848-57: *m* 1832, Claire Hortense, who *d* 1882, da of the Duke of Bassano, Minister of Napoleon I; *d* 6 Sept, 1868; *s* by his son **(4)** ALEXANDER HUGH, 4th Baron: *b* 1835; sat as MP for Thetford (LC) 1857-67: *m* 1864, Hon Leonora Caroline, who *d* 1930, da of 9th Baron Digby: *d* 1889; *s* by his eldest son **(5)** FRANCIS DENZIL EDWARD, 5th Baron; *b* 1866: *m* 1st, 1889, Hon Mabel Edith Hood, who *d* 1904, da of 4th Viscount Hood; 2ndly, 1906, Frances, who *d* 1959, da of James Caryll Donnelly, of New York; *d* 1938; *s* by his only son **(6)** ALEXANDER FRANCIS ST VINCENT, KG, KCVO, 6th Baron; *b* 1898; Lieut Royal Scots Greys, and Group Capt AAF; Man Dir Baring Bros 1928-62, Dir 1962-68, etc; Lord Lieut and Custos Rotulorum Hants and Isle of Wight 1960-73, DL 1973, Receiver-Gen Duchy of Cornwall 1961-73, High Steward Winchester Cathedral 1967-78, etc; Trustee King George's Jubilee Trust 1949-68, Treasurer King Edward VII Hosp Fund for London 1955-64 (Gov 1971-75): *m* 1924, Hon Doris Mary Thérèse Harcourt, who *d* 1981, da of 1st Viscount Harcourt; *d* 1991; *s* by his elder son **(7)** JOHN FRANCIS HARCOURT, 7th Baron and present peer.

ASHBY, BARONY OF (Ashby) (Extinct 1992)

SONS LIVING OF LIFE BARON

Hon Michael Farries, CBE, FRS (51 Maids Causeway, Cambridge), *b* 1935; *ed* Campbell Coll, Belfast, and Queen's Coll, Camb (BA, PhD), Hon MA (Harvard); FRS; Prof of Engineering, Univ of Camb, Royal Society Prof since 1989; CBE (Civil) 1997: *m* 1962, Maureen, da of S. James Stewart, of White House, Montgomery, Powys.

Hon Peter (42 Bennington Heights Drive, Toronto, Ont M4G 1A6, Canada), *b* 1937; *ed* Campbell Coll, Belfast, and Queen's Univ, Belfast (MB, BCh, MD); Prof, Univ of Toronto: *m* 1967, Moya, da of Rear-Adm Maurice Henry Adams, CB, of Canberra, Rock, Cornwall.

ASHCOMBE, BARON (Cubitt) (Baron UK 1892)

Happy is the prudent man

HENRY EDWARD CUBITT, 4th Baron, *b* 31 March 1924; *s* 1962; *ed* Eton; 1939-45 War with RAF: *m* 1st, 1955 (*m diss* 1968), Ghislaine, only da of Cornelius Willem Dresselhuys, of Long Island, New York, USA, and formerly wife of Maj Denis James Alexander, Irish Gds (later 6th Earl of Caledon); 2ndly, 1973 (*m diss* 1979), Hon Virginia Carington, yr da of the 6th Baron Carrington; 3rdly, 1979, (Mary) Elizabeth, da of Dr Henry Davis Chipps, of Lexington, Kentucky, USA, and widow of Geoffrey Mark Dent-Brocklehurst, of Sudeley Castle, Winchcombe, Cheltenham, Glos (*see* B Trevor, 1962 Edn).

𝕬rms – Checky or and gules, on a pile argent, a lion's head erased sable. 𝕮rest – A column proper, in front two scimitars in saltire argent, pommel and hilt or. 𝕾upporters – *Dexter*, a stonemason proper, habited in brown coat and hat, apron argent, in his right hand a mallet sable; *sinister*, a carpenter proper, habited in brown vest, apron argent, in his left hand a pair of compasses or.
Residences – Sudeley Castle, Winchcombe, Cheltenham, Glos; Flat H, 14 Holland Park Rd, W14 8LZ. *Club* – White's.

COLLATERAL BRANCHES LIVING

Issue of late Hon Jeremy John Cubitt, yr son of 3rd Baron, *b* 1927, *d* 1958: *m* 1952 (*m diss* 1957), Diana Edith, elder da of late Com Peter Du Cane, OBE, RN (*see* Pole, Bt, *cr* 1628, 1985 Edn):—
Sarah Victoria, *b* 1953: *m* 1975 (*m diss* 1981), David Gray Hutton, elder son of Thomas Hutton. *Residence* – Flat 3, 13 Cranley Gdns, SW7 3BB.

Grandchildren of late Maj Hon Archibald Edward Cubitt (infra):—
Issue of late Alick John Archibald Cubitt, *b* 1927, *d* 1983: *m* 1st, 1956, Priscilla Rosemary, who *d* 1957, elder da of Thomas Cecil Gouldsmith (*see* Laurie, Bt, colls, 1957 Edn); 2ndly, 1961, Jennifer Faith (Chetwode Manor, Buckingham) (who *m* 2ndly, 1986, J.E.H. (Tim) Collins), da of late Lt-Gen William Henry Ewart Gott, CB, CBE, DSO, MC:—
(By 2nd *m*) Amanda Jane, *b* 1966: *m* 1995, C. Rupert R. Sweeting, elder son of Christopher Sweeting, of Churchill, Oxon. ——— Belinda Carey, *b* 1968.

Issue of late (Mark) Robin Cubitt, *b* 1936, *d* 1991; *m* 1962 (*m diss* 1984), Juliet Perpetua, da of Edward Corbet Woodall, OBE (*see* Crawley-Boevey, Bt, colls, 1964 Edn):—
MARK EDWARD, *b* 29 Feb 1964: *m* 1992, Melissa Mary, only da of Maj Charles Hay, of Boldre, Hants, and has issue living, Richard Robin Alexander, *b* 14 June 1995, — Ronald Charles Edward, *b* 1997. *Residence* – 8 Hartismere Rd, SW6 7TT. ——— David Antony, *b* 1966. ——— Hugo John, *b* 1967: *m* 1996, Onnalee Virginia, elder da of Richard Lewis Longfield, of The Old Rectory, Weston Patrick, Hants.

Issue of late Maj Hon Archibald Edward Cubitt, 5th son of 2nd Baron, *b* 1901, *d* 1972: *m* 1st, 1926 (*m diss* 1933), Lady Irene Helen Pratt, who *d* 1976, da of 4th Marquess Camden; 2ndly, 1934 (*m diss* 1949), Sibell Margaret, da of Ronald Collet Norman (*see* E Bradford, 1936 Edn):—
(By 2nd *m*) Priscilla Margaret (*Countess of Harrington*), *b* 1941: *m* 1964, as his 3rd wife, 11th Earl of Harrington, of The Glen, Ballingarry, co Limerick.

Issue of late Col Hon (Charles) Guy Cubitt, CBE, DSO, TD, 6th and yst son of 2nd Baron, *b* 1903, *d* 1979: *m* 1927, Rosamond Mary Edith, who *d* 1984, da of Capt Sir Montague Aubrey Cholmeley, 4th Bt:—

Sir Hugh Guy, CBE (Chapel House, West Humble, Dorking, Surrey RH5 6AY), *b* 1928; FRICS; *ed* RNC Dartmouth; JP; late Lieut RN; Lord Mayor of Westminster 1977-78; High Sheriff Surrey 1983, DL Greater London 1978; *cr* CBE (Civil) 1977, and Knt 1983: *m* 1958, Linda Ishbel, yst da of late Hon Angus Dudley Campbell, CBE (*see* B Colgrain, colls), and has issue living, Jonathan Guy, *b* 1962: *m* 1999, Emma Louise, yr da of Hon James Donald Diarmid Ogilvy (*see* E Airlie), — Joanna Mary, *b* 1960: *m* 1986, Charles William Smyth-Osbourne, and has issue (*see* Ramsden, Bt), — Victoria Jane, *b* 1964: *m* 1987, Crispin Martin Harding-Rolls, of Rock Cottage, Buckingham Rd, S Holmwood, Dorking, Surrey RH5 4LB, yr son of Maj Christopher A. Harding-Rolls, of Pwll-y-Cwm, The Hendre, Monmouth, Gwent, and has issue living, George Christopher *b* 1992, Sophie Elizabeth *b* 1990. —— Sylvia Rosemary, *b* 1930: *m* 1951, Maj Ronald James Grant Dallas, 3rd Hus, of Primrose Hill, Westonbirt, Tetbury, Glos, and has had issue, Nigel Alexander, *b* 1962, — Caroline Rosamond, *b* 1952: *m* 1981, Philip T. Shearing, and *d* 1992, — Jenifer Mary, *b* 1954: *m* 1st, 1975 (*m diss* 1986), Philip S. W. Hawkins; 2ndly, 1987 (*m diss* 1991), Roger Babington Hill; 3rdly, 1993, Simon King, of Southview, Sandford, nr Crediton, Devon. —— Celia Mary (*Baroness Carew*), *b* 1939: *m* 1962, 7th Baron Carew.

PREDECESSORS – (1) GEORGE Cubitt, PC, son of late Thomas Cubitt, of Denbies, Surrey, *b* 1828: sat as MP for W Surrey (*C*) 1860-85, and for Mid, or Epsom, Div of Surrey Dec 1885 to June 1892; cr PC 1880, and *Baron Ashcombe*, of Dorking, co Surrey, and Bodiam Castle, Sussex (peerage of United Kingdom) 1892: *m* 1853, Laura, who *d* 1904, da of late Rev James Joyce, V of Dorking; *d* 1917; *s* by his son (2) HENRY, CB, TD, 2nd Baron; *b* 1867; sometime Lt-Col and Hon Col Comdg Surrey Yeo; Lord-Lt of Surrey 1905-39; MP for Surrey S-E or Reigate Div (*C*) 1892-1906: *m* 1890, Maud Mariamne, who *d* 1945, da of late Col Archibald Motteaux Calvert, of Ockley Court, Dorking; *d* 1947; *s* by his 4th but eldest surviving son (3) ROLAND CALVERT, 3rd Baron, *b* 1899: *m* 1st, 1920 (*m diss* 1947), Sonia Rosemary, OBE, who *d* 1986, da of late Lt-Col Hon George Keppel, MVO (E Albemarle, colls); 2ndly, 1948, Idina Joan (MILLS), who *d* 1954, da of late Col Robert Edward Myddelton, TD, DL, JP, of Chirk Castle, Denbighshire, and formerly wife of John Charles Trueman Mills; 3rdly, 1959, Jean, who was *k* in an air crash 1973, da of late Charles Tuller Garland, of Moreton Hall, Warwickshire, and formerly wife of (i) Arthur Turberville Smith-Bingham, (ii) Sir Robert George Maxwell Throckmorton, 11th Bt, and (iii) Greville Pollard Baylis; *d* 1962; *s* by his eldest son (4) HENRY EDWARD, 4th Baron and present peer.

Ashley, Lord; son of Earl of Shaftesbury.

ASHLEY OF STOKE, BARON (Ashley) (Life Baron 1992)

JACK ASHLEY, CH, PC, son of late John Ashley; *b* 6 Dec 1922; *ed* Ruskin Coll, Oxford, and Gonville and Caius Coll, Camb (Pres Union 1951); Shop Steward Convenor and Nat Exec Cttee Member Chemical Workers' Union 1946; Councillor Borough of Widnes 1946; BBC Radio Producer 1951-57, Sr TV Producer 1957-66, Member Gen Advisory Council BBC 1967-69 and 1970-74; PPS to Sec of State for Economic Affairs 1967-68, and to Sec of State for Dept of Health and Social Security 1974-76; Member Lab Party Nat Exec Cttee 1976-78; author of *Journey into Silence* 1973; MP Stoke on Trent (*Lab*) 1966-92; *cr* CH 1975, PC 1979, and *Baron Ashley of Stoke*, of Widnes, co Cheshire (Life Baron) 1992: *m* 1951, Pauline Kay, da of Clarence Adley Crispin, of Liverpool, and has issue.
Address – c/o House of Lords, SW1.

DAUGHTERS LIVING

Hon Jacqueline, *b* 1954: *m* 1987, Andrew Marr, and has issue living, Harry Cameron, *b* 1989, — Isabel Claire, *b* 1991.
Hon Jane Elizabeth, *b* 1958: *m* 1992, Martin Rosenbaum, and has issue living, Ben, *b* 1992.
Hon Caroline, *b* 1966: *m* 1993, Richard Dewdney.

ASHTON OF HYDE, BARON (Ashton) (Baron UK 1911)

With faith and valour

THOMAS JOHN ASHTON, TD, 3rd Baron; *b* 19 Nov 1926; *s* 1983; *ed* Eton, and at New Coll, Oxford (MA); formerly Lieut 11th Hussars, and Maj R Glos Hus (TA); a JP of Oxon; Dir of Barclays Bank 1968-86: *m* 1957, Pauline Trewlove, eldest da of late Lt-Col Robert Henry Langton Brackenbury, OBE, of Yerdley House, Long Compton, Shipston on Stour, and has issue.

ᴀrms – Sable, on a pile between two crescents in base argent, a mullet pierced of the first. Crest – On a mount vert, a mower proper, vested paly argent and sable, in the act of whetting his scythe also proper. Supporters – *Dexter*, a mower proper, vested paly argent and sable, holding in the exterior hand a scythe also proper; *sinister*, a boar argent semée of mullets sable pierced.
Residence – Fir Farm, Upper Slaughter, Bourton on the Water, Glos. *Club* – Boodles.

SONS LIVING

Hon (THOMAS) HENRY, *b* 18 July 1958; *ed* Eton, and Trin Coll, Oxford; late Royal Hussars (PWO), Lieut Royal Wessex Yeo: *m* 1987, Emma Louise, da of Colin Allinson, of Bath, and has issue living, Harriet Emily, *b* 1990, — Isabel Louise, *b* 1992, — Flora Juliet, *b* 1995. *Residence* – Broadwell Hill, Moreton-in-Marsh, Glos. *Club* – Boodle's.
Hon John Edward, *b* 1966.

DAUGHTERS LIVING

Hon Charlotte Trewlove, *b* 1960: *m* 1987, Andrew D. Bartlett, only son of late D. W. Bartlett, and of Mrs J. D. Potts, of Macclesfield, Cheshire, and has issue living, Oliver William, *b* 1991, — Hugh Alastair, *b* 1994.
Hon Katharine Judith, *b* 1962: *m* 1987, Douglas J. Lawson, son of Harry D. Lawson, of 58 Seafield Rd, Broughton Ferry, Dundee, and has issue living, James Alexander, *b* 1988, — Robert Douglas, *b* 1991, — Anna Katharine, *b* 1994.

PREDECESSORS – (1) THOMAS GAIR Ashton, son of late Thomas Ashton, JP, DL, of Hyde, Cheshire; *b* 1855; MP for Hyde Div of Cheshire (*L*) 1885-6, and for S, or Luton, Div of Bedfordshire 1895-1911; cr *Baron Ashton of Hyde*, co Chester (peerage of United Kingdom) 1911; *m* 1886, Eva Margaret, who *d* 1938, da of late John Henry James, of Kingswood, Watford, Herts: *d* 1933; *s* by his yr son (2) THOMAS HENRY RAYMOND, 2nd Baron, Maj R Glos Hus (TA); a JP and DL for Glos: *m* 1925, Marjorie Nell, who *d* 1993, da of late Hon Marshall Jones Brooks (*see* B Crawshaw, colls); *d* 1983; *s* by his only son (3) THOMAS JOHN, 3rd Baron and present peer.

ASHTOWN, BARON (Trench) (Baron I 1800)

Fortune is the companion of virtue

NIGEL CLIVE COSBY TRENCH, KCMG, 7th Baron; *b* 27 Oct 1916; *s* 1990; *ed* Eton, and Corpus Christi Coll, Camb; 1939-45 War as Maj KRRC (despatches); entered HM Foreign Ser (now Dip Ser) 1946; Counsellor Tokyo 1961-63, Washington 1963-67, and Cabinet Office 1967-69, HM Ambassador to Republic of Korea 1969-71, Assist Under-Sec Civil Ser Selection Board 1971-73, Ambassador to Portugal 1974-76; Member of Police, Prison and Fire Ser Selection Boards 1977-86; CMG 1966, KCMG 1976; Order of Diplomatic Service Merit, Rep of Korea, 1984: *m* 1st, 1939, Marcelle Catherine, who *d* 1994, yst da of Johan Jacob Clotterbooke Patyn van Kloetinge, of Zeist, The Netherlands; 2ndly, 1997, (Dorothea) Mary Elizabeth, Princess of Pless, elder da of late Lt-Col Richard George Edward Minchin, of Busherstown, co Tipperary, and formerly wife of HSH Hans Heinrich XVII Wilhelm Albert Eduard, 4th Prince of Pless, and has issue by 1st *m*.

Arms – Argent, a lion passant gules, between three fleurs-de-lis, azure, on a chief of the last a sun in splendour or. Crest – A dexter arm embowed in armour, the hand grasping a scimitar, all proper. Supporters – *Dexter*, a lion gules, semée-de-lis, and ducally crowned or; *sinister*, a stag proper, attired, unguled, ducally collared and lined or. Second Motto – Dieu pour la Tranche, qui contre (*"God for the Trench, whoever may oppose!"*). *Residence* – 4 Kensington Court Gdns, W8 5QE.

SON LIVING *(By 1st marriage)*

Hon RODERICK NIGEL GODOLPHIN, *b* 17 Nov 1944; *ed* Eton, and Stanford Univ, USA: *m* 1st, 1967, Janet, who *d* 1971, da of Harold Hamilton-Faulkner, of Redwood City, Calif, USA; 2ndly, 1973, Susan Barbara, da of Lewis Frank Day, FRCS, DLO, of Cooden, Sussex, and formerly wife of Michael R. J. Wright, and has issue living (by 1st *m*), Timothy Roderick Hamilton, *b* 29 Feb 1968; *ed* Sherborne, and London Univ, — (by 2nd *m*) Victoria Susan, *b* 1977. *Residence* – Bassetts, Coggins Mill Lane, Mayfield, Sussex.

SISTER LIVING

Lois Eileen, *b* 1910: *m* 1937, Capt Charles Algernon Mackintosh-Walker, MBE, of Geddes, Nairn, and has issue living, Charles James (Geddes, Nairn), *b* 1939; *ed* Rugby: *m* 1967, Elizabeth Margaret, da of Charles Stewart, CMG, OBE, of The Cottage, Dunvegan, Skye, and has had issue, Ewen Charles *b* 1970; *d* 1980, Andrew Eneas *b* 1976, Maria Jane *b* 1968, Sarah Emily *b* 1972, — Serena Mary, *b* 1946: *m* 1st, 1968 (*m diss* 1976), Hugh Robert Norton, 2nd son of Leslie C. Norton; 2ndly, 1976, Dr Kenneth Mitchell Nuttall.

DAUGHTER LIVING OF FIFTH BARON

Hon Jacqueline Noël, *b* 1940: *m* 1966, Alastair Gordon Eadie, of Bourne Orchard, Brickendon, Hertford, and has issue living, James Alastair, *b* 1967: *m* 1998, Rebecca, da of Prof David Morgan, of The Old Nursery, Hill Chorlton, Staffs, — Christopher John, *b* 1969, — Edward Charles, *b* 1972: *m* 1997, Emily J. V., da of James Tait Laurenson, of Hill House, Kirknewton, Midlothian.

COLLATERAL BRANCHES LIVING *(male line in remainder to barony)*

Granddaughters of late Hon William Cosby Trench, brother of 3rd Baron:—
Issue of late Walter Frederick Oliver Trench, *b* 1899, *d* 1960: *m* 1st, 1921, Norah Maude, who *d* 1958, da of Ven John Richard Hedges Becher, Archdeacon of Ross; 2ndly, 1960, Marion Gwendolyn, da of Robert Young, of Woolley, Yorks:—
(By 1st *m*) Olga Ann Oliver (PO Box 377, Richmond, Natal), *b* 1922: *m* 1948 (*m diss* 19—), William Hugh Hindley, and has issue living, Michael Edward Oliver, *b* 1951: *m* 1977, Jane Mary Brimacombe, of Devizes, Wilts, and has issue living, Alexander William Oliver (John) *b* 1980, Lawrence Hugh John *b* 1982, Thomas Henry Walter *b* 1984, Caroline Jane *b* 1988, — Douglas William John, *b* 1963, — Sheila Rachel, *b* 1949: *m* 1981, Christopher Davis. —— Norah Susan Oliver, *b* 1936: *m* 1957, Walter Stuart Gash, MBE, of Rocklea, Mitchell Rd, Walliston, W Aust 6076, and has issue living, Maureen Susan, *b* 1959: *m* 1980, Gregory John Gittos, of 5 Cooper Ridge, Winthrop, W Australia 6150, and has issue living, Michael John *b* 1987, Lisa Marie *b* 1988, — Sheila Ann (Sydney, Australia), *b* 1960: *m* 1981 (*m diss* 1985), Kevin John McDowall.

Branch from 2nd brother of 1st Baron

Granddaughter of late Charles Steuart Trench, 2nd son of late Henry Trench (b 1806), 4th son of late Very Rev Thomas Trench, Dean of Kildare, 2nd brother of 1st Baron:—
Issue of late Henry Marryat Trench, b 1876, d 1948: m 1904, Juliet Benham, who d 1946, eldest da of late William Seaman, of Staten Island, New York, USA:—
Edith Katharine, b 1905: m 1930, Albert Irwin Dorr, who d 1947.

Granddaughters of late John Townsend Trench, son of William Steuart Trench, 5th son of late Very Rev Thomas Trench (ante):—
Issue of late Rev George Frederick Trench, b 1881, d 1966: m 1919, Muriel Leonore, who d 1974, da of late Leslie Stephen Robertson, MICE:—
Leonore Elisita, b 1920; ed Girton Coll, Camb (BA): m 1945, Henry Denis Whitwell Powell, FRCS, MB, ChB, of Old Fox Cottage, Heath End Rd, Gt Kingshill, Bucks HP15 6HS, and has issue living, John Denis Trench (25 Hall Drive, Middleton, Manchester), b 1951; MA, ARCM, — Margaret Leonore, b 1945: m 1968, Frank William Taylor, and has issue living, Michael John b 1970: m 1996, Katrin Heidi Willcocks, Peter Hugh b 1972: m 1994, Naomi Hester Starbuck (and has issue living, Rebekah Joy b 1997, Hannah Rose b 1999), Christopher David b 1979, — Janet Elisita, b 1949: m 1st, 1972 (m diss 1990), Derek Peacock; 2ndly, 1990, Murray Roy Frankland, and has issue living (by 1st m), Timothy Simon b 1978, Antony Robert b 1980, — Clare Louise, b 1954: m 1979, Philip Marshall Garside, and has issue living, Douglas Paul b 1982, Alan Nigel b 1984, Ian Richard b 1987. —— Bridget Wray, b 1928; a Member of Assocn of Occupational Therapists, and Canadian Occupational Therapy Assocn: m 1959, Robin Blakeway Dickens, of 35, 6111 Sayward Rd, Duncan, BC, Canada V9L 5J4, and has issue living, Mark Lester, b 1961, — Lynn Catherine, b 1963: m 1985, Mark Hayden Lane, and has issue living, Jeremy b 19—, Daniel b 19—.

Branch from 3rd brother of 1st Baron

Granddaughter of late Louis Trench, yst son of late Rev Frederic Fitz-William Trench, son of late William Trench, 3rd brother of 1st Baron:—
Issue of late Geoffrey FitzLouis Trench, b 1885, d 1971: m 1927, Olive Muriel, who d 1984, da of George Constance:—
Joanna Mary, b 1937: m 1959, Timothy Francis Cox, of Priors Mesne, Aylburton, Lydney, Glos, and has issue living, Dermot Francis, b 1963: m 1989, Heather Ann, da of Anthony Jackson, of The Fields, Maesbury, Shropshire, and has had issue, Peter Francis b 1998, Naomi Josephine b 1995, — Miranda Josephine, b 1961: m 1985, Andrew Thomas Doran, of The Old Presbytery, Lower High St, Chipping Campden, Glos GL55 6DZ, and d 1994, leaving issue, Dominic Henry b 1988, Fionnghuala Mary b 1987.

Branch from 2nd son of 5th brother of 1st Baron

Grandchildren of late Col Charles Chenevix Trench, 3rd son of late Most Rev and Rt Hon Richard Chenevix Trench, DD, 2nd son of late Richard Trench, 5th brother of 1st Baron:—
Issue of late Lt-Col Sir Richard Henry CHENEVIX TRENCH, CIE, OBE, IA, and Indian Political Ser, b 1876, d 1954: m 1913, Evelyn May, who d 1977, da of late Capt Harry Evelyn Stracy Pocklington, 15th Hus:—
Charles Pocklington, MC (Lisnamoe House, Ballymackey, Nenagh, co Tipperary), b 1914; ed Winchester, and Magdalen Coll, Oxford; Maj (ret) IA; author of The Royal Malady and other works; 1939-45 War in Italy (MC): m 1st, 1946, Patricia Jane, who d 1963, da of late Maj George Foster Gretton, of 62 Melton Court, SW7; 2ndly, 1954, Mary Elizabeth, da of Lt-Col George Kirkbride, of Mullion, Cornwall, and has had issue (by 1st m), †Richard Hugh Roger, b 1949: m 1st, 1977, Eleni Leoussi; 2ndly, 1986, Johanna Davis, and d 1997, leaving issue (by 1st m), Jack Ferdinand b 1978, (by 2nd m), Alexander Ryland b 1986, Rose Alexandra (Anna) b 1988, — Charlotte Ann (106 Blvd de Rochechouart, Paris 75018), b 1946, — Priscilla Jane (42 Corbyn St, N4 3BZ), b 1947, — (by 2nd m) Lucy, b 1956: m 19—, Robert Collingwood, and has issue living, Patrick b 1990, Elizabeth b 1988, — Georgia, b 1959: PhD, NHMRC; Senior Research Fell, The Queensland Inst of Medical Research: m 1983, Prof Nicholas Gordon Martin, of 37 Burns Rd, Toowong, Qld 4066, Australia, and has issue living, Hilary Chenevix b 1985, Felicity Chenevix b 1991. —— (Evelyn) Jane Chenevix, b 1917: m 1950, Richard Christian Allhusen, who d 1998, and has issue living, Christian Henry (Manor House, Bradenham, Thetford, Norfolk IP25 7QU), b 1956: m 1986, Penelope Amanda, yr da of Colin G. C. Rae, of Littleweston House, Littleweston, Yeovil, Som BA22 7HP, and has issue living, Benjamin Christian Thomas b 1989, Matthew John Oliver b 1991, Natasha Sophie Tamsin b 1993, Sabrina Isabel India b 1996, — Richard Frederick (The Old Parsonage, Hinxton, Cambs CB10 1RS), b 1960: m 1989, Katrina Jane, yr da of I. R. P. Haig, of Brockstone House, Dunley, Worcs, and has issue living, Harry Alexander b 1994, Frederick James b 1998, — Elizabeth Mary, b 1952: m 1977, William P. Durlacher, of Whalebone House, Langham, Colchester, Essex CO4 5PX, son of late Jack Durlacher, and has issue living, Emma Jane b 1980, Susanna Mary b 1982, — Rosalind Jane, b 1954: m 1985, Nicholas Charles Thoresby Pawson, only son of Kenneth Vernon Frank Pawson, and has issue living, Iona Elizabeth b 1988, Georgia Catherine b 1991. Residence – Bradenham Hall, Thetford, Norfolk.

Grandchildren of late Charles Godfrey Chenevix Trench, CIE (infra):—
Issue of late Christopher John CHENEVIX TRENCH, MBE, b 1911, d 1971: m 1936, Mary Elizabeth Catherine, who d 1990, eldest da of late G. H. Allen, of Branksome, Poole:—
Timothy Christopher John (196 Broom Rd, Teddington, Middx), b 1938; ed King's Sch, Canterbury, and Corpus Christi Coll, Oxford: m 1st, 1961 (m diss 1973), Penelope Mary Travers Walton; 2ndly, 1977, Stella-Maris Melhuish, who d 1997, da of late Edwin Samuel Henderson, Supt CID, Burma; 3rdly, 1998, Mrs Rivka Osborne, and has issue living (by 1st m), Katherine Rae, b 1964: m 1984, Dr Robert Neil Summers Slater, only son of Robert Slater, of Childswickham, Worcs, and has issue living, Thomas Alexander b 1986, — Alison Mary, b 1965: m 1983, Jonathan Robert Hill, son of Fl-Lt F. G. Hill, — Phillida Clare, b 1969. —— John Richard (Glenalmond Coll, Perthshire), b 1948: m 1970, Pauline, da of late James Stephen Alexander, of 2 Seawood Place, Grange over Sands, Cumbria, and has issue living, Christopher Hamish b 1977, — Alix (a da), b 1983. —— Elizabeth Mary, b 1941: m 1964, Dr Anthony Savile Stephen Rowe, FRCP, of Woodtown Cottage, Sampford Spiney, Yelverton, Devon, and has issue living, Jonathan Stephen, b 1969, — James Benedict, b 1970; Dr: m 1997, Rebecca Sophie Wichmann Rowlatt, — Antonia Jane, b 1967; Dr: m 1993, Dr Jonathan Katz, and has issue living, Oliver James b 1994, James Sebastian b 1997.

Issue of late Lt-Cdr Richard Blakesley CHENEVIX TRENCH, RN, b 1912, d 1979: m 1939, Nancy Carey (21 Church Rd, Davenport Green, Wilmslow, Cheshire), only da of James Munro, of Shanghai:—

Fenella Anne, *b* 1943: *m* 1969, Richard Law Townsend, of 129 Broadleaf Cres, Ancaster, Ontario, Canada L9G 3T6, and has issue living, Simon Andrew, *b* 1974.

Issue of late Anthony CHENEVIX TRENCH, FRSE, FRSA, *b* 1919, *d* 1979: *m* 1953, Elizabeth Chalmers, who *d* 1991, da of Capt Sir Stewart Dykes Spicer, 3rd Bt, RN:—
Richard Thomas Chalmers (20 Hill Crest, 22 Plunketts Rd, The Peak, Hong Kong), *b* 1958: *m* 1985, Sarah Jane, eldest da of Raglan Charles Wykeham, of Northroyd, Crimphill, Englefield Green, Egham, Surrey, and has issue living, Harry Chalmers, *b* 1988, — James William Reynolds, *b* 1990, — Marcus, *b* 1993. ——Jonathan Charles Stewart (Flat 11, 7 Chelsea Embankment, SW3 4LF), *b* 1961: *m* 1998, Margaret Lucy, yr da of Gerald John Ward, CBE (*see* E Dudley, colls). ——Josephine Dykes, *b* 1954: *m* 1978, John George Richards Homfray, only son of Maj Herbert Franklen Richards Homfray, of Penllyn Court, Cowbridge, Glamorgan, and has issue living, Matthew Anthony, *b* 1980, — Thomas Richards, *b* 1983, — Virginia, *b* 1987.

Grandchildren of late Col Charles Chenevix Trench (ante):—
Issue of late Charles Godfrey CHENEVIX TRENCH, CIE, *b* 1877, *d* 1964: *m* 1910, Margaret May, who *d* 1981, eldest da of late John Holmes Blakesley, CE:—
Godfrey Maxwell, DSC (Kelling, Holt, Norfolk), *b* 1917; *ed* Shrewsbury; Cdr RN (ret); 1939-45 War (DSC and bar); history teacher: *m* 1945, Nancy Louise, da of Rev A. Clarkson Birch, of Cloughton, Scarborough, and has issue living, Juliet, *b* 1947: *m* 1973, Graham Duncan Campbell, of Perth, W Australia, and has issue living, Ian Neil *b* 1977, Duncan Alastair *b* 1981, — Frances Claire CHENEVIX-TRENCH (Brookside, The Street, Kelling, Holt, Norfolk), *b* 1949; has resumed her maiden name: *m* 1972 (*m diss* 1985), Christopher Maurice White, and has issue living, Colin Stephen Maxwell *b* 1974.

Issue of late Col Lawrence CHENEVIX TRENCH, CMG, DSO, *b* 1883, *d* 1958: *m* 1908, Winifred Ross, who *d* 1969, da of late Edward Henry Tootal:—
Katherine Anne, *b* 1912: *m* 1st, 1932, Lt-Col George William Frederic Leicester, Cheshire Regt, who *d* 1944 (*see* Leicester, Bt, colls, ext 1968); 2ndly, 1945, Lt-Col A. Frankland, who *d* 1969, and has issue (by 1st *m*) (*see* Leicester, Bt, colls, ext 1968), — (by 2nd *m*) Philip, *b* 1946; *ed* Tonbridge, — John, *b* 1949; *ed* King's Sch, Canterbury: *m* 1975, Mary Faith Elizabeth Townsend, da of Lionel Becher Somerville-Large, MRIA, of Blackrock, co Dublin, and has issue living, William Becher Chenevix *b* 1983, Anna *b* 1978, — Sarah FRANKLAND (preferred style), *b* 1947: *m* 1969, Dr Peter Morris, of Elm House, Matching Green, Essex CM17 0PZ, and has issue living, Patrick *b* 1982, Leila *b* 1980. *Residence* – The Gables, Hopton Cangeford, Ludlow, Shropshire.

Issue of late Brig Ralph CHENEVIX TRENCH, CB, OBE, MC, *b* 1885, *d* 1974: *m* 1916, Meriel Edith, who *d* 1985, da of late Rev George Edward Jelf, DD, Master of Charterhouse:—
John Gordon (Windmill Farm, Coleshill, Amersham, Bucks), *b* 1920; *ed* Wellington Coll; late Capt R Signals; FSA: *m* 1944, Ann Patricia, who *d* 1997, da of late Norman Moore, of 34 Jubilee Place, SW3, and has had issue, Maxwell John (Windmill Farm, Coleshill, Amersham, Bucks), *b* 1952: *m* 1991 (*m diss* 1998), Chou Ern, da of Lam-Tai Lim, of Selangor, Malaysia, — Jessica, *b* 1949: *m* 1st, 1970 (*m diss* 1976), Jonathan Yardley; 2ndly, 1976, George Frederick Laurence, QC, and *d* 1999, leaving issue (by 1st *m*), Thomas James *b* 1974, (by 2nd *m*) Benjamin George *b* 1981, Catherine Ann *b* 1978. ——Susan Meriel, *b* 1925: *m* 1950, Oscar Patrick Wood, who *d* 1994, of Christ Church, Oxford, and has issue living, Charles William Chenevix, *b* 1955: *m* 1985, Mary Rose, da of Rex Cooper, of E Bergholt, Suffolk, and has issue living, Oscar Giles Chenevix *b* 1986, Amelia Claire Lucy *b* 1988, Georgia Charlotte *b* 1991, — Silas James London, *b* 1965, — Lucy Melesina, *b* 1956.

Issue of late Alfred Saward CHENEVIX TRENCH, MC, *b* 1887, *d* 1963: *m* 1st, 1920, Helen Winifred, who *d* 1945, da of George Fowler; 2ndly, 1949, Sylvia Mary Crawford, who *d* 1978, twin da of late Francis Crawford Caffin:—
(By 1st *m*) Dudley Alfred Chenevix, *b* 1928; *ed* Bradfield Coll; late Lieut RA: *m* 1955, Isobel Margaret Logie, da of William Low McDonald, of Port Elizabeth, S Africa, and has issue living, Jennifer Elizabeth Chenevix, *b* 1957, — Helen Winifred Chenevix, *b* 1959. ——Gillian Chenevix, *b* 1920: *m* 1947, Maj James Thomas Benedictus Notley, DSO, late Duke of Cornwall's LI, of Redcote, 48 Port Hill Gdns, Shrewsbury, and has issue living, Christopher John Marwood, *b* 1949; Maj 1st Bn LI: *m* 1st, 1977 (*m diss* 1982), Christine Louise, da of Patrick Hugh Ash, of Haughley, Suffolk; 2ndly, 1987, Alison Jane Leila, da of Colin Biggs, of IoW, — Helen Ann Hamilton, *b* 1950: *m* 1971 (*m diss* 1987), Timothy Rowland Hunt, and has issue living, Benjamin Rowland *b* 1973, Nina Kathryn *b* 1974.

Grandchildren of late Rev Herbert Francis Chenevix Trench, 6th son of late Most Rev and Rt Hon Richard Chenevix Trench, DD (ante):—
Issue of late Col Arthur Henry CHENEVIX TRENCH, CIE, *b* 1884, *d* 1968: *m* 1913, Dorothy Pauline, who *d* 1950, da of late Allan Gibson Steel, KC, Recorder of Oldham:—
Reginald Allan (Lee's Orchard, Amberley, Arundel, Sussex BN18 9NN), *b* 1920; Maj RE (ret): *m* 1957, Sophie Sybella Strathern, da of Air Chief Marshal Sir Douglas Claude Strathern Evill, GBE, KCB, DSC, AFC, RAF (ret) (*see* Kleinwort, Bt, 1980 Edn), and has issue living, Ivo Richard, *b* 1959: *m* 1982, Joelle, da of René Bézert, of Marseilles, France, and has issue living, Maxwell *b* 1992, Sophie Armelle Françoise *b* 1982, — Angus, *b* 1960, — Katharine, *b* 1964, — Jessica Sophie, *b* 1966: *m* 1994, James H. Hunter, yr son of late S/Ldr Ewan Hunter, of Jersey, CI, and has issue living, George James Havard *b* 1994, Douglas Ewan Havard *b* 1996. ——Margaret Georgina (Farthings, School Lane, Fittleworth, Pulborough, W Sussex RH20 1JB), *b* 1915; formerly in FANY: *m* 1944, Patrick Millington Synge, late Maj Intelligence Corps, who *d* 1982, and has issue living, Arthur Hugh Millington, *b* 1951, — Robert Patrick, *b* 1957: *m* 1992, Susan Jean Frances Wixley. ——Dorothy Anne (3 The Old School House, Fittleworth, Pulborough, W Sussex), *b* 1916; formerly in WRNS: *m* 1942, Roderick Peter Garratt Wilson, who *d* 1994, son of Sir Roderick (Roy) Wilson, and has issue living, *Sir* Nicholas Allan Roy (*Hon Mr Justice Wilson*), *b* 1945; BA (Oxon); Bar Inner Temple 1967, QC and Recorder of Crown Court 1987-93, since when a Judge of High Court of Justice (Family Div); Ktd 1993: *m* 1974, Margaret (Bar Middle Temple 1966), da of late Reginald Francis Higgins, and has issue living, Matthew Roderick Benjamin *b* 1977, Camilla Jessica *b* 1981, — *Rev* Francesca Dorothy, *b* 1952: MA (Cantab), Dip Theol: *m* 1985, John Dudley Dixon, MBE, DSC, who *d* 1996.

Issue of late Maj Charles Reginald CHENEVIX TRENCH, *b* 1888, *ka* 1918: *m* 1915, Clare Cecily, who *d* 1989, da of late Henry Blunt Howard, of Bark Hart, Orpington, Kent:, —

Isabel Clare (48 The Cloisters, Pegasus Grange, Whitehouse Rd, Oxford OX1 4QQ), *b* 1915; Dip Social Studies, London: *m* 1939, (Clarence) John Molyneux Fletcher, FSA, who *d* 1986, and has issue living, *Prof* Anthony John (Old Farm, S Newington, Banbury, Oxon OX15 4JW), *b* 1941; *ed* Wellington Coll, and Merton Coll, Oxford (MA): *m* 1967, Tresna Dawn, da of Charles Henry Railton Russell, of 25 Minchenden Crescent, Southgate, N4, and has issue living, Crispin Hilary Trench *b* 1970: *m* 1994, Mary, da of Peter Louis, Dickon Anthony Railton *b* 1972, — Martin Chenevix (Westbrook, Rhinefield Rd, Brockenhurst, Hants SO42 7SR), *b* 1942: *m* 1972, Diana, da of John Edward Patrick Cantillon, of Blueberry Downs, Budleigh Salterton, Devon, and has issue living, Nicholas Cantillon *b* 1975, Alison Chenevix *b* 1973, — Joanna Delle, *b* 1946: *m* 1992, Cmdr Robert Walker, RN (ret), of 33 Batoum Gdns, W6 7QB, — Hilary Clare, *b* 1951: *m* 1976, John Bennett, of 13 Bramley Close, Kingswood, Wotton-under-Edge, Glos GL2 8JF, and has issue living, Peter David John *b* 1989, Charlotte Louise *b* 1981, Rowena Clare *b* 1982.

Issue of late Herbert CHENEVIX TRENCH, *b* 1892, *d* 1971: *m* 1922, Marjorie, who *d* 1962, da of R. C. Bell, of Melbourne, Vic, Australia:—
Frances Robina Chenevix, *b* 1925: *m* 1953, R. Raymond Lockyer, ARIBA, of The Old Manor Cottage, Broadwell, nr Lechlade, Glos, and has issue living, Sarah Frances Chenevix, *b* 1954: *m* 1982, Peter Hickman, of Wormley West End, Broxbourne, Herts, son of W. J. Hickman, and has issue living, Emma Charlotte *b* 1985, Lucy Elizabeth *b* 1987, — Victoria Robina Chenevix, *b* 1957: *m* 1995, Tim Atkinson, of Askernish, South Uist, Scotland, and has issue living, Brighde Anne Chenevix *b* 1998. —— Valerie Hester Chenevix, *b* 1929: *m* 1959, David McKie Kerslake, OBE, of Lime Tree Cottage, Yateley, Hants GU46 7SP, and has issue living, Michael John Chenevix, *b* 1962: *m* 1997, Michelle Mithra Theobald, — Caroline Julia Chenevix, *b* 1961.

Branch from 3rd son of 5th brother of 1st Baron

Grandchildren of late Richard Bayley Chenevix Trench, yst son of late Philip Charles Chenevix Trench, 3rd son of late Richard Trench (ante), 5th brother of 1st Baron:—
Issue of late Capt Hugo CHENEVIX TRENCH, *b* 1890, *d* 1965: *m* 1920 (*m diss* 1933), Emma Margaret Florence, who *d* 1948, da of Sir Robert McAlpine, 1st Bt:—
Brian Robert David (13 Holland Park, W11), *b* 1927: *m* 1st, 1956 (*m diss* 19—), Bridget, da of K. R. J. Saxon, of Boscombe, Hants; 2ndly, 1963, Elspeth Charlesworth, yr da of late Thomas Douglas Ross, OBE, of Stamford.

Issue of late Ivor CHENEVIX TRENCH, *b* 1892, *d* 1960: *m* 1918, Doris Mary, who *d* 1951, da of late John Francis Gaskell, of Cambus O'May, Aberdeenshire:—
Diana Doris, *b* 1920: *m* 1st, 1943 (*m diss* 1947), Capt Brodie Knight, WG; 2ndly, 1947, Gilbert Younghusband, late Capt RHG.

Issue of late Lionel CHENEVIX TRENCH, *b* 1901, *d* 1930: *m* 1925, Doris Maud (who *m* 2ndly, 1933, George Sweeting, who *d* 1956, and *d* 1980), da of late Charles D. Turrall, of Downes, Torrington, N Devon:—
(Keith Everard) George (The Old Mill, Worton, Devizes, Wilts), *b* 1926; *ed* Stowe; 1939-45 War as Sub-Lieut RNVR: *m* 1st, 1952 (*m diss* 1972), Bridget, da of late Lt-Col K. R. O'Brien, MC, late R Ulster Rifles; 2ndly, 1982, Mrs Daphne Du Sautoy (née Hazlewood), and has issue living (by 1st *m*), Guy Charles, *b* 1955: *m* 1982, Sarah A., yr da of John Speakman, of Maldon, Essex, and has issue living, Olivia Katie *b* 1985, Poppy *b* 1987, — Rupert George (42 California, Woodbridge, Suffolk), *b* 1957: *m* 1988, Susannah Rainey, da of Robert Craik, of Mill Cottage, Waldringfield, Woodbridge, Suffolk, and has issue living, Frederic George *b* 1989, Fleur Melesina *b* 1992.

Branch from 6th brother of 1st Baron

Granddaughters of late Wilbraham FitzJohn Trench (infra):—
Issue of late Patrick Mackenzie FitzJohn Trench, *b* 1905, *d* 1948: *m* 1st, 1926 (*m diss* 1930), Frances Cautley, who *d* 1982, da of late Cecil Cautley Baker; 2ndly, 1930, Evelyn, who *d* 1945, da of late John Hayden; 3rdly, 1948, Winifred Frances, who *d* 1992, da of late Arthur Edward Stidolph:—
(By 2nd *m*) Eveline Mary, *b* 1932: *m* 1952 (*m diss* 1987), Thomas William Lane, and has issue living, William, *b* 1955: *m* 1980, Janet Ellinor, da of Thomas Merville de Blois, of Toronto, and has issue living, Helen Eilís de Blois *b* 1984, Heather Fiona de Blois *b* 1988, — Patricia Sheela, *b* 1954: *m* 1993, Kenneth Malcolm Maclure, of Victoria, BC, Canada, and has issue living, Troy Liam Chalmers Alexander *b* 1994. *Residence* – 2571 Heron St, Victoria, BC, Canada V8R 5Z9. —— (By 3rd *m*) Brid, *b* 19—: *m* 1962, Michael Frederick Strutt, son of Frederick Strutt, of Pontypool, Gwent, and has issue living, Patrick *b* 1962, — Catherine, *b* 1964, — Anna, *b* 1965, — Siân, *b* 1978.

Grandson of late John Alfred Trench, eldest son of late Rev Frederic FitzJohn Trench, eldest son of late John Trench, 6th brother of 1st Baron:—
Issue of late Wilbraham FitzJohn Trench, *b* 1873, *d* 1939: *m* 1903, Mary Alicia, who *d* 1930, eldest da of late Edward Cross, formerly Lieut RA, of Hollywood, Portishead, Somerset:—
Chalmers Edward FitzJohn, *b* 1909: *m* 1940, Beatrice Esther, who *d* 1980, da of late Charles St George Orpen, of Lisheens, Carrickmines, co Dublin, and has issue living, Fiachra Terence Wilbraham McMAHON TRENCH (Easton House, Delgany, co Wicklow), *b* 1941; M Mus Cincinnati; assumed additional surname of McMahon 1983: *m* 1st, 1965 (*m diss* 1980), Micaela Fredericka, da of late Edgar H. Maus, of Hamilton, Ohio, USA; 2ndly, 1983, Hanora Carmel, yst da of late Joseph McMahon, of Nenagh, co Tipperary, and has issue living (by 1st *m*), Michael Chalmers Wilbraham *b* 1966, (by 2nd *m*) Oisín Patrick *b* 1984, Rian Charles *b* 1986, — Brian Arthur Wilbraham (529 Griffith Av, Dublin 11), *b* 1945; has issue (by Judith Carolyn, yr da of late E. A. Bowles, of Melton, Humberside), Danny Eric Trench BOWLES *b* 1993, Nora Trench BOWLES *b* 1987, — Patrick Chalmers Wilbraham (259 Lea Bridge Rd, E10), *b* 1955: *m* 1988, Julia Catherine, da of Dorian Cresswell Cooke, and has issue living, Liam Patrick Alexander *b* 1988, James Chalmers Dorian *b* 1991, — Beatrice Mary Wilbraham (18 Bellwood Av, Ottawa, Ontario, Canada), *b* 1948: *m* 1st, 1968 (*m diss* 1976), Sydney Douglas Saunders; 2ndly, 1983, Gerald Adrian Bol, elder son of late Gerrit Bol, of Utrecht, Netherlands, and Essex, Ontario, and has issue living (by 2nd *m*), Kieran Gerrit *b* 1986. *Residence* – Killrian, Slane, co Meath.

Grandchildren of late Frederic Herbert Trench, elder son (but only son by 1st *m*) of late William Wallace Trench, 2nd son of late Rev Frederick FitzJohn Trench (ante):—

Issue of late Waldo Trench Fox, MC, b 1892, d 1954, having assumed by deed poll 1934 the names of Waldo Trench Fox in lieu of Wallace Talbot Trench: m 1933, Janet Mary Kennedy, who d 1987, da of MacIvor Bassett, of Lelant, Cornwall:—

Robert Trench Fox, CBE (Cheriton House, Alresford, Hants), b 1937; ed Winchester, and Univ Coll, Oxford (MA); CBE (Civil) 1993: m 1962, Lindsay Garrett, DL Hants 1997, da of Sir Donald Forsyth Anderson, of The Manor, Notgrove, Glos, and has issue living, Barclay Trench, b 1971, — Caspar Lloyd, b 1972, — Fenella Garrett, b 1964: m 1990, John Francis Dernie, of Cirencester, and has issue living, Oliver Garrett b 1995, Joshua Garrett b 1997, Alexander Llewellyn b 1999, — Tamara Forsyth, b 1967: m 1995, Robert Denzil Onslow, and has issue (see E Onslow, colls). —— Jill Trench, b 1935; High Sheriff Cornwall 1996-97, DL 1999: m 1st, 1955, Lieut Rodney Francis Power Carne, RN, who d 1959; 2ndly, 1961, Capt Donald Barns Morison, RN, and has issue living (by 1st m), Rupert Barclay Power, b 1958: m 1994, Julie Evans, of Chichester, Sussex, and has issue living, Jerrick Achilles b 1996, Joel Jonah b 1997, — Nicola Trench, b 1957: m 1985, Eric McClean, of co Tyrone, and has issue living, Angus Carne b 1990, Kirsten Valentine b 1988, — (by 2nd m) Barnaby Daniel Barns, b 1964: m 1998, Sarah Louise Sutherland Pilch, of Pulborough, Sussex, — Candida Trench, b 1963: m 1990, Robin Spencer, of The Wirral, and has issue living, Samuel Peter Nelson b 1992, Freya Jill b 1995, Zanna Elizabeth b 1999. Residence – Boskenna, St Martin in Meneage, Helston, Cornwall. —— Rachel Trench, b 1943: m 1965, Raymond Joseph Morin, of 52 Bellevue Av, Haverhill, Mass, USA.

Issue of late Desmond Patrick Trench, b 1893, d 1967: m 1st, 1916, Elfrida Mary Eliott, who d 1942, da of Rev Daniel Eliott Young, sometime V of St Mary's Penzance; 2ndly, 1947, Hilda Olive, who d 1993, da of A. A. J. Akhurst, of Lyncrest, Southbourne, Hants:—

(By 1st m) Anthony Barclay (c/o Trench Electrics Ltd, 390 Midwest Rd, Scarborough, Ontario, Canada M1P 3B5), b 1919; AMIEE (England); Consulting Engr, Ontario; 1939-45 War as Fl-Lieut RAFVR (prisoner): m 1st, 1940, Sheila Mary, da of Lawrence Lois Keith, of Hastings, Sussex; 2ndly, 1981, Doris Lynne, da of Alvin Radcliffe James, of St Elizabeth, Jamaica, and has issue living (by 1st m), Simon Patrick, b 1946. —— Heather Mavis, b 1925: m 1948, Robin Krohn Pooley, sometime Headmaster of Dane Court Sch, Pyrford, Woking, Surrey, and has issue living, Peter John, b 1950; ed Bryanston: m 1986, Lynn Rachel Kimber, and has issue living, Alice Jane b 1990, Rachel Jane Sarah b 1996, — Catherine Susan (adopted da), b 1958: m 1958, Robert Darke, of Cour de la Bruyère, 27210 Manneville la Raoult Beuzeville, France, and has issue living, Jason Paul b 1980, Georgia b 1985, Jessica b 1989, Madeleine Barbara b 1991. Residence – Auburn, 48 Belmore Lane, Lymington, Hants SO41 3NN.

Granddaughter of late William Wallace Trench (ante):—
Issue of late Claud Llewellyn (Pomeroy) Trench, b 1881, d 1945: m 1911, Annie Elizabeth, who d 1972, eldest da of late William Charles Davis, of Cheltenham, Glos:—

Eileen Elizabeth, b 1917: m 1937, Cecil H. F. Knight, and has issue living, Bernard Cecil Frank, b 1939; Coldm Gds: m 1965, Jacqueline Ann, da of William John Rudkin, of 94 Heacham Drive, Leicester, and has issue living, Paul b 1968, — Elizabeth Ann (The Birches, 11A Willow Park Drive, Wigston, Leicester), b 1937: m 1956 (m diss 1973), John David Heighton, and has issue living, David Peter b 1957, Brian John b 1958: m 1977, Ellen Lucell Glover (and has issue living, Richard James Brian b 1981, Alexander Charles Luke b 1983, Claire Samantha Lucell b 1978), Suzanne Elizabeth b 1961, — Catherine Beryl, b 1945: m 1968, Patrick James Roddy, of 5 Highcroft, Husbands Bosworth, Leics, and has issue living, Christopher James b 1970, Paula Louise b 1972, — Hazel Mary, b 1949: m 1975, Martin Oliver, of 9 Dalby Rd, Anstey, Leics, and has issue living, Neil Edward Llewellyn b 1985, Heidi Joanne b 1974, Gwen Georgina b 1976, Jaqui Eve Marie b 1979, Ruth Christina b 1982. Residence – 51 Oadby Rd, Wigston Magna, Leicester LE18 3RP.

Grandchildren of late Col Ernest Frederic Crosbie Trench, CBE, TD, eldest son of late George Frederick Trench (infra):—
Issue of late Dermot George Crosbie Trench, b 1904, d 1984: m 1938, Nancy Muriel (O'NEIL) (El Mirador, MG-CA19, Javea, Alicante, Spain), da of late Dr Stewart Arthur Smith, of Sydney, NSW:—

Anthony Crosbie, b 1941. —— Patricia Ann, b 1944: m 1976, Roger A. Nuttall, of 48 Grayton Rd, NW3, and has issue living, Tom Oliver, b 1977, — Peggy Ellen Nan, b 1980.

Issue of late Brian Morley Crosbie Trench, b 1908, d 1979: m 1938, Harriett Milward, who d 1981, da of late John Lyons Agnew, of Ontario:—

Jonathan Agnew (40 Havelock Rd, Norwich), b 1939; ed Gordonstoun, and Ch Ch, Oxford (BA 1963): m 1969 (m diss 1987), Sarah, da of Don Cameron Williams, of Kansas City, USA, and has issue living, Mary Olivia, b 1972. —— Amanda Milward (12A Caithness Rd, W14 0SB), b 1941: m 1961 (m diss 1979), Jonathan Radice, and has issue living, James Heneage, b 1961, — Daniel Brett, b 1967.

Issue of late Fl-Lieut Desmond Ernest Crosbie Trench, b 1911, ka 1941: m 1937, Dorothy Waugh (who m 2ndly, 1953, Maj William Spencer), da of late Maj H. C. Shewell, RGA:—

Josephine Crosbie, b 1938: m 1965, David McCowan, and has issue living, Jonathan David, b 1965, — Deborah Kate, b 1967. —— Kerry Deborah (posthumous), b 1941: m 1965, Michael Honnor, of Wilkeysmoor, Cornwood, Ivybridge, Devon, and has issue living, Julius Desmond, b 1973, — Seth Michael, b 1976.

Issue of late Peter Crosbie Trench, b 1912, d 1969: m 1st, 1941 (m diss 1946), Nan Dorice Hunter; 2ndly, 1947, Joy Seymour (26 Manor Drive, Wembley Park, Middx), da of late H. Shave, of Calcutta:—

(By 2nd m) Colin Crosbie, b 1949: m 1st, 1972 (m diss 1975), Susan Ann Saunders; 2ndly, 1976, Susan Wooldridge, and has issue living (by 2nd m), Jacqueline, b 1979, — Joanna, b 1984, — Michelle, b 1985.

Grandchildren of late William Launcelot Crosbie Trench, CIE, 4th and yst son of late George Frederick Trench, 3rd son of late Rev Frederic Trench (ante):—
Issue of late Lt-Col George Shan Crosbie Trench, b 1913, d 1995: m 1945, Myrtle Sheila (105 Walsall Rd, Four Oaks, Sutton Coldfield, Warwicks B74 4NP), da of H. Jerrett, of Meols, Cheshire:—

Barney George Crosbie (83 Rue Marie Therese, Brussels 1040), b 1947; ed St Edward's Sch, Oxford, and St Catherine's Coll, Oxford (BA): m 1982, Marjorie (Midge) Shirley, and has issue living, Felix William Crosbie, b 1986. —— Margaret Felicity, b 1953: m 1982, Martin Christopher Colledge, and has issue living, Joanna Margaret b 1984.

Issue of late Sir David Clive Crosbie Trench, GCMG, MC, b 1915, d 1988: m 1944, Margaret, who d 1993, da of late Jay D. Gould, of New York, USA:—

Katherine Elizabeth, *b* 1956: *m* 1984, Christopher John Down, of 5a Bronsart Rd, SW6 6AJ, son of late Frederick William Down.

Granddaughter of late John Trench, 6th brother of 1st Baron:—
Issue of late James Currie Trench, *b* 1848, *d* 1936: *m* 1883, Annie Gertrude, who *d* 1944, elder da of late John Haughton, of Ardreigh, Athy, co Kildaire:—
Amy Feodora, *b* 1896: *m* 1922, James Alfred Stuart Watt, who *d* 1975, and has issue living, Lionel Robert (3 Ystrad Buildings, Trethomas, Newport, Mon), *b* 1924: *m* 1959, Elizabeth Maureen Buckley. *Residence* – 36 Castlwood Park, Rathmines, Dublin 6.

PREDECESSORS – (1) FREDERIC Trench, MP for Portarlington in the Irish Parliament, was cr *Baron Ashtown* (peerage of Ireland) 1800, with remainder to the heirs of his deceased father; *d* 1840; *s* by his nephew (2) FREDERIC MASON, 2nd Baron, *b* 1804: *m* 1st, Harriet, who *d* 1845, da of Thomas Phillips Cosby, of Stradbally Hall, Queen's co; 2ndly, 1852, Elizabeth, who *d* 1893, da and co-heir of Richard Oliver Gascoigne, of Parlington, Yorkshire; *d* 1880; *s* by his grandson (3) FREDERIC OLIVER (son of late Hon Frederic Sydney Charles Trench eldest son of 2nd Baron), 3rd Baron, *b* 1868: was a Representative Peer for Ireland 1908-15: *m* 1894, Violet Grace, who *d* 1945, yst da of Col Robert Ushworth Godolphin Cosby, of Stradbally Hall, Queen's co; *d* 1946; *s* by his eldest surviving son (4) ROBERT POWER, 4th Baron, *b* 1897: *m* 1st, 1926 (*m diss* 1938), Geraldine Ida, who *d* 1940, da of Sir Henry Foley Grey, 7th Bt; 2ndly, 1950, Oonah Anne, who *d* 1984, eldest da of late Brig-Gen Lewis Frederic Green-Wilkinson, CMG, DSO; *d* 1966; *s* by his brother (5) Dudley Oliver, OBE, 5th Baron, *b* 1901; Lt-Col KRRC; OBE (Civil) 1961: *m* 1st, 1932, Ellen Nancy, who *d* 1949, da of late William Garton, of Brixedon, Bursledon, Hants; 2ndly, 1955, Sheelah Adrienne Sarah, who *d* 1963, yr da of late Brig-Gen Lewis Frederic Green-Wilkinson, CMG, DSO; 3rdly, 1966, Frances Natalie, who *d* 1979, da of Maj Hermon Barker-Hahlo, and widow of Maj James Fenwick de Sales La Terriere; *d* 1979; *s* by his kinsman (6) CHRISTOPHER OLIVER (son of late Algernon Oliver Trench, 3rd son of late Hon William Cosby Trench, brother of 3rd Baron), 6th Baron, *b* 1931; Canadian Imperial Bank of Commerce 1950-57; *dunm* 1990; *s* by his kinsman (7) NIGEL CLIVE COSBY, KCMG (son of late Clive Newcome Trench, son of late Capt Hon Cosby Godolphin Trench, 2nd son of 2nd Baron), 7th Baron and present peer.

Asquith, family name of Earl of Oxford and Asquith.

Asquith, Viscount; son of Earl of Oxford and Asquith.

Asquith of Bishopstone, Barony of (Asquith) (Extinct 1954) (see E Oxford and Asquith, colls)

ASQUITH OF YARNBURY, BARONY OF (Bonham Carter) (Extinct 1969) (see also E Oxford and Asquith)

SON LIVING OF LIFE BARONESS

Hon Raymond Henry (7 West Heath Av, NW11), *b* 1929; Lt Irish Gds: *m* 1958, Elena, da of late Don Eduardo Propper de Callejon, and has issue living, Edward Henry, *b* 1960: *m* 1994, Victoria, da of Clifford Studd, of Aberdeen, and has issue living, Harry Raymond *b* 1996, — Thomas David, *b* 1961: *m* 1994, Virginia Catherine Elizabeth, 2nd da of Nigel Sharp, of Brick House, Gt Bardfield, Essex, and has issue living, Frederick David *b* 1990, Rose Violet *b* 1992, — Helena, *b* 1966; actress.

Assheton, family name of Baron Clitheroe.

Astley, family name of Baron Hastings.

ASTOR, VISCOUNT (Astor) (Viscount UK 1917)

WILLIAM WALDORF ASTOR, 4th Viscount; *b* 27 Dec 1951; *s* 1966; *ed* Eton; a Lord in Waiting 1990-93; Dept of National Heritage 1992-93; Parly Under Sec, Dept of Social Security 1993-94, Parly Under Sec, Dept of National Heritage 1994-95: *m* 1976, Annabel Lucy Veronica, da of Timothy Angus Jones (*see* B Clifford of Chudleigh, colls, 1985 Edn), and formerly wife of Reginald Adrian Berkeley Sheffield (now Sir Reginald Sheffield, 8th Bt), and has issue.

ᴀrms – Or, a falcon resting on a dexter hand couped at the wrist, proper and gauntleted gules in chief two fleurs-de-lys of the last. Crest – From a mount vert a falcon rising proper, ensigned by three mullets gold. Supporters – *Dexter*, a North American Indian; *sinister*, a North American fur trapper; each habited, accoutred, and holding in the exterior hand a rifle, all proper.
Residence – Ginge Manor, Wantage, Oxon OX12 8QT.

SONS LIVING

Hon WILLIAM WALDORF, *b* 18 Jan 1979.
Hon James Jacob, *b* 1981.

DAUGHTER LIVING

Hon Flora Katherine, *b* 1976.

To the stars

HALF-SISTERS LIVING (*Daughter of 3rd Viscount by 2nd marriage*)

Hon Emily Mary, *b* 1956; photographer: *m* 1st, 1984, Alan McL. Gregory, elder son of Donald Gregory, of San Francisco, California, USA; 2ndly, 1988, as his 2nd wife, James Ian Anderson (*see* E Perth). *Residence* – 2 St Albans Grove, W8.

(*Daughters of 3rd Viscount by 3rd marriage*)

Hon Janet Elizabeth (*Countess of March and Kinrara*), *b* 1961; *ed* New Coll, Oxford (BA), and King's Coll, London (MA): *m* 1993, as his 2nd wife, Charles Henry, Earl of March and Kinrara, only son of 10th Duke of Richmond, and has issue (see that title). *Residences* – Goodwood, Chichester, W Sussex PO18 0PX; 7 Charles St, W1X 7HB.
Hon Pauline Marian, *b* 1964: *m* 1990, George C. V. Case, son of late Denis Case, of Marlow, Bucks, and has issue living, Magdalena Beatrice, *b* 1994, — Nancy Mary, *b* 1996. *Residence* – Turville Lodge, Turville Heath, Oxon.

UNCLES LIVING (*Sons of 2nd Viscount*)

Hon (Francis) David Langhorne, CH, *b* 1912; *ed* Eton, and Balliol Coll, Oxford; late Capt RM; Editor of *The Observer* 1948-75; 1939-45 War (Croix de Guerre) CH 1994: *m* 1st, 1945 (*m diss* 1951), Melanie, da of Philip Hauser, of Berne, Switzerland; 2ndly, 1952, Bridget Aphra, da of Maj Cyril Wreford, of Yew Tree House, Goosey, Faringdon, Berks, and has issue living (by 1st *m*), Frances Christine Langhorne, *b* 1947: *m* 1970, Dr Miles Frankel, of Kilbrack House, Doneraile, co Cork, — (by 2nd *m*), Richard David Langhorne, *b* 1955: *m* 1990, Sarah G. H., da of James Skinner, and has issue living, Bonny Jane *b* 1992, — Thomas Robert Langhorne, *b* 1962, — Alice Margaret Frances, *b* 1953: *m* 1st, 1972 (*m diss* 1985), Lawrence Woodward; 2ndly, 1987, Mark Thomas Luke Grindon-Welch, of Stockadon Farm, Loddiswell, Kingsbridge, Devon TQ7 4EQ, and has issue living (by 1st *m*), William Lawrence *b* 1978, Jessica Alice *b* 1980, (by 2nd *m*) Adam Thomas Richard *b* 1988, Rose Aphra Elizabeth *b* 1991, — Lucy Aphra Nancy, *b* 1958, — Nancy Bridget Elizabeth, *b* 1960: *m* 1990, Séan V. Naidoo, of 89 Carlton Mansions, Randolph Av, NW1 8UG, son of Stanley Naidoo, of Johannesburg, and has issue living, Cara Mary *b* 1992. *Residences* – 9 Cavendish Av, NW8 9JD; Manor House, Sutton Courtenay, Oxon.
Hon Sir John Jacob, MBE, *b* 1918; *ed* Eton, and New Coll, Oxford; Maj Life Gds; DL Cambs 1962; Chm, Agric Research Council 1968-78; N-W Europe 1944-45 (MBE, Legion of Honour, French Croix de Guerre); MP for Sutton Div of Plymouth (*C*) 1951-59; MBE (Mil) 1945; Kt 1978: *m* 1st, 1944 (*m diss* 1972), Ana Inez, who *d* 1992, da of late Sr Dr Don Miguel Angel Carcano, KCMG, KBE, sometime Argentine Ambassador in London; 2ndly, 1976 (*m diss* 1985), Mrs Susan Sheppard, who *d* 1997, da of late Maj Michael Eveleigh, 3rdly, 1988, Mrs Marcia de Savary, and has issue living (by 1st *m*), Michael Ramon Langhorne, *b* 1946: *m* 1979, Daphne, da of late Edward Mortimer Morris Warburg, of Westport, Conn, USA, — Stella Ines, *b* 1949: *m* 1st, 1974 (*m diss* 1989), Martin Wilkinson, of Cwm Hall, Clunton, Craven Arms,

Shropshire; 2ndly, 1989, William Wells, of Venice Beach, California, USA, and has issue living, (by 1st *m*) Matthew MiguelAngel *b* 1977, Alice AnaMaria *b* 1975, (by 2nd *m*) Delilah Diamond Montana Tempest Respect *b* 19—. *Residence* – The Dower House, Hatley Park, Hatley St George, Sandy, Beds SG19 3HL.

MOTHER LIVING

Hon Sarah Katherine Elinor Norton (42 Melton Court, Old Brompton Rd, SW7 3JH), da of 6th Baron Grantley: *m* 1st, 1945 (*m diss* 1953), the 3rd Viscount Astor, who *d* 1966; 2ndly, 1953 (*m diss* 1965), Maj Thomas Michael Baring, Derbyshire Yeo (*see* B Northbrook, colls).

WIDOW LIVING OF SON OF SECOND VISCOUNT

Judith Caroline Traill, da of Paul Innes, and formerly wife of John Moynihan (son of late Rodrigo Moynihan, CBE, portrait painter): *m* 1970, as his 3rd wife, Hon Michael Langhorne Astor, 3rd son of 2nd Viscount, who *d* 1980, and has issue (see colls infra).

WIDOW LIVING OF THIRD VISCOUNT

Janet Bronwen Alun (*Bronwen, Viscountess Astor*) (Tuesley Manor, Tuesley, Godalming, Surrey); psychotherapist; da of late His Honour Sir (John) Alun Pugh: *m* 1960, as his 3rd wife, the 3rd Viscount, who *d* 1966.

COLLATERAL BRANCHES LIVING

Descendants of late Hon John Jacob Astor, 2nd son of 1st Viscount, who was cr *Baron Astor of Hever* 1956 (see that title.)

Issue of late Hon Michael Langhorne Astor, 3rd son of 2nd Viscount, *b* 1916, *d* 1980: *m* 1st, 1942 (*m diss* 1961), Barbara Mary Colonsay, who *d* 1980, only da of late Capt Ronald Frank Rous McNeill; 2ndly, 1961 (*m diss* 1968), (Patricia David) Pandora, who *d* 1987, 2nd da of late Hon Sir Bede Edmund Clifford, GCMG, CB, MVO, FRGS (*see* B Clifford of Chudleigh, colls, 1985 Edn), and formerly wife of Timothy Angus Jones; 3rdly, 1970, Judith Caroline Traill (ante), da of Paul Innes, and formerly wife of John Moynihan (son of late Rodrigo Moynihan, CBE, portrait painter):—
(By 1st *m*) David Waldorf, CBE (Bruern Grange, Milton-under-Wychwood, Oxon), *b* 1943; *ed* Eton, and Harvard Univ; CBE 1994: *m* 1968, Clare Pamela, da of Cdr Michael Beauchamp St John, DSC, RN (*see* B St John of Bletso, colls), and has issue living, Henry Waldorf, *b* 1969; has issue living by Alexandra Jean, da of late Francis Ryan, of Brooks, Maine, USA), George Francis *b* 1998, — Thomas Ludovic David, *b* 1972, — Joanna Colonsay Clare, *b* 1970, — Rose Nancy Langhorne, *b* 1979. —— James Colonsay Langhorne, *b* 1945; *ed* Eton, and Univ Coll, London (BSc): *m* 1972, Jane M. S., da of Charles de Chazal, of 4 Thames Reach, 80 Rainville Rd, W6, and has issue living, Tobias, *b* 1980, — Katharine Tamsin, *b* 1976. —— (Kathleen Nancy) Jane, *b* 1949. —— Georgina Mary, *b* 1952: *m* 1st, 1973 (*m diss* 1979), Hon Anthony Ramsay, 2nd son of 16th Earl of Dalhousie; 2ndly, 1979, (Thomas) Lorne Nelson, of Kilmaronaig, Connel, Argyll (*see* By Queenborough, 1990 Edn), and has issue living (by 1st *m*) (*see* E Dalhousie), — (by 2nd *m*) Thomas Michael, *b* 1979, — Alice Catherine, *b* 1981, — Clare Emma, *b* 1983. —— (By 3rd *m*) Polly Michael, *b* 1971. —— The Hon Michael Astor also adopted his stepson, Joshua Paul Michael ASTOR, *b* 1966.

PREDECESSORS – (1) WILLIAM WALDORF Astor, only son of John Jacob Astor, of New York; *b* 1848; United States Min to Italy 1882-5; naturalised 1899; cr *Baron Astor*, of Hever Castle, co Kent (peerage of United Kingdom) 1916, and *Viscount Astor*, of Hever Castle, co Kent (peerage of United Kingdom) 1917: *m* 1878, Mary Dahlgren, who *d* 1894, da of James W. Paul, of Philadelphia; *d* 1919; *s* by his eldest son (2) WALDORF, 2nd Viscount, *b* 1879; Chm of Directors of *The Observer*, and High Steward of Maidenhead; European War 1914-17 as temporary Major and Inspector of QMG Sers (despatches); Parliamentary Private Sec to Prime Min 1917-18, Parliamentary Sec to Min of Food 1918, and to Local Govt Board Jan to June 1919 (also Chm National Health Insurance Joint Committee Feb to June 1919), and first Parliamentary Sec to Min of Health 1919-21; appointed Hon Col Devon and Cornwall, Heavy Brig RA (TA) 1933; Chm of R Institute of International Affairs 1939-49, and of League of Nations Committee on Nutrition 1936-37; Lord Mayor of Plymouth 1939-44; MP for Plymouth (C) 1910-18, and for Sutton Div thereof 1918-19: *m* 1906, Nancy Witcher, CH, DLitt (first woman to sit in the House of Commons), who *d* 1964, da of late Col Chiswell Dabney Langhorne, of Mirador, Greenwood, Virginia, USA, and formerly wife of Robert Gould Shaw; *d* 1952; *s* by his eldest son (3) WILLIAM WALDORF, 3rd Viscount; *b* 1907; PPS to First Lord of the Admiralty 1936-37, and for Wycombe (C) 1939-45, and for Wycombe 1951-52: *m* 1st, 1945 (*m diss* 1953), Hon Sarah Katharine Elinor Norton, da of 6th Baron Grantley; 2ndly, 1955 (*m diss* 1960), Philippa Victoria, da of Lt-Col Henry Philip Hunloke (*see* D Devonshire, 1980 Edn); 3rdly, 1960, Janet Bronwen Alun, da of His Honour Sir (John) Alun Pugh; *d* 1966; *s* by his only son (4) WILLIAM WALDORF, 4th Viscount, and present peer; also Baron Astor.

ASTOR OF HEVER, BARON (Astor) (Baron UK 1956)

To the stars

JOHN JACOB ASTOR, 3rd Baron, *b* 16 June 1946; *s* 1984; *ed* Eton; Life Gds 1966-70: *m* 1st, 1970 (*m diss* 1990), Fiona Diana Lennox, da of Capt Roger Edward Lennox Harvey, of Parliament Piece, Ramsbury, Wilts (*see* Mainwaring, Bt, ext, 1990 Edn); 2ndly, 1990, Hon Mrs Elizabeth Constance Chagrin, yr da of 2nd Viscount Mackintosh of Halifax, and has issue by 1st and 2nd *m*.

𝔄rms – Argent eight barrulets sable over all resting on a dexter hand couped at the wrist proper gauntleted gules a falcon also gules in chief two fleurs de lys of the last. 𝔠rest – Rising from a mount vert a falcon proper ensigned by three mullets or. 𝔖upporters – *Dexter*, the figure of Aesculapius, and *sinister*, that of Mercury, both proper.
Residence – Frenchstreet House, Westerham, Kent TN16 1PW. *Clubs* – White's, Riviera Golf.

SON LIVING (*By 2nd marriage*)

Hon CHARLES GAVIN JOHN, *b* 10 Nov 1990.

DAUGHTERS LIVING (*By 1st marriage*)

Hon Camilla Fiona, *b* 1974.
Hon Tania Jentie, *b* 1978.
Hon Violet Magdalene, *b* 1980.

(*By 2nd marriage*)

Hon Olivia Alexandra, *b* 1992.

BROTHER LIVING

Hon Philip Douglas Paul, *b* 1959; *ed* Eton, and Ch Ch, Oxford; Bar Inner Temple 1989. *Residences* – Tillypronie, Tarland, Aboyne, Aberdeenshire AB34 4XX; Flat 3, 6 Embankment Gdns, SW3 4LJ.

SISTERS LIVING

Hon Bridget Mary, *b* 1948: *m* 1st, 1980 (*m diss* 1986), Count Arthur Tarnowski, yr son of late Count Hieronim Tarnowski, of Rudnik nad Sanem, Poland; 2ndly, 1989, Geofrey Richard Smith, 4th son of late James William Smith, of Eywood House, Titley, Hereford, and has issue living (by 1st husband), (John) Sebastian Gavin, *b* 1981, — Lucian Francis Philip, *b* 1984, — (by 2nd husband) Moya Morvenna Irene, *b* 1987. *Residence* – Sellack House, Sellack, Ross-on-Wye, Herefords HR9 6QP.
Hon (Elizabeth) Louise, *b* 1951: *m* 1st, 1979 (*m diss* 1981), David John Shelton Herring; 2ndly, 1985, David Joseph Ward, FRCS, son of Joseph Ward, FRCOG, of Tancrey, Fordwich, Canterbury, Kent, and has issue living (by 2nd *m*), Oliver Gavin Joseph, *b* 1985, — Victoria Mary, *b* 1987. *Residence* – Sauvey Castle Farm, Withcote, Oakham, Leics LE15 8DT.
Hon Sarah Violet, *b* 1953: *m* 1975, Hon George Edward Lopes, and has issue (*see* B Roborough). *Residence* – Gnaton Hall, Yealmpton, Plymouth, Devon PL8 2HU.

WIDOWS LIVING OF SONS OF FIRST BARON

Emily Lucy, da of Sir Alexander Davenport Kinloch, 12th Bt: *m* 1950, Hon Hugh Waldorf Astor, 2nd son of 1st Baron, who *d* 1999. *Residences* – Folly Farm, Sulhamstead, Berks RG7 4DF; 79 Ashley Gdns, Thirleby Rd, SW1P 1HG.
Penelope Eve (*Marchioness of Lansdowne*), da of late Cdr George Francis Norton Bradford, RN, and formerly wife of late David Rolt: *m* 2ndly, 1982, as his 2nd wife, Hon John Astor, yst son of 1st Baron, who *d* 1987; 3rdly, 1995, as his 4th wife, 8th Marquess of Lansdowne, PC. *Residence* – Meikleour House, Perthshire.

WIDOW LIVING OF SECOND BARON

Lady IRENE VIOLET FREESIA JANET AUGUSTA HAIG (*Irene, Baroness Astor of Hever*), da of Field Marshal 1st Earl Haig, KT, GCB, OM, GCVO, KCIE: *m* 1945, the 2nd Baron Astor of Hever, who *d* 1984. *Residences* – 11 Lyall St, SW1X 8DH; Hollytree House, Frenchstreet, Westerham, Kent, TN16 1PW.

COLLATERAL BRANCHES LIVING

Issue of late Hon Hugh Waldorf Astor, 2nd son of 1st Baron, *b* 1920, *d* 1999: *m* 1950, Emily Lucy (ante), da of Sir Alexander Davenport Kinloch, 12th Bt:—

Robert Hugh, *b* 1958: *m* 1991, Diana M., da of late Dr Louis Murray, of Johannesburg, and has issue living, Nicholas Louis Robert, *b* 1996, — Jonathan Hugh, *b* 1997. —— James Alexander Waldorf, *b* 1965: *m* 1996, Janine D., eldest da of James Valentine, of Reading, Mass, USA, and has issue living, Lucy Valentine, *b* 1998. —— Virginia Lucy (*Madam McGillycuddy of the Reeks*), *b* 1951: *m* 1984, Richard Denis Wyer McGillycuddy, The McGillycuddy of the Reeks, and has issue living, Tara Virginia, *b* 1985, — Sorcha Alexandra, *b* 1990. —— Rachel Mary (*Hon Mrs Nicholas Ward*), *b* 1955: *m* 1985, Hon (Edward) Nicholas Ward, yr son of 7th Viscount Bangor, and has issue (see that title). —— Jean Violet, *b* 1961: *m* 1982, John Maximilian Halford-Thompson, of Le Manoir du Grand Gennetay, 49640 Morannes, France, yr son of Lt-Col Peter Halford-Thompson, MC, of Manor Lodge, Longworth, Abingdon, and has issue living, Guy, *b* 1986, — Hugh Maximilian, *b* 1988, — Ralph Mark, *b* 1993.

Issue of late Hon John Astor, yst son of 1st Baron, *b* 1923, *d* 1987: *m* 1st, 1950, Diana Kathleen, who *d* 1982, da of late George Henry Drummond (*see* E Perth, colls, 1980 Edn); 2ndly, 1982, Penelope Eve (*Marchioness of Lansdowne*) (ante) (who *m* 3rdly, 1995, as his 4th wife, 8th Marquess of Lansdowne, PC), da of late Cdr George Francis Norton Bradford, RN, and formerly wife of late David Rolt:—
(By 1st *m*) (John) Richard, *b* 1953: *m* 1977, Katherine Mary, da of Brig Sir Jeffrey Lionel Darell, 8th Bt, MC, and has issue living, Charles John, *b* 1982, — Emily Mary, *b* 1980, — Tamara Sarah Diana, *b* 1989. *Residence* – Kirby House, Inkpen, nr Newbury, Berks. —— (George) David, *b* 1958: *m* 1983, Marianne Piroska Julia, only da of John Hurleston Leche, of Carden, Cheshire, and has issue living, Thomas David, *b* 1987, — Amy Violet, *b* 1989. *Residence* – The Old Vicarage, Ashbury, nr Swindon, Wilts. —— Elizabeth Kathleen, *b* 1951.

PREDECESSORS – (1) *Hon* JOHN JACOB Astor, 2nd son of 1st Viscount Astor, *b* 1886; Ch Proprietor of *The Times Newspaper* 1922-66, Chm of Middx Hosp 1938-62, and of Middx Hosp Med Sch 1945-62; MP for Dover (U) 1922-45; cr *Baron Astor of Hever*, of Hever Castle, Kent (peerage of (UK) 1956): *m* 1916, Lady Violet Mary Elliot, who *d* 1965, da of 4th Earl of Minto, and widow of Maj Lord Charles George Francis Mercer-Nairne, CVO (M Lansdowne); *d* 1971; *s* by his eldest son (2) GAVIN, 2nd Baron, *b* 1918; Chm Times Publishing Co 1959-66, and Co-Chief Proprietor *The Times* 1962-66, Life Pres Times Newspapers Ltd 1967-84, Dir Alliance Assurance Co Ltd 1954-84, Pres of Council Commonwealth Press Union 1972-75 (Chm 1959-72), Chm of Council R Commonwealth Soc 1972-75; Lord Lieut of Kent 1972-82, High Sheriff of Sussex 1955-56, Seneschal of Canterbury Cathedral 1973-83, Prime Warden Worshipful Co of Goldsmiths 1981-82; 1939-45 War as Capt Life Gds: *m* 1945, Lady Irene Violet Freesia Janet Augusta Haig, da of FM 1st Earl Haig, KT, GCB, OM, GCVO, KCIE; *d* 1984; *s* by his elder son (3) JOHN JACOB, 3rd Baron and present peer.

ATHOLL, DUKE OF (Murray) (Duke S 1703)

JOHN MURRAY, 11th Duke; *b* 19 Jan 1929; *s* 1996; *ed* Witwatersrand Univ; BScEng (land surveying): *m* 1956, Margaret Yvonne, only da of late Ronald Leonard Leach, of Louis Trichardt, N Transvaal, and has issue.

Arms – Not exemplified at time of going to press.
Estate Office — Blair Castle, Blair Atholl, Perthshire. *Address* – PO Box 137, Haenertsburg 0730, South Africa.

SONS LIVING

BRUCE GEORGE RONALD (*Marquess of Tullibardine*), *b* 6 April 1960; *ed* Saasveld Forestry Coll: *m* 1984, Lynne Elizabeth, eldest da of Nicholas Andrew, of Bedfordview, South Africa, and has issue.

SONS LIVING — Michael Bruce John (*Earl of Strathtay and Strathardle*), *b* 5 March 1985.
Lord David Nicholas George, *b* 1986.
DAUGHTER LIVING — *Lady* Nicole, *b* 1987.

Residence – Blair, Clouds End (PO Box 3548), Louis Trichardt 0920, S Africa.
Lord Craig John, *b* 1963: *m* 1988, Inge, 2nd da of Auke Bakker, of Bedfordview, S Africa, and has issue living, Carl, *b* 1994, — Shona, *b* 1995. *Residence* – Hurlyvale, Gauteng Province, S Africa.

DAUGHTER LIVING

Lady Jennifer, *b* 1958: *m* 1st, 1979 (*m diss* 1985), — Purdon; 2ndly, 1995, Martin Glodek, and has issue living (by 1st *m*), Grant Clive, *b* 1981, — Charlene, *b* 1983. *Residence* – 22 Loerie Town House, Lt G du Toit Crescent, Welgelegen, Pietersburg, S Africa. *Postal Address* — Box 11065, Bendor, 0699 S Africa.

MOTHER LIVING

Joan, da of late William Eastwood, of Buffelspoort, Mara, N Transvaal: *m* 1928, Maj George Murray, who *d* on active ser in S Africa 1940. *Address* – PO Box 111, Louis Trichardt 0920, N Transvaal.

COLLATERAL BRANCHES LIVING

Branch from 2nd son of 3rd Duke

Granddaughters of late Col Arthur Mordaunt Murray, CB, MVO, 2nd son of late Rev George Edward
Murray, eldest son of late Rt Rev George Murray, DD, Bishop of Rochester, 2nd son of late Rt Rev
Lord George Murray, DD, Bishop of St David's, 2nd son of 3rd Duke:—
Issue of late Lt-Col Godfrey Pemberton Murray, DSO, Seaforth Highlanders, b 1901, d 1985: m 1934, Mary
Isabel, who d 1995, da of J. Brownlee, of Middlesbrough:—
Susan Elizabeth, b 1935: m 1959, David Hill, of 95 Clarendon Rd, W11, son of Cdr George Walter Hill, RN, of Orlestone
Grange, Ham St, Kent, and has issue living, Simon Sebastian, b 1961, — David Alexander, b 1964, — Tobias Hunter, b
1967. —— Mary Jennifer, b 1939: m 1964, James Vickers, of 45 Beever Rd, Ashford, Kent, and has issue living, Sandra,
b 1965.

Granddaughters of late Col Walter Murray, OBE, MC, RE (infra):—
Issue of late Donald Stuart Murray, b 1917, d 1984: m 1948, Margaret Ann, da of Ernest Simmons, of The Glebe
House, Boughton Aluph, Ashford, Kent:—
Elizabeth Anne, b 1949: m 1978, John Kneafsey Kelsey, of Maitlands, 117 Manchester Rd, Chapel-en-le-Frith, High Peak,
and has issue living, Emily Jane, b 1981. — Victoria Louise, b 1983, — Henrietta Jean, b 1987. —— Jean Margaret, b
1951: m 1975, Nils Bertil Eidestedt, of Liljegatan 16, 75324 Uppsala, Sweden, and has issue living, Richard Nils Donald, b
1987, — Jessica Maria, b 1976, — Karin Marie, b 1981.

Grandchildren of late Rev Douglas Stuart Murray, 3rd son of Rev George Edward Murray (ante):—
Issue of late Col Walter Murray, OBE, MC, RE, b 1882, d 1945: m 1911, Evelyn, who d 1976, da of William E.
Adie, of The Rowans, Buxton, Derbyshire:—
Jean Pamela, b 1920: m 1947, Col James Andrew Fraser, MC, of Tomuaine, Tomich, by Beauly, Inverness-shire, and has
issue living, Simon John, b 1950, — Donald James, b 1951, — Jean Catherine, b 1954: m 1973, Daniel Letts.

Granddaughter of late Sir Herbert Harley Murray, KCB, 4th son of late Rt Rev George Murray, DD,
Bishop of Rochester (ante):—
Issue of late Major Stewart Lygon Murray, b 1863, d 1930: m 1895, Harriet Sophia, who d 1948, da of late Col
John Clark Kennedy, CB (see E Brownlow, colls, 1914 Edn):—
Christian Charlotte (1 Verandah Cottages, Cricket Green, Hartley Wintney, Hants), b 1904: m 1937, Ronald Peers
Williams, who d 1968, and has issue living, Richard Murray, b 1947: m 1980, Linda, da of Dennis Akehurst, of Denbury,
199 Loxley Rd, Stratford-upon-Avon, and has issue living, David b 1983, Benjamin b 1984, — Jennifer Mary, b 1940: m
1965, Colin Willmott, of 43 Princess Rd, NW1, and has issue living, Giles Benedict Paddington b 1967, Victoria b 1965,
— Susan b 1942, — Penelope Ann, b 1944: m 1971, Abraham Wax, of 219 E 69th St, New York 10021, NY, USA, and
has issue living, David Israel b 1980, Rebecca b 1981.

Grandchildren of late Gerald Otway Hay Murray, yr son of late Sir Herbert Harley Murray, KCB
(ante):—
Issue of late Herbert Frederick Murray, b 1906, d 1971: m 1942, Doris Mary Rowsel:—
Kathleen Elizabeth, b 1943: m 1969, Richard John May, Capt 2nd Bn LI, and has issue living, Amanda Jane, b 1969, —
Emma Louise May, b 1972.

Issue of late Douglas Gerald Murray, b 1907, d 1980: m 1940, Brenda, who d 1986, da of Earle R. Waight:—
Julian Charles, b 1946. Address – c/o Royal South Australian Yacht Sqdn, 161 Oliver Rogers Rd, Outer Harbour, S
Australia 5018.

Issue of late Stewart Hay Murray, b 1909, d 1988: m 1939, Freda Woodland (Folly House, Folly Lane, Lacock,
Wilts):—
John Stewart (Houndall Wood, Sparkwell, Plymouth), b 1940: m 1970, Alison, da of Humphrey Trembath, of Bath, and
has issue living, Charles Humphrey Stewart, b 1971, — Jennifer Mary Ellen, b 1974: m 1998, Mark Edgar John
Anderson, Lieut RN, of 4 Dunstone Cottages, Dunstone, Yealmpton, Devon. —— Peter Gerald Stewart (31 Priory Av,
W4), b 1944: m 1967, Jane, da of Alexander Wood, of Ashtead, and has issue living, Rupert Hay b 1969: m 19—, Chantal
Esin, da of Robert Dusting, of Brisbane, Queensland, — William Alexander, b 1972, — Sophie Elizabeth, b 19—, — Alice
Adelaide, b 1981. —— Geoffrey Charles Stewart (46 Rylett Rd, W12 9ST), b 1948: m 1983, C. Lynne, da of Stewart
Murray, of Ealing, and has issue living, James Stewart, b 1983, — George Andrew Stewart, b 1986.

Issue of late Arthur Frank Murray, b 1911, d 1997: m 1937, Ruby Joyce Hooper, who d 1996:—
Ann Jennifer, b 1939: m 1959, Neil Jarman, of 21 Middleton Rd, Ringwood, Hants BH24 1RN, and has issue living, Ian, b
1960: m 1989, Elizabeth Caroline Foster, and has issue living, Stephen Andrew b 1994, Sarah Jane b 1998, — Frances
Ann, b 1962: m 1989, Richard Allen, and has issue living, Jennifer Helen b 1992, — Rebecca, b 1965: m 1994, Jonathan
Percival, and has issue living, Alexander James b 1997.

Issue of late Keith Robert Murray, b 1912, d 1997: m 1941, Ellen Woodland, who d 1996:—
Andrew Keith (64 Shakespeare Rd, Eynsham, Oxford), b 1946: m 1969, Carole Yvonne Fear, and has issue living,
Nicholas Andrew, b 1971, — Sarah Anne b 1974: m 1992, Sean Donnelly, and has issue living, Charlotte Louise b 1993,
Chloë Siobhan b 1995. —— Joan Ursula, b 1945: m 1966, Peter Copeman Newell, of 42 Wroslyn Rd, Freeland, Witney,
Oxon OX8 8HH, and has issue living, Katherine Lara, b 1973.

Grandchildren of late Rev Frederick Auriol MURRAY-GOURLAY (who assumed the additonal surname of
Gourlay), eldest son of late Rev Frederick William Murray, yst son of Rt Rev George Murray, DD
Bishop of Rochester (ante):—

Issue of late (George) Ronald Auriol MURRAY-GOURLAY, *b* 1900, *d* 1961: *m* 1926, Phyllis, who *d* 1978, da of late
    Walter Langford Rowley, of Edgbaston, and Birlingham Grange, Worcs:—
†Brian Austin Walter MURRAY-GOURLAY *b* 1927; late RN: *m* 1st, 1953 (*m diss* 1962), Margaret, yr da of William Bryant, of
Elmsleigh, Cribbs Causeway, Glos; 2ndly, 1973, Patricia Mary (1 Old Brewery Court, High St, Chard, Som), yr da of
Daniel Eric Fewtrell, of Dudley, Worcs, and formerly wife of Charles Desmond Small, and *d* 1996, leaving issue (by 1st
m), Hugh William Auriol (Ivy Cottage, The Green, Poulshot, Devizes, Wilts), *b* 1960; *ed* St Edward's Sch, Oxford: *m*
1987, Fiona Joan, yst da of late Capt John Rumble, of 88 Wroughton Rd, SW11, and of Lymington, Hants, and has issue
living, Alice Auriol *b* 1992, Georgina Margaret *b* 1995. —— Auriol Mary, *b* 1933: *m* 1957, Capt Frederick Ernest
Herring, R Norfolk Regt, of Sentry Cottage, Sentry Rd, Swanage, Dorset, and has issue living, Jonathan James Auriol, *b*
1959: *m* 1995, Beverley Jane, elder da of Edward Gordon Peter Setter, of 45 Argyll Rd, Exeter, and has issue living,
Amanda Jane *b* 1997, — Christopher John Murray, *b* 1962: *m* 1998, Rowena Cabigas Garcia, da of Wilfredo Garcia, of
The Philippines, and has issue living, Monica Mary *b* 1998.

Grandchildren of late Rev Charles Hay Murray, 2nd son of late Rev Frederick William Murray (ante):—
    Issue of late Sir (Francis) Ralph Hay Murray, KCMG, CB, *b* 1908, *d* 1983: *m* 1935, Countess Mauricette
    Vladimira, who *d* 1996, only child of late Count Bernhard Kuenburg, of Payerbach, Austria:—
Ingram Bernard Hay, TD (23 Dunton Rd, Stewklcy, Leighton Buzzard, Beds LU7 0HY), *b* 1937; *ed* Bedford Sch, and St
Edmund Hall, Oxford; Lt-Col RE, TARO: *m* 1963, Juliet Anne Thackeray, da of late Capt J. M. T. Ritchie, and has issue
living, Alastair James Hay, *b* 1968: *m* 1995, Katherine Ann, da of John Perry, — Xenia Margaret Thackeray, *b* 1966, —
Francesca Helen Anne, *b* 1970. —— Nicholas Julyan Edward (The Old Vicarage, Aston Abbots, Aylesbury, Bucks), *b*
1939: *m* 1973, Caroline Anne, eldest da of Capt Alan McClintock, of Prospect House, Nenagh, co Tipperary, and has
issue living, Anstice Aileen Thérèse, *b* 1981. —— Simon Anthony (Eastern Hill House, Dunsford, Exeter, Devon EX6
7BW), *b* 1948: *m* 1975, Lesley-Ann, JP, da of Robert Freeman-Wright, of Larks Cottage, Treen, Cornwall, and has issue
living, Joshua Robert Darroch, *b* 1980, — Hannah Lisl, *b* 1982. —— Georgina Teresa, *b* 1942: *m* 1965, Roy Ashworth, of
55 Half Moon Lane, Dulwich, SE24, and has issue living, Simon, *b* 1966, — Jessica, *b* 1968.

Issue of late Stephen Umfreville Hay Murray, RASC and ABCA, actor (Stephen Murray), *b* 1912, *d* 1983: *m*
    1937, Joanna Alestha, da of John Joseph Moy Butterfield, of London:—
Amanda, *b* 1942; actress: *m* 1975, George Tarry, of The Old Stables, Roeheath, Chailey, Lewes, E Sussex BN8 4HR.

Granddaughter of late Rev Frederick William Murray (ante):—
    Issue of late Rev Maurice William Murray, *b* 1870, *d* 1943: *m* 1909, Eva Margaret, who *d* 1958, da of Charles
    Hubback Watson, formerly of Stone Castle, Greenhithe, Kent:—
Ursula Mary (89 High St, Tenterden, Kent), *b* 1919: *m* 1941, Alan A. White, late Maj Border Regt, who *d* 1993, and has
issue living, Christopher Douglas (11 Cornwall Mews South, Grenville Place, SW7 4RZ), *b* 1943: *m* 1987, Maria Eulalia
Pessoa, and has issue living, Douglas Alan Pessoa *b* 1987, — David Ian (2 Balliol Cottages, Wadhurst, E Sussex), *b*
(twin) 1943: *m* 1972, Margaret Ann Griffith, and has issue living, Jonathan Alan *b* 1974, Daniel Edmund *b* 1977.

Grandsons of late Capt Rupert Auriol Conant Murray, Seaforth Highlanders, 4th son of late Col Charles
    Edward Gostling Murray (infra):—
    Issue of late Col Anthony Ian Rupert Murray, OBE, Seaforth Highlanders, *b* 1914, *d* 1993: *m* 1944, Alexandra
    Elizabeth Barbara Patience, who *d* 1991, only da of late Lt-Col Douglas William Alexander Dalziel Mackenzie,
    CVO, DSO, of Farr, Inverness:—
John Rupert (Old Cardinham, Bodmin, Cornwall PL30 4ED), *b* 1945; *ed* Eton, and Sorbonne: *m* 1977, Valerie Margaret,
da of late Eric V. Sanders, and has issue living, Edward Ian, *b* 1977, — George John, *b* 1979. —— (Ian) James (Farr
Mains, Farr, Inverness-shire IV2 6XB), *b* 1947; *ed* Eton, and RMA Sandhurst; Lt-Col Queen's Own Highlanders: *m* 1976,
Christina Anne, yr da of late Arthur Carr, MC, and has issue living, Emma Juliette, *b* 1977, — Clare Patience Frances, *b*
1979, — Alice Christina, *b* 1983. —— Andrew Edward, *b* 1950; *ed* Gordonstoun, and Dijon Univ.

Grandsons of late Col Charles Edward Gostling Murray, yr son of late Rev Edward Murray, 4th son of
    late Rt Rev Lord George Murray, DD, Bishop of St David's (ante):—
    Issue of late Stracey Montagu Atholl Murray, *b* 1888, *d* 1970: *m* 1926, Irene Margaretta, who *d* 1972, yr da of
    Capt William W. Waring:—
Edward William Atholl (Highfield, Derby Rd, Haslemere, Surrey), *b* 1927: *m* 1st, 1959, Anne Oakeley, who *d* 1972, da of
late Maj Loraine Macgregor Kerr, MC (*see* Oakeley, Bt, 1967 Edn); 2ndly, 1974, Elizabeth Dawn, da of late H. D. Har-
man, MC, and has issue living (by 1st *m*), James Henry Atholl, *b* 1960, — Charlotte Melloney Loraine, *b* 1964.
—— Fane Robert Conant (Park House Farm, Baldersdale, Barnard Castle, co Durham), *b* 1929: *m* 1962, Margaret
Carsina, da of late Lt-Col Leslie George Gray-Cheape, MBE, JP, DL, of Carse Gray, Forfar, Angus, and has issue living,
Rupert Charles, *b* 1963, — Emma Jane, *b* 1965.

Branch from 3rd son of 3rd Duke

Grandson of late George Delmé-Murray, 3rd son of Vice-Adm James Arthur Murray, only son of Lord
    William Murray, 3rd son of 3rd Duke:—
    Issue of late Major George Arthur Delmé Murray, DSO, *b* 1879, *d* 1944: *m* 1906, Dorothea Emily Anne, who *d*
    1938, da of late T. Alexander Webb, of Waynwern, Monmouthshire:—
George Philip Alexander DELMÉ MURRAY, DSO, MBE, *b* 1921; Lt-Col KSLI; formerly Maj IA; Burma 1943-45 (wounded,
DSO); DSO 1945, MBE (Mil) 1966; *m* 1951, Alison Elizabeth, yr da of Col William John Beddows, MC, TD, JP, DL, of
Ackleton House, nr Wolverhampton, and has issue living, Caroline Alison, *b* 1953: *m* 1979, John William Howson, of The
Dingle, Ditton Priors, Bridgnorth, Shropshire, and has issue living, William George Frederick *b* 1982, Edward James
Philip *b* 1985, — Rosemary Janet, *b* 1956: *m* 1979, James Frederick Budgett, of Park Farm, Kirtlington, Oxon OX5 3JQ,
and has issue living, Charles George Arthur *b* 1981, Georgina Patricia Alison *b* 1985. *Residence* – Yew Tree Cottage,
Knowbury, Ludlow, Shropshire.

Branch from 4th son of 3rd Duke

Granddaughters of late Rev Richard Paget Murray, eldest son of Col Henry Murray, RA (infra):—

Issue of late Capt Henry James Stewart Murray, RE, b 1874, d 1942: m 1919, Maude Amelia (who d 1974, having m 2ndly, 1947, Thomas Rosser-Dummer, of Cape Town, S Africa), yst da of George Jonathan Mills, of Norwich:—

Margaret Dorothea, b 1926: m 1946, Stanley Alastair Miller, and has issue living, Pamela Ann (No 1 Shiraz, 26 Arum Rd, Bloubergrant, CP, S Africa), b 1949, — Sheila Frances, b 1950: m 1981, Anthony John Foxcroft, of Roodepoort, Transvaal, S Africa, and has issue living, Samantha Elizabeth b 1986, — Wendy Margaret, b 1954: m 1st, 1977 (m diss 1982), David Foxcroft; 2ndly, 1989, Mark Everingham, and has issue living (by 1st m), Neil Alastair b 1979, Debrin Eileen b 1981, (by 2nd m) Katherine b 1991. Residence – La Tremouille, 104 Third Ave, Bredell, Transvaal 1623. Address – PO Box 14204, Bredell, Transvaal, S Africa.

Issue of late Rev Athole Evelyn Murray, b 1881, d 1962: m 1917, Ellen Emily, who d 1960, da of Henry Frederic Tiarks:—

Anne (67B High St, Codford, nr Warminster, Wilts), b 1920; BMus Durham: m 1954, John Edward Page, who d 1964, and has issue living, Edward John Atholl, b 1956, — Henry Stewart Murray (twin), b 1956, — Thomas Patrick Murray, b 1960, — Susan Margaret, b 1955: m 1974 (m diss 1986), Julian Marc Piers Bryant, and has issue living, Polly Louise b 1976, Sophie Katherine b 1978, Emma Charlotte b 1980.

Granddaughters of late Maj Henry Francis Farquharson Murray, Black Watch, only son of late Lt-Col Henry Murray, 2nd son of late Col Henry Murray, RA, only son of Lt-Col Richard Murray, only son of Lord Henry Murray, 4th son of 3rd Duke:—

Issue of late Lt-Col Ian Henry Murray, MC, RHF, b 1916, d 1990: m 1940, Eleanor Fownes, who d 1983, da of late Rev Geoffrey Lionel Porcher, formerly R of Weston-super-Mare:—

Alison Fownes, b 1941: m 1970, Oliver William Wilkins, of Victoria House, St Keyne, Liskeard, Cornwall PL14 4SG, and has issue living, Geoffrey James Murray, b 1976, — Andrea Caroline Fownes, b 1975. ——— Jacqueline Dorothea Fownes (13 Wheatley Way, Chalfont St Peter, Bucks SL9 0JE), b 1942.

Grandchildren of late Rev Arthur Silver Murray, 6th son of late Col Henry Murray, RA (ante):—

Issue of late Arthur Evelyn Francis Murray, b 1888, d 1972: m 1927, Louise Isabelle, who d 1996, da of Lt-Col Addis Delacombe, DSO, of Shrewton Manor, nr Salisbury:—

James Stewart, b 1941; ed Stellenbosch Univ (BSc Agric): m 1979, Susan Janet Elizabeth, widow of Air Vice Marshal Thomas James Hanlon, CB, CBE, and da of Wyndham John Williams, of Great Oak, Gwent, and has issue living, Duncan William, b 1980, — Henry Stewart, b 1983, — Angus Iain, b 1983 (twin). Residence – Lewtrenchard Manor, Lewdown, nr Okehampton, Devon. ——— Jean Evelyn Louise (White Lodge, Startley, Chippenham, Wilts), b 1932; ed Stellenbosch Univ (BA): m 1959, Maj Jonathan Beresford Oliphant, 7th Duke of Edinburgh's Own Gurkha Rifles (ret), and has issue living, Angus Laurence (219a Stephendale Rd, SW6), b 1966: m 1995, Siobhan Alexandra Forbes, and has issue living, Frederick James b 1997, — Catriona Jane (21a Mountgrove Rd, N5), b 1960, — Janet Elizabeth, b 1963: m 1994, William Kerrison Gotch Hutchings, of Knoll House, Pen-y-Clawdd, Monmouth, and has issue living, Eleanor Charlotte Margaret b 1995, Octavia Frances Evelyn b 1999.

Issue of late Douglas Vivian Murray, b 1905, d 1976: m 1st, 1932 (m diss 1958), Isabel Mary Farquhar, da of Dr Andrew Grierson Fausset-Farquhar, of Bridgeton House, St Cyrus, Kincardineshire; 2ndly, 1958, Beryl Violet (No 6 Courtmead, South Stoke, Bath BA2 7EB), da of late Col John Henry Wybergh, Sherwood Foresters (ret), of Heath Brow, Ewshot, Farnham, Surrey:—

(By 2nd m) Hamish Douglas (Horse-shoe Cottage, Faulkland, Bath, Som BA3 5XA), b 1959; Merchant Navy: m 1993, Kate, only da of late Albert Edward Watson, of Combe Hay, Bath, and has issue living, Imogen Ann, b 1995. ——— Andrew Vivian (No 2 Cottages, Newbarns, Inverkeilor, Arbroath, Angus), b 1961; RM: m 1988, Anne Towns, and has issue living, James Andrew, b 1988, — Claire Beryl, b 1991. ——— Anne Beryl Charlotte de la Trémoïlle, b 1963: m 1988, George Coronis, and has issue living, Douglas Michael, b 1990, — Seymour Luke, b 1996, — Clementine Aspasia, b 1989, — Portia Marie Violet, b 1993.

Branch from 5th son of 3rd Duke

Grandchildren of late Charles Percy MURRAY-AYNSLEY (infra):—

Issue of late Francis Percy MURRAY-AYNSLEY, b 1924, d 1991: m 1950, Diana Deans (Wi Waka, Eketahuna, NZ), da of W. Gray Young, of Lowry Bay, Wellington, NZ:—

Charles William Percy MURRAY-AYNSLEY (Wi Waka, Eketahuna, NZ), b 1955. ——— Susan Jane, b 1951: m 1978, John Gerard Urry, of 135 Arcadia Rd, Arcadia, NSW 2159, Australia, and has issue living, Nicholas John, b 1982, — Alexandra Jane, b 1979, — Georgina Elizabeth, b (twin) 1982. ——— Bridget Anne, b 1952: m 1971, Richard William Hughes, of 36 Messines Rd, Karori, Wellington 5, NZ, and has issue living, Jason William, b 1971, — Emma Frances, b 1974: m 1995, Nicholas Alan Boettcher, of Wellington, NZ.

Granddaughter of late Hugh Percy MURRAY-AYNSLEY, son of John Murray-Aynsley, son of Very Rev Lord Charles Murray-Aynsley (who assumed by Royal Licence the additional surname of Aynsley), 5th son of 3rd Duke:—

Issue of late Charles Percy MURRAY-AYNSLEY, b 1862, d 1936: m 1st, 1911, Ina Winifred, who d 1917, da of late H. H. Prins, MD; 2ndly, 1921, Gladys, who d 1959, da of late Francis Turnor:—

(By 1st m) Elizabeth, b 1912: m 1935, John Duncan Simpson, and has issue living, Charles William, b 1936, — Duncan Murray, b 1938: m 1961, Judith Margaret Mary, da of H. Simmons, of Hawkes Bay, NZ, and has issue living, Michael Paul b 1961, Toby Duncan b 1963, — Patricia Mary, b 1940. Residence – Dalvey, Turakina, New Zealand.

(In special remainder to Dukedom)

Descendants of Lord Charles Murray (2nd son of 1st Marquess), who was cr Earl of Dunmore (see that title).

PREDECESSORS – **(1)** *Sir* JOHN MURRAY, PC, 12th feudal Baron of Tullibardine, was cr *Lord Murray of Tullibardine* (peerage of Scotland) 1604, and *Earl of Tullibardine* (peerage of Scotland) 1606; *d* 1613; *s* by his eldest son **(2)** WILLIAM, 2nd Earl; appointed Hereditary Sheriff of Perthshire 1600 for rescuing the King at Perth from the attempt of the Earl of Gowrie; he *m* Lady Dorothea Stewart, da of John, 5th and last Earl of Atholl, Charles I having on petition agreed to revive the Earldom of Atholl on the issue of the Countess of Tullibardine, the Earl by consent of the crown resigned his dignities to his brother Patrick (see * infra); *d* 1626; *s* by his son **(3)** JOHN, cr *Earl of Atholl* (peerage of Scotland) 1629: *d* 1642; *s* by his son **(4)** JOHN, KT, 2nd Earl, who on the death of his cousin James in 1670 became 5th Earl of Tullibardine; cr *Marquess of Atholl, Earl of Tullibardine, Viscount of Balquhidder,* and *Lord Murray, Balvany and Gask* (peerage of Scotland with remainder to heirs male of his body) 1676; *d* 1703; *s* by his eldest son **(5)** JOHN, KT, 2nd Marquess; cr (in his father's lifetime) *Earl of Tullibardine, Viscount Glenalmond, and Lord Murray* (peerage of Scotland for life) 1696, *Lord Murray, Balvenie and Gask, Viscount of Balwhidder, Glenalmond, and Glenlyon, Earl of Strathtay and Strathardle, Marquess of Tullibardine* and *Duke of Atholl* (peerage of Scotland) 1703, with special remainder failing heirs male of his body to those of his father; his eldest surviving son having joined the Earl of Mar 1715, was charged with high treason, and attainted by Parliament; *d* 1724; *s* by his 2nd son **(6)** JAMES, KT, 2nd Duke, upon whom the family honours were settled by Act of Parliament; on the death of the 10th Earl of Derby, he *s* through his grandmother to the *Barony of Strange* (peerage of England, cr 1628), and the Sovereignty of the Isle of Man; *d* 1764, when the Barony of Strange and the Sovereignty of the Isle of Man devolved upon his da Charlotte, and the Scotch honours reverted to his nephew (eldest son of Lord George Murray, 5th son of the 1st Duke) **(7)** JOHN, KT, 3rd Duke, who *m* his cousin Charlotte, Baroness Strange (ante); the Duke and Duchess disposed of their Sovereignty in the Isle of Man to the British Govt for £70,000; *d* 1774; *s* by his eldest son **(8)** JOHN KT, 4th Duke, cr *Baron Murray of Stanley* and *Earl Strange* (peerage of Great Britain) 1786, and *s* to English Barony of Strange 1805; he disposed of his remaining property and privileges in the Isle of Man to the crown for £409,000; *d* 1830; *s* by his son **(9)** JOHN, 5th Duke; *d* 1846; *s* by his nephew (eldest son of James, 1st *Baron Glenlyon* (peerage of United Kingdom, cr 1821), 2nd son of 4th Duke) **(10)** GEORGE AUGUSTUS FREDERICK JOHN, KT, 6th Duke, *b* 1814; *s* his father as 2nd *Baron Glenlyon* 1837: *m* 1839, Anne, VA, who *d* 1897, da of late Henry Home Drummond, of Blair Drummond, Perth; *d* 1864; *s* by his son **(11)** JOHN JAMES HUGH HENRY, KT, 7th Duke, *b* 1840; in 1865 inherited *Barony of Percy* (cr by writ 1722, peerage of Great Britain) and registered at Lyon Court his assumption of the surname of Stewart before his patronymic; was Lord-Lieut of Perthshire 1878-1917; in 1893 reverted to the original form of spelling the title ("Atholl" instead of "Atholc"): *m* 1863, Louisa, who *d* 1902, eldest da of Sir Thomas Moncrieffe, 7th Bt; *d* 1917; *s* by his eldest son **(12)** JOHN GEORGE, KT, GCVO, CB, DSO, TD, PC, 8th Duke *b* 1871; Lord-Lieut of Perthshire; appointed Lord High Commr to Gen Assembly of Ch of Scotland 1918, 1919, and 1920; was Lord Chamberlain of the Household 1921-2; Nile Expedition 1898 (DSO), South Africa 1899-1902, in command of two Regts of Scottish Horse (which he raised) with rank of Lieut-Col, European War 1914-19 in Gallipoli and Egypt, with Regts of Scottish Horse (which he raised), and Comdg a Scottish Horse Brig, and subsequently 8th and 10th Cyclist Brigs (CB); an ADC to HM 1920-31; sat as MP for Perthshire, W Div (C) 1910-17: *m* 1899, Katharine Marjory, DBE, LLD, DCL, MP, who *d* 1960, da of Sir James Henry Ramsay, 10th Bt, of Banff; *d* 1942; *s* by his brother **(13)** JAMES THOMAS, 9th Duke; *b* 1879; formerly Major Queen's Own Cameron Highlanders; *d* 1957, when the Barony of Strange (peerage of England cr 1628) fell into abeyance (*see* Bs Strange); the Barony of Percy, cr by writ 1722 (peerage of Great Britain) passed to the Duke of Northumberland, and the Earldom of Strange (peerage of Great Britain) 1786, and the Baronies of Murray of Stanley (peerage of Great Britain) 1786, and of Glenlyon (peerage of UK), 1821, became ext; *s* in his other peerages by his kinsman **(14)** GEORGE IAIN (son of late Lt-Col George Anthony Murray, OBE, RA, son of late Sir (George) Evelyn Pemberton Murray, KCB, grandson of late Rev George Edward Murray, grandson of Rt Rev Lord George Murray, DD, 2nd son of 3rd Duke), 10th Duke; *b* 1931; a Representative Peer for Scotland 1958-63; Chm RNLI 1979-89; *dunm* 1996; *s* by his kinsman **(15)** JOHN (only son of late Maj George Murray, 2nd son of late Rev Douglas Stuart Murray, 3rd son of late Rev George Edward Murray, grandson of Rt Rev Lord George Murray, DD, 2nd son of 3rd Duke), 11th Duke and present peer; also Marquess of Atholl, Marquess of Tullibardine, Earl of Atholl, Earl of Tullibardine, Earl of Strathtay and Strathardle, Viscount of Balwhidder, Glenalmond and Glenlyon, Lord Murray, Balvenie, and Gask, and Lord Murray of Tullibardine.

*(1) *Hon* PATRICK MURRAY was cr *Earl of Tullibardine* and *Lord Murray of Gask* (Peerage of Scotland) 1628, with remainder to his heirs male whatsoever, presumably with original precedence of 1606 and 1604 respectively, in consequences of resignation of that Earldom and Lordship by his brother, 2nd Earl of Tullibardine; *b* 15—: *m* Elizabeth, who *d* before 1656, da and co-heir of John Dent, of London, and widow of Francis Vere; *d* 1644; *s* by his son **(2)** JAMES, 4th Earl of Tullibardine, *b* 1617: *m* 1st, 1643, Lady Lilias Drummond, da of 2nd Earl of Perth; 2ndly, 1664, Lady Anne Murray, da of 1st Earl of Atholl (ante); 3rdly, 1667, Lilias (who *m* 2ndly, 16—, James Drummond, 4th Earl of Perth), da of Sir James Drummond of Machany; *d* 1670; *s* by his kinsman **(3)** JOHN Murray, 2nd Earl of Atholl (ante).

Atkins, surname of Barony of Colnbrook.

ATTENBOROUGH, BARON (Attenborough) (Life Baron 1993)

RICHARD SAMUEL ATTENBOROUGH, CBE, son of late Frederick Levi Attenborough; *b* 29 Aug 1923; *ed* Wyggeston Gram Sch for Boys, Leicester, and at RADA; Hon DLitt Leicester 1970, Kent 1981, and Sussex 1987, Hon DCL Newcastle 1974, Hon LLD Dickinson Penn 1983, Fellow BAFTA 1983, BFI 1992 and King's Coll, London 1993; served RAF 1943-46 as Flt Sgt Airgunner and Cameraman; Actor, Film Producer and Dir; appeared in more than fifty films inc *In Which We Serve* 1942, *Brighton Rock* 1948, *The Angry Silence* 1959, *The Great Escape* 1962, *Seance on a Wet Afternoon* 1963, *Guns at Batasi* 1964, *The Flight of the Phoenix* 1965, *The Sand Pebbles* 1966, *10 Rillington Place* 1970, *Jurassic Park* 1992, and *Miracle on 34th Street* 1994; Producer *Whistle Down The Wind* 1961,

The L-Shaped Room 1962, (and Dir) *Oh! What A Lovely War* 1969; Dir *Young Winston* 1972, *A Bridge Too Far* 1977, *Magic* 1978; Producer and Dir *Ghandi* 1980-81, *A Chorus Line* 1985, *Cry Freedom* 1987, *Chaplin* 1992, *Shadowlands* 1993; Chm BAFTA 1969-70 (Vice-Pres since 1971), RADA since 1970, Capital Radio 1972-92, Help A London Child since 1975, UK Trustees Waterford-Kamhlaba Sch, Swaziland since 1976, Duke of York's Theatre 1979-82, BFI 1982-92, Goldcrest Films and TV 1982-87, Channel 4 TV 1987-92; Dir Young Vic 1974-84, Gov National Film Sch 1970-81; Trustee Tate Gallery 1976-82, Tate Foundation since 1986, and Foundation for Sport and the Arts since 1991; Pro-Chancellor Sussex Univ since 1970; Freeman City of Leicester 1990; associated with many artistic and charitable fund-raising organisations; Cdr Ordre des Arts et des Lettres, Chevalier Légion d'Honneur, France; *cr* CBE (Civil) 1967, Knt 1976, and *Baron Attenborough*, of Richmond upon Thames in the London Borough of Richmond upon Thames (Life Baron) 1993: *m* 1945, Sheila Beryl Grant, JP (actress Sheila Sim), da of late Stuart Grant Sim, of Hove, Sussex, and has issue.
Clubs – Garrick, Beefsteak.

SON LIVING

Hon Michael John, *b* 1950; *ed* Westminster, and Sussex Univ (BA); Principal Associate Dir RSC: *m* 1st, 1971 (*m diss* 1976), Jane (actress as Jane Seymour), da of late Benjamin John Frankenberg, MRCS, LRCP, FRCOG, of Hillingdon, Middx; 2ndly, 1984, Karen Esther, yr da of late Sydney Victor Lewis, of SW1, and has issue living (by 2nd *m*), Thomas Frederick Richard, *b* 1986, — William Grant Oliver, *b* 1991. *Address* – c/o Royal Shakespeare Company, Barbican, EC2Y 8BQ.

DAUGHTERS LIVING

Hon Jane Mary, *b* 1955; *ed* Lady Eleanor Holles Sch and Sussex Univ; arts admin: *m* 1982, Michael Holland, 2nd son of George Holland, of Heathfield, Sussex, and has issue living, Samuel George William, *b* 1984, — Alice Jane, *b* 1987, — Lucy Elizabeth, *b* 1989.

Hon Charlotte Isabel, *b* 1959; *ed* Lady Eleanor Holles Sch, Bristol Univ, and RADA; actress: *m* 1993, Graham Sinclair, son of Edward Frederick Smith, of Hursley, Hants, and has issue living, Tobias George, *b* 1995, — Charles Edward, *b* 1997.

ATTLEE, EARL (Attlee) (Earl UK 1955)

JOHN RICHARD ATTLEE, 3rd Earl; *b* 3 Oct 1956; *s* 1991; *ed* Stowe; Major REME (TAVR); Opposition Whip and Spokesman for Defence, Transport and N Ireland since June 1997: *m* 1993, Celia Jane, yst da of Dexter Plummer, of Bishops Stortford, Herts.

Arms – Azure, on a chevron, or, between three hearts of the last winged argent, as many lions rampant sable. **Crest** – On a mount vert two lions rampant addorsed or. **Supporters** – On either side a Welsh terrier sejant proper.
Address – c/o House of Lords, SW1A 0PW.

SISTER LIVING

Lady Jane Elizabeth, *b* 1959.

AUNTS LIVING (*daughters of 1st Earl*)

Labour conquers all

(*Lady*) Janet Helen, *b* 1923; does not use courtesy title having taken American citizenship 1973: *m* 1947, Harold William Shipton, and has issue living, Ann Helen, *b* 1948: *m* 1st, 1969 (*m diss* 1994), Charles William Nandell; 2ndly, 1994, Michael George Zateslo, son of late George Zateslo, of Juno Beach, Florida, USA, and has issue living (by 1st *m*), one son and four das. *Residence* – 4 North Kingshighway, St Louis, MO 63108, USA.

Lady Felicity Ann, *b* 1925: *m* 1955, John Keith Harwood, OBE, who *d* 1989, and has issue living, Richard James Attlee, *b* 1963: *m* 1997, Miranda, da of Alan Kemp, of Wickham Bishops, Essex, and has issue living, Grace Elinor *b* 1998, — Penelope Ann, *b* 1956: *m* 1990, Richard Charles Anthony Robertson, only son of late A. H. Robertson, of Strasbourg, France, and has issue living, Joseph Keith *b* 1993, — Joanna Patricia, *b* 1958: *m* 1st, 1979 (*m diss* 1984), Philip Michael Darcey Pinniger, yst son of late T. Keith Pinniger; 2ndly, 1988, Martin Roundell Greene, only son of late George Roundell Greene, of Beaconsfield, Bucks, and has issue living (by 1st *m*), Thomas George *b* 1981, (by 2nd *m*) Charles George *b* 1988, — Sally Alexandra, *b* 1960: *m* 1985, Michael Paul Camps, elder son of David Camps, of Bosham, W Sussex, and has issue living Alice Beatrice *b* 1990, Elizabeth Ann *b* 1994. *Residence* – Appledore, 6 Hubert Day Close, Beaconsfield, Bucks HP9 1TL.

Lady Alison Elizabeth, *b* 1930: *m* 1952, Richard Lionel Lance Davis, and has issue living, Jennifer Alison, *b* 1953: *m* 1978, Christopher James Lochen, elder son of Harald Olaf Lochen, of Sevenoaks, Kent, — Tessa Meriel, *b* 1955: *m* 1976, Michael Robert Dormon, son of Jack Barrett Dormon, of Hadley Wood, Herts, and has issue living, Oliver Lance Barrett *b* 1983, Joshua Henry Edward *b* 1994, Felicity Meriel *b* 1981, Katherine Louise *b* 1987, Alexandra Mary *b* 1990, Sophie Jane *b* (twin) 1994, — Belinda Jane, *b* 1957: *m* 1979, Atholl Christopher Johnston, yr son of Christopher Kitchen Johnston, of Belfast. *Residence* – Westcott, Beacon Rise, Sevenoaks, Kent TN13 2NJ.

MOTHER LIVING

Anne Barbara, eldest da of late James Henderson, CBE, of Bath; *m* 1955 (*m diss* 1988), as his 1st wife, the 2nd Earl Attlee, who *d* 1991.

WIDOW LIVING OF SECOND EARL

MARGARET DEANE (*Margaret, Countess Attlee*), only da of late Geoffrey Gouriet, CBE, of Paper House, Hampton Court, Middx: *m* 1988, as his 2nd wife, the 2nd Earl Attlee, who *d* 1991.

PREDECESSORS – (1) *Rt Hon* CLEMENT RICHARD Attlee, KG, OM, CH, PC, 4th son of Henry Attlee, Solicitor, of Westcott, Putney, SW; *b* 1883; MP for Limehouse (*Lab*) 1922-50, and W Walthamstow 1950-55; Leader of Labour Party 1935-55, Dep Prime Min 1943-45, Prime Min 1945-51, and Leader of Opposition 1951-55; cr *Earl Attlee*, and *Viscount Prestwood*, of Walthamstow, co Essex (peerage of UK) 1955: *m* 1922, Violet Helen, who *d* 1964, yst da of Henry Edward Millar, of Heathdown, Hampstead, NW; *d* 1967; *s* by his only son (2) MARTIN RICHARD, 2nd Earl, *b* 1927; late Merchant Navy; Assist Public Relations Officer S Region British Rail: *m* 1st, 1955 (*m diss* 1988), Anne Barbara, eldest da of late James Henderson, CBE, of Bath; 2ndly, 1988, Margaret Deane, only da of late Geoffrey Gouriet, CBE, of Paper House, Hampton Court, Middx; *d* 1991; *s* by his only son (3) JOHN RICHARD, 3rd Earl and present peer; also Viscount Prestwood.

AUCKLAND, BARON (Eden) (Baron I 1789 and GB 1793)

ROBERT IAN BURNARD EDEN, 10th Baron; *b* 25 July 1962; *s* 1997; *ed* Blundells, and Dublin City Univ (BBS): *m* 1986, Geraldine, da of Charles Caroll, of Dublin, and has issue.

𝔄rms – Gules, on a chevron argent, between three garbs or, banded vert, as many escallops sable. 𝔈rest – A dexter arm embowed in armour proper, the hand grasping a garb or, the upper part of the arm encircled by an annulet gules. 𝔖upporters – *Dexter*, a horse guardant argent, charged on the shoulder with a fleur-de-lis or; *sinister*, a horse argent, charged on the shoulder with a tower or.
Residence – Tudor Rose House, 30 Links Rd, Ashtead, Surrey KT21 2HF.

DAUGHTER LIVING

Hon Alanna Margaret, *b* 1992.

SISTERS LIVING

Hon (Margaret) Fiona, *b* 1955: *m* 1979, Michael Shouler, yr son of John Richard Shouler, of Wollaton Nottingham, and has issue living, Benjamin, *b* 1987, — Elizabeth, *b* 1982,   Katherine, *b* 1983, — Abigail, *b* 1989.
Hon Rachel Audrey, *b* 1959: *m* 1981, Bramwell M. Paton, of 22 Penwortham Rd, Streatham, SW16 6RE, son of John B. Paton, of Maidenhead, Berks, and has issue living, Alexander Robert, *b* 1983, — Joe Bramwell, *b* 1986, — Charlotte Jane, *b* 1985.

If there be but prudence

UNCLE LIVING (*son of 8th Baron*)

Hon RONALD JOHN, *b* 5 March 1931; *ed* Glenalmond, and Ch Ch Oxford: *m* 1957, Rosemary Dorothy Marion, da of late Sir John (Frederick) Ellenborough Crowder (*see* B Petre, colls, 1980 Edn), and has issue living, Henry Vane, *b* 1958: *m* 1988, Alicia Claire, yr da of Christopher James Blois Needham (*see* E Kilmorey, colls), and has had issue, †Harry *b* and *d* 1989, Oliver *b* 1990, Roseanna *b* 1992, Annabel *b* 1995, — Edward John (Southview Cottages, Freefolk, Whitchurch, Hants RG28 2QS), *b* 1959; *ed* Glenalmond: *m* 1990, Victoria M. C., eldest da of late Maj D. P. T. Deshon, of Hartley Mauditt House, Alton, Hants, and has issue living, William *b* 1991, Charlotte *b* 1996. *Residence* – Cromlix, Dunblane, Perthshire FK15 9JT.

DAUGHTERS LIVING OF SEVENTH BARON

Hon Joan Edith, *b* 1920; JP of Essex: *m* 1st, 1941, Rev Alfred Lisinea Pond, V of Potten End and Nettleden, who *d* 1947; 2ndly, 1948, Rev Arthur Harrington Franklin, MBE, TD, who *d* 1996, and has issue living (by 1st *m*), Rosemary Jane, *b* 1942: *m* 1966, John Edward Rendall, of Sherborne Lodge, Adelaide Rd, Teddington, Middx, and has issue living, Angus Mark *b* 1975, Amelia Jane *b* 1969, Sophie Charlotte *b* 1971, — Sarah Joan, *b* 1945: *m* 1972, David Alexander Platts, of 6 Eddiscombe Rd, SW6 4UA, and has issue living, Charles Alexander *b* 1976, — (by 2nd *m*) Elizabeth, *b* 1949: *m* 1970, Dr Michael Peter Withycombe Lance, of 85 Ayer Rd, Williamsville, New York 14221, USA, and has issue living, Tom *b* 1979, Emma *b* 1977, — Caroline, *b* 1952: *m* 1979, Lt-Cdr Kenneth J. Leafe, RN, of Ivy House, Broughton, nr Huntingdon, Cambs, and has issue living, Alistair James Farquahar *b* 1984, Emily Jane *b* 1982, Charlotte Alice *b* 1993. *Residence* – Hea Corner, Mill Rd, Felsted, Dunmow, Essex CM6 3HQ.
Hon Elizabeth, *b* 1928: *m* 1954, Maj Frederic Edward Isdale (Robin) Mason, late Welsh Guards, Parachute Regt and 1st R Anglian Regt, who *d* 1995, and has issue living, Timothy Robin (The Anchorage, Bristol Hill, Shotley, Ipswich), *b* 1957, — Edward Geoffrey (Bridge Farm, Kettlebaston, nr Ipswich), *b* 1961: *m* 1987, Joanna Elizabeth, yr da of J. H. Beckly, of Manor Farm, Bowerchalke, Salisbury, Wilts, and has issue living, Hector Frederic Beckly *b* 1994, Georgina Sophie *b* 1991, — Catherine Elizabeth, *b* 1955: *m* 1989, Charles Robins Shelbourne, of Caswell, Walnut Hill, Surlingham, Norwich,

elder son of G. R. Shelbourne, of Langore, Cornwall, and has issue living, Freya Anna *b* 1992. *Residence* – Gable Cottage, Alton Hall Lane, Stutton, nr Ipswich.

DAUGHTER LIVING OF SIXTH BARON

Hon Susan Constance, *b* 1918: *m* 1st, 1942 (*m diss* 1956), Jose Diaz de Rivera; 2ndly, 1957, Guillermo Pakenham Bridges, OBE, who *d* 1980, sometime HM's Hon Vice-Consul at Rio Grande, Argentina, and has issue living (by 1st *m*), Jose Diaz, *b* 1944; has assumed the forenames names of Denis Pakenham in lieu of Jose Diaz, and the surname of Bridges in lieu of his patronymic.

WIDOW LIVING OF NINTH BARON

DOROTHY MARGARET, JP (*Dowager Baroness Auckland*), yr da of Henry Joseph Manser, of Beechwood, Friday Street, East-bourne, Sussex: *m* 1954, the 9th Baron Auckland, who *d* 1997. *Residence* – Tudor Rose House, 30 Links Rd, Ashtead, Surrey KT21 2HF.

COLLATERAL BRANCHES LIVING

Grandchildren of late William Annesley Eden, yr son of late Hon Robert Henley Shaw Eden, 4th son of 3rd Baron:—
Issue of late Edward Hildyard Eden, *b* 1898 *d* 1968: *m* 1942, Annie Sylvester who *d* 1981:—
Ernest John (RRH 2, Barrhead, Alberta, Canada), *b* 1943: *m* 1967, Allison Carolyne Wilde, and has issue living, Buckley John, *b* 1974, — Heidi Anne, *b* 1969: *m* 1991, Dereck Spence. —— William Edward (Box 13, Newbrook, Alberta, Canada), *b* 1945: *m* 1967, Maureen T. O'Hagan, and has issue living, Joseph Edward, *b* 1970.

Issue of late Maj George Henley Eden, TD, RA, *b* 1904; *d* 1982: *m* 1st, 1928 (*m diss* 1949), Avril Edith, who *d* 1966, da of late R. O. Simmons; 2ndly, 1951 (*m diss* 1974), Doreen Rosamund Averil Tobeason; 3rdly, 1974, Stella Frances, da of late W. H. Duplock:—
(By 1st *m*) Annesley Kathleen (Hill House, Hill Rd, Wangford, Beccles, Suffolk NR34 8AR), *b* 1928: *m* 1949, David George Warre Yeats Brown, who *d* 1990, and has issue living, Richard Andrew (63 Bell St, Fitzroy, Melbourne, Vic 3065, Australia), *b* 1955: *m* 1997, Mrs Gillian Winifred Graham (née Scott Mackenzie), — Caroline, *b* 1950, — Sarah Kate (*Hon Mrs Edward Noel*), *b* 1961: *m* 1997, Hon Edward Andrew Noel, yst son of 5th Earl of Gainsborough. —— Avril Jane, *b* 1930: *m* 1957, Peter Milne Horley, and has issue living, Rupert, *b* 1958. —— Sally Mabel Henley (*Lady Crofton*), *b* 1932: *m* 1st, 1964 (*m diss* 1988), Johann Leusink; 2ndly, 1998, as his 2nd wife, Sir Malby Sturges Crofton, 5th Bt (*cr* 1838), of 12 Caithness Rd, W14, and has issue living (by 1st *m*), Andrew Hamilton Henley EDEN, *b* 1968; has assumed the surname of Eden in lieu of his patronymic.

Issue of late Frederick Reeve Eden, *b* 1908, *d* 1989: *m* 1953, Beatrice Helena, da of late Montague Smith:—
Sarah Ursula, *b* 1954: *m* 1977, Michael Adam James Adams, of 91 The Common, Earlswood, Birmingham B94 5SJ, and has issue living, Ross Henley, *b* 1983, — Euan George, *b* 1986.

PREDECESSORS – (1) *Rt Hon* WILLIAM Eden, PC, 3rd son of Sir Robert Eden, 3rd Bt; *b* 1744; was Ch Sec for Ireland, and Ambassador to Versailles, Madrid, etc: *m* 1776, Eleanor, who *d* 1818, da of the Rt Hon Sir Gilbert Elliot, PC, 3rd Bt; cr *Baron Auckland* (peerage of Ireland) 1789, and *Baron Auckland* (peerage of Great Britain) 1793; *d* 1814; *s* by his eldest son (2) GEORGE, GCB, 2nd Baron; *b* 1784; Gov-Gen of India 1836-41; cr *Baron Eden* and *Earl of Auckland* (peerage of United Kingdom) 1839; *dsp* 1849, when the earldom became extinct; *s* in peerages of 1789 and 1793 by his brother (3) *Rt Rev* ROBERT JOHN, 3rd Baron, *b* 1799; was Lord Bishop of Sodor and Man 1847-54, and of Bath and Wells 1854-69: *m* 1825, Mary, who *d* 1872, eldest da of Francis Edward Hurt, of Alderwasley, co Derby; *d* 1870; *s* by his eldest son (4) WILLIAM GEORGE, 4th Baron, *b* 1829; in Diplo Ser 1847-61: *m* 1st, 1857, Lucy Walbanke, who *d* 1870, da of John Walbanke Childers, of Cantley, Yorkshire; 2ndly, 1872, Lady Mabel Emily Finch-Hatton, who *d* 1872, da of 11th Earl of Winchilsea; 3rdly, 1875, Edith, who *d* 1931, da of Sir William Eden, 6th Bt; *d* 1890; *s* by his eldest son (5) WILLIAM MORTON, 5th Baron, *b* 1859: *m* 1891, Sybil Constance, who *d* 1955, eldest da of late George Morland Hutton, CB, *d* 1917; *s* by his only surviving son (6) FREDERICK COLVIN GEORGE, 6th Baron; *b* 1895; Flight-Lieut RAF Vol Reserve: *m* 1st, 1917 (*m diss* 1925), Susan Livingstone, only da of Augustus Griffin Hartridge, of Jacksonville, Florida, USA; 2ndly, 1939, Constance Caroline, who *d* 1946, da of Benno Hart, of San Francisco, California, USA; *d* as a result of enemy action during European War 1941; *s* by his cousin (7) GEOFFREY MORTON, MBE (son of late Hon George Eden 3rd son of 4th Baron), 7th Baron; *b* 1891; Capt RASC (retired); European War 1914-18 (despatches twice, MBE), European War 1939-41: *m* 1919, Dorothy Ida, who *d* 1964, da of Rev Francis Clyde Harvey, V of Hailsham, and Preb of Chichester; *d* 1955; *s* by his brother (8) TERENCE, MC, 8th Baron; *b* 1892; Major Roy Armoured Corps (TA); European War 1914-18 as Capt Machine Gun Corps (despatches, MC with Bar); European War 1939-41: *m* 1925, Evelyn Vane (DRUMMOND OF CROMLIX), who *d* 1971, da of late Col Arthur William Henry Hay Drummond; *d* 1957; *s* by his eldest son (9) IAN GEORGE, 9th Baron, *b* 1926; served Royal Sigs 1945-48, and Sharpshooters (TA) 1948-53; Master Worshipful Co of Borderers 1967-68, Pres Inst of Insurance Consultants 1977-89, and Royal British Legion for Surrey; Knight (1st Class) White Rose (Finland) 1984: *m* 1954, Dorothy Margaret, yr da of Henry Joseph Manser, of Beechwood, Friday Street, Eastbourne, Sussex; *d* 1997; *s* by his only son (10) ROBERT IAN BURNARD, 10th Baron and present peer.

AUDLEY, BARONY OF (Souter) (Baron E 1312-13) (Abeyant 1997)

RICHARD MICHAEL THOMAS SOUTER, 25th Baron, *d* 1997, when the Barony fell into abeyance between his three daughters.

DAUGHTERS LIVING OF TWENTY-FIFTH BARON (*Co-heiresses to the Barony*)

Hon PATRICIA ANN, *b* 10 Aug 1946: *m* 1969, Carey Leigh Mackinnon, of Yew Trees, Bells Yew Green, Tunbridge Wells, Kent, and has issue living, Angus-Carey, *b* 1974, — Tamsin Sarah, *b* 1976.

Hon JENNIFER MICHELLE, *b* 23 May 1948: *m* 1978, Michael William Carrington, and has issue living, Jesse Michael, *b* 1978, — Jonah David, *b* 1980, — Holly Rosina, *b* 1975. *Residence* – 620 Vista Del Mar, Aptos, California 95003, USA.

Hon AMANDA ELIZABETH, *b* 5 May 1958; has issue living, Angelina, *b* 1996.

STEP-MOTHER LIVING OF TWENTY-THIRD BARON, AND OF ROSINA LOIS VERONICA, BARONESS AUDLEY

Lillie Kathleen, da of late George Ross, of co Monaghan: *m* 1st, 1923, as his 2nd wife, Thomas Touchet Tuchet-Jesson, who *d* 1939, having assumed by deed poll 1937 the additional surname of Tuchet; 2ndly, 1941, George Wynter Gray, who *d* 1945; 3rdly 19—.

WIDOW LIVING OF TWENTY-FIFTH BARON

(LILY) PAULINE (*Baroness Audley*), da of Dallas Louis Eskell: *m* 1941, the 25th Baron Audley, who *d* 1997. *Residence* – The Lodge, Uckfield Lane, Hever, Kent TN8 7LJ.

COLLATERAL BRANCH LIVING

Issue of late Charlotte Pamela Souter, sister of 25th Baron, *b* 1916, *d* 1990: *m* 1954, William Francis Harvey, who *d* 1995:—
John Richard HARVEY (Brambles, Perks Lane, Prestwood, Gt Missenden, Bucks), *b* 1959: *m* 1994, Alison Linda, da of Dennis William Upton, of 220 Osbourne Rd, Willesborough, Ashford, Kent. —— Katharine Mary, *b* 1955: *m* 1977, Prof Kenneth Ernest Evans, of 5 Harrington Lane, Pinhoe, Exeter, and has issue living, Colin Edward, *b* 1984, — Graham Malcolm, *b* 1992, — Janet Eileen, *b* 1987, — Marion Charlotte, *b* 1990. —— Amelia Anne, *b* 1957: *m* 1977, John Barry Hall, of Yewsfold Cottage, Main Rd, Dungworth, Sheffield S6 6HF, and has issue of living, Gregory John, *b* 1983, — Alastair William, *b* 1986, — Jennifer Elaine, *b* 1981.

PREDECESSORS – (1) NICHOLAS Audley, or Aldithley, of Heleigh, Staffordshire; *b* 1298; summoned to Parliament by writ as *Baron Audley* 1312-13: *m* 1312, Joan, only child of 1st Baron Martin, and widow of 6th Earl of Lincoln (cr circa 1147); *d* 1316; *s* by his son (2) JAMES, 2nd Baron; *b* 1313: *m* 1st, 13—, Joan, da of 1st Earl of March; 2ndly, 13—, Isabel, da of 5th Baron Strange of Knokin; *d* 1386; *s* by his son (3) NICHOLAS, 3rd Baron; *b* 13—; *m* 13—, Elizabeth, who *d* 1400, da of 1st Baron Beaumont; *d* 1391, when the Barony fell into abeyance between his sisters; this abeyance was terminated in 1405 in favour of his great-nephew (4) JOHN Tuchet (son of John Tuchet, son of Sir John Tuchet, by Joan, da of 2nd Baron), 4th Baron; *b* 1371: *m* 13—, Isabel, da of —; *d* 1408; *s* by his son (5) JAMES, 5th Baron; *b* 1398: *m* 1st, 14—, Margaret, da of 7th Baron de Ros; 2ndly, 14—, Eleanor, natural da of Thomas Holland, Earl of Kent, by Constance, da of Edmund of Langley, Duke of York, 5th son of King Edward III; *d* 1459; *s* by his son (6) JOHN, PC, 6th Baron; *b* 14—; sometime Lord Treasurer: *m* 14—, Anne, who *d* 1498, a of Sir Thomas Echingham, and widow of John Rogers, of Bryanston, Dorset; *d* 1490; *s* by his son (7) JAMES, KB, 7th Baron; *b* 1463: *m* 1st, 14—, Margaret, da of Sir Richard Dayrell; 2ndly, 14—, Joan, who *d* 1532, da of Fulk, Lord Fitz-Warine; joined Cornish insurrection and was beheaded 1497, when the title became forfeited; *s* by his son (8) JOHN, 8th Baron; *b* 1483; secured restoration of the title 1512: *m* 15—, Mary, da of John Griffin, of Braybrooke, Northants; *d c* 1557; *s* by his son (9) GEORGE, 9th Baron; *b* 15—: *m* 1st, 15—, Elizabeth, da of Sir Brian Tuke; 2ndly, 1560, Joan Platt; *d* 1560; *s* by his son (10) HENRY, 10th Baron; *b* 15—: *m* 15—, Elizabeth, da of Sir William Sneyd, of Bradwell, Staffordshire; *d* 1563; *s* by his son (11) George, 11th Baron; *b* 1551; sometime Gov of Utrecht, Netherlands, and of Kells, co Meath; cr *Baron Audley*, of Orier, co Armagh, and *Earl of Castlehaven*, co Cork (peerage of Ireland) 1616: *m* 1st, 15—, Lucy, only da of Sir James Mervyn; 2ndly, 1611, Elizabeth (who *m* 2ndly, 1619, Sir Piers Crosby), da of Sir Andrew Noel; *b* 1617; *s* by his son (12) MERVYN, 2nd Earl; *b* 1593: *m* 1st, 1619, Elizabeth, da of Benedict Barnham, of London; 2ndly, 1624, Anne, who *d* 1647, da of 5th Earl of Derby, and widow of 5th Baron Chandos of Sudeley; convicted of felony and beheaded 1631, when the English Barony became forfeited; *s* (in the Irish Earldom and Barony) by his son (13) JAMES, 3rd Earl; *b* 16—; cr *Baron Audley* of Hely (with precedence of the former Barony (cr 1312-13)) 1633, subsequently confirmed by Act of Parliament 1678: *m* 1st, 16—, Elizabeth, who *d* 1679, da of 5th Baron Chandos of Sudeley; 2ndly, 1679, Elizabeth, da of —; *d* 1684; *s* by his brother (14) MERVIN, 4th Earl; *b* 16—: *m* 16—, Mary, da of Sir Francis Fortescue, and widow of 10th Earl of Shrewsbury; *d* 1686; *s* by his son (15) JAMES, 5th Earl; *b* 16—: *m* 16—, Anne, who *d* 1733, da of Richard Pelson, of St George's-in-the-Fields, Middlesex; *d* 1700; *s* by his son (16) JAMES, 6th Earl; *b* 16—: *m* 1722, Elizabeth, who *d* 1743, da of 4th Baron Arundell of Wardour; *d* 1740; *s* by his son (17) JAMES, 7th Earl; *b* 1723; *d* 1769; *s* by his brother (18) JOHN, 8th Earl; *b* 17—: *m* 17—, Susanna, who *d* 1789, da of Henry Drax, of Ellerton Abbey, Yorkshire, and widow of William Cracraft; *d* 1777, when the Earldom of Castlehaven, and the Barony of Audley of Orier, became extinct, and the Barony of Audley of Hely devolved upon his kinsman (19) GEORGE (son of Philip Thicknesse, by Elizabeth, da of 5th Earl), 19th Baron; *b* 1758: assumed by R licence 1783, the additional surname of Tuchet after that of Thicknesse: *m* 1st, 1781, Elizabeth, who *d* 1785, da of Sir John Hussey Delaval, 1st Bt; 2ndly, 1792, Augusta Henrietta Catherina, who *d* 1844, yst da of the Rev André Boisdaune, and widow of Col Moorhouse; *d* 1818; *s* by his son (20) GEORGE JOHN, 20th Baron; *b* 1783: *m* 1816, Anne Jane, who *d* 1855, da of Vice-Adm Sir Ross Donnelly, KCB; *d* 1837; *s* by his son (21) GEORGE EDWARD, 21st Baron; *b* 1817: *m* 1st, 1857, Emily, who *d* 1860, da of Sir Thomas Livingstone Mitchell; 2ndly, 1868, Margaret Anne, who *d* 1888, widow of James William Smith; *d* 1872, when the Barony fell into abeyance between his two daughters, on the death of the yr of whom in 1937, the title devolved upon the elder (22) MARY, *b* 1858; *d* 1942; *s* by her kinsman (23) THOMAS PERCY HENRY TOUCHET *Tuchet-Jesson, MBE*, son of late Thomas Touchet Tuchet-Jesson, son of late Thomas Jesson, by Charlotte Anna, da of late Hon John Nicholas Thicknesse-Tuchet, son of 20th Baron, *b* 1913; Maj Worcestershire Regt; assumed by deed poll 1937, the additional surname of Tuchet: *m* 1st, 1952 (*m diss* 1958), June Isabel, MBE, who *d* 1977, da of Lt-Col Reginald Chaplin, and formerly wife of Rudolph Edgar de Trafford, OBE (later Sir Rudolph de Trafford, 5th Bt), who *d* 1983: 2ndly, 1962, Hon Sarah Millicent Hermione Spencer-Churchill, who *d* 1982, da of Rt Hon Sir Winston Leonard Spencer-Churchill, KG, OM, CH, TD, MP (D Marlborough, colls), and formerly wife of (i) Vic Oliver (né Victor von Samek), of Vienna; actor; and (ii) Antony Beauchamp, photographer; *d* 1963; *s* by his sister (24) ROSINA LOIS VERONICA, *b* 1911; assumed by deed poll 1937 additional surname of Tuchet; *m* 1943, John Archibald Joseph Macnamee; *d* 1973; *s* by her cousin (25) RICHARD MICHAEL THOMAS *Souter* (son of late Sir Charles Alexander Souter, KCIE, CSI, and his wife, late Charlotte Dorothy Jesson, aunt of 23rd Baron), 25th Baron, *b* 1914; Lieut RA: *m* 1941, Lily Pauline, da of Dallas Louis Eskell; *d* 1997, when the Barony fell into abeyance between his three daughters.

AVEBURY, BARON (Lubbock) (Baron UK 1900, Bt UK 1806)

The author makes the value

ERIC REGINALD LUBBOCK, 4th Baron, and 7th Baronet; *b* 29 Sept 1928; *s* 1971; *ed* Upper Canada Coll, Harrow and Balliol Coll, Oxford (BA); Lt Welsh Gds; MP for Orpington (*L*) 1962-70, and Liberal Ch Whip 1963-70: *m* 1st, 1953 (*m diss* 1983), Kina Maria, da of Count Joseph Henry O'Kelly de Gallagh, 2ndly, 1985, Lindsay Jean, da of Gordon Neil Stewart and of late Pamela Hansford Johnson (Lady Snow), writer, and has issue by 1st and 2nd *m*.

ᴀrms – Argent, on a mount vert a stork close ermine, on a chief gules three estoiles of the field. Crest – A stork, wings elevated ermine, supporting an antique shield azure, bordered or, charged with a lion rampant-guardant argent. Supporters – Two storks, wings elevated ermine, each gorged with a chain or, and pendent therefrom an escutcheon gules charged with an estoile argent.

SONS LIVING (*By 1st marriage*)

Hon LYULPH AMBROSE JONATHAN, *b* 15 June 1954: *m* 1977, Susan Carol MacDonald, and has issue living, Alexander Lyulph Robert, *b* 17 Jan 1985, — Vanessa Adelaide Felicity, *b* 1983. *Residence* – 53 Worlds End Lane, Orpington, Kent.
Hon Maurice Patrick Guy, *b* 1955: *m* 1982, Diana Rivia Tobin, and has issue living, Olivia Adelaide, *b* 1990.

(*By 2nd marriage*)

Hon John William Stewart, *b* 1985.

DAUGHTER LIVING (*By 1st marriage*)

Hon Victoria Sarah Maria, *b* 1959: *m* 1983, Alan Binney of 225 Evering Rd, E5 8AL, and has issue living, Archie, *b* 1983, — Alastair, *b* 1985.

SISTER LIVING

Alice Olivia Maureen (19 Beach Rd, Collaroy, NSW 2097, Aust), *b* 1926: *m* 1951 (*m diss* 1974), William Geoffrey Keighley, MLC, and has issue living, Francis Stephen, *b* 1953, — John William, *b* 1959, — Pamela Jane, *b* 1956, — Josephine Clare, *b* 1961.

DAUGHTER LIVING OF THIRD BARON

Hon Emma Rachel, *b* 1952: *m* 1977, Michael Charles Page, of Lepe House, Exbury, Southampton, and has issue living, Sophie Elizabeth, *b* 1982, — Natasha Diana, *b* 1984.

WIDOW LIVING OF THIRD BARON

BETTY GAY (*Betty, Baroness Avebury*), da of late William Oscar Ingham, and formerly wife of — Goode: *m* 1955, as his 3rd wife, the 3rd Baron Avebury, who *d* 1971.

COLLATERAL BRANCHES LIVING

(In remainder to Baronetcy only)

Grandchildren of late Maj Geoffrey Lubbock, 2nd son of late Henry James Lubbock, 2nd son of 3rd baronet:—
Issue of late David Miles Lubbock, *b* 1911, *d* 1992: *m* 1939, Hon Helen Anne Boyd Orr, who *d* 1994, da of 1st Baron Boyd Orr (ext):—
Geoffrey Orr (Marblehead, Mass, USA), *b* 1946; *ed* Eton, and Magdalene Coll, Camb: *m* 1981, Fiona Constance, yst da of Col Homer E. Harris, of Mass, USA, and has issue living, Francesca Eriminta Alessandra, *b* 1985, — Caroline Angelica, *b* 1989. —— John Nicholas Andrew (Harwood, Bonchester Bridge, Hawick, Roxburghshire), *b* 1948; *ed* Eton: *m* 1977, Jane Louisa, da of Col Charles King, OBE, of Hale House, Cuckington, Som, and has issue living, Hamish Percy Elliot, *b* 1977, — James Alexander George, *b* 1982, — Sammie Elizabeth Ursula, *b* 1980. —— Kenneth Miles Boyd, *b* 1950; *ed* Eton: *m* 1975, Moira Baillie, of Helensburgh, Dunbartonshire, and has issue living, John Angus Elliot, *b* 1981, — Julia Janet Roxanne, *b* 1989. —— Ann Patricia, *b* 1941: *m* 1972, John Daniel Gooch, VRD, of The Schoolhouse, Oathlaw, Forfar, Angus, and has issue *(see* Gooch, Bt, colls, *cr* 1866).

Grandsons of late Henry James Lubbock (ante):—
Issue of late Capt Rupert Egerton Lubbock, RN, *b* 1886, *ka* 1943: *m* 1912, Vera Isabel, who *d* 1962, da of G. R. Wingrove, of Shanghai:—
†Rupert James, *b* 1916; Capt 5th Batn Leics Regt (TA); 1939-45 War (prisoner): *m* 1954, Jeanette Patricia, who *d* 1976, only da of A. van Beugen Bik, of Broughton, Esher, Surrey, and *d* 1981, leaving issue, Rupert Guy Anthony, *b* 1956, — David Alexander, *b* 1958: *m* 1981 *(m diss* 1990), Nicky Francis, and has issue living, Rupert Henry James *b* 1984, Toby Anton Edward *b* 1988, — Fiona Jeannette Ariane, *b* 1960: *m* 1984 *(m diss* 1994), John Morley, and has issue living, Adam Bryan James *b* 1987, Zara Susan Jeannette *b* 1985. —— Christopher William Stuart, *b* 1920; *ed* Charterhouse, and at Brasenose Coll, Oxford; 1939-45 War as Lieut RNVR: *m* 1947, Hazel Gordon Chapman, and has issue living, (Rupert) James Gordon (139 Ramsden Rd, SW12), *b* 1948: *m* 1982, Miranda Jane, eldest da of Stephen St Clair McNeile, of Redvers, Hinderclay, Diss, Norfolk, and has issue living, Richard Christopher Sinclair *b* 1983, Sophie Caroline *b* 1986, — Victoria Margaret, *b* 1950: *m* 1977, Geoffrey Richard Edwards, of 44 St Barnabas Rd, Cambridge, and has issue living, Charles David Christopher *b* 1979, Guy William Humphrey *b* 1983, Chloë Elizabeth Rose *b* 1981. *Residence* – New Barn House, Great Horkesley, Essex.

Grandchildren of late Hugh Nevile Lubbock, 2nd son of late Sir Nevile Lubbock, KCMG, 3rd son of 3rd baronet:—
Issue of late Ralph Hugh Lubbock, MC, *b* 1891, *d* 1961: *m* 1st, 1914 *(m diss* 1922), Adelaide Margaret Constance, who *d* 1940, da of late Samuel Hynman Montgomerie *(see* E Eglinton, 1940 Edn); 2ndly, 1923, Louise, who *d* 1987, da of James Charles Vogel, of Durban:—
(By 2nd *m*) John Ralph (Cavalry and Guards' Club), *b* 1925; *ed* Malvern; 1939-45 War as Capt Coldm Gds: *m* 1st, 1950 *(m diss* 1957), Patricia Helen Winifred, da of late Brig-Gen Hon Roger Brand, CMG, DSO *(see* V Hampden, colls); 2ndly, 1957 *(m diss* 1961), Jane Marjorie, da of Maj Evelyn Ronald Moncrieff Fryer, MC, Gren Gds *(see* E Peel, colls, 1985 Edn); 3rdly, 1963 *(m diss* 1966), Helene Gladys Frances, only da of late Maj William Ferguson Thomson; 4thly, 1967 *(m diss* 1975), Anne Elizabeth, da of late Frank Colville Pearce; 5thly, 1980, Margaret Dorothy, da of Alan Pearce, and has had issue (by 1st *m*), †Hugh Roger, *b* 1951; *ed* Eton, and Churchill Coll, Camb (PhD, Fellow); *k* in a motor accident in Rio de Janeiro 1981, — (by 2nd *m*), Thomas Nevile, *b* 1957; journalist, — (by 4th *m*) Stephen Henry Ralph, *b* 1970; Lieut Coldstream Gds: *m* 1997, Melissa Caroline, eldest da of Ian Yates, of Steeple Bumpstead, Essex, — Elizabeth Serena, *b* 1967, — (by 5th *m*) Roderick John, *b* 1981, — Rosemary Margaret, *b* 1984. —— (By 1st *m*) Ursula Egidia, *b* 1919: *m* 1941, Peter Bellamy, of West End Cottage, Eythorne, nr Dover, and has issue living, Geraldine Anne, *b* 1943: *m* 1964, Michael Wyant, of Littlebourne, Canterbury, Kent.

Grandson of late Frederic Lubbock, 6th son of 3rd baronet:—
Issue of late Brig-Gen Guy Lubbock, CMG, DSO, *b* 1870, *d* 1956: *m* 1912, Lettice Isabella, who *d* 1980, da of Robert Harvey Mason, of Necton Hall, Swaffham:—
Joseph Guy, *b* 1915; *ed* Eton, and Trin Coll, Camb (BA 1937); late Capt RE (TA): *m* 1941, Ruth Cecilia, da of Major Quintin Edward Gurney, of Bawdeswell Hall, Norfolk, and has had issue, Jennifer LUBBOCK (2 Rectory Lane, Mulbarton, Norwich NR14 8AG), *b* 1942; has resumed her maiden name: *m* 1st, 1966 *(m diss* 1974), Marchese Ciaralli-Parenzi; 2ndly, 1975 *(m diss* 1990), Michael Wynne-Parker, and has issue living (by 1st *m*), Andrew *b* 1969, Elena *h* 1967: *m* 1994, Giuseppe Pizzini (and has issue living, Alexander *b* 1998, Vixen *b* 1994) (by 2nd *m*), Sarah Ruth Isabella *b* 1978, Fiona Alice Elizabeth *b* 1981, — Catherine, *b* 1944: *m* 1968, Stuart Jennings, MB, BS, of The Moat House, Church St, Blackmore, Essex, and has issue living, Mark *b* 1970: *m* 1993, Sarah Louise Hesketh (and has issue living, Eve *b* 1996), Samuel *b* 1971, — Lucinda, *b* 1948: *m* 1st, 1974, Thomas Henry Carew, who *d* 1978 *(see* B Carew); 2ndly, 1983, John Martin Harkness, of Hill House, Geldeston, Beccles, Suffolk, and *d* 1999, leaving issue (by 1st *m*) *(see* B Carew) (by 2nd *m*), Edward John *b* 1984, Alice Elizabeth *b* 1986. *Residence* – High Elms, Waldringfield, Suffolk; Carlton Club.

Grandchildren of late Cecil Lubbock, 2nd son of late Frederic Lubbock (ante):—
Issue of late Lt-Col Michael Ronald Lubbock, MBE, *b* 1906, *d* 1989: *m* 1st, 1929 *(m diss* 1956), Diana Beatrice, who *d* 1976, da of late Henry Ernest Crawley *(see* Crawley-Boevey, Bt, colls, 1976 Edn); 2ndly, 1957 *(m diss* 1975), Inga Olga, da of late Eugene Ivan de Rudez, of Zagreb, Jugoslavia, and widow of Col Geoffrey Moule; 3rdly, 1976, Elizabeth Christina (30/655 Richmond Rd, Ottawa, Ontario, Canada), da of John Sutherland, of Ontario, Canada:—
(By 1st *m*) Jeremy Michael (1390 Kelton Av, Apt 301, Los Angeles, Calif 90024, USA), *b* 1931: *m* 1st, 1956 *(m diss* 1959), Jill Caroline, da of late Eric Nicholls; 2ndly, 1963, Shelagh Mary, da of Richard Lang, MB, of Kenilworth, Cape, S Africa; 3rdly, 1974 *(m diss* 1987), his cousin, Philippa Harriet, da of Lt-Col Sir Charles Arthur Chadwyck-Healey, 4th Bt, OBE, TD, and has issue living, (by 2nd *m*) Justin Roger, *b* 1965, — (by 3rd *m*) Rowan Mark, *b* 1981, — Holly Andrée, *b* 1976. —— John David Peter (7 Warborough Rd, Shillingford, Oxon OX10 7SA), *b* 1945: *m* 1st, 1977 *(m diss* 1991), Eleanor Sloane; 2ndly, 1991, Christine Wilson Cairns, and has issue living (by 1st *m*), Daniel John, *b* 1978, — Patrick, *b* 1980, — (by 2nd *m*) Adam Thomas, *b* 1991, — Alexander Michael, *b* 1993. —— Judith Caroline Gurney, *b* 1934: *m* 1956, Martin Marriott, of Morris Farm House, Baverstock, nr Dinton, Salisbury, Wilts SP3 5EL, and has issue living, Charles John Phillip, *b* 1964, — Virginia Elizabeth, *b* 1958: *m* 1987, Patrick Francis O'Conor, of 51 Downs Park West, Westbury Park, Bristol, Avon, and has issue living, Harry Michael *b* 1993, Katherine Rosemary *b* 1989, Lucy Joanna *b* 1991, — Rebecca Jane, *b* 1960. —— Jessica Rose, *b* 1937: *m* 1961, Air Vice-Marshal

David Brook, CBE, RAF, and has issue living, William, *b* 1965, — Julie Nicola, *b* 1961. ——Joanna, *b* 1941: *m* 1965, Michael Coleridge Seligman, of Crown Lodge, Newnham, Basingstoke, Hants RG27 9AN, and has issue living, Simon Michael Hugo, *b* 1966, — Thomas Reginald James, *b* 1975, — Kate Sophie, *b* 1968. ——(By 2nd *m*) Inga Cecilia, *b* 1957.

Grandchildren of late Frederic Lubbock (ante):—
Issue of late Samuel Gurney Lubbock, *b* 1873, *d* 1958: *m* 1915, Irene Scharrer, who *d* 1971:—
Rachel Gurney, *b* 1920; actress (as Rachel Gurney): *m* 1945 (*m* annulled 1950), Denys Gravenor Rhodes (*see* B Plunket, 1968 Edn), and has issue living, Sharon Gurney, *b* 1950: *m* 1970, Simon Peter Gough, of Old Hall Farmhouse, Barney, Norfolk, son of Michael Gough, actor, and has issue living, Samuel Gurney *b* 1975, Dickon Graves *b* 1979, Tamasin Rachel *b* 1973, Daisy Diana *b* 1976.

Issue of late Roy Lubbock, *b* 1892, *d* 1985: *m* 1919, Yvonne, who *d* 1987, da of late Sydney George Vernham:—
†Jocelyn Roy, *b* 1920; *ed* Eton, and Peterhouse, Camb (BA 1941, MA 1945, MusB 1946): *m* 1st, 1948 (*m diss* 1976), Frances Georgette Coningsby, da of late Capt George Ashmead-Bartlett, and formerly wife of George Derek Pepys Whiteley; 2ndly, 1976, Adriana Camarca, of via Lucrino 41, Rome 00199, Italy, and *d* 1992, leaving issue (by 1st *m*), Annina Nicolette Mary, *b* 1949. —— †Hubert Timothy, *b* 1923; *ed* Eton, and Peterhouse, Camb (MA 1948): *m* 1958, Barbara Anne Caruth (Beech Mount, Bircham Rd, Reepham, Norwich), and *d* 1991, leaving issue, Catherine Fiona, *b* 1960: *m* 1986, Neil Atkinson, of Lytham St Ann's, Lancs, and has issue living, Samuel Lawrence *b* 1990, Rebecca Louise *b* 1987, Elizabeth Anne *b* 1994, — Lucinda Anne, *b* 1964: *m* 1987, Christopher Copage, of Bawburgh, Norfolk.

Issue of late Sir Alan Lubbock, *b* 1897, *d* 1990: *m* 1918, Helen Mary, who *d* 1987, only child of late John Bonham-Carter, of Adhurst St Mary, Petersfield, Hants:—
Roger John, DSC (Weatherall Lodge, Well Rd, NW3), *b* 1922; *ed* Eton, and King's Coll, Camb (MA); Lt-Cmdr RNR, served 1939-45 War (DSC): *m* 1955, Moyra, da of John Newton Mappin Fraser, and formerly wife of Maj Douglas Sutherland, and has issue living, Guy John, *b* 1957, — Paul Nigel, *b* 1960: *m* 1984, Lucinda, only da of late Ronald Simms, of St John's Wood, NW8, and has issue living, Oliver Guy *b* 1990, Jason Edward *b* 1994, Alice Helen *b* 1988. —— Martin (Brown's Copse, Heyshott, Midhurst, Sussex), *b* 1925; *ed* Eton, and King's Coll, Camb; Lieut RNVR; European War 1943-45: *m* 1957, Elizabeth, da of Ronald Marshall, of W Kirby, Yorks, and formerly wife of late Rt Hon Selwyn Lloyd, MP (later Baron Selwyn-Lloyd), and has issue living, Toby Mark *b* 1959: *m* 1990, Bridget A., da of Geoffrey Sleddon, of Deopham, Norfolk, — Robin Alan, *b* 1961.

PREDECESSORS – **(1)** JOHN Lubbock, *bapt* 1744, son of the Rev William Lubbock, R of Lammas, Norfolk; an opulent banker of the City of London; cr a *Baronet* 1806: *m* 1771, Elizabeth Christiana, da of Frederick Commerell, of Hanwell; *dsp* 1816; *s* by his nephew **(2)** JOHN WILLIAM, 2nd Bt; *b* 1773; an eminent banker: *m* 1799, Mary, da of James Entwistle, of Rusholme, Manchester; *d* 1840; *s* by his son **(3)** JOHN WILLIAM, 3rd Bt; *b* 1803; a banker, a distinguished scientific author, and Vice-Pres of R So: *m* 1833, Harriet, da of Lieut-Col George Hotham, of York; *d* 1865; *s* by his son **(4)** JOHN, PC, DCL, LLD, 4th Bt; *b* 1834; cr *Baron Avebury*, of Avebury, Wilts (peerage of United Kingdom) 1900; was head of London banking firm of Robarts, Lubbock, and Co, of 15 Lombard Street, EC (now amalgamated with Coutts and Co), Pres of So of Antiquaries, of R Microscopical So, of Royal So, of Central Asso of Bankers, and of London Chamber of Commerce; sat as MP for Maidstone (*L*) 1870-80, when he was defeated, and for the Univ of London 1880-1900: *m* 1st, 1856, Ellen Frances, who *d* 1879, da of late Rev Peter Horden, of Chorlton-cum-Hardy; 2ndly, 1884, Alice Augusta Laurentia, who *d* 1947, da of late Maj-Gen Augustus Henry Lane Fox-Pitt-Rivers; *d* 1913; *s* by his eldest son **(5)** JOHN BIRKBECK, 2nd Baron, *b* 1858; a Director of Coutts and Co, and of National Provincial and Union Bank of England; *d* 1929; *s* by his nephew **(6)** JOHN, son of late Capt Hon Harold Fox Pitt Lubbock (4th son of 1st Baron) *ka* 1918, 3rd Baron, *b* 1915: *m* 1st, 1938 (*m diss* 1945), Cicely Kathleen, da of late Dr N. A. K. Sparrow; 2ndly, 1946 (*m diss* 1955), Diana Mary Margaret Westcott, who *d* 1993, having *m* 2ndly, 1959 (*m diss* 1967), Charles Fletcher-Cooke, QC (later Sir Charles Fletcher-Cooke), da of late Capt Edward Westcott King, RA; 3rdly, 1955, Betty Gay, da of late William Oscar Ingham, and formerly wife of — Goode; *d* 1971; *s* by his cousin **(7)** ERIC REGINALD (only son of late Hon Maurice Fox Pitt Lubbock, yst son of 1st Baron), 4th Baron and present peer.

AVON, EARLDOM OF (Eden) (Extinct 1985)

WIDOW LIVING OF FIRST EARL

CLARISSA (*Countess of Avon*) (32 Bryanston Sq, W1), only da of late Maj John Strange Spencer-Churchill, DSO (*see* D Marlborough, colls): *m* 1952, as his 2nd wife, the 1st Earl of Avon, who *d* 1977.

AVONMORE, VISCOUNTCY OF (Yelverton) (Dormant 1910)

This peerage has been dormant since the death of the 6th Viscount in 1910. The senior male descendant in the male line of Hon Augustus Yelverton, 3rd son of 2nd Viscount, presumably is heir to the title.

COLLATERAL BRANCHES LIVING

Grandsons of late Barry Augustus Yelverton (infra):—
Issue of late Barry Goring Yelverton, *b* 1923, *d* 1985: *m* 1950, Frances Winifred (28 Karamu St, Wanganui, New Zealand) (who *m* 2ndly, 1988, Alan Mangan), da of late William Francis Battersby, of Glasgow Terr, Feilding, New Zealand:—
Ian Foster (13 Ward St, Kurnell, NSW 2231, Australia), *b* 1950; *ed* Palmerston North Boys High Sch: *m* 1985, Robyn Anne, da of late Aubrey Shearer, of 68 Tasman St, Kurnell, NSW, Australia, and has issue living, Lee Barry, *b* 1981, — Damian Talbot, *b* 1989, — Kursha May, *b* 1986. —— Avon Barry, *b* 1954: *m* 1983, Lisa Adele, da of William Johnstone, of Sandy Point, NSW, and has issue living, Nicholas William, *b* 1985, — Andrew Christion, *b* 1988, — Kimberley Rose, *b* 1990.

Grandchildren of late Foster Goring Yelverton (infra):—
Issue of late Barry Augustus Yelverton, *b* 1895, *d* 1960: *m* 1921, Margaret Ethel, who *d* 1970, da of John Thomas Green, of Christchurch, NZ:—
Michael Curran, *b* 1928: *m* 1949, Marjory Ruth, da of Arthur William Hall, of Gisborne, NZ, and has issue living, Kevin Barry (11 Armitage Court, Geelong, Victoria, Australia), *b* 1949; LTh, ThM, DMin: *m* 1972, Cherry Belle, da of Rodger Thomas Keane, of Tauranga, NZ, and has issue living, John Mark *b* 1980, Tracy Anne *b* 1978, — Mark Amour (23 Albert Mansions, Albert Bridge Rd, London SW11 4QB), *b* 1961: *m* 1985, Siobhan, da of Barry Hannan, of Christchurch, NZ, and has issue living, William George Hannan *b* 1998, Emily Alice Hannan *b* (twin) 1998, — Sharon Anne, *b* 1950: *m* 1969, John Charles Meehan, of 15 Corry Av, Napier, NZ, and has issue living, Clive Richard *b* 1970 (has issue living (by Pauline Mary Grant), Jordan Grant *b* 1994, Liam Charles *b* 1998), Richard John *b* 1978, Deborah Gaye *b* 1972. *Residence* – 19 Coverdale St, Napier, NZ.

Issue of late Hermann Stratton Yelverton, *b* 1896, *d* 1973: *m* 1923, Janetta Ferguson, who *d* 1963, da of John McEwen, of Palmerston North, NZ:—
Stratton Barton (28 Strowan Rd, Strowan, Christchurch 5, NZ), *b* 1926: *m* 1st, 1962 (*m diss* 1981), Jill Marion, da of late Colin Fergus Tennent-Brown; 2ndly, 1988, Margaret Alxiere, MBE, da of late Lionel Gordon Malcolm, and has issue living (by 1st *m*), John Stratton, *b* 1962: *m* 1995, Lorna Faye, da of Gordon Carey, — Andrew Colin, *b* 1964: *m* 1993, Karen Lee, da of L. M. Makings, — Bruce Avonmore, *b* 1966: *m* 1997, Bronwyn Terri, da of Neville Claughton, — Sally Janetta, *b* 1969. —— June Avonmore (3 Bretton Terrace, Hillcrest, Hamilton, NZ), *b* 1924: *m* 1944, Charles Herbert Dudley Scantlebury, who *d* 1997, and has issue living, Dudley Addison, *b* 1945: *m* 1976, Mary, da of Peter Shelling, of Nelson, NZ, and has issue living, Matthew James *b* 1982, Brent Dudley *b* 1985, Jodi Marie *b* 1977, — Gavin Stratton, *b* 1946: *m* 1971 (*m diss* 19—), Vivienne Mary, da of Wilfred John Westbury, of Adelaide, S Australia, and has issue living, Paul Gavin *b* 1974, Antoinette *b* 1973, — Gerald Avonmore (57 Kulim Av, Tauranga, NZ), *b* 1955: *m* 1982, Angela Therese, da of George Osca McMonogle, of Waihi, NZ, and has issue living, Giselle Sarah *b* 1983, — Mark Jonathan, *b* 1958: *m* 1978, Janet Anne, da of Douglas John Hemi, of Hamilton, NZ, and has issue living, Luke Douglas *b* 1980, John Mark *b* 1987, Benjamin Samuel *b* 1993, Samuel David *b* 1995, Anna Jane *b* 1982, Sarah Michelle *b* 1984, — Rosamond Karen Jane, *b* 1948: *m* 1973, Lester Thur Banfield, and has issue living, Rhys Ewen *b* 1977, Aaron Lester *b* 1978, — Jennifer Marie, *b* 1956: *m* 1st, 1988, Raúl Casto Pardo, of Madrid, Spain, who *d* 1995; 2ndly, 19—, Eduardo Almagro Muñoz, of Ceuta, Spain, and has issue living (by 1st *m*), Scfora *b* 1990, Raquel *b* 1992. —— Matel, *b* 1928: *m* 1951, Raymond William Watson, of 36B Goldie, St, St Heliers Bay, Auckland, NZ, and has issue living, Christopher Raymond (11 Arthur Crescent, Takapuna, Auckland 9, NZ), *b* 1952: *m* 1978, Penelope Winifred St John, da of Stanley Raymond Worth, Lt Cmdr RN (ret), of Takapuna, NZ, and has issue living, James Christopher Avonmore *b* 1991, Katherine Fiona Matel *b* 1981, Alexandra Penelope Alice *b* (twin) 1981, — Nicholas Stratton (1 Iona St, Black Rock, Melbourne, Australia), *b* 1956: *m* 1980, Nella, da of Antonio Colasacco, of Melbourne, and has issue living, Renée Clare *b* 1984, Elisa Laura *b* 1987, — Nigel Alexander (10 Woodward St, Taupo, NZ), *b* 1963.

Granddaughter of Foster Goring Yelverton, son of Augustus Barrymore Yelverton, son of Hon Augustus Yelverton, 3rd son of 2nd Viscount:—
Issue of late Macey Goring Yelverton, *b* 1898, *d* 1980: *m* 1922, Pauline, who *d* 1986, da of Jarrett Owen Allen, of Nottingham:—
Enid, *b* 1929: *m* 1952, Arthur Joseph Byrne, of Maple Lodge, Knightwood Av, Lyndhurst, Hants, and has issue living, Stephen Martin, *b* 1953, — Carol Patricia, *b* 1954: *m* 1975 (*m diss* 1980), Richard Mortimer, — Vanessa Elaine, *b* 1963: *m* 1st, 1990 (*m diss* 1994); 2ndly, 1997, Ian Teague, and has issue living (by 1st *m*), Regan Melissa BYRNE *b* 1991, (by 2nd *m*) Macey James Byrne *b* 1998.

AYLESFORD, EARL OF (Finch-Knightley) (Earl GB 1714)

To live with will unfettered

CHARLES IAN FINCH-KNIGHTLEY, 11th Earl; *b* 2 Nov 1918; *s* 1958; *ed* Oundle; Capt Black Watch, a JP for Warwickshire (Vice-Lieut 1964-74); Lord Lieut of W Midlands 1974-93; Warwickshire Co Commr for Boy Scouts Assocn 1949-74, since when Patron; a KStJ; a Member of Advisory Cttee World Wild Life Fund since 1970; 1939-45 War (wounded): *m* 1946, Margaret Rosemary, who *d* 1989, only da of late Maj Austin Arnold Tyer, MVO, TD, of Tunstall, Wadhurst, and has issue.

Arms – Argent, a chevron between three griffins passant sable. **Crest** – A griffin passant sable. **Supporters** – *Dexter*, a griffin sable, ducally gorged or; *sinister*, a lion or, ducally gorged azure.
Seat – Packington Old Hall, Meriden, Coventry, CV7 7HG.

SON LIVING

CHARLES HENEAGE (*Lord Guernsey*) (Packington Hall, Meriden, Coventry CV7 7HF) *b* 27 Mar 1947; *ed* Oundle, and Trin Coll, Camb: *m* 1971, Penelope Anstice, yr da of late Kenneth Arnold Gibbs Crawley, TD (*see* Crawley-Boevey, Bt, colls, 1968 Edn), and has issue:—

SON LIVING — *Hon* (Heneage) James Daniel, *b* 29 April 1985.
DAUGHTERS LIVING — *Hon* Rachel Louise, *b* 1974, — *Hon* Kate Pamela, *b* (twin) 1974, — *Hon* Alexandra Rosemary, *b* 1977, — *Hon* Laura Charlotte, *b* 1982.

DAUGHTERS LIVING

Lady Sarah Elizabeth Jane, *b* 1950: *m* 1974, Angus Nigel Garnet Maclean, 8th of Kilmoluaig, and has issue living, Angus Charles, *b* 1976, — Ian Andrew, *b* 1980.
Lady Clare Charlotte Rosemary, *b* 1959: *m* 1985, James Remington-Hobbs, son of C. Remington-Hobbs, of Normandy, France, and has issue living, Jonathan Ian, *b* 1986, — Alexander Charles, *b* 1988. *Residence* – Steyne House, Bembridge, Isle of Wight.

WIDOW LIVING OF SON OF TENTH EARL

Susan Mary, da of Capt Maj-Gen Geoffrey Woodroffe Palmer, CB, CBE: *m* 1948, Hon Anthony Heneage Finch-Knightley, who *d* 1995, and has issue (see colls, infra). *Residence* – Broomleigh, Huntingdon Rd, Brampton, Hunts.

COLLATERAL BRANCHES LIVING

Issue of late Capt Hon Anthony Heneage Finch-Knightley, yr son of 10th Earl, *b* 1920, *d* 1995: *m* 1948, Susan Mary (ante), da of late Maj-Gen Geoffrey Woodroffe Palmer, CB, CBE:—
Minette Jane FINCH-KNIGHTLEY, MBE (Broomleigh, Huntingdon Rd, Brampton, Hunts), *b* 1950; has resumed her maiden name; MBE (Civil) 1990: *m* 1983 (*m diss* 1986), Nicholas Redfern, and has issue living, James Heneage Stuart, *b* 1983. —— Joanna Elizabeth, *b* 1954: *m* 1987, (Christopher) Paul Anthony, of The Old Coach House, 45a Huntingdon Rd, Brampton, Hunts PE18 8PB, 2nd son of Kenneth Anthony of Oxted, Surrey, and has issue living, Harrington Arthur Heneage, *b* 1992, — Charles Henry, *b* 1996, — Charlotte Susan, *b* 1990.

Grandchildren of late Lt-Col Charles Arthur Wynne Finch, eldest son of late Charles Wynne Finch, MP, eldest son of late Charles Wynne Griffith-Wynne, eldest son of Hon Charles Finch, 2nd son of 3rd Earl:—
Issue of late Col John Charles Wynne Finch, CBE, MC, *b* 1891; *d* 1982: *m* 1914, Alice Mary Sybil, who *d* 1970, da of late Rt Rev Hon Edward Carr Glyn, DD (*see* B Wolverton, colls, 1970 Edn):—
Charles Edward Ifan (Cefnamwlch, Tudweiliog, Pwlheli, Caerns), *b* 1929; late Coldm Gds; Sheriff of Denbighshire: *m* 1967, Rosemary Dorothea, da of Lt-Col Clive Grantham Austin, JP, DL, RHA (*see* E Scarbrough, 1980 Edn), and has issue living, David Heneage, *b* 1970: *m* 1999, Henrietta Charlotte Anne, da of John Thring, of Lingfield, Surrey, — Mary Davina, *b* 1968, — Harriet Jane, *b* 1971. —— Elizabeth Jane Myfanwy, *b* 1918: *m* 1948, Alexander Dougal Malcolm, who *d* 1994, of Phillip's House, Much Marcle, Ledbury, and has issue living, James Ronald *b* 1951: *m* 1978, Sandra Lee, da of Charles Wilson Thomas, of Salt Lake City, Utah, USA, and has issue living, Peter Thomas *b* 1979, Lucy Caitlin *b* 1983, — Janet Mary, *b* 1949: *m* 1984, James Anthony Hume Greenfield, and has issue living, Harry Alexander Hume *b* 1985, Katharine Mary *b* 1987, — Elizabeth Anne, *b* 1960. —— Olwen Mary (The Bantam House, White Roding, Dunmow, Essex), *b* 1924: *m* 1944 (*m diss* 1969), Roger Wake (*see* Wake, Bt), who *d* 1988.

Granddaughter of late Edward Heneage Wynne Finch, yr son of late Charles Wynne Finch, MP (ante):—
Issue of late Arthur Wynne Finch, *b* 1878, *d* 1936: *m* 1926, Florence, who *d* 1978, da of late Very Rev Charles Thomas Ovenden, Dean of St Patrick's, Dublin:—
Anne, *b* 1927: *m* 1954 (*m diss* 1968), John Vavasour Earle, MB, BCh, and has issue living, Belinda Diana, *b* 1957, — Jenny Ruth, *b* 1959; has issue living (by Jonathan James Cornish, of Topcliffe House, Low Green, Gt Ayton, Middlesbrough), Sam Benjamin CORNISH *b* 1994, Chloe Nina CORNISH *b* 1992, — Polly Joan, *b* 1961. *Residence* – 9 Romany Rd, Gt Ayton, Stokesley, Middlesbrough, Yorks.

PREDECESSORS – (1) *Rt Hon* HENEAGE Finch, PC, 2nd son of the 1st Earl of Nottingham and brother of 6th Earl of Winchilsea; was Solicitor-Gen 1678-86, when he was removed by James II, and MP for Oxford Univ 1678-9, and for Guildford 1685; cr *Baron Guernsey* (peerage of Great Britain) 1702, and *Earl of Aylesford* (peerage of Great Britain) 1714; *d* 1719; *s* by his eldest son **(2)** HENEAGE, 2nd Earl; *d* 1757; *s* by his son **(3)** HENEAGE, 3rd Earl, LLD; MP for Leicestershire 1732-41, and for Maidstone 1754; *d* 1777; *s* by his eldest son **(4)** HENEAGE, 4th Earl, Lord Steward of the Household; *d* 1812; *s* by his eldest son **(5)** HENEAGE, 5th Earl; *d* 1859; *s* by his eldest son **(6)** HENEAGE, 6th Earl, *b* 24 Dec 1824; was MP for Warwickshire South 1849-57: *m* 1846, Jane Wightwick, who *d* 1911, da of John W. Knightley, of The Bury, Leamington Spa; *d* 10 Jan 1871; *s* by his eldest son **(7)** HENEAGE, 7th Earl; *b* 1849: *m* 1871, Edith, who *d* 1897, da of late Lieut-Col Peers Williams, MP, of Temple House, Great Marlow; *d* 1885; *s* by his brother **(8)** CHARLES WIGHTWICK, 8th Earl; established his claim to the Earldom and Barony July 1885; *b* 1851: *m* 1st, 1873, Hon Georgina Agnes, who *d* 1874, da of 3rd Baron Bagot; 2ndly, 1879, Ella Victoria, who *d* 1939, da of late John Ross, of Benena, and widow of Capt J. H. Linton, of Hemingford Abbots, Hunts; *d* 1924; *s* by his grandson **(9)** HENEAGE MICHAEL CHARLES, son of late Capt Heneage Greville, Lord Guernsey, Irish Gds (eldest son of 8th Earl), *ka* 1914, 9th Earl, *b* 1908; Capt RA (TA): *m* 1940, Pamela Elizabeth (DUGDALE), who *d* 1990, da of late Col Hon John Charles Coventry; *ka* 1940; *s* by his uncle **(10)** CHARLES DANIEL FINCH-KNIGHTLEY (2nd son of 8th Earl), 10th Earl; *b* 1886; assumed the additional surname of Knightley 1912; late Capt Rifle Brig (Prince Consort's Own): *m* 1918, Aileen Jane Chartres, who *d* 1977, da of late William McCormac Boyle; *d* 1958; *s* by his eldest son **(11)** CHARLES IAN, 11th Earl and present peer; also Baron Guernsey.

AYLESTONE, BARON (Bowden) (Life Baron 1967)

HERBERT WILLIAM BOWDEN, CH, CBE, PC, son of Herbert Henwood Bowden, of Cardiff; *b* 20 Jan 1905; *ed* Canton High Sch, Cardiff; Member of Leicester City Council 1938-45, PPS to Postmaster-Gen 1947-49, a Lord Commr of the Treasury 1950-51, Dep Ch Opposition Whip 1951-55, Ch Opposition Whip 1955-64, Lord Pres of Council and Leader of the House, 1964-66, Sec of State for Commonwealth Affairs 1966-67; Dep Speaker House of Lords 1983-93; Chm of IBA (formerly ITA) 1967-75 (Gold Medal Royal Television Soc 1975); MP for S Leicester (*Lab*) 1945-50, and for SW Leicester 1950-67: served World War II RAF 1940-45; cr CBE (Civil) 1953, PC 1962, *Baron Aylestone*, of Aylestone, City of Leicester (Life Baron) 1967, and CH 1975: *m* 1st, 1928, Louisa Grace, da of William Brown of Cardiff; 2ndly, 1993, Vicki Clayton, who *d* 1996, and has issue by 1st *m*.

Address – c/o House of Lords, SW1.

DAUGHTER LIVING (*By 1st marriage*)

Hon Brenda Dolores, *b* 1929: *m* 1951 (*m diss* 1983), John Leonard Billingham, and has issue.

AYLMER, BARON (Aylmer) (Baron I 1718, Bt I 1662)

MICHAEL ANTHONY AYLMER, 13th Baron, and 16th Baronet; *b* 27 March 1923; *s* 1982; *ed* Trin Hall, Camb (Exhibitioner, BA 1944, LLB 1945, MA 1948); admitted Solicitor 1948: *m* 1950, Countess Maddalena Sofia Maria Gabriella Cecilia Stefania Francesca, da of late Count Arbeno Maria Attems di Santa Croce, of Aiello del Friuli (*see* By Pirbright, 1954 Edn), and has issue.

Arms – Argent, a cross sable, between four Cornish choughs proper. **Crest –** Out of a ducal coronet or a Cornish chough rising proper. **Supporters –** Two marines vested with fur caps, brown jackets and blue breeches, their waists girt with hunting and dressed at all points like complete sailors, the *dexter* holding in his exterior hand a forestaff, and the *sinister* a deep-sea line, the plummet pendent, all proper.
Residence – Dovecote House, Jesse's Lane, Long Crendon, Bucks HP18 9AG.

SON LIVING

Hon (ANTHONY) JULIAN, *b* 10 Dec 1951; *ed* Westminster, and Trin Hall, Camb (MA); admitted Solicitor 1976: *m* 1990, Belinda Rosemary, only da of Maj Peter Henry Parker (*see* E Macclesfield, colls), and has issue living, Michael Henry, *b* 21 March 1991, — Rosemary Sofia, *b* 1993. *Residence –* 16 Edgarley Terrace, SW6.

DAUGHTER LIVING

Hon Gioia Francesca, *b* 1953: *m* 1991, Andrew Robert Shaw, and has issue living, Elizabeth Margaret Louise, *b* 1993, — Imogen Madeleine Rose, *b* 1995. *Residence* – 25 Littleworth Rd, Wheatley, Oxon OX33 1NW.

DAUGHTER LIVING OF TWELFTH BARON

Hon Ann Kathleen *b* 1941: *m* 1972, Gregor Byron Miller, of 6-1701 Chesterfield Av, N Vancouver, BC, Canada V7M 2N9, and has issue living, Jonathan Brown Aylmer, *b* 1975.

WIDOW LIVING OF TWELFTH BARON

ALTHEA (*Althea, Baroness Aylmer*), eldest da of late Lt-Col John Talbot, IA: *m* 1939, the 12th Baron Aylmer, who *d* 1982. *Residence* – 601-1159 Beach Drive, Victoria, BC V8S 2N2, Canada.

COLLATERAL BRANCHES LIVING

Grandchildren of late Col Frederick Arthur Aylmer, 2nd son of late Maj-Gen Henry Aylmer, grandson of Rev Hon John Aylmer, 4th son of 2nd Baron:—
Issue of late Capt Edward Arthur Aylmer, DSC, RN, *b* 1892, *d* 1974: *m* 1925, Gwladys Phoebe, who *d* 1968, da of late David Evans, of Brecon:—
Gerald Edward (St Peter's Coll, Oxford), *b* 1926; *ed* Winchester, and Balliol Coll, Oxford (BA); served in RN 1944-47; Master of St Peter's Coll, Oxford Univ 1978-91; Pres R Historical Soc 1984-88, Chm R Commn on Historical MSS 1989-94: *m* 1955, Ursula Adelaide, only da of late Maj Brian George Michael Frederick Nixon, and has two adopted children, Thomas Bartholomew, *b* 1962, — Emma Clare, *b* 1964. *Residences* – The Old Captains, Hereford Rd, Ledbury, Herefords HR8 2PX; 18 Albert St, Jericho, Oxford OX2 6AZ.

Issue of late Maj Henry Gerald Aylmer, *b* 1896, *d* 1978: *m* 1927, Nancy, who *d* 1991, da of late Drake Hollick, of The Old House, Sheering, Harlow, Essex:—
John Henry (Russetts, Orchard Close, Buckland Faringdon, Oxon SN7 8RJ), *b* 1936; *ed* Radley: *m* 1st, 1959 (*m diss* 1970), Venetia Mary, el da of Ian Thomson Henderson (*see* Verner, Bt, 1962 Edn); 2ndly, 1971, Mrs Margaret Gillian Elliot, da of John Musker, and has issue living (by 1st *m*), Miranda Jane, *b* 1962: *m* 1987, Simon M. A. Webster, of Mayfield House, Church Lane, Laughton, Lewes, E Sussex BN8 6AH, eldest son of P. M. Webster, of Blackstone Grange, Henfield, W Sussex, and has issue living, Sophie Charlotte Monica *b* 1990, Alexandra Jane *b* 1995, — Juliet Rose, *b* 1965: *m* 1997, Robert Taylor, of 2/15 Carpenter St, Brighton, Melbourne, Victoria 3186, Australia, eldest son of Brian Taylor, of Albany Creek, Queensland, and of Mrs Graeme Noble, of Tweed Heads, NSW. —— Rachel Moyra (*Lady Pauncefort-Duncombe*), *b* 1930: *m* 1951, Maj Sir Philip Digby Pauncefort-Duncombe, 4th Bt, Gren Gds (ret).

Issue of late Lt-Col Claud Aylmer, RA, *b* 1900, *d* 1952: *m* 1928, Margaret Victoria (who *m* 2ndly, 1954, Com John Rudolf Perronet Thompson, RN, who *d* 1965) (she *d* 1998, having resumed the surname of AYLMER by deed poll 1982), da of late Frank Hemming, of Franklyns, Great Waltham, Chelmsford:—
Richard Grenfell (Cromwell's House, 17 Mill Lane, Old Marston, Oxford OX3 0PY), *b* 1932; *ed* Wellington Coll, and London Univ (BA 1952); Capt (ret) RA: *m* 1964, Marelyn Joyce, only da of Sir James Miller, GBE, and has issue living, Christopher James, *b* 1966: *m* 1992, Cheryl Janice, yr da of Clive Perrett, of Stratford-upon-Avon, — Kenneth Malcolm (Flat 4, 11 Colville Terrace, W11 2BE), *b* 1970: *m* 1996, Illona R. M., yr da of S. C. Dixon, of Oxford.

PREDECESSORS – (1) MATTHEW Aylmer, 2nd son of Sir Christopher Aylmer, 1st Bt (*cr* 1662); was MP for Portsmouth 1695-8, and for Dover 1698-1718, Gov of Deal Castle 1710, Com-in-Ch of the Fleet 1709, Master of Greenwich Hospital, and Rear-Adm of Great Britain, etc; *cr Lord Aylmer, Baron of Balrath* (peerage of Ireland) 1718; *d* 1720; *s* by his son (2) HENRY, 2nd Baron; *d* 1754; *s* by his son (3) HENRY, 3rd Baron, Capt RN; *d* 1766; *s* by his son (4) HENRY, 4th Baron, who *s* his kinsman as 7th Bt 1780; *d* 1785; *s* by his son (5) MATTHEW, GCB, 5th Baron; a Gen in the Army and Col 18th Foot; assumed 1825 by R licence the additional surname of Whitworth; was Gov Gen of Canada 1830-35; *dsp* 1850; *s* by his brother (6) FREDERICK WILLIAM, KCB, 6th Baron; was an Adm; *d* 5 Mar 1858; *s* by his cousin (7) UDOLPHUS (el son of Capt John Athalmer Aylmer, RN, el son of Adm John Aylmer, son of the Rev Hon John Aylmer, 4th son of 2nd Baron), 7th Baron; *b* 1814: *m* 1841, Mary Eliza, who *d* 1881, da of Edward Journeaux, of Melbourne, Canada; *d* 1901; *s* by his el son (8) MATTHEW, 8th Baron; *b* 1842; Maj-Gen; sometime A-G and Inspector-Gen Canadian Forces: *m* 1875, Amy Gertrude, who *d* 1935, da of late Hon John Young, of Montreal; *d* 1923; *s* by his el son (9)JOHN FREDERICK WHITWORTH, 9th Baron; *b* 1880: *m* 1928, Gertrude Emma, who *d* 1977, da of late Colin Black, CE, of Vic, BC; *d* 1971; *s* by his brother (10) KENNETH ATHALMER, 10th Baron; *b* 1883: *m* 1924, Eleanor Katharine, who *d* 1970, da of late John Francis Rogers, of Swanington, Norfolk; *d* 1974; *s* by his brother (11) BASIL UDOLPHUS, 11th Baron; *b* 1886; 1914-18 War as Capt Canadian Forces: *m* 1st, 1916, Bessie Irving, ARRC, who *d* 1956, da of late Joseph Watson, of Westward Park, Cumberland; 2ndly, 1960, Helen Cooper, da of late Thomas Hogg, of Toronto, and widow of Frederick Gordon Riseborough; *d* 1977; *s* by his kinsman (12) HUGH YATES (only son of Arthur Lovell Aylmer, grandson of Maj Gen Harry Aylmer, 2nd son of Adm John Aylmer, ante), 12th Baron, *b* 1907: *m* 1939, Althea, eldest da of Lt-Col John Talbot, IA; *d* 1982; *s* by his cousin (13) MICHAEL ANTHONY (only son of Christopher Aylmer, grandson of Maj-Gen Harry Aylmer, ante), 13th Baron and present peer.

BACH, BARON (Bach) (Life Baron 1998)

WILLIAM STEPHEN GOULDEN BACH, son of Stephen Craine Goulden Bach, CBE; *b* 25 Dec 1946; *ed* Westminster, and New Coll, Oxford (BA); Bar, Middle Temple, 1972; Memb Leicester City Council (Lab) 1976-87, and Harborough District Council since 1995; Mayor of Lutterworth 1993-94; Treasurer, Leics West Constituency Labour Party 1974-87; Chm Harborough District Labour Party 1989-95; Chm Northants and Blaby Euro Constitutency Labour Party since 1992; Memb Labour Party Economic Commn since 1998, and Labour Party Nat Policy Forum since 1998; *cr Baron Bach*, of Lutterworth, co Leics (Life Baron) 1998: *m* 1st, ...; 2ndly, 1984, Caroline Jones, and has issue, (by 1st *m*), one son and one da, (by 2nd *m*), one da.
Address – c/o House of Lords, SW1A 0PW.

BADEN-POWELL, BARON (Baden-Powell) (Baron UK 1929, Bt UK 1922)
(Name and Title pronounced "Bayden Poell")

ROBERT CRAUSE BADEN-POWELL, 3rd Baron, and 3rd Baronet; *b* 15 Oct 1936; *s* 1962; *ed* Bryanston; RN 1955-57; Ch Scouts Commr Scout Assocn 1963-82, since when Vice-Pres Scout Assocn, World Scout Foundation 1978-88; Pres Camping & Caravan Club since 1993: *m* 1963, Patience Hélène Mary, CBE, da of Maj Douglas Myers Batty, of Zimbabwe.

𝕬rms – Quarterly: 1st and 4th, per fesse or and argent, a lion rampant guardant gules between two tilting spears erect proper, *Powell*; 2nd and 3rd, argent, a lion rampant proper, on the head a crown vallary or between four crosses patée gules and as many fleur-de-lis azure alternately, *Baden*. 𝕮rest – 1st, a lion passant or, in the paw, broken tilting spear in bend proper, pendent therefrom by a riband gules and escutcheon resting on a wreath sable, charged with a pheon, or, *Powell*; 2nd, out of a crown vallary or a demi-lion rampant gules, on the head a like crown, charged on the shoulder with a cross patée argent, and supporting with the paws a sword erect proper, pommel and hilt gold, *Baden*. 𝕾upporters – *Dexter*, an officer of 13th/18th Hussars in full dress, his sword drawn over his shoulder proper; *sinister*, a boy scout holding a staff also proper.
Residence – Weston Farmhouse, The Street, Albury, Surrey GU5 9AY.

BROTHER LIVING

Hon DAVID MICHAEL (18 Kalang Rd, Camberwell, Victoria 3124, Australia), *b* 11 Dec 1940; *ed* Pierrepont House; a Member of Mercers' Co, and a Freeman of City of London: *m* 1966, Joan Phillips, da of late Horace William Berryman, of Camberwell, Melbourne, Australia, and has issue living, David Robert, *b* 6 Jan 1971, — Alexander Peter, *b* 1973, — Myles Warrington, *b* 1975.

SISTER LIVING

Hon Wendy Dorothy Lillian (4/16 Allambee Av, Camberwell, Victoria 3124, Australia), *b* 1944; *ed* Clare Park, Hants, St Cyprians, S Africa, and the Sorbonne; Patron Baden-Powell Guild of GB.

AUNT LIVING (*Daughter of 1st Baron*)

Hon Betty St. Clair, CBE, *b* 1917; CBE (Civil) 1997: *m* 1936, Gervas Charles Robert Clay, late Provincial Commr, Colonial Service, N Rhodesia, and has issue living, Robin Baden, *b* 1939; *ed* Michaelhouse, Natal, and Loughborough Coll: *m* 1971, Susan, el da of late Rev Charles de Candole, of Witchampton Rectory, Dorset, and has issue living, Toby *b* 1973, Annarella *b* 1975, — Nigel Gerard Arden, *b* 1943; *ed* Peterhouse, and Rhodesia Univ: *m* 1969, Elaine, da of late Albert Hughes, of Bournemouth, and has issue living, Gerard *b* 1970: *m* 1997, Allison, da of Geoffrey Dickie, of Redbank, Queensland, Australia, Adam *b* 1975, Olivia *b* 1973: *m* 1998, Ian Walton, son of Arthur Walton, of Beerwah, Queensland, Australia, — Crispin David Powell, *b* 1944; *ed* Peterhouse, St David's Coll, Lampeter, and Univ of Wales: *m* 1973, Ortrud Wiese, of Windhoek, S-W Africa, and has issue living, Eric *b* 1974, — Gillian Ella St Clair, *b* 1937: *m* 1968, William Leigh Strudwick Clay, and has issue living, Rawley *b* 1971, Daphne *b* 1970: *m* 1995, Ewart Schofield, son of

David Ewart Schofield, of Purton, Wilts (and has issue living, Bertram *b* 1997). *Residence* – Ford Lodge, Wiveliscombe, Taunton, Som.

PREDECESSORS – The Powell family were resident in Suffolk until David Powell (*d* 1784) became a merchant in London. He *m* 1723, Susanna, da and heiress of Edward Thistlethwaite, Registrar to the Bishop of Salisbury, by Susanna, da and heiress of Andrew Baden, of Salisbury. His eldest son, David Powell, Treasurer St Luke's Hosp, London, *b* 1725: *m* 1761, Laetitia, who *d* 1801, da and heiress of John Clark, of St Botolph's, Bishopsgate, and *d* 1810, leaving issue, a yr son, Baden Powell, of Tunbridge Wells, Kent; High Sheriff Kent 1831; *b* 1767: *m* 1795, Hester, who *d* 1848, da of James Powell, of Clapton, and *d* 1844, leaving issue, three sons and two das. His eldest son, Rev Prof Baden Powell, was Vicar of Plumstead, Kent, and Savilian Prof of Geometry to Oxford Univ, FRGS, etc; *b* 1796, married thrice, and *d* 1860, leaving issue (by his 3rd wife, *m* 1846, Henrietta Grace, who *d* 1914, da of Vice-Adm W. H. Smyth), a 5th surv son **(1)** *Lieut-Gen Sir* ROBERT STEPHENSON SMYTH Baden-Powell, OM, GCMG, GCVO, KCB (assumed addl surname of Baden by Public Notice 1869, and the arms of Baden by Royal Licence 1902), *b* 1857; Lt-Gen late 13th Hussars; Afghanistan 1880-81, Zululand 1888, Ashanti Expedition 1895-96, in command of Native Contingent, which he raised, Matabeleland 1896, S Africa 1898-1900, raising Rhodesian Frontier Force, then Comdg troops defending Mafeking during memorable siege of that place; founded Boy Scouts Organization 1908, and Girl Guides Organization 1910; became Ch Scout of the World 1920; *cr* a *Baronet* 1922, and *Baron Baden-Powell*, of Gilwell, Essex (peerage of United Kingdom) 1929: *m* 1912, Olave St Clair, GBE, (World Ch Guide 1930-77), who *d* 1977, da of late Harold Soames, of Parkstone, Dorset; *d* 1941; *s* by his only son **(2)** ARTHUR ROBERT PETER, 2nd Baron, *b* 1913; in British S Africa Police 1934-37, and Native Affairs Dept, S Rhodesia 1937-45: *m* 1936, Carine, who *d* 1993, da of late Clement Hamilton Crause Boardman, of Johannesburg; *d* 1962; *s* by his el son **(3)** ROBERT CRAUSE, 3rd Baron and present peer.

BAGOT, BARON (Bagot) (Baron GB 1780, Bt E 1627)

HENEAGE CHARLES BAGOT, 9th Baron, and 14th Baronet; *b* 11 June 1914; *s* 1979; *ed* Harrow; late Maj 6th Queen Elizabeth's Own Gurkha Rifles: *m* 1939, Muriel Patricia, da of late Maxwell James Moore Boyle, of Tullyvin House, co Cavan, and Lareen House, co Leitrim, and has issue.

𝕬rms – Ermine, two chevronels azure. Crest – Out of a ducal coronet of five leaves or, a goat's head argent, armed gold. Supporters – Two goats argent, armed and bearded or. *Residences* – Tyn-y-Mynydd, nr Llithfaen, Gwynedd, N Wales LL53 6PD; 16 Barclay Rd, SW6.

SON LIVING

Hon (CHARLES HUGH) SHAUN (16 Barclay Rd, SW6), *b* 23 Feb 1944; *ed* Abbotsholme: *m* 1986, Mrs Sally A. Stone, da of D. G. Blunden, of Farnham, Surrey, and has issue living, Grace Lorina Kitty, *b* 1993.

DAUGHTER LIVING

Hon Caroline Patricia, *b* 1942: *m* 1st, 1962 (*m diss* 1985), Hugh Alexander James Cameron-Rose, who *d* 1993; 2ndly, 1991 (*m diss* 1997), Peter Garner-Clarke, and has issue living (by 1st *m*), Hugh Charles, *b* 1962, — Georgina Louise Stella, *b* 1968: *m* 1996, Simon J. D. Toogood, son of Michael Toogood, of Morcombelake, Dorset.

Possessing antiquity

ADOPTED DAUGHTER LIVING OF SIXTH BARON

Caryl Rosemary, *b* 1960. *Residence* – Blithfield Hall, Rugeley, Staffs WS15 3NL.

WIDOW LIVING OF SIXTH BARON

NANCY CONSTANCE BAGOT, da of late Francis Aldborough Spicer, of Sydney; resumed the surname of Bagot by deed poll 1971: *m* 1st, 1940, as his 2nd wife, the 6th Baron Bagot, who *d* 1961; 2ndly, 1965 (*m diss* 1972), George Kenneth Whitehead. *Residence* – Blithfield Hall, Rugeley, Staffs WS15 3NL.

COLLATERAL BRANCHES LIVING

Grandchildren of late Mrs Henry Melville Gaskell (infra):—
Issue of late Thomas Josceline Gaskell, *b* 1906, *d* 1982: *m* 1st, 1941 (*m diss* 1948), Barbara, who *d* 1998, da of late Percy Hague Jowett, CBE, Principal Royal Coll of Art, London; 2ndly, 1953, Daphne Joy, who *d* 1988, da of late E. C. E. Hemsted:—
(By 1st *m*) Josceline Rose (18 Ashchurch Park, Villas, W12), *b* 1943; *ed* Cranborne Chase, and Guildhall Sch of Music; cookery writer and broadcaster: *m* 1967, David Dimbleby, and has issue living, Henry Melville, *b* 1970, — Liza Lucasta, *b* 1968, — Kate, *b* 1973. ⸺ (By 2nd *m*) Benjamin Henry (38 Guildford Rd, SW8 2BU), *b* 1955; *ed* Bryanston, and New Coll, Oxford: *m* 1991, Hon Jessica Anne Mills, da of 4th Baron Hillingdon, and has issue living, Walter, *b* 1994, — Ruby, *b* 1992. ⸺ Joanna Mary, *b* 1957.

Grandson of late Lt-Col Josceline FitzRoy Bagot, MP, of Levens Hall, Westmorland, who was nominated a *baronet* Jan 1913, but *d* March 1913 before the patent passed the Great Seal, grandson of late Rt Hon Sir Charles Bagot, GCB, 2nd son of 1st Baron:—
Issue of late Dorothy Bagot, *b* 1886, *d* 1974: *m* 1905, Henry Melville Gaskell, JP, who *d* 1954:—
Oliver Robin BAGOT, TD (Levens Brow, Kendal, Cumbria), *b* 1914; *ed* Eton, and Trin Coll, Camb; JP Westmorland 1948, DL Cumbria 1967; Lieut 4th Bn Border Regt (TA); FRICS; 1939-45 War (prisoner); assumed by royal licence 1936 the surname of Bagot in lieu of his patronymic, and the arms of Bagot quarterly with those of Gaskell: *m* 1938, Annette Dorothy, da of Paymaster-Cdr F. R. Stephens, RN, of 2 Clarence Terr, Leamington Spa, and has issue living, Charles Henry (Levens Hall, Kendal, Cumbria), *b* 1946; FRICS; JP Cumbria 1991: *m* 1975, Susan Elizabeth, da of Ian Alexander Ross, of Aros Cottage, Gullane, E Lothian, and has issue living, Richard Alexander *b* 1981, Harry Josceline *b* 1983, Jessica Mary *b* 1977, Laura Elizabeth *b* 1979, — Priscilla, *b* 1939: *m* 1st, 1960 (*m diss* 1964), (Edward) Humphry Tyrrell Wakefield (afterwards 2nd Bt); 2ndly, 1967, Erik George Sebastian Smith, of Tithe Barn, Forde Abbey, Chard, Somerset TA20 4HN, and has issue living (by 2nd *m*), Miranda *b* 1968, Susanna *b* 1970, — Elizabeth Dorothy, *b* 1947: *m* 1967, Mark Roper, of Forde Abbey, Chard, Somerset (*see* E Lovelace, colls, 1985 Edn), and has issue living, Katherine Alice *b* 1968, Victoria Jane *b* 1970, Lucinda *b* 1972, — Lucinda Rose Mary (Cook House, Levens, Kendal, Cumbria), *b* 1950: *m* 1969 (*m diss* 1993), Michael Victor Sclater, and has issue living, Josceline Mark *b* 1972, Henry Rupert *b* 1976.

Grandchildren of late Cecil Villiers Bagot (infra):—
Issue of late Lt-Col Charles Frederic Villiers Bagot, OBE, *b* 1912, *d* 1986: *m* 1939, Lucy Violet Kathleen de la Cloche, who *d* 1972, da of late Harold Marriott, of 60 Great Cumberland Pl, WI; 2ndly, 1975, Mrs Anne Elisabeth Dyke (DRABBLE) (The Red House, Brockdish, Diss, Norfolk), elder da of Arthur Calver, of Docking, Norfolk, and formerly wife of James Drabble, of Bow Brickhill, Bucks:—
(By 1st *m*) Richard Charles Villiers, *b* 1941. —— Julian William D'Arcy, *b* 1943. —— Harriet Anne Elizabeth, *b* 1951: *m* 1978, Julian Patrick Ashley Greene, only son of late Col J. S. Greene, OBE, MC, of Grange House, Long Melford, Suffolk, and has issue living, John Charles Henry, *b* 1985, — Lucy Diana Sylvia, *b* 1989. *Residence* – 27 Brockwell Park Gdns, SE24 9BJ. —— Patricia Mary, *b* 1953: *m* 1984, Terence B. A. Maguire. *Residence* – 87 Lea St, Kidderminster, W Midlands DY10 1SN.

Granddaughter of late Rev Frederic Bagot, DCL, 8th son of late Rt Rev Hon Richard Bagot, DD, Bishop of Bath and Wells, 3rd son of 1st Baron:—
Issue of late Cecil Villiers Bagot, *b* 1865, *d* 1940: *m* 1903, Ethel, who *d* 1944, yr da of late Jesse Garratt, of Wateringbury, Kent:—
Milicent Jessie Eleanor, CBE, *b* 1907; *ed* Lady Margaret Hall, Oxford (MA); formerly attached to Min of Defence; MBE (Civil) 1949; CBE (Civil) 1967. *Residence* – 5 Putney Heath Lane, SW15 3JG.

In remainder to baronetcy only

Grandsons of late Rev John Greville Chester, 4th son of late Lt-Col Charles Montagu Chester, 2nd son of late Rev William Chester, 3rd son of Charles Bagot-Chester (who assumed the surname of Chester in lieu of his patronymic by act of parliament 1755), 2nd son of 5th baronet:—
Issue of late Maj Anthony James Bagot Chester, MC, *b* 1892, *d* 1952: *m* 1924, Gladys Mabel, who *d* 1974, eldest da of late Rev Frederick Charles Stamer (*see* Stamer, Bt, colls, 1972-73 Edn):—
John Greville Bagot, MC, *b* 1925; 1939-45 War as Maj Coldstream Gds (MC); DL Bucks. *Residence* – The Old Rectory, N Crawley, Newport Pagnell, Bucks.

Issue of late Henry Montagu Bagot Chester, *b* 1896, *d* 1969: *m* 1924, Alyce Amy Maude Tranchell, who *d* 1934:—
Hugh Malcolm, *b* 1929: *m* 1972, Mrs Pauline Lillian Butt, da of late Thomas Nicholls, of Bishopsworth, Bristol, and formerly wife of Lionel Butt. *Residence* – 76 Aylesbury Crescent, Bedminster Down, Bristol BS3 5NN.

Grandchildren of late Reginald Warham Antony St Leger (*d* 1952), of New Dorp Beach, Staten Is, NY, yst son of late John St Leger (who assumed the surname of St Leger in lieu of his patronymic 1863), eldest son of late Lt-Gen John Chester, 4th son of Charles Bagot-Chester (ante):—
Issue of late Gaspard Douglas Anthony St Leger, *b* 1890, *d* 1974: *m* 1914, Ivy, who *d* 1945, da of late William S. West:—
Ivy, *b* 1915: *m* 1939, Charles P. Leonard, of 23 Twin Hills Rd, Poughkeepsie, NY 12603, USA, and has issue living, Ann Carol, *b* 1940: *m* 1962, William Denno, and has issue living, Nicole *b* 1963, Lori *b* 1967. —— Virginia May, *b* 1922: *m* 1964, David Hunter, of 3616 Lone Wolf Trail, St Augustine, Florida 32086, USA.

Issue of late Geoffrey Bayard St Leger, *b* 1892, *d* 1961: *m* 1919, Grace Elizabeth, who *d* 1934, da of late Robert Baylor:—
Claire Amy, *b* 1928: *m* 1952, H. Charles McNally, and has issue living, Robert Charles, *b* 1953: *m* 1977, Jacqueline Port, and has issue living, Austin Charles *b* 1986, Ashley Jacqueline *b* 1983, Caroline Taylor *b* 1987, — Jan Barbara *b* 1955, — Jane Hoefer, *b* 1959: *m* 1982, Douglas E. Brandt, of 354 S Maple Av, Basking Ridge, NJ 07920, USA.

Issue of late Roderic Craufurd St Leger, *b* 1894, *d* 1949: *m* 1916, Cora Irene, who *d* 1932, da of late Giles Curtis Gass:—
(Roderic) Harry (25 Dirks Terrace, Highland, NY 12528, USA), *b* 1919: *m* 1950, Doris J., da of late Eugene Geary, and has had issue, †Thomas E., *b* and *d* 1951, — Nancy J., *b* 1953: *m* 1st, 1978 (*m diss* 1990), Roy L. Post; 2ndly, 1997, Leonard C. Ritchie, of 380, Plutarch Rd, Highland, NY 12528, USA. —— Beverly Cora (25 Dirks Terrace, Highland, NY 12528, USA), *b* 1917: *m* 1955, George Howard Hurd, who *d* 1987.

Granddaughter of late Col Heneage Charles Bagot-Chester, yr son of late Lt-Gen John Chester (ante):—
Issue of late Capt Hugh Augustus Bagot-Chester, *b* 1876, *d* 1938: *m* 1st, 1895 (*m diss* 1908), Margaret Kathleen

Julia, who *d* 1951, only da of late Col Richard E. Oakes, BSC; 2ndly, 1913, Clotilde Mary Hamilton, who *d* 1964, da of late Hon Arthur Henry Browne (*see* B Kilmaine, colls, 1963 Edn):—
(By 2nd *m*) Peggy Mary Clotilde, *b* 1914: *m* 1st, 1937 (*m diss* 1946), Wallace Stuart Finlayson, actor and stage dir (as Wallace Douglas), who *d* 1990; 2ndly, 1947 (*m diss* 1954), Edward Ralph Harley, CBE. *Residence* – 16 Swan Court, Flood St, Chelsea, SW3.

PREDECESSORS – This family descends from Bagod who held Bramshall, Staffs from Robert de Stafford at the time of the Domesday Survey in 1086. The Staffords, Dukes of Buckingham, descended from the same male stock, Hervey Bagot changing his name to Stafford in late 12th century as his mother was heiress of that family. (1) Sir HERVEY Bagot, Sheriff of Staffordshire 1626, a staunch loyalist; *cr* a Bt 1627; *d* 1660; *s* by his el son (2) Sir EDWARD, 2nd Bt, MP for Stafford in the Restoration Parliament; *d* 1673; *s* by his son (3) Sir WALTER, 3rd Bt, MP for Staffordshire in seven Parliaments; *d* 1704; *s* by his son (4) Sir EDWARD, 4th Bt, MP for co Stafford; *d* 1712; *s* by his son (5) Sir WALTER WAGSTAFFE, LLD, 5th Bt, successively MP for Newcastle-under-Lyme, Staffordshire, and Oxford Univ; *d* 1768; *s* by his el son (6) Sir WILLIAM, 6th Bt, MP for co Stafford 1754-80; *cr* Baron Bagot (peerage of Great Britain) 1780; *d* 1798; *s* by his el son (7) WILLIAM, LLD, 2nd Baron; distinguished for scientific attainments: *m* 1st, 1799, Hon Emily FitzRoy, who *d* 1800, da of 1st Baron Southampton; 2ndly, 1807, Lady Louisa Legge, who *d* 1816, da of 3rd Earl of Dartmouth, *d* 1856; *s* by his el son (8) WILLIAM, 3rd Baron; sat as MP for Denbighshire (C) 1835-52: *m* 1851, Hon Lucia Caroline Elizabeth Agar-Ellis, el da of 1st Baron Dover, and sister of 3rd Viscount Clifden; *d* 1887; *s* by his el son (9) WILLIAM, 4th Baron, *b* 1857; a Gentleman Usher of Privy Chamber to HM Queen Victoria 1885-7, and a Lord-in-Waiting to HM Queen Victoria 1896-1901: *m* 1903, Lilian Marie, who *d* 1958, da of late Henry May, of Maryland, USA; *d* 1932; *s* by his cousin (10) GERALD WILLIAM (son of late Vice-Adm Henry Bagot, son of 3rd son of 1st Baron), 5th Baron, *b* 1866; *d* 1946; *s* by his cousin (11) CARYL ERNEST (son of late Rev Lewis Richard Charles Bagot, son of late Rev Charles Walter Bagot, 4th son of late Rt Rev the Hon Richard Bagot, DD, Bishop of Bath and Wells, 3rd son of 1st Baron), 6th Baron; *b* 1877; Lieut Irish Guards; European War 1914-19: *m* 1st, 1911, Margaret, who *d* 1937, da of James McMenemy; 2ndly, 1940, Nancy Constance, da of late Francis Aldborough Spicer of Sydney, NSW; *d* 1961; *s* by his cousin (12) HARRY ERIC (son of late Charles Frederick Heneage Bagot, 4th son of late Rev Charles Walter Bagot (ante)) 7th Baron; *b* 1894: *m* 1st, 1951, Kathleen Elizabeth Saddler, who *d* 1972, widow of Noel Murray Puckle, of Melbourne, Aust; 2ndly, 1972, Mary Frances, who *d* 1997, da of late Lt-Col George Frederick Hibbert, late 7th Fus, and widow of Lt-Col (Albert) Claud Hewitt, late R Fus; *d* 1973; *s* by his brother (13) REGINALD WALTER, 8th Baron; *b* 1887: *m* 1st, 1922 (*m diss* 1934), Winifred Gwyneth Bowen; 2ndly, 1934, Millicent Brenda, who *d* 1980, only da of late Henry White Bowden, of Mobwell House, Gt Missenden, Bucks; *d* 1979; *s* by his half-brother (14) HENEAGE CHARLES, 9th Baron and present peer.

BAGRI, BARON (Bagri) (Life Baron 1997)

RAJ KUMAR BAGRI, CBE, son of late Sohan Lal Bagri; *b* 24 Aug 1930; Chm The Metdist Group since 1970; Memb Board of The London Metal Exchange since 1987, Vice-Chm 1990-93, since when Chm; Chm of Trustees The Rajiv Gandhi (UK) Foundation; Memb Governing Body of SOAS, and Advisory Cttee Princes Youth Business Trust; *cr* CBE 1994, and *Baron Bagri*, of Regent's Park in the City of Westminster (Life Baron) 1997: *m* 1954, Usha, da of late Ganesh Prashad Maheshwary, and has issue.

Arms – Per pale sable and gules six sword blades three bendsinisterwise issuant from the dexter three bendwise issuant from the sinister their points crossing in saltire or. **Crest** – A demi-kalasa pot sable garnished or a lotus flower also or. **Supporters** – Two elephants the dexter gules with housings on the back and forehead garnished tasselled and fringed or the sinister sable with like housings gules garnished tasselled and fringed or each semy of cinquefoils tusked and unguled argent the tusks banded or and holding aloft with the trunk a lotus flower slipped or.
Residence – Ionic Villa, Outer Circle, Regent's Park, NW1 4HB. *Club* – MCC.

SON LIVING

Hon Apurv, *b* 1959: *m* 1982, Alka, da of Nirmal Kumar Rakyan, and has issue living, Aditi (da), *b* 1985, — Amisha (da), *b* 1988.

DAUGHTER LIVING

Hon Amita, *b* 1956: *m* 1975, Chandrakant Birla, son of G. P. Birla, of New Delhi, India, and has issue living, Avani (da), *b* 1985, — Avanti (da), *b* 1988.

Bailey, family name of Baron Glanusk.

Baillie, family name of Baron Burton.

BAILLIEU, BARON (Baillieu) (Baron UK 1953)

Without changing

JAMES WILLIAM LATHAM BAILLIEU, 3rd Baron; *b* 16 Nov 1950; *s* 1973; *ed* Radley; *s* 1973; B Econ Monash, Melbourne; late 2nd Lt Coldm Gds; Man Banque Nationale de Paris 1978-82, since when Man Rothschild Australia Ltd: *m* 1st, 1974 (*m diss* 1985), Cornelia Masters, yst da of late William Conkling Ladd, of 61 Cadogan Sq, SW1; 2ndly, 1987, Clare, da of Peter Stephenson, and has issue by 1st *m*.

Arms – Sable on a pile between two eagles' heads erased or, three escutcheons gules, each charged with a fleur-de-lis of the second. **Crest** – Upon a billet fessewise azure, charged with three plates, a martlet sable, holding in the beak a fleur-de-lis as in the Arms. **Supporters** – *Dexter*, a yellow Labrador dog; *sinister*, a Kangaroo, both proper.
Residence – 56 Rose St, Armadale, Melbourne 3143, Australia.

SON LIVING (By 1st marriage)

Hon ROBERT LATHAM, *b* 2 Feb 1979.

BROTHER LIVING

Hon David Clive Latham, *b* 1952; *ed* Radley; Solicitor.

UNCLES LIVING (Sons of 1st Baron)

Hon Robert Latham, MBE, TD, *b* 1917; *ed* Winchester, and Magdalen Coll, Oxford (MA); Solicitor 1954; formerly Dir Banque Belge Ltd, Man Dir of Henry Ansbacher Co Ltd, C. H. Goldrei, Foucard and Son Ltd, and View Forth Investment Trust Ltd; 1939-45 War as Major Middx Yeo (despatches, MBE); MBE (Mil) 1945: *m* 1949, Delphine Mary, yr da of late Edgar Hastings Dowler (*see* Reynolds, Bt, 1980 Edn), and has issue living, Simon, *b* 1951: *m* 1977, Jane Brebner, of Dunkeld, Johannesburg, and has issue living, James *b* 1982, Nicole *b* 1986, — Anthony Robert *b* 1956, *m* 1980 (*m diss* 1988), Clare Veronica, da of Richard Gubbins, of The Old Post House, Phoenix Green, Hartley Wintney, Hants, and has issue living, Emma Louise *b* 1986, — Mary Clare, *b* 1950: *m* 1st, 1974 (*m diss* 1985), James Neil Percival Cranston; 2ndly, 1996, Antony St G. Gribbon, and has issue living (by 1st *m*), Sophie *b* 1976, Georgina *b* 1978, — Celia Maria, *b* 1953: *m* 1977, William Bryant Style, and has issue (*see* Style Bt, colls).

Hon Edward Latham, *b* 1919; *ed* Winchester, and Brasenose Coll, Oxford (BA 1942, MA 1947); formerly a Member of London Stock Exchange, Chm of Nat Mutual Life Assurance Assocn of Australasia (London Branch), Dir ANZ Bank, RTZ and other Cos; Past Dep Grand Master of United Grand Lodge of England; 1939-45 War as Capt RA and RHA (invalided): *m* 1942, Betty Anne Jardine, da of late Henry Leslie Jardine Taylor, of Crofton Lodge, Sunningdale, Berks, and has issue living, Christopher Latham, *b* 1949. *m* 1984, Jane E., only da of Robert Bowie, of Bayford, Somerset, and has issue living, Charles Latham *b* 1985, Edward Latham *b* 1990, Olivia Clare *b* 1987 , — Philip Latham, *b* 1958: *m* 1985, Lucinda Rosalie, el da of Francis Rokeby Black (*see* B Cadman), and has issue living, Sacha Frances *b* 1989, Francesca Caroline *b* 1994, — Annette Leslie, *b* 1955: *m* 1986, Christopher G. A. Aylwin, el son of late John Aylwin, FRCS, of Clos Nicolle, St Lawrence, Jersey, CI, and has issue living, Patrick John *b* 1990, Emma Alice *b* 1987, Camilla Louise *b* 1993.

AUNT LIVING (Daughter of 1st Baron)

Hon Yvette Latham, *b* 1922: *m* 1946, Robert Ruttan Wilson, of Durford Knoll, Upper Durford Wood, Petersfield, Hants (*see* Bs Berners, colls).

MOTHER LIVING

Anne Bayliss, el da of Leslie William Page, of Southport, Queensland, Australia: *m* 1st, 1945 (*m diss* 1961), Hon William Latham Baillieu, later 2nd Baron Baillieu, who *d* 1973; 2ndly, 1964, (Harry) Anthony Rupert Dodd, of Ridgewood, Parry Inlet, via Denmark, W Australia 6333.

WIDOW LIVING OF SECOND BARON

DELIA MURIEL (*Delia, Baroness Baillieu*), da of —, and formerly wife of — Champion: *m* 1962, and his 2nd wife, the 2nd Baron Baillieu, who *d* 1973.

PREDECESSORS – (1) Sir CLIVE LATHAM Baillieu, KBE, CMG, son of late Hon William Lawrence Baillieu, of Melbourne, Australia; *b* 1889; Dir-Gen British Purchasing Commn, Washington 1941-42; Head of British Raw Materials Mission, Washington, and British Repres on Combined Raw Materials Board 1942-43, Pres of FBI 1945-47, Chm of Dunlop Rubber Co 1949-57, and Pres 1957-67; *cr Baron Baillieu*, of Sefton Commonwealth of Australia and of Parkwood, co Surrey (peerage of UK) 1953: *m* 1915, Ruby Florence Evelyn, who *d* 1962, da of William Clark, of Windlesham Moor, Surrey; *d* 1967; *s* by his el son (2) WILLIAM LATHAM, 2nd Baron; *b* 1915: *m* 1st 1945 (*m diss* 1961), Anne Bayliss, el da of Leslie William Page, of Southport, Qld; 2ndly, 1962, Delia Muriel, Mrs Champion; *d* 1973; *s* by his elder son (3) JAMES WILLIAM LATHAM, 3rd Baron and present peer.

BAKER, BARONY OF (Baker) (Extinct 1985)

DAUGHTERS LIVING OF LIFE BARON

Hon Joanna MacAlister, *b* 1933: *m* 1962, Dr David Michael Ritchie Park, of 6 Saxe Coburg St, Edinburgh.
Hon Dinah, *b* 1936: *m* 1960, Nigel Esmond Recordon, of Bush Farm, Colwall, nr Malvern, Worcs.

BAKER OF DORKING, BARON (Baker) (Life Baron 1997)

KENNETH WILFRED BAKER, CH, PC, son of late Wilfred Michael Baker, OBE, of Twickenham, Middx; *b* 3 Nov 1934; *ed* St Paul's, and Magdalen Coll, Oxford; Memb Twickenham Borough Council 1960-62; MP (*C*) Acton 1968-70, St Marylebone 1970-83, and Mole Valley 1983-97; Parliamentary Sec, Civil Service Dept 1972-74, PPS to Leader of Opposition 1974-75, Min of State for Industry (with special responsibility for info technology) 1981-84, Minister for Local Government, Department of the Environment 1984-85, Sec of State for the Environment 1985-86, and for Education and Science 1986-89, Chm of the Conservative Party and Chancellor of the Duchy of Lancaster 1989-90, Hone Secretary 1990-92; Memb Public Accounts Cttee 1969-70, and Executive 1922 Cttee 1975-81; Chm Hansard Soc 1978-81; Sec Gen of UN Conference of Parliamentarians on World Population and Development 1978; Dir Inter-Hopper Ltd since 1998, Hanson plc since 1992, and Millennium Chemicals Inc since 1996; Nat Service Lt with Gunners in N Africa 1953-55, artillery instructor to Libyan Army; author; *cr* PC 1984, CH 1992, and *Baron Baker of Dorking*, of Iford, co E Sussex (Life Baron) 1997: *m* 1963, Mary Elizabeth, da of late William Gray Muir, WS, of Edinburgh, and has issue, one son and two das.

Arms – Gyronny of eight gules and azure a roundel also azure surmounted by an annulet enfiling the rings of the chains of three portcullises in pairle points inwards or. **Crest** – Upon two closed books each fesswise the upper azure the lower gules both garnished and titled or a cock also or combed jelopped and legged gules. **Supporters** – On either side a male griffin reguardant azure armed forelegged and rayed or the dexter grasping in the beak a thistle flowered gules slipped and leaved or and the sinister a daffodil slipped and leaved or. **Motto** – Bene Tentare
Address – House of Lords, SW1A 0PW. *Clubs* – Athenaeum, Carlton, Garrick.

Balcarres, Earl of; see Earl of Crawford and Balcarres.

BALDWIN OF BEWDLEY, EARL (Baldwin) (Earl UK 1937)

With the help of my God I leap over the wall

EDWARD ALFRED ALEXANDER BALDWIN, 4th Earl; *b* 3 Jan 1938; *s* 1976; *ed* Eton, and Trin Coll, Camb: *m* 1970, Sarah MacMurray, el da of Evan James, of Upwood Park, Abingdon, Berks, and has issue.

𝕬rms – Argent, on a saltire sable a quatrefoil or. 𝕮rest – A cockatrice sejant, wings addorsed argent, combed, wattled, and beaked or, gorged with a crown vallary, lined and reflexed over the back gold and charged on the shoulder with a rose gules, barbed and seeded proper. 𝕾upporters – On either side a white owl proper, that on the sinister holding in the beak a sprig of broom also proper.
Residence – Manor Farm House, Godstow Rd, Upper Wolvercote, Oxford OX2 8AJ.

SONS LIVING

BENEDICT ALEXANDER STANLEY (*Viscount Corvedale*), *b* 28 Dec 1973; *ed* Bryanston.
Hon James Conrad, *b* 1976.
Hon Mark Thomas Maitland, *b* 1980.

PREDECESSORS – (1) *Rt Hon Sir* STANLEY Baldwin, KG, son of late Alfred Baldwin (MP for W, or Bewdley, Div of Worcestershire), of Wilden House, Stourport; *b* 1867; a Junior Lord of the Treasury Jan to June 1917; Joint Financial Sec to the Treasury 1917 to April 1921, Pres of Board of Trade April 1921 to Oct 1922, Chancellor of the Exchequer Oct 1922 to Aug 1923, Leader of the Conservative Party May 1923 to May 1937, Prime Min and First Lord of the Treasury May 1923 to Jan 1924, again Prime Min and First Lord of the Treasury Nov 1924 to June 1929, Lord Pres of the Council Aug 1931 to June 1935 (also Lord Privy Seal Sept 1932 to Jan 1934), and again Prime Min and First Lord of the Treasury June 1935 to May 1937; acted as a Counsellor of State during HM King George V's absence abroad 1925, and during HM's illness 1928-29; *cr Viscount Corvedale*, of Corvedale, co Salop, and *Earl Baldwin of Bewdley* (peerage of United Kingdom) 1937: *m* 1892, Lucy, GBE (a DGStJ), who *d* 1945, el da of late Edward Lucas J. Ridsdale, of Rottingdean, Sussex; *d* 1947; *s* by his son (2) OLIVER RIDSDALE, 2nd Earl; *b* 1899; an Author and Journalist; sometime Parliamentary Private Sec to Sec of State for War; was Gov and Com-in-Ch of Leeward Islands 1948-50; sat as MP for Dudley (*Lab*) 1929-31, and for Paisley 1945-47, *d* 1958; *s* by his brother (3) (ARTHUR) WINDHAM, 3rd Earl; *b* 1904: *m* 1936, (Joan) Elspeth who *d* 1980, yst da of late Charles Alexander Tomes, of New York; *d* 1976; *s* by his son (4) EDWARD ALFRED ALEXANDER, 4th Earl and present peer.

BALERNO, BARONY OF (Buchanan-Smith) (Extinct 1984)

SONS LIVING OF LIFE BARON

Rev the Hon Robert Dunlop (Isle of Eriska, Oban, Argyll), *b* 1936; *ed* Edinburgh Acad, Trin Coll, Glenalmond, Pembroke Coll, Camb (BA), New Coll, Edinburgh, and Princeton Theological Seminary, New Jersey (ThM); Min of Christ's Church, Dunollie, Oban, 1962-66; Chap to 8th Bn Argyll and Sutherland Highlanders 1963, and of 3rd Bn Argyll and Sutherland Highlanders, and of 51st Highland Volunteers 1967-68; Chap of St Andrew's Univ 1966-73, Preacher to USA for British Council of Churches 1968, Chancellor's Assessor, St Andrew's Univ 1981-85, and Dir Scottish Television 1982-96: *m* 1966, Sheena Mary, da of late Alexander W. Edwards, and has issue.

Hon Jock Gordon (Pitcaple Farm, RR2, Cambridge, Ontario N3C 2V4, Canada; Royal Northern (Aberdeen) and Caledonian Clubs), *b* 1940; *ed* Trin Coll, Glenalmond, Aberdeen Univ, and Iowa State Univ, USA, PhD, Oklahoma: Lt Gordon Highlanders; TA (Res); Prof Univ of Guelph: *m* 1964, Virginia Lee, el da of John S. Maxson, of Dallas, Texas, and has issue.

DAUGHTER LIVING OF LIFE BARON

Hon Dame Mary Drummond, DBE, *b* 1927; *ed* St Denis, and Edinburgh Univ (MA 1949); FRSE 1997; Dep Ch Commr Girl Guides, Scotland 1972-77, Chm WRVS 1988-93, Member Parole Board for Scotland 1982-89, Chm Trustee Savings Bank Foundation, Scotland 1994-98, Gov Fettes Coll since 1982, Memb Convocation Heriot Watt Univ since 1986, and Visiting Cttee Glenochil Young Offenders Inst 1972-94; *cr* DBE 1993: *m* 1953, Col Charles Herbert Kenneth Corsar, LVO, OBE, TD, JP, DL, of Burg, Torloisk, Isle of Mull, and 11 Ainslie Pl, Edinburgh, and has issue.

WIDOWS LIVING OF SONS OF LIFE BARON

(Isobel Angela) Margaret, da of Edward Bowden, of Oxshott, Surrey, and widow of Stuart McIntosh: *m* 1961, Rev the Hon George Adam Buchanan-Smith, who *d* 1983. *Residence* – Woodhouselea, Milton Bridge, Pencuik, Midlothian.

Janet Delahoy, CBE, da of late Thomas Lawrie, CBE: *m* 1956, Rt Hon Alick Laidlaw Buchanan-Smith, MP, who *d* 1991. *Residence* – Cockeden, Cockburn, Balerno, Midlothian EH14 7JE.

BALFOUR, EARL OF (Balfour) (Earl UK 1922)

Virtue strives towards heaven

GERALD ARTHUR JAMES BALFOUR, 4th Earl; *b* 23 Dec 1925; *s* 1968; *ed* Eton; Master Mariner; Co Councillor (1960-74) and a JP for E Lothian; Merchant Navy (1944-53); farmer since 1969: *m* 1956, Mrs Natasha Georgina Lousada, who *d* 1994, da of late Capt George Anton, of Archangel, Russia, and formerly wife of late J. C. Lousada.

𝕬rms – (as recorded at Lyon Office), — Argent, on a chevron engrailed between three mullets sable as many otters' heads erased of the field. 𝕮rest - A palm tree proper. 𝕾upporters – Two otters proper, collared or.
Residence – Whittingehame Tower, Haddington, East Lothian EH41 4QA. *Clubs* – International Assocn of Cape Horners; English Speaking Union.

SISTERS LIVING

Lady Evelyn Jean Blanche, *b* 1929: *m* 1948 Michael William Brander, and has issue living, Andrew Michael, *b* 1949: *m* 1988, Mrs Donna Spielman, — Kathleen Jean, *b* 1950: *m* 1976, Ian McCall, BSc, Dir Game Conservancy Advisory Ser, Scotland, and has issue living, Angus *b* 1979, Andrew *b* 1980, — Evelyn Ann, *b* 1952.
Lady Alison Emily, *b* 1934: *m* 1963, Thomas Kremer, MA, and has issue living, David Lytton *b* 1964: *m* 1995, Karen, 2nd da of ...... Holloway, of Belmont, Surrey, and has issue living, Jack Lytton *b* 1997, — Amanda Lili, *b* 1966, — Kim Madeleine, *b* 1969. *Residence* – Widworthy Barton, Honiton, Devon.

COLLATERAL BRANCH LIVING (*In special remainder*)

Issue of late Lt-Col Francis Cecil Campbell Balfour, CIE, CVO, CBE, MC, el son of Col Eustace James Anthony Balfour, yst brother of 1st Earl, *b* 1884, *d* 1965: *m* 1920, Hon Phyllis Evelyn Goschen, who *d* 1976, da of 2nd Viscount Goschen:—
EUSTACE ARTHUR GOSCHEN (Le Pavillon, Ancenis-les-Bois, 44440 Riaillé, France; Savignac, Nanteuil de Bourzac, 24320 Verteillac, France), *b* 26 May 1921; *ed* Eton; 1939-45 War as Capt Scots Gds in N Africa and Italy (wounded): *m* 1st, 1946 (*m diss* 1971), Anne, da of late Maj Victor Yule; 2ndly, 1971, Mrs Paula Susan Cuene-Grandidier, da of late John Maurice Davis, MBE, and has issue living (by 1st *m*), Roderick Francis Arthur (Burpham Lodge, Burpham, Arundel, Sussex; *Clubs* – White's, City of London, Hurlingham, Lord's Taverners), *b* 1948; *ed* Eton; Memb London Stock Exchange 1975-81, Dir Union Discount Co of London plc 1983-90, since when Dir Rothschild Trust Corpn Ltd; Liveryman Clothworkers' Co 1986: *m* 1971, Lady Tessa Mary Isabel Fitzalan Howard, el da of 17th Duke of Norfolk, KG, GCVO, CB, CBE, MC, and has issue living, Willa Anne *b* 1973: *m* 1997, George William Franks, yst son of Anthony Kenric Stapleton Franks, of Becketts Grove, Matfield, Kent (and has issue living, Arthur Anthony *b* 1999), Kinvara Clare Rachel *b* 1975, Maria Alice Jubilee *b* 1977, Candida Rose *b* 1984, — Charles George Yule (15 Oakley St, SW3; Wedhampton, Devizes, Wilts), *b* 1951; *ed* Eton; Man Dir NASDAQ; Member Queen's Body Guard for Scotland (Royal Company of Archers): *m* 1st, 1978, Audrey Margaret, da of late Henry Peregrine Rennie Hoare, of Stourton, Wilts (*see* M Bristol, 1955 Edn); 2ndly, 1987, Reichsgräfin Svea Maria Cecily Lucrezia, elder da of Reichsgräf Ernst Friedrich von Goëss, of Schloss Ratzenegg, Carinthia, Austria, and has issue living (by 2nd *m*), George Eustace Charles *b* 1990, Eleanor Cecily Isabelle *b* 1989. *Clubs* – White's, Puffins.

PREDECESSORS – (1) *Sir* ARTHUR JAMES Balfour, KG, OM, PC, LLD, DCL, DPh, FRS, el son of late James Maitland Balfour, of Whittingehame, by his wife, Lady Blanche Mary Harriett Cecil, who *d* 1872, 2nd da of 2nd Marquess of Salisbury; *b* 1848; was employed on Special Mission of Lords Beaconsfield and Salisbury to Berlin 1878, Assist Private Sec to Sec of State for Foreign Affairs (Marquess of Salisbury) 1878-80, Pres of Local Govt Board June 1885 to Jan 1886, Sec for Scotland July 1886 to March 1887 (with a Seat in the Cabinet from Nov 1886), Ch Sec for Ireland March 1887 to Oct 1891, First Lord of the Treasury and Leader of the House of Commons Oct 1891 to Aug 1892, Leader of the Opposition 1892-5, again First Lord of the Treasury and Leader of the House of Commons 1895-1900 and 1900-1902, Prime Min, First Lord of the Treasury, and Leader of the House of Commons 1902-5 (also Lord Privy Seal 1902-3), Leader of the Opposition 1905-11, First Lord the the Admiralty May 1915 to Dec 1916 (also a Member of Cabinet War Council), Sec of State for Foreign Affairs in National Min 1916-19, Lord Pres of the Council 1919-22 and 1925-9, and Pres British Acad 1921-8; appointed a Member of Munitions of War Committee 1915, a British Representative at Peace Conference 1919, and British Delegate to Washington Conference 1921; Chm Med Research Council 1924-9; MP for Hertford (*C*) 1874-85, for E Div of Manchester 1885-1906, and for City of London Feb 1906 to April 1922; went as Head of Special Mission to USA 1917; a British Representative on League of Nations up to 1923; *cr Earl of Balfour*, and *Viscount Traprain*, of Whittingehame, co Haddington (peerage of United Kindom) 1922, with special remainder in default of heirs male of his body, to (1) his brother, *Rt Hon* Gerald William Balfour, and the heirs male of his body; (2) to his nephew, Francis Cecil Campbell Balfour, and the heirs male of his body; and (3) to his nephew, Oswald Herbert Campbell Balfour, and the heirs male of his body; *d* 1930; *s* under the special remainder by his brother (2) GERALD WILLIAM, PC, 2nd Earl; *b* 1853; was Ch Sec for Ireland 1895-1900, and Pres of Board of Trade 1900-1905; MP for Central Division of Leeds (*C*) 1885-1906: *m* 1887, Lady Elizabeth Edith Bulwer-Lytton, who *d* 1942, da of 1st Earl of Lytton; *d* 1945; *s* by his son (3)

ROBERT ARTHUR LYTTON 3rd Earl; b 1902; Chm Scottish Div NCB 1946-51: m 1925, Jean Lily, who d 1981, da of late Rev John James Cooke-Yarborough (Cooke, Bt, colls); d 1968; s by his son (4) GERALD ARTHUR JAMES, 4th Earl and present peer; also Viscount Traprain.

BALFOUR OF BURLEIGH, LORD (Bruce) (Lord S 1607)

Every land is the home of a brave man
We have been

ROBERT BRUCE, 8th (de facto) (and 12th but for the attainder) Lord; b 6th Jan 1927; s 1967; ed Westminster; CEng; FIEE, FRSE 1986 (Treasurer 1989-94), Hon FRIAS; Chancellor Stirling Univ 1988-98; Treas the Royal Scottish Corpn since 1967; a Dir of Bank of Scotland 1968-91 (Dep-Gov 1977-91), and The Scottish Investment Trust Ltd, Edinburgh since 1970; Chm of Scottish Arts Council 1970-78, and Viking Oil Ltd 1971-80; Commnr Forestry Commn 1971-74; Foreman and Supt The English Electric Co Ltd, Stafford & Liverpool 1952-57, Gen Manager The English Electric Co India, Ltd 1957-64, of English Electric Netherton Works 1964-66, and of D. Napier and Son, Ltd 1967-68; Dir Tarmac plc 1981-90, and Turing Inst 1983-92: m 1st, 1971 (m diss 1993), Jennifer, da of late E. S. Manasseh, and formerly wife of John Brittain Catlin; 2ndly, 1993, Dr Janet Morgan, da of Dr Frank Morgan, and has issue by 1st m.

Arms – Quarterly: 1st and 4th argent, on a chevron sable, an otter's head erased of the field, *Balfour*; 2nd and 3rd or, a saltire and chief gules, the latter charged with a mullet argent, *Bruce*. Crest – 1st, upon a rock a mermaid, holding in the dexter hand an otter's head, erased at the neck, and in the sinister hand a swan's head also erased, all proper; 2nd, a dexter arm in fesse, embowed, in armour, couped at the shoulder, the hand holding a sceptre in bend sinister, or. Supporters – *Dexter*, an otter proper; *sinister*, a swan also proper.

Residence – Brucefield, Clackmannan.

DAUGHTERS LIVING (By 1st marriage)

Hon VICTORIA, b 7 May 1973. *Residence* – 23 Callis Court Rd, Broadstairs, Kent CT10 3AG.
Hon Ishbel, b 1976. *Residence* – 23 Callis Court Rd, Broadstairs, Kent CT10 3AG.

BROTHER LIVING

(Hon) George John Done (does not use courtesy title) (6 Pembroke Walk, W8 6PQ; Athenaeum), b 1930; Past Pres of Royal Soc of Portrait Painters.

SISTERS LIVING

Hon Lætitia Mary, b 1920; MB, ChB St Andrews 1946; Vice-Pres NE Council on Addictions since 1983, Pres W Northumberland Branch NSPCC since 1980; Memb Inst of Advanced Motorists, JP for Newcastle upon Tyne: m 1955, Dr Ian Metcalfe Telfer, MRCGP, JP, who d 1988, and has issue living, John Bruce, b 1956; BA, — George Metcalfe, b 1961; Dip RSA, MD: m 1992, Susan Elizabeth, da of Michael Bernard Allen, of Rose Cottage, 11 Stoneheads, Whaley Bridge, Stockport, — Mary Daubeny, b 1958; BSc, MSc: m 1990, Kenneth Francis Douthwaite, and has issue living, Matthew Geoffrey Ian b 1991, Christopher Robert b 1993. *Residence* – 5 Ruthven Court, Adderstone Crescent, Newcastle upon Tyne, NE2 2HH.

(Hon) Katherine Gordon (does not use courtesy title) (25 Kew Green, Kew, Richmond, Surrey TW9 3AA), b 1922; reverted by deed poll 1975 to the surname of Bruce, and subsequently resumed the surname of Bland by deed poll 1995: m 1946 (m diss 1961), Thomas Riviere Bland, MC, and has issue living, Charles Riviere, b 1949: m 1980, Julie Louise, da of Sir Edgar Charles Beck, CBE, and has issue living, William Riviere b 1990, Jemima Katherine Agnes b 1983, Daisy Prudence Harriet b 1986, Harriet Cressida b 1994, — Susanna Katherine, b 1947: m 1986, Général Philippe Saint-Loubert Bié, of 49 Avenue de Versailles, 75016 Paris, and has issue living, Thomas Georges Bland b 1988, — Louise Margaret, b 1953.

Hon Jean, b 1924; formerly in WRNS: m 1st, 1949 (m diss 1971), John Shirley Ward, Jr; 2ndly, 1974, John Herbert Poole, who d 19—, and has issue living (by 1st m), John Shirley, b 1960: m 1987 (m diss 1994), Monica Lanz, — Lætitia, b 1951: m 1980, Dr Paul Buehrens, and has issue living, Thomas b 1984, Daniel b 1986, — Reavis Mary, b 1955: m 1987, Gottfried Hilz Ward, and has issue living, Sonia b 1988, Christine b 1993. *Residence* – 2194 Cooley Place, Pasadena, Cal 91104, USA.

Hon Margaret, b 1934: m 1967, David Graham Worthy, of Keepers Cottage, Hare Warren Hollow, Merrow Downs, Guildford, Surrey GU1 2HJ, and has issue living, Henry Jonathan David Bruce b 1971.

COLLATERAL BRANCHES LIVING

Descendants of Hon Mary Bruce, OBE, el da of 6th Lord, who *m* Sir John Augustus Hope, 16th Bt (*cr* 1628):—
See Hope, Bt (*cr* 1628).

Grandchildren of late Francis Balfour, elder son of late Maj Francis Walter Balfour, eldest son of Francis Balfour, great-grandson of Lt-Col Hon John Balfour, 2nd son of 3rd Lord:—
Issue of late Patrick Small Keir Balfour, *b* 1910, *d* 1967: *m* 1936, Lila Camilla (103 Greenleaf Gdns, Polgate, E Sussex BH6 6PH), da of Basil Edward Spicer:—
Robert William Keir (6 Millicent St, Leongatha, Vic 3953, Australia), *b* 1942: *m* 1964, Evelyn Mary Douglas, and has issue living, Michael Patrick Keir, *b* 1965. —— Frances Norah, *b* 1941: *m* 1965, Hugh Manning Tregarthen, of 10 Lawson St, Paddington, NSW 2021, Australia, and has issue living, Carolyn Mary, *b* 1967: *m* 1991, Stephen Noel Manns, and has issue living, James Stephen Buckley *b* 1996, Emelia Jean *b* 1994, — Sarah Jane, *b* 1970, — Susan Manning, *b* 1971. —— Sheila Katharine, *b* 1946: *m* 1st, 1966 (*m diss* 1975), Yan Owen Sikorski; 2ndly, 1989, Ronald Leslie Patterson, late RAAOC, of 67 Comer St, Henty, NSW 2658, Australia, and has issue living (by 1st *m*), Ian Patrick, *b* 1971, — Tanya Mary, *b* 1966: *m* 1988, Phillip Pitt, and has issue living, Christopher Leigh *b* 1983, Flynn Edward James *b* 1990, Kirsten Mary Marie *b* 1988, — Katharine Louise, *b* 1968.

PREDECESSORS – **(1)** *Sir* MICHAEL Balfour, KB, PC, Ambassador to the Duke of Tuscany and Lorraine, was *cr Lord Balfour of Burleigh* (peerage of Scotland) 1607; *d* 1619; *s* by his only da **(2)** MARGARET, who *m* Robert Arnot, who assumed the name of Balfour, and sat as Lord Balfour of Burleigh in the Scottish Parliament, of which he was President 1640-1; she *d* 1663; *s* by son **(3)** JOHN, 3rd Lord; *d* about 1696; *s* by his son **(4)** ROBERT, 4th Lord; *d* 1713; *s* by his son **(5)** ROBERT, 5th Lord, who previously to the death of his father had in 1709 been condemned to death for murder, but escaped from prison by exchanging clothes with his sister; he subsequently engaged in the rebellion of 1715, and in 1716 was attainted by Act of Parliament; *dsp* 1757; *s* (but for the attainder) by his sister **(6)** MARGARET, *b* 16— *d* 1769; *s* by her nephew **(7)** ROBERT (son of the Hon Mary Balfour, who *m* 1714, Brig-Gen Alexander Bruce of Kennet), *b* 1718; a Judge of Court of Session with title of *Lord Kennet* 1764: *m* 1754, Helen, who *d* 1786, da of George Abercromby of Tullibody; *d* 1785; *s* by his son **(8)** ALEXANDER, *b* 1755: *m* 1793, Hugh, who *d* 1851, da of Hugh Blackburn, of Glasgow; *d* 1808; *s* by his son **(9)** ROBERT, who claimed the lordship before the Committee for Privileges, House of Lords, but *d* before a decision was made; *b* 1794: *m* 1st, 1825, Anne, who *d* 1846, da of William Murray, of Touchadam; 2ndly, 1848, Jane Dalrymple Hamilton, who *d* 19—, da of Sir James Fergusson of Kilkerran, 4th Bt; *d* 1864; *s* by his son **(10)** ALEXANDER HUGH, KT, GCMG, GCVO, PC, 6th Lord, whose peerage was allowed by House of Lords 1868, the attainder of 1715 having been reversed by Act of Parliament 1869; *b* 1849; a Lord-in-Waiting to HM Queen Victoria 1887-88, Parliamentary Sec to Board of Trade 1888-92. Sec for Scotland with a seat in the Cabinet 1895-1903, and Lord Warden of the Stannaries and Rider and Master Forester of Dartmoor 1908-21; Capt Roy Co of Archers (HM Body Guard for Scotland): *m* 1876, Lady Katherine Eliza Gordon, who *d* 1931, da of 5th Earl of Aberdeen; *d* 1921; *s* by his son **(11)** GEORGE JOHN GORDON, 7th Lord, *b* 1883; Pres of Inst of Bankers 1948-49; Chm of Kensington Housing Trust 1926-49, of Medical Research Council 1936-48, of Cttee, of London Clearing Bankers 1950-52, and of Lloyds Bank 1946-54; a Representative Peer for Scotland 1922-63: *m* 1919, Violet Dorothy Evelyn, MBE, who *d* 1976, da of late Richard Henry Done, of Tarporley, Ches; *d* 1967; *s* by his el son **(12)** ROBERT, 8th Lord and present peer.

BALFOUR OF INCHRYE, BARON (Balfour) (Baron UK 1945)

God be with me

Laosit Deus

IAN BALFOUR, 2nd Baron; *b* 21 Dec 1924; *s* 1988; *ed* Eton, and Magdalen Coll, Oxford; European War 1942-45 with RN: *m* 1953, Josephine Maria Jane, da of late Morogh Wyndham Percy Bernard (*see* E Bandon, colls, ext), and has issue.

Arms – Argent, on a chevron indented sable between in chief a rose gules and in base a saltire couped azure, an otter's head erased of the first, a bordure engrailed of the third. **Crest** – A dexter hand grasping an olive branch, all proper. **Supporters** – *Dexter*, an otter per fess or and azure; *sinister*, a peregrine falcon proper, bells argent, jesses sable.
Residence – 4 Marsh End, Ferry Rd, Walberswick, Suffolk IP18 6TH.

DAUGHTER LIVING

Hon Roxane, *b* 1955: *m* 1978, Adrian Laird Craig, and has issue living, Robert Joseph, *b* 1982, — Mary Ann Josephine, *b* 1984, — Alethea Katharine, *b* 1986. *Residence* – 30 Coltbridge Terr, Edinburgh EH12 6AE.

HALF SISTER LIVING

Hon Mary Ann, *b* 1949: *m* 1974, Hon Martin Dearman Sutherland Janson (*see* Cs Sutherland). *Residence* – Uppat House, Brora, Sutherland KW9 6NL.

PREDECESSORS – (1) *Rt Hon* HAROLD HARINGTON Balfour, MC, son of Col Nigel Harington Balfour, OBE, of Belton, Camberley, Surrey; *b* 1897, European War 1914-19 with 60th Rifles, RFC, and RAF (MC and bar, 1914-15 star, two medals), was Parliamentary Under Sec of State for Air 1938-44, and Min Resident in W Africa 1944-45, Freeman City of London, MP for Isle of Thanet Div of Kent (*C*) May 1929-June 1945, *cr* PC 1941, and *Baron Balfour of Inchrye*, of Shefford, co Berks (peerage of United Kingdom) 1945: *m* 1st, 1921 (*m diss* 1946), Diana Blanche, who *d* 1982, da of Sir Robert Grenville Harvey, 2nd Bt (*cr* 1868, ext); 2ndly, 1947, Mary Ainslie, who *d* 1999, da of late Baron Albert Profumo, KC; *d* 1988; *s* by his only son **(2)** IAN, 2nd Baron and present peer.

Balfour, family name of Baron Kinross.

Balfour, family name of Baron Riverdale.

Balgonie, Lord; son of Earl of Leven and Melville.

Ballantrae, Barony of (Fergusson) (Extinct 1980) (see Fergusson, Bt)

Balniel, Lord; son of Earl of Crawford and Balcarres.

BALOGH, BARONY OF (Balogh) (Extinct 1985)

SONS LIVING OF LIFE BARON (*By 1st marriage*)

Hon Stephen Bernard, *b* 1946; *ed* Westminster, and Balliol Coll, Oxford.
Hon Christopher Thomas, *b* 1948; *ed* Westminster, and King's Coll, Camb.

DAUGHTER LIVING OF LIFE BARON (*By 1st marriage*)

Hon Penelope Kathryn Teresa, *b* 1957; *ed* Camden Sch for Girls, and Lancaster Univ: *m* 1988, Ian Henghes, only son of late Heinz Henghes, sculptor, and has issue living, Leo, *b* 1991.
5HE.

WIDOW LIVING OF LIFE BARON

CATHERINE, MRCS, LRCP (*Baroness Balogh*), da of late Arthur Cole, Fell of King's Coll, Camb, and formerly wife of Anthony Storr: *m* 1970, as his 2nd wife, Baron Balogh (Life Baron), who *d* 1985.

Bampfylde, family name of Baron Poltimore.

BANBURY OF SOUTHAM, BARON (Banbury) (Baron UK 1924, Bt Uk 1902)

I warn and I protect

CHARLES WILLIAM BANBURY, 3rd Baron and 3rd Baronet; *b* 29 July 1953; *s* 1981; *ed* Eton: *m* 1st, 1984 (*m diss* 1986), Lucinda Elizabeth Scarlett, elder da of John Frederick Edward Trehearne (*see* B Harvington); 2ndly, 1989, Mrs Inger Marianne Norton, da of — Wiegert, and has issue by 2nd *m*.

Arms – Ermine, a cross patée between five mullets of six points each within an annulet, three in chief and two in base, all gules. **Crest** – A demi-antelope proper, supporting between its feet a cross patée as in the arms and charged on the shoulder with a garb gules. **Supporters** – On either side a collie dog proper, each charged on the shoulder with a cross patée gules.
Residence – The Mill, Fossebridge, Cheltenham, Glos.

DAUGHTERS LIVING (*By 2nd marriage*)

Hon Charlotte Rosa, *b* 1990.
Hon Poppy Isobel, *b* 1991.

SISTERS LIVING

Hon Carolyn, *b* 1947: *m* 1977, Christopher (Kim) J. A. North, who was *k* in a motor accident 1988. *Residence* – Moyles Cottage, Quenington, Cirencester, Glos.
Hon Anna Josephine, *b* 1950: *m* 1970 (*m diss* 1981), Michael Gordon Croose Parry, and has issue living, Sophie Ruth Flora, *b* 1976.

Residence – Cross Cottage, Quenington, Cirencester, Glos.

MOTHER LIVING

Hilda Ruth, da of late A.H.R. Carr, of Malone, Belfast: *m* 1st, 1945 (*m diss* 1958), the 2nd Baron Banbury, who *d* 1981; 2ndly, 1959, Maj Robert O. G. Gardner, MC, who *d* 1987; 3rdly, 1988, as his 3rd wife, Richard Frederick Norman (*see* Collet, Bt, ext 1944, 1950 Edn).

PREDECESSORS – (1) *Rt Hon* FREDERICK GEORGE Banbury, PC, el son of late Frederick Banbury, of Shirley House, Surrey; *b* 1850; MP for Peckham Div of Camberwell (C) 1892-1906, and for City of London 1906-1924; *cr Baron Banbury of Southam*, of Southam, co Warwick (peerage of United Kingdom) 1924: *m* 1873, Elizabeth Rosa, who *d* 1930, da and co-heiress of late Thomas Barbot Beale, of Brettenham Park, Suffolk; *d* 1936; *s* by his grandson (2) CHARLES WILLIAM, son of late Capt Charles William Banbury, Coldstream Guards (only son of 1st Baron), *ka* 1914, 2nd Baron, *b* 1915; 1939-45 War (despatches): *m* 1945 (*m diss* 1958), Hilda Ruth (who *m* 2ndly, 1959, Maj Robert O. G. Gardner, MC, who *d* 1987, and 3rdly, 1988, as his 3rd wife, Richard Frederick Norman (*see* Collet, Bt, ext 1944, 1950 Edn)), da of late A. H. R. Carr, of Malone, Belfast; *d* 1981; *s* by his only son (3) CHARLES WILLIAM, 3rd Baron and present peer.

BANCROFT, BARONY OF (Bancroft) (Extinct 1996)

SONS LIVING AND DECEASED OF LIFE BARON

Hon Simon Powell *b* 1953; *ed* Kings Coll Sch, Wimbledon, and LSE (BSc); Vice Pres of Swett and Crawford USA: *m* 1985, Vicki Lynn, da of Glenn Rosenquist, of Dallas, Texas, and has issue living, Nicholas Glenn Powell, *b* 1990, — Megan Louise, *b* (twin) 1990. *Residence* – 11231 Dwarfs Circle, Dallas, Texas 75229, USA.

†*Hon* Adam David Powell (113 Pepys Rd, SW20); *b* 1955; *ed* Kings Coll Sch, Wimbledon, and LSE (BSc); wine merchant: *m* 1985, Amanda Claire, da of late A. J. McCance, of London SW19, and *d* 1999, leaving issue, Alexander Joseph Powell, *b* 1993, — Jessica Claire, *b* 1991.

DAUGHTER LIVING OF LIFE BARON

Hon Emma Charlotte, *b* 1959; *ed* Canterbury Coll of Art (BA); graphic designer: *m* 1984, Jeremy Guy Minton Haines, of 24 Santos Rd, SW18, son of G. D. M. Haines, of Pippins, Duddleswell, Uckfield, Sussex, and has issue living, Louis George Bancroft, *b* 1990, — Oscar Edward Bancroft, *b* 1993, — Phoebe Alice Bancroft, *b* 1988, — a da, *b* 1996.

WIDOW LIVING OF LIFE BARON

JEAN HILDA PATRICIA (*Baroness Bancroft*), da of David Richard Swaine: *m* 1950, Baron Bancroft, GCB (Life Baron), who *d* 1996.

BANDON, EARLDOM OF (Bernard) (Extinct 1979)

DAUGHTERS LIVING OF FIFTH EARL

Lady Jennifer Jane, *b* 1935. *Residence* – Castle Bernard, Bandon, co Cork.

Lady Frances Elizabeth, *b* 1943: *m* 1967, Paul Mark Carter, and has issue living, Philip Bernard, *b* 1979, — Emma Margaret, *b* 1969, — Annabelle Petria, *b* 1971; *m* 1997, Gary William Henry Abbott, son of P. M. Abbott, of Groesfford, Powys. *Residence* – Hill House, Birds Lane, Midgham, Reading, Berks RG7 5UL.

SISTER LIVING OF FIFTH EARL (*Raised to the rank of an Earl's daughter* 1925)

Lady Cynthia Lettice Margaret, *b* 1905: *m* 1st, 1925 (*m diss* 1936), Lt-Col Francis Christian Darby Tothill, Rifle Bde, who *d* 1992; 2ndly, 1947, A/Cdre Lionel Guy Stanhope Payne, CBE, MC, AFC, who *d* 1965, and has issue living (by 1st *m*), Betsann, *b* 1927: *m* 1947, Capt Matthew Page Page Wood, Coldstream Gds, who *d* 1999 (*see* Page-Wood, Bt). *Residence* – 31 Halsey St, SW3.

WIDOW LIVING OF FIFTH EARL

LOIS (*Countess of Bandon*) (Castle Bernard, Bandon, co Cork), da of Francis Russell, of Victoria, Australia, formerly wife of S/Ldr Frederick Arthur White, RAF: *m* 1946, as his 2nd wife, the 5th Earl of Bandon, GBE, CB, CVO, DSO, who *d* 1979.

COLLATERAL BRANCH LIVING

Granddaughter of late Percy Brodrick Bernard, el son of late Rt Rev Hon Charles Brodrick Bernard, DD, Lord Bishop of Tuam, 2nd son of 2nd Earl:—
Issue of late Morogh Wyndham Percy Bernard, *b* 1902, *d* 1977: *m* 1929, Hon Diana Pearl Dundas, who *d* 1979, da of 7th Viscount Melville:—
Josephine Maria Jane (*Baroness Balfour of Inchrye*), *b* 1934: *m* 1953, 2nd Baron Balfour of Inchrye.

BANGOR, VISCOUNT (Ward) (Viscount I 1781)

Salvation beneath the Cross

WILLIAM MAXWELL DAVID WARD, 8th Viscount; *b* 9 Aug 1948; *s* 1993; *ed* Univ Coll, London: *m* 1976, Mrs Sarah Mary Malet Bradford, biographer, da of late Brig Hilary Anthony Hayes, DSO, OBE, and formerly wife of Anthony John Bradford, of Lisbon, Portugal.

🏰rms – Quarterly: 1st and 4th azure, a cross patonce or, *Ward*; 2nd and 3rd gules, three cinquefoils ermine, on a chief of the second a man's heart of the first, *Hamilton*. Crest – A man's head couped at the shoulders affrontée proper, wreathed about the temples or and azure, and adorned with three ostrich feathers. Supporters – *Dexter*, a Knight in complete armour proper, charged on the breast with a cross moline gules, behind him a flowing crimson robe, a cross moline argent on its sinister side. On the helmet a plume of feathers of the last, his dexter hand resting on a drawn sword point downwards proper, pommel and hilt or; *sinister*, a Turkish prince vested in robes of blue and gold, white stockings, yellow sandals, gold sash and fringe round the waist, behind him a loose brown robe of fur, on the head a white turban with black feathers, and his hands in fetters proper. *Residence* – 31 Britannia Rd, SW6.

HALF-BROTHER LIVING

Hon (EDWARD) NICHOLAS, *b* 16 Jan 1953; *ed* Westminster, and Edinburgh Univ (MA); formerly Investment Analyst, Smith New Court Securities Ltd, since when an independent TV Prod: *m* 1985, Rachel Mary, da of late Hon Hugh Waldorf Astor (*see* B Astor of Hever, colls), and has issue living, Anna Roxelana, *b* 1987, — Zoë Rachel, *b* 1990. *Residence* – 9 Kildare Terrace, W2.

HALF-SISTER LIVING

Hon Sarah, *b* 1951; actress (as Lalla Ward): *m* 1st, 1980 (*m diss* 1982), Tom Baker, actor; 2ndly, 1992, Dr (Clinton) Richard Dawkins, DSc, of New College, Oxford. *Residences* – Savile House, Mansfield Rd, Oxford; 13 Durham Terrace, W2.

AUNTS LIVING (*Daughters of 6th Viscount*)

Hon Helen Elizabeth, *b* 1912. *Residence* – 7 Chelsea Lodge, 58 Tite St, SW3.
Hon Margaret Bertha Meriel (ERIC SMITH), *b* 1914: *m* 1st, 1938 (*m diss* 1947), Lt-Col Desmond Charles Forde, Coldstream Gds, who *d* 1961; 2ndly, 1947 (*m diss* 1962), Gavin Robert Sligh; 3rdly, 1969, Maj Dennis Eric Smith, of 21 Chesil Court, Chelsea Manor St, SW3, and has issue living (by 1st *m*), Patrick Mathew Desmond (Seaforde, co Down), *b* 1940; *ed* Eton; JP and DL co Down: *m* 1965, Lady Anthea Geraldine Lowry-Corry, da of 7th Earl Belmore, and has issue living, Mathew Galbraith *b* 1967: *m* 1998, Alice Albertine, yst da of John Seymour Dudley Madden, of Hilton Park, co Monaghan, Charles Patrick *b* 1972, Finnian Nicholas *b* 1982, Emily Louise *b* 1966: *m* 1995, Peter T. W. Mackie, yr twin son of William Denis Grenville Mackie, of Lissanoure, co Antrim, — Sylvia Helena (Flat 9, 110 Elm Park Gdns, SW10), *b* 1938.

COLLATERAL BRANCHES LIVING

Grandson of late Maxwell William Bernard Ward (infra):—
Issue of late Maj Bernard Maxwell Ward, LVO, late RHA, *b* 1921, *d* 1991: *m* 1948, Sunniva, who *d* 1962, elder da of Maj Sir Basil Hamilton Hebden Neven-Spence:—
Maxwell Colin Bernard, *b* 1949; *ed* Harrow, and St Catharine's Coll, Camb: *m* 1982, Sarah, yr da of late Lt-Col Peter William Marsham, MBE (*see* E Romney, colls), and has issue living, Charles Bernard Maxwell, *b* 1986, — Frederick Peter Neven, *b* 1989, — Laura Sunniva, *b* 1984, — Antonia Hersey, *b* 1993. *Residence* – Stobshiel House, Humbie, E Lothian EH36 5PD.

Grandson of late Lt-Gen Hon Bernard Matthew Ward, CB, 4th son of 3rd Viscount:—
Issue of late Maxwell William Bernard Ward, *b* 1889, *d* 1960: *m* 1st, 1919 (*m diss* 1931), Ruth Elizabeth, who *d* 1994, only da of late John Flasby Lawrance Whittingdale, OBE, MD, of Sherborne, Dorset, and Thornton-in-Lonsdale, Yorkshire; 2ndly, 1934, Josephine, yst da of Rev Hugh Robert Coulthard, Hon Canon of Truro, and V of Breage, Cornwall, and widow of Guy Nelson Brown:—
(By 1st *m*) John Maxwell *b* 1922; *ed* Sherborne; MRCS England, and LRCP London 1945: *m* 1948, Evelyn Millicent, da of J. P. Usher, and has issue living, Peter Evan, *b* 1949, — Michael John, *b* 1951, — Nicholas Crosbie, *b* 1956, — Philippa Jane, *b* 1957. *Address* – PO Box 72, Que Que, Zimbabwe.

Grandsons of late Edward Crosbie Ward, 2nd son of late Maj-Gen Sir Edward Wolstenholme Ward, KCMG, eldest son of late Hon John Petty Ward, BCS (infra):—
Issue of late Maj John Crosbie Ward, S Wales Borderers, *b* 1911, *d* 1952: *m* 1935, Margaret Llewellyn, who *d* 1983, da of late Rev Llewellyn Christopher Watson Bullock, of Gt Wigborough, Colchester:—
Christopher John Robert Crosbie (The Old House, Longbridge Deverill, Warminster, Wilts BA12 7DJ), *b* 1937; *ed* Wellington Coll; Maj 2nd Goorkhas: *m* 1979, Caroline Fiona, da of late Maj James Alan Gerald Harley, MC, of Lower Lodge, Wyck Rissington, nr Cheltenham, Glos, and has issue living, Robert James Crosbie, *b* 1986, — Arabella Louise Crosbie,

b 1980, — Sophie Ann Crosbie, *b* 1982. ——— David Edward Crosbie (St Olaf, Sellafirth, Yell, Shetland), *b* 1941; *ed* Wellington Coll: *m* 1976, Christine Julia, da of late Travers Burnell Christopher Christie, of Nelson, NZ.

Grandchildren of late John Petty Ward (*b* 1871) (infra):—
Issue of late Gen Sir Richard Erskine Ward, GBE, KCB, DSO, MC, *b* 1917, *d* 1989: *m* 1947, Stella Elizabeth (*Lady Ward*) (Bellsburn, 18 Lower St, Rode, Somerset BA3 6PU), da of late Brig Philip Neville Ellis, RA, of Rhyllech, nr Pwlheli, Caerarvon:—
Anthony Richard Bangor (Lower Bowden House, Pangbourne, Berks RG8 8JL), *b* 1960: *m* 1989, Mrs Carolyn WALLACE, eldest da of Giles Walker, of IoM, and has issue living, Archie Erskine Bangor, *b* 1990, — Maximilian Richard Petty, *b* 1992. ——— Jeremy Neville (266 Camberwell New Rd, SE5 0RP), *b* 1961: *m* 1984, Elizabeth, only da of Vernon Butterworth, of Thornton, Cleverlys, Lancs, and has issue living, Oliver Richard Xavier, *b* 1985, — Frederick, *b* 1988. ——— Léonie, *b* 1949: *m* 1982, David James Chalmers Brown, of Berrycroft Farmhouse, Ashbury, Swindon, Wilts SN6 8LX, son of late W. Chalmers Brown, of Balerno, Midlothian, and has issue living, Alexandra, *b* 1985, — Isobel, *b* 1988. ——— Stephanie Rachel, *b* 1952: *m* 1981, John David Lace, of 58 Duke's Av, W4 2AF, and has issue living, William John Edward, *b* 1985, — Thomas Charles, *b* 1988, — Toby Richard, *b* (twin) 1988, — Jessica Elizabeth Rachel, *b* 1983.

Grandchildren of late Noel Edward Ward (infra):—
Issue of late Maj James Palmer Ward, *b* 1902, *d* 1976: *m* 1931, Yvonne Lockington (who *m* 2ndly, 1977, Arthur George Kelly, who *d* 1983), da of Cedric Lockington Flood, of Dublin:—
Michael James (20 Cluny Grove, Killiney, co Dublin), *b* 1934; *ed* Aldenham: *m* 1959, Jocelyn Mary, da of late Arthur George Kelly, of Athlone (ante), and has had issue, †Jeremy Charles Arthur James, *b* 1960; *ed* St Andrew's Univ; *d* 1983, — Alexandra Rowena, *b* 1963; *ed* Glengara Park, and Trin Coll, Dublin. ——— Patrick Erskine, RD (57 Intwood Rd, Cringleford, nr Norwich NR4 6AA), *b* 1937: *ed* Nautical Coll, Pangbourne; Capt RNR (ret): *m* 1st, 1962 (*m diss* 1972), Eldrith Janet, da of John Bararis Delbridge, of Bulawayo; 2ndly, 1972, Sarah Elizabeth, da of late John Williams, of Ash, Bocking, Surrey, and has issue living (by 1st *m*), Richard John Rudall Bangor, *b* 1967: *m* 1997, Elizabeth May, yr da of Derek Thom, of Cheltenham, — Julia Helen Yvonne, *b* 1963: *m* 1992, John McGregor Moulton, and has issue living, Harriet Eldrith *b* 1995, India Fiona *b* 1998, — Janette Elizabeth Barwis, *b* 1964: *m* 1988, Andrew George Britton, and has issue living, Aaron David George *b* 1989, Sophie Britton *b* 1994, — (by 2nd *m*) James Julien Erskine, *b* 1977, — Timothy John, *b* 1979

Issue of late Jack Lionel Ward, OBE, *b* 1910, *d* 1986: *m* 1939, Beatrice Mary Caroline (Hope Cottage, Church Rd, Rotherfield, E Sussex TN6 3LE), da of George Austin Wareham, of King's Langley, Herts:—
Edward Raymond (Hookwood House, Shipbourne, Tonbridge, Kent), *b* 1945; *ed* Winchester, and Trin Coll, Camb: *m* 1973, Felicity Lilian Beatrice, da of John Richard Gibbs, of Bromley, Kent, and has had issue, Lucy Beatrice Alice, *b* 1974; *ed* Sevenoaks, and St Andrews Univ, — Emily Charlotte Holly, *b* 1982, — Holly (twin), *b* and *d* 1982. ——— Gillian Elizabeth, *b* 1939.

Grandchildren of late Sir William Erskine Ward, KCSI, 4th and yst son of late Hon John Petty Ward, BSC, 1st brother of 3rd Viscount:—
Issue of late John Petty Ward, *b* 1871, *d* 1956: *m* 1906, Rose Gladys May, who *d* 1937, da of Rev Richard Marsh Marsh-Dunn, V of St Nicholas', Shaldon, Devon:—
Myrtle Josephine, *b* 1907: *m* 1st 1929 (*m diss* 1972), Donald Stuart Denholm Fraser, who *d* 1986; 2ndly, 1972, Theodore Alfred Raymond, who *d* 1988, of Horizons Ord, Banff, Grampian, and has issue living (by 1st *m*), June, *b* 1930; ARCA: *m* 1963, Allen Hans Cull, of 5 Combemartin Rd, Southfields, SW18 5PP, and has issue living, Zoë Gail *b* 1970; BA, — Sally, *b* 1936: *m* 1971, Clive Freshwater, of The Hall, Kincraig, Inverness-shire, and has issue living, Duncan *b* 1971, Andrew *b* 1973, Jonathan *b* 1977, — Joanna (1021 Elliot Rd S, Lethbridge, Alberta, Canada), *b* 1950.

Issue of late Noel Edward Ward, *b* 1872, *d* 1944: *m* 1st, 1898 (*m diss* 1922), Jessie Mabel Wood, who *d* 1968, da of James B. Wood, of Woodbine Tea Estate, Assam; 2ndly, 1922, Muriel, who *d* 1983, da of Edward Dalton, of Leeds, Yorks:—
(By 2nd *m*) Noel Nicholas (Penrowan, New Rd, Boscastle, N Cornwall), *b* 1925; *ed* Marlborough; a Co Dir: *m* 1st, 1948, June Margaret, da of Albert Ellerton-Long, of Gravesend; 2ndly, 1977, Mrs Jacqueline Ann Aylwin, who *d* 1990, da of James Cyril Lodge, and has issue living (by 1st *m*), Jonathan Philip (109a Tankerton Rd, Tankerton, Whitstable, Kent), *b* 1951; *ed* St Edmund's Sch: *m* 1980, Pauline, da of Howard Moore Gentry, and has issue living, Michael John *b* 1983, Sarah-Jane *b* 1981, — Graeme David, *b* 1953; RN: *m* 1977, Mrs Janet Gates, da of Sidney Brewer, and has issue living, Colin *b* 1977, Michelle *b* 1980.

Grandsons of late Edward Robert Ward, elder son of late John Hamilton Ward, 4th son of late Rev Hon Henry Ward, 2nd brother of 3rd Viscount:—
Issue of late Albert Edward Hamilton Ward, *b* 1902, *d* 1976: *m* 1932, Violet Kate, who *d* 1998, da of John Henderson Jones:—
John Albert (Buzon No1, Urbanisation El Capso, 16 Cami els plans, Orba, 03791 Alicante, Spain), *b* 1933: *m* 1956, Judith Mary, da of Richard R. Lamdin, and has issue living, Stuart John (Avda, Valencia 33 2p pta 7, 03700 Denia, Alicante, Spain), *b* 1964: *m* 1991, Joaquina Donderis Oliver, — Fiona Maryon (115 Stanley Rd, Forest Field, Nottingham NG7 6HQ), *b* 1959: *m* 1984, — Weller, and has issue living, Harriette Judy *b* 1989.

Issue of late John Hamilton Ward, *b* 1907, *d* 1990: *m* 1939, Peggy Elizabeth Louise (Roseland, Garratts Lane, Banstead, Surrey SM7 2EQ), da of William Allen Hazeldine:—
Edward Hamilton (2 Cowdray Drive, Rustington, W Sussex BN16 3SJ), *b* 1944: *m* 1971, Jean Audrey, da of Alfred Hudson. ——— Roger Hamilton (23 Warren Rd, Banstead, Surrey SM7 1LG), *b* 1947: *m* 1993, Alison, da of Kenneth Spindler.

Granddaughter of late Thomas Lawrence Frederick Ward, 5th son of late Rev Hon Henry Ward (ante):—
Issue of late Frederic Valentine Ward, *b* 1878, *d* 1960: *m* 1908, Florence Grace, who *d* 1961, da of James Dalziel, of Auckland, NZ:—
Doreen Mabel Valerie, *b* 1915: *m* 1939, "Blondie" Henderson, of 15 Mason St, Lower Hutt, Wellington, NZ.

Granddaughter of late Francis Michael Ward, 7th son of late Rev Hon Henry Ward (ante):—
Issue of late Basil Edward Ward, *b* 1886, *d* 1953: *m* 1912, Hazel C. Smith, who *d* 1948:—
Caroline Anne (624 San Miguel Av, Berkeley, Calif 94707, USA), *b* 1914: *m* 1st, 1939, Robert Frederick McKean, who *d* 1966; 2ndly, 1967, Darrell Wiltse Walker, and has issue living (by 1st *m*), Robert Basil (540 41st St, Richmond, Calif 94805, USA), *b* 1943: *m* 1967, — , and has issue living, Jacob Frederick *b* 1969, Aaron Robert *b* 1970, Nathaniel Ward *b* 1973, — Barbara Ann, *b* 1940: *m* 1960, Ray Donald Konig, and has issue living, Kathleen Ann *b* 1966, Colleen Ann *b* 1970, — Patricia Ann, *b* 1951: *m* 1979, Ramish Ramchandani, of 2503 Lincoln Av, Alameda, Calif 94501, USA.

Grandson of late Lt-Col Bernard Edward Ward, 2nd son of late Rev Bernard John Ward, 3rd son of late Col Rt Hon Robert Ward, 3rd son of 1st Viscount:—
Issue of late Capt Bernard John Hamilton Ward, OBE, RN, *b* 1875, *d* 1938: *m* 1908, Annie Lilias, who *d* 1978, da of late Ralph Dalyell, CB (*see* E Warwick, colls, 1924 Edn):—
Bernard Ralph Henry, OBE (Trotts Close, Trotts Lane, Westerham, Kent TN16 1SD), *b* 1911; Lt-Cdr RN (ret); entered Executive Class, Home Civil Ser 1957; OBE (Mil) 1946: *m* 1st, 1943 (*m diss* 1951), Tamara Estya Jasvoin; 2ndly, 1955, Marian Violet, who *d* 1958, da of late Capt Percy William Rimington, OBE, RN; 3rdly, 1961, Daphne Thalia, who *d* 1999, da of John Lumsden, MBE, Vice-Consul, Casablanca, and has issue living (by 3rd *m*), Nicholas Ralph Dalyell (7 Abbots Close, Highcliffe-on-Sea, Dorset BH23 5BH), *b* 1964: *m* 1991, Victoria Anne, da of Leslie Francis Carr, of Highcliffe on Sea, and has had issue living, Emily Stephanie *b* 1992, *d* 1996, — Annie Christabel, *b* 1965: *m* 1992, Andrew Peter Forbes, of 70 Hillingdon Av, Sevenoaks TN13 3RA, and has issue living, Frances Rose *b* 1988, Ruby Ann *b* 1993, — John Louis Frederic (adopted son), *b* 1959, *ed* Univ of E Anglia (BA 1981); Royal Hong Kong Police 1982: *m* 1985, Melanie Bayoneta, da of Salcedo Isidro, of Camalines Sur, Philippines, and has issue living, Ralph Louis Frederic Junior *b* 1995, James Nicholas Bernard *b* 1997, Louisa Marie Christabel *b* 1986, (and an adopted son, Dean Salcedo *b* 1984).

Grandchildren of late Capt John Richard Le Hunte Ward, CBE, RN (infra):—
Adopted daughters of late Lt-Col Edward Le Hunte Ward, *b* 1906, *d* 1987: *m* 1946, Flora (Linney Water, Eastern Rd, Ashburton, S Devon TQ13 7AP), da of late Capt William Balfour Macdonald, DSO, RN:—
Antonia Janet Elizabeth, *b* 1947: *m* 1975, Daryl George Youé, of Linney Water, Eastern Rd, Ashburton, S Devon, and has issue living, André, *b* 1978, — Dominic, *b* 1980. —— Fynvola Mary Isabel, *b* 1949; BA, LLB: *m* 1975, Carlo Angelo Bernabucci, of 28 via Anton Cechov, Rome 00142, and has issue living, Ivan, *b* 1976, — Matteo, *b* 1978.

Grandchildren of late Maj Michael Bernard John Ward, yr son of late Capt John Richard Le Hunte Ward, CBE, RN, only son of late Adm Thomas Le Hunte Ward, CB, 3rd and yst son of late Rev Bernard John Ward (ante):—
Issue of late John Michael Barrie Ward, *b* 1945, *d* 1992: *m* 1974, Anne Christine Hotchkiss (The Cedars, Fairthorne Way, Shrivenham, Swindon, Wilts):—
Thomas Edward John Le Hunte, *b* 1980. —— Charlotte Jane, *b* 1977. —— Catherine Sophia, *b* 1979.

Grandchildren of late Maj Hamilton Frederick Ward (infra):—
Issue of late Capt John Frederick Ward, late Irish Gds, *b* 1923, *d* 1989: *m* 1950, Pamela Swinton (Kabazi, PO Box 153, Nakuru, Kenya), da of late Lt-Col George Archibald Swinton Home, of Soy, Kenya:—
Edward, *b* 1958: *m* 19—, Katherine Rundle, and has issue living, Luke Howard, *b* 1997. —— Sarah, *b* 1953: *m* 19—, Derek Miller, of Karen, Nairobi, and has issue living, Tanya, *b* 1982, — Katrina, *b* 1985.

Granddaughter of late Lt Robert Frederick Ward, RN only son of late Vice-Adm James Hamilton Ward, 5th son of late Col Rt Hon Robert Ward (ante):—
Issue of late Maj Hamilton Frederick Ward, *b* 1880, *d* 1971: *m* 1913, Violet Enid Jane, who *d* 1972, da of late Sir Henry Conway Belfield, KCMG:—
Sheila Marie Jane, *b* 1914: *m* 1939, Alexander Frederick Reynard, of 675 Pretorius, St, Arcadia, Pretoria 0083, S Africa, and has issue living, Edward Anthony, *b* 1945: *m* 1969, Margaret Marian, da of Thomas Allan Fairbairn, of Millbrae Head, Kirkton Manor, Peebles, and has issue living, Iain Michael *b* 1971, Robert Neil *b* 1974, — John William, *b* 1947: *m* 1974 (*m diss* 1989), Sandra Dianne, da of Willacy Guy Goulding, of 273 Pasteur Rd, Rembrandt Park, S Africa, and has issue living, Angela Lynne *b* 1979, Jennifer Susan *b* 1983, — Monica Mary, *b* 1942: *m* 1983, Michael William Atkinson, Civil Engr, son of William Charles Atkinson, of Johannesburg.

Granddaughter of late William Robert Ward, 6th son of late Col Rt Hon Robert Ward (ante):—
Issue of late Lt-Col Edward Ward, MBE, *b* 1852, *d* 1929; *m* 1900, Harriette Caroline Adeline (Etta), who *d* 1937, da of late John Steuart Maconchy:—
Charlotte Hazel, *b* 1900. *Residence* – 54 Crossgar Rd, Saintfield, co Down.

PREDECESSORS – (1) BERNARD Ward, MP for co Down 1749-70; cr *Baron Bangor* (peerage of Ireland) 1770, and *Viscount Bangor* (peerage of Ireland) 1781; *d* 1781, and was *s* by his el son (2) NICHOLAS, 2nd Viscount; *dsp* 1827; *s* by his nephew, el son of Hon Edward Ward, 2nd son of 1st Viscount (3) EDWARD SOUTHWELL, 3rd Viscount: *m* 1826, Harriet Margaret, who *d* 1880, da of 6th Baron Farnham; *d* 1837; *s* by his el son (4) EDWARD, 4th Viscount, a Representative Peer; *dsp* 1881; *s* by his brother (5) HENRY WILLIAM CROSBIE, 5th Viscount, *b* 1828; a Representative Peer: *m* 1st, 1854, Mary, who *d* 1869, da of late Rev Henry King, of Ballylin, King's co; 2ndly, 1874, Elizabeth, who *d* 1919, da of late Major Hugh Eccles, of Cronroe, co Wicklow; *d* 1911; *s* by his son (6) MAXWELL RICHARD CROSBIE, PC, OBE, 6th Viscount, *b* 1868; a Representative Peer for Ireland; sometime Parliamentary Private Sec to Prime Min of N Ireland; was a Member of Senate, N Ireland 1921-50, and Speaker 1930-50: *m* (Jan) 1905, Agnes Elizabeth, who *d* 1972, da of late Dacre Mervyn Archdall Hamilton, *d* 1950; *s* by his son (7) EDWARD HENRY HAROLD, 7th Viscount, *b* 1905; Broadcaster and Journalist: *m* 1st, 1933 (*m diss* 1937), Elizabeth, da of Thomas Balfour, JP, of Wrockwardine Hall, Wellington, Shropshire; 2ndly, 1937 (*m diss* 1947), May Kathleen, who *d* 1969, da of William Middleton, of Shanghai; 3rdly, 1947 (*m diss* 1951), Leila Mary, who *d* 1959, da of David Rimington Heaton, DSO, of Brookfield, Crowhill, S Devon; 4thly, 1951, Marjorie Alice, who *d* 1991, da of late Peter Banks, of St Leonards-on-Sea, and formerly wife of Reginald Forbes Simpson; *d* 1993; *s* by his elder son (8) WILLIAM MAXWELL DAVID, 8th Viscount and present peer; also Baron Bangor.

BANKS, BARONY OF (Banks) (Extinct 1997)

SONS LIVING OF LIFE BARON

Hon Alistair Richard Harvie, b 1950: m 1977, Loretta Ann Owen.
Hon Graham Thornton Harvie, b 1953.

WIDOW LIVING OF LIFE BARON

BARBARA (Baroness Banks), da of Richard Taylor Wells: m 1948, Baron Banks, CBE (Life Baron), who d 1997. Residence –
58 The Ridgeway, Kenton, Harrow, Middx.

BANNERMAN OF KILDONAN, BARONY OF (Bannerman) (Extinct 1969)

SONS LIVING OF LIFE BARON

Hon John Walter MacDonald, b 1932; MA (Hons) Glasgow; BA (Hons) Camb; PhD Camb, and has issue living, two sons
and one da.
Hon Calum Ruairi Mundell, b 1936; BA Camb: m 1962, Mary (neé Parker), and has issue living, one son and two das.

DAUGHTERS LIVING OF LIFE BARON

Hon (Janet) Ray, MP, b 1934; LCST; MP (Lib Dem) Argyll and Bute since 1987: m 1957, Lt-Col Iain Michie, RAMC, of
Tigh an Eas, Oban, Argyll, and has issue living, three das.
Hon Elizabeth Mary (The Braes, Uplawmoor, Renfrewshire), b 1938; resumed surname of Monro 1980: m 1st, 1960 (m
diss 1971), D. S. Munro; 2ndly, 1972 (m diss 1980), Iain Buchanan Anderson; 3rdly, 1990, John Daniel Scott, and has
issue living, one son and one da.

BARBER, BARON (Barber) (Life Baron 1974)

ANTHONY PERRINOTT LYSBERG BARBER, TD, PC, son of late John Barber, CBE; b 4 July 1920; ed
Retford Sch, and Oriel Coll, Oxford (MA, Hon Fellow 1971); LLB London; 1939-45 War as Lt RA
and pilot RAF (prisoner, despatches); a DL for W Yorks (1987); Bar Inner Temple 1948; PPS to
Under-Sec of State for Air 1952-54, Govt Whip 1953-57, Lord Commr of Treasury 1957-58, PPS to
PM 1958-59, Economic Sec to Treasury 1959-62, and Financial Sec to same 1962-63, and Min of
Health 1963-64; Chm Conservative Party Orgn 1967-70; Chancellor of the Duchy of Lancaster June
to July 1970, and Chancellor of the Exchequer 1970-74; Chm of Standard Chartered Bank 1974-87;
Chm Council of Westminster Med Sch 1975-84; Member Franks Committee on Falklands 1982-83;
British Member Eminent Persons Group on S Africa 1986; cr PC 1963, and Baron Barber, of Went-
bridge, W Yorks (Life Baron) 1974: m 1st, 1950, Jean Patricia, who d 1983, da of Milton Asquith, of
Wentbridge, W Yorks; 2ndly, 1989, Mrs Rosemary Surgenor, da of Canon Youens, of Brodsworth,
W Yorks, formerly wife of John Surgenor, and has issue by 1st m.
Club - Carlton.

DAUGHTERS LIVING (By 1st marriage)

Hon Louise Patricia Lysberg, b 1951.
Hon Josephine Julia Asquith, b 1953: m 1989, William J. L. Bradby, son of James Bradby, of Spetisbury, Dorset.
Residence – Hollesley Lodge, nr Woodbridge, Suffolk, IP12 3RT.

BARBER OF TEWKESBURY, BARON (Barber) (Life Baron 1992)

DEREK COATES BARBER, son of late Thomas Smith-Barber, of The Thatched House, nr Stradbroke, Suffolk; *b* 17 June 1918; *ed* RAC Circencester; Hon FRASE 1986; Hon DSc Bradford 1986; served 1939-45 War (invalided); Farmer and Land Consultant; Founder Member Farming & Wildlife Advisory Group 1969, Environment Consultant to Humberts, Chartered Surveyors, since 1972, Chm BBC's Central Agricultural Advisory Cttee 1974-80, Consultant to Humberts Landplan plc 1974-89, Chm RSPB 1976-81, and Pres 1990-91, Chm Countryside Commn 1981-91, Chm Booker plc Country-side Advisory Board since 1990, Pres Glos Naturalists' Soc since 1982, Patron Lancs Heritage Trust since 1990, Council Member Rare Breeds Survival Trust since 1987 (Pres 1991-99), Pres Royal Agricultural Soc of England 1991-92, Chm New Nat Forest Advisory Board 1991-94; author, and recipient of several agricultural and conservation awards; *cr* Kt Bach 1984, and *Baron Barber of Tewkesbury*, of Gotherington, co Glos (Life Baron) 1992: *m* 1st, 19- (*m diss* 1981), —, da of —, of —; 2ndly, 1983, Rosemary Jennifer Brougham, da of late Lt-Cdr Randolph Brougham Pearson, RN. *Residence* – Chough House, Gotherington, Glos GL52 4QU. *Club* – Farmers'.

Baring, family name of Baron Ashburton.

Baring, family name of Earl of Cromer.

Baring, family name of Baron Howick of Glendale.

Baring, family name of Baron Northbrook.

Baring, family name of Baron Revelstoke.

Barker, family name of Baroness Trumpington.

BARNARD, BARON (Vane) (Baron E 1698)

HARRY JOHN NEVILLE VANE, TD, 11th Baron; *b* 21 Sept 1923; *s* 1964; *ed* Eton; MSc Durham Univ; patron of 10 livings; JP co Durham 1961, DL 1956-70, Lord Lieut and Custos Rotulorum 1970-88; Lt-Col comdg Northumberland Hussars 1964-66, Hon Col 7th (Durham) Bn LI 1979-89; a Co Councillor for Durham 1952-61; Pres Durham County Branch BRCS 1969-87, Patron 1993, Vice-Chm of Council BRCS 1987-93 (Memb of Council 1982-85); Sr Grand Warden United Grand Lodge of England 1970-71, Provincial Grand Master for Durham 1969-98; Pres North of England TAVR Assocn 1974-77; KStJ; 1939-45 War as F/O RAFVR: *m* 1952 (*m diss* 1992), Lady Davina Mary Cecil, DStJ, el da of 6th Marquess of Exeter, and has issue.

Arms – Azure, three sinister gauntlets or. **Crest** – A dexter hand in armour couped at the wrist grasping a sword in bend all proper, pommel and hilt or. **Supporters** – *Dexter*, a griffin argent, gorged with a collar azure thereon three sinister gauntlets or as in the arms; *sinister*, an antelope or, gorged with a collar azure, thereon three martlets or.
Seat – Raby Castle, PO Box 50, Staindrop, Darlington, co Durham, DL2 3AY. *Clubs* – Brooks's, Durham County, Northern Counties (Newcastle).

SON LIVING

Hon HENRY FRANCIS CECIL, *b* 11 March 1959, *ed* Eton, and Edinburgh Univ (BSc): *m* 1998, Lydia Katharine (Kate), yr da of Christopher William Robson, of Rudd Hall, Richmond, N Yorks.

DAUGHTERS LIVING

Hon Carolyn Mary, *b* 1954; has issue living, Nicola Lauren VANE, *b* 1988.

Hon Elizabeth Anne, *b* 1956: *m* 1982 (*m diss* 1996), Glyn M. Deacon, elder son of late A. Deacon, and has issue living, Jessica Anne, *b* 1982, — Laura Sophie, *b* 1984.

Hon Sophia Rosalind, *b* 1962, *ed* Cobham Hall, and Westfield Coll, Univ of Lond (BSc): *m* 1986, Simon B. Phillips, yst son of late Peter J. Phillips, of Gustard Wood, Wheathampstead, Herts, and has issue living, Oliver John, *b* 1989, — Benjamin James, *b* 1994, — Emily Josephine, *b* 1992.

Hon Louise Cicely, *b* 1968; *ed* Cobham Hall, and Central St Martins' Sch of Art and Design (BA).

SISTER LIVING

Hon Rosemary Myra, *b* 1921; a Member of Barnard Castle RDC (Chm 1972-73); Chm Durham Co Fedn of Women's Insts: *m* 1948 (*m diss* 1954), Angus Josslyn Gore-Booth (later 8th Bt), who *d* 1996, and has issue (*see* Gore-Booth, Bt). *Residence* – The White House, Gainford, Darlington DL2 3DN.

COLLATERAL BRANCH LIVING

Grandsons of late Col Hon William Lyonel Vane (*who was raised to the rank of a Baron's son* 1892), brother of 9th Baron:—
Issue of late William Morgan FLETCHER VANE, TD (*Baron Inglewood*) (see that title).

PREDECESSORS – (1) *Rt Hon* CHRISTOPHER Vane, *b* 1653, 5th and only surviving son of Sir Henry Vane, the younger, who was beheaded for treason 1662; *cr Baron Barnard*, of Barnard Castle, in the County Palatine of Durham (peerage of England) 1698; *d* 1723; *s* by his son (2) GILBERT, 2nd Baron, *b* 1678, *d* 1753; *s* by his son (3) HENRY, 3rd Baron, *b* 1705, successively MP for Launceston, St Mawes, Ripon, and co Durham, Paymaster in Ireland, a Lord of the Treasury, and Lord-Lieut and Vice-Adm of Durham; *cr Viscount Barnard* and *Earl of Darlington* (peerage of Great Britain) 1754; *d* 1758; *s* by his son (4) HENRY, 2nd Earl, *b* 1726, MP for Downton and for co Durham; Lord-Lieut and Vice-Adm of County Palatine of Durham, Master of the Jewel Office, and Gov of Carlisle; *d* 1792; *s* by his son (5) WILLIAM HARRY, KG, 3rd Earl, *b* 1766; Lord-Lieut and Vice Adm of Co Durham; MP for Totnes 1788-90 and for Winchelsea 1790-92; *cr Marquess of Cleveland* (peerage of United Kingdom) 1827 and *Baron Raby* and *Duke of Cleveland* (peerage of United Kingdom) 1833: *m* 1st, 1787, Lady Katharine Margaret Powlett, who *d* 1807, da and co-heir of Harry, 6th and last Duke of Bolton; 2ndly, 1813, Elizabeth, who *d* 1861, da of Robert Russell; *d* 1842; *s* by his el son (by 1st *m*) (6) HENRY, KG, 2nd Duke; *b* 1788; a Lieut-Gen in the Army; MP 1812-42; *dsp* 1864; *s* by his brother (7) WILLIAM JOHN FREDERICK, 3rd Duke; *b* 1792, assumed the surname of Powlett by R licence 1813, and resumed his patronymic, Vane, by R licence 1864; MP 1812-31 and 1846-57; *d* 1864; *s* by his brother (8) HARRY GEORGE, KG, 4th Duke, *b* 1803; MP for S Durham (*L*) 1841-59, and for Hastings 1859-64; assumed in 1864 the name and arms of Powlett in lieu of Vane: *m* 1854, Catherine Lucy Wilhelmina, who *d* 1901, da of 4th Earl Stanhope, and widow of Lord Dalmeny, el son of 4th Earl of Rosebery; *d* 1891, when all his honours became extinct with the exception of the Barony of Barnard, which devolved upon (9) HENRY DE VERE (son of Sir Henry Morgan Vane, a descendant of the 2nd Baron), who was adjudged 9th Baron by Cttee for Privileges, House of Lords, 1892; *b* 1854; DCL, Hon Col 4th Bn Durham LI: *m* 1881, Lady Catherine Sarah Cecil, who *d* 1918, da of 3rd Marquess of Exeter; *d* 1918; *s* by his son (10) CHRISTOPHER WILLIAM, CMG, OBE, MC, TD, 10th Baron, *b* 1888, Lt-Col and Brevet-Col 6th DLI; served World War I 1914-18 as Maj Westmorland and Cumberland Yeo; Lord-Lieut of co Durham 1958-64 and JP co Durham: *m* 1920, Sylvia Mary, who *d* 1993, da of Herbert Straker, late of Hartforth Grange, Richmond, Yorks; *d* 1964; *s* by his el son (11) HARRY JOHN NEVILLE, 11th Baron and present peer.

Barnes, family name of Baron Gorell.

BARNETSON, BARONY OF (Barnetson) (Extinct 1981)

SON LIVING OF LIFE BARON

Hon (William) Denholm, *b* 1955.

DAUGHTERS LIVING OF LIFE BARON

Hon Astraea Joan Denholm, *b* 1941: *m* 1963, John R. D. Moore, of Nether Soonhope House, Peebles, and has issue living.
Hon Louise Jane Denholm, *b* 1952: *m* 1982 (*m diss* 1992), Bernard Rolfe, and has issue living.
Hon Julia Claire Denholm, *b* 1963: *m* 1990, Dr Timothy R. Cave, yr son of Maj Leslie Cave, of Eridge, Sussex, and has issue living.

BARNETT, BARON (Barnett) (Life Baron 1983)

JOEL BARNETT, PC, son of late Louis Barnett, of Manchester; *b* 14 Oct 1923; *ed* Central High Sch, Manchester; Hon Visiting Fellow Strathclyde Univ (1980), Hon LLD Strathclyde 1983, Hon Fellow Birkbeck Coll 1993; FCCA; 1939-45 War; Consultant J. C. Allen & Co (now Hacker Young), Manchester (Sr Partner 1954-74); Chm Parl Labour Party Economic & Financial Gp 1967-70; Ch Sec HM Treasury 1974-79 (Cabinet Member 1977-79), Chm Public Accounts Cttee 1979-83; Member Cttee Hallé Society of Manchester 1982-93, Trustee Victoria and Albert Museum 1983-96, Vice-Chm BBC 1986-93, Pres Royal Inst of Public Administrators 1988-92, Chm Birkbeck Coll Appeal Cttee 1992-95, Chm Hansard Soc 1985-91; MP for Heywood and Royton Div of Lancs (*Lab*) 1964-83; *cr* PC 1975, and *Baron Barnett*, of Heywood and Royton, in Greater Manchester (Life Baron) 1983: *m* 1949, Lilian Stella, da of Abraham Goldstone, and has issue.
Residences – 7 Hillingdon Rd, Whitefield, Lancs M45 7QQ; Flat 92, 24 John Islip St, Westminster, SW1.

DAUGHTER LIVING

Hon Erica Hazel, *b* 1951.

Barnewall, family name of Baron Trimlestown.

Barrie, family name of Abertay Barony.

BARRINGTON, VISCOUNTCY OF (Barrington) (Dormant or Extinct 1990)

SISTER LIVING OF ELEVENTH VISCOUNT

Priscilla Mary, *b* 1907.

COLLATERAL BRANCH LIVING

Granddaughter of late Hon Percy Evelyn Barrington, yst son of 9th Viscount:—
Issue of late Miguel O'Brien Shute Barrington, *b* 1909, *d* 1937: *m* 1935, Yvonne Guary-Dommergues, who *d* 1948, da of Madame Nebel, of Paris:—
Michaelle Susan (*posthumous*), *b* 1937; *ed* Somerville Coll, Oxford: *m* 1968, Renato Zanatta, of Savona, Italy.

BASING, BARON (Sclater Booth) (Baron UK 1887)
(Name pronounced "Slater Booth")

NEIL LUTLEY SCLATER BOOTH, 5th Baron; *b* 16 Jan 1939; *s* 1983; *ed* Eton, and Harvard Univ (BA); Dir Akroyd & Smithers Inc (New York City): *m* 1967, Patricia Ann, da of late George Bryan Whitfield, of 598 Prospect St, New Haven, Conn, USA, and has issue.

Arms – Quarterly; 1st and 4th gules a chevron, between in chief two bezants, and in base a portcullis chained or, *Booth*; 2nd and 3rd, argent a cross gules between two penguins proper in the first and fourth quarters, and two martlets azure in the second and third quarters, *Sclater*. **Crests** – *Dexter*, a horse's head erased proper, bridled and reined or, charged with a roundel argent, thereon a boar's head erect and erased sable, *Booth; sinister*, Between two sprigs of oak proper, fructed or, a woodcock's head erased proper, gorged with a collar argent, charged with a saltire azure, *Sclater*. **Supporters** – *Dexter*, winged a lion queue fourchee; *sinister*, an eagle sable; each gorged with a saltire azure affixed to the collar a chain reflexed over the back argent, the wings charged on the covert and secondary feathers with three cogwheels in chevron or.
Club – Harvard.

SONS LIVING

Hon STUART ANTHONY WHITFIELD, *b* 18 Dec 1969; *ed* The Collegiate Sch: *m* 1997, Kirsten Erica, da of Eric Henry Oxboel.
Hon Andrew Limbrey, *b* 1973; *ed* The Collegiate Sch.

DAUGHTERS LIVING OF THIRD BARON

Hon Diana Penelope Florence *b* 1925: *m* 1946, James Tennant Bailward, and has issue living, Christopher John (Horsington Manor, Horsington, Templecombe, Som), *b* 1949: *m* 1974, Anne, da of Lt-Col G. E. Gray, of Colehill, Wimborne, Dorset, and has issue living, James Richard *b* 1978, Thomas William *b* 1981, Robert John *b* (twin) 1981, Kate Louise *b* 1976, — Clare Penelope, *b* 1947: *m* 1973, Brian Jayes, of Wayside, Old Horsley Rd, Nailsworth, Glos, son of P. H. Hayes, of Lindfield, Sussex, and has issue living, Andrew Patrick Harris *b* 1977, Rosamund Sarah *b* 1974. *Residence* – 5 Park Farm Close, Martinstown, Dorchester, Dorset DT2 9TW.

Hon Barbara Amy, *b* 1926: *m* 1961, Peter Michell Luttman-Johnson, and has issue living, William Michell (Waldegrave Farm, Hartest, Bury St Edmunds, Suffolk IP29 4EA), *b* 1963: *m* 1992, Lucilla Jane, eldest da of David Adams, of Earls Colne, Essex, — Anne Elizabeth, *b* 1962, — Catherine Mary, *b* 1966: *m* 1996, Ian Guiver, elder son of P. Guiver, of Leigh on Sea, Essex, and has issue living, Eleanor Jane *b* 1999. *Residence* – Woodmancote, Lodsworth, Petworth, W Sussex.

Hon Gabrielle Mary, *b* 1929: *m* 1953, Cdr Martin Parnell Seth-Smith, RN, and has issue living Nicholas John, *b* 1961: *m* 1994, Sally Anne, da of late David Wright, and has issue living, Oliver Parnell *b* 1998, Maximilian David *b* (twin) 1998, — Imogen Gabrielle, *b* 1963: *m* 1996, Jeremy James Charles-Jones, of Charlham Farmhouse, Ampney St Peter, Cirencester, Glos GL7 5SJ, eldest son of Hugh Charles-Jones, and grandson of late Maj Francis Jones, Wales Herald Extraordinary. *Residence* – The Triangle, Wildhern, Andover.

PREDECESSORS – (1) George Sclater, PC, el son of late William Lutley Sclater, of Hoddington House, Hants; *b* 1826; assumed by R licence 1856 the additional surname of Booth; MP for N Hants (C) 1857-85, and for Hants N, or Basingstoke, Div 1885-7; Parliamentary Sec to Poor Law Board 1867-8, Financial Sec to Treasury 1868, and Pres of Local Govt Board 1874-80; *cr Baron Basing* (peerage of United Kingdom) 1887: *m* 1857, Lydia Caroline, who *d* 1881, da of late Major George Birch, of Clare Park, Hants; *d* 1894; *s* by his el son (2) GEORGE LIMBREY, CB, *b* 1860; Lt-Col and Brevet-

Col 1st (R) Dragoons, and Brig-Gen: *m* 1889, Mary, who *d* 1904, da of late John Hargreaves, of Maiden Erlegh Berks, and Whalley Abbey, Lancashire; *d* 1919; *s* by his only son (3) JOHN LIMBREY ROBERT, TD, 3rd Baron, *b* 1890: *m* 1924, Mary Alice Erle, who *d* 1970, da of late Lt-Col Richard Erle Benson, E Yorks Regt; *d* 1969, *s* by his cousin (4) GEORGE LUTLEY (son of Hon Charles Lutley Sclater Booth, 2nd son of 1st Baron), 4th Baron, *b* 1903: *m* 1st, 1938 (*m diss* 1944), Jeanette, who *d* 1957, da of late Neil Bruce MacKelvie, of New York; 2ndly, 1951, Cynthia, who *d* 1982, da of late Charles W. Hardy, of Salt Lake City, Utah, and widow of Carl H. Beal, of Los Angeles; *d* 1983; *s* by his only son (5) NEIL LUTLEY, 5th Baron and present peer.

Bass, Hastings-, family name of Earl of Huntingdon.

BASNETT, BARONY OF (Basnett) (Extinct 1989)

WIDOW LIVING OF LIFE BARON

KATHLEEN JOAN MOLYNEAUX (*Baroness Basnett*): *m* 1956, Baron Basnett (*cr* Life Baron 1987), who *d* 1989, and has issue, two sons. *Residence* – Windrush, St John's Av, Leatherhead, Surrey.

BASSAM OF BRIGHTON, BARON (Bassam) (Life Baron 1997)

(JOHN) STEVEN BASSAM, son of late Sydney Stevens and Enid Bassam, of Colchester, Essex; *b* 11 June 1953; *ed* Univ of Sussex (BA 1975), and Univ of Kent (MA 1979); Social Worker, E Sussex CC 1976-77; Legal Adviser, N Lewisham Law Centre 1979-83; Policy Adviser, LB Camden 1983-84, GLC (Police Cttee) 1984-86, and London Strategic Policy Unit (Policing) 1986-87; Assist Sec, Police, Fire, Environmental Health and Consumer Affairs, AMA 1988-97, since when Head of Environmental Health and Consumer Affairs, Local Government Assoc; Memb Brighton BC (Lab) 1983-97 (Leader 1987-97); Memb Brighton and Hove Unitary Council since 1996 (Leader since 1996); *cr Baron Bassam of Brighton*, of Brighton, co E Sussex (Life Baron) 1997: partner, Jill, da of June Whittaker, of London, and has had issue.
Residence – Longstone, 25 Church Place, Brighton, E Sussex BN2 5JN.

SONS LIVING AND DECEASED

Thomas Harry, *b* 1988.
Gregory John, *b* (Sept) 1994, *d* (Oct) 1994.

DAUGHTER LIVING

Lauren Stephanie, *b* 1990.

Bateson, de Yarburgh-, family name of Baron Deramore.

BATH, MARQUESS OF (Thynn and Thynne) (Marquess GB 1789, Bt E 1641)
(Name pronounced "Thin")

I have good reason

ALEXANDER GEORGE THYNN, 7th Marquess, and 10th Baronet; *b* 6 May 1932; *s* 1992; *ed* Eton, and Ch Ch, Oxford (MA); formerly Lieut Life Guards and Royal Wilts Yeo; has reverted to spelling of Thynn since 1976; contested (Wessex Regionalist) Westbury 1974, Wells 1979; contested (Wessex Regionalist and European Federal Party) Wessex, European Election 1979; mural artist, and composer; author of *The Carry Cot, Lord Weymouth's Murals, A Regionalist Manifesto, The King is Dead, Pillars of the Establishment*, etc; Dir Longleat Enterprises 1964: *m* 1969, Anna (Anna Gael, actress and journalist), da of Laszlo Izsak Gyarmarthy, of Los Angeles, Calif, USA, and has issue.

Arms – Quarterly: 1st and 4th, barry of ten or and sable, *Botteville*; 2nd and 3rd argent, a lion rampat tail nowed and erect gules, *Thynne*. Crest – A reindeer statant or. Supporters – *Dexter*, a reindeer or, gorged with a plain collar sable: *sinister*, a lion tail nowed and erect gules.
Seat – Longleat, Warminster, Wilts BA12 7NN.

SON LIVING

CEAWLIN HENRY LASZLO (*Viscount Weymouth*), *b* 6 June 1974; *ed* Kingdown Comprehensive Sch, Warminster, Bedales, Cambridge Coll, Richmond Univ, Va, USA, and Univ Coll London.

DAUGHTER LIVING

Lady Lenka Abigail, *b* 1969; *ed* Kingdown Comprehensive Sch, Warminster, and Univ Coll, Oxford.

BROTHER LIVING

Lord Christopher John, *b* 1934; *ed* Eton; late 2nd Lieut Life Guards: *m* 1968, Antonia Mary, da of Maj Sir Anthony Frederick Mark Palmer, 5th Bt (*cr* 1886), and has issue living, Sophie Emma, *b* 1968. *Residence* – Britmore House, Donhead St Andrew, Shaftesbury, Dorset SP7 9EB.

HALF-SISTER LIVING

Lady Silvy Cerne, *b* 1958: *m* 1989, Iain McQuiston, only son of Iain McQuiston, of London, and has issue living, Milo Henry Cerne, *b* 1992, — Eve Iris, *b* 1990.

WIDOW LIVING OF SON OF SIXTH MARQUESS

Liese Maria (*Lady Valentine Thynne*), da of Kenneth William Dennis, of Bristol, and formerly wife of Karl Martin Weschke; is an artist: *m* 1977, as his 3rd wife, Lord Valentine Charles Thynne, who *d* 1979. *Residence* – 16 Bedford St, Bath BA1 6AF.

WIDOW LIVING OF SIXTH MARQUESS

VIRGINIA PENELOPE (*Dowager Marchioness of Bath*), da of late Alan Parsons, of The Baas, Broxbourne, Herts, and formerly wife of Hon David Francis Tennant (*see* B Glenconner, colls): *m* 1953, as his 2nd wife, the 6th Marquess of Bath, ED, who *d* 1992. *Residence* – Job's Mill, Crockerton, Warminster, Wilts.

COLLATERAL BRANCHES LIVING

Issue of late Lord Valentine Charles Thynne, yst son of 6th Marquess, *b* 1937, *d* 1979: *m* 1st, 1961 (*m diss* 1971), Veronica Ann, only da of Col G. E. Jackson, of Stratford, NZ; 2ndly, 1971 (*m diss* 1976), Susanne Caroline, da of Edgar Harold Alder, of Primrose Farm, Little Wilbraham, Cambs, and formerly wife of Christopher Hodgson Moore; 3rdly, 1977, Liese Maria (ante), da of Kenneth William Dennis, and formerly wife of Karl Martin Weschke:—
(By 1st *m*) Lucien Henry Valentine, *b* 1965; *ed* Milton Abbey: *m* 1998, Henrietta Yvery, elder da of Nicholas Victor Hunloke (*see* E Sandwich). —— Xenia Laura, *b* 1962: *m* 1989, Joshua David Mason, who *d* 1991, son of Richard Mason. *Residence* – 20 Ingate Terrace, SW8 3RR.

Grandchildren of late Col Ulric Oliver Thynne, CMG, CVO, DSO, TD, yst son of Rt Hon Lord Henry
Frederick Thynne, 2nd son of 3rd Marquess:—
Issue of late Lt-Col Oliver St Maur Thynne, TD, b 1901, d 1978: m 1936, Mary Wroughton, who d 1992,
formerly wife of Maj Richard Wale Gordon Dill, MC, and da of late Herbert Francis Morris:—
Sheridan Ulric (Patterdale, S Stoke, nr Reading), b 1939; ed Eton; late Lt R Wilts Yeo: m 1964, Eve Clare, da of Lt-Cdr
George Jameson Cardew, RN, and has issue living, Piers Mark, b 1977, — Louise Sarah, b 1965: m 1994, Christopher
Gordon Marston, yst son of Maj Philip Marston, of Wings House, Farnham, and has issue living, Tilly Florence b 1996,
Flora Tatiana b 1998, — Marika Helen, b 1973: m 1997, Daniel J. Hortop, son of John Hortop, of Sudbury, Suffolk, —
Tamara Jane, b 1974.

Issue of late Group Capt Brian Sheridan Thynne, CBE, AFC, AE, RAAF, b 1907, d 1985: m 1st, 1940 (m diss
1948), Mrs Naomi Bourn, who d 1997, only da of C. E. Waters, of Sydney, Australia; 2ndly, 1952, Maria
Fernanda Herrero, who d 1987, da of the Marques de Aledo, of Madrid:—
(By 1st m) Harriet Anne (General Gallegos 1, Madrid 28036), b 1941. ——— (By 2nd m) Ulrica Maria Teresa, b 1954.
——— Jane Georgiana, b 1955: m 1979, Javier Arzola, of Reno 4, Los Monteros, Marbella, Malaga, Spain, and has issue
living, David, b 1981, — Raquel, b 1982, — Esther, b 1990.

Grandson of late Francis John Thynne, 2nd son of Rev Lord John Thynne, DD, 3rd son of 2nd
Marquess:—
Issue of late Capt George Augustus Carteret Thynne, late R N Devon Yeo, b 1869, d 1945: m 1915, Hon Gladys
Isabel Annette Adderley, who d 1960, da of 2nd Baron Norton:—
John Grenville (Hays House, Shaftesbury, Dorset), b 1917; ed Stowe; late Maj RHG; European War 1939-45 in Iraq, Syria,
Persia, Egypt, Italy, Holland, and Germany: m 1st, 1946, Baroness Marianne Madeleine, who d 1990, da of late Baron H.
R. de Jenner, of Château de Landshut, Berne; 2ndly, 1991, Mrs Yvonne Watkins, da of late Maj Cuthbert Augustine
Edward Chudleigh, of Rolandsfield, Bude, Cornwall, and has issue living (by 1st m), Bevil Grenville de Jenner, b 1947;
ed Stowe: m 1970, Gertrude Dagnie, da of Arvid G. Ekman, of Skansen, Lodöse, Sweden, and has issue living, Christ-
opher John Grenville b 1972, Richard Charles Grenville b 1977, — Richard George Grenville (Tads Cottage, Froxfield,
Petersfield, Hants), b 1950: m 1st, 1973, Elizabeth Lydia Jill, da of Geoffrey Edward Courtney Barton, of Casa Nuevo,
Aldosa, La Massana, Andorra; 2ndly, 1990, Mrs Penelope Jane Radmall, da of Cdr E. M. Halley, of Wickham, Hants, and
has issue living (by 1st m), Piers James Carteret b 1976, Serena Katherine Nora b 1980, — Joanna Sybil Marcia, b 1949:
m 1985, Graham Gordon, and has issue living, Edward Alexander b 1986, Jenna Elizabeth b 1988.

PREDECESSORS – (1) Sir HENRY FREDERICK Thynne, cra Baronet 1641; s by his el son (2) Sir THOMAS, PC, 2nd Bt;
Pres of Board of Trade 1702-7; sometime MP for Oxford University and Tamworth; inherited Longleat after the murder
of his kinsman, and was cr Baron Thynne of Warminster and Viscount Weymouth (peerage of E) 1682, with remainder to
his brother Henry Frederick; d 1714; s by his grand-nephew, grandson of Henry Frederick (ante) (3) THOMAS, 2nd
Viscount; Ranger of Hyde and St James's Parks; d 1751; s by his son (4) THOMAS, KG, 3rd Viscount: was Lord of the
Bedchamber 1760-63, Master of the Horse to Queen Charlotte 1765, Lord-Lieut of Ireland 1765, Sec of State for Northern Depart 1768, and Groom of the Stole 1782-96; cr Marquess of Bath (peerage of Great Britain) 1789; d 1796; s by his
el son (5) THOMAS, KG, 2nd Marquess, Lord-Lieut of co Somerset; d 1837; s by his son (6) HENRY FREDERICK, 3rd
Marquess, b 1797; Capt RN: m 1830, Hon Harriet, da of 1st Baron Ashburton; d 1837; s by his el son (7) JOHN
ALEXANDER 4th Marquess, b 1831; Lord-Lieut of Wilts: m 1861, Hon Frances Isabella Catherine Vesey, who d 1915, el da
of 3rd Viscount de Vesci; d 1896; s by his el son (8) THOMAS HENRY, KG, CB, TD, PC, 5th Marquess, b 1862; Lord-Lieut
for Somerset; Under-Sec of State for India 1905; Chm of Wilts County Council 1906-46, and Master of the Horse 1922-4;
MP for Frome Div of Somerset (C) 1886-92 and 1895-6: m 1890, Violet Caroline, who d 1928, da of Sir Charles
Mordaunt, 10th Bt; d 1946; s by his son (9) HENRY FREDERICK, ED, 6th Marquess; b 1905; Major Royal Wilts Yeo;
European War 1939-44 (wounded), Memb of Council of HRH the Prince of Wales 1933-36, MP Frome Div of Som (C)
Oct 1931-Oct 1935: m 1st, 1926 (m diss 1953), Hon Daphne Winifred Louise Vivian, who d 1997, da of 4th Baron Vivian;
2ndly, 1953, Virginia Penelope, da of late Alan Parsons, of The Baas, Broxbourne, Herts, and formerly wife of Hon David
Francis Tennant (see B Glenconner); d 1992; s by his eldest surviving son (10) ALEXANDER GEORGE, 7th Marquess and
present peer; also Viscount Weymouth, and Baron Thynne of Warminster.

BATHURST, EARL (Bathurst) (Earl GB 1772)

Keep thy faith

HENRY ALLEN JOHN BATHURST, 8th Earl; *b* 1 May 1927; *s* 1943; *ed* Ridley Coll, Canada, Eton, and Ch Ch Oxford; Capt R Glos Hus (TA Res); DL Glos 1960-86; formerly Lieut 10th R Hus; appointed Gov of Hospital of St Lawrence, Cirencester 1944, and of RAC Cirencester 1948, and Chancellor of Primrose League 1959; a Lord-in-Waiting to HM 1957-61, and Joint Parl Under-Sec of State, Home Office 1961-2; a Member of Councils, Country Landowners' Assocn, and Timber Growers Orgn; Pres of R Forestry Soc 1976-78, Pres Institute of Sales and Marketing Management from 1981, and of the Assoc of Professional Foresters 1983-87, and 1995-98: *m* 1st, 1959 (*m diss* 1976), Judith Mary, only da of late Amos Christopher Nelson; 2ndly, 1978, Gloria Wesley, only da of Harold Edward Clarry, of Vancouver, BC, and widow of David Rutherston, and has issue by 1st *m*.

𝕬rms – Sable, two bars ermine, in chief three crosses patée, or. 𝕮rest – A dexter arm embowed, armed in mail, the hand, proper, grasping a spiked club or. 𝕾upporters – Two stags, argent, each gorged with a collar gemellé ermine.
Residence – Manor Farm, Sapperton, nr Cirencester, Glos. *Clubs* – White's, Cavalry and Guards.

SONS LIVING (*By 1st marriage*)

ALLEN CHRISTOPHER BERTRAM (*Lord Apsley*), *b* 11 March 1961: *m* 1st, 1986 (*m diss* 1995), Hilary Jane, yr da of John F. George, of Weston Lodge, Albury, Surrey; 2ndly, 1996, Sara Lucille, da of Christopher Chapman, of Ilminster, Som, and has issue:—

SON LIVING (*by 1st marriage*) — *Hon* Benjamin George Henry, *b* 6 March 1990.

DAUGHTER LIVING (*by 1st marriage*) — *Hon* Rosie Meriel Lilias, *b* 1992.

Seat – Cirencester Park, Cirencester, Glos GL7 2BT.
Hon Alexander Edward Seymour, *b* 1965; *ed* Harrow, and RMA Sandhurst; Capt Royal Hussars (Prince of Wales's Own) (commn'd 1985): *m* 1992, Emma G., da of J. L. Sharpe, FRCS, and of Mrs Fiona Jackson, and has issue living, Harry John Seymour, *b* 1996, — Georgina Mary Viola, *b* 1997. *Residence* – Tarlton Farmhouse, Tarlton, Cirencester, Glos GL7 6PD.

DAUGHTER LIVING (*By 1st marriage*)

Lady Henrietta Mary Lilias, *b* 1962.

BROTHER LIVING

Hon George Bertram, *b* 1929, *ed* Eton, and Trin Coll, Oxford (MA); late Capt R Wilts Yeo; late Lt 10th Hus: *m* 1973 (*m diss* 1989), Susan Mary, da of Malcolm Messer, of Tarlton, Glos, and has issue living, William Malcolm, *b* 1978. *Residence* – Edgeley Barn, Tarlton, Glos. *Club* – Cavalry and Guards'.

COLLATERAL BRANCH LIVING

Grandsons of late Lt-Col Hon (Allen) Benjamin Bathurst, 3rd son of 6th Earl:—
Issue of late Group Capt Peter Bathurst, *b* 1903, *d* 1970: *m* 1927, Lady Elizabeth Ann (12A Northanger Court, Grove St, Bath), da of late Capt Hon Chandos Graham Temple-Gore-Langton (*see* E Temple of Stowe):—
Admiral of the Fleet Sir (David) Benjamin, GCB (c/o Coutts & Co, 440 Strand, WC2. *Clubs* – Boodle's, Army and Navy, and MCC), *b* 1936; *ed* Eton: Adm and C in C, Fleet, Allied C in C, Channel, and C in C Eastern Atlantic since 1989; Vice-Chief Defence Staff 1990-93, Chief of Naval Staff and First Sea Lord 1993-95, since when Admiral of the Fleet; DL Som 1996, Vice Lord-Lieut since 1999; *cr* KCB (Mil) 1987, GCB (Mil) 1991: *m* 1959, Sarah Christian Pandora, yst da of late Maj (Basil Arthur) John Peto (*see* Peto, Bt (*cr* 1927), colls), and has issue living, Benjamin John, *b* 1964; Maj Welsh Gds: *m* 1996, Katherine M., da of late S/Ldr Peter Ellison, and of Mrs John Lendrum, of Canterbury, Kent, — Alice Patricia, *b* 1962, — Anna Christian, *b* 1968, — Lucilla Ruby, *b* 1970. —— Timothy Seymour (College Farm, Tetbury Rd, Cirencester, Glos; Brooks's Club, and MCC), *b* 1939; *ed* Eton; late 2nd Lt Rifle Bde; a Dir of David Carritt Ltd and Artemis Fine Arts (UK) Ltd: *m* 1st, 1960 (*m diss* 1973), (Elizabeth) Mary, da of Philip Michael Armitage; 2ndly, 1973, Charlotte Anne, da of late Capt Richard Formby, RM, of Firwood, Formby, Lancs, and formerly wife of Richard Belloc Lowndes, and has issue living (by 1st *m*), Jonathan Chandos Seymour, *b* 1965: *m* 1994, Sharon E., da of Anthony Chinnery, of Frampton Cotterell, Bristol, and has issue living, Lara Elizabeth *b* 1997, — Joanna Mary, *b* 1963: *m* 1989, Hugh Simon Nevile, of 21 Cromwell Grove, W6 7RQ, and has issue (*see* B Mowbray, colls), — Elizabeth Sarah, *b* 1968: *m* 1993, Simon Dale Reid, of 15 Brackenbury Gdns, W6 0BP, son of Hubert Reid, and has issue living, George Frederick *b* 1999, Imogen Elizabeth *b* 1997, — (by 2nd *m*) James Seymour, *b* 1976; *ed* Eton.

PREDECESSORS – *Sir* Benjamin Bathurst, MP, Gov of the HEIC 1688-9, Treasurer of the Household to Princess Anne, and on her accession Cofferer of the Household, had with other issue (1) ALLEN, PC; sat as MP for Cirencester 1705-11; *cr Baron Bathurst* (peerage of Great Britain) 1711, and *Earl Bathurst* (peerage of Great Britain) 1772; *d* 1775; *s* by his el son (2) HENRY, PC, who in 1771 had been appointed Lord High Chancellor and *cr* 1771 *Baron Apsley* (peerage of Great Britain); sat as MP for Cirencester 1735-54; was sometime a Justice of the Common Pleas and Lord Pres of the Council; *d* 1794; *s* by his son (3) HENRY, KG, PC, 3rd Earl; was Pres of Board of Trade 1807-12, Sec of War and Colonies 1812-27, and Pres of the Council 1828-30; *d* 1834; *s* by his el son (4) HENRY GEORGE, 4th Earl; was MP for Cirencester 1812-34, and a Commr of India Board 1812-18; *dsp* 1866; *s* by his brother (5) WILLIAM, 5th Earl; was Clerk of the Privy Council 1827-60; *dsp* 1878; *s* by his nephew (6) ALLEN ALEXANDER (son of Lt-Col Hon Seymour Thomas Bathurst, 3rd son of 3rd Earl), 6th Earl, *b* 1832; MP for Cirencester (C) 1857-78: *m* 1st, 1862, Hon Meriel Leicester Warren, who *d* 1872, da of 2nd Baron de Tabley; 2ndly, 1874, Evelyn, who *d* 1927, da of George James Barnard Hankey, of Fetcham Park, Leatherhead; *d* 1892; *s* by his el son (7) SEYMOUR HENRY, CMG, TD, 7th Earl, *b* 1864; Hon Col Gloucestershire Regt: *m* 1893, Hon Lilias Margaret Frances Borthwick, who *d* 1965, da of 1st Baron Glenesk (ext); *d* 1943; *s* by his grandson (8) HENRY ALLEN JOHN (son of late Lt-Col Allen Algernon Bathurst, DSO, MC, TD, MP, Lord Apsley (*ka* 1942), el son of 7th Earl), 8th Earl and present peer; also Baron Bathurst, and Baron Apsley.

Bathurst, family name of Viscount Bledisloe.

BAUER, BARON (Bauer) (Life Baron 1983)

PETER THOMAS BAUER, son of Aladar Bauer who *d* 1944, of Budapest, Hungary; *b* 6 Nov 1915; *ed* Scholae Piae, Budapest, and Gonville and Caius Coll, Camb (MA); FBA; Reader in Agricultural Economics, Lond Univ 1947-48, Univ Lect in Economics, Camb Univ 1948-56, Smuts Reader in Commonwealth Studies, Camb Univ 1956-60, Prof of Economics at LSE, Lond Univ 1960-83, since when Prof Emeritus; author of *Indian Economic Policy and Development*, 1961; *Markets, Market Control and Marketing Reform* (co-author), 1968; *Dissent on Development*, 1972; *Aspects of Nigerian Development*, 1974; *Equality, The Third World of Economic Delusion*, 1981; *Reality and Rhetoric: Studies in the Economics of Development*, 1984, *The Development Frontier*, 1991; *cr Baron Bauer*, of Market Ward, City of Cambridge (Life Baron), 1983.

Arms – Gules a serpent erect between two escallops or on a chief also or a lion passant guardant gules between two open books argent bound gules. **Crest** – Between two feathers argent quilled or an escallop perched thereon a nightingale also or. **Supporters** – *Dexter*, a Malayan rubber tapper wearing a sarong of checked design argent and gules holding in the exterior hand a knife proper; *sinister*, an African market woman habited in a blouse sarong and headscarf of Batik design or and gules holding with her exterior hand a basket proper.
Address – House of Lords, SW1. *Clubs* – Garrick, Beefsteak.

Beach, Hicks-, family name of Earl St Aldwyn.

BEARSTED, VISCOUNT (Samuel) (Viscount UK 1925, Bt UK 1903)

Deeds, not words

NICHOLAS ALAN SAMUEL, 5th Viscount, and 5th Baronet; *b* 22 Jan 1950; *s* 1996; *ed* Eton, and New Coll, Oxford: *m* 1975, Caroline Jane, da of Dr David Sacks, and has issue.

𝕬rms – Gules, on a chevron between two lions' heads erased in chief and in base a naval crown or, a heart gules. 𝕮rest – A dexter arm embowed proper, grasping a battle-axe argent, the head charged with two triangles interlaced sable. 𝕾upporters – *Dexter*, a horse argent; *sinister*, a dragon gules; each charged on the shoulder with a heart or.
Residences – Farley Hall, Farley Hill, RG7 1UL; Acacia Rd, NW8 6AB. *Club* – White's.

SON LIVING

Hon HARRY RICHARD, *b* 23 May 1988.

DAUGHTER LIVING

Hon Eugenie Sharon, *b* 1977.
Hon Natalie Naomi, *b* 1979.
Hon Zoe Elizabeth, *b* 1982.
Hon Juliet Samantha, *b* 1986.

BROTHER LIVING

Hon Michael John, *b* 1952; *ed* Eton: *m* 1980, Julia Aline, yst da of James Edward Alexander Rundell Guinness, and has issue living, Benjamin Peter Marcus, *b* 1989, — Natasha Vivienne, *b* 1981, — Emily Elizabeth, *b* 1983, — Sophie Alexandra, *b* 1986. *Residences* – 24 Hyde Park Gate, SW7; The Dower House, Farley Hill, Berks RG7 1UL.

SISTER LIVING

Hon Sarah Virginia, *b* 1947: *m* 1st, 1969 (*m diss* 1978), Duncan John Lloyd Fitzwilliams, yr son of late Charles Collinsplatt Fitzwilliams, TD, JP, DL, of Cilgwyn, Newcastle Emlyn, S Wales; 2ndly, 1980, Brian Mullins. *Residence* – Moorhill House, Brannockstown, Naas, co Kildare.

UNCLE LIVING (*son of 2nd Viscount*)

Hon Anthony Gerald, *b* 1917; *ed* Eton, and New College, Oxford; European War 1939-45 as Lt Intelligence Corps: *m* 1st, 1946 (*m diss* 1961), Mary Eve, who *d* 1999, da of late John Comyn Higgins, CIE, of Alford, Lincs; 2ndly, 1962 (*m diss* 1966), Jenifer, da of Major Kenneth Alfred Bridge Puckle, RM (ret) of Farnham: 3rdly, 1966, (Jane) Mercy, da of Malcolm Charles Haystead, and has issue living (by 1st *m*), Jacqueline Eve (Rue a l'Eau 46, 1380 Maransart, Belgium), *b* 1948: *m* 1st, 1978 (*m diss* 19—), Robert Rusk; 2ndly, 1988, Jack O'Halloran, of California, USA, and has issue living (by 2nd *m*), Slaine Aoife *b* 1988, — Daphne Lavinia (L'Eden Tower, 25 Boulevard de Belgique, MC 98000, Monaco), *b* 1951: *m* 1980 (*m diss* 1985), Leo Petro; and has issue living, Marco Antonio CERRETO *b* 1985. *Residences* – 29 St Leonard's Terr, SW3 4QG; Woodbury House, Longparish, Hants SP11 6PB. *Clubs* – White's, Anglers' (New York).

DAUGHTER LIVING OF THIRD VISCOUNT (*By 1st marriage*)

Hon Felicity Ann, *b* 1948: *m* 1975, Robert Bernard Waley-Cohen, and has issue (*see* Waley-Cohen, Bt). *Residence* – 18 Gilston Rd, SW10.

WIDOW LIVING OF FOURTH VISCOUNT

NINA ALICE HILARY (*Nina, Viscountess Bearsted*), da of Reginald John Hearn, of London, and widow of Carmichael (Michael) Charles Peter Pocock, CBE: *m* 1984, as his 3rd wife, Maj the 4th Viscount Bearsted, MC, TD, who *d* 1996. *Residence* – 9 Campden Hill Court, W8 7HX.

PREDECESSORS – (1) *Sir* MARCUS Samuel, 2nd son of late Marcus Samuel, of 18 Upper Bedford Place, W; *b* 1853; was a Shipowner and Merchant; Lord Mayor of London 1902-3 (Sheriff 1894-5); Founder (many years Chm) of Shell Transport and Trading Co (Limited); cr a *Baronet* 1903, *Baron Bearsted*, of Maidstone, co Kent (peerage of United Kingdom) 1921, and *Viscount Bearsted*, of Maidstone, co Kent (peerage of United Kingdom) 1925: *m* 1881, Fanny Elizabeth, who *d* 16 Jan 1927, only da of late Benjamin Benjamin; *d* 17 Jan 1927; *s* by his son (2) WALTER HORACE, MC, 2nd Viscount; *b* 1882; was a Trustee of National Gallery 1936-43 (Chm 1942-3), and again 1947-8, and of the Tate Gallery 1938-42: *m* 1908, Dorothea Montefiore, who *d* 1949, da of late Edward Montefiore Micholls, Bar-at-Law, of 11 Queen's Gate, SW; *d* 1948; *s* by his son (3) MARCUS RICHARD, 3rd Viscount; *b* 1909, DL Warwicks, served European War 1939-45 in Middle East (wounded) Chm Hill Samuel Gp 1948-66, etc: *m* 1st, 1947 (*m diss* 1966), Elizabeth Heather, who *d* 1993 (having *m* 2ndly, 1966, Sir Ronald Hugh Grierson), elder da of late Geoffrey Firmston-Williams, of Clunie House, Hans Pl, SW1; 2ndly, 1968, Jean Agnew, who *d* 1978, da of late Robert Agnew Wallace, of 10 Eton Terr, Edinburgh, and formerly wife of Maj John Somerville; *d* 1986; *s* by his brother (4) PETER MONTEFIORE, MC, TD, 4th Viscount, *b* 1911; Maj Warwickshire Yeo (TA), served European War 1939-45 in Middle East (despatches, MC): *m* 1st, 1939 (*m diss* 1942),

Deirdre du Barry; 2ndly, 1946, Hon Elizabeth Adelaide Cohen, who *d* 1983, da of Baron Cohen (Life Baron), and widow of Capt Arthur John Pearce-Serocold, WG (Supplementary Res) (*see* B Sheffield, 1942 Edn); 3rdly, 1984, Nina Alice Hilary, da of Reginald John Hearn, of London, and widow of Carmichael (Michael) Charles Peter Pocock, CBE; *d* 1996; *s* by his elder son (5) NICHOLAS ALAN, 5th Viscount and present peer; also Baron Bearsted.

BEATTY, EARL (Beatty) (Earl UK 1919)

Not by force but by art

DAVID BEATTY, 3rd Earl; *b* 21 Nov 1946; *s* 1972; *ed* Eton: *m* 1st, 1971 (*m diss* 1983), Anne, yr da of A. Please, of Wokingham, Berks; 2ndly, 1984, Anoma Corinne, da of Ray Wijewardene, of Colombo, Sri Lanka, and has issue by 1st *m*.

Arms – Azure, a beehive beset with nine bees volant or a chief argent charged with the Cross of St George gules. Crest – A demi-lion gules holding in the dexter paw a crescent or. Supporters – *Dexter*, a Sailor of the Royal Navy; *sinister*, a Soldier of the Royal Marines, both proper.

SONS LIVING (*By 1st marriage*)

SEAN DAVID (*Viscount Borodale*), *b* 12 June 1973.
Hon Peter Wystan, *b* 1975.

HALF-BROTHER LIVING (*Son of 2nd Earl by 4th marriage*)

Hon Nicholas Duncan, *b* 1961; *ed* Eton, and Exeter Univ (BA): *m* 1990, Laura Mary Catherine, da of Charles William Lyle Keen (*see* E Howe), and has issue living, David Brin Charles, *b* 1992, — Ivo Maurice John, *b* 1998, — Emily Mary Violet, *b* 1994. *Residence* – Chicheley House, Newport Pagnell, Bucks.

HALF-SISTERS LIVING (*Daughter of 2nd Earl by 3rd marriage*)

Lady Diana Adrienne (*Viscountess Gage*), *b* 1952: *m* 1974, 8th Viscount Gage. *Residences* – Firle Place, Lewes, E Sussex; The Cottage, Charwelton, Daventry, Northants.

(*Daughter of 2nd Earl by 4th marriage*)

Lady Miranda Katherine, *b* 1963: *m* 1989, (Iain) Alan Stewart, yst son of late Sir Dugald Leslie Lorn Stewart of Appin, KCVO, CMG, 16th Chief of Clan Stewart of Appin, and has issue living, Alexandra Katherine, *b* 1991, — Augusta Lileas, *b* 1994.

MOTHER LIVING

Dorothy Rita, da of late Michael James Furey, of New Orleans, and widow of Sgt Edward Bragg, RAF: *m* 2ndly, 1946 (*m diss* 1950), as his 2nd wife, the 2nd Earl Beatty, DSC, who *d* 1972; 3rdly, 1951, Abram Stevens Hewitt, who *d* 1987. *Address* –

WIDOW LIVING OF SECOND EARL

DIANE (*Lady Nutting*), OBE, da of John Rutherford Blundell, of Havant, Hants, and adopted da of Capt Duncan Kirk: *m* 1st, 1959, as his 4th wife, the 2nd Earl Beatty, who *d* 1972; 2ndly, 1973, Sir John Grenfell Nutting, 4th Bt, of Chicheley Hall, Newport Pagnell, Bucks.

PREDECESSORS – (1) Adm of the Fleet Sir DAVID Beatty, GCB, OM, GCVO, DSO, PC, 2nd son of late David Longfield Beatty, of Borodale, Enniscorthy; *b* 1871; Dongola Expedition, 1896 (despatches DSO), Nile Expedition 1897 and 1898 (despatches twice, 4th class Order of Medjidie, promoted Com), China 1900 (despatches, wounded, promoted Capt), European War 1914-19, Comdg Battle Cruiser Squadron and Naval Forces in Heligoland Bight and Dogger Bank actions, and Battle Cruiser Fleet at battle of Jutland, and finally as Com-in-Ch of Grand Fleet (despatches, KCVO, GCB, Grand Cross of Order of Redeemer of Greece, Grand Officer Legion of Honour, GCVO, Mil Order of Savoy, Grand Cordon of Japanese Order of the Rising Sun (with Paulowina), Croix de Guerre, Orders of Leopold of Belgium and Star of Roumania, Grand Cordon (preciously brilliant) of Excellent Crop (China), Adm of the Fleet, thanked by Parliament, *cr* Earl, granted £100,000); was First Sea Lord of the Admiralty 1919-27; had 4th class of Russian Order of St George; elected Lord Rector of Edinburgh Univ 1917; *cr Earl Beatty, Viscount Borodale*, of Wexford, co Wexford, and *Baron Beatty*, of the North Sea, and of Brooksby, co Leicester (peerage of United Kingdom) 1919: *m* 1901, Ethel, who *d* 1932, da of Marshall Field, senr, of Chicago, USA; *d* 1936; *s* by his son (2) DAVID FIELD, DSC, 2nd Earl; *b* 1905; Lt-Cdr RN (ret); PPS to Parl and Financial Sec of the Admiralty 1931-36, and Joint Under-Sec of State for Air 1945; MP for Peckham (C) 1931-36: *m* 1st, 1937 (*m diss* 1945), Dorothy Sands, who *d* 1966, da of Thomas Sarsfield Kent Power, of Va, USA, and formerly wife of late Harry Ester Reynolds Hall; 2ndly, 1946 (*m diss* 1950), Dorothy Rita, da of late Michael James Furey, of New Orleans, and widow of Sgt Edward Bragg, RAF; 3rdly, 1951 (*m diss* 1958), Adelle, who *d* 1990 (having *m* 3rdly, 1960, Stanley Donen, film dir), da of M. Dillingham, of Oklahoma City, USA, and formerly wife of William V. O'Connor; 4thly, 1959, Diane (who *m* 2ndly, 1973, Sir John Grenfell Nutting, 4th Bt), da of John Rutherford Blundell, of Havant, Hants, and adopted da of Capt Duncan Kirk; *d* 1972; *s* by his el son (3) DAVID, 3rd Earl and present peer; also Viscount Borodale, and Baron Beatty.

BEAUCHAMP, EARLDOM (Lygon) (Extinct 1979)

(Title pronounced "Beecham" *Name Pronounced* "Liggon")

DAUGHTERS LIVING OF SEVENTH EARL

Lady Sibell, *b* 1907: *m* 1939, Flight-Lieut Michael Richard Bernard Rowley, AAF (*see* Corbet, Bt, 1945 Edn), who *d* 1952. *Residence* – 1 Stable Cottages, Barton House, Guitting Power, nr Cheltenham, Glos GL54 5UH.

Lady Dorothy, *b* 1912; late Section Officer WAAF: *m* 1985, as his 2nd wife, Robert Vernon Heber-Percy (*see* D Northumberland, colls), who *d* 1987. *Residence* – Lime Tree Cottage, 7 Coach Lane, Faringdon, Oxon SN7 8AB.

WIDOW LIVING OF SON OF SEVENTH EARL

Patricia Janet (Pyndar House, Hanley Castle, Worcester), da of late Rev Thomas Kensit Norman: *m* 1939, Hon Richard Edward Lygon, who *d* 1970, and has issue (see colls infra).

COLLATERAL BRANCHES LIVING

Issue of late Hon Richard Edward Lygon, yr son of 7th Earl, *b* 1916, *d* 1970: *m* 1939, Patricia Janet (ante), da of late Rev Thomas Kensit Norman:—
Lettice Patricia Mary, *b* 1940. ——— Rosalind Elizabeth (*Hon Lady Morrison*), *b* 1946: *m* 1st, 1967 (*m diss* 1984), Gerald John Ward (*see* E Dudley, colls); 2ndly, 1984, Hon Sir Charles Andrew Morrison, 2nd son of 1st Baron Margadale. *Seat* – Madresfield Court, Malvern, Worcs WR13 5AU.

Granddaughters of late Lt-Col Hon Robert Lygon, MVO, MC, Gren Gds, 3rd son of 6th Earl:—
Issue of late Reginald Arthur Lygon, *b* 1904, *d* 1976: *m* 1930, Agnes Mary Louise, who *d* 1969, da of late Rev George Fancourt Bell, V of Riverhead, Sevenoaks, and Hon Canon of Rochester:—
Margaret Annora Mary, *b* 1931: *m* 1955, Michael Richard West de Wend Fenton, of Ebberston Hall, Yorks (*see* E Buchan, colls, 1935 Edn), and has issue living, Jonathan Lygon West, *b* 1958: *m* 1988, Pamela Jane, yr da of G. A. Wood, of Ossett, W Yorks, and has issue living, William Osborne West *b* 1988, Lewis Charles Ross *b* 1992, Millicent Alexandra May *b* 1989, — Ross Mathew Mark, *b* 1960: *m* 1983, Helen Louise, elder da of Rev Charles Clifford Forster, of The Vicarage, Pudding Lane, Snainton, Scarborough, and has issue living, Charlotte Alice Rose *b* 1988, Amelia Jane *b* 1990, — Roselie Marye Margaret, *b* 1957: *m* 1981, Carlo Francis Tailleux, son of Francis Tailleux, of 27 rue de Longchamps, Neuilly sur Seine, and has issue living, Pierre Tancred *b* 1988, Tiphaine Eileen *b* 1984, — Clarissa Emily, *b* 1962: *m* 1986, Patrick Daulby, elder son of George Daulby, of Denmark Av, Wimbledon, and has issue living, Eleanor Clare *b* 1990, Emily Margaret *b* 1995. ——— Anne Juliet (12 The Quadrangle, Newland, Malvern, Worcs WR13 5AX), *b* 1937. ——— Eleanor Barbara Muriel, *b* 1938: *m* 1st, 1960 (*m diss* 1965), William James Cavendish-Bentinck, who *d* 1966 (*see* D Portland, colls, 1966 Edn); 2ndly, 1966, Robert Gore Langrishe (*see* Langrishe, Bt), who *d* 1982; 3rdly, 1983 (*m diss* 1987), Hugh Curran. *Residence* – 12 Knowsley Rd, SW11.

Beauclerk, family name of Duke of St Albans.

BEAUFORT, DUKE OF (Somerset) (Duke E 1682)

I scorn to change or to fear

DAVID ROBERT SOMERSET, 11th Duke; *b* 23 Feb 1928; *s* 1984; *ed* Eton; is Hereditary Keeper of Raglan Castle; late Lt Coldstream Gds; Pres British Horse Soc 1988-91: *m* 1950, Lady Caroline Jane Thynne, who *d* 1995, da of 6th Marquess of Bath, and has issue.

𝔄rms – Quarterly, 1st and 4th azure, three fleurs-de-lis or, *France*; 2nd and 3rd gules, three lions passant guardant in pale or, *England*; all within a bordure compony argent and azure. ℭrest – A portcullis or, nailed azure, chains gold. 𝔖upporters – *Dexter*, a panther argent, flames issuing from his mouth and ears proper, plain collared and chained or, and semée of torteaux, hurts and pommes alternately; *sinister*, a wyvern, wings endorsed vert, in the mouth a sinister hand, couped at the wrist gules.
Seat – Badminton House, Gloucestershire, GL9 1DB. *Club* – White's.

SONS LIVING

HENRY JOHN FITZROY (*Marquess of Worcester*), *b* 22 May 1952; *ed* Eton: *m* 1987, Tracy Louise, yr da of Hon Peter Alistair Ward (*see* E Dudley), and has issue:—

    SONS LIVING — Robert (*Earl of Glamorgan*), *b* 20 Jan 1989, — *Lord* Alexander, *b* 1995.
    DAUGHTER LIVING — *Lady* Isabella Elsa, *b* 1991.

Lord Edward Alexander, *b* 1958; *ed* Millfield: *m* 1982, Hon (Georgina) Caroline Davidson, 2nd da of 2nd Viscount Davidson, and has issue living, Francesca Anne, *b* 1984, — Rose Victoria, *b* 1992.

Lord John Robert, *b* 1964; *ed* King's Sch, Bruton: *m* 1990, Lady Cosima Maria Gabriella FRY, yr da of 9th Marquess of Londonderry, and has issue living, Lyle David, *b* 1991, — Romy Caroline, *b* 1993.

DAUGHTER LIVING

Lady Anne Mary, *b* 1955; writer: *m* 1988, Matthew Xavier Maillard Carr, and has issue (*see* Strickland-Constable, Bt, colls).

COLLATERAL BRANCHES LIVING

Branch from 2nd son of 5th Duke

    Grandchildren of late Henry Plantagenet Somerset, 2nd son of late Col Charles Henry Somerset, CB, eldest son of late Lieut-Gen Sir Henry Somerset, KCB, KH, eldest son of Gen Lord Charles Henry Somerset, MP, 2nd son of 5th Duke:—
Issue of late Capt Charles William Henry Rollo Somerset, MC, *b* 1895, *d* 1936: *m* 1925, Glory Kathleen, who *d* 1973, da of late Frederick Albert Turner, of Glenbardi, Toogoolawah, Queensland (infra):—
Arthur Henry, *b* 1926; S-W Pacific 1944-5 with R Australian Navy, and has issue living, Arthur Rollo Henry Plantagenet, *b* 1953; *ed* Queensland Univ (B Commerce); late Capt Royal Australian Inf: *m* 1st, 1979 (*m diss* 1998), Marion Lyle, da of D. V. Graham, of Brisbane; 2ndly, 1998, Alison Claire, eldest da of D. Spencer, of Atherton, Lancs, and has issue living (by 1st *m*), Katherine Lee *b* 1981, Victoria Anne *b* 1984, — John William Plantagenet, *b* 1965; *ed* Queensland Univ (B Commerce): *m* 1989, Margaret Judith, da of Ivan Bowen, of Brisbane, and has issue living, Justin Mitchell Plantagenet *b* 1993, Kristina Margaret Somerset *b* 1996, — Andrea Helen, *b* 1957: *m* 1988, Andrew L. M. Todd, and has issue living, Phillip William Andrew *b* 1994, Oliver James *b* 1996, Naima Louise Somerset *b* (triplet) 1994, Rachelle Alexandra Somerset *b* (triplet) 1994. *Residence* – 31 Rangeview St, Aspley, Brisbane, Queensland 4034, Australia. —— Patricia Honor, *b* 1928: *m* 1953, Norman David Thomas Butler, and has issue living, Luke Norman, *b* 1954: *m* 1988, Margaret, el da of J. R. R. D. Field, of Brisbane, and has issue living, Micah *b* 1989, — Robert David, *b* 1957; LLB: *m* 1995, Gayle Karen, 2nd da of M. W. H. Bice, of Maleny, Qld, and has issue living, Elizabeth Kathleen *b* 1997, — Glory Patricia, *b* 1962: *m* 1982 (*m diss* 1995), Trevor John Kennedy, and has issue living, Brendan James *b* 1986, Lachlan Gene *b* 1987. *Residence* – 110 Esplanade, Golden Beach, Queensland 4551, Australia. —— Barbara Joan, *b* 1933. *Residence* – 110 Esplanade, Golden Beach, Queensland 4551, Australia.

    Issue of late Hereward Henry Plantagenet Somerset, *b* 1900, *d* 1989: *m* 1923, Jean Castle, who *d* 1987, 2nd da of late Frederick Albert Turner, of Glenbardi, Toogoolawah, Qld (ante):—
Edward Plantagenet (79 Guy St, Warwick, Qld 4370, Australia), *b* 1924; European War 1942-44 with RAAF: *m* 1952, Elsie Joy, only da of Stanley Morrow, of Lismore, NSW, and has had issue, Richard John Plantagenet, *b* 1960: *m* 1982, Elizabeth Mary, da of Frank Neal, of Tara, Qld, and *d* 1991, leaving issue, Gillian Maree *b* 1985, Sarah Jane *b* 1987, Heidi Louise *b* 1990, — Pru-Ellen, *b* 1956: *m* 1976, Stuart Charles Barkla, of Rosscoe Downs, Cunnamulla, Qld 4490, and has issue living, Alina Jane *b* 1983, Zoë Ann *b* 1986. —— David Plantagenet (Peek-A-Doo, Taroom, Qld 4420, Australia), *b* 1926: *m* 1953, Margaret Pamela, 2nd da of David Victor Staines, of Jandowae, Qld, and has issue living, Jennifer Margaret, *b* 1954: *m* 1976, Stuart James Stirling, of Willwood, Pittsworth, Qld 4356, and has issue living, Jillian Elizabeth *b* 1978, Rebecca Lynn *b* 1981, Roslyn Ann *b* 1984, — Kerri Jane, *b* 1957, — Erica Jan, *b* 1959: *m* 1983, Harry Sibun Perrett, of Cattle Downs, Wandoan, Qld 4419, and has issue living, Edward Sibun *b* 1984, Hilary Elizabeth *b* 1986, Jessica Victoria *b* 1989, Sophie Jayne *b* 1993. —— Robert Plantagenet, AM (Caboonbah, Proston, Qld 4613, Australia), *b* 1930; AM 1992, JP: *m* 1952, Leslie Rawdon, only da of late Rawdon Briggs, JP, of Swindon, Mt Perry, Qld, and has had issue, Robert Plantagenet, *b* 1959: *m* 1990, Georgina Jane Persse, yst da of David Rokeby Robinson, of Lorraine, Longreach, Qld, — Leslie Ann, *b* 1953; JP: *m* 1974, Ian Robert Haselwood, of South Westgrove, Injune, Qld 4454, and has

issue living, Georgina Leslie *b* 1984, — Katherine Nina, *b* 1957: *m* 1978, Lindsay George Joseph Marshall, of Yurunga Farms, Beechmont, via Nerang, Qld 4211, and has issue living, Lachlan Colvin *b* 1981, Adam Lindsay *b* 1983, — Victoria Joyce, *b* 1967: *m* 1993, Paul Arthur Bartlett, of Annandale, Trangie, NSW 2823, — Jane Elizabeth, *b* 1968, *d* 1973. —— William Plantagenet (Warra Willa, Brolga Rd, Beaudesert, Qld 4285, Australia), *b* 1934; late RAN: *m* 1961, Marion Helene, elder da of Maiben Hay Blackman, of Brisbane, and has issue living, Mark William Plantagenet, *b* 1965: *m* 1990, Anne Marie Murphy, 2nd da of Terrence Michael Murphy, of Dalby, Qld, and has issue living, Brent Michael John Plantagenet *b* 1991, — Steven Plantagenet, *b* 1968, — Christine Helene, *b* 1963: *m* 1988, Nicholas John Case, and has issue living, Stephanie Helene *b* 1988. —— Charles Plantagenet (Caraweena MS 612, Kingaroy, Qld 4610, Australia), *b* 1944: *m* 1978, Pamela Dorothy, da of Guy Oakes McIver, of Braeside Bell, Qld, and has issue living, Myles Plantagenet, *b* 1979, — Scott Plantagenet, *b* 1981. —— Susan Somerset (53 Laguna St, Boreen Point, Qld 4565), *b* 1945; JP: *m* 1969 (*m diss* 1991), Heath Hill Hassall, and has issue living, Rem Hill, *b* 1970: *m* 1999, Anita Maree, only da of Lawrence John Welsh, of Taroom, Qld, — Martine Dione, *b* 1974.

Granddaughter of late Maj Henry Calthorpe Somerset, elder son of late Col Henry George Edward Somerset (infra):—
Issue of late Henry George FitzRoy Somerset, *b* 1885, *d* 1958: *m* 1913, Honore, who *d* 19—, da of J. Olive, of Ravenswood, Queensland:—
Margot, *b* 1916: *m* 1943, Donald Campbell, 9/11 Lovett St, Manly Vale, NSW, and has issue living, Bruce Ronald, *b* 1946, — Anne-Marie, *b* 1944.

Grandchildren of late Brig-Gen Charles Wyndham Somerset, CB, CMG, MVO, yr son of late Col Henry George Edward Somerset, 2nd son of late Lt-Gen Sir Henry Somerset, KCB, KH (ante):—
Issue of late Major Alan Fitz Roy Somerset, *b* 1902, *d* 1940: *m* 1927, Nell Lauder, who *d* 1951, da of late Harold E. Pyman:—
Robin Fitzroy, MBE (91 Edgar Rd, Winchester), *b* 1930; *ed* Eton, and Balliol Coll, Oxford; late Capt Rifle Bde; MBE (Mil) 1997: *m* 1977, Sarah Marguerite, da of Vice-Adm Sir Charles Piercy Mills, KCB, CBE, DSC, and has issue living, Charles Fitzroy, *b* 1981, — Anne Marguerite, *b* 1978. —— Barbara Carol (Aldehaven, Leiston Rd, Aldeburgh, Suffolk), *b* 1933.

Grandchildren of late Fitz Roy Maclean Henry Somerset, 3rd son of late Lt-Gen Sir Henry Somerset, KCB, KH, (ante):—
Issue of late Fitz Roy Henry Somerset, *b* 1881, *d* 1946: *m* 1902, Martha Johanna, da of Philip Watermeyer, of Hanover, S Africa:—
Raglan Henry, *b* 1903; a boilermaker, Daggafontein Mines: *m* 1928, Hendrica Alida Van der Burg, of Bloemfontein, S Africa, and has issue living, Eugene, *b* 1929: *m* 1951, Valerie Rene Stewart, of Benoni, S Africa, and has issue living, Sharon *b* 1952, Geraldine *b* 1954, — John Fitzroy, *b* 1933, — Eunice, *b* 1931. —— Philip Arthur, *b* 1905. —— Harry Edward (1 Raydora Mansions, Roxburgh Rd, Selection Park, Springs 1568, S Africa), *b* 1914: *m* 1939, Muriel Elizabeth Watkins, and has issue living, Ronald Arthur (8 Raydora Mansions, Roxburgh Rd, Selection Park, Springs 1567, S Africa), *b* 1940: *m* 1966 (*m diss* 1973), Lesley Drummond, and has issue living, Grant Bradford Somerset *b* 1967, — Beryl Louise, *b* 1946: *m* 1966, Arie David de Lange, of 19 Rogers Rd, Selection Park, Springs 1567, S Africa, and has issue living, David Jon *b* 1969, Shaye Beryl *b* 1967. —— Lilian Blanche, *b* 1906: *m* 1st, 1933, Richard Flagg, who *d* 1940; 2ndly, 1949, Thomas Grieve, and has issue living (by 1st *m*), John Richard, *b* 1937, — Marjorie, *b* 1935. *Residence –* Floreat, 8 Paschendale Rd, Delville, Germiston, S Africa. —— Winifred Mary, *b* 1925: *m* 1948, Derrick Egerton Moult, and has issue living, Adrian Thomas, *b* 1951, — Kathleen Dawn, *b* 1949.

Granddaughter of Rev Henry Plantagenet Somerset, elder son of Rev Villiers Henry Plantagenet Somerset, 3rd son of Gen Lord Charles Henry Somerset, MP (ante):—
Issue of late Capt Noel Henry Plantagenet Somerset, *b* 1885, *d* 1921: *m* 1915, Helen Barbara, who *d* 1952, da of late Joseph Arderne Ormerod, MD, FRCP, of Greenhill, Upham, Hants, and 25 Upper Wimpole Street, W:—
Mary Arderne Frances (Lavenders, 151 Elsley Rd, Battersea, SW11), *b* 1920.

Grandchildren of late William Francis Somerset (infra):—
Issue of late Lionel Francis Somerset, *b* 1903, *d* 1981: *m* 1937, Wanda Gertrude, da of Arthur W. Clarke, of Port Sydney, Ontario:—
Lionel Vere, *b* 1938: *m* 1970, Janet Mary, da of Maj David Colin Heggie, MD, GM, of Brampton, Ont, and has issue living, Scott Edward, *b* 1973, — Steven Arthur, *b* 1975, — Tammy Lee, *b* 1978. —— Cyril Henry, *b* 1940: *m* 1st, 1963 (*m diss* 1972), Bonnie Erin, da of Lloyd W. Wood, of Port Sydney; 2ndly, 1981, Gale Eileen, da of John William Russell, of Moncton, New Brunswick, and has issue living (by 1st *m*), Robin Marie, *b* 1964: *m* 1982, John Joseph Fiorini, of Shannon Hall, and has issue living, John Cyrle *b* 1984, Joey Michael *b* 1985, Matthew Dominic *b* 1988, Mikhele Erin *b* 1987, — (by 2nd *m*) Ashley Gale, *b* 1982. —— William John, *b* 1944: *m* 1978, Beverly Ann, da of George Robert Stewart, of 37 Wright Av, Toronto, Ont, and has issue living, Trevor John Stewart *b* 1985, Amanda Carol, *b* 1981.

Grandchildren of late Vere Francis John Somerset, elder son of late Col Poulett George Henry Somerset, CB, MP, 4th son of late Gen Lord Charles Henry Somerset, MP (ante):—
Issue of late William Francis Somerset, *b* 1876, *d* 1942: *m* 1st, 1899, Laura Helen, who *d* 1926, da of W. H. Thoms, of Port Sydney, Muskoka, Ontario, Canada; 2ndly, 1927, Ann Margaret Vibert, who *d* 1955, da of C. V. Lawrence, of Allensville, Ontario, Canada:—
(By 1st *m*) Jessie Catherine, *b* 1907: *m* 1944, Brodie Kay, of Port Sydney, Muskoka, Ontario, Canada, and has issue living, William Douglas, *b* 1949: *m* 1979, Cynda Campbell, and has issue living, Courtney Eileon *b* 19—. — Lenora Mary, *b* 1909: *m* 1936, George Simmens, who *d* 1973, and has issue living, Donald Wayne, *b* 1938: *m* 1970, Elaine Mary, da of Robert Bailey, of Cartier, Ontario, and has issue living, David Robert *b* 1974, Kirk William *b* 1976, Donald Glenn *b* 1980, — Norma Helen, *b* 1944. *Residence –* 129 Whitney Av, North Bay, Ontario, Canada.

Issue of late Charles Somerset, *b* 1878, *d* 1941: *m* 1913, Doris Amy (16 Allenby Rd, Dalkeith 6009, W Australia), da of Edward George Cronin:—
Henry Charles Fitzroy (16 Allenby Rd, Dalkeith 6009, W Australia), *b* 1919: *m* 1946, Patricia Barr, da of late Rudolph George Barr Goyder, and has issue living, Charles Nigel Fitzroy, *b* 1953, — Virginia Fitzroy, *b* 1947, — Suzette Fitzroy,

b 1950, — Mary Ursula Fitzroy, *b* 1958, — Georgina Patricia Fitzroy, *b* 1963. —— Claud Edward Ralph, *b* 1925. —— Mary Poulett, *b* 1916. —— Diana, *b* 1918. —— Susette, *b* 1920. *Residence* – Ferndale, Balingup, W Australia.

Issue of late Vere Edward Somerset, MRCS, LRCP, *b* 1884, *d* 1961: *m* 1910, Gladys Mildred, who *d* 1980, da of Richard Baker, of Dolton, Devon:—
Vere Murielle Cecily Idina SOMERSET, *b* 1912; has resumed the surname of Somerset: *m* 1st, 1934, Fl-Lt Dudley Scorgie, AFC; 2ndly, 1959 (*m diss* 1978), Capt Alan Abraham, late RASC, and has issue living (by 1st *m*), Vere Roderick (27 Bicton St, Exmouth, Devon), *b* 1938, — Annette Idina, *b* 1939: *m* 1966, Alan Peter Crow, of Cherrington Manor, Newport, Salop, and has issue living, Christopher John *b* 1973, Timothy *b* 1975, Camille Bettina *b* 1970.

Granddaughter of late Capt Henry Charles FitzRoy Somerset, yr son of Col Poulett George Henry Somerset, CB, MP (ante):—
Issue of late Capt Charles Alexander Somerset, RA, *b* 1901, *d* 1981: *m* 1st, 1926, Audrey Vernon, who *d* 1935, 2nd da of George W. L. Thompson, of Olton, Warwicks; 2ndly, 1955, Winifred May, who *d* 1996, 2nd da of late J. A. Helyar, of Windyridge, E Coker, Som:—
(By 1st *m*) (Audrey) Barbara, AMIA (Seal, Kent), *b* 1929: *m* 1954 (*m diss* 1960), Jeremy Paul Ellingham, and has issue living, Hugh Vere Alexander (Seal, Kent), *b* 1957; *ed* Marlborough, and Reading Univ (BSc), ARICS: *m* 1979, Angela, el da of late T. A. Jackson, of Lincoln, and has issue living, Marcus Charles Anthony *b* 1988, Luke William Alexander *b* 1990, Hugo Robert Vere *b* 1992, — (Charles Henry) Mark (7 Parliament Hill, Hampstead, NW3 2SY), *b* 1959; *ed* Marlborough, and Bristol Univ (BA): *m* 1991, Natania Maria, yst da of Dr Clifford Jansz, of London, and has issue living, Miles Arthur Almo *b* 1996.

Branch from 6th son of 5th Duke

Grandson of late FitzRoy William Henry Somerset, 2nd son of late Col Henry Charles Capel Somerset, eldest son of late Rev Lord William George Henry Somerset, 6th son of 5th Duke:—
Issue of late Henry Charles FitzRoy Somerset, *b* 1870, *d* 1940: *m* 1920, Winifred Marion, da of late George Bartram, of London, N:—
Francis Charles, *b* 1921: *m* 1945, Sheila Marion, da of Aldred Davis, of Yass, NSW, and has issue living, Susan, *b* 1952.

Grandson of late Raglan Somerset (*b* 1872), yr son of late FitzRoy William Henry Somerset (ante):—
Issue of late Fitzroy Raglan Somerset, *b* 1901, *d* 1985: *m* 1924, Alma Lauderdale, da of Henry Lauderdale Maitland, of Melbourne:—
Raglan Fitzroy, *b* 1925; MB BS: 1939-45 War in S-W Pacific with 2/10 Australian Commando Sqdn (despatches): *m* 1954, Lenore Beatrice, da of Oswald William Miller, of Brisbane, and has issue living, Stephen Raglan (112 Arundel St, Park Orchards, Victoria 3114), *b* 1956: *m* 1980, Antoinette Rose Briggs, and has issue living, Elise Ann *b* 1987, Olivia Rose *b* 1991. *Residence* – 67 Westering Rd, Christmas Hills, Victoria 3775, Australia.

Granddaughter of late Raglan Turberville Henry Somerset, 4th son of Rev William Somerset, 2nd son of Rev Lord William George Henry Somerset (ante):—
Issue of late Raglan Horatio Edwyn Henry Somerset, QC, *b* 1885, *d* 1956: *m* 1915, Adelaide Millicent Blanche Gwendolen, who *d* 1958, only da of late Arthur William FitzRoy Somerset (infra):—
Anna Millicent Horatia FitzRoy, OBE, *b* 1929: *m* 1950, William John Francis Tribe, and has issue living, William John Raglan Horatio, *b* 1955: *m* 1st, 1975 (*m diss* 1983), Maria Magdalena Hernas, of Wroclaw, Poland; 2ndly, 1983 (*m diss* 1987), Ana, da of Dr Janet Rutherford Esquivel; 3rdly, 1987, Ruth, da of Lawrence Corner, and has issue living (by 2nd *m*), Charles William Edward *b* 1986, — Raglan Horatio Andrew Harold, *b* 1961: *m* 1987, Susan Elizabeth, da of John Bennett, of Cheshire, and has issue living, William Nicholas Horatio *b* 1991, Toby John Raglan *b* (twin) 1991, Emma Louise Harriet *b* 1993, — Mary Anna Kathleen Horatia, *b* 1958: *m* 1982, Ian Geoffrey Arthur, son of Colin Arthur, of Llangibby, Gwent, and has issue living, Owain Colin Nelson *b* 1991, Rebecca Horatia Jean *b* 1988. *Residence* – Hill House, Raglan, Gwent.

Granddaughter of late Rev William Somerset (ante):—
Issue of late Charles Edward Henry Somerset, *b* 1862, *d* 1939: *m* 1908, Edith, who *d* 1932, da of Lionel Alexander Weatherly, MD, of Winsley House, Stourwood Bournemouth:—
Charlotte Georgiana Rose Mary (Pilatus Str. 12, 8916 Jonen, Switzerland), *b* 1909; *ed* Oxford Univ (MA): *m* 1933, Jules Omer Malfroy, LLM, who *d* 1973, and has had issue, Jules Michael Charles Somerset (The Old School House, Boxworth, Cambridge), *b* 1939; *ed* Downside, and Fitzwilliam Coll, Camb (MA); ARICS, AMTPI: *m* 1967, Moira Gore, and has issue living, Benedict Charles Jules Somerset *b* 1976, Emma Charlotte Mary *b* 1968, Kate Emily Rose *b* 1971, — Deborah Mary Somerset, *b* 1934; MA Camb; Solicitor 1960: *d* 1987, — Louise Georgiana Somerset, *b* 1942; BSc St Andrews Univ: *m* 1965, Richard Kent Percival, BSc, of Pilatus Str. 12, 8916 Jonen, Switzerland, and has issue living, Richard Eyre Somerset *b* 1979, Charlotte Georgiana *b* 1970, Lucy Margaret *b* 1972, Alice Louise *b* 1977.

Grandchildren of late Charles Edward Henry Somerset (ante):—
Issue of late William Raglan Henry Guy Somerset, *b* 1912, *d* 1981: *m* 1st, 1932 (*m diss* 1950), Edna Margaret, da of Ernald Drybrough Smith, MD, FRCS, of Hastings: 2ndly, 1955, Evelyn, da of William Lee, of Bradford:—
(By 1st *m*) William Michael John Charles (Somerville, 9 Overslade Close, E Hunsbury, Northampton NN4 0RZ), *b* 1934: *m* 1967, Pearl Constance Langley, and has issue living, John Reginald, *b* 1970. —— Margaret Drybrough (Northfield, 44 North St West, Uppingham, Leics LE15 9S6), *b* 1933: *m* 1951, Herbert Paul Liquorish, RHG, and has had issue, Michael Paul, *b* 1952; RN; murdered in Antigua 1973, — Susan Carlotta Anne, *b* 1953, — Deri Jane, *b* 1957: *m* 1987, Tyrone Maloney, of St Peter's, Barbados, and has issue living, Antoine Michael Bevan *b* 1992, Tamara Chantel *b* 1985, Tiahra Charmain *b* 1986, — Cherillyn Mary, *b* 1959: *m* 1978 (*m diss* 1981), Terrance Carr, and has issue living, Cheryl Marie *b* 1978, — Karin Melinda, *b* 1963. —— (By 2nd *m*) †Nicholas Anthony, *b* 1956, *d* 1981. —— Stephanie Lynn, *b* 1960. —— Amanda Jayne, *b* 1961, *d* 1971.

Grandchildren of late Arthur William FitzRoy Somerset, son of late Col FitzRoy Molyneux Henry Somerset, RE, 3rd son of late Rev Lord William George Henry Somerset (ante):—
Issue of late Arthur Plantagenet Francis Cecil Somerset, b 1889, d 1957; m 1916, Mary Frances Elizabeth, who d 1993, el da of late Felton George Randolph (see Nepean, Bt, colls, 1950 Edn):—
John FitzRoy Pechell, b 1923; ed Wellington Coll, and London Univ (BSc 1949): is a qualified Asso of Chartered Land Agents So, and an ARICS; European War 1942-45 with King's Roy Rifle Corps (wounded): m 1952, Daphne Marigold, yr da of late Col Clement Topham, OBE, MC, and has issue living, Clement Charles FitzRoy (Longdean House, Clapham, nr Worthing, Sussex), b 1956: m 1986, Sara Ann, da of Roy James Lally, of Worthing, Sussex, and has issue living, William Henry FitzRoy b 1994, Georgina Katherine Ella b 1987, — Annabel Mary, b 1953: m 1979 Robert Matthew Smyth, of Altmover House, Dungiven, co Derry, and has issue living, Emily Margaret b 1980, — Philippa Margaret, b 1965. Residence – Holt Farm House, Clapham, nr Worthing, Sussex. —— Cecily Mary Adelaide, b 1919: m 1946, Maj Laurence James Howe-Ely, 60th Rifles, and has issue living, Christopher Laurence Somerset, b 1946: m 1984, Linda Gilbee, of Port Elizabeth, S Africa, and has issue living, Michael b 1987, — Michael James FitzRoy, b 1950: m 1980, Mary Anne, da of George Piers, of Pregrave Farm, Harare, Zimbabwe, and has issue living, Piers Lawrence b 1985, Caroline Louise b 1982, — Anne Diana Mary (25 Kew Dr, Highlands, Harare, Zimbabwe), b 1948: m 1972, George Constantine Papasavvas, who d 1983, and has issue living, Alexander Lawrence b 1979, Christina Helena b 1978, Georgina Zoe b 1983, Suzanna Cecily b (twin) 1983. Residence – Piras Gdns, Oxford Rd, Avondale, Zimbabwe.

Grandchildren of late Rev Boscawen Thomas George Henry Somerset, 5th son of late Rev Lord William George Henry Somerset (ante):—
Issue of late William Horace Boscawen Somerset, b 1880, d 1946: m 1921, Rubie Drummond-Nairne, who d 1977, da of late William Redston Warner:—
FitzRoy Douglas Boscawen (Thackit Eaves, Highclere, Newbury), b 1923; ed Marlborough, and Exeter Coll, Oxford (BA 1949, MA 1957); formerly Lt King's Shropshire LI; in Colonial Administrative Ser, Nigeria 1950-57, and Assist Adviser, Aden Protectorate 1957-68; Assist Master Cheam Sch 1970-86; 1939-45 War (wounded): m 1962, Sheila Jean, da of Dr D. J. B. Wilson, of High Wycombe, Bucks, and has issue living, Douglas William Boscawen, b 1965; ed Marlborough, Bristol Univ (BSc) and Queen's Coll, Oxford (PhD): m 1995, Dr Mary Joan, da of Rev J. MacLeod, of Stornoway, Lewis, and has issue, living Sarah Joan Beaufort b 1998, — Eirene Helen Giffard b 1963; ed Downe House; RGN & RM. —— Helen Jane Boscawen, b 1925; ed Oxford Univ (MA 1950): m 1950, Henry Ensor Fossett Lock, of Winterborne, W Stafford, Dorchester, Dorset, and has issue living, Edward Henry Somerset, b 1953; ed Marlborough and London Univ (BA): m 1987, Caroline Metcalfe, and has issue living, Anthony Henry b 1989, Emma Ruth b 1991, — Charles John Somerset, b 1955; ed Marlborough and Keble Coll, Oxford (BA, PhD): m 1st, 1979 (m diss 1991), Helen Mogilansky; 2ndly, 1993, Nicoletta Isar, and has issue living (by 1st m), Nicholas Walter b 1981, Nadezhda Caroline b 1980, Persephone b 1987, — Richard Michael Somerset, b 1959; ed Marlborough and Balliol Coll, Oxford (BA): m 1991, Julia Bernhardt, — Amanda Mary Somerset, b 1966; ed Sherborne Sch for Girls: m 1996, Alan Victor Hill, of Brisbane, Queensland, Australia, and has issue living, Lily Ruby b 1999.

Branch from 8th son of 5th Duke

Descendants of late Field Marshal Lord FitzRoy James Henry Somerset GCB (8th son of 5th Duke), who was cr Baron Raglan 1852 (see that title).

PREDECESSORS – (1) Sir CHARLES Somerset, KG, natural son of Henry Beaufort, 3rd Duke of Somerset, who was 3rd in descent from John of Gaunt and Catherine Swynford; Sir Charles was summoned to Parliament in right of his wife, as Lord Herbert (peerage of England, cr 1461); cr Baron Herbert of Raglan, Chepstow and Gower (peerage of England) 1506, and Earl of Worcester (peerage of England) 1513; appointed Lord Chamberlain for life; d 1526; s by his el son (2) HENRY, 2nd Earl; d 1549; s by his el son (3) WILLIAM, KG, 3rd Earl; d 1589; s by his son (4) EDWARD, KG, 4th Earl; was Master of the Horse 1601-15; his 3rd son, cr Viscount Somerset, was Master of the Horse to Queen Anne, consort of James I, the Earl d 1628; s by his el son (5) HENRY, 5th Earl; a devoted royalist; garrisoned Raglan Castle, and at his own expense held it for nearly four years against the Parliamentary forces; cr Marquess of Worcester (peerage of England) 1642; d 1646; s by his el son (6) EDWARD, 2nd Marquess; a zealous partisan of Charles I, who addressed him as Earl of Glamorgan before he s as Marquess; d 1667; s by his son (7) HENRY, KG, PC, 3rd Marquess; Lord Pres of Wales; cr Duke of Beaufort (peerage of England) 1682: on the accession of William and Mary he refused to take the oath of allegiance and afterwards lived in retirement; d 1699; s by his grandson (8) HENRY, KG, 2nd Duke; d 1714; s by his el son (9) HENRY, KG, 3rd Duke; d 1746; s by his brother (10) CHARLES NOEL, 4th Duke: m Elizabeth, sister of 4th Baron Botetourt; d 1756; s by his son (11) HENRY, KG, 5th Duke; was Master of the Horse to Queen Charlotte 1768-80; s as Baron Botetourt (see that title); d 1803; s by his el son (12) HENRY CHARLES, 6th Duke, Lord-Lieut of cos Gloucester, Monmouth, and Brecon; d 1835; s by his el son (13) HENRY, KG, 7th Duke; b 1792; served with distinction in Peninsula War: m 1st 1814, Georgiana Frederica, who d 1821, da of Hon Henry FitzRoy (B Southampton); 2ndly, 1822, Emily Frances, da of Culling Charles Smith; d 1853; s by his son (14) HENRY CHARLES FITZROY, KG, PC, 8th Duke, b 1824; Lord-Lieut of Monmouthshire; MP for E Gloucestershire (C) 1842-56; was Master of the Horse 1858-59 and 1866-8: m 1845, Lady Georgiana Charlotte Curzon, el da of 1st Earl Howe, GCH; d 1899; s by his el son (15) HENRY ADELBERT WELLINGTON FITZROY, 9th Duke, b 1847; High Steward of Gloucester and Bristol; bore Curtana at Coronation of King George V 1911: m 1895, Louise Emily, who d 1945, da of late William Henry Harford, JP, DL, of Oldtown, Tockington, and widow of Baron Carlo de Tuyll; d 1924; s by his only son (16) HENRY HUGH ARTHUR FITZROY, KG, GCVO, PC, 10th Duke, b 1900; Lord Lieut of Bristol and Gloucester; Master of the Horse to HM 1936-78, High Steward of Bristol and Gloucester and of Tewkesbury; founded Badminton Horse Trials 1949; Chm Masters of Foxhounds Assocn, Pres British Field Sports Soc: m 1923, Lady (Victoria Constance) Mary Cambridge, who d 1987, da of 1st Marquess of Cambridge; d 1984; s by his kinsman (17) DAVID ROBERT (only surv son of Capt Henry Robert Somers FitzRoy de Vere Somerset, DSO, only surv son of Henry Charles Somers Augustus Somerset, OBE, only son of Rt Hon Lord Henry Richard Charles Somerset, 2nd son of 8th Duke), 11th Duke and present peer; also Marquess of Worcester, Earl of Worcester, and Baron Herbert of Raglan, Chepstow and Gower.

BEAUMONT OF WHITLEY, BARON (Beaumont) (Life Baron 1967)

I can do no other

Rev TIMOTHY WENTWORTH BEAUMONT, son of late Maj Michael Wentworth Beaumont, TD (*see* V Allendale, colls), *b* 22 Nov 1928; *ed* Eton, Gordonstoun, and Ch Ch, Oxford (MA); V of Ch Ch Kowloon, Hong Kong 1957-59; resigned Holy Orders 1973 and resumed 1984, V of St Philip and All Souls, Kew, and St Luke's, Kew, 1986-91; Proprietor of *Prism* 1960-65 and *New Christian*, 1965-70, Chm of Studio-Vista Ltd 1963-68, Hon Treasurer of Liberal Party 1962-63, Head of Liberal Party Organisation 1965-66, Chm of Liberal Party 1967-68, and Pres 1969-70; Liberal Spokesman on Education, Arts and Environment 1971-85, and on Conservation and the Countryside 1993-98; Member Liberal Democrat Federal Policy Cttee 1992-94; Chm of Inst for Research into Mental Retardation 1972-74; Proprietor and Editor of *New Outlook* 1972-74; Pres British Fedn of Film Socs 1974-80; Leader of British Liberal Delegation to Parl Assemblies Council of Europe & Western European Union 1977-79; Vice-Chm Liberal Group, Council of Europe 1978; co-ordinator The Green Alliance 1977-80; author of *The End of The Yellowbrick Road* (1997); *cr Baron Beaumont of Whitley*, of Child's Hill, Greater London, (Life Baron) 1967: *m* 1955, Mary Rose, da of Lt-Col Charles Edward Wauchope, MC, of Sandhill House, Rogate, Sussex, and has issue.

Arms – Gules, a lion rampant or, armed and langued azure, between eights crescents in orle of the second. Crest – A bull's head erased quarterly argent and gules, charged with a mullet sable. Supporters – *Dexter*, a phoenix; *sinister*, a pelican vulning herself proper.
Residence – 40 Elms Rd, SW4 9EX.

SON LIVING

Hon Hubert Wentworth (Harristown House, Brannockstown, Kildare), *b* 1956; *ed* Gordonstoun, and South Bank Polytechnic: *m* 1st, 1980 (*m diss* 1998), Katharine Emma, only da of Col Richard Francis Abel Smith, of Blidworth Dale, Notts (*see* ROYAL FAMILY); 2ndly, 1998, Noella Anne, 2nd da of Noel Murphy, of Barrettstown, Newbridge, co Kildare, and has issue living (by 1st *m*), George Wentworth, *b* 1985, — Richard Christian, *b* 1989, — Michael Patrick, *b* 1991, — Amelia May *b* 1983.

DAUGHTERS LIVING

Hon Atalanta Armstrong, *b* 1961: *m* 1987, Dr Stephen Francis Bungay, elder son of E. W. G. Bungay, of Chester, Cheshire, and has issue living, Felix Nicholas, *b* 1990, — Caspar Stephen, *b* 1994.

Hon Ariadne Grace, *b* 1963: *m* 1990, Mario Calvo-Platero, yr son of late Guido Calvo-Platero, of Milan, Italy, and has issue living, Oliver Guido, *b* 1991, — Milo Alaric, *b* 1992, — Clio Gemma Beaumont, *b* 1995.

Beaumont, family name of Viscount Allendale.

BEAVERBROOK, BARON (Aitken) (Baron UK 1917, Bt UK 1916)

Things for me, not I for things

MAXWELL WILLIAM HUMPHREY AITKEN, 3rd Baron and 3rd Baronet; *b* 29 Dec 1951; *s* 1985; *ed* Charterhouse, and Pembroke Coll, Camb; Chm Beaverbrook Foundation since 1985, and Highway One Corp Ltd since 1996; Lord in Waiting 1986-87; Dep Treas Conservative Party 1988-90, Treas 1990-92: *m* 1974, Susan Angela, el da of late Francis Ambrose Joseph More O'Ferrall (*see* Jackson, Bt, *cr* 1869), and has issue.

Arms – Argent, two barrulets wavy azure between in chief two maple leaves slipped and in base a thistle eradicated gules, a border sable charged with eight besants. **Crest** – Upon a drum proper a cock gules, wattled, armed and legged or. **Supporters** – On either side a beaver reguardant holding in the mouth a fish proper.
Seat – Cherkley Court, Leatherhead, Surrey. *Address* – 11 Old Queen St, SW1H 9JA. *Clubs* – White's, Royal Yacht Sqdn.

SONS LIVING

Hon MAXWELL FRANCIS, *b* 17 March 1977.
Hon Alexander Rory, *b* 1978.

DAUGHTERS LIVING

Hon Charlotte Susanna, *b* 1982.
Hon Sophia Violet Angela, *b* 1985.

HALF-SISTERS LIVING (*Daughters by 2nd marriage of 2nd Baron, who disclaimed the peerage for life 1964*)

Hon Kirsty Jane, *b* 1947: *m* 1st, 1966 (*m diss* 1973), Jonathan Derek Morley, yr son of late Brig Michael Frederick Morley, MBE, of Biddestone Manor, Chippenham, Wilts; 2ndly, 1975, Christopher Marten Smallwood, of Manor House, Southwood, nr Glastonbury, Som, son of Canon Graham Marten Smallwood, of Brook House, Childswickham, Worcs, and has issue living (by 1st *m*), Dominic Max Michael, *b* 1967: *m* 1995, Lesley Margaret, da of John Clark, and has issue living, Natasha Primrose Emma *b* 1998. — Sebastian Jake Finch, *b* 1969: *m* 1993, Victoria Clare Helen, only da of Samuel Charles Whitbread (*see* B Clinton, colls), — (by 2nd *m*), Eleanor Bluebell, *b* 1982.
Hon Lynda Mary Kathleen, *b* 1948: *m* 1st, 1969 (*m diss* 1974), Nicholas Saxton, son of Robert Saxton, of La Jolla, Calif; 2ndly, 1977, Jonathan James Dickson, and has issue living (by 2nd *m*), Joshua James, *b* 1977, — Leo Casper, *b* 1981.

SISTER LIVING

Hon Laura, *b* 1953; journalist; resumed her maiden name 1989: *m* 1st, 1984 (*m diss* 1989), David Victor Mark Mallet, yst son of late Sir Victor Alexander Louis Mallet, GCMG, CVO; 2ndly, 1992, Martin K. Levi, son of R. Levi, and has issue living (by 1st *m*), David Sonny Victor Maxwell, *b* 1984, — (by 2nd *m*), Louis Max Adam, *b* 1994, — Lucci Violet, *b* 1993.
Residence – The Prospect, 83 High St, Cowes, I of Wight.

WIDOW LIVING OF SECOND BARON (*who disclaimed the peerage for life 1964*)

VIOLET (*Lady Aitken*) (Mickleham Downs House, Dorking, Surrey), 3rd da of late Sir Humphrey Edmund de Trafford, 4th Bt, MC; Chancellor Univ of New Brunswick 1982-92 (Hon LLD), Chancellor Emeritus since 1992, Chm Beaverbrook Canadian Foundation: *m* 1951, as his 3rd wife, Sir Max (John William Maxwell) Aitken, 2nd Bt, DSO, DFC, who disclaimed the peerage for life 1964, and *d* 1985.

COLLATERAL BRANCH LIVING

Issue of late Capt Hon Peter Rudyard Aitken, R Fus, 2nd son of 1st Baron, *b* 1912, *d* 1947: *m* 1st, 1934 (*m diss* 1939), Janet Ruth Murrene, da of Prof Murray Macneill, of Dalhousie Univ, Halifax, Nova Scotia; 2ndly, 1942, (Marie) Patricia (who *d* 1995, having *m* 2ndly, 1948 (*m diss* 1956), Richard David Rafe Lycett Green, who *d* 1969) (*see* Green, Bt, *cr* 1886, colls), da of Michael Joseph Maguire, of Melbourne, Australia:—
(By 2nd *m*) Timothy Maxwell, *b* 1944; *ed* Repton, and McGill Univ; Chief Exec TV-am 1983-88: *m* 1st, 1966, Annette, da of Claus Hansen, of Denmark; 2ndly, 1972, Julie Ruth, da of Charles Filstead, and has issue living (by 2nd *m*), Theodore Maxwell, *b* 1976, — Charles Howard Filstead, *b* 1979. ———— Peter Michael, *b* 1946; *ed* Malvern: *m* 1980 (*m diss* 1985), Hon (Joan) Elizabeth Rees-Williams, only da of 1st Baron Ogmore, and formerly wife of (i) Richard Harris, actor, and (ii) Rex Harrison (afterwards Sir Rex Harrison), actor. *Residence* – 14 Lowndes Sq, SW1. ———— (By 1st *m*) Caroline Anne Christine, *b* 1935: *m* 1957, Conyers Collingwood Massy Baker, Lt, RCNR, of 28 Whitney Av, Toronto 5, Ontario, Canada, and has issue living, William Hugh Massy, *b* 1958, — Philip Massy, *b* 1960, — Jonathan Piers Massy, *b* 1967.

PREDECESSORS – (1) (WILLIAM) MAXWELL Aitken, CD, PC, son of Rev William Cuthbert Aitken Presbyterian Min of Newcastle, New Brunswick, Canada; *b* 1879; MP for Ashton-under-Lyne (*C*) 1910-16, with Canadian Expeditionary Force 1915, and Canadian Govt Representative at Front 1916, Chancellor of Duchy of Lancaster, and Min of Information 1918; formerly proprietor of *Daily Express*, *Sunday Express* (which he founded 1920), and *Evening Standard*; Min of Aircraft Production 1940, Min of State and Min of Supply 1941, a Member of War Cabinet 1940-42, Lord Privy Seal 1943-45; *cr a*

Baronet 1916, and *Baron Beaverbrook*, of Beaverbrook, Prov of New Brunswick, Canada, and of Cherkley, co Surrey (peerage of UK) 1917: *m* 1st, 1906, Gladys, who *d* 1927, da of Brig-Gen Charles William Drury, CB, of Halifax, Nova Scotia; 2ndly, 1963, Marcia Anastasia, who *d* 1994, da of John Christoforides, of Leyswood, Groombridge, Sussex, and widow of Sir James Hamet Dunn, QC, 1st Bt (*cr* 1921); *d* 1964; *s* by his el son (2) JOHN WILLIAM MAXWELL, DSO, DSC, 2nd Baron (until he disclaimed his peerage for life 12 June 1964); Group Capt Aux Air Force, 1939-45 War (despatches, DFC, DSO, Czechoslavakian Mil Cross); Chm Beaverbrook Newspapers Ltd 1968-77, Life Pres 1977-85; MP for Holborn (C) 1945-50: *m* 1st, 1939 (*m diss* 1944), Cynthia Helen Glencairn, da of Col Hugh Glencairn Monteith, DSO, OBE; 2ndly, 1946 (*m diss* 1950), Ursula Jane, da of late Maj Robert Orlando Rudolph Kenyon-Slaney (*see* B Kenyon, colls), and formerly wife of late Lt-Col (David Ludovic) Peter Lindsay, DSO (*see* E Crawford, colls); 3rdly, 1951, Violet, da of late Sir Humphrey Edmund de Trafford, 4th Bt, MC; *d* 1985; *s* by his only son (3) MAXWELL WILLIAM HUMPHREY, 3rd Baron and present peer and 3rd Baronet.

Beckett, family name of Baron Grimthorpe.

Bective, Earl of; son of Marquess of Headfort.

BEDFORD, DUKE OF (Russell) (Duke E 1694)

What will be, will be

JOHN ROBERT RUSSELL, 13th Duke; *b* 24 May 1917; *s* 1953; European War 1939-40 in Coldstream Gds (invalided): *m* 1st, 1939, Clare Gwendolen, who *d* 1945, da of John Bridgman, and formerly wife of Maj Kenneth Chamney Walpole Hollway, MC; 2ndly, 1947 (*m diss* 1960), Hon Lydia Yarde-Buller, da of 3rd Baron Churston, and widow of Capt Ian Archibald de Hoghton Lyle, Black Watch, el son of Sir Archibald Moir Park Lyle, 2nd Bt, MC; 3rdly, 1960, Madame Nicole Milinaire, da of Paul Schneider, of Paris, and has issue by 1st and 2nd *m*.

Arms – Argent, a lion rampant gules; on a chief sable, three escallops of the first. Crest – A goat statant argent, armed and unguled or. Supporters – *Dexter*, a lion rampant gules, gorged with a collar argent, charged with three escallops sable; *sinister*, a goat argent, armed, unguled and bearded or.
Residence – Les Ligures, 2 rue Honoré Labande, MC98000, Monaco.

SONS LIVING (By 1st marriage)

HENRY ROBIN IAN (*Marquess of Tavistock*), *b* 21 Jan 1940; *ed* Le Rosey, and Harvard Univ; DL Beds 1985; Dir Trafalgar House Ltd 1977-92, United Racecourses Ltd 1977-94, and Berkeley Govett & Co Ltd 1986-95; Chm TR Property Invest Trust 1982-91, and Berkeley Development Capital Ltd 1984-92; Pres Woburn Golf Country Club since 1976; Chm of Trustees Kennedy Memorial Trust 1985-90: *m* 1961, Henrietta Joan, only da of late Henry Frederic Tiarks, and has issue:—

SONS LIVING — ANDREW IAN HENRY (*Lord Howland*), *b* 30 March 1962, — *Lord* Robin Loel Hastings, *b* 1963: *m* 1994, Stephanie, yst da of Kurt Niklas, of Beverly Hills, Calif, USA, — *Lord* James Edward Herbrand, *b* 1975.

Seat – Woburn Abbey, Bedfordshire MK43 0TP. *Clubs* – White's, Brook (New York)
Lord Rudolf, *b* 1944; *ed* Gordonstoun: *m* 1989, Farah, yr da of R. Moghaddam. *Residence* – 3 Lyall St, SW1X 8DW.

(By 2nd marriage)

Lord Francis Hastings, *b* 1950; *ed* Eton; BSc (Land Admin); ARICS: *m* 1st, 1971, Mrs Faith Diane Charrington, da of late Dr S. I. M. Ibrahim, of Singapore; 2ndly, 1996, Sarah-Jane, da of Terence J. Clemence, of Wilton Crescent, SW1, and has issue living (by 1st *m*), Czarina Lydia, *b* 1976, — (by 2nd *m*), John Francis, *b* 1997. *Residence* – 26A Cadogan Sq, SW1X 0JP.

BROTHER LIVING

Lord Hugh Hastings, *b* 1923: *ed* Christ's Coll, Camb; an ARICS: *m* 1957, Rosemary, yr da of late Keith Freeling Markby, of Treworder, Blisland, Bodmin, Cornwall, and has issue living, Mark Hugh (Churchtown Farm, Lanteglos-by-Fowey, Cornwall PL23 1NR), *b* 1960: *m* 1987, Charlotte E. A., da of late J. W. D. Stewart, of Kingston upon Thames, Surrey, and has issue living, Laurie Stewart *b* 1990, Chloe Ruth *b* 1988, Hester Mae *b* 1994, — Karen Diana, *b* 1961: *m* 1991, Hugh Yelverton Scott Barrett, of Manor Farmhouse, Dinton, Salisbury, Wilts SP3 5ER, son of late John Scott Barrett, of Henfield, Sussex, and has issue living, Alexander *b* 1992, Katya *b* 1991, Alice Farrar *b* 1996. *Residence* – The Bell House, Dolau, Llandrindod Wells, Powys LD1 5UN.

COLLATERAL BRANCHES LIVING

Grandchildren of late Harold John Hastings Russell, eldest son of late Lord Arthur John Edward Russell (*infra*):—
Issue of late Anthony Arthur Russell, *b* 1904, *d* 1978: *m* 1947, Alicia Charlotte (The Ridgeway, Shere, Guildford, Surrey), only da of late Seton Eustace, of Stoodwell, Merrow, Surrey:—
Francis Anthony, *b* 1948; *ed* Crookham Court, Newbury. —— Hugo Eustace Arthur, *b* 1951; *ed* Milton Abbey: *m* 1991, Caroline L., eldest da of late Donald Grant, OBE, of Molino de la Hoz, Las Rozas de Madrid, Spain, and has issue living, Arthur Donald Anthony, *b* 1994, — William Hugo Alexander, *b* 1995, — Catherine Lucy, *b* 1992. —— Julia Alicia, *b* 1950; *ed* Downe House, Newbury: *m* 1985, Prof Ian Rutherford Sanderson, of 6 Markham St, SW3 3NP, and has issue living, Vita Frances, *b* 1988. —— Victoria Evelyn Elizabeth, *b* 1953; *ed* Downe House, Newbury.

Grandson of late Lord Arthur John Edward Russell, next brother of 9th Duke:—
Issue of late Maj Gilbert Byng Alwyne Russell, *b* 1875, *d* 1942: *m* 1917, Maud Julia Augusta, who *d* 1982, da of late Paul Nelke:—
Martin Basil Paul, *b* 1918; *ed* Eton, and King's Coll, Camb (MA); with KRRC 1939-40; Assist Private Sec to Rt Hon Duff Cooper (later 1st Viscount Norwich), when Min of Information 1940-41, and to Brendan Bracken (later Viscount Bracken) 1941, and Private Sec to Rt Hon Duff Cooper when Chancellor of Duchy of Lancaster, on Mission to Far East 1941-42; HQ Ceylon Army Command 1942-43 and HQ Allied Land Forces SE Asia, Kandy and Singapore 1943-46, with rank of Capt; author of *The Art of George Keyt*, 1949; with British S Africa Co 1954-61, Minerals Separation 1961-63; Ionian Bank 1964-66; founded M. B. P. Russell & Co Ltd 1967; a Member of Council of R Soc for India, Pakistan and Ceylon; FRAS: *m* 1954, Anne Swinton (Croix de Guerre), da of late Brig Stanlake Swinton Lee, CBE, DSO, and has issue living, Julian Hugh (86 South Hill Park, NW3 2SN; Brooks's Club), *b* 1955; *ed* Harrow, — Stephen Raymond (twin), *b* 1955; *ed* Harrow, — Laura Diana, *b* 1959; *ed* Essex Univ (BA), and Way Colls of Biblical Research, USA: *m* 1989, Colin Beresford, and has issue living, Helen Anne *b* 1992, — Emily Esther, *b* 1962; *ed* Manchester Univ (BA). *Residence* – Dungrove Farm House, Tarrant Gunville, Blandford, Dorset DT11 8JS. *Clubs* – White's, Brooks's, Buck's, Travellers' (Paris).

Descendants of late Rt Hon Lord Odo William Russell, GCB, GCMG (yr brother of 9th Duke), who was *cr Baron Ampthill* 1881 (see that title).

Descendants of late Lord John Russell (3rd son of 6th Duke), who was *cr Earl Russell* 1861 (see that title).

Grandchildren of late Maj-Gen Sir Thomas Wentworth Russell, KBE, CMG, Pasha in Egypt, 2nd son (and co-heir to Baronies of Beauchamp and Mordaunt) of Rev Henry Charles Russell, son of Lt-Col Lord Charles James Fox Russell, 6th son of 6th Duke:—
Issue of late Sir John Wriothesley Russell, GCVO, CMG, sometime Amb to Ethiopia, Brazil and Spain, *b* 1914, *d* 1984: *m* 1945, Aliki (*Lady Russell*) (The Vine Farm, Northbourne, nr Deal, Kent; Flat 1, 48 Queen's Gate Gdns, SW7 5ND), da of George Diplarakos, of Athens, and formerly wife of Paul-Louis Weiller (*d* 1993):—
Alexander Charles Thomas Wriothesley, *b* 1950; *ed* Eton, and Trin Coll, Camb: *m* 1986, Elizabeth (Libby) Diana, el da of Lord John Manners, of Knipton, Grantham, Lincs (*see* D Rutland), and has issue living, John, *b* 1995, — Sophie Camilla Mary, *b* 1989, — Rose Isobel Aliki, *b* 1991. —— Georgiana Alexandra (*Lady Boothby*), *b* 1947: *m* 1976, Sir Brooke Charles Boothby, 16th Bt, and has issue. *Residence* – Fonmon Castle, Barry, S Glamorgan CF6 9ZN.

PREDECESSORS – (1) JOHN Russell, KG, one of the most accomplished gentlemen of his time, attended the Archduke Philip of Austria (who had been stranded on the coast near Weymouth) to the Court of Henry VII, in 1506, where he was appointed a Gentleman of the Privy Chamber; accompanied Henry VIII in his French Wars, and having held various high appointments, was *cr Baron Russell* (peerage of England) 1539, and in 1540 obtained a grant of the site of Tavistock Abbey and of the extensive possessions belonging thereto; in 1550, *temp* Edward VI, he received a grant of the Monastery of Woburn and was *cr Earl of Bedford* (peerage of England); was Lord Privy Seal to Queen Mary, and went as Ambassador to Spain to conduct HM's royal consort, Philip II, into England; *d* 1555; *s* by his son (2) FRANCIS, KG, PC, 2nd Earl, a nobleman of great eminence, *temp* Elizabeth I; *d* 1585; *s* by his grandson (3) EDWARD, 3rd Earl; *dsp* 1627; *s* by his cousin, son of Sir William, *cr Baron Russell of Thornhaugh* (peerage of England) 1603, (4) FRANCIS, 4th Earl, who had previously *s* as 2nd Baron Russell; *d* 1641; *s* by his son (5) WILLIAM, KG, 5th Earl, *cr Marquess of Tavistock* and *Duke of Bedford* (peerage of England) 1694; his el son, William, the celebrated Lord Russell, was executed 21 July 1683, for high treason, as a participator in the Rye-House conspiracy; he *d* 1700, and the attainder upon Lord Russell having been annulled, he was *s* by his grandson (6) WRIOTHESLEY, KG, 2nd Duke; summoned to Parliament as *Baron Howland* (peerage of England) 1695; *d* 1711; *s* by his son (7) WRIOTHESLEY, 3rd Duke; *dsp* 1732; *s* by his brother

(8) JOHN, KG, 4th Duke; successively Lord-Lieut of Ireland and Ambassador to France: *d* 1771; *s* by his grandson (9) FRANCIS, 5th Duke; *d* unmarried 1802; *s* by his brother (10) JOHN, KG, 6th Duke; *d* 1839; *s* by his son (11) FRANCIS, KG, 7th Duke; summoned to Parliament in his father's Barony of Howland 1833; *d* 1861; *s* by his son (12) WILLIAM, 8th Duke; *dsp* 1872; *s* by his cousin (13) FRANCIS CHARLES HASTINGS, KG, 9th Duke (el son of Maj-Gen Lord George William, GCB, 2nd son of 6th Duke, by Elizabeth Anne, da of Hon John Theophilus Rawdon, brother of 1st Marquess of Hastings), *b* 1819; MP for Bedfordshire (*L*) 1847-72 Lord-Lieut of Hunts: *m* 1844, Lady Elizabeth Sackville-West, VA, who *d* 1897, el da of 5th Earl De La Warr; *d* 1891; *s* by his el son (14) GEORGE WILLIAM FRANCIS SACKVILLE, 10th Duke, *b* 1852; MP for Bedfordshire (*L*) 1875-85: *m* 1876, Lady Adeline Marie Somers-Cocks, GBE, who *d* 1920, da of 3rd Earl Somers (*ext*); *d* 1893; *s* by his brother (15) HERBRAND ARTHUR, KG, KBE, 11th Duke; *b* 1858; was Lord-Lieut of Middlesex 1898-1926: *m* 1888, Dame Mary Du Caurroy, DBE, RRC, who *d* 1937, da of the Ven W. H. Tribe, formerly Archdeacon of Lahore; *d* 1940; *s* by his son (16) HASTINGS WILLIAM SACKVILLE, 12th Duke; *b* 1888; formerly Lieut 10th Batn Duke of Cambridge's Own (Middlesex) Regt: *m* 1914, Louisa Crommelin Roberta Jowitt, who *d* 1960, da of late Robert Jowitt Whitwell, of Thornbury Lodge, 70 Banbury Rd, Oxford; *d* 1953; *s* by his el son (17) JOHN ROBERT, 13th Duke and present peer; also Marquess of Tavistock, Earl of Bedford, Baron Russell, and Baron Howland.

BEECHING, BARONY OF (Beeching) (Extinct 1985)

WIDOW LIVING OF LIFE BARON

ELLA MARGARET (*Baroness Beeching*), da of William J. Tiley, of Maidstone: *m* 1938, Baron Beeching (Life Baron), who *d* 1985. *Residence* – Barnlands, 97 High St, Lindfield, W Sussex RH16 2HN.

Belfast, Earl of; son of Marquess of Donegall.

BELHAVEN and STENTON, LORD (Hamilton) (Lord S 1647)

ROBERT ANTHONY CARMICHAEL HAMILTON, 13th Lord; *b* 27 Feb 1927; *s* 1961; *ed* Eton; Cmdr Cross of the Order of Merit, Poland, 1995; commn'd Cameronians 1947; Farmer 1950-72: *m* 1st, 1952 (*m diss* 1973), (Elizabeth) Ann, da of late Col Arthur Henry Moseley, DSO, of Hastings Rd, Warrawee, NSW; 2ndly, 1973 (*m diss* 1986), Rosemary, who *d* 1992, da of late Sir Herbert Geraint Williams, 1st Bt, MP (*cr* 1953), and formerly wife of late Sir Ian (John) Auld Mactaggart, 3rd Bt; 3rdly, 1986, Malgorzata Maria, da of Tadeusz· Pobog Hruzik-Mazurkiewicz, of Krakow, Poland, and has issue by 1st and 3rd *m*.

𝔄rms – Quarterly, 1st and 4th, gules, a mullet argent between three cinquefoils ermine *Hamilton of Udston*; 2nd and 3rd gules, a man's heart proper, shadowed or, between three cinquefoils ermine, all within a bordure argent *Hamilton of Raploch*. 𝔠rest – A horse's head couped argent, bridled gules. 𝔖upporters – Two horses argent, bridled gules.
Residence – 16 Broadwater Down, Tunbridge Wells, Kent, TN2 5NR.
Club – Army and Navy.

SON LIVING (*By 1st marriage*)

Hon FREDERICK CARMICHAEL ARTHUR (*Master of Belhaven*), *b* 27 Sept 1953; *ed* Eton: *m* 1st, 1981 (*m diss* 1989), (Elizabeth) Anne da of late Stephen Victor Tredinnick, of Naldretts Court, Wisborough Green, Sussex; 2ndly, 1991, Philippa Martha Gausel, da of Sir Rowland John Rathbone Whitehead, 5th Bt, and has issue living (by 1st *m*), William Richard, *b* 30 Dec 1982, — James Frederick, *b* 1984, — (by 2nd *m*) Olivia Martha, *b* 1993.

DAUGHTERS LIVING (*By 1st marriage*)

Hon Julia Elizabeth Heather HAMILTON, *b* 1956; novelist; resumed her maiden name 1992: *m* 1st, 1975, Richard Newbury; 2ndly, 1979, Stephen Hobbs, and has issue living (by 2nd *m*), Sophie Louise Ann, *b* 1981, — Arabella Leonie, *b* 1983.

(*By 3rd marriage*)

Hon Alexandra Maria, *b* 1987.

HALF-AUNTS LIVING (*Daughters of 11th Lord*)

Hon Margaret de Hauteville, *b* 1939: *m* 1st, 1964 (*m diss* 1981), C. Keith W. Schellenberg; 2ndly, 1983, James Frank Williams, of Udny Castle, Aberdeenshire, and has issue living (by 1st *m*), Nicholas Udny, *b* 1966, — Amy Julia Udny, *b* 1971: *m* 1996, Nicholas C. M. Roscoe, only son of Marshall Roscoe, of North Deighton Manor, Wetherby, N Yorks, and has issue living, Jasper Felix Udny Marshall *b* 1997, — Rose Camilla Joan Udny, *b* 1973.
Hon Victoria Edith, *b* 1941; PhD: *m* 1976, Nicholas Tufnell, of 990 Hanley Av, Los Angeles, Calif 90049, USA, and has issue living, Samuel, *b* 1978.

WIDOW LIVING OF TWELFTH LORD

CYRILLA MARY (Copper Cottage, New Galloway, Castle Douglas), da of late Raymund Louis Binns: *m* 1st, 1942, as his 2nd wife, the 12th Lord Belhaven and Stenton, who *d* 1961; 2ndly, 1969 (*m diss* 19—), Dennis Beaumont Vale, OBE.

COLLATERAL BRANCHES LIVING

Grandchildren of late Arthur Richard Hamilton, uncle of 10th Lord:—
Issue of late Arthur Henry Hamilton, *b* 1872, *d* 1930: *m* 1906, Mabel, who *d* 1918 da of John Harrower, of Baldur, Manitoba:—
Gladys Dorothy, *b* 1908: *m* 1928, Walter Booth Jorgenson, who *d* 1978, and has issue living, Robert Arthur, *b* 1929, — Allen Edward, *b* 1932, — Lynda Dorothy, *b* 1940, — Ellen Jean, *b* 1942.

Issue of late Charles Augustus Hamilton, *b* 1874, *d* 1960: *m* 1906, Alice May, who *d* 1956, da of Benjamin Thorn, of Souris, Manitoba:—
Frederick William, MC, *b* 1910; 1939-45 War as Maj R Canadian Engineers (MC): *m* 1945, Alice Elizabeth, who *d* 1969, da of George A. Stevenson, of Morris, Manitoba, and has issue living, Mary Ellen, *b* 1947: *m* 1st, 1969 (*m diss* 1982), Donald Keith Trueman, of Winnipeg, Canada; 2ndly, 1985, Michael Anthony Halligan, of 119 Balliol St, Toronto, Ontario, Canada MHS 1C2, and has issue living (by 1st *m*), Catherine Martha *b* 1973, — Catherine Alice, *b* 1949: *m* 1979, Robert Webster, and has issue, Paul Robert *b* 1981. —— Richard Terrick (Baldur, Manitoba), *b* 1912: *m* 1933, Muriel, da of John Mcleod, of Belmont, Manitoba, and has issue living, Betty Lorraine, *b* 1934: *m* 1961, W. Lexton Young, of Killarney, Manitoba, Canada, and has issue, Candis *b* 1961, Lana *b* 1963, Lisa *b* 1964, Jan *b* 1966, — Margaret Rose, *b* 1935: *m* 1955, Clare Vrooman, of Belmont, Manitoba, Canada, and has issue, Terry *b* 1956, Kevin *b* 1957, Dean *b* 1960, Patricia *b* 1958, Brenda *b* 1961, Kathy *b* 1962, Shelly *b* 1965, — Gertrude Joan, *b* 1936: *m* 1955, Neil Cline, of Wawanesa, Manitoba, Canada, and has issue, Bradley *b* 1956, Perry *b* 1959, Francis *b* 1965, Laurie *b* 1955, Pamela *b* 1958, — Joyce Elaine, *b* 1938: *m* 1956, Owen Vrooman, of Belmont, Manitoba, Canada, and has issue living, Darrel *b* 1956, Gordon *b* 1964, Debbie *b* 1957, Vicki *b* 1960. —— Rose Aileen, *b* 1908: *m* 1st, 1954, George Walter Easter, who *d* 1958; 2ndly, 1964, Rt Rev William Henry Howes Crump, DD, late Bishop of Saskatchewan.

Granddaughters of late Ven Anthony Hamilton (infra):—
Issue of late Clement Edward Hamilton, *b* 1854, *d* 1923: *m* 1898, Fanny, who *d* 1955, da of James Winch, JP, of Rochester:—
Eleanor Clara Roby, *b* 1902. —— Marjorie Francis Roby, *b* 1907.

Grandchildren of late Terrick Alfred Hamilton (infra):—
Issue of late Terrick Elyston Scott Hamilton, *b* 1881, *d* 1969: *m* 19—, Agnes, who *d* 1944, da of W. Lynch:—
Anthony Elyston John, *b* 1905: *m* 1928, Helen Margaret Doherty, and has issue living, Patrick, *b* 1928: *m* 1952, Dulcie Emily Hafey, and has issue living, Patrick William *b* 1953: *m* 1977, Maree Helen Fitzgerald, formerly wife of — Ward (and has issue living, Brendan James *b* 1979, Michelle Susan *b* 1978), Anthony John *b* 1955: *m* 1977, Suzanne Sylvia Heineman (and has issue living, Allison Madelene Natasha *b* 1975, Janie Leigh *b* 1978), Terrick Daniel *b* 1957: *m* 1979, Heather-Anne Watson, Dale Thomas *b* 1958. — Elyston William, *b* 1936: *m* 1960, Norma Merion Ilott, and has issue living, Jeanette *b* 1962, Kathleen *b* 1964, — Reginald John, *b* 1940: *m* 1962, Thelda Rose Park, and has issue living, Glen *b* 1963, Bradley *b* 1965, Ashley Regnald *b* 1969, Steven *b* 1971. — Margaret, *b* 1930: *m* 1st, 1951, Brian George Denny, who *d* 1959; 2ndly, 1966, Roy Palmer Carige, and has issue living (by 1st *m*), Annette Margaret *b* 1952: *m* 1971, Thomas William Kitchiner (and has issue living, Kellie Maree *b* 1974, Necia Ann *b* 1976, Suzanne *b* 1980), Denise *b* 1958: *m* 1975, Mark William Owttrim (and has issue living, Ryan Mark *b* 1981) (by 2nd *m*), Toni Maree *b* 1970, — Marjorie Jean, *b* 1935: *m* 1954, Donald Allan McKnight, and has issue living, Michael James *b* 1956: *m* 1980, Barbara Guascoine, Allan Douglas Thomas *b* 1967, Teresa Margaret *b* 1955, Tracy Ann *b* 1973, — Helen Margaret, *b* 1938: *m* 1957, Russell McQuie, and has issue living, Russell Scott *b* 1959: *m* 1981, Dana Cheree Mills, Larry *b* 1964, Wendy Ann *b* 1961, — Rita Grace, *b* 1941: *m* 1962, Allan Benjamin Park, and has issue living, Jenny Lorraine *b* 1964: *m* 1982, Neville Allen (and has issue living, Melissa Lorraine *b* 1981), Julie Maree *b* 1965, Allison Jane *b* 1969. —— Vernon Harvey, *b* 1914: *m* 1943, Gloria Volk, and has issue living, Ian Vernon, *b* 1944: *m* 1976, Patti Marie O'Neil, and has issue living, Roderick Joseph *b* 1969, Simon John *b* 1974, Ashley James *b* 1980, — Joy Agnes, *b* 1947: *m* 1967, Geoffrey Francis O'Neil, and has issue living, Lindsay Francis Louis *b* 1968, — Peter Sean *b* 1973, Renée Rose *b* 1975. —— John Edward, *b* 1917: *m* 1937, Olive Amy Florence Hannah Russell, and has issue living, Peter John, *b* 1939: *m* 1960, Joan Adele Kuln, and has

issue living, Geoffrey *b* 1962, Peter Scott *b* 1966, — Alan Patrick, *b* 1952, *m* 1973, Marilyn Anne Ward, and has issue living, John Allan *b* 1976, Michael Frederick *b* 1981, Rosalea Anne *b* 1975, Jantelle Maree *b* 1978, — Margaret, *b* 1938: *m* 1st, 1957 (*m diss* 1969), Colin Miller; 2ndly, 1970 (*m diss* 19—), William John Dolgner, and has issue living (by 1st *m*), Kimberley Mark *b* 1957, Rodney John *b* 1961, Kara Lea *b* 1964, (by 2nd *m*) Jason Ashley *b* 1970, Clayton Scott *b* 19—, — Mary Rose, *b* 1948: *m* 1964, William John Eckel, and has issue living, William John *b* 1965, Raymond Francis *b* 1967. —— William Robert, *b* 1921: *m* 1947, Jean Elsie Higgins, and has issue living, Diane Carol, *b* 1946: *m* 1965, Daniel Cameron, and has issue living, Andreena Louise *b* 1978, — Maree Estelle, *b* 1947: *m* 1966 (*m diss* 1978), Dale McDonald, and has issue living, Michael John *b* 1967, — Lynda Agnes, *b* 1949: *m* 1969, Robert Sing, and has issue living, Sharlene Maree *b* 1971, Bronwyn Anne *b* 1981, — Mary Anne, *b* 1950: *m* 1978, John King, and has issue living, Aeron James *b* 1971, — Charmaine Lee, *b* 1962; *m* 1983, Steven Bailey. —— Julia Agnes, *b* 1908: *m* 1938, John Edward Whitman, of Hamilton, Rundle-Jardine Sts, Wandal, Rockhampton, Queensland, Australia, and has issue living, Barry John (Kerrigan St, N Rockhampton, Queensland, Australia), *b* 1944: *m* 1969, Margaret Collins, and has issue living, Mark John *b* 1975, Joanne Maree *b* 1970, Louise Margaret *b* 1977, — Michael John (Houlihan St, N Rockhampton, Queensland, Australia), *b* 1948: *m* 1971, Lynette Wallace, and has issue living, Karl Anthony *b* 1975, Clint Andrew *b* 1977, Luke Phillip *b* 1980, Emily May *b* 1983, — Paulanne Mary, *b* 1939: *m* 1961, Edward John Kelly, of 49 Blenheim St, Chermside West, Brisbane, Queensland, Australia, and has issue living, Chris James *b* 1965, Kim Edward *b* 1967, Lee Michael *b* 1969, Jason John *b* 1974, Julie Maree (twin) *b* 1974, — Julie Anne, *b* 1941; JP: *m* 1964, Phillip J. Walsh, of 129 Rundle St, Rockhampton, Queensland, Australia, and has issue living, Anthony John *b* 1965: *m* 1990, Verena Finocchiaro, Justin Philip *b* 1966, John Edward *b* 1969. —— Mary Alice, *b* 1911: *m* 1939, Thorwald Harold Widt, of 22 Boowgala Rd, Florida Gdns, Gold Coast, Quensland, Australia, and has issue living, Peter Anthony, *b* 1945: *m* 1969, Diane McCallum, and has issue living, Stephen Anthony *b* 1968, — Helen Margaret, *b* 1940. —— Eileen Marjorie, *b* 1925: *m* 1947, Roland Mervyn Smith, who *d* 1975, and has issue living, Terrick Elystan Scott, *b* 1953: *m* 1982, Yasmine Hartmann, — Lynda Ngaio, *b* 1949: *m* 1974, Sqdn Ldr Gordon Maxwell Bennett, — Ruth Bronwen, *b* 1954: *m* 1973, Capt Roland Francis Bagshaw, and has issue living, Kristi Leanne *b* 1973, Alison Louise *b* 1975, Veronica Lauren *b* 1978.

Grandson of late Edward William Terrick Hamilton, son of late Ven Anthony Hamilton (*b* 1778), Archdeacon of Taunton, great-uncle of 10th Lord:—
Issue of late Terrick Alfred Hamilton, *b* 1851, *d* 1925: *m* 1878, Alice, da of John Scott, of Newcastle, NSW:—
John Helenus, *b* 1888.

Grandchildren of late Terrick Alfred Hamilton (ante):—
Issue of late Charles Hamilton, *b* 1885, *d* 1961: *m* 1911, Olivia Abbott Palmer:—
Charles Clive, *b* 1919: *m* 19—, Nellie Olive Watson, and has issue living, Noel Peter, *b* 1953, — Judith Helen, *b* 1945, — Lexie Mae, *b* 1949. —— Olivia Jessie, *b* 1913: *m* 19—, Edmund Rockett, and has issue living, James Edward, *b* 1947. —— Margaret Jean, *b* 1915: *m* 1st, Ernest Henry Bellingham; 2ndly, 1965, William Edward McCulloch, and has issue living (by 1st *m*), Alan Ward, *b* 1941: *m* 1966, Lynette Fawcett. —— Kepple Osborne, *b* 1917: *m* 19—, Dudley Halliwell Milton, and has issue living, Raymond Charles, *b* 1945.

PREDECESSORS – (1) JOHN HAMILTON, of Broomhill (son of James Hamilton, of Broomhill, *cr* a Bt of Nova Scotia 1635), was *cr Lord Belhaven and Stenton*, of co Haddington (peerage of Scotland) 1647. In 1675 he surrendered his Lordship to the crown, and received a new patent with remainder to John Hamilton, of Pressmannan, husband of his granddaughter Margaret, and in failure of that line to his heirs male whatsoever; *d* 1679; *s* by his son-in-law (2) JOHN, 2nd Lord, a Lord of the Treasury 1704, and a zealous opponent of the Union; was imprisoned in the Tower of London as an ally of the Chevalier St. George; *d* 1708; *s* by his son (3) JOHN, 3rd Lord, a Representative Peer; having been appointed Gov of Barbados, was drowned in his passage out 1721; *s* by his son (4) JOHN, 4th Lord; *dsp* 1764; *s* by his brother (5) JAMES, 5th Lord; *dsp* 1777, when the title was incorrectly assumed by Capt. William Hamilton (descended from John Hamilton of Coltness, el great-uncle of 2nd Lord), who voted at the election of Scottish Peers in 1790; it was resolved by the Committee for Privileges 1793 that his vote was not valid, and the title in 1790 was determined in favour of (6-7) WILLIAM, 7th Lord, son of Robert Hamilton, of Wishaw (great-great grandson of William Hamilton, 2nd great-uncle of 2nd Lord) who was *de jure* 6th Lord, William *d* 1814; *s* by his (8) ROBERT MONTGOMERY, KT, 8th Lord; Lord-Lieutenant of Lanarkshire; *cr Baron Hamilton*, of Wishaw (peerage of United Kingdom) 1831; *dsp* 1868, when the barony of Hamilton became extinct, and the Lordship of Belhaven and Stenton became dormant, and remained so until 1875, when the House of Lords adjudged it to (9) JAMES, 9th Lord, (son of late Archibald Hamilton, Surgeon 92nd Regt), *b* 1822: *m* 1877, Georgina, who *d* 1940, da of Sir John Watson, Bt, of Earnock and Neilsland, Lanarkshire; *d* 1893, when the Lordship was claimed by (10) ALEXANDER CHARLES (son of late William John Hamilton, MP, a descendant of late William Hamilton (ante), through whom the 9th Lord was descended), *b* 1840; was served heir to his kinsman, voted at the election of Scottish Representative Peers, matriculated Arms at the Lyon Office as 10th Lord, and was elected a Representative Peer for Scotland in the House of Lords: *m* 1880, Georgina Katherine, who *d* 1932, da of late Legh Richmond; *d* 1920; *s* by his nephew (11) ROBERT EDWARD ARCHIBALD, CIE (son of late Archibald William Hamilton, RN, yr brother of 10th Lord), 11th Lord, *b* 1871; Lieut-Col (ret) 4th Gurkhas (Indian Army); was Representative Peer for Scotland 1922-45; assumed the additional surname of Udny 1934: *m* 1st, 1898, Kathleen Gonville, who *d* 1935, da of Sir Benjamin Parnell Bromhead, CB, 4th Bt; 2ndly, 1938, Sheila de Hauteville, who *d* 1962, only da of Capt Algernon George Pearson, DSO, late Roy Berkshire Regt; *d* 1950; *s* by his son (12) ROBERT ALEXANDER BENJAMIN, 12th Lord; *b* 1903; Hon Lieut-Col, Roy Scots Fusiliers, an author, and an authority on S-W Arabia; was Political Officer Aden Protectorate 1934-9: *m* 1st, 1926 (*m diss* 1941), Heather Mildred Carmichael (who *d* 1992, having *m* 2ndly, 1944, Maj Basil William Seager, CMG, OBE, who *d* 1977), da of Lieut-Col Richard Carmichael Bell, DSO, OBE, late Central India Horse; 2ndly, 1942, Cyrilla Mary, who *m* 2ndly, 1969 (*m diss* 19—), Dennis Beaumont Vale, OBE, da of late Raymund Louis Binns; *d* 1961; *s* by his only son (13) ROBERT ANTHONY CARMICHAEL, 13th Lord and present peer.

BELL, BARON (Bell) (Life Baron 1998)

TIMOTHY JOHN LEIGH (TIM) BELL, son of late Arthur Leigh Bell, of South Africa; *b* 18 Oct 1941; *ed* Queen Elizabeth's Gram Sch, Barnet; with ABC TV 1959-61, Colman Prentis & Varley 1961-63,

Hobson Bates 1963-66, Geers Gross 1966-70; Chm and Man Dir Saatchi & Saatchi, Compton 1975-85 (Man Dir 1970-75); Group Chief Exec, Lowe Howard-Spink Campbell Ewald 1985-87; Dep Chm Lowe Howard-Spink & Bell 1987-89; Chm Bell Pottinger Communications and Chime Communications plc; Memb board of sundry charities, etc; FIPA; *cr* Kt Bach 1990, and *Baron Bell*, of Belgravia in the City of Westminster (Life Baron) 1998: *m* 1988, Virginia Wallis, da of Dr John Wallis Hornbrook, of Sydney, Australia, and has issue.

Address – c/o Chime Communications plc, 7 Hertford St, W1Y 8LP. *Clubs* – RAC, St Edward Yacht (Sydney).

SON LIVING

Hon Harry Leigh, *b* 1991.

DAUGHTER LIVING

Hon Daisy Alicia Wallis, *b* 1988.

BELLEW, BARON (Bellew) (Baron I 1848, Bt I, 1688)

JAMES BRYAN BELLEW, 7th Baron and 13th Baronet; *b* 5 Jan 1920; *s* 1981; late Lt IG: *m* 1st, 1942, Mary Elizabeth, who *d* 1978, el da of Rev Edward Eustace Hill; 2ndly, 1978, Gwendoline, da of late Charles Redmond Clayton-Daubeny, of Bridgwater, Som, and Bihar, India, and formerly wife of Maj P. Hall, and has issue by 1st *m*.

𝔄rms – Sable, fretty or. 𝔈rest – An arm embowed, in armour, holding a sword proper. 𝔖upporters – *Dexter*, a leopard or, gorged with a mural crown azure; *sinister*, a wolf azure, gorged with a ducal coronet or.
Seat – Barmeath Castle, Togher, co Louth.

SONS LIVING (*By 1st marriage*)

Hon BRYAN EDWARD, *b* 19 March 1943; *ed* Eton, and RMA Sandhurst; Maj IG (ret): *m* 1968, Rosemary Sarah, da of Maj Reginald Kilner Brasier Hitchcock, of Meers Court, Mayfield, Sussex, and has had issue, †Patrick Edward, *b* 1969; *d* as the result of an accident 1997, — Anthony Richard Brooke, *b* 1972.
Hon Christopher James, *b* 1954; *ed* Eton, and Durham Univ (BA 1976): *m* 1984 (*m diss* 1991), Hon Rose Griselda Eden, yst da of 7th Baron Henley, and formerly wife of Stuart Ballin. *Residence* – 56 Margravine Gdns, W6.

All from above

DAUGHTER LIVING (*By 1st marriage*)

Hon Angela Mary, *b* 1944: *m* 1964, Capt Simon Hugh Walford, 17th/21st Lancers, of Summerstown House, Trim, co Meath, and has issue living, Jeanie Anne, *b* 1966: *m* 1993, Timothy Hugo Pollock (*see* B Londesborough, 1995 Edn), — Caroline Sarah, *b* 1968: *m* 1997, Anthony Lionel Brockbank (*see* Findlay, Bt, ext 1979).

COLLATERAL BRANCHES LIVING

Issue of late Hon Sir George Rothe Bellew, KCB, KCVO, FSA, Garter Principal King of Arms 1951-61 (raised to the rank of a Baron's son 1935), half-brother of 6th Baron, *b* 1899, *d* 1993: *m* 1935, Ursula Kennard, who *d* 1994, da of late Anders Eric Knös Gull, of Warfield House, Berks.—
Richard George, *b* 1936; *ed* Eton; late 2nd Lieut Irish Guards; OStJ: *m* 1965, Shona, only da of late Col John Edward Mercer Ewart Clark Leask, MBE, IA, and formerly wife of Roderic Marshall Knowles, and has issue living, Henry Edward Courtenay, *b* 1973, — Aidan Nicholas, *b* 1980, — Serena Leonie Georgia, *b* 1969.

Issue of late Hon Patrick Herbert Bellew (raised to the rank of a Baron's son 1935), half-brother of 6th Baron, *b* 1905, *d* 1984: *m* 1st, 1936 (*m diss* 1947), Hon Catherine Moya de la Poer Beresford, who *d* 1967, da of 5th Baron Decies; 2ndly, 1954, Helen Carol, who *d* 1980, da of late Walter Clinton Louchheim, of New York:—
(By 1st *m*) John Jeremy de la Poer, *b* 1937; *ed* Princeton Univ; Chase Manhattan Bank, NA 1961-87: *m* 1966, Cynthia Annette, da of Ernest J. Saunders, of Johannesburg, and has issue living, John Patrick, *b* 1966, — Catherine Moyra, *b* 1969.

(In remainder to Baronetcy only)

Sir Edward Bellew, 6th Bt, had eight brothers, Mathew, John, William, Patrick, Michael, Richard, Robert and Francis. Some of these married, and their male descendants, if any, are in remainder to the Baronetcy.

PREDECESSORS – **(1)** *Sir* Patrick Bellew, son of Sir John Bellew, Knt, MP for co Louth 1639; *cr* a *Baronet* 1688; *d* 1716; *s* by his son **(2)** John, 2nd Bt; *d* 1734; *s* by his son **(3)** Edward, 3rd Bt; *d* 1741; *s* by his el son **(4)** John, 4th Bt; *d* 1750; *s* by his brother **(5)** Patrick, 5th Bt; *d* 1795; *s* by his son **(6)** Edward, 6th Bt; *d* 1827; was *s* by his son **(7)** *Rt Hon* Sir Patrick, PC, 7th Bt; *b* 1798; *cr Baron Bellew* (peerage of Ireland) 1848, was Lord-Lieut of co Louth: *m* 1829, Anna Femina, da of Don José Maria de Mendoza y Rios; *d* 1866; *s* by his son **(8)** Edward Joseph, 2nd Baron, *b* 1830: *m* 1853, Augusta Mary, who *d* 1904, da of Col George Bryan, of Jenkinstown, Kilkenny; *d* 1895, without having established his right to vote at the Elections of Irish Representative Peers; *s* by his el son **(9)** Charles Bertram, 3rd Baron, *b* 1855: *m* 1883, Mildred Mary Josephine, who *d* 1934, da of Sir Humphrey de Trafford, 2nd Bt, *d* 1911; *s* by his brother **(10)** George Leopold Bryan, 4th Baron, *b* 1857; a Representative Peer for Ireland; sometime Major 10th Hussars and Yorkshire Regt (TF); Afghan War 1878-9, Nile Expedition 1884-5, S Africa 1900, European War 1914-18; assumed by R licence 1881 the surname of Bryan in lieu of his patronymic: *m* 1927, Elaine Carlisle, who *d* 1973, da of late John B. Leach, of Queenstown, S Africa, and widow of Herbert Lloyd-Dodd, of Johannesburg, Transvaal, *d* 1935: *s* by his nephew **(11)** Edward Henry, MBE (son of late Hon Richard Eustace Bellew, 4th son of 2nd Baron), 5th Baron; *b* 1889: *m* 1912, Barbara Helen Mary, who *d* 1967, da of late Sir Henry Farnham Burke, KCVO, CB, Garter Principal King of Arms; *d* 1975; *s* by his brother **(12)** Bryan Bertram, MC, 6th Baron, *b* 1890: *m* 1918, Jeanie Ellen Agnes, who *d* 1973, da of late James Ormsby Jameson, of Dolland, Clonsilla, co Dublin; *d* 1981; *s* by his son **(13)** James Bryan, 7th Baron and present peer.

Bellow, family name of Lord Bellwin.

BELLWIN, BARON (Bellow) (Life Baron 1979)

Irwin Norman Bellow, son of Abraham Bellow; *b* 7 Feb 1923; *ed* Leeds Grmr Sch, and Leeds Univ (LLB); DL W Yorks 1991; Parl Under Sec of State, Dept of the Environment 1979-83, Min of State for Local Gvt and Environmental Services 1983-84; Leeds City Council Leader 1975-79; Chm Leeds Housing Cttee 1967-72; an Alderman of Leeds City Council 1968-73; JP since 1969; Pres Moor Allerton Golf Club since 1979; *cr Baron Bellwin*, of the City of Leeds (Life Baron) 1979: *m* 1948, Doreen Barbara, da of Myer Saperia, and has issue.

Arms – Azure in chief two bellows argent garnished or and in base a rose argent barbed and seeded proper, a border or fetty azure. Crest – Upon a wreath an owl guardant azure beaked, legged, murally crowned and holding in the dexter claws a bell bendwise gold. Supporters – *Dexter*, A ram azure armed, langued and tailed or; *sinister*, a lion rampant azure armed, crined, langued and the tail tufted or, both with a collar argent, charged with triangles interlaced in pairs azure.
Residence – Woodside Lodge, Ling Lane, Scarcroft, Leeds LS14 3HX.

SON LIVING

Hon Stephen Jeremy (The Oval, 25a Bracken Park, Scarcroft, Leeds LS14 3HZ), *b* 1953; *ed* Leeds Gram Sch, and Leeds Poly: *m* 1974, Marilyn Stern, and has issue living, Adam, *b* 1989, — Milena, *b* 1986.

DAUGHTERS LIVING

Hon Frances Rochelle, *b* 1951: *m* 1971, Stephen Taylor, of Balboa, 12 Fern Chase, Scarcroft, Leeds LS14 3JL, and has issue living, Daniel Mark, *b* 1973, — Edward David, *b* 1976.
Hon Linda Carol, *b* 1956: *m* 1st, 1976 (*m diss* 1988), Leslie Harris; 2ndly, 1990, Steven Porter, and has issue living (by 2nd *m*), Alexander, *b* 1993, — Robert, *b* 1993, — Eleanor, *b* 1992. *Residence* – 30 Ventnor Drive, Totteridge, N20 8BP.

BELMORE, EARL (Lowry-Corry) (Earl I 1797)

JOHN ARMAR LOWRY-CORRY, 8th Earl; *b* 4 Sept 1951; *s* 1960: *m* 1984, Lady Mary Jane Meade, 2nd da of 6th Earl of Clanwilliam, and has issue.

Arms – Quarterly: 1st grand quarter quarterly, 1st and 4th gules, a saltire argent, in chief a rose of the last, *Corry*: 2nd and 3rd sable, a cup argent, with a garland between two laurel branches issuing therefrom vert, *Lowry*; 2nd grand quarter gules, a saltire argent, on a bend azure, three buckles or, *Leslie*; 4th grand quarter or, a lion rampant gules, over all a bend sable, *Abernethy*. **Crest** – 1st, a cock proper; 2nd, a garland of laurel, between two branches of the same, all proper. **Supporters** – Two tiger cats, guardant proper, ducally collared and chained or.
Seat – Castle Coole, Enniskillen, co Fermanagh BT74 6JY.

SONS LIVING

JOHN ARMAR GALBRAITH (*Viscount Corry*), *b* 2 Nov 1985.
Hon Montagu Gilford George, *b* 1989.

DAUGHTER LIVING

Lady Martha Catherine, *b* 1992.

SISTERS LIVING

Lady Anthea Geraldine, *b* 1942: *m* 1965, Patrick Mathew Desmond Forde, of Seaforde, co Down (*see* V Bangor).
Lady Sarah Lillian, *b* 1945: *m* 1979, Gary McNulty, of 4131, County Rd 103, Carbondale, Colorado 81623, USA, and has issue living, Katherine, *b* 1979, — Margaret, *b* 1984.

AUNT LIVING (*Raised to the rank of an Earl's daughter,* 1951)

Lady Doreen Stella, *b* 1916; formerly 2nd Officer WRNS: *m* 1948, Rev John Gwinnett, MC, Chap to the Forces, who *d* 1977, and has issue living, Adrian John, *b* 1949: *m* 1971, Jane Elliot Allen, and has issue living, Giles Marcus *b* 1974, Verity Jane *b* 1977.

WIDOW LIVING OF SEVENTH EARL

GLORIA ANTHEA (Dar Sellum, Triq-is-Sellum, Zebbug GRB 103, Gozo, Malta), da of late Herbert Bryant Harker, of Melbourne, Australia: *m* 1st, 1939, the 7th Earl Belmore, who *d* 1960; 2ndly, 1963, Col Robert James Thompson Irwin, MC, R Inniskilling Fus, who *d* 1984.

COLLATERAL BRANCHES LIVING

Grandchildren of late Col Hon Henry William Lowry-Corry, 4th son of 3rd Earl:—
Issue of late Lt-Col Sir Henry Charles Lowry-Corry, MC, *b* 1887, *d* 1973: *m* 1920, Betty Alice Adeline, who *d* 1978, da of late Col Douglas James Proby (*see* D Abercorn, colls, 1976 Edn):—
Frederick Henry (Edwardstone Hall, Boxford, Suffolk), *b* 1926; *ed* Eton; Lt RN (ret); 1939-45 War: *m* 1949, Hon Rosemary Diana Lavinia Plumer, da of 2nd Viscount Plumer, and has issue living, Charles Frederick Armar, *b* 1951; *m* 1980, Elizabeth Jean, twin da of J. W. A. Andrews, of Ridge End, Highridge, Alton, Hants, and has issue living, Michael Henry Charles *b* 1983, Robert Galbraith *b* 1990, Joanna Elizabeth Louise *b* 1982, Angela Rosemary *b* 1987, — James Leopold Vincent, *b* 1955: *m* 1984, Judith, yr da of F. A. Lodge, of Overtrees, Foxhill, Leeds, Yorks, and has issue living, Charlotte *b* 1989. —— Elizabeth Margaret, *b* 1921. —— Edith (*Baroness Carver*), *b* 1923: *m* 1947, FM Baron Carver, GCB, CBE, DSO, MC (Life Baron), of Wood End House, Wickham, Hants, and has issue.

Granddaughter of late Brig-Gen Noel Armar Lowry-Corry, DSO (infra):—
Issue of late Montagu William Lowry-Corry, *b* 1907, *d* 1977: *m* 1st, 1929 (*m diss* 1938), Hon Mary Constance, who *d* 1991, da of 2nd Baron Biddulph; 2ndly, 1969, Jean Trefusis (Clover Farm, Shalden, Alton, Hants), da of late Hon Arthur Owen Crichton (see E Erne, colls), and widow of Lt-Col Eton James Henry Merry, MC:—
(By 1st *m*) Josephine Clare, *b* 1931: *m* 1957, Prince Rupert Ludwig Ferdinand zu Löwenstein-Wertheim-Freudenberg (*see* By Pirbright, 1963 Edn), of Petersham Lodge, River Lane, Richmond, Surrey, and has issue living, *Prince* Rudolf Amadeus, *b* 1957, — *Prince* Konrad Friedrich Ferdinand Johannes Ottokar Sylvester, *b* 1958, — *Princess* Maria Theodora Marjorie, *b* 1966: *m* 1998, Count Palatine Manfredi della Gherardesca, son of Count Palatine Guelfo della Gherardesca, of Florence, Italy.

Granddaughter of late Armar Henry Lowry-Corry, son of Rt Hon Henry Thomas Lowry-Corry, MP, 1st Lord of the Admiralty, 2nd son of 2nd Earl:—
Issue of late Brig-Gen Noel Armar Lowry-Corry, DSO, *b* 1867, *d* 1935: *m* 1st, 1895, Rosalind Gertrude, who *d* 1903, da of Lt-Col Robert Hamilton Lloyd-Anstruther (Anstruther, Bt, colls); 2ndly, 1904, Hon Clare O'Brien, who *d* 1950, da of 14th Baron Inchiquin:—

(By 2nd *m*) Patricia, *b* 1905. *Residence* – 33 Wynnstay Gdns, Allen St, W8 6UT.

PREDECESSORS – Galbraith Lowry, MP for co Tyrone; assumed in 1764 the additional surname of Corry; *d* 1769, having had with other issue **(1)** ARMAR, MP for co Tyrone, *cr Baron Belmore* 1781, *Viscount Belmore* 1789, and *Earl Belmore* (peerage of Ireland) 1797; *d* 1802; *s* by his son **(2)** SOMERSET, 2nd Earl; was Custos Rotulorum of co Tyrone; sometime MP for co Tyrone, Gov of Jamaica and a Representative Peer for Ireland; *d* 1841; *s* by his son **(3)** ARMAR, 3rd Earl, *b* 1801; was MP for co Fermanagh: *m* 1834, Emily Louise, who *d* 1904, da of William Shepherd, of Bradbourne, Kent; *d* 17 Dec 1845; was *s* by his son **(4)** SOMERSET RICHARD, GCMG, PC, MRIA, 4th Earl; *b* 1835; for fifty-six years a Representative Peer; Under-Sec of State for Home Depart 1866-7, Gov of NS Wales 1867-72, and one of the Lords Justices of Ireland during the absence of Lord-Lieut in 1885, 1890, 1891, 1895, 1896, 1897 and 1898; Lieut for co Tyrone 1892-1913: *m* 1861, Anne Elizabeth Honoria, who *d* 1919, 2nd da of late Capt John Neilson Gladstone, RN, MP; *d* 1913; *s* by his el son **(5)** ARMAR, 5th Earl; *b* 1870; Bar Inner Temple 1897; High Sheriff of co Fermanagh 1895, and of co Tyrone 1901; *d* 1948; *s* by his brother **(6)** CECIL, 6th Earl; *b* 1873,; was High Sheriff of co Tyrone 1916, and of co Fermanagh 1922, and Chm of Fermanagh Co Council 1943; *d* 1949; *s* by his cousin **(7)** GALBRAITH ARMAR (son of late Major Adrian Lowry-Corry, 5th son of late Adm Hon Armar Lowry-Corry, 2nd son of 3rd Earl), 7th Earl; *b* 1913; Major R Inniskilling Fusiliers, and a DL and JP for co Fermanagh: *m* 1939, Gloria Anthea, da of late Herbert Bryant Harker, of Melbourne, Australia; *d* 1960; *s* by his only son **(8)** JOHN ARMAR, 8th Earl and present peer; also Viscount Belmore, and Baron Belmore.

BELOFF, BARONY OF (Beloff) (Extinct 1999)

SONS LIVING OF LIFE BARON

Hon Michael Jacob, *b* 1942; *ed* Eton, and Magdalen Coll, Oxford; Bar Gray's Inn 1967; QC 1981; Recorder 1985; Bencher (Gray's Inn) 1988, Dep Judge of High Court 1989; Judge of the Courts of Appeal, Jersey and Guernsey, since 1995; Memb of Court of Arbitration for Sport since 1996; Pres Trin Coll, Oxford, since 1996: *m* 1969, Judith Mary Arkinstall, and has issue living, Rupert, *b* 1973, — Natasha, *b* 1976. *Residence* – The President's Lodgings, Trinity College, Oxford OX1 3BH.

Hon Jeremy Benjamin, *b* 1943; *ed* Rugby, and Oxford Univ: *m* 1973, Carol Macdonald, and has issue living, Nicholas, *b* 1975, — Jonathan Max, *b* 1986, — Catherine, *b* 1978. *Residence* – Glenwood, Templewood Lane, Farnham Common, Bucks, SL3 3HW.

WIDOW LIVING OF LIFE BARON

HELEN (*Baroness Beloff*), da of Samuel Dobrin: *m* 1938, Baron Beloff (Life Baron), who *d* 1999. *Residence* – Flat 9, 22 Lewes Crescent, Brighton BN2 1GB.

BELPER, BARON (Strutt) (Baron UK 1856)

(ALEXANDER) RONALD GEORGE STRUTT, 4th Baron, *b* 23 April 1912; *s* 1956; is Major Coldstream Gds, and patron of two livings; European War 1939-44 (wounded): *m* 1940 (*m diss* 1949), Zara Sophie Kathleen Mary, da of Sir Harry Stapleton Mainwaring, 5th Bt (ext), and has issue.

𝕬rms – Per pale sable and azure, two chevronels engrailed, between three cross crosslets fitchée or. ℭrest – In front of rays of the sun proper, a cubit arm erect, vested, bendy of six or and sable, cuffed argent, in the hand a roll of paper proper. 𝕾upporters – On either side a leopard proper, gorged with a collar gemellé azure, therefrom pendant an escutcheon also azure, charged with a cross crosslet fitchée or.
Seat – Kingston Hall, Nottingham.

SON LIVING

Hon RICHARD HENRY (The Park, Kingston on Soar, Nottingham NG11 0DH), *b* 24 Oct 1941; *ed* Harrow: *m* 1st, 1966 (*m diss* 19—), Jennifer Vivian, da of late Capt Peter Winser; 2ndly, 1980, Mrs Judith Mary de Jonge, da of James Twynam, of Kitemore House, Faringdon, Oxon, and has issue living (by 1st *m*), Michael Henry, *b* 1969, — Henrietta Lavinia, *b* 1970.

HALF-BROTHER LIVING

Hon Peter Algernon, MC, *b* 1924; *ed* Eton; Chm Tollemache & Cobbold Breweries Ltd; 1943-45 War as Lt Coldm Gds (MC); DL Suffolk 1988: *m* (Jan) 1953, Gay Margaret, da of Sir (Frank Guy) Clavering Fison, of Crepping Hall, Stutton, Suffolk, and has issue living, Henry Clavering Tollemache (Stutton Hall, Stutton, Ipswich), *b* (Dec) 1953: *m* 1979, Athena, only da of Jeremy Maas, of Suffolk House, Montpelier Row, Twickenham, and has issue living, Algy Jeremy Valentine *b* 1983, Leo Edward Orlando *b* 1988, Sam Jedediah *b* 1993, Daniel *b* 1998, Scarlett *b* 1985, — Martin Andrew (Church Westcote, Chipping Norton, Oxon), *b* 1985: *m* 1985, Mrs Emma Lithgow, da of late Jeremy John Holt and of Mrs Richard Cobbold, of Holbrook Lodge, nr Ipswich, Suffolk, and has issue living, Laurence *b* 1986, Luke *b* 1988, Lara *b* 1992, Imogen *b* 1995, — Jane Mariota, *b* 1956: *m* 1979, Dr Murdoch Laing, of Scardroy, Inverness-shire, and has issue living, Mungo Peter *b* 1984, Jash Murdoch (a son) *b* 1987, Tara *b* 1981, Alice Caitlin *b* 1982, — Elisabeth, *b* 1963: *m* 1995, Jonathan M. J. Burge, 2nd son of Ian Burge, of Glen Usk, Llanhennock, Gwent, and has issue living, Jack Valentine, *b* 1997, Georgia Rose *b* 1999. *Residence* – The Garden House, Stutton, Ipswich, Suffolk.

WIDOW LIVING OF SON OF THIRD BARON

Arielle, da of Joseph Washington Fraser, of Newport, Rhode Island, USA: *m* 1st, 1939, Hon Michael Strutt, P/O, RCAF, who was *ka* 1942; 2ndly, 1947 (*m diss* 1967), Eric Eweson.

COLLATERAL BRANCH LIVING

Issue of late Capt Hon (Desmond) Rupert Strutt, yr son (by 2nd *m*) of 3rd Baron, *b* 1926, *d* (27 Feb) 1993: *m* 1st, 1951 (*m diss* 1961), Jean Felicity, who *d* 1984, da of late Hon Francis Walter Erskine (*see* E Mar and Kellie, colls, 1985 Edn); 2ndly, 1964, Lucy Gwendolen, who *d* (16 Sept) 1993, only da of late Maj James William Stirling Home Drummond Moray, late Scots Guards (*see* D Buccleuch, colls, 1995 Edn):—
(By 1st *m*) Jeremy Bevil (Barn Pightle, Rotten Row, Tutts Clump, Pangbourne, Berks RG7 6LQ), *b* 1954; *ed* Eton: *m* 1979, Petrina, MP, twin da of Peter Neville Smith, DFC, of Fir Tree Cottage, Henbury, Macclesfield, Cheshire, and has issue living, Toby Charles, *b* 1981, — Julian Rupert *b* 1983, — Rupert Peter, *b* 1987. —— Christopher Charles (88 Broughton Rd, SW6 2LB), *b* 1955. —— (By 2nd *m*) Dominick James (The Wing, Chavenage, Tetbury, Glos GL8 8XP), *b* 1966. —— James Edward (82 Faroe Rd, W14 0EP), *b* 1969: *m* 1997, Georgina Julia, elder da of John Francis Pope (*see* Ewart, Bt, colls).

PREDECESSORS – **(1)** EDWARD Strutt, PC, FRS, LLD, son of William Strutt, of St Helen's House, Derby; *b* 1801; sat as MP (*L*) for Derby 1830-48, for Nottingham 1852-6; was Chancellor of Duchy of Lancaster 1852-4, and Lord-Lieut of Nottinghamshire 1864-80; *cr Baron Belper* (peerage of United Kingdom) 1856; *m* 1837, Amelia Harriet, da of late Right Rev William Otter, DD, Lord Bishop of Chichester; *d* 30 June 1880, and was *s* by his son **(2)** HENRY, PC, FRS, 2nd Baron; *b* 1840; MP for Derbyshire East (*L*), 1868-74, and for Berwick-on-Tweed in 1880; was Capt of HM's Corps of Gentlemen-at-Arms 1895-1906; *m* 1874, Lady Margaret Coke, who *d* 1922, da of 2nd Earl of Leicester; *d* 1914; *s* by his only son **(3)** ALGERNON HENRY, 3rd Baron; *b* 1883; Capt Household Cav and Major Reserve of Officers: *m* 1st, 1911 (*m diss* 1922), Hon Dame Eva Isabel Marian Bruce, DBE, JP, who *d* 1987, da of 2nd Baron Aberdare; 2ndly, 1923, Angela Mariota, who *d* 1995, having *m* 2ndly, 1958, Rev (Harry) Norman Tollemache (formerly Wrigley), who *d* 1981, da of late Hon Douglas Alfred Tollemache (*see* B Tollemache); *d* 1956; *s* by his el son **(4)** (ALEXANDER) RONALD GEORGE, 4th Baron and present peer.

BELSTEAD, BARON (Ganzoni) (Baron UK 1938, Bt UK 1929)

JOHN JULIAN GANZONI, PC, 2nd Baron and 2nd Baronet; *b* 30 Sept 1932; *s* 1958; *ed* Eton, and Ch Ch, Oxford; a JP of Ipswich, Lord Lieut Suffolk since 1994; a Parl Under-Sec of State, Dept of Education and Science 1970-73, and Parl Under Sec of State for N Ireland 1973-74; Chm of Governing Bodies Assocn since 1974; Under Sec of State, Home Office, 1979-82; Min of State, Foreign Office 1982-83, Min of Agriculture, Fisheries & Food 1983-87, Min of State, Dept of Environment, 1987-88; Deputy Leader House of Lords 1984-88, Leader of House of Lords and Privy Seal 1988-90, Min of State for N Ireland and Paymaster Gen 1990-92, since when Chm Parole Board; *cr* PC 1981.

Arms – Per fesse azure and argent a gentian plant, flowered and eradicated proper, between in chief a mullet and an increscent both or. **Crest** – A demi-lion or supporting a gentian plant as in the arms. **Supporters** – On either side a seahorse proper, gorged with a collar pendent therefrom a portcullis chained or.
Clubs – All England Lawn Tennis, MCC.

Fidelity overcomes

FIDELITAS · VINCIT

DEBRETT'S ILLUSTRATED PEERAGE

Hon Mary Jill, *b* 1931; a DL Suffolk 1988; Memb Gen Synod of Church of England 1970-95, a Church Commr 1978-93. *Residence* – Rivendell, Spring Meadow, Playford, nr Ipswich, Suffolk.

PREDECESSORS – **(1)** (FRANCIS) JOHN CHILDS Ganzoni, only son of late Julius Charles Ganzoni, of Prince's Gardens, SW7; *b* 1882; was Parliamentary Private Sec to Postmaster Gen 1924-9, temporary Chm of Committees, House of Commons 1932-34, and Chm of Private Bills Committee, House of Lords 1940-58; sat as MP for Ipswich (*C*) 1914-23, and 1924-37; *cr* a *Baronet* (UK, of Ipswich) 1929, and *Baron Belstead*, of Ipswich, Suffolk (peerage of UK) 1938: *m* 1930, Gwendolen Gertrude, who *d* 1962, el da of late Arthur Turner, of Ipswich; *d* 1958; *s* by his only son **(2)** JOHN JULIAN, 2nd Baron and present peer.

Bennet, family name of Earl of Tankerville.

BENSON, BARONY OF (Benson) (Extinct 1995)

SONS LIVING OF LIFE BARON

Hon Peter Macleod (53 Waterside Point, 2 Anhalt Rd, SW11 4PD; *Clubs* – Brooks's, Hurlingham, MCC), *b* 1940; *ed* Eton, and Edinburgh Univ (MA): *m* 1st, 1970 (*m diss* 1987), Hermione Jane Boulton; 2ndly, 1989, Maria de los Angeles Martin, da of Don Victoriano Martinez Latasa, and has issue living (by 1st *m*), Edward Henry, *b* 1975, — Candida Jane, *b* 1972, — Hermione Emily, *b* 1980.

Hon Michael D'Arcy (Grange Farm, Westour, York YO60 7NS), *b* 1943; *ed* Eton: *m* 1969, Rev Rachel Candia, da of Rt Rev Robin Woods, KCMG, KCVO, formerly Bishop of Worcester, and has issue living, Charles D'Arcy, *b* 1976, — Catherine Rachel, *b* 1971, — Harriet Anne, *b* 1974.

DAUGHTER LIVING OF LIFE BARON

Hon Phyllida Anne, *b* 1943; Personal Assist to HRH The Prince of Wales since 1996: *m* 1967, Simon John Dare, of The Old Bakery, Broadwell, Moreton-in-Marsh, Glos GL56 0TW, and has issue living, James Alexander, *b* 1973, — Camilla Jane, *b* 1969, — Nichola Lucy, *b* 1971.

Bentinck, family name of Earl of Portland.

Beresford, family name of Baron Decies.

Beresford, family name of Marquess of Waterford.

BERKELEY, EARLDOM OF (Berkeley) (Dormant or Extinct 1942)

Grandsons of late Capt Hastings George Fitzhardinge Berkeley, RN (not in remainder to Earldom as *b* before his parents' *m*), eldest son of late George Lennox Rawdon, 7th Earl of Berkeley, only surv son of Gen Sir George Henry Frederick Berkeley, KCB, eldest son of Adm Hon Sir George Cranfield Berkeley, GCB, 2nd son of 4th Earl:—
     Issue of late Sir Lennox Randal Berkeley, CBE, *b* 1903, *d* 1989: *m* 1946, Elizabeth Freda (*Lady Berkeley*) (12 Hereford Mansions, Hereford Rd, W2 5BA), da of late Isaac Bernstein, of London:—
Michael Fitzhardinge (49 Blenheim Crescent, W11 2EF), *b* 1948; *ed* Westminster Cathedral Choir Sch, Oratory Sch and Royal Academy of Music; composer and broadcaster: *m* 1979, Deborah Jane, da of late Guy Coltman-Rogers, DL, of Stanage Park, Radnorshire, and has an adopted da, Jessica Rose, *b* 1986. —— Julian Lennox (The Pottery, Ham Lane, Ramsdell, nr Basingstoke, Hants RG26 5SD), *b* 1950; *ed* Westminster Cathedral Choir Sch, Oratory Sch and Royal Coll of Music; man dir, Berkeley Guard Ltd. —— Nicholas Eadnoth (Darby House, Burton Bradstock, Dorset), *b* 1956; *ed* Oratory Sch, and Bournemouth & Poole Coll of Art & Design; photographer and lecturer; has issue living (by Tessa Moffatt), Jack Hastings, *b* 1984, — Flora Eve, *b* 1979.

BERKELEY, BARON (Gueterbock) (Baron E 1421)

ANTHONY FITZHARDINGE GUETERBOCK, OBE, 18th Baron; *b* 20 Sept 1939; *s* 1992; *ed* Eton, and Trin Coll, Camb (MA); MICE; OBE (Civil) 1989: *m* 1st, 1965 (*m diss* 1999), Diana Christine (Dido), eldest da of Eric William John Townsend, MRCS, LRCP; 2ndly, 1999, Rosalind Julia Georgina, da of Michael John Clarke, of Walnut Tree House, Didbrook, Winchcombe, Glos, and has issue by 1st *m*.

𝕬rms – Not exemplified at time of going to press.
Residence – 166 Banbury Rd, Oxford OX2 7BT.

SONS LIVING (By 1st marriage)

Hon THOMAS FITZHARDINGE, *b* 5 Jan 1969; *ed* St Paul's: *m* 1995, Helen Ruth, elder da of Lt-Cdr Brian Walsh, RN, and has issue living, Sam, *b* 20 Feb 1996, — William, *b* 1998.
Hon Robert William, *b* 1970; *ed* St Paul's, and Univ of Kent at Canterbury.

DAUGHTER LIVING (By 1st marriage)

Hon Philippa Louise, *b* 1975; *ed* Godolphin & Latymer, and Brighton Univ.

COLLATERAL BRANCHES LIVING

Grandsons of late Gen Sir (Frederick) Ivor Maxse, KCB, CVO, DSO, elder son of Adm Frederick Augustus Maxse, yr son of Lady Caroline FitzHardinge Berkeley (who *m* 1829, James Maxse), 2nd da of 5th Earl of Berkeley:—
     Issue of late Maj John Herbert Maxse, Coldm Guards, *b* 1901, *d* 1978: *m* 1931, Dorinda Mary, who *d* 1988, da of William Hobart Houghton Thorne, a Judge of Mixed Courts of First Instance, Egypt:—
Anthony John MAXSE (Homestead Farm, Selborne, Alton, Hants), *b* 1932; *ed* Eton; late Capt Coldm Guards; ADC to Gov of Cyprus 1959-60: *m* 1961, Susan Jane, da of late Frederick James Emson, MC, and has had issue, John James Ivor, *b* 1968; *ed* Eton, — †Georgina Anne, *b* 1962: *m* 1989, Hugh Stanley Keith Knowles (*see* Dewey, Bt, colls), and *d* 1998, leaving issue, Alicia *b* 1991, Claudia Rose *b* 1993, — Sarah Charlotte, *b* 1964: *m* 1990, George J. C. Bingham, of Peak House, W Meon, Hants, only son of late Cmdr George Edward Bingham, of Grenville House, Droxford, Hants, and has issue living, George *b* 1992, Charlotte *b* 1994. —— Martin William Frederick, LVO (Hall, Barnstaple, N Devon; Boodle's, Pratt's), *b* 1935; *ed* Eton; late Col Coldm Guards; LVO 1977: *m* 1959, Penelope Ann, da of late Maj Charles Chichester (*see* Fowke, Bt, 1995 Edn), and has issue living, Charles John Chichester, *b* 1962; *ed* Harrow: *m* 1995, Naomi H., da of Michael Joseph Bennett Parker, of Gooderstone, Norfolk (*see* M Winchilsea, 1976 Edn), and has issue living, a da *b* 1997, — Edward William, *b* 1969; *ed* Bradfield, — Clare Caroline, *b* 1960: *m* 1987, Capt Michael Patrick Campbell-Lamerton, SG, 2nd son of Col Michael John Campbell-Lamerton, of Shipston-on-Stour, Warwicks, and has issue living, Rory Patrick Chichester *b* 1989, William Michael John *b* 1991, Alexander Charles Martin *b* 1996. —— Christopher James Ivor (King's Paddock, Meonstoke, Southampton; *Club* – Boodle's), *b* 1942; *ed* Eton, and Open Univ (BA).

Grandchildren of late Ella Henrietta Maxse (who *d* 1916, having *m* 1862, as his 2nd wife, Lt-Gen Hon Edward Thomas Gage, CB, who *d* 1889), da of Lady Caroline Fitz Hardinge Berkeley (who *m* 1829, James Maxse), 2nd da of 5th Earl of Berkeley:—

See V Gage, colls.

Grandchildren of late Mrs Winifred Laura Capel Fookes (infra):—
Issue of late Sydney Faber Fookes, *b* 1906, *d* 1983: *m* 1939, Lorna Kathleen Joblin:—
Timothy Faber FOOKES (Darnell, Paekakariki Hill Rd, RD 1 Plimmerton, NZ), *b* 1940; Bar and Solicitor: *m* 1972, Sandra Jane Field, and has issue living, Kate Faber, *b* 1974, — Jane Faber, *b* 1977. —— Sally Faber, *b* 1941: *m* 1965, Barrie Miles Owen, of 10 Benjamin Place, Matua, Tauranga, NZ, and has issue living, Simon John, *b* 1972, — Angela Jane, *b* 1967: *m* 19—, Wilson Mellow, of 25B Mac Ville Rd, Mount Maunganus, NZ, and has issue living, Benjamin George *b* 1992, Matthew Barrie *b* 1994, Samantha Jane *b* 1998, — Philippa Ann, *b* 1969: *m* 1995, Andrew Pollock, of 1/43 Auld St, Torbay, Auckland, NZ.

Issue of late Kenneth Faber Fookes, *b* 1907, *d* 1984: *m* 1936, Constance Joyce Christian Boden:—
†Patrick Faber FOOKES, *b* 1937: *m* 1961, Anna Maree Tracy, and *d* 1982, leaving issue, John Faber *b* 1962, — Paul Faber, *b* 1966, — Stephen Faber, *b* 1967, — Joanna Tracy, *b* 1970. —— Alister Faber (4A Dunholme Rd, Remuera, Auckland, NZ), *b* 1941. —— Russell Faber, *b* 1947: *m* 1971, Margaret Edith Wilson, of 61 Dyers Pass Rd, Christchurch, NZ, and has issue living, Craig, *b* 1976, — Kerry, *b* 1975, — Megan Joy, *b* 1978. —— Jennifer Faber, *b* 1942: *m* 1964, David Aiken Olson, of 38 McMeekan Av, Hamilton, NZ, and has issue living, Carl David, *b* 1966, — Dean William, *b* 1969: *m* 1999, Nicola Marie Frecklington.

Granddaughter of late Capt Sydney Augustus Berkeley Capel, son of Lady Emily Elizabeth FitzHardinge Capel, 3rd da of 5th Earl of Berkeley:—
Issue of late Winifred Laura, *b* 1875, *d* 1927: *m* 1905, Dr Ernest Faber Fookes, who *d* 1948:—
Ernestine Emily Faber, *b* 1912: *m* 1940, Stuart Alexander Black, and has issue living, Anna Catherine, *b* 1946: *m* 19—, — Orr. *Residence* – 31 Beach St, Fitzroy, New Plymouth, NZ.

Grandchildren of late Maude Harold Capel Nolan, yr da of late Capt Sydney Augustus Berkeley Capel (ante):—
Issue of late David Nolan, *b* 1912, *d* 1975: *m* 1940, Elsa Isabel Mooney:—
Robert Leslie NOLAN (11 Fairearth St, The Gap, Brisbane, Queensland 4061, Australia), *b* 1941: *m* 1967, Maureen Anne Heffernan, and has issue living Brent Robert, *b* 1972, — Kim Kathleen, *b* 1974. —— Susanne Margaret, *b* 1944: *m* 1970, David Thomas Thorp, of Mountain Rd, RD3, New Plymouth, NZ, and has issue living, Nicholas Adam, *b* 1973, — Jane Victoria, *b* 1974. —— Elizabeth Mary, *b* 1945: *m* 1969, Charles Miles Brown, of 13 Konini St, Riccarton, Christchurch, NZ. —— Catherine Ruth, *b* 1947: *m* 1971, Ian James Robinson, of 125 Coronation Av, New Plymouth, NZ, and has issue living, Anna May, *b* 1973, — Lisa Letitia, *b* 1975.

Issue of late Nina Leslie Nolan, *b* 1908, *d* 1992: *m* 1935, John Dixon Law, of 14 Takomaru St, New Plymouth, NZ:—
†Barry LAW, *b* 1936: *m* 1961, Faith Georgina Gordon Glassford, and *d* 1980, leaving issue, Michael Barry (129 Fisher Parade, Pakuranga, Auckland, NZ), *b* 1963, — Stephanie Jane, *b* 1968. —— John Berkeley (8 Cracroft St, New Plymouth, NZ), *b* 1941: *m* 1970, Janet Elizabeth Slater, and has issue living, Richard Berkeley, *b* 1973, — Catherine Muriel, *b* 1975. —— Janet Capel (41 Frank Wilson Terrace, New Plymouth, NZ), *b* 1947: *m* 1969, Bryan Alexander Cleland, and has issue living, Scott Law, *b* 1971: *m* 1991, Angela Lisa Rule, — Benjamin John Stewart, *b* 1984, — Sarah Jane Capel, *b* 1974: *m* 1993, Dean Roy Garrod, and has issue living, Dylan Roy *b* 1994, Jacob Thomas *b* 1996.

Grandchildren of late Robert Valentine Berkeley (*b* 1853), eldest son of late Robert Berkeley (*b* 1823), eldest son of late Robert Berkeley (*b* 1794), 10th in descent from Hon Thomas Berkeley, 4th son of James, 1st Baron:—
Issue of late Capt Robert George Wilmot Berkeley, *b* 1898, *d* 1969: *m* 1927, Hon Myrtle Emmeline Theresa Dormer, who *d* 1982, da of 14th Baron Dormer:—
Robert John Grantley BERKELEY, TD (Berkeley Castle, Glos; Spetchley Park, Worcs), *b* 1931; *ed* Oratory Sch, and Magdalen Coll, Oxford; late Maj Queen's Own Warwicks and Worcs Yeo; late Lt 10th R Hus; JP Glos; and DL Hereford, Worcester and Glos, High Sheriff Worcs 1967, and Glos 1982; Joint Master Berkeley Foxhounds 1960-84: *m* 1967, Georgina Bridget, el da of late Maj Andrew Charles Stirling Home Drummond Moray, of Easter Ross, Comrie, Perthshire, and has issue living, Robert Charles Grantley, *b* 1968; *ed* Ampleforth, — Henry John Mowbray, *b* 1969; *ed* Ampleforth, and RMA Sandhurst; commn'd Queen's Own Hussars 1992. —— Rosalind Magdalen Ellen, *b* 1928; is a nun. —— Juliet Elizabeth Mary, *b* 1930.

Grandchildren of late Lt-Col Christopher Robert Berkeley, CMG, DSO, OBE, late Welch Regt, 2nd son of late Maj Henry William Berkeley, 3rd son of Robert Berkeley (*b* 1794) (ante):—
Issue of late Lt-Col Maurice Berkeley, RA, *b* 1921, *d* 1993: *m* 1950, Sylvia Mary Close (21 Chancellor House, Mount Ephraim, Tunbridge Wells, Kent TN4 8BT), da of late M. B. Tennant Maudsley:—
Hugh Christopher, *b* 1952; *ed* Stonyhurst. —— †John Henry, *b* 1956; *ed* Worth, and LCP (BA): *m* 1980, Nina Elaine, yr da of A. R. S. Pritchard-Davies, of 46 Borkum Close, Andover, and *d* 1998, leaving issue, Luke Dominic, *b* 1981, — Milo Thomas, *b* 1983, — Benn Alexander, *b* 1986. —— Michael Frederick (14 Prebend Gdns, W4 1TW), *b* 1958; *ed* Worth, Magdalene Coll, Camb (MA), and SDA Bocconi, Milan (MBA): *m* 1989, Caroline Jane, elder da of Sydney Riddell, of 31 Belmont Gdns, Edinburgh, and has issue living, Oscar Frederick Robert, *b* 1991, — Thomas Bertram Maurizio, *b* 1993.

Issue of late Capt Edward Henry Berkeley, *b* 1923, *d* 1962: *m* 1951, Joyce Louise (who *m* 2ndly, 1965, Charles Michael Philips, of 63 Larkhall Rise, SW4), da of late D. C. Duncan, of Valparaiso, Chile:—
†Mowbray Thomas, *b* 1952; *ed* Stonyhurst; *d* 1970. —— Grantley William Andrew, *b* 1954; *ed* Stonyhurst, and South-ampton Univ (LLB): *m* 1985, Sally Ann Stenson, da of late C. A. S. Webb, of Sutton Coldfield, Warwicks, and has issue living, Edward Charles Mowbray, *b* 1986, — Alice Mary, *b* 1989, — Sophie Louise, *b* 1991. —— Wulstan Hubert, *b* 1956; *ed* Stonyhurst, and Worcester Coll, Oxford. —— Thurstan Timothy Edward, *b* 1961; *ed* Stonyhurst, and Hatfield Coll, Durham: *m* 1992, Karen Ann Theresa, eldest da of Norman Goodale, of Beaconsfield, Quebec, Canada. —— Fiona

Maria Louise, *b* (twin) 1956; *ed* St Mary's, Ascot, and Bristol Univ: *m* 1990, Laurent Fauquex, of Geneva, Switzerland, and has issue living, Zoe, *b* 1990.

Issue of late Capt Basil Robert Berkeley, IG, *b* 1925, *d* 1994: *m* 1953, Gillian Rosamond Wellesley (Irvings Cottage, Fletching St, Mayfield, E Sussex TN20 6TJ), yst da of late Dr R. H. Spencer, of Alcester:—
Giles Robert (Christmas Cottage, Upper Green, Hawkley, Liss, Hants GU33 6LX), *b* 1959; *ed* Downside, and Durham Univ: *m* 1990, Alexandra Louise, yst da of Anthony Love, of Beggars Bush, Wadhurst, Sussex, and has issue living, Benedict Robert, *b* 1992, — Anthony Basil, *b* 1994. —— Roger Maurice (Hoggeshaws, Milstead, Sittingbourne, Kent ME9 0SA), *b* 1961; *ed* Downside: *m* 1986, Victoria, only da of John Russell Selmon, of Hemingfold Grange, Battle, E Sussex, and of Mrs William D. Hargraves, of Brickwall Bredgar, Sittingbourne, Kent, and has issue living, Rupert Charles, *b* 1988, — Robert Francis, *b* 1989.

PREDECESSORS – (1) THOMAS de Berkeley, 6th Feudal Lord, was summoned to Parliament as a Baron 1295-1321: *d* 1321; *s* by his son (2) MAURICE, summoned to Parliament of England as *Lord Berkeley*; having joined Thomas Plantagenet, Earl of Lancaster, he was imprisoned in Wallingford Castle, where he *d* 1326; *s* by his son (3) THOMAS, summoned to Parliament 1329-60: was sometime Custodian of Edward II, and after the murder of that King was arraigned as a participator in the deed and honourably acquitted; *d* 1361; *s* by his son (4) MAURICE, summoned to Parliament 1342; was wounded at Poitiers; *s* by his son (5) THOMAS, *d* 1417; *s* by his nephew (6) JAMES, summoned to Parliament by writ as *Baron Berkeley* 1421-61, *d* 1463; *s* by his el son (7) WILLIAM, 2nd Baron; *cr Viscount Berkeley* 1481, *Earl of Nottingham* 1483, and *Marquess of Berkeley* (peerage of England) 1489; the castle, lands, and lordships composing the Barony of Berkeley he settled upon Henry VII and his heirs male, failing which to descend to his own rightful heirs, a circumstance that had its origin in his next brother having married the da of a Bristol Alderman; *d* 1491, when his own honours became extinct and his brother (8) MAURICE *de jure* 3rd Baron was in consequence of the settlement referred to, deprived of the Barony; *d* 1506; *s* by his son (9) Sir MAURICE *de jure* 4th Baron; *d* 1526; *s* by his brother (10) Sir THOMAS *de jure* 5th Baron; *d* 1533; *s* by his son (11) THOMAS, 6th Baron: summoned to Parliament 1534; *d* 1534; *s* by his son (12) HENRY, 7th Baron, to whom the Barony and lands of Berkeley descended on the death of Edward VI, the last heir male of Henry VII; *d* 1613; *s* by his grandson (13) Sir GEORGE, 8th Baron; *d* 1658; *s* by his son (14) GEORGE, 9th Baron; *cr Viscount Dursley* and *Earl of Berkeley* (peerage of England) 1679; *d* 1698; *s* by his son (15) CHARLES, 2nd Earl, who in 1698 had been summoned to Parliament as Baron Berkeley; *d* 1710; *s* by his son (16) JAMES, 3rd Earl, a distinguished naval officer, who in 1704 had been summoned to Parliament as Lord Dursley; *d* 1736; *s* by his son (17) AUGUSTUS, KT, 4th Earl; a distinguished military officer; *s* by his son (18) FREDERICK AUGUSTUS, 5th Earl; Lord Lieut of Gloucester: *m* 1796, Miss Mary Cole, who *d* 1844 (a previous *m* to the same lady in 1785 was unsuccessfully attempted to be proved in the House of Lords 1811); *d* 1810; *s* by his el son born after the marriage in 1796 (19) THOMAS MORETON FITZHARDINGE, 6th Earl *de jure*; *d* 27 Aug 1882, *unm*, without having assumed the title or taken his seat in the House of Lords; at his decease the Earldom devolved upon his kinsman, George Lennox Rawdon Berkeley (upon the death of whose son, the Earldom became *ext* or dormant), and the Barony upon his niece (20) LOUISA MARY Milman (only da of late Hon Craven Fitzhardinge Berkeley, 3rd son of 5th Earl of Berkeley), to whom the title was confirmed by Roy Warrant 1893; *b* 1840: *m* 1872, Maj-Gen Gustavus Hamilton Lockwood Milman, RA, who *d* 1915; *d* 1899; *s* by her da (21) EVA MARY FITZ-HARDINGE, *b* 1875: *m* 1903, Col Frank Wigram Foley, CBE, DSO; R Berks Regt, who *d* 1949; *d* 1964, when the Barony fell into abeyance between her two daughters, Hon Mary Lalle Foley Berkeley and the Hon Mrs Cynthia Ella Gueterbock, and so continued until 1967, when the abeyance was terminated in favour of the elder (22) MARY LALLE Foley Berkeley; *b* 1905, assumed by deed poll 1951 the additional surname of Berkeley; *dunm* 1992; *s* by her nephew (23) ANTHONY FITZHARDINGE Gueterbock (son of late Hon Mrs Cynthia Ella Gueterbock, yr da of EVA MARY FITZ-HARDINGE, Baroness Berkeley), 18th Baron and present peer.

Berkshire, Earl of; see Earl of Suffolk and Berkshire.

BERNERS, BARONESS (Kirkham) (Baron E 1455)

PAMELA VIVIEN KIRKHAM (*Baroness Berners*), *b* 30 Sept 1929; *s* (on termination of abeyance) 1995: *m* 1952, Michael Joseph Sperry Kirkham, and has issue.

Arms – Quarterly of ten: 1st, argent a chevron reversed per pale azure and gules per chevron reversed counterchanged (*Williams*); 2nd, quarterly, 1st and 4th, gules three pewits two and one or (*Tyrwhitt*), 2nd and 3rd, argent a lion rampant vert vulned in the mouth proper (*Jones*); 3rd, Tyrwhitt as above; 4th, argent three boars' heads erect and erased sable (*Booth*); 5th, sable a wolf salient or in chief a fleur-de-lis argent between two bezants (*Wilson*); 6th, argent a bend sable a bordure engrailed sable (*Knyvett*); 7th, argent a cross engrailed gules between four water bougets sable over all a label azure of three points charged with three lions rampant or (*Bourchier*); 8th, gules a fess argent between seven billets in chief four and three and seven in base four and three or (*Lovayne*); 9th, quarterly, 1st and 4th, France modern, 2nd and 3rd, England all within a bordure argent (*Thomas of Woodstock*); 10th, quarterly or and vert (*Berners*). Supporters – Dexter, a falcon rising wings elevated argent jessed and belled or; *sinister*, a greyhound proper gorged with a collar gules studded or.
Residence – Ashwellthorpe, 103 Charlton Lane, Cheltenham, Glos.

SONS LIVING

Hon RUPERT WILLIAM TYRWHITT, *b* 18 Feb 1953; *ed* New Coll Choir Sch, Oxford, and Lord Williams Sch, Thame: *m* 1994, Lisa Carol (Judy), da of Col Edward Gibson Lipsey, USAF (ret) of Phoenix, Arizona, USA, and has issue living, Edward Michael Tyrwhitt, *b* 7 July 1994.
Hon Robin Raymond Tyrwhitt, *b* 1958; *ed* Queen Elizabeth Gram Sch, Ashbourne: *m* 1992, Jennifer Ann, da of Eric Gaynor Eller, of Johannesburg, S Africa, and has issue living, Tess Natalie, *b* 1994, — Annie Rose, *b* 1997. *Residence* – 26 Rosyntjiebos St, Randpark Ridge X41, 2194 Johannesburg, S Africa.

DAUGHTER LIVING

Hon Caroline Rosemary Tyrwhitt, *b* 1956: *m* 1981, Robert Francis Gordon, and has issue living, John Francis, *b* 1986, — Sally Grace Tyrwhitt, *b* 1984. *Residence* – Swiss Cottage, Alsop Rd, Parwich Lees, Ashbourne, Derbys DE6 1QN.

SISTER LIVING

Hon Rosemary Tyrwhitt, *b* 1931: *m* 1959, Kelvin Alexander Pollock, and has issue living, Simon Kelvin Tyrwhitt, *b* 1962: *m* 1998, Susan Lynne Elizabeth (Sandy), only da of Dr Alan Powell, of Christchurch, Dorset, — Alastair Michael Tannahill, *b* 1964. *Residence* – The Malthouse, Hollingbourne, Kent ME17 1UW.

COLLATERAL BRANCHES LIVING

Grandchildren of late Hon Ardyn Mary Tyrwhitt (*m* 1887, 1st Viscount Knollys, GCB, GCVO, KCMG, ISO, PC), eldest da of Emma Harriet, Baroness Berners:—
See V Knollys, and Mackenzie, Bt (*cr* 1890).

Grandchildren of late Hon Sibyl Grace Tyrwhitt (*m* 1895, James Volant Wheeler), da of Emma Harriet, Baroness Berners:—
Issue of late W/Cdr Vashon James Wheeler, MC, DFC, *b* 1898, *ka* 1944: *m* 1930, Josephine Hermione, who *d* 1977, da of Maj John Charles Spencer-Phillips, DSO, of Ridley House, Kingswear, Devon:—
John Vashon Tyrwhitt WHEELER, *b* 1931; *ed* Eton, and Trin Coll, Camb (BA 1953, MA 1960): *m* 1st, 1957, Geraldine Noel, who *d* 1970, yr da of late William Noel Jones, of Little Gables, Glasllwch Lane, Newport, Gwent; 2ndly, 1978, Mrs Caroline Susan Chance, da of Patrick Edward Michael Holmes, MBE, of 47 Pittville Lawn, Cheltenham, and has issue living (by 1st *m*), James Vashon, *b* 1960: *m* 1995, Katharine, 2nd da of James Trotter, of The White House, Ardingly, Sussex, and has issue living, George Vashon James *b* 1996, Miles John Tyrwhitt *b* (twin) 1996, — Nicholas Charles Tyrwhitt, *b* 1965: *m* 1995, Christian, da of P. A. S. Rucker, and of Mrs J. S. K. Calcutt, of Redlands, Crockham Hill, Kent, and has issue living, Thomas Charles Tyrwhitt *b* 1996, Isabella Noel *b* 1998, — Justin Alexander Noel, *b* 1970, — Susan Verity, *b* 1958: *m* 1983, Jean Marc Cummings, and has issue living, Oliver Michael John *b* 1984, Edward John Thomas *b* 1990, Georgia Grace *b* 1986. *Residence* – Bitterley Court, Ludlow, Shropshire. — Peter James WHEELER, *b* 1933: *m* 1960, Eileen Mary, only da of A. E. Larcombe, of Brierley, Livesey Rd, Ludlow, and has issue living, Gavin Vashon *b* 1972, — Karen Wanda Grace *b* 1970: *m* 1994, Mark John Hackett, and has issue living, Piers Timothy James *b* 1997, — Amanda Hermione (twin), *b* 1972. *Residence* – Llwyngoras, Velindre, nr Crymych, Pembs.

Issue of late Lt-Cdr Hugh Volant Wheeler, DSC, RN, *b* 1901, *d* 1990: *m* 1st, 1938, Pauline Johnstone; 2ndly, 1947, Diana Joan (Little Calgary, 211 1st St, Voëlklip, CP 7203, S Africa), da of Maj Albert Herbert MacIlwaine, DSO, MC, of Larkhill, Marandellas, S Zimbabwe:—
(By 2nd *m*) David Hugh WHEELER (Calgary, PO Box 27, Harare, Zimbabwe), *b* 1949: *m* 1981, Tessa Mary Hunter, da of

Prof Richard Hunter Chirstie, of Mapes Close, Mt Pleasant, Harare, and has issue living, Rory Vashon, *b* 1985, —
Timothy Tyrwhitt, *b* 1986.

Issue of late Col Gilbert Tyrwhitt Wheeler, DSO, *b* 1902, *d* 1984: *m* 1st, 1932, Beryl Audrey, who *d* 1974, da of
   H. J. Landon, of New England Hill, W Cobham; 2ndly, 1975, Kathleen, who *d* 1987, da of Herbert Sessions, of
   Quedgeley Court, Gloucester:—
(By 1st *m*) Audrey Julia, *b* 1933: *m* 1960, Capt William G. McC. Burn, RN, of 4 Clarence Crescent, Windsor, Berks SL4
5DT, and has issue living, Peter William, *b* 1960: *m* 1993, Sandra Georgina Parker, and has issue living, James Tyrwhitt
b 1996, Emma Harriet *b* 1995, — Hugh Tyrwhitt, *b* 1965, — Jenifer Julia, *b* 1962: *m* 1993, Clive Murray Norris, and has
issue living, Paul William *b* 1998. ——— Jacqueline Mary, *b* 1935: *m* 1960, Don H. Olson, of 7 The Green, Woodstock,
Vermont 05091, USA, and has issue living, Sven Tyrwhitt, *b* 1967, — Sonja Landon, *b* 1964: *m* 1991, James St Amand.

Issue of late A/Cdre Allen Henry Wheeler, CBE, RAF, *b* 1903, *d* 1984: *m* 1st, 1934 (*m diss* 1946), Ruth
   Margaret, da of George Ballard, of The Lowe, Stockton, Worcester; 2ndly, 1949, Barbara Agnes (Whistley
   Bridge Field, Twyford, Berks), da of late Basil Alfred Slade, of Whistley Bridge House, Twyford, Berks (*see*
   Slade, Bt, colls):—
(By 1st *m*) Ardyn Margaret, *b* 1937: *m* 1972, Eric Griffin, who *d* 1980, of Conifer Cottage, Pipers End, Longdon, Tewkes-
bury, Glos GL20 6AP, and has issue living, Robert, *b* 1974. ——— Meris Ann, *b* 1939.

Issue of late Dorothy Sibyl Wheeler, *b* 1897, *d* 1977: *m* 1929, E. Brande Don:—
Volant Geoffrey Vincent DON, *b* 1930. *Residence* – No 1, Blake, 4 Avenue Rd, Wimborne, Dorset BH21 1BT.

Grandchildren of late Oriana Mary Bracebridge Wilson (*m* 1894, Lt-Col Albert Finchett Garrard, VD,
   Australian Forces), da of late John Bracebridge Wilson, el son of Rev Edward Wilson, el son of Rev
   George Wilson, brother of 9th and 10th Barons:—
Issue of late Edith Mary Bracebridge Garrard, *b* 1895, *d* 1992: *m* 1926, Harold Bruce Adair, Lieut Australian
   Army Med Corps, who *d* 1986:—
John Bracebridge Garrard ADAIR (21 Collins St, Werribee, Vic 3030, Australia), *b* 1933: *m* 1954, Joy Isabel Balcombe, and
has issue living, Robyn Maree, *b* 1957: *m* 1978, Graeme Stephen Ball, and has issue living, Stephen John *b* 1981, David
Graeme *b* 1985, Katherine Maree *b* 1983, — Tracey Anne, *b* 1960: *m* 1982, Rolando Carmine Milone, and has issue
living, Daniel Robert *b* 1985, Kayla Rose *b* 1988, — Kerri Frances, *b* (twin) 1960: *m* 1982, Michael Clifford Newman, and
has issue living, Maddison Adair *b* 1993, — Helen Therese, *b* 1965. ——— Helen Becher Bracebridge, *b* 1930.

Grandchildren of late Henry Fletcher Wilson, son of late Capt Frederick Wilson, Merchant Navy, 10th
   son of Rev George Wilson (ante):—
Issue of late Knyvet McDonald Wilson, *b* 1909, *d* 1983: *m* 1937, Ethel, da of James W. McKnight, of St Louis,
   Mo, USA:—
Knyvet Robert WILSON (1810 Taylor St, Kenner, La, USA), *b* 1942: *m* 1967, Alice Ann, da of John Alexander Neely, of
Anderson, SC, USA, and has issue living, Michael Patrick, *b* 1969, — Christine Suzanne, *b* 1970: *m* 1994, Kerin Todd
Tanner. ——— Barbara Ethel, *b* 1938: *m* 1965, Robert Wayne Raley, of 804 Downing Drive, Richardson, Texas, and has
issue living, Kevin Wayne, *b* 1967, — Craig Wade, *b* 1968: *m* 1996, Baby Nene Mina Barbo Reyes, — Kathleen Elaine, *b*
1971.

Issue of late Maude Alice Wilson, *b* 1899, *b* 1996: *m* 1929, Hugh Francis Hart (2809 Law St, New Orleans, La,
   USA 70117):—
Gerard Hugh HART (610 Fos St, Harvey, La, USA), *b* 1930: *m* 1951, Lela, da of Wallace Chaisson, of Harvey, La, USA,
and has issue living, Gerard Maurice, *b* 1953, — Stephen Francis, *b* 1955, — David Sidney, *b* 1959, — Susan Louise, *b*
1957, — Cindy Ann, *b* 1965. ——— Maurice Henry HART (4616 Dreyfous Av, Metairie, La, USA), *b* 1932: *m* 1956, Audrey,
da of Leonce Gaudet, of Paincourtville, La, USA, and has issue living, Brian David, *b* 1959, — Keith Michael, *b* 1965: *m*
19—, and has issue living, Korin Michael *b* 1987, — Jo Ann, *b* 1957.

Grandchildren of late Archdale McDonald Wilson (*b* 1860), son of late Capt Frederick Wilson,
   Merchant Navy (ante):—
Issue of late Maj Arthur Knyvet Wilson, MC, *b* 1895, *d* 1979: *m* 1923, Dorothy Enid, da of late Lt-Col Walter W.
   Stewart:—
John Knyvet WILSON (339 Camelot Court, Burlington, Ont, Canada L7L 2G2), *b* 1933: *m* 1956, Marian Culham, and has
issue living, David Knyvet, *b* 1961: *m* 19—, Sharon, — Peter John, *b* 1964. ——— Nancy Margaret, *b* 1928: *m* 1953,
William Arnold Parker, and has issue living, Jeffrey Stewart, *b* 1955: *m* 1979, Katherine Beckett, of Ancaster, Ont, and
has issue living, Wilson Beckett *b* 1985, James Thomas *b* 1987, Kelly Coburn *b* 1990, — Gregory, *b* 1957: *m* 1982,
Sheilagh Ann O'Brien, of Halifax, NS, and has issue living, James O'Brien *b* 1986.

Issue of late Archdale McDonald Wilson, *b* 1899, *d* 1960; *m* 1930, Norah Elizabeth, who *d* 1994, da of Dr W. T.
   Connell, of Kingston, Ontario:—
Walter Archdale WILSON (158 Adio St, Sudbury, Ontario P3C 2C8, Canada), *b* 1936: *m* 1963, Freda Dian, da of late
Wallace Frederick Bond Roberts, of Toronto. ——— William Martin Connell WILSON (82 King St East, Bolton, Ont,
Canada L7E 3G2), *b* 1942; a Member of Canadian Inst of Planners: *m* 1968, Sandra May, da of Elwood C. Bobzien, of
5995 Lincoln Court, Newfane, New York, and has issue living, Mark Alexander, *b* 1975.

Issue of late Roland Frederick Wilson, QC, *b* 1901, *d* 1988: *m* 1934, Adelaide Bernice Sill, da of Dr W. T. Lan-
   grill, of Hamilton, Ont, Canada:—
Donald Langrill WILSON (284 Inglewood Drive, Toronto 7, Ont, Canada), *b* 1935; Member Royal Arch Inst of Canada, and
MArch Harvard: *m* 1960, Judie Jean Arnold, da of R. F. Chisholm, of Toronto, and has issue living, Robert Frederick, *b*
1962: *m* 1st, 1987, Nancy Alexander; 2ndly, 1992, Gale Withey, and has issue living (by 2nd *m*), Christopher *b* 1995, —
Wendy Jean, *b* 1964. ——— Stephen Roland WILSON, *b* 1941; BA W Ont Univ; LLB Osgood Law Sch, and MBA Stanford;

CA. —— Frances Elizabeth, b 1939: m 1969, Todd John Edgar, of 187 Glengrove Av W, Toronto, Canada, and has issue living, Wilson Gordon, b 1973, — Marnie Elizabeth, b 1978.

Issue of late Marion Alice Wilson, b 1893, d 1974: m 1920, Lt-Col Harold Brownlee Stuart, MBE, ED, RCE, who d 1946:—
Ronald Samuel STUART (26, Strathenden Rd, Toronto, Ont M4N 1E4, Canada), b 1927; BA 1950; MBA 1951; FCIS; formerly Lt RCN (Reserve): m 1954, Marjorie Irene, only da of Albert Parker Willis, of Mount Royal, Quebec, and has issue living, William Hugh Knyvet, b 1966, and two adopted children, Ronald Ian Knyvet, b 1964, — Marjorie Elizabeth Knyvet, b 1963; BA (1986).

Grandson of late Alice (who m 1871, Charles J. S. Naftel), b 1845, d 1940, da of late Capt Frederick Wilson, Merchant Navy (ante):—
Issue of late Frederick John Naftel, b 1871, d 1943: m 1900, Caroline Mabel, who d 195—, da of R. J. Drummond:—
Frederick Robb Knyvet NAFTEL (182 Gillard Av, Toronto, Roslen, Ontario, Canada M4J 4N8), b 1903: Cdr RCN (ret); b 1903: m 1933, Ruth Short, and has issue living, William, b 1940, — Dorothy Carolyn Drummond NAFTEL (57 Withrow Av, Toronto, Canada M4K IC8) (resumed maiden name 1975), b 1936: m 1964 (m diss 1975), M. E. Higgins, and has issue living, Benjamin b 1966.

Grandchildren of late Knyvett Eustace Naftel (infra):—
Issue of late Charles Knyvett Naftel, b 1910, d 1969: m 1937, Elizabeth, da of Cuthbert Bur:—
Paul NAFTEL (4006 Hill Av, Regina Saskatchewan, Canada S4S OX5), b 1939; ed Western Univ, London, Ontario (MSc): m 1967, Lillian Armbruster, of Prince Albert. —— Judith, b 1943: m 1965, David Mackintosh, CAF, and has issue living, Todd, b 1968, — Brian, b 1972.

Issue of late James Eustace Naftel, b 1913, d 1983: m 1938, Pearl (19 St Vincent St, Goderich, Ontario, Canada), da of Thomas Sandy:—
Sandy James NAFTEL, b 1939. —— Kathryn, b 1943: m 1967, James Lachlan Carson.

Grandchildren of late Alice Naftel (ante):—
Issue of late Knyvett Eustace Naftel, b 1881, d 1951: m 1907, Marion Grace, who d 1966, da of Andrew Crawford:—
Leslie Roland NAFTEL, b 1917; ed Wayne State Univ, Detroit (BSc); Fl Lt (ret) RCAF; 1939-45 War (despatches, King's Commendation): m 1942, Anna Kathleen, da of William A. Logan, and has issue living, Logan, b 1943: m 1974, Carol Howard, and has issue living, Christopher b 1979, Judi b 1982, Tara b 1985. —— Marion Alice Grace, b 1908: m 1930, Joseph L. Kulp, who d 1965, and has issue living, Joan Grace, b 1932: m 1952, Earl Roth, who d 1984, of 9274, Big Lake Rd, Clarkston, Mich 48016, USA, and has issue living, Lawrence Knyvet b 1953, Earl Lee b 1956, Leslie Ann b 1958; ed Michigan State Univ (BSc).

Grandsons of late Horace Alling Wilson, son of late John Coombe Wilson, 12th son of Rev George Wilson (ante):—
Issue of late Arthur Alling Wilson, b 1881, d 1934: m 1st, 1908, Lucie Nenon, who d 1924, el da of R. A. Ruttan, of Port Arthur, Ontario; 2ndly, 1926, Caroline Argyll (who m 2ndly, 1938, Julian Parks Hartley), da of John Roberts Allen, of Kentucky and New York City, USA:—
(By 1st m) Robert Ruttan WILSON (Durford Knoll, Upper Durford Wood, Petersfield), b 1913: m 1946, Hon Yvette Latham Baillieu, only da of 1st Baron Baillieu, and has issue living, Nenon Baillieu, b 1948: m 1979 (m diss 1992), (George) Martin Antony Bonham, el son of Maj Sir Anthony Lionel Thomas Bonham, 4th Bt, — Elizabeth Ruttan b 1950, — Merilyn Yvette, b 1953, — Deborah Baillieu, b 1955: m 1981, Philip Wingate Robert Carpenter, of Greenmead, Cumbers Lane, Rogate, nr Petersfield, Hants. —— (By 2nd m) Clarke Knyvet WILSON (5216 Harvest Loop, Eugene, Oregon 97402, USA) b 1929: m 1954, Sydney Ann Richardson, of Tacoma, Wash, USA, and has issue living, Robert Carroll (2151 de Vos St, Eugene, Oregon 97402, USA), b 1962, — Loree Ann, b 1957: m 19—, Thompson Allan Holmes, of 1746 Ridgefield St, Eugene, Oregon 97404, USA, and has issue living, Dylan Thompson b 1989, Julian Wilson b 1993, — Caroline Allen (2020 Brewer Ave, Eugene, Oregon 97401, USA), b 1959.

Granddaughters of late Brereton Knyvet Wilson, yr son of late Rev Herbert Wilson, yst son of Rev George Wilson (ante):—
Issue of late Dorothy Beatrice Knyvet Wilson, b 1893, d 1979: m 1917, Lt-Col Henry Marshall, Royal Lincs Regt, who d 1952:—
Patricia Robena Knyvet (5 Ravenscroft Rd, Henley-on-Thames, Oxon RG9 2DH), b 1918: m 1942, Maj David Young, MC, RA, who d 1990, and has issue living, Julian David Knyvet (2 Geoffrey St, Turramurra, NSW 2074, Australia), b 1946; ed Rannoch: m 1978, Margret, da of Gerhardt Krause, of Adelaide, S Australia, and has issue living, David Angus Knyvet b 1983, Lucy Elizabeth Julia Knyvet b 1981, — Anthony Charles Mayne (4 Fairfield Terr, Havant, Hants PO9 1BA), b 1948; ed Malvern, and RNC Dartmouth; late Lieut RN; BA, Dip Arch (1981), RIBA; JP Hants 1986: m 1973, Jane Lindsay, da of Richard Anthony Orton, of Instow, Devon, and has issue living, Thomas Anthony b 1983, Polly Elizabeth Jane b 1978, Sarah Josephine Lindsay b 1980, — Simon John, MC (Durweston House, Durweston, Blandford, Dorset DT11 0QA), b 1950; ed Bradfield; late Royal Green Jackets; MC 1972; FRICS 1979; JP Dorset 1987: m 1973, Henrietta Harriet Patricia, da of late Maj Gen (George) Douglas Gordon Dufferin Heyman, CB, CBE, of Appleshaw, Hants, and has had issue, Henry David Archdale Heyman b 1978, George Thomas Benedict Atkin b 1981, Clementine Beatrice Patricia b 1976, †Florence Eliza b 1979; d 1980. —— Leslie Philippa Knyvet (Wynchard, Durweston, Blandford, Dorset DT11 0QA), b 1926; Maj (ret) QARANC.

PREDECESSORS – (1) Sir John Bourchier, KG, 4th son of Sir William Bourchier, Count of Eu, was summoned to the Parliament of England as John Bourchier de Berners 1455-72: m 14—, Margery, who d 1475, da of Sir Richard Berners, and widow of John Ferreby; d 1474; s by his grandson (2) JOHN, 2nd Baron (son of Sir Humphrey Bourchier), b ca 1467; summoned to Parliament 1495-1529: m 14—, Lady Katharine Howard, who d 1536, da of 1st Duke of Norfolk; d 1533; s by his only surviving da (3) JANE, de jure Baroness Berners, b 15—; did not assume the title: m 15—, Edmund Knyvet, of Ashwellthorpe, who d 1539; d 1561; s by her grandson (4) Sir THOMAS, de jure 4th Baron (son of John

Knyvet), *b* 1539; obtained 1616 a certificate from the Commrs for the Office of Earl Marshal of his right to the Barony, but *d* before obtaining the King's confirmation: *m* 15—, Muriel, who *d* 1616, da of Sir Thomas Parry, Treasurer of the Household; *d* 1618; *s* by his grandson **(5)** THOMAS, *de jure* 5th Baron (son of Sir Thomas Knyvet), *b* 1596: *m* 1620, Katherine, who *d* 1658, da of 3rd Baron Burgh; *d* 1658; *s* by his el son **(6)** *Sir* JOHN, KB, *de jure* 6th Baron; *b* 16—: *m* 1655, Mary, who *d* 1713, el da of Sir Thomas Bedingfield; *d* 1673; *s* by his el son **(7)** THOMAS, *de jure* 7th Baron, *b* 1656; MP for Dunwich 1685-7, and for Eye 1689-90; *d* unm 1693, when the barony fell into abeyance between his sisters, Elizabeth, wife of Thomas Glenham, and Katharine, wife of John Harris, and so continued until 1711, when on the death without issue of Capt. Thomas Glenham, only child of Elizabeth Glenham, the barony devolved on **(8)** KATHERINE, Baroness Berners; *b* 1658; her title was confirmed by resolution of House of Lords 1720: *m* 1st, 1685, John Harris, who *d* 1686: 2ndly, 1696, Richard Bokenham, who *d* 1721; *d* 1743, when the Barony again fell into abeyance between the heirs of (i) Elizabeth Knyvet (wife of Henry Wilson, of Ashwellthorpe), and (ii) Lucy Knyvet (wife of Thomas Holt, and 2ndly, of John Field), granddaughters of John Knyvet, yr brother of *de jure* 6th Baron, and remained so until 1832, when the abeyance was terminated in favour of **(9)** ROBERT Wilson, 9th Baron, grandson of Elizabeth Knyvet (ante); *b* 1761, *d* unm 1838; *s* by his brother **(10)** *Rev* HENRY, 10th Baron, *b* 1762; summoned to Parliament by writ dated April 23rd, 1838: *m* 1788, Elizabeth, who *d* 1845, da of Thomas Sumpter; *d* 1851: *s* by his son **(11)** HENRY WILLIAM, 11th Baron, *b* 1797: *m* 1st, 1823, Mary Letitia, da and co-heir of Col George Crump, of Alexton Hall; 2ndly, 1857, Hon Henrietta Charlotte Cholmondeley, who *d* 1874, da of 1st Baron Delamere; *dsp* 27 June 1871; *s* by his son **(12)** EMMA HARRIET, Baroness Berners, da of late Rev Hon Robert Wilson, R of Ashwellthorpe, by Harriet, widow of John Sheppard, of Campsey Ash, and da and co-heir of Col George Crump (ante), *b* 1835: *m* 1853, Sir Henry Thomas Tyrwhitt, 3rd Bt, who *d* 1894; *d* 1917; *s* by her el son **(13)** *Sir* RAYMOND ROBERT TYRWHITT-WILSON, 13th Baron, *b* 1855; assumed the additional surname of Wilson and the arms of Wilson only by R licence 1892, and had *s* as 4th Bt in 1894; *d* 1918; *s* by his nephew **(14)** GERALD HUGH, 14th Baron (son of late Capt Hon Hugh Tyrwhitt, CVO, CSI, RN, 3rd son of late Emma Harriet, Baroness Berners), *b* 1883; assumed by R licence 1919 the additional surname of Wilson and the arms of Wilson quarterly with those of Tyrwhitt; *d* 1950, when the Baronetcy became ext, and he was *s* in the Barony by his kinswoman **(15)** VERA RUBY, Baroness Berners (da of late Major Hon Rupert Tyrwhitt, 5th son of Emma Harriet, Baroness Berners), *b* 1901: *m* 1927, Harold Williams, who *d* 1971; *d* 1992, when the barony again fell into abeyance between her daughters and remained so until 1995, when the abeyance was terminated in favour of the elder da **(16)** PAMELA VIVIEN, present peeress.

BERNSTEIN, BARONY OF (Bernstein) (Extinct 1993)

SON LIVING OF LIFE BARON *(By 2nd marriage)*

Hon David, *b* 19—: *m* 1995, Mrs Anne Christine Adriane Cockerell, da of Julian Tufnell Faber *(see* E Stockton*)*.

DAUGHTERS LIVING OF LIFE BARON *(By 2nd marriage)*

Hon Charlotte, *b* 19—.
Hon Jane, *b* 1958: *m* 1986, Jonathan R. Wells, son of Arnold Wells, of New York, USA.

Berriedale, Baron; son of Earl of Caithness.

Berry, family name of Viscount Camrose.

Berry, family name of Baron Hartwell.

Berry, family name of Viscount Kemsley.

Bertie, family name of Earl of Lindsey and Abingdon.

BESSBOROUGH, EARL OF (Ponsonby) Sits as BARON PONSONBY OF SYSONBY (GB 1749) (Earl I 1739)
(Name pronounced "Punsonby")

For the king, the law, and the people

ARTHUR MOUNTIFORT LONGFIELD PONSONBY, 11th Earl; *b* 11 Dec 1912; *s* 1993; *ed* Harrow, and Trin Coll, Camb (BA); served in World War II as Capt Welsh Gds 1940-46: *m* 1st, 1939, Patricia, who *d* 1952, da of Col Fitzhugh Lee Minnigerode, of Virginia, USA; 2ndly, 1956 (*m diss* 1963), Anne-Marie (GALITZINE), da of late Lt-Gen Sir Rudolf Carl Slatin, Pasha (Baron von Slatin), GCVO, KCMG, CB; 3rdly, 1963, Madeleine Lola Margaret, da of late Maj-Gen Laurence Douglas Grand, CB, CIE, CBE, of Delaford Manor, Iver, and has issue by 1st and 3rd *m*.

Arms – Gules, a chevron between three combs argent. Crest – Out of a ducal coronet azure, three arrows, points downwards, one in pale and two in saltire, entwined at the intersection by a snake proper. Supporters – Two lions reguardant proper.
Residence – Roche Court, Winterslow, Wilts.

SONS LIVING (*By 1st marriage*)

MYLES FITZHUGH LONGFIELD (*Viscount Duncannon*) (27 Wandsworth Bridge, Rd, SW6 2TA), *b* 16 Feb 1941; *ed* Harrow, and Trin Coll, Camb (MA); FCA: *m* 1972, Alison Marjorie, 3rd da of late William Storey, OBE, of Playford Mount, Gt Bealings, Suffolk, and has issue:—

SONS LIVING—*Hon* Frederick Arthur William, *b* 9 Aug 1974; *ed* Harrow, and E Anglia Univ.

Hon Henry Shakerley, *b* 1977; *ed* Harrow, and Birmingham Univ.

DAUGHTER LIVING—*Hon* Chloë Patricia, *b* 1975, *ed* Bedales, and Manchester Univ.

(*By 3rd marriage*)

Hon Matthew Douglas Longfield, *b* 1965; *ed* Marlborough, and Manchester Univ (BSc): *m* 1993, Jamilie Emett, eldest da of Graham Searle, of Thurloe Place, SW7, and has issue living, Douglas Arthur William, *b* 1998. *Residence* – 281 New King's Rd, SW6 4RD.
Hon Charles Arthur Longfield, *b* 1967; *ed* Marlborough, and Downing Coll, Camb: *m* 1996, Jenny M., da of Gerard Waghorn, of Nutfield, Woldingham, Surrey. *Residence* – 36 St Maur Rd, SW6 4DP.

DAUGHTER LIVING (*By 1st marriage*)

Lady Sarah, *b* 1943; painter and sculptress. *Residence* – Le Manoir du Moulin de Marolles, 14100 Lisieux, Calvados, France.

DAUGHTER LIVING OF TENTH EARL

Lady Charlotte Mary Roberte Paul, *b* 1949: *m* 1974, Yanni Petsopoulos, and has issue living, Alexis Anthony Frederick Ponsonby, *b* 1975; *ed* St Paul's, — Eric Demetri, *b* 1994. *Residence* – 43 Pembridge Villas, W11.

SISTER LIVING OF TENTH EARL

Lady Moyra Blanche Madeleine, DBE, *b* 1918; State Enrolled Nurse 1946; Chm, Hospitality Cttee, Victoria League 1956-62, and Vice-Chm, Central Council Victoria League 1961-65; Dep Supt-in-Ch, St. John Ambulance Bde 1964-70 (Supt-in-Ch 1970-83), Vice Pres R Coll of Nursing 1970-85, Nat Chm Support Group Research into Ageing 1987-93 (Gov since 1988); a DGStJ; OBE (Civil) 1962, DBE (Civil) 1977: *m* 1945, as his 2nd wife, Sir Denis John Wolko Browne, KCVO, FRCS, who *d* 1967, and has issue living, Desmond John Michael, QC (5 Raymond Buildings, Gray's Inn, WC1R 5BP), *b* 1947; *ed* Eton, and New Coll, Oxford; Bar Gray's Inn 1969; QC 1990, Recorder 1994: *m* 1973, Jennifer Mary, da of Frank Wilmore, of Brierfield, Lancs, and has issue living, Natasha Clare *b* 1974, Harriet Francesca *b* 1976, — Rosemary Anne Roberte (16 Wilton St, SW1X 7AX), *b* 1950: *m* 1974, Count Franco Aleramo Lanza, of Dronero, Italy, and has issue living, Aleramo Denis *b* 1979, Riccardo Vere (twin) *b* 1979. *Residence* – 16 Wilton St, SW1 7AX.

WIDOW LIVING OF TENTH EARL

MARY (*Dowager Countess of Bessborough*), da of Charles A. Munn, of New York, and of Paris: *m* 1948, the 10th Earl of Bessborough, who *d* 1993. *Residences* – Stansted Park, Rowlands Castle, Hants; 4 Westminster Gdns, SW1.

COLLATERAL BRANCHES LIVING

Grandchildren of late Violet Louise Ponsonby (Mrs Edward Archer Bolton Clive), only da of late John Henry Ponsonby-Fane, of Brympton d'Evercy, Som, eldest son of late Rt Hon Sir Spencer Cecil Brabazon Ponsonby-Fane, GCB, ISO (infra):—
Issue of late Nicholas Brabazon CLIVE-PONSONBY-FANE, *b* 1913, *d* 1963; assumed by Royal Licence 1935 the addl surname and arms of Ponsonby-Fane: *m* 1936, Petronilla (who *d* 1984, having *m* 2ndly, 1967, Walter Maurice Flower), only da of late Graham Eardley Dunsterville, Devonshire Regt (*see* Goldney, Bt, ext, 1980 Edn):—
Charles Edward Brabazon, *b* 1941; *ed* Harrow, l'Institut de Touraine, France, and RAC Cirencester; JP Som 1978, High Sheriff 1984: *m* 1974, Judy Barbara, da of Denis Bushby, of The Lodge, Unsted Park, Godalming, Surrey, and has issue living, Edward Nicholas Brabazon, *b* 1982; *ed* Harrow, — Lisa Charlotte, *b* 1976; *ed* North Foreland Lodge, Millfield, and St Edmund Hall, Oxford (BA), — Clementina Rose, *b* 1978; *ed* North Foreland Lodge, Sherborne Sch for Girls, and Newcastle Univ. *Residence* – Little Brympton, Yeovil, Som BA22 8TD. —— Georgiana, *b* 1937: *m* 1958, (Donald) William Formby Tulloch, who *d* 1994, and has issue living, Frederick William, *b* 1969, — (Diana) Kishanda, *b* 1960: *m* 1991, Francis Christopher Fulford, of Great Fulford, Devon, and has issue living, (Francis) Arthur, *b* 1994, Edmund Baldwin *b* 1996, Matilda Louisa, *b* (twin) 1992, — Catherine Serena, *b* 1961: *m* 1997, Hugh P. Lewin, and has issue living, Thomas Henry Hugh *b* 1998, — Louise Hermione, *b* 1964: *m* 1994, Gavin G. Trotman-Pitt, of Krugersdorp, S Africa. *Residence* – The Glebe House, Hannington, Highworth, Wilts SN6 7RP. —— Helen, *b* 1940: *m* 1962, John David Hay Mackenzie, and has issue living, Graham Alexander, *b* 1963, — Charlotte, *b* 1964: *m* 1988 (*m diss* 1997), Theodore Anthony Koziarz, of Long Beach, NJ, USA. *Residence* – Baldromma House, Maughold Village, I of Man. —— Isobel Victoria, *b* 1944. *m* 1976, Simon Parkes, yr son of late Sir Roderick Parkes, KCMG, OBE, and has issue living, Roderick Henry Edward Alexander, *b* 1980; *ed* Eton, and Edinburgh Univ, — Caroline Sophia Kerenhappuch, *b* 1978; *ed* North Foreland Lodge, St Clare's, Oxford, and Edinburgh Univ. *Residence* – Traiheen, Port Lewaigue, Maughold, I of Man IM7 1AG.

Granddaughter of late Robert Charles Ponsonby, 3rd son of Rt Hon Sir Spencer Cecil Brabazon Ponsonby-Fane, GCB, ISO, 6th son of 4th Earl:—
Issue of late Sir George Arthur Ponsonby, KCVO, *b* 1878, *d* 1969: *m* 1st, 1906, Julia Winifred Maitland (Sheila), who *d* 1918, da of late Phineas A. R. Oldfield; 2ndly, 1921, Elisa (Lady-in-Waiting to late Queen Maud of Norway), who *d* 1977, da of late Capt Hendrick Andreas Broch, of Oslo:—
(By 2nd *m*) Maud Elisabeth, *b* 1922: *m* 1957, Lt-Cdr William Hutton-Attenborough, RN (32 Maidenhead Rd, Stratford-upon-Avon), and has issue living, George William, *b* 1958: *m* 1988, Julie, elder da of J. B. Davidge, of The Bryn, Pontllanfraith, Gwent, — John Frederick, *b* 1960: *m* 1987, Helen Louise, da of John T. Brewer, of Rickmansworth, Herts, and has issue living, Matthew George *b* 1993, Robert William *b* (twin) 1993, Emma Eileen Maud *b* 1988, Katherine Elisabeth *b* 1991, Julia Claire *b* 1998.

Descendants of late Gen Rt Hon Sir Henry Frederick Ponsonby, GCB, son of Maj-Gen Hon Sir Frederick Cavendish Ponsonby, GCMG, KCB, KCH, 2nd son of 3rd Earl:—
Issue of late Rt Hon Sir Frederick Edward Grey Ponsonby, GCB, GCVO, who was *cr Baron Sysonby* 1935 (see that title).

Issue of late Arthur Augustus William Harry, who was *cr Baron Ponsonby of Shulbrede* 1930 (see that title).

Descendants of late Hon William Francis Spencer Ponsonby (3rd son of 3rd Earl), who was *cr Baron de Mauley* 1838 (see that title).

Grandchildren of late Chambré Brabazon Ponsonby, son of late Chambre Brabazon Ponsonby-Barker, grandson of 1st Viscount:—
Issue of late Thomas Brabazon Ponsonby, *b* 1878, *d* 1946: *m* 1909, Frances May, who *d* 1978, da of late Maj George Paynter, of Eaton Grange, Grantham, and 21 Belgrave Sq, SW:—
Chambré Brabazon (Low Port, Linlithgow, W Lothian), *b* 1911; Lt-Col (ret) 10th Hus; Comptroller to Gov-Gen of Australia 1936-37: *m* 1st, 1941, Merelina, who *d* 1993, only da of late Lt-Col James Tindal Ives Bosanquet; 2ndly, 1954, Diana Wray Hurt, who *d* 1999, of Reigate, Surrey, and has issue living (by 1st *m*), Merelina Karen PONSONBY (10 Lansdowne Gdns, S Lambeth, SW8 2EG), *b* 1946; has resumed her maiden name: *m* 1971 (*m diss* 1977), John Dymoke White, who *d* 1998, and has issue living, Merelina Rosanne (22 Offley Rd, SW9 0LS) *b* 1973, Lucinda Jane *b* 1974, — (by 2nd *m*), Richard Brabazon (6 Dene Walk, Lower Bourne, Farnham, Surrey GU10 3PL), *b* 1955; BScEng(Hons); Capt RE (ret) (despatches): *m* 1978, Diana Louise, da of A. R. Moodie, of Bonnytown House, Linlithgow, and has issue living, Tristan *b* 1984, Lorna Anne *b* 1980, Marianne Jane *b* 1982, — Miles Chambré, *b* 1957: *m* 1987, Jane Elizabeth, yr da of

(Oliver) Barrie Hopton, and has issue living, Simon Chambré *b* 1990, Jason Chambré *b* 1992. —— †George Thomas, MC, *b* 1913; Maj (ret) 17th/21st Lancers; 1939-45 War in N Africa and Italy (severely wounded, MC and bar): *m* 1948, Elizabeth Penelope Melville (The Threshing Barn, Grange Farm, Stratton, Cirencester, Glos GL7 2LR), da of Capt Walter Douglas Melville Wills, CBE, and *d* 1984, leaving issue, Thomas Charles George (28 Brook Green, W6 7BL), *b* 1950: *m* 1980 (*m diss* and annulled 1989), Elisabeth Marie Philippine, da of Jean Jules Marie Masurel, of 15 Avenue de Verzy, Paris 17, and has issue living, Sebastian Jean *b* 1983, — Henry Brabazon (Ballynatray, Youghal, co Cork), *b* 1952: *m* 1977, Elizabeth Fiona Mary, eldest da of Peter Bedford Brotchie, of Boxlands, Dorking, Surrey, and has issue living, Thomas George Peter *b* 1981, Rose *b* 1988, — Peter Douglas (Kilcooley Abbey, Thurles, co Tipperary), *b* 1955: *m* 1982, Faith Primrose Orr, only child of Rev Canon Ernest Arthur Brandon, of The Rectory, Foulksmills, co Wexford, and has issue living, Emma Rebecca Brandon *b* 1984, Sarah Georgina Brandon *b* 1986, Julia Nicola Brandon *b* 1992. —— Henry Jeffrey, *b* 1930: *m* 1960, Rosemary Jane, da of Ernest Sydney Wells, of Buxted Sussex, and has issue living, Julian Henry, *b* 1963: *m* 1993, Patricia Lynn, da of Dr Robert Alexander Ingram, of Washington, DC, USA, and has issue living, George Thomas *b* 1996, Lindsey Rose *b* 1998, — Jane Frances, *b* 1965: *m* 1994, Simon D. Marsh, only son of Hugh Marsh, of Westmill, Buntingford, Herts, and has issue living, Harry Duncan *b* 1995, Peter Nicholas *b* 1997, — Rosanna, *b* 1966. *Residence* – Grove, Fethard, co Tipperary. —— Noreen de Vere, *b* 1917: *m* 1939, Brig Henry Lawrence Savill Young, DSO, late Irish Gds (*see* Young, Bt, *cr* 1769, colls). *Residence* – End House, Pilton, Som.

PREDECESSORS – **(1)** WILLIAM Ponsonby, PC, MP for co Kilkenny, *temp* Anne and George I, was *cr Baron Bessborough* 1721, and *Viscount Duncannon* 1722 (peerage of Ireland); *d* 1724; *s* by his el son **(2)** BRABAZON, 2nd Viscount; MP for co Kildare 1704 and for Newtown 1713-15; *cr Earl of Bessborough* 1739 (peerage of Ireland), and *Baron Ponsonby of Sysonby* 1749 (peerage of Great Britain); *d* 1758; *s* by his el son **(3)** WILLIAM, PC, 2nd Earl, successively MP for Kilkenny, Derby, Saltash and Harwich, a Lord of the Treasury and Joint Postmaster-Gen; *d* 1793; *s* by his son **(4)** FREDERICK, 3rd Earl, MP for Knaresborough, and a Lord of the Admiralty; *d* 1844; *s* by his son **(5)** JOHN WILLIAM, 4th Earl, *b* 1781, sometime Lord-Lieut of Ireland and Ch Commr of Woods and Forests: *m* 1805, Lady Maria Fane, da of 10th Earl of Westmorland, KG; *cr Baron Duncannon* (peerage of Great Britain) 1834; *d* 1847; *s* by his el son **(6)** JOHN GEORGE BRABAZON, 5th Earl; was Lord Lieut of co Carlow, Master of HM's Staghounds, and Lord Steward of the Household; *d* 1880; *s* by his brother **(7)** FREDERICK GEORGE BRABAZON, 6th Earl, *b* 1815; *dsp* 1895; *s* by his brother **(8)** *Rev* WALTER WILLIAM BRABAZON, 7th Earl, *b* 1821; R of Stutton, Ipswich 1884-94: *m* 1850, Lady Louisa Susan Cornwallis Eliot, who *d* 1911, da of 3rd Earl of St. Germans, GCB; *d* 1906; *s* by his son **(9)** EDWARD, KP, CB, CVO, 8th Earl, *b* 1851; Sec to Speaker of House of Commons 1884-95: *m* 1875, Blanche Vere, CBE, who *d* 1919, yst da of Sir Josiah John Guest, 1st Bt; *d* 1920; *s* by his el son **(10)** VERE BRABAZON, GCMG, PC, 9th Earl; *b* 1880; Gov-Gen and Com-in-Ch, Dominion of Canada 1931-5; sat as MP for Cheltenham (C) Jan-Nov 1910, for Dover 1913-18, and for Dover Div of Kent (CoU) 1918-20; *cr Earl of Bessborough* (peerage of United Kingdom) 1937: *m* 1912, Roberte, JP (a DGStJ), who *d* 1979, only da of Baron de Neuflize, of Paris; *d* 1956; *s* by his el son **(11)** FREDERICK EDWARD NEUFLIZE, 10th Earl, *b* 1913; Capt 98th (Surrey and Sussex Yeo), ADC to GOC 1st Canadian Corps, Field Brig RA (TA Reserve), DL W Sussex, HM Foreign Ser 1944, Merchant Banker 1950-56, Dir ATV Ltd 1955-60, etc, Parl Sec for Science 1963-64, etc, Member European Parl 1972-79, Vice-Pres and Dep Leader European Conservative Group 1973-77, Pres Chichester Festival Theatre Trust and Playwright: *m* 1948, Mary, da of Charles A. Munn, of New York, and of Paris; *d* 1993, when the UK Earldom became ext, and he was *s* in his other titles by his cousin **(12)** ARTHUR MOUNTIFORT LONGFIELD (only son of late Maj Hon Cyril Myles Brabazon Ponsonby, MVO, Gren Gds, 2nd son of 8th Earl), 11th Earl and present peer; also Viscount Duncannon, Baron Duncannon, Baron Bessborough, and Baron Ponsonby of Sysonby.

Best, family name of Baron Wynford.

BESWICK, BARONY OF (Beswick) (Extinct 1987)

SON LIVING OF LIFE BARON

Hon Frank Jesse, *b* 1949; *ed* Latymer Upper Sch. *Residence* – 28 Skeena Hill, SW18.

DAUGHTER LIVING OF LIFE BARON

Hon Patricia Ann (202 Lakedale Rd, Plumstead, SE18), *b* 1939: *m* 1962, Anthony Woodbridge Atkinson, and has issue.

BETHELL, BARON (Bethell) (Baron UK 1922, Bt UK 1911)

I will keep faith

NICHOLAS WILLIAM BETHELL, 4th Baron, and 4th Baronet; *b* 19 July 1938; *s* 1967; *ed* Harrow, and Pembroke Coll, Camb; a Lord-in-Waiting to HM 1970-71; Member of European Parl, 1975-94 (elected rep June 1979): *m* 1st, 1964 (*m diss* 1971), Cecilia Mary Lothian, who *d* 1977, el da of Prof Alexander Mackie Honeyman, of Cowan's Rigg, St. Andrews; 2ndly, 1992, Bryony Lea Morgan, da of Brian David Griffiths, of Llanrhystyd, Dyfed, and has issue by 1st and 2nd *m*.

ꮇrms – Or, a chevron azure charged with an estoile of the first, in chief two boars' heads couped of the second. Crest – Upon a rock proper a boar's head couped azure. Supporters – *Dexter*, a wolf proper charged on the shoulder with an estoile or; *sinister* a wolf proper charged with a portcullis or.
Residence – Manor Farm, Brill, Bucks HP18 9SL.

SONS LIVING (By 1st marriage)

Hon JAMES NICHOLAS, *b* 1 Oct 1967.
Hon William Alexander, *b* 1969: *m* 1997, Tania J., elder da of Iain McDonald, of Weston Underwood, Bucks.

(By 2nd marriage)

Hon John Andrew Roland, *b* 1995.

SISTER LIVING

Sally Ann, *b* 1943: *m* 1965, Anthony Francis Wigram, of 16 Porchester Terr, W1, and has issue living, Maximilian John Lionel, *b* (March) 1966, — Camilla Ann, *b* (Dec) 1966: *m* 1989, Rupert Alister Peter John Cordle (*see* V Powerscourt, colls, 1985 Edn), and has issue living, Alexander Anthony *b* 1993, Hugo Andrew *b* 1995, — Lucy Olga (twin), *b* (Dec) 1966: *m* 1990, Benjamin V. Sangster, son of Robert Sangster, of The Nunnery, Douglas, IoM, and of Mrs Ian Strathearn Gordon, of Angeston Grange, Uley, Glos, and has had issue, James *b* and *d* 1995, Oliver Robert James *b* 1997, Eliza Camilla *b* 1992.

DAUGHTERS LIVING OF SECOND BARON

Hon Jennifer Mary, *b* 1930: *m* 1954, (Edward) Peter Moncrieff Brown, and has issue living, Alistair Peter, *b* 1955; *ed* Gordonstoun: *m* 1977, Eva Jacobsen, of Norway, and has issue living, Alexander *b* 1977, Charlotte *b* 1982, — Craig Edward, *b* 1957; *ed* Eton, and Bristol Univ; writer: *m* 1987, Frances J. M., da of late (James) Colin Ross Welch, of Aldbourne, Wilts, and has issue living, Silas *b* 1990, Tallulah *b* 1988, — James David, *b* 1959; *ed* Eton, and Oxford Univ: *m* 1990, Tracey, yr da of John Gadd, of Torrington, Devon, and has issue living, Daisy *b* 1991, Florence *b* 1996, — David Francis, *b* 1960; *ed* Stoneyhurst. *Residence* – 48 Prior's Acre, Boxgrove, Chichester, W Sussex PO18 0ER.

Hon Patricia Catherine, *b* 1933: *m* 1956, Michael William Nesbitt, DFC, and has issue living, William Patrick (Church House, Clapton on the Hill, Cheltenham, Glos), *b* 1963: *m* 1989, Caroline L., yr da of Dr D. Charlton-Smith, of Wellesbourne, Warwicks, and has issue living, Frederick William *b* 1993, Clementine Rose *b* 1991, — Anna Catherine, *b* 1957: *m* 1985, Kerry James McDonagh, of Manor Farmhouse, Wendlebury, nr Bicester, Oxon, elder son of James McDonagh, of Runcorn, Cheshire, and has issue living, Thomas *b* 1988, Edward *b* 1989, — Caroline Mary, *b* 1959. *Residence* – Rotherwood, Fittleworth, Pulborough, Sussex, RH20 1EW.

PREDECESSORS

– (1) JOHN HENRY BETHELL, son of late George Bethell, of South Woodford, Essex; *b* 1861: a Director of Barclays Bank Ltd; sat as MP for S or Romford Div of Essex (*L*) 1906-18, and for N Div of East Ham 1918-22; *cr* a *Baronet* (UK of Park House) 1911, and *Baron Bethell*, of Romford, co Essex (peerage of UK) 1922: *m* 1895, Florence, who *d* 1945, da of James Woolley Wyles; *d* 1945; *s* by his el surviving son (2) JOHN RAYMOND, 2nd Baron; *b* 1902: *m* 1st, 1927 (*m diss* 1948), Veronica Eileen, who *d* 1981, da of late Hon Sir James Daniel Connolly; 2ndly, 1948, Joan, who *d* 1966, da of late Brig-Gen Norman William Webber, CMG, DSO, and widow of Lt-Cdr H. N. Reid, RN; *d* 1965; *s* by his only son (3) GUY ANTHONY JOHN, 3rd Baron; *b* 1928; *d* 1967; *s* by his cousin (4) NICHOLAS WILLIAM (only son of late Hon William Gladstone Bethell, 3rd son of 1st Baron), 4th Baron, and present peer.

Bethell, family name of Baron Westbury.

Bethune, Lindsay-, family name of Earl Lindsay.

BICESTER, BARON (Smith) (Baron UK 1938)
(Title pronounced "Bister")

ANGUS EDWARD VIVIAN SMITH, 3rd Baron; *b* 20 Feb 1932; *s* 1968; *ed* Eton.

Steadfast in the faith

TENAX·IN·FIDE

Arms – Or, a chevron cottised sable, between three demi-griffins couped of the last, the two in chief respecting each other. **Crest** – An elephant's head erased or, charged on the neck with three fleurs de lis, one and two azure. **Supporters** – On either side a griffin sable charged on the shoulder with a horse-shoe inverted or.

BROTHER LIVING

HUGH CHARLES VIVIAN, *b* 8 Nov 1934; *ed* Eton, and Worcester Coll, Oxford; late 2nd Lt RAC.

DAUGHTER LIVING OF SECOND BARON

Hon Jane Beatrix Randal, *b* 1928: *m* 1949 (*m diss* 1991), John Richard Daniel Green, and has issue living, John James Randal (Foxboro Hall, Melton, nr Woodbridge, Suffolk, IP12 1ND) *b* 1953: *m* 1980, Hon Claerwen Gibson-Watt, el da of Baron Gibson-Watt (Life Baron), and formerly wife of Enrique Ulvert, and has issue living, Toby James Ralph *b* 1982, Richard John Sebastian *b* 1984, David Peter Julian *b* (twin) 1984, — Elizabeth Jane, *b* 1950: *m* 1982 (*m diss* 1991), Ian Mackinnon, only son of late Maj C. N. Mackinnon, of Old Garth, Bembridge, Isle of Wight, — Amanda Carol, *b* 1957: *m* 1986, Charles Thomas Bunbury, who *d* 1997, 2nd son of Sir (John) William Napier Bunbury, 12th Bt, and has issue (see that title). *Residence* – Taylors Mead, Sparsholt, Winchester, Hants SO21 2NR.

WIDOW LIVING OF SON OF FIRST BARON

Mabel, Mus Bac, da of late A. W. R. Lovering: *m* 1948, as his 2nd wife, Lt-Col Hon Stephen Edward Vivian Smith, late Coldm Gds, who *d* 1952. *Residence* – 6 Ravenscar Lodge, 22 The Downs, Wimbledon, SW20 8HT.

MOTHER LIVING

Elenor Anderson (Resides in USA), da of Edward Shepherd Hewitt, of New York City: *m* 1929 (*m diss* 1947), as his 1st wife, Lt-Col Hon Stephen Edward Vivian Smith, late Coldm Gds, who *d* 1952, 2nd son of 1st Baron.

COLLATERAL BRANCH LIVING

Issue of late Maj Hon Hugh Adeane Vivian Smith, MBE, 3rd son of 1st Baron Bicester, *b* 1910, *d* 1978: *m* 1933, Lady Helen Dorothy Primrose, who *d* 1998, da of 6th Earl of Rosebery:—
George Harry Vivian, *b* 1934: *m* 1st, 1962, June Rose Jager, da of Basil William Foster-Towne, of S Africa; 2ndly, 1966, Susan Mary, da of Frank Goodfellow, of Johannesburg, and has had issue (by 1st *m*), Charles James Vivian, *b* 1963, — (by 2nd *m*) Sarah Helen, *b* 1968; *d* 1995, — Amanda Mary, *b* 1972. ⸺ Elizabeth Vivian, *b* 1939: *m* 1960 (*m diss* 1991), (Alexander) James Macdonald-Buchanan (*see* By Woolavington, 1985 Edn), and has issue living, Hugh James, *b* 1961, — James Iain Harry (25 Brynmaer Rd, SW11 4EN), *b* 1963: *m* 1996, Julia, yr da of late Anthony Everard Savile Crossley (*see* B Somerleyton, colls), and has issue living, Angus Anthony *b* 1997, — Nicholas Mark, *b* 1967: *m* 1996, Vanessa L., da of late William Bates, and has issue living, Archie Nicholas *b* 1998, — Charles Alexander, *b* 1970. *Residence* – Inveran, Poolewe, Ross-shire.

PREDECESSORS – (1) VIVIAN HUGH Smith, son of late Hugh Colin Smith; *b* 1867; Chm of Morgan Grenfell, Ltd, and an Hon Freeman of Oxfordshire; was Lord-Lieut of Oxfordshire 1934-54; *cr Baron Bicester*, of Tusmore, co Oxford (peerage of United Kingdom) 1938: *m* 1897, Lady Sybil Mary McDonnell, who *d* 1959, da of 6th Earl of Antrim; *d* 1956; *s* by his el son (2) RANDAL HUGH VIVIAN, 2nd Baron; *b* 1898; High Sheriff of Oxon 1945: *m* 1922, Hon Dorothea Gwenllian James, who *d* 1974, da of 3rd Baron Northbourne; *d* 1968; *s* by his nephew (3) ANGUS EDWARD VIVIAN (2nd son of late Lt-Col Hon Stephen Edward Vivian Smith, 2nd son of 1st Baron), 3rd Baron, and present peer.

BIDDULPH, BARON (Maitland Biddulph) (Baron UK 1903)

Let us aim at loftier things

(ANTHONY) NICHOLAS COLIN MAITLAND BIDDULPH, 5th Baron; *b* 8 April 1959; *s* 1988; *ed* Cheltenham, and RAC Cirencester; an Armourer and Freeman of City of London; assumed addl surname of Maitland 1978: *m* 1993, Hon Sian Diana Gibson-Watt, yr da of Baron Gibson-Watt, MC, PC (Life Baron), and has issue.

Arms – Quarterly, 1st and 4th vert an eagle displayed and a canton argent (*Biddulph*); 2nd and 3rd or a lion rampant gules couped at all his joints of the field within a double tressure flory counterflory azure (*Maitland*). **Crest** – A wolf salient argent, charged on the shoulder with a trefoil slipped gules. **Supporters** – On either side a wolf argent, semée of trefoils slipped gules.
Seat – Makerstoun, Kelso, Roxburghshire. *Clubs* – Cavalry and Guards', White's.

SONS LIVING

Hon ROBERT JULIAN WATT, *b* 8 July 1994.
Hon David Michael William, *b* 1997.

BROTHER LIVING

Hon William Ian Robert Maitland Biddulph, *b* 1963; *ed* Loretto; an Armourer and Freeman of City of London; assumed addl surname of Maitland 1978. *Residence* – Fair Oak, Ashford Hill, Newbury, Berks RG19 8BJ. *Club* – Caveat Corpus.

SISTER LIVING

Hon Fiona Mary, *b* 1961; *ed* Courtauld Inst; an Armourer and Freeman of City of London; co-author of *Paris: Portrait of a City* 1994; assumed addl surname of Maitland 1981: *m* 1994, Anthony Henry Joseph Fraser, and has issue (*see* L Lovat, colls). *Residences* – 4 Wilmington House, Highbury Crescent, Islington, N5 1RU; Keepers House, Deene Rd, nr Corby, Northants NN17 3AB.

UNCLE LIVING (*son of 3rd Baron*)

Hon Edward Sidney, *b* 1934; *ed* Eton; Lt RHG (ret). *Residence* – Ribston Lawn, Much Marcle, Ledbury, Herefords, HR8 2ND. *Club* – White's

AUNTS LIVING (*daughters of 3rd Baron*)

Hon Marjorie Amy, *b* 1927: *m* 1947, Thomas Ian Michael Walker-Munro, who *d* 1965 (*see* Munro, Bt, *cr* 1825, colls).
Hon Susan Louise, *b* 1929.

WIDOW LIVING OF FOURTH BARON

Lady MARY HELENA MAITLAND (*Lady Mary Biddulph*), da of late Ivor Colin James, Viscount Maitland, son of 15th Earl of Lauderdale: *m* 1958, the 4th Baron Biddulph, who *d* 1988. *Residence* – Greatridgehall, Makerstoun, Kelso, Roxburghshire TD5 7PD. *Clubs* – Cavalry and Guards', Sloane.

COLLATERAL BRANCH LIVING

Grandchildren of late Hon Claud William Biddulph (*infra*):—
Issue of late Maj Anthony Biddulph, TD, *b* 1910, *d* 1984: *m* 1938, Mary Dearman, who *d* 1991, da of Maj Sir John Dearman Birchall, MP:—
Simon, TD (Rodmarton Manor, Rodmarton, Cirencester), *b* 1942; *ed* Eton: *m* 1970, Christina, da of George McCorquodale (*see* B Luke, 1990 Edn), and has issue living, John Simon, *b* 1971; *ed* Eton: *m* 1999, Hon Sarah Margaret Gretton, only da of 3rd Baron Gretton, — (Anthony) George, *b* 1973; *ed* Eton, and RMA Sandhurst, commn'd King's Royal Hus, — Sarah Rose, *b* 1980. —— (Anthony) Jasper (Manor Farm, Tarlton, Cirencester), *b* 1946; *ed* Eton: *m* 1975, Louise Perrett, da of William Sandeman Cox, of Coff's Harbour, NSW, and has issue living, James Jasper, *b* 1977, — Emily Selena Mary, *b* 1979. —— Clarissa Mary (28 Laxford House, Cundy St, SW1W 9JU), *b* 1939: *m* 1962, James Richard Ferard, and has issue living, Richard Anthony Agace, *b* 1963: *m* 1994, Lucilla Fleur Scott, elder da of late Hon (John) Greville Napier (*see* L Napier and Ettrick, colls), — (Charles) Edward, *b* 1970, — Susan Mary, *b* 1965.

Issue of late Hon Claud William Biddulph, yr son of 1st Baron, *b* 1871, *d* 1954: *m* 1906, Margaret, who *d* 1970, da of late Alfred John Howard (*see* E Carlisle, colls, 1970 Edn):—
Marjory Mary (*Lady Findlay*), *b* 1915: *m* 1st, 1938 (*m diss* 1962), as his 2nd wife, Maj Philip Wilfred Cripps, son of Maj Sir Frederick William Beresford Cripps, DSO; 2ndly, 1964, as his 2nd wife, Lt-Col Sir Roland Lewis Findlay, 3rd Bt, who *d* 1979, and has issue living (by 1st *m*), John Philip, *b* 1940; *ed* Eton: *m* 1975, Aileen Elizabeth, da of William Alexander

Hamilton, — Diana Josephine, *b* 1953: *m* 1984, Richard P. Turner, yr son of John Turner, of Lound, Retford, Notts. *Residence* – Lyddington, Uppingham, Leics.

PREDECESSORS – (1) MICHAEL Biddulph, son of late Robert Biddulph, MP, of Ledbury; *b* 1834; a partner in London banking firm of Cocks, Biddulph and Co; MP for Herefordshire (*L*) July 1865 to Nov 1885, and S, or Ross, Div of Here-fordshire (LU) 1885-1900; *cr Baron Biddulph*, of Ledbury, co Hereford (peerage of United Kingdom) 1903: *m* 1st, 1864, Adelaide Georgiana, who *d* 1872, da of late Gen Rt Hon Jonathan Peel, MP; 2ndly, 1877, Lady Elizabeth Philippa, VA, who *d* 1916, widow of Henry John Adeane, MP, and da of 4th Earl of Hardwicke; *d* 1923; *s* by his el son **(2)** JOHN MICHAEL GORDON, 2nd Baron, *b* 1869: *m* 1896, Marjorie Caroline Susan, who *d* 1961, da of late Col William Mure; *d* 1949; *s* by his el son **(3)** MICHAEL WILLIAM JOHN, 3rd Baron, *b* 1898: *m* 1925, Lady Amy Louise Agar, who *d* 1983, da of 4th Earl of Normanton; *d* 1972; *s* by his el son **(4)** ROBERT MICHAEL CHRISTIAN, 4th Baron, *b* 1931: a Tweed Commr: *m* 1958, Lady Mary Helena Maitland, da of late Ivor Colin James Viscount Maitland, son of 15th Earl of Lauderdale; *d* 1988; *s* by his elder son **(5)** (ANTHONY) NICHOLAS COLIN, 5th Baron and present peer.

BIFFEN, BARON (Biffen) (Life Baron 1997)

(WILLIAM) JOHN BIFFEN, son of Victor William Biffen, of Otterhampton, Som; *b* 3 Nov 1930; *ed* Dr Morgan's Gram Sch, Bridgwater, and Jesus Coll, Camb (BA 1953); with Tube Investments Ltd 1953-60; Economist Intelligence Unit 1960-61; MP (*C*) Oswestry 1961-83, and Shropshire North 1983-97; Chief Sec to the Treasury 1979-81; Sec of State for Trade 1981-82; Lord Pres of the Council 1982-83; Leader, House of Commons 1982-87; Lord Privy Seal 1983-87; DL Shropshire 1993; Dir Glynwed International plc since 1987, J. Bibby & Sons plc since 1988, and Rockware Group plc 1988-91; Trustee, The London Clinic since 1995; *cr* PC 1979, and *Baron Biffen*, of Tanat, co Shropshire (Life Baron) 1997: *m* 1979, Mrs Sarah Wood, da of J. A. Cyril Drew, of La Colline Court, Le Mont de Couray, St Martin, Jersey, CI.
Address – House of Lords, SW1A 0PW.

Bigham, family name of Viscount Mersey.

Bigham, family name of Lord Nairne.

Bingham, family name of Baron Clanmorris.

Bingham, family name of Earl of Lucan.

Bingham, Baron; title of Earl of Lucan on Roll of HL

Bingham, Lord; son of Earl of Lucan.

BINGHAM OF CORNHILL, BARON (Bingham) (Life Baron 1996)

THOMAS HENRY BINGHAM, PC, son of Dr Thomas Henry Bingham, of Reigate, Surrey; *b* 13 Oct 1933; *ed* Sedbergh, and Balliol Coll, Oxford (MA 19—); late Royal Ulster Rifles; Hon Fell of King's Coll, London 1992, and of Queen Mary and Westfield Coll, London 1993, Visitor, Balliol Coll (and Hon Fell), Hon LLD Birmingham Univ 1993, Hon DCL Oxford 1994, Hon DUniv Essex 1997, Hon LLD Wales 1998, Hon LLD London 1998; Bar, Gray's Inn 1959; junior counsel, Dept of Employment 1968-72; QC 1972; High Court Judge (Queen's Bench Division) 1980-86, Lord Justice of Appeal 1986-92, Master of the Rolls 1992-96, since when Lord Chief Justice of England and Wales; *cr* Kt 1980, PC 1986, and *Baron Bingham of Cornhill* [full territorial designation withheld] (Life Baron) 1996: *m* 1963, Elizabeth Patricia, only da of late Peter Noel Loxley, by his wife Elizabeth Lavender, da of late Major-Gen Guy Payan Dawnay, CB, CMG, DSO, MVO (*see* V Downe, colls, 1995 Edn), and has issue.
Address – Royal Courts of Justice, Strand, WC2A 2LL.

SONS LIVING

(*Hon*) (Thomas) Henry (does not use courtesy title), *b* 1967.
(*Hon*) Christopher Toby (does not use courtesy title), *b* 1969.

DAUGHTER LIVING

(*Hon*) Catherine Elizabeth (does not use courtesy title), *b* 1965.

Binning, Lord; son of Earl of Haddington.

Birch, family name of Baron Rhyl.

BIRDWOOD, BARON (Birdwood) (Baron UK 1938, Bt UK 1919)

Calm in action

MARK WILLIAM OGILVIE BIRDWOOD, 3rd Baron, and 3rd Baronet; *b* 23 Nov 1938; *s* 1962; *ed* Radley, and Trin Coll, Camb (MA 1970); late 2nd Lt RHG; Chm Martlet Ltd since 1986, Dir Scientific Generics Ltd 1989-97; Chm Worthington & Co 1994-97, and Fiortho Ltd since 1992; Dir Character Group plc since 1997, IMS plc since 1997, and Jasmin plc since 1998; Memb House of Lords Select Cttee on Science and Technology since 1999; Member Glaziers' Co: *m* 1963, Judith Helen, el da of Reginald Gordon Seymour Roberts, of Newton Aycliffe, co Durham, and has issue.

Arms – Azure, five martlets, two, two and one within an inescutcheon voided a representation of the Southern Cross, all argent. **Crest** – Out of a mural crown gules, a martlet argent between two branches of laurel proper. **Supporters** – *Dexter*, a Sergeant of the XIIth (Prince of Wales's Royal) Lancers, mounted on a bay horse; *sinister*, a Sikh Daffadar of the XIth (Prince of Wales's Own) Bengal Lancers mounted on a chestnut horse both habited and accoutred proper.
Residences – 5 Holbein Mews, SW1W 8NW; Russell House, Broadway, Worcs WR12 7BU. *Club* – Brooks's.

DAUGHTER LIVING

Hon Sophie Frederika, *b* 1964: *m* 1st, 1987 (*m diss* 1997), 3rd Earl of Woolton; 2ndly, 1998, David John Montgomery.

SISTER LIVING

Hon Sonia Gina Ogilvie, *b* 1933: *m* 1956, Geoffrey Thynne Valentine Archer, and has issue living, David Birdwood, *b* 1959: *m* 1984, Gwenyth Daphne, da of Ian Highley, of Stanford Dingley, Berks, and has issue living, Thomas Benjamin *b* 1988, James Birdwood *b* 1990, Isabel Gwenyth *b* 1992, — Sarah-Jane Birdwood, *b* 1957: *m* 1997, Don Fernando Muñoz-Gomez, PhD (Med), of Bilbao, and has issue living, Marcos Fernando Geoffrey *b* 1999, Marina *b* 1998, Paula Regina Sonia *b* (twin) 1999. *Residence* – Renson Mill, Ashwater, Devon EX21 5ER.

WIDOW LIVING OF SECOND BARON

JOAN POLLOCK (*Dowager Baroness Birdwood*), da of Christopher Norman Graham, of Ealing: *m* 1954, as his 2nd wife, the 2nd Baron Birdwood, who *d* 1962.

PREDECESSORS – (1) FM Sir WILLIAM RIDDELL Birdwood, GCB, GCSI, GCMG, GCVO, CIE, DSO, DCL, LLD, el surviving son of late Herbert Mills Birdwood, CSI, LLD, JP, ICS; *b* 1865; Field-Marshal; Hazara Expedition 1891 (medal with clasp), Isaza Expedition 1892, Tirah Expedition 1897-8 (despatches, medal with three clasps), S Africa 1899-1902, as Staff Officer, Brig Maj Mounted Brig (Natal) and DAAG, and Mil Sec to Com-in-Ch (Gen Lord Kitchener) (severely wounded, despatches five times, Queen's medal with six clasps. King's medal with two clasps, Brevets Major and Lieut-Col), Mohmand Expedition 1908, as Ch of Staff, present at action of Kargha (despatches, medal with clasp, DSO), European War 1914-18 with Mediterranean Expeditionary Force, first Comdg Australian and New Zealand Army Corps, then Com-in-Ch Mediterranean Expeditionary Force, and Comdg Dardanelles Army during Evacuation, and subsequently Comdg Australian and New Zealand troops and 5th Army in France (wounded, despatches many times, KCMG, Lieut-Gen, KCB, Grand Cordon of Legion of Honour, French Croix de Guerre with Palm, Belgian Order de la Couronne and Croix de Guerre, DSM of USA, Order of the Nile, Order of Aviz and of Christ and Grand Cordon of Tower and Sword of Portugal, 1st class of Orders of Rising Sun of Japan and Timsa of Persia, Order of Star of Nepal, GCMG, thanked by Parliament, *cr* Baronet, granted £10,000); was QMG, India May to Nov 1912, Sec to Govt of India, Army Depart, and a Member of Legislative Council of Gov-Gen of India 1912-14, Gen Officer Comdg Australian Imperial Forces 1915-20, ADC to King Edward VII 1906-10 and to King George V 1910-11, an ADC Gen to HM 1917-22, and Gen Officer Comdg-in-Ch, N Army, India 1920-24; acted as Com-in-Ch in India 1924, Com-in-Ch in India 1925-30, and Master of Peterhouse, Camb 1931-8; *cr a Baronet* (UK, of Anzac and Totnes) 1919, and *Baron Birdwood*, of Anzac, and of Totnes, co Devon (peerage of UK) 1938: *m* 1894, Janetta Hope Gonville, CI, who *d* 1947, el da of Col Sir Benjamin Parnell Bromhead, 4th Bt, CB; *d* 1951; *s* by his son (2) CHRISTOPHER BROMHEAD, MVO, 2nd Baron; *b* 1899; Lt-Col Probyn's Horse, Indian Army, a Commentator, Lecturer, and Author on International Affairs: *m* 1st, 1931 (*m diss* 1954), (Elisabeth) Vere Drummond, CVO, who *d* 1997, da of Lieut-Col Sir George Drummond Ogilvie, KCIE, CSI; 2ndly, 1954, Joan Pollock, da of Christopher Norman Graham; *d* 1962; *s* by his son (3) MARK WILLIAM OGILVIE, 3rd Baron and present peer.

BIRK, BARONY OF (Birk) (Extinct 1996)

SON LIVING OF LIFE BARONESS

Dr the Hon David Barry Wilson (28 Charlbury Rd, Oxford OX2 6UU), *b* 1943: *ed* Clifton Coll, Jesus Coll, Camb, and Hull, London and Australian Nat Univs; PhD: *m* 1969, Kate, da of Joseph Green, of London, NW8, and has issue living, Rebecca, *b* 1970, — Antonia, *b* 1971, — Georgina, *b* 1974.

DAUGHTER LIVING OF LIFE BARONESS

Hon Angela Felicity, *b* 1947; *ed* Camden Sch for Girls and London Univ; JP; *m* 1970, Richard Camber, of 28 Heath Drive, Hampstead, NW3, and has issue living, Thomas, *b* 1980, — Alice, *b* 1974, — Chloe, *b* 1980.

BIRKENHEAD, EARLDOM OF (Smith) (Extinct 1985)

SISTER LIVING OF THIRD EARL

Lady Juliet Margaret, LVO, *b* 1941; a Lady-in-Waiting to HRH The Princess Margaret, Countess of Snowdon 1965-71, since when an Extra Lady-in-Waiting; Lord Lieut Northants 1998; LVO (1981): *m* 1970, John Richard Townsend, of Newbottle Manor, Banbury, Oxon OX17 3DD, and has issue living, Eleanor Mary, *b* 1971, — Alice Jane, *b* 1974, — Margaret Ann, *b* 1978.

BIRKETT, BARON (Birkett) (Baron UK 1958)

MICHAEL BIRKETT, 2nd Baron; *b* 22 Oct 1929; *s* 1962; *ed* Stowe, and Trin Coll, Camb; film producer; Dep Dir National Theatre since 1974; Dir Greater London Council Recreation and Arts since 1979: *m* 1960, Mrs Junia Crawford, who *d* 1973, da of Harold Elliott; 2ndly, 1978, Gloria, da of Thomas Taylor, of Queen's Gate, SW, and has issue by 2nd *m*.

Arms – Gules three full bottomed wigs argent. **Crest** – Between two wings gules a Viking ship proper charged on the sail with a raven close sable. **Supporters** – *Dexter*, a lion or semee of roses gules; *sinister*, a wolf sable semee of mullets gold.
Address – c/o House of Lords, SW1.

The Law is my light

SON LIVING *(By 2nd marriage)*

Hon THOMAS, *b* 25 July 1982.

SISTER LIVING

Hon Linnea, *b* 1923: *m* 1949, Gavin Cliff Hodges (Croix de Guerre), who *d* 1998, and has issue living, Marcus Birkett Adam, *b* 1959, — Victoria Françoise, *b* 1951, — Gabrielle, *b* 1953, — Charmian Sophie, *b* 1957: *m* 1981, Christopher John Allwright, of 17 East Common, Harpenden, Herts. *Residence* – Willow Cottage, Stourton Caundle, Sturminster Newton, Dorset DT10 2JW.

PREDECESSOR – (1) WILLIAM NORMAN Birkett, PC, son of late Thomas Birkett, of Ulverston, Lancashire; *b* 1883; sat as MP for E Div of Nottingham (*L*) 1923-24, and 1929-31; Judge of High Court of Justice (King's Bench Div) 1941-50, and a Lord Justice of Appeal 1950-57; *cr Baron Birkett*, of Ulverston, co Palatine of Lancaster (peerage of UK) 1958: *m* 1920, Ruth, who *d* 1969, da of Emil Nilsson; *d* 1962; *s* by his son (2) MICHAEL, 2nd Baron and present peer.

Bishop, family name of Baroness O'Cathain.

BISHOPSTON, BARONY OF (Bishop) (Extinct 1984)

WIDOW LIVING OF LIFE BARON

WINIFRED MARY, JP; da of Frank Bryant, of Bristol: *m* 1945, Baron Bishopston, PC (Life Baron), who *d* 1984, leaving issue, four das. *Residence* – 11 Challoner Court, Merchants Landing, Redcliffe, Bristol BS1 4RG.

BLACK, BARONY OF (Black) (Extinct 1985)

DAUGHTER LIVING OF LIFE BARON

Hon Patricia Margaret, *b* 1919: *m* 1942, Leslie John Smyth, of Goudie's Farm, Lower Hamswell, Bath, Avon, and has issue.

BLACKETT, BARONY OF (Blackett) (Extinct 1974)

SON LIVING OF LIFE BARON

Hon Nicolas Maynard (18 Farquhar Rd, SW19), *b* 1928; *ed* Bristol Univ (BSc, PhD): *m* 1951, Patricia, da of Henry William Tankins, of Bristol, and has issue living, Peter, *b* 1962.

DAUGHTER LIVING OF LIFE BARON

Hon Giovanna, *b* 1926: *m* 1950, Kenneth Bloor, of 9 Queenston Rd, W Didsbury, Manchester M20.

BLACKFORD, BARONY OF (Mason) (Extinct 1988)

SISTER LIVING OF FOURTH BARON

Hon Elizabeth-Anne (St Luke St, SW3), *b* 1965.

BLACKSTONE, BARONESS (Blackstone) (Life Baroness 1987)

TESSA ANN VOSPER BLACKSTONE, da of late Geoffrey Vaughan Blackstone, CBE, GM, of Bures, Suffolk, by his wife Joanna, da of Maj Stanley Vosper; *b* 27 Sept 1942; *ed* Ware Gram Sch, and London Sch of Economics (BSc Soc, PhD); Associate Lect Enfield Coll 1965-66, Assist Lect, then Lect, Dept of Social Admin LSE 1966-75; Adviser Central Policy Review Staff, Cabinet Office, 1975-78; Prof of Educational Admin, Univ of London Inst of Educn, 1978-83; Dep Educn Officer (Resources), then Clerk and Dir of Educn, ILEA 1983-87; Master Birkbeck Coll 1987-97; since when Min of State Dept of Educn and Employment; Dir Royal Opera House 1987-97, and Chm Royal Opera House Ballet Board 1991-97; Founder Memb and Chm of Trustees Inst for Public Policy Research 1988-97; Trustee Natural History Museum 1992-97; *cr Baroness Blackstone*, of Stoke Newington, Greater London (Life Baroness) 1987: *m* 1963 (*m diss* 1975), Tom Evans, and has issue.
Residence – 17 Lloyd Sq, WC1X 9AJ.

SON LIVING

Hon Benedict Blackstone, *b* 1963: *m* 1987, Suzi, da of Donal Godson, of Dublin, and has issue living, Scarlet Eloise, *b* 1991, — Amber, *b* 1994, — Ruby, *b* (twin) 1994.

DAUGHTER LIVING

Hon Liesel Morwenna, *b* 1966: *m* 1996, Leo Burley.

BLACKWELL, BARON (Blackwell) (Life Baron 1997)

NORMAN ROY BLACKWELL, son of late Albert Edward Blackwell, of Blackheath; *b* 29 July 1952; *ed* Latymer Upper Sch, Hammersmith, Royal Academy of Music, Trinity Coll, Camb (BA 1973, MA 1978), and Wharton Business Sch, Univ of Pennsylvania (Thouron Scholar, MBA 1975, PhD 1976); Strategic Planning, Plessey Co 1976-78; with McKinsey & Co 1979-86, and 1988-94; Special Adviser to Prime Minister's Policy Unit 1986-87, Head of Policy Unit 1995-97; Dir Group Development, Nat West Group since 1997; *cr Baron Blackwell*, of Woodcote, co Surrey (Life Baron) 1997: *m* 1974, Brenda, da of Thomas Clucas, of Barrow-in-Furness, and has issue.

Arms – Sable between two chevronels argent five garbs or. **Crest** – A badger sejant erect proper gorged with a plain collar or and holding in the dexter forepaw a rose gules barbed seeded slipped and leaved or. **Supporters** – On either side a beaver sejant erect gules the tail or holding in the interior paw and blowing a trumpet also or.
Address – c/o House of Lords, Westminster, SW1A 0PW. *Clubs* – Carlton, RAC.

SONS LIVING

Hon Simon, *b* 1981; *ed* King's Coll Sch, Wimbledon.
Hon Richard, *b* 1987.
Hon William, *b* 1989.

DAUGHTERS LIVING

Hon Jane, *b* 1979; *ed* Sutton High Sch, and Edinburgh Univ.
Hon Sarah, *b* 1983; *ed* Rosebery Sch, Epsom.

Blackwood, family name of Baron Dufferin and Clandeboye.

BLAKE, BARON (Blake) (Life Baron 1971)

ROBERT NORMAN WILLIAM BLAKE, FBA, son of William Joseph Blake, of Brundall, Norfolk; *b* 23 Dec 1916; *ed* King Edward VI Sch, Norwich, and Magdalen Coll, Oxford (MA, DLitt); Hon DLitt Glasgow, E Anglia, Westminster Coll, Fulton, Missouri, USA, and Buckingham; 1939-45 War as Capt, RA; N Africa 1942, POW Italy 1942-44, escaped 1944, despatches 1944; a JP of Oxford; a Member of Oxford City Council 1957-64; Lecturer in Politics Ch Ch Oxford 1946-47, Student and Tutor in Politics Ch Ch 1947-68; Censor 1950-55, Senior Proctor 1959-60; Ford's Lecturer in English History 1967-68; Provost of Queen's Coll, Oxford 1968-87, Pro-Vice-Chancellor of Oxford Univ 1971-87; Member of Board of Channel Four TV Co 1983-87; author of *The Private Papers of Douglas Haig* 1952, *The Unknown Prime Minister (Life of Andrew Bonar Law)* 1955, *Disraeli* 1966, *The Conservative Party from Peel to Churchill* 1970, *The Office of Prime Minister* 1975; ed, with John Patten, *The Conservative Opportunity* 1976, *A History of Rhodesia* 1977, *Disraeli's Grand Tour* 1982; ed *The English World* 1982, *The Decline of Power 1915-64* 1985, *The Conservative Party from Peel to Thatcher* 1985; ed *Dictionary of National Biography*; ed, with Roger Louis, *Churchill* 1993; Chm R Commn on Historical Manuscripts from 1982; Chm Rhodes Trust 1983-87; Trustee Brit Museum 1978-88; Prime Warden Dyers' Co 1976-77; High Steward of Westminster since 1989; *cr Baron Blake*, of Braydeston, co Norfolk (Life Baron) 1971: *m* 1953, Patricia Mary, who *d* 1995, el da of Thomas Richard Waters, of Great Plumstead, Norfolk, and has issue.

Residence – Riverview House, Brundall, Norwich, Norfolk. *Clubs* – Brooks's, Beefsteak, Pratt's, United Oxford and Cambridge University, and Norfolk County.

DAUGHTERS LIVING

Hon Deborah Cicelie, *b* 1955.
Hon Letitia Lindley, *b* 1960.
Hon Victoria Mary, *b* 1963.

BLAKENHAM, VISCOUNT (Hare) (Viscount UK 1963)

I hate whatever is profane

MICHAEL JOHN HARE, 2nd Viscount; *b* 25 Jan 1938; *s* 1982; *ed* Eton, and Harvard Coll, USA (AB Econ); late 2nd Lt Life Gds; Man Dir S Pearson 1979-83, Chm since 1983; Chm of RSPB since 1982; Pres Sussex Trust for Nature Conservation since 1983; Chm *Financial Times* since 1984: *m* 1965, his cousin, Marcia Persephone, da of late Maj Hon Alan Victor Hare, MC (*see* E Listowel, colls), and has issue.

Arms – Gules, two bars and a chief indented or. Crest – A demi-lion rampant argent, ducally gorged or. Supporters – *Dexter*, a dragon ermine armed and langued gules; *Sinister*, a Guernsey cow proper.

SON LIVING

Hon CASPAR JOHN, *b* 8 April 1972.

DAUGHTERS LIVING

Hon Cressida, *b* 1966: *m* 1996, Simon M. Cowell, yr son of Barry Cowell, of Deal, Kent.
Hon Emily, *b* 1967.

SISTERS LIVING

Hon Mary Anne *b* 1936: *m* 1964, Timothy Mark Sergison-Brooke (*see* V Brookeborough, colls).

Hon Joanna Freda, *b* 1942: *m* 1967, Judge Stephen Breyer.

PREDECESSORS – (1) *Rt Hon* JOHN HUGH HARE, OBE, PC, 3rd son of 4th Earl of Listowel; *b* 1911; an Alderman LCC 1937-52, Chm of London Municipal Soc 1947-52, Vice-Chm of Conservative Party 1952-55; Min of State for Colonial Affairs 1955-56, Sec of State for War 1956-58, Min of Agriculture, Fisheries and Food 1958-60, Min of Labour 1960-63, and Chancellor of Duchy of Lancaster 1963-4, Dep Leader of House of Lords 1963-64, and Chm of Conservative Party Organisation 1963-5; Chm of Toynbee Hall 1966-82; Chm of Horticultural Soc 1970-82 (VMH 1974); Chm of Gov Peabody Donation Fund 1967-82; 1939-45 War in N Africa and Italy (despatches, MBE, OBE, Legion of Merit USA); MP for Woodbridge Div of E Suffolk (*C*) 1945-50, and for Sudbury and Woodbridge Div of E Suffolk 1950-63; *cr Viscount Blakenham*, of Little Blakenham, co Suffolk (peerage of UK) 1963: *m* 1934, Hon (Beryl) Nancy Pearson, who *d* 1994, da of 2nd Viscount Cowdray; *d* 1982; *s* by his only son (2) MICHAEL JOHN, 2nd Viscount and present peer.

BLAKER, BARON (Blaker) (Life Baron 1994)

PETER ALLAN RENSHAW BLAKER, KCMG, PC, son of late Cedric Blaker, CBE, MC, ED, of Scaynes Hill, Sussex; *b* 4 Oct 1922; *ed* Shrewsbury, Trinity Coll, Toronto (BA 1943), and New Coll, Oxford (MA 1953); 1939-45 War Capt Argyll and Sutherland Highlanders of Canada (wounded); Solicitor 1948, Bar 1952; HM Foreign Service 1953-64; MP for Blackpool S (C) 1964-92; Parly Under-Sec of State, Army 1972-74, FCO 1974, Min of State, FCO 1979-81, Armed Forces 1981-83; Chm Conservative Parly Foreign and Commonwealth Affairs Cttee 1983-92; *cr* KCMG 1983, PC 1983, and *Baron Blaker*, of Blackpool, co Lancs, and of Lindfield, co W Sussex (Life Baron) 1994: *m* 1953, Jennifer Nina Athenais Flora Mary, elder da of late Sir Pierson John Dixon, GCMG, CB, and has issue.

Arms – Per pale argent and or on a chevron sable between three martlets volant azure each holding in the beak a rose slipped gules seeded or two blackamoor heads couped argent the ears tinged or between three ermine spots argent. **Crest** – A horse's head sable maned or bridled argent reined ermine. **Supporters** – *Dexter*, a wild cat guardant or; *sinister*, a Chinese dragon also or.
Address – House of Lords, SW1A 0PW.

SON LIVING

Hon Adam Pierson Renshaw, *b* 1963; *ed* Eton: *m* 1996, Sophie R., eldest da of Thomas Colvill Holmes (Toby) Lyons, of Stansted, Essex, and of Mrs Heather Loxton, of Bere Regis, Dorset.

DAUGHTERS LIVING

Hon Antonia Helena Renshaw, *b* 1957; *ed* Benenden, St Andrews Univ, and Harvard Univ.
Hon Candida Juliet Renshaw, *b* 1961; *ed* Benenden, and Bristol Univ.

BLANCH, BARONY OF (Blanch) (Extinct 1994)

SON LIVING OF LIFE BARON

Hon Timothy Julian Yarworth, *b* 1953; *ed* King's Sch, Rochester, and Keble Coll, Oxford: *m* 1982, Monica Mary, da of late H. M. Keeble, and has issue living, Joseph Hugh, *b* 1987, — Rosa Katherine, *b* 1984. *Residence* – Ty Wrth Yr Eglwys, Glynogwr, Blackmill, nr Bridgend, Mid Glamorgan, S Wales.

DAUGHTERS LIVING AND DECEASED OF LIFE BARON

Hon Susan Elizabeth, *b* 1946; *d* 1992.

Hon Hilary Jane, *b* 1948.

Hon Angela Francesca Hayward, *b* 1950: *m* 1974, Timothy Michael Ambrose, and has issue living, Bethany, *b* 1978, — Emily, *b* 1981. *Residence* – 7 Plewlands Av, Edinburgh.

Hon Alison Sarah, *b* 1955.

WIDOW LIVING OF LIFE BARON

BRENDA GERTRUDE (*Baroness Blanch*), da of late William Arthur Coyte: *m* 1943, Baron Blanch, PC, DD (Life Baron), who *d* 1994. *Residence* – Bryn Celyn, The Level, Shenington, nr Banbury, Oxon OX15 6NA.

Blandford, Marquess of; son of Duke of Marlborough.

BLATCH, BARONESS (Blatch) (Life Baroness 1987)

EMILY MAY BLATCH, CBE, PC, da of Stephen Joseph Triggs; *b* 24 July 1937; *ed* Secondary Sch for Girls, Prenton, Birkenhead, and Huntingdonshire Coll; Air Traffic Control Assist WRAF 1955-59, and A&AEE Boscombe Down 1959-63; Member Board of Peterborough Devpt Corpn 1984-88, Cambs CC 1977-89 (Leader 1981-85), Association of County Councils 1981-85, European Econ and Social Cttee 1986-87; Chm Anglo-American Community Relations Cttee RAF Alconbury 1985-92; Baroness in Waiting Jan-Sept 1990, Under Sec of State Dept of the Environment 1990-91, Min of State Dept of the Environment 1991-92, Min of State for Educn and Science 1992-94, Min of State Home Office 1994-97; FRSA 1985; Rotarian Award of Paul Harris Fellow 1992; *cr* CBE 1983, PC 1993 and *Baroness Blatch*, of Hitchingbrooke, co Cambs (Life Baroness) 1987: *m* 1963, John Richard Blatch, AFC, and has issue (with one son deceased).
Residence – Red House, High St, Spaldwick, Cambridgeshire.

SONS LIVING

Hon James Richard, *b* 1967.

Hon Andrew Edward, *b* 1968.

DAUGHTER LIVING

Hon Elizabeth Anne, *b* (twin) 1968.

BLEASE, BARON (Blease) (Life Baron 1978)

WILLIAM JOHN BLEASE, son of William John Blease, *b* 28 May 1914; *ed* McClure Public Elementary Sch, New Univ of Ulster (Hon DLitt), and Queen's Univ, Belfast (Hon LLD); MBIM; Hon Fell BIM; N Ireland Officer, Irish Congress of Trade Unions 1959-76; a Member of Standing Advisory Commn for Human Rights, N Ireland 1977-79, and of Indep Broadcasting Authority 1974-79; a Member of N Ireland Economic Council 1964-76; a JP for Belfast; *cr Baron Blease*, of Cromac, City of Belfast (Life Baron) 1978: *m* 1939, Sarah Evelyn, who *d* 1995, da of William Caldwell, and has issue.

SONS LIVING

Hon William Victor, *b* 1942: *m* 1969, Rose Mary, da of Alan Seaton, and has issue.
Hon Maurice Caldwell, *b* 1944: *m* 1967, Mary, da of Philip Carrol, and has issue.
Hon Paul Charles, *b* 1953: *m* 1979, Ann, da of Howard Jennings, and has issue.

DAUGHTER LIVING

Hon Gillian Sarah, *b* 1948: *m* 1972, John Compton, and has issue.

BLEDISLOE, VISCOUNT (Bathurst) (Viscount UK 1935)

Hold to thy faith

CHRISTOPHER HILEY LUDLOW BATHURST, QC, 3rd Viscount; *b* 24 June 1934; *s* 1979; *ed* Eton, and Trin Coll, Oxford; Bar Gray's Inn 1959; QC 1978; late Lt 11th Hus; Pres San Moritz Tobogganing Club since 1991; is Lord of the Manors of Lydney, Purton and Aylburton: *m* 1962 (*m diss* 1986), Elizabeth Mary, da of Sir Edward Walter Thompson, of Gatacre Park, Bridgnorth, Shropshire (*see* E Coventry, colls, 1968 Edn), and has issue.

Arms – Sable, two bars ermine, in chief three crosses-patée or. Crest – A dexter arm in mail embowed, the hand proper grasping a club with spikes or. Supporters – One either side a bull guardant, ringed and a line therefrom reflexed over the back or.
Seat – Lydney Park, Gloucestershire. *Chambers*, Fountain Court, Temple, EC4. *Club* – Garrick.

SONS LIVING

Hon RUPERT EDWARD LUDLOW, *b* 13 March, 1964; *ed* Eton; painter.
Hon Otto Benjamin Charles, *b* 1971.

DAUGHTER LIVING

Hon Matilda Blanche, *b* 1967: *m* 1995, Charles L. H. Clark, son of Leslie Clark, of Merle Common, Surrey, and has issue living, a son, *b* 1998.

WIDOW LIVING OF SECOND VISCOUNT

JOAN (*Viscountess Bledisloe*) (East Wing, Lydney Park, Glos; 14 Mulberry Walk, SW3), da of late Otto Krishaber: *m* 1933, the 2nd Viscount, QC, who *d* 1979.

WIDOW LIVING OF SON OF SECOND VISCOUNT

(Mary) Cornelia, da of Andrew Kirkwood McCosh, of Culter Allers, Biggar, Lanarkshire: *m* 1967, Hon David Charles Lopes Bathurst, who *d* 1992, and has issue (see colls, infra). *Residence* – South Lodge, East Heath Rd, NW3.

COLLATERAL BRANCH LIVING

Issue of late Hon David Charles Lopes Bathurst, yr son of 2nd Viscount, *b* 1937, *d* 1992: *m* 1967, (Mary) Cornelia (ante), da of Andrew Kirkwood McCosh, of Culter Allers, Biggar, Lanarkshire:— Arabella Rose, *b* 1969. —— Lucy Celeste, *b* 1974. —— Flora Elizabeth, *b* 1977.

PREDECESSORS – **(1)** CHARLES BATHURST, GCMG, KBE, PC, son of late Charles Bathurst, of Lydney Park, Gloucestershire; *b* 1867; Bar Inner Temple 1892; was Parliamentary Sec, Min of Food 1916-17, Chm of Central Chamber of agriculture 1915, Director of Sugar Distribution 1918-19, Parliamentary Sec to Min of Agriculture 1924-28, Gov-Gen and Com-in-Ch of New Zealand 1930-35, and Pro-Chancellor of Bristol Univ 1934-47; *cr Viscount Bledisloe*, of Lydney, co Gloucester (peerage of United Kingdom) 1935: *m* 1st, 1898, Hon Bertha Susan Lopes, who *d* 1926, da of 1st Baron Ludlow; 2ndly, 1928, Hon Alina Kate Elaine (a DGStJ), who *d* 1956, da of 1st Baron Glentawe, and widow of Thomas Cooper-Smith; *d* 1958; *s* by his el son **(2)** BENJAMIN LUDLOW, 2nd Viscount, *b* 1899; QC and a Bencher Lincoln's Inn: *m* 1933, Joan, only da of late Otto Krishaber; *d* 1979; *s* by his el son **(3)** CHRISTOPHER HILEY LUDLOW, 3rd Viscount and present peer.

Bligh, family name of Earl of Darnley.

BLYTH, BARON (Blyth) (Baron UK 1907, Bt UK 1895)
(Name and Title pronounced "Bly")

I hope for better things

ANTHONY AUDLEY RUPERT BLYTH, 4th Baron and 4th Baronet: *b* 3 June 1931; *s* 1977: *m* 1st, 1954 (*m diss* 1962), Elizabeth Dorothea, da of Robert T. Sparrow, of Vancouver, BC, Canada; 2ndly, 1963, Oonagh Elizabeth Ann, yr da of late William Henry Conway, of Dundrum, Dublin, and has had issue by 1st and 2nd *m*.

Arms – Azure, on a mount vert a bull statant argent, ringed and chained or, on a chief arched of the fourth, a stag's head erased proper between two annulets gules. **Crest** – In front of a stag's head erased, gorged with a wreath of vine leaves proper, three roses argent. **Supporters** – Two stags proper, semée of annulets or, each gorged with a wreath of vine leaves, fructed proper.
Residence – Blythwood Estate, Athenry, co Galway.

SONS LIVING AND DECEASED (By 1st marriage)

†*Hon* Riley Audley John, *b* 4 March 1955; *ed* Portora Royal Sch: *m* 1st, 1979 (*m diss* 1984), Peggy, da of John Scanlon; 2ndly, 1986, Ernestine I. Ranking; *d* 23 June 1996.

(By 2nd marriage)

Hon JAMES AUDLEY IAN, *b* 13 Nov 1970.

DAUGHTERS LIVING (By 1st marriage)

Hon Marcia Edna Dorothea, *b* 1956.
Hon Alexandra, *b* 1957.

(By 2nd marriage)

Hon Lucinda Audley Jane, *b* 1966.

BROTHER LIVING

Hon Adrian Ulrick Christopher David, *b* 1944; *ed* Sebright Sch, and Northants Coll of Agric, Engine Reconditioner: *m* 1966, Patricia Maureen, da of Desmond C. Southey, of Northampton, and has issue living, Mark Terence, *b* 1969, — Ian Christopher, *b* 1975, — Sarah Ursula, *b* 1967, — Verena Rosemary, *b* 1971, — Natasha Rachael, *b* 1973: *m* 1996, William J. C. Hemmings, elder son of Peter Hemmings, of Pasadena, Calif, USA.

SISTERS LIVING

Hon Tanya Ormonde Audley, *b* 1929; SRN. *Residence* – Rockfield House, Athenry, co Galway.

Hon Barbara Edna Patricia, *b* 1936: *m* 1966, Aidan William Doyle, MRCVS, who *d* 1991, yst son of Martin E. Doyle, of Hill View, Athy, co Kildare, and has issue living, Nicholas Richard, *b* 1968, — Fiona Sarah, *b* 1971.

Hon Anne Shelagh Jennifer (twin), *b* 1936. *Residence* – Rockfield House, Athenry, co Galway.

PREDECESSORS – **(1)** JAMES Blyth, el son of late James Blyth, of Chelmsford, Essex by Caroline, da of late Henry Gilbey (Gilbey, Bt), of Bishop's Stortford, Herts; *b* 1841; was a Director of W. and A. Gilbey, wine merchants, of The Pantheon, Oxford Street, W, and Vice-Pres R So of Arts; deeply interested in agriculture and farming, and a recognized authority on vine culture and commerce connected therewith; *cr* a Baronet (UK, of Blythwood) 1895, and *Baron Blyth*, of Blythwood, Stansted Mountfitchet, co Essex (peerage of UK) 1907: *m* 1865, Eliza, who *d* 1894, da of William Mooney, of Clontarf, co Dublin; *d* 1925; *s* by his el son **(2)** HERBERT WILLIAM, 2nd Baron; *b* 1868: *m* 1927, Sylvia Mary (COLE), who *d* 1974 (having *m* 3rdly, 1947, Major Chave Charles Nainby Luxmoore, who *d* 1984), da of late Edwin E. Dennis; *d* 1943; *s* by his nephew **(3)** IAN AUDLEY JAMES (son of late Hon JAMES Audley Blyth, 2nd son of 1st Baron), 3rd Baron, *b* 1905: *m* 1928, Edna Myrtle, who *d* 1952, da of Ernest Lewis, of Wellington, NZ, *d* 1977; *s* by his el son **(4)** ANTHONY AUDLEY RUPERT, 4th Baron and present peer.

BLYTH OF ROWINGTON, BARON (Blyth) (Life Baron 1995)

JAMES BLYTH, son of Daniel Blyth, of Kilbirnie, Ayrshire; *b* 8 May 1940; *ed* Spiers Sch, and Glasgow Univ (MA 1963); Hon LLD Nottingham 1992; Mobil Oil Ltd 1963-69; General Foods Ltd 1969-71, Mars Ltd 1971-74, Dir and Gen Manager Lucas Batteries Ltd 1974-77, Lucas Aerospace Ltd 1977-81, Dir Joseph Lucas Ltd 1977-81, Head of Defence Sales, Ministry of Defence 1981-85, Man Dir Plessey Electronic Systems 1985-86, Ch Exec The Plessey Co plc 1986-87, Chief Executive The Boots Co plc 1987-98, since when Chm; non-exec Dir Imperial Group plc 1984-86, Cadbury-Schweppes plc 1986-90, British Aerospace 1990-94, Anixter Inc since 1995, Nat West Bank since 1998, and Diageo plc since 1999; Memb Council SBAC 1977-81, Chm Advisory Panel on Citizens' Charter 1991-97, Pres ME Assoc 1988-93, Gov London Business Sch 1987-96 (Fellow 1997), FRSA, Liveryman, Coachmakers' and Coach Harness Makers' Co; *cr* Kt 1985, and *Baron Blyth of Rowington*, of Rowington, co Warwicks (Life Baron) 1995: *m* 1967, Pamela Anne Campbell, da of Thomas Campbell Dixon, of Stoke-on-Tern, Shropshire, and has had issue.

Arms – Gyronny of twelve gules and argent a horse rampant sable langued gules. **Crest** – Out of an eastern crown gules a dexter arm embowed in armour the hand gauntletted proper grasping by its blade a sword pointing downwards all argent and holding to the blade by its stalk leaved vert a double rose argent upon gules barbed and seeded proper. **Supporters** – On either side a unicorn reguardant argent armed and unguled or in the mouth a double rose argent upon gules barbed seeded and leaved proper.
Address – c/o House of Lords, SW1A 0PW. *Clubs* – East India, Queen's, Royal Automobile.

SON DECEASED

Campbell Frederik, *b* and *d* 1970.

DAUGHTER LIVING

Hon Abigail Ann, *b* 1976.

BLYTON, BARONY OF (Blyton) (Extinct 1987)

DAUGHTERS LIVING OF LIFE BARON

Hon Jane (139 Brockley Av, S Shields, Tyne and Wear), *b* 1920: *m* 1943, John Johansen, who *d* 1955, and has issue.
Hon Marion Rose, *b* 1926: *m* 1948, John Plank, of 36 Gerald St, S Shields, Tyne and Wear, and has issue.
Hon Rita, *b* 1930: *m* 1954, Andrew Scott, of 67 Australia Grove, S Shields, Tyne and Wear, and has issue.

BOARDMAN, BARON (Boardman) (Life Baron 1980)

THOMAS GRAY BOARDMAN, MC, TD, son of John Clayton Boardman; *b* 12 Jan 1919; *ed* Bromsgrove Sch; DL Northants 1977, High Sheriff 1979-80; admitted a solicitor 1947; Min for Industry, Dept of Trade and Industry 1972-74; Chief Sec to Treasury 1974; Chm Chamberlain Phipps Ltd 1968-72; Dir Allied Breweries Ltd 1968-72 and 1974-1976 (Vice-Chm since 1975); Pres Assoc of British Chambers of Commerce 1977-80; Dir The Steetley Co Ltd 1975-83, Chm 1978-83; Dir National Westminster Bank plc since 1979 (Chm 1983-89); Dir MEPC Ltd 1980-89; Advisory Board LEK Partnership 1990-97; Chm Cttee of London and Scottish Bankers 1987-89; Chm Heron International NV 1993-95; HM Lieut City of London since 1989; Lt-Col Comdg Northants Yeo; served in NW Europe (MC 1944); MP (*C*) for Leicester SW 1967-74, and for Leicester S Feb-Sept 1974; *cr Baron Boardman*, of Welford, co Northants (Life Baron) 1980: *m* 1948, Norah Mary Deirdre, only da of late Hubert Vincent Gough, of Pangbourne, Reading, Berks, and widow of John Henry Chaworth-Musters, and has issue.

Arms – Azure on a fesse embattled between in chief two horses salient and in base a boar's head couped argent three roses gules barbed and seeded proper. **Crest** – A demi-horse argent maned crined and hooved or about its neck by the strings of a purse azure tasselled gold, mantled azure doubled or. **Supporters** – Dexter, a lion reguardant or head and mane gules gorged with a collar sable bezanty. Sinister, a horse rampant argent and maned crined and hooved or with a collar sable bezanty.
Residences – The Manor House, Welford, Northants NN6 6HX; 29 Tufton Court, Tufton St, London SW1P 3QH. *Club* – Cavalry and Guards.

SONS LIVING

Hon Anthony Hubert Gray (Lodge Farm, Hall Lane, Welford, Northants), *b* 1949; *m* 1977, Catherine, da of T. W. Penn, of Denton, Northants, and has had issue, three das.
Hon Nigel Patrick Gray (Tufnell Park, N7), *b* 1950; *m* 1975, Sarah, da of T. A. Coslett, of Cambridge, and has had issue, Hugo, *b* 1990, — Tamsin, *b* 1980, — Charlotte, *b* 1981, — Rebecca, *b* 1984, — Victoria, *b* and *d* 1985, — Cordelia, *b* 1987, — Elizabeth, *b* 1992.

DAUGHTER LIVING

Hon Grania Janet Gray, *b* 1955; *m* 1981, Capt Hon Rupert Edward Henry Law, late Coldm Gds, el son of 8th Baron Ellenborough, and has issue (see that title).

BOLINGBROKE and ST JOHN, VISCOUNT (St John) (Viscount GB 1712, Bt E 1611)
(Name and Title pronounced "Bullingbrook and Sinjun")

NEC·QUÆRERE·NEC·SPERNERE·HONOREM

Neither to seek nor to despise honours

KENNETH OLIVER MUSGRAVE ST JOHN, 7th Viscount, and 11th Baronet; *b* 22 March 1927; *s* 1974; *ed* Eton; patron of one living; a Fellow of Aust Inst of Travel; Pres of Travel Agents Assocn of NZ 1966-68; Dir of World Assocn of Travel Agencies 1968-75, and Chm of Australian Council of Tour Wholesalers 1972-74; Dir of Italian Importing Co: *m* 1st, 1953 (*m diss* 1972), Patricia Mary, da of B. J. McKenna, of Christchurch, NZ; 2ndly, 1972 (*m diss* 1987), Jainey Anne, da of the late Alexander Duncan McRae, of Timaru, NZ, and has issue by 1st and 2nd *m*.

𝔄rms – Argent, on a chief gules two mullets or. 𝔆rest – On a mount vert, a falcon rising or, ducally gorged gules. 𝔖upporters – *Dexter*, a falcon, wings displayed, or, ducally gorged gules; *sinister*, an eagle, wings displayed, or, charged on the breast with the hames, an ancient badge of the family of *Tregoze*.
Residence – 15 Tonbridge Mews (PO Box 25.069), Shrewsbury St, Christchurch, NZ. *Club* – Christchurch (Christchurch, NZ).

SONS LIVING (*By 1st marriage*)

Hon HENRY FITZROY, *b* 18 May 1957.

(By 2nd marriage)

Hon Oliver John Beauchamp, *b* 1972.
Hon Nicholas Alexander Mowbray, *b* 1974.

SISTER LIVING

Antonia Josephine (c/o Midland Bank, 799 Fulham Rd, SW6), *b* 1933: *m* 1st, 1955 (*m diss* 1966), Henry Wilson; 2ndly, 1967, Peter Johnson, and has issue living (by 2nd *m*), Melanie Joanne, *b* 1967.

COLLATERAL BRANCHES LIVING

Grandchildren of late Maj John Henry St John, 2nd son of Hon Ferdinand St John (infra):—
Issue of late Henry Warren St John, *b* 1860, *d* 1931: *m* 1916, Justina Margaret, who *d* 1969, da of late Duncan Mackenzie, of Hill View, East Grinstead:—
Margaret Irene, *b* 1917: *m* 1939 (*m diss* 1947), Gerald Francis William Matthews, and has issue living, Texicia (Scatwell, 41 Brook Rd, Horsham, W Sussex), *b* 1940: *m* 1974, Tony Hodson, and has issue living, Caroline Rose *b* 1975, Sophie Louise *b* 1977, — Wendy (Flat C, 11 The Goffs, Eastbourne, Sussex), *b* 1941. *Residence* – Ibstock, Rowplatt Lane, Felbridge, nr East Grinstead RH19 2NY.

Issue of late Walter Cecil Hompesch St John, *b* 1867, *d* 1955: *m* 1908, Maria Salome Rodrigues, who *d* 1930:—
Walter Warren (Bº JM Paz-Ed 7-4º P-Dpto 27 (cp 1772), Villa Celina, Buenos Aires, Argentina), *b* 1921: *m* 1949, Lida Goicoechea, and has issue living, Henry William, *b* 1950: *m* 1977 (*m diss* 1981), Silvia Mazzoni, and has issue living, German Andres *b* 1980, — Alice, *b* 1950; doctor: *m* 1974, Dr Alejandro Funes Lorea, of Congreso 643, Haedo, Prov Buenos Aires, Argentina, and has issue living, Paulo *b* 1978, Tristan *b* 1989, Clara *b* 1976, Maria Guadalupe *b* 1980, Marianna *b* 1982. —— Lila Ramona del Rosario, *b* 1910: *m* 1935, Dr Ernesto Christensen, of Entre Rios 166, Santiago del Estero, Argentina, and has issue living, Eduardo Ernesto (Entre Rios 166, Santiago del Estero, Argentina), *b* 1936; a lawyer: *m* 1974, Olga Vieyra, and has issue living, Alexander *b* 1976, Edward *b* 1979, — Lilian Margarita, *b* 1943: *m* 1965, Rodolfo Diedrich, forest engr, of San Isidro 1737, Bº San Francisco, 4400 Salta, Argentina, and has issue living, Rodolfo Guillermo *b* 1967: *m* 19—, Fabina Ledesma (and has issue living, Emilia *b* 1997), Alejandro Emilio *b* 1973, Eduardo Ernesto *b* (twin) 1973, Lilian Constanza *b* 1966: *m* 19—, Gastón Duba (and has issue living, Gastón *b* 1990, María Constanza *b* (twin) 1990), María Cristina *b* 1971: *m* 19—, Alvaro Arce (and has issue living, María del Pilar *b* 1993). —— Rosa Pastora (Madero 755, CP 1408 Buenos Aires, Argentina), *b* 1916: *m* 1940, Ubaldo Casimiro García, agron engr (Inter-American Agric Medal of OAS, Croix de Mérite Agric, France, Hon Agric Economist Texas Univ), and has issue living, Guillermo Ubaldo, *b* 1946; industrialist: *m* 1st, 1975 (*m diss* 1985), Norma Isabel Diez; 2ndly, 1985, Patricia Mónica Casto, and has issue living (by 2nd *m*), Christian Guillermo *b* 1989, Cintia Analía *b* 1986, — Graciela Salomé, *b* 1941: *m* 1970, Alfredo Pinto, of Cochicó 781, CP 1408, Buenos Aires, and has issue living, Paula Marcela *b* 1971, María Alejandra *b* 1972, Natalia Virginia *b* 1973, María Constanza *b* 1979, — María Rosa del Cármen, *b* 1942: *m* 1964, Guillermo Teijo, of Calle 16 No 785, Balcarce, Prov de Buenos Aires, and has issue living, Alejandro *b* 1966, Esteban Guillermo *b* 1977, Alfonso Ezequiel *b* 1978, María Victoria *b* 1971; Prof of English, — Teresa Pastora, *b* 1945: *m* 19—, Germán Aznar, Capitan de Fragata, Argentine Navy, who *d* 1986, of Cantilo 155, Haedo, Prov de Buenos Aires, and has issue living, Germán Agustín *b* 1971, Federico *b* 1972, María Lidia *b* 1970, María Lucila *b* 1975.

Issue of late Edward Archibald St John, *b* 1876, *d* 1949: *m* 1922, Clare Esmeralda Magno, of Buenos Aires, Argentina:—
Zeline Mabel Alice, *b* 1923: *m* 19—, — Morán, who *d* 19—, of Olazabal 3650-7ºD, Capital Federal, BA, Argentina. —— Gloria Alida, *b* 1924: *m* 1953, Prof Cesar Guerresi, who *d* 19—, and has issue living, Eduardo, *b* 1968. *Residence* – Calle Perú 1350, Buenos Aires 3ᵉʳᵒB, Argentina.

Grandchildren of late Sir Frederick Robert St John, KCMG, yst son of late Hon Ferdinand St John, 2nd son of 3rd Viscount:—

See E Orkney.

Granddaughters of late Major George Frederick Berkeley St John, 3rd son of late Gen Hon Frederick St John, 2nd son of 2nd Viscount:—
Issue of late Henry Augustus Bolingbroke St John, *b* 1847, *d* 1921: *m* 18—, Anna, da of late Maj — Henderson, HEICS:—
Mary Constance, *b* 1889. *Residence* – 1171 Newport Avenue, Victoria, British Columbia. —— Margaret, *b* 1896: *m* 1928, Gordon Sweet.

Grandchildren of late Alexander Storey St John, 3rd son of late Frederick Charles St John, eldest son of late Charles William George St John, 5th and yst son of late Gen Hon Frederick St John (ante):—
Issue of late Alexander Bolingbroke St John, *b* 1910, *d* 1968: *m* 1937, Gladys Spencer, who *d* 1981:—
Stewart Bolingbroke, *b* 1942. —— Janet Eleanor, *b* 1938: *m* 1962, Michael Stanley Hall, of 38 The Ridgeway, Tonbridge, Kent TN10 4NJ, and has issue living, Stephen Philip St John, *b* 1969, — Wendy Deborah, *b* 1964, — Alison Judith, *b* 1967.

Grandchildren of late Adm Henry Craven St John, 2nd son of late Charles William George St John (ante):—
Issue of late Vice-Adm Francis Gerald St John, CB, MVO, *b* 1869, *d* 1947: *m* 1st, 1898, Winifred Jessie, who *d* 1898, da of George Haward Trollope; 2ndly 1902, Emily Frances Louise, who *d* 1969, el da of late Allan Turner, of Bombay:—
(By 2nd *m*) Stratford Allan Gerald (Thornbury, Shamley Green, Guildford, Surrey), RN, *b* 1911; Capt 1956; European War 1939-44, operations off Norway and Sicily (despatches twice): *m* 1942, Honor Madeleine, who *d* 1997, da of Philip Smiles, of Belfast. —— Betty Allane, *b* 1905. —— Peggy Katharine Mary, *b* 1908: *m* 1st, 1939 (*m diss* 1948), Maj Leslie Fairfax d'Arch Smith; 2ndly, 1988, Colin Rosser Crickmay, of 2 Lynchen's Close, Bembridge, Isle of Wight, and has issue living (by 1st *m*), Nicola Lesley, *b* 1940: *m* 1962, Charles Quentin James, of Sandy Lane Farm, Parkmill, Swansea, W Glam, and has issue living, Andrew Thurstan Trewartha *b* 1965: *m* 1997, Deborah Lee, Simon Charles Trewartha *b* 1969, Emma Charlotte *b* 1963: *m* 1994, Douglas Smith, Sophie Louise *b* 1971.

Descendants, if any, of Edward George St John (*b* 1870), only son of late Edward George St John (*b* 1840), of Nebraska, USA, 3rd son of late Charles William George St John (ante).

PREDECESSORS – OLIVER St John (a descendant of Oliver St John, second son of Sir Oliver St John of Bletso (*see* B St John of Bletso)), who obtained considerable renown in the wars of Elizabeth and James in Ireland, was *cr Viscount Grandison* 1620, in peerage of Ireland (with remainder to the issue of his niece Barbara, wife of Sir Edward Villiers), and *Baron Tregoze* (peerage of England) 1626; *dsp*, when the Barony became ext and the Viscountcy (now merged in the Earldom of Jersey) descended to William, son of Barbara (ante). His nephew **(1)** JOHN, brother of Barbara (ante), a zealous royalist, had three sons slain in fighting under the royal standard; *cr* a *Baronet* 1611; *s* by his grandson **(2)** *Sir* JOHN, 2nd Bt, *dsp* 1656; *s* by his uncle **(3)** *Sir* WALTER, 3rd Bt, MP for co Wilts; *d* 1708; *s* by his son **(4)** *Sir* Henry, 4th Bt; *cr Baron St John of Battersea* and *Viscount St John* (peerage of Great Britain) 1716, with remainder to his 2nd and 3rd sons, his el son Henry, a famous statesman and writer, having in 1712 been *cr Baron St John*, of Lydiard Tregoze, and *Viscount Bolingbroke* (peerage of Great Britain), with remainder to his father and his father's issue; in 1714 Viscount Bolingbroke was attainted, but in 1723 he was restored in blood, and in 1725 his estates were restored without his honours; Viscount St John *d* 1742, and was *s* by his 2nd son **(5)** JOHN, 2nd Viscount St John; *d* 1748; *s* by his son **(6)** FREDERICK, 3rd Viscount St John, who in 1751, on the demise of his uncle Henry without issue, *s* to the Barony of St John of Lydiard Tregoze and the Viscountcy of Bolingbroke; *d* 1787; *s* by his son **(7)** GEORGE RICHARD, 3rd Viscount Bolingbroke; *d* 1824; *s* by his son **(8)** HENRY, 4th Viscount Bolingbroke, *b* 1786: *m* 1812, Maria, da of Sir Henry Paulet St John Mildmay, 3rd Bt; *d* 1851; *s* by his son **(9)** HENRY MILDMAY, 5th Viscount Bolingbroke, *b* 1820: *m* 1893, Mary Emily Elizabeth, who *d* 1940, da of Robert Howard; *d* 1899; *s* by his son **(10)** VERNON HENRY, 6th Viscount Bolingbroke and St John, *b* 1896 (claim admitted by Cttee of Privileges of House of Lords 1922, and writ of summons issued April 1926): *m* 1950 (*m diss* 1952), Valenzina, da of late Frederick William Frohawk, of Sutton, Surrey; *d* 1974; *s* by his kinsman **(11)** KENNETH OLIVER MUSGRAVE (el son by 2nd *m* of Capt Geoffrey Robert St John, MC, el son of Henry Percy St John, el son of Rev Maurice William Ferdinand St John, DD, el son of Hon Ferdinand St John, 2nd son of 3rd Viscount), 7th Viscount and present peer; also Baron St John of Lydiard Tregoze, and Baron St John of Battersea.

BOLTON, BARON (Orde-Powlett) (Baron GB 1797)
(Name pronounced "Ord-Pawlett")

Love loyalty

RICHARD WILLIAM ALGAR ORDE-POWLETT, 7th Baron; *b* 11 July 1929; *s* 1963; *ed* Eton, and Trin Coll, Camb (BA 1951); JP N Riding of Yorks 1959-78; Chm, Yorks Branch, R Forestry Soc 1963-64; a Dir of Yorkshire General Life Assurance Ltd, late Chm of Waterers Group, and Yorks Soc of Agric: *m* 1st, 1951 (*m diss* 1981), Hon Christine Helena Weld-Forester, da of the 7th Baron Forester; 2ndly, 1981, Masha Anne, only da of Maj Francis Edward Hudson, TD, of Winterfield House, Bedale, Yorks; 3rdly, 1991, Mrs Lavinia Fenton, da of late William Edward Wright, and has issue by 1st *m*.

Arms – Sable: three swords in pile, points downwards argent, pommels and hilts or, on a canton argent, an escutcheon sable, charged with a salmon hauriant proper. **Crest** – A falcon rising or, ducally gorged azure, charged on the breast and on each wing with an estoile gules, and holding in the beak a salmon proper. **Supporters** – *Dexter*, a hind proper, ducally gorged or, and charged on the shoulder with a white rose; *sinister*, a Cornish chough proper, also charged on the shoulder with a white rose proper.
Seat – Bolton Hall, Leyburn, Yorkshire DL8 4UF. *Clubs* – Turf, Flyfishers', Central African Deep Sea Fishers', White's, Sloane.

SONS LIVING (By 1st marriage)

Hon HARRY ALGAR NIGEL (The Corner House, Wensley, Leyburn, N Yorks), *b* 14 Feb 1954; *ed* Eton: *m* 1977, Philippa A., da of Maj Peter L. Tapply, of Wanstead, Essex, and has issue living, Thomas, *b* 16 July 1979, — William Benjamin, *b* 1981, — Nicholas Mark, *b* 1985.
Hon Michael Brooke, *b* 1959: *m* 1985, Kate Mary, da of George William Laing, of Newsham, N Yorks, and has issue living, James Michael, *b* 1987, — Emma Katherine, *b* 1988. *Residence* – Springdale, Cove, Tiverton, Devon.

DAUGHTER LIVING (By 1st marriage)

Hon Rosemary Victoria, *b* 1952: *m* 1974, (John) Richard Bentley North, of RMB 590 Boddington, W Australia 6390, and has issue living, Charles Richard, *b* 1975, — James William, *b* 1981, — Veronica Caroline *b* 1977.

BROTHER LIVING

Hon Patrick Christopher (Little Bordeaux, Little Chesterford, Saffron Walden, Essex), *b* 1931; *ed* Eton, and Jesus Coll, Camb (MA), ARICS; Council Member Timber Growers' Organisation, E England, until 1993; Partner J. Rothschild Partnership since 1994: *m* 1962, Elizabeth Jane, da of A. S. Kent, and has issue living, Rosamund Jane, *b* 1964: *m* 1999, Martin G. F. Lupton, elder son of Geoffrey Lupton, of Twickenham, — Heather Victoria, *b* 1966.

PREDECESSORS – (1) *Rt Hon* THOMAS Orde, son of late John Orde, DL, of Morpeth: *m* 1778, Jean Mary Powlett, natural da of Charles, 5th Duke of Bolton (*see* M Winchester), and having *s* to his estates, assumed in 1795 by sign manual the additional surname of Powlett; *cr Baron Bolton* (peerage of Great Britain) 1797; *d* 1807; *s* by his el son (2) WILLIAM, 2nd Baron: *m* 1810, Hon Maria, who *d* 1863, da of 1st Baron Dorchester; *d* 1850; *s* by his nephew (3) WILLIAM HENRY, 3rd Baron (son of late Hon Thomas Orde-Powlett, 2nd son of 1st Baron), *b* 1818: *m* 1844, Letitia, who *d* 1882, da of Col Crawfurd, of Newfield, Ayrshire; *d* 1895; *s* by his el son (4) WILLIAM THOMAS, 4th Baron, *b* 1845: *m* 1868, Lady Algitha Frederica Mary Lumley, who *d* 1919, el da of 9th Earl of Scarbrough; *d* 1922; *s* by his son (5) WILLIAM GEORGE ALGAR, 5th Baron; *b* 1869; Lord-Lieut for N Riding of Yorkshire; MP for Yorkshire, N Riding, Richmond Div (C) 1910-18: *m* 1893, Hon Elizabeth Mary Gibson, who *d* 1943, da of 1st Baron Ashbourne, *d* 1944; *s* by his son (6) NIGEL AMYAS, 6th Baron; *b* 1900: *m* 1928, Victoria Mary, who *d* 1933, da of Henry Montagu Villiers, MVO (E Clarendon, colls); *d* 1963; *s* by his el son, (7) RICHARD WILLIAM ALGAR, 7th Baron and present peer.

BONHAM-CARTER, BARONY OF (Bonham Carter) (Extinct 1994)

DAUGHTERS LIVING OF LIFE BARON

Hon Jane Mary, *b* 1957.

Hon Virginia Leslie, *b* 1959: *m* 1992, Charles David William Brand, of 1 Kingswood Av, NW6 6LA, and has issue (*see* V Hampden, colls).
Hon Elizabeth Cressida, *b* 1961.

WIDOW LIVING OF LIFE BARON

LESLIE (*Baroness Bonham-Carter*), da of late Condé Nast, of New York, USA, and formerly wife of 2nd Baron St Just: *m* 1955, Baron Bonham-Carter (Life Baron), who *d* 1994. *Residence* – 13 Clarendon Rd, W11 4JB.

Booth, Sclater-, family name of Baron Basing.

BOOTHBY, BARONY OF (Boothby) (Extinct 1986)

WIDOW LIVING OF LIFE BARON

WANDA (*Baroness Boothby*), da of Giuseppe Sanna, of Sardinia: *m* 1967, as his 2nd wife, Baron Boothby, KBE (Life Baron), who *d* 1986.

Boringdon, Viscount; son of Earl of Morley.

Borodale, Lord; son of Earl Beatty.

BORRIE, BARON (Borrie) (Life Baron 1995)

GORDON JOHNSON BORRIE, son of Stanley Borrie, of Croydon, Surrey; *b* 13 March 1931; *ed* John Bright Gram Sch, Llandudno, and Manchester Univ (LLB 1950, LLM 1952), Hon LLD City of London Poly (now City of London Univ) 1989, Manchester Univ 1990, Hull Univ 1991, Dundee Univ 1993, W of England Univ 1997; Hon DUniv Nottingham Trent Univ 1996; Bar Middle Temple 1952; National Service with Army Legal Services, HQ British Commonwealth Forces, Korea 1952-54; in law practice 1954-57; Lecturer then Senior Lecturer, Coll of Law 1957-64; Senior Lecturer, Birmingham Univ 1965-68, Prof of English Law and Dir Inst of Judicial Administration 1969-76, Dean of Law Faculty 1974-76; Dir-Gen of Fair Trading 1976-92; Chm Commn on Social Justice 1992-94, Pres of Inst of Trading Standards Admin since 1992; Dir: Woolwich Building Soc since

1992, Three Valleys Water plc since 1992, Mirror Group plc since 1993, TeleWest plc since 1994, and General Utilities plc since 1998; Gov Birmingham Coll of Commerce 1966-70; formerly Memb of Law Commn Advisory Panel for Contract Law; Memb: Parole Board 1971-74, Council of Consumers' Assoc 1972-75, and Equal Opportunities Commn 1975-76; Hon Memb SPTL 1989, FRSA 1982; author of *Commercial Law* 1962, 6th edn 1988, *The Development of Consumer Law and Policy* 1984, and other works in joint authorship; QC 1986; *cr* Knt 1982, and *Baron Borrie*, of Abbots Morton, co Hereford and Worcester (Life Baron) 1995: *m* 1960, Dorene, da of Herbert Toland, of Toronto, Canada.

Residence – Manor Farm, Abbots Morton, Worcs WR7 4NA.

BORTHWICK, LORD (Borthwick of that Ilk) (Lord S ca 1450)

JOHN HUGH BORTHWICK OF THAT ILK, 24th Lord; *b* 14 Nov 1940; *s* 1996; Baron of Heriotmuir, Midlothian, and Laird of Crookston; Hereditary Falconer of Scotland to HM; *ed* Gordonstoun, and Edinburgh Coll of Agriculture: *m* 1974, Adelaide, only da of Archy Birkmyre, of Lower Dalchonzie, Comrie, Perthshire (*see* Birkmyre, Bt, colls), and has issue.

Arms – Argent, three cinquefoils sable. **Crest** – A moor's head couped proper wreathed argent and sable. **Supporters** – Two angels proper winged or. **Motto** – Qui conducit.
Seat – Borthwick Castle, Midlothian. *Residence* – Crookston, Heriot, Midlothian. *Club* – New (Edinburgh).

DAUGHTERS LIVING

Hon Georgina, *b* 1975.
Hon Alexandra, *b* 1977.

BROTHER LIVING

Hon (JAMES) HENRY ALEXANDER BORTHWICK OF GLENGELT (*Master of Borthwick*), *b* (twin) 14 Nov 1940; *ed* Gordonstoun, and Heriot-Watt Univ: *m* 1972, Elspeth, da of Lt-Col Allan Dunn MacConachie, of Lauder, Berwicks (*see* V Molesworth, colls, 1990 Edn), and has issue living, Malcolm Henry, *b* 1973. *Residence* – Channelkirk Cottage, Oxton, Lauder, Berwicks TD2 6PT.

COLLATERAL BRANCH LIVING

Granddaughters of late Francis Borthwick, yst son of John Borthwick of Borthwick, 13th of Crookston, who repurchased Borthwick Castle 1812 to which, had it not been alienated, he would have *s* under a settlement of 1538, 12th in descent from Hon John Borthwick, 2nd son of 1st Lord:—
Issue of late Francis John Gordon Borthwick, WS, *b* 1871, *d* 1948: *m* 1912, Eugenie Helen Franklyn, da of Edmund Stow Thompson:—
Mary Alice (*Hon Mrs Douglas D. E. Vivian*): *m* 1943, Lt-Com Hon Douglas David Edward Vivian, DSC, RN (*see* B Vivian), who *d* 1973. —— Margaret Eugenie. *m* 1944, Maj Ian Rupert Farquhar, Gren Gds (*see* Farquhar, Bt, colls).
Residence – Hamlyns, Chudleigh, S Devon.

PREDECESSORS – *Sir* William Borthwick of Borthwick, Knt, a substitute hostage for James I 1424-27, had a Crown Charter of the Lands of Borthwick 1410; his 3rd son Sir William Borthwick, 2nd of Borthwick, Knt, has a licence to build the Castle of Borthwick 1430; his son (1) Sir WILLIAM Borthwick, 3rd of Borthwick, *cr Lord Borthwick* in the Peerage of Scotland 1450-54, sat as Lord of Parliament 1455-57, was Commissioner to treat with England 1459; *d* 1483; *s* by his son (2) WILLIAM, 2nd Lord, knighted in his father's lifetime, Master of the Household to James III 1485; *d* 1503; *s* by his son (3) WILLIAM, 3rd Lord: *m* 1491, Margaret, da of John, Lord Hay of Yester; *k* at Battle of Flodden 1513; *s* by his son (4) WILLIAM, 4th Lord, to whom was entrusted the Castle of Stirling after Flodden; *d* 1543; *s* by his son (5) JOHN, 5th Lord, opposed Reformation of 1560: *m* before 1544, Isobel (who *m* 2ndly, George Preston, of Cameron, and *d* 1577), da of 8th Earl of Crawford; *d* 1566; *s* by his son (6) WILLIAM, 6th Lord; a zealous supporter of Mary, Queen of Scots: *m* before 1570, Grissel (who lodged a complaint against him for desertion and cruelty 1581, and *m* 2ndly, Walter Cairncross, of Colmslie), da of Sir Walter Scott, of Branxholm; *d* "of the French disease" 1582; *s* by his 2nd son (7) JAMES, 7th Lord, *b* 1570: *m* 1582, Margaret, el da of William, Lord Hay of Yester; *d* 1599; *s* by his son (8) JOHN, 8th Lord: *m* before 1616, Lilias, 5th da of 1st Earl of Lothian; *d* 1623; *s* by his son (9) JOHN, 9th Lord, *b* 1616; held the Castle of Borthwick against Protector Cromwell until he obtained terms of honourable surrender 1650: *m* 1649, Elizabeth, 2nd da of 3rd Earl of Lothian; *dsp* 1672, when the male line of the 4th Lord failed and his estates passed to his nephew, John Dundas, son of his sister, who was served as his heir; the title remained dormant until 1762, but the right of succession passed to the descendants of Alexander Borthwick, 3rd son of 2nd Lord, his cousin and heir male (10) WILLIAM, *de jure* 10th Lord, Major in the army: *m* 1665, Marion Moorhead; *d ca* 1687-90; *s* by his only son (11) WILLIAM, *de jure* 11th Lord, *bapt* 1666, Capt Cameronian Regt 1689, Col in the army: *m* Jean, da of Robert Ker, of Kersland; *dsp* being slain at battle of Ramillies 1706; *s* by his cousin (12) HENRY, *de jure* 12th Lord: *m* Mary, da of Sir Robert Pringle of Stitchill, 1st Bt; *d* of wounds received at battle of Ramillies 1706; *s* by his son (13) WILLIAM, *de jure* 13th

Lord; *dsp* before 1723; *s* by his brother **(14)** HENRY, 14th Lord, his right to the title was admitted by the House of Lords 1762; *dsp* 1772, when the title again became dormant, the right of succession, however, passing to his cousin and heir male **(15)** PATRICK, *de jure* 15th Lord, a merchant in Leith: *m* Marian Scott; *d* 1772; *s* by his only son **(16)** ARCHIBALD, *de jure* 16th Lord, *b* 1732, a merchant in Christiansund, Norway, and afterwards a banker in Edinburgh: *m* 1777, Margaret Nicolson, who *d* 1833, da of James Scott, CS; *s* by his son **(17)** PATRICK, *de jure* 17th Lord, *b* 1779, sometime manager of National Bank of Scotland, Edinburgh; claimed the peerage 1816: *m* 1804, Ariana, who *d* 1836, 2nd da of Cunninghame Corbet, of Tolcross and of Glasgow; *d* 1840; *s* by his el son **(18)** ARCHIBALD, *de jure* 18th Lord, *b* 1811: *m* 1840, Mary Louisa, who *d* 1868, da of John Home Home, of Longformacus; *dspms* 1863; *s* by his brother **(19)** CUNNINGHAME, 19th Lord, *b* 1813; his claim to the Lordship was allowed 1870, a Representative Peer for Scotland: *m* 1865, Harriet Alice, who *d* 1911, da of Rev Thomas Hermitage Day, of Frinsbury, Kent; *d* 1885; *s* by his only son **(20)** ARCHIBALD PATRICK THOMAS, 20th Lord, *b* 1867, a Representative Peer for Scotland, and a JP for Wigtownshire: *m* 1901, Susanna Mary (DStJ) (who *m* 2ndly, 1916, as his 2nd wife, 18th Duke of Grafton (*d* 1930), and *d* 1961), da of Sir Mark John MacTaggart Stewart, 1st Bt; *d* 1910, when the title again became dormant, the right of succession, however, passing to his kinsman **(21)** WILLIAM HENRY, 15th of Crookston (14 in descent from Hon John Borthwick, 1st of Crookston, yr son of 1st Lord Borthwick), *de jure* 21st Lord, *b* 1832: *m* 1864, Rebecca, who *d* 1887, da of Robert Cathcart; *d* 1928: *s* by his el son **(22)** HENRY, *de jure* 22nd Lord, *b* 1868: *m* 1902, Melena Florence, who *d* 1962, 4th da of Capt James Thomas Pringle of Torwoodlee, RN: *d* 1937; *s* by his only son **(23)** JOHN HENRY STUART, TD, 23rd Lord, *b* 1905; claim to Lordship admitted by Lord Lyon 1986; one of the four representative Scottish barons in HM's post-Coronation State Visit to Edinburgh, carrying the Crown Canopy; Maj RA (TA), Lt-Col 1946: *m* 1938, Margaret Frances, who *d* 1976, da of Alexander Campbell Cormack; *d* 1996; *s* by his elder (twin) son **(24)** JOHN HUGH, 24th Lord and present peer.

BORWICK, BARON (Borwick) (Baron UK 1922, Bt UK 1916)

It passes

JAMES HUGH MYLES BORWICK, MC, 4th Baron, and 4th Baronet; *b* 12 Dec 1917; *s* 1961; *ed* Eton; is Maj (ret) Highland LI; European War 1939-45 (MC): *m* 1954, Hyllarie Adalia Mary, da of late Lt-Col William Hamilton Hall Johnston, DSO, MC, DL, of Bryn-y-Groes, Bala, N Wales, and has issue.

𝕬rms – Argent, three escarbuncles fesseways sable between three bears' heads erased of the last, muzzled or. 𝕮rest – Upon a mount proper, in front of a staff raguly erect azure, a stag browsing or, attired sable. 𝕾upporters – On either side a bear sable, muzzled and charged on the shoulder with an escarbuncle or.
Residence – Leys Farm, Bircher, Leominster, Hereford HR6 0AU. *Club* – Royal Ocean Racing.

DAUGHTERS LIVING

Hon Angela Jane BORWICK, *b* 1955; has resumed her maiden name: *m* 1988 (*m diss* 1991), Charles William Heathcoat Amory, yr son of late Lt-Col Sir William Heathcoat Amory, 5th Bt. *Residence* – The Cider Mill, Bircher, Leominster, Hereford HR6 0AZ.
Hon Mary-Anne, *b* 1957. *Residence* – Mill Farm, The Fox, Purton, Swindon, Wilts SN5 9EF.
Hon Diana, *b* 1959: *m* 1995 (*m diss* 1999), Giles R. Newman, son of Lt-Col Nigel Newman, of Windsor, Berks. *Residence* – Newton Cottage, Whiteparish, Salisbury, Wilts SP5 2QQ
Hon Amanda Gwyneth Rosemary, *b* 1965: *m* 1987, Brian Wynn Parry, eldest son of P. Owen Parry, of Llandderfel, N Wales, and has issue living, Robert James William, *b* 1990, — Caroline Hyllarie Wynn, *b* 1988, — Helen Rebecca Louise Wynn, *b* 1999. *Residence* – 3 Trem Berwyn, Llandderfel, Bala, Gwynedd, N Wales LL23 7HU.

HALF-BROTHER LIVING

Hon ROBIN SANDBACH, *b* 22 March 1927; *ed* Eton; late Lt The Life Guards: *m* 1950, Hon Patricia Garnett, only da of late Baron McAlpine of Moffat (Life Baron), and has issue living, (Geoffrey Robert) James (Jamie) (1 Love Lane, EC2), *b* 7 March 1955; *ed* Eton: *m* 1981, Victoria Lorne Peta, only da of late W/Cdr Roger Dennistoun Poore, of 33 Phillimore Gdns, W8 (*see* Poore, Bt, colls), and has issue living, Edwin Dennis William *b* 1984, Thomas James Robert *b* 1987, William Robert Hugh *b* 1997, Alexandra Victoria *b* 1990, — Richard David, *b* 1960; *ed* Eton: *m* 1983, Nicole D., da of late Group Capt Ronald M. Kerr, MVO, of Westwinds, Moulsford, Oxon, and has issue living, Christian Richard Sandbach *b* 1985, Fraser James Montgomery *b* 1992, Summer Louise Molly *b* 1987, Charlotte Alexandra Nicole *b* 1989, Skye Isabella Paula *b* 1994, Lily *b* 1997, — Judith Patricia, *b* 1952: *m* 1971, Padraic Desmond Curry-Towneley-O'Hagan, 29 Barons Court Rd, W14 9DZ, and has issue (*see* B O'Hagan). *Residence* – Neptune House, Newells Lane, Bosham, Sussex PO18 8PS.

SISTERS LIVING

Hon Katharine Hilda, *b* 1914: *m* 1938, Ashton Jack Ulyate, and has had issue, Stanley Ian Robert Borwick (11 Farforth Ness Rd, Waipapa, Keri Keri, Bay of Islands, NZ), *b* 1939: *m* 1973, Margaret Mary Anne Morling, and has issue living, William Robert *b* 1975, James Ashton *b* 1976, — Raymond Grant (342B The East Coast Rd, Mairangi Bay, Auckland, NZ) *b* 1955: *m* 1979, Shelley Diana, da of Alfred Bryan Stent, of 34 Maygrane Dr, Orewa, Hibiscus Coast, NZ, and has issue living, Angus Bryan *b* 1985, Genevieve Kathryn *b* 1987, — Jacqueline Borwick, *b* 1942 *d* 1951, — Sandra Irene Borwick, *b* 1945: *m* 1972, Peter Leslie Berry, of 18 Phipson Rd, Scottsville, Pietermaritzburg 3201, Natal, S Africa, and has issue living, Cynthia Jacqueline *b* 1972, Bruce Sidney, *b* 1975.

Hon Phyllis Dorothy (16 Wood Lane, Falmouth, Cornwall), *b* 1916: *m* 1963, John A'Court Bergne, who *d* 1978.

PREDECESSORS – (1) ROBERT HUDSON Borwick, last surviving son of late George Borwick, of Morven, Torquay; *b* 1845; was a Director of George & Sons, Ltd, and a JP for co London; *cr* a *Baronet* 1916, and *Baron Borwick*, of Hawkshead, co Lancaster (peerage of United Kingdom) 1922: *m* 1872, Caroline Smith, who *d* 1936, da of late Richard Daniel Johnston, of Kurnool, Madras; *d* 1936; *s* by his el son **(2)** GEORGE, 2nd Baron, *b* 1880: *m* 1st, 1908 (*m diss* 1913), Mary Mason, da of Lewis Cruger Hassell, of New York; 2ndly, 1918 (*m diss* 1938), Dorothea Gertrude, who *d* 1986, da of late Charles Gray, of Anerley, SE; *d* 1941; *s* by his brother **(3)** ROBERT GEOFFREY, 3rd Baron; *b* 1886; formerly Lieut 20th Hus; European War 1914-18 as Capt Hertfordshire Regt and Lt RFA: *m* 1st, 1913 (*m diss* 1920), Irene Phyllis, who *d* 1969, da of late Thomas Main Patterson, of Littlebourne House, Canterbury; 2ndly, 1920, Margaret Elizabeth, who *d* 1969, da of late Gilbert Robertson Sandbach, of Stoneleigh, Rossett, Denbighshire; *d* 1961; *s* by his el son **(4)** JAMES HUGH MYLES, 4th Baron and present peer.

Boscawen, family name of Viscount Falmouth.

Bossom, Barony of (Bossom) (Extinct 1965) (see Bosson, Bt)

BOSTON, BARON (Irby) (Baron GB 1761, Bt E 1704)

TIMOTHY GEORGE FRANK BOTELER IRBY, 10th Baron, and 11th Baronet; *b* 27 March 1939; *s* 1978; *ed* Clayesmore Sch Dorset, and Southampton Univ (BSc): *m* 1967, Rhonda Anne, da of Ronald Albert Bate, of Balgowlah, NSW, and has issue.

𝔄rms – Argent, fretty sable, on a canton gules, a chaplet or. 𝔠rest – A Saracen's head in profile proper, wreathed round the temples argent and sable. 𝔖upporters – Two antelopes gules, each gorged with a chaplet or.
Residence – Cae'r Borth, Moelfre, Anglesey LL72 8NN.

SONS LIVING

Hon GEORGE WILLIAM EUSTACE BOTELER, *b* 1 Aug 1971.
Hon Jonathan Charles Timothy, *b* 1975.

DAUGHTER LIVING

Hon Rebecca Frances Anne, *b* 1970.

HALF SISTER LIVING

Hon Anne Pauline, *b* 1927: *m* 1951, Sydney James Crews, MB, BChir, FRCSE, who *d* 1994, of 86 Wentworth Rd, Harborne, Birmingham B17 9SY, and has issue living, Francis Robert, *b* 1953, — Emma Rosemary Joanna, *b* 1956, — Bridget Harriet, *b* 1963.

Honour is the reward of fidelity

DAUGHTERS LIVING OF SEVENTH BARON

Hon Rachel Elizabeth Cecily, *b* 1914: *m* 1940, Lt Darsie Rawlins, RNVR, and has issue living, Adrian Drake, *b* 1942: *m* 1st, 1968 (*m diss* 1975), Julianna, da of Eugene Simor, of Budapest; 2ndly, 1980, Jill Catharine, da of Charles William Pays, of Gillingham, Kent, and has issue living (by 1st *m*), Titus Nicholas Gabriel *b* 1968, Alexander Francis Edward *b* 1971, — Anthony Irby (14 Island Close, Staines, Middx TW18 4YZ), *b* 1944: *m* 1992, Joseline Wilson, — Diana Caroline Zoë, *b* 1949: *m* 1976, Colin Cyril Ind, of Langton Cottage, 78 Gretton Rd, Winchcombe, Glos GL54 5EL, and has issue living, Christopher Edward *b* 1980, Charlotte Emily *b* 1984, — Christina Elizabeth, *b* 1955: *m* 1st, 1983 (*m diss* 1991), Graham Joseph Tayar; 2ndly, 1992, Seamus Mulvihill, of 27 Ashmead Rd, SE8 4DY, and has issue living (by 2nd *m*), Thomas James Irby *b* 1992, Theodore Anthony Irby *b* 1997. *Residence* – 11 Framers Court, Lane End, High Wycombe HP14 3LL.

Hon Isobel Caroline, *b* 1917: *m* 1st, 1946 (*m diss* 1950), Major Vernon Owain Roberts, The Buffs; 2ndly, 1950, Edward Horatio Sales, who *d* 1988, and has issue living (by 2nd *m*), Christian Caroline (18 The Crescent, Barnes, SW13 0NN), *b* 1950: *m* 1973, David Wyndham Hughes, who *d* 1989, and has issue living, Alexander Wyndham *b* 1977, Ben Cressall *b* 1979, Alice Irby *b* 1982, Holly Irby *b* 1988, — Alexandra Josephine (27 Rowan Av, Hangleton, Hove, E Sussex), *b* 1952: *m* 1st, 1973 (*m diss* 1980), Daniel Sean Devaney; 2ndly, 1991, Martin Paul Doyle, who *d* 1993, and has issue living (by 1st *m*), Damian Julian *b* 1977, Fleur Josephine *b* 1978. *Residence* – 18 Fourth Av, Hove, E Sussex BN3 2PJ.

WIDOW LIVING OF BROTHER OF NINTH BARON (*who was raised to the rank of Baron's son* 1976)

Mrs Beryl Harrison, yst da of late Harold Mayman, of Bramsgore, Hants: *m* 1957, as his 2nd wife, Hon Anthony Paul Irby, TD, who *d* 1986. *Residence* – 44 Rosebank, Holyport Rd, SW6 6LQ.

COLLATERAL BRANCHES LIVING

Issue of late Hon Anthony Paul Irby, TD, brother of 9th Baron, *b* 1908, *d* 1986: *m* 1st, 1934, Countess Mary Apponyi, who *d* 1952, elder da of late Count Anton Apponyi; 2ndly, 1957, Mrs Beryl Harrison (ante):—
(By 1st *m*) Paul Anthony (Garth House, Highclere, Newbury, Berks RG20 9ME), *b* 1935; *ed* Eton; late 2nd Lieut KRRC: *m* 1982, Emma Mary, formerly wife of (i) Hugh Leopold Seymour (*see* M Hertford, colls), and (ii) John Laurence David Aschan, and only da of Robert Alister Henderson (*see* Lowther, Bt, *cr* 1824, colls), and has issue living, Rupert Paul Anthony, *b* 1983, — Harry Robert Paul Anthony, *b* 1985. —— (George Anthony) Peter (Hill House, 64 Honor Oak Rd, SE23 3RZ), *b* 1942; *ed* Eton; late Maj RGJ: *m* 1981, Ginger Kay Patricia Wanda May, da of late Frank Edward Wallace, of Texas, USA, and has had issue living, Edward Peter Anthony Wallace, *b* 1986, — †Richard Peter Anthony Wallace, *b* 1988, *d* 1989, — Mary Charlotte Alexandra Wallace, *b* and *d* 1983, — Katharine Mary Louise Wallace, *b* 1984; *ed* Marlborough. —— Charles Leonard Anthony (125 Blenheim Crescent, W11 2EQ), *b* 1945; *ed* Eton: *m* 1971, Sarah Jane, da of David Sutherland, and has issue living, Nicholas Charles Anthony, *b* 1975, — Caroline Sarah, *b* 1977.

Grandchildren of late Edward de Crespigny Irby, el son of late Edward Irby (*b* 1821), 4th son of Rev Hon Paul Anthony Irby, 5th son of 2nd Baron:—
Issue of late Francis Edward Irby, *b* 1877, *d* 1960: *m* 1925, Katie Lorna, who *d* 1981, da of late W. Tibbits, of Gilgandra, NSW:—
Edith Elizabeth (210 High St, Lismore, NSW, Australia), *b* 1927: *m* 1953, Richard E. Wratten, who *d* 1969, and has issue living, Nigel Richard Irby, *b* 1955. —— Isla Frances, *b* 1930: *m* 1954, Wilfred Charles Tibbits, JP, of Cottage Green, Gilgandra, NSW, Australia, who *d* 1985.

Issue of late Paul Anthony Irby, *b* 1882: *d* 1968: *m* 1914, Mabel, who *d* 1960, da of Mrs Olive, of Casino, Sydney, NSW:—
Paul Anthony (2 Ray St, Bray Park, Murwillumbah, NSW 2484, Australia), *b* 1916; New Guinea and Solomon Islands 1944-45 with AIF: *m* 1948, Dorothy Mary, da of R. H. Hogg, of Wahroonga, Cecil Plains, Queensland, and has issue living, Paul Anthony Richard, *b* 1949; BEcon, — Ross James, *b* 1959; BA, — Judith Jessie, *b* 1951: *m* 1982, Geoffrey Robert Williams, of 28 Carlton St, Highgate, Adelaide, and has issue living, Benjamin Robert *b* 1984, Courtney Jayne *b* 1987. —— †Gordon Edward, *b* 1922: *m* 1950, Beryl Margaret (Weerona, Mooball, NSW, Australia), da of C. D. Mills, and *d* 1979, leaving issue living, Leonard Edward (12 Opal Place, Golden Links Estate, Murwillumbah, NSW, Australia 2484), *b* 1951: *m* 1981, Judith Ann, da of Robert B. Noble, of Murwillumbah, NSW, and has issue living, Mark Edward *b* 1983, Melissa Jan *b* 1986, Suzanne Marie *b* 1988, — Kenneth Francis *b* 1954: *m* 1973, Robyn M. Shillan, and has issue living, Peter Richard *b* 1978, Felica Lea *b* 1974, — Stephen Victor, *b* 1960: *m* 1989, Robyn, da of Horace Alfred Martin, of 4 Ewing St, Murwillumbah, NSW, and has issue living, Benjamin Anthony *b* 1992, Jacinta Elizabeth *b* 1990, — Robyn Joyce, *b* 1953: *m* 1998, Robert Michael Buckley, of Bangalow, NSW 2479, Australia, — Sharon Lea, *b* 1966: *m* 1989, Geoffrey David Grace, of Burringbar, NSW, Australia 2483, and has issue living, Zachary James *b* 1995, Maddison Lea *b* 1998. —— John Charles (Weerona, Mooball, NSW, Australia), *b* 1928: *m* 1952, Orene Ethel, da of W. D. Scott, of Burringbar, NSW, and has issue living, Douglas John (Greenvale Estate, Burringbar, NSW 2483), *b* 1953: *m* 1975, Barbara Anne, da of W. Murray, of Sydney, NSW, and has issue living, David John *b* 1978, Joanne Louise *b* 1977, Rachael Elizabeth *b* 1982, — Michael Anthony (43 Guildford Rd, Guildford, NSW 2161), *b* 1961: *m* 1994, Carolina, da of Manuel Baca, of Concord W, Sdyney, NSW, — Delmay Orene, *b* 1955: *m* 1996, Terrence John Brady, of 38 Sunbakers Drive, Forster, NSW 2428, — Janelle May, *b* 1957: *m* 1984, John Butturini, of Mooball, NSW 2483, and has issue living, Matthew John *b* 1987, Nicholas James *b* 1989, Andrew Anthony *b* 1993, — Elsie Maree, *b* 1959: *m* 1986, Mark Richardson Clapham, of Lismore, NSW 2480, and has issue living, Thomas Anthony *b* 1991, Melanie Alice *b* 1988, — Shirley Ellen, *b* 1963: *m* 1987, Gregory Craig King, of Pottsville, NSW 2484, and has issue living, Lucas Scott *b* 1990, Stacey Mary *b* 1992. —— Florence Mabel, *b* 1919; a JP: *m* 1947, Dalley Leslie Griffin, JP, of 15, Napier Cres, N Ryde, 2113, NSW, Australia, and has issue living, David Leslie Paul *b* 1947; JP: *m* 1978, Wendy, da of E. R. Raynor, of Manly, NSW, and has issue living, Jacqueline Lea *b* 1982, Lauren Jane *b* 1986, — Brian Arthur Charles, *b* 1948; BA; Aust Forces, 3rd Cav Regt, Vietnam; a JP: *m* 1972, Cheryl, da of K. Trescott, of Baulkham Hills, Sydney, NSW, and has issue living, Fiona Leigh *b* 1978, Kate Michelle *b* 1980, Sara Louise *b* 1984, — Elizabeth, Ann, *b* 1951; SRN. —— Nancy, *b* 1926: *m* 1946, Mervyn James Carthy, who *d* 1976, of Myponga, via Adelaide, S Australia 5202, and has issue living, Terry James, *b* 1947: *m* 1971, Maxine, da of K. Hutchinson of Myponga, S Australia, and has issue living, Todd Lee *b* 1978, Lisa Jane *b* 1975, — Peter, *b* 1949; served Austn Forces, Vietnam: *m* 1972, Wendy, da of Robert Rossiter, of Victor Harbour, S Australia, and has issue living, Meagan Emma *b* 1978, Belinda Abbie *b* 1980, — Graeme, *b* 1956, — Anne, *b* 1953: *m* 1973, Graham McKinley, of Jerramungup, W Australia, and has issue living, Ryan James *b* 1976, Amie Louise *b* 1978.

Grandchildren of late Edward de Crespigny Irby (ante):—
Issue of late Llewellyn George Irby, *b* 1883, *d* 1964: *m* 1914, Mary Louisa, el da of late Rev R. W. Stockdale, of Grafton, NSW:—
Kenneth Allan (1 Gibbons St, Wynward, Tasmania), *b* 1920; 1939-45 War in Middle East and S Pacific with RAAF: *m* 1948, Mary Rushton, da of the Rev E. E. Johnson, R of Carrick, Tas, and has issue living, Philip Anthony Kenelm, *b* 1951, — Judith Mary, *b* 1949: *m* 1971, Rev Ross Flint, of Wynyard, Tasmania, and has issue living, Andrew Mark *b* 1979, Janine Ruth *b* 1974, Natasha *b* 1976. —— Mary Edith (Rosemary) (Pond Garth, RMB 2545, Greens Rd, Upper Lurg, via Benalla, Victoria, Australia) *b* 1915: *m* 1943, George Philip MacDonell, who *d* 1980. —— Elspeth Douglas (3 Ivanhoe Court, Newcomb, Vic 3219 Australia), *b* 1917, late Sister in Australian Army Nursing Ser: *m* 1948, Rev Frederick Searle Ingoldsby, ThL, DipRE, who *d* 1976, and has issue living, James Douglas, *b* 1949; BA: *m* 1980, Leonie Christine Praetz,

and has issue living, Sophie Sky *b* 1981, Liria Vida *b* 1982, — David Llewellyn, *b* 1954: *m* 1987, Rosemary Crosby, and has issue living, Jonathan Dale *b* 1990, Clare Elizabeth *b* 1988, — Marilyn Margaret, *b* 1950; BFA, — Pamela Jean, *b* 1952; BA: *m* 1974, Rev M. J. Vercoe, and has issue living, Stephen Philip *b* 1980, Alison Mary *b* 1982, — Janet Elspeth Irby, *b* 1959; BA: *m* 1981, Michael John Down, and has issue living, John Philip Frederick *b* 1982, Elizabeth Winsome Mary *b* 1984, Deborah Lyn Emily *b* 1986.

Grandson of late Charles Augustus Irby (infra):—
Issue of late Arthur Algernon Irby, *b* 1890, *d* 1967: *m* 1927, Mary Isabel Marsden, who *d* 1953:—
Brian Keith (3 Banyeena Place, Belrose 2085, Sydney, NSW, Australia), *b* 1931; JP: *m* 1952, June Eve Hutton, and has issue living, Peter Brian Edward, *b* 1956: *m* 1985, Ruth Helen Goven, and has issue living, Nicholas Roland *b* 1989, Cameron Peter *b* 1993, — Donna-Elizabeth, *b* 1953.

Grandsons of late Edward Irby (*b* 1821), 4th son of Rev Hon Paul Anthony Irby, 5th son of 2nd Baron (ante):—
Issue of late Charles Augustus Irby, *b* 1861, *d* 1941: *m* 1888, Eva Georgiana, da of Richard Roberts, of Sydney, NS Wales:—
Beverley Keith, *b* 1899: *m* 1942, Kathleen Pilley, of Mudgee. *Residence* – 7 Alfred St, Campsie, NSW, Australia. —— Richard Wilfred, *b* 1901: *m* 1939, Margery McMillan, of Bathurst, Australia, and has issue living, Jenny Eva, *b* 1942: *m* 1964, Raymond Thomas Connell, of 27 Hope St, Penrith, NSW, Australia. —— Roland Frank, *b* 1906: *m* 1938, Mary Brown. *Residence* – Kar-Mar, Wallacia, NSW, Australia.

Granddaughters of late Rev George Powell Irby, 7th son of Rev Hon Paul Anthony Irby (ante):—
Issue of late Lewis Michael Aubert Irby, *b* 1882, *d* 1974: *m* 1914, Isabel Kate, who *d* 1972, da of late G. M. Thornton:—
Audrey Cynthia Yvette, *b* 1915: *m* 1955, Christopher Lucian Chamberlin, TD, who *d* 1996, of Withybed Cottage, Butleigh Wootton, Glastonbury, Som BA6 8TX. —— Beryl Diana Noël, *b* 1919: *m* 1951, Henry John Bunting, of 5 Cambray Court, Cheltenham G50 1JU, and has issue living, George Irby, *b* 1952: *m* 1974, Julia Angela Davey, and has issue living, Samuel Charles *b* 1979, Timothy George *b* 1984, — James Walter Irby, *b* 1954: *m* 1982, Hisaka Margaret Hiraoka, and has issue living, Paul Shu *b* 1985, Mark Rhu *b* 1990, Sarah Mai *b* 1992, — Edward Irby, *b* 1959: *m* 1991, Boika Spasova, — Richard Irby, *b* 1962.

PREDECESSORS – **(1)** EDWARD Irby, son of late Anthony Irby; MP for Boston; *cr* a *Baronet* 1704; *d* 1718; *s* by his son **(2)** *Sir* WILLIAM, MP, 2nd Bt, Lord Chamberlain 1761; *cr Baron Boston* (peerage of Great Britain) 1761; *d* 1775; *s* by his son **(3)** FREDERICK, DCL, 2nd Baron, for fifty years a Lord of the Bedchamber to George III; *d* 1825; *s* by his son **(4)** GEORGE, 3rd Baron; *b* 1777; *d* 1856; *s* by his son **(5)** GEORGE IVES, 4th Baron; *b* 1802; *d* 1869: *m* 1st, 1830, Fanny Elizabeth, who *d* 1860, da of W. R. Hopkins-Northey; 2ndly, 1861, Hon Caroline Amelia, who *d* 1927, da of 3rd Baron de Saumarez; *d* 1869; *s* by his son **(6)** FLORANCE GEORGE HENRY, 5th Baron; *b* 1837· *m* 1859, Hon Augusta Caroline, who *d* 1929, da of 3rd Baron de Saumarez; *d* 1877; *s* by his son **(7)** GEORGE FLORANCE, 6th Baron; *b* 1860; a Lord-in-Waiting to HM Queen Victoria 1885-6; *m* 1890, Cecilia Constance, who *d* 1938, da of late Hon Augustus Anthony Frederick Irby; *d* 1941; *s* by his nephew **(8)** GREVILLE NORTHEY (son of late Hon Cecil Saumarez Irby, 2nd son of 5th Baron); *b* 1889; Hon Capt (ret) Oxford and Bucks LI; sometime Principal in Colonial Office: *m* 1st, 1913, Constance Beryl, who *d* 1969, da of late William Richard Lester, of Alderley, Llandudno; 2ndly, 1954, Irene Frances, who *d* 1987, da of late Francis Holt, of Ewell, Surrey, and widow of Harry Mills; *d* 1958; *s* by his brother **(9)** CECIL EUSTACE, MC, 8th Baron, *b* 1897, *d* 1972; *s* by his kinsman **(10)** GERALD HOWARD BOTELER, MBE (el son of Lt-Col Leonard Paul Irby, OBE, son of Lt-Col Leonard Howard Loyd Irby, son of Rear-Adm Hon Frederick Paul Irby, CB, 2nd son of 2nd Baron), 9th Baron, *b* 1897; 1914-18 War (MBE 1918); 1939-45 War as Maj RASC: *m* 1st, 1926 (*m diss* 1931), Katherine Gertude, da of Capt C. M. H. Edwards, RASC; 2ndly, 1936, Erica Nelly, who *d* 1990, da of T. H. Hill; *d* 1978: *s* by his son **(11)** TIMOTHY GEORGE FRANK BOTELER, 10th Baron and present peer.

BOSTON OF FAVERSHAM, BARON (Boston) (Life Baron 1976)

TERENCE GEORGE BOSTON, yr surviving son of late George Thomas Boston; *b* 21 March 1930; *ed* Woolwich Polytechnic Sch, and Kings Coll, Univ of London; Bar Inner Temple 1960, and Gray's Inn 1973; QC 1981; Fl Lt RAF 1950-52; BBC News Sub-Editor, External Sers 1957-60; Snr BBC Producer (Current Affairs) 1960-64; MP for Faversham, Kent (*Lab*) 1964-70; PPS to Min of Public Building and Works 1964-66, to Min of Power 1966-68, and to Min of Transport 1968-69; Assist Govt Whip 1969-70; UK Delegate to UN General Assembly 1976-78; Minister of State, Home Office 1979; Opposition Spokesman on Home Office Affairs 1979-84, on Defence 1984-86; Chm TVS (TVS Entertainment plc) 1980-90; Principal Dep Chm of Cttees and Chm Select Cttee on the European Communities, House of Lords, 1992-94, since when Chm of Cttees; *cr Baron Boston of Faversham*, of Faversham in co Kent (Life Baron) 1976; *m* 1962, Margaret Joyce, el da of late Rowley Henry Jack Head, and step-da of late Henry Fermin Winters, of Melbourne, Victoria, Australia.

ᴀrms – per pale gules and azure a lion passant guardant dimidiated with a ship's hull or on a chief argent a duck-billed platypus statant proper between two cats' faces sable; Crest – a chapeau gules turned up ermine thereon a boar's head couped azure; Supporters – *Dexter*, a lion sejant erect guardant or; *Sinister*, a kangaroo guardant proper each resting the exterior foreleg on a fasces erect the axe facing outwards sable the whole upon a compartment comprising a grassy mount vert growing therefrom roses gules and argent barbed seeded slipped and leaved proper
Address – House of Lords, SW1A 0PW.

BOTETOURT AND HERBERT, BARONIES OF (Baron Botetourt, E 1305 and Baron Herbert, E 1461) (Abeyant 1984)

HENRY HUGH ARTHUR FITZROY SOMERSET, KG, KCVO, PC, 10th DUKE OF BEAUFORT, also 10th BARON BOTETOURT and 18th BARON HERBERT (*cr* 1461), *d* 1984, when the latter Baronies fell into abeyance between the descendants of his late sister Lady Blanche Linnie Somerset (infra).

CO-HEIRS TO BARONIES

Granddaughter of late Lady Rosemary Alexandra Eliot, el da of Lady Blanche Linnie Somerset (infra):—
Issue of late Davina Rosemary Enid NUTTING (*see* Nutting, Bt, colls, 1976 Edn), *b* 1940, *d* 1976, in a motor accident: *m* 1960 (*m diss* 1969), as his 2nd wife, John Martin Brentnall Cope, who *d* 1991:—
FREDERICA SAMANTHA MARY COPE, *b* 23 Sept 1963; co-heiress to Baronies of Botetourt and Herbert (quarter share); legally assumed forename of Frederica 1991. *Residence* – Flat D, 46 Sutherland St, SW1V 4JZ.

Grandchildren of late Lady Blanche Linnie Somerset (el da of 9th Duke of Beaufort): *m* 1st, 1918, 6th Earl of St Germans, who *d* 1922; 2ndly, 1924, Capt George Francis Valentine Scott Douglas, who *d* 1930 (*see* Douglas, Bt, *cr* 1786, 1969 Edn):—
Issue of late Lady Rosemary Alexandra Eliot, *b* 1919, *d* 1963: *m* 1st, 1939, Capt Edward Christian Frederick Nutting, RHG, who *d* on active service 1943, 2nd son of late Sir Harold Stansmore Nutting, 2nd Bt; 2ndly, 1945 (*m* annulled 1949), Lt-Cdr David Frederick Hew Dunn, RN; 3rdly, 1949, Col Ralph Alexander Rubens, Sherwood Foresters, who *d* 1995:—
(By 3rd *m*) ALEXANDRA LOUISE PEYRONEL, *b* 9 Oct 1951; *ed* St Martin's Sch of Art (BA); co-heiress to Baronies of Botetourt and Herbert (quarter share): *m* 1976, Daniel Augusto Peyronel, and has issue living, Jesse Alexander, *b* 1977; *ed* New York Univ, and Tisch Sch of The Arts (BFA). *Residence* – 27 Gertrude St, SW10 0JF.

Issue of late Lady Cathleen Blanche Lily Eliot, *b* 1921, *d* 1994: *m* 1st, 1946 (*m diss* 1956), Capt John Seyfried, RHG; 2ndly, 1957, Sir Havelock Henry Trevor Hudson, who *d* 1996:—
(By 1st *m*) DAVID JOHN SEYFRIED (39 Chiddingstone St, SW6 3TQ), *b* 3 March 1952; co-heir to Baronies of Botetourt and Herbert (half share); *ed* Harrow: *m* 1975, Jane Angela Bishop, and has issue living, Oliver Richard, *b* 1976; *ed* Harrow, — Charlotte Sophia Caroline, *b* 1977. —— Sarah Diana, *b* 1949: *m* 1975, Peter Michael Smith, and has issue living,

Benjamin Peter Havelock, b 1977, — Matthew William Eliot, b 1981. —— (By 2nd m) (Michael) Guy Havelock HUDSON, b 1962: m 1992, Sarah Heidi, da of Anthony Ehrler, of Lychpit, Basingstoke, and has issue living, Havelock Henry Eliot, b 1996, — Christian Alexander Havelock, b 1998. —— Louise Deborah, b 1958; has issue living, Jonathan, b 1986, — Eliot, b 1988.

Botreaux, Barony of; see Loudoun, Countess of.

Bourke, family name of Earl of Mayo.

BOURNE, BARONY OF (Bourne) (Extinct 1982)

SON LIVING OF LIFE BARON

Hon Michael Kemp (50 Bradbourne St, SW6), b 1937: m 1st, 1963 (m diss 1980), Penelope Jane, da of Capt H. W. Blyth, of Wyncombe Hill, Fittleworth, Sussex, 2ndly, 1985, Marian Lockhart, eldest da of Maj John Francis Leatham Robinson, MC (see Barran, Bt, colls), and has issue living (by 1st m) John Kemp, b 1969: m 1997, Kate E. S., yr da of Michael Robertson, of Weston Underwood, Bucks, and has issue living, Olivia Jane b 1998, — Amanda Caroline, b 1966: m 1987, Hugh Charles Gordon Garrod, son of Kenneth Garrod, of Whatton, Notts, and has issue living, George Charles b 1992, Edward b 1994, — Lucy Claire, b 1968.

DAUGHTER LIVING OF LIFE BARON

Hon Elizabeth Anne (Belmont House, Donhead St Mary, Shaftesbury, Dorset), b 1931: m 1952, Ian McKay Robertson, The Gordon Highlanders, who d 1984, and has issue four sons.

Bouverie, Pleydell-, family name of Earl of Radnor.

BOWDEN, BARONY OF (Bowden) (Extinct 1989)

SON LIVING OF LIFE BARON (By 1st marriage)

Hon Robin (19 Kirkbrae Av, Cults, Aberdeen AB1 9RF), b 1945; ed Old Swinford Hosp Sch, and Loughborough Univ; m 1978, Jess, da of W. MacPherson-Duncan, and has issue living, Alastair Robin, b 1982, — Lindsay Catherine, b 1979.

DAUGHTERS LIVING OF LIFE BARON (By 1st marriage)

Hon Mary BOWDEN (4 Martin Av, Dorval, H9S 3R3, Prov Quebec, Canada), *b* 1940; teacher of deaf children; has resumed her maiden name: *m* 1964 (*m diss* 19—), Dr Roger George Davey, and has issue, Lisa, *b* 1969, — Julie, *b* 1971.

Hon Virginia, *b* 1943; *ed* E Anglian Girls' Sch, and Reading and Manchester Univs: *m* 1967, David Ian Murray, of 61 Woburn Drive, Hale, Cheshire, and has issue living, Tanya, *b* 1973: *m* 1998, Phil Buchanan, and has issue living, Robert James Murray *b* 1999, — Louise, *b* 1976.

Bowden, family name of Baron Aylestone.

Bowmont and Cessford, Marquess of; son of Duke of Roxburghe.

BOWNESS, BARON (Bowness) (Life Baron 1995)

PETER SPENCER BOWNESS, CBE, son of late Hubert Spencer Bowness, of Cardiff; *b* 19 May 1943; *ed* Whitgift Sch, Croydon; DL (Greater London) 1982; Solicitor; partner Weightman Sadler, Solicitors, Purley since 1970; Leader of Croydon Council 1976-79 and 1980-94, Leader of Opposition Croydon Council 1994-96; Chm of London Boroughs Assoc 1978-94, Dep Chm Assoc of Metropolitan Authorities 1978-80; Memb of Audit Commn England and Wales 1983-95, of London Residuary Body 1985-93, National Training Task Force 1989-92, Standing Congress of Local and Regional Authorities of Europe (Council of Europe) 1990-98, UK Delegation Cttee of Regions European Union 1994-98, Bureau COR 1994-98; Memb Board of London First/London Forum 1993-94; Gov of Whitgift Foundation; Freeman of City of London 1987; Hon Col 151 (Greater London) Transport Regt (V) 1988-93; *cr* CBE 1981, Knt 1987, and *Baron Bowness*, of Warlingham, co Surrey, and of Croydon, in the London Borough of Croydon (Life Baron) 1995: *m* 1st, 1969 (*m diss* 1983), Marianne, da of Robert Hall, of Croydon; 2ndly, 1984, Mrs Patricia Jane Cook, da of John Cullis, of Abergavenny, and has issue by 1st *m*.

Arms – Argent, four pallets sable over all within a cross flory nowy round pierced and parted a roundel or. **Crest** – A demi bull argent armed and unguled and holding in the mouth a sword point downwards in bend or. **Supporters** – *Dexter*, a dachshund regardant sable holding in the mouth a daffodil slipped and leaved or; *sinister*, a dachshund regardant tenne holding in the mouth a daffodil slipped and leaved or. **Motto** – Never give up.
Address – Three Gables, 10 Westview Rd, Warlingham, Surrey CR6 9JD.

DAUGHTER LIVING (By 1st marriage)

Hon Caroline, *b* 1978; *ed* Croham Hurst Sch, Croydon.

Bowyer, family name of Baron Denham.

Boyd, family name of Baron Kilmarnock.

BOYD-CARPENTER, BARONY OF (Boyd-Carpenter) (Extinct 1998)

SON LIVING OF LIFE BARON

Hon Sir Thomas Patrick John, KBE, *b* 1938; *ed* Stowe; Lieut-Gen, Dep Ch of Staff, Programmes, Min of Defence since 1992-96, since when Chm Kensington & Chelsea and Westminster Health Authority; MBE (Mil) 1973, KBE (Mil) 1993: *m* 1972, Mary Jean, da of John Elwes Duffield, BM, BCh, of The Tithe House, Church St, Marcham, Berks, and has issue living, Harry, *b* 1973, — Emily, *b* 1975, — Clare, *b* 1977.

DAUGHTERS LIVING OF LIFE BARON

Hon Anne Mary, *b* 1942.
Hon Sarah Elizabeth Mary (*Baroness Hogg*), *b* 1946; *cr* Baroness Hogg (Life Baroness) 1995: *m* 1968, Rt Hon Douglas Martin Hogg, MP, son of Baron Hailsham of St Marylebone, KG, CH, PC (Life Baron), and has issue (*see* Bs Hogg).

WIDOW LIVING OF LIFE BARON

MARGARET MARY (*Baroness Boyd-Carpenter*), da of late Lt-Col George Leslie Hall, OBE, RE (*see* E Coventry, colls, 1976 Edn): *m* 1937, Baron Boyd-Carpenter, PC (Life Baron), who *d* 1998. *Residence* – 12 Eaton Terrace, SW1.

BOYD OF MERTON, VISCOUNT (Lennox-Boyd) (Viscount UK 1960)

SIMON DONALD RUPERT NEVILLE LENNOX-BOYD, 2nd Viscount; *b* 7 Dec 1939; *s* 1983; *ed* Eton, and Ch Ch, Oxford; Dep-Chm Arthur Guinness & Sons plc 1981-86; Chm Save the Children 1987-92, Chm Stonham Housing 1992-98: *m* 1962, Alice Mary, High Sheriff of Cornwall 1987-88, DL 1995, da of late Maj Meysey George Dallas Clive (*see* E Longford), and has issue.

Arms – Azure a fess chequy argent and gules, between an abbatical mitre simplex of the second filleted of the third in chief, and in base a rose of the second, seeded vert and barbed of the third. **Crest** – A dexter hand erect in pale, having two fingers turned in and the rest pointing upwards proper the wrist habited in a close sleeve azure, with cuff chequy argent and gules. **Supporters** – Two squirrels proper, having collars chequy argent and gules. *Residences* – 9 Warwick Sq, SW1; Ince Castle, Saltash, Cornwall.

SONS LIVING

Hon BENJAMIN ALAN, *b* 21 Oct 1964; *ed* Millfield: *m* 1993, Mrs Sheila Mary Margaret Carroll, da of Harold Emmanuel George Williams, of 343 North Rd, W Plymouth, and formerly wife of Michael Carroll, of Saltash, Cornwall, and has issue living, Alan George Simon, *b* 11 March 1993, — Henry Simon, *b* 1997, — Mary Alice, *b* 1994. *Residence* – South Broadmoor, Saltash, Cornwall.
Hon Edward George, *b* 1968; *ed* Eton, and Ch Ch, Oxford: *m* 1994, Tamsin S., only da of Antony Hichens, of Nether-

bury, W Dorset, and has issue living, Jago George Antony, *b* 1997, — William Enys, *b* 1998. *Residence* – 43 Brunswick Gdns, W8.

DAUGHTERS LIVING

Hon Charlotte Mary, *b* 1963; *ed* Cheltenham Ladies Coll, and Univ Coll, London: *m* 1992, Charles C. J. Mitchell, eldest son of late James Mitchell, of Wilsford-cum-Lake, Wilts, and has issue living, Albert James Edward, *b* 1996, — Reginald Alexander Philip, *b* 1998, — Gwendolen Charlotte Julia, *b* 1994.

Hon Philippa Patricia, *b* 1970; *ed* St Mary's, Calne: *m* 1998, Hon Patrick Nathaniel George Spens, elder son of 3rd Baron Spens. *Residence* – Beech House, 33a Pembroke Rd, W8.

BROTHERS LIVING

Hon Christopher Alan (42 Upper Brook St, W1), *b* 1941; *ed* Eton, and Ch Ch, Oxford.

Hon Sir Mark Alexander (3 Bloomfield Terr, SW1; Gresgarth Hall, Caton, Lancs), *b* 1943; *ed* Eton, and Ch Ch, Oxford; Bar Inner Temple 1968; MP for Morecambe and Lonsdale (*C*) 1979-83, MP for Morecambe and Lunesdale (*C*) 1983-97; PPS to Chancellor of Exchequer 1983-84, Assist Govt Whip 1984-86; Lord Commr of the Treasury 1986-88; PPS to Rt Hon Margaret Thatcher, Prime Minister, 1988-90, Parl Under-Sec, Foreign and Commonwealth Office 1990-92, Under-Sec of State, Dept of Foreign and Commonwealth Affairs 1992-94; Knt 1994: *m* 1974, Mrs Arabella Lacloche, only da of Piero Parisi, of Rome, and has issue living, Patricia Irene, *b* 1980.

WIDOW LIVING OF FIRST VISCOUNT

Lady Patricia Florence Susan Guinness (*Patricia, Viscountess Boyd of Merton*), da of 2nd Earl of Iveagh: *m* 1938, the 1st Viscount Boyd of Merton, CH, PC, who *d* 1983. *Residence* – Ince Castle, Saltash, Cornwall PL12 4RA.

PREDECESSOR – Alan Tindal Lennox-Boyd, CH, PC, son of Alan Walter Lennox-Boyd; *b* 1904; Parliamentary Sec to Min of Labour 1938-39, to Min of Home Security 1939, to Min of Food 1939-40, and to Min of Aircraft Production 1943-45; Min of State for Colonial Affairs 1951-52, Min of Transport and Civil Aviation 1952-54, and Sec of State for the Colonies 1954-59; Man Dir Arthur Guinness, Son & Co Ltd 1960-67, Joint Vice-Chm 1967-83; a Dir ICI; MP for Mid Div of Bedfordshire (*C*) Oct 1931-July 1960; *cr* PC 1951, and *Viscount Boyd of Merton*, of Merton-in-Penninghame, co Wigtown (peerage of UK) 1960: *m* 1938, Lady Patricia Florence Susan Guinness, da of 2nd Earl of Iveagh; *d* 1983; *s* by his el son **(2)** Simon Donald Rupert Neville, 2nd Viscount and present peer.

Boyle, Viscount; son of Earl of Shannon.

Boyle of Marston, Baron; title of Earl of Cork and Orrery on Roll of HL.

Boyle, family name of Earl of Cork and Orrery.

Boyle, family name of Earl of Glasgow.

Boyle, family name of Earl of Shannon.

BOYNE, VISCOUNT (Hamilton-Russell) Sits as BARON BRANCEPETH (UK 1866) (Viscount I 1717)

I neither fear nor despise

GUSTAVUS MICHAEL STUCLEY HAMILTON-RUSSELL, 11th Viscount; *b* 27 May 1965; *s* 1995; *ed* Harrow, and RAC Cirencester; ARICS: *m* 1991, Lucy, da of George Potter, of Foxdale, Bunbury, Cheshire, and has one son and one da.

Arms – Quarterly: 1st and 4th argent, between two chevronels a cinquefoil, the whole between three cross crosslets fitchée sable, *Russell*; 2nd and 3rd gules, three cinquetoils pierced ermine, *Hamilton*. Crests – 1st, a goat passant argent, collared gemelle, and charged on the body with an escallop sable, *Russell*; 2nd, out of a ducal crown, or, an oak tree fructed proper, and penetrated transversely in the main stem by a frame-saw proper, the frame gold, above the motto, "Through," *Hamilton*. Supporters – Two mermaids proper, hair dishevelled or, each holding in the exterior hand a mirror, of the last.
Seat – Burwarton, Bridgnorth, Shropshire. *Club* – Turf.

SON LIVING

Frederick Gustavus George, *b* 1997.

DAUGHTER LIVING

Hon Emelia Rose, *b* 1994.

SISTERS LIVING AND DECEASED

Hon Caroline Veronica, *b* 1957: *m* 1st, 1975 (*m diss* 1990), David George Fothergill Banks, FRICS; 2ndly, 1997, Maj R. C. R. (Bertie) Cotterell, and has issue living (by 1st *m*), Richard George Fothergill, *b* 1977; *ed* Milton Abbey, — Georgina Emma, *b* 1980. *Residence* – Upper Norton, Bromyard, Herefords.
Hon Sara Emma, *b* 1959: *m* 1981 (*m diss* 1987), Nigel Anthony Twiston-Davies (*see* Archdale, Bt, colls), and *d* as the result of an accident 1989.
Hon Lucy Jane, *b* 1961: *m* 1st, 1983 (*m diss* 1986), Patrick James Bailey, yst son of Sir Derrick Thomas Louis Bailey, 3rd Bt; 2ndly, 1989, Simon Edward Harlackendon Sherwood, 2nd son of late Nathaniel Edward Carwardine Sherwood, of Easthorpe Hall, Colchester, Essex, and has issue living (by 2nd *m*), Jack Edward, *b* 1992, — Anna Lucinda, *b* 1993. *Residence* – Sheepdrove, Lambourn, Hungerford, Berks.

GREAT AUNT LIVING (only daughter of 9th Viscount)

Hon Rosemary Katharine (*Lady Forbes*), *b* 1921: *m* 1942, 22nd Lord Forbes. *Residence* – Balforbes, Alford, Aberdeenshire.

WIDOW LIVING OF TENTH VISCOUNT

ROSEMARY ANNE (*Rosemary, Viscountess Boyne*), 2nd da of Maj Sir Dennis Frederic Bankes Stucley, 5th Bt: *m* 1956, the 10th Viscount Boyne, KCVO, who *d* 1995. *Residence* – The Old Dairy, Burwarton, Bridgnorth, Shropshire WV16 6QH.

COLLATERAL BRANCHES LIVING

Issue of late Brig Hon Richard Gustavus Hamilton-Russell, DSO, LVO, 2nd son of 9th Viscount, *b* 1909, *d* 1999: *m* 1939, Hon Pamela Penelope Cayzer, who *d* 1987, elder da of 1st Baron Rotherwick:—
BRIAN GUSTAVUS (Hardwickforge, Stottesdon, Kidderminster DY14 8TL), *b* 8 May 1940; *ed* Eton; Col 17th/21st Lancers: *m* 1st, 1967, Lea, only child of Col Harry Noël Havelock Wild, of Shelley Court, Tite St, Chelsea; 2ndly, 1982, Sarah Julianne, da of late Reginald Waugh Harris, of Greenside Cottage, Wombleton, N Yorks, and formerly wife of Richard Jeremy Colebrook-Robjent, and has issue living (by 1st *m*), Henry William Gustavus, *b* 28 Feb 1969; *ed* Milton Abbey, — Victoria Essex Lea, *b* 1976. —— Richard Desmond (Mincinbury, Barley, Royston, Herts), *b* 1943; *ed* Eton; commn'd

17th/21st Lancers 1962: *m* 1965, Prudence Sophia, only da of late Maj Ronald Penrhyn Pockney, of The Old Barn, Bishopthorpe, York, and has issue living, Charles Richard, *b* 1965; *ed* Stowe, and Exeter Univ (BSc); Maj Queen's Royal Lancers (ret): *m* 1993, Claire Fiona, da of Ian James Dussek, OBE, of Little Allens, Plaxtol, Kent, — Emma Sophia, *b* 1968: *m* 1996, Jonathan C. Bray, son of Geoffrey Bray, of Lilbourne, Warwicks, and has issue living, George Arthur *b* 1998, — Katharine Roseanna, *b* 1972. —— Veronica Anne, *b* 1949: *m* 1971, Nicholas Michael Houssemayne Jones, of The Manor, Coln St Denys, Cheltenham, Glos GL54 3JU, and has issue living, Oliver Mark, *b* 1977; *ed* Wellington Coll, — Rowena Rose, *b* 1975.

Issue of late Major Hon John Hamilton-Russell, MC, 3rd son of 9th Viscount, *b* 1911, *ka* 1943: *m* 1937, Lady Diana Legge (who *d* 1970, having *m* 2ndly, 1946, Lt-Col Adrian Lewis Matthews), da of 7th Earl of Dartmouth:—
James Gustavus, MBE, *b* 1938; *ed* Eton; Col Household Cavalry (ret); MBE (Mil) 1976; FIMgt: *m* 1965, Alison, da of late Dr Sydney Haydn Heard, MBE, Lieut Bailiff and Jurat of R Court of Albecq, Guernsey, and has issue living, Mark John Gustavus, *b* 1969; *ed* Stowe, and RMA Sandhurst; commn'd RHG/D 1989, — Edward Haydn James, *b* (twin) 1969; *ed* Stowe, and RMA Sandhurst; commn'd Life Guards 1990, — Julia Mary, *b* 1967: *m* 1998, Victor Huntington Jaques, son of Ralph Jaques, of Hampton, Middx.

Granddaughter of late Hon Claud Eustace Hamilton-Russell, 4th son of 8th Viscount:—
Issue of late Edric Claud Hamilton-Russell, *b* 1904, *d* 1984: *m* 1932, Helen Rosa, who *d* 1996, da of late William Humble, of Skellow Grange, Doncaster:—
Ann Katharine, *b* 1933: *m* 1953, Lt-Col William Frank Philip Currie, Queen's R Irish Hus, of Rollington House, Redlynch, Salisbury, Wilts, and has issue living, Richard William, *b* 1955; *ed* Radley; Lt-Col Queen's Royal Hussars, — Joanna, *b* 1959.

Granddaughters of late Maj Hon Arthur Hamilton-Russell, 5th son of 8th Viscount:—
Issue of late David Henry Gustavus Hamilton-Russell, *b* 1911, *d* 1988: *m* 1950, Pauline Albinia, MBE (103 Rowan House, Greycoat St, SW1P 2QD; 7 Beach Crescent, Littlehampton, W Sussex), da of late George Penkivil Slade, KC, of St Michael's, Painswick, Glos:—
Marion Albinia, *b* 1952: *m* 1975, (Frederick) Simon Arden Armson, of Broad Oak, Hurley, Maidenhead, Berks SL6 5LW, and has issue living, Patrick David Arden), *b* 1982, — Meriel Albinia, *b* 1979, — Katherine Geraldine, *b* 1984. —— Georgiana Mary, *b* 1955: *m* 1983, John Kenrick Hayward, of Upper Siddington House, Cirencester, Glos GL7 6HL, 2nd son of late Surg-Col Edwin William Hayward, OBE, of Erskine, Fairford, Glos, and has issue living, Cicely Albinia, *b* 1985, — Edwina Mary, *b* 1987, — Antonia Katharine, *b* 1994. —— Annette Katharine, *b* 1958: *m* 1989, Brian D. Lanaghan, of Thornhill Field, Passfield, Liphook, Hants, son of Richard Lanaghan, of Bath, and has issue living, James Henry David, *b* 1993, — Marina Katharine Albinia, *b* 1991. —— Margaret Louisa, *b* 1960.

Descendants, if any, of Henry Hamilton-Cox (*b* 1831), and his brother, Richard Sackville Hamilton-Cox (*b* 1834, *d* 1926, in USA), sons of Sackville Hamilton-Cox, 2nd son of Henry Hamilton-Cox (*d* 1821) (infra).

Descendants, if any, of Henry Alfred Hamilton-Cox (*b* 1842), and his brother, James Wellesley Hamilton-Cox (*b* 1844), both of Chicago, Illinois, USA, sons of Henry Wellesley Hamilton-Cox, 3rd son of Henry Hamilton-Cox (*d* 1821) (infra).

Granddaughters of late William George Cox (infra):—
Issue of late Walter Cox, *b* 1915, *d* 1993: *m* 1938, Lola, da of Clarence Bradley:—
Carolyn Jane, *b* 1940: *m* 1964, Francis Donovan, of 6 Apple Tree Lane, E Peoria, Illinois 61611, USA, and has issue living, Michael William, *b* 1970. —— Linda Jean, *b* 1947: *m* 1st, 1967, Charles Entwistle; 2ndly, 1981, James Krysiak, of Wenona, Illinois 61377, USA, and has issue living (by 1st *m*), Scott Alan, *b* 1972, — Melissa Ann, *b* 1969.

Granddaughter of late Henry Augustus George Cox, only son of William John Hamilton-Cox, yst son of Henry Hamilton-Cox (*d* 1821), grandson of Hon Henry Hamilton, 3rd son of 1st Viscount:—
Issue of late William Cox, *b* 1884, *d* 1970: *m* 1910, Caroline, who *d* 1977, da of late William Colling:—
Louise Rose, *b* 1916: *m* 1942, Clinton Carlton King, Horologist, of 1115 Herbert St, Peru, Illinois, USA, and has issue living, James Hamilton, MD, FACP (93 Victoria Av, Galesburg, Illinois 61401, USA), *b* 1944: *m* 1968, Mary, da of late Kenneth Gibson, and has issue living, John Hamilton *b* 1971, James Thaddeus *b* 1973.

Grandchildren of late Sackville Berkeley Hamilton, el son of Sackville Deane Hamilton, grandson of Rt Hon Sackville Hamilton, 3rd son of Hon Henry Hamilton, MP, 3rd son of 1st Viscount:—
Issue of late Col Sackville William Sackville Hamilton, DSO, MBE, *b* 1882, *d* 1956: *m* 1920, Margaret Dowell, who *d* 1993, da of S. C. Hester, of Laleham, Isle of Thanet:—
James Berkeley Sackville (Acklam Grange, Acklam, Malton, Yorks YO17 9RG), *b* 1923; *ed* Wellington Coll, and King's Coll, Camb (MA); Lt-Col RE (ret) (despatches 1946); Bursar Pocklington Sch, nr York 1972-88: *m* 1947, Mary Grizel, da of late Col Cecil Alexander Boyle, CIE, DSO (*see* E Glasgow, colls), and has issue living, Charles Patrick Sackville (Thrussendale Farm, Acklam, Malton, N Yorks), *b* 1949; *ed* Wellington Coll; MA (Camb): *m* 1980, Heather, da of T. Goodwin, of Mow Cop, Staffs, — Andrew James Sackville (Colorado Univ, USA), *b* 1951; *ed* Wellington Coll; MA (Oxon), MSc (Liverpool), MSc (London), PhD (Virginia Univ, USA), FRAS: *m* 1978, Catherine Clare, da of Dr R. A. Davidson, of Mombassa, Kenya, and has issue living, Jamie Wildrose Sackville *b* 1988, Jessica Liberty Sackville *b* 1984, — Nigel Ruaraidh Sackville (Bronwydd, Cross St, Bow St, Dyfed), *b* 1953; *ed* Wellington Coll; MA, PhD (Camb): *m* 1983, Dr Charmian A. G., da of Col J. J. G. Hunter, of Middle Farm, Codford St Mary, Wilts, and has issue living, Henry James Sackville *b* 1989, Alice Charlotte Sackville *b* 1991, — Patricia Margaret Sackville (Old Manor Farm, Helperthorpe, Malton, N Yorks), *b* 1956; *ed* Tudor Hall: *m* 1982, Richard Hall, son of W. W. L. Hall, of Burythorpe, N Yorks, and has issue living, Jonathan *b* 1983, Nicholas *b* 1984. —— Anne Margaret Sackville, *b* 1925; MA Camb: *m* 1950, David MacEwen, and has issue living, Diana Cushla, *b* 1951; has issue living, Mark Angus MacEwen *b* 1986, — Helen Margaret, *b* 1953, — Penelope Anne Georgina, *b* 1965; has issue living, Melissa Ariadne Clio MacEwen *b* 1992. *Residence* – 8 Cannon Hill Gdns, Colehill, Wimborne, Dorset BH21 2TA.

Issue of late Maj Charles Sackville Hamilton, *b* 1885, *d* 1971: *m* 1918, Averina Jane, who *d* 1973, eldest da of William Richardson Oliver, of Kil-na-Mulla, Buttevant, co Cork:—
Patricia May Sackville (The Garden Cottage, Fritham Court, Lyndhurst, Hants SO43 7HH), *b* 1924; ARCA: *m* 1948, Lt Derek Richard Spooner, RN, who *d* 1978, and has issue living, Richard Hamilton (Orchard House, Elkins Rd, Hedgerley, Bucks SL2 3YY), *b* 1952; *ed* The King's Sch, Ely; BA, ACA: *m* 1978, Susan Elizabeth Ann, yr da of John Rowntree, of Kidford, Sussex, and has issue living, Victoria Emily Barbara *b* 1985, Catherine Esmé Averina *b* 1987, Elizabeth Sackville *b* 1990, — Jane Rosemary Eleanor, *b* 1955: *m* 1979, Lt-Col John Malcolm Carmichael Watson, The Queen's Own Hus, of The Presbytery, Lulworth Castle Park, Wareham, Dorset, elder son of John Watson, of Northallerton, Yorks, and has issue living, Anna Patricia Louise *b* 1983, Edwina Rose Jane *b* 1986, Fenella Margaret Grace *b* 1990.

PREDECESSORS – (1) GUSTAVUS Hamilton, PC, son of the Hon Sir Frederick Hamilton, KB, youngest son of 1st Lord Paisley (D Abercorn), a distinguished military commander and MP for co Donegal 1703, was *cr Baron Hamilton of Stackallan* 1715, and *Viscount Boyne* 1717 (peerage of Ireland); *d* 1723, *s* by his grandson (2) GUSTAVUS, PC, 2nd Viscount; sat as MP for Newport, I of W, 1735; *d* unmarried 1746; *s* by his cousin (3) FREDERICK, 3rd Viscount; *dsp* 1772; *s* by his brother (4) RICHARD, 4th Viscount; *d* 1789, *s* by his son (5) GUSTAVUS, 5th Viscount; *d* 1826; *s* by his son (6) GUSTAVUS, 6th Viscount; *d* 1855; *s* by his son (7) GUSTAVUS FREDERICK, 7th Viscount, *b* 1797; assumed by R licence the additional surname of Russell, and was *cr Baron Brancepeth* (peerage of United Kingdom) 1866: *m* 1828, Emma Maria, da of Matthew Russell, MP, of Brancepeth Castle; *d* 1870; *s* by his son (8) GUSTAVUS Russell, 8th Viscount, *b* 1830: *m* 1858, Lady Katherine Frances Scott, who *d* 1903, da of 2nd Earl of Eldon; *d* 1907; *s* by his son (9) GUSTAVUS WILLIAM, 9th Viscount, *b* 1864: *m* 1906, Lady Margaret Selina Lascelles, CBE, who *d* 1978, da of 5th Earl of Harewood; *d* 1942; *s* by his grandson (10) GUSTAVUS MICHAEL GEORGE, KCVO, son of late Hon Gustavus Lascelles Hamilton-Russell, Lieut Gren Gds (el son of 9th Viscount), who was *ka* 1940, 10th Viscount, *b* 1931; JP, DL and Lord Lieut Shropshire; Lord in Waiting to HM; Dir National Westminster Bank 1976-90: *m* 1956, Rosemary Anne, 2nd da of Maj Sir Dennis Frederic Bankes Stucley, 5th Bt; *d* 1995; *s* by his only son (11) GUSTAVUS MICHAEL STUCLEY, 11th Viscount and present peer; also Baron Hamilton of Stackallan, and Baron Brancepeth.

Brabazon, family name of Earl of Meath.

BRABAZON OF TARA, BARON (Moore-Brabazon) (Baron UK 1942)

My life is vowed

IVON ANTHONY MOORE-BRABAZON, 3rd Baron, *b* 20 Dec 1946; *s* 1974; *ed* Harrow; a Lord-in-Waiting 1984-86; DL Isle of Wight 1993; Under-Sec for Transport (Min for Aviation and Shipping) 1986-89, Min of State Foreign and Commonwealth Office 1989-90, Min of State for Transport 1990-92; a Member of London Stock Exchange 1972-84: *m* 1979, Harriet Frances, da of Mervyn Peter de Courcy Hamilton, of Harare, Zimbabwe, and has issue.

Arms – Quarterly; 1st and 4th gules on a bend or three martlets sable, *Brabazon*; 2nd and 3rd azure on a chief per pale argent and or three mullets gules, *Moore*. **Crests** – 1st a falcon rising, belled or, Brabazon; 2nd issuant from a coronet composed of eight mullets set upon a rim or a Moor's head and shoulders proper wreathed about the temples argent and azure, *Moore*. **Supporters** – On either side a gull volant over water supporting the shield with its beak all proper.
Address – House of Lords, SW1A 0PW.
Clubs – White's, Royal Yacht Sqdn.

SON LIVING

Hon BENJAMIN RALPH, *b* 15 March 1983.

DAUGHTER LIVING

Hon Anabel Mary, *b* 1985.

PREDECESSORS – (1) JOHN THEODORE CUTHBERT Moore-Brabazon, GBE, MC, PC, son of Col Arthur Henry Moore-Brabazon, of Tara Hall, co Meath; *b* 1884; pioneer in aviation; made first flight by any Briton in Great Britain 1909; received first pilot's certificate issued by Roy Aero Club; PPS to Sec of State for Air 1919-21, Parl Sec, Min of Transport 1923-27, Min of Transport 1940-41, and Min of Aircraft Production 1941-42; MP for Chatham Div of Rochester (*U*) 1918-29, and for Wallasey 1931-42: *cr Baron Brabazon of Tara*, of Sandwich, co Kent (peerage of UK 1942): *m* 1906, Hilda Mary, who *d* 1977, da of Charles Henry Krabbé, of Buenos Aires; *d* 1964, *s* by his el son (2) DEREK CHARLES, CBE, 2nd Baron, *b* 1910; Member of London Stock Exchange; Chm S Kensington Conservative Assocn 1952-54, and Pres Kensington Conservative Assocn 1966-74: *m* 1939, Henrietta Mary, who *d* 1985, da of late Sir (Alfred) Rowland Clegg, and widow of Ivor Krabbé; *d* 1974; *s* by his only son (3) IVON ANTHONY, 3rd Baron and present peer.

BRABOURNE, BARON (Knatchbull) (Baron UK 1880, Bt E 1641)
(Title pronounced "Braybn")

My glory is in the cross

JOHN ULICK KNATCHBULL, CBE, 7th Baron, and 16th Baronet; *b* 9 Nov 1924; *s* 1943; *ed* Eton and Oxford Univ; a film and television producer; formerly Capt Coldstream Gds; Pres Kent Trust for Nature Conservation, formerly Chm Caldecott Community, formerly Chm of Govs of Norton Knatchbull Sch, Provost Wye Coll, Gov Gordonstoun Sch 1964-94, and United World Colls; formerly Pro Chancellor, Univ of Kent; formerly Chm Thames Television; Fellow and Gov BFI; Member British Screen Advisory Council; formerly Trustee Science Museum, Trustee British Academy of Film & TV Arts, Vice-Pres Royal Soc for Nature Conservation; 1939-45 War in NW Europe and SE Asia (wounded); CBE (Civil) 1993: *m* 26 Oct 1946, Lady Patricia Edwina Victoria Mountbatten, CBE (*Countess Mountbatten of Burma* in her own right), elder da of 1st Earl Mountbatten of Burma, and has had issue.

Arms – Quarterly: 1st and 4th argent, on a mount vert, two boars' erect, respecting each other sable, their forelegs resting against an oak tree proper, *Hugessen*; 2nd and 3rd azure, three cross crosslets fitchée between two bendlets or, *Knatchbull*. **Crests** – 1st, an oak tree proper, between two wings elevated, pinions azure, feathered or, *Hugessen*; 2nd, on a chapeau azure, turned up ermine, an ounce statant argent, spotted sable, *Knatchbull*. **Supporters** – On either side a leopard argent pelletty, gorged with an oak wreath vert, fructed gold, and holding in the mouth a cross crosslet fitchée or.

Residences – Newhouse, Mersham, Ashford, Kent TN25 6NQ; 39 Montpelier Walk, SW7 1JH.

SONS LIVING AND DECEASED

NORTON LOUIS PHILIP (*Lord Romsey*) (Broadlands, Romsey, Hants SO51 9ZD), *b* 8 Oct 1947; *ed* Gordonstoun, and Univ of Kent; High Steward of Romsey since 1980: *m* 20 Oct 1979, Penelope Meredith, only da of Reginald Eastwood, of Son Vida, Palma de Mallorca, Spain, and has had issue (*see* Ctss Mountbatten of Burma).

Hon Michael-John Ulick (1 Horbury Mews, W11 3NL), *b* 24 May 1950; *ed* Gordonstoun, and Reading Univ: *m* 1st, 1 June 1985 (*m diss* 1997), Melissa Clare, only da of Hon Mr Justice (Sir John Arthur Dalziel) Owen, of Bickerstaff House, Idlicote, Shipston-on-Stour, Warwicks; 2ndly, 6 March 1999, Mrs Susan Penelope Henderson, da of Cedric Coates, of The Old Rectory, Epperstone, Notts, and formerly wife of William Dalton Alexander Henderson, and has issue (by 1st *m*) (*see* Ctss Mountbatten of Burma).

Hon Philip Wyndham Ashley (41 Montpelier Walk, SW7 1JH), *b* 2 Dec 1961; *ed* Gordonstoun, Kent Univ, and London Internat Film Sch: *m* 16 March 1991, Mrs Atalanta Vereker, da of late John Cowan, and formerly wife of Hugo Dominic Charles Medlicott Vereker (*see* V Gort, colls), and has issue (*see* Ctss Mountbatten of Burma).

†*Hon* Nicholas Timothy Charles, *b* 18 Nov 1964; *k* with his grandfather, Earl Mountbatten of Burma, and grandmother, Doreen Lady Brabourne, 1979.

Hon Timothy Nicholas Sean, *b* (twin)18 Nov 1964; *ed* Gordonstoun, Atlantic Coll, Christ's Coll, Camb, and Kennedy Sch, Harvard Univ, USA: *m* 1998, Isabella Julia, 2nd da of David Mark Norman (*see* Sheffield, Bt).

DAUGHTERS LIVING

Lady Joanna Edwina Doreen, *b* 5 March 1955; *ed* Benenden, Atlantic Coll, Kent Univ, and Columbia Univ, USA: *m* 1st, 3 Nov 1984 (*m diss* 1995), Baron Hubert Henry François du Breuil, yr son of Baron Bertrand Pernot du Breuil, of 52 Avenue d'Iena, 75116 Paris; 2ndly, 19 Nov 1995, Azriel Adrian Sorin Zuckerman, elder son of Bercu Zuckerman, of Bucharest, Rumania, and has issue (by 1st *m*) (*see* Ctss Mountbatten of Burma).

Lady Amanda Patricia Victoria, *b* 26 June 1957; *ed* Benenden, Gordonstoun, Kent Univ, Peking Univ, and Goldsmith Coll, London: *m* 31 Oct 1987, Charles V. Ellingworth, eldest son of William Ellingworth, of Laughton, Leics, and has issue (*see* Ctss Mountbatten of Burma).

COLLATERAL BRANCHES LIVING

Grandchildren of Hon Adrian Norton KNATCHBULL-HUGESSEN, QC (infra):—
Issue of late Edward Herrick KNATCHBULL-HUGESSEN, b 1923, d 1955: m 1947, Mary Louise, who d 1969, da of
Walter Asahel Newton, of Montreal:—
Kenneth Norton (31 Russell Hill, Toronto, Ontario, Canada M4V 2S9), b 1949: m 1969, Karen, da of Olaf Wolff, of
Montreal, and has issue living, Arlo Edward, b 1970. —— Kathleen Mary, b 1950. —— Patricia Margaret, b 1952: m
19—, — Osgoode.

Issue of late Hon Adrian Norton KNATCHBULL-HUGESSEN, QC, 3rd son of 1st Baron, b 1891, d 1976: m
1922, Margaret Cecilia Ross, who d 1980 da of George Herrick Duggan, of 3636 McTavish St,
Montreal:—
Andrew John (5 Beacon Rd, Kirkland, Quebec, Canada H9J 2E9), b 1926: m 1952, Jane Frances, da of Douglas Gilfillan
Currie, of Montreal, Canada, and has issue living, Brian Andrew, b 1954, — John, b 1958, — Wendy Jane (twin), b 1954,
— Martha, b 1960. —— Hon James Cornelius (31 Elmdale Av, Ottawa, Canada K1M 1A1; Rideau Club), b 1933; ed
Balliol Coll, Oxford, and McGill Univ, Montreal; Bar Quebec 1958; Puisne Judge of Superior Court and Court of Queen's
Bench, Quebec 1972-73, Asso Ch Justice, Superior Court of Quebec 1973-83, since when Puisne Justice of Federal Court
of Appeal of Canada: m 1958, Mary Rosamond, da of R. Ewart Stavert, of Montreal, and has issue living, Jaime William,
b 1959, — Alexander Ewart, b 1965, — Ross Adrian, b 1969, — Kathleen Jill, b 1960, — Alicia Mary, b 1962. —— Mary
Cecelia, b 1929: m 1955, Stephen John Keynes, of 16 Canonbury Park South, N1, yr son of Sir Geoffrey Langdon Keynes, and has issue living, Gregory Robert Edward, b 1956, — Toby William, b 1959, — Zachary Edmund, b 1962, —
Elizabeth Harriet, b 1957, — Martha Paganel, b 1961.

(In remainder to Baronetcy only)

Granddaughters of late Rev Reginald Bridges Knatchbull-Hugessen, 7th son of 9th baronet:—
Issue of late Major Everard Knatchbull-Hugessen; b 1871; d 1946: m 1908, Grace Marshall, who d 1937, da of
James Arthur Hindmarsh, of Ayr:—
Pleasance Anne, b 1920: m 1948, John Stuart Comery, MC, of Home Farm, Upper Hayesden, Tonbridge, Kent, and has
issue living, William Knatchbull, b 1952, — Patricia Mary, b 1950.

Issue of late Sir Hughe Montgomery Knatchbull-Hugessen, KCMG, b 1886, d 1971: m 1912, Mary, who d 1978,
da of Brig-Gen Sir Robert Gordon Gilmour, 1st Bt, CVO, CB, DSO, cr 1926:—
Alethea (23 Emden House, Barton Lane, Old Headington, Oxford), b 1918.

Grandchildren of late Brig Gen George Wyndham Chichester Knatchbull, CMG, 4th son of late Lieut-
Gen Reginald Edward Knatchbull (infra):—
Issue of late Lt-Col Wyndham Marsden Knatchbull, b 1901, d 1977: m 1934, Eileen Mary, who d 1986, el da of
late Lt-Col William Chapman Croly, DSO, RAMC:—
Patrick Wyndham (16 Seafront Rd, Cultra, co Down BT18 OBB), b 1936; Cdr RD: m 1966, Mary, da of late L. F. Kelly,
of Tile Hatch, Bishops Down Park Rd, Tunbridge Wells, and has issue living, Simon Marsden, b 1967: m 1996, Jane
Spolton, and has issue living, William Marsden b 1999, — Andrew Wyndham, b 1969: m 1997, Sandra Jefferys, and has
issue living, Rachael Betty b 1998, — Felicity Jane, b 1972. —— Michael Walter (Gambles Lodge, Upper Mountown,
Dun Laoghaire, co Dublin) (twin), b 1936: m 1959, Rhona Dorothy, da of late John Sinclair Gunning, of Holywood, co
Down, and has issue living, Richard Edward Walter, b 1971, — Mark Wyndham John, b 1978, — Fiona Bridgid, b 1962:
m 1987, David Holmes, and has issue living, Philip Edward Knatchbull b 1993, Michael John Wyndham b 1995, Polly
Amanda b 1991, — Lucy Rhona, b 1964: m 1988, Robert O'Riordan, and has issue living, Samson Robert b 1992, Andrew
James b 1994, Rosie Katharine b 1997, — Gillian Mary, b 1966: m 1996, William Paul McChesney, of Chicago, USA.
—— Bridget Eileen Mary, b 1943: m 1st, 1964 (m diss 1971), James Seymour Emerson (see Keane, Bt); 2ndly, 1974,
Robert Ernest Somekh, of 6 Lyndewode Rd, Cambridge CB1 2HL.

Descendants, if any, of Reginald Edward Knatchbull (b 1893), late Capt IA Res of Officers, only son of
Owen Edward Knatchbull, 6th and yst son of Lieut-Gen Reginald Edward Knatchbull, 8th son of 8th
baronet.

Granddaughters of late Lt-Col Francis Knatchbull, 3rd son of Rev Wadham Knatchbull, LLD, 3rd son of
4th Bt:—
Issue of late Maj Wyndham Persse Knatchbull, b 1873, d 1967: m 1911, Sybil Mathilde, who d 1957, da of late
Ulick Burke (Burke, Bt, colls):—
Angela Alice, b 1912: m 1948, Reginald Cyril Neville Owbridge, who d 1975, and has issue living, Anthony Wyndham
(112 Grenville Rd, Aylesbury, Bucks HP21 8EZ), b 1949: m 1972, Barbara Jean, only da of Lawrence Lacy, of Chesham,
Bucks. —— Zara Eleanor (93 Livermore Green, Werrington, Peterborough PE4 5DQ), b 1920; 1939-45 War with ATS: m
1st, 1942 (m diss 1953), John Mackay; 2ndly, 1953, Christopher Jocelyn Lapage, who d 1990, and has issue living, (by
2nd m) Fiona Anne, b 1954: m 1976, Hamdy Taha.

Grandsons of late Maj Wyndham Persse Knatchbull (ante):—
Issue of late Charles Norton Knatchbull, b 1918, d 1980: m 1940, Jacqueline Nora (Batch Farm, Kilmersdon,
Bath), da of Henry Presland Veall, of Netley, Hants:—
Henry Norton (19 Riverside Rd, Westmoors, Ferndown, Dorset), b 1942; ed Stanbridge Earls Sch, Romsey: m 1988,
Jenny Elizabeth, yst da of Roy Brown, of Ferndown, Dorset. —— Richard Wyndham (Batch Farm, Kilmersdon, Bath), b
1947; ed Hurn Court, Christchurch: m 1970, Susan Ann Russell, only da of Arthur Candy, of Mells, Somerset, and has
issue living, Paul Wyndham, b 1973, — James Wyndham, b 1975.

(Not in remainder to Baronetcy)

Grandchildren of Herbert Thomas KNATCHBULL-HUGESSEN, MP, 9th son of 9th baronet:—
Issue of late Paul Lionel Knatchbull-Hugessen, *b* 1874, *d* 1958: *m* 1906, Marie Blanche, who *d* 1945, yst da of
Remi Poullin, of St Boniface, Manitoba:—
Herbert Clifford, *b* 1907: *m* 1936, Violet, el da of Samuel Oliver Emily Sutherland, of Edson, Alberta, Canada, and has
issue living, Darolyn, *b* 1941.

Issue of late Edward Knatchbull-Hugessen, *b* 1877, *d* 1969: *m* 1920, Edith Elizabeth, who *d* 1957, da of Charles
Edward Chatfield, of Bloomsbury:—
Christina Pauline (11 Greville Lodge, Avenue Rd, Highgate, N6 5DP), *b* 1931.

Issue of late George Knatchbull-Hugessen, *b* 1883, *d* 1966: *m* 1910, Jessie, who *d* 1961, da of John Downie Kay,
of Brinkley, Newmarket, Suffolk:—
Peter Merrick (Ropley House, Ropley, Hants), *b* 1915; *ed* Wadham Coll, Oxford; late Capt RA; served World War II with
111th Field Regt, and 6th Indian Field Regt; formerly Headmaster Papplewick Sch, Ascot: *m* 1992, Anna-Rose, da of late
Maj Henry Bramwell, of The White House, Mallow, co Cork (*see* B Rathdonnell, 1962 Edn), and widow of Lord James
Charles Crichton-Stuart (*see* M Bute).

Grandchildren of late Edward Knatchbull-Hugessen (*ante*):—
Issue of late Denis Norton Knatchbull-Hugessen, *b* 1923, *d* 1982: *m* 1947, Mavis Josephine, who *d* 1980, elder da
of Henry Albert Peard, of Bath:—
Mark Wyndham (11 Frayslea, Cowley Rd, Uxbridge, Middx), *b* 1953. —— Bernice Simone, *b* 1949: *m* 1975, Raymond
Charles Morley, of 112 Springdale Rd, Corfe Mullen, Wimborne, Dorset, and has issue living, Joseph Ronan Charles, *b*
1983, — Jessica Natasha, *b* 1985. —— Teresa Frances, *b* 1951: *m* 1971, Donald Pooley, of 145 Cowley Rd, Uxbridge,
Middx, and has issue living, Matthew Lee, *b* 1970. — Damon Ross, *b* 1972.

Grandchildren of late George Knatchbull-Hugessen (*ante*):—
Issue of late Robin John Kay Knatchbull-Hugessen, *b* 1921, *d* 1986: *m* 1st, 1945 (*m diss* 1956), Enid Mabel, da of
Thomas Marlow, of Highgate, N6; 2ndly, 1958, Barbara Anne Wilcox (Cilwern, Talley, Llandeilo, Dyfed):—
(By 1st *m*) Peter Wyndham (Grove Barn, Beckley, Oxford), *b* 1947: *m* 1st, 1975 (*m diss* 1988), Henrietta Frances, da of
Col John Ellis Spencer, of Hill Farm, Swalcliffe, Oxon; 2ndly, 19—, Mrs Marilyn F. Barrett, da of late Alan E. Higgs, of
Dorridge, Warwicks, and formerly wife of A. W. Barrett, and has issue living (by 1st *m*), Thomas Michael, *b* 1977, —
William Peter, *b* 1979, — Lydia Victoria, *b* 1982, — Holly Frances, *b* 1984. —— (By 2nd *m*) Simon Stephen (Lychpit,
Hants), *b* 1960: *m* 1990 (*m diss* 1996), Tracy Helen, eldest da of G. Burns, of Hook, Hants. —— Sally Anne, MVO, *b*
1959; MVO 1989: *m* 1987, Dr Thomas P. O'Brien, of 103 Ridgewood Rd, Baltimore, Maryland 21210, USA, and has issue
living, William Thomas Robin, *b* 1991. —— Jane Elizabeth, *b* 1962.

PREDECESSORS – (1) *Rt Hon* EDWARD HUGESSEN Knatchbull, PC, 6th son of the Rt Hon Sir Edward Knatchbull, MP,
9th Bt; *b* 1829; assumed by R licence the additional surname of Hugessen 1849; MP for Sandwich (*L*) 1857-80; was a
Lord of the Treasury 1859-66, Under-Sec of State for Home Depart 1866, and 1868-71, and Under Sec for Colonies 1871-
4; *cr Baron Brabourne*, of Brabourne, co Kent (peerage of United Kingdom) 1880: *m* 1st, 1852, Anna Maria Elizabeth,
who *d* 1889, da of late Rev Marcus R. Southwell, of St Stephen's Herts; 2ndly, 1890, Ethel Mary, who *d* 1929, da of Col
Sir George Gustavus Walker, KCB, of Crawfordton, Dumfriesshire, *d* 1893: *s* by his el son (2) EDWARD, 2nd Baron, *b*
1857; MP for Rochester (*L*) 1889-92; *m* 1880, Hon Amy Virginia Beaumont, who *d* 1949, da of 1st Baron Allendale: *d*
1909; *s* by his son, (3) WYNDHAM WENTWORTH, 3rd Baron; *b* 1885; Lt Gren Gds; *ka* 1915; *s* by his uncle (4) CECIL
MARCUS, 4th Baron; *b* 1863; *s* in 1917 his cousin as 13th *Baronet* of Mersham Hatch (*cr* 1641): *m* 1893, Helena Regina
Frederica, who *d* 1919, da of late Hermann von Flesch-Brunningen, Imperial Councillor of Vienna; *d* 1933: *s* by his only
son (5) MICHAEL HERBERT RUDOLPH, GCSI, GCIE, MC, 5th Baron; *b* 1895; assumed by deed poll 1919, the surname of
Knatchbull only; was MP for Ashford Div of Kent (*C*) 1931-3, and Gov of Bombay 1933-7, and of Bengal 1937-9 (acted as
Viceroy of India, June-Sept 1938): *m* 1919, Lady Doreen Geraldine Browne, CI, who *d* 1979, da of 6th Marquess of Sligo:
d 1939; *s* by his son (6) NORTON CECIL MICHAEL, 6th Baron: *b* 1922; Lt Gren Gds; served 1939-45 War (wounded,
prisoner); *k* on active service (shot by the Germans after he had escaped from a prison train in N Italy and had been
recaptured) 1943; *s* by his brother (7) JOHN ULICK, 7th Baron and present peer.

BRADBURY, BARON (Bradbury) (Baron UK 1925)

Justice, equity, and good faith

JOHN BRADBURY, 3rd Baron; *b* 17 March 1940; *s* 1994; *ed* Gresham's Sch, Holt, and Bristol Univ: *m* 1968, Susan, da of late William Liddiard, of E Shefford, Berks, and has issue.

Arms – Sable, a chevron ermine, between in chief two buckles and in base a fleur-de-lis argent **Crest** – In front of two ostrich feathers in saltire argent, a boar's head erect proper. **Supporters** – *Dexter*, a raven; *sinister*, a dove; both proper.
Residence – 10 Clifton Hill, NW8.

SONS LIVING

Hon JOHN, *b* 1973.
Hon Benjamin, *b* 1975.

SISTER LIVING

Hon Elizabeth Joan (twin), *b* 1940: *m* 1965, Warren Hansen, and has issue living, Karl Geoffrey, *b* 1971, — Christine Joan, *b* 1967.

HALF-SISTER LIVING

Hon Anne, *b* 1947: *m* 1970, Alastair James Ker-Lindsay, of 3 Temple Mews, Stour St, Canterbury, Kent CT1 2PQ, and has issue living, James *b* 1972, — Mark *b* 1973, — John Alexander, *b* 1977, — Adam, *b* 1979, — Laura, *b* 1985.

WIDOW LIVING OF SON OF FIRST BARON

Margaret Amy, da of late J. W. Stammers, of Purley, Surrey: *m* 1940, Hon Paul Bradbury, who *d* 1999, and has issue (see colls, infra). *Residence* – 32 Priory Court, Glasshouse Hill, Stourbridge, Worcs DY8 1NJ.

MOTHER LIVING

Joan, only da of Walter Dingle Knight, of Darley, Addlestone Surrey: *m* 1939 (*m diss* 1946), Hon John Bradbury (later 2nd Baron Bradbury), who *d* 1994. *Residence* –

WIDOW LIVING OF SECOND BARON

GWERFYL (*Dowager Baroness Bradbury*), da of late E. Stanton Roberts, of Gellifor, nr Ruthin, Denbighshire: *m* 1946, as his 2nd wife, the 2nd Baron Bradbury, who *d* 1994. *Residence* – 10 St Margarets, London Rd, Guildford, Surrey GU1 1TJ.

COLLATERAL BRANCH LIVING

Issue of late Hon Paul Bradbury, yr son of 1st Baron, *b* 1915, *d* 1999: *m* 1940, Margaret Amy (ante), da of late J. W. Stammers, of Purley, Surrey:-
Richard (Milcote House, Long Wood Drive, Jordans, Beaconsfield, Bucks), *b* 1941: *m* 1966, Elizabeth Mary Auchinleck, da of late Douglas C. L. Love, of Richmond, Surrey, and has issue living, Clare, *b* 1967, — Jane, *b* (twin) 1967, — Philippa, *b* 1972. —— James (Barnford, Holy Cross, Clent, Worcs DY9 9QD), *b* 1945: *m* 1967, Patricia Mary, da of late Hedley A. Funnell, of Bybrook House, Longdean, Yatton Keynell, Chippenham, Wilts, and has issue living, Anthony James, *b* 1969, — Jonathan Paul, *b* 1971, — Charlotte Ann, *b* 1973. —— David (Pencot, Tresham, Wotton-under-Edge, Glos), *b* 1950: *m* 1973, Janet Ann Salier, da of David H. Davidson, of Battramsley Cottage, Boldre, Lymington, Hants, and has issue living, Caroline Salier, *b* 1978. — Anna Sarah, *b* 1980.

PREDECESSORS – (1) *Sir* JOHN SWANWICK Bradbury, GCB, son of late John Bradbury, of Winsford, Cheshire; *b* 1872; Under Treasurer of Natal 1904-5, Private Sec to Chancellor of Exchequer (Rt Hon Herbert H. Asquith, MP) 1905-8, Principal Clerk in the Treasury, and First Treasury Officer of Accounts 1908-11, Joint Permanent Sec to the Treasury 1913-19, Principal British Delegate to Reparation Commn (Paris) 1919-25, Chm of International Relief Credits Committee 1920, of National Food Council 1925-9, and of Bankers' Clearing House Committee and British Bankers' Asso 1929-30 and 1935-6; *cr Baron Bradbury*, of Winsford, co Chester (peerage of United Kingdom) 1925: *m* 1911, Hilda Maude, who *d* 1949, 2nd da of William Arthur Kirby, of Goldhurst Terrace, Hampstead, NW; *d* 1950; *s* by his son (2) JOHN, 2nd Baron, *b* 1914: *m* 1st, 1939 (*m diss* 1946), Joan, only da of Walter Dingle Knight, of Darley, Addlestone, Surrey; 2ndly, 1946, Gwerfyl, da of late E. Stanton Roberts, of Gellifor, nr Ruthin, Denbighshire; *d* 1994; *s* by his only son (3) JOHN, 3rd Baron and present peer.

BRADFORD, EARL OF (Bridgeman) (Earl UK 1815, Bt E 1660)

RICHARD THOMAS ORLANDO BRIDGEMAN, 7th Earl, and 12th Baronet; *b* 3 Oct 1947; *s* 1981; *ed* Harrow, and Trin Coll, Camb; patron of five livings: *m* 1979, Joanne Elizabeth, el da of Benjamin Miller, of 42 Pembroke Rd, W8, and has issue.

𝕬rms – Sable, ten plates, four, three, two, and one; on a chief argent, a lion passant ermine. 𝕮rest – A demi-lion rampant argent, holding in the paws a wreath of laurel proper. 𝕾upporters – Two leopards guardant gules pelletée.
Seat – Weston Park, Shifnal, Shropshire. *Residence* – Woodlands House, Weston-under-Lizard, Shifnal, Shropshire TF11 8PX.

SONS LIVING

ALEXANDER MICHAEL ORLANDO (*Viscount Newport*), *b* 6 Sept 1980.
Hon Henry Gerald Orlando, *b* 1982.
Hon Benjamin Thomas Orlando, *b* 1987.

DAUGHTER LIVING

Lady Alicia Rose, *b* 1990.

BROTHER LIVING

Hon Charles Gerald Orlando (Albion Hayes Farm, Bomere Heath, Shrewsbury, Shropshire), *b* 1954; *ed* Harrow, Warwick Univ, and RAC Cirencester; ARICS 1993: *m* 1982, Nicola Marie-Thérèse, only da of Brian Sales, of Congleton, Cheshire, and has issue living, James Edward Charles Orlando, *b* 1978, — Robert Gerald Orlando, *b* 1983, — Nicholas Francis Orlando, *b* 1991.

Neither rashly nor timidly

SISTERS LIVING

Lady Serena Mary BRIDGEMAN, *b* 1949; has resumed her maiden name: *m* 1978 (*m diss* 1989), Richard Arnold Andrew. *Residences* – Dell House, Whitebridge, Inverness-shire IV1 2UN; Flat 1, 3 Westgate Terr, SW10 9BT.
Lady Caroline Louise, *b* 1952: *m* 1974, Brian Martin Garnell, of 16 Holland Park Av, W11 3QU, and has issue living, Thomas Henry Michael *b* 1986, — Benedict Charles Orlando, *b* 1990, — Daniel Gerald Orlando, *b* 1993, — Tara Serena Clare, *b* 1983.

AUNT LIVING (*Daughter of 5th Earl*)

Lady Anne Pamela (*Lady Anne Cowdray*), *b* 1913: *m* 1939 (*m diss* 1950), 3rd Viscount Cowdray, who *d* 1995, and has issue (see that title). *Residence* – Broadleas, Devizes, Wilts.

COLLATERAL BRANCHES LIVING

Issue of late Col Hon Henry George Orlando Bridgeman, DSO, MC, yst son of 4th Earl, *b* 1882, *d* 1972: *m* 1930, Joan, who *d* 1991, da of late Hon Bernard Constable-Maxwell (*see* L Herries of Terregles, colls):—
Peter Orlando Ronald, TD (Fallodon Hall, Embleton, Alnwick, Northumberland), *b* 1933; Lt-Col R Northumberland Fus (TA); TD 1968, DL Northumberland 1983; *m* 1967, Sarahjane, da of Patrick Corbett, of Silverlands, Boar's Head, Crowborough, and has issue living, Mark George Orlando, *b* 1968: *m* 1997, Lucia M. B., da of Russell Hawkes, of Saffron Walden, Essex, — Emma Virginia, *b* 1969, — Davina Sacha, *b* 1972. —— John Henry Orlando (Boreland House, Lockerbie, Dumfriesshire), *b* 1938: *m* 1970, Susan Gay, da of late A. Leonard Hill, of Boreland of Dryfe, Lockerbie, Dumfriesshire, and has issue living, Camilla Jane, *b* 1971, — Alexandra Mary, *b* 1973. —— Mary Helena, *b* 1932: *m* 1960, William Simon Rodolph Kenyon-Slaney, and has issue (*see* B Kenyon, colls). —— Alice Christina, *b* 1936: *m* 1967, Bruce Mckenzie, of Haselbech Hall, Northants NN6 9LG; Min of Agric, Kenya, and has issue living, Kim Alexander, *b* 1969, — James Malcolm, *b* 1971.

Grandchildren of late Brig-Gen Hon Francis Charles Bridgeman, 2nd son of 3rd Earl:—
Issue of late Reginald Francis Orlando Bridgeman, CMG, MVO, *b* 1884, *d* 1968: *m* 1923, Olwen Elizabeth, who *d* 1985, da of Maurice Jones, MPS:—
Henry Clive Orlando, *b* 1946; *ed* Harrow, and Trin Coll, Camb. —— Victoria Mary (71 Lauderdale Mansions, Lauderdale Rd, W9 1LX), *b* 1926: 1939-45 War with WRNS. —— Olwen Valery, *b* 1928: BA London: *m* 1962, Anthony Mark Barrington Golding, MB, FFPHM, of 12 Clifton Hill, NW8, and Keepers Cottage, Byworth, Petworth, Sussex, and has issue living, Richard Mark Orlando, *b* 1965; MEng & Man: *m* 1990 (*m diss* 1992), Sarah Dolman, and has issue living, Leo Dolman *b* 1991, — Rosemary Victoria Anne, *b* 1963; LLB; Solicitor: *m* 1996, Christopher Chilton, of 8 Milton Court, Ickenham, Middx UB10 8ND, and has issue living, Jasmine Rebecca Anne *b* 1997, Imogen Sarah Jane *b* 1999, — Catherine Elizabeth Marian, *b* 1967; BMedSc, MB BS, MRCP: *m* 1997, Sean James Connell, of 15 Stanhope Gdns, N6 5TT, — Charlotte Valery Patricia, *b* 1970; BA, BSc.

Issue of late Com Francis Paul Orlando Bridgeman, RN, *b* 1888, *d* 1930: *m* 1922, Alice, who *d* 1979, da of Herman Greverus Kleinwort, of 45 Belgrave Square, SW1:—

DEBRETT'S ILLUSTRATED PEERAGE P 195

Gerald William Paul Orlando, *b* 1929; *m* 1965, Mrs Rosemarie Ingrams, da of Willis Tomlinson. *Residences* – Dowdeswell Rookery, Andoversford, Glos; 43 Cheval Place, SW7; 51 Mixnam's Lane, Chertsey, Surrey. —— Jeannine Patricia, *b* 1923: *m* 1st, 1951 (*m diss* 1955), Alan Forde Scott, late Tanganyika Admin Ser; 2ndly, 1969, Rear Adm Josef Czeslaw Bartosik, CB, DSC, of Well House, Donnington, Moreton-in-Marsh, Glos, and of 33 Cheval Place, SW7. —— Marigold Helen, *b* 1925. *Residences* – Never End, Foxcote, Andoversford, Cheltenham, Glos GL54 4LP; 43 Cheval Place, SW7 1EW.

Grandchildren of late Maj Roger Orlando Bridgeman, only son of Charles George Orlando Bridgeman, yr son of Rev Hon George Thomas Orlando Bridgeman, 2nd son of 2nd Earl:—
Issue of late Richard Lynedoch Orlando Bridgeman, *b* 1931, *d* 1982: *m* 1965, Romayne Georgette Ord, who *d* 1985, only da of late Ingram Ord Capper, of The Mill, Polstead, Suffolk:—
(Leopold) Orlando, *b* 1968; *ed* Harrow. *Residence* – 8 Cranbourne Court, Albert Bridge Rd, SW11 4PE. —— Constantine Orlando, *b* 1970. *Residence* – 52 Ebury Mews, SW1. —— Celestine Victoria, *b* 1966: *m* 1988, Roger D. Bramley, son of late Richard Bramley, of Unstone, Derbys, and has issue living, Edward Orlando, *b* 1995, — Cressida Romayne, *b* 1994. *Residences* – 40 Anhalt Rd, SW11 4NX; Chedglow Barn Cottage, Crudwell, Malmesbury, Wilts.

Grandsons of late Rev Hon John Robert Orlando Bridgeman, 3rd son of 2nd Earl:—
Issue of late Rt Hon William Clive Bridgeman, who was *cr Viscount Bridgeman* 1929 (see that title).

PREDECESSORS – (1) Sir ORLANDO Bridgeman, successively Lord Chief Baron of Exchequer, Lord Chief Justice of Common Pleas, and Lord Keeper of Great Seal; *cr* a *Baronet* 1660; *d* 1674; *s* by his son (2) Sir JOHN, 2nd Bt; *d* 1710; *s* by his son (3) Sir JOHN, 3rd Bt; *d* 1747; *s* by his son (4) Sir ORLANDO, 4th Bt, MP for Shrewsbury, who *m* Lady Ann Newport, da of Richard, 2nd Earl of Bradford (title extinct 1762, on death of 4th Earl); *d* 1764; *s* by his son (5) Sir HENRY, 5th Bt, *cr Baron Bradford* (peerage of Great Britain) 1794; *d* 1800; *s* by his son (6) ORLANDO, 2nd Baron, *cr Viscount Newport* and *Earl of Bradford* (peerage of United Kingdom) 1815; *d* 1825; *s* by his son (7) George Augustus Frederick Henry, 2nd Earl, *b* 1789: *m* 1st, 1818, Georgina Elizabeth, who *d* 1842, da of Sir Thomas Moncreiffe, 5th Bt; 2ndly, 1849, Helen, who *d* 1869, da of Æneas Mackay, of Scotston, and widow of Sir David Moncreiffe, 6th Bt; *d* 1865; *s* by his son (8) ORLANDO GEORGE CHARLES, PC, 3rd Earl, *b* 1819; sometime Lord-Lieut of Salop; MP for S Shropshire (C) 1842-65; Vice-Chamberlain of HM Queen Victoria's Household 1852 and 1858-9, Lord Chamberlain 1866-8, and Master of the Horse 1874-80 and 1885-6: *m* 1844, Hon Selina Louisa Forester, who *d* 1894, da of 1st Baron Forester: *d* 1898; *s* by his el son (9) GEORGE CECIL ORLANDO, 4th Earl, *b* 1845; Lieut 1st Life Guards 1864-7, and Capt Shropshire Yeo 1867; MP for N Shropshire (C) 1867-85: *m* 1869, Lady Ida Frances Annabella Lumley, who *d* 1936, 2nd da of 9th Earl of Scarbrough; *d* 1915; *s* by his el son (10) ORLANDO, 5th Earl; *b* 1873; was Assist Private Sec of State for Foreign Affairs (Marquess of Salisbury) 1898-1900, and to Prime Min (Marquess of Salisbury) 1902, Private Sec to Prime Min (Rt Hon A. J. Balfour, MP) 1902-5, and a Lord-in-Waiting to HM 1919-24: *m* 1904, Hon Margaret Cecilia Bruce, who *d* 1949, el da of 2nd Baron Aberdare; *d* 1957; *s* by his only son (11) GERALD MICHAEL ORLANDO, 6th Earl, *b* 1911; Vice-Lieut for Salop 1970-74; a Crown Estate Commr 1956-67; Pres of Country Landowners' Assocn 1955-57, and of Timber Growers Organisation 1962-64, and Chm of Forestry Cttee of Great Britain 1964-66; received Freedom of Shrewsbury 1957; 1939-45 War (despatches): *m* 1946, Mary Willoughby, who (*d* 1986), da of late Lt-Col Thomas Hassard Montgomery, DSO, of Cadogan House, Shrewsbury; *d* 1981; *s* by his el son (12) RICHARD THOMAS ORLANDO, 7th Earl and present peer; also Viscount Newport, and Baron Bradford.

BRAGG, BARON (Bragg) (Life Baron 1998)

MELVYN BRAGG, son of Stanley Bragg, of Wigton, Cumbria; *b* 6 Oct 1939; *ed* Nelson Thomlinson Gram Sch, Wigton, and Wadham Coll, Oxford (MA), Hon DUniv Open Univ 1988, Hon LLD Univ of St Andrews 1993, Hon DLitt Liverpool 1986, Lancaster 1990, CNAA 1990, Hon DCL Univ of Northumbria 1994; writer and broadcaster; presenter and editor, South Bank Show since 1978; controller Arts Dept, LWT since 1990; recipient of many awards; FRSL, FRTS; *cr Baron Bragg*, of Wigton, co Cambria (Life Baron) 1998: *m* 1st, 1961, Marie-Elisabeth Roche (*dec*); 2ndly, 1973, Catherine Mary (the writer, broadcaster and tv producer Cate Haste), da of Eric L. Haste, of Crantock, Almondsbury, Som, and has issue by 1st and 2nd *m*.
Residence – 12 Hampstead Hill Gdns, NW3 2PL. *Club* – Garrick.

SON LIVING (*By 2nd marriage*)

Hon Tom, *b* 1980.

DAUGHTERS LIVING (*By 1st marriage*)

Hon Marie-Elsa, *b* 1965.

(*By 2nd marriage*)

Hon Alice, *b* 1977.

BRAIN, BARON (Brain) (Baron UK 1962, Bt UK 1954)

I am, therefore I think

The mind the star of the brain

CHRISTOPHER LANGDON BRAIN, 2nd Baron and 2nd Baronet; *b* 30 Aug 1926; *s* 1966; *ed* Leighton Park Sch, and New Coll, Oxford (MA), ARPS: *m* 1953, Susan Mary, da of George Philip Morris, and has issue.

Arms – Per pale or and argent, three cats' heads erased gules. **Crest** – A falcon sable armed and belled or, supporting with the dexter claw a representation of the silver staff of office of the President of the Royal College of Physicians of London proper. **Supporters** – *Dexter*, a lion rampant guardant or, gorged with a coronet composed of fleurs-de-lis argent, set upon a rim gobony silver and azure, holding in the interior paw a pomegranate slipped proper; *sinister*, a griffin gold beaked gules, gorged with a like coronet, holding in the interior claw a poppy slipped also proper. *Residence* – Alexandra House, 8 Cross St, Moretonhampstead, Devon TQ13 8NL.

DAUGHTERS LIVING

Hon Nicola Dorothy, *b* 1955; MB, ChB, MRCP, FRCP: *m* 1994, Dr Stephen Bashforth, elder son of G. P. Bashforth, of Norton, Sheffield, and has issue living, Rowena Elizabeth, *b* 1997.

Hon Fiona Janice, *b* 1958, BSc: *m* 1977, Rev Andrew John Proud, BD, of The Rectory, 136 Church Hill Rd, E Barnet, Herts EN4 8XD, and has issue living, Justin Dominic Edward, *b* 1979, — Emma Jane Chrysogen, *b* 1977.

Hon Naomi Melicent, *b* 1960; MA, MB BS: *m* 1990, Malcolm Hugh David Kemp, elder son of Prof C. D. Kemp, of St Andrews, Fife.

BROTHER LIVING

Hon MICHAEL COTTRELL, *b* 6 Aug 1928: *ed* Leighton Park Sch, and New Coll, Oxford (MA, BCh DM); FRCP, FRCP (C); late Cpt RAMC: *m* 1960, Dr Hon Elizabeth Ann Herbert, el da of late Baron Tangley (Life Baron), and has issue living, Thomas Russell, *b* 1965, — Hilary Catherine, *b* 1961: *m* 1986, Guido Dino de Luca, — Philippa Harriet, *b* 1963: *m* 1991, Armando Teves. *Residence* – Calgary, Alberta, Canada.

SISTER LIVING

Hon Janet Stella, *b* 1931; BA: *m* 1954, Leonard John Henry Arthur, MB, BCh, FRCP, who *d* 1983, of Royal Oak Cottage, Church Broughton, Derby (*see* Arthur, Bt, colls).

PREDECESSOR – (1) (WALTER) RUSSELL BRAIN, son of Walter John Brain, of Reading; *b* 1895; DM, FRCP, FRCPI, FRCPE; Pres of R Coll of Physicians 1950-57, and of British Assocn 1963-64; *cr* a *Baronet* (UK of Reading) 1954, *Baron Brain*, of Eynsham, co Oxford (peerage of UK) 1962: *m* 1920, Stella, who *d* 1993, da of Reginald Langdon Langdon-Down, MB, BCh; *d* 1966; *s* by his el son (2) CHRISTOPHER LANGDON, 2nd Baron, and present peer.

BRAINE OF WHEATLEY, BARON (Braine) (Life Baron 1992)

BERNARD RICHARD BRAINE, PC, son of late Arthur Ernest Braine, of Kew Gdns, Surrey; *b* 24 June 1914; *ed* Hendon County Gram Sch; DL Essex 1978; FRSA; 1939-45 War N Staffs Regt in W Africa, NW Europe and SE Asia, Camberley Staff Coll, Temp Lt-Col SEAC; Parly Sec Min of Pensions and Nat Insurance 1960-61, Under-Sec of State Commonwealth Relations 1961-62, Parly Sec Min of Health 1962-64, Chm Parly Cttee on Overseas Aid 1970-74, Dep-Chm Commonwealth Parly Assocn 1963-64 and 1970-74, Chm Nat Council on Alcohol 1974-82, British-German Parly Group 1970-92, British-Greek Parly Group 1979-92, UK Chapter Soc for Internat Development; Leader of several Parly Missions Abroad and Human Rights Mission to Soviet Union 1991; Father of the House of Commons 1987-92; Chm All Party Pro-Life Group 1983-91, since when Pres; Trustee and former Gov Commonwealth Inst, Visiting Prof Baylor Univ Texas; KStJ 1985, European Peace Medal 1979, Cdr Polonia Restituta (Polish Govt in Exile) 1983 (Grand Cross 1991), Kt Cdr Order of Merit (W Germany) 1984, KCSG (Papal) 1987, Grand Cdr Order of Honour (Greece) 1987; MP Billericay (*C*) 1950-55, Essex SE 1955-83, and Castle Point 1983-92; *cr* Kt Bach 1972, PC 1985, and *Baron Braine of Wheatley*, of Rayleigh, co Essex (Life Baron) 1992: *m* 1935, Kathleen Mary, who *d* 1982, da of late Herbert William Faun, of E Sheen, Surrey, and has issue.
Address – c/o House of Lords, SW1A 0PW.

Arms – Or a raven sable on a chief azure between two wheatsheaves a spur gold. **Crest** – Rising from a circlet of four chained portculises or alternating with pairs of tailor's scissors an arm embowed in armour holding a sword the blade proper hilt quillons and pommel or striking an arc of fetters also proper. **Supporters** – On either side a fawn proper that to the dexter gorged with a collar agent fimbriated gules and charged on each shoulder with an ostrich plume proper spined or (one manifest) that to the sinister gorged with a like collar argent fimbriated or and similarly charged with like ostrich plumes.

SONS LIVING

Hon Richard Laurence, *b* 1939.
Hon Michael Rodney, *b* 1942.
Hon Brendan Timothy, *b* 1945.

BRAINTREE, BARONY OF (Crittall) (Extinct 1961)

DAUGHTERS LIVING OF FIRST BARON

Hon Valentine Ellen MacDermott, *b* 1918: *m* 1939, Karl Stewart Richardson, and has issue living, Peter Valentine, *b* 1942, — Jeremy Stewart, *b* 1946. *Residence* – Hungry Hall, Witham, Essex.
Hon Jane Olive, *b* 1921: *m* 1947, Thomas Anthony Inglis Hall, and has issue living, Barnaby Inglis, *b* 1948; photographer, — Thomas Valentine Inglis, *b* 1949, — Sophia Charlotte, *b* 1954. *Residence* – 6 Windsor Terrace, Clifton, Bristol.
Hon Mary Frances, *b* 1922: *m* 1950, Germano Facetti, and has issue living, Lucia Olivia Josephine, *b* 1954.

BRAMALL, BARON (Bramall) (Life Baron 1987)

EDWIN NOEL WESTBY BRAMALL, KG, GCB, OBE, MC, son of late Maj Edmund Haseldon Bramall, late RA, of 2 Symons St, Sloane Sq, SW3; *b* 18 Dec 1923; *ed* Eton; commn'd KRRC 1943; served NW Europe 1944-45 (MC 1945), occupation of Japan 1946-47, Instructor Sch of Inf 1949-51, psc 1952, Middle East 1953-58, Instructor Army Staff Coll 1958-61, on Lord Mountbatten's staff with responsibility for reorganization of MoD 1963-64, Comdg Officer 2nd Green Jackets, KRRC, Malaysia 1965-66, comd 5th Airportable Bde 1967-69, idc 1970, GOC 1st Div BAOR 1971-73, Lt-Gen 1973, Comdr British Forces Hong Kong 1973-76, Gen 1976, C-in-C UK Land Forces 1976-78, Vice-Chief of Defence Staff 1978-79, Chief of General Staff 1979-82, Chief of Defence Staff 1982-85; ADC (Gen) to HM 1979-82, Col Comdt 3rd Bn RGJ 1973-84, Col 2nd Goorkhas 1976-86, Field Marshal 1982; Lord Lieut Greater London 1986-98; Trustee Imperial War Museum 1983-98 (Chm 1989-98); Pres MCC 1988-89; Pres London Playing Fields Assocn since 1990, Order of St John for London 1986-98, and Army Pressclub Not Forgotten Assocn since 1985, Chm Travellers' Club since 1998; *cr* OBE 1965, KCB 1974, GCB 1979, KG 1990, and *Baron Bramall*, of Bushfield, Hants (Life Baron) 1987: *m* 1949, Dorothy Avril Wentworth, only da of late Brig-Gen Henry Albemarle Vernon, DSO, late of Stoke Bruerne Park, Northants, and has issue.

Address – c/o National Westminster Bank, 34 Sloane Sq, SW3. *Clubs* – Travellers', Army and Navy, Pratts', MCC, I Zingari.

SON LIVING

Hon Nicolas, *b* 1952: *m* 1976 (*m diss* 1986), Janet Livingston, and has issue living, one son and one da.

DAUGHTER LIVING

Hon Sara, *b* 1951: *m* 1987, Dr Edwin R. Bickerstaff.

Brancepeth, Baron; title of Viscount Boyne on Roll of HL.

Brand, family name of Viscount Hampden.

Brandon, Duke of; see Duke of Hamilton and Brandon.

BRANDON OF OAKBROOK, BARONY OF (Brandon) (Extinct 1999)

SONS LIVING OF LIFE BARON

Hon James Roderick Vivian, *b* 1956; LLB, ACA: *m* 1991, Amelia Mary Hungerford, elder da of Maj Peter Hungerford Jackson (*see* Jackson, Bt, *cr* 1815, colls). *Residence* – 50 Richmond Rd, SW20 0PQ

Hon Richard Henry, *b* 1961: *m* 1988, Jean Patricia, 2nd da of R. B. Horsfield, of Eccles, Manchester.
Hon William Roland, *b* 1964: *m* 1991, Polly Jennifer Miriam, da of Janos Nyiri.

DAUGHTER LIVING OF LIFE BARON

Hon Juliet Mary, *b* 1958: *m* 1978, William Patrick Neill-Hall.

WIDOW LIVING OF LIFE BARON

JEANETTE ROSEMARY (*Baroness Brandon of Oakbrook*), eldest da of late Julian Vivian Breeze Janvrin: *m* 1955, Baron Brandon of Oakbrook, MC, PC (Life Baron), who *d* 1999. *Residence* – 6 Thackeray Close, SW19.

BRASSEY OF APETHORPE, BARON (Brassey) (Baron UK 1938, Bt UK 1922)

Often in difficulties, never in fear
ARDUIS · SÆPE · METU · NUNQUAM
H·N·E·

DAVID HENRY BRASSEY, OBE, 3rd Baron, and 3rd Baronet; *b* 16 Sept 1932; *s* 1967; *ed* Stowe; Maj (ret) Gren Gds; JP and DL Northants; OBE (Civil) 1994; *m* 1st, 1958, Myrna Elizabeth, who *d* 1974, only da of Lt-Col John Baskervyle-Glegg, of 9 The Gateways, Chelsea, SW3; 2ndly, 1978, Caroline, da of late Lt-Col Godfrey Ariel Evill, and of the Dowager Lady Duntze, of 55 Elm Park Gdns, SW10, and has issue by 1st and 2nd *m*.

Arms – Quarterly; 1st, per fesse indented sable and argent, in the first quarter a mallard of the second; 2nd, gules, in chief three mullets argent, and in base a dexter hand apaumée couped at the wrist of the last; 3rd, sable, a chevron between three bulls' heads cabossed argent; 4th, argent, on a chevron gules, three trefoils slipped of the field. **Crest** – A mallard proper. **Supporters** – On either side a mallard holding in the beak an ear of wheat slipped and leaved proper.
Residence – The Manor House, Apethorpe, Peterborough.

SON LIVING (*By 1st marriage*)

Hon EDWARD, *b* 9 March 1964.

DAUGHTERS LIVING (*By 2nd marriage*)

Hon Zara, *b* 1980.
Hon Chloe, *b* 1982.

BROTHER LIVING

Hon Thomas Ian (The Coach House, Duncote, Towcester, Northants NN12 8AQ), *b* 1934; *ed* Stowe; formerly Lt Gren Guards: *m* 1960, Valerie Christine, da of Alan David Finlason, and has issue living, (Thomas) Hugh, *b* 1971: *m* 1998, Leonie E., da of Allan Boardman, of Moree, NSW, Australia, — Miranda, *b* 1963: *m* 1988, Andrew Robinson Rawlin, eldest son of Dr Michael Rawlin, of North Anston, Sheffield, Yorks, and has issue living, William Bradbury *b* 1994, Alexandra Catherine *b* 1996, — Louise, *b* 1964: *m* 1995, Jeremy C. Wilkins, of Paddock Gate, Ogbourne Maizey, Marlborough, Wilts SN8 1RY, son of Denis Thomas Wilkins, of Amesbury Croft, Maidstone, Kent, — Davina Christine, *b* 1969: *m* 1994, Christopher Robert Merriman, yst son of late Patrick Merriman, of Rearsby House, Rearsby, Leics, and has issue living, Harriet Charlotte Nell *b* 1997.

WIDOW LIVING OF SON OF FIRST BARON

Lady Romayne Elizabeth Algitha Cecil, OBE, ARRC, da of 5th Marquess of Exeter: *m* 1944, Lt-Col Hon Peter Esmé Brassey, who *d* 1995, and has issue (see colls, infra). *Residence* – Pond House, Barnack, Stamford, Lincs.

WIDOW LIVING OF SECOND BARON

BARBARA (*Barbara, Baroness Brassey of Apethorpe*) (23 Bull Lane, Ketton, Stamford, Lincs), da of late Leonard Jorgensen, and formerly wife of Lt-Col Herbert Campbell Westmorland: *m* 1963, as his 2nd wife, the 2nd Baron Brassey of Apethorpe, who *d* 1967.

COLLATERAL BRANCH LIVING

Issue of late Lt-Col Hon Peter Esmé Brassey, yst son of 1st Baron, *b* 1907, *d* 1995: *m* 1944, Lady Romayne Elizabeth Algitha Cecil, OBE, ARRC (ante), da of 5th Marquess of Exeter:—
Henry Charles (Close House, Barnack, Stamford, Lincs PE9 3DY), *b* 1947; *ed* Milton Abbey: *m* 1972, Linda, da of Geoffrey Pinnock, of Fern Cottage, Ripley, Surrey, and has issue living, Thomas Charles, *b* 1974, — Elizabeth Jane, *b* 1978. —— Richard Edwin (116 Lots Rd, SW6), *b* 1949; *ed* Eton: *m* 1st, 1971 (*m diss* 1979), Tania, da of Norman William Duckworth; 2ndly, 1986, Pamina, da of Robert Caruso, of New York, and has issue living (by 1st *m*), Pikka (a da), *b* 1973, — (by 2nd *m*), George Peter, *b* 1987. —— Rowena Jane, LVO, *b* 1945; a Lady-in-Waiting to HRH The Princess Royal since 1970; LVO 1974: *m* 1977, Andrew James Feilden, of The Old Manor House, Minster Lovell, Oxon, and has issue (*see* V Hampden, colls).

PREDECESSORS – **(1)** (HENRY) LEONARD (CAMPBELL) Brassey, son of late Henry Arthur Brassey (formerly MP for Sandwich), of Preston Hall, Kent; *b* 1870; Major W Kent Yeo; Sheriff of Northants 1907; sat as MP for N Div of Northampton 1910-18, and for Peterborough Div thereof 1918-29; *cr* a *Baronet* 1922, and *Baron Brassey of Apethorpe*, of Apethorpe, co Northampton (peerage of United Kingdom) 1938: *m* 1894, Lady Violet Mary Gordon-Lennox, who *d* 1946, da of 7th Duke of Richmond and Gordon; *d* 1958; *s* by his 5th son **(2)** BERNARD THOMAS, MC, TD, 2nd Baron, *b* 1905: *m* 1st, 1931, Crystal Gloria, who *d* 1962, da of late Lt-Col Francis William George Gore (E Sondes); 2ndly, 1963, Mrs Barbara Westmorland, da of late Leonard Jorgenson; *d* 1967; *s* by his el son **(3)** DAVID HENRY, 3rd Baron, and present peer.

BRAYBROOKE, BARON (Neville) (Baron GB 1788)

ROBIN HENRY CHARLES NEVILLE, 10th Baron; *b* 29 Jan 1932; *s* 1990; *ed* Eton, and Magdalene Coll, Camb; DL Essex 1980, Lord Lieut 1992; an Hereditary Visitor of Magdalene Coll, Camb; patron of three livings: *m* 1st, 1955 (*m diss* 1974), Robin Helen, only da of late Thomas Adolph Brockhoff, of Rose Bay, Sydney, NSW; 2ndly, 1974 (*m diss* 1998), Linda, 2nd da of Arthur Norman, of Saffron Walden, Essex; 3rdly, 1998, Mrs Perina Fordham, elder da of late Augustine Courtauld (*see* L Napier and Ettrick, colls, 1985 Edn), and formerly wife of Christopher Jeremy King Fordham, and has had issue by 1st and 2nd *m*.

𝕬rms – Quarterly: 1st and 4th gules, on a saltire argent, a rose of the field, barbed and seeded proper; 2nd and 3rd or, fretty gules; on a canton of the first a lymphad sable. 𝕮rest – A bull statant argent, collared and chained or. 𝕾upporters – Two lions reguardant argent, maned sable, and gorged with wreaths of olive proper.
Residence – Abbey House, Audley End, Saffron Walden, Essex. *Club* – Boodle's.

Incline to nothing base

DAUGHTERS LIVING AND DECEASED (*By 1st marriage*)

Hon Amanda Muriel Mary, *b* 1962: *m* 1989, Stephen Christopher Jerningham Murray, only son of Christopher Mark Henry Murray, of La Glinette, St Aubin, Jersey, CI (*see* Jerningham, Bt (ext), 1955 Edn), and of late Mrs Michael P. Wyndham, and has issue living, Alexander Henry Jerningham, *b* 1992, — Isabella, *b* 1994.
Hon Caroline Emma (*Countess of Derby*), *b* 1963: *m* 1995, 19th Earl of Derby, of Knowsley, Prescot, Merseyside, and has issue (see that title).
Henrietta Jane, *b* 1965; *d* 1980.
Hon Victoria, *b* 1970: *m* 1995, Edward A. Bromet, elder son of John A. Bromet, of Wighill, N Yorks.

Hon Arabella, *b* (twin) 1970: *m* 1999, Duncan Potter, son of Geoffrey Potter, of Liskeard, Cornwall.

(By 2nd marriage)

Hon Sara Lucy, *b* 1975.
Hon Emma Charlotte, *b* 1979.
Hon Lucinda Octavia, *b* 1984.

DAUGHTER LIVING OF SEVENTH BARON

Hon Catherine Dorothy, OBE (Asherne, Strete, Dartmouth, Devon), *b* 1922; OBE (Civil) 1993: *m* 1954, Gordon Alexander Egerton Ruck, who *d* 1977, and has issue living, Louise Dorothy Catherine, *b* 1959: *m* 1992, Richard Claude Newman (*see* Newman, Bt, *cr* 1836).

COLLATERAL BRANCHES LIVING

Grandchildren of late Adm Sir George Neville, KCB, CVO, 2nd son of late Ralph Neville-Grenville, MP, son of late Very Rev Hon George Neville-Grenville, 3rd son of 2nd Baron:—
Issue of late Capt Philip Lloyd Neville, CVO, RN, *b* 1888, *d* 1976: *m* 1942, Eleanor, who *d* 1972, da of Duncan Fellowes, of Toronto, Canada:—
GEORGE, *b* 23 March 1943; *ed* Eton: *m* 1972, Patricia, da of late Patrick Quinn, and has issue living, Richard Ralph, *b* 1977, — Eleanor Anne, *b* 1975. ——John (Welgoer, Poyntington, Sherborne, Dorset), *b* 1944; *ed* Eton, and McGill Univ (MBA 1971): *m* 1980, Frances Jane, da of John Stuart Lomax, and has issue living, Edward Grey, *b* 1982, — Cicely Georgia, *b* 1984.

Issue of late Brig Alfred Geoffrey Neville, CBE, MC, RA, *b* 1891, *d* 1955: *m* 1922, Philippa, who *d* 1981, da of late Vice-Adm Sir George Price Webley Hope, KCB, KCMG (*see* M Linlithgow, colls):—
Caroline Philippa, *b* 1935: *m* 1st, 1960, Sir Gerard Robert Henry Sigismund Newman, 3rd Bt, who *d* 1987; 2ndly, 1996, Andrew F. B. Crawshaw. *Residence* – The Manor House, Fowlmere, Royston, Herts SG8 7SJ.

Granddaughter of late Louis Neville, 4th son of late Ralph Neville-Grenville, MP (*ante*):—
Issue of late Bertram Neville, *b* 1880, *d* 1950: *m* 1919, Gertrude May Thompson:—
Edith May, *b* 1925: *m* 1954, Derek George Rands, and has issue living, Margaret Elizabeth, *b* 1957, — Pauline Jane, *b* 1961. *Residence* – 51 Wychwood Av, Luton, Bedfordshire.

PREDECESSORS – **(1)** *Field-Marshal Sir* John Griffin-Whitwell (heir-general of 3rd and last Baron Griffin of Braybrooke) was summoned to Parliament 1784 as 4th Baron Howard de Walden, and in 1788 was *cr Baron Braybrooke* (peerage of Great Britain), with remainder to Richard Neville-Aldworth, of Billingbere; *d* 1797, when the Barony of Howard de Walden fell into abeyance and the Barony of Braybrooke devolved upon **(2)** RICHARD Aldworth-Neville, 2nd Baron; *b* 1750; was Lord Lieut and Vice-Adm of Essex, Provost-Marshal of Jamaica, etc; assumed by R licence 1798 the additional and principal surname of Griffin: *m* 1780, Catherine, who *d* 1796, da of Rt Hon George Grenville, PC; *d* 1825; *s* by his son **(3)** RICHARD NEVILLE, LLD, 3rd Baron, *b* 1783; editor of the *Diary of Samuel Pepys*: *m* 1819, Lady Jane, who *d* 1856, da of 2nd Marquess Cornwallis; *d* 1858; *s* by his son **(4)** RICHARD CORNWALLIS, 4th Baron; *d* 1861; *s* by his brother **(5)** CHARLES CORNWALLIS, 5th Baron, *b* 1823: *m* 1849, Hon Florence Priscilla Alicia Maude, who *d* 1914, 3rd da of 3rd Viscount Hawarden; *d* 1902; *s* by his brother **(6)** *Rev* LATIMER, 6th Baron, *b* 1827; Master of Magdalene Coll Camb: *m* 1853, Lucy Frances, who *d* 1918, el da of John Le Marchant; *d* 1904; *s* by his el son **(7)** HENRY, 7th Baron; *b* 1855: *m* 1st, Emelie Pauline, who *d* 1912, da of Antoine Gonin, of Château de Condemine, Mâcon; 2ndly, 1917, Dorothy Edith, who *d* 1973, yst da of late Sir George Lawson, KCB; *d* 1941; *s* by his el son **(8)** RICHARD HENRY CORNWALLIS, 8th Baron; *b* 1918; Lieut Gren Gds; *ka* 1943; *s* by his cousin **(9)** HENRY SEYMOUR (son of late Rev Hon Grey Neville, 2nd son of 6th Baron), 9th Baron, *b* 1897; European War 1915-19 as Flight-Com RNAS and Capt RAF; DL Essex: *m* 1st, 1930, Muriel Evelyn, who *d* 1962, da of late William Charles Manning, and widow of Euan C. Cartwright; 2ndly, 1963, Angela Mary, who *d* 1985, da of late William Herbert Hollis, and widow of John Ree; *d* 1990; *s* by his only son **(10)** ROBIN HENRY CHARLES, 10th Baron and present peer.

BRAYE, BARONESS (Aubrey-Fletcher) (Baron E 1529)

Beware. One alone.

·GARDEZ·

Beware.

Badge of the Barons Braye

MARY PENELOPE AUBREY-FLETCHER (*Baroness Braye*), *b* 28 Sept 1941; *s* 1985; High Sheriff of Northants 1983; heir-gen of the Earls Verney of Claydon (ext 1791): *m* 1981, as his 2nd wife, Lt-Col Edward Henry Lancelot Aubrey-Fletcher, Gren Gds (*see* Aubrey-Fletcher, Bt).

𝕬rms – Quarterly, 1st and 4th azure, fretty argent *Cave*; 2nd and 3rd azure, on a cross argent five mullets gules, *Verney*. 𝕾upporters – Two lions guardant or, winged vaire. 𝕭adge – A Hemp-breaker.
Seat – Stanford Hall, Lutterworth, Leics, LE17 6DH.

COLLATERAL BRANCH LIVING (*co-heiresses to the barony*)

Granddaughters of late Hon Cecilia Violet (Hon Mrs von Gratzy), elder da of 5th Baron:—
Issue of late Vera Cecilia, *b* 1906, *d* 1981: *m* 1929, Claude Henry Browne, who *d* 1997 :—
LINDA KATHLEEN CECILIA, *b* 2 May 1930: *m* 1965, Cdr Christopher Henry Fothergill, RN (*see* E Radnor, colls, 1966 Edn), of Otway House, Chobham, Surrey, and has issue living, Nicholas Henry, *b* 29 Nov 1965: *m* 1995, Lucy Victoria, da of late Timothy Sicks, — Alexander Verney Edmund, *b* 1967: *m* 1997, Joanna Frances, only da of Francis McGinn, of Monkswell House, Beaulieu, Hants, and has issue living, Matilda Alice *b* 1998. —— THERESA BEATRICE, *b* 9 Aug 1934. *Residence* – 10 Broomfield Drive, Broomfield Park, Sunningdale, SL5 0JP.

PREDECESSORS – (**1**) *Sir* Edmund Braye, Knt, of Eaton Braye, co Bedford, nephew of Sir Reginald Braye, KG, Lord High Treas to Henry VII, summoned to Parl as a *Baron* of England 1529; *d* 1539; *s* by his son (**2**) JOHN, 2nd Baron, summoned to Parliament 1545-55; was Master of the Ordnance to Queen Mary; *d* without issue 1557, when the Barony became abeyant, and remained so until 1839, when it was terminated in favour of (**3**) SARAH, only da of Sir Thomas Cave, 6th Bt, of Stanford Hall, co Leicester, and wife of Henry Otway, she being the descendant of Elizabeth, 2nd da of the 1st Baron, and wife of Sir Ralph Verney, Knt, of Claydon; she resumed in 1819 by R licence the additional surname of Cave, and *d* 1862, leaving four das, among whom the title again remained abeyant until 13 May 1879, when it passed to the last survivor of them (**4**) HENRIETTA: *m* 1844, Edgell Wyatt-Edgell, who *d* 1888, 2nd son of late Edgell Wyatt-Edgell, of Milton Place, Egham, Surrey; *d* 14 Nov 1879; *s* by her son (**5**) ALFRED THOMAS TOWNSHEND, 5th Baron; *b* 1849; assumed in 1880 by R licence the surnames of Verney-Cave in lieu of Wyatt-Edgell: *m* 1873, Harriet Cecilia, who *d* 1935, da of late William Gerard Walmesley, of Westwood House, Wigan; *d* 1928; *s* by his son (**6**) ADRIAN VERNEY, 6th Baron; *b* 1874; Lieut-Com RNVR: *m* 1900, Ethel Mary, who *d* 1955, da of late Capt Edward Bouverie Pusey, RN; *d* 1952; *s* by his son (**7**) THOMAS ADRIAN, 7th Baron, *b* 1902; Maj 13th/18th R Hus, and formerly F/O RAF: *m* 1934, Dorothea, who *d* 1994, da of late Daniel C. Donoghue, of Philadelphia, USA; *d* 1985; *s* by his only da (**8**) MARY PENELOPE, Baroness Braye, present peeress.

BRAYLEY, BARONY OF (Brayley) (Extinct 1977)

DAUGHTERS LIVING OF LIFE BARON

Hon Avril Gay, *b* 19—: *m* 19—.

Hon Tessa Ann, *b* 1948: *m* 1st, 1967 (*m diss* 1974), Gerald Conway; 2ndly, 1974 (*m diss* 1978), Anthony Forrest; 3rdly, 1982 (*m diss* 1988), John Smart, and has issue living (by 1st husband), Gerrard Curtis, *b* 1966. *Residence* – Tree House, Stratford Rd, Wootton Wawen, Warwicks B95 6BY.

BREADALBANE AND HOLLAND, EARLDOM OF (Campbell) (Earl S 1677, Bt S 1625)
(Dormant 1995)

(Title pronounced "Bredawlben")

COLLATERAL BRANCHES

Grandchildren of late John Breadalbane Campbell, of Florida, USA, only surviving son of late George Andrew Campbell, 2nd son of John Campbell of Boreland, great-uncle of 6th Earl:—
Issue, if any, of late Janos Breadalbane Campbell, *b* 1886 (Enterprise, Florida, USA), was living in Budapest, Hungary, 1941: *m* 19—, Illona Szalasi. *No further information available at the time of going to press.*

Descendants, if any, of late Colin Campbell, Surg 39th Regt, el son of Capt Robert Campbell, great-great-uncle of 6th Earl, *d* in Guadeloupe 1794.

Descendants, if any, of William Campbell (*d* before 30 Aug 1784) (4th son of Robert Campbell of Glenfalloch, great-great-uncle of 6th Earl), whose son Archibald, Sgt Middlesex Militia, had a son, Colin.

Descendants, if any, of Duncan Campbell, yst son of Robert Campbell of Glenfalloch (ante), of whom Colin Campbell went to America, and James Campbell was bookbinder to the Queen.

Brecknock, Earl of; son of Marquess Camden.

BRECON, BARONY OF (Lewis) (Extinct 1976)

DAUGHTERS LIVING OF FIRST BARON

Hon Rosalind Helen Penrose, CBE, *b* 1938; *ed* Cheltenham Ladies' Coll; High Sheriff Powys 1997; CBE 1994: *m* 1963, Arthur Leolin Price, CBE, QC, of 32 Hampstead Grove, NW3 6SR, and Moor Park, Llanbedr, Crickhowell, Powys NP8 1SS, and has issue living, Evan David Lewis, *b* 1976, — Thomas Leolin Alfred, *b* 1971, — Mary Ceridwen, *b* 1964: *m* 1992, Anthony Donald Hunt, 4th son of late Donald Hunt, of Holt, Norfolk, — Sophie Katharine, *b* 1966.
Hon Janet Mary Penrose, *b* 1944; *ed* Cheltenham Ladies' Coll: *m* 1969, Christopher John Foss, of Naish Hill House, Lacock, Wilts, and has issue living, Penrose Margaret Helen, *b* 1970, — Charlotte Sophia Louise, *b* 1975.

WIDOW LIVING OF FIRST BARON

MABEL HELEN, CBE (*Baroness Brecon*), (Greenhill, Cross Oak, Talybont-on-Usk, Powys, LD3 7UJ); a JP; High Sheriff of Breconshire 1971-72; CBE (Civil) 1964; da of late John McColville, of Abergavenny: *m* 1933, the 1st Baron, who *d* 1976, when the title became ext.

BRENTFORD, VISCOUNT (Joynson-Hicks) (Viscount UK 1929, Bt UK 1919)

CASSIS · TVTISSIMA VIRTVS

Virtue is the safest helmet

CRISPIN WILLIAM JOYNSON-HICKS, 4th Viscount, 4th Baronet of Holmsbury and 2nd Baronet of Newick, *b* 7 April 1933; *s* 1983; *ed* Eton, and at New Coll, Oxford; Solicitor 1960; a partner in the legal firm of Taylor Joynson Garrett (formerly Joynson-Hicks); late Lt 9th Lancers: *m* 1964, Gillian Evelyn, OBE (High Sheriff E Sussex 1998), el da of late Gerald Edward Schluter, OBE, of Nairobi, Kenya, and has issue.

𝔞rms – Gules, on a fesse wavy between three fleurs-de-lis or, a portcullis sable, all within a bordure of the second. Crest – A stag's head proper gorged with a collar or, thereon five roses gules, and charged on the neck with a fleur-de-lis gold. Supporters – On either side a stag proper gorged with a collar or, thereon five roses gules and charged on the neck with a fleur-de-lis gold.
Residence – Cousley Place, Wadhurst, East Sussex, TN5 6HF.

SON LIVING

Hon PAUL WILLIAM, *b* 1971.

DAUGHTERS LIVING

Hon Emma Rosalie, *b* 1966.
Hon Rowena Phyllis, *b* 1967: *m* 1989, Simon J. Banks, yr son of M. J. Banks, of Bishop's Stortford, Herts, and has issue living, James Thomas, *b* 1994, — Jack Samuel, *b* 1996, — Oliver Jeremy, *b* 1999.
Hon Amy Gillian, *b* 1978.

PREDECESSORS – (1) WILLIAM Joynson-Hicks, PC, son of late Henry Hicks, of Plaistow Hall, Kent; *b* 1865; founder of legal firm of Joynson-Hicks, solicitors; Parliamentary Sec (Overseas Trade Depart) to Board of Trade Oct 1922 to March 1923, Postmaster-Gen (also Paymaster-Gen) March to May 1923, Financial Sec to the Treasury (with a seat in the Cabinet), May to Sept 1923, Min of Health Sept 1923 to Jan 1924, and Sec of State for Home Depart Nov 1924 to June 1929; MP for NW Div of Manchester (*C*) April 1908 to Jan 1910, for Brentford Div of Middlesex March 1911 to Nov 1918, and for Twickenham Div thereof Dec 1918 to May 1929; *cr* a *Baronet* 1919, and *Viscount Brentford*, of Newick, Sussex (peerage of United Kingdom) 1929: *m* 1895, Grace Lynn, who *d* 1952, da of Richard Hampson Joynson, JP (whose surname he assumed), formerly of Chasefield, Bowdon, Cheshire; *d* 1932; *s* by his son (2) RICHARD CECIL, 2nd Viscount, *b* 1896; sometime on Staff of Gov of Jamaica: *m* 1st, 1920, Evelyn Mary Rothery, who *d* 1954, only da of late John F. McNellan, of Dollar, Clackmannanshire; 2ndly, 1955, Grace Esther, who *d* 1984, da of late A. E. A. Tothill, of Cape Town, and widow of D. S. T. McNellan, of Johannesburg, S Africa; *d* 1958; *s* by his brother (3) LANCELOT WILLIAM, 3rd Viscount, *b* 1902; solicitor 1926; Parliamentary Sec Min of Fuel and Power Nov 1951-Dec 1955; European War 1939-45 as acting Lt-Cdr RNVR; Senior Partner in the legal firm of Joynson-Hicks & Co 1938-66; Chm of Automobile Assocn 1957-74; MP for Chichester Div of W Sussex (*C*) May 1942-June 1958; *cr* a *Baronet* (of Newick) 1956: *m* 1931, Phyllis, who *d* 1979, only da of late Maj Herbert Allfrey, of Newnton House, Tetbury, Glos; *d* 1983; *s* by his only son (4) CRISPIN WILLIAM, 4th Viscount and present peer.

Brett, family name of Viscount Esher.

BRIDGE OF HARWICH, BARON (Bridge) (Life Baron 1980)

NIGEL CYPRIAN BRIDGE, PC, son of late Cdr Cyprian Dunscomb Charles Bridge, RN; *b* 26 Feb 1917; *ed* Marlborough; Bar Inner Temple 1947; Bencher 1964, Junior Counsel to HM Treasury in Common Law 1964-68, and a Judge of High Court of Justice (Queen's Bench Div) 1968-75; Presiding Judge, Western Circuit 1972-74; Lord Justice of Appeal 1975-80; Lord of Appeal in Ordinary since 1980; Member Security Commn 1977-82, Chm 1982-85; Treas Inner Temple 1986; 1939-45 War as Capt KRRC in Italy, France and Germany; *cr* Knt 1968, PC 1975, and *Baron Bridge of Harwich*, of Harwich, co Essex (Life Baron) 1980: *m* 1944, Margaret, da of Leonard Heseltine Swinbank, of Weybridge, Surrey, and has issue.

𝕬rms – Azure issuant from the centre of a bar wavy of water proper in the nombril point of a bridge of three arches embattled argent masoned sable the whole between as many sealions naiant guardant and each crowned with a mural crown gold. 𝕮rest – An eagle rising proper the beak or holding therein a sprig of lilac also proper. 𝕾upporters – *Dexter*, a winged horse in trian aspect argent hooved or resting the dexter hoof upon a portcullis chained also or; *sinister*, a sealion in trian aspect all argent resting the sinister forepaw on a portcullis chained gold, the compartment comprising a grassy mount growing therefrom on a rose gules barbed stalked and leaved proper another rose argent barbed and seeded also proper between on the dexter a rose argent and on the sinister a rose gules both barbed seeded stalked and leaved proper on the sinister side of the mount a flat rock proper.
Address – c/o House of Lords, SW1.

SON LIVING

Hon Charles Cyprian, *b* 1951: *m* 1971, Sheila Marie Street.

DAUGHTERS LIVING

Hon Jane Elizabeth, *b* 1944: *m* 1978, Prof J. M. Kister.
Hon Rachel Ann, *b* 1946: *m* 1975, Martin Pick.

BRIDGEMAN, VISCOUNT (Bridgeman) (Viscount UK 1929)

Neither rashly nor timidly

ROBIN JOHN ORLANDO BRIDGEMAN, 3rd Viscount; *b* 5 Dec 1930; *s* 1982; *ed* Eton; 2nd Lieut Rifle Bde 1950-51; CA 1958: *m* 1966, (Victoria) Harriet Lucy, da of Ralph Meredyth Turton, of Kildale Hall, Whitby (*see* V Chetwynd, colls), and has issue.

𝕬rms – Sable, ten plates, four, three, two, and one, on a chief argent, a lion passant ermines. 𝕮rest – A demi-lion rampant argent, holding in the paws a wreath of laurel proper. 𝕾upporters – On either side a leopard guardant gules pelletée, charged on the shoulder with a portcullis or.
Residences – Watley House, Sparsholt, Hants; 19 Chepstow Rd, W2 5BP.

SONS LIVING

Hon WILLIAM ORLANDO CASPAR, *b* 15 Aug 1968; *ed* Eton, and Bristol Univ.
Hon Luke Robinson Orlando, *b* 1971; *ed* Eton, and New Coll, Oxford: *m* 1996, Victoria Rose, yst da of late Henry Frost, and of Mrs William Mellen, of Moors Farm, W Farndon, Daventry, Northants.
Hon Esmond Francis Ralph Orlando, *b* 1974; *ed* Bryanston.
Hon Orlando Henry Geoffrey, *b* 1983.

SISTERS LIVING (*raised to the rank of a Viscount's daughters* 1996)

Hon Helena Mary, *b* 1932: *m* 1st, 1953 (*m diss* 1963), Hon Paul Asquith, who *d* 1984, son of Baron Asquith of Bishopstone, PC (Life Baron); 2ndly, 1963, James Francis Leslie Bayley, and has issue living (by 1st *m*) (*see* E Oxford and Asquith, colls), — (by 2nd *m*) Thomas Francis, *b* 1966, — Rachel Helena, *b* 1964.

Hon Daphne, *b* 1940: *m* 1965, William Howard Clive Montgomery, and has issue living, Hugh Geoffrey Clive, *b* 1966, — Rose Evelyn, *b* 1968, — Frances Mary, *b* 1970: *m* 1994, Mark H. L. Adams, of 27 Coningham Rd, W12 8BP, son of Nicholas Adams, of Crowland, Lincs., — Flora Anne Selina, *b* 1974. *Residence* – Grey Abbey, Newtownards, co Down.

DAUGHTERS LIVING OF SECOND VISCOUNT

Hon Anne Caroline Mary, *b* 1932: *m* 1955, Rev Nicolas David Stacey, and has issue living, David Robert, *b* 1958: *m* 1992, Annabel M. E., da of Maj Michael Edwards, of Norwood Farm, Corscombe, Dorset, — Caroline Jill, *b* 1956, — Mary Elizabeth, *b* 1961. *Residence* – The Old Vicarage, Selling, Faversham, Kent.

Hon Susan Elizabeth, *b* 1935; JP; was Lady-in-Waiting to Lady May Abel Smith, wife of H E Gov of Queensland 1958-60: *m* 1962, David Kenneth Dudley Foster, and has issue living, Robert Peter Dudley, *b* 1966, — Edward Kenneth Clive, *b* 1967, — Simon David Thomas, *b* 1969. *Residence* – The Spicer's House, 101 Corve St, Ludlow, Shropshire.

Hon Mary Selina, *b* 1940; JP: *m* 1962, Jeremy David Bagot Bayliss, of Sheepbridge Court, Swallowfield, Reading, and has issue living, Jonathan Andrew Bagot (6 Netheravon Rd, W4 2NA), *b* 1964: *m* 1992, Sarah E., elder da of Richard Bowes, of Enton, Surrey, and has issue living, Walter Richard Bridgeman *b* 1993, Casper Jeremy Lyle *b* 1995, Charles Robert Bowes *b* 1996, Cecily Mary Elizabeth *b* 1999, — Richard Charles, *b* 1965: *m* 1996, Anna, da of late Maurice Lidstone, of Gerrards Cross, Bucks, and has issue living, William Maurice Orlando *b* 1998, — Patrick Thomas Clive (15 Pindock Mews, W9 2PY), *b* 1968: *m* 1995, K. Rebecca de M., da of Jeremy Woodhouse, of Lockeridge, Wilts.

COLLATERAL BRANCH LIVING

Issue of late Hon Sir Maurice Richard Bridgeman, KBE, yst son of 1st Viscount, *b* 1904, *d* 1980: *m* 1933, Diana Mary Erica, who *d* 1979, da of late Humphrey Minto Wilson, of 9 S Audley St, W1:—
Erica Jane (*Lady Harman*) (Brook House, Highclere, Newbury, Berks), *b* 1934: *m* 1960 (*m diss* 1987), Sir Jeremiah Le Roy Harman, son of Rt Hon Sir Charles Eustace Harman, and has issue living, Charles Richard Le Roy, *b* 1963, — Toby John, *b* 1967: *m* 1992, Joanne L., da of Neville Boxer, of Maidenhead, Bucks, and has issue living, Isobel Leigh *b* 1997, — Sarah Jane, *b* 1962: *m* 1993, Hugh Lewis Evans, only son of Maj-Gen John Alan Maurice Evans, CB, of Salisbury, Wilts, and has issue living, Juliet Anne Elizabeth *b* 1998. ——Teresa Anne, CBE, *b* 1937; CBE (Civil) 1998: *m* 1960, Peter Baring, of 29 Ladbroke Sq, W11 (*see* B Revelstoke, colls). ——Elizabeth Caroline, *b* 1944: *m* 1971, Martin Dru Drury, of 3 Victoria Rise, SW4, and has issue living, Matthew Orlando Dru, *b* 1972, — Joseph Walter Richard Minto Dru, *b* 1977, — Augusta Daisy Elizabeth, *b* 1974. ——Rachel Diana, *b* 1947: *m* 1972, (Philip) Benjamin Hay, of Plummer, Tenterden, Kent, and has issue living, Thomas Alexander, *b* 1974, — Tara Caroline, *b* 1976.

PREDECESSORS – (1) *Rt Hon* WILLIAM CLIVE Bridgeman, PC, son of late Rev Hon John Robert Orlando Bridgeman, 3rd son of 2nd Earl of Bradford; *b* 1864; Chm of BBC, and of Govs of Shrewsbury Sch, a Fellow of Eton Coll and an Elder Brother of Trinity House; Assist Private Sec to Sec of State for Colonies 1889-92, Private Sec to Chancellor of Exchequer 1895-9, Junior Lord of the Treasury 1915-16, Assist Director, War Trade Depart 1916, Parliamentary Sec to Min of Labour 1916-18, and to Board of Trade 1919-20, Sec of Mines Aug 1920 to Oct 1922 Sec of State for Home Depart Oct 1922 to Jan 1924, and First Lord of the Admiralty Nov 1924 to June 1929; MP for Salop, W or Oswestry Div (C) 1906-29: *cr Viscount Bridgeman* of Leigh, co Salop (peerage of United Kingdom; 1929): *m* 1895, *Dame* Caroline Beatrix, DBE, who *d* 1961, da of late Hon Cecil Thomas Parker (E Macclesfield, colls); *d* 1935; *s* by his son (2) ROBERT CLIVE, KBE, CB, DSO, MC, 2nd Viscount, *b* 1896; Maj-Gen Rifle Bde (Prince Consort's Own); Lord Lieut for co Salop 1951-69, and Alderman of Salop Co Council 1951-75; Private Sec to his father when Parliamentary Sec to Min of Labour 1918; served in World Wars I and II; Dir-Gen Home Guard 1941-45, and DAG 1944-45: *m* 1930, Hon Mary Kathleen Lane Fox, JP, who *d* 1981, da of 1st Baron Bingley (ext); *d* 1982; *s* by his nephew (3) ROBIN JOHN ORLANDO, only son of late Brig Hon Geoffrey John Orlando Bridgeman, MC, MB, FRCS, LRCP, 2nd son of 1st Viscount, 3rd Viscount and present peer.

Bridgeman, family name of Earl of Bradford.

BRIDGES, BARON (Bridges) (Baron UK 1957)

THOMAS EDWARD BRIDGES, GCMG, 2nd Baron; *b* 27 Nov 1927; *s* 1969; *ed* Eton, and New Coll, Oxford; HM Diplo Ser 1951-87 (ret); seconded as Private Sec for Overseas Affairs to Prime Min 1972-74; HM Ambassador to Italy 1983-87; CMG 1975, KCMG 1983, GCMG 1988: *m* 1953, Rachel Mary, yst da of Sir Henry Nöel Bunbury, KCB, and has issue.

Arms – Argent a cross sable charged with a wreath of laurel fructed of the field a chief chequy also sable and of the first. **Crest** – A man's head and shoulders couped proper wreathed about the temples argent the ribands gules, vested paly of six sable and argent. **Supporters** – On either side a swan wings elevated and addorsed proper gorged with a collar chequy sable and argent.
Residence – 56 Church St, Orford, Woodbridge, Suffolk IP12 2NT.

To act without speaking

SONS LIVING

Hon MARK THOMAS (66 Lincolns Inn Fields, WC2A 3LH), *b* 25 July 1954; *ed* Eton, and Corpus Christi, Camb; solicitor (Partner Farrer & Co): *m* 1978, Angela Margaret, da of J. L. Collinson, of Mansfield, Notts, and has issue living, Miles Edmund Farrer, *b* 1 July 1992, — Venetia Rachel Lucy, *b* 1982, — Camilla Frances Iona, *b* 1985, — Drusilla Katharine Anne, *b* 1988.

Hon Nicholas Edward (6 Oakhill Park Mews, NW3 7LH), *b* 1956; *ed* Eton, and Bath Univ; ARIBA; Partner, Blee Ettwein Bridges: *m* 1985, Susan, eldest da of Peter Guggenheim, of Woodbury Salterton, Devon, and has issue living, Matthew Orlando, *b* 1988, — Alice Clementine, *b* 1986.

DAUGHTER LIVING

Hon Harriet Elizabeth BRIDGES, *b* 1958; *ed* Bryanston, and York Univ; resumed her maiden name 1983: *m* 1981 (*m diss* 1983), John Charles Eells. *Residence* – 20 Highland Ave, Beverly, Mass 01915-4911, USA.

BROTHER LIVING

Hon Robert Oliver *b* 1930; *ed* Eton, Magdalen Coll, Oxford, and Architectural Assocn Sch of Architecture; an ARIBA: *m* 1963, Rosamund Theresa, yr da of late Roger C. V. de Wesselow, and has issue living, John Edward, *b* 1968, — James George Robert, *b* 1970. *Residence* – Goodmans Furze, Headley, Epsom, Surrey KT18 6NQ.

SISTERS LIVING

Hon Shirley Frances, *b* 1924: *m* 1957, Hilary Topham Corke, and has issue living, William Edward Orlando, *b* 1961: *m* 1995, Sophie Denia, da of Michael John Wigram (*see* E Iddesleigh, colls), — Emma Lucy, *b* 1958, — Cicely Catharine, *b* 1960, — Georgiana Phoebe, *b* 1963.

Hon Margaret Evelyn, *b* 1932; PhD, FBA: *m* 1st, 1954 (*m diss* 1969), Trevor Henry Aston; 2ndly, 1971, Paul William Jex Buxton, of Castle House, Chipping, Ongar, Essex, and has issue (by 2nd *m*) (*see* Buxton, Bt, colls).

PREDECESSOR – **(1)** *Rt Hon Sir* EDWARD ETTINGDENE BRIDGES, KG, GCB, GCVO, MC, PC, FRS, son of late Robert Seymour Bridges, OM (Poet Laureate), (of Chilswell, Oxford); *b* 1892; Sec to the Cabinet 1938-46; Permanent Sec to HM Treasury and Head of Civil Ser 1945-56; Chm of British Council 1954-67; *cr Baron Bridges*, of Headley, co Surrey, and of St Nicholas at Wade, co Kent (peerage UK) 1957: *m* 1922, Hon Katharine Dianthe Farrer, who *d* 1986, da of 2nd Baron Farrer; *d* 1969; *s* by his son **(2)** THOMAS EDWARD, 2nd Baron and present peer.

BRIDPORT, VISCOUNT (Hood) (Viscount UK 1868)

ALEXANDER NELSON HOOD, 4th Viscount; *b* 17 March 1948; *s* 1969; *ed* Eton, and the Sorbonne; 7th *Duke of Bronte* in Sicily (*cr* 1799): *m* 1st, 1972 (*m diss* 1979), Linda Jacqueline, da of Lt-Col Vincent Rudolph Paravicini, of Nutley Manor, Basingstoke; 2ndly, 1979 (*m diss* 1999), Nina, da of Curt Lincoln, formerly wife of Phillip Martyn, and widow of Jochen Rindt, racing driver, and has issue by 1st and 2nd *m*.

Arms – Quarterly: 1st and 4th azure, a fret argent; on a chief or three crescents sable, *Hood;* 2nd and 3rd, or, a cross patonce sable, a bend gules surmounted of another engrailed of the field charged with three bombs fired proper, on a chief undulated argent, waves of the sea from which a palm tree issuant between a disabled ship on the dexter, and a battery in ruins on the sinister all proper, over all a fess wavy azure, thereon inscribed the word "Trafalgar" or, *Nelson.* **Crest** – A Cornish chough proper, the dexter foot resting on the fluke of an anchor in bend sinister or.
Supporters – *Dexter,* a figure of Neptune, crowned with an Eastern crown or a green robe flowing round his loins, holding a trident in the left hand, and resting the right on an anchor, also or; *Sinister,* a sea lion argent, the back fin and top of the tail gules, resting the sinister paw on an anchor or.
Residence – Rue des Trois Fontaines 1, 1266 Duillier, Switzerland. *Club* – Brooks's

SONS LIVING (*By 1st marriage*)

Hon PEREGRINE ALEXANDER NELSON, *b* 30 Aug 1974.

(*By 2nd marriage*)

Hon Anthony Nelson, *b* 1983.

PREDECESSORS – (1) *Adm Sir* ALEXANDER Hood, MP (yr brother of 1st Viscount Hood) a celebrated naval commander, was *cr Baron Bridport* (peerage of Ireland) 1794 with remainder to his great-nephew, Hon Samuel Hood, 2nd son of 2nd Viscount Hood, and in failure thereof to the heirs male of his uncle, Alexander Hood; *cr Baron Bridport,* of Cricket St Thomas, Som (peerage of GB) 1796, and *Viscount Bridport,* of Cricket St Thomas (peerage of GB) 1800; *d* without issue 1814, when the English honours expired, and the Irish peerage devolved upon his great-nephew (ante) (2) SAMUEL, 2nd Baron, *b* 1788: *m* 1810, Lady Charlotte Mary Nelson, Duchess of Bronte, who *d* 1873, only surviving child and heiress of 1st Earl Nelson; *d* 1868; *s* by his son (3) *Gen* ALEXANDER NELSON, GCB, 1st Viscount, *b* 1814; *cr Viscount Bridport* (peerage of United Kingdom) 1868; Groom-in-Waiting to HM Queen Victoria 1841-58, Clerk Marshal to late Prince Consort 1853-61, an Equerry to HM Queen Victoria 1858-84, a Lord-in-Waiting to HM Queen Victoria 1884-1901, and an Extra Equerry to HM Queen Victoria 1884-1901; was an Hon Equerry to HM King Edward VII: *m* 1838, Lady Mary Penelope Hill, who *d* 1884, da of 3rd Marquess of Downshire; *d* 1904; *s* by his son (4) Col ARTHUR WELLINGTON ALEXANDER NELSON, CB, 2nd Viscount, *b* 1839; MP for W Somerset (*C*) 1868-80: *m* 1872, Lady Maria Georgiana Julia Fox-Strangways, who *d* 1922, sister of 5th Earl of Ilchester; *d* 1924; *s* by his grandson (5) ROWLAND ARTHUR HERBERT NELSON (only son of late Lieut Hon Maurice Henry Nelson Hood, R Naval Div (*ka* 1915), 2nd son of 2nd Viscount), 3rd Viscount, *b* 1911; Lord-in-Waiting to HM 1939-40: *m* 1st, 1934 (*m diss* 1945), Pamela Aline Mary, only da of late Charles J. Baker; 2ndly, 1946, Sheila Jeanne Agatha (who *d* 1996, having *m* 3rdly, 1988, Alexei V. Haieff), only da of Johan Hendrik van Meurs, and widow of W/Cdr J. H. Little, DFC, AuxAF; *d* 1969; *s* by his son (6) ALEXANDER NELSON, 4th Viscount and present peer; also Baron Bridport.

BRIGGS, BARON (Briggs) (Life Baron 1976)

ASA BRIGGS, son of William Walker Briggs, of Keighley, Yorks; *b* 7 May 1921; *ed* Keighley Gram Sch, and Sidney Sussex Coll, Camb (MA); MA Oxford; BSc (Econ) London; Hon LLD York, Canada, New England, and Open University; Hon DLitt E Anglia, Strathclyde, Leeds, Liverpool, Bradford, Sussex, Birmingham, Cincinnati, George Washington and Tulane; FBA and Fellow American Academy; Hon Fellow, Sidney Sussex Coll and St Catharine's Coll, Camb, and Worcester Coll, Oxford; Hon DSc Florida Presbyterian; a Fellow of Worcester Coll, Oxford 1945-55, Prof of History, Leeds Univ 1955-61, Vice-Chancellor, Sussex Univ 1967-76, Provost of Worcester Coll, Oxford 1976-91, Chancellor, the Open Univ 1979-94; Chm European Inst of Educn 1975-85; Chm Commonwealth of Learning 1988-93; *cr Baron Briggs,* of Lewes, in co of E Sussex (Life Baron) 1976: *m* 1955, Susan Anne, da of Donald William Banwell, of Keevil, Wilts, and has issue.

Residences – The Tower, Tyninghame House, Tyninghame, E Lothian; The Caprons, Keere St, Lewes, Sussex. *Clubs* – Beefsteak, Oxford and Cambridge.

SONS LIVING

Hon Daniel Nicholas, *b* 1958: *m* 1989, Anabel E. M., yst da of Harvey Ziegler, of Chiddingfold, Surrey, and has issue living, Henry Nathaniel, *b* 1994, — Wilkie Arthur, *b* 1995, — Arthur Asa, *b* 1997, — Honor Johanna, *b* 1999.
Hon Matthew William Banwell, *b* 1964: *m* 1996, Susannah W., 2nd da of Alec E. H. Worster, of Hampstead Garden Suburb, NW11.

DAUGHTERS LIVING

Hon Katharine Jane, *b* 1956: *m* 1980, David Robert Wheeler, of 30 Alexandra Rd, Epsom, Surrey, and has issue living, Timothy Robert, *b* 1985, — Caroline Jane, *b* 1982, — Charlotte Rose, *b* 1987, — Georgina May, *b* 1991.
Hon Judith Susanna, *b* 1961: *m* 1985, Philip G. F. Preston, only son of W. Preston, of Folkestone, Kent, and has issue living, Jonathan, *b* 1989, — Samuel, *b* 1993, — Thomas (twin), *b* 1993.

BRIGHTMAN, BARON (Brightman) (Life Baron 1982)

JOHN ANSON BRIGHTMAN, PC, son of William Henry Brightman, of St Albans, Herts; *b* 20 June 1911; *ed* Marlborough, and St John's Coll, Camb (Hon Fellow 1982); Bar Lincoln's Inn 1932, QC 1961, a Bencher 1966; Member Gen Council of the Bar 1955-60 and 1966-70; Attorney-Gen of Duchy of Lancaster, and Attorney and Serjeant within the County Palatine of Lancaster 1969-70; Judge of Nat Industrial Relations Court 1971-74; Judge of High Court of Justice 1970-79; Lord Justice of Appeal 1979-1982, a Lord of Appeal in Ordinary 1982-86; FRGS 1994; Able Seaman, Merchant Navy, 1939-40, RNVR as Lt-Cdr 1940-46; Assist Naval Attaché, Ankara 1944; *cr* Knt 1970, PC 1979, and *Baron Brightman*, of Ibthorpe, co Hants, 1982 (Life Baron): *m* 1945, Roxane, da of Gerasimo Ambatielo, of Cephalonia, and has issue.

𝕬rms – Per fess wavy azure and argent in chief two dolphins naiant or and in base the stern of a man of war of circa 1805 proper. 𝕮rest – Upon a wreath argent and gules, a herring gull statant wings elevated and addorsed proper, supporting with the dexter foot a rose gules, barbed and seeded proper. 𝕾upporters – Two otters each on a grassy mount encircled by water proper and collared with a crown rayonny gold.
Residences – Ibthorpe, Hants SP11 0BY; 30 Onslow Gdns, SW7 3AH.

SON LIVING

Hon Christopher Anthony John, *b* 1948; *ed* Marlborough, and St John's Coll, Camb (MA); MB, BChir, MSc, MRCPath, FRGS: *m* 1975, Elisabeth, yr da of Jonkheer Willem de Beyer, and has issue living, Louisa, *b* 1978, — Justina, *b* 1980, — Eugénie, *b* 1982.

BRIGSTOCKE, BARONESS (Brigstocke) (Life Baroness 1990)

HEATHER RENWICK BRIGSTOCKE, da of Sqdn Leader John Renwick Brown, DFC; *b* 2 Sept 1929; *ed* Abbey Sch, Reading, and Girton Coll, Camb; Hon Bencher Inner Temple 1992; Classics Mistress Francis Holland Sch, SW1, 1951-53, and (part-time) Godolphin and Latymer Sch 1954-60, Latin Teacher Nat Cathedral Sch, Washington DC 1962-64, Headmistress Francis Holland Sch, NW1, 1965-74, and High Mistress St Paul's Girls' Sch 1974-89; Council Member London House for Overseas Graduates 1965-91 (Vice-Chm 1975-80), Middlesex Hosp Medical Sch 1971-80, Royal Holloway Coll 1977-85, City Univ 1978-83, Member The Royal Soc of Arts 1983-87, St George's House, Windsor, 1984-90, Modern Foreign Languages Working Group 1989-90, Museums and Galleries Commn since 1992, and Health Education Authority since 1989; Trustee National Gallery 1975-82, Kennedy Memorial Trust 1980-85, and City Technology Colls Trust since 1987; Pres Bishop Creighton House Settlement, Fulham, since 1977, and Girls' Schs Assocn 1980-81; Gov Wellington Coll 1975-87, The Royal Ballet Sch 1977-92, Forest Sch 1982-90, Museum of London 1986-92, and Gordonstoun Sch 1991-93; Chm English-Speaking Union of the Commonwealth since 1993; Non-Exec Dir LWT 1982-90, Member Programme Advisory Bd, LWT 1990-93; Chm Autistic Care & Training Devpt Appeal 1990, Trustees Geffrye Museum since 1990, Thames LWT Telethon Trust 1990, and The Menerva Educational Trust 1991-93; Independent Nat Dir The Times Newspaper Holdings since 1991; Member Governing Body Imperial Coll since 1991; Chm Landau Forte City Technology Coll, Derby since 1993 (Gov since 1992); Assoc Dir Great Universal Stores since 1993; Vice Pres City & Guilds of London Inst since 1993; Non-Exec Dir Burberrys since 1993; Cttee Member Automobile Assocn 1975-90; Special Advisor Kays 1989-90, and Burberrys 1989-92; *cr Baroness Brigstocke*, of Kensington, Royal Borough of Kensington and Chelsea (Life Baroness) 1990: *m* 1952, Geoffrey Brigstocke, who *d* 1974, and has issue.

Address – House of Lords, SW1A 0PW.

SONS LIVING

Hon David Hugh Charles, *b* 1953.
Hon Julian Renwick, *b* 1955.
Hon Thomas James Jefferson, *b* 1961: *m* 1998, Nicola A., yr da of Robert Sutton, of Sydney, Australia.

DAUGHTER LIVING

Hon Emma Persephone, *b* 1957.

BRIMELOW, BARONY OF (Brimelow) (Extinct 1995)

DAUGHTERS LIVING OF LIFE BARON

Hon Alison Jane, *b* 1949.
Hon Elizabeth Anne, *b* 1951.

BRISTOL, MARQUESS OF (Hervey) (Marquess UK 1826)
(Name pronounced "Harvy")

I shall never forget

FREDERICK WILLIAM AUGUSTUS HERVEY, 8th Marquess; *b* 19 Oct 1979; *s* 1999; *ed* Eton, and Edinburgh Univ; Hereditary High Steward of the Liberty of St Edmund, patron of thirty livings.

Arms – Gules, on a bend argent, three trefoils slipped vert. **Crest** – An ounce passant sable, spotted, ducally collared, and chain reflexed over the back or, holding in the dexter paw a trefoil slipped vert. **Supporters** – Two ounces sable, bezantée, ducally collared, and chain reflexed over the back or.
Property – Ickworth, Bury St Edmunds, Suffolk. *Residence* – 15 Chapel St, Belgrave Sq, SW1.

SISTERS LIVING

Lady Victoria Frederica Isabella, *b* 1976.
Lady Isabella Frederica Louisa, *b* 1982.

WIDOW LIVING OF SIXTH MARQUESS

YVONNE MARIE (*Marchioness of Bristol*) (Rosa-Maris, 29 Avenue des Papalins, Fontvieille, Monaco), only da of Anthony Sutton, of Woodstock, The Glen, Farnborough Park, Kent: *m* 1974, as his 3rd wife, the 6th Marquess of Bristol, who *d* 1985.

COLLATERAL BRANCHES LIVING

Granddaughter of late Sir George William Hervey, KCB, el son of late Lord William Hervey, CB, 3rd son of 1st Marquess:—
Issue of late Claude Arthur Hervey, *b* 1891, *d* 1927: *m* 1920, Edith Kathleen, who *d* 1972, da of late Humphry B. Lamb, of Penn, Staffordshire:—
Cecilia Dora, *b* 1923: *m* 1945, John Quay, and has issue living, Jacqueline Teresa, *b* 1950. *Residence* – 30 Forest Lodge, Portland Rd, East Grinstead, Sussex RH19 4EZ.

Grandchildren of late Alec Francis Hervey, 3rd son of late Francis Arthur Hervey, yr son of late Lord William Hervey, CB (ante):—
Issue of late Ronald Frederick William Hervey, *b* 1919, *d* 1997: *m* 1st, 1943 (*m diss* 1948), Constance Mary, who *d* 196—, da of late James David Bunce, of Seaway Mount, Torquay, and widow of Alexander Zatonski, F/O RAF; 2ndly, 1958 (*m diss* 1969), Jeanne Patricia, da of late Rev Archibald Wynne Esmonde Dowse, of Bexhill-on-Sea, E Sussex:—
(By 2nd *m*) TIMOTHY HUGH (Brambledown, Friston Hill, East Dean, E Sussex BN20 0EB), *b* 5 Feb 1960: *m* 1992, Susan Mary, da of Sidney Arthur Peacham, of Bexhill-on-Sea, E Sussex, and has issue living, Benjamin James William Peacham, *b* 1997, — Rebecca Maria, *b* 1992, — Hannah Rachel Louisa, *b* 1994. —— Jennifer Charlotte (Church Farm Barn, Ninfield, E Sussex TN33 9JX), *b* 1962: *m* 1987 (*m diss* 1997), Kevin Allen Moon, and has issue living, Robert William, *b* 1988, — Richard Charles, *b* 1990.

Granddaughter of late Douglas George Hervey (infra):—
Issue of late Edward George Hervey, *b* 1917, *d* 1959: *m* 1956, Sheila Mary Howard, who *m* 2ndly, 1965 (*m diss* 1984), as his 2nd wife, Sir Hugo Giles Edmund Sebright, 14th Bt, who *d* 1985, da of Walter Howard Rocke, of Salisbury, Rhodesia:—
Elizabeth Lepel Howard, *b* 1957.

Grandchildren of late George Henry William Hervey, 2nd son of Rt Rev Lord Arthur Charles Hervey, DD, Lord Bishop of Bath and Wells, 4th son of 1st Marquess:—
Issue of late Douglas George Hervey, *b* 1880, *d* 1965: *m* 1913, Ida Constance, who *d* 1972, da of late Rev Edward Clowes, of Colworth, Bexhill-on-Sea:—
Constance Valentine, *b* 1920: *m* 1951, Duncan C. Lamsdale, who *d* 1993, of 51 Priory Rd, Hastings, E Sussex, and has issue living, Judith, *b* 1952: *m* 1974, Robert Boyle, of 25 The Avenue, Loughton, Essex, and has issue living, Adam Simon *b* 1985, Nicola Alison *b* 1982, Caroline Suzanne *b* 1989, Helen Gillian *b* (twin) 1989, — Susan Sarah (94 Emmanuel Rd, Hastings, E Sussex), *b* 1956: *m* 1985 (*m diss* 1994), James Leighton Sullivan, and has issue living, Sarah Caroline *b* 1986, Poppy Emma *b* 1997. —— Margery, MBE, *b* 1921; MBE (Civil) 1981: *m* 1945, Arthur Thomas Hingle, of PO Box 1067, Wimberley, Texas 78676, USA, and has had issue, Michael George, *b* 1949; *d* 1978, — Peter John Benedict (526 Carol Court, Richardson, Texas 75081, USA), *b* 1956: *m* 1984 (*m diss* 1988), Elizabeth Ann Hobbs, and has issue living, Audrey Ninette *b* 1985, — Margery Jane, *b* 1947: *m* 1972, Allan Ronald Lerner, of 6 Shadow Lawn, Houston, Texas 77005, USA, and has issue living, Jeffrey Michael *b* 1979, — Gillian Mary (9700 Glenfield Court No. 225, Houston, Texas 77096, USA), *b* 1950: *m* 1982 (*m diss* 1990), William Harvey Brown, and has issue living, Duncan O'Donnell *b* 1984, — Veronica Anne (PO Box 799, Lewistown, Montana 59457, USA), *b* 1954: *m* 1983 (*m diss* 1997), Allan Dale Williams, — Margaret Mary Bridget, *b* 1959: *m* 1993, Thomas A. Tisthammer, of 9843 Rist Canyon Rd, Bellevue, Colorado 80512, USA, and has issue living, Taylor Michael *b* 1997, Alexandra Kathleen *b* 1994.

Issue of late Gerald Arthur Hervey, Lieut (TF) RGA, *b* 1881, *ka* 1917: *m* 1912, Dorothy, who *d* 1949, da of late Alfred Symes, of Tendring, Essex:—
Anthony Gerald, *b* 1915; *ed* Marlborough, and Pembroke Coll, Camb: *m* 1948, Aileen Margaret, da of late Dr L. R. Pickett, of 167 Cooden Sea Rd, Cooden, Sussex, and has issue living, Gerald Edward (12 Bucknalls Lane, Garston, Watford, Herts), *b* 1949: *m* 1974, Mary Agnes, da of late Michael Dore, of co Limerick, and has issue living, Simon

Anthony *b* 1985, — Christopher Symes (5 Burlington Gds, W4; 5820 Countrywood Drive, Sarasota, FL 34232-6001, USA), *b* 1952: *m* 1st, 1977 (*m diss* 1984), Christina Ann, da of Watson Failes, of Chorleywood, Herts; 2ndly, 1984 (*m diss* 1989), Nicole, da of Colin Charters, of Caterham, Surrey; 3rdly, 1992, Lesley, da of John Exley, of Stratford upon Avon, and has issue living (by 2nd *m*), Toby James Symes *b* 1987, Tanya Maria *b* 1985. *Residence* – 3825 Sarasota Golf Club Blvd, Sarasota, Florida, USA.

Descendants of late Frederick Anne Hervey-Bathurst, next brother of late Felton Elwell Hervey-Bathurst (el son of late Felton Lionel Hervey, son of late Hon Felton Hervey, 8th son of 1st Earl of Bristol), who was *cr* a *Baronet* 1818, and whom he *s* (under special remainder) 1819:—
See Hervey-Bathurst, Bt.

PREDECESSORS – (1) JOHN Hervey, of Ickworth, Suffolk, MP for Bury St Edmunds 1690-1 and 1695-1703, was *cr Baron Hervey of Ickworth* (peerage of England) 1703, and *Earl of Bristol* (peerage of GB)1714: *m* 1st, 1688, Isabella, who *d* 1693, da and heir of Sir Robert Carr, 3rd Bt; 2ndly, 1695, Elizabeth, who *d* 1741, da and co-heir of Sir Thomas Felton, 4th Bt, by Lady Elizabeth Howard, da and co-heir of 3rd Earl of Suffolk, and 3rd Lord Howard de Walden; his el son by 2nd *m*, John, who had been summoned to Parl as Lord Hervey 1733, *d* 1743, leaving, by his wife Mary Lepel, issue of whom three sons succeeded to the title; the Earl *d* 1751; *s* by his grandson (2) GEORGE WILLIAM, 2nd Earl; Ambassador to Spain 1758-61; Lord Lt of Ireland 1766-67; *d* unm 1775; *s* by his brother (3) AUGUSTUS JOHN, 3rd Earl, Vice-Adm of the Blue, and a Lord of the Admiralty in 1799; *dsp* 1779; *s* by his brother (4) *Rt Rev* FREDERICK AUGUSTUS, 4th Earl, *b* 1730; Bishop of Derry, who by descent from his grandmother *s de jure* to the Barony of Howard de Walden, which title was in 1806 confirmed upon his great-grandson, the 2nd Baron Seaford; the Bishop *m* 1752, Elizabeth, who *d* 1800, sister and heir of Sir Charles Davers, 5th Bt (and gt-grandda of 2nd Baron Jermyn); *d* 1803; *s* by his el surv son (5) FREDERICK WILLIAM, 5th Earl; *cr Earl Jermyn and Marquess of Bristol* (peerage of UK) 1826; *m* 1798, Elizabeth Albana, who *d* 1844, da of 1st Baron Templetown, *d* 1859; *s* by his son (6) FREDERICK WILLIAM, 2nd Marquess, *b* 1880; MP for Bury St Edmunds 1826-59; Treasurer of R Household 1841-46: *m* 1830, Lady Katharine Isabella Manners, who *d* 1848, da of 5th Duke of Rutland; *d* 1864; *s* by his son (7) FREDERICK WILLIAM JOHN, 3rd Marquess, *b* 1834; MP for W Suffolk (C) 1859-64, and Lord-Lt of Suffolk 1886-1907: *m* 1862, Geraldine Georgina Mary, who *d* 1927, da of Gen Hon George Anson; *d* 1907; *s* by his nephew (8) FREDERICK WILLIAM FANE, MVO (son of Lord Augustus Henry Charles Hervey, MP, 2nd son of 2nd Marquess), 4th Marquess, *b* 1863; Rear-Adm; MP for Bury St Edmunds (C) 1906-07: *m* 1896, Alice Frances Theodora, who *d* 1957, da of George Edward Wythes, of Copt Hall, Epping; *d* 1951, *s* by his brother (9) HERBERT ARTHUR ROBERT, 5th Marquess, *b* 1870; Min and Consul-Gen to Colombia 1919-23, and Min to Peru and Equador 1923-29: *m* 1st, 1914 (*m diss* 1933), Lady Jean Alice Elaine Cochrane, who *d* 1955, da of 12th Earl of Dundonald; 2ndly, 1952, Dora Frances Emblin, who *d* 1953, widow of Don Pedro de Zulueta; *d* 1960; *s* by his only son (10) VICTOR FREDERICK COCHRANE, 6th Marquess, *b* 1915; Chancellor Monarchist League: *m* 1st, 1949 (*m diss* 1959), Pauline Mary, who *d* 1996, da of late Herbert Coxon Bolton; 2ndly, 1960 (*m diss* 1972), Lady Anne Juliet Dorothea Maud Wentworth Fitzwilliam, only child of 8th Earl Fitzwilliam; 3rdly, 1974, Yvonne Marie, only da of Anthony Sutton, of Woodstock, The Glen, Farnborough Park, Kent; *d* 1985; *s* by his el son (11) FREDERICK WILLIAM JOHN AUGUSTUS, 7th Marquess, *b* 1954: *m* 1984 (*m diss* 1987), Francesca, da of Douglas H. Fisher, of Marbella, Spain, and formerly wife of Phillip Jones, of USA; *d* 1999; *s* by his half-brother (12) FREDERICK WILLIAM AUGUSTUS, 8th Marquess and present peer; also Earl of Bristol, Earl Jermyn, and Baron Hervey of Ickworth.

BROADBRIDGE, BARON (Broadbridge) (Baron UK 1945, Bt UK 1937)

By industry and perseverance

PETER HEWETT BROADBRIDGE, 3rd Baron and 3rd Baronet; *b* 19 Aug 1938; *s* 1972; *ed* Hurstpierpoint, and St Catherine's Coll, Oxford (MA, BSc): *m* 1st, 1967 (*m diss* 1980), Mary, only da of W. O. Busch, of An Der Brücke, Dittershausen, Kassel, W Germany; 2ndly, 1989, Sally Frances Finn, and has issue by 1st *m*.

𝕬rms – Gules, in chief two pens in saltire or and in base over water a stone bridge of a single span embattled proper. ℭrest – A dolphin hauriant argent between two gilly-flowers gules slipped and leaved vert. 𝕾upporters – On either side a dolphin proper charged with a sword erect gules. *Address* – c/o House of Lords, SW1.

DAUGHTERS LIVING (By 1st marriage)

Hon Jemima Louise, *b* 1970.
Hon Sophie Mary, *b* 1972.

UNCLE LIVING (son of 1st Baron)

Hon Howard Eustace (12 Texel, Alexandra Rd, Pietermaritzburg, Natal), *b* 1904: *m* 1935, Margaret Ada Marion, da of Capt H. H. Witherington, and has had issue, †George Witherington, *b* 1939; BSc: *m* 1962, Joan Margaret (Gablemere, Gable Rd, Durban, Natal, S Africa), da of Cyril Ridge, of Pietermaritzburg, S Africa, and *d* 1968, leaving issue, Ann Magaret *b* 1967, — Sally Kathleen, *b* 1937: *m* 1966, Peter Jeremy Chadwick Horne, and has issue living, Lance Chadwick *b* 1969, Timothy George Chadwick *b* 1971.

WIDOWS LIVING OF SONS OF FIRST BARON

Anne Marjorie, da of J. Locke Elfick: *m* 1927, Hon Hugh Trevor Broadbridge, who *d* 1979, and has issue (*see* colls infra).

Margaret Ada Marion, da of Capt H. H. Witherington: *m* 1935, Hon Howard Eustace Broadbridge, who *d* 1989, and has issue (see colls infra). *Residence* – 12 Texel, Alexandra Rd, Pietermaritzburg, Natal.

Margaret Anne, da of George S. Cumming, of Bloemfontein, S Africa: *m* 1948, Hon Rupert Guy Broadbridge, who *d* 19—, and has issue (*see* colls infra).

COLLATERAL BRANCHES LIVING

Issue of late Hon Ralph George Cameron Broadbridge, 2nd son of 1st Baron, *b* 1901; *d* 1983: *m* 1925, Emma Rose Hancock, who *d* 195-, da of Henry Van der Weydon:—
Enid Rose, *b* 1926: *m* 1948, Alexander Rolland, and has issue living, Andrew, *b* 1949, — Martin, *b* 1951, — Nigel, *b* 1955. —— June, *b* 1927. —— Anita, *b* 1928: *m* 1949, Dennis Robert Hutchins, and has issue living, Anthony David, *b* 1953, — Lucy Jane, *b* 1955.

Issue of late Hon Hugh Trevor Broadbridge, 3rd son of 1st Baron, *b* 1903, *d* 1979: *m* 1927, Anne Marjorie, da of J. Locke Elfick:—
MARTIN HUGH (23A Westfield Rd, Barton-on-Humber, N Lincs DN18 5AA), *b* 29 Nov 1929: *m* 1954, Norma, da of late Maj Herbert Sheffield, MC; 2ndly, 1968, Elizabeth, da of J. E. Trotman, and has issue living (by 1st *m*), Richard, *b* 1959, — Katharine, *b* 1956. —— Jill, *b* 1932: *m* 1954, John Damment, RAF (c/o Lloyds Bank, 6 Pall Mall, SW1 5NH), and has issue living, Stephen, *b* 1957, — Helen, *b* 1956, — Deborah, *b* 1958, — Louise, *b* 1959, — Susan, *b* 1962.

Issue of late Hon Howard Eustace Broadbridge, 4th son of 1st Baron, *b* 1904, *d* 1989: *m* 1935, Margaret Ada Marion (ante), da of Capt H. H. Witherington:-
†George Witherington, *b* 1939; BSc: *m* 1962, Joan Margaret (Gablemere, Gable Rd, Durban, Natal, S Africa), da of Cyril Ridge, of Pietermaritzburg, and *d* 1968, leaving issue, Ann Margaret, *b* 1967. —— Sally Kathleen, *b* 1937: *m* 1966, Peter Jeremy Chadwick Horne, and has issue living, Lance Chadwick, *b* 1969, — Timothy George Chadwick, *b* 1971.

Issue of late Hon Rupert Guy Broadbridge, 5th son of 1st Baron, *b* 1906, *d* 19—: *m* 1948, Margaret Anne, da of George S. Cumming, of Bloemfontein, S Africa:—
Beverley, *b* 1949: *m* 19—, Maurice Roger Descroizilles, and has issue living, Lee, *b* 1975, — Andrew Vivian, *b* 1977, — Corinne, *b* 1980.

PREDECESSORS – (1) *Sir* GEORGE Broadbridge, KCVO, son of late Henry Broadbridge, of Brighton; *b* 1869; an Alderman (Candlewick Ward) for City of London (Sheriff 1933-34), Lord Mayor of London 1936-37; sat as MP for City of London (C) 1938-45; *cr* a *Baronet* (UK, of Wargrave Place) 1937, and *Baron Broadbridge*, of Brighton, co Sussex (peerage of United Kingdom) 1945: *m* 1st 1895, Fanny Kathleen, who *d* 1928, da of late Richard Brigden, of Brighton; 2ndly, 1929, Clara Maud, who *d* 1949, da of late John Swornsbourne, of Bognor Regis, Sussex; *d* 1952; *s* by his el son (2) ERIC WILBERFORCE, 2nd Baron, *b* 1895: *m* 1924, Mabel Daisy, who *d* 1966, da of Arthur Edward Clarke; *d* 1972, *s* by his only son (3) PETER HEWETT, 3rd Baron and present peer.

Brocas, Viscount; son of Earl Jellicoe.

BROCK, BARONY OF (Brock) (Extinct 1980)

DAUGHTERS LIVING OF LIFE BARON

Hon Mary Rose, *b* 1933; *ed* Wycombe Abbey Sch: *m* 1959, Keith Vanstone, of Blakes Farm, Ashurst, Steyning, W Sussex, and has issue.

Hon Margaret Louise (Owl Cottage, Laurel Lane, Queen Camel, Som BA22 7NV), *b* 1936; *ed* Malvern Girls' Coll: *m* 1962 (*m diss* 1988) (John Alexander) Simon Cary Mayhew (*see* V Falkland, colls, 1990 Edn), and has issue living, Ella Rose Louise, *b* 1963, — Matilda Jane, *b* 1965: *m* 1990, James R. M. McMaster, son of Dr Brian Master, of W Coker, Som, and has issue living, George James *b* 1998, Charles William *b* (twin) 1998.

BROCKET, BARON (Nall-Cain) (Baron UK 1933, Bt UK 1921)

The cat stroked is meek

CHARLES RONALD GEORGE NALL-CAIN, 3rd Baron, and 3rd Baronet; *b* 12 Feb 1952; *s* 1967; *ed* Eton; late 14th/20th King's Hussars: *m* 1982 (*m diss* 1995), Isabell Maria only da of Gustavo Lorenzo, of Whaleneck Drive, Merrick, Long Island, New York, and has issue.

Arms – Quarterly: 1st and 4th argent, three salmon haurient gules, in chief an oak tree eradicated proper, *Cain;* 2nd and 3rd per chevron barry of six gules and or and of the first, in chief two stags' heads caboshed proper and in base a lion rampant guardant of the second, *Nall.* **Crest** – 1st, a cat salient guardant erminois holding between the paws a dexter hand couped gules, *Cain;* 2nd, within a leather garter buckled gules a bee or, *Nall.* **Supporters** – Two cats guardant erminois.

SONS LIVING

Hon ALEXANDER CHRISTOPHER CHARLES, *b* 30 Sept 1984.
Hon William Thomas Anthony, *b* 1991.

DAUGHTER LIVING

Hon Antalya Stephanie Lauren, *b* 1987.

BROTHERS LIVING *(Raised to the rank of a Baron's sons 1969)*

Hon Richard Philip Christopher (Potters Hall, Dane End, Ware, Herts SG12 0JU; MCC) *b* 1953; *ed* Eton; late Lieut 2nd Bn, RGJ: *m* 1978, Juliet Paula Vivian, da of J. E. V. Forester, of Villa Mont Gras d'Eau, St Brelade, Jersey, CI, and has had issue, †Sam Christopher Philip, *b* and *d* 1987, — Rebecca Elizabeth Emily, *b* 1981, — Claire Antonia Louise, *b* 1982.
Hon David Michael Anthony (Attington Stud, Tetsworth, Oxon), *b* 1955; *ed* Harrow: *m* 1992, Albertine Hungerbühler.

UNCLE LIVING *(Son of 2nd Baron)*

Hon David Lawrence Robert (Cairnfold, Wooler, Northumberland NE71 6QT; Cavalry Club), *b* 1930; *ed* Eton, and Magdalene Coll, Camb (BA 1953, MA 1957), late 12th Roy Lancers and Derbyshire Yeo; FRICS; JP Cheshire 1964; Gov St Patrick's Hosp Dublin 1973-77: *m* 1958, Lady Katherine Elizabeth Palmer, sister of 4th Earl of Selborne, and has issue living, James Alexander (Waterend House, Wheathampstead, Herts AL4 8EP), *b* 1961: *m* 1992, Sarah-Jane, elder da of Anthony Bremner, of Llorts, Andorra, and has issue living, Andrew David Bremner *b* 1995, Susan Beatrix Eloise *b* 1998, — Caroline Davina, *b* 1959: *m* 1986, Paul David Cherry of Weston Park, Weston, nr Hitchin, Herts SG4 7DR, yr son of Peter Harold Cherry, of Weston Manor, Hitchin, Herts, and has issue living, Alexander *b* 1988, Harriet *b* 1989, — Annabel Priscilla Angela (*Lady Anthony Hill*), *b* 1963: *m* 1992, Lord Anthony Ian Hill, of Ingram House, Powburn, Alnwick, Northumberland NE66 4LT, yr son of 8th Marquess of Downshire, and has issue (see that title).

AUNT LIVING *(Daughter of 2nd Baron)*

Hon Elizabeth Angela Veronica Rose, *b* 1938: *m* 1st, 1958 (*m diss* 1969), 6th Marquess of Headfort; 2ndly, 1970 (*m diss* 1987), William Murless Knight, and has issue living (by 1st *m*) (*see* M Headfort), — (by 2nd *m*), Peregrine Robert Christian Murless, *b* 1971. *Residence* – 1A Park Lane, Woodstock, Oxon OX20 1UD.

MOTHER LIVING

Elizabeth Mary, da of late R. J. Stallard, of Le Shakespeare, 12 Blvd Princess Charlotte, Monte Carlo, Monaco: *m* 1st, 1950, Hon Ronald Charles Manus Nall-Cain, who *d* 1961, el son of 2nd Baron; 2ndly, 1964, Colin John Richard Trotter, of Attington Stud, Tetsworth, Oxon.

PREDECESSORS – The family of O'Chan was settled in Northern Ireland from the earliest times, owning a large territory there called O'Cahan's country. The O'Cahans, who trace their descent from Niall of the Nine Hostages, King of Ulster in the 5th century (also ancestor of the O'Neills) were Lords of the Route and Princes of Limavady. They owned the fishing rights in the three rivers, Bann, Foyle, and Roe prior to the Plantation of Ulster, hence the three salmon in the Cain Arms, while the wild cat now used as a crest and supporters in the Arms is reputed to have been used on the shield of The O'Cahan in 850. Manus Cathan an Duin, Prince of Limavady, was killed in the Battle of Down in 1260. Sir Donall O'Cahan of Limavady was knighted in 1607. His grandson, Eanagh, was deprived of his lands on the Plantation of Ulster and settled in co Galway in 1631, Joseph O'Cahan, great-grandson of Eanagh, *d* in Ballybane, co Galway in 1756 and his 2nd son, William, *m* Catherine O'Malley, and was the father of James O'Cahan, *b* (in the parish of St Nicholas, Galway) 1787. James changed his name to Cain, joined the 88th Regiment of Foot (later the Connaught Rangers), and fought in the Penninsular War. He *m* Mary, da of Alexander Deane of Cork, and sister of Sir Thomas Deane, the well-known Architect and Lord Mayor of Cork. Their son, Robert Cain, *b* on Spike Island, Cork, 1826, emigrated to England in 1844: *m* 1848, Ann, da of James Newall, of Lowton. He founded the firm of Robert Cain & Sons, and had with other issue a 2nd son, William Ernest, *b* 1864, *cr* 1st Baronet of Wargrave, and a 4th **(1)** CHARLES ALEXANDER, *b* 1866; Chm of Walker Cain, Ltd, a JP and DL for Herts (High Sheriff 1925), Pres of Hitchin Dist of League of Mercy, and a KGStJ; assumed additional surname of Nall; *cr a Baronet* 1921, and *Baron Brocket*, of Brocket Hall, co Hertford (peerage of United Kingdom) 1933: *m* 1st, 1888, Florence, who *d* 1927, yst da of late William Nall, of Kegworth, Derbyshire; 2ndly, 1928, Anne Page, JP, who *d* 1949, da of late Richard Benyon Croft, JP, DL, of Fanhams Hall, Ware; *d* 1934; *s* by his son **(2)** ARTHUR RONALD NALL, 2nd Baron, *b* 1904; a JP for Herts; MP for Wavertree Div of

Liverpool (C) 1931-34: *m* 1927, Angela Beatrix, who *d* 1975, yr da of late Rev Preb William Geoffrey Pennyman, of Ormesby Hall, Yorks (Walker, Bt, *cr* 1868), *d* 1967; *s* by his grandson **(3)** CHARLES RONALD GEORGE (el son of late Hon Ronald Charles Manus Nall-Cain, el son of 2nd Baron) 3rd Baron, and present peer.

BROCKWAY, BARONY OF (Brockway) (Extinct 1988)

SON LIVING OF LIFE BARON (*By 2nd marriage*)

Hon Christopher Fenner, *b* 1946: *m* 1st, 1974 (*m diss* 1979), — ; 2ndly, 1981, Sophie Marie-Luc, da of Luc Bernhard Niggli, of Switzerland, and has issue living (by 1st *m*), Steven, *b* 1974, — (by 2nd *m*) David Mehdi, *b* 1985, — Laylah Suzanne, *b* 1982.

DAUGHTERS LIVING OF LIFE BARON (*By 1st marriage*)

Hon Joan Vera, *b* 1921: *m* 1944, Capt Everett Samuel Pover, and has issue.

Hon Olive Fenna, *b* 1924: *m* 1944 (*m diss* 1986), Cecil Outrim, and has issue. *Residence* – 14 Appletons, Hadlow, Kent.

WIDOW LIVING OF LIFE BARON

EDITH VIOLET (*Baroness Brockway*), da of late Archibald Herbert King, of Catford, SE6: *m* 1946, as his 2nd wife, Baron Brockway (Life Baron), who *d* 1988.

Brodrick, family name of Viscount Midleton.

Brooke, Lord; son of Earl Brooke and of Warwick (see Warwick)

Brooke, family name of Viscount Alanbrooke.

Brooke, family name of Viscount Brookeborough.

Brooke and of Warwick, Earl (see Warwick)

BROOKE OF ALVERTHORPE, BARON (Brooke) (Life Baron 1997)

CLIVE BROOKE son of John Brooke, of Wakefield; *b* 21 June 1942; *ed* Thornes House Sch, Wakefield; Assist Sec, Inland Revenue Staff Fedn 1964-82, Dep Gen Sec 1982-88, Gen Sec 1988-95; Jt Gen Sec Public Services Tax and Commerce Union since 1996; Memb Gen Council, Trade Union Congress since 1989, Exec Cttee since 1993; Memb Council of Civil Service Unions (Major Policy Cttee), Inland Revenue, Deptl Whitley Council, TUS 1976-88 (Chm 1986-88), House of Commons Speaker's Commn on Citizenship 1988, Exec Cttee, Involvement and Participation Assoc since 1991; Tstee, Duke of Edinburgh Study Conference since 1993 (Memb Canada Conference 1980); Community Services Volunteers since 1989; Memb Labour Party, Exec Cttee of Fabian Soc, and Churches Enquiry on Employment and Future of Work; *cr Baron Brooke of Alverthorpe*, of Alverthorpe, co W Yorks (Life Baron) 1997: *m* 1967, Lorna Hopkin, da of Idris Roberts, of Treharris, S Wales.

Address – c/o House of Lords, Westminster, SW1A 0PW.

BROOKE OF CUMNOR, BARONY OF (Brooke) (Extinct 1984)

SONS LIVING OF LIFE BARON

Rt Hon Peter Leonard, CH, MP (110A, Ashley Gdns, SW1; The Old Vicarage, W Lavington, Devizes, Wilts; *Clubs* – Brooks's, City Livery, I Zingari, MCC, St George's, Conservative), *b* 1934, *ed* Marlborough, Balliol Coll, Oxford and Harvard Business Sch, Assist Govt Whip House of Commons 1979-83; a Lord Commr of HM Treasury 1983, a Parliamentary Under Sec of State, Dept of Educn & Science, 1983-87, Paymaster Gen and Min of State 1987-89, Sec of State for N Ireland 1989-92, Sec of State for National Heritage 1992-94, Chm Churches Conservation Trust since 1995, Chm Conservative Party 1987-89; MP for City of London and Westminster South (*C*) since 1977; PC 1988, CH 1992: *m* 1st, 1964, Joan, da of late Frederick George Smith, of São Paulo, Brazil; 2ndly, 1991, Mrs Lindsay Allinson, and has issue (by 1st *m*), of whom the 3rd son, Sebastian H., *b* 19—: *m* 1995, (Owen) Beatrice, da of Roger Nichols.

Rt Hon Sir Henry (*Rt Hon Lord Justice Brooke*), *b* 1936; *ed* Marlborough, and Balliol Coll, Oxford; a Judge of the High Court of Justice (Queen's Bench Div) 1988-96, since when a Lord Justice of Appeal; Chm Law Commn 1993-95; Kt 1988, PC 1996: *m* 1966, Bridget Mary, da of Wilfrid George Kalaugher, of Appledene, Marlborough, and has issue living, Michael John, *b* 1967, — Nicholas George, *b* 1968, — Christopher Robert, *b* 1973, — Caroline Mary, *b* 1973. *Address* – Royal Courts of Justice, Strand, WC2.

DAUGHTERS LIVING OF LIFE BARON

Hon Honor Leslie, *b* 1941; *ed* St Mary's Calne, St Thomas's Hosp (Nightingale Nurse), and Nottingham and Warwick Univs; art historian: *m* 1966, Dr (Thomas) Nigel Miller, FRCP, of Laurel Hill, Repton, Derby, and has issue, three sons and two das.

Hon Margaret Hilary Diana, *b* 1944: *m* 1971, James Douglas Pulfer, c/o University of Papua New Guinea, and has issue.

WIDOW LIVING OF LIFE BARON

BARBARA MURIEL, (*Baroness Brooke of Ystradfellte*), DBE (Life Baroness) (see that title).

BROOKE OF YSTRADFELLTE, BARONESS (Brooke) (Life Baroness 1964)

BARBARA MURIEL BROOKE, DBE, da of late Rev Canon Alfred Augustus Mathews, of Llanwern, Gwent; *b* 14 Jan 1908; *ed* Queen Anne's Sch, Caversham, and Glos Training Coll of Domestic Science; a Member of Hampstead Borough Council 1948-65, and Vice-Chm of Conservative Party Organization 1954-64; a Member of N-W Metropolitan Regional Hosp Board 1955-66; Chm of Governing Body of Godolphin and Latymer Sch since 1960, and of Exec Cttee of Queen's Inst of Dist Nursing 1961-71; a Member of Management Cttee, King Edward's Hosp Fund for London 1967-70; Hon Fellow of Westfield Coll; *cr* DBE (Civil) 1960, and *Baroness Brooke of Ystradfellte,* of Ystradfellte, co Brecknock (Life Baroness) 1964: *m* 1933, Baron Brooke of Cumnor, (Life Baron), who *d* 1984, and has issue (see that title, ext).
Residence – Romans Halt, Mildenhall, Marlborough, Wilts. *Club* – University Women's.

BROOKEBOROUGH, VISCOUNT (Brooke) (Viscount UK 1952 Bt UK 1822)

Glory is the end

ALAN HENRY BROOKE, 3rd Viscount, and 7th Baronet; *b* 30 June 1952; *s* 1987; *ed* Harrow, and Millfield; DL co Fermanagh 1987; 17th/21st Lancers, Capt 4th Bn Ulster Defence Regt 1977, Maj 4th Bn UDR and Co Cmdr (part time) 1988, Lt-Col Royal Irish Regt 1993; Hon Col 4th/5th Rangers 1997; Memb House of Lords EEC Agric Cttee 1988; Memb House of Lords EU Select Cttee 1998; a Lord in Waiting to HM since 1997: *m* 1980, Janet Elizabeth, only da of John Cooke, of Ballyvoy Lodge, Doagh, co Antrim.

Arms – Or, a cross engrailed per pale gules and sable, a crescent for difference. **Crest** – A brock, or badger, passant argent. **Supporters** – *Dexter*, a dolphin sable; *sinister*, a lion double queued gules langued azure.
Seat – Colebrooke, Brookeborough, co Fermanagh. *Club* – Cavalry and Guards.

BROTHER LIVING

Hon CHRISTOPHER ARTHUR, *b* 16 May 1954; *ed* Gordonstoun; Lt 5th Inniskilling Drag Gds: *m* 1990, Amanda M., da of G. N. R. Hodges, of Lowlands, Trinity, Jersey, CI, and has issue living, Archie Alan John, *b* 17 Dec 1991, — Henry Arthur Oliver, *b* 1993, — Matthew Victor Francis, *b* 1995. *Residence* – Galgorm Castle, Ballymena, co Antrim.

SISTERS LIVING

Hon (Rosalind) Juliana, *b* 1950: *m* 1st, 1973, Maj Nigel Cowie, who *d* 1991, 2nd son of Lt-Col Howard Elphinstone Cowie, of South Poorton, Powerstock, Bridport, Dorset; 2ndly, 1994, Christopher James Grose, only son of late Brig James Grose, of Bicknoller, Som, and has issue living (by 1st *m*), Alexander John, *b* 1975, — Rosalind Mary, *b* 1977. *Residence* – The Old Bakery, Aldsworth, Cheltenham, Glos.
Hon Melinda Charlotte, *b* 1958: *m* 1982, Nicholas Ronald Taylor, eldest son of Ronald Taylor, of Brighton Wood, Alresford, Hants, and has issue living, Christopher Martin John, *b* 1990, — Alice Melinda, *b* 1988. *Residence* – Bradley Fields Farm, Lillingstone Lovell, Buckingham MK18 5BH.
Hon Susanna Cynthia, *b* 1962: *m* 1989, Richard John Hamilton Stubber, 2nd son of late Col John Henry Hamilton Stubber, of Aughentaine, Fivemiletown, co Tyrone, and has issue living, Thomas Richard, *b* 1991, — Iona Rose, *b* 1993. *Residence* – Foley Hill, Aghalee, co Antrim BT67 0DZ.

WIDOW LIVING OF SECOND VISCOUNT

ROSEMARY HILDA (*Rosemary, Viscountess Brookeborough*), da of late Lt-Col Arthur O'Neill Cubitt Chichester, OBE, MC (*see* M Donegall, colls): *m* 1949, the 2nd Viscount Brookeborough, PC, who *d* 1987. *Residence* – Ashbrooke, Brookeborough, co Fermanagh.

COLLATERAL BRANCHES LIVING (*In remainder to Baronetcy only*)

Issue of late Sir Alan Francis Brooke, KG, GCB, OM, GCVO, DSO, 6th son of 3rd Baronet, who was *cr Viscount Alanbrooke* 1946 (see that title).

Granddaughters of late Col Arthur Brooke, IA, 2nd son of late Capt Sir Harry Vesey Brooke, KBE, 2nd son of 2nd baronet:—
Issue of late Maj Basil Arthur Brooke, MC, late Gordon Highlanders, *b* 1917, *d* 1992: *m* 1st, 1946, Mora Allison, da of late Col James Alexander Stewart Balmain, of Alford House, Somerset; 2ndly, 1968, Jane, da of — Lane, and widow of Howard Samuel:—
(By 1st *m*) Patricia Alison, *b* 1946. —— Sheelah Anne, *b* 1949. —— Diana Eva, *b* 1951.

Grandson of Arthur Basil Brooke, 3rd son of 2nd baronet:—
Issue of late Lt-Gen Sir Bertram Norman SERGISON-BROOKE, KCB, KCVO, CMG, DSO, *b* 1880, *d* 1967: *m* 1st, 1915, Prudence Ida Evelyn, who *d* 1918, da of late Capt Charles Warden Sergison, of Cuckfield Park, Sussex (*see* B Sudeley, 1911 Edn); 2ndly, 1923, Hilda, who *d* 1954, da of Mark Fenwick, of Abbotswood, Stow-on-the-Wold:—
(By 2nd *m*) Timothy Mark (Chipping Warden Manor, Banbury, Oxon), *b* 1924; *ed* Eton; 1939-45 War with Gren Gds: *m* 1964, Hon Mary Anne Hare, el da of 1st Viscount Blakenham, and has issue living, Nicholas Mark, *b* 1966: *m* 1996, Clare F., da of John Nicholson, and has issue living, a son *b* 1999, — Kate Constantia, *b* 1968: *m* 1997, Stephen A. Lovegrove, son of John Lovegrove, of Gt Alne, Warwicks.

Grandson of late Brig-Gen Henry Francis Brooke, el son of late George Augustus Frederick Brooke, 8th son of 1st baronet:—
Issue of late Maj George Cecil Brooke, *b* 1870, *ka* at Gallipoli 1915: *m* 1912, Barbara, who *d* 1979, only child of late Capt W. H. Allen, of Dhuarigle Castle, co Cork:—
Henry John Allen, MBE, DSC, RN, *b* 1913; *ed* Wellington Coll; Com; acting Capt and Senior Officer Reserve Ships, Portsmouth 1960-61; MOD (Navy Dept) 1961-79 (ret); Nyon Patrol, Spanish Civil War, 1937-38, 1939-45 War in Mediterranean, N African Landings, with Arctic Convoys OPs Norway, and in Pacific (despatches, DSC); MBE (Civil) 1974: *m* 1946, Lesley Mary, 2nd da of late Capt Eric Noble, of Harpsden Court, Henley-on-Thames, and has issue living, Michael Henry Hastings, OBE, *b* 1948; *ed* Pangbourne; Col, late RE; OBE (Mil) 1991: *m* 1971, Philippa Wendy, da of Brig Rupert Crowdy, OBE, and has issue living, Simon Mark Hastings *b* 1974; *ed* Pangbourne, and Durham Univ (BA), James Matthew Crowdy *b* 1976; *ed* Pangbourne, and Univ of Wales, Swansea, — George John (45 Brookfield Av, Poynton, Stockport, Cheshire SK12 1JE), *b* 1952; *ed* Wellington Coll, St Peter's Coll, Oxford (MA); St John's Coll, Camb, and Claremont Graduate Sch, USA (PhD); staff of Salisbury & Wells Theo Coll 1978-84, Vice-Prin 1982; staff of Manchester Univ since 1984, Rylands Prof of Biblical Criticism and Exegesis since 1998: *m* 1976, Rev Rosemary Jane, da of Rev Dr Arthur R. Peacocke, MBE, DSc, DD, formerly Dean of Clare Coll, Camb, and has issue living, Peter George *b* 1979, David John *b* 1981, Rachel Mary *b* 1982, — Sarah Lesley, *b* 1949: *m* 1973, John Nigel Pointing, of 81 Spitalfield Lane, Chichester PO19 4SJ, son of late Leslie Arthur Pointing, and has issue living, Edward Hugh *b* 1983, Toby Richard *b* 1990, Clare Isabel *b* 1985, and two adopted children, Benjamin John *b* 1980, Jane Louise *b* 1978, — Mary Barbara, *b* 1954; BEd, MA. *Residence* – Benbow, Bosham, Chichester, W Sussex PO18 8QL. *Clubs* – Army and Navy, Civil Service; Royal Yacht Squadron.

Grandsons of late Lt-Col George Frank Brooke, DSO, elder son of late Rt Hon Frank (Francis) Theophilus Brooke, yst son of late George Augustus Frederick Brooke (ante):—
Issue of late Maj-Gen Frank Hastings Brooke, CB, CBE, DSO, *b* 1982: *m* 1st, 1935, Helen Edith Mary, who *d* 1973, da of late Maj Rupert Berkeley; 2ndly 1974, Mrs Sheila N. Carson:—
(By 1st *m*) George Hugo Hastings, TD (Hawthorne Cottage, Biddestone, Chippenham, Wilts SN14 7DG), *b* 1936; *ed* Blundell's, and RMA Sandhurst; Maj (ret) late RTR: *m* 1st 1962 (*m diss* 1978), Sarah, yr da of late Robert Blackburn, of Bowcliffe Hall, Boston Spa; 2ndly, 1983, Mrs Elizabeth Paula Minty, da of late Herbert Edwin Foxwell Morris, and has issue living (by 1st *m*), Andrew Robert Hastings, *b* 1969, — Belinda Jane, *b* 1965, — (by 2nd *m*) Emily, *b* 1985, — Rebecca, *b* 1987. —— Nigel Francis, *b* 1937; *ed* Blundell's.

PREDECESSORS – (1) HENRY Brooke, son of Francis Brooke, of Whibrooke, Ireland, and Hanna, da of Henry Prittie, and sister of 1st Lord Dunally; *b* 1770; *cr a Baronet* 1822: *m* 1792, Harriet, da of Hon John Butler, 4th son of 1st Viscount Lanesborough: *d* 1834; *s* by his son (2) *Sir* ARTHUR BRINSLEY, 2nd Bt; *b* 1797; MP for Fermanagh (C) 1840-54: *m* 1841, Hon Julia Henrietta Anson, who *d* 1886, da of Gen Sir George Anson, GCB; *d* 1854; *s* by his son (3) *Sir* VICTOR ALEXANDER, 3rd Bt; *b* 1843: *m* 1864, Alice Sophia, who *d* 1920, da of Sir Alan Edward Bellingham, 3rd Bt; *d* 1891; *s* by his son (4) *Sir* ARTHUR DOUGLAS, 4th Bt; *b* 1865; a JP and DL for Fermanagh: *m* 1887, Gertrude Isabella, who *d* 1918, da of Stanlake Batson; *d* 1907; *s* by his son (5) *Sir* BASIL STANLAKE, 5th Bt, KG, CBE, MC, *b* 1888; Member of Senate NI 1921-29, MP for Lisnaskea (U) NI 1929-68; Min of Commerce and Production 1941-45 and PM 1943-63; *cr Viscount Brookeborough*, of Colebrooke, co Fermanagh (peerage of UK 1952): *m* 1st, 1919, *Dame* Cynthia Mary, DBE, who *d* 1970, da of late Capt Charles Warden Sergison (*see* B Sudeley, 1911 Edn); 2ndly, 1971, Sarah Eileen Bell, who *d* 1989, da of Henry Healey, of Belfast, and widow of Cecil Armstrong Calvert, FRCS, Dir of Neurosurgery, R Victoria Hosp, Belfast; *d* 1973; *s* by his only surv son (6) JOHN WARDEN, PC (NI) 1972, 2nd Viscount, *b* 1922, MP for Lisnaskea (U) NI 1968-72, Ch Whip and Min of State for Finance NI 1971-72, *cr* Member NI Assembly (UPNI) 1972-74, and of N Ireland Convention 1975-87, Chm Co Council co Fermanagh, High Sheriff 1955: *m* 1949, Rosemary Hilda, da of late Lt-Col Arthur O'Neill Cubitt Chichester, OBE, MC (*see* M Donegall, colls); *d* 1987; *s* by his elder son (7) ALAN HENRY, 3rd Viscount and present peer.

BROOKES, BARON (Brookes) (Life Baron 1975)

RAYMOND PERCIVAL BROOKES, son of William Percival Brookes, of W Bromwich, W Midlands; *b* 10 April, 1909; *ed* Kenrick Tech Coll, W Bromwich; Chm and Ch Exec Guest Keen & Nettlefolds Ltd, 1965-74, and Life Pres since 1975; *cr* Knt 1971, and *Baron Brookes*, of W Bromwich, co of W Midlands (Life Baron) 1975: *m* 1937, Florence Edna, da of Isaac William Sharman, and has issue.

Arms – Or, on a pale sable between in chief two crosses crosslet gules, a sword the point upwards and enfiling a Stafford knot the blade charged above with guard with a sun in splendour over all all or. **Crest** – a demi-bear rampant proper beside and resting its sinister paw on an anvil sable. **Supporters** – *Dexter*, a dragon sable, armed gules; *sinister*, a figure habited as Vulcan standing in front of an anvil resting his exterior hand on a hammer, all proper. *Residence* – Mallards, Santon, Isle of Man.

SON LIVING

Hon John David, *b* 1940: *m* 1st, 1970, Faith, da of late John Rees Redman, of Blythe, Bidford on Avon, Warwicks; 2ndly, 1986, Susan Nemeth, and has issue.

BROOKMAN, BARON (Brookman) (Life Baron 1998)

(DAVID) KEITH BROOKMAN, son of late George Henry Brookman, MM, of Ebbw Vale, Gwent; *b* 3 Jan 1937; *ed* Nantyglo Gram Sch, Gwent; steel worker with Richard Thomas and Baldwin Ltd, Ebbw Vale 1953-73; Divisional Organiser, Iron and Steel Trades Confederation 1973, Assist Gen Sec 1985-93, Gen Sec 1993-99; Memb Exec Cncl, Confederation of Shipbuilding and Engineering Unions 1989-95; Chm Nat Trade Union Steel Co-ordinating Cttee 1993 (Memb 1991-93); Memb TUC Education Advisory Cttee for Wales 1976-82, Steel Cttee 1985-90, and Gen Council since 1992; Memb British Steel Joint Accident Prevention Advisory Cttee (JAPAC) 1985-93, Advisory Cttee on Education and Training (ACET) 1986-93, Operatives' Sec, Long Products Gen Steels Joint Standing Cttee 1993-98, Operatives' Sec, Strip Trade Board 1993-98, and Board British Steel (Industry) Ltd since 1993; Mem Labour Party Executive Cttee, Wales 1982-85 and Nat Constitutional Cttee 1987-91; Memb NEC 1991-92; Hon Sec British Section, Internat Metalworkers' Federation since 1993; Pres IMF Iron and Steel and Non-Ferrous Metals Dept since 1993; Operatives' Sec, Joint Industrial Cncl for the Slag Industry 1985-93; European Metalworkers' Federation Executive Council 1985-95; Steel Cttee since 1994; Euro Coal and Steel Community Consultative Cttee since 1993; Employees' Sec, Euro Works Council, British Steel since 1996; Govr Gwent Coll of Higher Education 1980-84; Trustee, Julian Melchett Trust 1985-95; *cr Baron Brookman*, of Ebbw Vale, co Gwent (Life Baron) 1998: *m* 1958, Patricia, da of late Lawrence Worthington, of Eddw Vale, and has issue.
Residence – 4 Bassett Close, Redbourn, Herts AL3 5JY.

DAUGHTERS LIVING

Hon Beverley, *b* 1960; *ed* Ebbw Vale Gram Sch, Croesyceiliog Comprehensive Sch, and Univ Coll of Wales, Bangor: *m* 1983, Michael John Gosling, and has issue living, Thomas David, *b* 1991, — Joseph Edward, *b* 1993, — Alice Catherine, *b* 1995.
Hon Louise, *b* 1964; *ed* Croesyceiliog Comprehensive Sch, and Plymouth Polytechnic; has issue (by Michael Saunders Burton), Lewis James BURTON, *b* 1998.
Hon Clare, *b* 1968; *ed* Croesyceiliog Comprehensive Sch, Loreta College, St Albans, and Univ Coll of Wales, Aberystwyth.

BROOKS OF TREMORFA, BARON (Brooks) (Life Baron 1979)

JOHN EDWARD BROOKS, son of Edward George Brooks; *b* 12 April 1927; *ed* Coleg Harlech and Univ Coll, Cardiff; Field Officer, Council of Social Sers, Wales; Sec Cardiff SE, Constituency Labour Party; Leader of S Glamorgan County Council 1974-78; Chm of Labour Party Wales 1978-79; *cr Baron Brooks of Tremorfa,* of Tremorfa in the county of Glamorgan (Life Baron) 1979: *m* 1st, 1948 (*m diss* 1956); 2ndly, Margaret Pringle, and has issue by both *m*.
Residence – 46 Kennerleigh Rd, Rumney, Cardiff CF3 9BJ.

Brooks, family name of Baron Crawshaw.

BROUGHAM and VAUX, BARON (Brougham) (Baron UK 1860)
(Name and Title pronounced "Broom")

For the king, the law, and the people

MICHAEL JOHN BROUGHAM, CBE, 5th Baron; *b* 2 Aug 1938; *s* 1967; *ed* Lycée Jaccard, Lausanne, Millfield, and Northampton Inst of Agric; Pres Royal Soc for the Prevention of Accidents 1986-89 (Vice Pres since 1990), Chm Tax Payers' Soc 1989-91, and European Secure Vehicle Alliance since 1992, Pres National Health & Safety Groups Council since 1994; Dep Speaker House of Lords since 1993; a Dep Chm of Committees House of Lords 1993-97; CBE (Civil) 1995: *m* 1st, 1963 (*m diss* 1967), Olivia Susan, who *d* 1986, only da of late Rear-Adm Gordon Thomas Seccombe (Peter) Gray, CB, DSC; 2ndly, 1969 (*m diss* 1981), Catherine Jill, el da of William Gulliver, and has issue by 1st and 2nd *m*.

ᴀ𝔯𝔪𝔰 – Gules, a chevron between three lucies hauriant argent. ℭ𝔯𝔢𝔰𝔱 – A dexter arm in armour embowed proper the hand holding a lucy fessewise argent, and charged on the elbow with a rose gules. 𝔖𝔲𝔭𝔭𝔬𝔯𝔱𝔢𝔯𝔰 – *Dexter*, a lion vert, armed and langued gules, gorged with a Vaux collar checky or and of the second; *sinister*, a stag argent, attired and unguled or, holding in the mouth a rose gules, barbed and seeded vert.
Residence – 11 Westminster Gdns, Marsham St, SW1P 4JA.

SON LIVING (*By 2nd marriage*)

Hon CHARLES WILLIAM, *b* 9 Nov 1971; *ed* Radley, and Reading Univ. *Residence* – 53A Quarrendon St, SW6 3ST.

DAUGHTER LIVING (*By 1st marriage*)

Hon Henrietta Louise, *b* 1965.

BROTHER LIVING

Hon David Peter (Folly House, Bampton, Oxon), *b* 1940; *ed* Sedbergh: *m* 1st, 1969 (*m diss* 1976), Moussie Christina Margareta Hallström, da of Sven Hörnblad, of Stockholm, Sweden; 2ndly, 1977, Caroline Susan, only da of Maj James Michael Heigham Royce Tomkin, MC, of Red House, Wissett, Halesworth, Suffolk (*see* Bunbury, Bt), and formerly wife of Julian Dixon, of Grantham, Lincs, and has issue living, (by 1st *m*) Henry Peter, *b* 1971, — (by 2nd *m*), Oliver Michael, *b* 1978.

WIDOW LIVING OF FOURTH BARON

EDITH ELLALINE (*Edith, Baroness Brougham and Vaux*), da of Leonard Teichman, and formerly wife of Richard Vaughan Hart-Davis: *m* 1942, as his 3rd wife, the 4th Baron Brougham and Vaux, who *d* 1967.

COLLATERAL BRANCH LIVING

Grandsons of late Capt Henry Brougham, only son of 3rd Baron:—
Issue of late Hon Anthony Charles Brougham (raised to the rank of the son of a Baron 19—), *b* 1915, *d* 1981: *m* 1st, 1940 (*m diss* 1961), Sonya, who *d* 1970, da of late Ivan Salzman; 2ndly, 1961, Doreen Margaret, who *d* 1972, da of late Roland Billington, and formerly wife of Richard Francis Warren:—
(By 1st *m*) Christopher Anthony Henry, *b* 1941; *ed* privately, and Univ Coll of Rhodesia (BSc Econ): *m* 1967, Ann Elizabeth, el da of Cecil Goldridge, of 72 Savernake Road NW3, and has issue living, Benjamin Paul, *b* 1972, — Guy Christopher, *b* 1975. —— Adrian Charles, *b* 1945; *ed* Downside: *m* 1967, Jan, da of R. J. Westhorpe, of Lees Lane, Little Norton, Wirral, Cheshire.

PREDECESSORS – (1) *Rt Hon* HENRY Brougham, PC, an eminent statesman, orator philosopher and writer; Attorney-Gen for Queen Caroline 1820; successively MP for Camelford, Winchilsea, Knaresborough and Yorkshire, and Lord High Chancellor 1830-4 *cr Baron Brougham and Vaux* 1830, and *Baron Brougham and Vaux* (peerage of United Kingdom) 1860, with remainder to his brother; *d* 1868; *s* by his brother (2) WILLIAM, 2nd Baron, *b* 1795; sat as MP for Southwark 1835-40; *m* 1834, Emily Frances, who *d* 1884, da of Sir Charles William Taylor, 1st Bt; *d* 3 Jan 1886; *s* by his son (3) HENRY CHARLES, KCVO, 3rd Baron, *b* 1836; a Clerk in House of Lords 1857-70: *m* 1882, Adora Frances Olga, who *d* 1925, da of Peter Wells, of Forest Farm, Windsor Forest, and widow of Sir Richard Courtenay Musgrave, MP, 11th Bt: *d* 1927; *s* by his grandson (4) VICTOR HENRY PETER (son of late Capt Hon Henry Brougham, son of 3rd Baron), 4th Baron *b* 1909: *m* 1st, 1931 (*m diss* 1934), Violet Valerie, who *d* 1997, da of late Lt-Col Hon Edward Gerald Fleming French, DSO (E Ypres); 2ndly, 1935 (*m diss* 1942), Jean, who *d* 1992, da of late Brig-Gen Gilbert Burrell Spencer Follet, DSO, MVO (E Dunmore); 3rdly, 1942, Edith Ellaline, da of Leonard Teichman, and formerly wife of Richard Vaughan Hart-Davis; *d* 1967; *s* by his elder surviving son (5) MICHAEL JOHN, 5th Baron, and present peer.

BROUGHSHANE, BARON (Davison) (Baron UK 1945)

Strength consists in action

(WILLIAM) KENSINGTON DAVISON, DSO, DFC, 3rd Baron; *b* 25 Nov 1914; *s* 1995; *ed* Shrewsbury, and Magdalen Coll, Oxford; Bar Inner Temple 1939; formerly W/Cdr RAF Vol Res; European War 1939-45 (DFC, DSO 1945).

Arms – Gules a stag trippant and in chief a celestial crown and a fleur-de- lis or. **Crest** – Upon a billet fessewise, a stag's head between two wings or. **Supporters** – On either side a stag, or gorged with a chain gules, and a pendant therefrom torteau the dexter charged with a portcullis and the sinister with a grenade fired or.
Residence – 3 Godfrey St, SW3 3TA. *Club* – Garrick.

WIDOW LIVING OF SON OF SECOND BARON

(Daphne) Bridget, only da of late Thomas Walter Jones, of Cawston, Norfolk, and formerly wife of Anthony John Nelson-Sullivan: *m* 1988, Hon Alexander Davison, who *d* 1988. *Residence* – 29 Queen St, Kings Lynn, Norfolk.

COLLATERAL BRANCH LIVING

Issue of late Hon Alexander Davison, only son of 2nd Baron, *b* 1936, *dvp* 1988: *m* 1st, 1961 (*m diss* 1966), Teresa Clare, only da of James Guy Bramwell (*see* Smith-Marriott, Bt, colls, 1990 Edn); 2ndly, 1970 (*m diss* 1977), Cecilia Ann, who *d* 1977, da of J. W. Ingrams, of Furlong, Patchings, Sussex; 3rdly, 1988, (Daphne) Bridget (ante), da of late Thomas Walter Jones, of Cawston, Norfolk, and formerly wife of Anthony John Nelson-Sullivan:—
(By 1st *m*) Emma Bettine (68 Cobbold Rd, W12 9LW), *b* 1961. —— Harriet Laura, *b* 1964. —— (By 2nd *m*) Arundell, *b* 1972.

PREDECESSORS – (1) WILLIAM HENRY DAVISON, KBE, only son of late Richard Davison, of Beechfield, Ballymena, co Antrim; *b* 1872; an Alderman of Roy Borough of Kensington (Mayor 1913-19), a FSA, Vice-Pres Roy So of Arts, a Gov of Foundling Hospital, a Freeman of City of London, a Member of Clothworkers' Co (Master 1941-42), and Pres Kensington Chamber of Commerce; during European War 1914 19 raised and equipped 22nd Batn R Fusiliers and assisted in raising 2 Territorial Batns; Chm of Metropolitan National Union of Conservative Assocns 1928-30; sat as MP for Kensington, S Div (C) 1918-45; *cr Baron Broughshane*, of Kensington, co London (peerage of United Kingdom) 1945: *m* 1st, 1898 (*m diss* 1929), Beatrice Mary, who *d* 1971, da of late Sir Owen Roberts, DCL, LLD, FSA, DL; 2ndly, 1929, Louisa Mary Constance, who *d* 1971, da of late Maj Charles Frederick Mariott (B Stafford, colls), *d* 1953; *s* by his son (2) PATRICK OWEN ALEXANDER, 2nd Baron, *b* 1903; Bar Inner Temple 1926, served with Irish Guards 1939-42, Assist Sec (Mil) War Cabinet 1942-45, American Legion of Merit: *m* 1929, Bettine, who *d* 1994, da of Sir Arthur Edward Ian Montague Russell, 6th Bt (*cr* 1812); *d* 1995; *s* by his brother (3) (WILLIAM) KENSINGTON, 3rd Baron and present peer.

Broughton, family name of Baron Fairhaven.

BROWN, BARONY OF (Brown) (Extinct 1985)

SONS LIVING OF LIFE BARON *(By 2nd marriage)*

Hon Richard Banks Duncan, *b* 1942; *ed* Bryanston and Brunel Univ: *m* 1968, Gillian Mary, da of late John Kennedy Cater, of Chichester, Berks, and has issue.

Hon Michael Colin Duncan, *b* 1944; *ed* Bryanston; AA, RIBA, Memb Chartered Soc of Designers: *m* 1970, Fenella, da of Peter Barnard, of White House, Rose Hill, Dorking. *Residence* – Palgrave House, Burnham Market, Norfolk PE31 8EJ, and has issue.

Hon Angus John Duncan, *b* 1951; *ed* Bryanston, and Newcastle Univ: *m* 1974, Polonca, da of Janez Baloh, of Ljublijana, Yugoslavia, and has issue. *Residence* – 39 Clifton Rd, N8 8JA.

WIDOW LIVING OF LIFE BARON

MARJORIE HERSHELL (*Baroness Brown*), da of late John Hershell Skinner, Ealing, W5: *m* 1939, as his 2nd wife, Baron Brown, MBE, PC (Life Baron), who *d* 1985.

Brown, see Baron George-Brown.

Browne, family name of Baron Kilmaine.

Browne, family name of Baron Oranmore and Browne.

Browne, family name of Marquess of Sligo.

BROWNE-WILKINSON, BARON (Browne-Wilkinson) (Life Baron 1991)

NICOLAS CHRISTOPHER HENRY BROWNE-WILKINSON, PC son of late Rev Canon Arthur Rupert Browne-Wilkinson, MC; *b* 30 March 1930; *ed* Lancing, and Magdalen Coll, Oxford (BA); Bar Lincoln's Inn 1953, QC 1972, Bencher 1977, a Judge of Courts of Appeal Jersey and Guernsey 1976-77, a High Court Judge Chancery Div 1977-83, Lord Justice of Appeal 1983-85, Vice-Chancellor Supreme Court 1985-91, since when a Lord of Appeal in Ordinary (Sr Lord of Appeal in Ordinary since 1998); Pres Senate of the Inns of Court and the Bar 1984-86; *cr* Knt 1977, PC 1983, and *Baron Browne-Wilkinson*, of Camden in the London Borough of Camden (Life Baron) 1991: *m* 1st, 1955, Ursula, who *d* 1987, da of Cedric de Lacy Bacon; 2ndly, 1990, Mrs Hilary Isabella Jane Tuckwell, da of Prof James Wilfred Warburton, and has issue by 1st *m*.
Address – Royal Courts of Justice, Strand, WC2

SONS LIVING *(By 1st marriage)*

Hon Adam, *b* 1957.
Hon Simon, *b* (twin)1957.
Hon Oliver, *b* 1962: *m* 1991, Carla R., da of Charles Smith, of Hong Kong.

DAUGHTERS LIVING *(By 1st marriage)*

Hon Henrietta, *b* 1960.
Hon Martha, *b* 1964.

BROWNLOW, BARON (Cust) (Baron GB 1776, Bt E 1677)

To be, rather than to seem

EDWARD JOHN PEREGRINE CUST, 7th Baron, and 10th Baronet: *b* 25 March 1936; *s* 1978; *ed* Eton; late Gren Gds; patron of ten livings; a Member of Lloyd's; a Dir of Hand-in-Hand Fire and Life Insurance Soc, and of Harris & Dixon (Underwriting Agencies) Ltd; High Sheriff of Lincs 1978-1979; Chm Council of Order of St John, Jersey, since 1996; OStJ 1997: *m* 1964, Shirlie, 2nd da of late John Yeomans, of Manor Farm, Hill Croome, Upton-on-Severn, Worcs, and has issue.

Arms – Ermine, on a chevron sable, three fountains proper. **Crest** – A lion's head erased sable, gorged with a collar paly wavy of six, argent and azure. **Supporters** – Two lions reguardant argent, each gorged with a collar paly wavy of six argent and azure.
Residence – La Maison des Prés, St Peter, Jersey CI. *Club* – Whites.

SON LIVING

Hon PEREGRINE EDWARD QUINTIN, *b* 9 July 1974.

SISTER LIVING

Hon Caroline Elizabeth Maud (68 Scarsdale Villas, W8 6PP), *b* 1928: *m* 1954 (*m diss* 1973), John Arthur Partridge, and has issue living, Frank David Peregrine (7 Thurloe Sq, SW7 2TA), *b* 1955: *m* 1982, Susan Anne, yr da of Brig Charles Hince, of Stretton House, Benington, Herts, and has issue living, Charlotte Iris *b* 1985, Annabel Lucy *b* 1987, — Claude Edward, *b* 1962: *m* 1999, Elizabeth Ann, yst da of Sir Peter Drury Haggerston Gadsden, GBE, AC, FEng (*see* Maxwell Scott, Bt, 1642), — Sophia Josephine, *b* 1969: *m* 1993, Anthony John Waltham, elder son of Donald Waltham, of Fleet, Lincs.

COLLATERAL BRANCHES LIVING

Granddaughters of late Sir Lionel Henry Cust, KCVO, LittD, son of late Sir Reginald John Cust, son of late Rev Hon Henry Cockayne Cust, 2nd son of 1st Baron:—
Issue of late Col Sir (Lionel George) Archer Cust, CBE, *b* 1896, *d* 1962: *m* 1925, Margaret Violet Louisa, who *m* 2ndly, 1975, 5th Viscount Templetown (*d* 1981), and *d* 1988, el da of late Lt-Col Henry Arthur Clowes, 1st Life Gds (B Hatherton, colls):—
Elizabeth Jemima Mary (28 St Mary's Mead, Witan Way, Witney, Oxon), *b* 1926: *m* 1947, Jack Musson Benn, who *d* 1992, and has issue living, Anthony Christopher, *b* 1948, — Michael Robert (Melbourne, Vic, Australia), *b* 1950: *m* 1st,

1977 (*m diss* 1986), Zvia Silverman, of Israel; 2ndly, 1992, Bridene Forest, of Melbourne, Australia, and has issue living (by 1st *m*), Shandy *b* 1977, (by 2nd *m*) James Edward *b* 1993, Samantha Kate *b* 1996, — Elizabeth Philippa, *b* 1952: *m* 1970, Istvan Benedek de Ujfalussy, of Greenacres, New Rd, Shiplake, Henley-on-Thames, Oxon RG9 3LA, and has issue living, Nicholas *b* 1981, Catherine *b* 1970, Louisa *b* 1972, Andrea *b* 1984. —— Margaret Sybil, *b* 1928: *m* 1950, (Paul) Oliver Ziegler, of Hightown Farm, Hightown Hill, Ringwood, Hants, and has issue living, Adam Charles (24-26 Braeside Rd, St Leonards, Ringwood, Hants), *b* 1952: *m* 1st, 1974 (*m diss* 1979), Christine Margaret Codling, of Ibsley, Hants; 2ndly, 1984, Trudi Lynette, da of Clayton William John Burt, and has issue living (by 1st wife), Nathaniel Oliver *b* 1977, (by 2nd wife) Amy Louise *b* 1983, Joanna Margaret *b* 1986, — William James Archer (Lords Oak Cottage, Landford, Salisbury, Wilts), *b* 1956: *m* 1979, Sarah Elizabeth, elder da of Com Ian Rochfort Johnston, RN (*see* B Vernon, colls), and has issue living, Polly Laura *b* 1983, Daisy Alice *b* 1985, Harriet Louise *b* 1988.

Grandchildren of late Rev William Arthur PUREY-CUST, el son of Very Rev Arthur Perceval PUREY-CUST, DD, 1st son of Hon William Cust, 4th son of the 1st Baron:—
Issue of late Brig Richard Brownlow PUREY-CUST, CBE, DSO, MC, *b* 1888, *d* 1958: *m* 1928, Gertrude Patricia Zoë, who *d* 1993, only da of late Francis Julian Laurence Birch:—
John Richard (c/o 12 Palliser Rd, Roseneath, Wellington, NZ), *b* 1934; *ed* Eton, and Edinburgh Univ (BSc). —— Veronica Caroline *b* 1937: *m* 1969, Herman Portmann, of C12, Site 3, RR7, Vernon, BC, Canada V1T 7Z3, and has issue living, Robert Purey, *b* 1974, — Heidi Patricia, *b* 1976.

PREDECESSORS – **(1)** RICHARD CUST, MP for co Lincoln 1635: *cr* a *Baronet* 1677; *d* 1700; *s* by his grandson **(2)** *Sir* RICHARD, 2nd Bt; *d* 1734; *s* by his son **(3)** *Sir* JOHN, PC, MP, 3rd Bt, was Speaker of House of Commons 1761-70; inherited the estates of his uncle Viscount Tyrconnel (*ext*); *d* 1770; *s* by his son **(4)** *Sir* BROWNLOW, 4th Bt; *cr Baron Brownlow* (peerage of United Kingdom) 1776; *d* 1807; *s* by his son **(5)** JOHN, 2nd Baron, *b* 1779; *cr Viscount Alford* and *Earl Brownlow* (peerage of United Kingdon) 1815; was Lord Lt of co Lincoln; his el son John Hume, Viscount Alford, MP, who *m* 1841, Lady Marian Margaret Compton, da of 2nd Marquess of Northampton, assumed by R licence the surname of Egerton, and pre-deceased him 1851; *d* 1853; *s* by his grandson **(6)** JOHN WILLIAM SPENCER, 2nd Earl; assumed by Roy licence 1853 the surname of Egerton, and in 1863 the additional surname of Cust; *d* 1867; *s* by his brother **(7)** ADELBERT WELLINGTON BROWNLOW, GCVO, PC, 3rd Earl; *b* 1844; Lord-Lt of Lincolnshire 1867-1921, Parliamentary Sec to Local Govt Board 1885-86, Paymaster-Gen 1887-89, and Under-Sec of State for War 1889-92: *m* 1868, Lady Adelaide Talbot, who *d* 1917, 3rd da of 18th Earl of Shrewsbury; *d* 1921, when the Earldom became ext, and the barony devolved upon his kinsman **(8)** ADELBERT SALUSBURY COCKAYNE, 5th Baron (2nd son of late Capt Henry Francis Cockayne Cust, MP, grandson of 1st Baron), 5th Baron; *b* 1867; *m* 1895, Maud, who *d* 1936, da of late Capt S. Buckle, RE; *d* 1927; *s* by his son **(9)** PEREGRINE FRANCIS ADELBERT, 6th Baron; *b* 1899; Lt and Adjt Gren Gds, 1939-45 War as Sqdn-Ldr RAF VR; Mayor of Grantham 1934-35; Lord in Waiting (personal) to HM King Edward VIII July-Dec 1936; Lord Lieut Lincs; PPS to Min of Aircraft Production 1940-1941; *m* 1st, 1927, Katherine Hariot, who *d* 1952, yr da of Brig-Gen Sir David Alexander Kinloch, 11th Bt, CB, MVO; 2ndly, 1954, Dorothy, who *d* 1966, yr da of Thomas Sarsfield Kent Power, of Norfolk, Virginia, USA, and formerly wife of (i) Harry Ester Reynolds Hall, (ii) 2nd Earl Beatty, DSC, (iii) John Gordon Baragwanath; 3rdly, 1969, Leila who *d* 1983, only da of late Maj Philip Guy Reynolds, DSO, formerly wife of late Maj John Dane Player, and widow of 2nd Baron Manton; *d* 1978; *s* by his son **(10)** EDWARD JOHN PEREGRINE, 7th Baron and present peer.

Brownlow, family name of Baron Lurgan.

Broxbourne, Barony of (Walker-Smith) (Extinct 1992) (see Walker-Smith, Bt)

Bruce, Lord; son of Earl of Elgin.

BRUCE OF DONINGTON, BARON (Bruce) (Life Baron 1974)

DONALD WILLIAM TREVOR BRUCE, son of the late William Trevor Bruce, of Norbury, Surrey: *b* 3 Oct 1912; *ed* Donington Gram Sch, Lincs; FCA; economist; 1939-45 War as Maj with R Signals (despatches); MP for N Portsmouth (*Lab*) 1945-50; PPS to Min of Health 1945-50; a Member of Min of Health delegation to Sweden and Denmark 1946, and of House of Commons Select Cttee on Public Accounts 1948-50; a Member of European Parl 1975-79; *cr Baron Bruce of Donington*, of Rickmansworth, Herts (Life Baron) 1974: *m* 1st, 1939 (*m diss* 1980), Joan Letitia, da of Hamilton Claude Butcher, of Maida Vale, W9; 2ndly, 1981, Mrs Cyrena Heard (*née* Shaw) and has issue by 1st *m*.

Address – 2 Bloomsbury St, WC1B 3ST.

SON LIVING (*By 1st marriage*)

Hon Michael Gordon, *b* 1952.

DAUGHTERS LIVING (*By 1st marriage*)

Hon Ann, *b* 1942; *m* 19—, T. Samuels.
Hon Mary Trevor, *b* 1945: *m* 1968, Shuhada Hilmi.

BRUCE-GARDYNE, BARONY OF (Bruce-Gardyne) (Extinct 1990)

SONS LIVING OF LIFE BARON

Hon Thomas Andrew, *b* 1962; *ed* Marlborough: *m* 1994, Catherine Clare, da of E. A. Mackenzie, of Blackheath, and has issue living, Molly Charlotte, *b* 1994, — Chloe Elizabeth, *b* 1996, — Flora Harriet Mary, *b* 1999.
Hon Adam George John, *b* 1967; *ed* Marlborough, Oxford Univ, and Cranfield Univ.

DAUGHTER LIVING OF LIFE BARON

Hon Roselle Sarah, *b* 1959; *ed* St Paul's Girls' Sch, Durham Univ, and INSEAD: *m* 1987, David Heckendorn, only son of C. H. Heckendorn, of Beaux Arts Village, Washington, USA, and has issue living, John Henry, *b* 1990, — Marianna Elizabeth, *b* 1993. *Residence* – 11 Lincoln St, Andover, Mass, USA.

WIDOW LIVING OF LIFE BARON

SARAH LOUISA MARY (*Baroness Bruce-Gardyne*), only da of late Cmdr Sir John Francis Whitaker Maitland, RN, of Harrington Hall, Spilsby, Lincs; High Sheriff Lincs 1997, DL 1997: *m* 1959, Baron Bruce-Gardyne (Life Baron), who *d* 1990. *Residence* – 13 Kelso Place, W8; Aswardby, Spilsby, Lincs.

Bruce, family name of Baron Aberdare.

Bruce, family name of Lord Balfour of Burleigh.

Bruce, family name of Earl of Elgin.

Bruce, Brudenell-, family name of Marquess of Ailesbury.

Bruce, Hovell-Thurlow-Cumming-, family name of Baron Thurlow.

BRUNTISFIELD, BARON (Warrender) (Baron UK 1942, Bt GB 1715)

Industry promotes

JOHN ROBERT WARRENDER, OBE, MC, TD, 2nd Baron, and 9th Baronet; *b* 7 Feb 1921; *s* 1993; *ed* Eton; DL Som 1965; Col RARO; Brig Queen's Body Guard for Scotland (Royal Company of Archers) (ret 1985), late Capt 2nd Dragoons, Royal Scots Greys; ADC to Gov of Madras 1946-48, and Comdg N Som Yeo 44th; Royal Tank Regt 1957-62 (OBE); 1939-45 War in Middle East, Italy and NW Europe (MC 1943); OBE (Mil) 1963: *m* 1st, 1948, Ann Moireen, who *d* 1976, 2nd da of late Lt-Col Sir Walter Fendall Campbell, KCIE, 2ndly, 1977, Mrs Shirley Crawley, who *d* 1981, da of J. L. Ross, and formerly wife of Jonathan James Crawley; 3rdly, 1985, Mrs Joanna (Jan) Kathleen Campbell Graham, da of late David Chancellor, of Pencaitland, E Lothian, and formerly wife of Capt Colin Hugh Campbell Graham (*see* Graham, Bt, *cr* 1906, colls), and has issue by 1st *m.*

Arms – Quarterly: 1st and 4th, argent, on a bend wavy, between six roses gules, three plates, *Warrender*; 2nd, or, a lion rampant gules, couped in all joints of the field, within a double tressure flory counter flory azure, *Maitland*; 3rd grand quarter, counter-quartered 1st quarter 1st and 4th vert, a lion rampant argent; 2nd and 3rd argent, three papingoes vert, beaked and membered gules, *Hume*; 2nd quarter gyronny of eight gules and ermine, *Campbell of Cessnock*; third quarter azure, on a fesse between three mascles argent, as many cinquefoils of the first, *Purves of Purves*; 4th quarter, 1st and 4th gules, three piles engrailed argent, *Polwarth of that ilk*; 2nd and 3rd argent, a cross engrailed azure, *Sinclair of Hermiston*, on surtout of the grand quarter an inescutcheon argent charged with an orange imperially crowned and slipped all proper. Crest – A hare sejant proper. Supporters – Two lions reguardant argent.
Residence – 18 Warriston Crescent, Edinburgh EH3 5LB. *Club* – New (Edinburgh).

SONS LIVING (By 1st marriage)

Hon MICHAEL JOHN VICTOR, *b* 9 Jan 1949; *ed* Downside, RMA Sandhurst, and Hatfield Coll, Durham (BA); Maj Irish Guards 1967-86; Dir Jardine Fleming Investment Mgmt Ltd since 1993: *m* 1978, Baroness Walburga, yr da of Baron Johannes von Twickel, of Schloss Lembeck, Lembeck, Germany, and has issue living, John, *b* 1 June 1996. *Address* – c/o Jardine Fleming Investment Management Ltd, PO Box 70, GPO Hong Kong. *Club* – White's.

Hon Jonathan James, *b* 1954; *ed* Downside, and Camberwell Sch of Art (BA); Artist: *m* 1979, Fiona Mary, yr da of late Alexander Grant Laing, MC, of Logie House, Forres, Moray (*see* E Stair, colls), and has issue living, George Alexander, *b* 1981, — Jonathan Hew, *b* 1985, — Alice Julian, *b* 1983. *Residence* – Minuntion, Pinmore, Girvan, Ayrshire KA26 0TE.

DAUGHTERS LIVING (By 1st marriage)

Hon Julian Mary WARRENDER, *b* 1950; resumed her maiden name by deed poll 1997: *m* 1974 (*m diss* 1997), Francis Alexander Moreton Akers-Douglas, and has issue (*see* V Chilston, colls). *Residence* – Barham Farmhouse, E Hoathly, Lewes, Sussex BN8 6QL.

Hon Sarah Jane, *b* 1952: *m* 1971, Anthony David Bune, and has issue living, Delius Jonathan, *b* 1976, — Tertius Alexander, *b* 1978, — Eloise Anne Moireen, *b* 1977. *Address* – PO Box 467, Chapel Rd, Waccabuc, NY 10597, USA.

BROTHERS LIVING

Hon Simon George, DSC, *b* 1922: *ed* Eton, Co Director and Aviation Consultant, Founder and Chm Australian World Airways; Asso Royal Aeronautical Soc, Fellow British Interplanetary Soc, Consul for Uruguay in State of Victoria; late Lieut RNVR; 1939-45 War (DSC 1944), Star of Russia 1945-85: *m* 1950, Pamela, only da of late Sir Norman Myer, of Toorak, Victoria, Australia, and has had issue, Alexander Victor Simon, *b* 1955, *d* 1976, — Simon Hamilton Angus Norman, *b* 1962, — Edwina, *b* 1952, — Alicia Gizelle, *b* 1953. *Residence* – 35 Barkly Av, Armadale, Victoria 3143, Australia. *Clubs* – Bath, Turf, Royal Aero RNVR, Melbourne.

Hon Robin Hugh *b* 1927; *ed* Eton, and Trin Coll, Oxford: *m* 1951, Gillian Elizabeth, only da of Leonard Lewis Rossiter (*see* Oppenheimer, Bt, 1985 Edn), and has issue living, Hugh Mark, *b* 1968, — Carolyn Robin, *b* 1953: *m* 1985, Francis I. M. Hazeel, of 54 Alderney St, SW1V 4EX, yr son of late Capt Harry Hazeel, of 28 Ormonde Gate, SW3, and has issue living, James Albert Victor *b* 1989, Geordie Alexander Robin *b* 1993, — Annabel Rose (*Hon Mrs Alastair Campbell*), *b* 1956: *m* 1979, Hon Alastair Colin Leckie Campbell, of The Stables, Everlands, Sevenoaks, Kent TN14 6HU, only son of 3rd Baron Colgrain, and has issue (see that title). *Residence* – Capps Lodge House, Fulbrook, Burford, Oxon OX18 4DB. *Club* – White's.

HALF-BROTHER LIVING

Hon Anthony Michael, *b* 1950; *ed* Eton, and Ch Ch Oxford; FCA: *m* 1st, 1976, Christine, da of Serge Semeneko, of Boston, Mass; 2ndly, 1983, Mrs Patricia Connors Kelly, da of Philip Connors, of Middleburg, Virginia, and has issue living (by 2nd *m*), Patrick Victor Anthony, *b* 1984. *Residence* – Oak Ridge Farm, PO Box 1431, Middleburg, Virginia 20118, USA. *Clubs* – Turf, White's.

HALF-SISTER LIVING

Hon Victoria Isabella (*Lady Reay*), *b* 1952: *m* 1980, as his 2nd wife, 14th Lord Reay, and has issue. *Residences* – Kasteel Ophemert, Ophemert in Gelderland, Netherlands; 98 Oakley St, SW3.

WIDOW LIVING OF FIRST BARON

TANIA (*Dowager Baroness Bruntisfield*), da of late Dr Michel Kolin, of St Jacob, Dubrovnik, Yugoslavia: *m* 1948, as his 2nd wife, the 1st Baron Bruntisfield, MC, who *d* 1993. *Residence* – Résidence le Village B1, CH-1837, Château-d'Oex, Switzerland.

PREDECESSORS – (1) GEORGE Warrender, son of late George Warrender; a Merchant and MP for Edinburgh 1715-21; *cr* a *Baronet* 1715: *m* 1st, 16—, Margaret Lawrie, of Edinburgh; 2ndly, Grizel, da of Hugh Blair of Edinburgh; *d* 1721; *s* by his el son (2) JOHN, 2nd Bt: *m* 1720, Henrietta, da of late Sir Patrick Johnston, MP, sometime Lord Provost of Edinburgh; *d* 1772; *s* by his only surviving son (3) PATRICK, 3rd Bt; *b* 1731; Lieut-Col 11th Dragoons; MP for Haddington Burghs 1768-74, and King's Remembrancer of Court of Exchequer 1771-91: *m* 1780, Miss H. Blair, who *d* 1838; *d* 1799; *s* by his el son (4) *Rt Hon* GEORGE, PC, 4th Bt *b* 1782: MP for Haddington Burghs 1807-12, for Truro 1812-18, for Sandwich 1818-26, for Westbury 1826-30, and for Honiton 1830-32; a Lord of the Admiralty 1812-22, and a Commr of Board of Control 1822-8: *m* 1810, Hon Anne Evelyn Boscawen, who *d* 1871, da of 3rd Viscount Falmouth; *d* 1849; *s* by his brother (5) JOHN, 5th Bt; *b* 1786; Capt in the Army: *m* 1st, 1823, Lady Julian Jane Maitland, who *d* 1827, da of 8th Earl of Lauderdale; 2ndly, 1831, Hon Frances Henrietta, who *d* 1852, da of 1st Baron Alvanley; *d* 1867; *s* by his only son (6) GEORGE, 6th Bt; *b* 1825; sometime Capt Coldstream Gds: *m* 1854, Helen, who *d* 1875, da of Sir Hugh Purves-Hume-Campbell, 7th Bt; *d* 1901; *s* by his el surviving son (7) GEORGE JOHN SCOTT, KCB, KCVO, 7th Bt; *b* 1860; Vice-Adm: *m* 1894, Lady Ethel Maud Ashley-Cooper, who *d* 1945, da of the 8th Earl of Shaftesbury; *d* 1917: *s* by his el son (8) VICTOR ALEXANDER GEORGE ANTHONY, MC, 1st Baron, *b* 1899; 2nd Lieut Gren Guards, European War 1917-18 (MC, Orders of St Stanislas and St Anne of Russia with Swords, Order of Star of Roumania); Vice-Chamberlain of the Household Sept 1932, Comptroller HM Household May 1935, Parl and Financial Sec to the Admiralty June 1935, Financial Sec to War Dept and a Member of Army Council Nov 1935, Parl Sec to Admiralty April 1940-July 1945; MP for Kesteven and Rutland, Grantham Div (C) Dec 1923-Feb 1942; *cr Baron Bruntisfield*, of Boroughmuir, City of Edinburgh (peerage of UK) 1942: *m* 1st, 1920 (*m diss* 1946), Dorothy Etta, who *d* 1975, da of late Col Richard Hamilton Rawson, MP (*see* E Lichfield, 1919 Edn); 2ndly, 1948, Tania, da of late Dr Michel Kolin, of St Jacob, Dubrovnik; *d* 1993; *s* by his eldest son (9) JOHN ROBERT, 2nd Baron and present peer.

BUCCLEUCH and QUEENSBERRY, DUKE OF (Montagu Douglas Scott) (Duke S 1663, Duke S 1684)

(Title pronounced "Buckloo")

I love

WALTER FRANCIS JOHN MONTAGU DOUGLAS SCOTT, KT, VRD, 9th Duke of Buccleuch, and 11th of Queensberry; *b* 28 Sept 1923; *s* 1973; *ed* Eton, and Ch Ch, Oxford; served RNVR and RNR 1942-46 Lt-Cdr, Hon Capt RNR 1988; Capt and Pres of Council Queen's Body Guard for Scotland (Royal Company of Archers); Lord-Lieut of Roxburghshire 1974-75, of Selkirk 1975, and of Roxburgh, Ettrick and Lauderdale 1975-98; JP 1974, Roxburghshire CC 1958; PPS to Sec of State for Scotland 1962-64; Pres of Royal Highland and Agric Soc 1969-70; East of England Agric So 1976; Pres St Andrew's Ambulance Assocn since 1969, Pres Malcolm Sargent Cancer Fund for Children in Scotland 1975-98, Commoneath Forestry Assocn since 1979, and Royal Blind Asylum & School; Vice-Pres RSSPCC, and King George's Fund for Sailors; received Countryside Commn and Country Landowners' Assocn annual jt award 1983; Chm of Royal Assocn for Disability & Rehabilitation (CCD) 1973-93 (since when Pres), Buccleuch Heritage Trust since 1985, Living Landscape Trust since 1986, and Assocn of Lord Lieuts 1990-98; Pres of Royal Scottish Agric Benevolent Instn, Royal Highland & Agric Soc of Scotland, Scottish Nat Instn for the War Blinded, and Pres Royal Scottish Forestry Soc 1994-96; Heritage Educn Trust Sandford Awards for Boughton 1989 and 1994, Drumlanrig 1991, and Bowhill 1994; Fellow Royal Agricultural Socs 1996; Chancellor Order of the Thistle since 1992; MP for N Div of Edinburgh (C) 1960-73; 1939-45 War; KT 1978: *m* 1953, Jane, only da of late John McNeill, QC, of Drumavuic, Appin, Argyllshire, and has issue.

Arms – Quarterly: 1*st grandquarter for the Earldom of Doncaster*, quarterly 1st and 4th, quarterly (i) and (iv) azure, three fleur-de-lis or; (ii) and (iii) gules, three lions passant guardant in pale or; 2nd, or, a lion rampant gules within a double tressure flory-counter-flory of the second; 3rd, azure, a harp or; all debruised by a baton sinister argent; 2*nd grand-quarter for the Dukedom of Argyll*, quarterly, 1st and 4th gyrony of eight or and sable (*Campbell*); 2nd and 3rd, argent, a lymphad, sails furled sable flags and pennons flying gules, and oars in action of the second (*Lorne*); 3*rd grandquarter for the Dukedom of Queensberry*, quarterly, 1st and 4th, argent, a human heart gules, crowned with an imperial crown or, on a chief azure three mullets of the field (*Douglas*); 2nd and 3rd azure, a bend between six cross crosslets fitchee or (*Mar*); the whole of this grandquarter within a border or, charged with a double tressure flory-counter-flory gules; 4*th grandquarter for the Dukedom of Montagu*, quarterly, 1st argent, three fusils conjoined in fess gules, a bordure sable (*Montagu*); 2nd, or a griffin displayed vert, beaked and membered gules (*Monthermer*); 3rd, sable, a lion rampant argent, on a canton of the last a cross gules (*Churchill*); 4th, argent, a chevron gules between three caps-of-maintenance, their fronts turned to the sinister azure, furred ermine (*Brudenell*); over the grandquarters, at the fess point an inescutcheon or, a bend azure mullet of six points between two crescents of the field (*Scott*). **Crest** – A stag trippant proper, attired and unguled or. **Supporters** – Two female figures proper, habited from the waist downwards in kirtles azure gathered up at the knees, the arms and bosoms uncovered, around the shoulders flowing mantles as before suspended by the exterior hand, girdles and sandals gules, and their heads adorned with a plume of three ostrich feathers argent.
Seats – Bowhill, Selkirk; Boughton House, Kettering; Drumlanrig Castle, Thornhill, Dumfriesshire.

SONS LIVING

RICHARD WALTER JOHN (*Earl of Dalkeith*) (Dabton, Thornhill, Dumfriesshire DG3 5AR), *b* 14 Feb 1954; *ed* Eton, and Ch Ch, Oxford; a Page of Honour to HM Queen Elizabeth the Queen Mother 1967-69; Member Queen's Body Guard for Scotland (Royal Company of Archers); DL Nithsdale, Annandale and Eskdale 1987; District Councillor Nithsdale 1984-90; Dir Border Television 1989-90, Memb Nature Conservancy Council 1989-91, Nature Conservancy Council for Scotland 1991-92, Scottish Natural Heritage (Chm SW Board) 1992-95; National Memb for Scotland, Independent Television Commn 1990-95, Dep Chm 1996-98; Pres East of England Agric Soc 1990, Pres Royal Smithfield Club 1992; Hon Patron Northants Co Cricket Club since 1986; Regimental Trustee King's Own Scottish Borderers since 1987; Council Memb Winston Churchill Memorial Trust since 1993; Memb Millennium Commn since 1994; IBA 1990, ITC 1991: *m* 1981, Lady Elizabeth Marian Frances Kerr, yst da of 12th Marquess of Lothian, and has issue:—

SONS LIVING— Walter John Francis (*Lord Eskdaill*) *b* 2 Aug 1984: Page of Honour to HM 1996-99, — Hon Charles David Peter, *b* 1987.
DAUGHTERS LIVING— *Lady* Louisa Jane Therese, *b* 1982, — *Lady* Amabel Claire Alice, *b* 1992.

Lord (William Henry) John, *b* 1957: *m* 1990, Mrs (Hafize) Berrin Torolsan, only da of Halil Torolsan, of Istanbul. *Residence* – CC480, Mecidiyeköy, 80303 Istanbul, Turkey.

Lord Damian Torquil Francis Charles, *b* 1969.

DAUGHTER LIVING

Lady Charlotte-Anne, *b* 1966: *m* 1991, Comte Bernard de Castellane, son of late Comte Albert de Castellane, of Provence, France, and has issue living, Boniface Louis Albert Charles, *b* 1993, — Rose Jane Michèle Elizabeth, *b* 1996 *Residence* – Château d'Esparron, 04800 Esparron-de-Verdon, France.

SISTERS LIVING

Lady Elizabeth Diana (*Elizabeth, Duchess of Northumberland*), *b* 1922; 1939-45 War in WRNS; Hon D Univ Newcastle Polytechnic (now Northumbria Univ) 1992; Hon Col 6th Bn Northumberland Fusiliers: *m* 1946, 10th Duke of Northumberland, who *d* 1988. *Residences* – Alnwick Castle, Northumberland; Syon House, Brentford, Middx TW8 8JF; Clive Lodge, Albury, Surrey.

Lady Caroline Margaret (*Baroness Gilmour of Craigmillar*), *b* 1927: *m* 1951, Baron Gilmour of Craigmillar, PC (Life Baron), of The Ferry House, Old Isleworth, Middx.

AUNTS LIVING (*Daughters of 7th Duke*)

Lady Alice Christabel, GCB, CI, GCVO, GBE (*HRH Princess Alice, Duchess of Gloucester*), *b* 1901, a GCStJ, Air Chief Marshal WRAF, Col-in-Ch of KOSB, Dep Col-in-Ch Royal Anglian Regt, and The King's Royal Hussars, and a Member of Council of British Red Cross Soc; received Freedom of City of Edinburgh 1937, of Gloucester 1939, and of Belfast 1952; GBE (Civil) and CI 1937, GCVO 1948, GCB (Civil) 1975: *m* 6 Nov 1935, HRH Prince Henry William Frederick Albert, 1st Duke of Gloucester, KG, KT, KP, GCB, GCMG, GCVO, PC, who *d* 10 June 1974, 3rd son of HM King George V (*see* ROYAL FAMILY). *Residence* – 1 Kensington Palace W8.

Lady Angela Christine Rose, *b* 1906: *m* 1936, Vice-Adm Sir Peter Dawnay, KCVO, CB, DSC (*see* V Downe, colls), who *d* 1989. *Residence* – 8 Sutton Manor Mews, Sutton Scotney, Winchester, Hants SO21 3JR.

COLLATERAL BRANCHES LIVING

Issue of late Lord William Walter Montagu Douglas Scott, MC, 2nd son of 7th Duke, *b* 1896, *d* 1958: *m* 1937, Lady Rachel Douglas-Home, who *d* 1996, da of 13th Earl of Home (*see* B Home of the Hirsel):—
Walter William, *b* 1946; *ed* Eton, and Keble Coll, Oxford: *m* 1991, Mrs Teresa Fisher, only da of Anatole Urbaniak, of Cape Town, S Africa. *Residence* – Chesterhall, Eildon, Melrose TD6 9HE. — Margaret Elizabeth, *b* 1938. —— Frances Henrietta (*Baroness Cranworth*), *b* 1940: *m* 1968, 3rd Baron Cranworth. —— Rosemary Alice (twin), *b* 1940: *m* 1978, (Samuel Alexander) Mark Collins, son of late Sir William Collins, and has issue living, Sampson William Francis, *b* 1982, — Benjamin Mark Timothy, *b* 1984. —— Jean Louise (*Lady Tapps-Gervis-Meyrick*), *b* 1943: *m* 1968, Sir George Christopher Cadafael Tapps-Gervis-Meyrick, 7th Bt.

Issue of late Col Lord George Francis John Montagu Douglas Scott, yst son of 7th Duke, *b* 1911, *d* 1999: *m* 1938, Mary Wina Mannin (Molly Bishop, the artist), who *d* 1998, only da of late Lt-Col Harry Oswald Bishop, of Harewood, Andover, Hants:—
David Henry George (19 Petworth St, SW11), *b* 1945; *ed* Eton: *m* 1967, Laura Jane, yst da of late St John Bernard Vyvyan Harmsworth, of Horsted Keynes, Sussex (*see* Boothby, Bt, colls, 1980 Edn), and has issue living, Lucy Rose, *b* 1969, — Harriet Mary, *b* 1972. —— Georgina Mary (*Baroness O'Neill*), *b* 1940: *m* 1963, 4th Baron O'Neill, of Shane's Castle, Antrim, and has issue (see that title). —— Charmian Rachel, *b* 1942: *m* 1st, 1964 (*m diss* 1977), Archibald Hugh Stirling, yr of Keir (*see* Stirling-Maxwell, Bt, colls); 2ndly, 1987, Colin Guy Napier Campbell, of 23 Lansdowne Gdns, SW8 (*see* Campbell, Bt, *cr* 1815, colls), and has issue (by 1st *m*) (*see* Stirling-Maxwell, Bt, colls).

Grandchildren of late Lt-Col Lord George William Montagu Douglas Scott, OBE, 3rd son of 6th Duke:—
Issue of late Lt-Col John Henry Montagu Douglas Scott, MC, 9th Lancers, *b* 1911, *d* 1991: *m* 1954, Anne Peace Arabella (Arbell) (Kirklands, Ancrum), da of late Capt Angus Alexander Mackintosh, RHG (*see* D Devonshire, 1973-74 Edn), and formerly wife of Maj John Antony Warre, MC, 12th Royal Lancers:—
James George, *b* 1959. —— (Elizabeth) Arabella, *b* 1956: *m* 1987, Peregrine J. Lewis, son of late Maj Raymond Lewis, 12th Royal Lancers, of Morden, Surrey, and has issue living, Merlin John Lewis, *b* 1991, — Arbell Eleanora, *b* 1993. *Residence* – Cotfield, Lilliesleaf, Melrose, Borders.

Issue of late Lt-Col Claud Everard Walter Montagu Douglas Scott, MC, *b* 1915, *d* 1994: *m* 1941, Margaret Francis (Bourton Hill House, Moreton-in-Marsh, Glos), da of late Brig-Gen Lewis Francis Philips, CB, CMG, CBE, DSO (*see* E Ducie, colls, 1970 Edn):—
Thomas Walter, *b* 1943; *ed* Eton: *m* 1973 (*m diss* 1985), (Marion) Miranda, da of Hon Claud Stephen Phillimore (later 4th Baron Phillimore), and has issue living, Alice, *b* 1978. —— Katharine Margaret, *b* 1946: *m* 1975, Robert Vere Spencer Bernard (*see* D Marlborough, colls). *Residence* – Nether Winchendon House, Aylesbury, Bucks HP18 0DY.

Grandchildren of late Lt-Col Lord Herbert Andrew Montagu Douglas Scott, CMG, DSO (infra):—
Issue of late Brig (Claud) Andrew Montagu Douglas Scott, DSO, *b* 1906, *d* 1971: *m* 1st, 1929 (*m diss* 1951), Lady Victoria Doris Rachel Haig, who *d* 1993, da of 1st Earl Haig; 2ndly, 1951, Zalia, who *d* 1986, yst (twin) da of late Sir Harold Edward Snagge, KBE (*see* B Avebury, colls, 1955 Edn), and formerly wife of late Lt-Col Esmond Charles Baring, OBE (*see* B Ashburton):—
(By 1st *m*) Douglas Andrew, OBE (Stonefield, Bemersyde, Melrose TD6 9DP), *b* 1930; late Capt IG; OBE (Civil) 1994: *m* 1st, 1954 (*m diss* 1977), Bridget Elizabeth, da of late Air Vice-Marshal Sir Robert Allingham George, KCVO, KBE, CB, MC; 2ndly, 1977, Daphne Maureen, only da of Dr Cyril de Vere Shortt, of Winchcome, Glos, and formerly wife of William George Fearnley-Whittingstall, and has had an adopted son, Adam, *b* 1961, *d* 1969, — and has two adopted das, Emily, *b* 1970, — Lucy Rosemary, *b* 1972. —— Henrietta (*Lady Griffin*), *b* 1934: *m* 1962, Maj Sir (Arthur) John Stewart Griffin, KCVO, of Barton's Cottage, Bushy Park, Teddington, Middx, and has issue living, Andrew Michael Stewart

(Mount Pleasant Farmhouse, Mount Pleasant Lane, Lamberhurst, Kent TN3 8LX), *b* 1963: *m* 1989, Maria Diane Cordelia, da of Royston James Vavasseur-Williams, of Childwall, Liverpool L15 6US, and has issue living, Alexander William Michael Stewart *b* 1992, Henry Edward Ralph Stewart *b* 1995, — Phillip Anthony Stewart, *b* 1965: *m* 1992, Heather A., elder da of late Gerald Kent, and of Mrs Malcolm Prescott, of Polstead, Suffolk, and has issue living, Hamish Andrew Lewis Stewart *b* 1994, Maximilian Benjamin Oliver Stewart *b* 1998. —— (By 2nd *m*) Nicholas Herbert, *b* 1954.

Issue of late Lt-Col Lord Herbert Andrew Montagu Douglas Scott, CMG, DSO, 5th son of 6th Duke, *b* 1872, *d* 1944: *m* 1905, Marie Josephine, who *d* 1965, da of late James Edwards, of Dovercourt, Essex:— Patricia Katharine (*Patricia, Countess of Dundee*), *b* 1910: *m* 1st, 1931, Lt-Col Walter Douglas Faulkner, MC, Irish Gds, who was *ka* (May) 1940; 2ndly (Sept) 1940, Lt Col (Hon) David Scrymgeour Wedderburn, DSO, Scots Gds, who *d* (of wounds received in action) 1944 (*see* E Dundee); 3rdly, 1946, 11th Earl of Dundee, who *d* 1983, and has had issue (by 1st *m*) David James, *b* 1932; Maj late IG: *m* 1958, Victoria Mary Rose (Haugh House, Longworth, Abingdon, Oxon), el da of late Robert James Buxton, MB, BChir, MRCS LRCP, DOMS (*see* Buxton, Bt, colls), and *d* 1993, leaving issue, John Douglas *b* 1959, Thomas Patrick *b* 1965, Matthew James *b* 1968, Robert David *b* 1970, Katharine Rose *b* 1960, — Hermione Patricia (*Lady Moncreiffe of that Ilk*) (24 Gordon Place, W8 4JE), *b* 1937: *m* 1966, as his 2nd wife, Sir Rupert Iain Kay Moncreiffe of that Ilk, 11th Bt, CVO, QC, who *d* 1985, — (by 2nd and 3rd *m*) (*see* E Dundee). *Residence* – Coultra Farm House, Newport-on-Tay, Fife.

Issue of late Lt-Col Lord Francis George Montagu Douglas Scott, KCMG, DSO, yst son of 6th Duke, *b* 1879, *d* 1952: *m* 1915, Lady Eileen Nina Evelyn Sibell Elliot, who *d* 1938, da of 4th Earl of Minto:— Moyra Eileen, *b* 1919; 1939-45 War with ATS (FANY) (despatches): *m* 1st, 1942, Maj Hugo Douglas Tweedie, Scots Gds, *ka* NE Europe 1945; 2ndly, 1947, Col David de Crespigny Smiley, LVO, OBE, MC, RHG (The Blues) (ret), of 30 Kensington Mansions, Trebovir Rd, SW5 9TQ (*see* Smiley, Bt), and has issue living (by 1st *m*), Gavin Hugo, *b* 1944; MA (Oxon); Maj The Blues & Royals (ret): *m* 1974, Philippa Mary, da of late Maj Michael Andrews, of Quarry House, Shepton Mallet, Som, and has issue living, Esmond Michael Xan *b* 1976, Alexander *b* 1978, — Anna Bridget Eileen, *b* 1942; MCSP: *m* 1971 (*m diss* 1986), Peter Robert McFerran, and has issue living, Hugo *b* 1975, Lucinda *b* 1972, — (by 2nd *m*) (*see* Smiley, Bt).

Issue of late Lord Henry John Douglas-Scott-Montagu, 2nd son of the 5th Duke of Buccleuch, who was *cr Baron Montagu of Beaulieu* 1885 (see that title).

PREDECESSORS – **(1)** *Sir* WALTER Scott, Knt, a powerful chieftain, and a military commander of renown in the Netherlands under the Prince of Orange, was in 1606 *cr Lord Scott of Buccleuch* (peerage of Scotland); *d* 1611; *s* by his son **(2)** WALTER, 2nd Lord: *cr Lord Scott of Whitchester and Eskdaill* and *Earl of Buccleuch* (peerage of Scotland) 1619, with remainder to his heirs whatsoever; *d* 1633; *s* by his only son **(3)** FRANCIS, 2nd Earl; *d* 1651; *s* by his da **(4)** MARY, when 11 years of age she *m* Walter Scott (then 14 years old) afterwards Earl of Tarras for life; *d* without issue; *s* by her sister **(5)** ANNE: *m* 1st, 1663, James, KG, Duke of Monmouth, who assumed on his marriage the surname of Scott; in 1663 he and his wife were *cr Lord and Lady Scott of Whitchester and Eskdaill, Earl and Countess of Dalkeith*, and *Duke and Duchess of Buccleuch* (peerage of Scotland), with remainder to the heirs male whatsoever descending from the Dukes's body; the Duke was executed 15 July 1685, when all his honours were forfeited, but the honours vested in the Duchess were not attainted; Her Grace *m* 2ndly, Charles, 3rd Baron Cornwallis, by whom she had issue; *d* 1732; *s* by her grandson **(6)** FRANCIS, KT, 2nd Duke, son of James, Earl of Dalkeith, a Representative Peer; in 1743, was restored by Act of Parliament to the English honours of his grandfather, and became *Earl of Doncaster and Baron Scott of Tynedale* (peerage of England, *cr* 1663); *d* 1751; *s* by his grandson **(7)** HENRY, KG, KT, 3rd Duke; by the death, in 1810, of 4th Duke of Queensberry, he became, under a special remainder (granted in 1706), *Lord Douglas of Kinmont, Middlebie and Dornoch, Viscount of Nith, Thorthorwald and Ross, Earl of Drumlanrig and Sanquhar, Marquess of Dumfriesshire*, and *Duke of Queensberry* (peerage of Scotland); *d* 1812; *s* by his son **(8)** CHARLES WILLIAM, KT, 4th Duke of Buccleuch and 6th Duke of Queensberry; called up in his father's Barony of Tynedale 1807: *d* 1819; *s* by his son **(9)** WALTER FRANCIS, KG, PC, DCL, LLD, FRS, 5th Duke of Buccleuch and 7th Duke of Queensberry; *b* 1806; was Lord Privy Seal 1842-6, President of the Council 1846, Lord-Lieut of Midlothian and Roxburghshire, and Chancellor of Glasgow Univ: *m* 1829, Lady Charlotte Anne Thynne, VA, who *d* 1895, 3rd da of 2nd Marquess of Bath: *d* 16 April 1884; *s* by his son **(10)** WILLIAM HENRY WALTER, KG, KT, PC, 6th Duke of Buccleuch and 8th Duke of Queensberry, *b* 1831; MP for Edinburghshire (C) 1853-68 and 1874-80; Lord-Lieut of co Dumfries 1858-1914; *m* 1859, Lady Louisa Jane Hamilton, VA, who *d* 1912, da of 1st Duke of Abercorn, KG; *d* 1914; *s* by his el son **(11)** JOHN CHARLES, KT, GCVO, 7th Duke of Buccleuch, and 9th Duke of Queensberry: *b* 1864; MP for Roxburghshire (U) 1895- 1906; Lord Lieut of co Dumfries: *m* 1893, Lady Margaret Alice Bridgeman, who *d* 1954, da of 4th Earl of Bradford; *d* 1935; *s* by son **(12)** WALTER JOHN, KT, GCVO, TD, PC, 8th Duke of Buccleuch and 10th Duke of Queensberry, *b* 1894; Lord Steward of the Household 1937-40, Lord Clerk Register of Scotland, and Keeper of the Signet 1956-73, Capt-Gen Queen's Body Guard for Scotland (R Company of Archers), and Gold Stick for Scotland 1962-73, Chancellor of Order of the Thistle 1966-73, MP for Roxburghshire and Selkirkshire (C) 1923-35, and Lord Lt of Roxburghshire 1932-73: *m* 1921, (Vreda Esther) Mary, who *d* 1993, da of late Maj William Frank Lascelles (E Harewood, colls); *d* 1973; *s* by his son **(13)** WALTER FRANCIS JOHN, KT, VRD, 9th Duke of Buccleuch, and 11th Duke of Queensberry, present peer; also Marquess of Dumfriesshire, Earl of Dumfriesshire, Earl of Drumlanrig and Sanquhar, Earl of Buccleuch, Earl of Doncaster, Earl of Dalkeith, Viscount Nith, Thorthorwald and Ross, Lord Douglas of Kinmont, Middlebie and Dornoch, Lord Scott of Buccleuch, Lord Scott of Whitchester and Eskdaill, and Baron Scott of Tynedale.

BUCHAN, EARL OF (Erskine) (Earl S 1469)

MALCOLM HARRY ERSKINE, 17th Earl; *b* 4 July 1930; *s* 1984; *ed* Eton; Chm The Dogs' Home, Battersea, and Member Rare Breeds Survival Trust: *m* 1957, Hilary Diana Cecil, da of late Sir Ivan McLannahan Power, 2nd Bt, and has issue.

𝕬rms – Quarterly of four; 1st azure, a barrulet en crancelin of four strawberry leaves between three garbs or *Buchan*; 2nd argent, a pale sable, in dexter canton a rose gules, barbed and seeded vert. *Erskine*; 3rd or, a lymphad sable, sails furled and oars in action and at the masthead a beacon all proper, surmounted of a fess chequy azure and argent charged with a mullet of the second, *Stewart of Buchan*; 4th argent, a lion passant guardant gules, crowned with an imperial and gorged with an open crown or, a label of three points of the second, the centre point charged with a crescent of the third, *Ogilvie of Auchterhouse*, on an inescutcheon en surtout gules, an eagle displayed or, armed and members azure, looking towards the sun in his splendour in dexter chief for lordship of *Cardross*. 𝕮rest – A dexter arm issuant from the wreath attired in a manche gules doubled ermine, the hand proper and grasping a club or. 𝕾upporters – Two ostriches proper, armed, beaked and membered or. *Residence* – Newnham House, Newnham, Hook, Hants.

SONS LIVING

HENRY THOMAS ALEXANDER (*Lord Cardross*), *b* 31 May 1960: *m* 1987, Charlotte Catherine Lucinda, da of Hon Matthew Henry Beaumont (*see* V Allendale), and has issue:—.

SONS LIVING - *Hon* Alexander, *b* 26 April 1990, — *Hon* Frederick Alastair, *b* 1992.

Hon Montagu John, *b* 1966: *m* 1997, Rachel Elizabeth, only da of Stephen Charles Archibald Pryor (*see* Vyvyan, Bt, colls), and has issue living, Iona Nancy, *b* 1998.

DAUGHTERS LIVING

Lady Seraphina Mary, *b* 1961: *m* 1990, Steven K. Berry, elder son of Maj Roy Berry, of Witham, Essex, and has issue living, Katherine Aphra, *b* 1990, — Eleanor India, *b* 1994.

Lady Arabella Fleur, *b* 1969; resumed her maiden name until remarriage: *m* 1st, 1992, Francis Robin Charles Salvesen; 2ndly, 1996, Mark A. Biddle, yr son of Donald Frank Biddle, of Milton on Stour, Dorset, and has issue living (by 2nd *m*), Milo Charles, *b* 1998.

SISTERS LIVING

Lady Sarah Louisa (Redlands Row Cottage, Little Compton, Moreton-in-Marsh, Glos), *b* 1931: *m* 1957 (*m diss* 1972), Major Norman Neill-Fraser, and has issue living, James Montagu Nicholas, *b* 1959.

Lady Caroline Flower, *b* 1935: *m* 1963, John Robin William Lingard, of Semley Grange, Shaftesbury, Dorset, and has issue living, Christina Helen, *b* 1964, *m* 1st, 1981 (*m diss* 1987), Murad Teja, son of late M. P. Teja; 2ndly, 1987, (John) Gawaine Maxwell, and has issue living (by 1st *m*), Alexandra Sophie *b* 1984, (by 2nd *m*) Jessica Loveday *b* 1987, Eloise Jane *b* 1990, — Victoria Margaret, *b* 1966.

COLLATERAL BRANCHES LIVING

Issue of late Hon (Richard) Alastair Erskine, yr son of 6th Baron Erskine, *b* 1901, *d* 1987: *m* 1933, Patricia, who *d* 1989, da of late Maj Paul FitzGerald Norbury, DSO, formerly of the Lench House, Stratford-on-Avon:—

Duncan FitzGerald, *b* 1936; *ed* Malvern: *m* 1st, 1964 (*m diss* 1984), Jillian Lavinia Mary, da of Brig Vincent Alexander Prideaux Budge, CBE, MVO; 2ndly, 1986, Susan, da of late Maj Leslie Frederick Buckholt, and has issue living (by 1st *m*), Rory Alistair, *b* 1972, — Alexander FitzGerald *b* (quadruplet) 1972, — Charlotte Annabel, *b* (quadruplet) 1972. —— Melanie (adopted da), *b* 1938: *m* 1st, 1957 (*m diss* 1967), Sir John Patrick McLannahan Power, 3rd Bt, who *d* 1984; 2ndly, 1968, William Barnsley Allen, who *d* (7 April) 1974; 3rdly, (5 Sept) 1974, Douglas Reginald Joseph Patrick Ward, of 19 St Keyna Av, Hove, E Sussex BN3 4PN, and has issue (by 1st *m*) (*see* Power, Bt, *cr* 1924), — (by 2nd *m*), Wendy Jane, *b* 1970.

Grandsons of Thomas Edward Erskine, 2nd son of late Rev Thomas Erskine, 2nd son of Rt Hon Thomas Erskine, 3rd son of 1st Baron Erskine:—

Issue of late John Steuart Erskine, *b* 1900, *d* 1981: *m* 1928, Rachel Diana Mary, who *d* 1997, da of Lt-Col Arthur Wilmot Rickman:—

David Steuart (71 Green Bush Rd, Willowdale, Ontario, Canada), *b* 1929; *ed* Acadia Univ (BSc 1948), and Toronto Univ (MA 1952): *m* 1957, Elizabeth Fyodorovna, da of late Fyodor Ivanovitch Kramarev, and has issue living, John David, *b* 1958, — Maria, *b* 1960: *m* 1981 (*m diss* 1990), Brian Clow, of Pickering, Ontario. —— Anthony John (16 Richardson St, Sackville, New Brunswick, Canada E4L 4H6), *b* 1931; *ed* Acadia Univ (BSc 1952), Queen's Univ (MA 1955, PhD 1957), and BC Univ (MA 1960): *m* 1955, Janet Madeline Clarke, of Canning, Nova Scotia, and has issue living, Thomas Edward, *b* 1957: *m* 1st, 1981, Judith Rosemary, da of James Reynolds, of Woodstock, Ontario; 2ndly, 1996, Leslie Clark, and has issue living (by 1st *m*), Sarah Laurel *b* 1982, Bronwynn Rebecca *b* 1985, — Rachel Julia Andrée, *b* 1958: *m* 1988,

Frank Collins, of Toronto, Canada, and has issue living, Julia Erskine *b* 1991, — Sally Eileen, *b* 1961: *m* 1980, Glenn Doucette, formerly of Hubbards Point, Nova Scotia, and has issue living, John Anthony Erskine *b* 1988, Madeleine Zoe *b* 1991, Clara Frances *b* 1993.

Grandchildren of late John Steuart Erskine (ante):—
Issue of late Roger Thomas Erskine, *b* 1933, *d* 1975: *m* 1956, Florence Elizabeth (RR3 Box 809, Bathurst, New Brunswick), da of late C. P. Taylor, of Windsor, Nova Scotia:—
Gerald Conrad, *b* 1957: *m* 1978, Carolyn, da of Clifford White, of Bathurst, New Brunswick, and has issue living, John Andrew, *b* 1981, — Ian Ross, *b* 1985. —— Neil Steuart, *b* 1960: *m* 1989, Ava, da of Stephen Czapalay, formerly of Barrington, Nova Scotia, and has issue living, Julian Benedict, *b* 1993, — Rachel Joanna, *b* 1995. —— Joseph Christian, *b* 1962: *m* 1992, Donna Macdonald. —— Jane Elizabeth, *b* 1966: *m* 1994, Shawn Branch, formerly of Bathurst, new Brunswick.

Grandchildren of late Edward John Erskine, yst son of late Rev Thomas Erskine (ante):—
Issue of late Steuart Edward Erskine, *b* 1902, *d* 1992: *m* 1930, Marjorie Luxton Clendening, who *d* 1991:—
John Steuart (9448 Olympia Fields Drive, San Ramon, California 94583, USA), *b* 1937: *m* 1967, Sharyl Tomes, of Omaha, Nebraska, and has issue living, Karen, *b* 1968, — and an adopted da, LeAnn, *b* 1965 (adopted 1968). —— Patricia Louise (Le Petit Dixcart, Sark, Channel Islands), *b* 1934: *m* 1968, Stanley Falle, and has issue living, Marie Claire Erskine, *b* 1971.

Grandchildren of late St Vincent Whitshed Erskine 2nd son of Maj Hon David Erskine, 21st Fus, 3rd son of 2nd Baron Erskine:—
Issue of late Charles Howard Erskine, *b* 1871, *d* 1918: *m* 1900, Charlotte Mildred, who *d* 1947, da of William Wright Greathead:—
George St Vincent (961 Pershing Av, San José, California 95126, USA), *b* 1905: *m* 1936, Ruth Genevieve, who *d* 1992, da of Iver Nelson, and has issue living, Charles Nelson (9205 Jura Rd, RR2, Sidney, BC, Canada V8L 3S1), *b* 1938: *m* 1969, Linda Ruth, da of Thomas G. McReynolds, and has issue living, George Lindley *b* 1973, Gyneth Alice *b* 1971.

Issue of late Maj Esmé Erskine, CMG, MC, *b* 1884, *d* 1962: *m* 1909, Elisabeth Susan Matilda, who *d* 1973, da of late Herman Reinders:—
Swanzie (*Lady Agnew of Lochnaw*), *b* 1916; *ed* Edinburgh Univ, (MA): *m* 1937, Sir Fulque Agnew of Lochnaw, 10th Bt, who *d* 1975.

Grandsons of Maj Esmé Erskine, CMG, MC (ante):—
Issue of late Esmé Stephenson Erskine, *b* 1914, *d* 1982: *m* 1941, Jean Meriel (Kingscliffe Farm, PO Glenside, 3477 Natal, S Africa), da of Harry Crawford Boyd, of Chobham, Surrey:—
Stephen St Vincent (Kingscliffe Farm, PO Glenside, 3477 Natal, S Africa), *b* 1947: *m* 1975, Bridget Grey, da of Derrick G. Norton, of Pietermaritzburg, Natal, and has issue living, Byron Thomas, *b* 1977, — Angela Jane, *b* 1979, — Paula Swanzie, *b* 1982. —— Andrew Stuart (Bosch Hoek, Balgowan, Natal, S Africa), *b* 1949: *m* 1972, Margaret Ann, da of Austin V. Johnson, of Howick, Natal, and has issue living, Stuart Graeme, *b* 1974, — Chad Esmé, *b* 1980, — Sarah Margaret, *b* 1976. —— David Boyd (335 Cowey Rd, Durban, Natal, S Africa), *b* 1954: *m* 1981, Marilyn-Gene, da of Harold Dodd, of Australia, and has issue living, Catherine Ann, *b* 1983, — Jennifer Lynn, *b* 1986.

Grandsons of late Capt Sir (Henry) David Erskine, KCVO, son of late James Erskine, el son of David Erskine, 3rd in descent from the Hon John Erskine, 3rd son of 2nd Lord Cardross:—
Issue of late Col Sir Arthur (Edward) Erskine, GCVO, DSO, *b* 1881, *d* 1963: *m* 1921, Rosemary Freda, who *d* 1970, da of late Brig-Gen Edward William David Baird, CBE:—
Donald Seymour (Cleish House, Cleish, Kinross-shire). *Club* – New (Edinburgh), *b* 1925; *ed* Wellington Coll; FRICS; DL Kinross-shire, and a Member of Queen's Body Guard for Scotland (Royal Company of Archers); 1939-45 War as Capt RA: *m* 1953, Catharine Annandale, only da of late Kenneth McLelland, of Wester Housebyres, Melrose, Roxburghshire, and has issue living, James Malcolm Kenneth, MBE (New (Edinburgh) Club), *b* 1957; *ed* Wellington Coll; Maj The Black Watch (Royal Highland Regt); Memb Queen's Body Guard for Scotland (Royal Company of Archers): MBE (Mil) 1995: *m* 1987, Jennifer, elder da of Donald MacLellan, of Stockbridge, Symington, Ayrshire, and has issue living, Harry Charles David *b* 1988, Geordie James Donald *b* 1990, — Caroline Janet, *b* 1954: *m* 1982, Lt-Col Alan Keith McCulloch Miller, OBE, Argyll & Sutherland Highlanders, and has issue living, Kirstie Araminta Jane *b* 1983, Jennifer Catharine Susanne *b* 1985, Iona Caroline *b* 1988, — Fiona Catharine, *b* 1956: *m* 1991, Christopher Brendan Still, of Australia, and has issue living, Alexander Christopher *b* 1992, Harriet Angela *b* 1994, — Julia Rosemary, *b* 1962: *m* 1995, Jonathan P. Flory, elder son of Peter Flory, of Wheathamstead, Herts, and has issue living, James Jonathan Anthony *b* 1998, Susanna Catharine *b* 1997, — Joanna Christian, *b* 1968: *m* 1996, (Newton) Edward John Bruce (*see* E Elgin and Kincardine). —— Angus Bruce (16 Braid Farm Rd, Edinburgh EH10 6LF), *b* 1928; Cdr RN: *m* 1961, Alison Gillian, yr da of late Dr Comyn Duthie, of Welkom, Orange Free State, S Africa, and has issue living, Alexander David, *b* 1964, — Keith Malcolm, *b* 1967.

Grandchildren of late Maj-Gen George Elphinstone Erskine, el son of Capt George Keith Erskine, 4th son of David Erskine (ante):—
Issue of late Gen Sir George Watkin Eben James Erskine, GCB, KBE, DSO, *b* 1899, *d* 1965: *m* 1930, Ruby, who *d* 1974, da of Sir Evelyn Andros de la Rue, 2nd Bt:—
Philip Niel (Ida's Valley Homestead, PO Box 132, Stellenbosch, Cape, S Africa), 1933; *ed* Charterhouse, and RMA Sandhurst; Maj Scots Gds; Equerry to HRH Duke of Gloucester 1962-64: *m* 1960, Alice Fiona, da of late Capt Edward Copleston Radcliffe, late 9th Lancers, of Derriford, Devon, and has issue living, Rupert Alexander (The Auld House, Swellendam, Cape Prov, S Africa), *b* 1961: *m* 1986, Alida Maria, yr da of Gabriël Fagan, of Cape Town, and has an adopted son, Malcolm John *b* 1997, — George Edward (Ridley Hall, Kenilworth, Cape Town, S Africa), *b* 1966: *ed* Diocesan Coll, Cape Town, RMA Sandhurst, and Natal Univ; Lt RGJ: *m* 1992, Deborah Jane, only da of Paul Bennett, of Hilton, Natal, and has issue living, Thomas David *b* 1998, — Lucy Rose, *b* 1962: *m* 1994, Patrick James Lumley Caruth, of 62 Crescent Lane, SW4 9PU, son of Maj Michael Caruth, of Hardington Lodge, Hardington-Mandeville, Som, and has issue living, George Alexander *b* 1998, Catherine Alice *b* 1996. —— Robert Keith (4 The Steadings, Walkmilton Farm, Linlithgow, nr Lothian EH49 7PU), *b* 1936; author of *Business Management*, and *Blueprint to Absorb National Debt*: *m* 1964, Susan Morag, da of Sir Archibald Charles Edmonstone, 6th Bt, and has issue living, Hamish Robert Coll Charles,

b 1967: *m* 1991, Anne Nicola Parsons, and had issue living, Jonathan *b* 1994, Thomas *b* 1996, Katie *b* 1998, — Alexander William Ian Marshall, *b* 1970: *m* 1991, Carina Gustafsson, and has issue living, Carl *b* 1994, Robert *b* 1996, Emmy *b* 1999, — Iona Mary, *b* 1965: *m* 1990, John Hunter Andrews, and has issue living, Tommie *b* 1996, Morna *b* 1993. —— Elizabeth Polly, *b* 1945: *m* 1967, Paul L. H. Bristol, and has issue living, Pollyanna, *b* 1969, — Sophy Louisa, *b* 1972, — Georgiana, *b* 1982.

PREDECESSORS – Buchan was one of the seven original Mormaerships (or Earldoms) of Scotland. In 1469 **(1)** *Sir* JAMES STEWART, 2nd son of Sir James Stewart of Lorn (the Black Knight of Lorn), by Joan, widow of James I of Scotland, was *cr Earl of Buchan* and *Lord Auchterhouse*; High Chamberlain of Scotland and Ambassador to France: *m* (before) 1466, Margaret, da of Sir Alexander Ogilvy, of Auchterhouse; *s* by his son **(2)** ALEXANDER, 2nd Earl; *d* 1505; *s* by his son **(3)** JOHN, 3rd Earl; *s* by his granddaughter **(4)** CHRISTIAN: *m* Robert Douglas, of Lochleven, who in right of his wife became Earl of Buchan; *s* by his son **(5)** JAMES, 5th Earl; *d* 1601; *s* by his da **(6)** MARY: *m* James Erskine, 2nd son of John, KG, 2nd Earl of Mar, who thereupon assumed the Earldom of Buchan; his wife resigned the dignity, and in 1617 she and her husband were *cr* by royal charter *Earl and Countess of Buchan* (peerage of Scotland), with remainder to the heirs-male of the marriage, whom failing, to the legitimate and nearest heirs-male and assignees of the Earl; in 1625 they had a further charter with similar limitation of the Earldom; in 1633 the precedency of the Earldom was established by Act of Parliament as 1469; the Countess *d* 1628, and the Earl 1640; *s* (under the charters of 1617 and 1625) by his son **(7)** JAMES, 7th Earl; *d* 1664; *s* by his son **(8)** WILLIAM, 8th Earl; *d* unmarried 1695; *s* by the heir male of 6th Earl **(9)** DAVID, PC, 9th Earl, and 4th Lord Cardross (see infra†), described in the Rolls of Parliament as 4th Earl of Buchan; right to this Earldom acknowledged by Parliament 1698; was a Representative Peer and Lord-Lieut of cos Stirling and Clackmannan; *d* 1745; *s* by his son **(10)** HENRY DAVID, 10th Earl; *d* 1767; *s* by his son **(11)** DAVID STEWART, 11th Earl: *d* 1829; *s* by his nephew **(12)** HENRY DAVID, 12th Earl; was *m* three times, 1st, 1809, to Elizabeth Cole who *d* 1828, da of Maj-Gen Sir Charles Shipley: he *d* 1857, and was *s* by his 2nd son by 1st *m* **(13)** DAVID STUART, 13th Earl, *b* 1815: *m* 1st, 1849, Agnes Graham who *d* 1875, da of James Smith, of Craigend Castle, Stirlingshire; 2ndly, 1876, Maria, da of William James, and widow of Jervoise Collas, of St Martin's House, Jersey; *d* 1898; *s* by his el son **(14)** SHIPLEY GORDON STUART, 14th Earl, *b* 1850: *m* 1876, Rosalie Louisa, who *d* 1943, da of late Capt Jules Alexandre Sartorius, of Hopsford Hall, Coventry; *d* 1934; *s* by his only son **(15)** RONALD DOUGLAS STUART MAR, 15th Earl; *b* 1878; formerly Lieut Argyll and Sutherland Highlanders, Scots Gds and E Riding Yeo; S Africa 1900-1902, European War 1915-17 in Egypt, Salonika and Palestine as Lieut RASC; *d* 1960; *s* by his kinsman **(16)** DONALD CARDROSS FLOWER, 7th Baron Erskine (see infra†), 16th Earl; Lt-Col 9th Lancers; *b* 1899: *m* 1927, Christina, who *d* 1994, da of late Hugh Woolner, and adopted da of late Lloyd Harry Baxendale, JP, of Greenham Lodge, Newbury, Berks; *d* 1984; *s* by his only son **(17)** MALCOLM HARRY, 17th Earl and present peer; also Lord Cardross, Lord Auchterhouse and Baron Erskine.

****(1)** JOHN, 2nd Earl of Mar, was *cr Lord Cardross* (peerage of Scotland) 1610, and acquired the right to assign the Lordship to whomsoever he might select, which privilege he exercised by Charter 1617 in favour of Henry, his 2nd son by his 2nd *m* ; *d* 1634; *s* by his grandson **(2)** DAVID, 2nd Lord *d* 1671; *s* by his son **(3)** HENRY, PC, 3rd Lord; suffered from religious persecution and was heavily fined and imprisoned; established a colony in Carolina, USA; was Gov of the Mint; *d* 1693; *s* by his son **(4)** DAVID, 4th Lord, afterwards 9th Earl of Buchan (ante).

†**(1)** The *Hon* THOMAS ERSKINE, KT, 3rd son of 10th Earl of Buchan, having served both in Army and Navy was called to the English Bar and became a distinguished Advocate; Attorney-Gen to HRH the Prince of Wales 1783, Chancellor of Duchy of Cornwall 1802, and Lord High Chancellor 1806; *cr Baron Erskine*, of Restormel Castle, co Cornwall (peerage of United Kingdom) 1806: *m* 1st, 1770, Frances, who *d* 1805, da of David Moore, MP; 2ndly, 18—, Sarah Buck; *d* 1823, *s* by his son **(2)** DAVID MONTAGU, 2nd Baron *b* 1777: *m* 1st, 1799, Frances, who *d* (March) 1843, da of Gen John Cadwalader, of Philadelphia, USA; 2ndly (July), 1843, Ann Bond, who *d* 1851, da of late John Travis; 3rdly, 1852, Anna, who *d* 1886 (having *m* 3rdly, 1856, the Ven J. Sandford, BD, Archdeacon of Coventry), widow of Thomas Calderwood Durham, of Largo; *d* 1855; *s* by his el son **(3)** THOMAS AMERICUS, 3rd Baron, *b* 1802: *m* 1830, Louisa, who *d* 1867, da of G. Newnham, of New Timber Place, Sussex, and widow of Thomas Legh, of Adlington; *d* 1877; *s* by his brother **(4)** JOHN CADWALLADER, 4th Baron; *b* 1805; served in BCS 1826-53: *m* 1st, 1829, Margaret, who *d* 1862, da of John Martyn, of co Tyrone; 2ndly, 1865, Mary Louisa, who *d* 1889 (having *m* 2ndly, 1886, Philip Henry Egerton), da of Col Alexander Campbell, CB, KH, of Blackburn House, Ayrshire; *d* 28 Mar 1882; *s* by his son **(5)** WILLIAM MACNAGHTEN, 5th Baron, *b* 1841: *m* 1864, Caroline Alice Martha, who *d* 1922, da of late William Grimble; *d* 1913; *s* by his son **(6)** MONTAGU, 6th Baron; *b* 1865; formerly Lt-Cdr RNVR: *m* 1895, Florence, who *d* 1936, 4th da of Edgar Flower, JP, formerly of Middlehill Park, Broadway, Worcestershire; and The Hill, Stratford-on-Avon; *d* 1957; *s* by his el son **(7)** DONALD CARDROSS FLOWER, 7th Baron and afterwards 16th Earl of Buchan (ante).

Buchan, family name of Baron Tweedsmuir.

Buckhurst, Lord; son of Earl De La Warr.

BUCKINGHAMSHIRE, EARL OF (Hobart-Hampden) (Earl GB 1746, Bt 1611)

(GEORGE) MILES HOBART-HAMPDEN, 10th Earl and 14th Baronet; *b* 15 Dec 1944; *s* 1983; *ed* at Clifton Coll, Exeter Univ (BA), and London Univ (MA): *m* 1st, 1968, Susan Jennifer, only da of late Raymond W. Adams, of Halesowen, Worcs; 2ndly, 1975, Alison Wightman, DL Bucks 1995, da of late William Forrest, of Edinburgh, and previously wife of late D. A. (Tim) Wishart, of Edinburgh.

Arms – Quarterly: 1st and 4th argent, a saltire gules, between four eagles displayed azure, *Hampden*: 2nd and 3rd sable, an estoile of six rays or, between two flaunches ermine, *Hobart*. **Crests** – 1st, a talbot statant ermine, collared and line reflexed thereto, tied in a knot over the back gules, *Hampden*; 2nd, a bull statant per pale sable and gules, bezantée, in the nose a ring or, *Hobart*. **Supporters** – *Dexter*, a buck; *sinister*, a talbot, both reguardant proper, each gorged with a radiant collar, and a line reflexed over the back or. **First Motto** – Auctor pretiosa facit (*The giver makes valuable*); **Second Motto** – Vestigia nulla retrorsum (*No steps backward*).
Address – House of Lords, SW1.

SISTER LIVING

Helen Moncreiff, *b* 1937: *m* 1962, Hugues Motteux, and has issue living, Thierry, *b* 1968, — Jean Paul, *b* 1973, — Nicole, *b* 1970. *Address* – Private Bag V7410, Mutare, Zimbabwe.

WIDOW LIVING OF NINTH EARL

MARGOT (*Margot, Countess of Buckinghamshire*) (c/o Barclays Bank, 6 Hanover Sq, W1), da of John Storey Rodger, of NSW, Australia, and widow of F. C. Bruce Hittman, MD, FRACS, of Sydney Australia: *m* 1972, the 9th Earl of Buckinghamshire, who *d* 1983.

COLLATERAL BRANCHES LIVING

Descendants of Sir Robert Henry Hobart KCVO, CB, *cr* a *Baronet* 1914, el son of Very Rev Hon Henry Lewis Hobart, 4th son of 3rd Earl:—
Of whom *Sir* JOHN VERE HOBART, 4th *Baronet*, *b* 9 April 1945, is *hp* to the Earldom.

Grandchildren of late Charles Guy Reginald Vivian Beauchamp Hobart, yr son of late Charles Hobart (*b* 1842), eldest son of Lt-Col Charles Robert Hobart, 2nd son of Rev Henry Charles Hobart, only son of Hon Henry Hobart, yst son of 1st Earl:—
Issue of late John Bertram Hobart, *b* 1911, *d* 1982: *m* 1st, 1944 (*m diss* 1971), June Mary, da of Franklin George Barnes; 2ndly, 1972, Leone, da of —:—
(By 1st *m*) †Roger John *b* 1956; *d* as the result of a motor accident 1978. —— Hilary Rosamond (14 Stirling St, Kew, Victoria 3101, Australia), *b* 1958: *m* 1988, Carl Bethridge Topp, and has issue living, Matthew HOBART-TOPP, *b* 1987, — Annika Alexandra HOBART-TOPP, *b* 1990.

Issue of late Wallace Elliot Hobart, MB, BS, *b* 1922, *d* 1972: *m* 1st, 1946 (*m diss* 1956), Joyce Stella Hussey; 2ndly, 1957, Halina Zofia Bobinska, MB, ChB, of 1, 23 Alma St, Essendon, Victoria 3040, Australia:—
(By 2nd *m*) Mark Michael (3 Derry St, Essendon, Victoria 3040, Australia), *b* 1958; *ed* Melbourne Univ (MB, BS): *m* 1990, Patricia Mildred Blair, and has issue living, Michael Wallace, *b* 1991, — Benedict William Conrad, *b* 1993. —— Pauline Ann, *b* 1960; BSc: *m* 1982, Bruce Maxwell Twite, of 67 Research-Warrandyte Rd, Research, Victoria 3095, Australia, and has issue living, Adam Alexander, *b* 1988, — Elin Andrea, *b* 1990, — Hannah Gabrielle, *b* 1992.

Grandsons of late Rev William Henry Hobart, 4th and yst son of late Lt-Col Charles Robert Hobart (ante):—
Issue of late Rev Charles Hampden Hobart, *b* 1886, *d* 1961: *m* 1924, Alice, who *d* 1960, da of Samuel Plumbly, of Findon Valley, Worthing:—
John Hampden (Brandon, Buckland, Oxon SN7 8QW), *b* 1925; Maj (ret) late 5th R Inniskilling Drag Gds: *m* 1961, Maureen, da of Alfred Clowes, of Stoke-on-Trent, and has issue living, Andrew Hampden, *b* 1962, — Jeremy Charles, *b* 1963. —— Christopher Beauchamp, MBE (The Old Stables, The Coppice, Clifton Hampden, Oxon OX14 3DF), *b* 1927; *ed* St John's Leatherhead, and New Coll, Oxford; MBE (Civil) 1997: *m* 1st, 1953 (*m diss* 1970), Margaret, da of Gilbert Reed, of Lingfield, Surrey; 2ndly, 1970, Joanna Margaret, da of Rear Adm Anthony Davies, CB, CVO, of Witt's Piece, Aldbourne, Marlborough, Wilts, and has issue living (by 1st *m*), Richard Hampden, *b* 1960, — Simon Vere, *b* 1964, — (by 2nd *m*) Edward Andrew Beauchamp, *b* 1971, — Robert Anthony, *b* 1973, — John Henry *b* 1976.

PREDECESSORS – (1) *Sir* HENRY HOBART, successively MP for Norwich and Yarmouth, and Lord Chief Justice of the Common Pleas; was *cr* a *Baronet* 1611; *d* 1625; *s* by his son (2) *Sir* JOHN, MP, 2nd Bt; *d* 1647; *s* by his nephew (3) *Sir* JOHN, MP, 3rd Bt; *d* 1683; *s* by his el son (by his 1st *m* with Mary, da of the patriot John Hampden) (4) *Sir* HENRY, MP, 4th Bt; Equerry to King William III at the Battle of the Boyne 1690; killed in a duel by Oliver le Neve, 1698; *s* by his son (5) *Sir* JOHN, 5th Bt; *cr* *Baron Hobart* of Blickling (peerage of Great Britain) 1728, and *Earl of Buckinghamshire* (Peerage of Great Britain) 1746; *d* 1756; *s* by his son (6) JOHN, 2nd Earl; was Ambassador to Court of Russia 1762, and Viceroy of Ireland 1777; *d* 1793; *s* by his brother (7) GEORGE, 3rd Earl; *d* 1804; *s* by his son (8) ROBERT, PC, 4th Earl;

was successively MP for Bramber, Sussex, and Armagh, Gov of Madras, Ch Sec for Ireland, Sec of State for War, and Sec of State for the Colonies, &c; summoned to Parliament as Baron Hobart 1797; *d* 1816; *s* by his nephew (**9**) GEORGE ROBERT, 5th Earl (son of Hon George Vere Hobart by Jane, da of Horace Cataneo, Esq); sat as MP for St Michael 1812-3; assumed by R licence in 1824 the surname of Hampden in lieu of Hobart; *d* 1849; *s* by his brother (**10**) *Rev* AUGUSTUS EDWARD, 6th Earl; *b* 1793; assumed by R licence 1878 the additional surname of Hampden, *m* 1st, 1816, Mary, who *d* 1825, da of John Williams, King's Sergeant; 2ndly, 1826, Maria Isabella, who *d* 1873, da of Rev Godfrey Egremont; *d* 1885; *s* by his grandson (**11**) SIDNEY CARR, OBE (son of Frederic John, Lord Hobart, 2nd son of 6th Earl, by Catherine Annesley, da of Rt Rev Thomas Carr, DD, formerly Bishop of Bombay), 7th Earl, *b* 1860; a Lord-in-Waiting to Queen Victoria 1895; assumed, by R licence 1903, the additional surnames of Mercer-Henderson for himself and issue: *m* 1888, Georgina Wilhelmina (authorised by R licence 1903, to use the surnames of Mercer-Henderson only and to subscribe herself by the surnames and title Mercer-Henderson-Buckinghamshire) who *d* 1937, da of late Hon Hew Adam Dalrymple Haldane Duncan-Mercer-Henderson; *d* 1930; *s* by his son (**12**) JOHN HAMPDEN, 8th Earl, *b* 1906; Dep-Chm of Cttees House of Lords 1952-4, and Dep Speaker House of Lords 1954-63; assumed by R licence 1938 the surname of Mercer-Henderson only in lieu of Hobart-Hampden-Mercer-Henderson; *d* 1963; *s* by his kinsman (**13**) VERE FREDERICK CECIL Hobart-Hampden (2nd son of late Arthur Ernest Hobart-Hampden, 2nd son of late Capt Hon Charles Edward Hobart-Hampden, 4th son of 6th Earl), 9th Earl *b* 1901; 1939-45 War with RAAF; *m* 1972, Margot Macrae, da of John Storey Rodger, of NSW, Aust, and widow of F. C. Bruce Hittman, MD, FRACS, of Sydney, Aust; *d* 1983; *s* by his kinsman (**14**) GEORGE MILES (only son of late Cyril Langel Hobart-Hampden, el son of Ernest Miles Hobart-Hampden, CMG, yst son of Hon George Augustus Hobart-Hampden, 5th son of 6th Earl), 10th Earl and present peer; also Baron Hobart.

Buckley, family name of Baron Wrenbury.

BUCKMASTER, VISCOUNT (Buckmaster) (Viscount UK 1933)

Equanimity, magnanimity

MARTIN STANLEY BUCKMASTER, OBE, 3rd Viscount; *b* 11 April 1921; *s* 1974; *ed* Stowe; FRGS entered FO 1946, Political Officer, Abu Dhabi, 1955-58, First Sec (Information), British Embassy, Benghazi 1958-62, and Tripoli, 1962-63, First Sec (Political) Bahrain 1963-67, FO 1967-69; First Sec and British High Commn, Kampala 1969-71, British Embassy, Beirut 1971-73; FCO 1973-77, HM Chargé d'Affaires and Head of Chancery, Yemen Arab Republic, 1977-81 (ret); Capt R Sussex Regt (TA) 1939-46, served in Middle East; OBE (Civil) 1979.

Arms – Or, semée of fleurs-de-lis azure, a lion rampant of the last, on a chief of the second a portcullis of the first. Crest – A demi-lion azure, holding in the dexter paw a fleur-de-lis and charged on the shoulder with a portcullis, both or. Supporters – On either side a bulk proper, each gorged with a chain pendant therefrom a portcullis or.
Residence – 90 Cornwall Gdns, SW7 4AX.
Club – Travellers'.

BROTHER LIVING

Hon COLIN JOHN (Ryece Hall, Brettenham, Ipswich), *b* 17 April, 1923; *ed* Winchester; late Fl Lt RAF: *m* 1946, May only da of Charles Henry Gibbon, of The Lodge, Great Bentley, Essex, and has issue living, Adrian Charles, *b* 1949: *m* 1975, Dr Elizabeth M, only da of Norman Mark, MB, Bch, of Downings, Prinsted, Emsworth, Hants, and has issue living, Andrew Nicholas *b* 1980, Clare May *b* 1979, Nicola Mary *b* 1986, — Simon John, *b* 1956: *m* 1983, Emma Elizabeth, da of Field Marshal Sir John Wilfred Stanier, KCB, MBE, of Whitewater House, Dipley, Hartley Wintney, Hants, and has issue living, George John *b* 1984, Hugo Denis *b* 1987, Toby Colin *b* 1991, Rachel May *b* 1988, — Michael Anthony Stanley, *b* 1959, — Ann Susan, *b* 1950: *m* 1976, Nicholas J. W. Tavener, and has issue living, Thomas Henry *b* 1980, Geoffrey John *b* 1985, Sarah Georgina *b* 1979, — Sarah Janet *b* 1952.

WIDOW LIVING OF SECOND VISCOUNT

DIANA CONSTANCE (Ringwold House, Middle Wallop, nr Stockbridge, Hants) da of late Maj Kenneth Arthur Seth-Smith, and formerly wife of Charles Stewart McDonnell Vane-Tempest (*see* M Londonderry, colls): *m* 1961, and 2nd wife, the 2nd Viscount Buckmaster, who *d* 1974; *m* 3rdly, 1982, as his 2nd wife, Roderick Edward Faure Walker.

PREDECESSORS – (**1**) *Rt Hon Sir* STANLEY OWEN Buckmaster, GCVO, PC, son of late John Charles Buckmaster, of Ashleigh, Hampton Wick; *b* 1861; sat as MP for Camb Borough (*L*) 1906-10, and for Keighley Div of N Part of W Riding of Yorkshire 1911-15; was Solicitor-Gen Oct 1913 to May 1915, and Lord High Chancellor of England May 1915 to Dec 1916; *cr Baron Buckmaster*, of Cheddington, Buckinghamshire (peerage of United Kingdom) 1915 and *Viscount Buckmaster*, of Cheddington, Buckinghamshire (peerage of United Kingdom) 1933: *m* 1889, Edith Augusta, who *d* 1935 da of S. R. Lewin, of Widford, Herts: *d* 1934: *s* by his son (2) OWEN STANLEY, 2nd Viscount, *b* 1890; Bar at law and underwriting member of Lloyds; Member of Cttee, London Stock Exchange 1938-42: *m* 1st, 1916 (*m diss* 1944), Joan, who *d* 1976, da of George Augustus Gary Simpson, MRCS; 2ndly, 1961, Diana Constance (VANE-TEMPEST) (who *m* 3rdly, 1982, as his 2nd wife, Roderick Edward Faure Walker), da of late Maj Kenneth Arthur Seth-Smith; *d* 1974; *s* by his el son (3) OWEN STANLEY, 3rd Viscount and present peer: also Baron Buckmaster.

Buckton, Barony of (Storey) (Extinct 1978) (see Storey, Bt)

Buller, Manningham-, family name of Viscount Dilhorne.

Buller, Yarde-, family name of Baron Churston.

BULLOCK, BARON (Bullock) (Life Baron 1976)

ALAN LOUIS CHARLES BULLOCK, FBA, son of Rev Frank Allen Bullock, of Bradford, Yorks; *b* 13 Dec 1914; *ed* Bradford Gram Sch, and Wadham Coll, Oxford (MD DLitt); Hon Fellow of St Catherine's Coll, New Coll, Merton Coll, Wadham Coll, Linacre Coll, and Wolfson Coll; Foreign Member of American Acad of Arts and Sciences; Hon Dr Univ Aix-Marseilles; Hon DLitt Bradford, Reading, Leicester, Sussex, Essex, Warwick, Newfoundland and Open University; Historian and Writer; FBA; Fellow, Dean and Tutor of New Coll, Oxford 1945-52, Censor of St Catherine's Soc Oxford 1952-60; Founding Master of St Catherine's Coll, Oxford 1960-80; Vice-Chancellor of Oxford Univ 1969-73; author of *Hitler, A Study in Tyranny* 1952, *The Liberal Tradition* 1956, *The Life and Times of Ernest Bevin* Vol I 1960, Vol II 1967, Vol III (*Ernest Bevin, Foreign Secretary*) 1983, *Hitler & Stalin: Parallel Lives* 1991 (revised edn 1993), and *The Twentieth Century* 1970, co-editor *Fontana Dictionary of Modern Thought* 1977 (2nd edn 1988), and *Fontana Biographical Companion to Modern Thought* 1983: *cr* Knt 1972, and *Baron Bullock*, of Leafield, co Oxfordshire (Life Baron), 1976: *m* 1940, Hilda Yates, da of Edwin Handy, of Bradford, and has issue.
Residence – The Old Manse, Leafield, Oxon.

SONS LIVING

Hon (Oliver) Nicholas Alan (King's College, Cambridge), *b* 1942: *m* 1st, 1967 (*m diss* 1972), — ; 2ndly, 1972 (*m diss* 1984), Ellen J. Blatt; 3rdly, 1984, Sally Todd, da of late Sinclair Holmes, of Bolden.
Hon Adrian Charles Sebastian (12 Brookside, Headington, Oxford OX3 7PJ), *b* 1944: *m* 1st, 1970 (*m diss* 1984), Susan Elizabeth Swindlehurst; 2ndly, 1992, Bernadette Lucia Maria, da of James Ferry, of Glasgow.
Hon Matthew Peter Dominic, *b* 1949: *m* 1970, Anna-lena Margareta, da of Sven Hansson, of Uppsala, Sweden.

Bunbury, McClintock-, family name of Baron Rathdonnell.

BURDEN, BARON (Burden) (Baron UK 1950)

ANDREW PHILIP BURDEN, 3rd Baron; *b* 20 July 1959; *s* 1995.
Address – c/o Barclays Bank plc, 26-30 Regent St, Weston-super-Mare, Somerset BS23 1SH.

BROTHERS LIVING

Hon FRASER WILLIAM ELSWORTH, *b* 6 Nov 1964.
Hon Ian Stuart, *b* 1967.

SISTERS LIVING

Hon Carol Mary, *b* 1952.
Hon Corynne Lesley, *b* 1955: *m* 1977, William D-Day Peters, of Greenland, Royston Water, Churchinford, Taunton, Som TA3 MEF, son of late Leonard Thomas Peters, and has issue living, Alexander, *b* 1983, — Lindsey Jane, *b* 1988.
Hon Adrienne Gail, *b* 1957.

WIDOW LIVING OF SECOND BARON

AUDREY ELSWORTH (*Baroness Burden*), da of Maj Wilfred Elsworth Sykes, of Kirk Ella, Hull: *m* 1951, the 2nd Baron Burden, who *d* 1995.
Residence –

PREDECESSORS – **(1)** THOMAS WILLIAM Burden, CBE, son of Thomas Burden, of Mile End, E; *b* 1885; 2nd Church Estates Commr 1945-50, a Member of House of Laity of Church Assembly 1947-50 and Lord in in Waiting to HM 1950-51; MP for Park Div of Sheffield (*Lab*) 1942-50; *cr Baron Burden*, of Hazlebarrow, co Derby (peerage of UK) 1950: *m* 1910, Augusta, who *d* 1976, da of David Sime, of Aberdeen; *d* 1970; *s* by his only son **(2)** PHILIP WILLIAM, 2nd Baron; *b* 1916: *m* 1951, Audrey Elsworth, da of Maj Wilfred Elsworth Sykes, of Kirk Ella, Hull; *d* 1995; *s* by his eldest son **(3)** ANDREW PHILIP, 3rd Baron and present peer.

Burford, Earl of; son of Duke of St Albans.

BURGH, BARON (Leith) (E 1529)
(Title pronounced "Borough")

ALEXANDER PETER WILLOUGHBY LEITH, 7th Baron; *b* 20 March, 1935; *s* 1959; *ed* Harrow, and Magdalene Coll, Camb; formerly in RAF: *m* 1st, 1957 (*m diss* 1982), Anita Lorna, novelist (as Anita Burgh), da of late Frederick Clements Eldridge, of Gillingham, Kent; 2ndly, 1984, Wilma, da of Bruno Schramm, of Germany, and has issue by 1st and 2nd wives.

ᴀrms – Quarterly, 1st and 4th or, a cross-crosslet fitchée sable between three crescents in chief and as many fusils in base barwise gules, all within a bordure azure, *Leith*; 2nd azure, three fleur-de-lis ermine, *Burgh*; 3rd, quarterly, 1st and 4th or, a lion rampant azure, armed and langued gules, *Percy*; 2nd and 3rd semée of six or and sable, *Strabolgi*. ℭrest – 1st, a cross-crosslet fitchée sable, *Leith*; 2nd, a falcon argent, beaked, legged and ducally gorged or, *Burgh*. ℭupporters – On either side a stag azure charged with three fleur-de-lis ermine in pale.
Address – c/o House of Lords, SW1. *Residence* – Santa Cruz, California, USA.

SONS LIVING (*By 1st wife*)

Hon (ALEXANDER) GREGORY DISNEY, *b* 16 March 1958: *m* 1st, 1984 (*m diss* 1999), Catherine Mary, da of David Parkes, of The Old Rectory, Wrington, Bristol; 2ndly, 1999, Emma Jane, da of Martin Burdick, of Sparrows Nest, The Strand, Shaldon, Devon, and has issue living (by 1st *m*), Alexander James Strachan, *b* 11 Oct 1986, — Benjamin David Willoughby, *b* 1988.
Hon Patrick Simon Vincent, *b* 1964.

DAUGHTERS LIVING (*By 1st wife*)

Hon Rebecca Moraigh Eveleigh LEITH, *b* 1959; has resumed her maiden name: *m* 1978 (*m diss* 1983), David K. O. Brandler. *Residence* – Ceneuil, 43800 St Vincent, France.

(*By 2nd wife*)

Hon Alexandra Nadja, *b* 1977.

HALF-BROTHER LIVING

Hon John Barnabas (24 Gardiner Close, Abingdon, Oxon OX14 3YA), *b* 1947; *ed* Wellington Coll, and Exeter Univ: *m* 1970, Erica Jane, da of David M. Lewis, of Winchester, and has issue living, Alexander David Kalimat, *b* 1973, — Thomas Magnus Abad, *b* 1976, — Angharad Jane, *b* 1977.

WIDOW LIVING OF SIXTH BARON

JOYCE WATTS, da of W. Wilson Wilson, of 10 Curzon Road, Hoylake, Cheshire: *m* 1st, 1947, as his 2nd wife, the 6th Baron Burgh, who *d* 1959; 2ndly, 1960, Rupert Walter Westmacott, who *d* 1989. *Residence* – Oaken Holt, Farmoor, Oxford.

PREDECESSORS – **(1)** THOMAS Burgh, *de jure* 5th Baron Strabolgi, son of Sir Edward Burgh, MP for co Lincoln (who is held to have succeeded to the Barony of Strabolgi as 4th Baron in 1496); summoned to Parliament as Lord Burgh, of Gainsborough, co Lincoln 1529: *m* 1st, 1496, Agnes, da of Sir William Tyrwhitt; 2ndly, 15—, Alice, da of William London, and widow (1) of Sir Thomas Bedingfeld, and (2) of Edmund Rokewood; *d* 1550; *s* by his el surviving son **(2)** WILLIAM, 2nd Baron Burgh, and *de jure* 6th Baron Strabolgi; summoned to Parliament as Lord Burgh 1551-80: *m* 15—, Catherine, da of Edward, Earl of Lincoln; *d* 1584; *s* by his el surviving son **(3)** THOMAS, KG, 3rd Baron Burgh, and *de jure* 7th Baron Strabolgi; summoned to Parliament as Lord Burgh 1584- 97; Ambassador to Scotland 1593, and Lord Dep of Ireland 1597: *m* 15—, Frances, da of John Vaughan, of Sutton-on-Derwent, and his da Elizabeth *m* George Brooke (see B Cobham); *d* 1597; *s* by his el surviving son **(4)** ROBERT, 4th Baron Burgh, and *de jure* 8th Baron Strabolgi; *dsp* (about) 1600, when the Baronies fell into abeyance between his four sisters, among whose decendants they so remained until the abeyances were determined in 1916, the Barony of Burgh being called out of abeyance in favour of **(5)** ALEXANDER HENRY Leith, 5th Baron son of late Gen Robert William Disney Leith, CB, by Mary Charlotte Julia, who *d* 1926, da of Sir Henry Percy Gordon, 2nd Bt, FRS, *cr* 1818 (*ext*), by Lady Mary Agnes Blanche, da of 3rd Earl of Ashburnham, *b* 1866: also established his claim before Committee for Privileges of House of Lords as senior co-heir to the Baronies of Burgh and Cobham 1912, and to the Barony of Strabolgi 1914, and in 1916 the abeyance in the Barony of Burgh was determined in his favour: *m* 1st, 1893, Mildred Catherine, who *d* 1894, el da of late Gen Stuart Nicholson, CB: 2ndly, 1902, Phyllis, who *d* 1972, da of Col Mark Goldie, RE; *d* 1926: *s* by his son **(6)** ALEXANDER LEIGH HENRY, 6th Baron; *b* 1906; Lieut Black Watch: *m* 1st 1934 (*m diss* 1943), Elizabeth Rose, who *d* 1981 (having *m* 2ndly, 1943 (*m diss* 19—), Sqdn-Ldr Herbert Benjamin (Micky) Bell-Syer, AFC, who *d* 1999), da of late Arthur Rose Vincent, CBE; 2ndly, 1947, Joyce Watts (who *m* 2ndly, 1960, Rupert Walter Westmacott), da of W. Wilson Wilson, of 10 Curzon Rd, Hoylake, Cheshire; *d* 1959; *s* by his el son **(7)** ALEXANDER PETER WILLOUGHBY 7th Baron and present peer.

Burghley, Lord; son of Marquess of Exeter.

Burlington, Earl of; grandson of Duke of Devonshire.

BURLISON, BARON (Burlison) (Life Baron 1997)

THOMAS HENRY (TOM) BURLISON, son of Robert Burlison, of Sacriston, co Durham; *b* 23 May 1936; *ed* Edmondsley, co Durham; panel beater 1951-57; professional footballer 1953-65; served in RAF 1959-61; General and Municipal Workers' Union, then General, Municipal, Boilermakers and Allied Trades Union, later GMB; Regional Officer 1965-78, Regional Sec 1978-91, Dep Gen Sec GMB 1991-97; Treasurer, Labour Party 1992-96; DL Tyne and Wear 1997; *cr Baron Burlison*, of Rowlands Gill, co Tyne and Wear (Life Baron) 1997: *m* 1981, Valerie, da of Robert Stephenson, of Newcastle upon Tyne, and has issue, two sons and one da.
Residence – c/o House of Lords, Westminster SW1A 0PW.

BURNHAM, BARON (Lawson) (Baron UK 1903, Bt UK 1892)

OF · OLD · I · HOLD

HUGH JOHN FREDERICK LAWSON, 6th Baron, and 6th Baronet; *b* 15 Aug 1931; *s* 1993; *ed* Eton, and Balliol Coll, Oxford (MA); late Lieut Scots Guards: *m* 1955, Hilary Margaret, yr da of late Alan Hunter, of Huntingtowerfield House, Almondbank, Perthshire, and has issue.

Arms – Quarterly: 1st and 4th azure, three bars geme, argent, over all a winged morion or; 2nd and 3rd gules, a saltire double parted and fretted or between in fesse two rams' heads, couped in fesse argent. **Crests** – 1st, in, front of a terrestrial globe proper a winged morion or; 2nd a ram argent holding in the mouth a trefoil slipped vert and resting the dexter fore leg on a quatrefoil or. **Supporters** – *Dexter*, the figure of Clio, the Muse of history proper; *sinister*, the figure of Hermes vested argent, mantled azure; on the head a winged morion, on his heels wings, and in his exterior hand a caduceus or.
Residence – Woodlands Farm, Beaconsfield, Bucks HP9 2SF. *Clubs* – Pratt's, Royal Yacht Squadron.

SON LIVING

Hon HARRY FREDERICK ALAN, *b* 22 Feb 1968; *ed* Eton.

DAUGHTERS LIVING

Hon Charlotte Ann, *b* 1960.
Hon Emma Lucia, *b* 1961.

DAUGHTERS LIVING OF FIFTH BARON

Hon Jenefer Anne, *b* 1949: *m* 1985, Andrew David Farncombe, son of George Frank Farncombe, of Ipswich, Suffolk, and has issue living, Frederick Alexander Edward, *b* 1987, — Joanna Abigail, *b* 1990. *Residence* – Hall Barn, Windsor End, Beaconsfield, Bucks HP9 2SG.

Hon Harriet Mary, *b* 1954: *m* 1984, Marino Sain, only son of Silvano Sain, of Trieste, Italy, and has issue living, Thomas Andrea, *b* 1987, — Giacomo Julian Lawson, *b* 1991, — Harry Benjamin, *b* 1994, — Teresa Anna, *b* (twin) 1994. *Residence* – via Ciamician 10, Trieste 34124, Italy.

Hon Sarah Jane, *b* 1955; resumed her maiden name 1991 until remarriage: *m* 1st, 1982 (*m diss* 1991), Michael Ian Grade; 2ndly, 1992, David Patrick Maher, and has issue living (by 2nd *m*), Edward James Lawson, *b* 1997. *Residences* – 5 Sussex Mews East, W2 2TS; Ardbraccan House, Navan, co Meath.

SISTER LIVING

Hon Lucia Edith, (Hallin, 18 Burnham Av, Beaconsfield, Bucks HP9 2JA), *b* 1922; European War 1939-45 in France and Germany as Co Sergeant-Maj ATS (despatches): *m* 1st, 1946 (*m diss* 1953), Hon Roger David Marquis (later 2nd Earl of Woolton), who *d* 1969; 2ndly, 1966, John Whitehead, who *d* 1982.

PREDECESSORS

PREDECESSORS – **(1)** *Sir* EDWARD Levy-Lawson, KCVO, son of late Joseph Moses Levy, JP, one of the principal founders of the Cheap Press in London; *b* 1833; was principal proprietor of the *Daily Telegraph*; assumed by R Licence 1875 the surname of Lawson in addition to and after that of Levy; *cr* a *Baronet* 1892, and *Baron Burnham*, of Hall Barn, Beaconsfield, Buckinghamshire (peerage of United Kingdom) 1903: *m* 1862, Harriette Georgiana, who *d* 1897, da of late Benjamin N. Webster, of Pen-y-craig, co Denbigh; *d* 1916; *s* by his eldest son **(2)** HARRY LAWSON WEBSTER, GCMG, CH, 2nd Baron, *b* 1862; sometime Principal Proprietor of the *Daily Telegraph*, and Chm of Newspaper Proprietors' Asso; Pres of Institute of Journalists 1910, and a Member of Indian Statutory Commn 1927-30; *cr Viscount Burnham*, of Hall Barn, co Buckingham (peerage of United Kingdom) 1919: *m* 1884, Olive, who *d* 1939, da of Gen Sir Henry Percival de Bathe, 4th Bt; *d* 1933, when the Viscountcy became ext and the Barony and Baronetcy passed to his brother **(3)** WILLIAM ARNOLD WEBSTER, DSO, 3rd Baron, *b* 1864; Capt Scots Guards and Lieut-Col and Brevet Col Bucks Yeo; S Africa 1900-1901 (DSO): *m* 1887 (*m diss* 1912), Sybil Mary, who *d* 1933, da of late Lieut-Gen Sir Frederick Marshall, KCMG; *d* 1943, *s* by his el son **(4)** EDWARD FREDERICK, CB, DSO, MC, TD, 4th Baron, *b* 1890; Maj-Gen TA; CRA 48th (S Midland Div) TA 1938-41, and GOC Yorkshire Div 1941-2, and Dir of Public Relations War Office and Senior Mil Adviser, Min of Information 1942-5: *m* 1920, Marie Enid, CBE, who *d* 1979, da of Hugh Scott Robson, of London, and Buenos Aires; *d* 1963; *s* by his el son **(5)** WILLIAM HARRY EDWARD, 5th Baron, *b* 1920; Lt-Col Scots Gds, comdg 1st Bn 1959-62; 1939-45 War in France, Middle East, N Africa and Italy; Malaya 1950-51 (despatches); DL Bucks: *m* 1942, Anne, who *d* 1998, 2nd da of late Maj George Gerald Petherick (*see* E Radnor, 1976 Edn); *d* 1993; *s* by his brother **(6)** HUGH JOHN FREDERICK, 6th Baron and present peer.

BURNS, BARON (Burns) (Life Baron 1998)

TERENCE BURNS, GCB, son of Patrick Owen Burns, of Hetton-le-Hole, co Durham; *b* 13 March 1944; *ed* Houghton-le-Spring Gram Sch, Manchester Univ (BA 1965), and London Business Sch; Chief Economic Adviser to HM Treasury and Head of Govt Economic Service 1980-91; Permanent Sec, HM Treasury 1991-98; Vice-Pres Soc of Business Economists since 1985, and Royal Economic Soc since 1992; Memb Board of Management, Manchester Business Sch 1993-98; Fell of London Business Sch since 1989; Visiting Fell, Nuffield Coll, Oxford 1991-97; Dir Queens Park Rangers FC; CIMgt 1992; *cr* Kt 1983, GCB 1995, and *Baron Burns*, of Pitshanger in the London Borough of Ealing (Life Baron) 1998: *m* 1969, Anne Elizabeth, da of William Morgan Jones Powell, of Brecon, and has issue.

Address – House of Lords, Westminster, SW1A 0PW. *Club* – Reform.

SON LIVING

Hon Thomas Michael, *b* 1973.

DAUGHTERS LIVING

Hon Katharine, *b* 1971.
Hon Emily Sarah, *b* 1976.

BURNTWOOD, BARONY OF (Snow) (Extinct 1982)

DAUGHTER LIVING OF LIFE BARON

Hon Harriet Louise Julia, *b* 1950; assumed the forenames of Flavia Hazlitt in lieu of Louise Julia by deed poll 1982.

BURTON, BARON (Baillie) (Baron UK 1897)

What is brighter than the stars ?

MICHAEL EVAN VICTOR BAILLIE, 3rd Baron; *b* 27 June 1924; *s* 1962; *ed* Eton; late Lieut Scots Gds and Lovat Scouts: *m* 1st, 1948 (*m diss* 1977), (Elizabeth) Ursula Forster, who *d* 1993, da of late Capt Anthony Forster Wise; 2ndly, 1978, Coralie Denise, da of late Claud R. Cliffe, and has had issue by 1st *m.*

Arms – Quarterly, 1st and 4th azure, nine stars, three, three, two and one argent, within a border engrailed or, charged with six cinquefoils of the field, *Baillie*; 2nd and 3rd, gules on a chevron cottised argent between three plates each charged with a fleur-de-lys azure, a demi lion couped of the first, *Bass*. **Crest** – A boar's head couped argent, armed or, langued gules. **Supporters** – On either side a lion reguardant sable each charged on the shoulder with a plate thereon a fleur-de-lys azure and resting the inner hind leg on a stag's head caboshed proper.
Residence – Dochgarroch Lodge, Inverness. *Clubs* – Cavalry and Guards', New (Edinburgh) and Pratt's.

SONS LIVING (By 1st marriage)

Hon EVAN MICHAEL RONALD *b* 19 March 1949; *ed* Harrow: *m* 1970 (*m diss* 1984), Lucinda Anne, el da of Robert Law, of Turnpike House, Withersfield, Haverhill, Suffolk, and has issue living, James Evan, *b* 3 Dec 1975, — Hamish Michael, *b* 1979, — Emma Elizabeth, *b* 1977. Resides in Australia.

Hon Alexander James, *b* 1963; *ed* Eton: *m* 1998, Gigina PARENTE-ADDISON, da of Dr John Thomas Parente, of Palm Beach, Florida, USA, and of late Mrs Archibald Randall George Addison, of Monikie, Angus, and has issue living, Isabella Victoria *b* 1999. *Residences* – The Gables, Rangemore, Burton-on-Trent, Staffs; Dochfour, Inverness.

DAUGHTERS LIVING AND DECEASED (By 1st marriage)

Hon Elizabeth Victoria, *b* 1950: *m* 1970, Hon Angus Grenfell Maclay, of Whitelee, Newtown St Boswells, Roxburghshire, and *d* 1986, leaving issue (*see* B Maclay).

Hon Philippa Ursula Maud, *b* 1951: *m* 1980, R. Ian McCowen, and has issue living, Ewan, *b* 1981, — Christopher Richard, *b* 1983. *Residence* – Polwarth Manse, Greenlaw, Berwickshire.

Hon Georgina Frances, *b* 1955: *m* 1998, Hugh Leopold Seymour (*see* M Hertford, colls). *Residence* – Home Farm, Stobo, Peebles.

Hon Fiona Mary, *b* 1957: *m* 1982, Alasdair Malcolm Douglas Macleod Hilleary (*see* D Hamilton and Brandon, 1985 Edn), and has issue living, Geordie, *b* 1991, — Flora Elizabeth Macleod, *b* 1985, — Rosannagh Catriona, *b* 1988. *Residence* – Greenhill House, Redcastle, Muir of Ord, Ross-shire.

BROTHER LIVING (Raised to the rank of a Baron's son 1964)

Hon Peter Charles, *b* 1927; *ed* Eton; late Maj The Life Gds; a JP of Hants: *m* 1955, Jennifer Priscilla, da of late Com Harold Reginald Newgass, GC, of Winterborne, W Stafford, Dorset, and has issue living, Catriona Margaret, *b* 1956: *m* 1998, Christakis Charalambous, — Elizabeth Mary Eilidh, *b* 1959: *m* 1st, 1982, Michael Halstead-Morton, who *d* 1995; 2ndly, 1998, Philip John Clabburn, of Knold, Lymore Lane, Keyhaven, Lymington, Hants, and has issue living (by 1st *m*), Hannah Elizabeth *b* 1983, Emily Victoria *b* 1985, — Susan Jennifer, *b* 1960: *m* 1989, Capt Christopher Rushworth, RAOC, and has issue living, William Christopher *b* 1993, — Rachel Emma, *b* 1963. *Residence* – Wootton Hall, New Milton, Hants BH25 5SJ.

SISTER LIVING (Raised to the rank of a Baron's daughter 1964)

Hon Judith Evelyn Maud, *b* 1925; formerly in ATS: *m* 1949, Lt-Col Angus Cameron, MC, Scots Gds, and has issue living, Angus Iain (Drummond, Dores, by Inverness), *b* 1952: *m* 1973, Candida, da of late Ronald T. Fryer Smith, of 8 Fulwood Park, Liverpool 17, and has issue living, Lorien *b* 1975, Fiona *b* 1978, — Hester Caroline, *b* 1950. *Residence* – Aldourie Castle, Inverness.

COLLATERAL BRANCH LIVING

Granddaughters of late Maj Hon Arthur Malcolm Augustus Baillie, yr son of late Nellie Lisa, Baroness Burton:—
Issue of late Lt-Col Ian Bruce Baillie, *b* 1928, *d* 1978: *m* 1962, June Marion Cloudesley (Congham Lodge, Hillington, King's Lynn, Norfolk PE31 6BZ), da of Arthur Cloudesley Smith, FRCS, and widow of (Arthur) Henry Bellingham (*see* Bellingham, Bt, colls):—
Katherine Victoria Harriet, *b* 1962: *m* 1990, (John) Benjamin Agnew Wallace, of Old Farm, Potsgrove, Beds MK17 9HQ, only son of (John) Malcolm Agnew Wallace, of Lochryan, Stranraer, Wigtownshire (*see* B Bagot, colls, 1965 Edn), and has issue living, Alexander Ian Agnew, *b* 1992, — Hewie Malcolm Agnew, *b* 1993, — Lara, *b* 1996. ———— Sarah Rosemary Caroline, *b* 1964.

PREDECESSORS – (1) Sir MICHAEL ARTHUR BASS, KVCO, el son of late Michael Thomas Bass, MP for Derby 1848-83; *b* 1837; a Director of Bass, Ratcliff, Gretton and Co (Limited), of Burton-on-Trent; MP for Stafford (*L*) 1865-8, for E Staffordshire 1868-85, and for Burton Div of Staffordshire 1885-6; *cr* a *Baronet* 1882, *Baron Burton*, of Rangemore and Burton-on-Trent, co Stafford (peerage of United Kingdom) 1886, and *Baron Burton*, of Burton-on-Trent, and of Rangemore, co Stafford (peerage of United Kingdom) 1897, with special remainder, in default of issue male, to his da and her male issue: *m* 1869, Harriet Georgina, who *d* 1931, da of late E. Thornewill, of Dove Cliff, co Stafford; *d* 1909; when the Barony (*cr* 1896) became *ext*, the baronetcy passed to his nephew, William Arthur Hamar Bass, and the Barony (*cr* 1897) devolved under the special remainder upon his da (2) NELLIE LISA, *b* 1873: *m* 1st, 1894, Col James Evan Bruce Baillie, MVO, RHA (TF), who *d* 1931; 2ndly 1932, Maj William Eugene Melles, who *d* 1953; *d* 1962; *s* by her grandson (3) MICHAEL EVAN VICTOR (son of late Brig Hon (George) Evan Michael BAILLIE, MC, TD, who *d* on active ser 1941), 3rd Baron and present peer.

BUSCOMBE, BARONESS (Buscombe) (Life Baroness 1998)

PETA JANE BUSCOMBE, da of Terence O'Flynn; *b* 12 March 1954; *ed* Hinchley Wood Sch, Rosebery Gram Sch, and Inns of Court Sch of Law; Bar 1977; Legal Adviser to The Dairy Trade Federation 1980; Lawyer with Barclays Bank International 1980-83; Institute of Practitioners in Advertising 1983-87; Memb S Oxfordshire Dist Council (C) since 1995; Vice-Chm S Oxfordshire Conservative Assoc 1995-98; Pres Slough Conservative Assoc since 1997; Patron Inns of Court Sch of Law Conservative Soc since 1998; Vice-Patron Abbeyfield House Appeal on Behalf of Abbeyfield Reading Soc Ltd since 1998; Pres S Oxfordshire Conservative Policy Forum since 1998; *cr Baroness Buscombe*, of Goring, co Oxfordshire (Life Baroness) 1998: *m* 1980, Philip John Buscombe, son of John Henry Buscombe, of Frensham, Surrey, and has issue.
Address – c/o House of Lords, Westminster, SW1A 0PW. *Clubs* – Carlton, Sloane.

SONS LIVING

Hon Christopher John Henry, *b* 1988.
Hon Leo Nicholas Philip, *b* (twin) 1988.

DAUGHTER LIVING

Hon Nathalie Jane, *b* 1987.

BUTE, MARQUESS OF (Crichton-Stuart) (Marquess GB 1796, Bt S 1627)

He flourishes in an honourable ancestory

JOHN COLUM CRICHTON-STUART, 7th Marquess, and 12th Baronet; *b* 26 April 1958; *s* 1993; Hereditary Sheriff and Coroner of co Bute, Hereditary Keeper of Rothesay Castle, and patron of nine livings; professional racing driver (as Johnny Dumfries) 1980-91, British Formula 3 Champion, and runner up in FIA European Formula 3 Championship 1984, joint winner Le Mans 1988: *m* 1st, 1984 (*m diss* 1993), Carolyn, da of late Bryson Waddell; 2ndly, 1999, Serena, da of Maj Jac Wendell, Grenadier Gds, and of Lady Rees, and formerly wife of Robert Delisser, and has issue by 1st and 2nd *m*.

Arms – Quarterly: 1st and 4th or a fesse checky azure and argent, within a double tressure flory counterflory gules, and in dexter chief of the first quarter a canton of Nova Scotia, *Stuart*; 2nd and 3rd argent, a lion rampant azure, armed and langued gules, *Crichton*; behind the shield are placed in saltire a key or, having within its handle a fesse checky azure and argent, and a rod gules surmounted of a tower argent masoned sable, conically capped loopholes and port gules (*Insignia of Office of Heritable Keeper*) a coronet. **Crests** – 1st a dragon vert, crowned with an open crown of four strawberry leaves langued or, *Crichton*; 2nd, a demi-lion rampant gules, armed and langued azure *Stuart*; 3rd, argent and azure, a wyvern proper, holding in the mouth a sinister hand couped gules (*for the Lordship and Fief of Cardiff*). **Supporters** – *Dexter*, a stag proper, attired or, gorged with an Earls coronet also proper, having therefrom a chain reflexed over the back gules ; *sinister*, a horse argent, bridled gules.
Seat – Mount Stuart, Rothesay, Isle of Bute.

SON LIVING (By 1st marriage)

JOHN BRYSON (*Lord Mount Stuart*), *b* 21 Dec 1989.

DAUGHTERS LIVING (By 1st marriage)

Lady Caroline, *b* 1984.
Lady Cathleen, *b* 1986.

(By 2nd marriage)

Lady ......, *b* 1999.

BROTHER LIVING

Lord Anthony, *b* 1961; *ed* Ampleforth, and Durham Univ; with Christie's, New York: *m* 1990, Alison J., yr da of Keith Bruce, of Highgate, NW6, and has issue living, Flora Grace, *b* 1994, — Eliza Rose, *b* 1996 .

SISTERS LIVING AND DECEASED

Lady Sophia Anne, *b* 1956; resumed her maiden name 1988 until remarriage: *m* 1st, 1979 (*m diss* 1988), Jimmy Bain; 2ndly 1990, as his 2nd wife, Alexius John Benedict Fenwick (*see* B Lilford, colls), and has issue living (by 1st *m*), Samantha Ella, *b* 1981, — (by 2nd *m*) Georgia Jessie, *b* 1990.
Lady (Eileen) Caroline, *b* 1957; *k* in a motor accident 1984.

AUNT LIVING (daughter of 5th Marquess)

Lady (Caroline Moira) Fiona, *b* 1941: *m* 1959, Capt Michael Lowsley-Williams, 16/5th Lancers (*see* Makins, Bt, 1967 Edn), and has issue living, Patrick David Edward, *b* 1960, — Mark Ogden Francis, *b* 1961, — Paul John Fermin, *b* 1964, — Michael Charles Javier, *b* 1967.

WIDOWS LIVING OF SONS OF FIFTH MARQUESS

Helen (*Lady David Crichton-Stuart*) (Kames Court, Cronkbourne, Braddan, Isle of Man), da of William Kerr McColl: *m* 1972, Lord David Ogden Crichton-Stuart, who *d* 1977, and has issue (see colls, infra).

Anna-Rose, da of late Maj Henry McClintock Bunbury Bramwell, of The White House, Mallow, co Cork (*see* B Rathdonnell, 1962 Edn): *m* 1st, 1970, as his 2nd wife, Lord James Charles Crichton-Stuart, who *d* 1982; 2ndly, 1992, Peter Merrick Knatchbull-Hugessen (*see* B Brabourne, colls), and has issue (by 1st *m*) (see colls, infra). *Residence* – Ropley House, Ropley, Hants SO24 0EB.

WIDOW LIVING OF SON OF FOURTH MARQUESS

Lady Janet Egidia Montgomerie (*Lady Robert Crichton-Stuart*) (Wards Cottage, Gartocharn, Dunbartonshire), da of 16th Earl of Eglinton and Winton: *m* 1934, Capt Lord Robert Crichton-Stuart, who *d* 1976, and has issue (see colls, infra).

MOTHER LIVING

(Beatrice) Nicola Grace, only da of late Lt-Cdr Wolstan Beaumont Charles Weld-Forester, CBE, RN (*see* B Forester, colls): *m* 1955 (*m diss* 1977), as his 1st wife, the 6th Marquess of Bute, who *d* 1993.

WIDOW LIVING OF SIXTH MARQUESS

JENNIFER (*Marchioness of Bute*), da of late John Brougham Home-Rigg, of Tarvit, Cupar, Fife, and formerly wife of Gerald Percy (*see* D Northumberland, colls): *m* 1978, as his 2nd wife, the 6th Marquess of Bute, KBE, who *d* 1993. *Residence* – 2 Cottesmore Gdns, W8 5PR.

COLLATERAL BRANCHES LIVING

Issue of late Lord David Ogden Crichton-Stuart, 2nd son of 5th Marquess, *b* (twin) 1933, *d* 1977: *m* 1972, Helen (ante), da of William Kerr McColl:—
Kenneth Edward David, *b* 1975. —— Elizabeth Rose, *b* 1973.

Issue of late Lord James Charles Crichton-Stuart, 3rd son of 5th Marquess, *b* 1935, *d* 1982: *m* 1st, 1959 (*m diss* 1968), Sarah Frances, only da of Lt-Col Arthur Edward Croker-Poole, of 19 Launceston Place, W8; 2ndly, 1970, Anna-Rose (ante) (who *m* 2ndly, 1992, Peter Merrick Knatchbull-Hugessen) (*see* B Brabourne, colls), da of late Maj Henry McClintock Bunbury Bramwell, of The White House, Mallow, co Cork (*see* B Rathdonnell, 1962 Edn):—
(By 2nd *m*) William Henry, *b* 1971. —— Hugh Bertram, *b* 1973. —— Alexander Blane, *b* 1982.

Issue of late Capt Lord Robert Crichton-Stuart, 2nd son of 4th Marquess, *b* 1909, *d* 1976: *m* 1934, Lady Janet Egidia Montgomerie (ante), da of 16th Earl of Eglinton and Winton:—
†Ninian, *b* 1935; *d* 1992. —— Henry Colum (19 Milton St, Edinburgh 8), *b* 1938: *m* 1963 (*m diss* 1985), Patricia Margaret, only da of late Brig Hugh Ronald Norman, DSO, of Lower St Clere, Kemsing, Kent, and has issue living, Alexander Colum, *b* 1967, — Camilla, *b* 1964: *m* 1994, Capt Andreas M. F. Carleton-Smith, MC, RGJ, 2nd son of Maj-Gen Sir Michael Edward Carleton-Smith, CBE, and has issue living, Joshua Michael *b* 1998, — Serena, *b* 1965: *m* 1993, Morgan Jonathan Watts, son of Dennis Watts, — Teresa Clare, *b* 1971: *m* 1995, Toby P. C. Mermagen, yst son of late Flight Lieut T. F. H. Mermagen, and of Mrs Alistair Kilburn.

Issue of late Lord David STUART, 3rd son of 4th Marquess, *b* 1911; discontinued use of surname of Crichton by decree of Lord Lyon 1934; *d* 1970: *m* 1940, Ursula Sybil CLIFTON, who *d* 1989, formerly wife of Peter Thomas Clifton (*see* Bruce, Bt, *cr* 1904), and da of late Sir Edward Hussey Packe, KBE (By Colebrooke):—
Flora, *b* 1941. *Residence* – The Old Place of Mochrum, Wigtownshire.

Issue of late Lord Patrick Crichton-Stuart, 4th son of 4th Marquess, *b* 1913, *d* 1956: *m* 1st, 1937, Jane, who *d* 1944, da of Capt von Bahr, of Stockholm, Sweden; 2ndly, 1947, Linda Irene, who *d* 1974, only da of William Evans, of St Mellons, Monmouth:—
(By 1st *m*) Charles Patrick Colum Henry (16 Douglas Court, West End Lane, NW6), *b* 1939; *ed* Ampleforth; late RAF; Flying Instructor, London Sch of Flying, Elstree, and Racing Driver: *m* 1st, 1967 (*m diss* 19—), Shirley Anne Field, the actress; 2ndly, 1980, Jennifer A. A. Collie, and has issue living (by 1st *m*), Nicola Jane, *b* 1967, — (by 2nd *m*) Patrick James, *b* 1982, — Sophie, *b* 1980. —— Angela Mary Monica (Watermans Lodge House, Charlbury, Oxon), *b* 1940: *m* 1963, Simon Mark Pilkington (*see* B Faringdon, colls).

Issue of late Capt Lord Rhidian Crichton-Stuart, RA, yst son of 4th Marquess, *b* 1917, *d* 1969: *m* 1939, Selina, who *d* 1985, da of Frederick Gerth Van Wijk, late Min Plen for the Netherlands in Paris:—
Frederick John Patrick (6 Huntly St, Edinburgh), TD, *b* 1940; a Kt of Sovereign Mil Order of Malta: *m* 1964, Elizabeth Jane Douglas, el da of Ernest J. Whitson, and has issue living, Rhidian Colum, *b* 1967: *m* 1997, Claire F. Stead, — Edward Neil James, *b* 1974, — Ione Jane, *b* 1965, — Amanda Mary, *b* 1968. —— (Jerome) Niall Anthony (2 Oake Court, Portinscale Rd, SW15 2HU), *b* 1948; Maj Scots Gds; a Kt of Sovereign Mil Order of Malta; Memb Queen's Body Guard for Scotland (Royal Co of Archers); Chevalier du Wissam Alouite (Royaume du Maroc): *m* 1971, Susan, el da of Prof Patrick Dwyer-Joyce, of Errislannan, Sandycove, co Dublin, and has issue living, Rhidian Charles Patrick, *b* 1974, — Niall Rollo Robert, *b* 1977, — Archie Michael John, *b* 1984. —— (Mary) Margot Patricia, *b* 1942: *m* 1962, Edward Henry Lovell, and has issue living, Peter Henry James, *b* 1965; *ed* Ampleforth, — Nicola Mary, *b* 1963, — Henrietta Margaret, *b* 1971.

Grandchildren of late Lt-Col Lord Ninian Edward Crichton-Stuart, MP, Welch Regt, 2nd son of 3rd Marquess:—
Issue of late Maj Michael Duncan David Crichton Stuart, MC, b 1915, d 1981: m 1941, Barbara, who d 1985, only da of late Lt-Col Sir (George) Stewart Symes, GBE, KCMG, DSO:—
Ninian John (Moncreiff House, High St, Falkland, Fife KY7 7BP), b 1957; Hereditary Keeper of Falkland Palace: m 1982, Anne Marie, da of Neil O'Donnell, of Dowanhill, Glasgow, and has issue living, Francis Paul, b 1984, — Christina Marie, b 1983. —— Elspeth Ann, b 1954: m 1981, Prof Thomas Puttfarken, of Annandale, Anglesea Rd, Wivenhoe, nr Colchester, Essex. —— The late Maj Michael D. D. Crichton Stuart also adopted two das, Mary (Marietta) Frances (4 Fitzwilliam Rd, Clapham Old Town, SW4), b 1951. —— Frances Elizabeth (6 Cadogan House, Beaufort St, SW3), b 1951; painter.

Grandchildren of late Capt Patrick James Crichton-Stuart, Gren Gds, only son of late Lt-Col James Frederick Dudley Crichton-Stuart, MP, Gren Gds, elder son of Lord Patrick James Herbert Crichton-Stuart, MP (who was granted the rank and precedence of the younger son of a Marquess 1817), 2nd son of John, Lord Mountstuart, eldest son of 1st Marquess:—
Issue of late Maj Patrick Dudley Crichton-Stuart, b 1909, d 1978: m 1948, Sheila Mary, who d 1999, da of Lt Col James Douglas Kendall Restler, OBE:—
(Patrick) James (1 Sloane Gdns, SW1W 8EA), b 1954; ed Downside; Lieut Scots Gds (Res): m 1st, 1978 (m diss 1982), Amanda Mary Howell, eldest da of Michael Pollock Howell Williams, of Cosford House, Thursley, Surrey; 2ndly, 1991, Lady Rowena Katherine Meade, elder da of 7th Earl of Clanwilliam, and has issue living (by 1st m), Frederick James, b 1981, — Katherine Rose, b 1979, — (by 2nd m), Rory Torquhil, b 1995. —— Caroline Mary Katherine, MVO, b 1949; MVO 1990: m 1993, Antony Frederick Gandolfi Hornyold, 4th Duke Gandolfi (see B Mowbray, colls).

Granddaughter of late Lt-Col Henry John Richard Villiers-Stuart, el son of Capt William Villiers-Stuart, MP, 2nd son of Lord Henry Stuart, 5th son of 1st Marquess:—
Issue of late Col John Patrick Villiers-Stuart, CB, DSO, OBE, b 1879, d 1958: m 1st, 1914, Phyllis Mary, who d 1933, da of late James Read; 2ndly, 1933, Eileen Nora, who d 1995, da of late Col Alexander John Maunsell MacLaughlin, CIE, of Derryheen, Hook Heath, Woking:—
(By 1st m) Stella, b 1918; formerly Assist Section Officer, WAAF: m 1st, 1941, Squadron-Leader Donald Maitland Wellings, DFC, RAF (ka during 1939-45 War) 1944; 2ndly, 1949, Lt-Col Anthony Hamilton Gerald Barton, MC, late RA, of Manesty Cottage, The Green, Fernhurst, Haslemere, Surrey, and has issue living, (by 1st m) Donald James (98 Netherwood Rd, W14), b 1942, — (by 2nd m) Patrick Anthony Richard (Langmere Hall, Langmere, Diss, Norfolk IP21 4PF), b 1956: m 1980, Jennifer Ann, da of Anthony R. Lucas, of Moyles Wood, Farnham Lane, Haslemere, Surrey, and has issue living, Hamish Anthony b 1987, Angus Patrick b 1990, Sophie Caroline b 1993, — Julia Penelope Susan (Flat 3, 1 Veronica Rd, SW17 8QR), b 1950.

Grandchildren of late Col John Patrick Villiers-Stuart, CB, DSO, OBE (ante):—
Issue of late Maj John Michael Villiers-Stuart, b 1927, d 1986: m 1960, Bridget Mary (11 East St, Wareham, Dorset), da of Lt-Col Patrick Grant, of Knockie, Whitebridge, Inverness-shire:—
Michael Patrick (Gothic Cottage, 393 Harborne Rd, Edgbaston B15 3LB), b 1961: m 1986, Caroline Mary, elder da of David Richard Marsh, of Middleton-by-Youlgreave, Derbys, and has issue living, Archie James, b 1992, — Angus Theodore b 1994, — Katharine Amelia, b 1990. —— Marianne Serena, b 1963: m 1st, 1986 (m diss 1993), Oliver John Nicholson; 2ndly, 1994, Michael Thomas Donnelly, of Tunbridge Wells, Kent, and has issue living (by 1st m), Natasha Elizabeth, b 1986.

Grandchildren of late Com Dudley Charles Stuart, RN, elder son of late Henry Stuart, only son of Rear-Adm Lord George Stuart, CB, 7th son of 1st Marquess:—
Issue of late Com Evclyn Charles Henry Stuart, RN, b 1875, d (16 Dec) 1944: m 1906, Anna Maria Knutzen Grane, who d (14 June) 1944:—
Dudley Evelyn, b 1907. —— Amy Ingeborg Sybil Eda, b 1911.

Issue of late Eric Hoy Stuart, b 1890, d 1950: m 1918 (Dorothie) Primrose (who d 1982, having m 2ndly, 1958, as his 3rd wife, Hon Michael Scott, OBE, who d 1959 (see E Eldon) and 3rdly, 1969, Surg Vice-Adm Sir Clarence Edward Greeson, KBE, CB, who d 1979), da of Maj Murray-Stewart:—
(Patricia) Elizabeth b 1923: m 1st, 1946 (m diss 1950), Thomas Daniel; 2ndly, 1972, Lt-Cmdr Philip Baxendale, OBE, RD, who d 1986, and has issue living (by 1st m), Timothy Hugh, b 1946: m 1973, Sara Nancy Hood-Daniel, and has issue living, Hugo Charles b 1983, Emily Sara b 1975, Josephine Polly b 1977, Olivia Zoe b 1984.

In remainder to the Earldom of Bute only.

Descendants of late Rt Hon James Archibald STUART-WORTLEY (son of Hon James Archibald Stuart, 2nd son of 3rd Earl of Bute), who was cr Baron Wharncliffe 1820 (see E Wharncliffe).

In remainder to the Earldom of Dumfries only.

Grandchildren of late John Crichton Stuart McDouall, OBE b (1878) (infra):—
Issue of late Maj John Crichton Stuart McDouall, R Sigs, b 1920, d 1951: m 1945, Dorothy Anne (who m 2ndly, 1954, Maj J. H. A. Bryden, RA, 61 Swanston Av, Edinburgh, EH10 7BZ), da of late Rev C. A. H. Going, of Shrewsbury:—
John Crichton Stuart (Flat 23, Block 8, Mansfield Rd, The Peak, Hong Kong), b 1950; Sr Superintendent Hong Kong Police: m 1975, Susanna Sze Wing-Lai, and has issue living, John Crichton Stuart, b 1976, — Patrick, b 1978. —— Philip Lewis (twin) (Box 580, RR2, Woodlawn, Ont, Canada K0A 3M0), b 1950; Marketing Dir Newbridge Networks Corp, Ottawa, Canada: m 1976, Marlis Bartels, and has issue living, Andrew Philip, b 1977, — James Stephen, b 1979, — Joanna Marie, b 1984. —— Patricia Anne, b 1945: m 1971, James Downing, of 106 Beauvista Drive, Sherwood Park, Alberta, Canada T8A 3X1, and has issue living, Frederick James, b 1972, — Timothy John, b 1979, — Sarah Frances, b

1975. —— Elizabeth Jean (4 Impasse Tarantaise 69300, Lyons, France), *b* 1947: *m* 1971 (*m diss* 1994), Jean Labaye, and has issue living, Jean Simon, *b* 1972, — Georges-Antoine, *b* 1982, — Victoria Anne, *b* 1974.

Grandchildren (by 1st *m*) of late Willoughby Crichton McDouall (*b* 1852), 5th son of John Crichton Stuart McDouall (*b* 1818), eldest son of Rev William M'Douall (*b* 1775), only son of John M'Douall, brother of 6th Earl of Dumfries:—
Issue of late John Crichton Stuart McDouall, OBE, *b* 1878; *d* 1941: *m* 1914, Marguerite Lavinia, who *d* 1950, da of Frank Garrett, of Highgate, N:—
Lewis Willoughby, *b* 1924: *m* 1964, Madeline, da of George Hall. *Address* – c/o Lloyds Bank, Sutton, Surrey. —— Marguerite Lavinia, *b* 1922: *m* 1941, Capt Ian Sibbald McCormick, MB, who *d* 1967, and has issue living, John Sibbald, *b* 1944: *m* 1975, Irene Marilyn, and has issue living, John Steven *b* 1981, David Charles *b* 1983, Jill Elaine *b* 1976, — Jennifer Anne, *b* 1943: *m* 1969, Kenneth Anthony Fleming, and has issue living, Stuart Kenneth *b* 1972, Andrew Michael *b* 1978, Anne Margaret *b* 1970, — Marguerite Lavinia, *b* 1948: *m* 1975, John Glen Abercromby, and has issue living, Andrew Frank *b* 1980, Jane *b* 1977, Carol Marguerite *b* 1983. *Residence* – 19 Durham Gdns, Lower Largo, Leven, Fife Y86 DU.

Grandchildren of late Rev Crichton Willoughby McDouall (infra):—
Issue of late John Crichton McDouall, CMG, *b* 1912, *d* 1979: *m* 1946, Kathleen Glover (4 Bicester House, King's End, Bicester, Oxon OX6 7DT), da of late Archibald Black Moir, of Isle of Wight:—
Brian John, *b* 1952: *m* 1978 (*m diss* 1989), Barbara May, da of Arnold Worth, of Manchester. —— Anne Glover (26 Barrett St, Oxford OX2 0AT), *b* 1948: *m* 1968 (*m diss* 1982), David Thomas Douglas James, PhD, and has issue living, Simon Alan, *b* 1969, — Annabel Louise, *b* 1971. —— Heather Crichton, *b* 1949; D Phil: *m* 1979, Robert Norman Swanson, PhD, of 106 Northfield Rd, Kings Norton, Birmingham, and has issue living, John Crichton Norman, *b* 1981, — Elizabeth Eleanor Crichton, *b* 1983.

Issue of late Kenneth Willoughby McDouall, *b* 1914, *d* 1995: *m* 1958, Edith Joan Sears (Greenways, 3 Mill Lane, Chinnor, Oxon OX9 4QU):—
Rhoda Mary, *b* 1959; PhD: *m* 1st, 1982 (*m diss* 1984), her 2nd cousin, Jeremy Stuart Stevenson (infra); 2ndly, 1992, Andrew Neil David Eagles, and has issue living (by 2nd *m*), Ellen Joanna, *b* 1996. *Residence* – Cotswold, 14 St John's Rd, Tylers Green, Penn, Bucks HP10 8HW.

Grandchildren of late Willoughby Crichton McDouall (*b* 1852) (ante):—
Issue of late Rev Crichton Willoughby McDouall, *b* 1881, *d* 1966: *m* 1st, 1911, Florence Charlotte, who *d* 1923, da of late William Bampfield Cogan, of Bristol; 2ndly, 1935, Jessie Kentish, who *d* 1979, da of late George Rudolf Cole, of Sheffield:—
(By 2nd *m*) David Christopher (8 Cranmer Rd, Cambridge), *b* 1936; *ed* Radley, and Jesus Coll, Camb (MA): *m* 1969, Veronica Mary, da of H. Earl Heighway, of Wyre Piddle, Worcs, and has issue living, Jonathan Crichton Stuart, *b* 1976, — Sara Frances, *b* 1972, — Fiona Mary, *b* 1974.

Issue of late Philip Hastings McDouall, *b* 1884, *d* 1978: *m* 1917, Ivy Harrie, who *d* 1987, da of Henry Charles Sanders, formerly PWD India:—
Philip John (8 Eastfield Orchard, Uffculme, Devon EX15 3AS), *b* 1924: *m* 1950, Hazel Rosemary, who *d* 1992, da of Charles Frederick Bowring, late RN, and has issue living, Andrew Crichton, *b* 1951: *m* 1977 (*m diss* 1984), Katherine, da of Rev G. Hardy, — Janet Mary (Bay Tree Cottage, Pit Court, N Nibley, Dursley, Glos), *b* 1953; has issue living, Hannah Caroline *b* 1993, — Ellen Margaret, *b* 1963. —— Margaret Heather (Rua do Rio da Bica 7, S Pedro de Sintra, Portugal), *b* 1920: *m* 1946, Leonardo Rey Colaço de Castro Freire, who *d* 1970, and has issue living, Martin Anthony (Rua Alexandre Herculano 91, Tomar, Portugal), *b* 1952: *m* 1982, Filipa Macedo, and has issue living, Manuel Felipe *b* 1984, Martim Afonso *b* 1986, — Jorge Leonardo (Rua Garcia de Orta 70-3°, Lisbon, Portugal), *b* 1956: *m* 1979, Ana Simões Pinto, and has issue living, Diogo *b* 1986, — Alexander Anthony (Rua Garcia de Orta 70, Lisbon, Portugal), *b* 1959: *m* 1984, Paula Vieira, and has issue living, Carolina *b* 1986, — Philippa Maria, *b* 1949: *m* 1972, João Manuel Rocheta, of Rua Garcia de Orta 70-2°, Lisbon, Portugal, and has issue living, Gonçalo *b* 1975, Rita *b* 1978, — Catarina Maria *b* 1954. —— Mabel Frances Harrie (1 Woodlands, Budleigh Salterton, Devon), *b* 1926: *m* 1985, Peter Haynes.

Issue of late Eric Oldfield McDouall, *b* 1886, *d* 1918: *m* 1913, Elizabeth Carpenter, who *d* 1954, da of Richard Morrish, of Lincoln, Canterbury, New Zealand:—
Ella Barbara (72 Wiggins St, Sumner, Christchurch 8, NZ), *b* 1914: *m* 1937, Rev Henry Jackson Eaton, who *d* 1991 and has issue living, Michael McDouall (Mountford, Wapara, N Canterbury, NZ), *b* 1937; *ed* Univ of NZ (Diplo in Fine Arts); FRSA: *m* 1st, 1962, Lynne Eleanor, who *d* 1986, da of Lester Heyward; 2ndly, 1993, Elizabeth Savill, and has issue living (by 1st *m*), Jonathan Heyward McDouall *b* 1964; LLB: *m* 1994, Fiona Smith, Benjamin Herriot McDouall *b* 1967, Penelope Jane *b* 1962: *m* 1985, William David Thomas (and has issue living, James William Grigg *b* 1986, Georgina Lynne *b* 1988, Rosa Virginia *b* 1990), Sarah Lynne *b* 1969, — Rt Rev Derek Lionel, QSM, *b* 1941; MA, Dip Theol, TTC, Bishop of Nelson, NZ; QSM 1985: *m* 1964, Alice Janice, da of George Maslin, and has issue living, Simeon Michael *b* 1968, Stephen Daniel *b* 1969, Rebecca Ann *b* 1971: *m* 1992, Andrew Robert Burgess.

Issue of late Gerald William McDouall, *b* 1887, *d* 1969: *m* 1920, Dora Olive, who *d* 1975, da of Arthur Alexander McKinnon of Oamaru, NZ:—
Eric Willoughby (5 Catamaran Close, Warsash, Southampton SO31 9AS), *b* 1921: *m* 1944, Marion Maud, da of J. Holder, of Tetbury, Glos, and has issue living Maurice Willoughby (37 Birchway Place, Acton, Ont, Canada L7J 2X4), *b* 1945: *m* 1st, 1967 (*m diss* 1990), Bernice Towers, da of Lindon Towers Cunliffe, of Fareham; 2ndly, 1995, Sharon Janice Laff, and has issue living (by 1st *m*), Fiona Bernice *b* 1968: *m* 1995, David Tanti (and has issue living, Emilie Marie *b* 1996), Rebecca Jane *b* 1972, — Geraldine Ann, *b* 1950: *m* 1976, Martin Rex Challis, and has issue living, Christopher Martin *b* 1986, Kirsty Ann *b* 1983. —— Gerald Ian Crichton, OBE (Freugh, 54 Oakland Av, Wanganui, NZ), *b* 1929; JP 1981, OBE 1984: *m* 1963, Shirley Maureen, QSM, da of late Thomas Sanson, of Wanganui, and has issue living, Gerald Andrew, *b* 1964: *m* 1992, Denys Ann, da of John Fotheringham, of Auckland, and has issue living, Alice Jane Timpany *b* 1995, Molly Anne Sanson, *b* 1998, — Hamish Crichton, *b* 1968, — Rachael Deborah, *b* 1963: *m* 1994, Michael Patrick Hay, PhD, of Napier, and has issue living, Thomas Patrick *b* 1999. —— Patricia Ellen, *b* 1923: *m* 1947, W/Cdr George Stuart Alexander Stevenson, DFC, RNZAF, who *d* 1993, of 25 Repton St, Merivale, Christchurch, NZ and has issue living, Hugh William, *b* 1951: *m* 1978, Jillian Margaret, da of late Melville James Pitt Glasgow, and has issue living,

David James *b* 1985, Sarah Jane *b* 1983, — Jeremy Stuart (99 Darragh's Rd, Otumoetai, Tauranga, NZ), *b* 1956 Lt RNZN: *m* 1st, 1982 (*m diss* 1984), his 2nd cousin, Rhoda Mary, da of late Kenneth Willoughby McDouall (ante); 2ndly, 1990, Melinda Jane Ferguson, of Auckland, and has issue living (by 2nd *m*), Timothy Alexander Stuart *b* 1992, Samuel Nicholas Ivan *b* 1995, — Helen Patricia, *b* 1953: *m* 1st, 1982 (*m diss* 1984), Michael John Fowler, of Wellington, NZ; 2ndly, 1986, Robert Stephen Schaffel, of NJ, USA. ———Alison Crichton, *b* 1926: *m* 1957, Philip John Poulett Wells, of 14B Broadshard Lane, Ringwood, Hants BH24 1RR,and has issue living, Philip David Crichton (5 Collins Lane, Ringwood, Hants), *b* 1961: *m* 1990, Sally Henrietta, da of Peter Collings, of Denham, Middx, and has issue living, Oliver Philip Collings *b* 1994, Millie Charlotte *b* 1998. — Diana Jane, *b* 1958: *m* 1984, Richard David Trinick, of 3 Bucklands Drive, Nailsea, N Som, and has issue living, Chester Michael *b* 1987, Robert John *b* 1989, Laurence James *b* 1990, — Elizabeth Joanna (15 Chanctonbury Drive, Shoreham-by-Sea, Sussex), *b* 1966.

Issue of late Alan Edward Crichton McDouall, *b* 1895, *d* 1962: *m* 1922, Doris Annie, who *d* 1984, da of Joseph Preston of Oamaru:—
Stuart Preston (28 Ure St, Oamaru, NZ), *b* 1922: *m* 1951, Winifred Edith Jones, who *d* 1985, and has issue living, Philip Stuart, *b* 1955: *m* 1978, Alison Nicholas, and has had issue, Daniel Stuart *b* 1980, James Murray *b* 1984, Timothy Philip *b* 1987, Melissa *b* 1982, *d* 1983, — Patricia Mary, *b* 1952: *m* 1973, Atholl Campbell, and has issue living, Hamish Iain *b* 1979, Sarah Leigh *b* 1976, — Judith Anne, *b* 1954: *m* 1976, Rex Ormandy, and has issue living, Michael Stuart *b* 1987, Haylee Jan *b* 1984, Lisa Jane *b* (twin) 1987, — Heather, *b* 1959: *m* 1981, Bruce Reilly, and has issue living, Megan Jayne *b* 1983, Anna Marie *b* 1985, Rachel Dawn *b* 1988. ———Willoughby Alan (43 Gordon St, Kurow, N Otago, NZ), *b* 1935: *m* 1963, Pamela Ann Rudduck, and has issue living, John Alan Crichton, *b* 1971, — Fiona Mary, *b* 1969: *m* 19—, Nigel Humphries, and has issue living, Nicholas John Alan *b* 1996, Emily Josephine Ann *b* 1993, Sophia Nancy Margaret *b* 1998, — Joanna Louise, *b* 1974. ———Doris Mary, *b* 1924: *m* 1947, Ernest Benjamin Lyons, of Woodbury RD21, Geraldine, NZ, and has had issue, Alan Mark, *b* 1950: *m* 1973, Vivienne Lorna McPhail of Wellington, NZ, and has issue living, Nathan John *b* 1979, — Valerie Anne *b* 1976, — John McDouall, *b* 1952: *m* 1982, Sue Hodgson, of Christchurch, NZ, and *d* 1991, leaving issue, Jai Douglas *b* 1985, Charlie John *b* 1987, — David Wayne, *b* 1954: *m* 1st, 1974 (*m diss* 1982), Frances Margaret O'Connell, of Invercargill, NZ; 2ndly, 1986, Margaret Shirley Bain, of Kawerau, NZ, and has issue living (by 1st *m*), Jeremy Rhys *b* 1974, Rachael Jane *b* 1978, Megan Aimee *b* 1980, (by 2nd *m*) Vanessa Lee *b* 1987, Samantha Renee *b* 19—, Amanda Kay *b* 1992, — Anthony Bruce, *b* 1956: *m* 1979 (*m diss* 1982), Gwen Haigh, of Perth, — Kenneth Brett, *b* 1957: *m* 1981 (*m diss* 1990), Jill Fowler, of Perth, — Susan Mary, *b* 1948: *m* 1972, Graeme Norris Sherwood, of Palmerston N, NZ, who *d* 1985, and has issue living, Jacalyn Anne *b* 1979, Joanne Lisa *b* 1982. ———Josephine Anne (16 Holly Rd, Christchurch, NZ) *b* 1926. ———Ellen Coverdale, *b* 1928: *m* 1952, James Bruce Anderson, of Monuina, Tripp Settlement Rd, RD 21, Geraldine, S Canterbury, NZ, and has issue living, Duncan Bruce, *b* 1955, — Ian James, *b* 1959: *m* 1st, 1980 (*m diss* 1986), Carol Ruth Lynette Williams, of Geraldine, NZ; 2ndly, 1989, Rose-Marie Anne Birnie, of Oamaru, NZ, and has issue living (by 1st *m*), Steven Ian *b* 1981, Karen Lynette *b* 1984, Katherine Ruth *b* (twin) 1984, (by 2nd *m*) Lisa Rose *b* 1998, — Helen Mary, *b* 1954: *m* 1975, Halene Kupa Magatogia, of Alofi, Box 211, Niue Island, NZ, and has issue living, James Kupa *b* 1977, Charles Bruce Tali *b* 1979, Tani Mary Pua *b* 1981: *m* 1999, Emani Haile Selassie Lui, — Barbara Ellen, *b* 1958: *m* 1981, Gerard Patrick Scott, of Kerrytown, RD4, Timaru, NZ, and has issue living, Finian Patrick *b* 1990, Conor William *b* 1996, Lucy Bridget *b* 1984, Ingrid Jane *b* 1989, — Susan Grace, *b* 1960: *m* 1981, Geoffrey Ronald Taylor, of Taieri NZ; 2ndly, 1989, Brian John Close, of Oamaru, NZ, and has issue living (by 1st *m*), Scott James *b* 1981, Mark Ronald *b* 1984, (by 2nd *m*) Catherine Grace *b* 1990.

Granddaughter of late John Crichton Stuart McDouall (*b* 1818) (ante):—
Issue of late Herbert Crichton M'Douall, MRCS, LRCP, DPH, *b* 1860, *d* 1947: *m* 1899, Hester Maria Corry, who *d* 1942, da of late C. S. Hartigan, of Blackheath SE:—
Mary Crichton Stuart (74 Ruth Place, Dalmeny, NSW 2546, Australia), *b* 1909: *m* 1938, Alexander Bain, Master Mariner, who *d* 1996, and has issue living, Roderick Alexander Crichton, *b* 1940: — John Herbert Crichton (28 Stapylton St, Holder, ACT), *b* 1944: BSc (New England), MSc (James Cook Univ, N Queensland): *m* 1969, Peta Jane, da of F. W. Holdsworth, of Somerton Park, Adelaide, S Aust, and has issue living, Scott James *b* 1971, Timothy Ross *b* 1974; *ed* Univ of Canberra.

Granddaughter of late Rev William Sutherland M'Douall, 2nd son of Rev William M'Douall (*b* 1775) (ante):—
Issue of late Claud Hay M'Douall, *b* 1864, *d* 1905: *m* 1904, Alice May, who *d* 1955, da of George Redding:—
Joan Alma, *b* 1905: *m* 1931, Brian Miller, who *d* 1992, of Witches Moon, Stony Lane, Little Kingshill, Gt Missenden, Bucks HP16 0DS, and has issue living, Ian Claud (4 Fryer Close, Chesham, Bucks HP5 1RD), *b* 1932: *m* 1st, 1955, Violet Grace Waters, who *d* 1987; 2ndly, 1994, Hazel Gwendolyn Wray, and has issue living (by 1st *m*), Nicola Anne, *b* 1960: DPhil, — Peter Gerald (3 Nicolas Av, Glen Eden, Auckland 8, NZ), *b* 1934: *m* 1955, Patricia Ann Collins, and has issue living, Rogan Edward Oliver *b* 1966: *m* 1986, Christine Lynette Alice Simpson (and has issue living, Jordan Rogan Peter *b* 1993, Amy Joy *b* 1989, Holly Eva *b* 1991), Cameron Peter *b* 1970, Carolyn Jane *b* 1959: *m* 1986, Robert Peter Coenradi (and has issue living, Peter Nathan *b* 1989, Benjamin Matthew *b* 1991, Samuel Luke *b* 1995, Sarah Anna *b* 1993), Philippa Jane *b* 1961: *m* 1982, David Peter Colman (and has issue living, Stephen James *b* 1988, Jason John *b* 1995, Catherine Louise *b* 1983, Melanie Ruth *b* 1985).

Grandchildren of late Kenneth Gilbert M'Douall, 3rd son of late Rev William Sutherland M'Douall (ante):—
Issue of late Ferdinand Huth M'Douall, *b* 1905, *d* 1990: *m* 1931, Lillian Hall, who *d* 1999, da of late W. J. Saville:—
Kenneth Hugh (2 West St, Denbury, Newton Abbot, S Devon TQ12 6DP), *b* 1935: *m* 1964, Jean, only da of W. Leonard Crouch, and has issue living, Duncan Hugh, *b* 1969, — Justin Ian, *b* 1972. ———Sidney Morris (75 Hill St, Richmond, Nelson, NZ), *b* 1944: *m* 1974, Virginia Helen, eldest da of M. N. Charters, of Rangiona, NZ, and has issue living, (Michael) Guy, *b* 1977, Simon Geoffrey, *b* 1981 ———(Evelyn) Susan, *b* 1937: *m* 1st, 1962 (*m diss* 1968), Stuart Wallace MacGregor; 2ndly, 1977, Andrew John Barr-Sim, of Blair House, 3 New St, Henley-on-Thames, Oxon, and has issue living (by 1st *m*), Fiona Judith, *b* 1964, — Alison Catherine, *b* 1966.

Grandchildren of late Alan Patrick M'Douall, 4th and yst son of late Rev William Sutherland M'Douall (ante):—
Issue of late Patrick Sutherland M'Douall, *b* 1904, *d* 1950: *m* 1941, Esther Mary (who *m* 2ndly 1952, George Black, of 3 Front Street, Cassop, Ferryhill, co Durham), da of late Jack William Albutt, of Newcastle:—
Alan Sutherland, *b* 1946: *m* 1970, Jennifer Ann Lingard, da of Kenneth John Jarvis, and has issue living, Alec Douglas Sutherland, *b* 1971, — Morwenna Jane, *b* 1973. ———Joy Mary, *b* 1942: *m* 1963, John Wilson, of 1 Tythe Pl, Fenstanton, Huntingdon, Cambs, and has issue living, Anthony John, *b* 1966, — Ian Patrick, *b* 1969.

Issue of late Alan Reeves M'Douall, *b* 1906, *d* 1971: *m* 1930, Hilma Hornfelt, who *d* 1994, of Saskatchewan:—
Katherine, *b* 1931; adopted the surname of McDouall 1961: *m* 1st, 1947 (*m diss* 1961), Raymond Frederick Flood; 2ndly, 1962, Royden Gilbert Young, of 956 Quadling Av, Coquitlam, New Westminster, BC, Canada, and has issue living (by 2nd *m*), Robert James, *b* 1967, — Douglas Alan, *b* 1968. —— Audrey Ethel (105, 9295 122nd St, Surrey, BC, Canada V3V 4L4), *b* 1933: *m* 1st, 1955 (*m diss* 1969), Ronald O'Day; 2ndly, 1971 (*m diss* 1992), Fred Charlton, and has issue living (by 1st *m*), Frederick Alan, *b* 1956, — Ronald Patrick (2491 11th Av, Port Alberni, BC, Canada V9Y 2S2), *b* 1957: *m* 1st, 1977 (*m diss* 1980), Shelley Mackenzie; 2ndly, 1989, Cheryl Eaglestad, and has issue living (by 1st *m*), Shane Ronald *b* 1978, Lucas *b* 1983, (by 2nd *m*) Cody Reeves *b* 1989, — Kathryn Rosanne, *b* 1958: *m* 1977, Steven Joseph Yaciw (Camp 37 Site 16, Kamloops, BC, Canada V2C 2J3, and has issue living, Angela Kristy *b* 1979, Lisa Marie *b* 1981, — Lorraine Janet, *b* 1959: *m* 1st, 1983 (*m diss* 1986)), —; 2ndly, 1994, Dereck Ross Dawe (11352 Glenavon Drive, Surrey, BC, Canada V3R 4V5), and has issue living (by 2nd husband), Colton Frederick *b* 1990, Levi Dereck Ron *b* 1992, Kaileigh Andra *b* 1989, Allison Mary Barbara *b* 1993:—

Granddaughter of late Rev William Sutherland M'Douall (ante):—

Issue of late Alan Patrick M'Douall, *b* 1872, *d* 1947: *m* 1902, Frances Ethel, who *d* 1968, da of late Edward Reeves, of Wellington, NZ:—
Mary Grace (Flat 5, Joan Nightingale House, Bolnore Rd, Haywards Heath, Sussex RH16 4AB), *b* 1908.

Grandchildren of late Rawdon M'Douall, 5th son of Rev William M'Douall (*b* 1775) (ante):—

Issue of late Rawdon George Herbert M'Douall, *b* 1852, *d* 1919: *m* 1906, Mary Somerville Townshend, who *d* 1968:—
†Rawdon Townshend, OAM, *b* 1907; OAM (1983), JP: *m* 1933, Elizabeth, who *d* 1983, da of late A. Cameron, of Glencoe, Narrabri, NSW, and *d* 1998, leaving issue, David Rawdon (Dunbeacon, Upper Horton, NSW 2347), *b* 1937: *m* 1962, Margaret Joan, da of Keith McDonald, of Strathallan Warialda, NSW, and has issue living, Rawdon Angus *b* 1963: *m* 1987, Melinda Mary, da of Watkin Williams, of Wattombri, Garah, NSW (and has issue living, Thomas Rawdon *b* 1991, Henry Angus *b* 1995, Polly Gwendoline *b* 1993), Ian Alexander *b* 1968, Helen Annette *b* 1964: *m* 1st, 1988 (*m diss* 1990), Timothy James Ross, of St Ives, NSW; 2ndly, 1992, Stephen Andrew Ninnes, of Ipswich, Qld (and has issue living (by 2nd *m*), James Frazer *b* 1995, Lucy Elizabeth *b* 1997). —— Lucy Katherine Shawford, *b* 1913: *m* 1946, Thomas Clark Capel, of The Oaks, Narrabri, NSW, who *d* 1986, and has issue living, Donald Gilbert, *b* 1949: *m* 19—, Jennifer Anne, da of Eric Bone, of Maitland, and has issue living, Angus Donald *b* 1985, Louise Anne *b* 1983, — Katherine Shawford (*Hon Mrs Alexander Erskine*), *b* 1950: *m* 1977, Hon Alexander David Erskine, 2nd son of 13th Earl of Mar and Kellie, — Nancy Patricia, *b* 1953. —— Patricia Hastings, *b* 1916: *m* 1954, Eric Limburg, of Windi, Bingara, NSW, and has issue living, Richard Eric *b* 1955: *m* 1988, Ann Margaret Simpson, — David Patrick Rawdon, *b* 1957: *m* 1981, Lea Ellen, da of Brian Forth, of Telarah, NSW, and has issue living, Nichole Ellen *b* 1983, Katrina Lea (twin) *b* 1983, Alyce Patricia *b* 1986, — Elizabeth Mary, *b* 1960: *m* 1981, Steven Mark Adams, of Gawler, S Australia, and has issue living, Kris *b* 1987, Naomi *b* 1984. —— Margaret Somerville, *b* 1918: *m* 1951, Jack Lattimore, who *d* 1988, of 21 Trelawney St, Thornleigh 2120, Sydney, NSW, and has issue living, Andrew Stuart, *b* 1958: *m* 1989, Bronwyn Gae Macpherson, da of Brig Brian Edwards, of Canberra, ACT, and has issue living, Jack Edward Macpherson *b* 1992, Angus William Macpherson *b* 1996, Sarah Claire Macpherson *b* 1994, — Mary-Ann Elizabeth, *b* 1954: *m* 1979, Hugh Geoffrey Beecher, of Rosedale, Narrandera, NSW, and has issue living, Nicholas Hugh Lattimore *b* 1991, Emma Louise Lattimore *b* 1988, — Margaret Louise, *b* 1960: *m* 1st, 1991, Christopher Allan Murphy, who *d* 1992; 2ndly, 1996, Grant Robert Clark, of Sydney, NSW, and has had issue (by 2nd *m*), Oscar Lattimore, *b* and *d* 1996, Molly Katherine Lattimore *b* 1997, Harriett Leslie *b* 1998.

Granddaughters of late Daniel Crichton Stuart M'Douall (infra):—

Issue of late Peter Crichton Stuart M'Douall, *b* 1933, *d* 1988: *m* 1959, Kay Margaret (Bald Hill, Narrabri, NSW), da of Kenneth Field Clemson, of Wyndella, Collarenebri, NSW:—
Sandra Anne, *b* 1961: *m* 1988, Richard Alexander Dillon, of Nass's Rd, Preston, Toowoomba, Qld. —— Nicki Jane, *b* 1963. —— Angela Susan, *b* 1967.

Grandchildren of late William Edward M'Douall (infra):—

Issue of late Daniel Crichton Stuart M'Douall *b* 1905, *d* 1961: *m* 1930, Jean (4 Bowen St, Narrabri, NSW), da of P. A. McAlister, of Narrabri, NSW:—
Judith, *b* 1931: *m* 1954, Allan Richard McMaster, of Violet Downs, Narrabri 2390, NSW, and has issue living, Stuart Allan, *b* 1955: *m* 1979, Deborah, da of David Mackay, of Brisbane, Queensland, and has issue living, Richard Stuart *b* 1982, Alec Bruce *b* 1985, Abby Jane *b* 1981, — Margaret Jean, *b* 1957: *m* 1979, Stephen Leslie Frost, of Toowoomba, NSW, and has issue living, Samuel Allan *b* 1986, Melanie Alaire *b* 1980, Angela Judith *b* 1982, — Cathryn Mary, *b* 1960: *m* 1984, John Charles Edmondson, of Sydney, NSW, and has issue living, Allan Gordon *b* 1988, Andrew John *b* 1990, Sally Louise *b* 1992.

Issue of late Hastings Uchrid M'Douall, *b* 1907, *d* 1992: *m* 1938, Nancy May (Lowana, Upper Horton, Via Barraba, NSW 2347), da of Ernest Capel, of Burren Junction, NSW:—
Richard Hastings (Kildare, Upper Horton, NSW 2347), *b* 1940: *m* 1966, Susan Anne Etheridge, and has issue living, Stuart John, *b* 1966: *m* 1992, Jayne Vickery, and has issue living, Toby Mathew *b* 1994, Samantha Vickery *b* 1996, Tabitha Vickery *b* (twin) 1996, — Graham Richard, *b* 1968: *m* 1997, Lisa Simpson, and has issue living, Luke Graham *b* 1998, Alexis Jessica *b* 1997. —— Donald Hastings (Boundary Creek, Bingara, NSW 2404), *b* 1946: *m* 1973, Bronwyn Lee, da of late W. Cupitt, of Bowral, NSW, and has issue living, Benjamin Donald, *b* 1975, — Samuel Hastings, *b* 1977, — Serena Lee, *b* 1981. —— Pamela Hastings, *b* (twin) 1940: *m* 1st, 1963, Roderick Warren Scotton, MB BS, of Grafton, NSW, who *d* 1981; 2ndly, 1983, Fergus McMaster Fysh, of 4 Breimba St, Grafton, NSW 2460, and has issue living (by 1st *m*), Richard Stuart, *b* 1966: *m* 1992, Melissa Gail Simpson, and has had issue, Thomas Warren, *b* 1995, William Peter *b* 1998 *d* 1999, Alysse Marie *b* 1994, Emma *b* (twin) 1998, — Peter Roderick, *b* 1969, — Sandra Louise, *b* 1965: *m* 1994, Benjamin Wellington Bundock, and has issue living, Henry Wellington *b* 1994, George McBean *b* 1997.

Grandchildren of late Rawdon M'Douall (ante):—

Issue of late William Edward M'Douall, *b* 1865, *d* 1936: *m* 1904, May Edna, who *d* 1961, da of Robert Scholes:—
Robert William (Eungai, Upper Horton, NSW 2347), *b* 1909: *m* 1934, Nancy Spencer, and has issue living, William Robert *b* 1939: *m* 1963, Louise, da of Eric Lauric, of Walcher NSW, and has issue living, James William *b* 1965, Andrew Alexander (twin) *b* 1965, Jonathon Laurie *b* 1967: *m* 1995, Felicity Vina, da of Gregory John Banks (and has issue living, Harrison George *b* 1998), — Arthur Frank, *b* 1942: *m* 1963, Beverley Ann, da of Clive Pyke, of Inverell, NSW, and has issue living, Baden Robert *b* 1964: *m* 1991, Jennifer Ann, da of Francis John Moulton, of Goondiwindi, Qld (and has issue living, Daniel Robert *b* 1993, William John *b* 1995), Gavin John *b* 1966: *m* 1994, Lisa Jane, da of Kelvin McAllister,

of Dubbo, NSW (and has issue living, Isabelle Grace *b* 1997), — Phillipa May, *b* 1937: *m* 1957, Andrew Ellis Wauch, of Barraba, NSW, and has issue living, John Andrew Robert *b* 1958: *m* 19—, Toni Ann, da of William Ronald Saunders (and has issue living, Thomas Robert Andrew *b* 1994), Wendy Ann *b* 1959, Sally May *b* 1966: *m* 1994, Martin Tremain (and has issue living, Laura May *b* 1996). —— Noel Edward (Peri, Caroda, via Barraba, NSW, Australia), *b* 1911: *m* 1942, Amy Patricia Hawke, and has issue living, Malcolm Noel (50 Post Office Rd, Glenorie, NSW), *b* 1943: *m* 1968, Louise, da of late R. A. Pedlingham, of Pymble, NSW, and has issue living, Matthew Richard Stuart *b* 1970, — Jillian May, *b* 1946: *m* 1967 (*m diss* 1978), Michael Thomas Mahony, and has issue living, Jake Thomas *b* 1975, Camilla *b* 1972. *Residence* – 66 Liverpool St, Paddington, NSW, Australia. —— Harold Stuart (Ulumbarella, Upper Horton, Via Barraba, NSW 2347) *b* 1920; Fl-Lt (ret) RAAF: *m* 1st, 1947, Doris Marion, who *d* 1970, da of Maj W. Squires; 2ndly, 1974, Gloria Geraldine, da of late Capt W. G. F. Leadbeater, MN, and has issue living (by 1st *m*), Garry Stuart (Yarraman, Bingara, NSW 2404), *b* 1949: *m* 1971, Linda Anne, da of Richard Littlejohn, of The Meadows, Harden, NSW, and has issue living, Scott Stuart *b* 1978, Hamish Richard *b* 1981, — Michael William (Coolowie, Bingara, NSW 2404), *b* 1953: *m* 1982, Julie Kay, da of Dr E. S. Hughson, and has issue living, Cameron Stuart *b* 1983, Mich William *b* 1985, Jenna Marion *b* 1986, — Diane Marion, *b* 1950: *m* 1st, 1971 (*m diss* 1977), Peter Russell Jones; 2ndly, 1983, Phillip Arthur Kelly, of Blue Nobby, Cobbadah, NSW 2347, and has issue living (by 1st *m*), Heulwen *b* 1973, (by 2nd *m*) Dustin Phillip *b* 1986, Alana Mae *b* 1984, Kylie Elizabeth *b* 1988. —— Edna May, *b* 1918: *m* 1941, John Murray Bowman, of Tarpoly, Upper Manilla, NSW 2346, and has issue living, Roger Murray, *b* 1943: *m* 1973, Sara Wilkin Smith, and has issue living, Thomas Murray *b* 1976, Katherine Sara *b* 1974, Susan Wilkin *b* 1979, — Graham Edward, *b* 1945: *m* 1972, Nanette Mary Mahony, and has issue living, Luke Edward *b* 1974, Jonathan Graham *b* 1980, Anna Nannatte *b* 1977, — Christopher George, *b* 1953: *m* 1978, Sharron Hubbard, and has issue living, Samuel James *b* 1984, Laura Emily *b* (twin) 1984, Angela Jane *b* 1986, — Julie May, *b* 1950.

PREDECESSORS – (1) *Sir* JAMES Stuart of Ardmaleish, Bute, 7th in descent from John Stuart, "The Black Stewart", natural son of Robert II, sided with Charles I; in 1640 his estates were sequestrated, but he was Commr for Bute 1643-8 and attended sittings in Parliament; dispossessed of custody of Rothesay Castle by Cromwell; *cr a Baronet* of Nova Scotia 1627: *m* Grizel, da of Sir Dugall Campbell of Auchinbreck, 1st Bt: *d* 1662; *s* by his son (2) *Sir* DUGAL, 2nd Bt: *m* 1658, Elizabeth, da of John Ruthven, of Dunglass; *d* 1670; *s* by his son (3) *Sir* JAMES, PC; a Commr to treat for a Union between Scotland and England; *cr Earl of Bute, Viscount Kingarth, Lord Mount Stuart, Cumra, and Inchmarnock* (peerage of Scotland) 1703, with remainder to heirs male whatsoever: *m* 1st, 1680, Agnes, da of Sir George MacKenzie of Rosehaugh; 2ndly, Christian, da of William Dundas of Kincavel; *d* 1710; *s* by his son (4) JAMES, 2nd Earl; Representative Peer 1715-23; Lord of the Bedchamber 1721-3: *m* 1711, Lady Anne Campbell (who *d* 1736, having *m* 2ndly, 1731, Alexander Fraser of Strichen), da of 1st Duke of Argyll; *d* 1723; *s* by his son (5) JOHN, KG, 3rd Earl; *b* 1713; Representative Peer 1737-41, and 1761-80; First Lord of the Treasury 1762-3: *m* 1736, Mary (*cr Baroness Mount Stuart of Wortley*, co York (peerage of Great Britain) 1761, with remainder to heirs male by her then marriage), who *d* 1794, da of Edward Wortley-Montagu; *d* 1792; *s* by his son (6) JOHN, 4th Earl, who in 1776 had been *cr Baron Cardiff*, of Cardiff Castle (peerage of Great Britain), and in 1796 was *cr Marquess of Bute, Earl of Windsor* and *Viscount Mountjoy*, of Isle of Wight, with remainder to heirs male of his body: *m* 1st, 1766, Charlotte Jane Windsor, who *d* 1800, da and heir of 2nd Viscount Windsor of Blackcastle, and Baron Mountjoy, of Isle of Wight (through whom the Welsh estates of the Earls of Pembroke passed to the House of Bute); 2ndly, 1800, Frances, who *d* 1832, da of Thomas Coutts, banker; *d* 1814; *s* by his grandson (7) JOHN, KT, (son of John, Viscount Mount Stuart by his wife Elizabeth Penelope, da and heir of 6th Earl of Dumfries), 2nd Marquess; *b* 1793; *s* his maternal grandfather as 7th Earl of Dumfries (see infra*); assumed in 1805 by Roy licence the additional surname of Crichton before Stuart: *m* 1st, 1818, Maria, who *d* 1841, el da of 3rd Earl of Guildford; 2ndly, 1845, Sophia, who *d* 1859, da of 1st Marquess of Hastings; *d* 1848; *s* by his only son (8) JOHN PATRICK, KT, LLD, 3rd Marquess; *b* 1847; Lord-Lieut of Buteshire: *m* 1872, the Hon Gwendolene Mary Anne Fitzalan-Howard, who *d* 1932, el da of 1st Baron Howard of Glossop; *d* 1900; *s* by his el son (9) JOHN, KT, 4th Marquess; *b* 1881: *m* 1905, *Dame* Augusta Mary Monica, DBE, who *d* 1947, da of Sir (Alan) Henry Bellingham, 4th Bt; *d* 1947; *s* by his son (10) JOHN, 5th Marquess; *b* 1907; Vice-Lieut for co Bute 1948-56: *m* 1932, Lady Eileen Beatrice Forbes, who *d* 1993, da of 8th Earl of Granard; *d* 1956; *s* by his el son (11) JOHN, KBE, 6th Marquess; *b* 1933; DL Bute 1961, Lord Lieut 1967-75, and Argyll and Bute 1990-93, Convenor Buteshire CC 1967-70, Lieut Scots Guards (Res), Member Countryside Commn for Scotland 1970-78, Chm Council and Exec Cttee National Trust for Scotland 1969-84 (Pres 1991-93), and Historic Buildings Council for Scotland 1983-88; FRSE, etc: *m* 1st, 1955 (*m diss* 1977), Beatrice Nicola Grace, only da of late Lt-Cdr Wolstan Beaumont Charles Weld-Forester, CBE, RN (*see* B Forester, colls); 2ndly, 1978, Jennifer, da of John Brougham Home-Rigg, and formerly wife of Gerald Percy (*see* D Northumberland, colls): *d* 1993; *s* by his elder son (12) JOHN COLUM, 7th Marquess and present peer; also Earl of Windsor, Earl of Dumfries, Earl of Bute, Viscount Mountjoy, Viscount Kingarth, Viscount of Air, Baron Mount Stuart of Wortley, Baron Cardiff, Lord Crichton, and Lord Mount Stuart, Cumra and Inchmarnock.

*(1) *Sir* ROBERT CRICHTON, of Sanquhar, co Dumfries, probably descended from a son of Alexander Crichton of Crichton, co Edinburgh 1296; *cr Lord Crichton of Sanquhar* (peerage of Scotland) 1488: *m* 1st, Margaret May; 2ndly *c* 1457, Christian, da of Sir John Erskine of Kinnoull, and widow of John Crichton; *d* 1494-95; *s* by his grandson (2) ROBERT (son of Robert Crichton by Marion Stewart, da of 1st Earl of Lennox), 2nd Lord; *mc* 1491, Marion Maxwell; *d* 1513; *s* by his son (3) ROBERT, 3rd Lord: *m* Elizabeth, (who *m* 2ndly Herbert Maxwell), da of Cuthbert Murray of Cockpool; *d* 1516-20; *s* by his son (4) ROBERT, 4th Lord: *m ca* 1534, Elizabeth (who *m* 3rdly the 4th Earl of Glencairn), da and heir of John Campbell of W Loudoun, and widow of William Wallace of Craigie; *d* a minor *ca* 1535; *s* by his brother (5) WILLIAM, 5th Lord: *m ca* 1540, Elizabeth, da of 3rd Lord Fleming; *d* (stabbed by Robert, Master of Sempill) 1550; *s* by his son (6) ROBERT, 6th Lord: *m* Margaret, da of John Cunningham of Caprington, and widow of Gilbert Kennedy; *d* 1561; *s* by his his brother (7) EDWARD, 7th Lord: *m* 1561, Margaret (who *m* 2ndly, 1571, 5th Earl of Menteith), da of Sir James Douglas of Drumlanrig; *d* 1569; *s* by his son (8) ROBERT, 8th Lord; *b ca* 1568; *m* 1608, Anne (who *d* 1675, having *m* 2ndly, 1615, 6th Earl of Thomond), da of Sir George Fermor, of Easton Neston, Northants; having connived at the murder of a fencing master John Turner, who had deprived him of the sight of an eye, was hanged in Great Palace Yard, Westminster, 1612; *s* by his kinsman (9) WILLIAM, (son of William, son of 5th Lord) 9th Lord; *cr Viscount of Air* and *Lord of Sanquhar* (peerage of Scotland) 1622, and *Earl of Dumfries, Viscount of Air*, and *Lord Crichton of Sanquhar and Cumnock* (peerage of Scotland) 1633, this creation with remainder to heirs male bearing the name and arms of Crichton: *m* 1st, Eupheme, da of James Seton of Touch, and widow of Patrick Hamilton; 2ndly, Ursula, da of Stephen Barnham, and widow of Sir Robert Swift; *d* 1642-3; *s* by his son (10) WILLIAM, PC (Scotland), 2nd Earl; resigned his honours to the Crown 1690, and obtained a new grant with same precedence, and with remainder to his grandson, then the four daughters of his deceased son Charles, Lord Crichton, failing whom to the latter's nearest heirs: *m* 1618, Penelope, da of Sir Robert Swift, and sister of 1st Viscount Carlingford; *d* 1691; *s* by his grandson (11) WILLIAM (son of Charles, Lord Crichton, by Sarah, da of 1st Viscount Stair), 3rd Earl; *d* young 1694; *s* by his sister (12) PENELOPE: *m* 1698, the Hon William Dalrymple, 2nd son of 1st Earl of Stair; *d* 1742; *s* by her son (13) WILLIAM Dalrymple- Crichton, KT (who also *s* as 4th Earl of Stair 1760: *m* 1st 1731, Lady Anne Gordon, who *d* 1755, da of 2nd Earl of Aberdeen; 2ndly, 1762, Anne, da of William Duff, of Crombie Advocate); *d* 1768; *s* in Earldom of Dumfries by his nephew (14) PATRICK MacDouall Crichton (el son of Elizabeth Dalrymple-Crichton who *m* John MacDouall of Freugh); *b* 1726, Capt 3rd Foot Guards; Representative Peer 1790-1803: *m* 1771, Margaret, who *d* 1799, da of Ronald Crauford of Restalrig; *d* 1803; *s* by his grandson (15) JOHN, 2nd Marquess of Bute (ante) (son of Elizabeth Penelope, who *m* 1792, John Stuart, Viscount Mount Stuart, el son of 1st Marquess of Bute).

BUTLER OF BROCKWELL, BARON (Butler) (Life Baron 1998)

(FREDERICK EDWARD) ROBIN BUTLER, GCB, CVO, son of Bernard Daft Butler, of St Annes on Sea, Lancs; *b* 8 Jan 1938; *ed* Harrow, and Univ Coll, Oxford (BA 1961); Private Sec to Rt Hon Edward Heath 1972-74, and Rt Hon Harold Wilson 1974-75; Principal Private Sec to Rt Hon Margaret Thatcher 1982-85; Second Perm Sec, HM Treasury 1985-87; Sec of the Cabinet and Head of the Home Civil Service 1988-98; Master of Univ Coll, Oxford since 1998; Chm of Govrs of Dulwich Coll since 1997; Hon Memb Worshipful Co of Salters; *cr* CVO 1986, KCB 1988, GCB 1992, and *Baron Butler of Brockwell*, of Herne Hill in the London Borough of Lambeth (Life Baron) 1998: *m* 1962, Gillian Lois, da of Dr Robert Galley, of Teddington, Middx, and has issue.
Residence – The Master's Lodgings, University College, Oxford OX1 4BH. *Clubs* – Anglo-Belgian, Athenaeum, Brooks's, Beefsteak.

SON LIVING

Hon Andrew, *b* 1968; *ed* Harrow, and Univ Coll, Oxford: *m* 1998, Catriona McLaren.

DAUGHTERS LIVING

Hon Sophie, *b* 1964; *ed* The Mary Datchelor Sch, Marlborough Coll, and Warwick Univ: *m* 1991, Nicholas Trend, and has issue living, William Oliver, *b* 1993, — Eleanor Rose, *b* 1995.
Hon Nell, *b* 1967; *ed* Alleyn's Sch, and Oriel Coll, Oxford: *m* 1996, Justin Rushbrooke, and has issue living, Thibault Stanley Arthur, *b* 1998.

Butler of Mount Juliet, Baron; title of Earl of Carrick on Roll of HL.

Butler, family name of Earl of Carrick.

Butler, family name of Baron Dunboyne.

Butler, surname of Earldom of Lanesborough.

Butler, family name of Viscount Mountgarret.

Butler, surname of Marquessate of Ormonde.

BUTLER OF SAFFRON WALDEN, BARONY OF (Butler) (Extinct 1982)

SONS LIVING OF LIFE BARON

Hon Sir Richard Clive (Gladfen Hall, Halstead, Essex CO9 1RN), *b* 1929; *ed* Eton, and Pembroke Coll, Camb (MA); late 2nd Lt RHG; High Sheriff Essex 1969-70, DL Essex 1972; a Farmer; Pres NFU 1979-86 (Dep-Pres 1971-78, Vice-Pres 1970); Dir Nat Westminster Bank plc 1986-96, and NFU Mutual Insurance Soc Ltd 1985-97, and Sir Richard and Lady Butler's Farms Ltd; Liveryman of Skinners' Co (Master 1994-95), and Farmers' Co (Master 1997-98); Kt Bach 1981: *m* 1952, Susan Anne Maud, only da of late Maj Patrick Bruce Walker, MBE, late RA, of Barry's Close, Long Crendon, Bucks (*see* Walker, Bt, *cr* 1868), and has issue living, (Richard) Michael (Froyz Hall, Halstead, Essex), *b* 1956: *m* 1st, 1984 (*m diss* 1994), Christina Anne, yst da of Robert B. Blackwell, of Gatehouse Farm, Earls Colne, Colchester, Essex; 2ndly, 1997, Judi M., da of R. J. Brooks, of Ely, Cambs, and has issue living (by 1st *m*), (Richard) Benjamin *b* 1986, Charles Robert *b* 1987, Rosie Olivia *b* 1993, (by 2nd *m*), Sophia Katie *b* 1998, — Christopher Patrick (twin), *b* 1956: *m* 1983, Tania G., 4th da of David Clarabut, of St Mary's Hoo, Kent, and has issue living, David Mark *b* 1987, Anna Louise *b* 1985, Kimberley Jane *b* 1988, — Antonia Mary, *b* 1954: *m* 1st, 1978 (*m diss* 1983), Nicholas Henry Seymour Lees; 2ndly, 1983, Timothy P. Finch, of Ruecastle, Lanton, Jedburgh, Roxburghshire, and has issue living (by 2nd *m*), Sophie Amanda *b* 1985, Lucy Charlotte *b* 1986.

Rt Hon Sir Adam Courtauld, FRSA (The Old Rectory, Lighthorne, Warwick CV35 0AR), *b* 1931; *ed* Eton and Pembroke Coll, Camb (BA); late 2nd Lt KRRC; DL Warwicks 1993, Vice Lord Lieut since 1998; ADC to Gov-Gen of Canada 1954-55; with Courtaulds Ltd 1955-73, Dir H. P. Bulmer (Holdings) plc 1988-97; an FRSA, and an Assist of Goldsmiths' Co; Chm Airey Neave Trust since 1990, Samuel Courtauld Trust, and Pres British Horse Soc 1990-92; a Conservative Whip 1974-75, PPS to Leader of Opposition (Rt Hon Margaret Thatcher) 1975-79; Min of State, Dept of Industry 1979-81, N Ireland Office 1981-84, and Defence Procurement 1984-85, MP for Bosworth (*C*) 1970-83, *cr* PC 1984, Kt 1986: *m* 1955, Felicity Sybil (High Sheriff Warwicks 1997), only da of Guy Kemyel Molesworth-St Aubyn, of Larks Hill, Braughing, Ware, Herts (*see* Molesworth-St Aubyn, Bt), and has issue living, Samuel Montagu Guy, *b* 1957: *m* 1982, Amanda J., da of Anthony H. B. Hart, of Bagendon, Glos, and has issue living, George Percy Kemyel *b* 1985, Henry Courtauld *b* 1987, — Edward Adam, *b* 1962; Maj The Royal Green Jackets: *m* 1991, Sophie Caroline, yr da of Capt Alec Rose, RN, of Petersfield, Hants, and has had issue, Robin Augustus *b* 1994, Augusta Rose *b* and *d* 1993, Octavia Grace *b* 1995, — Alexandra Katharine *b* 1959: *m* 1st, 1985 (*m diss* 1988), Dominick James Alexander Ashe, son of Sir Derick Rosslyn Ashe, KCMG; 2ndly, 1990, Comte Charles Henri du Luart, elder son of Comte Charles du Luart, of Paris, and has issue living (by 2nd *m*), Emily Marie-Madeleine *b* 1991, Eloise Jeanne Felicity *b* 1993.

Hon (Samuel) James (4E 355 King's Rd, SW3 5ES), *b* 1936; *ed* Eton, and Pembroke Coll, Camb; late 2nd Lt RHG: *m* 1st, 1960 (*m diss* 1977), Lucilla Blanche, yr da of late Algernon Malcolm Borthwick, MC, TD, of Wethersfield Place, Braintree, Essex (*see* Borthwick, Bt, colls); 2ndly, 1986, Jennifer, only da of Dr George Gladston, of Almera, NY, USA, and has issue living (by 1st *m*), Malcolm James, *b* 1964, — George Victor, *b* 1969, — Sydney Louise, *b* 1962, — Fleur Josephine, *b* 1967: *m* 1991, Richard Charles Selwyn Sharpe, of Low Fields, Exelby, Bedale, N Yorks, only son of Canon Roger Sharpe, of The Rectory, Warminster, Wilts, and has issue living, Thomas Richard Gildart *b* 1992, George James Augustus *b* 1994, Jasper William *b* 1995, — Lucilla Katherine Joan, *b* 1973: *m* 1998, Zaccariah Corbetts, — Emily Rebecca (twin), *b* 1973, — (by 2nd *m*), Georgina Elizabeth *b* 1989.

DAUGHTER LIVING OF LIFE BARON

Hon Sarah Theresa Mary, *b* 1944: *m* 1969, Anthony John Willis Price, of Manor House, Snarestone, nr Burton-on-Trent, Staffs, and has issue living, Jack Jerome, *b* 1972, — Edward Mulligan, *b* 1973, — Theodore William, *b* 1979.

WIDOW LIVING OF LIFE BARON

MOLLIE (*Baroness Butler of Saffron Walden*) (Spencers, Gt Yeldham, Essex), da of late Frank Douglas Montgomerie, of Castle Hedingham, Essex (*see* L Napier and Ettrick, colls, 1985 Edn), and widow of Augustine Courtauld: *m* 1959, as his 2nd wife, Baron Butler of Saffron Walden, KG, CH, PC (Life Baron), who *d* 1982.

BUTTERFIELD, BARON (Butterfield) (Life Baron 1988)

(WILLIAM) JOHN HUGHES BUTTERFIELD, OBE, son of late William Hughes Butterfield; *b* 28 March 1920; *ed* Solihull Sch, Exeter Coll, Oxford (DM 1968, Hon Fell 1978), and John Hopkins Univ (MD 1951), MA, MD Cantab 1975; FRCP; Hon Fell NY Acad Science 1962, NY Acad of Medicine 1987, Hon LLD Nottingham 1977, Hon DMedSci Keio Univ, Tokyo, 1983, Hon DSc Florida Internat Univ, Miami, 1985, Hon LLD Bristol 1994; late Maj RAMC; Medical Research Council 1946-58; Prof of Experimental Medicine Guy's Hosp 1958-63, Prof of Medicine Guy's Hosp Med Sch 1963-71; Prof Fell 1975-78, Master Downing Coll, Camb, 1978-87, Vice Chancellor Camb Univ 1983-85; Chm of many Medical, Scientific and Educational Cttees; Chm Jardine Educational Trust 1982-90, Health Promotion Research Trust 1983-97; GB-Sasakawa Fndn 1991-97 (since when a Trustee), and Croucher Fndn, Hong Kong, since 1979 (now Pres), etc; Pres British Univs Sports Fedn, Council St George's House Windsor 1987-92; Visitor King Edward's Hosp Fund 1964-71, Examiner in Medicine Oxford Univ 1960-66, Univ of E Africa 1966, and Camb Univ 1967-75, etc; Visiting Prof Yale 1966, Harvard 1978; Rock Carling Fell, Royal Coll of Physicians 1968; Lecturer; FRSA 1971; *cr Baron Butterfield*, of Stechford, co W Midlands (Life Baron) 1988: *m* 1st, 1946, Ann, who *d* 1948, da of late Robert Sanders, of New York City, USA; 2ndly, 1950, Isabel-Ann, da of late Dr Foster Kennedy, of New York City, and has issue by 1st and 2nd *m*.

Arms – Azure a pale ermine per fesse counterchanged on a fesse gules between three lozenges or a lion passant in trian aspect also or and between on the dexter a domed tower proper ensigned by an increscent argent and on the sinister a like tower ensigned by an estoile gold. **Crest** – A cubit arm vested azure semy of pentacles or the hand proper holding a pair of keys fesswise the bows interlaced gold. **Supporters** – *Dexter*, a greyhound statant erect argent gorged with an open crown or; *Sinister*, a griffin also statant erect gold.
Residence – 39 Clarendon St, Cambridge CB1 1JX. *Clubs* – Athenaeum, MCC, Queen's.

SONS LIVING (By 1st marriage)

Hon Jonathan West Sanders, *b* 1948; BA; has issue living, two sons and one da. *Residence* – Dulwich, SE24.

(By 2nd marriage)

Hon Jeremy John Nicholas, *b* 1954; PhD, MA; has issue living, one son and one da. *Residence* – All Souls Coll, Oxford.
Hon Toby Michael John, *b* 1965; BA; with Kay, Collyer & Boose, New York.

DAUGHTER LIVING (By 2nd marriage)

Hon Sarah Harriet Ann, *b* 1953; BSSc, ARIBA: *m* 1986, David Lindsay Willetts, MP, Paymaster Gen July 1996-May 1997, since when Shadow Min for Education, of Ashchurch Grove, W12, and has issue living, one son and one da.

BUTTERWORTH, BARON (Butterworth) (Life Baron 1985)

JOHN BLACKSTOCK BUTTERWORTH, CBE, only son of John William Butterworth, by his wife, Florence, da of John Blackstock, of Dumfries; *b* 13 March 1918; *ed* Queen Elizabeth's Gram Sch, Mansfield, and The Queen's Coll, Oxford; Hon DCL Sierra Leone 1976, Hon DSc Aston Univ 1985, Hon LLD Warwick 1986; served RA 1939-46; Bar Lincoln's Inn 1947 (Hon Bencher 1989); Fellow New Coll, Oxford 1946-63, Faculty Fellow Nuffield Coll 1953-58, Managing Trustee Nuffield Foundation 1964-85, since when Trustee; Chm Univs Cttee for Non-teaching Staffs 1970-85, Memb Board of British Council 1981-86; First Vice Chancellor Warwick Univ 1963-85; Gov R Shakespeare Theatre since 1964, Memb Jarratt Cttee on Univ Efficiency since 1986, Crohan Cttee on review of Univ Grants Cttee since 1987, Univ Commr (under Educn Reform Act 1988) since 1988; Pres Council for Science and Technology 1997 (Chm 1990-97); a DL Warwicks 1967-74, since when W Midlands; JP City of Oxford 1962, and Coventry since 1963; *cr* CBE (Civil) 1982, and *Baron Butterworth*, of Warwick, co Warwick (Life Baron) 1985: *m* 1948, Doris Crawford, da of George Elder, of Edinburgh, and has issue.

Arms – Sable on a fess argent a representation of a DNA double helix spirals azure lined gules with connecting lines or and in chief two bears erect argent muzzled gules and in base an elephant also erect each standing against a ragged staff argent and collared and chained or the chain reflexed over the back round the foot of the staff and ending in a ring gold. **Crest** – Rising from a tree stock couped sable a phoenix or in flames proper grasping in the dexter claw a millrind sable. **Supporters** – Upon a compartment comprising a grassy mount strewn with buttercups proper on either side a little owl proper charged on the neck with a representation of a DNA double helix as in the arms.
. *Residence* – The Barn, Guiting Power, Glos GL54 5US. *Club* – Athenaeum.

SON LIVING

Hon John William Blackstock (5a Montpelier Grove, NW5 2XD), *b* 1952; *ed* Winchester, and New Coll, Oxford.

DAUGHTERS LIVING

Hon Anna Elizabeth Blackstock, *b* 1951; *ed* Benenden, and Lady Margaret Hall, Oxford: *m* 1983, Timothy Edward Hanson Walker, of 24 Old Park Av, SW12 8RH.

Hon Laura Blackstock, *b* 1959; *ed* Benenden, Dean Close Sch, Cheltenham, and Westfield Coll, London: *m* 1985, John Laughton Burley, of College Farm House, Millington, Pocklington, Yorks, son of John Burley, of Pocklington, York.

BUXTON, EARLDOM (Extinct 1934)

DAUGHTER LIVING OF FIRST EARL (By 2nd marriage)

Lady Alethea Constance Dorothy Sydney, *b* 1910: *m* 1934, Ven Peter Charles Eliot, MBE, TD, late Lt-Col RA (TA), who *d* 1995, of The Old House, Kingsland, Leominster, Herefordshire HR6 9QS (*see* E St Germans, colls, 1995 Edn).

BUXTON OF ALSA, BARON (Buxton) (Life Baron 1978)

AUBREY BUXTON, KCVO, MC, son of late Leland William Wilberforce Buxton (*see* Buxton, Bt, colls); *b* 15 July 1918; *ed* Ampleforth, and Trin Coll, Camb; Maj Sup Reserves; DL Essex 1975, High Sheriff 1972; Extra Equerry to HRH The Duke of Edinburgh since 1964; 1939-45 War (despatches, MC); Dir Anglia Television since 1958, Treas, London Zoological Soc 1977-83; British Vice-Pres World Wildlife Fund since 1968; Pres Royal Television Soc 1973-77; Ch Exec Anglia TV Group (Dir 1955-88, Chm 1986-88), Chm Independent TV News Ltd 1981-86; Chm UPITN Internat TV News Agency since 1981; Chm Survival Anglia since 1986; Member Countryside Commn, etc; *cr Baron Buxton of Alsa*, of Stiffkey, co Norfolk (Life Baron) 1978: KCVO 1996: *m* 1st, 1946, Pamela Mary, who *d* 1983, da of Sir Henry Ralph Stanley Birkin, 3rd Bt, and widow of Maj Samuel Luckyn Buxton, MC, 17th/21st Lancers (*see* Buxton, Bt, colls); 2ndly, 1988, Mrs Kathleen Peterson, of Maine, USA, and has issue by 1st *m*.

Arms – Argent a lion rampant the tail elevated and turned over the head between two mullets in fesse sable. Crest – A stag's head couped gules attired or gorged with a collar of the last pendent therefrom an escutcheon argent charged with a negro's head couped at the shoulders in profile proper. Supporters – *Dexter*, a crowned crane (Balearica Pavonina); *Sinister*, a flamingo proper.
Residence – Old Hall Farm, Stiffkey, Wells-next-the-Sea, Norfolk. *Club* – White's.

SONS LIVING (By 1st marriage)

Hon Timothy Leland (The Dairy, Castle Howard, York YO4 7BY), *b* 1948; *ed* Ampleforth: *m* 1st, 1972 (*m diss* 1986), Julie Mary, da of Lt-Cdr (John) Michael Avison Parker, CVO; 2ndly, 1994, Mrs Amanda Evelyn Dickinson, da of A/Cdre Anthony Walkinshaw Fraser (*see* Feilden, Bt), and has issue living (by 1st *m*), Edward Leland, *b* 1976, — Alexandra Louise (Zanna), *b* 1973: *m* 1998, James A. C. Scrimgeour, son of Simon Scrimgeour, of Rozel, Jersey, CI.

Hon (Aubrey) James Francis (Church Farm, Carlton, Suffolk CB8 9LD), *b* 1956; *ed* Ampleforth, and RAC Cirencester: *m* 1981, Melinda, da of Peter Henry Samuelson, of Sigors, Clare, Suffolk, and has issue living, Henry James Aubrey, *b* 1988, — Emma Lucie Maria, *b* 1984, — Olivia Louise, *b* 1986. *Clubs* – White's, Norfolk (Norwich).

DAUGHTERS LIVING (By 1st marriage)

Hon Nicola Mary Caroline, *b* 1947: *m* 1970, Adrian William Guy Sykes, of Cook's Mill, Fordham Heath, Colchester, Essex CO3 5TF, and has had issue, Samuel Adrian Aubrey, *b* 1974, — Eleanor Mary Fiona, *b* 1972, — Miranda Pamma Lucinda, *b* 1982, — Daisy Maria Hester, *b* and *d* 1985, — Pandora India Nicola, *b* 1987.
Hon Lucinda Catherine, *b* 1950; Wildlife Photographer; FRGS.
Hon Veronica Frances *b* 1953: *m* 1975, William Robert Charles Williams-Wynne of Talybont, Peniarth, Gwynedd, and has issue (*see* Williams-Wynn, Bt, colls).
Hon Victoria Jane, *b* 1960.

Buxton, family name of Baron Noel-Buxton.

BYERS, BARONY OF (Byers) (Extinct 1984)

SON LIVING OF LIFE BARON

Hon Charles William, *b* 1949; *ed* Westminster, and Ch Ch Oxford, Bar (Gray's Inn) 1973; Recorder Crown Court since 1993: *m* 1972 (*m diss* 1995), Suzan Mary, da of late Aubrey Kefford Stone, and has issue living, Jonathan Charles, *b* 1975, — George William, *b* 1977. *Chambers* – 23 Essex St, WC1.

DAUGHTERS LIVING OF LIFE BARON

Hon Elizabeth Frances, *b* 1941: *m* 1st, 1961 (*m diss* 1977), Charles Alasdair Ronald Malcolm; 2ndly, 1978, Peter Gaff, and has issue living (by 1st *m*), Alasdair James, *b* 1968; has issue living, David James *b* 1998, Rhomi Elizabeth *b* 1996, — Catherine Luise, *b* 1965; has issue living, Christopher James *b* 1998, Anna Elizabeth *b* 1995.

Hon (Ann) Luise, *b* 1946: *m* 1st, 1972 (*m diss* 19—), Dipak Nandy; 2ndly, 19—, Ray Fitzwalter, and has issue living (by 1st *m*), Francesca, *b* 1977, — Lisa, *b* 1979.

Hon Sara Margaret, *b* 1952: *m* 1979, Simon John Somers, and has issue living, Laura Sian, *b* 1982, — Amy Rowena, *b* 1984.

BYFORD, BARONESS (Byford) (Life Baroness 1996)

HAZEL BYFORD, DBE, da of late Sir Cyril Osborne, MP; *b* 14 Jan 1941; *ed* St Leonard's Sch, St Andrews, and Moulton Agric Coll, Northampton; joined WRVS, Leicester 1961, County Organiser 1972-76; Chm Nat Cttee, Conservative Women 1990-93; Memb Transport Users' Consultative Cttee 1984-94, and Rail Users' Consultative Cttee 1994-95; Vice-Pres Nat Union of Conservative and Unionist Assoc 1993-96, and Pres 1996-97; *cr* DBE 1994, and *Baroness Byford*, of Rothley, co Leics (Life Baroness) 1996: *m* 1962, Charles Barrie Byford, CBE, son of late Donald Byford, CBE, of Thurcaston, Leics, and has had issue.

Arms – Per chevron azure and purpure in chief two garbs or and in base a pierced cinquefoil ermine. Supporters – On either side a hippocampus argent gorged with an ancient crown attached to the back thereof a chain flexed or.

Address – House of Lords, Westminster, SW1A 0PW. *Club* – Farmers'.

SON DECEASED

Hon (David) Charles, *b* 1968; *ed* Rugby; *d* 1999.

DAUGHTER LIVING

Hon (Margaret) Elizabeth, *b* 1965; *ed* Cheltenham Ladies' College.

Byng, family name of Earl of Strafford.

Byng, family name of Viscount Torrington.

BYRON, BARON (Byron) (Baron E 1643)

Trust Byron

ROBERT JAMES BYRON, 13th Baron; *b* 5 April 1950; *s* 1989; *ed* Wellington Coll, and Trin Coll, Camb; Bar Inner Temple 1974, Solicitor 1978, Ptnr Holman, Fenwick & Willan since 1984: *m* 1979, Robyn Margaret, da of John McLean, of Hamilton, NZ, and has issue.

𝕬rms – Argent, three bendlets enhanced gules. 𝕮rest – A mermaid proper. 𝕾upporters – Two horses of a brown bay colour unguled or. *Residence* – 155 Ashley Gdns, SW1.

SON LIVING

Hon CHARLES RICHARD GORDON, *b* 28 July 1990.

DAUGHTERS LIVING

Hon Caroline Anne Victoria, *b* 1981.
Hon Emily Clare, *b* 1984.
Hon Sophie Georgina, *b* 1986.

AUNT LIVING *(sister of 12th Baron)*

Sheila Margaret, *b* 1903: *m* 1st, 1923 (*m diss* 1929), James Roy Notter Garton, Capt KRRC, who *d* 1939; 2ndly, 1929, Edward William Standish, of Marwell Hall, Winchester, who *d* 1933; 3rdly, 1935, George Munro Kerr, who *d* 1970, and has issue living (by 2nd *m*), Anthony Edward Byron (Paternoster House, Ipplepen, Newton Abbot, S Devon), *b* 1931; *ed* Eton: *m* 1956, Diana Huguette, only da of late Dr Hugh Gordon, of 3 High St, Kirkcudbright, and has issue living, Miles Anthony *b* 1958: *m* 1989, Juliette Ellis, Alexander Hugh *b* 1959: *m* 1984, Caroline Lo, Edward Pery *b* 1968: *m* 1992, Anna Margaret, yr da of John Raymond Perring, TD (*see* Perring, Bt), Caroline Lucy *b* 1963: *m* 1992, Mark Gawor, — Susan Felicity, *b* 1929: *m* 1949, Capt Derek Russell de Courcy Trasenster, 4th/7th R Drag Gds, of Compton House, Upton Grey, Basingstoke, Hants, and has issue living, Mark William de Courcy, *b* 1954: *m* 1983, Elisabeth Ross (and has issue living, Sophie Georgina *b* 1984, Georgina Sarah *b* 1986, Sara Elisabeth *b* 1989, Cordelia Camilla de Courcy *b* 1991), Camilla de Courcy *b* 1951: *m* 1974, Brig Clendon Daukes, late 4th/7th R Drag Gds (and has issue living, Anthony Clendon, *b* 1976, Thomas Clendon *b* 1978, Rose-Anna *b* 1981). *Residence* – 52 Eresby House, Rutland Gate, SW7 1BG.

DAUGHTER LIVING OF ELEVENTH BARON

Hon (Isobel) Ann, *b* 1932: *m* 1st, 1951, Robert Reford Corr, who *d* 1980; 2ndly, 1983, Norman James Woods, son of late James Park Woods, VC, of W Australia, and has issue living, (by 1st *m*), John Byron Reford, *b* 1953: *m* 1982, Suzette Margaret Brackenridge, and has issue living, Alexandra Isobel *b* 1987, Georgina Elizabeth *b* 1992, — Anthony Byron Reford, *b* 1956: *m* 1984 (*m diss* 1996), Joanne Lee Cruickshank, and has issue living, Louisa Ann *b* 1988, Alana May *b* 1991, — Helen Jane, *b* 1961. *Residence* – 55A Mayfair St, Mount Claremont, W Australia.

PREDECESSORS – (1) *Sir* JOHN BYRON, KB, MP for Nottingham, a faithful adherent of Charles I, Gov to HRH the Duke of York, and FM Gen of the Forces is Worcester, Salop, Chester, and N Wales; was *cr Baron Byron*, of Rochdale, co Lancaster (peerage of England) 1643, with remainder to his brothers Richard, William, Thomas, Robert, Gilbert, and Philip; *dsp* 1652; *s* by his brother (2) RICHARD, KB, 2nd Baron, Gov of Appleby Castle, Westmorland, and of Newark: *d* 1679; *s* by his son (3) WILLIAM, 3rd Baron; *d* 1695; *s* by his son (4) WILLIAM, 4th Baron, gentleman of the Bedchamber to George, Prince of Denmark; *d* 1736; *s* by his son (5) WILLIAM, 5th Baron; having killed William Chaworth, Esq, in a duel, 26 Jan 1765, was arraigned before his peers and found guilty of manslaughter, but claiming the benefit of the statute of Edward VI, was discharged by simply paying the fees; *d* without surviving issue 1798; *s* by his great-nephew (6) GEORGE GORDON, 6th Baron, grandson of Hon John, 2nd son of 4th Baron; celebrated as a poet; *d* 1824, without male issue; *s* by his cousin (7) GEORGE ANSON, 7th Baron, an Adm and an Extra Lord-in-Waiting to HM Queen Victoria; *d* 1868; *s* by his son (8) GEORGE ANSON, 8th Baron: *m* 1844, Lucy Elizabeth Jane, who *d* 1912, da of late Rev William Westcomb, R of Langford; *dsp* 1870; *s* by his nephew (9) GEORGE FREDERICK WILLIAM, 9th Baron, *b* 1855: *m* 1901, *Dame* Fanny Lucy, DBE, who *d* 1936, da of late Thamas Radmall, of St Margarets, Twickenham (Brinckman, Bt), and formerly wife of Lt-Col Theodore Francis Brinckman (afterwards 3rd Bt) (she *m* 3rdly, 1924, Sir Robert Paterson Houston, 1st Bt, who *d* 1926); *d* 1917; *s* by his brother (10) *Rev* FREDERICK ERNEST CHARLES (son of Hon Frederick Byron, 2nd son of 7th Baron), 10th Baron, *b* 1861; sometime V of Thrumpton and R of Barton-in-Fabis: *m* 1921, Lady Anna Ismay Ethel, who *d* 1966, da of late Lord Charles Edward Fitzroy (D Grafton); *d* 1949; *s* by his kinsman (11) RUPERT FREDERICK GEORGE (son of late Col Wilfrid Byron, son of Rev Hon William Byron, 4th son of 7th Baron), 11th Baron, *b* 1903: *m* 1931, Pauline Augusta, who *d* 1993, da of late T. J. Cornwall, of Wagin, W Australia; *d* 1983; *s* by his kinsman (12) RICHARD GEOFFREY GORDON (son of late Col Richard Byron, DSO, son of late Maj-Gen John Byron, son of late Rev John Byron, son of Rear-Adm Richard Byron, CB, el son of Rev Hon Richard Byron, 3rd son of 4th Baron), 12th Baron, *b* 1899; Lt-Col 4th/7th R Drag Gds, European War 1939-45 in France (DSO 1944), ADC to Gov of Bombay 1921-22, Mil Sec to Gov-Gen and C-in-C New Zealand: *m* 1st, 1926 (*m diss* 1946), Margaret Mary, only da of late Francis Gerald Steuart, of Fyfhyde, Winchester, Hants; 2ndly, 1946, Dorigen Margaret, who *d* 1985, only da of Percival Kennedy Esdaile; *d* 1989; *s* by his yr son (his elder son, Hon Richard Noel Byron, *b* 1948, was *k* in an air accident in W Africa 1985, *unm*), (13) ROBERT JAMES, 13th Baron and present peer.

CACCIA, BARONY OF (Caccia) (Extinct 1990)
(Name pronounced "Catch-a")

SON DECEASED OF LIFE BARON

†*Hon* David Anthony Lawrence, *b* 1936; *ed* Eton, and Trin Coll, Oxford; HM Foreign Ser: *m* 1962 (*m diss* 1973), Angela Margaret, da of Edward James Read, of Johannesburg, and *d* 1983, leaving issue, Alexander Orlando Harold (The Lady Cottage, Notgrove, Glos; Abernant, Builth Wells, Powys LL2 3YR), *b* 1963: *m* 1994, Fiona C., da of Brian Reid, of Holland Park, W8, and has issue living, Antony *b* 1998, Laura *b* 1995, Lilian *b* 1996, — Arabella Sabina Lilian, *b* 1965: *m* 1990, Anthony James Hamilton-Russell, of Braemar House, P.O. Box 158, Hermanus, Cape, S Africa (*see* B Ashbourne).

DAUGHTERS LIVING OF LIFE BARON

Hon Clarissa Sabina, *b* 1939: *m* 1959, David Eugene Henry Pryce-Jones, of Pentwyn, Gwenddwr, Powys, and Phillimore Lodge, 1 Phillimore Terr, W8 6BJ, only son of Alan Payan Pryce-Jones, TD, and has had issue, Adam, *b* 1973, — Jessica Therese, *b* 1961: *m* 1988, David Roderick Shukman, elder son of Prof Harold Shukman, of St Antony's Coll, Oxford, and has issue living, Jack Nicholas Oliver *b* 1989, Harold David *b* 1992, Kitty Térèse *b* 1994, — Candida Zoe, *b* 1963: *m* 1989, Owen William Luxardo Mostyn-Owen, elder son of William Mostyn-Owen, of Woodhouse, Rednal, Shropshire, and has issue living, Gemma Clare *b* 1992, Poppy Hannah *b* 1994, Beatrice Lucia *b* 1998, — Sonia, *b* 1970, *d* 1972.

Hon Antonia Catherine CACCIA (21 Westwood Rd, Barnes, SW13), *b* 1947; has resumed her maiden name: *m* 1970 (*m diss* 1974), Barton Midwood, and has issue living, Jacob CACCIA, *b* 1972.

WIDOW LIVING OF LIFE BARON

ANNE CATHERINE (NANCY) (*Baroness Caccia*), da of Sir George Lewis Barstow, KCB (*see* B Trevethin and Oaksey, 1970 Edn): *m* 1932, Baron Caccia, GCMG, GCVO (Life Baron), who *d* 1990. *Residence* – Abernant, Builth Wells, Powys LD2 3YR.

CADMAN, BARON (Cadman) (Baron UK 1937)

Always ready

JOHN ANTHONY CADMAN, 3rd Baron; *b* 3 July 1938; *s* 1966; *ed* Harrow, Selwyn Coll, Camb, and RAC Cirencester: *m* 1975, Janet, da of late A. Hayes, of Laneside, Walton Av, Bare, Lancs, and has issue.

Arms – Azure, three fleur-de-lys in pale between four endorses indented argent. *Crest* – A stork's head holding in the beak a sprig of columbine proper. *Supporters* – *Dexter* a stork, and *Sinister* a peacock agent beaked gules, each gorged with a collar azure charged with a fleur-de-lys also argent. *Address* – c/o House of Lords, SW1.

SONS LIVING

Hon NICHOLAS ANTHONY JAMES, *b* 18 Nov 1977.
Hon Giles Oliver Richard, *b* 1979.

BROTHER LIVING

Hon James Rupert, *b* 1944; *ed* Harrow.

UNCLE LIVING (*Son of 1st Baron*)

Hon Arthur Denys, *b* 1911; *ed* Harrow, and Harvard Univ: *m* 1933, Cary, da of Burke Baker, of Texas, USA, and has issue living, John Denys (QL 26 Conj 6 Casa 1, Lago Sul, Brasilia, Brazil 74665-165), *b* 1941; *ed* Princeton Univ (BSE), and Univ of California (MS, PhD): *m* 1st, 1964, Judith Ann, da of Warren Whittaker, of Miami; 2ndly, 1984, Lais Moreira de Castro, of Rio de Janeiro, and has issue living (by 1st *m*), Cynthia, *b* 1965, Cary Anne *b* 1968, — David Baker (1732 McSpadden, Vancouver, BC V5N 1L4, Canada), *b* 1948; *ed* Univ of The South, Sewanee, Tennessee (BA): *m* 1980, Marie, da of Henrick C. Orth-Pallavicini, of New York, and has issue living, Darcy Eryn *b* 1984, — Anne, *b* 1935: *m* 1957, John Edward McCrea Lawrence, of 98 Ruskin, Ottawa, Canada, and has issue living, Edward Burke *b* 1959: *m* 1995, Lori Ann Eva Hickling, John Cadman *b* 1960: *m* 1980, Robyn Mooney (and has issue living, Jy Maya *b* 1989, Rohja Raina *b* 1991, Beniya Lalo *b* 1996), Denys McCrea *b* 1962: *m* 1988, Mona Stiffler (and has issue living, Noah Denys *b* 1989), Cary Edwina *b* 1964: *m* 1992, Thomas Christopher Paul LaPierre (and has issue living, Paige Beryl Polly *b* 1997), — Mary Betty, *b* 1937; BA Smith Coll, MDiv Trin Coll, Toronto Univ: *m* 1958, Robert Alexander Calvin, of 464 Oriole Parkway, Toronto, Canada, and has issue living, Robert Denys *b* 1960: *m* 1986, Barbara Patricia Lee (and has issue living, Graham Denys *b* 1992, Sarah Emily *b* 1990), John Collamer *b* 1962, Isobel Anne *b* 1965: *m* 1990, Justin Gray Bonar (and has issue living, Leonard George *b* 1999), — Cary *b* 1945; BA, Chatham Coll, Pittsburgh, USA: *m* 1984, Robert A. Johnson, of 324 Elm St, Duxbury, Mass 02332, USA, and has issue living, Marlana Rose *b* 1988. *Residence* – 4100 Jackson Apt 503, Austin, Texas 78731, USA.

AUNT LIVING (*Daughter of 1st Baron*)

Hon Sybil Mary (Bryn-Dedwydd, Maerdy, Corwen, Clwyd LL21 9NY), *b* 1916: *m* 1st, 1938, Maj-Gen William Pat Arthur Bradshaw, CB, DSO late Scots Gds, who *d* 1966; 2ndly 1968, James Simon Cadman, who *d* 1986, and has issue living (by 1st *m*); Christopher Patrick Cadman (Llwynon, Parrog Rd, Newport, Pembs SA42 0RF), *b* 1941; *ed* Eton, and St Andrews Univ (BSc): *m* 1973 (*m diss* 1998), Susan Elizabeth, da of D. W. Vasey, of Downways, Old Bosham, Sussex, and has issue living, Benjamin Patrick *b* 1975; *ed* Ardingly, Philippa Mary *b* 1977, Emma Judith *b* 1979, — (Francis) John Cadman, LVO (Rhagatt Hall, Carrog, Corwen, Clwyd LL21 9NY), *b* 1946; *ed* Pangbourne Nautical Coll; Cdr RN; LVO 1984: *m* 1981, Frances Mary Christine, only da of Col Robert Hugh Cuming, MBE (*see* B Robertson of Oakridge, 1995 Edn), and has issue living, Anna Mary Christine *b* 1983, Juliet Frances *b* 1985, Isabel Fiona *b* 1987, — Caroline *b* 1939: *m* 1959, Francis Rokeby Black, FCA, of The Old Vicarage, Wing, Leighton Buzzard, Beds LU7 0NU, and has issue living, James Pat Rokeby *b* 1963; *ed* Eton, and Exeter Univ (BSc): *m* 1990, Susan Elizabeth Bone (and has issue living, Charles Joshua Rokeby *b* 1995, Oliver Sebastian *b* 1998), Alexander William Francis *b* 1967; *ed* Harrow, and Exeter Univ (BSc); ACA, CEng, MIEE: *m* 1998, Sarah Gertrude O'Brien, Lucinda Rosalie *b* 1960; *ed* Exeter Univ (BA): *m* 1985, Philip Latham Baillieu (and has issue) (*see* B Baillieu), Natasha Caroline *b* 1976; *ed* Oxford Brookes Univ (BEd), — Rosalie Annette *b* 1944: *m* 1965, David Bernard Butler Adams, of The Old Rectory, Holtby, York, YO1 3UD, and has issue living, William David *b* 1974; *ed* Rugby, Sophie Anne *b* 1966, Amanda Jane *b* 1968, Fiona Mary *b* 1972.

WIDOW LIVING OF SECOND BARON

MARJORIE ELIZABETH (*Marjorie, Baroness Cadman*) (Overlands, 157 Church Rd, Combe Down, Bath), da of Byron William Bunnis: *m* 1936, the 2nd Baron Cadman, who *d* 1966.

PREDECESSORS – (1) JOHN CADMAN, GCMG, DSc, FRS, son of the late James Cope Cadman, MICE, of Newcastle-under-Lyme; *b* 1877; a Mining Engineer and Petroleum Technologist; *cr Baron Cadman*, of Silverdale, co Stafford (peerage of United Kingdom) 1937: *m* 1907, Lilian Julia, who *d* 1963, da of the late John Harragin of Trinidad; *d* 1941; *s* by his son (2) JOHN BASIL COPE, 2nd Baron; *b* 1909: *m* 1936, Marjorie Elizabeth, da of Byron William Bunnis; *d* 1966; *s* by his son (3) JOHN ANTHONY, 3rd Baron, and present peer.

CADOGAN, EARL (Cadogan) (Earl GB 1800)
(Name pronounced "Caduggan")

QUI INVIDET MINOR EST

He who envies is the inferior

CHARLES GERALD JOHN CADOGAN, 8th Earl; *b* 24 March 1937; *s* 1997; *ed* Eton; Chm Cadogan Estates and Group of Cos; Chm Leukaemia Research Fund; DL Greater London 1996; Freeman City of London; Hon Fellow Royal Veterinary Coll, and Incorporated Soc of Valuers and Auctioneers; patron of four livings: *m* 1st, 1963, Lady Philippa Dorothy Bluett Wallop, who *d* 1984, da of 9th Earl of Portsmouth; 2ndly, 1989 (*m diss* 1994), Jennifer Jane Greig, da of J. E. Keith Rae, and of Mrs Sebastian Z. de Ferranti; 3rdly, 1994, Dorothy Ann, MVO, yr da of late Dr W. E. Shipsey, and has issue by 1st *m*.

Arms – Quarterly: 1st and 4th gules, a lion rampant reguardant or, *Cadogan*: 2nd and 3rd argent, three boars' heads couped sable. **Crest** – Out of a ducal coronet or, a dragon's head vert. **Supporters** – *Dexter*, a lion reguardant or, gorged with a collar gemeflory counterflory gules; *sinister*, an eagle wings elevated sable, beaked, membered, and navally crowned or, gorged with a riband argent, fimbriated gules, pendent therefrom a representation of the cross of Imperial Austrian military order of Maria Theresa.
Office - The Cadogan Office, 18 Cadogan Gdns, SW3 2RP. *Clubs* – White's, RAC.

SONS LIVING (*By 1st marriage*)

EDWARD CHARLES (*Viscount Chelsea*), *b* 10 May 1966; *ed* St David's Coll, Llandudno; commn'd RAF 1988; served Gulf War: *m* 1990, Katharina Johanna Ingeborg, da of Rear Adm Diether P. H. Hülsemann, German Navy, and has issue:—
SONS LIVING— *Hon* George Edward Charles Diether, *b* 24 Sept 1995, — *Hon* Charles William LLywellyn, *b* 1998.
DAUGHTER LIVING— *Hon* Philippa Katharina, *b* 1992.
Hon William John, *b* 1973; *ed* Eton, and Glasgow Univ (MA).

DAUGHTER LIVING (*By 1st marriage*)

Lady Anna-Karina, *b* 1964: *m* 1992, Gary Andrew Thomson, son of Dr Colin Thomson, of St Andrews, Fife, and has issue living, Alexander Rory, *b* 1998.

SISTERS LIVING

Lady Sarah Primrose Beatrix (*Baroness Rockley*), *b* 1938: *m* 1958, 3rd Baron Rockley, of Lytchett Heath, Poole, Dorset BH16 6AE.

Lady Daphne Magdalen, *b* 1939: *m* 1961, David Malcolm Graham Bailey, of The Manor House, Dry Sandford, Abingdon, Oxon OX13 6JP, and has issue living, Alexander Graham (34 Twining Av, Twickenham, Middx TW2 5UR), *b* 1962; *ed* Eton: *m* 1986, Meriam Atsede Ambaye, and has issue living, Antony Francis Christopher Graham *b* 1987, Antoinette Catonia Mia Lydia Alga *b* (twin) 1987, — Kevin David, *b* 1964; *ed* Eton, — Leonie Daphne, *b* 1965: *m* 1988, Brian Sharrock, eldest son of Kevin Sharrock, of MacArthur, Victoria, Australia, and has issue living, a son *b* 1997.

Lady Caroline Ann TAHANY, *b* 1946 (assumed surname of Tahany 1981): *m* 1965 (*m diss* 1975), Euan Woodroffe Foster, and has issue living, Guy Peter Woodroffe, *b* 1968: *m* 1999, Nicola S. K., da of Nicholas Mackenzie-Charrington, of Alresford, Hants, — Hugo Woodroffe, *b* 1971. *Residence* – 11 Oakley Gdns, SW3.

AUNT LIVING (*daughter of 6th Earl*)

Lady Beatrix Lilian Ethel, *b* 1912: *m* 1st, 1931 (*m diss* 1941), Henry Peregrine Rennie Hoare (*see* M Bristol, 1955 Edn), who *d* 1981; 2ndly, 1942, Col Edward Leighton Fanshawe, who *d* 1982, el son of late Lt-Gen Sir Edward Arthur Fanshawe, KCB, and has issue living (by 1st *m*), Henry Cadogan, *b* 1931; *ed* Eton, and Trin Coll, Camb (MA): *m* 1st, 1959 (*m diss* 1970), Pamela Saxon, da of late Col George Francis Bunbury, OBE; 2ndly, 1977, Caromy, da of Robert Jenkins, CBE, and formerly wife of Donald Maxwell Macdonald (*see* E Ducie, colls), and has issue living (by 1st *m*), Henry Timothy *b* 1960, Nicholas Colt *b* 1964; *ed* Eton, and Trin Coll, Camb: *m* 1995, Sara, yr da of Gerard Keane (and has issue living, Bertram Arthur *b* 1996), Arabella S. *b* 1968: *m* 1995, Richard A. P. Hopewell (and has issue living, Thomas Henry Prince *b* 1997), — Melanie Beatrix, *b* 1937: *m* 1963, Charles Henry Petre (*see* B Petre, colls), — (by 2nd *m*) Ann Erika (5 Clareville Court, Clareville Grove, SW7), *b* 1943, — Clodagh Frances, *b* 1945: *m* 1985, Leslie Waddington, of 2 Cheyne Gdns, SW3. *Residence* – 74 Cranmer Court, Sloane Av, SW3 3HF.

COLLATERAL BRANCHES LIVING

Issue of late Rt Hon Sir Alexander George Montagu Cadogan, OM, GCMG, KCB, yst son of 5th Earl, *b* 1884, *d* 1968: *m* 1912, Lady Theodosia Acheson, who *d* 1977, da of 4th Earl of Gosford:—
Ambrose Alec Patrick George (6 Maitland Rd, Reading, Berks RG1 6NL), *b* 1914: *m* 1955 (*m diss* 1961), Mrs Pamela Maud Hope-Johnstone, who *d* 1994, da of late Lt-Col John Murray Cobbold, Scots Gds (*see* D Devonshire, 1985 Edn). — Cynthia (*Lady Goschen*), *b* 1918; formerly Co Assist ATS: *m* 1946, Maj Sir Edward Christian Goschen, 3rd Bt, DSO.

Grandchildren of late John Cecil Cadogan, 2nd son of late Hon Charles George Henry Cadogan, yst son of 4th Earl:—
Issue of late Erik Cadogan, *b* 1913, *d* 1990: *m* 1939, (Lory) Caroline Elisabeth, da of Count Hans Gotthard Wachtmeister, of Malmö:—
Charles John, *b* 1954. — (Caroline) Monica (*Hon Mrs Peter H. Lewis*), *b* 1942: *m* 1974, Maj Hon Peter Herbert Lewis, and has issue (*see* B Merthyr). — Patricia Elisabeth, *b* 1945: *m* 1974, Simon Mark Corbett, of The Hall, Great Wratting, Suffolk CB9 7HQ, and has issue living, Camilla Louise, *b* 1978, — Lucy Miranda, *b* 1980.

Issue of late Peter Cadogan, *b* 1918, *d* 1962: *m* 1st, 1940 (*m diss* 1955), Joan, who *d* 1979, only da of late Adm Frederick Arthur Frith Banbury; 2ndly, 1955, Pamela Mary, da of late Alexander Henry Burman, OBE:—
(By 1st *m*) Gerald (Culworth, Banbury, Oxon OX17 2AT), *b* 1942: *m* 1968, Lucy Dodd, da of Walter Ramberg, of Washington, DC, and has issue living, Leo, *b* 1975, — Nancy, *b* 1979. — Sarah (*Lady Burns*), *b* 1944: *m* 1st, 1966 (*m diss* 1970), Geoffrey Hugh Kenion; 2ndly, 1973, Sir (Robert) Andrew Burns, KCMG, c/o FCO, King Charles St, SW1A 2AH, and has issue living (by 1st *m*), Ella Jane, *b* 1968, — (by 2nd *m*) Robert Duncan, *b* 1975, — Thomas Alexander Luckwell *b* 1977.

Granddaughter of Cdr Francis Charles Cadogan, RN (infra):—
Issue of late Capt Christopher Michael Cadogan, R Berks Regt, *b* 1917, *ka* 1941: *m* 1940, Stella Irena (who *d* 1998, having *m* 2ndly, 1943 (*m diss* 1955), David Rhys Ellias, and 3rdly, 1958, Sir Geoffrey Arnold Wallinger, GBE, KCMG, who *d* 1979), da of late Konrad Zilliacus, MP:—
Catharine (38 Perrymead St, SW6), *b* 1941.

Granddaughter of late Hon Charles George Henry Cadogan (ante):—
Issue of late Cdr Francis Charles Cadogan, RN, *b* 1885, *d* 1970: *m* 1913, Ruth Evelyn, who *d* 1962, da of late Sir (Edward) Stafford Howard, KCB (D Norfolk, colls), and widow of Gardner Sebastian Bazley (Bazley, Bt):—
Henriette Alice, DCVO (*Lady Abel Smith*) (The Garden House, Quenington, Cirencester, Glos) *b* 1914; JP; appointed a Lady-in-Waiting to HM The Queen when HRH Princess Elizabeth 1949, a Woman of the Bedchamber to HM The Queen 1952, an Extra Woman of the Bedchamber 1953-73, since when again Woman of the Bedchamber; CVO 1964, DCVO 1977: *m* 1st, 1939, Maj Sir Anthony Frederick Mark Palmer, 4th Bt (*cr* 1886), RA, who was *ka* 1941; 2ndly, 1953, Brig Sir Alexander Abel Smith, TD, JP (D Somerset, colls), who *d* 1980, and has issue living (by 1st *m*), (*see* Palmer, Bt, *cr* 1886), — (by 2nd *m*) Christopher Abel, *b* 1954: *m* 19—, Catherine, da of Paul Berger, of Nancy, France, and has issue living, Lyam Paul Alexander *b* 1988, a da *b* 1985, — Juliet Sarah, *b* 1955: *m* 1979, Christopher Graham Stainforth, son of Maj-Gen Charles Herbert Stainforth, CB, OBE, of Powderham House, Dippenhall, Farnham, Surrey, and has issue living, Charles Alexander *b* 1989.

PREDECESSORS – (1) *Gen the Rt Hon Sir* WILLIAM CADOGAN, KT, PC, successively MP for Woodstock, Ambassador to Brussels, Master of the Robes, Ambassador to the States Gen, Master-Gen of the Ordnance and Com-in-Ch of HM's Forces, was *cr Baron Cadogan*, of Reading, co Berks (peerage of Great Britain) 1716, a *Baron Cadogan*, of Oakley, co Bucks with remainder to his brother Charles, and *Viscount Caversham* and *Earl Cadogan* (peerage of Great Britain) 1718; *d* 1726, without male issue, when the Barony of Cadogan of Reading 1716, and the Earldom and Viscountcy of 1718 became ext; *s* in Barony of Cadogan of Oakley by his brother (2) CHARLES, 2nd Baron; was a Gen of Horse, MP and Gov of Sheerness, etc; *d* 1776; *s* by his son **(3)** CHARLES SLOANE, 3rd Baron; was MP for Cambridge 1749-76, and Master of the Mint, etc; cr *Viscount Chelsea* and *Earl Cadogan* (peerage of Great Britain) 1800; *d* 1807; *s* by his son **(4)** CHARLES HENRY SLOANE, 2nd Earl; *d* 1832; *s* by his half-brother **(5)** GEORGE, CB, 3rd Earl, a distinguished Adm, who in 1831 had been cr *Baron Oakley*, of Caversham, co Oxford (peerage of United Kingdom); *d* 1864; *s* by his son **(6)** HENRY CHARLES, PC, 4th Earl, *b* 1812; was MP for Reading 1841-7 and for Dover 1852-7, and Capt of Yeomen of the Guard 1866-68; *m* 1836, his cousin, Mary Sarah who *d* 1873, da of late Rev Hon Gerald Valerian Wellesley, DD (E Cowley); *d* 8 June, 1873; *s* by his son **(7)** GEORGE HENRY, KG, PC, 5th Earl, *b* 1840; MP for Bath (*C*) 1873; Under-Sec for War 1875-8, and for the Colonies 1878-80, Lord Privy Seal 1886-92, and Lord-Lieut. of Ireland with a Seat in the Cabinet 1895-1902; held Canopy at Coronation of King George V 1911: *m* 1st, 1865, Lady Beatrix Jane Craven, VA, who *d* 1907, da of 2nd Earl of Craven: 2ndly, 1911, Countess Adele Palagi, who *d* 1960, da of Lippo Neri, Count Palagi, a Florentine Patrician; *d* 1915, *s* by his third but el surviving son **(8)** GERALD OAKLEY, CBE, 6th Earl, *b* 1869; sometime Lt 1st Life Gds, and Capt 3rd Batn Suffolk Regt: *m* 1911, Lilian Eleanor Marie, who *d* 1973, da of George Steward Coxon, formerly of Craigleith, Cheltenham; *d* 1933, *s* by his son **(9)** WILLIAM GERALD CHARLES, MC, 7th Earl, *b* 1914; Capt Coldm Gds (Res), Lt-Col R Wilts Yeo (TA), Mayor of Chelsea 1964, Member Chelsea Borough Council 1954-59; 1939-45 War in Middle East and Italy: *m* 1st, 1936 (*m diss* 1959), Hon Primrose Lilian Yarde-Buller, who *d* 1970, da of 3rd Baron Churston; 2ndly, 1961, Cecilia Margaret, who *d* 1999, yst da of late Lt-Col Henry Kellerman Hamilton-Wedderburn, OBE, Scots Gds; *d* 1997; *s* by his only son **(10)** CHARLES GERALD JOHN, 8th Earl and present peer; also Viscount Chelsea, Baron Cadogan of Oakley, and Baron Oakley.

Cain, Nall-; family name of Baron Brocket.

CAIRNS, EARL (Cairns) (Earl UK 1878)

I flourish

SIMON DALLAS CAIRNS, CBE, 6th Earl; *b* 27 May 1939; *s* 1989; *ed* Eton, and Trin Coll, Camb; Receiver-Gen Duchy of Cornwall since 1990; CBE (Civil) 1992: *m* 1964, Amanda Mary, only da of late Maj Edgar Fitzgerald Heathcoat-Amory (*see* Heathcoat-Amory, Bt, colls), and has issue.

Arms – Gules, three martlets, argent within a bordure of the second, charged with three trefoils slipped vert. **Crest** – A martlet argent, charged on the breast with a trefoil slipped vert. **Supporters** – On either side a hawk, wings expanded proper, collared belled and chained or, holding in its beak a trefoil slipped vert.
Residence – Bolehyde Manor, Allington, Chippenham, Wilts SN14 6LW.

SONS LIVING

HUGH SEBASTIAN (*Viscount Garmoyle*) (11 Lonsdale Rd, W11 2BY), *b* 26 March 1965; *ed* Eton, and Edinburgh Univ: *m* 1991, Juliet, only da of Andrew Eustace Palmer, CMG, CVO, of Little Missenden, Bucks, and has issue living, *Hon* Oliver David Andrew, *b* 7 March 1993, — *Hon* Tara Davina Amanda, *b* 1995, — *Hon* Harriet, *b* 1998.

Hon (David) Patrick, *b* 1967; *ed* Eton, and Bristol Univ: *m* 1993, Francesca L., da of Oliver Rena, of Little Venice, W2, and has issue living, Oscar, *b* 1996, — Felix Timothy, *b* 1998.

Hon Alistair Benedict, *b* 1969; *ed* Eton, and LSE: *m* 1998, Arabella (Bee) L., da of Campbell Sim, of Four Elms, Kent, and of Mrs Louisa Harmer, of Brook Green, W6.

BROTHER LIVING

Hon Hugh Andrew David (Knowle Hill Farm, Ulcombe, Maidstone, Kent), *b* 1942; *ed* Wellington Coll, and Dublin Univ: *m* 1966, Elizabeth, da of Lt-Col F. C. L. Bell, of Cross Glades, Chiddingfold, Surrey, and has issue living, Bertram Wilfrid Arthur, *b* 1972, — Katherine Frances, *b* 1974.

SISTER DECEASED

Lady Elisabeth Olive, *b* 1944: *m* 1965, Capt Martin Ralph Lowe, 9th/12th R Lancers (ret), of Castle End, Ross-on-Wye, Herefords HR9 7JY, and *d* 1998, leaving issue, Alexander Charles, *b* 1970.

AUNT LIVING (*Daughter of 4th Earl*)

Lady Sheila Mary, *b* 1905: *m* 1930, Maj Charles Ivor Patrick Holroyd, late Rifle Bde, who *d* 1976, and has issue living, Charles John (Providence Cottage, Chute Cadley, Andover), *b* 1933; Lt-Col RGJ (ret): *m* 1969, Amanda Jane, da of Col Sir Richard Hamilton Glyn, 9th Bt, OBE, TD, MP, and has issue living, Charles Wilfrid *b* 1970; *ed* Eton, New Coll, Oxford, and Univ of Geneva; Bar Gray's Inn 1997, George Alexander James *b* 1974; *ed* Eton, Durham Univ, and Univ of S Calif, Joanna Mary Ursula *b* 1972; *ed* Sherborne, and Exeter Univ, — Richard Norton (Les Lausiers, Condillac, Montelimar, France), *b* 1946: *m* 1977, Karine, da of Raymond Phèlip, and has issue living, Wilfrid Andrew *b* 1980, Alistair Hugo *b* 1985, Alexander Ivor *b* 1987, Annabel Juliette *b* 1983, — Alice Elizabeth, *b* 1936: *m* 1961, Ronald L. Lilburne, of 6c Battys Rd, Blenheim, NZ, and has issue living, David Milton *b* 1964, Linda Robyn *b* 1962, — Serena Jane, *b* 1939: *m* 1978, Dr Thomas D. Gledhill, of 5 Oakwood Rd, Henleaze, Bristol BS9 4NP, and has issue living, Stephen Mark *b* 1981; *ed* Clifton, Sheona Grace *b* 1979; *ed* Badminton, and KIAD Canterbury, — Susan Virginia, *b* 1943. *Residence* – Providence Cottage, Chute Cadley, Andover, Hants.

WIDOW LIVING OF FIFTH EARL

BARBARA JEANNE HARRISON (*Dowager Countess Cairns*), yst da of late Sydney H. Burgess, of Heathfield, Bowdon, Chesh: *m* 1936, Adm the 5th Earl Cairns, GCVO, CB, who *d* 1989. *Residence* – The Red House, Clopton, Woodbridge, Suffolk.

COLLATERAL BRANCH LIVING

Grandchildren of late Hon Douglas Halyburton Cairns, 5th son of 1st Earl:—
Issue of late Lt-Col Hugh William Cairns, MC, *b* 1911, *d* 1996: *m* 1939, Diana Katherine, yr da of late Capt Arthur Granville Soames, OBE, of Hays Lodge, Chesterfield Hill, W1:—
Peter Granville, *b* 1940; *ed* Eton: *m* 1991, Mrs Ann Camilla Carlton, da of late J. B. Leworthy, of Beacon Hill, Westerham, Kent. —— Francis John Hugh, *b* 1942; *ed* Eton, and Trin Coll, Camb: *m* 1983, Ulla Agneta, yr da of Sten Bylander, of Gothenburg, Sweden, and has issue living, Catriona Helen, *b* 1984. —— Celia Helen (Cherry), *b* 1944: *m* 1968, David William Barclay, of Higham, Bury St Edmunds, Suffolk, and has issue living, Robin David, *b* 1969; Capt Royal Hussars: *m* 1997, Juliet Emma, 2nd da of Christopher Allanson, of Rotherfield, Sussex, — Katharine Elizabeth, *b* 1971.

PREDECESSORS – **(1)** *Rt Hon Sir* HUGH MacCALMONT CAIRNS, DCL, LLD, 2nd son of late William Cairns, of Cultra, co Down; *b* 1819; sat as MP for Belfast (C) 1852-66; was Solicitor-Gen 1858-59, Attorney-Gen 1866, a Lord Justice of Appeal 1866-68, and Lord High Chancellor 1868 and 1874-80; cr *Baron Cairns*, of Garmoyle, co Antrim (peerage of United Kingdom) 1867, and *Viscount Garmoyle* and *Earl Cairns* (peerage of United Kingdom) 1878: *m* 1856, Mary Harriet, who *d* 1919, da of late John McNeile, of Parkmount, co Antrim; *d* 1885; *s* by his son **(2)** ARTHUR WILLIAM, 2nd Earl, *b* 1861: *m* 1887, Olivia Elizabeth, OBE, who *d* 1951, having *m* 2ndly, 1899, Major Roger Cyril Hans Sloane Stanley (*d* 1944), da of late Alexander Augustus Berens, of Castlemead, Windsor; *d* 1890; *s* by his brother **(3)** HERBERT JOHN, 3rd Earl; *b* 1863; *d* 1905; *s* by his brother **(4)** WILFRID DALLAS, CMG, 4th Earl; *b* 1865; sometime Capt Rifle Brig and Lt-Col Comdg London Rifle Brig; S Africa 1902, European War 1914-19 (CMG): *m* 1894, Olive, who *d* 1952, da of late J. P. Cobbold, MP, of The Cliffe, Ipswich; *d* 1946; *s* by his son **(5)** DAVID CHARLES, GCVO, CB, 5th Earl, *b* 1909; Rear Adm, Pres Naval Coll, Greenwich 1958-61, Marshal of Diplomatic Corps 1961-71, Prime Warden Fishmongers' Co 1972-73, Pres Navy League 1966-77, an Extra Equerry to HM 1972-89; 1939-45 War (despatches), DL Suffolk: *m* 1936, Barbara Jeanne Harrison, yst da of late Sydney H. Burgess, of Heathfield, Bowdon, Chesh; *d* 1989; *s* by his elder son **(6)** SIMON DALLAS, 6th Earl and present peer; also Viscount Garmoyle, and Baron Cairns.

CAITHNESS, EARL OF (Sinclair) (Earl S 1455, Bt S 1631)

MALCOLM IAN SINCLAIR, PC, 20th Earl and 15th Baronet; *b* 3 Nov 1948; *s* 1965; *ed* Marlborough, and RAC, Cirencester; FRICS; a Lord-in-Waiting to HM 1984-85, Under-Sec for Transport 1985-86, Min of State, Home Office 1986-88, Min of State, Dept of Environment 1988-89, Paymaster Gen 1989-90, Min of State, Foreign and Commonwealth Office 1990-92, Min of State for Transport 1992-94; Co Dir, Co-Founder Victoria Soames Ltd 1995; PC 1990: *m* 1975, Diana Caroline, who *d* 1994, da of Maj Richard Lovel Coke, DSO, MC (*see* F. Leicester, colls), and has issue.

Arms – Quarterly; 1st azure, a lymphad at anchor or, flagged gules sails furled argent oars erect in saltire, within a double tressure flory of the second, *Earldom of Orkney*; 2nd and 3rd or, a lion rampant gules armed and langued azure, *Sparr-Nithsdale*; 4th azure, a three-masted ship or, flagged gules under sail argent, *Earldom of Caithness*; over all dividing the quarters a cross engrailed and countercharged argent and sable, *Sinclair* **Crest** – A cock proper armed and beaked or. **Supporters** – Two griffins gules wings elevated, armed beaked and winged or.
Seat – Girnigoe Castle, Caithness. *Address* – c/o House of Lords, SW1A 0PW.

SON LIVING

Alexander James Richard (*Lord Berriedale*), *b* 26 March 1981.

DAUGHTER LIVING

Lady Iona Alexandra, *b* 1978.

HALF-SISTERS LIVING

Lady Jean Elizabeth, *b* 1936; *m* 1961, David Peere Williams-Freeman, of Glendean Farm, Nottingham Rd, Natal, and has issue living, Andrew Frederick Peere, *b* 1962: *m* 1991, Fiona, da of Walter Hinds, of Nairobi, Kenya, — Juliet Margaret, *b* 1964: *m* 1994, Clive King, of Natal, S Africa, — Theresa Jean, *b* 1966: *m* 1991, Robert Wilson, of Howick, Natal, — Kim Jannette, *b* (twin) 1966: *m* 19—, Neil Roberts, of Shunigwi, Zimbabwe.

Lady Margaret Nicola, *b* 1937: *m* 1st 1959, Capt David Colin Kirkwood Brown, late Gordon Highlanders; 2ndly, 1983, John James Maxwell Glasse (High Sheriff Beds 1996), of The Old Rectory, Milton Bryan, Beds, and has issue living (by 1st *m*), Nicola Jane Kirkwood, *b* 1960: *m* 1983, Duncan A. Clark, son of Michael Clark, CBE, of Braxted Park, Witham, Essex, — Olivia Grizel Kirkwood (*Hon Mrs Rupert Edwards*), *b* 1962: *m* 1990, Hon Rupert Timothy Guy Edwards, only son of Baron Crickhowell, PC (Life Baron).

Lady Fiona Catharine, *b* 1941: *m* 1969, Capt Michael Stephen Whitfield, late R Scots Drag Gds (*see* Renshaw, Bt), of PO Box 721, Marondera, Zimbabwe.

SISTER LIVING

Lady Bridget Sarah, *b* 1947: *m* 1976, Nicholas Anthony Oppenheim, of 46 Lysia St, SW6 6NG, son of Sir Duncan Morris Oppenheim, and has issue living, Christopher Duncan, *b* 1981, — Leonora Emily *b* 1977, — Zerlina Gabrielle, *b* 1979.

AUNT LIVING (*Raised to the rank of an Earl's daughter* 1948)

Lady (Euphemia) Meredith, *b* 1915. *Residence* – The Triangle Nursing Home, Wheatley, Oxon OX33 1YW.

DAUGHTER LIVING OF EIGHTEENTH EARL

Lady Lucy BUCHAN, *b* 1902: *m* 1928, Sir Thomas Innes of Learney, GCVO, LLD, FSA (Scot), who *d* 1971 (*see* Innes, Bt cr 1628, colls). *Residence* – 56 Darnell Rd, Edinburgh EH5 3PJ.

COLLATERAL BRANCH LIVING

Descendants of late James Sinclair (grandson of late Alexander Sinclair, youngest son of Hon George Sinclair, 3rd son of 4th Earl), who was cr a *Baronet* 1704.

PREDECESSORS – *Sir* William Sinclair, of Roslin, sat in the Scottish Parliament at Scone 1283-4; his great-grandson, *Sir* Henry Sinclair, was admitted to be Earl of Orkney in 1379, by Haakon VIth King of Norway, and his grandson **(1)** WILLIAM, 3rd Earl of Orkney, and Lord High Chancellor of Scotland, was cr *Earl of Caithness* (peerage of Scotland) 1455, and styled Earl of Orkney and Caithness; James III, having acquired the islands of Orkney in marriage with Margaret of Denmark, the Earl surrendered to the king the Earldom of Orkney in 1471; passing over his el son (ancestor of the Lords Sinclair), was *s* by his 2nd son **(2)** WILLIAM, 2nd Earl, slain at Flodden 1513; *s* by his son **(3)** JOHN, 3rd Earl; killed 1529 in attempting to take possession of the Orkneys, to which he asserted a right; *s* by his grandson **(4)** GEORGE, 4th Earl, who resigned his Earldom to James V, who in 1545 granted a charter thereof to John, the Earl's heir-apparent, with remainder to his heirs male and assigns, whom failing to his faither's heirs male whatever; *d* 1582; *s* by his grandson **(5)** GEORGE, 5th Earl; resigned Earldom and obtained a novodamus 1592 with remainder to his el son William (subsequently known as *Lord Berriedale*) and his heirs male and assigns whatsoever; in 1606 received charter of land forming Barony of Berriedale; *d* 1643; *s* by his great-grandson **(6)** GEORGE, 6th Earl; being heavily indebted to Sir John Campbell, 5th Bt, of Glenorchy, he assigned his estates and "Earldom of Caithness" (as held under a charter of apprizing) to that gentleman; *d* 1676, and Sir John Campbell (ante) was cr Earl of Caithness 1677, which honour he resigned then 1681 (see E. Breadalbane), the apprizing and assignation carrying only the land of the Earldom, whilst the honours then passed to the rightful heir **(7)** GEORGE, 7th Earl, son of Francis (of Northfield), 2nd son of 5th Earl; *dsp* 1698; *s* by his kinsman **(8)** JOHN, 8th Earl, lineal descendant of 4th Earl; *d* 1706; *s* by his son **(9)** ALEXANDER, 9th Earl; *d* 1765; *s* by his kinsman **(10)** WILLIAM, 10th Earl, heir male of Sir John, grandson of 4th Earl; *d* 1779; *s* by his son **(11)** JOHN, 11th Earl; *d* 1789; *s* by his kinsman **(12)** *Sir* JAMES SINCLAIR (7th Bt, cr 1631, of Canisbay), 12th Earl, heir male of George, of Mey, youngest son of 4th Earl; Lord-Lieut of Caithness, a Representative Peer, and Postmaster-Gen of Scotland; *d* 1823; *s* by his son **(13)** ALEXANDER, 13th Earl; Lord-Lieut of Caithness; *d* 1855; *s* by his son **(14)** JAMES, FRS, 14th Earl, *b* 1821; Lord-Lieut and Vice-Adm of Caithness, and Lord-in-Waiting to HM Queen Victoria 1856 and 1859-66; cr *Baron Barrogill* (peerage of United Kingdom) 1866: *m* 1st, 1847, Louisa Georgiana, who *d* 1870, da of Sir George Richard Philips, Bt; 2ndly 1872, Marie, who *d* 1895 (having been cr in her own right Duchess de Pomár by Pope Leo XIII in 1879), da of Don Antonio José de Mariategui, of Santa Catalina Macuriges, and widow of Gen the Count de Pomár; *d* 1881; *s* by his son **(15)** GEORGE PHILIPS ALEXANDER, 15th Earl, *d* 1889, the title remaining dormant until 1890, when the nearest heir male of the 15th Earl was adjuged to be **(16)** JAMES AUGUSTUS (son of Lt-Col John Sutherland Sinclair, RA, a descendant of Robert Sinclair, of Durran, younger son of Sir James Sinclair, 1st Bt, of Mey), 16th Earl, *b* 1827: *m* 1855, Janet, da of Roderick Macleod, MD, of London; *d* 1891; *s* by his el son **(17)** JOHN SUTHERLAND, 17th Earl, *b* 1857; *d* 1914; *s* by his brother **(18)** NORMAN MACLEOD, CBE, 18th Earl, *b* 1862; admitted a Solicitor 1887; a Representative Peer for Scotland 1918-29; Lieut-Col late Gordon Highlanders (TA); assumed 1911, the surname and arms of Buchan in lieu of his patronymic: *m* 1893, Lillian, who *d* 1933, da of late Higford Higford, of 23 Eaton Place, SW; *d* 1947; *s* by his nephew **(19)** (JAMES) RODERICK, CVO, CBE, DSO (son of late Rev Hon Charles Augustus Sinclair, 3rd son of 16th Earl), 19th Earl *b* 1906; a Representative Peer for Scotland 1950-63; Brig and Col Gordon Highlanders; Comdg Ceylon Army 1949-52; *m* 1st, 1933, Grizel Margaret, who *d* 1943, da of Sir George Miller-Cunningham, KBE, CB; 2ndly, 1946, Madeleine Gabrielle, who *d* 1990 (having *m* 3rdly, 1977, David Frederick Ewen, CBE, who *d* 1986), da of Herman Edward de Pury, and widow of Capt George Wareing Drewry Ormerod, RA; *d* 1965; *s* by his only son **(20)** MALCOLM IAN, 20th Earl and present peer; also Lord Berriedale.

CALDECOTE, VISCOUNT (Inskip) (Viscount UK 1939)

ROBERT ANDREW INSKIP, KBE, DSC, 2nd Viscount; *b* 8th Oct, 1917; *s* 1947; *ed* Eton (Fellow 1952-69), and King's Coll, Camb (MA, Fellow 1948-55); FRINA, Hon FIMechE, Hon FIEE, Hon FICE, FEng, Pres of Dean Close Sch 1960-90, a Vice-Pres of St Lawrence Coll, 1939-45 War as Lt-Cdr RNVR; DL Hants 1991; a Member of House of Laity, Church Assembly 1949-55, and of UK delegation to UN Assembly 1952; Vice-Pres of Eurospace 1961-68, Pres of Soc of British Aerospace Cos 1965-66, of AICMA 1966-68, and of Parl and Scientific Cttee 1966-69; Dir of English Elec Co 1955-69, and Dep Man Dir of British Aircraft Corpn 1960-67; Chm of EDC for Movements of Exports 1965-71, and of Export Council of Europe 1970-71; Exec Dir Delta Metal Co 1969-82 (Chm 1972), Dir Consolidated Goldfields, Ltd 1969-78, and of Lloyds Bank 1974-88, a Member of Review Board for Govt Contracts 1969-75, and of Inflation Accounting Cttee 1975-74; Dir of Legal and Gen Assurance of Soc 1976-80 (Chm 1977); Pro-Chancellor, Cranfield Inst of Technology 1976-84; Member British Rail Board 1979-85; Chm Investors in Industries Gp 1980-87; Chm Mary Rose Trust 1983-92; Dir W. S. Atkins Ltd 1985-92; KBE (1987): *m* 1942, Jean Hamilla, da of late Rear-Adm Hugh Dundas Hamilton, of Limes, Haddenham, Bucks, and has issue.

Arms – Per chevron azure and argent in chief two crosses pattée or and in base an eagle displayed of the first. **Crest** – Upon the battlements of a tower a grouse's leg erased proper. **Supporters** – *Dexter*, a talbot; *sinister*, a pegasus proper; each charged on the shoulder with a garb or.
Residence – Orchard Cottage, South Harting, Petersfield, Hants GU31 5NR. *Clubs* – Athenaeum Pratt's, Royal Ocean Racing, Royal Yacht Squadron.

SON LIVING

Hon PIERS JAMES HAMPDEN *b* 20 May 1947; *ed* Eton: *m* 1st, 1970, Susan Bridget, da of late W. P. Mellen, of Hill Farm, Gt Sampford, Essex; 2ndly, 1984, Kristine Elizabeth, da of Harvey Holbrooke-Jackson, of 12 Abbots Close, Ramsey, Cambs, and has issue living (by 2nd *m*), Thomas James, *b* 22 March 1985.

DAUGHTERS LIVING

Hon Serena Helen Christian, *b* 1943: *m* 1965 (*m diss* 1979), John Andrew Brodie Armit, and has issue living, Jerome Nathan, *b* 1971, — Vashti Imogen, *b* 1969.
Hon Antonia Jane Hamilla, *b* 1952: *m* 1972, Piers Rowlandson, and has issue living, Titus, *b* 1973.

PREDECESSOR – **(1)** *Rt Hon Sir* THOMAS WALKER HOBART Inskip, CBE, son of late James Inskip, of Clifton Park House, Bristol; *b* 1876; was Chancellor of Diocese of Truro 1920-22, Solicitor-Gen Oct 1922 to Jan 1924 and Nov 1924 to March 1928, Attorney-Gen March 1928 to June 1979, Solicitor-Gen in National Govt Sept 1931 to Jan 1932, again Attorney-Gen Jan 1932 to March 1936, Min for Co-ordination of Defence March 1936 to Jan 1939, Sec of State for Dominion Affairs Jan to Sept 1939, Lord High Chancellor Sept 1939 to May 1940, again Sec of State for Dominion Affairs (also Leader of the House of Lords) May to Oct 1940, and Lord Ch Justice of England 1940-46; MP for Central Div of Bristol 1918-29 and for Fareham Div of Hampshire 1931-9; cr *Viscount Caldecote*, of Bristol, co Gloucester (peerage of United Kingdom) 1939: *m* 1914, Lady Augusta Helen Elizabeth, who *d* 1967, da of 7th Earl of Glasgow, and widow of Charles Lindsay Orr-Ewing, MP; *d* 1947; *s* by his son **(2)** ROBERT ANDREW, 2nd Viscount and present peer.

Calder, family name of Baron Ritchie-Calder.

CALEDON, EARL OF (Alexander) (Earl I 1800)

By sea and by land

NICHOLAS JAMES ALEXANDER, 7th Earl, *b* 6 May 1955; *s* 1980; *ed* Gordonstoun; Lord Lieut co Armagh 1989: *m* 1st, 1979 (*m diss* 1985), Wendy Catherine, da of Spiro Nicholas Coumantaros, of Athens; 2ndly, 1989, Henrietta Mary Alison, elder da of John Francis Newman (*see* Newman, Bt, *cr* 1912), and has issue by 2nd *m*.

Arms – Per pale argent and sable, a chevron, and in base a crescent counterchanged; on a canton azure, a harp or stringed argent. Crest – A dexter arm embowed in armour, the hand holding a sword proper. Supporters – *Dexter*, a mermaid with a mirror in her right hand proper; *sinister*, an elephant argent.
Seat – Caledon Castle, co Tyrone.

SON LIVING (*By 2nd marriage*)

FREDERICK JAMES (*Viscount Alexander*), *b* 15 Oct 1990.

DAUGHTER LIVING (*By 2nd marriage*)

Lady Leonora Jane, *b* 1993.

SISTER LIVING

Lady (Elizabeth) Jane, *b* 1962; resumed maiden name by deed poll 1987 until remarriage: *m* 1st, 1981 (*m diss* 1987), Rory F. A. Peck, a war cameraman, who was *k* in the Moscow riots 1993, son of Julian Peck, of Prehen House, co Londonderry; 2ndly, 1990 (*m diss* 1999), Richard Francis Andrew Dobbs, eldest son of Richard Arthur Frederick Dobbs, of Castle Dobbs, co Antrim, and has issue living (by 1st *m*), James Julian, *b* 1982, — Alexander Nicolas de Graevenitz, *b* 1984, — (by 2nd *m*) Louisa Valla Joan, *b* 1992, — Elizabeth Calixta Leslie, *b* 1994, — Victoria Natasha Jane, *b* 1996.

HALF-SISTER LIVING

Lady Tana Marie, *b* 1945: *m* 1973, His Honour Judge (Paul Everard Justus) Focke, QC, of 7 Cheyne Walk, SW3, and has issue living, Diana Natasha, *b* 1974, — Victoria Justine *b* 1976.

WIDOW LIVING OF SIXTH EARL

MARIE ELISABETH BURTON (*Elisabeth, Countess of Caledon*), da of Maj Richard Burton Allen, and formerly wife of Maj Hon Iain Maxwell Erskine (later 2nd Baron Erskine of Rerrick): *m* 1964, as his 3rd wife, the 6th Earl of Caledon, who *d* 1980.

COLLATERAL BRANCHES LIVING

Issue of late Harold Rupert Leofric George Alexander (*Earl Alexander of Tunis*), KG, GCB, OM, GCMG, CSI, DSO, MC, PC 3rd son of 4th Earl, *b* 1891, *d* 1969 (see that title).

Issue of late Col Hon William Sigismund Patrick Alexander, DSO, yst son of 4th Earl, *b* 1895, *d* 1972: *m* 1934, Jane Hermione, who *d* 1967, da of late Cdr Bernard Buxton, DSO (Buxton, Bt, colls):—
Alastair Patrick Lindsay (2665 Laguna St, San Francisco, California 94123, USA), *b* 1935; *ed* Eton; late Lt IG: *m* 1961, Evelyn, da of Massimimo Forte, of 28 Via San Sebastiano, Rome, and has issue living, Simone Eugenia, *b* 1962. —— Desmond Charles Bernard, *b* 1938; *ed* Eton, Univ of British Columbia (B Com), and Lancaster Univ (MA). —— Annabella Elizabeth Hero, *b* 1943.

Granddaughters of Lt-Col Hon Charles Alexander, 3rd son of 3rd Earl:—
Issue of late Capt Conn Alexander, *b* 1883, *d* 1970: *m* 1st, 1906, Gladys Constance, who *d* 1944, da of late Thomas Wrigley Grimshaw, CB; 2ndly 1944, Doris Minnie, who *d* 1983, da of late Robert Pacey, of Hove:—
(By 1st *m*) Mona, *b* 1909: *m* 1939, Col Richard Michael Aylmer, who *d* 1975, and has issue living, Justin Michael (Flat 1, 149 Rathgar Rd, Dublin 6), *b* 1940; *ed* Wellington: *m* 1981, Bridget Frances Georgina, elder da of Rev Canon George Alfred Salter, of St Luke's Rectory, Cork, and Lakka House, Castletownshend, co Cork, and has issue living, William George Algernon *b* 1984, Christopher Fenton Alexander *b* 1987, — Dennis Fenton (Valley House, Knocksink, Enniskerry, co Wicklow), *b* 1942; *ed* Wellington; Dir Lyons & Co (Ireland) Ltd: *m* 1976, Dorothy Margaret, da of Thomas Anthony Fleming, and has issue living, Richard Thomas *b* 1978, Elizabeth Mona *b* 1982. —— Marjorie (The

Manor House, Rathlin I, co Antrim), *b* 1912: *m* 1931, Brig Richard Francis O'Donnell Gage, CBE, MC, who *d* 1973, and has issue living, Ezekiel Conn, *b* 1933; *ed* Wellington; Lt-Col RA: *m* 1965, Frances Elizabeth, elder da of Maj Frederick George Bolam, and has issue living, Matthew James George *b* 1967, Alexander Richard *b* 1972, Victoria Louise *b* 1968, — Patrick Richard (Old Angel, Woodhill, Stoke St Gregory, Taunton, Som), *b* 1938; *ed* Wellington; Cdr RN: *m* 1962, Annette Daphne, only da of late John Charles William Staveley, of Gloynes House, Yealmpton, Devon, and has issue living, Rory James *b* 1965, Nicola Jane *b* 1964, Lucinda Georgina *b* 1970.

PREDECESSORS – (1) JAMES Alexander (of whose family the Alexanders of Milford, co Carlow, are the senior branch), having filled several important offices in India, was cr *Baron Caledon*, of Caledon, co Tyrone (peerage of Ireland) 1790, *Viscount Caledon* (peerage of Ireland) 1797, and *Earl of Caledon* (peerage of Ireland) 1800; *d* 1802; *s* by his son (2) DU PRE, KP, 2nd Earl; first Gov of Cape of Good Hope; a Representative Peer; *d* 1839; *s* by his son (3) JAMES DU PRE, 3rd Earl, *b* 1812; a Representative Peer, Capt Coldstream Gds, and Col of Tyrone Militia: *m* 1845, Lady Jane Frederica Harriot Mary Grimston, VA, who *d* 1888, 4th da of 1st Earl of Verulam; *d* 1855; *s* by his son (4) JAMES, KP, 4th Earl, *b* 1846; a Representative Peer for Ireland: *m* 1884, Lady Elizabeth Toler, who *d* 1939, da of 3rd Earl of Norbury; *d* 1893; *s* by his elder son (5) ERIK JAMES DESMOND, 5th Earl; *b* 1885, *d* 1968; *s* by his nephew (6) DENIS JAMES (son of Lt-Col Hon Herbrand Charles Alexander, DSO, who *d* 1965), 6th Earl, *b* 1920; Maj Irish Gds and Ulster Defence Regt: *m* 1st, 1943 (*m diss* 1948), Ghislaine, only da of Cornelius Willem Dresselhuys, of The Hague, and of late Edith, Viscountess Kemsley; 2ndly, 1952, Baroness Anne Louise, who *d* 1963, only child of late Baron Nicholas Werner Alexander de Graevenitz; 3rdly, 1964, Marie Elisabeth Burton, da of late Maj Richard Burton Allen, and formerly wife of Maj Hon Iain Maxwell Erskine (*see* B Erskine of Rerrick); *d* 1980; *s* by his only son (7)NICHOLAS JAMES, 7th Earl and present peer; also Viscount Caledon, and Baron Caledon.

CALLAGHAN OF CARDIFF, BARON (Callaghan) (Life Baron 1987)

(LEONARD) JAMES CALLAGHAN, KG, PC, son of late James Callaghan, Ch Petty Officer, of Portsmouth; *b* 27 March 1912; *ed* Portsmouth Sec (Northern) Sch; Visiting Fellow Nuffield Coll, Oxford 1959-67, Hon Life Fellow 1967, Hon Fellow Univ Coll Cardiff 1978, Portsmouth Univ 1981, and Swansea Univ Coll 1993, Hon LLD Wales Univ 1976, Sardar Patel Univ, India 1978, Birmingham Univ 1981, Meisei Univ, Japan, 1984, and Sussex Univ 1987; Parl Sec to Min of Transport 1947-50, Parl and Financial Sec to Admiralty 1950-51, Chancellor of the Exchequer 1964-67, and Home Office 1967-70, Sec of State for Foreign and Commonwealth Affairs 1974-76, Min of Overseas Dvpt 1975-76, Prime Minister and First Lord of the Treasury 1976-79; Leader of Labour Party 1976-80, Leader of Opposition 1979-80; Treasurer Labour Party 1967-76, Vice-Chm 1973, Chm 1974; Father of House of Commons 1983-87; Pres Univ Coll Swansea since 1986; Hon Bencher Inner Temple 1976, Hon Life Fell, Cardiff Inst of Higher Education 1991, Hon Freeman City of Cardiff 1974, City of Sheffield 1979, City of Portsmouth 1991, and City of Swansea 1993; Grand Cross 1st class Order of Merit of Federal Republic of Germany 1979; author of A House Divided: the dilemma of Northern Ireland (1973), Time and Chance (Memoirs) 1987; MP (*Lab*) S Cardiff 1945-50, SE Cardiff 1950-83, and Cardiff South and Penarth 1983-87; *cr* PC 1964, KG 1987, and *Baron Callaghan of Cardiff*, of the City of Cardiff, co S Glamorgan (Life Baron) 1987: *m* 1938, Audrey Elizabeth, da of Frank Moulton, of Loose, Kent, and has issue.

Arms – Quarterly vert and azure in the former a portcullis or in the latter a lymphad with an anchor at its prow and masted or the sail set argent and pennants flying gules overall a fess or to the sinister thereof a grassy mount with a hurst of oak trees and issuing therefrom passant to the dexter a wolf proper. Crest – A seadragon sejant gules langued and scaled or its tail of the last and scaled gules the dorsal fin also gules about the neck a mural crown or masoned gules and supporting to the front with the fin of the dexter foreleg a portcullis gold. Motto – Malo laborare quam languere.
Residences – Upper Clayhill Farm, Ringmer, E Sussex; 5 Temple West Mews, West Sq, SE11 4TJ.

SON LIVING

Hon Michael James, *b* 1945; *ed* Dulwich, Univ of Wales Cardiff, and Manchester Business Sch: *m* 1968, Jennifer Mary Morris, and has issue living, Joseph Edwin James, *b* 1981, — Kate Elizabeth, *b* 1970, — Sarah Jane, *b* 1972. *Residence* – 18 Brentwood Rd, Ingrave, Brentwood, Essex CM13 3QZ.

DAUGHTERS LIVING

Hon Margaret Ann (*Baroness Jay of Paddington*), *b* 1939; *cr* Baroness Jay of Paddington (Life Baroness) 1992: *m* 1961 (*m diss* 1986), Peter Jay, son of Rt Hon Douglas Patrick Thomas Jay (later Baron Jay, Life Baron), and has issue (*see* Bs Jay of Paddington). *Residence* – 44 Blomfield Rd, W9 2PF.

Hon Julia Elizabeth, *b* 1942: *m* 1967, Ian Hamilton Hubbard, and has issue living, Tobin James Hamilton, *b* 1970, — Tom Ian, *b* 1975, — Sam Jonathan, *b* 1976, — Joanna Jane, *b* 1971. *Residence* – Nettleslack Farm, Lowick Green, Ulveston, Cumbria.

Calne and Calstone, Viscount; grandson of Marquess of Lansdowne.

CALTHORPE, BARONY OF (Gough-Calthorpe) (Extinct 1997)

(Title pronounced "Callthorpe") (Name pronounced "Goff-Callthorpe")

WIDOW LIVING OF TENTH BARON

ELIZABETH SIBYL (*Baroness Calthorpe*), da of James Young, of Bandol, Cranley Rd, Guildford, Surrey: *m* 1979, as his 2nd wife, the 10th Baron Calthorpe, who *d* 1997, when the title became extinct.

CALVERLEY, BARON (Muff) (Baron UK 1945)

CHARLES RODNEY MUFF, 3rd Baron; *b* 2 Oct 1946; *s* 1971; *ed* Moravian Sch for Boys, Fulneck, Pudsey; Member of W Yorks Police (formerly City of Bradford Police): *m* 1972 Barbara Ann, da of Jonathan Brown, and has issue.

Arms – Azure, within two barrulets wavy argent between in chief a rose of the second barbed and seeded proper, and in base a fleece or, three ducal coronets of the last. **Crest** – In front of two miners' picks in saltire a miner's safety lamp all proper. **Supporters** – On either side a calf proper. *Residence* – 110 Buttershaw Lane, Wibsey, Bradford BD6 2DA.

LABOR OMNIA VINCIT
Labour conquers all

SONS LIVING

Hon JONATHAN EDWARD, *b* 16 April 1975.
Hon Andrew Raymond, *b* 1978.

BROTHER LIVING

Hon Peter Raymond (Oakhurst, 377 Shadwell Lane, Leeds LS17 8AH), *b* 1953.

WIDOW LIVING OF SECOND BARON

MARY (*Mary, Baroness Calverley*), da of Arthur Farrar, of Halifax: *m* 1940, the 2nd Baron Calverley, who *d* 1971.

PREDECESSORS – (1) GEORGE MUFF, son of late George Muff, miner, of Bradford; *b* 1877; sat as MP for E Div of Kingston-upon-Hull (*Lab*) 1929-31, and 1935-45; cr *Baron Calverley*, of City of Bradford, W Riding of Yorkshire (peerage of United Kingdom) 1945: *m* 1909, Ellen Eliza, who *d* 1965, elder da of late Charles W Orford, of Bath; *d* 1955; *s* by his only son **(2)** GEORGE RAYMOND ORFORD, 2nd Baron *b* 1914: *m* 1940, Mary, da of Arthur Farrar, of Halifax; *d* 1971; *s* by his elder son **(3)** CHARLES RODNEY, 3rd Baron and present peer.

CAMBRIDGE, MARQUESSATE OF (Extinct 1981)

DAUGHTER LIVING OF SECOND MARQUESS

Lady Mary Ilona Margaret, *b* 1924; *m* 1950, Peter Whitley, only son of Sir Norman Henry Pownall Whitley, MC, and has issue living, Charles Francis Peter, *b* 1961: *m* 1991, Diana M., elder da of Mrs Diana Hewitt, of Hurtmore, Godalming, Surrey, — Sarah Elizabeth, *b* 1954: *m* 1982, Timothy J. F. Felton, and has issue living, Emily Ilona *b* 1985, Chlöe Amelia *b* 1987. *Residence* – Leighland House, Roadwater, Watchet, Som TA23 0RP.

CAMDEN, MARQUESS (Pratt) (Marquess UK 1812)

The judgement of my peers, or the law of the land

DAVID GEORGE EDWARD HENRY PRATT, 6th Marquess; *b* 13 Aug 1930; *s* 1983; *ed* Eton; late 2nd Lieut Scots Gds: *m* 1961 (*m diss* 1985), Virginia Ann, only da of Francis Harry Hume Finlaison, of Arklow Cottage, Windsor, Berks, and has issue.

Arms – Quarterly: 1st and 4th sable, on a fesse between three elephants' heads erased argent as many mullets of the field, *Pratt*; 2nd and 3rd sable, a chevron between three spears' heads argent, the points embrued, *Jeffreys*. Crests – 1st, an elephant's head erased argent; 2nd, a dragon's head erased vert,holding in the mouth a sinister hand couped at the wrist gules, and about the neck a gold chain, and pendant therefrom a portcullis or. Supporters – *Dexter*, a griffin sable; beak and claws gules, gorged with a plain collar argent, charged with three mullets sable; *sinister*, a lion or, collared as the dexter. *Residence* – Wherwell House, Andover, Hants.

SON LIVING

JAMES WILLIAM JOHN (*Earl of Brecknock*), *b* 11 Dec 1965; *ed* Eton.

DAUGHTER LIVING

Lady Samantha Carolina, *b* 1964.

HALF-BROTHER LIVING

Lord Michael John Henry, *b* 1946; *ed* Eton, and Balliol Coll, Oxford: *m* 1999, ND Janet Giannuzzi Savelli, of Tenuta di Monteverdi, Paganico, Grosseto, Italy. *Residence* – 16 Coulson St, SW3.

SISTER LIVING

Lady Mary Clementine, *b* 1921; is a DStJ: *m* 1st, 1940, Fl-Lt Hon (Herbert) Oswald Berry, who *d* 1952 (*see* V Kemsley); 2ndly, 1953, (Shafto) Gerald Strachan Pawle, who *d* 1991. *Residence* – Trehiven House, Madron, Penzance, Cornwall.

WIDOW LIVING OF FIFTH MARQUESS

ROSEMARY CECIL (*Rosemary, Marchioness Camden*); artist; da of late Brig Hanbury Pawle, CBE, TD, DL, and formerly wife of (1) Gp-Capt Peter Wooldridge Townsend, CVO, DSO, DFC (*d* 1995), and (2) John de Laszlo (*d* 1990): *m* 3rdly, 1978, as his 3rd wife, the 5th Marquess Camden, who *d* 1983.

COLLATERAL BRANCH LIVING

Issue of late Maj Lord Roderic Arthur Nevill Pratt, yr son of 4th Marquess, *b* 1915, *d* 1997: *m* 1945, Ursula Eva, who *d* 1993, elder da of late Capt Hon Valentine Maurice Wyndham-Quin, RN (*see* E Dunraven, 1990 Edn):—
Adrian John Charles, *b* 1952; *ed* Eton; late Capt Blues and Royals; Member of Lloyds since 1977; Man Dir British Equestrian Insurance Brokers since 1985, Dir Plumpton and Fontwell Park Racecourses since 1994; Dir British Horse-racing Board since 1998; Chm St Margaret's Insurances Ltd since 1999; Pres Equisure Inc (USA) since 1997: *m* 1984, Leanora Rosemary, da of Maj Peter Murray Lee. *Residence* – Orchard Lodge, Wadhurst, E Sussex. —— Zara Elizabeth, *b* 1955: *m* 1988, John Weir Johnstone, of The Old Rectory, Lidgate, Newmarket, Suffolk, son of late Andrew Johnstone, of Bonshaw Mains, Kirtlebridge, Lockerbie, Dumfriesshire, and has issue living, Harry Andrew, *b* 1989.

PREDECESSORS – (1) *Sir* CHARLES Pratt, Knt, MP for Downton, an eminent lawyer, was successively Attorney-Gen and Ch Justice of the Common Pleas; cr *Baron Camden*, of Camden Place, co Kent (peerage of Great Britain), 1765; appointed Lord High Chancellor 1766, and Lord Pres of the Council 1784; cr *Viscount Bayham* and *Earl Camden* (peerage of Great Britain 1786); *d* 1794; *s* by his son (2) JOHN JEFFREYS, KG, 2nd Earl; successively MP, a Lord of the Treasury, a Lord of the Admiralty, Viceroy of Ireland, and Chancellor of Univ of Camb; cr *Earl of Brecknock* and *Marquess Camden* (peerage of United Kingdom) 1812; *d* 1840; *s* by his son (3) GEORGE CHARLES, KG, 2nd Marquess; summoned to House of Lords 1835 as Baron Camden; *d* 1866; *s* by his son (4) JOHN CHARLES, 3rd Marquess; *b* 1840; MP for Brecon 1866: *m* 1866, Lady Clementine Augusta Spencer-Churchill, who *d* 1886, da of 6th Duke of Marlborough; *d* 1872; *s* by his son (5) JOHN CHARLES, GCVO, TD, 4th Marquess, *b* 1872; late Maj W Kent Yeo and Hon Col 58th (Kent) Brig RA (TA); Lord-Lieut for Kent 1905-43; *m* 1898, Lady Joan Marion Nevill, CBE, who *d* 1952, da of 3rd Marquess of Abergavenny; *d* 1943; *s* by his son (6) JOHN CHARLES HENRY, 5th Marquess, *b* 1899; 1939-45 War Comdg 45th Battery (which he raised), Maj Reserve of Officers Scots Gds Hon Col Light Anti-Aircraft Regt RA; a DL and JP for Kent; a member of Fedn Internationale des Automobiles, Patron of Coll of Automobile and Aeronautical Training, Chelsea, a Vice-Pres and Member of Cttee of Management of RNLI, Vice-Pres of Marine Motoring Assocn, Chm of Segrave Trophy Awarding Cttee, etc; a Gold Staff Officer at Coronation of King George VI: *m* 1st, 1920 (*m diss* 1941), Marjorie Minna, DBE, who *d* 1989, only child of Col Atherton Edward Jenkins, of Wherwell Priory, Andover; 2ndly, 1942, Averil, who *d* 1977, formerly wife of John Prescott Hallett, and elder da of late Col Henry Sidney John Streatfield, DSO, TD (E Lichfield); 3rdly, 1978, Rosemary Cecil, artist, formerly wife of (1) Gp-Capt Peter Wooldridge Townsend, CVO, DSO, DSC, and (2) John de Laszlo, and da of late Brig Hanbury Pawle, CBE, TD; *d* 1983; *s* by his elder son (7) DAVID GEORGE EDWARD HENRY, 6th Marquess and present peer; also Earl Camden, Earl of Brecknock, Viscount Bayham, and Baron Camden.

CAMERON OF BALHOUSIE, BARONY OF (Cameron) (Extinct 1985)

SON LIVING OF LIFE BARON

Hon Neil, *b* 1949; *ed* Dean Close Sch, London Univ (External, BA), and Bath Univ (Dip Ed).

DAUGHTER LIVING OF LIFE BARON

Hon Fiona Jane, *b* 1950; *ed* Birmingham Univ (MA).

WIDOW LIVING OF LIFE BARON

PATRICIA LOUISE (*Baroness Cameron of Balhousie*), da of late Maj Edward Asprey, RE: *m* 1947, Marshal of the RAF Baron Cameron of Balhousie, KT, GCB, CBE, DSO, DFC, AE (Life Baron), who *d* 1985. *Address* – King's College, Strand, WC2.

CAMERON OF LOCHBROOM, BARON (Cameron) (Life Baron 1984)

KENNETH JOHN CAMERON, PC, son of late Hon Lord (John) Cameron, KT, DSC, LLD (Scottish Lord of Session), of 28 Moray Place, Edinburgh, by his 1st wife, Eileen Dorothea, who *d* 1943, da of late Harry Milburn Burrell; *b* 11 June 1931; *ed* The Edinburgh Acad, Corpus Christi Coll, Oxford (MA) and Edinburgh Univ (LLB); admitted Faculty of Advocates 1958; QC (Scot) 1972; Hon Bencher Lincoln's Inn; Hon Fell Corpus Christi Coll, Oxford, Hon Fell RIAS, Fell RSE; Standing Junior to Dept of Transport 1964-71, to DoE 1971-72; Chm Industrial Tribunals in Scotland 1966-81; Advocate Depute 1981-84, Chm Pensions Appeal Tribunal (Scotland) 1975 (Pres 1976-84), Chm Cttee for Investigation in Scotland of Agricultural Marketing Schemes 1980-84, Lord Advocate 1984-89, since when Senator of Coll of Justice; served RN 1950-52 (comm'd RNVR 1951); *cr* PC 1984, and *Baron Cameron of Lochbroom*, of Lochbroom, in the District of Ross and Cromarty (Life Baron) 1984: *m* 1964, Jean Pamela, da of late Col Granville Murray, and has issue.

Arms – Gules, three bars Or, overall two flanches Ermine, at the honour point, also overall, a fleur de lys Sable. Crest – A kittiwake alighting wings expanded Proper. Motto – Et Regi Et Legi Servire.
Residence – Stoneyhill House, Musselburgh EH21 6RP. *Clubs* – Scottish Arts, New (Edinburgh).

DAUGHTERS LIVING

Hon Victoria Christian, *b* 1965: *m* 1991, James Annand Fraser, son of Sir Charles Annand Fraser, KCVO, DL, WS, of Shepherd House, Inveresk, Midlothian, and has issue living, Tabitha Christian Annand, *b* 1993.

Hon Camilla Louise, *b* 1967.

CAMOYS, BARON (Stonor) (Baron E 1383)

RALPH THOMAS CAMPION GEORGE SHERMAN STONOR, GCVO, PC, 7th Baron; *b* 16 April 1940; *s* 1976; *ed* Eton, and Balliol Coll, Oxford; a Lord in Waiting to HM 1992-98, since when Lord Chamberlain HM's Household, and Chancellor Royal Victorian Order; DL Oxon 1994; Dir Perpetual PLC since 1994, and 3i Group plc since 1991; formerly Member House of Lords EEC Select Cttee, and formerly Member Royal Commn on Historical MSS; formerly Chm Robert Jackson & Co Ltd, Man Dir Barclays Merchant Bank Limited, Chief Exec Barclays de Zoete Wedd Ltd, and Dir Barclays Bank plc; Consultor to the Patrimony of the Holy See; Member Exec Cttee The Pilgrims since 1990; Order of Gorkha Dakshina Bahu, 1st Class (Nepal); PC 1997, GCVO 1998: *m* 1966, Elisabeth Mary Hyde, da of late Sir William Stephen Hyde Parker, Bt (cr 1681), and has issue.

Arms – 1st and 4th azure, two bars dancettée or, a chief argent, *Stonor*; 2nd and 3rd, or, on a chief gules, three bezants, *Camoys*. Crest – A falcon standing on a rock and regarding a projection of that rock argent, all semee of hurts, bezants, torteaux and pommeis, the rock tufted with grass vert and the falcon holding in his beak a ruby proper. Supporters – *Dexter*, a lion rampant or; *sinister*, a lion rampant sable.
Seat – Stonor Park, Henley-on-Thames, Oxon RG9 6HF.

SON LIVING

Hon (RALPH) WILLIAM ROBERT THOMAS, *b* 10 Sept 1974; *ed* Eton, and Manchester Univ.

DAUGHTERS LIVING

Hon Alina Mary, *b* 1967; *ed* St Mary's Convent, Ascot, and Balliol Coll, Oxford; ACA: *m* 1994, Simon Derek Barrowcliff, ARICS, yst son of Dr Derek Barrowcliff, and has issue living, Thomas Simon Marmaduke, *b* 1994, — Louis Edmund Ford, *b* 1995, — Ines Honor, *b* 1998. *Residence* – 39 Abinger Rd, W4 1EX.

Hon Emily Mary Julia, *b* 1969; *ed* St Mary's Convent, Ascot, and Durham Univ. *Residence* – Stonor Park, Henley-on-Thames, Oxon RG9 6HF.

Hon Sophia Ulla STONOR, *b* 1971; has resumed her maiden name: *m* 1993 (*m diss* 1997), Hon James Alastair Stourton, yr son of 26th Baron Mowbray. *Residence* – 233 Sussex Gdns, W2 2RL.

SISTERS LIVING

Hon Julia Maria Cristina Mildred STONOR (90 Burnthwaite Rd, Fulham, SW6), *b* 1939; *ed* St Mary's Convent, Ascot, and Reading Technical Coll; resumed surname of Stonor by deed poll 1978: *m* 1963 (*m diss* 1977 and annulled 1978), Donald Robin Slomnicki Saunders, and has issue living, Alexander William Joseph STONOR SAUNDERS, *b* 1964; *ed* Worth, and St Andrew's Univ, — Frances Hélène Jeanne STONOR SAUNDERS *b* 1966; *ed* St Mary's Convent, Ascot, and St Anne's Coll, Oxford.

Hon Georgina Mary Hope (112 West St, Henley-on-Thames, Oxon RG9 2EA) *b* 1941; OStJ; Golden Cross of Merit (Poland).

Hon Harriet Pauline Sophia, *b* 1943: *m* 1965, (Jonathan) Julian Cotterell, and has issue living, Edmund Julian Francis, *b* 1967: *m* 1993, Angelica I. L., eldest da of Humphrey Stone, of Lower Lawn House, Tisbury, Wilts, and has issue living, Luke Aubrey *b* 1994, Archie James *b* 1996, — Rupert Sherman John, *b* 1969, — Alice Ellinor Mary, *b* 1966: *m* 1992, Thomas Bernard Constable Maxwell, and has issue (*see* L Herries, colls). *Residence* – Steeple Manor, Steeple, nr Wareham, Dorset.

AUNTS LIVING (*Daughters of 5th Baron*)

Hon (Pamela Sophia) Nadine, *b* 1917: *m* 1941, Lt-Col Charles Donald Leslie Pepys, King's Own Yorkshire LI (*see* E Cottenham, colls). *Residence* – 30 Lyefield Court, Kidmore End Rd, Emmer Green, nr Reading, Berks.

Hon (Mildred Sophia) Noreen, *b* 1922: *m* 1941, John R. Drexel (III), and has issue living, John Nicholas (IV) (40 E 94th St, New York, NY, USA), *b* 1945: *m* 1st, 1969 (*m diss* 1976), Pamela, da of Bernardo Rionda Braga; 2ndly, 1984, M. Jacqueline, da of John Jacob Astor, and has issue living (by 2nd *m*), Nicholas Astor 1987, — Pamela Sandra Noreen (3685 Upton St NW, Washington DC 20008, USA), *b* 1942: *m* 1966 (*m diss* 1977), Bradford Hastings Walker, and has issue living, Andrew *b* 1968, James Drexel *b* 1971, — Noreen Elizabeth Mildred, *b* 1961: *m* 1990, William J. O'Farrell, of 76 Taber Av, Providence, RI, USA, and has issue living, William (Liam) James *b* 1992, Fergus John *b* 1994, Aidan Thomas *b* 1996, Finnian Drexel *b* 1997. *Residence* – Stonor Lodge, Bellevue Av, Newport, Rhode Island 02840, USA.

COLLATERAL BRANCHES LIVING

Grandson of late Hon Edward Maurice Stonor, 2nd son of 4th Baron:—
Issue of late Betty Joyce Stonor, *b* 1910, *d* 1982: *m* 1938, Benjamin Rudolf Bonas, who *d* 1965:—
Benjamin Reginald Francis Stonor BONAS (16 Hereford Sq, SW7 4TS), *b* 1940; *ed* Marlborough, and Worcester Coll, Oxford: *m* 1967 (*m diss* 1994), Jacqueline A. J., eldest da of Jacques de Brabant, of Torcy, Seine-et-Marne, France, and has issue living, Charles Benjamin, *b* 1969, — Oliver Henry, *b* 1971.

Grandchildren of late Oswald Francis Gerard Stonor, CMG, 3rd son of late Charles Joseph Stonor (infra):—
Issue of late Joan Florence Mary Stonor, *b* 1907, *d* 1956: *m* 1st, 1927 (*m diss* 1948), John Colburn Bennett, CMG, CBE, who *d* 1969; 2ndly, 1948, John Keith Macara, who *d* 1978 (Macara, Bt):—
(By 1st *m*) Jill Mary (48 Peel St, W8 7PD), *b* 1929: *m* 1954 (*m diss* 1967), David Noel Templer Scott, who *d* 1989, and has issue living, John Andrew Templer (49 Telford Av, Streatham Hill, SW2 4XL), *b* 1960; *ed* Downside: *m* 1984, Catharine Frances, da of Cdr William John Macnamara Faulkner, RN (*see* de Trafford, Bt, colls, 1995 Edn), and has issue living, Rory David Templer *b* 1993, Alice Emily Cecilia *b* 1989, — Virginia Jane, *b* 1957: *m* 1985, Charles Leofric Thomas Temple-Richards, of 92 Huron Rd, SW17 8RD (*see* Temple, Bt, colls, 1990 Edn), and has issue living, Alec Thomas Leofric *b* 1995, Cornelia Florence *b* 1989, Juliana Virginia, *b* 1991. —— Veronica Anne (Old House, Llanigon, Hay on Wye, Hereford HR3 5RH), *b* 1942: *m* 1964 (*m diss* 1981), Michael Edward Rudman, and has issue living, Amanda Joan, *b* 1967, — Katherine Rose, *b* 1970.

Issue of late Evelyn Mary Stonor, *b* 1911, *d* 1995: *m* 1935 (*m diss* 1954), Cmdr Denis Hugh Bryan Barrett, CB, DSC, RN (*see* B Kensington, 1935 Edn):—
Michael Patrick Denis BARRETT, *b* 1937; *ed* Downside, and Trin Coll, Camb: *m* 1951 (*m diss* 19—), Kytia Buchs. —— Bryan Nicholas BARRETT, *b* 1940; *ed* Downside: *m* 1964 (*m diss* 19—), Sally Lois, yr da of Arthur Maxwell Hankin, CMG, and has issue living, Claire Fiona, *b* 1966, — Georgina Mary, *b* 1968.

Grandchildren of late Charles Joseph Stonor, only son of late Charles Henry Stonor, brother of 3rd Baron:—
Issue of late Charles Henry Joseph Stonor, *b* 1874, *d* 1930: *m* 1912, Hylda, who *d* 1968, da of Henry Lloyd-Carter, formerly of Bryn Seiont, Caernarvon:—

Henry Anthony (10 The Green, Marlborough, Wilts), *b* 1926; *ed* Downside, and Shrewsbury; late Lieut Royal Welch Fus. —— †Beatrice Maude, *b* 1913: *m* 1949, Ralph Aldersey, who *d* 1971, and *d* 1997, leaving issue, William Ralph (Manor House, Hampton, Malpas, W Cheshire), *b* 1950; *ed* Oswestry Sch. —— Pamela Mary, *b* 1915; OStJ Serving Sister, British Red Cross Soc (despatches). —— †Sheila Mary, *b* 1916: *m* 1946, Brig Ernest James Cholmeley Harrison, OBE, Royal Sigs, of Bramdown House, S Litchfield, Basingstoke, Hants RG25 3BP, son of late Sir Charlton Scott Cholmeley Harrison, CIE, and *d* 1994, having had issue, (James) Hugh Cholmeley (Sherwood, Ashtead Lane, Godalming, Surrey GU7 1SY), *b* 1947: *m* 1980, Amanda Elizabeth Fairtlough, — †Robert Mark Cholmeley, *b* 1950: *m* 1973, Lark Constance Newman (Midwinter House, Castle St. Mere, nr Warminster, Wilts BA12 6JF), and *d* 1987, leaving issue, Mark Sebastian Cholmeley *b* 1979, Charlotte Louise Monamie *b* 1985, — Sally Ann Monamy, *b* 1951: *m* 1973, Nicholas Armstrong, of Bramdown House, S Litchfield, Basingstoke, Hants RG25 3BP, and has issue living, Alexander Martin Cholmeley *b* 1978, James Nicholas Rinian *b* 1980, Thomas Bernard Martin *b* 1983, Isobel Harriet Marta *b* 1986. —— †Anne, *b* 1929: *m* 1955, Peter B. Sawdy, of 20 Smith Terrace, SW3 4DL, and *d* 1995, leaving issue, Caroline Ann, *b* 1957: *m* 1985, Symon Fraser Bridle, of 291 Yung Kung Rd, Yangmingshan, Taipeh, Taiwan, and has issue living, James Peter *b* 1987, Andrew Colin *b* 1990, — Susan Angela Lumley, *b* 1962: *m* 19—, Terry Alfred Warren, of 3 Olde Well Cottage, Oxbridge, Bridport, Dorset DT6 3UA, and has issue living, Fredrich *b* 1997, Mini Edwige Mickey *b* 1993.

Grandchildren of late Francis Cyril Stonor, 7th son of late Charles Joseph Stonor (ante):—
Issue of late Bernard Francis Stonor, *b* 1909; *d* 1982: *m* 1935, Elsie Graham:—
Mortimer (Bernie), *b* 1941: *m* 19—, Erika, da of —, and has issue living, Jamus, *b* 19—, — Brendon, *b* 19—, — Emily, *b* 19. —— Pride Cynthia (abandoned christian name of Anne), *b* 1935: *m* 1st, 1957, C. Killa, of Perth, W Australia; 2ndly, 1969, Douglas G. Maclean, and has issue living (by 1st *m*), Deborah Anne, *b* 1958: *m* 1981, Bruce Wishart Smith, of Bressay, Shetland Islands, and has issue living, Jody Kimberley *b* 1985. —— Juliana, *b* 1938: *m* 1st, 1960 (*m diss* 1978), Michael Carter; 2ndly, 1981, Colin Keith Pember, of 31/201 Albert St, Osborne Park, W Australia 6107, and has issue living (by 1st *m*), David Michael, *b* 1961: *m* 1994, Katrina ……, — Brian John STONOR, *b* 1964; assumed surname of Stonor by deed poll 1986 in lieu of his patronymic: *m* 1989, Leah, elder da of John Gadenne of 14 Chadwin Place, Padbury, W Australia 6025, and has issue living, Daniel James *b* 1996, Amy Louise *b* 1993, — Jennifer Dawn, *b* 1962: *m* 1981, Allan Burke, and has issue living, Zara Sheree *b* 1982, Karleah Marie *b* 1985, — Tania Gaye, *b* 1971: *m* 1998, Damon Smirke, of 8 Moody Glen Palmyra, W Australia 6157. —— Virginia, *b* 1946: *m* 19—, Desmond —, and has issue living, Stephen, *b* 19—, — Philip *b* 1973, — Raelene *b* 1978.

PREDECESSORS – **(1)** *Sir* THOMAS de CAMOYS, KG, an eminent warrior, commanded the left wing of the English army at Agincourt 1415; summoned to Parliament as a Baron of England 1383-1421; *d* 1421; *s* by his grandson **(2)** HUGH, 2nd Baron; *d* 1426, when the title went into abeyance between his sisters Margaret and Alianora, and it remained abeyant until 1839, when it was terminated in favour of the descendant of Margaret **(3)** THOMAS Stonor, 3rd Baron; sat as MP for Oxford 1832-3; was a Lord-in-Waiting to HM Queen Victoria 1846-52, 1853-8, 1859-66, and 1868-74; *d* 18 Jan 1881, and was *s* by his grandson **(4)** FRANCIS ROBERT, 4th Baron (son of late Hon Francis Stonor, 2nd son of 3rd Baron); *b* 1856; Lord-in-Waiting to HM Queen Victoria 1886 and 1892-5: *m* 1881, Jessie Philippa, who *d* 1928, 2nd da of late Robert Russell Carew, of Carpenders. Herts; *d* 1897; *s* by his elder son **(5)** RALPH FRANCIS JULIAN, 5th Baron; *b* 1884; *m* 1911, Mildred, who *d* 1961, da of late William Watts Sherman, of New York; *d* 1968; *s* by his only son **(6)** (RALPH ROBERT WATTS) SHERMAN, 6th Baron; *b* 1913: *m* 1938, Mary Jeanne, who *d* 1987, da of late Capt Herbert Marmaduke Joseph Stourton, OBE (B Mowbray colls); *d* 1976; *s* by his elder son **(7)** RALPH THOMAS CAMPION GEORGE SHERMAN, 7th Baron, and present peer.

Campbell, family name of Duke of Argyll.

Campbell, surname of Earldom of Breadalbane and Holland.

Campbell, family name of Earl Cawdor.

Campbell, family name of Baron Colgrain.

Campbell, family name of Baron Stratheden and Campbell.

CAMPBELL OF ALLOWAY, BARON (Campbell) (Life Baron 1981)

ALAN ROBERTSON CAMPBELL, ERD, QC, son of late John Kenneth Campbell; *b* 24th May 1917; *ed* Aldenham, and Trinity Hall, Camb. (MA); Bar Inner Temple 1939, QC 1965, Bencher 1972; Memb Carlton Club Political Cttee 1967-79, Law Advisory Cttee British Council 1974-82, House of Lords Cttee for Privileges since 1982; Recorder of Crown Court 1976-89; Chm Legal Research Cttee of Soc of Conservative Lawyers 1968-80; Memb of Management Cttee UK Assocn for European Law 1975-90; Patron Inns of Court Conservative Soc since 1996; Pres Colditz Assocn since 1998; commissioned 2nd Lieut RA (SR) 1939, served in France and Belgium (PoW Colditz 1940-45); cr *Baron Campbell of Alloway*, of Ayr, in the District of Kyle and Carrick (Life Baron) 1981: *m* 1957, Vivien da of late Comd A. H. de Kantzow, DSO, RN.

Chambers – 2 King's Bench Walk, Temple, EC4 7DE. *Clubs* – Carlton, Pratt's, Beefsteak.

CAMPBELL OF CROY, BARON (Campbell) (Life Baron 1974)

GORDON THOMAS CALTHROP CAMPBELL, MC, PC, son of late Maj-Gen James Alexander Campbell, DSO and bar; *b* 8 June 1921; *ed* Wellington; Maj (ret) RA; 1939-45 War in NW Europe, OC 320 Field Bty, 15th (Scottish) Div 1942-45 (MC and Bar, wounded and disabled); Vice Lieut for Nairn since 1988; Diplo Ser 1946-57; UK Mission at UN New York 1949-52; Private Sec to Sec of Cabinet 1954-56, First Sec, Vienna 1956-57, Govt Whip 1961-63, Under-Sec of State for Scotland 1963-64, and Sec of State for Scotland 1970-74; Consultant to Chevron Cos 1975-94, Chm Stoic Insurance Services 1979-93, Dir Alliance Building Soc since 1983, and Alliance and Leicester Building Soc 1985-92; Chm for Scotland, Internat Year of Disabled People 1981; Pres Anglo-Austrian Soc since 1991; MP for Moray and Nairn (*C*) 1959-74; cr PC 1970, and *Baron Campbell of Croy*, of Croy, co Nairn (Life Baron) 1974; *m* 1949, Nicola Elizabeth Gina, da of late Capt Geoffrey Spencer Madan (*see* Noble, Bt, *cr* 1902, 1985 Edn), and has issue.

ᴀrms – Gyronny of eight or and sable, overall on a fess ermine two pheons points upwards gules. Crest – Between two sprays of red roses barbed and leaved proper and tied in base with a riband or, a lyre sable. Supporters – Dexter an osprey and sinister a curlew both proper. *Residence* – Holme Rose, Cawdor, Nairn.

SONS LIVING

Hon Colin Ian Calthrop, *b* 1950; *ed* Eton (King's Scholar), and Trin Coll, Camb (Scholar).

Hon Alastair James Calthrop, *b* 1952; *ed* Eton, and Wadham Coll, Oxford (MA); commn'd Queen's Own Highlanders 1973, Col 1998; a Member of Queen's Body Guard for Scotland (Royal Company of Archers); FRGS: *m* 1993, Primrose Felicia, elder da of William Henry Tugwell Palmer (*see* E Longford, 1995 Edn), of Nun Monkton, York, and has issue living, Ferdinand James Marc, *b* 1994, — Edward Henry Brunel, *b* 1996, — Leonora Mary Felicia, *b* 1995, — Hermione Violet Celia, *b* 1998. *Residence* – Holme Rose, Cawdor, Nairn.

DAUGHTER LIVING

Hon Christina Marjorie, *b* 1953: *m* 1980, Mark Michael Clarfelt, of 30 Blomfield Rd, W9 1AA, son of Jack Clarfelt, of Linhay Meads, Timsbury, Romsey, Hants, and has issue living, Max Barnaby David, *b* 1986, — Alice Nicola Irene, *b* 1982, — Tessa Dorothy Florence, *b* 1984, — Harriet Lily Beatrice, *b* 1990, — Kate Calypso Rose, *b* 1994.

CAMPBELL OF ESKAN, BARONY OF (Campbell) (Extinct 1994)

SONS LIVING OF LIFE BARON

Hon John Charles Middleton, *b* 1940; *ed* Eton: *m* 1965, Patricia Ann, elder da of late Tom Webster, and has issue, two das and one adopted da. *Residence* – 39 Gondar Gardens, NW6.

Hon Peter Mark Middleton, *b* 1946; *ed* Eton: *m* 1st, 1972 (*m diss* 1989), Anne Susan, da of John E. Cuthbert, of Enfield, Middx; 2ndly, 1995, Belinda Lois Thornhill, elder da of James Shann, and has issue, two sons and one da. *Residence* – 148 Bennerley Rd, SW11 6DY.

DAUGHTERS LIVING OF LIFE BARON

Hon Rosalind Leonora Middleton, *b* 1942. *Residence* – 13 Alma Green, Stoke Row, Henley-on-Thames, Oxon.

Hon (Agneta) Joanna Middleton, *b* 1944: *m* 1966 (*m diss* 1985), Jonathan Geoffrey William Agnew (*see* Agnew, Bt, colls, *cr* 1895). *Residence* – 4 Brookville Rd, SW6 7BJ.

Campden, Viscount; son of Earl of Gainsborough.

CAMROSE, VISCOUNTCY OF (Berry) (Viscount UK 1941, disclaimed 1995, Bt UK 1921)

(WILLIAM) MICHAEL BERRY, MBE, TD; *Life Baron*, and 3rd Baronet; *b* 18 May 1911; *cr Baron Hartwell*, of Peterborough Court, City of London (Life Baron) 1968; *s* as 3rd Viscount Camrose 15 Feb 1995; disclaimed his hereditary peerages for life 9 March 1995. [For full particulars, *see* B Hartwell].

WIDOW LIVING OF SON OF FIRST VISCOUNT

(Janet Frances) Denise, elder da of late Maj (John) Leslie Rowan-Thomson, of Sayers, Great Somerford, Wilts: *m* 1946, Col Hon Julian Berry, OBE, JP, DL, who *d* 1988, and has issue (see colls infra).

COLLATERAL BRANCHES LIVING

Adopted da of late Hon Rodney Mathias Berry, TD, 3rd son of 1st Viscount, *b* 1917, *d* 1963: *m* 1955, Susan Jenifer (who *d* 7 Nov 1998, having *m* 2ndly, 1964 (*m diss* 1978), Henry Lambert Middleton (*see* Middleton, Bt, colls), who *d* 17 Jan 1998), da of late William Arthur Fearnley-Whittingstall, TD, QC, of The Old Manor House, Melbourn, Cambs:—
Emma Louise, *b* 1961: *m* 1984, Jeremy N. Oakley, of Millbrook House, Burghclere, Hants, son of Capt Neville Oakley, of Golf Drive, Camberley, Surrey, and has issue living, Joshua, *b* 1986, — Georgia Alice, *b* 1988.

Issue of late Col Hon Julian Berry, OBE, yst son of 1st Viscount, *b* 1920, *d* 1988: *m* 1946, (Janet Frances) Denise (The Old Rectory, Tunworth, nr Basingstoke, Hants), elder da of late Maj (John) Leslie Rowan-Thomson, of Sayers, Great Somerford, Wilts:—
Simon Ewert (Cortington Manor, Corton, Warminster, Wilts BA12 0SY), *b* 1955; *ed* Eton: *m* 1st, 1981 (*m diss* 1997), Martha Davidson, yst da of Louis Davidson Sage, of New York City; 2ndly, 1998, Mrs Krystyna Pretty, and has issue living (by 1st *m*), Lucy Elizabeth, *b* 1985, — Tara Edwina, *b* 1988, — Alexa Eloise, *b* 1992 . —— Caroline Denise, *b* 1948: *m* 1969, Jeremy James Wagg (*see* Horlick, Bt, 1969 Edn), and has issue living, Julian James, *b* 1972, — Katharine Denise, *b* 1974. *Residence* – 18 Eaton Mews South, Eccleston St, SW1.

PREDECESSORS – (1) WILLIAM EWERT BERRY, 2nd son of late Alderman John Mathias Berry, JP of Gwaelodygarth, Merthyr Tydfil; *b* 1879; a journalist and Newspaper Proprietor, Editor-in-Ch of *Daily Telegraph* and *Morning Post*, and Chm of Amalgamated Press Ltd; founder of Advertising world 1901, Editor-in-Ch *Sunday Times* 1915-36, Chm of Financial Times Ltd 1919-45, and of Allied Newspapers Ltd 1924-36: cr a *Baronet 1921, Baron Camrose*, of Long Cross,

Surrey (peerage of United Kingdom) 1929, and *Viscount Camrose*, of Hackwood Park, co, Southampton 1941: *m* 1905, Mary Agnes, who *d* 1962, elder da of late Thomas Corns, of 2 Bolton St Piccadilly, W1; *d* 1954; *s* by his eldest son (2) (JOHN) SEYMOUR, 2nd Viscount, *b* 1909; Dep Chm *Daily Telegraph and Morning Post* (ret 1987), a Younger Brother of Trinity House; Maj City of London Yeo, RA (TA), served 1939-45 War in N Africa and Italy (despatches); MP for Hitchin Div of Herts (C) 1941-45: *m* 1986, Princess Joan Aly Khan, who *d* 1997, eldest da of 3rd Baron Churston (*see* B Churston, 1995 Edn, and By Grey de Ruthyn, colls), and formerly wife of (i) W/Cdr Thomas Loel Evelyn Bulkeley Guinness, OBE (*see* B Ardilaun, ext, 1944 Edn), and (ii) Prince Aly Khan; *d* 1995; *s* by his brother (3) WILLIAM MICHAEL, 3rd Viscount until he disclaimed his peerages 1995.

Canning, family name of Baron Garvagh.

Capell, family name of Earl of Essex.

CARADON, BARONY OF (Foot) (Extinct 1990)

SONS LIVING OF LIFE BARON

Hon Paul Mackintosh (14 Canfield Gdns, NW6), *b* 1937; *ed* Univ Coll, Oxford; is a Journalist: *m* 1st, 1962 (*m diss* 1970), Monica, da of Dr Robert P. Beckinsale, of Oxford; 2ndly, 1971 (*m diss* 1995), Roseanne, da of Robert Harvey, and has issue living (by 1st *m*), John Mackintosh, *b* 1964, — Matthew Isaac, *b* 1966, — (by 2nd *m*) Tom, *b* 1979.

Hon Oliver Isaac (Higher Pendruffle Cottage, Duloe, nr Liskard, Cornwall), *b* 1947; *ed* Leighton Park Sch, RAC Cirencester, and Goddard Coll, Vermont, USA: *m* 1967 (*m diss* 1975), Nancy Foot, of New York City, USA, and has issue living, Jesse Isaac, *b* 1973, — Mary Rachel, *b* 1971.

Hon Benjamin Arthur, MBE, *b* 1949; *ed* Leighton Park Sch, and Univ Coll, Swansea; MBE (Civil) 1992: *m* 1981, Sally Jane, only da of late Maj Mark Francis Swain Rudkin, MC, and has issue living, Alexander Mark Isaac, *b* 1986, — Joanna Dingle, *b* 1983.

DAUGHTER LIVING OF LIFE BARON

Hon Sarah Dingle, *b* 1939: *m* 1961, Maj Timothy Nicholas Percival Winter Burbury, The Blues & Royals, of Ince Barton, Saltash, Cornwall, and has issue living, Charles Alexander Winter, *b* 1964, — Camilla Jane Winter, *b* 1962: *m* 1988, Mark Lindfield, of Orchard Cottage, Erth Barton, Elmgate, Saltash, Cornwall, and has issue living, Joshua Robert Isaac *b* 1988, Oliver Perran *b* 1994, Hannah-Kate *b* 1991, Lamorna Rose Winter *b* 1992.

CARBERY, BARON (Evans-Freke) (Baron I 1715, Bt I 1768)

Liberty

PETER RALFE HARRINGTON EVANS-FREKE, 11th Baron, and 7th Baronet; *b* 20 March 1920; *s* 1970; *ed* Downside; MICE; a Member of London Stock Exchange 1955-67; 1939-45 War as Capt RE in India and Burma: *m* 1941, Joyzelle Mary, only da of late Herbert Binnie, of Sydney, NSW, and has issue.

Arms – Quarterly: 1st and 4th sable, two bars, and in chief three mullets or, *Freke*; 2nd and 3rd argent, three boars' heads couped sable, *Evans*. Crests – 1st, a bull's head couped at the back sable, collared and chained or, *Freke*; 2nd, a demi-lion rampant reguardant or, holding in the paws a boar's head sable, *Evans*. Supporters – Two lions reguardant or, ducally crowned azure. *Residence* – 2 Hayes Court, Sunnyside, Wimbledon SW19 4SH.

SONS LIVING

Hon MICHAEL PETER, *b* 11 Oct 1942; *ed* Downside, Ch Ch Oxford (MA), Univ of Strathclyde (MBA), and King's Coll, London (PGCE): *m* 1967, Claudia Janet Elizabeth, only da of late Capt Percy Lionel Cecil Gurney, of Little Chart, Pen-shurst, and has issue living, Dominic Ralfe Cecil, *b* 1969, — Richenda Clare, *b* 1971, — Isabel Lucy, *b* 1973, — Anna-Louise Rachel, *b* 1979. *Residence* – 3 Westmead, Rock Rd, Chilcompton, Bath BA3 4HX.

Hon John Anthony (Lynturk Home Farm, Alford, Aberdeenshire AB33 8DU), *b* 1949; *ed* Downside, and RAC Cirencester; FRICS, formerly Agent to the Duke of Northumberland: *m* 1972, Veronica Jane, yst da of late Maj Eric Williams, of House of Lynturk, Alford, Aberdeenshire, and has issue living, James Eric, *b* 1976, — Charles William Anthony, *b* 1981, — Flora Mary, *b* 1979.

Hon Stephen Ralfe (The Corner House, Norfolk, Conn 06058, USA; Casa Niños, 1320 Marlborough Rd, Hillsborough, Calif 94010, USA), *b* 1952; *ed* Downside, and Trin Coll, Camb (BA); Pres PaineWebber Devpt Corpn, etc (USA): *m* 1990, Valerie BEATTIE JOHNSON, eldest da of Russell Beattie, of Stonington, Conn, USA, and has issue living, Yorick Peter, *b* 1992, — Roland Charles Goodheart, *b* 1993.

DAUGHTERS LIVING

Hon Maura Clare, *b* 1946; formerly Admin Assist Roy Coll of Music: *m* 1966, Richard Henry William Fanshawe, of Rafters, Waldron, Heathfield, E Sussex TN21 0QY, and has issue (*see* E Lindsey and Abingdon, colls).

Hon Angela Mary, *b* 1954: *m* 1975, Martin David Tomlins, of 96 Wormholt Rd, W12, and has issue living, Alexander Peter David, *b* 1978, — William John Anthony, *b* 1981.

HALF SISTER LIVING

Anne Mary Elizabeth, *b* 1933: *m* 1957, Ross Young, of Easters, Sandhills, Cattistock, Dorchester, Dorset, DT2 0HQ, and has issue living, Paul Ralfe, *b* 1958, — Clare Elizabeth, *b* 1960: *m* 1986, Stephen Delevante, and has issue living, Andrew Edward *b* 1988, Patrick Ross *b* 1991, — Diana Mary, *b* 1967.

DAUGHTERS LIVING OF TENTH BARON

Hon Fabienne José, *b* 1916: *m* 1st, 1936 (*m diss* 1946), Com John Dudley Dowse-Finnemore, RN, who *d* 1971, having assumed by R licence 1938, the additional surname and arms of Finnemore; 2ndly, 1947, Philip Claridge, of Cloonagh, Monkstown, co Cork.

Juanita Virginia Sistare CARBERY (does not use courtesy title), *b* 1925. *Residence* – Flat 5, Brunel House, 105 Cheyne Walk, SW10 0DF.

COLLATERAL BRANCHES LIVING

(Male line in special remainder to the Barony)

Grandchildren of late Eyre Frederick FitzGeorge Evans, eldest son of Maj George Thomas Evans, 3rd son of Eyre Evans (*b* 1773), only son of Eyre Evans, of Miltown Castle, co Cork, eldest son of Thomas Evans, MP, yr brother of 1st Baron:—
Issue of late Percy Evans, *b* 1871, *d* 1959: *m* 1916, Ethel Margaret, who *d* 1951, da of T. Dickson, formerly of Wanganui, NZ:—
Margaret Lees (16 Te Maku Grove, Waikanae, Kapiti Coast, NZ), *b* 1925: *m* 1947 (*m diss* 1991), Clifford Roy Dewe.

Issue of late Savage Corry Evans, *b* 1878, *d* 1968: *m* 1st, 1902 (*m diss* 1920), Jane Ann, da of H. Healey, of Naseby, NZ; 2ndly, 1927, Alicia Madeleine Isabel Gifford, only da of late Charles Gifford Moore, of Oamaru, NZ; 3rdly, 19—, Lilian Amelia (20 Phrosso Rd, W Worthing, Sussex), da of Joseph Fair, of Headford, co Galway:—
(By 1st *m*) Trevor George Corry, OBE, TD (9 St Swithin's Close, Sherborne, Dorset), *b* 1910; *ed* abroad, and RAC Cirencester; JP, FRICS, formerly Chief Agent to Duke of Norfolk; 1939-45 War as Lt-Col Royal Sussex Regt; OBE (Mil) 1946: *m* 1937, Sara Gwendolyn, da of R. C. Drummond, of Masterton, NZ, and has issue living, Michael George Corry (10 Moor Lane, Clevedon, Avon BS8 4LJ), *b* 1938; *ed* Rugby, and RAC Cirencester, — Stephen Telford Eyre (c/o Border Farm, Closworth, Yeovil, Som BA22 9SZ), *b* 1939; *ed* Rugby, and RAC Cirencester: *m* 1970, Susan Biron, da of Michael Pallister Young, of Bishopsbourne, Kent, — Patrick Heugh Robert Eyre (Border Farm, Closworth, Yeovil, Som BA22

9SZ), *b* 1944; *ed* Nautical Coll, Pangbourne: *m* 1970, Jennifer Robin, da of late Capt Brian Granville White, RM, of Chaldon, Surrey, and has issue living, James Richard Eyre *b* 1975, Caroline Nicola Corry *b* 1974. ——— Kathleen Ann, *b* 1906: *m* 1943, Capt Edward Copus, late RASC, of Spring Cottage, Harnett St, Sandwich, Kent CT13 9ES.

Grandchildren of late Rev Eric Evans (infra):—
Issue of late Rev Phillip Eyre Evans, *b* 1910, *d* 1980: *m* 1935, Florence Anne (15 Harrison Av, Burwood, Vic, Australia), da of Richard S. U. Reeves, of Melbourne:—
Rodger Eyre (13 Templemore Drive, Templestowe, Vic 3106, Australia), *b* 1937: *m* 1962, Noreen Lorraine, da of late James Alexander Cook, of Pascoe Vale South, Vic, and has issue living, Stephen Rodger Eyre (7 McCubbin Terrace, Doncaster East, Vic 3109), *b* 1970: *m* 1995, Carolyn Sandra, da of Rev Allan Dunn, of Templestowe, Vic, — Robyn Anne, *b* 1963: *m* 1988, Rodney David Johnson, of Unit 2, 131 Main Rd, Blackburn South, Vic 3103, Australia, — Melinda Joy, *b* 1967: *m* 1993, Peter John McMullen, of 108 Oban Rd, Ringwood North, Vic 3134, Australia, and has issue living, Joshua James *b* 1994, Benjamin Joel *b* 1997. ——— Wendy Jillian, *b* 1940: *m* 1962, Dr Gilbert Wilson Turnbull, of 51 Harrison Av, Burwood, Vic 3125, Australia, and has issue living, Leeanne Jane, *b* 1963: *m* 1988, Andrew Graham Edwin Cooke, of 142 Prospect Hill Rd, Canterbury, Vic 3126, and has issue living, Benjamin Andrew *b* 1990, Samuel Phillip *b* 1994, Elizabeth Anne *b* 1992, — Melissa Frances, *b* 1965: *m* 1991, Rodney Peter Endall, of 4 Finlayson St, Forest Hill, Vic 3131, and has issue living, Zachary Wilson *b* 1995, Luke Rodney *b* 1997, — Penelope Jillian, *b* 1967: *m* 1989, Timothy James Joyce, of 15 Ferris Av, Mitcham, Vic 3132, and has issue living, David George Gilbert *b* 1992, Sarah Jillian *b* 1994, Hannah Catherine Rose *b* 1997, — Rosemary Ferelith, *b* 1969: *m* 1993, John Gerard Cincotta, of 122 Through Rd, Camberwell, Vic 3125, and has issue living, Thomas John *b* 1994, Patrick James *b* 1995, Amelia-Rose *b* 1999.

Grandchildren of late Eyre Frederick FitzGeorge Evans (ante):—
Issue of late Rev Eric Evans, *b* 1882, *d* 1970: *m* 1910, Dora Handforth, who *d* 1980, of Onerahi, Auckland, NZ:—
Lewellyn Handforth (62 Kernot St, Spotswood, Vic 3015, Australia), *b* 1913: *m* 1st, 1940, Ivy Edith, who *d* 1949, da of William Elliot, of Melbourne; 2ndly, 1951, Una Jessie, who *d* 1979, da of late Charles A. Drew, of Melbourne, and has issue living (by 1st *m*), *Rev* Peter Handforth (34 Cuba St, Petone, Wellington, NZ), *b* 1941: *m* 1967, Merlyne Leslie, da of Henry Graeme Chambers, of 41a Kirkbrae, 749 Mt Dandanong Rd, Kilsythe, Vic, and has issue living, Yona Leslie *b* 1968: *m* 1990, Michael Heyward, Megan Joan *b* 1970, — Corry Margrett, *b* 1942: *m* 1964, Peter Owen Skilbeck, of Lot 27 Juliet Crescent, Healesville, Vic 3777, Australia, and has issue living, Finlay Grant *b* 1969, Bryn Andrew *b* 1976, Trudy Anne *b* 1970: *m* 1992, Mark Edmondson, — Jean Rebecca, *b* 1949: *m* 1972, Bruce David Glover, of 6 Finlay Court, Lesmurdie 6076, W Australia, and has issue living, Katherine Grace *b* 1976, Leonie Joy *b* 1977. ——— Raymond Austin (42 Jopling St, N Ryde, NSW 2113, Australia), *b* 1915: *m* 1958, Lucy Margaret, da of late Walter George Blomfield, of Killara, NSW, and has issue living, Bruce Raymond Blomfield, *b* 1962; BSc, BE Sydney Univ: *m* 1995, Vanessa Kelso, of Bathurst, NSW, and has issue living, Hugh Samuel *b* 1996, Annabel Elizabeth *b* 1998, — Kathryn Margaret, *b* 1959; BEd Hobart Univ: *m* 1989, Murray Gerrard Wilson, of Lot 2 Cedar Creek Rd, Corner Morrison Rd, Cedar Creek, via Samford, Qld 4520, and has issue living, Timothy Oliver *b* 1989, Joshua Thomas *b* 1997, Sophia Kathryn *b* 1991. ——— Denison Anthony (1 Gardiner Rd, Hawthorn, Vic 3122, Australia), *b* 1925: *m* 1962, Janette Relleen, da of Brian William Peacocke, of Hove, Sussex, and has issue living, Charles Anthony (10 Flint St, Eltham, Vic 3095, Australia), *b* 1963: *m* 1989, Jane, da of John Spiers, of Mosman, NSW, and has issue living, Elizabeth Clare *b* 1991, Catherine Rose *b* 1993, — John Andrew (70 John St, Williamstown, Vic 3016, Australia), *b* 1966: *m* 1993, Marcia, da of Joseph Meilak, of Altona, Vic, and has issue living, Joshua Jesse *b* 1996, Jessica Jamie *b* 1998, — Sarah Louise (7 Odette Court Ringwood, Vic 3134, Australia), *b* 1965: *m* 1988, Mark Anderson, and has issue living, Benjamin William *b* 1992. ——— Rhoda Caroline, *b* 1916: *m* 1945, Joseph Emerson Gibson, of 1 Joyce St, Nunawading, Vic 3131, Australia, and has issue living, David Warwick (Cona, PO Box 115, Port Fairy, Vic 3284), *b* 1947: *m* 1st, 1969 (*m diss* ca 1984), Miriam Felicia, da of Rev Philip Neilson Simmons, of Box Hill, Vic; 2ndly, 1991, Ivy Virginia, da of William Gordon Lockhart, of Ballarat, Vic, and has issue living (by 1st *m*), Timothy James *b* 1970, Kathryn Ruth *b* 1972, Bronwyn Fiona *b* 1975, — Janet Katherine (1/10 Hotham St, Mont Albert, Vic 3127), *b* 1951.

Issue of late Thomas Charles Evans, *b* 1890, *d* 1960: *m* 1st, 1919, Elsa Phyllis Heckler, who *d* 1925, of Mangamahoe, NZ; 2ndly, 1925, Elsie Edith Smith, who *d* 1964, of Hawke's Bay, NZ:—
(By 1st *m*) Francis Eyre Ogilvie (71A Polkinghorne Drive, Whangapararoa, Auckland, NZ), *b* 1919: *m* 1942, Marjorie Ahradsen, and has had issue, David James Ogilvie, *b* 1953: *m* 1977, Helen Anne Cowie, and has issue living, Jeremy David Ogilvie *b* 1980, Gabrielle Helen *b* 1978, Miriam Elizabeth *b* 1982, Michaela Frances *b* 1987, — †Christopher Paul Ogilvie, *b* 1954: *m* 1991, Bettina Susanne Richter, and *d* 1994, leaving issue, Nicholas Stefan *b* 1992, Brendan Christopher *b* 1994, — Jacqueline Susan, *b* 1947: *m* 1969, Dr James Robert Crush, of 1 Sheriff Place, Hillcrest, Hamilton, NZ, and has issue living, Alexandra Frances Hope *b* 1981, Stephanie Elizabeth Helen *b* 1985, — Elizabeth Frances, *b* 1948; *d* 1952. ——— †Thomas Corry Ogilvie, *b* 1921: *m* 1951, Marian Jean McIndoe (Forest Downs, RD2, Masterton, NZ), and *d* 1994, leaving issue, James Peter McIndoe, *b* 1958. — Corry Rhys Walter, *b* 1962. — Elsa Corrine *b* 1952: *m* 1973, Ian Vincent Morgan, of 129 Apollo Parade, Palmerston North, NZ, and has issue living, Craig Ian *b* 1973, Blair Evan *b* 1981, Deborah Corrine *b* 1974: *m* 1997, Andrew Gordon Trembath, of River Rd, Palmerston North, NZ, — Marilyn Brenda, *b* 1953: *m* 1979, John Frederick David Peach, and has issue living, Isaac Corry John Enavold *b* 1984, Julia Nina Eileen *b* 1979, Olivia Hope Marian *b* 1980, Fleur Amy Charlotte *b* 1982, Genevieve Angelicia Marilyn *b* 1989, — Helen Jean Magdalene, *b* 1956. ——— William Phillip Ogilvie (Linden Downs, Rangitumau, Masterton, NZ), *b* 1924: *m* 1950, Fay St Clair Rawlins, and has had issue, Lloyd Phillip, *b* 1955, — †Stephen William, *b* 1958; *d* 1982, — Susan Phyllis, *b* 1952: *m* 1979, Graeme Edmond Millow, and has issue living, Belinda Jane, *b* 1982, — Hannah Susan, *b* 1987. ——— (By 2nd *m*) Ashley Ogilvie (4 Tui Crescent, Manurewa, Auckland, NZ), *b* 1926: *m* 1950, Ruth Martin Napier, and has issue living, Neil Martin, *b* 1951, — Robert Denis, *b* 1954, — Philip Leslie, *b* 1958, — Allan Ashley, *b* 1960, — Bruce Raymond, *b* 1962. ——— Lees Ogilvie (14 Pacific View Rd, Papamoa 3003, NZ), *b* 1932: *m* 1954, Rae Irene Anne Croudis, and has issue living Lawrence Thomas (37 Albert St, Hamilton, NZ), *b* 1958: *m* 1st, 1979 (*m diss* 19—), Robyn Reynolds; 2ndly, 1993, Teresa Timms, of Hamilton, NZ, — Suzanne Mary, *b* 1955: *m* 1976, Gary Matthews, of 84 Insoll Av, Hamilton, NZ, and has issue living, Luke Gary *b* 1983, Clinton John *b* 1984, Katie Belinda *b* 1979, — Cynthia Anne (Manley St, Paraparaumu, Wellington, NZ), *b* 1957: *m* 1975, Tariana Wharakura, and has issue living, Andrew Mark *b* 1975, Paul Michael *b* 1977, Daniel William *b* 1982, — Catherine Pauline EVANS-MILLER, *b* 1962: *m* 1983, Dennis Peter Miller, of Garfield St, Gordonston, RD1, Hamilton, NZ, and has issue living, Nicholas George *b* 1987, Alice Emma *b* 1985, — Helen Lucy (991 Omanawa Rd, RD1, Tauranga, NZ), *b* 1964; has issue living (by James Easton, of Tauranga, NZ), Jacob EASTON *b* 1991, Christopher EASTON *b* 1995, — Patricia Frances EVANS-CASEY *b* 1966: *m* 1995, Michael Casey, of Plimerton, Wellington, NZ. ——— Olwyn Ogilvie, *b* 1927: *m* 1952, Eion John Davies, and has issue living, Garth Raynsley, *b* 1953, — Mark Thomas, *b* 1955, — Tracey Elizabeth, *b* 1958. ——— José Ogilvie, *b* 1929. ——— Fabienne Ogilvie, *b* (twin) 1932: *m* 1953, Neale Thomas Grenfell, and has issue living, Peter Andrew (263 Innes Rd, St Albans, Christchurch, NZ), *b* 1954: *m* 19—, Michelle Louise Kuilder, and has issue living, Andrew Joseph *b* 1987, Thomas Peter *b* (twin) 1997, — Frank James (2 Wrights Rd, Sheffield 8173, NZ), *b* 1956: *m* 19—, Alyson May Edwards, and has issue living, Ben James *b* 1981, Tim Frank *b* 1982, Millie May *b* 1989.

Grandchildren of late Capt George William Wallace D'Arcy-Evans (b 1860), son of late John D'Arcy-Evans (b 1817) (infra):—
Issue of late Cdr Hardress Waller Eyre D'Arcy-Evans, RN, b 1898, d 1962: m 1934, Mary Frideswide Leslie, who d 1997, da of late W. W. Jessopp Sharpe:—
John Hardress Waller (8 De Villiers Av, Rosebank 7700, S Africa), b 1938: m 1965, Janet Barbara, da of Francis Spencer Ware, and has issue living, Andrew Hardress Eyre, b 1966: m 1996, Georgina Watts, and has issue living, Nicholas David b 1999, — Stephen Elystan Waller, b 1973, — Jennifer Frances, b 1968. ——— Wendy Nina Mary, b 1940: m 1970, Capt M. B. Fowkes, of Riverside, Lismore Av, Tokai, Cape, S Africa, and has issue living, Jeremy Matthew Michael, b 1973, — Sarah Isobel Mary, b 1970.

Grandchildren of late Eyre Waller D'Arcy-Evans (infra):—
Issue of late Eyre Henry D'Arcy-Evans, b 1892, d 1957: m 1923, Mary Eleanor, who d 1959, da of John Garmony, of Killylea, co Armagh:—
Trevor Wallace (Belgrove Farm, RMB 806, Jennapullin, W Australia 6401), b 1926: m 1952, Shirley June Lovatt, and has issue living, Andrew Thomas, b 1956, — Clive Hugh, b 1958, — Alan William, b 1959: m 1981, Gaye-Ann Michelle French, and has issue living, Simon b 1982, Belinda b 1984, Shona b 1987, — Christopher Michael, b 1960: m 1987, Marie Louise Caroline Schreurs, and has issue living, Luke b 1987, Brad b 1989. ——— Joy, b 1924: m 1949, Dr (Eric) Brian Jeffcoat Smith, of 11 Dorward Court, Kardinya, W Australia 6163, and has issue living, Nicola, b 1953, — Deirdre, b 1955; BSc: m 1st, 1982, Leighton Brunn; 2ndly, 1988, Peter Baldock, of Margaret River, W Australia, — Vanessa, b 1960. ——— Ethne Elizabeth, b 1931: m 1964, Ronald James Manton who d 1993, of 5 Deane St, Mosman Park, W Australia 6012.

Grandchildren of late John Wallace D'Arcy-Evans (infra):—
Issue of late John D'Arcy-Evans, b 19—, d 1990: m 19—, Christina, da of —:—
Martin J. (1 MacLeod Rd, Applecross, Perth, W Australia 6015), b 19—; MB BS, MRCOG: m 19—, Lindy —, and has issue living, Elaine, b 19—. ——— Anne, b 1956: MAPsS: m 1990, Rev John Patton, Master, King's Coll, Upland Rd, St Lucia, Qld, Australia, and has issue living, Sean Kieran D'Arcy, b 1994, — Kiri-Anne, b 1992.

Grandchildren of late Eyre Waller D'Arcy-Evans (b 1864), son of late John D'Arcy-Evans (b 1817), 2nd son of James D'Arcy-Evans, of Knockaderry, co Limerick, 2nd son of Rev Thomas Waller Evans, LLD, Rector of Dunmanway, co Cork, 2nd son of Thomas Evans, MP (ante):—
Issue of late John Wallace D'Arcy-Evans, b 1894, d 19—: m 19—, Anne Kaye Fairfield (57 Osborne Rd, E Fremantle, W Australia 6160):—
Eyre James (139 Moreing Rd, Attadale, W Australia 6156), b 19—: m 19—, — da of —, and has issue living, one son. ——— Trevor Hugh, b 19—: m 1965, Priscilla Pang, and has issue living, Yergyeni Trevor, b 1965, — Mark Siegfried, b 1966. ——— Ida, b 19—. ——— A da, b 19—.

Issue of late Capt George William D'Arcy-Evans, b 1898, d 1967: m 1923, Flora Eleanor Thorpe Edwardes:—
Peter (1 Interman Rd, Boronia 3155, Victoria, Australia), b 1924: m 1953, Isabel Blair, and has had issue, †Paul William, b 1955: m 1982, Catherine Kennedy, and d 1989, leaving issue, Simon b 1985, Kylie b 1987, — John, b 1959: m 1983, Margaret Borger, and has issue living, Nicholas John b 1990, Tara Kate b 1987, — Ian, b 1961: m 1987, Judith Hayes, and has issue living, Brendan b 1986, Tegen b 1988, Cassandra Jane b 1990, — Clare Louise, b 1966: m 1990, Frederick Grey Kohlman, and has issue living, Darcy John b 1999. ——— John Eyre (14 Jubilee Court, Leacroft, Staines, Middx TW18 4NQ), b 1932: m 1959, Susan Kathleen, da of Henry Gerard de Visme Gipps, and has issue living, Guy William, b 1961: m 1986, Elizabeth —, and has issue living, Thomas Benjamin b 1990, Alex James b 1993, — Richard Henry, b 1962, — Patrick John, b 1965, — Jane, b 1968, — Kate, b 1971.

Issue of late Elystan Cecil D'Arcy-Evans, b 1906, d 1960: m 1953, Rosemonde Lovell Pryor Rainbird (Bland Rd, York, W Australia):—
Donald Hugh, b 1955: m 1982, Pamela Verena Hocking, and has issue living, Andrew Eyre, b 1983. Residence – 34 Stanley St, Morpeth Vale, S Australia 5136. ——— Ainslie Jean, b 1957; BSc: m 1982, Michael John Slack-Smith, BSc, of Lot 7, Lyon Rd, Jandakot, W Australia, and has issue living, David, b 1986, — Matthew, b 1988.

PREDECESSORS – George Evans, Bar-at-law, a zealous promoter of the Revolution of 1688, was after the accession of William III sworn of the Privy Council, and returned as MP for Charleville, co Cork, and subsequently declined a peerage offered by George I, an honour however, that was accepted by his son (1) GEORGE, MP, cr Baron Carbery, of Carbery, co Cork (peerage of Ireland) 1715, with remainder to the male issue of his father; d 1749; s by his son (2) GEORGE, MP, 2nd Baron; d 1759; s by his son (3) GEORGE, 3rd Baron; d 1783; s by his son (4) GEORGE, 4th Baron, MP for Rutland, dsp 1804: s by his uncle (5) GEORGE, 5th Baron (2nd son of 2nd Baron); d 1807, without surviving male issue; s by his kinsman (6) Sir JOHN EVANS-FREKE, 6th Baron (whose father, grandson of the 1st Baron, had been cr a Baronet (1) 1768, and assumed the additional surname of Freke); was a Representative Peer; dsp 1845; s by his nephew (7) GEORGE PATRICK, 7th Baron (son of Percy Evans-Freke, 3rd son of 1st Bt), by Dorothea, da of the Rev Christopher Harvey, DD, of Kyle, co Wexford, b 1807: m 1852, Harriet Maria Catherine, who d 1884, da of Lt-Gen Edward William Shuldham, HEIC, of Dunmanway, co Cork; d 1889; s by his son (8) WILLIAM CHARLES, 8th Baron, b 1812; a Representative Peer for Ireland: m 1st, 1840, Lady Sophia Sherard, who d 1851, da of 5th Earl of Harborough (ext), and widow of Sir Thomas Whichcote, 6th Bt, 2ndly, 1866, Lady Victoria Cecil, who d 1932, da of 2nd Marquess of Exeter; d 1894; s by his elder son (9) ALGERNON WILLIAM GEORGE, 9th Baron, b 1868; m 1890, Mary, who d 1949, da of late Henry J. Toulmin, of The Prè St Albans; d 1898; s by his son (10) JOHN, 10th Baron, b 1892; assumed name of John Evans Carberry by deed poll in Nairobi 1920: m 1st, 1913 (m diss 1919), José, da of Evelyn James Metcalfe; 2ndly 1922, Maia Ivy, who d 1928, da of Alfred Anderson, of Nairobi; 3rdly, 1930, June Weir Mosley, who d 1980; s by his nephew (11) PETER RALFE HARRINGTON, only son of late Hon Ralfe Evans-Freke, MBE (d 1969), 2nd son of 9th Baron, 11th Baron and present peer.

Cardigan, Earl of; son of Marquess of Ailesbury.

Cardross, Lord; son of Earl of Buchan.

CAREW, BARON (Conolly-Carew) (Baron I 1834, and UK 1838)

NIL ADMIRARI

To wonder at nothing

PATRICK THOMAS CONOLLY-CAREW, 7th Baron; *b* 6 March 1938; *s* 1994; *ed* Harrow, and RMA Sandhurst; late Capt RHG; Pres Irish Horse Trials Soc 1998; Hon Bureau Memb Federation Equestre Internationale 1996; Memb Irish Olympic Three Day Event Team 1968 and 1972; Pres Ground Jury Olympic Games 1992 and 1996: *m* 1962, Celia Mary, yr da of late Col Hon Charles Guy Cubitt, CBE, DSO, TD (*see* B Ashcombe), and has issue.

ᵃᵣᵐˢ Arms – Or, three lions passant in pale sable. Crest – An heraldic antelope passant sable, horned and tufted or. Supporters – Two heraldic antelopes gules, horned and tufted or.
Residence – Donadea House, Naas, co Kildare. *Clubs* – Kildare St, and University.

SON LIVING

Hon WILLIAM PATRICK, *b* 27 March 1973.

DAUGHTERS LIVING

Hon Virginia Mary, *b* 1965: *m* 1985, Neil S. McGrath, 3rd son of Dr Patrick McGrath, of Brownstown Stud Farm, Curragh, co Kildare, and has issue living, William James Thady, *b* 1987, — Christopher Neil, *b* 1990.
Hon Nicola Rosamond, *b* 1966: *m* 1st, 1991 (*m diss* 1992), Peter C. G. Schwerdt; 2ndly, 1998, Piers Louis Tottenham de Montfort, 2nd son of Archibald Lowry de Montfort, OBE, of 30 Dawson Place, W2, and of Sundial House, Castletownshend, co Cork, and has issue living (by 2nd *m*), Thomas Guy Archibald, *b* 1999.
Hon Camilla Sylvia, *b* 1969.

BROTHER LIVING

Hon Gerald Edward Ian MAITLAND-CAREW (Thirlestane Castle, Lauder, Berwickshire), *b* 1941; Capt (ret) 15th/19th Hus; assumed by deed poll 1971 the surname of Maitland-Carew: *m* 1972, Rosalind Averil, da of late Lt-Col Neil Hanning Reed Speke, MC, and has issue living, Edward Ian Conolly, *b* 1976, — Peter Gerald Speke, *b* 1979, — Emma Rosalind, *b* 1974.

SISTERS LIVING

Hon Diana Sylvia, *b* 1940: *m* 1985, Baron Alexis Wrangel, of Lone End, Oberstown Cross, Tara, co Meath.
Hon Sarah Catherine, *b* 1944: *m* 1966, Ian Arthur Cluny Macpherson, of Round Ash, E Worlington, Crediton, Devon EX17 4TZ, and has issue living, John Gavin, *b* 1967, — Caroline Emma Louisa, *b* 1969: *m* 1998, Richard Edmund John Gray, late Capt Coldstream Gds, elder son of Edmund Gray, of Elmbridge, Worcs, — Katharine Heather Elizabeth, *b* 1974.

COLLATERAL BRANCHES LIVING

Issue of late Hon Gavin George Carew, MBE, TD, 2nd son of 5th Baron, *b* 1906, *d* 1997: *m* 1932, Aileen Hilda Frances, who *d* 1974, da of late Ean Francis Cecil (*see* M Exter, colls, 1973-74 Edn):—
Anne Hilda Kathleen, *b* 1933: *m* 1953, John Dix, and has issue living, Stephen Gavin, *b* 1955, — Julia Anne, *b* 1954, — Anita Frances, *b* 1957. *Residence* – Gellillyndu, Llanio, Tregaron, Dyfed.

Issue of late Lt-Cdr Hon Peter Cuthbert Carew, RN, yst son of 5th Baron, *b* 1908, *d* 1980: *m* 1937, Barbara, who *d* 1999, da of late Henry Wolley Leigh-Bennett (Price, Bt, cr 1815, colls):—
†David Edward, *b* 1942; *d* 1997. —— Susan Catherine (*Lady Madel*), *b* 1944: *m* 1971, Sir (William) David Madel, MP, of 120 Pickford Rd, Markyate, Herts, and has issue living, Christopher William, *b* 1977, — Louise Iona, *b* 1975.

Granddaughter of late Lt-Cdr Hon Peter Cuthbert Carew, RN (ante):—
Issue of late Thomas Henry Carew, *b* 1947, *d* 1978: *m* 1974, Lucinda (who *d* 1999, having *m* 2ndly, 1983, John Martin Harkness, of Hill House, Geldeston, Beccles, Suffolk), yst da of Joseph Guy Lubbock (*see* B Avebury, colls):—

Rachel Catherine, *b* 1978 (*posthumous*).

PREDECESSORS – (1) ROBERT SHAPLAND Carew, Lord-Lt of co Wexford; cr *Baron Carew* (peerage of Ireland) 1834, and *Baron Carew*, of Castle Boro, co Wexford (peerage of United Kingdom) 1838; *d* 1856; *s* by his son (2) ROBERT SHAPLAND, KP, *b* 1818; Lord Lt of co Wexford, and MP for Waterford (*L*) 1840-7: *m* 1844, Emily Anne, da of Sir George Richard Philips, MP, 2nd Bt: *d* 1881; *s* by his son (3)ROBERT SHAPLAND GEORGE JULIAN, 3rd Baron; *b* 1860: *m* 1888, Julia Mary, who *d* 1922, da of late Albert Arthur Erin Lethbridge (Lethbridge, Bt colls); *d* 1923; *s* by his brother (4) GEORGE PATRICK JOHN, 4th Baron; *b* 1863; *m* 1888, Maud Beatrice, who *d* 1955, da of late John Ramsay; *d* 1926; *s* by his cousin (5) GERALD SHAPLAND (son of late Hon Shapland Francis Carew, son of 1st Baron), 5th Baron; *b* 1860: *m* 1904, Catherine, who *d* 1947, only da of late Thomas Conolly, MP, of Castletown, co Kildare; *d* 1927 *s* by his eldest son (6) WILLIAM FRANCIS, CBE, 6th Baron; *b* 1905; Maj Duke of Cornwall's LI, served 1939-45 War (wounded), ADC to Gov and Com-in-Ch of Bermuda 1931-36; Nat Chm British Legion 1963-66, Trustee Irish Sailors and Soldiers Land Trust; assumed by deed poll 1938 the additional surname of Conolly: *m* 1937, Lady Sylvia Gwendoline Eva Maitland, who *d* 1991, da of 15th Earl of Lauderdale; *d* 1994; *s* by his elder son (7) PATRICK THOMAS, 7th Baron and present peer.

Carington, family name of Baron Carrington.

Carleton, Baron, title of Earl of Shannon on Roll of HL.

CARLISLE, EARL OF (Howard) (Earl E 1661)

I am willing, but not able

GEORGE WILLIAM BEAUMONT HOWARD, 13th Earl; *b* 15 Feb 1949; *s* 1994; *ed* Eton, and Balliol Coll, Oxford (MA); Maj 9/12th Royal Lancers (resigned commn 1987).

Arms – Quarterly of six: 1st gules, a bend between six cross crosslets fitchée argent, on the bend an escutcheon or, charged with a demi-lion rampant, pierced through the mouth with an arrow, within a double tressure flory counterflory, all gules, and above the escutcheon a mullet sable, for difference, *Howard*; 2nd gules, three lions passant guardant or in pale, and in chief a label of three points argent, *Thomas of Brotherton*, son of Edward I; 3rd checky, or and azure, *Warren*, Earl Warren and Surrey; 4th gules, a lion rampant argent; *Mowbray*, Duke of Norfolk; 5th gules, three escallops argent, *Dacre*; 6th barry of six argent and azure over all, three chaplets gules proper, *Greystock*. **Crest** – On a chapeau gules, turned up ermine, a lion statant guardant, with the tail extended or, ducally gorged argent, a mullet sable for difference. **Supporters** – *Dexter*, a lion argent, charged with a mullet sable for difference; *sinister* a bull gules, armed unguled, ducally gorged and lined or.
Seat – Naworth Castle, Brampton, Cumbria CA8 2HF.

BROTHER LIVING

Hon PHILIP CHARLES WENTWORTH, *b* 25 March 1963; *ed* Eton, and Reading Univ; *m* 1992, Mrs Elizabeth Harrison, only da of John Moore, and has issue living, William Philip Alexander, *b* 9 Aug 1994, — Alexandra Jane Elizabeth, *b* 1997. *Residences* – The Gatehouse, Naworth, Brampton, Cumbria, and Naworth Castle, Brampton, Cumbria CA8 2HF.

SISTERS LIVING (*In remainder to Lordship of Ruthven of Freeland*)

Lady Jane Annabelle, *b* 1947: *m* 1st, 1968 (*m diss* 1977), John David Vaughan Seth-Smith; 2ndly, 1983 (*m diss* 1999), Rodney Spencer Ledward, and has issue living (by 1st *m*), Gemma Bridget Annabel, *b* 1972, — (by 2nd *m*) Bertie Arthur Ruthven, *b* 1985. *Residence* – Beaulieu Cottage, The Riviera, Sandgate, Folkestone, Kent CT20 3AB.

Lady Emma Bridget, *b* 1952: *m* 1st, 1974 (*m diss* 1981), John Philip Charles Langton-Lockton; 2ndly, 1983 (*m diss* 1988), Robie Patrick Maxwell Uniacke; 3rdly, 1988, Guy Mark Sisson, and has issue living (by 1st *m*), Maximillian, *b* 1980, — Tabitha Jane, *b* 1978, — (by 2nd *m*) Robie Jonjo, *b* 1984, — (by 3rd *m*) Ned John Hamilton, *b* 1989. *Residence* – North Wonson Farm, Throwleigh, nr Okehampton, Devon.

AUNT LIVING (*Daughter of 11th Earl by 1st marriage*)

Lady Carolyn Bridget Dacre (16 Brunswick Rd, Penrith, Cumbria), *b* 1919; 1939-45 War as Subaltern ATS (transferred to FANY Ambulance Corps 1941).

HALF-AUNT LIVING (*Daughter of 11th Earl by 2nd marriage*)

Lady Susan Ankaret, *b* 1948: *m* 1st, 1967 (*m diss* 1978), Charles James Buchanan-Jardine (*see* Buchanan-Jardine, Bt); 2ndly, 1978, Count Hubert Charles de Meyer, of 50 Hasker St, SW3, and Tracey Farm, Great Tew, Oxon, and has issue living (by 1st *m*) (*see* Buchanan-Jardine, Bt), — (by 2nd *m*), Alexander Charles Benedict, *b* 1979.

WIDOW LIVING OF TENTH LORD RUTHVEN OF FREELAND

JUDITH GORDON (Denbigh, Foreland Rd, Bembridge, Isle of Wight), yr da of late Bertie E. Bell, of Guernsey: *m* 1st, 1953, as his 2nd wife, the 10th Lord, who *d* 1956; 2ndly, 1965, Maj Digby Robert Peel, MC, RA, who *d* 1971.

WIDOW LIVING OF TWELFTH EARL

Hon ELA HILDA ALINE BEAUMONT (*Countess of Carlisle*), only da of 2nd Viscount Allendale: *m* 1945, the 12th Earl of Carlisle, MC, who *d* 1994. *Residence* – St Mary's Vale, Lanercost, Brampton, Carlisle.

COLLATERAL BRANCHES LIVING

Grandchildren of late Hon Oliver Howard, 4th son of 9th Earl:—
Issue of late Hubert Arthur George Howard, *b* 1901, *d* 1986: *m* 1930, Moira, who *d* 1986, da of late Rev John Arthur Victor Magee, V of St Mark's, Hamilton Terr, W (Wilson, Bt, *cr* 1874):—
David Charles Hubert (Le Petit Relai, 37800 Sepmes, Indre et Loire, France), *b* 1940; *ed* Eton: *m* 1st, 1962 (*m diss* 1969), Pamela Mary, da of Frederick Thomas Rose, of Kenilworth; 2ndly, 1978, Norma Ellen, da of Norman William Sparks, of Bridgwater, Som, and has issue living (by 1st *m*), Susan Mary, *b* 1963, — Rosalind Emma, *b* 1966, — (by 2nd *m*) Oliver Charles Frederick, *b* 1980. —— Lavinia Moira, *b* 1944: *m* 1963, Christopher Thomas Bernard Turville-Constable-Maxwell (*see* L Herries of Terregles, colls).

Grandsons of late Hon Geoffrey William Algernon Howard, 5th son of 9th Earl:—
Issue of late George Anthony Geoffrey Howard (*Baron Howard of Henderskelfe*), *b* 1920, *d* 1984; *cr* Baron Howard of Henderskelfe (Life Baron) 1983: *m* 1949, Lady Cecilia Blanche Geneviève FitzRoy, who *d* 1974, da of 8th Duke of Grafton:—
Hon Henry Francis Geoffrey, *b* 1950. —— *Hon* Nicholas Paul Geoffrey, *b* 1952; *ed* Eton, and Oxford Univ: *m* 1st, 1983 (*m diss* 1990), Amanda Kate Victoria, only da of late Derek Robert Nimmo, actor, of Kensington; 2ndly, 1992, Victoria, da of late Thomas E. Barnsley, OBE, of The Old Rectory, Llanelidan, N Wales, and has issue living (by 1st *m*), George Fulco Geoffrey, *b* 1985, — (by 2nd *m*), Blanche Mary, *b* 1994. *Residence* – 20 St Petersburgh Place, W2. —— *Hon* Simon Bartholomew Geoffrey, *b* 1956; *ed* Eton, and RAC Cirencester; High Sheriff N Yorks 1995: *m* 1983, Annette Marie, formerly wife of Spencer Douglas David, Earl Compton (later 7th Marquess of Northampton), and da of late Charles Antony Russell Smallwood, of Storrington, Sussex. *Seat* – Castle Howard, York. —— *Hon* (Anthony) Michael Geoffrey, *b* 1958: *m* 1985 (*m diss* 1997), Linda Louise, yr da of Alexander McGrady, of Broughty Ferry, Angus, and has issue living, Arabella Blanche Geneviève, *b* 1986, — Grania Alexandra Louise, *b* 1988. *Residence* – Spring House, Fairfield Farm, Skelton, York.

Granddaughter of late Richard Fitzroy Howard (infra):—
Issue of late Richard Frederick Robert Howard, Capt Green Howards, *b* 1916, *d* 1978: *m* 1946, Jean McBride (Cottage 82, Doone Village, Pinetown 3610, S Africa), da of Cyril Taylor:—
Jane Anne McBride (8 Cleveland Rd, Westville, Durban, S Africa), *b* 1951: *m* 1969 (*m diss* 1984), Andrew Hugh Ross MacLennan, and has issue living, Angus Howard, *b* 1972, — Morag Jean, *b* 1970, — Shannon Fiona, *b* 1976.

Grandchildren of late Col Frederick Compton Howard, 3rd son of late Frederick John Howard, son of late Hon Frederick Howard, 3rd son of 5th Earl:—
Issue of late Richard Fitzroy Howard, *b* 1879, *d* 1962: *m* 1914, Elsie Anne, who *d* 1936, elder da of late Robert Clarkson, of Scarborough:—
George William, *b* 1924; CEng, FIMechE: *m* 1952, Barbara Enid, da of Reginald Edgar Everett, and has issue living, Katherine Margaret, *b* 1954; BA: *m* 1st, 19— (*m diss* 19—), Peter Kay; 2ndly, 1989, Thomas Idris Bowen, — Lesley Jane, *b* 1957: *m* 1987, Stephen Hutty, of Elloughton, E Yorks, and has issue living, William Robert *b* 1988, Katharine Jane *b* 1990, Helen Rose *b* 1992, — Sarah Barbara, *b* 1960; MA Vet, MB MRCVS: *m* 1987 (*m diss* 1997), Geoffrey van-der-Walt, of Sussex. *Residence* – 109 Southella Way, Kirkella, E Yorks. —— Bertha Frances Grace (73 Silkham Rd, Oxted, Surrey), *b* 1914: *m* 1943 (*m diss* 1960), Douglas Haley, and has issue living, Ian Richard, *b* 1944: *m* 1965, Elizabeth Rose O'Reilly, of co Cavan, and has issue living, Damien Michael Douglas *b* 1974, Siobhan Geraldine *b* 1972, — Helen Veronica, *b* 1946: *m* 1974, Brian S. Liddell of 16 Pitford Rd, Woodley, Reading, and has issue living, Stephen *b* 1975, David *b* 1979. —— Kathleen Victoria, *b* 1918: *m* 1941, John Alan Lake, who *d* 1977, and has issue living, Ann Cecilia Mary, *b* 1942: *m* 1967, Stephen John Curtis, of Upton House, Beeford, Driffield, Yorks, and has issue living, Matthew

John *b* 1968, Amelia Ann *b* 1971, Madeleine Ann *b* 1975, — Susan Margaret, *b* 1949: *m* 19—, David Christopher Lavender, of 2 Lea Way, Huntington, York, and has issue living, Rachael *b* 1970. *Residence* – 44 Alton Park, Beeford, Driffield, Yorks. ——Elsie Anne, *b* 1927: *m* 1951, William Byass Temple, and has issue living, Janet, *b* 1954: *m* 1977, Bjornsten, of Norwkapsgatan II, 163-55, Spånga, Stockholm, — Wendy, *b* 1956, — Diane, *b* 1962. *Residence* – Oak Wood, 19 Throxenby Lane, Newby, Scarborough, Yorks

Issue of late George Frederick Howard, *b* 1894, *d* 1957: *m* 1919, Jane Anne Scott, who *d* 1961, da of John Young Myrtle, of Edinburgh:—
Margaret Anne Myrtle, MB, ChB, DPH, *b* 1921; formerly Capt RAMC: *m* 1946, Ralph Kenyon Hardy, who *d* 1993, and has issue living, Christopher Nigel (15 St Mary's Rd, Ditton Hill, Surbiton, Surrey), *b* 1947: *m* 1977, Carol, 2nd da of Peter Barnes, of 3 Heathfield Rd, Hersham, Surrey, and has issue living, Gemma Elizabeth *b* 1980, Annabel Frances *b* 1984, — Peter Ralph Howard, *b* 1953. *Residence* – 13 Denleigh Gdns, Thames Ditton, Surrey.

Grandchildren of late Alfred John Howard, 4th son of late Frederick John Howard (ante):—
Issue of late Capt William Gilbert Howard, CBE, RN, *b* 1877, *d* 1960: *m* 1912, Hon Agnes Caroline Sophia Parnell, JP, who *d* 1968, da of 4th Baron Congleton:—
Frederick Henry, DSO, MC, *b* 1915; Lt-Col (ret) 3rd Hus; Palestine 1936 (MC); European War 1939-45 in N Africa and N-W Europe (Bar to MC, DSO); DSO 1946: *m* 1st, 1941 (*m diss* 1946), Estelle Georgette da of Capt Sharp, of Londjani Kenya; 2ndly, 1952, Hon Jean Margaret Parnell, da of 6th Baron Congleton, and has issue living (by 2nd *m*), Henry James, *b* 1956; *ed* Eton, and RMA; Capt R Scots Drag Gds; Capt Scottish Yeo, and Memb Queen's Body Guard for Scotland (Royal Company of Archers): *m* 1983, Philippa Charlotte, 3rd da of Maj Lyon Balfour Paul, of Eskdale, Beauly, Inverness, and has issue living, William Henry *b* 1986, Kiloran Rose *b* 1988, — John Dugald, *b* 1958; *ed* Gordonstoun and RMA; 2nd Lt R Scots Drag Gds, — Rose, *b* 1953. *Residence* – Isle of Ulva, Aros, Mull, Argyll PA73 6LZ. *Clubs* – Naval and Military, Army and Navy, New (Edinburgh), Royal Highland Yacht. —— †John William, *b* 1917; *ed* Gresham's, and Magdalene Coll, Camb (MA); Colonial Admin Ser, Kenya, 1939-63, etc; 1939-45 War in Abyssinia and Madagascar as Capt 5th King's African Rifles (despatches twice): *m* 1949, Elizabeth Bligh (Appletree Cottage, Staplecross, Robertsbridge, Sussex), yst da of Capt Robert Francis Veasey, RN (*see* E Darnley, colls, 1951 Edn), and *d* 1988, leaving issue, Jonathan Arthur Francis (Royal Oak, Donhead St Mary, Shaftesbury, Dorset), *b* 1955; *ed* Eton, and Nottingham Univ (BA); Lt-Col King's Royal Hussars: *m* 1984, Louise Maria Theodora, elder da of late Richard Miles Backhouse (*see* Backhouse, Bt, colls), and has issue living, William Richard Michael *b* 1986, George Jonathan Henry *b* 1988, Henry John Arthur *b* 1989, — Sarah Elizabeth Anne, *b* 1951; BA London Univ; resumed maiden name 1978: *m* 1st, 1973 (*m diss* 1978), Robert James Rogers; 2ndly, 1989, Rev Charles Patrick Sherlock, elder son of late Niall Patrick Sherlock, of Ewhurst, Surrey, and has issue living (by 2nd *m*), Patrick John Howard *b* 1991, Francis Alexander Howard *b* 1994, — (Eva) Jane Agnes, *b* 1953: *m* 1979, Lt-Col Hugh Charles Gregory Willing, RGJ, and has issue living, Edward John David *b* 1982, Richard Hugh *b* 1984, Arabella Jane *b* 1987. —— Mark Alfred, *b* 1919; is a Grazier; N Africa and Greece 1939-45 as Lt Australian Forces (prisoner): *m* 1950, Judith Ruth, who *d* 1994, da of F. E. Selwyn Scott, MBE, JP, of Scotsburn, Victoria, Australia, and has had issue, †Michael Gilbert, *b* 1950; *ed* Geelong Gram Sch, and Australian Nat Univ (BA); *dunm* 1994, — William Mark, *b* 1959; *ed* Geelong Gram Sch, and Glenormiston Agric Coll: *m* 1994, Anne Townsend, — Margaret Jean, *b* 1953: *m* 1980, Colin McLeod Campbell, of Rockgedgicl, Quirnidi, NSW 2343, Australia, and has issue living, Henry Mark *b* 1982; *ed* The Scots Coll, Sydney, Andrew Colin *b* 1985. *Residence* – War Veterans Hostel, 59 Ferguson Av, Myrtle Bank, S Australia 5064; *Clubs* – Naval and Military (Melbourne), Melbourne. —— Margaret, *b* (twin) 1919; formerly Subaltern ATS: *m* 1945, Brig Christopher Charles Lloyd Browne, OBE, late RA, who *d* 1972, and has had issue, Andrew William Lloyd, *b* 1948; *d* 1967, — Elizabeth, *b* 1947; *ed* London Univ (BSc): *m* 1978, Lt-Cdr Quentin Parker, RN, and has issue living, Jonathan *b* 1980, Charles Godfrey *b* 1981, — Felicity, *b* 1954: *m* 1974, Rev Charles William Granville Dobbie, OBE, Lt-Col late KOSB, and has issue living, William Arthur Charles *b* 1980; *ed* Eton, George Galahad Christopher *b* 1986, Alice Felicity *b* 1982, — Carolyn, *b* 1958; BSc, DPhil (Oxon). *Residence* – Dean House, W Dean, Salisbury, Wilts. —— Agnes, *b* 1921; BA Open Univ; formerly Leading Wren WRNS: *m* 1945, Maj John Singleton Hattersley, RE, who *d* 1992, and has had issue, Charles William, *b* 1949; *ed* Marlborough, and Durham Univ (BA); FRGS; Lt-Cdr RN (ret): *m* 1988, Rebecca Jane, only da of David Smith, of Puttenham, Surrey, and has issue living, Elizabeth Maryse *b* 1989, Antonia Sarah *b* 1993, Caroline *b* 1996, — Margaret Sarah, *b* 1950; *ed* Lond Univ (BA); late Capt WRAC: *m* 1979, John Martyn Ford, son of late Rev Basil Ford, and has issue living, Michael John *b* 1986, Alexandra Margaret *b* 1982, — Anne Agnes, *b* 1952; *d* 1974, — Victoria Vera, *b* 1955; *ed* Aberystwyth Univ (LLB), and Edinburgh Univ (CQSW): *m* 1985, Peter Francis Harris, and has issue living, Sophia Victoria *b* 1997, — Helen Jean, *b* 1961; *ed* Sheffield Univ (BA). *Residence* – 20 Longview Close, Snettisham, Kings Lynn, Norfolk PE31 7RD.

Issue of late Vice-Adm Ronald Howard, *b* 1878, *d* 1959: *m* (Jan) 1913, Ruth Evelyn, who *d* 1968, da of late William Coryton (Parker Bt, cr 1884, colls):—
†Roger Alexander, TD, *b* 1919; Maj (ret) RAOC: *m* 1944, Jean (11 Knightsbridge Court, Sloane St, SW1), da of late Vice-Adm A. H. Alington, and *d* 1998, leaving issue, Alexandra Nancy, *b* 1946: *m* 1971, Christopher Skidmore Taylor, of Yorton House, Harmer Hill, Shrewsbury, and has issue living, Charles Argentinc Weston, *b* 1981, Emily Clare *b* 1973, Alexia Lucy *b* 1974, — Miranda Jane *b* 1948: *m* 1973, Petar Djedovic, of 12 Sedlescombe Rd, SW6 1RD, and Petrovac Na Moru, Montenegro, and has issue living, Natasha Kate *b* 1975, — Elvina Lucy *b* 1949: *m* 1974, Peter Robert Siddons, of 49 Clarendon Rd, Holland Park, W11 4JD, and has issue living, Alastair Mark *b* 1978, Philippa Sarah *b* 1977, Melanie Sarah *b* 1980. —— Millicent, *b* (Dec) 1913: *m* 1937, Col Charles Richard Spencer, OBE, DL, 12th R Lancers, of Elfordtown, Yelverton. S Devon, and has issue living, Edward Charles, *b* 1946: *m* 1974, Sarah Elizabeth Dewhurst, and has issue living, Oliver Charles Wyndham *b* 1978, Caroline Tana *b* 1976, Rebecca Victoria *b* 1983, — Elizabeth Janet (*Lady Kitson*), *b* 1938: *m* 1962, Gen Sir Frank Edward Kitson, GBE, KCB, MC, and has issue living, Catherine Alice *b* 1963: *m* 1993, Edward George Truman Knowles, of Fritton Old Hall, Church Lane, Fritton, Yarmouth, Norfolk (and has issue living, George Edward Kitson *b* 1994, Tilly *b* 1996, Isobel Flora *b* 1999), Rosemary Diana *b* 1966: *m* 1996, Orlando Campbell, Marion Ruth (Chiggy) *b* 1969: *m* 1996, D. Rupert P. Little.

Grandsons of late Gerald Richard Howard, 5th and yst son of late Frederick John Howard (ante):—
Issue of late Bertram Marcus Howard, *b* 1890, *d* 1970: *m* 1924, Phyllis Maude, who *d* 1988, da of Robert James Lamb, of Surbiton, Surrey:—
Michael Cavendish (24 South View, Letchworth Garden City, Herts), *b* 1926; *ed* King's Coll, Taunton; C Chem MRSC; W Africa 1944-45 with REME: *m* 1st, 1956, Muriel, who *d* 1978, widow of W. T. Mullings, BSc, MD; 2ndly, 1980, Patricia Ellen Millicent Gwatkin, da of William James Sandiford, of Woodford, Essex. —— Richard Cavendish (Pigeonhouse Barn, Dingle Rd, Brockamin, Leigh, Worcs WR6 5JX), *b* 1936; *ed* King's Coll, Taunton; MBIM, MIIM: *m* 1st, 1959 (*m diss* 1979), Diana Mary, da of Frank B. Wharton, of Lichfield, Staffs; 2ndly, 1998, Wendy Anne Gladwin, da of John Charles Houghton, of Leamington Spa, Warwicks, and has issue living (by 1st *m*), Dale Robin Cavendish (Moora-Moora Co-operative, PO Box 214, Healville, Victoria 3777, Australia), *b* 1960; BSc Manchester Univ: *m* 1993, Michelle Redman, and has an adopted stepson, Jacob Lee *b* 1989, — Timothy Richard Cavendish (139 Marley Fields, Leighton Buzzard, Beds LU7 8WJ), *b* 1962: *m* 1986, Anne Marcia, da of late Malcolm John McAlistair Bennett, of Harrogate, N Yorks, and

has issue living, Daniel Timothy Cavendish *b* 1989, Ellen Francesca *b* 1988, — James David Cavendish (Rosecroft, 12 Haynes Close, Thorne, Doncaster DN8 5HR), *b* 1968: *m* 1994, Leanda Clare Porter, and has issue living, Tyler James Cavendish *b* 1995, Tavia Shan Cavendish *b* 1997, — Angela Claire, *b* 1961: *m* 1992, Martin John Korchinsky, of 45 Keswick Rd, Heaton Chapel, Stockport, SK4 5JU, and has issue living, Benjamin John *b* 1990, Josef James *b* 1993.

      Grandson of late Capt John Henry Howard, RN, 2nd son of late Very Rev Hon Henry Edward John
      Howard, DD, Dean of Lichfield, 4th son of 5th Earl:—
      Issue of late Com Charles Wilbraham John Howard, RN *b* 1880, *d* 1959: *m* 1909, Dorothy Ida Leigh, who *d*
      1968, da of Sir Thomas Leigh Hare, 1st Bt, MVO (cr 1905):—
Geoffrey Charles (Stow House, Great Somerford, Wilts SN15 5HU), *b* 1910; Maj (ret) Black Watch; 1939-45 War; *m* 1939, Katharine, da of late Adm Sir Eric John Arthur Fullerton, KCB, DSO (B Fisher).

      Granddaughter of late Rev Henry Frederick Howard, 5th and yst son of late Very Rev Hon Henry
      Edward John Howard, DD, Dean of Lichfield (ante):—
      Issue of late Major Bernard Henry Howard, *b* 1879, *ka* 1916: *m* 1909, Margaret Ellen Edith McLean, who *d*
      1984, da of late Lt-Col Donat Edmund McMahon:—
Marjorie Isabella, *b* 1910: *m* 1st, 1938, Lt-Cdr Robert Lampard, RN, who was *ka* 1941; 2ndly, 1945, Lt-Cdr Roger Hoyle, RN, who *d* 1988, and has issue living (by 2nd *m*), Hugo Charles John, *b* 1949: *m* 1979, Susan Elizabeth Haynes, and has issue living, Joshua Roger *b* 1985, Sarah *b* 1984, — Angela Felicity, *b* 1947. *Residence* – Swandown, Axford, Marlborough, Wilts.

                      (*In remainder to Lordship of Ruthven of Freeland only.*)

      Issue of late Hon Alison Mary Ruthven, 3rd da of 10th Lord Ruthven, *b* 1902, *d* 1973: *m* 1929, Cdr Sir
      John Leighton Barran, 3rd Bt, RNVR, who *d* 1974:—
Sir John Napoleon Ruthven Barran, 4th Bt (see that title.)

      Issue of late Hon Margaret Leslie Ruthven, 4th da of 10th Lord Ruthven, *b* 1902 (twin), *d* 1970: *m*
      1932, Peter Llewelyn Davies, MC, who *d* 1960:—
George Caesar, *b* 1938; *ed* Eton.

      Grandson of late Rt Hon Sir Alexander Gore Arkwright Hore-Ruthven, VC, GCMB, CB, DSO, PC (2nd
      son of 9th Lord), who was cr *Earl of Gowrie* 1945 (see that title.)

      Issue of late Col Hon Christian Malise Hore-Ruthven, 3rd son of 9th Lord, *b* 1880, *d* 1969: *m* 1925, Hon
      Angela Margaret, RRC, who *d* 1970, da of 3rd Baron Manners:—
James John Malise (42 Westminster Gdns, Marsham St, SW1 4JD), *b* 1935; *ed* Eton: *m* 1965, Helen Dron, el da of John S. Craig, of Flat 1, Buckland Court, 37 Belsize Park NW3 4EB, and has issue living, Alexander Malise, *b* 1972, — Angela Dron, *b* 1976. —— Sarah Constance Anne, *b* 1930: *m* 1962, James Baynard-Smith, of 44 Sunderland Ave, Oxford, and has issue living, Peter James, *b* 1966: *m* 1993, Julia Woodley, and has issue living, Ben Richard *b* 1998, Rebekah Clare *b* 1996, — Christopher Ruthven, *b* 1972.

      Granddaughter of late Hon Charles Edward Stewart Hore-Ruthven, OBE, brother of 8th Lord:—
      Issue of late Charles Hore-Ruthven, *b* 1876, *d* 1963: *m* 1910, Elyned Rhona, who *d* 1965, da of late Thomas
      Wood (B Tollemache):—
Elyned Barbara, MBE, *b* 1915; MBE (Mil) 1946: *m* 1940, John Allan Legh Barratt, TD, of Upgate House, Swannington, Norfolk, and has had issue, David John (Manor House, Gt Witchingham, Norwich, Norfolk NR9 5PG) *b* 1947: *m* 1982, Penelope Constance Isabel Lloyd, and has issue living, Fergus Ralph Legh *b* 1984, Frederick David Nicholas *b* 1987, — Charles William Legh (Ollands Farm, Heydon, Norfolk), *b* 1949: *m* 1976, Caroline, da of Maj James Clifford Wilson, of Warren Farm, Ingoldisthorpe, Kings Lynn, and has issue living, William James *b* 1979, Samuel Charles Legh *b* 1982, — Anita Elyned, *b* 1952, *d* 1973.

PREDECESSORS – **(1)** CHARLES Howard, PC, great-grandson of Lord William Howard, 3rd son of 4th Duke of Norfolk; cr Viscount Howard of Morpeth by Oliver Cromwell 1657, and *Baron Dacre of Gillesland, Viscount Howard of Morpeth*, and *Earl of Carlisle* 1661; was subsequently Ambassador to the Czar of Muscovy and Gov of Jamaica; *d* 1686; *s* by his son **(2)** EDWARD, 2nd Earl; *d* 1692; *s* by his son **(3)** CHARLES, 3rd Earl; was First Lord of the Treasury, Constable of the Tower, and Gov of Windsor Castle; *d* 1738; *s* by his son **(4)** HENRY, KG; *d* 1758; *s* by his son **(5)** FREDERICK, KG, KT; Viceroy of Ireland 1780-2; *d* 1825; *s* by his son **(6)** GEORGE, KG, 6th Earl; *b* 1773; was Lord-Lieut of E Riding of York: *m* 1801, Lady Georgiana Dorothy Cavendish, da of 5th Duke of Devonshire; *d* 1848; *s* by his elder son **(7)** GEORGE WILLIAM FREDERICK, KG, PC; was Ch Sec for Ireland 1835-41, Ch Commr of Woods and Forests 1846-50, Chancellor of Duchy of Lancaster 1850-2, and Lord-Lieut of Ireland 1855-8 and 1859-64; *d* unmarried 1864; *s* by his brother **(8)** WILLIAM GEORGE, 8th Earl, *b* 1808; R of Londesborough 1832-77; *d* unmarried 1889; *s* by his nephew **(9)** GEORGE JAMES (son of late Hon Charles Wentworth George Howard, MP, 5th son of 6th Earl), 9th Earl; *b* 1843; MP for E Cumberland (*L*) 1879-80, when he was defeated and 1881-5: *m* 1864, Hon Rosalind Frances, who *d* 1921, da of 2nd Baron Stanley of Alderley; *d* 1911; *s* by his son **(10)** CHARLES JAMES STANLEY, 10th Earl; *b* 1867; sat as MP for Birmingham, S Div (LU) 1904-11; *m* 1894, Rhoda Ankaret, who *d* 1957, da of Col Paget W. L'Estrange, formerly RA; *d* 1912; *s* by his only son **(11)** GEORGE JOSSLYN L'ESTRANGE, 11th Earl, *b* 1895; Chm of UK Commercial Corporation, Ankara, 1941-3; *m* 1st, 1918 (*m diss* 1947), Hon Bridget Helen Hore-Ruthven, CBE (who *s* as Lady Ruthven of Freeland 1956, and *d* 1982), da of 10th Lord Ruthven of Freeland; 2ndly, 1947, Esme Mary Shrubb, who *d* 1997, da of Charles Edward Iredell; *d* 1963; *s* by his only son **(12)** CHARLES JAMES RUTHVEN, MC, 12th Earl; *b* 1923; *s* to Lordship of Ruthven of Freeland (Peerage of Scotland) 1982; 1939-45 War as Lieut Rifle Bde (twice severely wounded); DL Cumbria, Forestry Commr and FRICS: *m* 1945, Hon Ela Hilda Aline Beaumont, only da of 2nd Viscount Allendale; *d* 1994; *s* by his elder son **(13)** GEORGE WILLIAM BEAUMONT, 13th Earl and present peer; also Viscount Howard of Morpeth, and Baron Dacre of Gillesland; also Lord Ruthven of Freeland (see * infra).

*(1) *Sir* THOMAS Ruthven (great-grandson of William, 2nd Lord Ruthven, cr 1487-8, who was grandfather of 1st Earl of Gowrie), Col of Regt, a Commr for the Treaty of Ripon 1641, and a Commr of Exchequer 1649, was cr *Lord Ruthven of*

Freeland (peerage of Scotland) 1651; the patent is stated to have been burnt with the house of Freeland in 1750, and the limitations are not accurately known, nevertheless as the dignity was retained (together with many extinct titles) on the Union Roll, it has been presumed that the honour was to heirs-general; *d* 1673; *s* by his son (2) DAVID, 2nd Lord; was a Lord of the Treasury in Scotland; *d* ummarried 1701, when the estates devolved by entail upon his yst sister (3) Jean, and at her death in April 1722 they passed to her nephew Sir William Cunningham, Bt (only son of her elder sister Anne, and also heir of line), who *d* Oct 1722, having assumed the surname of Ruthven upon the death of the 2nd Lord, but (living only six months after his accession to the estates) without ever having assumed the title; his cousin, however, (4) ISABELLA (da of Hon Elizabeth (2nd da and heir of line of 1st Lord) by her marriage with Sir Francis Ruthven, Knt), was summoned as a Lady to the Coronation of George II, and recognized in the Lordship of Ruthven of Freeland: *m* Col James Johnson, who assumed the name of Ruthven; *d* 1730; *s* by her son (5) JAMES, 5th Lord; *d* 1783; *s* by his son (6) JAMES, 6th Lord; *d* 1789; *s* by his son (7) JAMES, 7th Lord; *dsp* 1853; *s* by his sister (8) MARY ELIZABETH THORNTON: *m* 1806, Walter Hore, who assumed the additional surname of Ruthven *d* 1864; *s* by her grandson (9) WALTER JAMES, 9th Lord Ruthven of Freeland (*b* 1838), who, like his predecessors, voted at the Election of Representative Peers for Scotland, and was cr *Baron Ruthven of Gowrie* (peerage of United Kingdom) 1919: *m* 1869, Lady Caroline Annesley Gore, who *d* 1914, da of 4th Earl of Arran; *d* 1921; *s* by his elder son (10) WALTER PATRICK, CB, CMG, DSO, 10th Lord; *b* 1870; Maj-Gen late Scots Guards; commanded Bangalore Brig 1920-24, and London Dist 1924-8, and was Lieut-Gov of Guernsey 1929-34: *m* 1st, 1895, Jean Leslie who *d* 1952, da of late Norman George Lampson (Lampson Bt, colls); 2ndly, 1953, Judith Gordon (who *m* 2ndly, 1965, Maj Digby R. Peel), da of late Bertie E. Bell, of Guernsey; *d* 1956; *s* in the Barony of Ruthven of Gowrie (peerage of United Kingdom) by his great-nephew the 2nd Earl of Gowrie, and in the Lordship of Ruthven of Freeland by his elder da (11) BRIDGET HELEN, CBE, Lady Ruthven of Freeland, *b* 1896; her petition as heir of line and heir tailzie of 1st Lord allowed in Lyon Court 1967 and her *s* to Peerage recognised: *m* 1st, 1918 (*m diss* 1947), 11th Earl of Carlisle, who *d* 1963; 2ndly, 1947, as his 2nd wife, 1st Viscount Monckton of Brenchley, who *d* 1965; *d* 1982; *s* by her only son (12) CHARLES JAMES RUTHVEN, MC, 12th Earl of Carlisle, and 12th Lord Ruthven of Freeland (ante).

CARLISLE OF BUCKLOW, BARON (Carlisle) (Life Baron 1987)

MARK CARLISLE, PC, QC, 2nd son of late Philip Edmund Carlisle; *b* 7 July 1929; *ed* Radley, and Manchester Univ (LLB); Bar Gray's Inn 1953, Bencher 1980 Northern Circuit, Judge of the Courts of Appeal of Jersey and Guernsey since 1990; Member Home Office Advisory Council on Penal System 1966-70, Recorder of Crown Court 1976-79 and since 1981; Joint Hon Sec Conservative Home Affairs Cttee 1965-69, Conservative Front Bench Spokesman on Home Affairs 1969-70, Parl Under-Sec of State Home Office 1970-72, Min of State Home Office 1972-74, Sec of State for Educn and Science 1979-81; Chm Conservative Home Affairs Cttee 1983-87, Parole Review Cttee 1987, Chm Criminal Injuries Compensation Bd since 1988; DL for Cheshire 1983; MP for Runcorn (C) 1964-83, and Warrington South 1983-87; QC 1971, PC 1979; *cr Baron Carlisle of Bucklow*, of Mobberley, co Cheshire (Life Baron) 1987: *m* 1959, Sandra Joyce, da of John Hamilton des Voeux, of St Ives, Cornwall, and has issue.

Residence – 3 Holt Gdns, Mobberley, Cheshire. *Club* – Garrick.

DAUGHTER LIVING

Hon (Vanessa) Lucy, *b* 1968: *m* 1994, Angus W. W. P. von Schoenberg, yr son of Baron Witold von Schoenberg, of Lower Heyford, Oxon.

Carlow, Viscount; son of Earl of Portarlington.

Carlton, Viscount; son of Earl of Wharncliffe.

CARMICHAEL OF KELVINGROVE, BARON (Carmichael) (Life Baron 1983)

NEIL GEORGE CARMICHAEL, son of James Carmichael, of Glasgow; *b* Oct 1921; *ed* Eastbank Acad, and Royal Coll of Science and Technology, Glasgow; PPS to Min of Technology 1966-67; Parl Under-Sec of State, Min of Transport 1967-69, Parl Sec, Min of Technology 1969-70, Parl Under-Sec of State, Dept of Environment 1974-75, and Dept of Industry 1975-76; Member Select Cttee on Transport since 1980; MP Woodside Div of Glasgow (*Lab*) 1962-74, and Kelvingrove Div of Glasgow (*Lab*) 1974-83; *cr Baron Carmichael of Kelvingrove*, of Camlachie, District of Glasgow (Life Peer) 1983: *m* 1948, Catherine McIntosh, da of John Dawson Rankin, of Glasgow, and has issue.
Residence – 53 Partickhill Rd, Glasgow G11 5AB.

DAUGHTER LIVING

Hon Sheena MacIntosh CARMICHAEL, *b* 1949; has resumed her maiden name: *m* 1974 (*m diss* 1988), Thomas Anthony Edward Sharpe, and has issue, one son and one da.

CARNARVON, EARL OF (Herbert) (Earl GB 1793)

One I will serve

HENRY GEORGE REGINALD MOLYNEUX HERBERT, KCVO, KBE, 7th Earl; *b* 19 Jan 1924; *s* 1987; *ed* Eton; late RHG; Hon Col 115th (Hampshire Fortress) Engineer Regt (TA) 1963; DL Hants 1965; appointed Racing Manager to HM 1970; KBE (Civil) 1976, KCVO (Civil) 1982: *m* 1956, Jean Margaret, da of Hon Oliver Malcolm Wallop (*see* E Portsmouth), and has issue.

Arms – Per pale azure and gules, three lions rampant argent, a crescent for difference. Crest – A wyvern, wings elevated, vert, in the mouth a sinister human hand couped at the wrist gules. Supporters – *Dexter*, a panther argent, incensed proper, spotted with hurts and torteaux alternately; *sinister*, a lion argent; both ducally gorged per pale azure and gules, with chain reflexed over the back or, and charged on the shoulder with an ermine spot sable.
Seat – Highclere Castle, Newbury, Berks, RG15 9RN. *Residence* – Milford Lake House, Newbury, Berks. *Clubs* – White's, Portland.

SONS LIVING

GEORGE REGINALD OLIVER MOLYNEUX (*Lord Porchester*), *b* 10 Nov 1956; *ed* Eton, and St John's Coll, Oxford; a Page of Honour to HM 1969-73: *m* 1st, 1989 (*m diss* 1998), Jayne M., eldest da of Kenneth A. Wilby, of Cheshire, and of Princess Prospero Colonna di Stigliano, of Ashford, co Wicklow; 2ndly, 1999, Fiona J. M., eldest da of late Ronnie Aitken, of SW1, and has issue:—

SON LIVING (by 1st *m*) — *Hon* George, *b* 13 Oct 1992.
DAUGHTER LIVING (by 1st *m*) — *Hon* Saoirse, *b* 1991.

Residence – Dairy Cottage, Highclere Park, Newbury, Berks RG15 9RN.

Hon Henry Malcolm, *b* 1959; *ed* Eton: *m* 1992, Francesca (Chica) V., yr da of Jonathan Stuart Vaughan Bevan, of 17 Eaton Terr, SW1, and of Mrs Roger Dalzell, of W Wratting Hall, Cambridge, and has issue living, Chloe Victoria, *b* 1994, — Francesca Jeanie, *b* 1995. *Residence* – Field House, Highclere Park, Newbury, Berks RG15 9RN.

DAUGHTER LIVING

Lady Carolyn Penelope, *b* 1962: *m* 1985, John Frederick Rufus Warren, son of John Warren, of Harlow, Essex, and has issue living, Jakie James, *b* 1986, — Alexander Edward, *b* 1994, — Susanna, *b* 1988. *Residence* – The Priory, Moulton, Newmarket, Edmunds, Suffolk.

COLLATERAL BRANCHES LIVING

Issue of late Lt-Col Hon Aubrey Nigel Henry Molyneux Herbert MP, 2nd son of 4th Earl, *b* 1880, *d* 1923: *m* 1910, Hon Mary Gertrude Vesey, who *d* 1970, da of 4th Viscount De Vesci:—
Anne Brigit Domenica, *b* 1914: *m* 1935, Capt Allaster Edward George Grant, MC, late 9th Lancers (*see* E Malmesbury, 1909 Edn), who *d* 1947, and has had issue, Robert John David (Nutcombe Manor, Clayhanger, Tiverton, Devon), *b* 1942; *ed* Ampleforth, and New Coll, Oxford: *m* 1970, Harriet, da of late Markway Roope Reeve, of Lower Brook House, Kings Somborne, Hants, and has issue living, Charles Edward *b* 1971, Peter Mark Haddon *b* 1981, Katherine Bridget *b* 1972,

Emma Philippa *b* 1973, — Mary Christina, *b* 1937: *m* 1962, Michael Edward Melotte, who *d* 1994, of 102 Talfourd Rd, SE15 6NZ, and has issue living, Edward John *b* 1965; Maj Irish Guards, Victoria Mary *b* 1963: *m* 1985, Jonathan Clark, of 17 Crescent Grove, SW4, — Evelyn Elizabeth Anne, *b* 1938: *m* 1958, Ian James Fraser, CBE, MC (later Sir Ian Fraser), and *d* 1984, leaving issue (*see* L Lovat, colls).

Grandchildren of late Hon Mervyn Robert Howard Molyneux Herbert, 3rd son of 4th Earl:—
Issue of late Edward Alan Mervyn Henry Molyneux Herbert, *b* 1926, *d* 1994: *m* 1966, Bridget Anne, who *d* 1976, da of late Maj Hugh Washington Hibbert (*see* B Mowbray, colls):—
Alan Mervyn Edward Hugh, *b* 1971. —— Mary Patricia, *b* 1967. ——Elizabeth Anne, *b* 1968: *m* 1997, David Colin Buxton Carter, and has issue living, Alexander Ivo, *b* 1999, — Isadora Lucie, *b* 1996. —— Penelope Gabrielle Serena, *b* 1969. *Residence* – Tetton House, Taunton, Som.

PREDECESSORS – Maj-Gen Hon William Herbert, 5th son of 8th Earl of Pembroke, MP for Wilton 1734-37; *d* 1756, leaving with other issue **(1)** HENRY; cr *Baron Porchester*, of High Clere, co Southampton (peerage of Great Britain), 1780, and *Earl of Carnarvon* (peerage of Great Britain) 1793; was Master of the Horse 1806; *d* 1811; *s* by his son **(2)** HENRY GEORGE, 2nd Earl, *d* 1833; *s* by his son **(3)** HENRY JOHN GEORGE, 3rd Earl; *b* 1800: *m* 1830, Henrietta Anna, who *d* 1876, da of Lord Henry Thomas Molyneux-Howard (D Norfolk); *d* 1849: *s* by his son **(4)** HENRY HOWARD MOLYNEUX, PC, 4th Earl, *b* 1831; Under Sec of State for colonies 1857-9, Sec of State thereof 1866-7 and 1874-8, and Lord-Lieut of Ireland 1885-6: *m* 1st, 1861, Lady Evelyn Stanhope, da of 6th Earl of Chesterfield; 2ndly, 1878, Elizabeth Catharine, who *d* 1929, elder da of late Henry Howard; *d* 1890; *s* by his elder son **(5)** GEORGE EDWARD STANHOPE MOLYNEUX, 5th Earl, *b* 1866; the discoverer, with Howard Carter, of Tutankhamun's tomb: *m* 1895, Almina Victoria Maria Alexandra, who *d* 1969 (having *m* 2ndly, 1923, Lt-Col Ian Onslow Dennistoun, MVO, who *d* 1938), da of late Frederick Charles Wombwell; *d* 1923; *s* by his son **(6)** HENRY GEORGE ALFRED VICTOR FRANCIS, 6th Earl *b* 1898; Lt-Col 7th (Queen's Own) Hus; European War 1916-19 in Mesopotamia: *m* 1st, 1922 (*m diss* 1936), Anne Catherine Tredick, who *d* 1977 (having *m* 2ndly, 1938, as his 2nd wife, Lt-Cdr Geoffrey Seymour Grenfell, RN, who *ka* 1940, and 3rdly, 1950, Don Stuart Mommand), elder da of late Jacob Wendell, of New York; 2ndly, 1939 (*m diss* 1947), Ottilie (Tillie Losch, the dancer), who *d* 1975, da of Eugene Losch of Vienna, and formerly wife of late Edward Frank Willis James, of West Dean Park, Sussex; *d* 1987; *s* by his only son **(7)** HENRY GEORGE REGINALD MOLYNEUX, 7th Earl and present peer; also Baron Porchester.

Carnegie, family name of Duke of Fife.

Carnegie, family name of Earl of Northesk.

Carnegie, Lord; grandson of Duke of Fife.

CARNEGY OF LOUR, BARONESS (Carnegy of Lour) (Life Baroness 1982)

Spot without spot

ELIZABETH PATRICIA CARNEGY OF LOUR, elder da of late Lt-Col Ughtred Elliott Carnegy of Lour, DSO, MC, JP, DL, 12th of Lour (*see* E Northesk, colls); *b* 28 April 1925; *ed* Downham Sch, Essex; DL Angus 1988; with Girl Guides Assoc 1947; Co Commr Angus 1956-63; Training Adviser Scotland 1958-62, and Commonwealth HQ 1963-65, Pres Council for Scotland 1979-89; Member Educn Cttee Angus CC 1967-75; Councillor Tayside Region 1974-82; Convenor Recreation and Tourism Cttee 1974-76; Educn Cttee 1976-82; Commr Manpower Services Commn 1979-82; Chm Working Party on Prof Training for Community Educn in Scotland 1975-77, of Manpower Services Commn Cttee for Scotland 1981-93, and of the Scottish Community Educn Council 1981-88, Member Scottish Economic Council 1981-93, Administrative Council Royal Jubilee Trusts 1984-88, Council Open Univ 1984-96; Trustee Nat Museums of Scotland 1987-91; Member of Court, Univ of St Andrews 1991-96; served in 1939-45 War in Cavendish Laboratory, Camb 1943-46; Hon Sheriff 1969-84; Hon LLD Dundee 1991, Hon LLD St Andrews 1997, Hon DUniv Open Univ 1998; *cr Baroness Carnegy of Lour*, of Lour in the District of Angus (Life Baroness) 1982.

𝕬rms – Or, an eagle displayed azure, beaked and membered sable, within a bordure gules. 𝕮rest – A demi leopard rampant proper. 𝕾upporters – Dexter, a leopard proper having a collar argent charged with three torteaux. Sinister, a greyhound proper having a collar gules charged with three escallops argent.
Residence – Lour, by Forfar, Angus DD8 2LR. *Clubs* – Lansdowne, New (Edinburgh).

CARNOCK, BARON (Nicolson of that Ilk) (Baron UK 1916, Bt NS 1629 and 1637)

Nothing to stand against

DAVID HENRY ARTHUR NICOLSON OF THAT ILK, 4th Baron, 16th Baronet of Lasswade and 14th Baronet of Carnock; Chief of Clan Nicolson; *b* 10 July 1920; *s* 1982; *ed* Winchester, and Balliol Coll, Oxford, admitted a Solicitor 1949; European War 1940-45 R Devon Yeo, Artillery and Staff (Major); ptnr Clifford Turner 1955-86.

𝕬rms – Or three falcons' heads erased gules armed argent in fess point an inescutcheon argent a saltire azure surmounted of an inescutcheon or charged with a lion rampant within a double tressure flory counterflory gules ensigned of an Imperial Crown proper being the addition of the arms of Nova Scotia as a Baronet. 𝕮rest – A lion issuant or armed and langued gules. 𝕾upporters – Two eagles or armed gules. 𝕸ottoes – (above the shield) - Generositate; (below the shield) - Nil sistere contra.
Residences – 90 Whitehall Court, SW1; Ermewood House, Harford, Ivybridge, Devon.
Clubs – Travellers', Beefsteak.

COLLATERAL BRANCH LIVING

Issue of late Hon Sir Harold George Nicolson, KCVO, CMG, yst son of 1st Baron, *b* 1886, *d* 1968: *m* 1913, Hon Victoria Mary Sackville-West, CH, who *d* 1962, da of 3rd Baron Sackville:—

†(Lionel) Benedict, CBE, MVO, FBA, *b* 1914; *ed* Eton, and Balliol Coll, Oxford; Dep Surveyor of the King's Pictures 1939-47; Editor the *Burlington Magazine* 1947-78; 1939-45 War as Capt Intelligence Corps: MVO (4th class) 1947, CBE (Civil) 1971: *m* 1955 (*m diss* 1962), Luisa, da of Prof Giacomo Vertova, of Florence, and *d* 1978, leaving issue, Vanessa Pepita Giovanna, *b* 1956: *m* 1991, Andrew Cunningham Churchill Davidson, of Horserace House, Sissinghurst, Cranbrook, Kent, son of Harry Churchill Davidson, of Hove, Sussex, and has issue living, Elena Rose *b* 1987, Rosa Ilaria *b* 1989. —— NIGEL, MBE (Sissinghurst Castle, Cranbrook, Kent), *b* 19 Jan 1917; *ed* Eton, and Balliol Coll, Oxford; 1939-45 War as Capt Gren Gds (despatches, MBE); MP for Christchurch and E Div of Bournemouth (*C*) 1952-59; MBE (Mil) 1945: *m* 1953 (*m diss* 1970), Philippa Janet, who *d* 1987, da of Sir (Eustace) Gervais Tennyson-d'Eyncourt, 2nd Bt, and has issue living, Adam (Perch Hill Farm, Brightling, nr Robertsbridge, E Sussex), *b* 1957: *m* 1st, 1982 (*m diss* 1992), Olivia Mary Rokeby, eldest da of Lt Cdr Antony Charles Reynardson Fane, RN (*see* E Westmorland, colls); 2ndly, 1993, Sarah Clare, da of John Earle Raven, of King's Coll, Camb, and has issue living (by 1st *m*), Thomas *b* 1984, William *b* 1986, Benedict *b* 1988, (by 2nd *m*) Rose Raven *b* 1993, Molly Raven *b* 1996, — Juliet, *b* 1954: *m* 1977 (*m diss* 1995), James Macmillan-Scott, and has issue living, Clementine *b* 1981, Flora *b* 1985, — Rebecca NICOLSON (5 Malvern Terr, N1 1HR), *b* 1963; has resumed her maiden name: *m* 1988 (*m diss* 1996), Hon Guy Wogan Philipps, eldest son of 3rd Baron Milford.

PREDECESSORS – Alexander Nicolson, by tradition from Isle of Skye, settled in Aberdeen 1444. From him descended John Nicolson, of Edinburgh, who *d* 1605, leaving issue four sons. Of these the eldest, John, was cr a *Baronet* (Nicolson of Lasswade) of Nova Scotia 1629, with remainder to heirs male whatsoever. Although this title was thought to have become extinct upon the death of the 7th Bt in 1743, the 4th Baron Carnock successfully petitioned the Lord Lyon to be recognised in the baronetcy of Nicolson of Lasswade, and as Chief of Clan Nicolson, and was so recognised in an interlocutor dated 3 Sept 1984. The 3rd son of John Nicolson of Edinburgh (ante) was **(1)** THOMAS Nicolson of Carnock, was cr a *Baronet* of Nova Scotia, with remainder to heirs-male whatsoever 1636; *d* 1646; *s* by his son **(2)** THOMAS, 2nd Bt, *d* 1664; *s* by his son **(3)** THOMAS, 3rd Bt, *d* 1670; *s* by his son **(4)** THOMAS, 4th Bt, *b* 1669; *s* as 4th Lord Napier of Merchistoun 1683; *d* 1686, when the peerage devolved upon his maternal aunt, and the baronetcy passed to his cousin and heir-male **(5)** THOMAS, 5th Bt, son and heir of Sir John Nicolson of Tillicoultry; *d* 1699; *s* by his son **(6)** GEORGE, 6th Bt (of Carnock) and *de jure* 8th Bt (of Lasswade) (ante), at which point the two baronetcies merged: *m* Charlotte Halkett; *d* 1771; *s* by his son **(9)** WALTER PHILIP, 9th and 7th Bt: *m* Helen Carpenter; *d* 1786; *s* by his brother **(10)** DAVID, 10th and 8th Bt; *d* 1808; *s* by his cousin and heir-male **(11)** WILLIAM, 11th and 9th Bt (only son of George Nicolson of Tarviston), *b* 1758; Maj-Gen in the Army: *m* 1804, Mary Russell; *d* 1820; *s* by his son **(12)** FREDERICK WILLIAM ERSKINE, 12th and 10th Bt; Adm, and sometime Chm Thames Conservancy Board: *m* 1st, 1847, Clementina Maria Marion, da of James Loch, of Drylaw; 2ndly, 1855, Augusta Sarah, da of Robert Cullington, and widow of Capt Hay; 3rdly, 1867, Anne, da of R. Cross; *d* 1899; *s* by his son **(13)** ARTHUR, GCB, GCMG, GCVO, KCIE, PC, 13th and 11th Bt, *b* 1849; was Assist Private Sec to Earl Granville at Foreign Office 1872-4; on Staff of Earl of Dufferin in Egypt 1882, acting Chargé d'Affaires at Athens 1882-5, Sec of Legation at Teheran, and Acting Chargé d'Affaires in Persia 1885-8, Consul-Gen for Hungary 1888-93, Sec of Embassy at Constantinople 1893-4, and Agent and Consul-Gen in Bulgaria 1894-5, Envoy Extraor and Min Plen at Tangier and Consul-Gen in Morocco 1895-1904, Ambassador Extraor and Plen to Spain 1904-5, and at St Petersburg 1906-10, and Permanent Under-Sec of State for Foreign Affairs 1910-16; British Representative at Algeciras Conference 1905-6; cr *Baron Carnock*, of Carnock co Stirling (peerage of United Kingdom) 1916: *m* 1882, Mary Catherine, who *d* 1951, da of late Archibald Rowan Hamilton of Killyleagh Castle, co Down; *d* 1928; *s* by his elder son **(2)** FREDERICK ARCHIBALD, MC, 2nd Baron; *b* 1883; Bar Inner Temple 1924; Major 15th King's Hussars; sometime ADC to Viceroy of India; *d* 1952; *s* by his brother **(3)** ERSKINE ARTHUR, DSO, 3rd Baron; *b* 1884; Capt RN: *m* 1919, Hon Katharine Frederica Albertha Lopes, who *d* 1968, da of 1st Baron Roborough; *d* 1982; *s* by his only surv son **(4)** DAVID HENRY ARTHUR, 4th Baron and present peer.

CARR OF HADLEY, BARON (Carr) (Life Baron 1975)

(LEONARD) ROBERT CARR, PC, son of late Ralph Edward Carr; *b* 11 Nov 1916; *ed* Westminster and Gonville and Caius Coll, Camb (MA); PPS to Sir Anthony Eden, as Sec of State for Foreign Affairs 1951-55, and as PM 1955, Parl Sec to Min of Labour 1955-58; Sec for Tech Co-operation 1963-64; Sec of State for Employment and Productivity June to Oct 1970, for Employment 1970-72, Lord Pres of the Council and Leader of House of Commons April to Nov 1972, and Sec of State for Home Affairs 1972-74; MP for Mitcham (C) 1950-74, and Sutton (Carshalton) 1974-75; a Dir, Metal Closure Group 1959-63, and 1965-70 (Dep Chm 1958-63), Chm John Dale Ltd 1958-63, and 1965-70, Dir Securicor Ltd and Security Services plc 1961-63, 1965-70 and 1974-85, SGB Group plc 1974-86, Cadbury Schweppes plc 1979-87, Prudential Assurance Co Ltd 1976-85 (Dep Chm 1979-80, Chm 1980-85), and Prudential Corpn plc 1978-89 (Dep Chm 1979-80, Chm 1980-85); Pres Consultative Council of Professional Management Organisations since 1976; cr PC 1963, and *Baron Carr of Hadley*, of Monken Hadley in Greater London (Life Baron) 1975: *m* 1943, Joan Kathleen, da of Dr E. W. Twining, and has issue.

Address – c/o House of Lords, SW1. *Club* – Brooks's.

DAUGHTERS LIVING

Hon Susan Elizabeth, *b* 1947: *m* 1972, (Alun) Rhodri Bradley-Jones, of Gardener's Cottage, Kingscote, Glos.

Hon Virginia Sarah, *b* 1957: *m* 1984, Michael Frederick Fox.

Carpenter, see Baron Boyd-Carpenter.

CARRICK, EARL OF (Butler) Sits as BARON BUTLER OF MOUNT JULIET (UK 1912)
(Earl I 1748)

Be steadfast

DAVID JAMES THEOBALD SOMERSET BUTLER, 10th Earl; *b* 9 Jan 1953; *s* 1992; *ed* Downside: *m* 1975, Philippa Janice Victoria, yr da of Wing Cmdr Leonard Victor Craxton, RAF (ret), of Mills Lydgate One, West Rd, Milford on Sea, Lymington, Hants, and has issue.

Ꚉrms – Or, a chief indented azure, a crescent for difference. Ꚉrest – Out of a ducal coronet or, a plume of ostrich feathers, and issuant therefrom a demi-falcon rising all argent. Ꚉupporters – *Dexter*, a falcon, wings inverted argent, beaked, membered, and belled, or; *sinister*, a male griffin argent, beaked, membered, armed, collared and chained, or; on each supporter a crescent for difference.
Residence – Pant yr Eos, Moelfre, Llansilin, Oswestry, Shropshire SY10 7QR.

SONS LIVING

(ARION) THOMAS PIERS HAMILTON (*Viscount Ikerrin*), *b* 1 Sept 1975.
Hon Piers Edmund Theobald Lismalyn, *b* 1979.
Hon Lindsay Simon Turville Somerset, *b* (twin) 1979.

SISTER LIVING

Lady Juliana Mary Philomena, *b* 1960. *Residence* – 31 Greenbank Av, Saltdean, Brighton BN2 8QS.

WIDOW LIVING OF SON OF SEVENTH EARL

Dorothea, yst da of late Thomas Warwick Bennett, of 40 Bishop's Rd, E2: *m* 1957, as his 2nd wife, Maj Hon Pierce Alan Somerset David Butler, TD, who *d* 1964. *Residence* – .

WIDOW LIVING OF NINTH EARL

GILLIAN IRENE (*Gillian, Countess of Carrick*), da of Leonard Grimes: *m* 1986, as his 2nd wife, the 9th Earl of Carrick, who *d* 1992. *Residence* – 10 Netherton Grove, SW10.

COLLATERAL BRANCHES LIVING

Issue of late Hon (Horace) Somerset Edmond Butler, CIE, 2nd son of 7th Earl, *b* 1903, *d* 1962: *m* 1928, Barbara, who *d* 1977, da of M. S. Jacomb-Hood:—
Georgina Carolin Eve (designer Gina Fratini), *b* 1931: *m* 1st, 1954, David Goldberg; 2ndly, 1961, Renato Fratini; 3rdly, 1969, James Allan Short (actor Jimmy Logan).

Issue of late Maj Hon Guy Somerset Lionel Butler, 3rd son of 7th Earl, *b* 1905, *d* 1983: *m* 1st, 1939 (*m diss* 1961), Mrs Patricia Anne (Paddianne) Tennant, who *d* 1982, da of late William Dunne; 2ndly, 1961, Mrs Janet Frances Parker, who *d* 1984, da of late Alexander Gordon Preston:—
(By 1st *m*) Rupert Lionel Somerset (Lily Bank Farm, Lily Bottom Lane, Parslows Hillock, Princes Risborough, Bucks HP27 0RN), *b* 1940, *ed* Tonbridge, Quintin Sch, and RAF Coll Cranwell: Fl-Lt RAF (ret) *m* 1968, Jenifer Mary, da of late Norman James Rush, FCA, of High Wood, Henley, Haslemere, Surrey, and has issue living, Piers Somerset Patrick, *b* 1970, — Eli Somerset James, *b* 1971, — Matthew Somerset Guy, *b* 1972, — Sebastian Somerset Lionel, *b* 1979. ——— Dermot Somerset Launcelot (Prospect House, Newcastle, co Wicklow), *b* 1941; *ed* Tonbridge, and Quintin Sch: *m* 1st, 1970 (*m diss* 1983), Lorna Ailsa Graham, da of Maj Ian Graham Menzies; 2ndly, 1986, Mrs Victoria Marsland Nabarro, da of John Lloyd Owen, and has issue living (by 1st *m*), Tara Siobhan Somerset, *b* 1974.

Issue of late Maj Hon Pierce Alan Somerset David Butler, TD, 5th son of 7th Earl, *b* 1909, *d* 1964: *m* 1st, 1933 (*m diss* 1957), Leri, who *d* 1985, elder da of Dr Gruffydd Llywelyn-Jones, of Bryn Glas, Llangefni, Anglesey; 2ndly, 1957, Dorothea (ante), yst da of late Thomas Warwick Bennett:—
(By 1st *m*) David Llywelyn Somerset (Brook Farm, Wethersfield, Braintree, Essex), *b* 1937; *m* 1966, Anne, da of A. S. Haigh of White Roding, Essex, and has issue living, Michael Somerset, *b* 1969, — Hilary Mary, *b* 1971. ——— Helen Sarah Ann (Fosters Buildings, Hartest, Bury St Edmunds, Suffolk), *b* 1936: *m* 1957 (*m diss* 1969), Anthony Thomas Colley.

Granddaughters of late Theobold Rollo Pierce Butler, BEM (infra):—
Issue of late Jeremy Somerset Pierce Butler, *b* 1944, *d* 1997: *m* 1968, Grete, da of late Soren Thogersen:—
Juliet Pierce, *b* 1973. ——— Camilla Pierce, *b* 1977.

Grandchildren of late Rev Pierce Rollo Butler (infra):—
Issue of late Theobald Rollo Pierce Butler, BEM, Detective Sgt, Metropolitan Police Force, *b* 1913, *d* 1983: *m* 1st, 1940 (*m diss* 1963), Christine Helen, da of Gilbert William Harding; 2ndly, 1964, Gwendoline May Emily (who *m* 2ndly, 1985 (*m diss* 19—), Anthony J. Doy), formerly wife of Arthur Robert Lane, and da of Frederick George Jennings:—
(By 1st wife) Charlotte Veronica Pierce, *b* 1942: *m* 1st, 1962 (*m diss* 1974), John Allen Kirby; 2ndly, 1975, David John Chatfield, of Priory Villa, Peppercorn Lane, Brecon, Powys LD3 9EG, and has issue living (by 1st *m*), Rupert Charles Allen (246 Victoria Drive, Old Town, Eastbourne, Sussex BN20 8QT), *b* 1966: *m* 1988, Lisa Jane Fuller, and has issue living, Myles Oliver Allen *b* 1991, James Douglas Allen *b* 1993, — Douglas Richard Allen, *b* 1968: *m* 1992, Gillian Porter, and has issue living, Hannah Grace *b* 1995, — Oliver John Allen, *b* 1970; Fl Lt RAFVR(T). —— (By 2nd wife) Mark Pierce (85 Beulah Rd, Walthamstow, E17 9LD), *b* 1960; serving Constable, Metropolitan Police: *m* 1983, Jane, da of Alfred Reginald Gill, and has issue living, Scarlett Frances, *b* 1986.

Issue of the late James Armar Cory Butler, *b* 1916, *d* 1973: *m* 1944, Marjorie Wells (140 Broom Rd, Teddington, Middx):—
Sandra Leigh, *b* 1945: *m* 19—, Charles Devine, and has issue living, Anthony Michael, *b* 1969, — Sarah Louise, *b* 1976. —— Melanie Ann, *b* 1949: *m* 1978, Terence Patrick Cook, and has had issue, Coralie Joanna, *b* 1979; *d* 1985, — Natalie Jane, *b* 1982, — Genevere Eloise, *b* 1987, — Daniella, *b* 1990.

Grandchildren of late Rev Pierce Armar Butler, only son of late Rev Pierce Butler, 3rd son of late Lt-Gen Hon Henry Edward Butler, 2nd son of 2nd Earl (infra):—
Issue of late Rev Pierce Rollo Butler, *b* 1885, *d* 1950: *m* 1911, Ethel Florence, who *d* 1943, da of Rev Thomas Legge Symes:—
Kenelm Somerset Priaulx, *b* 1917; late Lt-Col Falkland Islands Defence Force, and Admin Officer, S Georgia; formerly Capt R Sigs (TA): *m* 1954, Janet Cooper, da of James Gilmour. *Residence* – 16 Penny Lane, Durbanville, CP 7550, S Africa.

Issue of late Maj Hubert Blennerhassett Butler, *b* 1887, *d* 1986: *m* 1919, Sophie Marie, who *d* 1985, da of Jules Castravelli, of Bacos, Alexandria, Egypt:—
Marjorye Marie (Batchelors, Tyning, Heytesbury, Warminster, Wilts), *b* 1921: *m* 1944, Maj Peter Quentin Logan, S Staffordshire Regt, who *d* 1992, and has issue living, Michael Roderic Quentin, *b* 1947: *m* 1971 (*m diss* 1981), Gillian, da of Cdr J. McC. Rutherford, RNVR, of Henley-on-Thames, Oxon. —— Noreen May, *b* 1923: *m* 1944, Col Frank Hilary Bristowe, RM, of 18 Archery Sq, Walmer, Deal, Kent, and has issue living, Rosamund Gillian, *b* 194?: *m* 1969, Charles Vivian Parry, of 2 Queen's Terr, King's Rd, Windsor, Berks, and has issue living, Giles Hubert *b* 1974, Julian Charles *b* 1976, — June Hilary, *b* 1949: *m* 1969, William Magnus Jamieson, of 53 Loxley Rd, SW18, and has issue living, Henry William Ashton *b* 1979, James Nicholas Rupert *b* 1986, Francesca Catherine Sophie *b* 1977, Leanda Georgina Hilary *b* 1983, — Nicola Catherine Diana, *b* 1960: *m* 1984, Courtenay Charles Ilbert Inchbald, 54 Elmfield Rd, SW17, and has issue living, Isabella Catherine Noreen *b* 1991, Venetia Presiley Alice *b* 1996.

PREDECESSORS – (1) *Sir* PIERCE Butler, Knt; Lt-Gen of the Irish Army under Lord Mountgarret, was cr *Viscount Ikerrin* (peerage of Ireland) 1629; *s* by son (2) PIERCE, 2nd Viscount; *s* by his son (3) JAMES, 3rd Viscount; *d* 1688; *s* by his son (4) PIERCE, 4th Viscount; *d* 1710; *s* by his son (5) JAMES, 5th Viscount; *d a* minor 1712; *s* by his uncle (6) THOMAS, 6th Viscount, Chaplain-Gen to Army in Flanders under James, Duke of Ormonde; *d* 1719; *s* by his son (7) JAMES, 7th Viscount; *d* 1721; *s* by his brother (8) SOMERSET HAMILTON, 8th Viscount; cr *Earl of Carrick* (peerage of Ireland) 1748; *d* 1774; *s* by his son (9) HENRY THOMAS, 2nd Earl; *d* 1813; *s* by his son (10) SOMERSET RICHARD, 3rd Earl; *b* 1779: *m* 1st, 1811, Anne, who *d* 1829, da of Owen Wynne, of Haslewood, co Sligo; 2ndly, 1833, Lucy, who *d* 1884, da of late Arthur French, of French Park; *d* 1838, *s* by his elder son (11) HENRY THOMAS, 4th Earl; *d a* minor 1846; *s* by his brother (12) SOMERSET ARTHUR, 5th Earl, *b* 1835; *d* 1901; *s* by his cousin (13) CHARLES HENRY SOMERSET (son of late Capt Charles George Butler, 86th Regt, grandson of 2nd Earl), 6th Earl, *b* 1851; present during repulse of an incursion of Fenians into Canada 1870: *m* 1st, 1873, Kathleen Emily Hamilton, who *d* 1888, da of Lieut-Col Albert Ernest Ross, 5th Fusiliers; 2ndly, 1896, Emily Codrington, who *d* 1915, da of late Mark Jones; *d* 1909; *s* by his son (14) CHARLES ERNEST ALFRED FRENCH SOMERSET, OBE, 7th Earl, *b* 1873; Comptroller of the Household to Lord-Lieut of Ireland 1913-15; cr *Baron Butler of Mount Juliet*, co Kilkenny (peerage of United Kingdom) 1912: *m* 1898, Ellen Rosamond Mary, who *d* 1946, da of late Lieut-Col Henry Gore Lindsay, *d* 1931; *s* by his son (15) THEOBALD WALTER SOMERSET HENRY, 8th Earl; *b* 1903; European War 1939-44 as acting Com RNVR, British Naval Liaison Officer in USA and Senior RN Officer: *m* 1st, 1930 (*m diss* 1938), Marion Caher (EDWARDS), who *d* 1973, da of Daniel C. Donoghue, of Philadelphia, USA; 2nd, 1938, Margaret (DRUM), who *d* (July) 1954, da of Charles B. Power, of Helena, Montana, USA; 3rdly, Oct 1954, Ruth, who *d* 1992, da of Francis T. M. McEnery, Chicago, Ill, USA, *d* 1957; *s* by his son (16) BRIAN STUART THEOBALD SOMERSET CAHER, 9th Earl; *b* 1931; Co Dir: *m* 1st, 1951 (*m diss* 1976), (Mary) Belinda, who *d* 1993, da of late Maj David Turville-Constable-Maxwell, TD, RA (*see* L Herries of Terregles, colls); 2ndly, 1986, Gillian Irene, da of Leonard Grimes; *d* 1992; *s* by his only son (17) DAVID JAMES THEOBALD SOMERSET, 10th Earl and present peer; also Viscount Ikerrin, and Baron Butler, of Mount Juliet.

CARRINGTON, BARON (Carington) (I 1796, GB 1797)

Persevering and faithful

PETER ALEXANDER RUPERT CARINGTON, KG, GCMG, CH, MC, PC, 6th Baron; *b* 6 June 1919; *s* 1938; *ed* Eton (Fellow 1966); Hon LLD Cantab 1981, Leeds 1981, Aberdeen 1985, Nottingham 1993, Birmingham 1993; Hon Dr Laws Philippines Univ 1982, S Carolina Univ 1983, Harvard 1986, Reading 1989, Sussex 1989; Hon DUniv Essex 1983, Buckingham 1989; Hon DSc Cranfield 1988, and Hon DCL Newcastle 1998; Maj (ret) Gren Gds; Parl Sec Min of Agriculture and Fisheries 1951-54, Parl Sec Min of Defence 1954-56, High Commr for UK in Australia 1956-59, First Lord of the Admiralty 1959-63, Min without Portfolio and Leader of House of Lords 1963-64, Leader of the Opposition in House of Lords 1964-70, and 1974-79; Sec of State for Defence 1970-74, and Sec of State Dept of Energy Jan to Feb 1974; Min of Aviation Supply 1971-74; Chm of Conservative Party 1972-74; Sec of State, Foreign and Commonwealth Affairs and Min of Overseas Development 1979-82; Sec-Gen NATO 1983-88; a Dir Amalgamated Metal Corpn, Ltd, 1965-70, Hambros Bank 1967-70, Barclays Bank 1967-70, and 1974-79, Cadbury Schweppes, Ltd 1968-70, and 1974-79, Chm Christies 1988-92, Dir The Telegraph plc since 1990; Joint Dep Chm Aust & NZ Bank 1965-67, Chm 1967-69; a Dir Rio Tinto-Zinc Corpn 1974-79; Chm Trustees Victoria and Albert Museum since 1983; Pres The Pilgrims 1983, Trustee Tradescant Trust since 1990, Chm European Community Peace Conference on Yugoslavia 1991-92, since when Chancellor Reading Univ; Chancellor of the Order of St Michael and St George 1984-95, since when Chancellor of the Order of the Garter; 1939-45 War (MC); KCMG 1958, PC 1959, CH 1983, KG 1985, GCMG 1988: *m* 1942, Iona, da of Lt-Col Sir Francis Kennedy McClean, AFC, and has issue.

ᴁrms – Or, a chevron cottised, between three demi-griffins, the two in chief respectant sable. ℭrest – An elephant's head erased or, eared gules, charged on the neck with three fleurs-de-lis, two and one azure. ᴤupporters – Two griffins' wings elevated sable, the *dexter* charged with three fleurs-de-lis palewise or, the *sinister* with three trefoils slipped palewise of the last.
Seat – The Manor House, Bledlow, near Aylesbury, Bucks. *Town Residence* – 32A Ovington Square, SW3 1LR. *Clubs* – Pratt's, White's.

SON LIVING

Hon RUPERT FRANCIS JOHN, *b* 2 Dec 1948; *ed* Eton, and Bristol Univ: *m* 1989, Daniela, da of Flavio Diotallevi, of Madrid, and has issue living, Robert, *b* 7 Dec 1990, — Francesca, *b* 1993, — Isabella Iona, *b* 1995. *Residence* – 16 Mallord St, SW3 6DU.

DAUGHTERS LIVING

Hon Alexandra, *b* 1943: *m* 1965, Maj Peter Noel de Bunsen, Coldm Gds (ret), eldest son of Charles de Bunsen (*see* Buxton, Bt, 1953 Edn), and has issue living, Charles Rupert, *b* 1970, — Peter James, *b* 1973, — Victoria, *b* 1968: *m* 1991, Andrew Falcon (*see* D Wellington, colls, 1995 Edn), and has issue living, William *b* 1994, Frank *b* 1998, Ruby *b* 1993. *Residence* – The Old Rectory, Kirby Bedon, Norwich, Norfolk.
Hon Virginia CARINGTON, *b* 1946; has resumed her maiden name: *m* 1973 (*m diss* 1979), 4th Baron Ashcombe. *Residence* – 5 Rutland Gate Mews, SW7.

SISTER LIVING

Hon Elizabeth, *b* 1917: *m* 1943, William Lionel Dove, MB, ChB, MRCS, LRCP, and has issue living, Anthony Edward (Little House, Common Lane, Lower Stretton, Cheshire), *b* 1946: *m* 1st, 1983 (*m diss* 1988), Jane Susan, only da of A. H. Smith, of Dundrum, Queens Rd, Ilkley, Yorks; 2ndly, 19—, Julie Maria, da of G. Williams, of Warrington, Cheshire, — (John) Andrew (14 Guion Rd, SW6), *b* 1951: *m* 1st, 1980 (*m diss* 1984), Jane Esther, da of Denis Horace Holland, of Park Farm, Lavenham, Sudbury, Suffolk; 2ndly, 19—, Jacqueline Clare, da of Anthony Scott, of Chebsey, Staffs, and has issue (by 2nd *m*), Florence *b* 1995. *Residence* – 6 Woolton Hill Rd, Liverpool, L25 6HX.

PREDECESSORS – (1) ROBERT Smith, MP for Nottingham 1779-96; cr *Baron Carrington*, of Bulcot Lodge (peerage of Ireland) 1796, and *Baron Carrington*, of Upton, Notts (peerage of Great Britain) 1797; *d* 1838; *s* by his son (2) ROBERT JOHN, 2nd Baron; *b* 1796; MP for Wendover 1818-20, Buckinghamshire 1820-30, and High Wycombe 1831-8; Lord-Lieut of Bucks; assumed surname of Carington in lieu of Smith by R licence 1839: *m* 1st, 1822, Hon Elizabeth Katherine, who *d* 1832, da of 1st Baron Forester; 2ndly, 1840, Hon Augusta Annabella Drummond-Willoughby, who *d* 1879, da of 21st Baron Willoughby D'Eresby; *d* 1868; *s* by his son (3) CHARLES ROBERT, 3rd Baron; *b* 1843; Joint Hereditary Lord Great Chamberlain (appointed to act for Reign of King George V); sat as MP for Wycombe (L) 1865-8; surname of Carington confirmed by R licence 1880; subsequently granted R licence 1896 to assume the surnames of Wynn-Carrington; was Gov and Com-in-Ch of New South Wales 1885-90, Lord Chamberlain to Queen Victoria's Household 1892-5, Pres of Board of Agriculture Dec 1905 to Oct 1911, and Lord Privy Seal Oct 1911 to Feb 1912; bore St Edward's Staff at Coronation of King Edward VII; cr *Viscount Wendover*, of Chepping Wycombe, Bucks, *Earl Carrington* (peerage of United Kingdom) 1895, and *Marquess of Lincolnshire* (peerage of United Kingdom) 1912: *m* 1878, Hon Cecilia Margaret Harbord, elder da of 5th Baron Suffield; *d* 1928, when the Marquessate of Lincolnshire, the Earldom of Carrington, and the Viscountcy of Wendover became ext (his only son, Albert Edward Samuel Charles Robert, *Viscount Wendover, b*

1895; Lt RHG, *d* of wounds in action during WW I 1915), while the two Baronies of Carrington devolved upon his brother **(4)** RUPERT CLEMENT GEORGE Carington, CVO, DSO, 4th Baron, *b* 1852; MP for Buckinghamshire (*L*) 1880-85; surname of Carington confirmed by R licence 1880; *m* 1891, Edith, who *d* 1908, da of John S. Horsfall, of Widglewa, NS Wales; *d* 1929; *s* by his son **(5)** RUPERT VICTOR JOHN, 5th Baron, *b* 1891: *m* 1916, Hon Sybil Marion Colville, who *d* 1946, da of 2nd Viscount Colville of Culross; *d* 1938; *s* by his son **(6)** PETER ALEXANDER RUPERT, 6th Baron, and present peer.

CARRON, BARONY OF (Carron) (Extinct 1969)

DAUGHTERS LIVING OF LIFE BARON

Hon Hilary Mary, *b* 1933: *m* 1959, John Simon Weidemann, of The Gables, 27 Bromley Rd, SE6 2TS, and has issue.
Hon Patricia Ann, *b* 1945: *m* 1970 (*m diss* 1982), Victor Albert Hull, and has issue.

CARSON, BARONY OF (Carson) (Extinct 1935)

WIDOW LIVING OF SON OF LIFE BARON (*By 2nd marriage*)

Heather, da of late Frank Arthur Sclater, OBE, MC, of Milford, Surrey: *m* 1943, Hon Edward Carson, who *d* 1987, and has issue living, Edward Rory (Perseverence Cottage, Harpsden, Henley-on-Thames, Oxon), *b* 1949: *m* 1975, Araminta, yr da of Sir John James Macdonald Horlick, 5th Bt, and has issue (*see* Horlick, Bt). — Patricia Margaret, *b* 1945: *m* 1st, 1971 (*m diss* 1980), Colin Fyfe-Jamieson; 2ndly, 1981, Michael Raymond Coulman, of Bainden Farmhouse, Horsmonden, Kent, and has issue living (by 1st *m*), Lucy Jane *b* 1972, Georgina Alice *b* 1976, Sophie Patricia *b* (twin)1976. *Residence –* Crossways, Westfield, nr Hastings, Sussex.

CARTER, BARON (Carter) (Life Baron 1987)

DENIS VICTOR CARTER, PC, son of late Albert William Carter; *b* 17 Jan 1932; *ed* Xaverian Coll, Brighton, E Sussex Agric Coll, Essex Coll of Agric, and Worcester Coll, Oxford (B Litt); agricultural consultant and farmer since 1957, founder AKC Ltd (agricultural accounting and management) 1957, partner Drayton Farms since 1975, and a Dir W.E. & D.T. Cave Ltd since 1976; Exec Prod Link TV (programmes for the disabled); Capt HM Body Guard of Hon Corps of Gentlemen at Arms (Ch Govt Whip, House of Lords) since 1997; Sgt RASC, in Central Zone, Egypt; PC 1997; *cr Baron Carter*, of Devizes, co Wilts (Life Baron) 1987: *m* 1957, Teresa Mary, da of late Cecil William Greengoe, and has had issue.
Address – c/o House of Lords, SW1. *Club –* Farmers'.

SON DECEASED

Andrew Peter, *b* 1963; *d* 1982.

DAUGHTER LIVING

Hon Catherine Mary, *b* 1959.

CARVER, BARON (Carver) (Life Baron 1977)

(RICHARD) MICHAEL POWER CARVER, GCB, CBE, DSO, MC, son of late Harold Power Carver; *b* 24 April 1915; *ed* Winchester, RMC Sandhurst; commd R Tank Corps 1935; GSO1, 7th Armd Div 1942; OC 1st RTR 1943; Cmd 4th Armd Bde 1944; GOC 3rd Div 1962-64; C-in-C Far East 1967-69; GOC Southern Command 1969-71; CGS 1971-73; Chief of Defence Staff 1973-76; Field Marshal 1973; British Commr designate for Rhodesia 1977; DSO 1943 (Bar 1944), CBE (Mil) 1945, CB (Mil) 1957, KCB (Mil) 1966, GCB (Mil) 1970; 1939-45 War in Middle East, Italy and NW Europe (despatches twice, MC, DSO and Bar, CBE); Kenya (despatches, CB); *cr Baron Carver*, of Shackleford, co Surrey (Life Baron) 1977: *m* 1947, Edith, da of late Lt-Col Sir Henry Lowry-Corry, MC (*see* E Belmore, colls) and has issue.

Residence – Wood End House, Wickham, Hants. *Clubs* – Cavalry & Guards, Anglo-Belgian.

SONS LIVING

Hon Andrew Richard (Bayswater Mill House, Headington, Oxford OX3 9SB), *b* 1950: *m* 1st, 1973, Anne Rosamunde, da of Brian Stewart, of the Broich, Crief, Perthshire; 2ndly, 1989, Patricia, da of Jack Taffe, of Marco Is, Florida, USA.

Hon John Antony, *b* 1961: *m* 1992, Susan E., only da of Alexander Graham, of Kirkcaldy, Fife, and has issue living, Henry Paul, *b* 1995.

DAUGHTERS LIVING

Hon Susanna Mary (57A Broughton Rd, SW6 2LE), *b* 1948.

Hon Alice Elizabeth (33 The Green, Brill, Aylesbury, Bucks HP18 9RU), *b* 1954: *m* 1976 (*m diss* 1989), Capt Claude Walters, Gren Gds.

Cary, family name of Viscount of Falkland.

CASEY, BARONY OF (Casey) (Extinct 1976)

SON LIVING OF LIFE BARON

Hon Donn (141 Newmarket Rd, Cambridge), *b* 1931; relinquished by deed poll 1970 the forenames Richard Charles.

DAUGHTER LIVING OF LIFE BARON

Hon Jane Alice Camilla (5 Darley Place, Darlinghurst, NSW 2010, Australia), *b* 1928: *m* 1955 (*m diss* 1981), Murray W. Macgowan.

Cassel, family name of Baroness Mallalieu.

CASTLE, BARONY OF (Castle) (Extinct 1979)

WIDOW LIVING OF LIFE BARON

BARBARA ANNE (*Baroness Castle of Blackburn*), PC; *cr* Baroness Castle of Blackburn (Life Baroness) 1990; da of Frank Betts: *m* 1944, Baron Castle (Life Baron), who *d* 1979.

CASTLE OF BLACKBURN, BARONESS (Castle) (Life Baroness 1990)

BARBARA ANNE CASTLE, PC, da of late Frank Betts; *b* 6 Oct 1910; *ed* Bradford Girls' Gram Sch, and St Hugh's Coll, Oxford (Hon Fellow 1966), Hon DTech Bradford 1968, and Loughborough 1969, Hon Fellow Bradford and Ilkley Community Coll 1985, Hon Fellow Umist 1991, Hon LLD Lancaster Univ 1991, Hon Fellow Humberside Polytechnic 1991, Hon Fellow York Univ 1992, Hon LLD Manchester Univ 1993, Hon LLD Camb 1998, Hon DLitt De Montfort 1998, Hon DUniv N London 1998; Cross of Order of Merit (Germany) 1990; Member Nat Exec Cttee of Labour Party 1950-85, Chm Labour Party 1959, Min of Overseas Devpt 1964-65, Min of Transport 1965-68, First Sec of State and Sec of State for Employment and Productivity 1968-70, Sec of State for Social Services 1974-76; Co-Chm Women's Nat Commn 1975-76; MP Blackburn (*Lab*) 1945-50, Blackburn East 1950-55, and Blackburn 1955-79, MEP Greater Manchester North 1979-84, and Greater Manchester West 1984-89; *cr* PC 1964, and *Baroness Castle of Blackburn*, of Ibstone, co Bucks (Life Baroness) 1990: *m* 1944, Edward Cyril Castle, who was *cr* Baron Castle (Life Baron) 1974, and who *d* 1979.
Address – House of Lords, SW1A 0PW.

CASTLEMAINE, BARON (Handcock) (Baron I 1812)

VIGILATE ET ORATE

Watch and pray

ROLAND THOMAS JOHN HANDCOCK, 8th Baron; *b* 22 April, 1943; *s* 1973; Maj Army Air Corps: *m* 1st, 1969, Pauline Anne, el da of John Taylor Bainbridge, of The Moat House, Burstow, Surrey; 2ndly, 1988, Lynne Christine, eldest da of Maj Justin Michael Gurney, RAEC, and has issue by 2nd *m*.

Arms – Ermine, on a chief sable, a dexter hand between two cocks argent, armed, crested, and jelloped gules. **Crest** – a demi-lion rampant azure, holding a lozenge argent, charged with a cock gules. **Supporters** – *Dexter*, a lion guardant azure; *sinister*, a cock, proper. *Address* – Keepers Cottage, Winterbourne Stoke, Salisbury.

SON LIVING (By 2nd marriage)

Hon RONAN MICHAEL EDWARD, *b* 27 March 1989.

SISTERS LIVING

Hon Eileen Esther, *b* 1931: *m* 1959, Fl Lt Terence Frank Adams, RAF (ret), and has issue living, Patrick Joseph John, *b* 1960, — Niall Michael, *b* 1968, — Siobhan Mary, *b* 1962.
Hon Edith Deirdre, *b* 1936: *m* 1st, 1957 (*m diss* 1974), Keith Moss, BEM; 2ndly, 1975, Terence Hook, and has issue living (by 1st *m*), Julian Duncan, *b* 1962.

COLLATERAL BRANCHES LIVING

Grandchildren of late Henry Handcock (infra):—
Issue of late Richard Henry Algernon Handcock, *b* 1895, *d* 1974: *m* 1943, Catherine, who *d* 1971, da of late Emmanuel Breham, of Pont de l'Arche, France, and widow of John Morgan Keeley Knight, Lt RFC:—
Clifford Marcel, *b* 1925; late CQMS, KOSB; 1939-45 War with 1st Airborne Div: *m* 1944, Joyce Morton, and has issue living, Linda, *b* 1945. —— Claude Desmond Richard, *b* 1928: *m* 1948, Enid Perry, and has issue living, Andre Patrick James, *b* 1950, — Peter Michael Roland, *b* 1951, — Teresa Catherine Rose, *b* 1954. —— Sheila Annette Kathleen, *b* 1927: *m* 19—, Brinley Aurelius, of 143 Humber Way, Langley, Slough, Berks, and has issue living, Geoffrey, *b* 1955, — Heather, *b* 1947: *m* 19—, Stanley Rush, of The Random Stack, Parsonage Lane, Farnham Common, Bucks SL2 3PA.

Issue of late Terence Robin Handcock, *b* 1902, *d* 1998: *m* 1933, Eva Mary, da of Charles Taylor:—
Michael Robin, *b* 1934: *m* 1961, Jean Anne, only da of J. T. Smoker, and has issue living, Jenny Samantha, *b* 1969.

Grandson of late Hon Robert John Handcock, 2nd son of 3rd Baron:—
Issue of late Henry Handcock, *b* 1869, *d* 1917: *m* 1892, Charlotte, who *d* 1922, da of late Richard Cole:—
Patrick Francis Denys (White Lodge, Restronguet Point, Feock, Truro, Cornwall), *b* 1913: *m* 1st, 1933, Kathleen Joan,
who *d* 1972, da of Frederick Lyle; 2ndly, 1972, Hilary Maybelle, widow of Sqd-Ldr D. W. Willis, RAF, and has issue
living (by 1st *m*), Patrick Michael, *b* 1934.

Grandson of late Rev John Harward Jessop Handcock, son of late Rev John Gustavus Handcock, 4th
son of 2nd Baron:—
Issue of late Harward Devereux Handcock, *b* 1874, *d* 1944: *m* 1907, Eleanor Winifred, who *d* 1966, da of late
Henry John Potts, of Glan-yr-afon, Mold, Flintshire, and Ollerton, Cheshire:—
John Harward (Anderida, Brook Green, Cuckfield, Sussex) *b* 1924: *m* 1949, Brenda Tenrill, da of Donald Stewart
Alexander Simpson, and has issue living, Jeremy John, *b* 1953: *m* 1978, Elfie, eldest da of H. Hallaschek, of Stuttgart, W
Germany, and has issue living, Alexander John *b* 1981, Thomas William Heinz *b* 1983, — Timothy Charles, *b* 1964, —
Fiona Elizabeth Jane, *b* 1956; has issue living, Oscar *b* 1984, Jonathan *b* 1988.

Grandchildren of late Robert Harris Temple Handcock, only son of Edward Stanley Handcock, yst son
of late Lt-Col Hon Robert French Handcock, 8th son of 2nd Baron:—
Issue of late Cdr William Stanley Handcock, RN, *b* 1908, *d* 1964: *m* 1933, Joan Mary (Sparshott House,
Hambledon, Hants), da of late Sir Ralph Molyneux Combe:—
Timothy Stannus (Holmwood Cottage, Stroud, Petersfield, Hants), *b* 1938. —— Deirdre Elizabeth, *b* 1935: *m* 1960, Capt
Colin Prinsep James, MC, late Rifle Bde, of Madford House, Hemyock, Cullompton, Devon, and has issue living, Emma
Louise, *b* 1962, — Belinda Anne Nonie, *b* 1964. —— Luleen Annette, *b* 1946: *m* 1st, 1977, Michael Poynder; 2ndly, 1981,
Frederick Moseley Wanklyn, of Rose Cottage, PO Box N7776, Lyford Cay, Nassau, Bahamas.

PREDECESSORS – **(1)** WILLIAM Handcock, Constable and Gov of Athlone; *cr Baron Castlemaine*, of Moydrum, co
Westmeath (peerage of Ireland) 1812, with remainder to his brother and *Viscount Castlemaine* (peerage of Ireland) 1822;
d 1839, when the Viscountcy became extinct; *s* in Barony by his brother **(2)** RICHARD, 2nd Baron; *d* 1840; *s* by his son
(3) RICHARD, 3rd Baron; *b* 1791; a Representative Peer: *m* 1822, Margaret, da of Michael Harris, of Dublin; *d* 1869; *s* by
his son **(4)** RICHARD, 4th Baron, *b* 1826; a Representative Peer, and Lord-Lieut of co Westmeath: *m* 1857, Hon Louisa
Matilda, who *d* 1892, da of 2nd Baron Harris; *d* 1892; *s* by his el son **(5)** ALBERT EDWARD, 5th Baron; *b* 1863; a
Representative Peer: *m* 1895, Annie Evelyn, who *d* 1955, da of late Col Thomas Joseph Barrington; *d* 1937; *s* by his
brother **(8)** ROBERT ARTHUR, 6th Baron; *b* 1864; a DL for co Westmeath; European War 1914-19 as Lieut RASC: *m* 1894,
Ethel Violet, who *d* 1934, da of late Col Sir Edmond Bainbridge, KCB, of Sheringham Norfolk; *d* 1954; *s* by his kinsman
(7) JOHN MICHAEL SCHOMBERG STAVELEY (only son of late Robert John Handcock, 2nd son of late Hon Robert John Handcock, 2nd son of 3rd Baron), 7th Baron, *b* 1904: *m* 1930, Rebecca Ellen, who *d* 1978, only da of William T. Soady, RN; *d*
1973; *s* by his son **(8)** ROLAND THOMAS JOHN, 8th Baron and present peer.

Castlereagh, Viscount; son of Marquess of Londonderry.

CASTLE STEWART, EARL (Stuart) (Earl I 1800, Bt S 1628)

ARTHUR PATRICK AVONDALE STUART, 8th Earl and 15th Baronet; *b* 18 Aug 1928; *s* 1961; *ed* Eton, and Trin Coll, Camb (BA 1950); late Lieut Scots Gds; is a Farmer; FBIM (1978): *m* 1952, Edna, da of William Edward Fowler, of Harborne, Birmingham, and has issue.

Arms – Quarterly of four: 1st the Royal arms of *Scotland*; 2nd or, a fesse checky azure and argent, and in chief a label of three points gules, *Stuart*; 3rd argent, a saltire between four roses gules, barbed and seeded proper, *Lennox*; 4th or, a lion rampant gules, *Macduff*; the whole within a bordure compony argent and azure. **Crest** – An unicorn's head couped at the neck argent, armed, crined, and tufted or. **Supporters** – Two wyverns, their tails, nowed or, armed proper and langued gules. **Seat** – Stuart Hall, Stewartstown, co Tyrone. *Residence* – Manor Farm, Babcary, Somerset TA11 7DT.

SON LIVING

ANDREW RICHARD CHARLES (*Viscount Stuart*), (Combehayes Farm, Buckerell, nr Honiton, Devon), *b* 7 Oct 1953; *ed* Millfield, and Exeter Univ; lecturer: *m* 1973, Annie Yvette, da of Robert le Poulain, of 65 Av de Marville, St Malo, France, and has issue:—

DAUGHTER LIVING— *Hon* Celia Elizabeth, *b* 1976.

DAUGHTER LIVING

Lady Bridget Ann (Stone House, E Pennard, Shepton Mallet, Somerset) *b* 1957; *ed* Wynstones Sch, Whaddon, Glos; MHort (RHS) 1983; DMS 1989; cider apple grower: *m* 1990, Robert W. Wadey, only son of Thomas Wadey, of 12 Marine Gdns, Brighton, and has issue living, Miriam Sarah, *b* 1997.

BROTHER LIVING

Hon Simon Walter Erskine (Windyridge, Wych Cross, Forest Row, Sussex RH18 5JP), *b* 1930; *ed* Eton, and Trin Coll, Camb (BA 1953, MA 1957); late 2nd Lt Scots Gds; an Assist Master at Haberdashers' Aske's Sch 1961-78 formerly at King's Canterbury, and Stowe, since when a writer: *m* 1973, Deborah Jane, da of late Michael Mounsey, of Backhouse, Murton, Appleby, Cumbria, and has issue living, Thomas Harry Erskine, *b* 1974, — Corin Edward Leveson, *b* 1975, — Tristram James Avondale, *b* 1977.

COLLATERAL BRANCHES LIVING

Granddaughter of late Richard Wingfield Stuart (infra):—
Issue of late John William Wingfield Stuart, *b* 1901, *d* 1983: *m* 1930, Dorothy Eleanor, da of T. Baker Insoll, of Hamilton, NZ:—
Mary Rose Dorothy Wingfield, *b* 1931: *m* 1st, 1954, Leonard Russell Goggs, who *d* 1977; 2ndly, 1979, Percy Wilbur Collom, Jr, of 2/182 Gover St, N Adelaide, S Australia 5006, and has issue living (by 1st *m*), Stephen John (14 Nelson Place, Curtin, ACT, Australia), *b* 1962: *m* 1990, Jillian, da of William Scrymgour, of 2 Violet Court, Novar Gdns, S Australia, and has issue living, Alistair Michael Dominic *b* 1996, — Brenda Margaret, *b* 1955: *m* 1976 (*m diss* 1990), Edmund John Attridge, and has issue living, Antony Hugh *b* 1986, Eleanor Charlotte *b* 1981, Sophie Irene *b* 1983, Vanessa Selina *b* 1985, — Catherine Mary, *b* 1956: *m* 1st, 1980 (*m diss* 1986), Peter Louis Baratosy; 2ndly, 1986, W/ Cmdr Norman Melville Goodall, DFC, RAAF, of Paradale Too, Strathalbyn, S Australia, and has issue living (by 2nd *m*), Emma *b* 1986, — Ursula Anne, *b* 1958: *m* 1988, Alexander Edward Jeakins, of 2 Starsmead, Haresfield, Stonehouse, Glos GL10 3EG, and has issue living, Adrian Edward *b* 1989, Humfrey Francis *b* 1990, Isabel Rose *b* 1994, — Sarah Louise, *b* 1963: *m* 1st, 1986 (*m diss* 1988), John Dostal; 2ndly, 1992, Graeme Russell George French, of 5 Fifth Av, Kensington, W Australia, and has issue living (by 2nd *m*), Hamish Russell Douglas *b* 1994, Elliott Stuart Jackson *b* 1996.

Grandson of late Rev Hon Andrew Godfrey Stuart, 4th son of 2nd Earl:—
Issue of late Richard Wingfield Stuart, *b* 1843, *d* 1914: *m* 1st, 1869, Jeannie Miriam, who *d* 1889, da of John Macdermott, of Gayfield, Sydney; 2ndly, 1891, Isabel Clare, who *d* 1953, el da of Charles Lee, MLA, of NS Wales for Tenterfield:—
(By 2nd *m*) Godfrey Richard Wingfield, *b* 1905. *Residence* 2/182 Gover St, N Adelaide, S Australia 5006.

Descendants, if any, of Andrew William Godfrey Stuart (*b* 1869), and his brother, George Sydney Stuart (*b* 1871), sons of Andrew Godfrey Stuart, of Hobart, Tasmania, eldest son of Andrew Thomas Stuart (infra).

Descendants, if any, of Arthur Burleigh Stuart (*b* 1876), only son of George Joseph Stuart, 2nd son of Andrew Thomas Stuart (infra).

Granddaughter of late Robert Walter Stuart, 3rd son of Andrew Thomas Stuart, eldest son of Hon Andrew Godfrey Stuart, 2nd son of 1st Earl:—
Issue of late Burleigh Stuart, *b* 1875, *d* 1912: *m* 1901, Helen Gertrude (who *d* 1956, having *m* 2ndly, 1913, John Martin Muir, of Sorell, Tasmania, who *d* 1943), da of Edward Mace, of Burnie, Tasmania:—
Sylvia Annie, *b* 1902.

Grandchildren of Walter Burleigh Stuart, eldest son of late Robert Walter Stuart (ante):—
Issue of late Burleigh Athol Stuart, *b* 1904, *d* 1982: *m* 1927, Winifred May, da of Ernest Kerrison, of Beaconsfield, Tasmania:—
Ernest Martin, *b* 1935: *m* 1965, June Rosalyn, da of Stanley Bastian, of Como, W Australia, and has issue living, Conway Athol, *b* 1968, — Kym Robina, *b* 1967. —— Claire Leila, *b* 1928: *m* 1951, Reginald Edward Johnston, of 19 Rialannah Rd, Mount Nelson, Hobart, Tasmania, and has issue living, Kent Reginald, *b* 1952: *m* 1975, Marlene Irene Baier, and has issue living, Nathan James *b* 1975, Alycia Irene *b* 1979, Caitlin Laine *b* 1989, — Vivienne Claire, *b* 1955: *m* 1980, Kenneth Ross Watts, and has issue living, Samuel Neil *b* 1984, Emma Claire *b* 1982, Amanda Joan *b* 1988, — Celia Anne, *b* 1963, — Dianne Ruth, *b* 1965. —— Winifred Ellen, *b* 1929: *m* 1950, John Robert Sinclair Mackey, of 460 Doran's Rd, Sandford, Tasmania 7020, and has issue living, Andrew John Sinclair (56 Terrina St, Lauderdale 7020, Tasmania), *b* 1956: *m* 1978, Debbie Lee Robson, and has issue living, Courtney Lee *b* 1986, Kurt Marcus Sinclair *b* 1992, — Denise Claire, *b* 1952: *m* 19— (*m diss* 19—), Robert John Wells. —— Alma Elaine, *b* 1931: *m* 1955, James Maxwell Carter, of 1500 S Arm Rd, Clifton Beach, Tasmania 7020, and has issue living, Stuart James, *b* 1958: *m* 1984 (*m diss* 19—), Eleni Atzamoglou, — Michael Jackson, *b* 1960, — Lee Andrea, *b* 1956: *m* 1978, Ian Cameron Tremayne, and has issue living, Ben Cameron *b* 1981, Emma Kate *b* 1983.

Grandson of late Andrew Thomas Stuart (ante):—
Issue of late Audley Mervyn Stuart, *b* 1860, *d* 1942: *m* 1892, Alice Anne Rogers, of Hobart, Tasmania, who *d* 1897:—
Audley Andrew Mervyn, *b* 1897: *m* 1934, Beryl Elizabeth, da of Edward Alfred Irwin, of Hobart, Tasmania, and has issue living, Elizabeth Anne Castle *b* 1937, — Helen Christine Castle, *b* 1939, — Margaret Lyndsay Castle, *b* 1942.

Grandchildren of late Maj Godfrey Richard Conyngham Stuart, CB, eldest son of late Maj Burleigh William Henry Fitz-Gibbon Stuart, 4th son of Hon Andrew Godfrey Stuart (ante):—
Issue of late Lt-Col Godfrey Walter Burleigh Stuart, *b* 1901, *d* 1996: *m* 1933, Christine Valerie, who *d* 1997, da of late Col Stephen Simpson, TD, DL, of Bowerswood, nr Garstang, Lancs:—
Jane Christine, *b* 1934: *m* 1st, 1960 (*m diss* 1972), Anthony Rossington Vickers; 2ndly, 1974, Herbert Jackson Daniel, who *d* 1974; 3rdly, 1982, Wayne Locksley Kines, of RR3, Ottawa, Ont, Canada K0E 1T0, and has issue living (by 1st *m*), Robin Daniel STUART, *b* 1964; has legally assumed the surname of Stuart in lieu of his patronymic: *m* 1988, Kathleen Nielsen, and has issue living, Christopher Anthony *b* 1995, Samantha Anne *b* 1992, Nicole Christine *b* 1993, Michaela Marie *b* 1997, — Helena Jane Stuart, *b* 1969: *m* 1992, Rev Dr Philip Ziegler, and has issue living, Karl Gordon *b* 1999. —— Wendy Mary, *b* 1935: *m* 1st, 1955 (*m diss* 1972), William Joynson; 2ndly, 1983 (*m diss* 1990), John Remmett-Smith; 3rdly, 1995, Edward Stuart-Murphy, of Hillbrook House, 47 Queen's Rd, Chorley, Lancs PR7 1LA, and has issue living (by 1st *m*), Timothy William Stuart, *b* 1958: *m* 1989, Linda Spencer, — Nicholas George Stuart, *b* 1960: *m* 1998, Katryn Ahrens, and has issue living, Connor Liam *b* 1998, — Jeremy Duncan Stuart, *b* 1963, — Andrew Douglas Stuart, *b* 1965.

Issue of late Lt-Col Robin Charles Burleigh Stuart, *b* 1907, *d* 1970: *m* 1939, Evelyn Alice, who *d* 1996, da of Harry Freegard, of Charlton Kings, Glos:—
Douglas Charles Burleigh, *b* 1940; *ed* Cheltenham, and Nautical Coll, Pangbourne; formerly with Air Traffic Control, Melbourne; Past Pres Internat Fedn of Air Traffic Controllers; Man Dir Stuart Aviation Internat Ltd: *m* 1st, 1962 (*m diss* 1990), Pamela, da of Gordon Sivyer, of Wembley, W Australia; 2ndly, 1992 (*m diss* 1999), Roslyn Harriet, da of late Roy Jennings, of Brighton, Vic, and has issue living (by 1st *m*), Andrew John Burleigh, *b* 1967; *ed* Eltham Coll, and Melbourne Univ (BComm): *m* 1996, Joanne Aisha, eldest da of William Mellor, of Mosman, NSW, and has issue living, Aisha Alexandra *b* 1997, — Joanna Mary, *b* 1965; *ed* Eltham Coll, and Latrobe Univ (BA). *Residence* – 370 Maintongoon Rd, Bonnie Doon, Vic 3720, Australia.

Grandsons of late Maj Burleigh William Henry Fitz-Gibbon Stuart (ante):—
Issue of late Brig-Gen Burleigh Francis Brownlow Stuart, CB, CMG, *b* 1868, *d* 1952: *m* 1916, Evelyn Margaret, JP, who *d* 1970, da of Lt-Col Sir Edward Henry St Lawrence Clarke, 4th Bt, CMG, DSO (*cr* 1804, ext):—
John William Brownlow, MBE, MC (Corner Cottage, Radford, Inkberrow, Worcs WR7 4LR), *b* 1917; *ed* Rugby; Col Worcestershire Regt (ret); OC 1st Bn 1959-61; Palestine 1939 (MC), Sudan and Eritrea 1940-41 W Desert and Egypt 1941-43 (despatches), Italy 1944-45 (MBE), Kenya 1956-57 (Africa Gen Ser Medal with clasp); MBE (Mil) 1945: *m* 1954, Anthea Joan, who *d* 1977, el da of late Ashley Ernest Herman, OBE, FRCS, of Shipton Hill, Hambledon, Godalming. —— Burleigh Edward St Lawrence (Hunter's Close, Ickford, Aylesbury, Bucks), *b* 1920; *ed* Rugby, Peterhouse, Camb and Trin Coll, Oxford (MA); Malayan Civil Ser 1951-52, E African High Commn (Forestry Research) 1952-56, Colonial Forest Ser, Kenya, 1956-63, and Commonwealth Forestry Bureau, Oxford 1964-76; formerly Capt Worcs Regt; India 1940-44, Burma 1944-45: *m* 1952, Joan Elizabeth, da of Col Matthew George Platts, CIE, OBE, MC, of The Down Wood, Blandford, Dorset, and has issue living, Edward John Burleigh (28 Sinnels Field, Shipton-under-Wychwood, Oxon), *b* 1953; horologist: *m* 1976, Alison Ann, yst da of James Steel, of Paddock Gate, Clanfield, Oxon, and has issue living, Simon Francis Brownlow, *b* 1980, Henry George Burleigh, *b* 1982, — Elizabeth Helen (*Countess Howe*), *b* 1955: *m* 1983, 7th Earl Howe, of Penn House, Amersham, Bucks, — Catherine Frances (98 Sunningwell Rd, Oxford OX1 4SY), *b* 1958: *m* 1982 (*m diss* 1995), Graham Ian Briggs.

PREDECESSORS – **(1)** ANDREW Stuart, *cr Lord Avondale* (peerage of Scotland) 1459, was afterwards Chancellor of Scotland; *d* 1488; *s* by his nephew **(2)** ALEXANDER, 2nd Lord; one of the Lords Auditors; *d* 1489; *s* by his son **(3)** ANDREW, 3rd Lord; fell at Flodden 1513; *s* by his son **(4)** ANDREW, 4th Lord; exchanged his Lordship with Sir James Hamilton for that of Ochiltree, and by Act of Parliament 1542 was ordained to be styled *Lord Stuart of Ochiltrie*; *d* 1548; *s* by his son **(5)** ANDREW, 2nd Lord Stuart of Ochiltrie; *d* 1592; *s* by his grandson **(6)** ANDREW, 3rd Lord Stuart of Ochiltrie, a Lord of the Bedchamber to James I of England; resigned his title to his cousin, Sir James Stuart with the consent of the Crown, and was himself *cr Baron Castle Stuart* (peerage of Ireland) 1619, and received from the King considerable estates in co Tyrone; *d* 1628; *s* by his son **(7)** *Sir* ANDREW, 2nd Baron, who in 1628 had been *cr* a *Baronet* (Nova Scotia): *d* 1639; *s* by his son **(8)** ANDREW, 3rd Baron; *d* 1650; *s* by his brother **(9)** JOSIAS, 4th Baron, *dsp* 1652. *s* by his uncle **(10)** JOHN, 5th Baron; *d* unmarried 1678, when the Peerage and Baronetcy became dormant, and remained so until 1774, when they were successfully claimed by **(11)** ANDREW THOMAS, 9th Baron, the descendant in the 4th generation of Col Hon Robert, 3rd son of 1st Baron; *cr Viscount Castle Stuart* (peerage of Ireland) 1793, and *Earl Castle Stewart* (peerage of Ireland) 1800; *d* 1809; *s* by his son **(12)** ROBERT, 2nd Earl; *d* 1854; *s* by his el son **(13)** EDWARD, 3rd Earl; *d* 1857; *s* by his brother **(14)** CHARLES KNOX, 4th Earl; *b* 1810: *m* 1835, Charlotte Raffles Drury, da of late Quintin Thompson; *d* 1874; *s* by his son **(15)** HENRY JAMES, 5th Earl, *b* 1837; assumed in 1867, by Roy licence, the additional surname of Richardson: *m* 1866, Augusta le Vicomte Massy Richardson, who *d* 1908, widow of Major Hugh Massy (85th Foot), yst da and heiress of late Major Richardson-Brady, of Drum Manor, co Tyrone; *d* 1914; *s* by his cousin **(16)** ANDREW JOHN (2nd son of late Rev Hon Andrew Godfrey Stuart, 4th son of 2nd Earl), 6th Earl; *b* 1841; in MCS: *m* 1876, Emma Georgiana, who *d* 1949, da of Maj-Gen Arthur Stevens; *d* 1921; *s* by his son **(17)** ARTHUR, MC, 7th Earl; *b* 1889; Bar Inner Temple 1943; European War 1914-18 as Major Machine Gun Corps and a GSO (MC); sat as MP for Harborough Div of Leicestershire (*U*) 1929-33: *m* 1920, Eleanor May, who *d* 1992, da of Solomon R Guggenheim, of New York, USA; *d* 1961; *s* by his son **(18)** ARTHUR PATRICK AVONDALE, 8th Earl and present peer; also Viscount Castle Stuart, and Baron Castle Stuart.

CATHCART, EARL (Cathcart) (Lord S about 1452, Earl UK 1814)

CHARLES ALAN ANDREW CATHCART, 7th Earl; *b* 30 Nov 1952; *s* 1999; *ed* Eton; late Scots Guards: *m* 1981, Vivien Clare, only da of Francis Desmond McInnes Skinner, of North Farm, Snetterton, Norfolk, and has issue.

Arms – Azure, three cross crosslets fitchée issuing out of as many crescents argent. Crest – A dexter hand couped above the wrist and erect proper, grasping a crescent argent as in the arms. Supporters – Two parrots wings inverted proper.
Residences – Gateley Hall, Dereham, Norfolk; 18 Smith Terrace, SW3.

I·HOPE·TO·SPEED

SON LIVING

ALAN GEORGE (*Lord Greenock*), *b* 16 March 1986.

DAUGHTER LIVING

Lady Laura Rosemary, *b* 1984.

SISTERS LIVING

Lady Louisa, *b* 1948: *m* 1975, Norman Kirkpatrick Cosgrave, of Totterdown Lodge, Inkpen, nr Hungerford, Berks, who *d* 1991.
Lady Charlotte Mary, *b* 1951: *m* 1972, Capt Anthony C. McCallum, late 1st The Queen's Drag Gds, and has issue living, Charles Colin, *b* 1973, — Anthony James, *b* 1977, — Sophie Charlotte, *b* 1975. *Residence* – Week Green Farm, Froxfield, Petersfield, Hants.

WIDOW LIVING OF SIXTH EARL

MARIE ISOBEL (*Dowager Countess Cathcart*), da of late Hon William Joseph French (*see* B de Freyne, colls), and widow of Sir Thomas Brian Weldon, 8th Bt: *m* 1984, as his 2nd wife, Major General the 6th Earl Cathcart, CB, DSO, MC, who *d* 1999. *Residence* – Moor Hatches, W Amesbury, Salisbury, Wilts.

COLLATERAL BRANCHES LIVING

Grandchildren of late Maj Frederick Adrian Cathcart, el son of Hon Augustus Murray Cathcart, yr son of 2nd Earl:—
Issue of late Alan Reginald Cathcart, *b* 1908, *d* 1967: *m* 1934, Daphne Victoria Catherine, who *d* 1993, da of late Maj-Gen John Archibald Henry Pollock, CB (*see* Montagu-Pollock, Bt, colls, 1990 Edn):—
Charles Alan (Culraven, Borgue, Kirkcudbright), *b* 1940: *m* 1973, Carol Ann, yr da of late A. E. Jenner, and has issue living, Daniel Edward, *b* 1974, — Emma Katherine, *b* 1976. — Julia Mary, *b* 1936: *m* 1959, Angus George Millar, WS, who *d* 1996, of 24 Buckingham Terr, Edinburgh EH4 3AE, and has issue living, James George, *b* 1961: *m* 1992, Katharine Ann, yr da of late John Danielson, and has issue living, Hector George Danielson *b* 1994, Ludovic Angus Danielson *b* 1996, — Charles Angus, *b* 1963, — Roderick Alan, *b* 1967.

Issue of late Lt-Col Charles Frederick Cathcart, DSO, *b* 1912, *d* 1971: *m* 1st, 1939 (*m diss* 1954), Pamela Violet, who *d* 1996, da of late Lt-Col Patrick Douglas Stirling, OBE, MC, JP, of Kippendavie, Kippenross, Dunblane, Perths; 2ndly, 1955, Pamela Vera, who *d* 1987, da of late Maj Harry Sebastian Garrard, of Welton Place, Daventry, and widow of Maj Sir Arthur Ralph Wilmot, 7th Bt:
(By 1st *m*) Clovannis Jane, *b* 1942: *m* 1961, Maj Colin Berowald Innes, Black Watch (*see* Innes, Bt (*cr* 1628) colls). —— (Sarah) Camilla (*Baroness Jauncey of Tullichettle*), *b* 1946: *m* 1977, Baron Jauncey of Tullichettle (Life Baron), and has issue (see that title). *Residence* – Tullichettle, Comrie, Perthshire PH6 2HU.

PREDECESSORS – **(1)** *Sir* ALAN Cathcart, Knt, Warden of the West Marches and Master of Artillery, *cr Lord Cathcart* (peerage of Scotland) 1447; *d* 1499; *s* by his grandson **(2)** JOHN, 2nd Lord; *d* 1535; *s* by his grandson **(3)** ALAN, 3rd Lord; *k* at battle of Pinkie 1547; *s* by his grandson **(4)** ALAN, 4th Lord; *d* 1618; *s* by his grandson **(5)** ALAN, 5th Lord; *d* 1628; *s* by his son **(6)** ALAN, 6th Lord; *s* by his son **(7)** ALAN, 7th Lord; *d* 1732; *s* by his son **(8)** CHARLES, 8th Lord, a Representative Peer and a Lord of the Bedchamber to George II; appointed Com in Ch of the British Forces in America 1740, but *d* during the passage out; *s* by his son **(9)** CHARLES, KT, PC, 9th Lord, a Representative Peer, Lieut-Gen in the Army, First Lord of Police, Ambassador to Russia, etc; *d* 1776; *s* by his son **(10)** WILLIAM SCHAW 10th Lord, a

Representative Peer, a Gen in the army, and Ambassador to St Petersburg 1805-06 and 1812-20; *cr Baron Greenock*, of Greenock, co Renfrew and *Viscount Cathcart*, of Cathart, co Renfrew (peerage of United Kingdom) 1807, and *Earl Cathcart* (peerage of United Kingdom) 1814; *d* 1843; *s* by his son **(11)** CHARLES MURRAY, GCB, 2nd Earl; *b* 1783; a Gen in the Army, and Gov-Gen and Com-in-Ch in British N America, etc; *m* 1818, Henrietta da of Thomas Mather, *d* 1859; *s* by his son **(12)** ALAN FREDERICK, 3rd Earl; *b* 1828; Chm of N Riding Quarter Sessions 1858-68: *m* 1850, Elizabeth Mary, who *d* 1902, el da and co-heiress of Sir Samuel Crompton, Bt (ext); *d* 1905; *s* by his **(13)** ALAN, 4th Earl, *b* 1856; *d* 1911; *s* by his brother **(14)** GEORGE, 5th Earl, *b* 1862: *m* 1919 (*m diss* 1922), Vera Estelle, who *d* 1993, da of late John Fraser, of Cape Town, and widow of Capt de Grey Warter, 4th Dragoon Guards; *d* 1927; *s* by his son **(15)** ALAN, CB, DSO, MC, 6th Earl, *b* 1919; Maj-Gen; Lt Col Comdg Scots Gds 1960-62, Col AQ Scottish Command 1962-63, Imperial Defence Coll 1964, Commander 152nd Highland Inf Bde (TA) 1965-66, Brig Operations Div SHAPE 1967-69, GOC Yorks Dist 1969-70, and GOC Berlin (British Sector) 1970-73; Brig Queen's Body Guard for Scotland (Royal Company of Archers), Lord Prior Order of St John 1985-88: *m* 1st, 1946, Rosemary Clare Marie Gabrielle, who *d* 1980, da of late Air-Commodore Sir Henry Percy Smyth-Osbourne, CMG, CBE; 2ndly, 1984, Marie Isobel, da of late Hon William Joseph French (*see* B de Freyne, colls), and widow of Sir Thomas Brian Weldon, 8th Bt; *d* 1999; *s* by his only son **(16)** CHARLES ALAN ANDREW, 7th Earl and present peer; also Viscount Cathcart, Lord Cathcart, and Baron Greenock.

CATTO, BARON (Catto) (Baron UK 1936, Bt UK 1921)

STEPHEN GORDON CATTO, 2nd Baron, and 2nd Baronet; *b* 14 Jan 1923; *s* 1959; *ed* Eton, and Trin Coll, Camb; formerly Flt Lt RAF VR; a Member of Advisory Council of Export Credits Guarantee Dept 1959-65; a part-time Member of London Transport Board 1962-68; farmer; Pres Morgan Grenfell Group plc, Chm Yule Catto & Co plc, a Dir Times Newspapers Ltd, and of other cos; Chm of RAF Benevolent Fund 1978-91: *m* 1st, 1948 (*m diss* 1965), Josephine Innes, el da of George Herbert Packer, of Alexandria, Egypt; 2ndly, 1966, Margaret, who *d* 1998, da of James Stuart Forrest, of Dilston, Tasmania, and has issue by 1st and 2nd *m*.

Arms – Or, on a chevron between three lymphads sable as many boars' heads couped of the field, **Crests** – A wild cat sejant proper, resting the dexter paw on a garb or. **Supporters** – On either side a tiger proper, charged on the shoulder with an ivy leaf or.
Residences – 41 William Mews, Lowndes Sq, SW1X 9HQ; House of Schivas, Ythanbank, Aberdeenshire.

SONS LIVING (*By 1st marriage*)

Hon INNES GORDON, *b* 7 Aug 1950. *Residence* – Flat 17, Centre Point Flats, St Giles High St, WC2.
Hon Alexander Gordon, *b* 1952; *ed* Westminster: *m* 1981, Elizabeth Scott, twin da of Maj T. P. Boyes, of Brookvale Cottage, Whitford, Devon, and has issue living, Thomas Innes Gordon, *b* 1983, — Alastair Gordon, *b* 1986, — Charlotte Gordon, *b* 1988. *Residence* – Holmdale, Holmbury St Mary, Dorking, Surrey RH5 6NR.

(*By 2nd marriage*)

Hon James Stuart Gordon, *b* 1966: *m* 1997, Kathryn M., da of Robert Lawton, of Aldbourne, Wilts, and has issue living, Hamish Robert Forrest, *b* 1998. *Residence* – Lower Lutheredge Farm, Shortwood, Nailsworth, Stroud, Glos GL6 0SJ.

DAUGHTERS LIVING (*By 1st marriage*)

Hon Christian Victoria Gordon, *b* 1955: *m* 1983, Charles N. Menzies-Wilson, eldest son of W. N. Menzies-Wilson, of Holland Park, W11, and has issue living, Richard Napier, *b* 1988, — James Benedict, *b* 1991, — Cathryn Lucy, *b* 1986. *Residence* – Newport House, Newport Lane, Braishfield, nr Romsey, Hants SO51 0PL.
Hon Ariane Madeleine Gordon, *b* 1960.

(*By 2nd marriage*)

Hon Georgina Lucinda Gordon, *b* 1969: *m* 1993, Robert Alistair Newman, elder son of Alistair Newman, of Sutton Green, Guildford, and has issue living, Charles Guy Gordon, *b* 1994, — Tobias James Gordon, *b* 1997. *Residence* – Sandford House, Avening, Tetbury, Glos GL8 8NF.

SISTER LIVING

Hon Ruth Gordon, *b* 1919: *m* 1947, Francis Ernest Herman Bennett, CBE, son of late Sir Ernest Nathaniel Bennett, MP, and has issue living, David Francis, *b* 1948: *m* 1980, Lynn D., da of Lt-Col Allan Burton, DSO, ED, of Limestone Hall, Milton, Ontario, Canada, and has issue living, Nicholas Gordon *b* 1982, Audrey Claire *b* 1984, — Adam Gordon Greverus, *b* 1954: *m* 1986, Zoë Diana, da of late Prof Terence John Bew Spencer, of Birmingham Univ, and has issue living, Oscar Francis *b* 1986, Isabel Diana *b* 1989, — Olivia Gay, *b* 1950.

PREDECESSOR – (1) *Rt Hon Sir* THOMAS SIVEWRIGHT CATTO, CBE, son of William Catto, of Peterhead, Aberdeenshire; *b* 1879; E India Merchant and Banker, and Managing Director of Morgan Grenfell & Co Ltd, of London, of Yule Catto & Co Ltd, of London, and of Andrew Yule & Co, of Calcutta; was Gov of Bank of England 1944-9; *cr* a *Baronet* 1921, and *Baron Catto*, of Cairncatto, co Aberdeen (peerage of UK) 1936: *m* 1910, Gladys Forbes, who *d* 1980, da of Stephen Gordon, of Elgin; *d* 1959; *s* by his son (2) STEPHEN GORDON, 2nd Baron and present peer.

Caulfeild, family name of Viscount Charlemont.

CAVAN, EARL OF (Lambart) (Earl I 1647)

Prepared on every side

ROGER CAVAN LAMBART, 13th Earl (has not yet established his right to the Peerage); *b* 1 Sept 1944; *ed* Wilson's Sch, Wallington, Surrey.

Arms – Gules, three gillieflowers pierced argent **Crest** – On a mount vert a centaur argent drawing a bow or. **Supporters** – Two knights in complete armour sable, garnished or, with an under habit gules, fringed of the second, the beaver up, and on the helmet seven plumes alternately of the third and argent.

HALF-SISTERS LIVING

Issue of late Frederick Cavan Lambart, *b* 1902, *d* 1963: *m* 1st, 1924 (*m diss* 1942), Adelaide Constance, da of late Ottywell Butler:—
Olivia Marianne LAMBART (abandoned the christian name of Olive), *b* 1925; has resumed her maiden name: *m* 1950 (*m diss* 1970), Ernest Ephraim Corrett, and has issue living, Paul (2 Erskine Mews, Regent's Park, NW3), *b* 1952; *ed* Stowe: *m* 1984, Anne Margaret, da of late Ernest Joseph Ferridge, of 35 Dunbar Rd, N22, and has issue living, Catherine Marianne *b* 1986, — Graham, *b* 1954; *ed* Corona Stage Sch: *m* 1982 (*m diss* 1988), Kelly Elaine, da of late Seymour Arnold Hoppen, of 7 Egerton Place, SW3, and formerly of S Africa, and has issue living, Natasha *b* 1983.

Issue of late Frederick Cavan Lambart, *b* 1902, *d* 1963: *m* 3rdly, 1958, (Kathleen) Elizabeth (who *m* 2ndly, 1965, Frederick Rufus Lawrence, who *d* 1969; 3rdly, 1970, John Armstrong Wiggin, formerly of The Anchor Hotel, Shepperton, Middx), elder da of Edward James Henry Darvill, of Port Vale House, Hertford:—
Elizabeth, *b* 1959. *Residence* – .

DAUGHTERS LIVING AND DECEASED OF TWELFTH EARL

Lady Sarah Audrey, *b* 1948: *m* 1968, Capt Alistair Charles Sinclair, late 17th/21st Lancers, of Piccadilly Cottage, Kingston Lisle, Wantage, Oxon OX12 9QU, and *d* 1981, leaving issue, Harry Charles Lambart, *b* 1972; *ed* Radley, — Rupert Alistair Grenville, *b* 1973; *ed* Radley.

Lady Jane Mary, *b* 1949; *d* 1954.

Lady Katherine Lucy LAMBART, *b* 1955; has resumed her maiden name: *m* 1978 (*m diss* 1986), Don Lorenzo Ruiz Barrero, yr son of Don Lorenzo Ruiz Jimenez, of Madrid, and has issue living, Lorenzo Cavan, *b* 1980, — Natasha Pepa, *b* 1982. *Residence* – 174 Broomwood Rd, SW11 6JY.

DAUGHTERS LIVING OF TENTH EARL (By 2nd marriage)

Lady Elizabeth Mary (The Old Rectory, Todenham, Moreton-in-Marsh, Glos GL56 9PA), *b* 1924: *m* 1949, Mark Frederic Kerr Longman, who *d* 1972, and has issue living, Caroline Elizabeth, *b* 1951: *m* 1982, Peter Jan Zevenbergen, of Netton House, Bishopstone, nr Salisbury SP5 4AE, son of Jan Zevenbergen, and has issue living, Frederik Edmund Christian *b* 1985, Raphael James Christian *b* 1991, — Jane, *b* 1955, — Emma, *b* 1959: *m* 1980, Timothy James Hanbury, son of late James Robert Hanbury, of Burley-on-the-Hill, Oakham, Rutland (*see* Birkin, Bt, 1976 Edn), and has issue living, David Mark James *b* 1986, Marina Jane *b* 1982, Rose Sarah *b* 1984.

Lady Joanna, *b* 1929: *m* 1955, Maj Michael Godwin Plantagenet Stourton, Gren Gds (ret), of The Old Rectory, Great Rollright, Chipping Norton, Oxon (*see* B Mowbray).

MOTHER LIVING

Audrey May, da of late Albert Charles Dunham: *m* 1942 (*m diss* 1948), as his 2nd wife, Frederick Cavan Lambart, who *d* 1963. *Residence* – 34 Woodleigh Gdns, SW16.

STEPMOTHER LIVING

(Kathleen) Elizabeth, elder da of Edward James Henry Darvill, of Port Vale House, Hertford: *m* 1st, 1958, as his 3rd wife, Frederick Cavan Lambart, who *d* 1963; 2ndly, 1965, Frederick Rufus Lawrence, who *d* 1969; 3rdly, 1970, John Armstrong Wiggin, of The Anchor Hotel, Shepperton, Middx.

WIDOW LIVING OF TWELFTH EARL

Essex Lucy (*Countess of Cavan*), only da of late Henry Arthur Cholmondeley (*see* B Delamere, colls): *m* 1947, Col the 12th Earl of Cavan, TD, who *d* 1988. *Residence* – The Glebe House, Stockton, Shifnal, Shropshire TF11 9EF.

COLLATERAL BRANCHES LIVING

       Granddaughter of late Com Hon Octavius Henry Lambart, 5th son of 8th Earl:—
       Issue of late Howard Frederick John Lambart, *b* 1880, *d* 1946: *m* 1st, 1908, Helen Marianne, who *d* 1932, da of late Samuel Shelley Wallbridge, LLB; 2ndly, 1938, May, who *d* 19—, da of late Hon Robert Bickerdike, of Montreal, Canada:—
(By 1st *m*) Evelyn Mary, *b* 1914.

       Granddaughter of late Maj Frederick Richard Henry Lambart, 2nd son of late Cdr Hon Oliver William Matthew Lambart, RN, son of 7th Earl:—
       Issue of late Capt Richard Frederick Lacon Lambart, DSO, *b* 1875, *d* 1924: *m* 1st, 1899 (*m diss* 1909), Enid, who *d* 1963, da of Spencer Brunton; 2ndly, 1913 (*m diss* 19—), Faith Bevan; 3rdly, 1922, Kitty (who *m* 2ndly, 1924 (*m diss* 19—), Herbert Alfred Rich; 3rdly, 1941, Capt Horace Lacy Bullimore, RQMS S Wales Borderers, who *d* 1969), da of Henry Edward Gibbens, of Stanmore, Essex:—
(By 3rd *m*) (Kathleen) Joy Lydia Lacon, *b* 1923. *Residence* – Canada.

       Descendants, if any, of Arthur Oliver Reid Lambart (*b* 1909), only son of Ford Augustus Oliver Lambart, only son of Arthur Oliver Lambart, of E London, S Africa, 5th son of Cdr Hon Oliver William Matthew Lambart, RN (ante).

       Grandchildren of late Cyril Henry Edward Lambart (infra):—
       Issue of late Terence Edward William Lambart, *b* 1903, *d* 1965: *m* 1946, Valma Verdun Johnson, who *m* 2ndly, 1973, Philip John Richardson, of Coomera Gorge Drive, Tamborine Mountain, Queensland, Australia:—
Cavan Cyril Ernest (*presumed heir*) (19 Andrea St, Tarragindi, Brisbane, Qld 4121, Australia), *b* 27 March 1957; *ed* Queensland Inst of Technology (BE, MIEA): *m* 1989, Janita Sandona (BSc), and has issue living, Julian Stuart, *b* 26 Dec 1993, — Carla Thomasine, *b* 1991. —— Diana (21 Jersey St, Morningside, Qld 4170, Australia), *b* 1948: *m* 1968 (*m diss* 19—), Peter Athol McLauchlan, and has issue living, Fraser Burnett *b* 1968; BA, — Ashley Lambart, *b* 1970; BE, — Burnett Hunter, *b* 1972. —— Vivienne, *b* 1950; *ed* Queensland Univ (BA Hons; Dip Ed; M Litt Stud): *m* 1976, Donald William Muller, LLB, of 55 Sugars Rd, Bellbowrie, Brisbane, Queensland, and has issue living, Daniel Richard, *b* 1980, — Samuel Edward, *b* 1984, — Victoria Louise, *b* 1978. —— Rosalind, *b* 1952; *ed* Wollongong Univ (BCom): *m* 1973, Michael Angus Robinson (BSc, Dip Comp Sci), of Barton Place, Wombarra, NSW, and has issue living, Danielle, *b* 1983, — Emma, *b* 1986.

       Issue of late Cyril Alwyn Lawrence Lambart, *b* 1910, *d* 1985: *m* 1940, Claire Gilmore, who *d* 1985:—
Charles Dennis (17 Bodalla St, Norman Park, Qld 4170, Australia), *b* 1943: *m* 1st, 1967, Mary Bambrick; 2ndly, 19—, Margaret Phyllis Beagrie, and has issue living (by 1st *m*), Sally Ann, *b* 1970, — Juliette, *b* 1972, — (by 2nd *m*) Charles James Cyril George, *b* 1992. —— Richard Gilmore, *b* 1947: *m* 1979, Michelle Pluskovits, and has issue living, Robin Stephen, *b* 1980, — Nicholas, *b* 1985, — Rebecca Kim, *b* 1981. —— Jacqueline Ann, *b* 1945: *m* 19—, Paul Grima, of Mena Creek, Innisfail, Qld 4860, Australia, and has issue living, Jason Paul, *b* 1973, — Matthew Thomas, *b* 1975, — David Julian, *b* 1977, — Tristan Jose, *b* 1980.

       Grandson of late Gustavus William Lambart, 5th in descent from the Hon Oliver Lambart, MP, 2nd son of 1st Earl:—

Issue of late Cyril Henry Edward Lambart, *b* 1866, *d* 1955: *m* 1900, Ethel Caroline Annie, who *d* 1960, da of Albert Thomas Ward, of Newton Hall, Rosebery Topping, Yorks:—
George Desmond Richard (27 Richmond St, Chelmer, Brisbane, Queensland 4068, Australia), *b* 1912.

PREDECESSORS – (1) *Sir* OLIVER LAMBART, PC, Knt, Gov of Connaught 1601, and MP for co Cavan 1613, etc; *cr Lord Lambart, Baron of Cavan* (peerage of Ireland) 1617; *d* 1618; *s* by his son (2) CHARLES, PC, 2nd Baron, MP for Bossiney, Cornwall, 1625-7, and Com-in-Ch of Forces in City of Dublin 1642, etc; *cr Viscount Kilcoursie* and *Earl of Cavan* (peerage of Ireland) 1647; *d* 1660; *s* by his son (3) RICHARD, 2nd Earl; *s* by his son (4) CHARLES, 3rd Earl; *d* 1702; *s* by his son (5) RICHARD, 4th Earl; *d* 1741; *s* by his son (6) FORD, 5th Earl; *d* 1772; *s* by his cousin (7) RICHARD, 5th Earl, son of Hon Henry Lambart, 3rd son of 3rd Earl; *d* 1778; *s* by his son (8) RICHARD FORD WILLIAM, 7th Earl; a Gen in the Army; commanded a Div under Sir Ralph Abercrombie in Egypt 1800; *d* 1837; *s* by his grandson (9) FREDERICK JOHN WILLIAM, 8th Earl, son of George Frederick Augustus, Viscount Kilcoursie, by Sarah, da of J. P. Coppin, of Cowley, Oxfordshire, *b* 1815: *m* 1838, Hon Caroline Augusta, who *d* 1892, da of 1st Baron Hatherton; *d* 1887; *s* by his el son (10) FREDERICK EDWARD GOULD, KP, PC, 9th Earl, *b* 1839; Vice-Chamberlain of the Household 1886; served throughout siege of Sebastopol 1854; present at bombardment of Canton 1856, and with "forlorn hope" at attack of Pieho Forts 1858; MP for S Div of Somersetshire (L) 1885-92: *m* 1863, Mary Sneade, who *d* 1905, only child of late Rev John Olive; *d* 1900; *s* by his el son (11) FREDERIC RUDOLPH, KP, GCB, GCMG, GCVO, GBE, 10th Earl, *b* 1865; Field-Marshal; sometime Lieut of Tower of London; Ch of Imperial Gen Staff 1922-6; Capt of Hon Corps of Gentlemen-at-Arms 1929-31; S Africa 1899-1902 (despatches), European War 1914-19 in France and Comdg British Troops in Italy (despatches seven times, CB, KCB, GCMG, Orders of St Maurice and St Lazarus of Italy, Crown of Belgium and Wen Hu of China, Legion of Honour, Mil Order of Savoy, French and Italian Croix de Guerre): *m* 1st, 1893, Caroline Inez, who *d* 1920, da of late George Baden Crawley; 2ndly, 1922, Lady (Hester) Joan Byng, DBE, who *d* 1976, da of 5th Earl of Strafford, and widow of Capt Hon Andrew Edward Somerset Mulholland; *d* 1946; *s* by his brother (12) HORACE EDWARD SAMUEL SNEADE, 11th Earl; *b* 1878; Archdeacon Emeritus of Salop, Preb Emeritus and Provost of Denstone; sometime V of St Mary-the-Virgin, Shrewsbury: *m* 1907, Audrey Kathleen, who *d* 1942, da of late Alfred Basil Loder; *d* 1950; *s* by his son (13) MICHAEL EDWARD OLIVER, TD, 12th Earl *b* 1911; Lt-Col Shropshire Yeo (Comdg 1955-58), 1939-45 War (despatches), Vice Lord-Lieut for Salop 1975-87: *m* 1947, Essex Lucy, da of late Henry Arthur Cholmondeley (*see* B Delamere, colls); *d* 1988, *s* by his kinsman (14) ROGER CAVAN (only son of late Frederick Cavan Lambart, only son of late Maj Charles Edward Kilcoursie Lambart, 4th son of late Maj Frederick Richard Henry Lambart, 2nd son of late Com Hon Oliver Matthew Lambart, RN, 2nd son of 7th Earl), 13th Earl and present peer; also Viscount Kilcoursie, and Lord Lambart, Baron of Cavan.

Cavendish, family name of Baron Chesham.

Cavendish, family name of Duke of Devonshire.

Cavendish, family name of Baron Waterpark.

CAVENDISH OF FURNESS, BARON (Cavendish) (Life Baron 1990)

(RICHARD) HUGH CAVENDISH, elder son of late Capt Richard Edward Osborne Cavendish (*see* D Devonshire, colls); *b* 2 Nov 1941; *ed* Eton; High Sheriff Cumbria 1978, DL 1988, Member Cumbria CC 1985-90, and Commn on Historic Buildings and Monuments (English Heritage) 1992-98; a Lord in Waiting to HM 1990-92; Titular Abbot of Furness; Chm Holker Estate Group of Cos since 1971, Morecambe and Lonsdale Conservative Assocn 1975-78, and Chm of Govs St Anne's Sch, Windermere 1983-89; Dir UK Nirex Ltd since 1993; FRSA 1988; *cr Baron Cavendish of Furness*, of Cartmel (Life Baron) 1990: *m* 1970, Grania Mary, da of Brig Toby St George Caulfeild, CBE (*see* V Charlemont, colls), and has issue.

Arms – Sable, three bucks' heads cabossed argent. Crest – A serpent nowed proper.
Seat – Holker Hall, Cark-in-Cartmel, Cumbria LA11 7PL. *Clubs* – Brooks's, White's, Pratt's, Beefsteak.

SON LIVING

Hon Frederick Richard Toby, *b* 1972.

DAUGHTERS LIVING

Hon Lucy Georgiana, *b* 1973.
Hon Emily Moyra, *b* 1980.

CAWDOR, EARL (Campbell) (Earl UK 1827)

COLIN ROBERT VAUGHAN CAMPBELL, 7th Earl, and 25th Thane of Cawdor; *b* 30 June 1962; *s* 1993; *ed* Eton, and St Peter's Coll, Oxford: *m* 1994, Lady Isabella Rachel Stanhope, yst da of 11th Earl of Harrington, and has issue.

Arms – Quarterly of four: 1st or, a stag's head cabossed sable attired gules, *Calder*; 2nd, gyronny of eight, or and sable, *Campbell*; 3rd argent, a lymphad or ancient galley sable, *also Campbell*, 4th per fesse azure and gules, a cross or, *Lort*. Crest – A swan proper, crowned or. Supporters – *Dexter*, a lion guardant gules; *sinister*, a stag proper.
Seat – Cawdor Castle, Nairn.

SON LIVING

JAMES CHESTER (*Viscount Emlyn*), *b* 8 July 1998.

BROTHER LIVING

Hon Frederick William, *b* 1965; *ed* Eton, E Anglia Univ, and Heriot Watt Univ: *m* 1996, Katherine J. M., 3rd da of Richard Barrett, of Dallas, Texas. *Residence* – 13 Prince's Rd, Harfield Village, Claremont, 7700 Cape Town, S Africa.

SISTERS LIVING

Lady Emma Clare, *b* 1958: *m* 1983, David Marrian, son of Peter Marrian, of Nairobi, and has issue living, Jack Alexander Wolf, *b* 1985, — Hunter James, *b* 1988, — Finlay David, *b* 1991. *Address* – PO Box 45465, Nairobi, Kenya.
Lady Elizabeth (Liza) CAMPBELL *b* 1959; has resumed her maiden name: *m* 1990, William Robert Charles Athill, 3rd son of Maj Andrew Athill, Royal Norfolk Regt, of The Cottage, Morston, Norfolk, and has issue living, Atticus Ocean, *b* 1992, — Storm (a da), *b* 1990. *Residence* – 14 Almeric Rd, SW11.
Lady Laura Jane, *b* 1966. *Residence* – Flat 5, 60 St Stephen's Gdns, W2 5NJ.

UNCLE LIVING (*son of 5th Earl*)

Hon James Alexander, *b* 1942; *ed* Eton; ARCA: *m* 1st, 1964 (*m diss* 1973), Brigid Carol Dolben, da of late Capt Patrick Owen Lyons, RA; 2ndly, 1973 (*m diss* 1986), Ann Elizabeth, da of late Col Argyle Henry Gillmore, OBE, and has issue living (by 1st *m*), Slaine Catherine, *b* 1966, — Cara Jenny, *b* 1968, — (by 2nd *m*), Lucy Georgia Elizabeth, *b* 1973, — Sarah Ann, *b* 1977. The Hon James Campbell also has issue, Isabella Grace, *b* 1994.

MOTHER LIVING

Cathryn, 2nd da of late Maj-Gen Sir (William) Robert Norris Hinde, KBE, CB, DSO, of Shrewton House, Shrewton, Salisbury, Wilts: *m* 1957 (*m diss* 1979), as his 1st wife, the 6th Earl Cawdor, who *d* 1993. *Residences* – 30 Rawlings St, SW3 2LS; Kennt House, Ramsbury, nr Marlborough SN8 2QN.

WIDOW LIVING OF SIXTH EARL

Countess ANGELIKA (*Dowager Countess Cawdor*), da of Count Prokop Lazansky von Bukowa: *m* 1979, as his 2nd wife, the 6th Earl Cawdor, who *d* 1993. *Residence* – Cawdor Castle, Nairn IV12 5RD.

COLLATERAL BRANCHES LIVING

Issue of late Lt-Col Hon Ralph Alexander Campbell, CBE, 3rd son of 3rd Earl, *b* 1877, *d* 1945: *m* 1st, 1906, Marjorie Theophila, who *d* 1911, da of Sir John Arthur Fowler, 2nd Bt; 2ndly, 1914, Marjorie Edith, who *d* 1984, da of Horace George Devas:—
(By 2nd *m*) David Archibald, CBE, TD, *b* 1915; *ed* Eton, and Trin Hall, Camb; FRICS; is Lt-Col and Brevet Col late Berks Yeo; OBE (Mil) 1954, CBE (Civil) 1988. *Residence* – Paxton House, Bucklebury, Reading, Berks. —— Angus Mervyn, TD, *b* 1918; *ed* Eton; late Maj Surrey Yeo; 1939-45 War (despatches): *m* 1950, Rosemary Madeline Hamilton, only da of Hugh Alastair Hamilton Fraser (D Somerset, colls), and has issue living, Ian Angus Ralph (Church House, Aldworth Rd, Compton, Newbury, Berks RG20 6RD), *b* 1951; *ed* Bradfield: *m* 1984, Jacqueline, da of John Jowett, and has issue living, Edward Alastair Ian *b* 1988, Frederick Hugh *b* 1990, Laura Beatrice *b* 1995, — *Rev* James Malcolm (Holy Cross Vicarage, Binsted, Alton, Hants GU34 4NX), *b* 1955; *ed* Eton, RAC Cirencester, and Wycliffe Hall, Oxford; ordained 1991: *m* 1984, Mary, eldest da of John Rolston, and has issue living, John (Jack) Alexander *b* 1988, Harry David *b* 1990, Chloe Elizabeth *b* 1992, Alice Violet *b* 1994, — Catherine Rosemary, *b* 1964. *Residence* – Wasing Lodge, Aldermaston, Reading, Berks RG7 4LZ. —— Rosemary Edith, *b* 1921. *Residence* – Pond Cottage, Padworth Common, Reading, Berks RG7 4QG.

Issue of late Hon Elidor Ronald Campbell, 4th son of 3rd Earl, *b* 1881, *d* 1957: *m* 1913, Violet, who *d* 1975, da of Octavius Edward Bulwer-Marsh, of Bryngwyn Manor, Raglan, Monmouthshire:—
Fiona Mary, *b* 1925: *m* 1973, Iain Alastair MacDonald. *Residence* – 2 Blaen-y-Myarth, Llangynidr, nr Crickhowell, Powys.

Grandsons of late Capt Hon Ronald George Elidor Campbell, 2nd son of 2nd Earl:—
Issue of late Lt-Col Robert Campbell, DSO, *b* 1878, *d* 1945: *m* 1926, Mary Emelda, who *d* 1979, da of late William Robert Wood:—
Robin John Ronald, *b* 1927; *ed* Eton; Maj (ret) Queen's Own Highlanders; Malaya 1951 (despatches): *m* 1954, Alison Barbara Rose, da of late Major Horace Cave-Browne (*see* Cave-Browne-Cave, Bt, colls), and has issue living, Ian Robert, *b* 1956; *ed* abroad; Northern Constabulary, — James Farquhar Robin (Old Cowpastures Farm House, Hook Norton, Oxon), *b* 1958; *ed* Gordonstoun; late Capt Queen's Own Highlanders: *m* 1985, Marina Caroline Vere, elder da of late Maj Charles Pepler Norton, of Coldstone House, Ascott-under-Wychwood, Oxon (*see* Ogilvy, Bt, colls), and has issue living, Guy James Farquhar *b* 1991, Hugh Robin Farquhar *b* 1997, Ishbel Elizabeth Rose *b* 1988, Isla Sophia Rose *b* (twin) 1997. *Residence* – Kinrara, Aviemore, Inverness-shire. —— Alan, *b* 1929; *ed* Eton; Lt-Col (ret) Queen's Own Highlanders (formerly The Cameronians) (Scottish Rifles); Malaya 1952 (despatches): *m* 1963, Sylvia, da of late Richard Hermon, CBE, and has issue living, Alexander, *b* 1964; *ed* Eton, — James, *b* 1967; *ed* Eton; Capt Queen's Own Highlanders, — Andrew, *b* 1969; *ed* Eton, — Nicholas, *b* 1971; *ed* The King's Sch, Ely, — Theresa Ann, *b* 1965. *Residence* – Crossways House, Bartlow, Cambridge.

Grandson of late Capt Hon Alexander Francis Henry Campbell, 3rd son of 2nd Earl:—
Issue of late Major Duncan Elidor Campbell, DSO, *b* 1880, *d* 1930: *m* 1914, Hon Florence Evelyne Willey, who *d* 1978, da of 1st Baron Barnby:—
Ian Robert, CB, CBE, AFC, *b* 1920; *ed* Eton; Air Vice-Marshal RAF (ret); Ch of Staff, No 18 Gp RAF 1973-75; 1939-45 War in Middle East, Italy, and Germany (prisoner); CBE (Mil) 1964; CB (Mil) 1976: *m* 1st, 1953, Beryl Evelyn, who *d* 1982, da of late Brig Thomas Kennedy Newbigging, MC; 2ndly, 1984, Mrs Elisabeth Owen, yst da of Maj Richard Kennedy Lingard-Guthrie (*see* B Maclean, colls, 1980 Edn), and formerly wife of Tim Owen, of Fifield, Glos, and has issue living (by 1st *m*), Alister Neil, *b* 1955; *ed* Eton: *m* 1982, Ceril Diana, only da of A. Barnato-Kahan, of 12 Grove Court, Drayton Gardens, SW10, and has issue living, Rory Dominic Alexander *b* 1987, Arabella Louise Evelyn *b* 1984. *Residence* – Pike Farm, Fossebridge, Cheltenham, Glos. *Clubs* – Boodle's, RAF.

PREDECESSORS – Pryse Campbell, MP (a descendant of Sir John Campbell, 3rd son of 2nd Earl of Argyll), had with other issue (1) JOHN, MP for Nairnshire 1777-80 and for Cardigan 1780-96; *cr* Baron Cawdor (peerage of Great Britain) 1796; *d* 1821; *s* by his son (2) JOHN FREDERICK, FRS, DD, 2nd Baron; *b* 1790; *cr* Viscount Emlyn and Earl Cawdor (peerage of United Kingdom) 1827: *m* 1816, Lady Elizabeth Thynne, da of 2nd Marquess of Bath; *d* 1860; *s* by his son (3) JOHN FREDERICK VAUGHAN, 2nd Earl, *b* 1817, MP for Pembrokeshire (LC) 1841-59; Lord-Lieut of Carmarthenshire: *m* 1842, Sarah Mary, who *d* 1881, da of late Gen Hon Henry Frederick Compton Cavendish (D Devonshire); *d* 1898; *s* by his el son (4) FREDERICK ARCHIBALD VAUGHAN, PC, 3rd Earl, *b* 1847; Chm of Great Western Railway 1895-1905, and Lord-Lieut of Pembroke 1896-1911; MP for Carmarthenshire (C) 1874-85; First Lord of the Admiralty 1905: *m* 1868, Edith Georgina, who *d* 1926, el da of late Christopher Turnor, of Stoke Rochford; *d* 1911; *s* by his el son (5) HUGH FREDERICK VAUGHAN, 4th Earl, *b* 1870: *m* 1898, Joan Emily Mary, who *d* 1945, da of John Charles Thynne (*see* M Bath, colls); *d* 1914; *s* by his el son (6) JOHN DUNCAN VAUGHAN, 5th Earl, *b* 1900; Lt-Col Queen's Own Cameron Highlanders (TA); Chm Historic Buildings Council for Scotland; FSA: *m* 1st, 1929 (*m diss* 1961), Wilma Mairi, who *d* 1982, el da of late Vincent C. Vickers, of 38 Prince's Gate, SW7; 2ndly, 1961, Elizabeth, who *d* 1985, da of J. Topham Richardson, JP, of Harps Oak, Merstham, Surrey, and widow of Maj Sir Alexander Penrose Gordon Cumming, 5th Bt, MC; *d* 1970; *s* by his elder son (7) HUGH JOHN VAUGHAN, 6th Earl, *b* 1932; FSA, FRICS, FRSA, High Sheriff Carmarthenshire 1964: *m* 1st, 1957 (*m diss* 1979), Cathryn, 2nd da of late Maj-Gen Sir (William) Robert Norris Hinde, KBE, CB, DSO; 2ndly, 1979, Countess Angelika, da of Count Prokop Lazansky von Bukowa; *d* 1993; *s* by his elder son (8) COLIN ROBERT VAUGHAN, 7th Earl and present peer; also Viscount Emlyn, and Baron Cawdor.

CAWLEY, BARON (Cawley) (Baron UK 1918, Bt UK 1906)

I desire, I believe, I have

FREDERICK LEE CAWLEY, 3rd Baron, and 3rd Baronet; *b* 27 July 1913; *ed* Eton, and New Coll, Oxford (MA); Bar Lincoln's Inn 1938; Capt RA (Leics Yeo), 1939-45 War (wounded); Dep Chm of Cttees, House of Lords 1958-67: *m* 1944, Rosemary Joan, da of late Reginald Edward Marsden (*see* V Dillon, 1990 Edn), and has issue.

Arms – Sable, three swans heads erased argent, guttée de poix, a chief arched or, thereon a rose gules, barbed and seeded proper, between two garbs azure. Crest – Upon a mount vert, a swan's head erased argent between six bullrushes stalked and leaved, three on either side, or. Supporters – On either side a swan, wings surgeant tergiant argent, guttée de poix, each standing upon a garb fessewise or.
Seat – Berrington Hall, Leominster. *Residence* – Bircher Hall Leominster, Herefordshire, HR6 0AX.

SONS LIVING

Hon JOHN FRANCIS (Castle Grounds, Ashton, Leominster, Herefordshire HR60 DN), *b* 28 Sept 1946; *ed* Eton, *m* 1979, Regina Sarabia, el da of the late Marqués de Hazas, of Madrid, and has issue living, William Robert Harold, *b* 2 July 1981, — Thomas Frederick José-Luis, *b* 1982, — Andrew David, *b* 1988, — Susan Mary, *b* 1980.

Hon William Frederick, *b* 1947; *ed* Eton, and New Coll, Oxford (MA): *m* 1979 (*m diss* 1988), Philippa J., el da of Philip Hoare, DFC, of The Playle, Weycombe Rd, Haslemere, Surrey, and has issue living, Edward Frederick, *b* 1980, — Elizabeth Lena, *b* 1982.

Hon Richard Kenneth, *b* 1949; *ed* Eton, Durham Univ (BA), and City Univ Business Sch (MBA); MBIM: *m* 1976, Tsugumi, 2nd da of S. Ota, of Takarazuka, Japan.

Hon Justin Robert, *b* 1953; *ed* Milton Abbey Sch: *m* 1986 (*m diss* 1995), Margaret Lee Greatorex-Davies. *Residence* – 24 Malta Close, Popley, Basingstoke, Hants RG24 9PD.

Hon Charles Michael, *b* 1955; *ed* Milton Abbey Sch, and Manchester Univ (BA): *m* 1980 (*m diss* 1987), Justine J., da of J. F. B. Parry, of Hockley, Essex.

Hon Mark Andrew, *b* 1957; *ed* Eton, New Coll, Oxford (MA), and INSEAD (MBA).

DAUGHTER LIVING

Hon Vanessa Mary, *b* 1951; BA Open Univ: *m* 1971, Dr John Anthony Marston, of Gorwell House, Barnstaple, N Devon, and has issue living, Cicely Alice, *b* 1973, — Emma Elizabeth, *b* 1975, — Camilla Vere, *b* 1977, — Annabel Sarah, *b* 1979.

WIDOW LIVING OF SON OF SECOND BARON

Iris Edrica, da of late Reginald Edward Marsden (*see* V Dillon, 1990 Edn): *m* 1952, Hon Stephen Robert Cawley, who *d* 1995, and has issue (see colls, infra).

COLLATERAL BRANCH LIVING

Issue of late Hon Stephen Robert Cawley, yr son of 2nd Baron, *b* 1915, *d* 1995: *m* 1952, Iris Edrica (ante), da of late Reginald Edward Marsden (*see* V Dillon, 1990 Edn):—
Robin Alexander, *b* 1954; *ed* Eton: *m* 1982, Roslyn, only da of George Latham, of Newport, Gwent, and has issue living, Hugh Edward, *b* 1984, — Timothy James, *b* 1987. —— James Edward, *b* 1956: *m* 1984, Mary Fiona, only da of Lt-Cdr E. J. Wright, of Elm House, Ampleforth, York, and has issue living, Joseph Edward John, *b* 1989. —— Martin Harold, *b* 1959. —— Yoland Diana, *b* 1957: *m* 1988, Prof Mark Jonathan Dodgson, of Australian Nat Univ.

PREDECESSORS – **(1)** *Rt Hon* FREDERICK Cawley, PC, son of late Thomas Cawley, of Priestland, Cheshire; *b* 1850; Chancellor of the Duchy of Lancaster in National Min 1916-18; MP for Prestwich Div of Lancashire (SE) (*L*) 1895-1918; *cr a Baronet* 1906, and *Baron Cawley*, of Prestwich, co Palatine of Lancaster (peerage of United Kingdom) 1918: *m* 1876, Elizabeth, who *d* 1930, da of John Smith, of Kynsal Lodge, Audlem; *d* 1937; *s* by his son **(2)** ROBERT HUGH, 2nd Baron, *b* 1877; S Africa 1900-01: *m* 1912, Vivienne, who *d* 1978 (aged 100), da of Harold Lee, of Broughton Park, Manchester; *d* 1954; *s* by his son **(3)** FREDERICK LEE, 3rd Baron and present peer.

CAYZER, BARONY OF (Cayzer) (Extinct 1999)

(WILLIAM) NICHOLAS CAYZER, *Life Baron* and 2nd *Baronet*; *d* 1999, when the Life Peerage and the Baronetcy became extinct.

DAUGHTERS LIVING OF LIFE BARON

Hon Nichola, *b* 1937: *m* 1956, Michael Keith Beale Colvin, MP, late Lieut Gren Gds, and has issue living, James Michael Beale CAYZER-COLVIN, *b* 1965: *m* 1992, Esther Anne Mary, adopted da of Michael Tree, of Shute House, Donhead St Mary, Dorset (*see* D Devonshire), and has issue living, Molly Isabella Elizabeth *b* 1995, Lily Georgia Daphne *b* 1999, — Amanda, MBE, *b* 1957; MBE (Civil) 1990: *m* 1985, Rupert Spencer Ponsonby, 2nd son of Sir Ashley Charles Gibbs Ponsonby, 2nd Bt, KCVO, MC, and has issue (*see* Ponsonby, Bt), — Arabella Nichola, *b* 1960: *m* 1983, James Gaggero, only son of Joseph Gaggero, CBE, of King's Yard Lane, Gibraltar, and has issue living, Nicholas James *b* 1985, Alexander Charles *b* 1987. *Residences* – 73 Westminster Gdns, SW1; Tangley House, nr Andover, Hants.

Hon Elizabeth, *b* 1946: *m* 1992, Nigel Christopher Gilmour, MD.

Cayzer, family name of Baron Rotherwick.

Cecil, family name of Baron Amherst of Hackney.

Cecil, family name of Marquess of Exeter.

Cecil, family name of Baron Rockley.

Cecil, Gascoyne-, family name of Marquess of Salisbury.

Cecil, Baron; title of Viscount Cranborne on Roll of HL.

CHADLINGTON, BARON (Gummer) (Life Baron 1996)

PETER SELWYN GUMMER, son of late Rev Canon Selwyn Gummer, of Winston Grange, Debenham, Suffolk; *b* 24 Aug 1942; *ed* King's Sch, Rochester, and Selwyn Coll, Camb (BA 1964, MA 1971), FRSA, FInstD, FIPR, Fell Inst of Marketing; Portsmouth and Sunderland Newspaper Group 1964-65, Viyella International 1965-66, Hodgkinson & Partners 1966-67, Industrial & Commercial Finance Corporation (later 3i Group) 1967-74; Chm Shandwick International plc since 1974; Non-executive Dir CIA Group PLC 1990-94, and Halifax Building Soc since 1994 (Non-exec Dir London Board 1990-94); Non-exec Member NHS Policy Board 1991-95, Arts Council of Great Britain 1991-94, Arts Council of England 1994-96 (Chm Arts Council Lottery Board until 1996); Chm Understanding Industry Trust 1991-95 and Royal Opera House 1996-97; *cr Baron Chadlington*, of Dean, co Oxon (Life Baron) 1996: *m* 1982, Lucy Rachel, da of late Antony Ponsonby Dudley-Hill, of Sandle Manor, Fordingbridge, Hants, and has issue.

Arms – Gules a cross potent nowy quadrate argent between four escallops fukes inwards or. Crest – A cock wings elevated and addorsed or beaked combed jelloped and legged gules grasping in the dexter claws a lily of the valley argent slipped and leaved or. Supporters – On either side a falcon reguardant argent beaked and legged gules belled or and holding in the beak a rose gules barbed seeded slipped and leaved or.
Address – c/o Shandwick International plc, 61 Grosvenor St, W1X 9DA. *Clubs* – Garrick, MCC, Carlton.

SON LIVING

Hon James, *b* 1990.

DAUGHTERS LIVING

Hon Naomi, *b* 1984.
Hon Chloe, *b* 1985.
Hon Eleanor, *b* 1988.

CHALFONT, BARON (Gwynne Jones) (Life Baron 1964)

Arms yield to the toga

ALUN ARTHUR GWYNNE JONES, OBE, MC, PC, son of Arthur Gwynne Jones, of Cwmbran, Newport, Mon; *b* 5 Dec 1919; *ed* W Monmouth Sch; Brevet Lt-Col (ret) S Wales Borderers (Regular Army Officer 1940-61); Defence and Mil correspondent, *The Times* 1961-64; Min of State, Foreign Office 1964-70, and British Permanent Representative to WEU 1969-70; 1939-45 War in Burma (MC); *cr*, OBE (Mil) 1961, PC 1964, and *Baron Chalfont*, of Llantarnam, co Monmouth (Life Baron) 1964: *m* 1948, Mona, MB, ChB, da of Harry Douglas Mitchell, of Grimsby.

Arms – Gules a sword point downwards proper pommel and hilt or within an orle of two branches of olive fructed gold. Crest – A dragon sejant gules supporting a column sable charged with nine bars argent, the capital also argent. Supporters – *Dexter*, a private of the Grenadier Company, 24th Foot (South Wales Borderers) in the uniform of circa 1751, supporting with the exterior hand a bamboo cane leaved proper; *sinister*, a herald vested in a tabard of the arms proper and holding in the exterior hand a sprig of olive fructed or.
Address – House of Lords, SW1A 0PW. *Clubs* – Garrick, City Livery, MCC.

CHALKER OF WALLASEY, BARONESS (Landa) (Life Baroness 1992)

LYNDA CHALKER, PC, da of late Sidney Henry James Bates; *b* 29 April 1942; *ed* Roedean, Heidelberg Univ, Westfield Coll, London, and Central London Poly; Statistician, Research Bureau Ltd (subsidiary of Unilever) 1963-69, Market Researcher Shell Mex and BP Ltd 1969-72, Chief Exec of Internat Div Louis Harris Internat 1972-74; Chm Greater London Young Conservatives 1969-70, National Vice-Chm 1970-71; Member BBC Gen Advisory Cttee 1975-79; Parly Under Sec of State Dept of Health and Social Security 1979-82, Transport 1982-83, Min of State Transport 1983-86, and FCO 1986, Dep Foreign Sec 1987-89, Min of State FCO and Min Overseas Devpt 1989-97; Advisory Dir Unilever plc since 1998, Non-Exec Dir Freeplay since 1997, Non-Exec Dir Landell Mills Ltd since 1999, Non-Exec Dir Capital Shopping Centres since 1997, Advisor on Africa and Development to Business and Governments, The World Bank and The Global Coalition on Africa; MP Wallasey (*C*) 1974-92; *cr* PC 1987, and *Baroness Chalker of Wallasey*, of Leigh-on-Sea, co Essex (Life Baroness) 1992: *m* 1st, 1967 (*m diss* 1973), Eric Robert Chalker; 2ndly, 1981, Clive Landa.
Address – c/o House of Lords, SW1A 0PW.

Chaloner, family name of Baron Gisborough.

CHAMPION, BARONY OF (Champion) (Extinct 1985)

DAUGHTER LIVING OF LIFE BARON

Hon Barbara, *b* 1931: *m* 1957, Trevor Chubb. *Residence* – 160 Redland Rd, Redland, Bristol, BS6 6YG.

WIDOW LIVING OF LIFE BARON

MARY EMMA (*Baroness Champion*) (22 Lanelay Terr, Pontypridd, Mid Glamorgan CF37 1ER), da of William Williams: *m* 1930, Baron Champion, PC (Life Baron), who *d* 1985.

CHANDOS, VISCOUNT (Lyttelton) (Viscount UK 1954)

Do what must be done, come what may

THOMAS ORLANDO LYTTELTON, 3rd Viscount; *b* 12 Feb 1953; *s* 1980; *ed* Eton, and Worcester Coll, Oxford (BA): *m* 1985, Arabella Sarah Lucy, da of John Adrian Bailey (*see* E Haddington), and has issue.

𝔄rms – Argent, a chevron between three escallops sable a cross moline for difference. ℭrest – A Moor's head in profile couped at the shoulders proper, wreathed round the temples argent and sable. 𝔖upporters – On either side a merman proper holding in the outer hand a trident pendant from a rope around the inner shoulder an escutcheon or charged with a pile gules.
Residence – 149 Gloucester Av, NW1.

SONS LIVING

Hon OLIVER ANTONY, *b* 21 Feb 1986. ⸺ *Hon* Benedict, *b* 1988.

DAUGHTER LIVING

Hon Rosanna Mary, *b* 1990.

BROTHER LIVING

Hon Matthew Peregrine Antony, *b* 1956; *ed* Eton, and Trin Coll, Camb (BA): *m* 1988, Gillian N. Rudd, and has issue living, Thomas Ivan, *b* 1988, — Joshua Anthony, *b* 1991. *Residence* – 43 High St, Hallaton, Market Harborough, Leics LE16 8UD.

SISTERS LIVING

Hon Laura Katharine, *b* 1950; *ed* Cranborne Chase Sch, St Anne's Coll, Oxford (BA), and London Univ (BSc).
Hon Deborah Clare, *b* 1963.

UNCLE LIVING (*Son of 1st Viscount*)

Hon (Nicholas) Adrian Oliver, *b* 1937; *ed* Eton: *m* 1960, Margaret, who *d* 1993, da of late Sir Harold Hobson, the drama critic, and has issue living, Francis Sebastian Jasper, *b* 1967, — Celia Melissa Francesca, *b* 1960: *m* 1985, Dr Andrew Rae, eldest son of John Rae, of Brook House, Johannesburg. *Residence* – 79 Oxford Gdns, W10.

AUNT LIVING (*Daughter of 1st Viscount*).

Hon Rosemary (*Viscountess Chaplin*), *b* 1922: *m* 1951, as his 2nd wife, 3rd Viscount Chaplin, who *d* 1981. *Residence* – Flat 7, 15 Pembridge Sq, W2 4EH.

WIDOW LIVING OF SECOND VISCOUNT

CAROLINE MARY (*Hon Mrs David Erskine*), da of late Rt Hon Sir Alan Frederick Lascelles, GCVO, KCB, CMG, MC (*see* E Harewood, colls): *m* 1st, 1949, the 2nd Viscount, who *d* 1980; 2ndly, 1985, as his 2nd wife, Hon David Hervey Erskine, of Felsham House, Felsham, Bury St Edmunds, Suffolk, brother of 13th Earl of Mar and Kellie.

PREDECESSORS – (1) Rt Hon OLIVER LYTTELTON, KG, DSO, MC, PC, son of late Rt Hon Alfred Lyttelton, KC, MP, 8th son of 4th Baron Lyttelton (V Cobham), *b* 1893; Pres of Board of Trade 1940-41 and 1945, Min of State Cairo and Member of War Cabinet 1941, Min of Production 1942-45, and Sec of State for Colonies, of Aldershot, co Southampton (peerage of UK) 1954: *m* 1920, Lady Moira Godolphin Osborne, who *d* 1976, da of 10th Duke of Leeds; *d* 1972; *s* by his son (2) ANTONY ALFRED, 2nd Viscount, *b* 1920: *m* 1949, Caroline Mary, who *m* 2ndly, 1985, as his 2nd wife, Hon David Hervey Erskine, of Felsham House, Felsham, Bury St Edmunds, Suffolk (*see* E Mar and Kellie), da of late Rt Hon Sir Alan Frederick Lascelles, GCVO, KCB, CMG, MC (*see* E Harewood, colls); *d* 1980; *s* by his el son (3) THOMAS ORLANDO, 3rd Viscount and present peer.

Channon, family name of Baron Kelvedon.

CHAPLIN, VISCOUNTCY OF (Chaplin) (Extinct 1981)

DAUGHTERS LIVING OF THIRD VISCOUNT (*By 1st marriage*)

Hon (Oenone) Clarissa, *b* 1934: *m* 1958, Michael Charles Deane Luke, son of late Sir Harry Charles Luke, KCMG, and has issue living, Igor Charles de Zander, *b* 1965, — Chloe Oleanda Alvilde, *b* 1959, — Œnone Jemima, *b* 1960: *m* 1992, Richard C. Gladstone, of via Lombarda 355, Lammari, Lucca 55013, Italy, son of David Gladstone, of Menai Bridge, Anglesey, — Cressida Eugénie, *b* 1961. *Residence* – 22 Eaton Sq, SW1.

(*By 2nd marriage*)

Hon Miranda Amadea, *b* 1956: *m* 1980, Brian Corran, and has issue living, Hereward, *b* 1981, — George, *b* 1989.

Hon Christina Susanna, *b* 1958.

WIDOW LIVING OF THIRD VISCOUNT

Hon Rosemary (*Viscountess Chaplin*), da of 1st Viscount Chandos: *m* 1951, as his 2nd wife, the 3rd Viscount Chaplin, who *d* 1981, when the title became ext. *Residence* – Flat 7, 15 Pembridge Sq, W2 4EH.

Chapman, family name of Baron Northfield.

CHAPPLE, BARON (Chapple) (Life Baron 1985)

FRANCIS (FRANK) JOSEPH CHAPPLE, son of Frank Chapple, of Shoreditch, by his wife Emily, da of Joseph Rook, of Hoxton; *b* Aug 1921; *ed* elementary sch; Member Electrical Trade Union Confederation 1937-83; Shop Steward and Branch Official; Member Exec Council 1958; Assist Gen Sec 1963-66; Gen Sec Electrical, Electronic, Telecommunication and Plumbing Union 1966-83; Member Gen Council of TUC 1971-83 (Chm 1982-83), Member Labour Party Exec; Gold Badge of Congress 1983; *cr Baron Chapple*, of Hoxton, Greater London (Life Baron) 1985: *m* 1944, Joan Jeanette, who *d* 1994, da of James Nicholls, and has issue.
Address – c/o Electrical, Electronic, Telecommunication and Plumbing Union, Hayes Court, West Common Rd, Bromley BR2 7AU.

SONS LIVING

Hon Roger Francis, *b* 1947; *ed* Brooke House Comprehensive Sch: *m* 1969, Susan Audrey, da of Charles F. W. Brown.

Hon Barry Joseph, *b* 1951; *ed* Hawes Down Comprehensive Sch: *m* 1980, Angela Christine, da of Kenneth R. Medgett.

CHARLEMONT, VISCOUNT (Caulfeild) (Viscount I 1665)
(Title pronounced "Char-le-mont")

DEO DUCE FERRO COMITANTE

God my leader, the sword my companion

JOHN DAY CAULFEILD, 14th Viscount; *b* 19 March 1934; *s* 1985: *m* 1st, 1964, Judith Ann, who *d* 1971, da of late James E. Dodd, of Islington, Ontario; 2ndly, 1972, Janet Evelyn, da of late Orville R. Nancekivell, of Mount Elgin, Ontario, and has issue by 1st *m*.

Arms – Quarterly, 1st and 4th, barry often argent and gules, on a canton of the second a lion passant guardant or, *Caulfeild*; 2nd and 3rd, or, a chevron checky argent and azure between three martlets sable. *Houston.* **Crest** – A dragon's head erased gules, gorged with a bar gemelle argent. **Supporters** – Two dragons gules, wings elevated, each gorged with a bar gemelle argent.
Residence – 820 Burnhamthorpe Rd No 1009, Etobicoke, Ontario, Canada M9C 4W2.

SON LIVING (By 1st marriage)

Hon JOHN DODD, *b* 15 May 1966: *m* 1991, Nadea Stella, da of Wilson Fortin, of 308 Wallenberg Crescent, Mississauga, Ontario, and has issue living, Shane Andrew, *b* 19 May 1996. *Residence* – 3749 Densbury Drive, Mississauga, Ontario, Canada L5N 6Z2.

DAUGHTER LIVING (By 1st marriage)

Hon Janis Ann, *b* 1968.

SISTER LIVING

Edith Jane, *b* 1941: *m* 1963, Edward John Cobean, of 106 Brown's Av, Walkerton, Ontario, Canada N0G 2V0, and has issue living, Robert Edward, *b* 1967, — Stephen John, *b* 1971, — Susan Jane, *b* 1966.

UNCLE LIVING (Brother of 13th Viscount)

Ven Arthur Edward Lampay, CD, *b* 1906; *ed* Bishop's Univ (BA); DD King's Coll, R of Trin Church, Saint John, New Brunswick 1957-73; Chap R Canadian Air Force 1941-51: *m* 1940, Emilie Kathleen Irene, da of Rev Edgar Frank Salmon, DD, of Philadelphia, USA, and has issue living, David Arthur, *b* 1942; BArch, MASc, MRAIC, PEng; architect: *m* 1965, Diane, da of late Frederick Parker Du Vernet, of Ottawa, and has issue living, Sean David *b* 1966, Derek Arthur *b* 1969, — Charles Patrick (883 Safari Rd, Kingston, Ontario K7M 6W2, Canada), *b* 1946; BEng: *m* 1968, Marjorie Agnes, da of late Robert Reid, of Saint John, New Brunswick.

DAUGHTERS LIVING OF TWELFTH VISCOUNT

Hon Dorothy Frances Lucy St George, *b* 1915: *m* 1945, Robert Hender Trowbridge, late Fl-Lt RAAF, who *d* 1993, of Drumcairn, Lane End, Elmstead Market, Essex C07 7BB, and has issue living, Mark Robert, *b* 1947, — Richard Keith Giles, *b* 1950: *m* 1980, Pamela Mary, da of Philip N. Bradshaw, of Gt Driffield, NE Yorks, and has issue living, Laura Frances *b* 1986, Emma Kathryn *b* 1988. *Clubs* – Royal Over-Seas, St James's.
Hon Alicia St George, *b* 1918: *m* 1939, Gp Capt Gordon Hackworth Stuart, MD, RAF, of 3 Lovel Hill, Windsor Forest, Berks, and has issue living, Colin, *b* 1940: *m* 1st, 1965 (*m diss* 1970), Jane Susan, da of Maj Dennis Mitchel, Kings African Rifles; 2ndly, 1981, Eve Lin-Yau, da of Yau Shan Shan, of Peking, and has issue living (by 2nd *m*), Alicia Frances Sarah, *b* 1983.

DAUGHTERS LIVING OF ELEVENTH VISCOUNT

Hon Constance Ada, *b* 1918: *m* 1943, Henry Edward Pearce, of 254 Mooroondu Rd, Thorneside, Queensland 4158, Aust, and has issue living, Edward Charles (44 Dawson Rd, Ormiston Heights, Queensland 4163), *b* 1943; AAIA: *m* 1967, Beverley Ellen Cooper, and has issue living, Rodney Edward *b* 1975, Sandra Ellen *b* 1970: *m* 1995, Andrew Deane Freeman, — Donald John, *b* 1947; BEng: *m* 1971, Rasa Janina Zvirblis, and has issue living, Scott Ramon *b* 1975, Kristie Louise *b* 1977, — Pamela Ann, 1946: *m* 1966, Hendrik Wouter Veenstra, of 18 Gallang St, Rochedale, Qld 4123, Australia, and has two adopted children, Wade Hendrick *b* 1971, Annelies Pamela *b* 1973: *m* 1999, Gary John Cowin, — Janet May, *b* 1950; BEd, — Wendy Roslyn, *b* 1958; DipT: *m* 1998, David Ray.
Hon Janie St George, *b* 1921: *m* 1942, David Dominic Moore, BSc; MIE (Aust), of 30 Maxwell St, Turramurra, Sydney, NSW, and has issue living, Colleen Janie, *b* 1944: *m* 1967, Alan Charles Watts, MB, ChB, LRCP, MRCS, and has issue living, Tracey Colleen *b* 1968, Kellie Mary Jane *b* 1972, Christine Judith *b* 1975, Sarra Alaine *b* 1979, — Margaret Louise, *b* 1947: *m* 1972, Keith Douglas Brodie, LLB, CA, of Sydney, NSW, and has issue living, Barry *b* 1977, Paula Louise *b* 1975, Claire Elizabeth, *b* 1980.

DAUGHTER LIVING OF NINTH VISCOUNT

Hon Patricia St George (55 New Rd, Lewes, E Sussex), *b* 1920; 1939-45 War as 3rd Officer WRNS.

WIDOW LIVING OF THIRTEENTH VISCOUNT

DOROTHY JESSIE (*Dowager Viscountess Charlemont*), da of late Albert Allan Johnston, of Ottawa, Canada: *m* 1930, the 13th Viscount Charlemont, who *d* 1985.

MOTHER LIVING

Edith Evelyn (5, 4th St, Walkerton, Ontario, Canada NOG 2VO), da of Frederick William Day, of Ottawa: *m* 1933, Eric St George Caulfeild, who *d* 1975.

COLLATERAL BRANCHES LIVING

Granddaughter of late Francis John Rothe Toby St George Caulfeild, ISO, MICE, 6th son of Rt Rev Charles Caulfeild, DD, Bishop of Nassau, elder son of late Rev Hans Caulfeild (*d* 1854), son of late Rev Charles Caulfeild, 3rd son of late Rev Hon Charles Caulfeild, 5th son of 2nd Viscount:—
Issue of late Major Harry Frowd St George Caulfeild, *b* 1881, *d* 1961: *m* 1914, Geraldine Marguerite, who *d* 1922, da of Lt-Col Charles Purvis Boyd:—
Geraldine St George (Orchard Leigh, Prinsted, Emsworth, Hants PO10 8HR), *b* 1918: *m* 1st, 1947, Maj Peter Lawry Matthews, TD, RASC, who *d* 1970; 2ndly, 1975, Hugh Alan Mason, who *d* 1992, and has issue living (by 1st *m*), Toby St George, *b* 1950, — Helen Brontë, *b* 1953: *m* 1st, 1980 (*m diss* 1988), Charles Koller, of California, USA; 2ndly, 1989, Phillip Warren Kunz, and has issue living (by 2nd *m*), Sarah Kaitlyn *b* 1990.

Grandson of late Capt Alfred Hans Waring Caulfeild, MB, only son of late Hans James Caulfeild (infra):—
Issue of late Evan Michael St George Caulfeild, *b* 1918, *d* 1993: *m* 1948, Shirley Joyce, who *d* 1995, da of Harry Scutt Burt, of Richmond Hill, Ontario, Canada:—
Toby Michael Hans, *b* 1949; *ed* Univ of Toronto (BA and BEd). *Residence* – Apt 1810 7 Jackes Av, Toronto, Ont, Canada M4T 1E3

Grandchildren of late Hans James Caulfeild, el son of late Hans Caulfeild, MD, 6th son of Rev Hans Caulfeild (*d* 1854) (ante):—
Issue of late (James) Gordon Caulfeild, *b* 1917, *d* 1975: *m* 1943, Olive (Irene), da of late Thomas Henry Bradley, of Goderich, Ontario:—
Roddy Terence, MD (Tavistock, Ontario, Canada NOB 2RO), *b* 1946; *m* 1969, Patricia Ann Rogers, and has issue living, Stephen Michael, *b* 1972, — Jonathan David, *b* 1975. —— Caroline Diane, *b* 1948: *m* 1969, Peter Stanley Wardell, of 74 Derby Court, Newmarket, Ontario, Canada L3Y 5Z9, and has issue living, Peter Alexander, *b* 1975, — Stephanie Suzanne, *b* 1978.

Grandchildren of late Edwin James Stuart Widdrington Caulfeild, only son (by 2nd *m*) of Cmdr Edwin Toby Caulfeild, RN, el son of Wade Toby Caulfeild (*b* 1732) (infra):—
Issue of late Edwin Vivian Stuart Caulfeild, *b* 1874, *d* 1958: *m* 1903, Edith Helen, who *d* 1966, aged 89, da of Claude L. Ferneley, formerly of Loughborough:—
Stewart Frederick Barry, *b* 1907. —— Leonore Alicia, *b* 1906.

Descendants, if any, of Charles St George Stewart Hanvey Caulfeild (*b* 1874), only son of late Charles Caulfeild, only son of late Rev Abraham St George Caulfeild, DD, Rector of Windsor, 7th son of Rev Hans Caulfeild (*d* 1854) (ante).

Grandchildren of late Vice-Adm Francis Wade Caulfeild, CBE, elder son of late Francis William Caulfeild, only son (by 2nd *m*) of Rev Edward Warren Caulfeild, yr son of Wade Toby Caulfeild (*b* 1732), el son of Col William Caulfeild, 2nd son of Hon Toby Caulfeild, 3rd son of 1st Viscount:—
Issue of late Wade Toby Caulfeild, *b* 1902, *d* 1991: *m* 1935, Philippa Mary, who *d* 1996, da of Capt H. C. R. Brocklebank, of Charlton House, Shaftesbury, Dorset:—
James Alexander Toby, *b* 1937; *ed* Eton, and New Coll, Oxford; late 2nd Lieut KRRC. *m* 1976, Diana Penelope, da of Col Martin Pound, RM, and has issue living, Harriet Katharine, *b* 1980, — Victoria Louise, *b* 1982, — Charlotte Frances, *b* 1984, — Sophie Elizabeth, *b* 1987. *Residence* – Hookland, Redford, Midhurst, Sussex. —— Charlotte Antonia, *b* 1939: *m* 1975, Rev David Burton Evans, Rector of St Michael's, Cornhill, EC3. *Residence* – 59 Walcot Sq, Kennington, SW11 4UB.

Granddaughter of late Col Robert Caulfeild, 2nd son of Lt-Col John Caulfeild, el son of Col William Caulfeild (*d* 1831), el son of Ven John Caulfeild, 2nd son of Col William Caulfeild (ante):—
Issue of late Col Gordon Napier Caulfeild, DSO, *b* 1862, *d* 1922: *m* 1902, Mildred, who *d* 1963, yst da of Philip O'Reilly, DL, of Colamber, Westmeath:—
Irene Mildred, *b* 1909; a Nun at St Cecilia's Abbey, Ryde, Isle of Wight.

Granddaughter of late Brig-Gen Charles Trevor Caulfeild, CMG, 3rd son of late Col Robert Caulfeild (ante):—
Issue of late John Trevor Caulfeild, b 1908, d 1968: m 1948, Elisabeth Allie Madeleine, who d 1968, da of late Gerard de Mestral, of Berne and Mont sur Rolle, Switzerland:—
Catherine Norah (28 New Close, Knebworth, Herts SG3 6NU), b 1949: m 1985, Nicholas William Hall, yr son of Francis George Hall, of Sharmans How, Digswell, Hertfords, and has issue living, Andrew Nicholas Francis William, b 1988, — Clare Elisabeth Alexandra, b 1987.

Grandchildren of late Brig-Gen James Edward Wilmot Smyth Caulfeild, CMG, 2nd son of Rev William Caulfeild, only son of Commodore Thomas Gordon Caulfeild, 2nd son of the Ven John Caulfeild (ante):—
Issue of late Col St George Frederick Gordon Caulfeild, RM, b 1881, d 1973: m 1917, Eila Rosslyn, who d 1973, da of Reginald John, of Colombo:—
Toby St George, CBE, b 1919; ed Wellington, Brig (reg), late RA; MBE (Mil) 1952, CBE (Mil) 1974: m 1st, 1942 (m diss 1951), Mary, da of late Sir William Lindsay Murphy, KCMG; 2ndly, 1959, Agnes Sheila, da of Edward Buckmaster Robinson, of Tankerton, Kent, and has issue living (by 1st m), Toby John St George (Newlands Grange, Shotley Bridge, Consett, co Durham), b 1943: m 1st, 1967, Gillian, da of C. M. Rhead; 2ndly, 1980, Joanna, da of Arthur R. Yates Hunter, of Saskatoon, Canada, and has issue living (by 1st m), Patrick William St George b 1968, — Grania Mary (Baroness Cavendish of Furness), b 1947: m 1970, Baron Cavendish of Furness (Life Baron), of Holker Hall, Cark-in-Cartmel, Cumbria.

Issue of late Lt-Col Wilmot Smyth Caulfeild, MC, RA, b 1887, d 1980: m 1st 1923, Meredith de Lisle, who d 1924, yr da of late Reginald John, of Merryworth Lawn, Wrotham; 2ndly, 1928, Shellah, who d 1992, da of late John J. Bevan, of Dublin:—
(By 1st m) Pamela Ann de Lisle, b 1924; a JP of Shropshire: m 1st, 1944 (m diss 1970), Maj Philip Hugh Godsal, 52nd LI, who d 1982; 2ndly, 1970, Capt Walter Edward Browning Godsal, RN, of Edbrooke, Winsford, Som (yr brother of her 1st husband), and has issue living (by 1st m), Philip Caulfeild (Iscoyd Park, Whitchurch, Shropshire), b 1945; ed Eton; High Sheriff Clwyd 1993; FRICS; Land Agent: m 1st, 1969 (m diss 1985), Lucinda Mary, da of late Lt-Cdr Percival Royston Dancey, RNVR, of Old Shalesbrook, Forest Row, Sussex; 2ndly, 1986, Mrs Selina Baber, da of Thomas William Brooke-Smith, of Canford Cliffs, Dorset, and has issue living (by 1st m), Philip Langley b 1971, Benjamin Rupert Wilmot b 1976, Thomas Henry b 1973 (has issue living, Arthur Benjamin Francis GODSAL b 1997), — David Hugh, MBE, b 1947; ed Eton, and Exeter Univ (BA); Brig late RGJ; MBE (Mil) 1983: m 1971, Tamsin Annette, da of Capt Thomas Keppel Edge-Partington, RN, of Arnoldsfield, Fairfield Rd, Quenington, Cirencester, Glos GL7 5RT, and has issue living, James Keppel b 1977, Jonathan Hugh b 1981, Nicola Jane b 1974, — Rupert Charles, b 1952; ed Eton; Dep Headmaster, Horris Hill Preparatory Sch, Newtown, Newbury, Berks, — Caroline Mary, b 1950: m 1974, Robert Thornewill Miller, of Stowbridge House, Moreton-in-Marsh, Glos, and has issue living, David Robert b 1982, Clare Serena b 1983, — Meredith Jane, b 1956: m 1981, Maj Adam H. C. MacMillan-Scott, MBE, KOSB, son of W. T. R. MacMillan-Scott, of 2 Grove Meadow, Sticklepath, Okehampton, Devon, and has issue living, Katherine Rachel Sarah b 1982, Charlotte Meredith Lucy b 1984, Isobel Sophie de Lisle b 1986. —— (By 2nd m) Eileen Ruth Morley, b 1929: m 1952, Henry Edward Percy, who d 1985, and has issue (see D Northumberland, colls). Residence – Ballygate House, Beccles, Suffolk NR34 9ND. —— Barbara Joan Shellah, b 1932: m 1969, Preston Caradoc Hardinge Mostyn Prichard, of The Croft, Says Lane, Upper Langford, Bristol (see V Hardinge, colls, 1980 Edn), and has issue living, Julian Caulfeild Mostyn, b 1970; ed Milton Abbey, — Diana Mostyn, b 1973.

Grandchildren of late Capt George Blake Caulfeild, yr son of late George Caulfeild, 4th son of Lt-Gen James Caulfeild, CB, yst son of Ven John Caulfeild (ante):—
Issue of late Leslie Alexander Caulfeild, b 1902, d as a result of enemy action 1940: m 1930 (m diss 1936), Jennie Ida, da of late Charles Deering Manson:—
A son, b 193—.

Issue of late William Henry Caulfeild, b 1911, d on active service in Burma 1943: m 1935, Lorna, who d 1998, da of late Cuthbert Wilkinson:—
Anne Marie, b 1941: m 1965, Rupert Alan Travis, of Manor Farmhouse, Glandford, nr Holt, Norfolk NR25 7JP, and has issue living, Benjamin William Norman, b 1973, — Toby Rupert Dale, b 1979, — Amanda Tiffany, b 1972.

PREDECESSORS – (1) Rt Hon Sir TOBY Caulfeild, PC, a distinguished soldier, MP for Armagh 1613, Master of the Ordnance 1614, &c, was cr Lord Caulfeild, Baron of Charlemont (peerage of Ireland) 1620, with remainder to his nephew Sir William Caulfeild, Knt; d unmarried 1627; s by his nephew (2) Sir WILLIAM, 2nd Baron: Master Gen of the Ordnance 1627-34; d 1640; s by his son (3) TOBY, 3rd Baron; when Governor of Charlemont, during the Rebellion of 1641, he was surprised and taken prisoner and subsequently shot by the order of Sir Phelim O'Neile; d unmarried; s by his brother (4) ROBERT, 4th Baron; d 1642, from an over-dose of opium; s by his brother (5) WILLIAM, 5th Baron; apprehended Sir Phelim O'Neile, and had him executed for the murder of his brother the 3rd Baron; cr Viscount Charlemont (peerage of Ireland) 1665; d 1671; s by his son (6) WILLIAM, 2nd Viscount; zealously opposed the cause of James II, by whose parliament he was attainted, but King William, after the rebellion was quelled, gave him a regt of foot and made him Gov of cos Tyrone and Armagh, &c; d 1726; s by his son (7) JAMES, 3rd Viscount, MP for Charlemont 1727; d 1734; s by his son (8) JAMES, KP, 4th Viscount; cr Earl of Charlemont (peerage of Ireland) 1763; was Com in Ch of Vol Army in Ireland 1779; d 1799; s by his son (9) FRANCIS WILLIAM, KP, 2nd Earl, b 1775; a Representative Peer; cr Baron Charlemont (peerage of United Kingdom) 1837, with remainder to his brother: m 1802, Anne, da and co-heir of William Bermingham, of Ross Hill, co Galway; d 1863; s by his nephew (10) JAMES MOLYNEUX, KP, 3rd Earl (son of Hon Henry, 2nd son of 1st Earl), b 1820; Lord-Lieut of co Tyrone; MP for Armagh co (L) 1847-67: m 1st, 1856, Hon Elizabeth Jane Somerville, who d 1882, da of 1st Baron Athlumney; 2ndly, 1883, Anna Lucy, who d 1925, da of the Rev Charles James Lambart; d 1892, when the Earldom (1763) and the Barony (1837) became extinct, and the Peerages of 1620 and 1665 devolved upon his cousin (11) JAMES ALFRED, CB (son of Edward Houston Caulfeild, great-grandson of Rev Hon Charles Caulfeild, 5th son of 2nd Viscount), 7th Viscount, b 1830; Capt Coldstream Guards; served in Crimean War 1854-6; Comptroller of Household to successive Viceroys of Ireland 1868-95; Usher of Black Rod to Order of St Patrick: m 1858, Hon Annette Handcock, who d 1888, da of 3rd Baron Castlemaine; d 1913; s by his nephew (12) JAMES EDWARD, PC (son of late Hon Marcus Piers Francis Caulfeild, brother of 7th Viscount), 8th Viscount, b 1880; Vice-Lieut for co Tyrone 1923-39; a Member of Senate of N Ireland 1925-37, and Min of Education and Leader of the Senate 1926-37: m 1st, 1914 (m diss April 1940), Evelyn, who d as a result of enemy action Oct 1940, da of Edmund Charles Pendleton Hull, of Park Gate House, Ham Common, Surrey; 2ndly, 1940, Hildegarde, who d 1969, da of Rodolphe Slock-Cottell, of Malstapel, Buysselede, Belgium; d 1949; s by his kinsman (13) CHARLES EDWARD ST GEORGE (only son of late Hans St George Caulfeild, 2nd son of late Rt Rev Charles Caulfeild, DD, Bishop of Nassau, el son of Rev Hans Caulfeild, grandson of

Rev Hon Charles Caulfeild, 5th son of 2nd Viscount), 9th Viscount: *m* 1911, Mabel, who *d* 1965, el da of James Hawthorn; *d* 1964; *s* by his kinsman **(14)** ROBERT TOBY ST GEORGE (2nd son of late Henry St George Caulfeild, 1st son of late James Caulfeild, 2nd son of late Rev Hans Caulfeild (ante)), 10th Viscount; *b* 1881; *d* 1967; *s* by his brother **(15)** CHARLES ST GEORGE, 11th Viscount, *b* 1884: *m* 1915, Lydia Clara, who *d* 1973, da of Charles James Kingston, of Aramac; *d* 1971; *s* by his brother **(16)** RICHARD WILLIAM ST GEORGE, 12th Viscount, *b* 1887: *m* 1914, Dorothy Laura, who *d* 1961, da of Frank Giles, ICS; *d* 1979; *s* by his kinsman **(17)** CHARLES WILBERFORCE (el son of the Rev Wilberforce Caulfeild, Rector of St Mary, Kilkenny, 4th son of the Rev Hans Caulfeild (ante)), 13th Viscount, *b* 1899: *m* 1930, Dorothy Jessie, da of late Albert Allan Johnston, of Ottawa, Canada; *d* 1985; *s* by his nephew **(18)** JOHN DAY (son of late Eric St George Caulfeild), 14th Viscount and present peer; also Lord Caulfeild, Baron of Charlemont.

Charteris, family name of Earl of Wemyss.

CHARTERIS OF AMISFIELD, BARON (Charteris) (Life Baron 1978)

Behold my charter

MARTIN MICHAEL CHARLES CHARTERIS, GCB, GCVO, QSO, OBE, PC, yr son of late Capt Hugo Francis Charteris, Lord Elcho, and brother of the 12th Earl of Wemyss and March; *b* 7 Sept 1913; *ed* Eton, and RMC Sandhurst; Lt-Col (ret) KRRC; Private Sec to HM the Queen when HRH Princess Elizabeth 1950-52; Assist Private Sec to HM 1952-72, and Private Sec and Keeper of the Queen's Archives 1972-77; an extra Equerry to HM 1956, and a permanent Lord in Waiting to HM since 1978; Provost of Eton Coll 1978-91; Chm Nat Heritage Memorial Fund 1980-92; a trustee Police Convalescence and Rehabilitation Trust since 1987; Pres Prayer Book Soc since 1987; Grand Officer of the Legion of Honour; 1939-45 War in Middle East; OBE (Mil) 1946, MVO (4th class) 1953, KCVO 1962, PC 1972, KCB (Civil) 1972, GCVO 1976, GCB (Civil) 1977, Royal Victorian Chain 1992; *cr Baron Charteris of Amisfield*, of Amisfield, E Lothian (Life Baron) 1978: *m* 1944, Hon (Mary) Gay Hobart Margesson, da of 1st Viscount Margesson, and has issue.

Arms – Quarterly; 1st and 4th, argent, a fess azure within a double tressure flory counterflory gules, *Charteris*; 2nd and 3rd, or, a lion rampant gules, armed and langued azure, *Wemyss*; over all at the fess point a crescent sable for difference. **Crest** – a dexter hand issuant paleways holding between the thumb and forefinger in bend sinister a pair of sulptor's callipers, all proper. **Supporters** – Dexter, a scribe soberly attired holding in his exterior hand a quill pen proper; *sinister*, an Officer of the King's Royal Rifle Corps in the uniform worn circa 1904, proper.
Residences – 11 Kylestrome House, Cundy St, SW1W 9JT; Wood Stanway House, Wood Stanway, Cheltenham, Glos GL54 5PE.

SONS LIVING

Hon Andrew Martin (11 Grove Rd, Hitchin, Herts), *b* 1947; *ed* Milton Abbey.

Hon Harold Francis (94 Talfourd Rd, SE15 5NZ), *b* 1950; *ed* Eton, and Pembroke Coll, Oxford: *m* 1984, Blandine Marie, elder da of Roger Desmons, of 14 rue Wilhelm, Paris 16me, and has issue living, Zoe France, *b* 1984, — Julia Marie, *b* 1985.

DAUGHTER LIVING

Hon Francesca Mary, *b* 1945: *m* 1977, as his 2nd wife (*m diss* 1995), Baron Pearson of Rannoch (Life Baron), and has issue. *Residence* – 3 Shepherd's Close, W1Y 3RT.

CHATFIELD, BARON (Chatfield) (Baron UK 1937)

For our altars and our hearths

ERNLE DAVID LEWIS CHATFIELD, 2nd Baron; *b* 2 Jan 1917; *s* 1967; *ed* Trin Coll, Camb; late Hon Lt RNVR; an ADC to Gov Gen of Canada 1940-45: *m* 1969, (Felicia Mary) Elizabeth, da of late Dr John Roderick Bulman, of Hereford.

𝔄rms – Or, a griffin segreant sable, on a chief purpure an anchor between two escallops of the first. ℭrest – An heraldic antelope's head erased, argent, gorged with a naval crown or. Supporters – *Dexter*, an Admiralty Messenger holding in the exterior hand his staff; *sinister*, a Seaman Gunner of the Royal Navy resting the exterior hand on a shell all proper.
Address – 535 Island Rd, Victoria, BC V8S 2T7, Canada.

SISTER LIVING

Hon (Mary) Katharine Medina, OBE, *b* 1911; with Women's Vol Sers 1939-46; OBE (Civil) 1946: *m* 1947, Henry George Austen de L'Etang Herbert Duckworth, RA, who *d* 1992, son of late Sir George Herbert Duckworth, CB, FSA (*see* E Carnarvon, 1958 Edn), and has issue living, Sarah Margaret Katharine, *b* 1951: *m* 1974, Hector William Munro of Foulis (*see* Munro Bt, *cr* 1634, colls), — Harriet Angela Victoria (twin) (63 Wood Vale, SE23), *b* 1951: *m* 1979 (*m diss* 1992), Count Andreas Jean-Paul von Einsiedel, son of Count Wittigo von Einsiedel, of Frankfurt, W Germany, and has issue living, (*Count*) Orlando Ernle Benedict *b* 1980, (*Count*) Evelyn *b* 1982, (*Count*) Robin *b* 1988, (*Countess*) Gwendolen *b* 1985. *Residence* – Dalingridge Place, Sharpthorne, Sussex.

PREDECESSOR – (1) *Adm of the Fleet Sir* (ALFRED) ERNLE MONTACUTE Chatfield, GCB, OM, KCMG, CVO, PC, son of late Adm Alfred John Chatfield, CB; *b* 1873; Present at actions of Heligoland Bight 1914, Dogger Bank 1915, and Jutland 1916, as Flag Capt HMS Lion, Third Sea Lord and Controller of Navy 1925-28, C-in-C Atlantic Fleet 1929-30; and Med Fleet 1930-32 First Sea Lord 1933-38, and Min for Co-ordination of Defence 1939-40; *cr Baron Chatfield*, of Ditchling, co Sussex (peerage of UK) 1937: *m* 1909, Lilian Emma (CStJ), who *d* 1977, da of late Maj George L. Matthews, TF; *d* 1967; *s* by his son (2) ERNLE DAVID LEWIS, 2nd Baron and present peer.

Chaworth, Baron; title of Earl of Meath on Roll of HL.

CHELMER, BARONY OF (Edwards) (Extinct 1997)

SON LIVING OF LIFE BARON

Hon Robin Ernest, *b* 1940: *m* 1967, Carol Mayes, and has issue.

WIDOW LIVING OF LIFE BARON

ENID (*Baroness Chelmer*), da of Frank William Harvey: *m* 1939, Baron Chelmer, MD, TD (Life Baron), who *d* 1997. *Residence* – Peacocks, Margaretting, Essex.

CHELMSFORD, VISCOUNT (Thesiger) (Baron UK 1858, Viscount UK 1921)

Hope and fortune

FREDERIC JAN THESIGER, 3rd Viscount; *b* 7 March 1931; *s* 1970; late Lt Inns of Court Regt: *m* 1958, Clare Rendle, da of Dr George Rendle Rolston, of Bambers, Haslemere, Surrey, and has issue.

Arms – Gules, a griffin segreant or, within an orle of roses argent, barbed and seeded proper. **Crest** – A cornucopia fessewise, the horn or, the fruit proper, thereon a dove holding in the beak a sprig of laurel also proper. **Supporters** – On either side a griffin or, winged vaire.
Residence – 26 Ormonde Gate, SW3

SON LIVING

Hon FREDERIC CORIN PIERS (KIM), *b* 6 March 1962; TV Producer. *Residence* – 4/4 Hampstead Hill Gardens, NW3 2PL.

DAUGHTER LIVING

Hon Tiffany Gay, *b* 1968.

SISTERS LIVING

Hon Dawn Loraine (Hazelbridge Court, Chiddingfold, Surrey), *b* 1934.
Hon Philippa Merryn (Hazelbridge Court, Chiddingfold, Surrey), *b* 1939.

COLLATERAL BRANCHES LIVING (*In remainder to Barony only*)

Granddaughters of late Hon Percy Mansfield Thesiger, MBE, 2nd son of 2nd Baron:—
Issue of late Donald Adrian Wallace Thesiger, *b* 1901, *d* 1978: *m* 1927, Frances Nina, who *d* 1968, da of late Brig-Gen Sylvester Bertram Grimston, CMG:—
Nina Frances, *b* 1928. —— Zara Jane, *b* 1933: *m* 1969, Arthur Mark Farrer, DL, of The Brick House, Finchingfield, Essex, and E12, Sloane Av Mansions, SW3, and has issue living, Lucy Frances, *b* 1971.

Granddaughters of late Capt Hon Wilfrid Gilbert Thesiger, DSO (*infra*):—
Issue of late Col Brian Peirson DOUGHTY-WYLIE, MC, who assumed the surname of Doughty-Wylie by deed poll 1933 in lieu of his patronymic, *b* 1911; *d* 1982: *m* 1937, Diana, who *d* 1976, only child of late Maj Vere de Hoghton (de Hoghton, Bt, colls):—
Daphne Susan, *b* 1940: *m* 1st, 1961, Capt Jonathan Reeves, R Welch Fus; 2ndly, 1983, Jeremy David Michael Case, of New Marton Hall, New Marton, Oswestry, Shropshire, and has issue living (by 1st *m*), Thomas Somerville Thesiger, *b* 1969, —— Emma de Hoghton, *b* 1963: *m* 1988, Richard Charles Farquhar (*see* Farquhar, Bt, colls), —— Katherine Rebecca, *b* 1966. —— Philippa Vere Thesiger, *b* 1942: *m* 1964, Major John Lewarne Harvey, SCLI, of Halston, Whittington, Oswestry, Shropshire SY11 4NS, and has issue living, Rupert Lewarne, *b* 1965, —— James Thesiger, *b* 1969, —— Pippa Vere Karenza, *b* 1971, —— Joanna Demelza, *b* 1975.

Issue of late Capt Hon Wilfred Gilbert Thesiger, DSO, 3rd son of 2nd Baron, *b* 1871, *d* 1920: *m* 1909, Kathleen, CBE, who *d* 1973, having *m* 2ndly, 1931, as his 2nd wife, Reginald Basil Astley, who *d* 1942 (B Hastings, colls), da of late Thomas Mercer Cliffe Vigors, of Burgage, co Carlow (B Castlemaine, colls):—
Sir Wilfred Patrick, KBE, DSO (Woodcote Grove House, Meadow Hill, Coulsdon, Surrey CR5 2XL; Beefsteak, Travellers', Pratt's Clubs), *b* 1910, *ed* Eton, and Magdalen Coll, Oxford (MA); Hon DLitt Leics, and Bath 1992, Hon Fell British Acad 1982, Hon Fell Magdalen Coll, Oxford 1983; author of *Arabian Sands, The Marsh Arabs, Desert, Marsh and Mountain, The Life of my Choice, Visions of a Nomad, My Kenya Days, The Danakil Diary, Among the Mountains*; Sudan Civil Ser 1935-44; 1939-45 War in Abyssinia as Bimbashi Sudan Defence Force, and in Middle East as Maj with Special Air Ser (despatches, DSO); attached to HRH the Duke of Gloucester's Mission to Ethiopia 1930 (Star of Ethiopia 3rd class); Founder's gold medal of R Geographical Soc, R Central Asian Soc's Lawrence of Arabia Medal, Livingstone Gold Medal of R Scottish Geographical Soc, R Soc of Literature Award, and R Asiatic Soc Burton Gold Medal; DSO 1941, CBE (Civil) 1968, KBE 1995. —— Roderic Miles Doughty (Lucton, Leominster, Herefordshire), *b* 1915; *ed* Eton, and Ch Ch, Oxford (BA 1938); 1939-45 War as Capt Welsh Gds, and Parachute Regt (twice wounded): *m* 1st, 1940 (*m diss* 1946), Mary Rose, who *d* 1962, da of Hon Guy Lawrence Charteris (E Wemyss and March); 2ndly, 1946, Ursula Joan, da of Aymer William Whitworth (M Bristol, colls), and has issue living, (by 2nd *m*) Simon Dermot (Old Manor Cottage, Stapley, Taunton, Som), *b* 1950: *m* 1973, Concepción, da of Pérez Chavez, of Coyuca de Catalan, Mexico, and has issue living, Rebecca Maria *b* 1980, —— Sarah Elizabeth, *b* 1947: *m* 1974, Christopher Simon Wintle, of 40 Stradella Rd, SE24, and has issue living, Alice Marina *b* 1977, Emily Miranda *b* 1981.

Grandsons of late Lt-Col Hon Eric Richard Thesiger, DSO, yst son of 2nd Baron:—
Issue of late Osric Wilfrid Thesiger, *b* 1905, *d* 1977: *m* 1934, Cecily Mary, who *d* 1988, da of late F. Vandertaelen:—
Michael Eric (Ridgecrest, Church Rd, St John's, Redhill, Surrey), *b* 1936; *ed* Downside; FCA; Kt of Grace and Devotion of Sovereign Mil Order of Malta: *m* 1964, Patricia Low, da of G. Waddington, and has issue living, Edward Osric, *b* 1967; *ed* Downside, RMA Sandhurst, and Nottingham Univ (BA); commn'd RGJ 1992: *m* 1997, Joanna C., elder da of Peter Woolley-Stafford, of Little Kingshill, Gt Missenden, Bucks, —— Antony Martin, *b* 1968; *ed* Downside, and Oxford Polytechnic (BA); ARICS, —— Justin Michael, *b* 1970; *ed* Downside, and Oxford Polytechnic (BSc): *m* 1998, Joanna M. Ll., only da of late Innes Lloyd, of Richmond, Surrey, —— Robert Cedric, *b* (twin) 1970; *ed* Downside, and Exeter Univ (BA),

— Georgina Mary, *b* 1965: *m* 1993, David Charles Dowden, son of Lt-Col Ronnie Dowden, of Axminster, Devon, and has issue living, Charles Edward *b* 1995, William George *b* 1997.

Issue of late Cedric Paul Thesiger, *b* 1915, *d* 1987: *m* 1942, Barbara Cecilia (1/31 Dominion St, Takapuna, Auckland, NZ), da of late Maj Hubert Cecil Delacour Jarrett, IA:—
Peter Hubert (4934-2A Av, Delta, BC, Canada), *b* 1943; *ed* The Oratory, and Simon Fraser Univ (MBA 1977): *m* 1969, Jill Patricia, da of Lt-Cdr E. J. Worthy, RCN (ret), and has issue living, James Edward, *b* 1980, — Julia Mary, *b* 1983. ——— Richard Paul (Box 14-530, Panmure, Auckland, NZ), *b* 1945; *ed* The Oratory: *m* 1st, 1971 (*m diss* 1981), Susan, da of J. Sydes; 2ndly, 1981, Jennifer Diane, da of Jonathan David Sharp, RNZAMC, of 12 Stewart Av, Panmure, Auckland, NZ, and has issue living (by 1st *m*), Robin Bruce, *b* 1973, — Clare Louise, *b* 1975. ——— John Bede (9 Castleton St, Birkenhead, Auckland, NZ), *b* 1947; *ed* Blackfriars: *m* 1981, Christine Joyce, da of late G. A. Edmond, BEM, and has issue living, David George, *b* 1986, — Kevin Ryan, *b* 1988.

Granddaughters of late Maj-Gen George Handcock Thesiger, CB, CMG, elder son of Lt-Gen Hon Charles Wemyss Thesiger, 2nd son of 1st Baron:—
Issue of late Sir Gerald Alfred Thesiger, MBE, *b* 1902; *d* 1981; Judge of High Court of Justice, Queen's Bench Div 1958-78: *m* 1932, Marjorie Eileen, who *d* 1972, da of late Raymond Guille, of Long Island NY:—
Oonah Caroline, *b* 1936: *m* 1957, Vincent Vine, and has issue living, Peter Gerald, *b* 1958, — Juliet Mary, *b* 1960, — Anita Oonah, *b* 1962. ——— Juliet Elizabeth, *b* 1943: *m* 1st, 1966 (*m diss* 1977), Roderick Carl Warwick Neville; 2ndly, 1977, David Halliwell Sutcliffe, and has issue (by 1st *m*), Roderick Thomas Gerald, *b* 1968: *m* 1993, Frances Johnson, — Nicola Ingalisa, *b* 1967.

Grandchildren of His Honour late Arthur Lionel Bruce Thesiger (infra):—
Issue of late Lt-Col Richard Edward Knight Thesiger, OBE, *b* 1984: *m* 1st, 1934 (*m diss* 1947), Carolin Sophie, da of Norman M. Grant, of New York; 2ndly, 1947, Eileen Alice, who *d* 1991 only da of late John Still:—
(By 1st *m*) David Arthur Grant (74 Herne Rd, Surbiton, Surrey KT6 5BP), *b* 1934; *ed* Winchester, and Trin Hall, Camb; solicitor 1965: *m* 1963, Margaret Evelyn, da of A. E. Thomas, and has issue living, Amanda Carolin Thomas, *b* 1964: *m* 1996, Timothy Meacham, and has issue living, Milo Douglas THESIGER-MEACHAM *b* 1997, — Clare Margaret Thomas (33 rue du Chevalier de la Barre, 59175 Templemars, France), *b* 1966; has issue living, Madeleine Patience TISON-THESIGER *b* 1992, Leah Emilienne TISON-THESIGER *b* 1995. ——— (By 2nd *m*) John Still (7 Herne Rd, Surbiton, Surrey KT6 5BX), *b* 1948; *ed* Winchester, and Magdalen Coll, Oxford (MA); social worker (CQSW 1975): *m* 1979, Nefise Serpil, da of Mehmet Bayböri, of Küçükyali, Istanbul, and has issue living, Osman Richard Bayböri, *b* 1987, Hatice Emma *b* 1989. ——— Anne Alice Florita, *b* 1951; *ed* Bristol Univ (BA): *m* 1973, Rev Preb Paul Towner, of 102 Green St, Hereford HR1 2QW, and has issue living, Andrew Paul John, *b* 1976, — Katherine Anne, *b* 1975, — Elizabeth Marjorie, *b* 1979. ——— Frances Georgina (107 Upper Brook St, Winchester, Hants), *b* 1956.

Granddaughter of late Hon Sir Edward Peirson Thesiger, KCB, yst son of 1st Baron:—
Issue of His Honour late Arthur Lionel Bruce Thesiger, *b* 1872, *d* 1968: *m* 1902, Florita Maria Engracia, OBE, who *d* 1966, da of late Edward J. Knight of Tregroes, Pencoed, Glam:—
Patience Elizabeth Florita, MBE, TD (Eleven Plus, Hungershall Park, Tunbridge Wells), *b* 1908; a Borough Councillor; Mayor of R Tunbridge Wells 1969-70, Vice Chm Kent CC 1982-84; served ATS 1939-45; MBE (Civil) 1994.

PREDECESSORS – (1) Rt Hon Sir FREDERIC Thesiger, KB, DCL, FRS; *b* 1794; served as a Midshipman, RN, at battle of Copenhagen 1807; called to the bar at Gray's Inn 1818; became a KC 1834; was Solicitor-Gen 1844-5, Attorney-Gen 1845-6 and 1852, MP for Woodstock (C) 1840-4, for Abingdon 1844-52, and for Stamford 1852-8, and Lord High Chancellor 1858-9 and 1866-8; *cr. Baron Chelmsford* of Chelmsford, co Essex (peerage of United Kingdom) 1858: *m* 1822, Anna Maria, da of William Tinling, of Southampton, *d* 1878; *s* by his son **(2)** FREDERIC AUGUSTUS, GCB, GCVO, 2nd Baron; *b* 1827; a Gen in the Army, and Col 2nd Life Guards; served in Crimea, during Indian Mutiny, and in Abyssinia; commanded forces during Kaffir and Zulu Campaigns; an ADC to HM Queen Victoria 1868-77, and Lieut of Tower of London 1884-9: *m* 1867, Adria Fanny, who *d* 1926, da of late Maj-Gen Heath, Bombay Army; *d* 1905; *s* by his son **(3)** Rt Hon FREDERIC JOHN NAPIER, GCSI, GCMG, GCIE, GBE, 3rd Baron; *b* 1868; Gov of Queensland 1905-9, and of NS Wales 1909-13, Viceroy of India 1916-21, and First Lord of the Admiralty Jan to Nov 1924; a KJStJ; *cr. Viscount Chelmsford,* of Chelmsford, co. Essex (peerage of United Kingdom) 1921: *m* 1894, Hon Frances Charlotte Guest, CI, GBE, who *d* 1957, da of 1st Baron Wimborne; *d* 1933; *s* by his son **(4)** ANDREW CHARLES GERALD, 2nd Viscount; *b* 1903: *m* 1927, Gillian, who *d* 1978, da of late Arthur Nevile Lubbock (B Avebury, colls); *d* 1970; *s* by his son **(5)** FREDERIC JAN, 3rd Viscount, and present peer; also Baron Chelmsford.

Chelsea, Viscount; son of Earl Cadogan.

CHELWOOD, BARONY OF (Beamish) (Extinct 1989)

DAUGHTERS LIVING OF LIFE BARON (*By 1st marriage*)

(*Hon*) Claudia Hamilton (does not use courtesy title), *b* 1952. *Residence* – Westraw House, Pettinain, Lanark ML11 8SL
Hon Andrea Tufton, *b* 1955: *m* 1985, Christopher C. Plowman.

WIDOW LIVING OF LIFE BARON

MARIA PIA (*Baroness Chelwood*), da of Baron Ernest von Roretz, of Schloss Breiteneich, bei Horn, Austria, and formerly
wife of Alan McHenry: *m* 1975, as his 2nd wife, Baron Chelwood, MC (Life Baron), who *d* 1989.

CHESHAM, BARON (Cavendish) (Baron UK 1858)

Secure by caution

NICHOLAS CHARLES CAVENDISH, 6th Baron; *b* 7 Nov 1941; *s* 1989;
ed Eton; ACA; Patron of two livings; Capt Queen's Body Guard
of the Yeomen of the Guard (Dep Ch Whip, House of Lords)
1995-97: *m* 1st, 1965 (*m diss* 1969), Susan Donne, eldest da of
late Frederick Guy Beauchamp, MD, MRCS (*see* By North);
2ndly, 1973, Suzanne Adrienne, elder da of late Alan Gray
Byrne, of Sydney, NSW, and has issue by 2nd *m*.

𝔄rms – Sable three stags' heads cabossed argent. 𝔠rest – A snake, nowed
proper. 𝔖upporters – *Dexter*, a buck proper, gorged with a chaplet of roses
argent and azure; *sinister*, a greyhound argent gorged with a plain collar
gules, thereon three buckles or.
Residence – Manor Farm, Preston Candover, nr Basingstoke, Hants RG25
2EN. *Clubs* – Pratt's, Australian (Sydney).

SON LIVING (*By 2nd marriage*)

Hon CHARLES GRAY COMPTON, *b* 11 Nov 1974; *ed* King's Sch, Parramatta, and Durham Univ.
Hon William George Gray, *b* 1980.

BROTHER LIVING

Hon John Charles Gregory (Hall Farm, Farringdon, Alton, Hants), *b* 1952; *ed* Eton, and Jesus Coll, Camb: *m* 1976,
Lucinda Mary, da of late Richard Hugh Corbett, of Manor Farm, Beauworth, Hants.

SISTERS LIVING

Hon Joanna Mary, *b* 1938: *m* 1960, Peter Henry Mabille Price, of Pinn Hill Farm, Sidbury, Sidmouth, Devon, son of late
Cmdr Maurice Price, RN, of Sutton, Surrey, and has issue living, Nicholas Henry Maurice, *b* 1971: *m* 1996, Celina, da of
Charles Llewellyn, of Leigh, Surrey, and of Mrs Nova Williamson, of Aldeburgh, Suffolk, and has issue living, Daisy May
b 1998, — Caroline Mary, *b* 1967: *m* 1st, 1988 (*m diss* 19—), Christopher G. Marler, son of late Geoffrey Marler; 2ndly,
1997, Henry William St John Symes Bullen, son of Michael Fitzherbert Bullen, of Borough Court, Hartley Wintney,
Hants.
Hon Georgina Mary, *b* 1944: *m* 1967, (Michael) Wynne Tufnell, of High Dell Farmhouse, Bighton, Alresford, Hants, only
son of late Capt Michael Neville Tufnell, DSC, RN (ret), of Curdridge Grange, Botley, Hants, and has issue living,
Christopher Wynne, *b* 1969, — Michael Greville, *b* 1971: *m* 1997, Katharine Louise, yr da of David Ronald Adam, of Halland, E Sussex (*see* McAlpine Bt), — Simon Charles *b* 1977.

WIDOW LIVING OF FIFTH BARON

MARY EDMUNDS (*Dowager Baroness Chesham*), 4th da of late David Gregory Marshall, MBE, of White Hill, Cambridge: *m*
1937, the 5th Baron Chesham, TD, PC, who *d* 1989. *Residence* – Meadow House, Preston Candover, Basingstoke, Hants.

COLLATERAL BRANCH LIVING

Grandchildren of late Brig-Gen Hon William Edwin Cavendish, MVO 3rd of 2nd Baron:—
Issue of late Capt Evan George Charles Cavendish, OBE, RNVR, *b* 1891, *d* 1955: *m* 1923, Esmé Frances Sylvia
IRBY, who *d* 1959, da of late Hon Gilbert Neville Smyth (B Boston, colls):—

Greville Adrian (Hope Town, Abaco, Bahamas; Moretown, Vermont, USA), *b* 1925; Lt-Cdr RN (ret): *m* 1st, 1952 (*m diss* 1974), Hazel Colleen Elizabeth, only da of late John Henry May, of Jersey; 2ndly, 1974, Gillian, da of late Leslie George Webb, of W. Hagley, Worcs, and has issue living (by 1st *m*), Rupert Edward Greville, *b* 1955, — Piers Antony Charles (58 St John's Hill Grove, SW11 2RG), *b* 1956: *m* 1986, (Rose Vivien) Louise, eldest da of late Gerard Dacres (Dickie) Olivier, and of Mrs Hester St John Ives, of Chain House, Modbury, S Devon, and has issue living, Patrick Alexander *b* 1990, Georgia Claire *b* 1989, — Kiloran Arabella, *b* 1959. —— Susan, *b* 1924: *m* 1st, 1951 (*m diss* 1955), David Murray Martin; 2ndly, 1955, Leslie Gordon Graham, and has issue living, (by 1st *m*) Trudy Carol, *b* 1952, — Amanda Jane, *b* 1954, — (by 2nd *m*) Sarah Frances, *b* 1956. *Residence* – Mount Farm, nr Ringwood, Hants.

PREDECESSORS – (1) *Hon* CHARLES COMPTON CAVENDISH, 4th son of 1st Earl of Burlington (*see* D Devonshire), MP for E Sussex (*L*) 1832-41, for Youghal 1841-47, and for Buckinghamshire 1847-57; *cr Baron Chesham* (Peerage of United Kingdom) 1858; *d* 1863; *s* by his son (2) WILLIAM GEORGE, 2nd Baron, *b* 1815; MP for Peterborough (*L*) 1847, and for Buckinghamshire 1857-63: *m* 1849, Henrietta Frances, who *d* 1884, da of late Right Hon William Saunders Sebright Lascelles (E Harewood); *d* 26 June 1882; *s* by his son (3) CHARLES COMPTON WILLIAM, 3rd Baron, KCB, PC, *b* 1850; Master of the Buckhounds 1900-1901, and a Lord of the Bedchamber to HRH the Prince of Wales 1901-7: *m* 1877, Lady Beatrice Constance Grosvenor, RRC, who *d* 1911, 2nd da of 1st Duke of Westminster; *d* 1907; *s* by his son (4) JOHN COMPTON, MC, 4th Baron; *b* 1894; Capt 10th Hussars and Squadron Leader RAF Vol Reserve: *m* 1st 1915 (*m diss* 1937), Margot, who *d* 1985, da of late John Layton Mills of Tansor Court, Oundle; 2ndly, 1938, Marion Caher (EDWARDS), who *d* 1973, da of Daniel C. Donoghue, of Philadelphia, USA, and formerly wife of 8th Earl of Carrick; *d* 1952; *s* by his only son (5) JOHN CHARLES COMPTON, TD, PC, 5th Baron, *b* 1916; Capt RA (TA); a Lord in Waiting to HM The Queen 1955-59, Joint Parl Sec Min of Transport 1959-64, Exec Vice-Chm RAC 1966-70, etc: *m* 1937, Mary Edmunds, 4th da of late David Gregory Marshall, MBE, of White Hill, Cambridge; *d* 1989; *s* by his elder son (6) NICHOLAS CHARLES, 6th Baron and present peer.

Cheshire, Barony of (Cheshire) (Extinct 1992) (see Bs Ryder of Warsaw)

CHETWODE, BARON (Chetwode) (Baron UK 1945, Bt E 1700)

CORONA MEA CHRISTUS

Christ is my crown

PHILIP CHETWODE, 2nd Baron and 8th Baronet; *b* 26 March 1937; *s* 1950; *ed* Eton; Capt (ret) RHG: *m* 1st, 1967 (*m diss* 1979), Susan Janet, el da of late Capt Voltelin James Howard Van der Byl, DSC, RN (ret) and formerly wife of Alwyn Richard Dudley Smith; 2ndly, 1990, Fiona, da of late Christos Tsintsaris, of Greece, and formerly wife of Sam James Sydney Holt (son of late Rt Hon Harold Edward Holt, CH, sometime Prime Minister of Australia), and has issue by 1st *m*.

Arms – Quarterly argent and gules, four crosses patée counterchanged. **Crest** – Out of a ducal coronet or, a demi-lion rampant gules. **Supporters** – *Dexter*, a Crusader in chain armour and surcoat resting the exterior hand proper on a shield of the arms of Chetwode; *sinister*, an Officer of the 19th R Hus resting his exterior hand on the hilt of his sword proper. *Residence* – The Mill House, Chilton Foliat, Hungerford, Berks.

SONS LIVING (By 1st marriage)

Hon ROGER, *b* 29 May 1968: *m* 1998, Miranda J., yst da of Cmdr Graeme Rowan-Thomson, RN, of Corton Denham, Sherborne, Dorset.
Hon Alexander, *b* 1969: *m* 1998, Alexandra Louise Neville, yr da of Maj-Gen Christopher Neville Last, CB, OBE, of Abergele, N Wales.

DAUGHTER LIVING (By 1st marriage)

Hon Miranda, *b* 1974.

BROTHER LIVING

(Raised to the rank of a Baron's son 1951)

Hon Christopher Roger (Hill House, Cheriton, Alresford, Hants), *b* 1940; *ed* Eton: *m* 1961, Hon Philippa Mary Imogen Brand, da of 5th Viscount Hampden, and has issue living, Michael Walhouse David, *b* 1962: *m* 1986, Louise Ann, da of R. W. Wood, of Maldon, Essex, and of Mrs Trevor R. Robins, of Bocking, Essex, and has issue living, George *b* 1992, Emma Louisa Patricia *b* 1987, Holly *b* 1989, Daisy *b* (twin) 1992, — Richard Christopher *b* 1964: *m* 1993, Sheelagh Maria, da of Desmond Francis Boylan, of Marion, Mas, USA (*see* O'Brien, Bt, 1980 Edn), and has issue living, Harry Thomas Christopher *b* 1996, Lucy Imogen Brigid *b* 1998, — Charles Philip, *b* 1967, — William Robin, *b* 1973, — James Nicholas, *b* 1975.

COLLATERAL BRANCHES LIVING *(In remainder to Baronetcy only)*

Granddaughter of late Adm Sir George Knightley Chetwode, KCB, CBE (infra):—
Issue of late Paymaster-Lt John Chetwode, RNR, *b* 1909, *ka* 1941: *m* 1934, Joan Muriel (who *d* 1951, having *m* 2ndly, 1947, Capt Joseph Anthony Collings, MBE, late N Somerset Yeo, who *d* 1954), da of Lt-Col Frederick George Glyn Bailey (E Inchcape):—
Janet Amanda Alice, *b* 1937; *ed* Westonbirt, and St Clare's Coll, Oxford. *Club* – Lansdowne.

Grandson of late Lt-Col Sir George Chetwode, 6th baronet:—
Issue of late Adm Sir George Knightley Chetwode, KCB, CBE, *b* 1877, *d* 1957: *m* 1st, 1908, Alice, who *d* 1937, da of late Maj Vaughan Hanning Vaughan-Lee, MP for W Div of Somersetshire; 2ndly, 1939, Elizabeth, who *d* 1979, da of Frederick Taylor, of Jericho, Queensland, and formerly wife of Capt Lionel Dawson, RN:—
(By 1st *m*) George David, MBE, *b* 1914; *ed* RNC Dartmouth, and RMC Sandhurst; Maj Coldsteam Gds; sometime ADC to Gov of Bombay; European War 1939-45 in N Africa and Italy (wounded, MBE); MBE (Mil) 1944: *m* 1946, Lady Willa Elliot, da of 5th Earl of Minto, and has issue living, Joshua Lariston Knightley, *b* 1967: *ed* Eton, and LSE, — Davina Marion (33 Summer St, Northampton, Mass 01060, USA), *b* 1947: *m* 1st, 1968 (*m diss* 1975), William John N. Moore, son of William Moore, of Thornhill House, Stalbridge, Dorset; 2ndly, 1977, Joshua Miller, son of Prof Irving Miller, of New York, and has issue living (by 1st *m*), Lucy *b* 1970 (by 2nd *m*), Corina Emily *b* 1979, Sophie Claire *b* 1983, — Sarah Alice (94 Cambridge Gdns, W10 6HS), *b* 1948: *m* 1969 (*m diss* 1983), Andrew Donald Cox, son of late Donald Cox, of Gourdie, Fife, and has issue living, Damian *b* 1975, Indiajane *b* 1970, Alice Dawn *b* 1972: *m* 1998, Andreas John Kodell, son of Demetre Kodellas, of Melbourne, Victoria, Australia, Flora Eileen Gian *b* 1976, — Emma Bridget *b* 1950: *m* 1971, Simon Lindley Keswick, of Rockcliffe, Upper Slaughter, Cheltenham, Glos GL54 2JW, yst son of late Sir William Keswick, of Glenkiln, Shawhead, Dumfries (*see* By Lindley, 1950 Edn), and has issue living, Benjamin William *b* 1972, Archibald David *b* 1980, Poppy Teresa *b* 1978, Willa Mary China *b* 1984, — Willa Mary Gabriel (*Lady Elphinstone*), *b* 1954: *m* 1978, 18th Lord Elphinstone, who *d* 1994, — Georgina Caroline, *b* 1955: *m* 1983, Edward Charles Markes, of 67 Drakefield Rd, SW17, 2nd son of late John Edward Markes, of Recess, co Galway, and has issue living, Dominic John *b* 1989, Gerard David *b* 1991, Araminta Victoria *b* 1987, Sylvie Elise *b* 1996. *Residence* – Swiss Farm House, Upper Slaughter, Cheltenham, Glos GL54 2JP.

PREDECESSORS – (1) JOHN Chetwode, el son of late Philip Chetwode, of Oakley, Staffs, *b* 1666; *cr Baronet* 1700: *m* 1st, 1695, Mary, who *d* 1702, da of late Sir Jonathan Raymond, of Barton Court, Berks; 2ndly, 17—, Catherine, who *d* 1717, da of late John Tayleur, of Rodington, Shropshire; *d* 1733; *s* by his son (2) *Sir* PHILIP TOUCHET, 2nd Bt; *b* 1700: *m* 1727, Elizabeth, who *d* 1745, only da of late George Venables, of Agdon, Cheshire; *d* 1764; *s* by his el son (3) *Sir* JOHN, 3rd Bt; *b* 1732: *m* 1756, Dorothy, who *d* 1769, da of late Tobias Bretland, of Thorncliffe, Cheshire; *d* 1779; *s* by his only surviving son (4) *Sir* JOHN, 4th Bt; *b* 1764: *m* 1st, Lady Elizabeth Grey, who *d* 1826, da of 5th Earl of Stamford and 1st Earl of Warrington; 2ndly, 1827, Elizabeth, who *d* 18— (having *m* 2ndly, 1848, Andrew Kennedy Hutchinson, of Chester Square, Pimlico, SW); *d* 1845; *s* by his el son (5) *Sir* JOHN, 5th Bt; *b* 1788; assumed by R licence 1826 the additional surnames of Newdigate-Ludford: *m* 1st, 1821, Elizabeth Juliana, who *d* 1859, el da of late John Newdigate-Ludford, of Ansley Hall, Warwickshire; 2ndly, 1861, Arabella Phyllis, only child of late Samuel Denton, and widow of James Reade, of Lower Berkeley Street, W; *d* 1873; *s* by his nephew (6) *Sir* GEORGE (2nd son of late Rev George Chetwode, 2nd son of 4th Bt), 6th Bt; *b* 1823; Lt-Col 8th Hus: *m* 1868, Alice Jane, who *d* 1919, da of late Michael Thomas Bass, MP, of Rangemore, Staffs, *d* 1905: *s* by his el son (7) *Sir* PHILIP WALHOUSE, GCB, OM, GCSI, KCMG, DSO, 7th Bt; *b* 1869; became Field-Marshal 1933; Chin Hills Expedition 1892-3, S Africa 1899-1902 (despatches thrice, DSO), European War 1914-18 in France Comdg 5th Cav Brig (original) and 2nd Cav Div, in Sinai Comdg Desert Corps, and in Palestine and Syria Comdg 20th Army Corps which captured Jerusalem (wounded, despatches eight times, CB, promoted Maj-Gen and Lt-Gen KCMG, KCB); Assist Mil Sec, Aldershot 1906-8; commanded London Mounted Brig, Territorial Force 1912-14; appointed Mil Sec to Sec of State for War, and Sec of Selection Board 1919, Dep Ch of Imperial Gen Staff and a Member of Army Council 1920, AG to the Forces 1922, Gen Officer Comdg-in-Ch, Aldershot Command 1923, Col R Scots Greys (2nd Drag) 1925, ADC-Gen to HM 1927, Ch of Gen Staff in India 1928, Col 8th King George's Own Light Cav (Indian Army) 1932, and Hon Col 2nd/10th Dragoons, Canadian Mil 1938; Com-in-Ch in India and a MEC 1930-35; Constable of Tower of London 1943-8; Col 15th/19th King's R Hus 1944-7; received Grand Cross of Orders of St Olav of Norway, and of George I of Greece, and Order of Brilliant Star of China with Grand Cordon; a Knight Grand Cross of Order of Orange-Nassau of the Netherlands; *cr Baron Chetwode*, of Chetwode, co Buckingham (peerage of United Kingdom) 1945: *m* 1899, Alice Hester Camilla, who *d* 1946, da of late Col Hon Richard Southwell George Stapleton-Cotton (*see* B Combermere, 1946 Edn); *d* 1950; *s* by his grandson (8) PHILIP (son of late Capt Roger Charles George Chetwode, son of 1st Baron), 8th Baronet and present peer.

CHETWYND, VISCOUNT (Chetwynd) (Viscount I 1717)

Probity is true honour

ADAM RICHARD JOHN CASSON CHETWYND, 10th Viscount; *b* 2 Feb 1935; *s* 1965; *ed* Eton; Lt Queen's Own Cameron Highlanders; New Business Man, The Prudential Assurance Co of SA Ltd, Harland House Branch, Johannesburg: *m* 1st, 1966 (*m diss* in Rhodesia 1974), Celia Grace da of Cdr Alexander Robert Ramsay, DSC, RNVR (*see* Ramsay, Bt, colls, *cr* 1806); 2ndly, 1975, Angela May, only da of Jack Payne McCarthy, of 21 Llanberis Grove, Aspley, Nottingham, and has issue by 1st *m*.

🛡️rms – Azure, a chevron between three mullets or. Crest – A goat's head erased argent, horns gold. Supporters – Two unicorns argent, gorged with chaplets of roses gules, and having a chain of the same reflexed over their backs.
Address – c/o J. G. Ouvry, Esq, Lee Bolton & Lee, 1 Sanctuary, Westminster SW1P 3JT.

SONS LIVING (*By 1st marriage*)

Hon ADAM DOUGLAS, *b* 26 Feb 1969.
Hon Robert Duncan (twin), *b* 1969.

DAUGHTER LIVING (*By 1st marriage*)

Hon Emma Grace, *b* 1967: *m* 1989, Peter William Cabot, of 6 Pym St, Belair, S Australia 5052, and has issue living, Samantha Grace, *b* 1998.

SISTER LIVING

Hon Philippa Mary Agnes Joan, *b* 1930: *m* 1959, Major John Anthony Hawtrey Luard, Coldstream Gds, of Maidenford, Goodleigh, nr Barnstaple, Devon EX32 7NG, and has issue living, David Andrew John, *b* 1961, — Sophia Mary, *b* 1960: *m* 1982 (*m diss* 1987), Gianfranco Goddi, only son of Sra Mele-Goddi, of Rome, and has issue living, Lucrezia Ruth Jessica *b* 1983.

HALF-SISTERS LIVING

Hon Catherine Sophia Marianne, *b* 1956.
Hon Frances Diana Dorothea, *b* 1959: *m* 1997, Keith Cowieson, and has issue living, two das.

COLLATERAL BRANCHES LIVING

Grandchildren of late Hon John Julian Chetwynd (infra):—
Issue of late Richard Walter Chetwynd, *b* 1938, *d* 1990: *m* 1964, Judith Mary, who *d* 1998, only da of late Capt Selwyn Victor Jephson, RN, of The Red House, Hambledon, Hants:—
Mark Richard, *b* 1972. —— Katharine Margaret, *b* 1965: *m* 1990, Michael William Toogood, eldest son of James Anthony Gordon Toogood, of Riversdale, Malmesbury, Wilts, and has issue living, William Richard Stanley, *b* 1996, — Emma Georgina, *b* 1994, — Alexandra Kate, *b* (twin) 1994. —— Sarah Alexandra, *b* 1967.

Issue of late Hon John Julian Chetwynd, 2nd son of 8th Viscount, *b* 1906, *d* 1966: *m* 1937, Margaret Agnes, who *d* 1993, da of late Maj-Gen Hugh Clement Sutton, CB, CMG (*see* Sutton, Bt, colls):—
John Hugh, *b* 1942; *ed* Stowe: *m* 1st, 1966 (*m diss* 1971), Denyse Jacqueline, da of H. de Frisching, of Berne, Switzerland; 2ndly, 1973 (*m diss* 1977), Caroline, elder da of John Fitzwilliams; 3rdly, 1983, Mrs Lorna Butler (*née* Menzies), and has issue living (by 1st *m*), Hugh Nigel, *b* 1967, — Philip Mark, *b* 1969, — (by 3rd *m*) Fleur Alicia Camilla, *b* 1983.

Granddaughter of late Capt Hon Henry Weyland Chetwynd, RN, 3rd son of 6th Viscount:—
Issue of late Henry Goulburn Willoughby Chetwynd, AMICE, el brother of 8th Viscount, *b* 1858, *d* 1909: *m* 1893, Eva Constance Elizabeth Fanny, who *d* 1936, da of late Augustus Berney (Berney, Bt, colls):—
Sylvia Evelyn, *b* 1902: *m* 1931, Anthony Makower, who *d* 1984, and has issue living, Peter (2 Lillian Rd, Barnes, SW13), *b* 1932; *ed* Trin Coll, Camb (MA); FRIBA; MRTPI: *m* 1960, Katharine, da of late James Howarthe Paul Chadburn, MBE, and has had issue, Andrew *b* 1961: *m* 1991, Alison Grace Astley, da of John Weston (and has issue living, Timothy Edward *b* 1998, Eleanor Ruth *b* 1992, Agnes Rose *b* 1995), Timothy *b* 1965: *m* 1994, Sibella Caroline, eldest da of Sir Richard Baker Wilbraham, 8th Bt (and has issue living, Noah *b* 1997), Mary *b* 1963; *d* 1979, — Michael Stanley (Gogar House, Blairlogie, by Stirling), *b* 1936: *m* 1960, Selina Elizabeth, da of late Henry Vernon Flower Barran (*see* Barran, Bt, colls), and has issue living, Sophia Galiena *b* 1962, Janet Elizabeth Agnes *b* 1964: *m* 1991, Darby Edwards (and has issue living, Florence Isabel *b* 1993, Phoebe Mary *b* 1996, Emily Frances *b* 1999), Margaret Eleanor *b* 1966, — *Rev Canon Dr* Malory (9 Duverlin Close, Eaton, Norwich NR4 6HS), *b* 1938; *ed* Dublin Univ (MA), and St John Coll, Oxford (MA, DPhil): *m* 1967 (*m diss* 1987), Mary Noel, da of Ralph Edward Stokes, and has issue living, Philip *b* 1969, William *b* 1976, Caroline *b* 1968, Sandra *b* 1972, — Anne (8 Richmond Hill, Monkstown, Dublin), *b* 1934, *ed* Dublin Univ (BA): *m* 1964, Christopher O'Connell Fitz-Simon, and has issue living, Adrian Christopher *b* 1967, Vanessa Una *b* 1965.

Grandsons of late Capt Hon Louis Wentworth Pakington Chetwynd, RN, brother of 8th Viscount:—
Issue of late Maj (Wentworth) Randolph Chetwynd, MBE, *b* 1903, *d* 1985: *m* 1st, 1931 (*m diss* 1964), Bridget, da of late Col Theobald Alfred Walsh, DSO; 2ndly, 1964, Mary, da of Francis Rosser:—
(By 1st *m*) Rupert Milo Talbot (The New Stables, Ingestre, nr Stafford), *b* 1934; *ed* Stowe: *m* 1st, 1956 (*m diss* 1970), Antonia, only child of late Denis Clark, DFC; 2ndly, 1970, Luciana Maria, el da of late Count Ernest Arrighi, and has issue living (by 1st *m*), Rupert Jonathan Richard, *b* 1957, — Dominic Jeremy, *b* 1959, — Crispin, *b* 1961, — Alexander Anthony, *b* 1964, — Persephone Catherine, *b* 1965: *m* 1995, John A. Madley, — (by 2nd *m*) Aaron St George Francesco Arrighi, *b* 1971, — Alalia, *b* 19—. —— Tom Wentworth Guy (12 Mornington Terr, NW1), *b* 1938; 2nd Lieut RAC: *m* 1959, Helene, da of Baron Pierre de Bosmelet, and has issue living, Yolanda, *b* 1960, — Natasha, *b* 1961, — Bridget, *b* 1966.

Grandchildren of late Miles Chetwynd-Stapylton, yr son of late Henry Edward Chetwynd-Stapylton, el son of Maj Henry Richard Chetwynd-Stapylton, el son of Maj-Gen Hon Granville Anson Chetwynd-Stapylton, 2nd son of 4th Viscount:—
Issue of late Philip Miles Chetwynd-Stapylton, *b* 1889, *d* 1965: *m* 1920, Esmé, who *d* 1990, da of late W. G. Eveleigh:—
Henry Philip (8 Jubilee Terr, Chichester, W Sussex PO19 1XL), *b* 1921; *ed* Radley; late Capt IA (1939-45 War); B Arch 1952; an ARIBA, FRSA: *m* 1962, Elizabeth Bentinck, who *d* 1992, yst da of late E. E. Chambers, of Ringwood, Hants, and has issue living, (Henry) Edward, *b* 1966; *ed* Radley; BSc, Dip TP, FRGS: *m* 1995, Nicola A., elder da of Martin Wilberforce, of Thames Ditton, Surrey, — Diana Rachel, *b* 1970. —— Esmé Elizabeth, *b* 1927: *m* 1954, Col Robert Edward Waight, OBE, late LI, and has issue living, Richard Edward Charles, *b* 1960; Maj LI, — Deborah Anne, *b* 1957. *Residence* – Charcroft, Maddington St, Shrewton, Wilts.

Grandchildren of late Lt-Gen Granville George Chetwynd Stapylton, 2nd son of late Maj Henry Richard Chetwynd-Stapylton (ante):—
Issue of late Maj Granville Joseph Chetwynd Stapylton, *b* 1871, *ka* 1914: *m* 1906, Elizabeth Grace, who *d* 1930, da of late Christopher Lethbridge, of 19 Chester Square, SW:—
Granville Richard (1a Shelton Fields, Shrewsbury), *b* 1909, *ed* Charterhouse; Lt-Col (ret) Somerset LI: *m* 1934, Emma, yst da of late Col W. A. Young, and has issue living, Richard Granville Hugh (Beckets House, Lapford, Crediton, Devon EX17 6PZ), *b* 1939; *ed* Charterhouse; Lt-Col (ret) LI: *m* 1968, Janet Mary Agnes, da of Cdr Alastair Shand Cumming, RN, and has issue living, (Margot) Emma *b* 1969: *m* 1995, Matthew Alan Walton, of Crumble Cottage, The Fosseway, Stow-on-the-Wold, Glos GL54 1EG, son of Michael Walton, of Toothill, Romsey (and has issue living, Poppy Olivia *b* 1997), Polly Rose *b* 1971, — Sarah Elizabeth, *b* 1936: *m* 1962, Lt-Col Ian Guy Mathews (ret), SCLI, and has issue living, Nicola *b* 1963: *m* 1996, Frederick David Richard Coupe, of 147 Vaughan Rd, Harrow, Middx, son of Thomas Bryan Coupe, of Gt Cheverill, Wilts (and has issue living, Alastair Guy Winter *b* 1998), Amanda *b* 1965: *m* 1994, Andrew Robert Greig, of Bench Hill, Woodchurch, Tenterden, Kent TN26 3TL, son of late Victor Stuart Greig. —— Barbara Mary Elizabth, *b* 1907: *m* 1934, Ronald Anthony Edward Birch, and has issue living, George Anthony, *b* 1935, — William *b* 1938, — John Montagu, *b* 1941.

Issue of late Col Bryan Henry Chetwynd-Stapylton, CBE, *b* 1873, *d* 1958: *m* 1905, Dorothy Constance, who *d* 1942, da of late Chambré Brabazon Ponsonby (E Bessborough, colls):—
Mary Blanche, *b* 1910: *m* 1936, Ralph Meredith Turton, of Kildale Hall, Whitby, N Yorks, who *d* 1988, and has had issue, Cecilia Mary, *b* 1936: *m* 1959, John Harold Vick Sutcliffe, CBE, DL, of Chapelgarth, Gt Broughton, Middlesbrough, and *d* 1998, leaving issue, Andrew Harold Wentworth (Kildale Hall, Whitby, N Yorks) *b* 1960: *m* 1988, Emma Elisabeth, elder da of Sir Angus Duncan Æneas Stirling (*see* E Dunmore) (and has had issue, Ralph Andrew Æneas *b* 1991, *d* 1992, Rose Cecilia *b* 1990, Helena Tertia Morar *b* 1993, Laura Mary *b* 1995), John Ralph Beaumont (16 Beauclerc Rd, W6 0NS) *b* 1964: *m* 1991, Marcella, yr da of Giovanni Pellegrino, of Milan (and has issue living, Edward John Ralph *b* 1995, Francesca Renata *b* 1993, Cecilia Marcella *b* 1999), Mark David Chetwynd (12 Aquinas St, SE1 8AE) *b* 1967: *m* 1997, Henrietta Katherine, da of Ian Wallace, of Edinburgh, Henrietta Cecilia *b* 1961: *m* 1987, Matthew Williams, elder son of Sir John Williams, of Hanging Langford, Wilts (and has issue living, Joshua John Ralph *b* 1989, Jonathan Frederick Matthew *b* 1991, Katherine Mary Elizabeth *b* 1994), — Lavinia Rose (*Lady Horsbrugh-Porter*), *b* 1939: *m* 1964, Sir John Simon Horsbrugh-Porter, 4th Bt, of Bowers Croft, Coleshill, Amersham, Bucks, — Victoria Harriet Lucy (*Viscountess Bridgeman*), *b* 1942; *ed* Trin Coll, Dublin (MA): *m* 1966, 3rd Viscount Bridgeman, of Watley House, Sparsholt, Hants, and 19 Chepstow Rd, W2, — Sylvia Dorothy, *b* 1947, *m* 1st, 1977, David Laurence (Jeremy) Booth; 2ndly, 1983, Martin Oakley, of 24 Warnborough Rd, Oxford, and has issue living (by 2nd *m*), Oliver Ronald *b* 1984, Edmund Ralph *b* 1986, Esther Amelia Blanche *b* 1990.

Granddaughter of late Maj Granville Joseph Chetwynd-Stapylton (ante):—
Issue of late Lt-Col Christopher George Chetwynd-Stapylton, RA, *b* 1913, *d* 1988: *m* 1952, Bridget, formerly wife of Ian Urquhart Wilson, and da of late Harry Selwyn Dixon-Spain, of Little Massingham Manor, King's Lynn, Norfolk:—
Elizabeth Alice, *b* 1954: *m* 1979, Lt-Col Michael Anthony Hart, MBE, QGM, The Cheshire Regt, elder son of late Maj R. F. S. Hart, of Gt Clacton, Essex, and has issue living, Christopher James Seymour, *b* 1984, — Rebecca Louise, *b* 1981.

Grandson of late Col Bryan Henry Chetwynd-Stapylton, CBE (ante):—
Issue of late Maj Edward Henry Chetwynd-Stapylton, *b* 1912, *d* 1992: *m* 1957, Priscilla, da of Maj Robert Gerald Wright, of Tunstall Grange, Richmond, N Yorks:—
Miles Edward, *b* 1958; *ed* Bradfield: *m* 1987, Caroline, da of late Jan Siwy, of Bedford Park, London, and has issue living, Thomas Edward *b* 1996, — Rachel Caroline, *b* 1992, — Anna Jessica, *b* 1996. *Residence* – 38 Minster Rd, Oxford.

Granddaughters of late Richard Chetwynd-Stapylton, elder son of late Edward Chetwynd-Stapylton (infra):—
Issue of late Maj Edward Mark Chetwynd-Stapylton, KRRC, *b* 1919, *d* 1995: *m* 1946, Anne Phillida (formerly WRNS) (110 Western Rd, Lewes, E Sussex BN7 1RR), da of Sir Alfred Edward Pease, 2nd Bt (*cr* 1882):—
Judy Anne (5 Bridgefield Rd, Cheam, Surrey SM1 2DG), *b* 1948: *m* 1977, John Trevor Lambert, and has issue living, Sophie Alice Doanda, *b* 1977, — Hannah Madeleine Harriet, *b* 1983. —— Phillida Helen (Brack Mound House, Castle Precincts, Lewes, E Sussex BN7 1YT), *b* 1949. —— Joanna Elizabeth (30 Lansdown Place, Lewes, E Sussex BN7 2JU), *b* 1951: *m* 1978 (*m diss* 1983), Kim Stephen Fuller, and has issue living, Jessie Alison, *b* 1980.

Granddaughter of late Edward Chetwynd-Stapylton, eldest son of Rev Canon William Chetwynd-Stapylton, 3rd son of Maj Henry Richard Chetwynd-Stapylton (ante):—
Issue of late William Eric Chetwynd-Stapylton, *b* 1895, *d* 1978: *m* 1st, 1924, Vivienne, who *d* 1961, da of Harry Spurling, formerly of Upton Park, Slough; 2ndly, 1962, Audrey Margaret, who *d* 1983, da of Percival Hardy, of London, and widow of Ian T. B. Cash:—
(By 1st *m*) Violet Mary, *b* 1926; late WRNS: *m* 1955, Richard Nevill Vaughan Fairbank, TD, late Capt Hon Artillery Co, of Coopers Green, Windlesham, Surrey, and has issue living, David Richard Stapylton (Perry Leigh, Grove Rd, Selling, Faversham, Kent ME13 9RN), *b* 1956: *m* 1981, Clare Arabella, elder da of late Peter Leonard Eckersley, and has issue (*see* Hardy, Bt, colls), — Anthony William Vaughan, *b* 1963: *m* 1989, Harriet Caroline, elder da of Com Oliver Lascelles, MBE, DSC, RN (*see* E Harewood, colls), and has issue living, Emily Rose *b* 1991, Olivia Alice *b* 1992, — Victoria Mary Nevill, *b* 1959: *m* 1983, James Harman Thompson, late Major, Queen's Royal Irish Hussars, of Milton Bank Farm, Sandfield Lane, Acton Bridge, Northwich, Cheshire, and has issue living, William James Richard *b* 1986, Jack Peter *b* 1992, Rosanna Patricia Mary *b* 1988.

Granddaughters of late Granville Chetwynd-Stapylton, yst son of late Rev Canon William Chetwynd-Stapylton (ante):—
Issue of late Col Granville Brian Chetwynd-Stapylton, CB, OBE, TD, *b* 1887, *d* 1964: *m* 1922, Catherine, who *d* 1981, da of late Herbert Lyne, of Newport, Mon:—
Lucy (Jesus Fellowship Community, Festal Grange, Church Rd, Pattishall, nr Towcester, Northants), *b* 1923: *m* 1945 (*m diss* 1980), Paul Anthony Robinson, Fl-Lt late RAFVR, and has issue living, Nigel Anthony, *b* 1946: *m* 1971 (*m diss* 1986), Sandra Ann Coggs, and has issue living, Howard Charles *b* 1978, Suzanne Louise *b* 1974, — Jennifer Chetwynd, *b* 1949: *m* 1st, 1974 (*m diss* 1986), Malcolm Colin Bowden; 2ndly, 1997, Edward Dudley, and has issue living (by 1st *m*), David *b* 1981, Josephine *b* 1980. —— Mary Elizabeth (6 The Cloisters, 55 Kenilworth Rd, Leamington Spa, Warwicks CV32 6JL), *b* 1926: *m* 1949, Grahame Archer Nicholls, BSc, who *d* 1997, and has issue living, Granville Richard, *b* 1952: — David Chetwynd, *b* 1957: *m* 1988, Karen Jane Hodgkinson, — Janet Archer, *b* 1950.

PREDECESSORS – (1) WALTER Chetwynd, son of late John Chetwynd; MP for boroughs of Stafford and Lichfield 1703-35, and sometime Ambassador at Turin and Master of the Stag hounds; *cr Baron of Rathdown*, co Dublin and *Viscount Chetwynd*, of Bearhaven, co Kerry (peerage of Ireland) 1717, with remainder to the issue male of his father; *d* 1735; *s* by his brother (2) JOHN, 2nd Viscount; Ambassador to Madrid 1717; *d* 1767; *s* by his brother (3) WILLIAM RICHARD, 3rd Viscount; Resident at Republic of Genoa 1708-12, MP 1714, Cmmr of the Admiralty 1717-27, and Master of the Mint 1727: *d* 1770; *s* by his son (4) WILLIAM, 4th Viscount, *b* 1721: *m* 1751: *d* 1791; *s* by his son (5) RICHARD, 5th Viscount: *d* 1821; *s* by his son (6) RICHARD WALTER, 6th Viscount, *b* 1800: *m* 1st, 1822, Mary, who *d* 1857, da of Robert Moss; 2ndly, 1861, Mary, who *d* 1901, da of late John Hussey; *d* 6 Dec 1879; *s* by his son (7) RICHARD WALTER, 7th Viscount, *b* 1823: *m* 1858, Harriet Johanna, who *d* 1898, da of late Walter Campbell; *d* 1911; *s* by his nephew (8) GODFREY JOHN BOYLE, CH (2nd son of late Capt Henry Weyland Chetwynd, RN, 3rd son of 6th Viscount), 8th Viscount, *b* 1863; was Managing Director of National Shell Filling Factory at Chilwell, Notts 1915-19: *m* 1st, 1893 (*m diss* —), Baroness Hilda von Alvensleben, da of Baron George von Alvensleben-Rusteberg; 2ndly, 1904, Hon Mary Eden, who *d* 1925, da of 4th Baron Auckland; *d* 1936; *s* by his son (9) ADAM DUNCAN, TD, 9th Viscount *b* 1904; a FSA, and Lt-Col RA: *m* 1st, 1928 (*m diss* 1951), Joan Gilbert (FINDLAY), and who *d* 1979, only child of late Herbert Alexander Casson, CSI; 2ndly, 1952, Dorothea Marianne, MBE, CStJ, who *d* 1990, da of Lt-Col Angus Colin Duncan-Johnstone, MBE, ED; *d* 1965; *s* by his only son (10) ADAM RICHARD JOHN CASSON, 10th Viscount and present peer; also Baron Rathdown.

Chewton, Viscount; son of Earl Waldegrave.

CHEYLESMORE, BARONY OF (Eaton) (Extinct 1974)

COLLATERAL BRANCH LIVING

Issue of late Hon Herbert Edward Eaton, 2nd son of 3rd Baron, *b* 1895, *d* 1962: *m* 1st, 1921 (*m diss* 1944), Sheila Marguerite, who *d* 1967, da of Alan Southey Dumbleton, of Victoria, BC, and formerly wife of John Aloysius Ashton Case; 2ndly, 1944, Barrie Kinghorn (WILLIAMS), who *d* 1972, da of Walter Grey, of Edinburgh:—
(By 1st *m*) Elizabeth Valerie EATON-CROSS, *b* 1922; 1939-45 War with WAAF: *m* 1949, Edward John Kynaston Cross, and has issue living, Richard Anthony Kynaston, *b* 1951: *m* 1978, Pauline Elizabeth, da of Herbert Leonard Tewkesbury, of Warnham, Sussex. *Residence* – 11 Holmbrook Gdns, Farnborough, Hants GU14 9SH.

CHICHESTER, EARL OF (Pelham) (Earl UK 1801, Bt E 1611)

The love of my country prevails

JOHN NICHOLAS PELHAM, 9th Earl and 14th Baronet; *b* (*posthumous*) 14 April 1944; *s* 1944: *m* 1975, Mrs June Marijke Hall, da of Group Capt E. D. Wells, DSO, DFC, of Marbella, Spain, and has issue.

𝕬rms – Quarterly: 1st and 4th azure, three pelicans vulning themselves argent; 2nd and 3rd gules, two pieces of belts with buckles, erect in pale, the buckles upwards argent. 𝕮rest – A peacock in pride argent. 𝕭adges – The buckle of a belt or. 𝕾upporters – *Dexter*, a horse of a mouse dun colour; and *sinister*, a bear proper, each collared with a belt, buckle and pendant or.
Residence – Little Durnford Manor, Salisbury.

DAUGHTER LIVING

Lady Eliza Catherine, *b* 1983.

SISTER LIVING

Lady Georgina Jocelyn, *b* 1942: *m* 1974, Helios Alberto Caranci, of La Catalina, Diego de Alvear, Santa Fe, Argentina, son of Helios Jorge Caranci, of Arredondo 2015, Castelar, Buenos Aires, Argentina, and has issue living, Helios Nicolas, *b* 1983, — Cecilia Catalina, *b* 1976, — Ursula Claudia, *b* 1978.

COLLATERAL BRANCHES LIVING

Grandchildren of Hon Henry George Godolphin Pelham, 2nd son of 5th Earl:—
Issue of late Maj Anthony George Pelham, *b* 1911, *d* 1969: *m* 1938, Ann-Margret, who *d* 1990, da of late Axel Bergengren, of Borås, Sweden:—
RICHARD ANTHONY HENRY (Studley House, Wanstrow, Som), *b* 1 Aug 1952; *ed* Eton: *m* 1987, Georgina, da of David Gilmour, of Ringshall Grange, Suffolk, and has issue living, Duncan James Bergengren, *b* 24 Nov 1987, — Christopher (Kit), *b* 1990. —— Ella Christine (*Lady Perring*), *b* 1940: *m* 1961, Sir John Raymond Perring, 2nd Bt, of 21 Somerset Rd, Wimbledon, SW19, and has issue (*see* Perring, Bt). —— Judith Henrietta, *b* 1943: *m* 1968, Christopher John Chetwood, who *d* 1990, and has issue living, Thomas William, *b* 1970: *m* 1998, Rachel, da of Matthew Bultman, of Robertsbridge, Sussex, — Henry Jonathan, *b* 1972, — Matthew James, *b* 1981, — Henrietta Rose, *b* 1983.

Grandchildren of late Rev Walter Henry Pelham, only son of late Hon Thomas Henry William Pelham, CB, 3rd son of 3rd Earl:—
Issue of late Rev Thomas Bertram Pelham, *b* 1915, *d* 1984: *m* 1948, Gudrun Elisabeth (2 Upper Grange, Love-days Mead, Stroud, Glos GL5 1XB), da of late Rev Uno Axel Valdemar Almgren, of Goteborg, Sweden:—
Philip Henry (15 Ethelbert Rd, Canterbury, Kent), *b* 1949; *ed* Lushington Boys Sch, Ootacamund, Malmesbury Gram Sch, and Sch of Herbal Medicine, Tunbridge Wells: *m* 1983, Mrs Jennifer B. Wellington, da of Col J. D. Power, of Tetherings, Mystole, nr Canterbury, Kent, and has issue living, Andrew Timothy, *b* 1984, — Annabel Claire, *b* 1985, — Elizabeth Rose, *b* 1990. —— David Almgren (28 York Rd, Colwyn Bay, Clwyd), *b* 1950: *ed* Lushington Boys Sch, Ootacamund, Malmesbury Gram Sch, Derby Univ, and Rhodes Univ, Grahamstown, S Africa (MSc): *m* 1980, Julie Ann, da of D. G. Killingley, of 19 Trysull Gdns, Merry Hill, Wolverhampton, and has issue living, Thomas James, *b* 1982, — Lucy Jane, *b* 1985. —— Peter Thomas (48 Leighton Hill Flats, 16 Link Rd, Happy Valley, Hong Kong), *b* 1952; *ed* Lushington Boys Sch, Ootacamund, Malmesbury Gram Sch, and Manchester Univ: *m* 1974 (*m diss* 1994), Linda Margaret, da of late Capt P. H. Phillips, of Benallack, Grampound Rd, Truro, Cornwall, and has issue living, Henry William, *b* 1983, — and an adopted da Suyin, *b* 1985. —— Erik John Christopher, *b* 1954: *ed* Lushington Boys Sch, Ootacamund, Malmesbury Gram Sch, and Lancaster Univ: *m* 19—, Jane, da of John Souter Henley, and has issue living, Alexander *b* 1990, Joseph *b* 1992, Laura, *b* 1988. —— (James) Richard (27 Hill Head, Glastonbury, Somerset), *b* (twin) 1955; *ed* Lushington Boys Sch, Ootacamund, and Bremilham Sch, Malmesbury; has issue (by Mary Chipper), Isaac Roy, *b* 1994. —— Astrid Louisa, *b* (twin) 1955: *m* 1978 (*m diss* 1994), Richard Michael Flaye (formerly Fleay), of Kettlehouse, Chapel Lane, Belchford, Lincs, son of Martin Fleay, of Rydon Acres, Stoke Gabriel, Totnes, Devon, and has issue living, Thomas Charles, *b* 1983, — Tobias Pelham, *b* 1985, — Ella, *b* 1988. —— Susan Margaret (1 Wraxhill Rd, Street, Somerset), *b* 1959; has issue, Robin David Pelham, *b* 1985, — (by Jonny Green) Maia, *b* 1992.

Issue of late Capt Robert Henry Pelham, RA, *b* 1919, *d* 1980: *m* 1951, Anne Farebrother Dalziel, who *d* 19—, da of Capt Geoffrey Dalziel Mayer, of Abinger, Surrey:—
Michael Henry, *b* 1953. —— Sarah Mary, *b* 1955.

Grandsons of Sir (Edward) Henry Pelham, KCB (infra):—
Issue of late Maj Eric Thomas Pelham, WG, *b* 1915, *d* 1984: *m* 1940, Barbara Hilda, who *d* 1909, yst da of Henry John Fordham, of Therfield, Royston, Herts:—
Henry Thomas (Kilmington House, Kilmington, nr Warminster, Wilts), *b* 1943; *ed* Harrow: *m* 1978, Sarah E., yr da of John Charlton, of Culworth Fields, Banbury, Oxon, and has issue living, Charles Thomas, *b* 1987, — Sophie, *b* 1980, — Clare, *b* 1981. —— Richard John (Flat 3, 1 Catherine Rd, Newbury, Berks RG14 7NA), *b* 1945; *ed* Harrow. —— Charles Herbert, *b* 1947; *ed* Harrow: *m* 1st, 1972 (*m diss* 1979), Thérèse Annabella, elder da of Maj James Richard Edwards Harden, DSO, MC (*see* B Rayleigh, colls); 2ndly, 1985 (*m diss* 1999), Sarah Carter, and has issue living (by 2nd *m*), Henry Edward Charles, *b* 1986, — Kate Isobel, *b* 1984. —— William Robert (50 Holland Park Av, W11 3QY), *b* 1950; *ed* Harrow: *m* 1990, Anjuli Krista, da of Krisham Chandra Dosaj.

Granddaughters of late Henry Francis Pelham, Pres Trin Coll, Oxford, eldest son of Rt Rev Hon John Thomas Pelham, DD, Bishop of Norwich 1857-93, 4th son of 2nd Earl:—

Issue of late Sir (Edward) Henry Pelham, KCB, *b* 1876, *d* 1949: *m* 1905, Hon Irene Lubbock, who *d* 1961, da of 1st Baron Avebury:—

Irene Joan, *b* 1912: *m* 1961, Brig Maurice Leslie Hayne, CBE, who *d* 1971. *Residence* – Woodlands, 174 Reading Rd South, Church Crookham, Fleet, Hants GU13 0AE. —— Susan, *b* 1918: *m* 1940, Air Vice-Marshal Cresswell Montagu Clementi, CB, CBE, who *d* 1981, only son of late Sir Cecil Clementi, GCMG, and has issue living, Christopher Pelham, *b* 1943; *ed* Bradfield: *m* 1st, 1976, Pamela Juliette Nollan, who *d* 1992; 2ndly, 1994, Frances Kathleen Chivers (*née* Parr), and has issue living (by 1st *m*), Richard Adam *b* 1978, — David Cecil, *b* 1949; *ed* Winchester, Lincoln Coll, Oxford, and Harvard Business Sch: *m* 1972, Sarah Louise, da of late Dr A. B. Cowley, of E Molesey, Surrey, and has issue living, Thomas Cowley *b* 1979, Anna Lucy *b* 1976, — Nancy, *b* 1946: *m* 1972, Peter Lambert Tribe, and has issue living, Mark Lambert *b* 1978, Howard Clementi *b* 1981, Natalie Clare *b* 1975. *Residence* – Navigator's Cottage, 44 Strand-on-the-Green, Chiswick W4.

PREDECESSORS – (1) THOMAS Pelham, MP for Sussex 1586, and Sheriff of Surrey and Sussex 1589; *cr* a *Baronet* 1611; *d* 1624; *s* by his son (2) *Sir* THOMAS, 2nd Bt, MP for Sussex; *d* 1654; *s* by his son (3) *Sir* JOHN, 3rd Bt, MP for Sussex in five parliaments; *d* 1703; *s* by his son (4) *Sir* THOMAS, 4th Bt, MP for many years; *cr Lord Pelham, Baron of Pelham*, of Laughton, co Sussex (peerage of Great Britain); *d* 1712; *s* by his son (5) THOMAS, KG, 2nd Baron, *cr Viscount Houghton* and *Earl of Clare* (peerage of Great Britain) 1714, with remainder to his brother Henry; Marquess of Clare and Duke of Newcastle (peerage of Great Britain) 1715, with similar limitation; Duke of Newcastle-under-Lyme (peerage of Great Britain) 1756, with remainder to Henry, 9th Earl of Lincoln, who had *m* Catherine, da of his brother Henry (ante); and *Baron Pelham of Stanmer* (peerage of Great Britain) 1762, with remainder to his cousin Thomas, grandson of Henry, 3rd son of 3rd Bt; *d* without male issue 1768, when the peerages of 1712, 1714, 1715 became extinct, the dukedom of 1756 passed to the Earl of Lincoln, and the peerage of 1762 devolved upon his kinsman (6) THOMAS, PC, 2nd Baron Pelham; was successively MP for Sussex, Commr of Trade and Plantations, a Lord of the Admiralty, and Comptroller of the Household; *cr Earl of Chichester* 1801; *d* 1805; *s* by his son (7) THOMAS, 2nd Earl; *b* 1756; MP for Sussex 1780-90; was successively Sec to Lord-Lieut of Ireland, and Sec of State for Home Depart, Chancellor of Duchy of Lancaster, and Postmaster Gen; called to House of Lords in his father's barony 1801: *m* 1801, Mary Henrietta Juliana, who *d* 1862, da of 5th Duke of Leeds; *d* 1826; *s* by his son (8) HENRY THOMAS, 3rd Earl; *b* 1804; was Lord-Lieut of Sussex: *m* 1828, Lady Mary Brudenell, who *d* 1867, da of 6th Earl of Cardigan; *d* March 1886; *s* by his son (9) WALTER JOHN, 4th Earl; *b* 1838; MP for Lewes (*L*) 1865-74: *m* 1861, Elizabeth Mary, who *d* 1911, da of late Hon Sir John Duncan Bligh, KCB (*see* E Darnley, 1911 Edn); *d* 1902; *s* by his brother (10) *Rev* FRANCIS GODOLPHIN, 5th Earl; *b* 1844: *m* 1870, Hon Alice Carr Glyn, who *d* 1934, da of 1st Baron Wolverton; *d* 1905; *s* by his son (11) JOCELYN BRUDENELL, OBE, 6th Earl, *b* 1871; a Public Works Loan Commr 1904-26: *m* 1898, Ruth, da of late Francis William Buxton; *d* 14 Nov 1926; *s* by his el son (12) FRANCIS GODOLPHIN HENRY, 7th Earl, *b* 1905; *d* 22 Nov 1926: *s* by his brother (13) JOHN BUXTON, 8th Earl, *b* 1912; Capt Scots Guards: *m* 1940, Ursula, who *d* 1989, having *m* 2ndly, 1957 (*m diss* 1971), Ralph Gunning Henderson, da of late Walter de Pannwitz, of Hartekamp, Benebroek, Holland; *d* on active service 1944; *s* by his son (14) JOHN NICHOLAS, 9th Earl and present peer; also Baron Pelham of Stanmer.

Chichester, family name of Marquess of Donegall.

Chichester, Viscount; grandson of Marquess of Donegall.

CHILSTON, VISCOUNT (Akers-Douglas) (Viscount UK 1911)

Wisdom and Truth

ALASTAIR GEORGE AKERS-DOUGLAS, 4th Viscount; *b* 5 Sept 1946; *s* 1982; *ed* Eton; patron of one living: *m* 1971, Juliet Anne, da of Lt-Col Nigel Lovett, of The Old Rectory, Inwardleigh, Okehampton, Devon, and has issue.

Arms – Quarterly: 1st and 4th argent, a man's heart gules, ensigned with an imperial crown and pierced by an arrow fessewise, the pheon to the dexter, proper; on a chief azure, three mullets of the field, *Douglas*; 2nd and 3rd, gules, three escallops or within a bordure argent, charged with eight acorns proper, *Akers*. **Crests** – 1st, an arm in armour embowed proper, garnished or, the gauntlet grasping a dagger also proper, *Douglas*; 2nd, an arm in armour embowed proper, garnished or, the gauntlet grasping a pennon barry of four azure and argent, *Akers*. **Supporters** – *Dexter*, a horse argent, supporting a banner azure charged with three mullets also argent; *sinister*, a like horse supporting a similar banner ermine, charged with a man's heart gules, ensigned with an imperial crown, and pierced by an arrow fesse wise, the pheon to the dexter, proper.
Seats – Chilston Park, Sandway, Maidstone, Kent; Craigs, near Dumfries. *Residence* – The Old Rectory, Twyford, Winchester, Hants.

SONS LIVING

Hon OLIVER IAN, *b* 13 Oct 1973.
Hon Alexander Hugh, *b* 1975.
Hon Dominic, *b* 1979.

SISTER LIVING (*Raised to the rank of a Viscount's daughter* 1995)

Hon Diana, *b* 1948: *m* 1969, Simon Richard Harrap, and has issue (*see* Darell, Bt). *Residence* – Perryland, Bentley, Farnham, Hants.

HALF-SISTER LIVING (*Raised to the rank of a Viscount's daughter* 1995)

Hon Jennifer, *b* 1938: *m* 1st, 1958, George David Henry Wiggin (*see* Wiggin, Bt, colls), who *d* 1990; 2ndly, 1993, Charles Arthur Smith-Bingham. *Residence* – Stag Cottage, Bagnor, Newbury, Berks.

MOTHER LIVING

Phyllis Rosemary, da of late Arthur David Clere Parsons (*see* E Rosse, colls): *m* 1st, 1945, as his 2nd wife, Capt Ian Stanley Akers-Douglas, who *d* 1952; 2ndly, 1965, John Anthony Cobham Shaw (*see* By Cobham). *Residence* – 1 Garden Cottages, Amesbury Abbey, Amesbury, Wilts SP4 7EX.

COLLATERAL BRANCH LIVING

Grandchildren of late Lt-Col Hon George Alexander Akers-Douglas, Royal Fusiliers, 2nd son of 1st Viscount:—

Issue of late Maj Anthony George Akers-Douglas, late 13th/18th Royal Hussars, *b* 1914, *d* 1991: *m* 1941, Dorothy Louise (23 Mytten Close, Cuckfield, W Sussex RH17 5LN), da of late Brig-Gen Moreton Foley Gage, DSO (*see* V Gage, colls):—

Adrian Anthony (PO Box 257, Limassol, Cyprus), *b* 1943; *ed* Eton: *m* 1st, 1974 (*m diss* 1994), Janet (Penny), da of Sir Frederick Cecil Mason, KCVO, CMG, of The Old Forge, Ropley, Alresford, Hants; 2ndly, 1996, Artemis, eldest da of Louis Coudounari, and widow of George Yiordamli, and has issue living (by 1st *m*), Lara Victoria, *b* 1983, — Nicola Antonia, *b* 1991. —— Francis Alexander Moreton (Warrie Wood House, Windmill Hill, St Mary's Platt, Sevenoaks, Kent TN15 8QR), *b* 1948; *ed* Eton: *m* 1st, 1974 (*m diss* 1997), Hon Julian Mary Warrender, elder da of 2nd Baron Bruntisfield; 2ndly, 1998, Mrs Lorna Anne Stables, yr da of John Farquharson, of Aberdeen, and has issue living (by 1st *m*), Joseph Michael Aretas, *b* 1979, — James George, *b* 1989, — (by 2nd *m*), Maxwell Alastair Edward, *b* 1998. —— Laura Dorothy, *b* 1957: *m* 1985, Nicholas James Bell, of Old Post Office, Upton, nr Andover, Hants SP11 0JS, elder son of Dr Anthony Bell, of Woodruffs Farm, Fittleworth, Sussex, and has issue living, Joshua Anthony Fernie, *b* 1988, — Benedict William James *b* 1991, — Eliza Dorothy Thalia, *b* 1994.

PREDECESSORS – (1) ARETAS Akers-Douglas, GBE, PC, son of late Rev Aretas Akers, of Malling Abbey, Kent; *b* 1851; Patronage Sec to the Treasury June 1885 to Jan 1886, July 1889 to Aug 1892, and June to July 1895, First Commr of Works, with a seat in the Cabinet July 1895 to Aug 1902, and Sec of State for Home Depart Aug 1902 to Dec 1905; assumed in 1875, by Roy licence, the additional surname of Douglas; MP for E Kent (*C*) 1880-85, and for St Augustine's Div of Kent 1885-1911; *cr Baron Douglas of Baads*, co Midlothian, and *Viscount Chilston*, of Boughton Malherbe, co Kent (peerage of United Kingdom) 1911: *m* 1875, Adeline, who *d* 1929, da of Horatio Austen Smith, of Hayes Court, Kent; *d* 1926; *s* by his el son (2) ARETAS, GCMG, PC, 2nd Viscount, *b* 1876; was Envoy Extraor and Min Plen at Vienna 1921-28, and at Budapest 1928-33, and Ambassador at Moscow 1933-38: *m* 1903, Amy, who *d* 1962, da of J. R. Jennings Bramley, RHA; *d* 1947; *s* by his 2nd son (3) ERIC ALEXANDER, 3rd Viscount, *b* 1910: *m* 1955, Marion, who *d* 1970, da of late Capt Charles William Howard, RE; *d* 1982; *s* by his cousin (4) ALASTAIR GEORGE (son of late Capt Ian Stanley Akers-Douglas, el son of Lt-Col Hon George Alexander Akers-Douglas, yr son of 1st Viscount), 4th Viscount and present peer; also Baron Douglas of Baads.

CHILVER, BARON (Chilver) (Life Baron 1987)

(AMOS) HENRY CHILVER, FRS, eldest son of Amos Henry Chilver, of Southend-on-Sea, Essex; *b* 30 Oct 1926; *ed* Southend High Sch, and Bristol Univ; lectr Bristol Univ 1952-54, and Camb Univ 1956-61; Fell CCC 1958-61 (Hon Fell 1981); FRS (1982), FEng (1977), CIMgt, Hon DSc Bath, Bristol, Buckingham, Compiegne, Cranfield, Leeds, Salford and Strathclyde Univs; Prof of Civil Engrg Univ Coll London 1961-69; Dir Centre for Environmental Studies 1967-69, Vice Chancellor Cranfield Inst of Technology 1970-89; Chm ECC Group plc 1989-95, Milton Keynes Development Corpn 1983-92, RJB Mining 1993-97, and Chiroscience 1995-98; author and contributor to various papers on structural theory in engineering journals; *cr* Kt 1978, and *Baron Chilver*, of Cranfield, co Beds (Life Baron) 1987: *m* 1959, Claudia Mary Beverley, only da of late Sir Wilfrid Grigson, CSI, of Pelynt, Cornwall, and has issue.

Residence – Lanlawren House, Trenewan, Looe, Cornwall PL13 2PZ. *Clubs* – Athenaeum, and United Oxford and Cambridge.

SONS LIVING

Hon John, *b* 1964; *ed* Bedford Sch.
Hon Mark, *b* 1965; *ed* Bedford Sch.
Hon Paul, *b* 1967; *ed* Bedford Sch.

DAUGHTERS LIVING

Hon Helen, *b* 1960: *m* 1979, Geoffrey Prentice.
Hon Sarah, *b* 1962: *m* 1991, Francis Vaughan.

CHITNIS, BARON (Chitnis) (Life Baron 1977)

PRATAP CHIDAMBER CHITNIS, son of late Chidamber Chitnis; *b* 1 May 1936; *ed* Stonyhurst, Birmingham Univ (BA), and Kansas Univ (MA); Head of Liberal Party Organisation 1966-69; Chief Exec Rowntree Social Ser Trust 1969-88; Member of Community Relations Comn 1971-77; *cr Baron Chitnis*, of Ryedale, co N Yorks (Life Baron) 1977: *m* 1964, Anne, da of Frank Mansell Brand, and had issue (one son deceased).

Address – Beverley House, Shipton Rd, York.

CHOLMONDELEY, MARQUESS OF (Cholmondeley) (Marquess UK 1815)
(Name and Title pronounced "Chumley")

Virtue is the safest helmet

DAVID GEORGE PHILIP CHOLMONDELEY, 7th Marquess; *b* 27 June 1960; *s* 1990; *ed* Eton, and La Sorbonne; a Page of Honour to HM 1974-76; Joint Hereditary Lord Great Chamberlain of England (acting for reign of Queen Elizabeth II since 1990).

Arms – Gules, in chief two esquires' helmets argent, and in base a garb or. **Crest** – A demi-griffin segreant sable, beaked, winged, and membered or, holding between the claws a helmet as in the arms. **Supporters** – *Dexter*, a griffin sable, beaked, winged, and membered or, langued gules; *sinister*, a wolf or, collared vaire, armed and langued gules.
Seats – Cholmondeley Castle, Malpas, Cheshire; Houghton Hall, King's Lynn, Norfolk.

SISTERS LIVING

Lady Rose Aline, *b* 1948. *Residence* – 44 Bassett Rd, W10 6JL.
Lady Margot Lavinia, *b* 1950: *m* 1978 (*m diss* 19—), (Walter) Anthony Huston, only son of late John Huston, film director, of Las Caletas, Puerto Vallarta, Mexico, and has issue living, Matthew Horatio, *b* 1979, — Jack Alexander, *b* 1982, — Laura Sybil, *b* 1981. *Residence* – Village Farm, Houghton, King's Lynn, Norfolk.
Lady Caroline Mary, *b* 1952: *m* 1982, Rodolphe d'Erlanger, son of late Leo Frederic Alfred d'Erlanger, and has issue living, Leo Frederic Hugh, *b* 1983, — David Joshua Robert, *b* 1987.

AUNT LIVING *(daughter of 5th Marquess)*

Lady Aline Caroline, *b* 1916. *Residence* – 39B Eaton Sq, SW1.

WIDOW LIVING OF SON OF FIFTH MARQUESS

Maria Cristina (*Lady John Cholmondeley*), only da of late Giorgio Solari, of Genoa: *m* 1957, Lord John George Cholmondeley, who *d* 1986, and has issue (see colls, infra). *Residence* – 22 Hyde Park Gdns, W2.

WIDOW LIVING OF SIXTH MARQUESS

LAVINIA MARGARET (*Marchioness of Cholmondeley*), only da of late Lt-Col John Leslie, DSO, MC, of Brancaster, Norfolk (*see* Skipwith, Bt, colls, 1934 Edn); DL Cheshire 1992: *m* 1947, Maj the 6th Marquess of Cholmondeley, GCVO, MC, who *d* 1990. *Residences* – Cholmondeley Castle, Malpas, Cheshire; Houghton Hall, King's Lynn, Norfolk.

COLLATERAL BRANCHES LIVING

Issue of late Lord John George Cholmondeley, yr son of 5th Marquess, *b* 1920, *d* 1986: *m* 1957, Maria Cristina (ante), only da of late Giorgio Solari, of Genoa:—
CHARLES GEORGE, *b* 18 March 1959. —— Joanna Antonia, *b* 1958.

Issue of late Lord George Hugo Cholmondeley, OBE, MC, son of 4th Marquess, *b* 1887, *d* 1958: *m* 1st, 1911 (*m diss* 1921), Clara Elizabeth, who *d* 1925, da of Charles Henry Taylor, of Washington, USA, and formerly wife of Maj John Alexander Stirling, DSO, MC; 2ndly, 1921 (*m diss* 1948), Ina Marjorie Gwendoline, OBE, who *d* 1969, da of late Rev Canon Raymond Percy Pelly (Pelly, Bt, colls), and formerly wife of Maj Hon Christopher Lowther (*see* V Ullswater, 1935 Edn); 3rdly, 1948, Diana, who *d* 1965, da of late Hon Rupert Evelyn Beckett (*see* B Grimthorpe, colls, 1955 Edn), and widow of Albany Kennett Charlesworth, MC (*see* Laurie Bt, 1941 Edn):—
(By 1st *m*) Irene, *b* 1913: *m* 1937, Stanislaw Falkowski, MD, late Maj RAMC, who *d* 1986, having assumed 1949 the names of Stephen Falkland, and has issue living, Priscilla Susan, *b* 1948: *m* 1974, Robert A. I. Dicketts, of Rosemary Cottage, Claphatch Lane, Wadhurst, Sussex TN5 6HN, and has issue living, Oliver Simon *b* 1979.

PREDECESSORS – Robert Cholmondeley; *cr* a Baronet 1611, *Viscount Cholmondeley of Kells* (peerage of Ireland) 1628, *Baron Cholmondeley*, of Wiche Malbank (peerage of England) 1645 and *Earl of Leinster* (peerage of England) 1646; *dsp* 1659, when the honours became extinct and his estates passed to his nephew **(1)** ROBERT Cholmondeley; *cr Viscount Cholmondeley*, of Kells, 1661; *s* by his son **(2)** HUGH, 2nd Viscount; *cr Baron Cholmondeley*, of Namptwich (peerage of England) 1689, with remainder to his brother George, and *Viscount Malpas* and *Earl of Cholmondeley* (peerage of Great Britain) 1706, with similar remainder; *d* unmarried 1724; *s* by his brother **(3)** GEORGE, 2nd Earl, who had previously been *cr Baron Newborough*, of Newborough, co Wexford (peerage of Ireland) 1715, and *Baron Newburgh* in the Isle of Anglesey (peerage of Great Britain) 1716; a distinguished military officer; commanded Horse Guards at battle of the Boyne; *d* 1733; *s* by his son **(4)** GEORGE, KB, PC, 3rd Earl; MP for East Looe 1724 and Windsor 1727; successively Master of the Robes; Chancellor of Duchy of Lancaster, Keeper of Privy Seal, Paymaster Gen, and Treasurer of War for Ireland; *d* 1770; *s* by his grandson **(5)** GEORGE JAMES, KG, 4th Earl; *b* 1749; was Lord Steward of the Household; *cr Earl* *of Rocksavage* and *Marquess of Cholmondeley* (peerage of United Kingdom) 1815; *d* 1827; *s* by his son **(6)** GEORGE HORATIO, PC, 2nd Marquess; *b* 1792; summoned to House of Lords in his father's Barony of Newborough 1821; *s* his mother as Joint Hereditary Great Chamberlain of England 1838; *dsp* 1870; *s* by his brother **(7)** WILLIAM HENRY HUGH, 3rd Marquess; *b* 1800; sat as MP for Castle Rising 1822-32, and for S Hampshire (C) 1852-57; *d* 1884; *s* by his grandson **(8)** GEORGE HENRY HUGH (son of late Charles George Cholmondeley, by his wife, Susan Caroline, who *d* 1891, da of Sir George Dashwood, 4th Bt), PC, 4th Marquess, *b* 1858; Joint Hereditary Lord Great Chamberlain (acted for reign of King Edward VII): *m* 1879, Winifred Ida, OBE, who *d* 1938, da of late Col Sir Robert Nigel Fitzhardinge Kingscote, KCB, of Kingscote, Wotton-under-Edge (E Howe); *d* 1923; *s* by his son **(9)** GEORGE HORATIO CHARLES, GCVO, 5th Marquess *b* 1883; Joint Hereditary Lord Great Chamberlain (acted for reign of King Edward VIII, and for reign of Queen Elizabeth II 1952-66): *m* 1913, Sybil Rachel Betty Cécile, CBE, who *d* 1989, da of Sir Edward Albert Sassoon, 2nd Bt (*cr* 1890) ext; *d* 1968; *s* by his son **(10)** (GEORGE) HUGH, GCVO, MC, 6th Marquess, *b* 1919; Joint Hereditary Lord Great Chamberlain (acted for reign of Queen Elizabeth II 1966-90): *m* 1947, Lavinia Margaret, only da of late Lt-Col John Leslie, DSO, MC, of Brancaster, Norfolk (*see* Skipwith, Bt, colls, 1934 Edn); *d* 1990; *s* by his only son **(11)** DAVID GEORGE PHILIP, 7th Marquess and present peer; also Earl of Rocksavage, Earl of Cholmondeley, Viscount Malpas, Baron Cholmondeley, Baron Newborough, and Baron Newburgh.

Cholmondeley, family name of Baron Delamere.

CHORLEY, BARON (Chorley) (Baron UK 1945)

ROGER RICHARD EDWARD CHORLEY, 2nd Baron, *b* 14 Aug 1930; *s* 1978; *ed* Stowe, and Gonville and Caius Coll, Camb; Hon DSc Reading 1990, and Kingston 1992; Pres RGS 1987-90; Chm The National Trust 1991-95: *m* 1964, Ann, yr da of A. S. Debenham, of Ingatestone, Essex, and has issue.

𝔄rms – Per chevron argent and vert, in chief two blue-bottles proper and in base a fountain. 𝔠rest – In front of two torches in saltire or and inflamed, a teazle stalked and leaved proper. 𝔖upporters – On either side a buzzard proper.
Residence – Field Head House, Hawkshead, Cumbria. *Club* – Alpine.

SONS LIVING

Hon NICHOLAS RUPERT DEBENHAM, *b* 15 July 1966: *m* 1996, Morag Jane, yr da of W. S. Smith, of St Andrews.
Hon Christopher Robert Hopkinson, *b* 1968.

BROTHER LIVING

Hon (Geoffrey) Patrick Hopkinson, *b* 1933; *ed* Stowe, and New Coll, Oxford: *m* 1st, 1955 (*m diss* 1972), Daria Antonia Maria, da of the Marquis de Merindol; 2ndly, 1975, May Amaryllis, da of Prof A. Ashmore, of 24 Pine Rd, Didsbury, Manchester, and has issue living (by 1st *m*), Alexandra (Asya) Maria, *b* 1956: *m* 1981, Hugh Bett, son of Cdr R. T. Bett, of Paxtons, E Lavant, Sussex, — Elizabeth Henrietta Marianne, *b* 1961. *Residence* – Briar House, Briar Rd, Twickenham, Middx.

PROPOSITI TENAX
Tenacious of purpose

SISTER LIVING

Hon Gillian Theodora Marianne, *b* 1929; *ed* Liverpool Coll for Girls, and St Anne's Coll, Oxford; *m* 1965, F. Godfrey Goodwin of 29 Chalcot Sq, NW1, and has issue living, Robert Theodore Chorley, *b* 1969.

PREDECESSOR – **(1)** ROBERT SAMUEL THEODORE CHORLEY, QC, 1st Baron, son of Richard Fisher Chorley, of Kendal; *b* 1895; *cr Baron Chorley* of Kendal, co Westmorland (Peerage of UK) 1945; Bar Inner Temple 1920, QC 1961; a Principal, Home Office 1940-41, Assist-Sec Min of Home Security 1941-42, Dep Regional Commr for Civil Defence (NW Region) 1942-44; a Lord-in-Waiting to HM 1945-50: *m* 1925, Katharine Campbell, who *d* 1986, only da of Edward Hopkinson, DSc, of Alderley Edge, Cheshire; *d* 1978; *s* by his son **(2)** ROGER RICHARD EDWARD, 2nd Baron and present peer.

CHRISTOPHER, BARON (Christopher) (Life Baron 1998)

ANTHONY MARTIN GROSVENOR CHRISTOPHER, CBE, son of late George Russell Christopher, of Bath, by his late wife, Helen Kathleen Milford (née Rowley); *b* 25 April 1925; *ed* Cheltenham Gram Sch, and Westminster Coll of Commerce; Chm Trades Union Unit Trust Managers Ltd 1983; Public Affairs Consultant since 1989; Assist Sec, Inland Revenue Staff Fedn 1957-60, Assist Gen Sec 1960-74, Jt Gen Sec 1975, Gen Sec 1976-88; Vice-Pres Building Societies Assoc 1985-90; Dir Civil Service Building Soc 1958-87, and Birmingham Midshires Building Soc 1987-88; Pres TUC Gen Council 1988-89 (Memb 1976-89); Memb Bd Civil Service Housing Assoc 1958-96 (Vice-Chm 1988-96), Council of Nat Assoc for Care and Resettlement of Offenders 1956 (Chm 1973-98), Home Secretary's Advisory Council for Probation and After-Care Cttee 1966-79, Home Secretary's Working Party on Treatment of Habitual Drunken Offenders 1969-71, Council of Policy Studies Inst, Council Inst of Manpower Stations, Royal Commn on Distribution of Income and Wealth 1978-79, IBA 1978-83, Economic Social Research Council 1985-88, Gen Medical Council 1989-94, Tyre Industry EDC (Chm) 1983-86, TUC Gen Council 1976-89, TUC Economic Cttee 1977-89, TUC Education Cttee 1977-85, TUC Employment Policy and Organisation Cttee 1979-89, TUC Int Cttee 1982-89, TUC Media Working Group 1979-89 (Chm 1985-89), and other cttees; author; FRSA 1989; *cr* CBE 1984, and *Baron Christopher*, of Leckhampton, co Glos (Life Baron) 1998: *m* 1962, Adela Joy Thompson. *Address* – c/o TU Fund Managers Ltd, Congress House, Great Russell St, WC1B 3LQ. *Clubs* – Beefsteak, Wig and Pen, and RAC.

Chubb, family name of Baron Hayter.

CHURCHILL, VISCOUNT (Spencer) (Viscount UK 1902)

God defend the right

VICTOR GEORGE SPENCER, 3rd Viscount; *b* (*posthumous*) 31 July 1934; *s* 1973; *ed* Eton, and New Coll, Oxford (MΛ); Lt Scots Gds 1953-55.

Arms – Quarterly argent and gules, in the 2nd and 3rd quarters a fret or, over all on a bend sable, three escallops of the first. **Crest** – Out of a ducal crest coronet or, a griffin's head, between two wings expanded argent, gorged with a bar gemelle gules. **Supporters** – *Dexter*, a griffin wings elevated per fesse argent and or, gorged with a collar or, charged with three escallops sable, line reflexed over the back also or; *sinister*, a wyvern wings elevated gules, gorged with a collar or, charged with three escallops sable.
Residence – 6 Cumberland Mansions, George St, W1.

SISTER LIVING

Hon Sarah Faith Georgina, MBE *b* 1931; MBE (Civil) 1997: *m* 1951, Richard John Palmer, JP, DL, and has issue living, David Charles, *b* 1955: *m* 1989, Lucy Belinda, elder da of late Capt Patrick John Boteler Drury-Lowe (*see* Earle, Bt), and has issue living, George Richard Charles *b* 1992, Shamus Patrick John *b* 1993, a son *b* 1996, — James Nicholas (49 Fernside Rd, SW12 8LN), *b* 1963: *m* 1988, Cybele I., da of Francis Bullock, of Egypt Farm, Hamptons, Kent, and has issue living, Oliver Victor George *b* 1990, Sophie Rose *b* 1995, — Christopher Richard, *b* 1967, — Caroline Mary, *b* 1952: *m* 1st, 1975 (*m diss* 1991), Maj Hon Richard Nicholas Bethell, MBE, elder son of 5th Baron Westbury; 2ndly, 1992, as his 2nd wife, Mark Chaytor Dickinson, of The Courtyard, Newbrough, Hexham, Northumberland (*see* Chaytor, Bt, 1990 Edn). *Residence* – Queen Anne's Mead, Swallowfield, Berks

COLLATERAL BRANCHES LIVING (*In remainder to Barony only*)

Granddaughter of late Col John Winston Thomas MUNRO-SPENCER, who assumed the additional surname of Munro 1911, son of late Lt-Col Hon George Augustus Spencer, 2nd son of 1st Baron:—
Issue of late Capt Almeric Stuart John Spencer, *b* 1885, *d* 1960: *m* 1912 (*m diss* 1928), Phyllis Margaret, who *d* 1971, da of late Charles Richard Rivers, of 20 Palmeira Square, Hove, and Orrell, Lancashire:—
Synolda Joan Margaret (Church View, West St, Hinton St George, Crewkerne, Somerset TA17 8SA), *b* 1914: *m* 1949, Capt Cecil Campbell Hardy, DSO, RN, who *d* 1963, and has issue living, Charles Rupert Almeric, *b* 1951; *ed* Wellington Coll, and Magdalene Coll, Camb (BA); MBA (Insead): *m* 1982, Helen, da of Lt-Col R. C. Orgill, OBE, and has issue

living, Robin Campbell Richard *b* 1984, Jack Spencer *b* 1986, Christopher Munro *b* 1992, — Theodora Margaret, *b* 1953; LCST: *m* 1989, Jeremy Gilson Lowe, and has issue living, Nicholas Jasper *b* 1994, Jessamy Synolda *b* 1991.

Grandchildren of late Lt-Col Augustus Campbell Spencer, son of Gen Hon Sir Augustus Almeric Spencer, GCB, 3rd son of 1st Baron:—
Issue of late Col Richard Augustus Spencer, DSO, OBE, *b* 1888, *d* 1956: *m* 1925, Maud Evelyn, who *d* 1989, da of late Lieut-Col Henry Lushington Ramsay (*see* E Dalhousie, colls, 1990 Edn):—
(RICHARD) HARRY RAMSAY (The Old Vicarage, Vernham Dean, Hants SP11 0EN), *b* 11 Oct 1926; *hp* to Barony of Church-ill; late Lt Coldm Gds; ARIBA, AADipl: *m* 1958, Antoinette Rose-Marie, who *d* 1994, da of Godefroy de Charrière, of Pervenrenges, Lausanne, Switzerland, and has issue living, Michael Richard de Charrière, *b* 1960: *m* 1995, Elisabeth Monk, — David Anthony, *b* 1970. ———— Charles Geoffrey Campbell (Stokke Common, Marlborough, Wilts), *b* 1928; late Lt Coldm Guards; served in Malaya 1948-50, and Kenya 1954-56: *m* 1964, Cherry Elizabeth, da of William Carlyle Clarke.

Issue of late Lt-Col (Edward) Almeric Spencer, OBE, RA, *b* 1892, *d* 1984: *m* 1918, Elsie Winifred, who *d* 1969, da of Arthur Macan, DL, of Drumcashel, co Louth:—
Guinevere Elsie (Lower House, Ashley, Box, Corsham, Wilts), *b* 1920: *m* 1945 (*m diss* 1975), Charles Arthur Wellesley Williamson, MC, TD, late Maj Sherwood Foresters, and has issue living, Richard Almeric Spencer, *b* 1949; *ed* Winchester: *m* 1st, 1970 (*m diss* 1982), June, da of Wilfrid Mansfield; 2ndly, 1982, Aura Figueroa, and has issue living, (by 1st *m*) Sasha *b* 1971, Damian *b* 1974, Mischa *b* 1977, — Michael Anthony Wellesley (4 Somer's Place, Leamington Spa, Warwicks), *b* 1952; *ed* Winchester, and Durham Univ (BA); ARCM: *m* 1981, Pascale Eyre, — Francis Charles Fitzroy, *b* 1959; *ed* Wellington Coll; MSc, — Patrick Alexander Campbell, *b* 1960; *ed* Wellington Coll, — Sarah Lavinia, *b* 1946: *m* 1976, Michael Danny, of The Manor House, Wellow, Bath, and has issue living, William *b* 1979, Christopher *b* 1981, Melissa *b* 1976.

Grandchildren of late Brig-Gen John Almeric Walter Spencer, CMG, DSO, son of late Capt William Francis Spencer, elder son of late Rev Hon William Henry Spencer, 4th son of 1st Baron:—
Issue of late Capt John Lawrence Spencer, DSO, MC, *b* 1917, *d* 1967: *m* 1943, Jane Lilian (Ghyllas, Sedbergh, Cumbria), da of late Col Granville Duff, MC, of Heydon, Norfolk:—
John William James, *b* 1957; *ed* Sedbergh, and Magdalene Coll, Camb: *m* 1st, 1982 (*m diss* 1987), Leonie Margaret, da of Ralph Jameson, 2ndly, 1987, Jane Elizabeth, da of late Andrew Young, and has issue living (by 2nd *m*), Charles William Alexander, *b* 1990, — Rosanagh Jane Katharine, *b* 1991, — Caitlin Anne Sophia, *b* 1996. *Residence* – Ghyllas, Sedbergh, Cumbria LA10 5LT. ———— Caroline Mary, *b* 1948: *m* 1969, Robin Peter Sandys-Clarke, son of late Lt W. A. Sandys-Clarke, VC, of Bolton, and has issue living, Peter Edward David, *b* 1981, — Jessica Jane, *b* 1975, — Lucinda Mary *b* 1977.

Granddaughter of late Col Almeric George Spencer, yr son of late Rev Hon William Henry Spencer (ante):—
Issue (by 2nd *m*) of late Lt-Col Almeric Arthur William Spencer, *b* 1874, *d* 1934: *m* 1st, 1907 (*m diss* 1927), Sybil da of Frederick William Lawson, formerly of Oaklands, Adel, Leeds; 2ndly, 1930, Charlotte (34 Ashgarth Court, Harrogate, N Yorks) (who *m* 2ndly, 1941, Cecil Trevor Hamilton Whiteside, MC, MRCS, who *d* 1965 (*see* L Belhaven, colls, 1980 Edn), da of late Rev John Lesley Parker, V of Lanteglos, Fowey:—
Ann Frances, *b* 1931; resumed her maiden name 1963: *m* 1st, 1957 (*m* annulled 1963), Rev Leslie Vandernoll Wright; 2ndly, 1979, Patrick Joseph Healy.

Grandson of late Col Francis Elmhirst Spencer, DSO, MC (infra):—
Issue of late Francis Tracey Spencer, *b* 1917, *d* 1989: *m* 1962, *Rev* Diana (3013 Josette Place, Victoria, BC, Canada V8T 4Z9), eldest da of Dennis Haines, of Wattisfield Croft, Suffolk:—
Philip Henry (15-8 High Park Av, Toronto, Ont, Canada M6P 2R9), *b* 1966; *ed* Glenlyon Sch, Victoria, Univ of Victoria (BSc), and Harvard (PhD).

Granddaughter of late Lt-Col Charles Francis Henry Spencer, el son of late Rev Hon Charles Frederic Octavius Spencer, 8th son of 1st Baron:—
Issue of late Col Francis Elmhirst Spencer, DSO, MC, *b* 1881, *d* 1972: *m* 1916, Augusta (Vera), who *d* 1956, da of late Col Arthur Tracey, formerly RGA:—
Joan Elizabeth, *b* 1921; late QARNNS (Res): *m* 1949, Surg-Cdr Geoffrey Norman Shell, RN, who *d* 1999, of Gomorin, Court Woods, Newton Ferrers, Plymouth, and has issue living, Peter Geoffrey, *b* 1951; *ed* Haileybury: *m* 1984, Marianne Jane, elder da of Paul Pierre Tissier, FRSS, of 97 Oxford Rd, Abingdon, and has issue living, Timothy Geoffrey *b* 1987, Jonathan Paul *b* 1992, — David Spencer, *b* 1954; *ed* Milton Abbey: *m* 1998, Clare Crofts, and has issue living, Lucy Jane *b* 1998.

PREDECESSORS – **(1)** *Lord* FRANCIS ALMERIC Spencer, DCL, 2nd son of 4th Duke of Marlborough; *b* 1779; *cr Baron Churchill*, of Wychwood, co Oxford (peerage of United Kingdom) 1815: *d* 1845; *s* by his son **(2)** FRANCIS GEORGE, DCL, 2nd Baron; *b* 1802: *m* 1849, Lady Jane Conyngham, VA, who *d* 1900, da of 2nd Marquess Conyngham; *d* 24 Nov 1896; *s* by his son **(3)** VICTOR ALBERT FRANCIS CHARLES, GCVO, 3rd Baron, *b* 1864; was a Page of Honour to Queen Victoria 1876-81, and a Lord-in-Waiting to Queen Victoria 1889-92, and 1895-1901, and to King Edward VII, 1901-5; Chm of Great Western Railway Co, and of British Overseas Bank; Master of the Buckhounds 1900, Lord Chamberlain 1902, and Master of the Robes at Coronation of King George V 1911; KCVO 1900, GCVO 1902; *cr Viscount Churchill*, of Rolleston, co Leicester (peerage of United Kingdom) 1902: *m* 1st, 1887, Lady Verena Maude, VA, who *d* 1938 (from whom he had obtained a divorce for desertion in the Scottish Courts 1927), da of 3rd Earl of Lonsdale; 2ndly, 1927, Christine McRae, who *d* 1972, having *m* 2ndly, 1937 (*m diss* (Reno)) 1938), Lt-Col Ralph Heyward Isham, CBE, who *d* 1955, and 3rdly, 1939, Sir Lancelot Oliphant, KCMG, CB, who *d* 1965, da of William Sinclair; *d* 1934; *s* by his son **(4)** VICTOR ALEXANDER, 2nd Viscount; *b* 1890; FRAS: *m* 1st, 1916, Kathleen, who *d* 1943, da of late Hon Robert Beaven, formerly Premier of Victoria, BC, Canada, and widow of Capt Stanley Venn Ellis, RN; 2ndly, 1949, Joan, who *d* 1957, da of late Joseph Baron Black; *d* 1973; *s* by his half-brother **(5)** VICTOR GEORGE, 3rd Viscount and present peer; also Baron Churchill.

Churchill, Spencer-, family name of Duke of Marlborough.

CHURSTON, BARON (Yarde-Buller) (Baron UK 1858, Bt GB 1790)

AQVILA NON CAPIT·MUSCAS

The eagle does not catch flies

JOHN FRANCIS YARDE-BULLER, 5th Baron and 7th Baronet; *b* 29 Dec 1934; *s* 1991; *ed* Eton; is patron of two livings; late 2nd Lieut RHG: *m* 1973, Alexandra Joanna, only da of Anthony Contomichalos, of 23 Eaton Place, SW1, and has issue.

Arms – Quarterly; 1st and 4th sable, on a cross argent quarterly, pierced of the field, four eagles displayed of the first, *Buller*; 2nd and 3rd argent, a chevron gules, between three water-bougets sable, *Yarde*. Crest – A Saracen's head couped, proper. Supporters – *Dexter*, an ostrich proper, in the beak a horse-shoe or; *sinister*, an eagle sable.
Residence – Yowlestone House, Puddington, Tiverton, Devon. *Clubs* – Buck's, White's.

SON LIVING

Hon BENJAMIN FRANCIS ANTHONY, *b* 13 Sept 1974; *ed* Eton, and ...... Coll, Oxford.

DAUGHTERS LIVING

Hon Katherine Marina, *b* 1975.
Hon Francesca Elizabeth, *b* 1980.

SISTER LIVING

Hon Nicole, *b* 1936: *m* 1st, 1958 (*m diss* 1962), Richard Wilfred Beauvoir Berens, who *d* 1998; 2ndly, 1963, Michael Russell, and has issue living (by 1st *m*), Thomas Richard, *b* 1960; *ed* Bishop Wordsworth Sch, — Jessica Primrose, *b* 1959; *ed* Cranbourne Chase; journalist, — (by 2nd *m*) Francis, *b* 1966; *ed* Harrow: *m* 1993, Penelope G., yr da of late Maj J. I. L. Syddall, of Puddletown, Dorset, — Alexander, *b* 1969; *ed* Eton, and Edinburgh Univ: *m* 1997, Rose M., twin da of John Sydney Fairbairn, DL, of Harvest Hill, Cuckfield, W Sussex, and has issue living, Hector John *b* 1998, — Lorna, *b* 1963; *ed* St Mary's Calne. *Residence* – Wilby Hall, Wilby, Norwich, Norfolk.

AUNTS LIVING AND DECEASED (*daughters of 3rd Baron*) (*in remainder to Barony of Grey of Ruthyn*)

†Hon Joan Barbara, *b* 1908: *m* 1st, 1927 (*m diss* 1936), W/Cdr (Thomas) Loel Evelyn Bulkeley Guinness, OBE, Auxiliary Air Force (Res), who *d* 1988 (*see* By Ardilaun, 1944 Edn); 2ndly, 1936 (*m diss* 1949), Aly Khan, who *d* in a motor accident 1960, son of HH late Rt Hon the Aga Khan, GCSI, GCIE, GCVO; 3rdly, 1986, 2nd Viscount Camrose, who *d* 1995, and *d* 1997, having had issue (*see* B Grey de Ruthyn, colls).
Hon Denise Margaret *b* 1916: *m* 1941 (*m diss* 1954), as his 2nd wife, 5th Baron Ebury, who *d* 1957. *Residence* – 10 Froxfield, Eversholt, Bletchley, Bucks MK17 9DP.
Hon Lydia, *b* 1917: *m* 1st, 1938, Capt Ian Archibald de Hoghton Lyle, Black Watch; who was *ka* 1942 in the Middle East, el son of Sir Archibald Moir Park Lyle, 2nd Bt, MC; 2ndly, 1947 (*m diss* 1960), 13th Duke of Bedford. *Residence* – Little Ribsden, Windlesham, Bagshot, Surrey.

COLLATERAL BRANCHES LIVING

Issue of late Hon John Reginald Henry Yarde-Buller, 2nd son of 3rd Baron, *b* 1915, *d* 1962: *m* 1939, Gwendolen, who *d* 1999, da of late Rev Charles Roots, of Heathfield, Sussex:—
Roger Charles John, *b* 1942. *Residence* – Le Vallon, Mont Félard, Jersey, CI. —— Anthony Reginald Lawrence, *b* 1946. *Residence* – Le Vallon, Mont Félard, Jersey, CI.

Grandchildren of late Hon Geoffrey Yarde-Buller, brother of 2nd Baron:—
Issue of late Geoffrey Yarde-Buller, *b* 1894, *d* 1993: *m* 1st, 1919, Hortensia Naboulet Pajot, who *d* 1957, da of Leon Naboulet, of Parana, Argentina; 2ndly, 19— (*m diss* 1972), Elsa Cejas:—
(By 1st *m*) Norberto (La Tribuna 1705, Castelar, Buenos Aires), *b* 1922: *m* 1946, Yolanda Adela, da of Carlos Devillier, of Florida, Argentina, and has issue living, Daniel Carlos, *b* 1954: *m* 1976, Elda Beatriz Martinez, and has issue living, Soledad Jorgelina *b* 1980, — Norberto Luis, *b* 1959: *m* 1987, Viviana Sandra Masseo, and has issue living, Alexis *b* 1988, Jimena *b* 1989, — Rita Adela, *b* 1947: *m* 1979, Ingeniero Jorge Daniel Balan, and has issue living, Gonzolo Daniel *b* 1992, — Susan Hortensia, *b* 1952: *m* 1985, Marcelo Esteban Gilberto. —— Eduardo (Luis Maria Campos 4029, Villa Insuperable, La Matanza, Buenos Aires), *b* 1926: *m* 1953, Isabel Esther, da of Francisco Hinojosa, of Buenos Aires, and has issue living, Eduardo Guillermo, *b* 1972, — Liliana Beatriz, *b* 1955: *m* 1976, Luciano Dal Cin, and has issue living,

Mariano *b* 1983, Ignacio *b* 1985, Dario *b* 1988, Luciana *b* 1991, — Jaquelina Ines, *b* 1968: *m* 1985, Marcelo Romero, and has issue living, Federico *b* 1991, Maria Azul *b* 1987. —— Lilian (Arias 1955-5° Piso, Dto C, Buenos Aires), *b* 1920: *m* 1st, 1944, Osvaldo Federico Alizeri, who *d* 1962; 2ndly, 1968, Victor Antonio Olivera, Capitan de Corbeta de la Armada Argentina, and has had issue (by 1st *m*), Stella Maria, *b* 1945; *d* 1967, — Diana, *b* 1947: *m* 1973, Juan Jose Molero, and *d* 1980, leaving issue, Federico Jose *b* 1977, Enrique Marcelo *b* 1979. —— Delia (Av Maipu 1864-2° Piso, Vicente Lopez, Buenos Aires), *b* 1932: *m* 1949, Rafael Maria Parravicini Piaggio, who *d* 1967, and has issue living, Octavio Horacio, *b* 1950: *m* 1972, Raquel O. Melgarejo Dutra, and has issue living, Octavio Ovidio *b* 1976, Mercedes *b* 1980, Florencia Soila *b* 1985, Delmira Soita *b* (twin) 1985, — Rafael Guido, *b* 1952: *m* 1980, Ana Maria Liria Laurant, and has issue living, Alejo Andres *b* 1989, Lucia Florencia *b* 1981, — Denise Oriental, *b* 1959. —— Doris (Av Maipu 1468-2° Piso, Vicente Lopez, Buenos Aires), *b* 1934: *m* 1962, Jorge Gattino Cuesta, and has issue living, Gabriela Amalia, *b* 1965: *m* 1988, Ingeniero Leonardo Omar Lanzilotta. —— Estela (Feliciano Chiclana 61, 1708 Morón, Buenos Aires), *b* 1939: *m* 1961, Prof Ismael Sabino Salvatierra, and has issue living, Alejandro Ismael, *b* 1962; Ingeniero, — Eduardo Pablo, *b* 1964; Prof: *m* 1993, Adrioma Marcela Viggiano, — Gustavo Fabian, *b* 1968, — Adriana Hortensia, *b* 1970. —— (By 2nd *m*) Silvia Veronica, *b* 1966: *m* 1984, Luis Cosenza, and has issue living, Alexis, *b* 1985.

       Issue of late Edmond Yarde-Buller, *b* 1897, *d* 19—: *m* 19—, Adela Jmelnisky:—
Reinaldo Alberto, *b* 19—: *m* 19—, Martha Elena Melgar, and has issue living, Christian, *b* 1964. —— Jorge, *b* 19—. —— Anita Sofia, *b* 19—: *m* 19—, Rodolfo Juan Carlos Nux. —— Cecilia Olegaria, *b* 19—: *m* 19—, Eduardo Tirado.

       Descendants, if any, of John Yarde-Buller (1893-1990), Henry Yarde-Buller (*b* 1899), Manuel Yarde-Buller (*b* 1901), Albert Yarde-Buller (*b* 1908), and Reginald Yarde-Buller (*b* 1911), sons of late Hon Geoffrey Yarde-Buller (ante).

                    (*In remainder to Baronetcy only*)

       Descendants of Sir Edward Manningham-Buller (who assumed the additional surname and arms of Manningham) 3rd son of 2nd Bt (*see* V Dilhorne).

PREDECESSORS – **(1)** *Sir* FRANCIS Buller, KB, KC, a very eminent lawyer and a Justice of the Common Pleas; *cr* a *Baronet* 1790; *d* 1800; *s* by his son **(2)** *Sir* FRANCIS, 2nd Bt, MP for Totnes; assumed the additional and final surname of Yarde by Roy licence 1800; *d* 1833; *s* by his son **(3)** JOHN, DCL, 3rd Bt; MP for S Devon (C) 1835-58; assumed the surname of Yarde-Buller by Roy licence 1860; *cr Baron Churston*, of Churston Ferrers, and Lupton, Devon (peerage of United Kingdom) 1858; *d* 1871; *s* by his grandson **(4)** JOHN, 2nd Baron, son of Hon John, el son of 1st Baron, by Charlotte, da of Edward Sacheverell Chandos-Pole, of Radborne, co Derby, *b* 1846: *m* 1872, Hon Barbara, who *d* 1924, da of late Adm Sir Hastings Reginald Yelverton, GCB, and of late Barbara (in her own right) Baroness Grey de Ruthyn, widow of 2nd Marquess of Hastings; *d* 1910; *s* by his son **(5)** JOHN REGINALD LOPES, MVO, OBE, 3rd Baron; *b* 1873; an ADC to Viceroy of India (Baron Curzon of Kedleston) 1902-3, and ADC to Inspector-Gen of the Forces (F-M HRH the Duke of Connaught) 1904-6; sometime Inspector of QMG Sers: *m* 1907 (*m diss* 1928), Jessie, who *d* 1960, only da of late Alfred Smither, *d* 1930; *s* by his son **(6)** RICHARD FRANCIS ROGER, VRD, 4th Baron, *b* 1910; Lt-Cdr RNVR; bore one of the Golden Spurs at the Coronations of King George VI and Queen Elizabeth II: *m* 1st, 1933 (*m diss* 1943), Elizabeth Mary (who *d* 1951, having *m* 2ndly, 1943, Maj Peter Laycock, who *d* 1978), da of late Lt-Col William Baring Du Pree, JP, DL, of Wilton Park, Beaconsfield, Bucks; 2ndly, 1949, Sandra, who *d* 1979, da of Percy Needham, and formerly wife of (i) Claud Harold Bertram Arthur Griffiths, and (ii) Jack Dunfee; 3rdly, 1981, Mrs Olga Alice Muriel Blair, who *d* 1992, natural da of 2nd Baron Rothschild (by Marie Barbara, da of Maximilian Fredenson, of Newton Sq, Bayswater, W2), and formerly wife of Bryce Evans Blair; *d* 1991; *s* by his only son **(7)** JOHN FRANCIS, 5th Baron and present peer.

CITRINE, BARON (Citrine) (Baron UK 1946)

RONALD ERIC CITRINE, 3rd Baron; *b* 19 May 1919; *s* 1997, but does not use the title; *ed* Univ Coll, London; MRCS, LRCP: *m* 1945, Mary, who *d* 1995, da of Reginald Williams, of Wembley, Middx.

𝔄rms – Argent, on waves of the sea in base, an ancient three-masted ship in full sail proper, on a chief gules a Saxon crown between two seaxes points downwards or, the dexter in bend, the sinister in bend sinister. 𝔠rest – A cubit arm habited azure cuffed argent, the hand grasping a citrine proper. 𝔰upporters – *Dexter*, an alsatian wolfhound proper, on the shoulder a terrestial globe or, charged with a human heart; *sinister*, a lion proper, on the shoulder a torteau charged with a spade and pickaxe in saltire and pen-nib in pale or.
Residence – 1 Rosella Place, Maunu, Whangarei, Bay of Islands, New Zealand.

Strive for right

DAUGHTER LIVING OF SECOND BARON

Hon Patricia Deirdre, *b* 1939. *Residence* – 22 Kath Hopper Drive, Orewa, Hibiscus Coast, Northland, NZ.

PREDECESSORS – WALTER MCLENNAN CITRINE, GBE, PC, 1st Baron, son of Alfred Citrine, of Wallasey, *b* 1887; *cr Baron Citrine*, of Wembley, co Middlesex (peerage of UK) 1946; was Gen Sec of Trades Union Congress 1926-46, Pres of Internat Fedn of Trade Unions 1928-45, and Pres of World Fedn of Trade Unions 1945-46; Pres World Anti-Nazi Council 1936-46; first Chm Central Electricity Authority 1947-57: *m* 1913, Doris Helen, who *d* 1973, da of Edgar Slade; *d* 1983; *s* by his el son (2) NORMAN ARTHUR, 2nd Baron, *b* 1914; admitted Solicitor 1937; author of legal textbooks, etc; Legal Adviser to Trades Union Congress 1946-51, and Pres Devon and Exeter Law Soc 1971-72: *m* 1939, Kathleen Alice, who *d* 1993, da of late George Thomas Chilvers, of Saxmundham, Suffolk; *d* 1997; *s* by his brother (3) RONALD ERIC, 3rd Baron and present peer.

CLANCARTY, EARL OF (Le Poer Trench) Sits as VISCOUNT (UK 1823) (Earl I 1803)

NICHOLAS POWER RICHARD LE POER TRENCH, 9th Earl, and Marquis of Heusden in The Netherlands; *b* 1 May 1952; *s* 1995; *ed* Ashford Gram Sch, Plymouth Polytechnic, and Univ of Colorado, Boulder; Artist and Film-Maker.

𝔄rms – Quarterly: 1st and 4th argent, a lion passant gules, between three fleurs-de-lis azure, on a chief azure, a sun in splendour, *Trench*; 2nd and 3rd argent, a chief indented sable, *Le Poer*. Over all an escutcheon or, ensigned with the coronet of a Marquis of the Netherlands and charged with a wheel of six spokes gules. 𝔠rest – 1st, a dexter arm embowed in armour, the hand grasping a scimitar proper; 2nd, a lion rampant or, imperially crowned, holding in the dexter fore paw a naked sword argent, pommel and hilt gold, and in the sinister a sheaf of arrows also or; 3rd, a stag's head cabossed argent, attired or, and between the attires a crucifix. 𝔰upporters – *Dexter*, a lion gules, semée of fleurs-de-lis or; *sinister*, a stag guardant proper, attired or, between the attires a crucifix, and supporting with the sinister fore paw a lance resting bendwise over the shoulder proper, and thereon a banner of the arms of Le Poer.
Address – c/o House of Lords, SW1.

By counsel and prudence

SISTER LIVING

Caroline Jessica Mary LE POER TRENCH, *b* 1954; *ed* St Paul's Girls' Sch, and Wadham Coll, Oxford; painter and print-maker; has retained her maiden name: *m* 1st, 1981 (*m diss* 1984), Alan Rodger; 2ndly, 1991, Robert Richard Hill, and has issue living (by 2nd *m*), Theodore Alexander, *b* 1994. *Residence* – 21 Bullingdon Rd, Oxford OX4 1QQ.

DAUGHTERS LIVING OF SIXTH EARL

Lady Maureen Isabel (No 5 Orchard Cottage, Sutton Manor, Sutton Scotney, Winchester SO21 3JX), *b* 1923: *m* 1949, Christopher Colin Cooper, and has issue living, Simon Richard Colin (Furners Farm, Elcombe, nr Stroud, Glos GL6 7LA), *b* 1956; wood sculptor: *m* 1979, Julia C., yst da of Edmund B. Teesdale, of Little Mullions, Aldsworth, Glos, — Claudia (36 Hurst St, Oxford OX41 8HB), *b* 1952; Univ lecturer, Muscat, Oman.

Lady Caragh Seymour LE POER TRENCH, *b* 1933; has resumed her maiden name: *m* 1st, 1953 (*m diss* 1961), Lt-Cdr John Anthony Lake, RN; 2ndly, 1961, Capt Arthur Jay Oken, USAF; 3rdly, 1966, Capt Donald Van Horn Lee, USAF; 4thly, 19—; 5thly, 19—, — Jefferson, and has issue living (by 1st *m*), Henry John Challoner, *b* 1955, — Catherine Challoner, *b* 1957, — Jean Challoner, *b* 1959. *Address* – PO Box 47788, San Antonio, Texas 78265, USA.

MARY AGNES (*Countess of Clancarty*), da of E. Radonicich, and widow of Cmdr Frank M. Beasley, RN (ret): *m* 1976, as his 4th wife, the 8th Earl of Clancarty, who *d* 1995. *Residence* – Flat 2, 51 Eaton Place, SW1X 8DE.

PREDECESSORS – (1) WILLIAM POWER KEATING Trench, MP for Galway 1768-97; *cr Baron Kilconnel*, of Garbally, co Galway (peerage of Ireland) 1797, *Viscount Dunlo* (peerage of Ireland) 1801, and *Earl of Clancarty* (peerage of Ireland) 1803; *d* 1805; *s* by his son (2) RICHARD, GCB, 2nd Earl; *cr Baron Trench* (peerage of United Kingdom) 1815, and *Viscount Clancarty* (peerage of United Kingdom) 1823; appointed Ambassador to the Hague 1813; *cr Marquis of Heusden*, in the Kingdom of the Netherlands 1818, and in 1824 received the royal permission to bear the title in this country; *d* 1837; *s* by his son (3) WILLIAM THOMAS, 3rd Earl; *b* 1803: *m* 1832, Lady Sarah Juliana Butler, da of 3rd Earl of Carrick; *d* 1872; *s* by his son (4) RICHARD SOMERSET, 4th Earl, *b* 1834: *m* 1866, Lady Adeliza Georgiana Hervey, who *d* 1911, da of 2nd Marquess of Bristol; *d* 1891; *s* by his el son (5) WILLIAM FREDERICK, 5th Earl, *b* 1868: *m* 1st, 1889, Isabel Maude Penrice, who *d* 1906, da of John George Bilton, of Charlton, Kent; 2ndly, 1908, Mary Gwatkin, who *d* 1974, da of late W. F. Rosslewin Ellis, Bar-at-Law, of Fulford, Yorkshire; *d* 1929; *s* by his son (6) RICHARD FREDERICK JOHN DONOUGH, 6th Earl, *b* 1891: *m* 1st, 1915 (*m diss* 1918), Edith Constance, who *d* 1950, da of Maj Alexander Albemarle Rawlinson; 2ndly, 1919, Cora Marie Edith, who *d* 1993, aged 100, da of late H. H. Spooner, of Thornton Hall, Surrey; *d* 1971; *s* by his brother (7) GREVILLE SYDNEY ROCHFORT, 7th Earl; *b* 1902: *m* 1926, Beatrice Georgiana, who *d* 1979, yst da of late Capt James Gordon Miller, of Thurlow Hall, Suffolk; *d* 1975; *s* by his half-brother (8) WILLIAM FRANCIS BRINSLEY, 8th Earl, *b* 1911; sometime Editor *Flying Saucer Review*, and Founder the International Unidentified Object Observer Corps; author (as Brinsley Le Poer Trench) of *The Sky People, Men Among Mankind, Forgotten Heritage*, etc: *m* 1st, 1940 (*m diss* 1947), Diana Joan, da of Sir William Robert Younger, 2nd Bt; 2ndly, 1961 (*m diss* 1969), Wilma Dorothy Millen, da of S. R. Vermilyea, of USA, and formerly wife of William Burke Belknap, Jr; 3rdly, 1974, Mrs Mildred Alleyn Spong, who *d* 1975, da of R. Bensusan; 4thly, 1976, Mary Agnes, da of E. Radonicich, and widow of Cdr Frank M. Beasley, RN (ret); *d* 1995; *s* by his nephew (9) NICHOLAS POWER RICHARD (son of late Hon Power Edward Ford Le Poer Trench, 6th and yst son of 5th Earl), 9th Earl and present peer; also Viscount Dunlo, Viscount Clancarty, Baron Kilconnel, and Baron Trench.

Clanfield, Viscount; son of Earl Peel.

CLANMORRIS, BARON (Bingham) (Baron I 1800)

Christ is my hope

SIMON JOHN WARD BINGHAM, 8th Baron; *b* 25 Oct 1937; *s* 1988; *ed* Downside, and Queens' Coll, Camb (MA); FCA: *m* 1971, Gizella Maria, only da of late Sandor Zverkó, of Budapest, and has issue.

𝕬rms – Azure, a bend cottised or between six crosses-patée or. ℭrest – On a mount a falcon rising all proper. 𝕾upporters – Two lions azure.

DAUGHTER LIVING

Hon Lucy Katherine Gizella, *b* 1974.

SISTER LIVING

Hon Charlotte Mary Thérèse, *b* 1942; *ed* The Priory, Haywards Heath, and the Sorbonne, Paris; novelist and scriptwriter: *m* 1964, Terence Joseph Brady, writer and actor, of Hardway House, Hardway, Bruton, Som BA10 0LR, and has issue living, Matthew Joseph Mulligan, *b* 1972, — Candida Marie Thérèse, *b* 1965: *m* 1994, Titus M. Ogilvy, only son of Ian Ogilvy, actor.

COLLATERAL BRANCHES LIVING

Issue of late Lt-Col Hon (John) Denis Yelverton Bingham, DSO, 2nd son of 5th Baron, *b* 1880, *d* 1940: *m* 1926, Vera, who *d* 1972, da of late Major Norman Darbyshire, of Sefton Park, Liverpool:—

Elizabeth Rosemary, *b* 1927: *m* 1949, Maxwell John Denham, MBE, of Lock Farm, Tixall, Stafford ST18 0XR, and has issue living, (John) Alistair Campbell (19 Vanderbilt Rd, Earlsfield, SW18 3BG), *b* 1955; has issue living (by Fiona Anne, da of Michael Pirie, of Edinburgh), Ella Iona Alice *b* 1994, — Iain Maxwell (The Old Barn, The Green, Fernhurst, nr Haslemere, Surrey GU27 3HY), *b* 1957: *m* 1988, Wendy Ann, da of Albert Edward Johnson, of Hastings, Sussex, and has issue living, Jonathan Maxwell *b* 1991, Jessica Sarah *b* 1989. —— (Mary) Mavourneen Denise, *b* 1931: *m* 1951, Albert Schiff, and has had issue, Robert John Denis, *b* 1958; *ed* Eton: *m* 1983, Lucinda Mary (who *m* 2ndly, 1992 (*m diss* 1996), Andrew Nigel Crosbie Bengough (*see* Albu, Bt, 1980 Edn); 3rdly, 1998, Richard Huxley Cowen, of Newdown Farm, Micheldever, Winchester), elder da of Capt John Geoffrey Sherston, of Terry House, Warehorne, Ashford, Kent, and drowned 1990, leaving issue, Frederick John Albert *b* 1984,

Maximilian Robert Denis *b* 1986, Robert Edmund Bingham *b* (*posthumous*) 1990, — Miranda Caroline, *b* 1952: *m* 1980, Derek Hearn, of Muntins, The Gardens, Adstock, Bucks. *Residence* – Ambrose Farm House, Ramsbury, Wilts SN8 2PW.

Issue of late Rear-Adm Hon Edward Barry Stewart Bingham, VC, OBE, 3rd son of 5th Baron, *b* 1881, *d* 1939: *m* 1915 (*m diss* 1937), Vera, da of Edward Temple Patterson, formerly of 10 Culford Gdns, SW:— Lavinia Mary, *b* 1921: *m* 1946, Simon Campbell (*see* V Hawarden, colls, 1973-74 Edn), and has issue living, Luke Bingham, *b* 1948; *ed* Lancing, — Julian Simon, *b* 1949; *ed* Lancing, — Roderick Barry, *b* 1951; *ed* Lancing, — Nicholas Edward Angus, *b* 1956, — Thomas Neil, *b* 1961: *m* 1994, Rosemary, da of late Maurice Phelan, and has issue living, Eoin Simon *b* 1992, Cormac Barry *b* 1997. *Residence* – Inchivore, Old Connaught Av, Bray, co Wicklow.

Grandchildren of late Hon Hugh Terence de Burgh Bingham (infra):— Issue of late (John) Peter Derrick Bingham, *b* 1913, *d* 1978: *m* 1st, 1939 (*m diss* 1954), Mary Machen, who *d* 1995, eldest da of late Robert Morehead Rose, of Sydney, NSW; 2ndly, 1954, Jean (25/177 Penquite Rd, Launceston, Tas 7250), eldest da of late Robert Harold Hogarth, of Waverley, Tas:— (By 1st *m*) †(Robert) Michael Terence, *b* 1941; *m* 1981, Alison Mary Powell (7/4 Livingstone Place, Newport, NSW 2106, Australia), and *d* 1988, leaving issue, Hannah Catherine Rose, *b* 1983. —— Angela Rose, *b* 1944: *m* 1969, Anthony William Steyn, MB, BS, of Sydney, NSW. *Address* – RR6, Claremont, Ontario, Canada L1Y 1A3.

Issue of late Capt Hugh Denis Sinclair Bingham, Royal Inniskilling Fus, *b* 1914, *d* 1946: *m* 1939, Margaret Douglas (who *m* 2ndly, 1948 (*m diss* 1953), George Lennox Barrow, resumed the surname of Bingham by deed poll 1951, and *d* 1980), da of late Robert Stevenson, of Aloha, Dungannon, co Tyrone:— (ROBERT) DEREK DE BURGH (Cooks Barn, Chillesford Lodge, Sudbourne, Woodbridge, Suffolk IP12 2AN), *b* 29 Oct 1942; *ed* Stowe; formerly Ed *The Field*: *m* 1969, Victoria Mary, yr da of Peter Athelwold Pennant-Rea, MBE, of Laurel Tree Cottage, Guiting Power, Glos, and has issue living, Alexandra Louise Clare, *b* 1974, — Georgina Mary Margaret, *b* 1976, — Rosamunde Jessica Elizabeth, *b* 1979. —— (Jane) Victoria Clare BINGHAM, *b* 1941; has resumed her maiden name: *m* 1966 (*m diss* 1985), Béla Peter de Daranyi, and has issue living, Imre Patrick Béla, *b* 1973, — Katherine Emma Margaret, *b* 1967: *m* 1991, Angus W. Jurkschat, and has issue living, Rudi Béla MacGregor *b* 1997, Natasha Clare Mac-Gregor *b* 1998, — Sophie Jane Clare, *b* 1968: *m* 1995, Gareth G. B. Hudd, 2nd son of Glyn Hudd, of Gravesend, Kent, and has issue living, Isabella Victoria *b* 1998.

Issue of late Hon Hugh Terence de Burgh Bingham, 4th son of 5th Baron, *b* 1885, *d* 1957: *m* 1912, Dorothea Minnie, who *d* 1976, da of late J. A. Sinclair, Bar-at-Law, of Lahore:— Elizabeth Maude, *b* 1922: *m* 1944, Jelle Roel Hogeveen Veenbaas, and has issue living, Peter Hans, *b* 1946: *m* 1978, Veronica Anne, da of Carl Christian Moore, of Warminghurst, Storrington, W Sussex. *Residence* – Erwarton Hall Farm, nr Ipswich, Suffolk.

PREDECESSORS – (1) JOHN Bingham, son of late Henry Bingham, of Newbrook, co Mayo; *b* 1762; *cr Baron Clanmorris*, of Newbrook, co Mayo (peerage of Ireland, 1800); *d* 1821; *s* by his son (2) CHARLES BARRY, 2nd Baron; *dsp* 1829; *s* by his brother (3) DENIS ARTHUR, 3rd Baron; *d* 1847: *m* 1825, Maria Helena, who *d* 1899, da of Robert Persse, of Roxborough; *s* by his son (4) JOHN CHARLES ROBERT, 4th Baron; *b* 1826: *m* 1849, Sarah Selina, who *d* 1907, da of Burton Persse, of Moyode Castle, co Galway; *d* 1876; *s* by his son (5) JOHN GEORGE BARRY, 5th Baron; *b* 1852: *m* 1878, (Maude) Matilda Catherine, who *d* 1941, only child and heiress of late Robert Edward Ward, of Bangor Catle, co Down; *d* 1916; *s* by his son (6) ARTHUR MAURICE ROBERT, 6th Baron; *b* 1879; Capt Lancers: *m* 1907, Leila, who *d* 1969, da of late Gordon Cloete, JP, of Rosebank, Cape Town, S Africa; *d* 1960; *s* by his son (7) JOHN MICHAEL WARD, 7th Baron, *b* 1908; spy and crime novelist (as John Bingham), author of *My Name is Michael Sibley*, *Five Roundabouts to Heaven*, *The Third Skin*, etc: *m* 1934, Madeleine Mary (biographer as Madeleine Bingham), who *d* 16 Feb 1988, da of late Clement Ebel, of Copyhold Place, Cuckfield, Sussex; *d* 6 Aug 1988; *s* by his only son (8) SIMON JOHN WARD, 8th Baron and present peer.

This family descends from the Binghams of Melcombe Bingham, Dorset. Sir George, 3rd son of Robert Bingham of Melcombe (*d* 1561), was father of Sir Henry Bingham, 1st baronet, ancestor of the Earls of Lucan, and of John Bingham of Foxford, co Mayo, ancestor of Barons Clanmorris.

CLANWILLIAM, EARL OF (Meade) Sits as BARON (UK 1828) (Earl I 1776, Bt I 1703)

Always ready

JOHN HERBERT MEADE, 7th Earl and 10th Baronet; *b* 27 Sept 1919; *s* 1989; *ed* RNC Dartmouth: *m* 1956, Maxine, only da of late James Adrian Hayden Scott, and formerly wife of Michael John Willson Levien, and has issue.

ᴀrms – Quarterly, 1st and 4th gules a chevron ermine between three trefoils slipped argent, *Meade*; 2nd and 3rd quarterly, 1st and 4th azure, three peewits argent, *Magill*, 2nd and 3rd per chevron argent and vert, three stags trippant proper, *Hawkins*. ᴄrest – An eagle with two heads displayed sable, armed or. ꜱupporters – *Dexter*, an eagle close sable; *sinister*, a falcon close proper, both plain collared and chained or.
Residence – Blundells House, Tisbury, Wilts. *Club* – Turf.

SON LIVING

PATRICK JAMES (*Lord Gillford*), *b* 28 Dec 1960; *ed* Eton, and RMA Sandhurst; Coldstream Guards 1979-83; Cllr Royal Borough of Kensington & Chelsea 1990-98: *m* 1st, 1989 (*m diss* 1992), Serena Emily, adopted da of late Lt-Col Brian Joseph Lockhart (*see* L Gray, colls); 2ndly, 1995, Cara J., da of Paul de la Peña, of Elmley Castle, Pershore, Worcs, and has issue:—

> SON LIVING (*by 2nd m*) — *Hon* John Maximillian, *b* 28 Jan 1998.
> DAUGHTER LIVING (*by 1st m*) — *Hon* Tamara Louise, *b* 1990.

Residence – 51 Causton St, SW1P 4AT.

DAUGHTERS LIVING

Lady Rowena Katherine, *b* 1957: *m* 1991, as his 2nd wife, (Patrick) James Crichton-Stuart, and has issue (*see* M Bute, colls). *Residence* – 1 Sloane Gdns, SW1W 8EA.
Lady Tania Frances, *b* 1963: *m* 1989, as his 2nd wife, James Alwyne Compton, and has issue (*see* M Northampton, colls). *Residence* – Spilsbury Farm, Tisbury, Salisbury, Wilts SP3 6RW.

SISTER LIVING (*Raised to the rank of an Earl's daughter, 1990*)

Lady Jean Mary, *b* 1917: *m* 1943, Brig Michael James Babington Smith, CBE, TD, who *d* 1984, eldest son of late Sir Henry Babington Smith, GBE, CH, KCB, CSI (*see* E Elgin, 1944 Edn), and has issue living, Alan Babington, *b* 1946; *ed* Eton, and Trin Coll, Camb, — Louisa, *b* 1944: *m* 1967, Lt-Col James Richard Macfarlane, Coldm Gds, of Riverwood, Wickham, Hants PO1Y 5AY, and has issue living, Edward Michael Richard *b* 1969; Capt Coldm Gds, David Peter *b* 1970, — Sukie Mary, *b* 1950: *m* 1979, John Henry Hemming, CMG, of 10 Edwardes Sq, W8, and has issue living, Henry Sebastian *b* 1979, Beatrice Margaret Louisa *b* 1981.

DAUGHTERS LIVING OF SIXTH EARL

Lady Selina Catherine, *b* 1950: *m* 1972, Nicholas George Lawrence Timpson, and has issue (*see* Houstoun-Boswall, Bt). *Residence* – Ardington Croft, Wantage, Oxon.
Lady Mary Jane (*Countess Belmore*), *b* 1952: *m* 1984, 8th Earl Belmore, and has issue (see that title). *Residence* – Castle Coole, Enniskillen, co Fermanagh BT74 6JY.
Lady Julia Elizabeth, *b* 1953: *m* 1985, as his 2nd wife, Robert Ralph Scrymgeour Hiscox, son of late Ralph Hiscox, CBE, and has issue living, Milo Edmund, *b* 1987, — Henry Charles, *b* 1989, — Sidney John, *b* 1993. *Residence* – Rainscombe Park, Oare, Marlborough, Wilts SN8 4HZ.
Lady Laura Louise, *b* 1957: *m* 1981, W. Scott B. Reid, son of Howard A. Reid, of Bronxville, New York, USA, and has issue living, Nicholas John Howard, *b* 1982, — Amelia Louise Catherine, *b* 1984, — Clementine Julia, *b* 1988.
Lady Katharine Anne, *b* 1959: *m* 1987, Christopher Aubrey Hamilton Wills, elder son of Hon Victor Patrick Hamilton Wills, and has issue (*see* B Dulverton). *Residence* – Litchfield Down, Whitchurch, Hants.
Lady Sophia Hester, *b* 1963: *m* 1990, Jonathan G. Heywood, son of Brig Anthony Heywood, of Monkton House, Monkton Deverill, Wilts, and has issue living, Richard Garnett, *b* 1993, — Alec Garnett, *b* 1996.

WIDOW LIVING OF SIXTH EARL

CATHERINE (*Dowager Countess of Clanwilliam*), yst da of late Arthur Thomas Loyd, OBE, of Lockinge, Wantage, Berks: *m* 1948, Maj the 6th Earl of Clanwilliam, who *d* 1989. *Residence* – Maizley Cottage, Oare, Marlborough, Wilts SN8 4HZ.

COLLATERAL BRANCHES LIVING

Granddaughters of late Adm Hon Sir Herbert MEADE-FETHERSTONHAUGH, GCVO, CB, DSO (who assumed by Royal licence 1932 the surname of Fetherstonhaugh after Meade, and the arms quarterly), 3rd son of 4th Earl:—
Issue of late Richard James MEADE-FETHERSTONHAUGH, b 1913, d 1958: m 1948, Jean Phyllis (14 Limerston St, SW10; Uppark, Petersfield), da of late Maj Basil Falkner:—
Harriet Sarah (Uppark, Petersfield, Hants; 6 Darlan Rd, SW6 5BT), b 1949: m 1969, John de Bianchi Cossart, of Madeira, and has had issue, Charles Richard, b 1972; ed Downside; d 1997, — Edward James, b 1984, — Henrietta-Maria b 1974. ——Emma Mary, b 1951: m 1976, Geoffrey Wanklyn Goad, of Deerkeepers, Uppark, Petersfield, Hants, and has issue living, Oliver Edward, b 1977, — Harry Frederick, b 1978, — Matilda Rose, b 1989. ——Sophia Theresa, b 1954: m 1985, Angus Warre, of Dalcross Castle, Croy, Inverness, eldest son of Maj John Antony Warre, MC, of Barrowden, Oakham, Rutland (see D Devonshire, 1973-74 Edn), and has issue living, Theodora, b 1986.

Grandchildren of late Sir Robert Henry Meade, GCB, 2nd son of 3rd Earl:—
Issue of late Charles Francis Meade, b 1881, d 1975: m 1913, Lady Aileen Hilda Brodrick, who d 1970, da of 1st Earl of Midleton:—
Simon Robert Jasper (Pen-y-lan, Meifod, Montgomeryshire), b 1928: m 1957, Lady Sophia Catherine Gathorne-Hardy, da of 4th Earl of Cranbrook, and has issue living, Jasper, b 1962, — Benjamin, b 1963, — Camilla, b 1958, — Rachel b 1965. ——Evelyn Clodagh, b 1916: m 1940, Colin Hercules Mackenzie, CMG, who d 1986, of Kyle House, Kyleakin, I of Skye, only son of late Maj-Gen Sir Colin John Mackenzie, KCB, and has issue living, Christian Fiona, b 1941: m 1966, (Charles) Nicholas Phipps (see D Buccleuch, 1990 Edn), and has issue living, Charles Mackenzie b 1967, Alice Christian b 1969. ——Flavia Mary (Baroness Ebbisham), b 1920: m 1949, 2nd Baron Ebbisham, who d 1991.

Granddaughters of late Francis Henry Meade, CBE, only son of late Rev Hon Sidney Meade, 3rd son of 3rd Earl:—
Issue of late Lt-Col Robert Sidney Stuart Meade, b 1901, d 1971: m 1st, 1930, Veronica Augusta, who d 1968, da of Lt-Col Herbert Vere Wilbraham; 2ndly, 1970, Baroness Maria Elisabeth Johanna Rosalia Ottilia, da of late Baron August Hermann Georg Victor Ramberg, Capt Imperial Austrian Navy, and widow of Count Ferdinand Zdenko Karl Emmerick Maria von Thun und Hohenstein:—
(By 1st m) Daphne Theresa, b 1936. ——Jane Cecilia (New English Art Club), b 1940: m 1967, Col David Henry George Corsellis, c/o Nat Westminster Bank, Bishops Stortford, Herts, and has issue living, Nicholas Robert Alexander, b 1968; Bar, Lincoln's Inn 1993, — James Henry Merrick, b 1970.

Grandchildren of late Capt John Percy Meade, elder son of Capt John Meade, of Earsham Hall, Norfolk, and Burrenwood, co Down, yr son of Lt-Gen Hon Robert Meade, 2nd son of 1st Earl:—
Issue of Maj John Windham Meade, b 1894, d 1984: m 1932, Grace Dorothea, JP, who d 1977, da of late Sir Cecil Fane De Salis, KCB:—
John Michael (Manor Farm House, Hedenham, Bungay, Suffolk), b 1935; ed Stowe: m 1967, Princess Valentine, 2nd da of late Prince Nicholas Galitzine, and has issue living, Nicholas, b 1969; ed Stowe, — Catherine, b 1968: m 1994, Gary Donald Meyer, yst son of Donald Meyer, of Leigh on Sea, Essex, and has issue living, Joseph b 1998, Anastasia b 1995, Kira b 1996, — Tatiana, b (twin) 1968: m 1994, Prince Andrei Mikhailovitch Galitzine, son of Prince Mikhail V. Galitzine, of Moscow, and has issue living, Alexei b 1997, Helena b 1994, — Elizabeth, b 1971. ——Francis Windham (39 Courtlands, Patchinghall Lane, Chelmsford, Essex), b 1941; ed Stowe, and London Univ (BSc 1962). ——Theodosia Frances (18 Quaves Lane, Bungay, Suffolk), b 1932.

PREDECESSORS – **(1)** *Sir* JOHN Meade, KB; MP successively for Dublin Univ and co Tipperary, and Attorney-Gen to James, Duke of York; cr a *Baronet* of Ireland 1703; d 1711; s by his son **(2)** *Sir* PIERCE, 2nd Bt; dsp; s by his brother **(3)** *Sir* RICHARD, 3rd Bt; d 1744; s by his son **(4)** *Sir* JOHN, 4th Bt; cr *Baron Gillford* and *Viscount Clanwilliam* (peerage of Ireland) 1766, and *Earl of Clanwilliam* (peerage of Ireland) 1776; d 1800; s by his son **(5)** RICHARD, 2nd Earl; d 1805; s by his son **(6)** RICHARD, GCH, 3rd Earl; b 1795; Under-Sec for Foreign Affairs 1822, and Ambassador at Berlin 1823-8; cr *Baron Clanwilliam, co Tipperary* (peerage of United Kingdom) 1828: m 1830, Lady Elizabeth Herbert, who d 1858, da of 11th Earl of Pembroke; d 1879; s by his son **(7)** RICHARD JAMES, GCB, KCMG, 4th Earl; b 1832; an Adm of the Fleet; a Naval ADC to HM Queen Victoria 1872-6, and a Lord of the Admiralty 1874-80: m 1867, Elizabeth Henrietta, who d 1925, el da of late Sir Arthur Edward Kennedy; d 1907; s by his second son **(8)** ARTHUR VESEY, MC, 5th Earl, b 1873; was Capt and Adj Roy Horse Guards, and Assist Provost Marshal; S Africa 1900-02, European War 1914-18 (MC): m 1909, Muriel Mary Temple, MBE, who d 1952, da of Russell Stephenson and widow of Hon Oliver Howard (E Carlisle); d 1953; s by his only son **(9)** JOHN CHARLES EDMUND CARSON, 6th Earl; b 1914; Maj Coldm Gds, Lord Lieut co Down; European War 1939-45 in Middle East (despatches twice): m 1948, Catherine, yst da of late Arthur Thomas Loyd, OBE, of Lockinge, Wantage, Berks; d 1989; s by his cousin **(10)** JOHN HERBERT (yr son of late Adm Hon Sir Herbert Meade-Fetherstonhaugh, GCVO, CB, DSO, 3rd son of 4th Earl), 7th Earl and present peer; also Viscount Clanwilliam, Baron Clanwilliam, and Baron Gillford.

CLARENDON, EARL OF (Villiers) (Earl GB 1776)
(Name pronounced "Villers")

The cross, the test of faith

GEORGE FREDERICK LAURENCE HYDE VILLIERS, 7th Earl; *b* 2 Feb 1933; *s* 1955; *ed* Eton, and Madrid Univ; Page of Honour to HM King George VI 1948-49; Managing Dir of Seccombe, Marshall and Campion plc 1962-93 (and Chm 1985-93); Lt RHG (AER): *m* 1974, Jane Diana, da of Edward William Dawson, of Idmiston, Salisbury, Wilts, and has issue.

Arms – Argent, a cross gules, charged with five escallops or. Crest – A lion rampant argent ducally crowned or. Supporters – Two eagles, wings expanded and inverted sable, beaked, membered, and ducally crowned or, and charged on the breast with a plain cross argent.
Residence – Holywell House, Swanmore, Hants SO32 2QE.

SON LIVING

GEORGE EDWARD LAURENCE (*Lord Hyde*), *b* 12 Feb 1976; Page of Honour to HM The Queen 1988-90.

DAUGHTER LIVING

Lady Sarah Katherine Jane, *b* 1977.

SISTER LIVING (*Raised to the rank of an Earl's daughter* 1956)

Lady Rosemary Verena Edith (*posthumous*), *b* 1935: *m* 1959, Richard Hugh Jordan Steel, el son of Sir Christopher Eden Steel, GCMG, MVO (Buxton, Bt, colls), and has issue living, James Thomas Jordan (Barrowfield House, Much Hadham, Herts), *b* 1960: *m* 1989, Lindsay J., elder da of Michael Farrell, of Much Hadham, Herts, and has issue living, Frederick James Edward *b* 1993, Toby Patrick Richard *b* 1998, Sophie Mary Verena *b* 1991, — Oliver George Nigel, *b* 1962: *m* 1992, Jacqueline E., yr da of Colin Quaife, of Lea, Wilts, — Arabella Rosemary Louise, *b* 1966: *m* 1998, Rupert S. H. Sawyer, yr son of Dr Roger Sawyer, of Bembridge, I of Wight. *Residence* – Glebe House, Notgrove, Cheltenham, Glos.

UNCLE LIVING (*Son of 6th Earl*)

Hon (William) Nicholas Somers Laurence Hyde, *b* 1916; *ed* Eton, and at New Coll, Oxford; Maj Gren Gds (SR), ERD; a JP for Hants, and an OStJ: *m* 1939, Mary Cecilia Georgina, da of Maj Hon Edric Alfred Cecil Weld-Forester, CVO (*see* B Forester), and has issue living, Caroline Jane (21 Glycena Rd, SW11 5TP), *b* 1940: *m* 1964 (*m diss* 1974), J. Kenneth Havard, — Nerena Anne Hyde (Old Posting House, Didmarton, nr Badminton, Glos), *b* 1941: *m* 1966 (*m diss* 1980), Timothy Congreve Stephenson (V Hawarden, colls), and has issue living Guy Congreve *b* 1969, Henry Frederick *b* 1978, Lucinda Mary Pamela *b* 1967, Henrietta Cecilia *b* 1975, — (Elizabeth) Georgina Gail, *b* 1952: *m* 1980, Edward Rivers R. Jewson, of Wacton House, Norwich, Norfolk NR15 2UF, only son of late Col John Howlett Jewson, MC, of Mergate Hall, Norwich, and has issue living, Sophie Emily Josceline *b* 1987, Isobel Mary Elizabeth *b* 1988. *Residence* – Firs Farm, Milbourne, Malmesbury, Wilts.

COLLATERAL BRANCHES LIVING

Branch from 4th son of 4th Earl

Grandsons of late Rt Hon Sir Francis Hyde Villiers, GCMG, CB, 4th son of 4th Earl:—
Issue of late Eric Hyde Villiers, DSO, Capt Highland LI, *b* 1881, *d* 1964: *m* 1928, Joan Ankaret, who *d* 1986, da of late John Edward Talbot (*see* E Shrewsbury, colls):—
Henry Hyde (Icknor House, South Green, Sittingbourne, Kent; *Club* – Boodle's), *b* 1931; *ed* Wellington Coll; JP Kent and High Sheriff 1992: *m* 1959, Mary Elizabeth Cavan, da of late Robert Hugh Swan Corbett, of Yalding, Kent, and has issue living Charles James Hyde, *b* 1967, — Robert Henry Hyde, *b* 1969, — Charlotte Amelia, *b* 1961: *m* 1988, Christopher H. C. Figg, eldest son of Sir Leonard Clifford William Figg, KCMG, of Great Missenden, Bucks, and has issue living, Orlando *b* 1992, Jake *b* 1996, — Henrietta Barbara, *b* 1962: *m* 1986, Alastair Henderson Scott, son of Paul Henderson Scott, CMG, of 109 Keyes House, Dolphin Sq, SW1. —— †James Michael Hyde, *b* 1933; *ed* Wellington Coll; actor: *m* 1st, 1966 (*m diss* 1984), Patricia, da of William Victor Donovan, of Fern House, Pembroke; 2ndly, 1994, Lucinda Clare Noelle (59 Maltravers St, Arundel, Sussex), da of Alan Jex, and *d* 1998, leaving an adopted son, Alan Michael Hyde, *b* 1961 (adopted 1967). —— John Francis Hyde (21 Overstrand Mansions, Prince of Wales Drive, SW11 4EZ; *Club* – Royal Over-Seas League), *b* 1936; *ed* Winchester, and King's Coll, Camb (MA, PhD); Fellow Royal Asiatic Soc, and FRSA: *m* 1958 (Myee) Miranda, el da of Lt-Col David McKenna, CBE (*see* E Albemarle), and has issue living, Daniel James Hyde, *b* 1960, — Cecilia Ankaret, *b* 1962: *m* 1983, David Michael Holdsworth, of Vigeau, St Mézard, Lectoure, 32700 France, yr son of G. M. Holdsworth, of Seal, Kent, — Antonia Aniela, *b* 1965, — Susanna Sophia (twin), *b* 1965.

Granddaughters of late Algernon Hyde Villiers, Lieut Yeo, attached Machine Gun Corps (*ka* 1917), 3rd and yst son of late Rt Hon Sir Francis Hyde Villiers, GCMG, CB (ante):—
Issue of late Lt-Col Sir Charles English Hyde Villiers, MC, sometime Chm British Steel Corpn, *b* 1912, *d* 1992: *m* 1st, 1938, Pamela Constance, who *d* 1943, da of late Maj John Flower, 60th Rifles; 2ndly, 1946, Marie José (*Lady Villiers*) (Blacknest House, Sunninghill, Berks), da of Comte Henri de la Barre d'Erquelinnes, of Jurbise, Belgium:—

(By 2nd *m*) Diana Mary, *b* 1947: *m* 1976, Ambassador John Dimitri Negroponte, US Foreign Ser. —— Anne Hyde, *b* 1950: *m* 1st, 1973, Paul Nuttall Kesterton; 2ndly, 1993, Thomas Martin, and has issue living (by 1st *m*), Toby, *b* 1977, —— Lara Beatrice, *b* 1979.

Branch from 4th brother of 4th Earl

Grandchildren of late Edward Ernest Villiers, only son of late Col Ernest Villiers, eldest son of Hon Edward Ernest Villiers, 4th brother of 4th Earl:—
Issue of late Capt Algernon Edward Villiers, *b* 1892, *d* 1991: *m* 1924, Annie Augusta Merewether, who *d* 1978, da of late George Latham Massy, of Berridge, Sunningdale:—
George Edward, TD (73 Carlton Hill, NW8; *Club* – Boodle's), *b* 1931; *ed* Wellington Coll, and Brasenose Coll, Oxford (MA); late Maj Berks and Westminster Dragoons (TA), late Lieut RHA: *m* 1962, Anne Virginia, elder da of late Cuthbert Raymond Forster Threlfall, of Warstone House, Bewdley, Worcs, and has issue living, Edward Richard (56 Kensington Park Rd, W11 3BJ), *b* 1963; *ed* Highgate, and Bristol Univ: *m* 1995, Lisa Alexandra, eldest da of Lionel Bryer, of Sloane St, SW1, and has issue living, James *b* 1997, Frederick *b* (twin) 1997, — Henry Raymond, *b* 1965; *ed* Central St Martin's Sch of Art, — Theresa Anne, *b* 1968; LLB Bristol, BCL Jesus Coll, Oxford; Memb Inner Temple. —— Elizabeth Anne, *b* 1925. —— Barbara Jane (Flat 17, 55 Shepherd's Hill, N6 5QP), *b* 1927.

Branch from elder son of 5th brother of 4th Earl

Granddaughter of late Rev Henry Montagu Villiers (*b* 1837), el son of Rt Rev Hon Henry Montague Villiers, DD, Bishop of Durham, 5th brother of 4th Earl:—
Issue of late Henry Montagu Villiers, MVO, *b* 1863, *d* 1948: *m* 1896, Carmen, who *d* 1953, da of late Dr Luhrsen, Envoy Extraor, and Min Plen for German Empire in Colombia, S America:—
Margaret Anne Theresa (twin), *b* 1913: *m* 1940, Ronald Basil Strickland, of Bow River, W Australia, and has issue living, John Montague, *b* 1940; Fl Cdr and Sqdn Ldr RAAF: *m* 1967, Elsa Rosen, — Mark Henry (Bull Creek, W Australia), *b* 1947: *m* 1972, Margaret Walker, and has issue living, Stuart *b* 1976, Margaret *b* 1974, — Neil William (Bedford, W Australia), *b* 1948: *m* 1968, Wendy Baker, and has issue living, Paulette *b* 1969, Cassandra *b* 1972, — Edward George (Canberra, Australia), *b* 1949: — Robert Clive, *b* 1956; BA W Australia Univ: *m* 1975, Linda Williams, — Tora Lillian, *b* 1944: *m* 1963, Terence McNamara, of Newman, W Australia, and has issue living, Michelle, *b* 1967, Marina *b* 1969, — Thea *b* 1973, — Ronda Christine, *b* 1951: *m* 1968, Robert Kemmers, of Girrawheen, W Australia, and has issue living, Robert *b* 1972, Catherine *b* 1968, — Terri Ann, *b* 1952: *m* 1970, Frank Ebbett, of Bow River, W Australia, and has issue living, Neil *b* 1975, Debra *b* 1971, Sandra *b* 1973.

Grandchildren of late Henry Montagu Villiers, MVO (*b* 1863) (ante):—
Issue of late Cdr George Dumba Villiers, RN, *b* 1900, *d* 1977: *m* 1926, Anne Hilda Whellens, who *d* 1990, da of late James Barton Hall, of Longframlington, Northumberland:—
Simon William George (16 Harmony St, Rusthall, Tunbridge Wells, Kent), *b* 1927; Maj RA (ret), attached to Malay Regt, Malaya 1958 (despatches, Order of Ali Manghu Negra): *m* 1956, Patricia de Lacey, and has issue living, Clive Matthew George, *b* 1957, — Virginia Anne *b* 1959: *m* 1979, Nigel Mark Batchelor, of 55 Old Exeter St, Chudleigh, Devon, and has issue living, Matthew Joseph *b* 1979, Christopher Luke *b* 1981, — Moira Lillian, *b* 1963: *m* 1st, 1983 (*m diss* 19—), Terence Michael Rodden; 2ndly, 1994, Michael Rudd, of 7 Cypress Way, Gillingham, Dorset, and has issue living (by 1st *m*), Sally Anne *b* 1985, (by 2nd *m*), Sean *b* 19—. —— Janet Mary (Tormead, Daddyhole Plain, Torquay, Devon TQ1 2EQ) *b* 1929; formerly Head Mistress of Middle Sch, Tormead Sch for Girls, Guildford.

Issue of late Edmund Rollo Stanley Villiers, *b* 1909, *d* 1960: *m* 1st, 1934 (*m diss* 1957), Margit Cleland, da of late Robert Rogerson, of Marchmount, Dumfries; 2ndly, 1957, Christine Joan (The Old School Hall, Mill Rd, W Ashling, nr Chichester, W Sussex PO18 8EA), da of late Com W. O. H. Lambert, RN, of The Toll, Buxted, Sussex:—
(By 1st *m*) Charles Russell (Wargrave Lodge, Wargrave-on-Thames, Berkshire), *b* 1938; *ed* Cheltenham, and Corpus Christi Coll, Camb (BA), MB, BChir, DMRD, FFR, FRCR: *m* 1971, Barbara Clare, 3rd da of Fredwin R. McMaster, of Nottinghill, Belfast.

Grandchildren of late John Russell Villiers, 2nd son of late Rev Henry Montagu Villiers (*b* 1837) (ante):—
Issue of late Arthur Henry Villiers, MC, *b* 1894, *d* 1975: *m* 1919, Vera Adeline, who *d* 1976, da of late Charles Howe, of Durban, Natal:—
Peter William (9 Havelock Rd, Sheringham, Norfolk NR26 8QD), *b* 1922; *ed* Lancing Coll; late Lt KRRC; film producer: *m* 1st, 1945 (*m diss* 1958), June, only child of W. Friedhoff; 2ndly, 1959, Alice, da of A. J. Startup, and has had issue (by 1st *m*), Roger Peter, *b* 1946: *m* 1975, Julia Helen, da of A. S. Rymer, and has issue living, Mark Roger *b* 1980, Helen Fiona *b* 1977, — Jennifer Ann, *b* 1948; *d* 1970. —— Geoffrey Richard (1301 Jefferson St, Napa, Calif, USA), *b* 1924; *ed* Lancing Coll; 1939-45 War as Sub-Lt RNVR: *m* 1948, Janet Myra, who *d* 1998, da of Dr Leonard W. Trott, of Adelaide, S Aust, and has issue living, Mary Jane, *b* 1954: *m* 1996, Edward Norman Harris, son of Samuel Richard Harris, of The Olde Dairy House, Longburton, Sherborne, Dorset DT9 5PG, and has issue living, Robert Edward *b* 1976, — Lisa Kathleen, *b* 1959: *m* 1988, George Emerson Smith, of Punga Cove, Endeavor Inlet, Marlborough, NZ, and has issue living, Heather Michelle *b* 1991, Kendra Nicole *b* 1993. —— Christopher Nigel, *b* 1929; *ed* Lancing Coll: *m* 1053 (*m diss* 1964), Brenda Margaret, yr da of D. R. Penny, of Ferring, Sussex, and has issue living, Nigel Richard, *b* 1956: *m* 1980, Valerie Reeling, and has issue living, Kirstie June, *b* 1982, — Gillian Grace, *b* 1958: *m* 1977 (*m diss* 1984), Alan Lawrence, Sussex, and has issue living, Charlene Louise *b* 1978.

Issue of late Brig Richard Montagu Villiers, DSO, *b* 1905, *d* 1973: *m* 1932, Nancy (4 Orford Mews, Puddletown, Dorchester, Dorset DT2 8TL), el da of late Lt-Gen Sir Charles Alexander Campbell Godwin, KCB, CMG, DSO:—
Timothy Charles *b* 1943; *ed* Eton, and RMA; Lt-Col 15th/19th Hus: *m* 1971, Maureen, da of late Ven R. G. H. McCahearty, and has issue living, Nicholas Charles, *b* 1976, — Richard Henry *b* 1980, — Louise Elizabeth, *b* 1973. —— Judith Annette, *b* 1935: *m* 1960, Brig Rupert H. G. McCarthy, 15th/19th KRH, of Rew Cottage, Buckland Newton, Dorchester DT2 7DN, and has issue living, William Rupert, *b* 1963: *m* 1997, Louise Gwendoline Squire Stickland, —

Sarah Victoria, *b* 1961: *m* 1997, Simon Robert Thornton James, of Treyone, Hassenford, Cornwall PL11 3HE, — Meriel Anne, *b* 1966: *m* 1995, Andrew David Lane, of Ashe Park Cottages, Steventon, Hants RG25 3AF, and has issue living, Henry George Harold *b* 1997. —— Victoria Belinda, *b* 1938: *m* 1963, Robert Quentin Yeatman, of 9 Clarendon Rd, Cambridge CB2 2BH, and has issue living, Catherine Victoria, *b* 1964, — Lucy Belinda, *b* 1966, — Rosanna Charlotte, *b* 1973. —— Carol Elspeth, *b* 1944: *m* 1st, 1965, Gerald Charles Mordaunt (*see* Mordaunt, Bt, colls); 2ndly, 1984, as his 3rd wife, Maj Charles Cyril Willmott Hammick (*see* Hammick, Bt, colls), who *d* 1990. *Residence* – Waterston Manor, Dorchester, Dorset DT2 7SP.

Grandchildren of late Com Thomas Hyde Villiers, RN (infra):—
Issue of late Nicholas Lister Villiers, RN, *b* 1926, *d* 1984: *m* 1954, Betty Midelton (Heatherlands, Orford Rd, Bromeswell, nr Woodbridge, Suffolk IP12 2PP), 2nd da of Sidney Ralph Midelton Barlow, of Wayside, Chalfont St Giles, Bucks:—
Derek Midelton Lister (Willows End, Orford Rd, Bromeswell, nr Woodbridge, Suffolk IP12 2PP), *b* 1958: *m* 1984, Deborah, da of Christopher John Randall, of 34 Redwald Rd, Rendlesham, Suffolk, and has issue living, Nicholas Christopher Lister, *b* 1985, — George Alexander, *b* 1991, — Charles Fredrick Hyde, *b* 1994, — Catriona Sarah, *b* 1987. —— Caroline Patricia (16 Gloucester Rd, Newbury, Berks RG14 5JP), *b* 1960.

Grandson of Sir Thomas Lister Villiers, 3rd son of Rev Henry Montagu Villiers (*b* 1837) (ante):—
Issue of late Com Thomas Hyde Villiers, RN, *b* 1902, *d* 1955: *m* 1925, Eleanor, who *d* 1958, da of late Francis Edgar Croft (Croft, Bt, *cr* 1818, colls):—
Stephen Hyde (Clump House, Dummer, nr Basingstoke, Hants RG25 2RF), *b* 1931; *ed* Eton: *m* 1958, Elizabeth Jill, da of John Stewart Jeffrey Chapple, of Clayton, Hadham Rd, Bishop's Stortford, Herts, and has issue living, Harry Hyde, *b* 1959, — Timothy Stewart, *b* 1960, — Hugo James, *b* 1962, — Lucinda Victoria, *b* 1961.

Grandchildren of late Rev Henry Montagu Villiers (*b* 1837) (ante):—
Issue of late Godfrey Robert Randall Villiers, *b* 1877, *d* 1925: *m* 1967, Sylvia, who *d* 1926, da of late Dr James Moore Bennett, formerly of Princes Rd, Liverpool:—
Sylvia Betty, *b* 1915: *m* 1934, Stavros Sirakos, and has issue living, Denise Catherine, *b* 1935: *m* 1961, Philippe Moulierac, and has issue living, Christopher *b* 1964, Pascale *b* 1967.

Issue of late Maj Paul Frederick Villiers, DSO, *b* 1884, *d* 1968: *m* 1912, Evelyn, who *d* 1973, da of late Edward Webb:—
Pauline Mary Lethbridge (8 St Lucia, West Parade, Bexhill on Sea, E Sussex TN39 3DT), *b* 1914: *m* 1936, Dennis Estyn Dunnill, MB BS, MRCS, LRCP, DA, who *d* 1986, and has issue living, Richard Paul Hyde (Dairy Farm House, Avon, nr Christchurch, Dorset, BH23 7BG), *b* 1945; MB BS, LRCP, MRCS, FFARCS; *ed* Charterhouse, and Guy's Hosp: *m* 1st, 1971 (*m diss* 1977), Rosamund Strange; 2ndly, 1978, Charlotte Gorter, and has issue living (by 1st *m*), Robert James Hyde *b* 1975, (by 2nd *m*) Charles William Hyde *b* 1981, Elizabeth Anna *b* 1979, Sarah Denise *b* 1986, — Veronica Mary, *b* 1937: *m* 1st, 1963 (*m diss* 1973), Timothy Mawdsley Welch; 2ndly, 1982, Andrew Charles Gottlieb, of Eastbourne, Sussex, and has issue living (by 1st *m*), Andrew Ronald Mawdsley *b* 1968, Nicola Mary *b* 1966, — Angela Evelyn, *b* 1939; JP W Yorks: *m* 1966, William Raymond Barker, of 109 Tadcaster Rd, Dringhouses, York YO2 1XA, and has issue living, Christopher Paul Howard *b* 1967: *m* 1998, Zoë Alice, da of John Lomax, Caroline Susan *b* 1969.

Issue of late Capt Gerald Berkeley Villiers, OBE, RN, *b* 1885, *d* 1959: *m* 1918, Rachel Joan, da of late Rev Henry Vernon Heber Percy (*see* D Northumberland, colls):—
Anthony Henry Heber, *b* 1921; Capt late Gren Gds; 1939-45 War: *m* 1948, Rosemary Elizabeth, da of late Maj (William) Bertram Bell, 12th Lancers (By Barrymore), and has had issue, (Anthony James) Valentine (The Kennels, Petworth Park, Petworth, W Sussex GU28 9LR), *b* 1949: *m* 1st, 1974, Sally Wilson; 2ndly, 1984, Sara A., da of Basil Gotto, of Willowhill House, Carrigaline, co Cork, and has issue living, (by 1st *m*) Henry Anthony Edward *b* 1978, (by 2nd *m*) Delia Dorothy *b* 1989, Geraldine Olive *b* 1990, — †Charles Henry, *b* 1954; *ed* Milton Abbey; *d* 1980, — (Rosemary) Henrietta Dorothy, *b* 1950: *m* 1st, 1973 (*m diss* 1978), (Nigel Graham Cedric) Peregrine Banbury; 2ndly, 1978, William Murray Lucas, who *d* 1982, and has an adopted da, Elizabeth Jacquetta *b* 1981, — Emma Helen, *b* 1963: *m* 1988, Richard Henry Ronald Benyon, and has issue (*see* Shelley, Bt, colls). *Residence* – The Old Priory, N Woodchester, Stroud, Glos. *Club* – Guards'.

Grandchildren of late Maj Oliver George Graham Villiers, DSO (infra):—
Issue of late W/Cdr David Hugh Villiers, DFC, *b* 1921, *d* 1962: *m* 1st, 1942 (*m diss* 1948), Patricia, only child of late Richard Payne; 2ndly, 1954, Elizabeth Barbara (who *m* 2ndly, 1992, Capt John B. Rumble, who *d* 1996, of White Horse Cottage, School St, Stoke-by-Nayland, Suffolk CO6 4QY) (assumed by deed poll 1949 the surname of Prideaux in lieu of her patronymic), da of late Horace Leonard Hobbins:—
(By 1st *m*) Robin Julian, *b* 1945: *m* 1974, Birgitte, da of Peter Stafford. —— (By 2nd *m*) Christopher Francis (100 Elsenham St, SW18 5NT), *b* 1958; actor: *m* 1985, Katherine, only da of William Threlfall, of SW6, and has issue living, Charles Sebastian, *b* 1987, — Frederick James, *b* 1988. —— Jonathan Paul, *b* 1961; actor. —— Catherine Judith, *b* 1955; film prod.

Granddaughter of late Rev Henry Montagu Villiers (*b* 1837) (ante):—
Issue of late Maj Oliver George Graham Villiers, DSO, *b* 1886, *d* 1981: *m* 1918, Aleen Judith, who *d* 1976, da of late Rev Henry Vernon Heber-Percy (D Northumberland, colls):—
(Judith) Rosemary (3 West End, Spilsby, Lincs PE23 5ED), *b* 1919: *m* 1949, Peter George Locke-Wheaton, who *d* 1981, and has issue living, Henry George (36 Medgbury Rd, Swindon, Wilts SN1 2AS), *b* 1950: *m* 1st, 1973 (*m diss* 1986), Cynthia Jane, da of Eric Bagley; 2ndly, 1995, Christine Elizabeth Pollard (*née* Mulcock), and has issue living (by 1st *m*), David George *b* 1983, Sarah Jane *b* 1977, Annabelle *b* 1980, — John Antony Charles (18 Evergreen Drive, Calcot, Reading, Berks), *b* 1952; MA (Cantab): *m* 1977, Margaret Patricia, da of late Rev George Clifford Hunt, and has issue living, Stephen Antony *b* 1983, Jennifer Anne *b* 1981, — Philip James (64 Baldwin Rd, Kidderminster, Worcs), *b* 1955: *m* 1980, Janet Rosemary, da of George Danks, and has issue living, Daniel Philip *b* 1981, Luke Peter *b* 1983, Simon George *b* 1990, Naomi Janet *b* 1985, Miriam Rachel *b* 1988, — Richard Oliver (Mill Cottage, Toynton-all-Saints, Lincs), *b* 1957: *m* 1979, Janice Sheila, da of Peter Rothery, and has issue living, Christopher James *b* 1985, Nicola Claire *b* 1983, — (Henrietta) Mary-Anne, *b* 1951: *m* 1st, 1970 (*m diss* 1975), Richard Peter Noble; 2ndly, 1982, Graham Roy Elliker, of Roburs, The Common, W Chiltington, W Sussex, and has issue living (by 1st *m*), Sarah Louise *b* 1974: *m* 1998, Andrew

Charles Goodwin, of Lynwood, W Keal, Spilsby, Lincs, (by 2nd *m*) Hallam Piers Oliver *b* 1983, Camilla Aleen *b* 1987, — Caroline Susan-Ann (76 Newmarket Rd, Bulwell, Nottingham), *b* 1953: *m* 1979 (*m diss* 1989), Capt Paul Hendy (Salvation Army), and has issue living, Stuart James *b* 1982, Corrine Louise *b* 1981.

Branch from yr son of 5th brother of 4th Earl

Grandson of late Lt-Col Charles Walter Villiers, CBE, 2nd son of late Capt Frederick Ernest Villiers (infra):—
Issue of late Lt-Col (Francis) Berkeley Hyde Villiers, OBE, *b* 1906, *d* 1991: *m* 1938, Rose Marie (Stone House, Stone, nr Kidderminster, Worcs), da of Consul Gen von Passavant, of Vienna:—
Nicholas Hyde, *b* 1939; *ed* Eton. *Residence* – Stone House, Stone, nr Kidderminster, Worcs.

Grandson of late Capt Frederick Ernest Villiers, yr son of Rt Rev Hon Henry Montagu Villiers, DD, (ante):—
Issue of late Reginald Hyde Villiers, DSO, *b* 1876, *d* 1953: *m* 1906, Florence Marianne, who *d* 1937, da of Dr George Stockwell, formerly of Dunedin, New Zealand:—
Frederick Montagu Hyde (Braemar, 13 Dixon Rd, Buderim, Queensland 4556, Australia), *b* 1907; late Maj Ceylon LI: *m* 1st, 1936 (*m diss* 1947), Maisie Marguerite Hunt; 2ndly, 1948 (*m diss* 1959), Ann Sybella, da of Rev Nixon Chetwode Ram, of Petersfield, Hants, and formerly wife of Count Carl Otto Werner Schimmelmann, of Ahrensburg, Holstein; 3rdly, 1959, Sheila Joyce, 3rd da of late Charles Alexander Squair, of Reigate, Surrey, and widow of Douglas Montague Baird, and has living issue (by 1st *m*), Judith Marianne, *b* 1937: *m* 1st, 1958 (*m diss* 1973), David Price; 2ndly, 1991, Geoffrey Alan Hill, of Ferndale, Limestone Rd, Yea, Victoria 3717, Australia, and has issue living (by 1st *m*), Brett Alexander Hyde (Bayswater, Melbourne, Victoria 3153, Australia) *b* 1960: *m* 1986, Lindy Sue Ferry (and has issue living, Maddison Hyde *b* 1988), James Stuart (Bayswater, Melbourne, Victoria 3153, Australia) *b* 1961: *m* 1991, Roslyn Anne Dimech (and has issue living, Brock David *b* 1987, Tasmin Jean *b* 1992).

Granddaughter of late Reginald Hyde Villiers, DSO (ante):—
Issue of late George Pelham Villiers, *b* 1909, *d* 1989: *m* 1st, 1937 (*m diss* 1945), Gladys Mildred Moehr, who *d* 1977; 2ndly, 1945, Ursula Alison Paterson, who *d* 1957, da of John Hodgson, of Kotapala, Ceylon; 3rdly, 1959, Kathleen Cooke, who *d* 1984:—
(By 1st *m*) Ursula Georgette Victoria Maria, *b* 1943: *m* 1st, 1965, Lieut John Philip Bear, RN, who *d* 1967; 2ndly, 1976, Rear Adm Jonathan Alexander Burch, CBE, RN, and has issue living (by 1st *m*), Alexander George Philip Villiers, *b* 1966: *m* 1995, Clare Louise Tyrrell-Smith. *Residence* – St James's Grange, West Littleton, Chippenham, Wilts.

Grandchildren of late Evelyn Charles Arthur Villiers, 4th and yst son of late Capt Frederick Ernest Villiers (ante):—
Issue of late Capt Robert Alexander Villiers, CBE, RN, *b* 1908, *d* 1990: *m* 1st, 1933, Leila Alexandra, who *d* 1938, eldest da of late Lt-Col William Alexander Victor Findlater, Royal Irish Fus, of The Croft, Tenterden, Kent; 2ndly, 1939 (*m diss* 1958), Elizabeth Mary, da of late Maj-Gen Arthur Leslie Irvine Friend, CB, CBE, MC, of Dynes Farm, Bethersden, Kent; 3rdly, 1960, (Irene) Mary (Robinsgreen, Warham, Sussex; 33 Ennismore Gdns, SW7), da of William Ellis-Jones, of W Kirby, Cheshire:—
(By 1st *m*) Diana Susan, *b* 1935: *m* 1963, Ian Buchanan Watt, CMG, who *d* 1988, of Kingswood House, 8 Lower Green Rd, Esher, Surrey, and has issue living, James Alexander Macdonald, *b* 1965, — Robert John Macdonald, *b* 1969, — Harriet Leila Elizabeth, *b* 1970. —— (By 2nd *m*) †Michael Alexander *b* 1941; *ed* Eton, RMA Sandhurst, and Cranfield (MBA); commn'd 11th Hus 1959: *m* 1st, 1968 (*m diss* 1982), Annabel Vanessa, da of F. R. G. N. Sherrard, of South Lodge, Dorchester; 2ndly, 1989, Jean Annette Mary, da of late Brig Robert Angus Graham Binny, CBE, of Pitt Farm House, Skilgate, Taunton, Som (*see* E Coventry, colls, 1963 Edn), and formerly wife of Lt-Col William Robert Wilson FitzGerald, Royal Dragoons (*see* E Harrington, colls, 1941 Edn), and *d* 1996, having had issue (by 1st *m*), †Patrick George Alexander Hyde, *b* 1970; *d* 1972, — Annabell Jane (Longhill Farm, Cucklington, nr Wincanton, Som BA9 9PT), *b* 1974. —— Charles Nigel (8 Sutherland St, SW1; Grove House, Selling, Faversham, Kent), *b* (twin) 1941; *ed* Winchester, and New Coll, Oxford; FCA; Dir National Westminster Bank plc 1995-98, Dir Abbey National plc 1989-99, since when Dep Chm: *m* 1970, Sally Priscilla, da of late Capt D. H. Magnay, RN, and has issue living, Christopher Frederick Pelham, *b* 1976; *ed* Winchester, and Edinburgh Univ, — Caroline Harriet, *b* 1974; *ed* St Mary's, Calne, Charterhouse, and Edinburgh Univ. —— Sarah Jane Amanda, *b* 1956.

PREDECESSORS – (1) *Rt Hon* THOMAS Villiers, 2nd son of 2nd Earl of Jersey; successively Ambassador to Dresden, Poland, and Vienna, a Lord of the Admiralty, Joint Postmaster-Gen-Chancellor of the Duchy of Lancaster, and Ambassador to Berlin; *cr Baron Hyde*, of Hindon, Wilts (peerage of Great Britain) 1756, with remainder to the heirs male of his body by his then wife (Charlotte), da of 3rd Earl of Essex by Jane Hyde, da of 4th Earl of Clarendon (*cr* 1661), and in default to his said wife and the heirs male of her body, *Earl of Clarendon* (peerage of Great Britain) 1776, and a Baron of the Kingdom of Prussia 1782, which honour he received the Roy licence to enjoy; *d* 1786; *s* by his son (2) THOMAS, 2nd Earl; *d* unmarried 1824; *s* by his brother (3) JOHN CHARLES, 3rd Earl; *d* 1838; *s* by his nephew (4) GEORGE WILLIAM FREDERICK, KG, GCB, DCL, 4th Earl, el son of the Hon George, 3rd son of 1st Earl; *b* 1800; was First Commr of Excise 1824-33, Ambassador at Madrid 1833-9, Lord Privy Seal 1840-41, Pres of Board of Trade 1846-7, Viceroy of Ireland 1847-52, Sec. for Foreign Affairs 1853-8 and 1868-70, and Chancellor of Duchy of Lancaster 1864-5: *m* 1839, Lady Katherine Grimston, da of 1st Earl of Verulam, and widow of John Barham; *d* 27 June 1870; *s* by his el surviving son (5) EDWARD HYDE, GCB, GCVO, 5th Earl, *b* 1846; MP for Brecon (*L*) 1869-70; a Lord-in-Waiting to Queen Victoria 1895-1901, and Lord Chamberlain of the Household to King Edward VII 1901-5 and Lord-Lieut for Herts 1902-14: *m* 1st, 1876, Lady Caroline Elizabeth Agar, who *d* 1894, da of 3rd Earl of Normanton; 2ndly, 1908, Emma Mary Augusta, who *d* 1935, da of late Lt-Gen George Cliffe Hatch, CSI, and widow of Hon Edward Roden Bourke (E Mayo); *d* 1914; *s* by his el son (6) GEORGE HERBERT HYDE, KG, GCMG, GCVO, PC, 6th Earl; *b* 1877; Lord-in-Waiting to HM 1921-2, Ch Govt Whip in House of Lords, and Capt of HM Corps of Gentlemen-at Arms 1922-4 and 1924-5, Parliamentary Under-Sec of State for Dominion Affairs 1925-7, Chm British Broadcasting Corporation 1927-30, Gov-Gen and Com-in-Ch, Union of S Africa 1931-7, Lord Chamberlain of the Household and Chancellor of Roy Victorian Order 1938-52, Chancellor of Order of St Michael and St George 1942-55, and a permanent Lord-in-Waiting to HM 1952-5; *m* 1905, Adeline Verena Ishbel, LLLD, JP, who *d* 1963, da of late Herbert Haldane Somers-Cocks, and sister of 6th Baron Somers; *d* 1955; *s* by his grandson (7) GEORGE FREDERICK LAURENCE HYDE (son of late George Herbert Arthur Edward Hyde, Lord Hyde (*d* 1935) (who *m* 1932, Hon Marion Feodorovna Louise Glyn, DCVO, who *d* 1970, da of 4th Baron Wolverton), el son of 6th Earl), 7th Earl and present peer; also Baron Hyde.

CLARK, BARONY OF (Clark) (Extinct 1983)

SONS LIVING OF LIFE BARON

Rt Hon Alan Kenneth McKenzie (Saltwood Castle, Kent), *b* 1928: *ed* Eton, and Ch Ch, Oxford: Bar Inner Temple 1955; Gov St Thomas Hosp; Mil-Historian; Parliamentary Under Sec of State, Dept of Employment, 1983-86, Min for Trade 1986-90, Min for Defence 1990-92; MP for Plymouth, Sutton (*C*) Feb 1974-92, and for Kensington and Chelsea (*C*) since 1997; PC 1991; *m* 1958, Caroline Jane, da of Col Leslie Brindley Bream Beuttler, and has issue (*see* E Seafield, colls).

Hon Colin MacArthur (Paço da Glória, 4970 Arcos de Valdevez, Portugal), *b* 1932; *ed* Eton, and Ch Ch, Oxford: *m* 1st, 1961 (*m diss* 1969), Violette Verdy; 2ndly, 1971 (*m diss* 19—), Faith Beatrice, formerly wife of Julian Shuckburgh (*see* V Esher), and da of Sir Paul Hervé Giraud Wright; 3rdly, 1984, Helena Siu Kwan, da of late Cheung Wan Li, of Hong Kong, and has issue living (by 3rd *m*), Christopher Ming, *b* 1986.

DAUGHTER LIVING OF LIFE BARON

Hon Colette Elizabeth Dickson, *b* (twin) 1932; *ed* Cheltenham Coll, and Lady Margaret Hall, Oxford (BA); has issue living, Samuel CLARK, *b* 19—: *m* 1996, Samantha M., da of Edward Clarke, of Pentrehobyn, Mold, Flintshire.

Clark, Chichester-, family name of Baron Moyola.

CLARK OF KEMPSTON, BARON (Clark) (Life Baron 1992)

WILLIAM GIBSON CLARK, PC, son of Hugh Clark, of Cautley Av, SW4; *b* 18 Oct 1917; *ed* in London; 1939-45 War in UK and India; Wandsworth Borough Cllr; Chm Clapham Conservative Assocn 1949-52, and Mid-Beds Conservative Assocn 1949-52, Nat Hon Dir Lord Carrington Conservative Appeal 1967-68, Joint Dep-Chm Conservative Party 1975-77 (Joint Treasurer 1974-75), Chm Conservative Finance Cttee 1979-92; Chm Anglo-Austrian Soc 1983-98; Pres City Cttee Smaller Companies (CISCO) 1992-98; ACA 1941; Freeman City of London; Fellow Industry and Parliament Trust; Austrian Grand Gold Cross 1989, Grand Decoration of Honour in Gold (Austria) 1994; MP Nottingham S (*C*) 1959-66, E Surrey 1970-74, and S Croydon 1974-92; *cr* Kt Bach 1980, PC 1990, and *Baron Clark of Kempston*, of Kempston, co Beds (Life Baron) 1992: *m* 1944, Irene Dorothy Dawson, da of Edward Francis Rands, of Grimsby, Lincs, and has had issue.

ᴀrms – Erminois, on a pile azure between two quills pilewise points in base argent penned or, a portcullis chained in centre in chief or and five roundels in pile of the last. Crest – A demi unicorn azure winged, armed, crined and unguled or, collared chequy argent and azure and supporting with the forelegs a thistle plant flowered proper. Supporters – *Dexter*, a lion gules gorged with a collar chequy argent and azure, pendent therefrom by a cord or an escallop argent and resting the interior hind paw on a portcullis gold; *sinister*, an unicorn azure, winged, horned, unguled and crined or, gorged with a collar chequy argent and azure, pendent therfrom by a cord gold an escallop argent and resting the interior hoof on a bezant. *Residences* – 3 Barton St, SW1; The Clock House, Box End, Bedford. *Clubs* – Buck's, Carlton.

SONS LIVING AND DECEASED

Hon Richard Anthony, *b* 1947; *ed* Charterhouse, and Sorbonne; Solicitor: *m* 1st, 1973, Susan Kirstie Macgregor, da of late Hamish Edgar Donaldson Adamson; 2ndly, 1996, Mrs Sue Gregory, yr da of Michael Haslam, and widow of Oliver Gregory, and has issue living (by 1st *m*), Oliver Hamish William, *b* 1978, — Lucy Caroline, *b* 1976, — Polly Catherine Isabel, *b* 1981. *Residence* – Manor Farmhouse, Potterne, Devizes, Wilts SN10 5PR.

Hon David William Francis, *b* 1948; *ed* Charterhouse, and Sorbonne; FCA: *m* 1972 (*m diss* 19—), Elizabeth Grace, da of late Cdr Thomas Woodrooffe, and has issue living, Serena Elizabeth, *b* 1974, — Camilla Georgina Grace, *b* 1977. *Residence* – 3 Godmersham Park, Godmersham, Kent CT4 7DT.

Hon Charles Edward Hugh, *b* 1959; *ed* Haileybury: *m* 1991, Nicoletta Luisa Caroline, da of Dr Mario Lentati, of Ave de Fabron, Nice, France, and *d* 1997.

DAUGHTER DECEASED

Hon Angela Margaret Grayson, *b* 1950: *m* 1st, 1971, Hugh Duncan Sinclair, who *d* 1987; 2ndly, 1992, Peter Thomas Labey, and *d* 1998, leaving issue (by 1st *m*), Hugh, *b* 1973, — Harriet Emily Margaret, *b* 1975.

CLARKE OF HAMPSTEAD, BARON (Clarke) (Life Baron 1998)

ANTHONY JAMES CLARKE, CBE, son of Henry Walter Clarke, of Hampstead; *b* 17 April 1932; *ed* St Dominic's Roman Catholic Sch, Kentish Town, and Ruskin Coll (TU Education Course 1954); joined Post Office as a Telegraph Boy 1946, worked as Postman and Postman Higher Grade (Sorter) until 1979; Editor UPW Journal (The Post) 1979; Dep Gen Sec UPW (now CWU) 1982-93 (ret); Trustee Post Office Pension Funds 1991-97; Chm Labour Party 1992-93; Govr Westminster Foundation for Democracy 1992-98; awarded Papal Knighthood (KSG) for services to the community, international affairs and politics 1994; *cr* CBE 1998, and *Baron Clarke of Hampstead*, of Hampstead in the London Borough of Camden (Life Baron), 1998: *m* 1954, Josephine Ena, da of Charles Douglas Turner, of Wandsworth, and has issue.
Residence – 83 Orchard Drive, Park St, St Albans, Herts AL2 2QH.

SON LIVING

Hon Alan John, *b* 1958; *ed* Quintin Kynaston Sch, London: *m* 1997, Caroline Dixon, da of David Eckford, of Edinburgh.

DAUGHTER LIVING

Hon Ann-Marie, *b* 1961; *ed* La Sainte Union Convent, London: *m* 1988, John Wale, son of Gordon Wale, of London.

CLEDWYN OF PENRHOS, BARON (Hughes) (Life Baron 1979)

CLEDWYN HUGHES, CH, PC, son of late Rev Henry David Hughes; *b* 14 Sept 1916; *ed* Holyhead Gram Sch, and Univ Coll of Wales, Aberystwyth (LLB), Hon LLD Sheffield 1992, Hon LLD Univ of Wales 1970, Hon LLD Glamorgan Univ 1993; Pres Univ Coll of Wales, Aberystwyth 1975-84, Pro-Chancellor Univ of Wales 1984-94, Pres Univ of Wales, Bangor, since 1995; Solicitor 1940; Min of State for Commonwealth Affairs 1964-66, Sec of State for Wales 1966-68, Min of Agric, Fisheries and Food 1968-70; Chm of Parl Labour Party 1974-79; PM's Emissary to Southern Africa 1978; Opposition Leader of House of Lords 1982-92; MP for Anglesey (*Lab*) 1951-79; 1939-45 War as Fl Lt RAFVR; *cr* PC 1966, CH 1977, and *Baron Cledwyn of Penrhos*, of Holyhead in Isle of Anglesey (Life Baron) 1979: *m* 1949, Jean Beatrice, JP, da of Capt Jesse Hughes, and has issue.
Residence – Penmorfa, Trearddur, Anglesey. *Clubs* – Travellers, RAF.

SON LIVING

Hon Harri Cledwyn, *b* 1955: *m* 1986, Jennifer Meryl, da of R. P. Hughes, of Coedlys Valley, Anglesey, and has issue.

DAUGHTER LIVING

Hon Emily Ann, *b* 1950: *m* 1976, Peter Wright, and has issue.

CLEMENT-JONES, BARON (Clement-Jones) (Life Baron 1998)

TIMOTHY FRANCIS CLEMENT-JONES, CBE, son of late Maurice Llewelyn Clement-Jones, of Haywards Heath, Sussex; *b* 26 Oct 1949; *ed* Haileybury, and Trinity Coll, Camb (MA 1975); Solicitor 1974; Associate Joynson-Hicks & Co 1974-76; Corporate Lawyer, Letraset International Ltd 1976-80; Assist Head and later Head Legal Services LWT Ltd 1980-83; Legal Dir, Retailing Division, Grant Met plc 1984-86; Group Co Sec and Legal Adviser, Kingfisher plc (formerly Woolworth Holdings plc) 1986-95; Dir Political Context Ltd since 1996; Co-founder and Partner, Independent Corporate Mentoring (ICM) since 1996; Vice-Pres Eurocommerce (Euro Retail Federation) 1992-95; Chm Assoc of Liberal Lawyers 1982-86, and Liberal Party 1986-88; Chm Federal Finance Cttee, Liberal Democrats 1991-98, Dir Euro Election Campaign 1992-94, and Vice-Chm General Election Group 1994-97; Liberal Democrat Health Spokesman House of Lords since 1998; Tstee Cancer BACUP since 1986; Chm Crime Concern Advisory Bd 1991-95; *cr* CBE 1988, and *Baron Clement-Jones*, of Clapham in the London Borough of Lambeth (Life Baron) 1998: *m* 1st, 1973, Vicky Veronica, who *d* 1987, da of Teddy Yip, of Hong Kong; 2ndly, 1994, Jean Roberta, da of late Robert Whiteside, of Liverpool, and has issue by 2nd *m*.

Residence – 10 Northbourne Rd, SW4 7DJ. *Clubs* – National Liberal, RAC, Royal Society of Arts.

SON LIVING (By 2nd marriage)

Hon Harry Alexander, *b* 1998.

CLIFFORD OF CHUDLEIGH, BARON (Clifford) (Baron E 1672)

Always ready

THOMAS HUGH CLIFFORD, 14th Baron, *b* 17 March 1948: *s* 1988; *ed* Downside; late Capt Coldm Guards: *m* 1st, 1980 (*m diss* 1993), (Muriel) Suzanne, da of Maj Campbell Austin, of The Old Rectory, Muff, co Donegal; 2ndly, 1994, Clarissa Anne, elder da of His Honour Anthony Charles Goodall, MC, DL, of Mardon, Moretonhampstead, Devon, and has issue by 1st *m*.

Arms – Checky or and azure, a fease gules. **Crest** – Out of a ducal coronet or, a demi-wyvern gules. **Supporters** – Two wyverns purpure.
Seat – Ugbrooke Park, Chudleigh, S Devon TQ13 0AD.

SONS LIVING (By 1st marriage)

Hon ALEXANDER THOMAS HUGH, *b* 24 Sept 1985.
Hon Edward George Hugh, *b* 1988.

DAUGHTER LIVING (By 1st marriage)

Hon Georgina Apollonia, *b* 1983.

BROTHER LIVING

Hon Rollo Hugh, *b* 1954; *ed* Downside: *m* 1st, 1977, Fiona Margaret, only da of Richard Andrew Palethorpe Todd, OBE, actor; 2ndly, 1989, Mrs Caroline Peta Versen, only da of Peter Marshall Roberts, of Sydney, Australia, and has issue living (by 1st *m*), Christopher Rollo, *b* 1982, — Alasdair Rollo, *b* 1986, — Elizabeth Alice, *b* 1981, — (by 2nd *m*) Sophie Katharine Rose, *b* 1991. *Residence* – Worthy Manor, Porlock Weir, Minehead, Som TA24 8PG.

SISTERS LIVING

Hon Cecilia Alice KIRBY CLIFFORD, *b* 1945: *m* 1968 (*m diss* 1998), Capt Nicholas Breakspear Kirby, RN, of Melbury Bubb, nr Dorchester, Dorset, and has issue living, Julian Breakspear Bede, *b* 1975, — Samantha Mary, *b* 1969, — Christina Mary Anna, *b* 1971, — Caroline Mary Julia, *b* 1977. *Residence* – 43 Wilson Rd, Blairgowrie, Victoria 3942, Australia.

Hon Sarah Amy, *b* 1956: *m* 1981, Robert Carwithen Richardson, of Greatcombe, Holne, Devonshire TQ13 7SP, 2nd son of Christopher Richardson, of Dartmouth, Devon, and has issue living, Amy Natasha, *b* 1984, — Jessie Katharine, *b* 1987, — Polly, *b* 1994.

AUNTS LIVING (*daughters of 12th Baron*)

Hon Mary, *b* 1919: *m* 1943, Major Jack Philip Albert Galvin Clifford Wolff, MBE, of Hunters Lodge, Hunts Common, Hartley Wintney, Hants RG27 8AA, and has issue living, Rosamund Elizabeth, *b* 1944: *m* 1966, John David Arnold Wallinger, of The Manor House, Upton Grey, Basingstoke, Hants, son of late Sir Geoffrey Arnold Wallinger, GBE, KCMG, — Antoinette Mary, *b* 1946: *m* 1970, David Brian Parkes, of Ashcombe House, Tollard Royal, Wilts, and has issue living Harry *b* 1971, Sam *b* 1974.

Hon Rosamund Ann (*Baroness Fisher*) (Marklye, Rushlake Green, Heathfield, Sussex); *b* 1924; formerly zoo director and author; *m* 1st, 1946 (*m diss* 1965), Geoffrey Forrester Fairbairn; 2ndly, 1970, 3rd Baron Fisher, and has issue living (by 1st *m*), James Clifford, *b* 1950: *m* 1979, Catherine Elizabeth, da of Prof E. K. Cruickshank, of Ore, Wilts, and has issue living, Paul *b* 1982, Julia *b* 1984, — Charles Marcus Clifford, *b* 1955: *m* 1984, Sarah Jane, da of P.A. Coveney, of Burgess Hill, Sussex, and has issue living, Rory Tobias *b* 1987, Chloe Rebecca *b* 1985, — Katrina Elizabeth, *b* 1947: *m* 1st, 1968 (*m diss* 1982), Robert Moss; 2ndly, 1986, Peter Laurence Wise, of 38 Perryn Rd, W3, and has issue living (by 1st *m*), Pandora *b* 1971, Candida Rebecca *b* 1978, (by 2nd *m*) Serena Alice *b* 1988.

COLLATERAL BRANCHES LIVING

Issue of late Capt Hon Sir Bede Edmund Hugh Clifford, GCMG, CB, MVO, yst son of 10th Baron, *b* 1890, *d* 1969: *m* 1925, Alice Devin, who *d* 1980, da of John Murton Gundry, of Cleveland, Ohio, USA:—

Anne Frances May, *b* 1929: *m* 1952 (*m diss* 1985), 2nd Viscount Norwich. —— (Patricia David) Pandora, *b* 1930: *m* 1st, 1948 (*m diss* 1960), Timothy Angus Jones, son of late Sir (George) Roderick Jones, KBE; 2ndly, 1961 (*m diss* 1968), Hon Michael Langhorne Astor (*see* V Astor, colls), who *d* 1980; 3rdly, 19—, Phillip Lebon, and *d* 1987, leaving issue (by 1st *m*), Alexander Roderick, *b* 1955, — Annabel Lucy Veronica (*Viscountess Astor*), *b* 1948: *m* 1st, 1969 (*m diss* 1975), Reginald Adrian Berkeley Sheffield (later 8th Bt); 2ndly, 1976, 4th Viscount Astor. —— (Alice Devin) Atalanta, *b* 1932: *m* 1st, 1955, Richard Fairey, who *d* 1960, son of Sir (Charles) Richard Fairey, MBE; 2ndly, 1963 (*m diss* 19—), W/Cdr Timothy Ashmead Vigors, DFC; 3rdly, 1972, Michael Henry Dennis Madden, of 21A Barclay Rd, SW6 1EJ, and has issue living (by 1st *m*) Leanda Alice Devin Joan, *b* 1957, — (by 2nd *m*), Thomas Ashmead Murton, *b* 1969, — (by 3rd *m*) Henry George Bede, *b* 1973.

Descendants of late Sir Charles Clifford (el son of late George Lambert Clifford, 5th son of late Hon Thomas Clifford, 2nd son of 3rd Baron), who was *cr* a Baronet 1887:—
See Clifford, Bt, *cr* 1887.

PREDECESSORS – **(1)** *Rt Hon* THOMAS Clifford, PC; MP for Totnes, Comptroller of the Household 1666, Treasurer of the Household 1668, and Principal Sec of State and Lord High Treasurer 1672; *cr Baron Clifford of Chudleigh*, co Devon, 1672; *d* 1673; *s* by his son **(2)** HUGH, 2nd Baron; *d* 1730; *s* by his son **(3)** HUGH, 3rd Baron; *d* 1732; *s* by his son **(4)** HUGH, 4th Baron; *d* 1783; *s* by his el son **(5)** HUGH EDWARD HENRY, 5th Baron; *dsp* 1793; *s* by his brother **(6)** CHARLES, 6th Baron: *m* Hon Eleanor Mary (a Countess of the Holy Roman Empire), da of 8th Baron Arundell of Wardour; *d* 1831; *s* by his son **(7)** HUGH CHARLES, 7th Baron, and in right of his mother, a *Count of the Holy Roman Empire; d* 1858; *s* by his son **(8)** CHARLES HUGH, 8th Baron, *b* 1819: *m* 1845, Hon Agnes Catherine Louisa, who *d* 1891, da of 11th Baron Petre; *d* 1880; *s* by his son **(9)** LEWIS HENRY HUGH, 9th Baron, *b* 1851: *m* 1890, Mabel Anne, who *d* 1921, da of Col John Towneley, of Towneley, Lancashire; *d* 1916; *s* by his brother **(10)** WILLIAM HUGH, 10th Baron, *b* 1858: *m* 1st, 1886, Catherine Mary, who *d* (March) 1943, da of R. Basset; 2ndly, (May) 1943, Grace Muriel, who *d* 1963, da of late W. St Clair Munro, of Glasgow; *d* (July) 1943; *s* by his el son **(11)** CHARLES OSWALD HUGH, 11th Baron; *b* 1887; Lieut 5th Batn Devon Regt (TA) and Sub-Lieut RNVR: *m* 1st, 1917, Dorothy, who *d* 1918, da of late Alfred Joseph Hornyold; 2ndly, 1940, Clare Mary, who *d* 1975, da of late Capt Jasper Graham Mayne, CBE, and widow of Charles Struthers White Ogilvie; *d* 1962; *s* by his brother, **(12)** LEWIS JOSEPH HUGH 12th Baron; *b* 1889: *m* 1st, 1914, Amy, who *d* 1926 el da of John A. Webster, MD; 2ndly, 1934, Mary Elizabeth, da of late Rt Hon Sir Adrian Knox; *d* 1964; *s* by his only son **(13)** LEWIS HUGH, OBE, 13th Baron, *b* 1916, Col Devonshire Regt, Hon Col Devon Territorials (R Devon Yeo/1st Rifle Vol) T & AVR, Dep Hon Col Wessex Yeo RAC, TAVR, served European War 1939-45 (prisoner, escaped), ADC to HM 1964-69, DL Devon: *m* 1945, Hon Katharine Vavasseur Fisher, who *d* 1999, da of 2nd Baron Fisher; *d* 1988; *s* by his elder son **(14)** THOMAS HUGH, 14th Baron and present peer.

Clifton of Leighton Bromswold, Baron; title of Earl of Darnley on Roll of House of Lords.

Clifton of Rathmore, Lord; son of Earl of Darnley.

CLINTON, BARON (Fane Trefusis) (Baron E 1299)

GERARD NEVILE MARK FANE TREFUSIS, 22nd Baron; *b* 7 Oct 1934; *s* (on termination of abeyance) 1965; assumed by deed poll 1958 the surname of Trefusis after his patronymic; JP Bideford 1963, and DL Devon 1977; Memb Prince of Wales Councils 1968-79: *m* 1959, Nicola Harriette, da of late Maj Charles Robert Purdon Coote (*see* Coote, Bt, colls), and has issue.

Arms – Argent semy of cross crosslets fitchy sable in a chief azure two mullets or pierced gules, *Clinton*, charged with a inescutcheon quarterly, 1st, argent, on a fess azure three dexter gauntlets appaumy or, *Fane*, 2nd, argent, a chevron between three spindles sable, *Trefusis*, 3rd, azure, three boars' heads couped argent, muzzled gules, a cross crosslet argent, for distinction, *Forbes of Pitsligo*, 4th, or, a bend gules, surmounted by a fess checky azure and argent, in chief a crescent azure, a canton ermine for difference, *Stuart*. **Crest** – A bull's head erased sable armed, and about the neck an ancient crown attached thereto a line or, in the mouth a rose gules barbed seeded slipped and leafed proper. **Supporters** – On either side a greyhound argent collared with line reflexed over the back gules, in the mouth a gauntlet as in the arms, *Clinton*. *Residence* – Heanton Satchville, Okehampton, Devon EX20 3QE.

SON LIVING

Hon CHARLES PATRICK ROLLE, *b* 21 March 1962: *m* 1992, Rosanna E., yr da of (Alexander) John Rennie Izat, of High Cocklaw, Berwick upon Tweed, and has issue living, Edward Charles Rolle, *b* 26 Feb 1994. — James Henry Rolle, *b* 1996.

DAUGHTERS LIVING

Hon Caroline Harriet, *b* 1960: *m* 1995, Charles S. Fowle, elder son of Lt-Col Anthony Fowle, of Broughton, Hants, and has issue living, Thomas Trefusis, *b* 1997.
Hon Henrietta Jane, *b* 1964.

SISTERS LIVING

Carol, *b* 1937: *m* 1959, Hugo Peter Charles Bevan, of The Old House, Little Everdon, Daventry, Northants, and has issue living, Rupert Charles, *b* 1965: *m* 1992, Sophie Louise, only da of Clement Michael Charles Royds, of Armathwaite, Cumbria, and has issue living, Orlando *b* 1994, a son *b* 1999, Matilda *b* 1996, — Georgina Lucy, *b* 1963: *m* 1991, Rupert Patrick Fordham, of Wappenham Manor, Wappenham, nr Towcester, Northants NN12 8SH eldest son of late John Rupert Fordham, of 94 Portland Rd, W11, and has issue living, Patrick Hugo John *b* 1993, William Herbert *b* 1995, Henry Rupert Livingston *b* 1997, — Charlotte Adèle, *b* 1967, — Sophie Alexandra, *b* 1968.
Fiona, *b* 1939: *m* 1963, Sylvanus John Connolly, of 29 Blvd Pierre Alard, 31310 Montesquieu Volvestre, Haute-Garonne, France, and has issue living, Daniel Charles, *b* 1970, — Nicola Jane, *b* 1964: *m* 1991, Michael Leslie John Beck, of 111 Disraeli Rd, SW15, only son of Roger Beck, of Dinton, Wilts, — Alice Louise, *b* 1965, — Claudia Gay, *b* 1969: *m* 1997, Nicholas Lucien Richardson, of 6 Rue de la Folie Mericourt, Paris, eldest son of David Richardson, of Spetisbury, Dorset, and has issue living, Lucien Hector *b* 1996.

AUNT LIVING (*Daughter of Hon Harriet Fane, elder da of 21st Baron*)

Idonea Elizabeth, *b* 1912.

COLLATERAL BRANCHES LIVING

Grandchildren of late Hon Harriet Fane, elder da of 21st Baron:—
Issue of late John Henry Mark FANE, MBE, *b* 1917, *d* 1995: *m* 1st, 1939 (*m diss* 1954), Catherine Adelaide Anne, who *d* 19—, only child of late Gabriel Noel Dyer (*see* Legard, Bt, colls, 1971 Edn); 2ndly, 1954 (*m diss* 1962), Eleanor Sybil Ruth, da of late Albert Henry Archdeacon, of Hastings; 3rdly 1964, Elizabeth (6 Ollivier St, Alderney, CI), da of Kenneth W. Cowell, of Les Butes, Alderney:—
(By 2nd *m*) Simon John Nevile, *b* 1954. —— Robert Trefusis, *b* 1958. —— Harriet Jane, *b* 1956. —— Briony Ann, *b* 1957.

Issue of late Anne Charmian Fane, *b* 1916, *d* 1990: *m* 1st, 1937 (*m diss* 1949), Maj Robert Henry Arthur Rivers-Bulkeley, Scots Guards (*see* E Wemyss, colls, 1985 Edn); 2ndly, 1949, Peter Richard Hampton, MC:—
(By 1st *m*) Miranda Jane, *b* 1938: *m* 1963, John Goglis (actor, as John Voglis), of Psaron 4, Glyfada, Athens, and has issue living, Dimitri, *b* 1965, — Robertos Nicholas, *b* 1969.

Issue of late Hon Fenella Hepburn-Stuart-Forbes-Trefusis, yr da of 21st Baron, *b* 1889, *d* 1966: *m* 1914, Hon John Herbert Bowes-Lyon, who *d* 1930, 2nd son of 14th Earl of Strathmore:—
Katherine, *b* 1926.

Grandchildren of late Hon Fenella Hepburn-Stuart-Forbes-Trefusis (ante):—
Issue of late Anne Ferelith Fenella Bowes Lyon, *b* 1917, *d* 1980: *m* 1st, 1938 (*m diss* 1948), Maj Thomas William Arnold, Viscount Anson, who *d* 1958; 2ndly, 1950, HH Prince Georg of Denmark, who *d* 1986:—
(By 1st *m*) (*see* E Lichfield)

Issue of late Diana Cinderella Bowes Lyon, *b* 1923, *d* 1986: *m* 1960, Peter Gordon Colin Somervell, who *d* 1993, of Fettercairn House, Fettercairn, Kincardineshire, only surv son of Maj Sir Arnold Colin Somervell, OBE:—
Katherine Elizabeth SOMERVELL, *b* 1961; has resumed her maiden name: *m* 1991 (*m diss* 1996), Robert W. P. Lagneau, son of Michel Lagneau, and of Mrs Jane Few Brown.

Grandchildren of late Maj Hon Henry Walter Hepburn-Stuart-Forbes-Trefusis, Scots Gds, 2nd son of 20th Baron:—
Issue of late Henry TREFUSIS, late Lt Cdr RNVR, who relinquished the surnames of Hepburn-Stuart-Forbes by statutory declaration 1939, *b* 1908, *d* 1975: *m* 1940, Sheila Margaret (20 Tregew, Flushing, Falmouth), da of late Herman Bryan, of Lanthwaite, Eaton Hill, Norwich:—
Nicholas John TREFUSIS (Trefusis, Falmouth); *b* 1943; Lt-Cdr RN; JP for Cornwall: *m* 1973, Servane, yst da of late Louis Mélénec, of Brest, and Landévennec, and has issue living, Jan Henry Nicholas, *b* 1977, — Tamara Jane *b* 1974. —— Thomasine Mary, *b* 1942: *m* 1970, Philip Henry Faudel Heycock, of 62 Hamilton Park West, N5 1AB, and has issue living, Thomas Henry Trefusis, *b* 1971, — Eleanor Rachel, *b* 1974, — Sarah Kerensa Faudel, *b* 1977. —— Morwenna Jane, *b* 1945: *m* 1973, Robin Orton, of 11 Radlett Av, SE26 4BZ, and has issue living, Magdalen Jane Dorothy, *b* 1975, — Ann Emily, *b* 1977. —— (Ann) Kerensa, *b* 1949: *m* 1973, Andrew Michael Pearson, of 7 Gussiford Lane, Exmouth EX8 2SD, and has issue living, Timothy Mark, *b* 1977, — William Hugh, *b* 1979.

Issue of late Hon Robert Henry Hepburn-Stuart-Forbes-Trefusis, yst son of 20th Baron, *b* 1888, *d* 1958: *m* 1914, Lady Dorothy Marguerite Elizabeth, OBE, who *d* 1956, da of late Col Edward William Herbert, CB (E Powis):—
Helen Beatrice Margaret, *b* 1917: *m* 1936, Maj Simon Whitbread, KRRC (*see* E Mayo, colls, 1985 Edn), who *d* 1985, and has issue living, Samuel Charles (Southill Park, Biggleswade, Beds), *b* 1937; *ed* Eton, and Trin Coll, Camb; a CC 1974-81, JP 1969-83, DL Beds, High Sheriff 1973-74, Lord Lieut since 1991; Chm Whitbread & Co 1984-92: *m* 1961, Jane Mary, da of Charles Hugh Hayter, and has issue living, Charles Edward Samuel *b* 1963: *m* 1991, Jane Elizabeth, da of David Evans, of Warsash, Hants (and has issue living, Samuel David, *b* 1995, Emily Victoria *b* 1992, Catherine Helen *b* 1994), Henry George Simon *b* 1965: *m* 1994, Serena Caroline, da of Anthony J. Barclay, of Nineveh Farm, Nuneham Courtenay, Oxon (and has issue living, Edward Charles James *b* 1996, Thomas Anthony William *b* 1998), William John Howard *b* 1966, Victoria Clare Helen, *b* 1969: *m* 1993, Sebastian Jake Finch Morley (*see* B Beaverbrook), — Elizabeth Anne (65 Eccleston Sq Mews, SW1), *b* 1939: *m* 1962, James Carthew Cavendish Bennett, Diplo Ser, who *d* 1969, and has issue living, Nicholas James *b* 1964, Simon Patrick *b* 1965: *m* 1996, Natasha Jane, da of Gilles Turle, of Nairobi, Kenya (and has issue living, Amanda Sarah *b* 1996), Charles David *b* 1969.

Issue of late Hon Margaret Adela Hepburn-Stuart-Forbes-Trefusis, 3rd da of 20th Baron, *b* 1866, *d* 1939: *m* 1897, Rt Rev Leonard Jauncey White-Thomson, Bishop of Ely, who *d* 1933:—
(*See* 1939 Edn).

Issue of late Hon Harriet Margaret Hepburn-Stuart-Forbes-Trefusis, 6th and yst da of 20th Baron, *b* 1891, *d* 1975: *m* 1914, Lt-Col Eustace Widdrington Morrison-Bell, who *d* 1947:—
(*See* Morrison-Bell, Bt, *cr* 1905 colls).

Issue of late Katherine Helen Elizabeth Trefusis (who *m* 1906, Hon Arthur Owen Crichton), 3rd da of late Col Hon Walter Rodolph Trefusis, CB, 3rd son of 19th Baron:—
(*See* E Erne, colls).

Issue of late Marion Gertrude Trefusis (who *m* 1905, 4th Earl of Leicester), 4th da of late Col Hon Walter Rodolph Trefusis, CB (ante):—
(*See* E Leicester).

Grandchildren of late Margaret Harriet Trefusis (who *m* 1911, Lt-Col Edgar Hugh Brassey, MVO), 5th and yst da of late Col Hon Walter Rodolph Trefusis, CB (ante):—
Issue of late Col Sir Hugh Trefusis Brassey, KCVO, OBE, MC, *b* 1915, *d* 1990: *m* 1939, Joyce Patricia (Smokey Cottage, Little Somerford, Chippenham, Wilts), da of Capt Maurice John Kingscote (*see* B Gifford, 1947 Edn):—
Antony Hugh Owen BRASSEY (Hill Court, Shipton Moyne, Tetbury, Glos), *b* 1945; *ed* Eton; served Royal Scots Greys 1964-67: *m* 1980, Mrs Susan Sigri Burgoyne, da of late Robin Robsahm Fuglesang, of Lacock, Wilts, and has issue living, Hugo Timothy, *b* 1982, — Louisa Fiona, *b* 1984. —— Kim Maurice BRASSEY (High Farm House, Finches Lane, Baydon, Marlborough, Wilts), *b* 1955; financial consultant: *m* 1st, 1981, Alison Sarah, who *d* 1990, da of Edwin James Cracknell; 2ndly, 1992, Joanna, da of late Capt Colin Gowans, MN, and has issue living (by 1st *m*), Fiona Elizabeth, *b* 1985, — Lily Patricia, *b* 1988, — (by 2nd *m*) Jack William, *b* 1992, — Ellie *b* 1994. —— †Fiona Gillian, *b* 1942; *d* 1958. —— Jane Margaret, *b* 1946: *m* 1971, John Morrison Rogers, who *d* 1995, of Riverhill House, Sevenoaks, Kent, son of late Maj

David Morrison Rogers (*see* Morrison-Bell, Bt, 1919 Edn), and has issue living, John Edward, *b* 1974, — Daniel Hugh, *b* 1976. —— Sarah Patricia, *b* 1949: *m* 1980, John Moorehead, of 10 Egbert St, NW1, son of late Alan Moorehead, author and war correspondent, and has issue living, Alexander Patrick, *b* 1979, — Benjamin Christopher, *b* 1982.

Issue of late Marjorie Eva Brassey, *b* 1911, *d* 1975: *m* 1933, Hugh Myddleton Peacock, TD, DL, of The Ferry, Milton, Peterborough:—
Michael Hugh PEACOCK, *b* 1946; *ed* Eton: *m* 1974, Caroline Mary, yst da of Maj Robert Hoare, MC, of Hambleton Hall, Oakham. —— Idina Caroline, *b* 1933: *m* 1957, Col James William Gordon Pirie, 60th Rifles, who *d* 1994, of 38 Kew Green, Richmond, Surrey, and has issue living, James Hugh Pirie, *b* 1959, — Amanda Caroline, *b* 1962. —— Susan Margaret, *b* 1938: *m* 1964, Michael Andrieus Jones, of 24 Sunswyck Rd, Darien, Connecticut 06820, USA, and has issue living, Philip Andrieus, *b* 1966: *m* 1994, Susan Anne, da of Franklyn Ayres, of Winnetka, Illinois, USA, and has issue living, Tristan Ayres *b* 1998, — Idina Maria, *b* 1968: *m* 1995, Frank Roberston Holden, of Traverse City, Michigan, USA, and has issue living, Duncan Peter *b* 1997, Ian Roberston *b* 1998.

Granddaughter of late Col Hon John Schomberg TREFUSIS, CMG, 4th son of 19th Baron:—
Issue of late Elizabeth Katharine Mary Trefusis, *b* 1887, *d* 1976, Capt Garth Neville Walford, VC, RHA, who was *ka* 1915:—
Phyllida *b* 1915: *m* 1944, Kenneth Ellis, who *d* 1972. *Residence* – Gapperies, W Porlock, Som TA24 8NX.

Grandchildren of late Maj George Rodolph Trefusis, eldest son of late Rt Rev Robert Edward Trefusis, DD, Bishop of Crediton, yr son of late Capt Hon George Walpole Rolle Trefusis, RN, 3rd son of 17th Baron:—
Issue of late Maj Robert John Rodolph Trefusis, *b* 1914, *d* 1997: *m* 1955, Shirley Adeline Scott (Longmeadows Lodge, Feniton, Honiton, Devon EX14 0BE), da of late Charles Scott Barton, of Sullington, Sussex:—
Rev Charles Rodolph, *b* 1961; V of Christ Church, Purley, Surrey, since 1994: *m* 1989, Catherine, da of late Brian Dudgeon, of Guildford, Surrey, and has issue living, William Henry Rodolph, *b* 1997, — Harriet Sarah Patricia, *b* 1991, — Charlotte Rosanna, *b* 1993, — Eleanor Rachel, *b* 1995. —— Rosemary Jane, *b* 1959: *m* 1988, David Richard Fry, late Lt-Cdr RN, of 3 Ormsby Rd, Southsea, Hants PO5 2AL, eldest son of Capt R. G. Fry, OBE, RN, of Whitchurch Canonicorum, Bridport, Dorset, and has issue living, Edward James, *b* 1993, — Emma Katherine, *b* 1991, — Georgina Sarah, *b* 1996.

PREDECESSORS – **(1)** JOHN de Clinton, summoned to Parliament of England 1299; his grandson **(2)** JOHN, 2nd Baron, summoned to Parliament 1332-35; *s* by his son **(3)** *Sir* JOHN, Knt, 3rd Baron, summoned to Parliament 1357-97; *d* 1397; *s* by his grandson **(4)** WILLIAM, 4th Baron; *d* 1432; *s* by his son **(5)** JOHN, 5th Baron; a staunch Yorkist, was attainted 1461, and subsequently restored; *d* 1464; *s* by his son **(6)** JOHN, 6th Baron; *d* 1488; *s* by his son **(7)** JOHN, 7th Baron; *d* 1514; *s* by his son **(8)** THOMAS, 8th Baron; *d* 1517; *s* by his son **(9)** EDWARD, KG, PC, 9th Baron, Lord High Adm; *cr Earl of Lincoln* (peerage of England) 1572; *d* 1585; *s* by his son **(10)** HENRY, KB, 2nd Earl; *d* 1616; *s* by his son **(11)** THOMAS, 3rd Earl; *d* 1618; *s* by his son **(12)** THEOPHILUS, KB, 4th Earl; *d* 1667; *s* by his grandson **(13)** EDWARD, 5th Earl; *dsp* 1692, when the Earldom devolved upon his cousin (*see* D Newcastle), and the barony became abeyant between the issue of his aunts; in 1721 the abeyance was terminated in favour of **(14)** HUGH Fortescue, 14th Baron; *cr Baron Fortescue*, of Castlehill, co Devon, with limitation to his half-brother Matthew, and *Earl of Clinton* (peerage of Great Britain) 1746, *dsp* 1751, when the Earldom of Clinton became extinct, the Barony of Fortescue passed to his half-brother (*see* E Fortescue), and the Barony of Clinton devolved upon his cousin **(15)** MARGARET, widow of 2nd Earl of Orford, and wife of Hon Sewallis Shirley (E Ferrers); *d* 1781; *s* by her son **(16)** GEORGE, 3rd *Earl of Orford* and 16th Baron Clinton; *dsp* 1791, when the Earldom passed to his nephew, and in 1794 the Barony of Clinton was sucessfully claimed by his cousin **(17)** ROBERT GEORGE WILLIAM Trefusis, the descendant of Lady Arabella Rolle, 2nd da of 4th Earl of Lincoln; *d* 1797; *s* by his el son **(18)** ROBERT COTTON ST. JOHN, 18th Baron; a Lord of the Bedchamber to George III; *d* 1832; *s* by his brother **(19)** CHARLES RODOLPH, 19th Baron, *b* 1791: *m* 1831, Lady Elizabeth Georgiana Kerr, who *d* 1871, da of 6th Marquess of Lothian; *d* 1866; *s* by his son **(20)** CHARLES HENRY ROLLE, 20th Baron, *b* 1834; sat as MP for N Devon (LC) 1857-66; Under-Sec of State for India 1867-68, a Charity Commr 1874-80, and Lord-Lieut of Devonshire 1887-1904; assumed by Roy licence 1867, the additional surnames of Hepburn-Stuart-Forbes; *m* 1st, 1858, Harriet Williamina, who *d* 1869, da and heiress of Sir John Stuart Forbes, 8th Bt; 2ndly, 1875, Margaret, who *d* 1930, da of Sir John Walrond Walrond, 1st Bt; *d* 1904; *s* by his son **(21)** CHARLES JOHN ROBERT, GCVO, PC, 21st Baron; *b* 1863; High Steward of Barnstaple; was Joint Parliamentary Sec to Board of Agriculture and Fisheries 1918, a Member of Council of Cornwall (1911-33) and Keeper of the Privy Seal (1913-33) of HRH the Prince of Wales, and Lord Warden of the Stannaries 1921-33; Chm of Forestry Institute 1924-29, and of Forestry Commn 1927-29: *m* 1886, Lady Jane Grey McDonnell (a CStJ), who *d* 1953, da of 5th Earl of Antrim; *d* 1957, when the Barony fell into abeyance between his two daughters, Hon Harriet, who *d* 1958, having *m* Maj Henry Nevile Fane, and Hon Fenella, who *d* 1966, having *m* Hon John Herbert Bowes Lyon, and so continued until 1965, when the abeyance was terminated in favour of the senior co-heir **(22)** GERARD NEVILE MARK (only son of late Capt Charles Nevile Fane, el son of late Hon Harriet Fane), 22nd Baron and present peer.

Clinton, Fiennes-, family name of Earl of Lincoln.

CLINTON-DAVIS, BARON (Clinton-Davis) (Life Baron 1990)

STANLEY CLINTON-DAVIS, PC, son of Sidney Davis; *b* 6 Dec 1928; *ed* Hackney Downs Sch, Mercers' Sch, and King's Coll, London (Fellow 1996); Parly Under Sec Trade 1974-79, Opposition Front Bench Spokeman Trade 1979-81, Foreign and Commonwealth Affairs 1981-83; Member Assocn of Professional, Executive, Clerical and Computer Staffs, Pres British Multiple Sclerosis Soc (Hackney Branch), Councillor (Hackney) 1959-71, Mayor Hackney 1968-69, Solicitor since 1953; Member Commn of European Communities 1985-89, Vice-Pres Soc of Lab Lawyers since 1987; Trustee Bernt Carlsson Trust, Hon Member Exec Council of Justice, Member UN Selection Cttee Sasakawa Environment Project since 1989; Dir Jewish Chronicle since 1989; Consultant on European Law and Affairs, S. J. Berwin & Co, since 1989, Senior Advisor on European Affairs with Hill & Knowlton Int since 1989; Min of State for Trade 1997-98; MP Hackney Central (*Lab*) 1970-83; assumed by deed poll 1990 the surname of Clinton-Davis in lieu of his patronymic; *cr Baron Clinton-Davis*, of Hackney, in the London Borough of Hackney (Life Baron) 1990, and PC 1998: *m* 1954, Frances Jane, da of late Marcus Gershon Lucas, and has issue.
Residence – 22 Bracknell Gate, Hampstead, NW3.

SON LIVING

Hon Henry, *b* 1960.

DAUGHTERS LIVING

Hon Joanna, *b* 1955: *m* 19—, — Lavell.
Hon Susanna, *b* 1962: *m* 19—, — Fox.
Hon Melissa, *b* 1964.

CLITHEROE, BARON (Assheton) (Baron UK 1955, Bt UK 1945)

I am neither proud nor afraid

RALPH JOHN ASSHETON, 2nd Baron and 3rd Baronet; *b* 3 Nov 1929; *s* 1984; *ed* Eton (Oppidan Scholar), and Ch Ch, Oxford (Scholar, MA); late The Life Guards; DL Lancs 1986; Chm Yorkshire Bank plc since 1990, Dir Halliburton Co, Texas since 1987; formerly Dep Ch Exec RTZ Corpn plc, and Dir First Interstate Bank of California, of Touche Remnant Natural Resources, of American Mining Congress, of Chemical Industries Assocn, and other Cos; a Liveryman of Skinners' Co; Pres Assocn of Lancastrians in London 1990: *m* 1961, Juliet, da of late Lt-Col Christopher Lionel Hanbury, MBE, TD, of Juniper Hill, Burnham, Bucks, and has issue.

Arms – Argent a mullet sable pierced of the field. **Crest** – On a cap of maintenance, a mower, vested and capped quarterly, argent and sable, sleeves and stockings counter changed, holding a scythe azure, handled or, the point of the blade towards the dexter. **Supporters** – *Dexter*, a Labrador dog sable; *sinister*, a bull argent armed or.
Residence – Downham Hall, Clitheroe, Lancs BB7 4DN.
Clubs – Boodle's, Pratt's, RAC.

SONS LIVING

Hon RALPH CHRISTOPHER, *b* 19 March 1962; *ed* Eton; Lord of the Honor of Clitheroe: *m* 1996, Olivia Sarah, only da of Capt John Anthony Cromek Warrington (*see* B Hastings, colls), and has issue living, Ralph Anthony, *b* 3 Dec 1998.
Hon John Hotham (Bridge House, Broughton, Banbury, Oxon OX15 5ED), *b* 1964; *ed* Harrow: *m* 1989, Amanda E., da of Geoffrey Freeman, of Red Lion House, Nettlebed, Oxfordshire, and has issue living, William Hotham, *b* 1992, — James Charles, *b* 1999, — Charlotte, *b* 1994.

DAUGHTER LIVING

Hon Elizabeth Jane, *b* 1968; *ed* Wycombe Abbey, and Edinburgh Univ (MA): *m* 1995, Robin Anthony Edward Tarling, late Maj The Life Guards, son of Timothy Tarling, of Dulverton, Som, and has issue living, Eleanor Katherine, *b* 1998.

BROTHER LIVING

Hon Nicholas, *b* 1934; *ed* Eton, and Ch Ch, Oxford (MA); FSA; Lord of the Manor and Liberty of Slaidburn, Grindleton and Bradford; formerly Member of London Stock Exchange (Member of Council 1968-88), formerly partner and sr partner Montagu, Loebl, Stanley & Co, formerly Dep Chm Coutts & Co; Treasurer and Extra Equerry to HM Queen Elizabeth the Queen Mother since 1998; Memb of Council Soc of Antiquaries of London since 1998; a Liveryman of Vintners' Co; late 2nd Lt The Life Gds, and Lt Inns of Court of Regt: *m* 1960, Jacqueline Jill, da of Marshal of the RAF Sir Arthur Travers Harris, 1st Bt, GCB, OBE, AFC, and has issue living, Thomas (Manor Farm, Longborough, Moreton-in-Marsh, Glos. *Clubs* – White's, Pratt's), *b* 1963; *ed* Eton, and Reading Univ (BSc); late Capt The Life Gds: *m* 1989, Katharine Sophie, da of David Alphy Edward Raymond Peake (*see* V Ingleby, colls), and has issue living, Noah Frederick *b* 1991, Molly *b* 1992, — Caroline, *b* 1961, — Mary Thérèse, *b* 1967; has issue living, Arthur Travers GORDON *b* 1994, Alice GORDON *b* 1988. *Residence* – 15 Hammersmith Terrace, W6 9TS. *Clubs* – White's, Pratt's, City of London.

SISTER LIVING

Hon Bridget (*Hon Lady Worsley*), *b* 1926; late WRNS: *m* 1955, Sir (William) Marcus John Worsley 5th Bt, and has issue (see that title). *Residence* – Hovingham Hall, York.

AUNT LIVING (*Daughter of 1st Baronet*)

Eleanor, CBE, *b* 1907; was Vice-Chm of the Yorkshire Provincial Area of National Union of Conservative and Unionist Assoc 1952-5; CBE (Civil) 1956: *m* 1926, Maj John Edward Evelyn Yorke, JP, who *d* 1997, and has issue living, David John, *b* 1927; *ed* Eton, and Trin Coll, Camb (MA); late The Life Gds; FRICS; a JP and DL of Lancs: *m* 1957, Susan Alexandra, da of Lt-Col Scrope Arthur Francis Sutherland Egerton, Highland LI (ret) (*see* D Sutherland, colls), and has issue living, John Alexander *b* 1959; *ed* Eton, Charles Scrope Edward *b* 1965; *ed* Eton, Sophia Caroline Annabel *b* 1961: *m* 1984, Nicholas Anthony Bevil Acland, yr son of Sir Antony Arthur Acland, GCMG, GCVO (*see* Acland, Bt, *cr* 1890, colls), — Felicity Anne, *b* 1931: *m* 1955, James Patrick Ashley Cooper, son of Sir Patrick Ashley Cooper, of Hexton Manor, Hitchin, Herts, and has issue living, Patrick John Ashley *b* 1957; *ed* Eton, and Trin Hall, Camb: *m* 1989, Belinda Jane, da of Christopher Firth, of Brantingham Hall, Brough, E Yorks (and has issue living, Christopher Patrick Ashley *b* 1990, Thomas James Ashley *b* 1992, Amelia Clare *b* 1994), Edward James Ashley *b* 1966, Katharine Mary *b* 1956: *m* 1991, Dr Peter Foot (and has issue living, Sarah *b* 1993), Felicity *b* 1961: *m* 1997, Ian Reid Gorton. *Residence* – Halton Place, Hellifield, Skipton, Yorks.

PREDECESSORS – (1) Ralph Cockayne Assheton, son of late Ralph Assheton, MP, of Downham Hall, Clitheroe, Lancashire, and Cuerdale, Lancashire; *b* 1860; High Sheriff of Lancashire 1919; was a Co Councillor for Lancashire 1892-1902, and a Co Alderman 1902-49; *cr* a *Baronet* 1945: *m* 1898, Mildred Estelle Sybella, CBE, JP, who *d* 1949, da and co-heiress of John Henry Master, JP, of Montrose House, Petersham, Surrey; *d* (Sept) 1955; *s* by his only son (2) RALPH, 2nd Bt; *b* 1901; MP for Rushcliffe Div of Notts 1934-45, for City of London 1945-50 and for W Div of Blackburn 1950-55; Fin Sec to Treas 1942-44; *cr* PC 1944, *Baron Clitheroe*, of Downham, co Lancaster (peerage of UK) 1955, and KCVO 1977: *m* 1924, Hon Sylvia Benita Frances Hotham, FRICS, who *d* 1991, da of 6th Baron Hotham; *d* 1984; *s* by his elder son (3) RALPH JOHN, 2nd Baron and present peer, also 3rd Baronet.

Clive, Viscount; son of Earl of Powis

Clive, Windsor-, family name of Earl of Plymouth.

CLWYD, BARON (Roberts) (Baron UK 1919, Bt UK 1908)
(Title pronounced "Cloo-id")

(JOHN) ANTHONY ROBERTS, 3rd Baron and 3rd Baronet; *b* 2 Jan 1935; *s* 1987; *ed* Harrow, and Trin Coll, Camb; Bar Gray's Inn 1970: *m* 1969, (Linda) Geraldine, yr da of Charles Eugene Cannons, of Sanderstead, Surrey, and has issue.

Arms – Per fesse azure and argent, a lion rampant between three ostrich feathers all counter-changed. **Crest** – A lion rampant per fesse argent and azure, holding in its paws on ostrich feather. **Supporters** – *Dexter*, a dragon proper, collared or; *sinister*, a sable bear, also collared or.
Residence – 24 Salisbury Av, Cheam, Surrey SM1 2DJ.

SONS LIVING

Hon (JOHN) MURRAY, *b* 27 Aug 1971.
Hon Jeremy Trevor, *b* 1973.
Hon Hugh Gerald Arthur, *b* 1977.

SISTER LIVING

Hon Alison de Bois, *b* 1939: *m* 1st, 1965 (*m diss* 1972), George Stricevic; 2ndly, 1972, Anthony H. Brown, of 9 Royal Terr, Glasgow, G3 7NT, and has issue living (by 1st *m*) Milorad, *b* 1967, — (by 2nd *m*) Barnaby Joseph, *b* 1973, — Benedict Joseph, *b* 1975, — Lionel Trevor, *b* 1978.

WIDOWS LIVING OF SONS OF FIRST BARON

Aileen Mary, da of late Charles Edward Burrow, of Sale, Cheshire: *m* 1936, Hon David Stowell Roberts, who *d* 1956, and has issue (see colls, infra). *Residence* – 24 Long Ashton Rd, Long Ashton, Bristol BS18 9LB.

Eileen Margaret, da of late Alfred Thomas Easom, of Hillside, Abergele: *m* 1947, Hon (William Herbert) Mervyn Roberts, who *d* 1990, and has issue (see colls, infra). *Residence* – 54 April Close, Horsham, W Sussex RH12 2LN.

COLLATERAL BRANCHES LIVING

Issue of late Hon David Stowell Roberts, 2nd son of 1st Baron, *b* 1900, *d* 1956: *m* 1936, Aileen Mary (ante), da of late Charles Edward Burrow, of Sale, Cheshire:—
(Hugh) Martin (29 Chalfont Rd, Oxford OX2 6TL), *b* 1941; *ed* Christ's Hosp Sch, and Merton Coll, Oxford; Headmaster Cherwell Comprehensive Sch, Oxford: *m* 1966, Diana, da of Denis C. Cochran, of Cape Town, and has issue living, Thomas Owen, *b* 1973, — Sarah Megan *b* 1971. —— Peter Gareth, *b* 1947; *ed* Christ's Hosp Sch, and Univ of E Anglia: *m* 1982, Susan Browne, and has issue living, Matthew Lewis, *b* 1984. —— Fenella, *b* 1940: *m* 1968, Peter Rosenwald, and has issue living, David Joseph, *b* 1972, — Celia Janet, *b* 1974.

Issue of late Hon (William Herbert) Mervyn Roberts, 3rd and yst son of 1st Baron, *b* 1906, *d* 1990: *m* 1947, Eileen Margaret (ante), da of late Alfred Thomas Easom, of Hillside, Abergele:—
Catherine Angela, *b* 1950: *m* 1984, David James Arnold, of 37 Springfield Park, N Parade, Horsham, W Sussex RH12 2BF.

PREDECESSOR – (1) JOHN HERBERT Roberts, el son of late John Roberts (sometime MP for Flint Dist) of Bryngwenallt, Abergele, N Wales; *b* 1863; Chm of Welsh Liberal Parliamentary Party 1912-18 (formerly Sec); MP for W Div of Denbighshire (*L*) 1892-1918; *cr a Baronet* 1908, and *Baron Clwyd*, of Abergele, co Denbigh (peerage of United Kingdom) 1919: *m* 1893, Hannah Rushton, who *d* 1951, da of late William Sproston Caine, MP, of 33 North Side, Clapham Common, SW; *d* 1955: *s* by his el son (2) (JOHN) TREVOR, 2nd Baron, *b* 1900, bar Gray's Inn; assist sec of Commons, Lord Chancellor's Dept, House of Lords 1949-61: *m* 1932, Joan de Bois, who *d* 1985, da of late Charles R. Murray, of Woodbank, Partickhill, Glasgow; *d* 1987; *s* by his only son (3) JOHN ANTHONY, 3rd Baron and present peer.

CLYDE, BARON (Clyde) (Life Baron 1996)

JAMES JOHN CLYDE, PC, son of late Rt Hon Lord Clyde (James Latham McDiarmid Clyde), PC, DL, Lord Justice General of Scotland and Lord President of the Court of Session; *b* 29 Jan 1932; *ed* Edinburgh Acad, Corpus Christi Coll, Oxford (BA 1954), and Edinburgh Univ (LLB 1959), Hon DUniv Heriot-Watt 1991, Hon DLitt Napier Univ 1995, Hon DUniv Edinburgh 1997, Hon Fellow of Corpus Christi Coll, Oxford 1996, Hon Bencher, Middle Temple 1996; Advocate, Scotland 1959, QC (Scot) 1971, Advocate-Depute 1973-74, Chancellor to Bishop of Argyll and the Isles 1972-85, Member Scottish Valuation Advisory Council 1972-96 (Vice-Chm 1980-87, Chm 1987-96), Leader, UK Delegation to the CCBE 1981-84, Chm Medical Appeal Tribunals 1974-85, Judge in the Courts of Appeal for Jersey and Guernsey 1979-85, a Senator of the College of Justice in Scotland 1985-86, a Lord of Appeal in Ordinary since 1996; Trustee of St Mary's Music Sch 1978-93, Dir Edinburgh Acad 1979-88, Vice-Pres The Royal Blind Asylum and Sch since 1987, Pres Scottish Young Lawyers' Assoc 1988-97, Chm of Council, St George's Sch for Girls 1989-97, Gov of Napier Univ (formerly Napier Poly) 1989-93; Assessor to Chancellor of Edinburgh Univ 1989-97, Vice-Chm of Council 1993-96; Pres Scottish Universities Law Inst 1991-98; Trustee of National Library of Scotland 1977-94; *cr Baron Clyde*, of Briglands and Perthshire and Kinross (Life Baron) 1996, and PC 1996: *m* 1963, Ann Clunie, da of late Donald Robert Armstrong Hoblyn, of Tunbridge Wells, Kent, and has issue.

𝕬rms – Per fess argent and azure a fess wavy per fess wavy azure and argent, two bushes upon mounds vert in chief, and a tower or window and port gules in base. 𝕮rest – A tree with branch of mountain ash, of beech and cherry proper. 𝕸otto – Diligens integer laetus.
Residence – 12 Dublin St, Edinburgh EH1 3PP. *Club* – New (Edinburgh).

SONS LIVING

Hon James, *b* 1969; *ed* Edinburgh Acad, and Durham Univ.
Hon Timothy, *b* 1973; *ed* Edinburgh Acad, Fettes Coll, and Durham Univ.

Clydesdale, Marquess of (Marquess of Douglas and Clydesdale); son of Duke of Hamilton and Brandon.

CLYDESMUIR, BARON (Colville) (Baron UK 1948)

I cannot forget

DAVID RONALD COLVILLE, 3rd Baron; *b* 8 April 1949; *s* 1996; *ed* Charterhouse: *m* 1978, Aline Frances, eldest da of Peter Merriam, of Holton Lodge, Holton St Mary, Suffolk (*see* M Ailsa, 1985 Edn), and has issue.

𝔄rms – Argent, a cross moline sable, on a chief of the last a thistle slipped proper between two bulls' heads also argent. 𝔠rest – A hind's head erased proper. 𝔖upporters – A roebuck and a doe, both proper.

SONS LIVING

Hon RICHARD, *b* 21 Oct 1980.
Hon Hamish, *b* 1989.

DAUGHTERS LIVING

Hon Rachel, *b* 1983.
Hon Harriet, *b* 1985.

BROTHER LIVING

Hon Andrew John, *b* 1953; *ed* Harrow, and Magdalene Coll, Camb (MA); Solicitor 1976-80, since when a Merchant Banker: *m* 1978, Elaine Geneviève, yst da of E. G. Davy, of Corner Farm, Holton St Peter, Suffolk, and has issue living, Patrick Edwin Ronald, *b* 1988, — Emily Christine Rose, *b* 1986. *Residence* – 40 Pembroke Rd, W8.

SISTERS LIVING

Hon Diana Mary, *b* 1947; temporary Lady in Waiting to HRH The Duchess of Gloucester 1980-83: *m* 1973, Christopher I. C. Munro, and has issue living, Andrew James William, *b* 1979, — Fiona Mary, *b* 1976. *Residence* – 26 Pembroke Sq, W8 6PB.
Hon Elizabeth Anne *b* 1955: *m* 1983, Christopher J. V. R. Baker, and has issue living, Lucy Florence, *b* 1986.

AUNT LIVING (*daughter of 1st Baron*)

Hon Rosemary Anne Heather, *b* 1927: *m* 1954, Philip Arthur Whitcombe, of Green Cross Farm, Churt, Farnham, Surrey, and has issue living, Robert John (Berry Grove Farm, Liss, Hants), *b* 1955: *m* 1988, Sophie Emma, da of Trefor Owen Roberts, of Petersfield, Hants, — Susan Anne Clare, *b* 1957: *m* 1985, Robin R. Marriott, yr son of Anthony Marriott, of Park View Farm, Headley, Hants.

WIDOW LIVING OF SECOND BARON

JOAN MARGUERITA (*Joan, Baroness Clydesmuir*), da of late Lt-Col Ernest Brabazon Booth, DSO, MD, of Darver Castle, Dundalk, co Louth: *m* 1946, 2nd Baron Clydesmuir, KT, CB, MBE, TD, who *d* 1996. *Residence* – Langlees House, Biggar, Lanarkshire ML12 6HP.

PREDECESSORS – (1) *Rt Hon Sir* DAVID JOHN Colville, GCIE, TD, PC, son of late John Colville, MP, JP, of Cleland House, Lanarkshire; *b* 1894; was Parliamentary Sec to Depart of Overseas Trade 1931-5, Under-Sec of State for Scotland 1935-36, Financial Sec to the Treasury 1936-8, Sec of State for Scotland 1938-40 and Gov of Bombay 1943-48 (acted as Viceroy and Gov-Gen of India on four occasions); a Gov of British Broadcasting Corporation 1950-4 and National Gov for Scotland 1952-4, sat as MP for N Div of Midlothian and Peeblesshire (*U*) 1929-43; *cr Baron Clydesmuir*, of Braidwood, co Lanark (peerage of United Kingdom) 1948: *m* 1915, Agnes Anne, CI, who *d* 1970, da of Sir William Bilsland, 1st Bt, LLD, *d* 1954; *s* by his only son (2) RONALD JOHN BILSLAND, KT, CB, MBE, TD, 2nd Baron, *b* 1917; Capt-Gen Queen's Body Guard for Scotland (Royal Company of Archers), Pres of Council 1974-81; Pres of Lowlands of Scotland TA & VR Assocns 1968-73, Hon Col 6th/7th (Territorial) Bn, The Cameronians (Scottish Rifles); Gov Bank of Scotland 1972-81; Lord High Commr to Gen Assembly of Church of Scotland 1971 and 1972; Lord Lieut for Lanarks 1963-96: *m* 1946, Joan Marguerita, da of late Lt-Col Ernest Brabazon Booth, DSO, MD, of Darver Castle, Dundalk, co Louth; *d* 1996; *s* by his elder son (3) DAVID RONALD, 3rd Baron and present peer.

COBBOLD, BARON (Lytton Cobbold) (Baron UK 1960)

Brave in adversity

DAVID ANTONY FROMANTEEL LYTTON COBBOLD, 2nd Baron; *b* 14 July 1937; *s* 1987; *ed* Eton, and Trin Coll, Camb (BA 1960); assumed by deed poll 1960 the additional surname of Lytton before his patronymic; DL Herts 1993; Fellow Assocn of Corporate Treasurers; BP Finance Internat 1979-87, Gen Manager Treasury, TSB England & Wales plc 1987-88, Dir Hill Samuel Bank Ltd 1988-89, Chm Lytton Enterprises Ltd since 1971, Hon Treasurer Historic Houses Assocn 1988-97, Managing Dir Gaincorp UK Ltd 1989-94, Dir Close Brothers Group plc since 1993, Pres Univ of Hertfordshire Development Cttee since 1992, Memb Board of Governors, Univ of Hertforshire since 1993, Trustee, The Pilgrim Trust since 1993, Chm Stevenage Community Trust since 1992: *m* 1961, Christine Elizabeth, 3rd da of Maj Sir Dennis Frederick Bankes Stucley, 5th Bt, and has issue.

Arms – Sable a chevron or between in chief two bezants and in base a lion passant guardant gold on a chief dancetty of the last two ducal coronets azure. Crest – A lion statant guardant argent crowned with a ducal coronet azure supporting with the dexter paw an escutcheon vert thereon three escutcheons also argent each having a bordure engrailed or. Supporters – On either side a yellow labrador dog proper each resting the interior hind foot on a battering ram fessewise the head inward also proper headed and garnished azure.
Seat – Knebworth House, Herts. *Town Residence* – 2d Park Place Villas, W2.

SONS LIVING

Hon HENRY FROMANTEEL, *b* 12 May 1962; *ed* Eton, and Kent Univ (BA 1983): *m* 1987, Martha Frances, da of James Buford Boone, Jr, of Tuscaloosa, Alabama, USA, and has issue living, Edward Stucley Fromanteel, *b* 23 April 1992, — Morwenna Gray, *b* 1989.

Hon Peter Guy Fromanteel, *b* 1964; *ed* Eton, and Durham Univ (BA 1986): *m* 1988, Ginette Elizabeth, da of Bernard Keigher, of Holland Park, W11, and has issue living, Frederick Alexander, *b* 1992, — Natasha Elizabeth, *b* 1994.

Hon Richard Stucley Fromanteel, *b* 1968; *ed* Eton, and Bristol Univ; a Page of Honour to HM 1980-82: *m* 1994, Frankie May, da of Jeremy Lancaster, of Broadwell, Glos, and has issue living, Sam Arthur Fromanteel, *b* 1997.

DAUGHTER LIVING

Hon Rosina Kim, *b* 1971; has issue living, Lily Tofina, *b* 1998.

BROTHER LIVING

Hon Rowland John Fromanteel COBBOLD, *b* 1944; *ed* Eton, and Trin Coll, Camb (MA); Dir Cathay Pacific Airways Ltd since 1987: *m* 1969, Sophia Augusta, da of B. N. White-Spunner, of Lansdowne, Nenagh, co Tipperary, and has issue living, Patrick Alexander Fromanteel, *b* 1974, — Lorna Bridget, *b* 1971. *Residence* – 30 Astell St, SW3.

SISTER LIVING

Hon Susan Victoria, *b* 1933; High Sheriff Herts 1989: *m* 1957, S/Ldr Christopher Charles Blount, MVO, RAF and has issue living, James Hubert Rowland, *b* 1958, — Oliver Charles, *b* 1959: *m* 1994, Vivien A., yr da of Cdr Peter Barton, RN, of Monks Eleigh, Suffolk, and has issue living, Guy Henry *b* 1995, William Hubert *b* 1997, Fergus Charles *b* (twin) 1997, — Catherine Victoria Jane, *b* 1962: *m* 1988, Richard M. Glaister, 5th son of Thomas Glaister, of Crofthead, Kentmere, Kendal, Cumbria, and has issue living, Cosima Susan Ruth *b* 1990, Davina Millicent Jane *b* 1991, Genevieve Pamela Rose *b* 1995, — Pamela Jane, *b* 1965: *m* 1991, Rupert A. W. Goodman, elder son of Nigel Goodman, of Eton Coll, Berks, and has issue living, Felix Christopher Woodward *b* 1993, Polly Rachel *b* 1996, Lucy Catherine *b* 1998. *Residence* – Manor Farm, Barkway, Herts.

WIDOW LIVING OF FIRST BARON

Lady (Margaret) Hermione (Millicent) Lytton (*Lady Hermione Cobbold*), da of 2nd Earl of Lytton: *m* 1930, the 1st Baron Cobbold, KG, GCVO, PC, who *d* 1987. *Residence* – Stables Cottage, Knebworth, Herts.

PREDECESSOR – (1) *Rt Hon* CAMERON FROMANTEEL Cobbold, KG, GCVO, son of late Lt-Col Clement John Fromanteel Cobbold; *b* 1904, Lieut for City of London, DL for Herts, High Sheriff for Co of London 1946-47, Gov of Bank of England 1949-61, Chm Middx Hosp and Medical Sch Council 1963-74, Pres British Heart Foundation 1969-76, Lord Chamberlain of HM Household 1963-71, a Lord-in-Waiting to HM 1971-87; *cr* PC 1959, and *Baron Cobbold*, of Knebworth, co Herts (peerage of UK) 1960: *m* 1930, Lady (Margaret) Hermione (Millicent) Lytton, da of 2nd Earl of Lytton; *d* 1987; *s* by his elder son (2) DAVID ANTONY FROMANTEEL, 2nd Baron and present peer.

COBHAM, BARONY OF (Alexander) (Baron E 1312-13) (Abeyant 1951)

ROBERT DISNEY LEITH ALEXANDER, 13th Baron (16th but for the attainder), *s* his brother, GERVASE DISNEY ALEXANDER, 1933 (in whose favour the abeyance was determined 1916); *d* 1951, when the Barony again fell into abeyance.

WIDOW LIVING OF THIRTEENTH BARON

CHRISTINA JEAN (*Baroness Cobham*), da of Albert Edward Honeybone: *m* 1923 (*m diss* 1934), and whom she re-married 1949, the 13th Baron, who *d* 1951. *Address* – c/o 246 Metella Rd, Prospect, NSW 2149, Australia.

COLLATERAL BRANCHES LIVING

Issue of late Hon Mary Isabel Alexander, el sister of 13th Baron, *b* 1882, *d* 1978: *m* 1st, 1916, Capt John Leslie Morton Shaw, Duke of Wellington's (W Riding Regt), who *d* 1925; 2ndly, 1927, John Bazley Bazley-White, MC (*d* on active service 1940) (E Rothes):—
(By 1st *m*) John Anthony Cobham SHAW, MC (1 Garden Cottages, Amesbury Abbey, Amesbury, Wilts SP4 7EX), *b* 1917; *ed* Eton; 1939-45 War as Maj RA (MC and Bar): *m* 1st, 1945, Rhondda, who *d* 1964, da of late Brig-Gen Charles Herbert Rankin, CB, CMG, DSO (Rankin, Bt, *cr* 1898, colls); 2ndly, 1965, Phyllis Rosemary, da of late Arthur David Clere Parsons (*see* E Rosse, colls), and widow of late Capt Ian Stanley Akers-Douglas, Berks Yeo (*see* V Chilston, colls), and has issue living (by 1st *m*), Simon Rhys (40 James St, Oxford OX4 1ET), *b* 1949: *m* 1976, Christine, da of Alfred Morton Hind, — Veronica Mary (5 Dorchester Way, Greywell, Basingstoke, Hants), *b* 1946: *m* 19— (*m diss* 1988), Peter Kamerling, and has issue living, Henri Alexander *b* 1975, Henrietta Herina *b* 1978, Vancessa Johanna *b* 1980. —— Cynthia Mary (12 Heather Close, Taunton TA1 3XJ), *b* 1920: *m* 1946, Sidney James Fulton, CMG, who *d* 1993, and has issue living, Robert Henry Gervase, *b* 1948: *m* 1975, Midge Free, and has issue living, James Anthony Gervase *b* 1977, Mark William Miller *b* 1980, — Ann Elizabeth, *b* 1947, — Jane Louisa, *b* 1954: *m* 1979, Denis Anthony Tocher, and has issue living, Alastair James *b* 1985, Lydia Josephine *b* 1987. —— Margaret Daphne, *b* 1923: *m* 1947, Charles Herbert Fowler Ransom, who *d* 1988, of Porter's Farm, Wyck Rissington, Cheltenham, Glos, and has issue living, Andrew Charles D'Oyley (35 Arlington Sq, N1), *b* 1948: *m* 1971, Elizabeth Magaret Gee, of Kingston-upon-Hull, E Yorks, — Mark Anthony (Church Farm, Idbury, Oxfordshire), *b* 1952: *m* 1st, 1979, Jane Eason, who *d* 1991, of Broadway, Worcs; 2ndly, 1995, Katherine Mary HINTON, da of late Peter Rutherford Aston, of Barnbarroch Lodge, Kippford, Dalbeattie, Kirkcudbrightshire, and has issue living (by 1st *m*), Christopher James *b* 1982, Nicholas Charles *b* 1984, Edward Jeremy *b* 1987, — Jeremy Peter Scott (Church Farm Cottage, Idbury, Oxfordshire), *b* 1953: *m* 1984, Marie-Pierre Köhl, of Villeneuve-Loubet, France.

Issue of late Hon Muriel Helen Alexander, yr sister of 13th Baron, *b* 1887, *d* 1978: *m* 1916, Maj John Edmund Burnet Thornely, OBE, who *d* 1978:—
(Gervase) Michael (Cobham) THORNELY (High Stangerthwaite, Killington, Sedbergh, Cumbria), *b* 1918; *ed* Rugby, and Trin Hall, Camb (MA); Headmaster of Sedbergh Sch 1954-75: *m* 1954, Jennifer Margery, da of Sir (Charles) Hilary Scott, of Knowle House, Bishops Walk, Addington, Surrey, and has issue living, Richard Michael Gervase (Blencathra, Pondtail Drive, Horsham, W Sussex RH12 4HY), *b* 1957: *m* 1987, Janet Anne, da of late Peter Francis Martin Turberville, of 16 Greenways, Beckenham, Kent, and has issue living, Michael Alistair *b* 1987, Andrew Peter *b* 1989, James Nicholas *b* 1994, — Charles William Alexander, *b* 1958, — Elizabeth Miranda, *b* 1960: *m* 1983, Edmund Nigel Ronald Hosker, and has issue living, Lucy Abigail *b* 1988, Josephine Rose *b* 1989, Katharine Amy *b* 1992, — Jacqueline Sarah, *b* 1965: *m* 1987, Bruce Andrew Walkom, and has issue living, Samuel Francis *b* 1990, Benjamin Oliver *b* (twin) 1990.

COBHAM, VISCOUNT (Lyttelton) (Viscount GB 1718, Bt E 1618)

One God, one king

JOHN WILLIAM LEONARD LYTTELTON, 11th Viscount, and 14th Baronet, *b* 5 June 1943; *s* 1977; *ed* Eton, Christ's Coll, NZ, and RAC Cirencester: *m* 1st, 1974 (*m diss* 1995), Penelope Ann, el da of Roy Cooper, of Moss Farm, Knutsford, Cheshire; 2ndly, 1997, Dr Lisa R. Clayton, da of Daniel Clayton, of Bromsgrove, Worcs.

Arms – Argent, a chevron between three escallops sable. Crest – A Moor's head in profile couped at the shoulders proper, wreathed round the temples argent and sable. Supporters – Two mermen proper, each holding in the exterior hand a trident or.
Seat – Hagley Hall, Stourbridge, W Midlands DY9 9LG; 20 Kylestrome House, Cundy St, Ebury St, SW1.

BROTHERS LIVING

Hon CHRISTOPHER CHARLES (28 Abbey Gdns, NW8), *b* 23 Oct 1947; *ed* Eton: *m* 1973, Tessa Mary, da of late Col Alexander George Jeremy Readman, DSO (*see* Curtis, Bt, colls), and has issue living, Oliver Christopher, *b* 1976, — Sophie Emma, *b* 1978.
Hon Richard Cavendish (5 Queen's Gate Place Mews, SW7 5BG), *b* 1949; *ed* Eton: *m* 1971, Romilly, da of Michael Barker, of 14 Harley Gdns, SW10, and has issue living, Thomas Charles Henry, *b* 1986, — Mary Viola, *b* 1976.
Hon Nicholas Makeig, *b* 1951; *ed* Shiplake Court, Oxon: *m* 1980 (*m diss* 1993), June Carrington, and has issue living, David Charles, *b* 1981.

SISTERS LIVING

Hon Juliet Meriel, *b* 1944: *m* 1967, John Michael Dugdale, of Birch Farm, Kinlet, Bewdley, Worcs, DL12 3DS, son of John E. M. Dugdale, of Lower Cefn Perfa, Kerry, Newtown, Powys, and has issue living, Mark Rupert Marshall, *b* 1968, — Helen Riba, *b* 1970, — Clare Lucinda, *b* 1973, — Rowena Sarah, *b* 1976.
Hon Catherine Elizabeth (*Baroness Forester*), DStJ, *b* 1946; High Sheriff Shropshire 1997: *m* 1967, 8th Baron Forester, of Willey Park, Broseley, Shropshire TF12 5JJ.
Hon Lucy, *b* 1954: *m* 1980, Mark N. Kemp-Gee, of Park House, Upper Wield, Alresford, Hants SO24 9RU, yr son of late Bernard Kemp-Gee, of 16 Airlie Gdns, W8, and has issue living Henry Alfred, *b* 1981, — Robert Arthur, *b* 1984, — John Andrew, *b* 1987.
Hon Sarah, *b* (twin) 1954: *m* 1976, C. Nicholas Bedford, of Armsworth Hill Cottage, Old Alresford, Hants, and has issue living, Minna Lucy, *b* 1978, — Olivia Alison, *b* 1982.

AUNTS LIVING (*Daughters of 9th Viscount*)

Hon Audrey Lavinia (Poplar Cottage, Fore St Hill, Budleigh Salterton, Devon), *b* 1918: *m* 1950, as his 3rd wife, David Edsell Thomas Lindsay, who *d* 1968 (*see* E Crawford, colls)
Hon Lavinia Mary Yolande (Cannon Cottage, Fore St, Budleigh Salterton, Devon), *b* 1921; Subaltern ATS 1941-45: *m* 1st, (Feb) 1945, Capt Cecil Francis Burney Rolt, 23rd Hus, who was *ka* April 1945; 2ndly, 1949, Maj John Edward Dennys, MC, who *d* 1973, and has issue living (by 2nd *m*), Nicholas Charles Jonathan, QC (The Old Rectory, Arborfield, Berks RG2 9HZ) *b* 1951; *ed* Eton, and Brasenose Coll, Oxford (BA); Bar, Middle Temple 1975; QC 1991: *m* 1977, Frances Winifred, da of Rev Canon Gervase William Markham, of Morland House, Penrith, and has issue living, Harriet *b* 1979, Sophie *b* 1981, Romilly Mary *b* 1984, Katharine *b* 1986.

COLLATERAL BRANCHES LIVING

Issue of late Hon George William Lyttelton, 2nd son of 8th Viscount, *b* 1883, *d* 1962: *m* 1919, Pamela Marie, who *d* 1975, da of late Charles Robert Whorwood Adeane, CB (B Leconfield, colls):—
Humphrey Richard Adeane, *b* 1921; musician and writer; Pres Soc for Italic Handwriting since 1990: *m* 1st, 1948 (*m diss* 1952), Patricia Mary Braithwaite, da of late J. Wellesley Gaskell; 2ndly, 1952, Elizabeth Jill, da of Albert F. Richardson and has issue living (by 2nd *m*), (Anthony) Stephen, *b* 1955: *m* 1989, Emma, da of J. de Vere Hunt, of Kensington, London, and has issue living, Charles *b* 1991, Oliver Stephen *b* 1993, Lucy Elizabeth Joanie *b* 1989, — David George, *b* 1958, — (by 1st *m*) Henrietta Marie, *b* 1949, — (by 2nd *m*), Georgina Pamela, *b* 1963. *Residence* – Alyn Close, Barnet Rd, Arkley, Herts. —— Diana Maud (*Viscountess Hood*), CVO, *b* 1920; was Assist Press Sec to HM late King George VI 1947-52, and to HM The Queen 1952-7; MVO (4th Class) 1952, CVO 1957: *m* 1957, 7th Viscount Hood. *Residences* – 67 Chelsea Sq, SW3; Loders Court, Bridport, Dorset. —— Helena Frances, *b* 1923: *m* 1940, Peter Stafford Hayden Lawrence, of Simeons, Little Milton, Oxford (*see* Lawrence, Bt, *cr* 1867, colls). —— (Margaret) Rose, *b* 1926: *m* 1949, Robert Morice Antony Bourne, who *d* 1995, an Assist Master at Eton 1947-84, of 25 Nine Mile Ride, Finchampstead, Wokingham, Berks (*see* E Cairns, 1985 Edn), and has issue living, (Robert) Humphrey Lyttelton, *b* 1954, — George Julian, *b* 1960, — Harriet Madeline, *b* 1950, — Charlotte Elizabeth, *b* 1952, — Lucy Jane, *b* 1956, — Emily Hester, *b* 1963. —— Mary Pamela, *b* 1929: *m* 1953, Maj-Gen Arthur George Ernest Stewart Cox, DFC, RA, and has issue living, Rupert Lyttelton (Downside Abbey Home Farm, Chilcompton, Bath BA3 4HX), *b* 1956: *m* 1984, Mary Catherine, yst da of J. M. Mitchell, of Tullymurdoch, Alyth, Perthshire, and has issue living, Georgina Helen *b* 1987, Phoebe *b* 1991, — Jonathan May (Bound Oak, Gare Hill Rd, Witham Friary, Frome, Som BA11 5EX), *b* 1957, — Charles Arthur, *b* 1960: *m* 1996, Jacqueline L., elder da of George Donaldson of Edinburgh, — Belinda Jane (67a Chelsea Sq, SW3), *b* 1954. *Residence* – Long Mead, Brixton Deverill, Warminster, Wilts.

Issue of late Hon Richard Glynne Lyttelton, yst son of 8th Viscount, *b* 1893, *d* 1977: *m* 1931, Judith, who *d* 1993, da of late Lt-Col Percy Archer Clive, MP, Gren Gds:—
Thomas Glynne (7 The Grove, Highgate Village, N6 6JU), *b* 1940; *ed* Eton, and Trin Coll, Camb; Assist Master, Eton Coll 1968-94.

Grandchildren of late Rt Rev Hon Arthur Temple Lyttelton, DD, 5th son of 4th Baron Lyttelton:—
Issue of late Cdr Stephen Clive Lyttelton, OBE, DSC, RN, *b* 1887, *d* 1959: *m* 1st, 1919 (*m diss* 1933), Maureen Nina, who *d* 1980, da of Harold Anthony Smith, formerly of 6 Dean's Yard, Westminster, SW; 2ndly, 1938, Mary Cicely, who *d* 1945, da of Brig-Gen Sir (Ernest) Frederick (Orby) Gascoigne, KCVO, CMG, DSO; 3rdly, 1947, Phoebe Hermione (3 The Croft, Old Headington, Oxford), da of A. K. Graham:—
(By 2nd *m*) Edward Gascoigne, *b* 1944; *ed* Eton, King's Coll, Camb, and Ripon Hall Theological Coll. *Residence* – 306 Delaware Av, Toronto, Ontario, Canada M6H 2T6. —— (By 1st *m*) Barbara Meriel, *b* 1921: *m* 1947, Charles Russell Fawcus, who *d* 1985, and has had issue, Mark Russell, *b* 1951; *ed* Clifton: *m* 1975, Cynthia (22 Hill View Rd, Hildenborough, Kent), da of Ronald Stephen Blair, and *d* 1998, leaving issue, Philip Russell *b* 1981, James Russell *b* 1989, — Meriel Clare, *b* 1949: *m* 1974, Benjamin J. I. Carver, of Two Ways Cottage, Kington Magna, Gillingham, Dorset, and has issue living, Annabel Jane *b* 1976, Victoria Meriel *b* 1978. *Residence* – High Drive House, Woldingham, Surrey. —— (By 2nd *m*) Mary Kathleen, *b* 1939: *m* 1970, Malcolm Robert Fraser of Reelig (Reelig House, Kirkhill, Invernessshire). —— (By 3rd *m*) (Cicely Phoebe) Lavinia, *b* 1950: *m* 1979, Peter John Northrop, of Moor of Clunes, Kirkhill, Inverness, son of D. F. Northrop, of Teynham, Kent.

Descendants of late Rt Hon Alfred Lyttelton, KC, MP, 8th son of 4th Baron Lyttelton:—
Issue of late Rt Hon Oliver Lyttelton, DSO, MC, PC (*Viscount Chandos*), *b* 1893, *d* 1972:—
(*See* V Chandos).

PREDECESSORS – (1) *Sir* Richard Temple, 4th Bt, of Stowe, a military commander of renown under the 1st Duke of Marlborough, was *cr Baron Cobham*, of Cobham, Kent 1714, and *Baron Cobham*, Kent, and *Viscount Cobham* (peerage of Great Britain) 1718, with special remainder failing heirs male of his body, to his sister Hester, wife of Richard Grenville, MP, and her heirs male, and failing such to his 3rd sister, Christian, wife of Sir Thomas Lyttelton, 4th Bt (*see* infra), and her issue male; *d* 1740; *s* by his sister (2) HESTER GRENVILLE, *cr Countess of Temple* (peerage of Great Britain) 1749, with remainder to her heirs male; *d* 1752; *s* by her son (3) RICHARD, KG, 2nd Earl, a leading statesman, *temp* George III; *d* without issue 1779; *s* by his nephew (4) GEORGE, 3rd Earl; was Viceroy of Ireland 1782 and 1787: *m* Mary Elizabeth (who *d* 1812, having in 1800 been *cr Baroness Nugent* (peerage of Ireland), with remainder to her 2nd son George, who *d* 1850 without issue), da and heiress of Robert, Earl of Nugent, in the peerage of Ireland; assumed by R licence the additional surnames of Nugent and Temple; was *cr Marquess of Buckingham* 1784, and in 1788 *s* by special remainder his father-in-law, as *Earl Nugent* (peerage of Ireland, *cr* 1776); *d* 1813; *s* by his son (5) RICHARD, KG, 2nd Marquess; assumed 1799, by R licence, the additional surnames of Brydges-Chandos; *cr Earl Temple* (with remainder to his grandda Anne Eliza Mary, afterwards wife of W. H. Powell Gore-Langton, Esq, MP), *Marquess of Chandos* and *Duke of Buckingham* (peerage of United Kingdom) 1822; *d* 1839; *s* by his son (6) RICHARD PLANTAGENET, KG, 2nd Duke; *d* 1861; *s* by his son (7) RICHARD PLANTAGENET CAMPBELL, 3rd Duke, *b* 1823: *m* 1st, 1851, Caroline, who *d* 1874, da of Robert Harvey, of Langley Hall, Bucks; 2nd, 1885, Alice Anne, who *d* 1931, el da of Sir Graham Graham-Montgomery, 3rd Bt; *d* 1889, when the Dukedom of Buckingham and the Earldoms of Temple (*cr* 1749) and Nugent became extinct, the Lordship of Kinloss (to which he had established his right in 1868) devolving on his el da, Lady Mary Morgan, the Earldom of Temple (*cr* 1822) on William Stephen Gore-Langton, and the Viscountcy of Cobham (under special remainder) as heir male of Christian, wife of Sir Thomas Lyttelton, 4th Bt, on (8) CHARLES GEORGE, 5th Baron Lyttelton (see *infra), 8th Viscount Cobham, *b* 1842; High Steward of Bewdley; MP for Worcestershire, E (*L*) 1868-74: *m* 1878, Hon Mary Susan Caroline Cavendish, who *d* 1937, da of 2nd Baron Chesham; *d* 1922; *s* by his son (9) JOHN CAVENDISH, KCB, TD, 9th Viscount, *b* 1881; Lt-Col RA (TA), High Steward of Bewdley, and Lord-Lieut for City and co of Worcester; Under-Sec of State for War 1939-40; MP for Worcestershire Mid or Droitwich Div (*U*) 1910-16: *m* 1908, Violet Yolande, who *d* 1966, da of Charles Leonard; *d* 1949; *s* by his son (10) CHARLES JOHN, KG GCMG, GCVO, TD, PC, 10th Viscount; *b* 1909; Lt-Col RA (TA); Hon Col (Warwicks and Worcs Yeo Sqdn), The Mercian Yeo 1972-77; Pres MCC 1954, Gov Gen NZ 1957-62; Lord Lieut Worcs 1963-74; Lord Steward of HM Household 1967-72, Chancellor of Order of the Garter 1972-77: *m* 1942, Elizabeth Alison (CStJ), who *d* 1986, da of John Reeder Makeig-Jones, CBE, late ICS; *d* 1977; *s* by his el son (11) JOHN WILLIAM LEONARD, 11th Viscount and present peer; also Baron Cobham, Lord Lyttelton, Baron of Frankley, and Baron Westcote.

*(1) *Sir* THOMAS Lyttelton, Knt; Sheriff of Worcester 1613, and MP for Worcestershire 1620-8 and 1639-40 (name spelt Littleton in records of Parliament); was a zealous partisan of Royalty during the Civil Wars, and suffered imprisonment in the Tower; *cr a Baronet* 1618; *d* 1650; *s* by his el son (2) *Sir* HENRY, 2nd Bt; was imprisoned in the Tower seventeen months for his attachment to the Royal cause; *dsp* 1703; *s* by his brother (3) *Sir* CHARLES 3rd Bt, also an active partisan of Royalty; was incarcerated in Colchester; *d* 1716; *s* by his son (4) *Sir* THOMAS, 4th Bt successively MP for Worcestershire and Camelford; a Lord of the Admiralty 1727-41: *m* Christian, da of Sir Richard Temple, Bt, of Stowe (*see* ante); *d* 1751; *s* by his son (5) *Sir* GEORGE, PC, 5th Bt, MP for Okehampton, Principal Sec to Prince of Wales 1737, a Lord of the Treasury 1744-55, Cofferer to the Household 1754-5, and Chancellor and Under Treasurer of Court of Exchequer 1755; *cr Lord Lyttelton, Baron of Frankley*, co Worcester 1756; *d* 1773; *s* by his son (6) THOMAS, 2nd Baron; *dsp* 1779, when the Barony became extinct, and the Baronetcy devolved upon his uncle (7) WILLIAM HENRY, 7th Bt; MP for Bewdley 1748-54, Gov of S Carolina 1755-60, Gov of Jamaica 1760-6, and Envoy Extraor to Portugal; *cr Baron Westcote*, of Balamere, co Longford (peerage of Ireland) 1766, and *Lord Lyttelton, Baron of Frankley* (peerage of England) 1794; *d* 1808; *s* by his son (8) GEORGE FULKE, 2nd Baron; *d* unmarried 1828; *s* by his half-brother (9) WILLIAM HENRY, 3rd Baron; was Lord-Lieut of co Worcester; *d* 1837; *s* by his son (10) GEORGE WILLIAM, KCMG, PC, FRS, 4th Baron; *b* 1817; was Lord-Lieut of co Worcester, Under Sec for Colonies 1846, and Ch Commr of Endowed Schools 1869-74: *m* 1st, 1839, Mary, who *d* 1857, da of Sir Stephen Richard Glynne, 8th Bt; 2ndly, 1869, Sybella Harriet, who *d* 1900, da of George Clive, and widow of Humphrey Francis Mildmay; *d* 1876; *s* by his son (11) CHARLES GEORGE, 5th Baron, who *s* (under special remainder) as 8th *Viscount Cobham* 1889 (ante).

Cochrane, family name of Earl of Dundonald.

Cochrane, Lord; son of Earl of Dundonald.

COCHRANE OF CULTS, BARON (Cochrane) (Baron UK 1919)

By virtue of labour

(RALPH HENRY) VERE COCHRANE, 4th Baron; *b* 20 Sept 1926; *s* 1990; *ed* Eton, and King's Coll, Camb (MA); late Lieut RE, served 1945-48; Member Queen's Body Guard for Scotland (Royal Company of Archers); DL Fife: *m* 1956, Janet Mary Watson, da of late William Hunter Watson Cheyne, MB, MRCS, LRCP (*see* Cheyne, Bt, colls), and has issue.

Arms – Quarterly, 1st Argent, a chevron gules between three boars' heads erased azure, armed and langued of the second, within a bordure contre-ermine, *Cochrane*; 2nd, Gules, a fess ermine, in chief a stag's antler or, fessways, *Crawford of Kilbirnie*; 3rd, Gules, a fess chequy argent and azure, in chief three mullets of the second *Lindsay of the Byres*; 4th, Argent, on a saltire sable nine lozenges of the field, in centre chief a mullet gules, *Blair*, **Crest** – A horse passant argent, between two stag's attires gules. **Supporters** – Two ermines ermine.
Seat – Cults, Cupar, Fife KY15 5RD *Club* – New (Edinburgh).

SONS LIVING

Hon THOMAS HUNTER VERE, *b* 7 Sept 1957, *ed* Eton, and Exeter Univ; Bar Inner Temple 1980; ACII. *Clubs* – Royal and Ancient, New (Edinburgh).
Hon Michael Charles Nicholas, *b* 1959; *ed* Glenalmond, and RNC Dartmouth; Lt Cdr RN. *Clubs* – Naval and Military, Royal Yacht Sqdn.

BROTHER LIVING

Hon (John Douglas) Julian, *b* 1929; *ed* Eton: *m* 1965, Vaila Rose, da of late Cdr Robert Dalby, RN (ret), of Castle Donnington, Leics, and has issue living, John Colin, *b* 1969, — Julietta Anne, *b* 1966, — Alice Georgina, *b* 1974. *Residence* – Hopton, Derbys.

COLLATERAL BRANCHES LIVING

Issue of late Capt Hon Sir Archibald Douglas Cochrane, 2nd son of 1st Baron, GCMG, KCSI, DSO, RN, *b* 1885, *d* 1958: *m* 1926, Hon Julia Dorothy Cornwallis, CBE, who *d* 1971, da of 1st Baron Cornwallis:—
Douglas Fiennes (1 West Warwick Place, SW1V 2DH), *b* 1928: *ed* Eton, and Trin Coll, Camb: *m* 1969 (*m diss* 1987), Patricia Ann, da of late Frank Renshaw, of Puddletown, Dorset, and has issue living, Alexander Douglas, *b* 1972: *m* 1998, Kirsty, da of Gilbert Wood, of Glasgow, — James Archibald, *b* 1976. —— Mabel Dorothy, *b* 1932: *m* 1958, Col Geoffrey Douglas Gill, MBE, King's Regt, who *d* 1990, and has a son, Peter Geoffrey Fiennes, *b* 1966. *Residence* – Camino Son Toells 5, San Agustin, 07015 Palma de Mallorca, Spain.

Issue of late Air Ch Marshal Hon Sir Ralph Alexander Cochrane, GBE, KCB, AFC, 3rd son of 1st Baron, *b* 1895, *d* 1977: *m* 1930, Hilda Frances Holme, who *d* 1982, 3rd da of late Francis Holme Wiggin:—
John Alexander (Fairspear House, Leafield, Oxford, OX8 5NY), *b* 1935; *ed* Eton, and Balliol Coll, Oxford (BA): *m* 1966 Margaret Minna, da of Sir Charles Henry Rose, 3rd Bt (*cr* 1909), and has issue living, Thomas Hugh, *b* 1973, — Phoebe Clare, *b* 1967, — Alexandra, *b* 1969, — Katherine Grizel Rose, *b* 1975. —— Malcolm Ralph (Grove Farmhouse, Shipton-under-Wychwood, Oxon), *b* 1938; *ed* Eton; DL Oxon 1998, and Vice Lord Lieut 1998: *m* 1972, Mary Anne, da of Ralph Henry Scrope (E Mexborough), and has issue living, William Ralph, *b* 1974, — Alice Anne, *b* 1976, — Harriet Mary, *b* 1979. —— Ann Grizel, *b* 1932: *m* 1953, Lt-Col Robert Christie Stewart, CBE, TD, Argyll and Sutherland Highlanders, HM Lord Lieut Kinross-shire 1966-74, Lord Lieut Clackmannshire since 1994 (*see* Lighton, Bt, 1980 Edn), and has issue living, Alexander Christie (Clarehaven, Newmarket, Suffolk), *b* 1955: *m* 1986, Katherine Lake, elder da of Denys Barry Herbert Domvile (*see* B Bellew, 1995 Edn), and has issue living, Archie Christie *b* 1989, Georgina Elizabeth *b* 1987, — John Cochrane, *b* 1957: *m* 1989, Lucy, da of Maj Michael Parton, — Catriona Ann, *b* 1954: *m* 1975, Julian Charles Marsham (*see* E Romney, colls), — Sara Jane, *b* 1966: *m* 1996 (*m diss* 1998), Anthony Craufurd Scott (*see* Bagge, Bt). *Residence* – Arndean, by Dollar, Clackmannshire.

PREDECESSORS – **(1)** THOMAS HORATIO ARTHUR ERNEST Cochrane, yr son of 11th Earl of Dundonald; *b* 1857; Maj and Hon Lt-Col 4th Batn Princess Louise's (Argyll and Sutherland Highlanders), Lt-Col cmdg 2/7th Black Watch 1914-17; Parliamentary Private Sec of State for the Colonies 1895-1901, and Under Sec of State for the Home Depart 1902-1905; MP for Ayrshire, N Div (LU) 1892-1910; *cr Baron Cochrane of Cults*, of Crawford Priory, co Fife (peerage of United Kingdom) 1919: *m* 1880, Lady Gertrude Julia Georgina Boyle, OBE, who *d* 1950, da of 6th Earl of Glasgow; *d* 1951; *s* by his son **(2)** THOMAS GEORGE FREDERICK, DSO, 2nd Baron; *b* 1883; Maj Black Watch; 1914-18 War (DSO 1919): *m* 1st, 1920,

Hon Elin Douglas-Pennant, who *d* 1934, da of 2nd Baron Penrhyn; 2ndly, 1948, Millicent Agnes Mary, who *d* 1981, da of late Alexander Duckham, PhD, and formerly wife of Wilfred Neill Foster; *d* 1968; *s* by his son **(3)** Thomas Charles Anthony, 3rd Baron, *b* 1922; founder and trustee The Gardners' Memorial Trust; *d* 1990; *s* by his brother **(4)** (Ralph Henry) Vere, 4th Baron and present peer.

COCKFIELD, BARON (Cockfield) (Life Baron 1978)

(Francis) Arthur Cockfield, son of late Lt Charles Francis Cockfield; *b* 28th Sept 1916; *ed* Dover Gram Sch and LSE (LLB, BSc (Econ)); Hon LLD Fordham (NY), Hon LLD Sheffield, Hon DUniv Surrey; Bar Inner Temple 1942; Dir of Statistics and Intelligence, Board of Inland Revenue 1945-52, Commr of Inland Revenue, Member of Board of Inland Revenue 1951-52; Finance Dir, Boots Pure Drug Co Ltd 1953-61, and Man Dir and Chm, Exec Managing Cttee, 1961-67; Member NEDC 1962-64 and 1982-83, Pres, R Statistical Soc 1968-69; Adviser on Taxation Policy to Chancellor of the Exchequer 1970-73, and Chm Price Commn 1973-77; Min of State HM Treasury 1979-82; Sec of State for Trade 1982-83; Chancellor of Duchy of Lancaster 1983-84, Vice-Pres European Commn 1985-88; Grand Cross Order of Leopold II, Belgium; cr Knt 1973, PC 1983, and *Baron Cockfield*, of Dover, co Kent (Life Baron) 1978: *m* 1st, 1943 (*m diss* ca 1968), Ruth Helen, da of late Henry Solomon Simonis, LLD; 2ndly, 1970, Aileen Monica Mudie, choreographer, who *d* 1992, and has issue by 1st *m*.
Address – c/o House of Lords, SW1.

SON LIVING (By 1st marriage)

Hon Roger Edmund (7 Ringwood Close, Wigston, Leics LE18 2JL), *b* 1947: *m* 1975 (*m diss* 1989), Susan Vineall, and has issue living, Catherine, *b* 1977, — Emma, *b* 1981.

DAUGHTER LIVING (By 1st marriage)

Hon Hilary Ann, *b* 1944: *m* 1st, ca 1964 (*m diss* ca 1985), Frederick Williams; 2ndly, 19—, Bernard English, and has issue living (by 1st *m*), Christopher, *b* 1973, — Patrick, *b* 1976, — Juliet, *b* 1966. *Residence* – ......

Cocks, family name of Baron Somers.

COCKS OF HARTCLIFFE, BARON (Cocks) (Life Baron 1987)

Michael Francis Lovell Cocks, PC, son of late Rev Harry F. Lovell Cocks, of Amersham, Oxon; *b* 19 Aug 1929; *ed* Bristol Univ; Assist Govt Whip 1974-76, Parl Sec to Treasury and Govt Whip 1974-79; MP (*Lab*) Bristol South 1970-87; *cr* PC 1976, and *Baron Cocks of Hartcliffe*, of Chinnor, co Oxfordshire (Life Baron) 1987: *m* 1st, 1954, Janet Macfarlane; 2ndly, 1979, Valerie Davis, and has issue, two sons and two das, by 1st *m*.
Address – c/o House of Lords, SW1.

COGGAN, BARON (Coggan) (Life Baron 1980)

Rt Rev and *Rt Hon* (FREDERICK) DONALD COGGAN, PC, DD, son of the late Cornish Arthur Coggan, of London; *b* 9 Oct 1909; *ed* Merchant Taylors' Sch, St John's Coll, Camb (MA), and Wycliffe Hall, Oxford; BD Toronto 1941; DD Lambeth 1957; Hon DD Toronto, Leeds, Cambridge, Hull, Aberdeen, Tokyo, Saskatoon, Huron, and Manchester, Moravian Theol Seminary; HHD Westminster Choir Coll, Princeton, NJ, Hon D Litt Lancaster 1967, STD New York, Hon LLD Liverpool; Hon DCL Canterbury 1975; D Univ York 1975; Assist Lecturer in Semitic Languages and Literature, Manchester Univ 1931-34; Curate of St Mary's, Islington N 1934-37, Prof of New Testament, Wycliffe Coll, Toronto 1937-44, Prin of London Coll of Divinity 1944-56, and Examining Chap to Bishop of Lincoln 1946-56, to Bishop of Manchester 1951-56, to Bishop of Southwark 1954-56, and to Bishop of Chester 1955-56; select Preacher of Oxford Univ 1961; consecrated 3rd Bishop of Bradford 1956, enthroned 93rd Archbishop of York, Primate of England, and Metropolitan 1961, 101st Archbishop of Canterbury, Primate of All England and Metropolitan 1974-80; Sub-Prelate of Order of St John 1960 and Prelate 1967-90; Pro-Chancellor of York Univ 1962-74, and Hull Univ 1968-74 and Chm of Coll of Preachers; Chm exec cttee of Council of Christians and Jews 1983-87; author of *A People's Heritage* 1944, *The Ministry of the Word* 1945, *The Glory of God* 1950, *Stewards of Grace* 1958, *Five Makers of the New Testament* 1962, *Sinews of Faith* 1969, *Word and World* 1971, *Convictions* 1975, *Paul: Portrait of a Revolutionary* 1984, *The Sacrament of the Word* 1987, *Cuthbert Bardsley: Bishop, Evangelist, Pastor* 1989, *The Voice from the Cross* 1993, *The Servant-Son* 1995, *Meet Paul* 1998, and *Psalms 1-72* 1998; *cr* PC 1961 and *Baron Coggan*, of Canterbury and Sissinghurst, co Kent (Life Baron) 1980; received Royal Victorian Chain 1980: *m* 1935, Jean Braithwaite, da of Dr William Loudon Strain, and has issue.
Residence – 28 Lions Hall, St Swithun St, Winchester SO23 9HW. *Club* – Athenaeum.

DAUGHTERS LIVING

Hon Dorothy Ann, *b* 1938. *Residence* – 1 King Alfred Place, Hyde, Winchester SO23 7DF.
Hon Ruth Evelyn, *b* 1940. *Residence* – 15 Plough Way, Badger Farm, Winchester.

COHEN, BARONY OF (Cohen) (Extinct 1973)

SON LIVING OF LIFE BARON

Hon Leonard Harold Lionel, *b* 1922; *ed* Eton, and New Coll, Oxford (BA 1945, MA 1946); Bar Lincoln's Inn 1948; European War 1941-45 with Rifle Brig (wounded): *m* 1949, Eleanor Lucy da of late Philip Q. Henriques, and has issue. *Residence* – Dovecote House, Swallowfield Park, nr Reading, Berks RG7 1TG. *Club* – White's.

WIDOW LIVING OF SON OF LIFE BARON

Jane, da of late Rt Hon Sir Seymour Edward Karminski (*see* Lewis, Bt, *cr* 1902, ext, 1955 Edn): *m* 1953, Hon Hugh Lionel Cohen, who *d* 1992, and has issue, three sons. *Residence* – Overbrook House, Devil's Highway, Crowthorne, Berks RG45 6BJ.

COHEN OF BRIGHTON, BARONY OF (Cohen) (Extinct 1966)

SON LIVING OF LIFE BARON (*By 1st marriage*)

Hon John Christopher Coleman, *b* 1940; *ed* Stowe, and McGill Univ (PhD): *m* 1965, Anne-Marie, da of Eugene Krauss, of Paris, and has issue.

DAUGHTERS LIVING OF LIFE BARON (*By 1st marriage*)

Hon Christine Coleman, *b* 1942: *m* 1965 (*m diss* 19—), David Maxwell Park, MRCP, and has issue, one da.

Hon Madeleine Coleman, *b* 1946; assumed by deed poll 19— the surname of Coleman in lieu of Coleman-Cohen: *m* 1978, Ross King, of 3222, 3rd Street SW, Calgary, Alberta T2S 1V3, Canada, and has issue, one son and one da.

Cokayne, family name of Baron Cullen of Ashbourne.

Coke, family name of Earl of Leicester.

Coke, Viscount; son of Earl of Leicester.

COLE, BARONY OF (Cole) (Extinct 1979)

SON LIVING OF LIFE BARON

Hon Jonathan Dare, *b* 1946; *ed* Eton, and Hertford Coll, Oxford.

DAUGHTER LIVING OF LIFE BARON

Hon Juliet Anthea, *b* 1951.

Cole, family name of Earl of Enniskillen.

COLERAINE, BARON (Law) (Baron UK 1954)

JAMES MARTIN BONAR LAW, 2nd Baron; *b* 8 Aug 1931; *s* 1980; *ed* Eton, and Trin Coll, Oxford: *m* 1st, 1958 (*m diss* 1966), Emma Elizabeth, only da of late Nigel Richards; 2ndly, 1966, Anne Patricia, who accidentally drowned in Portugal 1993, yr da of late Maj-Gen Ralph Henry Farrant, CB, of Wareham, Dorset; 3rdly, 1998, Mrs Marion Robina (Bobbie) Smyth, da of late Sir Thomas Robinson Ferens, CBE, of Sunderlandwick, Driffield, Yorks, and widow of Frederick Peterson (Peter) Smyth, and has had issue by 1st and 2nd *m*.

ᚷrmꜱ – Argent a saltire azure between four cocks proper. Ꞓreꜱt – Issuant from a chaplet of maple leaves vert, a demi salmon proper. ᚄupporterꜱ – *Dexter*, a Basenji dog; *Sinster*, a kid, both proper.
Residences – Flat 3, 5 Kensington Park Gdns, W11; The Dower House, Sunderlandwick, Driffield, E Yorks.

SON LIVING (*By 2nd marriage*)

Hon (JAMES) PETER BONAR, *b* 23 Feb 1975; *ed* Eton, and LSE.

DAUGHTERS LIVING AND DECEASED (*By 1st marriage*)

Thy law my thought

Hon Elizabeth Mary, *b* 1961; *ed* Sussex Univ: *m* 1985, Hon Charles Edmund Grenville Ironside, only son of 2nd Baron Ironside.
Hon Sophia Anne, *b* 1964; *ed* Leeds Univ.

(*By 2nd marriage*)

Hon Henrietta Margaret, *b* 1968; *ed* Manchester Univ; accidentally drowned in Portugal 1993.
Hon Juliana Caroline Matilda, *b* 1971; *ed* LSE.

BROTHER LIVING

Hon Andrew Bonar, *b* 1933; *ed* Rugby, and Trin Coll, Dublin: *m* 1961, Joanna Margarette, da of Raymond Neill, of Fairview, Delgany, co Wicklow, and has issue living, Richard Pitcairn Bonar, *b* 1963, — Charlotte Mary de Montmorency Bonar, *b* 1964: *m* 1993, Robert Otway-Norwood, and has issue living, Phoebe *b* 1999. *Residence* – Shankill Castle, Shankill, co Dublin.

PREDECESSOR – (1) *Rt Hon* RICHARD KIDSTON Law, PC, son of late Rt Hon Andrew Bonar Law, MP; Prime Minister 1922-23; *b* 1901; Min of State 1943-45, Min of Educn May-June 1945; Chm Standing Advisory Cttee on Pay of Higher Civil Service 1957-61, and Chm of Nat Youth Employment Council 1955-62; MP for SW Div of Kingston-upon-Hull (*C*) 1931-45, for S Div of Kensington 1945-50 and for Haltemprice Div of Kingston-upon-Hull 1950-54; *cr* PC 1943, and *Baron Coleraine*, of Haltemprice, E Riding of Yorks (peerage of UK) 1954: *m* 1929, Mary Virginia, who *d* 1978, yr da of late Abraham Fox Nellis, of Rochester, NY USA; *d* 1980; *s* by his el son (2) JAMES MARTIN BONAR, 2nd Baron and present peer.

COLERIDGE, BARON (Coleridge) (Baron UK 1873)

WILLIAM DUKE COLERIDGE, 5th Baron, *b* 18 June, 1937; *s* 1984; *ed* Eton; Maj Coldm Gds, served King's African Rifles and Kenya Army 1961-63, Commanded Guard's Independent Parachute Co 1970-72: *m* 1st, 1962 (*m diss* 1977), Everild Tania, only child of Lt-Col Beauchamp Hamborough, of Wispers Farm, Nairobi, Kenya; 2ndly, 1977, Pamela, da of late George William Baker, CBE, VRD, and has issue by 1st and 2nd *m*.

ᚷrmꜱ – Argent, on a mount vert in base an otter proper, a chief gules, charged with a dove of the first between two crosses patée fitchée or. Ꞓreꜱt – On a mount vert therefrom issuing ears of wheat proper, in front of a cross gules an otter also proper. ᚄupporterꜱ – *Dexter*, an otter proper; *sinister*, a lion sable; each gorged with a garland of roses gules, leaved vert.
Seat – The Chanter's House, Ottery St Mary, S Devon.

As life so the end

SON LIVING (By 1st marriage)

Hon JAMES DUKE, b 5 June 1967.

DAUGHTERS LIVING (By 1st marriage)

Hon Tania Rosamund, b 1966: m 1993, William George Harcourt Cooze, son of late William Harcourt Cooze, and of Mrs Pryor, of W11, and has issue living, Sophia Khin, b 1998.
Hon Sophia Tamsin, b 1970.

(By 2nd marriage)

Hon Vanessa Leyla, b 1978.
Hon Katharine Suzannah, b 1981.

BROTHER LIVING

Hon Samuel John Taylor (17 Bourne St, SW1), b 1942; ed Winchester, and Trin Coll, Oxford; Brig Gren Gds; attached Army Air Corps 1964-68, Mil Attaché Algiers and Tunis 1985-88: m 1973, Patricia Susan, yr da of John Basil Edwards, CBE, of Cradley, nr Malvern, Worcs, and has issue living, Jessica Alice Seymour, b 1974, — Clara Emily Taylor, b 1976.

COLLATERAL BRANCHES LIVING

Issue of late Hon (Ronald) James Duke Coleridge, yst son of 3rd Baron, b 1911, d 1972: m 1937, Ursula Mary, who d 1987, da of late Rev William Turner Long, of Cheltenham:—
Syndercombe James Duke, b 1941; ed King's Sch, Worcester, and RNC Dartmouth; Lt RN (ret): m 1st, 1964 (m diss 1969), Barbara June, da of F. L. Dawson, of Rio de Janeiro; 2ndly, 1969 (m diss 1972), Deborah Coburn, da of the Rev Marcus Brown Hall, of Vermount, USA; 3rdly, 1977, Susan Elizabeth, only da of Derrick Vernon Littlejohn, of St Alban's Mansions, Kensington, W8, and has issue living (by 1st m), Christina Joanne, b 1965: m 1992, Charles Rupert Cosmo Verner, son of James William Hay Verner, of Stembridge, Som, and of Countess Helen Benckendorff, of Clare, Suffolk, — (by 3rd m) Robert James Duke, b 1979, — Nicholas John, b 1981.   Sara Louise Sidney, b 1945: m 1st, 1964, Alexander Arthur Luttrell Reid, PhD; 2ndly, 1988, Alexander Milne, and has issue living (by 1st m), Anna Louise, b 1965, — Katharine Louise, b 1967.

Grandchildren of late John Duke Coleridge, eldest son of late Hon Stephen William Buchanan Coleridge (infra):—
Issue of late Peter Duke Coleridge, b 1905, d 1958: m 1936 (m diss 1953), Sigrid Stahl Christensen:—
John Duke, MD, b 1940 (11644 N 52nd St, Scottsdale, Arizona 285254, USA); ed Univ of Göteborg Med Sch: m 1963, Carin Eva Christina, da of Karl Olaf Lennart Cassmark, and has issue living, Peter John, b 1966: m 1994, Rosemary Widroe, and has issue living, Samuel John b 1997, — Christina b 1964, — Malin Charlotta, b 1970.

Issue of late Arthur Nicholas Coleridge, b 1915, d 1988: m 1941, Lady (Marguerite) Georgina Hay (33 Peel St, W8), da of 11th Marquess of Tweeddale:—
Frances Marguerite Katharine, b 1943: m 1964, Neil Lindsay Vaughan Smith, of Park Hill, Appledore, Kent, and has issue living, Julian Arthur Vaughan, b 1969: m 1994, Suzanne Elaine, elder da of Michael David Hearne, and has issue living, Emma Frances Vaughan b 1998, Katherine Grace Vaughan b (twin) 1998, — Candida Louise Vaughan, b 1967: m 1992, Robert Lindsay Machin, and has issue living, Miles Robert Arthur b 1996, Tabitha Eleanor Frances b 1994, Natasha Louise Emilia b 1997.

Grandson of late Hon Stephen William Buchanan Coleridge, 2nd son of 1st Baron:—
Issue of late Paul Humphrey Coleridge, MC, b 1888, d 1955: m 1914, Margaret Frances, who d 1964, da of late George Campbell Giffard, JP, of Bulkeley House, Englefield Green:—
Antony Duke, b 1915; Capt late Queen's Bays; European War 1939-45 (despatches): m 1947, June Marian, da of George Frederick Charles Caswell, and has had issue, Jeremy Charles Duke, b 1949, d 1955, — Nicholas Antony, b 1955: m 1983, Gayl June, yr da of Clive O. J. Grove-Palmer, of 64 Staunton Rd, Oxford, and has issue living, Matthew Oliver Duke b 1984, Laura Claire May b 1986, — David George, b 1957: m 1981, Naomi Jean, 2nd da of Dr Harry Vere White, of 3 Elmfield Grove, Gosforth, Newcastle upon Tyne, and has issue living, Katherine Natasha b 1989, Hannah Lucy b 1991, Emily Claire b 1994, — Geraldine Margaret, b 1948: m 1974, David Roger Leeming, and has issue living, Robert Antony Dundas b 1978, Toby Alexander David b 1981. Residence – Ottery, Harwood Rd, Marlow, Bucks.

Grandchildren of late Paul Humphrey Coleridge, MC (ante):—
Issue of late Maj James Bernard Coleridge, b 1919, d 1991: m 1946, Jane Evelina (85 Erpingham Rd, SW15), da of Campbell Walter Giffard, of 4 Melina Place, NW8:—
Paul James Duke, QC, b 1949; ed Cranleigh; Bar Middle Temple 1970, QC 1993: m 1973, Judith Elizabeth, da of Hugh Trenchard Rossiter, and has issue living, William Paul Hugh Duke, b 1976, — Edward James, b 1980, — Alice Evelina, b 1974.   Susan Margaret Ethel, b 1947: m 1970, Peter John Cunard, and has issue living, Nicholas Peter, b 1971, — Sebastian James, b 1972, — Catherine Jane, b 1976.   Lucy Veronica, b 1954: m 1977, Stuart John Selleck, and has issue living, Samuel George, b 1978, — Leo James, b 1986, — Georgina Jane, b 1980.

Issue of late Francis Stephen Coleridge, DSC, b 1920, d 1992: m 1st, 1948 (m diss 1973), Jane Dealtry, 3rd da of

late Maj George Arthur Howson, MC; 2ndly, 1980, Mrs Jean Roberts McFadyean (*née* Ogden) (Sontut, Camino de San Vicente, Pollensa, Mallorca):—
(By 1st *m*) Stephen John, *b* 1953. —— Harriet Sibell, *b* 1959: *m* 1st 1988 (*m diss* 1994), Martin F. Wright; 2ndly, 1994 Alexander Victor Akoulitchev. *Residence* – Cherry Tree Pottery, Common Rd, Headley, Newbury, Berks.

PREDECESSORS – (1) *Rt Hon* JOHN DUKE Coleridge, PC, el son of late Rt Hon Sir John Taylor Coleridge; *b* 1820; MP for Exeter (*L*) 1865-73; Recorder of Portsmouth 1855-66, Solicitor-Gen 1868-71, Attorney-Gen 1871-3 Lord Ch Justice of Common Pleas 1873-80, and Lord Ch Justice of England 1880-94; *cr Baron Coleridge*, of Ottery St Mary, Devon (peerage of United Kingdom) 1873: *m* 1st, 1846, Jane Fortescue, who *d* 1878, da of Rev George Turner Seymour, of Farringford Hill, Isle of Wight; 2ndly, 1885, Amy Augusta Jackson, who *d* 1933, da of Henry Baring Lawford, BCS; *d* 1894; *s* by his el son (2) BERNARD JOHN SEYMOUR, 2nd Baron, *b* 1851; MP for Sheffield, Attercliffe Div (*L*) 1885-94; was a Judge of High Court of Justice 1907-23: *m* 1876, Mary Alethea, who *d* 1940, da of late Rt Rev John Fielder Mackarness, DD, sometime Lord Bishop of Oxford; *d* 1927; *s* by his son (3) GEOFFREY DUKE, 3rd Baron; *b* 1877; sometime Capt Devonshire Regt: *m* 1904, Jessie Alethea, who *d* 1957, da of late Evelyn Mackarness, of Lahard, co Cavan; *d* 1955; *s* by his son (4) RICHARD DUKE, KBE, 4th Baron, *b* 1905; Capt RN; French Gen Headquarters, Vincennes, France 1940, in War Cabinet Office 1940-41, Dep Sec to British Joint Staff and Combined Chiefs of Staff 1941-46, United Kingdom Sec, Mil Staff Committee of United Nations Organization, New York 1946-48, with British Joint Staff Mission, Washington, USA 1950-51, and Ch Staff Officer to Marshal of the RAF Lord Tedder 1950-51; represented British Chiefs of Staff on temporary Committee of Council of NATO Paris 1951, Exec Sec NATO 1952-70; attended Conferences of Washington, Quebec 1943/44, Cairo, Teheran 1943, Malta and Yalta 1945; DL of Devon; has American Legion of Merit; OBE (Mil) 1944, CBE (Mil) 1951, KBE (Civil) 1971: *m* 1936, Rosamund, who *d* 1991, el da of late Adm Sir William Wordsworth Fisher, GCB, GCVO; *d* 1984; *s* by his elder son (5) WILLIAM DUKE, 5th Baron and present peer.

COLGRAIN, BARON (Campbell) (Baron UK 1946)

Act and Hope

DAVID COLIN CAMPBELL, 3rd Baron; *b* 24 April 1920; *s* 1973; late 9th Lancers: *m* 1st, 1945 (*m diss* 1964), Veronica Margaret, da of late Col William Leckie Webster, RAMC; 2ndly, 1973, Sheila, da of late Robert McLeod Mitchell, and formerly wife of M. M. Hudson, and has issue by 1st *m*.

Arms – Gyronny of eight or and sable, on a chief azure a bezant between two crescents of the first. **Crest** – A boar's head erect and erased azure issuant from a wreath of myrtle leaved and flowered proper. **Supporters** – *Dexter*, a horse argent; *sinister*, a boar azure. *Residence* – Bushes Farm, Weald, Sevenoaks, Kent.

SON LIVING (*By 1st marriage*)

Hon ALASTAIR COLIN LECKIE, *b* 16 Sept 1951; *ed* Eton, and Trin Coll, Camb: *m* 1979, Annabel Rose, yr da of Hon Robin Hugh Warrender, of Widcombe Manor, Church St, Bath (*see* B Bruntisfield), and has issue living, Thomas Colin Donald, *b* 9 Feb 1984, — Nicholas Robin, *b* 1986.

DAUGHTER LIVING (*By 1st marriage*)

Hon Virginia Charlotte Angela, *b* 1948: *m* 1973, Maj Jonathan Charles Mackay-Lewis, son of late Maj-Gen Kenneth Frank Mackay Lewis, CB, DSO, MC, of Stamps and Crows, Layer Breton, Essex, and has issue living, James Edward, *b* 1978, — George Mungo Pyne, *b* 1985, — Gemma Elizabeth, *b* 1977. *Residence* – Gattertop, Leominster, Herefords HR6 0JY.

BROTHERS LIVING

Hon Robert (Robin) Dudley, *b* 1921; late Scots Gds: *m* 1st, 1954 (*m diss* 1978), Cecilia Barbara, el da of late Cdr Alexander Leslie, RN (ret), of Old Manor Cottage, Lympne Hill, Kent; 2ndly, 1983, Mrs Muriel Anne Kandal, da of late George Tuson, RN, of Loughborough, Leics, and has issue living (by 1st *m*), Lenore Robina Cecilia, *b* 1957: *m* 1985, Michael C. Maynard, of The Old Bakery, Poughill, Crediton, Devon EX17 4DQ, son of late Ronald Maynard, of Epping, Essex, and has issue living, Chantal Robina *b* 1987, Alexandra Samantha *b* 1992, — Zephyrine Alexandra, *b* 1967: *m* 1996, Christopher R. Bennett, son of Peter Bennett, of Hanslope, Bucks, and has issue living, Maximilian Dudley James *b* 1998. *Residence* – Sharp's Place, Boughbeech, Edenbridge, Kent.

Hon Neil Donald, DSC, *b* 1922; late Lt RN: *m* 1951, Angela Louise Vereker, da of Rt Hon Sir Ronald Hibbert Cross, KCMG, KCVO, 1st Bt (ext), and has had issue, †Andrew Donald, *b* 1954; *ed* Harrow; *m* 1974, Dominique, eldest da of Peter Juul, of Copenhagen, and *d* 1980, having had issue, Claire *b* 1974; *d* 1978, — Roderick Hugo, *b* 1960: *m* 1988, Sophie Louise, da of Richard Hicks, and has issue living, Arthur Frederick *b* 1988, Edie Blanche *b* 1990, Olympia Louise Kathleen *b* 1995, — Martin Emmott, *b* 1963; has issue living (by Penelope Wilson), Kiloran Diana Claire *b* 1990, — Joanna Louise, *b* 1953: *m* 1st, 1980 (*m diss* 1987), Michael L. Wennink, yr son of Cornelis Wennink; 2ndly, 1992, Robert M. Tennant, son of late Cecil Tennant, and has issue living (by 1st *m*), Oliver Neil *b* 1981, (Jonathan Roelof) Donald *b* 1982, (by 2nd *m*), Hugh Campbell *b* 1992. *Residence* – Yorks Hill, Ide Hill, Sevenoaks, Kent.

SISTER LIVING

Hon Gillian Margaret, *b* 1925: *m* 1951, Peter Scott Young, who *d* 1988, and has issue living, Robert James Campbell, *b* 1954: *m* 1986, Josyane Noelle, da of Jean Pierard, of Le Figueret, Flayosc, Haut-Var, France, and has issue living, Sam Peter Antoine *b* 1987, Yannick Robert Pierard *b* 1989, — Mark Peter, *b* 1961: *m* 1990, Andrea C. S., da of Maj Geoffrey Browne, MBE, of Jasmine Cottage, Harwell, Didcot, Oxon, and has issue living, Fergus Scott Antony *b* 1993, Luke Peter James *b* 1997, Pollyanna (Polly) Gillian *b* 1995, — Bridget Margaret, *b* 1952: *m* 1983, Patrick L. Macdougall, of 40 Stevenage Rd, SW6 6EJ, son of late J. A. Macdougall, of Midhurst, and has issue living, Laura Margaret Valerie, *b* 1984, Nicola Elizabeth Bridget *b* 1987, Vanessa Emily Hope *b* 1990, — Deborah Mary, *b* 1957: *m* 1983, Steven H. Hewlett, son of Maurice Hewlett, of 9 The Old Nurseries, Grange-over-Sands, Cumbria, and has issue living, Jacob (Jake) Robert *b* 1986, Adam James *b* 1988, Megan Ruth *b* 1991. *Residence* – Orchard House, Langton Green, Tunbridge Wells, Kent.

COLLATERAL BRANCH LIVING

Issue of late Hon Angus Dudley Campbell, CBE, yr son of 1st Baron, *b* 1895, *d* 1967: *m* 1926, Joan Esther Sybella, JP, who *d* 1998, da of late Col Hercules Arthur Pakenham, CMG (*see* E Longford, colls):—
Judith Averil, *b* 1927; DL Fife 1997: *m* 1954, Lt-Cmdr Gerard St John Roden Buxton, RN, of Pitteadie House, Kirkcaldy, Fife KY2 5UN (*see* Buxton, Bt). —— Linda Ishbel (*Lady Cubitt*), *b* 1934: *m* 1958, Sir Hugh Guy Cubitt, CBE, JP, of Chapel House, W Humble, Dorking, Surrey (*see* B Ashcombe).

PREDECESSORS – (1) COLIN FREDERICK Campbell, son of George William Campbell; *b* 1866; Pres of British Bankers' Asso 1938-46, and a Director of National Provincial Bank, London Assurance, and other cos; *cr Baron Colgrain*, of Everlands, co Kent (peerage of United Kingdom) 1946: *m* 1890, Lady Angela Mary Alice Ryder, MBE, who *d* 1939, da of 4th Earl of Harrowby; *d* 1954; *s* by his eldest son (2) DONALD SWINTON, MC, 2nd Baron; *b* 1891; Chm of Grindlays Bank 1949: *m* 1917, Margaret Emily, who *d* 1989, da of late Percy William Carver, of Courtlands, W Hoathly, Sussex: *d* 1973; *s* by his eldest son (3) DAVID COLIN, 3rd Baron and present peer.

Collins, family name of Baron Stonham.

COLNBROOK, BARONY OF (Atkins) (Extinct 1996)

SON LIVING OF LIFE BARON

Hon Charles Edward Spencer, *b* 1952; *ed* Eton: barrister-at-law; *m* 1980, Clare Margaret, da of Henry Neville Hemsley, and has issue living, Edward Oliver, *b* 1982, — Nicholas Charles, *b* 1985, — Matthew Spencer, *b* 1988, — Katherine Margaret Lucy, *b* 1992.

DAUGHTERS LIVING OF LIFE BARON

Hon Sheila Kathleen, *b* 1944: *m* 1st, 1964 (*m diss* 1974), Peter Thornycroft Romer-Lee; 2ndly, 1975 (*m diss* 1978), Keith Allen Manners; 3rdly, 1982, Royston Joseph Schroeder, of Ellimore Farm, Lustleigh, Devon, and has issue living (by 1st *m*), Richard Peter, *b* 1965; ed Sherborne: *m* 1991, Kirsten, da of Col Richard Smith, — Anthony James, *b* 1967; *ed* Sherborne.
Hon Julia Margaret, *b* 1946; *m* 1st, 1966 (*m diss* 1972), David Charles Roderick; 2ndly, 1972, John Stanley Melville Keay, of Succoth, Dalmally, Argyll, and has issue living, (by 2nd *m*), Alexander John Melville, *b* 1973, — Samuel Michael Cosmo, *b* 1979, — Anna Julia, *b* 1974, — Nell Christina, *b* 1977.
Hon Sally Mary, *b* 1948: *m* 1970, William Field Clegg, of Homer House, Ipsden, Oxford, and has issue living, William Humphrey, *b* 1975, — Islay Mary, *b* 1973: *m* 1999, Henry John Gilbey (*see* B Vaux of Harrowden).

WIDOW LIVING OF LIFE BARON

ADELA MARGARET (*Baroness Colnbrook*), da of late Maj Sir Robert Spencer-Nairn, 1st Bt: *m* 1944, Baron Colnbrook, KCMG, PC (Life Baron), who *d* 1996. *Residence* – Tuckenhams, Waltham St Lawrence, Reading, Berks.

Colville, family name of Baron Clydesmuir.

COLVILLE OF CULROSS, VISCOUNT (Colville) (Viscount UK 1902, Lord precedence S 1609)

OUBLIER NE PUIS

I can not forget

JOHN MARK ALEXANDER COLVILLE (*His Honour The Viscount Colville of Culross*), QC, 4th Viscount and 13th Lord (*cr* 1609); *b* 19 July 1933; *s* 1945; *ed* Rugby, and New Coll, Oxford (MA, Hon Fellow 1997); Bar Lincoln's Inn 1960, QC 1978, a Bencher 1986; Chm Parole Board 1988-92; Recorder 1990, Circuit Judge 1993-99; Lt Gren Gds (Reserve), and a Member of Queen's Body Guard for Scotland (Royal Company of Archers); Member of Council, Univ of E Anglia 1968-72; Min of State Home Office 1972-74: *m* 1st, 1958 (*m diss* 1973), Mary Elizabeth, da of Col M. H. W. Webb-Bowen, RM; 2ndly, 1974, Margaret Birgitta (LLB King's Coll, Lond; JP Inner Lond), da of Maj-Gen Cyril Henry Norton, CB, CBE, DSO, and formerly wife of 2nd Viscount Davidson, and has issue by 1st and 2nd *m*.

Arms – Quarterly: 1st and 4th argent, a cross moline sable, *Colville*; 2nd and 3rd gules, a fesse, checky, argent and azure, *Lindsay*. Crest – A hind's head couped at the neck argent. Supporters – *Dexter*, a rhinoceros proper; *sinister*, a savage habited in a bearskin and supporting on his left shoulder with his exterior hand a club all proper.
Address – House of Lords, SW1.

SONS LIVING (By 1st marriage)

Hon CHARLES MARK TOWNSHEND (*Master of Colville*), *b* 5 Sept 1959; *ed* Rugby, and Durham Univ (BA).
Hon (Richmond) James Innys, *b* 1961; *ed* Rugby, Bristol Univ (BSc), and London Univ (MSc); MB, BS, FRCS England: *m* 1993, (Aurea) Katharine, da of Sir Philip Manning Dowson, CBE, PRA (*see* Bacon, Bt, 1995 Edn), and has issue living, Alexander Richmond Philip, *b* 1995, — Oliver Mark Sherban, *b* 1996.
Hon Alexander Fergus Gale, *b* 1964; *ed* Wellington Coll, and Nottingham Poly (BSc): *m* 1993, Elizabeth, yst da of John Desmond O'Hare, of Liverpool.
Hon Rupert George Streatfeild, *b* 1966; *ed* Milton Abbey.

(By 2nd marriage)

Hon Edmund Carleton, *b* 1978.

BROTHER LIVING

Hon (Charles) Anthony (Rydes, Nevill Court, Tunbridge Wells, Kent), *b* 1935; *ed* Rugby, and Magdalen Coll, Oxford (BA); late Sub-Lt RNR; Solicitor 1969; Overseas Civil Ser, Kenya 1958-64: *m* 1965, Katherine, da of late Humphrey John Sankey, of Kinangop, Kenya, and has issue living, Robert Quintin Oxnam, *b* 1971, — Charles Alexander, *b* 1974.

COLLATERAL BRANCHES LIVING

Grandchildren of late Adm Hon Sir Stanley Cecil James Colville (Vice Adm of UK), GCB, GCMG, GCVO, 2nd son of 1st Viscount:—
Issue of late Capt George Cecil Colville, CBE, RN, *b* 1903, *d* 1983: *m* 1935, Gabrielle, who *d* 1987, da of late Gen Sir Arthur Power Palmer, GCB, GCIE, and widow of Col Leger Livingstone-Learmonth, of Southover, Tolpuddle, Dorset:—
Rona Alice Gabrielle, *b* 1936: *m* 1959 (*m diss* 1975), Maj Hon Thomas Robin Valerian Dixon, MBE, Gren Gds (later 3rd Baron Glentoran). *Residence* – Gazebo, The Plantation, Curdridge, nr Southampton.

Issue of late Maj-Gen Edward Charles Colville, CB, DSO, *b* 1905, *d* 1982: *m* 1934, Barbara Joan, who *d* 1983, da of late Edward Henry Marland Denny, of Staplefield Place, Staplefield, Sussex:—
Jane, *b* 1936: *m* 1st, 1957 (*m diss* 1967), Sir Archibald Bruce Charles Edmondstone, 7th Bt; 2ndly, 1967, HSH Prince Martin Lubomirski, who *d* 1977; 3rdly, 1983, Capt John Holliday Bingham Hartley, late Coldm Gds, of 19 Cliveden Place, SW1. —— Antonia (*Princess Carol of Roumania*), *b* 1939: *m* 1st, 1962 (*m diss* 1973) Garry Lacon Jock Ropner (*see* Ropner, Bt (*cr* 1904), colls); 2ndly, 1984, (HRH) Prince Carol of Roumania (*see* Royal Family), of 36 Doria Rd, SW6.

Issue of late Cdr (S) Sir Richard Colville, KCVO, CB, DSC, RN (ret), *b* 1907, *d* 1975: *m* 1933, Dorothy, who *d* 1972, da of Brig-Gen Halhed Brodrick Birdwood:—
Peter Alan (Golden Hill House, Stourton Caundle, Sturminster Newton, Dorset DT10 2JW), *b* 1935; late Lt RM: *m* 1964, Jane, el da of late Capt Thomas Harland, of Walton House, Kineton, Warwicks, and has issue living, James Richard, *b* 1976, — Julia Mary, *b* 1965: *m* 1995, Jeremy P. Minchin, yr son of Peter Minchin, of Wadhurst, Sussex, and has issue living, Thomas Peter *b* 1998, — Annabel Clare, *b* 1967: *m* 1997, Humphrey J. Nokes, yr son of Julian Nokes, of Kensington, W8, and of Mrs Alastair Shaw, of Suffolk and London, and has issue living, Ben *b* 1999, — Joanna Elizabeth, *b* 1969: *m* 1992, Nicholas Alexander Waite, of Sawmills Cottage, Forde Abbey, Chard, Som TA20 4LT, elder son of Michael Waite, of E Coker, Som, and has issue living, Rosalind Emma Corlyon *b* 1996, Georgina Kate Corlyon *b* 1998, — Sarah Dorothy Louise, *b* 1972. ——Anne Bridget (The Manse, Iden Green, nr Cranbrook, Kent), *b* 1939: *m* 1963 (*m diss* 19—), Oliver Spankie, late Capt RM, and has issue living, Hugh Nicholas, *b* 1967, — Rosemary Bridget, *b* 1964. ——June Claire, *b* 1948: *m* 1977, Anthony Barrington Prowse, of Rose Cottage, Coombe Shute, Stoke Gabriel, S Devon, and has issue living, Sebastian Irwin Barrington, *b* 1978, — Nicholas Richard Barrington, *b* 1982, — Alexandra Rose Adelaide Barrington, *b* 1979.

Grandchildren of late Hon George Charles Colville, MBE, 3rd son of 1st Viscount:—
Issue of late David Richard Colville, *b* 1909, *d* 1986: *m* 1933, Lady Joan Child-Villiers (Hollybush Farm, Stoneyheath, Ramsdell, nr Tadley, Hants RG26 5SL), da of 8th Earl of Jersey:—
†Robert John, *b* 1941; *ed* Harrow; Liveryman Fishmongers' Co: *m* 1997, Elizabeth Mary (Duxhams, Dulverton, Som TA22 9EJ), da of late Leonard White, of Dulverton, Som, and *d* 1999. ——James Richard Charles (Windflower House, Halfway Pitch, Pitchcombe, Glos GL6 6LJ), *b* 1952; *ed* Harrow: *m* 1982, (Mary) Virginia Louise, yr da of late Timothy Walter Horn (*see* E Carnarvon, colls, 1990 Edn), and has issue living, Charles David James, *b* 1987, — Edward Timothy George, *b* 1988, — Emma Virginia Anne, *b* 1987 (twin), — Sophia Antonia Louise, *b* 1994. ——Sarah Anne (*Sarah, Lady Pigot*), *b* 1933: *m* 1968, Maj-Gen Sir Robert Anthony Pigot, 7th Bt, CB, OBE, DL, of Garden House, St Luke's Drive, Bembridge, I of Wight, who *d* 1986. ——Catherine, *b* 1935: *m* 1958, Cdr Warren Llewellyn Russell Euan Gilchrist, RN (ret), of Rook Hill, Monk Sherborne, Basingstoke, Hants, and has issue living, Charles Warren, *b* 1962, — David Warren, *b* 1967, — Catherine Anne, *b* 1960, — Julia Mary, *b* 1969. ——Mary Julia, *b* 1947: *m* 1969, Aubrey Francis Houston Bowden, of The Old Vicarage, Winkfield, Windsor, Berks (*see* Bowden, Bt).

Issue of late Sir John Rupert Colville, CB, CVO, *b* 1915, *d* 1987: *m* 1948, Lady Margaret Egerton, CVO (The Close, Broughton, Stockbridge, Hants), da of 4th Earl of Ellesmere (*see* D Sutherland):—
Alexander George, *b* 1955; *ed* Harrow; a Page of Honour to HM 1968-71. ——Rupert Charles, *b* 1960; *ed* Harrow, and Trin Coll, Oxford (MA): *m* 1991, Sarah Catherine, da of Richard Russell, of Cherington, Warws. ——(Elizabeth) Harriet, *b* 1952; *ed* St Mary's, Wantage, and London Univ (BA); a Lady-in-Waiting to HRH The Princess Royal since 1990: *m* 1976, David James Bowes-Lyon, of Heriot Water, Heriot, Midlothian (*see* E Strathmore, colls).

PREDECESSORS – (1) *Sir* JAMES Colville, Knt; served with distinction in the French War under Henry of Navarre, afterwards Henry IV of France, and in 1589 received a charter of the Abbey of Culross as a feudal barony, and was *cr* (by charter and investiture) *Lord Colville of Culross* 1604 with remainder to his heirs male whatsoever; on the resignation of his kinsman the Commendator of Culross, the Abbey Estates were in 1609 re-erected with a Lordship and he was *cr Lord Colville of Culross* (peerage of Scotland) 1609, with remainder to heirs male whatsoever; *d* 1620; *s* by his son (2)JAMES, 2nd Lord, *d* 1624; *s* by his son (3) WILLIAM, 3rd Lord; *d* 1656; *s* by his brother (4) JOHN, 4th Lord; *s* by his kinsman (5) ALEXANDER, 5th Lord; *d* 1721; *s* by his son (6) JOHN, 6th Lord; in 1722, at the Gen Election of Scottish Peers his name was excluded from the Peers' Roll on the ground that it was not on the roll at the time of the Union; but on petition to the House of Lords, when the Charter of 1609 was the instrument acted on, he was declared, in 1723, to be entitled to the dignity, and his name was placed on the roll as *Lord Colville of Culross* next to Lord Cardross; *d* 1741; *s* by his eldest son (7) ALEXANDER, 7th Lord, a distinguished Vice-Adm; *d* 1770; *s* by his brother (8) JOHN, 8th Lord; *d* 1811; *s* by his son (9) JOHN; Adm of the White, and a Representative Peer; *d* 1849; *s* by his nephew (10) CHARLES JOHN (son of Gen Sir Charles Colville, GCB, 2nd son of 9th Lord), PC, KT, GCVO, 10th Lord, *b* 1818; Lord Chamberlain to Queen Alexandra 1873-1903; *cr Baron Colville of Culross* (peerage of United Kingdom) 1885, and *Viscount Colville of Culross*, co Perth (peerage of United Kingdom) 1902: *m* 1853, Hon Cecile Katherine Mary Carington, who *d* 1907, da of 2nd Baron Carrington; *d* 1903; *s* by his el son (11) CHARLES ROBERT WILLIAM, 2nd Viscount, *b* 1854; Lieut-Col late Grenadier Guards; was Mil Sec to Gov-Gen of Canada (Baron Stanley of Preston) 1888-92; Zulu War 1879 (despatches, medal with clasp): *m* 1885, Ruby, who *d* 1943, da of late Lt-Col Henry Dorrien Streatfeild, of Chiddingstone, Kent; *d* 1928; *s* by his son (12) CHARLES ALEXANDER, 3rd Viscount; *b* 1888; Com RN; European War 1914-19 (despatches), European War 1939-45: *m* 1931, Kathleen Myrtle, OBE, who *d* 1986, da of late Brig-Gen Henry Richmond Gale, CMG, RE; *k* in a flying accident on active service in the Azores 1945; *s* by his el son (13) JOHN MARK ALEXANDER, 4th Viscount and present peer; also Baron Colville of Culross, and Lord Colville of Culross.

COLWYN, BARON (Smith) (Baron UK 1917, Bt UK 1912)

I give thanks

IAN ANTHONY HAMILTON SMITH, CBE, 3rd Baron, and 3rd Baronet; *b* 1 Jan 1942; *s* 1966; *ed* Cheltenham, and London Univ (BDS), LDS RCS, CBE (Civil) 1989: *m* 1st, 1964 (*m diss* 1977), Sonia Jane, el da of P. H. G. Morgan, of Malvern, Worcs; 2ndly, 1977, Nicola Jeanne, da of Arthur Tyers, of The Avenue, Sunbury-on-Thames, Middx, and has issue by 1st and 2nd *m*.

Arms – Per chevron gules and argent, in chief two cocks of the second, in base a whale spouting proper. Crest – Upon a whale a cock, both as in the arms. Supporters – *Dexter*, a miner holding in his exterior hand and resting on his shoulder a pick-axe, suspended from his belt a miner's lamp, all proper; *sinister*, a female weaver holding in her exterior hand a shuttle also proper.

SON LIVING (*By 1st marriage*)

Hon CRAIG PETER, *b* 13 Oct 1968.

DAUGHTERS LIVING (*By 1st marriage*)

Hon Jacqueline Jane, *b* 1967: *m* 1999, Sean C. R. Pertwee, only son of late Jon Pertwee.

(by 2nd marriage)

Hon Kirsten Antonia, *b* 1981.
Hon Tanya Nicole, *b* 1983.

BROTHER LIVING

Hon Timothy Hamilton (Diocesan Coll, Rondebosch 7700, Cape, S Africa), *b* 1944; *ed* Cheltenham; MA, Oxford: *m* 1967, Carolyn, da of late Bernulf Llewelyn Hodge, MRCS, LRCP, of The Old Cottage, Jac-na-Parc, Polperro, S Cornwall, and has issue living, Annabel, *b* 1972, — Fiona, *b* 1974.

AUNT LIVING (*sister of 2nd Baron*)

Elisabeth Joan Babette Hamilton (Ashcraig, The Croft, Bures, Essex), *b* 1919: *m* 1939, Lt-Col John Baddeley Bagot Ferguson, R Tank Regt, and has issue, Nicholas John (Ashcraig, The Croft, Bures, Essex), *b* 1941: *m* 1965, Karen Elisabeth Svanso, and has issue living, James Fergus *b* 1966, Kate Elisabeth Venetia *b* 1967.

COLLATERAL BRANCH LIVING

Issue of late Hon (Hubert) Constantine Smith, yr son of 1st Baron, *b* 1890, *d* 1956: *m* 1917, Majorie Methwold, OBE, who *d* 1984, da of late Arthur Birkett, of Langford Lodge, Southwold, Suffolk:—
Michael Constantine (Maes Nant, Pant Glas, Garndolbenmaen, Gwynedd), *b* 1919; is Capt RA: *m* 1st, 1945 (*m diss* 1970), Veronica, only da of Thomas Flanagan, of Tralee; 2ndly, 1970, Marie Therese, yr da of Patrick Stuart Martin, of Glasgow, and has had issue (by 1st *m*), †Christopher Michael Constantine, *b* 1953; *d* 1998, — Sally Constantine, *b* 1947, — Judy Jennifer Constantine, *b* 1951. —Anthony Methwold Constantine (Beech Lawn Cottage, South Entrance, Saxmundham, Suffolk), *b* 1923: *m* 1955, Susan Muriel, only da of Frederick B. Staveacre, of Braeside, Colwyn Bay, and has issue living, David Anthony Constantine, *b* 1962: *m* 1986, Anita Simpson, and has issue living, Frederic Thomas *b* 1995, Sophie Louise *b* 1987, Rose Elizabeth *b* 1990, Kitty Patience *b* 1993, — Caroline Constantine, *b* 1957: *m* 1983, Quentin Muir Russell, and has issue living, Rory Angus *b* 1990, Jessica Clare *b* 1984, Fenella Louise Mimosa *b* 1986, Jemima Stephanie Rona *b* 1987, — Nicola Constantine, *b* 1959: *m* 19—, Gordon Macdonald, and has issue living, Meghan Rowen *b* 1992. —— Elizabeth Pamela Constantine, *b* 1918: *m* 1945, Michael William Malim, who *d* 1974, and has issue living, Flavia Constantine Eve, *b* 1949, — Lydia Elisabeth Constantine *b* 1952: *m* 1985, Nicholas David Umney, of 62 London Rd, Riverhead, Sevenoaks, Kent TN13 2DJ, and has issue living, Michael David *b* 1987, Georgina Alice Daisy *b* 1995, — Julia Pamela Constantine, *b* 1955, — Delia Constantine, *b* 1959: *m* 1990, David Allan Robinson, of 1 Lime Tree Cottages, The Street, Erpingham, Norwich, Norfolk NR11 7QD, and has issue living, Martha Pamela Malim *b* 1994, Constance Alix Malim *b* 1997. *Residence* – Little Court, High St, Stock, Ingatestone, Essex CM4 9BA.

PREDECESSORS – (1) *Rt Hon* FREDERICK HENRY SMITH, el son of late Joshua Smith, JP, of Eccles; *b* 1859; was Dep Chm of Martin's Bank, Ltd, and a Director of Railway Cos; High Sheriff of Carnarvonshire 1917; *cr* a *Baronet* 1912, and *Baron Colwyn*, of Colwyn Bay, co Denbigh (peerage of United Kingdom) 1917: *m* 1882, Elizabeth Ann, who *d* 1945, da of late Hamilton Savage, of Eccles; *d* 1946; *s* by his grandson (2) FREDERICK JOHN VIVIAN (son of late Hon Frederick Henry Hamilton Smith, el son of 1st Baron), 2nd Baron; *b* 1914: *m* 1st, 1940 (*m diss* 1951), Miriam, who *d* 1996, da of late Victor Ferguson; 2ndly, 1952 (*m diss* 1954), Hermione Sophia O'Bryen, who *d* 1989, da of late Cyril Bertie Edward Hoare (Hoare, Bt, *cr* 1784); 3rdly, 1955, Beryl (who *d* 1987, having *m* 4thly, 1969, Sir George Taylor, FRS, who *d* 1993), da of the late Harvey Walker, formerly wife of Edward Chorley Cookson, and widow of Mortimer Reddington, FRCS; *d* 1966; *s* by his eldest son (3) IAN ANTHONY HAMILTON, 3rd Baron.

COLYTON, BARON (Hopkinson) (Baron UK 1956)

Look forward

ALISDAIR JOHN MUNRO HOPKINSON, 2nd Baron *b* 7 May 1958; *s* 1996; *ed* Shiplake Coll: *m* 1980, Philippa Jane, yr da of Peter John Bell, of Harefield, Itchen Abbas, Hants, and has issue.

🛡rms – Azure, on a chevron argent between three mullets of six points or as many mascles gules a bordure engrailed of the third. Crest – A demi-lion sable between two mullets of six points or. Supporters – On either side an angel proper habited azure winged or, the dexter holding in the exterior hand a Saxon Crown and the sinister likewise holding a trumpet gold.

SONS LIVING

Hon JAMES PATRICK MUNRO, *b* 8 May 1983.
Hon Thomas Charles Robert, *b* 1985.

DAUGHTER LIVING

Hon Katherine Alice, *b* 1988.

BROTHER LIVING (*Raised to the rank of a Baron's son* 1997)

Hon Charles Henry Kenneth, *b* 1960; *ed* Eton: *m* 1988, Karen Anne, eldest da of Eric Snowdon, of Melbourne, Australia, and has issue living, Frederick Nicholas Hugo, *b* 1990, — Henry Jonathan Arthur, *b* 1992, — Camilla Fiona Rose, *b* 1994.

WIDOW LIVING OF FIRST BARON

BARBARA ESTELLA ADDAMS (*Dowager Baroness Colyton*), da of late Stephen Barb, of New York, USA, and formerly wife of Charles Samuel Addams, the cartoonist: *m* 1956, as his 2nd wife, the 1st Baron Colyton, CMG, PC, who *d* 1996. *Residence* – Le Formentor, Av Princess Grace, Monte Carlo, Monaco.

PREDECESSOR – (1) HENRY LENNOX D'AUBIGNÉ Hopkinson, CMG, PC, son of late Sir Henry Lennox Hopkinson, KCVO; *b* 1902; Diplo Ser 1924-46, Head Conservative Parl Secretariat and Joint Dir Conservative Research Dept 1946-49, Sec Overseas Trade 1951-52, Min of State Colonial Affairs, and Delegate to Gen Assembly of UN 1952-55; Royal Humane Soc's Award for Saving Life (from drowning) 1919; MP (C) Taunton Div of Somerset 1950-56; *cr Baron Colyton*, of Farway, co Devon, and Taunton, co Somerset (peerage of UK) 1956: *m* 1st, 1927, Alice Labouisse, who *d* 1953, da of Henry Lane Eno, of Bar Harbour, Maine, USA; 2ndly, 1956, Mrs Barbara Estella Addams, da of late Stephen Barb, of New York, USA, and formerly wife of Charles Samuel Addams, the American cartoonist; *d* 1996; *s* by his grandson (2) ALISDAIR JOHN MUNRO (elder son of late Hon Nicholas Henry Eno Hopkinson, only son of 1st Baron), 2nd Baron and present peer.

COMBERMERE, VISCOUNT (Stapleton-Cotton) (Viscount UK 1826, Bt E 1677)
(Title pronounced "Cumbermeer")

Prepared in all circumstances

MICHAEL WELLINGTON STAPLETON-COTTON, 5th Viscount, and 10th Baronet; *b* 8 Aug 1929; *s* 1969; *ed* Eton, and King's Coll London Univ; BD, MTh London; Lecturer in Biblical and Religious Studies, Dept of Extra-Mural Studies, London Univ since 1972, Sr Lecturer in Religious Studies, Birkbeck Coll, London Univ, Centre for Extra Mural Studies since 1988; Chm World Congress of Faiths 1983-88; Fl Lt RAF (Reserve); served Palestine Police Force 1947-48 Roy Canadian Mounted Police 1948-50 and RAF 1950-58: *m* 1961, Pamela, Elizabeth, da of Rev Robert Gustavus Coulson, R of Stansted, Kent, and has issue.

Arms – Quarterly: 1st and 4th azure, a chevron between three hanks of cotton argent palewise, and in chief pendant from a ribbon gules, a representation of the medal and clasps presented to the 1st Viscount, *Cotton*; 2nd and 3rd argent, a lion rampant sable, *Stapleton*. **Crests** – 1st a falcon, wings expanded and inverted proper, beaked, membered, and belled or, holding in the dexter claw part of a belt proper, buckled gold; 2nd, on a mount vert, a dragoon of the 20th Regiment, mounted on a black horse, and in the act of charging, and over the crest in an escrol azure, the word "Salamanca", in gold letters; 3rd, out of a ducal coronet or, a Saracen's head couped at the shoulders affrontée wreathed round the temples, argent and sable. **Supporters** – Two falcons, wings expanded and endorsed proper, beaked, membered, and belled or, the *dexter* supporting a spear, also proper, therefrom flowing to the dexter a standard swallow-tailed vert, semée of estoiles or, streamers and tassels of the last, and the *sinister* supporting a like spear, therefrom flowing a yellow standard, swallow-tailed streamers and tassels of the last.
Residence – Vanners, Bucklebury, nr Reading, Berks RG7 6RU. *Club* – RAC

SON LIVING

Hon THOMAS ROBERT WELLINGTON, *b* 30 Aug 1969.

DAUGHTERS LIVING

Hon Tara Christabel, *b* 1961: *m* 1992, Laurent Saglio, and has issue living, Clementine Lily, *b* 1995.
Hon Sophia Mary, *b* 1963: *m* 1995, Greville Thomas Worthington (*see* Howard-Lawson, Bt).

BROTHER LIVING

Hon David Peter Dudley (The Old Buffers, Station Rd, Darling, Cape, S Africa), *b* 1932; *ed* Eton; Capt Life Gds (Res): *m* 1955, Susan Nomakepu, da of Sir George Werner Albu, 2nd Bt, and has issue living, Simon, *b* 1959: *m* 1993, Tessa, da of Dr John Cummings, of Cape Town, and has issue living, Oliver Dudley *b* 1994, James Peter George *b* 1996, — Toby James, *b* 1966, — Nicola Caroline Louisa, *b* 1957: *m* 1994, Martin Street, son of Brian Street, of Evesham, Worcs, and has issue living, Rhiannon Madeleine *b* 1995, — Polly, *b* 1961: *m* 1990, Bernard John Harton, son of Mrs D. Barker, of Worcester.

COLLATERAL BRANCHES LIVING

(*In remainder to Baronetcy only*)

Grandchildren of late Capt Frederick Arthur Stapleton Cotton, eldest son of late Rev James Stapleton Cotton, 2nd son of late Rev Henry James Cotton, elder son of late Very Rev James Henry Cotton, 2nd son of late Rev George Cotton, LLD, 3rd son of 4th Bt:—
  Issue of late Hugh Philip Stapleton Cotton, *b* 1913, *d* 1979: *m* 1938, Mary Josephine, da of Frederick Thomas Wheeler:—
Stephen Hugh Stapleton (Chailey Moat, Chailey, E Sussex BN8 4DA), *b* 1949; *ed* Tonbridge, and Reading Univ (BSc Estate Management); FRICS: *m* 1970, Josephine Katharina, da of Owen Eric Goddard, HM British Consul in Oporto, and has issue living, Rufus Tom Stapleton, *b* 1976, — Gabriele Pippa, *b* 1974: *m* 1997, Jamie C. J. Stein, eldest son of John Stein, of Stirling, — Hannah Stephanie, *b* 1977, — Olivia Jo, *b* 1979. ——— Jennifer Mary (Whistle Cottage, Cowden, Edenbridge, Kent), *b* 1943: *m* 1964 (*m diss* 1983), Peter Ivan Chettle, and has issue living, Dominic Mark, *b* 1967, — Deborah Jane Emma, *b* 1970. ——— Marilyn Elizabeth, *b* 1946; *ed* Sussex Univ (BEd), Dip RSA: *m* 1st, 1977 (*m diss* 1988), Christopher David Jones; 2ndly, 1989, Steven John Linehan, of 30 Stanford Av, Hassocks, W Sussex, and has issue living (by 1st *m*), Benjamin Kester, *b* 1973, — Daniel Ian, *b* 1975.

Grandchildren of late Charles Calveley Cotton, eldest son of late Charles Robert Cotton, son of late Henry Calveley Cotton (*b* 1750), 6th son of 4th Bt:—
Issue of late Lt-Col Arthur Egerton Cotton, DSO, *b* (twin) 1876; *d* 1922; *m* 1909, Beryl Marie, who *d* 1966 (having *m* 2ndly, 1922, John Lee Booker, JP, who *d* 1942), da of late Henry Jack Cumming, of Foston Hall, Derby:—
Diana Sara, *b* 1914: *m* 1936, Ernest Addenbrooke Crutchley, CBE, who assumed by deed poll 1945, the name of Brooke in lieu of his christian names of Ernest Addenbrooke, and has issue living, Edward Brooke, *b* 1950: *m* 1982, Eugenie Tsirmoula, and his issue living, James Edward Brooke *b* 1986, — Christopher Miles, *b* 1951, — Anna Maria, *b* 1954. *Residence* – 39 High Street, Great Shelford, Cambs.

Issue of late Lt-Col Vere Egerton Cotton, CBE, TD, *b* 1888; *d* 1970: *m* 1922, Elfreda Helen, JP, who *d* 1992, aged 100, da of William Francis Moore:—
Simon Arthur (28 Sauncey Av, Harpenden, Herts) *b* 1924; *ed* Repton, and Magdalene Coll, Camb (Scholar, BA); Bar Gray's Inn 1951; JP: *m* 1960, Barbara Helen Ralston, da of late Albert James Sutcliffe, of Dodleston, Ches, and has issue living, William Andrew Calveley, *b* 1962; *ed* Radley, and Bristol Univ (BA), — Emma Jane, *b* 1961; *ed* Sidney Sussex Coll, Camb (BA), — Helen Clare, *b* 1965; *ed* Durham Univ (BA). —— Robert Charles (The Cherry Orchard, Badgemore, Henley on Thames), *b* 1925; *ed* Repton, and Magdalene Coll, Camb (MA): *m* 1954, Nicolette Anne, da of Capt Robert Lionel Brooke Cunliffe, CBE, RN (*see* Cunliffe, Bt, colls), and has issue living, Richard Robert (The Malthouse, Bramdean, Alresford, Hants), *b* 1956; *ed* Bradfield, and E Anglia Univ (BA): *m* 1984, Corin, da of Carel Wevers, of The Hague, and has issue living, Oliver Charles *b* 1987, Anthony Vere *b* 1988, Pavinia Sarah *b* 1991, — Philip Egerton (15 Kyrle Rd, SW11 6BD), *b* 1960; *ed* Shiplake Coll: *m* 1st, 1987 (*m diss* 1996), Rosie Louise, da of Capt James Pack, OBE, RN, of Wickham, Hants; 2ndly, 1998, Juliet, da of Barry Edwards, of Over Alderley, Ches, and has issue living (by 1st *m*), Charles Rupert Egerton *b* 1989, (by 2nd *m*), Cosmo Alexander *b* 1998, — Penelope Clare, *b* 1957; *ed* Queen Anne's, Caversham, and Royal Free Med Sch (MB BS): *m* 1983, John Christopher Arnold, of 1 Deepdene Park Rd, Dorking, Surrey, son of late Rev Eric Joseph Arnold, of Tiverton and has issue living, William Henry *b* 1991, Hugh James *b* 1993, Frances Helen *b* 1996, — Caroline Harriet, *b* 1963; *ed* St Mary's, Calne, and Manchester Univ (BA): *m* 1992, Thomas R. Emlyn Jones, of 40 Lady Somerset Rd, NW5 1TU, son of J. H. Emlyn Jones, of Ivinghoe, Bucks, and has issue living, Jack *b* 1995, Sam *b* 1998, Kate *b* 1993.

Grandchildren of late Lt-Col Vere Egerton Cotton, CBE, TD (ante):—
Issue of late Henry Egerton Cotton, JP, Lord-Lieut Merseyside 1989-93; *b* 1929, *d* 1993: *m* 1955, (Elizabeth Margaret) Susan, JP, DL (Norwood, Grassendale Park, Liverpool 19), da of late Clifford James Peard, DSO, JP, of North Curry, Som:—
Timothy James Egerton, *b* 1958; *ed* Bredon Sch, Tewkesbury. —— Catherine Susan, *b* 1956; *ed* Benenden, and Camb Coll of Art & Technology: *m* 1996, Yiannis Psillos, of Kritsa, Crete, and has issue living, Natalie Sofia, *b* 1999.

Grandson of late Maj Gilbert Francis Egerton Cotton (infra):—
Issue of late Maj Francis Brian Egerton Cotton, *b* 1916, *d* 1989: *m* 1955, Ruth, MBE, da of late Richard Stratton, CBE, of Kingston Deverill, Wilts:—
Charles Egerton (34 Stockton, Warminster, Wilts BA12 0SQ), *b* 1958: *m* 1991, Catherine Clea, da of Col Terence Thomas Taylor, of Ashfield, Parsons Lane, Crockerton, Warminster, and has issue living, Rilla Catherine Egerton, *b* 1994, — Ellen Ruth Egerton, *b* 1996, — Kitty Frances Egerton, *b* 1998.

Granddaughter of Maj Francis Egerton Cotton, 2nd son of Charles Robert Cotton, 5th son of Henry Calverley Cotton (*b* 1750) (ante):—
Issue of late Maj Gilbert Francis Egerton Cotton, *b* 1880, *d* 1971: *m* 1913, Nora, who *d* 1956, da of Mathew Williams:—
Helen Viola Egerton, *b* 1917: *m* 1st, 1940, Capt Sir John Hargreaves Pigott-Brown, 2nd Bt, Coldm Gds, who was *ka* in Tunisia 1942; 2ndly, 1948, Capt Charles Raymond Radclyffe, late R Scots Greys, of Lew, Oxon, and has issue living (by 1st *m*) (*see* Pigott-Brown, Bt), — (by 2nd *m*) Sarah (15 Shirlock Rd, NW3 2HR), *b* 1950; film producer: *m* 1996, W. P. (Bill) Godfrey, son of John Godfrey, of Neen Sollars, Shropshire, and has issue living, Sam Charles Radclyffe *b* 1989, Callum *b* 1995.

Granddaughter of late William Gordon Lynch Cotton, MICE, son of late Col Hugh Calveley Cotton, 6th son of Henry Calveley Cotton (*b* 1750) (ante):—
Issue of late Hugh Gordon Cotton, *b* 1869, *d* 1942: *m* 1903, Gertrude Mary, da of late Charles Parsons:—
Vivien Mary, *b* 1903.

PREDECESSORS – (1) *Sir* ROBERT COTTON, MP for Cheshire; *cr* a *Baronet* 1677; *d* 1712; *s* by his son (2) *Sir* ROBERT SALUSBURY, 3rd Bt, MP for Cheshire; *dsp*; *s* by his brother (4) *Sir* LYNCH SALUSBURY, MP 4th Bt; *d* 1775; *s* by his son (5) *Sir* ROBERT SALUSBURY, 5th Bt, MP for Cheshire; *d* 1807; *s* by his son (6) *Sir* STAPLETON, GCB, GCH, KSI, *b* 1772; served with remarkable distinction in Peninsular War 1791-1814, and at siege of Bhurtpore 1826, when Com in Ch in India; was a Field Marshal, Constable of the Tower, Lord-Lieut of Tower Hamlets, Gold Stick-in-Waiting, and Col 1st Life Guards; *cr* *Baron Combermere*, of Combermere, co Chester (peerage of United Kingdom) 1814, and *Viscount Combermere*, of Bhurtpore, E Indies, and of Combermere, co Chester (peerage of United Kingdom) 1827: *m* 2ndly, 1814, Caroline, da of William Fulke Greville; *d* 1805, *s* by his son (7) WELLINGTON HENRY, 2nd Viscount, *b* 1818, MP for Carrickfergus (C) 1847-57: *m* 1844, Susan Alice who *d* 1869, da of Sir George Sitwell, 2nd Bt; *d* 1891; *s* by his eldest son (8) ROBERT WELLINGTON, 3rd Viscount, *b* 1845: *m* 1st 1866 (*m diss* 1879), Charlotte Anne, only child of late J. Fletcher Ellis Fletcher, of Pool Hall, Lancashire; 2ndly, 1880, Isabel Marian, who *d* 1930, yst da of Sir George Chetwynd, 3rd Bt; *d* 1898; *s* by his only son (9) FRANCIS LYNCH WELLINGTON, 4th Viscount; *b* 1887: *m* 1st, 1913 (*m diss* 1926), Hazel Louisa who *d* 1943, da of late Henry de Courcy Agnew (Agnew, Bt, *cr* 1629, colls); 2ndly, 1927, Constance Marie Katherine, who *d* 1968, da of late Lt-Col Sir Francis Dudley Williams-Drummond, KBE, of Hafodneddyn, Carmarthenshire (Williams-Drummond, Bt, colls): *d* 1969; *s* by his son (10) MICHAEL WELLINGTON, 5th Viscount and present peer; also Baron Combermere.

Compton, family name of Marquess of Northampton.

Compton, Earl; son of Marquess of Northampton.

CONGLETON, BARON (Parnell) (Baron UK 1841, Bt I 1766)

TE DIGNA · SEQVERE

Honours have followed thee

CHRISTOPHER PATRICK PARNELL, 8th Baron, and 11th Baronet; *b* 11 March 1930; *s* 1967; *ed* Eton, and New Coll, Oxford: *m* 1955, Anna Hedvig, da of G. A. Sommerfelt, of Oslo, Norway, and has issue.

Arms – Gules: two Chevronels, and in chief three escallops argent. **Crest** – A boar's head erased or, between two wings gules, each charged with two chevronels argent. **Supporters** – *Dexter*, an angel vested argent, wings and the head radiated gold; *sinister*, a hermit vested, the exterior hand supporting his staff proper, the hat ensigned with an escallop or.
Residence – West End Lodge, Ebbesbourne Wake, Salisbury, Wilts SP5 5JR.

SONS LIVING

Hon JOHN PATRICK CHRISTIAN, *b* 17 March 1959; *ed* Eton, and Edinburgh Univ: *m* 1985, Marjorie-Anne (Annie), only da of John Hobdell, of The Ridings, Cobham, Surrey, and has issue living, Christopher John Edward, *b* 1987, — Harry Gustav Willem, *b* 1990, — Phoebe Anna Hedvig, *b* 1992.
Hon Thomas David Howard, *b* 1963.

DAUGHTERS LIVING

Hon (Anne) Cathrine, *b* 1956: *m* 1980, (Michael) Robin Long, and has issue living, Richard Per, *b* 1981, — Willum Jan, *b* 1984.
Hon Elizabeth Dagny, *b* 1960.
Hon Mary-Clare, *b* 1965.

SISTERS LIVING

Hon Mary Elizabeth, *b* 1919: *m* 1956, Percy Purves Turnbull, who *d* 1976. *Residence* – 74 St Ann St, Salisbury, Wilts SP1 2DX. *Club* – Special Forces, New Cavendish.
Hon Jean Margaret, *b* 1922: *m* 1952, as his 2nd wife, Lt-Col Frederick Henry Howard, DSO, MC and bar, late 3rd Hus (*see* E Carlisle colls). *Residence* – Isle of Ulva, Aros, Mull, Argyll PA73 6LZ.
Hon Sheila Helen, *b* 1923: *m* 1959 (*m diss* 1979), Roger Henry Duvollet, and has had issue, Annette Frances, *b* 1961, *d* 1982.
Hon Ann Bridget, *b* 1927: *m* 1947 (*m diss* 1967), Maj Derek Campbell Russell, RE. *Residence* – Lyscombe, Piddletrenthide, Dorset.
Hon Heather Doreen, *b* 1929: *m* 1960, Robert Peter Mangin Bell, and has issue living, (Robert) Simon Parnell, *b* 1961: *m* 1986, Fiona J., MD, elder da of David Sanders, of Winchester, and has issue living, (Robert) Edward Sanders *b* 1989, Jack Digby *b* 1993, Alice Seymour *b* 1990, — Aidan William George, *b* 1967: *m* 1997, Judith L., da of R. F. Harrison, of Cheltenham, Glos, and has issue living, Sophie Seymour *b* 1998, — Penelope Edith, *b* 1963: *m* 1991, Peter M. Melville, elder son of Rev P. K. Melville, of Albury, NSW, Australia, and has issue living, Catriona Constance *b* 1993, Eliza Macdonald *b* 1995, Tamsin Edith *b* 1998. *Residence* – Sarsen House, 5 Mead Rd, St Cross, Winchester.

COLLATERAL BRANCHES LIVING

Grandchildren of late Bertram Damer Parnell, playwright, 2nd son of late Col Hon Arthur Parnell, 3rd son of 3rd Baron:—
Issue of late Desmond Damer Parnell, *b* 1900, *d* 1972: *m* 1930, Ivy Maude, who *d* 1972, da of late Mark Hunt Harding:—
John Desmond (3 Edwin Ware Court, Crossway, Pinner, Middx HA5 3UJ), *b* 1930: *m* 1961, Barbara Jean, da of Laurence Chapell, of Leeds, and formerly wife of Coleson John King, and has issue living, Sally Dee, *b* 1966: *m* 1998, Robin Jeremy Peake. —— Jean Pamela, *b* 1943: *m* 1976, Ronald James Johnson, of 28 Castleview Road, E Slough, Berks SL3 7NQ, and has issue living, Philip Andrew, *b* 1981, — Joanna, *b* 1976.

Grandchildren of late Myles Bligh Damer FARMILOE (infra):—
Issue of late Michael John FARMILOE, b 1931, d (27 Feb) 1983: m 1953, Mary Elizabeth, who d 1980, only da of
Vivian Ewart Berry, of 118 Berkeley Court, NW1:—
Simon Charles FARMILOE, b 1961. —— Sarah Elizabeth, b 1959: m 1986, John Kiddell, son of Percy Edgar Kiddell, and
has issue living, Jamie Michael, b 1992, — Lewis Edward, b 1994. *Residence* – Quorndon, Newlands Drive, Maidenhead,
Berks SL6 4LL.

Grandson of late Bertram Damer Parnell (ante):—
Issue of late Myles Bligh Damer FARMILOE (assumed surname of Farmiloe in lieu of his patronymic by deed poll
1929), b 1903, d (11 Oct) 1983: m 1929, Cynthia Joyce, who d 1990, da of Maj Henry Percy Holt:—
Timothy Miles FARMILOE, b 1935; ed Winchester, and New Coll, Oxford (MA). *Residence* – Little Brookwood, 30
Woodfield Lane, Ashtead, Surrey KT21 2BE.

Grandson of late Hon Lionel Charles Nugent Parnell, 7th son of 3rd Baron:—
Issue of late Harold Charles Stewart Parnell, b 1900, d 1973: m 1938, Marjorie J. Carvell, who d 1990:—
Christopher Charles Stewart (213a Northfield Av, Ealing, W13 9QU), b 1946: m 1982, Joy E. Johnson.

PREDECESSORS – (1) JOHN PARNELL, MP for Maryborough 1761; cr a *Baronet* 1766; d 1782; s by his son (2) *Sir*
JOHN, PC, 2nd Bt, MP for Queen's co 1783-1801, Chancellor of the Exchequer in Ireland 1787, and a Lord of the
Treasury 1793-9; d 1801; s by his eldest son (3) *Sir* JOHN AUGUSTUS, 3rd Bt; *dsp* 1812; s by his brother (4) *Sir* HENRY
BROOKE, 4th Bt; s to the paternal estates by special Act of Parliament 1789, upon the demise of his father; was MP for
Maryborough 1797, Queen's co 1802-6, and Dundee (L) 1833-41, a Lord of the Treasury, Sec at War 1831-2. Paymaster-
Gen of the Forces, and Treasurer of the Navy and Ordnance 1835-41; cr *Baron Congleton,* of Congleton, Cheshire
(peerage of United Kingdom) 1841: m 1801, Lady Caroline Elizabeth Dawson, da of 1st Earl of Portarlington; d 1842; s
by his eldest son (2) JOHN VESEY, 2nd Baron, b 1805: d 1883; s by his brother (5) HENRY WILLIAM, 3rd Baron, b 1809;
present as Midshipman at battle of Navarino: m 1st, 1835, Sophia, who d 1846, da of late Col Hon William Bligh; 2ndly,
1851, Hon Caroline Margaret, who d 1912 (sometime a Maid of Honour to HM Queen Victoria), da of late Hon Lionel
Charles Dawson; d 1896; s by his eldest surviving son (4) HENRY, CB, 4th Baron, b 1839; Maj-Gen in Army; served
during Zulu Campaign 1879, Comdg 3rd Batn Buffs, ed Kent Regt (despatches, CB): m 1885, Elizabeth Peter, who d
1931, yst da of late Dugald Dove, of Nutshill, co Renfrew; d 1906; s by his son (5) HENRY BLIGH FORTESCUE, 5th Baron, b
1890; Lt Gren Gds; ka 1914 (despatches); s by his brother (6) JOHN BROOKE MOLESWORTH, 6th Baron, b 1892: m 1918,
Hon Edith Mary Palmer Howard, who d 1979, da of late Baroness Strathcona and Mount Royal (in her own right); d
1932: s by his son (7) WILLIAM JARED, RN, 7th Baron, b 1925; d 1967; s by his brother (8) CHRISTOPHER PATRICK, 8th
Baron and present peer.

CONSTANTINE, BARONY OF (Constantine) (Extinct 1971)

DAUGHTER LIVING OF LIFE BARON

Hon Gloria, b 1928; ed St Andrew's Univ (MA), and Inst of Education, London Univ (Dip Ed): m 1954, André Valère,
barrister of 202A, Terrace Vale Rd, Goodwood Park, Point Cumana, Trinidad and Tobago, and has issue.

CONSTANTINE OF STANMORE, BARON (Constantine) (Life Baron 1981)

THEODORE CONSTANTINE, CBE, son of late Leonard Constantine, of London; b 15 March 1910; ed
Acton Coll; High Sheriff and DL of Greater London 1967; Master of Worshipful Co of Coachmakers
1975; Freeman of City of London 1949, a Trustee of Sir John Wolstenholme Charity; Chm Nat
Union of Conservative and Unionists Assocns since 1968 (Pres 1980); served in 1939-45 War with
RAuxAF (AE 1945); DL Greater London; cr CBE (Civil) 1956; Kt 1964 and *Baron Constantine of
Stanmore*, in Greater London (Life Baron) 1981: m 1935, Sylvia Mary, who d 1990, da of Wallace
Henry Legge-Pointing, of London, and has issue.
Residence – 12 Gleneagles, Gordon Av, Stanmore, Middlesex HA7 3BQ.

SON LIVING

Hon Roy, b 1936. *Residence* – 11 Grove Park Terr, W4.

DAUGHTER LIVING

Hon Jill Diane, *b* 1938: *m* 1965, Geoffrey Murray, and has issue living, Guy John, *b* 1968, — Tracy Diane, *b* 1966.

Conwy, Rowley-, family name of Baron Langford.

CONYNGHAM, MARQUESS (Conyngham) (Marquess I 1816) sits as BARON MINSTER (UK 1821)
(Title pronounced "Cunningham")

Boodle's, R St George Yacht.

FREDERICK WILLIAM HENRY FRANCIS CONYNGHAM, 7th Marquess; *b* 13 March 1924; *s* 1974; *ed* Eton; late Capt Irish Gds; patron of one living: *m* 1st, 1950 (*m diss* 1970), Eileen Wren, da of Capt Clement Wren Newsam, of Ashfield, Beauparc, co Meath; 2ndly, 1971, Elizabeth Ann, yr da of late Frederick Molyneux Hughes, of Fareham, Hants, and formerly wife of David Sutherland Rudd; 3rdly, 1980, Daphne Georgina Adelaide, who *d* 1986, eldest da of R. C. Armour, formerly of Kenya, and formerly wife of C. P. V. Walker, of Nairobi; 4thly, 1987, (Emma Christianne) Annabel, only da of (Denys) Martin Agnew, of Grosvenor Court, 22 Grove Rd, East Cliffe, Bournemouth (*see* Agnew, Bt, *cr* 1895, colls), and has issue by 1st *m*.

Arms – Argent, a shake fork between three mullets sable. Crest – A unicorn's head erased argent, armed or crined and tufted sable. Supporters – *Dexter*, a horse argent, hoofs and mane or, and charged on the breast with an eagle displayed or; *sinister*, a stag, proper, attired, unguled and charged on the breast with a griffin's head erased or.
Residence – Myrtle Hill, Andreas Rd, Ramsey, Isle of Man. *Clubs* –

SONS LIVING (*by 1st marriage*)

HENRY VIVIAN PIERPOINT (*Earl of Mount Charles*), *b* 23 May 1951; *ed* Harrow: *m* 1st, 1971 (*m diss* 1985), Juliet Ann, yr da of Robert R. B. Kitson, of Churchtown, Morval, Cornwall; 2ndly, 1985, Lady Iona Charlotte Grimston, yst da of 6th Earl of Verulam, and has issue by 1st and 2nd *m*:—

    SON LIVING (by 1st *m*) Alexander Burton (*Viscount Slane*), *b* 30 Jan 1975.
    DAUGHTERS LIVING (by 1st *m*) *Lady* Henrietta Tamara Juliet, *b* 1976, — (by 2nd *m*), *Lady* Tamara Jane, *b* 1991.

Seats – Slane Castle, co Meath; Beau Parc, Navan, co Meath. *Clubs* – Kildare Street and University.
Lord Simon Charles Eveleigh Wren (49 Oxberry Av, SW6), *b* 1953; *ed* Harrow: *m* 1st, 1978 (*m diss* 19—), Emma S., da of late W/Cdr F. W. Breeze; 2ndly, 1990, Mrs Carole Crossman Yorke, yst da of late Eldon F. le Poer Power, of Ashfield, Beauparc, co Meath, and formerly wife of Nicholas Roger Yorke (*see* E Hardwicke, colls), and has issue living (by 1st *m*), Chloe Wren, *b* 1980, — (by 2nd *m*) Frances, *b* 1991.
Lord (Frederick William) Patrick (Dundrocken, Tallanstown, co Louth), *b* 1959: *m* 1st, 1990, Charlotte Mary Temple Gordon, elder da of (Michael) Donald Gordon Black, MC, of Edenwood, Cupar, Fife; 2ndly, 1995, Mrs Siobháin Ramos.

WIDOW LIVING OF SON OF SIXTH MARQUESS

Olivia Phoebe (has reverted to her former style of *Lady John Conyngham*), da of late Capt Percy Neave Leathers, of Fayre Cottage, Robertsbridge, Sussex: *m* 1st, 1950, Lord John Victor Albert Blosse Conyngham, who *d* 1963; 2ndly, 1963,

Hon Francis Alexander Innys Eveleigh-Ross-de-Moleyns, who *d* 1964 (*see* B Ventry). *Residence* – Windmill Cottage, Yapton Rd, Barnham, Bognor Regis, W Sussex.

COLLATERAL BRANCH LIVING

Descendants of late Lord Albert Conyngham, KCH, FRS (3rd son of 1st Marquess), was *cr Baron Londesborough* 1850 (see that title).

PREDECESSORS – (1) *Rt Hon* HENRY Conyngham, PC, MP 1737-53, Vice-Adm, of Ulster and Gov of cos Donegal and Londonderry; *cr Baron Conyngham* (peerage of Ireland) 1953, *Viscount Conyngham* (peerage of Ireland) 1756, *Earl Conyngham* (peerage of Ireland) 1781, and *Baron Conyngham* (peerage of Ireland) 1781, with remainder to his nephew Francis Pierpont-Burton, MP; *d* 1781; *s* by his nephew (2) FRANCIS Pierpont-Burton, 2nd Baron, who assumed by R licence the surname and arms of Conyngham; *d* 1787; *s* by his son (3) HENRY, KP, 3rd Baron; was a Gen in the Army and a Representative peer for Ireland; *cr Viscount Conyngham* (peerage of Ireland) 1789, *Viscount Mount Charles*, and *Earl of Conyngham* (peerage of Ireland) 1797, *Viscount Slane, Earl of Mount Charles* and *Marquess Conyngham* (peerage of Ireland) 1816, and *Baron Minster* (peerage of United Kingdom) 1821; *d* 1832; *s* by his son (4) FRANCIS NATHANIAL, KP, PC, GCH, 2nd Marquess; a Gen in the Army and Lord-Lieut of co Meath; *d* 1876; *s* by his son (5) GEORGE HENRY, 3rd Marquess; *b* 1825; was a Lieut-Gen in the Army, a JP for Kent and Hon Col E Kent Yeo Cav: *m* 1854, Lady Jane St Maur Blanch Stanhope, da of 4th Earl of Harrington; *d* 2 June 1882; *s* by his son (6) HENRY FRANCIS, 4th Marquess, *b* 1857: *m* 1882, Hon Frances Elizabeth Sarah Eveleigh-de Moleyns, who *d* 1939, (having *m* 2ndly 1899, Major John Russell Bedford Cameron), da of 4th Baron Ventry; *d* 1897; *s* by his el son (7) VICTOR GEORGE HENRY FRANCIS, 5th Marquess, *b* 1883; *d* 1918; *s* by his brother (8) FREDERICK WILLIAM BURTON, 6th Marquess, *b* 1890: *m* 1st 1914 (*m diss* 1921), Elizabeth Alice, who *d* 1933, da of late William Andrew Tobin, of Australia; 2ndly, 1922, Antoinette Winifred, who *d* 1966, da of John William Howard Thompson; 3rdly, 1966, Stella, who *d* 1985, el da of late Francis Barrallier Thompson, MRCS, LRCP, and window of Robert Newton Tory; *d* 1974; *s* by his son (9) FREDERICK WILLIAM HENRY FRANCIS, 7th Marquess and present peer; also Earl Conyngham, Earl of Mount Charles, Viscount Slane, Viscount Mount Charles, Viscount Conyngham, Baron Conyngham, and Baron Minster.

COOKE OF ISLANDREAGH, BARON (Cooke) (Life Baron 1992)

VICTOR ALEXANDER COOKE, OBE, son of (Norman) Victor Cooke, of The Ingles, Greenisland, co Antrim; *b* 18 Oct 1920; *ed* Marlborough, and Trin Coll, Camb (MA); Lieut (E) RN 1940-46; DL co Antrim 1970; Henry R. Ayton Ltd, Belfast 1946-89 (Chm 1970-89), Chm Springvale EPS (formerly Polyproducts) Ltd since 1964, Belfast Savings Bank 1963, and Harland & Wolff Ltd 1980-81 (Dir 1970-87); Dir NI Airports 1970-85; Member of Senate NI Parliament 1960-68, NI Economic Council 1974-78; Commr Irish Lights 1983-95 (Chm 1990-92); CEng, FIMechE; *cr* OBE (Civil) 1981, and *Baron Cooke of Islandreagh*, of Islandreagh, co Antrim (Life Baron) 1992: *m* 1951, Alison Sheila, only da of late Maj-Gen Francis Casement, DSO, of Craigtara, Ballycastle, co Antrim, and has issue. *Address* – c/o House of Lords, SW1. *Club* – Naval.

SONS LIVING

Hon Michael John Alexander, *b* 1955, *ed* Marlborough, and Van Mildert Coll, Durham (BSc): *m* 1983, Anne Helen Madeleine, eldest da of late Maj Michael Henry Armstrong, MBE, DL, of Dean's Hill, co Armagh, and has issue living, Robert Michael James, *b* 1990, — Helen Frances Alice, *b* 1985, — Katharine Elizabeth Mary, *b* 1987, — Susannah Madeleine Jane, *b* 1993.

Hon James Victor Francis, *b* 1960; *ed* Marlborough, Trin Coll, Camb (MA), and Cranfield Business Sch (MBA).

DAUGHTER LIVING

Hon Victoria Sally, *b* 1956; *ed* Cobham Hall, Marlborough, and Edinburgh Univ (MA): *m* 1982, Nicholas Patrick Yonge, yst son of Cmdr Philip Evelyn Yonge, OBE, DSC, RN (ret), and has issue living, Cyprian Alexander, *b* 1990, — Charlotte Emma Rosealeen, *b* 1988.

COOKE OF THORNDON, BARON (Cooke) (Life Baron 1995)

ROBIN BRUNSKILL COOKE, KBE, PC, son of late Hon Mr Justice (Philip Brunskill) Cooke, MC; *b* 9 May 1926; *ed* Wanganui Collegiate Sch, Victoria Univ Coll, Wellington, NZ (LLM 1950), and Gonville and Caius Coll, Camb (MA 1952, PhD 1954, Hon Fell 1982), Hon LLD Victoria Univ 1989, Univ of Camb 1990, Hon DCL Univ of Oxford 1991; bar NZ 1950, Inner Temple 1954 (Hon Bencher 1985); practised in NZ 1955-72, QC 1964; Judge of Supreme Court of NZ 1972-76, Court of Appeal of NZ 1976-96 (Pres 1986-96); Visiting Fell of All Souls Coll, Oxford 1990; Memb Internat Commn of Jurists since 1993; Special Status Memb of American Law Inst since 1993; Overseas Judge Hong Kong Court of Final Appeal since 1997; Judge of Court of Appeal, Samoa, and Superior Court, Fiji; a Lord of Appeal; *cr* Knt 1977, PC 1977, KBE 1986, and *Baron Cooke of Thorndon*, of Wellington, New Zealand, and of Cambridge, co Cambs (Life Baron) 1995: *m* 1952, Phyllis Annette, da of late Malcolm Balgownie Miller, of Wellington, and has issue.

𝕬rms – Sable on a cross engrailed or between four volcanoes argent inflamed or a cross ermine. 𝕮rest – In front of a black robin counterstatant a black robin statant proper. 𝕾upporters – *Dexter*, a mid-nineteenth century Captain in the Royal Navy proper; *sinister*, a Maori warrior proper cloaked skirted and holding in the exterior hand a spear or and adorned with two head feathers argent.
Residence – 4 Homewood Crescent, Karori, Wellington, New Zealand. *Clubs* – United Oxford and Cambridge University, Wellington (NZ).

SONS LIVING

Hon Philip Malcolm Brunskill, *b* 1957; *ed* Wanganui Collegiate Sch, and Wellington Polytechnic Central Sch of Technology.
Hon Christopher Monckton Duthie, *b* 1959; *ed* Wanganui Collegiate Sch.
Hon Francis Morland Robin, *b* 1965; *ed* Wanganui Collegiate Sch, Victoria Univ of Wellington, and Gonville and Caius Coll, Camb.

Cooper, family name of Viscount Norwich.

Cooper, Ashley-, family name of Earl of Shaftesbury.

COOPER OF STOCKTON HEATH, BARONY OF (Cooper) (Extinct 1988)

DAUGHTERS LIVING OF LIFE BARON (*By 1st marriage*)

Hon Brenda, *b* 1937: *m* 1st, 1958, (*m diss* 1967), John Abbott; 2ndly, 1968, Pereric Astrom. *Residence* – 9 Rathen Rd, Withington, Manchester M20 9QJ.

Hon Marjorie *b* 1941: *m* 1st 1959 (*m diss* 1969), Neville Finch; 2ndly, 1974 (*m diss* 1979), Robert Dennis Menpes, and has issue living, two sons and two das. *Residence* – 102 Douglas Rd, Esher, Surrey KT10 8BG.

Hon Jacqueline, *b* 1946: *m* 1972, J. Bradford Thomas, and has issue living, three sons. *Residence* – 54 Stanley Rd, East Sheen, SW14 7DZ.

WIDOW LIVING OF LIFE BARON

JOAN (*Baroness Cooper of Stockton Heath*), fomerly wife of — Rogers: *m* 1969, as his 2nd wife, Baron Cooper of Stockton Heath (Life Baron), who *d* 1988. *Address* – 23 Kelvin Grove, Chessington, Surrey.

COPE OF BERKELEY, BARON (Cope) (Life Baron 1997)

JOHN AMBROSE COPE, PC, son of late George Arnold Cope, MC, FRIBA, of Leicester; *b* 13 May 1937; *ed* Oakham; Chartered Accountant; MP for S Glos (C) 1974-83, and for Northavon 1983-97; Assist Govt Whip 1979-81; a Lord Commissioner of the Treasury 1981-83; Dep Chief Whip and Treasurer HM's Household 1983-87; Min of State, Dept of Employment and Min for Small Firms 1987-89; Min of State, Northern Ireland 1989-90; Dep Chm Conservative Party 1990-92; HM Paymaster Gen and Senior Commissioner of the Royal Hosp, Chelsea 1992-94; FCA; *cr* PC 1988, Kt 1991, and *Baron Cope of Berkeley*, of Berkeley, co Glos (Life Baron) 1997: *m* 1969, Djemila, da of late Col P. V. Lovell Payne, of Martinstown, Dorset, and late Mrs Tanetta Blackden, of the American Colony, Jerusalem, and has issue.

Address – c/o House of Lords, Westminster, SW1A 0PW.

DAUGHTERS LIVING

Hon Lucinda Catherine Lovell, *b* 1971: *m* 1991, Giacomo LoPresti, son of Domenico LoPresti, of Bristol, and has issue living, Domenic Ambrose, *b* 1992, — Michael John David, *b* 1997, — Sophie Margaret Grace, *b* 1995.
Hon Nicola Louise, *b* 1976.

Copley, Bewicke-, family name of Baron Cromwell.

Corbett, family name of Baron Rowallan.

CORK and ORRERY, EARL OF (Boyle) Sits as BARON BOYLE OF MARSTON (GB 1711)
(Earl I 1620)

JOHN WILLIAM BOYLE, DSC, VRD, 14th Earl; *b* 12 May 1916; *s* 1995; *ed* Harrow, and King's Coll, London (BSc); CEng, FICE; 1939-45 War as Lt-Cdr RNVR (despatches twice, DSC), VRD 19—: *m* 1943, Mary Leslie, only da of late Gen Sir Robert Gordon Finlayson, KCB, CMG, DSO, and has issue.

𝕬rms – Per bend embattled argent and gules 𝕮rest – Out of a ducal coronet or, a lion's head per pale embattled, argent and gules. 𝕾upporters – Two lions the *dexter* per pale embattled, gules and argent; the *sinister*, per pale embattled, argent and gules. *Residence* – Nether Craigantaggart, Dunkeld, Perthshire PH8 0HQ. *Club* – Lansdowne.

SONS LIVING

JOHN (JONATHAN) RICHARD (*Viscount Dungarvan*), *b* 3 Nov 1945; *ed* Harrow, and RNC Dartmouth; Lt-Cdr RN (ret); Dir E. D. & F. Man Sugar Ltd: *m* 1973, Hon Rebecca Juliet Noble, da of Baron Glenkinglas (Life Baron) (extinct), and has issue:—

SON LIVING — *Hon* Rory Jonathan Courtenay, *b* 10 Dec 1978.
DAUGHTERS LIVING — *Hon* Cara Mary Cecilia, *b* 1976, — *Hon* Davina Claire Theresa, *b* (twin) 1978.
Residence – Lickfold House, Petworth, W Sussex GU28 9EY. *Club* – Boodle's.

Hon Robert William, *b* 1948; *ed* Harrow, and Ch Ch, Oxford (MA); Partner PricewaterhouseCoopers; FCA: *m* 1987, Fiona Mary, da of Hon (Oliver) Piers St Aubyn, MC (*see* B St Levan), and has issue living, Richard Piers, *b* 1988. *Residence* – 30 Durand Gdns, SW9 0PP. *Club* – Brooks's.

Hon (Charles) Reginald, *b* 1957; *ed* Harrow, and RMA Sandhurst; Vice Pres Morgan Stanley Dean Witter & Co; late Coldstream Gds: *m* 1987, Susan Shields, da of Philip Hoene, of Duluth, Minnesota, USA, and has issue living, John Arthur Hoene, *b* 1994, — Georgina Margaret, *b* 1989. *Residence* – 6840 West 83rd St Terrace, Minneapolis, MN 55438, USA.

COLLATERAL BRANCHES LIVING

Grandsons living of late Maj Charles John Boyle, 2nd son of Rev Hon Richard Cavendish Boyle, 4th son of 8th Earl:—
Issue of late Capt Edmund Michael Gordon Loeventhorpe Boyle, RN, *b* 1895, *d* 1982: *m* 1927, Maida Cecil, who *d* 1995, da of late Lt-Col Hon Percy Cecil Evans-Freke (*see* B Carbery, colls):—
George Hamilton (Nozieres, 07270 Lamastre, France), *b* 1928; *ed* Canford, and Imp Coll, Lond (BSc); ARSM; High Sheriff Rutland 1964, and Leics and Rutland 1976, DL Leics 1980, and Rutland 1998: *m* 1953, Alathea Henriette Mary, da of John Adrian Frederick March Phillipps de Lisle, of Stockerston Hall, Leics, and has issue living, Robert Edmund John (Bisbrooke Hall, Uppingham, Rutland), *b* 1954; *ed* Eton, and RMA Sandhurst; late Capt Irish Gds: *m* 1985, Gabrielle Georgiana, only da of late Patrick Tobias Telfer Smollett, MC, DL, of Bonhill, Cameron, Alexandria, Dunbartonshire (*see* Fox, Bt, ext 1959), and has issue living, Patrick Gordon Tobias *b* 1991, Albinia Mary *b* 1988, — Richard William (The Priory, Gt Milton, Oxford), *b* 1959; *ed* Gordonstoun, and Wanganui Coll, NZ: *m* 1990, Suzanna Jean, eldest da of Charles Bingham, of Warrens Cross, Tavistock, Devon, and has issue living, Clementine Pamela *b* 1996, — Rupert Lancelot Cavendish (The Park House, Laxton, Northants), *b* 1960; *ed* Gordonstoun: *m* 1986, Sarah Daphne, eldest da of Simon Anthony Berry, of Cloggs Hall, Great Cornard, Suffolk, and has issue living, Angus Hugo Edmund *b* 1989, Christopher Simon Hamilton *b* 1992, Jocelyn William Rupert *b* 1998. —— Patrick Stephen Crispin, *b* 1935: *m* 1975, Heather Ann Williamson, and has issue living, Edmund Charles Thomas, *b* 1976, — Katharine Anna Cecil, *b* 1978. *Residence* – 5 Weech Rd, NW6.

Grandchildren of late Col Lionel Richard Cavendish Boyle, CMB, MVO, 2nd son of late Charles John Boyle, 2nd son of late Vice-Adm Hon Sir Courtenay Boyle, KCH, 3rd son of 7th Earl:—
Issue of late Capt Richard Courtenay Boyle, DSC, RN, *b* 1902, *d* 1986: *m* 1936, Guendolen Mabel Maclean (DL Herts) (14 Mandeville Close, Broxbourne, Herts EN10 7PN), da of late Lt-Col Edward Hugh Griffith, CBE:—
John Richard (40 Drayton Gdns, SW10), *b* 1938; *ed* Eton, and Trin Coll, Camb: *m* 1st, 1964 (*m diss* 1978), Jeannine Mary, da of Capt Timothy John Gurney, Coldm Gds, of The White House, Hare St, Buntingford, Herts (*see* De Bathe, Bt, ext); 2ndly, 1978, Mrs Lena Jupp, yst da of Maj G. B. Rahr, and has issue living (by 1st *m*), Richard Burlington, *b* 1966, — Charles Robert, *b* 1969; *ed* Eton, and Edinburgh Univ: *m* 1997 (*m diss* 1999), Laura J., da of late John Shaw, of Edinburgh, — Patrick William, *b* 1971, — (by 2nd *m*) Harry Courtenay, *b* 1979, — Olivia Mary, *b* 1982. —— William Robert Cavendish (21 Sussex St, SW1), *b* 1944; *ed* Eton: *m* 1994, Janet Ann, da of late John Bainbridge. —— Belinda, *b* 1940: *m* 1963, Brig Thomas Neil McMicking, The Black Watch, who *d* 1998, of Miltonise, New Luce, Wigtownshire DG8 0LY, elder son of late Maj-Gen Neil McMicking, CB, CBE, DSO, MC, and has issue living, Charles Neil, *b* 1965: *m* 1993, Diana J., eldest da of John Hall, of Chathill, Northumberland, — James Richard, *b* 1968, — Henrietta Sophia, *b* 1972.

PREDECESSORS – **(1)** *Rt Hon Sir* RICHARD BOYLE, PC, embarked for Ireland as an adventurer, and having eventually amassed considerable wealth, sat as MP for Lismore 1615; was knighted 1603, and *cr Baron Boyle of Youghal* (peerage of Ireland) 1616, and *Viscount Dungarvan* and *Earl of Cork* (peerage of Ireland) 1620, and was afterwards Lord High Treasurer of Ireland, and known as the "Great Earl"; Cromwell is reported to have said of him that "if there had been an Earl of Cork in every province, it would have been impossible for the Irish to have raised a rebellion"; *d* 1643; *s* by his son (2) RICHARD, 2nd Earl, who in 1642 had by special remainder *s* by his brother Lewis as 2nd *Baron of Bandon Bridge* and *Viscount Boyle of Kinalmeaky* (peerage of Ireland), *cr* 1627: *m* Elizabeth, da and heiress of Henry Clifford, 5th and last Earl of Cumberland, who had in 1628 been summoned by writ as Baron Clifford: he was *cr Baron Clifford*, of Lanesborough, co York (peerage of England) 1644, and *Earl of Burlington* (peerage of England) 1664; *d* 1697; *s* by his grandson (3) CHARLES, 3rd Earl; *d* 1703, *s* by his son (4) RICHARD, 4th Earl; an eminent patron of literature and the fine arts; claimed and was allowed the Barony of Clifford by writ, *cr* 1628; *d* 1753, without male issue, when the Barony of Clifford, *cr* 1628, devolved upon his da Charlotte, wife of William Marquess of Hartington, afterwards 4th Duke of Devonshire; the Barony of Clifford of Lanesborough, *cr* 1644, and the Earldom of Burlington became extinct, and the Irish honours reverted to his kinsman (5) JOHN, 5th Earl, who had in 1731 *s* as 5th *Earl of Orrery*, 5th *Lord Boyle, Baron of Broghill*, and 2nd *Baron Boyle of Marston* (see *infra); d* 1762; *s* by his son (6) HAMILTON, 6th Earl; *dsp* 1764: *s* by his half-brother (7) EDMUND, 7th Earl; *d* 1798; *s* by his son (8) EDMUND, KP; a Gen in the Army; *d* 1856; *s* by his grandson (9) RICHARD EDMUND ST LAWRENCE, KP, PC (son of Charles, Viscount Dungarvan, by Lady Katherine St Lawrence, da of 2nd Earl of Howth), 9th Earl; *b* 1829; Lord-Lieut Somerset; Master of the Buckhounds 1866, 1868, and 1880-85, and Master of the Horse 1886 and 1894-5: *m* 1853, Lady Emily Charlotte De Burgh, who *d* 1912, da of 1st Marquess of Clanricarde, KP; *d* 1904; *s* by his son (10) CHARLES SPENCER CANNING, 10th Earl, *b* 1861: *m* 1918, Rosalie Gray, who *d* 1930, da of William Waterman de Villiers, of Romscy, Hants; *d* 1925; *s* by his brother (11) ROBERT JOHN LASCELLES, 11th Earl, *b* 1864: *m* 1890, Josephine Catherine, who *d* 1953, da of J. P. Hale, of San Francisco, USA; *d* 1934; *s* by his kinsman (12) WILLIAM HENRY DUDLEY, GCB, GCVO, son of late Col Gerald Edmund Boyle (by Lady Elizabeth Theresa Pepys, da of 1st Earl of Cottenham), (grandson of 8th Earl), 12th Earl, *b* 1873; Adm of the Fleet; C in C Home Fleet 1933-35, and at Portsmouth 1937-39; commanded combined expedition for capture of Narvik 1940: *m* 1902, Lady Florence Cecilia Keppel, who *d* 1963, da of 7th Earl of Albemarle; *d* 1967, *s* by his nephew (13) PATRICK REGINALD (son of Maj Hon Reginald Courtenay Boyle, MBE, MC, by his wife, Violet, who *d* 1974, da of late Arthur Flower (*see* Pauncefort-Duncombe, Bt, 1936 Edn), brother of 12th Earl), 13th Earl, *b* 1910; 1939-45 War with Royal Ulster Rifles and Parachute Regt; S-E Asia 1941-45 with Burma Rifles and Cameronians (Scottish Rifles) in Special Force (Chindits) (severly wounded); a Dep Speaker and Dep Chm of Cttees House of Lords 1973-78, Pres and Chm of Exec Cttee, British Cancer Council, and a Member of Council Cancer Research Campaign 1973-77: *m* 1st, 1952, Mrs Dorothy Kate Scelsi, who *d* 1978, only da of late Robert Ramsden, of Meltham, Yorks, and formerly wife of (i) Marquis Demetrio Imperiali dei Principe di Francavilla, and (ii) G. F. Scelsi; 2ndly, 1978, Mary Gabrielle, who *d* 1999, only da of late Louis Ginnett, and widow of Kenneth McFarlane Walker; *d* 1995; *s* by his brother (14) JOHN WILLIAM, 14th Earl and present peer; also Viscount Dungarvan, Viscount Boyle of Kinalmeaky, Baron Boyle of Youghal, Baron of Bandon Bridge, and Lord Boyle, Baron of Broghill, and Baron Boyle of Marston.

*(1) Sir ROGER BOYLE, PC, 3rd son of 1st Earl of Cork, *cr* when seven years of age *Baron Boyle of Broghill* (peerage of Ireland) 1621, with remainder to heirs of his father; was sometime MP for co Cork and for Arundel; substantially assisted to quell the rebellion in Ireland 1642-3, and after the death of Cromwell planned the restoration of Charles II in Ireland; *cr Earl of Orrery* (peerage of Ireland) 1660; *d* 1679; *s* by his son (2) ROGER, 2nd Earl; *d* 1682; *s* by his son (3) LIONEL, 3rd Earl; attainted by this Parliament of James II 1689; sometime MP for E Grinstead, Sussex; *dsp* 1703; *s* by his brother (4) CHARLES, KT, 4th Earl; and Lt-Gen in the Army, MP for Huntingdon 1700, Ambassador to Brabant and, Flanders, and a Lord of the Bedchamber to George I; *cr Baron Boyle of Marston*, Somerset 1711; in 1722 was imprisoned for six months in the Tower on suspicion of high treason; the astronomical instrument invented by George Graham was named "Orrery" after this peer: *d* 1731; *s* by his son (5) JOHN, 5th Earl, who *s* as 5th Earl of Cork (ante).

Cornwall, Duke of; title borne by the Prince of Wales.

CORNWALLIS, BARON (Cornwallis) (Baron UK 1927)

FIENNES NEIL WYKEHAM CORNWALLIS, OBE, 3rd Baron; *b* 29 June, 1921; *s* 1982; *ed* Eton; formerly in Coldm Gds; Pres Nat Assocn of Agric Contractors 1958-63, and 1986-98; Memb of Board of Trustees Chevening Estate 1979-99; Chm Small Firms Council CBI 1978-81; DL; OBE (Civil) 1963: *m* 1st, 1942 (*m diss* 1948), Judith, only da of Lt-Col Lacy Scott, of Ashcroft, Wadhurst, Sussex; 2ndly, 1951, Agnes Jean, yr da of Capt Henderson Russell Landale, of Ewell Manor, W Farleigh, Maidstone, and has issue by 1st and 2nd *m*.

Arms – Quarterly 1st and 4th, sable, guttée d'eau, on a fesse argent three martlets of the field, *Cornwallis*; 2nd and 3rd, sable on a fesse embattled counter-embattled between three goats passant argent, as many pellets, *Mann*. **Crest** – On a mount vert, a stag lodged reguardant argent, attired or, vulned in the shoulder proper, and gorged with a wreath of laurel also proper. **Supporters** – On either side a stag argent, attired or and gorged with a chaplet of oak fructed vert.
Residences – Ruck Farm, Horsmonden, Tonbridge, Kent; 25B Queen's Gate Mews, SW7.

Virtue overcomes envy

SONS LIVING (*By 1st marriage*)

Hon (FIENNES WYKEHAM) JEREMY *b* 25 May, 1946; *ed* Eton, and RAC Cirencester: *m* 1969, Sara Gray de Neufville, da of Lt-Col Nigel Stockwell, of Benenden, Kent, and has issue living, (Fiennes) Alexander Wykeham Martin, *b* 25 Nov 1987, — Anna Julia Gray, *b* 1971, — Charlotte Louise, *b* 1972. *Residence* – Dundurn, St Fillans, Crieff, Perthshire PH6 2NH.

(*By 2nd marriage*)

Hon (Patrick Wykeham) David (Hamnish Court, Hamnish, Leominster, Herefords) *b* 1952; *ed* Lancing, and Aiglon, Switzerland: *m* 1977, Susannah, da of William Edward Guest, of The Old Vineyard, Rufford Abbey, Notts, and widow of Stephen Thursfield, and has issue living, (Patrick Wykeham) James, *b* 1977, — Thomas Wykeham Charles, *b* 1980, — William Wykeham George, *b* 1982.

DAUGHTERS LIVING (*By 2nd marriage*)

Hon Cecily Mary Clare, *b* 1954: *m* 1980, Ian McCulloch, yr son of Mrs E. McCulloch, and has issue living, Ruari Alexander Fiennes, *b* 1982, — Rohan Grey, *b* 1984, — Fiennes, *b* 1989, — Skye, *b* 1987.

Hon Vanessa Rachel, *b* 1958: *m* 1986, H. Jeremy Middleton, of 104 Prince Albert Rd, Mosman, Sydney, NSW, Australia.

Hon (Susan Patricia) Rose, *b* 1963: *m* 1986, Scott Simon Crolla, designer, son of Romano Crolla, of Queen's Gate, London.

COLLATERAL BRANCH LIVING

Issue of late Capt Hon Oswald Wykeham Cornwallis, OBE, RN, yst son of 1st Baron; *b* 1894, *d* 1974: *m* 1923, Hon Venetia Jane Digby, who *d* 1956, da of 10th Baron Digby:—
Michael Wykeham (10 Ravelston House Rd, Edinburgh, EH4 3LW), *b* 1924: *ed* Eton; Lt-Cdr RN (ret): *m* 1953, Margaret Dorothy, da of late J. W. Cannon, MB, ChB, and has issue living, Richard Wykeham, *b* 1959, — Diana Margaret, *b* 1957: *m* 1991, David Casey, of 23 Baird Rd, Alloway, Ayr KA7 4PN, son of A. Casey, of Dunblane, and has issue living, Colin Wykeham *b* 1994. —— Venetia Mabel, *b* 1928: *m* 1956, Lt-Cdr Geoffrey Arthur George Brooke, DSC, RN, and has issue (*see* Brooke, Bt, colls *cr* 1903).

PREDECESSORS – (1) FIENNES STANLEY WYKEHAM Cornwallis, CBE, son of late Major Fiennes Cornwallis, of Chacombe Priory, near Banbury; *b* 1864; was Col late W Kent Imperial Yeo, a JP for Kent (Chm of County Council 1910-30), and MP for Maidstone (*C*) 1888-95 and 1898-1900; *cr Baron Cornwallis* of Linton, co Kent (peerage of United Kingdom) 1927: *m* 1886, Mabel, who *d* 1957, da of late Capt Oswald Peter Leigh, of Belmont Hall, Cheshire; *d* 1935; *s* by his son (2) WYKEHAM STANLEY, KCVO, KBE, MC, 2nd Baron, *b* 1892; Capt Scots Greys; Lord-Lieut of Kent 1944-72; Chm Co Council 1935-36, Lieut for City of London and Lord-Lieut for City and Co of Canterbury 1944-72; Pro-Chancellor Kent Univ 1965-72; Chm Kent War Agric Exec Cttee 1939-46; Pres MCC 1947-48; Hon Col 8th Bn (T) The Queen's Regt TAVR (W Kent); 1914-18 War in France and Belgium (wounded, despatches, MC, 1914 star, two medals): *m* 1st, 1917, Cecily Etha Mary, who *d* 1943, da of Sir James Heron Walker, 3rd Bt (*cr* 1868); 2ndly, 1948, Esme Ethel Alice, who *d* 1969, da of late Capt J. Montmorency de Beaumont, 5th Royal Irish Lancers, of Hove, Sussex, and widow of Maj Sir Robert James Milo Walker, 4th Bt (*cr* 1868); *d* 1982; *s* by his son (3) FIENNES NEIL WYKEHAM, and present peer.

Corry, Viscount; son of Earl Belmore.

Corry, Lowry-, family name of Earl Belmore.

Corvedale, Viscount; son of Earl Baldwin of Bewdley.

COTTENHAM, EARL OF (Pepys) (Earl of UK 1850, Bt GB 1784 and UK 1801)
(Name pronounced "Pepp-iss")

·MENS·CUJUSQUE·IS·EST·QUISQUE·

Mind makes the man

(KENELM) CHARLES EVERARD DIGBY PEPYS, 8th Earl, and 11th Baronet (*cr* 1784) and 10th (*cr* 1801); *b* 27 Nov 1948; *s* 1968; *ed* Eton: *m* 1975, Sarah, yr da of Capt Samuel Richard Le Hunte Lombard-Hobson, CVO, OBE, RN, and has issue.

Arms – Sable, on a bend or, between two nags' heads erased argent, three fleurs-de-lis of the field. Crest – A camel's head erased or, bridled, lined, ringed, and gorged with a ducal coronet sable. Supporters – On either side a horse argent, bridled, and gorged with a ducal coronet sable; pendent therefrom an escutcheon or, charged with a fleur-de-lis of the second.

SONS LIVING

MARK JOHN HENRY (*Viscount Crowhurst*), *b* 11 Oct 1983; *ed* Eton. *Hon* Sam Richard, *b* 1986.

DAUGHTER LIVING

Lady Georgina Marye, *b* 1981.

SISTER LIVING

Lady Gillian Angela (*Baroness McGowan*), *b* 1941: *m* 1962, 3rd Baron McGowan. *Residences* – Highway House, Lower Froyle, Alton, Hants; 12 Stanhope Mews East, SW7.

DAUGHTERS LIVING OF SIXTH EARL

Lady Rose Edith Idina (19 Warwick Sq, SW1V 2AB), *b* 1927: *m* 1994, Col Oliver Charles Berger, Royal Scots Greys, who *d* 1998. *Lady* Paulina Mary Louise, *b* 1930: *m* 1973, Denis Bernard Hadley, of White Hill House, Upham, Hants, SO3 1JL.

COLLATERAL BRANCHES LIVING

Grandchildren of late Hon Henry Leslie Pepys, 3rd son of 1st Earl:—
Issue of late Lt-Col Arthur Guy Leslie Pepys, MC, Essex Regt, *b* 1875, *d* 1953: *m* 1915, Olive Grace, who *d* 1961, da of late John Frederick Starkey, JP, DL, of Bodicote House, Banbury:—
Iris Leslie, *b* 1918; late Flight Officer WRAF: *m* 1953, W/Cdr Norman Maxwell Boffee, DFC, RAF (ret), and has issue living, Mark Guy, *b* 1956: *m* 1982, Jean, da of Noshir Rumwalla, of Hounslow, Middx. *Residence* – 1B Little Green Lane, Chertsey, Surrey.

Issue of late Col Gerald Leslie Pepys, CB, DSO, *b* 1879, *d* 1936: *m* 1907, Charlotte Helen, who *d* 1965, da of late Charles W. Lambe Forbes, formerly of Auchrannie, Forfarshire:—
Charles Donald Leslie, *b* 1909: *ed* Radley; Lt-Col KOYLI: *m* 1941, Hon (Pamela Sophia) Nadine Stonor, da of 5th Baron Camoys. *Residence* – 30/31 Lyefield Court, Kidmore End Rd, Emmer Green, Reading, Berks RG4 8AP. *Club* – Naval and Military. —— Geraldine Mary Leslie, *b* 1908: *m* 1935, Lt-Col William Louis Barnard, Oxford and Bucks LI, who *d* 1953, and has issue living, Simon William Leslie (92B Underhill Rd, SE22), *b* 1938: *m* 1962, Joy, da of Thomas Frank Prior Pavely, and has issue living, Jonathan James *b* 1969, Emma Louise *b* 1966. *Residence* – 8 Royston Court, Burbage Rd, SE24.

Granddaughter of late Hon George Pepys, 4th son of 1st Earl:—
Issue of late George Digby Pepys, CBE, *b* 1868, *d* 1957: *m* 1902, Margaret Mary Humphry, who *d* 1954, da of late George Walter Davidson, of 167 Queen's Gate SW:—
Anna Margaret, *b* 1906: *m* 1931, Peter Pryor, who *d* 1980, and has issue living, Roderick (Weston Lodge, Hitchin, Herts), *b* 1932: *m* 1959, Carolyn Vaughan, el da of late Donald Smith of Old Mill House, Sandwich, Kent, and has issue living, Peter David *b* 1965: *m* 1993, Melanie Ruth, da of Malcolm Palmer, of Woodsford Sq, W14 (and has issue living, Edwin Roderick *b* 1998, Rose Elizabeth *b* 1995), Louise Margaret *b* 1960, Victoria Jane *b* 1962: *m* 1987, Denis Henry Clough, of Old Vicarage, Braughing, Herts, son of Peter Clough, of Hampsthwaite, Yorks (and has issue living, Hugh Peter *b* 1993, Alice Eleanor *b* 1991, Clare Helen *b* 1996), — George (Rte de Porte de Castet, 64260 Castet, France), *b* 1936: *m* 1960, Virginia Anne, da of late Rev Charles M. Jones, of Chapel Hill, N Carolina, USA, and has had issue, Richard *b* 1965: *m* 1993, Philippa, da of Colin Brannigan, OBE (and has issue living, Harriet Nicola *b* 1997), Mark *b* 1967, Nicola *b* 1963, *d* 1066, Catherine Eleanor *b* 1970: *m* 1994, Alan Roy Jones (and has issue living, Charles Alan *b* 1995) — Clova Margaret, *b* 1935: *m* 1st, 1960 (*m diss* 1983), Glyn Tudor; 2ndly, 1990, David Elwyn Morris, of 42 Frenchay Rd, Oxford, son of late Rev S. M. Morris, and has issue living (by 1st *m*), Adam *b* 1966, Anna Morwenna *b* 1962: *m* 1992, Marcel Goudsblom, of Amsterdam (and has issue living, Isadora Jane *b* 1994), Gay Elizabeth *b* 1964: *m* 1997, Carlos Caruncho, of Oregon House, Calif, USA (and has issue living, Milo Adam *b* 1998), — Mary, *b* 1944: *m* 1969, Roy Hodges, of Newnham Grounds, Daventry, Northants NN11 3EP, and has issue living, Jeremy George *b* 1972, Jonathan Francis *b* 1976. *Residence* – Weston Lodge, Hitchin, Herts.

Grandchildren of late Rev Charles Sidney Pepys, BD (infra):—
Issue of late Rt Rev (George) Christopher Cutts Pepys, Bishop of Buckingham, *b* 1914, *d* 1974: *m* 1947, Elizabeth Margaret (who *m* 2ndly, 1991, Rt Rev Michael A. Mann, sometime Dean of Windsor, of Lower End Farm Cottage, Eastington, Northleach, Glos), da of Maj-Gen Roger Gillies Ekin, CIE:—

(Charles) Richard Ekin (Highfield School, Liphook, Hants GU31 7EQ), *b* 1951; *ed* Winchester; BA: *m* 1979, Jane Elizabeth Cracroft, da of late Lt-Cdr Gervis Frere-Cook, RN, of Exton, Hants (*see* Brown, Bt, colls, 1995 Edn), and has issue living, (George) Oliver Frere, *b* 1982, — Suzannah Mary Elizabeth, *b* 1985, — Clemency Rosemary Eleanor, *b* 1987. —— Caroline Elizabeth (53 Hayfield Rd, Oxford), *b* 1948. —— Sarah Priscilla, *b* 1950: *m* 1980, William Howard Davies, of Norcott, 68 Foreland Rd, Bembridge, Isle of Wight, and has issue living, William Christopher Pepys, *b* 1985, — Holly Pepys, *b* 1983. —— Frances Mary (12A Clifford Gdns, NW10 5JD), *b* 1954. —— Anna Margaret, *b* 1956: *m* 1982, Robert Peter Agnew, of Hillhead of Letter, Dunecht, Westhill, Aberdeenshire AB32 7EQ, son of Dr Sydney Alexander Agnew, of South Molton, Devon, and has issue living, Alexander Christian Pepys, *b* 1984, — Thomas Robert Pepys, *b* 1987, — Eleanor Josephine, *b* 1990.

Granddaughters of late Hon George Pepys (ante):—
Issue of late Rev Charles Sidney Pepys, BD, *b* 1875, *d* 1927: *m* 1913, Adelaide Mary Elizabeth, who *d* 1968, da of late Charles Duncan Cutts, of Buenos Aires:—
Elizabeth Sidney, *b* 1915: *m* 1939, Rev (Arthur) Guy St John Daniel, and has had issue, (Arthur) Jeremy Pepys, *b* 1940; *ed* St Paul's Sch; *d* as the result of a motor accident 1964, — Nicholas Guy (24 Third Ave, Ottawa, Ont, Canada K1S 2J6), *b* 1942; *ed* St Paul's Sch: *m* 1st, 1974 (*m diss* 1983), Menna Matthews; 2ndly, 1984, Susan Cartwright, — Timothy Peter Charles (37 St Gabriel's Rd, NW2 4DT), *b* 1944; *ed* St Paul's Sch, and Bristol Univ: *m* 1974, Rosalie Horner, and has two adopted children, Christopher Rupert Guy *b* 1983, Laura Narmeen *b* 1980. *Residence* – 2 Gervis Court, Penwerris Av, Osterley, Middx TW7 4QU. —— (Phyllis) Ann Jennifer, *b* 1924: *m* 1947, Alexander Paton, MD, FRCP, and has had issue, Alexander, *b* 1948; *ed* Sebright Sch, Wolverley: *m* 19—, Alison Kirkland McGilp, and has issue living, Rose *b* 1984, Eleanor *b* 1986, Anna *b* 1990, — Charles Pepys, 1950; *ed* Solihull Sch; RN; *d* 1973, — Antony Grimwood, *b* 1954; *ed* Solihull Sch: *m* 1983, Pauline Marion Gibbins, and has issue living, Benjamin Charles *b* 1985, Nicola Marion *b* 1990, — Clare Jennifer, *b* 1952: *m* 1st, 1972 (*m diss* 1983), Terence Patrick Mead; 2ndly, 1988, George Albert Kitcher, and has issue living (by 1st *m*), Samuel James *b* 1979, Jessica Ann *b* 1976, (by 2nd *m*) Nathan John *b* 1991, Naomi Mary *b* 1993, — Rachel Mary, *b* 1953; has issue living, Christopher James *b* 1994. *Residence* – Knollbury, Chadlington, Oxon.

(In remainder to Baronetcy only)

Grandchildren of Herbert Frederick Pepys, eldest son of Rev Herbert George Pepys, yr son of Rt Rev Henry Pepys, DD, Bishop of Worcester, 3rd son of 1st Baronet:—
Issue of late Frederick (Eric) Courtenay Pepys, *b* 1904, *d* 1983: *m* 1935, Mary Caroline Bradley, who *d* 1996, of Los Angeles, California, USA:—
Eric Courtenay (jr) (526 S Bayfront, Newport Beach, California 92662-1039, USA), *b* 1936: *m* 1964, Shirley Ann Dietrich, and has issue living, Noel Dietrich, *b* 1970, — Maximillian Paul, *b* 1972, — Renée Catherine, *b* 1964, — Tiffany Ann, *b* 1968. —— Mark Bradley (6065 Via Sonoma, Rancho Palos Verdes, California 90274, USA), *b* 1937: *m* 1970, Anne Claire Bowden, and has issue living, Craig Brian, *b* 1974, — Kirsten Anne, *b* 1976. —— Keith Alan (8223 Woodland Drive, Buena Bark, California 90620, USA), *b* 1948. —— Christine (1816 Lark Ellen Drive, Fullerton, California 92635, USA), *b* 1939: *m* 1960, Ronald Vincent Heusser, and has issue living, Melinda Christine, *b* 1965, — Noelle Pepys, *b* 1968, — Hilary Dawn, *b* 1971. —— Mary Noel (2222 Leavonworth, Apt 504, San Francisco, California 94133-2239, USA), *b* 1946; Attorney-at-Law.

PREDECESSORS – **(1)** WILLIAM WELLER Pepys, a Master in Chancery; *cr a Baronet* 801 of Wimpole Street; *d* 1825; *s* by his son **(2)** WILLIAM WELLER, 2nd Bt; *dsp* 1845; *s* by his brother **(3)** *Sir* CHARLES CHRISTOPHER, PC, KB, DCL, 3rd Bt; an eminent lawyer, was Queen's Solicitor-Gen 1830, Solicitor-Gen 1834, Master of the Rolls 1834, High Commr of the Great Seal 1835, and Lord High Chancellor 1836-41 and 1846-50; *cr Baron Cottenham* (peerage of United Kingdom) 1836; by special remainder *s* by his cousin, Sir Henry (Pepys) Leslie, as 4th Bt, *cr* 1784 (of Upper Brook Street); *cr Viscount Crowhurst* and *Earl of Cottenham* 1850: *m* 1821, Caroline Elizabeth, da of William Wingfield, QC; *d* 1851; *s* by his son **(4)** CHARLES EDWARD, 2nd Earl; *dsp* 1863; *s* by his brother **(5)** WILLIAM JOHN, 3rd Earl; *b* 1825: *m* 1870, Theodosia Selina, who *d* 1919, da of Sir Robert Charles Dallas, 2nd Bt; *d* 1881; *s* by his son **(6)** KENELM CHARLES EDWARD, 4th Earl; *b* 1874: *m* 1st 1899, Lady Rose Nevill, who *d* 1913, da of 1st Marquess of Abergavenny; 2ndly, 1916, Patricia, who *d* 1962, da of late John Humphry Burke, of Galway and California; *d* 1919; *s* by his el son **(7)** KENELM CHARLES FRANCIS, 5th Earl; *b* 1901, *d* 1922, *s* by his brother **(8)** MARK EVERARD, 6th Earl; *b* 1903: *m* 1927 (*m diss* 1939), Sybil Venetia, da of Capt John Vickris Taylor, of North Aston Manor Oxford; *d* 1943; *s* by his brother **(9)** JOHN DIGBY THOMAS, 7th Earl; *b* 1907: *m* 1933, Lady Angela Isabel Nellie Nevill, who *d* 1980, da of 4th Marquess of Abergavenny; *d* 1968; *s* by his son **(10)** KENELM CHARLES EVERARD DIGBY, 8th Earl and present peer; also Viscount Crowhurst, and Baron Cottenham.

COTTESLOE, BARON (Fremantle) (Baron UK 1874, Bt UK 1821)
(Title pronounced "Cotslo")

Neither by entreaty nor bribery

JOHN TAPLING FREMANTLE, 5th Baron, 5th Baronet, and a Baron of the Austrian Empire; *b* 22 Jan 1927; *s* 1994; *ed* Eton; Cdr RN (ret); High Sheriff Bucks 1969-70, Lord Lieut 1984-(Jan) 1997; Pres Bucks Co Scout Assocn, Royal British Legion, SSAFA and FHS, Bucks Branch CLA (Chm 1976-79), Bucks Historic Churches Trust, Bucks Council for Voluntary Ser, Bucks Assocn of Local Councils, Bucks Playing Fields Assocn, Bucks Record Soc, and Bucks Assocn for Care of Offenders; a Vice-Pres BASC, RASE, Eastern Wessex TAVR, The Hospital Saving Assocn, Bucks Co Show (Chm 1977-82, Pres 1983), and National Soc for Epilepsy; Manager Swanbourne; Ch of England First (Aided) Sch; Hon Treas Aylesbury Vale Assocn of Local Councils 1974-84; Vice-Chm CLA Game Fair 1971 and 1981, and of Winslow RDC 1971-74; a Gov Stowe Sch 1983-89, and a Radcliffe Trustee; Chm Oxon Bucks Div Royal Forestry Soc 1982-84; Memb Bucks Farming and Wildlife Advisory Group, Trustee Bucks Fedn of Young Farmers' Clubs, Bucks Military Museum Trust, and Bucks Assocn for the Blind; Hon DUniv Buckingham 1993; KStJ 1984: *m* 1958, Elizabeth Ann, elder da of late Lt-Col Henry Shelley Barker, DSO, of Walcote House, nr Rugby, and has issue.

𝔄rms – Vert, three bars ermine, surmounted by a lion rampant gules, murally crowned or and in chief two plates. ℭrest – Out of a mural coronet or, a demi-lion gules, charged on the shoulder with a plate and holding in the paws a banner quarterly argent and vert. 𝔖upporters – Two eagles, wings expanded in inverted, sable. *Residence* – The Old House, Swanbourne, Milton Keynes, Bucks MK17 0SH. *Clubs* – Travellers', RN, and Royal Albert Yacht (Portsmouth).

SON LIVING

Hon THOMAS FRANCIS HENRY, *b* 17 March 1966; *ed* St Edward's Sch, Oxford, and RAC Cirencester.

DAUGHTERS LIVING

Hon Elizabeth (Betsy) Wynne, *b* 1959: *m* 1982, (George) Iain Duncan Smith, MP, and has issue living, Edward St Alban, *b* 1987, — a son, *b* 19—, — Alicia Cecilia, *b* 1989, — a da, *b* 19—.

Hon Frances (Fanny) Ann, *b* 1961: *m* 1984, Shaun Richard Stanley (*see* B Haden-Guest, 1990 Edn), and has issue living, Joshua John, *b* 1988, — Theo Peter, *b* 1996, — Isabelle, *b* 19—.

HALF-BROTHER LIVING

Hon Edward Walgrave, *b* 1961: *m* 1991, Sara Elizabeth, da of late Lt Cmdr Harry Chillingworth, of Bembridge, I of Wight, and has issue living, Henry John, *b* 1996, — Louisa Clare, *b* 1994. *Residence* – 4 Merivale Rd, SW15 2NW.

SISTER LIVING

Hon Ann, *b* 1930: *m* 1951, Timothy Gerald Martin Brooks, and has issue (*see* B Crawshaw, colls). *Residence* – Wistow, Leicester.

HALF-SISTERS LIVING

Hon Elizabeth Cecilia Jane FREMANTLE (4 Summerfield Av, NW6 6JU), *b* 1962; assumed additional forename of Elizabeth 1977; journalist; has resumed her maiden name: *m* 1991, Olivier Philippe Haguenauer, eldest son of Dr Pierre Haguenauer, of Neuilly-sur-Seine, France, and has issue living, Raphael John, *b* 1996, — Alice Flora Vivette, *b* 1994.

Hon Flora Catherine (167 Leander Rd, SW2 2LP), *b* 1967: *m* 1993, Dan Miyonga, of Kisumu, Kenya, and has issue living, Rose Allal, *b* 1994, — Arabella Poppy, *b* 1995.

AUNTS LIVING *(daughters of 3rd Baron)*

Hon Bride Faith Louisa, *b* 1910; *ed* Girton Coll, Camb (BA 1935, MA 1938): *m* 1936, John Berry, CBE, DL, PhD, LLD, DSc, FRSE, and has issue living, William (Tayfield House, Newport-on-Tay, Fife), *b* 1939; *ed* Eton, St Andrews Univ (MA), and Edinburgh Univ (LLB), WS: *m* 1973, Elizabeth Margery, da of Sir Edward Redston Warner, KCMG, OBE, of Old Royal Oak, Blockley, Glos, and has issue living, John *b* 1976, Robert Edward Alexander *b* 1978, — Peter Fremantle, CMG (58 Pyrland Rd, N5), *b* 1944; *ed* Eton, and Lincoln Coll, Oxford (MA); Crown Agent 1988; CMG 1999: *m* 1972, Paola, da of late Giovanni Padovani, and has issue living, Richard John *b* 1979, Sara *b* 1974; *ed* St Andrews Univ (BSc), Anna *b* 1977; *ed* St Catherine's Coll, Oxford (BA), — Margaret Wilhelmina, *b* 1937; Dip Arch Edinburgh: *m* 1962, Ronald Lindsay Alexander, ARIBA, of 81 Balfour Rd, N5, and has issue living, Adam George *b* 1971; BA, Jane Louise *b* 1969; BA Oxon: *m* 1992, Duncan Arthur Spencer MacLaren. *Residence* – The Garden House, Tayfield, Newport-on-Tay, Fife DD6 8HA.

Hon Katharine Dorothy Honor, *b* 1919; *ed* Girton Coll, Camb (BA 1941); PhD London 1956. *Residence* – Dennenlaan 48, Hollandsche Rading, Netherlands.

WIDOW LIVING OF SON OF THIRD BARON

Anne-Marie Huth (St Wilfred's Convent, 29 Tite St, SW3), 2nd da of late Rt Hon Frederick Huth Jackson (*see* Jackson, Bt, colls): *m* 1930, Hon Christopher Evelyn Fremantle, who *d* 1979, and has issue (*see* colls infra).

WIDOW LIVING OF FOURTH BARON

GLORIA JEAN IRENE DUNN (*Dowager Baroness Cottesloe*), adopted da of late W. E. Hill, of Barnstaple, N Devon: *m* 1959, as his 2nd wife, the 4th Baron Cottesloe, GBE, TD, who *d* 1994. *Residence* – 78 Orbel St, SW11 3NY.

COLLATERAL BRANCHES LIVING

Issue of late Hon Christopher Evelyn Fremantle, yst son of 3rd Baron, *b* 1906, *d* 1978: *m* 1930, Anne-Marie Huth (ante), 2nd da of late Rt Hon Frederick Huth Jackson (*see* Jackson, Bt, colls, cr 1869):—
Adam Augustus (178 East 93rd St, New York, NY 10128, USA), *b* 1934; *ed* Eton, and Balliol Coll, Oxford (MA), and Fordham Univ NYC (JD); Bar Inner Temple 1957: *m* 1963 (*m diss* 1978), Mary Christine, da of late Prince Paul Sapieha, and has issue living, Christopher Nicholas, *b* 1965; *ed* Worth, and Aberdeen Univ (MA, MLitt); Gov Dr Johnson's House Trust, Memb Children's Panel: *m* 1989, Gillian, yst da of Peter Hainey, of Bitterne, Southampton, — Paul Zachary, *b* 1968; *ed* Worth, and Balliol Coll, Oxford: *m* 1991, Jane Pamela, da of Rev John William Hunwicke, Chaplain of Lancing Coll. —— Richard Christian Wynne (via Matteo Palmieri 9, Florence 50122, Italy), *b* 1936; *ed* Portsmouth Priory, RI, and Columbia Univ, USA (MA): *m* 1971 (*m diss* 1984), Chloë Sarabella, yr da of late Sir Geoffrey Cecil Ryves Eley, CBE (*see* Walker, Bt, colls, cr 1856), and has issue living (by Camilla Baines), Oskar Frederick Cornelius BAINES, *b* 1990. —— (Dominic Christopher) Hugh (1082 Park Ave, New York, NY 10128, USA), *b* 1944; *ed* Georgetown Univ, USA: *m* 1993, Susan Faye, da of late Bryant M. Stevens.

Issue of late Hon Reginald Scott Fremantle, 2nd son of 2nd Baron *b* 1863, *d* 1956: *m* 1900, Hilda Lucy, who *d* 1953, da of late E. M. Barry, RA:—
Joan Lucy, *b* 1904: *m* 1930, Caleb Henry Trevor, and has issue living, Malcolm Henry, *b* 1932. *Residence* – 72 Talbot Rd, Highgate, N6.

Grandchildren of late Sir Francis Edward Fremantle, OBE, TD, MD, MCh, FRCS, FRCP, DPH, MP, 4th son of Very Rev Hon William Henry Fremantle (Dean of Ripon) 2nd son of 1st Baron:—
Issue of late Lt-Col Francis David Eardley Fremantle, TD, JP, DL, *b* 1906, *d* 1968: *m* 1936, Emmeline Amy, who *m* 2ndly, 1973, Lt-Col Edward Peter Fletcher Boughey, OBE (*d* 1986) (*see* Boughey, Bt, colls, 1985 Edn), da of late Brig-Gen Vigant William de Falbe, CMG, DSO, of Whittington House, Lichfield:—
Edward Vigant Eardley (4 Sutherland St, SW1V 4LB), *b* 1942; *ed* Eton, and Balliol Coll, Oxford (MA): FCA: *m* 1973, Sarah Maud, yst da of late Col William Henry Whitbread, TD, of Hazelhurst, Bunch Lane, Haslemere, Surrey, and has issue living, Anna Elizabeth, *b* 1981, — Katherine Fiona, *b* 1984. —— Thomas David (Wayside Cottage, E Markham, Newark, Notts), *b* 1944: *ed* Eton, and RNC Dartmouth; late Lt RN: *m* 1971, Alice Marian, da of late Cyril Reginald Egerton, of Hall Farm, Newmarket (*see* D Sutherland, colls), and has issue living, Mark Thomas, *b* 1975; *ed* Eton, and Edinburgh Univ, — Christopher Richard, *b* 1978; *ed* Eton, and Trin Coll, Oxford, — Emily Teresa Alice, *b* 1981; *ed* Wycombe Abbey. —— Richard Francis, *b* 1946; *ed* Eton, and Keble Coll, Oxford; *d* 1976. —— Marion Jane, *b* 1948: *m* 1972, David Christopher Hanbury, of The Old Rectory, Ruckinge, Ashford, Kent, and has issue living, Jonathan Christopher, *b* 1975, — Susannah Mary *b* 1977, — Caroline Jane, *b* 1981.

Grandson of late Ronald Aubrey Fremantle, 3rd son of late Hon Sir Charles William Fremantle, KCB, 3rd son of 1st Baron:—
Issue of late Maj Maurice Alan (Pat) Fremantle, *b* 1900, *d* 1972: *m* 1928, Ida Thelma Gordon, who *d* 1976, da of late Edward Reginald Stirling Bloxsome, of The Rangers, Copthorne, Sussex:—
Robin Patrick (Fannyfield, Evanton, Ross & Cromarty IV16 9XA), *b* 1930: *ed* Wellington Coll; Capt late 4th Queen's Own Hussars, and Ayrshire (ECO) Yeo (TA); Chm The Economic League 1989-93; Principal Fremantle & Co since 1980: *m* 1st, 1962 (*m diss* 1980), June Helen, yr da of late Brig Ereld Boteler Wingfield Cardiff, CB, CBE, of Easton Court, Ludlow, Shropshire; 2ndly, 1985, Honor Diana, yr da of late Sir (Coles) John Child, 2nd Bt, and widow of Noel H. Matterson, and has issue living (by 1st *m*), Charles Ereld Patrick, *b* 1964: *m* 1996, Samantha C., da of late Richard Beale, of Drumlanford, Ayrshire, — Serena Katherine, *b* 1967.

Grandchildren of late Sir Sydney Robert Fremantle, GCB, MVO, eldest son of late Adm Hon Sir Edmund Robert Fremantle, GCB, GCVO, CMG, 4th son of 1st Baron:—

Issue of late Cdr Edmund Seymour Denis Fremantle, DSC, RN, *b* 1904, *d* 1980: *m* 1st, 1928 (*m diss* 1944), Dorothy Clare Haldane, who *d* 1980, el da of Col W. M. Sinclair, OBE, RM; 2ndly, 1946, Edna Maud (Redlands, Hookhills Rd, Churston Ferrers, Paignton, Devon), da of late Albert John Tweed Cusselle, of Dartford, Kent, and formerly wife of James Richard Lyddon:—
(By 1st *m*) Charles Alan (Langley Corner, Langley Burrell, Chippenham, Wilts), *b* 1935; *ed* Sutton Valence, and RNC Dartmouth; Cdr RN; Memb N Wilts District Council 1987-91: *m* 1960, Caroline Mary, da of Cdr Sydney Andrew Boyd Morant, OBE, DSC, RN, and has issue living, Timothy Charles, *b* 1967; *ed* Plymouth Poly (BSc), — James Justin, *b* 1971; *ed* Portsmouth Univ (BA), — Naomi Juliet, *b* 1961; *ed* Keele Univ (BA): *m* 1990, Stuart John Hill, of Hammonds Cottage, Waltham Chase, Hants SO3 2LQ, son of Michael John Hill, of Eastleigh, Hants, and has issue living, Matthew Augustus Fremantle *b* 1992, Georgina Elizabeth *b* 1994, Hannah Juliet *b* 1996. —— Sydney Walter, CBE, *b* 1936; *ed* Sherborne, and Oriel Coll, Oxford (BA): *m* 1961, Susan Delia Aiton, da of the late Brig John Aiton Bell, CBE, and has had issue, Samuel Patrick, *b* 1967, — Joanna Mary Aiton, *b* 1964; *d* 1986. —— Ann Penelope, *b* 1931: *m* 1966, Sirio Morgia, of Summerfields, Via Tito Poggi 21, Via Ardeatina, Rome 00134. —— (By 2nd *m*) Richard William (40 Denmark Rd, W13), *b* 1948: *m* 1975, Alison, da of Arnold Cruse, and has issue living, Edmund Richard, *b* 1979, — Peter Thomas, *b* 1985, — Mary Grace, *b* 1980. —— Stephen Antony (9 Stavordale Way, Weymouth, Dorset), *b* 1950: *m* 1st, 1972 (*m diss* 1976), Hanna Elizabeth Fiona, da of K. Sierakowski, of Bickley, Kent; 2ndly, 1976, Patricia Mary, adopted da of Miss Margaret Lewin, and has issue living, (by 1st *m*) Melanie Leila, *b* 1973, — (by 2nd *m*) Holly, *b* 1978.

Issue of late Lt-Cdr David Robert Fremantle, RNVR, *b* 1906, *d* 1989: *m* 1st, 1939 (*m diss* 1951), Patience Ann, da of late Lt-Cdr Evelyn Culme-Seymour (*see* Culme-Seymour, Bt, colls); 2ndly, 1954 (*m diss* 1976), Mrs Rosabel Stewart-Liberty, da of late Arthur H. Fynn, of Helston, Cornwall, and formerly wife of late Arthur Ivor Stewart-Liberty, MC, TD:—
(By 1st *m*) Francesca Mary, *b* 1941; *ed* London Univ (PhD). *Residence* – 13 Child's St, SW5 9RY.

Granddaughter of late Alfred Ernest Albert Fremantle, yst son of late Adm Hon Sir Edmund Robert Fremantle, GCB, GCVO, CMG (ante):—
Issue of late Maj Paris Oscar (Réné) Francesco Fremantle, *b* 1908, *d* of wounds 1944: *m* 1934, Rosamond Carnegie of 4 Ravens Court, St John's Rd, Eastbourne, who *m* 2ndly, 1947, Brig Gordon de Bruyne, OBE, late 60th Rifles (who *d* 1972), da of late Arthur Knox, of Fairfield, Wargrave, Berks:—
Valerie Rosamond Christina, *b* 1942. *Residence* – 39 Kensington Mansions, Trebovir Rd, SW5 9TQ.

PREDECESSORS – (1) *Rt Hon* THOMAS FRANCIS FREMANTLE, PC, son of Vice Adm Sir Thomas Francis Fremantle, GCB (*cr* Baron of Austrian Empire 1816); *b* 1798; sat as MP for Buckingham (*C*) 1827-46, and was successively Sec of the Treasury, Sec at War, Ch Sec for Ireland, and Chm of Board of Customs; received Royal licence for himself and issue to bear his father's Austrian title of Baron 1822; *cr* a *Baronet* 1821 (with remainder to his father's heirs), and *Baron Cottesloe*, of Swanbourne and Hardwick, co Bucks (peerage of UK) 1874: *m* 1824, Louisa Elizabeth, who *d* 1875, da of F-M Sir George Nugent, GCB, 1st Bt; *d* 1890; *s* by his el son (2) THOMAS FRANCIS, 2nd Baron; *b* 1830; MP for Buckinghamshire (*C*) 1876-85; sometime Chm of London, Brighton and South Coast Railway: *m* 1859, Lady Augusta Henrietta Scott, who *d* 1906, da of 2nd Earl of Eldon; *d* 1918; *s* by his el son (3) THOMAS FRANCIS, CB, VD, TD, 3rd Baron; *b* 1862; Hon Col (formerly Lieut-Col Comdg) Bucks Batn, Oxfordshire and Buckinghamshire LI; Assist Sec to Sec of State for War (Rt Hon W. St J. Brodrick, MP) 1900-1903; Lord Lieut of Bucks 1923-54: *m* 1896, Florence, who *d* 1956, da of late Thomas Tapling, of Kingswood, Dulwich; *d* 1956; *s* by his el surviving son (4) JOHN WALGRAVE HALFORD, GBE, TD, 4th Baron, *b* 1900; 1939-45 War as GSO (I), Sr Mil Liaison Officer and Lt-Col Comdg 20th Light Anti-Aircraft Regt RA (TA); Lt-Col RA (TA Reserve); DL co London 1951 (Chm of DL's Cttees in Bermondsey and Deptford), Memb LCC 1945-55, Port of London Authority 1949-67 (Vice-Chm 1955-67), etc; Trustee Tate Gallery 1953-60, Chm 1959-60, Chm Advisory Council and Reviewing Cttee on Export of Works of Art 1954-72, Chm Arts Council of GB 1960-65, Gov Old Vic and Sadler's Wells 1957-60, Chm South Bank Theatre Board 1962-77; Gov King Edward's Hosp Fund for London 1973-83, etc; Chm The Dogs Home, Battersea 1970-82: *m* 1st, 1926 (*m diss* 1944), Lady Elizabeth Harris, who *d* 1983, only da of 5th Earl of Malmesbury; 2ndly, 1959, Gloria Jean Irene Dunn, adopted da of late W.E. Hill, of Barnstaple, N Devon: *d* 1994; *s* by his elder son (5) JOHN TAPLING, 5th Baron and present peer.

Cotton, Stapleton-, family name of Viscount Combermere.

Courtenay, family name of Earl of Devon.

Courtenay, Lord; eldest son of Earl of Devon.

COURTOWN, EARL OF (Stopford) Sits as BARON SALTERSFORD (GB 1796) (Earl I 1762)

Faithful to an unhappy country

JAMES PATRICK MONTAGU BURGOYNE WINTHROP STOPFORD, 9th Earl; *b* 19 March 1954; *s* 1975; *ed* Eton, Berkshire Coll of Agric, and RAC Cirencester; a Lord in Waiting to HM 1995-97; ARICS: *m* 1985, Elisabeth Dorothy, yr da of Ian Rodger Dunnett, of Broad Campden, Glos, and has issue.

Arms – Azure, semée of cross crosslets and three lozenges or. **Crest** – A wyvern, wings elevated proper. **Supporters** – Two stags proper, plain collared and chained, and each charged on the shoulder with a lozenge or.
Residence – The Paddock, Ampney Crucis, Cirencester, Glos.

SON LIVING

JAMES RICHARD IAN MONTAGU (*Viscount Stopford*), *b* 30 March 1988.

DAUGHTER LIVING

Lady Rosanna Elisabeth Alice, *b* 1986.

BROTHER LIVING

Hon Jeremy Neville, LVO *b* 1958; *ed* Eton; Capt Irish Gds; Temporary Equerry to HM Queen Elizabeth the Queen Mother 1982-84; LVO 1984: *m* 1984, Bronwen, da of Lt-Col David MacDonald Milner, of Ashford Hill, Newbury, Berks, and has issue living, Clementine Lucy Patricia, *b* 1986, — Matilda Rose Philippa, *b* 1988, — Violet Mary Renée, *b* 1992.

SISTER LIVING

Lady Felicity Aileen Ann, *b* 1951: *m* 1st, 1977 (*m diss* 1981), Leslie Edward Archer-Davis; 2ndly, 1982, John Andrew McIndoe, of 9 Franche Court Rd, SW17, and has issue living (by 2nd *m*), Harry James, *b* 1985.

HALF SISTERS LIVING

Lady Mary Christina, *b* 1936; JP, Lord Lieut Cornwall 1994; DStJ: *m* 1959, Geoffrey Jermyn Holborow, OBE, High Sheriff Cornwall 1977, and has issue living, Crispin David Jermyn, *b* 1963: *m* 1994, Louise Cecilia Middleton, da of Maj John Middleton Neilson Powell, of Corscombe, Dorset (*see* Kennard, Bt), and has issue living, George Maunsell Jermyn *b* 1997, William *b* 1999, — Katharine Mary, *b* 1961: *m* 1990, Robert Anstey Preston Wild, of 22 Brackenbury Rd, W6 0BH, son of Anstey Wild, of The White Cottage, Brailsford, Derbys, and issue living, James *b* 1991, Madeleine *b* 1993, Isobel *b* 1997. *Residence* – Ladock House, Ladock, Truro, Cornwall.
Lady Elizabeth Cameron, *b* 1939; High Sheriff Berks 1990, DL 1994; Chief Pres St John Ambulance 1990-96, High Steward of Wokingham since 1992: *m* 1962, Alan Anthony Colleton Godsal, and has issue living, Hugh Colleton, *b* 1965: *m* 1994, Samantha Jane, elder da of Ian Angus, of Soto Grande, Spain, and has issue living, Clover Christina Hope *b* 1998, — Lucy Violet, *b* 1964: *m* 1992, Christopher J. Zeal, 2nd son of Michael Zeal, of Westcott, Surrey, and has issue living, Hugo Henry *b* 1994, Toby Alan *b* 1996, Kitty Cameron *b* 1998, — Laura Christina, *b* 1968. *Residence* – Haines Hill, Twyford, Berks.

AUNTS LIVING (*Daughters of 7th Earl*)

Lady Patricia Mary, *b* 1906: *m* 1934, Maurice John Hayward, Malayan Civil Ser (ret), only son of late Sir Maurice Henry Weston Hayward, KCSI, and has issue living, Maurice Richard (28 Weymouth Drive, Four Oaks, Sutton Coldfield), *b* 1939: *m* 1968, Christina, da of Matthew Hyland, of the Glebe, Coolrain, co Leix, and has issue living, David Maurice *b* 1970, Philip Matthew *b* 1973, Jane Margaret *b* 1969, — Bridget Mary, *b* 1935: *m* 1964, John Everard Kitchin (18 Gloucester Rd, Hampton, Middx), and has issue living, Hugh Everard *b* 1965, Simon John *b* 1967, — Caroline Patricia, *b* 1936: *m* 1960, Myles Anthony Clive Saker, of Rose Cottage, Cuddington, Aylesbury, Bucks, and has issue living, John Anthony *b* 1962: *m* 1998, Saeko, da of K. Sasaki, of NJ, USA, Deborah Ann *b* 1967, — Sarah Elizabeth (Church Square Cottage, Islip, Oxon), *b* 1946. *Residence* – White Hart House, Haddenham, Aylesbury, Bucks.
Lady Moyra Charlotte, BEM *b* 1917: *m* 1943, Lt-Cdr David Henry Champion Streatfeild, RN, and has issue living, David Anthony (63 Roehampton Lane, SW15), *b* 1945: *m* 1971, Jill Katherine, da of late William Macfarlane, of The Old Cottage, Potters Lane, Send, Surrey and has issue living, James Anthony *b* 1973, Charles David *b* 1979, Katherine Moyra *b* 1975, — Timothy James (The Former Vicarage, North Stoke, Wallingford, Oxon), *b* 1947: *m* 1976, Jane, da of late Denis McVicar Merritt, MRCS, LRCP, of Grove House, Birchington, Kent, and has issue living, Rupert Champion *b* 1980, Anna Eleanor *b* 1978, — Peter Stopford (Royal Cottage, Kew Green, Kingston-upon-Thames, Surrey), *b* 1954: *m* 1981, Caroline J, da of D. S. M. (Roy) Webster, of Farnham, Surrey, and has issue living, Alexander David Stopford *b* 1988, Henry Peter Champion *b* 1990, Emma *b* 1998, — Cicely Mary, *b* 1950: *m* 1975, Dr Michael R. Smith, of Redlands, Clifton Rd, Chesham Bois, Bucks, son of Bryan Crossley Smith, CBE, of Wendover, Bucks, and has issue living, Harriet May Crossley *b* 1982, Lucy Patricia Streatfeild *b* 1985. *Residence* – Redberry House, Bierton, Aylesbury, Bucks.
Lady Cecilia Norah (twin), *b* 1917; formerly Junior Com ATS: *m* 1947, Cdr Thomas Philip Frederick Urquhart Page, RN, who *d* 1994, son of late Sir Leo Francis Page, and has issue living, Nicholas Leo Thomas, *b* 1948: *m* 1971, Sarah June, el da of Leslie Bramhall, and has issue living, Thomas Leslie *b* 1973: *m* 1998, Isabelle Mary Rosa, yr da of Anthony Bolton, Alexia Frances *b* 1976, — Victoria Cecilia, *b* 1951: *m* 1979, Robin E. Furber, son of Dr Stanhope Furber, of Somerton Cottage, Winkfield, Berks, and has issue living, George *b* 1986, Eleanor Primrose *b* 1988, — Juliet Mary, *b* 1955.

WIDOW LIVING OF SON OF SEVENTH EARL

Mrs Millicent DAVIES, elder da of late Geoffrey Watt, and previously wife of late Trevor Waterson: *m* 1978, as his 2nd wife, Hon Edward Richard Barrington Stopford, who *d* 1990. *Residence* – 8 Turner's Lane, N Ferriby, N Humberside HU14 3JP.

WIDOW LIVING OF EIGHTH EARL

Patricia (*Patricia, Countess of Courtown*) (Threeways, Jordans, Bucks), da of late Harry Stephen Winthrop, of Auckland, NZ: *m* 1951, as his 2nd wife, the 8th Earl of Courtown, who *d* 1975.

COLLATERAL BRANCHES LIVING

Issue of late Hon Edward Richard Barrington Stopford, 2nd son of 7th Earl, *b* 1914, *d* 1990: *m* 1st, 1946, Ann Marie Elizabeth Douglas, who *d* 1976, only da of late Brig Harold Gordon Henderson, CBE, of Hyde House, Chalford, Glos; 2ndly, 1978, Mrs Millicent DAVIES (ante), previously wife of late Trevor Waterson, and elder da of late Geoffrey Watt:—
(By 1st *m*) Michael James Patrick (Pilgrim Cottage, Morchard Bishop, Devon), *b* 1950: *m* 1985, Mrs Prudence Jane Louise FAYERS, eldest da of late Noel Scott Unsworth, of Morchard Bishop, Devon. —— Christopher Gordon Edward, *b* 1953. —— Penelope Ann, *b* 1948: *m* 1977, Philip Henry Leigh, of 28 Great Cob, Chelmsford, Essex, and has issue living, Rosemary Ann, *b* 1980, — Alice Margaret, *b* 1983.

Issue of late Capt Hon Terence Victor Stopford, RN, 3rd and yst son of 7th Earl, *b* 1918, *d* 1998: *m* 1951, Sheila Adèle, who *d* 1994, only da of Philip Page:—
(Henry) Philip Terence (2 Ralston Rd, SW3 4DS), *b* 1953; *ed* Eton, Brunel Univ (LLB), and Virginia Univ, USA (LLM); Harkness Fellowship: *m* 1981, Michele Susan, da of Orlando Hyndman Lobo, of Bethesda, Maryland, USA, and has issue living, Philip Christian Andrew, *b* 1983, — Susannah Louise Adèle, *b* 1985, — Alexandra Frances Ileara, *b* 1991. —— Robert Edward James, *b* 1958; *ed* Pangbourne: *m* 1987, Anne Louise, da of Lt-Cmdr P. J. Patrick, of Bedford Lodge, Bourne End, and has issue living, James Charles Frederick, *b* 1996, — Louise Frances Catherine, *b* 1994. —— James Richard Hugh, *b* 1961; *ed* Pangbourne; Maj Irish Gds: *m* 1989, Michelle, yr da of Michael N. Reeves, of St Catherines, Iver, and has issue living, Milo Victor Michael, *b* 1995, — Isabella Frances, *b* 1992. —— Catherine Mary Adèle, *b* 1965.

Grandson of late Capt Hon Edward Barrington Lewis Henry Stopford, 2nd son of 5th Earl:—
Issue of late Lt-Cdr Barrington George Dashwood Stopford, RN, *b* 1889, *d* 1930: *m* 1918, Muriel Florence Mary, who *d* 1980, el da of late Rev Nathaniel Nicholas Lewarne, formerly V of Yealmpton, S Devon:—
Brian Barrington Dashwood, LVO, *b* 1923; *ed* Stowe, and Trin Coll, Camb (BA); Solicitor 1948; Solicitor to Duchy of Cornwall 1954-72; LVO 1971: *m* 1st, 1948, Alison Honor, who *d* 1986, da of late Maurice Sylvester Gibb, CBE; 2ndly, 19—, Heather Mary Sally, da of John Basil Collingwood, and has issue living (by 1st *m*), Justin Montagu Dashwood (10 Lindop Rd, Hale, Altrincham, Cheshire), *b* 1949; *ed* Salford Univ: *m* 1972, Gillian, da of Eric Heatherington, and has issue living, Jeremy Lewis Dashwood *b* 1982, Nicola Louise *b* 1979, — Yolande Honor, *b* 1951; *ed* Dartford Coll of Ed: *m* 1982, Owen Arthur Reynolds, of Lower Ellenden Farm, Water Lane, Hawkhurst, Kent, and has issue living, Thomas *b* 1984, Oliver *b* 1986. *Residence* – 122 High St, Lewes, Sussex. *Club* – English-Speaking Union.

Grandchildren of late George Christian Noel Stopford (infra):—
Issue of late Edward Montagu Stopford, *b* 1917, *d* 1988: *m* 1941, Dora (Innisfail, Queensland, Australia), da of late T. W. Flood, of Warwick, Qld:—
Peter (PO Box 59, Innisfail 4860, Queensland, Australia), *b* 1942: *m* 1965, Lorraine Dawn, da of Percy Dinman Day, of Atherton, Qld, and has issue living, Mark Peter, *b* 1968, — Tracey Dawn, *b* 1966. —— Robin, *b* 1946. —— Wendy, *b* 1944: *m* 1965, Allan David Stephens, of Toowoomba, Qld, and has issue living, David Allan, *b* 1966, — Peter Brian, *b* 1974, — Christine Louise, *b* 1968.

Granddaughter of late Hon George Frederick William Stopford, 3rd son of 5th Earl:—
Issue of late George Christian Noel Stopford, *b* 1891, *d* 1969: *m* 1915, Mary Georgina, who *d* 1967, da of late Rev Canon Edward Newland, of Buncara, co Donegal:—
Claire, *b* 1922: *m* 1948, James Gordon McIlwraith, who *d* 1984, and has issue living, James Edward, *b* 1955: *m* 1990, Claire Elizabeth Davis, and has issue living, Jesse (a son) *b* 1989, — Duncan George, *b* 1956: *m* 1986, Yoshiko Hiramatsu, and has issue living, Ria Asuka *b* 1987, Ellie *b* 1989, — Margaret Anne (known as Annie Stopford), *b* 1951: *m* 1st, 1975, Dennis Morrison, who *d* 19—; 2ndly, 1989, Ayi Mensah, of Ghana, and has issue living (by 2nd *m*), Nii-ayitey (a son) *b* 1990, — Janet Claire, *b* 1953: *m* 1973, Roger O'Shannessy, and has issue living, Nye (a son) *b* 1974, Tristan *b* 1978, Keely (a da) *b* 1976, — Judith Pamela, *b* 1958: *m* 1977, Stuart Tutchen, and has issue living, Bradley (a son) *b* 1978, Duane (a son) *b* 1982, Shari (a da) *b* 1980. *Address* – Unit 10, Cascade Walk, 56 Burnett St, Buderim, Queensland 4556, Australia.

Grandchildren of late Rear-Adm Hon Walter George Stopford, 6th son of 4th Earl:—
Issue of late Rear-Adm Frederick Victor Stopford, CBE, *b* 1900; *d* 1982: *m* 1924, Mary Guise (Varndean House, St Leonards, Ringwood, Hants), da of Capt Frederick Charles Ulick Vernon-Wentworth, CB, RN (Guise Bt, colls):—
John Walter (Amberley, N Canterbury, NZ), *b* 1926; Capt R Canadian Armd Corps (ret): *m* 1960, Barbara, only da of Maj W. H. McHaffie, of Aberdour on Spey, and has issue living, Michael John, *b* 1966, — Susan Caroline, *b* 1961, — Jennifer Claire, *b* 1965. —— †Robin Frederick, *b* 1929: *m* 1960, Patricia Ann, who *d* 1997, el da of Lt-Col Leo Dominic Gleeson, DSO, and *d* 1996, leaving issue, Jonathan Paul Michael, *b* 1964, — Sarah Frances Ann, *b* 1969. —— Timothy Patrick (17 Allington Drive, Strood, Rochester, Kent), *b* 1935; author of *Admiralty Ships' Badges 1919-1994*. —— Catherine Jill, *b* 1939: *m* 1961, Capt (N) Garry Joseph Oman, CD, RCNR, of 17 Duncairn Drive, Toronto, Ont, Canada M9B 2P2, and has issue living, Christopher David, *b* 1966, — Catherine Mary, *b* 1964, — Elizabeth Frances Anne, *b* 1972.

Grandson of late Rev Frederick Manners Stopford, son of late Lt-Col Hon Edward Stopford, 2nd son of 3rd Earl:—
Issue of late Walter Montagu Stopford, b 1874, d 1933: m 1919, Mary Josephine, da of late Patrick O'Neill, of Enniscorthy, co Wexford:—
Lionel Frederick John, b 1921; European War 1944-5 in Welsh Gds: m 1950 (m diss 1960), Violet Eira, da of Harold Dart, of Cefn, Murch Rd, Dinas Powis, Glamorgan, and has issue living, John Martin, b 1958, — Linda Mary, b 1951, — Wendy Margaret, b 1953. Residence – 153 Fraser St, Kenilworth Johannesburg, 2190, S Africa.

Grandson of late Maj-Gen Sir Lionel Arthur Montagu Stopford, KCVO, CB, son of Adm Hon Sir Montagu Stopford, KCB, 6th son of 3rd Earl:—
Issue of late Capt Lionel Montagu Phipps Stopford, Seaforth Highlanders, b 1897, d 1985: m 1934, Sheila Frances, MBE, who d 1978, da of Gen Sir Cecil Francis Romer, GCB, KBE, CMG:—
Robert Cecil Montagu (Kintail, Hobhole Bank, Old Leake, Boston, Lincs PE22 9RX), b 1935; ed Radley: m 1958, Elizabeth Ann, da of late Alexander Krott, of Terskaya, Russia, and has issue living, Andrew Alexander Montagu (Zakres, Situ da Ribeira, S João da Boa Vista, 3420 Tabua, Portugal), b 1959, — Sara Elizabeth Fiona, b 1967.

Granddaughter of late Vice-Adm Frederick George Stopford, 4th son of Adm Robert Fanshawe Stopford, eldest son of Adm Hon Sir Robert Stopford, GCB, GCMG, 3rd son of 2nd Earl:—
Issue of late Robert Edward Wilbraham Stopford, b 1897, d 1982: m 1925, Alicia Ellen Saunders, who d 1967:—
Mona Alicia STOPFORD, b 1926; has resumed her maiden name: m 19— (m diss 19—), — Anderson, and has issue living, Robert Edward, b 1952, — Alec, b 1954, — Susan Jean STOPFORD, b 1956; assumed surname of Stopford by Court Order, — Ellen Pegeen STOPFORD, b 1960; assumed surname of Stopford by Court Order.

Grandchildren of late Col Lionel Richard STOPFORD SACKVILLE, 2nd son of late William Bruce Stopford Sackville (who assumed by Royal Licence 1870 the additional surname and arms of Sackville), 4th son of late Rev Hon Richard Bruce Stopford, 4th son of 2nd Earl:—
Issue of late Col Nigel Victor Stopford Sackville, CBE, TD, b 1901: m 1st, 1929 (m diss 1943), Beatrix Helen Constance, who d 1990, da of late Col Hercules Arthur Pakenham, CMG (see E Longford, colls): 2ndly, 1946, Lilah Mary (The Weirs, Chilton Foliat, Hungerford, Berks), da of late Capt Percy Richard Hare (see E Listowel, colls), and formerly wife of Maj George Seton Wills, R Wilts Yeo (see Wills, Bt, cr 1904):—
(By 1st m) Lionel Geoffrey STOPFORD SACKVILLE (Drayton House, Lowick, Kettering) (Clubs - White's, Pratt's), b 1932 ed Eton; Chm of Union Jack Oil plc, Lowick Manor Farms Ltd, J. Goedhuis & Co Ltd; Dir of Mercury World Mining Trust plc, Dartmoor Investment Trust plc, Pantheon International Participations plc and Can Gold Resources Inc; FCA; Late Lt Northants Yeo; former Lt 14/20 Hus, served in Libya: m 1st, 1960, Susan J., only da of late Jenkin Coles, of the Abbey, Knaresborough, Yorks; 2ndly, 1980 (m diss 1995), Hon (Mary) Teresa Pearson, el da of 3rd Viscount Cowdray, TD; 3rdly, 1997, Mrs Eleanor Mary Stoddart, el da of Lt-Col Samuel Soames, RA, of Sunningdale, Berks, and has had issue (by 1st m), Charles Lionel, b 1961: m 1992, Shona, yst da of late Donald McKinney, CBE, of Nassau, Bahamas, and of Mrs Philip Harari, of Albany, Piccadilly, W1, and has issue living, Luke Mordaunt b 1993, Ela Lucinda b 1995, Islay b 1998, — Thomas Nigel, b 1968, — Lucinda Mary, b 1963; k in a motor accident 1992, — (by 2nd m), Camilla Anne, b 1981. —— Venetia Mary (50 Vera Rd, SW6), b 1930: m 1952 (m diss 1968), Maj Benjamin Robert Chetwynd Talbot, TD, who d 1999, and has issue living, Benjamin Simon Robert, b 1956, — Victoria Mary, b 1958: m 1986, Jeremy Jennings, and has issue.

Grandchildren of late Maj Heneage Frank Stopford, 4th son of James Sydney Stopford, 5th son of Rev Hon Richard Bruce Stopford (ante):—
Issue of late Capt James Coverley Stopford, OBE, RN, b 1909, d 1985: m 1936, (Katherine) Sheila Hope, who d 1986, da of late Capt G. C. S. MacLeod, Black Watch:—
Robert Heneage (Cool Bank Cottage, Winson, Cirencester, Glos), b 1945; ed Wellington. —— Serena Margaret, b 1939: m 1964, Christopher H. M. Holmes, Fl Lt RAF, of Allergarth, Burswell Villas, Hexham, Northumberland, eldest son of W/Cdr K. E. M. Holmes, RAF, of Great Leighs, Essex, and has issue living, Andrew David, b 1965, — Richard Mark, b 1967, — Bridget Constantia, b (twin) 1967.

Issue of late Edward Kennedy Stopford, CB, b 1911, d 1983: m 1952, Patricia Iona Mary, who d 1989, da of late W. Howard Carrick, and widow of Duncan George Stewart, CMG:—
Michael John (1645 Westchester Court, Annapolis, Maryland, USA), b 1953; ed Radley, and New Coll, Oxford: m 1995, Susan Elizabeth, da of Leonard Navrat, of Wichita, Kansas, USA, and has issue living, Michael Edward b 1996.

Grandchildren of the late Capt Wyndham Horace Stopford, 5th and yst son of James Sydney Stopford (ante):—
Issue of the late Wyndham Horace Stopford, b (posthumous) 1904, d 1984: m 1st 1928, May, who d 1967, da of Col John White Craig, of Manila, Philippine Islands; 2ndly, 1968, Charlotte, da of Rev James Graham Clark, of Barrhead, Glasgow:—
(By 1st m) Neville Craig (2 Briarcliff Rd, Larchmont, NY, USA), b 1932: m 1963, (Helen) Alison, 2nd da of William Leslie Baty, of Cheviot View, Ponteland, Northumberland, and has issue living, Wyndham Leslie (200 West 15th St, New York, NY, USA), b 1965, — Angus Craig (33 Marino Av, Port Washington, NY 11050, USA), b 1967: m 1994, Jeannine Catherine, da of John Whitfield Daly, of New York, NY, and has issue living, Wyndham John b 1996. —— Craig Leeson (Marbridge Foundation, Manchaca, Texas, USA), b 1939. —— Ann, b 1935: m 1959, Michael William Frewen Jenkin, of Queen Anne House, Dukes Lane, Kensington, W8 4JL, 3rd son of the late Charles Oswald Frewen Jenkin, and has issue living, Andrew Wyndham, b 1960, — Richard Frewen, b 1962.

Grandchildren of late Cdr Robert Maurice Stopford, DSC, RN (infra):—
Issue of late Maj Michael Robert Horace Stopford, b 1921, d 1995: m 1945, Megan (The Glebe, E Morden, Dorset BH20 7DS), da of late Arthur Reyner Williams:—
Robert Michael Hastings, b 1949; ed Downside: m 1st, 1976, Jennifer, da of late Maj J. H. Walmesley-Cotham; 2ndly, 1984, Alexandra E., da of Douglas G. Hartley, and has issue living (by 2nd m), Joshua Gordon, b 1984, — Benjamin Charles, b 1986, — Zoë Megan Patience, b 1989. —— †Charles Michael Reyner, b 1950; ed Downside; Capt 9th/12th Royal Lancers (Prince of Wales's): m 1979, J. Clare (who m 2ndly, 1986, Jonathan J. Harris, of 50 Barclay Rd, SW6), yst da of late M. H. J. Villeneuve, of Byway House, Fordwich, Kent, and d 1980, as the result of a flying accident.

—— Laura Cecilia Mary, *b* 1947: *m* 1969, Capt Kenneth Andres Courtenay, RN, of Henstridge, Som, and has issue living, Edward Michael Andres, *b* 1970, —— Tamsin Mary Andres, *b* 1972. —— Teresa Megan Marguerite, *b* 1955: *m* 1st, 1975, Nigel A. S. Healey; 2ndly, 1984, Anton D. Simon, of 8 Chepstow Villas, W11 2RB, 2nd son of Arthur G. Simon, of Portsmouth, and has had issue (by 2nd *m*), Charles Stephen, *b* 1987, —— Harry Eugene, *b* and *d* 1991, —— Eugene Michael, *b* 1992, —— Fleur Megan Margaret, *b* 1995.

Grandchildren of late Lt-Col Horace Robert Stopford, only son of late Robert Stopford, 7th and yst son of Rev Hon Richard Bruce Stopford (ante):—
Issue of late Cdr Robert Maurice Stopford, DSC, RN, *b* 1890, *d* 1977: *m* 1920, Elsie, who *d* 1967, da of late Capt Francis William Lawson, Connaught Rangers:—
Stephen Robert Anthony, CB, MBE (c/o Child & Co, 1 Fleet St, EC4), *b* 1934; Maj-Gen late Scots DG; MBE (Mil) 1971, CB (Mil) 1988: *m* 1963, Vanessa, da of late Theodore Baron, of 18 Rex Place, W1. —— Rosemary Dolores, *b* 1926: *m* 1963, John Walter Mills, TD, KSS, High Sheriff of Warwicks 1959-60, who *d* 1997.

PREDECESSORS – (1) JAMES Stopford, son of late James Stopford, MP, of Courtown, MP for co Wexford 1721-7, and for Fethard 1727-58; *cr Baron Courtown*, of co Wexford (peerage of Ireland) 1758, and *Viscount Stopford* and *Earl of Courtown* (peerage of Ireland) 1762; *d* 1770; *s* by his son (2) JAMES, 2nd Earl; *cr Baron Saltersford*, of Saltersford, co Chester (peerage of Great Britain) 1796; *d* 1810; *s* by his son (3) JAMES GEORGE, KP, PC, 3rd Earl; *d* 1835; *s* by his son (4) JAMES THOMAS, 4th Earl; *b* 1794: *m* 1st, 1822, Lady Charlotte Montagu-Scott, who *d* 1828, da of the 4th Duke of Buccleuch; 2ndly, 1850, Dora, who *d* 1859, da of late Right Hon Edward Pennefather, Ch Justice of the Queen's Bench in Ireland; *d* 1858; *s* by his son (5) JAMES GEORGE HENRY, 5th Earl; *b* 1823: *m* 1846, Hon Elizabeth Frances Milles, who *d* 1894, 2nd da of 4th Baron Sondes; *d* 1914; *s* by his el son (6) JAMES WALTER MILLES, 6th Earl, *b* 1853; High Sheriff of co Wexford 1877 and of co Carlow 1878, and Lieut for co Wexford 1901: *m* 1st, 1876, Hon Catherine Elizabeth Neville, who *d* 1884, da of 4th Baron Braybrooke; 2ndly, 1886, Gertrude, who *d* 1934, da of late Gen Charles James Conway Mills, of Cardington, Beds; *d* 1933; *s* by his el son (7) JAMES RICHARD NEVILLE, OBE, 7th Earl; *b* 1877; Major Gen List; S Africa 1900-1901, European War 1915-19, Mayor of Aylesbury 1927-8, DAAG, War Office 1941-7: *m* 1905, Cicely Mary, OBE, JP, who *d* 1973, yr da of late John Arden Birch; *d* 1957; *s* by his el son (8) JAMES MONTAGU BURGOYNE, OBE, TD, 8th Earl; *b* 1908; Lt Col and Brevet Col London Irish Rifles, R Ulster Rifles; N Africa 1943 and Italy 1943-45: *m* 1st, 1934 (*m diss* 1946), Christina Margaret, da of Adm John Ewen Cameron CB, MVO, of Brunton House, Christon Bank, Northumberland; 2ndly, 1951, Patricia, da of Harry Stephen Winthrop, of Auckland, NZ; *d* 1975; *s* by his el son (9) JAMES PATRICK MONTAGU BURGOYNE WINTHROP, 9th Earl, and present peer; also Viscount Stopford, Baron Courtown, and Baron Saltersford.

COUTANCHE, BARONY OF (Coutanche) (Extinct 1973)

SON LIVING OF LIFE BARON

Jurat the Hon John Alexander Gore, OBE, *b* 1925; Lt-Cdr RNR; Lieut Bailiff and Jurat of Royal Court, Jersey; OBE (Civil) 1997: *m* 1st, 1949, Jean Veronica, who *d* 1977, da of late Alexander Thomson Dawson, of Portelet House, Jersey; 2ndly, 1978, Gillian Margaret, da of late Brig John Douglas Fellowes Fisher, CBE, of Ravenscroft, Val de la Mare, Jersey, and has issue living (by 1st *m*), Christopher John Alexander *b* 1959, Michelle Jane *b* 1953: *m* 19—, —— Lucas, Madeleine Isobel *b* 1956: *m* 19—, —— Poole. *Residence* – Clos Des Tours, St Aubin, Jersey.

Coutts, Money-, family name of Baron Latymer.

COVENTRY, EARL OF (Coventry) (Earl E 1697)

Candidly and constantly

GEORGE WILLIAM COVENTRY, 11th Earl; *b* 25 Jan 1934; *s* 1940; *ed* Eton; late 2nd Lt Gren Gds: *m* 1st, 1955 (*m diss* 1963), Marie Farquhar, da of late William Sherman Medart, of St Louis, USA; 2ndly, 1969 (*m diss* 1975), Ann, da of Frederick William James Cripps, of Bickley, Kent; 3rdly, 1980 (*m diss* 1988), Valerie Anne Birch; 4thly, 1992, Rachel Wynne, da of Jack Mason, and has had issue by 1st *m*.

Arms – Sable, a fesse ermine, between three crescents or. **Crest** – A cock gules, comb, wattles, and legs or, standing on a garb fesse-wise or. **Supporters** – Two eagles, wings expanded and inverted argent, beaked and membered or.
Seat – Earls Croome Court, Earls Croome, Worcester WR8 9DE.

SON DECEASED (*By 1st marriage*)

†Edward George William Omar (*Viscount Deerhurst*), *b* 24 Sept 1957; *d* 4 Oct 1997, in Hawaii, USA.

SISTERS LIVING

Lady Anne Donne, *b* 1922.
Lady Maria Alice COVENTRY (Levant Lodge, Earls Croome, Worcester), *b* 1931: *m* 1954 (*m diss* 1968), John Richard Lewes.

COLLATERAL BRANCHES LIVING

Issue of late Col Hon Charles John Coventry, 2nd son of 9th Earl, CB, *b* 1867, *d* 1929: *m* 1900, Lily, who *d* 1970, yr da of late Fitz Hugh Whitehouse, of Eastbourne Lodge, Newport, USA:—
FRANCIS HENRY, *b* 27 Sept 1912; *ed* Eton, and New Coll, Oxford (BA 1934); is Lt-Cdr RNVR; formerly Lieut Worcestershire Yeo (TA): *m* 1945, Yolande Lucienne, da of P. di Benedetto, of Alexandria and has issue living, Patricia Caroline Mary, *b* 1950: *m* 1st, 1969 (*m diss* 1984), Antonio Morisani; 2ndly, 1986, Raymond P. Bianchi, of Castel S Pietro, and has issue living (by 1st *m*), Gian-Marco *b* 1970. *Residence* – 6987 Caslano, Switzerland.

Issue of late Hon Sir Reginald William Coventry, KC, 4th son of 9th Earl, *b* 1869, *d* 1940: *m* 1st, 1911, Gwenllian Pascoe, who *d* 1925, da of Edward Vaughan Morgan, formerly of 22 Harrington Gardens, SW; 2ndly, 1926, Frances Constance, who *d* 1943, widow of Walter P. Jeffreys, of Cynghordy:—
(By 1st *m*) Mary Gwenllian, *b* 1912: *m* 1935, George Albert Finegan, LRCPI, LRCSI, who *d* 1965, and has issue living, Barbara Jane, *b* 1936, — Sonia Mary, *b* 1939: *m* 19—, Graham Meredith, of Keeper's Cottage, Soalwood Lane, Froxfield, Petersfield, Hants GU32 1DP. *Residence* – 274 Cooden Drive, Bexhill, Sussex.

Issue of late Hon Thomas George Coventry, yst son of 9th Earl, *b* 1885, *d* 1972: *m* 1910 (*m diss ca* 1930), Alice Ann, who *d* 1961, da of Thomas Ward, of Hasketon, Woodbridge, Suffolk:—
Victor Gerald, CD (1739-148 A St, Surrey, BC, Canada V4A 6G5), *b* 1917; Lt (QW) Cdn Militia, Sup Customs-Excise, Govt of Canada (ret): *m* 1943, Constance Hilda, da of late Henry Edward Green, of S Tottenham, N15, and has had issue, †John Stephen, *b* 1949; *d* 1972, — Angela Barbara, *b* 1944: *m* 1974, Robert Arthur Chapman, of 553 Schoolhouse, Coquitlam, BC, V3J 5P2, Canada, and has issue living, Lloyd Steven *b* 1979, Susan Teresa *b* 1977.

Granddaughter of late Hon Thomas George Coventry (*ante*):—
Issue of late Flight-Lieut Robert George Coventry, RAF, *b* 1913, *ka* 1940: *m* 1936, Olga, who *d* 1985, only da of late John Henry Warhurst:—
(Monica) Anne (c/o National Westminster Bank, 27 Cannon St, EC4), *b* 1939: *m* 1967, James Stuart Underhill.

Granddaughter of late Henry Robert Beauclerk Coventry, only son of late Capt Henry Amelius Beauclerk Coventry, son of late Hon Henry Amelius Coventry, 2nd son of 8th Earl:—
Issue of late Capt Arthur Beauclerk Coventry, OBE, DSC, RN, *b* 1900, *d* 1971: *m* 1928, Muriel Ethel Francis, who *d* 1986, da of late Hugh B. Craven, of Wheathills House, Kirk Langley, Derbys:—
Auriol Susan, *b* 1932: *m* 1966, Wallace McMillan Reid, of 36 Peter's Sq, W6, and has issue living, Caspar James Beauclerk, *b* 1971, — Frances Elizabeth, *b* 1967.

Grandson of late Gilbert William Coventry (*infra*):—
Issue of late Cdr Cecil Dick Bluett Coventry, DSC, RD, RNR, *b* 1905, *d* 1952: *m* 1939, Anne Josephine Hale, who *d* 1974, da of late Maj H. J. Sherwood, RE:—
George William (21 Malvern Rd, Hampton, Middx), *b* 1939; *ed* Prince of Wales Sch, Nairobi: *m* 1965, Gillian Frances, da of late Frank W. R. Randall, of Wyke Regis, Weymouth, Dorset, and has issue living, Diana Elizabeth Sherwood, *b* 1980.

Grandchildren of late Cdr Cecil Dick Bluett Coventry, DSC, RD, RNR (*ante*):—

Issue of late Peter Harold Sherwood Coventry, *b* 1941, *d* 1985: *m* 1969, Kay Sandra (Rebecca's Cottage, Sampford Courtenay, Okehampton, Devon EX20 2SZ), da of late Lt-Cdr Roy S. Baker-Falkner:—
David Duncan Sherwood, *b* 1973. —— Lynn Karen Sherwood, *b* 1970.

Grandchildren of late Gilbert William Coventry (infra):—
Issue of late Arthur John Clifford Coventry, *b* 1909, *d* 1965: *m* 1st, 1937 (*m diss* 1947), Dulcie Alice Saxon; 2ndly, 1952, Margaret Nancy, who *d* 1986, only da of W. E. Gell, of Gosford, NSW:—
(By 1st *m*) Gilbert John Henry (15 Queen St, Guildford, NSW 2161, Australia), *b* 1939: *m* 1961, Patricia Anne, da of Reginald Charles Deeley, of Balgowaie, NSW, and has issue living, Wesley John, *b* 1965, — Anne Maree, *b* 1962: *m* 1993, Xavier Hogan, and has issue living, Nicholas *b* 1996, — Robyne Michelle, *b* 1971; has issue living, Justin Alan COVENTRY *b* 1992. —— †Geoffrey Robert, *b* 1941: *m* 1964, Lynette, da of Patrick Salmon, of Corrimal, NSW, and *d* 1964. —— Margaret Elaine, *b* 1943: *m* 1964, Barrie Robert Stanford, of 10 Jennifer Crescent, Thirroul, NSW 2515, Australia, and has issue living, Cheryn Lee, *b* 1968: *m* 1st, 1992 (*m diss* 1994), Charles Goudman; 2ndly, 1996, David Craig Porter, — Karlyn Leslie, *b* 1970: *m* 1992, Sean Cameron Johns, and has issue living, Matheson Sean *b* 1998, Alexandra Lee *b* 1995. —— (By 2nd *m*) Richard William (29 Munro Rd, Queanbeyan, NSW 2620, Australia), *b* 1953: *m* 1st, 19—, —; 2ndly, 1984, Carolyn, da of William John Dray, of 11-13 Frederick St, Marburg, Qld, and has issue living (by 1st *m*), Richard John, *b* 1972, — (by 2nd *m*), Sarah Margaret, *b* 1986. —— Elizabeth Nancy, *b* 1955: *m* 1986, Colin Hickey, of 9 Marston Close, Macarthur, ACT 2905, Australia; has issue living, Penelope Lee COVENTRY, *b* 1973.

Grandchildren of late William George Coventry, eldest son of late Hon William James Coventry, 4th son of 7th Earl:—
Issue of late Gilbert William Coventry, *b* 1868; *d* 1947: *m* 1st, 1902, Georgina Blanche, who *d* 1922, da of late Major William H. P. G. Bluett (formerly Lincolnshire Regt), of Paignton; 2ndly, 1923, Margaret Charlotte, who *d* 1981, widow of Major G. D'Arcy Elliott-Cooper:—
(By 1st *m*) (Gilbert) Hugo Gordon (Fermoy Cottage, Vermont Drive, E Preston, Sussex), *b* 1911; formerly Lt-Cdr R Indian Navy; sometime Rubber Planter; formerly Manager of Eng Kee Kundong Estates, Tangkah, Johore, Malaysia: *m* 1st, 1948 (*m diss* 1953), Alice, widow of Frank Tabrum; 2ndly, 1959, Mary, who *d* 1991, widow of Gordon Graham, of Mile End House, Aberdeen. —— (By 2nd *m*) Anne, *b* 1925: *m* 1951, Stanley A. Peter Keevil, and has issue living, Sarah Anne, *b* 1952: *m* 1975, Paul Kane, of Three Oaks, 65 Worthing Rd, Horsham, Sussex, — Charlotte Fiona, *b* 1956: *m* 1990, Anthony Ferens, of Château de Béysserat, Monségur, 33580 Gironde, France. *Residence* – The Barn, W Ogwell, Newton Abbot, Devon.

Grandchildren of late Rev Henry William Coventry, 2nd son of Hon William James Coventry (ante):—
Issue of late Fulwar Cecil Ashton Coventry, OBE, *b* 1874, *d* 1944: *m* 1917, Lorna Mary, who *d* 1965, da of late Capt Peregrine H. T. Fellowes, Ch Constable of Hants:—
Digby Colquitt (Norris Castle, E Cowes, I of Wight), *b* 1919; 1939-45 War (despatches, Chevalier of Order of Leopold with palm, Belgian Croix de Guerre with palm): *m* 1946, Marina, only da of Wilhelm Georg Viktor von Wahl, and formerly wife of Willie Goss, and has issue living, Sebastian, *b* 1946: *m* 1965, Helene Kozlow, of Paris, and has issue living, Adrian *b* 1967: *m* 1991, Sharon Elizabeth, da of Ivan Richard Leslie Jackman (and has issue living, Adam *b* 1996, Natalia *b* 1994), Alexandra *b* 1966: *m* 1994, Steven Douglas Price (and has issue living, Christian Coventry *b* 1997), Christine *b* 1971: *m* 1994, Denys Clément (and has issue living, Sarah *b* 1996), Catherine *b* 1976, — Mark, *b* 1952, — Elizabeth, *b* 1947: *m* 1st, 1967, Henry J. C. Pauwels; 2ndly, 19—, Patrick Corbett, and has issue living (by 1st *m*), Catherine I. C. *b* 19—: *m* 1995, Karim R. M. Derrough (and has issue living, Gregoire Malik Digby *b* 1996), — Xenia (60 Wesley Av, Park Royal, NW10 7BN), *b* 1949: *m* 1st, 1969, Richard Aubrey Cox; 2ndly, 1981, Christin William Gillan, and has issue living. —— Lorna Peggy Maria (32A St Catherine's Way, Gorleston, Gt Yarmouth, Norfolk NR31 7QB), *b* 1922.

Grandchildren of late Harry Coventry, eldest son of late Henry Halford Coventry, CE, yst son of late Frederick Coventry, eldest son of late Hon John Coventry, 2nd son of 6th Earl:—
Issue of late St John Coventry, *b* 1901, *d* 1963: *m* 1930, Caroline Gertrude, who *d* 1993, da of John David Hocking:—
Henry John (Smithfield Rd, Ashburton, NZ), *b* 1932; BCA Victoria; Sqdn-Ldr RNAZF; Queen's Commendation 1964: *m* 1st, 1958, Rev Frances Winifred, da of Marcus Davenport Clarke; 2ndly, 1991, Frances Anne, da of William Carl Olsen; 3rdly, 1997, Jennie Lynn, da of Andre Louis Rieper, and has issue living (by 1st *m*), Simon St John, *b* 1963: *m* 1991, Esther Ruth, da of Edward Alan Ashby, and has issue living, David Henry St John *b* 1996, Danielle Francie Ruth *b* 1994, — David Henry Halford, *b* 1969, — Rosalyn Barbara, *b* 1959; BA Victoria: *m* 1989, Rev Dr Uili Feleterika Nokise, and has issue living, Tualagi Christopher Pepe *b* 1989, Fetuao O Le Malama St David Henry *b* 1994, Samoana Lilia Kiwi *b* 1991, — Adrienne Claire, *h* 1960: *m* 1988, Niel Douglas Brown, — Anna Louise *b* 1967; BA Canterbury. —— Roger Michael (Merrivale, Battersea Line, Greytown, NZ), *b* 1934; Asso of RSH: *m* 1961, Margaret Ann Cooke, and has issue living, Geoffrey Alan, *b* 1969: *m* 1992, Laurence, da of Martial Henri Placide Lamy, of France, and has issue living, David *b* 1995, Audrey *b* 1993, — Jennifer Beryl, *b* 1965: *m* 1988, Bill Biber, — Sylvia Ann, *b* 1967: *m* 1993, Seck Lok Lee, of Singapore, — Marilyn Gay, *b* 1968: *m* 1991, Robin Griffith. —— Alan Francis (46 Reesville Rd, Maleny, Qld 4552, Aust), *b* 1940; a Radio Technician: *m* 1st, 1961 (*m diss* 1972), Patrina Rathbride, da of Patrick Francis Dwan; 2ndly, 1972, Alison Leslie, da of Dallas Evans, and has issue living (by 1st *m*), Charles Raymond St John, *b* 1963: *m* 19—, Pauline Wendy Dyer, and has issue living, Sean James St John *b* 1985, Benjamin St John *b* 1987, Alyson Patrina *b* 1983, — Andrew Patrick Francis, *b* 1964: *m* 1988, Irene Florence, da of David Alan Parr, and has issue living, Christian Francis Richard *b* 1994, Grace Elizabeth Katherine *b* 1992, — Charmaine Louise, *b* 1961: *m* 19—, Andrew Bryan Duxfield, and has issue living, Michael Thomas *b* 1984, Timothy Edward *b* 1986, Amy Georgiana *b* 1988, — (by 2nd *m*) Richard Alan Penrose, *b* 1971, — Katherine Margaret, *b* 1973. —— Bernadine Helen Mary, *b* 1945: *m* 1964, Enda Francis McBride, of 27 Tennyson St, Trentham, Upper Hutt, NZ, and has issue living, Lenore Frances, *b* 1965: *m* 1989, Michael Cunningham, — Joanna Claire, *b* 1967: *m* 1988, Robert Stuart Nicol.

Issue of late Frederick Halford Coventry, *b* 1905, *d* 1997: *m* 1940, Dolores Rosamund Christine, who *d* 1994, yr da of late Léon Dominic Ashton, of Cairo, Egypt:—
Edward Bernard Halford St John (103 Castelnau, SW13 9EL), *b* 1943; BSc London. —— Elizabeth Mary Hephzibah, *b* 1947; Dip AD: *m* 1st, 1968 (*m diss* 1980), Terence Carville; 2ndly, (Jan) 1981, John Henry Brierley, of 125 Ipswich Rd, Woodbridge, Suffolk IP12 4BY, and has issue living (by 2nd *m*), Alexandra Frances Mary, *b* (Dec) 1981.

Granddaughters of late John Coventry (*b* 1845), eldest son of late Rev John Coventry (*b* 1819), eldest son of late John Coventry (*b* 1793) (infra):—

Issue of late John Joseph Coventry, *b* 1882, *d* 1950: *m* 1910, Margaret Camilla (who *d* 1958, having *m* 2ndly, 1955, Adrian Leonard Moreton, MS, FRCS, of Wilton House, Hungerford, Berks), da of Carlyle Henry Hayes Macartney, formerly of Foxhold, Newbury:—

Catherine Margaret Mary, *b* 1915: *m* 1936, Herbert Alan Jones, who *d* 1998, and has issue living, Charles Alan (32 Cromer Villas Rd, SW18 1PN), *b* 1937: *m* 1961, Margaret Elizabeth Cowper, and has issue living, Timothy Charles *b* 1963, Nicholas Alan *b* 1967, Patricia Margaret *b* 1965, — Celia Margaret, *b* 1948. ⸺ Dorothea Olivia, *b* 1918: *m* 1937 (*m diss* 1952), Adrian Charles Enthoven, and has issue living, Stephen Andrew (15 Ladbroke Sq, W11 3NA), *b* 1939: *m* 1965, Fiona Valerie Maclean, and has issue living, Thomas Samuel Donald *b* 1974, John Henry William *b* 1978, — John Christopher, *b* 1945: *m* 1968, Valerie Kathleen Roberts, and has issue living, Andrew James *b* 1975, Alexandra Louise *b* 1973.

Grandson of late Bernard Seton Coventry, 2nd son of late John Coventry (*b* 1845) (ante):—

Issue of late Anthony James Seton Coventry, *b* 1913, *d* 1955: *m* 1942, Mollie Rosina (9 Parish Court, Lymington, Hants), who *m* 2ndly, 1961, Harold J. Hayles, who *d* 1972, da of J. Grummett, of St Abbs Head, Coldingham, Berwickshire:—

John James Seton, *b* 1955: *m* 1993, Naomi Elizabeth Margaret, only da of late J. S. Jones, of Dawlish, Devon, and has issue living, Isobelle Florence Elisabeth, *b* 1997. *Residence* – Chapel House, Tregawne, nr Withiel, Bodmin, Cornwall PL30 5NR. ⸺ The late Anthony James Seton Coventry also had an adopted da, Margaret Elizabeth, *b* 1946: *m* 1978, Nigel James Brooks, of Shilton House, Pitmore Lane, Lymington, Hants, son of late Lt-Cdr F. L. Brooks, MBE, RD, RN, of Lymington, Hants, and has issue living, Richard John, *b* 1981, — Anthony James, *b* 1982, — Nicola Kate, *b* 1985.

Granddaughter of late John Coventry (*b* 1793), 2nd son of late Hon John Coventry, 2nd son of 6th Earl:—

Issue of late Francis Martin Coventry, *b* 1863, *d* 1917: *m* 1896, Amy Maud, who *d* 1949, da of Henry W. J. Hill, formerly of 17 Cleveland Square, W, and Turcoliah, Bengal:—

Catherine Nora, *b* 1906: *m* 1926, Hubert de Burgh Williams, who *d* 1949, and has issue living, Evan John, *b* 1926: *m* 1952, Janet, da of Boyd Hill, of Ross-on-Wye, and has issue living, Alan Christopher *b* 1956, Sheila Anne *b* 1954, — Hubert Michael, *b* 1927. *Residence* – 71 Castle Rd, Colchester, Essex CO1 1UN.

Grandchildren of late Gilbert Walter Coventry, 4th son of late Thomas William Coventry, only son of late Hon Thomas William Coventry, 3rd son of 6th Earl:—

Issue of late Francis Gilbert Coventry, *b* 1892, *d* 1960: *m* 1929, Clara Dorothy, who *d* 1970, da of late Robert Charles Brown:—

Noel, *b* 1933: *m* 1960, Nola Elsie May, da of Robert Archibald Lindsay. *Residence* – 72 Station Rd, Paeroa, New Zealand. ⸺ Francis Henry, *b* 1934: *m* 1961, Shirley Ann, da of late Thomas Henry Lionel Turner.

Issue of late Arthur Roger Coventry, *b* 1894, *d* 1975: *m* 1938, Alma Rata Williams, who *d* 1980:—

Bevan R...... (92b Halifax St East, Nelson, NZ), *b* 1944: *m* 1st, 1964 (*m diss* 1976), ...; 2ndly, 1986, Annetta (Sally) Haul Shilling, and has issue living (by 1st *m*), Richard John (now known as Wolff), *b* 19—, — Daniel Martin (now known as Wolff), *b* 19—, — (by 2nd *m*), Lindsay Ross, *b* 1988, — Hayden Douglass, *b* 1992, — Trent Gideon, *b* 1994, — Blair Ralph, *b* 1997, — Kimberley Joy, *b* 1990. ⸺ Margaret, *b* 1938. ⸺ Shirley, *b* 1940. ⸺ Adle, *b* 1944.

PREDECESSORS – (1) *Sir* THOMAS Coventry, KB (whose ancestor John Coventry was Lord Mayor of London 1426), Recorder of London 1615, Solicitor and Attorney-Gen 1616, and Lord Keeper of the Great Seal 1625; *cr Baron Coventry*, of Aylesborough, co Worcester (peerage of England) 1628; *d* 1640; *s* by his son (2) THOMAS, 2nd Baron; *d* 1661; *s* by his son (3) GEORGE, 3rd Baron; *s* by son (4) JOHN, 4th Baron; *d* unmarried 1687; *s* by his uncle (5) THOMAS, 5th Baron, 2nd son of 2nd Baron; *cr Viscount Deerhurst* and *Earl of Coventry* (peerage of England) 1697, with limitation to the grandson of Walter, yst brother of 1st Baron; *d* 1699; *s* by his son (6) THOMAS, 2nd Earl; *d* 1710; *s* by his son (7) THOMAS, 3rd Earl *d* a minor 1712; *s* by his uncle (8) GILBERT, 4th Earl, 2nd son of 1st Earl; *dsp* 1719, when the Barony became extinct, and the other honours reverted to his kinsman (9) WILLIAM, PC, 5th Earl, grandson of Walter Coventry (ante); successively a Clerk of the Green Cloth, MP for Bridport, and Lord-Lieut of Worcestershire; *d* 1751; *s* by his son (10) GEORGE WILLIAM, 6th Earl, *d* 1809; *s* by son (11) GEORGE WILLIAM, 7th Earl, Recorder of Worcester and High Steward of Tewkesbury; *d* 1831; *s* by his son (12) GEORGE WILLIAM, 8th Earl; Lord-Lieut of Worcestershire; *d* 1843; *s* by his grandson (13) GEORGE WILLIAM, PC (son of George William, Viscount Deerhurst, el son of 8th Earl), 9th Earl *b* 1838; Capt and Gold Stick of Corps of Gentlemen at Arms 1877-80 and 1880-85, Master of the Buckhounds 1886-92 and 1895-1890, and Lord-Lieut of Worcestershire 1891-1903: *m* 1865, Blanche, who *d* 1930, da of 2nd Earl of Craven, *d* 1930; *s* by his grandson (14) GEORGE WILLIAM REGINALD VICTOR (son of late George William, Viscount Deerhurst, el son of 9th Earl), 10th Earl, *b* 1900: *m* 1921, Hon Nesta Donne Philipps (who *d* 1997, having *m* 2ndly, 1953, Major Terrance Vincent Fisher-Hoch), da of 1st Baron Kylsant (ext); *ka* 1940; *s* by his only son (15) GEORGE WILLIAM, 11th Earl and present peer, also Viscount Deerhurst.

COWDRAY, VISCOUNT (Pearson) (Viscount UK 1917, Bt UK 1894)

MICHAEL ORLANDO WEETMAN PEARSON, 4th Viscount, and 4th Baronet; *b* 17 June 1944; *s* 1995; *ed* Gordonstoun: *m* 1st, 1977 (*m diss* 1984), Ellen (Fritzi), da of late Hermann Erhardt, of Munich; 2ndly, 1987, Marina Rose, 2nd da of John Howard Cordle, of Malmesbury House, The Close, Salisbury, Wilts (*see* V Powerscourt, colls, 1985 Edn), and has issue by 2nd *m*.

𝕬rms – Per fesse indented gules and or, in chief two suns in splendour and in base a demi-gryphon couped, all counter-changed. 𝕮rest – In front of a demi-gryphon gules holding between its claws a millstone proper thereon a mill-rind sable, a sun in splendour. 𝕾upporters – *Dexter*, a diver holding in his exterior hand his helmet; *sinister* a Mexican peon; both proper.
Seat – Cowdray Park, Midhurst, W Sussex GU29 0AY.

SONS LIVING (*By 2nd marriage*)

Hon PEREGRINE JOHN DICKINSON, *b* 27 Oct 1994.
Hon Montague Orlando William, *b* 1997.

DAUGHTERS LIVING (*By 2nd marriage*)

Hon Eliza Anne Venetia, *b* 1988.
Hon Emily Jane Marina, *b* 1989.
Hon Catrina Sophie Lavinia, *b* 1991.

THE FOURTH VISCOUNT ALSO HAS ISSUE (*by Barbara Page*)

Sebastian William Orlando PEARSON, *b* 1970.

HALF-BROTHER LIVING

Hon Charles Anthony, *b* 1956; *ed* Harrow: *m* 1992, Baroness Benedicte (Lila) Blixen-Finecke, da of Ifver Iuul, of Fyn, Denmark, and of Mrs Gerald Barry, of Cookham, Berks, and has issue living, George Frederick, *b* 1995, — Carinthia Alexandra, *b* 1993. *Residences* – 31 Jubilee Place, SW3; Dunecht House, Dunecht, Skene, Aberdeenshire AB32 7DD.

SISTERS LIVING

Hon Mary Teresa, *b* 1940: *m* 1980 (*m diss* 1995), as his 2nd wife, Lionel Geoffrey Stopford Sackville, and has issue (*see* E Courtown, colls). *Residence* – Idbury House, Idbury, Chipping Norton, Oxon OX7 6RU.

Hon (Liza) Jane, *b* 1942: *m* 1967, Malcolm MacNaughton, and has issue living, Justin John, *b* 1972, — Natasha Anne, *b* 1969. *Residence* – Old Law House, 395 Miramontes Rd, Woodside, Calif 94062, USA.

HALF-SISTERS LIVING

Hon Lucy, *b* 1954: *m* 1st, 1972 (*m diss* 1978), Luis Hector Juan Sosa Basualdo, of Buenos Aires; 2ndly, 1988, Charles Torquil de Montalt Fraser, late The Life Guards, elder son of Maj Michael Quintin Fraser, late 7th Hussars (*see* V Molesworth, colls, 1958 Edn), and has issue living (by 1st *m*), Rupert Peregrine PEARSON, *b* 1976, — Charlotte PEARSON, *b* 1974, — (by 2nd *m*) Emerald Chloe, *b* 1989, — Iona Violet, *b* 1991, — Iolanthe Maude, *b* 1993, — Nairne Constance, *b* 1995. *Residence* – Blackdown Park, Lurgashall, Petworth, W Sussex.

Hon Rosanna, *b* 1959: *m* 1988, Palma Taylor, of Jamaica, and has issue living, Annie Glennah, *b* 1990, — Dora Georgiana Joan, *b* 1994. *Address* – PO Box 11, Green Island, Hanover, Jamaica.

AUNT LIVING (*daughter of 2nd Viscount*)

Hon (Helena) Daphne, *b* 1918: *m* 1939, Lt-Col John Lakin, TD, late Warwickshire Yeo, who *d* 1989, and has issue (*see* Lakin, Bt colls).

MOTHER LIVING

Lady Anne Pamela Bridgeman (*Lady Anne Cowdray*), da of 5th Earl of Bradford: *m* 1939 (*m diss* 1950), as his 1st wife, the 3rd Viscount Cowdray, who *d* 1995. *Residence* – Broadleas, Devizes, Wilts.

ELIZABETH GEORGIANA MATHER (*Elizabeth, Viscountess Cowdray*), 2nd da of Sir Anthony Henry Mather Mather-Jackson, 6th Bt (*cr* 1869): *m* 1953, as his 2nd wife, the 3rd Viscount Cowdray, who *d* 1995. *Residence* – Orchard House, Easebourne St, Midhurst, W Sussex.

COLLATERAL BRANCHES LIVING

Issue of late Hon (Bernard) Clive Pearson, 2nd son of 1st Viscount, *b* 1887, *d* 1965: *m* 1915, Hon Alicia Mary Dorothea Knatchbull-Hugessen, who *d* 1974, da of 1st Baron Brabourne:—
Elisabeth Dione (*Baroness Gibson*), *b* 1920: *m* 1945, Baron Gibson (Life Baron), of Penn's Rocks, Groombridge, Sussex.

Issue of late Hon Francis Geoffrey Pearson, 3rd son of 1st Viscount, *b* 1891, *ka* 1914: *m* 1909, Ethel Elizabeth PEARSON (who *m* 2ndly, 1918 (*m diss* 1926), Air-Commodore Henry John Francis Hunter, CBE, MC, RAF (B Dormer), and *d* 1982, having resumed the surname of Pearson 1928), da of John Lewis, of Hove:—
Joan Cinetta, *b* 1912: *m* 1932, William Antony Acton, who *d* 1993, and has issue living, Caroline Jane (*Lady Dawson*) (11 Burton Court, Franklin's Row, SW3), *b* 1933: *m* 1955, Maj Sir Hugh Halliday Trevor Dawson, 3rd Bt (*cr* 1920), late Scots Gds, who *d* 1983. *Address* – Post Box 31, Poste Restante, Corfu, Greece.

PREDECESSORS – **(1)** *Right Hon Sir* WEETMAN DICKINSON Pearson, GCVO, PC, son of late George Pearson, of Brickendonbury, Hertford; *b* 1856; was Pres of the firm of S Pearson & Son Ltd, of Westminster, SW, and High Steward of Colchester 1897-1927; Pres of Air Board Jan to Nov 1917; MP for Colchester (Lib) 1895 to 1910; Lord Rector of Aberdeen Univ 1918-21; Hon Freeman of Aberdeen and Colchester; *cr* a *Baronet* 1894, *Baron Cowdray*, of Midhurst, co Sussex (peerage of United Kingdom) 1910, and *Viscount Cowdray*, of Cowdray, Sussex (peerage of United Kingdom) 1917: *m* 1881, Annie, GBE, who *d* 1932, da of late Sir John Cass, of Bradford, Yorkshire; *d* 1927; *s* by his son **(2)** WEETMAN HAROLD MILLER, 2nd Viscount, *b* 1882; MP for N-E or Eye, Div of Suffolk (Lib) 1906-18: *m* 1905, Agnes Beryl, who *d* 1948, da of late Lord Edward Spencer-Churchill; *d* 1933; *s* by his only son **(3)** WEETMAN JOHN CHURCHILL, TD, 3rd Viscount, *b* 1910; Capt 98th (Surrey and Sussex) Field Regt RA (TA); European War 1939-40 (severely wounded); Parl Private Sec to Under-Sec of State for Air 1941-42; Chm S. Pearson & Son Ltd 1954-77, Pres Pearson plc: *m* 1st, 1939 (*m diss* 1950), Lady Anne Pamela Bridgeman, da of 5th Earl of Bradford; 2ndly, 1953, Elizabeth Georgiana Mather, 2nd da of Sir Anthony Henry Mather Mather-Jackson, 6th Bt (*cr* 1869); *d* 1995; *s* by his elder son **(4)** MICHAEL ORLANDO WEETMAN, 4th Viscount and present peer; also Baron Cowdray.

Cowdrey, family name of Lady Herries of Terregles.

COWDREY OF TONBRIDGE, BARON (Cowdrey) (Life Baron 1997)

(MICHAEL) COLIN COWDREY, CBE, son of late Ernest Arthur Cowdrey, of Banglore, India; *b* 24 Dec 1932; *ed* Tonbridge, and BNC, Oxford; former cricketer; Capt Kent CCC 1957-71 (awarded county cap 1951); 114 England test caps 1954-75 (Capt 23 times); scored 107 centuries in first class cricket (22 in test matches); conslt Barclays Bank plc SE Region; Memb Cttee MCC (Pres 1986-87); Chm Internat Cricket Cncl 1989-93; Pres The Lord's Taverners 1995, 1996 and 1997; Freeman of the City of London 1962; Memb Court of Assistants, Worshipful Co of Skinners (Master 1986); author of books on cricket; *cr* CBE 1970, Kt 1992, and *Baron Cowdrey of Tonbridge*, of Tonbridge, co Kent (Life Baron) 1997: *m* 1st, 1956 (*m diss* 1985), Penelope Susan, da of late (Cecil) Stuart Chiesman, of Calderwood, Chislehurst, Kent; 2ndly, 1985, Lady Anne Elizabeth Fitzalan Howard (*Lady Herries of Terregles* in her own right), eldest da of 16th Duke of Norfolk, KG, GCVO, GBE, TD, PC, and has issue by 1st *m*.

Arms – ......
Residence – Angmering Park, Littlehampton, W Sussex BN16 4EX. *Clubs* – Boodle's, MCC.

SONS LIVING *(By 1st marriage)*

Hon Christopher Stuart, *b* 1957; *ed* Tonbridge; professional cricketer: *m* 1988, Christel Margareta, da of Carl-Johan Arne Holste-Sande, of Sweden, and has issue living, Fabian Kruuse, *b* 1993, — Julius Lindahl, *b* (twin) 1993.
Hon Jeremy Colin, *b* 1960; *ed* Tonbridge; stockbroker, partner Cazenove & Co: *m* 1989, Philippa Telford, and has issue living, Robert, *b* 1990, — Charles, *b* 1993, — Kate, *b* (twin) 1990, — Lara Elizabeth, *b* 1998.
Hon Graham Robert, *b* 1964; *ed* Tonbridge; professional cricketer: *m* 1993, Maxine, da of late Terence Juster and Mrs Ann Jones, of Leamington Spa, Warwickshire.

DAUGHTER LIVING *(By 1st marriage)*

Hon Carolyn Susan, *b* 1961: *m* 19—, Alastair Keith, son of ...... Keith, of ......, and has issue living, James, *b* 1992, — Lucy, *b* 1994.

COWLEY, EARL (Wellesley) (Earl UK 1857)

Moreover, one thing is necessary

GARRET GRAHAM WELLESLEY, 7th Earl; *b* 30 July 1934; *s* 1975; *ed* Univ of S California (BS), and Harvard Univ (MBA); US Army Counter-Intelligence Corps, France 1957-60; Investment Analyst, Wells Fargo Bank, San Francisco 1962-64, Investment Counsel Dodger Cox 1964-66, Research Dir, Wells Fargo Bank 1966-67, Vice-Pres, Investment Council, Thorndike, Doran, Paine & Lewis, Los Angeles 1967-69; Sr Vice-Pres (Dir securities, real estate and acquisitions), Shareholders Capital Corpn, Los Angeles 1969-74; Sr Vice-Pres (Investment Mgr), Bank of America, San Francisco 1974-78; Gp Vice-Pres (Man Dir), Internat Investment Management Service, Bank of America, London 1978-85, Ch Investment Offr (Private Banking Div), Bank of America, London 1978-85: Dir Bank of America Internat Ltd 1978-83, etc; Sr Inv Partner, Thos. R. Miller & Son (Bermuda) since 1990; Member Assocn of Conservative Peers: *m* 1st, 1960 (*m diss* 1967), Elizabeth Suzanne, da of late Haynes Lennon, of S Carolina; 2ndly, 1968 (*m diss* 1981), Isabelle O'Bready, of Sherbrooke, Quebec, Canada; 3rdly, 1981, Paige Deming, of Reno, Nevada, USA, and has issue by 1st *m*.

𝕬rms – Quarterly: 1st and 4th gules, a cross argent, between twenty plates, five in each quarter saltirewise, *Wellesley*; 2nd and 3rd or, a lion rampant gules, ducally gorged gold, *Cowley*. 𝕮rest – Out of a ducal coronet or, a demi-lion rampant gules, holding a spear erect proper, and thereon flowing a pennon argent, charged with the cross of St George. 𝕾upporters – Two lions, gules, ducally gorged and chained or, and charged on the shoulder with an annulet for difference.
Address – c/o House of Lords, SW1A 0PW. *Clubs* – Brooks's, Philippics, Harvard.

SON LIVING *(By 1st marriage)*

Hon GARRET GRAHAM (*Viscount Dangan*), *b* 30 March 1965: *m* 1990, Claire L., only da of Peter W. Brighton, of Stow Bridge, Norfolk, and has issue:-

SON LIVING — *Hon* Henry Arthur Peter, *b* 3 Dec 1991.
DAUGHTER LIVING — *Hon* Natasha Rose, *b* 1994.

Residence – Ashbourne Manor, High St, Widford, Herts SG12 8SZ.

DAUGHTER LIVING *(By 1st marriage)*

Lady Tara Lennon, *b* 1962.

BROTHER LIVING

Hon Brian Timothy, *b* 1938; *ed* Arizona State Coll, Denver Univ, Colorado, and Nevada Univ (BS); Internat Consultant KPMG Peat Marwick: *m* 1st, 1961 (*m diss* 1964), Patricia Tribbey; 2ndly 1966 (*m diss* 1980), Karen Elizabeth Bradbury, of Reno, Nevada, USA; 3rdly, 1988, Katherine Samaniego, of New Mexico, USA. *Address* – PO Box 70904, Reno, Nevada, USA 89570-0904.

SISTER LIVING

Lady Colleen, *b* 1925: *m* 1945, Paul A. Hanlon, MD, late Capt US Army, and has issue living, Paul Christian, *b* 1946, — Gavin Edward, *b* 1948, — Christopher Peter, *b* 1951, — Timothy Patrick, *b* 1955, — Richard Francis, *b* 1957, — Colleen Patricia, *b* 1958, — Jennifer Mary, *b* 1960. *Residence* – ....

DAUGHTERS LIVING OF SIXTH EARL

Lady Alexia Anne Elizabeth, *b* 1973.
Lady Caroline Maria Frances *b* (*posthumous*), 1976.

WIDOW LIVING OF SON OF THIRD EARL

Valerie Rose (Doynton House, Doynton, nr Bristol), 2nd da of late Christian Ernest Pitman, CBE, of Doynton House, Doynton, nr Bristol: *m* 1969, as his 4th wife, Hon Henry Gerald Valerian Francis Wellesley, 2nd son of 3rd Earl, who *d* 1981, and has issue (*see* colls infra).

MOTHER LIVING OF SIXTH EARL

Elizabeth Anne, da of late Lt-Col Pelham Rawstorn Papillon, DSO, of Crowhurst, Sussex, and widow of Fl-Lt Stephen Alers Hankey, RAF: *m* 2ndly, 1944 (*m diss* 1950), Denis Arthur, Viscount Dangan (later the 5th Earl Cowley), who *d* 1968; 3rdly, 1953, Freeman Winslow Hill, who *d* 199—. *Address* – PO Box 119 Westport Point, MA 02791-0119, USA.

WIDOWS LIVING OF FOURTH, FIFTH AND SIXTH EARLS

MARY (ELSIE) MAY HIMES (*Elsie, Countess Cowley*), of San Francisco, California, USA: *m* 1933, the 4th Earl Cowley who *d* 1962. *Residence* – 3201 Plumas St, Reno, Nevada 89509, USA.

JANET ELIZABETH MARY, da of late Ramiah Doraswamy Aiyar, FRCS, of Ystrad, Denbigh, N Wales: *m* 1st, 1961, as his 3rd wife, the 5th Earl Cowley, who *d* 1968; 2ndly, 1976 (*m diss* 1981), Piers (Pierson John Shirley) Dixon, son of late Sir Pierson Dixon, GCMG, CB.

MARIA DELIA, yr da of late Enrique Buenaño, of Buenos Aires: *m* 1st, 1971, the 6th Earl Cowley, who *d* 1975; 2ndly, 1980, as his 2nd wife, Lt-Col Robin James Stirling Bullock-Webster, OBE, Irish Gds. *Residence* – 5 Stanhope Gdns, SW7 5RG.

COLLATERAL BRANCHES LIVING

Issue of late Hon Henry Gerald Valerian Francis Wellesley, 2nd son of 3rd Earl, *b* 1907; *d* 1981: *m* 1st, 1929 (*m diss* 1953), Sabia, da of late Edward Robert Kennedy; 2ndly, 1954 (*m diss* 1955), Nancy Joan, only da of late Bentley Collingwood Hilliam, of The White Cottage, Bank, Lyndhurst, Hants; 3rdly, 1957 (*m diss* 1969), Maria Isobel Sherlock, da of late Capt Rowland Francis Eustace, of Doric House, Bath, formerly wife (i) Capt George James Wellwood Moncreiffe, and (ii) Cmdr John Bremer Richards Horne, DSC, RN, and widow of Lt Robert Charles Dundas; 4thly, 1969, Valerie Rose (Doynton House, Doynton, nr Bristol), 2nd da of late Christian Ernest Pitman, CBE, of Doynton House, Doynton, nr Bristol:—
(By 4th *m*) Henry Arthur Winston Butler, *b* 1970. ──── Richard Valerian, *b* 1972.

(In remainder to Barony of Cowley of Wellesley)

Grandchildren of late Capt Gerald Valerian Wellesley, MC, son of late Gerald Edward Wellesley, son of late Hon William Henry George Wellesley, 2nd son of 1st Baron Cowley of Wellesley:—
Issue of late Julian Valerian Wellesley, *b* 1933, *d* 1996: *m* 1965, Mrs Elizabeth Joan Hall (who *m* 3rdly, 1998, as his 2nd wife, Charles Henry David Denning, of Northgate House, Church St, Ticehurst, E Sussex TN5 7AE), da of Cyril Stocken, and formerly wife of David Hall:—
William Valerian (403 Fulham Rd, SW10 9TU), *b* 1966: *m* 1994, (Marjorie) Emma, da of Sir (Maurice Arthur) Brian Jenks, 3rd Bt, and has issue living, Julian Valerian Arthur, *b* 1997, — Daisy Elizabeth Susan, *b* 1999. ──── Kate Elizabeth, *b* 1970.

PREDECESSORS – (1) *Hon Sir* HENRY Wellesley, GCB, 5th son of 1st Earl of Mornington, and brother of Marquess Wellesley and 1st Duke of Wellington: *b* 1773: an eminent diplomatist; *cr Baron Cowley of Wellesley* (peerage of United Kingdom) 1828: *m* 1st, 1803 (*m diss* 1810), Lady Charlotte Cadogan, who *d* 1853; she *m* 2ndly, 1810, (1st Marquess of Anglesey), da of 1st Earl Cadogan; 2ndly, 1816, Lady Georgiana Charlotte Augusta Cecil, who *d* 1860, da of 1st Marquess of Salisbury; *d* 1847; *s* by his son (2) HENRY RICHARD CHARLES, 2nd Baron, KG, GCB, PC, DCL; *b* 1804; was Min Plen in Switzerland 1848-49; Envoy Extraor, and Min Plen at Frankfort 1849-51, and to Germanic Confederation 1851-52, and Ambassador Extraor, and Min Plen to France 1852-67; *cr Viscount Dangan* and *Earl Cowley* (peerage of United Kingdom) 1857: *m* 1833, Hon Olivia Cecilia Fitzgerald de Ros, who *d* 1885, da of Charlotte (in her own right), Baroness de Ros; *d* 15 July 1884; *s* by his son (3) WILLIAM HENRY WELLESLEY, 2nd Earl, *b* 1834; Lieut-Col Coldstream Guards: *m* 1863, Emily Gwendolin, who *d* 1932, da of Col Thomas Peers Williams, MP, of Temple House, Great Marlow; *d* 1895; *s* by his son (4) HENRY ARTHUR MORNINGTON, 3rd Earl, *b* 1886: *m* 1st, 1889 (*m diss* 1897), Lady Violet Nevill, who *d* 1910, da of 1st Marquess of Abergavenny; 2ndly, 1905 (*m diss* 1913), Hon Millicent Florence Eleanor, da of the 1st Baron Nunburnholme, and formerly wife of Sir Charles Edward Cradock-Hartopp, 5th Bt; 3rdly, 1914, Clare Florence Mary, who *d* 1949, da of Sir Francis George Stapleton, 8th Bt; *d* 1919; *s* by his son (5) CHRISTIAN ARTHUR, 4th Earl, *b*

1890: *m* 1st (in New York, USA), 1914 (*m diss* 1933), Mae Pickard (an actress), of Memphis, Tennessee, USA, who *d* 1946; 2ndly (at Reno, Nevada) 1933, Mary (Elsie) May HIMES, of San Francisco, Calif, USA; *d* 1962; *s* by his son **(6)** DENIS ARTHUR, BEM, 5th Earl, *b* 1921; Chm and Managing Dir of City Prudential Building Soc 1962-65: *m* 1st, 1944 (*m diss* 1950), Elizabeth Anne, da of late Pelham Rawstorn Papillon, DSO, of Crowhurst, Sussex, and widow of Fl-Lt Stephen Alers Hankey, RAF; 2ndly, 1950, Mrs Annette Nancy Doughty Simmonds, who *d* as the result of a motor accident 1959, da of Maj J. J. O'Hara; 3rdly, 1961, Janet Elizabeth Mary (who *m* 2ndly, 1976 (*m diss* 1981), Piers Dixon), da of Ramiah Doraswamy Aiyar, FRCS, of Ystrad, Denbigh, N Wales; *d* 1968; *s* by his only son **(7)** RICHARD FRANCIS, 6th Earl, *b* 1946: *m* 1971, Maria Delia (who *m* 2ndly, 1980, Lt-Col Robin James Stirling Bullock-Webster), yr da of late Enrique Buenaño, of Buenos Aires; *d* 1975; *s* by his uncle **(8)** GARRET GRAHAM, 7th Earl, and present peer; also Viscount Dangan, and Baron Cowley of Wellesley.

COX, BARONESS (Cox) (Life Baroness 1983)

CAROLINE ANNE COX, da of late Robert John McNeill Love, of Sewards, Brickendon, Hertford; *b* 7 July 1937; *ed* Channing Sch, Highgate, and Lond Univ (BSc Hons Sociology, MSc Economics); Head of Sociology Dept, N Lond Polytechnic, 1974-77, Dir Nursing Educn Research Unit, Chelsea Coll, Lond Univ 1977-84; a Baroness in Waiting April-Aug 1985; *cr Baroness Cox*, of Queensbury, in Greater London (Life Baroness) 1983: *m* 1959, Dr Murray Newell Cox, who *d* 1997, and has issue.

Arms – Azure a sword in fess the blade couped at the point argent the hilt pommel and quillons to the sinister or between two ancient lamps also or enflamed proper. **Supporters** – *Dexter*, a horse argent crined and hoofed or: *sinister*, an unicorn argent its horn or crined and unguled gold.
Residences – The White House, Wyke Hall, Gillingham, Dorset SP8 4NS; 1 Arnellan House, 144-146 Slough Lane, Kinsbury, NW9. *Club* – Royal Commonwealth Society.

THINK·AND·THANK

SONS LIVING

Hon Robin Michael COX McNEILL LOVE, *b* 1959; *ed* Kingsbury High Sch, and The Royal Free Hosp Sch of Medicine (MB BS); Surg Lt Cdr RN, Prin Med Officer HMY Britannia: *m* 1985, Penelope Jane, da of Dr Richard Michael Griffin, of 64 Warwick Rd, Bishops Stortford, Herts.

Hon Jonathan Murray, *b* 1962; *ed* Kingsbury High Sch.

DAUGHTER LIVING

Hon Philippa Ruth Dorothy, *b* 1965; *ed* Channing Sch, Highgate.

Cox, Roxbee, surname of Barony of Kings Norton.

COZENS-HARDY, BARONY OF (Cozens-Hardy) (Extinct 1975)

(Name and Title pronounced "Kuzzens-Hardy")

DAUGHTERS LIVING OF THIRD BARON

Hon Beryl Gladys, OBE, *b* 1911; formerly JP for Norfolk; Chm of World Cttee, World Assocn of Girl Guides and Girl Scouts 1972-75; OBE (Civil) 1971. *Residence* – The Glebe, Letheringsett, Holt, Norfolk NR25 7YA.

Hon Helen Rosemary, *b* 1918: *m* 1953, Brig Douglas Vandeleur Phelps, TD, JP, DL, who *d* 1988, and has an adopted son and da, John Edward Vandeleur, *b* 1961, — Laura Douglas, *b* 1959. *Residence* – Grove Farm House, Langham, Holt, Norfolk NR25 7BU.

Craig, family name of Viscount Craigavon.

CRAIG OF RADLEY, BARON (Craig) (Life Baron 1991)

DAVID BROWNRIGG CRAIG, GCB, OBE, son of late Maj Francis Brownrigg Craig, of Dublin; *b* 17 Sept 1929; *ed* Radley, and Lincoln Coll, Oxford; Commn'd RAF 1951, AOC No 1 Gp RAF Strike Command 1978-80, Vice-Chief of Air Staff 1980-82, AOC-in-C Strike Command and C-in-C UKAF 1982-85, Chief of Air Staff 1985-88, Chief of Defence Staff 1988-91, and Marshal of the RAF 1988; *cr* OBE 1967, CB 1978, KCB 1980, GCB 1984, and *Baron Craig of Radley*, of Helhoughton, co Norfolk (Life Baron) 1991: *m* 1955, Elisabeth June, da of late Charles James Derenburg, of W Byfleet, Surrey, and has issue.

𝕬rms – Ermine, an arrow in bend gules feathered or, the point upwards proper, transfixing a mullet vert, over all on a chevron sable three delta figures argent. 𝕮rest – Rising from an astral crown or a knight on horseback in full armour, his dexter hand holding a broken tilting spear, all proper, his helm surmounted by three ostrich plumes gules, argent and sable. 𝕾upporters – On either side a double-headed eagle wings displayed per pale gules and azure, beaked and legged or, that to the dexter charged on the breast with two keys in saltire wards upwards also gold and that to the sinister charged on the breast with a rose argent barbed and seeded proper; a compartment comprising a grassy mount traversed palewise by a runway both proper bordered by four crosses formy gules.
Address – House of Lords, SW1A 0PW.

SON LIVING

Hon Christopher Charles Brownrigg, *b* 1957; *ed* Radley, and Jesus Coll, Camb: *m* 1981, Marilyn Ashmead. *Address* – c/o Royal Bank of Scotland, 9 Pall Mall, SW1Y 5LX.

DAUGHTER LIVING

Hon Susan Elisabeth, *b* 1960: *m* 1997, Michael A. N. Tomlin, son of C. S. N. Tomlin, of Binham, Norfolk.

CRAIGAVON, VISCOUNT (Craig) (Viscount UK 1927, Bt UK 1918)
(Title pronounced "Craigavvon")

JANRIC FRASER CRAIG, 3rd Viscount, and 3rd Baronet; *b* 9 June 1944; *s* 1974; *ed* Eton, and London Univ (BA, BSc); FCA.

Arms – Gules, a fesse ermine between three bridges of as many arches proper. **Crest** – A demi-lion rampant per fesse gules and sable, holding in the dexter paw a mullet or. **Supporters** – *Dexter*, a Constable of the Ulster special Constabulary, his hand resting on a rifle; *sinister* a Private of the Royal Ulster Rifles, armed and accoutred, both proper.
Address – House of Lords, London SW1.

SISTERS LIVING

Hon Janitha Stormont, *b* 1940: *m* 1965, Gordon Robert MacInnes, ICSA, and has issue living, Avila, *b* 1967, — Córdova, *b* 1971, — Jimena, *b* 1975.
Hon Jacaranda Fiona, *b* 1949: *m* 1972 (*m diss* 1983), Dudley Francis MacDonald, and has issue living, Toby James Francis, *b* 1975, — Rose Carole, *b* 1978.

WIDOW LIVING OF SECOND VISCOUNT

(ANGELA) FIONA (*Viscountess Craigavon*), da of late Percy Tatchell, MRCS, LRCP: *m* 1939, the 2nd Viscount Craigavon, who *d* 1974.

COLLATERAL BRANCH LIVING

Issue of late Maj Hon (Patrick William) Dennis Craig, MBE, yr son of 1st Viscount, *b* 1906, *d* 1972: *m* 1st, 1931 (*m diss* 1935), Aline Margaret Mary McLaren, da of late J. Cumming; 2ndly, 1947, Marjorie Joy, who *d* 1974, da of Algernon Cecil Newton, RA, and formerly wife of late Igor Vinogradoff:—
(By 1st *m*) Deirdre, *b* 1931: *m* 1st, 1951 (*m diss* 1959), Jonathan Craven, late 9th Lancers; 2ndly, 1959, Cyril Vernon Connolly, CBE, writer, who *d* 1974; 3rdly, 1977, Peter Chad Tigar Levi, Prof of Poetry at Oxford Univ since 1984, of Austin's Farm, Stonesfield, Oxford, and has issue living (by 1st *m*), Simon James (Field Cottage, Elmley, Castle, Worcs), *b* 1954; *ed* Eton, — Sarah, *b* 1952: *m* 1973 (*m diss* 1983), Martin J. Bradbury, and has issue living, Arthur John *b* 1976, Jack Daniel *b* 1978, — (by 2nd *m*), Matthew Vernon, *b* 1970 — Cressida Louisa Vernon, *b* 1960; writer: *m* 1st, 1982 (*m diss* 1983), Adrian A. Gill; 2ndly, 1985, Charles Alexander Burnell Hudson, of Wick Manor, Wick, Pershore, Worcs, and has issue living, Gabriel Charles More *b* 1994, Violet Isobel Connolly *b* 1988, Ellen Rose *b* 1990.

PREDECESSORS – **(1)** JAMES CRAIG, PC, LLD, DCL, DL, 6th son of late James Craig, JP, of Craigavon and Tyrella, co Down; *b* 1871; was Treasurer of HM Household 1916-18, Parliamentary Sec to Min of Pensions 1919-20, Financial Sec to Admiralty 1920-21, and Prime Min of N Ireland 1921-40; sat as MP for E Down Div of Down Co (*U* and *Tariff Reformer*) 1906-18, and for Mid Div thereof 1918-21, and for Down co (*U*) in Parliament of N Ireland 1921-29, and for N Down Div of Down co 1929-40; cr a *Baronet* 1918, and *Viscount Craigavon*, of Stormont, co Down (peerage of United Kingdom) 1927: *m* 1905, *Dame* Cecil Mary Nowell Dering, DBE, who *d* 1960, da of late Sir Daniel Alfred Anley Tupper, MVO, formerly Assist Comptroller of Lord Chamberlain's Depart and Sergeant-at-Arms to HM King George V; *d* 1940; *s* by his son **(2)** JAMES, 2nd Viscount; *b* 1906: *m* 1939, (Angela) Fiona da of late Percy Tatchell, MRCS, LRCP; *d* 1974; *s* by his son **(3)** JANRIC FRASER, 3rd Viscount and present peer.

CRAIGMYLE, BARON (Shaw) (Baron UK 1929)

Mercy, Fidelity, Right

THOMAS COLUMBA SHAW, 4th Baron; *b* 19 Oct 1960; *s* 1998: *m* 1987, (Katharine) Alice, 2nd da of David Floyd, OBE, of Priory Close, Combe Down, Bath, and has issue.

Arms – Ermine, a fir tree issuing out of a mount in base proper, between two piles azure, issuing from a chief gules charged with a scroll argent, its seal pendant proper between two lymphads or. Crest – A demi-savage holding in his dexter hand a club resting on his shoulder proper. Supporters – *Dexter*, a lion rampant gules; *sinister*, a kangaroo proper.

SONS LIVING

Hon ALEXANDER FRANCIS, *b* 1 July 1988.
Hon Finnian Donald, *b* 1990.
Hon Calum Edward, *b* 1993.
Hon Joseph Thomas, *b* 1996.

BROTHERS LIVING

Hon Justin Edward Magnus, *b* 1965; *ed* Eton, and Gonville and Caius Coll, Camb (MA). *Residence* – 32 Thurloe Sq, SW7 2SD.
Hon (Alexander) Joseph (Ranald), *b* 1971; *ed* Ampleforth, and St Benet's Hall, Oxford (BA), Dip Theol (D), BPhil.

SISTERS LIVING

Hon Alison Margaret, *b* 1956; *ed* Harvard Univ (BA 1979), and Antioch Univ (MA 1991): *m* 1995, Oliver G. Heggs, yr son of Geoffrey Ellis Heggs. *Residence* – 6/6 Collingham Gdns, SW5 0HW.
Hon Catriona (Kate) Mary, *b* 1958: *m* 1986, Dr Brian Irial Patrick MacGreevy, elder son of late Dr Brian MacGreevy, of Onslow Sq, SW7, and has issue living, Ivo Alexander Patrick, *b* 1987, — Hubert Donald Brian, *b* 1989, — Christabel Elizabeth Anthea, *b* 1991, — Flora Catherine Mary, *b* 1993, — Madeleine Sarah Isabel, *b* 1996. *Residence* – 1 Fernshaw Rd, SW10 0TB.
Hon Madeleine Claire, *b* 1963.

AUNTS LIVING (*Daughters of 2nd Baron*)

Hon Thalia Mary, *b* 1918: *m* 1939, Winton Basil Dean, and has issue living, Stephen Nicholas Winton (Fairnilee, Galashiels, Selkirkshire TD1 3PR), *b* 1946; *ed* Seaford Coll, and Kent Univ, — Diana Rosamund Thalia (adopted da), *b* 1955: *m* 1978, Michael William Bracewell, of 49 Windsor Rd, Kew, Surrey TW9 2EJ. *Residence* – Hambledon Hurst, Godalming, Surrey GU8 4HF.
Hon Elspeth Ruth, *b* 1921: *m* 1945, Archibald James Florence Macdonald, JP, who *d* 1983, and has issue living, Michael Christopher Archibald, *b* 1947; *ed* Univ Coll Sch, and Merton Coll, Oxford: *m* 1979 (*m diss* 1989), C. Ann, da of Rodney G. Searight, — Ian Alexander James (Coldred Court Cottage, Coldred, nr Dover, Kent CT15 5AQ), *b* 1950; *ed* Univ Coll Sch, and Atlantic Coll.

WIDOW LIVING OF THIRD BARON

ANTHEA ESTHER CHRISTINE THERESA (*Anthea Baroness Craigmyle*), da of late Edward Charles Rich, of 31 Yeomans Row, SW3: *m* 1955, the 3rd Baron Craigmyle, who *d* 1998. *Residences* – 18 The Boltons, SW10 9SY; Scottas, Knoydart, Inverness-shire PH41 4PL.

PREDECESSORS – **(1)** *Rt Hon* THOMAS Shaw, PC, KC, LLD, son of Alexander Shaw, of Dunfermline, Fifeshire; *b* 1850; was Solicitor-Gen for Scotland 1894-5, and Lord Advocate 1905-9: MP for Hawick Dist (*L*) 1892-1909; became a Lord of Appeal in Ordinary with title of *Baron Shaw*, of Dunfermline, co Fife (Life Baron) 1909; *cr Baron Craigmyle*, of Craigmyle, co Aberdeen (Peerage of United Kingdom) 1929: *m* 1879, Elsie Stephen, who *d* 1939, da of George Forrest, of Ludquharn, Aberdeenshire; *d* 1937; *s* by his son **(2)** ALEXANDER, 2nd Baron; *b* 1883; sat as MP for Kilmarnock Dist (*L*) 1915-18, and for Kilmarnock Div of Buteshire and Ayrshire 1918-23; *m* 1913, Lady Margaret Cargill Mackay, who *d* 1958, el da of 1st Earl of Inchcape; *d* 1944; *s* by his son **(3)** THOMAS DONALD MACKAY, 3rd Baron; *b* 1923; 1939-45 War as Sub-Lt (A) RNVR; Kt Grand Cross of Obedience, Sovereign Mil Order of Malta (Pres British Assocn 1989-95), Kt Cmdr with Star, Order of Pius IX 1993, KStJ: *m* 1955, Anthea Esther Christine Theresa, da of late Edward Charles Rich, of 31 Yeomans Row, SW3; *d* 1998; *s* by his eldest son **(4)** THOMAS COLUMBA, 4th Baron and present peer.

Cranborne, Viscount; son of Marquess of Salisbury.

CRANBROOK, EARL OF (Gathorne-Hardy) (Earl UK 1892)
(Name pronounced "Gaythorn-Hardy")

Armed with hardy faith

GATHORNE GATHORNE-HARDY, 5th Earl; *b* 20 June 1933; *s* 1978; *ed* Eton, and Corpus Christi Coll, Camb (BA, MA), PhD Birmingham 1960, Hon DSc Aberdeen 1989, Hon DSc Cranfield 1996; late Lt RA (TA); OStJ, FLS, FZS, C Biol; DL Suffolk; JBS(K) (Sarawak); Assist Sarawak Museum 1956-58, and Fellow Jajasan Siswa Lokantara, Indonesia 1960-61, and Lect in Zoology, Univ of Malaya, Kuala Lumpur 1961-70; editor of *Ibis* 1973-80; Suffolk Coastal District Councillor 1976-83; Chm Panel of Enquiry into Shooting and Angling 1976-79; Pres Suffolk Trust for Nature Conservation since 1979, Member R Commn on Environmental Pollution 1981-92; Chm English Nature (Nature Conservancy Council for England) 1990-98; Memb UK Round Table on Sustainable Development 1995-99; Chm Entrust, Regulator of Environmental Bodies under Landfill Tax Regulations, since 1996; author of *Mammals of Borneo*, *Wild Mammals of Malaya*, *Riches of the Wild: Mammals of SE Asia*, and *Wonders of Nature of SE Asia*; ed *Key Environments: Malaysia*, and co-author of *Birds of the Malay Peninsula*, vol 5, and *Belalong: a tropical rainforest*; Trustee BM (Nat Hist) 1982-86; Member Natural Environmental Research Council 1982-88, Board of Anglian Water 1987-98, Broads Authority 1988-99, and Harwich Haven Authority 1989-97: *m* 1967, Caroline, da of late Col Ralph George Edward Jarvis, of Doddington Hall, Lincoln (E Clanwilliam, colls), and has issue.

𝕬rms – Quarterly, 1st and 4th argent, on a bend invected plain, cottised gules, three catherine wheels or; on a chief of the second as many leopards' faces of the third, *Hardy*; 2nd and 3rd, per pale argent and or, a bend compony azure and gules between two pellets, each within an annulet sable, *Gathorne*. 𝕮rest – 1st, a dexter arm embowed in armour proper, garnished or entwined with a branch of oak vert, charged with two catherine wheels, the one above and the other below the elbow gules, the hand grasping a dragon's head erased proper, *Hardy*; 2nd, in front of a wolf's head erased argent, a staff reguly fessewise or, *Gathorne*. 𝕾upporters – On either side a leopard guardant proper, gorged with a collar gules, therefrom suspended an escutcheon of the last, charged with a catherine wheel or.
Address – c/o House of Lords, SW1A 0PW.

SONS LIVING

(JOHN) JASON (*Lord Medway*), *b* 26 Oct 1968; *ed* Woodbridge Sch, and Pembroke Coll, Oxford (BA).

Hon Argus Edward, *b* 1973; *ed* Woodbridge Sch, Gresham's Sch, King's Coll, London, Trin Coll, Dublin (BA), and Prince of Wales Coll of Architecture.

DAUGHTER LIVING

Lady Flora, *b* 1971; *ed* Woodbridge Sch, Bryanston, Emmanuel Coll, Cambridge (BA), and Newnham Coll, Camb (PhD).

BROTHER LIVING

Hon Hugh, *b* 1941; *ed* Eton and Corpus Christi Coll,Camb (MA): *m* 1971, Caroline Elisabeth, da of William Nigel Ritchie, of Mariners, Bradfield, Berks (*see* B Ritchie of Dundee, colls), and has issue living, Frederick Jasper, *b* 1972, — Alfred, *b* 1978, — Alice, *b* 1974, — Daisy, *b* 1977. *Residence* – The Hall Farm, Great Glemham, Saxmundham, Suffolk.

SISTERS LIVING

Lady Juliet (The White House, Rooks Hill, Underriver, Sevenoaks, Kent), *b* 1934: *m* 1958 (*m diss* 1970), Charles Colin Simpson, TD, and has issue living, Charles Duncan, *b* 1962, — Edward Colin, *b* 1965, — Fidelity Anne, *b* 1960, — Amanda Juliet, *b* 1964.

Lady Sophia Catherine, *b* 1936: *m* 1957, Simon Robert Jasper Meade, of Pen-y-lan, Meifod, Powys, and has issue (*see* E Clanwilliam, colls).

Lady Christina, *b* 1940: *m* 1967, Stanley Edward Letanka, MRCS, LRCP, of Stonehill Farmhouse, Horam, Heathfield, E Sussex, and has issue living, Peter Edward, *b* 1974, — Stella LETANKA-JEFFS, *b* 1968: *m* 1996, Richard Jeffs, and has issue living, Xenan Peter LETANKA-JEFFS *b* 1997, — Florence Ruth, *b* 1969: *m* 1998, Mark Pettit, and has issue living Laurence Edgar *b* 1999.

AUNT LIVING (*daughter of 3rd Earl*)

Lady Anne Catherine Dorothy, *b* 1911: *m* 1938, George Heywood Hill, of Snape Priory, Saxmundham, Suffolk (*see* Johnstone, Bt, colls, 1959 Edn), who *d* 1986, and has issue living, Harriet, *b* 1943: *m* 1st, 1963 (*m diss* 1981), Timothy John

Behrens; 2ndly, 1985, Simon Frazer, and has issue living (by 1st *m*), Algernon Kenneth *b* 1966, Charlie Corrado Hey-
wood *b* 1979, Frances Anne *b* 1963, — Rabea (Lucy), *b* 1946: *m* 1970, Abdul Azis (George James) Redpath, of The Tithe
Barn, Stoke Holy Cross, Norwich, and has issue living, Justin Abd'Allah *b* 1971, Abdul Razzaq *b* 1977, Hafidha *b* 1975,
Aisha Iman *b* 1983, Khayria *b* 1985.

WIDOW LIVING OF SON OF THIRD EARL

Mary Catherine (21 Cranebrook, Manor Rd, Twickenham, Middx), da of late Bernard Joseph Smartt: *m* 1974, as his 2nd
wife, Surg Cdr Hon Antony Gathorne Gathorne-Hardy, RN, MB, ChB, who *d* 1976 (infra).

WIDOW LIVING OF FOURTH EARL

FIDELITY (*Dowager Countess of Cranbrook*), OBE, JP (Red House Farm, Great Glemham, Saxmundham, Suffolk), da of
Hugh Exton Seebohm, JP, of Poynders End, Hitchin: *m* 1932, as his 2nd wife, the 4th Earl of Cranbrook, CBE, JP, DL,
who *d* 1978.

COLLATERAL BRANCHES LIVING

Issue of late Surg Cdr Hon Antony Gathorne Gathorne-Hardy, RN, MB, ChB, yst son of 3rd Earl, *b*
1907, *d* 1976: *m* 1st 1931, Ruth Elizabeth, who *d* 1973, da of Cdr Arthur Penton Napier Thorowgood,
DSO, RN (*see* Hunter-Blair, Bt, colls, 1936 Edn); 2ndly, 1974, Mary Catherine (ante), da of late Bernard
Joseph Smartt:—
(By 1st *m*) Jonathan Gathorne (31 Blacksmith's Yard, Binham, Fakenham, Norfolk NR21 0AL) *b* 1933: writer, author of
The Rise & Fall of the British Nanny, The Public School Phenomenon, Love, Sex, Marriage & Divorce, Doctors, etc: *m* 1st,
1963 (*m diss* 1977), Sabrina Viola, da of late Hon David Francis Tennant, of El Palomar, Mijas, Malaga, Spain (*see* B
Glenconner, colls); 2ndly, 1985, Nicolette, da of Dr Kenneth William Cripps Sinclair-Loutit, MBE, and has issue living
(by 1st *m*), Benjamin, *b* 1967: *m* 1992, Philippa, yr da of David Heimann, and of Mrs Desmond Corcoran, and has issue
living, a da *b* 1994, — Jenny, *b* 1965: *m* 1996, Joseph (Joe) Chase Hurt Mellen, and has issue living, Rudy Blu (a son) *b*
1996. —— Samuel Gathorne (Old Bullock Sheds, Great Glemham, Saxmundham), *b* 1936: *m* 1965, Grace D'Cruz, and
has issue living, Robert Dee, *b* 1973, — Lydia, *b* 1964, — Penelope Rose, *b* 1965. —— Elizabeth Rose, *b* 1949: *m* 1974,
Ian Richmond Battye, MB, BS, and has issue living, Thomas Gathorne, *b* 1975, — Nell Aurore, *b* 1977.

Issue of late Lt-Col Hon Nigel Charles Gathorne-Hardy, DSO, yst son of 2nd Earl, *b* 1880, *d* 1958: *m*
1910, Doris Cecilia Featherston, who *d* 1973, da of late Hon Sir Charles John Johnston, MLC, of Karori,
Wellington, New Zealand:—
Margaret Doris (*Lady Cameron of Lochiel*), *b* 1913: *m* 1939, Col Sir Donald Hamish Cameron of Lochiel, KT, CVO, TD,
late Comdg Lovat Scouts (*see* D Montrose, 1976 Edn), and has issue living, Donald Angus yr of Lochiel, *b* 1946; *ed*
Harrow, and Ch Ch, Oxford; DL Lochaber, Inverness, and Badenoch and Strathspey 1986, Vice Lord Lieut since 19—: *m*
1974, Lady Cecil Nennella Therese Kerr, 2nd da of 12th Marquess of Lothian, KCVO, and has issue living, Donald
Andrew John *b* 1976, Catherine Mary *b* 1975, Lucy Margot Therese *b* 1980, Emily Frances *b* 1986, — John Alastair
Nigel, *b* 1954: *m* 1982, Julia R., da of R. C. Wurtzburg, of Kensington Court Place, W8, and has issue living, Hamish *b*
1985, Robert Andrew *b* 1991, Kirsty Anne *b* 1987, — Margaret Anne, *b* 1942: *m* 1968, Timothy E. Nott-Bower, of Buckwood, Chisbury Lane, nr Marlborough, Wilts, son of late Sir John Reginald Hornby Nott-Bower, KCVO, and has issue
living, John William *b* 1972, Katherine Margot *b* 1970, — Caroline Marion, *b* 1943: *m* 1967, Blaise Noel Anthony Hardman, of Farley House, Farley Chamberlayne, Romsey, Hants, son of Air Ch Marshal Sir (James) Donald Innes Hardman,
GBE, KCB, DFC, and has issue living, Thomas *b* 1977, Jane *b* 1969, Annabel *b* 1971, Elizabeth *b* 1974, Rosanna *b* 1979.
Residence – Achnacarry, Spean Bridge, Inverness-shire.

PREDECESSORS – (1) *Right Hon* GATHORNE Hardy, GCSI, PC, DCL, LLD, third son of late John Hardy, MP; *b* 1814;
Under-Sec of State for Home Depart 1858-9, Pres of Poor Law Board 1866-7, Sec of State for Home Depart 1867-8, for
War 1874-8, and for India 1878-80, and Lord Pres of the Council 1885-6 and 1886-92; assumed in 1878, by Roy licence,
the additional surname of Gathorne; MP for Leominster (C) 1856-65, and for Univ of Oxford 1865-78; GCSI 1880; cr.
Viscount Cranbrook, of Hemsted, co Kent (peerage of United Kingdom) 1878, and *Earl of Cranbrook* and *Baron Medway*,
of Hemsted, co Kent (peerage of United Kingdom) 1892: *m* 1838, Jane, CI, who *d* 1897, da of James Orr, of Hollywood
House, co Down; *d* 1906: *s* by his el son (2) JOHN STEWART, 2nd Earl, *b* 1839; MP for Rye (C) 1868-80, for Mid-Kent
1884-5, and for Kent, Mid, or Medway, Div 1885-92: *m* 1867, Cicely Marguerite Wilhelmina, who *d* 1931, da and heiress
of late Joseph Ridgway, of Fairlawn, Kent: *d* 1911: *s* by his el son (3) GATHORNE, 3rd Earl; *b* 1870: *m* 1899, Lady Dorothy
Montagu Boyle, who *d* 1968, da of 7th Earl of Glasgow; *d* 1915; *s* by his el son (4) JOHN DAVID, CBE, JP, DL, 4th Earl, *b*
1900; Trustee of British Museum (Natural History), and Member of Nature Conservancy: *m* 1st, 1926 (*m diss* 1931), his
cousin, Bridget Cicely, DBE, who *d* 1985, da of Rupert D'Oyly Carte, impressario (*see* E Cranbrook, 1976 Edn); 2ndly,
1932, Fidelity, OBE, JP, da of Hugh Exton Seebohm, JP, of Poynders End, Hitchin; *d* 1978; *s* by his el son (5)
GATHORNE, 5th Earl and present peer; also Viscount Cranbrook, and Baron Medway.

Cranley, Viscount; son of Earl of Onslow.

CRANWORTH, BARON (Gurdon) (Baron UK1899)

Virtue flourishes in adversity

PHILIP BERTRAM GURDON, 3rd Baron; *b* 24 May 1940; *s* 1964; *ed* Eton, and Magdalene Coll, Camb; late Lt R Wilts Yeo: *m* 1968, Frances Henrietta, da of late Lord William Walter Montagu Douglas Scott, MC (*see* D Buccleuch, colls), and has issue.

𝕬rms – Sable, three leopards' faces jessant-de-lis or ℭrest – A goat climbing up a rock, all proper. 𝕾upporters – On either side a rock thereon a goat proper, collared gemelle or
Seat – Grundisburgh Hall, Woodbridge, Suffolk.

SONS LIVING

Hon (SACHA WILLIAM) ROBIN, *b* 12 Aug 1970.
Hon Brampton Charles, *b* 1975.

DAUGHTER LIVING

Hon Louisa-Jane, *b* 1969: *m* 1999, Simon D. K. Hanbury, 3rd son of Benjamin John Hanbury, of Cogans, Piltdown, Sussex.

SISTER LIVING

(Raised to the rank of a Baron's daughter 1964)

Hon Jeryl Marcia Sarah, DL (*Hon Lady Smith-Ryland*), *b* 1932; DL Warwicks 1990; CStJ 1981, DStJ 1990: *m* 1952, Sir Charles Mortimer Tollemache Smith-Ryland, KCVO, who *d* 1989, of Sherbourne Park, Warwick, and has issue (*see* B Tollemache, colls). *Residence* – Medbourne Old Hall, Market Harborough, Leics LE16 8DZ.

PREDECESSORS – (1) ROBERT THORNHAGH Gurdon, el son of late Brampton Gurdon, MP, of Letton Hall, Norfolk, and Grundisburgh, Suffolk; *b* 1829; MP for S Norfolk (*L*) 1880-85, and for Norfolk Mid Div (*L*) 1885-6, and (*LU*) 1886-92 and April to July 1895; *cr* Baron Cranworth, of Letton and Cranworth, co Norfolk (peerage of UK) 1899: *m* 1st, 1862, Harriott Ellin, who *d* 1864, da of Sir William Miles,MP, 1st Bt; 2ndly, 1874, Emily Frances, who *d* 1934, da of Robert Boothby Heathcote; *d* 1902; *s* by his son (2) BERTRAM FRANCIS, KG, MC, 2nd Baron; *b* 1877; Vice-Lieut for Suffolk 1947-64: *m* 1903, Vera Emily, CBE, who *d* 1966, el da of late Arthur William Ridley (V Ridley, colls); *d* 1964; *s* by his grandson (3) PHILIP BERTRAM (yr son of late Hon Robert Brampton Gurdon, who was *ka* in Libya 1942), 3rd Baron, and present peer.

CRATHORNE, BARON (Dugdale) (Baron UK 1959, Bt UK 1945)

By persevering

CHARLES JAMES DUGDALE, 2nd Baron and 2nd Baronet; *b* 12 Sept 1939; *s* 1977; *ed* Eton, and Trin Coll, Camb (MA); FRSA; DL Cleveland 1983, Lord Lieut N Yorks since 1999; Assist to Pres Parke-Bernet, New York 1965-69; James Dugdale & Associates, London, Independent Fine Art Consultancy Service, since 1969; James Crathorne & Associates since 1980; Member, Productions Cttee Georgian Theatre Royal, Richmond since 1969, and Yorks Regional Cttee Nat Trust 1978-84, and 1988-94; Member Court of Leeds Univ 1985-97, Conservative Advisory Group on Arts and Heritage since 1988, Hon Sec All Party Parliamentary Arts & Heritage Group since 1981, and Chm The Georgian Group since 1990, etc; Chm Captain Cook Trust since 1978, and Nat Heritage Memorial Fund 1992-95; Dir Blakeney Hotels Ltd 1981-93, Dir Cliveden plc 1993-98, Dir Cliveden Ltd since 1999, and Woodhouse Securities Ltd since 1989; author *Edouard Vuillard* (1967), and co-author *Tennant's Stalk* (1973), *History of Crathorne* (1989), *Cliveden The Place and the People* (1995), and *The Royal Crescent Book of Bath* (1998); Pres of numerous local organisations, including the Cleveland and N Yorks Branch Magistrates' Assocn since 1997: *m* 1970, Sylvia Mary, yr da of late Brig Arthur Montgomery, OBE, TD (*see* Montgomery, Bt, colls) and has issue.

𝕬rms – Ermine a cross moline gules between four hurts. 𝕮rest – A gryphon's head ermine wings endorsed erminois gorged with a collar azure therefrom pendant a cross moline gules. 𝕾upporters – *Dexter*, a crow sable beaked and membered or in the beak a sprig of blackthorn flowered proper; *sinister*, a stag also sable attired unguled and gorged with a mural crown gold charged on the shoulder with a thistle slipped and leaved also proper. *Residence* – Crathorne House, Yarm, N Yorks TS15 0AT.

SON LIVING

Hon Thomas Arthur John, *b* 30 Sept 1977.

DAUGHTERS LIVING

Hon Charlotte Patricia, *b* 1972.
Hon Katharine Feodora Nicola, *b* 1980.

BROTHER LIVING

Hon David John (Park House, Crathorne, Yarm, N Yorks), *b* 1942; *ed* Eton, and Trin Coll, Camb (MA); High Sheriff Cleveland 1995, DL N Yorks 1998: *m* 1972, Susan Louise, yr da of late Lewis A. Powell, and has issue living, Jonathan William Shaun, *b* 1980, — Clare Nancy Louise, *b* 1978.

PREDECESSOR – **(1)** *Rt Hon Sir* Thomas Lionel Dugdale, TD, PC, son of James Lionel Dugdale, of Crathorne, Yorks; *b* 1897; PPS to Rt Hon Sir Philip Cunliffe-Lister, MP 1931-35 and to Rt Hon Stanley Baldwin, MP 1935-37, a Junior Lord of the Treasury 1937-40, Dep Ch Govt Whip and Vice-Chm of Conservative Party Orgn 1941-42 and Chm 1942-44, Min of Agric and Fisheries 1951-54, and UK Member of Gen Assembly, Council of Europe 1958-59 and 1961-65 (Vice-Pres 1962-64); MP for Richmond Div, N Riding of Yorks (C) 1929-59; *cr* a Baronet 1945, PC 1951 and *Baron Crathorne*, N Riding of Yorks (peerage of UK) 1959: *m* 1936, Nancy (Gates), OBE, who *d* 1969, da of Sir Charles Tennant, 1st Bt (B Glenconner); *d* 1977; *s* by his el son **(2)** Charles James, 2nd Baron, and present peer.

CRAVEN, EARL OF (Craven) (Earl GB 1801)

Benjamin Robert Joseph Craven, 9th Earl; *b* 13 June 1989; *s* 1990.

𝕬rms – Argent, a fesse, between six cross crosslets fitchée, gules. 𝕮rest – On a chapeau gules, turned up ermine, a griffin statant wings elevated ermine, beaked and membered or. 𝕾upporters – Two griffins, wings elevated ermine, beaked and membered or.

AUNT LIVING *(daughter of 6th Earl by 2nd marriage)*

Lady Ann Mary Elizabeth, *b* 1959; *ed* — Univ (BA): *m* 1978, Prof Lionel Tarassenko, MA, DPhil, CEng, MIEE, of 68 Old Rd, Headington, Oxford, elder son of Sergei Tarassenko, of Swanage, Dorset, and has issue living, Luke Ivan Thomas, *b* 1988, — Simon Robert Serge, *b* 1991, — Naomi Rachel Elizabeth, *b* 1989.

HALF-AUNT LIVING *(daughter of 6th Earl by 1st marriage)*

Lady Sarah Jane, *b* 1940: *m* 1961, David John Trail Thomson Glover, of La Gratitude, 6 De Villiers St, Cape Province 7130, S Africa, and has had issue, Suzanne Gwendoline, *b* 1964, — Priscilla, *b* 1967, *d* 1971, — Vanessa Kate, *b* 1972.

WIDOW LIVING OF SIXTH EARL

Elizabeth Gwendolen Teresa, da of late Robert Sholto Johnstone-Douglas (*see* M Queensberry, colls): *m* 1st, 1954, as his 2nd wife, the 6th Earl, who *d* 1965; 2ndly, 1966, Kenneth Kruger Harmood Banner, of Peelings Manor, Pevensey, Sussex, who *d* 1995.

WIDOW LIVING OF EIGHTH EARL

Teresa Maria Bernadette (*Countess of Craven*), da of Arthur John Downes, of Black Hall, Clane, co Kildare: *m* 1988, the 8th Earl, who *d* 1990, following a motor accident. *Residence* – Hawkwood House, Hawkhurst Lane, Waldron, E Sussex.

Virtue consists in action

VIRTUS · IN · ACTIONE · CONSISTIT

COLLATERAL BRANCHES LIVING

Issue of late Major Hon Rupert Cecil Craven, OBE, 2nd son of 3rd Earl, *b* 1870, *d* 1959: *m* 1st, 1898 (*m diss* 1908), Inez, da of George Broom; 2ndly, 1925, Josephine Marguerite, who *d* 1971, da of José Reixach, and widow of Capt Charles William Banbury (B Banbury):—

(By 2nd *m*) RUPERT JOSE EVELYN (Swordly, Bettyhill by Thurso, Caithness KW14 7TA), *b* 22 March 1926; Lt-Cdr RN: *m* 1955, Margaret Campbell, who *d* 1985, da of Alexander Smith, MBE, of Glasgow, and Alness.

Granddaughter of late William George Craven, el son of Hon George Augustus Craven, yr son of 1st Earl:—
Issue of late Augustus William Craven, *b* 1852, *d* 1929: *m* 1st, 1880, Florence Champagné, who *d* 1899, da of Gen Corbet Cotton (V Combermere); 2ndly, 1900, Lilian, da of John Hearn:—
(By 2nd *m*) Violet Lilian Mary (Lullington Manor, Alfriston, Sussex), *b* 1906: *m* 1935, Roland Crosley Wimbush, who *d* 1964, and has issue living, Jennifer, *b* 1940: *m* 1965, James Charles Tempest Bouskell, and has issue living, James Henry Tempest *b* 1968, Louisa Jane *b* 1967: *m* 1994, James Richard Symington (and has issue living, Thomas Tempest *b* 1998).

(In Special remainder to Barony only)

Grandchildren of late Edmund Filmer Craven, grandson of late Fulwar Craven (*b* 1782), grandson of late Charles Craven, brother of 2nd Baron:—
Issue of late Fulwar Craven, *b* 1873, *d* 1956: *m* 1916, Elizabeth A. Wheatley:—
Edmund Filmer (11 Buckley Av, Mount Isa 4825, Cloncurry, Queensland, Australia), *b* 1917; late RAAF: *m* 1944, Ada Clemence Adelaide, da of C. Richardson, of Cloncurry, Queensland, Australia, and has issue living, John Edmund (Unit 2 No 471 6th Av, Kedron 4031, Queensland, Australia), *b* 1946: *m* 1980 (*m diss* 1987), Julie Ann Airie, and has issue living, Jillian Lee *b* 1980. —— Evelyn Caroline, *b* 1929: *m* 1952, Donald Leslie Whitehouse, who *d* 1981, of 58 Alma Rd, Clayfield, Brisbane 4011, Queensland, Australia, and has had issue, Gregory Thomas, *b* 1954: *m* 1990, Kerryn Wilson, and has issue living, Edward Anthony *b* 1991, — Jennifer Lynette, *b* 1953: *m* 1976, Clive Baylis, of London, and *dsp* 1979.

PREDECESSORS – (1) *Sir* WILLIAM Craven, Knt, a soldier of renown in the Netherlands under Henry, Prince of Orange, under Gustavus Adolphus, King of Sweden, and in the service of the States of Holland, was a zealous partisan of Charles I and Charles II; *cr Baron Craven*, of Hamstead Marshall, co Berks (peerage of England) 1626, with remainder to his brothers, John and Thomas, *Viscount Craven*, of Uffington, co Berks, with remainder to Sir William Craven, Knt, and Sir Anthony Craven, *Earl of Craven* (peerage of England), 1663, and *Baron Craven*, of Hamstead Marshall, Berks, 1665, with remainder to Sir William Craven, Knt, of Combe Abbey, Warwickshire, son of Thomas Craven, brother of Sir Anthony (ante); *d* unmarried 1697, when all the peerages became extinct except the *cr* of 1665, which devolved upon (2) WILLIAM, 2nd Baron, son of Sir William, Knt (ante); *d* 1711; *s* by his son (3) WILLIAM, 3rd Baron; *dsp* 1739; *s* by his brother (4) FULWAR, 4th Baron; *d* unmarried; *s* by his cousin (5) WILLIAM, 5th Baron, son of John, 2nd son of 2nd Baron; *d* 1769; *s* by his nephew (6) WILLIAM, 6th Baron; *d* 1791; *s* by his son (7) WILLIAM, 7th Baron; a Maj-Gen in the Army, and Lord-Lieut of Berks; *cr Viscount Uffington* and *Earl of Craven* (peerage of Great Britain) 1801; *d* 1825; *s* by his son (8) WILLIAM, 2nd Earl; *b* 1809; Lord-Lieut of Warwickshire; *d* 1866; *s* by his son (9) GEORGE GRIMSTON, 3rd Earl; *b* 1841; Lord-Lieut of Berks: *m* 1867, Hon Evelyn Laura, who *d* 1924, da of 7th Viscount Barrington; *d* 1883; *s* by his son (10) WILLIAM GEORGE ROBERT, 4th Earl; *b* 1868; Lord-Lieut of Warwickshire: *m* 1893, Cornelia, who *d* 1961, da of late Bradley Martin, of New York, USA; *d* 1921; *s* by his son (11) WILLIAM GEORGE BRADLEY, 5th Earl, *b* 1897; European War 1915-18, as Lieut Hampshire Regt (wounded): *m* 1916, Wilhelmina Mary, who *d* 1974, da of William George, OBE, JP, Town Clerk of Invergordon, Scotland; *d* 1932; *s* by his son (12) WILLIAM ROBERT BRADLEY, 6th Earl, *b* 1917: *m* 1st, 1939 (*m diss* 1954), Irene, 6th da of late Ferdinand Richard Holmes Meyrick, MD, of 59 Kensington Court, W8; 2ndly, 1954, Elizabeth Gwendolen Teresa (who *m* 2ndly, 1966, Kenneth Kruger Harmood Banner, who *d* 1995), da of late Robert Sholto Johnstone-Douglas (*see* M Queensberry, colls); *d* 1965; *s* by his el son (13) THOMAS ROBERT DOUGLAS, 7th Earl, *b* 1957; *dspl* 1983; *s* by his brother (14) SIMON GEORGE, 8th Earl, *b* 1961; student nurse: *m* 1988, Teresa Maria Bernadette, da of Arthur John Downes, of Black Hall, Clane, co Kildare; *d* 1990, following a motor accident; *s* by his only son (15) BENJAMIN ROBERT JOSEPH, 9th Earl and present peer; also Viscount Uffington, and Baron Craven.

CRAWFORD and BALCARRES, EARL OF (Lindsay) (Earl S 1398 and 1651)

Endure bravely

ROBERT ALEXANDER LINDSAY, KT, PC, 29th Earl of Crawford (Premier Earl on Union Roll of Scotland), and 12th Earl of Balcarres; *b* 5 March, 1927; *s* 1975; *ed* Eton, and Trin Coll, Camb; late Lt Gren Gds; PPS to Financial Sec to the Treasury 1955-57, and to Min of Housing and Local Govt 1957-59, Prin Opposition Front Bench Spokesman on Health and Social Security 1967-70; Min of State, Defence 1970-72, and Min of State for Foreign and Commonwealth Affairs 1972-74; Lord Chamberlain to HM Queen Elizabeth the Queen Mother since 1992; MP for Hertford Div of Herts (*C*) 1955-74, and for Welwyn and Hatfield Feb to Oct 1974; Pres Rural Dist Councils Assocn for England and Wales 1959-65; Chm National Assocn of Mental Health 1963-70, Lombard North Central Ltd 1976-80, and Historic Buildings Council for Scotland 1976-83; a Dir of National Westminster Bank Ltd 1975-88, Vice-Chm Sun Alliance and London Insurance Group 1975-91, and Dir of Scottish American Investment Trust 1978-88; First Crown Estate Commissioner 1980-85, Chm Royal Commn on Ancient and Historical Monuments of Scotland 1985-95, Crown Trustee and Chm of Board of Nat Library of Scotland since 1990; *cr* PC 1972, *Baron Balniel*, of Pitcorthie, co Fife (Life Baron), 1974, and KT 1996: *m* 1949, Ruth Beatrice, da of Leo Meyer-Bechtler, of 49 Keltenstrasse, Zürich, Switzerland, and has issue.

Arms – Quarterly: 1st and 4th gules, a fesse checky argent and azure, *Lindsay;* 2nd and 3rd or, a lion rampant gules, debruised of a ribbon in bend sable, *Abernethy.* **Crest** – Out of an antique ducal coronet a swan's neck and wings proper. **Supporters** – Two lions rampant guardant gules.
Seat – Balcarres, Colinsburgh, Fife.

SONS LIVING

ANTHONY ROBERT (*Lord Balniel*) (6 Pembridge Place, W2 4XB; *Club* – New (Edinburgh)), *b* 24 Nov 1958; *ed* Eton, and Edinburgh Univ: *m* 1989, Nicola A., yst da of Antony Bicket, of Derwas, Dolwen, N Wales, and has issue:—

     SONS LIVING— *Hon* Alexander Thomas (*Master of Lindsay*), *b* 5 Aug 1991.
     Hon James Antony, *b* 1992.
     DAUGHTER LIVING— *Hon* Katherine Ruth Vere, *b* 1996.

Hon Alexander Walter, *b* 1961; *ed* Eton; Endure Pursuivant to his father. *Residence* – Studio 5, Neckinger Mills, 162 Abbey St, SE1.

DAUGHTERS LIVING

Lady Bettina Mary, *b* 1950: *m* 1975, Peter Charles Hay Drummond-Hay, of 86 Rowayton Av, Rowayton, Conn 06853, USA, and Le Pestou, Castelsagrat, France, and has issue (*see* E Kinnoull, colls).
Lady Iona Sina, *b* 1957: *m* 1983, Charles Gerard Mackworth-Young, of 18 The Chase, SW4 0NH, and has issue (*see* Young, Bt, *cr* 1813, colls).

BROTHER LIVING

Hon Thomas Richard, *b* 1937; *ed* Eton; late 2nd Lieut Scots Gds: *m* 1961, Sarah Virginia, only da of George Nigel Capel Cure, TD, JP, DL (*see* Barry, Bt, colls), and has issue living, Ivan James, *b* 1962: *m* 1992, Julie, da of Mads Gad, of Rolighedsvej 11, 2942 Skodsborg, Denmark, and has had issue, †Maximilian James *b* 1993; *d* 1995, — Constantine David, *b* 1966: *m* 1996, Samantha, yst da of Harry Asprey, of York Av, Sheen, Surrey, and has issue living, Clara Mary *b* 1998, — Jason Richard, *b* 1968, — Alexandra Mary, *b* 1964: *m* 1990, Marcus Basil Ziani de Ferranti (*see* E Eglinton, 1990 Edn), and has issue living, Thomas Ziani *b* 1994, Augustus Ziani *b* 1997, Polly Ziani *b* 1992, — Sophia Victoria, *b* 1971. *Residence* – The Old Rectory, Ashmore, Salisbury, Wilts, SP5 5AG. *Club* – Brook's.

AUNTS LIVING (*Daughters of 27th Earl*)

Lady Mary Lilian (*Dowager Viscountess Dilhorne*), *b* 1910: *m* 1930, 1st Viscount Dilhorne, who *d* 1980, and has issue (see that title).
Lady Barbara, *b* 1915: *m* 1939, Col Richard Lumley Hurst, R Sussex Regt TA, Bar-at-law, who *d* 1962, son of Sir Cecil James Barrington Hurst, GCMG, KCB, and has issue living, Robert Andrew, *b* 1945: *m* 1977, Cristina, el da of J. J. Couper Edwards, of Rusper Nunnery, Horsham, W Sussex, and has issue living, Andrew *b* 1981, Sarah *b* 1978, Mary *b*

1982, — Elizabeth, *b* 1940: *m* 1967, Angus Hugh Gilroy, Member Queen's Body Guard for Scotland (Royal Company of Archers), of Grainingfold, Five Oaks, Billingshurst, W Sussex, and has issue living, Fergus Hugh *b* 1969, Margaret Cecilia *b* 1970, — Cecilia Barbara (*Lady Goodlad*), *b* 1944: *m* 1968, Rt Hon Sir Alastair Robertson Goodlad, KCMG, MP, Ch Whip 1995-97, of Common Farm, Rhuddal Heath, Tarporley, Cheshire, and has issue living, Magnus James *b* 1972; *ed* Eton, and Oriel Coll, Oxford, William Duff *b* 1974; *ed* Eton and Pembroke Coll, Oxford, — Katharine Constance, *b* 1948: *m* 1st, 1975, Donald M. Corbett, who *d* 1987; 2ndly, 1991, as his 2nd wife, (Peter) Noel (Houldsworth) Gibbs (*see* B Dulverton, colls), of Combend Manor, Elkstone, Cheltenham, Glos GL53 9PT, and has issue living (by 1st *m*), Alexander James *b* 1977, Clare Barbara *b* 1978. *Residence* – Powerswood, Elkstone, Cheltenham, Glos GL59 9PT.

WIDOW LIVING OF SON OF TWENTY-EIGHTH EARL

Lady Amabel Mary Maud YORKE (*Lady Amabel Lindsay*) (12 Lansdowne Rd, W11), eldest da of 9th Earl of Hardwicke: *m* 1955, Hon Patrick Lindsay, who *d* 1986, and has issue (see colls, infra).

WIDOW LIVING OF SON OF TWENTY-SEVENTH EARL

Hon Bronwen Mary Scott-Ellis, eldest da of 8th Baron Howard de Walden: *m* 1933, Maj Hon James Louis Lindsay, who *d* 1997, and has issue (see colls, infra). *Residence* – Sutton Manor, Sutton Scotney, nr Winchester, Hants SO21 3JX.

COLLATERAL BRANCHES LIVING

Issue of late Hon Patrick Lindsay, 2nd son of 28th Earl of Crawford, *b* 1928, *d* 1986: *m* 1955, Lady Amabel Mary Maud Yorke (ante), eldest da of 9th Earl of Hardwicke:—
(Alexander) Ludovic, *b* 1957: *m* 1994, Lucy J. elder da of Richard Davenhill, of Belbroughton, Stourbridge, Worcs, and has issue living, Merlin Edward, *b* 1997, — Cosmo Simon, *b* 1999. —— James Richard, *b* 1961: *m* 1995, Arabella Kate Louise, da of Gavin Nicholas Tait (*see* D Northumberland, colls), and has issue living, Luke Jai *b* 1996. —— Valentine, *b* 1962: *m* 1990, Hayley, elder da of Rex Whittome, of Willowhayne House, Sutton, nr Wansford, Peterborough, and has issue living, Patrick, *b* 1995, — Orlando, *b* 1998. —— Laura Mary, *b* 1956.

Issue of late Maj Hon James Louis Lindsay, yr son of 27th Earl, *b* 1906, *d* 1997: *m* 1933, Hon Bronwen Mary Scott-Ellis (ante) eldest da of 8th Baron Howard de Walden:—
Hugh John Alexander (The Old Rectory, Litton Cheney, Dorchester, Dorset DT2 9AH), *b* 1934; *ed* Eton, and Magdalen Coll, Oxford; FCA; late 2nd Lieut Black Watch: *m* 1961, (Constance) Carolyn, yr da of Sir Charles James Buchanan, 4th Bt, and has issue living, David Charles (26 Avondale Park Gdns, W11), *b* 1962; *ed* Eton, and Southampton Univ; ACA, — Alastair James (Alexander Wood House, Sotterley, Beccles, Suffolk), *b* 1964; *ed* Eton, and Southampton Univ; CA: *m* 1992, Heather J., da of Denis Adair, of Newtownabbey, co Antrim, and has issue living, James Oliver *b* 1995, Polly Alexandra *b* 1997, — Robert Hugh, *b* 1967; *ed* Eton, and Reading Univ; Major Scots Gds: *m* 1995, Joanna, da of Stuart Shoesmith, of Haslemere, Surrey, and has issue living, Alec Guy Sebastian *b* 1998, Eliza Sophie Paget *b* 1996, — (Serena) Clare, *b* 1970; *ed* St Andrews Univ, and Homerton Coll, Camb: *m* 1996, Dr Matthew Jones, of 59 Oakworth Rd, W10 6DF, and has issue living, Samuel Glyndwr *b* 1999. —— Alexander Thomas (Cavalry and Guards' Club), *b* 1936; *ed* Eton, and Magdalen Coll, Oxford; Col 17/21st Lancers: *m* 1966, Jessie Miranda Cecilia, da of Col John Anthony Tristram Barstow, DSO, TD, DL, and has issue living, James Alexander Tristram, *b* 1968; *ed* Eton, — Roderick Charles, *b* 1970; *ed* Eton. —— Stephen James (Invermoidart, Acharacle, Argyll), *b* 1940; *ed* Eton; Lt-Col Black Watch: *m* 1966, Margaret Ann, yr da of late Maj John Henry Courthope Powell (*see* Spencer-Nairn, Bt), and has issue living, Richard Stephen, *b* 1969; *ed* Eton, and St Catherine's Coll, Oxford: *m* 1997, Xanthe Clare Lorraine, da of Sir Ian George Lorraine Critchett, 3rd Bt, and has issue living, Oscar James Montague *b* 1998, — Charles Ludovic, *b* 1974; *ed* Eton, and St Andrews Univ, — Andrew James Ronald, *b* 1977; *ed* Eton, — Jane Margaret, *b* 1966; *ed* Edinburgh Univ: *m* 1991, Charles R. S. Graham, of 43 Moreton Terr, SW1W 2NS, son of Maj Stephen Graham, of Flint House, Goodworth, Clatford, Andover, Hants, and has issue living, Cosmo Stephen Buckle *b* 1995, Ludovic James Buckle *b* 1997. —— Julia Margaret, *b* 1941: *m* 1963, (Malcolm) Peter Speight Barton, of Sydenhams, Bisley, Glos GL6 7BU, and has issue living, Henry James, *b* 1967; *ed* Eton, and Durham Univ: *m* 1998, Alison, da of Dr Peter Mitchell, of Meopham, Kent, — Christopher Charles, *b* 1970; *ed* Eton, and Durham Univ, — Fenella Jane, *b* 1965; *ed* Exeter Univ, The Coll of Law, and Trin Coll of Music: *m* 1996, Nicholas Clements, of Keeper's Cottage, Chewton Mendip, Bath BA3 4NY, son of Arthur Clements.

Granddaughter of late Hon Walter Patrick Lindsay, 2nd son of 26th Earl of Crawford:—
Issue of late Kenneth Andrew Lindsay, *b* 1903, *d* 1970: *m* 1928, Kathleen Mary, who *d* 1975, da of H. E. Lovemore, formerly of Queenstown, S Africa:—
Patricia Jane, *b* 1932: *m* 1956, Noël Gwynne Harpur, of 19 Surrey St, Claremont, Cape Town 7700, and has issue living, Patrick Leslie Gwynne, *b* 1957, — Colin Andrew Lindsay, *b* 1959.

Issue of late Maj Hon Robert Hamilton Lindsay, 3rd son of 26th Earl of Crawford, *b* 1874, *d* 1911: *m* 1903, Mary Janet, who *d* 1960, da of Sir William John Clarke, 1st Bt:—
Robert William Ludovic, OBE (12 Fairlie Court, S Yarra, Victoria 3141, Australia), *b* 1905; *ed* Eton, and RMC Sandhurst; Gren Gds 1925-45, Trans-Jordan Frontier Force 1932-34 (ret as Maj): a Member of House of Representatives of Australia 1954-66; ret 1966; OBE (Civil) 1971: *m* 1946, Rosemary Catherine Marion, only da of Sir Robert Wilson Knox (*see* Clarke, Bt, *cr* 1882, 1963 Edn), and has had issue, †Robin David, *b* 1947; *d* 1965, — Andrew William Michael, *b* 1949; has issue living, Sarah Ivy *b* 1997, — Ian Alexander, *b* 1957: *m* 1995, Susan (Suzie) Margaret, da of Peter Robert Scott, of Melbourne, Vic, and of Mrs Elinor Margaret Sloan, and has issue living, Robert Peter David *b* 1996, Nikita Elinor Rosemary *b* 1997, — James Malcolm, *b* 1961. *Clubs* – Guards, Melbourne (Vic).

Issue of late Hon Lionel Lindsay, MC, 6th and yst son of 26th Earl of Crawford, *b* 1879, *d* 1965: *m* 1921, Kathleen Yone, who *d* 1970, da of late Sir John Gordon Kennedy, KCMG (M Ailsa, colls):—
Colin Paul (Hambrook House, Chichester, W Sussex PO18 8UD), *b* 1922; *ed* Eton, and at New Coll, Oxford; is a FCA: *m* 1955, Jennifer Ann, da of late Capt Thomas Marcus Brownrigg, CBE, DSO, RN (ret), and has issue living, Christopher Ronald, *b* 1957: *m* 1986, Anna Giulia, da of Andrea Orsini Baroni, of Via della Scala, Florence, and has issue living,

Alexander *b* 1995, Giulia *b* 1988, Francesca *b* 1993, — Andrew Mark, *b* 1962: *m* 1995, Katherine, eldest da of David Weaver, of Guildford, Surrey, and has issue living, Thomas *b* 1997.

      Grandchildren of late Lt-Col Henry Edith Arthur Lindsay, OBE, 4th and yst son of Col Hon Charles Hugh Lindsay, CB, 3rd son of 24th Earl of Crawford:—
Issue of late Lt-Col (David Ludovic) Peter Lindsay, DSO, *b* 1900, *d* 1971: *m* 1st, 1940 (*m diss* 1946), Ursula Jane, da of late Robert Orlando Rodolph Kenyon-Slaney (*see* B Kenyon, colls); 2ndly, 1950, Barbara J., da of Edward Dunn:—
(By 2nd *m*) David Michael, *b* 1956: *m* 1991, Sarah Jane, eldest da of Anthony Poat, of Salisbury, and has issue living, Jack Christopher, *b* 1993, — Charles Frederick, *b* 1999, — Alice Georgina, *b* 1996. *Residence* – The New House, Wilton, Wilts SN8 3ER. ——— Jane Caroline, *b* 1951. ——— Sarah Jacqueline (*Hon Mrs James Jauncey*), *b* 1952: *m* 1988, as his 2nd wife, Hon James Malise Dundas Jauncey, elder son of Baron Jauncey of Tullichettle (Life Baron).

      Grandson of late Maj Francis Howard Lindsay, 4th son of late William Alexander Lindsay, CVO, KC (infra):—
Issue of late Major John Stewart LINDSAY-MacDOUGALL, DSO, MC, Argyll and Sutherland Highlanders, *b* 1911, *d* (of wounds while a prisoner in Italy) 1943, having assumed the additional surname of MacDougall 1932: *m* 1934, Sheila Marion Roma (6 Laverockbank Rd, Edinburgh EH5 3DG) (who *m* 2ndly, 1949, Lt-Col Aubrey Wynter Gibbon, OBE, Argyll and Sutherland Highlanders, who *d* 1978), da of late Capt J. W. L. Sprot, Black Watch:—
Colin John Francis (Lunga, Ardfern, Lochgilphead, Argyll), *b* 1939; *ed* Radley: *m* 1961 (*m diss* 1978), Hon Frances Phœbe, da of late Capt Hon Anthony Francis Phillimore (*see* B Phillimore), and has issue living, James Alexander, *b* 1964, — Lucien Coll, *b* 1966, — Aidan John, *b* 1968, — Antonia Frances, *b* 1961, — Joanna Theresa, *b* 1962.

      Granddaughter of late William Alexander Lindsay, CVO, KC, el son of late Hon Colin Lindsay, 4th son of 24th Earl of Crawford:—
Issue of late Maj Francis Howard Lindsay, *b* 1876; *ka* 1916: *m* 1910, Helen Margaret, who *d* 1941, el da and co-heir of the late Lt-Col Stewart MacDougall, Gordon Highlanders (formerly Maj Argyll and Sutherland Highlanders), one of HM's Corps of Gentlemen-at-Arms, of Lunga, Ardfern, Argyll:—
Katherine Frances LINDSAY-MacDOUGALL, *b* 1915; *ed* St Hilda's Coll, Oxford (MA, BLitt, Dip Archive Admin); Curator of Manuscripts, Nat Maritime Museum, Greenwich 1949-59; educational work in Zambia 1964-69; 1939-45 War as 1st Officer WRNS; assumed the additional surname of MacDougall 1949. *Residence* – Innisaig, Ardfern, Lochgilphead, Argyll PA31 8QN.

      Grandchildren of late Maj Sir George Humphrey Maurice BROUN LINDSAY, DSO, only son of late Alfred Lindsay, 3rd son of late Hon Colin Lindsay (ante):—
Issue of late Colin George BROUN LINDSAY, *b* 1926, *d* 1989: *m* 1952, Countess Beatrice Marie Thérèse Ferdinande Yvonne Ghislaine (*Madam Broun Lindsay*) (Colstoun, Haddington), da of Count Conrard Marie Joseph Gaspard Melchior Baltasar Ghislain d'Ursel, of Château de Moulbaix, Belgium:—
Ludovic David, *b* 1954; *ed* Ampleforth. *Residence* – Colstoun, Haddington. ——— Christian Georgeana, *b* 1956.

      Grandsons of late Capt Claud Frederic Thomas Lindsay, RFA, 2nd son of late Col Henry Edzell Morgan Lindsay, CB, eldest son of late Lt-Col Henry Gore Lindsay (infra):—
Issue of late Maj George Morgan Thomas Lindsay, *b* (*posthumous*) 1918, *d* 1990: *m* 1954, Jennifer Mary (Glanmor, Southerndown, nr Bridgend, Glamorgan), only da of late Col John Geoffrey Ferry, RA (ret), of Wymering Lodge, Farnborough, Hants:—
David Charles Thomas, *b* 1955; *ed* Wellington Coll: *m* 1987 (*m diss* 1991), Alexandra Wendy, da of late Robert Emmas. ——— William George Thomas, *b* 1958; *ed* Wellington Coll.

      Grandchildren of late Col Henry Edzell Morgan Lindsay, CB (ante):—
Issue of late David Edzell Thomas Lindsay, *b* 1910, *d* 1968: *m* 1st, 1933 (*m diss* 1939), Kathleen Mary, yr da Austin Green; 2ndly, 1940 (*m diss* 1947), Eleanor Margaret, da of Kenneth Campbell, of Foxcote House, Andoversford, Glos; 3rdly, 1950, Hon Audrey Lavinia Lyttelton (Poplar Cottage, Fore St Hill, Budleigh Salterton, Devon), da of 9th Viscount Cobham:—
(By 1st *m*) David Claud (38 Bassingham Rd, SW18 3AG), *b* 1934; *ed* Eton: *m* 1964, Sheela Mary, da of late Michael Edward FitzGerald, of Brougham House, Newcastle, co Galway. ——— (By 3rd *m*) † Hugh Charles Lyttelton, MVO, *b* 1953; *ed* Millfield; Maj 9th/12th Lancers (Prince of Wales's); Equerry to HM 1984: *m* 1987, Sarah Patricia, MVO (who *m* 2ndly, 1996, Paul M. Horsley), da of late Brian John (Tim) Brennan, MC, of Weybank House, Godalming, Surrey, and *d* in a skiing accident 1988, leaving issue, Alice Rose Lyttelton, *b* (*posthumous*), 1988. ——— Andrew Edzell Thomas (8 Ash-grove Rd, Redland, Bristol BS6 6LY), *b* 1956; *ed* Millfield: *m* 1991, Patricia May, da of David Thesen, of Bath, and has issue living, Charles Edzell Thesen, *b* 1994, — Ellinor Viola, *b* 1996. ——— Emma Katrina, *b* 1955; *ed* Millfield: *m* 1986, Lt-Col Ian M. Daniell, RE, elder son of Dr B. L. Daniell, of Farnham, Surrey, and has issue living, Tobias Hugh, *b* 1989, — Amy Meriel, *b* 1987.

      Granddaughters of late Lt-Col Henry Gore Lindsay, 2nd son of late George Hayward Lindsay, 4th son of late Rt Rev Hon Charles Dalrymple Lindsay, Bishop of Kildare, 6th son of 5th Earl of Balcarres:—
Issue of late Maj David Balcarres Lindsay, *b* 1863, *d* 1943: *m* 1898, Grace Maud, who *d* 1945, da of George Mill-er, of Brentry House, Westbury-on-Trym:—
Winifred Laura, *b* 1907. *Residence* – Newtown Anner, Clonmel, co Tipperary.

      Issue of late Maj-Gen George Mackintosh Lindsay, CB, CMG, CBE, DSO, *b* 1880, *d* 1956: *m* 1907, Constance, who *d* 1974, da of George Stewart Hamilton:—
Joan Mary, *b* 1911: *m* 1938, Charles Holwell Thomas, OBE, who *d* 1990 (*see* E Lauderdale, colls, 1968 Edn), and has had issue, Robert Heriot Lindsay, *b* 1941, — David Charles Morgan, *b* 1942: *m* 1970, Ann Tresina, da of R. H. B. Benger, of Johannesburg, and *d* 1987, leaving issue, Rupert James Morgan *b* 1972; *k* in a motor accident 1992, Camilla Jane Beringer *b* 1976, — George Francis Maitland *b* 1944: *m* 1976, Geraldine, da of Adrian van der Kwast, of Curacao, Netherlands Antilles, and has issue living, Morgan Adrian Maitland *b* 1979, Georgiana Elaine Lindsay *b* 1980, — Sarah

Elizabeth Lindsay, *b* 1946: *m* 1971, Henry Charles Alfred Rowe, of Winfrith House, Winfrith Newburgh, Dorset, and has issue living, Charles Edward Kingsley *b* 1973, Louise Arabella Lindsay *b* 1975, Serena Elizabeth Henrietta *b* 1977. *Residence* – Southwick House, Kirkcudbrightshire.

PREDECESSORS – **(1)** WALTER de Lindesay (1113), son of Gilbert de Ghent; *s* by his son **(2)** WILLIAM, of Ercildun, 2nd Lord of his name, *s* by his son **(3)** WALTER, 3rd Lord; *s* by his son **(4)** WILLIAM, 4th Lord; *s* by his son **(5)** WALTER, 5th Lord (Lord of Lamberton); *s* by his son **(6)** WILLIAM, 6th Lord (1247); *s* by his son **(7)** WALTER, 7th Lord; *s* by his son **(8)** WILLIAM, 8th Lord (1282); *s* by his kinsman **(9)** *Sir* ALEXANDER, 9th Lord (grandson of Sir David of Brenevil and the Byres, a Regent of Scotland 1255), companion of King Robert Bruce, and a Baron 1308; *s* by his son **(10)** *Sir* DAVID, 10th Lord, one of the Barons who signed the famous letter to Pope John XXII asserting the independence of Scotland; *s* by his son **(11)** *Sir* JAMES, 11th Lord; *s* by his son **(12)** *Sir* JAMES, 12th Lord, High Justiciary of Scotland; *s* by his cousin **(13)** *Sir* DAVID, 13th Lord, a valiant knight, was *cr*, proclaimed and belted *Earl of Crawford* (peerage of Scotland) at Perth, April 21, 1398, his lordship being at the same time erected into a regality; was Ambassador to England 1406; *s* by his son **(14)** ALEXANDER, 2nd Earl; a Commr to treat for the release of James I; was detained as a hostage for his ransom 1424-7; *s* by his son **(15)** DAVID, 3rd Earl; *k* 1446 while endeavoring to prevent the Battle of Arbroath; *s* by his son **(16)** ALEXANDER, 4th Earl; Hereditary Sheriff of Aberdeenshire; fought in rebellion at Battle of Brechin 1452; was attainted and afterwards restored; *s* by his son **(17)** DAVID, 5th Earl; having held numerous high offices, was *cr Duke of Montrose* (peerage of Scotland) 1488, a dignity that has not since been assumed by any of his successors; *d* 1495; *s* by his 2nd son **(18)** JOHN, 6th Earl; accused of murdering his el brother, but was killed at Flodden before the accusation was heard; *s* by his uncle **(19)** ALEXANDER, 7th Earl; *s* by his son **(20)** DAVID, 8th Earl; his son Alexander being found guilty of constructive parricide, was by the law of Scotland attainted; *s* by his kinsman **(21)** DAVID, 9th Earl, grandson of Walter, son of 3rd Earl; by consent of the crown he reconveyed his earldom to the son of Alexander (ante), but in failure of his issue the title to be in remainder to his son, Sir David (Lord Edzell), a Lord of Session; John, the 2nd son of this peer, Lord Menmuir, a Lord of Session, had issue, David, *cr* 1st Lord Lindsay of Balcarres (infra): *s* by his kinsman **(22)** DAVID, 10th Earl; a faithful adherent of Queen Mary's cause; *s* by his son **(23)** DAVID, 11th Earl; *s* by his son **(24)** DAVID, 12th Earl, who alienated the greater portion of the estates; *s* by his uncle **(25)** HENRY, 13th Earl, son of 10th Earl; *s* by his son **(26)** GEORGE, 14th Earl; *s* by his half-brother **(27)** ALEXANDER, 15th Earl; *s* by his brother **(28)** LUDOVIC, 16th Earl; during the Civil Wars commanded a Regt of Horse, and fought at Marston Moor, Philiphaugh, and Newcastle, where he was taken prisoner, and in exchange, it is supposed, for his liberty, resigned with the sanction of the Crown, his Earldom to Charles I for a re-grant (failing his own issue) to John, 10th Earl of Lindsay, with remainder to his own collateral heirs; *dsp*, when the Earldom passed to John, 10th Earl of Lindsay, in whose family it continued until 1808, when the line failed (see E Lindsay). **(29)** DAVID, son of Lord Menmuir (refer to 9th Earl), was *cr Lord Lindsay of Balcarres* (peerage of Scotland) 1633; *s* by his son **(30)** ALEXANDER, 2nd Lord; rendered valuable service to the royal cause; *cr Lord Lindsay and Balniel* and *Earl of Balcarres* (peerage of Scotland) 1651; for taking part with the Earl of Glencairn his estates were sequestrated; *s* by his son **(31)** CHARLES, 2nd Earl of Balcarres; *d* unm 1662; *s* by his brother **(32)** COLIN, a staunch Royalist; *s* by his son **(33)** ALEXANDER, 4th Earl of Balcarres; became in 1744, on the death of David Lindsay of Edzell, *de jure* Lord Lindsay of Crawford, and Chief of his house: *m* 1718, Elizabeth, who *d* 1768, da of David Scott, of Scotstarvet; *d* 1746; *s* by his brother **(34)** JAMES, 5th Earl of Balcarres; *d* 1768; *s* by his son **(35)** ALEXANDER, 6th Earl of Balcarres; a Representative Peer, a Gen in the Army and Gov of Jamaica; in 1808, *s* as 23rd Earl of Crawford; *d* 1828; *s* by his son **(36)** JAMES, 24th Earl of Crawford and 7th of Balcarres; *b* 1783: *m* 1811, Hon Maria Margaret Frances Pennington, who *d* 1850, da of 1st Baron Muncaster; *cr Baron Wigan*, of Haigh Hall, co Lancaster (peerage of United Kingdom) 1826, and had Earldom of Crawford and Lordship of Lindsay confirmed to him 1848; *d* 1869; *s* by his son **(37)** ALEXANDER WILLIAM CRAWFORD, 25th Earl of Crawford and 8th of Balcarres, and 33rd Lord Lindsay of Crawford; *b* 1912: *m* 1846, Margaret, who *d* 1909, da of Lt-Gen James Lindsay, of Balcarres; *d* 1880; *s* by his son **(38)** JAMES LUDOVIC, KT, LLD, FRS, 26th Earl of Crawford and 9th of Balcarres; *b* 1847; MP for Wigan (*C*) 1874-80; acted as Dep for Great Steward of Scotland at Coronations of King Edward VII, and King George V: *m* 1869, Emily Florence, who *d* 1934, da of late Col Hon Edward Bootle-Wilbraham; *d* 1913; *s* by his el son **(39)** DAVID ALEXANDER EDWARD, KT, PC, DCL, 27th Earl of Crawford and 10th of Balcarres; *b* 1871; was a Junior Lord of the Treasury 1903-5, Pres of Board of Agriculture and Fisheries July to Dec 1916, Lord Privy Seal 1916-19, Chancellor of Duchy of Lancaster 1919-21, First Commr of Works 1921-2 and Min of Transport 1922; MP for Lancashire (N), Chorley Div (*C*) 1895-1913: *m* 1900, Constance Lilian, who *d* 1947, da of Sir Henry Carstairs Pelly, MP, 3rd Bt; *d* 1940; *s* by his el son **(40)** DAVID ALEXANDER ROBERT, KT, GBE, FSA, 28th Earl of Crawford and 11th Earl of Balcarres; *b* 1900; Chm of National Gallery 1938-41, and again 1945-49, Roy Fine Art Commn 1943-57, National Trust 1945-65, National Art Collections Fund 1945-70, National Gallery of Scotland 1952-72, and National Library of Scotland 1944-74; R of St Andrews Univ 1952-55; MP for Lancs, Lonsdale Div (*U*) 1924-40: *m* 1925, Mary Katherine, who *d* 1994, da of late Col Rt Hon Lord Richard Frederick Cavendish, CB, CMG (D Devonshire); *d* 1975; *s* by his el son **(41)** ROBERT ALEXANDER, PC, 29th Earl of Crawford, and 12th Earl of Balcarres and present peer; also Lord Lindsay (of Crawford), Lord Lindsay of Balcarres, Lord Lindsay and Balniel, Baron Wigan, and Baron Balniel (Life Baron).

CRAWLEY, BARONESS (Crawley) (Life Baroness 1998)

CHRISTINE MARY CRAWLEY, da of ......, of ......; *b* 9 Jan 1950: *ed* Notre Dame Catholic Secondary Girls' Sch, Plymouth, and Digby Stuart Training Coll, Roehampton; drama teacher and youth theatre leader; Town and District Councillor in Oxford; MEP for Birmingham E (Lab) since 1984; Chm Women's Rights Cttee 1989-94, Dep Leader Euro Parliamentary Labour Party since 1994; Memb Civil Liberties Cttee and Women's Rights Cttee; Memb Fabian Soc, Co-operative Party, CND, etc; FRSA; *cr Baroness Crawley*, of Edgbaston, co West Midlands (Life Baroness) 1998: *m* 19—, ... Crawley, son of ...... Crawley, of ......, and has issue.

Arms – ......
Address – c/o House of Lords, Westminster, SW1A 0PW.

CRAWSHAW, BARON (Brooks) (Baron UK 1892, Bt UK 1891)

Consider the end

DAVID GERALD BROOKS, 5th Baron, and 5th Baronet; *b* 14 Sept 1934; *s* 1997; *ed* Eton, and RAC Cirencester; High Sheriff Leics 1985; Lord of the Manor of Long Whatton: *m* 1970, Belinda Mary, da of George P. H. Burgess, of 14 Kirkwood Av, Sandringham, Melbourne, Australia, and has issue.

Arms – Argent, three bars wavy azure, a cross fleury erminois, in chief a fountain. Crest – A demi-lion proper, maned argent, charged on the shoulder with a fountain, and holding in the paws a pheon in bend sinister proper, stringed or. Supporters – *Dexter*, a stag argent; *sinister*, a horse argent; each collared wavy azure, and suspended from the collar an escutcheon erminois charged with a fountain.
Seat – Whatton House, Long Whatton, Loughborough, Leicestershire LE12 5BG.

DAUGHTERS LIVING

Hon Susanna Jane, *b* 1974.
Hon Amanda Mary, *b* 1975.
Hon Elisabeth Joan, *b* 1976.
Hon Katharine Sheila, *b* 1978.

BROTHER LIVING

Hon JOHN PATRICK (25 Cadogan St, SW3), *b* 17 March 1938; *ed* Loughborough Coll: *m* 1967, Rosemary Vans Agnew, only da of late C. Vans Agnew Frank, of Greenways, Hunmanby, E Yorks, and has issue living, Edward Samuel, *b* 1969, — Caroline Miranda, *b* 1972.

SISTER LIVING

Hon Mary Aletheia, *b* 1931.

COLLATERAL BRANCHES LIVING

Grandchildren of late Hon Herbert William Brooks (*infra*):—
Issue of late Capt Christopher John Brooks, Coldm Gds, *b* 1925, *d* 1991: *m* 1st, 1951 (*m diss* 1957), Patricia Evelyn Beverley, who *d* 1992, el da of John William Matthews, of Heathcroft, Hertford Heath, Herts; 2ndly, 1958, Gwendoline Helen (10 Tonsley Rd, SW18 1BG), el da of Louis D. Evans:—
(By 1st *m*) Sarah Jane, *b* 1956: *m* 1988, Maj Harry St John Holcroft, The Blues and Royals, yst son of late Oliver Holcroft, of Upton-on-Severn, Worcs, and has issue living, Harry Christopher Esmond, *b* 1990, — Christopher Nicholas, *b* 1991. —— (By 2nd *m*) Timothy Allan William, *b* 1962: *m* 1986, Christine, da of Leonard Pugh, of Adelaide, Australia. —— Georgina Helen, *b* 1960: *m* 1985, Peter Myrtle, of 115 Golfers Drive, Covington, Louisiana 70433, USA, son of Giles Myrtle, of Dalreagle, Wigtownshire, and has issue living, Frederick Giles Christopher, *b* 1988, — Christopher Thomas John, *b* 1992, — Victoria Gwendoline Virginia, *b* 1987.

Issue of late Hon Herbert William Brooks, yr son of 2nd Baron, *b* 1890, *d* 1974: *m* 1922, Hilda Muriel, who *d* 1967, da of late A. G. Steel, KC:—
Timothy Gerald Martin (Wistow, Leicester), *b* 1929; NDA; JP Leics 1960, High Sheriff 1980, DL 1984, Lord Lieut 1989: *m* 1951, Hon Ann Fremantle, da of 4th Baron Cottesloe, and has issue living, Richard Allan Halford, *b* 1958: *m* 1985, Diana Elizabeth, yr da of Sir Godfrey Michael David Thomas, 11th Bt (*cr* 1694), and has issue living, Charles John Halford *b* 1989, Michael *b* 1994, Sabrina *b* 1991, — Andrew Herbert John, *b* 1966, — Michael Julian, *b* 1969, — Lucinda Jane, *b* 1953: *m* 1978, Keith Charlton, and has issue living, three sons and two das, — Nicola Frances, *b* 1955: *m* 1978, Gerald A. Michel, and has issue living, two das.

Grandchildren of late Hon Marshall Jones Brooks, yr son of 1st Baron:—
Issue of late Lt-Col Thomas Marshall Brooks, MC, TD; *b* 1893; *d* 1967: *m* 1920, Evelyn Sylvia, who *d* 1967, da of Rev Hon Archibald Parker, Preb of Lichfield (E Macclesfield, colls):—
Ronald Marshall (Heath Hill, Bourton-on-the-Water, Glos), *b* 1924; *ed* Eton; 1939-45 War as Lt Queen's Bays: *m* 1950, Dorothy Valerie, da of Geoffrey Freer, of Ditchford Hill, Moreton-in-Marsh, Glos.

Issue of late Maj Noel Brand Brooks, MC, TD, *b* 1896, *d* 1984: *m* 1921, Joan Margaret, JP, who *d* 1984, da of Brig-Gen Sir Edward Thomas Le Marchant, 4th Bt, CB, CBE:—
Anne, *b* 1922. —— Betty Rosamond, *b* 1924: *m* 1950, Maj Nigel Steuart Kearsley, late Welsh Gds (Ramsay, Bt, *cr* 1806, colls), of The Old Vicarage, Asthall, nr Burford, Oxon OX18 4HW, and has issue living, Rosamond Joanna, *b* 1955, — Grania Anne, *b* 1957: *m* 1983, Lt-Col Patrick John Tabor, MVO, The Blues and Royals, and has issue, two sons and two das.

Grandchildren of Maj Noel Brand Brooks, MC, TD (ante):—
Issue of late Robert Noel Brand Brooks, *b* 1927, *d* 1976: *m* 1955, Caroline Diana (Castle Barn, Churchill, Oxon), only da of Brig George Herbert Norris Todd, MC, DL, of Court House, Stretton-on-Fosse, Moreton-in-Marsh, Glos:—

Christopher George, b 1959: m 1989, Miranda, eldest da of John Sergeant, of Phoenix Farm, Widford, nr Ware, Herts. —— Charles Patrick Evelyn, b 1963; ed Eton; former racehorse trainer. —— Annabel Joan, b 1958: m 1981, Damian David Harris (see B Ogmore).

PREDECESSORS – (1) THOMAS BROOKS, son of late John Brooks, of Crawshaw Hall, Lancashire, b 1825; High Sheriff of Lancashire 1884; cr a Baronet 1891, and Baron Crawshaw, of Crawshaw, co Lancaster and of Whatton, co Leicester (peerage of the United Kingdom) 1892: m 1851, Catherine, who d 1917, da of late John Jones, of Kilsall Hall, Shropshire; d 1908; s by his son (2) WILLIAM, 2nd Baron, b 1853: m 1882, Mary Ethel, who d 1914, da of Sir Michael Hicks-Beach, 8th Bt; d 1929; s by his son (3) GERALD BEACH, 3rd Baron, b 1884: m 1930, Marjory Sheila, da of late Lieut-Col Percy Robert Clifton, CMG, DSO, TD; d 1946; s by his son (4) WILLIAM MICHAEL CLIFTON, 4th Baron, b 1933; DL Leics 1992, Treas Loughborough Div Conservative Assocn; dunm 1997; s by his brother (5) DAVID GERALD, 5th Baron and present peer.

CRAWSHAW OF AINTREE, BARONY OF (Crawshaw) (Extinct 1986)

WIDOW LIVING OF LIFE BARON

AUDREY FRANCES (Baroness Crawshaw of Aintree), da of Francis Augustine Lima, of Liverpool: m 1960, Baron Crawshaw of Aintree, OBE (Life Baron), who d 1986. Residence – The Orchard, Aintree Lane, Liverpool L10 8LE.

CREWE, MARQUESSATE OF (Crewe-Milnes) (Extinct 1945)

DAUGHTER LIVING OF FIRST MARQUESS (By 2nd marriage)

Lady Mary Evelyn Hungerford, b 1915; bore the Queen's Canopy at Coronation of King George VI: m 1935 (m diss 1953), 9th Duke of Roxburghe, who d 1974. Residence – 15 Hyde Park Gardens, W2.

Crichton, family name of Earl of Erne.

Crichton, Viscount; son of Earl of Erne.

CRICKHOWELL, BARON (Edwards) (Life Baron 1987)

(ROGER) NICHOLAS EDWARDS, PC, son of late (Herbert Cecil) Ralph Edwards, CBE, FSA, of Suffolk House, Chiswick Mall, W4, and of Pont Esgob Mill; *b* 25 Feb 1934; *ed* Westminster, and Trin Coll, Camb (MA 1968); Pres Cardiff Univ 1988-98; a Member of Lloyds since 1965, Dir Wm Brandts Sons & Co Ltd 1974-76, and Chief Exec Brandts Insurance Div; Chm Nat Rivers Authority 1989-96, Chm HTV Group plc, Associated British Ports Holdings plc 1988-99, Anglesey Mining plc and Member of Cttee of Automobile Assocn 1988-98; Chm ITNET plc; Dir Anglesey Mining plc; Opposition Spokesman on Welsh Affairs 1975-79, Sec of State for Wales 1979-87; MP for Pembroke (*C*) 1970-87; *cr* PC 1979, and *Baron Crickhowell*, of Pont Esgob in the Black Mountains and co of Powys (Life Baron) 1987: *m* 1963, Ankaret, da of William James Healing, of Kinsham House, nr Tewkesbury, Glos, and has issue.

Residences – Pont Esgob Mill, Fforest, Abergavenny NP7 7LS; 4 Henning St, SW11 3DR.

SON LIVING

Hon Rupert Timothy Guy, *b* 1964; *ed* Radley, and Trin Coll, Camb: *m* 1990, Olivia Grizel Kirkwood, yr da of Capt David Colin Kirkwood Brown (*see* E Caithness), and has issue living, Joshua James, *b* 1991, — Camilla Sophie, *b* 1994, — Eliza Nicola, *b* 1996.

DAUGHTERS LIVING

Hon Sophie Elizabeth Ankaret, *b* 1966.
Hon Olivia Caroline, *b* 1970.

Cripps, family name of Baron Parmoor.

CROFT, BARON (Croft) (Baron UK 1940, Bt UK 1924)

BERNARD WILLIAM HENRY PAGE CROFT, 3rd Baron, and 3rd Baronet; *b* 28 Aug 1949; *s* 1997; *ed* Stowe, and Wales Univ (BSc): *m* 1993, Mary Elizabeth, da of late James Richardson, of co Tyrone.

Arms – Quarterly per fesse indented azure and argent; in the 1st quarter a lion passant guardant or. **Crests** – 1st, a lion passant guardant argent; 2nd, a wyvern sable vulned in the side gules. **Supporters** – *Dexter*, a lion rampant quarterly per fesse indented azure and argent; *sinister*, a wyvern sable, vulned in the side gules.
Seat – Croft Castle, Leominster, Herefordshire HR6 9PW. *Town Residence* – 5 Comeragh Mews, Comeragh Rd, W14 9HW. *Clubs* – Hurlingham, Naval and Military.

SISTER LIVING

Hon Charlotte Elizabeth Ann, *b* 1952; *ed* Benenden: *m* 1975 (*m diss* 1995), Emrys Thomas Devonald, and has issue living, James Emrys, *b* 1979, — Jennifer Ann, *b* 1977. *Residence* – 1 Kingfisher Close, Prestwood, Great Missenden, Bucks HP16 0UA.

AUNTS LIVING (*daughters of 1st Baron*)

Hon Hilda Elizabeth Mary, *b* 1909: *m* 1934, Richard Hayter Bayford, Bar-at-Law, Capt R Berks Regt, who *d* 1982, and has issue living, Robert Michael Croft (65B Belsize Park Gdns, NW3), *b* 1936, — Gillian Sara Carolyn *b* 1935: *m* 1958, Flight-Lieut

To be rather than to seem

Michael R. Holmes, RAF, of 113 St Pancras, Chichester PO19 4LH, — Mary Elizabeth (9 North Hill Av, Highgate, N6), *b* 1944. *Residence* – Croft Lodge, Croft Rd, Goring on Thames, Oxon.

Hon Nancy Diana Joyce, *b* 1912: *m* 1936, Manfred Uhlman, who *d* 1985, and has issue living, Francis Raymond Croft, *b* 1943, — Caroline Ann, *b* 1940: *m* 1966 (*m diss* 1976), Albert Charles Compton, and has issue living, Tristram Ludovic Archer *b* 1968, Sarah Harriet *b* 1972. *Residence* – Croft Castle, Leominster, Herefords HR6 9PW.

Hon Anne Rosemary Dorothea, *b* 1918: *m* 1946, Flight-Lieut Herbert Edmund Poole, RAF, who *d* 1984, and has issue living, Herbert Benyon (Knight's Hill, 19 Knight St, Sawbridgeworth, Herts CM21 9AT), *b* 1947, — Jeremy Henry Borwick (Thorn's Orchard, East Mill Lane, Sherborne, Dorset DT9 3DP), *b* 1949, — Hugo Edmund (26A Bell St, Sawbridgeworth, Herts CM21 9AN), *b* 1952: *m* 1st, 1977 (*m diss* 1992), Christina Susan de Jong Cleyndert; 2ndly, 1992, Anne Margaret Lovell, and has issue living (by 1st *m*), Charlotte Annalika *b* 1979, Jessica Margery Anne *b* 1981, Kate Antonia *b* 1982. *Residence* – Dower House, 17A Knight St, Sawbridgeworth, Herts.

PREDECESSORS – (1) *Rt Hon Sir* HENRY PAGE Croft, CMG, TD, PC, son of late Richard Benyon Croft, of Fanhams Hall, Ware (*see* Croft, Bt, *cr* 1671, colls); *b* 1881; European War 1914-16 as Brig-Gen late Herts Regt (CMG); was Joint Under-Sec of State for War 1940-45; sat as MP for Christchurch (C) 1910-18, and for Bournemouth 1918-40; *cr a Baronet* 1924, and *Baron Croft*, of Bournemouth, co Southampton (peerage of United Kingdom) 1940: *m* 1907, Hon Nancy Beatrice Borwick, who *d* 1949, yst da of 1st Baron Borwick; *d* 1947; *s* by his son (2) MICHAEL HENRY GLENDOWER PAGE, 2nd Baron, *b* 1916; Bar Inner Temple 1952; OStJ, FRSA; 1939-45 War, Hon Capt RASC; Art Collector, Hon Keeper of Contemporary Art, Fitzwilliam Museum: *m* 1948, Lady Antoinette Fredericka Hersey Cecilia Conyngham, who *d* 1959, da of 6th Marquess Conyngham; *d* 1997; *s* by his only son (3) BERNARD WILLIAM HENRY PAGE, 3rd Baron and present peer.

CROFTON, BARON (Crofton) (Baron I 1797, Bt I 1758)

God gives the increase

GUY PATRICK GILBERT CROFTON, 7th Baron and 10th Baronet; *b* 17 June 1951; *s* 1989; *ed* Theresianistische Akademie, Vienna, and at Midhurst Gram Sch; Lt-Col 9th/12th Royal Lancers (POW): *m* 1985, Gillian Susan Burroughs, only da of Harry Godfrey Mitchell Bass, CMG, of Reepham, Norfolk, and has issue.

Arms – Per pale indented or and azure, a lion passant guardant counterchanged. **Crest** – Seven ears of wheat growing on one stalk or. **Supporters** – *Dexter*, a lion azure: *sinister*, a stag proper. *Address* – c/o Home HQ 9/12 L, TA Centre, Saffron Rd, Wigston, Leics LE18 4UX. *Club* – Cavalry and Guards'.

SONS LIVING

Hon (EDWARD) HARRY (PIERS), *b* 23 Jan 1988.
Hon (Charles) Marcus (George), *b* (twin) 1988.

BROTHERS DECEASED

Hon Brian St George, *b* and *d* 1950.
Hon Arthur Blaise Adrian, *b* 1957; *d* 1987.

SISTER LIVING

Hon Georgiana Ann CROFTON, *b* 1955; has resumed her maiden name: *m* 1980 (*m diss* 1986), Brent Hutchinson, son of Ivan Hutchinson, and has issue living, Blaise Peter Louis, *b* 1982, — Louisa Beatrice, *b* 1981. *Address* – 11 Shalcomb St, SW10 0HZ.

DAUGHTER LIVING OF SIXTH BARON

Hon Freya Charlotte, *b* 1983.

WIDOW LIVING OF SON OF FOURTH BARON

Madeleine Barbara (PRATT), da of late William James Heath, of London: *m* 1951, as his 4th wife, Hon (Arthur) Marcus (Lowther) Crofton, Maj Irish Guards, who *d* 1962. *Residence* – 401, 1430 Newport Av, Victoria, BC, Canada.

MOTHER LIVING

Ann Pamela TIGHE, elder da of late Gp Capt Charles Herbert Tighe, OBE, DFC, RAF (ret), of The Red House, Inistioge, co Kilkenny; has resumed her maiden name: *m* 1st, 1948 (*m diss* 1963), 5th Baron Crofton, who *d* 1974; 2ndly 1964 (*m diss* 1972), Robert Thomas Francis Flach, Bar-at-law, of London; 3rdly, 1973 (*m diss* 1976), Guy Brooke, of New York City. *Residence* – 12 Curzon St, Calne, Wilts SN11 0DD.

WIDOW LIVING OF FIFTH BARON

MARY (*Mary, Baroness Crofton*), eldest da of late Maj James Irvine Hatfeild Friend, OBE, MC, DL, of Northdown, Thanet, Kent: *m* 1st, 1951 (*m diss* 1963), Robert Thomas Francis Flach, Bar-at-law (ante), of London; 2ndly, 1964, as his 2nd wife, the 5th Baron Crofton, who *d* 1974. *Residence* – Flat 1, 123 Gloucester Terr, W2.

WIDOW LIVING OF SIXTH BARON

MAUREEN JACQUELINE (*Maureen, Baroness Crofton*), da of Stanley James Bray, of Taunton, Som: *m* 1976, the 6th Baron, who *d* 1989. *Residence* – Briscoe Cottage, Ford St, nr Wellington, Somerset.

COLLATERAL BRANCHES LIVING (*In remainder to Barony and Baronetcy*)

Grandson of late Capt Hon Francis George Crofton, RN (infra):—
Issue of late George Crofton, *b* 1881, *d* 1943: *m* 1910, Elina, da of late K. Smith, of Natal:—
Francis George, *b* 1915.

Grandchildren of late Alfred Gerald Crofton (infra):—
Issue of late Dermott Kenneth Crofton, *b* 1904, *d* 1994: *m* 1934, Doris Livingstone, el da of late J. W. Taylor, of Belfast:—
Patrick Dermott (Ballymurray Farm, 4010 Prospect Lake Rd, Victoria, BC, Canada V9E 1H7), *b* 1935; Lt-Cdr (S) CAF (ret): *m* 1958, Patricia Judith Mary, only da of Capt Trevor Williams, of Folly, The Walled Garden, Wargrave, Berks, and has issue living, Marietta Susan Annette, *b* 1959, — Virginia Margaret Adele, *b* 1961, — Susanne Catherine Mary, *b* 1962, — Tessa Penelope Sarah, *b* 1965. —— Marcus Livingstone (1809 Grandview Drive, Victoria, BC, Canada V8N 2T8), *b* 1937; Lt-Col CAF: *m* 1966, Elizabeth Jane, da of Lt-Col Geoffrey A. Churchill, of Victoria, BC, and has issue living, Dermott Marcus Churchill, *b* 1970, — Geoffrey Patrick, *b* 1973, — Laura Elizabeth, *b* 1967, — Jenny Livingstone, *b* 1969. —— Sharron Diana (1880 San Luis Place, Victoria, BC, Canada V8N 2H2), *b* 1940: *m* 1964 (*m diss* 1970), Robert Montagu Scott, and has issue living, Ian Dermott Montagu, *b* 1967, — Andrea Gillian, *b* 1966.

Issue of late Lt-Col Desmond Gerald Crofton, ED, *b* 1905, *d* 1977: *m* 1st, 1925, Ida, who *d* 1970, da of late Frank Hardcastle, DL, JP, and widow of Maj Frank Harvey Corbett, MC, RFA; 2ndly, 1971, Dorothea Herriet, yst da of Arthur George Wilson, and widow of Keith Edward Hook:—
(By 1st *m*) John Edward, CD, *b* 1925; Lt-Col CAF: *m* 1950, Marie White, and has issue living, Desmond, *b* 1951, — Kevin, *b* 1954, — Neil, *b* 1956. —— Sylvia Ida, *b* 1928: *m* 1954, Maj Arthur Leake Gale, CD, Princess Patricia's Canadian LI, and has issue living, Reginald Derek Leake, *b* 1956, — Rupert Arthur Leake, *b* 1962, — Deirdre Sylvia Leake, *b* 1957.

Grandchilden of late Capt Hon Francis George Crofton, RN, yr brother of 3rd Baron:—
Issue of late Alfred Gerald Crofton, *b* 1882, *d* 1942: *m* 1903, Frances Nona, who *d* 1951, da of Rev Edward Wilson:—
Donovan Patrick (10672 Madrona Drive, RR1, Sidney, BC, Canada V8L 3R9), *b* 1915; Italy and NW Europe 1943-45 as Maj Princess Patricia's Canadian LI (despatches): *m* 1946, Anne B., da of Harry Marshall Erskine Evans, OBE, of Edmonton, Alberta, and has issue living, Cameron P. L., *b* 1947, — Barry Gerald, *b* 1953, — Catherine Anne, *b* 1949. —— Denise Frances, *b* 1913.

Issue of late Francis Lowther Crofton, *b* 1883, *d* 1971: *m* 1st, 1917, Annie Rebecca, MM, who *d* 1956, da of late Robert Colhoun, of Londonderry; 2ndly, 1957, Nancy Esten, da of H. H. Nash, and widow of F. Arthur Inglis:—
(By 1st *m*) Francis David, *b* 1919; *ed* McGill Univ (MD); late Capt RCAMC: *m* 1st, 1948, Marguerite, who *d* 1994, da of Earl Hines, of Halifax, Nova Scotia; 2ndly, 1996, Mrs Joan Anthea Maciejewski Crofton, of Sydney, Australia, da of late John Ernest Crofton, of Nottingham, UK, and has issue living (by 1st *m*), Catherine Elizabeth Ellen, *b* 1950, — and adopted children, Kevin Christopher DREW, *b* 1953; *d* 1955, — Jaice David Lowther, *b* 1960, — Tighe Francis Lowther, *b* 1962, — Christine Leslie-Ann, *b* 1955, — Carol Ainslie-Ann, *b* (twin) 1955. *Residence* – 303 1250 Martin St, White Rock, BC, Canada V4B 3W3.

(*In remainder to Baronetcy only*)

Granddaughters of late Frederick Norris Lowther Crofton, elder son of Maj George Lowther Crofton, only son of Frederick Charles Edward Lowther Crofton, elder son of Frederick Lowther Crofton, grand-son of Capt John Frederick Crofton, 4th son of 1st baronet:—
Issue of late George Lowther Crofton, *b* 1905, *d* 1976: *m* 1928, Nea, who *d* 1981, da of Rev A. P. Cameron, Moderator of Church of Scotland, NSW, of The Manse, Glen Innes, NSW:—
Judith Mary, *b* 1932: *m* 1st, 1957 (*m diss* 1968), Les Hayna; 2ndly, 1970, Edgar Allen, of M/S 108 Windermere Rd, Bundaberg, Queensland 4670, Australia, and has issue living (by 1st *m*), Christine Nea (PO Box 620, Bundaberg, Qld 4670), *b* 1957: *m* 1977, Wayne Olsen, of Bundaberg, Queensland, and has issue living, Timothy Malcolm *b* 1981, Daniel Christopher *b* 1985, Kerri-Ann *b* 1977, — (by 2nd *m*) Geoffrey Edgar Howell, *b* 1971, — William George John, *b* (twin) 1971. —— Clare Edith, *b* 1936: *m* 1st, 1956 (*m diss* 1982), Alex Barry Mitchell; 2ndly, 1986, Desmond Fourro, of Bundaberg, Qld, and has issue living (by 1st *m*), Steven George, *b* 1957: *m* 1989, Lynette Mary Baker, of Mackay, Qld, and has issue living, Kirsty Leeanne *b* 1982, Kylie Marie *b* (twin) 1982, — Brian Alec, *b* 1961: *m* 1985, Jacqueline Davies, of Mackay, Queensland, and has issue living, Hayden Rhys *b* 1992, Kylie Nicole *b* 1986, Leah Suzanne *b* 1988, — Glenn Cameron, *b* 1965; has issue living (by Sharon Dawn McLean), Jias Nathan Braid *b* 1993, — Jennifer Jeanie, *b* 1959: *m* 1984 (*m diss* 1986), Guus Hoogland, of Mackay, Queensland; has issue living (by Wayne Robert King, of Mackay, Qld), Michelle Cori *b* 1991.

PREDECESSORS – (1) Catherine, da of Sir Edward Crofton, MP, 4th Bt, of the Mote (which title, *cr* 1661, became extinct on the death of the 5th Bt 1780): *m* MARCUS Lowther, MP for Roscommon, who assumed the surname of Crofton and was *cr* a Bt 1758; *d* 1774; *s* by his son **(2, 3)** *Sir* Edward, 2nd Bt; MP for co Roscommon: *m* Anne, da and heir of Thomas Croker, of Baxtown, co Kildare; *d* 30 Sept 1797, having a short time before his death been offered a peerage; on 1 Dec of the same year his widow ANNE, was *cr Baroness Crofton* (peerage of Ireland); she *d* 1817, and was *s* by her grandson; Sir Edward was *s* by his son **(4)** EDWARD, 3rd Bt; *d* 1816; *s* by his son **(5)** EDWARD, 4th Bt, *b* 1806; *s* his grandmother as 2nd Baron 1817; a Representative Peer, and a Lord-in-Waiting to HM Queen Victoria: *m* 1833, Lady Georgiana Paget, da of 1st Marquess of Anglesey; *d* 1869; *s* by his son **(6)** EDWARD HENRY Churchill, 3rd Baron; *b* 1834; a Representative Peer; Gentleman of the Bedchamber (1866-8) and State Steward (1880) to Viceroy of Ireland; *d* 1912; *s* by his nephew (7) ARTHUR EDWARD Lowther, 4th Baron, *b* 1866; a Representative Peer: *m* 1893, Jessie Castle, who *d* 1923, da of J. Hewitson and widow of Neville Paddon; *d* 1942; *s* by his grandson (8) EDWARD BLAISE (son of late Hon Edward Charles Crofton, el son of 4th Baron), 5th Baron, *b* 1926: *m* 1st, 1948 (*m diss* 1963) Ann Pamela, elder da of Gp Capt Charles Herbert Tighe, OBE, DFC, RAF (ret); 2ndly, 1964, Mary, el da of late Maj James Irvine Hatfeild Friend, OBE, MC, DL, and formerly wife of Robert Thomas Francis Flach; *d* 1974; *s* by his el son (9) CHARLES EDWARD PIERS, 6th Baron, *b* 1949; Ship Master, ·Member Nautical Inst: *m* 1976, Maureen Jacqueline, da of Stanley James Bray, of Taunton, Som; *d* 1989, *s* by his brother (10) GUY PATRICK GILBERT, 7th Baron and present peer.

CROHAM, BARON (Allen) (Life Baron 1978)

Always ready

DOUGLAS ALBERT VIVIAN ALLEN, GCB, son of late Albert John Allen; *b* 1917; *ed* Wallington County Boys, and LSE (BScEcon); Perm Sec, Dept of Economic Affairs 1966-68, Perm Sec, Treasury 1968-74, and Perm Sec, Civil Service Dept, and Head of Home Civil Ser 1974-77; Advisor to Gov of Bank of England 1978-83; Chm British Nat Oil Corpn 1982-86, and Guiness Peat Gp plc 1983-89; 1939-45 War as Capt RA, AA Command; *cr* CB 1963, KCB 1967; GCB 1973, and *Baron Croham*, of London Borough of Croydon (Life Baron) 1978: *m* 1941, Sybil Eileen, who *d* 1994, da of late John Marco Allegro, and has issue.

𝕬rms – Argent on a base checky or and azure an oak tree proper fructed or, the trunk supported by two crows respectant proper beaked and legged gold. 𝕮rest – An alaunt proper gorged with a crown or reposing its dexter paw upon a purse azure corded and tasselled the cords tied over the paw in a bow or 𝕾upporters – Dexter, a griffin azure semy of roundels or and argent winged beaked legged and tufted or. Sinister, a pantheon azure semy of mullets of six points or and argent winged and hooved or.
Residences – 9 Manor Way, South Croydon; Ashcroft, Crowborough Rd, Nutley, Sussex.

SONS LIVING

Hon John Douglas (Westfields, 23 Quaker Rd, Sileby, Leics), *b* 1945: *m* 1969, Sheila, only da of Dr A. J. Ward, of Hemingford Grey, Cambs, and has issue living, Gregory, *b* 1972, — Alexander, *b* 1975, — Sarah, *b* 1979.
Hon Richard Anthony (2 Mount Close, Kenley, Surrey), *b* 1950: *m* 1st, 1980 (*m diss* 1986), Karen, only da of F. Hughes, of Whetstone, London; 2ndly, 1988 (*m diss* 1995), Gillian, only da of R. Harraway, of Huddersfield, Yorks.

DAUGHTER LIVING

Hon Rosamund Sybil, *b* 1942: *m* 1974, Stephan Sulyák, of 8A Harewood Rd, S Croydon, Surrey CR2 7AL, son of late Laszló Sulyák, of Kunszentmartón, Hungary, and has issue living, Veronica Claire, *b* 1976.

CROMARTIE, EARL OF (Mackenzie) (Earl UK 1861)

LUCEO NON URO

I shine not burn

JOHN RUARIDH GRANT MACKENZIE, 5th Earl, *b* 12 June 1948; *s* 1989; *ed* Rannoch Sch, and Strathclyde Univ; recognized by Lord Lyon as Chief of Clan Mackenzie; discontinued the use of the forename and surname of Blunt 1962; author of *Selected Climbs in Skye*, etc; MIExpE: *m* 1st, 1973 (*m diss* 1983), Helen, da of John Murray; 2ndly, 1985, Janet Clare, da of Christopher James Harley, of Strathpeffer, Ross-shire, and has issue by 2nd *m*.

𝕬rms – Azure a buck's head cabossed or. 𝕮rest – The sun in his splendour. 𝕾upporters – On either side a wild man wreathed about the loins with oak, holding a club resting on the exterior shoulder proper.
Seat – Castle Leod, Strathpeffer, Ross and Cromarty. *Clubs* – Army and Navy, Pratt's, Scottish Mountaineering.

SONS LIVING (*By 2nd marriage*)

COLIN RUARIDH (*Viscount Tarbat*), *b* 7 Sept 1987.
Hon Alasdair Kenelm Stuart, *b* 1989.

HALF-SISTERS LIVING

Lady (Sibell Anne) Julia MACKENZIE, *b* 1934; has resumed her maiden name: *m* 1st, 1953 (*m diss* 1961), Francis Edward Lascelles-Hadwen; 2ndly, 1974, Apputhurai Jeyarama Chandran, and has issue living (by 1st *m*), James Brian Mackenzie, *b* 1957, — Georgina Frances, *b* 1959, — (by 2nd *m*) Anita Anne Dorothy, *b* 1977.
Lady Gilean Frances MACKENZIE, *b* 1936; has resumed her maiden name: *m* 1959 (*m diss* 1973), Rene Eugene Welter, and has issue living, Michael George, *b* 1964, — Nadia (Nadine) Christine, *b* 1960. *Residence* – Tigh na Otraich, Heights of Inchvannie, Strathpeffer, Ross and Cromarty IV14 9AE.

AUNT LIVING (*daughter of Sibell Lilian, Countess of Cromartie*)

Lady Isobel, *b* 1911: *m* 1947, Capt Oscar Linda. *Residence* – Assynt House, Evanton, Ross-shire.

WIDOW LIVING OF SON OF SIBELL LILIAN, COUNTESS OF CROMARTIE

Mary, da of Theophilus Dan Hix, of Holbech, Lincs: *m* 1st, 1946, as his 2nd wife, Hon Walter Osra Blunt-Mackenzie, who *d* 1951; 2ndly, 1964, Maj Clement Victor Palmer, who *d* 1969; 3rdly, 1982, Sijbren Tijmstra, and has issue living (by 1st *m*) (see colls, infra). *Address* – PO Box 14, White River, E Transvaal, S Africa.

WIDOW LIVING OF FOURTH EARL

LILIAS JANET GARVIE (*Dowager Countess of Cromartie*), MB, ChB Leeds, da of Prof James Walter McLeod, OBE, FRS, and formerly wife of Lt-Col D. S. Richard, MBE: *m* 1962, as his 3rd wife, Maj the 4th Earl, MC, TD, who *d* 1989. *Residence* – Castle Leod, Strathpeffer, Ross and Cromarty.

COLLATERAL BRANCHES LIVING

Issue of late Hon Walter Osra Blunt-Mackenzie, 2nd son of Sibell Lilian, Countess of Cromartie, *b* 1906, *d* 1951: *m* 1st, 1934 (*m diss* 1940), Pamela Lilian Ursula, da of Mr Justice Oliver; 2ndly, 1946, Mary (ante) (who *m* 2ndly, 1964, Maj Clement Victor Palmer, who *d* 1969, and 3rdly, 1982, Sijbren Tijmstra), da of Theophilus Dan Hix, of Holbech, Lincs:—
(By 2nd *m*) Roderick BLUNT-MACKENZIE, *b* 1947: *m* 1969, Yvonne, da of Bernard Arthur (Bill) Lemmon, of White River, S Africa, and has issue living, Craig Walter, *b* 1973, — Jacquelyn, *b* 1970, — Lara, *b* 1971, — Sarah Jane, *b* 1978. *Address* – 21 Crowned Eagle Way, Oak Park, Pietermaritzburg 3201, S Africa.

Descendants of late Lady Florence Leveson-Gower, eldest da of Anne, Duchess of Sutherland (Countess of Cromartie) *b* 1855, *d* 1881: *m* 1876, Rt Hon Henry Chaplin, afterwards 1st Viscount Chaplin (see that title, and Cs Sutherland, colls).

PREDECESSORS – **(1)** ANNE, VA, only child of John Hay Mackenzie of Cromartie, in direct descent from the 3rd Earl of Cromartie who was attainted in 1746: *m* 1849, 3rd Duke of Sutherland, and was *cr Countess of Cromartie, Viscountess Tarbat of Tarbat Baroness Castlehaven, of Castlehaven*, and *Baroness MacLeod, of Leod* (peerage of United Kingdom 1861), with remainder (1) to her second surviving son, Francis, and the heirs male of his body, (2) to each other of her yr sons in like manner in priority of birth, (3) to said Francis and the heirs of his body, (4) to each other her yr sons in like manner in priority of birth, (5) to her daughter Florence and the heirs of her body, and (6) to each other of her daughters (in like manner in priority of birth); she *d* 1888, when the Earldom of Cromartie devolved, in accordance with the special remainder, upon her second surviving son (2) FRANCIS, *b* 1852: *m* 1876, Hon Lilian Janet, who *d* 1926, da of 5th Baron Macdonald; *d* 1893, when the title fell into abeyance between his two surviving das, Sibell Lilian and Constance, and so remained until the abeyance was terminated in 1895 in favour of his eldest da and the heirs of her body, when the honours were confirmed to (3) SIBELL LILIAN, as Countess of Cromartie in her own right; *b* 1878: *m* 1899, Lieut-Col Edward Walter Blunt, DL, who *d* 1949, having assumed the additional surname of Mackenzie 1905; she subsequently discontinued the surname of Blunt; *d* 1962; *s* by her eldest son (4) RODERICK GRANT FRANCIS, MC, TD, 4th Earl, *b* 1904; Maj Seaforth Highlanders (TA), served N Ireland, India and European War 1939-45 as Maj 4th Bn in France (prisoner 1940-45), Hon Sheriff Ross and Cromarty, Convenor 1971-75, FSAS; discontinued surname of Blunt, recognised as Chief of Clan Mackenzie by Lord Lyon 1979: *m* 1st, 1933 (*m diss* 1945), Dorothy (PORTER), da of Grant Butler Downing, of Kentucky, USA; 2ndly, 1947, Olga (MENDOZA), who *d* 1996, da of Stewart Laurance, and formerly wife of Peter Mendoza; 3rdly, 1962, Lilias Janet Garvie (RICHARD), MB, ChB Leeds, da of Prof James Walter McLeod, OBE, FRS, and formerly wife of Lt-Col D. S. Richard; *d* 1989; *s* by his son (5) JOHN RUARIDH BLUNT GRANT, 5th Earl and present peer, also Viscount Tarbat, Baron Castlehaven, and Baron Macleod.

CROMER, EARL OF (Baring) (Earl UK 1901)

By probity and industry

EVELYN ROWLAND ESMOND BARING, 4th Earl; *b* 3 June 1946; *s* 1991; *ed* Eton; Man Dir Inchcape (China) Ltd, and Inchcape Vietnam Ltd, Dep-Chm Motor Transport Co of Guangdong & Hong Kong Ltd (China), and Land-Ocean Inchcape Container Transport Co Ltd (China): *m* 1st, 1971 (*m diss* 1992), Plern, da of late Dr Charanbadhana Isarankura na Ayudhya, of Thailand; 2ndly, 1993, Shelley Hu, da of Hu Guo-qin, of Shanghai, and has issue by 2nd *m*.

Arms – Quarterly, 1st and 4th azure, a fesse or, in chief a bear's head proper, muzzled and ringed or, differenced by an escallop azure; 2nd and 3rd gules, a cross-patée fitchée or between three fish haurient argent within an orle of eight cross-crosslets of the second. **Crest** – A mullet erminois between two wings argent. **Supporters** – Two bears proper, muzzled or, the dexter collared checky, argent and azure and charged on the shoulder with a lion's head erased or, the sinister collared azure, and charged on the shoulder with an escallop or.
Residence – Drayton Court, Drayton, Somerset. *Address* – GPO Box 36, Hong Kong. *Clubs* – Oriental, White's, Hong Kong.

SON LIVING (*By 2nd marriage*)

ALEXANDER ROWLAND HARMSWORTH (*Viscount Errington*), *b* 5 Jan 1994.

DAUGHTER LIVING (*By 2nd marriage*)

Lady ......, *b* 1998.

BROTHER LIVING

Hon Vivian John Rowland, *b* 1950; *ed* RAC Cirencester; Dir Northcliffe Newspapers Group Ltd; Chm of St John Ambulance Council, Kent 1985-87, Chm Council, Glos 1989-93: *m* 1974, Lavinia Gweneth, an Extra Lady-in-Waiting to HRH the Princess of Wales 1981-92, eldest da of late Maj Sir Mark Baring, KCVO (*see colls infra*), and has issue living, Rowley Mark Thomas, *b* 1977; a Page of Honour to HM 1989-91, — Thomas Patrick Vivian, *b* 1979. — Camilla Rose, *b* 1985. *Residence* – The Stone House, Lower Swell, Stow on the Wold, Glos GL54 1LQ. *Clubs* – White's, Royal Yacht Squadron.

SISTER DECEASED

Lady Lana Mary Gabriel, *b* 1943: *m* 1963, Anthony James Gray, son of late Prof Sir James Gray, CBE, MC, FRS, and *d* 1974, leaving issue, Ashley James Rowland, *b* 1964; *ed* Grenville Coll, Devon: *m* 1990, Annabel, yst da of John Ludovici, of East Woodhay, Berks, and has issue living, Theodore John Ashley *b* 1995, Louis Albert James *b* 1997, Lily Lana Patricia *b* 1993, — Tamara Mary Gabriel, *b* 1966.

AUNT LIVING (daughter of 2nd Earl)

Lady Rosemary Ethel, *b* 1908; FRGS: *m* 1932, Lt-Col John David Hills, MC, formerly Headmaster of Bradfield Coll, and has issue living, John Evelyn Baring (Stagg Mill, Uplowman, Tiverton, Devon EX16 7LY), *b* 1939; *ed* Eton; Maj 17/21st Lancers, Col Royal Wessex Yeo (TA), Hon ADC to HM 1990-93; High Sheriff Glos 1990, DL 1989; TD: *m* 1964, Katherine Adrian, yr da of late G. F. Alderson-Smith, of Bishopric Court, Horsham, Sussex, and has issue living, John George Baring *b* 1966; *ed* Bradfield, Veronica Adrian Harriet *b* 1968, — Jean Adini, *b* 1933: *m* 1955 (*m diss* 1990), Brig Hon (Henry Ernest) Christopher Willoughby, Coldm Gds, and has issue (*see* B Middleton), — Margaret Ruby, *b* 1934: *m* 1960, Michael Giles Neish Walker, of Shanwell House, Kinross-shire (*see* Nairn, Bt, 1980 Edn), and has issue living, Simon Giles David *b* 1961; *ed* Eton: *m* 1991, Corinne Rawstorne (and has issue living, a son *b* 1996, a da *b* 1993), Geordie Michael *b* 1966; *ed* Strathallan, Nicola Margaret *b* 1965: *m* 1995, Jeremy Bruce Sturgess. *Residence* – 15 Hanover Court, Dulverton, Som TA22 9HZ.

WIDOW LIVING OF THIRD EARL

Hon ESME MARY GABRIEL HARMSWORTH, CVO, da of 2nd Viscount Rothermere: *m* 1st, 1942, 3rd Earl of Cromer, KG, GCMG, MBE, PC, who *d* 1991; 2ndly, 1993, as his 2nd wife, (Reinier) Gerrit Anton van der Woude, late Capt Gren Guards, who *d* 1999. *Residences* – Heronden, Eastry, Sandwich, Kent CT13 0ET; 1 Douro Place, W8.

COLLATERAL BRANCHES LIVING

Grandchildren of late Hon Windham Baring, 2nd son of 1st Earl:—
Issue of late Robin Windham Baring, TD, *b* 1914, *d* 1994: *m* 1954, Anne Elizabeth, JP (Went House, W Malling, Kent), eldest da of Maj William Frederick Husband:—
James Windham (4 Tilton St, SW6), *b* 1957: *m* 1st, 1985, Suzy, da of John Barry Prendergast, of Oyster Bay, New York, and of Mrs Barbara Barnard, of North Lodge, Odiham, Hants; 2ndly, 1991, Mrs Angela P. Clarke, eldest da of Peter Halstead, of Cranmer Court, SW3, and has issue living (by 2nd *m*), Clementine Lara, *b* 1992. —— Clarissa, *b* 1955: *m* 1987, Michael Charles David Pilkington, of 20 Brackenbury Rd, W6 0BA, eldest son of Ronald Charles Leslie Pilkington, of Stanstead Abbots, Herts, and has issue living, Grace Cristabel Alice, *b* 1987, — Eleanor Scarlett Rose, *b* 1989, — Silvy Emerald Isabelle, *b* 1993. —— Rosemary Anne, *b* 1960: *m* 1989, Anthony M. Standing, of The Old Rectory, Sharrington, Melton Constable, Norfolk NR24 2PG, son of late Michael Frederick Cecil Standing, CBE, and has issue living, Michael Frederick Oliver, *b* 1990, — Archie Jonathan Guy, *b* 1992. —— Katherine Claire, *b* 1963: *m* 1st, 1992, Alexander T. H. Slack, yr son of Tom Slack, of Mousehole, Cornwall, and of Chelsea, SW3; 2ndly, 1995, Peter L. Walters.

Issue of late Maj Sir Mark Baring, KCVO, *b* 1916, *d* 1988: *m* 1949, Victoria Winifred (*Lady Michael Fitzalan Howard*) (66 Melton Court, SW7 3JH) (who *m* 2ndly, 1997, Maj-Gen Lord Michael Fitzalan Howard, GCVO, CB, CBE, MC (*see* D Norfolk)), da of late Col Reginald Edmund Maghlin Russell, CVO, CBE, DSO, of Hurst House, Church Crookham, Hants:—
Lavinia Gweneth (*Hon Mrs Vivian Baring*), *b* 1951; an Extra Lady in Waiting to HRH the Princess of Wales 1981-92: *m* 1974, Hon Vivian John Rowland Baring (ante). —— Juliet Victoria (Littleton House, W Littleton, Chippenham, Wilts SN15 3RJ), *b* 1953: *m* 1984, Gavin Adrian Alexander Henderson (*see* B Faringdon, colls), who *d* 1991.

Issue of late Hon Sir Evelyn Baring, KG, CMG, KCVO (who was *cr Baron Howick of Glendale* 1960), yst son of 1st Earl (see that title).

PREDECESSORS – (1) Rt Hon Sir EVELYN Baring, GCB, OM, GCMG, KCSI, CIE, yr son of late Henry Baring, MP (see B Northbrook, colls); was Commr of Egyptian Public Dept 1877-9, Comptroller-Gen in Egypt 1879-80, Financial Member of Council of Viceroy of India 1880-83, and Agent and Consul-Gen in Egypt and a Min Plen in Diplo Ser 1883-1907 (granted £50,000 by Parliament); cr *Baron Cromer*, of Cromer, co Norfolk (peerage of United Kingdom) 1892, *Viscount Cromer*, co Norfolk (peerage of United Kingdom) 1899, and *Viscount Errington*, of Hexham, co Northumberland, and *Earl of Cromer*, co Norfolk (peerage of United Kingdom) 1901: *m* 1st, 1876, Ethel Stanley, who *d* 1898, da of Sir Rowland Stanley Errington, 11th Bt; 2ndly, 1901, Lady Katherine Georgiana Louisa Thynne, who *d* 1933, da of 4th Marquess of Bath; *d* 1917; *s* by his eldest son (2) ROWLAND THOMAS, GCB, GCIE, GCVO, PC, 2nd Earl, *b* 1877; in Diplo Ser 1900-11; Private Sec to successive Permanent Under-Secs of State for Foreign Affairs (Lord Hardinge of Penshurst, and Lord Carnock) 1907-11; ADC to successive Viceroys and Govs-Gen of India (Lord Hardinge of Penshurst, and Viscount Chelmsford) 1915-16, Equerry and Assist Private Sec to HM 1916-20, and an Extra Equerry 1920-53; Ch of Staff to HRH the Duke of Connaught during visit to India 1920-21 (KCIE), and to HRH the Prince of Wales during tour of India 1921-22; Lord Chamberlain of the Household 1922-38; a Permanent Lord-in-Waiting 1938-53; Pres of Marylebone Cricket Club 1934-35; Chm Joint Red Cross and St John War Organisation 1939-40; Receiver-Gen of Order of St John of Jerusalem 1943-47; a British Govt Director of Suez Canal 1926-50: *m* 1908, Lady Ruby Florence Mary Elliot (a GCStJ), who *d* 1961, da of 4th Earl of Minto; *d* 1953; *s* by his only son (3) GEORGE ROWLAND STANLEY, KG, GCMG, MBE, PC, 3rd Earl, *b* 1918; Sr Partner and Man Dir Baring Brothers & Co Ltd, 8 Bishopsgate, EC2 1948-60 and 1967-70, Dir Daily Mail & General Trust Ltd 1948-58, and many other Cos, Chm IBM United Kingdom Ltd 1967-70 and 1974-79, Economic Min and Head of UK Treasury and Supply Delegation, Washington 1959-61, UK Exec Dir International Monetary Fund, International Bank for Reconstruction and Development, and International Finance Corporation 1959-61, Gov Bank of England 1961-66, HM Ambassador to Washington 1971-74; Trustee King George's Jubilee Trust, Dep Chm Queen's Jubilee Appeal Council, and Treas Canterbury Cathedral Appeal; HM Lieut City of London 1961, DL Kent 1968-79: *m* 1942, Hon Esme Mary Gabriel Harmsworth, CVO (who *m* 2ndly, 1993, as his 2nd wife, (Reinier) Gerrit Anton van der Woude, late Capt Gren Guards, who *d* 1999), da of 2nd Viscount Rothermere; *d* 1991; *s* by his elder son (4) EVELYN ROWLAND ESMOND, 4th Earl and present peer; also Viscount Cromer, Viscount Errington, and Baron Cromer.

CROMWELL, BARON (Bewicke-Copley) (Baron E 1375)

I conquer by the cross

GODFREY JOHN BEWICKE-COPLEY, 7th Baron; *b* 4 March 1960; *s* 1982; *ed* Eton, and Camb Univ: *m* 1990, Elizabeth A., da of John Hawksley, and has issue.

Arms – 1st and 4th, argent, a chief gules, over all a bend azure, *Cromwell*; 2nd and 3rd, chequy or and gules, a chief ermine, *Tateshall*; on an escutcheon of pretence, quarterly, 1st and 4th, argent a cross-moline sable, *Copley*; 2nd and 3rd, argent five lozenges conjoined in fesse gules, each charged with a mullet of the field, between three bears' heads erased sable, *Bewicke*. Crest – 1st, out of a ducal coronet or five ostrich feathers argent, *Copley*; 2nd, a goat's head erased at the neck argent, armed, maned and gorged with a mural crown gules, *Bewicke*. Supporters – On either side a lion sable charged on the shoulder with a representation of the Treasurer's Purse (being the Badge of Ralph, 3rd Baron Cromwell).
Address – c/o House of Lords, SW1.

SON LIVING

Hon DAVID GODFREY, *b* 21 Sept 1997.

DAUGHTER LIVING

Hon Helen Tatiana, *b* 18 March 1995.

BROTHER LIVING

Hon Thomas David, *b* 1964; *ed* Eton; actor (as Percy Copley). *Residence* – Res Clemenceaux Bat A1, 7 Bis Rue Victor Hugo, 77400 Thorigny sur Marne, France.

SISTERS LIVING

Hon Anne Elizabeth, *b* 1955: *m* 1982, David James McNaught Runciman, yst son of late Dr J. B. M Runciman, of Langbank, Renfrewshire, and has issue living, Findlay Redfers, *b* 1990, — Ruth Vivian, *b* 1987. *Residence* – Cross's Barn, Sherborne, Northleach, Cheltenham, Glos.

Hon Davina Mary, *b* 1958: *m* 1991, Anthony William Savile Birkbeck, and has issue (*see* B Somerleyton). *Residence* – Meddoms Farm Barn, Horton, Banbury, Oxon OX15 6EA.

AUNT LIVING (*daughter of 5th Baron*)

Hon Philippa Selina (*Hon Lady Mather*), *b* 1925: *m* 1951, Lt-Col Sir (David) Carol (MacDonell) Mather, MC, MP, Welsh Gds (ret), and has issue living, Nicholas David, *b* 1958: *m* 1985, Susan Alexandra, da of H. B. Thomas, of the Old Rectory, Harnhill, Glos, and has issue living, Toby Montgomery William *b* 1993, Leila Isabella Nadežhda *b* 1990, — Selina Jane, *b* 1952: *m* 1980, Maj Alastair Alexander Linton Watson, The Black Watch, of Old School House, Lower Swell, Stow-on-the-Wold, Glos, elder son of Maj-Gen Andrew Linton Watson, CB, of Royal Hospital, Chelsea, and has issue living, Harry William George *b* 1988, Sophia Arabella *b* 1981, Alice Selina *b* 1985, — Rose Amabel, *b* 1954: *m* 1986, David Benjamin Shepherd-Cross, elder son of late Maj Peter Shepherd-Cross, of Compton Bassett, Wilts, and has issue living, Maximilian Peter *b* 1989, George Alexander *b* 1991, — (Alice) Victoria, *b* 1960: *m* 1988, Edward Mortimer Harley, elder son of Christopher Charles Harley, of Brampton Bryan Hall, Herefordshire, and has issue living, (Leonora) Brilliana *b* 1992, Imogen Freda *b* 1994, Alice Ianthe *b* 1997. *Residence* – Oddington House, Moreton-in-Marsh, Glos.

WIDOW LIVING OF SIXTH BARON

(DORIS) VIVIAN (*Dowager Baroness Cromwell*) (The Oranges, Sherborne, Northleach, Cheltenham, Glos), yst da of Hugh de Lisle Penfold, of Isle of Man: *m* 1954, the 6th Baron Cromwell, who *d* 1982.

PREDECESSORS – (1) RALPH de Cromwell; summoned to Parliament 1375-97: *m* 1366, Maud, da of John Bernake, of Tattershall; *d* 1398; *s* by his son (2) RALPH, 2nd Baron; summoned to Parliament 1399-1417: *m* a widow (Joan), who *d* 1434; *d* 1417; *s* by his son (3) RALPH, PC, 3rd Baron; summoned to Parliament 1422-55; Lord High Treasurer 1433-43, Master of the King's' Mews and Falcons 1436, and Constable of Nottingham Castle 1444-5: *m* 1424, Margaret, da of John, Lord Deincourt; *d* 1454, when the Barony fell into abeyance between the co-heirs, his nieces Maud, widow of Robert, Lord Willoughby de Broke, and Joan, wife of Sir Humphrey, Bourchier; on the death of the latter without issue in 1490, the Barony devolved upon the former (4) MAUD; *dsp* 1497, when the Barony again passed into abeyance between co-heirs descendants of the das of the 1st Baron, and so remained until 1922, when the Committee for Privileges of the House of Lords reported in favour of the petition of Selina Frances, wife of Brig-Gen Sir Robert Calverley Alington Bewicke-Copley, KBE, CB, who *d* 1923 (she was da of Sir Charles Watson Copley, 3rd Bt (Watson, Bt, cr 1700), and one of the co-heirs of William Fitzwilliam, sole heir of Maud, wife of Sir William Fitzwilliam, of Sprotborough, and a da of the 1st Baron), for the determination of the abeyance; she *d* 1923, and the Barony was in July 1923 called out of abeyance in favour of her son (5) ROBERT GODFREY WOLSELEY Bewicke-Copley, DSO, MC, 5th Baron, *b* 1893; Lord Lieut of Leics 1949-65: *m* 1925, Freda Constance who *d* 1979, da of Maj Frederick William Beresford Cripps, DSO, of Ampney Park, Glos; *d* 1966; *s* by his only son (6) DAVID GODFREY, 6th Baron, *b* 1929; Barrister-at-law, Inner Temple, 1956, Senior Govt Broker 1981-82: *m* 1954, Doris Vivian, yst da of Hugh de Lisle Penfold, of Isle of Man; *d* 1982; *s* by his elder son (7) GODFREY JOHN, 7th Baron and present peer.

CROOK, BARON (Crook) (Baron UK 1947)

DOUGLAS EDWIN CROOK, 2nd Baron; *b* 19 Nov 1926; *s* 1989; *ed* Whitgift Sch, Croydon, and Imp Coll of Science and Technology; BSc (Eng) 1947, ACGI, DIC, MICE: *m* 1954, Ellenor, who *d* 1998, da of late Robert Rouse, and has issue.

ᄣrms – Or, on a bend vert between in chief two Tudor roses barbed and seeded proper, and in base a sprig of oak slipped and fructed of the second, a shepherd's crook of the field. Crest – Two crooks in saltire or, surmounted by a Tudor rose barbed and seeded proper. Supporters – *Dexter*, an antelope gorged with a collar of Tudor roses leaved proper; *sinister*, a greyhound argent collared or, with line reflexed over the back, the collar charged with three cross crosslets gules.
Residence – 15 Cordova Court, Seabrook Rd, Folkestone, Kent CT20 7HQ.

The cross a shield

SON LIVING

Hon ROBERT DOUGLAS EDWIN (12 Fairfax St, Redhill, Gap, Qld 4059, Australia), *b* 29 May 1955: *m* 1981, Suzanne Jane, da of Harold Robinson, of Farnsfield, Notts, and has issue living, Matthew Robert, *b* 28 May 1990, — James Nicholas, *b* 1992.

DAUGHTER LIVING

Hon Catherine Hilary CROOK, *b* 1960; resumed her maiden name 1993: *m* 1984, Christopher John Ramsdale, of Foinavon, Churn Rd, Compton, Newbury, Berks RG20 6PP, son of C. Ramsdale, of Coventry.

PREDECESSOR – (1) REGINALD DOUGLAS Crook, *b* 1901; Chm National Dock Labour Board 1951-65; *cr Baron Crook*, of Carshalton, co Surrey (peerage of UK) 1947: *m* 1922, Ida Gertrude, who *d* 1985, da of Joseph Haddon; *d* 1989; *s* by his only son (2) DOUGLAS EDWIN, 2nd Baron and present peer.

CROSS, VISCOUNT (Cross) (Viscount UK 1886)

ASSHETON HENRY CROSS, 3rd Viscount; *b* 7 May 1920; *s* 1932; *ed* Shrewsbury, and at Magdalene Coll, Camb; formerly Capt Scots Guards: *m* 1st, 1952 (*m diss* 1957), Patricia Mary, eldest da of Edward Pearson Hewetson, of The Craig, Windermere, Westmorland; 2ndly, 1972 (*m diss* 1977), Mrs Victoria Webb, who *d* 1997; 3rdly, 1983 (*m diss* 1987), Mrs Patricia Jean Rossiter, widow of John Rossiter, and has issue (by 1st *m*).

ᄣrms – Gules, a cross flory argent, charged with five passion nails sable, a bordure of the second. Crest – A griffin's head, erased argent, gorged with a double chain gold, therefrom pendant a mullet pierced sable, in the beak a passion nail also sable. Supporters – On either side a pegasus argent, holding in the mouth a passion nail sable, the dexter gorged with a chain or, therefrom pendant a cross flory gules, the sinister gorged with a double chain or, therefrom pendant a mullet pierced sable.

Trust in the Cross

Residence – Wildwood, Itchenor, Sussex. *Club* – Guards'.

DAUGHTERS LIVING (*By 1st marriage*)

Hon Venetia Clare, *b* 1953: *m* 1986, Rev Norman Hill, son of late Charles Hill, of Sheffield, and has issue living, Gregory, *b* 1989.

Hon Nicola, *b* 1954: *m* 1992, Audley George Parry Burnett, son of Lt-Col G. P. Burnett, of Winchester, Hants, and has issue living, Galen Assheton Parry, *b* 1992, — Rhodri Parry, *b* 1998, — Fay Natalie Cross, *b* 1995. *Residence* – Ty Hen, Drefach Felindre, Llandysul, Dyfed.

WIDOW LIVING OF SON OF SECOND VISCOUNT

Sybil Anne, da of late Thomas Prain Douglas Murray, MBE, TD, DL, JP, of Templewood, Brechin, Angus: *m* 1st, 1950, Hon John Michael Inigo Cross, who *d* 1951; 2ndly, 1956, Lt-Cdr James Parker-Jervis, RN (ret) (*see* V St Vincent, colls), and has issue living (by 1st *m*) (*see* colls infra). *Residence* – Templewood, Brechin, Angus DD9 7PT.

COLLATERAL BRANCH LIVING

Issue of late Hon John Michael Inigo Cross, 3rd son of 2nd Viscount, *b* 1923, *d* 1951: *m* 1950, Sybil Anne (ante); she *m* 2ndly, 1956, Lt-Cdr James Parker-Jervis, RN (ret) (*see* V St Vincent, colls), da of late Thomas Prain Douglas Murray, MBE, TD, DL, JP, of Templewood, Brechin, Angus:—

Mary Beatrice (*posthumous*) (*Lady Jardine of Applegirth*), *b* 1951: *m* 1982, Sir Alexander Maule Jardine of Applegirth, 12th Bt. *Residence* – Ash House, Millom, Cumbria LA18 5HY.

PREDECESSORS – (1) *Rt Hon Sir* RICHARD ASSHETON Cross, GCB, GCSI, PC, DCL, LLD, FRS, 3rd son of late William Cross, DL, of Red Scar, Preston; *b* 1823; Sec of State for Home Depart 1874-80 and 1885-6, one of the Committee of Council on Education in Scotland Aug 1885 to Jan 1886, Sec of State for India July 1886 to Aug 1892, and Lord Privy Seal June 1895 to Oct 1900; MP for Preston (*C*) 1857-62, for SW Lancashire 1868-85, and for Newton Div of SW Lancashire 1885-6; cr *Viscount Cross*, of Broughton-in-Furness (peerage of United Kingdom) 1886: *m* 1852, Georgiana, CI, who *d* 1907, da of late Thomas Lyon, JP, DL, of Appleton Hall, Cheshire; *d* 1914; *s* by his grandson (2) RICHARD ASSHETON, 2nd Viscount (only son of late Hon William Henry Cross, MP, 2nd son of 1st Viscount), by Mary da of late William Lewthwaite, JP, DL of Broadgate, Cumberland, *b* 1882; acted as Private Sec to successive Permanent Secs to the Treasury 1912-17, and was a Principal there 1917-32: *m* 1918, Maud Evelyn Inigo (who *d* 1976, having *m* 2ndly, 1944, as his second wife, Guy Hope Coldwell, who *d* 1948), da of late Maj-Gen Inigo Richmond Jones, CVO, CB; *d* 1932; *s* by his son (3) ASSHETON HENRY, 3rd Viscount and present peer.

CROSS OF CHELSEA, BARONY OF (Cross) (Extinct 1989)

DAUGHTER LIVING OF LIFE BARON

Hon Julia, *b* 1953: *m* 1st, 1973 (*m diss* 19—), Barney Walker; 2ndly, 19—, David Openshaw, and has issue living.

WIDOW LIVING OF LIFE BARON

MILDRED JOAN (*Baroness Cross of Chelsea*), da of late Lt-Col Theodore Eardley-Wilmot, DSO (*see* Eardley-Wilmot, Bt, colls): *m* 1952, Baron Cross of Chelsea, PC (Life Baron), who *d* 1989. *Residence* – The Bridge House, Leintwardine, Craven Arms, Shropshire.

Crossley, family name of Baron Somerleyton.

Crowhurst, Viscount; son of Earl of Cottenham.

DEBRETT'S ILLUSTRATED PEERAGE

CROWTHER, BARONY OF (Crowther) (Extinct 1972)

SONS LIVING OF LIFE BARON

Hon Charles Worth (Bourne Bank, Bourne End, Bucks), *b* 1939: *m* 1963, Barbara, yr da of Prof Norman Merrett Hancox, MD, of Barn End, Moorside Lane, Neston, Wirrall, Cheshire, and has issue, one son and da.

Hon David Richard Geoffrey, *b* 1943: *m* 1974, Martina, da of Martin Menn-Fink, of Ilanz, Switzerland.

DAUGHTERS LIVING OF LIFE BARON

Hon Anne Hallowell, *b* 1937: *m* 1958, Jonathan Sofer, Bar-at-Law, of 46 Regent's Park Rd, NW1, and has issue, two sons and one da.

Hon Felicity Margaret, *b* 1947: *m* 1978, Colin Rochfort Luke, of 18 Regent's Park Rd, NW1 7TX, and has issue, two sons and one da.

Hon Nicola Mary, *b* 1950.

CROWTHER-HUNT, BARONY OF (Crowther-Hunt) (Extinct 1987)

DAUGHTERS LIVING OF LIFE BARON

Hon Elizabeth Anne, *b* 1947; *ed* Headington Sch, Oxford, and Newnham Coll, Camb; Dir The Prince's Trust Volunteers since 1990: *m* 1976, Peter John Coulson, of 37 Deodar Rd, Putney, SW15 2NP, and has issue.

Hon Rosamund Shirley, *b* 1950: *m* 1978, John Christopher Hill, of 5 Aldwincle Rd, Thorpe Waterville, Kettering, Northamptonshire, and has issue.

Hon Penelope Carol, *b* 1955: *m* 1988, Andrew A. Barr, elder son of W. G. Barr, of Oxford, and has issue. *Residence* – 30 Upland Park Rd, Oxford.

WIDOW LIVING OF LIFE BARON

JOYCE (*Baroness Crowther-Hunt*), da of late Rev Joseph Stackhouse, of Walsall Wood, Staffs; Pres Oxfordshire Guides 1990, Lazo de Dama de Isabel la Católica 1991; DL Oxon: *m* 1944, Baron Crowther-Hunt (Life Baron), who *d* 1987. *Residence* – 14 Apsley Rd, Oxford.

Cubitt, family name of Baron Ashcombe.

CUCKNEY, BARON (Cuckney) (Life Baron 1995)

JOHN GRAHAM CUCKNEY, son of late Air Vice-Marshal Ernest John Cuckney, CB, CBE, DSC; *b* 12 July 1925; *ed* Shrewsbury, and Univ of St Andrews; Chm The Orion Publishing Group Ltd since 1994, Dir Brixton Estate plc since 1985, non-exec Vice-Chm Glaxo Holdings plc since 1993; *cr* Kt 1978, and *Baron Cuckney,* of Millbank, in the City of Westminster (Life Baron) 1995: *m* 1st, 19—, ..., da of ......, of .....; 2ndly, 1960, Muriel, da of late Walter Scott Boyd, of ....

Arms – Vert on each of two flaunches argent cotised rayonny on the outer edge or a flaunch vert. **Crest** – Two dragons heads addorsed the necks entwined and conjoined in base the whole winged or. **Supporters** – On either side a seadragon vert supporting a trident or.
Address – The Orion Publishing Group Ltd, 5 Upper St Martin's Lane, WC2H 9EA.

CUDLIPP, BARONY OF (Cudlipp) (Extinct 1998)

WIDOW LIVING OF LIFE BARON

JODI (*Baroness Cudlipp*), da of the late John L. Hyland, of Palm Beach, Florida, USA: *m* 1963, as his 3rd wife, Baron Cudlipp, OBE (Life Baron), who *d* 1998. *Residence* – 14 Tollhouse Close, Avenue de Chartres, Chichester, W Sussex PO19 1SF.

CULLEN OF ASHBOURNE, BARON (Cokayne) (Baron UK 1920)

Courage in Adversity

CHARLES BORLASE MARSHAM COKAYNE, MBE, 2nd Baron; *b* 6 Oct 1912; *s* 1932; *ed* Eton; is Major Roy Corps of Signals (TA); a Lord in Waiting to HM 1979-82, and a Lieut of City of London; MBE (Mil) 1945: *m* 1st, 1942, Valerie Catharine Mary, da of late W. H. Collbran; 2ndly, 1948, Patricia Mary, who *d* 1996, el da of late Col S. Clulow-Gray; 3rdly, 1998, Filiz Zeynep Sargent, yr da of late Lt-Gen Ali Merey, and has issue by 1st *m*.

Arms – Argent, three cocks gules, armed crested, and jelloped sable. **Crest** – A cock's head erased gules, beaked, crested, and jelloped sable. **Supporters** – *Dexter,* a lion guardant party per fesse or and argent; *sinister,* an ostrich argent holding in its beak a horseshoe proper; each gorged with a collar pendant therefrom an escutcheon argent, charged with two bars vert.
Residence – 75 Cadogan Gardens, SW3.

DAUGHTER LIVING (By 1st marriage)

Hon Julia Collbran, *b* 1943: *m* 1968 (*m diss* 1989), Don Francesco Costa Sanseverino di Bisignano; 2ndly, 1991 (*m diss* 1994), Michael G. M. Groves; 3rdly, 1994, Sture Wigart, and has issue living (by 1st *m*), Edoardo *b* 1969. — Alessandro, *b* 1071, — Sveva, *b* 1973. *Residence* – Oxleys, Dock Lane, Beaulieu, Hants SO42 7YJ; 20 St Luke's St, SW3 3RP.

BROTHERS LIVING

Hon EDMUND WILLOUGHBY MARSHAM (15-1901 Maxwell Av, Merritt, BC, Canada V1K 1L9), *b* 18 May 1916; *ed* Eton, and Royal Sch of Mines; Mining Engr in Australia, Canada and USA; late Fl Lt RAF: *m* 1943, Janet (MANSON), da of late William Douglas Watson, of Canterbury, and has an adopted da, Jean Charlotte, *b* 1935: *m* 1952 (*m diss* 1962), Harold Gordon Bell, and has issue living, Douglas Gordon *b* 1956, Thomas Edmund *b* 1958, Janet Catherine *b* 1953: *m* 1978, Merle L. Boley.

(Hon) John O'Brien Marsham (does not use courtesy title), *b* 1920; *ed* Eton: *m* 1948, Anne Frances, who *d* 1971, da of late Bertram Clayton, of Wakefield, Yorks, and has issue living, Michael John, *b* 1950: *m* 1st, 1976 (*m diss* 1985), Baudilia Medina Negrin, of Caracas, Venezuela; 2ndly 1986 (*m diss* 1994), Yvette Santana. *Residence* – 14 St Omer Rd, Cowley, Oxford OX4 3HB.

SISTER LIVING

Hon Barbara Mary, *b* 1905: *m* 1929, Maj Gilbert Edgar Francis Vandernoot, late Irish Gds, who *d* 1981, and has issue living, Anthea Caroline (22 Byfields Rd, Kingsclere, Newbury, Berks RG15 8TG), *b* 1936: *m* 1963, John Michael Ryan, who *d* 1990. *Residence* – Oak Cottage, Hartley Wintney, Hants.

PREDECESSOR – **(1)** *Sir* BRIEN IBRICAN Cokayne, KBE, son of late George Edward Cokayne, FSA, Clarenceux King of Arms; *b* 1864; a partner in the firm of Anthony Gibbs and Sons, merchants and bankers; appointed a Director of the Bank of England 1902, and was Dep Gov 1915-18, and Gov 1918-20; *cr Baron Cullen of Ashbourne*, of Roehampton, co Surrey (peerage of United Kingdom) 1920: *m* 1904, Grace Margaret, who *d* 1971, da of late Rev the Hon John Marsham (E Romney); *d* 1932; *s* by his son **(2)** CHARLES BORLASE MARSHAM, 2nd Baron and present peer.

CUMBERLEGE, BARONESS (Cumberlege) (Life Baroness 1990)

JULIA FRANCES CUMBERLEGE, CBE, da of Dr Lambert Ulrich Camm, of Appleton, Newick, Sussex; *b* 27 Jan 1943; *ed* Convent of the Sacred Heart, Kent; JP 1973-85, DL E Sussex 1986, Vice Lord Lieut 1991; Member Lewes District Council 1966-79 (Leader 1977-78), E Sussex CC 1974-85 (Chm Social Services Cttee 1979-82), E Sussex Area Health Authority 1977-81; Chm Brighton Health Authority 1981-88, Nat Assocn of Health Authorities 1987-88, and SW Thames Regional Health Authority 1988-92; Member NHS Policy Bd 1989-97, Council of St George's Medical Sch, Press Council 1977-83, and Appointments Commn since 1984; Chm Review of Community Nursing for England 1985, and Reports: Neighbourhood Nursing, and Changing Childbirth; Chm Review of Maternity Sers for England 1993; Vice-Pres Royal Coll of Nursing since 1988; Under-Sec of State, Dept of Health since 1992; *cr* CBE (Civil) 1985, and *Baroness Cumberlege*, of Newick, co E Sussex (Life Baroness) 1990: *m* 1961, Patrick Francis Howard Cumberlege (*see* Gibbons, Bt, 1995 Edn), and has issue.
Residence – Snells Cottage, The Green, Newick, Lewes, E Sussex BN8 4LA.

SONS LIVING

Hon (Christopher) Mark, *b* 1962; *ed* Sutton Valence.
Hon Justin Francis, *b* 1964; *ed* Haileybury.
Hon Oliver Richard, *b* 1968; *ed* Lancing.

CUNLIFFE, BARON (Cunliffe) (Baron UK 1914)

Faithfully

ROGER CUNLIFFE, 3rd Baron; *b* 12 Jan 1932; *s* 1963; *ed* Eton, and at Trin Coll, Camb (MA), Architectural Assocn (AA Dipl), and Open Univ; RIBA, MIMgt; Assist, Goldsmiths' Co: *m* 1957, Clemency Ann, el da of late Maj Geoffrey Benyon Hoare, of Clover House, Aldeburgh, Suffolk, and has issue.

Arms – Per chevron or and sable, three conies courant counterchanged. **Crest** – Upon a rock a greyhound sejant sable, collared or. **Supporters** – On either side a figure habited as a Gate Porter of the Bank of England, supporting in the exterior hand his staff of office. *Residence* – The Broadhurst, Brandeston, Woodbridge, Suffolk IP13 7AG.

SONS LIVING

Hon HENRY, *b* 9 March 1962, *ed* Eton; Freeman, Goldsmiths' Co.

Hon Luke, *b* 1965, *ed* Eton, and Bransons Coll; Freeman, Goldsmiths' Co: *m* 1992, Penelope A., da of Cmdr P. S. Wilson, RN (ret), of Chipstead, Surrey, and of Mrs J. H. Grantham, of Hampstead, London.

DAUGHTER LIVING

Hon Rachel Henrietta, *b* 1960; *ed* N London Collegiate Sch, Felsted Sch, Camb Univ (BA), Manchester Univ, Minnesota Univ (MEd), and Arizona Univ; Freeman, Goldsmiths' Co: *m* 1987, Roger David Hardesty, son of late R. D. Hardesty, of Belle Mead, NJ, USA.

BROTHER LIVING

Hon Merlin (Wills Rd, Dixon's Creek, Vic 3775, Australia), *b* 1935; *ed* Eton: *m* 1st, 1960 (*m diss* 19—), Deborah Rutherford Grimwade; 2ndly, 1978, Mrs Amanda June Foster, da of Samuel Rogers, and has had issue (by 1st *m*), Tamsin Elizabeth, *b* 1963; *d* 1982, — Sophia Catherine, *b* 1966: *m* 1995, Matthew Blake, son of Peter Blake, of Melbourne, and has issue living, Eliza Tamsin *b* 1996.

SISTERS LIVING

Hon Shirley Cynthia, *b* 1926: *m* 1959, Alan Desmond Wilson, and has issue living, Matthew Crispin, *b* 1961, — Richenda Catherine, *b* 1963. *Residence* – Ashbrook, Aston Tirrold, Didcot, Oxon OX11 9DL.
Hon Corinna, *b* 1929: *m* 1957, Frederick Starr Wildman, and has issue living, Tarik Charles, *b* 1959: *m* 1993, Susan O'Reilly. *Residence* – The Applehouse, 81 Rogers Rd, Dorset, Vermont 05251, USA.

COLLATERAL BRANCHES LIVING

Grandchildren (by 1st *m*) of late Hon Geoffrey Cunliffe (infra):—
Issue of late Peter Cunliffe, *b* 1925, *d* 1987: *m* 1955, Barbara Marion (La Maison de Leoville, Le Mont de La Greve de Lecq, Jersey, CI), da of H. F. Phillips, of Grouville Park, Jersey, CI:—
Robert, *b* 1958. —— Christopher, *b* 1960. —— Oliver, *b* 1966: *m* 1995, Amanda Jane, da of Philip Edward Couse, of Edgbaston, and of Mrs David Carr, and has issue living, Charlotte Jane, *b* 1999.

Issue of late Hon Geoffrey Cunliffe, 2nd son of 1st Baron, *b* 1903, *d* 1982: *m* 1st, 1922, Patrick Sidney, who *d* 1940, da of late Robert Benjamin Frend, of Ardsallagh, co Tipperary; 2ndly, 1941 (*m diss* 1947), Gavrelle, only da of Col William Arthur Thomas, of Hampstead, and widow of Christopher Bernard Hobhouse; 3rdly, 1947, Barbara Waring, who *d* 1990, da of Dr J. A. Gibb, of Maidstone, Kent, and formerly wife of Laurence A. Evans:—
(By 2nd *m*) Adam (17 Dorset Rd, Leeds 8, W Yorks), *b* 1946; *ed* Wellington Coll. —— Carol (7 Orchard St, Mendham, NJ 07945, USA), *b* 1944: *m* 1st, 1066 (*m diss* 1905), Joseph Francis Logan; 2ndly, 1992, Jay K. Dilley.

PREDECESSORS – (1) *Sir* WALTER Cunliffe, GBE, son of late Roger Cunliffe, of Tyrrells Wood, Surrey; *b* 1855; was head of the firm of Cunliffe Bros (afterwards Goschens and Cunliffe), of 12 Austin Friars, EC; Dep-Gov of Bank of England 1911-13, and Gov 1913-18; *cr Baron Cunliffe*, of Headley, co Surrey (Peerage of United Kingdom) 1914: *m* 1st, 1890, Mary Agnes, who *d* 1893, da of late Robert Henderson, of Randalls Park, Leatherhead; 2ndly, 1896, Edith Cunningham, who *d* 1965, da of Col Robert Tod Boothby, of St Andrews Fife; *d* 1920; *s* by his el son (2) ROLF, *b* 1899; Wing-Cdr RAFVR: *m* 1st, 1925 (*m diss* 1952), Joan Catherine, who *d* 1980, da of late Cecil Lubbock (B Avebury, colls); 2ndly, 1952, Kathleen Elsie, who *d* 1990, da of Ernest Brownfield Pope, of Wargrave, Berks, and widow of Capt Philip Robinson, RAMC, of Manor House, Wendover, Bucks (*ka* 1944); *d* 1963; *s* by his el son (3) ROGER, 3rd Baron and present peer.

CURRIE OF MARYLEBONE, BARON (Currie) (Life Baron 1996)

DAVID ANTHONY CURRIE, son of late Kennedy Moir Currie, of London; *b* 9 Dec 1946; *ed* Battersea Gram Sch, Manchester Univ (BSc 1968), Birmingham Univ (MSocSci 1972), and London Univ (PhD 1978); DLitt Glasgow (1998); Hon Fellow Queen Mary and Westfield Coll, London Univ, 1997; Lecturer, Queen Mary Coll, London 1972-79, Reader 1979-81, Professor of Economics 1981-88, since when Professor of Economics, London Business Sch; Dir of Centre for Economic Forecasting 1988-95 (Gov 1989-95), Deputy Principal 1992-95; Memb HM Treasury Panel of Independent Forecasters 1992-95, Memb Advisory Board for the Research Councils 1992-93, Memb Advisory Commn RPI 1992-93; Trustee, Joseph Rowntree Reform Trust since 1991; Sr Advisor Offer/Ofgas since 1998; Memb Royal Economic Society; *cr Baron Currie of Marylebone*, of Marylebone in the City of Westminster (Life Baron) 1996: *m* 1st, 1975 (*m diss* 1992), Shaziye, da of Hussein Gazioglu, of Nicosia, Cyprus; 2ndly, 1995, Angela Mary Piers, da of Maurice Francis Gerald Piers Dumas, of Clapham, London, and has issue by 1st *m*.

Address – c/o London Business School, Sussex Place, Regents Park, NW1 4SA.

SONS LIVING (*By 1st marriage*)

Hon James Mehmet, *b* 1979; *ed* Robert Gordon's Acad, Aberdeen, and Edinburgh Univ.
Hon Timothy Timur, *b* 1982; *ed* Robert Gordon's Acad, Aberdeen.

Curzon, Viscount; son of Earl Howe.

Curzon, family name of Earl Howe.

Curzon, family name of Viscount Scarsdale.

Curzon, Roper-, family name of Baron Teynham.

Curzon of Kedleston, Marquessate of (Curzon) (Extinct 1925) (see B Ravensdale)

Cust, family name of Baron Brownlow.

DACRE, BARONESS (Douglas-Home) (Baron E 1321)

RACHEL LEILA DOUGLAS-HOME (*Baroness Dacre*); *b* 24 Oct 1929; da of 4th Viscount Hampden; *s* (on termination of abeyance) 1970: *m* 1951, Hon William Douglas-Home, who *d* 1992 (*see* B Home of the Hirsel), and has issue.

Arms – Not exemplified at time of going to press.
Residence – Derry House, Kilmeston, nr Alresford, Hants.

SON LIVING

Hon JAMES THOMAS ARCHIBALD, *b* 16 May 1952: *m* 1979, Christine, da of William Stephenson, of The Ridings, Royston, Herts, and has issue living, Emily, *b* 7 Feb 1983.

DAUGHTERS LIVING

Hon Sarah, *b* 1954: *m* 1977, Nicholas Charles Dent, yst son of Maj J. C. Dent, of 51 Addison Rd, W14, and has issue living, Rose Bridget, *b* 1982.
Hon Gian Leila, *b* 1958.
Hon Dinah Lilian, *b* 1964: *m* 1989, Harry Marriott, 2nd son of John Marriott, of Gt Milton, Oxfordshire, and has issue living, Wilfred William J., *b* 1994, — a son, *b* 1998, — a da, *b* 1996.

SISTER LIVING

Hon Tessa Mary, *b* 1934: *m* 1956, Julian Ogilvie Thompson, of Froome, Froome Rd, Athol Extension, Sandton 2196, S Africa, and has issue living, Christopher William, *b* 1958: *m* 1984, Kathleen Jean, da of Alastair Blackstock, of Blairgowrie, Johannesburg, and has issue living, James Alastair *b* 1988, Luke Julian *b* 1991, — Anthony Thomas, *b* 1964: *m* 1992, Meredith, da of Harold James Jensen, of 828 Fifth Ave, New York, NY 10021, and has issue living, Harold Nicholas *b* 1996, David Theodore *b* (twin) 1996, — Rachel Amanda, *b* 1960: *m* 1985, Richard Miles Keene, of The Oast House, Mill Court, Upper Froyle, Hants, son of Douglas Keene, of Littlehampton, W Sussex, and has issue living, Harold Thomas *b* 1988, Justin Frederick *b* 1989, Oliver Stephen *b* 1993, Tessa Emily *b* 1995, — Leila Katharine, *b* 1965: *m* 1990, Hilton A. Barnett, of Froome Close, Froome Rd, Athol, Sandton 2196, son of G. G. Barnett, of Somerset W, Cape Town, and has issue living, Thomas Christopher *b* 1995, William Frederick *b* 1998

COLLATERAL BRANCHES LIVING (*See* V Hampden).

PREDECESSORS – (1) *Sir* RANDOLF de Dacre, son and heir of Sir William de Dacre of Dacre, Cumberland; summoned to Parliament 1321-38, whereby he is held to have become Lord Dacre: *m* Margaret, da and heir of Thomas de Multon, of Gilsland, Cumberland; *d* 1339; *s* by his son (2) WILLIAM, 2nd Baron: *m* Katherine, da of Sir Ralph Neville, of Raby, co Durham; *d* 1361; *s* by his brother (3) RANDOLF, 3rd Baron; *b* about 1322; murdered 1375; *s* by his brother (4) HUGH, 4th Baron: *m* 1354/55, Elizabeth, widow of Sir William Douglas, Earl of Atholl; *d* 1383; *s* by his son (5) WILLIAM, 5th Baron: (said to have married first, Joan Douglas): *m* Mary; *d* 1399; *s* by his son (6) THOMAS, 6th Baron; *b* 1387: *m* Philippa, da of Ralph Neville, Earl of Westmorland; *d* 1458; *s* by his grand-da (7) JOAN (da of Sir Thomas Dacre): *m* 1446, Sir Richard Fiennes, who was summoned to Parliament as Baron Dacre 1459; he *d* 1483 and his widow *d* 1486; he was *s* by his grandson, (8) THOMAS (son of Sir John Fiennes), 8th Baron; KB 1494: *m* about 1492, Anne, da of Sir Humphrey Bourchier; *d* 1533; *s* by his grandson (9) THOMAS (son of Sir Thomas Fiennes), 9th Baron: *m* 1536, Mary, da of George Nevill, Lord Abergavenny; having taken part in a deer hunt at Laughton Park, Sussex, when a park keeper was killed, he was found guilty of murder, hanged at Tyburn 1541, and his honours forfeited; his son (10) GREGORY, 10th Baron (whose elder brother Thomas, *d* 1553, aged 15, would have succeeded but for his father's forfeiture) was restored to his honours 1558: *m* about 1558, Anne Sackville, sister of 1st Earl of Dorset; *d* 1594; *s* by his sister (11) MARGARET, 9th Baron: *m* 1564, Sampson Lennard, who *d* 1615; *d* 1612; *s* by her son (12) HENRY, 12th Baron; *b* 1570: *m* 1589, Chrysogona, da of Sir Richard Baker of Sissinghurst; *d* 1616; *s* by his son (13) RICHARD, 13th Baron; *b* 1596: *m* 1st, 1617, Elizabeth, da of Sir Arthur Throckmorton; 2ndly, 1625, Dorothy North, da of 3rd Lord North; *d* 1630; *s* by his son (14) FRANCIS, 14th Baron; *b* 1619: *m* 1641, Elizabeth Bayning (who was *cr* Viscountess of Sheppey for life 1680), da of Paul 1st Viscount Bayning of Sudbury; *d* 1662; *s* by his son (15) THOMAS, 15th Baron, *b* 1654; *cr* Earl of Sussex 1674: *m* 1674, Anne Palmer or FitzRoy, da of Barbara Duchess of Cleveland; *d* 1715, when the Earldom became ext and the Barony of Dacre fell into abeyance between his two das, until 1741, when the yr (16) ANNE *s* on the death without issue of her sister Barbara; *b* 1684: *m* 1st, 1716, Richard Barrett, of Belhus, Essex, who *d* 1716; 2ndly, 1718, Henry Roper, 8th Baron Teynham, who *d* 1723; 3rdly, 1725, Hon Robert Moore, son of 3rd Earl of Drogheda, who *d* 1762; she *d* 1755; *s* by her son (17) THOMAS Barrett-Lennard, 17th Baron; *b* 1717: *m* 1739, Anna Maria, sister of 1st Earl Camden; *d* 1786; *s* by his nephew (18) TREVOR CHARLES Roper (son of Hon Charles Roper), 18th Baron; *b* 1773, Mary, da and heir of Sir Thomas Fludyer, of Lee, Kent; *d* 1794; *s* by his sister (19) GERTRUDE; *b* 1750: *m* 1771, Thomas Brand, who *d* 1794; *d* 1819; *s* by her son (20) THOMAS, 20th Baron; *b* 1774: *m* 1819, Barbarina, da of Adm Sir Chaloner Ogle, 1st Bt, and widow of Valentine Henry Wilmot; *d* 1851; *s* by his brother (21) HENRY OTWAY Trevor, 21st Baron; *b* 1777; Gen in the Army; assumed by R licence 1824 the surname of Trevor in lieu of Brand: *m* 1806, Pyne Crosbie, sister and co-heir of William, 4th Baron Brandon; *d* 1853; *s* by his son (22) THOMAS CROSBIE WILLIAM Trevor, 22nd Baron; *b* 1808; assumed by R licence 1851 the surname of Trevor in lieu of Brand: *m* 1837, Hon Susan Sophia Cavendish, da of 1st Baron Chesham; *d* 1890; *s* by his brother **(23)** HENRY BOUVERIE WILLIAM, GCB, PC, 23rd Baron; Speaker of the House of Commons, who in 1884 was *cr Viscount Hampden*, of Glynde, Sussex (peerage of UK); from that time the Barony of Dacre descended with the Viscountcy of Hampden **(25-27)** until the death of the 4th Viscount and 27th Baron in 1965, when the Barony fell into abeyance between his two das, Hon Mrs Rachel Leila Douglas-Home, and Hon Mrs Tessa Mary Ogilvie Thompson, and so continued until 1970, when the abeyance was terminated in favour of the el **(28)** RACHEL LEILA, present peeress.

DACRE OF GLANTON, BARON (Trevor-Roper) (Life Baron 1979)

Prof HUGH REDWALD TREVOR-ROPER, son of late Bertie William Trevor-Roper, MB, MRCS (*see* B Teynham, colls); *b* 15 Jan 1914; *ed* Charterhouse, and Ch Ch Oxford; Regius Prof of Modern History, Oxford 1957-1980; Master of Peterhouse, Camb 1980-87; *cr Baron Dacre of Glanton*, of Glanton, co Northumberland (Life Baron) 1979: *m* 1954, Lady Alexandra Henrietta Louisa Haig, who *d* 1997, da of 1st Earl Haig, and formerly wife of Rear Adm Clarence Dinsmore Howard-Johnston, CB, DSO, MC.

𝔄rms – Quarterly: *1st and 4th*, per fesse azure and or, a pale and three roebuck's heads erased counterchanged for *Roper*; *2nd and 3rd*, per bend sinister ermine and ermines a lion rampant or, and for distinction a canton sanguine, thereon an escallop argent charged with a cross flory of the fourth for *Trevor*. 𝔠rests – 1st, a lion rampant sanguine holding in his right paw a ducal coronet or for *Roper*; 2nd, on a chapeau gules turned up ermine a wyvern wings elevated sanguine and for distinction on the breast an escallop charged as in the arms. 𝔖upporters – *Dexter*, a bull gules armed and unguled crined and tufted eyed and langued or about the shoulders a collar of crowns joined at their circlets by three links gold; *sinister*, a lion sable about the shoulders a like collar of crowns, the compartment comprising a grassy mount and growing therefrom eight sprigs of oak fructed and leaved four gules and four gold.
Residence – The Old Rectory, Didcot, Oxon OX11 7EB.

DAHRENDORF, BARON (Dahrendorf) (Life Baron 1993)

RALF DAHRENDORF, KBE, son of late Gustav Dahrendorf; *b* 1 May 1929; *ed* Hamburg Univ (DPhil), and LSE (PhD), Hon DLitt Reading and Dublin, Hon LLD Manchester, Wagner Coll, NY, York (Ontario), and Columbia, NY, Hon DHL Kalamazoo Coll, and John Hopkins Univ Baltimore, Hon DSc Ulster, Bath and Bologna, Hon DUniv Open Univ, Maryland and Surrey, Hon Dr Université Catholique de Louvain, Hon DSSc Queen's Belfast and Birmingham, etc; Hon Fellow Imperial Coll and LSE; formerly Prof of Sociology at Hamburg, Tübingen and Konstanz Univs; Member EEC Commn Brussels 1970-74, Dir LSE 1974-84; Non-Exec Dir Glaxo Holdings plc 1984-92; Warden St Antony's Coll, Oxford, since 1987, Dir and Chm Newspaper Publishing plc 1992-93; FBA, FRSA; *cr* KBE 1982, and *Baron Dahrendorf*, of Clare Market, in the City of Westminster (Life Baron) 1993: *m* 1980, Ellen Joan, da of James Krug, of New York.
Address – House of Lords, Westminster, SW1A 0PW. *Clubs* – Reform, Garrick.

DAINTON, BARONY OF (Dainton) (Extinct 1997)

SON LIVING OF LIFE BARON

Prof the Hon John Bourke, *b* 1947. *Address* – c/o Dept of Physics, Univ of Liverpool, PO Box 147, Liverpool L69 3BX.

DAUGHTERS LIVING OF LIFE BARON

Dr the Hon Mary Crawford, *b* 1950: *m* 1981 (*m diss* 1988), David Whitehead, and has issue living, two children. *Residence* – 7 Veronica Rd, Didsbury, Manchester M20 0ST.
Hon Rosalind Hazlitt, *b* 1952: *m* 1981, Christopher Conway, and has issue living, one child. *Residence* – 58 Trinity St, Belle Vue, Shrewsbury SY3 7PQ.

WIDOW LIVING OF LIFE BARON

BARBARA HAZLITT (*Baroness Dainton*), JP, PhD, Hon DSc, only da of late Dr W. B. Wright, of Manchester: *m* 1942, Baron Dainton (Life Baron), who *d* 1997. *Residence* – 36 Charlbury Rd, Oxford OX2 6UX.

DALHOUSIE, EARL OF (Ramsay) (Earl S 1633)

Pray and labour

†SIMON RAMSAY, KT, GCVO, GBE, MC, 16th Earl; *b* 17 Oct 1914; *s* 1950; *ed* Eton, and Ch Ch, Oxford; KStJ; late Major 4th/5th Batn Black Watch (TA); Gov-Gen of Federation of Rhodesia and Nyasaland 1957-63; Lord Chamberlain to HM Queen Elizabeth the Queen Mother 1965-92; Lord Lieut co Angus (later Tayside Region) 1967-89, and Chancellor of Dundee Univ since 1977; Hon LLD Dalhousie Univ, Halifax, Nova Scotia, and Dundee; 1939-45 War (MC); an additional Conservative Whip 1946-50; MP for Forfarshire (*C*) 1945-50; GBE (Civil) 1957; KT 1971; GCVO 1978: *m* 1940, Margaret Elizabeth Mary, who *d* 1997, da of late Brig-Gen Archibald Stirling of Keir (*see* Stirling-Maxwell, Bt, colls), and has issue. The 16th Earl of Dalhousie *d* 15 July 1999.

Arms – Argent, an eagle displayed sable, beaked and membered gules. Crest – An unicorn's head, couped at the neck argent, armed, maned, and tufted or. Supporters – *Dexter*, a griffin argent; *sinister*, a greyhound argent, gorged with a collar gules, charged with three escallops of the first.
Seats – Brechin Castle, Brechin, Angus DD9 6SH; Dalhousie Castle, Bonnyrigg, Midlothian. *Clubs* – White's and Puffin's.

SONS LIVING

JAMES HUBERT (*Lord Ramsay*) (Brechin Castle, Brechin, Angus DD9 6SH; Flat 15, 41 Courtfield Rd, SW7 4DB), *b* 17 Jan 1948; *ed* Ampleforth; late 2nd Lt Coldm Gds; DL Angus 1993: *m* 1973, Marilyn Davina, da of Maj Sir David Henry Butter, KCVO, MC (*see* Wernher, Bt, ext), and has issue:—

SON LIVING— *Hon* Simon David, *b* 18 April 1981; Page of Honour to HM 1993-96.
DAUGHTERS LIVING— *Hon* Lorna Theresa, *b* 1975, — *Hon* Alice Magdalene, *b* 1977.

Hon Anthony, *b* 1949; *ed* Ampleforth, and Magdalen Coll, Oxford: *m* 1st, 1973 (*m diss* 1979), Georgina Mary, da of late *Hon* Michael Langhorne Astor (*see* V Astor); 2ndly, 1984, Vilma, da of late Raphael Salcedo, of Santa Martha, Colombia, and has issue living (by 1st *m*), Alexander Simon, *b* 1977, — (by 2nd *m*) Zoë Mary, *b* 1985, — Isabella, *b* 1987. *Residence* – 37 Anhalt Rd, SW11 4N2.
Hon John Patrick, *b* 1952; *ed* Ampleforth: *m* 1981, Louisa Jane, only da of late Robert Erland Nicolai d'Abo, of West Wratting Park, W Wratting, Cambs (*see* D Rutland), and has issue living, Christopher, *b* 1984, — Lucy Emma, *b* 1985. *Residence* – 1 Kassala Rd, SW11.

DAUGHTERS LIVING

Lady Elizabeth (*Countess of Scarbrough*), *b* 1941; a Lady of the Bedchamber to HM Queen Elizabeth the Queen Mother since 1994: *m* 1970, 12th Earl of Scarbrough. *Residence* – Sandbeck Park, Maltby, Rotherham S66 8PF.

Lady Sarah, *b* 1945: *m* 1966, Sir (John) Chippendale (Lindley) Keswick, of 1A Ilchester Place, W14, and Auchendolly House, Old Bridge of Urr, Castle Douglas, Kirkcudbrightshire, 2nd son of late Sir William Keswick, of Glenkiln, Shawhead, Dumfries (*see* Lindley, By, 1950 Edn), and has issue living, David, *b* 1967: *m* 1999, Samantha M., eldest da of Peter Shaw, of Huish Champflower, Som, — Tobias, *b* 1968, — Adam, *b* 1973.

COLLATERAL BRANCHES LIVING

Grandchildren of late Hon Sir Patrick William Maule Ramsay, KCMG, 2nd son of 13th Earl, *b* 1879, *d* 1962: *m* 1917, Cynthia, who *d* 1957, da of late Brig-Gen Sir Herbert Conyers Surtees, CB, and widow of Christopher Cecil Tower, of Weald Hall, Essex:—
Issue of late David Patrick Maule Ramsay, *b* 1919, *d* 1978: *m* 1948 (*m diss* ca 1958), Hélène (who *d* 1980, having *m* 2ndly, John Tod Horton), da of Leonidas Arvanitidi, of Paris:—
Sylvia Patricia (5617 South Dorchester Av, Chicago, 60637-1749 Illinois, USA), *b* 19—. —— David RAMSAY (recognised issue by Luisa Garcia Vega), *b* 1965 (Madrid); *ed* Sch of Medicine, Berne Univ, Switzerland (MD): *m* 1990, Anja, da of Hans-Ulrich Liechti, and has issue living, Jan (a son), *b* 1990, — Benjamin, *b* 1992.

Issue of late Adm Hon Sir Alexander Robert Maule Ramsay, GCVO, KCB, DSO, 3rd son of 13th Earl, *b* 1881, *d* 1972: *m* 1919, HRH Princess (Victoria) Patricia Helena Elizabeth, VA, CI, CD, GCStJ, who *d* 1974 (who on her marriage renounced by Royal permission the style and title of "HRH" and "Princess", and adopted that of "Lady", with precedence before Marchionesses of England), yr da of Field Marshal HRH the 1st Duke of Connaught and Strathearn (*see* ROYAL FAMILY):—
Alexander Arthur Alfonso David Maule RAMSAY OF MAR (Cairnbulg Castle, Fraserburgh, Aberdeenshire AB43 5TN; Inverey House, Braemar, Aberdeenshire; Flat 8, 25 Onslow Sq, SW7 3NJ; *Clubs* – Cavalry & Guards', New (Edinburgh), Turf); *b* 21 Dec 1919; *ed* Eton, and Trin Coll, Oxford (MA); FRICS; DL Aberdeenshire 1971; Baron of Kellie; Capt Gren Gds (ret); served 1938-47 (wounded Tunisia 1943); an ADC to HRH the Duke of Gloucester whilst Gov-Gen of Australia 1944-47; a Page of Honour at Coronation of King George VI; Chm of Exec Cttee of Scottish Life Boat Council, RNLI since 1965; Vice-Patron of RNMDSF, and of Braemar Royal Highland Soc: *m* 6 Oct 1956, Hon Flora Marjory Fraser (*Lady Saltoun* in her own right), da of 19th Lord Saltoun, and has issue (*see* L Saltoun).

Granddaughters of Capt Archibald Henry Maule Ramsay (infra):—
Issue of late Robert John Maule Ramsay, *b* 1920, *d* 1978: *m* 1st, 1948 (*m diss* 1961), Theodora Jean (2 Cliffield, Shalford, Essex CM7 5HP), da of Martyn Hewlett, of Cranham Hall, Little Waltham; 2ndly, 1961, Elizabeth Frances, who *d* 1972, da of A. F. Bultitude:—
(By 1st *m*) Theodora Alice Maule (8-2 Hailsland Grove, Wester Hailes, Edinburgh EH14 3BW), *b* 1950. —— Christian Ismay Maule, *b* 1952: *m* 1972, Juan Carlos Torres, of Santiago de Compostela, Spain, and has issue living, Aaron *b* 1976. —— Charlotte Maule, *b* 1954: *m* 1976, John Gentry, of 275 Peach Tree Lane, Newnan, Georgia 30263, USA, and *d* 1992, leaving issue, Nathan, *b* 1975, — Mathew, *b* 1982, — Andrew, *b* 1989.

Grandson of late Lt-Col Henry Lushington Ramsay, elder son of late Gen Hon Sir Henry Ramsay, KCSI, CB, brother of 12th Earl:—
Issue of late Capt Archibald Henry Maule Ramsay, *b* 1894, *d* 1955: *m* 1917, Hon Ismay Lucretia Mary, who *d* 1975, da of 14th Viscount Gormanston, and widow of Lord Ninian Edward Crichton-Stuart (M Bute):—
George Patrick Maule (The Old School House, The Square, Elham, Kent), *b* 1922; *ed* Eton; Col late Scots Gds: *m* 1st, 1947 (*m diss* 1977), Patricia Mary, da of Dr J. J. Morrin; 2ndly, 1980, Mrs Bridget Kelly, da of late Ronald Thomas Dyson Hornby, of 25 Elm Tree Green, Gt Missenden, Bucks, and formerly wife of late Capt Edward Kelly, and has issue living (by 1st *m*), Alexander John Patrick Maule (Flat A, 38 Dafforne Rd, SW17), *b* 1948, — Patrick William Maule (40 Elmbourne Rd, SW17 8JR), *b* 1951: *m* 1984, Fiona, da of Peter Stoddart, of North Rye House, Moreton-in-Marsh, Glos, and has issue living, Nicholas George *b* 1992, Emily May *b* 1986, Katie Olivia *b* 1988, — Catherine Mary Maule (The Stone House, Wyck Rissington, Cheltenham, Glos GL54 2PN), *b* 1950: *m* 1972 (*m diss* 1991), Capt Sir Peter Ralph Leopold Walker-Okeover, 4th Bt, Blues and Royals, — Diana Mary Maule, *b* 1957: *m* 1983, as his 2nd wife, Timothy J. P. Coghlan, of Weedon Lodge Cottage, Everdon, nr Daventry, Northants NN11 6BQ, son of late A. F. Coghlan, of Ludwell Grange, Horsted Keynes, Sussex, and has issue living, Louise Mary *b* 1985, Elizabeth Mary *b* 1987, — Fiona Elisabeth Maule, *b* 1964: *m* 1987, Robert Algernon Radcliffe Boyle, Maj Irish Gds (ret) (*see* E Shannon, colls).

PREDECESSORS

PREDECESSORS – (1) Sir GEORGE Ramsay of Dalhousie, Knt; on his own resignation had a charter of the Barony of Dalhousie; also of the Barony of Melrose on the resignation of John Ramsay, Earl of Holderness; *cr Lord Ramsay of Melrose* (peerage of Scotland) by charter 1618, but not liking the title obtained a letter from James VI to change it to *Lord Ramsay of Dalhousie* (with precedence of 1618); *d* 1629; *s* by his el son (2) WILLIAM, 2nd Lord; raised a Regt in Army of the Covenant, which he commanded at Marston Moor and Philliphaugh; *cr Lord Ramsay of Keringtoun*, and *Earl of Dalhousie* (peerage of Scotland) 1633; *d* 1674; *s* by his son (3) GEORGE, 2nd Earl; *d* 1675; *s* by his son (4) WILLIAM, 3rd Earl; 2nd in command of Earl of Mar's Regt at Bothwell Brig 1679; *d* 1682; *s* by his son (5) GEORGE, 4th Earl; (killed in a duel) 1696 unmarried; *s* by his brother (6) WILLIAM, 5th Earl; Col Scots Guards; (while on active ser in Spain during War of Succession) 1710; *s* by his kinsman (7) WILLIAM, 6th Earl, son of John 2nd son of 1st Earl; *d* 1739; *s* by his grandson (8) CHARLES, 7th Earl; *d* 1764 unmarried; *s* by his brother (9) GEORGE, 8th Earl; an Advocate; Lord High Commr to Gen Assembly of Church of Scotland 1777-82, and a Representative Peer 1774-87 (his 2nd son, William, *cr Baron Panmure*, peerage of United Kingdom 1831, assumed the surname and arms of Maule of Panmure, and *d* 1852); *d* 1787; *s* by his el son (10) GEORGE, GCB, 9th Earl; a Gen in the Army; served with distinction in Peninsular War, and commanded 7th and 6th Divs at Vittoria; Gov-Gen of Canada 1819-28, and Com-in-Ch in India 1829-32; *cr Baron Dalhousie*, of Dalhousie Castle, co Edinburgh (peerage of United Kingdom) 1815; *d* 1838; *s* by his son (11) JAMES ANDREW, KT, PC, 10th Earl; Gov-Gen of India 1847-56, Constable of Dover Castle, Lord Warden of the Cinque Ports, etc; assumed the additional surname of Broun of Coulstoun on succession to the Coulstoun estate; *cr Marquess of Dalhousie*, of Dalhousie Castle, co Edinburgh, and of the Punjab (peerage of United Kingdom) 1849; *d* 1860, when the UK Barony of Dalhousie and the Marquessate became ext; *s* in Scottish honours by his cousin (12) FOX, KT, GCB, PC, 11th Earl, who had in 1852 *s* his father as 2nd Baron Panmure; was an Under-Sec of State 1835-41, Vice-Pres of Board of Trade 1841, Sec at War 1846-52 and 1855-8, Lord-Lieut of co Forfar, and Keeper of the Privy Seal of Scotland, etc, assumed the surname and arms of Ramsay of Dalhousie after that of Maule; *dsp* 1874, when the UK Barony of Panmure expired; *s* by his cousin (13) GEORGE, CB, 12th Earl, son of Hon John Ramsay, 4th son of 8th Earl, *b* 1806; was an Adm; *cr Baron Ramsay*, of Glenmark, co Forfar (peerage of United Kingdom) 1875: *m* 1845, Sarah Frances, da of William Robertson, of Logan House, NB; *d* 1880; *s* by his son (14) JOHN WILLIAM, KT, PC, 13th Earl, *b* 1847: *m* 1877, Lady Ida Louisa Bennett, who *d* 1887, da of 6th Earl of Tankerville: *d* 1887; *s* by his el son (15) ARTHUR GEORGE MAULE, 14th Earl, *b* 1878; Capt Scots Guards, and Hon Col RGA (TA): *m* 1903, Lady Mary Adelaide Heathcote-Drummond-Willoughby, who *d* 1960, yst da of 1st Earl of Ancaster; *d* 1928; *s* by his son **(16)** JOHN GILBERT, 15th Earl; *b* 1904, *d* 1950; *s* by his brother **(17)** SIMON, 16th Earl and present peer; also Lord Ramsay of Dalhousie, Lord Ramsay of Keringtoun, and Baron Ramsay of Glenmark.

Dalkeith, Earl of; son of Duke of Buccleuch.

Dalmeny, Lord; son of Earl of Rosebery.

Dalrymple, family name of Earl of Stair.

Damer, Dawson-, family name of Earl of Portarlington.

Dangan, Viscount; son of Earl Cowley.

DARCY DE KNAYTH, BARONESS (Ingrams) (Baroness E 1332)

DAVINA MARCIA INGRAMS, DBE (*Baroness Darcy de Knayth*), *b* 10 July 1938; *s* 1943; a Member Gen Advisory Council IBA 1987-90; *cr* DBE (Civil) 1996: *m* 1960, Rupert George Ingrams, who was *k* in a motor accident 1964 (*see* Reid, Bt *cr* 1897, 1964 Edn), and has issue

Arms – Per pale azure and gules, three lions rampant argent. **Supporters** – *Dexter*, an heraldic tiger argent; *sinister*, a bull sable.
Residence – Camley Corner, Stubbings, Maidenhead, Berks SL6 6QW.

SON LIVING

Hon CASPAR DAVID, *b* 5 Jan 1962; *ed* Eton, and Reading Univ (BSc): *m* 1996, Catherine Ann, elder da of Bryan Baker, of Abingdon, Oxon, and of Mrs Bryan Barnes, of Pickering, N Yorks.

DAUGHTERS LIVING

Hon Miranda, *b* 1960.
Hon Catriona, *b* 1963.

WIDOW LIVING OF SEVENTEENTH BARON

VIDA, only da of late Capt James Harold Cuthbert, DSO, Scots Gds; is an OStJ; appointed a Lady-in-Waiting to HRH the Duchess of Gloucester 1944: *m* 1st, 1934, the 17th Baron Darcy de Knath (also Viscount Clive), who was *ka* 1943; 2ndly, 1945, Brig Derek Shuldham Schreiber, MVO, who *d* 1972 (*see* B Faringdon, 1946 Edn). *Residence* – Fir Hill, Droxford, Hants.

COLLATERAL BRANCHES LIVING

Issue of late Lady Hermione Gwladys Herbert, only da of Violet Ida Evelyn, Baroness Darcy de Knayth (Countess of Powis), *b* 1900, *d* 1995: *m* 1924, Conte Robert Lucchesi Palli, 11th Duca della Grazia, and 13th Principe di Campofranco, who *d* 1979:-
Donna Violet Maria Carolina Sidonie LUCCHESI PALLI, *b* 1930. *Residence* – Villa Rovera Molina, via Lunga 57, I 21020 Barasso, Varese, Italy.

Descendants of Sir William D'Arcy of Plattyn (*b* 1330), only surviving son (by 2nd *m*) of 1st Baron:—
See 1969 Edn.

PREDECESSORS – (1) JOHN DARCY DE KNAYTH was summoned to Parliament of England as *"Johanni Darcy le Cosin"* 1332; *d* 1347; *s* by his son (2) JOHN; summoned to Parliament as *Lord Darcy de Knayth*: *m* Elizabeth, in her own right *Baroness Meinill* (who *d* 1368), only child of Nicholas, Lord Meinill; *d* 1356, and was *s* by his son (3) JOHN, 3rd Baron; *d* unmarried, and *vita matris*; *s* by his brother (4) PHILIP, Lord Darcy de Knayth and Meinill; *d* 1398; *s* by his son (5) JOHN; *d* 1411; *s* by his el son (6) PHILIP, Lord Darcy de Knayth and Meinill, at whose death in 1418 the Baronies of Darcy de Knayth and Meinill fell into abeyance between his das, of whom the yr, Margery, *m* Sir John Conyers, of Hornby, and had a son Sir John Conyers, of Hornby, who *m* Alice, da and co-heir of William Nevill, Earl of Kent, and Lord Fauconberg (by Joan his wife *suo jure* Baroness Fauconberg); they had issue William, 1st Lord Conyers (*see* By of Fauconberg and Conyers), whose great-great-grandson (7) CONYERS DARCY (son of Thomas Darcy by Elizabeth, da and co-heir of the 3rd Baron Conyers) received in 1641 Letters Patent determining in his favour the abeyances then existing in the Baronies of Darcy de Knayth and Conyers; *d* 1653; *s* by his son (8) CONYERS, Baron Darcy de Knayth and Conyers; *cr Earl of Holderness* 1682; *d* 1688; *s* by his son (9) CONYERS, 2nd Earl; *d* 1692; *s* by his grandson (10) ROBERT 3rd Earl; *d* 1722; *s* by his son (11) ROBERT 4th Earl; *d* 1778, when the Earldom became ext, but the Baronies passed to his da (12) AMELIA, wife of 5th Duke of Leeds; *d* 1784; *s* by her son (13) GEORGE WILLIAM FREDERICK, 6th Duke; *d* 1838; *s* by his son (14) FRANCIS GODOLPHIN DARCY, 7th Duke; *d* 1859; *s* by his nephew (15) SACKVILLE GEORGE (son of Sackville Walter Lane Fox, Esq, MP), *b* 1827: in 1859 established his right to Barony of Conyers only, and was known by that title, his right to the Barony of Darcy de Knayth being established posthumously in 1903: *m* 1860, Mary, Lady Darcy de Knayth and Conyers, who *d* 1921, el da of Reginald Curteis, of Windmill Hill, Sussex; *d* 1888, when the Baronies fell into abeyance, this being determined as to the Barony of Conyers in 1892 in favour of the elder da Marcia Amelia Mary, Countess of Yarborough (in whose favour also the abeyance existing in the Barony of Fauconberg was determined 1903), and as to the Barony of Darcy de Knayth in 1903 in favour of the yr da (16) VIOLET IDA EVELYN, Countess of Powis, *b* 1865: *m* 1890, 4th Earl of Powis, who *d* 1952; *d* 1929; *s* by her yr son (17) MERVYN HORATIO, 17th Baron; *b* 1904; Squadron-Leader RAF: *m* 1934, Vida, only da of late Capt James Harold Cuthbert, DSO; *ka* 1943; *s* by his only child (18) DAVINA MARCIA, present peeress.

DARESBURY, BARON (Greenall) (Baron UK 1927, Bt UK 1876)
(Title pronounced "Darsbury")

I seek to rise

PETER GILBERT GREENALL, 4th Baron, and 5th Baronet; *b* 18 June 1953; *s* 1996; *ed* Eton, Magdalene Coll, Camb (MA), and London Business Sch; High Sheriff Cheshire 1992, DL 1994: *m* 1982, Clare Alison, only da of Christopher Nicholas Weatherby, MC, of Whaddon House, Whaddon, Bucks (*see* E Erne, colls, 1995 Edn), and has issue.

Arms – 1st and 4th or, on a bend benuly vert three bugle-horns stringed of the field, *Greenall*; 2nd and 3rd argent, five pallets sable, the centre pallet charged with an ermine spot of the field, *Griffith*. **Crest** – Between two wings or, a pomme surmounted by a bugle-horn as in the arms. **Supporters** – *Dexter*, a bull proper; *sinister*, a bay mare, mane and tail sable, charged on the shoulder with a sprig of two oak leaves or.
Residence – Hall Lane Farm, Daresbury, Warrington, Cheshire WA4 4AF.
Clubs – Jockey, White's, Turf, MCC.

SONS LIVING

Hon THOMAS EDWARD, *b* 6 Nov 1984.
Hon Oliver Christopher, *b* 1986.
Hon Toby Peter, *b* 1988.
Hon Jonathan James, *b* 1992.

BROTHERS LIVING

Dr the Hon Gilbert, CBE, *b* 1954; *ed* Eton; MB, ChB, MBA; CBE (Civil) 1993: *m* 1983, Sarah Elizabeth, elder da of Ian C. Mouat, of Stetchworth, Suffolk, and formerly wife of Robert Greville Kaye Williamson, and has issue living, Gilbert Edward, *b* 1984, — Frederick John, *b* 1986, — Alexander, *b* 1988, — Amelia Frances, *b* 1990. *Residence* – Bromesberrow Place, Ledbury, Herefordshire HR8 1RZ. *Club* – White's.

Hon John Edward, *b* 1960; *ed* Fettes; BSc Econ: *m* 1st, 1985 (*m diss* 1991), Gabrielle, da of Stephen James, of Lymington, Hants; 2ndly, 1998, Laura Anne, da of Nicholas Collin (*see* B Feversham), and has issue living (by 1st *m*), James Edward, *b* 1988, — Katie Laura, *b* 1986. *Residence* – Lullington House, Lullington, Swadlincote, Derbys DE12 8EG.

SISTER LIVING

Hon Susan Rosemary, *b* 1956: *m* 1st, 1978 (*m diss* 1989), David St Clare Oswald Bruton; 2ndly, 1989, Anthony St John Haden-Taylor, son of late Frank Pacey Haden-Taylor, of Broughton Gifford, Wilts, and has had issue (by 1st *m*), Alastair Edward Oswald, *b* 1985, — Natasha Charlotte, *b* 1983, — (by 2nd *m*) Pandora Eleanor Christine, *b* 1989, *d* 1990, — Annabella Margaret Christine, *b* 1995. *Residence* – White Oaks, Park Estate, St Brelade's, Jersey, CI JE3 8EQ.

MOTHER LIVING

Margaret Ada, yst da of late Charles John Crawford (*see* Anson, Bt, 1954 Edn): *m* 1952 (*m diss* 1986), Hon Edward Gilbert Greenall (later 3rd Baron Daresbury), who *d* 1996. *Residence* – Waltham House, Waltham, Melton Mowbray, Leics.

WIDOW LIVING OF THIRD BARON

MARY PATRICIA (*Molly, Baroness Daresbury*), da of late Lewis Parkinson: *m* 1986, as his 2nd wife, the 3rd Baron Daresbury, who *d* 1996. *Residence* – Crossbow House, Trinity, Jersey, CI.

PREDECESSORS – (1) GILBERT Greenall, 6th son of late Edward Greenall, of Wilderspool, co Chester, *b* 1806; MP for Warrington (C) 1847-68, 1874-80 and 1885-92; *cr* a *Baronet* 1876, *m* 1ot, 1836, Mary, who *d* 1861, da of David Claughton, of Haydock, Lancashire; 2ndly, 1864, Susannah, who *d* 1896, da of John Louis Rapp; *d* 1894; *s* by his only son (2) *Sir* GILBERT, CVO, 2nd Bt, *b* 1867; High Sheriff for Cheshire 1907; *cr Baron Daresbury* of Walton, co Chester (peerage of United Kingdom) 1927: *m* 1900, Frances Eliza, JP, who *d* 1953, da of late Capt Edward Wynne Griffith, formerly 1st R Dragoons; *d* 1938; *s* by his only surviving son (3) EDWARD, 2nd Baron, *b* 1902; Lieut Res of Officers, late Life Guards, Jt Master Belvoir Hounds 1934-47, Master co Limerick Hounds 1947-89: *m* 1st, 1925, Joan Madeline, who *d* 1926, elder da of late Capt Robert Thomas Oliver Sheriffe, of Goadby Hall, Melton Mowbray; 2ndly, 1927, Josephine, who *d* 1958, yst da of late Brig-Gen Sir Joseph Frederick Laycock, KCMG, DSO (*see* E Listowel, colls, 1952 Edn); 3rdly, 1966, Lady Helena Albreda Marie Gabriella, who *d* 1970, da of 7th Earl Fitzwilliam, and formerly wife of late Maj Chetwode Charles Hamilton Hilton-Green; *d* 1990; *s* by his only son (4) EDWARD GILBERT, 3rd Baron, *b* 1928; Chm Randall and Vautier Ltd, and Grunhalle Lager Internat: *m* 1st, 1952 (*m diss* 1986), Margaret Ada, yst da of late Charles John Crawford (*see* Anson, Bt, 1954 Edn); 2ndly, 1986, Mary Patricia, da of late Lewis Parkinson; *d* 1996; *s* by his eldest son (5) PETER GILBERT, 4th Baron and present peer.

DARLING, BARON (Darling) (Baron UK 1924)

ROBERT CHARLES HENRY DARLING, 2nd Baron; *b* 15 May 1919; *s* 1936; *ed* Wellington Coll; Major (ret) Somerset LI; DL for Somerset: *m* 1942, (Bridget) Rosemary Whishaw, who *d* 1997, da of Rev Francis Cyprian Dickson, formerly V of Emery Down, Lyndhurst, Hants, and has issue.

The gift of God

Arms – Argent, on a chevron engrailed between three flesh-pots sable a stirrup leathered or. **Crest** – In front of a dexter cubit arm proper holding in the hand a heart gules a chaplet of laurel vert. **Supporters** – On either side a Pegasus argent, charged on each wing with a chevron engrailed sable. **Badge** – A sprig of heather and a sprig of gorse in saltire proper, enfiled by a Baron's coronet.
Residence – Puckpits, Limpley Stoke, Bath, Somerset.

SON LIVING

Hon (ROBERT) JULIAN HENRY (Intwood Hall, Norwich), *b* 29 April 1944; *ed* Wellington Coll, and RAC Cirencester; FRICS: *m* 1970, Janet Rachel, yr da of Mrs D. M. E. Mallinson, of Richmond, Yorks, and has issue living, Robert James Cyprian, *b* 1972, — Henry Thomas Unthank, *b* 1978, — Rachel Pollyanna Margaret, *b* 1974.

DAUGHTERS LIVING

Hon Anna Josephine Bridget, *b* 1946: *m* 1971, Anthony Robert Pardoe, of Sharow Cottage, Sharow, Ripon, N Yorks, and has issue living, David Hugh Charles, *b* 1974, — Georgina Rosemary Jane, *b* 1977.
Hon Lucinda Mary Joan, *b* 1958: *m* 1982, Rory P. A. Macdiarmid, only son of late Col Peter Macdiarmid, and has issue living, George Peter Robert, *b* 1985, — Fergus Charles Ian, *b* 1987, — Philippa Rosemary Kate, *b* 1990.

PREDECESSOR – (1) *Rt Hon Sir* CHARLES JOHN Darling, PC, el son of late Charles Darling, of Langham Hall, Essex; *b* 1849; MP for Deptford (*C*) 1888-97; Judge of the High Court of Justice 1897-1923; *cr Baron Darling*, of Langham, Essex (peerage of United Kingdom) 1924: *m* 1885, Mary Caroline, who *d* 1913, el da of late Maj-Gen Wilberforce Harris Greathed, CB; *d* 1936; *s* by his grandson (2) ROBERT CHARLES HENRY (son of late Maj Hon John Clive Darling, DSO, only son of 1st Baron), 2nd Baron and present peer.

DARLING OF HILLSBOROUGH, BARONY OF (Darling) (Extinct 1985)

SON LIVING OF LIFE BARON

Hon Peter George, *b* 1950.

DAUGHTER LIVING OF LIFE BARON

Hon Isabel, *b* 1948.

DARNLEY, EARL OF (Bligh) Sits as BARON CLIFTON OF LEIGHTON BROMSWOLD (E 1608) (Earl I 1725)
(Name pronounced "Bly")

ADAM IVO STUART BLIGH, 11th Earl; *b* 8 Nov 1941; *s* 1980; *ed* Harrow, and Ch Ch Oxford; Vice-Chm of the Govs of Cobham Hall Sch since 1991: *m* 1965, Susan Elaine, JP, da of late Sir Donald Forsyth Anderson (*see* Llewellyn, Bt, *cr* 1922), and has issue.

Arms – Azure, a griffin segreant or, armed and langued gules, between three crescents argent. **Crest** – A griffin's head erased or. **Supporters** – Two griffins, wings expanded or, ducally gorged and chained azure.
Residence – Netherwood Manor, Tenbury Wells, Worcs WR15 8RT.

Look to the end

SON LIVING

IVO DONALD STUART (*Lord Clifton of Rathmore*), *b* 17 April 1968; *ed* Marlborough, and Edinburgh Univ: *m* 1997, Peta Martine, da of Robert Beard, of Scobbiscombe, S Devon, and of Mrs Penny Fletcher, of Axminster, Devon, and has issue living, *Hon* Henry Robert Stuart, *b* 23 April 1999.

DAUGHTER LIVING

Lady Katherine Amanda, *b* 1971; *ed* St Mary's Sch Calne, Marlborough Coll, and St Edmund Hall, Oxford.

SISTERS LIVING

Lady Melissa Geraldine Florence, *b* 1945: *m* 1st, 1965, Don Manuel Torrado y de Fontcuberta, who *d* 1980; 2ndly, 1985, as his 2nd wife, Rev Canon Colin Russell Levey and has issue living (by 1st *m*), Manuel Ivo, *b* 1966: *m* 1st, 1991 (*m diss* 1995), Audrey Elizabeth, da of Andrew Perratt; 2ndly, 1997, Alison Frances, da of Francis de Vroome, — Maria Melissa, *b* 1968: *m* 1998, Juan-Carlos de Camps Galobart, — Victoria Irene Anna, *b* 1973. *Residence* – The Vicarage, Orton, Penrith, Cumbria C10 3RQ.
Lady Harriet Esme Ghislaine, *b* 1949; *ed* Cobham Hall, and Somerville Coll, Oxford. *Residence* – Meadow House Cottage, Cobham, Gravesend, Kent DA12 3B2.

HALF-SISTERS LIVING (*Daughter of 9th Earl by 1st marriage*)

Lady Marguerite Rose (52 Redcliffe Gdns, SW10), *b* 1913: *m* 1st, 1934 (*m diss* Feb 1941), Claud Dobrée Strickland, F/O AAF, who was *ka* Oct 1941 (Strickland-Constable, Bt, colls); 2ndly, 1942 (*m diss* 1951), W/Cmdr Gordon Stanley Keith Haywood, RAF; 3rdly, 1951 (*m diss* 1963), as his 2nd wife, Nigel Trevithick Tangye, who *d* 1988, and has issue living (by 2nd *m*), Gareth Peter, *b* 1943: *m* 1965 (*m diss* 1969), Zehra Ipek, da of Prof Semseddin Talip Diler, of Taksmin, Istanbul, — Lucinda March (10 Hollywood Rd, SW10), *b* (twin) 1943: *m* 1964 (*m diss* 1983), James Hilary Glyn, and has issue (*see* B Wolverton, colls).

(*Daughter of 9th Earl by 2nd marriage*)

Lady Rose Amanda (*Lady Rose Hare*), *b* 1935: *m* 1961, Sir Thomas Hare, 5th Bt, who *d* 1993, of Stow Bardolph, King's Lynn, Norfolk PE34 3HU, and has issue (*see* Hare, Bt).

WIDOW LIVING OF SON OF EIGHTH EARL

Mrs Kathleen Weatherill Strickland (5 Sloane Gate Mansions, D'Oyly St, SW1): *m* 1973, as his 3rd wife, Lt-Col Hon Noel Gervase Bligh, DSO, who *d* 1984.

WIDOW LIVING OF NINTH EARL

ROSEMARY, da of late Basil Potter: *m* 1st, 1940, as his 3rd wife, the 9th Earl, who *d* 1955; 2ndly, 1963, as his 2nd wife, Pierre Trasenster, who *d* 1968. *Residence* – Meadow House, Cobham, Gravesend, Kent DA12 3BZ.

COLLATERAL BRANCH LIVING

Grandchildren of late Major Lodovick Edward Bligh, son of Rev Hon Edward Vesey Bligh, 2nd son of 5th Earl:—
Issue of late Algernon Stuart Bligh, *b* 1888, *d* 1952: *m* 1st, 1922 (*m diss* 1937), Dora Joan, da of T. Lovelace, of Bratton Court, Minehead; 2ndly, 1938, Dorothy, who *d* 1994, da of late J. F. V. Larway:—
(By 1st *m*) Noel Edward, *b* 1926; late Capt RASC, and Lt RN: *m* 1961, Jane Mary, da of Trevor Seymour-Smith, and has issue living, Victoria Joan, *b* 1962. *Residence* – Churchcombe, Yarnscombe, Barnstaple, N Devon. —— Audrey Diana, *b* 1924: *m* 1947, John Sefton Spencer Hawkins, of Osbornes, Upper Dicker, Hailsham, Sussex, and has issue living, Nigel

Bligh Spencer, b 1954, — David Stuart Spencer (Cairns Lodge, 2 Newlands Av, Bexhill-on-Sea, E Sussex), b 1956: m 1985, Elaine Mary Menhinick, and has issue living, Matthew Bligh Spencer b 1988, Melanie Joanne Spencer b 1990. —— (By 2nd m) Jennifer Wendy, b 1942: m 1st, 1963 (m diss 1974), Ronald Colin Board Webber; 2ndly, 1975 (m diss 19—), Alan Thomas Wormell; 3rdly, 1982, Peter MacDonell Prior-Wandesforde, of Ballylanigan House, Mullinahone, co Tipperary, and has issue living (by 1st m), Katrina Jane, b 1964: m 1991, Maj J. P. Stanhope-White, of Poundisford, Crowcombe, Taunton, Som, and has issue living, Atalanta Jasmine Bligh b 1998. —— Heather Rosalind, b 1945: m 1st, 1968 (m diss 1977), Arthur Keith Amor; 2ndly, 1983, Christopher James Dunn, of Staple Fitzpaine Manor, Staple-Fitzpaine, Taunton, Som, and has issue living (by 1st m), Jason Keith Bligh, b 1970, — Lucinda Jane Bligh, b 1969, — (by 2nd m), Harry James Bligh, b 1984.

PREDECESSORS – (1) JOHN BLIGH, MP for Athboy 1709-21; cr Baron Clifton of Rathmore (peerage of Ireland) 1721, Viscount Darnley (peerage of Ireland) 1723, and Earl of Darnley (peerage of Ireland) 1725; d 1728; s by his son (2) EDWARD, 2nd Earl, who in 1722 had s his mother as Baron Clifton of Leighton Bromswold (peerage of England) by writ of summons 1608; d unmarried 1747; s by his brother (3) JOHN, 3rd Earl; MP for Maidstone; d 1781; s by his son (4) JOHN, 4th Earl; in 1829 claimed as heir-gen the Scottish Dukedom of Lennox, but the House of Lords did not come to any decision; d 1831; s by his son (5) EDWARD, 5th Earl; b 1795; sat as MP for Canterbury 1818-30; was Lord Lieut of co Meath: m 1825, Emma Jane, who d 1884, da of 1st Baron Congleton; d 1835; s by his son (6) JOHN STUART, 6th Earl, b 1827: m 1850, Lady Harriet Mary Pelham, who d 1905, el da of 3rd Earl of Chichester; d 1896; s by his el son (7) EDWARD HENRY STUART, 7th Earl, b 1851: m 1899, Miss Jemima Adeline Blackwood; d 1900, when the Barony of Clifton of Leighton Bromswold passed to his da and only child Elizabeth Adeline Mary (see infra *), who d 1937, while he was s in the Earldom by his brother (8) IVO FRANCIS WALTER, 8th Earl; b 1859; a Representative Peer for Ireland: m 1884, Dame Florence Rose, DBE, who d 1944, da of late Stephen Morphy, of Beechworth, Victoria; d 1927; s by his son (9) ESME IVO, 9th Earl; b 1886: m 1st, 1912 (m diss 1920), Daphne Rachel, who d 1948, da of late Hon Alfred John Mulholland; 2ndly, 1923 (m diss 1936), Nancy, who d 1991, da of late Capt Glen Kidston, 3rd Batn Black Watch; 3rdly, 1940, Rosemary (who m 2ndly, 1963, as his 2nd wife, Pierre Trasenster, who d 1968), da of late Basil Potter; d 1955; s by his el son (10) PETER STUART, 10th Earl; b 1915; d 1980; s by his half-brother (11) ADAM IVO STUART, 11th Earl and present peer; also Viscount Darnley, Baron Clifton of Rathmore, and Baron Clifton of Leithton Bromswold.

*(1) Sir GERVASE Clifton, son of Sir John Clifton, of Barrington, Somerset, was summoned to Parliament as Baron Clifton of Leighton Bromswold (peerage of England) 1608: d 1618; s by his da (2) CATHERINE: m Lord Esme Stuart who was cr Baron Stuart of Leighton Bromswold (in her right), and Earl of March 1619, and s as 3rd Duke of Lennox, 1624; d 1637; s by her son (3) JAMES, 4th Duke of Lennox; d 1655; s by his son (4) ESME, 5th Duke; d 1660; s by his sister (5) MARY Butler, Countess of Arran; d 1667; s by her cousin (6) CHARLES, 6th Duke of Lennox; d 1672; s by his sister (7) CATHERINE O'Brien (wife of Henry, el son of 7th Earl of Thomond), who claimed and was allowed the barony in 1674 as grand-da of Catherine, da of 1st Baron; she m 2ndly, Sir Joseph Williamson; d 1702; s by her da (8) CATHERINE Hyde, Viscountess Cornbury; d 1706; s by her son (9) EDWARD, Viscount Cornbury; d 1712; s by his sister (10) THEODOSIA: m John Bligh, of Rathmore, co Meath, who was cr Baron Clifton of Rathmore (peerage of Ireland) 1721, Viscount Darnley (peerage of Ireland) 1723, and Earl of Darnley (peerage of Ireland) 1725; d 1722; s by her son (11) EDWARD, 2nd Earl of Darnely, who in 1722 had s his mother as Baron Clifton of Leighton Bromswold (peerage of England) by writ of summons 1608; d unmarried 1747; s by his brother (12) JOHN, 3rd Earl; MP for Maidstone; d 1781; s by his son (13) JOHN, 4th Earl; in 1829 claimed as heir-gen the Scottish Dukedom of Lennox, but the House of Lords did not come to any decision; d 1831; s by his son (14) EDWARD, 5th Earl; b 1795; sat as MP for Canterbury 1818-30; was Lord-Lieut of co Meath: m 1825, Emma Jane, who d 1884, da of 1st Baron Congleton; d 1835; s by his son (15) JOHN STUART, 6th Earl; b 1827: m 1850, Lady Harriet Mary Pelham, who d 1905, el da of 3rd Earl of Chichester; d 1896; s by his el son (16) EDWARD HENRY STUART, 7th Earl; b 1851: m 1899, Miss Jemima Adeline Blackwood; d 1900, when the Earldom of Darnley passed to his brother, while he was s in the Barony of Clifton of Leighton Bromswold by his da and only child (17) ELIZABETH ADELINE MARY, Baroness Clifton of Leighton Bromswold; b 1900; d 1937; s by her cousin (18) ESME IVO 9th Earl of Darnley (ante).

DARTMOUTH, EARL OF (Legge) (Earl GB 1711)

Virtue rejoices in trial

WILLIAM LEGGE, 10th Earl; b 23 Sept 1949; s 1997; ed Eton, Ch Ch, Oxford, and Harvard Business Sch; FCA.

Arms – Azure, a buck's head cabossed argent. Crest – Out of a ducal coronet or, a plume of five ostrich feathers argent and azure alternately. Supporters – Dexter, a lion argent semée of fleurs-de-lis sable, ducally crowned or, and issuing from the coronet a plume of five ostrich feathers argent and azure, alternately; sinister, a stag argent, unguled or, and semée of mullets gules. Residences – 16 Westbourne Terr, W2; Blakelea House, Marsden, nr Huddersfield, Yorks.

BROTHERS LIVING

Hon RUPERT, b 1 Jan 1951; ed Eton, and Ch Ch, Oxford (MA); Bar Inner Temple 1975; author of The Children of Light (1986), Fashionable Circles (1991), Playing With Fire (1993), A Dangerous Age (1995), etc: m 1984, M— Victoria S—, da of Lionel Edward Bruce Ottley, of Tichborne Park Cottage, Alresford, Hants (see B Avebury, colls, 1955 Edn), and has issue living, Edward Peregrine, b 14 Dec 1986, — Claudia Rose, b 1989. Residence – Hamswell House, nr Bath, Glos BA1 9DG.
Hon Henry, b 1968; ed Eton, and Worcester Coll, Oxford; Bar Lincoln's Inn 1996: m 1995, Cressida M—, yr da of Sir Christopher Anthony Hogg, of Mayfair, SW1. Residences – 11a Berkeley Gdns, W8; Llangunnock House, Three Ashes, St Leonards, Herefords.

SISTER LIVING

Lady Charlotte, *b* 1963: *m* 1990, Alexander Paternò Castello, 13th Duca di Cárcaci (*see* E Inchcape, 1973-74 Edn), and has issue living, *Don* Tancredi (Barone di Placa é Baiana), *b* 1997, — *Donna* Miranda, *b* 1993, — *Donna* Chiara, *b* 1995. *Residence* – 18 Cheyne Row, SW3.

AUNT LIVING (*daughter of 8th Earl*)

Lady Heather Margaret Mary (*Baroness Herschell*), *b* 1925: *m* 1948, 3rd Baron Herschell, and has issue. *Residence* – Westfield House, Ardington, Wantage, Berks.

DAUGHTERS LIVING OF SEVENTH EARL

Lady Mary Cecilia, *b* 1906: *m* 1929, Cdr Noel Charles Mansfeldt Findlay, RN, who *d* 1976, son of Sir Mansfeldt de Cardonnel Findlay, GBE, KCMG, CB, and has issue living, Jonathan Mansfeldt (Eden Lodge, Droxford, Hants), *b* 1933; Cdr RN: *m* 1962, Jutta, da of Gen Karl von Graffen, and has issue living, Christopher Mansfeldt Karl *b* 1967, Caroline Ilse *b* 1962, Angela Mary *b* 1964, — Martin Charles (Ledburn Manor, Leighton Buzzard, Beds), *b* 1935: *m* 1966, Davina Margaret, da of Maj Sir Thomas Calderwood Dundas, MBE, 7th Bt (*cr* 1898) (ext), and has issue living, Mark Simon *b* 1967, Adam James *b* 1969, — Jane Elizabeth, *b* 1930: *m* 1961, Jeremy Debenham, of Reeds Farm, Sayers Common, Hassocks, Sussex, and has issue living, Catherine Mary *b* 1962, Henrietta Jane *b* 1965: *m* 1991 Oliver George Curtis, Susannah Elizabeth *b* 1968: *m* 1998, David Ross Drummond. *Residence* – 2 South Close, The Precincts, Canterbury, Kent CT1 2EJ.
Lady Elizabeth, DCVO (67 Cottesmore Court, Stanford Rd, W8), *b* 1908; appointed an Extra Woman of the Bedchamber to HM Queen Elizabeth the Queen Mother 1955; CVO 19—, DCVO 1989: *m* 1931, Ronald Lambart Basset, who *d* 1972 (*see* Salusbury-Trelawny, Bt, 1947 Edn), and has issue living, Bryan Ronald, CBE (Quarles, Wells-next-the-Sea, Norfolk NR23 1RY), *b* 1932: *m* 1960, Lady Carey Elizabeth Coke, da of 5th Earl of Leicester, and has issue living, David Francis *b* 1961, Michael James *b* 1963: *m* 1996, Caroline J., elder da of late J. Philip Bailey, of Quakers, Lower Hazel, Bristol (and has issue living, Elizabeth Jane *b* 1998), James Bryan *b* 1968; formerly a Page of Honour to HM.
Lady Barbara, *b* 1916; formerly in First Aid Nursing Yeo: *m* 1945, Adam Kwiatkowski, Lieut Polish Army, and has issue living, Jan Witold (Bonham Farm, Stourton, nr Warminster, Wilts), *b* 1945: *m* 1968, Sarah Hope, da of Christopher Challis, of Pineways, Grays Park, Stoke Poges, Bucks, and has issue living, Adam Witold *b* 1974, Daniel Christopher *b* 1974, William *b* 1977, Alexander George *b* 1979, — Marek William, *b* 1947: *m* 1977, Belinda Mary Graham, el da of Maj John Cecil Graham Moon (*see* Moon, Bt *cr* 1855, colls), and has issue, Stefan Marek *b* 1981, — Christopher (The Stables, Patshull, Albrighton, Shropshire), *b* 1951: *m* 1978, Allison Porter, el da of R. P. Yates, of Hinnington Grange, Shifnal, Shropshire, and has issue living, Marek *b* 1987, Anna *b* 1989, — Michael Andrew Adam, *b* 1955: *m* 1978 (*m diss* 1981), Scylla Nina Antoinette, yst da of late Roderick W. Parkyn, of Pen-y-Lan, Hardwicke, Herefordshire. *Residence* – The Bothy, Patshull Park, Burnhill Green, Wolverhampton.

MOTHER LIVING

Raine (*Raine, Countess Spencer*), da of late Alexander George McCorquodale, of The White Lodge, Speen, Berks, and of Dame Barbara Cartland, DBE, of Camfield Place, Hatfield, Herts: *m* 1st, 1948 (*m diss* 1976), as his 1st wife, the 9th Earl of Dartmouth, who *d* 1997; 2ndly, 1976, as his 2nd wife, the 8th Earl Spencer, LVO, who *d* 1992; 3rdly, 1993 (*m diss* 1996), Count Jean-François de Chambrun; resumed her former style 1997. *Residence* – 24 Farm St, W1X 7RE.

WIDOW LIVING OF EIGHTH EARL

ROMA ERNESTINE (*Roma, Countess of Dartmouth*), da of Sir Ernest Burford Horlick, 2nd Bt: *m* 1923, the 8th Earl of Dartmouth, CVO, DSO, who *d* 1962. *Residence* – 15B Bedford Towers, Brighton, Sussex.

WIDOW LIVING OF NINTH EARL

Mrs GWENDOLINE MAY SEGUIN (*Countess of Dartmouth*), da of late Charles René Seguin: *m* 1980, as his 2nd wife, the 9th Earl of Dartmouth, who *d* 1997. *Residence* – 47 Grosvenor Square, W1.

COLLATERAL BRANCHES LIVING

Grandchildren of late Nigel Walter Henry LEGGE-BOURKE, only son of late Col Hon Sir Henry Charles Legge, GCVO, 2nd son of 5th Earl:—
Issue of late Maj Sir (Edward Alexander) Henry Legge-Bourke, KBE, DL, MP, *b* 1914, *d* 1973: *m* 1938, Catherine Jean (*Lady Legge-Bourke*) (121 Dovehouse St, SW3 6JZ), da of Col Sir Arthur Grant of Monymusk, 10th Bt, CBE, DSO:—
William Nigel Henry (Penmyarth, Glanusk Park, Crickhowell, Powys NP8 1LP), *b* 1939; *ed* Eton, and Magdalene Coll Camb (MA); late Capt RHG (The Blues); DL Powys 1997: *m* 1964, Hon (Elizabeth) Shân (Josephine) Bailey, LVO, da of 3rd Baron Glanusk, and has issue living, Harry Russell, *b* 1972; a Page of Honour to HM The Queen 1985-87; commn'd WG 1992, Capt (despatches 1994), — Alexandra Shân, *b* 1965, — Zara Victoria, *b* 1966: *m* 1985 (*m diss* 1997), Richard Grosvenor Plunkett-Ernle-Erle-Drax, and has issue (*see* B Dunsany, colls). —— Heneage (32 Quai d'Orléans, 75004 Paris, France), *b* 1948; *ed* Eton, and Ecole Hotelière, Lausanne; a Page of Honour to HM The Queen 1963-64: *m* 1978 (*m diss* 1997), Maria Clara, da of late Vasco de Sá-Carneiro, of Lisbon, and has issue living, Edward Alexander Heneage *b* 1984, — Eleanor Jean Maria, *b* 1980. —— Victoria Lindsay, LVO (21 Eccleston Sq, SW1V 1NS), *b* 1950; a Lady in Waiting to HRH The Princess Royal since 1974; LVO 1986.

Grandchildren of late Rev Hugh Legge, 3rd son of late Rev Hon George Barrington Legge, 2nd son of 4th Earl:—
Issue of late Maj John Barrington Legge, *b* 1918, *d* 1989: *m* 1940, Gertrude Sarah (The Porch House, Dodford, Northants), da of Frederick Wood, of Little Preston Capes, Northants:—
Hugh, *b* 1945; *ed* Haileybury; late Lieut RA: *m* 1977 (*m diss* 1995), Julia, da of J. H. Taylor, of Newcastle, Staffs, and has issue living, Robin Francis, *b* 1980, — Colin Brendan, *b* 1982. —— Jane, *b* 1941: *m* 1977, John Grace Day. —— Hannah, *b* 1947; *d* 1987.

Granddaughter of late Lt-Col the Hon Edward Henry Legge, 3rd son of 4th Earl:—
Issue of late John Douglas Legge, MC, *b* 1886, *d* 1954: *m* 1917, Haroldine, who *d* 1970, da of late Harold S. Peck, of Chicago, USA:—
Virginia Lois (*Hon Mrs Nial A. R. O'Neill*) (Crowfield House, Crowfield, Ipswich, Suffolk IP6 9TP), *b* 1922: *m* 1966, Maj Hon Nial Arthur Ramleh O'Neill, who *d* 1980 (*see* B Rathcavan).

Grandson of late Rt Rev Hon Augustus Legge, DD, Bishop of Lichfield, 5th son of 4th Earl:—
Issue of late Francis Augustus Legge, *b* 1880, *d* 1966: *m* 1909, Mabel Clara Arden, who *d* 1963, da of late Charles Lucena, of Westwick, Easthampstead:—
Christopher Augustus Sackville (c/o 1013 Mass Ave NE, Washington DC 20002, USA), *b* 1911; *ed* Eton, and Worcester Coll, Oxford (MA); Bar Inner Temple 1936: *m* 1st, 1952, Kari, who *d* 1971, da of the late Walther Brebeck, Pres of Senate, of Eutin, Germany; 2ndly, 1979, Signe White, and has issue living (by 1st *m*) Christopher Walter, *b* 1955, — Barbara Ingrid, *b* 1960.

Grandchildren of late Hon Charles Gounter Legge, 6th son of 4th Earl:—
Issue of late Brig-Gen William Kaye Legge, CMG, DSO, *b* 1869, *d* 1946: *m* 1902, Constance Adeline, who *d* 1964, da of late Hon James David Palmer, of Bloemfontein, Orange Free State Province, S. Africa:—
Peter, *b* 1910; *ed* Wellington Coll; Wing-Cdr (ret) RAF; 1939-45 War (despatches twice): *m* 1st, 1937 (*m diss* 1953), Mary Claire, da of William Dwyer, of Elmville, Rushbrooke, co Cork; 2ndly, 1955, Violet Bertha, da of late George Wallace, and has issue living (by 1st *m*), Michael William, *b* 1938; *ed* Downside: *m* 1965 (*m diss* 19—), Kim Hoang, and has issue living, Julian *b* 1969, Nicola *b* 1967, — David Anthony, *b* 1941; *ed* Downside: *m* 1966, Mary Roden, and has issue living, Christopher Dermot *b* 1970, Thomas David *b* 1974, Andrew *b* 1976, Jennifer Claire *b* 1968, Anna Constance *b* 1972, — Susan Noelle Ann, *b* 1943: *m* 1966, Paul Dempsey, and has issue living, Karen Jane *b* 1967, Joanna Ruth *b* 1969, Sophie Ann *b* 1972, Emma Claire *b* 1973, Rachel *b* 1978.

Issue of late Lt-Cdr John Augustus Legge, RD, RNR, *b* 1871, *d* 1945: *m* 1908, Grace Margaret, who *d* 1957, da of late Alexander Henderson Dunsmure, of 46 Egerton Crescent, SW3:—
John Michael Derek, *b* 1913; *ed* Eton: *m* 1945, Esmé Edith, da of the late Vice-Adm Cyril St Clair Cameron, CBE, and has had issue, †Derek Rupert Spicer, *b* 1949: *m* 1990, Jacqueline Ann Hollaway, and *d* 1996, leaving issue, Henry Rupert Cameron *b* 1993, Victoria Alice *b* 1990, — Elizabeth Angela, *b* 1946. *Residence* – Homefield, Nunney, Frome, Som BA11 4LG. —— David Alexander Keppel, CBE, *b* 1916; *ed* Eton; Col R Fus (ret); 1939-45 War (wounded); MBE (Mil) 1953, CBE (Mil) 1970: *m* 1944, Patria, da of late Lt-Col C.B.R. Hornung, DL, JP, of Ivorys, Cowfold, and has issue living, Richard Charles Gounter (Furneaux Farmhouse, Whatfield, Ipswich, Suffolk) *b* 1948: *m* 1972, Lesley Mayfield Finch, da of Frederick Ledger, of Brompton House, Malvern, and has issue living, Jonathan Alexander Heneage *b* 1979, Thomas Henry Finch *b* 1983, — Anthea Frances, *b* 1946: *m* 1969, Richard Charles Roundell, of Dorfold Hall, Nantwich, Cheshire (*see* Cs Dysart, colls, 1966 Edn), and has issue living, Charles Henry *b* 1975, Laura Ann (*Hon Mrs Orlando W. Montagu*) *b* 1972: *m* 1996, Hon Orlando William Montagu, yr son of 11th Earl of Sandwich. *Residence* – Sandwell, Marston Magna, Yeovil, Som. —— Margaret Elizabeth, *b* 1908. *Residence* – Tutton Hill House, Colerne, Wilts.

Issue of late Thomas Charles Legge, *b* 1872, *d* 1949: *m* 1904, Ivy Emily, who *d* 1961, yst da of J. Reid, of Zeerust, Transvaal:—
Mary Charlotte Lois, *b* 1905; BCom: *m* 1934, George Wilson Low, Colonial Vet Ser. *Address* – Cramond, Vipingo, via Mombasa, Kenya.

Grandson of late Thomas Charles Legge (ante):—
Issue of late (Gounter Heneage) Hugh Legge, *b* 1909, *d* 1992: *m* 1936, Joyce Kathleen, who *d* 19—, yst da of late Thomas Angus Brown:—
Traver Francis Hugh (20 Cherry Glebe, Mersham, Ashford, Kent TN25 6NL), *b* 1942; assumed the christian name of Traver in lieu of Thomas; *ed* Witwatersrand Univ (BSc(Eng)), and Imperial Coll, London (DIC, MSc): *m* 1972, Helen Dorothy, da of John Downie, of Johannesburg, and has issue living, Angela Claire, *b* 1975, — Janet Helen, *b* 1980.

Grandchildren of late Capt Ronald George Legge, 7th son of late Hon Charles Gounter Legge (ante):—
Issue of late Major Rupert Mortimer Legge, Roy Fusiliers, *b* 1911, *ka* in Italy 1944: *m* 1940, Anne, who *d* 1982, da of late Sir James Adam, CBE, KC:—
Rupert James (Croft Cottage, Firby, Bedale, N Yorks DL8 2PW), *b* 1944; *ed* Wellington Coll: *m* 1968, Jacqueline Hope, da of late Maj E. T. H. Ubsdell, and has issue living, Edward James *b* 1971: *m* 1998, Sarah, da of Alistair Lennox, — Philippa Georgina *b* 1972. —— (Christian Anne) Victoria (Ridgewood House, Brent Eleigh, Sudbury, Suffolk), *b* 1942: *m* 1973 (*m diss* 1993), Christopher T. Sharman, and has issue living, Matthew Rupert Derek *b* 1975, — Thomas Christopher James, *b* 1977, — Patrick William Adam, *b* 1979.

PREDECESSORS – (1) *Rt Hon* GEORGE Legge, an eminent naval commander, and Col of a regt of Foot; founded the Roy Fus; Gov of Portsmouth, Master of the Ordnance, and Master of the Horse and Gentleman of the Bedchamber to James, Duke of York, etc; *cr Baron Dartmouth*, of Devon (peerage of England) 1682; during the reign of James II held several important offices, but falling with his party at the Revolution, was been suspected of plotting against William III, was imprisoned in the Tower, where he *d* 1691; *s* by his son (2) *Rt Hon* WILLIAM, 2nd Baron; Sec of State 1710; Lord Privy Seal 1713, and after the death of Queen Anne, one of the Lords Justice of Great Britain; *cr Viscount Lewisham* and *Earl of Dartmouth* (peerage of Great Britain) 1711; *d* 1750; *s* by his grandson (3) WILLIAM, 2nd Earl; Sec of the Colonies; sponsor of Dartmouth Coll, Hanover, New Hampshire 1769; *d* July 1801; *s* by his son (4) GEORGE, KG, 3rd Earl, summoned to Parliament in his father's barony June 1801; *d* 1810; *s* by his son (5) WILLIAM, FRS, DCL, 4th

Earl; *b* 1784: *m* 1st, 1821, Lady Frances Charlotte, who *d* 1823, da of 2nd Earl Talbot; 2ndly, Hon Frances, who *d* 1849, da of 5th Viscount Barrington; *d* 22 Nov 1853; *s* by his son **(6)** WILLIAM WALTER, 5th Earl, *b* 1823; MP for S Staffordshire (*C*) 1849-53; Lord-Lieut of Staffordshire: *m* 1846, Lady Augusta Finch, who *d* 1900, el da of 5th Earl of Aylesford; *d* 1891; *s* by his el son **(7)** *Rt Hon* WILLIAM HENEAGE, GCVO, KCB, VD, TD, 6th Earl, *b* 1851; Vice-Chamberlain of HM Queen Victoria's Household 1885-6, and 1886-91, and Lord-Lieut of Staffs 1891-1927; MP for W Kent (*C*) 1878-85, and for Lewisham 1885-91: *m* 1879, Lady Mary Coke, CBE, who *d* 1929, da of 2nd Earl of Leicester; *d* 1936; *s* by his el son **(8)** WILLIAM, GCVO, TD, 7th Earl; *b* 1881; Co Councillor for London, 1907-10, Hon Col Duke of Wellington's (W Riding) Regt and Staffordshire Yeo; MP for West Bromwich (*C*) 1910-18; upon death of Marquess of Lincolnshire appointed 1928 by HM King George V to execute office of Lord Great Chamberlain for remainder of his reign: *m* 1905, Lady Ruperta Wynn-Carrington, who *d* 1963, da of 1st Marquess of Lincolnshire; *d* 1958; *s* by his brother **(9)** HUMPHRY, CVO, DSO, 8th Earl; *b* 1888; Cdr RN; present at Jutland 1916; Assist Ch Constable of Staffs 1929-32, and Ch Constable of Berks 1932-54: *m* 1923, Roma Ernestine, da of Sir Ernest Burford Horlick, 2nd Bt; *d* 1962; *s* by his only son **(10)** GERALD HUMPHRY, 9th Earl; *b* 1924; Capt Coldstream Gds (despatches); FCA; Dir Rea Brothers, Chm Ocean Wilson Holdings Ltd, Royal Choral Soc and Anglo-Brazilian Soc: *m* 1st, 1948 (*m diss* 1976), Raine, da of late Alexander George McCorquodale, of The White Lodge, Speen, Berks, and of Dame Barbara Cartland, DBE; 2ndly, 1980, Mrs Gwendoline May Seguin, of Rio de Janeiro, Brazil, da of late Charles René Seguin; *d* 1997; *s* by his eldest son **(11)** WILLIAM, 10th Earl and present peer; also Viscount Lewisham and Baron Dartmouth.

DARWEN, BARON (Davies) (Baron UK 1946)

ROGER MICHAEL DAVIES, 3rd Baron; *b* 28 June 1938; *s* 1988; *ed* Bootham Sch, York: *m* 1961, Gillian Irene, da of Eric G. Hardy, of Valley View, Leigh Woods, Bristol, and has issue.
Residence – Labourer's Rest, Green St, Pleshey, Chelmsford, Essex.

SONS LIVING

Hon PAUL *b* 1962.
Hon Benjamin, *b* 1966.

DAUGHTERS LIVING

Hon Sarah, *b* 1963.
Hon Naomi, *b* 1965.
Hon Mary, *b* 1969.

BROTHERS LIVING

Hon Stephen Humphrey, *b* 1945: *m* 1968, Kathleen Prestwood, and has issue living, Timothy Prestwood, *b* 1970, — Peter, *b* 1980, — Ruth Mary, *b* 1972, — Rachel, *b* 1976.
Hon Philip Cedric Mark, *b* 1951.

SISTER LIVING

Hon Catherine Joy, *b* 1948; *ed* Cardiff Univ (BA, PGCE), lecturer in Eng Lit and Lang: *m* 1st, 1970 (*m diss* 1976), Robert Nienhuis; 2ndly, 1976, Richard George Tipping, and has issue living, (by 2nd *m*) Damian Richard George, *b* 1977, — Gregory Luke Darius, *b* 1980.

UNCLE LIVING (*son of 1st Baron*)

Hon (Francis) Ronald, *b* 1920; *ed* Bootham Sch, and Queen's Coll, Oxford (BA 1942, MA 1946); Bar Gray's Inn 1948: *m* 1942, Margaret Phyllis, da of John George Cocksworth, and has issue living, Daniel Watson, *b* 1948, — John Russell, *b* 1950, — Helen Bronwen, *b* 1954. *m* 1979, Peter Johnson. *Residence* – 39 Parkside, Mill Hill, NW7.

AUNTS LIVING (*daughters of 1st Baron*)

Hon Joan Kathleen, *b* 1917: *m* 1940, Walter Higham Brindle, MBE, TD, and has issue living, Michael Patrick, *b* 1943, — Alison Lesley, *b* 1947. *Residence* – 27 Abbotsford Court, Colinton Rd, Edinburgh EH10 5EH.
Hon Marjorie Heather, *b* 1923; JP: *m* 1944, Frederick Joseph Adams, CBE, and has issue living, Christopher Stephen, *b* 1946: *m* 1st, 1968 (*m diss* 1987), Julia Helene Phipps; 2ndly, 1997, Sharon Andrea Harrison (*née* Holland), and has issue living, (by 1st *m*), Tamsin Ruth *b* 1973, Melanie Rachel *b* 1975. *Residence* – Birch House, Main St, Kniveton, Ashbourne, Derbys DE6 1JH.

WIDOW LIVING OF SON OF FIRST BARON

Doreen, da of Arthur James Allen: *m* 1941, Hon Thomas Barratt Davies, who *d* 1991, and has issue (see colls, infra).

WIDOW LIVING OF SECOND BARON

KATHLEEN DORA (*Kathleen, Baroness Darwen*), da of George Sharples Walker *m* 1934, the 2nd Baron Darwen, who *d* 1988. *Residence* – White Lodge, Sandelswood End, Beaconsfield, Bucks.

COLLATERAL BRANCH LIVING

Issue of late Hon Thomas Barratt Davies, 2nd son of 1st Baron, *b* 1916, *d* 1991: *m* 1941, Doreen (ante), da of Arthur James Allen:—
Alan John Barry, *b* (twin) 1949: *m* 1st, 1983 (*m diss* 1996), Kofo Worola Agbeke Williams; 2ndly, 1996, Ekasa Roseline Agha, and has issue living, (by 1st *m*) Oluwatobi Olumuyiwa Peter Barry, *b* 1990, — Titilola Eniola Caroline Ann, *b* 1985, — Ternitope Abiodun Eleanor Judith, *b* 1986, — (by 2nd *m*) John Benedict Kodjo, *b* 1998. ▬▬ Barbara Jean, *b* 1944: *m* 19— (*m diss* 19—), …… Kirke. ▬▬ Frances Hilary, *b* 1947: *m* 19—, Roy Ecclestone, of 19 Southfield Rd, Tubridge Wells, Kent TN4 9UH. ▬▬ Judith Ann (100 North Park Av, Roundhay, Leeds LS8 1HP), *b* (twin) 1949: *m* 1970 (*m diss* 1979), David John Merchant, who *d* 1998, and has issue living, Stephen Alan, *b* 1972, — Lucy Ann *b* 1974.

PREDECESSORS – **(1)** JOHN PERCIVAL Davies, son of late Thomas Pearce Davies, of Heatherfield, Darwen, and Pengarth, Grange-over-Sands; *b* 1885; a Cotton Manufacturer; a Lord-in-Waiting to HM 1949-50; *cr Baron Darwen*, of Heys-in-Bowland, W Riding of Yorkshire (peerage of UK) 1946: *m* 1914, Mary Kathleen, who *d* 1964, da of Alfred Kemp Brown, BD; *d* 1950; *s* by his son **(2)** CEDRIC PERCIVAL, 2nd Baron, *b* 1915 *m* 1934, Kathleen Dora, da of George Sharples Walker; *d* 1988; *s* by his elder son **(3)** ROGER MICHAEL, 3rd Baron and present peer.

DAVENTRY, VISCOUNT (FitzRoy Newdegate) (Viscount UK 1943)

FRANCIS HUMPHREY MAURICE FITZROY NEWDEGATE, 3rd Viscount, *b* 17 Dec 1921; *s* 1986; *ed* Eton; formerly Capt Coldm Gds (wounded); ADC to Viceroy of India 1946-48; JP 1960, DL 1970, High Sheriff of Warwicks 1970, Vice Lord Lieut 1974-90, Lord Lieut 1990-96; KStJ 1991: *m* 1959, Hon Rosemary Norrie, da of 1st Baron Norrie, and has issue.

Arms – Quarterly 1st and 4th, gules three lion's gambs two and one argent, *Newdegate*; 2nd and 3rd grand quarters quarterly: 1st and 4th, France and England quarterly; 2nd Scotland, 3rd Ireland; the whole debruised by a baton sinister compony argent and azure, *FitzRoy*. Crests – 1st, a fleur-de-lys argent, *Newdegate*; 2nd, on a chapeau gules, turned up ermine, a lion statant guardant or, ducally crowned azure, and gorged with a collar counter compony argent and azure, *FitzRoy*. Supporters – *Dexter*, a lion rampant guardant or crowned azure; *Sinister*, a greyhound argent; both gorged with a collar gobony ermine and azure a mullet argent in the azure, each collar edged also azure.
Residence – Temple House, Arbury, Nuneaton, Warwicks.

SONS LIVING

Hon JAMES EDWARD, *b* 27 July 1960; *ed* Milton Abbey, and RAC Cirencester: *m* 1994, Georgia, yr da of John Stuart Lodge, of Daglingworth Place, Cirencester, Glos, and has issue living, Humphrey John, *b* 23 Nov 1995, — Hester Anne, *b* 1997.
Hon Hugh Francis, *b* 1962; *ed* Eton.

DAUGHTER LIVING

Hon Joanna Norrie, *b* 1964: *m* 1990, Nicholas Yvone John Kirkpatrick, and has issue (*see* Loder, Bt, colls).

SISTER LIVING (*raised to the rank of a Viscount's daughter* 1988)

Hon Jocelyne, *b* 1929: *m* 1st, 1952 (*m* annulled 1953), Richard John Barton; 2ndly, 1957 (*m diss* 1980), Maj Henry John Allfrey, OBE, RA (ret), and has issue living (by 2nd *m*), Henry David, *b* 1959; *ed* Wellington Coll; Maj Scots DG: *m* 1985, Fiona Jean Hamilton, only da of Gen Sir Edward Burgess, KCB, OBE, and has issue living, Henry Edward *b* 1991,

Olivia *b* 1988, — Charles John, *b* 1963; *ed* Eton; Capt The Royal Hus (Prince of Wales's Own) (ret): *m* 1989, Caroline Margaret Violet, elder da of Sir Alastair Sturgis Aird, GCVO (*see* Aird, Bt, colls), and has issue living, Helena Idina *b* 1996, Isabel Anne *b* 1998, — Lucia Susan, *b* 1961: *m* 1988, Maj David St John Homer, MBE, RGJ, elder son of G/Capt Derek Homer, MVO, of Harpenden, Herts, and has issue living, Thomas David William *b* 1990, Charles St John *b* 1994, William Richard John *b* 1995. *Residence* – 3 New Cottages, Alnport, Andover, Hants.

DAUGHTERS LIVING OF SECOND VISCOUNT

Hon Barbara Helen, *b* 1928: *m* 1952, Col Peter Charles Ormrod, MC, 8th King's R Irish Hus, JP 1958, High Sheriff of Clwyd 1962, DL (1972), and has issue living, Emma Jane Caroline (Pen-y-Lan, Ruabon, Wrexham LL14 6HS), *b* 1958: *m* 1980 (*m diss* 1998), Julian Pendrill Warner Holloway, yr son of A. G. W. Holloway, of Boscobel, Burleigh, Stroud, Glos, and has issue living, James Oliver Pendrill *b* 1986, Thomas Henry Charles *b* 1988, Alexander Hugh George *b* 1991, Lavinia Sophie Olivia *b* 1984, — Alice Amelia, *b* 1964: *m* 1991, (Roger) James St George Hedley, of Butterfly Cottage, Gyfelia, Wrexham, LL13 0YH, son of Maj Roger St George Hedley, late Royal Fusiliers, of Corton, Wilts, and has issue living, Barbara Jane *b* 1992, Lilian Grace *b* 1994, Hermione Aurora *b* 1996. *Residence* – Bridge Lodge, Pen-y-Lan, Ruabon, Wrexham, Clwyd.

Hon Amelia Grace (Bridge Cottage, Stoke Charity, Winchester, Hants), *b* 1930; *m* 1950 (*m diss* 1978), Capt David Charles George Jessel, Coldstream Guards, and has issue (*see* Jessel, Bt), who *d* 1985.

PREDECESSORS – (1) Muriel, CBE, da of late Lt-Col Hon Archibald Charles Henry Douglas-Pennant (*see* B Penrhyn, colls), *b* 1869; *cr Viscountess Daventry*, of Daventry, co of Northampton (peerage of UK) 1943: *m* 1891, Capt Rt Hon Edward Algernon FitzRoy, MP (Speaker of House of Commons 1928-43), who *d* 1943 (two months before he was to have received a Viscountcy) (*see* B Southampton, colls); *d* 1962; *s* by her el son (2) (ROBERT) OLIVER, 2nd Viscount *b* 1893, Capt RN, High Sheriff of Rutland 1956, European Wars 1914-18, and 1939-45 (despatches): *m* 1916, Grace Zoe, who *d* 1978, da of late Claude Hume Campbell Guinness (E Westmeath, colls); *d* 1986; *s* by his nephew (3) FRANCIS HUMPHREY MAURICE (only son of late Cdr Hon John Maurice FitzRoy Newdegate, RN), *b* 1897, *d* 1976, who assumed by R Licence 1936, the addl surname and arms of Newdegate, by his wife, Lucia Charlotte Susan, OBE, who *d* 1982, da of late Sir Francis Alexander Newdigate-Newdegate, GCMG (*see* B Bagot, 1940 Edn), 3rd Viscount and present peer.

DAVID, BARONESS (David) (Life Baroness 1978)

NORA RATCLIFF DAVID, da of George Blockley Blakesley; *b* 23 Sept 1913; *ed* Ashby-de-la-Zouch Girls' Gram Sch, St Felix, Southwold, and Newnham Coll, Camb (MA, Hon Fellow 1986), Cambridge City Councillor 1964-67, and 1968-74; Cambs Co Councillor 1974-78; Member of Board, Peterborough Development Corpn 1976-78; Baroness-in-Waiting to HM 1978-79; JP Cambridge City; *cr Baroness David*, of Romsey, City of Cambridge (Life Baroness) 1978: *m* 1935, Richard William David, CBE, who *d* 1993, and has issue.
Residences – 50 Highsett, Cambridge CB2 1NZ; Cove, New Polzeath, Cornwall PL27 6UF.

SONS LIVING

Hon Nicholas Christopher (Dept of Archaeology, Univ of Calgary, Canada), *b* 1937: *m* 1st, 1962 (*m diss* 1975), Hilke Hennig; 2ndly, 1977 (*m diss* 1989), Iva Williams; 3rdly, 1905, Judy Sterner.

Hon (Richard) Sebastian (Box 820, Fort Macleod, Alberta, Canada), *b* 1940: *m* 1963, Eva Ross.

DAUGHTERS LIVING

Hon Teresa Katherine (50 Clarence Rd, Moseley, Birmingham B13 9UH), *b* 1944: *m* 1967, Llewelyn Anthony Davies.

Hon Elizabeth Sarah, *b* 1947: *m* 1st, 1966 (*m diss* 1977), Martin Anthony Potter; 2ndly, 1979, John Forder.

DAVIDSON, VISCOUNT (Davidson) (Viscount UK 1937)

Light out of darkness

JOHN ANDREW DAVIDSON, 2nd Viscount; *b* 22 Dec 1928; *s* 1970; *ed* Westminster, and Pembroke Coll, Camb; Capt Yeomen of the Guard (Dep Chief Whip) 1986-91, 1992: *m* 1st, 1956 (*m diss* 1974), Margaret Birgitta, da of late Maj-Gen Cyril Henry Norton, CB, CBE, DSO; 2ndly, 1975, Mrs Pamela Joy Dobb, da of John Vergette, and has had issue by 1st *m*.

Arms – Argent, on a fesse sable between in chief two pheons azure and in base a boar's head erased of the second a portcullis chained or. **Crest** – A lion passant gules charged on the shoulder with a pheon or and holding in the dexter paw a torch inflamed proper. **Supporters** – *Dexter*, a horse argent charged on the shoulder with a rose gules, barbed and seeded proper; *sinister*, a horse sable charged on the shoulder with a martlet or.

DAUGHTERS LIVING AND DECEASED (*by 1st marriage*)

Hon Alexandra Frances Margaret, *b* 1957: *m* 1982, Richard John Oldfield, only son of late Christopher Charles Bayley Oldfield, of 5 Ovington Gdns, SW3, and *d* 1995, leaving issue, Christopher, *b* 1986, — Henry, *b* 1991, — Leonora, *b* 1985. *Residence* – Doddington Place, Sittingbourne, Kent.

Hon (Georgina) Caroline (*Lady Edward Somerset*), *b* 1958: *m* 1982, Lord Edward Alexander Somerset, 2nd son of 11th Duke of Beaufort, and has issue (see that title).

Hon Camilla Birgitta, *b* 1963: *m* 1st, 1988 (*m diss* 1991), Simon Guthrie McNair Scott (*see* V Camrose, 1995 Edn); 2ndly, 1995, (Jonathan) Mark Bradford Gibson, and has issue living (by 2nd *m*), Katherine, *b* 19—.

Hon Kristina Louise (twin), *b* 1963.

BROTHER LIVING

Hon MALCOLM WILLIAM MACKENZIE, *b* 28 Aug 1934; *ed* Westminster, and Pembroke Coll, Camb: *m* 1970, Mrs Evelyn Ann Carew Perfect, yr da of William Blackmore Storey (M Queensberry, colls), and previously wife of late Alan Perfect, WS, and has issue living, John Nicolas Alexander, *b* 1971, — Sophie Ann Frances, *b* 1973. *Residence* – Las Cuadras, Monte de la Torre, Los Barrios, Prov de Cadiz, Spain. *Clubs* – Travellers', Pratt's.

SISTERS LIVING

Hon Margaret Joan, *b* 1922: *m* 1943, Ven Benjamin George Burton Fox, MC, TD, Archdeacon of Wisbech, who *d* 1978, and has issue living, *Rev* Colin George, TD (The Rectory, Church Street, Pewsey, Wilts SN9 5DL), *b* 1946: *m* 1975, Bridget Andrea Louise Willan, and has issue living, George Hugh *b* 1977, Henry Benjamin Andrew *b* 1983, Alice Frances *b* 1979, — Elizabeth Angela, *b* 1943 CStJ: *m* 1973, Prof Anthony R. Mellows, TD, GCStJ, LLD, of 22 Devereux Court, Temple Bar, WC2R 3JJ, — Catherine Anne (23 Mulberry Close, Cambridge CB4 2AS), *b* 1950: *m* 1977, James Lemon, who *d* 1992, — Penelope Margaret, *b* 1953: *m* 1979, Jonathan Hay Marland, of The Cottage, Morlys Lane, Gislingham, nr Eye, Suffolk IP23 8JS, — Rosemary Marjorie (twin), *b* 1953: *m* 1978, Michael George Peter Swiney of Orchard House, Chapel Rd, Cockfield, Bury St Edmunds, Suffolk IP30 0HE. *Residence* – 63 Arundell, Ely, Cambs CB6 1BQ.

Hon Jean Elizabeth, *b* 1924: late Capt WRAC (TA): *m* 1952, Hon Charles Richard Strutt, who *d* 1981 (*see* B Rayleigh). *Residence* – Berwick Place, Hatfield Peverel, Chelmsford, Essex.

PREDECESSOR – (1) *Rt Hon Sir* JOHN COLIN CAMPBELL Davidson, GCVO, CH, CB, PC, son of the late Sir James Mackenzie Davidson, MB, *b* 1889; MP for Hemel Hempstead (*U*) 1920-23 and 1924-37; Chancellor of Duchy of Lancaster 1923-24 and 1931-37; Chm of Conservative and Unionist Party Organisation 1927-30; *cr Viscount Davidson*, of Little Gaddesden, co Hertford (peerage of UK) 1937: *m* 1919, Hon Dame Frances Joan Dickinson, DBE (*Baroness Northchurch*), who *d* 1985, da of 1st Baron Dickinson; *d* 1970; *s* by his el son (2) JOHN ANDREW, 2nd Viscount, and present peer.

DAVIES, BARON (Davies) (Baron UK 1932)

DAVID DAVIES, 3rd Baron, *b* 2 Oct 1940; *s* 1944; *ed* Eton, and King's Coll, Camb: *m* 1972, Beryl, da of W. J. Oliver, and has issue.

Arms – Or, a lion rampant gules, between two fleurs-de-lis in fesse azure; on a chief azure, two pickaxes fessewise. **Crest** – An arm embowed proper, vested to the elbow argent, holding in the hand a miner's safety lamp proper. *Seat* – Plas Dinam, Llandinam, Powys.

SONS LIVING

Hon DAVID DANIEL, *b* 23 Oct 1975.
Hon Benjamin Michael Graham, *b* 1985.

DAUGHTERS LIVING

Hon Eldrydd Jane, *b* 1973.
Hon Lucy, *b* 1978.

BROTHER LIVING

Hon Jonathan Hugh (The Forest, Kerry, nr Newtown, Powys), *b* 1944; *ed* Eton, and Univ Coll, Oxford; a Member of Museums and Galleries Commn since 1985: *m* 1966, (Mary) Veronica, eldest da of late Sir (William) Godfrey Agnew, KCVO, CB, ot Pinehurst, S Ascot, Berks, and has issue living, Michael Edward, *b* 1968: *m* 1999, Sacha J., only da of Roderick Francis Loder-Symonds, of Denne Hill Farm, Canterbury, Kent, — Alexander William, *b* 1972: *m* 1994, Sophia Mary Clare, only da of (John) Robin Thistlethwayte, of Sorbrook Manor, Adderbury, Oxon, and has issue living, Orlando Harry Grasett *b* 1998, — Ruth Gwendoline, *b* 1969, — Gwendoline Christianne Mary, *b* 1975, — Christianne Eldrydd, *b* 1976, — Mary Theresa Ruth, *b* 1982.

HALF-UNCLE LIVING (*son of 1st Baron by 2nd marriage*)

Hon Islwyn Edmund Evan, *b* 1926; *ed* Gordonstoun; is a JP for Montgomeryshire, and a DL for Powys: *m* 1959, Camilla Anne, el da of late Col L. W. Coulden, of 14 Portsea Place, W2, and has issue living, Robin David (Lower Penrhyddlan, Llandinam, Powys SY17 5AX), *b* 1961: *m* 1988, Julie Hughes, and has issue living, Rupert Edmond David *b* 1988, Daisy Gemma *b* 1990, — Christopher William, *b* 1963: *m* 1988, Wendy Jones, — Richard Edward, *b* 1965. *Residence* – Perth-y-bu, Sarn, Newtown, Powys SY16 4EP.

HALF-AUNTS LIVING (*daughters of 1st Baron by 2nd marriage*)

Hon Mary Myfanwy, *b* 1923; formerly in Women's Roy Canadian Naval Ser; is a CStJ: *m* 1958 (*m diss* 1979), Hugh MacAskill Noble and has three sons, Robert David, *b* 1961, — Andrew Jonathan, *b* 1962: *m* 1992, — Hugh James, *b* 1965.
Hon Gwendoline Rita Jean, *b* 1929: *m* 1950 (*m diss* 1979), John McRae Cormack, AFC, and has had issue, Michael John, *b* 1962, *d* as the result of an accident 1980, — Shara Jane, *b* 1955: *m* 1983, Anthony J. Leonard, QC, of 5 Montana Rd, SW20, son of Hon Sir John Leonard, and has issue living, Olivia Mary *b* 1985, Stephanie Emma *b* 1989, — Amanda Caroline, *b* 1957: *m* 1982, Edward John Weston, of The Malt House, Coln St Aldwyns, Glos, and has issue living, Ruth Medina *b* 1984, Ella Jane *b* 1986, — Teresa Mary (*Hon Mrs Henry Tennant*), *b* 1959: *m* 1983, Hon Henry Lovell Tennant, who *d* 1990, 2nd son of 3rd Baron Glenconner, and has issue (*see* B Glenconner).

WIDOW LIVING OF SON OF FIRST BARON

Shirley, da of Le Grew Harrison, and formerly wife of John Gaze: *m* 1975, as his 2nd wife, Hon Edward David Grant Davies, who *d* 1997. *Residence* – ......

COLLATERAL BRANCH LIVING

Issue of late Hon Edward David Grant Davies, 2nd son of 1ot Baron (and eldest son by 2nd *m*), *b* 1925, *d* 1997: *m* 1st, 1949 (*m diss* 19—), Patricia Elizabeth, yr da of Clifford Roberts Musto, of Salisbury, Rhodesia; 2ndly, 1975, Shirley (ante), da of Le Grew Harrison, and formerly wife of John Gaze:—
(By 1st *m*) David Edmund Clifford (Inverpolly, Ullapool, Ross-shire IV26 2YB), *b* 1958: *m* 1988, Nicola Denise Miller, yst da of John Walter Maxwell Miller Richard, of Edinburgh, and has issue living, Annabel Emily, *b* 1990, — Mary Elizabeth Charlotte, *b* 1996. —— Mary Ann Margaret, *b* 1949: *m* 1970 (*m diss* 19—), Martin Lovegrove, of Boarden House, Hawkenbury, Headcorn, Kent, and has two children, Thomas, *b* 1983, — Amy, *b* 1979. —— Patricia Jean, *b* 1951: *m* 1977, Toby Douglas Everett, of Woodhill Farm, Frensham, Farnham, Surrey, and has issue living, James Douglas, *b* 1980, — Emma Patricia, *b* 1978, — Polly Victoria, *b* 1986. —— Penelope Eldrydd, *b* 1955: *m* 1983, Maj Peter Geoffrey Scrope, late 13/18th Royal Hussars (Queen Mary's Own) (*see* E Mexborough, 1972-73 Edn), of Langbaurgh Hall, Great Ayton, Middlesbrough, N Yorks TS9 6QQ, and has issue living, Edward Ralph William, *b* 1989, — Thomas Henry Aloysius, *b* 1994, — Alexandra Beatrice Mary, *b* 1985, — Victoria Emily Louise, *b* 1986, — Henrietta Perpetua Agnes, *b* 1991.

PREDECESSORS – (1) DAVID Davies, of Plâs Dinam, Llandinam; *b* 1880; a Director of Great Western Railway, and of Midland Bank; sat as MP for Montgomeryshire (*L*) 1906-29; *cr Baron Davies*, of Llandinam, co Montgomery (peerage of United Kingdom), 1932; *m* 1st, 1910, Amy, who *d* 1918, da of L. T. Penman, of Broadwood Park, Lanchester, and Gateshead; 2ndly, 1922, Henrietta Margaret, who *d* 1948, da of late James Grant Fergusson, of Baledmund; *d* June 1944; *s* by his son (2) DAVID MICHAEL, 2nd Baron; *b* 1915; Maj R. Welch Fusiliers (TA): *m* 1939, Ruth Eldrydd, who *d* 1966, da of late Maj W. M. Dugdale, of Glanyrafon Hall, Llanyblodwell, Salop; *ka* Sept 1944; *s* by his son (3) DAVID, 3rd Baron and present peer.

Davies, family name of Baron Darwen.

DAVIES OF COITY, BARON (Davies) (Life Baron 1997)

(DAVID) GARFIELD DAVIES, CBE, son of late David John Davies, of Bridgend, Glam; *b* 24 June 1935; *ed* Heolgam Secondary Modern Sch, Bridgend, Bridgend Technical Coll, and Port Talbot Sch of Further Education; joined British Steel Corporation 1950; RAF (Nat Ser) 1956-58; Electrician 1958-69; Area Organiser, Union of Shop Distributive and Allied Workers (USDAW) 1969-73, Dep Divisional Offr 1973-78, Nat Offr 1978-86, Gen Sec 1986-97; Memb Gen Cncl TUC 1986-97; Memb Employment Appeal Tribunal since 1991; Chm International Cttee TUC 1992-97; Councillor, Penybont RDC 1966-69; JP Ipswich 1972-78; *cr* CBE 1996, and *Baron Davies of Coity*, of Penybont, co Mid-Glamorgan (Life Baron) 1997: *m* 1960, Marian, da of Raymond Jones, of Trelewis, nr Treharris, Glam, and has issue.

𝔄rms – ......
Residence – 64 Dairyground Rd, Bramhall, Stockport, Cheshire SK7 2QW.

DAUGHTERS LIVING

Hon Helen Claire, *b* 1961.
Hon Susan Karen, *b* 1962.
Hon Karen Jayne, *b* 1965.
Hon Rachel Louise, *b* 1969.

DAVIES OF LEEK, BARONY OF (Davies) (Extinct 1985)

DAUGHTER LIVING OF LIFE BARON

Hon Harriet Olivia, *b* 1930; BScEcon London: *m* 1950, Derek Shephard, of 36 Clevenden Mansions, Lissenden Gdns, NW5.

DAVIES OF OLDHAM, BARON (Davies) (Life Baron 1997)

BRYAN DAVIES, son of late George William Davies, of Tredegar, Mon; *b* 9 Nov 1939; *ed* Redditch County High Sch, Univ Coll, London (BA 19—), Inst of Education, and LSE (BSc 19—); Teacher, Latymer Sch 1962-65; Lecturer, Middx Polytechnic 1965-74; MP for Enfield North (Lab) 1974-79, and for Oldham Central and Royton 1992-97; Sec, Parliamentary Labour Party 1979-92; PPS to Dep PM 1975-76, Dept of Education 1976, Treasury 1977; Govt Whip 1979; Memb Select Cttee on Overseas Devpt 1975-78, Public Expenditure 1975-78, and National Heritage 1992-93; Shadow Min for Higher Education 1993-97; Memb Medical Research Council 1977-79; *cr Baron Davies of Oldham*, of Broxbourne, co Herts (Life Baron) 1997: *m* 1963, Monica Rosemary Mildred, da of late Jack Shearing, of Stowmarket, Suffolk, and has issue.
Address – c/o House of Lords, Westminster, SW1A 0PW.

SONS LIVING

Hon Roderick Gareth, *b* 1964: *m* 1994, Sally Messenger.
Hon Gordon Huw, *b* 1966.

DAUGHTER LIVING

Hon Amanda Jane, *b* 1969.

DAVIES OF PENRHYS, BARONY OF (Davies) (Extinct 1992)

SONS LIVING OF LIFE BARON

Hon Gwynfor, *b* 1942: *m* 1969, Linda, da of late Anthony Henry, of Port Talbot, Glam, and has issue.
Hon David Daniel, *b* 1944: *m* 1969, Cheryl, da of Thomas Herbert, of Tylorstown, Rhondda, and has issue, one son.

DAUGHTER LIVING OF LIFE BARON

Hon Beryl, *b* 1947: *m* 1965, Colin James Powell, of Maesgwyn, Ton Pentre, Rhondda, and has issue one son.

Davies, see Baron Llewelyn-Davies.

Davies, see Baron Lovell-Davies.

Davison, family name of Baron Broughshane.

Dawick, Viscount; son of Earl Haig.

Dawnay, family name of Viscount Downe.

Dawnay, Baron, title of Viscount Downe on Roll of HL.

DAWSON OF PENN, VISCOUNTCY OF (Dawson) (Extinct 1945)

DAUGHTER LIVING OF FIRST VISCOUNT

Hon Ursula Margaret (*Hon Lady Bowater*), *b* 1907: *m* 1927, Lt-Col Sir Ian Frank Bowater, GBE, DSO, RA (TA), who *d* 1982, (*see* Bowater, Bt, *cr* 1939). *Residence* – 38 Burton Court, Franklin's Row, SW3 4SZ.

DEAN OF HARPTREE, BARON (Dean) (Life Baron 1993)

(ARTHUR) PAUL DEAN, PC, son of late Arthur Dean, of Weaverham, Cheshire; *b* 14 Sept 1924; *ed* Ellesmere Coll, and Exeter Coll, Oxford (MA, BLitt); served 1939-45 War as Capt WG, ADC to Cdr 1 Corps BAOR; formerly a farmer; Resident Tutor Swinton Conservative Coll 1958-64, Assist Dir Conservative Research Dept 1962-64; Parl Under-Sec Dept of Health and Social Security 1970-74, Chm Conservative Health and Social Security Cttee, and Memb Commons Services Select Cttee 1979-82, 2nd Dep Chm House of Commons, and Dep Chm Ways and Means 1982-87, 1st Dept Chm Ways and Means, and Dep Speaker 1987-92; Dir Charterhouse Pensions, and Watney Mann and Truman Holdings, Gov Commonwealth Inst 1981-89, and former Gov BUPA, Pres Oxford Univ Conservative Assocn; MP N Som (*C*) 1964-83, and Woodspring 1983-92; *cr* Knt 1985, PC 1991, and *Baron Dean of Harptree*, of Wedmore, co Somerset (Life Baron) 1993: *m* 1st, 1957, Doris Ellen, who *d* 1979, da of late Frank Webb, of Sussex; 2ndly, 1980, Mrs Margaret Frances Parker (*née* Dierden).

Address – House of Lords, SW1A 0PW. *Clubs* – Oxford Carlton, Oxford and Cambridge.

DEAN OF THORNTON-LE-FYLDE, BARONESS (McDowall) (Life Baroness 1993)

BRENDA DEAN, PC, da of Hugh Dean, of Thornton, Cleveleys, Lancs; *b* 29 April 1943; *ed* St Andrews, Eccles, and Stretford Gram Sch; Hon MA Salford 1986, Hon Fellow Lancashire Poly 1991, Hon Law Degree City Univ, London 1993; Admin Sec Manchester Branch SOGAT 1959-71, Assist Branch Sec 1971, Sec 1976, Pres SOGAT 1983-85, Gen Sec 1985-91, Dep Gen Sec GPMU 1991-92; Memb Women's National Commn NEDC 1985-92 (Co-Chm 1975-78), BBC Gen Advisory Council 1985-89, TUC Gen Council 1985-92, TUC Econ Cttee 1987-92, City Univ Council since 1991; Gov Ditchley Foundation since 1992; Chm ICSTIS since 1993, Memb Press Complaints Commn 1993-94, Memb Broadcasting Complaints Commn since 1993, non-exec dir Inveresh plc; *cr Baroness Dean of Thornton-le-Fylde*, of Eccles, co Greater Manchester (Life Baroness) 1993, and PC 1998: *m* 1988, Keith Desmond McDowall, CBE.

Address – c/o House of Lords, SW1A 0AA.

Deane, family name of Baron Muskerry.

DEARING, BARON (Dearing) (Life Baron 1998)

RONALD ERNEST (RON) DEARING, CB, son of late Ernest Henry Ashford Dearing, of Kingston upon Hull; *b* 27 July 1930; *ed* Doncaster Gram Sch, Hull Univ (BSc 1954), and London Business Sch (Sloane Fell); Hon Doctorates of Brighton, Durham, Exeter, Nottingham, Hull, Humberside, Northumbria, Open, and Staffordshire Univs, Hon Fell Sunderland Univ, and Trinity Sch of Music; Regnl Dir N Region, DTI 1972-74; Under-Sec DTI and Dept of Industry 1972-76; Dep Sec, Dept of Industry 1976-80; Chm Post Office 1981-87 (Dep Chm 1980-81), and Camelot Group plc 1994-95; Group Chm Nationalised Industries Chairmen's Group 1983-84; Non-Exec Dir Prudential Corpn 1987-91, Whitehead Co plc 1988-90, Ericsson Ltd 1988-93, British Coal Corpn 1988-91, IMI plc 1988-94, and SDX plc 1996 98; Chm Co Durham Devpt Corpn 1987-90, CNAA 1987-88, Polys and Colls Funding Cncl 1988-92, Northern Devpt Corpn 1990-94, Financial Reporting Cncl 1989-93, Review Cttee on Accounting Standards, Universities Funding Cncl 1991-92, Higher Education Funding Cncl for England 1992-93, Nat Curriculum Cncl, Sch Examinations and Assessment Cncl 1993, Sch Curriculum and Assessment Authority 1993-96, Nat Cttee of Inquiry into Higher Education 1996-97 and Write Away since 1996, Univ for Industry since 1999; Chancellor Nottingham Univ; Memb Governing Body of Melbourne Univ since 1997 (and Menzies Lecturer since 1998); first Pres Inst of Direct Marketing 1994-97; Tstee TRAC until 1997, and The Sascha Lasserson Memorial Trust; Gold Medallist Inst of Management 1994; Mackenzie Lecturer, Liverpool Univ 1995; Robert Menzies Oration, Melbourne Univ 1998; Hon FEng 1992; Hon FCGI; *cr* CB 1979, Kt 1984, and *Baron Dearing*, of Kingston upon Hull, co E Riding of Yorkshire (Life Baron) 1998: *m* 1954, Margaret Patricia, da of Richard William Riley, of Deal, Kent, and has issue, two das.

Address – c/o House of Lords, Westminster, SW1A 0PW.

DECIES, BARON (de la Poer Beresford) (Baron I 1812)
(Title pronounced "Deeshies")

NIL · NISI · CRUCE

Nothing without the Cross

MARCUS HUGH TRISTRAM DE LA POER BERESFORD, 7th Baron, *b* 5 Aug 1948; *s* 1992; *ed* St Columba's Coll, and Dublin Univ (M Litt): *m* 1st, 1970 (*m diss* 1974), Sarah Jane, only da of Col Basil Gunnell; 2ndly, 1981, Edel Jeannette, da of late Vincent Ambrose Hendron, of Dublin, and has issue by 2nd *m*.

Arms – Quarterly: 1st and 4th argent semée or cross-crosslets fitchée, three fleurs-de-lis within a bordure engrailed, all sable, *Beresford*; 2nd and 3rd argent, a chief indented sable, *de la Poer*; a mullet argent for difference. **Crest** – A dragon's head erased azure, transfixed in the neck with a broken tilting spear or, the point broken off argent transfixing the upper jaw, charged with a mullet for difference. **Supporters** – Two angels proper, vested argent, crined and winged or, each holding in the exterior hand a sword erect of the first, pommel and hilt gold and charged on the breast with a mullet for difference.
Residence – Straffan Lodge, Straffan, co Kildare.

SONS LIVING (*By 2nd marriage*)

Hon ROBERT MARCUS DUNCAN DE LA POER, *b* 14 July 1988.
Hon David George Morley Hugh de la Poer, *b* 1991.

DAUGHTERS LIVING (*By 2nd marriage*)

Hon Louisa Katherine de la Poer, *b* 1984.
Hon Jessica Laragh de la Poer, *b* 1996.

SISTERS LIVING

Hon Sarah Ann Vivien de la Poer, *b* 1949: *m* 1st, 1975 (*m diss* 1982), Joerg B. Schnapka, son of Dr Herbert Schnapka, of Bochum, W Germany; 2ndly, 1992, Andrew McMeekan, and has issue living (by 1st *m*), Roland Rufus, *b* 1976. *Residence* – 12A Malcolm Rd, Wimbledon, SW19 4AS.
Hon Clare Antoinette Gabrielle de la Poer, *b* 1956: *m* 1986, Jorge Koechlin, son of late Jose Edmondo Koechlin, of Lima, Peru, and has issue living, Michael Joseph Tristram, *b* 1986. *Address* – c/o Coutts & Co, 1 Old Park Lane, W1.

WIDOW LIVING OF SON OF THIRD BARON

Ida Kaye: *m* 1941, as his 4th wife, Hon William Arthur Horsley-Beresford, who *d* 1949, and has issue (see colls, infra).

WIDOW LIVING OF SIXTH BARON

DIANA (*Dowager Baroness Decies*), da of late W/Cdr George Turner-Cain, of Marsh House, Wells, Norfolk, and widow of Maj David W. A. Galsworthy, The Royal Fus: *m* (Sept) 1945, as his 2nd wife, the 6th Baron Decies, who *d* 1992. *Residence* – Little Barwick, Stanhoe, King's Lynn, Norfolk PE31 8PT.

COLLATERAL BRANCHES LIVING

Grandchildren of late Hon William Arthur de la Poer Horsley-Beresford (infra):—
Issue of late George Graham de la Poer Horsley-Beresford, *b* 1903, *d* 1974: *m* 1938, Sherman (Box 1085, Frederiksted, Isle of St Croix, US Virgin Islands 00841), da of Frank Olmsted of New York, NY, USA:—
Marcus Hughes (Frederiksted, St Croix, US Virgin Islands 00841), *b* 1943; late Capt USAF; Pilot Eastern Airlines: *m* 1st, 1962 (*m diss* 19-) Lynne Green, of East Millstone, NJ, USA; 2ndly, 1979, Diane Armstrong, and has issue living (by 1st *m*), Marcus Tyler de la Poer, *b* 1963, — Teresa Leigh, *b* 1965, — (by 2nd *m*) Julia Victoria de la Poer, *b* 1983. —— Peter Graham de la Poer (4501 15th St N, Arlington, VA 22207, USA), *b* 1956: *m* 1989, Carrie, da of John Peterson, of Naples, Florida, and has issue living, Graham Peterson de la Poer, *b* 1999. —— Holley Audrey, *b* 1939: *m* 1960 (*m diss* 1972), and has issue living, four sons and one da.

Issue of late Hon William Arthur de la Poer Horsley-Beresford, yst son of 3rd Baron, *b* 1878; *d* 1949: *m* 1st, 1901 (*m diss* 1919), Florence, who *d* 1969, da of Gardner L. Miller, MD, of Providence, Rhode Island, USA; 2ndly, 1919 (*m diss* 1928), Laura, who *d* 1958, da of late Capt St John Halford Coventry (E Coventry, colls); 3rdly, 1933 (*m diss* 1940), Georgina Leonora, who *d* 1969, only da of late Richard Frederik Hendrik Mosselmans, of the Hague, and formerly wife of Count Fernand de Bertier de Sauvigny; 4thly, 1941, Ida Kaye (ante):—
(By 2nd *m*) Patrick, *b* 1924: *m* 1st, 1953 (*m diss* in USA 1956), Miriam Morton, of Philadelphia, USA; 2ndly, 1959, Leslie Yvonne, who *d* 1985, da of late Leslie Robert McCaskey, of Wellington, NZ, and has issue living (by 2nd *m*) Marcus Dominic St John (Via dei Tirreni 16, 01015 Sutri (VT) Italy), *b* 1960: *m* 1984, Rossana, da of Angelo Zeppa, of Viterbo, Italy, and has issue living, Morgan John Ross *b* 1985, Jordan Milton Leslie *b* 1988. —— Hazel (Springfield, 32 Park Avenue, Old Basing, Basingstoke, Hants RG24 0HT), *b* 1920: *m* 1940, Gerald Herbert Incledon, who *d* 1990, and has had issue, Jonathan Guy, *b* 1963, — Margaret Anne, *b* 1941: *m* 1961, Anthony E. Hodson, of Spring Lanes, Holly Spring Lane, Bracknell, Berks, and has issue living, Christopher James *b* 1963, Lucy Alice *b* 1967: *m* 1995, Stephen David Head,

of 97 Lily Hill Rd, Bracknell, Berks RG12 2RY, and has issue living, Louise Catherine *b* 1998, — Heather, *b* 1943: *m* 1966, Christopher C. E. Stamford, of Grassmere, Mid St, S Nutfield, Surrey, and has issue living, Daniel Charles *b* 1967, Charlotte Anne *b* 1970, Louisa Emma *b* 1975, — Susan Amber *b* 1945: *m* 1st, 1968 (*m diss* 1976), David Ellis Green, MBE, R Regt Fus; 2ndly, 1979, Christopher Norman (Merton House, 7 Bath Rd, Camberley, Surrey), and *d* 1993, leaving issue (by 1st *m*), Rebecca Claire *b* 1973, (by 2nd *m*) Annabel Sarah *b* 1983, — Amanda Elizabeth, *b* 1947: *m* 1983, Richard Bailey, of 38 Robert Cecil Av, Swaythling, Southampton, Hants, — Moya Catherine, *b* 1956: *m* 1976, Charles Mellor, of 5 Sandpiper Close, Marchwood, Hants, and has issue living, Stephen Andrew *b* 1981, Gillian Leigh *b* 1984, Joanna *b* (twin) 1984. —— (By 4th *m*) Peter, *b* 1945; *ed* Emanuel Sch, and Univ Coll, Oxford (BA). —— Maureen, *b* 1942.

   Granddaughters of late Maj-Gen Sir George de la Poer Beresford, CB, MC, eldest son of late Henry   Tristam Beresford (infra):—
  Issue of late Benedict Henry de la Poer Beresford, *b* 1917, *d* 1997: *m* 1949, Dorothy Kate (3 Cambridge   Cottages, Kew, Richmond, Surrey), da of George Cooper, of Gt Bedwyn, Wilts:—
Margaret Jane, *b* 1963.

  Issue of late Lieut-Cdr Stephen Marcus de la Poer Beresford, DSC, RN, *b* 1920, *d* 1982: *m* 1952, Susan Wendy,   who *d* 1998, da of late Maj Tom Lees Dearbergh, of Hollywood Cottage, Lymington, Hants:—
Diana Margaret, *b* 1953: *m* 1976, Henry James Harmer, of 46 Blackborough Rd, Reigate, Surrey, and has issue living, Nicholas Benjamin, *b* 1983, — Claire Susan, *b* 1981, — Amy Diana, *b* 1986. —— Angela Susan (PO Box 830, Cooma, NSW 2630, Australia), *b* 1953 (twin).

   Grandchildren of late Henry Tristam Beresford, son of Rev George Hamilton de la Poer Beresford, 3rd   son of Rev Hon George Beresford, 2nd son of 1st Baron:—
  Issue of late William Coventry de la Poer Beresford, *b* 1887, *d* 1938: *m* 1921, Jessie, who *d* 1931, da of J.   Rowling, of NSW:—
(Charles) Marcus Tristram de la Poer (Deepdene, Coonabarabran, NSW), *b* 1923; 1942-45 War with RAAF: *m* 1st, 1948, Mary Frances, who *d* 1972, da of Hugh Buckingham Loveband, of Blenheim, Coonabarabran, NSW; 2ndly, 1973, Gwen Cornwell, and has issue living (by 1st *m*), Roslyn de la Poer, *b* 1949, — Julia de la Poer, *b* 1952. —— Patricia de la Poer, *b* 1922: *m* 1953, R. S. Meares, of 51 Bishop St, Goulburn, NSW, and has issue living, Richard Grant, *b* 1955, — Philip Marcus, *b* 1960.

  Issue of late Marcus Gervais de la Poer Beresford, *b* 1888, *d* 1967: *m* 1927, Susan Mildred (3 Hovel St, Manuka,   ACT 2603, Aust), da of late Edward Charles Campbell:—
Barrington Henry de la Poer (9 Melrose Av, Sylvania, NSW), *b* 1928: *m* 1952, Fleur Marie, da of late John Crisp, of Corowa, NSW, and has issue living, Sean Anthony de la Poer, *b* 1962, — Amanda de la Poer, *b* 1956.

PREDECESSORS – **(1)** *Rev Hon* WILLIAM Beresford, 3rd son of 1st Earl of Tyrone and brother of 1st Marquess of Waterford; Bishop of Dromore 1780-2, Bishop of Ossory 1782-94, and Archbishop of Tuam 1794-1819; *cr Baron Decies* (peerage of Ireland) 1812; *d* 1819; *s* by his son **(2)** JOHN, 2nd Baron; *b* 1773: *m* 1810, Charlotte Philadelphia, only da and heiress of Robert Horsley, of Bolam House, Morpeth, when he assumed the additional surname of Horsley; *d* 1 March 1855; *s* by his son **(3)** WILLIAM ROBERT JOHN DE LA POER, 3rd Baron, *b* 1811: *m* 1860, Catherine Anne, who *d* 1941, da of William Hedley-Dent, of Shortflatt Tower, Belsay; *d* 1893; *s* by his el son **(4)** WILLIAM MARCUS DE LA POER, 4th Baron, *b* 1865: *m* 1901, Maria Gertrude, who *d* 1939, da of Sir John Pollard Willoughby, 4th Bt; *d* 1910; *s* by his brother **(5)** JOHN GRAHAM HOPE DE LA POER, PC, DSO, 5th Baron, *b* 1866; Major (ret) 7th Hussars; Matebeleland 1896, S Africa 1902, Somaliland 1903-4 (DSO); Ch Press Censor in Ireland 1916-19: *m* 1st, 1911 Helen Vivien, who *d* 1931, da of late George Jay Gould, of New York USA; 2ndly, 1936, Elizabeth, who *d* 1944, da of George Drexel, and widow of Henry Symes Lehr; *d* 1944; *s* by his son **(6)** ARTHUR GEORGE MARCUS DOUGLAS DE LA POER, 6th Baron, *b* 1915; European War 1938-45 as Flying Officer RAFVR (American DFC): *m* 1st, 1937, Ann Christina, who *d* (March) 1945, da of late Sidney Walter Trevor, of Camperdown, Vic, Australia; 2ndly, (Sept) 1945, Diana, da of late W/Cdr George Turner-Cain, of Marsh House, Wells, Norfolk, and widow of Maj David W. A. Galsworthy, The Royal Hus; *d* 1992; *s* by his only son **(7)** MARCUS HUGH TRISTRAM DE LA POER, 7th Baron and present peer.

DE CLIFFORD, BARON (Russell) (Baron E 1299)

What will be, will be

JOHN EDWARD SOUTHWELL RUSSELL, 27th Baron; *b* 8 June 1928; *s* 1982; *ed* Eton, and RAC Cirencester: *m* 1959, Bridget Jennifer, yst da of Duncan Robertson, of Llantysilio Hall, Llangollen, Denbighshire (*see* Williams-Wynn, Bt).

Arms – Argent, a lion rampant gules, on a chief sable three escallops of the first. **Crest** – A goat statant argent, armed and unguled or. **Supporters** – *Dexter*, a wyvern gules; *Sinister*, a monkey proper, ringed round the loins and lined or.
Residence – Riggledown, Pennymoor, Tiverton, Devon EX16 8LR.

BROTHER LIVING

Hon WILLIAM SOUTHWELL (Gilboa Farmhouse, Brokenborough, Malmesbury, Wiltshire SN16 0HX), *b* 26 Feb 1930; *ed* Eton, and King's Coll, Camb: *m* 1961, Jean Brodie, da of Neil Brodie Henderson, of Glebe House, Little Hormead, Buntingford, Herts (*see* Madden, Bt, 1980 Edn), and has issue living, Miles Edward Southwell, *b* 1966: *m* 1995, Marion E., yr da of D. W. Arkley, of Bournville, Birmingham, and has issue living, Edward Southwell *b* 18 Nov 1998, — Mary-Jane Sophia, *b* 1963: *m* 1991, Matthew G. Howe, elder son of Philip Howe, of Sydney, Australia, and has issue living, Jack Henry *b* 1999, Ella Margaret *b* 1997, — Joanna Clare, *b* 1965.

WIDOW LIVING OF TWENTY-SIXTH BARON

MINA MARGARET (*Mina, Baroness de Clifford*), only da of George Edward Sands: *m* 1973, as his 2nd wife, Col 26th Baron de Clifford, who *d* 1982.

COLLATERAL BRANCHES LIVING

Issue of late Hon Diana Katharine Russell, only da of 25th Baron, *b* 1909, *d* 1978: *m* 1st, 1933 (*m diss* 1948), Mervyn Hesseltine Taylor; 2ndly, 1948, His Honour Judge Thomas Elder-Jones, who *d* 1988:—
(By 1st *m*) Christopher John TAYLOR (East Cottage, Bourton on the Hill, Morton-in-Marsh, Glos), *b* 1934: *m* 1st, 1959 (*m diss* 1971), Sarah Mary, only da of late Ewan Mews; 2ndly, 1972, Jane Seymour, yst da of late George Macdonald Brown, and has issue living (by 1st *m*), Vernon Edmund Christopher, *b* 1965, — Claire Virginia Mary, *b* 1962. —— Virginia Carol EDLER-JONES, *b* 1945; adopted by her mother and stepfather, whose name she assumed 1956.

Descendants of Frances Sophia Cholmondeley (da of George James Cholmondeley, by Hon Mary Elizabeth, da of John Thomas Townshend, 2nd Viscount Sydney, by his 1st wife, Hon Sophia Southwell, da of 20th Baron): *m* 1846, Rev Charles Riddell, of whom Rev John Charles Riddell was father of 11th Bt:—
(*see* Riddell, Bt).

Descendants of Robert Marsham-Townshend, only son of 2nd Earl of Romney, by his 2nd wife, Hon Mary Elizabeth Townshend, da of 2nd Viscount Sydney, and widow of George James Cholmondeley (ante):—
(*see* E Romney, colls).

Descendants of Hon Elizabeth Southwell, da of 20th Baron: *m* 1792 as his 1st wife, the 4th Earl of Albemarle:—
(*see* E Albemarle).

PREDECESSORS – (1) ROGER de Clifford: *m* Isabel, el da and co-heiress of Robert de Vipont, Lord of Westmorland, and in 1277 acknowledged the service of two fees and a half, for a moiety of the Barony of Westmorland; *d* 1282; *s* by his son (2) ROBERT, 2nd Lord of Westmorland, and *1st Baron de Clifford*; summoned to Parliament of England 1299-1313; Earl Marshal of England 1307, Warden of Scotland 1308; killed at Bannockburn 1314; *s* by his son (3) ROGER, 2nd Baron ; *dsp* 1327; *s* by his brother (4) ROBERT, 3rd Baron; *d* 1344; *s* by his son (5) ROBERT, 4th Baron; *dsp* 1362; *s* by his brother (6) ROGER, 5th Baron; *d* 1390; *s* by his son (7) THOMAS, 6th Baron ; *d* 1392; *s* by his son (8) JOHN, 7th Baron; *d* 1422; *s* by his son (9) THOMAS, 8th Baron; *d* 1455; *s* by his son (10) JOHN, 9th Baron; *d* 1461; *s* by his son (11) HENRY, 10th Baron; *d* 1524; *s* by his son (12) HENRY, 11th Baron; *cr Earl of Cumberland* (peerage of England) 1525; obtained large grants out of the monastic spoliations and had a principal command in the army which invaded Scotland; *d* 1543; *s* by his son (13) HENRY, KB, 2nd Earl; *d* 1569; *s* by his son (14) GEORGE, KG, 3rd Earl, an eminent naval commander and an ardent sportsman; *d* 1605, leaving issue one da (15) ANNE, wife of Richard Sackville, 2nd Earl of Dorset; in 1628 the Countess of Dorset claimed the title, but the House of Lords postponed the hearing, and the Barony remained dormant until 1691, when it was allowed to (16) NICHOLAS, 15th Baron, and 3rd Earl of Thanet, son of John, 2nd Earl of Thanet, by Lady Margaret, da of Anne, Countess of Dorset (ante); *s* by his brother (17) JOHN, 16th Baron, and 4th Earl of Thanet: *s* by his brother (18) RICHARD, 17th Baron, and 5th Earl of Thanet; *s* by his brother (19) THOMAS, 18th Baron, and 6th Earl of Thanet; *d* 1721, when the Earldom of Thanet devolved upon his nephew, and the Barony of de Clifford went into abeyance between his five das, and remained so until 1734, when the crown terminated it in favour of the 3rd da (20) MARGARET, wife of Thomas Coke, 1st Baron Lovel, who in 1744 was *cr* Earl of Leicester; *d* 1775, when the Barony again became abeyant, and it remained so until 1776, when it was terminated in favour of (21) EDWARD Southwell, 20th Baron (MP for co Gloucester), son of Edward Southwell, by the Hon Catherine, da of Edward, Viscount

Sondes (el son of 1st Earl of Rockingham) and Lady Catherine, el da of 6th Earl of Thanet; *d* 1777; *s* by his son **(22)** EDWARD, 21st Baron; *dsp* 1832, when the Barony became abeyant between his sisters, and remained so until 1833, when it was terminated in favour of the surviving issue of his el sister Catherine, by Col George Coussmaker, viz **(23)** SOPHIA, wife of Capt John Russell, RN (*see* D Bedford, colls); *d* 1874, *s* by her son **(24)** EDWARD SOUTHWELL, 23rd Baron; *b* 1824; MP for Tavistock (*L*) 1847-58: *m* 1853, Harriet Agnes, who *d* 1896, da of late Adm Sir Charles Elliot, KCB; *d* 1877; *s* by his son **(24)** EDWARD SOUTHWELL, 24th Baron; *b* 1855: *m* 1879, Hilda, who *d* 1895, da of Charles Balfour, of East-hampstead, Berks; *d* 1894; *s* by his son **(25)** JACK SOUTHWELL, 25th Baron; *b* 1884: *m* 1906, Evelyn Victoria Anne, who *d* 1979, having *m* 2ndly, 1913, Capt Arthur Roy Stock (*d* 1915), of Glenapp Castle, Ballantrae, Ayrshire, and 3rdly, 1922, George Vernon Tate, MC (*d* 1955) (*see* Tate, Bt, colls) da of Walter Robert Chandler; *d* 1909; *s* by his son **(26)** EDWARD SOUTHWELL, OBE, 26th Baron *b* 1907; Col REME, R Gloucestershire Hussars (TA) *m* 1st 1926 (*m diss* 1973), Dorothy Evelyn, who *d* 1987, da of Ferdinand Richard Holmes Meyrick, MD, of 59 Kensington Court, W8; 2ndly 1973, Mina Margaret, only da of George Edward Sands; *d* 1982; *s* by his el son **(27)** JOHN EDWARD SOUTHWELL RUSSELL, 27th Baron and present peer.

De Courcy, family name of Baron Kingsale.

DEEDES, BARON (Deedes) (Life Baron 1986)

WILLIAM FRANCIS DEEDES, MC, PC; *b* 1 June 1913, only son of late Herbert William Deedes, of Galt, Hythe, Kent, and formerly of Sandling Park and Saltwood Castle, Kent (*see* B Ashtown, colls, 1966 Edn); *ed* Harrow; Hon DCL (Univ of Kent at Canterbury 1988); Parliamentary Sec, Min of Housing and Local Govt 1954-55, Joint Parliamentary Under-Sec of State Home Office, 1955-57, and Min without Portfolio 1962-64; Editor, The Daily Telegraph 1974-86; served 1939-45 War as Maj KRRC (TA); a DL of Kent; MP for Ashford Div of Kent (*C*) 1950-74; *cr* PC 1962, and *Baron Deedes*, of Aldington, co Kent (Life Baron) 1986: *m* 1942, Evelyn Hilary, da of Clive Branfoot, of Stonegrave, Yorks, and has had issue.

Residence – New Hayters, Aldington, Kent. *Club* – Carlton.

SONS LIVING AND DECEASED

Hon Jeremy Wyndham, *b* 1943; *ed* Eton; journalist and Editorial Director The Daily Telegraph 1986-96, since when Man Dir The Telegraph plc: *m* 1973, Anna Rosemary, da of late Maj Elwin Clive Gray, Seaforth Highlanders, of Aldington, Kent, and has issue living, George William, *b* 1976, — Henry Julius, *b* 1978. *Residence* – Hamilton House, Compton, Newbury, Berks. *Club* – Boodle's.

Julius Brook, *b* 1947; journalist; *dunm* 1970.

DAUGHTERS LIVING

Hon Juliet Evelyn Mary, *b* 1948: *m* 1990, Robert Dale Means, eldest son of Robert Means, of Blythe, Calif. *Residence* – 92 North Rd, Hythe, Kent.

Hon Victoria Frances Jill, *b* 1950: *m* 1982, Jonathan Edward Southey, 3rd son of Sir Robert Southey, AO, CMG, of Mount Eliza, Australia, and has issue living, Samuel William Robert, *b* 1984, — Simon Raymond Julius, *b* 1986. *Residence* – Maben House, Llaneast St, Malvern 3144, Victoria, Australia.

Hon Lucy Rose, *b* 1955: *m* 1st, 1978 (*m diss* 1995), Hon Crispin James Alan Nevill Money-Coutts, son of 8th Baron Latymer; 2ndly, 1996, Jeremy Hagan Whaley, and has issue living (by 1st *m*) (*see* B Latymer), — (by 2nd *m*), Henry Francis, *b* 1998. *Residence* – Reedy Loch, Duns, Berwicks.

DE FREYNE, BARON (French) (Baron UK 1851)

FRANCIS ARTHUR JOHN FRENCH, 7th Baron; *b* 3 Sept 1927; *s* 1935; is a Knight of Sovereign Order of Malta: *m* 1st, 1954 (*m diss* 1978), Shirley Ann, da of late D. R. Pobjoy; 2ndly 1978, Sheelin Deirdre, da of late Col Henry Kane O'Kelly, DSO, of co Wicklow, and widow of William Walker Stevenson and has issue by 1st *m*.

Arms – Ermine, a chevron sable. **Crest** – A dolphin embowed proper. **Supporters** – *Dexter*, an ancient Irish warrior habited, supporting with his dexter hand a battle-axe, head downwards and bearing on his sinister arm a shield, all proper; *sinister*, a female figure vested proper and scarf flowing argent.
Address – c/o House of Lords, Westminster SW1.

MALO MORI QUAM FOEDARI

I had rather die than be dishonoured

SONS LIVING (By 1st marriage)

Hon FULKE CHARLES ARTHUR JOHN, *b* 21 April 1957: *m* 1986, Julia Mary, only da of Dr James H. Wellard, of Hampstead, NW3, and has issue living, Alexander James Charles, *b* 22 Sept 1988, — William Rory Francis, *b* 1991. *Residence* – 14 Langside Av, SW15 5QT.
Hon Patrick Dominick Fitzstephen Jude, *b* 1969.

DAUGHTER LIVING (By 1st marriage)

Hon Vanessa Rose Bradbury, *b* 1958: *m* 1991, Richard Leslie Phillips, of Oak Farm House, Stradsett, King's Lynn, Norfolk PE33 9HH, and has issue living, Toby Richard French, *b* 1994, — Hugo Francis French, *b* (twin) 1994, — Emma Elizabeth Ann French, *b* 1998.

SISTER LIVING

Hon Patricia Mary (4 Linley Court, Rouse Gdns, W Dulwich, SE21), *b* 1917: *m* 1941, Reginald Johnson, who *d* 1958, and has issue living, Michael Reginald (56 Pymers Mead, SE21), *b* 1943: *m* 1982, Marta Jablonska, and has issue living, Patrick Martin *b* 1983, Mark Conrad Eric *b* 1986, — Diana Mary, *b* 1942: *m* 1972, Frederick Robert Robinson, of 111 Gatley Ave, Westewell, Surrey, and has issue living, Nicholas Frederick *b* 1980, Victoria Jane *b* 1977.

WIDOW LIVING OF SON OF FOURTH BARON

Mary Frances, da of Charles Hasslacher, of 3 Kensington Park Gdns, W8: *m* 1937, the Hon Hubert John French, who *d* 1961, and has issue (see colls, infra).

COLLATERAL BRANCHES LIVING

Issue of late Capt Hon William Joseph French, 3rd son of 4th Baron, *b* 1885, *d* 1974: *m* 1920, Victoria Louise, who *d* 1989, da of late William Dalglish Bellasis, JP:—
Marie Isobel (*Dowager Countess Cathcart*), *b* 1923: *m* 1st, 1942, Capt Sir Thomas Brian Weldon, 8th Bt, who *d* 1979; 2ndly, 1984, as his 2nd wife, Maj Gen 6th Earl Cathcart, CB, DSO, MC, who *d* 1999. *Residence* – Moor Hatches, W Amesbury, Salisbury, Wilts. —— Eleanor Mary, *b* 1925: *m* 1946, Capt Patrick Munro of Foulis, TD (*see* Munro Bt, *cr* 1634), Seaforth Highlanders, who *d* 1995, of Foulis Castle, Evanton, Ross-shire.

Issue of late Hon Louis Richard French, 5th son of 4th Baron, *b* 1888, *d* 1952: *m* 1922, Margaret Eleanor, who *d* 1972, da of late Capt Maurice Kirk, 4th King's Own (Roy Lancaster) Regt:—
Sheila Mary, MBE, *b* 1924; MBE (Civil) 1987: *m* 1948, John Benedict Stilwell, MBE, Lieut Coldstream Guards (ret), and has had issue, Mark Andrew (Quinta de Alcalar, Alcalar, 8500-120 Mexilhoeira Grande, Portugal), *b* 1949: *m* 1974, Viviane de Gheldere, and has issue living, John Philip *b* 1975, Alexandra Mary *b* 1978, — Christopher John (Lote 74, Alto Golf, PO Box No 1, Alvor, 8500, Portimão, Portugal), *b* 1952: *m* 1982, Dr Ana Luiza Mendes Victor, and has issue living, John William *b* 1983, — John William, *b* 1954; *d* 1983, — Charles Louis (Brackenwood, 5 Plymouth Rd, Barnt Green, Worcs B45 8JE), *b* 1957: *m* 1986, Mary Elizabeth Baker, and has issue living, Simon Benedict *b* 1989, Christian Louis *b* 1992, Andrew Charles *b* (twin) 1992, — Philippa Ann, *b* 1950: *m* 1973, João Carlos Zilhão, of 41 Avenida do Restelo, Lisbon, Portugal, and has issue living, João Miguel *b* 1974, Antonio Carlos *b* 1976, Francisco *b* 1989, Ana Felipa *b* 1981. *Residence* – Casa dos Arcos, Tapada da Penina, 8500-336 Portimão, Portugal.

Issue of late Hon Hubert John French, 8th son of 4th Baron, *b* 1896, *d* 1961: *m* 1937, Mary Frances (ante), da of Charles Hasslacher, of 3 Kensington Park Gardens, W8:—
Christopher John (Brewerstreet Farm, Bletchingley, Surrey), *b* 1943: *m* 1966, Sacha, da of late Robert Wild, of 5 Ivy Mill Lane, Godstone, Surrey, and has issue living, Philip John, *b* 1968, — Julia Winifred, *b* 1971. —— Richard Charles (24 Detillens Lane, Limpsfield, Oxted, Surrey RH8 0DJ), *b* 1945: *m* 1969, Hilda Mary Felicity, el da of Lt-Col J. J. Pearson, of Tandridge, Surrey, and has issue living, Charles Peter, *b* 1974, — Helen Mary Luise, *b* 1969: *m* 1996, Benjamin John Christopher Moore, son of Dr John Moore, of Northwood, Middx, and has issue living, Daisy Eliza Mary *b* 1998, — Suzanna Frances, *b* (twin) 1974; *m* 1999, Matthew James Press, son of Dixon Press, of Uckfield, Sussex. —— Jane Mary, *b* 1938: *m* 1966, Donald John Lawlor, of 2 Elsenwood Crescent, Camberley, Surrey, and has issue living, Bernard John, *b* 1969, — Timothy Charles, *b* 1970, — Stephen Andrew, *b* 1976, — Elizabeth Mary, *b* 1967: *m* 1998, Van Charles Dare. —— Sarah Anne, *b* 1940 (6418 Dry Barley Lane, Columbia, Md 21045, USA), *b* 1940; BA (Oxon), MPhil, MEd,

PhD: *m* 1971, Clement Henry Lutterodt, PhD, and has issue living, Tobias Henry *b* 1973, — Isabelle Anne, *b* 1975, — Justine Frances, *b* 1979.

Issue of late Hon Bertram Leo French, 9th son of 4th Baron, *b* 1900, *d* 1941: *m* 1927, Maud Mary, who *d* 1974, only da of late Edmund FitzLaurence Dease (*see* B Stafford, colls):—
Maurice Aloysius, MBE (71 East St, Warminster, Wilts), *b* 1930; Maj R Regt Fus; Korea 1952 (despatches), MBE (Mil) 1976: *m* 1st (*m diss* 1965), Heather, da of late Arthur Charles Tarbutt, of Jantar, Joss, Nigeria; 2ndly, 1965, Lavinia Mary, da of late Maj Patrick Henry Anthony Burke, of Stackalan, co Meath, and has issue living, (by 1st *m*) Dominic Arthur, *b* 1959: *m* 1987, Miranda, da of late Philip Howden, and has issue living, Richard Maurice *b* 1988, James Philip *b* (twin) 1988, — Nicola Anne, *b* 1960: *m* 1984, David Stogdale, and has issue living, Sam Patrick *b* 1987, Will Benedict *b* 1994, Abigail Gaynor *b* 1990, — (by 2nd *m*), Patrick Rollo, *b* 1966; MA, FRGS: *m* 1992, Abigail Digna Joanna, da of Cmdr Eoin Ashton-Johnson, of East Orchard, Dorset, and has issue living, Thomas Tenzin *b* 1994, — Gerald Hugh, *b* 1975, — Claudia Rosemary, *b* 1973, — Emily Mary Lucia (twin), *b* 1975. —— Arthur Edmund (38 Belfield Rd, Didsbury, Manchester M20 6BH), *b* 1933; *ed* Trin Coll, Camb (BA 1957); Bar Inner Temple 1962; late Lt Irish Gds: *m* 1986, Charlotte Mary, 2nd da of Sir Simon Peter Edmund Cosmo William Towneley, KCVO, of Dyneley, Burnley, Lancs (*see* E Lindsey and Abingdon, colls), and has issue living, Edmund Peter *b* 1989, — Alice Cecilia, *b* 1987. —— Lavinia Marie, *b* 1928: *m* 1971, Maj John Norman Pembroke Watson, late RHG, of Pannett's, Shipley, Horsham, Sussex.

PREDECESSORS – (B)(1) ARTHUR French, MP, great-grandson of late Arthur French, of French Park, who *d* 1769; *cr* *Baron de Freyne*, of Artagh (peerage of United Kingdom) 1839, and *Baron de Freyne*, of Coolavin (peerage of United Kingdom) 1851, with remainder to his brothers; *d* 1856, when the 1st peerage expired; *s* in Barony of 1851 by his brother (2) *Rev* JOHN, 2nd Baron; *d* 1863; *s* by his brother (3) CHARLES, 3rd Baron: *m* 1851, by a Roman Catholic priest, to Catherine, da of Luke Maree; a question having arisen as to the validity of that marriage, she being a Roman Catholic and he a Protestant, they were again married in 1854 in the Established Church, having at that time had issue, Charles, MP for co Roscommon 1873-80, *b* 1851 (who *d* 1925), John *b* 1853 (who *d* 1916), and William *b* 1854 (who *d* 1929 in USA); *s* by his el son born after the marriage of 1854 (4) ARTHUR, 4th Baron; *b* 1855: *m* 1st, 1877, Lady Laura Octavia Dundas, who *d* 1881, sister of 3rd Earl of Zetland; 2ndly, 1882, Marie Georgiana, who *d* 1923, da of late Richard Westbrook Lamb, of West Denton, Northumberland; *d* 1913; *s* by his son (5) ARTHUR REGINALD, 5th Baron; *b* 1879; Capt 3rd Batn S Wales Borderers: *m* 1902, Annabel, who *d* 1962, da of William Angus; *ka* 1915 (despatches); *s* by his half-brother (6) FRANCIS CHARLES, 6th Baron, *b* 1884: *m* 1916, Lina Victoria, who *d* 1974, da of Sir John Alexander Arnott, 2nd Bt; *d* 1935; *s* by his son (7) FRANCIS ARTHUR JOHN, 7th Baron and present peer.

De Grey, family name of Baron Walsingham.

DELACOURT-SMITH, BARONY OF (Delacourt-Smith) (Extinct 1972)

SON LIVING OF LIFE BARON

Hon Stephen DELACOURT-SMITH (73 Athenlay Rd, SE15), *b* 1946.

DAUGHTERS LIVING OF LIFE BARON

Hon Carolyn DELACOURT-SMITH, *b* 1944: *m* 1969, Roger Martin Pudney, of Tanglewood, Manor Park, Hazlemere, Bucks and has issue, a son, *b* 1977, — a da, *b* 1975.
Hon Lesley DELACOURT-SMITH (6 Herrick Rd, N5), *b* 1948.

WIDOW LIVING OF LIFE BARON

MARGARET ROSALIND (*Baroness Delacourt-Smith of Alteryn*), da of Frederick James Hando of Newport, Mon; *cr* a Life Baroness 1974: *m* 1st, 1939, Baron Delacourt-Smith (Life Baron) who *d* 1972; 2ndly, 1978, Prof Charles Stuart Blackton.

DELACOURT-SMITH OF ALTERYN, BARONESS (Blackton) (Life Baroness 1974)

MARGARET ROSALIND DELACOURT-SMITH, da of Frederick James Hando, of Newport, Mon; *b* 5 April 1916; *ed* Newport High Sch, and St Anne's Coll, Oxford (MA); Councillor of Roy Borough of New Windsor 1962-65, and a JP 1962-67; *cr Baroness Delacourt-Smith of Alteryn*, of Alteryn, in co of Gwent (Life Baroness) 1974: *m* 1st, 1939, Baron Delacourt-Smith (Life Baron) who *d* 1972, and has issue (see that title); 2ndly, 1978, Prof Charles Stuart Blackton.
Address – c/o House of Lords, SW1.

DELAMERE, BARON (Cholmondeley) (Baron UK 1821)
(Name pronounced "Chumley")

Virtue is the safest helmet

HUGH GEORGE CHOLMONDELEY, 5th Baron; *b* 18 Jan 1934; *s* 1979; *ed* Eton, and Magdalene Coll, Camb (MA): *m* 1964, Ann Willoughby, only da of late Sir Patrick Muir Renison, GCMG, of Freeman's Farm House, Mayfield, Sussex, and formerly wife of Michael Patrick Tinné, and has issue.

Arms – Gules, two esquires' helmets in chief proper, and in base a garb or. **Crest** – A demi-griffin sejeant sable, beaked, membered, ducally gorged, and wings elevated or, holding between the claws a helmet, as in the arms. **Supporters** – Two griffins sable, beaked, membered, and wings elevated, ducally gorged and chained or.
Residence – Soysambu, Elmenteita, Kenya.

SON LIVING

Hon THOMAS PATRICK GILBERT, *b* 19 June 1968: *m* 1998, Dr Sally A., da of Prof Derrick Brewerton, of Westminster, SW1, and has issue living, Hugh, *b* 9 Nov 1998.

SISTER LIVING

Hon Anne Jeanetta Essex, *b* 1927: *m* 1951, Conrad Peter Almeric Garnett, and has had issue, Jeremy Paul, *b* 1953, — David Michael, *b* 1956, *d* 1981. *Residence* – Burnside House, Easter Balgedie, Kinross-shire KY13 7HQ.

COLLATERAL BRANCHES LIVING

Granddaughters of late Hon Thomas Grenville Cholmondeley, 2nd son of 1st Baron:—
Issue of late Brig-Gen Hugh Cecil Cholmondeley, CB, CBE, *b* 1852, *d* 1941: *m* 1st, 1885, Mary Stewart, who *d* 1929, da of late Horace Payne Townshend; 2ndly, 1931, Violet Maud, JP, who *d* 1993, aged 100, da of late Rev Hon Archibald Parker (*see* E Macclesfield, colls):—
(By 2nd *m*) (Violet) Essex, *b* 1932: *m* 1964, Maj William James Pinney, 11th Hussars, and has issue living, Hugh Charles William, *b* 1966. *Residence* – Lee Old Hall, Ellesmere, Shropshire SY12 9AE.

Issue of late Henry Arthur Cholmondeley, *b* 1855, *d* 1952: *m* 1920, Helen Mary, who *d* 1923, da of Harold Wrigley, of Ganton Hall, Scarborough:—
(Essex) Lucy (*Countess of Cavan*), *b* 1921: *m* 1947, 12th Earl of Cavan, who *d* 1988. *Residence* – The Glebe House, Stockton, Shifnal, Shropshire TF11 9EF.

Granddaughters of late Maj Henry Reginald Cholmondeley, DSO, son of late Rev Hon Henry Pitt Cholmondeley, 3rd son of 1st Baron:—
Issue of late Maj Anthony Pitt Cholmondeley, *b* 1908, *d* 1986: *m* 1936, Monica Irene, da of late Rev Albert Ernest Snow:—
Anne, *b* 1938. —— Gillian, *b* 1951. —— Faith, *b* 1953: *m* 1978, Nicholas John Vann, and has issue living, Antonia May, *b* 1990.

PREDECESSORS – (1) THOMAS Cholmondeley; *b* 1767; *cr Baron Delamere*, of Vale Royal, co Chester (peerage of United Kingdom) 1821: *m* 1810, Henrietta Elizabeth, da of Sir Watkin Williams-Wynn, 4th Bt; *d* 1855; *s* by his son (2) HUGH, 2nd Baron, *b* 1811; sat as MP for Denbighshire (*C*) 1840-1, and for Montgomery 1841-7: *m* 1st, 1848, Lady Sarah Hay, who *d* 1859, da of 10th Earl of Kinnoull: 2ndly, 1860, Augusta Emily, who *d* 1911, el da of late Rt Hon Sir George Hamilton Seymour, GCB, GCH, PC; *d* 1887; *s* by his son (3) HUGH, KCMG, 3rd Baron; *b* 1870; sometime a MLC of Kenya Colony: *m* 1st, 1899, Lady Florence Anne Cole, who *d* 1914, da of 4th Earl of Enniskillen; 2ndly, 1928, Gwladys Helen, who *d* 1943, da of Hon Rupert Evelyn Beckett; *d* 1931; *s* by his son (4) THOMAS PITT HAMILTON, 4th Baron, *b*

1900; Capt Welsh Gds: *m* 1st, 1924 (*m diss* 1944), Phyllis Anne, who *d* 1978, el da of late Lord George William Montagu-Douglas-Scott, OBE (*see* D Buccleuch, colls); 2ndly, 1944 (*m diss* 1955), Hon (Ruth) Mary Clarisse, who *d* 1986, yr da of 1st Baron Mount Temple (ext), and formerly wife of (i) Capt Alec Stratford Cunningham-Reid, DFC (*d* 1987), (ii) Maj (Ernest) Laurie Gardner; 3rdly, 1955, Diana, who *d* 1987, yr da of late Seymour Caldwell, and formerly wife of (i) Vernon Motion (*d* 1980); widow of Sir (Henry John) Delves Broughton, 11th Bt, and formerly wife of (ii) Gilbert de Préville Colvile (*d* 1966) (*see* B de Clifford, 1972-73 Edn); *d* 1979; *s* by his only son (5) HUGH GEORGE, 5th Baron and present peer.

DE LA WARR, EARL (Sackville) (Earl GB 1761)
(Title pronounced "De la Ware")

Days of my life!

WILLIAM HERBRAND SACKVILLE, 11th Earl; *b* 10 April 1948; *s* 1988; *ed* Eton; patron of four livings; *m* 1978, Anne Pamela, eldest da of Arthur Edmund Leveson, OBE, of Hall Place, Ropley, Hants, and formerly wife of Adrian John Charles, Earl of Hopetoun (later 4th Marquess of Linlithgow), and has issue.

Arms – Quarterly, 1st, argent, a fesse dancettée sable, *West*; 2nd, azure, three leopards' heads reversed jessant de lys or, *Cantelupe*; 3rd gules erusilly and a lion argeut, *la Warr*; 4th, quarterly or and gules, a bend vaire, *Sackville*. **Crest** – 1st, issuant from a ducal coronet or a griffin's head azure, beaked and eared gold. *West*; 2nd, upon a coronet composed of fleurs-de-lis or, an estoile argent, *Sackville*. **Supporters** – *Dexter*, a wolf cow-ard argent gorged with a collar or; *sinister*, a cockatrice or, winged azure. **Badge** – A Crampet or, he inside per pale azure and gules, charged with the letter R.
Seat – Buckhurst Park, Withyham, Sussex. *Town Residence* – 14 Bourne St, SW1. *Clubs* – White's, Turf.

SONS LIVING

WILLIAM HERBRAND THOMAS (*Lord Buckhurst*) *b* 13 June 1979.
Hon Edward Geoffrey Richard, *b* 1980.

BROTHER LIVING

Hon Thomas Geoffrey, *b* 1950; *ed* Eton, and Lincoln Coll, Oxford (BA); Under-Sec of State, Dept of Health 1992-97; MP (*C*) for Bolton West 1983-97; merchant banker: *m* 1979, Catherine, da of late Brig James Windsor Lewis, and has a son and da, Arthur Michael, *b* 1983, — Savannah Elizabeth, *b* 1986.

SISTER LIVING

Lady Arabella Avice Diana SACKVILLE, *b* 1958; has resumed her maiden name: *m* 1981 (*m diss* 1988), Conte Giovanni Emo Capodilista Maldura, son of Conte Gabriele Emo Capodilista Maldura, of Palazzo Grazioli, Rome (*see* E Newburgh, colls).

AUNT LIVING (*daughter of 9th Earl*)

Lady Katharine Pamela, *b* 1926: *m* 1946, Frank Thomas Robertson Giles, and has issue living, (Henry Frank) Sebastian (11 Junction Mews, W2), *b* 1952; *ed* Westminster: *m* 1988, Sarah, elder da of Brian Palmer, of Highgate Village, N6, and has issue living, Maxwell Joseph W. *b* 1989, Lucas Charles O. *b* 1992, — Sarah Elizabeth GILES (170 E 78th St, New York, NY 10025, USA), *b* 1950; has resumed her maiden name: *m* 1972 (*m diss* 1976), Rodolphe d'Erlanger, son of late Leo Frederic Alfred d'Erlanger, — Belinda Susan Mary GILES, *b* 1958; *ed* Girton Coll, Camb; has resumed her maiden name: *m* 1982 (*m diss* 1997), Christopher Simon Sykes, and has issue (*see* Sykes, Bt, 1783). *Residences* – 42 Blomfield Rd, W9 2PF; Bunns Cottage, Lye Green, Crowborough, E Sussex TN6 1UY.

WIDOW LIVING OF TENTH EARL

ANNE RACHEL (*Anne, Countess De La Warr*), only da of late Capt Geoffrey Charles Devas, MC (*see* E Cawdor, colls, 1924 Edn): *m* 1946, the 10th Earl De La Warr, who *d* 1988.

COLLATERAL BRANCHES LIVING

Descendants of Lt-Col Hon William Edward SACKVILLE-WEST, 6th son of 5th Earl, *b* 1830, *d* 1905: *m* 1860, Georgina, who *d* 1883, da of late George Dodwell, of Kevinsfort, Sligo (*see* B Sackville).

Descendants of Hon Leonard West, 5th son of 8th Baron De La Warr (*cr* 1342) (*not in remainder to Earldom and Barony of De La Warr cr* 1570):—
See 1969 and earlier edns.

PREDECESSORS – **(1)** *Sir* THOMAS West, Knt, accompanied Edward III to France 1329, and also in the wars with David Bruce, King of Scotland; summoned to Parliament of England as *Baron West* 1342; *d* 1342; *s* by his son **(2)** THOMAS, 2nd Baron; was not summoned to Parliament; served at Crecy 1346; *s* by his son **(3)** THOMAS, 3rd Baron; summoned to Parliament 1402; *d* 1405; *s* by his son **(4)** THOMAS, 4th Baron; took a distinguished part in the French wars of Henry V; *dsp* 1415; *s* by his brother **(5)** REGINALD, 5th Baron; summoned to English Parliament as 6th *Baron De La Warr* on the death of his uncle 1426 (see note *infra*); *d* 1451; *s* by his son **(6)** RICHARD, 7th Baron, a staunch supporter of the House of Lancaster in the War of the Roses; *d* 1497; *s* by his son **(7)** THOMAS, KG, 8th Baron; *d* 1525; *s* by his son **(8)** THOMAS, 9th Baron; not having male issue he adopted as his heir William, son of his half-brother Sir George West; his nephew, however, having attempted to poison his uncle was debarred by Act of Parliament from succeeding to his uncle's honours or estates; *d* 1554, when the baronies of West and De La Warr fell into abeyance. **(9)** WILLIAM West (ante), nephew of the 9th Baron, having served in the English Army at Picardy, was knighted Feb 1568, fully restored in blood by Act of Parliament in March following, and *cr Baron De La Warr* 1570; *d* 1595; *s* by his son **(10)** THOMAS, 11th Baron; restored to the place and precedence of his ancestors; *s* by his son **(11)** THOMAS, 12th Baron; Gov and Capt-Gen of Virginia; *d* 1618; *s* by his son **(12)** HENRY, 13th Baron; *d* 1628; *s* by his son **(13)** CHARLES, 14th Baron; *s* by his son **(14)** JOHN, 15th Baron; *d* 1723; *s* by his son **(15)** JOHN, KB, PC, 16th Baron; a Gen in the Army, Lord of the Bedchamber to George I, Gov and Capt-Gen of New York; *cr Viscount Cantelupe* and *Earl De La Warr* (peerage of Great Britain) 1761; *d* 1766; *s* by his son **(16)** JOHN, 2nd Earl; a Lt-Gen in the Army, Master of the Horse, and Vice-Chamberlain to the Queen; *d* 1777; *s* by his el son **(17)** WILLIAM AUGUSTUS, 3rd Earl; *d* unmarried 1783; *s* by his brother **(18)** JOHN RICHARD, 4th Earl; *d* 1795; *s* by his son **(19)** GEORGE JOHN, PC, DCL, 5th Earl; *b* 1791; Lord Chamberlain 1858-9; assumed by Roy licence 1845 the additional surname of Sackville: *m* 1813, Lady Elizabeth Sackville, who *d* 1870, yr da and co-heir of 3rd Duke of Dorset (title extinct); this lady was in 1864 *cr Baroness Buckhurst*, of Buckhurst, co Sussex (peerage of United Kingdom), with remainder to her yr sons and their male issue, but with a proviso that upon any Baron Buckhurst succeeded to the Earldom of Delawarr, the said Barony should devolve upon the heir next entitled to succeed, as if the person having so succeeding to the Earldom of De La Warr had died without male issue; *d* 1869; *s* by his son **(19)** CHARLES RICHARD, KCB, 6th Earl; a Maj-Gen in the Army distinguished himself in India and in the Crimea; *d* unmarried 1873, *s* by his brother **(20)** *Rev* REGINALD WINDSOR, 7th Earl, who *d* 1870 had *s* his mother as 2nd Baron Buckhurst, but a claim to that Barony under the above-mentioned proviso by his next brother was unsuccessful, and it has remained merged in the Earldom; *b* 1817; assumed by Roy licence 1871 the surname of Sackville only in lieu of Sackville-West: *m* 1867, Hon Constance Mary Elizabeth, who *d* 1929, el da of 1st Baron Lamington; *d* 1896; *s* by his second son **(21)** GILBERT GEORGE REGINALD, 8th Earl; *b* 1869: *m* 1st, 1891 (*m diss* 1902), Lady Muriel Agnes, who *d* 1930, da of 1st Earl Brassey; 2ndly, 1903, Hilda Mary Claveriny (who *d* 1963, having *m* 2ndly, 1922, John William Dennis, sometime MP), da of late Col C. Lennox Tredcroft, of Glen Ancrum, Guildford; *d* while on active service as Lieut RNVR 1915; *s* by his only son **(22)** HERBRAND EDWARD DUNDONALD BRASSEY, GBE, PC, 9th Earl; *b* 1900; Lord-in-Waiting to HM 1924 and 1929-30; Parl Under-Sec of State for the Colonies 1936-37, Lord Privy Seal 1937-38, Pres of Board of Education 1938-40, First Commnr of Works 1940, and PMG 1951-55: *m* 1st, 1920, Diana, who *d* 1966, da of late Capt Henry Gerard Leigh (*see* Antrobus, Bt, colls); 2ndly, 1968, Dame Sylvia Margaret, DBE, who *d* 1992, da of William Harrison, of Liverpool, and widow of 1st Earl of Kilmuir; *d* 1976; *s* by his son **(23)** WILLIAM HERBRAND, 10th Earl, *b* 1921, served 1939-45 war as Capt Parachute Regt, Hon Col Sussex ACF, a DL for E Sussex: *m* 1946, Anne Rachel, only da of late Capt Geoffrey Charles Devas, MC, of Hunton Court, Maidstone, Kent (*see* E Cawdor, colls, 1924 Edn); *d* 1988; *s* by his elder son **(24)** WILLIAM HERBRAND, 11th Earl and present peer; also Viscount Cantelupe, Baron De La Warr, and Baron Buckhurst.

*ROGER La Warr, summoned to English Parliament 1299-1311; *d* 1329; *s* by his son **(2)** JOHN, KB, 2nd Baron, a valiant soldier; summoned to Parliament of England 1307-47; *d* 1347; *s* by his son **(3)** ROGER, 3rd Baron; a renowned soldier, was present at Poitiers when John, King of France, surrendered to him and Sir John Pelham, in commemoration of which the crampet, or chape, of the king's sword was given to him as a badge: *m* 2ndly, Alianore, da of John, 2nd Baron Mowbray, and had an only da, Joanna, wife of 3rd Baron West, who had issue Thomas 4th Baron West, and Richard 5th Baron West and 6th Baron De La Warr; *d* 1370; *s* by his son **(4)** JOHN, 4th Baron, summoned to Parliament 1370-97; *d* 1398; *s* by his brother **(5)** THOMAS, 5th Baron; Rector of the Parish Church of Manchester; *d* 1426; *s* by his half-sister's son **(6)** REGINALD, 5th Baron West (ante).

DELFONT, BARONY OF (Delfont) (Extinct 1994)

SON LIVING OF LIFE BARON

Hon David Stephen, *b* 1953; *ed* Millfield: *m* 1981, Sarah, da of Peter Edgington, and has issue living, Ben, *b* 1973, — Joseph, *b* 1983, — Alexander, *b* 1985.

DAUGHTERS LIVING OF LIFE BARON

Hon Susan Jane, *b* 1947; stills photographer for films and TV: *m* 1982 (*m diss* 1992), Mark Derek Meddings, and has issue, Thomas, *b* 1983, — Lydia, *b* 1986.

Hon Jennifer, *b* 1949: *m* 1974 (*m diss* 1987), Andrew Morse, and has issue, Jamie, *b* 1975, — Samuel, *b* 1979.

WIDOW LIVING OF LIFE BARON

HELEN VIOLET CAROLYN (*Baroness Delfont*) (actress, as Carole Lynne), da of Victor Cecil Haymen, and formerly wife of Derek Farr, actor, who *d* 1986: *m* 1946, Baron Delfont (Life Baron), who *d* 1994. *Address* – 49 York Terrace West, Regents Park, NW1 4QA.

DE L'ISLE, VISCOUNT (Sidney) (Viscount UK 1956, Bt UK 1806 and 1818)
(Title pronounced "De Lyle")

QUO·FATA·VOCANT

Whither the Fates call me

PHILIP JOHN ALGERNON SIDNEY, MBE, 2nd Viscount, and 10th Baronet of Castle Goring (*cr* 1806) and 8th Baronet of Penshurst Place (*cr* 1818); *b* 21 April 1945; *s* 1991; *ed* Tabley House; late Maj Grenadier Guards; Hon Col 5th Bn Princess of Wales Royal Regt since 1992; DL Kent 1996; Freeman City of London, and Liveryman Goldsmiths' Co; MBE (Mil) 1977: *m* 1980, Isobel Tresyllian, yst da of late Sir Edmund Gerald Compton, GCB, KBE, and has issue.

𝔄rms – Quarterly: 1st and 4th or, a pheon azure, *Sidney*; 2nd and 3rd sable, on a fesse engrailed, between three whelk shells or, a mullet for difference, *Shelley*. 𝔠rests – 1st, a porcupine statant azure, quills, collar, and chain or; 2nd, a griffin's head erased argent, ducally gorged or. 𝔖upporters – *Dexter*, a porcupine azure, quills, collar, and chain or; *sinister*, a lion queue fourchée vert. *Seat* – Penshurst Place, Tonbridge, Kent.

SON LIVING

Hon PHILIP WILLIAM EDMUND, *b* 2 April 1985.

DAUGHTER LIVING

Hon Sophia Jacqueline Mary, *b* 1983.

SISTERS LIVING

Hon Elizabeth Sophia, *b* 1941: *m* 1st, 1959 (*m diss* 1966), George Silver Oliver Annesley Colthurst (*see* Colthurst, Bt); 2ndly, 1966 (*m diss* 1971), Sir (Edward) Humphry Tyrrell Wakefield, 2nd Bt; 3rdly, 1972 (*m diss* 1989), Capt James Silvester Rattray of Rattray, 28th Chief; 4thly, 1989, (Robert) Samuel Clive Abel Smith (*see* Buxton, Bt, colls, 1957 Edn), and has issue living (by 1st *m*) (*see* Colthurst, Bt), — (by 2nd *m*) (*see* Wakefield, Bt), — (by 3rd *m*) Robert, *b* 1972; *ed* Milton Abbey. *Residence* – The Old Hall, Langham, Oakham, Leics.

Hon Catherine Mary, OBE, *b* 1942; OBE (Civil) 1995: *m* 1st, 1964 (*m diss* 1983), (Martin) John Wilbraham; 2ndly, 1983, Nicholas Hyde Villiers (*see* E Clarendon, colls, 1995 Edn), who was lost at sea 1998, and has issue living (by 1st *m*), Alexander John, *b* 1965; *ed* Eton: *m* 1996, Fernanda Amaral Valentini, eldest da of Arnaldo Valentini, of São Paulo, Brazil, and has issue living, Marina *b* 1997, Camilla *b* (twin) 1997, — Rupert Edward Robert, *b* 1967; *ed* Eton, — Jocelyn Thomas Ralph, *b* 1970; *ed* Eton. *Residence* – St Leonard's Grange, Beaulieu, Hants.

Hon Anne Marjorie, *b* 1947: *m* 1967, David Alexander Harries, elder son of late Rear Adm David Hugh Harries, CB, CBE, and has issue living, (David) Henry, *b* 1970; *ed* Eton, — James Hugh, *b* 1972; *ed* Eton, — Alexandra Victoria Corinna, *b* 1968; *ed* Benenden, and Somerville Coll, Oxford. *Residence* – Lower Woolwich, Rolvenden, Cranbrook.

Hon Lucy Corinna Agneta, *b* 1953: *m* 1974, Hon Michael Charles James Willoughby, eldest son of 12th Baron Middleton, MC, and has issue (*see* B Middleton). *Residence* – North Grimston House, Malton, N Yorks.

WIDOW LIVING OF FIRST VISCOUNT

MARGARET ELDRYDD (*Dowager Viscountess De L'Isle*), da of late Maj-Gen Thomas Herbert Shoubridge, CB, CMG, DSO; High Sheriff Powys 1977: *m* 1st, 1942, as his 2nd wife, 3rd Baron Glanusk, DSO, who *d* 1948; 2ndly, 1966, as his 2nd wife, 1st Viscount De L'Isle, VC, KG, GCMG, GCVO, PC, who *d* 1991. *Residence* – Glanusk Park, Crickhowell, Powys.

COLLATERAL BRANCH LIVING

Granddaughter of late Capt George Ernest Shelley, brother of 5th Baronet:—
Issue of late Maj George Edward Shelley, MBE, *b* 1891, *d* 1961: *m* 1st, 1920 (*m diss* 1935), Cicely Alice Colquhoun, who *d* 1954, el da of late Lt-Col Lionel Arthur Bosanquet; 2ndly, 1935 (*m diss* 1941), Hon Lucy

Gwen, who *d* 1957, da of Baron Atkin (Life Peer); 3rdly, 1951, Freda Victoria (OHLSON), who *d* 1977, yr da of late F. H. L. Jeffery:—

(By 1st *m*) Iris Gwendolin (43 Victoria Rd, Cirencester, Glos GL7 1ES), *b* 1927: *m* 1954, Maj Philip Gordon Tanner, RA, who *d* 1994, and has issue living, Nicholas Shelley (The Coach House, Ampney Crucis, Glos GL7 5RY), *b* 1955: *m* 1980, Melanie Anne, elder da of late A. F. Challis, and has had issue, George William *b* 1982; *d* 1989, William Archie Bowen *b* 1988, Olivia Cicely Rose *b* 1990, Isabel Charlotte Alice *b* 1993, — Clare Theresa, *b* 1958: *m* 1987, Keith Evans, elder son of L. Evans and has issue living, Christopher *b* 1990, Daniel *b* 1992.

PREDECESSORS – (1) *Sir* JOHN Shelley-Sidney; *cr a Baronet* 1818; assumed additional surname of Sidney by Roy licence 1793 on succeeding to the estate of his maternal grandmother, Elizabeth (who *m* William Perry), da of Hon Thomas Sidney, 4th son of 4th Earl of Leicester; *d* 1849; *s* by his son (2) PHILIP CHARLES, GCH, DCL, who had in 1835 been *cr Baron De L'Isle and Dudley* (peerage of United Kingdom); *b* 1800; discontinued the surname of Shelley: *m* 1825, Lady Sophia Fitzclarence, natural da of King William IV, and sister of 1st Earl of Munster: *d* 4 March 1851; *s* by his son (3) PHILIP, 2nd Baron, *b* 1828: *m* 1st, 1850, Mary, who *d* 1891, da of Sir William Foulis, 8th Bt; 2ndly, 1893, Emily Frances, who *d* 1926, el da of late William Fermor Ramsay; *d* 1898; *s* by his el son (4) PHILIP, 3rd Baron, *b* 1853: *m* 1902, Hon Elizabeth Maria, da of 4th Viscount Gort, and widow of William Harvey Astell, JP, DL, (sometime Grenadier Guards), of Woodbury Hall, Beds; *d* 1922; *s* by his brother (5) ALGERNON, 4th Baron, *b* 1854; sometime Lieut-Col and Brevet Col RA; *d* April 1945; *s* by his brother (6) WILLIAM, 5th Baron, *b* 1859; Bar Inner Temple 1886; Mayor of Chelsea 1906 and 1907 and a County Councillor for London 1922-34: *m* 1905, Winifred Agneta Yorke, who *d* 1959, da of late Roland Yorke Bevan, *d* June 1945; *s* by his son (6) WILLIAM PHILIP, VC, KG, GCMG, GCVO, PC, 1st Viscount, *b* 1909, Capt Grenadier Guards (Reserve), 1939-45 War in France and Italy (VC), DL Kent, Parl Sec to Min of Pensions May-July 1945, Sec of State for Air 1951-55, Gov-Gen of Australia 1961-65, MP for Chelsea (C) Oct 1944-June 1945, Chm of Trustees Winston Churchill Memorial Trust, and sometime Chm Phoenix Assurance Co, Dir Phoenix Assurance Co of New York, Yorkshire Bank Ltd, and other Cos, Chm Board of Trustees of the Armouries 1983-86; *cr Viscount De L'Isle*, of Penshurst, co Kent (peerage of United Kingdom) 1956: *m* 1st, 1940, Hon Jacqueline Corinne Yvonne Vereker, who *d* 1962, da of F-M 6th Viscount Gort, VC, GCB, CBE, DSO, MVO, MC; 2ndly, 1966, Margaret Eldrydd, da of late Maj-Gen Thomas Herbert Shoubridge, CB, CMG, DSO, and widow of 3rd Baron Glanusk; *d* 1991; *s* by his only son (7) PHILIP JOHN ALGERNON, 2nd Viscount and present peer; also Baron De L'Isle and Dudley (see infra *).

*(1) *Sir* BYSSHE Shelley, of Castle Goring, Sussex son of Timothy Shelley, 7th in descent from Edward Shelley of Worminghurst Park, Sussex, yr son of John Shelley, of Michelgrove (*d* 1526) (*see* Shelley Bt, *cr* 1611); *b* 1731; *cr a Baronet* 1806: *m* 1st, Mary Catherine, who *d* 1760, da and heir of the Rev Theobald Mitchell; 2ndly, 1769, Elizabeth Jane Sidney, who *d* 1781, da and heir of William Perry by Elizabeth Sidney, heir of Penshurst Place, Kent; *d* 1815; *s* by his el son (2) *Sir* TIMOTHY, 2nd Bt, *b* 1753: *m* 1791, Elizabeth, da of Charles Pilfold, of Effingham, Surrey; *d* 1844; *s* by his grandson (3) *Sir* PERCY FLORENCE, 3rd Bt (son of Percy Bysshe Shelley the poet, who was drowned 1822); *b* 1819: *m* 1848, Jane, who *d* 1899, da of Thomas Gibson, and widow of Hon Charles Robert St John; *d* 1889; *s* by his cousin (4) *Sir* EDWARD, 4th Bt; *b* 1827; Capt 16th Lancers: *m* 1866, Mary, who *d* 1886, da of Henry Mitchell Smyth; *d* 1890; *s* by his brother (5) *Sir* CHARLES, 5th Bt; *b* 1838; Lt-Col Scots Fus Guards: *m* 1869, Lady Mary Jane Jemina Stopford, who *d* 1937, da of 3rd Earl of Courtown; *d* 1902; *s* by his el son (6) *Sir* JOHN COURTOWN EDWARD, 6th Bt, *b* 1871; Capt Scots Guards: *m* 1898, Hon Eleanor Georgiana Rolls, who *d* 1961, da and heir of 1st and last Baron Llangattock; they assumed by Royal Licence 1917, the additional name and arms of Rolls; *d* 1951; *s* by his brother (7) *Sir* PERCY BYSSHE, 7th Bt, *b* 1872, *d* 1953; *s* by his brother (8) *Sir* SIDNEY PATRICK, 8th Bt; Capt Hampshire Yeo; *d* 1965; *s* by his kinsman (9) 1st Viscount De L'Isle, descendant of Sir John Shelley-Sidney, 1st Bt (*cr* 1818), only son of 1st Bt (*cr* 1806) by his 2nd wife (ante).

Delvin, Lord; son of Earl of Westmeath.

DE MAULEY, BARON (Ponsonby) (Baron UK 1838)
(Name pronounced "Punsonby")

GERALD JOHN PONSONBY, 6th Baron; *b* 19 Dec 1921; *s* 1962; *ed* Eton, and Ch Ch, Oxford (BA 1941, MA 1947); Bar Middle Temple 1949; formerly Lieut Leicestershire Yeo, and Capt RA; European War 1939-45: *m* 1954, Helen Alice, da of late Hon Charles William Sholto Douglas (*see* E Morton), and widow of Lt-Col Brian Lynch Leslie Abdy Collins, OBE, MC, RE.

𝕬rms – Gules, a chevron between three combs argent. 𝕮rest – Out of a ducal coronet or three arrows, points downwards, one in pale and two in saltire, entwined at the intersection by a snake proper. 𝕾upporters – *Dexter*, a lion reguardant proper; *sinister*, a bull sable, armed, unguled, tufted, and ducally gorged or.
Residence – Langford House, Little Faringdon, Lechlade, Glos.

For the king, the law, and the people

BROTHER LIVING

Hon THOMAS MAURICE, TD, *b* 2 Aug 1930; *ed* Eton; Lt-Col The Wessex Yeo; Brevet Col TA; DL for Glos; High Sheriff of Glos 1978: *m* 1956, Maxine Henrietta, da of late William Dudley Keith Thellusson, and has issue living, Rupert Charles, *b* 1957, — Ashley George, *b* 1959. *Residence* – The Common, Little Faringdon, Lechlade, Glos.

SISTER LIVING

Hon June Mary (*Baroness Grimston of Westbury*), *b* 1924: *m* 1949, 2nd Baron Grimston of Westbury. *Residence* – The Old Rectory, Westwell, Burford, Oxon.

COLLATERAL BRANCHES LIVING

Grandchildren of late Hon Edwin Charles William Ponsonby, 5th son of 2nd Baron:—
Issue of late Col Sir Charles Edward Ponsonby, Bt TD, *b* 1879, *d* 1976; *cr* a Baronet 1956 (*see* Baronetage).

Issue of late Rev Maurice George Jesser Ponsonby, MC, *b* 1880, *d* 1943: *m* 1918, Lady Phyllis Sydney Buxton, OBE, who *d* 1942, da of 1st Earl Buxton:—
Elizabeth, *b* 1922: *m* 1952, John Lionel Clay, TD, Circuit Judge (retd), and has issue living, Andrew John Buxton, *b* 1962, — Fiona Elizabeth, *b* 1954: *m* 1982, Rev John Alexander Taylor, and has issue living, Simon Joseph *b* 1990, Lucy Alethea *b* 1988, — Catriona Mary, *b* 1955: *m* 1983, John Kendall Bush, — Joanna Penelope, *b* 1958. *Residence* – Newtimber Place, Hassocks, Sussex. —— Mary Veronica, *b* 1927: *m* 1961, William Peter Ward Barnes, HM Civil Service, 2nd son of Rt Rev Ernest William Barnes, Bishop of Birmingham, and has issue living, Peter Denis Ponsonby, *b* 1962, — Thomas William Ponsonby, *b* 1965, Susanna Barbara, *b* 1963: *m* 1987, Ian Hardy, of Lea Corner, Leasy Dell Drive, Wheathampstead, Herts AL3 4HS, and has issue James William Barnes *b* 1992, Christina Louise *b* 1990. *Residence* – 37 Oak Village, NW5 4QN.

Issue of late Capt Victor Coope Ponsonby, MC, *b* 1887, *d* 1966: *m* 1923, Gladys Edith, who *d* 1964, da of late Godfrey Walter, of Malshanger, Basingstoke:—
†Myles Walter, CBE, *b* 1924; *ed* Eton; late Capt KRRC; HM Consul-Gen at Hanoi 1964-65; Ambassador to Mongolian People's Republic 1974-77; 1939-45 War; CBE (Civil) 1966: *m* 1950, Ann Veronica Theresa (6 Hyde House Gdns, Hyde St, Winchester SO23 7EL), da of late Brig Francis Herbert Maynard, CB, DSO, MC, and *d* 1999, leaving issue, John Maurice Maynard, OBE, *b* 1955; Group Capt RAF; OBE (Mil) 19—: *m* 1980, Marie Jose (Cé) Antoinette, eldest da of W. M. van Huizen-Husselson, of Knoll House, Kilmersdon, nr Radstock, Bath, and has issue living, Luke Myles William *b* 1986, Charlotte Emma *b* 1982, Francesca Sarah *b* (twin) 1986, — Belinda Mary, *b* 1951: *m* 1973, John Mitchell, of West Lodge, Northington, Alresford, Winchester, Hants SO24 9TG, and has issue living, Jonathan Myles *b* 1976, Charles Edward *b* 1978, James *b* 1981, — Emma Christina, *b* 1959: *m* 1981, Capt Bryn St Pierre Parry, RGJ, elder son of late Lt-Col R. G. R. Parry, MC, and has issue living, Thomas Robin St Pierre *b* 1985, Sophie Laura *b* 1983, Louisa Mary *b* 1987. —— Sheila Mary (Bathurst Cottage, Teffont Magna, Salisbury SP3 5QP, Wilts), *b* 1927: *m* 1st, 1952 (*m diss* 1975), Cdr Michael Edward St Quintin Wall, RN (*see* E Peel, colls, 1972-73 Edn); 2ndly, 1976, Giles Aubrey Cartwright, who *d* 1988 (*see* Buxton, Bt, colls, 1990 Edn), and has issue living (by 1st *m*), Hugo St Quintin, *b* 1954, — Sarah Fenella, *b* 1955: *m* 1981 Michael Hugh Warwick Bampfylde, and has issue (*see* B Poltimore).

Grandchildren of late Claude Ashley Charles Ponsonby, el son of late Capt Hon Ashley George John Ponsonby, 2nd son of 1st Baron:—
Issue of late Harold Ashley Curzon Ponsonby, *b* 1891, *d* 1950: *m* 1941, Ruth Margaret, only da of James Miller, of Chippenham, Wilts:—
John Ashley Charles, *b* 1948. —— Sarah Haller, *b* 1944: *m* 1971, Phillip James Hilton, of Winishill, Nibley Lane, Yate, Bristol. —— Jane Caroline, *b* 1946: *m* 1966 (*m diss* 1969), Stephen Thornton Parr, and has issue living, Sally Jane Thornton, *b* 1965.

PREDECESSORS – (1) *Hon* WILLIAM FRANCIS SPENCER Ponsonby, 3rd son of 3rd Earl of Bessborough, *b* 1787: *m* 1814, Lady Barbara Ashley-Cooper, da of 5th Earl of Shaftesbury (a co-heir to Barony of Mauley *cr* 1295); *cr Baron de Mauley*, of Canford, co Dorset (peerage of United Kingdom) 1838; *d* 1855; *s* by his son (2) CHARLES FREDERICK ASHLEY COOPER, 2nd Baron, *b* 1815; MP for Poole (*L*) 1837-47 and for Dungarvan 1851-2: *m* 1838, Lady Maria Jane Elizabeth Ponsonby, da of 4th Earl of Bessborough; *d* 1896; *s* by his el son (3) WILLIAM ASHLEY WEBB, 3rd Baron; *b* 1843; *d* 1918; *s* by his brother (4) *Rev* MAURICE JOHN GEORGE, 4th Baron, *b* 1846; sometime V of Wantage: *m* 1875, Hon Madeleine Emily Augusta Hanbury-Tracy, who *d* 1938, da of 2nd Baron Sudeley; *d* 1945; *s* by his son (5) HUBERT WILLIAM, 5th Baron; Capt Gloucester Yeo, 1914-18 War: *m* 1920, Elgiva Margaret, who *d* 1987, da of late Hon Cospatrick Thomas Dundas (*see* M Zetland, colls); *d* 1962; *s* by his son (6) GERALD JOHN, 6th Baron and present peer.

de Moleyns, Daubeny, family name of Baron Ventry.

DENBIGH AND DESMOND, EARL OF (Feilding) (Earl E 1622)

Honour is the reward of virtue

ALEXANDER STEPHEN RUDOLPH FEILDING, 12th Earl; *b* 4 Nov 1970; *s* 1995; *ed* Stowe: *m* 1996, Suzanne Jane, yr da of Gregory R. Allen, of Mudberry House, Centry Rd, Brixham, Devon.

Arms – Argent, on a fesse azure, three lozenges or. Crest – A nuthatch pecking at a hazel branch, all proper. Supporters – Two stags proper, attired and unguled or.
Residence – Newnham Paddox, Monks Kirby, Rugby CV23 0RX.

SISTERS LIVING

Lady Samantha Clare Barbara, *b* 1966: *m* 1990, Guy John Desmond Hurley, elder son of David Hurley, of Ballydaheen, Port Salon, co Donegal, and has issue living, Charlotte Lauren Sasha, *b* 1992, — Constance Cora Anna, *b* 1994, — Cora Lucy Vivienne, *b* 1995. *Residence* – 17 Veronica Rd, SW17 8QL.
Lady Louisa Helen Sonia, *b* 1969: *m* 1995, Richard Henry Redfern Barton, elder son of Brian Barton, of The Daye House, Wilton Park, Salisbury, Wilts, and has issue living, Phoebe Isobel Antonia, *b* 1999. *Residence* – 121 Mallinson Rd, SW11 1BH.

AUNT LIVING (*daughter of 10th Earl*)

Lady (Imelda) Clare, *b* 1941: *m* 1st, 1966 (*m diss* 1979), David Rodney Doig, 2ndly, 1984, Jack Levon Simonian, and has issue living (by 1st *m*), Andrew William David, *b* 1969; *ed* Blundells, — Rowena Helen, *b* 1967, — Zoe Claire, *b* 1971. *Residence* – Grounds Farm, Monks Kirby, Rugby CV23 0RH.

WIDOWS LIVING OF BROTHERS OF TENTH EARL

Rosemary (The Park Cottage, Monks Kirby, Rugby CV23 0RB), only da of late Cdr (Frederick) Neville Eardley-Wilmot, RN (ret) (*see* Eardley-Wilmot, Bt): *m* 1939, Capt Hon Basil Egerton Feilding, who *d* 1970, and has issue (see colls, infra).
Sheila Katharine, only da of late Brig Charles Arthur Bolton, CBE: *m* 1944, Sqdn Ldr Hon Hugh Richard Feilding, RAFVR, who *d* 1996, and has issue (see colls, infra). *Residence* – Home Farm, Bainton, Driffield, E Yorks.
Dunia Maureen (Willow Tree House, Post House Gdns, Pailton, Rugby CV23 0QU), yr da of late Gordon Spencer, MD: *m* 1950, Capt Hon Henry Anthony Feilding, MC, who *d* 1994, and has issue (see colls, infra).

WIDOW LIVING OF ELEVENTH EARL

CAROLINE JUDITH VIVIENNE (*Dowager Countess of Denbigh and Desmond*), only da of Lt-Col Geoffrey Cooke, of Little Orchard, Sunningdale, Berks: *m* 1965, the 11th Earl of Denbigh and Desmond, who *d* 1995. *Residence* – Newnham Paddox, Monks Kirby, Rugby CV23 0RX.

COLLATERAL BRANCHES LIVING

Issue of late Hon David Charles Feilding (2nd son of late Lt-Col Rudolph Edmund Aloysius, Viscount Feilding, CMG, DSO, el son of 9th Earl), *b* 1913, *d* 1966: *m* 1938, Elizabeth Alice, who *d* 1990, da of late William Fletcher, of Cumberland:—
WILLIAM DAVID (Oristano Great House, Bluefields, PO Box 1, Westmoreland, Jamaica), *b* 12 Aug 1939; *ed* Downside; Artist: *m* 1980, Lydia Sarah, da of Martin Harding, of Chelsea. —— Michael Henry (107 Hartfield Rd, Wimbledon, SW19 3TJ), *b* 1946; *ed* Downside, and Oxford Univ (BSc): *m* 1970, Linnet, da of William Hale, of The Island, Hurstbourne Priors, Hants, and has issue living, Emily Linnet, *b* 1973, — Melissa Anne, *b* 1976. —— Charles Richard (47 Vista Barranca, Rancho Santa Margarita, California 92688, USA), *b* 1949; *ed* Downside, and Fordham Univ, New York: *m* 1st, 1972 (*m diss* 1980), Jeanne, da of Eugene Tanzillo, of New York; 2ndly, 1982, April Ann, da of late Chauncey Gaylord Street, of Orlando, Florida.

Issue of late Capt Hon Basil Egerton Feilding (3rd son of late Lt-Col Rudolph Edmund Aloysius, Viscount Feilding, CMG, DSO, el son of 9th Earl), *b* 1916, *d* 1970: *m* 1939, Rosemary (ante), da of late Cdr (Frederick) Neville Eardley-Wilmot, RN (ret) (*see* Eardley-Wilmot, Bt):—
Peter Rudolph (Highfields, 11 Marlow Rd, High Wycombe, Bucks HP11 1TA), *b* 1941; *ed* Ampleforth; FCA: *m* 1968, Diana Mourne, only da of C. C. Cox, TD, of 16 Albany House, Albany Court, Lansdown Rd, Cheltenham, Glos, and has issue living, Basil James, *b* 1974, — Chloë Louise, *b* 1972. —— Giles Anthony STEUART-FEILDING (The Manor House, Arnesby, Leics), *b* 1950; assumed surname of Steuart-Feilding in lieu of his patronymic by deed poll 1981: *m* 1977, Sara Jane, da of late Cdr D. E. Barton, MVO, DSC, RN, of 47 St Mary Abbot's Terr, W14, and has issue living, Thomas Assheton Henry, *b* 1980, — Imogen Clare, *b* 1978. —— Crispin Everard, *b* 1960. —— Jennifer Mary, *b* 1947: *m* 1st 1968 (*m diss* 1971), Graham F. Bond; 2ndly, 1974, Charles Eliot Crawley, and has issue living (by 2nd *m*) Tobias, *b* 1978. —— Imelda Jane, *b* 1958: *m* 1981, Piers L. Rendell, of Little Thatch, Woolage Green, Canterbury, Kent CT4 6SF, son of Brig D. B. Rendell, of West Street House, Selsey, and has issue living, Hugo Anthony, *b* 1983, — Sebastian James, *b* 1985.

Issue of late Sqdn Ldr Hon Hugh Richard Feilding, FAFVR (4th son of late Lt-Col Rudolph Edmund Aloysius, Viscount Feilding, CMG, DSO, el son of 9th Earl), *b* 1920, *d* 1996: *m* 1944, Sheila Katharine (ante), only da of late Brig Charles Arthur Bolton, CBE:—
John Henry Christopher (The Village Farm, Offchurch, Leamington Spa, Warwicks CV33 9AP), *b* 1945; *ed* Ampleforth: *m* 1st, 1971 (*m diss* 1989), Veronica, 2nd da of John Farmer; 2ndly, 1995, Mrs Patrice Heather Mary Hoyle, da of Dr Kenneth Flory Strachan, and formerly wife of Adrian William Hoyle, and has issue living (by 1st *m*), Michael John Richard, *b* 1975, — Andrew Francis Alexander, *b* 1977, — Natasha Frances Katharine, *b* 1973, — Alexandra Margaret Anne, *b* 1981.

Issue of late Capt Hon Henry Anthony Feilding (yst son of late Lt-Col Rudolph Edmund Aloysius, Viscount Feilding, CMG, DSO, el son of 9th Earl), *b* 1924, *d* 1994: *m* 1950, Dunia Maureen (ante), da of late Gordon Spencer, MD, of Putley, nr Ledbury, Herefordshire:—
Jasper Simon (Falstaff House, 33 Sheep St, Shipston-on-Stour, Warwicks), *b* 1953; *ed* Ampleforth, and RAC, Cirencester: *m* 1980, Diana Margaret, only da of Maj E. D. Lloyd-Thomas, of Maes-y-Crochan House, St Mellons, Cardiff, and has issue living, Katherine Louisa, *b* 1982, — Tessa Caroline, *b* 1985. —— Penelope Dunia, *b* 1954: *m* 1976, Maj Robert Hugh Power Goodwin, RGJ, of 6 Church Rd, Aspley Heath, Woburn Sands, Beds MK17 8TA, yst son of Lt-Gen Sir Richard Elton Goodwin, KCB, CBE, DSO, and has issue living, Lucy Dunia, *b* 1980, — Clare Penelope, *b* 1982, — Alice Elizabeth, *b* 1985.

Grandchildren of late Percy Henry Feilding, yr son of late Gen Hon Sir Percy Robert Basil Feilding, KCB, 2nd son of 7th Earl:—
Issue of late Basil Percy Terence Feilding, *b* 1907, *d* 1986: *m* 1931, Margaret Mary, who *d* 1989, da of Lt-Col Rowland Charles Feilding, DSO (infra):—
Jocelyn Roland Rupert Geoffrey (The Old Manor House, Whiteheads Lane, Bradford on Avon, Wilts BA15 1JU), *b* 1940; *ed* Downside: *m* 1st, 1963 (*m diss* 1983), Rowena Marion, da of Capt Simon Harvey Combe, MC, of the Manor House, Burnham Thorpe, Norfolk (*see* E Leicester); 2ndly, 1998, Harriet, da of James Earle, of Pattingham, Staffs, and has issue living (by 1st *m*), Emma Mary Clothilde, *b* 1964, — Lucy Silvia Margaret, *b* 1966. —— Julia Felicity Maria Gabrielle, *b* 1933; Dip Arch Oxford, ARIBA: *m* 1st, 1957 (*m diss* 1963), Leslie John Rebanks, ARIBA, of Toronto, Canada; 2ndly, 1963, Donald Rhind Morrison, Dip Arch, Dip TP (Dunelm), ARIBA, of Bridge End House, Dorchester-on-Thames, Oxon OX9 8JT, and has had issue (by 1st *m*), Leander Piers John, *b* 1960, — Alexander Basil, *b* 1961, — (by 2nd *m*) Justin Guy Stuart Feilding, *b* 1964: *m* 1992, Sarah Louise Gilbert, and has issue living, Daniel Josef *b* 1996, Eleanor Zuleika *b* 1998, — Zuleika Jane Feilding, *b* 1963: *m* 1994, Bruce Lionel Hawker, of Overshot, Cunnamulla, Queensland, and *d* 1998, leaving issue, Ruben James *b* 1995, Aden Harry *b* 1997. —— Chloë Mary Antonia (16 London Place, Oxford), *b* 1936: *m* 1962 (*m diss* 1973), David Coombes, and has issue living, Rowland William Sebastian, *b* 1967, — Victoria Roque-Rebecca, *b* 1963, — Connemara Alice Mary, *b* 1965. —— Amanda Claire Marion (*Lady Neidpath*), *b* 1943: *m* 1st, 1968 (*m diss* 1993), Joseph (Joe) Chase Hurt Mellen, son of William Mellen; 2ndly, 1995, as his 2nd wife, James Donald, Lord Neidpath, son of 12th Earl of Wemyss, KT, and has issue living (by 1st *m*), Rock Basil Hugo Feilding, *b* 1979, — Cosmo Birdie Feilding, *b* 1985.

Grandchildren of late John Basil Feilding, eldest son of Rev Hon Charles William Alexander Feilding (infra):—
Issue of late Rev Charles Rudolph Feilding, STD, *b* 1902, *d* 1978: *m* 1935, Ann, who *d* 1997, only da of late Ernest Truslow, of Southport, Conn, USA:—
Geoffrey Truslow (655 Grosvenor Av, Westmount, Quebec), *b* 1939: *m* 1966, Martha Anne, da of John S. Corrigan, of Toronto, and has issue living, Charles Corrigan, *b* 1968, — Jonathan Corrigan, *b* 1970. —— Goodith Mary (507 Hunter St West, Peterborough, Ont K9H 2M9), *b* 1936: *m* 1956, Rev Brian Heeney, DPhil, who *d* 1983, Vice-Pres, Trent Univ, Peterborough, Ontario, Canada, and has issue living, Michael Feilding, *b* 1957: *m* 1982, Hilary Meredith, and has issue living, Henry Meredith *b* 1988, Mark Meredith *b* 1996, Frances Meredith *b* 1991, — Timothy Charles, *b* 1966: *m* 1991, Shuna Baird, and has issue living, Duncan *b* 1995, Emma *b* 1997, — Matthew Macleod, *b* 1968: *m* 1999, Polly Collins, — Ann, *b* 1961: *m* 1987, Richard Johnston, and has issue living, Rachel Margaret Heeney *b* 1991.

Granddaughter of late Rev Hon Charles William Alexander Feilding, 4th son of 7th Earl:—
Issue of late Lt-Col Rowland Charles Feilding, DSO, *b* 1871, *d* 1945: *m* 1903, Edith Mary, who *d* 1961, da of late Frederick Stapleton-Bretherton, of The Hall, Rainhill, Lancs (B Petre):—
Prunella Mary Patricia, *b* 1916; late Junior Com ATS: *m* 1942, Charles Neil Howard, MC, late Major Black Watch, who *d* 1975, and has issue living, Simon Neil (11 Crescent Mansions, 122 Elgin Crescent, W11 2JN), *b* 1951, — Caroline Edith Mary (Lodge Farm, Stowood, nr Beckley, Oxford OX3 9SR), *b* 1947: *m* 1st, 1976 (*m diss* 1979), David Hugh Craig, MA; 2ndly, 1990 Simon Lachlan Gordon-Duff (*see* Baird, Bt, *cr* 1809), and has issue living (by 1st *m*), Nicholas Charles David *b* 1977, — Harriet Prunella Mary, *b* 1948. *Residence* – The Cottage, Lodge Farm, Stowood, Beckley, Oxon.

Grandsons of late Allen Fielding, son of late Rev Henry Fielding, el son of late Rev Allen Fielding (son of the famous novelist), grandson of the late Rev Hon John Fielding, DD, son of 1st Earl of Desmond and brother of 3rd Earl of Denbigh:—
Issue of late Geoffrey Kenmil Fielding, *b* 1884, *d* 1960: *m* 1917, Elsie, who *d* 1986, da of late John Edward Watkins, of Shrewsbury:—
Allen Henry (5/60 Pennington Terr, N Adelaide, S Australia 5006), *b* 1919; ARIBA, ARAIA; served 1939-46 War as Capt Royal Sussex Regt: *m* 1943, Estelle Teague, of The Old Hall, Builth Wells, and has issue living, David Henry, *b* 1944, — Barbara Ann, *b* 1950: *m* 1972, William Henderson, of P.O. Box 38 Clare, South Australia 5453, and has issue living, Andrew William Fielding *b* 1987. —— John Henry (twin), *b* 1919; 1939-45 War as Capt RA: *m* 1st, 1948, Pamela Mary, who *d* 1986, only da of John Alfred Spurle Barnard; 2ndly, 1900, Grace McInnes, da of William Collins, of Glasgow, and has issue living (by 1st *m*), Simon Henry (100 Beaconsfield Rd, Leicester), *b* 1949, — Geoffrey John (The Old Farmhouse, St Mary's Rd, Wrotham, Kent), *b* 1950. *Residence* – 113 Woodbrook Rd, Sidmouth, Devon.

Grandchildren of late Rev George Frederick Marshall Fielding, eldest son of late George Fielding (*b* 1827) (infra):—
Issue of late George Basil Fielding, *b* 1889, *d* 1959: *m* 1st, 1918 (*m diss* 1932), Esmé, who *d* 1961, da of late Outram Kellie McCallum; 2ndly, 1932, Gertrude, who *d* 1983, widow of G. A. Vickers:—
(By 1st *m*) Cecil Dolores, *b* 1922: *m* 1944, Maj Charles William Auchmuty, late Indian Army, of 53 Shepherd's Way, Liphook, Hants GU30 7HH, and has issue living, Susan Ann Esmé, *b* 1950: *m* 1972, David André Wavre, of Swevenings, Linersh Wood Rd, Bramley, Surrey GU5 0EF, and has issue living, Robert André Auchmuty *b* 1975, Thomas Marc *b*

1978, Natalie Chantal *b* 1982, — Jane Dolores, *b* 1955: *m* 1977, Richard David Lee Crowe, who *d* 1998, of 5 Stafford Oaks, Kernersville, N Carolina 27284, USA, and has issue living, David William *b* 1979, James Andrew *b* 1981.

Issue of late Henry Armitage Fielding, *b* 1892, *d* 1965: *m* 1914, Ethel Mary Baldock, who *d* 1975:—
Henry George (89 Chapel Lands, Alnwick, Northumberland NE66 1ES), *b* 1916: *m* 1st, 1940, Anne Scargill, who *d* 1965; 2ndly, 1965, Eirene Helen, only da of late George Sydney Sell, of Northumberland, and has issue living, (by 1st *m*) Henry Michael Clive, MSc (33 Woodstock Rd, Carlingford, Sydney, NSW 2188), *b* 1944: *m* 1971, Lorraine Patricia Kirton, and has issue living, Zoë Anne Clare *b* 1977, Sorrel Elizabeth May *b* 1979, Imogen Olivia Heather *b* 1981, — George Peter Keith (20 Ashwell Rd, Bygrave, Baldock, Herts SG7 5DT), *b* 1945; Lt RN (ret): *m* 1968, Gillian Margaret Stearn, and has issue living, James Marcus *b* 1977, Sarah Anne *b* 1970: *m* 1997, Daniel Ward, of 48 River Av, Palmers Green N13 5RN, Emma Jade *b* 1972, — John David Barry (19 Arnold Av, Camden, Sydney, NSW 2570), *b* 1946: *m* 1968, Pamela Margaret Cann, and has issue living, Maxine Anne *b* 1969, Chelsea Louise *b* 1974: *m* 1998, Harry Callinan, who has assumed the surname of Fielding, — Anthony Robert Max, *b* 1948; Lt RN (ret): *m* 1st, 1977 (*m diss* 1978), Stephanie Ann Johnson; 2ndly, 1980, Mrs Rachael Jane Thompson, da of Frederick Dodge, of Somerset, and has issue living (by 2nd *m*), Henry Lawrence Max *b* 1983, Amelia Anne *b* 1981. —— Barbara Jean, *b* 1917: *m* 1st, 1940 (*m diss* 1952), Frank St Omer; 2ndly, 1952, Godfrey Walter Allen Sweet, of 606 Rochester Way, Eltham, SE9 1RL, and has issue living, (by 1st *m*) Judy Mary (91 Hitchen Hatch Lane, Sevenoaks, Kent TN13 3BD), *b* 1942: *m* 1970 (*m diss* 1984), Martin Moseling, and has issue living, Mark Christian *b* 1973, Emma Jane *b* 1972, — (by 2nd *m*) John Simon (171 Tuckers Rd, Loughborough, Leics LE11 2PH), *b* 1954: *m* 1981, Kathleen Susan Cornell, and has issue living, Robbie Dylan John *b* 1993.

Grandchildren of late Percy Fielding, 4th son of late George Fielding (*b* 1827), 2nd son of late Rev Charles Fielding, LLB, 3rd son of late Rev Allen Fielding (ante):—
Issue of late George Rudolph Fielding, *b* 1889, *d* 1969: *m* 1926, Marya Nagazina, who *d* 1973:—
Ernest Rudolf (439 Willowdale Crescent SE, Calgary, Alberta, Canada T2J 1K2), *b* 1927: *m* 1956, Audrey Madge, da of Alex Mackie, of Calgary, and has issue living, Douglas Ernest (204 Woodmont Court SW, Calgary, Alberta, Canada T2W 4X1), *b* 1957: *m* 1985, Mary Ann Dibulskis, and has issue living, Mark Antantas *b* 1989, — Grant Alexander, *b* 1964, — Karen Lea, *b* 1962. —— Rosa Alice, *b* 1926: *m* 1944, John Boyd, of Box 843, Rosedale, Alberta, Canada T0J 2V0, and has issue living, Bryan Alexander, *b* 1955, — Kathleen Anne, *b* 1945, — Gloria Jean, *b* 1947. —— Vera Mary, *b* 1929: *m* 1946, John Mackenzie Adamson, of 3213 19th Av SE, Calgary, Alberta, Canada T2B 0A4, and has issue living, Gary Wesley (50 Sandringham Way NW, Calgary, Alberta, Canada), *b* 1951: *m* 1986, Catherine Elizabeth Kirkham, — Carol Anne, *b* 1948: *m* 1968, Larry Alexander Jones, of 2815 Dover Ridge Drive SE, Calgary, Alberta, Canada T2B 2L2.

Granddaughters of late Sir Charles William Fielding, KBE, only son of late Thomas Mantell Fielding, 3rd son of late Rev Charles Fielding, LLB (ante):—
Issue of late Rudolph Burton Fielding, *b* 1902, *d* 1970: *m* 1939, Frances Adelaide, who *d* 1996, da of George Greene, of Dublin:—
Daphne Claire, *b* 1942; MA, MRCS, LRCP: *m* 1980, Timothy Hugh Drabble, and has had issue, Oliver John Fielding, *b* 1981; *d* 1994. *Residence* – Okehurst, Billingshurst, W Sussex RH14 9HS. —— Jean Eleanora Leckie, *b* 1946: *m* 1966, Terence Michael O'Flynn, and has issue living, Caspar Michael, *b* 1969, — Emma Frances, *b* 1966: *m* 1996, Logan Vijayaratnam. *Residence* – Wyneshore House, West Lavington, Devizes, Wilts SN10 4LW.

Grandson of late Rev George Hanbury Fielding, son of late Rev George Fielding, 4th son of late Rev Allen Fielding (ante):—
Issue of late Major George Rudolf Fielding, Sherwood Foresters (Notts and Derbyshire Regt), *b* 1881, *ka* 1915: *m* 1914, Evelyn Carlota, da of Edward Jewell, formerly of Clifton Court, Bournemouth:—
George Rudolf Hanbury, DSO, *b* 1915; *ed* Shrewsbury; Major (ret) 3rd King's Own Hussars; European War 1939-45; DSO 1945: *m* 1940, Beatrice Georgina, who *d* 1997, da of Maj Maurice Pope, and has issue living, Martin George Rudolf (East Hall Gate Cottage, Middleton Tyas, nr Richmond, N Yorks DL10 6RE) *b* 1945; *ed* Eton; Capt (ret) The Queen's Own Hussars; ARICS: *m* 1992, Mrs Erica Mackay Agace, yr da of late Acland Mackay Geddes, of Cuesta de la Villa, Tenerife, Canary Is, — Sarah Georgina (*Hon Mrs Guy B. Norrie*), *b* 1947: *m* 1968, Hon Guy Bainbridge Norrie, of Old Church Farm, Broughton, nr Stockbridge, Hants SO20 8AA (*see* B Norrie). *Address* – Grevire d'Amont, 1837 Château d'Oex, Vaud, Switzerland.

PREDECESSORS – (1) *Sir* WILLIAM Feilding, Knt, was *cr Baron Feilding*, of Newnham Paddox, Warwickshire, *Viscount Feilding* (peerage of England) 1620, and *Earl of Denbigh* (peerage of England) 1622; a faithful adherent of Charles I; killed in a skirmish near Birmingham 1643; his 2nd son Sir George, KB, was in 1622 *cr Baron Feilding*, of Lecaghe, *Viscount Callan* and *Earl of Desmond* (peerage of Ireland); *s* by his el son (2) BASIL, 2nd Earl, was one of the most eminent of the Parliament's Mil Commanders; *cr* after the restoration of the monarchy *Baron St Liz* 1663, with remainder to the male issue of his father; *dsp* 1675: *s* by his nephew (3) WILLIAM, 3rd Earl, who had in 1665 *s* his father George (ante) as 2nd Earl of Desmond; *d* 1685; *s* by his son (4) BASIL, 4th Earl; *d* 1717; *s* by his son (5) WILLIAM 5th Earl; *d* 1755; *s* by his son (6) BASIL, 6th Earl, *b* 1719: *m* 1957, Mary, who *d* 1782, 3rd da of Sir John Bruce Cotton, 6th Bt; *d* 1800; *s* by his grandson (7) WILLIAM BASIL PERCY, DCL (el son of William Robert Basil, Viscount Feilding, el son of 6th Earl), 7th Earl, *b* 1796; Master of the Horse to Queen Adelaide: *m* 1822, Mary Elizabeth Kitty, who *d* 1842, el da of 1st Earl of Ducie; *d* 1865; *s* by his son (8) RUDOLPH WILLIAM BASIL, 8th Earl, *b* 1823: *m* 1st, 1846, Louise, who *d* 1853, da of David Pennant, of Downing, Flint; 2ndly, 1857, Mary, who *d* 1901, da of Robert Berkeley; *d* 1892; *s* by his el son (9) RUDOLPH ROBERT BASIL ALOYSIUS AUGUSTINE, GCVO, 9th Earl, *b* 1859; Col TA (ret); a Lord-in-Waiting to HM Queen Victoria 1897-1901 and to HM King Edward VII 1901-1905: *m* 1st, 1884, the Hon Cecilia Mary Clifford, who *d* 1919, da of 8th Baron Clifford of Chudleigh; 2ndly, 1923, Kathleen, who *d* 1952, da of late Thomas Addis Emmet, of New York, USA; *d* 1939; *s* by his grandson (10) WILLIAM RUDOLPH STEPHEN (el son of late Lieut-Col Rudolph Edmund Aloysius, Viscount Feilding, CMG, DSO, el son of 9th Earl), 10th Earl of Denbigh and 9th Earl of Desmond, *b* 1912: *m* 1940, Verena Barbara, who *d* 1995, da of William Edward Price, and widow of Lt-Col Thomas Paget Fielding Johnson; *d* 1966; *s* by his only son (11) WILLIAM RUDOLPH MICHAEL, 11th Earl of Denbigh and 10th Earl of Desmond, *b* 1943: *m* 1965, Caroline Judith Vivienne, only da of Lt-Col Geoffrey Cooke, of Little Orchard, Sunningdale, Berks; *d* 1995; *s* by his only son (12) ALEXANDER STEPHEN RUDOLPH, 12th Earl of Denbigh and 11th Earl of Desmond and present peer; also Viscount Callan, Viscount Feilding, Baron Feilding, and Baron St Liz.

DENHAM, BARON (Bowyer) (Baron UK 1937, Bt England 1660 and UK 1933)

Contentment surpasses riches

BERTRAM STANLEY MITFORD BOWYER, KBE, PC, 2nd Baron, 10th Baronet of Denham, and 2nd Baronet of Weston Underwood; *b* 3 Oct 1927; *s* to the Barony and Baronetcy of Bowyer of Weston Underwood (*cr* 1933) 1948, and to the Baronetcy of Bowyer of Denham (*cr* 1660) 1950; *ed* Eton, and King's Coll, Camb; a Lord-in-Waiting to HM 1961-64, and again 1970-71; Capt Yeomen of the Guard and Dep Chief Whip House of Lords 1971-74; Opposition Dep Chief Whip 1974-78, and again 1978-79, Capt Gentlemen at Arms (Chief Whip) 1979-92; Countryside Commr 1993-99; Black Rod 1997; Extra Lord in Waiting since 1998; author of *The Man Who Lost His Shadow* (1979), *Two Thyrdes* (1983) and *Foxhunt* (1988); PC 1980, KBE (Civil) 1991: *m* 1956, Jean, only da of Kenneth McCorquodale, MC, TD, of Fambridge Hall, White Notley, Essex, and has issue.

Arms – Or, a bend vaire cottised sable. **Crest** – A falcon rising, belled or. **Supporters** – *Dexter*, a golden retriever; *sinister*, a black greyhound proper, each charged on the shoulder with portcullis or.
Residence – The Laundry Cottage, Weston Underwood, Olney, Bucks MK46 5JZ. *Clubs* – White's, Garrick, Pratt's.

SONS LIVING

Hon RICHARD GRENVILLE GEORGE, *b* 8 Feb 1959: *m* 1988, Eleanor, only da of A. Sharpe, of Truemans Heath, Worcs.
Hon Henry Martin Mitford, *b* 1963: *m* 1994, Barbara H., yr da of J. H. Strachan, of Ednaston, Derbys, and has issue living, Edmund Hunter Mitford, *b* 1997.
Hon George Philip Paul, *b* 1964.

DAUGHTER LIVING

Hon Jocelyn Jane, *b* 1957.

SISTER LIVING

Hon Peggy, *b* 1925: *m* 1947 Cdr John David Latimer Repard, OBE, DSC, RN, and has issue living, Jennifer Ann, *b* 1948: *m* 1970, Peter William Allen, of Chearsley, Bucks, and has issue living, William John Kenneth *b* 1974, John Peter Clarkson *b* 1977, — Susan Elisabeth, *b* 1950: *m* 1976, Richard G. Algeo, son of late Sir Arthur Algeo, CBE, and has issue living, Nicholas Arthur *b* 1978, Jonathon Henry *b* 1985, Lucy Catharine *b* 1978, — Melinda Louise, *b* 1955: *m* 1993, Gerald Stone. *Residence* – Bridleway Cottage, Leafy Lane, Tring, Herts HP23 6JS.

COLLATERAL BRANCHES LIVING (*In remainder to Baronetcy of Bowyer of Denham* (*cr* 1660) *only*)

Grandchildren of late Lt-Cdr John Francis Bowyer, CB, RN (infra):—
Issue of late Maj Hugh Edward Wentworth Bowyer, Rifle Bdle, *b* 1921, *d* 1985: *m* 1942, Suzette, who *d* 1995, da of Capt Peter Longton, of Heatherwold, Burghclere, Newbury:—
James David Ross (9 Fairview Gdns, Woodford Green, Essex G98 7DG), *b* 1949; *ed* Harrow: *m* 1993, Susan Rymond. — Sally Anne, *b* 1945: *m* 1967, Brig Robert Stewart Tailyour, RM, of Boxfield, 15 Knowle Rd, Budleigh Salterton, Devon EX9 6AR, and has issue living, Helen Caroline, *b* 1971: *m* 1999, Richard J. Brain, son of Howard Brain, of Aberdeenshire, — Georgina Anne, *b* 1977.

Grandson of late Lt-Col Wentworth Grenville Bowyer, 2nd son of late Rev William Henry Wentworth Atkins-Bowyer, 2nd son of late Maj William Atkins-Bowyer, el son of late Richard Atkins-Bowyer, 5th son of 3rd baronet of Denham:—
Issue of late Lt-Cdr John Francis Bowyer, CB, RN (Emergency List), *b* 1893, *d* 1974: *m* 1919, Violet, da of Maj-Gen George Robert James Shakespear, Indian Army, and widow of Maj Egerton Lowndes Wright, MC:—
John Robert Patrick, *b* 1924: *m* 1948, Diana, da of late J. P. Longland, of Olney, Bucks, and has issue living, David John Hugh (Plain Farmhouse, E Tisted, Alton, Hants), *b* 1950: *m* 1977, Sarah Helen, da of Arthur Henry Mann, of Bovey Tracey, Devon, and has issue living, Daisy Georgina Sarah *b* 1978, Alessandra Diana Helen *b* 1981, Rosanna Claire Vienna *b* 1984, — Sabrina Violet Jane, *b* 1948: *m* 1970, Frank Yeoman Smith, of Life Boat House, 1 Island St, Salcombe, Devon TQ8 8DP, and has issue living, Peter Alexander *b* 1975, Helen Elizabeth *b* 1978, — Sarah Joy (Lake House, Frome Hall Lane, Rodborough, Stroud, Glos GL5 3JH), *b* 1958: *m* 1982 (*m diss* 19—), Christopher Gino Spencer-Chapman, and has issue living, Stephen Frederick *b* 1985, Hazel Diana *b* 1987, — Diana Jane, *b* 1965: *m* 1986, Ross John McMullen, of PO Box 655, Airlie Beach, Queensland 4802, Australia, and has issue living, Daniel John *b* 1991, Joshua David *b* 1993, Jessica Diana *b* 1997.

PREDECESSORS – **(1)** GEORGE EDWARD WENTWORTH Bowyer, MC, son of late Lieut-Col Wentworth Grenville Bowyer, el son of late Rev William Henry Wentworth Atkins-Bowyer, great-grandson of 3rd Bt of Denham (*cr* 1660); *b* 1886; Major late Oxfordshire and Bucks LI; Parliamentary Private Sec (unpaid) to Pres of Board of Trade 1921-24; Conservative Party Whip in House of Commons 1925-35, Vice-Chm Conservative and Unionist Party Organization 1930-36, a Junior Lord of the Treasury 1926-29, Comptroller of HM's Household June to Dec 1935, and Parliamentary Sec to Min of Agriculture and Fisheries 1939-40; a Conservative Whip in House of Lords 1945-47; European War 1914-18 (wounded, despatches, MC); sat as MP for Buckingham Div of Buckinghamshire (*U*) 1918-37; *cr* a Knt 1929, a *Baronet* 1933, and *Baron Denham* of Weston Underwood, co Buckingham (peerage of United Kingdom) 1937: *m* 1919, Hon Daphne Freeman-Mitford, who *d* 1996, aged 100, da of 1st Baron Redesdale; *d* 1948; *s* by his son **(2)** BERTRAM STANLEY MITFORD, 2nd Baron and present peer.

*(1) Sir WILLIAM Bowyer, el son of Sir Henry Bowyer, of Denham Court, Bucks; *b* 1612; MP for Bucks 1659-60, and 1661-79 (Sheriff 1646-47); *cr* a Baronet 1660: *m* 1634, Margaret, who *d* 1678, da of John Weld, of Arnolds, Edmonton, Middlesex; *d* 1679; *s* by his el son **(2)** WILLIAM, 2nd Bt; *b* 1639: *m* 1679, Hon Frances, who *d* 1723, da of Charles Cecil, Viscount Cranborne, son of 2nd Earl of Salisbury; *d* 1722; *s* by his grandson **(3)** WILLIAM (el son of late Cecil Bowyer, el son of 2nd Bt), 3rd Bt; *b* 1710: *m* 1733, Anne who *d* 1785, da of Rt Hon Sir John Stonehouse, MP, 7th and 4th Bt of Radley, Berks; *d* 1767; *s* by his el son **(4)** WILLIAM 4th Bt, *b* 1736; Capt The Guards: *m* 1776, Anne, who *d* 1802, da of — Carey, and widow of Capt James Baker, RN; *d* 1799; *s* by his brother **(5)** GEORGE, 5th Bt, *b* 1739; Adm; MP for Queenborough 1784-90; distinguished himself in Lord Howe's naval victory over the French, 1 June 1794, for which he was rewarded with an annual pension of £1,000, and was *cr* a *Baronet* 1794 (of Radley, Berks): *m* 1st, 1768, Margaret, who *d* 1778, da of Rev — Price, curate of Barrington, Gloucestershire, and widow of Sir Jacob Garrard Downing, 4th Bt; 2ndly, 1782, Henrietta, who *d* 1845, da of Adm Sir Piercy Brett, of Beckenham, Kent; *d* 1799; *s* by his el son **(6)** GEORGE, 6th Bt, *b* 1783; MP for Malmesbury 1807-10, and for Abingdon 1811-18: *m* 1808, Anne Hammond, who *d* 1844, da of Capt Sir Andrew Snape Douglas, RN; *d* 1860; *s* by his el son **(7)** GEORGE, 7th Bt, *b* 1811; MP (*L*) for Dundalk 1852-68, and for Wexford 1874-80; *d* 1883; *s* by his brother **(8)** WILLIAM, 8th Bt, *b* 1812: *m* 1857, Ellen Sarah, who *d* 1899, da of Shirley Foster Woolmer, Bar-at-law; *d* 1893; *s* by his nephew **(9)** GEORGE HENRY (only son of late Henry George Bowyer, yst son of 6th Bt), 9th Bt; *b* 1870; Lieut Cheshire Mil: *m* 1899 (*m diss* 1900), Ethel, da of Francis Hawkins; *d* 1950; *s* by his kinsman **(10)** BERTRAM STANLEY MITFORD (ante).

Denison, family name of Baron Londesborough.

DENMAN, BARON (Denman) (Baron UK 1834, Bt UK 1945)

CHARLES SPENCER DENMAN, CBE, MC, 5th Baron, and 2nd Baronet (of Staffield, co Cumberland); *b* 7 July 1916; *s* as 2nd Bt 1957, and as 5th Baron, 1971; *ed* Shrewsbury; late Maj DCLI (TA); 1939-45 War in Middle East (MC); CBE (Civil) 1976; Chm Arundell House Securities, Dir Close Bros, and Marine and Gen Mutual Life Assurance; Vice Pres of Middle East Assoc, Member Cttee of Middle East Trade, and of British Invisible Export Council: *m* 1943, Sheila Anne, who *d* 1987, da of late Lt-Col Algernon Bingham Anstruther Stewart, DSC (*see* E Galloway, colls), and has issue.

Arms – Argent, on a chevron between three lions' heads erased gules, as many ermine spots or. **Crest** – A raven rising proper, in the beak an annulet or. **Supporters** – On either side a lion gules, charged on the body with five ermine spots in cross or.
Address – c/o House of Lords. *Club* – Brooks's.

SONS LIVING

Hon RICHARD THOMAS STEWART, *b* 4 Oct 1946; *ed* Milton Abbey: *m* 1984, (Lesley) Jane, da of John Stevens, of 2 Shakespeare Drive, Hinckley, Leics, and has issue living, a son, *b* 19 Dec 1995, — Natasha Anne, *b* 1986, — Philippa Jane, *b* 1987, — Louisa Clare, *b* 1993. *Club* – Brooks's.

Hon James Stewart, *b* 1954; *ed* Stowe: *m* 1989, Philippa Jane Emma, da of late Lewis Ronald Frederick Trowbridge, of Falfield, Winchester, Hants, and has issue living, Olivia Anne Stewart, *b* 1992. *Residence* – 14 Prairie St, SW8 3PU.

Hon (Christopher) John, *b* 1955; *ed* Millfield: *m* 1984, Jenny Bridget, MVO, only da of Rupert Allen, of Head Hedgeside, Headley, Hampshire, and has issue living, Nicholas Thomas Stewart, *b* 1988, — Charles Rupert Pendarves, *b* 1990, — Thomas Oliver Pelham, *b* 1993. *Residence* – Hurston Street Farm, Hurston Lane, Storrington, W Sussex RH20 4HF.

DAUGHTER LIVING

Hon Gillian Patricia, *b* 1944: *m* 1971, William K. McCall, of Upper Old Park Farm, Farnham, Surrey, and has issue (*see* Laurie, Bt, colls).

BROTHERS LIVING

Harold (East Heath Barn, Stream Lane, Hawkhurst, Kent TN18 4RD), *b* 1922; *ed* Repton, and Balliol Coll, Oxford (BA); 1939-45 War with RA: *m* 1976, Lady Frances Esmé Curzon, da of 5th Earl Howe, and formerly wife of Derek Alan Whiting, and has issue living, Roland Sebastian Richard, *b* 1977.

George (Stratton House, Stoney Stratton, Shepton Mallet, Somerset BA4 6EA), *b* 1925; 1939-45 War with Border Regt: *m* 1960, Linda Louisa, yr da of David Fortune Landale, of Dalswinton, Dumfries, and has issue living, Louisa Anne, *b* 1961, — Carola Jane (*Lady Campbell*), *b* 1963: *m* 1993, Sir James Alexander Moffat Bain Campbell, 9th Bt, — Davina, *b* 1968.

SISTERS LIVING

Phyllis (Penberth, 41 Oakfield Rd, Ashtead, Surrey KT21 2RD), *b* 1919; MRCS England and LRCP London.

Catherine (Cherwell House, Old Kidlington, Oxford OX5 2EG), *b* 1920: *m* 1957, Philip Musgrave Cowburn, who *d* 1989, and has issue living, Stephen Denman, *b* 1959, — Anne Clare, *b* 1962: *m* 1986, Ieuan D. Hemlock.

COLLATERAL BRANCHES LIVING

(*Not in remainder to the Baronetcy*)

Grandchildren of late Sir Arthur Denman, 2nd son of late Rt Hon George Denman, 4th son of 1st Baron:—
Issue of late Lieut-Col Roderick Peter George Denman, Roy Corps of Signals, *b* 1894, *ka* 1941: *m* 1922, Charlotte Marie Mathilde, MBE, who *d* 1980, da of late Baron Raphael d'Erlanger (*see* Blennerhassett, Bt, 1963 Edn):—
Peter Frederick Arthur, *b* 1923; *ed* Eton, and Trin Coll, Camb (BA 19—): *m* 1957, Cornelia Rowena (JANSON), da of late Hon (Oscar) Montague Guest (*see* V Wimborne, colls), and has issue living, Philip, *b* 1961, — Benedict Raphael, *b* 1970, — Francesca Marie-Carola, *b* 1959. *Residence* – Duke's House, 23 Lawrence St, SW3. ——— Carol Antonia Rosaline, *b* 1928.

Issue of late Henry du Bourg Denman, *b* 1918, *d* 1938: *m* 1936, (Evelyn) Joy (who *d* 1998, having *m* 2ndly, 1947, William Herbert Hooper, barrister-at-law, who *d* 1974, of 75 Mill Lane, Herne Bay, Kent), da of late George Henry Hatton:—
Carol Julian du Bourg (son), *b* 1938. *Residence* – 70 Fiddlers Folly, Fordham Heath, Colchester, Essex.

Grandchildren of late Lewis William Eden Denman, son of late Rev Hon Lewis William Denman, 5th son of 1st Baron:—
Issue of late Joseph Alban Denman, *b* 1890, *d* 1965: *m* 1919, Annie Mary, who *d* 1954, da of Thomas Spicer, of Sask, Canada:—
George Lewis (c/o Mrs Robert Honeyman, RR2, Enderby, BC, Canada VOE 1V0), *b* 1920: *m* 1st, 1949, Emily Woodgate who *d* 1956; 2ndly, 1963, Catherine Woodgate, da of W. A. C. Batchelor, of Water Valley, Alberta, and has issue living, (by 1st *m*) Robert John, *b* 1952, — Ronald Dean, *b* 1954, — Dorothy Louisa, *b* 1951: *m* 1971, Robert Honeyman. ——— David Keith (7392 Giscome Rd, Prince George, BC, Canada V2N 6V1), *b* 1937: *m* 1957, Helen Balko, and has issue living, Stephen Lawrence (1817 Bachinski Crescent, Prince George, BC, Canada), *b* 1961: *m* 1994, Cora-Terry Miksch, and has issue living, David William *b* 1994, Kimberly Marie *b* 1996, — Stacey Eldon (1575 Steele Drive, Prince George, BC, Canada), *b* 1968: *m* 1990, Barbara Lynne Sarauer, and has issue living, Brittany Christine *b* 1990, Dayna Katelyn *b* 1993, — Shawn Lewis Eden (5430 Lehman, Prince George, BC, Canada), *b* 1973, — Debra Ann (838 Douglas, Prince George, BC, Canada), *b* 1958, — Denise Josephine, *b* 1965: *m* 1991, Paul Bernard Bergeron, of 2408 Lindsay Place, Prince George, BC, Canada, and has issue living, Brenden David *b* 1994, Kaitlynd Ellayne *b* 1997. ——— Joan Gwendoline, *b* 1925: *m* 1959, Maurice J. Parfitt, and has issue living, Dennis Lee, *b* 1946: *m* 1966, Lynn Stoddard, and has issue living, Michelle Lee *b* 1970: *m* 1991, Jacques Pelletier (and has issue living, Brandon Dennis Rudolphe *b* 1993), — Sydney Robert, *b* 1947: *m* 1969, Susan Strom, and has issue living, Rachael Andrea *b* 1971, Kirsten Jane *b* 1973, — Lee Roy, *b* 1949, — Gordon Douglas, *b* 1952: *m* 1973, Brenda Erickson, and has issue living, Spencer James *b* 1976, Amy Olan *b* 1978. *Residence* – RR#8, Site 5, Comp 3A9, Prince George, BC, Canada V2N 4M6.

PREDECESSORS – (1) *Sir* THOMAS Denman, *b* 1779; MP for Nottingham, Attorney-Gen 1830-2 and Lord Ch Justice of England 1832-50; *cr Baron Denman*, of Dovedale (peerage of United Kingdom) 1834: *m* 1804, Theodosia Anne, da of late Rev Richard Vevers, Rector of Saxby; *d* 1854; *s* by his son (2) THOMAS, 2nd Baron, *b* 1805; Bar Lincoln's Inn 1833; Marshal and Associate to his father 1832-50; assumed by Roy licence 1876 the additional surname of Aitchison: *m* 1st, 1829, Georgiana, who *d* 1871, el da of late Rev Thomas Roe; 2ndly, 1871, Marion, who *d* 1902, el da and coheiress of James Aitchison, of Alderston and Morham, NB; *d* 1894; *s* by his great nephew (3) THOMAS, GCMG, KCVO, PC (el son of late Richard Denman, grandson of 1st Baron), 3rd Baron; *b* 1874; was a Lord-in-Waiting to King Edward VII 1905-7, Capt of HM's Hon Corps of Gentlemen-at-Arms 1907-11, Dep Speaker in House of Lords, 1909, and Gov-Gen of Commonwealth of Australia 1911-14: *m* 1903, Hon *Dame* Gertrude Mary Pearson, GBE, who *d* 1954, da of 1st Viscount Cowdray; *d* 1954; *s* by his only son (4) THOMAS, 4th Baron; *b* 1905; *d* 1971; *s* by his cousin (5) CHARLES SPENCER (el son of the Hon Sir Richard Douglas Denman, who was *cr* a *Baronet* (UK) 1945), 5th Baron, and present peer.

DENNING, BARONY OF (Denning) (Extinct 1999)

Hon Robert Gordon, *b* 1938; *ed* Winchester, and Magdalen Coll, Oxford (Fellow 1968): *m* 1967, Elizabeth Carlyle Margaret, da of E. R. Chilton, of Oxford, and has issue.

DENTON OF WAKEFIELD, BARONESS (Denton) (Life Baroness 1991)

JEAN DENTON, CBE, da of Charles Moss, of Wakefield, W Yorks; *b* 29 Dec 1935; *ed* Rothwell Gram Sch, and LSE (BSc); Information Exec BBC News Div (Home and Overseas) 1958, Communications Exec Proctor & Gamble 1959-61, Marketing Consultant and Assist Ed Retail Business Economist Intelligence Unit 1961-64, Women's Magazine Div IPC 1964-66, Hotel and Catering Dept Surrey Univ 1966-68, Professional Racing and Rally Driver 1968-71; Marketing Dir Huxford Group 1971-78, Heron Motor Group 1978-80, Man Dir Herondrive 1980-85 (voted Female Exec of the Year 1983); Dir External Affairs Austin Rover Group 1985-86, Dir Burson-Marsteller since 1986, Dep Chm Black Country Development Corpn since 1987; Board Member British Nuclear Fuels plc, Triplex Lloyd plc, London & Edinburgh Insurance Group, and Think Green 1988-91; Member Interim Advisory Cttee on Teachers Pay and Conditions, The Engineering Council, The Royal Soc of Arts Council, and School Teachers Review Body since 1991; Board Member North West TV since 1991; Chm FORUM UK, Women on the Move Against Cancer, and formerly Chm Marketing Group of GB; Member of Worshipful Co of Marketors, Freeman City of London 1982; Baroness in Waiting 1991-92; Under-Sec of State, Dept of Trade and Industry 1992-94, Under-Sec N Ireland Office 1994-97; FCInstM 1972, FIMI 1974, FRSA 1987, CBIM 1988; *cr* CBE (Civil) 1990, and *Baroness Denton of Wakefield*, of Wakefield, co W Yorks (Life Baroness) 1991: *m* 19—, — Denton.

Clubs – Reform, British Women Racing Drivers.

DERAMORE, BARON (de Yarburgh-Bateson) (Baron UK 1885, Bt UK 1818)

We fly by night

RICHARD ARTHUR DE YARBURGH-BATESON, 6th Baron, and 7th Baronet; *b* 9 April 1911; *s* 1964; *ed* Harrow, and at St John's Coll, Camb (MA); 1939-45 War as Fl-Lt RAFVR; ARIBA; *m* 1948, Janet Mary (served 1939-45 War as 3rd Officer WRNS), da of late John Ware, MD, of Nether Close, Askam-in-Furness, and has issue.

᎓rms – Quarterly, 1st and 4th grand quarters, 1st and 4th argent, three bats' wings erect sable, on a chief gules, a lion passant or, *Bateson*; 2nd and 3rd per pale argent and azure, a chevron between three chaplets counter-changed, *de Yarburgh*, 2nd and 3rd grand quarters, argent three lions dormant in pale sable between two flaunches of the last, each charged with three mullets palewise of the first, *Lloyd*. ᒪrests – 1st, a bat's wing as in the arms; 2nd, a falcon close or, belled gold, preying on a mallard proper. ᒪupporters – Two lions or, each gorged wth a collar gemel gules, and pendant therefrom an escutcheon ermine, that on the dexter charged with a bat's wing as in the arms, and that on the sinister wth a raven proper. ᖲirst ᒪotto – "Nocte volamus" (*We fly by night*). ᒪecond ᒪotto – "Non est sine pulvere palma" (*The prize is not won without dust*).
Residence – Heslington House, Aislaby, Pickering, Yorks. *Clubs* – RAF and RAC

DAUGHTER LIVING

Hon Ann Katharine, *b* 1950: *m* 1982, Jonathan Henry Maconchy Peel, elder son of Walter Peel, of Knockdromin, Lusk, co Dublin (*see* Rugge-Price, Bt, colls, 1969 Edn), and has issue living, Nicholas Richard Yarburgh, *b* 1987, — Katharine Diana, *b* 1985. *Residence* – Sturdy Cottage, High Street, Thornborough, Bucks.

PREDECESSORS – **(1)** ROBERT BATESON; MP for Londonderry (C) 1830-42; *cr* a *Baronet* 1818; *b* 1782: *m* 1811, Catherine, da of late Samuel Dickson, of Ballynaguile, Limerick; *d* 1863; *s* by his son **(2)** *Sir* THOMAS, 2nd Bt, who was *cr Baron Deramore*, of Belvoir, co Down (peerage of United Kingdom) 1885, with remainder to his younger brother, George William Bateson de Yarburgh; *b* 1819; sat as MP for Londonderry (C) 1844-57, and for Devizes 1864-85; a Lord of the Treasury 1852: *m* 1849, Hon Caroline Elizabeth Anne Rice-Trevor, who *d* 1887, da of 4th Baron Dinevor; *d* 1890; *s* by his brother **(3)** GEORGE WILLIAM, 2nd Baron; *b* 1823; assumed by Roy Licence 1876, the additional surname of de Yarburgh, and in 1892 the surname of Bateson after, instead of before, that of de Yarburgh: *m* 1862, Mary Elizabeth, who *d* 1884, da of George John Yarburgh, of Heslington Hall, York; *d* 1893; *s* by his el son **(4)** ROBERT WILFRID, TD, 3rd Baron; *b* 1865; Lord-Lieut for E Riding of Yorkshire, and Lieut-Col late Yorkshire Hussars Yeo: *m* 1st, 1897, Lucy Caroline, who *d* 1901, da of late William Henry Fife, of Lee Hall, Northumberland; 2ndly, 1907, Blanche Violet, who *d* 1972, el da of Col Philips Saltmarshe, formerly RA, of Saltmarshe, East Yorkshire; *d* 1936; *s* by his brother **(5)** GEORGE NICHOLAS, 4th Baron: *b* 1870; *m* 1900, Muriel Katharine, who *d* 1960, da of late Arthur Grey; *d* 1943, *s* by his el son **(6)** STEPHEN NICHOLAS, 5th Baron, *b* 1903: *m* 1929, Nina Marion, OBE, who *d* 1979, da of late Alastair Macpherson-Grant; *d* 1964, *s* by his brother **(7)** RICHARD ARTHUR, 6th Baron and present peer.

DE RAMSEY, BARON (Fellowes) (Baron UK 1887)

Patience and perseverance with magnanimity

JOHN AILWYN FELLOWES, 4th Baron; *b* 27 Feb 1942; *s* 1993; *ed* Winchester; patron of four livings; DL Cambs 1993; Pres Country Landowners' Assocn 1991-93 Crown Estate Commr since 1994; Pres Assocn Drainage Authorities 1992-94; Chm Environment Agency 1995-2000: *m* 1st, 1973 (*m diss* 1983), Phyllida Mary, yr da of Philip Athelstan Forsyth, MRCS, LRCP, of The Poplars, Wickhambrook, Suffolk; 2ndly, 1984, Alison Mary, elder da of Sir Archibald Birkmyre, 3rd Bt, and has issue by 1st and 2nd *m*.

Arms – Azure, a fesse dancettée ermine between three lions' heads erased or, murally crowned argent. **Crest** – A lion's head as in the arms, charged with a fesse dancettée ermine. **Supporters** – On either side a ram proper gorged with a chain or, pendant therefrom and escutcheon ermine charged with a ram's eye also proper. *Seat* – Abbots Ripton Hall, Huntingdon, Cambs.

SONS LIVING (*By 1st marriage*)

Hon FREDDIE JOHN, *b* 31 May 1978; *ed* Eton.

(*By 2nd marriage*)

Hon Charles Henry, *b* 1986.

DAUGHTERS LIVING (*By 2nd marriage*)

Hon Daisy Lilah, *b* 1988.
Hon Flora Mary, *b* 1991.

BROTHER LIVING

Hon Andrew Edward (36 Charolais Crescent, Benowa, Qld 4217, Australia), *b* 1950: *m* 1974, Anne Mary, da of Roy Tweedy, of Mungle, North Star, NSW, and has issue living, Robert Andrew, *b* 1978, — Katherine Jane, *b* 1976, — Rachael Julie, *b* 1982.

SISTERS LIVING

Hon Sarah, *b* 1938: *m* 1972, Peter Shelton, of Le Castel de Perillac, 81140 Penne, Tarn, France, and has issue living, David, *b* 1977, — Fay, *b* 1973.
Hon Jennifer Julia FELLOWES (Hall Farm, Abbots Ripton, Huntingdon), *b* 1940; has resumed her maiden name: *m* 1964 (*m diss* 1986), John Frederick Moxon, and has issue living, Simon John, *b* 1965, — Matthew Sebastian, *b* 1967, — Christian Frederick, *b* 1974, — Alice Lavinia, *b* 1966: *m* 1989, Anthony Cripps, of Hatfield House, 4 MacBride Av, Huntershill, Sydney, NSW 2110, Australia, and has issue living, William John *b* 1990, Henry Anthony *b* 1992, Charlie Frederick *b* 1996, Daisy Jennifer Elizabeth *b* 1997, — Emily Faith Martha, *b* 1972.

WIDOW LIVING OF HALF-BROTHER OF THIRD BARON

Mervyn, da of late Reinold de Toll, and formerly wife of Peter Sherwood: *m* 1977, as his 3rd wife, Hon John David Coulson Fellowes, who *d* 1998, having been raised to the rank of a Baron's son 1933. *Residence* – Flat 3, 117 Elgin Crescent, W11.

COLLATERAL BRANCH LIVING

Issue of late Hon John David Coulson Fellowes, half-brother of 3rd Baron, who was raised to the rank of a Baron's son 1933, *b* 1915, *d* 1998: *m* 1st, 1946 (*m diss* 1962), Mrs Louise Mackay, who *d* 1975, yr da of Lt James Henry Domville, 5th Bt, RN, and formerly wife of Leslie Alexander Mackay; 2ndly, 1963, Mrs Joan Lynette Neame, who *d* 1965, only da of Edgar G. Rees of Llanelli, S Wales, and formerly wife of Richard Dewar Neame; 3rdly, 1977, Mrs Mervyn Sherwood (ante), da of late Reinold de Toll, and formerly wife of Peter Sherwood:—

(By 1st *m*) Peter Reginald (134 Belsize Rd, NW6), *b* 1948; *ed* privately: *m* 1980, Alison Elizabeth, 2nd da of Dr John Vance, of 1973 Rivermead Court, SW6, and has issue living, Charles Oliver Vance, *b* 1983, — Daisy Louise, *b* 1984. —— Jacqueline Denise, *b* 1955: *m* 1982, Michael Humfrey.

PREDECESSORS – (1) EDWARD Fellowes, *b* 1809; MP for Huntingdonshire (C) 1837-80; *cr Baron De Ramsey*, of Ramsey Abbey, Huntingdon (peerage of United Kingdom), 5 July 1887: *m* 1845, Hon Mary Julia Milles, el da of 4th Baron Sondes; *d* 9 Aug 1887; *s* by his el son (2) WILLIAM HENRY, 2nd Baron, *b* 1848; MP for Huntingdonshire (C) 1880-85, and for N, or Ramsey, Div of Huntingdonshire 1885-7; a Lord-in-Waiting to Queen Victoria 1890-92: *m* 1877, Lady Rosamond Jane Frances Spencer-Churchill, who *d* 1920, da of 7th Duke of Marlborough, KG; *d* 1925; *s* by his grandson (3) AILWYN EDWARD, KBE (son of late Capt Hon Coulson Churchill Fellowes, 1st Life Guards, el son of 2nd Baron), 3rd Baron, *b* 1910; Capt RA (TA), served 1939-45 War (prisoner), Lord-Lieut Hunts 1947-65, and Huntingdon and Peterborough 1965-68: *m* 1937, Lilah Helen Suzanne, who *d* 1987, da of late Francis Anthony Labouchere (*see* Stirling, Bt, *cr* 1800 (ext), 1940 Edn); *d* 1993; *s* by his elder son (4) JOHN AILWYN, 4th Baron and present peer.

DERBY, EARL OF (Stanley) (Earl E 1485, Bt E 1627)

Without changing

EDWARD RICHARD WILLIAM STANLEY, 19th Earl, and 13th Baronet; *b* 10 Oct 1962; *s* 1994; *ed* Eton, and RAC Cirencester; DL Merseyside 1999; commn'd Gren Gds 1982, ret 1985; Merchant Banker, Fleming Private Asset Management Ltd: *m* 1995, Hon Caroline Emma Neville, 2nd da of 10th Baron Braybrooke, and has issue.

Arms – Argent, on a bend azure, three bucks' heads, cabossed or. **Crest** – On a chapeau gules, turned up ermine, an eagle wings extended, or, preying on a child proper, swaddled gules, in a cradle laced or. **Supporters** – *Dexter*, a griffin, wings elevated, or, ducally collared, and line reflexed over the back azure; *sinister* a stag, or, collared and lined as the dexter. *Seat* – Knowsley, Prescot, Merseyside L34 4AF.

SON LIVING

EDWARD JOHN ROBIN (*Lord Stanley of Bickerstaffe*), *b* 21 April 1998.

DAUGHTER LIVING

Lady Henrietta Mary Rose, *b* 1997.

BROTHER LIVING (*Raised to the rank of an Earl's son* 1995)

Hon Peter Hugh Charles, *b* 1964; *ed* Eton: *m* 1990, Hon Frances Caroline Burke Roche, only da of 5th Baron Fermoy, and has issue living, (Richard) Hugh Edward, *b* 1993, — Algernon Edmund, *b* 1999, — (Portia Ruth) Isobel, *b* 1995. *Residence* – New England Stud, Newmarket, Suffolk CB8 OXA.

WIDOW LIVING OF GRANDSON OF SEVENTEENTH EARL

Mary, da of late Maj Vyvian Alfred Tylor, MC, of Sussex, formerly wife of W/Cdr P. H. M. Richey, DFC, and widow of William Herbert Harrison: *m* 1979, as his 2nd wife, Capt Hon Richard Oliver Stanley, who *d* 1983. *Residence* – Barn House, Ledwell, Chipping Norton, Oxon OX7 7AN.

MOTHER LIVING

Mary Rose, 2nd da of late Charles Francis Birch, of Rhodesia: *m* 1st, 1961, Hon Hugh Henry Montagu Stanley, who *d* 1971, 3rd son of late Rt Hon Edward Montagu Cavendish (*Lord Stanley*), MC; 2ndly, 1973, (Anthony) William Assheton Spiegelberg (DL Cheshire 1995). *Residence* – Oulton Park House, Tarporley, Cheshire CW6 9BL.

COLLATERAL BRANCHES LIVING

Grandsons of late Rt Hon Oliver Frederick George Stanley, MC, MP (infra):—
Issue of late Capt Michael Charles Stanley, MBE, b 1921, d 1990: m 1951, (Aileen) Fortune (Constance Hugh) (Halecat, Witherslack, Grange-over-Sands, Cumbria LA11 6RU), elder da of late Owen Hugh Smith, of Old Hall, Langham, Oakham, Rutland (yr brother of 1st Baron Bicester):—
Oliver Hugh, b 1952; ed Eton and — Coll Camb (MA, MD): m 1982, Bernadette, da of John McMullen, of Middlesbrough, and has issue living, John Michael, b 1982, — Aidan, b 1986, — Naomi Isabel, b 1989. —— Nicholas Charles, b 1954; ed Eton, and Univ Coll, Durham: m 1st, 1986 (m diss 1999), Sarah Louise Gilroy, only da of George Henry Gilroy Williams, of Warwick Rd, Maperley Park, Nottingham; 2ndly, 1999, Charlotte, da of Derek Willard, of Glebe House, Rue de l'Eglise, Bernieulles, Pas-de-Calais, France 62170, and has issue living (by 1st m), Thomas Michael Henry, b 1990, — Jack William Oliver, b 1993.

Issue of late Rt Hon Oliver Frederick George Stanley, MC, MP, 2nd son of 17th Earl, b 1896, d 1950: m 1920, Lady Maureen Helena Vane-Tempest-Stewart, who d 1942, da of 7th Marquess of Londonderry:—
Kathryn Edith Helen (Lady Dugdale), DCVO, b 1923; JP Shropshire 1964, DL 1995; a Woman of the Bedchamber (temporary) to HM the Queen 1955-60, Extra Woman of the Bedchamber 1960-72, Woman of the Bedchamber 1972-85; Cdr of Royal Order of North Star of Sweden 1956; 1939-45 in WRNS; CVO 1973; DCVO 1984: m 1956, Sir John Robert Stratford Dugdale, KCVO, who d 1994 (see Dugdale, Bt, cr 1936). Residence – Tickwood Hall, Much Wenlock, Shropshire.

Grandchildren of late Brig-Gen Hon Ferdinand Charles Stanley, CMG, DSO, 5th son of 16th Earl:—
Issue of late Col Frederick Arthur Stanley, OBE, TD, Cameron Highlanders (TA), b 1905, d 1978: m 1932, Ann Jane, who d 1997, only da of late Col Williams Fellowes Collins, DSO (D Roxburghe):—
Peter Henry Arthur (Cundall Hall, Helperby, York; White's Club); late 2nd Lt Gren Gds, b 1933; ed Eton: m 1st, 1965 (m diss 1985), Countess Gunilla Margaretha Antonia Sophie Douglas, da of Count Wilhelm Douglas, of Schloss Langenstein, Baden, Germany; 2ndly, 1990 (m diss 1992), Mrs Lucy Barnett Campbell, da of James A. Barnett, of Bel Air, Calif, USA, and formerly wife of (i) Clifford Smith, Jr, and (ii) Colin Guy Napier Campbell (see Campbell, Bt, cr 1815, colls); 3rdly, 1999, Hon Mrs Caroline Mary Parr, eldest da of Baron Renton, KBE, TD, PC, QC (Life Baron), and formerly wife of (i) Peter Dodds Parker, and (ii) Robin Warwick Antony Parr, and has issue living (by 1st m), Robin James Axel, b 1968, — Louisa Charlotte Ann, b 1966. —— Sarah, b 1935: m 1962, Simon Hawkshaw Creswell, of Markers, Cattistock, Dorset DT2 0JH, and has issue living, Alexander John Peter, b 1965: m 1995, Catharine Louise, da of Dr Alexander Reid, of Notting Hill Gate, W8, and of Mrs Sandy Milne, of Piddlehinton, Dorset, and has issue living, Jocelyn Arthur b 1999, — Miranda Ann Louise, b 1963: m 1994, Rory D. A. Carnegie, of 5 Longworth Rd, Oxford, and has issue living, Sholto Hector Hawkeshaw b 1995, Lorcan Fred Andrew b 1997, Cloudy Ann Hardy b 1993, — Sophia Alice Chrystal, b 1969.

Issue of late Col Hon Algernon Francis Stanley, DSO, 7th son of 16th Earl, b 1874, d 1962: m 1918, Lady Mary Cavendish Grosvenor, who d 1959, da of 1st Duke of Westminster, and widow of Viscount Crichton, MVO, DSO (E Erne):—
Constance Mary, b 1919: m 1946, Malcolm Weaver, Lieut US Army, and has issue living, Mark Marion, b 1960, — Mary Constance, b 1954: m 1978, Thomas Milton Crain, and has issue living, Allison Mary b 1982.

Grandchildren of late Lt-Col Hon (Frederick) William Stanley, DSO, 8th son of 16th Earl:—
Issue of late Maj David William Stanley, b 1906, d 1997: m 1937, Marjorie (Himeville, Natal, S Africa), only da of late Douglas Knox Homan, Indian Police:—
William Douglas (PO Box 318, Hilton, 3245, S Africa), b 1938; ed St Andrew's Coll, Grahamstown, and Trin Coll, Camb (BA): m 1963, Sally Avory, eldest da of late Stanley Harold Read, of Johannesburg, and has issue living, David Andrew, b 1964: m 1995, Nicole, da of Ross Bush, of Christchurch, NZ, and has issue living, Daniel b 1996, — Clare Alexandra, b 1967, — Nicola Avory, b 1969, — Fiona Anne, b 1972. Residence – 4 Cuckoo Lane, Winterskloof, Natal, S Africa. —— Patrick (Belstone Cottage, Badgworth, Som), b 1943; ed St Andrew's Coll, Grahamstown, and Trin Coll, Camb (BA): m 1968, (Margaret) Jane, eldest da of Denis Evers, of Four Winds, Wolverley, Kidderminster, and has issue living, Andrew, b 1969, — Deborah, b 1971, — Clare Rebecca, b 1973. —— Caroline Alexandra, b 1940: m 1968, Nigel Norman Proddow, of 27 Hertford Av, SW14 8EF, and has issue living, Charles William Nigel, b 1969, — Guy Edward Stanley, b 1971.

Grandchildren of late Charles Henry Stanley, DSM, elder son of Capt Charles Geoffrey Stanley, 2nd son of Hon Henry Thomas Stanley, MP, 2nd son of 13th Earl:—
Issue of late Very Rev Charles Geoffrey Nason Stanley, b 1884, d 1977: m 1st, 1914, Eileen Chapman, who d 1928; 2ndly, 1931, Violet Claire Baldwin (Glendonagh House, Dungourney, Midleton, co Cork):—
(By 1st m) †Rev Eric William (Cuanbeg, Ballycotton, co Cork), b 1922; ed Trin Coll, Dublin (MA): m 1949, Phoebe Elizabeth Mary Pollard, and d 1998, leaving issue, Joy, b 1950, — Katherine, b 1953. —— (By 2nd m) Rev Arthur Patrick (2081 S Av, Stanton, Iowa 51573, USA), b 1932; ed Trin Coll, Dublin (MA); late Chap to the Forces: m 1st, 1958, Kathleen Marjorie Ethel, who d 1981, da of Harold Victor Earl, of Waterford; 2ndly, 1983, Jessie Ernestine Fisher, née Tombleson, and has issue living (by 1st m), Stephen Patrick, b 1961, — Belinda Susan, b 1959. —— Sylvia Penelope, b 1936: m 1956, Rev William George Stanley Spence, MSc, of RR2, Box 20, 2494 Parker Rd, Nanoose Bay, BC V0R 2R0, Canada, and has issue living, Peter Edward, b 1959, — Janet, b 1962. —— Hazel Claire: m 1963, Richard John Armstrong (Dr Phil), of Nedre Markveg 1, Tromsø, Norway, and has issue living, Geoffrey James, b 1966, Charloo Ivan, b 1969, — Niall John, b 1974, — Claire Winifred, b 1964.

Issue of late Frederick George Stanley, b 1888, d 1979: m 1931, Grace Evelyn Thrower, who d 1988:—
Helen Audrey, b 1936: m 1966, George Watts, of 12 Greenways, Abbots Langley, Watford.

Issue of late Henry William Stanley, b 1903, d 1977: m 1930, Kathleen May Hardwick, who d 1981:—
Leslie Hugh (18 Heather Av, Bearsden, Glasgow), b 1931: m 1956, Marjorie Green, and has issue living, Christopher John, b 1958: m 1991, Sally Ann Morrison of The Barn, Balmore by Glasgow, and has issue living, Tessa Morrison b 1994, — Geoffrey Hugh, b 1962; BSc: m 1989, Catherine Anne Sheehan, BSc, of Knock Managh co Cork, — Lissa

Rachel, b 1963: m 1984, Mark Stephen Ferguson, and has issue living, Geoffrey Christopher b 1990. —— Norman Edward (Carraghan, Church St, Alcombe, Minehead, Som), b 1937: m 1961, Maxine Wyness, and has issue living, Adam, b 1969; BA (Camb), — Dominique, b 1965, — Mia, b 1966; BA (Edinburgh Coll of Art).

Grandson of late Lt-Col Charles Edward Henry Stanley, son of late Col Hon Charles James Fox Stanley, 3rd son of 13th Earl:—

Issue of late Charles Douglas Stanley, b 1878, d 1975: m 1909, Adela Grace, who d 1950, da of F. A. Walker-Jones, JP, formerly of Beddgelert, Gwynedd:—

Charles John Geoffrey (5 Shoreham Place, Shoreham, Sevenoaks, Kent TN14 7RX), b 1918; ed Eton, and St John's Coll, Camb (BA); formerly Capt RAC; France 1940, NW Europe 1944-45: m 1942, Marjorie Laura Awdry, da of J. F. Awdry Ball, and has issue living, Christopher Geoffrey Awdry (The Old Rectory, Knighton-on-Teme, Tenbury Wells, Worcs WR15 8LY), b 1949; ed Radley, and London Univ; BSc(Econ): m 1974, Anita Jane Keogh, and has issue living, Thomas Edward Christopher b 1983; ed Ampleforth, Ruth Mary Frances b 1987, — Martin John Llewelyn (Ruard, Neb Lane, Oxted, Surrey), b 1952; ed Radley, and St John's Coll, Oxford; m 1979, Philippa Alison Beauvais, yst da of late W. Beric Southwell, of Ide Hill, Sevenoaks, and has issue living, Charles Douglas Llewelyn b 1982, Max Wilfred Southwell b 1988, Isobel Beauvais b 1984.

Grandson of late Edward James Stanley, 5th in descent from Peter Stanley, yr son of Sir Thomas Stanley, 2nd Bt, and great-uncle of 11th Earl:—

Issue of late Capt Edward Arthur Vesey Stanley, b 1879, d 1941: m 1st, 1919 (m diss 1932), Sybil, who d 1972, da of late Maj Heathfield Butler Dodgson, DSO (B Vivian, colls); 2ndly, 1936, Marjorie Beatrice (8 Ash Court, Stanway Close, Taunton, Som) (who m 2ndly, 1942, Charles Langford Sidey, who d 1993), da of late A. R. Booth:—

(By 2nd m) John Alexander, b 1938; ed Repton: m 1983, Susan, da of Dennis Brown, and has issue living, Thomas Charles Edward, b 1984.

Descendants of the late Sir Thomas Stanley (el son of Sir Thomas Stanley 5th in descent from the Hon Sir John Stanley, 3rd son of 1st Baron Stanley), who was cr a Baronet 1660 (see B Stanley of Alderley).

(In remainder to the Barony of Stanley (cr 1456) only) (see Cs Loudoun.)

PREDECESSORS – (1) Sir THOMAS Stanley, KG; successively Lord Dep and Lord-Lt of Ireland, and Knight of the Shire of Lancashire 1447-51 and 1453-4; summoned to Parliament of England as Baron Stanley 1456; d 1458-9; s by his son (2) THOMAS, KG, 2nd Baron; Justice of Chester 1463-85, Steward of the Household 1474, and Constable of England for life; for the services he rendered at Bosworth Field, where he placed the crown of Richard III on the head of the victorious Richmond (Henry VII), was cr Earl of Derby (peerage of England) 1485; d 1504; s by his grandson (3) THOMAS, 2nd Earl, who in 1488 had s as 2nd Baron Strange, his father having been summoned to Parliament in right of his wife as Baron Strange of Knockyn 1482-97; d 1522; s by his son (4) EDWARD, KG, 3rd Earl; Lord High Steward at coronation of Queen Mary; celebrated for his magnificence and liberality; d 1593; s by his son (5) HENRY, KG; one of the peers who sat upon the trial of Mary, Queen of Scots: m 1555, Margaret, who d 1596, da of Henry Clifford, 2nd Earl of Cumberland, by his wife Eleanor, da of Charles Brandon, Duke of Suffolk (niece of King Henry VIII); d 1593; s by his el son (6) FERDINANDO, 5th Earl; is supposed to have been poisoned by certain conspirators who had suggested he should assume the title of king in right of his grandmother, a proposal he had indignantly rejected; d 1594, when the Baronies of Stanley and Strange fell into abeyance among his das, and the earldom devolved upon his brother (7) WILLIAM, KG, 6th Earl; purchased from his nieces their claims on the Isle of Man; d 1642; s by his son (8) JAMES, KG, 7th Earl, who in 1628 had been summoned to Parliament as Baron Strange under the impression that such a barony was enjoyed by his father; the summons cr a new peerage (see B Strange): during the Civil Wars was attached to the royal cause, and his wife Charlotte, da of Claude de la Trémouille, Duke of Thouars, is famed for her defence of Latham House when besieged by the Parliamentarians 1644, and for her energetic protection of the Isle of Man 1651; falling into the hands of the enemy after the battle of Worcester was decapitated at Bolton 1651; s by his son (9) CHARLES, 8th Earl; d 1672; s by his son (10) WILLIAM GEORGE RICHARD, 9th Earl; d 1702; s by his brother (11) JAMES, 10th Earl; dsp 1736 when the Isle of Man and the Barony of Strange, cr 1627, devolved upon the 2nd Duke of Atholl, the other baronies became abeyant between the co-heirs of the 5th Earl, and the earldom reverted to his kinsman (12) Sir EDWARD Stanley, 11th Earl and 5th Bt (see note *infra); d 1776, s by his grandson (13) EDWARD, 12th Earl; Lord-Lt Lancashire; after whom the greatest race in English Turf history is named; d 1834; s by his son (14) EDWARD SMITH, KG, 13th Earl; Lord-Lt Lancashire; cr Baron Stanley, of Bickerstaffe (peerage of United Kingdom) 1832; d 1851; s by his son (15) EDWARD GEOFFREY, KG, GCMG, PC, DCL, 14th Earl; b 1799; an eminent orator, scholar and statesman; MP for Stockbridge (C) 1820-6, for Preston 1826-30, for Windsor 1830-2, and for N Lancashire 1832-46; Ch Sec for Ireland 1830-3, Sec of State for Colonies and for War 1833-4 and 1841-5, First Lord of the Treasury 1852, 1858-9 and 1866-8, Chancellor of Univ of Oxford, &c; called to House of Lords in his father's Barony of Stanley 1846: m 1825, Hon Emma Caroline Wilbraham, who d 1876, da of 1st Baron Skelmersdale; d 28 Oct 1869; s by his son (16) EDWARD HENRY, KG, PC, 15th Earl; b 1826; MP for Lynn Regis (C) 1848-69; Under Sec for Foreign Affairs 1852, Sec for Colonies 1858, Pres of Board of Control 1858, Sec of State for India 1858-9, for Foreign Affairs 1866-8 and 1874-8, and Sec of State for the Colonies 1882-5: m 1870, Mary Catherine, who d 1900, da of 5th Earl De La Warr, and widow of 2nd Marquess of Salisbury; d 1893; s by his brother (17) FREDERICK ARTHUR, KG, GCB, GCVO, PC, 16th Earl; b 1841; Lord-Lt Lancashire; a Civil Lord of the Admiralty Aug to Nov 1868, Financial Sec to War Office 1874-7, Sec to Treasury 1877-8, Sec of State for War 1878-80, Sec of State for Colonies 1885-6, Pres of Board of Trade 1886-8, and Gov Gen of Canada and Com-in-Ch of Prince Edward Island 1888-93; MP for Preston (C) 1865-8 for N Lancashire 1868-85, and for Blackpool Div of Lancashire N 1885-6; cr Baron Stanley of Preston (peerage of United Kingdom) 1886: m 1864, Lady Constance Villiers, who d 1922, el da of 4th Earl of Clarendon; d 1908; s by his el son (18) EDWARD GEORGE VILLIERS, KG, GCB, GCVO, TD, PC, 17th Earl; b 1865; Lord-Lt Lancashire; was a Junior Lord of the Treasury 1895-1900, Financial Sec to War Office 1900-1903, Postmaster-Gen 1903-1905, Under Sec of State for War 1916, Sec of State for War 1916-18, Ambassador Extraor and Plen to France 1918-20, and again Sec of State for War 1922-4; sat as MP for Lancashire (SE) Westhoughton Div 1892-6; m 1889, Lady Alice Maud Olivia Montagu, who d 1957, da of 7th Duke of Manchester; d 1948; s by his grandson (19) EDWARD JOHN, MC (son of the late Rt Hon Edward Montagu Cavendish, Lord Stanley, MC, el son of 17th Earl), 18th Earl; b 1918; served 1939-45 War as Maj Gren Gds (MC), Pres Merseyside Chamber of Commerce, DL Lancs 1946, Lord Lieut and Custos Rotulorum 1951-68, Pro-Chancellor Lancaster Univ 1964-71, Constable Lancaster Castle, Chm Aintree Trust: m 1948, Lady Isabel Milles-Lade, who d 1990, sister of 4th Earl Sondes; dsp 1994; s by his nephew (20) EDWARD RICHARD WILLIAM (elder son of late Hon Hugh Henry Montagu Stanley, 3rd son of late Rt Hon Edward Montagu Cavendish (Lord Stanley, MC)), 19th Earl and present peer; also Baron Stanley of Bickerstaffe, and Baron Stanley of Preston.

*(1) EDWARD, of Bickerstaffe, great-grandson of Hon Sir James Stanley, Knt, brother of 3rd Earl; cr a Baronet 1627; s by

his son (2) *Sir* THOMAS, 2nd Bt; *d* 1653; *s* by his son (3) *Sir* EDWARD, 3rd Bt; *d* 1671; *s* by his son (4) *Sir* THOMAS, 4th Bt; *d* 1714; *s* by his son (5) EDWARD, 11th Earl of Derby and 5th Bt (*see* ante).

DE ROS, BARON (Maxwell) (Baron E 1264)
(Title pronounced "de Roos")

PETER TREVOR MAXWELL, 28th Baron (Premier Baron of England); *b* 23 Dec 1958; *s* 1983; *ed* Headfort Sch, Kells, Stowe, and Down High Sch, Downpatrick: *m* 1987, Angela Siân, da of late Peter Campbell Ross, and has issue.

𝔄rms – Quarterly, 1st and 4th, Argent a saltire gules, *Fitzgerald*, 2nd and 3rd, gules, three water bougets argent *de Ros*. 𝔖upporters – Two falcons wings expanded and inverted proper.
Residence – Old Court, Strangford, co Down.

SON LIVING

Hon FINBAR JAMES, *b* 14 Nov 1988.

DAUGHTERS LIVING

Hon Katharine Georgiana, *b* 1990.
Hon Jessye Macvc, *b* 1992.

SISTER LIVING

Hon Diana Elizabeth MAXWELL, *b* 1957; has resumed her maiden name: *m* 1st, 1976 (*m diss* 1978), Jonathan Watkins; 2ndly, 1978 (*m diss* 1981), Don Richard Bell; 3rdly, 1987 (*m diss* 1992), Eric Ford, and has issue living (by 3rd *m*), Nisha, *b* 1988.

AUNT LIVING (*Sister of* GEORGIANA ANGELA, BARONESS DE ROS)

Rosemary ROSS, *b* 1937: *m* 1973, Beresford George Edward Osborne, MIPA, and has issue living, Joanna Elizabeth, *b* 1975.

GRANDMOTHER LIVING

Hon Angela Ierne Evelyn Dixon, da of 1st Baron Glentoran: *m* 1st, 1929, Lt-Cdr Peter Ross, RN, who was *ka* 1940, el son of Una Mary, Baroness de Ros; 2ndly, 1943, Lt-Col Trevor Langdale Horn, MC, 16th/5th Lancers, who *d* 1966, and has issue living (by 2nd *m*), June Victoria Langdale, *b* 1946. *Residence* – Luckington Court, Chippenham, Wilts.

FATHER LIVING

Cdr (John) David Maxwell, RN; High Sheriff co Down 1981; DL: *m* 1st, 1954, Georgiana Angela, Baroness de Ros in her own right, who *d* 1983; 2ndly, 1984, Mrs Patricia Carolyn Coveney (*née* Ash). *Residence* – Old Court, Strangford, co Down.

COLLATERAL BRANCHES LIVING *(all in remainder)*

Issue of late Hon Charles Dudley Anthony Ross, yr son of Una Mary, Baroness de Ros, *b* 1907, *d* 1976: *m* 1st, 1940 (*m diss* 1949), Lady Elizabeth (ANNESLEY), who *d* 1982, da of 8th Earl of Roden; 2ndly, 1953, Mary Margaret, who *d* 1994, da of late Thomas Graham, of Monaghan:—
(By 1st *m*) Anthony Arthur (Casa Zabora, Brendon Av, Morningside Manor, Sandton, S Africa), *b* 1941; *ed* Winchester; FCA, CASA: *m* 1969, Joan, da of Herbert Cahn, of Highlands N, Johannesburg, and has issue living, Zara Gail, *b* 1971: *m* 1994, Stephen Mark Sanders, of 25 Whitehead Grove, Balsall Common, Warwicks CV7 7US, and has issue living, Devon James *b* 1995, Jadon Dean *b* 1996, Brandon Michael *b* 1998, — Deborah Kim, 1972.

Grandson of late Lady Eleanor Charlotte Augusta Dawson (who *m* 1st, 1906 (*m diss* 1920), Capt Aubrey Nugent Wade-Palmer), yr sister of Una Mary, Baroness de Ros:-

Issue of late Barbara Madeline Wade-Palmer, *b* 1907, *d* 1992: *m* 1923 (*m diss* 1936), Col Béla Domjan de Domjanszeg, of Hungary:-

Robert DOMJAN (Dene Hill, Beechenlea Lane, Swanley Village, Kent BR8 7PR), *b* 1924: *m* 1956, Countess Heilwig Freda Anna Helene Christa Hildegard, da of Count Gerhart von Büdingen, and has issue living, Nicholas Charles Robert, *b* 1960; *ed* Dulwich: *m* 1st, 1985 (*m diss* 1991), Margaret Mitchell; 2ndly, 1995, Deborah Susan, da of Godfrey George Hamilton, of Majorca, and has issue living (by 2nd *m*), Francis Robert *b* 1998, Charlotte Rose *b* 1995, Holly Eleanor *b* 1996.

PREDECESSORS – (1) ROBERT de Ros took an active part against Henry III and was one of the principal barons summoned to Parliament of England in the king's name 1264; was also again summoned as *Baron de Ros* 1285; *d* 1285; *s* by his son (2) WILLIAM, 2nd Baron; unsuccessfully competed for the crown of Scotland 1292 and 1296; *d* 1316; *s* by his son (3) WILLIAM, 3rd Baron; *d* 1343; *s* by his son (4) WILLIAM, 4th Baron; led a division of the English Army at Crecy; *d* in Palestine 1352; *s* by his brother (5) THOMAS, 5th Baron; *d* 1384; *s* by his son (6) JOHN, 6th Baron; *d* 1394; *s* by his brother (7) WILLIAM, KG, 7th Baron; Lord High Treasurer of England 1403; *d* 1414; *s* by his son (8) JOHN, 8th Baron; killed at battle of Baugé 1421; *s* by his brother (9) THOMAS, 9th Baron; *d* 1431; *s* by his son (10) THOMAS, 10th Baron; summoned to Parliament 1449-60; was attainted 1461 and his honours forfeited; *s* by his son (11) EDMUND, 11th Baron; obtained a reversal of attainder 1485, but was not summoned to Parliament; *d* 1508, when the title became abeyant between his two sisters; the abeyance was terminated 15— in favour of (12) GEORGE Manners (son of Eleanor, the el sister by Sir Robert Manners, Knt), 12th Baron; was not summoned to Parliament; *d* 1513; *s* by his son (13) THOMAS , KG, 13th Baron; summoned to Parliament 1515, and *cr Earl of Rutland* (peerage of England) 1525; *d* 1543; *s* by his son (14) HENRY, KG, 2nd Earl; *d* 1563; *s* by his son (15) EDWARD, 15th Baron; *d* 1587, when the earldom reverted to his brother (*see* D Rutland), and the barony devolved upon his da (16) ELIZABETH, wife of William Cecil, afterwards 2nd Earl of Exeter; *d* 1591; *s* by her son (17) WILLIAM CECIL, 17th Baron; *dsp* before his father 1618; *s* by his cousin (18) FRANCIS Manners, 18th Baron and 6th Earl of Rutland; *cr Baron Ros*, of Hamlake 1616; *d* 1632 without male issue, when the Barony of Ros, of Hamlake, expired, the earldom reverted to his brother, and the old barony devolved upon his da (19) KATHERINE: *m* 1st, 1620, 1st Duke of Buckingham, who was assassinated 1628; 2ndly, 1635, 1st Marquess of Antrim; *d* 1666; *s* by her son (20) GEORGE, KG, 20th Baron and 2nd Duke; noted for his profligacy and his wit; *d* 1687, when the dukedom expired, and the Barony of de Ros went into abeyance between the descendants of Bridget and Frances, das of John, 4th Earl of Rutland, and remained so until 1806, when it was terminated in favour of (21) CHARLOTTE (a descendant of Frances (ante), and da of Hon Robert Boyle-Walsingham, 5th son of 1st Earl of Shannon): *m* 1791, Lord Henry FitzGerald, son of 1st Duke of Leinster; assumed by Roy licence 1806 the additional surname of de Ros; *d* 1831; *s* by her son (22) HENRY WILLIAM, 22nd Baron; *d* 1839; *s* by his brother (23) WILLIAM LENNOX LASCELLES, PC, 23rd Baron, *b* 1797; a Gen in the Army, Capt Yeomen of the Guard 1852 and 1858-9, and Lieut-Gov of the Tower of London 1852-74, &c: *m* 1824, Georgiana, who *d* 1891, da of 4th Duke of Richmond; *d* 1874; *s* by his son (24) DUDLEY CHARLES, KP, KCVO, 24th Baron, *b* 1827; Equerry to the Prince Consort 1853-61, and Queen Victoria 1861-74, and a Lord in Waiting 1874-80, 1885-6, and 1886-92: *m* 1st, 1853, Lady Elizabeth Egerton, who *d* 1892, el da of 2nd Earl of Wilton, GCH; 2ndly, 1896, Mary Geraldine, who *d* 1921, da of Rev Sir William Vesey Ross Mahon, 4th Bt; *d* 1907; *s* by his only da (25) MARY FRANCES, *b* 1854: *m* 1878, 3rd Earl of Dartrey (who *d* 1933); she *d* 1939, when the Barony again fell into abeyance between her three daughters and so remained until 1943, when it was terminated in favour of the el (26) UNA MARY ROSS, *b* 1879: *m* 1904, Arthur John Ross, who was *ka* 1917; *d* 1956, when the Barony again fell into abeyance between her two granddaughters, and so remained until 1958, when it was terminated in favour of the el (27) GEORGIANA ANGELA (da of late Lieut-Com Peter Ross RN, el son of Una Mary, Baroness de Ros), *b* 1933: *m* 1954, Cdr (John) David Maxwell, RN; *d* 1983; *s* by her only son (28) PETER TREVOR, 28th Baron and present peer.

DERWENT, BARON (Vanden-Bempde-Johnstone) (Baron UK 1881, Bt GB 1795)
(Title pronounced "Darwent")

NUNQUAM NON PARATUS

ROBIN EVELYN LEO VANDEN-BEMPDE-JOHNSTONE, LVO, 5th Baron and 7th Baronet, *b* 30 Oct 1930; *s* 1986; *ed* Winchester, and Clare Coll, Camb; DL N Yorks 1991; late 2nd Lieut KRRC, and Lieut Queen Victoria's Rifles (TA Reserve); 3rd Sec Foreign Office 1954-55, and at Paris (Private Sec to British Ambassador) 1955-58, 2nd Sec 1958, at Foreign Office 1958-61, at Mexico City 1961-65, 1st Sec 1962, Washington 1965-68, and Foreign Office 1968-69; Dir N. M. Rothschild and Sons Ltd 1969-85, Man Dir Hutchison Whampoa (Europe) Ltd 1985-97, Dep Chm since 1998, Dir Foreign & Colonial (Pacific) Investment Trust, Scarborough Building Soc; former Chm London and Provincial Antique Dealers' Assocn, and Member Fine Arts and Antiques Export Cttee; Chev of Legion of Honour (France) 1957; LVO 1957; Officier de l'Ordre Nationale du Merite (France) 1978: *m* 1957, Sybille Marie Louise Marcelle, da of late Vicomte de Simard de Pitray, and has issue.

Arms – Quarterly: 1st and 4th argent, a saltire sable, in base a human heart ensigned with a regal crown or, on a chief gules, three woolpacks of the third; 2nd and 3rd per fesse, the 1st or, and the last per pale gules and vert, a demi-eagle with two heads displayed, issuing in chief sable, the dexter base charged with a tower, the sinister with five towers in saltire of the first, the gate and portcullis of each proper. Crests – 1st, a winged spur erect or,

Residences – Hackness Hall, Scarborough, N. Yorks; Flat 6, Sovereign Court, 29 Wrights Lane, W8 5SH.

SON LIVING

Hon FRANCIS PATRICK HARCOURT, *b* 23 Sept 1965; *ed* Eton, and Edinburgh Univ: *m* 1990, Cressida E., only da of Christopher Bourke, of 61 Kingsmead Rd, SW2.

DAUGHTERS LIVING

Hon Emmeline Veronica Louise, *b* 1958: *m* 1982, James John Winterbotham, son of Richard Winterbotham, of The Hall, Wittersham, Tenterden, Kent, and has issue living, Alexander William Harcourt, *b* 1988, — Frederick Charles Leo, *b* 1990, — Héloïse Sophie Laura, *b* (twin) 1990. *Residence* – 48 Oakley Rd, N1.

Hon Joanna Louise Claudia, *b* 1962: *m* 1991, Timothy Matthews, yr son of Rev Canon John Matthews, of Walberswick, Suffolk and has issue living, Leopold Kai Maximilian, *b* 1993. *Residence* – 12 Hawkwood Lane, Greenwich, CT 6830, USA.

Hon Isabelle Catherine Sophie, *b* 1968: *m* 1998, Nikola Tabain, only son of Hugo Tabain, of Melbourne, Vic, Australia. *Residence* – 2 Arkle St, Prahran, Melbourne, Vic 2181, Australia.

COLLATERAL BRANCHES LIVING

Grandson of late Hon Louis Vanden-Bempde-Johnstone, 5th son of 1st Baron:—
Issue of late Lt-Col Granville Henry Vanden-Bempde-Johnstone, DSO, RA, *b* 1891, *d* 1969: *m* 1923, Margarita Ruby, who *d* 1972, da of late Arthur Vernon O'Connell, of Buenos Aires:—
John Louis, *b* 1928: *ed* Eastbourne Coll; late Capt RA: *m* 1964, Eltis, da of W. Robinson, and has issue living, Louise Dorothy Ann, *b* 1967.

Granddaughters of late Hon Gilbert Vanden-Bempde-Johnstone, yst son of 1st Baron:—
Issue of late Lt-Col Mark Vanden-Bempde-Johnstone, *b* 1900, *d* 1956: *m* (Jan) 1928, Susan, who *d* 1993 da of late Geoffrey Head, OBE (Pauncefort-Duncombe, Bt) (and sister of 1st Viscount Head):—
Virginia Susan (127 Cranmer Court, Whiteheads Grove, SW3 3HE), *b* (Oct) 1928.

Issue of late Cdr Felix Gilbert Vanden-Bempde-Johnstone, RN, *b* 1904, *d* 1964: *m* 1st, 1938, Mrs June Estcourt, da of late H. W. Looker; 2ndly, 1945, Frances Elizabeth (Dove Cottage, 6 Orchard Thatch, Sutton Manor, Sutton Scotney, Hants SO21 3JX), da of late Charles McIntyre Brown:—
(By 1st *m*) Sarah June, *b* 1939: *m* 1961, Peter George Glossop, of The White House, 68 East St, Coggeshall, Essex CO6 1SL, and has issue living, Nicholas George, *b* 1971, — Georgemma Sarah, *b* 1963: *m* 1990, Richard Morgans, and has issue living, Max *b* 1993, Jed *b* 1998, Polly *b* 1994, — Lucy Maria, *b* 1966: *m* 1992, James Patrick Atherton, only son of Brig Maurice Alan Atherton, CBE, of Digges Place, Barham, Kent, and has issue living, Alexander *b* 1997, — Camilla June, *b* 1969: *m* 1997, Graham V. Appleyard, elder son of Robert Appleyard, of High Halden, Kent.

(In remainder to the Baronetcy only)

Descendants of late Col John Johnstone, 2nd son of 2nd baronet of Westerhall (*cr* 1700):—

Grandchildren of late Capt Charles Johnstone-Scott (infra):—
Issue of late Ronald Johnstone-Scott, *b* 1911, *d* 1967: *m* 1937, Winifred Joan Peck, who *d* 1994:—
Richard Anthony (124 Miladi Farm, Longueville, St Saviours, Jersey, CI), *b* 1946: *m* 1968, Jennifer Le Lerre, and has issue living, Iain Richard, *b* 1972, — Giles Edward, *b* 1978, — Emma Louise, *b* 1970: *m* 1990, Robert John Paul Thomas, of 77 School Rd, St Clement, Jersey, CI, and has issue living, Oliver Robert *b* 1991. —— Bruce Roger (19 Boleyn Drive, Eastcote, Ruislip, Middx), *b* 1956. —— Gillian Fenton, *b* 1938: *m* 1960, David Godfrey Kimsey, Detective Chief Supt, Met Police, of Squirrels Leap, 94 Broadwood Av, Ruislip, Middx HA4 7XT, and has issue living, Stephen David (The Castle, Huish Champflower, Taunton, Som), *b* 1962: *m* 1985, Sharon Ivy Elaine Crick, and has issue living, Frederick Arthur Stephen *b* 1995, Alyse Louis *b* 1991, Liberty Mae *b* 1996, — Mark Fenton (54 Boldmere Rd, Eastcote, Middx), *b* 1967; Barrister at Law (LLB): *m* 1994, Emma Jane Sykes, and has issue living, Thomas Fenton *b* 1995, Charlotte Emma *b* 1997, — Deborah Gillian, *b* 1964: *m* 1987, Michael Jon Hennessey, of 41 Seaford Close, Ruislip, Middx and has issue living, Callum Michael Charles *b* 1992, Emily Kate *b* 1989, Georgia Grace *b* 1995, — Sarah Cressida, *b* 1972; ALCM: *m* 1995, Michael Antony Grimmel, of 103 Aylsham Drive, Ickenham, Middx, and has issue living, Jessica Joan *b* 1997. —— Sandra Elizabeth Louise, *b* 1952: *m* 1974, Ivor Owen Tomrley, of Dellside, Dibden Hill, Chalfont St Giles, Bucks, and has issue living, Hannah Jane, *b* 1977, — Charlotte Louise, *b* 1979.

Grandchildren of late Henry Richard JOHNSTONE-SCOTT, 2nd son of 2nd baronet of Hackness (*cr* 1795), who assumed the additional surname of Scott by R licence 1860:—
Issue of late Capt Charles JOHNSTONE-SCOTT, *b* 1870, *d* 1948: *m* 1907, Elizabeth Irvine Matheson-Warrack, who *d* 1956:—
Aline, *b* 1908: *m* 1934, Errol Chapman Houston, who *d* 1977, and has issue living, Anthony Charles (225 Bree St, Vryheid, 3100, S Africa), *b* 1935: *m* 1960, Ryvés Dawn, only child of Joseph Geber, and has issue living, Murray James (12th Avenue, Parktown North, 2193, S Africa) *b* 1964: *m* 1998, Cindi Rayner-Fysh, Andrea Leigh *b* 1961: *m* 1984, Bruce John Murray-Reinders, of 11 Shelley Av, Willowild, 2196, S Africa (and has issue living, Scott Charles *b* 1986, Phillipa Claire *b* 1989), Nicola Brigid *b* 1967: *m* 1989, John Justin Hendry, of 8 Reeves Av, Epping, Sydney, Australia (and has issue living, Justin Rhys *b* 1992, Michael John *b* 1998), — Sally Patricia, *b* 1943: *m* 1965, Edward Carl William Meyer, of 9 Wood Rd, Rondebosch, Cape Town, S Africa, and has issue living, Graham Carl Alan (6 Isobel Av, Claremont, Cape Town), *b* 1966: *m* 1994, Tarron Grimmbacher, Craig Carl Anthony *b* 1973, Susan Belinda *b* 1968: *m* 1992, Chis Ronald Das, of 9 Claire Court, Strathroy, Ontario, Canada (and has issue living, James Peter William *b* 1996, Jonathan Brian *b* 1999). —— (Margaret) Cressida (34 Oldaker Rd, Newick, E Sussex BN8 4LP), *b* 1915: *m* 1947, Lt-Col Richard Melville

Brooker, who *d* 1994, and has had issue, Robin Nicholas (7 Tennyson Way, Basingstoke, Hants RG22 6BE), *b* 1948: *m* 1971, Roberta Cope, and *d* 1996, leaving issue, Caroline *b* 1972, — Richard David (31 Oldaker Rd, Newick, E Sussex BN8 4LN), *b* 1949: *m* 1976, Vivienne Smith, and has issue living, Julian Charles *b* 1981, Jonathan Ashley *b* 1984.

Granddaughter of late Charles Julius Johnstone, son of late Rev Vanden Bempde Johnstone, son of late Charles Philipps Johnstone, 2nd son of Charles John Johnstone, brother of 1st baronet:—
Issue of late Cmdr Richard Noel Johnstone, RN, *b* 1896, *d* 1989: *m* 1933, Mary Edmée, da of late Charles William Campbell, CMG:—
Susan Mary (*Lady Rowe*), *b* 1935: *m* 1957, Sir Jeremy Rowe, CBE, who *d* 1996, of Woodside, Peasmarsh, Rye, Sussex, and has issue living, Lucinda Mary, *b* 1958: *m* 1985, Richard J. Grant and has issue living, Robert Alexander Jeremy *b* 1992, Charlotte Mary *b* 1988, Henrietta Sarah *b* 1989, — Josephine Alice, *b* 1960: *m* 1991, Rev Richard Fothergill, of The Rectory 16 Waterloo Rd, Wynberg 7800, Cape Town, South Africa, son of Peter John Fothergill, and has issue living, Anna Sophie *b* 1993, Helena Kate *b* 1997, — Nicola Susan, *b* 1963: *m* 1989, John A. Herring, and has issue living, Anthony David *b* 1991, Edward John *b* 1997, Sarah Mary *b* 1993, Emily Lucinda *b* 1995, — (Harriet) Sarah, *b* 1966: *m* 1990, Barry W. Burles, and has issue living, George Thomas *b* 1995, Charles William *b* 1997.

Descendants, if any, of late Charles Frederick Dale Johnstone (*b* 1858) and late Richard James Annandale Johnstone (*b* 1865), sons of late Edmund John Johnstone, 3rd son of late Richard James Johnstone, 5th son of late Charles John Johnstone, brother of 1st baronet.

PREDECESSORS – **(1)** RICHARD Johnstone (son of late Col John Johnstone, 2nd son of Sir William Johnstone, 2nd Bt, of Westerhall), MP for Weymouth 1790-96; assumed by Act of Parliament 1793, the surnames of Vanden-Bempde, and in 1795 was authorized by Roy licence to resume the name of Johnstone; *m* 1st, 1756, Catherine, who *d* 1790, da of James Agnew, of Bishop Auckland; 2ndly, 1795, Margaret, who *d* 1853, da of John Scott, of London; *cr a Baronet* 1795, under the name of Bempde-Johnstone, with remainder to the male issue of his brother Charles John; *d* 1807; *s* by his son **(2)** *Sir* JOHN, successively MP for Yorkshire and Scarborough; *b* 1799: *m* 1825, Louisa Augusta Venables-Vernon, da of the Most Rev Edward Harcourt, Archbishop of York (B Vernon), *d* 1869; *s* by his son **(3)** *Sir* HARCOURT, 3rd Bt; *b* 1829; MP for Scarborough (*L*) 1869-80; *cr Baron Derwent, of Hackness, co York (peerage of United Kingdom)* 1881: *m* 1850, *Charlotte Mills, who d* 1903, sister of 1st Baron Hillingdon; *d* 1916; *s* by his son **(4)** FRANCIS, 2nd Baron, *b* 1851: *m* 1880, Ethel, who *d* 1891, da of Henry Strickland-Constable; *d* 1929; *s* by his nephew **(5)** GEORGE HARCOURT (son of late Hon Edward Henry Vanden-Bempde-Johnstone, 2nd son of 1st Baron), 3rd Baron, *b* 1899; Hon Attaché at Warsaw 1923, at Brussels 1927, at Madrid 1928, and at Berne 1939: *m* 1929, Comtesse Sabine Ozaykowska, who *d* 1941, da of Gen D. Iliesco (formerly Ch of Gen Staff, Rumanian Army), of 12 Rue Alexandre Lahovary, Bucharest, Rumania; *d* 1949; *s* by his brother **(6)** PATRICK ROBIN GILBERT, CBE, 4th Baron; Chm British Rd Fedn 1954-62, Min of State, Board of Trade 1962-63, and Min of State, Home Office 1963-64; Dep Speaker House of Lords 1970-85: *m* 1929, Marie-Louise Henriette, who *d* 1985, formerly wife of late Brig Phillip Stafford Myburgh, CBE, DSO and bar, MC, and da of late Albert Picard, of Paris; *d* 1986; *s* by his only son **(7)** ROBIN EVELYN LEO, 5th Baron and present peer.

DESAI, BARON (Desai) (Life Baron 1991)

MEGHNAD JAGDISHCHANDRA DESAI, son of late Jagdishchandra Chandulal Desai, of Baroda, India; *b* 10 July 1940; *ed* Bombay Univ (BA, MA), and Pennsylvania Univ (PhD 1964); Lecturer LSE 1965-77, Sr Lecturer 1977-80, Reader 1980-83, since when Prof of Economics; Head of Devpt Studies since 1990; Dir Centre for the Study of Global Governance, LSE; Council Member Royal Economic Soc, Exec Cttee Fabian Soc 1990-92; Chm Islington South and Finsbury Constituency Labour Party 1986-92; Pres Assocn of Univ Teachers in Economics 1987-90; author; *cr Baron Desai*, of St Clement Danes in the City of Westminster (Life Baron) 1991: *m* 1970, Gail Graham, da of late George Ambler Wilson, CBE, of Brandon House, North End Av, NW3, and has issue.
Residence – 606 Collingwood House, Dolphin Sq, SW1V 3NF.

SON LIVING

Hon Sven, *b* 1975.

DAUGHTERS LIVING

Hon Tanvi, *b* 1972.
Hon Nuala, *b* 1974.

DE SAUMAREZ, BARON (Saumarez) (Baron UK 1831, Bt UK 1801)
(Name and Title pronounced "Sommerez")

I hope in God

ERIC DOUGLAS SAUMAREZ, 7th Baron, and 7th Baronet (Premier Baronet of UK creation); *b* 13 Aug 1956; *s* 1991; *ed* Milton Abbey, Nottingham Univ, and RAC Cirencester: *m* 1982 (*m diss* 1990), Christine Elizabeth, yr da of Bernard Neil Halliday, OBE, of Woodford Green, Essex; 2ndly, 1991, Susan, da of late Joseph Hearn, and has issue by 1st *m*.

Arms – Argent, on a chevron gules, between three leopards' faces sable, as many castles triple-towered or. Crest – A falcon, displayed proper. Supporters – *Dexter*, an unicorn, tail between the legs argent, navally gorged azure, charged on the shoulder with a castle triple-towered or; *sinister*, a greyhound argent, collared gules, rimmed or, charged on the shoulder with a wreath of laurel vert, encircling an anchor sable.
Residence – Shrubland Park, Coddenham, Ipswich, Suffolk.

DAUGHTERS LIVING (By 1st marriage)

Hon Claire, *b* 1984.
Hon Emily, *b* 1985.

BROTHER LIVING

Hon VICTOR THOMAS, *b* (twin) 13 Aug 1956; *ed* Milton Abbey, and Exeter Univ (BA); MBA.

SISTER DECEASED

Hon Louisa, *b* 1955: *m* 1982 (*m diss* 1989), Duncan W. MacGregor, of Tregaer Mill, Monmouth, and *d* 1994, having resumed her maiden name.

AUNT LIVING (Daughter of 5th Baron)

Hon Veronica, *b* 1915; European War, Red Cross VAD 1940-43 attached RAF Hosps, 1943-5 with ATS: *m* 1945, Brigadier Anthony William Allen Llewellen Palmer, DSO, MC, King's Dragoon Guards, who *d* 1990 (M Lincolnshire ext). *Residence* – Old Pond Cottage, Shrubland Park, Coddenham, nr Ipswich, Suffolk IP6 9QQ.

WIDOW LIVING OF SIXTH BARON

JOAN BERYL (JULIA) (*Dowager Baroness de Saumarez*), da of Douglas Raymond Charlton, of Windlesham, Surrey; *m* 1953, the 6th Baron, who *d* 1991. *Residence* – Shrubland Park, Coddenham, Ipswich, Suffolk.

PREDECESSORS – (1) *Sir* JAMES Saumarez, GCB, 3rd son of late Matthew Saumarez; *b* 1757; Adm of the Red, Gen of the Marine Forces, and a most distinguished naval commander; 2nd in command at the battle of Nile; *cr* a *Baronet* 1801, and *Baron de Saumarez*, of Saumarez, Guernsey (peerage of United Kingdom) 1831: *m* 1788, Martha, who *d* 1849, da of Thomas Le Marchant, of Guernsey; *d* 1836; *s* by his son (2) *Rev* JAMES, 2nd Baron, *b* 1789; Rector of Huggate, co York: *m* 1814, Mary, who *d* 1849, da of Vice-Adm Lechmere, of Steeple Aston, Oxon; *dsp* 1863; *s* by his brother (3) JOHN ST VINCENT, 3rd Baron, *b* 1806: *m* 1st, 1838, Caroline Esther, who *d* 1846, el da of William Rhodes, of Kirskill and Bramhope Halls, York: *m* 2ndly, 1850, Margaret Antoinette, da of William Richard Hopkyns Northey, of Oving House, Bucks; *d* 1891; *s* by his el son (4) JAMES ST VINCENT, 4th Baron, *b* 1843: *m* 1882, Jane Anne, OBE, who *d* 1933, da of late Capt Charles Acton Vere-Broke, RE; *d* 1937; *s* by his son (5) JAMES ST VINCENT BROKE, 5th Baron; *b* 1889; Capt Scots Guards; Founded Rhodesia Fairbridge Coll 1946: *m* 1914, Gunhild, who *d* 1985, da of late Maj-Gen Viktor Gustaf Balck, KCMG, of Stockholm; *d* 1969; *s* by his son (6) JAMES VICTOR BROKE, 6th Baron, *b* 1924; 1939-45 War with Life Guards; Dir Shrubland Health Clinic: *m* 1953, Joan Beryl (Julia), da of Douglas Raymond Charlton, of Windlesham; *d* 1991; *s* by his elder (twin) son (7) ERIC DOUGLAS, 7th Baron and present peer.

Desmond, Earl of; see Earl of Denbigh and Desmond.

Devereux, family name of Viscount Hereford.

DE VESCI, VISCOUNT (Vesey) (Viscount I 1776, Baron I 1750, Bt I 1698)
(Name pronounced 'Veezy')

Under this sign thou shalt conquer

SUB HOC SIGNO VINCES

THOMAS EUSTACE VESEY, 7th Viscount, 9th Baronet; *b* 8 Oct 1955; *s* 1983; *ed* Eton, and Univ Coll, Oxford: *m* 1987, Sita-Maria Arabella, da of late Brian Michael Leese (later known as Brian de Breffny), of Castletown Cox, co Kilkenny, and of Maharaj Kumari Jyotsna Dutt, da of Maharajadhiraja Bahadur Sir Uday Chand Mahtab of Burdwan, KCIE, and has issue.

ᴀrms – Or, on a cross sable, a patriarchal cross of the field. Crest – A dexter hand erect in armour holding a laurel branch proper. Supporters – Two figures of Hercules, each clad in a lion's skin, and holding a club over the exterior shoulder proper.
Residence – 14 Rumbold Rd, SW6 2JA.

SONS LIVING

Hon Damian Brian John, *b* 1985.
Hon OLIVER IVO, *b* 16 July 1991.

DAUGHTER LIVING

Hon Cosima Frances, *b* 1988.

SISTERS LIVING

Hon Emma Frances, *b* 1951: *m* 1986, Norman Zalkind, of 186 Highland Av, Newton, Mass 02465, USA, and has issue living, Susan Clare, *b* 1987.
Hon Catherine Anne, *b* 1953: *m* 1984, Bruno Cretton, of Le Plot, 74570 Groisy, France, and has issue living, Matthew John, *b* 1985, — Alexis Pierre, *b* 1988, — Cecily Anne, *b* 1986, — Madeleine, *b* 1991.

AUNTS LIVING (*Sisters of 6th Viscount*)

Margaret Constance, *b* 1912: *m* 1946, Herbert William Quinton, of 6 Forest Field, Horsham, Sussex, and has issue living, Thomas William, *b* 1947: *m* 1975, Beverley Eileen, da of H. Lestor Price, — Christopher John, *b* 1948: *m* 1969, Carol, da of Clifford H. Green, and has issue living, William Alan John *b* 1972, Thomas Henry Alexander *b* 1973, Michael Patrick James *b* 1979, Catherine Sarah *b* 1969, — Peter Valentine, *b* 1953: *m* 1979, Deborah Helen, da of Bernard Boucher, — Caroline Mary, *b* 1950: *m* 1976, John Grinsted, and has issue, Mathew John *b* 1981, Sarah Margaret *b* 1979,
Bridget Georgina (*Lady Airey*), *b* 1915: *m* 1947, Lieut-Gen Sir Terence Sydney Airey, KCMG, CB, CBE, who *d* 1983. *Residence* – The White Cottage, Hempnall, Norwich NR15 2NG.

COLLATERAL BRANCHES LIVING

Granddaughter of late Maj-Gen George Henry Vesey, 5th son of Rev Hon Arthur Vesey, 2nd son of 1st Viscount:—
Issue of late Lieut-Col Charles Edward Gore Vesey, *b* 1871, *d* 1958: *m* 1920, Mary Dorothea, who *d* 1966, da of Arthur Henry Loring:—
Claudine Mary Rosalind, *b* 1925; MRCS England and LRCP London 1950, DCH England 1954: *m* 1959, William Anthony Barry Brown, of Red Wing, South Park, Sevenoaks, Kent, and has had issue, Martin Thomas Vesey, *b* 1960, — James Benedict, *b* 1961: *d* 1990, — Adrian Walter, *b* 1963, — Susan Mary Loring, *b* 1965: *m* 1993, Nicholas Stephen Wiltshire, and has issue living, Martha Constance *b* 1992.

Grandsons of late Gen Sir Ivo Lucius Beresford Vesey, KCB, KBE, CMG, DSO, yst son of Maj-Gen George Henry Vesey (ante):—
Issue of late Major Christopher Thomas Vesey, MC, RHA, *b* 1916, *d* 1956: *m* 1952, Helen Cynthia Mary (who *m* 2ndly, 1969, Brig Ferdinand Shaw Eiloart, OBE, who *d* 1993, of 16 Keepers Green, Braiswick, Colchester, Essex), da of late Brig Wilfrid Algernon Ebsworth, CB, CBE:—
Rev Nicholas Ivo (c/o Midland Bank plc, 69 Pall Mall, SW1Y 5EY), *b* 1954. —— Thomas Wilfrid, *b* 1956: *m* 1981, Marie-Christine Josiane Renée, yst da of late Roger Landon, of Pamiers, France, and has issue living, Alexander Thomas Ferdinand, *b* 1981, — Sebastien Guillaume, *b* 1989, — Olivia Denise Helen, *b* 1984.

PREDECESSORS – **(1)** *Right Rev* THOMAS Vesey; successively Bishop of Killaloe and Ossory; *cr* a *Baronet* 1698; *d* 1730; *s* by his son **(2)** *Sir* JOHN DENNY, 2nd Bt, MP for Newtown, co Down, and Custos Rotulorum of Queen's Co; *cr Baron Knapton (peerage of Ireland) 1750; d* 1761; *s by hs son* **(3)** THOMAS, 2nd Baron: *cr Viscount de Vesci* of Abbeyleix,

Queen's Co (peerage of Ireland) 1776; *d* 1804; *s* by his son **(4)** JOHN, 2nd Viscount: Lord-Lieut of Queen's Co and a Representative Peer; *d* 1855; *s* by his son **(5)** THOMAS, 3rd Viscount; *b* 1803; MP for Queen's Co (*C*) 1835-7; a Representative Peer: *m* 1839, Lady Emma Herbert, da of 11th Earl of Pembroke; *d* 1875; *s* by his son **(6)** JOHN ROBERT WILLIAM, 4th Viscount, *cr Baron de Vesci, of* Abbey Leix, Queen's Co (peerage of United Kingdom) 1884; *b* 1844: *m* 1872, Lady Evelyn Charteris, who *d* 1939, da of 8th Earl of Wemyss and March; *d* 1903, when the Barony became Ext and he was *s* in the Irish dignities by his nephew **(7)** IVO RICHARD (son of late Capt Hon Eustace Vesey, 2nd son of 3rd Viscount), 5th Viscount; *b* 1881; Major Irish Guards; an Irish Representative Peer: *m* 1st, 1906 (*m diss* 1919), Georgina Victoria, who *d* 1930, da of late Gerald Edward Wellesley (E Cowley, colls); 2ndly, 1920, Frances Lois, who *d* 1984, da of Sir Cecil Edmund Lister-Kaye, 4th Bt, and widow of 5th Earl of Rosse; *d* 1958; *s* by his nephew **(8)** JOHN EUSTACE (son of late Col the Hon Thomas Eustace Vesey, brother of 5th Viscount), 6th Viscount, *b* 1919; FRICS; Lieut IG (Supplementary Reserve), 1939-45 War in Norway, N Africa and Italy (wounded, prisoner): *m* 1950, Susan Anne, who *d* 1986, da of late Ronald Owen Lloyd Armstrong-Jones, MBE, QC; *d* 1983; *s* by his only son **(9)** THOMAS EUSTACE, 7th Viscount and present peer; also Baron Knapton.

DE VILLIERS, BARON (de Villiers) (Baron UK 1910)

ARTHUR PERCY DE VILLIERS, 3rd Baron; *b* 17 Dec 1911; *s* 1934; *ed* Magdalen Coll, Oxford (BA 1936); Bar Inner Temple 1938: *m* 1939 (*m diss* 1958), Edna Alexis Lovett, el da of late Rev Dr A. D. MacKinnon, of Peachland, British Columbia, and has issue.

Arms – Azure, a bend enhanced argent, on a mount in base a Paschal Lamb proper. **Crest** – Issuant from a circlet of gold embellished with nine pearls raised upon points, a dexter arm in armour embowed grasping in the hand a seax argent. **Supporters** – On either side a springbok proper, gorged with a circlet of gold, embellished with nine pearls raised upon points.
Address – PO Box 66, Kumeu, Auckland, NZ.

The hand to the work

SON LIVING

Hon ALEXANDER CHARLES, *b* 29 Dec 1940: *m* 1966.

DAUGHTERS LIVING

Hon Celia Yvonne Lovett, *b* 1942: *m* 1st, 1968 (*m diss* 1978), Robin Hastings Sancroft Beck; 2ndly, 1979, Alan McCallum, and has issue living (by 1st *m*), Donovan Henry, *b* 1969, — Robert Arthur, *b* 1974, — Honor Alexa Catherine, *b* 1970, — (by 2nd *m*) Georgina Kay Lovett, *b* 1983.
Hon Rosemary Aletta, *b* 1946: *m* 1st, 1967 (*m diss* 1979), Robin Anderson Elliott, TD; 2ndly, 1979 (*m diss* 1981), Craig Benthin, of Sangar Hill Farm, Magaliesburg, Transvaal, and has issue living, Robert Alexander Blyth, *b* 1970, — Hector de Villiers James, *b* 1973, — Conrad Lovat Johnston, *b* 1974.

SISTER LIVING

Hon Yvonne Aletta, *b* 1913; *ed* Lady Margaret Hall, Oxford: *m* 1939, James Kenneth Hill, and has issue living, Antony James de Villiers, *b* 1940, — Richard Lansley, *b* 1946, — Hamish Robert, *b* 1949, — Susan Felicity, *b* 1942. *Residence* – 2/7 Tyndall St, Surrey Hills, Vic 3127, Australia.

WIDOW LIVING OF SON OF SECOND BARON

Christine Mary, da of A. C. Buller, of Dwarsriviershoek, Stellenbosch, S Africa: *m* 1946, Hon John Maurice de Villiers, who *d* 1988, and has issue (see colls, infra). *Residence* – 61 Berg'n See, Hermanus 7200, Cape, S Africa.

COLLATERAL BRANCH LIVING

Issue of late Hon John Maurice de Villiers, yr son of 2nd Baron, *b* 1915, *d* 1988, *m* 1946, Christine Mary (ante), da of late A. C. Buller, of Dwarsriviershoek, Stellenbosch, S Africa:—
Jeanne Clair, *b* 1947: *m* 1st, 1968, Peter Puttick; 2ndly, 1972, Patrick Grierson, of 228 Erskine Av, Toronto, Canada M4P 1Z4. —— Michèle Jacqueline (1867 Rising Glen Rd, Los Angeles, Calif 90069, USA), *b* 1950.

PREDECESSORS – **(1)** *Rt Hon Sir* JOHN HENRY de Villiers, KCMG, son of Charles Christian de Villiers, of Paarl, Cape of Good Hope; *b* 1842; Attorney-Gen of Cape Colony 1872-4, and Ch Justice of Cape of Good Hope 1874-1910, and first Ch Justice of Union of South Africa 1910-14; *cr Baron de Villiers*, of Wynberg, Province of Cape of Good Hope and Union of South Africa (peerage of United Kingdom) 1910: *m* 1871, Aletta Johanna, who *d* 1922, da of Jan Pieter Jordaan, of Worcester, Cape of Good Hope; *d* 1914; *s* by his son **(2)** CHARLES PERCY, 2nd Baron, *b* 1871: *m* (Jan) 1911, Adelheid Helene Selma, who *d* 1968, da of Henri Christian Koch, formerly an Assist Judge, Supreme Court, Natal, of Pietermaritzburg, Natal; *d* 1934; *s* by his el son **(3)** ARTHUR PERCY, 3rd Baron and present peer.

DEVLIN, BARONY OF (Devlin) (Extinct 1992)

SONS LIVING OF LIFE BARON

Hon Gilpatrick (20 Bingham Place, W1M 3FH), *b* 1938; *ed* Winchester: *m* 1st, (Feb) 1967 (*m diss* 1995), Glenna, da of John Parry-Evans, MRCS, of Colwyn Bay; 2ndly, 1996, Mara, da of Alexandr Amats, of Latvia, and has issue living, Benedick, *b* (Nov) 1967: *m* 1995, Claudia Thomasina, da of Simon Ward (*see* Malcolm, Bt, colls).

Hon Dominick, *b* 1942; *ed* Winchester, and Univ Coll, London (LLB): *m* 1967, Carla, da of Lamberto Fulloni, of Rome, and has issue living, Daniel, *b* 1968, — Christopher, *b* 1972, — Maddalena, *b* 1969: *m* 1998, Riaz Rizvi.

Hon Timothy, *b* 1944; *ed* Winchester, and Univ Coll, Oxford: *m* 1967, Angela, elder da of A. J. G. Laramy, and has issue living, Sebastian, *b* 1973, — Fabian, *b* 1975, — Miranda, *b* 1969: *m* 1991, Neil McPherson and has issue living, one da, — Esmeralda, *b* 1971.

Hon Matthew, *b* 1946; *ed* Winchester, and New Coll, Oxford: *m* 1969, Rosemary Joan Boutcher, da of Lt-Col E. C. Van der Kiste, of The Old Rectory, Durrington, Wilts, and has issue living, William, *b* 1972, — Edward *b* 1975, — Beatrice, *b* 1970, — Mary, *b* 1977.

DAUGHTERS LIVING OF LIFE BARON

Hon Clare, *b* 1940: *m* 1961 (*m* annulled 1984), Julian Reginald Desgrand Jermy Gwyn, Prof in History, Univ of Ottawa, and has issue living, Christopher, *b* 1965, — Matthew, *b* 1978, — Frances, *b* 1962: *m* 19—, Robert Thorpe, and has issue living, one son and two das, — Anya, *b* 1963: *m* 19—, Jerry Knol, and has issue living, one son and two das, — Elin, *b* 1964: *m* 19—, Robert Vallé, and has issue living, two sons and one da.

Hon Virginia (*Hon Lady Kennedy*), *b* (twin) 1940: *m* 1965, Rt Hon Sir Paul Kennedy, a Lord Justice of Appeal, and has issue living, Christopher, *b* 1966: *m* 1992, Rebecca McCarthy, — John, *b* 1969, — Joanna, *b* 1968, — Brigid, *b* 1971: *m* 1998, James Robert Easton Turner.

WIDOW LIVING OF LIFE BARON

MADELEINE HILDA (*Baroness Devlin*), JP, da of Sir Bernard Oppenheimer, 1st Bt: *m* 1932, Baron Devlin, PC (Life Baron), who *d* 1992. *Residence* – West Wick House, Pewsey, Wilts.

DEVON, EARL OF (Courtenay) (Earl E 1553, Bt I 1644)

HUGH RUPERT COURTENAY, 18th Earl, and 14th Baronet; *b* 5 May 1942; *s* 1998; *ed* Winchester, and Magdalene Coll, Camb; patron of four livings; DL Devon 1991: *m* 1967, Dianna Frances, elder da of late Jack Watherston, of Menslaws, Jedburgh, Roxburghshire, and has issue.

𝕬rms – Quarterly: 1st and 4th or, three torteaux, *Courtenay*; 2nd and 3rd or, a lion rampant azure, *Redvers, Earl of Devon*. 𝕮rests – 1st, out of a ducal coronet or, a plume of seven ostrich feathers four and three argent; 2nd, a dolphin embowed proper. 𝕾upporters – Two boars argent, tusked, crined, and unguled or.
Seat – Powderham Castle, near Exeter, Devon EX6 8JQ.

QUOD VERUM TUTUM

What is true is safe

SON LIVING

CHARLES PEREGRINE (*Lord Courtenay*), *b* 14 Aug 1975; *ed* Eton, and St John's Coll, Camb.

DAUGHTERS LIVING

Lady Rebecca Eildon, *b* 1969: *m* 1994, Jeremy Lloyd Wharton, 2nd son of P. M. Wharton, of Monkton Farleigh, Wilts, and has issue living, Alice Lucinda, *b* 1998. *Residence* – 16 Delaford St, SW6 7LT.
Lady Eleonora Venetia, *b* 1971.
Lady Camilla Mary, *b* 1974.

SISTER LIVING

Lady Katherine Felicity, *b* 1940: *m* 1966, Antony Stephen Pope Watney, who *d* 1986, and has issue living, Michael Hugh Sanders (Nicholas Cottage, Brabourne, nr Ashford, Kent TN25 5LD), *b* 1966; *ed* Stowe, and RAC Cirencester: *m* 1995, Louise Mary, da of Anthony Winsborough, of Upham, Hants. *Residence* – 1 Playhatch Cottages, Playhatch, nr Reading, Berks RG4 9QX.

AUNTS LIVING (*Daughters of 16th Earl*)

Lady Mary Elizabeth, *b* 1910; is a State Registered Nurse. *Residence* – The Briary, Exton, Exeter.
Lady (Marguerite) Kathleen, *b* 1911: *m* 1933, Col Eugene St John Birnie, OBE, Indian Army (ret), who *d* 1976, and has issue living, Marguerite Susan, *b* 1934: *m* 1958, Jasper Meadows Clutterbuck, of Mottisfont House, nr Romsey, Hants,

and has issue living, Hugh Meadows *b* 1959: *m* 1987, Camilla, da of Richard Nicholson, of Woodcott House, Whitchurch, Hants (and has issue living, Jack Rupert Meadows *b* 1990, Henry Charles Meadows *b* 1992, Simon Alexander Meadows *b* 1994), Nichola Marguerite *b* 1961: *m* 1988, Geoffrey Wharton (and has issue living, Matthew Harry *b* 1994, Nell Marguerite *b* 1991), — Angela Patricia Jane, *b* 1936: *m* 1956, Michael Edmond Joly de Lotbinière, of Rougham House, Bury St Edmunds (B Hylton, 1990 Edn), and has issue living, Christopher David *b* 1957: *m* 1991, Victoria C., da of Graham Harvey Evers, of Domaine de la Rose, Opio, France AM (and has issue living, Sasha (a da) *b* 1995, Lucy Isabelle Joly *b* 1998), Giles Antony *b* 1959: *m* 1990, Veronica J., elder da of John Egerton Levett-Scrivener, of Sibton Abbey, Peasenhall, Suffolk, Tessa Jane *b* 1962: *m* 1984, Nigel N. V. Raywood. *Residence* – The Cottage, Longparish, Hants.

Lady Camilla Gabrielle, *b* 1913. *Residence* – The Briary, Exton, Exeter.

Lady Angela Leslie, *b* 1918: *m* 1947, Harold Cecil Moreton Horsley, MBE, Malayan Civil Ser (ret), who *d* 1969, and has issue living, Richard Geoffrey Courtenay (Elliotts Farmhouse, Adstone, Towcester, Northants NN12 8DY), *b* 1947: *m* 1983, Susan Philippa, only da of E. A. Trotman, of Lower Twinhoe Cottage, Midford, Bath, and has issue living, Moreton William Edward *b* 1985, Anna Gabrielle Susan *b* 1987, — William Frederick Moreton (Flat 1, 30 Bina Gdns, SW5 0LA), *b* 1949: *m* 1979, Noriko, elder da of Tetsuo Makuuchi, of 5-8-10 Ogikubo, Suginami-ku, Tokyo, Japan. *Residence* – Marwood House, Offwell, Honiton, Devon EX14 9RW.

WIDOW LIVING OF SEVENTEENTH EARL

SYBIL VENETIA (*Dowager Countess of Devon*), da of late Capt John Vickris Taylor (formerly Welsh Guards), of North Aston Manor, Oxford, and formerly wife of 6th Earl of Cottenham: *m* 1939, the 17th Earl of Devon, who *d* 1998. *Residence* – Powderham Castle, nr Exeter, Devon EX6 8JQ.

PREDECESSORS – (1) *Sir* HUGH de Courtenay, Knt, 6th feudal Baron of Okehampton, summoned as a Baron to all the Parliaments of Edward II, and to the Parliaments of Edward III 1327-35; was in 1335 summoned as *Earl of Devonshire*; *d* 1340; *s* by his son (2) HUGH, 2nd Earl; *d* 1377; *s* by his grandson (3) EDWARD, 3rd Earl; Earl Marshal; *d* 1419; *s* by his son (4) HUGH, 4th Earl; *d* 1422; *s* by his son (5) THOMAS, 5th Earl; a faithfull adherent to the "Red Rose"; *d* 1458; *s* by his son (6) THOMAS, 6th Earl, a strenuous upholder of the Lancastrian cause fell into the hands of the Yorkists at Towton Field, and was beheaded April 1462, his honours being attainted; *s* by his brother (7) HUGH; was restored to a part of his ancestral estates, but subsequently engaged in the Lancastrian quarrel, was attainted and beheaded 1466. (The greater part of the Courtenay estates having been conferred upon Humphry Stafford, Baron Stafford, of Southwicke, he was *cr Earl of Devon* 1469, and in the same year was beheaded as a traitor, when the earldom expired). Hugh (ante), was *s* by his brother (8) JOHN, 8th Earl, who was restored to his honours by the Parliament that replaced the crown upon the head of Henry VI; the subsequent defeat of the Earl of Warwick, at Barnet Field, 14 April 1471, again jeopardised his fortunes, and joining Margaret of Anjou he fell at Tewkesbury, 14 May, following, and his honours were attainted. The representation of the family then devolved upon (9) *Sir* EDWARD, Knt, grandson of Sir Hugh, next brother of 3rd Earl; participated in the victory of Bosworth and was *cr Earl of Devon* 1485, and obtained regrants of the greater part of the estates of Thomas, 6th Earl; *d* 1509; *s* by his son (10) *Sir* WILLIAM, *b* ca 1475: *m* 1495, Katherine, 6th da of King Edward IV; was attainted 1504 and doomed to incarceration during the reign of Henry VII; he was released by Henry VIII, but *d* before being formally restored to earldom; his son (11) HENRY, 2nd Earl (*cr* 1485), was restored in blood and honours, and *cr Marquess of Exeter* 1525; was subsequently committed to the Tower for conspiring to place Reginald Pole, Dean of Exeter, upon the throne, and was beheaded 9 Jan 1539, his titles being attainted and his estates annexed to the Duchy of Cornwall; *s* by his son (12) EDWARD; was committed to the Tower 1539 when twelve years of age, and remained there until 1553, when he was released by Queen Mary, and though restored in blood not any of the attainders were reversed; *cr Earl of Devon* 1553; was subsequently imprisoned in the Tower and in Fotheringay Castle for an alleged connection with Wyatt's rebellion, but was released on the marriage of the Queen with Philip of Spain; *d* unmarried at Padua 1556, when, in consequence of the limitations of the patent not being known, the honours became dormant, and remained so until 1831, when it was revived in favour of (13) WILLIAM, 3rd *Viscount Courtenay* (see note*infra), who became 9th Earl (of *cr* 1553); *d* unmarried 1835, when the viscountcy became extinct and his baronetcy and earldom devolved upon his cousin (14) WILLIAM, 10th Earl, son of the Right Rev Henry Reginald, Bishop of Exeter, who was son of Henry Reginald Courtenay, MP, 2nd son of 2nd Bt (see note^infra); *b* 1777: *m* 1st, 1804, Lady Harriet Leslie, da of Sir Lucas Pepys, Bt, and Jane Elizabeth, Countess of Rothes; 2ndly, 1849, Elizabeth Ruth, who *d* 1914, da of late Rev John Middleton Scott; *d* 1859; *s* by his son (15) WILLIAM REGINALD, PC, 11th Earl, *b* 1807; was MP for S Devon (C) 1842-48: *m* 1830, Lady Elizabeth Fortescue, who *d* 1867, da of 1st Earl Fortescue; *d* 1888; *s* by his son (16) EDWARD BALDWIN, 12th Earl, *b* 1836; MP for Exeter (C) 1864-68, and for Devonshire E 1868-70; *d* 1891; *s* by his uncle (17) *Rev* HENRY HUGH, 13th Earl, *b* 1811; R of Powderham: *m* 1835, Lady Anna Maria Leslie, who *d* 1897, da of late Henrietta Anne, Countess of Rothes; *d* 1904; *s* by his grandson (18) CHARLES PEPYS (son of late Henry Reginald, Lord Courtenay, el son of 13th Earl, by Lady Evelyn Pepys, da of 1st Earl of Cottenham), 14th Earl; *b* 1870; an Inspector in Board of Agriculture 1895-1904; *d* 1927; *s* by his brother (19) *Rev* HENRY HUGH, 15th Earl, *b* 1872; was R of Powderham 1904-27; *d* (Feb) 1935; *s* by his brother (20) *Rev* FREDERICK LESLIE, 16th Earl, *b* 1875; was R of Honiton: *m* 1907, Marguerite, who *d* 1950, da of late John Silva, of Itchen Abbas, Hants; *d* (June) 1935; *s* by his son (21) CHARLES CHRISTOPHER, 17th Earl, *b* 1916; Capt Coldstream Guards (Regular Army Reserve); served European War 1939-45 (wounded, despatches): *m* 1939, Sybil Venetia, da of late Capt John Vickris Taylor (formerly Welsh Guards), of North Aston Manor, Oxford, and formerly wife of 6th Earl of Cottenham; *d* 1998; *s* by his only son (22) HUGH RUPERT, 18th Earl and present peer.

*(1) *Sir* PHILIP Courtenay, Knt, 6th son of 2nd Earl of Devon of the original *cr*, Lord-Lieut of Ireland 1383-92; *s* by his son (2) RICHARD; Lord Bishop of Norwich; one of the Ambassadors sent by Henry V to the King of France to demand the crown of that kingdom; *d* 1415; *s* by his nephew (3) *Sir* PHILIP, Knt; *s* by his son (4) *Sir* WILLIAM, Knt; High Sheriff of Devon 1483; *d* 1485; *s* by his son (5) *Sir* WILLIAM, Knt; *d* 1512; *s* by his son (6) *Sir* WILLIAM, Knt; styled "The Great"; *d* 1535; *s* by his grandson (7) *Sir* WILLIAM, Knt, *de jure* 2nd Earl; killed at storming of St Quintin 1557; *s* by his son (8) *Sir* WILLIAM, Knt, *de jure* 3rd Earl; one of the undertakers to send over settlers for the better planting of Ireland, *d* 1630; *s* by his son (9) FRANCIS, *de jure* 4th Earl, *d* 1638; *s* by his son (10) WILLIAM, *de jure* 5th Earl; *cr a Baronet* 1644 (disdaining the title did not assume it, but was always styled "Sir" in commissions sent by the king); *d* 1702; *s* by his son (11) *Sir* WILLIAM, 2nd Bt *de jure* 6th Earl; MP for Devon; *d* 1736; *s* by his son (12) *Sir* WILLIAM, *de jure* 7th Earl; *cr Viscount Courtenay*, of Powderham Castle, co Devon (peerage of Great Britain, 1762); *d* 1762; *s* by his son (13) WILLIAM, 2nd Viscount, and *de jure* 8th Earl; *d* 1788; *s* by his son (14) WILLIAM, 3rd Viscount, who established his right to the Earldom of Devon (see ante).

DEVONPORT, VISCOUNT (Kearley) (Viscount UK 1917, Bt UK 1908)

The way is made through strength

TERENCE KEARLEY, 3rd Viscount, and 3rd Baronet; *b* 29 Aug 1944; *s* 1973; *ed* Aiglon Coll, Switzerland, and Selwyn Coll, Camb (MA); Dip Arch RIBA; BPhil (Newcastle); ALI; Landscape Architect, Architect-Developer, Farmer and Forester: *m* 1968 (*m diss* 1979), Elizabeth Rosemary, 2nd da of late John Gordon Hopton, Solicitor, of Chute Manor, Andover, and has issue.

Arms – Azure, in chief two mitres argent garnished or, and in base a square tower of the second. Crest – An ancient ship or, the mainsail azure charged with a sea lion gold. Supporters – On either side a sea lion argent, crined, finned, and tufted or, each gorged with a collar gules charged with three roses gold, and each supporting a spear erect proper.
Residence – Ray Demesne, Kirkwhelpington, Northumberland NE19 2RG. *Clubs* – Northern Counties (Newcastle), Beefsteak, RAC, Farmers, MCC and Royal Over-Seas League.

DAUGHTERS LIVING

Hon Velvet Jane, *b* 1975.
Hon Idonia Clare, *b* 1977.

SISTER LIVING

Hon Marilyn Whitson, *b* 1939.

WIDOW LIVING OF SECOND VISCOUNT

SHEILA ISABEL (*Viscountess Devonport*) (The Old Vicarage, Peasmarsh, Rye, E Sussex, TN31 6XB), el da of late Col Charles Hope-Murray, of Morishill, Beith, Ayrshire: *m* 1938, the 2nd Viscount Devonport, who *d* 1973.

COLLATERAL BRANCH LIVING

　　　Issue of late Hon Mark Hudson Kearley, yr son of 1st Viscount; *b* 1895, *d* 1977: *m* 1928, Mabel Florence, who *d* 1967, da of late John Francis Dagley:—
CHESTER DAGLEY HUGH, *b* 29 April 1932: *m* 1974, Josefa Mesquida. —— Patrick Richard Hudson, *b* 1935: *m* 1962, Susanna Brigitta, da of Carl Erik Ringberg, of Stockholm, and has issue living, Selina Anna-Karin, *b* 1967, — Cecilia Laura Anthea, *b* 1974. *Residence* – 9 Chemin Tavarnay, 1218 Geneva, Switzerland. —— Anthea, *b* 1929: *m* 1959, Luigi Triossi, of 141 Via del Babuino, Rome, Italy, and has issue living, Amanda Consuelo Fiorenza, *b* 1963.

PREDECESSORS – (1) *Rt Hon* HUDSON EWBANKE Kearley, son of George Ewbanke Kearley, of Uxbridge; *b* 1856; Parl Sec to Board of Trade 1905-09, Chm of Roy Commn on Sugar Supply 1917, Food Controller 1916-17, and First Chm of Port of London Authority 1909-25; sat as MP for Devonport (*L*) July 1892 to Jan 1910; *cr* a Baronet 1908, PC 1909, and *Baron Devonport*, of Wittington, co Buckingham (peerage of United Kingdom) 1910, and *Viscount Devonport*, of Wittington, co Bucks (peerage of United Kingdom) 1917: *m* 1888, Selina, who *d* 1931, da of Edward Chester, of Blisworth, Northampton; *d* 1934; *s* by his el son (2) GERALD CHESTER, 2nd Viscount, *b* 1890: *m* 1938, Sheila Isabel, da of late Col Charles Hope Murray, of Morishill, Beith, Ayrshire; *d* 1973; *s* by his son (3) TERENCE, 3rd Viscount and present peer; also Baron Devonport.

DEVONSHIRE, DUKE OF (Cavendish) (Duke E 1694)

CAVENDO · TVTVS

Secure by caution

ANDREW ROBERT BUXTON CAVENDISH, KG, MC, PC, 11th Duke; *b* 2 Jan 1920; *s* 1950; *ed* Eton, and Trin Coll, Camb; Hon LLD, Sheffield 1963; Vice-Lieut for Derbyshire 1957-87, and a KStJ; Parliamentary Under-Sec of State for Commonwealth Relations 1960-62, and Min of State, Commonwealth Relations Office 1962-64; Chancellor of Manchester Univ 1965-86; 1939-45 War as Capt Coldstream Guards in Italy (MC); PC 1964, KG 1996: *m* 1941, Hon Deborah Vivien Freeman-Mitford, DCVO, da of 2nd Baron Redesdale, and has issue.

ᵃrms – Sable, three bucks' heads cabossed argent. Crest – A serpent nowed proper. Supporters – Two bucks proper, each wreathed round the neck with a chaplet of roses, alternately argent and azure.
Seats – Chatsworth, Bakewell, Derbyshire; Bolton Abbey, Yorks; Lismore Castle, co Waterford.

SON LIVING

PEREGRINE ANDREW MORNY (*Marquess of Hartington*), CBE (Beamsley Hall, Skipton, N Yorks BD23 6HD), *b* 27 April 1944; *ed* Eton, and Exeter Coll, Oxford; Sr Steward The Jockey Club 1989-94; HM's Representative at Ascot since 1998; Pres Yorks Agric Soc 1998-99; Dir Sotheby's Holdings Inc since 1994 (Dep Chm since 1996); CBE (Civil) 1997: *m* 1967, Amanda Carmen, only da of late Cdr Edward Heywood-Lonsdale, RN, and has issue:—

SON LIVING — William (*Earl of Burlington*), *b* 6 June 1969.
DAUGHTERS LIVING—*Lady* Celina Imogen, *b* 1971: *m* 1995, Alexander Corfield Key Carter, only son of William George Key Carter, CBE, of The Old Rectory, Elmley Lovett, Worcs, and has issue living, Jake, *b* 1997, — *Lady* Jasmine Nancy, *b* 1973.

DAUGHTERS LIVING

Lady Emma, *b* 1943: *m* 1963, Hon Tobias William Tennant, of Shaws, Newcastleton, Roxburghshire (*see* B Glenconner).
Lady Sophia Louise Sydney, *b* 1957: *m* 1st, 1979 (*m diss* 1987), Anthony (Gurth) William Lindsay Murphy, elder son of Christopher Murphy; 2ndly, 1988, Hon Alastair John Morrison, eldest son of 2nd Baron Margadale.

SISTERS LIVING

Lady Elizabeth Georgiana Alice, CVO, *b* 1926; is a JP; appointed an Extra Lady-in-Waiting to HRH The Princess Margaret 1960; LVO 1976, CVO 1997. *Residences* – 19 Radnor Walk, SW3; Moor View, Edensor, Bakewell, Derbyshire.
Lady Anne Evelyn Beatrice, *b* 1927: *m* 1949, Michael Lambert Tree, of 29 Radnor Walk, SW3, and has two adopted das, Isabella Elizabeth Nancy, *b* 1964: *m* 1993, Charles Raymond Burrell, eldest son of Sir (John) Raymond Burrell, 9th Bt, — Esther Anne Mary, *b* 1966: *m* 1992, James Michael Beale Cayzer-Colvin (*see* B Cayzer).

COLLATERAL BRANCHES LIVING

Grandchildren of late Col Rt Hon Lord Richard Frederick Cavendish, CB, CMG (infra):—
Issue of late Capt Richard Edward Osborne Cavendish, JP, DL, *b* 1917, *d* 1972: *m* 1937, Pamela (The Dower House, Holker Hall, Cark-in-Cartmel, Cumbria), da of late Hugh Lloyd Thomas, CMG, CVO (*see* B Bellew, 1976 Edn):—
(Richard) Hugh, *b* 1941; *cr Baron Cavendish of Furness* (Life Baron) 1990 (see that title). —— Edward Osborne (Butley Priory, nr Woodbridge, Suffolk IP12 3NR), *b* 1955: *m* 1st, 1977 (*m diss* 1980), Kirsten, eldest da of Dr Ronald T. St Blaize-Molony, of Fordwich, Kent; 2ndly, 1983, (Anna) Frances, yr da of Spencer Shelley, of Mayhill Lodge, Mayhill, Glos (*see* Shelley, Bt, colls), and has issue living (by 2nd *m*), Elizabeth Angelica, *b* 1985, — Georgiana Rose, *b* 1988. —— Georgiana Elizabeth, *b* 1939: *m* 1968, Capt Andrew Henry Clowes, late Scots Gds, of 52 Bowerdean St, SW6, and has issue (*see* M Lothian, colls). —— Harriet Moyra Aline, *b* 1944: *m* 1972, Capt Anthony Peter Coote Sykes (*see* D Wellington, colls, 1955 Edn), late R Scots Greys, of Bellamont House, Long Bredy, Dorchester, Dorset DT2 9HN, and has issue living, Eyre William, *b* 1975, — Nina Aline, *b* 1973, — Evelyn Harriet, *b* 1980. —— Susan Anne CREWE, *b* 1949; Social Ed *Harpers & Queen* 1991-92, Ed *House & Garden* since 1993: *m* 1st, 1970 (*m diss* 1983), Quentin Hugh Crewe, writer and traveller, who *d* 1998 (*see* M Crewe, ext, 1948 Edn); 2ndly, 1984, (Christopher) Nigel John Ryan, CBE, eldest son of late Brig Charles Edmond Ryan, MC, of Uckfield, Sussex, and has issue living (by 1st *m*), Nathaniel Richard, *b* 1971, — Charity *b* 1972.

Granddaughter of late Rt Hon Lord Edward Cavendish, MP, 3rd son of 7th Duke:—
Issue of late Col Rt Hon Lord Richard Frederick Cavendish, CB, CMG, *b* 1871 (raised to rank of a Duke's son 1908), *d* 1946: *m* 1895, Lady Moyra de Vere Beauclerk, who *d* 1942, da of 10th Duke of St Albans:—
Sybil, *b* 1915: *m* 1941, Rev Lawrence Gregson Fell Dykes, who *d* 1993, and has issue living, Michael, *b* 1942, — Rose, *b* 1946, — Catherine Mary, *b* 1948. *Residence* – The Garden House, Holker Hall, Cark-in-Cartmel, Cumbria.

Grandchildren of late Maj Cecil Charles Cavendish, yst son of Lt-Col William Henry Frederick Cavendish, el son of Gen Hon Henry Frederick Compton Cavendish, MP (infra):—
Issue of late Maj Frederick George Cavendish, DSO, MC, *b* 1891, *d* 1936: *m* 1919, Milla Jean, who *d* 1976, da of late W. St Clair Grant, of Bhagalpur, Bengal:—
Jean Caroline, *b* 1932; *ed* Lady Margaret Hall, Oxford: *m* 1st, 1954 (*m diss* 1959), Anthony Richard Champion de Crespigny; 2ndly, 1974, George Charles Denis Lassalle, of 117 Irinis, Limassol, Cyprus, and has issue living (by 1st *m*), Camilla Georgiana, *b* 1955.

Issue of late Brig Ronald Valentine Cecil Cavendish, OBE, MC, *b* 1896, *ka* in Burma 1943: *m* 1923, Violet Helen, who *d* 1974, el da of late Arthur Sackville Boucher, of Sharpcliffe Hall, Staffordshire:—
Peter Boucher, CB, OBE (The Rock Cottage, Middleton, Bakewell, Derbys) *b* 1925; *ed* Winchester; Maj-Gen late 14th/20th King's Hus; Chm NATO Mil Agency for Standardisation; OBE (Mil) 1969; CB (Mil) 1981; MBIM: *m* 1952, Marion Loudon, da of late Robert Alfred Constantine, TD, JP, of Tanton Grange, Stokesley, Yorks, and has issue living, (Ronald) Simon Constantine (191 Annie St, New Farm, Brisbane, Qld 4005, Australia), *b* 1954; *ed* Wellington Coll: *m* 1990, Rosemary Alexandra, yr da of P. G. F. Lancaster, of Aston Flamville, Leics, and has issue living, Nicholas Peter Lancaster *b* 1993, Maia Marita *b* 1995, — Mark Francis, *b* 1955; *ed* Wellington Coll, — Rupert William, *b* 1962: *m* 1986, Lesley, el da of late J.K. Buckle, of Harlow, Essex, and has issue living, Sarah Frances *b* 1991. ——†Robin Francis, MBE, *b* 1930; *ed* Winchester; is late Capt King's Roy Rifle Corps; MBE (Civil) 1975: *m* 1957, Diana Mary, yr da of late Lt-Col Latham Valentine Stewart Blacker, OBE (E Peel), and *d* 1994, leaving issue, Jonathan Stewart, *b* 1959; *ed* Eton, and Oxford Univ: *m* 1992, Lesley A., da of Eric Rogers, and has issue living, Theodore *b* 1996, Polly *b* 1996, Willow *b* (triplets) 1996. *Residence* – Furlongs, Drayton St Leonard, Oxford.

Issue of the late (Charles) Vernon Balfour Cavendish, *b* 1902; *d* 1981: *m* 1st, 1938 (*m diss* 1950), Nancy Cranswick Neal, who *d* 1986, da of Ernest William Redstone; 2ndly, 1963, Eve, who *d* 1986, widow of Athelston Douglas Dempster Bonnor:—
(By 1st *m*) Rosalind, *b* 1945: *m* 1971, Alan Hugh Davidson, of 16A Clarendon Rd, Colliers Wood, SW19 2DU.

Grandchildren of late Capt Godfrey Lionel John Cavendish, 2nd (but eldest surv) son of late Reginald Richard Frederick Cavendish, eldest son of late Francis William Henry Cavendish (infra):—
Issue of late Capt Godfrey Herbert Richard Cavendish, *b* 1912, *d* 1958: *m* 1950, Angela Margaret Jervis (9 Oakhill Place, SW15 2QN), da of late Lt-Col William Gerald Officer, late Duke of Wellington's Regt, of 37 Lowndes St, SW1:—
Diana Grace Angela, *b* 1954: *m* 1975, (Frederick) John Reeves, of Kilmichael House, Kilmichael Glassary, by Lochgilphead, Argyll PA31 8QA, and has issue living, Henry Frederick Godfrey, *b* 1981, — Georgina Caroline Angela, *b* 1984, — Olivia Clare Lucy, *b* 1989. —— Caroline Elizabeth Clare (*Hon Mrs Philip Remnant*), *b* 1956: *m* 1977, Hon Philip John Remnant, of Ham Farm House, Baughurst, nr Basingstoke, Hants RG26 5SD, el son of 3rd Baron Remnant, and has issue (*see* B Remnant).

Issue of late (Hubert) Gordon Compton Cavendish, *b* 1913, *d* 1993: *m* 1942, Beaujolois Inez (Bosvathick, Constantine, Falmouth, Cornwall TR11 5RD), da of late Capt Philip George Wodehouse, DSO, RN (*see* E Kimberley, colls):—
Richard Gordon John (10 Basil Close, Earley, Reading, Berks), *b* 1949; *ed* Sherborne; Capt British Airways: *m* 1st, 1973 (*m diss* 1980), Jill Dare, da of Frank D. Baker, of Sunbury on Thames; 2ndly, 1981, Mrs Susan Denton, da of John Glyndwr Thomas, and has issue living (by 1st *m*), Charles William Gordon, *b* 1975, — Susanna Lucy, *b* 1974, — (by 2nd *m*) Theresa Louise, *b* 1983. —— (Beaujolois) Katharine, *b* 1947: *m* 1978, Stephen Charles Smyth-Tyrrell, of Bosvathick, Constantine, Falmouth, Cornwall TR11 5RD, and has issue living, Philip Charles, *b* 1981, — Eleanor Katharine Beaujolois, *b* 1979, — Josephine Clare, *b* 1983.

Grandson of late Ernest Lionel Francis Cavendish, 3rd son of late Francis William Henry Cavendish, 2nd son of Gen Hon Henry Frederick Compton Cavendish, MP, 3rd son of 1st Earl of Burlington, who was uncle of 7th Duke:—
Issue of late Maj Alwyn Lionel Compton Cavendish, *b* 1890, *d* 1928: *m* 1917, Muriel Cecil Harriotte, who *d* 1975, having *m* 3rdly, 1946, 2nd Baron Forteviot, who *d* 1947, da of late Lt-Col Sir Charles Henry Brabazon Heaton-Ellis, CBE, of Wyddiall Hall, Herts, and widow of Richard Charles Graves-Sawle, Lt Coldm Gds (Graves-Sawle, Bt (ext)):—
Charles Francis Alwyn Compton (6 King Alfred Terrace, Winchester, Hants SO23 7DE), *b* 1919; *ed* Eton, and at Fettes; is Lieut King's Own Scottish Borderers; formerly 2nd Lt 8th Hussars and Intelligence Corps; 1939-45 War in Middle East and NW Europe (wounded): *m* 1st, 1943 (*m diss* 1946), Margaret Savage (Section Officer, WAAF), who *d* 1961, da of Capt Philip Clayton Alcock, DL, JP, late Gloucester Regt, of Overton Lodge, Ludlow, Shropshire; 2ndly, 1947, Esther Marion, only da of Col Chichester de Windt Crookshank, of Johnstounburn, Humbie, East Lothian, and has issue living, (by 2nd *m*) William Alwyn Charles Chichester (Pippin Cottage, 3 Gastons Rd, Malmesbury, Wilts), *b* 1956: *m* 1985, Margaret Josephine, da of Joseph Benedict MacDonald, of Antigonish, Nova Scotia, and has issue living, Myles Joseph Charles *b* 1991, Monica Josephine Patricia *b* 1988, — Mark Andrew Lionel Compton (Benham Grange, Halfway, Newbury, Berks), *b* 1958: *m* 1988, Sarah Jane, elder da of Richard Formby, of Chartley Hall, Stafford, and has issue living, George Andrew Francis Stuart *b* 1989, Edward Charles Robert Pitcairn *b* 1994, Katharine Mary Louise *b* 1991. *Club* – Turf.

Grandson of late William Henry Alexander George Delmar Cavendish (infra):—
Issue of the late Charles Alfred William Delmar Cavendish, *b* 1878, *d* 1939: *m* 1st, 1914 (*m diss* 1926), Ruth Madeline, yst da of late Henry William Smith, of Sydney, NSW; 2ndly, 1926, Marguerite Florence, who *d* 1943, eldest da of Henri Moreau, of Paris, and Sydney, NSW:—
(By 1st *m*) Richard Blake Delmar, *b* 1916.

Grandchildren of late William Henry George Cavendish, yr son of late William Henry Alexander George Delmar Cavendish, only child of Capt George Henry Cavendish, 5th son of Gen Hon Henry Frederick Compton Cavendish, MP (ante):—
Issue of the late Capt Edwin Pearson Delmar Cavendish, *b* 1908, *d* 1970: *m* 1943, Daphne Joan (Banchory

Cottage, Hinton St George, Som), da of the late Maj William John Van de Weyer, MVO (V Powerscourt), and widow of Sqdn Ldr Charles Richard John Pink, RAF:—
Adrian Delmar (The Dairy House, 611 Merrimac Dr, Lexington, Kentucky, USA), *b* 1947; late LG: *m* 1982, Louise Russell, da of Thomas Allison Ray, Snr, of Ramona, California, USA, and has issue living, John Spencer, *b* 1987.

Issue of late Capt William Delmar Cavendish, *b* 1911, *d* 1997: *m* 1943, Luisa (Via Gramsci 36, 00197 Rome, Italy), da of Antonio Fusco, of Catania, Italy:—
William Anthony Delmar (157 East 72nd St, New York, NY, USA), *b* 1952; *ed* San Leone Magno Sch, and Columbia Univ, New York; Kt of Order of SS Mauritius and Lazarus: *m* 1979, Liliana De La Barbara, of New York, and has issue living, Edward William Henry Delmar, *b* 1987, — Georgiana Beatrice, *b* 1985. —— Jessica Luisa, *b* 1946.

Descendants of late Hon Charles Compton Cavendish (4th son of 1st Earl of Burlington), who was *cr Baron Chesham* 1858 (see that title).

PREDECESSORS – (1) Sir WILLIAM Cavendish, KB; *cr Baron Cavendish*, of Hardwicke (peerage of England) 1605, and *Earl of Devonshire* (peerage of England) 1618; *d* 1625; *s* by his son (2) WILLIAM, 2nd Earl; *d* 1628; *s* by his son (3) WILLIAM, 3rd Earl; *d* 1684; *s* by his son (4) WILLIAM, KG, PC, 4th Earl; MP for co Derby, Lord-Lieut of Derbyshire and Lord Steward of the Household; *cr Marquess of Hartington*, and *Duke of Devonshire* (peerage of England) 1694; *d* 1707; *s* by his son (5) WILLIAM, KG, 2nd Duke; *s* by his son (6) WILLIAM, KG, 3rd Duke; Lord Steward of the Household 1729, Lord-Lieut of Ireland 1737-44; *d* 1755; *s* by his son (7) WILLIAM, KG, 4th Duke; summoned to House of Lords in his father's Barony of Cavendish 1751; Lord-Lieut of Ireland 1755, First Lord of the Treasury 1756-7, Master of the Horse, Lord Chamberlain 1757, &c: *m* Charlotte Elizabeth, *Baroness Clifford*, da of Richard, 4th Earl of Cork, whose claim to the Barony of Clifford, of Lanesborough (peerage of England, *cr* 1628), had been allowed; his 3rd son, George Augustus Henry, was *cr Earl of Burlington* and *Baron Cavendish*, of Keighley (peerage of United Kingdom) 1831; *d* 1764; *s* by his el son (8) WILLIAM, KG, 5th Duke, who in 1754 had *s* his mother as Baron Clifford; *d* 1811; *s* by his son (9) WILLIAM SPENCER, KG, PC, 6th Duke, Lord-Lieut of co Derby *d* unmarried 1858, when the Barony of Clifford became abeyant between his two sisters, and the other honours devolved upon (10) WILLIAM, KG, 7th Duke, who had in 1834 *s* his grandfather as 2nd Earl of Burlington (el son of the Hon William Cavendish, MP, el son of 1st Earl of Burlington (ante), by Louisa, el da of 1st Baron Lismore), *b* 1808; Chancellor of London Univ 1836-56, and of Camb Univ 1862-91, and Lord-Lieut of Lancashire 1855-8, and of Derbyshire 1858-91; MP for Camb Univ (*L*) 1829-31, for Molton 1831, and for N Derbyshire 1831-4: *m* 1829, Lady Blanche Georgiana Howard, who *d* 1840, da of 6th Earl of Carlisle, KG; *d* 1891; *s* by his el son (11) SPENCER COMPTON, KG, GCVO, PC, DCL, LLD, 8th Duke, *b* 1833; attached to Earl Granville's Special Embassy to Russia 1856, and went to St Petersburg to attend the Coronation of Alexander II 1857; a Lord of the Admiralty 1863, Under-Sec for War 1863-6, Sec of State for War 1866, Postmaster-Gen 1868-70, Ch Sec for Ireland 1870-74, Lord Rector of Glasgow Univ 1877-80, Sec of State for India 1880-82 and for War 1882-5, Pres of Board of Education 1900-1902, and Lord Pres of the Council and Pres of Council of National Defence 1895-1903; Lord-Lieut of Derbyshire and High Steward of Derby; MP for N Lancashire 1857-68, for New Radnor (*L*) 1869-80, for Lancashire, NE 1880-85, and for Rossendale Div of NE Lancashire 1885-91 (LU): *m* 1892, Louise Frederica Augusta, who *d* 1911, da of the late Charles, Count von Alten, of Hanover, and widow of 7th Duke of Manchester, *d* 1908; *s* by his nephew (12) VICTOR CHRISTIAN WILLIAM, KG, GCMG, GCVO, TD, PC (el son of late Lord Edward Cavendish, MP, 3rd son of the 7th Duke), 9th Duke; *b* 1868; was Treasurer of HM's Household 1900-1903, Financial Sec to the Treasury 1903-5, a Civil Lord of the Admiralty 1915, Gov-Gen and Com-in-Ch, Dominion of Canada 1916-21, Sec of State for the Colonies 1922-4, and Chm of Executive Council of British Empire Exhibition 1924 and 1925; sat as MP for Derbyshire, W Div (LU) 1891-1908; bore Queen Consort's Crown at Coronation of King George V: *m* 1892, Lady Evelyn Emily Mary Fitzmaurice, GCVO, who *d* 1960, da of 5th Marquess of Lansdowne; *d* 1938; *s* by his el son (13) EDWARD WILLIAM SPENCER, KG, MBE, TD, 10th Duke; *b* 1895; Train Bearer at Coronation of King George V 1911; was Parliamentary Under-Sec of State for Dominion Affairs 1936-40, for India and Burma 1940-42, and for the Colonies 1942-45; sat as MP for W Div of Derbyshire (*U*) 1923-38: *m* 1917, Lady Mary Alice Gascoyne-Cecil, GCVO, CBE, who *d* 1988, da of 4th Marquess of Salisbury; *d* 1950; *s* by his only surviving son (14) ANDREW ROBERT BUXTON, 11th Duke and present peer; also Marquess of Hartington, Earl of Devonshire, Earl of Burlington, Baron Cavendish of Hardwicke, and Baron Cavendish of Keighley.

Dewar, family name of Baron Forteviot.

DHOLAKIA, BARON (Dholakia) (Life Baron 1997)

NAVNIT DHOLAKIA, OBE, son of Permananddas Mulji Dholakia, of Bhavnagar, India; *b* 4 March 1937; *ed* Home Sch and Inst of Science, Bhavnagar, Gujarat, and Brighton Technical Coll; Medical Laboratory Technician, Southlands Hosp, Shoreham-by-Sea 1960-66; Development Offr, Nat Cttee for Commonwealth Immigrants 1966-68, Senior Development Offr 1968-74, Principal Offr and Sec 1974-76, Community Relations Commn; with Commn for Racial Equality 1976-94; Memb Home Office and other Cttees; Memb Howard League for Penal Reform since 1992; Chm NACRO since 1998; Memb Governing Body of Commonwealth Inst since 1998; Chm Brighton Young Liberals 1959-62 and Brighton Liberal Assoc 1962-64; Memb Brighton CBC (Lib) 1961-64; Memb Cncl SCF since

1992; JP Mid-Sussex 1978; *cr* OBE 1994, and *Baron Dholakia*, of Waltham Brooks, co W Sussex (Life Baron) 1997: *m* 1967, Ann, da of Harold McLuskie, of London, and has issue.
Residence – 76 Penland Rd, Haywards Heath, W Sussex RH16 1PH.

DAUGHTERS LIVING

Hon Anjali, *b* 19—; *ed* Edinburgh Univ.
Hon Alene, *b* 19—; *ed* St Bartholomew's Medical Coll.

DIAMOND, BARON (Diamond) (Life Baron 1970)

JOHN DIAMOND, PC, son of late Rev Solomon Diamond, of Leeds; *b* 30 April 1907; *ed* Leeds Gram Sch; LLD (hc); FCA; PPS to Min of Works 1947, and Chm of Finance Cttee, Gen Nursing Council 1947-53; Hon Treas of Fabian Soc 1950-64, Dir Sadler's Wells Trust 1957-64; Hon Treas Labour Cttee for Europe 1961-64; Ch Sec to Treasury (and Member of Cabinet 1968-70) 1964-70; Prin Dep Chm of Cttees, House of Lords 1974; Chm Royal Commn on Distribution of Income and Wealth 1974-79, of Civil Ser Advisory Cttee on Business Appointments 1975-88, and of Industry and Parliament Trust 1976-81; Trustee Social Democratic Party 1981-82, Leader SDP in House of Lords 1982-88; MP for Blackley, Manchester (*Lab*) 1945-51, and for Gloucester 1957-70; *cr* PC 1965, and *Baron Diamond* in City of Gloucester (Life Baron) 1970: *m* 1st, 1932 (*m diss* 1947), Sadie Lyttleton (decd); 2ndly, 1948 (*m diss* 19—), Julie Malamuth (decd); 3rdly, 1976, Barbara Jean, da of late Joseph Blower, of Duffield, Derbys, and has issue by 1st and 2nd *m*.
Residence – Aynhoe, Doggetts Wood Lane, Chalfont-St-Giles, Bucks HP8 4TH.

SONS LIVING (By 1st marriage)

Hon Derek R. (9 Ashley Drive, Walton-on-Thames, Surrey KT12 1JL), *b* 1933: *m* 1957, Esme Grace ......, and has issue living, Andrew Richard, *b* 1961, — Stella Ruth, *b* 1963.
Hon Martin, *b* 1935.

DAUGHTERS LIVING (By 1st marriage)

Hon Ruth, *b* 1937.

(By 2nd marriage)

Hon (Patricia) Joan, *b* 1949.

DICKINSON, BARON (Dickinson) (Baron UK 1930)

RICHARD CLAVERING HYETT DICKINSON, 2nd Baron; *b* 2 March 1926; *s* 1943; *ed* Eton, and Trin Coll, Oxford; late Capt Coldstream Guards: *m* 1st, 1957 (*m diss* 19—), (Margaret) Ann, el da of late Brigadier Gilbert Reader McMeekan, CBE, DSO; 2ndly, 1980, Mrs Rita Doreen Moir, and has issue by 1st *m*.

Arms – Or, a bend cottised between two lions passant gules. **Crest** – Issuant from clouds a dexter cubit arm erect the hand holding an olive branch fructed all proper. **Supporters** – *Dexter*, a falcon proper, collared and lined or; *sinister*, a dove holding in the beak an olive branch fructed both proper.
Residence – Painswick House, Stroud, Gloucestershire.

SONS LIVING (*By 1st marriage*)

Hon MARTIN HYETT, *b* 30 Jan 1961: *m* 1995, Caroline Sally, da of Nigel Edwards, of Bristol.
Hon Andrew, *b* 1963.

BROTHERS LIVING (*Raised to the rank of a Baron's sons* 1944)

Hon Peter Malcolm de Brissac, *b* 1927; *ed* Eton, and at King's Coll, Camb: *m* 1st, 1953, Mary Rose, who *d* 1988, el da of late Vice-Adm Sir Geoffrey Barnard, KCB, CBE, DSO; 2ndly, 1992, Jennifer Carolyn Robin McKinley, of Blue Hill, Maine, USA, and has issue living (by 1st *m*), John Geoffrey Hyett, *b* 1962: *m* 1992, Philippa Ann, da of Michael Thomson, and has issue living, Rosemary Clare *b* 1994, — James Christopher Meade, *b* 1963: *m* 1988, Sarah Ann, da of John Reid, and has issue living, Samuel George Lambourne *b* 1992, Andrew Francis Southey *b* 1994, — Philippa Lucy Anne, *b* 1955: *m* 1983, Stephen West, son of Reginald West, and has issue living, Nicholas Oliver *b* 1988, — Polly, *b* 1956; assumed the name of Polly in lieu of her baptismal names of Dorothy Louise; has issue by former *m*, David ADELMAN *b* 1988. *Residence* – Bramdean Lodge, nr Alresford, Hants.
Very Rev Hon Hugh Geoffrey (22 St Peter's Rd, Cirencester, Glos GL7 1RG), *b* 1929; *ed* Westminster Sch, and Trin and Cuddesdon Colls, Oxford; Chap, Trin Coll, Camb 1958-63, and Winchester Coll 1963-69, Bishop's Adviser for Adult Education Coventry Diocese 1969-77, V of St Michael's, St Albans 1977-86, Dean of Salisbury 1986-96, since when Dean Emeritus: *m* 1963, Jean Marjorie, only da of Arthur Storey, of 25 Woodbourne Av, Leeds, 17, and has issue living, Benjamin Mark, *b* 1966, — Teresa, *b* 1964.
Hon David Christopher (Nanneys Bridge, Church Minshull, Nantwich, Ches), *b* 1935; *ed* Eton and Trin Coll, Oxford: *m* 1970, Caroline Mary, da of late Arthur Denton Toosey, and widow of Peter Yeoward.

MOTHER LIVING

May Southey, da of Charles Lovemore, of Melsetter, Cape Province, S Africa; is a JP: *m* 1924, Hon Richard Sebastian Willoughby Dickinson, DSO, who *d* 1935, only son of 1st Baron. *Residence* – The Poultry Court, Painswick, Gloucestershire.

PREDECESSOR – (1) *Rt Hon* WILLOUGHBY HYETT Dickinson, KBE, only son of late Sebastian Stewart Dickinson (MP for Stroud), of Brown's Hill, Stroud; *b* 1859; Chm of London County Council 1900; sat as MP for N Div of St Pancras (*L*) 1906-18; *cr Baron Dickinson*, of Painswick, co Gloucester (peerage of United Kingdom) 1930: *m* 1891, Minnie Elizabeth, who *d* 1967, da of late Gen Sir Richard John Meade, KCSI, CIE; *d* 1943; *s* by his grandson (2) RICHARD CLAVERING HYETT (el son of late Hon Richard Sebastian Willoughby Dickinson, DSO, only son of 1st Baron), 2nd Baron and present peer.

DIGBY, BARON (Digby) (Baron I 1620, and GB 1765)

EDWARD HENRY KENELM DIGBY, KCVO, 12th Baron, *b* 24 July 1924; *s* 1964; *ed* Eton, and Trin Coll,Oxford; Hon Fellow of Roy Agric Soc of the Commonwealth 1977; Capt late Coldm Gds; Hon Col 4th Bn Devonshire and Dorset Regt; Lord Lieut Dorset 1984; JP 1960; Pres Wessex Branch Inst of Directors, and Council of St John, Dorset; Patron Dorset Red Cross; Pres Royal Bath and West Soc 1976; Dep Chm SW Economic Planning Council 1972-79; Vice-Chm Dorset County Council 1974-81; Capt Lords and Commons Ski Club 1982-85; Dir Beazer plc, Gifford-Hill Inc, and Paccar (UK) Ltd; ADC to C-in-C Far East Forces 1950-51, and to C-in-C, BAOR 1951-52; 1939-45 War; Malaya 1948-50; KStJ 1985; KCVO 1999: *m* 1952, Dione Marian, DBE, DL Dorset, da of Rear-Adm Robert St Vincent Sherbrooke, VC, CB, DSO, and has issue.

Arms – Azure, a fleur-de-lis argent. Crest – An ostrich with a horse-shoe in its beak, all proper. Supporters – Two monkeys proper, environed round the loins and lined or.
Residence – Minterne, Dorchester, Dorset DT2 7AU. *Club* – Pratt's.

From God not Fortune

SONS LIVING

Hon HENRY NOEL KENELM, *b* 6 Jan 1954; *ed* Eton; ACA; Dir Jardine Fleming Investment Management Ltd: *m* 1980, Susan E., el da of Peter Watts, of 6 Albert Terr Mews, NW1, and has issue living, Edward St Vincent Kenelm, *b* 5 Sept 1985, — Alexandra Jane Kira, *b* 1987.
Hon Rupert Simon, *b* 1956; *ed* Eton, and Southampton Univ (BSc); Technical Mangr Vodafone Value Added and Data Services Ltd: *m* 1986, Charlotte Fleury, yr da of late Robert Hirst, of Durford Mill, nr Petersfield, and has issue living, Arabella Dione, *b* 1989, — Olivia, *b* 1991. *Residence* – Rookwood Farmhouse, Stockcross, nr Newbury, Berks RG16 8JX.

DAUGHTER LIVING

Hon Zara Jane, *b* 1958; dress designer: *m* 1993, as his 2nd wife, James Edward Caulfeild Percy (*see* D Northumberland, colls).

SISTERS LIVING

Hon Constance Sheila, *b* 1921; in ATS 1939-40, and with British Security Co-ordination 1943-45, *m* 1945, Charles Arthur Moore, who *d* 1989. *Residences* – Bearforest, Mallow, co Cork; 5310 Chemin de Vie, Atlanta, Georgia 30342, USA.
Hon Jaquetta Mary Theresa, *b* 1928; a Member of Mid-Sussex Hosp Cttee 1960-68, and of Dorset Area Health Authority 1974-81; Chm, Hamilton Lodge Sch for Deaf Children, Brighton 1962-80: *m* 1950, David Pelham James, MBE, DSC, MP, who *d* 1986, having assumed the addl surname of Guthrie before his patronymic 1979, el son of Wing-Com Sir Archibald William Henry James, KBE, MC, and has issue living, Peter Edward, *b* 1951; *ed* Downside, — Michael David Ashworth, *b* 1955; *ed* Downside: *m* 1996, Namrata Rai, and has issue living, Sahayavalle *b* 1998, — Christopher Leslie Donan (Torosay Castle, Isle of Mull, Argyllshire PA65 6AY), *b* 1957; *ed* Downside, and Edinburgh Univ: *m* 1997, Sarah Finlayson, and has issue living, Fenella *b* 1997, — Kenelm Henry Thomas, *b* 1962; *ed* Downside, — Patricia Bridget Edwina, *b* 1952; *ed* Mayfield, and York Univ: *m* 1989, Ian Maxwell, of 5 St Marks Place, Edinburgh, and has issue living, Rowan *b* 1992, Anna *b* 1989, — Diana Mary GUTHRIE JAMES, *b* 1953; has resumed her maiden name: *m* 1972 (*m diss* 1980), Alan Fry, and has issue living, Daniel James *b* 1972, Adam James *b* 1975, Susannah James *b* 1974; and has further issue, Mairina James *b* 1991. *Residence* – Torosay Castle, Isle of Mull, Argyllshire PA65 6AY.

COLLATERAL BRANCHES LIVING

Granddaughters of late Hon Robert Henry Digby (infra):—
Issue of late Henry Berkeley Digby, *b* 1933, *d* 1992: *m* 1st, 1960 (*m diss* 1983), Jacqueline Winifred, elder da of Charles A. Hussey, of Barking, Essex; 2ndly, 1983, Mrs Rosalie McLaren (5 Carlton House Terrace, W1; San Pedro de Alcantara, Prov Malaga, Spain), eldest da of Maj Richard Atkinson-Turner, of Worlington, Suffolk, and formerly wife of Andrew McLaren, of Coughton, Warwicks:—
(By 1st *m*) Jane Diana, *b* 1962: *m* 1987, Christoph D. Auer, eldest son of Ernst Auer, of Grunwald, Munich, Germany, and has issue living, Charles Felix Ernst, *b* 1991, — Hugo Henry Berkeley, *b* 1995. —— (Charlotte) Sophia, *b* 1964.

Issue of late Hon Robert Henry Digby, 2nd son of 10th Baron, *b* 1903; *d* 1959: *m* 1928, Diana Mary, who *d* 1969, da of Sir Berkeley Digby George Sheffield, 6th Bt:—
Caroline Theresa, *b* 1943: *m* 1963, Charles Dermot Fitzroy Musker (*see* V Daventry, 1985 Edn), and has issue living, Dermot Henry, *b* 1964, — Rupert Anthony, *b* 1975, — Emily Mary, *b* 1972, — Chloé Diana Leopoldine, *b* 1979. *Residence* – Sallowfield Cottage, Wattlefield, Wymondham, Norfolk NR18 9PA.

Grandson of late Sir Kenelm Edward Digby, GCB, KC, eldest son of late Rev Hon Kenelm Henry Digby (infra):—

Issue of late Com Edward Aylmer Digby, KC, *b* 1883, *d* 1935: *m* 1911, Winifred Digby, who *d* 1967, da of
Arthur George Watson, DCL, JP:—
Kenelm Hubert (3 Mount St, Wellington, NZ), *b* 1912: *m* 1946, Mutal Agnes Helen, only da of Bertram E. Fielder, of
Glebe Farm, Sherfield English, Romsey, and has issue living, Noel Kenelm (9 Montacute Close, Farnborough, Hants
GU14 7HG), *b* 1946: *m* 1993, Helen Anne, da of late Frank Hope, of London, and has issue living, Aleisha Grace *b* 1994,
— Geoffrey Aylmer, *b* 1957, — Rosalind Clare, *b* 1948.

Grandsons of late Algernon Digby, 6th and yst son of late Rev Hon Kenelm Henry Digby, brother of
9th Baron:—
Issue of late Thomas Hankinson Digby, *b* 1892, *d* 1985: *m* (Jan) 1938, Diana Broughton, who *d* 1998, only da of
Lt-Col Frederick Guy Knight, MC, of The Oaks, Queningborough, Leics:—
Simon Kenelm (12 Busby House, Aldrington Rd, SW16 1TZ), *b* (Dec) 1938; *ed* Marlborough: *m* 1st, 1961 (*m diss* 1965),
Ann Stallard, only da of Rev Geoffrey Kitson Walton; 2ndly, 1965 (*m diss* 1978), Sylvia Josephine, da of John Cheers, and
has issue living (by 2nd *m*), Oliver Francis, *b* 1966, — Roland Anthony, *b* 1969. —— Patrick Timothy (Bryngwyn,
Llandissilio, Clunderwen, Dyfed SA66 7UR), *b* 1941; *ed* Bradfield: *m* 1973, Lyneth Anne, da of David Clee, and has issue
living, Huw Timothy, *b* 1975, — Catrin Elizabeth, *b* 1978. —— Robin Paul (Ramlösavägen 124A, 25656 Helsingborg,
Sweden), *b* 1944; *ed* Radley: *m* 1966, Marja Birgitta, da of Helmer Hägglöf, of Njurunda, Sweden, and has issue living,
Christina Ruth, *b* 1967: *m* 1993, Paul Ellaby, and has issue living, Daniel Jacob Digby *b* 1998, — Joanna Isabel, *b* 1971,
— Rebecca Alice, *b* 1987.

PREDECESSORS – (1) ROBERT Digby, Gov of King's Co; *cr Baron Digby*, of Geashill, King's Co (peerage of Ireland)
1620; *d* 1642; *s* by his son (2) KILDARE, 2nd Baron; *s* by his son (3) ROBERT, 3rd Baron; *s* by his brother (4) SIMON, 4th
Baron; *d* 1686; *s* by his brother (5) WILLIAM, 5th Baron; *d* 1752; *s* by his grandson (6) EDWARD, 6th Baron; *d* unmarried
1757; *s* by his brother (7) HENRY, 7th Baron; *cr Baron Digby*, of Sherborne (peerage of Great Britain) 1765, with
remainder to the issue male of his father, and *Viscount Coleshill* and *Earl Digby* (peerage of Great Britain) 1790; *d* 1793;
s by his son (8) EDWARD, 2nd Earl; Lord-Lieut of Dorset; *d* unmarried 1856, when the viscountcy and earldom became
extinct, and the baronies devolved upon his kinsman (9) EDWARD St VINCENT, 9th Baron, *b* 1809: *m* 1837, Lady Theresa
Anne Maria Fox-Strangways, who *d* 1874, el da of 3rd Earl of Ilchester; *d* 1889; *s* by his el son (10) EDWARD HENRY
TRAFALGAR, 10th Baron, *b* 1846; sat as MP for Dorsetshire (C) 1876-85: *m* 1893, Emily Beryl Sissy, who *d* 1928, da of
Hon Albert Hood; *d* 1920; *s* by his el son (11) EDWARD KENELM, KG, DSO, MC, TD, 11th Baron, *b* 1894; Col late Cold-
stream Guards, Lord-Lieut of Dorset 1952-64, and Chm of Dorset Co Council 1955-64: *m* 1919, Hon Constance Pamela
Alice Bruce, OBE, JP, who *d* 1978, da of 2nd Baron Aberdare; *d* 1964; *s* by his only son (11) EDWARD HENRY KENELM,
12th Baron and present peer.

DILHORNE, VISCOUNT (Manningham-Buller) (Viscount UK 1964, Bt UK 1866)

The eagle does not catch flies

JOHN MERVYN MANNINGHAM-BULLER, 2nd Viscount,
and 5th Baronet; *b* 28 Feb 1932; *s* 1980; *ed* Eton;
formerly Lt Coldstream Gds; Barrister at Law (1979);
a Fellow of Inst of Taxation and a Member of Wilts
Co Council 1967-70: *m* 1st, 1955 (*m diss* 1973), Gillian
Evelyn, JP, da of Col George Cochrane Stockwell;
2ndly, 1981, Mrs Susannah Jane Gilchrist, formerly
wife of Colin Gilchrist, and da of Cmdr W. C. Eykyn,
RN, and has issue living by 1st *m*.

Arms – Quarterly: 1st and 4th, sable, on a cross argent quarterly
pierced of the field, four eagles displayed of the first, *Buller*; 2nd
and 3rd, sable, a fesse ermine in chief three griffins' heads
erased or, *Manningham*. **Crest** - 1st a Saracen's head affrontée
couped proper; 2nd, out of a ducal coronet gules, a talbot's head
or, collared gules, line terminating in a knot sable. **Supporters** –
Dexter, An Eagle wings elevated and addorsed ermine beaked and
legged or gorged with a ducal coronet gules therefrom a line
reflexed over the back and terminating in a knot sable; *sinister*, a
Pegasus azure winged crined unguled and queued argent both
charged on the shoulder with a Portcullis chained gold.
Residence - 164 Ebury St, SW1. **Clubs** - Buck's, Pratt's, MCC,
Beefsteak, Savage.

SONS LIVING (By 1st marriage)

Hon JAMES EDWARD, *b* 20 Aug 1956; formerly Capt WG: *m* 1985, Nicola Marion, el da of late Sven Mackie, of Ballydugan
House, Downpatrick, co Down, and has issue living, Edward John, *b* 25 Jan 1990, — Camilla Mary, *b* 1992. *Residence* –
Ballymote House, Downpatrick, co Down.

Hon Mervyn Reginald, *b* 1962: *m* 1st, 1989, Lucy Meriel, da of George Thurstan; 2ndly, 1996, Lara Caroline Dudley,
eldest da of James Calcraft Dudley Ryder (*see* E Harrowby, colls). *Residence* - 126 Hurlingham Rd, SW6 3NF.

DAUGHTER LIVING (*By 1st marriage*)

Hon Mary Louise, *b* 1970: *m* 1992, Capt James M. Cowan, The Black Watch (Royal Highland Regt), eldest son of Col Edward Cowan, of Marnhull, Dorset, and has issue living, Fergus Edward Napoleon, *b* 1996.

SISTERS LIVING

Hon Marian Cynthia, *b* 1934: *m* 1955, Edmund Crispin Stephen James George Brudenell (*see* M Ailesbury, colls). *Residences* – Deene Park, Corby, Northants NN17 3EW; 10 Lochmore House, Ebury St, SW1.
Hon Elizabeth Lydia, *b* 1948.
Hon Anne Constance, *b* 1951: *m* 1982, John Christopher Parsons, CVO (*see* E Rosse, colls).

AUNT LIVING (*Daughter of Lt-Col Sir Mervyn E. Manningham-Buller, 3rd Bt*)

Pamela Lilah (6 Glenthorne Rd, Torquay TQ1 1QL), *b* 1919; CC Devon 1973-85: *m* 1951, Norman Wilkinson-Cox, who *d* 1969, and has issue living, Gavia Lilah, *b* 1952.

WIDOW LIVING OF FIRST VISCOUNT

Lady MARY LINDSAY (*Dowager Viscountess Dilhorne*) 4th da of 27th Earl of Crawford and Balcarres: *m* 1930, Sir Reginald Edward Manningham-Buller, 4th Bt (*cr* Viscount Dilhorne 1964), PC, who *d* 1980.

PREDECESSORS – (1) EDWARD Manningham-Buller, of Dilhorne Hall, Staffs, 3rd son of Sir Francis Buller, 2nd Bt (*cr* 1790) and brother of 1st Baron Churston; *b* 1800; assumed by Roy Licence 1866 the additional surname of Manningham; MP for N Staffs 1833-42, 1867 and 1874, and for Stafford 1842-47; *cr* a Baronet 1866: *m* 1st, 1824, Mary Anne, who *d* 1860, da and heir of Maj-Gen Coote Manningham; 2ndly, 1863, Georgina Charlotte, who *d* 1875, da and heir of Adm of the Fleet Sir Charles Edmund Nugent, GCM, and widow of the Rt Hon George Bankes MP; *d* 1882; *s* by his el son (2) *Sir* MORTON EDWARD, 2nd Bt, *b* 1825: *m* 1865, Mary, who *d* 1923, da of William Davenport, of Maer Hall, Staffs; *d* 1910; *s* by his nephew (3) *Sir* MERVYN EDWARD (only son of Maj-Gen Edmund Manningham-Buller), 3rd Bt; Lt-Col Rifle Bde, and MP for Kettering 1924-29, and Northampton 1931-40: *m* 1903, Hon Lilah Constance Cavendish, OBE, who *d* 1944, da of 3rd Baron Chesham; *d* 1956; *s* by his only son (4) *Sir* REGINALD EDWARD, 4th Bt, *b* 1905; Solicitor-Gen 1951-54, Attorney-Gen 1954-62, Lord High Chancellor 1962-64 and Dep Leader of Opposition, House of Lords 1964-66; a Lord of Appeal in Ordinary 1969-80; MP for Daventry Div of Northants (*C*) 1943-50, and for S Div of Northants 1950-62; *cr* Knt 1951, PC 1954, *Baron Dilhorne*, of Towcester, co Northampton (peerage of UK) 1962, and *Viscount Dilhorne*, of Greens Norton, co Northampton (peerage of UK) 1964: *m* 1930, Lady Mary Lilian Lindsay, 4th da of 27th Earl of Crawford and Balcarres; *d* 1980; *s* by his only son (5) *Sir* JOHN MERVYN, 5th Bt, and present peer; also Baron Dilhorne.

DILLON, VISCOUNT (Dillon) (Viscount I 1622)

While I breathe I hope

HENRY (HARRY) BENEDICT CHARLES DILLON, 22nd Viscount; *b* 6 Jan 1973; *s* 1982; is *Count Dillon* in France (*cr* 1711).

Arms – Quarterly: 1st and 4th argent, a lion passant, between three crescents gules, *Dillon*; 2nd and 3rd argent, a fesse between three crescents sable, *Lee*. **Crest** – A demi-lion gules, holding in its paws an estoile argent. **Supporters** – Two angels proper, vested argent, winged and crined or, each holding in the exterior hand a branch of palm proper, and having a riband over the shoulder of the second. *Residence* – 28 Canning Cross, SE5 8BH.

SISTER LIVING

Hon Beatrice Inès Renée, *b* 1978.

UNCLES LIVING (*Sons of 20th Viscount*)

Hon RICHARD ARTHUR LOUIS (Brook House, Sudborough, nr Kettering, Northants NN14 3BX) *b* 23 Oct 1948; *ed* Downside, and RAC Cirencester; FSVA: *m* 1975, Hon Priscilla Frances Hazlerigg, da of 2nd Baron Hazlerigg, and has issue living, Thomas Arthur Lee, *b* 1 Oct 1983, — Charlotte Frances, *b* 1978.
Hon Patrick Dominic (14 St Mary's Cottages, Drogheda, co Louth), *b* 1956; *ed* Downside, and Trin Coll, Dublin.
Hon Michael Edmond (8 Keslake Rd, NW6 6DL), *b* 1957; *ed* Glenstal, and Hampshire Coll of Agric; painter: *m* 1983, Henrietta Catherine, yr da of Charles J. L. Elwell, of Bottrells Close, Chalfont St Giles, Bucks, and has issue living, Charles Augustus Henry, *b* 1985, — Emily Madeleine, *b* 1987, — Catherine Elizabeth, *b* 1989, — Henrietta Sophie, *b* 1993.

AUNTS LIVING AND DECEASED (Daughters of 20th Viscount)

Hon Isabel Anne Marie Henrietta, *b* 1942: *m* 1970, Richard Alexander Charles Cobbe, of The Manor House, Yattendon, Newbury, Berks RG16 0UH, and has issue living, Thomas Alexander Michael, *b* 1973, — Henry Frederick Hugh, *b* 1975, — Frances Henrietta, *b* 1971, — Rose Eleanor (twin), *b* 1973.

Hon Inès Marie Jeanne, *b* 1952.

Hon Rosaleen Marie Carmel, *b* 1953; *d* as a result of an accident 1960.

Hon Madeleine Marie, LVO (66 Westbourne Terrace, W2 3UJ), *b* (twin) 1957; Assist Private Sec to HRH The Princess Royal since 1988; LVO 1997: *m* 1989, Leonard Constantine Louloudis, only son of Constantine Louloudis, and has issue living, Constantine Michael, *b* 1991, — Theodora Catherine Lily, *b* 1993.

WIDOW LIVING OF TWENTIETH VISCOUNT

IRENE MARIE FRANCE (*Irène Viscountess Dillon*) (14 St Mary's Cottages, Drogheda, co Louth), da of René Merandon du Plessis, of Whitehall, Mauritius: *m* 1939, the 20th Viscount Dillon, who *d* 1979.

WIDOW LIVING OF TWENTY-FIRST VISCOUNT

(MARY) JANE (*Viscountess Dillon*) (28 Canning Cross, SE5 8BH), da of John Young, of Castle Hill House, Birtle, Lancs; designer: *m* 1972, the 21st Viscount Dillon, who *d* 1982.

COLLATERAL BRANCHES LIVING

Grandchildren of late Francis Noel Dillon, only son of late Philip Gerald Dillon, 2nd son of late Hon Constantine Augustus Dillon, 4th son of 13th Viscount:—
Issue of late Patrick Philip Lee Dillon, *b* 1912, *d* 1993: *m* 1937, Joan Elfie (Leefield, Blenheim, NZ), da of G. C. Williams, of Masterton, NZ:—
Patrick Francis (Waikirikiri, RD3, Leeston, Canterbury, NZ), *b* 1946: *m* 1974, Susan Lee, da of Dr Peter Thodey, of Timaru, NZ, and has issue living, Jonathan Patrick Lee, *b* 1977, — Mark Peter Lee, *b* 1981, — Lisa Francis, *b* 1975, — Brigid Louise Lee, *b* 1982. —— Rachel Anne, *b* 1939: *m* 1966, Robert Lionel Savory, of Bengeo Hall, Hereford, and has issue living, Charlotte Katharine Anne, *b* 1968, — Victoria Lucy Lee, *b* 1970, — Josephine Elizabeth, *b* 1972. —— Joanna Lee, *b* 1941: *m* 1963, David Cameron, of Waituna, Waikari, N Canterbury, NZ, and has issue living, Timothy Charles, *b* 1967: *m* 1995, Jo-Ann Mirielle, da of W. J. McKean, of Christchurch, NZ, and has issue living, Archibald William David *b* 1997, — Andrew Lee, *b* 1970, — Nicola Jane, *b* 1965: *m* 1994, Andrew Robert Davie, of Wellington, NZ, and has issue living, Oscar Wilson *b* 1998.

Issue of late Fl-Lt Michael Lee Dillon, RNZAF, *b* 1913, *d* 1968: *m* 1939, Gwendoline Reay (The Tummil, Blenheim, NZ), da of J. W. Trolove, of The Shades, Blenheim, NZ:—
Richard Lee (The Tummil, Blenheim, NZ), *b* 1941: *m* 1965, Elizabeth Campbell, da of J. B. Hay, of Pigeon Bay, Bank's Peninsular, NZ, and has issue living, Nicolas Lee, *b* 1966, — Samuel Hay, *b* 1967, — Sarah Elizabeth, *b* 1971. —— James Michael Lee (Tummil Flat, Blenheim, NZ), *b* 1947: *ed* Christ's Coll, Christchurch: *m* 1974, Maling Eve, da of Michael Joseph Nathan, of Wellington, NZ, and has issue living, Olivia Michal, *b* 1976, — Amber Maling, *b* 1978, — Honor Louisa, *b* 1982. —— Sarah Christine, *b* 1942: *m* 1965, Peter Wallace Coy, of Salt Creek, Woorndoo, Vic, Aust, and has issue living, Edward Francis Dillon, *b* 1974, — Rosa Susan, *b* 1966, — Sally Amanda, *b* 1968, — Georgina Anne, *b* 1971. —— Rosa Lee, *b* 1949: *m* 1975, Michael John Hawdon Davison, of Kaiwara, Culverdon, NZ, and has issue living, Frederick Michael Dillon, *b* 1980, — Antonia Frames Alice, *b* 1979, — Georgina Constance Lee, *b* 1982.

Issue of late Maj Gerald Francis Lee Dillon, NZ Forces, *b* 1917, *d* 1983: *m* 1946, Mary Ritson (Spelsbury, Blenheim, RD1, Marlborough, NZ), da of Cdr T. S. Critchley, RN, of Tirohunga, Blenheim, NZ:—
David Sandford Lee (The Throne, Blenheim, NZ), *b* 1946; late Lieut NZ Army; a farmer: *m* 1973, Susan Hamilton, da of late P. D. Reid, of Blenheim, NZ, and has issue living, Henry Gerald Lee, *b* 1976, — Thomas Patrick Lee, *b* 1979, — Hannah Frances, *b* 1982. —— Susan Ann Lee, *b* 1948: *m* 1974, Richard John Macfarlane, of Winterholme, Kekerengu, Marlborough, NZ, and has issue living, Sandford Samuel, *b* 1975, — Winston William, *b* 1977, — Clive Charles, *b* 1978, — Alexandra Augusta, *b* 1981.

Granddaughter of late Augustus Henry Fitz-Gibbon, 2nd son of late Hon Gerald Normanby Fitz-Gibbon, 6th son of 13th Viscount:—
Issue of late Capt Gerald Ernest George Fitz-Gibbon, MC, *b* 1884, *d* 1929: *m* 1st, 1908 (*m diss* 1912), Mary Monica, who *d* 1930, da of Lt-Col Hugh Marshall Hole, CMG, of 2 London Wall Buildings, EC2; 2ndly, 1914, Hélène, who *d* 1969, da of Etienne Niel, of Rouen, France and widow of Strentham Ford, of Cape Town:—
(By 1st *m*) Elizabeth Rosemary, *b* 1912: *m* 1934, Henry Bockholst Livingston, CBE, who *d* 1968, and has issue living, Nicholas Henry (Valfond, Chemin du Moulin Vieux, 84210 St Didier, Vaucluse, France), *b* 1942; *ed* King's Sch, Canterbury, and King's Coll, Camb (Foundation Scholar); Foreign Office 1964: *m* 1968, Ana Maria, da of late Dr Idilio Oneto, and has issue living, Barnaby *b* 1973, Emma Sophie *b* 1976.

Descendants, if any, of late Clare Valentine Fitz-Gibbon (*b* 1859), who was last heard of in Canada, 4th son of late Hon Gerald Normanby Fitz-Gibbon (infra).

Grandchildren of late Lt-Cdr Robert Francis Lee-Dillon, RN (*Count Robert F. Lee-Dillon* in France), elder son of late Louis Theobald Fitz-Gibbon (infra):—

Issue of late (Robert Louis) Constantine FITZ-GIBBON, the author, b 1919, d 1983: m 1st, 1939 (m diss 1944), Margaret Aye Moung; 2ndly, 1944 (m diss 1960), Theodora Rosling, cookery writer, who d 1991 (having m 2ndly, 19—, George Morrison, film archivist); 3rdly, 1960 (m diss 19—), Marion Gutmann; 4thly, 1967, Marjorie, formerly wife of (i) Huntington Hartford, and (ii) Dudley Sutton, actor, and da of Harold Wright Steele, of Cal, USA:—
(By 3rd m) Francis George Herbert Dillon, b 1961: m 1986, Camilla G. Beresford, and has issue living, Sam, b 1997, — Lily Theodora, b 1987. Residence – 46 Brondesbury Rd, NW6. —— (By 4th m) Oonagh Louise Dillon, b 1968.

Grandson of late Louis Theobald FITZ-GIBBON, 5th and yst son of late Hon Gerald Normanby FITZ-GIBBON, 6th son of 13th Viscount:—
Issue of late Lt-Cdr Robert Francis LEE-DILLON, RN (Count Robert F. Lee-Dillon in France), b 1884, d 1954; having resumed in 1925 the surname of Lee-Dillon: m 1st, (Feb) 1908 (m diss 1923), Georgette (who d 1972), da of George Winthrop Folsom, of Lenox, Mass, USA; 2ndly, 1924, Kathleen Clare, who d 1950, da of late James Aitchison, CE, of Belfast, and Cardigan, Lavender Bay, Sydney, NSW, and widow of Hon Henry Lee Stanton Lee-Dillon (only son of 17th Viscount Dillon) (see V Dillon, colls, 1985 Edn):—
(By 2nd m) Louis Theobald DILLON FITZGIBBON (Flat 2, 8 Portland Place, Brighton, Sussex BN2 1DG), b 1925; assumed by deed poll 1962, the surnames of Dillon FitzGibbon in lieu of Lee-Dillon; Lt RN (ret); Area Pres of St John Ambulance Bde; a Knt of Sovereign Mil Order of Malta; Kt Cdr of Order of Restitution of Poland; Polish Gold Cross of Merit; Cross of Merit (1st Class) of Germany: m 1st, 1950 (m diss 1962), Mrs Josephine McDonald, who d 1979, da of J. H. Webb; 2ndly, 1962, Madeleine Sally Hayward-Surry, who d 1980; 3rdly, 1980, Mrs Joan Elizabeth Jevons, and has issue living (by 2nd m), James Augustus b 1963, — Simone Frances, b 1962, — Michèle Clare, b 1965.

Grandchildren of late John Monro Dillon, 3rd son of late Rev Martin Dillon, 6th in descent from Hon Thomas Dillon, 4th son of 1st Viscount:—
Issue of late Capt Arnold Michael Dillon, b 1892, d 1955: m 1915, Esther Dorothy, da of William Currie Allen, of London, Ontario:—
Arnold Charles, b 1920: m 1947, Donalda Ruth, da of Arthur J. Cowie, of Caledonia, Ontario, Canada, and has issue living, John Michael b 1956, — Dorothy Nina, b 1954. —— Mary Louie Margarette, b 1917: m 1944, Dennis Bishop, late Flying Officer, RAF Vol Reserve, and has issue living, Dennis John, b 1945, — Caroline Mary Beverley Anne, b 1952. Residence –

Grandchildren of late Maurice Ashurst Dillon, 4th son of late Rev Martin Dillon (ante):—
Issue of late Brig Marmaduke Murray Dillon, MC, ED, b 1894, d 1976: m 1st, 1919, Muriel, da of the late Rev Canon Richard Hicks; 2ndly, 1956, Mildred Whitley (842 Wellington St, London, Ont, Canada), widow of Col Charles W. Jeffers, US Army:—
(By 1st m) Richard Maurice, MC, ED; b 1920; BA; Lt-Col (ret) Canadian Mil, Dean of Faculty of Eng Science, W Ont Univ; 1939-45 War in Sicily and Italy (MC); Coronation medal (1953): m 1945, Mary Elizabeth, da of Harry H. Dempsey, of Stratford, Ont, and has issue living, Kelly Elizabeth, b 1949, — Ann Dempsey, b 1952, — Katherine Talbot, b 1955. —— Michael Talbot, CD (Unit 73, 2 Cadeau Terrace, London, Ont N6K 4K7), b 1926; BA, MD; Lt-Col (ret) late RCAMC (M): m 1959, Margaret, da of Roy Kirk Hamilton, of Arthur, Ont, and has issue living, Timothy Arthur, b 1960; ed W Ontario Univ (BSc), and Queen's Univ (MBA), — Kirk Fitzgerald, b 1961; ed W Ontario Univ (BSc, MD): m 1989, Julie Anne, da of Charles Duncan, of London, Ont, and has issue living, Loghan Charles Michael b 1994, Rebecca Anne b 1990, Kate Elizabeth Margaret b 1992, — David Morgan, b 1963; ed W Ontario Univ (BA); has issue living (by Lisa Westalaken), Morgan Jane (who now bears the surname of PASSARELLI) b 1986. —— Shelagh Muriel, b 1924: m 1945, Neil Archibald Watters, MD, FRCS (Canada), of 172 Rosedale Heights Drive, Toronto, and has issue living, Douglas Bruce, b 1948, — James Murray, b 1952, — Michael Grant, b 1955, — Louise Shelagh, b 1959. —— Diana Mary Morgan, b 1926; BA, MD, FRCP: m 1956, Rev Gerald Cecil Johnson, BA, BTh (RR1, Haliburton, Ontario, Canada K0M 1S0), and has had issue, Patrick Bruce, b 1965; d 1988, — Kevin Sean (twin), b 1965: m 1991, Teri Dillon, and has issue living, Dillon Patrick b 1993, Seanna Lee b 1991, — Michele Ann Jean, b 1958: m 1989, Thomas William Stuart Journeaux, and has had issue Kala Jacqueline Diana b 1989, Brianna Angela Morgan b and d 1997, — Margaret Rebecca Morgan, b 1962; has issue living, Saba Patricia JOHNSON b 1989.

Grandson of late Luke Gerald Dillon, OBE, MD, eldest son of Charles Blake Dillon, son of late Luke Dillon, 5th in descent from Hon Thomas Dillon (ante):—
Issue of late Gerald Dormer Fitzgerald Dillon, b 1901, d 1979: m 1940, Maureen, who d 1992, da of Thomas Stewart, formerly of Cowdenbeath, Fife:—
Martin Luke Gerald (The Red House, Much Hadham, Herts), b 1942; ed Downside, and Queen's Coll, Oxford (BA): m 1965, Diana Mary, da of late Rev Arthur Robert Botting, BA, and has issue living, Anthony Hugh Patrick Martin, b 1965, — Clare Elizabeth Teresa, b 1968: m 1988, Robert James Ashcroft, and has issue living, Thomas Alexander b 1989, Matthew Robert b 1991, William James b 1994, Hugo Oliver b 1995.

PREDECESSORS – (1) Sir THEOBALD Dillon, Knt; Lord Pres of Connaught; cr Viscount Dillon, of Costello-Gallen (peerage of Ireland) 1622; d 1624; s by his grandson (2) LUCAS, 2nd Viscount; d 1629; s by his son (3) THEOBALD, 3rd Viscount; d an infant 1630; s by his uncle (4) THOMAS, 4th Viscount; b 1615; Joint Commr of Mayo Nov 1641, and Joint Pres of Connaught and Gov of Fort Athlone 1645-62; exempted from pardon for life by Cromwell 1652 (restored 1660); Custos Rotulorum of co Meath 1662; d 1673; s by his son (5) THOMAS, 5th Viscount; d 1674; s by his kinsman (6) LUCAS, 6th Viscount, el son of Sir Theobald, 3rd son of Sir Christopher el son of 1st Viscount; dsp 1682; s by his kinsman (7) THEOBALD, 7th Viscount, grandson of Sir Lucas, 2nd son of 1st Viscount; attached himself to the falling fortunes of James II, and was outlawed 1690; s by his son (8) HENRY, 8th Viscount, in whose favour the outlawry was reversed; d 1713; s by his son (9) RICHARD, 9th Viscount; d 1737; s by his cousin (10) CHARLES, 10th Viscount, el son of Hon Arthur Dillon (2nd son of 7th Viscount), who was cr Count Dillon by Louis XIV 1711, Earl Dillon by the Old Pretender 1721 and KT 1722; dsp 1741; s by his brother (11) HENRY, 11th Viscount; a Col in the French army; d 1787; s by his son (12) CHARLES, KP, 12th Viscount; conformed to the Established Church, and his claim to be 12th Viscount was allowed by the House of Lords in 1788 in the names of Dillon-Lee, which he had assumed in 1776 in accordance with the will of his maternal uncle, the 3rd Earl of Litchfield; d 1813; s by his son (13) HENRY AUGUSTUS, 13th Viscount; b 1777: m 1807, Henrietta, da of Dominick Geoffrey Browne, MP; d 1832; s by his el son (14) CHARLES HENRY, 14th Viscount; d 1865; s by his brother (15) THEOBALD DOMINICK GEOFFREY, 15th Viscount; d 1879; s by his brother (16) ARTHUR EDMUND DENIS, 16th Viscount, b 1812: m 1843, Ellen, da of James Adderly; d 1892; s by his el son (17) HAROLD ARTHUR, CH, 17th Viscount, b 1844; Pres of So of Antiquaries 1897-1904, Curator of the Tower Armouries 1895-1913, and a Trustee of British Museum 1897-1932; Senior Trustee of the National Portrait Gallery, Antiquary of Roy Acad and an Original Fellow of British Acad: m 1st, 1870, Julia (Order of Mercy), who d 1925, el da of late Isaac Brock Stanton, of the Canadian Civil Ser; 2ndly, 1926, his cousin, Margaret Louisa Everard, who d 1954, da of late Rev Henry Edward ffolkes, and widow of Rev John Erasmus Philipps; *d* 1932; *s* by his nephew **(18)** ARTHUR HENRY (el son of Hon Conrad Adderly Dillon, 2nd son of 16th Viscount), 18th Viscount, *b* 1875: *m* 1907, Hilda, who *d* 1966, da of Rt Hon Sir John Tomlinson Brunner, 1st Bt, PC, and widow of Charles Harold Broadbent, JP; *d* 1934; *s* by his brother **(19)** ERIC FITZGERALD, CMG, DSO, 19th Viscount, *b* 1881; Brig (ret) Roy Munster Fusiliers; S Africa 1900-01, 1914-18 War (DSO, CMG), 1939-45 War: *m* 1907, Norah Juanita Muriel, who *d* 1962, only child of late Brig-Gen Charles Edward Beckett, CB; *d* 1946; *s* by his son **(20)** MICHAEL ERIC, 20th Viscount; *b* 1911; Lt-Col RHG, sometime Lt-Col 15/19th The King's Royal Hussars, an Officer of Order of Orange Nassau of the Netherlands with Swords, and a Vice-Pres of Roy Stuart Soc: *m* 1939, Irène Marie France, da of René Merandon du Plessis, of Whitehall, Mauritius; *d* 1979; *s* by his son **(21)** CHARLES HENRY ROBERT, 21st Viscount; *b* 1945: *m* 1972, Mary Jane, da of John Young, of Castle Hill House, Birtle, Lancs; *d* 1982; *s* by his only son **(22)** HENRY BENEDICT CHARLES, 22nd Viscount and present peer.

Dinevor, Baron, see Dynevor.

Dingwall, Lord, see Baron Lucas of Crudwell and Dingwall.

DIXON, BARON (Dixon) (Life Baron 1997)

DONALD (DON) DIXON, PC, son of late (Christopher) Albert Dixon, of Jarrow; *b* 6 March 1929; *ed* Ellison Street Elementary Sch, Jarrow; shipyard worker 1947-74; Branch Sec, GMWU 1974-79; Councillor, S Tyneside MDC since 1963; MP (Lab) for Jarrow 1979-97; Labour Dep Chief Whip 1987-96; Freeman of Jarrow; DL co Tyne and Wear 1997; *cr* PC 1996, and *Baron Dixon*, of Jarrow, Co of Tyne and Wear (Life Baron) 1997: *m* 1979, Doreen, da of Sydney Morad, of Hebburn, and has issue one son and one da.

Arms – Gules between two flaunches voided or three crosses flory in pale argent. **Crest** – A sea-bee or winged proper. **Supporters** – On either side a sea-dragon reguardant argent gorged with a plain collar and supporting with the exterior foot a trident or.
Residence – 1 Hillcrest, Jarrow, Tyne and Wear NE32 4DP. *Clubs* – Jarrow Labour, Ex Servicemen's (Jarrow), Hastings (Hebburn).

Dixon, family name of Baron Glentoran.

DIXON-SMITH, BARON (Dixon-Smith) (Life Baron 1993)

ROBERT WILLIAM DIXON-SMITH, 2nd son of late Dixon Smith, of Lascelles, Braintree, Essex; *b* 30 Sept 1934; *ed* Oundle, and Writtle Agric Coll; 2nd Lieut King's Dragoon Gds 1955-57; DL Essex 1986; Farmer; Chm Essex CC 1986-89 (Councillor since 1965), Chm Assocn of CCs 1992-93 (Vice-Chm 1989-92), Chm of Govs Anglia Poly 1991-93; Freeman Farmers' Co 1988; *cr Baron Dixon-Smith*, of Bocking, co Essex (Life Baron) 1993: *m* 1960, Georgina Janet, da of George Cook, of Halstead, Essex, and has issue.

Arms – Argent a lion sejant erect azure gorged with a baron's coronet proper holding in the dexter forepaw a seax proper hilt pommel and quillons or and resting the sinister forepaw on a garb also gold. Crest – A garb or to the sinister and to the dexter resting its tail thereon a dolphin urinant vert fins and tail also gold. Supporters – Two lions sejant erect azure ermined or each resting the exterior forepaw upon a garb also gold.
Residence – Lyons Hall, Braintree, Essex CM7 6SH.

SON LIVING

Hon Adam William George, *b* 1962: *m* 19—, Anna Hogg, and has issue living, Guy, *b* 1994, — Kit, *b* (twin) 1994, — Harry, *b* 1996, — Archie George Theodore, *b* 1999.

DAUGHTER LIVING

Hon Sarah Jane, *b* 1960: *m* 1986, Christopher Henry St John (Toby) Hoare, son of J. Michael Hoare, and has issue living, Oscar, *b* 1988, — Giles, *b* 1990, — Camilla, *b* 1994. *Residence* – 130 Kensington Park Rd, W11 2EP.

Dodson, family name of Baron Monk Bretton.

DONALDSON OF KINGSBRIDGE, BARONY OF (Donaldson) (Extinct 1998)

SON LIVING OF LIFE BARON

Hon Thomas Hay, *b* 1936, *ed* Eton, Univ of Cincinnati and Trin Coll Camb (BA) *m* 1962, Natalie, da of Basil Wadkovsky, of Miami Beach, Florida, USA, and has issue. *Residence* – The Old Lodge, Mayertorne, Wendover Dean, Wendover, nr Aylesbury, Bucks HP22 6QA.

DAUGHTERS LIVING OF LIFE BARON

Hon Rose Albinia, *b* 1937: *m* 1961 (*m diss* 1988), Prof Nicholas Dampier Deakin, CBE, son of Sir (Frederick) William Dampier Deakin, DSO, and has issue.
Hon Catherine Frances, *b* 1945: *m* 1973, G. Mark Jennings, of 57 Winsham Grove, SW11, and has issue.

DONALDSON OF LYMINGTON, BARON (Donaldson) (Life Baron 1988)

JOHN FRANCIS DONALDSON, PC, son of late Malcolm Donaldson, FRCS, FRCOG, of Woodstock Rd, Oxford; *b* 6 Oct 1920: *ed* Charterhouse, and Trin Coll, Camb (Hon Fellow 1983), MA Cantab 1948, MA Oxon 1982, Hon DUniv Essex 1983, Hon LLD Sheffield 1984, Hon LLD Nottingham Trent 1992; served 1939-45 War in Roy Signals in NW Europe and Guards Armoured Divnl Signals (Hon Lt-Col 1946); Bar Middle Temple 1946, QC 1961, Dep Chm Hants Quarter Sessions 1961-66, Bencher 1966, Judge of High Court of Justice (Queen's Bench Div) 1966-79, Pres Nat Industrial Relations Court 1971-74, a Lord Justice of Appeal 1979-82, Master of the Rolls 1982-92; Pres Council of Inns of Court 1987-90, Carthusian Soc 1978-82, British Maritime Law Assocn since 1979 (Vice-Pres 1969-78), British Insurance Law Assocn 1979-81 (Dep-Pres 1978-79), British Records Assocn 1982-92; Chm Advisory Council on Public Records 1982-92, Magna Carta Trust 1982-92; FCIArb 1980 (Pres 1980-83), Financial Law Panel since 1993; Gov Sutton's Hosp in Charterhouse 1981-84; Visitor: Nuffield Coll, Oxford 1982-92, UCL 1982-92 and London Business Sch 1986-92; Hon Freeman Worshipful Co of Drapers 1984; *cr* Kt 1966, PC 1979, and *Baron Donaldson of Lymington*, of Lymington, co Hants (Life Baron) 1988: *m* 1945, (Dorothy) Mary, GBE, da of late Reginald George Gale Warwick, of Wickham, Hants, and has issue.

𝕬rms – Sable, two bars or, in chief three petasi argent winged gold. 𝕮rest – A sealion erect sable, scales, fins and tail or, holding a lymphad also or, the mainsail displaying the arms, viz sable, two bars or, in chief three petasi argent winged gold, each mast ensigned by a cross formy gules.

Address – c/o House of Lords, SW1A 0PW. *Clubs* – Royal Cruising, Bar Yacht, Royal Lymington Yacht.

SON LIVING

Hon Michael John Francis, *b* 1950; *ed* Stanbridge Earls: *m* 1972, Judith Margaret, da of Edgar William Somerville, FRCS, of Stone House, Garsington, Oxford, and has issue living, William Michael Somerville, *b* 1977, — James John Francis, *b* (twin) 1977. *Residence* – The Old Coach House, Westwood Rd, Windlesham, Surrey GU20 6LT.

DAUGHTERS LIVING

Hon Margaret-Ann Michelle, *b* 1946; *ed* St Paul's Girls' Sch, London Sch of Occupational Therapy (Dip OT), and Univ of Saskatchewan (MCEd and PhD): *m* 1969, Conal Tompson, and has issue living, Douglas Conal, *b* 1974, — Caroline Margaret, *b* 1975. *Residence* – 736 University Drive, Saskatoon, Saskatchewan S7N 0J4, Canada.

Hon Jennifer Mary, *b* 1948: *m* 1970, Michael Lodwig Williams, and has issue three sons.

DONEGALL, MARQUESS OF (Chichester) Sits as BARON FISHERWICK (GB 1790)
(Marquess I 1791)

DERMOT RICHARD CLAUD CHICHESTER, LVO, 7th Marquess; *b* 18 April 1916; *s* as 5th Baron Templemore 1953, and as 7th Marquess of Donegall 1975; *ed* Harrow and RMC; Maj (ret) late 7th Queen's Own Hussars; Standard Bearer of HM Body Guard of Hon Corps of Gentlemen at Arms 1984-86; Hereditary Lord High Admiral of Lough Neagh and Gov of Carrickfergus Castle; Grand Master Masonic Order (Ireland) 1981-92; 1939-45 War in Middle East and Italy (prisoner); LVO 1986: *m* 1946, Lady Josceline Gabrielle Legge, who *d* 1995, da of 7th Earl of Dartmouth, and has issue.

Arms – Quarterly: 1st and 4th checky, or and gules, a chief vaire, *Chichester;* 2nd and 3rd azure, fretty argent, *Etchingham.* **Crest** – A stork, with an eel in its bill proper. **Supporters** – Two wolves gules, ducally collared and chained or.
Seat – Dunbrody Park, Arthurstown, co Wexford. *Clubs* – Cavalry, Kildare St (Dublin).

SON LIVING

ARTHUR PATRICK (*Earl of Belfast*), *b* 9 May 1952; *ed* Harrow, and RAC Cirencester; Lt Coldm Gds: *m* 1989, Caroline Mary, elder da of Maj Christopher Roland Philipson, late Life Guards, of Lofts Hall, Saffron Walden, Essex (*see* By Woolavington, 1985 Edn), and has issue:

Honour follows, though unsought for

SON LIVING — James (*Viscount Chichester*), *b* 19 Nov 1990.

DAUGHTER LIVING — *Lady* Catherine Gabrielle, *b* 1992.

DAUGHTERS LIVING

Lady Jennifer Evelyn, *b* 1949: *m* 1971, John Robert Henry Fowler, of Rahinston, Enfield, co Meath, and has issue living, Robert Henry, *b* 1975, — Charles James, *b* 1977.
Lady Juliet Clare, *b* 1954: *m* 1983, Andrew David Frazer, of Hillmount, Cullybackey, co Antrim, and has issue living, William John Andrew, *b* 1985, — Mary Emma, *b* 1985 (twin).

BROTHER LIVING (Son of 4th Baron Templemore)

(*Raised to the rank of a Marquess's son,* 1977)

Lord Desmond Clive, MC, *b* 1920; *ed* Harrow, and Ch Ch, Oxford (BA 1944, MA 1945); Maj Coldm Gds (ret); was ADC to Gov-Gen of Canada 1948-50; 1939-45 War in N Africa and Italy (despatches MC); Dir Colne Valley Water Co since 1956 (Chm 1983): *m* 1st, 1946, Lorna Althea, who *d* 1948, da of Capt Montagu Hamer Ravenhill (Colleton, Bt), and widow of (i) Geoffrey Christopher Appleby Holt, Pilot Officer RAF, and (ii) Capt Richard Cecil Twining, Welsh Gds; 2ndly, 1951, Felicity Stella, da of late Maj John Fenwick Harrison (*see* B Burnham, 1969 Edn), and has issue living (by 1st *m*), (Desmond) Shane Spencer (Cygnet House, Martyr Worthy, nr Winchester, Hants SO21 1DZ), *b* 1948: *m* 1976, (Isabel) Jane, da of Michael George Thomas Webster, of The Vale, Windsor Forest, Berks (*see* M Conyngham, 1941 Edn), and has issue living, Patrick Michael Desmond *b* 1980, Henry Richard *b* 1981, Louisa Clare *b* 1978, — (by 2nd *m*) Dermot Michael Claud (Christie's Ltd, 8 King St, SW1), *b* 1953: *m* 1st, 1975 (*m diss* 1980), Frances Jane Berners, da of Michael Edward Ranulph Allsopp (*see* B Hindlip, colls); 2ndly, 1982, Shan, da of Alastair Ros McIndoe, of Heythrop Cottage, Wyck Rissington, Glos, and has issue living (by 2nd *m*), Rory Alastair St Clair *b* 1985, Ottilie *b* 1988, Sapphira *b* 1990. *Residence* – Preston Hill, Preston, Hitchin, Herts. *Club* – White's.

WIDOW LIVING OF SIXTH MARQUESS

MAUREEN (*Marchioness of Donegall*) (26 Queen's Court, Queen's Rd, Richmond, Surrey TW10 6LA), el da of late Maj Geoffrey C. Scholfield, MC, of Birkdale, Lancs, and formerly wife of Douglas McKenzie: *m* 1968, as his 2nd wife, the 6th Marquess of Donegall, who *d* 1975.

COLLATERAL BRANCHES LIVING

Granddaughter of late Hon Frederick Arthur Henry Chichester, 3rd son of 1st Baron Templemore, el son of Lord Spencer Stanley Chichester, of Dunbrody Park, co Wexford, 3rd son of 1st Marquess:—
Issue of late Maj Spencer Frederick Chichester, *b* 1854, *d* 1931: *m* 1892, Helen, who *d* 1948, da of Archibald Coats, of Woodside, Paisley:—
Verena Frances Elizabeth, *b* 1906: *m* 1931, Cdr Derek Howard Secker, LVO, RN, who *d* 1988, and has issue living, Malcolm Chichester (Flat 9, 10 Porchester Terr, W2) *b* 1934; *ed* Eton.

Grandsons of Hon Francis Algernon James Chichester, 5th son of 1st Baron Templemore (ante):—
Issue of late Shane Randolph Chichester, OBE, b 1883, d 1969: m 1914, Madeline Herschel, who d 1977, da of Henry Arthur Whately:—
(Oscar) Richard Herschel (Wiscombe Park, Southleigh, Colyton, Devon EX13 6JE; Clubs – Pratt's, Army and Navy), b 1915; ed Wellington Coll, and Trin Coll, Camb (BA); Maj (ret) Rifle Bde (Prince Consort's Own); ADC to High Commr for Palestine 1946-48; Palestine 1936 (medal), 1939-45 War (African Star): m 1951, Margaret Edmondson, da of Charles Edgar Farr, JP, of Weston Bury, Weston, nr Hitchin, Herts, and has issue living, Timothy Arthur Shane, b 1956: m 1983, Mary Frances, yr da of Frank Sebastian Cooksey, CBE, MD, FRCP, of Aldeburgh, Suffolk, and has issue living, John Francis Shane b 1985, — Jane Caroline Sheelah CHICHESTER, b 1952; has resumed her maiden name: m 1980 (m diss 1984), Richard Philip Palmer, son of Reginald H. Palmer, of Dawlish, and has issue living, Daniel b 1981, Thomas b 1983, — Sara Kathleen Arabella, b 1958: m 1988, Michael Constant John Raynor, elder son of R. D. Raynor, of Belford House, Four Marks, Hants, and has issue living, Madeline Jacqueline Kathleen b 1989. —— Desmond Shane (Holway House, Whatcombe, Blandford, Dorset; Club – MCC), b 1919; ed Wellington Coll, and Trin Coll, Camb (MA); Agent to the Earl of Radnor (ret); FRICS; Capt (ret), 80th Heavy Anti-Aircraft Regt RA and N Irish Horse; 1939-45 War in N Africa and Italy: m 1951, Patricia, who d 1987, yr da of late Lt-Col Henry George Moreton Pleydell-Railston, DSO (Mansel, Bt, colls), and has issue living, Piers Desmond Herschel (Kingston Farmhouse, Winterborne Kingston, Blandford, Dorset), b 1954; ed Wellington Coll, and RAC Cirencester; FRICS, FAAV: m 1989, Charlotte Anne, only da of Lt-Col Peter Richard Heaton-Ellis, OBE, of The Coach House, Chitterne, Warminster, Wilts, and has issue living, Harry Pleydell Whately b 1992, Sophia Patricia b 1990, — Jonathan Morton (twin) (46 Redway Drive, Whitton, Twickenham, Middx), b 1954; ed Wellington Coll: m 1982, Caroline Margaret, da of Peter Douglas Bird, of W Kirby, Wirral, and has issue living, Peter Shane b 1983, Benjamin Charles b 1986, Eleanor Madeline Patricia b 1987, — (Adrian) George (The Mount, Chieveley, Newbury, Berks RG20 8XG), b 1955; ed Wellington Coll, and Keble Coll, Oxford (MA); FRICS, FAAV: m 1988, Caroline Ann, only da of Dr John Richard Storer, of Westfield House, Blewbury, Oxon, and has issue living, Hugh Edmund b 1991, Tessa Ann b 1989, Camilla Emily b 1993, Iona Madeline b 1995, — Morna Rosemary b 1952; ed Westonbirt Sch, and Lady Margaret Hall, Oxford (MA): m 1982, Andrew David Wood Partridge, of 6 Beavers Rd, Farnham, Surrey GU9 7BD, son of late Simon Harry Wood Partridge, OBE, of Kilndown, Kent, and has issue living, Katharine Mary Emily b 1986, Verena Frances Herschel b 1987.

In remainder to the Earldom of Donegall, Viscountcy of Chichester, and Barony of Chichester of Belfast only

Descendants of late Rev William Chichester, el son of late Rev Edward Chichester, who was cr Baron O'Neill 1868, great-great-grandson of John Chichester, brother of 2nd Earl (see O'Neill, B).

Granddaughters of late Rev Edward Arthur Chichester, son of Rev George Vaughan Chichester, son of late Rev Edward Chichester (ante):—
Issue of late Lt-Col Arthur O'Neill Cubitt Chichester, OBE, MC, b 1889, d 1972: m 1924, Hilda Grace, who d 1980, da of late Rt Hon William Robert Young (Macnaghten, Bt):—
Rosemary Hilda (Rosemary, Viscountess Brookeborough) (Colebrooke, co Fermanagh, and Ashbrooke, Brookeborough, co Fermanagh), b 1926: m 1949, 2nd Viscount Brookeborough, who d 1987. —— Finola Margaret, b 1932: m 1st, 1959, William McWilliams, who d 1963; 2ndly, 1964, D. Herbison, of Ardvernis Farm, Cullybackey, Ballymena, co Antrim, and has issue living (by 1st m) Grace Mildred, b 1960, — Tracey Margaret Emily, b 1961, — (by 2nd m), John Patrick Arthur, b 1972, — Virginia Maria, b 1966, — Cathleen Laura, b 1968.

PREDECESSORS – Sir ARTHUR Chichester, Knt, PC, 2nd son Sir John Chichester, of Raleigh, Pilton Devon, and yr brother of Sir John, grandfather of 1st Bt (see Chichester, Bt); 1563; Lord Dep of Ireland 1605-15, Lord Treas of Ireland 1616-1625, and Ambassador to Palestine 1622; cr Baron Chichester of Belfast (peerage of Ireland) 1613: m 1605, Lettice, who d 1620, da of Sir John Perrott, of Haroldson, Pembrokeshire, Lord Dep of Ireland, and widow of (i) John Laugharne, and (ii) Walter Vaughan, of Golden Grove, Carmarthenshire; d 1625, when his peerage became ext, but was s in estates by his next brother (1) Sir EDWARD, Knt, PC, b circa 1568; Gov of Carrickfergus; Joint Commr of the Treasury, Ireland 1632; cr Viscount Chichester of Carrickfergus, and Baron Chichester of Belfast, both in co Antrim 1625-48: m 1st, 1605, Anne, who d 1616, da and heir of John Coplestone of Eggesford, Devon; 2ndly, 16—, Mary, who d 1637, da of — Denham, of Wortham, Devon, and widow of Otwell Hill; d 1648; s by his el son (2) ARTHUR, PC, b 1606; Gov of Carrickfergus 1660-1675; MP for co Antrim 1634 and 1640-47; being distinguished in Irish Rebellion, was cr Earl of Donegall, 1647, with remainder to heirs male of his father's body: m 1st, Dorcas, who d 1630, da of John Hill of Honiley, Warwicks; 2ndly, before 1638, Lady Mary Digby, who d 1648, da of 1st Earl of Bristol; 3rdly, 1651, Letitia (who m 2ndly Sir William Franklin, and d 1691), da of Sir William Hicks, 1st Bt; d 1675; s by his nephew (3) ARTHUR, PC, 2nd Earl, el son of Lt-Col John Chichester, of Dungannon, co Tyrone, 2nd son of 1st Viscount, b 18—; MP of Dungannon 1661-66, joint Clerk of the Pipe Roll 1668-78, and Gov of Carrickfergus 1675-78: m 1st, 1660/1, Jane, da and heir of John Etchingham, of Dunbrody, co Wexford, who d 1712, having m 2ndly, Richard Booth of Epsom; d 1678; s by his el son (4) ARTHUR, 3rd Earl; b 1666; Col 35th Regt Foot; Maj Gen of Spanish Forces 1704: m 1st before 1676, Lady Barbara Boyle, who d 1682, da of 1st Earl of Orrery; 2ndly, 1685, Lady Catherine Forbes, who d 1743, da of 1st Earl of Granard; killed at Fort Monjuich 1706; s by his son (5) ARTHUR, 4th Earl; b 1695; m 1716, Lady Lucy Ridgeway, who d 1732, da of 4th Earl of Londonderry; d 1757; s by his nephew (6) ARTHUR, 5th Earl, son of Hon John, MP, 2nd son of 3rd Earl; b 1739; cr Baron Fisherwick, of Fisherwick, co Stafford (peerage of Great Britain) 1790, Marquess of Donegall, and Earl of Belfast (peerage of Ireland) 1791: m 1st, 1761, Lady Anne, who d 1780, da of 5th Duke of Hamilton; 2ndly, 1788, Charlotte, who d 1789, da and co-heir of Conway Spencer, of Tremary, co Down, and widow of Thomas Moore; 3rdly, 1790, Barbara, who d 1829, da of Rev Luke Godfrey, DD, R of Midleton, York, d 1799; s by his son (7) GEORGE AUGUSTUS, KP, 2nd Marquess; b 1769; Lieut of co Donegal: m 1795, Anna, da of Sir Edward May, Bt; d 1844; s by his son (8) GEORGE HAMILTON, KP, GCH, PC, FRS, 3rd Marquess; b 1797; MP for Carrickfergus 1818-20, for Belfast 1820-30, and for Antrim (I) 1830-7; Vice-Chamberlain of the Household 1831-4, Capt of Yeomen of the Guard 1848-52, and Lord-Lieut of co Antrim; cr Baron Ennishowen and Carrickfergus (peerage of United Kingdom) 1841: m 1st, 1822, Harriet Anne who d 1860, da of 1st Earl of Glengall (ext); 2ndly, 1862, Harriet, da of Sir Dellingham Reginald Graham, 7th Bt, and widow of Lieut Gen Sir Frederick Ashworth, KCB; d 1883, when the barony of Ennishowen and Carrickfergus became extinct; s in the other honours by his brother (9) EDWARD, 4th Marquess, b 1799; Dean of Raphoe 1832-73; m 1821, Amelia Spread Deane, da of Henry Deane Grady; d 1889; s by his el son (5) GEORGE AUGUSTUS HAMILTON, 5th Marquess, b 1822; was Clerk of the Peace for co Antrim: m 1st, 1859 (m diss 1863), Lucy Elizabeth Virginia, da of Henry Holt Oliver, of Weston Priory, Somerset; 2ndly, 1865, Mary Ann Williams, who d 1901, da of late Edward Cobb, of Wright's Lane, Kensington, and of Arnold, Kent; 3rdly, 1902, Violet Gertrude, who d 1952, only da of late Henry St George Twining, of Halifax, Canada; d 1904; s by his son (7) EDWARD ARTHUR DONALD ST. GEORGE HAMILTON, 6th Marquess, b 1903; Lt-Col Army Cadet Force; Journalist; War Correspondent 1939-45: m 1st, 1943 (m diss 1968), (Gladys) Jean, who d 1991, yr da of late Capt Christian Combe (M Conyngham); 2ndly, 1968, Maureen, el da of late Maj Geoffrey C. Scholfield, MC, of Birkdale, Lancs, and formerly wife of Douglas McKenzie; d 1975; s by his kinsman (see infra*), Dermot Richard Claud, 5th Baron Templemore (5th in descent from Lord Spencer Stanley Chichester, 2nd son of 1st

Marquess), 7th Marquess and present peer; also Earl of Donegall, Earl of Belfast, Viscount Chichester, Baron Colchester of Belfast, and Baron Fisherwick.

*(1) ARTHUR Chichester, MP, of Durbrody Park, co Wexford (el son of Lord Spencer Stanley Chichester, 2nd son of 1st Marquess of Donegall); *b* 1797; MP for co Wexford; Lt-Col, a Lord of the Bedchamber to William IV, and a Lord-in-Waiting to HM Queen Victoria; *cr Baron Templemore*, of Templemore, co Donegal (peerage of United Kingdom) 1831: *m* 1820, Lady Augusta Paget, who *d* 1872, da of 1st Marquess of Anglesey; *d* 1837; *s* by his son (2) HENRY SPENCER, 2nd Baron; *b* 1821; *m* 1st, 1842, Laura Caroline Jane, who *d* 1871, 3rd da of late Right Hon Sir Arthur Paget, GCB; 2ndly, 1873, Lady Victoria Elizabeth Ashley, who *d* 1927, da of 7th Earl of Shaftesbury; *d* 1906; *s* by his son (3) ARTHUR HENRY, 3rd Baron, *b* 1854; High Sheriff of co Wexford 1890: *m* 1st, 1879, Evelyn, who *d* 1883, da of Rev William James Stracey (*see* Stacey Bt, colls); 2ndly, 1885, Alice Elizabeth, who *d* 1954, da of late Clinton George Augustus Dawkins; *d* 1924; *s* by his son (4) ARTHUR CLAUD SPENCER, KCVO, DSO, OBE, PC, *b* 1880; Col (ret) TA (formerly Comdg 5/7th Batn Hampshire Regt); formerly Major Irish Guards, and Capt Roy Fusiliers (City of London Regt); S Africa 1902, with Tibet Mission 1904, present at action of Gyantse and march to Lhassa, European War 1915-18; was Private Sec to Under-Sec of State for War 1927-28, and to Paymaster-Gen 1928-29, a Lord-in-Waiting to HM 1929, and 1931-34, and Capt of Yeomen of the Guard 1934-45; Ch Whip in House of Lords 1940-45: *m* 1911, Hon Clare Meriel Wingfield, who *d* 1969, da of 6th Viscount Powerscourt; *d* 1953; *s* by his son (5) DERMOT RICHARD CLAUD, 5th Baron, who *s* as 7th Marquess of Donegall (see ante).

DONERAILE, VISCOUNT (St Leger) (Viscount I 1785)
(Title pronounced "Dunnaral" Name Pronounced "Sentleger")

Great and good

RICHARD ALLEN ST LEGER, 10th Viscount (has not yet established his right to the Peerages); *b* 17 Aug 1946; *s* 1983; *ed* Orange Coast Coll, Cal; Air Traffic Control Specialist, Mississippi Univ: *m* 1970, Kathleen Mary, el da of Nathaniel Simcox, of Mallow, co Cork, and has issue.

Arms – Argent, fretty argent, a chief or Crest – A griffin passant or. Supporters – Two griffins or, wings elevated azure, fretty argent.
Residence – 44-445 San Jose Ave, Palm Desert, California 92260, USA.

SON LIVING

Hon NATHANIEL WARHAM ROBERT ST JOHN, *b* 13 Sept 1971.

DAUGHTER LIVING

Hon Maeve Isobel Melva, *b* 1974.

BROTHERS LIVING

Hon David Hugh, *b* 1950; *ed* Calif State Univ, Long Beach.
Hon Edward Hayes, *b* 1960; *ed* Univ of Calif, Riverside.

SISTERS LIVING

Hon Elizabeth Adele, *b* 1953. *Residence* –
Hon Karen Jean, *b* 1955: *m* 1977 (*m diss* 1981), Richard Lehman, and has issue living, Corey R., *b* 1980.

WIDOW LIVING OF NINTH VISCOUNT

MELVA JEAN (*Melva, Viscountess Doneraile*), da of George W. Clifton, of St Louis, Mo: *m* 1945, the 9th Viscount, who *d* 1983.

PREDECESSORS – (1) ST. LEGER Aldworth, MP, for Doneraile 1761-76, succeeded in 1767 to the estates of his maternal uncle, Hayes St Leger, 4th and last Baron Kilmadon, and Viscount Doneraile (*cr* 1703), and assumed the surname of St Leger in lieu of his patronymic; *cr Baron Doneraile* of Doneraile (peerage of Ireland) 1776, and *Viscount Doneraile* (peerage of Ireland) 1785; *d* 1797; *s* by his son (2) HAYES, 2nd Viscount; *d* 1819; *s* by his son (3) HAYES, 3rd Viscount; *b* 1786; a Representative Peer: *m* 1816, Lady Charlotte Esther Bernard, da of 1st Earl of Bandon; *d* 1854; *s* by his son (4) HAYES, 4th Viscount; *b* 1818; a Representative Peer: *m* 1851, Mary Anne Grace Louisa, who *d* 1907, da of late George Lenox-Conyngham; *d* 1887; *s* by his cousin (5) RICHARD ARTHUR, 5th Viscount, son of Rev Richard Thomas Arthur St Leger, and grandson of Hon Richard St Leger MP, 2nd son of 1st Viscount, *b* 1825; *d* 1891; *s* by his nephew (6) EDWARD (son of the Rev Edward Frederick St Leger, and great-grandson of Hon Richard St Leger, 2nd son of 1st Viscount), 6th Viscount, *b* 1886; Mayor of City of Westminster 1919-20, and Chm of Metropolitan Asylums Board 1928-30; *d* 1941; *s* by his brother (7) HUGH, 7th Viscount; *b* 1869; admitted a Solicitor 1893: *m* 1920, Mary Isobel, who *d* 1976, da of Francis Morice, JP, of Whakapunake, Poverty Bay, NZ; *d* 1956; *s* by his kinsman, (8) ALGERNON EDWARD (son of late Richard William St Leger, grandson of late Hon Richard St. Leger, MP, 2nd son of 1st Viscount), 8th Viscount; *b* 1878: *m* 1919, Sylvia Stephenson, who *d* 19——, da of Alexander Mitchell; *d* 1957; *s* by his only son (9) RICHARD ST JOHN, 9th Viscount, *b* 1923: *m* 1945, Melva Joan, da of George W. Clifton, of St Louis, Mo; *d* 1983; *s* by his el son (10) RICHARD ALLEN, 10th Viscount and present peer; also Baron Doneraile.

DONNET OF BALGAY, BARONY OF (Donnet) (Extinct 1985)

SONS LIVING OF LIFE BARON

Hon Gavin Alexander (9 Scotscraig Place, Broughty Ferry, Dundee DD5 3SU), *b* 1950; *ed* Hyndland Sec Sch, Glasgow: *m* 1976, Margaret Louise Scott, and has issue living, Jane, *b* 19—, — Fiona, *b* 19—.

Hon Stephen Christopher (9 Hollymount, Bearsden, Glasgow G61), *b* 1960, *ed* Jordanhill Coll Sch, and Strathclyde Univ: *m* 1989, Deborah Rae, da of Edward James Campbell, and has issue living, Alexander Edward, *b* 1992.

DAUGHTER LIVING OF LIFE BARON

Hon (Sandra) Lillias, *b* 1947: *m* 1971, Dr Nigel Duguid, of 8 Sackville St, St John's, Newfoundland, A1A 4R3, Canada, and has issue.

WIDOW LIVING OF LIFE BARON

MARY (*Baroness Donnet of Balgay*), da of Gavin Mitchell Black: *m* 1945, Baron Donnet of Balgay (Life Baron), who *d* 1985.

DONOUGHMORE, EARL OF (Hely-Hutchinson) Sits as VISCOUNT HUTCHINSON (UK 1821) (Earl I 1800)
(Title pronounced "Dunomore")

FORTITER GERIT CRUCEM

He bravely bears the cross

RICHARD MICHAEL JOHN HELY-HUTCHINSON, 8th Earl; *b* 8 Aug 1927; *s* 1981; *ed* Winchester, Groton, USA, and New Coll, Oxford (MA, BM and BCh); Capt RAMC; Chm Hodder Headline plc 1986-97: *m* 1951, Sheila, da of late Frank Frederick Parsons, and has issue.

Arms – Quarterly: 1st and 4th per pale gules and azure, a lion rampant, between eight cross-crosslets argent, *Hutchinson*; 2nd azure, a fesse between three bucks' heads erased in chief argent, and in base a demi-lion rampant or, *Hely*; 3rd azure, a garb or, between three wolves' heads erased argent, *Nickson*. **Crest** – Out of a ducal coronet a demi cockatrice, wings elevated azure. **Supporters** – Two cockatrices, wings elevated or, collared sable, combs and wattles gules, and charged on the breast with a wreath of laurel vert

Residence – The Manor House, Bampton, Oxon OX18 2LQ. *Clubs* – Sloane, Jockey (Paris).

SONS LIVING

JOHN MICHAEL JAMES (*Viscount Suirdale*) (38 Thornton Avenue, W4 1QG), *b* 7 Aug 1952; *ed* Harrow; Dir Burberry Ltd: *m* 1977, Marie-Claire, da of Gerard van den Driessche, and has issue:—

    SON LIVING— *Hon* Richard Gregory, *b* 3 July 1980.

    DAUGHTERS LIVING— *Hon* Marie-Pierre Joanna, *b* 1978, —

    Hon Tatiana Louise, *b* 1985.

Hon Timothy Mark, *b* 1953; *ed* Eton; Man Dir Hodder Headline plc since 1986.

Hon Nicholas David, *b* 1955; *ed* Harrow: *m* 1982, Fiona Margaret MacIntyre, yr da of the late Maj W. R. Watson, and has issue living, Seamus David, *b* 1987, — Flora Clare, *b* 1984.

Hon Ralph Charles, *b* 1961; *ed* Eton: *m* 1995, Caroline D., only da of John Rylance, and of Mrs Paul Davis, of Shiplake, Oxon, and has issue living, Ranulph Edward, *b* 1996.

BROTHER LIVING

Hon Mark, *b* 1934; *ed* Eton, at Magdalen Coll, Oxford (BSc, MA), and Mass Inst of Technology, USA (SM); late 2nd Lt Irish Guards: *m* 1962, Margaret, yr da of late Dr Robert Rowan Woods of 3 Fitzwilliam Place, Dublin, 2, and has issue living, Henry Peter, *b* 1963: *m* 1993, Susan Essex, and has issue living, Laura *b* 1996. — Walter James, *b* 1966, — Anna Doreen, *b* 1969: *m* 1997, Andrew Maltzoff, of 6 Carlisle Terrace, Malahide, co Dublin. *Residence* – Larch Hill, Coolock Lane, Dublin 17.

SISTER LIVING

Lady Sarah Elena, *b* 1930: *m* 1951, William Collins, and has issue living, William Noel, *b* 1952: *m* 1979, Lucinda Rosemary, eldest da of Michael Harper Gow (*see* Greenwell, Bt), and has issue living, Emily Lucinda Julian *b* 1981, Melissa Daisy *b* 1984, — Jane Margarita, *b* 1954, — Tiffany Anne, *b* 1964: *m* 1991, Peter L. Hall, son of W. L. Hall, of Dearham House, Esher, Surrey, — Bryony Mary Pierre, *b* 1974. *Residence* – High Coodham, Symington, Ayrshire.

WIDOW LIVING OF SON OF SIXTH EARL

Barbara Mary, 3rd da of Maj Hugh James Wyld, of Essendon Close, Hatfield, Herts: *m* 1934, Lt-Col Hon David Edward Hely-Hutchinson, who *d* 1984, and has issue (see colls, infra).

COLLATERAL BRANCHES LIVING

Issue of late Lt-Col Hon David Edward Hely-Hutchinson, yr son of 6th Earl, *b* 1911, *d* 1984: *m* 1934, Barbara Mary (ante), 3rd da of Maj Hugh James Wyld, of Essendon Close, Hatfield, Herts:—
Rose Mary, *b* 1935: *m* 1959, William Mackinnon Fernie, of Manor Farm, Tellisford, Bath, Avon BA3 6RL, and has issue living, James Mackinnon, *b* 1962: *m* 1987, Fiona Elizabeth Swann, and has issue living, David Mackinnon *b* 1994, — Barbara Alison, *b* 1960: *m* 1988, Colin Francis Smith, — Juliet Rose, *b* 1967: *m* 1993, Burton Simon Persse, and has issue living, Jessica Rose *b* 1995, Lucy Veronica *b* 1998, — Deborah Mary, *b* 1971: *m* 1996, Julian Murray Wakeham. —— Jean Elena, *b* 1939: *m* 1972, Bernard B. D. Kain, of Poplar Farm, Atworth, Melksham, Wilts. —— Pollyann Elise, *b* 1942: *m* 1970, Capt Hamish J. Lochore, R Scots Greys (ret) (*see* Brooke, Bt, *cr* 1919), of Burgie House, Forres, Moray, and has issue living, Alexander David, *b* 1971, — Hugh Mark, *b* 1974, — Clare Hermione, *b* 1977. —— Kathryn Gabriel, *b* 1944: *m* 1973, Maj Christopher Brian Amery, Blues and Royals (ret), of Flash Farm, Antrobus, Northwich, Cheshire, and has issue living, Edward Mark Richard, *b* 1975, — Nicholas John David, *b* 1979. —— Deborah Jane, *b* 1949: *m* 1971, William Backhouse, of Layer Marney Wick, Colchester, Essex, CO5 9UT, and has issue (*see* Backhouse, Bt, colls).

Grandchildren of late Rt Hon Sir Walter Francis Hely-Hutchinson, GCMG, 2nd son of 4th Earl:—
Issue of late Christopher Douglas Hely-Hutchinson, MC, *b* 1885, *d* 1958: *m* 1914, Gladys, who *d* 1974, da of William Beachy Head, of Johannesburg:—
Frances Anne (*Lady Stevens*), *b* 1917; Devon Rep of Nat Art Collections Fund 1977-88: *m* 1940, Sir John Melior Stevens, KCMG, DSO, OBE, who *d* 1973, and has issue living, John Christopher Courtenay, MEP, *b* 1955; MEP Thames Valley since 1989, — Jane Frances, *b* 1945; MD, — Mary Anne Victoria, *b* 1947; MA (London); Art Historian: *m* 1980, John Myerscough, of 39 Campden St, W8, and has issue living, John Claude *b* 1982, Catherine Anne *b* 1986. *Residence* – East Worlington House, Crediton, Devon EX17 4TS.

Issue of late Maurice Robert Hely-Hutchinson, MC, *b* 1887, *d* 1961: *m* 1920, Melita Agnes Mary, who *d* 1987, da of late Adm Sir Colin Richard Keppel, GCVO, KCIE, CB, DSO (*see* E Albemarle, colls, 1985 Edn):—
Henry Aymar, *b* 1925; *ed* Eton; late Lieut Coldstream Guards: *m* 1957, Maria Anna, da of late Charles de Erney, of Budapest, Hungary, and has issue living, Nicholas Charles (Polands Farm, Four Elms, Edenbridge, Kent TN8 6LT), *b* 1958: *m* 1986, Kate Johanna, elder da of Timothy Connolly, of Knockholt, Kent, and has issue living, Harry Thomas *b* 1992, Rose Mollie *b* 1990, Lily Matilda *b* 1994, — Colin Henry (Hopewell House, Marsh Green, Edenbridge, Kent TN8 5QS), *b* 1959: *m* 1983, Emma (Pipi), el da of T. Hugh T. Morton, of London and New York, and has issue living, James Alexander *b* 1986, Nicholas Henry *b* 1991, Victoria Sarah *b* 1984, Alexandra Melita *b* 1990, Lucinda Catherine *b* 1994, — Melita Louise, *b* 1962: *m* 1992, Stephen Blair Glaister, of Arlebury Park Farm Cottage, Alresford, Hants SO24 9ES, son of Thomas Glaister, of Cartmel, Cumbria, and has issue living, Henry Augustus *b* 1994, Albert Constantine *b* 1996, Jessica Louise *b* 1993. *Residence* – 22 Kylestrome House, Cundy St, SW1W 9JT. —— Colin Christopher (twin) (c/o 22 Kylestrome House, Cundy St, SW1W 9JT), *b* 1925; *ed* Eton; late Lt Irish Gds. —— Marie Elizabeth, *b* 1921. *Residence* – 35, Richmond Court, 200 Sloane St, SW1X 9QU. —— Diana Margaret, *b* 1928: *m* 1960, Walter von Halle, of 7 Condray Place, Battersea Church Rd, SW11 3PE. —— Patricia May *b* 1929, DL, JP: *m* 1950, Maj George Burrell MacKean, DL, JP, who *d* 1983, and has had issue, William Muir *b* 1954: *m* 1988, Charlotte, yr da of Paddy Davies, of Slinfold, Sussex, and has issue living, George Louis *b* 1992, William Patrick Oscar *b* 1996, Emily Rose *b* 1990, — Shane Charles Robert, *b* 1958: *m* 1983, Elizabeth A. Paul, of Maryland, USA, and has issue living, William Muir *b* 1987, Cassian Donald Burrell *b* 1988, Milo David Feargus *b* 1992, India May Frances *b* 1990, — Kirsten (Curzon) Henrietta, *b* 1951: *m* 1st, 1972 (*m diss* 1986), Sir (Robert) Nicholas Oliver Couper, 6th Bt; 2ndly, 1987, Michael Tussaud, of 6 Marlborough Rd, W4 4ET, elder son of late Angelo Tussaud, — Claudia Margaret Diana, *b* 1953: *d* 1957, — Georgia Isabella, *b* 1961: *m* 1983, Lt-Col Michael B. Stubington (ret), of Burnside House, 35 Burnside Rd, Antrim BT41 2HZ, and has issue living, Claudia Mary *b* 1990, Lucca Inez *b* 1995. *Residence* – Loughanmore, 51 Loughermore Rd, Antrim BT41 2HN.

Issue of late (Christian) Victor (Noel Hope) Hely-Hutchinson, DMus, *b* 1901, *d* 1947: *m* 1925, Marjorie Anna, who *d* 1988, da of Dr Dirk de Vos Hugo, of Cape Town, S Africa:—
John Richard (Moolmanshof, 217 Voortrek Str, Swellendam 6740, S Africa), *b* 1929; PhD, CEng: *m* 1957, Allison Joyce, only da of Ernest Simpson, of Paarl, S Africa, and has two adopted children, John Andrew, *b* 1960, — Teresa Mary, *b* 1963. —— Christopher Adrian, *b* 1931; Lt-Cdr RN (ret): *m* 1963, Beatrice Mary, yr da of late Stephen Harris, of Barbon, Westmorland, and has issue living, Adam Hugo, *b* 1968, — Henrietta Lucy, *b* 1973. *Residence* – The Garden House, Brand Lane, Ludlow, Shropshire.

Grandchildren of late John Hely-Hutchinson, son of late Capt Hon Coote Hely-Hutchinson, RN, brother of 3rd Earl:—
Issue of late Lieut-Col Coote Robert Hely-Hutchinson, OBE, *b* 1870, *d* 1930: *m* 1914, Julia, who *d* 1948, da of late William Browne-Clayton, of Browne's Hill, Carlow:—
Michael (Croft Cottage, New Marton, St Martins, Oswestry, Shropshire), *b* 1916; Maj (ret) Roy Norfolk Regt: *m* 1951, Ruth Somerled, da of late Kenneth Mackenzie, MD, FRCS, of Auckland, New Zealand, and has issue living, Caroline Anne, *b* 1954: *m* 1979, Timothy Neal Harlow, MB, ChB, of Whitley House, Bradninch, Exeter, Devon EX5 4LA, and has issue living, Alastair Michael *b* 1984, Jennifer Fiona *b* 1985. —— †David Coote, *b* 1918: *m* 1948, Geraldine Mary (Parteenalax, Limerick), da of late Donough Richard O'Brien (*see* B Inchiquin, colls), and *d* 1994, leaving issue, Fiona Kathryn O'Brien, *b* 1965. —— Mary Caroline, *b* (twin) 1914. —— Julia Louisa, *b* 1921.

PREDECESSORS – (1) CHRISTIANA, da of Abraham Nickson and wife of the Rt Hon John Hely-Hutchinson, an eminent lawyer and statesman of Ireland, was *cr Baroness Donoughmore*, of Knocklofty, co Tipperary (peerage of Ireland) 1783; *d* 1788; *s* by her son (2) RICHARD HELY, 2nd Baron; a Gen in the Army; *cr Viscount Donoughmore* of Knocklofty (peerage of Ireland) 1797, and *Earl of Donoughmore* (peerage of Ireland) 1801, with remainder to the heirs male of his mother, and while a Representative Peer was *cr Viscount Hutchinson* (peerage of United Kingdom) 1821, with limitation as in peerage of 1801; *d* unmarried, when all the honours devolved upon his brother (3) JOHN, GCB (2nd Earl, who in 1801 had been *cr Baron Hutchinson*, of Alexandria and Knocklofty peerage of UK); *d* 1832, when the Barony of Hutchinson became ext and the other honours, devolved upon his nephew (4) JOHN HELY, KP, 3rd Earl, son of Hon Francis Hely, MP, 3rd son of Baroness Donoughmore; *d* 1851; *s* by his son (5) RICHARD JOHN, PC, 4th Earl; *b* 1823; Pres of Board of Trade: *m* 1847, Thomasine Jocelyn, da of Walter Steele, of Moynalty, co Monaghan; *d* 1866; *s* by his son (6) JOHN LUKE GEORGE, KCMG, 5th Earl, *b* 1848: *m* 1874, Frances Isabella, who *d* 1925, da of late Gen Stephens, HEICS; *d* 1900; *s* by his son (7) RICHARD WALTER JOHN, KP, PC, 6th Earl; *b* 1875; Under-Sec of State for War 1903-1904; Civil Member of the Army Council 1904-1905, and Chm of Committees and Dep Speaker in House of Lords 1911-31; a Member of Senate of S Ireland 1921; *m* 1901, Elena Maria, who *d* 1944, da of late M. P. Grace, of New York, USA; *d* 1948: *s* by his son (8) JOHN MICHAEL HENRY, 7th Earl, *b* 1902; Col RAC; MP for Peterborough (C) 1943-45: *m* 1925, (Dorothy) Jean, MBE, who *d* 1995, da of late John Beaumont Hotham (*see* B Hotham, colls); *d* 1981; *s* by his el son (9) RICHARD MICHAEL JOHN, 8th Earl and present peer; also Viscount Donoughmore, Viscount Hutchinson, and Baron Donoughmore.

DONOUGHUE, BARON (Donoughue) (Life Baron 1985)

BERNARD DONOUGHUE, *b* 8 Sept 1934, son of late Thomas Joseph Donoughue, by his late wife, Maud Violet Andrews; *ed* Secondary Modern Sch, Gram Sch, Northampton, and Lincoln Coll and Nuffield Coll, Oxford (MA, DPhil); FRHistS; Sr Policy Advisor to PM 1974-79, Development Dir Economist Intelligence Unit 1979-81, Assist Ed The Times 1981-82, Head of Investment Policy and Research Grievson Grant & Co 1982-86, Head of Investment Policy and International Research 1986-88, since when Exec Vice Chairman London, Bishopsgate International plc; Parl Sec Agriculture, Fisheries and Food (farming and food) since 1998; author; *cr Baron Donoughue*, of Ashton, co Northants (Life Baron) 1985: *m* 1959, Carol Ruth, da of late Abraham Goodman, and has issue.

Residence – 7 Brookfield Park, NW5. *Address* – 1 Sloane Sq, SW1.

SONS LIVING

Hon Paul Michael David, *b* 1969; *ed* William Ellis Sch.
Hon Stephen Joel, *b* 1969; *ed* William Ellis Sch.

DAUGHTERS LIVING

Hon Rachel Anne, *b* 1965.
Hon Kate Miriam, *b* 1967.

DONOVAN, BARONY OF (Donovan) (Extinct 1971)

SONS LIVING OF LIFE BARON

Hon Hugh Desmond (40 Felden St, SW6 5AF), *b* 1934; *ed* Harrow, and New Coll, Oxford: *m* 1968, Margaret Mary, el da of late Hugh Forbes Arbuthnott, of Winterfold House, Chaddesley Corbett, Worcs (*see* V Arbuthnott, colls), and has issue living, Charles Edward Horatius Arbuthnott DONOVAN, *b* 1974; assumed addl forename of Arbuthnott before that of Donovan, and relinquished the forename of Horatius by deed poll 1993.

Hon John (Great Rissington Farm, Great Rissington, Glos), *b* 1938; *ed* Harrow, and Univ Coll, Oxford: *m* 1973, Pauline Nicole Christiane, yst da of H. A. Klene, of Wasennaar, The Hague, and has issue living, Florence, *b* 1977, — Miranda, *b* 1979.

DAUGHTER LIVING OF LIFE BARON

Hon Susan Elizabeth, *b* 1936: *m* 1960 (*m diss* 1984), Gerard Francis Horton, of 27 Weemala Rd, Northbridge, NSW, and has issue.

DORCHESTER, BARONY OF (Carleton) (Extinct 1963)

DAUGHTER LIVING OF SECOND BARON

Hon Lorraine Charmian Gabrielle, *b* 1919; formerly Dist Commr Girl Guides, Chelsea, and Hon Sec Chelsea Soc; formerly Chm West Dean Parish Meeting, and Editor FANY Gazette; Cllr Cuckmere Valley Parish Council 1990: *m* 1947, James Metcalfe Knowles, FRIBA, FRICS, MRTPI, who *d* 1993, and has issue living Thomas James Metcalfe, *b* 1952: *m* 1993, Colleen M. G., only da of Patrick Sullivan, of New York, — Elizabeth Charmian Carleton, *b* 1949: *m* 1976, Christopher J. A. Coleman. *Residence* – Sheep Pen Cottage, Friston Forest, West Dean, Seaford, E Sussex.

DORMAND OF EASINGTON, BARON (Dormand) (Life Baron 1987)

JOHN DONKIN DORMAND, son of Bernard Dormand, of Haswell, co Durham; *b* 27 Aug 1919; *ed* Bede Coll, Durham, Loughborough Coll, St Peter's Coll, Oxford and Harvard; Hon Fell St Peter's Coll, Oxford; teacher 1940-48; educn adviser 1948-52 and 1957-63, District Educn Offr Easington RDC 1963-70; Dep Chm Teesside Devel Corpn; Assist Govt Whip 1974, a Lord Commr of HM Treasury 1974-79, Chm Parl Labour Party 1981-87, MP (*Lab*) Easington 1970-87; *cr Baron Dormand of Easington*, of Easington, co Durham (Life Baron) 1987: *m* 1963, Doris, da of Thomas Robinson, of Houghton-le-Spring, co Durham.
  Address – c/o House of Lords, SW1

DORMER, BARON (Dormer) (Baron E 1615, Bt E 1615)

GEOFFREY HENRY DORMER, 17th Baron, and 17th Baronet; *b* 13 May 1920; *s* 1995; *ed* Eton, and Trin Coll, Camb; Lt-Cmdr RNR, served 1939-45 War as Lieut RNVR: *m* 1st, 1947 (*m diss* 1957), Janet, yr da of James F. A. Readman, of 16 Lennox St, Edinburgh; 2ndly, 1958, Pamela, da of late Wallace Levick Simpson, and has issue by 1st and 2nd *m*.

ᴁrms – Azure, ten billets, four, three, two, and one, or; on a chief of the second, a demi-lion issuant sable. ᴄrest – A falcon, wings displayed and inverted argent, beaked, membered, and belled or, standing on a falconer's right-hand glove fesseways argent. ᴘupporters – Two falcons, wings displayed and inverted argent, beaked, membered, and belled or.
Residence – Yew Tree Cottage, Dittisham, Devon TQ6 0EX.

SONS LIVING (*By 2nd marriage*)

Hon WILLIAM ROBERT, *b* 8 Nov 1960; *ed* King Edward VI Gram Sch, Southampton Univ, and Cranfield Univ: *m* 1985, Paula Sharon, da of Peter Robinson, of Heaton Mersey, Cheshire, and has issue living, Hugo Edward Geoffrey, *b* 7 July 1995, — a da, *b* 1998. *Residence* – ......
Hon Hugh Richard Cecil, *b* 1964; *ed* King Edward VI Gram Sch, Plymouth Polytechnic (BSc), and Plymouth Maritime Sch: *m* 1996, Denise Anne, da of Peter Anthony Lunt, of Maghull, Lancs. *Residence* – 2 Staplake Cottages, New Rd, Starcross, Exeter, Devon EX6 8GG.

What God wills I will

DAUGHTERS LIVING (*By 1st marriage*)

Hon Carol Susan, *b* 1949: *m* 1974, Patrick Howard Lynn, and has issue living, Iain Patrick, *b* 1978, — Joshua Alexander, *b* 1980, — Sarah Amy Janet, *b* 1986. *Residence* – Hockerwood Park, Southwell, Notts NG25 0PZ.
Hon Sally Ann Vanessa, *b* 1951: *m* 1973, Roger Arthur Skinner, who *d* 1995, and has issue living, Timothy Roger, *b* 1977, — Clare Vanessa, *b* 1975.

DAUGHTERS LIVING OF FIFTEENTH BARON

Hon Jane Maureen Thérèse, *b* 1945: *m* 1st, 1966 (*m diss* 1978), (Henry Alistair) Samuel Sandbach; 2ndly, 1980, Sqdn-Ldr Geoffrey Edward Meek, RAF, who *d* 1984; 3rdly, 1988, Lt-Cmdr Robert Nigel Forbes Glennie, RN (ret), and has issue living (by 1st *m*), James Peter Charles, *b* 1969; *ed* Ampleforth, and St Andrews Univ, — Emma Pauline Jane, *b* 1967: *m* 1993, Graham Defries, son of Nicholas Defries, of Merstham, Surrey, and has issue living, Charles Samuel Nicholas *b* 1996. *Residences* – 14 Langham Place, W4 2QL; Church Farm Cottage, East Wittering, Chichester, W Sussex PO20 8PT.
Hon Catherine Mary, *b* 1950: *m* 1st, 1972 (*m diss* 1989), Christopher John Godfrey Bird (*see* Vavasour, Bt); 2ndly, 1992, Michael Simon Stone, and has issue living (by 2nd *m*), Raphael Charles, *b* 1992. *Residence* – 81 Lakeside Rd, N13.

WIDOW LIVING OF FIFTEENTH BARON

Lady MAUREEN THERESE JOSEPHINE NOEL, only da of 4th Earl of Gainsborough: *m* 1st, 1944, the 15th Baron Dormer, who *d* 1975; 2ndly, 1982, as his 2nd wife, Peregrine Edward Launcelot Fellowes, who *d* 1999. *Residence* – The Court, Chipping Campden, Glos GL55 6JQ.

COLLATERAL BRANCHES LIVING

Grandchildren of late Hon Hubert Francis Dormer, 3rd son of 11th Baron, *b* 1837, *d* 1913: *m* 1865, Mary, who *d* 1938, da of Kenelm Digby:—
Issue of late John Hubert Aloysius Dormer, *b* 1874, *d* 1946: *m* 1900, Virginia Sinclair, who *d* 1956, da of late Charles Tankerville Chamberlaine Bey, of Paris:—
Charles Hubert Aloysius (PO Box 423, Hudson, Quebec J0P 1HO, Canada), *b* 1906: *m* 1st, 1930 (*m diss* 1946), Mary Johnson, of Ottawa, Canada; 2ndly, 1946 (*m diss* 1948), Jane Loutitt Ellis; 3rdly, 1948 (*m diss* 1991), Mary Johnson, his 1st wife, and has issue living, (by 2nd *m*) Anthony Fredrick Charles, *b* 1946: *m* 1966, Anita Lusick, of Melbourne, Australia, and has issue living, Aaron *b* 1972, Justine *b* 1974, — Lynn Elizabeth Jane, *b* 1944, — Susan Ann Sturrock, *b* 1948. *m* 1973, Peter James McNevern, of Queensland, Australia. —— Richard Joseph Thaddeus, DSC (Flat 6, The Manor Park Lands Gdns, Inner Park Rd, Wimbledon, SW19), *b* 1913; late RNVR. —— Hélène Venetia Anne, *b* 1907: *m* 1937, Frank R. Kelley, who *d* 1985, of 7 Ridgewood Lane, Westport, Conn 06880, USA, and has had issue, Christopher Francis Valentine (11818 Grey Birch Place, Reston, Virginia 22091-4223, USA), *b* 1939: *m* 1st, 1963 (*m diss* 1976), Ruth Jordan, of Bethesda, Maryland, USA; 2ndly, 1978, Elizabeth Ann Bowser, of Norfolk, Virginia, USA, and has issue living (by 1st *m*), Kevin Francis Dormer *b* 1966, Laura Anne *b* 1964, (by 2nd *m*) Patrick David Christopher *b* 1978, Matthew John Martin *b* 1980, — Peter John Dormer (10 Cranbrook Drive, Centerport, NY 11721, USA), *b* 1943: *m* 1967, Patricia F. Ruehle, of Chicago, and has issue living, Peter John *b* 1983, Elizabeth Louise Estelle *b* 1978, Margaret Evelyn Venetia *b* 1981, — David Richard Paul, *b* 1946; *d* 1972. —— Louise Cecilia Mary, *b* 1922 (*m diss* 1954), Maj Peter Bailward, RA; 2ndly, 1954, Maj William Goulding Petrie-Hay, RA, and has issue living (by 1st *m*), David John Aucher Michael (Maple Ridge, BC, Canada), *b* 1941; *ed* Ampleforth: *m* 1969, Charlotte Martha Petra, da of Herbert Frohberg, of Ottawa, and has issue living, Alan Jeffrey *b* 1975, — Sarah Jane Mary (Sally), *b* 1944: *m* 1965, Lt-Col Richard Grahame Dugard Showell,

TD, of The Old School House, Bishampton, Pershore, Worcs WR10 2LX, and has had issue, Jeremy Peter Dugard *b* 1965; *d* 1974, Alexander Geoffrey Dugard *b* 1971; *ed* Belmont Abbey, Claire Louise Dugard *b* 1966, — (by 2nd *m*) Rufus William, *b* 1955. *Address* – Lower Bouts Farm, Inkberrow, Worcs.

Issue of late Kenelm Everard Dormer, *b* 1879, *d* 1935: *m* 1910, Josephine, who *d* 1965, da of late Hon John T. Toohey, of Sydney:— ·
John Kenelm (Flat E, 36 Courtfield Gdns, SW5), *b* 1915; *ed* Downside; 1939-45 War as Capt KOYLI: *m* 1984, Kathleen, da of Frederick Rhys Michael, of Cairns, Australia.

Issue of late Capt Robert Stanhope Dormer, *b* 1880, *d* 1960: *m* 1927, Ebba, who *d* 1961, da of late Charles Cecil Beresford Whyte, of Hatley Manor and Newton Manor, co Leitrim, and widow of Sir Everard Alexander Hambro, KCVO:—
Michael Henry Stanhope, *b* 1930; is a Knight of Sovereign Order of Malta, and a Kt of Justice of the Constantinian Order of St George: *m* 1959, Daphne Margaret, el da of the late Capt O. J. Battine, and has issue living, Merlin Robert Colum Charles, *b* 1963, — Leanda Xenia Sophia Stanhope, *b* 1959: *m* 1984, Peter Andrew Paul March Phillipps de Lisle, of Osbaston Hall, Osbaston, Leics, 2nd son of Gerard Arnaud Amaury March Phillipps de Lisle, of Quenby Hall, Hungarton, Leics, and has issue living, Rupert Gerard Xavier *b* 1986, Christian Michael Frederick *b* 1988, Dominic Robert Peter *b* 1990, — Athena Cecilia Stanhope, *b* 1961: *m* 1993, David J. R. Defert, eldest son of Michel Defert, of Dijon, France. *Residence* – Bowdown House, Greenham, Newbury.

PREDECESSORS – (1) Sir ROBERT DORMER, Knt; *cr* a *Baronet* 10 June, 1615, and *Baron Dormer*, of Wenge (peerage of England) June 20th, 1615; *d* 1616; *s* by his grandson (2) ROBERT, 2nd Baron; a Gen of Horse; *cr Viscount Ascot and Earl of Carnarvon* (peerage of England) 1628; killed at first battle of Newbury 1643; *s* by his son (3) CHARLES, 2nd Earl; *d* 1709, when the ealdom and viscountcy expired, and the barony reverted to his kinsman (4) ROWLAND, 4th Baron, grandson of Hon Anthony, 2nd son of 1st Baron; *d* 1712; *s* by his cousin (5) CHARLES, 5th Baron, grandson of the Hon Robert, 3rd son of 1st Baron; *d* 1728; *s* by his son (6) *Rev* CHARLES, 6th Baron, a Priest of the Church of Rome; did not assume the title; *d* 1761; *s* by his brother (7) JOHN, 7th Baron; *d* 1785; *s* by his el son (8) CHARLES, 8th Baron; *d* 1894; *s* by his son (9) CHARLES, 9th Baron; *d* unmarried 1819; *s* by his half-brother (10) JOHN EVELYN PIERREPONT, 10th Baron; having conformed to the Church of England took his seat in the House of Lords; *d* 1826; *s* by his kinsman (11) JOSEPH THADDEUS, 11th Baron, son of John, 2nd son of 7th Baron; *b* 1790: *m* 1829, Elizabeth Anne, who *d* 1883, da of Sir Henry Joseph Tichborne, 8th Bt; at one time an officer of rank in the Austrian service: *d* 1871; *s* by his son (12) JOHN BAPTIST JOSEPH, 12th Baron, *b* 1830: *m* 1st, 1866, Louisa, who *d* 1868, da of late Col Edward King Tenison, of Kilronan Castle, Roscommon; 2ndly, 1871, Leonie, who *d* 1883, da of Mons Fortamps, a Senator of Belgium, and widow of Count Alfred de Beuren; 3rdly, 1885, Emily Constance Campbell, who *d* 1919, da of John Bald, of Monzie Castle, Perth; *s* by his nephew (13) ROLAND JOHN, 13th Baron, *b* 1862; sometime Sub-Director, Secretariat, Egyptian Ministry of Finance: *m* 1897, Marie Hanem, who *d* 1964, el da of late F. Eywaz, of Cairo; *d* 1920; *s* by his brother (14) CHARLES JOSEPH THADDEUS, CBE, 14th Baron; *b* 1864; Capt RN; a Gentleman Usher to HM King George V 1919-22: *m* 1903, Caroline Mary, who *d* 1951, da of late Sir Robert Cavendish Spencer Clifford, 3rd Bt (ext): *d* 1922: *s* by his el son (15) CHARLES WALTER JAMES, 15th Baron; *b* 1903; ADC to Gov-Gen of NZ 1939-41: *m* 1944, Lady Maureen Thérèse Josephine Noel (who *m* 2ndly, 1982, as his 2nd wife, Peregrine Edward Launcelot Fellowes), only da of 4th Earl of Gainsborough; *d* 1975; *s* by his brother (16) JOSEPH SPENCER PHILIP, 16th Baron; *b* 1914; late Capt Scots Guards; *dunm* 1995; *s* by his kinsman (17) GEOFFREY HENRY (2nd son of late Edward Henry Dormer, eldest son of late Hon Hubert Francis Dormer, 3rd son of 11th Baron), 17th Baron and present peer.

Douglas, family name of Earl of Morton.

Douglas, family name of Marquess of Queensberry.

Douglas, Akers-, family name of Viscount Chilston.

Douglas and Clydesdale, Marquess of; son of Duke of Hamilton and Brandon.

DOUGLAS OF BARLOCH, BARONY OF (Douglas) (Extinct 1980)

DAUGHTER LIVING OF FIRST BARON (*By 1st m*)

Hon Frances Margaret, MB and BS London 1943; Fellow of Royal College of Anaethetists 1957: *m* 1943, Kenneth Ulyatt, PhD, MSc, and has issue living, Charles Kenneth, *b* 1945, — James Francis, *b* 1950, — Mary Stella Miranda, *b* 1958: *m* 1994, Mark A. Carpenter, son of John Carpenter, of Leonard Stanley, Glos, and has issue living, Cecily Margaret Joy *b* 1997. *Residence* – 8 Cambridge Rd, Battersea Park, SW11.

DOUGLAS OF KIRTLESIDE, BARONY OF (Douglas) (Extinct 1969)

DAUGHTER LIVING OF FIRST BARON

Hon Katharine Ann, *b* 1957: *m* 1984, Geoffrey Andrews.

WIDOW LIVING OF FIRST BARON

HAZEL (*Baroness Douglas of Kirtleside*), da of late George Eric Maas Walker, of Mill Hill, NW, and widow of Capt W. E. R. Walker: *m* 1955, as his 3rd wife, the 1st Baron, who *d* 1969, when the title became ext.

DOUGLASS OF CLEVELAND, BARONY OF (Douglass) (Extinct 1978)

DAUGHTER LIVING OF LIFE BARON

Hon Jean, *b* 1928: *m* 1952, Garry Long, FCIS, of Malt House, Farm Lower Rd, Stoke Mandeville, Bucks and has issue.

Doune, Lord; son of Earl of Moray.

Douro, Marquess of; son of Duke of Wellington.

DOWDING, BARON (Dowding) (Baron UK 1943)

PIERS HUGH TREMENHEERE DOWDING, 3rd Baron; *b* 18 Feb 1948; *s* 1992; *ed* Fettes, and Amherst Coll, Mass, USA (BA); Prof of English at Okayama Shoka Univ, Japan since 1977: *m* 1973, Noriko Shiho, of Japan, and has issue.

Arms – Argent, three bars gemel sable, over all a fleur-de-lys azure, on a chief of the second, three Doric columns of the first. **Crest** – Upon a catherine wheel azure, a falcon rising or, belled and hooded gules.

DAUGHTERS LIVING

Hon Rosemary June, *b* 1975.
Hon Elizabeth Ann Yuki, *b* 1989.

BROTHER LIVING

Hon MARK DENIS JAMES, *b* 11 July 1949; *ed* Wymondham Coll, Norfolk: *m* 1982, Heather, da of Stanley Arter, of S Africa, and has issue living, Alexander, *b* 1983.

MOTHER LIVING

Alison Margaret, da of James Bannerman, LRCP, LRCS, of 158 Newmarket Rd, Norwich, and widow of Maj R. W. H. Peebles: *m* 2ndly, 1947 (*m diss* 1960), Wing-Cdr Hon Derek Hugh Tremenheere Dowding, RAF (later 2nd Baron Dowding), who *d* 1992; 3rdly 1963, David Hartnell-Beavis, who *d* 1992. *Residence* – Oakwood House, Old Watton Rd, Colney, Norwich, Norfolk NR4 7TP.

To work is to pray

WIDOW LIVING OF SECOND BARON

ODETTE LUCIE MARIE SOPHIE (*Odette, Baroness Dowding*), da of late Louis Joseph Houles, of Toulouse, France, and formerly wife of Brian Hughes: *m* 1961, as his 3rd wife, Wing-Cdr the 2nd Baron Dowding, RAF, who *d* 1992. *Residence* – 501 Gilbert House, Barbican, EC2Y 8BD.

PREDECESSORS – (1) *Air Ch Marshal Sir* HUGH CASWELL TREMENHEERE DOWDING, GCB, GCVO, CMG, son of Arthur John Caswall Dowding; *b* 1882; 1914-18 War (despatches); Dir of Training Air Min 1926-29, AOC Fighting Area, Air Defence of Gt Britain 1929-30, a Member of Air Council (Research and Development) 1930-36, and AOC-in-C Fighter Command 1936-40 *cr Baron Dowding*, of Bentley Priory, co Middlesex (peerage of UK) 1943: *m* 1st, 1913, Clarice Maud, who *d* 1920, da of Capt John Williams; 2ndly, 1951, Muriel, who *d* 1993, da of late John Albino, of Richmond, Surrey, and widow of Jack Maxwell Whiting, P/O RAFVR (*ka* 1944); *d* 1970; *s* by his son (2) DEREK HUGH TREMENHEERE, 2nd Baron; *b* 1919; Wing-Cdr RAF, 1939-45 War: *m* 1st, 1940 (*m diss* 1947), Joan Myrle, da of Donald James Stuart, of Nairn; 2ndly, 1947 (*m diss* 1960), Alison Margaret, da of James Bannerman, LRCP, LRCS, of 158 Newmarket Rd, Norwich, and widow of Maj R. W. H. Peebles; 3rdly, 1961, Mrs Odette Lucie Marie Sophie Hughes, da of late Louis Joseph Houles, of Toulouse, France, and formerly wife of Brian Hughes; *d* 1992; *s* by his elder son (3) PIERS HUGH TREMENHEERE, 3rd Baron and present peer.

DOWNE, VISCOUNT (Dawnay) Sits as BARON DAWNAY (UK 1897). (Viscount I 1681)

TIMET · PUDOREM

He fears shame

JOHN CHRISTIAN GEORGE DAWNAY, 11th Viscount; *b* 18 Jan 1935; *s* 1965; *ed* Eton and Ch Ch, Oxford; DL N Yorks: *m* 1965, Alison Diana, da of Ian Francis Henry Sconce, OBE, TD, of Brasted, Kent, and has issue.

𝕬rms – Argent, on a bend cottised sable, three annulets of the field. 𝕮rest – A demi-Saracen in armour couped at the thighs, wreathed about the temples proper, holding in the dexter hand a ring or, stoned azure, and in the sinister a lions' jamb erased gold, armed gules. 𝕾upporters – Two lions or, ducally crowned argent, each gorged with a collar cottised sable, charged with three annulets of the second.
Seat – Wykeham Abbey, Scarborough, Yorkshire. *Town Residence* – 5 Douro Place, W8.

SON LIVING

Hon RICHARD HENRY, 9 April 1967.

DAUGHTER LIVING

Hon Sarah Frances, *b* 1970.

WIDOW LIVING OF SON OF TENTH VISCOUNT

Gillian, yst da of late Maj James Cyril Aubrey George Dance, MP, of Moreton House, Moreton Morrell, Warwicks, and formerly wife of Capt Simon George Melville Portal (*see* Portal, Bt, colls): *m* 1976, Hon James Richard Dawnay, who *d* 1991, and has issue (see colls, infra).

COLLATERAL BRANCHES LIVING

Issue of late Hon James Richard Dawnay, yr son of 10th Viscount, *b* 1937, *d* 1991: *m* 1976, Gillian (ante), yst da of late Maj James Cyril Aubrey George Dance, MP, of Moreton House, Moreton Morrell, Warwicks, and formerly wife of Capt Simon George Melville Portal (*see* Portal, Bt, colls):—
Thomas Payan, *b* 1978.

Issue of late Maj Hon George William ffolkes Dawnay, MC, yr son of 9th Viscount, *b* 1909, *d* 1990: *m* 1945, Rosemary Helen, who *d* 1969, da of late Lord Edward Grosvenor (*see* D Westminster, 1969 Edn):—
Valentine George, *b* 1948; *ed* Eton. —— Edward William (Hillington Hall, King's Lynn, Norfolk PE31 6BW), *b* 1950; *ed* Eton: *m* 1996, his 2nd cousin, Lady Jane Meriel Grosvenor, da of 5th Duke of Westminster, and formerly wife of 10th Duke of Roxburghe. —— Elizabeth Rose, *b* 1946. —— (Mary) Isabel Dorothy, *b* 1955: *m* 1976, Victor Anthony Cazalet, and has issue (*see* Mainwaring, Bt, ext).

Grandchildren of late Maj Hon Hugh Dawnay, DSO, 2nd son of 8th Viscount:—
Issue of late Maj-Gen Sir David Dawnay, KCVO, CB, DSO, *b* 1903, *d* 1971: *m* 1926, Lady Katharine Nora de la Poer Beresford, who *d* 1991, da of 6th Marquess of Waterford:—
Hugh (Whitfield Court, Waterford), *b* 1932; *ed* Eton; Maj The Royal Hussars (ret): *m* 1971, Maria Ines, da of Dr D. Cermesoni, of Salta, Argentina, and has issue living, David Danton, *b* 1972, — Sebastian Hugo, *b* 1975. —— Peter (Pendene, Kale St, Batcombe, Somerset BA4 6AD), *b* (twin) 1932; *ed* Eton, and Ch Ch, Oxford (MA): *m* 1980, Caroline Mary, 2nd da of Gp Capt Nicolas Henry Joseph Tindal, RAF, of Terrybaun, Bofeenaun, Ballina, Mayo, and has issue living, Giles William, *b* 1981.

Issue of late Vice Adm Sir Peter Dawnay, KCVO, CB, DSC, *b* 1904, *d* 1989: *m* 1936, Lady Angela Christine Rose Montagu Douglas Scott (8 Sutton Manor Mews, Sutton Scotney, Winchester, Hants SO21 3JR), da of 7th Duke of Buccleuch:—
Charles John, *b* 1938; *ed* Eton; Lt-Col Welsh Guards: *m* 1968, Adrian Louise, da of Maj-Gen Godfrey John Hamilton, CBE, DSO (*see* Colthurst, Bt, 1973-74 Edn), and has issue living, Henry Marcus, *b* 1969, — George Edward, *b* 1970, — Nicholas St John, *b* 1978, — Sophia Penelope, *b* 1981. —— Moyra Jane, *b* 1946: *m* 1969, Timothy Rupert de Zoete, of 33 Pembridge Villas, W11, and has issue living, Alexandra Margot, *b* 1973.

Issue of late Lt-Col Ronald Dawnay, *b* 1908, *d* 1990: *m* 1st, 1932, Lady Elizabeth Katherine Grey, who *d* 1941, yr da of 5th Earl Grey; 2ndly, 1949, Sibell Margaret (The Glen, Dallingary, co Limerick), elder da of late Ronald Collet-Norman (*see* Collet, Bt, ext, 1950 Edn), and formerly wife of Maj Hon Archibald Edward Cubitt (*see* B Ashcombe):—
(By 1st *m*) Ann Josephine, *b* 1933; *ed* Somerville Coll, Oxford. —— Mary (*Lady Carew Pole*), LVO, JP, *b* 1936; a Lady-in-Waiting to HRH The Princess Royal since 1970; LVO 1983: *m* 1974, as his 2nd wife, Sir (John) Richard Walter Reginald Carew Pole, 13th Bt, of Antony House, Torpoint, Cornwall, PL11 2QA, and has issue (see that title).

Issue of late Wing-Cdr Michael Dawnay, RAF, *b* 1912, *d* 1946: *m* 1938, Julian Mary, who *d* 1979, adopted da of 1st Baron Brassey of Apethorpe:—
Patrick Julian (Château de Ragny, 14310 Tournay sur Odon, France; 38 St Stephen's Av, W12 8JH), *b* 1939; *ed* Eton: *m* 1966, Julie Katharine, da of late Lt-Col William Herbert Olivier, TD, DL, RA (*see* Jones, Bt, *cr* 1919), and has issue living,

Michael William (34 St Stephen's Av, W12 8JH), b 1969: m 1998, Gabriella K., da of Mrs A. M. Scott, of Holland Park, W11, and has issue living, Finn Julius Patrick b 1998, — Katharine Julian, b 1968: m 1996, Crispin D. Bonham Carter, actor, of 8 Cotleigh Rd, NW6 2ND, and has issue living, Arthur Thomas Patrick b 1997, Christopher Ruan (Kit) b 1999, — Evelyn Mary, b 1974. —— Romayne Julian, b 1940: m 1972, Peter Rowland Timms, of 198 Lake Rd, Ashburnham, Mass 01430, USA, and has issue living, Matthew Rowland Julian, b 1974, — Christopher Rowland Julian, b 1978, — Zoë Virginia Julian, b 1975.

(In remainder to Viscountcy only)

Grandchildren of late Maj-Gen Guy Payan Dawnay, CB, CMG, DSO, MVO, elder son of late Lt-Col Hon Lewis Payan Dawnay, 2nd son of 7th Viscount:—
Issue of late Lt-Col Christopher Payan Dawnay, CBE, MVO, b 1909, d 1989: m 1939, Patricia, who d 1989, da of late Maj-Gen Sir Hereward Wake, 13th Bt, CB, CMG, DSO:—
Rupert Payan (The Mill House, Longparish, Andover, Hants SP11 6QH), b 1940; ed Eton: m 1982, Carolyn, da of Chapman Marshall, of 7440 SW 117th St, Miami, Florida, USA, and has issue living, Nicholas Marshall, b 1986, — Lewis Payan, b 1986 (twin), — Thomas Payan, b 1988. —— Guy Payan, b 1944; ed Eton, and Lausanne Univ: m 1975 (m diss 1990), Charmian Rose, da of Lt-Col Alastair Neilson, of Dene House, Callaly, Northumberland, and has issue living, Christopher Payne, b 1977, — Mark Payne, b 1979. —— Gillian, b 1942: m 1966, Christopher Butler, of 18 Staverton Rd, Oxford, and has issue living, Sophie Rosalind, b 1968, — Josephine Laura, b 1970. —— Sarah (18 Wycombe Place, SW18 2LT), b 1947: m 1970 (m diss 1989), Jollyon Coombs, Welsh Guards, and has issue living, Charles E. Hardy, b 1976, — Arabella Sarah, b 1971, — Victoria Margaret, b 1974.

Issue of late Capt Oliver Payan Dawnay, CVO, b 1920, d 1988: m 1st, 1944 (m diss 1962), Lady Margaret Dorothea Boyle, da of 8th Earl of Glasgow; 2ndly, 1963, Hon Iris Irene Adele Peake, LVO (Wexcombe House, Marlborough, Wilts; Flat 5, 32 Onslow Sq, SW7), da of 1st Viscount Ingleby:—
(By 1st m) (Charles) James Payan, b 1946; ed Eton: m 1978, Sarah, elder da of (Edgar) David Stogdon, of Witchampton, Dorset (see Fergusson, Bt, 1971, Edn), and has issue living, David Frederick Payan, b 1985, — Olivia Margaret, b 1981, — Fenella Christian, b 1988. Residence – Symington House, nr Biggar, Lanarkshire. Clubs – Brooks's, Pratt's. —— Ivo Nicholas Payan, b 1952; ed Eton: m 1st, 1980 (m diss 1986), Chantal Mary Beatrice, da of Michael Rigby Bishop, of Combe House, Beckley, nr Rye, Sussex; 2ndly, 1992, Rachel S., da of Stanley Patrick Johnson, of W Nethercote, Winsford, Som, and has issue living (by 2nd m), Ludovic James Payan, b 1993, — Oliver Payan, b 1996, — Charlotte Millicent b 1994. —— Caroline Margaret, b 1950; Literary Agent; has issue living, Hugo Ronald Alexander MacPherson, b 1980. —— (By 2nd m) Emma Jane Clarissa, b 1964.

Granddaughters of late Hon Eustace Henry Dawnay, 5th son of 7th Viscount:—
Issue of late Lt-Col Cuthbert Henry Dawnay, MC, b 1891, d 1964: m 1921, Marjorie Kathleen, who d 1986, da of late Maj Reginald Bernard Loder (see Loder, Bt, colls, 1985 Edn):—
Eve Margaret, b 1926. —— Delia Mary, CVO (Lady Millar), b 1931; CVO 1996: m 1954, Sir Oliver Nicholas Millar, GCVO, FBA, FSA, Surveyor Emeritus of The Queen's Pictures, of The Cottage, Rays Lane, Penn, Bucks, and has issue living, Charles James, b 1965: m 1990, Alice Katherine, da of John W. P. Martin, of E Molesey, Surrey, and has issue living, Alfred Martin Parsifal b 1995, — Cynthia Mary, b 1956, — Lucy Anne, b 1958: m 1st, 1977 (m diss 1982), John E. L. Porter; 2ndly, 1983, Barnaby John Dickens, and has issue living (by 1st m), Roland Oliver b 1979, Max John b 1981, (by 2nd m) Archie b 1994, Marianna b 1985, — Beatrix Jane, b 1961: m 1987, Peter Andrew Flory, and has issue living, Oliver William b 1990, Nico Piers b 1993. —— Verena Joan, b 1936: m 1958, John Antony de la Cour Elliott, of 12 Cathcart Rd, SW10, and has issue living, Davina May, b 1962, — Bridget Victoria, b 1964: m 1988, Charles Holme Benthall, of Rectory Farm, W Heslerton, Malton, N Yorks, and has issue living, Thomas b 1995, — Felicity Jane, b 1966: m 1990, Ronald Bourlet, who d 1995, and has issue living, Michael b 1990, Christopher b 1995, Rebecca b 1993.

Grandchildren of late Nigel William Dawnay, only son of late Hon William Frederick Dawnay, 6th son of 7th Viscount:—
Issue of the late Frederick Cecil Dawnay, b 1905, d 1983: m 1st, 1929 (m diss 1955), Margaret Jean, who d 1989, da of the late William Coats Hutton, of Lexden Grange, Colchester; 2ndly, 1956, Betty Thora (2 Spring Grove, Sunningdale, Berks), da of the late Samuel Henry Darling, of Wentworth, Surrey:—
(By 1st m) Richard William, OBE (Courtside, Richmond Rd, Bath, Som BA1 5PU), b 1930; ed Sherborne; Brig The Parachute Regt; OBE (Mil) 1970: m 1962, Penelope Anne, da of late Col Norman West Finlinson, DSO, and has issue living, Rupert Charles Richard, b 1964, — Philippa Ruth, b 1963: m 1990 (m diss 1994), Peter Shepherd, yr son of J. A. Shepherd, of Wimborne, Dorset, and has issue living, Samuel Elliot b 1992, Jessica Kate b 1991, — Deborah Kate, b 1966: m 1997, Denis Colman Moloney, son of Michael Moloney, of Dungarvan, co Waterford, and has issue living, Bethany Kate b 1999. —— Christopher Ronald (19 Asher Drive, Mill Ride, Ascot, Berks SL5 8LJ), b 1933; ed Sherborne; late Capt 10th Hussars.

Issue of late William Richard Dawnay, b 1910, d 1977: m 1st, 1940 (m diss 1961), Olive Margaret, da of late Arthur James Barratt, of The Mile House, Oswestry (infra); 2ndly 1963, Pamela (Crouch Farm, Whatfield, Ipswich, Suffolk), da of late Charles Lester, of Piper's Croft, Harpenden, Herts:—
(By 1st m) Diana Margaret, b 1947.

Issue of late Capt Eric Christopher Dawnay, TD, b 1913, d 1999: m 1945, Vera Winifred (Llyndir, Dolgellau, Gwynedd), da of late Arthur James Barratt, of Mile House, Oswestry (ante):—
David Nigel (Llyndir, Dolgellau, Gwynedd), b 1946: m 1975 (m diss 1990), Hilary Jane, da of James W. Robins, MC, of Spinners, Lackford, Suffolk. —— Michael William, b 1950; ed Radley, and London Univ (BA).

Granddaughter of late Capt Hon Geoffrey Nicolas Dawnay, 7th son of 7th Viscount:—
Issue of late Capt Eric Geoffrey Dawnay, b 1890; d 1970: m 1930, Daisy, who d 1967, da of late Lt-Col Lewis Butler, of The Wilderness, Earley, Reading:—
Diana Buttercup, b 1931: m 1957, Hugh Rowland Murray Barran, of Hildenley, Malton, Yorks (see Barran, Bt, colls).

PREDECESSORS – (1) CHRISTOPHER DAWNAY; *cr* a *Baronet* 1642; *d* 1644; *s* by his son (2) *Sir* THOMAS, 2nd Bt; *d* 1644, aged 12. His uncle (3) *Sir* JOHN (MP for Yorkshire 1660, and for Pontefract 1661-88) was *cr Viscount Downe* (peerage of Ireland) 1681, and sat in James's Irish Parliament 1689; *d* 1695; *s* by his son (4) HENRY, 2nd Viscount, MP for Yorkshire in several parliaments; *d* 1741; *s* by his grandson (5) HENRY PLEYDELL, 3rd Viscount; MP for Yorkshire 1749-51; *dsp* 1760, from wounds received at battle of Campen, near Wesen, when in command of 25th Foot; *s* by his brother (6) JOHN, 4th Viscount; *d* 1780; *s* by his son (7) JOHN CHRISTOPHER BURTON, 5th Viscount; *cr Baron Dawnay*, of Cowick, co York (peerage of Great Britain) 1796; *d* 1832, when the barony expired; *s* by his brother (8) *Rev* WILLIAM HENRY, 6th Viscount; Rector of Sessay and Thormanby; *d* 1846; *s* by his son (9) WILLIAM HENRY, 7th Viscount; *b* 1812; *m* 1843, Mary Isabel, da of Rt Rev Hon Richard Bagot, Lord Bishop of Bath and Wells; *d* 1857; *s* by his son (10) HUGH RICHARD, KCVO, CB, CIE, 8th Viscount; *b* 1844: Hon Maj-Gen in the Army; Zulu Campaign 1879 (medal with clasp), and S Africa 1900, as ADC to FM Lord Roberts, and in charge of Foreign Mil Attachés (despatches twice, medal with seven clasps, CB), and 1901-2, in charge of Remount Depart; *cr Baron Dawnay*, of Danby, N Riding of York (peerage of United Kingdom) 1897: *m* 1st, 1869, Lady Cecilia Maria Charlotte Molyneux, VA (sometime Lady of the Bedchamber to HM Queen Victoria), who *d* 1910, da of 3rd Earl of Sefton; 2ndly, 1911, Florence Faith, who *d* 1958, (having *m* 2ndly, 1931, Rev Arthur Maxwell Bury, V, of Loose, who *d* 1937), da of late Rev Thomas Henry Dening, formerly V of Holy Trinity, Kilburn, NW, *d* 1924; *s* by his son (11) JOHN, CMG, DSO, 9th Viscount, *b* 1872; ADC to FM Lord French 1915-18, and Mil Sec to him in Ireland 1918-19: *m* 1902, Dorothy, who *d* 1957, only da of Sir William Hovell Browne ffolkes, 3rd Bt; *d* 1931 *s* by his el son (12) RICHARD, OBE, 10th Viscount; *b* 1903: Col and Hon Brig 5th Bn Green Howards; Comdg 69th Inf Bde and Assist A-G W Africa Command 1939-45 War: *m* 1928, Margaret Christine, who *d* 1967, da of Christian Bahnson, of Passiac, NJ, USA; *d* 1965; *s* by his el son (13) JOHN CHRISTIAN GEORGE, 11th Viscount and present peer; also Baron Dawnay.

Downpatrick, Baron; grandson of Duke of Kent.

DOWNSHIRE, MARQUESS OF (Hill) Sits as EARL OF HILLSBOROUGH (GB 1772)
(Marquess I 1789)

By God and my sword I have obtained

PER DEUM ET FERRUM OBTINUI

(ARTHUR) ROBIN IAN HILL, 8th Marquess; *b* 10 May 1929; *s* 1989; *ed* Eton; Hereditary Constable of Hillsborough Fort; *hp* to the Barony of Sandys: *m* 1st, 1957, Hon Juliet Mary Weld-Forester, who *d* 1986, da of 7th Baron Forester; 2ndly, 1989, Mrs Diana Marion Hibbert, who *d* 1998, 2nd da of late Rt Hon Sir Ronald Hibbert Cross, 1st Bt, KCMG, KCVO, and has issue by 1st *m*.

Arms – Quarterly: 1st sable, on a fesse argent between three leopards passant guardant or, spotted of the field, as many escallops gules, *Hill*; 2nd per bend sinister ermine and ermines, a lion rampant or, *Trevor*; 3rd gules, a quatrefoil or, *Rowe*; 4th argent, a chevron azure, between three trefoils slipped, per pale, gules and vert, *Rowe*. Crest – A reindeer's head couped gules, attired and plain collared or. Supporters – *Dexter*, a leopard or, spotted sable, ducally collared and chained gules; *sinister*, a reindeer gules, attired, unguled, and plain collared or.
Residence – High Burton House, Masham, Ripon, N Yorks HG4 4BS.

SONS LIVING (By 1st marriage)

(ARTHUR FRANCIS) NICHOLAS WILLS (*Earl of Hillsborough*) (High Burton, Masham, nr Ripon, N Yorks HG4 4BS), *b* 4 Feb 1959: *m* 1990, (Diana) Jane, only da of Gerald Leeson Bunting, of Otterington House, North-allerton, Yorks, and has issue:—

SON LIVING —Edmund Robin Arthur (*Viscount Kilwarlin*), *b* 21 May 1996.
DAUGHTERS LIVING —*Lady* Isabella Diana Juliet, *b* 1991, — *Lady* Beatrice Hannah Georgina, *b* 1994, — *Lady* Claudia Lucy Helena, *b* 1998.

Lord Anthony Ian, *b* 1961: *m* 1992, Annabel Priscilla Angela, yr da of Hon David Lawrence Robert Nall-Cain (*see* B Brocket), and has issue living, Marcus Robert Francis, *b* 1994, — Orlando Harry Wills, *b* 1997. *Residence* – Ingram House, Powburn, Alnwick, Northumberland NE66 4LT.

DAUGHTER LIVING (By 1st marriage)

Lady Georgina Mary, *b* 1964.

SISTERS LIVING

Venice Marigold (Rosie), *b* 1930: *m* 1954 (*m diss* 1989), 3rd Baron Kindersley. *Residence* – Ramhurst Manor, Tonbridge, Kent.

Lady Caroline Sylvia, *b* 1938; raised to the rank of a Marquess's daughter 1992: *m* 1976, Dr Alan Charles Nelson Borg, CBE, Dir Victoria and Albert Museum, and has issue living, Leonora Ishbel, *b* 1980, — Helen Olivia, *b* 1982. *Residence* – Telegraph House, 36 West Sq, SE11 4SP.

COLLATERAL BRANCHES LIVING

Descendants of late Lord Arthur Edwin Hill-Trevor, 3rd son of 3rd Marquess, who was *cr Baron Trevor* 1880 (see that title).

Descendants of late Lord George Augustus Hill, MP, 5th son of 2nd Marquess, and in remainder to his mother's *Barony of Sandys* (see that title).

PREDECESSORS – **(1)** TREVOR HILL, PC; successively MP for Aylesbury, Malmesbury and Downshire, and Lord-Lieut of co Down; *cr Baron Hill*, of Kilwarlin, and *Viscount Hillsborough* (peerage of Ireland) 1717, with remainder to the heirs male of his father; *d* 1742; *s* by his son **(2)** WILLS, PC, 2nd Viscount; MP for Huntingdon, and for Warwick 1742-56, Comptroller of Household to George II, Joint Postmaster-Gen, Sec of State for the Colonies 1768-72 and 1779-82, and Registrar of High Court of Chancery, Ireland; *cr Viscount Kilwarlin* and *Earl of Hillsborough* (peerage of Ireland) 1751, with remainder to his uncle Arthur (later Viscount Dungannon), *Baron Harwich*, of Harwich, co Essex (peerage of great Britain, 1756), *Viscount Fairford and Earl of Hillsborough* (peerage of Great Britain) 1772, and Marquess of Downshire (peerage of Ireland) 1789; *d* 1793; *s* by his son **(3)** ARTHUR, 2nd Marquess; his wife Mary, da of Hon Martyn Sandys, having succeeded to the estates of Edwin, 2nd and last Baron Sandys (*cr* 1743), was *cr Baroness Sandys*, of Ombersley (peerage of United Kingdom) 1802, with remainder to 2nd and younger sons successively; she *d* 1836, and was *s* by her 2nd son (*see* B Sandys): the Marquess *d* 1801; *s* by his son **(4)** ARTHUR BLUNDELL SANDYS TRUMBULL, KP, DCL, 3rd Marquess; Lord-Lieut of co Down; *d* 1845; *s* by his son **(5)** ARTHUR WILLS BLUNDELL SANDYS TRUMBULL WINDSOR, KP, 4th Marquess; *d* 1868; *s* by his son **(6)** ARTHUR WILLS BLUNDELL, 5th Marquess; *b* 1844; *m* 1870, Georgina Elizabeth, who *d* 1919, da of John Balfour, of Balbirnie, co Fife; *d* 1874; *s* by his son **(7)** ARTHUR WILLS JOHN WELLINGTON BLUNDELL TRUMBULL, 6th Marquess; *b* 1871: *m* 1st, 1893 (*m diss* 1902), Katherine Mary, who *d* 1959, da of Hon Hugh Henry Hare; 2ndly, 1907, Evelyn Grace May, who *d* 1942, da of Edmund Benson Foster; *d* 1918; *s* by his el son **(8)** ARTHUR WILLS PERCY WELLINGTON BLUNDELL TRUMBULL SANDYS, 7th Marquess; *b* 1894; Lieut Berks Yeo, attached to British Red Cross in France during European War: *m* 1953, Mrs Noreen Gray-Miller, who *d* 1983, only da of late William Barraclough; *d* 1989; *s* by his nephew **(9)** (ARTHUR) ROBIN IAN (only son of late Capt Lord (Arthur) Francis Henry Hill, The Greys (Reserve), yr son of 6th Marquess), 8th Marquess, and present peer; also Earl of Hillsborough, Viscount Hillsborough, Viscount Fairford, Viscount Kilwarlin, Baron Harwich, and Baron Hill.

DROGHEDA, EARL OF (Moore) (Earl I 1661, Baron UK 1954) Sits as BARON MOORE (UK 1954)
(Title pronounced "Droyeda")

HENRY DERMOT PONSONBY MOORE, 12th Earl; *b* 14 Jan 1937; *s* 1990; *ed* Eton, and Trin Coll, Camb; late 2nd Lieut Life Guards; photographer; Dir Derry Moore (Photography) Ltd: *m* 1st, 1968 (*m diss* 1972), Eliza, da of Stacy Barcroft Lloyd, Jr, of Philadelphia, and St Croix, Virgin Is; 2ndly, 1978, Alexandra, da of Sir Nicholas Henderson, GCMG, KCVO, and has issue by 2nd *m*.

Arms – Azure, on a chief indented or, three mullets pierced gules. **Crest** – Out of a ducal coronet or, a Moor's head in profile proper, wreathed round the temples argent and azure. **Supporters** – Two greyhounds argent.
Residence – 40 Ledbury Rd, W11. *Club* – Brooks's.

SONS LIVING (By 2nd marriage)

BENJAMIN GARRETT HENDERSON (*Viscount Moore*), *b* 21 March 1983.
Hon Garrett Alexander, *b* 1986.

DAUGHTER LIVING (By 2nd marriage)

Lady Marina Alice, *b* 1988.

A brave man may fall but cannot yield

COLLATERAL BRANCH LIVING

> Granddaughter of late Col Francis Moore, gt grandson of John Moore of Drumbanagher, co Armagh (*d* 1809), grandson of Hon Arthur Moore, 5th son of 1st Viscount:—
> Issue of late Col Francis Moore, DSO, OBE, *b* 1879, *d* 1938: *m* 1916, Anne Early, who *d* 1964, da of William Van Wyck, of New York:—

Kathleen Clifford, *b* 1918: *m* 1942, Lieut-Col Stephen Murfin Rose, OBE, R Fusiliers, who *d* 1992, and has issue living, Margaret Anne, *b* 1947: *m* 1975, Col O. Mark Roberts, OBE, R Regt of Wales, of Daisyfield Cottage, Rowledge, Farnham, Surrey, and has issue living, Camilla Margaret Rose *b* 1977, Katharine Frances Rose *b* 1980, — Mary Elizabeth, *b* 1951: *m* 1979, Cdr Jeremy G. Hurlbatt, OBE, RN, of Reaphay, W Buckland, Wellington, Somerset, and has issue living, Charles Henry *b* 1984, Claire Alice Rose *b* 1982. *Residence* – 10 The Cloisters, Sherborne, Dorset.

PREDECESSORS – (1) *Sir* GARRETT Moore, Knt, MP, *cr Baron Moore*, of Mellefont, co Louth (peerage of Ireland) 1616, and *Viscount Moore*, of Drogheda (peerage of Ireland) 1621; *d* 1627, *s* by his son (2) HENRY, 2nd Viscount; killed at Portlester in service of Charles I 1643; *s* by his son (3) HENRY, 3rd Viscount; *cr Earl of Drogheda* (peerage of Ireland) 1661; *s* by his son (4) CHARLES, 2nd Earl; *d* 1679; *s* by his brother (5) HENRY, 3rd Earl; assumed the name of Hamilton on succeeding to the estates of his brother-in-law Henry, 2nd and last Earl of Clanbrassill; *d* 1714; *s* by his grandson (6) HENRY, 4th Earl; inherited the Monasterevin estates of Arthur, 3rd and last Viscount Loftus, of Elye; *dsp* 1727; *s* by his brother (7) EDWARD, 5th Earl; drowned in passage from England to Dublin 1758; *s* by his son (8) CHARLES, KP; *cr Marquess of Drogheda* (peerage of Ireland) 1791, and *Baron Moore*, of Moore Place, co Kent (peerage of United Kingdom) 1801; *d* 1821; *s* by his son (9) CHARLES, 2nd Marquess; *d* unmarried 1837; *s* by his nephew (10) HENRY FRANCIS SEYMOUR, 3rd Marquess (son of late Lord Henry Seymour Moore, 2nd son of 1st Marquess), *b* 1825; Vice-Adm of Leinster, and Lieut of Kildare: *m* 1847, Hon Mary Caroline Stuart-Wortley, who *d* 1896, da of 2nd Baron Wharncliffe; *d* 1892, when the Marquessate of Drogheda (*cr* 1791) and Barony of Moore (*cr* 1801) became extinct, and the peerages of 1616, 1621 and 1661 devolved upon his cousin (11) PONSONBY WILLIAM (son of late Ponsonby Arthur Moore, great grandson of 5th Earl), 9th Earl, *b* 1846; a Representative Peer for Ireland: *m* 1879, Anne Tower, who *d* 1924, da of late George Moir, LLD, Sheriff of Stirlingshire; *d* 1908; *s* by his son (12) HENRY CHARLES PONSONBY, KCMG, PC, 10th Earl, *b* 1884; was Lieut of Co Kildare 1918-21, a Representative Peer for Ireland 1913-57, Director-Gen of Min of Economic Warfare 1942-5, and Chm of Committees and Dep Speaker of House of Lords 1946-57; *cr Baron Moore*, of Cobham, co Surrey (peerage of UK) 1954: *m* 1st, 1909 (*m diss* 1922), Kathleen, CBE, who *d* 1965, da of late Charles Maitland Pelham Burn, of Grange Park, Edinburgh; 2ndly, 1922, Olive Mary (formerly Lady Victor William Paget), who *d* 1947, da of George Meatyard; *d* 1957; *s* by his only son (13) CHARLES GARRETT PONSONBY, KG, KBE, 11th Earl, *b* 1910, Dir Economist Newspaper Ltd, and of Earls Court and Olympia Ltd, Chm Financial Times Ltd 1971-74 (Man Dir 1946-71), of Newspaper Publishers Assocn 1968-70, and of Royal Opera House, Covent Garden, Ltd 1958-74: *m* 1935, Joan Eleanor, who *d* (16 Dec) 1989, da of late William Henry Carr; *d* (24 Dec) 1989; *s* by his only son (14) HENRY DERMOT PONSONBY, 12th Earl and present peer: also Viscount Moore, and Baron Moore (peerage of Ireland 1616, and of UK 1954).

DRUMALBYN, BARONY (Macpherson) (Extinct 1987)

DAUGHTERS LIVING OF FIRST AND LAST BARON (*By 1st marriage*)

Hon Jean Stewart (*Hon Lady Weatherall*), *b* 1938: *m* 1962, Vice Adm Sir James L. Weatherall, KBE, of Craig House, Bishop's Waltham, Hants, and has issue living, Ian James Stewart, *b* 1976, — Annie Norah, *b* 1974: *m* 1996, David G. Sexton, elder son of Richard Sexton, of Cowbridge, S Glam, — Elizabeth Alwynne, *b* (twin) 1976. Adm and the Hon Lady Weatherall also have two adopted children, Niall Anthony Stewart, *b* 1967: *m* 1998, Joanne Louise, da of Steven Burroughs, of Calmore, Hants, — Sarah Margaret, *b* 1968.

Hon Mary Stewart MACPHERSON, *b* 1942; continues to be known by her maiden name: *m* 1st, 1967 (*m diss* 1991), Philip D. Wilson; 2ndly, 1994, Howard Alvine Rees. *Residence* – 62 Prospect Quay, Point Pleasant, SW18 1PR.

WIDOW LIVING OF FIRST AND LAST BARON

RITA (*Baroness Drumalbyn*), widow of Harry Edmiston: *m* 1985, as his 2nd wife, 1st Baron Drumalbyn, KBE, PC, who *d* 1987. *Residence* – 108 Montagu Mansions, W1H 1LE.

Drumlanrig, Viscount; son of Marquess of Queensberry.

Drummond, family name of Earl of Perth.

Drummond of Megginch, family name of Baroness Strange.

DUBS, BARON (Dubs) (Life Baron 1994)

ALFRED DUBS; *b* Dec 1932; *ed* LSE (BSc Econs); Memb Westminster City Council 1971-78; Chm Westminster Community Relations Council 1972-77; Memb Kensington, Chelsea and Westminster Area Health Authority 1975-78; MP for Wandsworth, Battersea S (*Lab*) 1979-83, Battersea 1983-87; Memb Home Affairs Select Cttee 1981-83, opposition spokesman on Home Affairs 1983-87; Dir of Refugee Council since 1988; Memb of Broadcasting Standards Council 1988-93; Under Sec of State N Ireland Office since 1998; *cr Baron Dubs*, of Battersea in the London Borough of Wandsworth (Life Baron) 1994: *m*, and has issue.
Address – c/o House of Lords, SW1A 0PW.

DUCIE, EARL OF (Moreton) (Earl UK 1837)

DAVID LESLIE MORETON, 7th Earl; *b* 20 Sept 1951; *s* 1991; *ed* Cheltenham, London Univ, and Wye Coll (BSc Agric): *m* 1975, Helen, da of M. L. Duchesne, of Langford, Bristol, and has issue.

Arms – Quarterly: 1st and 4th argent, a chevron gules, between three square buckles sable, *Moreton*; 2nd and 3rd or, two lions passant gules, *Ducie*. **Crest** – A moorcock's head or, combed and wattled gules, between two wings displayed azure. **Supporters** – Two unicorns argent, armed, unguled, maned, and tufted or, each gorged with a ducal coronet per pale gold and gules.
Seat – Tortworth, Wotton-under-Edge, Glos.

SON LIVING

JAMES BERKELEY (*Lord Moreton*), *b* 6 May 1981.

DAUGHTER LIVING

Lady Claire Alison *b* 1984.

BROTHERS LIVING

Hon Douglas Howard, *b* 1958; *ed* Bredon Sch. *Residence* – Tortworth, Wotton-under-Edge, Glos.
Hon Robert Matthew, *b* 1964; *ed* Malvern, and RAC Cirencester: *m* 1988, Heather Elizabeth (LLB Lincoln's Inn 1998), only da of Colin Lynton-Jenkins, of Alveston, Avon, and has issue living, Charles Henry Robert, *b* 1993, — Olivia Alexandra Rose, *b* 1991. *Residence* – North Nibley, Dursley, Glos.

By persevering

SISTER LIVING

Lady (Alison) Jeannette, *b* 1954: *m* 1986, Mark Allan Stewart, of Ottawa, Ontario, Canada, and has issue living, Derek Allan, *b* 1987, — Laura Jessica, *b* 1989. *Residence* – 1159 St Jerome Crescent, Orleans, Ontario, Canada K1C 2A7.

WIDOW LIVING OF SIXTH EARL

ALISON MAY (*Alison, Countess of Ducie*), da of Leslie Aitken Bates, of Pialba, Queensland: *m* 1950, the 6th Earl of Ducie, who *d* 1991. *Residence* – Tortworth, Wotton-under-Edge, Glos.

COLLATERAL BRANCHES LIVING

Grandchildren of late Henry John Moreton, 2nd son of late Capt Hon Reynolds Moreton, RN, 5th son of 2nd Earl:—
Issue of late Theodore Reynolds Moreton, b 1890, d 1970: m 1921, Marie Ann Josephine, who d 1965, da of David O. Anderson, of Duluth, Minnesota, USA:—
David Oral (Jackson Highlands Rd, Box 32, Jackson, NH 03846-0032, USA), b 1922: m 1948, Barbara Colby, da of late L. Graham Harris, of New York, and has had issue, Henry Packard (140 Phillip Rd, Woodside, CA 94062-2625, USA), b 1958: m 19—, Ann Woodward, da of Jay Sydeman, of Grass Valley, CA, and has issue living, Emily Woodward b 1996, Julia Packard b 1998, — Theodora, b 1954, d 1969.

Issue of late Hugh Berkeley Moreton, b 1891, d 1935: m 1923, Phyllis Mott, who d 1928:—
Henry John (PO Box 778, The Pas, Manitoba, Canada R9A 1K8), b 1926: m 1951, Patricia, da of William A. Russell, and has issue living, John Russell Berkeley (PO Box 2607, The Pas, Manitoba, Canada 9RA 1L5), b 1956: m 1984, Sheila Marian, da of David Bown, and has issue living, Dayton Kyle b 1991, Logan Quinn Russell b 1994, — Richard Steven, b 1963, — Brenda Leigh, b 1952: m 1973, Dennis Boiteau, of RRI, Shallow Lake, Ontario, Canada N0H 2K0, and has issue living, Mark Steven b 1976, Dereck Troy b 1979, Mathew Scott b 1982, — Patricia Ann, b 1954: m 1983, Colin Chopp, of 79 McDowell Drive, Winnipeg, Manitoba, Canada R3R 2T9, and has issue living, Colin Ryan b 1985, Kelsey Lauren b 1987. —— Carrie Ann, b 1924: m 1950, Charles William Schmidt, who d 1993, of 1950 Bosworth Lane, Northfield, IL 60093, USA, and has issue living, Charles William (III), b 1951: m 1975, Rebecca Lynn Hess, and has issue living, Christina Lynn b 1985, Katelyn Marie b 1988, — Stephen Berkeley (6813 Beckwith Rd, Morton Grove, IL 60053, USA), b 1957, — Susan Moreton (4927 Louise, Skokie, IL 60077, USA), b 1953, — Karin Marie (4927 Louise, Skokie, IL 60077, USA), b 1955.

Grandchildren of late Reginald Moreton, 4th son of late Capt Hon Reynolds Moreton, RN (ante):—
Issue of late Richard Beresford Reynolds Moreton, b 1909, d 1984: m 1929, Irene Beatrice, who d 1986, da of Maj M. Donnithorne, of Torquay:—
David Buckland REYNOLDS-MORETON (Cobb Cottage, 23 Fore St, Bovey Tracey, Devon), b 1931: m 1965, Cecilie Margaret Elswood, da of Lilian Elswood, of 91 Woodlands Gdns, Isleworth, Middx. —— Anthony (20 St George's Rd, W Harnham, Salisbury, Wilts), b 1938. —— Jennifer Anne, b 1941: m 1969, John Wrigley, of Manor Cottage, E Grimstead, Salisbury, Wilts.

Grandchildren of late John Ronald Moreton-Macdonald, only son of late Charles Moreton-Macdonald, elder son of late Hon Augustus Henry Macdonald-Moreton, MP, 2nd son of 1st Earl:—
Issue of late John Maxwell Macdonald; assumed the surname of Maxwell Macdonald in lieu of his patronymic 1930; b 1908, d 1995: m 1930, Anne (Largie, Taylinloan, Argyllshire), da and heir of tailzie of Sir John Maxwell Stirling-Maxwell, KT, 10th Bt:—
John Ronald MAXWELL MACDONALD, b 1936; is eventual heir to the baronetcy of Stirling-Maxwell (see that title). —— Donald (55 Park Walk, SW10 0AZ), b 1938; ed Winchester, and Ch Ch, Oxford: m 1st, 1962 (m diss 1976), Caromy, da of late Robert Jenkins, of The Manor House, Hooton Roberts, Yorks; 2ndly, 1977, Margaret Anne, da of late Alfred Kingerley, and has issue living (by 1st m), James Donald, b 1965, — Harriet Caromy Anne, b 1967.

Issue of late Maj Simon Foster Macdonald Lockhart of The Lee, Lovat Scouts; assumed the surname of Macdonald Lockhart of The Lee 1946; b 1916, d 1991: m 1942, Caitriona (Dunsyre House, Dunsyre, Lanark), elder da of late Seton Gordon, CBD, FZS, of Upper Duntullin, Isle of Skye:—
Angus Hew MACDONALD LOCKHART OF THE LEE (Newholm, Dunsyre, Lanark ML11 8NQ), b 1946; ed Rannoch, and Aberdeen Agric Coll: m 1970, Susan Elizabeth, da of late Hon William Normand (see B Normand, 1967 Edn), and has issue living, Ranald William Angus, b 1975, — Fiona, b 1972. —— Simon James (Thorntonhill, Fossoway, Kinross KY13 7PB), b 1949; ed Winchester: m 1973, Lavinia, da of late Col Peter William Marsham, MBE (see E Romney, colls) and has issue living, James Seton Alexander, b 1976, — Andrew Peter Robert, b 1978, — Davina, b 1981. —— Norman Philip, b 1954. —— Mairi Susan, b 1943: m 1st, 1962 (m diss 1965), Leslie Swan; 2ndly, 1965, Ian Hamilton Finlay; 3rdly, 1998, her former husband, Richard (formerly Leslie) Swan, of Stonypath, Dunsyre, Lanark, and has issue living (by 2nd m), Alexander, b 1966, — Aileen, b 1967.

Granddaughter of late Robert Moreton, 2nd surv son of Hon Percy Moreton, 3rd son of 1st Earl:—
Issue of late Maurice Fitzhardinge Reynolds Moreton, b 1884, d 1976: m 1917, Anna Margaretta, who d 1971, da of late Rev Edward Brown Charlton, R of Tatenhill:—
Berkeley John Reynolds (Wason House, Castle Cary, Somerset), b 1918: m 1945, Lois, yr da of late Louis Hardaker, of Ackworth, Yorks, and has issue living, Stephen Maurice, b 1950: m 1972, Lynn, da of Thomas Milford, of Swansea, — John Evelyn (Treetops, Leckhampton Hill, Cheltenham, Glos), b 1952: m 1981, Jennifer, yr da of David Davis, of Cheltenham, and has issue living, Robert Berkeley Reynolds b 1983, James Henry Fitzhardinge b 1984, — Jane Mary Margaretta, b 1956.

PREDECESSORS – (1) MATTHEW DUCIE Moreton; cr Lord Ducie, Baron of Moreton, co Stafford (peerage of Great Britain) 1720; d 1735; s by his son (2) MATTHEW, 2nd Baron; cr Baron Ducie of Tortworth, co Gloucester (peerage of Great Britain) 1763, with remainder to the sons of his sister Hon Elizabeth Reynolds; d 1770, when the Barony of Moreton expired, and the Barony of Ducie devolved upon his nephew (3) THOMAS Reynolds, 2nd Baron; assumed the surname of Moreton by Act of Parliament 1771; dsp 1785; s by his brother (4) FRANCIS Reynolds, 3rd Baron; assumed the surname of Moreton by Act of Parliament 1786; d 1808; s by his son (5) THOMAS REYNOLDS, 4th Baron; cr Baron Moreton, of Tortworth, and Earl of Ducie (peerage of United Kingdom) 1837; d 1840; s by his son (6) HENRY GEORGE FRANCIS, 2nd Earl; b 1802; m 1826, Hon Elizabeth Dutton, da of 2nd Baron Sherborne; d 1853; s by his son (7) HENRY JOHN, GCVO, FRS, 3rd Earl; b 1827; MP for Stroud (L) 1852-53; Lord-Lieut of Gloucestershire 1857-1911, and Lord Warden of the Stanneries and a Member of Council of Prince of Wales 1888-1908: m 1849, Julia, who d 1895, da of late James Haughton Langston, MP, of Sarsden, Chipping Norton; d 1921; s by his brother (8) BERKELEY BASIL, 4th Earl, b 1831; many years engaged in sheep and cattle farming in Queensland; Postmaster-Gen of Queensland 1885 Min of Public Instruction, Queensland 1885-86, and Colonial Sec and Min of Public Instruction 1886-88: m 1862, Emily Eleanor, who d 1921, da of John Kent, Commr of Crown Lands, Queensland; d 1924; s by his el son (9) CAPEL HENRY BERKELEY, 5th Earl; b 1875; many years engaged in dairy and fruit farming in Australia: m 1903 (Maria) Emma, who d 1958, da of Frederick Bryant, of Maryborough, Queensland; d 1952; s by his nephew (10) BASIL HOWARD (son of late Hon Algernon

Howard Moreton, 2nd son of 4th Earl), 6th Earl; *b* 1917: *m* 1950, Alison May, da of Leslie Aitken Bates, of Pialba, Qld; *d* 1991; *s* by his eldest son (11) DAVID LESLIE, 7th Earl and present peer; also Baron Ducie, and Baron Moreton.

DUDLEY, BARONESS (Hamilton) (Baron E 1439)

BARBARA AMY FELICITY HAMILTON, *Baroness Dudley*; *b* 23 April, 1907; *s* 1972: *m* 1st, 1929, Guy Raymond Hill Wallace, who *d* 1967; 2ndly, 1980, Charles Anthony Crosse Hamilton, and has issue by 1st *m*.

Arms – Azure two bars nebuly argent, each charged with as many crescents sable, a chief or, issuant therefrom a demi lion sable. **Supporters** – On either side, a lion double-queued vert armed and langued gules, gorged with a ducal coronet, attached thereto a cordon passing between the forelegs and reflexed over the back or.
Residence – Hill House, Napleton Lane, Kempsey, Worcs WR5 3PY.

SONS LIVING (*By 1st marriage*)

Hon JIM ANTHONY HILL WALLACE (Little Grange, Napleton, Kempsey, Worcs), *b* 9 Nov 1930; *ed* Lancing: *m* 1962, Nicola Jane, da of Philip William Edward Leslie Dunsterville, and has issue living, Jeremy William Guilford, *b* 1964, — Nicholas John Hill, *b* 1967.
Hon Robin Guy Hill WALLACE (Pond House, Ham Hill, Powick, Worcs WR2 4RD), *b* 1936; *ed* Malvern: *m* 1959, Jill Alexandra, da of late Herbert Williams, and has issue living, Simon Alexander Hill, *b* 1962, — Andrew George Hill, *b* 1964.
Hon William John Sutton WALLACE (Beechmount House, Hallow, Worcs), *b* 1938; *ed* Malvern: *m* 1962, Jean Carol Ann, da of late Albert Edward Shipton, and has issue living, Guy Edward John Sutton, *b* 1963, — Piers William Somery, *b* 1965.

DAUGHTER LIVING (*By 1st marriage*)

Hon Felicity Lilla, *b* 1944: *m* 1967, Philip Neil Faram, of Heath Hill, Queen Hill, Upton-on-Severn, Worcs, and has issue living, David Stephen, *b* 1968, — Michael Guy, *b* 1970, — Philip John, *b* 1976.

PREDECESSORS – (1) *Sir* JOHN Sutton de Dudley, KG, son of Sir John Sutton; *b* 1400; summoned to Parliament 1439-40; *d* 1487; *s* by his grandson (2) EDWARD (son of Sir Edmund Dudley), 2nd Baron; *b* 1459; knighted 1487; summoned to Parliament 1492-1529: *m* Cicely, da of Sir William Willoughby; *d* 1531; *s* by his son (3) JOHN, 3rd Baron; *d* 1553; *s* by his son (4) EDWARD, 4th Baron; summoned to Parliament 1584-86; Lieut of Hampnes Castle: *m* 1st, 1555, Katherine, da of 1st Baron Chandos of Sudeley; 2ndly, Jane, da of 3rd Earl of Derby; 3rdly, Mary, da of 1st Baron Howard of Effingham; *d* 1586; *s* by his son (by his 2nd *m*) (5) EDWARD, 5th Baron; *b* 1567; *dsp* 1643; *s* by his granddaughter (6) FRANCES (only da of Sir Ferdinando Sutton, by his wife Honora, only da of Edward Seymour, Lord Beauchamp, and grandda of Lady Katherine Grey, niece of King Henry VIII); *b* 1611: *m* 1628, Sir Humble Ward, who *d* 1670, having been *cr Baron Ward*, of Birmingham, co Warwick 1643, with remainder to the heirs-male of his body, by his wife, Frances; *d* 1697; *s* by her son (7) EDWARD Ward, 7th Lord Dudley and 2nd Baron Ward: *m* Frances, da of Sir William Gretton, 2nd Bt; *d* 1701; *s* by his grandson (8) EDWARD (son of William Ward), 8th Baron Dudley and 3rd Baron Ward; *b* 1683: *m* 1703, Diana, da of Sir Thomas Howard, of Ashtead, Surrey; *d* 1704; *s* by his son (9) EDWARD, 9th Baron Dudley and 4th Baron Ward; *b* (posthumous) 1704; *d* 1731; *s* by his uncle (10) WILLIAM, 10th Baron Dudley and 5th Baron Ward (yr brother of the 8th Baron); *b* 168-; *d* 1740, when the Barony of Ward devolved upon the heir-male, and that of Dudley on the heir-general, his nephew (11) FERDINANDO DUDLEY Lea, 11th Baron (son of William Lea, of Halesowen Grange, by Frances, sister of the 10th Baron); *b* 1710; *d* 1757, when the Barony of Dudley fell into abeyance between his sisters and co-heirs, and so remained until 1916, when the abeyance was determined in favour of the senior co-heir (12) FERDINANDO DUDLEY WILLIAM LEA SMITH (el and only surviving son of late Ferdinando Dudley Lea Smith), 12th Baron: *m* 1904, Sybil Augusta, who *d* 1958, da of late Rev Henry William Coventry (E Coventry, colls); *d* 1936; *s* by his only son (13) FERDINANDO DUDLEY LEA, 13th Baron, *b* 1910: *m* 1941 (*m diss* 1965), Kirsten Laura Hedvig, da of Lars Anton Albrechtson, of Vibsig, Denmark; *d* 1972; *s* by his sister (14) BARBARA AMY FELICITY, Baroness Dudley and present peeress.

DUDLEY, EARL OF (Ward) (Earl UK 1860)

WILLIAM HUMBLE DAVID WARD, 4th Earl; *b* 5 Jan 1920; *s* 1969; *ed* Eton, and Ch Ch, Oxford; late Lt and temp Capt 10th R Hussars; 1939-45 War in Italy (wounded): *m* 1st, 1946 (*m diss* 1961), Stella, el da of late Dr Don Miguel Angel Carcano, KCMG, KBE, sometime Argentine Ambassador in London; 2ndly, 1961, Maureen, da of James Swanson, and has issue by 1st and 2nd *m.*

𝕬rms – Checky, or and azure, a bend ermine. 𝕮rest – Out of a ducal coronet or, a lion's head azure. 𝕾upporters – Two angels proper, hair and wings or, under robe sanguine, upper robe azure.
Residence – 6 Cottesmore Gdns, W8. *Club* – White's, Pratt's, and Royal Yacht Squadron.

SONS LIVING (By 1st marriage)

WILLIAM HUMBLE DAVID JEREMY (*Viscount Ednam*) (Villa Montanet, Les Garrigues, 84220 Goult-Gordes, France), *b* 27 March 1947; *ed* Eton, and Ch Ch, Oxford: *m* 1st, 1972 (*m diss* 1976), Sarah Mary, da of Sir Alastair Francis Stuart Coats, 4th Bt; 2ndly, 1976 (*m diss* 1980), Debra Louise, da of George Robert Pinney, and has issue (by 2nd *m*):—

> DAUGHTER LIVING— (*By 2nd marriage*)— Hon Bethany Rowena, *b* 1977.

(By 2nd marriage)

Hon Leander Grenville Dudley, *b* 1971; *ed* Eton, and Univ of S California.

As I was

DAUGHTERS LIVING (By 1st marriage)

Lady Rosemary Millicent, *b* 1955: *m* 1980, Castor Cañedo, eldest son of late Castor Cañedo Pidal, and of Sra Maria del Carmen Angoso, of Madrid, and has issue living, Gabriela, *b* 1982. *Residence* – Jorge Juan 37, 28001 Madrid, Spain.

Lady Anne-Marie Ines (twin), *b* 1955: *m* 1978, Laureano Perez-Andujar Gimena, son of Don Laureano Perez de Andujar y Andujar, and of Sra Dona Caridad Gimena de Manas, of Madrid. *Residence* – Marques de Valdecilla 6, 28002 Madrid, Spain.

(By 2nd marriage)

Lady Susanna Louise, *b* 1963.

Lady Melissa Patricia Eileen, *b* 1964: *m* 1991, Dr Simon P. Puxley, and has issue living, India Ward, *b* 1991. *Residence* – The Mansard, Vention, Putsborough, nr Georgeham, N Devon EX33 1LD.

Lady Victoria Cecilia Larissa, *b* 1966.

Lady Amelia Maureen Erica, *b* 1967.

Lady (Emma Sophia) Cressida, *b* 1970: *m* 1996, Oliver N. Preston, son of Nicholas Preston, of Tetbury, Glos.

BROTHER LIVING

Hon Peter Alistair, *b* 1926; *ed* Eton, Univ of British Columbia, and Ch Ch, Oxford; Chm of Baggeridge Brick plc; 1943-45 War with Roy Canadian Air Force, and Fleet Air Arm: *m* 1st, 1956 (*m diss* 1974), Claire Leonora, da of Amyas Evelyn Giles Baring (*see* B Ashburton, colls); 2ndly, 1974, Elizabeth Rose, da of Richard Victor Charles Westmacott, of Ascona, Switzerland (*see* B St Oswald, 1966 Edn), and has issue living (by 1st *m*), Alexander Evelyn Giles (Cornwell Grove, Chipping Norton, Oxon), *b* 1961: *m* 1988, Lucy Rose, eldest da of Rupert Lycett Green (*see* Green, Bt, colls), and has issue living, Archibald Rupert William *b* 1993, Jasmine Carrie *b* 1990, — Rachel Claire, *b* 1957; actress; admitted to Australian Citizenship 1994: *m* 1983, Bryan Brown, actor, of Sydney, Australia, and has issue living, Joe *b* 19—, Rosie *b* 1985, Matilda *b* 1987, — Tracy Louise (*Marchioness of Worcester*), *b* 1958: *m* 1987, Henry John Fitzroy, Marquess of Worcester, eldest son of 11th Duke of Beaufort, — (by 2nd *m*), Jeremy Christopher, *b* 1975, — Benjamin Robin, *b* 1978. *Residences* – 7 Elm Park Lane, SW3; Cornwell Manor, Chipping Norton, Oxon. *Clubs* – White's, Pratt's, and Royal Yacht Squadron.

WIDOW LIVING OF SON OF SECOND EARL

Hon Alethea Gwendoline Alys Mary Fitzalan-Howard, da of 2nd Viscount FitzAlan of Derwent: *m* 1953, as his 2nd wife, Group Capt Hon Edward Frederick Ward, RAF, who *d* 1987. *Residence* – 21b Ave du Temple, Lausanne, Switzerland.

WIDOW LIVING OF THIRD EARL

GRACE MARIA (*Grace, Countess of Dudley*), da of Dr Michel Kolin, of St Jacob, Dubrovnik, and formerly wife of Prince Stanislas Radziwill: *m* 1961, as his 3rd wife, the 3rd Earl of Dudley, who *d* 1969.

COLLATERAL BRANCHES LIVING

Issue of late Lieut-Col Hon Roderick John Ward, 2nd son of 2nd Earl, *b* 1902, *d* 1952: *m* 1st, 1928 (*m diss* 1936), Eileen Patricia, da of Lieut-Col Marcus Michael Hartigan, CMG, DSO; 2ndly, 1940 (*m diss* 1947), Valerie Maud, who *d* 1989, da of late Robert Jeremiah Skelton, of Nairobi, Kenya Colony; 3rdly, 1947, Charlotte Anne Park, who *d* 1971, da of late Capt Charles Frederick Osborne, RD, RNR, of Broadstone, Dorset:—

(By 2nd *m*) Robert John Christopher BARWICK-WARD; *b* 1942; *ed* Millfield, and Grenoble Univ; assumed by deed poll 1952, the additional surname of Barwick: *m* 1st, 1968 (*m diss* 1974), Frances Pauline, who *d* 1975, el da of Sqdn-Ldr Mathieu Donald Einhorn, OBE, JP, RCAF, of Cragg Hill House, Killinghall, Yorks; 2ndly, 1976 (*m diss* 1985), Laura Madeleine, da of late Henry J. Sutcliffe, of Havercroft, Kearby, nr Wetherby, W Yorks, and has issue living (by 1st *m*), Annabel Jane, *b* 1970: *m* 1997, Simon D. Everett, of Northfield Cottage, Bulmer, N Yorks, yr son of Ronald H. Everett, of Restronguet Weir, Cornwall, and has issue living, Henry George Alfred *b* 1997, — (by 2nd *m*) Lucinda Marie Clare, *b* 1980. —— (By 3rd *m*) Rupert Michael, *b* 1947: *m* 1970, Frances Margaret Mary, el da of late J. C. Barry, of Adelaide House, Bruff, co Limerick, and has issue living, Eric Roderick Humble, *b* 1973.

Issue of late Rt Hon George Reginald Ward (*Viscount Ward of Witley*, PC), yst son of 2nd Earl, *b* 1907, *d* 1988; *cr* Viscount Ward of Witley 1960: *m* 1st, 1940 (*m diss* 1951), Ann Diana France Ayesha, da of late Capt Arthur Edward Capel, CBE (*see* By of Ribblesdale, 1980 Edn); 2ndly, 1962, Barbara Mary Colonsay, who *d* 1980, da of late Capt Ronald Frank Rous NcNeill, Irish Guards, and formerly wife of late Hon Michael Langhorne Astor (*see* V Astor):—

(By 1st *m*) †*Hon* Anthony Giles Humble, *b* 1943; *ed* Eton; *d* 1983. —— *Hon* Georgina Anne, *b* 1941; resumed her maiden name by deed poll 1971: *m* 1st, 1966 (*m diss* 1971), Alastair Cameron Forbes; 2ndly, 1978, Patrick Claude Henry Tritton, who *d* 1998. *Residence* – Quintana 23, Gustavo A Madero, Mexico DF ZP14.

Grandson of late Major Hon Sir John Hubert Ward, KCVO, 2nd son of 1st Earl:—
Issue of late Col Edward John Sutton Ward, LVO, MC, *b* 1909, *d* 1990: *m* 1st, 1934, Susan, who *d* 1981, eldest da of late Geoffrey Robert Josceline Corbett, DSO, of Rossferry, Enniskillen, co Fermanagh; 2ndly, 1986, Marion Elizabeth Jesse, who *d* 1997, da of late Charles M. Clover, formerly wife of Geoffrey Adams, and widow of (i) Capt Lionel Cecil (*see* M Salisbury, colls, 1963 Edn), and (ii) 4th Baron Romilly:—

(By 1st *m*) Gerald John, CBE, *b* 1938; *ed* Eton, RMA Sandhurst, and RMC Cirencester: *m* 1st, 1967 (*m diss* 1984), Rosalind Elizabeth, yr da of late Hon Richard Edward Lygon (*see* E Beauchamp, colls); 2ndly, 1984, Mrs Amanda Mildred Dinan, only da of late Sir Lacey Eric Vincent, 2nd Bt, and has issue living (by 1st *m*), Sarah Patricia, *b* 1968: *m* 1993, Adrian Richard Scrope (*see* Sykes, Bt, *cr* 1783, colls, 1990 Edn), and has issue living, Hugh Gerald Cuthbert *b* 1996, Rose Edith Lygon *b* 1994, — (Margaret) Lucy, *b* 1970: *m* 1998, Jonathan Charles Stewart Chenevix-Trench (*see* B Ashtown, colls). *Residence* – Chilton Park Farm, Hungerford, Berks.

Granddaughters of late Hon Robert Arthur Ward, OBE, 3rd son of 1st Earl:—
Issue of late Maj Julian Humble Dudley Ward, *b* 1908, *d* 1971: *m* 1st, 1946 (*m diss* 1954), Ann Elisabeth, only da of late Capt John Walter Wilson Bridges; 2ndly, 1962, Mary Rebecca Jane, da of Albert Edward Morris-Hadwell, of Kidderminster, Worcs, and Ballarat, Vic, Aust, and widow of Col Harry Latham, RHA:—

(By 1st *m*) Patricia Anne, *b* 1947. —— Georgina Mary, *b* 1950.

Granddaughter of late Capt William Humble Dudley Ward, 14th Hus, Herts Yeo Cav, only son of Hon Humble Dudley Ward, 2nd son of 10th Baron:—
Issue of late Rt Hon William Dudley Ward, *b* 1877, *d* 1946: *m* 1913 (*m diss* 1931), Winifred May (who *m* 2ndly, 1937, Wing-Com Marquis de Casa Maury (Spain), and *d* 1983), da of late Col Charles Wilfrid Birkin (*see* Birkin, Bt, 1980 Edn):—

Angela Clare Louise (*Lady Laycock*), *b* 1916; a DStJ, JP and Co Councillor for Notts: *m* 1935, Maj-Gen Sir Robert Edward Laycock, KCMG, CB, DSO, Roy Horse Guards, who *d* 1968 (E Listowel, colls), and has had issue, †Joseph William Peter, *b* 1938; *ed* Eton: *m* 1971, (Eve) Lucinda (actress as Lucy Fleming) (who *m* 2ndly, 1986, as his 2nd wife, Simon Williams, actor), yr da of late Lt-Col Peter Fleming, OBE, of Merrimoles House, Nettlebed, Oxon, by his late wife Dame Celia Johnson, DBE, actress, and was accidentally drowned 1980, leaving issue, Robert *b* 1973, Diggory *b* 1975, Flora *b* 1972, drowned with her father 1980, — Benjamin Richard (Kingwell Farmhouse, Old Hill, Wincanton, Som BA9 8BJ), *b* 1947: *m* 1971, Rose Cuninghame, and has issue, Samuel Edward *b* 1983, Bonny Mary *b* 1972, Josephine Clare *b* 1973, — Edwina Ottilie Jane (217 E 61st St, New York City, USA), *b* 1936: *m* 1st, 1955 (*m diss* 1963), Lt (Richard) Mark Walter Agnew, RN (*see* Agnew, Bt, *cr* 1895, colls); 2ndly, 1963, Sidney Davis, who *d* 1988, — Emma Rose, *b* 1943: *m* 1964, Richard Temple, of 6 Clarendon Cross, W11, el son of Sir Richard Antony Purbeck Temple, MC, 4th Bt, — Katherine Martha, *b* 1949: *m* 1969, David A Mlinaric, of 61 Glebe Place, SW3, and has issue living, Nicholas Maximilian *b* 1977, Jessica Rose *b* 1970, Frances Josepha Octavia *b* 1972: *m* 1996, Andrew M. D. Penn, 2nd son of late Michael Penn. *Residence* – La Canada Real, Soto Grande, Cadiz, Spain.

PREDECESSORS – (1) JOHN de Sutton; *d* 1359; *s* by his son (2) JOHN; *d* 1376; *s* by his son (3) JOHN; *d* 1407; *s* by his son (4) JOHN, KG; summoned to Parliament as *Baron Dudley*, or *Sutton of Dudley* 1439-87; *d* 1487; *s* by his grandson (5) EDWARD, KG, 2nd Baron; summoned to Parliaments 1492-29; *d* 1531; *s* by his son (6) JOHN, 3rd Baron; never summoned to Parliament; having suffered great pecuniary losses by the machinations of usurers he eventually lost Dudley Castle, and for many years subsisted upon the charity of friends, being styled "Lord Quondam"; *d* 1553; *s* by his son (7) EDWARD, KB, 4th Baron; summoned to Parliaments 1554-86; Queen Mary restored to him by patent Dudley Castle and other lands of great value, which had vested in the crown on the attainder of John Dudley, Duke of Northumberland; *d* 1586; *s* by his son (8) EDWARD, 5th Baron, summoned to Parliament 1593-1639; having lavished a large portion of his patrimony in profligacy, gave his grand-da and heir in marriage to Humble Ward, son of an opulent goldsmith and jeweller to Charles I; he *d* 1643, and was succeeded in the Barony by his grand-da (ante) (9) FRANCES WARD, whose husband, Humble Ward, having been knighted was in 1644 *cr Baron Ward*, of Birmingham (peerage of England); he *d* 1670; *s* by his son (10) EDWARD, 2nd Baron Ward, who also became on the death of his mother in 1697 7th Baron Dudley, and was styled Baron Dudley and Ward; *d* 1701; *s* by his grandson (11) EDWARD, 8th Baron Dudley and 3rd Baron Ward; *d* 1704; *s* by his son (12) EDWARD, 9th Baron Dudley and 4th Baron Ward; *d* unmarried 1731; *s* by his uncle (13) WILLIAM, 10th Baron Dudley and 5th Baron Ward; *d* unmarried 1740, when the Barony of Dudley passed to Ferdinando Dudley, son of his sister Frances, by her marriage with William Lea, and at his death, in 1757, that title fell into abeyance between his sisters (*see* B Dudley); *s* in Barony of Ward by his kinsman (14) JOHN, 6th Baron Ward, grandson of Hon Wiliam Ward, 2nd son of 1st Baron Ward; *cr Viscount Dudley and Ward* (peerage of Great Britain)

1763; *d* 1774; *s* by his son **(15)** JOHN, LLD, 2nd Viscount; *dsp* 1788; *s* by his half-brother **(16)** WILLIAM, 3rd Viscount; *d* 1823; *s* by his son **(17)** JOHN WILLIAM, 4th Viscount; *cr Viscount Ednam and Earl Dudley* (peerage of United Kingdom) 1827; *d* unmarried 1833, when the Viscountcies and Earldom became extinct, and the Barony of Ward passed to his kinsman **(18)** *Rev* WILLIAM HUMBLE, 10th Baron Ward; *b* 1781: *m* 1816, Amelia, da of William Gooch Pillans, of Bracondale, Norwich; *d* 1835; *s* by his son **(19)** WILLIAM, 11th Baron; *b* 1817: *m* 1st, 1851, Selina Constance, who *d* 1851, da of Hubert de Burgh, of West Drayton Manor, Middlesex; 2ndly, 1865, Georgina Elizabeth, who *d* 1929, da of Sir Thomas Moncreiffe, 7th Bt; *cr Viscount Ednam and Earl of Dudley* (peerage of United Kingdom) 1860: *d* 7 May 1885; *s* by his son **(20)** WILLIAM HUMBLE, 2nd Earl, GCB, GCMG, GCVO, PC, *b* 1867; Parliamentary Sec to Board of Trade 1895-1902; Lord-Lieut of Ireland 1902-5, and Gov-Gen of Commonwealth of Australia 1908-1911: *m* 1st, 1891, Rachel, CBE, RRC, who *d* 1920, da of late Charles Gurney; 2ndly, 1924, Gertrude, who *d* 1952, da of John Millar, widow of Lionel Monckton; *d* 1932; *s* by his el son **(21)** WILLIAM HUMBLE ERIC MC, TD, 3rd Earl, *b* 1894; PPS to Under-Sec of State for India 1922-24; High Sheriff of Worcs 1930; MP for Hornsey (*C*) 1921-24, and for Wednesbury 1931-32; *m* 1st, 1919, Lady Rosemary Millicent Sutherland-Leveson-Gower, RRC, who *d* 1930, da of 4th Duke of Sutherland; 2ndly, 1943 (*m diss* 1954), Frances Laura, who *d* 1990, da of Hon Guy Lawrence Charteris (*see* E Wemyss); 3rdly, 1961, Grace Maria, da of late Dr Michel Kolin, of Dubrovnik, and formerly wife of Prince Stanislas Radziwill; *d* 1969; *s* by his el son **(22)** WILLIAM HUMBLE DAVID, 4th Earl and present peer: also Viscount Ednam, and Baron Ward.

DUFFERIN AND AVA, MARQUESSATE OF (Hamilton-Temple-Blackwood) (Extinct 1988)

DAUGHTER LIVING OF FOURTH MARQUESS

Lady Perdita Maureen, *b* 1934; racehorse breeder. *Residence* – Cavallo Farm, Crawfordsburn Rd, Newtownards, co Down.

WIDOW LIVING OF FIFTH MARQUESS

SERENA BELINDA ROSEMARY (LINDY) (*Marchioness of Dufferin and Ava*), only da of late G/Capt (Thomas) Loel Evelyn Bulkeley Guinness, CBE, Auxiliary Air Force (Reserve) (*see* D Rutland): *m* 1964, the 5th Marquess of Dufferin and Ava, who *d* 1988, when the title became ext. *Residences* – Clandeboye, co Down; 4 Holland Villas Rd, W14.

COLLATERAL BRANCHES LIVING

Granddaughter of late Maj Price Frederick Blackwood, yst son of late Rev Hon William Stear Blackwood, 4th son of 2nd Baron Dufferin:—
Issue of late Lieut-Col Albemarle Price Blackwood, DSO (Border Regt), *b* 1881, *d* 1921: *m* 1920, Kyra, who *d* 1937, elder da of late Albert Llewelyn Hughes, and widow of Serge de Boursac:—
Kyra Henrietta, *b* 1921: late Sergeant WAAF: *m* 1st, 1945, Samuel Junior Marshall, US Army Air Force, who *d* 1948; 2ndly, 1951, Iain Gregor Finton Robertson, who *d* 1995, and has issue living (by 2nd *m*), James Paul (Druim Wood, Stratherrick Rd, Inverness IV2 4LQ), *b* 1952: *m* 1982, Judith Ellen Bull, and has issue living, Iain David *b* 1989, Kyra Frances *b* 1992, Alice Freda *b* 1997. *Residence* – Green Bank Cottage, 9 Langside, E Linton, E Lothian EH40 3AN.

Descendants of late Vice Adm Hon Sir Henry Blackwood, KCB, 7th and yst son of Baroness Dufferin and Clandeboye, who was *cr* a *Baronet* 1814:—
(See B Dufferin and Clandeboye.)

DUFFERIN AND CLANDEBOYE, BARON (Blackwood) (Baron I 1800, Bt I 1763 and UK 1814)

·PER·VIAS·RECTAS·

JOHN FRANCIS BLACKWOOD, 11th Baron, 12th Baronet of Ballyleidy and 8th Baronet of UK; *b* 18 Oct 1944; *s* his father 1991 (although his claim to the peerage has not yet been established); *ed* Barker Coll, Hornsby, and Univ of NSW (B Arch); ARAIA, architect in private practice: *m* 1971, Annette Kay, da of Harold Greenhill, artist, of Seaforth, Sydney, NSW, and has issue.

Arms – Azure a fess or in chief a crescent argent between two mullets of the second and in base a mascle of the third. Crest – On a cap of maintenance gules turned up ermine a crescent argent. Supporters – *Dexter*, a lion gules gorged with a tressure flory counterflory or; *sinister*, an heraldic tiger ermine gorged with a like tressure gules. Motto – Per Vias Rectas.
Address – PO Box 1815, Orange, NSW 2800, Australia.

SON LIVING

Hon FRANCIS SENDEN, *b* 6 Jan 1979.

DAUGHTER LIVING

Hon Freya Jodie, *b* 1975.

BROTHER LIVING

Hon Peter Maurice, *b* 1950; *ed* Knox Gram Sch, Wahroonga, and Macquarie Univ (BA); anthropologist: *m* 1979, Kay Lynette, da of William Maurice Winkle of Brisbane, Qld, and has issue living, Alexander Francis Winkle, *b* 1986, — Alice Kathleen Winkle, *b* 1982. *Residence* – 26 Jarda St, Smithfield Heights, Cairns, FNQ 4878, Australia.

SISTER LIVING

Hon Angela Margaret, *b* 1942; *ed* Sydney Univ (BSc), and Charles Sturt Univ (Dip Ed): *m* 1965, Clifton Elliott Barker, BSc, of 141 Campbell Drive, Wahroonga, NSW 2076, Australia, and has issue living, Stephen Michael, *b* 1969: *m* 1993, Sally Ann, da of Douglas Alan Farrington, and has issue living, Harry George *b* 1998, Emily Rose *b* 1996, — Zoë Frances, *b* 1971: *m* 1998, Jonathon Lloyd Caudrick, — Lucinda Alice, *b* 1975, — Karina Emily, *b* 1980.

UNCLES LIVING (*brothers of 10th Baron*)

George, OBE, DSC (c/o de La Pau 29, Andraitx, Mallorca, Spain), *b* 1920; Cdr RN; OBE (Mil) 1970: *m* 1950, Diana, da of late Lt-Col A. L. A. Flint, and has issue living, Robert George Temple, *b* 1953, — Michael Francis, *b* 1959, — Clare Mary, *b* 1956.
Henry (Babworth Gdns, 44/105A Darling Point Rd, Darling Point, NSW 2027, Australia), *b* 1922; *ed* Knox Gram Sch, Wahroonga; late Lieut RANR(S); Capt Merchant Marine: *m* 1948, Kathryn, da of D. T. Rankin, of Wyalong, NSW, and has issue living, Maurice Henry (Ebony Hall, Moreton Park Rd, Douglas Park, NSW, Australia), *b* 1954; *ed* Sydney C of E Gram Sch, NSW Univ, and Sydney Tech Coll (Assoc Dip Metallurgy); Co Dir: *m* 1982, Anne Edith, da of M. H. L. Macarthur, of Katoomba, NSW, and has issue living, James Maurice Henry *b* 1988, Jennifer Anne Halley *b* 1986.

AUNT LIVING (*sister of 10th Baron*)

Mary, *b* 1917: *m* 1st, 1940, John Frankcomb, who was *ka* as P/O RAAF 1942; 2ndly, 1945, Edward Lister Ifould, DSO, DFC and Bar, who *d* 1981, of 317 Peninsula Gdns, Bayview, NSW, Australia, and has issue living (by 1st *m*), Dorothy Pamela, *b* 1942, — (by 2nd *m*) William Edward, *b* 1947; *ed* Sydney C of E Gram Sch, — Marian, *b* 1946, — Frances Gay Lister, *b* 1953.

WIDOW LIVING OF SIXTH BARONET

LILIAN MARGARET (*Lilian, Lady Blackwood*), da of late Fulton J. MacGougan, of Vancouver: *m* 1921, Sir Francis Elliot Temple Blackwood, 6th Bt, who *d* 1979.

COLLATERAL BRANCH LIVING

Issue of late Neville Foster Blackwood, 4th son of 4th baronet, *b* 1884, *d* 1964: *m* 1919, Kathleen Nelly, who *d* 1959, da of late Henry Sidney Mosenthal:—
Robin Henry (5 Gurney Close, Caversham, Reading, Berks), *b* 1926.

PREDECESSORS – (1) ROBERT BLACKWOOD, el son of late John Blackwood, of Ballyleidy, co Down: *m* 1st, 1721, Joyce, da of late Joseph Leeson; 2ndly, 1729, Grace, who *d* 1788, da of Isaac Macartney, *cr* a *Baronet* 1763; *d* 1774; *s* by his son (2) *Sir* JOHN, 2nd Bt; MP in five Parliaments 1761-90; *d* 1799; in 1800 his widow DORCAS was *cr Baroness Dufferin and Clandeboye* (peerage of Ireland); she *d* 1808; *s* by her son (3) JAMES, 2nd Baron, who had in 1799 *s* his father as 3rd Bt; MP for Killyleagh in three Parliaments and a Representative Peer, *dsp* 1836; *s* by his brother (4) HANS, 3rd Baron; *d* 1839; *s* by his son (5) PRICE, 4th Baron; *b* 1794; Capt RN; *m* 1825, Helen Selina, da of late Thomas Sheridan; *d* 1841; *s* by his son (6) FREDERICK TEMPLE, KP, GCB, GCMG, GCIE, PC, DCL, LLD, FRS, 5th Baron, *b* 1826; a Lord-in-Waiting to HM Queen Victoria 1848-52, and 1854-8, Under-Sec for India 1864-6, and for War 1866, Chancellor of Duchy of Lancaster and Paymaster-Gen 1868-72, Gov-Gen and Com-in-Ch of Canada 1872-8 Ambassador Extraor and Min Plen at St Petersburg 1879-81, and at Constantinople 1881-4 Viceroy of India 1884-8, Ambassador Extraor and Plen at Rome 1888-91, and Ambassador at Paris 1891-6; assumed by Roy licenses 1862 the additional surname of Hamilton and 1872 that of Temple; *cr Baron Clandeboye* 1850, and *Viscount Clandeboye* and *Earl of Dufferin* (peerage of UK) 1871, and *Earl of Ava* and *Marquess of Dufferin and Ava*, of co Down and of Burmah (peerage of UK) 1888; *m* 1862, Dame Hariot Georgina, VA, CI, DBE, who *d* 1936, el da of late Archibald Rowan Hamilton, of Killyleagh Castle, co Down; *d* 1902; *s* by his son (7) TERENCE TEMPLE, 2nd Marquess; *b* 1866; a Clerk in Foreign Office 1906-18: *m* 1893, Florence (Flora), who *d* 1925, da of John H. Davis, of 24 Washington Sq, New York; *d* 1918; *s* by his brother (8) FREDERICK TEMPLE, DSO, PC, 3rd Marquess, *b* 1875; S Africa 1900 (wounded, despatches twice. Queen's medal with nine clasps DSO), European War 1914-17 as Staff-Capt Household Cav and with a Guards Div (twice wounded, 1914-15 star, two medals); Mil Sec to Gov-Gen of Commonwealth of Australia 1914, Speaker of Senate of N Ireland June 1921 and 1925-30, and Vice-Adm of Province of Ulster 1923-30: *m* 1908, Brenda, who *d* 1946, only da of late Robert Woodhouse, formerly of Orford House, Ugley, Bishop's Stortford; *d* 1930; *s* by his son (9) BASIL SHERIDAN, 4th Marquess, *b* 1909; Capt Roy Horse Guards; a Lord-in-Waiting to HM 1936-7, the Under-Sec of State for Colonies 1937-40: *m* 1930, Maureen Constance, da of Hon Arthur Ernest Guinness; *ka* in Burma 1945; *s* by his son (10) SHERIDAN FREDERICK TERENCE, 5th Marquess, *b* 1938; Trustee of Nat Gallery (London) and the Wallace Collection: *m* 1964, Serena Belinda Rosemary (Lindy), only da of late G/Capt (Thomas) Loel Evelyn Bulkeley Guinness, CBE, Auxiliary Air Force (Reserve) (*see* D Rutland); *d* 1988, when the Marquessate of Dufferin and Ava, the Earldoms of Dufferin and Ava and the Viscountcy and Barony of Clandeboye became extinct; he was *s* in the Barony of Dufferin and Clandeboye and the Baronetcy of Blackwood of Ballyleidy by his kinsman (11) FRANCIS GEORGE (infra), 10th Baron Dufferin and Clandeboye, *b* 1916; FIEAust, ARACI, Chemical and Consulting Engr: *m* 1941, Margaret, who *d* 1999, da of Hector Kirkpatrick, of Lindfield, NSW; *d* 1991; *s* by his elder son (12) JOHN FRANCIS, 11th Baron and present peer.

*The 1st baronet Hon Sir Henry Blackwood, KCB, 7th and yst son of Sir John Blackwood, 2nd Bt (ante), was a Vice Adm of the Blue, and the bearer of despatches announcing the victory of Trafalger; *cr* a baronet 1814. The 4th baronet, Sir Francis, was Capt RN, and served in the Crimea. His grandson was Sir Francis George, 7th Bt (ante), son of Capt Maurice Baldwin Raymond Blackwood, DSO, RN, who *d* on active service 1941.

Dugdale, family name of Baron Crathorne.

Duke, family name of Baron Merrivale.

DULVERTON, BARON (Wills) (Baron UK 1929, Bt UK 1897)

Wherever the light leads

(GILBERT) MICHAEL HAMILTON WILLS, 3rd Baron, and 4th Baronet; *b* 2 May 1944; *s* 1992; *ed* Gordonstoun: *m* 1980, Rosalind Johnny Maria, only da of J. van der Velde, of Rozenburg, Holland, and of Mrs R. D. Oliver, of Lochside, Kelso, Roxburgh, and has issue.

Arms – Gules, three estoiles flammant fessewise between two griffins passant wings expanded and inverted all or. Crest – Issuant from an annulet or, a demi-griffin gules, charged with an estoile as in the arms, and holding in the dexter claw a battle-axe also or. Supporters – *Dexter*, a trumpeter of the Royal North Devon Yeomanry; *sinister*, a huntsman of the Dulverton hunt; both proper.
Seat – Batsford Park, Moreton-in-Marsh, Gloucestershire.

SON LIVING

Hon ROBERT ANTHONY HAMILTON, *b* 20 Oct 1983.

DAUGHTER LIVING

Hon Charlotte Alexandra Hamilton, *b* 1981.

BROTHER LIVING

Hon (Robert) Ian Hamilton, *b* 1948; *ed* Harrow, and Warwick Univ (BA): *m* 1979, Elizabeth Jane, eldest da of Michael Taylor Downes, of The Old Parsonage, Lower Slaughter, Glos, and has issue living, James Douglas Hamilton, *b* 1984, — Emma Elizabeth Hamilton, *b* 1982. *Residence* – Soundborough Farm, Andoversford, Cheltenham, Glos.

SISTER LIVING

Hon Sarah May Hamilton, *b* 1942. *Residence* – 8 Montrose Court, Prince's Gate, SW7.

UNCLES LIVING (*sons of 1st Baron*)

Hon (Edward) Robert Hamilton, *b* 1918; *ed* Eton; Maj late Gren Gds, European War 1935-45 (wounded); Chm The Farmington Trust. *Residence* – Farmington Lodge, Northleach, Glos.

Hon (Victor) Patrick Hamilton, *b* 1926; *ed* Eton, and Coll of Estate Management; Lieut Gren Gds and Parachute Regt (ret); FLAS 1957; DL Hants 1975, Co Councillor 1965-73; Chm Hants Playing Fields Assocn 1969-79, Trustee Dulverton Trust 1949-81, Gov Internat Students' Trust 1965 (Vice-Pres 1979, Chm 1984), Vice-Chm Trident Trust 1972 (Chm 1978-80), Chm Atlantic Salmon Conservation Trust (Scotland) 1985-91: *m* 1st, 1948 (*m diss* 1962), Felicity Betty, da of late Maj Aubrey Thomas Jonsson, Royal Irish Rifles; 2ndly, 1963, Mrs Jean Felicity Strutt, who *d* 1984, yr da of late Hon Francis Walter Erskine (E Mar and Kellie); 3rdly, 1988 (*m diss* 1993), Mrs Elizabeth Gilmor Shaw, and has issue living (by 1st *m*), Christopher Aubrey Hamilton (Litchfield Down, Whitchurch, Hants), *b* 1953; *ed* Eton; Lieut Gren Gds (ret); a Trustee Dulverton Trust 1979: *m* 1987, Lady Katharine Anne Meade, 5th da of 6th Earl of Clanwilliam, and has issue living, Thomas Robert Hamilton *b* 1991, George Edmund Hamilton *b* 1993, a da *b* 1996, — Jeremy Robert Hamilton (Bevis Farm, Charlbury, Oxon), *b* 1955; *ed* Eton; Capt Gren Gds (despatches 1984): *m* 1982, Alison Mary, da of David Malkin, of Winnington Grange, Market Drayton, Shropshire, and has issue living, Nicholas Patrick Hamilton *b* 1986, Benjamin James Hamilton *b* 1988, — Penelope Margaret Hamilton, *b* 1950: *m* 1976 (*m diss* 1986), David J. Enthoven, and has issue living, James John *b* 1980, Belinda Margaret *b* 1977. *Residence* – Litchfield Manor, Whitchurch, Hants.

WIDOW LIVING OF SECOND BARON

RUTH VIOLET MARY (*Ruth, Baroness Dulverton*), only da of Sir Walter Randolph Fitzroy Farquhar, 5th Bt, and formerly wife of late Maj Richard Gennys Fanshawe, 16th/5th Lancers: *m* 1962, as his 2nd wife, the 2nd Baron Dulverton, CBE, TD, who *d* 1992. *Residence* – Barnbrook Cottage, Milton Lilbourne, Pewsey, Wilts SN9 5LQ.

COLLATERAL BRANCHES LIVING (*In remainder to the Baronetcy only*)

Grandsons of late Frederick Noel Hamilton Wills (infra):—
Issue of late Capt Michael Desmond Hamilton Wills, MC, Coldstream Guards; *b* 1915, *ka* in Middle East 1943: *m* 1939, Mary Margaret (*Lady Gibbs*) (who *m* 2ndly, 1947, Col Sir Martin St John Valentine Gibbs, KCVO, CB, DSO, who *d* 1992, of The Manor House, Ewen, Cirencester, Glos), da of Lt-Col Philip Mitford (*see* Fowler, Bt, ext, 1966 Edn):—
(Michael) Thomas Noel Hamilton (Miserden Park, Miserden, Stroud, Glos), *b* 1940; *ed* Eton; Maj late Coldm Gds (ret); High Sheriff Glos 1985, DL Glos 1991; Exon HM Body Guard of Yeomen of the Guard 1993: *m* 1982, Penelope A., el da of Ben Howard-Baker, of Glascoed Hall, Llansilin, Shropshire, and has issue living, Nicholas James Noel Hamilton, *b* 1983, — Camilla Jane Hamilton, *b* 1985. ——— Frederick Hugh Philip Hamilton (Anton's Hill, Coldstream, Berwicks TD12 4JD), *b* (twin) 1940; *ed* Eton; Capt 11th Hussars (ret); High Sheriff Glos 1995: *m* 1969, Priscilla Annabelle, da of late Capt Alec Francis, of The Grange, Malmesbury (*see* L Kinloss, colls), and has issue living, Michael James Hamilton, *b* 1972; *ed* Milton Abbey: *m* 1999, Juliet A., eldest da of Andrew Dixon, of Wolverton Farm, Basingstoke, Hants, — Edward Hamilton, *b* 1974, — Clare Alexandra, *b* (twin) 1974. ——— (Peter) John Hamilton, *b* 1941; *ed* Eton, and Magdalen Coll,

Oxford: *m* 1970, Elizabeth Jean, da of Maj J. J. Mann, of Oxleaze Farm, Filkins, Lechlade, Glos, and has issue living, Richard Henry, *b* 1974, — Grania Sarah, *b* 1972, — Emily Jane, *b* 1975.

        Issue of late Frederick Noel Hamilton Wills, 3rd son of 1st baronet, *b* 1887, *d* 1927: *m* 1912, Margery Hamilton (who *m* 2ndly, 1942, Wing-Com Huntly Macdonald Sinclair, RCAF, of Miserden Park, Stroud), el da of late Hon Sir Hugh Fraser, JP, a Judge of High Court of Justice, of Stromeferry House, Ross-shire:—

Sir (Hugh) David Alastair Hamilton, CBE, TD, *b* 1917; late Maj Queen's Own Cameron Highlanders; a DL of Oxford (High Sheriff 1961); 1939-45 War, MBE (Mil) 1946, CBE (Civil) 1971; *cr* Knt 1979: *m* 1949, Eva Helen McMorrough, da of late Maj Arthur Thomas McMorrough Kavanagh, MC (Buxton, Bt, colls), and has had issue, †Martin David Hamilton *b* 1952; *d* 1992, — Catherine Mary Hamilton, *b* 1950. *Residence* – Sandford Park, Sandford St Martin, Oxon. *Club* – Boodle's. —— Margery Angela Hamilton, *b* 1922: *m* 1st, 1948 (*m diss* 1971), Anthony Andrew Francis Tabor, late Capt Herts Yeo; 2ndly, 1972, Thomas Anthony Stainton, who *d* 1988; 3rdly, 1994, as his 2nd wife, Col Rodney Francis Maurice Windsor, CBE, DL, and has issue living (by 1st *m*), (Adrian Andrew) Hamish *b* 1960: *m* 1986, Carolina Giovanna, da of Conte Massimiliano Magnaghi, of Le Martinet, Lausanne, Switzerland, and of Mme Philippe Saint-Armand, of Auxerre, France, and has issue living, Francesca Giovana Angela *b* 1989, Julia Aloisa Allegra *b* 1992, — Marilyn Margery Hamilton, *b* 1949: *m* 1972, Anthony German-Ribon, of 57 Napier Av, SW6 3PS, and has issue living, Philip Anthony *b* 1973, Catriona Hamilton *b* 1976, — Nicola Mary Hamilton, *b* 1952: *m* 1974, Hugh Sherbrooke (*see* Bs Herries, colls). *Residence* – Mains of Warthill, Meikle Wartle, Aberdeenshire AB51 5AJ. —— Audrey Mackenzie Hamilton, *b* 1925: *m* 1946, Capt Peter Houldsworth Gibbs, Scots Gds, and has issue living, (Peter) Noel (Houldsworth) (Combend Manor, Elkstone, Cheltenham, Glos), *b* 1948; *ed* Eton, and Magdalen Coll, Oxford: *m* 1st, 1976 (*m diss* 1989), Clare, da of Nigel Viney; 2ndly, 1991, Katharine Constance, yst da of late Col Richard Lumley Hurst (*see* E Crawford), and widow of Donald M. Corbett, and has issue living (by 1st *m*), Hugo Houldsworth *b* 1984, Chlöe Lucy *b* 1982, Amelia Emma (twin) *b* 1982, — Linda Hamilton, *b* 1951: *m* 1st, 1973, Robert Bruce John Dunipace; 2ndly, 1991, Lt-Col Anthony Singer, KRH, and has issue living (by 1st *m*), Aulden Malcolm Bruce *b* 1975, Fergus Roland Fraser *b* 1981, Imogen Larissa *b* 1976, Flavia Iona Churchill *b* 1983. *Residence* – Hall's Grove, Elkstone, Glos.

PREDECESSORS – (1) FREDERICK Wills, son of late Henry Overton Wills, JP, of Bristol, and brother of Sir Edward Payson Wills, KCB, 1st Bt (*cr* 1904), *b* 1838; a Director of Imperial Tobacco Co (Limited); sat as MP for Bristol, N Div (LU) 1900-1906; *cr* a *Baronet* 1897: *m* 1867, Annie, who *d* 1910, el da of the Rev James Hamilton, DD, of Longridge, Stonehouse; *d* 1909; *s* by his son (2) GILBERT ALAN HAMILTON, OBE, 2nd Bt; *b* 1880; Pres of Imperial Tobacco Co (Limited), Parliamentary Private Sec to Postmaster-Gen 1921, High Sheriff of Gloucestershire 1928, MP for Taunton (*C*) 1912-18, and for Weston-super-Mare Div of Somerset 1918-22; *cr Baron Dulverton*, of Batsford (peerage of United Kingdom), 1929: *m* 1914, Victoria May, OBE, who *d* 1968, da of Rear-Adm Sir Edward Chichester, CB, CMG, 9th Bt; *d* 1956; *s* by his el son (3) (FREDERICK) ANTHONY HAMILTON, 2nd Baron, CBE, TD, *b* 1915; Maj Lovat Scouts; Pres Timber Growers' Assocn, and British Deer Soc; Chm Dulverton Trust, and Forestry Cttee of GB, Member Red Deer Commn, and Scottish Advisory Cttee Nature Conservancy; Waynflete Fell Magdalen Coll, Oxford; DL Glos: *m* 1st, 1939 (*m diss* 1960), Judith Betty, who *d* 1983, da of late Lt-Col Hon Ian Leslie Melville, TD (*see* E Leven and Melville); 2ndly, 1962, Mrs Ruth Violet Fanshawe, only da of Sir Walter Randolph Fitzroy Farquhar, 5th Bt; *d* 1992; *s* by his elder son (4) GILBERT MICHAEL HAMILTON, 3rd Baron and present peer.

Dumfries, Earldom of; see Marquess of Bute.

DUNALLEY, BARON (Prittie) (Baron I 1800)

IN·OMNIA·PARATUS·

Prepared for all things

(HENRY) FRANCIS CORNELIUS PRITTIE, 7th Baron; *b* 30 May 1948; *s* 1992; *ed* Gordonstoun, and Trin Coll, Dublin (BA): *m* 1978, Sally Louise, el da of late Ronald Vere, of Heaton Chapel, Cheshire, and has issue.

Arms – Per pale argent and gules three wolves' heads erased or. Crest – A wolf's head erased or. Supporters – *Dexter*, a man in armour proper, holding a tilting spear in the right hand; *sinister*, a stag proper, attired, unguled, ducally collared and chained, or.
Residence – 15 Barton Lane, Oxford OX3 9JR.

SON LIVING

Hon JOEL HENRY, *b* 29 April 1981.

DAUGHTERS LIVING

Hon Rebecca Louise, *b* 1979.
Hon Hannah Beatrice, *b* 1983.
Hon Rachel Sarah, *b* 1987.

BROTHER LIVING

Hon Michael Philip St John, *b* 1961; *ed* Stowe. *Address* – PO Box 95871, Seattle, Washington, USA.

SISTER LIVING

Hon Mary Rose Madeline, *b* 1953; has issue living, Flora Tamsine JOYCE, *b* 1981, — Pollyanna Felicity Rose JOYCE, *b* 1990, — Lily Philippa JOYCE, *b* 1992. *Residence* – Athry, Recess, co Galway.

WIDOW OF SIXTH BARON

(MARY) PHILIPPA (*Dowager Baroness Dunalley*), only child of late Hon Philip Plantagenet Cary (*see* V Falkland, colls): *m* 1947, Lt-Col the 6th Baron Dunalley, who *d* 1992. *Residence* – The Bridge Barn, Bampton, Oxon OX18 2HA.

COLLATERAL BRANCH LIVING

Issue of late Hon Terence Cornelius Farmer Prittie, MBE, yr son of 5th Baron, *b* 1913, *d* 1985: *m* 1946, Laura, who *d* 1988, only child of late G. Dreyfus Dundas, of Columbia:—
Oliver Alan Graham (9 Blithfield St, W8), *b* 1948; *ed* Eton: *m* 1st, 1973 (*m diss* 1983), Alison Victoria, da of Arnold Bertram Kingsley Tillie, of Harley Gdns, SW10; 2ndly, 1986, Krystyna Emilia, da of Michael Wasiukiewicz, of 18 Shelley Rd, Stratford-upon-Avon, Warwicks, and has issue living (by 1st *m*), Jemma Victoria, *b* 1975, — Kinvara Louise, *b* 1978, — (by 2nd *m*) Dominic Terence, *b* 1987, — Laura Zoe, *b* 1989. —— (James) Hugo Cameron (Le Breuilh, St-Meard-de-Dronne, 24600 Riberac, France), *b* 1950; *ed* Eton: *m* 1983, Mrs Helga Isolda Lachnitt, eldest da of late Robert Werthenbach, of Siegen, W Germany.

PREDECESSORS – (1) HENRY PRITTIE, *b* 1743; MP for Banagher 1767-8, for Gowran 1769-76, and for co Tipperary 1776-90; *cr Baron Dunalley*, of Kilboy, co Tipperary (peerage of Ireland) 1800; *d* 1801; *s* by his el son (2) HENRY SADLEIR, FSA, 2nd Baron, *b* 1775; MP for Carlow 1798-1801, and for Okehampton 1819-24; a Representative Peer; *d* 1854; *s* by his nephew (3) HENRY, 3rd Baron, *b* 1807: *m* 1841, Hon Anne Maria Louisa O'Callaghan, who *d* 1867, da of 1st Viscount Lismore; *d* 10 Sept, 1885; *s* by his son (4) HENRY O'CALLAGHAN, 4th Baron; *b* 1851; a Representative Peer for Ireland, and Lieut and Custos Rotulorum of co Tipperary: *m* 1876, Mary Frances, MBE, who *d* 1929, da of late Maj-Gen Reginald Onslow Farmer, RA, of Grove House, Aspley Guise; *d* 1927; *s* by his son (5) HENRY CORNELIUS O'CALLAGHAN, DSO, 5th Baron; *b* 1877; Major late Rifle Brigade; S African War; 1914-18 War (DSO): *m* 1911, Beatrix Evelyn, who *d* 1967, da of late James Noble Graham, JP DL, of Carfin, and Stonebyres, Lanarkshire; *d* 1948; *s* by his son (6) HENRY DESMOND GRAHAM, 6th Baron; *b* 1912; Lt-Col Rifle Bde, served with King's African Rifles 1937-40, 1939-45 War in E Africa, Middle East, Italy and Far East: *m* 1947, Mary Philippa, only child of late Maj Hon Philip Plantagenet Cary (*see* V Falkland colls); *d* 1992; *s* by his elder son (7) HENRY FRANCIS CORNELIUS, 7th Baron and present peer.

DUNBOYNE, BARON (Butler) (Baron I 1324 and 1541)

TIMOR·DOMINI·FONS·VITÆ

The fear of the Lord is the fountain of life

PATRICK THEOBALD TOWER BUTLER, 28th Baron (18th by patent); (*His Honour The Lord Dunboyne, VRD*); *b* 27 Jan 1917; *s* 1945; *ed* Winchester, and Trin Coll, Camb (Pres of Union; MA); Bar Middle Temple (Harmsworth Scholar) 1949, of Inner Temple 1962, and King's Inns, Dublin 1966, a JP; Foreign Office 1945-46; Dep Chm Middlesex Sessions 1963-65; Commissary Gen of Canterbury Diocese 1959-71; Recorder of Hastings 1961-71; Dep Chm Kent Sessions 1963-71, and Inner London Sessions 1971; a Circuit Judge 1972-86; Pres Wireless Telegraphy Appeal Tribunal for England and Wales 1967-70; Home Sec's Commr for ward-boundaries 1960-70; Fellow Irish Genealogical Research Soc (Pres 1971-91); founder-Sec Bar Lawn Tennis Soc 1950-62 (Vice-Pres since 1963), and of Irish Peers Assocn 1963-71 (Pres 1988-91); Lt late Irish Guards (SR); served European War 1939-44 (prisoner, repatriated); Lieut RNVR 1951-58, RNR 1958-60, VRD 1987: *m* 1950, Anne Marie, da of Sir Victor Alexander Louis Mallet, GCMG, CVO, and has issue.

Arms – Or, a chief indented azure, and three escallops in bend counterchanged. **Crest** – Out of a ducal coronet or, a plume of five ostrich feathers, and issuant therefrom a demi-falcon rising argent. **Supporters** – *Dexter*, a lion guardant argent; *sinister*, a horse sable, mane, tail and hoofs or. *Residences* – 36 Ormonde Gate SW3 4HA; The Flat, West Ilkerton Farm, Lynton, Devon EX35 6QA. *Clubs* – Irish, Pitt (Cambridge), Union (Cambridge), All England Lawn Tennis and Croquet (Wimbledon), International Lawn Tennis of Great Britain (Dep-Pres 1970-73, Pres 1973-83), and 45 Club (Pres 1974-91).

SON LIVING

Hon JOHN FITZWALTER (Argos Hill House, Rotherfield, E Sussex TN6 3QG), *b* 31 July, 1951; *ed* Winchester, and Trin Coll, Camb (MA); Sloan Fellow of London Business Sch: *m* 1975, (Diana) Caroline, da of late Sir Michael Sanigear Williams, KCMG, and has issue living, Richard Pierce Theobald, *b* 5 July 1983, — Genevieve Synolda, *b* 1977, — Imogen Katharine, *b* 1979, — Cleone Isolde, *b* 1986.

DAUGHTERS LIVING

Hon Mary Synolda, *b* 1954; *ed* Benenden, and Girton Coll, Camb (BA 1975, MA 1980); Solicitor 1980: *m* 1984, Alastair Henry Walton, only son of late Sir Raymond Henry Walton, and has issue living, Alexandra Mary, *b* 1985, — Christina Frances, *b* 1986, — Stephanie Katharine, *b* 1988, — Florence Lucy, *b* 1992. *Residence* – 26 Paradise Walk, SW3 4JL.

Hon Betty Quenelda, *b* 1956; *ed* Benenden, and Girton Coll, Camb (BA 1978, MA 1983); PGCE Cantab: *m* 1985, Edward Roland Haslewood Perks, yr son of His Honour Clifford Perks, MC, TD, FSA, and has issue living, Lawrence Patrick Haslewood, *b* 1989, — Candida Anne Quenelda, *b* 1986, — Sophie Maria Katharine, *b* 1994. *Residence* – 4 Broomwood Rd, SW11 6HT.

Hon Victoria Morina, *b* 1959; *ed* Benenden, St Andrew's Univ (BSc 1982), and Wye Agric Coll, Univ of London (MSc 1983): *m* 1986, Christopher J. P. Eveleigh, eldest son of John Eveleigh, of Croyde, N Devon, and has issue living, George Jethro, *b* 1987, — Sarah Victoria, *b* 1990. *Residence* – West Ilkerton Farm, Lynton, Devon EX35 6QA.

SISTERS LIVING

Hon (Doreen) Synolda Tower, *b* 1918: *m* 1945, Major Atholl Duncan, MC, RA, who *d* 1983, and has issue living, (Walter) Alastair, *b* 1947, — Patrick Atholl, MBE, *b* 1957; Lt-Col RHA: *m* 1987, Margrit Victoria, da of Franz Frefel, of Frampton, Dorchester, Dorset, and has issue living, Christopher Patrick *b* 1991, Alexander Edward *b* 1993, Charlotte Isabel *b* 1989, — Zara Synolda, *b* 1950: *m* 1979, David Firmin, FRIBA, of 38 Wandsworth Common Northside, SW18 2SL, son of E. H. Firmin, of Aldwick Bay Estate, Bognor Regis, W Sussex, and has issue living, Philip Duncan *b* 1981, Robert Charles *b* 1985, Zoe Charlotte *b* 1980. — Lorna Romayne, *b* 1956: *m* 1987, Lt-Col Bryan M. Elliott, MBE, LI, of 22 Pennard Rd, W12 8D5, son of late Cdr Charles Elliott, RN. *Residence* – 9 Marland House, 28 Sloane Street, SW1X 9NE.

Hon Maureen Maude Tower, *b* 1919: *m* 1946, Lieut-Col Robert Caradoc Rose Price, DSO, OBE, late Welsh Guards, who *d* 1988, and has issue (*see* Price, Bt, *cr* 1815, colls). *Residence* – 98 Old Church Street, SW3 6EP.

Hon (Isolde) Sheila Tower, *b* 1925: *m* 1949, Com Penryn Victor Monck, RNVR (E Peel), who *d* 1987, and has issue living, Rory Penryn, *b* 1951, — Tasha Penryn, *b* 1950: *m* 1st, 1976, Martin P. A. Travers: 2ndly, 1984, Rev William Donald, of 82 Forest View Rd, Tuffley, Gloucester GL4 0BY, and has issue living (by 1st *m*), Isabel Eileen *b* 1977, (by 2nd *m*) Jesse Michael Penryn *b* 1985, — Fiona Penryn, *b* 1957: *m* 1981, Andrew Pettinger, 2nd son of Eric J. C. Pettinger, of Watsons, Belsford, Harberton, Totnes, Devon TQ9 7SP.

COLLATERAL BRANCHES LIVING

Grandsons of late Brig-Gen Hon Lesley James Probyn Butler, CMG, DSO, 2nd son of 26th Baron:—
Issue of late Lt-Col James Dighton Butler, *b* 1911, *d* 1987: *m* 1943, Pamela, who *d* 1987, da of late William Alfred Pickwoad, OBE, and widow of Lt-Col A. J. F. Sugden, RA:—
(Michael) James (Morgans Bradley, Templeton, Tiverton, Devon EX16 8BJ), *b* 1944; *ed* Eastbourne Coll, RMA Sandhurst, and RAC Cirencester (Dip Rural Estate Mgmnt); FRICS; Fellow Western Counties Assocn of Agric Valuers; late 15th/19th King's Royal Hus: *m* 1981, Jennifer, da of late Percy Williams, of Dundee, and has issue living, Elizabeth Mary, *b* 1985. —— Robert Patrick, *b* 1947; *ed* Milton Abbey; late Queen's Royal Irish Hus: *m* 1972, Nicola Jane, da of P. W. R. Pope, of W Stafford, Dorchester, Dorset, and has issue living, Alexander Philip Dighton, *b* 1975, — Edward Patrick, *b* 1978.

Grandchildren of late St John Henry ARCEDECKNE-BUTLER, grandson of late Hon St John Butler, 6th (but 2nd surviving) son of 23rd Baron:—
Issue of late Maj-Gen St John Desmond Arcedeckne-Butler, CBE, *b* 1896, *d* 1959: *m* 1929, Ethel Helen Nesbitt, who *d* 1953, da of late Col Reginald Selby Walker, DSO, RE:—
St John Patrick (Parker's Pound, Walton Lane, Old Bosham, W Sussex, PO18 8QB), *b* 1930; Maj (ret), R Signals: *m* 1st, 1956, Jane (Frances Elizabeth Mary), who *d* 1983, da of late Lt-Col F. E. Massie, MC, of W Ayton, Scarborough; 2ndly, 1991, (Jacqueline) Jean, da of late H. C. Morris, of Dorchester, Dorset, and has issue living (by 1st *m*), St John Terence, *b* 1956, — Christopher Michael, *b* 1959, — John Patrick, *b* 1969, — Mark Piers, *b* 1972. —— †Michael Francis Peel, RN, *b* 1933; Lt-Cdr (ret): *m* 1961, Jacqueline (Cutlers, Wickham, Hants PO17 5AN), da of late Col George Leonard Carpenter-Garnier, OBE, of Wickham, Hants, and *d* 1993, leaving issue, Timothy Garnier, *b* 1962: *m* 1995, Nathalie Catherine, yr da of M. M. Rawoo, of London, and has issue living, James Michael *b* 1998, Emily Julia Garnier *b* 1996, — Nicola Catherine, *b* 1964; Master of Wine 1996: *m* 1996, J. James Longden, of The Old Stables, Northington Down, Alresford, Hants SO24 9TZ, son of late Capt John Longden. —— Christal Synolda, *b* 1938: *m* 1961, Geoffrey William Medcalf, of Malt Square House, 15 High St, S Witham, Grantham, Lincs, and has issue living, Richard William Desmond (2 Templars Way, S Witham, Grantham, Lincs), *b* 1966: *m* 1994, Nicola Jayne Watkins, and has issue living, William Richard Moses *b* 1993, Emily Ann Christal *b* 1989, — David Geoffrey (27 Moor Lane, S Witham, Grantham, Lincs), *b* 1969; has issue living, Cassandra Susan *b* 1996, — Sallie Jane, *b* 1962: *m* 1988, William Edmund Green, of 25 Kemp Close, Warwick, and has issue living, Jamie Daniel *b* 1990, Hannah Louise *b* 1993, — Helen Sheevaum Cristal, *b* 1963: *m* 1983, Russell John Trimble, of 65 Grantham Rd, Sleaford, Lincs, and has issue living, Martin Russell *b* 1983, Thomas Joseph *b* 1999, — Patricia Ann, *b* 1964: *m* 1987, Alan John Burton, of 13 Moor Lane, S Witham, Grantham, Lincs, and has issue living, Richard Alan John *b* 1991, Amy Jane *b* 1988, — Rosemary Janet Slaney, *b* 1970: *m* 1993, Colin John Baxter, of 3 Sproxton Rd, Buckminster, Grantham, Lincs, and has issue living, Yasmine Lucy *b* 1993.

Grandchildren of late Edward Arthur Butler, 3rd son of Hon Charles Lennox Butler, 7th son of 23rd Baron:—
Issue of late Charles Edward Butler, *b* 1874, *d* 1960: *m* 1919, Alice Elizabeth, who *d* 1984, da of late T. J. Worship, of North Walsham:—
Clarence Francis (West Winds, Baldhoon Rd, Laxey, IoM IM4 7QH), *b* 1920; 1939-45 War as Flight-Lieut RAF (despatches): *m* 1st, 1944, Pamela Constance, who *d* 1991, da of late F. J. Drakard, of Ingham House, Martlesham, Suffolk; 2ndly, 1996, Annette Dolors (Dawn), yr da of late Percy H. Froud, of Maidstone, Kent, and has issue living (by 1st *m*), Julia Rosemary, *b* 1945: *m* 1967, Dennis Curran, of Bishop's Stortford, Herts, — Denise Angela *b* 1947: *m* 1988, Christopher Bannister Simpson, of Baldhoon, Laxey, I of Man. —— †Brian Charles *b* 1924: *m* 1952, Joyce Caroline (Little Leigh, Holcombe, Dawlish, Devon), da of G. Hitchcock, of Kenton, Devon, and *d* 1992, leaving issue, Rosena Marie, *b* 1959. —— Rosalinda Maria, *b* 1921: *m* 1946, Douglas Kyrle Redgrave, who *d* 1992, of Pantiles, Woodland Av, Teignmouth, Devon TQ14 8UU, and has issue living, Michael Kyrle, *b* 1950, — Diana Lynne, *b* 1952.

Issue of late Henry Francis Butler, *b* 1877, *d* 1969: *m* 1908, Ethel Isabel Marion, da of late Allix Edward Pardoe, of Dawlish, Devon:—
Sheila Francis, *b* 1914: *m* 1940, Andrew McKenzie Stevens, of Sandspit Rd, RD 2, Warkworth, Auckland, NZ, and has issue living, Mary Louise (26 Whareora Rd, Whangarei, NZ), *b* 1945: *m* 1966 (*m diss* 1979), Johnny Bindner, of Copenhagen, and has an adopted son, Daniel *b* 1975.

Grandchildren of late Lieut-Col Charles James BUTLER-KEARNEY, DL, JP, son of William Butler, greatgrandson of Theobald Butler, el son of Richard Butler (*b* 1701), grandson of James Butler, el son of Hon Theobald Butler, 8th son of 12th Baron:—
Issue of late Theobald William Butler-Kearney, *b* 1876, *d* 1936: *m* 1914, Hester Louise, who *d* 1972, da of late Carew Davies Gilbert:—
James Davies Theobald (48 Ashdell Rd, Alton, Hants GU34 2TA), *b* 1916: *m* 1951 (*m diss* 1954), Gillian Mary Soltau, el da of late Maj W. H. Anketell; 2ndly, 1970, Juliet Mary, da of late Rev Andrew Hunt. —— Catherine Mary, *b* 1918. *Residence* – Flat 46, Mary Rose Mews, Adams Way, Alton, Hants GU34 2UU.

Issue of late Capt Trench Frank Butler-Kearney, *b* 1877, *d* 1954: *m* 1920, Shirley, who *d* 1971, da of late John Bailey Sequeira:—
Jean, *b* 1920. —— Norma, *b* 1924. *Residence* – 15 The Green, Burgh Heath, Surrey KT20 5NP.

Grandchildren of late Charles Herbert Jackson Butler (*b* 1870), 6th son of William Butler (*b* 1814), son of James Butler (*b* 1785), grandson of James Butler, of Park, co Tipperary, 3rd son of Richard Butler (*b* 1701) (ante):—
Issue of late George Herbert Butler, *b* 1901, *d* 1955: *m* 1929, Irene Rose, who *d* 1994, da of late Edward Sparnon:—
June Rose Margaret (637a Corinne St, Garsfontein, Pretoria, S Africa), *b* 1930: *m* 1961, Philip Clement Brown, who *d* 1984, and has issue living, Timothy Philip, *b* 1964; *ed* Natal Univ: *m* 1993, Paula Claire, da of John Raftesath, of Natal, — Rosalind June, *b* 1962: *m* 1984, Dr Bruce Gummow, and has issue living, Ian Andrew *b* 1994. —— (Patricia) Colleen (1103 Kensington, 311 North Ridge Rd, Durban 4001, S Africa), *b* 1938.

Issue of late Frederick William Webb Butler, *b* 1903, *d* 1946: *m* 1934, Nancy Anne O'Mahony:—
Patrick Barry Webb, *b* 1941. —— Michael Terence Webb, *b* 1943.

Grandchildren (by 1st *m*) of late Henry John Butler-Lloyd (*b* 1874) (infra):—
Issue of late William Francis Butler-Lloyd, *b* 1899, *d* 1956: *m* 1930, Mary Margaret, da of Thomas FitzGerald:—
Thomas Henry John Butler-Lloyd (Richmond, Templemore, co Tipperary), *b* 1932: *m* 1966, Veronica, da of Patrick
Harney, of Manna, Templemore, co Tipperary, and has issue living, William Francis, *b* 1969, — Audrey Veronica, *b* 1972.

Issue of late Henry John Butler-Lloyd, *b* 1910, *b* 19—: *m* 1947, Kathleen (Castleleiny Cottage, Templemore, co
Tipperary), da of — Leacky, of —:—
Henry John Butler-Lloyd (57 Maundeby Walk, NW10 2TG), *b* 1948: *m* 19—, Florence, da of Douglas Henry Lewis, of
Burnt Oak, Edgeware, Middx, and has issue living, Jason James, *b* 1977, — Katherine Geraldine, *b* 1973, — Jacqueline
Caroline *b* 1975. —— Mary, *b* 19—. —— Maggie-Jo, *b* 19—. —— Caroline, *b* 19—. ——Carmel, *b* 19—.
—— Geraldine, *b* 19—.

Grandson of late William Butler (*b* 1814) (ante):—
Issue of late Henry John Butler-Lloyd, *b* 1874, *d* 1946; assumed the additional surname of Lloyd 1896: *m* 1st,
1897, Catherine, who *d* 1907, da of late James Davoran; 2ndly, 1908, Jane, who *d* 1956, da of late Capt W. Head-
ech, 20th Regt:—
(By 2nd *m*) Charles Butler-Lloyd, *b* 1913.

Granddaughters of late Richard John Butler, 2nd son of Whitwell Butler (*b* 1798), 4th son of Rev
Richard Butler, DD (infra):—
Issue of late George Whitwell Butler, *b* 1888, *d* 1960: *m* 1918, Ada Isabel Dering, who *d* 1961, da of Arthur
Lucius Cary, of Swords, co Dublin:—
Mary Isabel, *b* 1919: *m* 1943, Carass Frederick Bladon Topham, of 25 Selwyn Cres, Radley, Abingdon, Oxon OX14 3AL,
and has issue living, Ronald Bladon, *b* 1945, — John Carass (114 Mid St, S Nutfield, Surrey), *b* 1951: *m* 1981, Christine
Allen, and has issue living, Laurence James Carass *b* 1982, Ralph Lewis Bladon *b* 1984, Phillip George Graham *b* 1987,
— Pamela Mary (twin), *b* 1951. —— Eileen Synolda, *b* 1926. *Residence* – 7 Fordhook Av, Ealing Common, W5 3LS.

Granddaughter of late George Butler (1859-1941) (infra):—
Issue of late Hubert Marshal Butler, *b* 1900, *d* 1991: *m* 1930, Susan Margaret (Maiden Hall, Bennettsbridge, co
Kilkenny), da of late Dr Thomas Clement Guthrie, of Annaghmakerrig, co Monaghan (and sister of late Sir
Tyrone Guthrie):—
Julia Mary Synolda, *b* 1935: *m* 1959, Dr Richard Savington Crampton, of 1106 Rugby Rd, Charlottesville, Va 22903, USA,
and has issue living, Thomas William Butler, *b* 1967, — Anne Cordelia, *b* 1960: *m* 1988, James Vaughan Gelly, of 41
Village Drive, Convent Station, NJ 07960, USA, and has issue living, Piers George Crampton *b* 1991, Bennett Butler
Vaughan *b* 1993, — Suzanna Louise, *b* 1963, — Katherine Synolda, *b* 1966.

Grandson of late John Butler, 6th son of late Rev Richard Butler, DD, el son of James Butler, of Pries-
town, co Meath, el son of Capt Theobald Butler, 2nd son of Pierce Butler, 2nd son of Hon Theobald
Butler (ante):—
Issue of late George Butler, *b* 1859, *d* 1941: *m* 1898, Harriet Neville, who *d* 1939, da of Marshal Neville Clarke,
of Graiguenoe Park, co Tipperary:—
(George) Gilbert, *b* 1910: *m* 1940, Norah Helen Pomeroy, who *d* 1997, da of late George Pomeroy Arthur Colley, of
Corkagh House, Clondalkin co Dublin (*see* V Harberton, colls), and has issue living, James George, *b* 1942: *m* 1972,
Diana Gillian, da of late John Hedges Becher, of Bagenalstown House, co Carlow, and has issue living, Thomas George
b 1973, John James *b* 1974, — Jessica Harriet (*Baroness Rathdonnell*), *b* 1940: *m* 1965, 5th Baron Rathdonnell. *Residence*
– Scatorish, Bennettsbridge, co Kilkenny.

Grandchildren of late James Edward Butler, son of late James Butler (*b* 1820), grandson of Whitwell
Butler (*b* 1736), 2nd son of Capt Theobald Butler (ante):—
Issue of late Maj James Whitwell Butler, *b* 1897, *d* 1971: *m* 1927, Hilda Winifred, who *d* 1978, da of Charles
Nason Haines:—
James Charles, MC (Belgrove, Cobh, co Cork), *b* 1928; late Lt King's R Irish Hussars; Korea 1951 (MC): *m* 1959,
Margaret Perry, da of Harold Perry Goodbody, of The Glen, Cobh, co Cork, and has issue living, James Perry George, *b*
1960, — Corinna Margaret, *b* 1962. —— †Edward Theobald *b* 1929: *m* 1952, Judith (Tullow, Fethard, co Tipperary), da
of Edward Webb, of Borris-in-Ossory, co Leix, and *d* 1992, leaving issue, Jennifer Mary, *b* 1954, — Diana Elizabeth, *b*
1956: *m* 1975, John Aloysius Taylor, of Boyertown, Pennsylvania, USA, and has issue living, Kerry Ann *b* 1978, — Caroline Eve, *b* 1960: *m* 1984, Hugh Christopher Stanhope Morshead, elder son of Christopher William Trelawny Morshead,
MC, TD, of Bellewstown House, co Meath, and has issue living, Christopher Edward *b* 1986, James Stanhope *b* 1989.
—— Hilda Elizabeth, *b* 1932: *m* 1956, Julius Pridden Jameson, of Shell Cove House, Teignmouth Rd, Dawlish, Devon,
and has issue living, Robert Julius Whitwell, *b* 1957: *m* 1997, Philomena Murphy, — James Leander, *b* 1964, — Linda
Rose, 1959: *m* 1991, Steven Osborne, and has issue living, Thomas Stanley Jameson *b* 19—.

Descendants of late Hon Peter (or Pierce) Butler, 2nd son of 10th Baron:—

Issue of late Theobald Blake Butler, el son of Theobald Fitzwalter Butler, JP, DL (infra), *b* 1888, *d*
1965: *m* 1st, 1921 (*m diss* 1930), Mary Gammell Stewart, da of William Smytton Davidson; 2ndly, 1933
(*m diss* 1942), Catherine Dorothy, da of Arthur Ashworth; 3rdly, 1962, Elsie, who *d* 1970, da of late
Albert Edward Keen:—
(By 1st *m*) James Roland Blake Fox-Andrews, QC (20 Cheyne Gdns, SW3), *b* 1922; *ed* Stowe, and Camb Univ (BA); Bar
Gray's Inn 1949, QC 1968, an ad eundem Member of Middle Temple 1972, and Bencher, Gray's Inn 1974; Recorder of
Winchester 1971, since when Hon Recorder; Dep Chm of Devon Quarter Sessions 1970-71; a Recorder of Crown Court
1972-85; Leader of Western Circuit 1982-84, Circuit Judge assigned to Official Referee business 1985-94; assumed the

surname of Fox-Andrews in lieu of his patronymic 1939: *m* 1950, Angela Bridget, who *d* 1991, da of Brig Charles Copley Swift, OBE, MC, and has issue living, (Jonathan) Mark (Piers), *b* 1952; *ed* Eton, and Trin Hall, Camb (BA): *m* 1984, Rosemary, da of Dennis Jenks, and has issue living, Maximillian George *b* 1987, Alfred James *b* 1993, Florence Ruth *b* 1989, Constance Augusta *b* 1992, — Piers Norman James, *b* 1954; *ed* Eton, and Bristol Univ: *m* 1985, Elizabeth Keith, da of Terence Allan, and has issue living, Charles Adam *b* 1986, Guy James *b* 1992, Emma Mary *b* 1988.

Grandson of late Theobald Blake Butler (ante):—
Issue of late John Stuart Blake Butler, *b* 1923, *d* 1957: *m* 1947, Stephanie Elizabeth (who *d* 1970, having *m* 2ndly, 1963, Guy Green), da of Thomas Swann, of The Old Vicarage, Thriplow, Cambs:—
Samuel Thomas Blake, *b* 1949.

Issue of late Fitzwalter Butler, *b* 1889, *d* 1979, 2nd son of Theobald Fitzwalter Butler, JP, DL, 6th and yst son of James Blake Butler, JP, great-grandson of James Butler (*d* 1746), el son of James Butler, of Doone, co Clare, great-great-grandson of late James Butler, el son of Hon Peter (or Pierce) Butler (ante):—
Theobald Fitzwalter (Little Croft, 7 Spooner Vale, Windermere, Cumbria LA23 1AU), *b* 1921: *m* 1951, Patricia Penelope, da of Richard Lowe, of Donaghadee, co Down, and has issue living, Simon Blake Fitzwalter, *b* 1958; *ed* Univ of Wales, Lampeter (BA) and Sheffield Univ (MA 1985, PhD 1992), — Judith Margaret, *b* 1953; *ed* Univ Coll, Cardiff (LLB), and Wolverhampton TTC (Cert Ed): *m* 1977, Paul Llewelyn Evans, BSc, of 20 Histons Dr, Codsall, Wolverhampton WV8 2ET, and has issue living, Ian Llewelyn *b* 1981, Richard Theobald *b* 1984, Edward Pierce *b* 1988.

Grandchildren of late Lieut-Col Walter Blake BUTLER-CREAGH (infra):—
Issue of late Richard BUTLER-CREAGH, *b* 1890, *d* 1955: *m* 1919, Ada Murray, who *d* 1949:—
Richard (PO Box 8951, Nairobi, Kenya), *b* 1922: *m* 1957, Therèse Agnes Spoorenberg, and has issue living, Michelle Edith, *b* 1957, — Simone Antoinette, *b* 1960. —— Vincent, *b* 19—. —— Walter, *b* 19—. —— Mary, *b* 19—: *m* 19—, William Witham. —— Sheila, *b* 19—: *m* 19—, Michael Baines, solicitor, and has issue living. —— Maureen, *b* 19—: *m* 19—, — Whittingham. —— Clara, *b* 1929: *m* 1953, William Craig, and has issue living, Albert, *b* 1954, — William Richard, *b* 1956, — Robert, *b* 1958. —— Ethanna, *b* 19—: *m* 1957, William Henry Harris. —— Joan, *b* 19—: *m* 19—, — Finn and has issue living, Anthony Richard, *b* 19—, — David *b* 1956, — Linda, *b* 19—, — Bernadette Marie, *b* 1952.

Granddaughter of late Nicholas Butler, son of late Walter Butler, el son of late William Butler, of Bunnahow, co Clare (*b* 1759), son of late Peter Butler, younger son of late James Butler, of Doon, co Clare (ante):—
Issue of late Lieut-Col Walter Blake BUTLER-CREAGH, King's Own Yorkshire LI, *b* 1859, *d* 1943 (having assumed 1889 by R Licence the additional surname and arms of Creagh after his patronymic): *m* 1888, Clara, who *d* 1928, da and co-heir of Cornelius Creagh, of Dangan, co Clare:—
Mary Gertrude, *b* 1892. *Residence* – 2 Waterloo Rd, Dublin.

PREDECESSORS – (1) *Sir* Thomas Butler, 3rd son of Theobald Butler or Botiller, 4th hereditary Chief Butler of Ireland (whose 2nd son Edmund was father of 1st Earl of Ormonde) (*see* Ormonde, M), was summoned as *Baron of Dunboyne* to Parliament of Ireland 1324: *m* 1320, Synolda, Lady of Dunboyne, da and heiress of William le Petit, 6th Baron of Dunboyne (by tenure), who was summoned to parliament as *Baron of Dunboyne* 1274; *d* 1329; *s* by his son (2) PETER, 2nd Baron: *m* before 1353, Katherine, da and heiress of John de Bermingham, Lord of Kiltenian; *d* 1370; *s* by his son (3) WILLIAM, 3rd Baron: *m* Elizabeth, da of Nicholas le Poer, of Kilmeaden, co Waterford; *d* 1405; *s* by his son (4) PETER, 4th Baron, *b* before 1398; *d* unm 1415; *s* by his brother (5) EDMUND, 5th Baron; *d* unm 1419; *s* by his brother (6) JAMES (3rd son of 3rd Baron) 6th Baron: *m* Morina Brien, of Thomond, who *d* 1476; *d* 1445; *s* by his son (7) WILLIAM, 7th Baron; attainted 1455; *d* circa 1459; *s* by his brother (8) EDMOND FITZ-JAMES, 8th Baron; his dignity and estates were restored by Act of Parliament 1471/2, and he received large grants from the Crown for his great services in the Irish Wars: *m* before 1468/9, Catherine, da of Richard Butler MacRichard, of Buolick, co Tipperary; *d* 1498/9; *s* by his son (9) JAMES, 9th Baron: *m* 1st, Elinor, da of Sir Laurence Taafe; 2ndly, Catherine, da of Fineen McCarthy Reagh, Chief of Carberry; *d* 1508; *s* by his son (10) JAMES, 10th Baron: *m* Lady Joan Butler, da of 1st Earl of Ossory and 8th Earl of Ormonde; *d* 1533; *s* by his son (11) EDMUND, KB, 11th Baron, *b* 1517; *cr* by patent *Baron Dunboyne*, of co Meath (peerage of Ireland) 1541: *m* before 1551, Cecilia (who *m* 2ndly, 1568, as his 3rd wife, Richard Bourke, 2nd Earl of Clanricarde), da of Cormac Oge Macarty, of Muskerry; *d* 1566; *s* by his son (12) JAMES, 12th Baron; summoned to Parliament 1569-71 and 1614: *m* 1st, about 1580, Margaret FitzPatrick, da and heiress of 2nd Baron of Upper Ossory; 2ndly, about 1591, Lady Margaret O'Brien, da of 3rd Earl of Thomond; *d* 1624; *s* by his grandson (13) EDMOND (son of late John Butler, son of 9th Baron), 13th Baron: *m* 1st 1625, Margaret Butler, who *d* 1632, da and heiress of 2nd Baron Caher; 2ndly, about 1637, Lady Ellen FitzGerald, who *d* 1660, da of 15th Earl of Desmond, and widow of (1) Sir Donough O'Connor, and (2) Sir Robert Cressy; *d* 1640; *s* by his son (14) JAMES, 14th Baron; twice outlawed in 1642 for his share in the Irish Rebellion 1641 (but the Solicitor-Gen reported in 1827 that as there were serious errors in the drawing up of writs of outlawry, he considered them invalid): *m* Ellen Butler, da of 1st Viscount Ikerrin; *d* 1662; *s* by his cousin (15) PIERCE (only son of late Edmund Butler, el son of late Piers Butler, 2nd son of 11th Baron), 15th Baron; ostensibly outlawed posthumously 1691 for rebelling against William and Mary's government (which the Lord Chancellor stated in 1859 was illegal, as such an outlawry could only have been made by the Lord Ch Justice acting as Coroner, and in this instance the outlawry was in the wrong Christian name, and Pierce, Baron Dunboyne, was not involved in this rebellion): *m* Catherine, da of Sir Thomas Hurley, 1st Bt; *d* 1690; *s* by his son (16) JAMES, *de jure* 16th Baron: *m* 1686, Elizabeth, da of Sir Redmond Everard, Bt; *d* 1701; *s* by his el son (17) PIERCE, *de jure* 17th Baron: *m* Anna, da and heir of Robert Cadell, of Dublin; *d* 1718; *s* by his brother (18) EDMOND, *de jure* 18th Baron: *m* Anne, da of Oliver Grace, of Shanganagh, co Tipperary, Ch Remembrancer of the Exchequer, Ireland, and widow of Richard Nagle; *d* 1732; *s* by his el son (19) JAMES; *de jure* 19th Baron; *dsp* 1768; *s* by his brother (20) PIERCE, *de jure* 20th Baron, *m* 1773, Maria (who *m* 2ndly, 1775, David Walsh), da of George Macnamara, of Cong, co Mayo; *d* 1773; *s* by his son (21) PIERCE EDMOND CREAGH, *de jure* 21st Baron; *d* umn 1785; *s* by his uncle (22) *Right Rev* JOHN, DD (3rd son of 8th Baron), *de jure* 22nd Baron, Roman Catholic Bishop of Cork 1763-86; he resigned his See after succession to the title and requested from the Pope a dispensation to marry, this being refused, he became a Protestant: *m* 1787, Maria (who *m* 2ndly, 1801, John Hubert Moore, of Shannon Grove, King's Co, Bar-at-law, and *d* 1860), da of Theobald Butler, of Wilford, co Tipperary; *dsp* 1800; *s* by his kinsman (23) JAMES (son of late James Butler, grandson of late Edward Butler, grandson of late Hon Edward Butler, 6th son of 11th Baron), *de jure* 23rd Baron; the outlawries of James, 14th Baron and Pierce, 15th Baron, were reversed by Royal Warrant, on the grounds of "the errors therein" 1827, and he was confirmed in the peerage: *m* 1st, 1799, Eleanor, who *d* 1817, da of David O'Connell, of Cork, 2ndly, 1843, Mary Anne Vincent Vaughan, who *d* 1847; *d* 1850; *s* by his son (24) THEOBALD FITZ-WALTER, 24th Baron; *b* 1806; his right to Barony of Dunboyne was confirmed by Committee for Privileges of House of Lords 1860; a Representative Peer: *m* 1832, Julia Celestina Maria, da of late William Brander, of Morden Hall, Surrey; *d* 1881; *s* by his son (25) JAMES FITZ-WALTER CLIFFORD, 25th Baron, *b*

1839: *m* 1860, Marion, who *d* 1919, da of Col Henry Morgan Clifford, of Llantilio Crossenny, Monmouthshire, whose surname he assumed in addition to that of Butler; *d* 1899; *s* by his brother **(26)** ROBERT ST JOHN FITZ-WALTER, 26th Baron, *b* 1844; a Representative Peer; sometime Senior Master of Supreme Court, and King's Remembrancer: *m* 1869, Caroline Maude Blanche, who *d* 1927, da of late Capt George Probyn (and sister of Gen Rt Hon Sir Dighton Probyn, VC, GCB, GCSI, GCVO, ISO); *d* 1913; *s* by his el son **(27)** FITZ-WALTER GEORGE PROBYN, 27th Baron, *b* 1874; Capt (ret) RN: *m* 1915, Dora Isolde Butler, who *d* 1977, da of late Cmdr Francis Fitzpatrick Tower, OBE, late RNVR; *d* 1945; *s* by his son **(28)** PATRICK THEOBALD TOWER, 28th Baron (and 18th by patent) and present peer.

DUNCAN-SANDYS, BARONY OF (Duncan-Sandys) (Extinct 1987)

SON DECEASED OF LIFE BARON (*By 1st marriage*)

(*Hon*) Julian George Winston SANDYS, QC (did not use courtesy title) (Charnwood, Shackleford, Godalming, Surrey) *b* 1936; Bar Inner Temple 1959 and Grays Inn 1970; QC (1983): *m* 1970, Elisabeth Jane, only da of John Besley Martin, CBE, of Kenton, and *d* 1997, leaving Duncan John Winston, *b* 1973, — Jonathan Martin Edwin, *b* 1975, — Roderick Julian Frederick, *b* 1977, — Lucy Diana, *b* 1971.

DAUGHTERS LIVING OF LIFE BARON (*By 1st marriage*)

Hon Edwina, MBE (131 E 66th St, New York, NY 10021, USA) *b* 1938; sculptress: *m* 1st, 1960 (*m diss* 1973), Piers (Pierson John Shirley) Dixon, MP, son of late Sir Pierson John Dixon, GCMG, CB; 2ndly, 1985, Richard D. Kaplan, and has issue living (by 1st *m*), Mark Pierson, *b* 1962; photographer, and co dir, — Hugo Duncan, *b* 1963; journalist.

Hon Celia Mary SANDYS (4 Bedwyn Common, Marlborough, Wilts SN8 3HZ), *b* 1943; has resumed her maiden name: *m* 1st, 1965 (*m diss* 1970), Michael Kennedy, who *d* 1990; 2ndly, 1970 (*m diss* 1979), Dennis Walters, MBE, MP (later Sir Dennis Walters); 3rdly, 1985, Maj-Gen Kenneth Perkins, CB, MBE, DFC, and has issue living (by 1st *m*), Justin, *b* 1967, — (by 2nd *m*) Dominic, *b* 1971, — (by 3rd *m*), Alexander Winston Duncan, *b* 1986, — Sophie Rachel, *b* 1988.

(*By 2nd marriage*)

Hon Laura Jane, *b* 1964. *Residence* – 30 Hesper Mews, SW5 0HH.

WIDOW LIVING OF LIFE BARON

MARIE-CLAIRE (*Baroness Duncan-Sandys*), da of Adrien Schmitt, of Paris, and formerly wife of 2nd Viscount Hudson: *m* 1962, as his 2nd wife, Baron Duncan-Sandys, CH, PC (Life Baron), who *d* 1987. *Residence* – Flat T, 12 Warwick Sq, SW1V 2AA.

Duncannon, Viscount; son of Earl of Bessborough.

Duncombe, family name of Baron Feversham.

Dundas, family name of Viscount Melville.

Dundas, family name of Marquess of Zetland.

DUNDEE, EARL OF (Scrymgeour) (Earl S 1660)

ALEXANDER HENRY SCRYMGEOUR OF DUNDEE, 12th Earl; *b* 5 June 1949; *s* 1983; *ed* Eton, and St Andrew's Univ; Hereditary Standard Bearer for Scotland; contested Hamilton by-election 1978 (*C*); a Lord in Waiting to HM 1986-89: *m* 1979, Siobhan Mary, da of David Llewellyn, and has issue.

Arms – Gules, a lion rampant or armed and langued azure holding in his dexter forepaw a crooked sword or scimitar argent and behind the shield in saltire two representations of the Royal Banner of Scotland viz a lion rampant gules armed and langued azure within a double tressure flory counter flory gules, ropes and tassels of the last (*as Bearer for the Sovereign of the Royal Banner of Scotland*). **Crest** – a lion's paw erased in bend or holding a crooked sword or scimitar argent. **Supporters** – two greyhounds argent collared gules.
Seat – Birkhill, Cupar, Fife. *Clubs* – White's, New (Edinburgh).

SON LIVING

HENRY DAVID (*Lord Scrymgeour*), *b* 20 June 1982.

DAUGHTERS LIVING

Lady Marina Patricia, *b* 1980.
Lady Flora Hermione Vera, *b* 1985.
Lady Lavinia Rebecca Elizabeth, *b* 1986.

Disperse

WIDOW LIVING OF ELEVENTH EARL

PATRICIA KATHARINE (*Patricia, Countess of Dundee*), da of late Lt-Col Herbert Andrew Montagu Douglas Scott, CMG, DSO (*see* D Buccleuch, colls), and widow of (i) Lt-Col Walter Douglas Faulkner, MC, Irish Guards, and (ii) Lt-Col (Hon) David Scrymgeour-Wedderburn, DSO, Scots Guards (see colls infra): *m* 1946, the 11th Earl of Dundee, who *d* 1983. *Residence* – Coultra Farm House, Newport-on-Tay, Fife.

COLLATERAL BRANCHES LIVING

Issue of late Lieut-Col (Hon) David Scrymgeour-Wedderburn, DSO, Scots Guards, younger son of the *de jure* 10th Earl, *b* 1912, *d* of wounds received in action 1944: *m* 1940, Patricia Katharine (*Patricia, Countess of Dundee*) (ante) (who *m* 3rdly, 1946, 11th Earl of Dundee (infra), who *d* 1983), da of late Lieut-Col Lord Herbert Andrew Montagu Douglas Scott, CMG, DSO (*see* D Buccleuch, colls), and widow of Lieut-Col Walter Douglas Faulkner, MC, Irish Guards:—
Janet Mary, *b* 1941: *m* 1962, Capt (Edward Arthur) Mervyn Fox-Pitt, Welsh Guards, of Grange Scrymgeour, Cupar, Fife, and has issue living, David William, *b* 1964, — Leonie Patricia, *b* 1962: *m* 1982, Aidan Joseph Merry Gibbs (*see* E Erne, colls), — Miranda Mary (*Hon Mrs Peregrine Moncreiffe of Moncreiffe*), *b* 1968: *m* 1988, Hon Peregrine David Euan Malcolm Moncreiffe of Moncreiffe (*see* E Erroll). —— Elizabeth (*Baroness Teynham*) *b* 1943: *m* 1964, 20th Baron Teynham, of Pylewell Park, Lymington, Hants, and The Walton Canonry, Cathedral Close, Salisbury, Wilts.

Grandchildren of late (Hon) Frederick Lewis Scrymgeour-Wedderburn, 2nd son of *de jure* 9th Earl:—
Issue of late William Alexander Scrymgeour-Wedderburn, DFC, *b* 1919, *d* 1995: *m* 1st, 1940, Mabel Kathleen, da of F. W. Rowe, of Torquay; 2ndly, 1951, Margaret Emily, who *d* 1988, da of William Henry Innes, of Largo, Fife:—
(By 2nd *m*) John Frederick (The West Lodge, Craigtoun, St Andrews, Fife) *b* 1955; PhD: *m* 1984, Sabine, BSc, yr da of Hubert Schauten, of Essen, Germany, and has issue living, Lewis Alexander, *b* 1994, — Georgina Emily, *b* 1997. —— Caroline Sarah, *b* 1954: *m* 1986, John Quentin Conway Ashton, of The Old Schoolhouse, Rathven, by Buckie, Morayshire AB56 4DD, and has issue living, Chloe Jane, *b* 1986. —— Grace Marion, *b* 1959; MA: *m* 1980, Jonathan W. Humphrey, of Myrtle Cottage, Orton, by Fochabers, Moray IV32 7QB, elder son of late D. W. Humphrey, of Cross Farm, Styal, Cheshire.

Issue of late (Hon) Charles Kenneth Scrymgeour-Wedderburn, 3rd son of *de jure* 9th Earl, *b* 1887, *d* 1963: *m* 1915, Gertrude Louisa Marie, who *d* 1957, only da of late James Carnegie Wemyss, younger, of Wemyss Hall:—
Rosemary (Strowan, by Crieff, Perthshire), *b* 1916: *m* 1st, 1937 (*m diss* 1947), Lt-Col Christian Landale Melville, DSO, who *d* 1984; 2ndly, 1949, Brig William Noel Roper-Caldbeck, DSO, who *d* 1965, and has issue living, (by 1st *m*), Robin Kenneth Christian, WS (Woodborough Manor, nr Pewsey, Wilts), *b* 1938: *m* 1st, 1961 (*m diss* 1984), Elizabeth Mary Melville, da of late Capt Melville Stewart Jameson; 2ndly, 1985, Loraine Sylvia Alice, widow of Benjamin Mark Weston Wells, and has issue living (by 1st *m*), James Landale *b* 1963; Capt Royal Scots Dragoon Gds: *m* 1991, Sophie E., yr da of Brig Peter Marsh, of Camberley, Surrey (and has issue living, Mary (Molly) Elizabeth *b* 1997), Christian Kenneth Bowring *b* 1965; Capt Royal Scots Dragoon Gds, — Edward Charles, WS (Holydean, Melrose, Roxburghshire), *b* 1940: *m* 1966, Alison Sinclair, da of Thomas Sinclair Fraser, and has issue living, Peter Charles Fraser *b* 1970, Rachel Anne Rosemary *b* 1972, — Anthony (7 Hagbourne Close, Woodcote, S Oxon RG8 0RZ), *b* 1942: *m* 1981, — Michael Landale (Strowan, Crieff, Perthshire), *b* 1943; Maj The Black Watch: *m* 1971, Susan Louise Margaret, da of Maj Edmund Robert Cox, TD, JP, and has issue living, Neil Edmund Landale *b* 1976, Alastair Michael Landale *b* 1987, Sarah Anne Louise *b*

1974, Julia Rosemary Susan *b* 1983, Nicola Jane *b* (twin) 1987. —— Lorna Mabel, *b* 1918: *m* 1966, Ian Miskelly, DSC, JP, who *d* 1993, of Glenara, Methven, Perthshire. —— Aimée Elspeth, *b* 1920: *m* 1945, James Ferrier Macfarlane, who *d* 1986, of Apt 507, 3495, Mountain St, Montreal, Quebec, Canada H3G 2A5, and has issue living, Charles Ferrier, *b* 1946: *m* 1970, Kathryn Anne Oppé, and has issue living, James Andrew *b* 1973, — Ian Fraser Oppé *b* 1975, — Jennifer Elspeth, *b* 1948: *m* 1975, William Lorne Lindsay, and has issue living, Christopher Lorne Ferrier *b* 1977, Gillian Aimée *b* 1980.

Issue of late Capt (Hon) William Ogilvy Scrymgeour-Wedderburn, DSC, RN, yst son of *de jure* 9th Earl, *b* 1894, *d* 1958: *m* 1921, Joyce, who *d* 1990, only da of late Col Robert Henry Jennings, CSI, RE:—
Ian Alexander, *b* 1923; Cdr RN (ret); FRIN: *m* 1947, Desirée, da of late Col Richard White, of Church Farm House, Smarden, Kent, and has issue living, James Ian (87 Howards Lane, SW15 6NZ), *b* 1951; *ed* Sherborne, and Hertford Coll, Oxford (MA): *m* 1981, Sarah M. A., da of late Col Michael Seys-Phillips, of The Malt House, Mereworth, Kent, and has issue living, Charles Richard *b* 1986, Alexander James *b* 1988, Catherine Juliet *b* 1984. *Residence* – Dunlichity Lodge, Farr, Inverness IV2 6AN. *Club* – Army and Navy. —— Fiona Marigold Joyce, *b* 1925: *m* 1951, Rev James Ainsworth Yates, and has issue living, Katherine Fiona, *b* 1958, — Veronica Margaret (twin), *b* 1958, — and an adopted da, Susannah Elizabeth, *b* 1956. *Residence* – 97 Grove Rd, Hitchin, Herts SG5 1SQ.

PREDECESSORS – (1) JOHN Scrymgeour, Hereditary Standard Bearer of Scotland and Constable of Dundee: *cr Viscount Dudhope* and *Lord Scrymgeour* (peerage of Scotland) 1641, with remainder to his heirs male whatsoever: *m* 1596, Margaret, da of George Seton, of Parbroath; *d* 1643; *s* by his el son (2) JAMES, 2nd Viscount, *b* 1597; commanded a Regt of Scottish Inf under the Earl of Leven: *m* 1618, Lady Isobel Kerr, 3rd da of 3rd Earl of Roxburghe; *d* (from wounds received at Battle of Marston Moor) 1644; *s* by his el son (3) *Rt Hon* JOHN, 3rd Viscount, *b* 1622; Col of Horse under Duke of Hamilton 1468 in attempt to rescue Charles I; accompanied Charles II at Battle of Worcester 1650, and was taken prisoner by the English; fought in Middleton's Campaign of 1654; *cr Earl of Dundee,* and *Lord Inverkeithing* (peerage of Scotland) 1660, with remainder to heirs male whatsoever: *m* 1644, Lady Anne Ramsay, da of 1st Earl of Dalhousie; *d* 1668, whereupon all the honours became dormant; *s* (as Viscount Dudhope according to the decision of the Committee for Privileges of House of Lords 1952, and as Earl of Dundee according to the decision of the Committee for Privileges of House of Lords 1953) by his kinsman and heir male, and of line (4) JOHN (son of John Scrymgeour of Kirkton, grandson of John Scrymgeour of Kirkton) (*d* 1629), great-grandson of James Scrymgeour of Kirkton (*d* 1513), grandson of David Scrymgeour, younger son of Sir James Scrymgeour of Dudhope, and brother of Sir John Scrymgeour of Dudhope, and a brother of Sir John Scrymgeour of Dudhope, great-grandfather of John Scrymgeour (*d* 1562), great-grandfather of 1st Viscount Dudhope, *de jure* 2nd Earl; *b* 1628; deprived of the Scrymgeour family estates by the influence of the Duke of Lauderdale with Charles II: *m* 1659, Magdalene, da of Alexander Wedderburn of Kingennie; *d* 1698; *s* by his son (5) JAMES, *de jure* 3rd Earl, *b* 1664; *d* 1699; *s* by his brother (6) ALEXANDER, *de jure* 4th Earl, *b* 1669, Lay Professor of Humanity, Philosophy and Theology, St Andrews Univ: *m* 1697, Janet, only da of David Falconer, Professor of Divinity, St Andrews Univ; 1739; *s* by his son (7) DAVID, *de jure* 5th Earl, *b* 1702; Advocate and Sheriff Depute of Inverness: *m* 1739, Katherine, da of Sir Alexander Wedderburn, 4th Bt of Blackness; *d* 1772; *s* by his son (8) ALEXANDER Scrymgeour-Wedderburn, *de jure* 6th Earl, *b* 1742; *s* to estates, name and arms of Wedderburn of Wedderburn 1778: *m* 1771, Elizabeth Ferguson, da of Lord Pitfour; *d* 1811; *s* by his brother (9) HENRY Scrymgeour-Wedderburn, *de jure* 7th Earl, *b* 1755, attended King George IV, as Hereditary Standard Bearer of Scotland at Holyrood 1822: *m* 1793, Mary Turner, el da of Capt Hon Frederick Lewis Maitland RN, 6th son of Earl of Lauderdale; *d* 1841; *s* by his only son (10) FREDERICK LEWIS, *de jure* 8th Earl, *b* 1808; a JP and DL for Fifeshire: *m* 1st, 1839, Hon Helen Arbuthnott, who *d* 1840, 5th da of 8th Viscount Arbuthnott; 2ndly, 1852, Selina Mary, who *d* 1902; da of Capt Thomas Garth, RN, of Haines Hill, Berks; *d* 1874; *s* by his el son (11) HENRY SCRYMGEOUR, *de jure* 9th Earl; *b* 1840; a JP and DL for Fifeshire and Capt 17th Regt, his right to the hereditary office of Roy Standard Bearer for Scotland was admitted by the Court of Claims at Coronation of Edward VII, when he bore the Standard of Scotland, and confirmed by the House of Lords 1910: *m* 1869, Juliana, who *d* 1921, yst da of Thomas Braddell, of Coolmelagh, co Wexford; *d* 1914; *s* by his son (12) HENRY, *de jure* 10th Earl; *b* 1872; Lieut-Col late TA Reserve and Capt Gordon Highlanders; bore Standard of Scotland at Coronation of George V in place of his father: *m* 1901, Edith, who *d* 1968, only da of John Moffat; *d* 1924; *s* by his son (13) HENRY JAMES Scrymgeour of Dundee (formerly Scrymgeour Wedderburn of Wedderburn), PC, 11th Earl; *b* 1902; claim to Viscountcy of Dudhope admitted by Committee for Privileges of House of Lords 1952, and *s* to Earldom of Dundee 1953; JP and DL for Fifeshire; Parl Under Sec of State for Scotland 1936-39, served with 7th Bn Black Watch 1939-41, and Joint Parl Under-Sec of State for Scotland 1941-42, Min without Portfolio 1958-61, and Mln of State, Foreign Office, 1961-63, Dep Leader of House of Lords 1962-64; bore Roy Standard of Scotland at Coronations of King George VI 1937, and of Queen Elizabeth II 1953; MP for W Div of Renfrew 1931-45; *cr Baron Glassary* or Glassary, co Argyll (peerage of UK) 1954: *m* 1946, Patricia Katharine, da of late Lt-Col Lord Herbert Andrew Montagu Douglas Scott, CMG, DSO (*see* D Buccleuch, colls), and widow of (1) Lt-Col Walter Douglas Faulkner, MC, Irish Guards, and (2) Lt-Col (Hon) David Scrymgeour-Wedderburn, DSO, Scots Guards (see ante); *d* 1983; *s* by his only son (14) ALEXANDER HENRY Scrymgeour of Dundee, 12th Earl, and present peer, also Viscount Dudhope, Lord Scrymgeour, Lord Inverkeithing, and Baron Glassary.

DUNDONALD, EARL OF (Cochrane) (Earl S 1669)

By courage and labour

(IAIN ALEXANDER) DOUGLAS BLAIR COCHRANE, 15th Earl; *b* 17 Feb 1961; *s* 1986; *ed* Wellington Coll, and RAC Cirencester; Dir Duneth Securities Ltd, and Associated Cos: *m* 1987, M. Beatrice L., da of Adolphus Russo, of Cumberland Rd, Gibraltar, and has issue.

Arms – Argent, a chevron gules, between three boar's heads erased azure. Crest – A horse passant argent. Supporters – Two greyhounds argent collared and lined or.
Seat – Lochnell Castle, Ledaig, Argyll.

SONS LIVING

ARCHIE IAIN THOMAS BLAIR (*Lord Cochrane*), *b* 14 March 1991.
Hon James Douglas Richard, *b* 1995.

DAUGHTER LIVING

Lady Marina Aphra Mariola, *b* 1992.

SISTER LIVING

Lady Tanya Jean Farquhar, *b* 1964; *ed* Benenden: *m* 1992, Anthony J. L. Peake, yr son of Peter Lowsley Peake, of Chantry Dene, Guildford, Surrey, and has issue living, Patrick Ian Lowsley, *b* 1994, — Francesca Mary Lowsley, *b* 1995, — Victoria Aphra Lowsley, *b* 1998. *Residence* – Stanton Waters Farm, Hannington, Highworth, Swindon, Wilts SN6 7RY.

AUNT LIVING (*sister of 14th Earl; raised to the rank of an Earl's daughter*, 1960)

Lady (Winifred) Anne Grizel, *b* 1923: *m* 1967, Alfred Ashford, who *d* 1981, and has issue living, Alexis, *b* 1969.

WIDOW LIVING OF FOURTEENTH EARL

(ANN) MARGARET (*Dowager Countess of Dundonald*), da of late Sir Joseph Welsh Park Harkness, CMG, OBE, MB, ChB, MA, BSc, and formerly wife of late C. F. E. Staib, of Las Palmas, Canary Islands: *m* 1978, as his 2nd wife, the 14th Earl of Dundonald, who *d* 1986. *Residence* – Beau Coin, La Haule, Jersey, CI.

COLLATERAL BRANCHES LIVING

Descendants of late Hon Thomas Horatio Arthur Ernest Cochrane (yr son of 11th Earl), who was *cr Baron Cochrane of Cults* 1919 (see that title).

Grandchildren of late Horace Egerton Cochrane, yst son of Capt Hon Ernest Grey Lambton Cochrane, 4th son of 10th Earl:—
Issue of late Richard Ernest Horace Cochrane, *b* 1909, *d* 1985: *m* 1939, Alma Josephine (c/o Mrs James Creamer, 3309 Hopewell Rd, Valley, Alabama 36864, USA), da of Albert Helland, of Powell River, BC, Canada:—
David Lambton Grey, *b* 1957; *ed* Camb Univ, and Ulster Poly: *m* 1991, Gillian Christine, da of Edwin O'Brien, of Salford, Lancs, and has issue living, Rachel Katherine, *b* 1991. *Residence* – 61 Great Dover St, SE1 4YF. ⸺ Gayle Patricia, *b* 1941: *m* 1977, James Creamer, of 3309 Hopewell Rd, Valley, Alabama 36864, USA. ⸺ Myrna Avice Ruth, *b* 1946: *m* 1971, James Eddison, and has issue living, David James, *b* 1974, — John Richard, *b* 1976.

Granddaughter of late Capt John Palmer Cochrane, 3rd son of late Col William Marshall Cochrane, only son of late Maj Hon William Erskine Cochrane, 3rd son of 9th Earl:—
Issue of late Basil William Dundonald Cochrane, *b* 1891, *d* 1954: *m* 1920, Anne, who *d* 1986, 2nd da of late William Robertson, of Edinburgh:—
Elizabeth Anne, *b* 1926: *m* 1951, Peter Dodds, son of late John William Dodds, of Farnborough, Hants, and has had issue, Peter John Cochrane, *b* 1953; *ed* Gresham's Sch, Norfolk; late Merchant Navy, engr with Dowty Engrg: *m* 1980, Catherine, da of John Stubbs, of Harare, Zimbabwe, and *d* 1993, leaving issue, Andrew John Cochrane *b* 1984, Richard David Cochrane *b* 1986, — David Michael Cochrane, *b* 1954; *ed* Gresham's Sch, Norfolk; photographer, — Anthony Palmer Cochrane, *b* 1962; *ed* Falcon Coll, Zimbabwe: *m* 1993, Mary Lucinda, only da of Clive Aggett, of Kifuku Ranch, Rumuruti, Kenya, and has issue living, George Ian *b* 1996, Chala Jane *b* 1994. *Address* – Box 318, Simon's Town 7995, S Africa.

Grandchildren of late Wing-Cdr John Erichsen Blair Cochrane (*infra*):—
Issue of late John Erskine Dundonald Cochrane, *b* 1920, *d* 1987: *m* 1st, 1943 (*m diss* 1958), Elizabeth Mary, who *d* 1995, da of late Capt Bertram Allgood; 2ndly, 1958, Bela (Lion Cottage, 24 Park Rd, Chislehurst, Kent BR7 5AY), eldest da of William Carlton, of Leeds:—
(By 1st *m*) Ian Michael Dundonald (1 Spinning Mill Cottage, Goulds Ground, Frome, Somerset BA11 3DW), *b* 1950: *m* 1973 (*m diss* 1995), Nicola Robina, da of Eric Wood, of Rowlands, Stour Provost, Dorset, and has issue living, Adam Thomas Dundonald, *b* 1977, — Katrin Emma, *b* 1975, — Lydia Rose, *b* 1983. ⸺ Alastair Charles Dundonald (Nutters Cottage, Nutters Wood, Cleeve Hill, Cheltenham, Glos), *b* 1956: *m* 1978, Julia, da of late George Alan Bedwell, MD,

MRCP, of Osgrove, Penn Lane, King's Stanley, nr Stroud, Glos, and has issue living, Charles Alexander Dundonald, *b* 1985, — Victoria Louise, *b* 1978, — Rebecca Frances, *b* 1981, — Francesca Emily, *b* 1990. —— Sarah Elizabeth (Basque House, Eaton Hastings, nr Faringdon, Oxon SN7 8BL), *b* 1946; has adopted the surname BULL: *m* 1971 (*m diss* 1981), Alastair John Milne Home (*see* E Minto, colls, 1970 Edn), and has issue living, Marcus John Hepburn, *b* 1975, — Camilla Marian Isobel, *b* 1973. —— (By 2nd *m*) David John Dundonald, *b* 1959. —— Peter John Dundonald, *b* 1963. —— Anthony Albert Dundonald, *b* 1967.

Grandchildren of late Capt John Palmer Cochrane (ante):—
Issue of late Wing-Cdr John Erichsen Blair Cochrane, *b* 1894, *d* 1949: *m* 1916, his cousin, Mary, who *d* 1958, eldest da of late Com Thomas Erskine Cochrane (*see* E Dundonald, colls, 1958 Edn):—
Basil Thomas Dundonald (Corner Cottage, 8 Resthaven Drive, Tokai 7945, Cape, S Africa), *b* 1924; late RAF: *m* 1st, 1955 (*m diss* 1973), Sally, only da of Henry Edmund Hounsell, of Livingstone, Zambia; 2ndly, 1974, Daphne Maureen Joyce, da of late Elliot Esmond Baxter, of Camberley, Surrey.

Issue of late Douglas Thomas Cochrane, *b* 1900, *d* 1988: *m* 1st, 1926, Ivy, who *d* 1928, eldest da of G. A. Massdorp, of Queenstown, Cape Province; 2ndly, 1935, Christine Marie Hammond (The Retreat, 4 Harris Rd, PO Highlands, Harare, Zimbabwe):—
(By 1st *m*) Edward Denzil Dundonald (11 Linda Rd, Claremont 7700, Cape Town, S Africa), *b* 1927; MSM, MSc, CEng: *m* 1953, Janet Ainslie, only da of late Robert Allan, OBE, MC, DCM, and has issue living, Michael Allan Dundonald, *b* 1957: *m* 1980, Fiona Jayne, elder da of Norman MacDonald, and has issue living, Daniel Dundonald *b* 1985, Bridget Jayne *b* 1982, — Susan Elizabeth, *b* 1954: *m* 1980, David William Butcher, only son of James Butcher, and has issue living, Joshua David *b* 1988, Sian Catherine *b* 1982, Clare Louise *b* 1985. —— Blair Douglas Dundonald (PO Box 101, Karoi, Zimbabwe), *b* 1928: *m* 1958, Thea Jean, eldest da of Norman R. Stevenson, and has issue living, Ian Dundonald, *b* 1959: *m* 1989, Joanne, only da of William John Kelley, and has issue living, Mark Ian Dundonald *b* 1993, Kelly Jane *b* 1991, — Robert Douglas Dundonald, *b* 1961: *m* 1991, Louise Gail, da of Norton Gebbie, and has issue living, Thomas Dundonald *b* 1995, — Jennifer Mary, *b* 1965: *m* 1989, Russell John Taylor, who *d* 1991, son of Greville Taylor, and has issue living, Russell David *b* 1991, — Sarah Alyson Jane, *b* 1972: *m* 1994, Shaun Vernon Madgwick, son of Hendry Madgwick, and has issue living, Stacey Jane *b* 1997. —— (By 2nd *m*) John Robert Colley (PO Box 650, Harare, Zimbabwe), *b* 1939: *m* 1960, Rosemary Josephine Anne, da of G. W. R. Caine, of Zimbabwe, and has issue living, Jeremy Robert (PO Box 351, Noordhoek, Cape Town 7985, S Africa), *b* 1962: *m* 1987, Sarah Lisa, da of late Ronald Thomas Tomlinson, and has issue living, Emma Lauren *b* 1990, Brittany Lisa *b* 1992, Elizabeth Tacy *b* 1995, — Samantha Caroline, *b* 1965. —— William Thomas (PO Box 650, Harare, Zimbabwe), *b* 1943: *m* 1969, Pamela Evelyn, da of Val Setzkorn, of 46 Danpienaar Drive, Amanzimtoti, Natal, and has issue living, Richard William, *b* 1974, — Ingrid Margaret, *b* 1971, — Lucille Pamela, *b* 1976. —— Richard Bruce (9 Plymouth Rd, Sandton, Johannesburg, S Africa), *b* 1948: *m* 1975, Pamela Brown, and has issue living, Douglas, *b* 1981, — Alexander Richard, *b* 1984, — Jennifer Leigh, *b* 1983. —— Steven David (33 Court Rd, Greendale North, Harare, Zimbabwe), *b* 1951; BSc (Agric): *m* 1st, 1973 (*m diss* 1987), Penelope Jane Lutley, eldest da of Denzil Awdry Randles; 2ndly, 1991, Evelyn Judy, da of John Rau, of Harare, and has issue living (by 1st *m*), William James Dundonald, *b* 1975, — Graham Douglas, *b* 1977, — James Denzil, *b* 1980, — Abigail Elizabeth, *b* 1982, — (by 2nd *m*) Michelle Cecily, *b* 1993. —— Cecily Mary Elizabeth, *b* 1935: *m* 1959, Kenneth Saywood, of PO Box 177, Karoi, Zimbabwe, and has issue living, Neil Frank, *b* 1960, — David, *b* 1961, — Peter John, *b* 1966, — Michael Anthony, *b* 1970. —— Una Patricia Louwina COCHRANE (8 Rue Cdt Mouchotte, 75014 Paris, France), *b* 1937; has resumed her maiden name: *m* 1958 (*m diss* 1975), Kenneth Davies, and has issue living, Patricia Clare Cochrane, *b* 1959: *m* 1981, Roy Alexander Brooks, and has issue living, William Sebastien *b* 1981, Lawrence Thomas *b* 1983, — Andrea Jane Cochrane, *b* 1962.

Grandsons of late Arthur Henry Douglas Cochrane, 4th and yst son of late Col William Marshall Cochrane (ante):—
Issue of late Arthur Blair Dundonald Cochrane, *b* 1888, *d* 1936: *m* 1918, Nancy, who *d* 1985, da of late Robert Barber, Bar-at-Law:—
Hugh Benjamin (Hope Cottage, 88 Newland, Sherborne, Dorset DT9 3DT), *b* 1925; *ed* Radley, and Queens' Coll, Camb (MA); CEng, FICE, MIMechE; late Lt RE: *m* 1953, Anne Deirdre, el da of late William Schoener Scott. —— Nicholas Baillie (Old Oak Farm, Easthampstead Park, Wokingham, Berks RG11 3DL) *b* 1929; late Capt King's African Rifles: *m* 1958, Diana Isabel, da of late Norman Balfour Craig, and has issue living, Amanda Elizabeth, *b* 1959: *m* 1993, Capt Jeremy Robert Shafto (Army Air Corps), elder son of Maj Robert Shafto, of SW11, and of Mrs Nicola Williamson, of Bath, Avon, and has issue living, Hamish Alexander Cochrane *b* 1993, Katharine Arabella Emily *b* 1995, — Susan Mary, *b* 1962.

Granddaughters of late Vice-Adm Basil Edward Cochrane, el son of late Basil Edward Arthur Cochrane, 2nd son of late Capt Hon Archibald Cochrane, RN, 4th son of 9th Earl:—
Issue of late Rear-Adm Archibald Cochrane, CMG, *b* 1874, *d* 1952: *m* 1904, Maye Amelie Lucile, who *d* 1954, da of late Col Alured de Vere Brooke, RE (Brooke, Bt, *cr* 1662, colls):—
Monica Frances Mary, *b* 1908: *m* 1950, George Worcester, who *d* 1969. *Residence* – Penny Cottage, Windlesham, Surrey GU20 6BP. —— Dorothea Stella, *b* 1913: *m* 1951, John Errington Rothwell Harrison, and has issue living, James Anthony Rothwell, *b* 1952: *m* 1975, Louise Marie, da of Louis Matarazzo, of Thunder Bay, Ont, Canada, and has issue living, Neil Owen *b* 1981, Thomas Louis *b* 1984, Laura Catherine *b* 1990, — Anne Lucile Rothwell, *b* 1953: *m* 1988, Robert Wallace Sargalis.

Granddaughter of Rear-Adm Sir Edward Owen Cochrane, KBE (infra):—
Issue of late Maj James Owen Cochrane, MC, RA, *b* 1914, *ka* 1943: *m* 1941, Margaret Angela Clare (who *m* 2ndly, 1950, Desmond Pertwee, who *d* 1991, of Rookery House, Great Horkesley, in Colchester, Essex), da of Vice-Adm Charles Wolfram Round-Turner, CB, CMG:—
Janet Owen (known as Jane COCHRANE), *b* 1942: *m* 1st, 1965 (*m diss* 1978), Paul Moore; 2ndly, 1992, Alec Kazantzis, and has issue living (by 1st *m*), Thomas Owen, *b* 1966: *m* 1993, Lisa Pool, and has issue living, Saul Owen *b* 1993, China Gwen *b* 1994, — Amy Clare MOORE, *b* 1969; has retained her maiden name: *m* 1997, Mark Draper, and has issue living, Maisie Angelica *b* 1997.

Granddaughter of late Vice-Adm Basil Edward Cochrane (ante):—
Issue of late Rear Adm Sir Edward Owen Cochrane, KBE, *b* 1881, *d* 1972: *m* 1908, Mary Lucy (Molly), who *d* 1955, da of S. K. George, of The Brackens, Ascot:—
Susanne Gloria, *b* 1918: *m* 1957, David Logan Howell. *Residence* – 23 Ashley Court, Morpeth Terrace, SW1P 1EN.

Grandchildren of late William Edward Cochrane, 4th son of Basil Edward Arthur Cochrane (ante):—
Issue of late Cdr Arthur FitzGerald Cochrane, RN, *b* 1888, *d* 1967: *m* 1913, Beryl Irma, who *d* 1954, da of Gen
Charles Frederick Thomas, of Excliffe, Exmouth, and widow of Percy Hugh Druce:—
Peter William FitzGerald (761 London Rd, Sarnia, Ontario N7T 4X7, Canada), *b* 1916; *ed* Ampleforth, and at McGill Univ;
1939-45 War with Atlantic Ferry Command and as Flying Officer RCAF with Bomber Command: *m* 1944, Margaret
Eunice, only da of Wesley William Rowley, of London, Ontario, Canada, and has issue living, Richard Arthur Wesley
Rowley, *b* 1948: *m* 1986, Andrina Maria, yst child of Peter Rull, of Hong Kong and New York, and has issue living,
Marie Margaret *b* 1987, — Stephen Bryce Rowley, *b* 1952: *m* 1980, Tracey, da of R. Gordon Henderson, of BC, Canada,
and has issue living, Sydney Margaret *b* 19—. —— Evelyn Jean FitzGerald, *b* 1914. —— Shelia Fitzgerald, *b* 1917: *m*
1942, Lt Cdr John Aarvold Loughlin Stubbs, RNVR, of 10 Dorset Close, Harrogate, and has issue living, Penelope Ann, *b*
1945; BSc: *m* 1966, Maj Patrick Joseph David Herberts, MD, of Brigend of Kildarroch, Borgue, Kirkcudbright, and has
issue living, Andrew John David *b* 1970, Alison Philippa *b* 1967, Catherine Elizabeth *b* 1972, — Gillian Mary *b* 1947.
—— Cecilia Florence Fitzgerald, *b* 1924: *m* 1955, John Gray Robertson, of Sunlaws, Parkhead, Dumfries, and has issue
living, Peter Arthur Cochrane (The Chase, 3 Kingsmeadow, Crudwell, Malmesbury, Wilts), *b* 1956; BSc Glasgow: *m*
1982, Shirley Margaret Bradford, and has issue living, Andrew George Cochrane *b* 1987, David John Cochrane *b* 1991,
— Philip John Cochrane, *b* 1962: *m* 1984 (*m diss* 1992), Rhonda Eleanor Kelly.

Granddaughter (by 2nd wife) of late Thomas Belhaven Henry Cochrane, MVO (infra):—
Issue of late Lt-Cdr John Cochrane, RN, *b* 1909, *ka* 1941: *m* 1937, Jocelyn Mary (who *d* 1988, having *m* 2ndly,
1946, Col Brian Leslie Sundius-Smith, who *d* 1965), da of late Capt John Francis Robins, RN:—
Vivien Mary Grisell, *b* 1939: *m* 1962, Anthony Cortlandt Richard Chappell, and has issue living, Richard John Anthony
(Poplar House, Flookersbrook, Chester CH2 3AF), *b* 1967; *ed* Oundle, and Bristol Univ: *m* 1997, Caroline Jane, elder da
of late Robert Harding, of Evington, Leicester, — Andrew Thomas Robert, *b* 1969; *ed* Oundle, and Leicester Univ: *m*
1998, Natasha Lucy, yr da of Anthony Baldwin, of Hartley Wespall, Hants, — Caroline Margaret Joan, *b* 1966: *m* 1995,
Edward Tom Atkinson, of 2 Melody Rd, SW18, and has issue living, Angus Alexander Patrick *b* 1998, Isobel Kitty
Lavinia *b* 1996. *Residence* – Croxton House, Fulmodeston, Fakenham, Norfolk NR21 0NJ.

Grandson of late Adm of the Fleet Sir Thomas John Cochrane, GCB, MP, eldest son of late Adm Hon
Sir Alexander Forester Inglis Cochrane, GCB, MP, 6th son of 8th Earl:—
Issue of late Thomas Belhaven Henry Cochrane, MVO, Lieut RN, *b* 1856, *d* 1925: *m* 1st, 1887, Lady Adela
Charlotte Rous, who *d* 1911, sister of 3rd Earl of Stradbroke; 2ndly, 1911, Beatrice, who *d* 1977, da of late
William Henry Knight:—
(By 2nd *m*) †Thomas Dundonald Hugh (157 Temelec Circle, Sonoma, Calif 95476, USA), *b* 1912; *ed* Oundle; Lieut RNVR
1940-46: *m* 1937, Margery, da of late Norman Rowe, and *d* 1998, leaving issue, Norman Thomas (12398 Copenhagen
Court, Reston, VA 22091, USA), *b* 1938: *m* 1965, Sarah Wills, and has issue living, Thomas Alexander *b* 1970, Ann Lee *b*
1972, — Sandra Ann, *b* 1946: *m* 1982, Graham Baker, of 7417 Continental Trail, N Richland Hills, Texas 76180, USA.

PREDECESSORS – (1) Sir WILLIAM Cochrane (of the family of Cochrane, which had been settled on the Barony of
Cochrane in W of Scotland for many centuries), PC, KB, MP for Ayrshire, and Col of Royalist Militia, who assisted in
sending the Scots Army into England, was *cr Lord Cochrane, of Dundonald* (Peerage of Scotland) 1647, with remainder
to the heirs male of his body, and *Earl of Dundonald* and *Lord Cochrane of Paisley and Ochiltree* (peerage of Scotland)
1669, with remainder to his heirs male, whom failing to his heirs female without division who should bear or assume
the name of Cochrane, and in failure to his heirs-gen; *d* 1686; *s* by his grandson (2) JOHN, PC, 2nd Earl; *d* 1690; *s* by his
el son (3) WILLIAM, 3rd Earl; *d* unmarried 1705; *s* by his brother (4) JOHN, 4th Earl; a Representative Peer; commanded
Scottish Horse Guards 1715; *d* 1720; *s* by his son (5) WILLIAM, 5th Earl; *d* unmarried 1725; *s* by his cousin (6) THOMAS ,
6th Earl, grandson of William, Lord Cochrane of Dundonald, el son of 1st Earl; *d* 1737; *s* by his son (7) WILLIAM, 7th
Earl; killed at Siege of Louisburg 1758; *s* by his cousin (8) THOMAS, 8th Earl (grandson of Col the Hon Sir John
Cochrane, 2nd son of 1st Earl), *b* 1691: sat as MP for Renfrewshire 1722-7; *d* 1778; *s* by his son (9) ARCHIBALD, 9th Earl;
b 1748; served in RN; an eminent Scientist, and inventor; made many beneficial discoveries connected with Chemistry; *s*
by his son (10) THOMAS, GCB, 10th Earl; *b* 1775; a distinguished Adm, and one of the greatest Naval Commanders of
any age; conducted attack on French Fleet in Basque Rds, with fire and explosion ships, 1809, and was also renowned
for many daring exploits in the RN; commanded the Chilian and Peruvian Navy (destroying Spanish Naval power in
Pacific), the Brazilian Navy against Portugal (completely successful), and the Greek Fleet, in the Wars of independence
of those countries; sat as MP for Westminster, and was an advanced Reformer, and an eminent scientist and inventor; *cr
Marquess of Maranham*, in Brazil, 1824; *d* 1860 (buried in Westminster Abbey); *s* by his son (11) THOMAS BARNES, 11th
Earl; *b* 1814; was a Representative Peer, and QMG to Forces in Chinese War: *m* 1847, Louisa Harriet, who *d* 1902, da of
late William Alexander-Mackinnon, MP, of Mackinnon; *d* 1885; *s* by his son (12) DOUGLAS MACKINNON BAILLIE HAMILTON,
KCB, KCVO, 12th Earl; *b* 1852; Lieut-Gen (retired); Nile Expedition 1884-5, S Africa 1899-1901 at Relief of Ladysmith
(promoted Maj-Gen for distinguished ser in the field); sometime a Representative Peer for Scotland: *m* 1878, Winifred,
who *d* 1924, only child of late Robert Bamford Hesketh, of Gwrych Castle, Abergele, N Wales; *d* 1935, *s* by his son (13)
THOMAS HESKETH DOUGLAS BLAIR, 13th Earl; *b* 1886; was a Representative Peer for Scotland 1941-55; *d* 1958; *s* by his
nephew (14) IAN DOUGLAS LEONARD (son of late Hon Douglas Robert Hesketh Roger Cochrane, 2nd son of 12th Earl)
14th Earl, *b* 1918; a Representative Peer for Scotland 1959-63, Maj Black Watch, Chm Anglo-Chilean Soc 1958-65: *m* 1st,
1960, Aphra Farquhar, who *d* 1972, da of late Cdr George Fetherstonhaugh, RNR, of The Beacon, Benenden, Kent;
2ndly, 1978, (Ann) Margaret, da of late Sir Joseph Welsh Park Harkness, CMG, OBE, MB, and formerly wife of late
C.F.E. Staib; *d* 1986; *s* by his only son (15) IAIN ALEXANDER DOUGLAS BLAIR, 15th Earl and present peer; also Lord
Cochrane of Dundonald, and Lord Cochrane of Pailsley and Ochiltree.

Dungarvan, Viscount; son of Earl of Cork and Orrery.

Dunglass, Lord; son of Earl of Home.

Dungarvan, Viscount; son of Earl of Cork and Orrery.

Dunglass, Lord; son of Earl of Home.

DUNLEATH, BARON (Mulholland) (Baron UK 1892, Bt UK 1945)

Always girt

BRIAN HENRY MULHOLLAND, 5th Baron, and 3rd Baronet; *b* 25 Sept 1950; *s* 1997; *ed* Eton: *m* 1976, Mary Joan, yst da of Maj Robert John Fuller Whistler, of Achaeon, Middleton Rd, Camberley, Surrey, and has issue.

𝕬rms – Azure, a stag's head erased argent between three escallops or. 𝕮rest – An escallop gules, 𝕾upporters – On either side an elk proper, charged on the shoulder with an escallop or, and holding in the mouth a trefoil slipped vert. *Seat* – Ballywalter Park, Newtownards, co Down BT22 2PA.

SONS LIVING

Hon ANDREW HENRY, *b* 15 Dec 1981; *ed* Portora Royal Sch, Enniskillen, and Methodist Coll, Belfast.
Hon William Alexander, *b* 1986; *ed* Methodist Coll, Belfast.

DAUGHTER LIVING

Hon Tara Miranda, *b* 1980; *ed* Victoria Coll, Belfast.

WIDOW LIVING OF FOURTH BARON

DORINDA MARGERY (*Dorinda, Baroness Dunleath*), da of late Lt-Gen Arthur Ernest Percival, CB, DSO, OBE, MC, of Bullards, Widford, Ware, Herts: *m* 1959, Lt-Col the 4th Baron Dunleath, TD, who *d* 1993. *Residence* – Killyvolgan House, Ballywalter, Newtownards, co Down BT22 2NX.

COLLATERAL BRANCHES LIVING

Issue of late Hon (Godfrey) John Arthur Murray Lyle Mulholland, MC, 4th son of 2nd Baron, *b* 1892; *d* 1948: *m* 1923, Hon Olivia Vernon Harcourt, DCVO, who *d* 1984, da of 1st Viscount Harcourt:—
Martin Edward Harcourt, *b* 1927; formerly Lieut Irish Guards; High Sheriff co Antrim 1961: *m* 1953, Lilian Diana Tindall, only da of Maj John de Blaquiere Tindall Lucas, MC, and has issue living, John Martin (Cautley Cottage, Slaley, Hexham, Northumberland), *b* 1953; late Capt 5th R Inniskilling Drag Gds: *m* 1981, Diana Margaret Sara, da of Geoffrey Walter Wilson, of Garden Lodge, Ballygarvey, Ballymena, co Antrim, and has issue living, Charles John *b* 1984, Sara Juliet *b* 1987, — Simon Edward, *b* 1955; a Page of Honour to HM Queen Elizabeth, The Queen Mother 1969-71: *m* 1991, Catriona M., yst da of J. B. C. Darroch, of Sevenoaks, Kent, — Giles Alexander, *b* 1959. *Residence* – North Hall, E Chiltington, Lewes. —— Mary Norah, *b* 1924; in WRNS 1943-45: *m* 1944, John William Owen Elliot, late Capt Scots Guards (*see* E Minto, colls).

Grandchildren of late Hon Alfred John Mulholland, 3rd son of 1st Baron:—
Issue of late John Llewellyn Mulholland, *b* 1908, *d* 1989 (in Brazil): *m* 1st, 1928 (*m diss* June 1930, in Hungary), Helen, da of Vladimir Moss; 2ndly, 1930 (in Hungary) (*m diss* 1937), Olga, da of Nicholas Kuznetzov; 3rdly,

1937 (in France) (*m diss* 1938), Colette, da of Georges Mounier; 4thly, 1944 (in Brazil), Lucia, da of Antonio Izaquirre:—
(By 1st *m*) John Peter Patrick (Chesterfield, Somerford Rd, Cirencester, Glos), *b* 1929; *ed* Berkhamstead, RMA Sandhurst, Trin Coll, Dublin, and Sch of Slavonic Studies (BA); Bar Middle Temple 1969; formerly Brazilian Organiser BBC; MRAC, ACIArb: *m* 1st, 1962 (*m diss* 1970), Suelly, da of Olympio Jose do Lindo; 2ndly, 1973, Rosemary Kathleen Vaughan, only da of late Charles Hawkins, MC, BDS, and has issue living (by 2nd *m*), John Charles, *b* 1975, — James Patrick, *b* 1977. —— (By 2nd *m*) Alexander Anatol (Rua Senador Vergueiro 237/501, 2230 Rio de Janeiro, Brazil), *b* 1931 (in Hungary); *ed* Colegio S Jose, Rio de Janeiro, Solihull Sch, and Trin Coll, Dublin (BA): *m* 1959, Judith, da of Domicio Francisco de Azevedo, and has issue living, Ines, *b* 1961. —— (By 3rd *m*) †Christian, *b* 1938 (in France): *m* 1964, Danielle Andrée (who *m* 2ndly, 19—, R. A. Turner), da of late André Emile Bombail, of Relizane, Algeria, and *d* 1968, leaving issue, Valentine Marie Danielle, *b* 1964; BA, — Hélène Marie Christine, *b* 1965.

Issue of late Maj Alfred Ivo Mulholland, *b* 1913, *d* 1998: *m* 1946, Monica Mary, da of late William Lowry Craig Knight, CMG:—
Mary-Rose Emma, *b* 1951; has issue living, Jeremy Jigne MULHOLLAND, *b* 1982. *Residence* – Lantern Lodge, Aish, S Brent, Devon TQ10 9JQ.

PREDECESSORS – **(1)** JOHN Mulholland, LLD, son of late Andrew Mulholland, JP, DL, of Ballywalter Park; *b* 1819; MP for Downpatrick (*C*) 1874-85; *cr Baron Dunleath,* of Ballywalter, co Down (peerage of United Kingdom) 1892: *m* 1851, Frances Louisa, who *d* 1909, da of Hugh Lyle, of Knocktarna, co Londonderry; *d* 1895; *s* by his second son **(2)** HENRY LYLE, 2nd Baron, *b* 1854; MP for Londonderry co, N Derry Div (*C*) 1885-95: *m* 1881 Norah Louisa Fanny, OBE, who *d* 1935, da of late Capt Hon Somerset Richard Hamilton Augusta Ward; *d* 1931; *s* by his son **(3)** CHARLES HENRY GEORGE, CBE, DSO, 3rd Baron; *b* 1886; Capt 11th Hussars; Mil Sec to Lord-Lieut of Ireland 1919-21, and Gov-Gen of Australia 1923-5: *m* 1st, 1920, Sylvia Henrietta, who *d* 1921, da of Sir Arthur Douglas Brooke, 4th Bt; 2ndly, 1932, Henrietta Grace, who *d* 1969, da of late Most Rev Charles Frederick D'Arcy (B Darcy de Knayth, colls); *d* 1956; *s* by his only son **(4)** CHARLES EDWARD HENRY JOHN, TD, 4th Baron; *b* 1933; Lt-Col cmdg N Irish Horse (T), Hon Col 'D' (N Irish Horse) Squadron Royal Yeomanry Regt, DL co Down, Nat Gov for N Ireland BBC, etc: *m* 1959, Dorinda Margery, only da of late Lt-Gen Arthur Ernest Percival, CB, CMG, DSO, MC; *d* 1993; *s* by his cousin **(5)** MICHAEL HENRY (son of late Rt Hon Sir Henry George Hill Mulholland, 1st Bt, 3rd son of 2nd Baron), 5th Baron; *b* 1915; Maj Oxford and Bucks LI; served Burma 1942-45: *m* 1st, 1942 (*m diss* 1948), Rosemary, only da of late Maj David Alfred William Ker, OBE, of Portavo, Donaghdee, co Down (*see* Barrington, Bt, 1947 Edn); 2ndly, 1949, Elizabeth M., who *d* 1989, twin da of late Laurence B. Hyde, of Bexhill-on-Sea; *d* 1997; *s* by his only son **(6)** BRIAN HENRY, 6th Baron and present peer.

The 1st baronet, Rt Hon Sir Henry George Hill Mulholland, 3rd son of 2nd Baron Dunleath, was speaker of Parliament of N Ireland 1929-45, *cr* PC 1930, and a baronet 1945.

Dunluce, Viscount; son of Earl of Antrim.

DUNMORE, EARL OF (Murray) (Earl S 1686)

MALCOLM KENNETH MURRAY, 12th Earl; *b* 17 Sept 1946; *s* 1995: *m* 1970, Joy Anne, da of late Arthur Partridge, of Launceston, Tasmania, and has two adopted children.

Arms – Quarterly of six in three ranks, first (in dexter chief) azure, three mullets argent within a double tressure flowered and counterflowered of fleurs de lys or (*Murray of Atholl*); second (in sinister chief) or, a fess chequy azure and argent (*Stewart*); third (in dexter fess) paly of six or and sable (*Atholl*); fourth (in sinister fess) argent, on a bend azure, three bucks' heads cabossed or (*Stanley, Earl of Derby*); fifth (in dexter base) gules, three legs in armour proper garnished and spurred or, flexed and conjoined in triangle at the upper part of the thigh (*Man*); sixth (in sinister base) gules, two lions passant in pale argent armed and langued azure (*Strange*); overall at the honour point a crescent sable. **Crest** – a demi wild man wreathed about the loins and temples with laurel charged on the breast of a crescent sable, holding in his dexter hand a sword proper hilted and pommelled sable and in his sinister hand a key also sable. **Supporters** – *dexter*, a savage proper wreathed about the loins charged on the breast of a crescent sable; *sinister*, a lion rampant gules, armed and langued azure gorged of a collar argent charged with three crescents sable. **Motto** – Furthward Fortune.
Address – PO Box 100E, East Devonport, Tasmania 7310, Australia.

ADOPTED SON LIVING

Leigh Kenneth, *b* 1978.

ADOPTED DAUGHTER LIVING

Elisa Anne, *b* 1981.

BROTHER LIVING

Hon GEOFFREY CHARLES, *b* 31 July 1949: *m* 1974, Margaret Irene, da of late Herbert Bullock, of Blackwall, Tasmania. *Residence* – 18 Newlands St, Trevallyn, Tasmania 7250.

AUNTS LIVING (*sisters of 10th and 11th Earls*)

Lorraine Edith, *b* 1914: *m* 1st, 1940, Hector Roy Bird, who *d* 1963; 2ndly, 1966, Stanley Millwood Farquhar, who *d* 1996, and has issue living (by 1st *m*), Grace Lucinda, *b* 1950: *m* 1969 (*m diss* 1995), Haydn Peter Borella, of 62 Talbot Rd, Launceston, Tasmania 7250, and has issue living, Paul Andrew *b* 1973, Angela Jayne *b* 1971; also has issue David John BARTLETT *b* 1968. *Residence* – 62 Talbot Rd, S Launceston, Tasmania 7250.
Constance Margaret, *b* 1922: *m* 1946, John Mallinson, and has issue living, Edward Arthur John, *b* 1955: *m* 1979, Janice Maree Shipp, and has issue living, Damian Edward *b* 1980, Erin Elizabeth *b* 1983, — David Andrew, *b* 1957. *Residence* – 12 Munford St, Kings Meadows, Launceston, Tasmania.

DAUGHTERS LIVING OF TENTH EARL

Lady Susan, *b* 1949: *m* 1980, Graham Price, of 15 Wandoo Rd, Duncraig, W Australia 6023.
Lady Elizabeth Mary, *b* 1951: *m* 1973, John Michael Parkinson, of 882 Cambridge Rd, Cambridge, Tasmania 7170, and has issue living, James Murray, *b* 1976, — Anna Louise, *b* 1978.

DAUGHTERS LIVING OF NINTH EARL

Lady Kate Rodel (38 Broadhinton Rd, SW4 0LT), *b* 1969; Graphic Designer, *Sunday Telegraph*.
Lady Rebecca Moulin (The Old Inn, Black Bourton, Bampton, Oxon OX18 2PF), *b* 1970; Freelance Artist: *m* 1997, Ben Wightman, son of Bev Wightman, of Finstock, Oxon.

DAUGHTERS LIVING OF EIGHTH EARL

Lady Marjorie Hilda, *b* 1904; has Order of Mercy: *m* 1926, Duncan Alexander Stirling, late Capt Coldstream Guards, and Chm National Westminster Bank, who *d* 1990, and has issue living, Alexander Murray (Hunterswood House, Chipperfield, Herts; *Clubs* – Brooks's, City Univ, Army and Navy), *b* 1927; *ed* Eton, and New Coll, Oxford; late Lieut Coldstream Guards; late Partner Thos R. Miller & Son: *m* 1951, Mary, da of late Maj Neville Wakefield, DSO, and has issue living, Robert Alexander (143 Elgin Crescent, W11 2JH) *b* 1959; *ed* Eton, and Lincoln Coll, Oxford: *m* 1988, Susan Mary, yr da of late Rear Adm James Humphrey Walwyn, CB, OBE (and has issue living, Alexander Humphrey *b* 1994, Rory James *b* (twin) 1994), Oliver John (7 Hartswood Rd, W12 9NQ) *b* 1961; *ed* Eton, and Oxford Sch of Architecture: *m* 1991, Susan Caroline, da of Henry Keith Foster, of Ingatestone, Essex (and has issue living, Rufus Alexander Algernon *b* 1993, Iona Grace Tean *b* 1995, Flora India Oriana *b* 1997), Annabel Mary Charlotte *b* 1963: *m* 1995, (Richard) Hugh Jolly, of Rose Cottage, Hellidon, Northants NN11 6LG, yr son of Alec Jolly of Yelvertoft, Northants (and has issue living,

Crispin Valentine *b* 1999, Venetia Charlotte *b* (twin) 1999), — *Sir* Angus Duncan Æneas (25 Ladbroke Grove, W11), *b* 1933; *ed* Eton, and Trin Coll, Camb; Chm Royal Opera House, Covent Garden, 1991-96; Dir-Gen National Trust 1983-95, Chm Greenwich Foundation for the Royal Naval Coll since 1996; Ktd 1994: *m* 1959, Armyne Morar Helen, da of late William George Broadbent Schofield (*see* B Hastings, colls), and has issue living, Duncan William Angus *b* 1963, Emma Elisabeth *b* 1960: *m* 1988, Andrew Harold Wentworth Sutcliffe, and has issue (*see* V Chetwynd, colls), Candida Helen *b* 1966. *Residence* – 20 Kingston House South, Ennismore Gdns, SW7.

Lady (Mary) Elisabeth, *b* 1918: *m* 1937, Major Peter Carlton Oldfield, OBE, Warwickshire Yeo, and has issue living, Sara Elizabeth (West Manor Stables, Standen, Hungerford, Berks RG17 0RB), *b* 1939: *m* 1961 (*m diss* 1983), William Thomson, late Scots Guards, and has issue living, Lucinda *b* 1965. *Residence* – Ham Cottage, Sydmonton, Newbury, Berks.

WIDOW LIVING OF NINTH EARL

ANNE AUGUSTA (*Anne, Countess of Dunmore*) (14 Regent Terr, Edinburgh EH7 5BN), da of Thomas Clouston Wallace, of Holodyke, Dounby, Orkney; Dir Edinburgh Tapestry Co: *m* 1967, the 9th Earl of Dunmore, who *d* 1980.

WIDOW LIVING OF TENTH EARL

PATRICIA MARY (Kooringal, 27 Beach Rd, Gravelly Beach, 7276, W Tamar, Tasmania), da of Frank Edwin Coles, of Robigana, W Tamar, Tasmania: *m* 1st, 1948, the 10th Earl of Dunmore, who *d* 1981; 2ndly, 1984, Geoffrey Howard Fitze.

COLLATERAL BRANCHES LIVING

　　　　Issue of late Alexander Edward Murray, yr brother of 10th and 11th Earls, *b* 1917, *d* 1994: *m* 1st, 1943 (*m diss* 1968), June Caroline Lucy, el da of late Boaz Rabinovitch, of E Moonah, Tasmania; 2ndly, 1970, Irene Maud Barwick, who *d* 1991, of Hobart, Tasmania:—
(By 1st *m*) Stephen Alexander (36 Newlands St, Riverside, Launceston, Tasmania 7250), *b* 1953: *m* 1979, Marilyn Ann Rose, da of James Sellers, of Trevallyn, Launceston, and has had issue, †Mathew James, *b* 1982; *d* 1995, — Anthony Victor, *b* 1989. —— Marilyn Joy (11 Leamington St, Reservoir, Vic 3073), *b* 1947: *m* 1st, 1964 (*m diss* 1971), Michael John Hankin; 2ndly, 1979, Brian Carson, and has issue living (by 1st *m*), Brett Michael, *b* 1967, — Tania Maree, *b* 1965, — Sharon Louise, *b* 1971. —— Wendy Lorraine, *b* 1951: *m* 1969, Maxwell Kevin Upton, of 122 Brent St, Glenorchy, Hobart, Tasmania, and has issue living, Jason Boaz, *b* 1971: *m* 19—, Vicki Ann Miller, and has issue living, Emily Ann *b* 1995, — Natasha Ruby Maree, *b* 1976.

　　　　Granddaughter of late Charles James Murray, son of late Rt Hon Sir Charles Augustus Murray, KCB, son of 5th Earl:—
　　　　Issue of late Charles Wadsworth Murray, *b* 1894, *d* 1945: *m* 1924, Elizabeth, who *d* 1993, da of Frank Grant, of Knockie, Inverness:—
Helen Rosemary, *b* 1928: *m* 1966, Hubert Zipperlen.

　　　　Grandchildren of late Reginald Augustus Frederick Murray, eldest son of Capt Virginius Murray, 2nd son of Lt-Col Hon Alexander Murray, 2nd son of 4th Earl:—
　　　　Issue of late Virginius Henry Randolph Murray, *b* 1872, *d* 1937: *m* 1910, Alice, who *d* 1966, da of William Clarke, MD, of Banff:—
Patricia Aimee, *b* 1916: *m* 1960, Peter Bayard Horne, of 42 Musgrave St, Mosman 2088, NSW, Australia

　　　　Issue of late Reginald Herbert Earn Murray, *b* 1893, *d* 1980: *m* 1928, Nina Clarendon, who *d* 1975, da of Clarendon James Seager:—
John Dunmore (Coonawarra, 2 Twin St, Stirling, S Australia 5152), *b* 1929; *ed* Adelaide Univ (B Eng); MIE Aust: *m* 1962 (*m diss* 1994), Geraldine Marjorie, da of late Col Rupert Edward Fanning, of S Yarra, Victoria, and has issue living, Catriona Dunmore Stewart, *b* 1965: *m* 1992, Michael David Mills, of 138 Mount Pleasant, Cockfosters, EN4 9HG, son of David Mills, of 9 Coppice Walk, Totteridge, N20, and has issue living, Ruaraidh Alexander *b* 1997, — Bridget Dunmore Stewart, *b* 1967, — Vanessa Dunmore Stewart, *b* 1969, — Kirsten Dunmore Stewart, *b* 1971: *m* 1998, David Little, of Sydney, NSW, son of Warwick Little, of Glenalta, S Aust, and has issue living, Ciaran Murray *b* 1998.

　　　　Grandchildren of late Capt Virginius Murray, son of late Lieut-Col Hon Alexander Murray (infra):—
　　　　Issue of late George Earn Murray, *b* 1850, *d* 1902: *m* 1889, Julia Mary McLeod, who *d* 1933, second da of late Gen C. B. Fuller, RHA (Col Comdt):—
Dudley Stewart, *b* 1892. —— Gladys, *b* 1890.

　　　　Grandchildren of late Henry Alexander Murray, 6th and yst son of Capt Virginius Murray (ante):—
　　　　Issue of late Lt-Col Henry Alexander Murray, MD, *b* 1893, *d* 1988: *m* 1st, 1916, Josephine Lee, who *d* 1962, da of Neal Rantoul, of Boston, Mass, USA; 2ndly, 1969, Caroline, da of Alfred Chandler, of Wilmington, Delaware, USA:—
(By 1st *m*) Josephine, *b* 1921; MA (1954), MD New York Univ (1961). *Residence* – 41 Concord Av, Cambridge, Mass 02138, USA.

　　　　Issue of late Cecil Dunmore Murray, *b* 1897, *d* 1935: *m* 1921, Veronica, who *d* 1988, da of Kenneth Frazier, of Garrison, New York:—
Rev Michael Hunt (301 Indian Springs Rd, Williamsburg, Va 23185, USA), *b* 1922; late Lt USA Naval Air Force: *m* 1st, 1943, Gloria Caruso; 2ndly, 1955, Eliane, da of Eugene Cadilhac, of Paris, France, and has issue living, (by 1st *m*) Eric Dunmore, *b* 1945, — Colin Duncan Alexander, *b* 1949. —— Julia Fannie, *b* 1924: *m* 1953, Robert Linfield Mackintosh,

and has issue living, Amy Rogers, *b* 1954, — Louisa Linfield, *b* 1956, — Susan Frazier, *b* 1958. *Residence* – Manchester, Mass, USA.

Grandchildren of late Charles Stewart Murray, CIE, 2nd son of Brig-Gen Alexander Henry Murray, yst son of Lt Col Hon Alexander Murray, 2nd son of 4th Earl:—
Issue of late Cdr Archie Alastair Stewart, RN, *b* 1892, *d* 1964: *m* 1925, Marie Louise Ravend de Martainville, who *d* 1990, da of late Alfred Taylor Pattison, of New Orleans, USA:—
Hugh Archie Stewart (Quinta Arca de Noé, Ferragudo, Algarve, Portugal), *b* 1927; *ed* Stowe, and Trin Coll Oxford (MA); late Lt Welsh Guards: *m* 1st, 1955 (*m* annulled 1963), Kathleen Mary, only da of late Clive Raymond Hargreaves; 2ndly, 1967, Eileen Jane Alexandra, da of late Charles Clement Lockhart Ross.

Issue of late Maj Alastair Donald Stewart Murray, MC, *b* 1898, *d* 1966: *m* 1st, 1922, Joan Ethel, da of late Robert Moore McMahon, of Holly Mount, Carlow; 2ndly, 1933 (*m* diss 1948), Marjory, who *d* 1959, da of late Capt Anthony Standidge Thomson, CB, CBE, and formerly wife of Capt Herbert Caryl Uniacke, RA; 3rdly, 1951, Oonah Tighe, only da of Thomas Tait, of Gatehouse-of-Fleet, Kirkcudbrightshire, and formerly wife of — McKellar:—
(By 3rd *m*) Alastair Stewart (31 Chater Hall, G/F, 1 Conduit Rd, Mid-Levels, Hong Kong), *b* 1952; Ch Inspector Royal Hong Kong Police; MIExpE, MIABTI: *m* 1973, Sheila, da of — Garvie, and has issue living, Struan Alastair Stewart, *b* 1977, — Ian Nairn, *b* 1980.

Issue of late Charles Stewart Murray, *b* 1900, *d* 1960: *m* 1st, 1926 (*m* diss 1933), Beryta, who *d* 1982, only da of Roland Allport, of Sydney, NSW; 2ndly, 1937, Alice Mary, 3rd da of late Robert Matthews, of Sydney, NSW:—
(By 1st *m*) Diana Stewart, *b* 1930: *m* 1st, 1948 (*m* diss 1960), Richard de Graaff Hunter; 2ndly, 1969, Arthur Eustace Farmiloe, and *d* 1992, leaving issue (by 1st *m*), Sarah Stewart, *b* 1949: *m* 1st, 1971 (*m* diss 1977), David Peter Edmund Harrington; 2ndly, 1984, Anthony John Beerbohm, of La Higuera, Calle Piedras, Gaucin (Malaga), Spain.

Granddaughter of late Lieut-Col Cyril Francis Tyrrell Murray, CB, MVO, 3rd son of late Brig-Gen Alexander Henry Murray (ante):—
Issue of late Brigadier Cyril Alexander George Octavius Murray, DSO, *b* 1887, *d* 1960: *m* 1922, Marjorie Lilias, who *d* 1965, da of late W. Jennings Milles, MD, FRCS of Shanghai:—
Anne Elizabeth (2 Mansfield Place, Moffat, Dumfriesshire DG10 9DS), *b* 1937.

Granddaughters of late Lt-Col Sir Malcolm Donald Murray, GCVO, CB, CIE, 4th son of late Brig-Gen Alexander Henry Murray (ante):—
Issue of late Lt-Col Iain Arthur Murray, DSO, *b* 1904, *d* 1986: *m* 1st, 1932 (*m* diss 1946), Angela Houssemayne, da of late Lt-Col Arthur Houssemayne du Boulay, DSO; 2ndly, 1947 (*m* diss 1957), Anne, who *d* 1985, da of late Vice-Adm Hon Edmund Rupert Drummond, CB, MVO (*see* F. Perth, colls):—
(By 1st *m*) Virginia Anne (45 Castle Rd, Isleworth, Middx TW7 6QR), *b* 1934: *m* 1st, 1955 (*m* diss 1963), Anthony Gordon Reid; 2ndly, 1964 (*m* diss 1977), D. Ricardo Saenz de Heredia, and has issue living (by 1st *m*), Iain Malcolm Gordon, *b* 1956: *m* 1980, Susan McLeod, who *d* 1998, and has issue living, Philippa Susanna *b* 1986, Serena Madeleine *b* 1994, — (by 2nd *m*) Ricardo, *b* 1968, — Roberto, *b* 1969, — Pedro, *b* 1970. —— Serena Jane, *b* 1939: *m* 1963, Konradin Geotte Vidigal, of Avenida do Brazil, 130 2E Lisbon 5, Portugal.

PREDECESSORS – **(1)** *Rt Hon Lord* Charles Murray, 2nd son of 1st Marquess of Athole; Master of the Horse to Queen Mary II of England; *cr Lord Murray of Blair, Moulin and Tillimet (Tullimet), Viscount Fincastle* and *Earl of Dunmore* (peerage of Scotland) 1686; *d* 1710; *s* by his cl son **(2)** JOHN, 2nd Earl; a Gen in the Army, and a Representative Peer; *d* 1752; *s* by his brother **(3)** WILLIAM, 3rd Earl, having taken part in the rebellion of 1745, was in 1746 tried for high treason and pleaded guilty, but obtained the King's pardon; *s* by his son **(4)** JOHN, 4th Earl; a Representative Peer 1761-84, Gov of New York 1769-70, Virginia 1770-76, and Bahamas 1787-96; *d* 1809; *s* by his son **(5)** GEORGE, 5th Earl; *cr Baron Dunmore*, of Dunmore (peerage of United Kingdom) 1831; *d* 1836; *s* by his son **(6)** ALEXANDER EDWARD, 6th Earl: *b* 1804: *m* 1836, Catherine who *d* 1886, da of 11th Earl of Pembroke; *d* 1845; *s* by his son **(7)** CHARLES ADOLPHUS, 7th Earl; *b* 1841; a Lord-in-Waiting to Queen Victoria 1874-80, and Lord-Lt of co Stirling 1875-85: *m* 1866, Lady Gertrude Coke, who *d* 1943, da of 2nd Earl of Leicester; *d* 1907; *s* by his son **(8)** ALEXANDER EDWARD, VC, DSO, MVO, 8th Earl; *b* 1871; Maj 16th Lancers; served with Soudan Field Force 1896, and Malakand Field Force 1897-98 (VC); S Africa 1899-1900; Comdg 31st Batn Imperial Yeo 1902; 1915-17 War (twice wounded, DSO); Capt Hon Corps of Gentlemen-at-Arms 1924, and a Lord-in-Waiting to HM 1930-36: *m* 1904, Lucinda Dorothea, who *d* 1966, el da of late Col Horace William Kemble, of Toravaig, Skye (Mackenzie, Bt, *cr* 1702, colls): *d* 1962; *s* by his grandson **(9)** JOHN ALEXANDER (son of late Capt Edward David, Viscount Fincastle, (*ka* 1940), only son of 8th Earl) 9th Earl, *b* 1939; Lt Queen's Own Cameron Highlanders: *m* 1967, Anne Augusta, da of Thomas Clouston Wallace, of Holodyke, Dounby, Orkney; *d* 1980; *s* by his kinsman **(10)** REGINALD ARTHUR (great great grandson of Lt-Col Hon Alexander Murray, 2nd son of 4th Earl) 10th Earl, *b* 1911: *m* 1948, Patricia Mary (who *m* 2ndly, 1984, Geoffrey Fitze), da of Frank Coles, of Robigana, W Tamar, Tasmania; *d* 1981; *s* by his brother **(11)** KENNETH RANDOLPH 11th Earl; *b* 1913; Sergeant 12th/50th Btn Australian Inf; JP: *m* 1938, Margaret Joy, who *d* 1976, da of P. D. Cousins, of Burnie, Tasmania; *d* 1995; *s* by his son **(12)** MALCOLM KENNETH, 12th Earl and present peer, also Viscount Fincastle, Lord Murray of Blair, Moulin and Tillimet (Tullimet).

DUNN, BARONESS (Thomas) (Life Baroness 1990)

LYDIA SELINA DUNN, DBE, da of late Yenchuen Yeh Dunn; *b* 29 Feb 1940; *ed* St Paul's Convent Sch, Hong Kong, and Univ of Calif at Berkeley (BS); Hon LLD Chinese Univ of Hong Kong 1984, Univ of Hong Kong 1991, and Univ of BC 1991; JP; Chm Swire & Maclaine Ltd since 1982, Exec Dir Swire Pacific Ltd since 1982; Chm Hong Kong Trade Devpt Council 1983-91; Dir Cathay Pacific Airways Ltd since 1985, Volvo 1991-93 (Memb Internat Advisory Board 1985-91), and Hong Kong Seibu Enterprise Co Ltd since 1989; Dep-Chm Hongkong & Shanghai Banking Corpn since 1992 (Dir 1981-92), and HSBC Holdings plc (formerly Hong Kong and Shanghai Banking Corpn Holdings (London)) since 1992 (Dir 1990-92); Chm Lord Wilson Heritage Trust since 1993, Hong King/Japan Business Co-operation Cttee since 1988 (Member since 1983); Memb Legislative Council 1976-88 (Sr Memb 1985-88), Hong Kong/US Econ Co-op Cttee 1984-93; Prime Minister of Japan's Trade Award 1987; Sr Member Exec Council Hong Kong since 1988; has retained her maiden name; *cr* OBE (Civil) 1978, CBE (Civil) 1983, DBE 1989, and *Baroness Dunn*, of Hong Kong Island in Hong Kong and of Knightsbridge in the Royal Borough of Kensington and Chelsea (Life Baroness) 1990: *m* 1988, Michael David Thomas, CMG, QC.

Addresses – John Swire & Sons (HK) Ltd, 5th Floor, Swire House, 9 Connaught Rd, Central Hong Kong; Somerford Keynes House, Cirencester, Glos. *Clubs* – Hong Kong, and Royal Hong Kong Jockey.

DUNRAVEN and MOUNT-EARL, EARL OF (Wyndham-Quin) (Earl I 1822 Bt GB 1781)

Head of the serpent for ever

THADY WINDHAM THOMAS WYNDHAM-QUIN, 7th Earl, and 7th Baronet; *b* Oct 27th, 1939; *s* 1965; *ed* Le Rosey: *m* 1969, Geraldine, da of Air Commodore Gerard Ward McAleer, CBE, of Wokingham, Berks, and has issue.

ꙮrms – Quarterly, 1st and 4th gules, a hand couped below the wrist grasping a sword all proper between in base two serpents erect and respecting each other, tails nowed or, in chief two crescents argent, *O'Quin of Munster*; 2nd and 3rd azure, a chevron between three lions' heads erased or, a mullet for difference, *Wyndham*. ꙮrest – 1st, wolf's head, erased argent, *Quin*; 2nd, a lion's head erased within a fetter-lock and chain or, *Wyndham*. ꙮupporters – Two ravens with wings elevated proper, collared and chained or.
Residence – Kilgobbin House, Adare, co Limerick. *Club* – Kildare Street.

DAUGHTER LIVING

Lady Ana, *b* 1972.

SISTERS LIVING

Lady Melissa Eva Caroline, *b* 1935: *m* 1959, Major Sir George Cecil Francis Brooke, 3rd Bt, MBE, of Glenbevan, Croom, co Limerick, who *d* 1982.
Lady Caroline Olein Geraldine (*Marchioness of Waterford*), *b* 1936: *m* 1957, 8th Marquess of Waterford, of Curraghmore, Portlaw, co Waterford, and Glenbride Lodge, Valleymount, co Wicklow.

COLLATERAL BRANCH LIVING

Issue of late Capt Hon Valentine Maurice Wyndham-Quin, RN, yr son of 5th Earl, *b* 1890, *d* 1983: *m* 1919, Marjorie Elizabeth, who *d* 1969, da of late Rt Hon Ernest George Pretyman (E Bradford):—
Marjorie Olein (*Marchioness of Salisbury*), *b* 1922: *m* 1945, 6th Marquess of Salisbury. —— Pamela (*Dowager Baroness Egremont*), *b* 1925: *m* 1947, 6th Baron Leconfield and 1st Baron Egremont, who *d* 1972. *Residence* – Cockermouth Castle, Cockermouth, Cumbria.

PREDECESSORS – (1) VALENTINE RICHARD Quin; *cr a* Baronet 1781, *Baron Adare* (peerage of Ireland) 1800, *Viscount Mount-Earl* (peerage of Ireland) 1816, and *Viscount Adare* and *Earl of Dunraven and Mount-Earl* (peerage of Ireland) 1822; *d* 1824; *s* by his son (2) WINDHAM HENRY, 2nd Earl; assumed the additional surname of Wyndham by Roy licence 1815; a Representative Peer; *d* 1850; *s* by his son (3) EDWIN RICHARD WINDHAM, KP, 3rd Earl; *b* 1812; MP for Glamorganshire (C) 1836-50; Lieut of co Limerick; *cr Baron Kenry*, of co Limerick (peerage of United Kingdom) 1866: *m* 1st 1836, Augusta, who *d* 1866, da of Thomas Goold, a Master in Changery; 2ndly 1870, Anne, who *d* 1917, da of Henry Lambert of Carnagh co Wexford; *d* Oct 6th, 1871; *s* by his son (4) *Rt Hon* WINDHAM THOMAS, KP, 4th Earl *b* 1841; Parliamentary Under-Sec of State for the Colonies 1885-86, and HM Lieut for co Limerick 1894-1926; a Senator of Irish Free State 1922-6: *m* 1869, Florence, who *d* 1916, da of late Lord Charles Lennox Kerr; *d* 1926, when the Barony of Kenry became ext, while the Irish titles and the Baronetcy devolved upon his cousin (5) WINDHAM HENRY, CB, DSO (el son of late Capt the Hon Windham Henry Wyndham-Quin, 2nd son of 2nd Earl), 5th Earl, *b* 1857; Major 16th Lancers,

Capt and Hon Major Gloucestershire Yeo Cav, and Lieut-Col Comdg and Hon Col Glamorganshire Yeo; Transvaal Campaign 1881, S Africa 1900-01 with Imperial Yeo (despatches, DSO); was ADC and Mil Sec to Gov of Madras 1886-89, and High Sheriff for co Kilkenny 1914; sat as MP for Glamorganshire, S Div (C) 1895-1906: *m* 1885, Lady Eva Constance Aline, who *d* 1940, da of 6th Earl of Mayo; *d* 1952; *s* by his son **(6)** RICHARD SOUTHWELL WINDHAM ROBERT, CB, CBE, MC, 6th Earl, *b* 1887; Master of the Horse and Mil Sec to Lords Lieut of Ireland 1918-21: *m* 1st, 1915 (*m diss* 1932), Helen, who *d* 1962, da of late John Swire, of Hillingdon House, Harlow; 2ndly, 1934, Nancy, who *d* 1994, da of Thomas Burks Yuille, of Halifax Co, Virginia; *d* 1965; *s* by his only son **(7)** THADY WINDHAM THOMAS, 7th Earl and present peer; also Viscount Mount-Earl, Viscount Adare, and Baron Adare.

DUNROSSIL, VISCOUNT (Morrison) (Viscount UK 1959)

JOHN WILLIAM MORRISON, 2nd Viscount, CMG; *b* 22 May 1926; *s* 1961; *ed* Fettes, and Oriel Coll, Oxford (BA 1950, MA 1952), Hon Fellow Magdalen Coll, Oxford 1994; DL Western Isles 1990, Lord Lieut of the Islands Area of the Western Isles 1993; formerly Flight-Lieut RAF, entered Commonwealth Relations Office 1951; was Assist Private Sec to Sec of State 1952-4, 2nd Sec, Canberra 1954-56, and 1st Sec and acting Dep High Commr, Dacca, E Pakistan 1958-60; 1st Sec, Pretoria and Capetown 1961-64, and FO 1964-68, and on loan to Intergovernmental Maritime Consultative Organisation 1968-70, and Counsellor and Head of Chancery, Ottawa, 1975-78, Brit High Commr to Fiji (and non-resident in Nauru and Tuvalu) 1978-82, Brit High Commr to Barbados (and non-resident to Antigua and Barbuda, and to St Lucia, Dominica, Grenada, St Vincent and the Grenadines, and St Kitts and Nevis) 1982-83, Gov and C-in-C of Bermuda 1983-88 (ret); CMG (1981); KSt J (1983): *m* 1st, 1951 (*m diss* 1969), Mavis Dawn, da of A. Llewellyn Spencer-Payne, LRCP, MRCS, LDS; 2ndly 1969, Diana Mary Cunliffe, da of C. M. Vise, and has issue by 1st and 2nd *m*.

Arms – Per bend sinister gules and argent a demi-lion rampant issuant or armed and langued azure holding in his paws a battleaxe the shaft curved of the third and the axehead of the fourth in chief, and in base, issuant from the sea undy vert and or, a tower sable windows and port or, over all a bend sinister embattled azure charged with an open crown or jewelled gules between two fleurs-de-lys argent; within a bordure vert for difference. Crest – Issuant from waves of the sea azure crested argent, a mount vert, thereon an ambatfled wall azure masoned argent, charged with a portcullis or, and issuant therefrom a cubit arm naked proper, the hand grasping a dagger azure hilted or. Supporters – Two lions regardant or armed and langued gules collared vert supporting between their exterior forepaws and interior hind paws battleaxes azure, the shafts embowed.
Residence – Dunrossil, Clachan Sands, by Lochmaddy, N Uist, Western Isles HS6 5AY.

SONS LIVING (By 1st marriage)

Hon ANDREW WILLIAM REGINALD, *b* 15 Dec 1953; *ed* Eton, and Univ Coll, Oxford: *m* 1986, Carla Marie Brundage, and has issue living, Callum Alasdair Brundage, *b* 12 July 1994, — Catriona Leslie, *b* 1986, — Meredith Marie, *b* 1988, — Camilla Brooke, *b* 1991. *Residence* – 132 Park Hill, San Antonio, Texas 78201, USA.

Hon Ranald John, *b* 1956; *ed* Westminster, and Univ Coll, London (BSc): *m* 1979, Henrietta Frances, da of late J. H. Wilson, of Addison Rd, W8, and of Mrs Carey-Wilson, of Halewell, Withington, Glos, and has issue living, Richard Donald, *b* 1983, — Alexander Thomas, *b* 1988, — Allison Catherine, *b* 1984, — Rebecca Louise, *b* 1987. *Residence* – 9 Hurlingham Rd, St Andrews, Bristol.

Hon Alasdair Godfrey, *b* 1962: *m* 1987, Tania M., only da of J. A. Redman, of Minehead, Som. *Residence* – 81 Fifth Cross Rd, Twickenham, Middx TW2 5UJ.

DAUGHTERS LIVING (By 1st marriage)

Hon Catriona Mary, *b* 1952: *m* 1973, John James Galt, and has issue living, Iain Robert, *b* 1978, — Malcolm David, *b* 1982, — Sarah Christine, *b* 1976, — Emma, *b* 1986, — Erin, *b* 1988.

(By 2nd marriage)

Hon Joanna Catherine, *b* 1971. *Residence* – 13 Bloemfontein Av, W12 7BJ.

Hon Mary Allison, *b* 1972. *Residence* – Callo 100, No 10.25 (Apto 604), Santa Fe de Bogota, Colombia.

BROTHER LIVING

Hon Alasdair Andrew Orr, *b* 1929; *ed* Fettes, and Balliol Coll, Oxford (MA); PhD, Chicago; High Sheriff of Glos 1983: *m* 1958, Frances Mary, da of Wilfrid Rippon Snow, of Adelaide, S Australia, and has issue living, William Alasdair Ewing, *b* 1960, — Alexandra Mary, *b* 1962: *m* 1989, David T. M. Young, son of late B. R. Young, of Shiplake, Oxfordshire, and has issue living, Ruaridh *b* 19—, Fergus *b* 19—, —, Joanna Allison, *b* 1964. *Residence* – Maisemore Lodge, Gloucester.

WIDOW LIVING OF SON OF FIRST VISCOUNT

Sheila Mary, MB BS Lond 1953, MRCS Eng, LRCP Lond 1953, da of Alexander Forbes, of 12 Denmark Rd, Gloucester: *m* 1959, Rev Hon Nial Ranald Morrison, who *d* 1991, following a road accident, and has issue (see colls, infra). *Residence* – 24 Fox Close, Stroud, Glos.

COLLATERAL BRANCH LIVING

Issue of late Rev Hon Nial Ranald Morrison, 3rd son of 1st Viscount, *b* 1932, *d* 1991, following a road accident: *m* 1959, Sheila Mary, MB BS, MRCS, LRCP (ante), da of Alexander Forbes, of 12 Denmark Rd, Gloucester:—
Neil William Alexander, *b* 1961: *m* 1992, Clare E., da of John Molloy, of Haslemere, Surrey. —— John Forbes, *b* 1963: *m* 1996, Rosette Muzigo, da of Joab Kawaaluko, of Nabarumba, Uganda. —— Hugh Robert Shepherd, *b* 1965. —— (Alison) Mary, *b* 1960: *m* 1992, Paul A. Broad, son of Richard Broad, of Dunkeswell, Devon. —— (Elizabeth) Iona, *b* 1969: *m* 1992, Dr Mark W. James, son of Kenneth James, of Birdwood, Glos.

PREDECESSORS – (1) *Rt Hon* WILLIAM SHEPHERD Morrison, GCMG, MC, PC, QC, son of late John Morrison, of Torinturk, Argyll; *b* 1893; Recorder of Walsall Feb to Nov 1935; Private Sec to Solicitor-Gen 1922-23 and 1924-27, and to Attorney-Gen 1927-28; again Parliamentary Private Sec to Attorney-Gen 1931-5, Financial Sec to Treasury 1935-6, Min of Agriculture and Fisheries 1936, Chancellor of Duchy of Lancaster and Min of Food 1939-40, and Postmaster-Gen 1940-43; Min for Town and County Planning 1943-45, Speaker of House of Commons 1951-9, and Gov-Gen and Com-in-Ch of Commonwealth of Australia 1960-61; European War 1914-19 as Capt RFA (Special Reserve) in France (wounded, despatches thrice, MC); sat as MP for Cirencester and Tewkesbury Div of Gloucestershire 1929-59; *cr Viscount Dunrossil*, of Vallaquie, Isle of North Uist, co Inverness (peerage of United Kingdom) 1959: *m* 1924, (Catherine) Allison (a C St J), who *d* 1983, da of late Rev William Swan, DD, Min of South Leith Parish; *d* 1961; *s* by his el son (2) JOHN WILLIAM, 2nd Viscount and present peer.

DUNSANY, BARON OF (Plunkett) (Baron I 1439)
(Title pronounced "Dunsayny")

FESTINA LENTE

Quick, without impetuosity

EDWARD JOHN CARLOS PLUNKETT, 20th Baron; *b* 10 Sept 1939; *s* 1999; *ed* Eton, Slade Sch of Fine Art, and Ecole des Beaux Arts, Paris: *m* 1982, Maria Alice Villela de Carvalho, and has issue.

𝕬rms – Sable, a bend, and in the sinister chief a tower argent. 𝕮rest – A horse passant argent. 𝔖upporters – *Dexter*, a pegasus per fesse or and argent; *sinister*, an antelope argent, armed, unguled, plain collared and chained, or.
Seat – Dunsany Castle, co Meath. *Town Residence* – 32 Margaretta Terrace, SW3 5NX.

SONS LIVING

Hon RANDAL, *b* 9 March 1983.
Hon Oliver, *b* 1985.

HALF-SISTER LIVING

Hon Beatrice Mary, *b* 1948.

WIDOW LIVING OF NINETEENTH BARON

SHEILA VICTORIA KATRIN (*Dowager Baroness Dunsany*), da of Capt Sir Henry Erasmus Edward Philipps, 2nd Bt (*see* Foley-Philipps, Bt, ext), and widow of Maj John Frederick Foley, Baron de Rutzen, Welsh Gds: *m* 1947, as his 2nd wife, Lt-Col the 19th Baron Dunsany, who *d* 1999. *Residence* – Dunsany Castle, co Meath.

COLLATERAL BRANCH LIVING

Issue of late Adm the Hon Sir Reginald Aylmer Ranfurly PLUNKETT-ERNLE-ERLE-DRAX, KCB, DSO (who assumed by Royal licence for himself and issue 1916, the additional surnames and arms of Ernle, Erle and Drax, after that of Plunkett), 2nd son of 17th Baron, *b* 1880, *d* 1967: *m* 1916, Kathleen, who *d* 1980, da of Quintin Chalmers, MD, JP:—

(Henry) Walter (Charborough Park, Wareham, Dorset), *b* 1928; Lt-Cdr RN (ret); a JP and DL of Dorset, High Sheriff 1988: *m* 1957, Hon Pamela Rose Weeks, da of 1st Baron Weeks, and has issue living, Richard Grosvenor, *b* 1958; late Coldstream Gds: *m* 1st, 1985 (*m diss* 1997), Zara Victoria, yr da of William Nigel Henry Legge-Bourke (*see* E Dartmouth, colls); 2ndly, 1998, Eliza Sarah, yst da of late Cmdr James George Greville Dugdale, RN, of Salterton, Salisbury, Wilts, and has issue living (by 1st *m*), Toby Henry *b* 1989, James William *b* 1995, Tamara Katherine *b* 1987, Natasha Shan *b* 1993, — Jeremy Ryton, *b* 1960, — Charles Ranfurly (High Fogrigg, Bardon Mill, Hexham, Northumberland), *b* 1962: *m* 1990, Camilla Mary, only da of Christopher Robin St Quintin Wall, of The Apple Orchard, Bradenham, High Wycombe, Bucks (*see* E Crawford, 1995 Edn), and has issue living, Michael Oliver *b* 1996, Katherine Anne *b* 1994, — Mark Wyndham, *b* 1967, — Edward Quintin, *b* 1971. —— Patricia Doreen, *b* 1919: *m* 1953, Col Neil Stanley Eustace Maude, RM (ret), who *d* 1987, of Priory Farmhouse, Wheathill, Somerton, Som, and has issue living, Nicholas John Eustace, *b* 1953; *ed* Winchester: *m* 1993, Alison, da of Donald Sword, of Yarnhams, Upper Froyle, Hants, and has issue living, Beatrice Belinda *b* 1994, — Julia Jane, *b* 1954: *m* 1st, 1986 (*m diss* 1988), Charles Miller, son of late Wladek Miller, of London; 2ndly, 1994, Thomas Walter Bullard King, of 37 Rodenhurst Rd, SW4 8AE, son of Peter King, of Bylaugh, Norfolk, and has issue living (by 2nd *m*), Olivia Clare Victoria *b* 1996, — Sarah Anne, *b* 1956: *m* 1981, Richard William James Parry, of 72 Ritherdon Rd, SW17 8QG, and has issue living, William *b* 1989, Edward *b* 1997, Sophie *b* 1983, Emily *b* 1985. —— Mary (*Baroness Robert Rothschild*) (43 Ranelagh Grove, SW1), *b* 1925: *m* 1st, 1948, Robert Gustaf Percy Hollond; 2ndly, 1973, Baron Robert Rothschild, who *d* 1998, and has issue living (by 1st *m*), Thomas Robert, *b* 1950; *ed* Milton Abbey, — John Ernle, *b* 1953; *ed* Eton, — James Nicholas, *b* 1959: *m* 1985, Beatrice Hannah Millicent, da of Brian Entwhistle Hare, of Chartley, Fleet, Hants, and has issue living, Oscar James St John *b* 1995, Leo Robert William *b* 1998, Phoebe Natasha Lara *b* 1989, Lara Blaise *b* 1991, — Eliza Jane, *b* 1965: *m* 1998, Edward S. C. Blood, only son of Peter Blood, of Stone, Staffs.

PREDECESSORS – (1) *Sir* CHRISTOPHER Plunkett, 2nd son of 1st Baron Killeen (E Fingall); *cr Baron of Dunsany* by writ (peerage of Ireland) 1439, and by patent 1461; *s* by his son (2) RICHARD, 2nd Baron; *s* by his son (3) JOHN, KG, 3rd Baron; *s* by his son (4) EDWARD, 4th Baron; *d* 1521; *s* by his son (5) ROBERT, 5th Baron; one of the Peers of Parliament held at Dublin 1541; *s* by his son (6) CHRISTOPHER, 6th Baron; *s* by his son (7) PATRICK, 7th Baron; *s* by his son (8) CHRISTOPHER, 8th Baron; *s* by his son (9) PATRICK, 9th Baron; summoned to Parliament 1625 and 1660-6; *s* by his grandson (10) CHRISTOPHER, 10th Baron; *d* unmarried; *s* by his brother (11) RANDAL, 11th Baron; for his adherence to James II, was outlawed, but by the treaty of Limerick his estates were restored, but neglecting the forms necessary to re-establish himself in the privileges of the peerage he had not a seat in Parliament; *d* 1735; *s* by his son (12) EDWARD, 12th Baron, conformed to the Established Church but took no step to confirm his right to a seat in Parliament; *d* 1781; *s* by his son (13) RANDAL, 13th Baron; claimed and was allowed his seat in Parliament 1791; *d* 1821; *s* by his son (14) EDWARD WADDING, 14th Baron; *b* 1773: *m* 1st, 1803, Hon Charlotte Louisa Lawless, who *d* 1819, da of 1st Baron Cloncurry; 2ndly, 1823, Hon Eliza, da of 7th Baron Kinnaird; *d* 1848; *s* by his el son (15) RANDAL EDWARD, 15th Baron, *dsp* 1852; *s* by his brother (16) EDWARD, 16th Baron; *b* 1808; an Adm and a Representative Peer: *m* 1846, Hon Anne Constance Dutton, who *d* 1858, da of 2nd Baron Sherborne; *d* 1889; *s* by his son (17) JOHN WILLIAM, 17th Baron; *b* 1853; a Representative Peer for Ireland; MP for Gloucestershire, S, or Thornbury, Div (*C*) 1886-92: *m* 1877, Ernle Elizabeth Louisa Maria Grosvenor, who *d* 1916 (having assumed by Roy licence 1906 the surnames of Plunkett-Ernle-Drax), only child of late Col Francis Augustus Plunkett Burton, Coldstream Guards; *d* 1899; *s* by his el son (18) EDWARD JOHN MORETON DRAX, 18th Baron; *b* 1878; a Poet, Playwright and Author; Byron Professor, Athens Univ 1941, Pres of Authors' Club 1953-57: *m* 1904, Lady Beatrice Child-Villiers, who *d* 1970, da of 7th Earl of Jersey; *d* 1957, *s* by his only son (19) RANDAL ARTHUR HENRY, 19th Baron, *b* 1906; Lt-Col Indian Cav (Guides), N-W Frontier of India 1930 (medal with clasp): *m* 1st, 1938 (*m diss* 1947), Vera, who *d* 1986, da of Col Genesio de Sà Sottomaior, of San Paolo, Brazil, and formerly wife of John Felix Charles (Ivar) Bryce; 2ndly, 1947, Sheila Victoria Katrin, da of Capt Sir Henry Erasmus Edward Philipps, 2nd Bt (*see* Foley-Philipps, Bt, ext), and widow of Maj John Frederick Foley, Baron de Rutzen, Welsh Gds; *d* 1999; *s* by his only son (20) EDWARD JOHN CARLOS, 20th Baron and present peer.

*Lord Dunsany is thought to be heir male and heir general to the Earls of Fingall (ext 1984), whereby he is also held to be Baron of Killeen.

Dunwich, Viscount; son of Earl of Stradbroke.

DU PARCQ, BARONY OF (du Parcq) (Extinct 1949)

SON LIVING OF LIFE BARON

Hon John Renouf (10 Anchor Quay, Norwich, Norfolk NR3 3PR), *b* 1917; *ed* Rugby, and Exeter Coll, Oxford (MA); MIEE: *m* 1940, Elizabeth Anne, da of late Evan Skull Poole, and has issue.

DAUGHTER LIVING OF LIFE BARON

Hon Catherine Simonne: *m* 1939, Leslie Twelvetrees, who *d* 1984. *Residence* – 115 Dover House, Dover Street, Leicester LE1 6PP, and has issue.

Dupplin, Viscount; son of Earl of Kinnoull.

DURHAM, EARLDOM OF (Lambton) (Earl UK 1833, disclaimed 1970)

The day will come

ANTONY CLAUD FREDERICK LAMBTON; *b* 10 July 1922; *s* as 6th Earl of Durham, 4 Feb 1970; disclaimed his peerages for life 23 Feb, 1970, but was allowed by Mr Speaker Lloyd to sit in the House of Commons as 'Lord Lambton' and later was so designated for three years while holding an office of profit under the Crown; patron of two livings; PPS to Min of Supply 1954, and to Foreign Sec 1955-57; an Under-Sec, Min of Defence 1970-73; MP for Berwick-upon-Tweed (*C*) 1951-73: *m* 1942, Belinda Bridget, da of late Capt Douglas Holden Blew-Jones, and has issue.

Arms – Quarterly: 1st sable, a fesse between three lambs passant argent, *Lambton*; 2nd argent, a fesse gules, between three popinjays vert, collared gules, *Lumley*; 3rd argent, an escutcheon sable, within an orle of eight cinquefoils gules, *Hedworth*; 4th argent, three cinquefoils gules, *D'Arcy*. **Crest** – A ram's head cabossed argent, horns sable. **Supporters** – (borne by Earls of Durham). Two lions, the *dexter* gules, the *sinister* azure, each ducally gorged or, and supporting a flagstaff or, therefrom flowing a banner azure, the dexter charged with a cross patonce and the sinister with a lion passant guardant or.
Seats – Lambton Castle, Fence Houses, co Durham; Fenton, Wooler, Northumberland. **Residences** – Biddick Hall, Lambton Park, Chester-le-Street, co Durham; Villa Cetinale, Sovicille, Siena, Italy.

SON LIVING

Hon EDWARD RICHARD (styled *Baron Durham*), *b* 19 Oct 1961: *m* 1st, 1983 (*m diss* 19—), Christabel Mary, yst da of late Roderick (Rory) McEwen, of Bardrochat, Colmonell, Ayrshire (*see* McEwen, Bt, colls); 2ndly, 1995, Catherine Celinda Leopoldine, eldest da of Desmond John Villiers FitzGerald, 29th Knight of Glin, of Glin Castle, co Limerick, and has issue living (by 1st *m*), Frederick, *b* 23 Feb 1985.

DAUGHTERS LIVING

Lady Lucinda, *b* 1943; writer, photographer, and television broadcaster as Lucinda Lambton: *m* 1st, 1965 (*m diss* 19—), Henry Mark Harrod, el son of Sir (Henry) Roy Forbes Harrod (*see* Ffolkes, Bt colls, 1976 Edn); 2ndly, 1986 (*m diss* 19—), as his 2nd wife, Sir Edmund John William Hugh Ramsay-Fairfax-Lucy, 6th Bt; 3rdly, 1991, as his 2nd wife, Sir Peregrine Gerard Worsthorne (*see* E Lindsey and Abingdon, colls), and has issue living (by 1st *m*), Henry Barnaby *b* 1965, — Huckleberry Nathaniel *b* 1967. *Residence* – The Old Rectory, Hedgerley, Bucks.

Lady Beatrix Mary, *b* 1949: *m* 1st, 1971, George William Bowdrey, son of Henry George Bowdrey; 2ndly, 1982, Guy Rupert Gerard Nevill (*see* M Abergavenny), who *d* 1993, and has issue living (by 1st *m*), Honey, *b* 19—; has issue living (by Andrew Pitkin), Amber *b* 1994, — Rose Violet, *b* 1973. *Residence* – The Garden House, Eridge Park, Tunbridge Wells, Kent.

Lady Rose Diana, *b* 1952: *m* 1979 (*m diss* 1989), (Herbert) Oliver FitzRoy Musker (*see* V Daventry, 1985 Edn), and has issue living, Claud, *b* 1977, — Sam, *b* 1982, — Lily, *b* 1981. *Residence* – Malcolm House, Batsford, Moreton-in-Marsh, Glos.

Lady Mary Gabrielle Ann, *b* 1954; actress (as Anne Lambton).

Lady Isabella, *b* 1958: *m* 1980, Sir Philip Vyvian Naylor-Leyland, 4th Bt, and has issue (see that title). *Residences* – Nantclwyd Hall, Ruthin, N Wales; Milton Hall, Milton Park, Peterborough, Cambs.

HALF-BROTHER LIVING

Hon John George, *b* 1932.

COLLATERAL BRANCHES LIVING

Issue of late Brig-Gen Hon Charles Lambton, DSO, 4th son of 2nd Earl, *b* 1857, *d* 1949: *m* 1912, Lavinia Marion, who *d* 1976, da of late William Henry Garforth, of The Brow, Malton, Yorks (B Middleton):—

Charles William, *b* 1921; *ed* Eton; Major (retired) Coldstream Guards: *m* 1950, Lady Elizabeth Mary Fitzmaurice, da of 6th Marquess of Lansdowne, and has issue living, William Henry Charles, *b* 1951: *m* 1st, 1975, Elizabeth Susan Kingdom; 2ndly, 1989, Sorrel M. G., da of Michael Pym, and has issue living (by 1st *m*), Lucy Marion *b* 1980, Sarah Isabella *b* 1982 (by 2nd *m*), a son *b* 1990, — Julian Edward (Pennybridge House, Pennybridge, Ulverston, Cumbria LA12 7RJ), *b* 1955: *m* 1986, Vanda Jane, yr da of late Lt-Col Charles David Agnew, of Bilborough, York (*see* Agnew, Bt, colls, *cr* 1895), and has issue living, Patrick David Charles *b* 1992, Georgina Marion *b* 1990, — Christopher John (Chapelgill, Broughton, by Biggar ML12 6JA), *b* 1960: *m* 1991, Julie, elder da of Dr James Kenneth Watt Morrice, of Aberdeen, and has issue living, Alexander Maurice *b* 1993, Kitty Norah *b* 1996, — Anne Elizabeth, *b* 1952: *m* 1979, Patrick John Wintour, of

Weavers House, Sandridge Lane, Bromham, Chippenham, Wilts, yr son of late Capt E. R. Wintour, and has issue living, Adam Richard *b* 1988, Laura Katherine *b* 1981, Mary Rose Cecilia *b* 1982, Isabel Martha *b* 1994. *Residence* – The Old Rectory, Calstone, Calne, Wilts SN11 8PZ.

Grandsons of late Hon George Lambton (infra):—
Issue of late John Lambton, Flying Officer RAF, *b* 1909, *ka* 1941: *m* 1934, Ethel Ruth (who *m* 2ndly, 1942, Edwin D. Ballard, of PO Box N9035, Bailey Drive, Coral Harbour, Nassau, Bahamas), only da of late Capt William Henry Nicholson, RN:—
Peter John George (1877 NE Jackson, Bend, Oregon 97701, USA), *b* 1935.

Issue of late Capt Edward George Lambton, RHG, *b* 1918, *d* 1983: *m* 1st, 1949 (*m diss* 1959), Anne, only da of late Col Lawrence Lees, of Cheswardine, Shropshire, and formerly wife of David Rawnsley; 2ndly, 1959, Pauline, who *d* 1996, da of late Herbert Coxon Bolton, and formerly wife of Victor Frederick Cochrane Hervey, Earl Jermyn (afterwards 6th Marquess of Bristol):—
(By 2nd *m*) George, *b* 1962: *m* 1992, Lise, only da of late Niels Blemmer, and has issue living, James, *b* 1994, — Thomas, *b* 1998.

Issue of late Hon George Lambton, 5th son of 2nd Earl, *b* 1860, *d* 1945: *m* 1980, Cecily, who *d* 1972, da of late Sir John (Francis Fortescue) Horner, KCVO:—
Ann Katharine Swynford, OBE (Gregory, Kirknewton, Wooler, Northumberland NE71 6XE), *b* 1912; BA, PhD, D Lit, FBA; Prof Emeritus London Univ; Press Attaché, British Embassy, Teheran 1939-46; OBE (Civil) 1943; Reader Emeritus in Diocese of Newcastle.

Grandchildren of Hon Claud Lambton, 7th son of 2nd Earl:—
Issue of late Cdr Hedworth Lambton, DSC, RN, *b* 1904, *d* 1983: *m* 1st, 1935 (*m diss* 1963), Iris Wynnfred Violet, who *d* 1997, formerly wife of Charles Caulfield Hewitt, and da of William Law Halpin, mining engr; 2ndly, 1963, Olivia, who *d* 1986, widow of Col Denys Redwood Vachell, MC, and da of Reginald Monckton:—
(By 1st *m*) Rosemary Ann, *b* 1936.

Issue of late D'Arcy Lambton, *b* 1908, *d* 1938: *m* 1933, Hon Monica Dorothy Brand (Saxon House, Shottisham, Woodbridge, Suffolk), da of 3rd Viscount Hampden:—
Michael Charles (6 Rosenau Cres, SW11), *b* 1934; *ed* Eton: *m* 1969, Nancy, da of John Gillespie, and has issue living, D'Arcy, *b* 1970: *ed* Eton, and Newcastle Univ: *m* 1997, Joanna, only da of Martin Wells, of Maldon, Essex.

PREDECESSORS – **(1)** *Rt Hon Sir* JOHN GEORGE Lambton, GCB; MP for co Durham 1813-28, Ambassador to Court of Russia, Lord Privy Seal 1830-33, and Gov-Gen of British N America, &c; *cr Baron Durham* (peerage of United Kingdom) 1828, and *Viscount Lambton* and *Earl of Durham* 1833; *d* 1840; *s* by his son **(2)** GEORGE FREDERICK D'ARCY, 2nd Earl; *b* 1828; Lord-Lieut of co Durham; *m* 1854, Lady Beatrix Frances Hamilton, da of 1st Duke of Abercorn; *d* 1879; *s* by his son **(3)** *Rt Hon* JOHN GEORGE, KG, GCVO, 3rd Earl, *b* 1855; bore Queens Consort's Ivory Rod with Dove at Coronation of King George V 1911; was Lord High Steward to HM during visit to India 1911-12: *m* 1882, Ethel Elizabeth Louisa, who *d* 1931, da of late Henry Beilby William Milner; *d* 1928; *s* by his twin brother **(4)** FREDERICK WILLIAM, 4th Earl, *b* 1855; sat as MP for Durham, S (*L*) 1880-85, and for Durham co S-E Div (LU) 1900-1910: *m* 1879, Beatrix, who *d* 1937, da of John Bulteel, of Pamflete, Ivybridge; *d* 1929; *s* by his el son **(5)** JOHN FREDERICK, 5th Earl, *b* 1884: *m* 1st, 1919, Diana Mary, who *d* 1924, da of late Granville Frederick Farquhar (Farquhar, Bt); 2ndly, 1931, Hermione, who *d* 1990, da of Sir George Bullough, 1st Bt; *d* 1970; *s* by his son **(6)** ANTONY CLAUD FREDERICK, 6th Earl, and Viscount Lambton and Baron Durham until he disclaimed his peerages 1970.

DYNEVOR, BARON (Rhys) (Baron GB 1780)

Secret and bold

RICHARD CHARLES URYAN RHYS, 9th Baron; *b* 19 June 1935; *s* 1962; *ed* Eton, and Magdalene Coll, Camb: *m* 1959 (*m diss* 1978), Lucy Catherine King, only da of late Sir John Knewstub Maurice Rothenstein, CBE, and has issue.

Arms – Argent, a chevron between three ravens sable. Crest – A raven sable. Supporters – *Dexter*, a griffin per fesse or and argent, wings addorsed and inverted, tail between the legs; *sinister*, a talbot argent, collared flory counterflory gules, ears ermine, and charged on the shoulder with a trefoil slipped vert.

SON LIVING

Hon HUGO GRIFFITH URYAN, *b* 19 Nov 1966.

DAUGHTERS LIVING

Hon Miranda Jane Caroline, *b* 1960: *m* 1986, David Rule, 2nd son of Ronald William Pritchard Rule, of Deal, Kent and has issue living, James Gareth, *b* 1986, — Rhiannon, *b* 1987.

Hon Sarah Sophia Rhiannon, *b* 1963: *m* 1987 (*m diss* 1998), Dyfrug Williams, eldest son of Daniel Thomas Williams, of Carmarthen, and has issue living, Stefan Orlando, *b* 1988, — Sophie Adeline, *b* 1993.

Hon Susannah Mair Elizabeth, *b* 1964: *m* 1993, Barnaby Stone, 3rd son of Ralph Neville Stone, of Oxford, and has issue living, Matthew Hugo Jonathan, *b* 1994, — Mair Hope Emily, *b* 1999.

AUNT LIVING (*Daughter of 7th Baron*)

Hon Imogen Alice (*Imogen, Viscountess Hampden*) (Old School, Glynde, Lewes), *b* 1903: *m* 1936, 5th Viscount Hampden, who *d* 1975.

WIDOW LIVING OF SON OF SEVENTH BARON

Sheila Mary, formerly wife of Christopher d'Ambrumenil, and only da of late Douglas J. Phillips, of Popley Fields, Basingstoke: *m* 1963, as his 2nd wife, Capt Hon David Reginald Rhys, who *d* 1991, and has issue (see colls infra). *Residence* – Southwick Court Chapel, Southwick, Trowbridge, Wilts BA14 9QB.

COLLATERAL BRANCHES LIVING

Issue of late Capt Hon Elwyn Villiers Rhys, 2nd son of 7th Baron, *b* 1900, *d* 1966: *m* 1931, Diana Sloane, who *d* 1994, da of Maj Roger Cyril Hans Sloane Stanley:—
Daphne Margaret, *b* 1933: *m* 1956, Maurice Brain, of Tower Farm, Whiteparish, Salisbury, and has issue living, Graham Stephen Maurice, *b* 1957, — Patrick John Elwyn, *b* 1959.

Issue of late Capt Hon David Reginald Rhys, yst son of 7th Baron, *b* 1907, *d* 1991: *m* 1st, 1933 (*m diss* 1963), Lady Anne Maud Wellesley, only da of 5th Duke of Wellington; 2ndly, 1963, Sheila Mary (ante), formerly wife of Christopher d'Ambrumenil, and only da of late Douglas J. Phillips, of Popley Fields, Basingstoke:—
(By 1st *m*) Llewelyn Arthur, *b* 1935; *ed* Eton: *m* 1961, Rosemary Martha Ann, elder da of late Rev Canon Robert Victor Sellers, of Burnham-on-Sea, Somerset, and has issue living, Robert David Arthur, *b* 1963, — Julian Nicholas James, *b* 1966, — Fiona Martha Alison, *b* 1962: *m* 1986, Capt R. D. C. James, and has issue living, Charles Richard Arthur *b* 1993, Thomas Valerian *b* 1997, Olivia Martha Alison *b* 1987, Lucinda Sophie Rose *b* 1989. —— Elizabeth Maud, *b* 1937: *m* 1966, Peter Matthew Doran, of 7 Killock, Martello Park, Canford Cliffs, Poole, Dorset BH13 7BA. —— (By 2nd *m*) George Dafydd, *b* 1965; *ed* Milton Abbey, and Caen Univ: *m* 1st, 1992 (*m diss* 1998), Vanessa Donald; 2ndly, 1999, Jayne Nicola Church, and has issue living, (by 1st *m*) Samuel David, *b* 1995.

Grandchildren of late Rev Hon William Talbot Rice, 3rd son of 5th Baron:—
Issue of late Mervyn Gurney Talbot Rice, *b* 1899, *d* 1979: *m* 1st, 1929, Eleanor Butler Adair, who *d* 1965, da of Andrew Williamson; 2ndly, 1969, Esther Lynette Sutherland, who *d* 1990, da of Maj James Reay Sutherland Mackay, of Doune, Perthshire, and widow of Ronald David Stewart-Brown, QC:—
(By 1st *m*) Andrew Gurney Talbot (33 Cornwall Gdns, SW7 4AP), *b* 1930; *ed* Eton, and Worcester coll, Oxford: *m* 1957, Helen Lalage (Gay), only da of late Charles Buchanan, of Chesterhill, Newport-on-Tay, Fife, and has issue living, Richard Bruce, *b* 1957; *ed* Radley, and Durham Univ: *m* 1995, Kathryn J. E., yr da of Dr David Owen, of Bryn y Mor, Fishguard, Pembrokeshire, and has issue living, William David *b* 1997, — Jonathan William Gurney, *b* 1961: *m* 1996, M. L. E. (Tina), da of late Dr Hans Sprinz, of Johannesburg, — Julia Margaret, *b* 1959: *m* 1990, Nicholas W. A. Bannister, eldest son of Michael Bannister, of Coniston Hall, Skipton, N Yorks, and has issue living, Harry Andrew Ayrton *b* 1994, Archibald William Rennie *b* 1995, — Catherine Helen, *b* 1964: *m* 1991, William H. M. Gibson, son of Colin Gibson, of Mare Hill House, Pulborough, W Sussex, and has issue living, Dominic John Mulholland *b* 1993, Angus Michael Mulholland *b* 1995, Tessa Mary *b* 1998. —— David Mervyn Talbot (43A Elizabeth St, SW1), *b* 1935; *ed* Charterhouse, and Worcester Coll, Oxford. —— Nigel Talbot (Yellow Wood, Ethelred Court, Headington, Oxford OX3 9DA) *b* 1938; *ed* Charterhouse, and Ch Ch, Oxford (MA, Dip Ed): *m* 1968, Joanna, da of late Air Commodore Frederick John Manning,

CB, CBE, and has issue living, Samuel Peter Gurney, b 1982, — Sarah Kate, b 1969, — Caroline Emma, b 1971: m 1996, Jonathan M. A. Bewes, eldest son of Michael Keith Bewes, of Lexden, Colchester, — Rebecca Mary, b 1973, — Helena Rachel, b 1977. —— Margaret Adair Talbot, b 1932: m 1956, Rev Edward George Humphrey Saunders, of The Hensol, Shires Lane, Chorleywood, Herts WD3 5NH, and has issue living, Hilary Margaret, b 1959.

Grandchildren of late Capt Henry Charles Talbot Rice, yr son of late Rev Hon Henry Rice, brother of 5th Baron:—
Issue of late Major Harry Talbot Rice, late Welsh Guards, b 1889, d 1948: m 1927, Hon Blanche Marion Devereux, who d 1976, da of 17th Viscount Hereford:—
(David) Arthur Talbot, b 1931; ed Eton, and Ch Ch, Oxford: m 1st, 1957 (m diss 1961), Annabella Frances Serena, da of late Major Cyril Augustus Drummond (see E Perth, colls); 2ndly, 1961, Sylvia Dorothea, da of P. B. Metaxas, of 71 Eaton Place, SW1, and has issue living (by 2nd m), Robert Harry Talbot, b 1963; ed Eton, and Durham Univ; Major WG: m 1991, (Alice) Elspeth Middleton, yr da of David Middleton Lindsley, of Springfield House, Fremington, Richmond, N Yorks, — Alexander Thomas Talbot, b 1969; ed Stowe, and Durham Univ, — Victoria Penelope Helen Talbot, b 1961: m 1994, Mark S. Thorniley, of 163 Engadine St, Southfields, SW18 5DU, yr son of Harold Thorniley, of Kensington, Johannesburg. Residence – Barnfield House, Cowfold, Sussex RH13 8AT. Club – Cavalry and Guards.

Issue of late Lt-Col Prof David Talbot Rice, CBE, TD, FSA, b 1903, d 1972: m 1927, Tamara, author and art historian, who d 1993, adopted da of Boris Abelson, of Paris:—
Nicholas Charles Talbot (Pigeon House, Coln Rogers, Glos, GL54 3LB; Boodle's and Pratt's Clubs), b 1944; ed Eton, and Ch Ch Oxford: m 1973, Jocelyn Mary, da of Maj Robert Higgens, and has issue living, David Henry Talbot, b 1975, — Sophia Elizabeth Talbot, b 1974. —— Elizabeth Roussoudana Talbot, b 1931; ed Edinburgh Univ (MA). —— Nina Violet Tamara Talbot, b 1941: m 1966, Hugh Bredin, and has issue living, Cosmo James, b 1970, — Zoë, b 1972.

PREDECESSORS – (1) WILLIAM Talbot, 1st Earl Talbot (see E Shrewsbury); cr, Baron Dinevor, of Dinevor (usually spelt Dynevor) (peerage of Great Britain) 1780, with remainder to his only da and the heirs male of her body; d 1782; s by his da (2) Lady CECIL, wife of the Rt Hon George Rice, PC, MP (10th descent from Sir Rhys ap Thomas, KG, who joined the Earl of Richmond, late Henry VII, after his landing and assisted him at Bosworth); assumed the surname of de Cardonnell only by Roy licence 1787; d 1793; s by her son (3) GEORGE TALBOT, 3rd Baron; assumed the surname of de Cardonnell by Roy licence 1793, and resumed the name of Rice by Roy licence 1817; Lord-Lieut of Carmarthenshire; d 1852; s by his son (4) GEORGE RICE, 4th Baron; assumed the additional surname of Trevor by Roy licence 1824; d 1869; s by his kinsman (5) FRANCIS WILLIAM, 5th Baron, 2nd son of Very Rev Hon Edward Rice, 2nd son of Baroness Dynevor; b 1804; V of Fairford; d 1878; s by his son (6) ARTHUR DE CARDONNEL, 6th Baron, b 1836: m 1869, Selina, who d 1889, da of late Hon Arthur Lascelles; d 1911; s by his son (7) WALTER FITZ-URYAN, 7th Baron, b 1873; was Assist Sec to Sec of State for India 1899-1903, an Assist Private Sec to First Lord of the Admiralty 1903-5, MP for Brighton (C) 1910-11, a Co Councillor for Carmarthenshire 1919-35, and Lord Lieut for Carmarthenshire 1928-49; re-assumed by Roy licence 1916 for himself and his issue the surname of Rhys in lieu of Rice: m 1898, Lady Margaret Child-Villiers, who d 1959, el da of 7th Earl of Jersey; d 1956; s by his el son (8) CHARLES ARTHUR URYAN, CBE, MC, 8th Baron; b 1899; Capt Gren Guards ; MP for Romford (C) 1923-29, and Guildford 1931-35; PPS to Financial Sec to War Office 1924-26, to Under-Sec of State for the Colonies 1926-27, and to Prime Min 1927-29; 1939-45 War; Pres of Univ Coll of S Wales and Monmouth 1960-62: m 1934, Hope Mary Woodbine, who d 1980, formerly wife of Capt Arthur Granville Soames, OBE, and da of late Charles Woodbine Parish, d 1962; s by his only son (9) RICHARD CHARLES URYAN, 9th Baron, and present peer.

DYSART, COUNTESS OF (Greaves) (Earl S 1643)

ROSAMUND AGNES GREAVES, Countess of Dysart, b 15 Feb 1914; s 1975.

Arms – Azure, and Imperial Crown proper between three mullets argent within a double tressure flory counterflory of. Supporters – Two lions gules collared azure, each collar charged with three mullets argent.
Residence – Bryn Garth Farm, Grosmont, Abergavenny, Gwent.

SISTER LIVING

Lady KATHERINE, b 1 June 1918: m 1941, Lieut-Col John Peter Grant of Rothiemurchus, MBE, Lovat Scouts, who d 1987, and has issue living, John Peter, b 1946; ed Gordonstoun: m 1971, (Wendy) Philippa, da of late John Wybergh Chance, of Llanvapley Court, Mon. and has issue living, James Patrick b 1977, Louisa Katherine b 1975, Alexandra Elizabeth Rose b 1985, — Jane Margery, b 1943: m 1965, Andrew Robert Fowell Buxton, of Bentley Park, Ipswich (see Buxton Bt, colls). Residence – Rothiemurchus, Aviemore, Inverness-shire.

COLLATERAL BRANCHES LIVING

(Descendants in the male line of William Tollemache Lord Huntingtower, who was cr a Bt 1793, are also in remainder to this Baronetcy).

Branch from yst da of Wenefryde Agatha, Countess of Dysart

Issue of late Lady Mary Greaves, yst da of late Wenefryde Agatha, Countess of Dysart, *b* 1921, *d* 1955: *m* 1942, Capt Bernard Albert Blanger, Sec French Legation, Lisbon, who *d* 1950:—
Brigitte BLANGER, *b* 1943; has resumed her maiden name by deed poll 19—: *m* 1st, 1964 (*m diss* 1967), John Fotheringham; 2ndly, 1969 (*m diss* 1976), Pavlos Athanasacopoulos. —— Beatrice Wenefryde, *b* 1945: *m* 1977, Robin Evans, and has issue living, Schuyler Benjamin Lionel, *b* 1978. — Beatrice Rosamund Louisa, *b* 1980. *Residence* – 5 Charlotte Rd, SW13 9QJ.

Branch from yst sister of 9th Earl

Grandchildren of late Lady Agatha Manners Tollemache (sister of 9th Earl), who *d* 1941, having *m* 1882, 3rd Lord Westbury, who *d* 1930:—
See that title.

Branch from 2nd son of William, Lord Huntingtower

Grandchildren of late Sir Lyonel Felix Carteret Eugene Tollemache, 4th Bt, eldest son of late Caroline Tollemache (only da of late Hon Felix Thomas Tollemache, 2nd son of William, Lord Huntingtower, el son of Louisa, Countess of Dysart), who *d* 1867, having *m* 1853, as his 1st wife, Rev Ralph William Lionel Tollemache-Tollemache (infra):—
Issue of late Sir Humphry Thomas Tollemache, 6th Bt, CB, CBE, *b* 1897, *d* (30 March) 1990: *m* 1926, Nora Priscilla, who *d* (24 Oct) 1990, da of John Taylor, of Broomhill, Eastbourne:—
See BARONETAGE.

Issue of late Cynthia Joan Caroline Tollemache, *b* 1890, *d* 1988: *m* 1918, Harry Scott Judd, who *d* 1948:—
Anthony Hubert Scott JUDD (94 Christchurch Av, NW6 7PE), *b* 1919; FRAM: *m* 1956, Gloria Michele, who *d* 1997, da of late Harry Solloway, of Los Angeles, Calif, USA, and has had issue, †Terence Dominic, *b* 1957; pianist; *d* 1979, — Diana Caroline, *b* 1963; LRAM: *m* 1999, Alastair John Brett. —— Barbara Hersilia, *b* 1926.

Grandchildren of late Cynthia Joan Caroline Tollemache (Mrs Judd) (ante):—
Issue of late John Harry Manners Judd, *b* 1924, *d* 1958: *m* 1954, Sarah (who *m* 2ndly, 1959, H. W. J. Cohen, who *d* 1991; and 3rdly, 19—, Maj T. B. Ellis, of Trinity Hall, Bungay, Suffolk NR35 1EX), yr da of Gerald Arthur Millar, of Tewes, Little Sampford, Essex:—
Christopher John Harry JUDD, *b* 1957: *m* 1980, Emma Mary Powell, da of late Paul Francis Powell Williams, and has issue living, Thomas Jack Francis, *b* 1984, — Harry Mark Christopher, *b* 1985, — Katherine Mary, *b* 1981. *Residence* – Tendrings, Debden, Saffron Walden, Essex CB11 3LT. —— Isabella Sarah Veronica, *b* 1955.

Branch from 3rd son of William, Lord Huntingtower

Grandson of late Emily Katherine Tollemache (Mrs George Fitz Roy Cole), da of late Arthur Lionel Tollemache, son of late Hon Arthur Caesar Tollemache, 3rd son of William, Lord Huntingtower (ante):—
Issue of late Derek Arthur Stephen Fitz Roy COLE, MC, *b* 1895, *d* 1971: *m* 1918, Joan Shirley, who *d* 1971, da of Walter Octavius Hudson:—
John Derek COLE, *b* 1920: *m* 1st, 1942 (*m diss* 1959), Beryl Portia Black; 2ndly, 1960, Penelope Ann Hyde-Hartley, and has had issue (by 1st *m*), †Nigel John, *b* 1943; *k* in a motor accident in Holland 1977, *unm*, — Clive Derek (36 Straid-a-Cnoc, Clynder, Helensburgh, Argyll G84 0QX), *b* 1944: *m* 1966, Jennifer, eldest da of Raymond Stanley Labbett, of 20 Laxton Close, Taunton, Som, and has issue living, Alan Derek *b* 1967: *m* 1991, Karen, eldest da of William Hamilton, of Paisley (and has issue living, Ryan Karl *b* 1994), Angela Suzanne *b* 1969: *m* 1991, Colin Oldroyd (and has issue living, Amy Michelle *b* 1995), — Nicholas Peter (3 Boyton Rd, Hollesley, Woodbridge, Suffolk IP12 3LD), *b* 1949: *m* 1972, Janet Barbara, da of late John Bloomfield Cornell, of Colchester, and has issue living, Julia Marie *b* 1972, — (by 2nd *m*), Jeremy Fitz Roy, *b* 1961: *m* 1985, Belinda Joan Elizabeth, da of Douglas Alfred Thomas Riggs, of South View, Piddletrenthide, Dorchester, and has issue living, Matthew James Fitz Roy *b* 1987, Rowanne Elizabeth *b* 1989, — Alicia Jane, *b* 1962. *Residence* – Goose Cottage, Duck St, Cerne Abbas, Dorchester, Dorset.

Descendants, if any, of late Melanie Sophia Tollemache, 2nd da of late Hon Arthur Caesar Tollemache (ante), *b* 1823, *d* 1894, having *m* 1849, Raymond Louis Abrial.

Descendants of late Laura Tollemache, 4th da of late Hon Arthur Caesar Tollemache (ante), *b* 1830, *d* 1908, having *m* 1859, Albert, Comte de Lastic St Jal, who *d* 1865:—
See 1995 Edn.

Branch from 4th son of William, Lord Huntingtower

Grandchildren of late Sir Lyonel Felix Carteret Eugene Tollemache, 4th Bt, eldest son of late Rev Ralph William Lionel Tollemache-Tollemache, eldest son of Rev Hon Hugh Francis Tollemache, 4th son of William, Lord Huntingtower (ante):—

Issue of Sir Humphry Thomas Tollemache, 6th Bt, CB, CBE, *b* 1897, *d* (30 March) 1990: *m* 1926, Nora Priscilla, who *d* (24 Oct) 1990, da of John Taylor, of Broomhill, Eastbourne:—
See BARONETAGE, and ante.

Grandchildren of late Lyulph Ydwallo Odin Nestor Egbert Lyonel Toedmag Hugh Erchenwyne Saxon Esa Cromwell Orma Nevill Dysart Plantagenet Tollemache-Tollemache, 4th son of late Rev Ralph William Lionel Tollemache-Tollemache (ante):—
Issue of late Lyulph Thomas Tollemache, *b* 1899, *d* 1977: *m* 1st, 1924 (*m diss* 1943), Mavis, da of late Rev Charles Tuke, of Ellerslie, NZ; 2ndly, 1946, his cousin, Phyllis Agnes Barham, who *d* 1994, da of late Maj Frederick Pitcairn Nunneley, OBE, MD (*see* Cs Dysart, colls, 1995 Edn):—
(By 1st *m*) Lyulph Hugh Tuke (4 Roland Hill, Glen Eden, Auckland 7, NZ), *b* 1933; *ed* at Wanganui Collegiate Sch; MSCP, London: *m* 1960, Nadja, OBE, el da of late U. Victor Benziger (*see* Cs Dysart, colls, 1990 Edn), and has issue living, Ralph Victor Hugh Thomas, *b* 1968, — Damon Leo, *b* 1969, — Nigel Robert Bentley, *b* 1972, — Rachel Eva, *b* 1961: *m* 1980 (*m diss* 19—), Andrew Thompson, — Amanda Beatrice, *b* 1963, — Melanie Ruth, *b* 1964, — Vanessa Mavis (twin), *b* 1964, — Althea Phyllis Jessica, *b* 1967. —— Diana Rosemary, *b* 1928; *ed* NZ Univ (BA); a JP Croydon: *m* 1949, Saiyad Zarbaft Shah, of Shalimar, 24 Oakfield Rd, West Croydon, Surrey, and has had issue, †Saiyad Mubarak, *b* 1959; Bar Inner Temple 1983: *m* 1988, Cheryl, da of late Paul Scroope, of NSW, Australia, and *d* 1992, leaving issue, Kitab Paul *b* 1989, — Layla Irene Zarbaft, *b* 1949; *ed* Univ of Newcastle upon Tyne; RIBA: *m* 1969, Terry Dawson, MICE, — Shireen Haseena, *b* 1952; *ed* Manchester Univ (BA): *m* 1980, Michael Drew, of 2 Vyvyan Terrace, Clifton, Bristol, and has issue living, Laurence Finn *b* 1983, Rory Capstan *b* 1988, Jay Latimer *b* 1990.

Issue of late Adrian Francis Tollemache, *b* 1903, *d* 1992: *m* 1938, Una Frances (Peggy) (11/59 Brighton Rd, Scarborough 6019, W Australia), da of Lionel Edward MacKenzie, of Perth, W Australia:—
John Jeffrey (146 Calais Rd, Wembley Downs, W Australia), *b* 1941: *m* 1969, Mary Monica Kerin, of Kent, England, and has issue living, Luke Jonathan, *b* 1971. —— Peter Clive, *b* 1948: *m* 1978, Nicola Jill Boyd, of Auckland, NZ, and has issue living, Jonathan Robert, *b* 1980, — Christina Kate, *b* 1983. —— Joan, *b* 1944; BEd: *m* 1st, 1968 (*m diss* 1973), Michael Harvey Blewitt; 2ndly, 1977, Ivan Pummer, BA (Hons), DipEd, of 24 Elphin St, Florcat, W Australia 6014, and has issue living (by 1st *m*), Amanda Jacqueline (9 Bramble Terr, Redhill, Qld 4059), *b* 1966; BA.

Issue of late Saxon George Tollemache, *b* 1904, *d* 1974: *m* 1933, Ruth Bell, who *d* 1975, da of late Frederick George Wayne, of Parawai, Thames, NZ:—
John Saxon Manners (Dysart Lane, Kumeu, NZ), *b* 1943: *m* 1971, Catherine Mary, da of Seymour Jack, and has issue living, Mark Seymour Manners, *b* 1975. —— Elizabeth Mary, *b* 1936: *m* 1966, Maurice John Arthur Fuller, MSc, of 113 Sunrise Av, Mairangi Bay, Auckland, NZ, and has issue living, Michael Arthur, *b* 1968, — Katherine Ruth, *b* 1969, — Louisa Elizabeth, *b* 1974. —— Suzannah Jane, *b* 1940: *m* 1962, John Brian Miller, PhD, ME, of 11 Chaucer Court, Ewelme, Oxford, and has issue living, Hugh Benjamin Tollemache, *b* 1965, — Jane Elizabeth, *b* 1963.

Issue of late Lyonel Dysart Tollemache, *b* 1908, *d* 1990: *m* 1942, Rita Janet Isabel Rowley, of Auckland, NZ:—
Roland Lionel, *b* 1948: *m* 1970, Sarah Norris, of Auckland, NZ, and has issue living, Peter Michael Dysart, *b* 1973, — Christopher Edwin, *b* 1976. —— Pamela Rita (3/18 Walmsley Rd, St Heliers Bay, Auckland, NZ), *b* 1952: *m* 1st, 1976 (*m diss* 1988), Alan John Pickering, LLB; 2ndly, 1994, Dennis Ian Crisp, and has issue living (by 1st *m*), Vanessa Jasmine, *b* 1981.

Issue of late Winifred Dora Tollemache, *b* 1898, *d* 1981: *m* 1926, Laurence Galwey Walker:—
See 1990 Edn.

Issue of late Celia Kathrine Mabel Tollemache, *b* 1901, *d* 1990: *m* 1935, Charles Tennant Smith, who *d* 1971:—
See 1990 Edn.

Grandchildren of late Rev Ralph William Lionel Tollemache-Tollemache (ante):—
Issue of late Lyulph Ydwallo Odin Nestor Egbert Lyonel Toedmag Hugh Erchenwyne Saxon Esa Cromwell Orma Nevill Dysart Plantagenet Tollemache-Tollemache *b* 1876, *d* 1961: *m* 1st, 1897, Winifred Frances, who *d* 1955, da of late Thomas Goldsborough Anderson, of Tauranga, New Zealand; 2ndly, 1957, Kathleen, who *d* 1981, da of Michael Hinge, of Northolt, Middlesex, and widow of Robert William Alexander Geoffrey Gordon, of Huia, New Zealand:—
(By 1st *m*) Archibald Douglas (104 Landscape Rd, Mt Eden, Auckland, NZ), *b* 1910: *m* 1935, Edna, da of late F. C. Willis, of Napier, NZ, and has issue living, Janet Winifred, *b* 1936: *m* 1957, William Winston Lewins, of 75 Belfast St, Hillsborough, Auckland, NZ, and has issue living, Robyn Ann *b* 1963, Denise Gay, *b* 1965, — Yvonne Dorothy, *b* 1938: *m* 1961, John Walker Robinson, c/o 75 Belfast St, Hillsborough, Auckland, NZ, and has issue living, Tania Anne *b* 1962: *m* 1st, 1982, Steven James Cleary who *d* 1989; 2ndly, 1990, Scott Donald Harrison, of 31 Tole St, Ponsonby, Auckland (and has issue living (by 1st *m*), Natalie Yvonne *b* 1985, Rachael Mary *b* (twin) 1985, (by 2nd *m*) Curtis Scott *b* 1991) Vicki Jan *b* 1964: *m* 1986, Jonathan Charles Poole, of 17 Wingrove Av, Epping 2121, Sydney, NSW, Australia, Angela Patricia *b* 1967: *m* 1994, Brett Keith Wilson, of 22 Halesowen St, Sandringham, Auckland (and has issue living, Ridge *b* 1997, Brooke Candice *b* 1995). —— Vivian Rosamund, *b* 1913: *m* 1934, Rev Harold Graham Titterton, of 37A Botanical Rd, Tauranga, NZ, and has issue living, Graham Richard (Gow's Rd, Opotiki, NZ) *b* 1947: *m* 1974, Gaylene, da of James Cooper, of Kati Kati, NZ, and has issue living, Richard Graham *b* 1979, Sandy James *b* 1985, Gretchen Richa *b* 1975, Jennifer Graham, *b* 1937: *m* 1964, John Yeeles, of 820 Idylwood Drive SW, Issaquah, Wash, 98027, USA, and has issue living, Christopher John *b* 1964, Peter Graham *b* 1967, Andrew Scott *b* 1971. —— Ruth Lorraine *b* 1915: *m* 1944, Ivan Edward Salter Bartlett, who *d* 1991, and has issue living, Timothy John (Hahei, NZ), *b* 1951; has issue (by Maxine Kavali), Sarah *b* 1979, Anna *b* 1981, — Jacqueline Jane (35B Wallace St, Herne Bay, Auckland, NZ), *b* 1949: *m* 1971 (*m diss* 1995), John Michael Cochrane Piper, of 50 Hamilton Rd, Herne Bay, Auckland, NZ, and has issue living, Michael David *b* 1980, Megan Emma *b* 1983.

Issue of late Capt Leo (Quintus Tollemache-Tollemache) de Orellana (Plantagenet) Tollemache, *b* 1879, *ka* 1914 (names in brackets were renounced by deed poll 1908): *m* 1906, Jessie Winifred, who *d* 1967, da of late Charles Bryant, of Highbury New Park, N:—
†Eva, *b* 1908. *m* 1935, U. Victor Benziger, who *d* 1962, and *d* 1992, leaving issue (*see* 1990 Edn).

Grandchildren of late Capt Leonè Sextus Denys Oswolf Fraudati Filius Tollemache-Tollemache de Orellana Plantagenet Tollemache, Leicestershire Regt, 6th son of late Rev Ralph William Lionel Tollemache-Tollemache (ante):—

Issue of late Denys Herbert George Tollemache, b 1915, d 1991: m 1st, 1939 (m diss 1948), Eileen Frances Mary, who d 1976, da of late Owen Phelim O'Conor, The O'Conor Don; 2ndly, 1972, Elizabeth Sheila, who d 1998, da of Cecil Hughes:—

(By 1st m) Peter Denys, b 1940. —— Stephen Patrick, b 1946. —— Susan Frances (Lough Urlaur, 13 Willbrook Grove, Rathfarnham, Dublin 14), b 1939. —— Linda Mary, b 1945: m 1975, William Mostyn Llewellyn, of 32 Cambridge Rd, Bexhill-on-Sea, E Sussex, and has issue living, Peter Mostyn Tollemache, b 1982, — Ursula Sarah Tollemache, b 1978.

Grandchildren of late Rev Ralph William Lionel Tollemache-Tollemache (ante):—

Issue of late Maj Lyonulph Cospatrick Bruce Berkeley Jermyn Tullibardine Petersham de Orellaña Dysart Plantagenet Tollemache-Tollemache, b 1892, d 1966: m 1916, Lilian May, who d 1969, da of late Ernest T. W. Pearse, Govt Agent, Kamloops, BC, Canada:—

Miles de Orellaña, b 1918; Lt RNVR: m 1st, 1942, Diana Muriel, da of late Clarence Charles Hatry, publisher; 2ndly, 1944, Margaret E. K., el da of late Henry Williams, of Llwyn Gern, Pontardulais; 3rdly, 1949, Joan Doreen, da of late G. Saxon, Civil Ser, and has issue living, (by 3rd m) Timothy Miles Saxon, b 1950, — Bruce Robert Saxon, b 1951, — Alistair Murray Saxon, b 1953, — Iain Stuart William Saxon (87 Oxford Rd, Cumnor, Oxford OX2 9PD), b 1960; BA: m 1991, Janet Ruth Eva, only da of late Ivor Michael Allen, of Oxford, and has issue living, Nicholas James de Orellaña b 1992, Hannah Ruth de Orellaña b 1996, — Elspeth Mary Joan, b 1956: m 1983, Mark Black.

Issue of late Lyona Decima Veronica Esyth Undine Cyssa Hylda Rowena Viola Adele Thyra Ursula Ysabel Blanche Lelias Dysart Plantagenet Tollemache, b 1878, d 1962: m 1909, Major Charles Cecil Stone, late Berks Yeo, who d 1951:—

†Lyonel Francis Tollemache STONE, b 1909; Capt Coldm Gds: m 1st, 1943 (m diss 1951), Mathilde, da of late G. Henry A. Thomas of New Orleans, USA; 2ndly, 1952 (m diss 1966), Marie Lod (MONTELEONE), da of late Frank Marion Attaway, of New Orleans, USA; 3rdly, 1972, Mrs Christiane Claire McRoberts (418 S Harbor Drive, Key Largo, Florida, USA), da of late Petrus Marthoud, of Lyons, France, and d 1998, leaving issue (by 1st m), Michael Tollemache (1 Cherokee Lane, Covington, La, USA), b 1949: m 19—, — , and has issue living, Barton McIntyre b 1975, Andrew Deslonde b (twin) 1975, Michael Tollemache b 1981, — Mathilde Thomas, b 1945: m 1967, Prieur James Leary, and has issue living, Prieur James b 1968, Ashley Baldwin b 1973, Mathilde Deslonde b 1971.

Issue of late Lyonella Fredegunda Cuthberga Ethelswytha Ideth Ysabel Grace Monica de Orellana Plantagenet Tollemache-Tollemache, b 1882, d 1952: m 1906, Major Frederick Pitcairn Nunneley, OBE, MD (Oxon), who d 1922, formerly Army Med Ser:—

†Lyonella Joan Tollemache, b 1907: m 1935, Ernest Robin Vladimir Kindersley, who d 1986, and d 1998, leaving issue, Patricia Dora Mary (Pond Cottage, Wallcrouch, Wadhurst, E Sussex TN5 7JN), b 1935: m 1966, John Pearman Spencer-Wood, who d 1982, and has issue living, Alexandra Carolina b 1967: m 1988, Richard Neeves, of 2 The Mount, Rotherfield Lane, Mayfield, E Sussex TN20 6AS (and has issue living, Thomas Joshua b 1992, Laura Bryony b 1987, Francesca Sophie b 1991), Sophie Maria b 1970.

Grandchildren of late Lyonetta Edith Regina Valentine Myra Polwarth Avelina Philippa Violantha de Orellana Plantagenet Tollemache (Mrs Adolph Paul Oppé), 8th and yst da of late Rev Ralph William Lionel Tollemache-Tollemache (ante):—

Issue of late Maj Denys Lyonel Tollemache Oppé, MBE, b 1913, d 1992: m 1949, Jean Mary, who d 1997, da of late Charles Struthers White Ogilvie, of Delvine, Murthly, Perthshire:—

John Simon Tollemache OPPÉ, b 1951; ed Ampleforth. —— Lucy Valentine Mary, b 1950. —— Charlotte Mary Clare, b 1954. —— Mary Josephine, b 1956: m 1991, Alexander D. D. Calf, of Chiswick, W4, and has issue living, Thomas Alexander, b 1991, — William, b 1995, — Rebecca Alice, b 1993.

Granddaughter of late Hugh Ernest Tollemache, el son of late Rev Ernest Celestine Tollemache, 3rd son of late Rev Hon Hugh Francis Tollemache, 4th son of William, Lord Huntingtower (ante):—

Issue of late Maj John Ernest Tollemache, b 1898, d 1969: m 1921, Violet Edith Gertrude, who d 1985, da of late W. Rae Sands:—

Lyona Violet Anne Tollemache, b 1929: m 1950, Lt-Cdr Richard Milford Power Carne, RN, of Tresahor Vean, Constantine, Cornwall and Nairobi, Kenya, and has issue living, William Lyonel Power, b 1957, — Caroline Julia Tollemache, b 1951: m 1970 (m diss 1973), D. A. Godley, — Karenza Lyona Tollemache, b 1953: m 1973, Gordon Taylor (c/o PO Box 2374, Randburg 2125, S Africa).

Grandchildren of late Henry Gilbert Tollemache, 2nd son of late Rev Ernest Celestine Tollemache (ante):—

Issue of late Cmdr Douglas Hugh Tollemache, RN, b 1898, d on active service 1941: m 1931, Alys Kynaston (who d 1992, having m 2ndly, 1943, Com Richard Tolson, DSC, RN, who d 1992), da of late Rev John Henry Bebbington, R of Slinfold, Sussex, and Canon of Chichester:—

Ian Henry Douglas (265 King's Rd, SW3), b 1936; ed Lancing: m 1st, 1973 (m diss 19—), Priscilla A. Coker; 2ndly, 1989, Joanna Wilson. —— (Sheila) Rosemary Edith, b 1939: m 1963, T. Barry Nightingale, FCA, of 5 Spinney View, Great Glen, Leics LE8 0EP, and has issue living, Lucy Frances, b 1964, — Kate Elizabeth, b 1965, — Anna Ruth, b 1967.

Issue of late Dorothy Clare Tollemache, b 1895, d 1949: m 1921, Arthur Edward Durling:—

John Alfred Osborne DURLING (5 Stapylton St, Holder, Canberra, ACT, Aust), b 1929: m 1960, Enid Joan Coling, and has issue living, Paul Edward Porttor b 1962, — Richard John, b 1965, — Jillian Clare, b 1969.

Granddaughters of late Dorothy Clare Tollemache (Mrs Durling) (ante):—

Issue of late Pauline Mary Tollemache Durling, b 1924, d 1972: m 1954, John Ingham Brooke, of Brewery House, Southstoke, Bath (see Hewett, Bt, 1990 Edn):—

Penelope Anne (5 The Cliff, Puddingmoor, Beccles, Suffolk), b 1955. —— Susan Miranda, b 1957: 1986, Alexander Marek Andrew Jan Gregor, of 3 Fairfield Rd, Bristol BS6 5JN, and has issue living, Andrzej Maximilian, b 1986.

Grandson of late Gwendoline Anna Tollemache (Mrs Gilbert Henderson Philips), only da of late Rev Ernest Celestine Tollemache (ante):—
Issue of late Constance Gwendoline Joyce, b 1908, d 1987: m 1934, Rev John William Harper Faulkner, who d 1982:—
Alan Henderson FAULKNER, b 1938: m 1964, Anita Diane, da of Harwood Arthur Bence, of Bedford, and has issue living, Lynn Deborah, b 1966, — Tracey Jane, b 1968: m 1996, Stephen Thomas Woods, and has issue living, Anna Katherine b 1997. Residence – 43 Oaks Drive, Colchester, Essex CO3 3PS.

Grandson of late Capt Anastasius Eugene Tollemache son of late Rev Hon Hugh Francis Tollemache (ante):—
Issue of late Louisa Ethelgiva Rowena, b 1878, d 1962: m 1910, as his 2nd wife, Lieut-Col Walter Francis Courtenay Chicheley Plowden, who d 1918:—
Cursham Chicheley PLOWDEN, b 1911; Capt (ret): m 1937, Joan Brown, and has issue living, Robert Henry Bowland Chicheley, b 1947. Residence – The Sun House, Kentsford Rd, Grand-over-Sands, Cumbria.

Grandchildren of late Louisa Harrington Tollemache, b 1833 (who d 1928, having m 1862, Col Rt Hon Thomas Edward Taylor, MP, who d 1883), 2nd da of late Rev Hon Hugh Francis Tollemache (ante):—
See M Headfort, colls.

Branch from 5th son of William, Lord Huntingtower

Descendants of late Ada Maria Katherine Tollemache, b 1848 (who d 1928, having m 1868, the 4th Baron Sudeley), younger da of late Hon Frederick James Tollemache, MP, 5th son of William, Lord Huntingtower (ante):—
See B Sudeley.

Branches from daughters of William, Lord Huntingtower

Descendants of late Louisa Maria Burke, who d 1863 (having m 1849, Rev John´Montagu Mason), el da of late Hon Louisa Grace Tollemache (who d 1830, having m 1816, Sir Joseph Burke, 11th Bt (ext)), el da of William, Lord Huntingtower (ante).

Descendants of late Hon Lady Catherine Camilla Tollemache, b 1792 (who d 1863, having m 1816, Sir George Sinclair, 2nd Bt), 2nd dau of William, Lord Huntingtower (ante).
See V Thurso.

Branches from younger children of Louisa, Countess of Dysart

Descendants, if any, of Algernon Montriou Tollemache (b 1884), Lieut Lancashire Hussars Yeo (ret 1919), only son of late Maj Algernon Seymour Tollemache, only son of William Tollemache, 5th son of Hon Charles Tollemache, 3rd son of Louisa, Countess of Dysart (in her own right).

Granddaughters of late Matilda Jane Tollemache (da of William Tollemache (ante)), who d 1918, having m 1873, Capt Marcus Augustus Stanley Hare, RN, who d 1878:—
Issue of late Ethel Lucy Hare, b 1875, d 1940: m 1901, Sir Herbert Charles Perrott, 6th Bt, CH, CB, who d 1922, when the title became ext:—
See Perrott, Bt (ext).

Descendants of late Lady Catherine Sophia Tollemache, b 1769, who d 1825 (having m 1793, Sir Gilbert Heathcote, 4th Bt), el da of Louisa (in her own right), Countess of Dysart (ante):—
See Heathcote, Bt (of London).

Branch from yst da of 4th Earl

Descendants of late John Jervis Tollemache, MP (el son of late Adm John Richard Delap Tollemache, who assumed by Roy Licence in 1821 that surname and Arms in lieu of Halliday, el son of late Lady Jane Halliday, youngest da and co-heir of 4th Earl) who was cr Baron Tollemache 1876 (see that title, and 1968 and earlier edns).

PREDECESSORS – (1) WILLIAM Murray, son of Rev William Murray, Min of Dysart co Fife (grandson of Anthony Murray, of Dollerie, Perthshire, whose elder brother Patrick was ancestor of the Murray baronets of Ochtertyre); MP for Fowrey 1626, and for E Looe 1628-9; cr by patent Lord Huntingtower and Earl of Dysart (peerage of Scotland) 1643: m 16—, Catherine, da of Col Norman Bruce, of Clackmannan; d 1654; s by his el da (2) ELIZABETH, Countess of Dysart, 16—; who in 1670 resigned the peerage and received a new grant thereof by patent with precedency of her father, and with remainder to her heirs of the body, failing which to her heirs whatsoever: m 1st, 1647, Sir Lionel Tollemache, 3rd Bt (cr 1611), who d 1669; 2ndly, 1672, John Maitland, 1st Duke of Lauderdale, by whom she did not have issue; the Duchess d 1698; s by her el son (3) LIONEL, 3rd Earl b 1648; s his father as 4th Bt in 1669; MP for Orford 1678-85 and for Suffolk 1698-1700; declined an English barony upon accession of Queen Anne: m 1680, Grace, who d 1740, da of Sir

Thomas Wilbraham, 3rd Bt; *d* 1727; *s* by his grandson **(4)** LIONEL, KT, 4th Earl (only son of Lionel, Lord Huntingtower), *b* 1708: *m* 1729, Hon Grace Carteret, who *d* 1755, da of 2nd Earl Granville; *d* 1770; *s* by his son **(5)** LIONEL, 5th Earl, *b* 1734: *m* 1st, 1760, Charlotte, who *d* 1789, natural da of Hon Sir Edward Walpole, KB; 2ndly 1791, Magdalene, who *d* 1823, da of David Lewis, of Malvern Hall, Warwickshire; *dsp* 1799; *s* by his brother **(6)** WILLIAM, 6th Earl, *b* 1739: *m* 1773, Anna Maria, who *d* 1804, da of David Lewis (ante); *d* 1821, when the Baronetcy (*cr* 1611) became ext; *s* in Earldom and Lordship by his sister **(7)** LOUISA; *b* 1745; assumed by Roy licence 1821 (the surname and Arms of Talmash in lieu of Manners): *m* 1765, John Manners, MP, of Grantham Grange, co Lincoln, who *d* 1792: *d* 1840; *s* by her grandson **(8)** LIONEL WILLIAM JOHN, 8th Earl (el son of William, Lord Huntingtower, who in 1793 was *cr* a *Baronet*, and in 1821 assumed by Roy licence the surname and Arms of Talmash only), *b* 1794; *s* by his father's Baronetcy 1833: *m* 1819, Maria Elizabeth, who *d* 1852, da of Sweeney Toone, of Keston Lodge, Kent: *d* 1878: *s* by his grandson **(9)** WILLIAM JOHN MANNERS, 9th Earl (only son of William Lionel Felix, Lord Huntingtower), *b* 1859: *m* 1885, Cecilia Florence, who *d* 1917, da of late George Onslow Newton, of Croxton Park, St Neots; *d* 1935; *s* in the Baronetcy by his kinsman, Lyonel Felix Carteret Eugene Tollemache, and in the Earldom and Lordship by his niece **(10)** WENEFRYDE AGATHA Greaves (da of late Charles Norman Lindsay Tollemache Scott, by Lady Agnes Mary Manners, who *d* 1912, da of William Lionel Felix, Lord Huntingtower), Countess of Dysart, *b* 1889: *m* 1913, Maj Owain Edward Whitehead Greaves, DL, RHG Machine Gun Regt, who *d* 1941, *d* 1975, *s* by her el da **(11)** ROSAMUND AGNES, Countess of Dysart, and present peeress; also Lady Huntingtower.

Eady, family name of Baron Swinfen.

EAMES, BARON (Eames) (Life Baron 1995)

Most Rev ROBERT HENRY ALEXANDER EAMES, son of late William Edward Eames, of Belfast; *b* 27 April 1937; *ed* Belfast Royal Acad, Methodist Coll, Belfast, Queen's Univ, Belfast (LLB 1960, PhD 1963), and Trinity Coll, Dublin (LLD 1992); Hon LLD Queen's Univ, Belfast 1989; Hon DLitt Greenwich Univ 1993; Hon DD Camb 1994; Hon LLD Lancaster 1994; Hon DD Aberdeen 1997; Hon DD Exeter 1999; Research Scholar and Tutor, Queen's Univ 1960-63; Curate of Bangor, co Down 1963-66; Incumbent of Gilnahirk, co Down 1966-74 and Dundela, co Down 1974-75; Bishop of Derry and Raphoe 1975-80, Bishop of Down and Dromore 1980-86, since when Archbishop of Armagh and Primate of All Ireland; Chm Archbishop of Canterbury's International Commn on Communion and Women in the Episcopate 1988; Gov Church Army since 1985; Chm Anglican Communion Theological and Doctrinal Commn, Anglican Communion Finance Cttee, and Armagh Observatory and Planetarium; author of *A Form of Worship for Teenagers* 1965, *The Quiet Revolution, Irish Disestablishment* 1970, *Through Suffering* 1973, *Thinking Through Lent* 1978, *Through Lent* 1984, *Chains to be Broken* 1992; *cr Baron Eames*, of Armagh, co Armagh (Life Baron) 1995: *m* 1966, (Ann) Christine, da of late Capt William Adrian Reynolds Daly, of London, and has issue.

Arms – Azure on a fess embattled counterembattled or between three Celtic crosses each dimidiated with a shamrock or a barrulet azure. **Crest** – Within a circlet of shamrocks or a mitre with infulae proper. **Supporters** – *Dexter*, a stag per fess sable and vert attired and unguled or gorged with a ribband tied purpure semy of shamrocks or; *sinister*, a stag per fess vert and sable attired unguled and gorged with a like ribband.
Address – c/o House of Lords, SW1A 0PW. *Clubs* – Strangford Yacht, Ringhaddy Yacht, Kildare St and University (Dublin).

SONS LIVING

Hon Niall, *b* 1967; *ed* Campbell Coll, Belfast, and Queen's Univ, Belfast.
Hon Michael, *b* 1969; *ed* Campbell Coll, Belfast, and Queen's Univ, Belfast.

EATWELL, BARON (Eatwell) (Life Baron 1992)

JOHN LEONARD EATWELL, son of Harold Jack Eatwell, of Swindon, Wilts; *b* 2 Feb 1945; *ed* Headlands
Gram Sch, Swindon, Queens' Coll, Camb (BA, MA), and Harvard Univ (AM, PhD), Teaching
Fellow Harvard Univ 1968-69; Research Fellow Queens' Coll, Camb 1969-70, Fellow and Dir of
Studies in Economics, Trin Coll, Camb 1970-96, since when Pres of Queens' Coll, Camb; Assist
Lecturer in Economics Camb Univ 1975-77, since when Lecturer; Visiting Prof of Economics, New
Sch for Social Research, NY 1980-96 and Economics Advisor to Rt Hon Neil Kinnock 1985-92; Chm
Crusaid 1993-96; Member Cambridge Constituency Labour Party, Royal Economics Soc, and
American Economics Assocn; Economist; *cr Baron Eatwell*, of Stratton St Margaret, co Wilts (Life
Baron) 1992: *m* 1970, Hélène, da of Georges Seppain, of Marly-le-Roi, France, and has issue.
Residence – Queens' College, Cambridge CB3 9ET.

SONS LIVING

Hon Nikolai, *b* 1971.
Hon Vladimir, *b* 1973.

DAUGHTER LIVING

Hon Tatyana, *b* 1978.

EBBISHAM, BARONY OF (Blades) (Extinct 1991)

DAUGHTERS LIVING OF SECOND BARON

Hon Susan Mary, *b* 1951: *m* 1980, Peter D. Stevenson, of The White House, Whitehouse Loan, Edinburgh EH9 2EY, son
of late Alexander Stevenson, of Westfield House, W Calder, Midlothian, and has issue living, George Dennistoun, *b* 1987,
— Mary Flavia, *b* 1984.

Hon Emma Caroline, *b* 1954: *m* 1977, Franklin Brooke-Hitching, of Osmington House, Kintbury, Hungerford, Berks, son
of late Desmond Brooke-Hitching, of 12 Porchester Terrace, W2 and has issue living, Edward Robert, *b* 1982, —
Matthew Thomas, *b* 1985, — William Franklin, *b* 1987, — Georgia Emma, *b* 1992.

Hon Catherine Anne, *b* 1955: *m* 1981, Charles J. Spencer, of Search Farm, Stourton, Warminster, Wilts, son of Kenneth
Spencer, of St Martin's Farm, Zeals, Wilts, and has issue living, Thomas James, *b* 1985, — Henry Charles Blades, *b*
1990, — Flora Antonia Blades, *b* 1987.

DAUGHTER LIVING OF FIRST BARON

Hon Janet Mary, *b* 1916: *m* 1952, Rear-Adm John Edwin Home McBeath, CB, DSO, DSC, DL, who *d* 1982, and has issue
living, John Rowland Blades, *b* 1954, — Rosemary Diana Jane, *b* 1957. *Residence* – Woodbury, 9 Annandale Drive, Lower
Bourne, Farnham, Surrey GU10 3JD.

WIDOW LIVING OF SECOND BARON

FLAVIA MARY (*Baroness Ebbisham*), yst da of late Charles Francis Meade (*see* E Clanwilliam, colls): *m* 1949, the 2nd
Baron Ebbisham, TD, who *d* 1991. *Residence* – St Ann's, Church St, Mere, Wilts BA12 6DS.

EBURY, BARON (Grosvenor) (Baron UK 1857)

Virtue, not ancestry

FRANCIS EGERTON GROSVENOR, 6th Baron; *b* 8 Feb 1934; *s* 1957; *ed* Eton, and Melbourne Univ; is *hp* to Earldom of Wilton: *m* 1st, 1957 (*m diss* 1962), Gillian Elfrida (Elfin), da of late Martin Roland Soames, of Hinton Ampner Place, Bramdean, Hants (*see* E Perth, colls, 1980 Edn); 2ndly, 1963 (*m diss* 1973), Kyra, da of late L. L. Aslin; 3rdly, 1974, Suzanne Jean, da of Graham Suckling, of Tai Tapu, NZ, and has issue by 1st and 3rd wives.

ᴀrms – Azure, a garb or, a mullet for difference. Crest – A talbot statant or. Supporters – On either side a talbot reguardant or, collared azure, charged on the shoulder with a mullet of the second.
Address – Moore Park PO, Box 466, Mt Macedon, Vic 3441, Australia.
Clubs – Melbourne, and Melbourne Savage, Hong Kong and Oriental.

SON LIVING (*by 1st wife*)

Hon JULIAN FRANCIS MARTIN, *b* 8 June 1959; *ed* Gordonstoun: *m* 1987 (*m diss* 1989), Danielle, 6th da of Theo Rossi, of Sydney, Australia. *Residence* – 101 Barcom Av, Rushcutters Bay, Sydney 2011, NSW.

DAUGHTER LIVING (*by 3rd wife*)

Hon Georgina Lucy, *b* 1973.

HALF-BROTHERS LIVING

Hon William Wellesley, *b* 1942; *ed* Eton, and Trin Coll, Oxford: *m* 1966, Ellen da of late Dr Gunter Seeliger, of Harlaching, Munich, and has issue living, Alexander Egerton, *b* 1968, — Petra Antonia Primrose, *b* 1970: *m* 1996, Peter Gavin Pinnock, son of Roger Pinnock, of Milton Malsor, Northants. *Residence* – Sheep Lane House, Potsgrove, Woburn, Beds.

Hon Richard Alexander, *b* 1946; *ed* Milton Abbey, and Univs of Perugia, Montpelier, Lyons, Tours and Munich: *m* 1st, 1970 (*m diss* 1986), Gabriella, da of Dr Xavier Speckert; 2ndly, 1989, Frances Ann, da of David Samuel Williams, of Newport, Mon, and has issue living (by 1st *m*), Bendor Robert Gerard, *b* 1977, — (by 2nd *m*) Letisah Emma, *b* 1989.

HALF-SISTERS LIVING

Hon (Laura Georgina) Kiloran (twin), *b* 1946; resumed the surname of Grosvenor by deed poll 1983: *m* 1st, 1969 (*m diss* 1979), G. R. Mark Cross; 2ndly, 1993, Brian Murrell. *Residence* – 30 Bedford St, Woburn, Beds MK17 9QB.

Hon Linda Denise, *b* 1948: *m* 1973, Christopher D. Vane Percy, and has issue living, Maximilian Egerton, *b* 1979, — Grace Dorothy Denise, *b* 1981, — Tryce Mary Susanne, *b* 1991. *Residence* – Island Hall, Godmanchester, Cambs.

UNCLE LIVING (*Son of 4th Baron*)

Hon Hugh Richard, *b* 1919; *ed* Radley Coll, and RMA Sandhurst; European War 1939-45 as Capt King's Shropshire LL: *m* 1st, 1939 (*m diss* 1952), Margaret, da of James L. Jacobs, of Neilsen, Pednolver Terr, St Ives, Cornwall; 2ndly, 1955, Victoria, only da of H. Wright, of Newport, Shropshire, and has issue living (by 1st *m*) Margaret Elizabeth, *b* 1947, — (by 2nd *m*) William Peter Wellesley, *b* 1959, — Rebecca Victoria, *b* 1975. *Residence* – River Ridge, Courtlands Park, Carmarthen.

AUNT LIVING (*Daughter of 4th Baron*)

Hon Maud Elizabeth, *b* 1909: *m* 1st, 1931 (*m diss* 1942), 2nd Viscount Harcourt, who *d* 1978; 2ndly, 1942, Lieut-Col Edward O'Shaughnessy, and has issue living, (by 1st *m*) (*see* V Harcourt), — (by 2nd *m*) Elizabeth Mary, *b* 1947, — Caroline Margaret (twin), *b* 1947. *Residence* – Bethavon, Duke St, Northam 6401, Western Australia.

WIDOW LIVING OF SON OF FIFTH BARON

Caroline, only da of late Ronald Harry Higham (*see* V Hampden): *m* 1959, Hon (Robert) Victor Grosvenor, who *d* 1993, and has issue (*see* colls, infra). *Residence* – Bennets, Grafton, Oxon OX18 2RY.

WIDOW LIVING OF FIFTH BARON

SHEILA WINIFRED (ANKER) (*Dowager Baroness Ebury*), yr da of Arthur Edward Dashfield, of Oxford: *m* 1954, as his 3rd wife, the 5th Baron Ebury, who *d* 1957. *Residence* – 37 Linkside Av, Oxford OX2 8JE.

COLLATERAL BRANCH LIVING

Issue of late Hon (Robert) Victor Grosvenor, 2nd son (by 1st *m*) of 5th Baron, *b* 1936, *d* 1993: *m* 1959, Caroline (ante), only da of late Ronald Harry Higham (*see* V Hampden):—
Rachel Egerton, *b* 1963: *m* 1986, Tobias S. Buckler, son of Humphrey Buckler, of Bledington, Oxon, and has issue living, Peregrine Humphrey, *b* 1988, — Valentine Robert, *b* 1993, — Kiloran Dorothea Anne, *b* 1989. *Residence* – Llwyn-on, Llanthony, Monmouthshire NP7 7NW. —— Virginia, *b* 1965: *m* 1988, Mark Quinton Graham, son of late John Graham, of Newcastle-upon-Tyne, and has issue living, Emily Charlotte, *b* 1990. *Residence* – 12 Macfarlane Rd, Bearsden, Glasgow G61.

PREDECESSORS – **(1)** *Rt Hon* ROBERT Grosvenor, 3rd son of 1st Marquess of Westminster, *b* 1801; MP for Shaftesbury 1822-6, for Chester 1826-47, and for Middlesex (*L*) 1847-57; Comptroller of HM's Household 1830-34, Treasurer thereof 1846-7, and Groom of the Stole to the Prince Consort; was *cr* Baron Ebury (peerage of United Kingdom) 1857: *m* 1831, Hon Charlotte Arbuthnott Wellesley, who *d* 1891, sister of 1st Earl Cowley; *d* 1893; *s* by his el son **(2)** ROBERT WELLESLEY, 2nd Baron, *b* 1834; Capt 1st Life Guards; MP for Westminster (*L*) 1865-74: *m* 1867, Hon Emilie Beaujolois White, who *d* 1923, da of 1st Baron Annaly; *d* 1918; *s* by his el son **(3)** ROBERT VICTOR, 3rd Baron, *b* 1868: *m* 1903, Florence, who *d* 1927, da of late Edward M. Padelford, of Savannah, USA; *d* 1921; *s* by his brother **(4)** FRANCIS EGERTON, DSO, MC, 4th Baron, *b* 1883; Chm Army and Navy Co-operative So, a Director of Union Bank of Australia, and of Roy Exchange Assurance Co (West End Branch), and Major Canadian Forces (Reserve of Officers); European War 1914-18 (wounded, despatches four times, MC with Bar, DSO with Bar, French Croix de Guerre with Palm): *m* 1902, Mary Adela, who *d* 1960, da of late G. Glasson: *d* 1932; *s* by his son **(5)** ROBERT EGERTON, DSO, 5th Baron; *b* 1914; Major Berkshire Yeo; was a Lord of Waiting to HM 1939-40: *m* 1st, 1933 (*m diss* 1941), Anne, who *d* 1982, da of late Major Herbert Walter Acland-Troyte, MC (*see* Acland, Bt, *cr* 1678, colls); 2ndly, 1941 (*m diss* 1954), Hon Denise Margaret Yarde-Buller, da of 3rd Baron Churston; 3rdly, 1954, Mrs Sheila Winifred (ANKER), yr da of Arthur Edward Dashfield, of Oxford; *d* 1957; *s* by his el son **(6)** FRANCIS EGERTON, 6th Baron and present peer.

ECCLES, VISCOUNT (Eccles) (Viscount UK 1964)

TRUTH AND BEAUTY

JOHN DAWSON ECCLES, CBE, 2nd Viscount; *b* 20 April 1931; *s* 1999; *ed* Winchester, and Magdalen Coll, Oxford; Dir Courtaulds Textiles plc since 1992 (non-exec Chm since 1995); CBE (Civil) 1985: *m* 1955, Diana Catherine (*Baroness Eccles of Moulton*) (Life Baroness), da of late Raymond Sturge, of Lords Mead, Ashmore, Salisbury, and has issue.

𝔄rm𝔰 – Chevronny argent and sable per pale counterchanged two torches erect or enflamed proper. ℭre𝔰t – A three masted ship sails furled pennons and flags flying or, between two wings addorsed sable. 𝔖upporter𝔰 – On either side a wolf sable armed and langued gules gorged with a plain collar attached thereto a chain reflexed over the back and resting the interior hind paw on a portcullis chained or.
Residences – Moulton Hall, Moulton, Richmond, Yorks DL10 6QM; 6 Barton St, SW1P 3NG. *Club* – Brooks's.

SON LIVING

Hon WILLIAM DAVID, *b* 9 June 1960; *ed* Winchester, and St John's Coll, Oxford: *m* 1984, Claire Margaret Alison, da of Brian Seddon, of 77 Lawn Rd, Hampstead, NW3, and has issue living, Peter David, *b* 2 Jan 1987, — Thomas Edward, *b* 1988, — Catherine Lucy, *b* 1991. *Residence* – 111 Howards Lane, SW15.

DAUGHTERS LIVING

Hon Alice Belinda, *b* 1958: *m* 1981, Rev Robert Charles Irwin Ward, eldest son of late John Ward, of The Old Vicarage, Salehurst, Robertsbridge, Sussex, and has issue living, Samuel John, *b* 1982, — James Nicholas, *b* 1984, — David Christopher, *b* 1994, — Susanna Mary, *b* 1988. *Residence* – 1 Hawthorn Villas, The Green, Wallsend-on-Tyne.

Hon Catherine Sara, *b* 1963: *m* 1990, Joseph Brendan Gannon, son of Patrick Gannon, of Dublin, and has issue living, Sorcha Margaret, *b* 1993, — Ella Catherine, *b* 1996. *Residence* – 18 Lynton Rd, NW6 6BL.

Hon Emily Frances, *b* 1970: *m* 1999, Patrick J. Irwin, only son of Rear Adm Richard Irwin, of Chichester, Sussex. *Residence* – 6 Donaldson Rd, NW6 6NB.

BROTHER LIVING

Hon Simon Dawson, *b* 1934; *ed* Repton: *m* 1961 (*m diss* 1986), Sheelin, da of late Henry E. Ryan, of Long Meadow, Goring on Thames, Oxon, and has issue living, Anthony James, *b* 1967, — Annabelle Charlotte, *b* 1964: *m* 1988, Leo Zinovieff, and has issue (*see* D Northumberland, colls). *Residence* – 27 Chestnut St, Boston, Mass 02108, USA.

SISTER LIVING

Hon (Selina) Polly Dawson (*Polly, Marchioness of Lansdowne*), *b* 1937; *ed* Sherborne Sch for Girls and London Univ: *m* 1st, 1962 (*m diss* 1968), Robin Andrew Duthac Carnegie, late Capt Queen's Dragoon Gds; 2ndly, 1969 (*m diss* 1978), 8th

Marquess of Lansdowne, and has issue living (by 1st *m*) Andrew James Duthac, *b* 1963. *Residence* – 32 Maunsel St, SW1P 2QN.

WIDOW LIVING OF FIRST VISCOUNT

MARY (*Dowager Viscountess Eccles*), da of ......, and widow of Donald Hyde, of Four Oaks Far, 350 Burnt Mill Rd, Somerville, NJ, USA: *m* 1984, as his 2nd wife, the 1st Viscount Eccles, CH, KCVO, PC, who *d* 1999. *Residences* – Dean Farm, Upper Chute, Wilts; 6 Barton St, SW1.

PREDECESSOR – **(1)** DAVID McADAM Eccles, CH, KCVO, PC, son of late Lt-Col W. C. McAdam Eccles, FRCS; *b* 1904; MP for Chippenham Div of Wilts (*C*) 1943-62; Min of Works 1951, Min of Education 1954, Pres of Board of Trade 1957, and again Min of Education 1959-62, Paymaster Gen and Min for The Arts 1970-73; Trustee British Museum 1963-70 (Chm of Trustees 1968-70); Chm Anglo-Hellenic League 1967-70; Chm British Library Board, and Pres World Craft Council 1973-78; *cr Baron Eccles*, of Chute, co Wilts (peerage of UK) 1962, and *Viscount Eccles*, of Chute, co Wilts (peerage of UK) 1964: *m* 1st, 1928, Hon Sybil Frances Dawson, who *d* 1977, da of 1st Viscount Dawson of Penn; 2ndly, 1984, Mary, widow of Donald Hyde, of Four Oaks Farm, 350 Burnt Mill Rd, Somerville, NJ, USA; *d* 1999; *s* by his elder son **(2)** JOHN DAWSON, 2nd Viscount and present peer; also Baron Eccles.

ECCLES OF MOULTON, BARONESS (Eccles) (Life Baroness 1990)

DIANA CATHERINE ECCLES (*Viscountess Eccles*), 2nd da of late Raymond Wilson Sturge, of Lords Mead, Ashmore, Salisbury, Wilts; *b* 4 Oct 1933; *ed* St James's Sch, W Malvern, and Open Univ (BA), Chm Ealing, Hammersmith & Hounslow Health Authority: *m* 1955, 2nd Viscount Eccles, CBE, and has issue (see preceding article).
Residences – Moulton Hall, Moulton, Richmond, Yorks; 6 Barton St, SW1.

Eddisbury, Baron, see Baron Sheffield.

Eden, family name of Baron Auckland.

Eden, family name of Earldom of Avon.

Eden, family name of Baron Henley.

EDEN OF WINTON, BARON (Eden) (Life Baron 1983, Bt (E) 1672 and (GB) 1776)

✱SI·SIT·PRUDENTIA✱

JOHN BENEDICT EDEN, PC, Life Baron, 9th *Baronet* of 1st creation, and 7th *Baronet* of 2nd creation; *b* 15 Sept 1925; *s* his father, *Sir* TIMOTHY CALVERT, in his baronetcies, 1963; *ed* Eton, and at St Paul's Sch, USA; a Member of House of Commons Estimates Cttee 1960-64, Delegate to Council of Europe and W European Union 1960-62, and to NATO Parliamentarians Conference 1962-66; Min of State for Technology June to Oct 1970, Min for Industry 1970-72, and Min of Posts and Telecommunications 1972-74; a Member of House of Commons Expenditure Cttee 1974-76; Chm Select Cttee on EEC Legislation etc 1976-79; Chm Select Cttee on Home Affairs 1980-83; Chm British Lebanese Assocn 1990-98; Chm R Armouries Museum 1986-94; Member Timken Co Internat Advisory Board; Chm Lady Eden's Schs Ltd; 1939-45 War as Lt Rifle Bde; 2nd KEO Gurkha Rifles and the Gilgit Scouts; MP for W Div of Bournemouth (*C*) 1954-83; *cr* PC 1972, and *Baron Eden of Winton*, of Rushyford, co Durham (Life Baron) 1983: *m* 1st, 1958 (*m diss* 1974), Belinda Jane, only da of late Sir (Frederick) John Pascoe; 2ndly, 1977, Margaret Ann, da of late Robin Gordon, and formerly wife of John Eric, Viscount Strathallan, son of 17th Earl of Perth, and has issue by 1st *m*.

𝕬rms – Gules, on a chevron argent between three garbs or, branded vert, as many escallops sable. 𝕮rest – A dexter arm embowed in armour, couped at the shoulder proper and grasping a garb fessewise as in the arms, banded vert. 𝕾upporters – Two lions rampant guardant gules about the mane of each a chain pendant therefrom a portcullis or that on the dexter side holding by the interior paw a cross patonce also or and that on the sinister side holding by the interior paw a rose branch proper having three double roses argent on gules barbed and seeded proper the compartment comprising a mount rising in the centre and growing therefrom fir trees and beech trees in the foreground a bay with cliffs proper and a rivulet wavy azure running across a sandy beach also proper into the sea barry wavy of four azure and argent.
Residence – 41 Victoria Rd, W8 5RH. *Clubs* – Boodle's, Pratt's.

SONS LIVING (*By 1st marriage*)

Hon ROBERT FREDERICK CALVERT, *b* 30 April 1964: *m* 1997, Encanaçion Garrido, and has issue living, Petrouchka, *b* 1997.
Hon John (Jack) Edward Morton, *b* 1966: *m* 1991, Joanna J., eldest da of Barrie D. Spears, of Hong Kong, and has issue living, Nicholas Cazenac, *b* 1997, — Madeleine Alexandra, *b* 1992. *Residence* – 118/2 Cotta Rd, Colombo 08, Sri Lanka.

DAUGHTERS LIVING (*By 1st marriage*)

Hon Emily Rose, *b* 1959: *m* 1984, Ronald Etienne Brown, yr son of James Brown, and has issue living, Nicholas James, *b* 1986, — Charlotte Lucy, *b* 1985. *Residence* – 15-2 Sarugaku-Cho, Shibuya-Ku, Tokyo 150, Japan.
Hon (Arabella) Charlotte, *b* 1960: *m* 1983, Hon Mungo Alexander Cansh McGowan, yst son of 2nd Baron McGowan, and has issue (*see* B McGowan). *Residence* – Bragborough Farm Braunston, Daventry, Northants.

SISTERS LIVING

Ann Caroline, *b* 1923: *m* 1951, Peter Noel Negretti, and has had issue, Alexandra Mary, *b* 1953: *m* 1981, David C. C. Maule, of 6 Criffel Av, SW2 4AZ, and has issue living, Robert Alexander Carteret *b* 1985, Oliver Raymond Carteret *b* 1990, Emma Charlotte *b* 1983, — Emma Frances, *b* 1954; *d* 1977, — Cristina Gabrielle, *b* 1956: *m* 1982, W. Guy R. Fearon, of Brook House, Gasper, Wilts, and has issue living, Christopher Nicholas William *b* 1991, Camilla Frances *b* 1989, — Sarah Ann *b* 1959: *m* 1984, Jonathan Paul Asquith, of 8 Colinette Rd, SW15 6QQ, and has issue (*see* E Oxford and Asquith, colls). *Residence* – The Old Stables, Gracious St, Selborne, Alton, Hants. ⸺ (Meriall) Rose, *b* 1927: *m* 1959, James Dalton Murray, CMG, who *d* 1984, and has issue living, William Andrew Eden, *b* 1960, — and an adopted son, Hugo Felix Dalton, *b* 1963: *m* 1989, Kaye Melanie Underhill, of Bridgewater, Som, and has issue living, Matthew James *b* 1993, Alaster Michael *b* 1995. *Residence* – 66500 Mosset, Prades, Pyrénées-Orientales, France. ⸺ Amelia Mary, *b* 1933: *m* 1958, Giovanni Borrelli, of Chapel Lane Cottage, Fritham, Lyndhurst, Hants, and has issue living, Timothy Raffaele, *b* 1962, — Matteo Francesco Antonio, *b* 1965, — Chiara Maria Concetta, *b* 1960. ⸺ Elfrida Charlotte *b* 1940: *m* 1963, Richard Gordon Fallowfield, of 78 West Side, Clapham Common, SW4, and has issue living, Timothy Gordon, *b* 1965, — Nicholas John, *b* 1967, — Laura Louise, *b* 1974.

COLLATERAL BRANCHES LIVING

Grandchildren of late Rowland Frederick Eden, 3rd son of late Frederick Morton Eden, eldest son of Rt Rev Robert Eden, DD, Primus of Scotland, and Bishop of Moray and Ross, 3rd son of 2nd baronet of Maryland:—
Issue of late Lt-Cdr Frederick Augustus Morton Eden, RN (Emergency List), *b* 1904, *d* 1985: *m* 1929, Everil Mary, who *d* 1993, eldest da of late John Stephen Lang Whiteaway, of Tankerville, Kingston Hill, Surrey:—

David Frederick Edward, MBE, *b* 1934; *ed* Ampleforth; W/Cdr RAF (ret); MBE (Mil) 1981: *m* 1957, Audrey Joan Wilson, and has issue living, Audrey Mary Caroline, *b* 1958. *Residence* – 31 Howard Court, Rutland Drive, Harrogate, N Yorks HG1 2PB. —— John Graham Walter, *b* 1948. *Residence* – 16 East MacKenzie Park, Inverness IV2 3SR. —— Mary Alexandra Morton, *b* 1945: *m* 1983, Robert S. Cameron, and has issue living, Neil Robert David, *b* 1987. *Residence* – Gallowa' View, Dockhead, Dumfries DG1 2RX.

Descendants of Sir Robert Eden, 1st baronet of Maryland, who was 2nd son of 3rd baronet of West Auckland:—

Grandson of late Charles Calvert Eden, son of late Lieut-Gen George Morton Eden, 4th son of 2nd baronet of Maryland:—
Issue of late Morton Frederic Eden, MBE, *b* 1865, *d* 1948: *m* 1909, Marie Therése MacMahon, who *d* 1962:—
Robert Charles Frederick, MBE, *b* 1916; *ed* Zuoz Coll, Switzerland and at Camb Univ (BA 1940); European War 1939-45 as Capt Intelligence Corps; MBE (Mil) 1948: *m* 1958, Barbara, 2nd da of late George Reginald Benson, and has issue living, Michael Anthony, *b* 1960: *m* 1990 (*m diss* 1996), Carolina Haydée Rodrigues-Valverde, of Lima, Peru, and has issue living, Linda Nicole *b* 1990. *Residence* – Märchligen, 3112 Allmendingen, Berne, Switzerland. *Club* – Alpine.

Descendants of late Rt Hon William Eden (3rd son of 3rd baronet of West Auckland), who was *cr Baron Auckland* 1789 (see that title).

Grandchildren of late Lt-Col John Henry Eden, Chief Constable of Durham 1892-1902, eldest son of Rev John Patrick Eden, son of Thomas Eden (*b* 1787), eldest son of Thomas Eden, 4th son of 3rd baronet of West Auckland:—
Issue of late Brig George Wilfrid Eden, CBE, *b* 1903, *d* 1986: *m* 1946, Katharine Margaret Dorothy, MBE (Norchard Farm, Stanton St Gabriel, Morcombelake, Bridport, Dorset), da of late Rev Edward Henry Good, Chap RN:—
John Patrick Edward (c/o Williams & Glyn's Bank, Holt's Whitehall Branch, SW1), *b* 1950; *ed* Charterhouse. —— Philippa Catherine, *b* 1948: *m* 1976, Stephen Lawrence McDonnell, of 49 St Catherine's Rd, Winchester, Hants, and has issue living, Catherine Claire, *b* 1981.

Grandchildren of late Sqdn Ldr Gerald Balfour Eden (infra):—
Issue of late John Hamilton Rodney Eden, RAF, *b* 1939, *d* 1992: *m* 1964, Sandra Anne, da of Dennis Rowland Toms:—
Anthony Winston Richard (22 Westbury Leigh, Westbury, Wilts), *b* 1965: *m* 1993, Catherine Mary, da of B. O'Connell, and has issue living, John Anthony Bernhard, *b* 1994. —— Jeremy Rodney Hugh, *b* 1967. —— Françoise Geraldine, *b* 1968: *m* 1993, James McLaren Eden-Hamilton (formerly Hamilton) (c/o Milton of Ruthven, Blairgowrie, Perthshire), and has issue living, John Alexander, *b* 1993.

Granddaughter of late Right Rev George Rodney Eden, DD (Lord Bishop of Wakefield 1897-1928), 3rd son of Rev John Patrick Eden (ante):—
Issue of late Sqdn Ldr Gerald Balfour Eden, *b* 1896, *d* 1970: *m* 1929, Anne, who *d* 1977, da of late Maj T Macey, late Indian Army:—
Margaret Anne, *b* 1929: *m* 1955, John William Howard Kirkbride, of 66 Swansfield Park Rd, Alnwick, Northumberland NE66 1AR, and has issue living, Nicholas George, *b* 1959: *m* 1989, Philipa Jane, da of Julian Ross Smith, and has issue living, Olivia Clare *b* 1990, — Amanda, *b* 1957: *m* 1980, Adrian Hardwick, of 7 Laverdene Av, Sheffield, Yorks, and has issue living, Mark Andrew *b* 1986, — Katherine, *b* 1961: *m* 1985, Nicholas Graham Clemo, of 23 York Rd, Windsor, Berks SL4 3NX, and has issue living, Andrew *b* 1990, Rachel *b* 1992.

Grandson of late Charles Hamilton Eden, OBE, 4th son of late Rev John Patrick Eden (ante):—
Issue of late Brig Henry Charles Hamilton Eden, CBE, MC, *b* 1889, *d* 1963: *m* 1st, 1916, Violet Alice, who *d* 1956, da of Capt Henry Percy Pulleine, of Sandford House, Richmond, Yorks; 2ndly, 1957, Penelope Glynne (Pine Close, Carroll Av, Ferndown, Dorset), da of H. W. Sitwell, of Leamington Hastings, and widow of Lt-Col R. Temple, RA:—
(By 1st *m*) Robert John Pulleine (Badlake Farm, West Anstay, S Molton, Devon), *b* 1920; Capt TA: *m* 1st, 1947 (*m diss* 1969), Hon Rosemary Winifred Vivian, who *d* 1981, da of 3rd Baron Swansea; 2ndly, 1969, Mrs Elizabeth Stanley Cleverly, da of Alan Crowe Rawlinson, and has issue living, (by 1st *m*) Sarah, *b* 1948: *m* 1982, Robin Fasola, — (by 2nd *m*), Catherine, *b* 1969, — Emily Rose, *b* 1972.

Grandson of late Brig Henry Charles Hamilton Eden, CBE, MC (ante):—
Issue of late Michael Charles Eden, *b* 1921, Lieut RE; *ka* at Arnhem 1944: *m* 1944, Patricia (who *m* 2ndly, 1946, Robert Everett, of Roeburn Scar, Roeburndale, Lancaster), da of late Col Reginald James Brook, CBE, DSO, ED:—
Peter Michael (*posthumous*) (Quinta dos Penedos, Elvas, Portugal), *b* 1944: *m* 1965, Rosemary Frances, da of Kenneth Charles Bishop, MBE, TD, Evans House, Sedbergh School, Yorks, and has issue living, Rupert Michael, *b* 1972, — Caroline Rose, *b* 1967, — Claire Louise, *b* 1969: *m* 1992, António Freire Dias da Costa, of Valverde, Evora, Portugal, and has issue living, Sophie Alexandra *b* 1993, — Lucy Catherine, *b* 1985.

Grandsons of Guy Ernest Morton Eden, son of Charles Henry Eden, son of Robert Eden, son of Thomas Eden, 4th son of 3rd baronet:—
Issue of late Charles Egerton Eden, *b* 1908, *d* 1957: *m* 1936, Eileen Antoinette, da of late H. H. Menzies, of Taplow:—
David Guy Egerton, *b* 1937. *Residence* – Essex.

Issue of late Rev Adrian Arthur Eden, *b* 1911, *d* 1980: *m* 1939, Margaret Anne, who *d* 1973, da of H. Edgar Bushell, of Golborne Manor, Tattenhall, Cheshire:—
Robin Guy (3 Othello Court, 50 Shakespeare Rd, Bedford MK40 2ED), *b* 1943; *ed* King's Sch, Canterbury; LTCL; schoolmaster. ——John Kenneth (Little Wootton, Church Rd, Scaynes Hill, Haywards Heath, Sussex RH17 7NH), *b* 1949; *ed* King's Sch Canterbury, and Dundee Univ (MA); stockbroker: *m* 1st, 1977 (*m diss* 1983), Margaret Elizabeth, da of William Alfred Noy, of 12 Hyacinth Rd, Strood, Rochester, Kent; 2ndly, 1992, Sophie Jane, da of Timothy John Green, of Kaines Orchard, Slugwash Lane, Scaynes Hill, Sussex RH17 7TD, and has issue living (by 1st *m*), Christopher Guy Eden, *b* 1978, — Kathleen Anne Elizabeth, *b* 1980, — (by 2nd *m*) Nicholas Morton, *b* 1996, — Daisy Charlotte, *b* 1998.

Descendants of late Morton Eden (5th son of 3rd baronet of West Auckland), who was *cr Baron Henley* 1799 (see that title).

PREDECESSORS – Sir Robert Eden, 1st Bt of W Auckland, co Durham, was son of Col John Eden, who raised a Regt for Charles I. Sir Robert Eden, Gov of Maryland 1776, the 2nd son of the 3rd baronet of West Auckland was created a baronet of Maryland, and the 3rd and 5th sons were respectively created Baron Auckland and Baron Henley. The 5th baronet of West Auckland assumed the additional surname of Johnson. On his death without issue in 1844, he was *s* by Sir William, 4th Bt, of Maryland, the two baronetcies thus becoming merged. Sir Timothy Calvert Eden, 8th Bt, *d* 1963, having *m* 1923, Patricia Edith, who *d* 1990, founder of Lady Eden's Schs, da of late Arthur Prendergast.

Edgcumbe, family name of Earl of Mount Edgcumbe.

Edinburgh, Duke of, see Royal Family.

Edmondson, family name of Baron Sandford.

EDMUND-DAVIES, BARONY OF (Edmund-Davies) (Extinct 1992)

DAUGHTERS LIVING OF LIFE BARON

Hon Ann, *b* 1936; JP 1979: *m* 1959, Frederick Cecil Worlock, MB, BChir, MRCS, LRCP, of Brooklands, Fladbury, Pershore, Worcs WR10 2QB, and has issue, one son and one da.
Hon Elisabeth, *b* 1939: *m* 1st, 1965 (*m diss* 1975), Richard Owen Roberts; 2ndly, 1987, Alan Large, of 7 Swaledale Av, Reedley, Burnley, Lancs BB10 2LJ.
Hon Shan, *b* 1940: *m* 1964, Prof Wolfram Schüffel, MD, of 3550 Marburg/Lahn, Kaffweg 17A, W Germany.

Ednam, Viscount; son of Earl of Dudley.

Edwardes, family name of Baron Kensington.

Edwards, family name of Baron Chelmer.

Edwards, family name of Baron Crickhowell.

EFFINGHAM, EARL OF (Howard) (Earl UK 1837)

Virtue is worth a thousand shields

DAVID MOWBRAY ALGERNON HOWARD, 7th Earl; *b* 29 April 1939; *s* 1996; *ed* Fettes, and RNC Dartmouth; Cmdr RN (ret); The Royal British Legion: *m* 1st, 1964 (*m diss* 1975), Anne Mary, da of late Harrison Sayer, of Cambridge; 2ndly, 1992, Mrs Elizabeth Jane Turner, da of late Dennis Eccleston, of Eccleshall, Staffs, and formerly wife of Peter Robert Easton Turner, and has issue by 1st *m*.

Arms – Quarterly: 1st gules, on a bend between six cross-crosslets fitchée argent an escutcheon or, charged with a demi-lion rampant pierced through the mouth with an arrow gules, within the Royal tressure of Scotland. *Howard*; 2nd England, with a label of three points for difference. *Thomas of Brotherton*; 3rd checky or and azure. *Warren*; 4th gules, a lion rampant argent. *Mowbray*; the whole charged with a mullet for difference. **Crest** – On a cheapan gules, turned up ermine, a lion statant guardant or, tail extended, ducally gorged argent, charged with a mullet sable. **Supporters** – Two lions argent, each charged on the shoulder with a mullet for difference.
Residence – Readings Farmhouse, Blackmore End, Essex CM7 4DH. *Clubs* – Royal Navy, Essex, Naval and Military.

SON LIVING (*By 1st marriage*)

EDWARD MOWBRAY NICHOLAS (*Baron Howard of Effingham*), *b* 11 May 1971; *ed* Oundle, and Bristol Univ. *Residence* – Miller's Cottage, Eades Mill, Gt Witchingham, nr Reepham, Norfolk NR9 5PQ.

HALF-BROTHER LIVING

Charles Anthony Frederick, *b* 1951; *ed* Sherborne, and St John's Coll, Camb (MA); Bar Inner Temple 1975; QC 1999: *m* 1st, 1978 (*m diss* 1999), Geraldine Margaret Theresa, da of Dr Thomas Dorman, of Morley, Derbys; 2ndly, 1999, Rosel (Rosie) Marie, da of Maj Charles Boycott, and formerly wife of David Leitch, and has issue living (by 1st *m*), Alexander Charles Frederick, *b* 1981, — Francesca Clare, *b* 1982. *Residence* – 16 Leamington Road Villas, W11 1HS. *Club* – Groucho.

WIDOW LIVING OF SIXTH EARL

(MABEL) SUZANNE MINGAY (*Suzanne, Countess of Effingham*), da of late Maurice Jules-Marie Le Pen, of Paris, and widow of Wing-Cdr Francis Talbot Cragg: *m* 1972, as his 3rd wife, the 6th Earl of Effingham, who *d* 1996. *Residence* – Apt 2409, The Hallmark, 2960 N Lake Shore Drive, Chicago, Illinois 60657, USA.

PREDECESSORS – (1) *Lord* WILLIAM Howard, KG, el son of his 2nd marriage of Thomas 2nd Duke of Norfolk; in 1542 found guilty of misprision of treason for concealing the misconduct of his niece Catherine, Queen of Henry VIII, and condemned with his wife to perpetual imprisonment (pardoned 1544); Lord Dep of Calais 1552-3, Lord High Adm 1553-7, Lord Chamberlain of the Household 1558-72, and Lord Privy Seal 1572; *cr Baron Howard of Effingham* (peerage of England) 1554, *d* 1572; *s* by his son (2) CHARLES, KG, 2nd Baron; was Com-in-Ch of the fleet that destroyed the Spanish Armada 1588; *cr Earl of Nottingham* (peerage of England) 1596; *d* 1624; *s* by his son (3) CHARLES, 2nd Baron; *dsp* 1642; *s* by his half-brother (4) CHARLES, KB, 3rd Earl; *d* 1681, when the earldom expired and the barony reverted to (5) FRANCIS, 5th Baron; *d* 1694; *s* by his son (6) THOMAS, 6th Baron; *dsp* 1725; *s* by his brother (7) FRANCIS, 7th Baron; a distinguished military officer; *cr Earl of Effingham* (peerage of Great Britain) 1731; *d* 1743; *s* by his son (8) THOMAS, 2nd Earl; Dep Earl Marshal; *d* 1763; *s* by his el son (9) THOMAS, 3rd Earl; Dep Earl Marshal; *dsp* 1791; *s* by his brother (10) RICHARD, 4th Earl; *d* 1816, when the earldom became extinct, and the barony devolved upon his kinsman (11) KENNETH ALEXANDER, GCB, 11th Baron; *b* 1767; a Gen in the Army; *cr Earl of Effingham* (peerage of United Kingdom) 1837; *m* 1800, Lady Charlotte Primrose, da of 3rd Earl of Rosebery; *d* 1845; *s* by his son (12) HENRY, 2nd Earl, *b* 1806; sat as MP for Shaftesbury (*L*) 1841-5; *m* 1832, Eliza, da of late Gen Sir Gordon Drummond, GCB; *d* 1889; *s* by his el son (13) HENRY, 3rd Earl, *b* 1837; *m* 1865, Victoria Francisca, who *d* 1899, el da of A. Boyer, of Paris; *d* 1898; *s* by his son (14) HENRY ALEXANDER GORDON, 4th Earl, *b* 1866; *d* 1927; *s* by his cousin (15) GORDON FREDERICK HENRY CHARLES (son of late Capt Hon Frederick Charles Howard, 2nd son of 2nd Earl), 5th Earl, *b* 1873; *m* 1st, 1904 (*m diss* 1914), Rosamond Margaret, who *d* 1957, da of late Edward H. Hudson, of Scarborough; 2ndly, 1924, Madeleine (Mrs Keleher), who *d* 1958, da of William D. Foshay, of USA; *d* 1946; *s* by his son (16) MOWBRAY HENRY GORDON, 6th Earl, *b* 1905; 1939-45 War with RA and 3rd Maritime Regts; *m* 1st, 1938 (*m diss* 1946), Manci Maria Malvina, da of Ferenz Joseph Gertler, of Hungary; 2ndly, 1952 (*m diss* 1971), Mrs Gladys Irene Kerry, da of late Capt William Freeman, Merchant Navy, and formerly wife of Frederick Charles Kerry (who *d* 1999); 3rdly, 1972, (Mabel) Suzanne Mingay, da of late Maurice Jules-Marie Le Pen, of Paris, and widow of Wing-Cdr Francis Talbot Cragg; *d* 1996; *s* by his nephew (17) DAVID MOWBRAY ALGERNON (elder son of late Hon John Algernon Frederick Charles Howard, yr son of 5th Earl), 7th Earl and present peer; also Baron Howard of Effingham.

Egerton, family name of Duke of Sutherland.

Egerton, family name of Earl of Wilton.

EGLINTON and WINTON, EARL OF (Montgomerie) (Earl S 1507, and UK 1859)
(Name pronounced "Muntgummery")

Take good care

ARCHIBALD GEORGE MONTGOMERIE, 18th Earl; *b* 27 Aug 1939; *s* 1966; *ed* Eton; Hereditary Sheriff of Renfrew: *m* 1964, Marion Carolina, only da of John Henry Dunn-Yarker, of Le Château, 1814 La Tour de Peilz, Vaud, Switzerland, and has issue.

𝔄rms – Quarterly, 1st and 4th grand quarters counter quartered, 1st and 4th azure, three fleurs-de-lys or, *Montgomerie*; 2nd and 3rd gules, three annulets or, stoned azure, *Eglinton*, all within a bordure or charged with a double tressure flory counterflory gules; 2nd and 3rd grand quarters counterquartered, 1st and 4th or, three crescents within a double tressure flory counterflory gules, *Seton*; 2nd and 3rd azure, three garbs or, *Buchan*; over all an escutcheon parted per pale gules and azure, the dexter charged with a sword in pale proper, pommelled and hilted or, supporting an imperial crown, the sinister charged with a star of twelve points argent, all within a double tressure flory counterflory gold. 𝔊rest – 1st, a lady dressed in ancient apparel azure, holding in her dexter hand an anchor or, and in her sinister the head of a savage couped suspended by the hair all proper; 2nd, a ducal coronet or, issuing therefrom a wyvern vomiting fire, his wings elevated proper. 𝔖upporters – Two wyverns vert, vomiting fire proper.
Residence – Balhomie, Cargill, Perth PH2 6DS.

SONS LIVING

HUGH ARCHIBALD WILLIAM (*Lord Montgomerie*), *b* 24 July 1966; RN (ret 1993); *m* 1991 (*m diss* 1998), S. Alexandra, eldest da of Niel Redpath, of Fulham, SW6. *Residence* – 17 Ormiston Grove, W12 0JR.

Hon William John, *b* 1968.

Hon James David, *b* 1972; *m* 1998, Philippa M. W., eldest da of Dr N. E. Williams, of Tinwell, Rutland.

Hon Robert Seton, *b* 1975.

SISTERS LIVING

Lady Susanna, *b* 1941: *m* 1963, Capt David Dundas Euing Crawford, and has issue living, Alexander William Euing, *b* 1967, — Daniel Dundas Euing (twin), *b* 1967, — Arabella Sara, *b* 1965: *m* 1995, Ewan Barford Christian, son of late Lt-Col John Monsell Christian, MC, and of Mrs John Henderson, of Newbury, Berks, and has issue living Charlie John *b* 1998. *Residence* – Newington House, Cupar, Fife KY15 4NW.

Lady Elizabeth Beatrice, *b* 1945: *m* 1976, Maj Christopher Miles Barne, The Blues and Royals, of Culeaze, Wareham, Dorset, and has issue living, Charles Miles, *b* 1978.

HALF-UNCLE LIVING (*Son of 16th Earl*) (*by 2nd marriage*)

Hon Roger Hugh, DFC, *b* 1923; *ed* Eton, and at New Coll, Oxford (MA); formerly Flight-Lt RAF; 1939-45 War (DFC). *Residence* – Lanehead, Dunscore, Dumfries.

AUNT LIVING (*Daughter of 16th Earl*)

Lady Janet Egidia, *b* 1911: *m* 1934, Capt Lord Robert Crichton-Stuart, Scots Gds, who *d* 1976 (*see* M Bute). *Residence* – Wards Cottage, Gartocharn, Dunbartonshire.

COLLATERAL BRANCHES LIVING

Grandchildren of late Alexander Montgomerie (*b* 1865), eldest son of late Capt Alexander Montgomerie (*b* 1824) (infra):—
Issue of late Alexander James Montgomerie, *b* 1892, *d* 1945: *m* 1919, Winifred Jane, who *d* 1993, aged 99, da of late George Gifford, of Bulls, Rangitikei, New Zealand:—
Alexander Kelvin (35 Washington Av, St Heliers, Auckland, NZ), *b* 1922; 1939-45 War with NZ Scottish Regt and RNZN: *m* 1958, Doreen Evelyn, da of Capt G. F. Price, 51 Woodfield Av, Farlington, Portsmouth, and has issue living, Roger James, *b* 1961, — Alexander Andrew (27 Robinson Terrace, Taupo, NZ), *b* 1962; *ed* Auckland Univ (BTP): *m* 1990, Sandra, only da of Edwin Baumann, of Burglen, Thurgau, Switzerland, and has issue living, Kristina Katherine *b* 1992, Stefanie Kim *b* 1994, Jessica Grace *b* 1996, Allison Jane *b* 1998, — Stuart Hugh (9/409 Sarawia St, Newmarket, Auckland, NZ), *b* 1966; *ed* Auckland Univ (BA): *m* 1995, Susanne, only da of Benny Rehder, of Frederiksberg, Copenhagen, Denmark. —— Seton Eglinton, *b* 1924: *m* 1960, Joan, da of late Harry Bladen, and has issue living, Seton Bladen *b* 1962, — Elsa Jane *b* 1964: *m* 1985, Philip Keith Belton, of Te Huia, RD2, Ngutuwera, Waverley, NZ, yst son of John Keith Belton, and has issue living, Christopher Reece *b* 1986, Sarah Jane *b* 1988, Emma Louise *b* 1993. *Residence* – 18 Tongariro St, Castlecliff, Wanganui, NZ. —— Zona Winifred, *b* 1920: *m* 1943, Norman Claude Nicholson, RNZAF, and has issue living, John Montgomerie (B8 Beryl Grove, Birchvale, Upper Hutt, NZ), *b* 1947: *m* 1977, Deborah Mary, da of W. J. Evenson, of 91 Pasadena Crescent, Upper Hutt, NZ, and has issue living, Jonathan Montgomerie *b* 1980, Victoria Rose *b* 1983, — Murray James (132 Oberon Rd, Chittaway Bay, Wyong, NSW 2259, Australia), *b* 1950: *m* 1971, Joy Louise, da of V. Frampton, of 1 Mundoora Av, Yattalunga, Gosford, NSW, and has issue living, Mathew James *b* 1974, Jodie Louise *b* 1972, Lisa Eileen *b* 1975, — Claudia Michele, *b* 1945: *m* 1966, Peter William Fitzsimmons, OBE (PO Box 33-369, Takapuna 1309, NZ), and has issue living, Timothy Peter *b* 1974, Megan Clare *b* 1977. *Residence* – Woodleigh, Jocelyn Cres, Pinehaven, Silverstream, Wellington, NZ. —— Rana Maude, *b* 1929: *m* 1951, Jack Rogers William Elder, RNZAF, and has issue living David Lawson James (74B Greerton Rd, Tauranga, NZ), *b* 1959: *m* 1989, Helen Margaret, da of R. A. Pond, of Papamoa, NZ, and has issue living, Kevin Robert James *b* 1992, Rachel Kawa Beth *b* 1995, — Raèwyne Janice, *b* 1955: *m* 1980, Stephen Hugh Allen, of 2 Greerton Rd, Tauranga, NZ, and has issue living, Matthew Stephen *b* 1983, Kimberley Jane *b* 1981. *Residence* – Broadview, 279 Bellevue Heights, Tauranga, NZ.

Issue of late Archibald William Montgomerie, *b* 1894, *d* 1969: *m* 1942, Barbara Mary (36 Brookvale Rd, Havelock North, NZ), da of Samuel Scott Linton:—
David William (460 Wegman Rd, RD7, PA 19606, USA), *b* 1944; *ed* McGill Univ, Montreal (PhD). —— Roger Linton (5 Thomas Av, Roseville, NSW 2069, Australia), *b* 1946; *ed* Massey Univ, NZ (B Tech, Dip BIA): *m* 1977, Judith Lorraine, da of R. A. R. Holland, of Sydney, Aust, and has issue living, Simon Holland, *b* 1980, — Andrew Scott, *b* 1987, — Kate Louise, *b* 1982. —— Barbara Mary (11 rue de l'Avenir, 91260 Juvisy sur Orge, France), *b* 1942: *m* 1973 (*m diss* 1982), Bernard Antoine Vollon, of Paris. —— Jeanne Elizabeth (29 Gordon Rd, Te Awanga, Hawkes Bay, NZ), *b* 1945: *m* 1969 (*m diss* 1982), Griffith Powell Richards, and has issue living, Nicholas Powell, *b* 1971, — Philip Powell, *b* 1972, — Michael Powell, *b* 1975, — Anna Elizabeth, *b* 1977. —— Barbara Hylda (39B Wright Rd, Pt Chevalier, Auckland, NZ), *b* 1950.

Issue of late John Eglinton Montgomerie, *b* 1899, *d* 1971: *m* 1921, Irene Agnes, da of Thomas Ross Cameron, of New Plymouth, NZ:—
Archibald William, *b* 1931: *m* 1962, Geraldine Anne, da of Gerald Cecil Davy, of Turanga, and has issue living, Michael William, *b* 1966, — Donna Marie, *b* 1962. —— Robert Patrick (24 Ihaia St, Waitara, Taranki, NZ), *b* 1934: *m* 1960, Mhyre Laughton, da of A. H. Collins, and has issue living, Leighton John, *b* 1966, — Wilson Bruce, *b* 1968, — Patricia Ann, *b* 1961: *m* 1984, Charles Thomas McAlister, and has issue living, Charles Luke *b* 1983, Kayla Maree *b* 1988, — Kerrie Lyn, *b* 1963; has issue living, Casey Brooke *b* 1995, — Jillian Beth, *b* 1964; has issue living, Conor Marie *b* 1994. —— Ian James, *b* 1935: *m* 1961, Diana Long, and has issue living, Paul Ian, *b* 1963, — Tracy Diana, *b* 1965, — Lisa Alayne, *b* 1967. —— Anita Mary, *b* 1921: *m* 1944, David Gordon Harrison, of 15 Whiteley St, New Plymouth, NZ, and has had issue, Errol John, *b* 1945: *m* 1970, Shirley Doreen Elwin, and *d* 1993, leaving, Sheree Ann *b* 1975, Melanie Jane *b* 1977, — Ira James (59B Manu Crescent, New Plymouth, NZ), *b* 1948, — Peter David (17A Divon St, Oakuru, NZ), *b* 1950: *m* 1970, Susan Wilson, who *d* 1993, and has issue living, Jason David *b* 1970, Kim Sheree *b* 1973, — Patrick Vivian (399 Main South Rd, Omata, Taranaki, NZ), *b* 1959: *m* 1986, Kay Walter, and has issue living, Greer Sam Walter *b* 1993, Reid *b* 1994, Carter *b* 1996, — Carrol Ann, *b* 1946: *m* 1967, Terry Arthur Jordan, of 28 Joseph Banks Drive, Whitby, Wellington, NZ, and has issue living, Rhys Craig *b* 1968, Carla Ann *b* 1970, — Shirley Mary, *b* 1953: *m* 1977, Marco Grandacci, of Camerino, Italy, and *d* 1986, leaving issue, Marco *b* 1977, Natalie Anita *b* 1978, — Yvonne Joan, *b* 1956: *m*

19—, Ronald Lance Wood, of 35 Matairo St, Titahi Bay, Wellington, NZ, and has issue living, Bianca Jay *b* 1978, Amber *b* 1980, Candice Skye *b* 1987. ——— Nola, *b* 1923: *m* 1941, Eric William Hopson, of RD3, Matamata, NZ, and has had issue, Kevin Eric (RD Mangakino, NZ), *b* 1943: *m* 1966, Shirley Anne Montague, and has issue living, Trevor John *b* 1968, Warrick David *b* 1972, Gareth Andrew *b* 1981, Janelle Marie *b* 1970, — Denis Michael (RD3, Matamata, NZ), *b* 1946: *m* 1980, Elizabeth Margaret Baker, and has issue living, Teresa Elizabeth *b* 1980, Catherine Anne *b* 1982, Bridget Alice *b* 1984, Rebecca Clare *b* 1985, — Graeme Patrick (RD1, Walton, NZ), *b* 1950: *m* 1972, Diane Elizabeth Hicks, and has issue living, Craig Patrick *b* 1975, Susan Marie *b* 1973, — Murray John, *b* 1953: *m* 1981, Sandra Daphne Brooks, and has issue living, Brendan Murray *b* 1989, Christine Sandra *b* 1983, Andrea Jane *b* 1985, — Allan David, *b* 1956: *m* 1978, Gillian Joy Christopher, and has issue living, Tanya Kirstin *b* 1978, Renee Jade *b* 1981, — Joan Frances, *b* 1941: *m* 1962, Peter Bruce Donnison, of RD3, Matamata, NZ, and has issue living, Bruce Stephen *b* 1962: *m* 1987, Adele Wilcockson (and has issue living, Rhys Francis *b* 1991, Hayley Petria *b* 1993), Paul David *b* 1963: *m* 1990, Kathryn Cuddihy (and has issue living, Callum Michael *b* 1992, Caitlin Joelle *b* 1993), Gregory James *b* 1965: *m* 1992, Kristin Evans, Martyn John *b* 1966: *m* 1993, Helen Conlon (and has issue living, Cam John McGrail *b* 1990, Hayley Francesca *b* 1994), Cameron Peter *b* 1975, Matthew Leighton *b* 1978, Regan Michael *b* 1981, Mylene Joanne *b* 1969, — Maureen Anne, *b* 1948: *m* 1966, Robin Bruce Lindsay, and has issue living, Gene Bruce *b* 1966: *m* 1994, Sherry Gillard (and has issue living, Troy Bruce *b* 1992), Shane Michael *b* 1970, Sharron Lee *b* 1968: *m* 1989, Kenneth Watkinson, Tracey Sharleen *b* 1972: *m* 1993, Gregory James (and has issue living, Hayden Charles *b* 1994), Kylie Maree *b* 1983, — Karen Irene, *b* 1960: *m* 1982, Warren Crawford, and has issue living, Holly Diane *b* 1991, — Diane Marie, *b* (twin) 1960: *m* 1982, Paul Moroney, and *d* 1982. ——— Peggy Agnes, *b* 1924: *m* 1945, Aubrey Edgar Hopson, of 170 Tukapo St, New Plymouth, NZ, and has issue living, Wayne Leighton, *b* 1946: *m* 1973, Heather Henderson, and has issue living, Candy Leighton *b* 1977, — Brian James, *b* 1948: *m* 1972, Elizabeth Lawson, and has issue living, Gareth Brian *b* 1982, Bryce James *b* 1985, Kieran Paul *b* 1989, — Valerie Margaret, *b* 1952: *m* 1975, Graeme McEldowney, and has issue living, Steven Craig *b* 1977, Dale Andrew *b* 1979, Aaron John *b* 1980, — Barbara Irene, *b* 1953: *m* 1973, Lindsay Gault, and has issue living, Shane David *b* 1978, Karen Maree *b* 1974, Julie Heather *b* 1976. ——— Barbara Winifred (70 Dundebar Rd, Wanneroo, Perth, W Australia 6065), *b* 1933: *m* 1954 (*m diss* 1978), David Walter Gosling, and has issue living, Ronald David (25 Celestine Rd, Wanneroo, Perth, W Australia 6065), *b* 1955: *m* 1978, Julie Dawn Bailey, and has issue living, Vicky Rachel *b* 1983, Donna Colette *b* 1987, — Ian Peter (70 Dundebar Rd, Wanneroo, Perth, W Australia 6065), *b* 1957: *m* 1980, Clare Lucy Knights, and has issue living, Thomas Iain *b* 1980, Matt Luke *b* 1981, James Patrick *b* 1985, Daniel Shane *b* 1986, Jessica Barbara *b* 1983, Rebecca Clare *b* 1989, — Claire Annette, *b* 1963: *m* 1st, 1980 (*m diss* 1983), Michael Currer; 2ndly, 1984 (*m diss* 1990), George Lubert, of Arkansas, USA; 3rdly 1993, Dale Jenkins, of 300 South Hospital Drive, Apt 805, Jacksonville, Arkansas, USA, and has issue living, (by 1st *m*) Gary Paul *b* 1980, (by 2nd *m*) Melissa Dawn *b* 1986, Tiffany Nicole *b* 1987.

Issue of late George Arnulph Montgomerie, *b* 1901, *d* 1980: *m* 1945, Peggy Patricia Greener, who *d* 1991, formerly of Wanganui, NZ:—
Wayne Arnold (4 Stanley Av, Palmerston North, NZ), *b* 1947: *m* 1971, Christina Mary, da of late Bernard Colin Williams, and has issue living, Darien Mary, *b* 1975, — Loren Patricia, *b* 1978. ——— Peter John (3 Brudenell Drive, Jerrabomberra, NSW 2619, Australia), *b* 1951: *m* 1977, Jennifer Joan, da of Hugh Carter Milroy, of 290 Great Western Highway, Warrimoo, NSW 2774, and has issue living, Shane Peter, *b* 1983, — Fiona Jenny, *b* 1982.

Grandchildren of late Roger Arnulph Montgomerie, 2nd son of late Capt Alexander Montgomerie (*b* 1824), el son of William Eglinton Montgomerie, el son of Alexander Montgomerie, brother of 12th Earl:—
Issue of late Roger Oswald Montgomerie, *b* 1896, *d* 1965: *m* 1940, Beryl Victoria, QSM (13 Laurence St, Tauranga, NZ), da of late Guy Carlton Clark, of Melbourne:—
John Clark (11 Gardiner Place, Havelock North, NZ) *b* 1943; *ed* Wanganui Collegiate, and Massey Univ: *m* 1972, Glenis Erina, only da of late Norman Cameron, of Masterton, NZ, and has issue living, Richard John, *b* 1974, — Meredith Jane, *b* 1977. ——— Roger Clark, *b* 1945; *ed* Wanganui Collegiate: *m* 1971, Patricia Clare, only da of late Vincent Patrick Donnelly, of Paeroa, NZ, and has issue living, Hayden James *b* 1979. ——— Edward William Gudopp, and has issue living, David Charles, *b* 1967: *m* 1998, Gretchen Elaine Wainwright, of Hamilton, NZ, — Deborah Jane, *b* 1965: *m* 1990, Brent William Lincoln, of 58 Panorama Drive, Tauranga, NZ, and has issue living, Daniel William *b* 1993, Samantha Victoria *b* 1991. ——— Helen Victoria, *b* 1959.

Issue of late Hew Seton Montgomerie, *b* 1898, *d* 1969: *m* 1938, Violet Muriel, who *d* 1976, da of late Donald Harry Rait, MRCVS, of Palmerston N, NZ:—
Susanna Seton, *b* 1940: *m* 1976, Michael Hensleigh Norris, of 10 Hillside Terrace, St John's Hill, Wanganui, NZ, and has issue living, Hew Seton Hensleigh, *b* 1977. ——— Egidia Seton *b* 1942: *m* 1980, Jerome Robert DesRoches, of 17 Morey Rd, Mangonui 0557, NZ.

Grandchildren of Hew Winton Montgomerie (infra):—
Issue of late Ian Hew de Greenlaw Montgomerie, *b* 1913, *d* 1981: *m* 1st, 1940 (*m diss* 1948), Elizabeth Isobella Gregg Stratford; 2ndly, 1948, Marjorie Thelma, who *d* 1975, da of Albert Eugene Brookes, of Auckland, New Zealand; 3rdly, 1977, his 1st wife, Elizabeth Isobella Gregg Stratford (51 Rawhiti Rd, Onehunga, Auckland, NZ):—
(By 1st *m*) Hew Winton Rowland (51 Rawhiti Rd, Onehunga, NZ), *b* 1941: *m* 1st, 1967 (*m diss* 1978), Carol Leonie, yst da of Stanley Rollingston Cromwell, Headmaster of Whangarei, NZ; 2ndly, 1984, Joana Tinisivo, da of Autiko Quna, of Fiji, and has issue living (by 1st *m*), Stuart Seton, *b* 1974, — Rachael Leonie, *b* 1970, — (by 2nd *m*) Ian Hew Mocewai, *b* 1992. ——— (By 2nd *m*) Lynetta Eugene, *b* 1952: *m* 1971, Albert John Bainbridge, and has issue living, Brent Albert, *b* 1976, — Tanya Lyn, *b* 1973, — Sacha Lee, *b* 1975.

Granddaughters of late Capt Alexander Montgomerie (*b* 1824) (ante):—
Issue of late Hew Winton Montgomerie, *b* 1872, *d* 1920: *m* 1906, Mary Laura, da of Charles J. G. de Greenlaw, of Syndey, NS Wales:—
Barbara de Greenlaw (49A Chipping Lane, Redwood, Christchurch, NZ), *b* 1915: *m* 1942, Ernest Clement Dawson, who *d* 1997, and has issue living, Ernest John Linnaeus (32 Bennett St, Christchurch, NZ), *b* 1945: *m* 1971, Lois Adrienne, da of Norman Farr, of Christchurch, NZ, and has issue living, Stephanie Justine *b* 1976, Julia Clare *b* 1978, — Bernard Stanley Winton (20 Waikuta Rd, Rotorua, NZ), *b* 1953; *ed* Univ of Canterbury, NZ (PhD Chemistry): *m* 1980, Sharon-May, da of Tan Hock Siang, of Singapore, and has issue living, Vivian Bernard *b* 1984, — Ann Michelle de Greenlaw, *b* 1943: *m* 1971, Lt-Cdr Edward Nigel Parry, RN, of Lowford House, School Rd, Bursledon, Hants SO3 8BU, — Linda Egidia Montgomerie, *b* 1949: *m* 1971, Miguel Zuniga, Chief Petty Offr, US Navy, of 955 N Gracia St, Camarillo, California 93010, USA, and has issue living, Dominick Miguel *b* 1972, Cheyenne Barbara *b* 1976.

Issue of late Archibald William Eglinton Montgomerie, *b* 1874, *d* 1951: *m* 1901, Elizabeth Grace, who *d* 1956, da of late Duncan Blair, of Wanganui, New Zealand:—
Nancy Edith, *b* 1903.

Issue (by 1st *m*) of late John Eglinton Montgomerie, *b* 1878, *d* 1930: *m* 1st, 1910, Edith Lillia, who *d* 1921, da of late Hon George Young, MLC, of Melbourne, Australia; 2ndly, 1928, Sarah (who *m* 2ndly, 19—, George Crowe, of Arbroath, Angus), da of — Mitchell, of Arbroath, Scotland:—
Bettie Winton, *b* 1916: *m* 1940, Thomas Charles Howden, and has issue living, Ann Montgomerie, *b* 1952, — Janet, *b* 1955. *Residence* – 2/119 Lumsden Rd, Hastings, New Zealand.

PREDECESSORS – **(1)** Sir ALEXANDER Montgomerie, Knt; *cr Lord Montgomerie* (peerage of Scotland) 1449; *d* 1451; *s* by his grandson **(2)** ALEXANDER, 2nd Lord; *s* by his son **(3)** HUGH, 3rd Lord; nominated after the fall of James IV at Flodden one of the Queen-Dowager's Councillors, and was afterwards Justice Gen of N parts of Scotland; *cr Earl of Eglinton* (peerage of Scotland) 1508; *d* 1545; *s* by his grandson **(4)** HUGH, 2nd Earl; *d* 1546; *s* by his son **(5)** HUGH, 3rd Earl; *d* 1585; *s* by his son **(6)** HUGH, 4th Earl; assassinated 1586; *s* by his son **(7)** HUGH, 5th Earl; obtained a charter settling the earldom upon his cousins, Alexander, Thomas and John, sons of his aunt Margaret, by Robert Seton, 1st Earl of Winton; *d* 1611; *s* by his cousin (ante) **(7)** ALEXANDER Seton, 6th Earl (3rd son of 1st Earl of Winton and 6th Lord Seton); took an active part against the crown, *temp* Charles I, fought on the Parliament side at Marston Moor; subsequently attached himself to Charles II, and falling into the hands of the enemy was imprisoned at Berwick 1651-60; *d* 1661; *s* by his son **(8)** HUGH, 7th Earl; espoused the royal cause during the civil wars and was opposed to his father at Marston Moor; *d* 1669; *s* by his son **(9)** ALEXANDER, 8th Earl; *d* 1701; *s* by his el son **(10)** ALEXANDER, PC, 9th Earl; a Representative Peer; *d* 1729; *s* by his son **(11)** ALEXANDER, 10th Earl; killed during a dispute 1769 by Mungo Campbell, whom the Earl had ordered off his lands and insisted upon the trespasser delivering up his gun; *s* by his brother **(12)** ARCHIBALD, 11th Earl; a Gen in the Army, MP for Ayrshire 1761, Dep Ranger of Hyde and St James's Parks, and a Representative Peer 1776-96; *d* 1796; *s* by his kinsman **(13)** HUGH, KT, 12th Earl, great grandson of the Hon James Seton, 4th son of 6th Earl; MP for Ayrshire 1780-9 and 1796, and a Representative Peer 1798-1806; *cr Baron Ardrossan* (peerage of United Kingdom) 1806; *d* 1819; *s* by his grandson **(14)** ARCHIBALD WILLIAM, 13th Earl, KT, PC, DCL, LLD; *b* 1812; in 1840 served heir male of George, 4th Earl of Winton (*cr* 1600), and 9th Lord Seton (*cr* 1448) (peerage of Scotland); *cr Earl of Winton*, and *Baron Seton and Tranent* (peerage of United Kingdom) 1859; Viceroy of Ireland 1852 and 1858-9, and Lord-Lieut of Ayrshire; inaugurated and carried out a celebrated tournament at Eglinton Castle 1839: *m* 1st, 1841, Theresa, who *d* 1853, widow of Com Richard Howe Cockerell, RN; 2ndly, 1858, Lady Adela Capel, who *d* 1860, da of 6th Earl of Essex; *d* 1861; *s* by his son **(15)** ARCHIBALD WILLIAM, 14th Earl, *b* 1841: *m* 1862, Lady Sophia Adelaide Theodosia Anderson-Pelham, who *d* 1886, da of 2nd Earl of Yarborough; *d* 1892; *s* by his brother **(16)** GEORGE ARNULPH, 15th Earl, *b* 1848; Lord-Lieut of Ayrshire: *m* 1873, Dame Janet Lucretia, DBE, LLD, who *d* 1923, da of Boyd Cunninghame, RN, of Craigends, co Renfrew; *d* 1919; *s* by his son **(17)** ARCHIBALD SETON, 16th Earl, *b* 1880: *m* 1st, 1908 (*m diss* 1922), Lady Beatrice Susan Dalrymple, who *d* 1962, da of 11th Earl of Stair; 2ndly, 1922, Marjorie, da of Thomas Walker McIntyre, and widow of Guy Fitzpatrick Vernon; *d* 1945; *s* by his son **(18)** ARCHIBALD WILLIAM ALEXANDER, 17th Earl, *b* 1914: *m* 1938, Ursula Joan, who *d* 1987, da of Hon Ronald Bannatyne Watson (*see* B Watson, ext, 1966 Edn); *d* 1966; *s* by his son **(19)** ARCHIBALD GEORGE, 18th Earl and present peer; also Earl of Winton, Lord Montgomerie, Baron Seton and Tranent, and Baron Ardrossan.

EGMONT, EARL OF (Perceval) Sits as BARON LOVEL AND HOLLAND (GB 1762) (Earl I 1733, Bt I 1661)

Under the white cross

FREDERICK GEORGE MOORE PERCEVAL, 11th Earl, and 15th Baronet; *b* 14 April 1914; established his claim to the Earldom 1939: *m* 1932, Ann Geraldine, da of Douglas Gerald Moodie, and has issue.

Arms – Quarterly; 1st and 4th argent, on a chief indented gules, three crosses patée of the field, *Perceval*; 2nd and 3rd barry nebulée of six, or and gules, *Lovel*. **Crest** – A thistle proper. **Supporters** – *Dexter*, an antelope argent, armed, unguled, ducally collared and chained or, holding in the mouth a thistle slipped proper; *sinister*, a stag sable, attired, unguled, ducally collared and chained or, holding in the mouth a thistle slipped proper.
Residence – Two-Dot Ranch, Nanton, Alberta, Canada.

SON LIVING

THOMAS FREDERICK GERALD (*Viscount Perceval*), *b* 17 Aug 1934.

DAUGHTER LIVING

Lady Geraldine Elizabeth Ursula, *b* 1939.

COLLATERAL BRANCH LIVING

Grandchildren of late Charles Spencer Perceval, LLD, son of late Dudley Montagu Perceval, son of 4th son of 2nd Earl:—
Issue of late Dudley Perceval, *b* 1874, *d* 1956: *m* 1914, Hon Mary Elizabeth Massey, who *d* 1960, da of 5th Baron Clarina:—

†Philip Edward, MD, *b* 1915; *ed* St John's Coll, Camb (BA 1936, MA 1940, MB and BCh 1940, MD 1950): *m* 1945, Joan Margaret, who *d* 1993, da of Lieut-Col Alfred Hacking, DSO, MC, of Dalmorton, Selsey, Sussex, and *d* 1996, leaving issue, Elizabeth Margaret, *b* 1947. *Residence* – 11 Condover Park, Condover, Shropshire SY5 7DU. ─── Mary Leonora, *b* 1916. *Residence* – Armadale, Aston St, Aston Tirrold, Didcot, Oxon OX11 9DJ.

PREDECESSORS – (1) *Rt Hon Sir* JOHN PERCEVAL; *cr* a *Baronet* 1661 with the exceptional privilege of allowing the el son or grandson when twenty-one years of age (and after notice given as provided) to receive the Order of Knighthood and have the rank and precedence of a Bt concurrently with the father or grandfather; *d* 1665; *s* by his el son (2) *Sir* PHILIP, 2nd Bt; *d* unmarried 1680; *s* by his brother (3) *Sir* JOHN, 3rd Bt; *d* 1686; *s* by his son (4) *Sir* EDWARD, 4th Bt; *d* a minor 1691; *s* by his brother (5) *Rt Hon Sir* JOHN, 5th Bt; successively MP for co Cork and Harwick, and 1st Pres of Georgia; *cr Baron Perceval*, of Burton, co Cork (peerage of Ireland) 1715, with remainder to the heirs male of his father, *Viscount Perceval* (peerage of Ireland) 1722, and *Earl of Egmont* (peerage of Ireland) 1733; *d* 1748; *s* by his son (6) *Rt Hon* JOHN, 2nd Earl; MP 1731-62, Lord High Adm and Postmaster-Gen; summoned to Parliament of Great Britain as *Lord Lovel and Holland*, of Enmore, co Somerst 1762: *m* 1st, 1737, Catherine, who *d* 1752, da of 5th Earl of Salisbury; 2ndly, 1756, Catherine, da of Hon Charles Compton (*see* M Northampton); she was *cr Baroness Arden*, of Lohort Castle, co Cork (peerage of Ireland) 1770; he *d* 1772; *s* by his son (7) JOHN JAMES, 3rd Earl; *d* 1822; *s* by his son (8) JOHN, 4th Earl; *d* 1835; *s* by his son (9) HENRY FREDERICK JOHN, 5th Earl; *d* 1841; *s* by his cousin (10) GEORGE JAMES, 6th Earl (2nd Baron Arden, of Arden), whose father CHARLES GEORGE (Baron Arden, of Lohort), el son of Catherine, Baroness Arden, of Lohort, had been *cr Baron Arden*, of Arden, co Warwick (peerage of United Kingdom) 1802; *dsp* 1874; *s* by his nephew (11) CHARLES GEORGE (son of late Rev Hon Charles George Perceval, 4th son of 2nd Baron Arden, of Lohort), 7th Earl, *b* 1845; MP for Midhurst (C) 1874: *m* 1869, Lucy, who *d* 1932, da of late Henry King; *d* 1897; *s* by his cousin (12) AUGUSTUS ARTHUR (son of late Charles John Perceval, grandson of 2nd Baron Arden, of Lohort), 8th Earl, *b* 1856: *m* 1881, Kate, who *d* 1926, da of late Warwick Howell, of S Carolina, USA; *d* 1910; *s* by his brother (13) CHARLES JOHN, 9th Earl, *b* 1858: *m* 1890, Florence, who *d* 1954, yst da of late George Gibson, MD; *d* 1929, when the title was claimed by (14) FREDERICK JOSEPH TREVELYAN (a descendant of late Rt Hon Spencer Perceval, MP, 7th son of 2nd Earl), *b* 1873: *m* 1911, Cecilia, who *d* 1916, da of James Burns Moore, of Montreal, Canada; *d* 1932, without having established his claim to the Earldom; his only son (15) FREDERICK GEORGE MOORE, *b* 1914; established his claim as 11th Earl 1939; also Baron and Viscount Perceval, Baron Arden, and Baron Lovel and Holland.

EGREMONT, BARON LECONFIELD AND (Wyndham) (Baron UK 1859 and 1963)

(JOHN) MAX HENRY SCAWEN WYNDHAM (*Baron Egremont*), 7th Baron Leconfield, and 2nd Baron Egremont; *b* 21 April 1948; *s* 1972; *ed* Eton, and Ch Ch, Oxford; Member Royal Commn on Historical Manuscripts since 1989; Chm The Friends of the National Libraries since 1985, Trustee Wallace Collection since 1988, and British Museum since 1990, Pres Action With Rural Communities since 1993; author (as Max Egremont), *The Cousins* 1977, *Balfour* 1980, *The Ladies' Man* 1983, *Dear Shadows* 1986, *Painted Lives* 1989, *Second Spring* 1993, and *Under Two Flags* 1997: *m* 1978, (Audrey) Caroline, elder da of Alexander Ronan Nelson, of Muckain, Taynuilt, Argyll (*see* Queenborough, By, 1990 Edn).

Arms – Azure, a chevron between three lions, heads erased or, within a bordure wavy of the last. **Crest** – A lion's head erased or, within a fetterlock, the lock gold, and the bow countercomponée or an azure; the head charged with a saltire wavy gules. **Supporters** – *Dexter*, a winged lion azure, wings, inverted and plain collared or, *sinister*, a griffin argent, gutté de sang, plain collared, gules. *Residences* – Petworth House, W Sussex GU28 0AE; Cockermouth Castle, Cumberland.

To the just, right

SON LIVING

Hon GEORGE RONAN VALENTINE, *b* 31 July, 1983.

DAUGHTERS LIVING

Hon Jessica Mary, *b* 1979.
Hon Constance Rose, *b* 1980.
Hon Mary Christian, *b* 1985.

BROTHER LIVING

Hon Harry Hugh Patrick, *b* 1957: *m* 1985, Susan Fiona McLean, eldest da of Bruce Woodall, of 7 Sheffield Terr, W8, and has issue living, Alexander, *b* 1986, — Richard, *b* 1990.

SISTER LIVING

Hon Caroline Elizabeth, *b* 1951: *m* 1976, Colin Chisholm, son of Archibald Hugh Tennent Chisholm, CBE, and has issue living, Hugh Archibald John, *b* 1976, — Mark Colin, *b* 1980, — Laura Carlyn, *b* 1978.

UNCLE LIVING *(Son of 5th Baron Leconfield)*

Hon Mark Hugh, OBE, MC (Newmans Cottage, ·Froxfield Green, Petersfield, Hants), *b* 1921: late Capt 12th R Lancers; Chm of C of E Children's Soc 1967-82; Chm of 999 Club Trust since 1993; 1939-45 War in Middle East and Italy. (twice wounded, MC): *m* 1st, 1947, Anne, da of late Hon Reginald Henry Winn (*see* B St Oswald); 2ndly, 1986, Patricia, formerly wife of Maj Henry Claude Lyon Garnett, CBE, and yr da of late Lt-Col Esmond Charles Baring, OBE (*see* B Ashburton, colls), and has issue living (by 1st *m*), Henry Mark (The Old Rectory, Southease, Lewes, E Sussex; *Clubs* – White's, MCC, Pratt's, Dilettanti Soc), *b* 1953; *ed* Eton, and Sorbonne, Paris; Christie's 1974-87, Art Dealer 1987-93; Chm Sotheby's UK since 1994; Chm Sotheby's Europe since 1997; *m* 1978, Rachel Sarah, yst da of late Lt-Col Leslie Francis Gordon Pritchard, MBE, TD (*see* Wheler, Bt), and has issue living, Ned Francis Reginald *b* 1983, Leo David *b* 1985, William Henry *b* 1988, — Elizabeth Jane (*Lady Charles Spencer-Churchill*) (81 Pimlico Rd, SW1), *b* 1948: *m* 1970, Lord Charles George William Colin Spencer-Churchill (*see* D Marlborough), — Melissa Anne (Flat 6, 3 Cranley Place, SW7 3AB), *b* 1949.

WIDOW LIVING OF SIXTH BARON LECONFIELD AND FIRST BARON EGREMONT

Pamela (*Dowager Baroness Egremont*) (Cockermouth Castle, Cockermouth, Cumbria), da of late Capt the Hon Valentine Maurice Wyndham Quin, RN (*see* E Dunraven): *m* 1947, the 6th Baron Leconfield and 1st Baron Egremont, who *d* 1972.

COLLATERAL BRANCHES LIVING

Issue of late Col Hon Everard Humphrey Wyndham, MC, yst son of 2nd Baron Leconfield, *b* 1888, *d* 1970: *m* 1920, Ruth Constance, who *d* 1984, da of late Hubert Delaval Astley, of Brinsop Court, Herefordshire (*see* B Hastings, colls):—
Michael Patrick (Quarry House, Ampney Crucis, Cirencester, Glos; *Clubs* – White's (Chm), MCC), *b* 1929; late Capt Life Guards: *m* 1st, 1957, Mrs Shelagh Anne Barker, who *d* 1967, da of late Dr Sydenham Frederick Moore, OBE, of Cairo; 2ndly, 1967, Mrs Laura Prudence Rosamund Murray, who *d* 1983, da of late Mervyn Stutchbury, of Gayles, Friston, E Sussex, and formerly wife of Christopher Mark Henry Murray (*see* Jerningham, Bt, ext 1935, 1955 Edn); 3rdly, 1985, Mrs Alison Dean, eldest da of Sir (Anthony) Reay Mackay Geddes, KBE, of 49 Eaton Place, SW1, and widow of Capt (Edward) Martin Dean, of Glen Usk, Gwent, and has issue living, (by 1st *m*) Samantha Madeline, *b* 1962, — Georgina Maria, *b* 1963: *m* 1990, Jimmy G. Penfold, son of late Graham Penfold. —— Mary Constance (*Baroness Peyton of Yeovil*), *b* 1921: *m* 1st, 1945 (*m diss* 1966), Ralph Hamilton Cobbold, who *d* 1987; 2ndly, 1966, Baron Peyton of Yeovil (Life Baron), and has issue living (by 1st *m*), David Anthony (13 Blvd des Frères Voisin, Paris 75015), *b* 1946: *m* 1972 (*m diss* 1982), Christine Elisabeth Pearcey, and has issue living, Melissa Eve *b* 1975, — Charlotte Ruth, *b* 1949: *m* 1st, 1979 (*m diss* 1984), George Michael Maguire; 2ndly, 1993, David Thomas Williams, and has issue living (by 1st *m*), Leo George *b* 1981, (by 2nd *m*) Rafe Thomas *b* 1993.

Granddaughters of late Col Guy Percy Wyndham, CB, MVO (infra):—
Issue of late Maj Guy Richard Charles Wyndham, MC, *b* 1896, *d* 1948: *m* 1st, 1920 (*m diss* 1925), Iris Winifred Youell, da of Andrew Percy Bennett, CMG, Envoy Extraor and Min Plen to Panama; 2ndly, 1930 (*m diss* 1941), Margeretha Wulfsberg:—
(By 1st *m*) Joan Olivia, *b* 1921: *m* 1st, 1947 (*m diss* 1952), Maurice Stansbury Rowdon; 2ndly, 1952, Alexander Shivarg, of 429 Fulham Rd, SW10, and has issue living, (by 1st *m*) Clare Viola, *b* 1947: *m* 1985, Joaquim Ferreira Soares, — (by 2nd *m*) Camilla Gabrielle (286 Earl's Court Rd, SW5 9AS), *b* 1953: *m* 1998, Jonathan Timothy de Beaurepaire Ross (*see* Fry, Bt, *cr* 1929). —— (By 2nd *m*) Ingrid Olivia Georgia (*Baroness Kelvedon*), *b* 1931: *m* 1st, 1951 (*m diss* 1963), Hon Jonathan Bryan Guinness (later 3rd Baron Moyne); 2ndly, 1963, Baron Kelvedon, PC (Life Baron), of 96 Cheyne Walk, SW10, and Kelvedon Hall, Brentwood, Essex, and has had issue (by 1st *m*) (*see* B Moyne), — (by 2nd *m*) (*see* B Kelvedon).

Grandsons of late Capt Hon Percy Scawen Wyndham, 3rd son of 1st Baron Leconfield:—
Issue of late Col Guy Percy Wyndham, CB, MVO, *b* 1865, *d* 1941: *m* 1st, 1892, Edwina Virginia Joanna, who *d* 1919, da of Rev Frederick Fitzpatrick, and widow of John Monck Brooks (*see* M Headfort); 2ndly, 1923, Violet Lutetia, who *d* 1979, da of late Ernest Leverson:—
(By 2nd *m*) Francis Guy Percy (530A Harrow Rd, W9) *b* 1924; *ed* Eton, and Ch Ch, Oxford; FRSL. —— Hugh Guy Osbert (64 Osborne St, Swindon), *b* 1926; *ed* Eton, and at Corpus Christi Coll, Oxford, Capt late Coldstream Guards: *m* 1961 (*m diss* 1966), Edith Elizabeth Creswick, el da of late John Watson, FRIBA, of Old Mains, Giffnock, Glasgow and has issue living, Rachel Olivia Violet, *b* 1963; ARCM.

PREDECESSORS – The 7th Duke of Somerset, who inherited the Percy estates, including the lands of Egremont, Cumberland, from his mother Elizabeth, da and heir of the 11th Earl of Northumberland, was *cr Earl of Egremont* 1749, with special remainder to his maternal nephew Sir Charles Wyndham, 4th baronet of Orchard Wyndham, Som. The Egremont estates passed to the 1st Earl of Northumberland (*cr* 1377) on his 2nd *m* to Maud (who *dsp*), sister and heir of Anthony, Lord Lucy. These, and the Sussex estates of the Percys, were devised to the 2nd Earl of Egremont. **(1)** Col GEORGE Wyndham, natural son and adopted heir of George O'Brien, 3rd Earl of Egremont: *b* 1787; a Col in the Army; *cr Baron Leconfield*, of Leconfield, E Riding of York (peerage of United Kingdom) 1859: *m* 1815, Mary Fanny, who *d* 1863, da of Rev William Blunt, of Crabbett, Sussex; *d* 1869; *s* by his son **(2)** HENRY, 2nd Baron, *b* 1830; MP for W Sussex (C) 1854-69: *m* 1867, Lady Constance Evelyn Primrose, who *d* 1939, having been raised to the rank of an Earl's da 1886, 2nd da of late Lord Dalmeny; *d* 1901; *s* by his el surviving son **(3)** CHARLES HENRY, GCVO, 3rd Baron; *b* 1872; Co Comdt Roy Sussex Vol 1917-18, and Lord-Lt of Sussex 1917-49: *m* 1911, Beatrice Violet, who *d* 1956, da of late Col Richard Hamilton Rawson, MP; *d* 1952; *s* by his brother **(4)** HUGH ARCHIBALD, 4th Baron, *b* 1877: *m* 1908, Hon Maud Mary Lyttleton, who *d* 1953, da of 8th Viscount Cobham; *d* 1963; *s* by his brother, **(5)** EDWARD SCAWEN, DSO, 5th Baron, *b* 1883: *m* 1907,

Gladys Mary, who *d* 1971, da of late Fitzroy James Wilberforce Farquhar (*see* Farquhar, Bt, colls), *d* 1967; *s* by his son **(6)** JOHN EDWARD REGINALD, MBE (who was *cr Baron Egremont*, of Petworth, co Sussex, 1963), 6th Baron, *b* 1920; Private Sec to PM 1957-63; a Trustee of Wallace Collection 1953-72; *m* 1947, Pamela, da of Capt Hon Valentine Maurice Wyndham Quin, RN (E Dunraven), *d* 1972; *s* by his el son **(7)** JOHN MAX HENRY SCAWEN, 7th Baron Leconfield, 2nd Baron Egremont, and present peer.

ELDON, EARL OF (Scott) (Earl UK 1821)

JOHN JOSEPH NICHOLAS SCOTT, 5th Earl; *b* 24 April 1937; *s* 1976; *ed* Ampleforth, and Trin Coll, Oxford; Lt Scots Gds Army Emergency Reserve: *m* 1961, Countess Claudine, yst da of Count Franz von Montjoye-Vaufrey and de la Roche, of 45 Hasenauerstrasse, Vienna 18, and has issue.

Arms – Argent, an anchor erect sable, between three lions' heads erased gules; on a chief wavy azure, a portcullis with chains or. **Crest** – A lion's head erased gules, gorged with a chain, and pendant therefrom a portcullis or. **Supporters** – Two lions guardant proper, each gorged with a double chain and a portcullis attached thereto gold, pendent from the portcullis a shield argent, charged with a civic wreath vert.

Let honour be without stain

SON LIVING

JOHN FRANCIS THOMAS MARIE JOSEPH COLUMBA FIDELIS (*Viscount Encombe*), *b* 9 July 1962: *m* 1993, Charlotte, da of Bob de Vlaming, and has issue:—.

SON LIVING - *Hon* John James R— C—, *b* 1996.

DAUGHTER LIVING - *Hon* Helena Rose C—, *b* 1994.

DAUGHTERS LIVING

Lady Tatiana Maria Laura Rose Columba Fidelis, *b* 1967: *m* 1989, Anthony C. Wilson, eldest son of Jeffery Graham Wilson, and has issue living, Shimi Fairne James Fidelis Columba, *b* 1995, — Merenna Louise Jane Fidelis Columba, *b* 1993.
Lady Victoria Laura Maria Magdalene, *b* 1968: *m* 1996, Mark C. A. Pougatch, son of late Michael Pougatch, and has issue living, Michael Columba (Sam), *b* 1998.

BROTHER LIVING

Hon Simon Peter (Frogden, Kelso, Roxburghshire TD5 8AB), *b* 1939; was a Page of Honour to HM 1953-56; *ed* Ampleforth Coll, Salamanca and Madrid Univs, and Sorbonne (Paris); Lt Scots Guards Army Emergency Reserve: *m* 1966, Mary Isabel, da of late Andrew Ramon Dalzell de Bertodano (*see* E Mexborough, 1948 Edn), and has issue living, Sebastian Andrew, *b* 1967, — Benedict Simon, *b* 1971, — James Joseph Michael, *b* 1974, — Maria Sylvia Rose, *b* 1968: *m* 1995, Gavin M. White.

COLLATERAL BRANCHES LIVING

Grandchildren of late Hon Michael Simon Scott (infra):—
Issue of late Michael Richard Scott, *b* 1937, *d* 1981: *m* 1964, Pamela Hanford (Long Lane, Far Hills, NJ 07931, USA) (who *m* 2ndly, 19—, Marshall Jeanes), da of Wellington Vandeveer:—
Michael Simon, *b* 1966. —— Andrew Fraser, *b* 1973. —— Wendy Vendeveer, *b* 1967. —— Katherine Brady, *b* 1970.

Granddaughter of late John, Viscount Encombe, el son of 3rd Earl:—
Issue of late Hon Michael Simon Scott, *b* 1900, *d* 1938: *m* 1928, Ruth (who *d* 1972, having *m* 2ndly, 1944, Lieut-Com Adams Batcheller, who *d* 1950), da of late James Cox Brady:—
Sheila Mary (Box 176, Far Hills, NJ 07931, USA), *b* 1932: *m* 1952, Philip Webster Smith, Jr, and has issue living, Philip Webster (III) (Box 944, Far Hills, NJ 07931, USA), *b* 1955: *m* 1983, Hillary, da of Vincent R. Bailey, and has issue living, Philip Webster (IV) *b* 1988, Courtney Converse *b* 1986, — Michael Simon (Box 56, Far Hills, NJ 07931, USA), *b* 1959: *m* 1987, Anne Marie, da of Cornelius Murray, and has issue living, Katherine Fraser *b* 1989, Elizabeth Clark *b* 1992, — Elizabeth Brady, *b* 1954: *m* 1979, Wayne Barry Lawrence, of 76 West St, Beverly Farms, Mass 01915, USA, and has issue living, Andrew Brady *b* 1986, Alexandra Webster *b* 1984, Elizabeth Hamilton *b* 1994.

Issue of late Hon Sir Ernest Stowell Scott, KCMG, MVO, 2nd son of 3rd Earl, *b* 1872, *d* 1953: *m* 1941, Winifred Kathleen Brodrick, who *d* 1990:—
Margaret Rachel (19 Lambourn Rd, SW4), *b* 1943: *m* 1964 (*m diss* 1973), David Edward Wyndham Tennant (*see* B Glenconner, colls).

Grandchildren of late Hon Osmund Scott (infra):—
Issue of late Lt-Col Harold Eldon Scott, *b* 1907, *d* 1997: *m* 1938, Daphne Josephine, who *d* 1985, da of Col Fitzhardinge Hancock, of Congham Hall, King's Lynn:—
David Eldon (Encombe House, Corfe Castle, Dorset), *b* 1939; *ed* Winchester, and RAC Cirencester: *m* 1966, Clover, da of His Honour Judge (Sidney Henry) Noakes, of 1 Paper Buildings, Temple, EC4, and has issue living, Rupert Eldon (The Stable House, Encombe, Corfe Castle, Dorset), *b* 1967: *m* 1994, Sophie Jane Wollen, and has issue living, Charles Eldon *b* 1995, Edward Eldon *b* 1997, — Henry Eldon, *b* 1969: *m* 1997, Sacha J., da of late Peter Domville-Musters, of E Grinstead, W Sussex. —— Verena Mary, *b* 1942: *m* 1963, Simon Norman Philips (*see* E Ducie, colls, 1956 Edn), of Huerta Alajate, 29691 Manilva, Malaga, Spain, and has issue living, Lucy Jane, *b* 1964, — Sophie Ann, *b* 1966. —— Angela Lindsay, *b* 1949: *m* 1st, 1978 (*m diss* 1987), Daniel Sicardi; 2ndly, 1987, Count Christopher Levin Orssich (*see* B Faringdon, colls, 1985 Edn), of Mayfield, W Grafton, Marlborough, Wilts, and has issue living (by 1st *m*), Rebecca Tania, *b* 1983, — (by 2nd *m*), Nicholas Robert, *b* 1988. —— Suzanne (14 Brunswick St, Bath BA1 6PQ), *b* 1952: *m* 1st, 1977 (*m diss* 1995), Peter Woloszynski; 2ndly, 1999, Francis Edward Gaius Davy, and has issue living, (by 1st *m*) Harry Maximilian Andrew, *b* 1982, — Emily, *b* 1980.

Issue of late Capt Alan Dudley Scott, *b* 1910, *d* 1951: *m* 1936, Dorothy Dulany (Thea) (who *d* 1988, having *m* 2ndly, 1953, Maj Alexander Soldatenkov, who *d* 1954), only da of late Lt-Col Sefton Dulany Brancker, of The Croft, Crowborough, Sussex:—
Dudley John Eldon (Patrijsstraat 49, 6971 VP Brummen, The Netherlands), *b* 1939: *m* 1st, 1961, Irene Florence, only da of Frederick James Smith, of 30 Old Lane, Chobham, Surrey; 2ndly, 1982, Annelies, da of late Jacobus Leonardus Arnoldus Hotz, and has issue living (by 1st *m*), Alan James, *b* 1964, — Maria Lynn, *b* 1963. —— Caroline Edith Mary, *b* 1946: *m* 1st, 1969 (*m diss* 1984), Michael John Theobald; 2ndly, 1992, Anthony Terrence Garrett, of 4 Castilian Mews, Ramleaze Drive, Shaw, Swindon, Wilts SN5 9PR, and has issue living (by 1st *m*), Emma Caroline Mary, *b* 1975, — Amelia Margaret Jennifer, *b* 1978. —— Jennifer Dorothy Dulany, *b* 1948.

Issue of late Hon Osmund Scott, 3rd son of 3rd Earl; *b* 1876, *d* 1948: *m* 1906, Mary Cecilia, who *d* 1941, da of late Com Dudley Charles Stuart, RN (M Bute, colls):—
Eric Surtees, MBE, *b* 1912; *ed* Bradfield, and RMC Sandhurst; Lt-Col (ret) The Buffs (Royal E Kent Regt); N-W Europe 1944-45 (MBE Mil 1945): *m* 1938, Rose Anne, who *d* 1994, only da of late Lt-Col Charles Edward Stewart, RA, and has issue living, Michael Ian Eldon, CB, CBE, DSO (c/o Royal Bank of Scotland, Whitehall, SW1), *b* 1941; *ed* Bradfield, and RMA Sandhurst; Maj-Gen late Scots Gds; Equerry to HRH The Duke of Gloucester 1965-66; served S Atlantic Campaign 1982 (DSO 1982); Gov Edinburgh Castle 1993-94; Military Sec 1995-96; CBE (Mil) 1987, CB (Mil) 1997: *m* 1968, Veronica Mary, yr da of late Capt J. H. Daniell, and of Mrs J. A. Hilton, of 106 Cranmer Court, SW3, and has issue living, Charles Daniell Eldon *b* 1970, Louisa Claire *b* 1971, — Veronica Susan, *b* 1944: *m* 1st, 1965, Michael Conway Phayre-Mudge, who *d* 1983; 2ndly, 1994, as his 2nd wife, Christopher William Kerr Devas (*see* M Lothian, colls), and has issue living (by 1st *m*), Marcus Andrew *b* 1968, Zoë Catherine *b* 1970: *m* 1997, Giles John Palmer (and has issue living, Grace Jasmine *b* 1999). *Residence* – Pound House, Wareham, Dorset. —— †Kenneth Bertram, MC, *b* 1915; served 1939-45 War (MC) as Maj Royal W Kent Regt: *m* 1939, Denise Primrose Garnet (Kim) (who *d* 1968, having *m* 2ndly, 1952, Alan Blackwell, of Laurel Farm, Little Barningham, Aldborough, Norwich), 2nd da of Garnet Leslie Clark, of The Red House, Tadworth, Surrey, and was *ka* in Sicily 1943, leaving issue, John Kenneth Eldon, *b* 1940; *ed* privately, and at Ruskin Sch of Art, Oxford.

Issue of late Capt Hon Denys Scott, 4th son of 3rd Earl, *b* 1877, *d* 1962: *m* 1907, Lillis Amy, who *d* 1970, da of late Com Dudley Charles Stuart, RN (M Bute, colls):—
John Ernest Dudley (Ridgeway, Eastacombe, nr Barnstaple, N Devon EX31 3NT), *b* 1908; AFRAeS; formerly Sqdn-Ldr RAFO: *m* 1st, 1934 (*m diss* 1937), Joan Gwendolen, da of R. Clayton-Cooper; 2ndly, 1937, Ethel Daphne Smith, who *d* 1956; 3rdly, 1957, Margaret Lila Monro, MRCS, LRCP, who *d* 1973, da of Bertram John Monro, of Rydal Mount, Hendon; 4thly, 1975, Barbara Anne Veit, who *d* 1990, and has had issue (by 1st *m*), Peter Denys John, QC (4 Eldon Rd, W8 5PU; Fountain Court, Temple, EC4), *b* 1935; *ed* Monroe High Sch, Rochester, NY, and Balliol Coll, Oxford (MA); late Lieut RHA; Bar Middle Temple 1960, QC 1978, Chm Bar Council 1987 (Vice-Chm 1985-86), — (by 2nd *m*) Roger John Stuart (Barn Owl, Holmacott, Instow, Bideford, N Devon EX39 4LR), *b* 1939; *ed* Uppingham, and RAF Tech Coll, Henlow; Sqdn-Ldr RAF: *m* 1st, 1967 (*m diss* 1991), Mary Alexandra, eldest da of late Alexander Lynch, of Limerick; 2ndly, 1991, Sally Constance, da of late Donald Golege-Steel, of Hurley Cottage, Hurley, Berks, and has issue living (by 1st *m*), Alexander John Stuart *b* 1968, Louise Katherine *b* 1973, — (Daphne) Charmian, *b* 1942: *m* 1964, Jeremy David Pickett-Heaps, and was *k* in a flying accidcent in Colorado, USA, 1971, leaving issue, David Angus *b* 1967, Rebecca *b* 1969, — Georgina Rosemary, *b* 1944.

PREDECESSORS – **(1)** *Rt Hon Sir* JOHN SCOTT, KB, one of the most distinguished lawyers of England, was son of a merchant at Newcastle, and yr brother of Baron Stowell (*cr* 1821, extinct 1836); was Solicitor-Gen 1788, Attorney-Gen 1793, Lord Chief Justice of the Common Pleas 1799-1801, and Lord High Chancellor 1801-6 and 1807-27; *cr Baron Eldon*, of Eldon, co Durham (peerage of Great Britain) 1799, and *Viscount Encombe* and *Earl of Eldon* (peerage of United Kingdom) 1821; *d* 1838; *s* by his grandson **(2)** JOHN, DCL, 2nd Earl, *b* 1805; MP for Truro 1828-31: *m* 1831, Hon Louisa Duncombe, da of 1st Baron Feversham; *d* 1854; *s* by his son **(3)** JOHN, 3rd Earl; *b* 1845: *m* 1869, Henrietta Minna, who *d* 1921, da of Capt Henry Martin Turner; *d* 1926; *s* by his grandson **(4)** JOHN, GCVO (son of late John, Viscount Encombe, el son of 3rd Earl), 4th Earl; *b* 1899; a Lord-in-Waiting to HM 1937-68: *m* 1934, Hon Magdalen Mary Charlotte Fraser, OBE, who *d* 1969, da of 14th Lord Lovat; *d* 1976; *s* by his el son **(5)** JOHN JOSEPH NICHOLAS, 5th Earl and present peer; also Viscount Encombe, and Baron Eldon.

ELGIN AND KINCARDINE, EARL OF (Bruce) (Earl S 1633)

We have been

ANDREW DOUGLAS ALEXANDER THOMAS BRUCE, KT, CD, 11th Earl of Elgin and 15th Earl of Kincardine; *b* 17 Feb 1924; *s* 1968; *ed* Eton, and Balliol Coll, Oxford (MA); Hon LLD Dundee and Glasgow, Hon D Litt St Mary's, Nova Scotia; JP and DL of co Fife, Lord Lieut since 1987; HM Lt-Col; Comdt Fife Bn, Army Cadet Force 1951-65; Grand Master Mason of Scotland 1961-65; Lord High Commr to General Assembly of Church of Scotland 1980-81; Ensign Queen's Body Guard for Scotland (Royal Co of Archers), and Bde Pres, Boys' Bde 1963-85; a Dir Scottish Amicable Life Assurance Soc; Chm Nat Savings Cttee for Scotland 1972-78; Hon Col The Elgin Regt (Canada); Hon Col 153(H) Regt RCT(V) TAVR 1980-87; 1939-45 War as Lt Scots Guards (wounded); KT 1981, CD 1985: *m* 1959, Victoria Mary, only da of Maj Dudley George Usher, MBE, TD, Scottish Horse (Hunter Blair, Bt, colls), and has issue.

Arms – Or, a saltire and chief gules, on a canton argent, a lion rampant azure, armed and langued of the second. Crest – A lion statant, tail extended azure, armed and langued gules. Supporters – Two wild men, proper, wreathed round the temples and loins with laurel vert.
Residence – Broomhall, Dunfermline, Fife KY11 3DU.

SONS LIVING

CHARLES EDWARD (*Lord Bruce*), *b* 19 Oct 1961; *ed* Eton, and St Andrews Univ (MA); a Page of Honour to HM Queen Elizabeth The Queen Mother 1975-77; Dir Environmental Trust for Scotland, Memb Exec Council Assocn for Protection of Rural Scotland: *m* 1990, Amanda Leigh, yr da of James Movius, of Fairbanks, Alaska, and has issue:—

> SONS LIVING - *Hon* James Andrew Charles Robert (*Master of Bruce*), *b* 16 Nov 1991, — *Hon* George Benjamin Thomas, *b* 1993.
> DAUGHTER LIVING - *Hon* Antonia Jean, *b* 1990.

Residence – The Abbey House, Culross, Fife KY12 8JB. *Club* – Brooks's.

Hon Adam Robert, *b* 1968; *ed* Glenalmond, Balliol Coll, Oxford (MA) (Pres Oxford Union 1989), and Edinburgh Univ (LLB); Solicitor and Notary Public. *Residence* – 8 Montgomery St, Edinburgh EH7 5JS. *Club* – New (Edinburgh).

Hon Alexander Victor, *b* 1971; *ed* Glenalmond, and Napier Univ: *m* 1998, Victoria M., elder da of David Bythell, of East Kirkland, Newton Stewart.

DAUGHTERS LIVING

Lady Georgiana Mary, *b* 1960.
Lady Antonia Katherine, *b* 1964: *m* 1989, Marcel Ballot, son of Jacques-Henri Ballot, of Paris.

BROTHERS LIVING

Hon James Michael Edward, CBE, *b* 1927; *ed* Eton; late Lt Scots Guards; a JP of Perthshire; FRSA, FInstD; a Member Home Grown Timber Advisory Cttee 1963-94; Chm SWOAC Holdings Ltd 1967-93; Hon Fellow Scottish Council for Development & Industry 1993, Hon Fellow Game Conservancy 1993; CBE 1992: *m* 1st, 1950 (*m diss* 1974), Hon (Margaret) Jean Dagbjørt Coats, da of 2nd Baron Glentanar (ext); 2ndly, 1975, Morven-Anne, who *d* 1994, da of Alistair Macdonald, of Lairg, Sutherlandshire, and has had issue (by 1st *m*), †Robert James Thomas, *b* 1953; *ed* Eton; *d* 1979, — John Edward (Balmanno Castle, Perth PH2 9HG), *b* 1958: *m* 1995, Caroline T., da of Peter Fitch, and of Mrs Kenneth Lumsden, of Marlee, Blairgowrie, and has issue living, George Robert *b* 1998, — Michael Andrew (Glen Tanar House, Aboyne, Aberdeenshire AB34 5EU), *b* 1961: *m* 1988, Claire M., eldest da of James Mattocks, of Edinburgh, and has issue living, Alasdair James Thomas *b* 1991, Angus William Robert *b* 1996, Eleanor Marie Jean *b* 1993, — (Janet) Clare, *b* 1954: *m* 1979, John Seton Burrell Carson, of Congalton, N Berwick, E Lothian EH30 5JL, elder son of Alan Carson, of Drumbain, Dumfrie, Ayrshire, and has issue living, David *b* 1986, Iona Jane *b* 1981, Rachel Anne *b* 1983, Alice Mary *b* 1989, Rosanna Jean *b* (triplet) 1989, Sophie Katherine *b* (triplet) 1989, — (by 2nd *m*) Alexander James, *b* 1977, — Simon Alistair, *b* 1979, — Katherine Ann, *b* 1980, — Emma Victoria, *b* 1987. *Residence* – Dron House, Balmanno, by Perth. *Clubs* – New (Edinburgh), Pratt's.

Hon Edward David, *b* 1936; *ed* Eton, and Balliol Coll, Oxford (BA 1960); late Lieut Intelligence Corps; Chm Bruce Stevenson Ltd; Chm Church of Scotland Insurance Co; Pres Youth Clubs Scotland: *m* 1st, 1960 (*m diss* 1998), Sara Elisabeth Wallop, yr da of late Capt Newton James Wallop William-Powlett, DSC, JP, RN (*see* E Portsmouth, colls); 2ndly, 1999, Jessie Mary, yr da of John Jephson Jones, and has issue living (by 1st *m*), (Newton) Edward John, *b* 1964: *m* 1996, Joanna Christian, yst da of Capt Donald Seymour Erskine, of Cleish House, Cleish, Kinross-shire (*see* E Buchan, colls), — Anna Catherine *b* 1962: *m* 1988, Edward H. Hocknell, of 5 Dundas St, Edinburgh, elder son of Peter Hocknell, of Willaston, Cheshire, and has issue living, Henrietta Jean Wallop *b* 1992, Catherine Elisabeth *b* 1994, Grizel Patience *b* 1998. *Residence* – Gallowridgehill, Dunfermline, Kinross.

SISTERS LIVING

Lady Martha Veronica, OBE, TD, *b* 1921: Gov HM Prison, Greenock 1970-75, Gov HM Institution, Cornton Vale, Stirling 1975-83, and a JP for co Fife; Lady-in-Waiting to HRH late Princess Royal Jan to March 1965; OBE (Mil) 1958. *Residence* – Gardener's Cottage, The Old Orchard, Limekilns, Dunfermline KY11 3HS.

Lady Jean Christian, *b* 1923; formerly in WAAF; DL Perth 1988: *m* 1945, Capt David Wemyss of Wemyss, late Roy Corps of Signals (*see* E Wemyss, colls). *Residence* – Invermay, Forteviot, Perthshire.

WIDOW LIVING OF SON OF NINTH EARL

Mary Patricia, da of late Maj Donald Ramsay Macdonald, DSO, MC, of Hollymount, co Carlow, and formerly wife of Gerald Francis Annesley, of Castlewellan, co Down: *m* 1976, as his 3rd wife, Maj Hon Bernard Bruce, MC, who *d* 1983. *Residence* – Auld Upper Cloan, Auchterarder, Perthshire.

COLLATERAL BRANCHES LIVING

Issue of late Major Hon Robert Bruce, CBE, 2nd son of 9th Earl, *b* 1882, *d* 1959: *m* 1910, Mary Katherine, who *d* 1982, da of late Maj-Gen Hon John Edward Lindley (*see* B Lindley):—
Veronica Mary (Finlarig House, Rafford, Morayshire), *b* 1911; Director of Cygnet Ballet Sch, Forres. —— Isobel Ursula, *b* 1920; sometime in WRNS. *Residence* – 114 Watchfield Court, Sutton Court Rd, Chiswick, W4 4ND.

Issue of late Col Hon David Bruce, 4th son of 9th Earl, *b* 1888, *d* 1964: *m* 1919, Jennet, OBE, who *d* 1982, da of late Rt Rev Atherton Gwillym Rawstorne, DD, Suffragan Bishop of Whalley:—
Rachel Mary, *b* 1922; HM Coastguard Ser 1940-45: *m* 1967, as his 2nd wife, Rear-Adm Bryan Cecil Durant, CB, DSO, DSC, who *d* 1983, of The Old House, Bighton, nr Alresford, Hants.

Issue of late Capt Hon John Bernard Bruce, RN, 5th son of 9th Earl, *b* 1892, *d* 1971: *m* 1923, Helen Rachel, who *d* 1983, 3rd da of late Henry Feilden Rawstorne, of Roche Court, Fareham, Hants:—
Henry Victor BRUCE OF SALLOCH (Rodfield Cottage, Ovington Down, Alresford, Hants SO24 0HS; 39 Ashley Gdns, Ambrosden Av, SW1; Farmers' Club, and MCC), *b* 1924; *ed* Eton and RAC, Cirencester: Lt-Cdr RN (ret), and a Farmer; recognised in the name of Bruce of Salloch by Lord Lyon 1985; JP and DL Hants 1984; Councillor of Winchester, Itchen Stoke and Ovington with Northington 1963-74; Chm of Hants Co Scout Council 1964-75, since when a Vice-Pres; a Gen Commr of Income Tax since 1966: *m* 1951, Helen Vernon Wallop, da of late Vice-Adm Sir Peveril Barton Reibey Wallop William-Powlett, KCB, KCMG, CBE, DSO (*see* E Portsmouth, colls), and has issue living, Peveril John (Hampage House, Ovington, nr Alresford, Hants), *b* 1953; *ed* Eton; ACA 1976, FCA 1981; Farmer: *m* 1986, Rosamond Cornelia McLay (Minna), yr da of Neil McLay Mills (*see* B Hazlerigg, 1990 Edn), and has issue living, Otto Feilden *b* 1989, Finn Cardigan *b* 1992, Todd Heron *b* 1996, — Alastair Andrew Bernard Reibey BRUCE OF CRIONAICH (22 Comeragh Rd, W14 9HP; Tigh na Feidh, Inverie, Knoydart, Inverness-shire; Cavalry and Guards Club), *b* 1960; *ed* Milton Abbey, and RMA Sandhurst; late Lt Scots Guards, served S Atlantic Campaign 1982; Maj SG (Media Operations Group (v)); recognised in the name of Bruce of Crionaich by Lord Lyon 1984; CStJ, Assist Dir of Ceremonies for the OStJ, Assist Vice-Pres Merrill Lynch 1983-89, since when a TV documentary maker and commentator; Gov Milton Abbey; Fitzalan Pursuivant Extraordinary since 1998, — Robina Helen, *b* 1952; SRN 1974; Member Nightingale Fund Council 1982: *m* 1977, Nigel Edward Charles Talbot-Ponsonby, and has issue (*see* E Shrewsbury, colls), — Lucinda Jane, *b* 1956: *m* 1981, Laurence Keith Scott, of Melbourne, Australia, and has issue living, Henry Edward Osborne *b* 1982, Toby Alexander Peveril *b* 1984, Oliver Charles Somerville *b* 1987, Barnaby Richard Laurence *b* 1989, Harvey Michael Luckman *b* 1991. —— *Rev* Francis Bernard (6 Gloucester St, Cirencester, Glos GL7 2DG; Gate Cottage, Mungrisdale, Penrith, Cumbria CA11 0XR), *b* 1930; *ed* Eton, Trin Coll, Oxford (MA), and Westcott House, Camb; Assist Curate of Bury 1954-58, and Sherborne Abbey, and Curate in charge of St Paul's, Sherborne 1958-61, R of St Michael and All Angels, Croston 1961-86, V of Bibury with Winson and R of Barnsley, Glos 1986-95: *m* 1957, Fiona Jane Beryl, da of Capt John Robert Sutherland Haines, CBE, RN, and has issue living, Simon Jock, *b* 1959: *m* 1988, Emma Félise, only da of Sir Martin Wakefield Jacomb (*see* Heathcoat-Amory, Bt, colls), and has issue living, Patrick Francis Martin *b* 1991, Dominic Simon Mark *b* 1993, Zoe Fiona Evelyn *b* 1995, — Jonathan Francis, *b* 1967. — Emma Cecilia Rachel, *b* 1960. —— Victor Robert (Eastwood, Altass, by Lairg, Sutherland IV27 4EU; Waterford, 8 Claremont Rd, Marlow, Bucks), *b* 1932; *ed* Eton; MB, BS London 1956; DRCOG 1958; Surg-Lt RN (ret): *m* 1956, Dorothy May, MBE, da of late Rev Arthur E. Pavey, and has issue living, Angus Robert John, *b* 1960: *m* 1985, Jill, da of Brian Moughtin, and has issue living, John Yardley *b* 1989, Ben River *b* 1995, Hannah May 1991, — Hamish Charles Victor, *b* 1962: *m* 1990, Susan Mary, da of Gordon Landreth, and has issue living, David Alexander *b* 1993, Jonathan Peter *b* 1996. —— Alexander Rawstorne (67 Av Ernest Solvay, 1310 La Hulpe, Belgium), *b* 1936; *ed* Eton: *m* 1st, 1962, Béatrice Germaine, who *d* 1995, da of Jacques-Etienne Rossier, of Champbabaud, Veytaux, Vaud, Switzerland; 2ndly, 1998, Julie Mary Horrocks, da of Eugene Maloney, of 5 Whalley Drive, Formby. —— The late Capt Hon John B. Bruce, RN, and Mrs Bruce, also adopted a son, Timothy Robertson BRUCE (The Old Rectory, Combs, Stowmarket, Suffolk IP14 2JS), *b* 1942; *ed* Radley: *m* 1st, 1972 (*m diss* 1983), (Diana) Olivia, da of late George Raymond Tibbitt (*see* Agnew, Bt, *cr* 1895, colls, 1970 Edn); 2ndly, 1988, Mrs Susan Mary Nicholson, da of John Fraser Carnegie, DFC (*see* D Fife, colls), and has issue living (by 1st *m*), Tania Romayne, *b* 1973, — Diana Iona, *b* 1975. —— Constance Madeline (Gloucester House, Landsdowne Rd, Sevenoaks, Kent TN13 3XU), *b* 1927: *m* 1949, Lt-Cdr Godfrey Joseph Hines, RN (ret), and has issue living, Catherine Angela, *b* 1950: *m* 1972, Clive Ward, and has issue living, Joanna *b* 1974, Diana *b* 1976, Emily *b* 1978, — Fiona Madeleine, *b* 1952: *m* 1972, David Reynolds, and has issue living, Johnathon Richard *b* 1973, Mark David *b* 1974. —— Mabel Cecilia Helen (Celia), *b* 1939: *m* 1962, Lt-Cdr Lachlan Ronald Duncan Mackintosh, 30th Chief of Mackintosh, OBE, JP, FSA (Scot), RN, late Lord Lieut Inverness, who *d* 1995, of Moy Hall, Tomatin, Inverness IV13 7YQ, and has issue living, John Lachlan, The Mackintosh of Mackintosh, *b* 1969, — Louisa Celia, *b* 1962: *m* 1987, Stuart Robert Cross, of 1 Riverside Rd, Wormit, Fife DD6 8LR, — Bridget Margaret, *b* 1966: *m* 1993, Paul W. Dickson, of 48 Pentland Drive, Comiston, Edinburgh EH10 6PX, and has issue living, Calum *b* 1996, Heather Mackintosh *b* 1994.

Grandsons of late Hon Frederick John Bruce (infra):—
Issue of late Lewis Bruce, *b* 1880, *d* 1961: *m* 1911, Anne Margaret Macdonald, who *d* 1961, da of late Robert Burt Ranken, WS, of Edinburgh:—
John Frederick Lambton, *b* 1912: *m* 1941, his cousin, Marjory Katherine Fernie, who *d* 1994, da of late Capt Charles Bruce (*see* E Elgin, colls, 1995 Edn), and has issue living, Penelope Margaret, *b* 1943: *m* 1974, Richard Barry Bigger,

and has issue living, Rachel Diana *b* 1976, — Juliet Louisa, *b* 1950: *m* 1979, David Frederick John Nokes, — Janet Marion, *b* 1956: *m* 1978, Colin Geoffrey Singer, and has issue living, Helen Nadine *b* 1982, Emma Louise *b* 1984, Stephanie Elise *b* 1989. *Residence* – Lambda Cottage, Wick Hill, Finchampstead, Berks. —— Robert Richard Fernie, DFC (1 Orchard Close, Hardwicke, Gloucester GL2 4SZ), *b* 1915; BMus 1938; 1939-45 War as Fl-Lt RAF Vol Reserve (DFC and Bar): *m* 1941, Beatrice, da of late A. Tombolini, and has issue living, Richard Stephen Witherington (347 Crawford Rd, Inglewood, W Australia 6052), *b* 1942, MB, BS London; FRCA, FANZCA, MRACMA: *m* 1st, 1965 (*m diss* 1969), Frances Mary, da of K. G. Morgan, MRCVS, of Lyttleton, Welsh St, Chepstow; 2ndly, 1969 (*m diss* 1984), Katherine Jane, da of late Mrs J. A. Hunter, of W Australia, and has issue living (by 1st *m*), Katherine Blanche Mary *b* 1966, — Anthony James Lewis (Sportmanstraat 10, 2341 JG, Oegstgeest, The Netherlands), *b* 1948; BSc: *m* 1st, 1972 (*m diss* 1991), Glenys Vaughan, da of late J. Jones, of Caernarvon; 2ndly, 1994, Veronica Ellen, da of late A. B. Seccombe, of Mansfield, and has issue living (by 1st *m*), Elgan Lewis *b* 1977, Lowri Ann *b* 1975, Catrin Ellen *b* 1981, — Katharine Anne Russell (66 The Willows, Quedgeley, Gloucester GL2 4XG), *b* 1945; MCSP: *m* 1968, John Mervyn Henry Clements, MA, ACA, who *d* 1998, and has issue living, Timothy Robert Henry *b* 1968, Charles Richard Edward *b* 1971, Victoria Penelope Louise *b* 1972. —— †James Alexander, *b* 1919: *m* 1952, Joan Beryl Marion Elizabeth (Hill Cottage, Hazeley Lea, Hartley Wintney, Hants RG27 8ND), da of Granville Alexander Silby, and widow of Group Capt Walter Donald Butler, RAF, and *d* 1989, leaving issue, Nigel Charles, *b* 1954, — Miranda Veronica, *b* 1953. —— Katharine Anne Doughty (Coriander Cottage, 1 Deer Park View, Odiham, Hook, Hants RG29 1JY), *b* 1921; ARCM: *m* 1971, Sidney John Doe, who *d* 1993.

Grandchildren of late Capt Charles Bruce (infra):—
Issue of late Lieut David Charles Richard Bruce, RN, *b* 1928; *d* 1957: *m* 1950, Georgina (PO Box 242, Paphos Post Office, Paphos, Greece) (who *m* 2ndly, 1968, Peter Joseph Bruce-Souster), da of G. E. Keay, of 5 Erith Rd, Bexleyheath, Kent:—
Roland Christopher, *b* 1956. —— Clarissa Jane Fernie, *b* 1952. —— Fiona Geraldine (Rosemullion, 54 Roman Way, Glastonbury, Som), *b* 1953. —— Miranda Jacqueline (Rosemullion, 54 Roman Way, Glastonbury, Som), *b* 1955.

Granddaughters of late Hon Frederick John Bruce, yst son of 8th Earl:—
Issue of late Capt Charles Bruce, *b* 1883, *d* 1958: *m* 1918, Joan, who *d* 1984, da of Isaac Newton Woodiwiss, of Trusthope Hall, Lincolnshire:—
Isobel Seaton, *b* 1921: *m* 1956, Joseph Henry Clift, who *d* 1986, and has issue living, Michael Charles David, *b* 1957, — Simon Paul, *b* 1963. *Residence* – 5 Lemin Parc, Reawla Lane, Gwinear, Hayle, Cornwall TR27 5HJ. —— Jill Rosalind Dodsworth (The Old Rectory, E Bridgford, Nottingham NG13 8PE), *b* 1927; BA, Oxford: *m* 1st, 1949 (*m diss* 1968), James Mayo Alastair Gunn; 2ndly, 1977, Bryan L. C. Dodsworth, and has issue living (by 1st *m*), Henry Alastair Bruce (The Bothy, West Gables, Hill Brow, Liss, Hants GU33 7QR), *b* 1951: *m* 1978 (*m diss* 1993), his 2nd cousin, Rosalind Claire, da of late J. Alexander Oxenford, of Shepherd's Purse, Ashprington, S Devon (*see* E Elgin, colls, 1958 Edn), and has issue living, Richard Henry Charles *b* 1982, Thomas Robert Alexander *b* 1985, Jessica Mary Veronica *b* 1980, — David James Paul (The School House, Ffestiniog, Gwynedd LL41 4NF), *b* 1956: *m* 1979, Sheila, da of James McGlasson, of 78 Forest Rd, Selkirk, and has issue living, Matthew David *b* 1981, Kester James *b* 1984, — Nicola Fernie (90 Hawksley Rd, N16 0TJ), *b* 1952, — Ann Veronica, *b* 1954: *m* 1987, Dr Brendan Francis Patrick, of 22 Nethergate, Crail, Fife KY10 3TY, and has issue living, Francesca Maria Julia *b* 1991, Olivia Clare Louise *b* 1994.

Granddaughter of Robert Charles Bruce, MC (infra):—
Issue of late David Bruce, *b* 1920, *d* 1978: *m* 1949 (*m diss* 1958), Elizabeth Joan, da of late Maj-Gen Philip Saxon George Gregson-Ellis, CB, OBE (*see* Lloyd, Bt (ext) 1975 Edn):—
(Cynthia) Penelope Helen, *b* 1951: *m* 1981, Charles Walter Bartholomew Pumphrey (*see* Riddell, Bt), of 23 Trinity Crescent, SW17 7AG, and has issue living, Oliver James, *b* 1986, — David Laurence, *b* 1989, — Katharine Elizabeth, *b* 1983.

Granddaughter of late Charles Thomas Bruce, el son of late Hon Thomas Charles Bruce, 5th son of 7th Earl:—
Issue of late Robert Charles Bruce, MC, *b* 1898, *d* 1953: *m* 1919, Hon Kate Mary Maugham, who *d* 1961, da of 1st Viscount Maugham:—
Katherine Mary (Garth House, Llangammarch Wells, Breconshire), *b* 1928: *m* 1st, 1948 (*m diss* 1960), John Scott; 2ndly, 1968, Francis Amcotts Wilson (*see* Wilson, Bt, *cr* 1874), and has issue living, (by 1st *m*) Caroline Judith, *b* 1950: *m* 1st, 1970 (*m diss* 1984), Michael David Sykes; 2ndly, 1990, Adrian Charles de Vries Owen-Smith, and has issue living (by 1st *m*), Jeremy James *b* 1974, Wiliam Oliver *b* 1978, (by 2nd *m*) Emily Florence *b* 1990, — Katherine Dinah (twin) *b* 1950: *m* 1971, John Hunter Pemberton, and has issue living, Michael Hunter *b* 1975, Susan Clare *b* 1973, — and has an adopted son and da (by 2nd *m*) (*see* Wilson, Bt, *cr* 1874).

PREDECESSORS – (1) Thomas BRUCE, of Clackmannan: *m* Marjorie Charteris; *d* 1359; *s* by their son (2) Robert, who had a Charter of King DAVID II of castle, lands and barony of Clackmannan 9 Dec 1359; *s* 1403 by his son (3) Robert; *s* 1405 by his son (4) David; *s* by his son (5) John; *s* by his son (6) Sir David, who made his second son (7) David, heir to Barony of Clackmannan 1481; *s* by his son (8) Sir David, who *m* Jean Blaccader of Tulliallan, and had 6 sons and 4 daughters, of whom 3rd son, (9) Edward Bruce was *m* to Alison Reid, and had 4 sons. This second son was (10) *Sir* EDWARD Bruce, Knt, PC, a Lord of Session 1597-1603, accompanied King James to England on his accession 1603, was naturalized that year, and appointed Master of the Rolls for life; *cr Lord Kinloss* (peerage of Scotland) 1602, with remainder to his heirs and assigns whatsoever, and *Lord Bruce of Kinloss* (peerage of Scotland) 1604 with remainder to his heirs male; *d* 1611; *s* by his el son (11) EDWARD, KB, 2nd Lord; *k* in a duel 1613; *s* by his brother (12) THOMAS, 3rd Lord; *cr Earl of Elgin* (peerage of Scotland) 1633 with remainder to heirs male whatever bearing the name and arms of Bruce, and *Baron Bruce*, of Whorlton, co York (peerage of England) 1640; *d* 1663; *s* by his son (13) ROBERT, 2nd Earl; *cr Baron Bruce*, of Skelton, co York, *Viscount Bruce*, of Ampthill, Beds, and *Earl of Ailesbury*, co Bucks (peerage of England) 1663; Lord Chamberlain 1685; *d* 1685; *s* by his son (14) THOMAS, 3rd Earl of Elgin and 2nd Earl of Ailesbury; *d* 1741; *s* by his son (15) CHARLES, 4th Earl of Elgin and 3rd Earl of Ailesbury; *cr Baron Bruce*, of Tottenham (peerage of Great Britain) 1746, with remainder to his nephew Hon Thomas-Brudenell, 4th son of 3rd Earl of Cardigan; *d* 1746, when the Lordship of Kinloss became abeyant (*see* Ly Kinloss), the Lordship of Bruce of Tottenham reverted to his nephew (ante) (*see* M Ailesbury), and the Earldom of Elgin and Lordship of Bruce of Kinloss devolved upon his kinsman and heir male (16) CHARLES BRUCE, 5th Earl, who in 1740 had *s* as 9th Earl of Kincardine (see note *), assumed the joint title of Earl of Elgin and Kincardine; *d* 1771; *s* by his el son (17) WILLIAM ROBERT, 6th Earl of Elgin and 10th Earl of Kincardine; *d* 1771; *s* by his brother (18) THOMAS, KC, PC, 7th Earl of Elgin and 11th Earl of Kincardine; a Gen in the Army, a Representative Peer 1790-1840, and successively Ambassador to Brussels, Berlin, and Constantinople; the "Elgin Marbles" deposited in the British Museum were collected by him during his residence in Turkey; *d* 1841; *s* by his son (19) JAMES, KT, GCB, KSI, 8th Earl of Elgin and 12th Earl of Kincardine, *b* 1811; MP for Southampton 1841-2,

Gov-Gen of Jamaica 1842-6, and of Canada 1846, Ambassador on special missions to China 1859 and 1860, Postmaster-Gen 1859, and Gov-Gen of India 1860-3; *cr Baron Elgin*, of Elgin (peerage of United Kingdom) 1849: *m* 1st, 1841, Elizabeth Mary, who *d* 1843, da of Charles Lennox Cumming-Bruce, MP, of Dunphail, Morayshire; 2ndly, 1846, Lady Mary Louisa Lambton, CI, da of 1st Earl of Durham; *d* 1863; *s* by his son (20) VICTOR ALEXANDER, KG, GCSI, GCIE, PC, 9th Earl of Elgin and 13th Earl of Kincardine, *b* 1849; Treasurer of the Household and Commr of Works and Buildings 1886, Viceroy of India 1894-9, and Sec of State for Colonies Dec 1905 to April 1908; Lord-Lieut of Fife 1886-1917: *m* 1st, 1876, Lady Constance Mary Carnegie, CI, who *d* 1909, da of 9th Earl of Southesk, KT; 2ndly, 1913, Gertrude Lilian, who *d* 1971, da of late Com William Sherbrooke, RN, of Oxton Hall, Notts, and widow of Capt Frederick Charles Ashley Ogilvy, RN; *d* 1917; *s* by his el son (21) EDWARD JAMES, KT, CMG, TD, CD, 10th Earl of Elgin and 14th Earl of Kincardine, *b* 1881; Lord High Commr to Gen Assembly of Ch of Scotland 1925-26, Pres and Chm of Scottish Development Council 1931-46; and Lord-Lieut of Fife 1935-65: *m* 1921, Hon Dame Katherine Elizabeth Cochrane, DBE, who *d* 1989, el da of 1st Baron Cochrane of Cults; *d* 1968; *s* by his son (22) ANDREW DOUGLAS ALEXANDER THOMAS, 11th Earl of Elgin, and 15th Earl of Kincardine, and present peer; also Lord Bruce of Kinloss, Lord Bruce of Torry, and Baron Elgin.

*(1) Sir EDWARD Bruce, Knt; *cr Lord Bruce of Torry*, and *Earl of Kincardine* (peerage of Scotland) 1647, with remainder to heirs general; *dsp*; *s* by his brother (2) ALEXANDER, PC, 2nd Earl; after the Restoration the Govt of Scotland was placed in his hands, and he was appointed an Extraordinary Lord of Session; *d* 1680; *b* by his son (3) ALEXANDER, 3rd Earl; *d* unmarried 1705, when the honours were claimed by his sister Lady Mary Cochrane, and also by his kinsman only son of Robert Bruce, uncle of 1st Earl; the competition terminated in favour of the latter (4) ALEXANDER, 4th Earl; *s* by his el son (5) ROBERT, 5th Earl; *dsp*; *s* by his brother (6) ALEXANDER, 6th Earl, *dsp*; *s* by his brother (7) THOMAS, 7th Earl; *s* by his el son (8) WILLIAM, 8th Earl; *s* by his son (9) CHARLES, 9th Earl, who *s* as 5th Earl of Elgin.

ELIBANK, LORD (Erskine-Murray) (Lord S 1643, Bt S 1628)
(Title pronounced "Ellibank")

ALAN D'ARDIS ERSKINE-MURRAY, 14th Lord and 14th Baronet; *b* 31 Dec 1923; *s* 1973; *ed* Bedford Sch and Peterhouse, Camb (MA); Bar Middle Temple 1949: *m* 1962, Valerie Sylvia, who *d* 1997, da of late Herbert William Dennis, of St Margarets, Middx, and has issue.

Arms – Quarterly; 1st and 4th or, a fetterlock azure, on a chief of the 2nd 3 stars argent, *Murray of Blackbarony*; 2nd and 3rd, azure, 3 stars within a double tressure counter-flowered argent and in the centre a martlet or. **Crest** – A lion rampant gules holding a battleaxe proper. **Supporters** – Two horses argent, bridled gules.
Residence – Flat 80, Pier House, Cheyne Walk, SW3 5HX.

SONS LIVING

Hon ROBERT FRANCIS ALAN (*Master of Elibank*), *b* 10 Oct 1964; *ed* Harrow, and Reading Univ: *m* 1996, Antonia S.W., yr da of Roger Carrington, of Rockbourne, Hants, and has issue living, Isabella Valerie Elibank, *b* 1997. *Residence* – 15 Ouseley Rd, SW12 8ED.

Hon Timothy Alexander Elibank, *b* 1967.

BROTHER LIVING

Patrick Elibank (3 Park View, Bakewell, Derbys DE45 1BS), *b* 1927; *ed* Bedford Sch and Pembroke Coll, Camb (MA); FICE: *m* 1957, Jenny Mary Margaret, da of late John Brown, of Bowbank, Middleton-in-Teesdale, co Durham, and has had issue, Vivien Mary, *b* 1958: *m* 1992, John David Jarvis, and has issue living, William Tom *b* 1996, — Clare Ruth, *b* 1960: *m* 1998, Matthew White, son of Stuart White, of Oxford, — Hilary Margaret, *b* 1965, *d* 1976.

SISTER LIVING

Helen Veronica, *b* 1931; MB, BS London: *m* 1958, Neil MacDonald, FRCS, of 22 Old Broadway, Manchester M20 3DF, and has issue living, Sally, *b* 1959, — Fiona *b* 1961, — Juliet, *b* 1964.

COLLATERAL BRANCHES LIVING

Grandson of late Alexander Erskine ERSKINE-MURRAY, son of late Hon James Murray, 4th son of 7th Lord:—
Issue of late Lieut-Col Arthur Erskine-Murray, CBE, DSO (uncle of 13th Lord), *b* 1877, *d* 1948: *m* 1906, Ena Nelson, who *d* 1942, da of late Henry Ernest Trestrail, FRCS, MRCP, of Mount Pleasant House, Longton, Staffordshire:—
Arthur Sydney Elibank, *b* 1909; *ed* Bedford Sch, and at Birmingham Univ BSc (Civil Eng); MICE; a Dir of Erskine, Murray & Co: *m* 1940, Florence Duncan, da of late William Duncan Robertson, and has issue living, Ann, *b* 1942; MA: *m* 1965, Anthony Peter Bartleet, of Bucklers Farm, Coggeshall, Essex CO6 1SB, and has issue living, James Murray *b* 1967, Thomas Anthony *b* 1969: *m* 1995, Joanna Louise Morrison (and has issue living, Henry Oliver *b* 1997), William

Arthur *b* 1971, — Susan, *b* 1945: *m* 1975, Godfrey Stuart Shocket, of 7 Genoa Av, Putney, SW15. *Residence* – Myrtle Bank, Gt Amwell, Ware, Herts SG12 9SN.

Grandchildren of late William Harry Elibank Murray, 2nd son of late Capt James Pulteney Murray (infra):—
Issue of late Douglas Elibank Murray, Australian Light Horse, *b* 1898, *d* 1989: *m* 1st, 1935 (*m diss* 1946), Rewa, da of Joseph Patrick O'Hara, of Fiji; 2ndly, 1947, Ngaio Milva Barnott, who *d* 1976:—
(By 1st *m*) William Eoin Elibank (Lot 8 Burraga Rd, Rockley, NSW 2795), *b* 1938: *m* 1970, Sheila Marion, da of Walter Robert Pont, of E Maitland, NSW, and has issue living, James Douglas Elibank, *b* 1970, — Alexandra Naomi, *b* 1974. —— Pamela Anna Elibank, *b* 1940: *m* 1967, C. T. McKenna, of 78 Fairfield Rd, Hamilton, NZ. —— Rita Gai Elibank, *b* 1942: *m* 1974, Graham John Horrigan Burns, of PO Box 213, Lindfield, NSW.

Granddaughter of late Capt James Pulteney Murray, son of Lieut James Edward Ferguson Murray, RN, el son of Maj-Gen James Patrick Murray, CB, MP, el son of late Gen the Hon James Murray, 5th son of 4th Lord:—
Issue of late Brig-Gen Edward Rushworth Blakiston Murray, *b* 1868, *d* as a result of enemy action 1942: *m* 1905, Hilda Dorothea, el da of late Reginald Paul, formerly of Woodgate, Loughborough:—
Elizabeth, *b* 1911. *Residence* – 4 Church Hill, Edinburgh EH10 4BQ.

Grandsons of late Brig-Gen Edward Rushworth Blakiston Murray (ante):—
Issue of late James Patrick Murray, CMG, *b* 1906, *d* 1993: *m* 1934, (Margaret) Ruth (Trewen, Shaftesbury Rd, Woking, Surrey GU22 7DU), da of late Rev Alfred Edward Buchanan, formerly R of Pedmore, Worcs:—
James Alexander Gideon (Selhurst, Selhurst Common, Bramley, nr Guildford, Surrey GU5 0LS), *b* 1936; *ed* Trin Coll, Glenalmond; FCA; Chm Standard Commercial Corporation, NC: *m* 1965, Gillian Mary, da of late H. Gordon Adcock, of St Albans, Herts, and has issue living, James Richard (Cottage on the Green, Meysey Hampton, Glos), *b* 1967; *ed* Bradfield, and Durham Univ; Schoolmaster, — Andrew Thomas, *b* 1968; *ed* Bradfield, and Exeter Univ (BSc); assist prod BBC. —— Patrick Edward (1 Chelsea Drive, Durban 4051, Natal), *b* 1939; *ed* Trin Coll, Glenalmond: *m* 1963, Marie-Danielle, da of Henri C. Du Cladier de Curac, of Lusaka, Zambia, and has issue living, Charles Patrick, *b* 1971; *ed* Hilton Coll, Natal, and Cape Town Univ, — Danielle Jeanne, *b* 1964: *m* 1994, Terence Lance Maritz, of Johannesburg, and has issue living, Tomika Jemma Danielle *b* 1996, — Diana Ruth, *b* 1965. —— Thomas Walter (The White House, Pembroke Rd, Woking, Surrey GU22 7EB), *b* 1942; *ed* Trin Coll, Glenalmond; Solicitor: *m* 1975, Annette Timms, da of Clifford Tapper, of Solihull, Warwicks, and has issue living, David Thomas, *b* 1976; *ed* St George's, Weybridge, and Durham Univ.

PREDECESSORS – (1) PATRICK Murray, el son of Sir Gideon Murray of Elibank, Lord of Session (3rd son of Andrew Murray of Blackbarony, and uncle of 1st Bt, *cr* 1628); *cr* a *Baronet* 1628, and *Lord Elibank*, of Ettrick Forest, co Selkirk (peerage of Scotland) 1643, with remainder to his heirs male whatsoever; one of the six peers who opposed the delivering up of Charles I to the Parliament of England; *d* 1649; *s* by his son (2) PATRICK, 2nd Lord; *d* 1661; *s* by his son (3) PATRICK, 3rd Lord; *d* 1687; *s* by his son (4) ALEXANDER, 4th Lord; *d* 1736; *s* by his el son (5) PATRICK, 5th Lord; *dsp* 1778; *s* by his brother (6) GEORGE, 6th Lord; an Adm; *d* 1785; *s* by his nephew (7) ALEXANDER, 7th Lord, son of Rev Hon Gideon, DD, 3rd son of 4th Lord; Lord-Lieut of co Peebles; *d* 1820; *s* by his son (8) ALEXANDER, 8th Lord; *d* 1830; *s* by his son (9) ALEXANDER, 9th Lord; *b* 1804: *m* 1838, Emily Maria, da of Archibald Montgomery; *d* 1871; *s* by his son (10) MONTOLIEU FOX OLIPHANT, 10th Lord; *b* 1840; was Lord-Lieut of Peeblesshire 1896-1908; *cr Viscount Elibank*, of Elibank, co Selkirk (peerage of United Kingdom) 1911: *m* 1868, Blanche Alice, who *d* 1936, da of late Edward John Scott, of Portland Lodge, Southsea; *d* 1927; *s* by his son (11) (CHARLES) GIDEON, 2nd Viscount; *b* 1877; was Private Sec to Commr for Native Affairs in S Africa 1901-2, Assist Private Sec to Permanent Under-Sec of State for the Colonies 1907-9, Administrator of St Vincent 1909-14, and of St Lucia 1914-17, and Lord-Lieut for Peeblesshire 1935-45; sat as MP for St Rollox Div of Glasgow (*U*) 1918-22: *m* 1908, Ermine Mary Katherine, JP, who *d* 1955, da of late Henry Robarts Madocks, of Glanywen, Denbigh, and widow of Lieut-Col James Henry Aspinwall; *d* 1951; *s* by his brother (12) ARTHUR CECIL, CMG, DSO, 3rd Viscount, *b* 1879; Capt King's Own Scottish Borderers and Lt-Col Special Reserve Cav; MP for Kincardineshire (*L*) 1908-23; PPS to Parliamentary Sec to Board of Trade 1909, to Under-Sec of State for India 1909-10, and to Sec of State for Foreign Affairs (Rt Hon Sir Edward Grey, Bt, MP) 1910-14, and Assist Mil Attaché at Washington 1917-18: *m* 1931, Faith Celli, who *d* 1942 (the dream da in Barrie's "Dear Brutus" 1916 and 1922), da of late Francis H. Standing; *d* 1962, when the UK Viscountcy became ext; *s* in the Lordship by his kinsman (13) JAMES ALASTAIR FREDERICK CAMPBELL Erskine-Murray (son of late Sqdn Leader James Robert Erskine-Murray, DSc, el son of late Alexander Erskine Erskine-Murray, el son of late Hon James Murray, 4th son of 7th Lord), 13th Lord; *b* 1902; Maj HLI; *d* 1973, *s* by his cousin, (14) ALAN D'ARDIS (son of Maj Robert Alan Erskine-Murray, OBE, uncle of 13th Lord), 14th Lord and present peer.

Eliot family name of Earl of St Germans.

Eliot, Lord; son of Earl of St Germans.

ELIS-THOMAS, BARON (Elis-Thomas) (Life Baron 1992)

DAFYDD ELIS ELIS-THOMAS, son of ...... Thomas, of .....; *b* 18 Oct 1946; *ed* Ysgol Dyffryn Conwy, and Univ Coll of N Wales; Tutor in Welsh Studies, Coleg Harlech 1971; Lecturer, Department of English, Univ Coll of N Wales, Bangor, Aberystwyth, Cardiff and Open Univ; Memb TGWU; MP (Plaid Cymru) for Merioneth 1974-83, and for Meirionydd Nant Conwy 1983-92; Pres Plaid Cymru 1984-92 (Vice-Pres 1979-81); Memb Parly Select Cttee on Education, Science and the Arts 1979-83; first Chm Welsh Language Board since 1993; *cr Baron Elis-Thomas*, of Nant Conwy in the County of Gwynedd (Life Baron) 1992: *m* 1st, 1970 (*m diss* 19—), Elen M......, da of ...... Williams, of ......; 2ndly, 1993, Mair, da of ...... Parry Jones, of ....., and has issue by 1st *m*, three sons.
Address – Welsh Language Board, Market Chambers, 5-7 St Mary St, Cardiff CF1 2AT.

ELLENBOROUGH, BARON (Law) (Baron UK 1802)

RICHARD EDWARD CECIL LAW, 8th Baron; *b* 14 Jan 1926; *s* 1945; *ed* Eton, and at Magdalene Coll, Camb; Pres, National Union of Ratepayers' Assos; Dir Towry Law plc: *m* 1st, 1953, Rachel Mary, who *d* 1986, only da of late Major Ivor Hedley, 17th Lancers; 2ndly, 1994, Mrs Frances Kimberley, and has issue by 1st *m*.

Arms – Ermine, on a bend engrained, between two cocks gules, three mullets pierced or. **Crest** – A cock gules, charged on the breast with a mitre pendant from a chain round the neck or. **Supporters** – Two eagles, wings elevated sable, each gorged with a chain or, and pendant therefrom on the breast of the *dexter* supporter a mitre, and on the *sinister* a covered cup gold.
Residence – Withypool House, Observatory Close, Church Rd, Crowborough, Sussex. *Club* – Turf.

SONS LIVING (By 1st marriage)

Hon RUPERT EDWARD HENRY, *b* 28 March, 1955; *ed* Eton; Maj Coldm Gds (ret); Coutts & Co since 1988: *m* 1981, Hon Grania Janet Grey, only da of Baron Boardman (Life Baron), and has issue living, James Rupert Thomas, *b* 8 March 1983, — Frederick George Towry Gray, *b* 1990, — Georgina Poppy, *b* 1984.
Hon Edmund Ivor Cecil, *b* 1956; *ed* Eton and Peterhouse, Camb (MA): *m* 1982, Susan Claire, el da of Derek Baker, of 5 Jermyn Close, Cambridge, and has issue living, David Christopher, *b* 1984,

Law and equity combined

— John Christian, *b* 1986.
Hon Charles Adrian Christian Towry, *b* 1960; *ed* Eton, and York Univ (BA).

BROTHER LIVING

Hon Cecil Towry Henry, *b* 1931; *ed* Eton; late Lieut King's Dragoon Guards (Reserve) and Chm of Towry Law plc, and all associated cos in Towry Law Group: *m* 1957, Daphne Mary Jean, 2nd da of late Hon Laurence Paul Methuen-Campbell (*see* B Methuen, colls), and has issue living, Edward Henry Towry, *b* 1971; *ed* Eton, and Exeter Univ (BA), — Cecilia Diana, *b* 1958: *m* 1985, James E. Chamberlain, son of E. J. R. Chamberlain, of Box, Glos and has issue living, Jasper Edward *b* 1992, Hector James David *b* 1998, Natasha Diana *b* 1990, — Marianne Jean, *b* 1960; *ed* St Hilda's Coll, Oxford (MA): *m* 1986, George Alexander Wheeler-Carmichael (*see* Gibson-Craig-Carmichael, Bt, colls, 1995 Edn), and has issue living, James Henry *b* 1990, Guy Thomas *b* 1992, — Catherine Rose, *b* 1962; *ed* Edinburgh Univ (MA): *m* 1985, Dr Anthony Charles Murray Ayles, 2nd son of Dr William Ayles, of Moray Pl, Edinburgh, and has issue living, William Anthony Carrington *b* 1992, Charlotte Catherine Mary *b* 1988, Emily Flora Isobel *b* 1990. *Residence* – 6 Sussex Sq, W2. *Club* – Cavalry.

WIDOW LIVING OF SEVENTH BARON

(HELEN) DOROTHY (*Dowager Baroness Ellenborough*), da of late H. W. Lovatt, formerly of Tiraun, Newcastle, co Down; a DStJ: *m* 1923, the 7th Baron Ellenborough, who *d* 1945. *Residence* – Shockerwick House, Shockerwick, Bath BA1 7LL

COLLATERAL BRANCHES LIVING

Grandsons of late Thomas Graves Law, LLD, 3rd son of Hon William Towry Law, 5th son of 1st Baron:—
Issue of late Henry Duncan Graves Law, CIE, *b* 1883, *d* 1964: *m* 1st, 1909, Jean, who *d* 1956, da of late Peter Graham, RA, of Westoun, St Andrews; 2ndly, 1958, Nancy Olive Legge, who *d* 1977, da of late Sir Henry Frederick Oswald Norbury:—
(By 1st *m*) Richard Graham (High Trees, Ramsay Wood, Gatehouse-of-Fleet DG7 2HJ), *b* 1918; *ed* Tonbridge, and at Peterhouse, Camb (BA 1940, MA 1947); MB 1947, MD 1952, FRCOG 1961: *m* 1944, Barbara, MB, BS, DPH, da of

Horace Wright, and has issue living, Nigel Graham, *b* 1949, — David Jocelyn Wright, *b* 1951, — Penelope Jane, *b* 1955. —— Christopher (Appleyard, Little Chart, Ashford, Kent), *b* 1921; *ed* Tonbridge, and at Peterhouse Camb; ARIBA: *m* 1954, Alison Mitchell, and has issue living, Jonathan, *b* 1958: *m* 1987, Diane Joyce French, — Ian Graham, *b* 1961; ARICS: *m* 1990, Fiona Mary McIntyre, and has issue living, Duncan Graham *b* 1989, Thomas Henry *b* 1993, Katrina Mary *b* 1988, — Fiona Jean, *b* 1955. —— Michael Haldane (90A Upper Tollington Park, N4 4NB), *b* 1925; *ed* Tonbridge, and at Peterhouse, Camb: *m* 1954, Dorothea von Schön-Kreuzenau, who *d* 1999, and has issue living, Richard Anthony *b* 1955, — Peter Andrew, *b* 1958: *m* 1979, Carol Rattee, and has issue living, Naomi Kirsten *b* 1986, Gemma Nicole *b* 1991, — John Martin, *b* 1961; has issue living (by Melanie Ruth Day), Jasper Johnson Day *b* 1999, Holly Katrina Day *b* 1996, — Stephen Francis, *b* 1966.

Grandchildren of late Capt William Victor Law (infra):—
Issue of late Frederick Henry Law, *b* 1912, *d* 1986: *m* 1937, Ruth, da of George H. Dill, of Toronto:—
Stephen Frederick (1657 Truscott Dr, Mississauga, Ont, Canada L5J 1Z5), *b* 1943: *m* 1966, Julika Fietius, and has issue living, Adrian Crawford, *b* 1979, — Alexandra Juliane Erika, *b* 1977. —— Sharron Constance, *b* 1937: *m* 1955, James Wilfred Brazier, of 106 Hawthorne Av, Stouffville, Ont, Canada L4A 7Z8, and has issue living, Frederick James, *b* 1955: *m* 1980, Mary Maresa, da of Gio Batta Garlatti, and has issue living, Ryan Garlatti *b* 1982, Jeremy Frederick *b* 1984, Nadine Constance *b* 1988, — Danny Allen (316 Lori Av, Stouffville, Ont, Canada L4A 6C2), *b* 1957: *m* 1990, Deborah Jane, da of Frank Clifford Carr, — Timothy Stewart, *b* 1960.

Grandchildren of late Cmdr Frederick Charles Law, RN, 4th son of Hon William Towry Law (ante):—
Issue of late John Crawford Law, *b* 1876, *d* 1919: *m* 1917, Eleanor Agnes Letitia, da of Rupert E. Kingsford, of Toronto:—
Margaret Augusta Eleanor, *b* 1918: *m* 1st, 1940, Capt Denys Symons, Roy Tank Regt; 2ndly, 1966, Oliver Bosshardt Bennett, CBE, who *d* 1983, and has issue living, (by 1st *m*) Ivor James, *b* 1944, — Dianna Venetia, *b* 1940.

Issue of late Capt William Victor Law, *b* 1880, *d* 1967: *m* 1912, Helen Violet who *d* 1971, da of late Henry Morris Watson, Assist Gen Manager of Bank of Hamilton:—
Mary Charlotte Violet (44 Valerie Drive, St Catherines, Ont, Canada L2T 3G5), *b* 1917: *m* 1st, 1939, Capt W. Marshal Cleland, Gov-Gen's, Horse Guards, Canadian Army, who *d* 1958; 2ndly, 1960, John Franklin Horne, who *d* 1974, and has issue living, (by 1st *m*), William Marshal *b* 1944: *m* 1st, 1967, Sheila, da of Jack M. Reid, of Kingston, Ont; 2ndly, 1979, Lois, da of Robert Charles Pettigrew, — Donald Law (RRI Vittoria, Ont, Canada), *b* 1947: *m* 1974, Kathryn, da of Ward E. Kitchen, of RRI, Vittoria, Ont, and has issue living, Eric William *b* 1978, Kimberley Dawn *b* 1982, — Calder Bruce (685 Sarah St, Gravenhurst, Ont, Canada), *b* 1949: *m* 1st, 1969, Sandra, da of Louis Melnyke, of Brantford, Ont; 2ndly, 1978, Wendy, da of Henry Collens, of Port Carling, Ontario, and has issue living (by 2nd *m*), Jeremy Marshal *b* 1978, Calder Daniel *b* 1981, — Peter Andrew (PO Box 1389, Waterford, Ont, Canada), *b* 1957: *m* 1st, 1981, Vicky, da of Stephen Kochany, of Simcoe, Ont; 2ndly, 1995, Ellen Catherine, da of David F. Watson, of Oakville, Ont, and has issue living, (by 1st *m*) Kristin Michele *b* 1984, Amanda Lindsay *b* 1986.

Granddaughter of late Maj Adrian Aloysius Sherwood Law, 5th and yst son of late Cmdr Frederick Charles Law, RN (ante):—
Issue of late Adrian Augustus Stuart Law, *b* 1918, *d* 1968: *m* 1st, 1942 (*m diss* 1951), Wilhelmina Noble Angus; 2ndly, 1952, Muriel Beverley (2582 MacDonald Drive, Victoria, BC, Canada), da of late Brooke Vaio:—
(By 1st *m*) Moira Jean (1 Luton Court, Broadstairs, Kent CT10 2DE), *b* 1943.

PREDECESSORS – **(1)** *Sir* EDWARD LAW, KB, PC, and eminent lawyer, was Attorney-Gen 1801-2, and Lord Ch Justice of England 1802-18; *cr Baron Ellenborough*, of Ellenborough, co Cumberland (peerage of United Kingdom) 1802; *d* 1818; *s* by his son **(2)** EDWARD, 2nd Baron, PC, GCB; Lord Privy Seal 1828-9, Pres of Board of Control 1829-30, 1834-5, 1841 and 1858, Gov-Gen of India 1841-4, and First Lord of the Admiralty 1846; *cr Viscount Southam* and *Earl of Ellenborough* (peerage of United Kingdom) 1844; *d* 1871, when the viscountcy and earldom became extinct and the barony devolved upon his nephew **(3)** CHARLES EDMUND TOWRY, 3rd Baron (son of late Hon Charles Ewan, 2nd son of 1st Baron, by Elizabeth Sophia, da of Sir Edward Nightingale, 6th Bt), *b* 1820; assumed in 1885 by Roy licence the additional surname of Towry: *m* 1st 1840, Lady Eleanor Cecil Howard, who *d* 1852, da of 4th Earl of Wicklow; 2ndly, 1855, Anna Elizabeth, who *d* 1860, da of Rev John Fitzgerald-Day of Beaufort House, Killarney; 3rdly, 1863, Isabella, who *d* 1874, da of Alexander Ogilby, of Pelipar, Londonderry; 4thly, 1874, Beatrice Joanna, who *d* 1932, da of Sir Norton Joseph Knatchbull, 10th Bt; *d* 1890; *s* by his son **(4)** CHARLES TOWRY HAMILTON, 4th Baron, *b* 1856; *dsp* 1902; *s* by his cousin **(5)** EDWARD DOWNES, 5th Baron, *b* 1841; Com RN; served in Baltic during Russian War 1855, in China Expedition 1859-61, and during Ashantee War 1870-74: *m* 1906, Hermione Octavia Courtenay, who *d* 1942, da of E. W. H. Schenley (Rifle Brig), of Little Warsash, S Hants; *d* 1915; *s* by his brother **(6)** CECIL HENRY, CB, 6th Baron, *b* 1849; entered 54th Regt 1869, and retired as Brevet Col 1906; Afghan Campaign 1878-80, S African War 1900-2: *m* 1884, Alice Caroline, who *d* 1916, da of late John Harvey Astell, of Woodbury Hall, Sandy, Beds; *d* 1931; *s* by his son **(7)** HENRY ASTELL, MC, 7th Baron, *b* 1889; Major (ret) King's Own Yorkshire LI; European War 1914-18 (MC): *m* 1923, Helen Dorothy, da of H. W. Lovatt, formerly of Tiraun, Newcastle, co Down; *d* 1945; *s* by his el son **(8)** RICHARD EDWARD CECIL, 8th Baron and present peer.

ELLES, BARONESS (Elles) (Life Baroness 1972)

DIANA LOUIE ELLES, da of late Col Stewart Francis Newcombe, DSO; *b* 19 July 1921; *ed* London Univ (BA); Bar Lincoln's Inn 1956 (Hon Bencher 1993); 1939-45 War as Flight Officer WAAF (Intelligence, Air Ministry); Member of Outside Organization Sub-Cttee, Conservative Women's Nat Advisory Cttee 1960-72, and of Women's Nat Advisory Cttee 1961-62, and since 1969 (Chm Sub-

Cttee on One Parent Families 1970); author of *The Housewife and the Common Market* 1971; Care Cttee Worker, Kennington SE 1956-72; UK Delegate to UN Gen Assembly 1972; a Member of UN Sub Commn on Prevention of Discrimination and Protection of Minorities 1973 and 74; Chm of Conservative Party International Office 1973-78; International Chm, European Union of Women 1973-79; a Member of UK Delegation to European Parl 1973-75; Opposition Spokesman, Foreign Affairs, House of Lords 1975-79; MEP for Thames Valley 1979-89; Vice-Pres European Parl 1982-87; Chm Legal Affairs Cttee European Parl 1987-89; Dep Chm Assocn of Conservative Peers 1995-99; *cr Baroness Elles*, of City of Westminster (Life Baroness) 1972: *m* 1945, Neil Moncrieff Elles, barrister, and has issue.

Arms – Not exemplified at time of going to press.
Residences – 75 Ashley Gdns, SW1; Villa Fontana, Ponte del Giglio, Lucca, Italy.

SON LIVING

Hon James Edmund Moncrieff (35 Rue Camille Lemonnier, 1050 Brussels, Belgium), *b* 1949 *ed* Eton, and Edinburgh Univ; MEP since 1994: *m* 1977 (*m diss* 1997), Françoise, da of François Le Bail, and has issue, Nicholas, *b* 1982, — Victoria, *b* 1980.

DAUGHTER LIVING

Hon (Elizabeth) Rosamund, *b* 1947; *ed* St Andrews Univ (MA) and Courtauld Inst, London Univ (MA): *m* 1971 (*m diss* 1992), Christopher John Lockhart-Mummery, QC, son of late Sir Hugh Evelyn Lockhart-Mummery, KCVO, and has issue (*see* V Hampden, colls). *Residence* – 26 Sheffield Terrace, W8 7NA.

Ellesmere, Earl of, see Duke of Sutherland.

ELLIOTT OF MORPETH, BARON (Elliott) (Life Baron 1985)

·IMPRIMIS·HONOR·

(ROBERT) WILLIAM ELLIOTT, son of Richard Elliott, of Morpeth, Northumberland, by his wife, Mary Elizabeth, da of William Fulthorpe, of Morpeth; *b* 11 Dec 1920; *ed* Morpeth Gram Sch; farmer since 1939; MP (*C*) Newcastle upon Tyne North 1957-83; PPS to joint Parliamentary Secs, Min of Transport & Civil Aviation 1958-59, to Under-Sec Home Office 1959-60, to Min of State Home Office 1960-61, to Sec for Technical Co-operation 1961-63, Assist Govt Whip 1963-64, Opposition Whip 1964-70; Comptroller of the Household June-Sept 1970; Vice-Chm Conservative Party 1970-74; Chm Select Cttee on Agriculture, Fisheries and Food 1980-83; *cr* Kt 1974, and *Baron Elliott of Morpeth*, of Morpeth, in the County of Northumberland and of the City of Newcastle upon Tyne (Life Baron) 1985: *m* 1956, Jane, da of John Burton Morpeth, of Newcastle upon Tyne, and has issue.

Arms – Gules on a bend or cotised dancetty argent bendwise in chief a triple-towered castle gules masoned argent the portal azure with portcullis down gold. **Crest** – Upon a mount vert in front of an oak tree proper fructed or a fountain ensigned by a crown flory azure. **Supporters** – *Dexter*, a stag proper attired and unguled gold; *sinister*, a seahorse erect argent scaled gold, the compartment comprising three grassy mounts proper with between that in the centre and those on either side water barry wavy of four argent and azure.
Residence – Hindley Hall, Stocksfield, Northumberland NE43 7RY.

SON LIVING

Hon Richard John, *b* 1959; *ed* Sedburgh Sch, Edinburgh Univ (BA), and RMA Sandhurst: *m* 1988, Susu, yr da of Lionel Robertson, of Abbey Lodge, Park Rd, London, and has issue living, William, *b* 1995, — Romy, *b* 1990, — Laura, *b* 1992, — Florence, *b* 1999.

DAUGHTERS LIVING

Hon Alison Mary, *b* 1957; *ed* Oxenford Castle Sch: *m* 1985, Hugh A. Campbell Adamson, yr son of Lt-Col William John Campbell Adamson, TD, JP, of Careston Castle, Brechin, Angus, and has issue living, James William, *b* 1989, — Rosemary Jane, *b* 1987, — Catherine Grace, *b* 1991.

Hon Catherine Victoria, *b* 1962; *ed* St Mary's Convent, Berwick-upon-Tweed, and Durham Univ (BA): *m* 1988, (Alexander) Julian Taylor, eldest son of J. A. Taylor, of Rumer Hall, Welford-on-Avon, Warwicks, and has issue living, Alexander William John, *b* 1990, — George Arthur James, *b* 1992, — Camilla (Millie) Rose, *b* 1996.

Hon Sarah Ann, *b* 1962 (twin); *ed* New Hall Sch, Essex, and Edinburgh Univ (BA): *m* 1986, George Evelyn Atkinson-Clark, and has issue (*see* B Suffield, colls).

Hon Louise Jane, *b* 1967; *ed* St Anne's, Windermere, and Durham Univ (BA).

Ellis, Scott-, family name of Baron Howard de Walden.

ELPHINSTONE, LORD (Elphinstone) (Lord S 1509, and Baron UK 1885)

ALEXANDER MOUNTSTUART ELPHINSTONE, 19th Lord; *b* 15 April 1980; *s* 1994; *ed* Eton.

𝕬rms – Quarterly: 1st grand quarter argent, a chevron sable, between three boars' heads erased gules, armed of the field, and langued azure, *Elphinstone*; 2nd, grand quarter, counterquartered; 1st, gules, a chevron, within a double tressure, flory counterflory, argent, *Fleming*; 2nd, azure, three frases argent, *Fraser*; 3rd, argent, on a chief gules, three pallets or, *Keith*; 4th, or, three bars wavy gules, *Drummond*; 3rd grand quarter, argent, a chevron, between three otters' heads erased gules, within a bordure of the last, *Fullerton*; 4th grand quarter, sable, on a cross argent, square pierced of the field, four eagles, displayed of the first, in the dexter canton an arm embowed proper, issuing out of a naval crown, the hand holding a trident or, *Buller*. 𝕮rest – A lady, from the waist upwards, richly habited in red, her arms extended, the right hand supporting a tower, and the left holding a branch of laurel, all proper. 𝕾upporters – Two wild men, wreathed about the temples and loins with laurel, and holding on their exterior shoulders clubs proper.
Residence – Whitberry House, Tyninghame, Dunbar, E Lothian EH42 1XL.

BROTHERS LIVING

Hon ANGUS JOHN *b* 7 July 1982.
Hon Fergus David, *b* 1985.

SISTER LIVING

Hon Clementina Rose, *b* 1989.

AUNT LIVING (*sister of 18th Lord*)

Rosemary Elizabeth, *b* 1947: *m* 1967, James Pigé Leschallas (*see* E Romney, colls), and has issue living, Andrew James, *b* 1970; *ed* Eton, — Alexander Charles, *b* 1978; *ed* Eton, — Sophie Elizabeth, *b* 1968: *m* 1993, James Dominic Auriol Gaselee, LG, son of Nicholas Auriol Digby Charles Gaselee, of Saxon Cottage, Lambourn, Berks, and has issue living, Olivia Rose *b* 1997. *Residence* – Maryland, Worplesdon, Guildford, Surrey.

GREAT AUNTS LIVING *(Daughters of 16th Lord)*

Hon Jean Constance, MVO, *b* 1915, Extra Lady-in-Waiting to HRH The Princess Margaret, 1970; MVO (1983): *m* 1936, Maj John Lycett Wills, Life Guards (ret) *(see* Wills, Bt, *cr* 1904, colls). *Residence* – Allanbay Park, Binfield, Berks.

Hon Margaret, *b* 1925; Extra Lady-in-Waiting to HM Queen Elizabeth the Queen Mother since 1991: *m* 1950, Denys Gravenor Rhodes *(see* B Plunket, 1968 Edn), who *d* 1981, and has issue living, Simon John Gravenor, *b* 1957: a Page of Honour to HM 1971-73: *m* 1983, Susan, eldest da of Eden Simon, of Tara Farm, Bindura, Zimbabwe, — Michael Andrew Gravenor, *b* 1960, — Annabel Margaret, *b* 1952: *m* 1st, 1978, Christopher J. D. Strickland-Skailes, twin son of Frank Strickland-Skailes, of Lea Hall, Hatfield Heath, Essex; 2ndly, 1986, G. V. (Charles) Cope, 2nd son of late Herbert Vallack Cope, of Rose Hill, Bideford, Devon, and has issue living (by 1st *m*), Andrew James Downing *b* 1980, — Victoria Ann, *b* 1953: *m* 1974, Nicholas Deans, who *d* 1991. *Residence* – The Garden House, Windsor Great Park, Windsor, Berks.

GRANDMOTHER LIVING

Jean Frances, CVO, da of late Capt Angus Valdimar Hambro, MP, and widow of Capt Hon Vicary Paul Gibbs, Gren Gds *(see* B Aldenham and Hunsdon of Hunsdon): *m* 2ndly, 1946, Rev Hon Andrew Charles Victor Elphinstone, who *d* 1975; 3rdly, 1980, Lt-Col John William Richard Woodroffe, who *d* 1990 *(see* E Ducie, colls, 1968 Edn). *Residence* – Maryland, Worplesdon, Guildford, Surrey.

WIDOW LIVING OF EIGHTEENTH LORD

WILLA MARY GABRIEL *(Lady Elphinstone)*, yr da of Maj George David Chetwode, MBE, Coldm Gds *(see* B Chetwode, colls): *m* 1978, the 18th Lord Elphinstone, who *d* 1994. *Residence* – Whitberry House, Tyninghame, Dunbar, E Lothian EH42 1XL.

PREDECESSORS – **(1)** ALEXANDER Elphinstone, son of Sir John Elphinstone, grandson of Sir Henry Elphinstone, of Pittendreich; *cr Lord Elphinstone*, of Elphinstone, co Stirling (peerage of Scotland) 1509; fell at Flodden Field 1513; *s* by his son **(2)** ALEXANDER, 2nd Lord; slain at Pinkie 1547; *s* by his son **(3)** ROBERT, 3rd Lord; *s* by his son **(4)** ALEXANDER, 4th Lord; Lord Treasurer of Scotland; *d* 1638; *s* by his son **(5)** ALEXANDER, 5th Lord; *d* 1648; *s* by his newphew **(6)** ALEXANDER, 6th Lord; *d* 1654; *s* by his el son **(7)** ALEXANDER, 7th Lord; *dsp* 1669; *s* by his brother **(8)** JOHN, 8th Lord; *d* 1720; *s* by his son **(9)** CHARLES, 9th Lord; *d* 1757; *s* by his son **(10)** CHARLES, 10th Lord; *d* 1781; *s* by his son **(11)** JOHN, 11th Lord; a Representative Peer 1784-94; *d* 1794; *s* by his son **(12)** JOHN, 12th Lord; a Lt-Gen in the Army, Lord-Lieut of Dunbartonshire, and a Representative Peer 1803-13; *d* 1813; *s* by his son **(13)** JOHN, GCB, GCH, PC, 13th Lord; a Representative Peer; was Gov of Bombay and of Madras during the Mutiny 1857; *cr Baron Elphinstone*, of Elphinstone, co Stirling (peerage of United Kingdom) 1859; *d* 1860, when the barony of 1859 became extinct, and the Scottish Lordship devolved upon his cousin **(14)** JOHN (el son of Adm Hon Charles Elphinstone-Fleeming, 2nd son of 11th Lord), 14th Lord; *d* unmarried 1861; *s* by his kinsman **(15)** WILLIAM (son of Lt-Col James Drummond Buller-Fullerton Elphinstone, 4th son of Hon William Elphinstone, 3rd son of 10th Lord), 15th Lord, *b* 1828; a Representative Peer for Scotland 1867-85, and a Lord-in-Waiting to HM Queen Victoria 1874-80, 1885-6, and 1886-9; *cr Baron Elphinstone*, of Elphinstone co Haddington (peerage of United Kingdom) 1885: *m* 1864, Lady Constance Euphemia Woronzow Murray, who *d* 1922, da of 6th Earl of Dunmore; *d* 1893; *s* by his el surviving son **(16)** SIDNEY HERBERT, KT, 16th Lord, *b* 1869; Lord High Commr to Gen Assembly of Church of Scotland 1923-4, Capt-Gen of Queen's Body Guard for Scotland (Roy Co of Archers) 1935-52, Clerk Register of Scotland and Keeper of the Signet 1944-55, and Chancellor of Order of the Thistle 1949-55: *m* 1910, Lady Mary Frances Bowes-Lyon, DCVO, who *d* 1961, da of 14th Earl of Strathmore; *d* 1955; *s* by his el son **(17)** JOHN ALEXANDER, 17th Lord; *b* 1914; Capt Queen's Body Guard for Scotland (Roy Co of Archers); *d* 1975; *s* by his nephew **(18)** JAMES ALEXANDER, 18th Lord; *b* 1953: *m* 1978, Willa Mary Gabriel, yr da of Maj George David Chetwode, MBE, Coldm Gds *(see* B Chetwode, colls); *d* 1994; *s* by his eldest son **(19)** ALEXANDER MOUNTSTUART, 19th Lord and present peer.

ELTON, BARON (Elton) (Baron UK 1934)

RODNEY ELTON, TD, 2nd Baron; *b* 2 March 1930; *s* 1973; *ed* Eton and New, Coll, Oxford (BA); late Capt Warwicks Yeo, and late Maj Leics and Derbys Yeo; Publisher of Yendor Books; Assist Master Loughborough Gram Sch 1962-67, Fairham Comprehensive Sch for Boys, Nottingham 1967-69, Lecturer Bishop Lonsdale Coll 1969-72; Conservative Whip House of Lords 1974-76; Spokesman for Opposition 1976-79; Under Sec of State, N Ireland Office, 1979-81, Parliamentary Under Sec for Health and Social Security 1981-82, at Home Office 1982-84, Min of State at Home Office 1984-85, and at Dept of Environment 1985-86, Member Exec Cttee Assocn of Conservative Peers 1986-93 and since 1994 (Dep Chm 1990-93); Chm Financial Intermediaries, Managers and Brokers Regulatory Assocn 1989-90, Vice-Chm Andry Montgomery Ltd since 1987, Member Panel on Takeovers and Mergers 1989-90, and Chm Enquiry into Discipline in Schs in England and Wales 1988-89 (Report 1989); Chm Intermediate Treatment Fund 1990-93, since when Chm The Divert Trust: *m* 1st, 1958 *(m diss* 1979), Anne Francis, el da of Brig Robert Adolphus George Tilney, CBE, DSO, TD, DL *(see* Paget, Bt, *cr* 1897 (ext) 1959 Edn); 2ndly, 1979, (Susan) Richenda,

CVO, a Lady-in-Waiting to HM since 1987, yst da of late Sir Hugh Gurney, KCMG, MVO (*see* E Southesk, colls, 1980 Edn), and has issue by 1st *m*.

Arms – Paly or and gules a bend and on a chief sable three pierced mullets or. **Crest** – Between two pierced mullets and out of a wreath of laurel fructed or a dexter arm embowed in mail proper, tied about the elbow a cord or, the gauntlet grasping a scimitar proper hilt and pommel or. **Supporters** – *Dexter*, a knight in mail and white surcoat supporting with the exterior hand a sword point downwards proper hilt and pommerl or; *sinister*, a Viking habited proper mantled azure supporting with the exterior hand a battleaxe head downwards and outwards proper. *Address* – House of Lords, SW1. *Clubs* – Cavalry, Beefsteak, Pratt's.

SON LIVING (*By 1st marriage*)

Hon EDWARD PAGET, *b* 28 May 1966.

DAUGHTERS LIVING (*By 1st marriage*)

Hon Annabel, *b* 1960: *m* 1986, Donald M. Peebles, eldest son of Dr Robert Anthony Peebles, of Hampton Court, Surrey, and has issue living, Emma Richenda, *b* 1988, — Rosalie, *b* 1990.

Hon Jane, *b* 1962: *m* 1989, James A. J. Cronin, son of Vincent Cronin.

Hon Lucy, *b* 1963: *m* 1993, Hon Andrew Godfrey Diarmid Stuart Campbell-Gray, Master of Gray, son of 22nd Lord Gray. *Residence* – Airds Bay House, Taynuilt, Argyll PA35 1JR.

SISTERS LIVING

Hon Audrey (Hill House, Enford, Pewsey, Wilts) *b* 1922: *m* 1948, the Rev Brian William Frere Goodrich, who *d* 1977, formerly Assist Commr, Singapore Police, and has issue living, John, *b* 1952, — Peter, *b* 1954, — Simon, *b* 1957, — Justin, *b* 1962, — Alexander, *b* 1968, — Sarah, *b* 1949.

Hon Rosemary, *b* 1925: *m* 1st, 1946 (*m diss* 1955), William Yates; 2ndly, 1955, David Charles Attlee, and has issue living, (by 1st *m*) Elizabeth Anne, *b* 1948: *m* 1975, Oliver Raymond Greene, of Holton Hall, Holton St Mary, Colchester, Essex, and has had issue, William Charles Raymond *b* 1979, Nicholas Graham Raymond *b* 1981, Charlotte Eleanor *b* and *d* 1983, Annabel Lucy Raymond *b* 1985, — Angela Faith, *b* 1950: *m* 1st, 1972 (*m diss* 1980), Denis Delahunt; 2ndly, 1983, G. Stafford, and has issue living (by 1st *m*), Christopher William *b* 1974, Thomas James *b* 1977, (by 2nd *m*), David Charles *b* 1986, — (by 2nd *m*) James Tristram, *b* 1956: *m* 1986, Charlotte de Courcy, and has issue living, Joseph *b* 1990, Grace 1988, — Helena Rosemary, *b* 1958: *m* 1986, Alexander Ronald Dalhousie Ramsay, FRGS, of Bryncalled, Bucknell, Craven Arms, Shropshire, elder son of Patrick George Alexander Ramsay, FRSA, of Abcott Manor, Abcott, Clungunford, nr Ludlow, Shropshire. *Residence* – Brockley House, Leintwardine, Craven Arms, Shropshire.

PREDECESSOR – (1) GODFREY Elton, el son of late Edward Fiennes Elton, of Ovington Park, Hants, and Burleigh Court, Glos; *b* 1892; Fellow of Queen's Coll, Oxford and Lecturer in Modern History 1919-39, Dean 1921-23; Hon Political Sec Nat Labour Cttee 1932, and Sec to Rhodes Trust 1939-59; author of "Life of James Ramsay MacDonald 1866-1919", 1939, and other works, *cr Baron Elton*, of Headington, co Oxford (peerage of UK) 1934: *m* 1921, Dedi, who *d* 1977, da of Gustav Hartmann, of Oslo, *d* 1973, *s* by his only son (2) RODNEY, TD, 2nd Baron and present peer.

ELWORTHY, BARONY OF (Elworthy) (Extinct 1993)

SONS LIVING OF LIFE BARON

Hon Timothy Charles, CVO, CBE (c/o Buckingham Palace, SW1A 1AA), *b* 1938; Air Cdre RAF (ret 1993); Capt The Queen's Flight 1989-94; Extra Equerry to HM 1991-97, since when Dir of Travel and Senior Air Equerry to HM; CBE 1986, CVO 1995: *m* 1st, 1961 (*m diss* 1969), Victoria Ann, eldest da of Lt-Col H. C. W. Bowring; 2ndly, 1971, Anabel, da of late Reginald Ernest Harding, OBE, and formerly wife of Nicholas Block, and has issue living, (by 1st *m*) Katharine Emma Victoria, *b* 1963: *m* 1st, 1991 (*m diss* 1993), Christopher David Cooke, elder son of David Cooke; 2ndly, 1995, Karl Sliver, eldest son of Keith Sliver, and has issue living, (by 2nd *m*) Sam Fraser *b* 1996, Hal James *b* 1998, — Lucinda Rose, *b* 1965: *m* 1997, John F. Comparelli, son of David Comparelli, of Vancouver, BC, Canada, and has issue living, Archangelo *b* 1998, — (by 2nd *m*) Edward Charles, *b* 1974.

Hon Anthony Arthur (Box 782404, Sandton 2146, S Africa), *b* 1940: *m* 1967, Penelope, who *d* 1988, da of E. J. W. Hendry, MBE, and has issue living, Alexander Julius, *b* 1973, — Tracy Lara, *b* 1971.

Hon Christopher Ashton (Gordon's Valley Station, RD2, Timaru, NZ); *b* 1946: *m* 1968, Ann, da of late Harry Bell Lewis Johnstone, and has issue living, Caroline Helen, *b* 1968, — Amanda Victoria, *b* 1970.

DAUGHTER LIVING OF LIFE BARON

Hon Clare Louise Katharine, *b* 1950: *m* 1975, Anthony Joyce Cary, CMG, of The Old Vicarage, Knatchbull Rd, SE5 9QU, son of late Sir (Arthur Lucius) Michael Cary, GCB, and has issue living, Sam Michael, *b* 1978, — Thomas Joyce, *b* 1980, — Arthur Lucius, *b* 1983, — Harriet Maude, *b* 1985.

ELWYN-JONES, BARONY OF (Jones) (Extinct 1989)

SON LIVING OF LIFE BARON

Hon Daniel ELWYN-JONES (196 Cable St, E1), *b* 1940; Head of Campaigns, Amnesty Internat: *m* 19—, Denise Turner, and has issue living, Davey Elwyn, *b* 19—, — Sam, *b* 19—, — Polly Elizabeth, *b* 19—.

DAUGHTER LIVING

Hon Josephine, *b* 19—: *m* 1972, James Francis Gladstone (*see* Gladstone, Bt).

ELY, MARQUESS OF (Tottenham) Sits as BARON LOFTUS (UK 1801) (Marquess I 1801, Bt I 1780)

CHARLES JOHN TOTTENHAM, 8th Marquess, and 9th Baronet; *b* 30 May 1913; *s* 1969; *ed* Queen's Univ, Kingston, Ontario (BA); formerly Headmaster, Boulden House, Trin Coll Sch, Port Hope, Ontario: *m* 1st, 1938, Katherine Elizabeth, who *d* 1975, da of Lt-Col W. H. Craig, of Kingston, Ontario; 2ndly, 1978, Elspeth Ann, who *d* 1996, only da of late P. T. Hay, of Highgate and has issue by 1st *m*.

Arms – Not yet confirmed at the College of Arms for the line of the present Marquess.
Residence – Trinity College School, Port Hope, Ontario, Canada.

SONS LIVING (By 1st marriage)

CHARLES JOHN (*Viscount Loftus*), *b* 2 Feb 1943; *ed* Trin Coll, Toronto Univ (MA): *m* 1969, Judith Marvelle, da of Dr J. J. Porter, of Calgary, Alberta, and has two adopted children, Andrew, *b* 1973, — Jennifer, *b* 1975.
Lord Timothy Craig, *b* 1948; *ed* Ottawa Teachers' Coll: *m* 1973, Elizabeth Jane, da of Grant McAllister, of Ottawa, Ont, and has issue living, Scott Craig, *b* 1977, — John Douglas, *b* 1981.
Lord Richard Ivor (819 Grace St, Newmarket, Ontario L3Y 2L6, Canada), *b* 1954; *ed* Univ of Western Ont (BA): *m* 1978, Virginia Murney, da of late William Murney Morris of Toronto, Ont, Canada, and has issue living, Elizabeth Murney, *b* 1983, — Katherine Ann, *b* 1985.

DAUGHTER LIVING (By 1st marriage)

Rt Rev Lady Ann Elizabeth, *b* 1940; *ed* Trin Coll, Toronto Univ (BA, STB, BEd, DDhon), and Union Seminary, New York (STM); Headmistress, Bishop Strachan Sch, Toronto, Ontario; Suffragan Bishop of Toronto since 1997.

SISTER LIVING (Raised to the rank of a Marquess's daughter 1973)

Lady Dora Elizabeth (24 The Gateways, SW3), *b* 1919; *ed* Queen's Univ, Kingston, Ont (BA); 1939-45 War, as Lt WRCNS: a JP for London: *m* 1st, 1946, Lt (E) Bernard Edgar Hall, RN, who *d* 1947; 2ndly, 1950, Sir Ivor Thomas Montague Pink, KCMG, who *d* 1966, and has issue living, (by 2nd *m*) Celia Elizabeth, *b* 1952.

WIDOW LIVING OF BROTHER OF EIGHTH MARQUESS

Jane Elizabeth (Trullwell, Box, nr Stroud, Glos, GL6 9HD), da of Arthur Martin: *m* 1944, Lord George Tottenham, who *d* 1975, and has issue (see colls infra).

THEA MARGARET GORDON (*Thea, Marchioness of Ely*), da of late Lars G. Gronvold, of 36 Wilbury Rd, Hove: *m* 1928, the 7th Marquess of Ely, who *d* 1969.

COLLATERAL BRANCHES LIVING

Granddaughter of George Leonard Tottenham, grandson of Charles John Tottenham, el son of late Rt Rev Lord Robert Ponsonby Tottenham, Bishop of Clogher, 2nd son of 1st Marquess:—
Issue of late Cdr Lord George Robert Tottenham, RCN, who was raised to the rank of a Marquess's son 1973, *b* 1914, *d* 1975: *m* 1944, Jane Elizabeth (ante), da of Arthur Martin:—
Jane Elizabeth, *b* 1945: *m* 1971, Capt Mark Graham Robinson, late RA, of Trullwell, Box, nr Stroud, Glos GL6 9HD, and has issue living, Nano Sophie Tottenham, *b* 1973.

Grandchildren of late Very Rev George Tottenham, 10th son of late Rt Rev Lord Robert Ponsonby Tottenham, Bishop of Clogher (ante):—
Issue of late Edward Loftus Tottenham, *b* 1867, *d* 1949: *m* 1899, Jessie Hilda, who *d* 1938, da of late John Honey Trace:—
George William Loftus, *b* 1911: *m* 1949, Margaret Mary Hamilton, da of late Thomas Valentine Powell, and has issue living, (Robert) Ashley Christopher, *b* 1953: *m* 1st, 1978, Philippa Jane, who *d* 1981, el da of Maj P. F. Stevens, of Cornmongers, Runwick, Farnham, Surrey; 2ndly, 1983, Gabriele Maria, da of Anton Schüle, of Rötenbach, Wolfegg, W. Germany, and has issue living (by 1st *m*), Joe *b* 1980, — Alison Margaret, *b* 1951: *m* 1976, Roger Jones, and has issue living. *Residence* – Blaney, Enniskillen, co Fermanagh. —— Emily Frances: *m* 1931, Henry Gordon Sansom and has issue living. *Residence* – 15 Old Rossopy Park, Enniskillen, co Fermanagh.

PREDECESSORS – (1) JOHN Tottenham, MP for New Ross, etc; *cr* a *Baronet* 1780; *d* 1786; *s* by his son (2) CHARLES, KP, PC (2nd Bt), who had in 1783 *s* to the estates of his uncle Henry Loftus (which surname he assumed), KP, 1st and last Earl of Ely (*cr* 1771), and in 1785 had been *cr Baron Loftus*, of Loftus (peerage of Ireland); was Postmaster-Gen 1789; *cr Viscount Loftus* (peerage of Ireland) 1789, *Earl of Ely* (peerage of Ireland) 1794, *Marquess of Ely* (peerage of Ireland) 1801, and *Baron Loftus*, of Long Loftus, co York (peerage of United Kingdom) 1801; *d* 1806; *s* by his son (3) JOHN, KP, 2nd Marquess; *d* 1845; *s* by his son (4) JOHN HENRY, 3rd Marquess; *b* 1814: *m* 1844, Jane, VA, da of James Hope-Vere, of Craigie and Blackwood, NB; *d* 1857; *s* by his son (5) JOHN HENRY WELLINGTON GRAHAM, 4th Marquess, *b* 1849: *m* 1875, Caroline Anne, who *d* 1917, da of late George Caithness; *d* 1889, *s* by his cousin (6) JOHN HENRY (el son of the Rev Lord Adam Loftus, 3rd son of 2nd Marquess), 5th Marquess, *b* 1851: *m* 1895, Margaret Emma, who *d* 1931, da of F. Aldridge Clark, of Lynton Court, Hove, Sussex, and Gracefield, Prince, Risborough, Bucks; *d* 1925; *s* by his brother (6) GEORGE HERBERT, 6th Marquess, *b* 1854: *m* 1st, 1884, Emily Harriet, who *d* 1886, da of Major Arthur Vandeleur, RA; 2ndly, 1902, Ethel Beatrice Lemprière, who *d* 1927, da of late Nigel Gresley, JP, of Hobart, Tasmania; *d* 1935; *s* by his son (7) GEORGE HENRY WELLINGTON, 7th Marquess, *b* 1903: *m* 1928, Thea Margaret Gordon, da of late Lars G. Gronvold, of Hove; *d* 1969; *s* by his kinsman (8) Charles John (el son of George Leonard Tottenham, grandson of Charles John Tottenham (*b* 1808), el son of the Rt Rev Lord Robert Ponsonby Tottenham, Bishop of Clogher (who resumed the name and arms of Tottenham), 2nd son of 1st Marquess), 8th Marquess and present peer; also Earl of Ely, Viscount Loftus, and Baron Loftus.

ELYSTAN-MORGAN, BARON (Morgan) (Life Baron 1981)

(DAFYDD) ELYSTAN MORGAN, son of late Dewi Morgan; *b* 7 Dec 1932; *ed* Ardwyn Gram Sch, Aberystwyth, Univ Coll of Wales, Aberystwyth; admitted a solicitor 1957; Chm Welsh Parly Party 1967-68; Parly under Sec of State Home Office 1968-70; Barrister at Law Grays Inn 1971; front bench spokesman on Welsh Affairs 1972-74; a Circuit Judge, Wales and Chester circuit since 1987; MP (Lab) Cardiganshire 1966-74; a Recorder 1983-87; Fellow of Univ of Wales Aberystwyth 1992, Pres since 1997; *cr Baron Elystan-Morgan*, of Aberteifi, co Dyfed (Life Baron) 1981: *m* 1959, Alwen, da of William E. Roberts, and has issue.
Residence – Careg Afon, Dolau, Bow Street, Dyfed.

SON LIVING

Hon Owain, *b* 1962.

DAUGHTER LIVING

Hon Eleri, *b* 1960; LLB: *m* 1989, Peter Gerard Hurt, 2nd son of Rudolph Hurt, of Hathern, Loughborough, Leics.

EMERTON, BARONESS (Emerton) (Life Baroness 1997)

AUDREY CAROLINE EMERTON, DBE, da of late George William Emerton, of Tunbridge Wells, Kent; *b* 10 Sept 1935; *ed* Tunbridge Wells Gram Sch, St George's Hosp (SRN 1956), SCM 1958, RNT 1964; Hon DCL Kent 1989, Hon DUniv Central England 1997, Hon DSc Brighton 1997; Senior Tutor, St George's Hosp 1965-68; Principal Nursing Offr, Education, Bromley HMC 1968-70; Chief Nursing Offr Tunbridge Wells and Leybourne HMC 1970-73; Regional Nursing Offr SE Thames RHA 1973-91; Chief Nursing Offr St John Ambulance Bde 1988-96; Chief Offr Care in the Community 1996-98, since when Ch Cmdr St John Ambulance; Chm English Nat Board for Nursing, Midwifery and Health Visiting 1983-85; Chm UK Central Council for Nursing Midwives and Health Visitors 1985-93; Hon Vice-Pres RCN since 1994; Trustee, Kent Community Housing Trust 1993-98; DL Kent 1992; DStJ 1994; *cr* DBE 1989, and *Baroness Emerton*, of Tunbridge Wells, co Kent, and of Clerkenwell in London Borough of Islington (Life Baroness) 1997.

Arms – ......
Residence – Carlton House, 3 Strettitt Gdns, East Peckham, Tonbridge, Kent TN12 5ES.

Emlyn, Viscount; family name of Earl Cawdor.

EMMET OF AMBERLEY, BARONY OF (Emmet) (Extinct 1980)

SON LIVING OF LIFE BARONESS

Hon David Alastair Rennell (Casilla de Correo 55174, San Carlos, Maldonado, Uruguay), *b* 1928; *ed* Ampleforth, and Worcester Coll, Oxford; a Member of British Community Council, Argentina 1964-68: FRGS: *m* 1967, Sylvia Delia, da of late Willis Knowles, of Buenos Aires, and has issue living, Thomas Ian David, *b* 1970, — Caroline Ann Gloria *b* 1968.

DAUGHTERS LIVING OF LIFE BARONESS

Hon (Gloria) Lavinia Eileen, *b* 1924: *m* 1950, Maj Mark Winton Slane Fleming, 10th R Hussars (PWO) (ret) and has issue living, Andrew Gerard James (Lower Farmhouse, Great Rissington, Cheltenham Spa GL54 2LH), *b* 1956; FBHI: *m* 1985, Kathryn Claire, only child of late John William Warner, DSC, and has issue living, Giles William Slane *b* 1989, Jack Francis Edmund *b* 1992, Lucinda Marion Kate *b* 1987, — Mary Georgina, *b* 1951: *m* 1972, Michael David Hardinge, of calle Pintor Gisbert 3, p2, 46006 Valencia, Spain and has issue living, Elizabeth Selene *b* 1972: *m* 1998, Iain Stephen Stewart Sainsbury, — Sarah Elizabeth Sophia, *b* 1953: *m* 1979, Jonathan Francis Bruce Ward, of 2 Olive Hill Cottages, Wyck Rissington, Cheltenham Spa, Glos GL54 2LH, and has issue (*see* Bruce, Bt, *cr* 1628, colls), — Charlotte Ann (Damside Cottage, Guthrie, Forfar, Angus DD8 2SN), *b* 1955.

Hon (Penelope) Ann Clare (Flat 4, 43 Onslow Sq, SW7), *b* 1932: *m* 1951 (*m diss* 1965), Hon Hugo Nevill Money-Coutts (later 8th Baron Latymer).

EMSLIE, BARON (Emslie) (Life Baron 1980)

GEORGE CARLYLE EMSLIE, MBE, PC, son of Alexander Emslie; *b* 6 Dec 1919; *ed* The High Sch of Glasgow, and Glasgow Univ (MA, LLB, Hon LLD); FRSE, 1939-45 War in N Africa, Italy, Greece and Austria (despatches); Bde Maj 1944-46; Advocate Scotland 1948; QC 1957; Advocate Depute to Sheriff Courts 1955-57; Junior Assessor to City of Edinburgh 1955-57; a Member of Scottish Cttee of Council on Tribunals 1962-70; Chm of Scottish Agricultural Wages Board 1968; Sheriff of Perth and Angus 1963-66; Dean of Faculty of Advocates 1965-70, and Senior Assessor to City of Edinburgh 1965-70; Senator of the College of Justice; a Lord of Session with the title of *Lord Emslie* 1970; Lord Justice Gen of Scotland and Lord Pres of the Court of Session 1972; Hon Bencher Inner Temple 1974; *cr* PC 1972, and *Baron Emslie*, of Potterton, in the District of Gordon (Life Baron) 1980: *m* 1942, Lilias Ann Mailer, who *d* 1998, da of Robert Hannington, of Glasgow, and has issue.

Arms – not exemplified at the time of going to press.
Residence – 47 Heriot Row, Edinburgh EH3 6EX. *Club* – New (Edinburgh).

SONS LIVING

Hon (George) Nigel Hannington (20 Inverleith Place, Edinburgh EH3 5QB), BA (Cantab), LLB (Edin), QC (Scot) 1986, *b* 1947; *ed* Edinburgh Acad, Trinity Coll, Glenalmond, and Gonville and Caius Coll Camb and Edinburgh Univ; QC: *m* 1973, Heather Ann, da of Arthur Frank Davis, of Bristol, and has issue.

Hon Derek Robert Alexander (*Hon Lord Kingarth*) (35 Ann St, Edinburgh EH4 1PL), BA (Cantab) LLB (Edin), QC (Scot) 1987, *b* 1949; *ed* Edinburgh Acad, Trinity Coll, Glenalmond, Gonville and Caius Coll Camb, and Edinburgh Univ; QC 1987; Senator of the College of Justice; a Lord of Session with the title of Lord Kingarth 1997: *m* 1974, Elizabeth Jane Cameron, da of Andrew McLaren Carstairs of Newport-on-Tay, and has issue.

Hon Richard Hannington, *b* 1957, *ed* Edinburgh Acad, Trinity Coll, Glenalmond, and Gonville and Caius Coll Camb (MA PhD).

Encombe, Viscount; son of Earl of Eldon.

ENERGLYN, BARONY OF (Evans) (Extinct 1985)

WIDOW LIVING OF LIFE BARON

JEAN THOMPSON (*Baroness Energlyn*), da of John Miller, of St Andrews Cres, Cardiff: *m* 1942, Baron Energlyn (Life Baron), who *d* 1985. *Residence* – 7 The Dentons, Denton Rd, Eastbourne, East Sussex BN20 7SW

Enfield, Viscount; son of Earl of Strafford.

ENNALS, BARONY OF (Ennals) (Extinct 1995)

SONS LIVING OF LIFE BARON (By 1st marriage)

Prof the Hon John Richard, *b* 1951; *ed* King's Coll Sch, Wimbledon, Phillip's Academy, Andover, USA, King's Coll, Camb, and London Univ Inst of Educn; Prof Kingston Business Sch since 1990: *m* 1975, Roberta Mary, da of Norman Robert Reedman, of Barnet, Herts, and has issue living, Robert Jonathan, *b* 1979, — Christopher Paul, *b* 1981. *Residence* – 19 Belgrade Rd, Hampton, Middx TW12 2AZ.
Hon Paul Martin, *b* 1957.
Hon Simon David, *b* 1959.

DAUGHTER LIVING OF LIFE BARON (By 1st marriage)

Hon Susan, *b* 1953.

WIDOW LIVING OF LIFE BARON

Mrs KATHERINE TRANOY (*Baroness Ennals*): *m* 1977, as his 2nd wife, Baron Ennals, PC, who *d* 1995. *Residence* – 6 Glenloch Rd, Belsize Park, NW3.

ENNISKILLEN, EARL OF (Cole) Sits as BARON GRINSTEAD (UK 1815) (Earl I 1789)

Worship God; honour the King

ANDREW JOHN GALBRAITH COLE, 7th Earl, *b* 28 April 1942; *s* 1989; *ed* Eton; late Capt Irish Guards: *m* 1964, Sarah Frances Caroline, only da of Maj-Gen John Keith-Edwards, CBE, DSO, MC, of Nairobi, and has issue.

Arms – Argent, a bull passant sable, armed and hoofed or, within a bordure of the second, charged with eight bezants; on a canton sinister per pale gules and azure, a harp of the third, stringed argent. **Crest** – A demi-dragon wings elevated vert, holding a dart in the dexter paw and resting the sinister on an antique buckler, charged as the canton. **Supporters** – Two dragons reguardant vert, each holding in the inner fore paw a dart.
Seat – Florence Court, Enniskillen, co Fermanagh. *Address* – c/o House of Lords, SW1A 0PW.

DAUGHTERS LIVING

Lady Amanda Mary, *b* 1966: *m* 1992, Jeffrey Arthur Hayward, and has issue living, Joshua Arthur, *b* 1994, — Jack Benjamin, *b* 1996.
Lady Emma Frances, *b* 1969.
Lady Lucy Caroline, *b* 1970.

SISTER LIVING

Lady Linda Mary, *b* 1944: *m* 1975, Sir Richard James Kay Muir, 4th Bt, of Park House, Blair Drummond, Stirling, Perths, and has issue (see that title).

UNCLE LIVING (brother of 6th Earl)

ARTHUR GERALD, *b* 15 Nov 1920; *ed* Eton; late Capt Irish Guards: *m* 1949, Prudence Tobina, da of late Algernon Richard Aubrey Cartwright (*see* Buxton, Bt, colls), and has issue living, Berkeley Arthur (151 Battersea Rise, SW11 1HP), *b* 1949; *ed* Milton Abbey: *m* 1978, Hon Cecilia Anne Ridley, eldest da of 4th Viscount Ridley, TD, and has issue living, Joshua Berkeley *b* 1986, Richard David *b* 1991, — Hugh Galbraith, *b* 1954; *ed* Milton Abbey, — Richard Lowry (1 Avon View, Upper Seagry, Chippenham, Wilts), *b* 1956; *ed* Eton: *m* 1st, 1977 (*m diss* 1988), Susan Elizabeth, da of David Allen, of Nairobi, Kenya; 2ndly, 1988 (*m diss* 19—), Karen, da of Ernest Robert Victor Ingram, of Chippenham, Wilts, and has issue living (by 1st *m*), Arthur Berkeley David *b* 1983, — Marian Rose, *b* 1951: *m* 1979, Bruce Hobson, of Rosslyn Estate, Box 34247, Nairobi, Kenya, and has issue living, Amelia Rose *b* 1986. *Residence* – 2 Orchard Brae, Edinburgh EH4 1NY.

DAUGHTER LIVING OF FIFTH EARL

Lady Frances Jane, *b* 1914; late Junior Com ATS: *m* 1954, as his 2nd wife, Group Capt Henry Ivan Hanmer, DFC, RAF, who *d* 1984 (*see* Hanmer, Bt, colls). *Residence* – 1 Church Way, Grendon, Northampton.

COLLATERAL BRANCHES LIVING

Grandchildren of late Claud CHALONER (who assumed the surname of Chaloner under the will of his uncle Richard Chaloner) son of Arthur Willoughby Cole-Hamilton, grandson of late Hon ARthur Cole-Hamilton, MP, 2nd son of 1st Baron Mountflorence:—
Issue of late Maj Claudius Willoughby CHALONER, *b* 1882, *d* 1963: *m* 1918, Winifred Adelaide, who *d* 1969 da of late Col Alexander Sinclair Grove, DSO, MSC:—
Desmond Willoughby Richard (High Bank, Chearsley, Aylesbury), *b* 1920; *ed* Shrewsbury, and at Trin Coll, Dublin (MA); 1939-45 War as Lt King's African Rifles. —— Nancy Winifred (Beechtree, Rathmore, Naas, co Kildare), *b* 1921: *m* 1st, 1945, Francis G. Cornwall, who *d* 1949; 2ndly, 1959, Prof John Seton Michael Pringle, FRCS, who *d* 1975, and has issue living (by 1st *m*), Francis David Willoughby, *b* 1947, — Ann Patricia (*posthumous*), *b* 1950: *m* 1973, Robert Tristram Rowan Woods, of Beechmount, Orwell Rd, Dublin 14, and has issue living, Robert Seton Rowan *b* 1986, John Francis Cornwall *b* (twin) 1986, Nicola Clare *b* 1982, Lucinda Ann *b* 1983.

Issue of late John Cole CHALONER, *b* 1889, *d* 1940: *m* 1922, Monica Katharine, who *d* 1975, da of late Rev William Ralph Westropp Roberts, DD:—
Charity Patricia (RRI, Naramata, BC, Canada), *b* 1923: *m* 1949 (*m diss* 1973), Henry FitzGibbon, MD, who *d* 1989, and has issue living, John (638 Monterey Ave, Victoria, BC, Canada), *b* 1951: *m* 1976, Paula Gammell, and has issue living, Fletcher *b* 1987, Gamelle (a da) *b* 1984, — Thomas (3/103 Beach St, Coogee, NSW 2034, Australia), *b* 1952; PhD, — Frances (RMB 396 Little Whiskas Rd, via Bungendore, NSW 2621, Australia), *b* 1954; PhD: *m* 1993, — Pamela Anne, *b* 1959: *m* 1994, Wayne Clayton, of 895 Alfriston Place, Victoria, BC, Canada. —— Mary Frances Jonet, *b* 1925: *m* 1950, Richard John Shackleton, and has issue living, Richard Chaloner, *b* 1953: *m* 1988, Sarah Caroline Benton, and has issue living, Christopher Mark *b* 1989, James Richard *b* 1991, Deborah Mary *b* 1993, — Michael Beattie, *b* 1959, — Christine Mary, *b* 1951: *m* 1988, Samir Habouch, — Jonet Rhoda, *b* 1956: *m* 1984, Thomas Mary Egan, of White Lodge, Kennedy Rd, Dunboyne, co Meath, and has issue living, Eoin Shackleton *b* 1987. *Residence* – Anna Liffey House, Lucan, co Dublin. —— Henrietta Sophia, *b* 1930: *m* 1959, Robert Frederick Twigg, and has issue living, Robert Chaloner (Amber Hill, Kilmeaden, co Waterford), *b* 1960: *m* 1985, Janet Beck, and has issue living, Nathan Robert *b* 1988, Katie Beck *b* 1986, Lucy Astrid *b* 1989, — Nicola *b* 1962: *m* 1993, Christopher Woods, and has issue living, John Rowan *b* 1995, Katharin Mary Sophie *b* 1998, — Fiona, *b* 1963: *m* 1987, Frank O'Reilly, of Granite Lodge, Enniskerry, co Wicklow, and has issue living, Stephen Peter *b* 1988, Alan Robert *b* 1990, Karen Sophie Anne *b* 1993, — Sarah *b* 1970. *Residence* – Newtownmountkennedy, co Wicklow.

Granddaughters of late Rev Arthur Henry Cole-Hamilton, son of late Arthur Willoughby Cole-Hamilton (ante):—
Issue of late George William Cole-Hamilton, *b* 1875, *d* 1946: *m* 1908, Katharine Edith, who *d* 1960, da of late William Clinton-Baker, of Bayfordbury, Herts:—
Mary, TD, *b* 1913; formerly Ch Comm ATS: *m* 1st, 1936 (*m diss* 1952), John Carew Jones; 2ndly, 1952, Col John Locke Lovibond, TD, MD, FRCP, RAMC (TA), who *d* 1954; 3rdly, 1956, Col Donald Barry Girling, MC, TD, RA (TA), who *d* 1986. *Residence* – Highworth Farm, Charlwood, Surrey. —— Elizabeth Peace, *b* 1918: *m* 1st, 1939, Lt-Com Rodney Athelstan Price, RN, who was *ka* 1943; 2ndly, 1945, Col Geoffrey Russell Armstrong, DSO, MC, TD, Hon Artillery Co, and has issue living, (by 1st *m*) David George (Woodcock, Thirsk, Yorks), *b* 1940; MA, Camb: *m* 1970, Diana Catherine Symington, da of late Alastair Symington Davie, of Grangehill, Beith, Ayrshire, and has issue living, Toby Charles Rodney *b* 1972, Simon James Edward *b* 1974, — (by 2nd *m*) Johny (Woodlands House, Colgate, Sussex), *b* 1946: MA Camb: *m* 1976, Elsie Borodale, da of Frederick S. Peters, of New Jersey, USA, and has issue living, Geoffrey Read *b* 1980, Graham Whitney *b* 1983, — Ruth Margaret, *b* 1949: *m* 1976, Henry Clifton Calvert (*see* Brown, Bt, colls), of Holmbush, Faygate, Sussex, and has issue living, Piers Henry *b* 1977, Henrietta Amelia *b* 1980. *Residence* – Axmas Cottage, Rusper, Sussex.

Grandsons of late Ven Richard Mervyn Cole-Hamilton (infra):
Issue of late Maj Richard Arthur Cole-Hamilton, *b* 1912, *d* 1992: *m* 1947, (Ruth Kathleen) Betty (Hawthorn Villa, 386 Ferry Rd, Edinburgh EH5 3QG), da of Sir William Lorenzo Parker, 3rd Bt, OBE:—
Robin (39 Fawnbrake Av, SE24 OBE), *b* 1948; *ed* Trin Coll, Glenalmond: *m* 1982, Helen, da of late Rev Canon Gerald Archer Luckett, of Meonstoke, Hants, and has issue living, Jonathan Archer, *b* 1986, — Katharine Faith, *b* 1983. —— Richard Simon (Elm Cottage, 54 Culcabock Av, Inverness IV2 3RQ), *b* 1951; *ed* Trin Coll, Glenalmond; CA: *m* 1982, Anni, da of J. G. M. Watt, of Edinburgh, and has issue living, Joanna Ruth, *b* 1983, — Sarah Constance, *b* 1985. —— William Mervyn John (Lethenty Cottage, Fyvie, Aberdeenshire AB53 8NE), *b* 1954; *ed* Trin Coll, Glenalmond: *m* 1978, Jill, yst da of late Dr K. C. Johnston, and has issue living, Richard James, *b* 1983, — Emma Judith, *b* 1985.

Issue of late Lieut David Edmund Cole-Hamilton, DSC, RN, *b* 1914; *k* on active service in the Mediterranean 1942: *m* 1938, Anne (who *d* 1995, having *m* 2ndly, 1959, Oswald Graham Noel Turnbull, MC, who *d* 1970), da of late George William Cole-Hamilton (ante):—
Michael Anthony (The Ridge, RR2 Lyndhurst, Ont K0E 1N0, Canada), *b* 1940; *ed* Bradfield; late Lieut RN: *m* 1963, Jane Elizabeth Mary, elder da of late Arthur Maurice Stewart-Wallace, MD, FRCP, of The Moot House, Ditchling, Sussex, and has issue living, William Michael David, *b* 1967, — Elen Susannah, *b* 1965: *m* 1993, Graham Lunt, elder son of Ronald Lunt, of Boscheok Farm, Duiwelskloof, S Africa, and has issue living, Stuart Alexander *b* 1997, — Alexandra Jane, *b* 1971.

Grandson of late Rev Arthur Henry Cole-Hamilton (ante):—
Issue of late Ven Richard Mervyn Cole Hamilton, *b* 1877, *d* 1959: *m* 1st, 1911, Margaret, JP, who *d* 1954, da of late Edmund Grove Bennett, of The Close, Salisbury; 2ndly, 1955, Elsie Irén (WARNER), who *d* 1975, da of W. H. Pendlebury, of Shrewsbury:—
(By 1st *m*) Anthony Mervyn, *b* 1919; Lt-Cdr RN (ret); 1939-45 War (despatches): *m* 1st, 1944, Monica Mary (3rd Officer WRNS), who *d* 1954, da of late Lt-Col John Rogers Cartwright, DSO; 2ndly, 1956 (*m diss* 1983), Angela Elizabeth, who *d* 1988, da of J. I. Baeza, FRCS, DPH, of Barbados, and formerly wife of M. A. G. Hanschell and has issue living (by 1st *m*), David John, *b* 1948; Irvine Prof of Chemistry, St Andrews Univ: *m* 1973, Elizabeth Ann, da of Bruce Lloyd Brown, of Vic, BC, Canada, and has issue living, Alexander Geoffrey *b* 1977, Nicholas Anthony Michael *b* 1986, Rose Monica Elizabeth *b* 1979, Sian Fiona Non *b* 1986, — Susan Joan COLE-HAMILTON, *b* 1945; has resumed her maiden name: *m* 1st, 1969 (*m diss* 1978), Andrew Wallace; 2ndly, 1978 (*m diss* 1998), Gerard Garra, — Isobel Margaret, *b* 1950, — Patricia Anne, *b* 1952: *m* 1982, F. Tomlin, and has issue living, Lucy Sarah Patricia *b* 1980, Alison Kirsty *b* 1982. *Residence* – Marine Cottage, Alleyn's Rd, Stevenage, Herts.

Granddaughter of late John Isaac Cole-Hamilton, yst son of late Arthur Willoughby Cole-Hamilton (ante):—

Issue of late Air Vice-Marshal John Beresford Cole-Hamilton, CB, CBE, *b* 1894, *d* 1945: *m* 1928, Hilda Violet Leslie, who *d* 1945, da of late Charles Leslie Fox, of Rumwell Hall, Taunton:—

Diana Patricia Selina, *b* 1932: *m* 1957 (*m diss* 1968), Stephen Wilbraham Ford, and has issue living, Jonathan Hugo (62 Charles St, Oxford OX4 3AS), *b* 1960: *m* 1991, Amanda Jane, da of John Stow, of University Farm, Bledington, Oxon, — Joanna Margaret Randle, *b* 1958. *Residence* – The Old Vicarage, The Street, Greywell, Hook, Hants RG29 1BZ.

Granddaughter of late Col Arthur Richard Cole-Hamilton, son of late Capt William Claude Cole-Hamilton, brother of late Claud Chaloner (ante):—

Issue of late Capt William Moore Cole-Hamilton, late RASC, *b* 1883, *d* 1948: *m* 1903, Ada Beatrice, yst da of late William Peter Huddle, of Dover:—

Nora Kathleen, *b* 1904: *m* 1st, 1926 (*m diss* 1944), Carl Rudolf Baltzar von Braun, MRCS, late Capt RAMC; 2ndly, 1944, John Mathew Shufflebotham.

PREDECESSORS – (1) JOHN COLE, MP for Enniskillen, 4th in descent from Sir William Cole, who settled in Co Fermanagh *temp* James I, was *cr Baron Mountflorence*, of Florence Court, co Fermanagh (peerage of Ireland) 1760; *d* 1767; *s* by his son (2) WILLIAM WILLOUGHBY, 2nd Baron; *cr Viscount Enniskillen* (peerage of Ireland), 1776, and *Earl of Enniskillen* (peerage of Ireland) 1789; *d* 1803; *s* by his son (3) JOHN WILLOUGHBY, 2nd Earl; *b* 1768; Lord-Lieut of co Fermanagh; *cr Baron Grinstead*, of Grinstead, Wilts (peerage of United Kingdom) 1815; *d* 1840; *s* by his son (4) WILLIAM WILLOUGHBY, DCL, LLD, FRS; *b* 1807; sat as MP for Fermanagh (C) 1831-40: *m* 1st, 1844, Jane, who *d* 1855, el da of late James Archibald Casamaijor; 2ndly, 1865, Hon Mary Emma Brodrick, who *d* 1896, da of 6th Viscount Middleton; *d* Nov 1886; *s* by his el son (5) LOWRY EGERTON, KP, 4th Earl, *b* 1845, MP for Enniskillen (C) 1880-5: *m* 1869, Charlotte Marion, who *d* 1937, da of late Douglas Baird, of Closeburn, NB; *d* 1924; *s* by his son (6) JOHN HENRY MICHAEL, CMG, 5th Earl, *b* 1876; Lt 7th Hussars, and Lt-Col N Irish Horse, and Chm N Ireland Transport Board: *m* 1st, 1907 (*m diss* 1931), Irene Frances, who *d* 1937, da of Alfred Edward Miller Mundy; 2ndly, 1932, Mary Cecily, da of late Hugh Nevill, and widow of Maj Thomas Syers, RA; *d* 1963; *s* by his nephew (7) DAVID LOWRY, MBE (son of late Hon Galbraith Lowry Egerton Cole, 3rd son of 4th Earl), 6th Earl, *b* 1918; 1939-45 War as Capt Irish Guards; Elected Member Kenya Leg Council (Mt Kenya Constituency) 1961-63, DL, JP co Fermanagh: *m* 1st, 1940 (*m diss* 1955), Sonia, who *d* 1982, da of late Maj Thomas Syers, RA (by his wife Mary Cicely Nevill, who *d* 1963, having *m* 2ndly, 1932, the 5th Earl of Enniskillen); 2ndly, 1955, Nancy Henderson, who *d* 1998, da of late Dr John Alexander MacLennan, of Bridgeport, Conn, USA; *d* 1989; *s* by his only son (8) ANDREW JOHN GALBRAITH, 7th Earl and present peer; also Viscount Enniskillen, Baron Mountflorence, and Baron Grinstead.

Erleigh, Viscount; son of Marquess of Reading.

ERNE, EARL OF (Crichton) Sits as BARON FERMANAGH (UK 1876) (Earl I 1789)
(Name pronounced "Cryton")

%% GOD · SEND · GRACE %%

HENRY GEORGE VICTOR JOHN CRICHTON, 6th Earl; *b* 9 July 1937; *s* 1940; *ed* Eton; was a Page of Honour to HM 1952-54; late Lieut N Irish Horse; a JP and Lord Lieut co Fermanagh: *m* 1st, 1958 (*m diss* 1980), Camilla Marguerite, el da of late Wing Com Owen George Endicott Roberts; 2ndly, 1980, Mrs Anna Carin Hitchcock, *née* Bjorck, and has issue by 1st *m*.

Arms – Argent, a lion rampant azure. Crest – A wyvern's head couped at the neck vert emitting flames proper from the mouth and ears. Supporters – Two lions azure, on the head of each an earl's coronet proper.
Seat – Crom Castle, Newtown Butler, co Fermanagh. *Clubs* – White's, Lough Erne Yacht Club.

SON LIVING (*By 1st marriage*)

JOHN HENRY MICHAEL NINIAN (*Viscount Crichton*), *b* 19 June 1971.

DAUGHTERS LIVING (*By 1st marriage*)

Lady Cleone Lucinda, *b* 1959: *m* 1989, Richard F. Versen, son of late Frederick Versen, of Rosewood Cottage, Ascot, Berks, and has issue living, Frederick James, *b* 1992. *Residence* – 23 Lochmorc House, Cundy St, SW1W 9JX.
Lady Davina Jane, *b* 1961: *m* 1990, Nicholas J. R. Scarr, elder son of late Peter R. R. Scarr, and has issue living, Oliver Peter Renforth, *b* 1992, — Sabrina Katherine Renforth, *b* 1993. *Residence* – Hatherden Manor, Hatherden, Andover, Hants SP11 0HL.
Lady Katherine Patricia, *b* 1962: *m* 1989, Jonathan C. Townsend-Rose, son of Colin Townsend-Rose, of W Printonan, Berwicks, and has issue living, Rory Dixon Crichton, *b* 1993, — Alexandra Lucy Flora, *b* 1992. *Residence* – Maxton Westend, Maxton, St Boswells, Roxburghshire TD6 0RL.
Lady Tara Guinevere, *b* 1967: *m* 1993, James William Loyd, yr son of Christopher Lewis Loyd, MC, of Lockinge, Wantage, Berks, and of Mrs Simon Burne, of Charlton, Malmesbury, and has issue living, William George, *b* 1996, — Eliza Rose, *b* 1999. *Residence* – St Andrew's Cottage, Shaftesbury, Dorset SP7 9LQ.

SISTERS LIVING

Lady Rosanagh Mary, *b* 1932: *m* 1956, Baron Michael Paul Raben-Levetzau, who *d* 1990, and has issue living, (Siegfried) Matthew (John) RABEN (35 Fontenoy Rd, SW12 9LX; *Club* – White's), *b* 1962; *ed* Eton: *m* 1987, Sarah Jane L., da of Vernon Gordon-Lennox Stratton, of St Helen's Station, IoW, and has issue living, Frederick Michael James *b* 1990, Timothy Peter William *b* 1995, Sophie Eleanor Rose *b* 1993, — Alexander Peter Vincent (31 Craddockstown Park, Naas, co Kildare), *b* 1964: *m* 1995, Amelia Kate, eldest da of John Seymour Dudley Madden, of Hilton Park, Clones, co Monaghan, — Christopher Victor Patrick, *b* 1968, — Seamus Julian Henry, *b* 1971. *Residence* – 23 Stack House, Cundy St, SW1.
Lady Antonia Pamela Mary, *b* 1934: *m* 1st, 1953, Timothy William Wardell (*see* Crossley, Bt, 1985 Edn); 2ndly, 1981, Charles William Beckwith, and has issue living (by 1st *m*), Michael John William (1/51 Sir Thomas Mitchell Rd, Bondi, NSW 2026, Australia), *b* 1956; *ed* Eton, and Australian Nat Univ: *m* 1980 (*m diss* 1991), Elizabeth O'Neil, and has issue living, Myles Timothy William *b* 1984, Francesca Mary Louise *b* 1986, Sophia Helen Mary *b* 1986, — Antony Henry Constantine, *b* 1959: *m* 1989, Nichola M. L., da of Thomas Wright, of Maudlin Farmhouse, Steyning, Sussex, and has issue living, Thomas William *b* 1993, a da *b* 1991, — David Stewart Timothy, *b* 1963, — Sabrina Mary Louise, *b* 1954: *m* 1974, Michael L. F. Smith, — Henrietta Pamela Mary, *b* 1967: *m* 1998, Antony C. Jackson, elder son of late Leonard Jackson, and of Mrs John Gough, of Moore Lodge, Newry, co Down. *Residence* – The Dower House, Kirklington, nr Bedale, N Yorks DL8 2LX.

COLLATERAL BRANCHES LIVING

Grandchildren of late Col Hon Sir George Arthur Charles Crichton, GCVO (infra):—
Issue of late Maj David George Crichton, LVO, *b* 1914, *d* 1997: *m* 1st, 1941, Joan Fenella (Susie), who *d* 1992, in a road accident, da of late Lt-Col Douglas Whyte Cleaver, DSO, of Park Palace, Monte Carlo; 2ndly, 1994, Betty (28C Thorney Crescent, Morgan's Walk, SW11 3TT), da of late Col Maurice George Lee, MC, RFC, and widow of Andrew George Hughes-Onslow (*see* E Onslow, colls):—
(By 1st *m*) Charles David Blayney (28 Linver Rd, SW6 3RB), *b* 1953; *ed* Eton: *m* 1st, 1977, Nicola Sian, da of Wing-Cdr Peter Berry, DFC, of Little Bookham, Surrey; 2ndly, 1988, Harriet E., yr da of Martin Monier-Williams, of Burrell House, Chiddingfold, Surrey, and has issue living, (by 2nd *m*) Oliver Charles Martin, *b* 1995, — Jessica Eloise, *b* 1991, Flora Susie, *b* 1993. —— Fenella Jane, *b* 1948: *m* 1st, 1969 (*m diss* 1974), Hon Anthony Henry Amherst Cecil (*see* B Amherst of Hackney); 2ndly, 1978, John Ernest, and has issue living (by 2nd *m*), Charlotte Matilda, *b* 1986.

Issue of late Col Hon Sir George Arthur Charles Crichton, GCVO, Coldstream Guards, 2nd son of 4th Earl, *b* 1874, *d* 1952: *m* 1913, Lady Mary Augusta Dawson, JP, who *d* 1961, da of 2nd Earl of Dartrey:—
Richard John Vesey, CVO, MC, *b* 1916; *ed* Eton; is Col late Coldstream Guards; Memb HM's Bodyguard of Hon Corps of Gentlemen-at-Arms 1966-86, Lieut since 1981; 1939-45 War (twice wounded, despatches, MC), CVO 1986: *m* 1948, Yvonne (OLIVER), da of late Dr H. E. Worthington, and has issue living, Vesey George (79 Cornwall Gardens, SW7 4AZ), *b* 1949; *ed* Eton, and E Anglia Univ, — Adrian David (2 Kersley St, SW11), *b* 1952; *ed* Eton, Bristol Univ, and INSEAD: *m* 1974, Janie, yr da of Duncan Wauchope, of Pinns Farm, Wellow, Romsey, Hants, and has issue living, Sophie *b* 1981,

Henrietta b 1983, Laura b 1985, — Simon Patrick (Shute End Farm House, Alderbury, Salisbury, Wilts), b 1956; ed Eton; JP: m 1983, Fiona Jane, da of late Colin Midwood, JP, of Grange Cottage, Funtington, W Sussex, and has issue living, Edward William Richard b 1989, Charles Patrick Vesey b 1992, Georgina Caroline Nicola b 1986. Club – Cavalry and Guards'. —— †Patrick Henry Douglas, OBE, b 1919; ed Eton, and at Oxford Univ; Maj Berks Yeo (TA); was a Page of Honour to HM 1932-36; 1939-45 War (despatches); OBE (1991): m 1948, Gillian Moyra, who d (30 Sept) 1998, da of late Rt Hon Sir Alexander George Montagu Cadogan, OM, GCMG, KCB (see E Cadogan, colls), and d (3 Sept) 1998, leaving issue, Hugh Patrick George, b 1949: m 1984, Kerry, elder da of L. M. Kyle-Little, of Brisbane, Australia, and has issue living, Georgina Jane b 1988, Laura Juliette b 1988 (twin), — Desmond Cadogan (6 Rumbold Rd, SW6 2JA), b 1953; ed Eton: m 1990, Emma Jane, elder da of Maj (Walter Brian) Julian Crawshay, of Tasburgh Grange, Norwich, and has issue living, a son b 1992, Hal Julian b 1995, Mary Euphane b 1994, — Jane Elizabeth (twin), b 1949: m 1977, Bevil Charles Fitz Ives Granville, of Ibworth, Tadley, Hants, yst son of late Maj Richard St Leger Granville, and has issue living, Harry Court Crichton b 1979, Camilla Jane b 1982. —— Mary Bridget Anne, b 1927: m 1951, Maj John William Burke Cole, Coldstream Guards (ret) (E Longford, colls), and has issue living, James William John (The Malt House, W Woodhay, Newbury, Berks RG15 0BJ), b 1952; ed Eton: m 1989, Yvonne, da of R. Hawkins, of Hitchin, Herts, and has issue living, Robert William James b 1990, Annabel Charlotte Mary b 1992, Emma Sophie Elizabeth b 1994. — Michael George, b 1955; ed Radley, — Elizabeth Anne, b 1961: m 1984, Simon Leigh Hayes, of The Barn, W Woodhay, Newbury, Berks, elder son of Roger Leigh Hayes, of Seaford, Sussex, and has issue living, Johnnie Kinloch de Vere b 1997. Residence – The Little Barn, W Woodhay, Newbury, Berks.

Issue of late Hon Arthur Owen Crichton, yst son of 4th Earl, b 1876, d 1970: m 1906, Katherine Helen Elizabeth, who d 1964, da of late Col Hon Walter Rodolph Trefusis, CB (B Clinton, colls):—
Jean Trefusis (Clover Farm, Shalden, Alton, Hants), b 1912: m 1st, 1933, Lt-Col Eion James Henry Merry, MC, R Horse Gds (see V Chetwynd, 1950 Edn), who d 1966; 2ndly, 1969, Capt Montagu William Lowry-Corry, who d 1977 (see E Belmore, colls), and has had issue (by 1st m), Davina Jean (Lady Gibbs) b 1934: m 1955, Field Marshal Sir Roland Christopher Gibbs, GCB, CBE, DSO, MC, late 60th Rifles, of Patney Rectory, Devizes, Wiltshire SN10 3QZ, and has issue living, Aidan Joseph Merry (Phoineas House, by Beauly, Inverness IV4 7BA) b 1957: m 1982, Leonie, el da of Capt (Edward Arthur) Mervyn Fox-Pitt (see E Dundee, colls) (and has issue living, Eion Roland Merry b 1992, Hermione Davina Janet b 1988, Jeanie Sinclair b 1998), James Roland Melvil b 1958, Melissa Margaret Jane b 1966, — Diana, b 1937; d 1980.

Grandchildren of late Hon Sir Henry George Louis Crichton, KCB, 3rd son of 3rd Earl:—
Issue of late Col Charles William Harry Crichton, DSO, b 1872, d 1958: m 1912, Dorothy Maud, who d 1959, da of late Hon Eustace Henry Dawnay (see V Downe, colls):—
Ronald Henry, b 1913; ed Radley, and Ch Ch, Oxford; late Capt Rifle Brig. Residence – Passatge Maluquer 7, Pral. 1, 08022 Barcelona, Spain. —— Brian John, OBE, b 1918; ed Radley, and at Trin Coll, Camb; OBE (Civil) 1977: m 1953, Anne Radclyffe, DL Gwynedd 1989, yr da of late Lt-Col Thomas Hassard Montgomery, DSO, of Cadogan House, Shrewsbury, and has had issue, Susan Jane, b 1955: m 1977, Michael Patrick York, of Colorado Springs, Col 80906, USA, and d 1991, leaving issue, Adam Patrick Crichton b 1980, Nicholas Brian Tyler b 1990, — Diana Mary, b 1957: m 1984, Richard John Charlton MacMullen, of The Verderers, Bradenham, Norfolk, 2nd son of James MacMullen, MC, of Laxey, I of Man, and has issue living, Patrick James Montgomery b 1989, — Judith Anne, b 1959: m 1st, 1983, Anthony Wall, who d 1989, eldest son of Lt-Col E. Wall, RE; 2ndly, 1996, Michael John Stewart Preece, of Ivy House, Leppington, Yorks, elder son of late Lt-Col James Preece, OBE, of Jersey, CI. Residence – Plas Trefor, Llansadwrn, Anglesey.

Issue of late Capt Reginald Louis Crichton, RN, b 1874, d 1929: m 1902, Hester Beatrix, who d 1961, da of late Rev Richard Allen White, R of Wing, Rutland:—
(Patricia) Jane (Lady Mount), b 1920: m 1st, 1946, John Herbert Mount, who d 1973; 2ndly, 1975, Sir James William Spencer Mount, CBE, of Woolton Farm, Bekesbourne, Canterbury, and has issue living (by 1st m), John Richard Herbert Crichton, b 1953; ed Gordonstoun: m 1977, Martha, only da of Prof Emeteus, of Cambridge, — Mark Donald Crichton b 1957; ed King's Sch, Canterbury, — Virginia Jane, b 1947: m 1968, Richard Henry Ringrose Latham, of Stowting Hill House, Ashford, Kent, and has issue (see E Jellicoe, colls), — (Selina) Clare, b 1950: m 1st, 1974 (m diss 1978), Alexander Brunton Badenoc; 2ndly, 1978, Andrew Pirie Stuart Robinson.

Granddaughters of late Capt Reginald Louis Crichton, RN (ante):—
Issue of late Cdr Marcus Henry Reginald Crichton, RN, b 1904, d 1985: m 1935, Elizabeth Frances, who d 1993, da of late Col Francis Holland Dorling, DSO, of The Crouch, Seaford, Sussex:—
Catherine Elizabeth, b 1937: m 1969, Christopher Bates, PhD, of 10 Station Rd, Harston, Cambridge, and has issue living, Gemma Clare Irene, b 1974. —— Frances Margaret, b 1942: m 1962, Maj Patrick Lloyd Ker Thompson, and has issue living, James Marcus Crichton, b 1966, — Bridget Clare, b 1964. —— Madelaine Louise, b 1944: m 1967, Peter George Ridley Dodds, of Meadow Ridge, Stockton, NJ 08559, USA, and has issue living, George Alexander Crichton, b 1970, — Lucy, b 1972.

PREDECESSORS – **(1)** Abraham Creighton; cr Baron Erne, of Crom Castle, co Fermanagh (peerage of Ireland) 1768; d 1772; s by his son **(2)** John, 2nd Baron; b 1738 (about); cr Viscount Erne (peerage of Ireland) 1781, and Earl Erne (peerage of Ireland) 1789: m 1761, Catherine, da of Rt Rev Robert Howard, Lord Bishop of Elphin, and sister of 1st Viscount Wicklow; d 1828; s by his son **(3)** Abraham, 2nd Earl; d unmarried 1842; s by his nephew **(4)** John, KP, 3rd Earl; b 1802; changed spelling of name to Crichton; was Lord-Lieut of co Fermanagh and a Representative Peer for Ireland; cr Baron Fermanagh, of Lisnaskea (peerage of United Kingdom) 1872: m 1837, Selina Griselda, who d 1884, da of late Rev Charles Cobbe Beresford; d 2 Oct 1885; s by his son **(5)** John Henry, KP, PC, 4th Earl; Lieut of co Fermanagh; MP for Enniskillen (C) 1868-80, and for co Fermanagh 1880-83; a Lord of the Treasury 1876-80: m 1870, Lady Florence Mary Cole, who d 1924, da of 3rd Earl of Enniskillen; d 2 Dec 1914; s by his grandson **(6)** John Henry George (only son of late Major (Henry William) Viscount Crichton, MVO, DSO, Roy Horse Guards (el son of 4th Earl), who was ka during European War 31 Oct 1914), 5th Earl; b 1907; Major N Irish Horse, and Lieut Roy Horse Guards (Reserve); was a Page of Honour to HM 1921-4, and a Lord-in-Waiting to HM 1936-9: m 1931, Lady Davidema Katharine Cynthia Mary Millicent Lytton, who d 1995 (having m 2ndly, 1945, Col Hon Christopher Montague Woodhouse, DSO, OBE (see B Terrington)), da of 2nd Earl of Lytton; d of wounds received in action during European War 1940; s by his son **(7)** Henry George Victor John, 6th Earl and present peer; also Viscount Erne, Baron Erne, and Baron Fermanagh.

Errington, Viscount; son of Earl of Cromer.

ERROLL, EARL OF (Hay) (Earl S 1452)

MERLIN SERELD VICTOR GILBERT HAY, 24th Earl; *b* 20 April 1948; *s* 1978; 28th Hereditary Lord High Constable of Scotland; *s* his father, *Sir* (Rupert) Iain Kay Moncreiffe of that Ilk, CVO, QC, as 12th holder of the Baronetcy, cr (NS) 1685, 1985; *ed* Eton, and Trin Coll, Camb, OStJ; Lt Atholl Highlanders; Member of Queen's Body Guard of Scotland (Royal Company of Archers): *m* 1982, Isabelle Jacqueline Laline, only child of Thomas Sidney Astell Hohler, MC, of Wolverton Park, Basingstoke (*see* V Gort, 1958 Edn), and has issue. [The LORD HIGH CONSTABLE has precedence in Scotland before Dukes and every other hereditary honour after the Blood Royal. He also maintains his own Officer of Arms, Slains Pursuivant, who first appears on record in 1404.]

Arms – Argent, three inescutcheons gules; above the shield, which is suspended from an ox yoke proper, bows gules, and behind which are set in saltire two batons argent tipped or, is placed His Lordship's coronet, thereon an helmet befitting his degree with a mantling gules doubled ermine. Crest – Issuing out of a coronet a falcon volant proper, armed, jessed and belled or. Supporters – Two savages wreathed about the middle with laurel, each bearing on his shoulders an ox yoke proper bows gules.

Residence – Woodbury Hall, Everton, Sandy, Beds SG19 2HR. *Clubs* – White's, Pratt's, Puffin's (Edinburgh).

SONS LIVING

HARRY THOMAS WILLIAM (*Lord Hay*), *b* 8 Aug 1984.
Hon Richard Merlin Iain, *b* 1990.

DAUGHTERS LIVING

Lady Amelia Diana Jacqueline, *b* 1986.
Lady Laline Lucy Clementine, *b* 1987.

BROTHER LIVING

Hon Peregrine David Euan Malcolm MONCREIFFE OF MONCREIFFE; 25th feudal Baron of Easter Moncreiffe since 1997, *b* 1951; *ed* Eton, and Ch Ch, Oxford; Chm Scottish Ballet: *m* 1988, Miranda Mary, yr da of Capt (Edward Arthur) Mervyn Fox-Pitt, WG (*see* E Dundee, colls), and has issue living, Ossian Peregrine T. G., *b* 1991, — Idina May, *b* 1992, — Elisabeth Miranda, *b* 1995, — a da, *b* 1996, — a da, *b* 1998. *Residence* – Easter Moncreiffe, Perthshire PH2 8QA. *Clubs* – Turf, White's, Pratt's, New (Edinburgh), Puffin's (Edinburgh), Royal and Ancient Golf (St Andrews), Leander (Henley), and Brook (New York).

HALF-BROTHER LIVING

Hon Jocelyn Jacek Alexander Bannerman CARNEGIE (Craggish, Comrie, Perthshire PH6 2JT), *b* 1966; *ed* Glenalmond: *m* 1990, Susie Mhairi, da of Thomas Mitchell Hastie Butler, of Eastmillhill, Crimond, and has had issue (*see* D Fife, colls).

SISTER LIVING

Lady Alexandra Victoria Caroline Anne, *b* 1955: *m* 1989, Jolyon Christopher Neill Connell, eldest son of late James Christopher Ferrier Connell, of Pitlochry, Perthshire; has issue living (by Sir Michael Iain Wigan, 6th Bt), Ivar Francis Grey de Miremont WIGAN, *b* 1979, — and further issue, Flora Diana Katharine Cecilia, *b* 1990, — Ciara Edith Elisabeth, *b* 1994. *Residence* – Spye Arch House, Spye Park, Lacock, Chippenham, Wilts SN15 2PR.

COLLATERAL BRANCHES LIVING

Issue of late Gilbert Allan Rowland Boyd (who *s* as 6th *Baron Kilmarnock* 1941), yr son of 21st Earl, *b* 1903, *d* 1975:—
See that title.

Grandchildren of late Gilbert Allan Rowland Boyd (6th *Baron Kilmarnock*) (ante):—
Issue of late Hon Laura Alice Boyd, *b* 1934, *d* 1999: *m* 1962, (Robert) Anthony Hyman:—
Anthony A. HYMAN, *b* 1962. —— Merlin M. HYMAN, *b* 1969, — Francesca M. D., *b* 1963: *m* 1994, Charles Mills, son of Capt K. H. Mills, of Chickerell, Dorset.

Grandchildren of late Lady Rosemary Constance Ferelith Hay, da of 21st Earl (*m* 1st, 1924 (*m diss* 1935), Lt-Col Rupert Sumner Ryan, CMG, DSO, who *d* 1952; 2ndly, 1935, Maj James Frank Gresham, DSO, Welsh Gds, who *d* 1983):—
Issue of late Patrick Victor Charles Ryan, *b* 1925, *d* 1989: *m* 1949, Rosemary Elizabeth (76 Park St, S Yarra, Vic 3141, Australia), eldest da of Francis Rupert Chesterman, of Orford, Tasmania:—
Dominic Rupert Charles RYAN (43 Otter St, Collingwood, Vic 3066, Australia), *b* 1956. —— Siobhan Ferelith, *b* 1959: *m* 1994, Mark Douglass, of 356 Glen Eira Rd, Elsternwick, Vic 3185, Australia, and has issue living, Hunter, *b* 1990.

Issue of late Capt Hon Ivan Josslyn Lumley Hay, MBE, 3rd son of 20th Earl, *b* 1884, *d* 1936: *m* 1921, Pamela, who *d* 1977, da of Francis George Burroughes (B Suffield and E Mayo, colls):—
Elizabeth Anne, *b* 1925; formerly in WRNS: *m* 1945 (*m diss* 1970), Jeremy Christopher Gurney, Lt RN, and has issue living, Michael Jeremy, *b* 1946; *ed* Eton. — William Ivan, *b* 1948; *ed* Eton. *Residence* – 22 Lennox Gdns, SW1. —— Penelope Constance, *b* 1930: *m* 1957, George Harold Armine Dare (*see* Morris, Bt, *cr* 1806, 1972-73 Edn), of 9 Launceston Place, W8, and has issue living, Henry James, *b* 1959; *ed* Stowe, and Keele Univ, — Amelia Alexandra Elizabeth, *b* 1961.

PREDECESSORS – William de la Haye, Butler of Scotland, was granted a charter of feudal Barony of Erroll c 1178-82; Sir Gilbert de la Haye, 3rd feudal Baron of Erroll, co-Regent of Scotland 1255: *m* Lady Idoine, da of William Comyn, Earl of Buchan, and sister of the Constable of Scotland. Their grandson, Sir Gilbert, was for his long adherence to Bruce *cr* by charter hereditary *Great Constable of Scotland* 1314 on the forfeiture of his Comyn cousins (his great-grandson, Sir Thomas, 3rd Constable: *m* Elizabeth, da of Robert II, King of Scots); his descendant in the 7th generation was **(1)** Sir WILLIAM Hay, 5th Great Constable of Scotland; *cr Lord Hay* (peerage of Scotland) 1449, and *Earl of Erroll* and *Lord Slains* (peerage of Scotland) 1452: *m* Beatrix, da of James, 7th Earl of Douglas; *d* 1463; *s* by his el son **(2)** NICHOLAS, 2nd Earl; *dsp* 1470; *s* by his brother **(3)** WILLIAM, 3rd Earl; *d* 1506; *s* by his son **(4)** WILLIAM, 4th Earl; (*ka* 1513); *s* by his son **(5)** WILLIAM, 5th Earl; *d* 1522; *s* by his son **(6)** WILLIAM, Earl; *d* 1541; *s* by his cousin **(7)** GEORGE (son of Thomas, 2nd son of 3rd Earl), 7th Earl; Lord Lieut of all Central Scotland from the Earn to the Spey 1559; *d* 1573; *s* by his son **(8)** ANDREW, 8th Earl; *d* 1585; *s* by his son **(9)** FRANCIS, 9th Earl; exiled for leading a Catholic rebellion 1594, but subsequently pardoned; *d* 1631; *s* by his son **(10)** WILLIAM, 10th Earl; *d* 1636; *s* by his son **(11)** GILBERT, 11th Earl; *dsp* 1674; *s* by his kinsman **(12)** JOHN (grandson of Sir George, 4th son of 8th Earl), 12th Earl; *d* 1704; *s* by his son **(13)** CHARLES, 13th Earl; *d* unmarried 1717; *s* by his sister **(14)** MARY, wife of Alexander Falconer (brother of 5th Lord Falconer), who assumed the name of Hay of Delgaty; *dsp* 1758; *s* by her grand-nephew **(15)** JAMES (son of William, 4th Earl of Kilmarnock, by Lady Anne Livingtone, da of Lady Margaret Hay (wife of James, 5th Earl of Linlithgow), sister of Mary, Countess of Erroll), 15th Earl; was Lord of Police 1767; *d* 1778; *s* by his el son **(16)** GEORGE, 16th Earl; having let drop a secret of Mr Pitt, committed suicide 1798; *s* by his brother **(17)** WILLIAM, 17th Earl; was Knight-Marischal of Scotland 1805, and Lord High Commr to Ch of Scotland; *d* 1819; *s* by his son **(18)** WILLIAM GEORGE, KT, PC, GCH, 18th Earl, *b* 1801; was Lord Steward of the Household, Master of the Buckhounds, and Lord-Lieut of Aberdeenshire; *cr Baron Kilmarnock*, of Kilmarnock, co Ayr (peerage of United Kingdom) 1831: *m* 1820, Lady Elizabeth Fitzclarence, who *d* 1856, sister of 1st Earl of Munster; *d* 1846; *s* by his son **(19)** WILLIAM HENRY, 19th Earl, *b* 1823; Major (ret) Rifle Brig; Crimea 1854-5 (wounded): *m* 1848, Eliza Amelia, VA, who *d* 1916 da of late Gen the Hon Sir Charles Gore, GCB; *d* 1891; *s* by his son **(20)** CHARLES GORE, KT, CB, LLD, 20th Earl, *b* 1852; Hon Maj-Gen in the Army; sometime Lieut-Col Comdg Roy Horse Guards; a Lord-in-Waiting to King Edward VII 1903-5: *m* 1875, Mary Caroline, who *d* 1934, da of late Edmund L'Estrange, of Tynte Lodge, co Leitrim; *d* 1927; *s* by his son **(21)** VICTOR ALEXANDER SERELD, KCMG, 21st Earl, *b* 1876; acted as Chargé d'Affaires at Berlin 1919-21; was British High Commr of Rhineland Commn 1921-28: *m* 1900, Mary Lucy Victoria, who *d* 1957, only da of Sir Allan Russell Mackenzie, 2nd Bt (*cr* 1890); *d* 1928; *s* by his son **(22)** JOSSLYN VICTOR, 22nd Earl, *b* 1901: *m* 1st, 1923 (*m diss* 1930), Lady (Myra) Idina (GORDON), who *d* 1955, da of 8th Earl De La Warr; 2ndly, 1930, Edith Mildred Mary (RAMSAY-HILL), who *d* 1939, da of late R. W. Maude, of Cleveland, Yorkshire; *d* 1941; *s* in the Barony of Kilmarnock by his brother the Hon Gilbert Allan Rowland Hay, and in the Earldom, and Lordships of Hay and Slains by his only child **(23)** DIANA DENYSE, Countess of Erroll, *b* 1926; retained her maiden name of Hay under Scots Law: *m* 1st, 1946 (*m diss* 1964), Capt Sir (Rupert) Iain Kay Moncreiffe of that Ilk, 11th Bt, who *d* 1985; 2ndly, 1964, Maj Raymond Alexander Carnegie (*see* D Fife); *d* 1978; *s* by her el son **(24)** MERLIN SERELD VICTOR GILBERT, 24th Earl and present peer; also Lord Hay and Lord Slains.

ERROLL OF HALE, BARON (Erroll) (Baron UK 1964)

FREDERICK JAMES ERROLL, TD, PC, 1st Baron, son of George Murison Erroll, of Glasgow, and London; *b* 27 May 1914; *ed* Oundle, and Trin Coll, Camb; Parl Sec to Min of Supply 1955-56, and to Board of Trade 1956-58, Economic Sec to HM Treasury 1958-59, Min of State, Board of Trade, 1959-61, Pres of Board of Trade 1961-63, and Min of Power 1963-64, a Member of National Economic Development Council 1962-63, and Pres of London Chamber of Commerce 1966-69; Dep Chm Decimal Currency Board 1966-71; Chm of Home Office Liquor Licensing Cttee, 1970-72, Pres Electrical Research Assocn since 1971, and Chm of Whessoe, Ltd, Darlington since 1970, Bowater Corpn since 1973, Automobile Assocn since 1974, and Consolidated Gold Fields Ltd since 1976; a Dir of other cos; MP for Altrincham and Sale (*C*) 1945-64; *cr* PC 1960, and *Baron Erroll of Hale*, of Kilmun, co Argyll (Peerage of UK) 1964: *m* 1950, Elizabeth, da of Richard Sowton Barrow, of Exmouth, Devon.

𝕬rms – Per bend azure and gules, on a bend embellished of six electric flashes or a fleur-de-lys and two lozenges sable. 𝕮rest – A chevronel round embattled sable. 𝕾upporters – *Dexter*, an elephant Guardant sable; *sinister*, a bear reguardant argent, muzzled azure, and from the muzzle cord sable, ringed or and reflexed over the back.
Address – House of Lords, SW1.

Erskine, Baron; see Earl of Buchan.

Erskine, family name of Earl of Buchan.

Erskine, family name of Earl of Mar and Kellie.

Erskine, St Clair-, family name of Earl of Rosslyn.

ERSKINE OF RERRICK, BARONY OF (Erskine) (Extinct 1995)

DAUGHTERS LIVING OF SECOND BARON (by 2nd marriage)

Hon Henrietta Cora, *b* 1975.
Hon Griselda Maxwell, *b* 1979.
Hon Cora McLeave, *b* 1981.

SISTER LIVING OF SECOND BARON

Hon Elizabeth Olson, *b* 1923; 1939-45 War as Subaltern ATS: *m* 1944, Gilbert Butler of Gatehouse, 8B Churchfields Av, Weybridge, Surrey KT13 9YA, and has issue living, David John Lister, *b* 1949; BA; Solicitor: *m* 1978, Celia Elizabeth, yst da of Prof Stephen D. Elek, of Lausanne, Switzerland, — Brian Robert Erskine (George), *b* 1960; Maj Army Air Corps, formerly Scots Dragoon Gds: *m* 1989, Nicola Mary, da of Col Keith S. Robson, of Babcary, Somerset, — Elizabeth Mary, *b* 1946: *m* 1978, Michael John Dickinson.

WIDOW LIVING OF SECOND BARON

DEBRA (*Baroness Erskine of Rerrick*), da of late Gordon Owen Knight, of Northants: *m* 1993, as his 3rd wife, the 2nd Baron Erskine of Rerrick, who *d* 1995.

ESHER, VISCOUNT (Brett) (Viscount UK 1897)

We have conquered

LIONEL GORDON BALIOL BRETT, CBE, 4th Viscount; *b* 18 July 1913; *s* 1963; *ed* Eton, and at New Coll, Oxford (MA); Hon DLitt Strathclyde; Hon D Univ of York; Hon DSc Edinburgh; Hon Fellow American Inst of Architects; Pres of RIBA 1965-67; a Member of Roy Fine Art Commn 1951-69, and of the Arts Council of GB 1972-77; Rector and Vice-Provost, Roy Coll of Art 1971-78; 1939-45 War as Maj RA (despatches); CBE (Civil) 1970: *m* 1935, Helena Christian Olive, da of late Col Ebenezer John Lecky Pike, CBE, MC, and has issue.

Arms – Quarterly: 1st and 4th or, a lion rampant gules holding in the dexter paw a fasces erect proper, within an orle of crosses bottonée fitchée of the second; 2nd, per pale or and gules three leopards' faces counterchanged; 3rd, azure three bears' heads couped argent, muzzled gules. Crest – A lion passant gules, charged on the shoulder with a cross bottonée fitchée or, and holding in the dexter paw a fasces proper. Supporters – Dexter, a boar sable; sinister, a lion sable; each charged on the shoulder with a cross bottonée fitchée or, and supporting a fasces proper.
Residence – Snowball Hill, Russell's Water, Henley-on-Thames, Oxford. Club – Arts.

SONS LIVING

Hon CHRISTOPHER LIONEL BALIOL (Watlington Park, Oxon), *b* 23 Dec 1936; *ed* Eton, and Magdalen Coll, Oxford: *m* 1st, 1962 (*m diss* 1970), Camilla Charlotte, da of Sir (Horace) Anthony Claud Rumbold, 10th Bt, KCMG, CB; 2ndly, 1971, Valerie, da of Maxwell Maurice Harrington, and has issue living, (by 1st *m*) Matthew Christopher Anthony (12 Dorville Crescent, W6 0HJ; *Club* – Pratt's), *b* 1963: *m* 1992, Hon Emma Charlotte Denison-Pender, elder da of 3rd Baron Pender, and has issue living, Jack *b* 14 June 1996, Eleanor Rose *b* 1994, Alice Martha *b* 1999, — Miranda Jane, *b* 1964: *m* 1990, Martin Nicholas Caleb Thomas, yr son of Prof (Antony) Charles Thomas, CBE, DL, of Lambessow, St Clement, Truro, Cornwall, and has issue living, Joseph Achilles Caleb *b* 1990, Frederick Jacob Theseus *b* 1992, Flora *b* 1994, Olivia Honey *b* 1997, — Rebecca Catherine, *b* 1966: *m* 1998, Samuel Riley, — (by 2nd *m*), Oliver Maxwell, *b* 1972, — William Falkland, *b* 1982, — Susannah Mary, *b* 1973, — Clare Christian (twin), *b* 1973.

Hon Michael Jeremy Baliol, *b* 1939; *ed* Eton; ARIBA: *m* 1971, Sarah Calloway, of Shelbyville, Kentucky, USA.

Hon Guy Anthony Baliol, *b* 1942; *ed* Eton: *m* 1975, Alexandra Altamirano, of Santiago, Chile, and has issue living, Luciana, *b* 1976.

Hon (Maurice) Sebastian Baliol, *b* 1944; *ed* Eton, and at Trin Coll, Oxford: *m* 1st, 1968 (*m diss* 1971), Pauline R., da of Lt-Cdr Paul Murray-Jones, RN (ret), of Cordwainers, Titchfield, Hants; 2ndly, 1971 (*m diss* 1980), Mary Maddox; 3rdly, 1980, Leticia Garrido, and has issue living (by 2nd *m*), Judd, *b* 1972, — (by 3rd *m*) Claudia, *b* 1985.

Hon Stephen Patrick Baliol, *b* 1952; *ed* Bryanston.

DAUGHTER LIVING

Hon Olivia Clare Teresa, *b* 1947: *m* 1970 (*m diss* 1985), Anthony Grey Gascoigne (*see* Wigan, Bt, colls), and has issue living, Fenn Jessie *b* 1977, — Elly May, *b* 1979.

SISTERS LIVING

Hon Nancy Mildred Gladys (*Hon Lady Shuckburgh*), *b* 1918: *m* 1937 Sir (Charles Arthur) Evelyn Shuckburgh, GCMG, CB, Diplo Ser, who *d* 1994, and has issue living, Julian John Evelyn (22 Ellingham Rd, W12 9PR), *b* 1940: *m* 1st, 1963 (*m diss* 1970), Faith Beatrice, da of Sir Paul Hervé Giraud Wright; 2ndly, 1975 (*m diss* 1992), Sarah Elizabeth, da of Sir David (Valentine) Willcocks, CBE, MC, and has issue living (by 1st *m*), Benjamin Evelyn *b* 1966: *m* 1991, Emma M., yr da of Sir Bernard Albert Ashley (and has issue living, Samuel *b* 1995, Rose *b* 1997), Matilda Ann *b* 1964: *m* 1st, 1983 (*m diss* 1988), Scott Ziegler; 2ndly, 1993, Lyle McCormick (and has issue living (by 1st *m*), Emma Dorothy *b* 1985), (by 2nd *m*) Alexander William *b* 1982, Amy Catherine Lorna *b* 1977, Hannah Jane Elizabeth *b* 1979, — Robin Anthony (Holton Place House, Holton, Oxford), *b* 1948: *m* 1972, Philippa Mary, da of Nicholas Spargo, of Maidensgrove, Henley-on-Thames, and has issue living, Jacob Nicholas Anthony *b* 1978, Laura Mary *b* 1983, — Catherine SHUCKBURGH, *b* 1939; has resumed her maiden name: *m* 1961 (*m diss* 1970), (John) David Caute, author and playwright, and has issue living, Edward Peter *b* 1963, Daniel Alexander *b* 1965. *Residence* – High Wood, Watlington, Oxon.

Hon Priscilla Léonie Helen (*Hon Lady Beckett*), *b* 1921: *m* 1941, Capt Sir Martyn Gervase Beckett, 2nd Bt, MC, Welsh Guards, and has issue (see that title). *Residences* – 3 St Alban's Grove, W8; Kirkdale Farm, Nawton, Yorks.

COLLATERAL BRANCH LIVING

Grandchildren of late Lt-Col Hon Maurice Vyner Baliol Brett, OBE, MVO (infra):—
　　Issue of late Maj Antony Reginald Forbes Baliol Brett, MBE, *b* 1913, *d* 1981: *m* 1939, Bay Helen, who *d* 1989, da of late Charles Neville Brownell, of Birkenhead:—
Simon Baliol (12 Blowhorn St, Marlborough, Wilts SN8 1BT), *b* 1943; *ed* Ampleforth, and St Martin's Sch of Art: *m* 1974, Mrs Juliet Shirley-Smith, da of Paul Hamilton Wood, OBE, MD Melb, FRCP, and has issue living, Emily Agnes, *b* 1977. — Vanessa Baliol, *b* 1947: *m* 1977, William Northrop Parker, and has issue living, Guy Hugo, *b* 1987, — Rebecca Brett, *b* 1980.

Issue of late Lieut-Col Hon Maurice Vyner Baliol Brett, OBE, MVO, 2nd son of 2nd Viscount, *b* 1882, *d* 1934: *m* (Jan) 1911, Florence Hariette Zena (the actress, Zena Dare), who *d* 1975, da of late Arthur Albert Dones:—
Angela Mariel Baliol, *b* (Oct) 1911: *m* 1934, Maj Kenneth Marcus Thornton, who *d* 1998, and has issue living, Timothy Kenneth (Juthware Hall, Halstock, nr Yeovil, Som), *b* 1935; *ed* Eton: *m* 1966, Mrs Jacqueline Green, da of David Hillman, and formerly wife of John Green, of Malmesbury, Wilts, and has issue living, Daniel Timothy *b* 1968; *ed* Eton, and Camb Univ, Katharine Zena *b* 1970, — Brian Maurice (Priors Mesne, Aylburton, Lydney, Glos), *b* 1937; *ed* Eton: *m* 1959, Verity, da of late Guy Gordon Lawrence, of Little Easton Manor, Dunmow, and has had issue, Guy Dominic *b* 1960; *ed* Gordonstoun: *m* 1st, 1983 (*m diss* 19—), Hon Diana Cara Broughton, elder da of 3rd Baron Fairhaven; 2ndly, 1996, Samantha N. D., eldest da of Capt Frederick Grant Barker, late 11th Hus, and of Viscountess Wimborne (and has issue living (by 1st *m*), Thomas George Cranbrook *b* 1986, (by 2nd *m*), Atalanta Nancy *b* 1998), Benjamin Douglas *b* 1965; *ed* Eton, Edinburgh Univ (BSc), and Cranfield Univ (MBA): *m* 1996, Emma J., 2nd da of late John Moss (and has issue living, Mia Katherine *b* 1998), Giles Marcus *b* 1966; *ed* Gordonstoun; *k* by robbers in Kenya 1998, Jolyon Kenneth *b* 1970; *ed* Harrow, and Warwick Univ: *m* 1996, Sarah L. E., da of Patrick Nicholls, Sam Fergus *b* 1976; *ed* Harrow, and Edinburgh Univ, Kim Marie *b* 1961: *m* 1986, Geoffrey Stuart Wheating (and has issue living, Tara Nel *b* 1988, Matilda Rose *b* 1990). *Residence* – Woodside Cottage, Windsor Forest, Berks. — Marie Louise, *b* 1916: *m* 1938, Cdr Archibald Rider Cheyne, RN, who *d* 1950, and has issue living, Mark Rider (38d Whistlers Avenue, SW11 3TS), *b* 1941; *ed* Rugby, FCA, — Angela Zena, *b* 1947. *Residence* – Spring Hill, Burleigh Rd, Ascot, Berks.

PREDECESSORS – (1) *Rt Hon Sir* WILLIAM BALIOL Brett, son of late Rev Joseph George Brett, of Ranelagh, Chelsea, SW; *b* 1815; MP for Helston (*C*) 1866-8; Solicitor-Gen 1868, a Justice of the Common Pleas 1868-75, a Judge of the High Court of Justice (Common Pleas Div) 1875-6, a Lord Justice of Appeal 1876-83, and Master of the Rolls 1883-97; *cr Baron Esher*, of Esher, co Surrey (peerage of United Kingdom) 1885, and *Viscount Esher*, of Esher, co Surrey (peerage of United Kingdom) 1897: *m* 1850, Eugenie, who *d* 1904, da of Louis Mäyer; *d* 1899; *s* by his eldest son (2) REGINALD BALIOL, GCB, GCVO, PC, 2nd Viscount, *b* 1852; Private Sec to Marquess of Hartington 1878-85, MP for Penryn and Falmouth (*L*) 1880-85 Sec to Office of Works and Public Buildings 1895-1902, Dep Constable and Lieut-Gov of Windsor Castle 1901-28, and Constable thereof 1928-30: *m* 1879, Eleanor, RRC, who *d* 1940, da of Sylvain Van de Weyer, of New Windsor, late Belgian Min at the Court of St James's; *d* 1930; *s* by his son (3) OLIVER SYLVAIN BALIOL, GBE, 3rd Viscount, *b* 1881; Private Sec to Sec of State for India 1905-10: *m* 1911, Antoinette, who *d* 1965, da of late August Heckscher of New York; *d* 1963; *s* by his only son (4) LIONEL GORDON BALIOL, CBE, 4th Viscount and present peer; also Baron Esher.

ESSEX, EARL OF (Capell) (Earl E 1661)

ROBERT EDWARD DE VERE CAPELL, 10th Earl; *b* 13 Jan 1920; *s* 1981 (claim admitted by Cttee for Privileges of House of Lords, and writ of summons issued 1989); 1939-45 War as Fl Sgt RAF: *m* 1942, Doris Margaret, da of George Frederick Tomlinson, of Morecambe, Lancs, and has issue.

Arms – Gules, a lion rampant between three cross-crosslets fitchée or. Crest – A demi-lion rampant holding in the dexter paw a cross-crosslet fitchée gules. Supporters – Two lions or, ducally crowned, gules.
Residence – 2 Novak Place, Torrisholme, Morecambe, Lancs.

SON LIVING

FREDERICK PAUL DE VERE (*Viscount Malden*), ACP, LLCM (TD) FRSA, *b* 29 May 1944; *ed* Lancaster Royal Gram Sch, Didsbury Coll of Educn, and Northern School of Music. *Residence* – 35 Pinewood Av, Brookhouse, Lancaster LA2 9NU.

SISTER LIVING

Elsie Elfreda (Flat 28, Raglan Lodge, 23 North Lodge Rd, Parkstone, Dorset), *b* 1921: *m* 1943, Ernest Walls, who *d* 1968, and has issue living, Derek Arthur, *b* 1950, — Jennifer Dawn, *b* 1948.

COLLATERAL BRANCHES LIVING

By fidelity and fortitude

Granddaughter of late Hon Adolphus Frederick Charles Molyneux Capell, brother of 6th Earl:—
Issue of late Rev Horatio Bladen Capell, *b* 1839, *d* 1933: *m* 1st, 1866, Ada Augusta, who *d* 1916, da of Theophilus Hawkins, formerly of Newton Abbot; 2ndly, 1916, Violet Annie, who *d* 1960, da of Robert Frost, formerly of Snape, Suffolk:—
(By 2nd *m*) Beatrix Violet de Vere, *b* 1919: *m* 1st, 1939 (*m diss* 1950), Raymond Smith; 2ndly, 1950, Edward Reginald Tranter, and has had issue, (by 1st *m*) Anthony Capel, *b* 1940: *m* 1968 (*m diss* 1980), Evelyn Hamilton Bentink Martin, adopted da of Charles Penryn Ackers, and formerly wife of Michael Charles Butler Johnson, and *d* 1993, leaving issue, Matilda Amelia *b* 1967, Emily Jane *b* 1969. *Residence* – Essex House, Great Easton, Dunmow, Essex.

Grandchildren of late Bladen Ozro Capell (*infra*):—
Issue of late Bladen Horace Capell, *b* 1922, *d* 1978: *m* 1945, Mae Elizabeth, who *d* 1981, da of late William J. Walley:—
William Jennings (867 Kelli Drive, Yuba City, CA 95991-6162, USA), *b* 9 Aug 1952: *m* 1971, Sandra Elaine, da of late Chester M. Matson, and has issue living, Kevin Devereux, *b* 24 Feb 1982, — Jennifer Elaine, *b* 1974. —— Dorita Mae (1750 Clayton Court, Yuba City, CA 95991-6162, USA), *b* 1948: *m* 1971 (*m diss* 1978), Robert Cooper, and has issue living, Michael Keith, *b* 1974; has issue living, Bladen Michael *b* 1998, — Bobby Ryan, *b* 1977; has issue living, Kirsten Ashley *b* 1995. —— Raylene Dee (1750 Clayton Court, Yuba City, CA 95991-6162, USA), *b* 1958: *m* 1976 (*m diss* 1993), Theodore Schwartz.

Granddaughter of late Horace Charles George Arthur Capell, eldest son of late Rev Horatio Bladen Capell (*ante*):—
Issue of late Bladen Ozro Capell, *b* 1897, *d* 1959: *m* 1st, 1920 (*m diss* 1929), Marjora Crawford, of Utah, USA, who *d* 1956; 2ndly, 19—, Hazel Kruse:—
(By 1st *m*) Helen Lucille, *b* 1926: *m* 1945, Leonard A. Sampson, and has issue living, David Andrew, *b* 1947, — Danny Jay, *b* 1957, — Barbara Jean, *b* 1956. *Residence* – PO Box 8116, Otis Orchard, Washington 99027, USA.

Grandsons of late Algernon Arthur Capell (*infra*):—
Issue of late Colin Algernon Andrew Essex Capell, *b* 1935, *d* on active service in Rhodesia 1977: *m* 1957, Cecily Ann (PO Box 3418, Pietersburg, S Africa), da of late Arend Smith, of Marlborough, Rhodesia:—
Clint Andrew Devereux (PO Box 66526, Kopje, Harare, Zimbabwe), *b* 1960: *m* 1981, Jeanne, da of Robert Bolton, of Sinoia, Zimbabwe, and has issue living, Joanne Victoria, *b* 1981. —— Craig Robert Lawrence (PO Box 3418, Pietersburg, S Africa), *b* 1962: *m* 1985, Janet, da of David Sloman, of Johannesburg, and has issue living, Dylan Colin David, *b* 1987, — Sherilyn May Ann *b* 1993.

Grandchildren of late Lt-Col Algernon Essex Capell, CBE, DSO, 2nd son of the Rev Horatio Bladen Capell (*ante*):—
Issue of late Algernon Arthur Capell, *b* 1903, *d* 1950: *m* 1933, Violet Mary, who *d* 1987, da of late Andrew Boyd, of Dumfries:—
Robert Devereux Boyd (961 Montcalm Dr, Kelowna, BC, Canada V1Y 3M8), *b* 1942: *m* 1967, Elin Rosemary, da of late Alan L. Earle, of Bulawayo, Rhodesia, and has issue living, Jennifer Rosemary, *b* 1975. —— Rosemary Susan Lois, *b* 1934: *m* 1958, Cyril Bryan Hughes, and has issue living, Barry William Vaughan, *b* 1961, — Kevin Bryan Vaughan, *b* 1962, — Ross Anthony Vaughan, *b* 1967, — Susan Anne Vaughan, *b* 1969. *Address* – PO Box 33, Plumtree, Zimbabwe.

Grandson of late Rev Horatio Bladen Capell (*ante*):—
Issue of late Henry Addison Devereux Capell, *b* 1873, *d* 1925: *m* 1901, Olive Mary, who *d* 1937, da of late William Richardson-Bunbury (*see* Richardson-Bunbury Bt, colls):—

Robert, *b* 1903.

Granddaughters of late Capt Terence Capel, RFC, son of late Col Arthur William Capel, Bengal Cav, eldest son of late Lt-Col Edward Samuel Capell, Bengal Army, yst son of Rev Hon William Robert Capell, yst son of 4th Earl:—
Issue of late Capt William Terence CAPEL, 11th Hussars (surname registered as CAPELL), *b* 1921; *d* 1993: *m* 1963, Petronella, da of late Maj Peter Beale Lewis, MC, late Royal Ulster Rifles:—
Georgina Mary Eveleen Penelope, *b* 1964: *m* 1997, Anthony J. V. Cheetham, yr son of Sir Nicolas Cheetham, KCMG.
—— Rosalind Elizabeth Maud, *b* 1968: *m* 1996, Mark A. Gray-Spencer, son of John Gray-Spencer, of Sydney, Australia.

PREDECESSORS – **(1)** ARTHUR Capell; MP for co Hertford in the Long Parliament; *cr Baron Capell of Hadham* 1641; for his loyalty to the King he was beheaded 1649; *s* by his son **(2)** ARTHUR, 2nd Baron, *cr Viscount Malden* and *Earl of the co of Essex* (peerage of England, 1661); Viceroy of Ireland 1672-7, and sometime First commr of the Treasury; being accused with Lord Russell of connection with "The Fanatic Plot" was committed to the Tower, where he was found with his throat cut 1683; *s* by his son **(3)** ALGERNON, 2nd Earl; a Lt-Gen in the Army and Constable of the Tower of London; *d* 1709; *s* by his son **(4)** WILLIAM, 3rd Earl; *d* 1743; *s* by his son **(5)** WILLIAM ANNE, 4th Earl; *d* 1799; *s* by his son **(6)** GEORGE, DCL, 5th Earl; assumed the surname of Coningsby; *d* 1839; *s* by his nephew **(7)** ARTHUR ALGERNON (son of Hon John Thomas, 2nd son of 4th Earl), 6th Earl, *b* 1803; assumed in 1880, by Royal licence, for himself and issue the surname of Capell in lieu of Capel; *d* 1892: *m* 1st, 1825, Lady Caroline Jeannetta Beauclerk, who *d* 1862, da of 8th Duke of St Albans; 2ndly, 1863, Lady Louisa Caroline Elizabeth Boyle, who *d* 1876, sister of 9th Earl of Cork, 3rdly, 1881, Louisa, who *d* 1914, da of late Charles Fieschi Heneage, and widow of Lord George Augustus Frederick Paget, KCB; *s* by his grandson **(8)** GEORGE DEVEREUX DE VERE (el son of Viscount Malden, el son of 6th Earl), 7th Earl, *b* 1857: *m* 1st, 1882, Ellenor Harriet Maria, who *d* 1885, da of late William Henry Harford, JP, of Oldown House, Almondsbury, Gloucestershire; 2ndly, 1893, Adele, who *d* 1922, el da of late Beach Grant, of New York; *d* 1916: *s* by his son, **(9)** ALGERNON GEORGE DE VERE, 8th Earl, *b* 1884: *m* 1st, 1905 (*m diss* 1926), (Mary) Eveline Stewart, who *d* 1955, el da of late William Russell Stewart Freeman, JP, DL, of The Old Manor House, Wingrave, Bucks; 2ndly, 1926 (*m diss* 1950), Alys Montgomery, who *d* 1977, da of Robert Hayes Falkiner, and formerly wife of Ernest Scott Brown; 3rdly, 1950 (*m diss* 1956), Zara Mildred Carson, of Los Angeles, Cal, USA; 4thly, 1957, Christine Mary Davis, who *d* 1985; *d* 1966; *s* by his son **(10)** Reginald George de Vere, TD 9th Earl, *b* 1906: *m* 1st, 1937 (*m diss* 1957), Mary Reeve, da of F. Gibson Ward, of Rosemount, Bermuda, and widow of Col George Ashton Strutt, of Brailsford, Derbys; 2ndly, 1957, Nona Isobel, who *d* 1997, da of David Wilson Miller, of Christchurch, NZ, and widow of Francis Sydney Smythe, of Yew Tree Cottage, Colgate, Sussex; *d* 1981; *s* by his kinsman **(11)** ROBERT EDWARD DE VERE (2nd son of late Arthur Algernon de Vere Capell, only son of late Charles Horatio Algernon Capell, 6th and yst son of late Capt Hon Algernon Henry Champagne Capell, RN, brother of 6th Earl), 10th Earl and present peer; also Viscount Malden and Baron Capell.

Ettrick, Baron, see Lord Napier and Ettrick.

Euston, Earl of; son of Duke of Grafton.

EVANS, BARONY OF (Evans) (Extinct 1963)

DAUGHTER LIVING OF FIRST BARON

Hon Jean Rosemary, *b* 1934: *m* (Jan) 1966, Eric Anthony Hathorn, of 51 Netherhall Gdns, NW3, and has issue living, James Horace Vans, *b* (Dec) 1966: *m* 1997, Olivia Jane Ariane, elder da of Brian Henry Tisdall, — Charles Thomas Vans, *b* 1972, — Helen Angela, *b* 1970.

Evans, family name of Baron Energlyn.

Evans, family name of Baron Mountevans.

EVANS OF CLAUGHTON, BARONY OF (Evans) (Extinct 1992)

SON LIVING OF LIFE BARON

Hon David Robert Cynlais, *b* 1964; *ed* Birkenhead Sch, and UCL (LLB); Solicitor.

DAUGHTERS LIVING OF LIFE BARON

Hon Elizabeth Ann Cynlais, *b* 1957: *m* 1989, Ian F. Johnson, only son of A. F. Johnson, of Oswestry, Shropshire, and has issue living, Lucy, *b* 1995, — Elise, *b* 1998.
Hon Sarah Louise Cynlais, *b* 1966; *ed* Liverpool Univ (BA), and Coll of St Paul and St Mary, Cheltenham (PGCE): *m* 1998, Stephen Foy, son of Thomas Foy, of Liverpool, and has issue living, Jacob, *b* 1999.
Hon Jane Lucy Cynlais, *b* 1968; *ed* Nottingham Univ (BA).

WIDOW LIVING OF LIFE BARON

MOIRA ELIZABETH (*Baroness Evans of Claughton*), da of late James Rankin: *m* 1956, Baron Evans of Claughton (Life Baron), who *d* 1992. *Residence* – Sunridge, 69 Bidston Rd, Claughton, Birkenhead, Merseyside L43 6TR.

EVANS OF HUNGERSHALL, BARONY OF (Evans) (Extinct 1982)

DAUGHTER LIVING OF LIFE BARON

Hon Hilary Ann (Duck Cottage, Puncknowle, Dorchester DT2 9BW), *b* 1931: *m* 1954 (*m diss* 1963), William John Barrow, and has issue.

EVANS OF PARKSIDE, BARON (Evans) (Life Baron 1997)

JOHN EVANS, son of late James Evans, of Jarrow, co Durham; *b* 19 Oct 1930; *ed* Jarrow Central Sch; Marine Fitter and Engineer, Tyneside Shipyard; Memb Hebburn UDC 1962-74 (Chm 1972-73, Leader 1969-74); Memb S Tyneside MDC 1973-74; MEP 1975-78 (Chm Regional Policy and Transport Cttee 1976-78); MP for Newton (Lab) 1974-83, and for St Helens N 1983-97; Assist Govt Whip 1978-79; Opposition Whip 1979-80; PPS to Rt Hon Michael Foot as Leader of the Opposition 1980-83; Memb Labour Party NEC 1982-96; Opposition Front Bench Spokesman on Employment

1983-87; Chm Nat Labour Party 1991-92; *cr Baron Evans of Parkside*, of St Helens, co Merseyside (Life Baron) 1997: *m* 1959, Joan, da of Thomas Slater, of Hebburn, co Durham, and has issue.
Address – c/o House of Lords, Westminster, SW1A 0PW.

SONS LIVING

Hon David John, *b* 1961; *ed* Culcheth Comprehensive Sch, Warrington: *m* 1987, Joy, da of Michael Anthony Spencer, of Culcheth, and has issue living, Louise, *b* 1982, — Mandy, *b* 1988.
Hon Alan Thomas, *b* 1967; *ed* Culcheth Comprehensive Sch.

DAUGHTER LIVING

Hon Judith Slater, *b* 1962; *ed* Culcheth Comprehensive Sch.

EVANS OF WATFORD, BARON (Evans) (Life Baron 1998)

DAVID CHARLES EVANS, son of Arthur Evans; *b* 30 Nov 1942; *ed* Hampden Secondary Sch, and Watford Coll of Technology (City and Guilds, Edward Hunter Medal); printer; Founder and Chm Centurion Press Group Ltd since 1971; Dir Centurion Press Ltd, Centurion Design Forum Ltd, The Hammond Organisation, Personnel Publications Ltd, Aero Space Com Ltd, Centurion Press International Ltd, Centurion Morgan Allen Partnership Ltd, Centurion Publishing Ltd, Centurion International Media Services Ltd, Associated Media Sales Ltd, Indigo Publishing Ltd, Centurion Media Services bv (Holland), Centurion Press bv (Holland), Centurion Press Inc (US), Aero-Space Com Inc (USA); Advisor, West Herts Coll; Life Govr Imperial Cancer Research Fund; Memb Worshipful Co of Marketors; FCIM, FInstD; *cr Baron Evans of Watford*, of Chipperfield, co Herts (Life Baron) 1998: *m* 1966, June Scaldwell, and has issue, one son and one da.
Address – Centurion Press Group, Centurion House, 34-36 High Street, Rickmansworth, Herts WD3 1ER.

Eve, family name of Baron Silsoe.

EWART-BIGGS, BARONY OF (O'Sullivan) (Extinct 1992)

SON LIVING OF LIFE BARONESS (*by 1st marriage*)

Hon Robin Thomas Fitzherbert EWART-BIGGS, *b* 1963: *m* 1993, Katherine Bonner.

DAUGHTERS LIVING OF LIFE BARONESS (*by 1st marriage*)

Hon Henrietta EWART-BIGGS, *b* 1961.

Hon Kate EWART-BIGGS, *b* 1967.

WIDOWER LIVING OF LIFE BARONESS

Kevin O'Sullivan: *m* 1st, (18 Sept) 1992, as her 2nd husband, (Felicity) Jane, Baroness Ewart-Biggs (Life Baroness), who *d* (8 Oct) 1992; 2ndly, 1996, Hon Victoria, CBE (the writer Victoria Glendinning), elder da of late Baron Seebohm (Life Baron), widow of Terence de Vere White, and formerly wife of Prof Oliver Nigel Valentine Glendinning. *Residence* – 38 Wynnstay Gdns, Allen St, W8 6UT.

EWING OF KIRKFORD, BARON (Ewing) (Life Baron 1992)

HARRY EWING, son of late William Ewing, of Cowdenbeath, Dunfermline; *b* 20 Jan 1931; *ed* Beath High Sch, Cowdenbeath; DL Region of Fife 1995; held various appointments Union of Post Office Workers 1962-71; Sec Scottish Lab Group 1972-74, Parly Under-Sec of State Scottish Office 1974-79, Sr Vice-Chm Trade Union Group of Lab MPs since 1979, Member Council of Europe and Western European Union since 1987; MP Stirling and Falkirk (*Lab*) 1971-74, Stirling, Falkirk and Grangemouth 1974-83, and Falkirk E 1983-92; *cr Baron Ewing of Kirkford*, of Cowdenbeath, District of Dunfermline (Life Baron) 1992: *m* 1954, Margaret, da of John Greenhill, of Leven, Fife, and has issue.

Residence – Gowanbank, 45 Glenlyon Rd, Leven, Fife KY8 4AA.

SON LIVING

Hon Alan William John, *b* 1961: *m* 1986, June, da of William Adamson, of Kirkcaldy, and has issue living, one son and one da.

DAUGHTER LIVING

Hon Alison Margaret, *b* 1966: *m* 1991, Ian Binnie, son of Sydney Binnie, of Arbroath.

Orr-Ewing, Baron, see Orr.

EXETER, MARQUESS OF (Cecil) (Marquess UK 1801)
(Name pronounced "Cissel")

CORUNUMVIAUNA

One heart, one way

(WILLIAM) MICHAEL ANTHONY CECIL, 8th Marquess; *b* 1 Sept 1935; *s* 1988; Hereditary Grand Almoner, Lord Paramount of the Soke of Peterborough: *ed* Eton: *m* 1st, 1967 (*m diss* 1993), Nancy Rose, da of late Lloyd Arthur Meeker, of Loveland, Colorado, USA; 2ndly, 1999, Barbara Anne, da of Eugene Magat, of Chapel Hill, N Carolina, USA, and has issue by 1st *m*.

𝕬rms – Barry of ten argent and azure, six escutcheons, three, two, and one, sable each charged with a lion rampant argent. 𝕮rest – On a chapeau gules, turned up with ermine, a garb or, supported by two lions rampant, the *dexter* argent, the *sinister* azure. 𝕾upporters – Two lions ermine.
Seat – Burghley House, Stamford, Lincs PE9 3JY. *Address* – RR3, Kelsey C21, Sechelt, BC, Canada V0N 3A0.

SON LIVING (*By 1st marriage*)

ANTHONY JOHN (*Lord Burghley*), *b* 9 Aug 1970; *ed* Eton, and Oxford Univ.

DAUGHTER LIVING (*By 1st marriage*)

Lady Angela Kathleen, *b* 1975.

HALF-SISTER LIVING

Lady Marina June, *b* 1956: *m* 1980, Peter Jules Workman Castonguay, son of Nelson Castonguay, of Ottawa, Canada, and has issue living, Dylan Martin Nelson, *b* 1984, — Majessa Lillian, *b* 1983. *Residence* – 100 Mile House, PO Box 2170, BC V0K 2E0, Canada.

DAUGHTERS LIVING OF SIXTH MARQUESS (*By 1st marriage*)

Lady Davina Mary (*Lady Davina Barnard*), *b* 1931; DStJ: *m* 1952 (*m diss* 1992), 11th Baron Barnard. *Residence* – The Yews, Barningham, Richmond, N Yorks DL11 7DU.

Lady Gillian Moyra Katherine, *b* 1935: *m* 1st, 1954 (*m diss* 1978), Sir Giles Henry Charles Floyd, 7th Bt; 2ndly, 1979, George Michael Kertesz, of Flat 6, 20 Pembridge Villas, W11, and Holly House, Northchapel, nr Petworth, West Sussex.

Lady Angela Mary Rose, LVO, *b* 1938; an Extra Woman of the Bedchamber to HM Queen Elizabeth The Queen Mother 1981-82, since when a Woman of the Bedchamber; LVO 1993: *m* 1958, Sir (William Richard) Michael Oswald, KCVO, The King's Own Royal Regt, Capt RF, Dir of the Royal Studs, and has issue living, William Alexander Michael, *b* 1962; appointed a Page of Honour to HM 1976; Capt The Life Guards: *m* 1994, Arabella V., da of Nicholas Sydney Cobbold, and has issue living, Marina Charlotte *b* 1996, Lucy Frances *b* 1997, — Katharine Davina Mary, *b* 1959: *m* 1983, Lt-Col Alexander Fergus Matheson, yr of Matheson, Coldm Gds, and has issue (*see* Matheson, Bt). *Residence* – Flitcham Hall, King's Lynn, Norfolk.

(*By 2nd marriage*)

Lady Victoria Diana, *b* 1947; Hon DUniv De Montfort Univ, Leicester; DL Cambs 1993; Hon Col 158 (Royal Anglian) Regt, The Royal Logistic Corps (Volunteers) TA; Trustee Courtauld Inst, and Stoneleigh Abbey Trust; author of *Burghley - The Life of a Great House*; broadcaster: *m* 1967, Simon Patrick Leatham (*see* By Buckland, 1976 Edn), and has issue living, Richard David, *b* 1971: *m* 1996, Georgina Susan, yst da of Simon Mounsey, of Barnes House, Piltdown, E Sussex and has had issue, Milo Charles Albert *b* and *d* 1997, Ludovic Simon *b* 1999, — Miranda Rosemary, *b* 1969: *m* 1997, Orlando William Adam Rock, yr son of Tim Rock. *Residences* – Burghley House, Stamford, Lincs PE9 3JY; Flat 18, Chelsea House, 24 Lowndes St, SW1.

AUNT LIVING (*daughter of 5th Marquess*)

Lady Romayne Elizabeth Algitha, OBE, ARRC, *b* 1915; late VAD (attached RN); European War 1939-44 (ARRC); OBE 1986: *m* 1944, Lieut-Col Hon Peter Esmé Brassey, Northants Yeo, who *d* 1995 (*see* B Brassey of Apethorpe). *Residence* – Pond House, Barnack, Stamford, Lincs PE9 3DN.

WIDOW LIVING OF SEVENTH MARQUESS

LILLIAN JANE (*Dowager Marchioness of Exeter*), eldest da of late Roy Peter Kopf Johnson, of Milwaukee, USA: *m* 1954, as his 2nd wife, the 7th Marquess of Exeter, who *d* 1988. *Residence* – 100 Mile House, PO Box 2054, BC V0K 2E0, Canada.

COLLATERAL BRANCHES LIVING

Granddaughter of late Richard William Francis Cecil, son of late Lieut Lord Francis Horace Pierrepont Cecil, RN, 2nd son of 3rd Marquess:—
Issue of late Lieut Richard Francis Bain Cecil, RN, *b* 1902, *d* 1929: *m* 1926, Marjorie Joan (who *d* 1993, having *m* 2ndly, 1939, B. Grosvenor Harris, who *d* 1993), da of late William Lloyd Evans, of Postlip Hall, Gloucestershire:—
Jean Frances, *b* (*posthumous*) 1929: *m* 1952, Com Henry Walton Jennings, RN, who *d* 1997, and has issue living, Dirmuid Brian Cecil (Studley Cottage, Haw Lane, Bledlow Ridge, Bucks), *b* 1957; late RN: *m* 1983, Angela, el da of W. Wilson, of Aughton, Lancs, — Stephen Francis, *b* 1960. *Address* – Eastwell, Upper Lansdown Mews, Bath, Avon.

Descendants of late Col Lord William Cecil, CVO, 3rd son of 3rd Marquess, *b* 1854, *d* 1943, who *m* 1st, 1885, Mary Rothes Margaret, who *d* 1919 (*Baroness Amherst of Hackney* in her own right) (see that title).

Grandchildren of late Col Lord John Pakenham JOICEY-CECIL (who assumed by Royal licence 1898 the additional surname of Joicey), 4th son of 3rd Marquess:—
Issue of late Edward Wilfrid George Joicey-Cecil, *b* 1912, *d* 1985: *m* 1945, Rosemary Lusia, who *d* 1989, da of late Capt Hon Fergus Bowes-Lyon, Black Watch (*see* E Strathmore, colls):—
James David Edward (49 Clapham Common South Side, SW4 9BX), *b* 1946; *ed* Eton: *m* 1975, Jane Susanna Brydon, da of late Capt P. W. B. Adeley, of Delcombe Manor, Milton Abbas, Dorset, and has issue living, Katherine Mary, *b* 1978, — Susanna Maud, *b* 1981. —— (Elizabeth) Anne, *b* 1950: *m* 1971, Alastair Richard Malcolm, of Hart Hill Farm, Woodfalls, Salisbury, Wilts, and has issue living, Colin Andrew Fergus, *b* 1973; *ed* Eton, and St Catherine's Coll, Oxford, — William James Ronald, *b* 1975; *ed* Eton, and St Hugh's Coll, Oxford.

(*In remainder to Barony of Burghley only*)

Descendants of late Rt Hon Sir Robert Cecil, KG, (yr son of 1st Baron Burghley), who was *cr Earl of Salisbury* 1605 (see M Salisbury).

PREDECESSORS – (1) *Sir* WILLIAM Cecil, KG, KB, PC, a lawyer and eminent statesman was Sec of State 1549, 1551, and 1558, Chancellor of Camb Univ 1558-98, Master of the Ward, 1561, and Lord High Treasurer 1572-98; *cr Baron of Burghley* (peerage of England) 1571; *d* 1598; *s* by his son (2) THOMAS, KG, KB; MP in five Parliaments; distinguished himself in the wars in the Low Countries; *cr Earl of Exeter* (peerage of England) 1605; *d* 1622; *s* by his son (3) WILLIAM, KG, 2nd Earl; *d* 1640; *s* by his nephew (4) DAVID, 3rd Earl, son of Sir Richard, MP, 2nd son of 1st Earl; *d* 1643; *s* by his son (5) JOHN, 4th Earl; *d* 1678; *s* by his son (6) JOHN, 5th Earl; *d* 1700; *s* by his son (7) JOHN, 6th Earl; *d* 1721, *s* by his el son (8) JOHN, 7th Earl; *d* 1722; *s* by his brother (9) BROWNLOW, 8th Earl; *d* 1754; *s* by his son (10) BROWNLOW, 9th Earl; *dsp* 1793; *s* by his nephew (11) HENRY, 10th Earl, son of the Hon Thomas Chambers, 2nd son of 8th Earl; *cr Marquess of Exeter* (peerage of United Kingdom) 1801; *d* 1804; *s* by his son (12) BROWNLOW, KG, 2nd Marquess; *b* 1795; Lord Lieut of cos Northampton and Rutland, Groom of the Stole to Prince Albert 1841-6, Lord Chamberlain 1852, and Lord Steward of the Household 1858-9: *m* 1824, Isabella, da of William Stephen Poyntz, of Cowdray House, Sussex; *d* 1867; *s* by his son (13) WILLIAM ALLEYNE, PC, 3rd Marquess, *b* 1825; MP for S Lincolnshire (*C*) 1847-57, and for N Northamptonshire 1857-67; was Treasurer of HM Queen Victoria's Household 1866-7, and Capt of Hon Corps of Gentleman-at-Arms 1867-8 and 1874-5: *m* 1848, Lady Georgiana Sophia Pakenham, who *d* 1909, da of 2nd Earl of Longford; *d* 1895; *s* by his el son (14) BROWNLOW HENRY GEORGE, PC, 4th Marquess, *b* 1849; MP for Northamptonshire N (*C*) 1877-85 and for Northamptonshire, N Div 1885-95; Vice-Chamberlain of HM Queen Victoria's Household 1891-2: *m* 1875, Isabella, who *d* 1917, da of Sir Thomas Whichcote, 7th Bt; *d* 1898; *s* by his son (15) WILLIAM THOMAS BROWNLOW, KG, CMG, TD, 5th Marquess; *b* 1876; Col RFA (TA); Chm of Govs of Stamford Endowed Schs 1899-1955, Mayor of Stamford 1909-10, Chm of Soke of Peterborough County council 1910-49, Lord Lieut of Northants 1922-52, an Additional ADC to HM 1922-32, and Pres of County Councils Asso 1943 and 1945: *m* 1901, the Hon Myra Rowena Sibell Orde-Powlett, who *d* 1973, only da of 4th Baron Bolton; *d* 1956, *s* by his el son (16) DAVID GEORGE BROWNLOW, KCMG, 6th Marquess, *b* 1905, Lt Col Gren Gds, Pres and Chm of Internat Amateur Athletic Fedn, of Amateur Athletic Asso, and of British Olympic Assocn (won an Olympic gold medal in 400 metre hurdles 1928), and Doyen Internat Amateur Athletic Cttee; Pres Burghley Horse Trials, British Empire Chambers of Commerce, and of Radio Industry Council 1952-54, and Vice-Pres of Internat Olympic Cttee 1954-66; Pres British Travel Assocn 1966-69; Assist Dir of Tank Supply 1941-42, Controller of Repair and Overseas Supplies of Aircraft 1942-43, and Gov and C-in-C of Bermuda 1943-45; R of St Andrews Univ 1949-52; Leader of UK Industrial Mission to Pakistan 1950 and to Burma 1954; Mayor of Stamford 1961-62; MP for Peterborough Div of Northants (*C*) 1931-43: *m* 1st, 1929 (*m diss* 1946), Lady Mary Theresa Montagu Douglas Scott, who *d* 1984, da of 7th Duke of Buccleuch; 2ndly, 1946, Diana Mary, who *d* 1982, da of late Hon Arnold Henderson (*see* B Faringdon, colls), and widow of Lt-Col David Walter William Forbes, MC, Coldstream Guards (*see* B Hotham, colls); *d* 1981; *s* by his brother (17) WILLIAM MARTIN ALLEYNE, 7th Marquess, *b* 1909; prominent Canadian cattleman, and leader of spiritual movement Emissaries of Divine Light: *m* 1st, 1934, Edith Lilian, who *d* 1954, only da of late Aurel Csanady de Telegd, of Budapest, Hungary; 2ndly, 1954, Lillian Jane, eldest da of late Roy P. K. Johnson, of Milwaukee, USA; *d* 1988; *s* by his only son (18) (WILLIAM) MICHAEL ANTHONY, 8th Marquess and present peer: also Earl of Exeter, and Baron of Burghley.

EXMOUTH, VISCOUNT (Pellew) (Viscount UK 1816, Bt GB 1796)

God being my helper

PAUL EDWARD PELLEW, 10th Viscount, and 10th Baronet; *b* 8 Oct 1940; *s* 1970; *ed* Downside; patron of one living: *m* 1st, 1964 (*m diss* 1974), Maria Krystina de Garay, da of late Don Recaredo de Garay y Garay, of Madrid; 2ndly, 1975, Rosemary Frances, only da of Francis Harold Scoones, MRCS, LRCP, JP, of 83 Abbotsbury Rd, W14, and formerly wife of Murray de Vere, Earl of Burford (later 14th Duke of St Albans), and has issue by 1st and 2nd *m*.

𝕬rms – Gules, a lion passant guardant, in chief two civic wreaths or, on a chief of augmentation wavy argent, a representation of Algiers, and on the dexter side a man-of-war bearing the flag of an admiral of the blue, all proper. 𝕮rest – Upon waves of the sea the stern of a wrecked ship, inscribed "Dutton" (East Indiaman), upon a rocky shore off Plymouth garrison (*ie* in the background a hill, upon the top of which a tower with a flag hoisted), all proper. 𝕾upporters – *Dexter*, a lion guardant or, navally crowned azure, his sinister hind paw resting on an increscent argent; *sinister*, a human figure intended to represent a Christian slave, naked from the waist upwards, a cloth round the loins, and thighs and legs habited in blue and white striped trousers, holding in the right hand a cross or, and in his left fetters broken proper. *Residence* – Canonteign, near Exeter, Devon.

SONS LIVING (*By 2nd marriage*)

Hon EDWARD FRANCIS, *b* 30 October 1978.
Hon Alexander Paul, *b* 1978 (twin).

DAUGHTER LIVING (*By 1st marriage*)

Hon Patricia Sofia, *b* 1966. *Residence* – Paseo de Rosales 3Z, Madrid, Spain.

BROTHER LIVING

Hon Peter Irving, *b* 1942; *ed* Downside.

SISTERS LIVING

Hon Mary Rose PELLEW, *b* 1938; retains her maiden name: *m* 1974, Don Roman Llanso. *Residence* – Pasaje Del Obispo 4,1,B, 28005 Madrid, Spain.
Hon Mary Elizabeth Josephine, *b* 1947: *m* 1969, Robin Gerard d'Erlanger, ACA, son of late Sir Gerard John Regis Leo d'Erlanger, CBE, and has issue living, Gerard Pownoll, *b* 1970, – Hugh Robin, *b* 1976, — Josephine Louise, *b* 1972, — Marietta Elizabeth, *b* 1974, – Emilia Mary Florence, *b* 1982. *Residence* – Hensleigh Cottage, Tiverton, Devon EX16 5NH.

COLLATERAL BRANCHES LIVING

Grandchildren of late Fleetwood Hugo Pellew, son of Rev Hon Edward Pellew, 4th son of 1st Viscount:—
  Issue of late Major Fleetwood Hugo Pellew, *b* 1871, *d* 1961: *m* 1909, Violet, who *d* 1964, da of late James Du Pre, of Wilton Park, Bucks:—
Fleetwood Hugo, *b* 1910; *ed* Malvern, and RMA Woolwich; Lieut-Col (ret) Roy Signals: *m* 1939, Geraldine Mildred, da of Major William Gerald Hole, of Parke, Bovey Tracey, S Devon, and has issue living, Pamela Geraldine, *b* 1946: *m* 1979, Brian E. Jones, and has issue. *Residence* – Waye Farm, Lustleigh, Devon. —— †Anthony Pownoll, *b* 1911; Cdr (ret) RN: *m* 1st, 1941 (*m diss* 1953), Margaret Julia, da of Clive Cookson, of Nether Warden, Hexham; 2ndly, 1957, Hilary Frances, da of Capt Alfred Garbett Pape, of 20 Northumberland St, Edinburgh, and *d* 1992, leaving issue (by 1st *m*), Mark Edward, LVO (4/51 St George's Sq, SW1), *b* 1942; *ed* Winchester, and Trin Coll, Oxford; HM Diplomatic Ser since 1965; HM Amb to Holy See since 1998; LVO 1980: *m* 1965, Jill Hosford, da of Prof Frank Thistlethwaite, CBE, of St John's Coll, Cambridge, and has issue living, Adam Lee *b* 1966, Dominic Stephen *b* 1968, — Robert (Robin) Anthony (2 Luard Rd, Cambridge CB2 2PJ), *b* 1945; *ed* Marlborough, and Edin Univ; Dir World Wildlife Fund: *m* 1975, Pamela, da of Dr P. D. MacLellan, and has issue living, Toby James Pownoll *b* 1982, Sophie Harriet *b* 1979, — Phoebe Sarah, *b* 1947: *m* 1974, Faisal Hamzah Ghoth, of Medina, Saudi Arabia, and has issue living, Arabi Faisal *b* 1974, Ibrahim *b* 1976, — (by 2nd *m*) Nicholas Charles (Burnham, Bucks), *b* 1959; *ed* Wellington Coll, Exeter Univ, and Camb Univ: *m* 1989, Doone Philippa, da of Robert Selbie, of Hurstbourne Priors, Hants, and has issue living, Christopher Anthony Lloyd *b* 1992, Timothy Mark Fleetwood *b* 1994, — Philip Esmond, *b* 1962. *Residence* – 3 Glencairn House, 70 Ridgway, Wimbledon, SW19. —— Myles Addington, *b* 1919; *ed* Malvern: *m* 1957, Jill Primrose Twentyman, yst da of late Capt Alfred Maurice Davis, OBE, of 124 Walton St, SW3, and has issue living, Simon Du Pre (92 Catford Hill, SE6 4PU), *b* 1959: *m* 1988, Shunu, da of late G. K. Chowdhury, and has issue living, Dominic Chowdhury *b* 1997, Sarah Chowdhury *b* 1994, — Alexandra Twentyman, *b* 1961: *m* 1st, 1987, Jeffrey G. Fowler, son of J. T. G. Fowler, of Lambeth, London; 2ndly, 1997, (Robert) Adam Pappworth, of Cotton Hall, Middlewich Rd, Holmes Chapel, Ches CW4 7ET, son of Sidney Pappworth, of Greenmoor, Sheffield, and has issue living (by 1st *m*), James Vernon Pellew *b* 1988, Olivia Lucinda *b* 1990, — Miranda Frances, *b* 1964: *m* 1996, Peter J. Seymour, of 58 Hanover Terrace, Brighton BN2 2SP. *Residence* – 2 Little Chesters, Beech Lane, Walton-on-the-Hill, Surrey. —— Timothy Winthrop, *b* 1921; *ed* Camb Univ (MA): *m* 1950, Margaret Richmond, da of late Edmund George Hamilton Mewburn, of 20 Norfolk House, Courtlands, Richmond, Surrey, and has issue living, Fleetwood Timothy (31 Churchill Av, Willowdale, Ont, Canada M2N 1Y6), *b* 1952, — Adrian Harold (88

Squire Drive, Richmond Hill, Ont, Canada L4F 1C7), *b* 1954: *m* 1991, Leanne Eileen, da of late Edmund C. Randell, of Mississauga, Ont, Canada, and has issue living, Mallory Anne *b* 1993, — Owen Simon (23 Uplands Av, Thornhill, Ont, Canada L4J 1J8), *b* 1958, — Colin David (41 Norhead Av, Scarborough, Ont, Canada M1S 3G8), *b* 1961, — Mabel Audrey, *b* 1955: *m* 1983, Milenko Milicev, of RR2, PO Box 213, Breslau, Ont, Canada N0B 1M0. *Residence* – 31 Churchill Av, Willowdale, Ont, Canada M2N 1Y6. —— Anne, *b* 1915: *m* 1st, 1941, Capt John Pearce Gould, RASC; 2ndly, 1947, Denis Owen Burns, of Clumps End, Lower Bourne, Farnham, Surrey.

PREDECESSORS – (1) *Sir* EDWARD Pellew, GCB: a celebrated Adm; *cr* a *Baronet* 1796, *Baron Exmouth*, of Canonteign, co Devon (peerage of United Kingdom) 1814, and *Viscount Exmouth* (peerage of United Kingdom) 1816; *d* 1833; *s* by his son **(2)** POWNOLL BASTARD, 2nd Viscount; *d* 1833; *s* by his son **(3)** EDWARD, 3rd Viscount; *d* 1876; *s* by his nephew **(4)** EDWARD FLEETWOOD JOHN, 4th Viscount (son of Hon Fleetwood John, 4th son of 2nd Viscount), *b* 1861: *m* 1884, Edith, who *d* 1914, da of late Thomas Hargreaves, of Arborfield Hall, Reading; *d* 1899; *s* by his son **(5)** EDWARD ADDINGTON HARGREAVES, 5th Viscount, *b* 1890; *d* 1922; *s* by his cousin **(6)** HENRY EDWARD (only son of late Very Rev the Hon George Pellew, DD, Dean of Norwich, 3rd son of 1st Viscount, by the Hon Frances Addington, da of 1st Viscount Sidmouth), 6th Viscount; *b* 1828; a naturalized American: *m* 1st, 1858, Eliza, who *d* 1869, da of late Hon William Jay, of Bedford, New York, a Judge in New York; 2ndly, 1873, Augusta, who *d* 1917, da of late Hon William Jay (ante); *d* 1923; *s* by his son **(7)** CHARLES ERNEST, 7th Viscount; *b* 1863: *m* 1st 1886, Margaret, who *d* 1922, da of late Professor C. F. Chandler, of New York; 2ndly 1923, Mabel, who *d* 1949, da of late Richard Gray, of San Francisco; *d* 1945; *s* by his kinsman **(8)** EDWARD IRVING POWNOLL, OBE, MRCS, LRCP (son of late Capt Pownoll William Pellew, RN, son of Rev Hon Edward Pellew, 4th son of 1st Viscount), 8th Viscount; *b* 1868: *m* 1902, Frances, who *d* 1963, da of Alfred Wells Edwards; *d* 1951; *s* by his son **(9)** POWNOLL IRVING EDWARD, 9th Viscount; *b* 1908: *m* 1938, Maria Luisa (Marquesa de Olias in Spain; *cr* 1652; *s* 1940), who *d* 1994, da of late Luis de Urquijo, Marques de Amurrio, of Madrid, and widow of Gonzalo Alvarez-Builla; *d* 1970; *s* by his son **(10)** PAUL EDWARD, 10th Viscount and present peer; also Baron Exmouth.

EZRA, BARON (Ezra) (Life Baron 1983)

DEREK EZRA, MBE, son of late David Ezra; *b* 23 Feb 1919; *ed* Monmouth Sch, and Magdalene Coll, Camb (MA, Hon Fell 1977); joined Nat Coal Board 1947, Regional Sales Manager 1958-60, Dir-Gen Marketing 1960-65, Board Member 1965-67, Dep-Chm 1967-71, Chm 1971-82; Vice-Pres Brit Inst of Management since 1978 (Chm 1976-78); Chm Assoc Heat Services plc since 1966; Dir of other Cos in Energy Sector; served in Army 1939-47; MBE (Mil) 1945; *cr* Kt 1974, and *Baron Ezra*, of Horsham, co W Sussex (Life Baron) 1983: *m* 1950, Julia Elizabeth, da of Thomas Wilkins, of Portsmouth, Hants.

Address – House of Lords, Westminster, SW1A 0PW.

FAIRFAX OF CAMERON, LORD (Fairfax) (Baron S 1627)

NICHOLAS JOHN ALBERT FAIRFAX, 14th Lord; *b* 4 Jan 1956; *s* 1964: *m* 1982, Annabel Ruth, el da of late Henry Lester Louis Morriss (*see* Jackson, Bt, *cr* 1869), and has issue.

Arms – Or, three bars gemelles gules, surmounted by a lion rampant sable. **Crest** – A lion passant guardant sable. **Supporters** – *Dexter*, a lion guardant sable; *sinister*, a bay horse proper.
Residence – 10 Orlando Rd, SW4 0LF. *Club* – Royal Yacht Squadron.

SONS LIVING

Hon EDWARD NICHOLAS THOMAS, *b* 20 Sept 1984.
Hon John Frederick Anthony, *b* 1986.
Hon Rory Henry Francis, *b* 1991.

BROTHERS LIVING

Hon Hugh Nigel Thomas (50 Streathbourne Rd, SW17 8QX. *Club* – Boodle's), *b* 1958; *ed* Eton: *m* 1984, Victoria Janet, elder da of Digby Sheffield Neave (*see* Neave, Bt), and has issue living, Alexander Thomas Digby, *b* 1986, — Laura Jane Ulla, *b* 1987, — Marina, *b* 1989.
Hon Rupert Alexander James, *b* 1961; addl assist Private Sec to HRH The Prince of Wales 1986-88.

FARE FAC

Speak and act

SISTER LIVING

Hon Serena Frances, *b* 1952: *m* 1976, William Robert Geoffrey Bell, elder son of William Archibald Ottley Juxon Bell (*see* By Wenlock, 1969 Edn), and has issue living, William Thomas Dawson, *b* 1986, — Francesca Rose, *b* 1982, — Martha Clare, *b* 1984.

UNCLE LIVING (*Son of 12th Lord*)

Hon Peregrine John Wishart, *b* 1925; *ed* Eton, and Trin Coll, Camb; late Lt 12th R Lancers; Northumberland Hussars 1955-61; High Sheriff of Northumberland 1971: *m* 1965, Virginia Alexandra de L'Etang, da of late Hon Philip Leyland Kindersley (*see* B Kindersley, colls), and has issue living, Thomas Philip, *b* 1966, — Doune Alexandra Wishart, *b* 1968. *Residence* – Mindrum, Northumberland. *Clubs* – Northern Counties (Newcastle), Whites.

WIDOW LIVING OF THIRTEENTH LORD

SONIA HELEN (*Sonia, Lady Fairfax of Cameron*), da of late Capt Cecil Bernard Gunston, MC (*see* M Dufferin and Ava, 1980 Edn); a JP of Berks; a temporary Lady of the Bedchamber to HM 1967-71: *m* 1951, the 13th Lord, who *d* 1964.

COLLATERAL BRANCHES LIVING

Grandchildren of late Raymond Fairfax, son of late Hon Henry Fairfax, 2nd son of 9th Lord:—
Issue of late Henry Reginald Fairfax, MD, *b* 1875, *d* 1955: *m* 1907, Nellie Virginia who *d* 1957, da of M. O. Randolph, of Williamson, West Virginia, USA:—
Reginald Randolph, *b* 1908: *m* 1934, Genevieve, da of J. W. McKee, of Brookhaven, Mississippi, USA. —— Ronald Cary, *b* 1915: *m* 1954, Judith Victoria, da of Jonathan Breckenridge Stovall, of Amherst co Virginia, USA. —— Marion Avery, *b* 1918: *m* 1943, Collin Freeman Baker, MD (Junior), and has issue living, Colin Freeman, *b* 1947, — Carey Leigh, *b* 1952, — Ann Fairfax, *b* 1949.

Grandchildren of Frederick Griffith Fairfax (infra):—
Issue of late Edmund Wharton Fairfax, *b* 1914, *d* 1966: *m* 1943, Nancy (Hague, Virginia, USA), da of James L. King, of Pittsburg, USA:—
Edmund Wharton, *b* 1944. —— Bryan Griffith, *b* 1959. —— Jean Ann, *b* 1951. —— Barbara Jane, *b* 1953.

Grandchildren of late William Henry Fairfax, MD, son of late Ferdinand Fairfax, MD, 3rd son of Hon Ferdinando Fairfax, 2nd son of 8th Lord:—
Issue of late Frederick Griffith Fairfax, *b* 1867, *d* 1948: *m* 1903, his cousin, Mary Fernando, who *d* 1961, da of Capt Edmund Wharton:—
Frederick Griffith, *b* 1916: *m* 1st, 1946 (*m diss* 1956) Dorothy Brooke; 2ndly, 1957, Annette Aiken, of Atlanta, Georgia, and has issue living (by 1st *m*), Frederick Griffith (RR1, Hague, Virginia 22469, USA), *b* 1947, — William Henry (RR1, Box 4, Hague, Virginia 22469, USA), *b* 1950, — (Dorothy) Eleanor, *b* 1946: *m* 19—, Robert Demastus, of Rt 1 Box 28, Callao, Virginia 22435, USA, — Ada Carter, *b* 1949: *m* 19—, — Wright, — Grace Kate FAIRFAX, *b* 1952; has retained her maiden name: *m* 19—, — —(by 2nd *m*) Mary Lynette, *b* 1960: *m* 19—, — Roane. *Address* – RR1, Box 4, Hague, Virginia 22469, USA. Fernando (da), *b* 1908. *Residence* – RR1, Hague, Virginia 22469, USA. —— Annie Staunton, *b* 1011: *m* 1933, Edward Greco, and has issue living, Edward Fairfax (4732 Browntown Rd, Front Royal, Va 22630, USA), *b* 1935: *m* 1st, 1966 (*m diss* 1995), Barbara Ruth Gomez; 2ndly, 1996, Polly Anna Wallin, of Canton, N Carolina, and has issue living (by 1st *m*), Michelle Anne *b* 1968, William Edward Fairfax *b* 1972, — Frederick Dominic (6618 Ivy Hill Drive, McLean, Va 22101, USA) *b* 1937: *m* 1962, Carole Ann Drake, of Falling Waters, W Va, and has issue living, William Scott *b* 1969, Michael Drake *b* 1972. *Address* – PO Box 661, McLean, Virginia 22101, USA. —— Katherine Rambsey *b* 1919. *Residence* – Culpeper Gdns, Arlington, Virginia, USA.

Granddaughters of late Lt-Col John Carlyle Fairfax, US Army, elder son of late Archibald Carlyle Fairfax, 3rd son of late Cmdr Archibald Blair Fairfax, 4th son of Hon Ferdinando Fairfax (ante):—
Issue of late John Pollock Fairfax, *b* 1911, *d* 1983: *m* 1935, Dorothy Elsa, who *d* 1991, da of late Reginald Charles Steeple, of San Mateo, Calif, USA:—
Dorothy Anne, *b* 1936: *m* 1st, 1956 (*m diss* 1960), Frederick W. Timby; 2ndly, 1961 (*m diss* 1973), Henry Mohr Hermann; 3rdly, 1974, Jack Margolis, of 1520 Middlefield Rd, Palo Alto, Calif 94301, USA, and has issue living (by 1st *m*), Jeffrey William Fairfax (1718 Constitution Ct, Fort Collins, CO 80526, USA), *b* 1957: *m* 1982, Denise Jackson, and has issue living, Benjamin Fairfax *b* 1988, Gregory Charles *b* 1996, Blair Elizabeth *b* 1996, Julia Anne *b* 1991, Katherine Marie *b* 1993, Sarah Abigail *b* 1998, — Christopher Corey (440 N Winchester Blvd No 102, Santa Clara, Calif 95050, USA), *b* 1959: *m* 1997, Cynthia Ann Garland, — (by 2nd *m*), Susan Mohr, *b* 1963: *m* 1988, James David Peisker, of 2402 Cranberry Cove, Cedar Park, Texas 78613, USA, and has issue living, Matthew James *b* 1990, Laura Ruth *b* 1991, Emily Janice *b* 1994. —— Jain Pollock, *b* 1937: *m* 1st, 1960 (*m diss* 1968), John Phillip de Angeles; 2ndly, 1968 (*m diss* 19—), Terry Ernest Jamison; 3rdly, 1983, Michael Langston, of 4050 Bayberry Drive, Santa Rosa, Calif 95404, USA, and has issue living (by 1st *m*), Melissa Jain, *b* 1962, — Jenna Lynne, *b* 1963.

PREDECESSORS – (1) *Sir* THOMAS Fairfax, Knt; *cr Lord Fairfax of Cameron* (peerage of Scotland) 1627; *s* by his son (2) FERDINANDO, KB, 2nd Lord; successively MP for Boroughbridge and Yorkshire; as Parliamentary Gen of the Northern Forces became eminently distinguished, and had a chief command at the Battle of Marston Moor, where he defeated the Royal Army; was subsequently Gov of York; *d* 1647; *s* by his son (3) THOMAS, KB, 3rd Lord, a distinguished Republican military leader; commanded a Cavalry wing at Marston Moor; appointed Gen in Ch of the Parliaments' Army 1645, and in that year gained the celebrated victory at Naseby; he afterwards defeated the Royalists in a series of engagements, but did not participate in the execution of the king; in 1650 resigned the command of the army to Cromwell, and in 1659 zealously assisted to restore the monarchy; was Constable of the Tower 1647, and Lord of the Isle of Man 1650, and sat as MP for Yorkshire 1660; *d* 1671; *s* by his cousin (4) HENRY, 4th Lord, son of Rev Hon Henry, 2nd son of 1st Lord; *d* 1685; *s* by his son (5) THOMAS, 5th Lord, MP for co York 1688-1707, when the Act of

Union he became ineligible; took an active part in promoting the revolution; *d* 1710; *s* by his el son (6) THOMAS, 6th Lord; inherited from his mother estates in England which he gave to his brother, and also inherited about 5,700,000 acres of land in Virginia, upon which he erected two mansions, where he resided in baronial splendour; *d* 1781; *s* by his brother (7) ROBERT, 7th Lord; *d* 1793; *s* by his kinsman (8) BRYAN, 8th Lord, grandson of Rev Hon Hnery, 2nd son of 4th Lord (title confirmed by House of Lords 1800); *d* 1802; *s* by his son (9) THOMAS, 9th Lord; *d* 1846; *s* by his grandson (10) CHARLES SNOWDEN, 10th Lord, son of Hon Albert el son of 9th Lord, by Caroline, da of Richard Snowden, of Oakland, Maryland; Speaker of House of Delegates of State of California 1854-7, and Clerk of Supreme Court of California 1857-62; *d* 1869; *s* by his brother (11) JOHN CONTEE, MD, 11th Lord; *b* 1830: *m* 1857, Mary, who *d* 1912, da of Col Edmund Kirkby, of USA: *d* 1900: *s* by his el son (12) ALBERT KIRBY, 12th Lord (confirmed by Committee for Privileges of the House of Lords 1908); *b* 1870; a Representative Peer for Scotland: *m* 1922, Maude Wishart (who *d* 1973, have *m* 2ndly, 1947, Maj Cecil Rookherst Wigan, MC, who *d* 1958; 3rdly, 1962, Brig Felix Alexander Vincent Copland-Griffiths, DSO, MC), da of James McKelvie, of Ducklys Park, East Grinsted, *d* 1939, *s* by his el son (13) THOMAS BRIAN McKELVIE, 13th Lord; *b* 1923; Lt Grenadier Guards; a Representative Peer for Scotland 1945-63; Assist Conservative Whip, House of Lords 1947-48, PPS to Lord Pres of the Council 1951-53, and to Min of Materials 1953-54, and a Lord-in-Waiting to HM 1954-57: *m* 1951, Sonia Helen, da of late Capt Cecil Bernard Gunston, MC (*see* M Dufferin and Ava, 1980 Edn); *d* 1964; *s* by his el son (14) NICHOLAS JOHN ALBERT, 14th Lord and present peer.

FAIRHAVEN, BARON (Broughton) (Baron UK 1961)

If I can

AILWYN HENRY GEORGE BROUGHTON, 3rd Baron; *b* 16 Nov 1936; *s* 1973; *ed* Eton, and RMA; Maj Blues and Royals; Vice Lord-Lieut of Cambs 1977-84: JP and DL for Cambs: *m* 1960, Kathleen Patricia, el da of Col James Henry Magill, OBE, of Moat Cottage, Kirtling, Newmarket, Suffolk, and has issue.

Arms – Argent, two bars and in the dexter chief point a saltire gules. **Crest** – In front of a bull's head erased sable, armed and collared and chained or, three fleur-de-lis gold. **Supporters** – On either side a winged bull sable, each armed and gorged with a chain or, pendant therefrom an escutcheon charged with the Arms of Broughton.
Residence – Anglesey Abbey, Cambridge. *Club* – Turf.

SONS LIVING

Hon JAMES HENRY AILWYN, *b* 25 May 1963; *ed* Harrow; late Maj The Blues and Royals: *m* 1990, Sarah Olivia, da of Harold Digby Fitzgerald Creighton, of Ryder St, SW1, and has issue living, George Ailwyn James, *b* 17 March 1997, — Sophie Rose, *b* 1992, — Emily Patricia, *b* 1995.

Hon Huttleston Rupert, *b* 1970.

Hon Charles Leander, *b* 1973; *ed* Eton, and RMA Sandhurst; commn'd Gren Gds 1996: *m* 1999, Nicola J., da of Quentin Goggs, of Easterton, Wilts.

Hon Henry Robert, *b* 1978.

DAUGHTERS LIVING

Hon Diana Cara, *b* 1961: *m* 1st, 1983 (*m diss* 19—), Guy Dominic Thornton (*see* V Esher, colls); 2ndly, 1991, as his 3rd wife, Alan Brodie Henderson, and has issue (by 1st *m*) (*see* V Esher, colls).

Hon Melanie Frances, *b* 1966: *m* 1st, 1989 (*m diss* 1992), Matthew Eric Smith; 2ndly, 1994, Andrew Edgar, and has issue (by 1st *m*) (*see* Hill-Wood, Bt, colls).

PREDECESSORS – (1) URBAN HUTTLESTON ROGERS Broughton, son of Urban Hanlon Broughton, of Park Close, Englefield Green, Surrey (*b* 1857, *d* 1929, before his intended elevation to the Peerage, and who gave Ashridge to Conservative Party), by Cara Leland (who, with her two sons presented Runnymede to the nation 1929, and who was granted by Roy Warrant 1929 the style and title as if her husband had received the barony of Fairhaven), da of Henry Huttleston Rogers, of New York; *cr Baron Fairhaven*, of Lode, co Camb (Peerage of UK 1929) with remainder to, heirs male of the body, and *Baron Fairhaven*, of Anglesey Abbey, co Camb (Peerage of UK) 1961, with remainder to his yr brother, and the heirs male of his body; *d* 1966, when the Barony *cr* 1929 became ext; *s* in the Barony *cr* 1961, by his brother (2) HENRY ROGERS, 2nd Baron, *b* 1900: *m* 1st, 1932, Hon Diana Rosamond, who *d* 1937, da of late Capt Hon Coulson Churchill Fellowes (B de Ramsey); 2ndly, 1953, Joyce Irene (who *d* 1989, having *m* 3rdly, 1982, Vice-Adm Sir Geoffrey Thistleton-Smith, KBE, CB, GM, DL), da of Edward Arthur Miller, and widow of Lt Gerald Henry Charles Dickens, RN; *d* 1973; *s* by his only son (3) AILWYN HENRY GEORGE, 3rd Baron, and present Peer.

FALCONER OF HALKERTON, LORDSHIP OF (Falconer) (Dormant 1966)

The Lordship of Falconer of Halkerton became dormant on the death of the 10th Earl of Kintore and 12th Lord Falconer of Halkerton in 1966. Owing to the Earls of Kintore not having taken any steps to vote as Lords Falconer for over forty years, the dignity was removed, by mistake, from the Union Roll after the death of the 7th Earl and 9th Lord in 1844. It will be necessary for the next male heir to the Lordship of Falconer of Halkerton to have this peerage restored to the Union Roll by resolution of the House of Lords.

COLLATERAL BRANCHES LIVING

Descendants of late George Falconer (who changed the spelling of his surname to Falconar), brother of 4th Lord:—

Granddaughter of late George Mercer FALCONAR-STEWART (who assumed the additional surname of Stewart after his patronymic), son of late George FALCONAR of Carlowrie, great-grandson of late George Falconer (ante):—
Issue of late Maj Cyril Falconar-Stewart, MC, b 1884, d 1962: m 1915, Nita, who d 1968, da of Bryce Allan, of Wemyss Bay, Renfrewshire:—
Grizel Anne, b 1917: m 1944, Wladyslaw Chlebowski, of 26 Greenhill Gdns, Edinburgh, EH10 4BP, and has issue living, Jan Ronald Stewart, b 1945, — Victor Tadeusz Stewart, b 1953: m 1988, Jean MacLellan, and has issue living, Amy Louisa b 1990, Isla Rose b 1992, — Alexandra Ewa Stewart, b 1948; m 1975, Dr William David Smith, of 4 St Margaret's Rd, Edinburgh, and has issue living, Robin Paul Stewart b 1977, Tamsin Louise Stewart b 1981.

Grandchildren of late John Egerton Falconer, son of Randle Wilbraham Falconer, MD, FRCP, DCL, 6th in descent from Patrick Falconer of Newton, uncle of 1st Lord:—
Issue of late Thomas Falconer, FRIBA, b 1879, d 1934: m 1912, Florence Edith, who d 1944, da of late Henry Campbell Serrell, of Brooke House, Hants:—
PETER SERRELL (presumed heir to the Lordship of Falconer of Halkerton), b 7 March, 1916; ed Bloxham; FRIBA: m 1941, Mary, da of late Rev C. B. Hodson, and has issue living, Thomas Serrell (Daisy Cottage, Fairseat, Kent), b 1946: m 1981, Philippa Mary, da of J. R. C. Sheldon, of Court House, Fairseat, Kent, and has issue living, Alexander Peter b 1989, Olivia Siena b 1983, Katharine Daisy b 1986, — Richard Alaric (St Davids, Kemps Lane, Painswick, Glos), b 1949; RIBA: m 1982, Virginia Suzanne Rowell, only da of Richard Francis Jarrett, FRCP, MA, MB, BCh, of Hamfield, Painswick, Glos, and has issue living, Holly Frances b 1984, Rosanna Frances b 1985, Venetia Frances b 1989, — William John (103 Princess Victoria St, Clifton, Bristol BS8 4DD), b 1952; RIBA: m 1983, Susan Mary, da of late Arthur Leslie Bill, of Roslyn, St John's Hill, Wimborne, Dorset, and has issue living, Phoebe Margaret b 1993, Alice Elizabeth b 1995, — Caroline Elisabeth, b 1942: m 1973, Maj Paul Beresford Weller, late Som LI, of Morcombe Farm House, Caudle Green, Cheltenham, Glos GL53 9PR, and has issue living, Victoria Mary Henrietta b 1976, Atalanta Catherine b 1978, Pandora May b 1983. Residence – St Francis, Minchinhampton, Gloucestershire. —— Peggie Florentia, b 1918: m 1941, Douglas Albert Guest, CVO, MA, MusD, Emeritus Organist and Master of Choristers, Westminster Abbey, who d 1996, and has issue living, Susan Jennifer b 1943: m 1966, Martin Hayward Garrett-Cox, of Shrubhill, Hill of Row, by Dunblane, Perthshire FK15 9PA, and has issue living, Jeremy Hayward (23 St Dunstan's Rd, W6 8RE) b 1968: m 1996, Katherine Lucy, da of Timothy Jenkins, of Crockerhill, W Sussex, and of Mrs Andrew Muir, of Itchen Lodge, Hants, Robin Guy b 1970, Sacha Clare b 1973: m 1996, Emmanuel Michel Marie Jan, of Coire-Domhain, Mangoëro, 56400 Plumergat, France (and has issue living, Béatrice Patricia Rose-Marie b 1998), — Penelope Anne, b 1946: m 1970, Prof Simon de Lange, MB BS, PhD, FRCA, of Diepstraat 48, 6245 BL Eijsden, Netherlands, and has issue living, Cara Michelle b 1974, Claire Louise b 1976. Residence – The Gables, Minchinhampton, Glos GL6 9JE.

Issue of late William Wilbraham Phillips Falconer, b 1883, d 1952: m 1911, Gladys, who d 1969, da of late David Howard Jones, of Carmarthen:—
Joan Egerton, MBE, b 1920; MBE (Civil) 1991: m 1st, 1940 (m diss 1944), Maj Gerrit Geel, Netherlands Army; 2ndly, 1945, Col James Bouverie-Brine, and has issue living (by 1st m), Marie Ann Falconer, b 1943: m 1st, 1963 (m diss 1986), Edward Alexander Caudwell; 2ndly, 1988, Wing Cdr A. Webb, AFC, RAF, and has issue living (by 1st m), Edward James b 1966: m 1993, Lucinda, da of Brig J. Alexander, of Andover, Hants (and has issue living, Camilla Delacour b 1997), Alexandra Jane Marie b 1969, – (by 2nd m), Christopher James Falconer, b 1946: m 1968, Ellen Agnes Maria, da of Henk Verkroost, of Utrecht, Holland, — Michael Pusey, b 1959: m 1984, Claire Andrée, da of Frederick G. Henley, of Swindon, Wilts, and has issue living, George James b 1993, Lucy Anne b 1992, — Kathleen Joan, b 1948: m 1968 (m diss 1994), Fl Lt Alexander Frederick Paul Rhodes, RAF, and has issue living, Paul William b 1969, Helen Kathleen (twin) b 1969, — Amelia Pusey, b 1953: m 1st, 1974 (m diss 1981), Edward Alfred Funnell; 2ndly, 1982, Lt-Cmdr Stephen Patrick Lacey, RN, and has issue living (by 1st m), Simon Edward b 1975, Louise Amelia b 1979, (by 2nd m) James Patrick b 1986, — Elizabeth, b 1956: m 1st, 1978 (m diss 1985), Dudley James Cox, of Nailsea, Avon; 2ndly, 1986, Michael McGaughrin. Residence – 9 St Mary's Close, Bradenstoke, Chippenham, Wilts SN15 4ET.

Issue of late John Philip Egerton Falconer (twin), b 1883, d 1970: m 1931, Florence Eleanor, who d 1957, da of late Alfred Attwood, of Yeovil, Som:—
David Dunbar (Iris Bank, 17 Cockhill, Trowbridge, Wilts BA14 9BG), b 1934; BA: m 1959, Gillian Mary, only da of late Wing-Cdr William Richard Owen, MBE, RAF, and has issue living, Jonathan Randle, b 1961; BA: m 1992, Tracy Anne Gronow, — Patrick Markham, b 1964; BA: m 1989, Deborah Anne Helena, da of late T. C. Close, of Bristol, and has issue living, James Patrick b 1994, John Douglas b 1997, Georgina Louise b 1991, Philippa Jane b 1993, — Henrietta Frances, b 1970; BA.

PREDECESSORS – (1) Sir ALEXANDER Falconer of Halkerton, Kincardineshire, whose family descended from Ranulf (c1185-1235), Falconer to William the Lion, from which office he assumed the surname of Falconer, was a Lord of Session 1639, MP for co Kincardine 1643, and a Commr of the Treasury 1645; cr Lord Falconer of Halkerton (peerage of Scotland) 1646, with remainder to his heirs male whatsoever: m 1619, Anne Lindsay, only da and heiress of John, 8th Lord Lindsay of the Byres, co Haddington; d 1671; s by his son (2) ALEXANDER, 2nd Lord: m 1666, Lady Margaret

Ogilvy, da of James, 2nd Earl of Airlie; *d* 1684; *s* by his son **(3)** DAVID, 3rd Lord; *d* unmarried 1724; *s* by his kinsman **(4)** DAVID (son of Sir David Falconar of Newton, Lord Newton, Lord Pres of Court of Session (who *m* 1678, Mary, da of George Norvell of Boghall, co Linlithgow), 2nd son of Sir David Falconar, brother of 1st Lord), 4th Lord: *m* 1703, Lady Katharine Margaret Keith, el da of William, 2nd Earl of Kintore, *d* 1751; *s* by his son **(5)** ALEXANDER, 5th Lord, *b* 1707: *m* 1757, Frances, da of Herbert Mackworth; *d* 1762; *s* by his brother **(6)** WILLIAM, 6th Lord; Col in Dutch Ser: *m* 1735, Rembertina-Maria van Iddekinge; *d* 1776; *s* by his son **(7)** ANTHONY ADRIAN, 7th Lord, who *s* as 5th Earl of Kintore 1778 (see that title). On the death of ARTHUR GEORGE, 10th Earl and 12th Lord Falconer of Halkerton 1966, the latter peerage became dormant.

FALCONER OF THOROTON, BARON (Falconer) (Life Baron 1997)

CHARLES LESLIE FALCONER, son of John Leslie Falconer, of Edinburgh; *b* 19 Nov 1951; *ed* Trinity Coll, Glenalmond, and Queens' Coll, Camb; Bar-at-law, Inner Temple, 1974 (Master of the Bench 1997); QC 1991; Solicitor-Gen 1997-98, since when Min of State Cabinet Office; *cr Baron Falconer of Thoroton*, of Thoroton, co Nottinghamshire (Life Baron) 1997: *m* 1985, Marianna Catherine Thoroton, only da of Sir David Henry Thoroton Hildyard, KCMG, DFC, and has issue.
Address – 70 Whitehall, SW1.

SONS LIVING

Hon Hamish, *b* 1985.
Hon Rocco, *b* 1988.
Hon Johnny, *b* 1993.

DAUGHTER LIVING

Hon Rosie, *b* 1990.

FALKENDER, BARONESS (Falkender) (Life Baroness 1974)

MARCIA MATILDA FALKENDER, CBE, da of Harry Field; *b* 1932; *ed* Queen Mary Coll, London Univ (BA); Sec to Mr Morgan Phillips, Gen Sec Labour Party 1955-56; Private Sec to Rt Hon Sir Harold Wilson, OBE, FRS, MP; Political Columnist, *The Mail on Sunday* 1982-88; Lay Gov Queen Mary Coll 1987-93; Pres UNIFEM UK, United Nations Development Fund for Women UK Cttee; Dir Peckham Building Soc 1986-91, S London Investment & Mortgage Corpn 1987; Memb British Screen Advisory Council since 1985; Trustee The Silver Trust; assumed by deed poll, 1974 the surname of Falkender in lieu of Williams; *cr* CBE (Civil) 1970, and *Baroness Falkender*, of West Haddon, co Northants (Life Baroness) 1974: *m* 1955 (*m diss* 1960), George Edmund Charles Williams; has issue, two sons.
Address – House of Lords, SW1.

FALKLAND, VISCOUNT OF (Cary) (Viscount S 1620)

Faithful in both

LUCIUS EDWARD WILLIAM PLANTAGENET CARY, 15th Viscount, *b* 8 May 1935; *s* 1984; *ed* Wellington Coll; late 2nd Lieut 8th Hus; formerly Ch Exec C. T. Bowring Trading (Holdings) Ltd; export marketing consultant; Deputy Whip SLD, House of Lords since 1988: *m* 1st, 1962 (*m diss* 1990), Caroline Anne, only da of late Lt-Cdr Gerald Butler, DSC, RN; 2ndly, 1990, Nicole, da of late Milburn Mackey, and has issue by 1st and 2nd *m*.

𝕬rms – Quarterly: 1st and 4th argent, on a bend sable, three roses of the field, barbed and seeded proper, *Cary;* 2nd sable, two bars nebulée ermine, *Spencer of Spencercombe;* 3rd, France and England quarterly, within a bordure componée argent and azure, *Beaufort,* Duke of Somerset. 𝕮rest – A swan, wings elevated proper. 𝕾upporters – *Dexter,* an unicorn argent, armed, crined, tufted and unguled or; *sinister,* a lion guardant proper, ducally crowned, and gorged with a plain collar or.
Address – House of Lords, SW1.

SONS LIVING *(By 1st marriage)*

Hon (LUCIUS) ALEXANDER PLANTAGENET (*Master of Falkland*), *b* 1 Feb 1963; *ed* Westminster, Loretto, and RMA Sandhurst; late Capt Scots Guards; Screenwriter and Film Producer since 1991: *m* 1993, Linda, da of Raymond Purl, of Colorado Springs, USA, and has issue living, a son, *b* 6 Feb 1995. *Residence* – 10417 Ravenwood Court, Bel Air, CA 90077, USA. *Club* – Cavalry and Guards'.

(By 2nd marriage)

Hon Charles Byron Milburn, *b* 1992.

DAUGHTERS LIVING AND DECEASED *(by 1st marriage)*

Camilla Anne, *b* 1965; *d* 1972.
Hon Samantha Anne, *b* 1973.
Hon Lucinda Mary, *b* 1974.

HALF-SISTERS LIVING *(Daughters of 14th Viscount by 1st m)*

Hon Elizabeth Ann Bevil (*Hon Lady Nelson*), *b* 1927: *m* 1945, Sir William Vernon Hope Nelson, 3rd Bt, OBE, who *d* 1991. *Residence* – The Old Post House, Chiselborough, Som.
Hon Jean Rosemary Vera, *b* 1928; artist: *m* 1950, Capt Henry Herman Evelyn Montagu Winch, late High Sheriff of Merioneth, who *d* 1987. *Residence* – Castle Barn, Minffordd, Gwynedd.

UNCLE LIVING *(son of 13th Viscount)*

Hon Richard Lorenzo Plantagenet, *b* 1915; *ed* Repton, and Downing Coll, Camb: *m* 1959, Dorothy Denise Lloyd.

COLLATERAL BRANCHES LIVING

Issue of late Hon Byron Godfrey Plantagenet Cary, 2nd son of 13th Viscount, *b* 1908, *d* 1971: *m* 1932, Daphne Helen, who *d* 1997, da of late Capt Edward Westcott King, RA:—
Robert Byron, *b* 1944; *ed* Repton. —— Rosemary Sally (118 High St, Wivenhoe, Essex), *b* 1935: *m* 1980, Neil Pugh. —— Susan Jane, *b* 1938: *m* 1960, Ronald Frederick Featherstone, of 20 Clinton Rd, Lower Buckland, Lymington, Hants, and has issue living, Angus Frederick, *b* 1962, — Penelope Helen *b* 1961: *m* 1986, Geoffrey Williams, — Louise, *b* 1964: *m* 1987, Mark Snodgrass, — Greta Jane, *b* 1965, — Katy Ann Lorraine, *b* 1967, — Ingrid Laura, *b* 1980.

Issue of late Hon Philip Plantagenet Cary, yst son of 12th Viscount, *b* 1895, *d* 1968: *m* 1920, Esther Mildred, who *d* 1972, da of Sir George Edward Leon, 2nd Bt:—
(Mary) Philippa (*Dowager Baroness Dunalley*) (Church End House, Swerford, Oxford OX7 4AX), *b* 1922: 1939-45 War, as 3rd Officer, WRNS: *m* 1947, Lt-Col 6th Baron Dunalley, who *d* 1992.

PREDECESSORS – (1) *Rt Hon Sir* HENRY CARY, PC, Comptroller of the Household 1617; MP for Hertfordshire 1620-1, and Lord Dep for Ireland 1622-9; *cr Viscount Falkland* and *Lord Cary* (peerage of Scotland) 1620; *d* 1633; *s* by his son (2) LUCIUS, 2nd Viscount; MP for Newport, and Sec of State to Charles I; *k* at first battle of Newbury 1643; *s* by his el son (3) LUCIUS, 3rd Viscount; d 1649; s by his brother (4) HENRY, 4th Viscount; MP for Arundell and Lord-Lieut of co Oxford; d 1663; s by his son (5) ANTHONY, PC, 5th Viscount; Treasurer of the Navy 1681-89, Commr of the Admiralty to William and Mary, and First Lord of the Admiralty 1693 until his death; committed to the Tower in 1693 by the House of Commons, of which he was a member, for begging and receiving £2,000 from HM, contrary to the ordinary method of issuing and bestowing the King's money; s by his cousin (6) LUCIUS HENRY CARY, 6th Viscount, grandson of Hon Patrick Cary, 5th son of 1st Viscount; d 1730; s by his son (7) LUCIUS CHARLES, 7th Viscount; d 1785; s by his grandson (8) HENRY THOMAS, 8th Viscount, el son of Hon Lucius Ferdinand, el son of 7th Viscount; d unmarried 1796; s by his brother (9) CHARLES JOHN, 9th Viscount; b 1768; Capt RN; killed in a duel 1809; s by his son (10) LUCIUS BENTINCK, GCH, PC, 10th Viscount; b 1803; was a Lord of the Bedchamber to William IV 1830, a Representative Peer for Scotland 1831-32, Gov of Nova Scotia 1840-46, Capt of Yeomen of the Guard 1846-48, and Gov of Bombay 1848-53; cr Baron Hunsdon of Scutterskelfe, co York (peerage of United Kingdom) 1832; d 1884, when the Barony of Hunsdon became extinct; s by his brother (11) PLANTAGENET PIERREPONT, 11th Viscount; was an Adm; d 31 Jan 1886; s by his nephew (12) BYRON PLANTAGENET (el son of Capt Hon Byron Charles Ferdinand Plantagenet Cary, 3rd son of 9th Viscount), 12th Viscount, b 1845; a Representative Peer: m 1879, Mary (a Lady of Grace of Order of St John of Jerusalem in England), who d 1920, da of late Robert Reade, of New York; d 1922; s by his el son (13) LUCIUS PLANTAGENET, OBE, 13th Viscount, b 1880; Capt and Brevet Major Grenadier Guards; Dep Gov of Wandsworth Prison 1910-14; European War 1914-19 (OBE); a Representative Peer for Scotland 1922-31; m 1904, Ella Louise, who d 1954, da of late Edward Walter Catford; d 1961; s by his el son (14) LUCIUS HENRY CHARLES PLANTAGENET, 14th Viscount, b 1905: m 1st, 1926 (m diss 1933), Joan Sylvia, da of Charles Bonham Southey; 2ndly, 1933 (m diss 1958), Constance Mary, who d 1995, da of late Capt Edward Berry; 3rdly, 1958 (m diss 1974), Charlotte Anne, elder da of late Bevil Granville, of Chadley, Wellesbourne, Warwicks (see Halsey, Bt, 1952 Edn); d 1984; s by his only son (15) LUCIUS EDWARD WILLIAM PLANTAGENET CARY, 15th Viscount and present peer; also Lord Cary.

FALMOUTH, VISCOUNT (Boscawen) (Viscount GB 1720)
(Name pronounced "Boscowen")

GEORGE HUGH BOSCAWEN, 9th Viscount; b 31 Oct 1919; s 1962; ed Eton, and at Trin Coll, Camb (MA); Capt Coldstream Guards, and patron of five livings; Lord Lieut of Cornwall 1977-94; 1939-45 War in Italy (wounded, despatches); m 1953, Elizabeth, el da of A. H. Browne, and has issue.

Arms – Ermine, a rose gules, barbed and seeded proper. Crest – A falcon close proper. Supporters – Two sea lions erect on their tails argent, gutte de larmes. Motto – Patience Passe Science.
Clubs – Athenaeum, Army and Navy.

SONS LIVING

Hon EVELYN ARTHUR HUGH, b 13 May 1955; ed Eton, and Royal Agric Coll, Cirencester; Chm Kent Branch Country Landowners' Assocn; Liveryman Clockmakers' Co: m 1st, 1977 (m diss 1995), Lucia Caroline, el da of Ralph William Vivian-Neal, of Poundisford Park, Som; 2ndly, 1995, Katharine Helen, eldest da of Mark Maley, of Nayland, Suffolk, and has issue living (by 1st m), (Evelyn George) William, b 1 Oct 1979, — Laura Frances, b 1982, — (by 2nd m), Frederick Mark, b 1996, — Archard (Archie) Hugh, b 1998. Residence – Tregothnan, Truro, Cornwall. Clubs – White's, Athenaeum.

Hon Nicholas John (Peckham Place, Peckham Bush, Tonbridge, Kent TN12 5NA), b 1957; ed Eton, and RAC Cirencester: m 1985, Virginia Mary Rose, yr da of Robin Beare, MB BS, FRCS, of Scraggs Farm, Cowden, Kent, and has issue living, Louisa Emily Chiara, b 1990, — Georgia Olivia Catharine, b 1992.

Hon Charles Richard (Moat Farm, Dennington, nr Framlingham, Suffolk), b 1958; ed Eton, and Trin Coll, Camb (MA): m 1985, Frances Diana, yst da of late Maj Hon George Nathaniel Rous, of Dennington Hall, Woodbridge, Suffolk (see E Stradbroke, colls), and has issue living, Arthur George, b 1991, — John Charles, b

Patience surpasses knowledge

1993, — Rosanna Frances, b 1989.

Hon Vere George (Bullock's Horn Place, Charlton, nr Malmesbury, Wilts), b 1964: m 1991, Catharine Mary, da of Christopher Halliday, of Whitton Hall, Westbury, Shropshire, and has issue living, Harry Christopher, b 1992, — Guy William, b 1997, — Isabella Catharine, b 1994.

BROTHERS LIVING

Hon (Henry) Edward, b 1921; ed Eton, and Peterhouse, Camb; is Lieut RE; European War 1940-45 in Italy and NW Europe; High Sheriff W Sussex 1979-80: m 1951, Anne Philippa, el da of Col Sir Edward Courtenay Thomas Warner, 2nd Bt, DSO, MC, and has issue living, Thomas Edward, b 1964, — Sarah Kathleen, b 1958: m 1986, Jeremy M. Bray, yr son of Christopher Bray, of Southwold, Suffolk, and has issue living, Alice Frances b 1988, Emily Sarah b 1991, Susannah Nesta b 1993, — Jessica Frances, b 1960: m 1990, Hubert Alastair Speare-Cole, son of Cdr M. B. Speare-Cole, of Fulham SW, and has issue living, Edward Arthur Bremer b 1995, Antonia Margaret b 1991, Rebecca Anne b 1993. Residence – The Garden House, High Beeches Lane, Handcross, Sussex.

Rt Hon Robert Thomas, MC, b 1923; ed Eton, and Trin Coll, Camb; late Lt Coldstream Guards; MP for Wells (C) 1970-83, and for Somerton and Frome 1983-92; a Lord Commr of HM Treasury 1980-83; Vice Chamberlain HM Household 1983-86, Comptroller HM Household 1986-88; Govt Whip 1979-88; served 1941-45 War in NW Europe (wounded, MC 1944); PC 1992: m 1949, Mary Alice, JP, el da of late Col Sir Geoffrey Ronald Codrington, KCVO, CB, CMG, DSO, OBE, TD (see Codrington, Bt, cr 1721), and has issue living, Hugh Geoffrey Robert, b 1954; ed Eton, and Bristol Univ (BA);

Lt-Col Coldm Gds, served Gulf War 1991: *m* 1981, Alexandra Marie-Monique, el da of Anthony Eden, of Torberry House, W Harting, Sussex, and has issue living, Veryan John Hugh *b* 1987, Aldwyn George Hugh *b* 1989, — Dozmary Carolyn Claire, *b* 1951: *m* 1984, David B. Keller, son of late Col Blanton S. Keller, and has issue living, Nicholas Francis David *b* 1988, — Karenza Pamela Mary, *b* 1961. *Residence* – 14 Tite St, SW3. *Clubs* – Pratt's, and Royal Yacht Squadron.

SISTER LIVING

Hon Mary Kathleen, *b* 1926; is a JP for Cornwall; European War 1944-45 in WRNS: *m* 1948, Lieut-Com David Verney (*see* Verney, Bt *cr* 1946), who *d* 1992. *Residence* – Trevella, St Erme, Truro, Cornwall.

COLLATERAL BRANCHES LIVING

(In remainder to the Viscountcy only)

Grandchildren of late Lt-Col John Hugh Boscawen, eldest son of late Rev Hon John Townshend Boscawen, brother of 6th Viscount:—
Issue of late Capt Spencer Boscawen, *b* 1887, *d* 1957: *m* 1919, Sydney Iris Kelly, who *d* 1982:—
John Roger, *b* 1922; late Flight Lieut Roy New Zealand Territorial Air Force; formerly with Seaport Operations Ltd; Auckland, New Zealand; SW Pacific 1943-5 (1939-45 star, Pacific star, two medals). *Residence* – Whitford Park Rd, Manurewa RD1, Auckland, NZ. ⸺ Owen Tremayne, *b* 1925; *ed* Otahuhu Coll, and NZ Univ (BSc, BA, DipEd); Prin of Otahuhu Coll; 1939-45 War as LAC, RNZAF: *m* 1st, 1954 (*m diss* 1981), Beverley Rose Wheeler, of Papatoetoe, Auckland, NZ; 2ndly, 1982, Mrs Mary Joan Hilford, and has had issue (by 1st *m*), John Spencer, *b* 1956, — Leanne Kay, *b* 1960; *d* 1980. *Residence* – 232 Whitford Park Rd, Manurewa RD1, Auckland, NZ. ⸺ Diana Margaret, *b* 1926: *m* 1950, Alan Frederick Arlington, of PO Box 9, Whitford, Auckland, NZ, and has issue living, Revel Miles, *b* 1957, — Lesley Joan, *b* 1953, — Pauline Gay, *b* 1954, — Fiona Fay, *b* 1958, — Karenza Margaret, *b* 1964. ⸺ Sydney Joy, *b* 1931: *m* 1959, Walter Flatz, of 864B Waiuku Rd, Mauku, RD3, Pukekohe, NZ, and has issue living, Roger Noel, *b* 1960, — Kenneth Frederick, *b* 1962, — Wallace Owen, *b* 1965, — Hayley June, *b* 1966. ⸺ Vanda Vivian, *b* 1935: *m* 1958, Clement Henry Harris, of 172 Whitford Park Rd, Manurewa RD2, Auckland, NZ, and has issue living, Bryce Henry, *b* 1959, — Mark Clement, *b* 1967, — Megan Sydney, *b* 1962, — Odette Vivian, *b* 1964.

Granddaughters of late Maj John Perceval Townshend Boscawen, MBE (infra):—
Issue of late James Townshend Boscawen, *b* 1932, *d* 1992: *m* 1955, Deirdre Elsie Elizabeth (*Lady Drinkwater*) (who *m* 2ndly, 1998, as his 2nd wife, Lt-Cmdr Sir John Muir Drinkwater, RN (ret), QC, of Meysey Hampton Manor, Cirencester), yr da of late Frederick Henry (Derek) Curtis-Bennett, QC:—
Caroline Elizabeth, *b* 1959: *m* 1982, Angus G. Fleming, of Pewitt House, Culworth, Banbury, Oxon OX17 2HJ, elder son Maj Richard Fleming, of Braemar Farm, Harare, Zimbabwe, and has issue living, James, *b* 1991, — George, *b* 1994, — Lucy, *b* 1984. ⸺ Diana Mary, *b* 1962: *m* 1991, Nigel R. Fielder, son of Geoffrey Fielder, of Wells, Som, and has issue living, Edward Townsend Farrar, *b* 1994, — Georgina Louise, *b* 1992.

Grandson of late Townshend Evelyn Boscawen, 4th son of late Rev Hon John Townshend Boscawen (ante):—
Issue of late Maj John Perceval Townshend Boscawen, MBE, *b* 1906, *d* 1972: *m* 1931, Lady Mary Helen Alma Graham (who *d* 1999, having *m* 2ndly, 1975, Brig Leslie Colville Dunn, TD, DL, who *d* 1990), elder da of 6th Duke of Montrose:—
Simon John Evelyn (Jackson's Cottage, Rudgwick, Sussex), *b* 1936; *ed* Eton: *m* 1961, Judith Perdita Rosemary, only da of Arthur Gregory George Marshall, of Horseheath Lodge, Linton, Cambs, and has issue living, Alistair John Evelyn (25 St Ann's Park Rd, SW18), *b* 1963: *m* 1st, 1990 (*m diss* 1997), Victoria A. M., da of late William Porter, of Queen Alexandra's Court, SW19; 2ndly, 1998, Katherine Louise, yst da of late Giles Witherington, of Bishops, Widdington, Saffron Walden, Essex, — David Simon Townshend, *b* 1965: *m* 1993, Clare Victoria, eldest da of John Edmund Kincaid Floyd (*see* Floyd, Bt), and has issue living, Megan Victoria *b* 1995, Flora Rose *b* 1997, — John Michael Arthur, *b* 1969: *m* 1995, Miranda Tracey, elder da of Timothy Finlow, of Dockenfield, Surrey, and has issue living, Benjamin Arthur John *b* 1997.

(In remainder to the Barony of Le Despencer only)

Descendants (now only surviving in the female line) of late Rev Hon Miles John Stapleton, 3rd son of 22nd Baron Le Despencer (infra).

Descendants (now only surviving in the female line) of late Rev Hon Francis Jarvis Stapleton (4th son of Sir Thomas Stapleton, 6th Bt and 22nd Baron Despencer), who *s* his father in the Baronetcy 1831.
See Stapleton, Bt (ext 1995).

PREDECESSORS – (1) HUGH Boscawen, PC, MP for Cornwall, Truro, and Penryn, Groom of the Bedchamber to Prince George, Comptroller of the Household, Warden of the Stanneries, and Vice-Treasurer of Ireland; *cr Baron Boscawen-Rose* and *Viscount Falmouth* (peerage of Great Britain) 1720; *d* 1734; *s* by his son (2) HUGH, 2nd Viscount, a Gen in the Army and Capt of the Yeomen of the Guard; *dsp* 1782; *s* by his nephew (3) GEORGE EVELYN, 3rd Viscount, son of Adm Hon Edward, 2nd son of 1st Viscount; Capt of Band of Gentlemen-at-Arms; *d* 1808; *s* by his son (4) EDWARD, 4th Viscount; *cr Earl of Falmouth* 1821; *d* 1841; *s* by his son (5) GEORGE HENRY, 2nd Earl; *d* 1852, when the earldom became extinct, and the viscountcy devolved upon his cousin (6) EVELYN, 6th Viscount, son of Rev Hon John Evelyn, 2nd son of 3rd Viscount, *b* 1819: *m* 1845, Mary Frances Elizabeth, in her own right Baroness Le Despencer; *d* 1889; *s* by his el son (7) EVELYN EDWARD THOMAS, KCVO, CB, 7th Viscount, *b* 1847; Maj-Gen in the Army; *s* as 24th Baron Le Despencer 1891 (see *infra*): *m* 1886, Hon Kathleen Douglas-Pennant, who *d* 1953, da of 2nd Baron Penrhyn; *d* 1918; *s* by his el son (8) EVELYN HUGH JOHN, 8th Viscount; *b* 1887; Alderman of London Co Council 1931-7: *m* 1915, Mary Margaret Desirée, CBE, who *d* 1985, da of late Hon Frederick George Lindley Meynell; *d* 1962; *s* by his 2nd son (9) GEORGE HUGH, 9th Viscount and present peer; also Baron Boscawen-Rose, and Baron Le Despencer.

*(1) HUGH Le Despencer, summoned to Parliament of England 1264 and constituted Justiciary of England; *k* at battle of Evesham 1265; *s* by his son (2) HUGH, 2nd Baron; summoned to Parliament 1283-1326; *cr Earl of Winchester* 1322; was banished the realm 1321; and being subsequently recalled was beheaded Oct 1326 without the formality of a trial; *s* by his son (3) HUGH, Knt, 3rd Baron; summoned to Parliament 1314-25, and *cr Earl of Gloucester*, was Lord Chamberlain to Edward II, and Warden of Forest of Dean; in Nov 1326 he was beheaded, and his honours forfeited; his el son (4) HUGH, commonly called Lord Glamorgan, was summoned to Parliament 1338-49; *dsp* 1349; *s* by his nephew (5) EDWARD, KG, 5th Baron; summoned to Parliament 1357-72; *d* 1375; *s* by his son (6) THOMAS, 6th Baron; summoned to Parliament 1396 and *cr Earl of Gloucester* 1397; declared a traitor and beheaded 1400 when his honours were forfeited; his sister, (7) ISABEL, *m* 1st, Richard Beauchamp, Earl of Worcester and Baron Bergavenny, and 2ndly, Richard, 5th Earl of Warwick; by her 1st *m* she had (8) ELIZABETH, who having obtained a reversal of the attainder became Baroness Le Despencer: *m* Sir Edward Neville, KG, 6th son of Ralph, 1st Earl of Westmorland, who was summoned to Parliament, in right of his wife, as Baron Bergavenny 1450-72; on the death of (9-11) HENRY, 4th Baron Bergavenny, that barony passed to the heir male and the Barony of Le Despencer reverted to his da (12) MARY, wife of Sir Thomas Fane, knt, and in 1604 the barony was confirmed to her by letters patent; *d* 1626; *s* by her el son (13-20) FRANCIS, 12th Baron; *cr Baron Burghersh* and *Earl of Westmorland* (peerage of England) 1624; the Barony of Le Despencer was merged in the earldom until 1762 when it became abeyant between the sisters of the 7th Earl; in 1763 the abeyance was terminated in favour of (21) FRANCIS Dashwood, 21st Baron, who had in 1724, *s* by his father as 2nd Bt; was Lord-Lieut of Bucks and Groom of the Stole to HRH the Prince of Wales; *dsp* 1781, when the barony again became abeyant, and continued so until 1788 when it was terminated in favour of (22) THOMAS Stapleton, 22nd Baron, who had in 1781 *s* his father as 6th Bt; *d* 1831; when the baronetcy reverted to his 4th son, and the barony descended to his granddaughter (23) MARY FRANCES ELIZABETH (only child of Hon Thomas, el son of 22nd Baron, by Maria Wynne, da of Henry Bankes, of Kingston Hall, Dorset), *b* 1822: *m* 1845, the 6th Viscount Falmouth, who *d* 1889; *d* 1891; *s* by her el son (24) EVELYN EDWARD THOMAS, KCVO, CB, 7th Viscount Falmouth (ante).

Fane, family name of Earl of Westmorland.

FANSHAWE OF RICHMOND, BARON (Royle) (Life Baron 1983)

ANTHONY HENRY FANSHAWE ROYLE, KCMG, el son of late Sir Lancelot Carrington Royle, KBE; *b* 27 March 1927; *ed* Harrow, and RMA Sandhurst; PPS to Under-Sec of State for the Colonies 1960, to Sec of State for Air 1960-62, and to Min of Aviation 1962-64; Conservative Whip 1967-70; Parly Under-Sec of State for Foreign and Commonwealth Affairs 1970-74; Vice-Chm Conservative Party Organisation and Chm Conservative Internat Office 1979-84; Member Assembly of Council of Europe and WEU 1965-67; late Capt Life Guards, served in Germany, Egypt, Palestine and Transjordan 1945-48, and with 21st SAS (TA) 1948-51; MP for Richmond, Surrey (*C*) 1959-83; has Most Esteemed Family Order of the State of Brunei (1st class); *cr* KCMG 1974, and *Baron Fanshawe of Richmond*, of South Cerney, co Glos (Life Baron) 1983: *m* 1957, Shirley, da of late John Ramsay Worthington, and has issue.

Arms – Quarterly, 1st and 4th, per pale or and sable on a chevron per pale sable and or between three fleurs-de-lys as many leopards' heads counterchanged, *Royle*; 2nd, or a chevron between three fleurs-de-lys sable, *Fanshawe*; 3rd, checky azure and argent overall a cross gules, *Fanshawe augmentation* 1649. Crest – on a chapeau sable turned up erminois, a dragon's head erased or, breathing flames of fire proper. Supporters – Two dragons or, winged sable each breathing flames of fire and gorged with a collar checky argent and azure rimmed gules. Motto – Dux Vitae Ratio in Cruce Victoria (Leadership in Life Depends on Victory in the Cross).
Residences – 42 Cadogan Place, SW1; The Chapter Manor, South Cerney, Glos.
Clubs – White's, Pratt's, Brooks's.

DAUGHTERS LIVING

Hon Susannah Caroline Fanshawe, *b* 1960: *m* 1992, Guy C. Lester, yr son of Gerald Lester, of Rowledge, Hants.
Hon Lucinda Katherine Fanshawe, *b* 1962.

FARINGDON, BARON (Henderson) (Baron UK 1916, UK 1902)

Virtue alone ennobles

CHARLES MICHAEL HENDERSON, 3rd Baron, and 3rd Baronet; *b* 3 July 1937; *s* 1977; *ed* Eton, and Trin Coll, Camb (BA); a Lord in Waiting to HM since 1998: *m* 1959, Sarah Caroline, da of late Maj John Marjoribanks Askew, CBE, Gren Gds (*see* D Sutherland), and has issue.

𝕬rms – Or, three piles issuant from the sinister vert, on a chief ermine three torteaux. 𝕮rest – A hand holding a torteau charged with a mullet of six points argent. 𝕾upporters – *Dexter*, a chevalier armed at all points, holding in his dexter hand a lance with his lordship's pennon, bearing the motto "Sursum corda," all proper; *sinister*, a centaur drawing his bow proper.
Seat – Buscot Park, Faringdon, Oxon.

SONS LIVING

Hon JAMES HAROLD, *b* 14 July 1961: *m* 1986, Lucinda Maria, yst da of late Desmond Hanson, of Knipton, nr Grantham, Lincs, and has issue living, George Alexander *b* 18 May 1992, — Frederick Walter, *b* 1995, — Annabel Rose, *b* 1989. *Residence* – Eaton Grange, Eaton, nr Grantham, Lincs NG32 1ET

Hon Thomas Alexander Gavin, *b* 1966: *m* 1997, Eve Caroline, only da of Jean-Pierre Crame, and Mme Michel Bridart. *Residence* – Barnsley Park, Cirencester, Glos.

Hon Angus George, *b* 1969: *m* 1997, Alexia Jane, only da of R. H. Hedley, of Chagford, Devon. *Residence* – 3a Clarendon Rd, W11.

DAUGHTER LIVING

Hon Susannah Jane, *b* 1963: *m* 1986, Aidan James Maitland-Robinson, yst son of late Joseph W. C. Maitland-Robinson, and has issue living, Joseph Charles, *b* 1989, — Samuel James, *b* 1994, — Joanna Alice, *b* 1987, — Sarah Florence, *b* 1990, — Helena Susan, *b* 1992.

COLLATERAL BRANCHES LIVING

Grandchildren of late Hon Alec Puleston Henderson (infra):—
Issue of late Capt Ian Alexander Henderson, *b* 1918, *d* 1968: *m* 1st, (*m diss* 1955), Patience, da of late Lt-Col John Charles Brand, DSO, MC (*see* V Hampden, colls); 2ndly 1955, Sarah Veronica (Westmeads, Butlers Marston, Warwickshire), da of late Cosmo Stafford Crawley (Crawley-Boevey, Bt, colls):—
(By 1st *m*) Veronica, *b* 1946: *m* 1967, Oliver Alexander Guy Baring (*see* B Ashburton, colls). —— (By 2nd *m*) Shamus Alec, *b* 1958: *m* 1986, Camilla Carolyn, da of Robert Ashton Adams, of 139 Prospect Terr, North Hill, N6, and has issue living, James Archie, *b* 1988, — Laura Natasha, *b* 1990.

Issue of late Adrian Donald Henderson, *b* 1922, *d* 1994: *m* 1st, 1944 (*m diss* 1958), Marieluz, da of late Capt Robert Peel Dennistoun-Webster, DSC, RN, of Hurst Grange, nr Twyford; 2ndly, 1959, Mrs Angela Mary Oriana Harrington Pollen, who *d* 1990, eldest da of Maj Felix John Russi, MC, 5th Royal Inniskilling Dragoons:—
(By 1st wife) †Gavin Adrian Alexander, *b* 1944; *ed* Eton: *m* 1984, Juliet Victoria (Littleton House, W Littleton, Chippenham, Wilts SN15 3RT), yr da of late Maj Sir Mark Baring, KCVO (*see* E Cromer, colls), and *d* 1991, leaving issue, Violet Gweneth, *b* 1985. —— Mark Alistair, *b* 1946; *ed* The Oratory Sch, Reading. —— (By 2nd wife) Alexander Jonathan, *b* 1962: *m* 1987, Fiona Mary, yr da of David McLeod, of Park House, Old Hunstanton, Norfolk, and has issue living, a da, *b* 1995. —— Victoria Angela, *b* 1956: *m* 1979, John Jeremy Campbell Underwood, of 39 Herondale Av, SW18 3JN, and has issue living, James Michael Campbell, *b* 1981, — Toby George Campbell, *b* 1984. —— Fiona Mary, *b* (twin) 1962: *m* 1988, Antony William Dodd-Noble (*see* E Cork, 1980 Edn).

Issue (by 2nd *m*) of late Hon Alec Puleston Henderson, 2nd son of 1st Baron, *b* 1876, *d* 1931: *m* 1st, 1905, Henrietta Emily Cecil, who *d* 1913, da of late Capt Frederick Arthur Bertie (E Abingdon, colls); 2ndly, 1915, Gladys Rhoda, who *d* 1953, having *m* 2ndly, 1934, as his 2nd wife, Sir Murrough John Wilson, KBE, of Cliffe Hall, Darlington (B Inchiquin, colls), only child of late Major Donald Maclean:—
Susan Violet, *b* 1915: *m* 1st, 1936, Capt Mark Leslie Pilkington, MC, Life Guards, who was *ka* 1942; 2ndly, 1943, Fl Lt Charles Pretzlik, RAFVR, and has issue living (by 1st *m*), Simon Mark (Orchard House, Little London, Broad Chalke, Salisbury, Wilts SP5 5HL), *b* 1938: *m* 1963, Angela Mary Monica, da of late Lord Patrick Crichton-Stuart (*see* M Bute, colls), and has issue living, Rupert Charles *b* 1964, Mark Patrick *b* 1965, Jane Susan *b* 1966, Kate Sophie *b* 1970, — (by 2nd *m*) Nicholas Charles (44 Hornton St W8), *b* 1945: *m* 1970, Ursula Scheuring, and has issue living, Charles Oliver *b* 1971, Luke Nicholas *b* 1972, — Jacqueline Susan, *b* 1944: *m* 1970, Peter Raine, of 57 Chesilton Rd, SW6, and has issue living, Simon Patrick Wallace *b* 1973, Nancy Susan Wallace *b* 1971. *Residence* – Millers House, Isington, Hants.

Grandsons of late Lt-Col Hon Philip Henderson (infra):—
Issue of late David Hope Henderson, *b* 1912, *d* 1977: *m* 1st, 1935 (*m diss* 1938), Alice Reed Rawle, da of Antony Geyelin, of Philadelphia, USA; 2ndly, 1945, Eleanora Anderson (Achie Farm, New Galloway, Kirkcudbrightshire), da of Maj David Anderson Spence, VD, Black Watch, of Dunninald Mains, Montrose:—
(By 2nd *m*) Philip David Hope (21 Bowerdean St, SW6), *b* 1947; *ed* Eton, and RAC Cirencester; FRICS. —— Ian Ramsay Hope (20 Westbourne Park Rd, W2), *b* 1949; *ed* Eton, and Edinburgh Univ (MA, LLB); FCA: *m* 1978, Virginia Phyllis Theresa, yr da of Lt-Col John Edward Broke Freeman (*see* D Norfolk), and has issue living, Alexander Storm David Hope, *b* 1982, — Charles John Bernard Hope, *b* 1984, — George Ian Henry Hope, *b* 1987.

Issue of late Lieut-Col Hon Philip Henderson, 4th son of 1st Baron, b 1881, d 1939: m 1908, Rachel
Magdaleine Mary, who d 1953, da of late James Charles Hope-Vere (M Linlithgow, colls):—
Ralph Alexander, b 1923; ed Eton, and Trin Coll, Camb; was 3rd Sec at British Embassy Lisbon 1945-46: m 1950,
Myriam, who d 1987, da of late Adm A. de Souza e Silva, Brazilian Navy, of Rio de Janeiro, and has had issue, Ralph
Peter, b 1951: m 1977, Maria Elisa, da of Luiz Pessoa de Luna, of Rio de Janeiro, — †Charles James (twin), b 1951: m
1983 (m diss 1989), Alice, da of Herly Sampaio Vitor, and d 1994, San Paulo, Brazil, — Lavinia Magdaleine Marie, b
1954: m 1975, Pedro Rabello Cotrim, and has issue living Nelson b 1977, Cecilia b 1978. Residence – Rua Santa Clara 47,
Apt 1201, Copacabana, Rio de Janeiro, Brazil. Club – Boodle's.

Grandchildren of late Hon Arnold Henderson, OBE, 5th son of 1st Baron:—
Issue of late Flight-Lieut Roger Arnold Henderson, RAF Vol Reserve, b 1909, d on active ser 1941: m 1934,
Judith Violet Christine (who d 1966, having m 2ndly, 1946, Robert Edward Manifold, of Wiridgil, Camperdown,
Victoria, Australia), da of Edmund Thornley, of Gnotuk, Camperdown, Australia:—
David Arnold Thornley (Koorrnong, Tarcutta, NS Wales 2652), b 1937: m 1962, Sophie Jacqueline Fern Welsh, and has
issue living, Roger David, b 1963, — Nicholas John Welsh, b 1964, — Anna Jacqueline Judith, b 1966. —— Davina
Christina, b 1935: m 1st, 1961 (m diss 1974), Dr Peter Kaye Bryan; 2ndly, 1974, Richard Lawrence Baillieu, of Clondrisse,
Flinders, Vic 3929, Aust, and has issue living (by 1st m), Roger Jon, b 1961: m 1998, Isabelle Ann, da of Frederick
Berglas, of Bardfield Place, Sunningdale, Ascot, — Christopher Peter, b 1968: m 1999, Emma Sarah, da of Robert Roland
Day, of Gate House Farm, Marden, Kent, — Rebecca Alexandra, b 1963: m 1990, Nigel Richard Drake Trinca, of 341
Auburn Rd, Hawthorn, Vic 3122, 3rd son of Dr Geoffrey Francis Trinca, and has issue living, Lucy Elizabeth Davina b
1993, Celia Madeline b 1995, Emily Rebecca b 1998.

Grandchildren of late Hon Eric Brand Butler-Henderson (infra):—
Issue of late Major Lionel Butler-Henderson, b 1911, d 1961: m 1936, Una, who d 1992, da of late Guy
Fenwick:—
Guy (Beckfield House, Sandon, Buntingford, Herts), b 1948: m 1st, 1968 (m diss 1975), Glynis, da of Kenneth Bladon;
2ndly, 1977, Valerie, elder da of late Thomas Taylor, of Cheshire, and formerly wife of John Arthur Handforth, and has
issue living (by 1st m) Timothy, b 1971, — Gemma, b 1975, — (by 2nd m) Charles Guy, b 1978. —— Jane, b 1938: m
1st, 1957 (m diss 1967), John Guy Mercer; 2ndly, 1968 (m diss 19—), George Frederick Hewitt; 3rdly, 1979, Albert
George Etheridge, of Wheelers Stud, Peasenhall, Suffolk, and has issue living (by 1st m), Christopher John, b 1960, —
Belinda, b 1958, — (by 2nd m) Antony George, b 1970, — (by 3rd m) Susan, b 1980.

Issue of late Patrick Butler-Henderson, RAFVR, b 1913, d 1979: m 1st, 1943 (m diss 1963), Kathleen Rebe Curtis
(Section Officer late WAAF), da of late Lt-Col Herman Curtis Clarke, CBE, DSO; 2ndly, 1968, Mrs Pamela L.
Godrich (Apple Tree Cottage, Quenington, Glos GL7 5BW):—
(By 1st m) Eric Alexander (The Old Thatch, Stanway, Cheltenham, Glos), b 1946: m 1st, 1970, Leslie Hallingan; 2ndly,
1993, Pauline Ann Lowe, and has issue living (by 1st m), Chad Stuart, b 1976, — Kerryn, b 1975. —— Christine, b 1944:
m 1st, 1971, Maj Neil James Cameron Sutherland, Queen's Own Highlanders; 2ndly, 1981, Julian Russell Sturgis (see
Borthwick, Bt, colls, 1995 Edn), and has issue living (by 1st m), Alasdair Patrick Cameron, b 1972, — Rachel Bridget, b
1974, — (by 2nd m), Hugh Russell, b 1983. —— Amalia Zoe, b 1945: m 1970, Capt Simon Brian Taylor, of Glenlivet
House, By Ballindalloch, Banffshire AB37 9DJ (see Smith-Dodsworth, Bt, 1990 Edn), and has issue living, Emma Amalia
Jane, b 1971: m 1993, Tswang Topgal, and has issue living, Tsering Edward b 1996, — Amanda Katherine Zoe, b 1973,
— (Hilda) Penelope Beatrice, b 1976.

Issue of late Hon Eric Brand BUTLER-HENDERSON, yst son of 1st Baron, b 1884, d 1953, having assumed
by deed poll 1910 the additional surname of Butler: m 1910, Hon Sophia Isabelle (Zoe) Butler-Massey,
who d 1977, da of 5th Baron Clarina:—
Edward, b 1916; ed Eton; late Lt-Col 99th (Royal Bucks Yeo) Field Regt, RA (TA): m 1939, Elizabeth Marjorie Dacres,
who d 1988, only da of late Henry George Dacres Dixon (see E Yarborough, colls, 1985 Edn), and has issue living, Alan
(The Ridings, Lot 1772 DD 221, Sha Ha Rd, Sai Kung, Hong Kong), b 1943: m 1st, 1964 (m diss 1975), Maria Cassy
Ugena; 2ndly, 1975, Jacqueline Wright, and has issue living (by 1st m), David James b 1967, Elizabeth Cassy b 1965, (by
2nd m) Benjamin b 1976, Jason b 1982, — Penelope, b 1940: m 1962, Ian Alan Douglas Pilkington, of Warennes Wood,
Mortimer, Berks, and has issue living, Rory Ian Douglas b 1968: m 1999, Alexandra Ormsby, of Sydney, NSW, Camilla
Douglas b 1966: m 1990, Angus Charles Gordon Lennox, and has issue (see D Richmond and Gordon, colls), Sarah
Douglas b 1973. Residence – 3 West Halkin St, SW1X 8JJ. —— Kenneth (11 Egerton Place, SW3 2EF), b 1929; ed Eton:
m 1952, Phyllis Daphne, da of late Lt-Col Alfred Edward Cartmel, CIE, MM, and has issue living, Julian, b 1956: m 1st,
1980 (m diss 1988), Bridget Anne, da of James Robert Patrick Sullivan, of Wyndrush, Stoke Orchard, nr Cheltenham,
Glos; 2ndly, 1990 (m diss 1996), Adina, da of late Peter Smallwood, of Witney, Oxon, and has issue living (by 1st m),
Oliver Stephen b 1982, — Serina, b 1953: m 1990, Arthur Eugene Burland, late Queen's Royal Irish Hus, and has issue
living, Heloise Alice b 1991, — Clare, b 1954. —— Doreen (The Old Post House, Mawley Rd, Quenington, Cirencester,
Glos GL7 5BH), b 1920: m 1st, 1939 (m diss 1961), John Gordon Wordsworth, OBE, late Lt-Col Suffolk Regt, who d
1995; 2ndly, 1962, Gp Capt William Digby Blackwood, OBE, DFC, RAF, who d 1993, and has issue living, (by 1st m)
Antony Christopher Curwen (Little Brockholds Farm, Radwinter, Saffron Walden, Essex CB10 2TF), b 1940: m 1962,
Rosamond Anne, eldest da of Maj John David Summers, and has issue living, Mark Edward Curwen (32 Flanchford Rd,
W12 9ND) b 1965: m 1991, Eleanor Margaret, only da of late Ian Mapherson, of Broughton, Hants (and has issue living,
Edward Ian Curwen b 1997, Alice Lucy b 1995), (Katherine) Lucy b 1968: m 1993, Nicholas A. K. Brown, elder son of
Michael Brown, of Edinburgh and Hong Kong (and has issue living, Patrick Alexander Kennedy b 1996), Evelyn Mary b
1972: m 1998, Jonathan Shillington, elder son of Anthony Shillington, of The Glebe House, Shalstone, Bucks, — Michael
(Marsh Court, Eldersfield, nr Gloucester GL19 4PN), b 1942: m 1966, Christine Stella Lear, and has issue living, Giles
Patrick John b 1969, Zara Caroline b 1972, — Charles William, b 1946: m 1968, Maria Reyes Garcia Contillo, and has
issue living Alexander Carlos b 1978, Cristina b 1970, Veronica b 1975, — Peter John, b 1949: m 1979, Joan, da of T. W.
Hannigan, of Newcastle-upon-Tyne, and has issue living, Caroline Louise b 1980, Emma Harriet b 1984.

PREDECESSORS – (1) ALEXANDER Henderson, CH, son of late George Henderson, of Langholm, Dumfries; b 1850; MP
for W Div of Staffordshire (LU) 1898-1906, and for St George, Hanover Square 1913-15; cr a Baronet 1902, and Baron
Faringdon, of Buscot Park, co Berks (peerage of United Kingdom) 1916: m 1874, Jane Ellen, who d 1920, da of late
Edward William Davis, d 1934; s by his grandson (2) ALEXANDER GAVIN (son of late Lieut-Col Hon Harold Greenwood
Henderson, CVO, el son of 1st Baron, and late Lady Violet Charlotte Dalzell, da of 12th Earl of Carnwath (ext)), 2nd
Baron, b 1902; a Member of LCC 1958-61 and an Alderman 1961-65: m 1927 (m annulled 1931), Hon Honor Chedworth
Philipps, who d 1961, da of 1st Baron Kylsant (ext); d 1977; s by his nephew (3) CHARLES MICHAEL (son of late Lt-Col
Hon Michael Thomas Henderson, 16th/5th Lancers, 2nd son of 1st Baron), 3rd Baron, and present peer.

FARNHAM BARON (Maxwell) (Baron I 1756, Bt NS 1627)

I am ready

BARRY OWEN SOMERSET MAXWELL, 12th Baron and 14th Baronet; *b* 7 July 1931; *s* 1957; *ed* Eton, and at Harvard Univ; late Lieut Roy Horse Guards; Chm of Brown, Shipley & Co, Merchant Bankers, EC2 1984-91 (Dir 1959-91); Chm Brown Shipley Holdings 1976-91; Chm Avon Rubber plc 1978-97 (Dir 1966-97); Chm Provident Mutual Life Assurance Assocn 1989-95 (Dir 1967-95); Dir The London Clinic since 1979; Pro Grand Master United Grand Lodge of England since 1991; Pres Tree Council since 1992: *m* 1959, Diana Marion, CVO, a Lady of the Bedchamber to HM since 1987, a JP, el da of late Nigel Eric Murray Gunnis, of Branden, Sissinghurst, Kent (*see* B Trevor, 1962 Edn), and has two adopted das.

𝕬rms – Quarterly: 1st and 4th, argent, a saltire sable, on a chief of the first three pallets of the second, *Maxwell*, 2nd and 3rd, barry of six argent and gules, *Barry*. 𝕮rest – A buck's head erased proper. 𝕾upporters – Two bucks proper.
Residences – Farnham, co Cavan; 11 Earls Court Gdns, SW5 0TD. *Clubs* – Boodle's, Kildare St, and University (Dublin).

ADOPTED DAUGHTERS LIVING

Harriet Virginia, *b* 1964: *m* 1990, James D. H. Naylor, eldest son of David Naylor, of Oakridge Lynch, Glos, and has issue living, Henry James Huntly, *b* 1995, — Araminta Sheelin Huntly, *b* 1993.
Sophia Mary, *b* 1967.

BROTHER LIVING (*Raised to the rank of a Baron's son* 1959)

Hon SIMON KENLIS, *b* 12 Dec 1933; *ed* Eton; late Lieut 10th Roy Hussars: *m* 1964, Karol Anne, da of late Maj-Gen George Erroll Prior-Palmer, CB, DSO, and has issue living, Robin Somerset, *b* 1965: *m* 1993, Tessa M., da of David Shepherd, of Stansted, Essex, and has issue living, James David Somerset *b* 1996, Isabella Emily *b* 1995, — Mark Erroll, *b* 1968, — Lorna Suzanna Katherine (twin) *b* 1968. *Residence* – The Dower House, Westcote, nr Chipping Norton, Oxon OX7 6SF.

SISTER LIVING (*Raised to the rank of a Baron's daughter* 1959)

Hon Sheelin Virginia (*Viscountess Knollys*), *b* 1937; DL Norfolk 1996: *m* 1959, 3rd Viscount Knollys. *Residence* – The Bailiff's House, Bramerton Hall Farm, Norwich, Norfolk NR14 7DN.

COLLATERAL BRANCH LIVING

Issue of late Vice-Adm Hon Sir Denis Crichton Maxwell, KCB, CBE, yst son of 10th Baron, *b* 1892, *d* 1970: *m* 1923, Theodora Mary, who *d* 1986, da of Arthur Hickling, of Wing Old Hall, Rutland:—
Elizabeth Crichton, *b* 1926: *m* 1953 (*m diss* 19—), Ivor Mabberley, of Wanborough, Wilts.

PREDECESSORS – (1) JOHN MAXWELL, MP for co Cavan 1727-56; *cr Baron Farnham*, of Farnham, co Cavan (peerage of Ireland) 1756; *d* 1759; *s* by his cl son (2) ROBERT, 2nd Baron; *cr Viscount Farnham* (peerage of Ireland) 1761, and *Earl of Farnham* (peerage of Ireland) 1763; *dsp* when the Viscountcy and Earldom expired, and the Barony reverted to his brother (3) BARRY, 3rd Baron; *cr Viscount Farnham* (peerage of Ireland) 1781, and *Earl of Farnham* (peerage of Ireland) 1785, *d* 1800, s by his son (4) JOHN JAMES, 2nd Earl; *dsp* 1823, when the Viscountcy and Earldom expired, and the Barony devolved upon his kinsman (5) JOHN MAXWELL BARRY, 5th Baron el son of the Most Rev Hon Henry, DD, PC, Lord Bishop of Meath, 3rd son of 1st Baron; *dsp* 1838; *s* by his brother (6) *Rev* HENRY, 6th Baron: *m* 1798, Lady Ann Butler, da of 2nd Earl of Carrick; *d* 1838; *s* by his el son (7) HENRY, KP, 7th Baron; successively MP for Cavan, and a Representative Peer; killed with his wife in a dreadful accident on NW Railway at Abergele, 20 Aug 1868; *s* by his brother (8) SOMERSET RICHARD, 8th Baron; *b* 1803; was MP for Cavan (C) 1838-40; *dsp* 1884; *s* by his brother (9) JAMES PIERCE, 9th Baron, *b* 1813; MP for Cavan 1843-65; *s* by his kinsman as 11th *Baronet* (*cr* 1627) of Calderwood 1885; *dsp* 1896; *s* by his nephew (10) SOMERSET HENRY (son of late Hon Richard Maxwell, 7th son of 6th Baron), 10th Baron; *b* 1849; Lieut of co Cavan, and a Representative Peer for Ireland: *m* 1875, Lady Florence Jane Taylour, who *d* 1907, da of 3rd Marquess of Headfort: *d* 1900; *s* by his son (11) ARTHUR KENLIS, DSO, 11th Baron; *b* 1879; Lieut-Col (ret) late N Irish Horse, and a Representative Peer: *m* 1903, Aileen Selina, who *d* 1964, da of late Charles Purdon Coote (*see* Coote, Bt, colls); *d* 1957; *s* by his grandson (12) BARRY OWEN SOMERSET (el son of late Lieut-Col Hon Somerset Arthur Maxwell, MP), 12th Baron and present peer.

FARRINGTON OF RIBBLETON, BARONESS (Farrington) (Life Baroness 1994)

JOSEPHINE FARRINGTON, da of late Ernest Joseph Cayless; *b* 29 June 1940; Memb of Preston Borough Council 1973-76, and of Lancashire County Council since 1977; Vice-Chm Association of County Councils 1990-94, since when Chm; Baroness in Waiting to HM (Govt Whip) since 1997; *cr Baroness Farrington of Ribbleton*, of Fulwood, co Lancs (Life Baroness) 1994: *m* 1960, Michael James Farrington, son of Leonard James Farrington, and has issue, three sons.
Residence – 114 Victoria Rd, Fulwood, Preston, Lancs PR2 4NN.

FAUCONBERG AND CONYERS, BARONIES OF (Pelham) (Baron E 1283 and 1509) (Abeyant 1948)

SACKVILLE GEORGE PELHAM, 5th Earl of Yarborough, 8th Baron Fauconberg, and 14th Baron Conyers; *d* 1948, when the Baronies fell into abeyance (see infra).

DAUGHTERS LIVING OF EIGHTH BARON FAUCONBERG AND FOURTEENTH BARON CONYERS (FIFTH EARL OF YARBOROUGH) (*Co-heiresses to the Baronies*)

Lady DIANA MARY (c/o Zimbank, Box 2270, Harare, Zimbabwe), *b* 5 July 1920; SRN: *m* 1952, Robert Miller, who *d* as the result of a motor accident in Harare 1990, and has issue living, Marcia Anne LYCETT, *b* 1954; adopted by Maj Michael H. L. Lycett (infra) (and renamed Anthea Theresa), whose surname she assumed, but retains right of succession to the Baronies, — Beatrix Diana, *b* 1955: *m* 1991, Simon William Jones Armstrong (Box 49, Gilgil, Kenya), only son of late Christopher Wyborne Armstrong, OBE, of Kwetu Farm, Gilgil, Kenya, and has issue living, Guy William Robert *b* 1996, Matthew Charles *b* 1998.

Lady (JUNE) WENDY, *b* 6 June 1924; late 3rd Officer WRNS; Joint Master Tynedale Hunt 1974-77: *m* 1959, Maj Michael Hildesley Lycett Lycett, CBE, late Royal Scots Greys, Joint Master Tynedale Hunt 1975-77. *Residence* – West Grange, Scots Gap, Morpeth, Northumberland NE61 4EQ.

COLLATERAL BRANCHES LIVING

> Grandchildren of late Charlotte Katherine Marcia Weld-Blundell, daughter of late Hon Charles Pierrepont D'Arcy Lane-Fox, brother of 15th Baron Darcy de Knayth and great-grandson of Amelia, Baroness Conyers and *de jure* Baroness Darcy de Knayth:—
> Issue of late Richard Shireburn Weld-Blundell, *b* 1887, *d* 1916: *m* 1915, Mary Angela (who *d* 1976, having *m* 2ndly, 1927, Alfred Noyes, CBE, who *d* 1958), da of late Capt Jasper Graham Mayne, CBE, Ch Constable of E Suffolk;—
> Agnes Mary (*Lady Grey*), *b* 1915: *m* 1936, Sir Paul Francis Grey, KCMG (*see* E Grey, colls). *Residence* – Holmwood, Elstead, Godalming, Surrey.

> Issue of late Alice Mary, *b* 1890, *d* 1947: *m* 1923, John Joseph Humphrey Weld, of Birkdale, Lancs, who *d* 1960, having assumed by Royal licence 1923, the additional surname of Blundell:—
> Charles Joseph Ignatius WELD-BLUNDELL (Pinehurst, Tongland, Kirkcudbright DG6 4NA), *b* 1928; *ed* Stonyhurst; Lt Gren Gds; High Sheriff Lancs 1989: *m* 1951, Veronica Mary, da of late Alfred Noyes, CBE (ante), and has issue living, John Joseph Thomas (Leagram Park, Chipping, nr Preston, Lancs PR3 2RD), *b* 1955; *ed* Stonyhurst, and RAC: *m* 1979, Geneveive Margaret, who *d* 1996, da of Charles Plunkett, of W Australia, and has issue living, Stacy John *b* 1984, Kimberley Joe (a son) *b* 1986, — Peter Alfred (7 Tamar St, Preston, Lancs PR1 4GX), *b* 1956; *ed* Stonyhurst: *m* 1977 (*m diss* 19—), Janet, da of — Lock, and has issue living, two children, — George Edric (Loud Mythom, Little Bowland Rd, Chipping, nr Preston, Lancs PR3 2TS), *b* 1960; *ed* Ampleforth, and Liverpool Univ (BSc): *m* 1985, Buddug L......, da of G...... Selwyn-Lloyd, of Grasmere, Linden Drive, Prestatyn, and has issue living, Joseph Charles *b* 1993, Laura Sian *b* 1987, Philippa Kate *b* 1989, — Richard Charles (16 Greville Rd, Rosanna, Vic 3084, Australia), *b* 1964; *ed* Ampleforth: *m* 1988, Julie Louise, only da of late Donald Stewart, of Melbourne, Australia, and has issue living, Charlotte May *b* 1992, Isabelle Veronica *b* 1998, — Thomas Andrew, *b* 1967; *ed* Ampleforth, — Mary Alice, *b* 1952, — Lucy Ann, *b* 1953: *m* 1979, Jean-Pierre Vidal Bartoli, of 14 Route de L'Annonciade, Menton, France, and has issue living, Christopher John *b* 1982, Kevin Michel *b* 1988, Stephanie Nicole *b* 1984, — Diana Celia, *b* 1958: *m* 1990, Charles E. Hothersall, of Windsmoor House, Calder Vale, Preston PR3 1SR, and has issue living, Lydia *b* 1996, Sophia Rose *b* 1999, — Fiona Ann, *b* 1962: *m* 1991, Robert Armstrong, of 13 Lodge Av, E Cosham, Portsmouth PO6 2AA, — Elizabeth, *b* 1969: *m* 1994, Gary Pollington, of Little Baddow, nr Chelmsford, Essex, and has issue living, Thomas *b* 1999, Victoria Louise *b* 1996.
> —— Theresa Mary Katharine (10 Archery Steps, St George's Fields, W2 2YF), *b* 1926; Dame of Honour and Devotion, Sovereign Mil Order of Malta. —— Mary Geraldine, *b* 1930: *m* 1957, Antony St John Davies, of 30 Glentham Rd, Barnes, SW13, and has issue living, Benedict Antony John Whitcliffe, *b* 1960. — Simon, *b* 1963. — Hermione Anne, *b* 1958. —— Anne Mary, *b* 1933: *m* 1960, Thomas Frederick de Pentheny-O'Kelly, of 2 Grange Rd, Yelverton, Devon PL20 6BJ, and has issue living, Edmund Thomas, *b* 1962, — Maureen Louise, *b* 1961, — Carmel Anne, *b* 1964, — Mary Clare, *b* 1967.

PREDECESSORS – (1) Walter de Fauconberg, son of Walter de Fauconberg of Ryse; summoned to Parliament by various writs, the earliest being in 1283, signed the famous letter of the Barons to the Pope in 1301; *d* 1304; *s* by his son (2) WALTER; summoned to Parliament 1303-1318; *d* 1318; *s* by his son (3) JOHN; *d* 1349; *s* by his son (4) WALTER; *d* 1362; *s* by his son (5) THOMAS; *d* leaving an only da and heiress (6) JOAN, *suo jure* Baroness Fauconberg: *m* Sir William Nevill, yr son of the Earl of Westmorland, who was summoned to Parliament and sat therein as *Lord Fauconberg* in right of his wife; distinguished himself greatly in the French Wars and at the siege of Orleans; KG and Adm of England; *cr Earl of Kent* 1461; *d* without male issue in 1463, when the Earldom became extinct; at the death of his wife (1491) the Barony of Fauconberg fell into abeyance between his da and co-heirs, and so remained until 1903, when it was determined by Letters Patent in favour of (7) MARCIA AMELIA MARY, OBE, Countess of Yarborough, she and her sister the Countess of Powis (in whose favour the Barony of Darcy de Knayth was at the same time determined) being the sole heirs of Alice, yr da and co-heiress of Joan, Lady Fauconberg and Countess of Kent, which Alice *m* Sir John Conyers of Hornby, and had issue William, 1st Baron Conyers (see *infra); b* 1863: *m* 1886, 4th Earl of Yarborough; *d* 1926; *s* by her yr son (8) SACKVILLE GEORGE, 8th Baron Fauconberg, 14th Baron Conyers, and 5th Earl of Yarborough; *b* 1888; Lieut-Col Comdg Notts Yeo (Sherwood Rangers); European War 1914-19 (MC), European War 1939-45: *m* 1919, Nancye, da of late Alfred Brocklehurst; *d* 1948, when he was *s* in the Earldom by his brother and the Baronies of Fauconberg and Conyers fell into abeyance between his two das (scc ante).

*(1) *Sir* WILLIAM Conyers; served at Flodden Field; summoned to the Parliament of England as *Baron Conyers* 1509; *d* 1524; *s* by his son (2) CHRISTOPHER, 2nd Baron; *d* 1538; *s* by his son (3) JOHN, 3rd Baron; *d* without male issue, when the title went into abeyance between his three daughters; the 2nd da, Elizabeth, *m* Thomas, 2nd son of Sir Arthur D'Arcy, 2nd son of Thomas, Baron D'Arcy, who was attainted and beheaded 1538, and had with other issue (4) CONYERS, 4th Baron, in whose favour the abeyance in the Baronies of Darcy de Knayth (*see* Bs Darcy de Knayth) and Conyers were determined by letters patent 1641; *d* 1653; *s* by his son (5) CONYERS, 5th Baron; *cr* 1682 *Earl of Holderness; d* 1689; *s* by his son (6) CONYERS, 2nd Earl; *d* 1692; *s* by his grandson (7) ROBERT, 3rd Earl; *d* 1722; *s* by his son (8) ROBERT, 4th Earl; *d* 1778, when the Earldom became extinct, and the Barony of Conyers reverted to his daughter (9) AMELIA, wife of 5th Duke of Leeds; *d* 1784; *s* by her son (10) GEORGE WILLIAM FREDERICK, 10th Baron Conyers and 6th Duke of Leeds; *d* 1838; *s* by his son (11) FRANCIS GODOLPHIN, 11th Baron and 7th Duke; *d* 1859; *s* by his nephew (12) SACKVILLE GEORGE, 12th Baron (son of Sackville Walter Lane-Fox, MP), *b* 1827: *m* 1860, Mary, who *d* 1921, el da of Reginald Curteis, of Windmill Hill, Sussex; *d* 1888, when the title remained in abeyance between his two das, until in 1892 the abeyance was terminated in favour of his el da (13) MARCIA AMELIA MARY, OBE, Countess of Yarborough (ante)

FAULKNER OF DOWNPATRICK, BARONY OF (Faulkner) (Extinct 1977)

SONS LIVING OF LIFE BARON

Hon (Brian) David Alexander, *b* 1951; *ed* Glenalmond, and Aberdeen Univ: *m* 1982, Belinda Gail, el da of James Elliott Wilson, OBE, DL, of White Lodge, Boardmills, co Down, and has issue, two sons, one da.
Hon (James) Michael Sewell, *b* 1956; *ed* Glenalmond, and Aberdeen Univ (LLB): *m* 1990, Lynn, da of John McGregor, of Anstruther, Fife.

DAUGHTER LIVING OF LIFE BARON

Hon Lucy Claire, *b* 1954.

FEATHER, BARONY OF (Feather) (Extinct 1976)

SON LIVING OF LIFE BARON

Hon Harry Alexander (The Mill, Sudborough, Northants), *b* 1938; Master Mariner. *m* 1972, Patricia Lesley, JP, da of Gilbert Victor Green.

DAUGHTER LIVING OF LIFE BARON

Hon Patricia Margaret (24 Wheathampstead Rd, Harpenden, Herts), *b* 1934: *m* 1957, Stanley Lawrence Palmer.

Feilding, family name of Earl of Denbigh.

Feilding, Viscount; son of Earl of Denbigh and Desmond.

FELDMAN, BARON (Feldman) (Life Baron 1995)

BASIL SAMUEL FELDMAN, son of Philip Feldman, of London; b 23 Sept 1926; ed Grocers' Sch; Member Nat Union of Conservative & Unionist Assocs since 1975, Greater London Area Dep Chm 1975-78, Chm 1978-81, Pres 1981-85; Vice Pres Nat Union 1982-85, Pres 1985-86, Chm 1991-96; Chaired 1985 Blackpool Conference; Chm Impact '80's 1982-87; Treas Conservative Party since 1996, among other Conservative appointments; Member GLC Arts Cttee 1976-81, Housing Management 1973-77; Chm Shopping Hours Reform Council 1988-94; Member POUNC 1978-81; Chm Clothing Little Neddy 1978-85, Founder and Chm Better Made in Britain since 1983, Better Business Opportunities since 1990, Quality Mark 1987-92, and Market Opportunities Advisory Group DTI 1991-93; Founder and Chm London Arts Season 1994, Chm Festival of Arts and Culture 1995; Trustee Salzburg Festival Trust since 1997; Member English Tourist Bd 1986-96; Gov Sports Aid Foundation since 1990; Freeman City of London 1984; FRSA 1987; cr Kt 1982, and Baron Feldman, of Frognal in the London Borough of Camden (Life Baron) 1995: m 1952, Gita, da of late Albert Julius, of London, and has issue.

Arms – Per chevron argent guttée de sang and gules guttée d'eau in chief two apple trees eradicated and fructed proper and in base a phoenix rising from flames also proper. Crest – A mount issuant therefrom between two sprigs of basil both flowered a dexter cubit arm the hand grasping a wreath of laurel all proper. Supporters – Dexter, a lion reguardant or holding in the dexter paw a copper handbell and in the mouth a sprig of pink camellia both proper; sinister, a hind reguardant or gorged with a portcullis attached to a chain sable and holding in the mouth a sprig of basil flowered proper.
Address – c/o House of Lords, SW1. Club – Carlton.

SONS LIVING

Hon Nicholas, b 1955; ed Highgate.
Hon Steven, b 1959; ed Highgate.

DAUGHTER LIVING

Hon Alexandra, b 1957; ed N London Collegiate Sch.

Fellowes, family name of Baron Ailwyn.

Fellowes, family name of Baron De Ramsey.

Fermanagh, Baron, title of Earl Erne on Roll of HL.

FERMOY, BARON (Roche) (Baron I 1856)

MON·DIEU·EST·MA·ROCHE

My God is my rock

(PATRICK) MAURICE BURKE ROCHE, 6th Baron; *b* 11 Oct 1967; *s* 1984; *ed* Eton; a Page of Honour to HM Queen Elizabeth The Queen Mother 1982-84; The Blues and Royals 1987-95; with Bass Taverns since 1995: *m* 1998, Mrs Tessa F. Ledger, and has issue.

𝕬rms – Gules, three roach naiant in pale argent, a canton of the last. Crest – Standing on a rock proper, an osprey, or sea eagle, with wings displayed argent, collared gemelle azure, membered or, holding a roach in its claw. Supporters – *Dexter*, a lion erminois, gorged with a collar sable, therefrom pendent an escutcheon gules, charged with three roach naiant in pale argent; *sinister*, a greyhound pean, gorged with a collar or, therefrom pendent an escutcheon per pale of the second and gules, charged with three lions passant guardant in pale counterchanged.
Residences – Nethercote House, Nethercote, Rugby, Warwicks CV23 8AS.

DAUGHTER LIVING

Hon Arabella Elizabeth Burke, *b* 1999.

BROTHER LIVING

Hon (EDMUND) HUGH BURKE, *b* 5 Feb 1972.

SISTER LIVING

Hon Frances Caroline Burke, *b* 1965: *m* 1990, Hon Peter Hugh Charles Stanley (*see* E Derby). *Residence* – New England Stud, Newmarket, Suffolk CB8 0XA.

AUNTS LIVING (*Daughters of 4th Baron*)

Hon Mary Cynthia Burke ROCHE, *b* 1934; resumed her maiden name 1987: *m* 1st, 1954 (*m diss* 1966), Hon Anthony George Berry (later Hon Sir Anthony Berry), who *d* 1984 (*see* V Kemsley); 2ndly, 1973 (*m diss* 1980), Denis Roche Geoghegan; 3rdly, 1981 (*m diss* 1989), Michael Robert Fearon Gunningham. *Residence* – 12M Warwick Sq, SW1V 2AA.
Hon Frances Ruth Burke, *b* 1936: *m* 1st, 1954 (*m diss* 1969), Edward John, Viscount Althorp, LVO (later 8th Earl Spencer), who *d* 1992; 2ndly, 1969 (*m diss* 1990), Peter Shand Kydd. *Residence* – Isle of Seil, by Oban, Argyll.

WIDOW LIVING OF FIFTH BARON

LAVINIA FRANCES ELIZABETH, only da of late Capt John Pitman, of Foxley House, Malmesbury: *m* 1st, 1964, the 5th Baron Fermoy, who *d* 1984; 2ndly, 1995, as his 2nd wife, Nigel Edward Corbally Stourton (*see* B Mowbray, colls). *Residence* – Axford House, nr Marlborough, Wilts.

COLLATERAL BRANCHES LIVING

Grandson of late Hon Alexis Charles Burke Roche, 3rd son of 1st Baron:—
Issue of late Capt George Denis Burke Roche, MC, *b* 1893, *d* 1954: *m* 1921, Aletta S., who *d* 1982, da of M. M. Venter, of Comodoro, Rivadavia, Argentine, and Cape Province:—
Alexis Martin Burke, *b* 1922; Capt RE: *m* 1st, 1945 (*m diss* 1974), Leonora Alice Hudson, who *d* 1985; 2ndly, 1974, Vera Haydee, da of Luis Uffenheimer, and has issue living (by 1st *m*), Rosalie Anne Burke, *b* 1945, — Caroline Jean Burke, *b* 1950, — Christine Lorna Burke, *b* 1956, — (by 2nd *m*) Peter Martin Burke, *b* 1974, — Vanessa Caroline Burke, *b* 1976. *Residence* – Rosales 2571, Olivos, Buenos Aires, Argentina.

Granddaughter of late Col Hon Ulick De Rupé Burke Roche, CB, 4th son of 1st Baron:—
Issue of late Maj Ulick Edmund Burke Roche, S Wales Borderers (24th/41st Foot), *b* 1906, *d* 1990: *m* 1949,

Primrose Eda (Ynysfor, Penrhyndeudraeth, Merionethshire), da of Sir John Karslake Thomas Buchan-Hepburn, 5th Bt:—

Rosemary Evelyn Sybil Burke, *b* 1951: *m* 1982 (*m diss* 1989), Michael Menelaou, and has issue living, Alexander Demitri Burke, *b* 1983, — Nicholas Edmund Burke, *b* 1986.

PREDECESSORS – (1) EDMUND BURKE Roche, *b* 1815; MP for co Cork (*L*) 1837-55, and for Marylebone 1859-65, and Lord Lieut for co Cork; *cr Baron Fermoy* (peerage of Ireland) 1856: *m* 1848, Elizabeth Caroline, who *d* 1897, da of James B. Boothby, Esq, of Twyford Abbey, near Acton; *d* 1874; *s* by his son (2) EDWARD FITZ EDMUND BURKE, 2nd Baron, *b* 1850; *m* 1877, Hon Cecilia O'Grady, who *d* 1919, da of 3rd Viscount Guillamore; *d* 1920; *s* by his brother (3) JAMES BOOTHBY BURKE, 3rd Baron, *b* 1852: *m* 1880 (*m diss* 1891, on her petition to Superior Court, Wilmington, Delaware, USA) Frances, who *d* 1947, da of Frank Work, of New York; *d* 1920; *s* by his el son (4) EDMUND MAURICE, 4th Baron; *b* 1885; sat as MP for King's Lynn Div of Norfolk (*U*) 1924-35, and 1943-5, and was Mayor of King's Lynn 1931-32: *m* 1931, Ruth Sylvia, DCVO, OBE, who *d* 1993, da of late Col William Smith Gill, CB, VD, of Dalhebity, Bieldside, Aberdeenshire; *d* 1955; *s* by his only son (5) EDMUND JAMES BURKE, 5th Baron; *b* 1939; Capt Royal Horse Guards; Dist Councillor (Hungerford), Newbury Dist Council 1975-79, and Mayor of Hungerford 1982-83: *m* 1964, Lavinia Frances Elizabeth (who *m* 2ndly, 1995, Nigel Edward Corbally Stourton) (*see* B Mowbray, colls), only da of late Capt John Pitman, of Foxley House, Malmesbury; *d* 1984; *s* by his elder son (6) (PATRICK) MAURICE BURKE, 6th Baron, 6th Baron and present peer.

Ferrard, Viscount, see Viscount Massereene and Ferrard.

FERRERS, EARL (Shirley) (Earl GB 1711, Bt E 1611)

Honour is the reward of virtue

ROBERT WASHINGTON SHIRLEY, PC, 13th Earl, and 19th Baronet; *b* 8 June 1929; *s* 1954: *ed* Winchester, and Magdalene Coll, Camb (MA Agriculture); late Lieut Coldstream Guards; Malaya 1950; a Lord-in-Waiting to HM 1962-64, and again 1971-74; DL Norfolk 1983; Parl Sec Min of Agric, Fisheries and Food Jan to March 1974; Joint Dep Leader of Opposition, House of Lords 1976-79 and since 1988, Min of State, Min of Agric, Fisheries and Food 1979-83; Dep Leader of House of Lords 1979-83, and 1988-97; Min of State, Home Office 1988-94, Dept of Trade and Industry 1994-95, Min for Environment and Countryside, Dept of Environment 1995-97; Member of Armitage Cttee on Political Activity of Civil Servants 1976; Trustee of Trustee Savings Bank of Eastern England 1975-79 (Chm 1977-79); a Dir of Central Trustee Savings Bank Ltd 1978-79; Dir of Norwich Union Insurance Group 1975-79 and 1983-88; a Member of Council, Hurstpierpoint Coll 1959-68; Dir Chatham Dockyard Historic Trust 1984-88; Chm R Commn on Historical Monuments (England) 1984-88; High Steward, Norwich Cathedral since 1979; Fellow Winchester Coll since 1988, Sub-Warden since 1988; *cr* PC 1982: *m* 1951, Annabel Mary, da of late Brig William Greenwood Carr, CVO, DSO, of Ditchingham Hall, Suffolk, and has had issue.

Arms – Paly of six or and azure, a quarter ermine. **Crest** – A Saracen's head in profile, couped at the neck, proper, wreathed round the temples or and azure. **Supporters** – *Dexter*, a talbot ermine, the ears gules, and ducally gorged or; *sinister*, a reindeer gules, attired and ducally gorged or, billettée and charged on the shoulder with a horse-shoe argent. *Seat* – Shirley, Brailsford, Derbyshire. *Residence* – Ditchingham Hall, Bungay, Suffolk. *Club* – Beefsteak.

SONS LIVING

ROBERT WILLIAM SASWALO (*Viscount Tamworth*) (The Old Vicarage, Shirley, Ashbourne, Derbys DE6 3AZ; *Club* – Boodles), *b* 29 Dec 1952; *ed* Ampleforth; FCA; Ernst and Whinney 1972-86, Group Auditor and Senior Treasury Analyst with BICC plc 1982-86, Financial Controller Viking Property Group Ltd 1986-92 (Dir 1987), Dir Norseman Holdings Ltd and assoc Cos 1987-92; Dir Ruffer Investment Management Ltd since 1994 (Man Dir since 1999); Dir Derbyshire Student Residences Ltd since 1997: *m* 1980, Susannah Mary, yst da of late Charles Edward William Sheepshanks, of Arthington Hall, Otley, W Yorks, and has issue:

SONS LIVING— *Hon* William Robert Charles, *b* 10 Dec 1984.

Hon Frederick James Walter, *b* 1990.

DAUGHTER LIVING— *Hon* Hermione Mary Annabel, *b* 1982.

Hon Andrew John Carr Sewallis (Collycroft House, Clifton, Ashbourne, Derbys DE6 2GN), *b* 1965; *ed* Ampleforth; ARICS: *m* 1992, Tamara R., da of Donald Halfpenny, of Sutton in Ashfield, Notts, and has issue living, Henry Benedict, *b* 1997.

DAUGHTERS LIVING AND DECEASED

Lady Angela Mary, *b* 1954: *m* 1975, Jonathan Felix Hugh Ellis, FCA (*see* By Hirst, 1995 Edn), of The Old Rectory, Thurning, Dereham, Norfolk NR20 5QX, and has issue living, Charles William Donald, *b* 1979, — Louise Mary, *b* 1977, — Georgina Hermione, *b* 1981.
Lady Sallyanne Margaret, *b* 1957.
Lady Selina Clare, *b* 1958: *m* 1989, Antoine Bertrand Robert Chenevière, yr son of Bertrand Chenevière, of Geneva, and *d* 1998, leaving issue, Alexandre, *b* 1995, — Francesca Mary, *b* 1990, — Tatiana Annabel Haritina, *b* 1992.

SISTER LIVING

Lady Jane Penelope Justice, *b* 1925: *m* 1944, Rev Canon John Maurice Robson, TD, Canon Emeritus of Derby Cathedral (Hon Canon Derby Cathedral 1975), who *d* 1989, of Bristow's Close, Southrop, Lechlade, Glos, and has issue living, David Edward Shirley (Slip of Wood, Cranleigh, Surrey GU6 7BE), *b* 1947: *m* 1st, 1973 (*m diss* 1976), Carol Diana, yr da of late Wilfrid Durose; 2ndly, 1980, Josephine Ann Charlotte, da of Richard Manwaring-White, and has issue living (by 2nd *m*), Oliver Charles Richard *b* 1986, Jonathan Hugo David *b* 1990, — Julia Phillida Shirley, *b* 1953: *m* 1972, James Douglas Jermain, of 7 Park Rd, Winchester, Hants SO22 6AA.

COLLATERAL BRANCHES LIVING

Grandchildren of late Sewallis Evelyn Shirley, son of Evelyn Philip Shirley, son of Evelyn John Shirley, MP, DCL, son of Evelyn Shirley (infra):—
Issue of late Lieut-Col Evelyn Charles Shirley, *b* 1889, *d* 1956: *m* 1921, Kathleen Mary Phillis, who *d* 1977, da of late Lieut-Col George Ambrose Cardew, CMG, DSO—
John Evelyn, *b* 1922; *ed* Eton; Major (ret) King's Roy Rifle Corps; 1939-45 War: *m* 1952, Judith Margaret, yr da of Sir William Francis Stratford Dugdale, 1st Bt (*cr* 1936), and has issue living, Philip Evelyn, *b* 1955: *m* 1989, Augusta M. R., elder da of Hugo Southern, of Yew Trees, Bratton, Wilts, and has issue living, Evelyn Robert *b* 1990, Horatio John *b* 1993, Nathaniel Guy *b* 1995, Perdita Rose *b* 1997, — Hugh Sewallis, *b* 1961, — Emily Margaret (*Hon Mrs Robin Grimston*), *b* 1957: *m* 1984, Hon Robert John Sylvester Grimston, elder son of 2nd Baron Grimston of Westbury. *Seats* – Ettington Park, Stratford-on-Avon; Lough Fea, Carrickmacross, co Monaghan. *Residence* – Ormly Hall, Ramscy, Isle of Man. —— Mary Louisa Phyllis, *b* 1931.

Granddaughter of late Rev William Shirley, son of late Rev Arthur George Sewallis Shirley, son of late Evelyn Shirley, son of late Hon George Shirley, 5th surviving son of 1st Earl:—
Issue of late Col Sewallis Robert Shirley, MC, *b* 1885, *d* 1969: *m* 1st, 1917, Hilda Grace, da of Harry Gavin Young, formerly Indian Army; 2ndly, 1940, Edna Blodwen (7 Minster House, Abbey Park Rd, Beckenham, Kent), da of Albert William Laking:—
(By 1st *m*) Eileen Diana, *b* 1922: *m* 1946, Malcolm Young, of Whyr Farm, Winterbourne Bassett, Swindon, Wilts, and has issue living, Peter Malcolm Gavin (22 Belmont Rd, Mosman, NSW 2088, Australia), *b* 1947: *m* 1989, Anne Elizabeth Sadleir, — Richard William Shirley (Whyr Farm, Winterbourne Bassett, Swindon, Wilts), *b* 1949: *m* 1973, Deborah Anne Greene French, and has issue living, James Malcolm Sewallis *b* 1985, Juliet Anne Verity *b* 1978, Stefanie Clare Elizabeth *b* 1980.

PREDECESSORS – (1) GEORGE Shirley; *cr* a *Baronet* 1611; *d* 1622; *s* by his son (2) Sir HENRY, 2nd Bt: *m* Lady Dorothy, da of Robert Devereux, 2nd Earl of Essex (*cr* 1572), who became on the death of her brother, Robert, 3rd and last Earl, yst co-heir to the Baronies of Ferrers of Chartley, and Bourchier; *d* 1632; *s* by his el son (3) Sir CHARLES, 3rd Bt; *d* unmarried 1646; *s* by his brother (4) Sir ROBERT, 4th Bt; *d* a prisoner in the Tower, where he had been committed by Cromwell; *s* by his el son (5) Sir SEYMOUR, 5th Bt; *s* at birth by his posthumous son (6) ROBERT, 6th Bt; *d* an infant; *s* by his uncle (7) Sir ROBERT, 7th Bt, in whose favour, in 1677, Charles II terminated the abeyance of one of the peerages of which his grandmother was co-heir (see ante), he thus became *Baron Ferrers of Chartley* (peerage of England) *cr* 1299 (see infra *), while his right to the Barony of Bourchier, *cr* 1342, was overlooked; *cr Viscount Tamworth*, and *Earl Ferrers* (peerage of Great Britain) 1711; *d* 1717, when the Barony of Ferrers of Chartley, reverted to his granddau (see infra *), and the viscountcy and earldom passed to his 2nd son (8) WASHINGTON, 2nd Earl; Lord-Lieut of Staffordshire; *dsp*; *s* by his brother (9) HENRY, 3rd Earl; *d* unmarried 1745; *s* by his nephew (10) LAURENCE, 4th Earl, son of Hon Laurence, 3rd surviving son of 1st Earl; having in a paroxysm of rage killed Mr Johnson, his land-steward, was tried and condemned for murder, and executed at Tyburn 5 May 1760; *s* by his brother (11) WASHINGTON, 5th Earl; Vice-Adm; *dsp* 1778; *s* by his brother (12) ROBERT, 6th Earl; *d* 1787; *s* by his son (13) ROBERT, 7th Earl; *dsp* 1827; *s* by his brother (14) WASHINGTON, 8th Earl; *d* 1842; *s* by his grandson (15) WASHINGTON SEWALLIS, 9th Earl, son of Robert William, Viscount Tamworth, el son of 8th Earl: *m* 1844, Lady Augusta Annabella Chichester, who *d* 1914, da of the 4th Marquess of Donegall; *d* 1859; *s* by his son (16) SEWALLIS EDWARD, 10th Earl, *b* 1847: *m* 1885, Lady Ina Maude White, who *d* 1907, da of 3rd Earl of Bantry (*ext*); *d* 1912; *s* by his kinsman (17) WALTER KNIGHT (great-great grandson of Rev Hon Walter Shirley, brother of 4th, 5th and 6th Earls), 11th Earl, *b* 1864: *m* 1890, Mary Jane, who *d* 1944, da of late Robert Moon, Bar-at-law, of 10 Prince's Gardens, SW: *d* 1937; *s* by his son (18) ROBERT WALTER, 12th Earl; *b* 1894; *m* 1922, Hermione Justice, who *d* 1969, da of late A. Noel Morley; *d* 1954; *s* by his only son (19) ROBERT WASHINGTON, 13th Earl and present peer; also Viscount Tamworth.

*(1) JOHN de Ferrers, only son of Robert de Ferrers, 8th and last Earl of Derby (*cr* 1138) whose title was forfeited was summoned to Parliament as *Baron Ferrers of Chartley*, co Stafford 1299; *d* 1312; *s* by his son (2) ROBERT, 2nd Baron; summoned to Parliament 1342; *s* by his son (3) JOHN, 3rd Baron; never summoned to Parliament; *d* 1367; *s* by his son (4) ROBERT, 4th Baron; never summoned to Parliament; *d* 1413; *s* by his son (5) EDMUND, 5th Baron; never summoned to Parliament; *d* 1435; *s* by his son (6) WILLIAM, 6th Baron; *d* 1450; his da Anne *m* (7) Sir Walter Devereux, who was summoned to Parliament in the dignity of his deceased father-in-law 1461; he *d* at Bosworth Field 1485, and was *s* by his son (8) JOHN, 8th Baron; summoned to Parliament 1488-95; *d* 1499; *s* by his son (9) WALTER, 9th Baron; *cr Viscount Hereford* (*see* V Hereford) in whose family it remained until 1646, when it became abeyant, and remained so until it was terminated in favour of (13) Sir ROBERT Shirley, 7th Bt (ante); *d* 1717; *s* by his granddau (14) ELIZABETH, wife of 5th Earl of Northampton (*see* M Northampton).

FERRIER, BARONY OF (Noel-Paton) (Extinct 1992)

SON LIVING OF LIFE BARON

Hon Frederick Ranald (Easter Dunbarnie, Bridge of Earn, Perthshire), *b* 1938; *ed* Rugby, Haverford Coll, Pa, USA, and McGill Univ: *m* 1973, Patricia, da of late Gen Sir William Gurdon Stirling, GCB, CBE, DSO, of Saxham Hall, Bury St Edmunds, and has issue.

DAUGHTERS LIVING OF LIFE BARON

Hon Amanda Mary (*Hon Lady Fergusson*), *b* 1933: *m* 1961, Sir Charles Fergusson of Kilkerran, 9th Bt, of Kilkerran, Maybole, Ayrshire, and has issue.

Hon Caroline (Kirsty), *b* 1934: *m* 1957, Michael Laird, OBE, FSIA, FRIAS, RIBA, who *d* 1999, of 22 Moray Place, Edinburgh, 3, and has issue.

Hon Fiona Margaret, *b* 1943: *m* 1967, Hon Leslie Bruce Hacking, of Burchetts, Lower Moushill Lane, Milford, Surrey (*see* B Hacking).

Ferris, Grant, family name of Baron Harvington.

FEVERSHAM, BARON (Duncombe) (Baron UK 1826)
(Title pronounced "Fevversham")

For God, my king and my country

(CHARLES ANTONY) PETER DUNCOMBE, 6th Baron; *b* 3 Jan 1945; *s* 1963; *ed* Eton; Chm of Yorks Arts Assocn 1969-1980, and Pres 1987-91; Chm Standing Conference of Regional Arts Assocns 1969-76; Chm Trustees of Yorkshire Sculpture Park since 1981; Pres Yorkshire Local Councils Assoc 1986-99, and Pres National Assocn of Local Councils 1986-99; author of *A Wolf in Tooth* 1967 and *Great Yachts* 1970: *m* 1st, 1966, Shannon, who *d* 1976, da of late Sir Thomas Arthur Wyness Foy, CSI, CIE; 2ndly, 1979, Pauline M., da of John Aldridge, of Newark, Notts, and has issue by 1st and 2nd *m*.

Arms – Quarterly, 1st and 4th, per chevron engrailed gules and argent three talbots heads counterchanged for *Duncombe*; 2nd and 3rd, argent a chevron sable between three crosses flory of the second for *Anderson*. **Crests** – For *Duncombe*, out of a ducal coronet or, a horse's hind leg sable, hoof upwards and shod argent. For *Anderson*, a water spaniel passant or. **Supporters** – *Dexter*, a horse of dark iron grey, guttee and ducally gorged or: *Sinister*, a lion argent semme of fleurs-de-lis sable, his head adorned with a plume of six ostrich feathers argent and azure alternately, issuant from a ducal coronet or.
Seat – Duncombe Park, Helmsley, York.

SONS LIVING (*By 1st marriage*)

Hon JASPER ORLANDO SLINGSBY, *b* 14 March 1968.
Hon Jake Barnaby, *b* 1972.

(*By 2nd marriage*)

Hon Patrick Charles Kildare, *b* 1981.

DAUGHTER LIVING (*By 1st marriage*)

Hon Melissa Rose, *b* 1973.

SISTER LIVING

Juliet Priscilla Mary, *b* 1937: *m* 1960, Wilfred Trevor Woodley, pianist, and has issue living, Karin Lee, *b* 1961.

DAUGHTER LIVING OF THIRD EARL

Lady Clarissa, *b* 1938; High Sheriff N Yorks 1998: *m* 1966, Nicholas Collin, of Whytherstone House, Pockley, York YO6 5TE, and has issue living, Frederick Slingsby, *b* 1967, — Laura Anne (*Hon Mrs John E. Greenall*), *b* 1969: *m* 1998, as his 2nd wife, Hon John Edward Greenall, yst son of 3rd Baron Daresbury.

COLLATERAL BRANCHES LIVING

Grandchildren of late William Arthur Duncombe-Anderson, OBE, JP, yr son of Capt Frederick William Duncombe, 3rd son of Adm Hon Arthur Duncombe, 4th son of 1st Baron Feversham:—
Issue of late Maj Roland Frederick DUNCOMBE-ANDERSON, *b* 1908, *ka* 1940: *m* 1935, Elizabeth Frances (who *m* 2ndly, 1952, Brig Howard Greene, CBE, DSO, MC (*d* 1985), of Glebe Cottage, Bishopstrow, Warminster, Wilts), da of late Algernon Mawson:—
Alastair Guy, *b* 1938; *ed* Sherborne: *m* 1961, Judith Anne, da of late F. E. Abbott, and has issue living, Alastair Mark, *b* 1962, — Nicholas, *b* 1963, — Timothy Guy, *b* 1965, — Rebecca Elizabeth, *b* 1966, — Justine Anne, *b* 1971.

Issue of late Wilfred George DUNCOMBE-ANDERSON, *b* 1911, *d* 1982: *m* 1st, 1942, Valerie, who *d* 1969, da of Capt S. M. Pemberton, of Byring, Washington, Sussex; 2ndly, 19—, Mrs Enid Mary Gabrielle Nicholl, who *d* 1998:—
(By 1st *m*) David Martin (Brookside, Milton Mills, Milton Abbas, Blandford, Dorset DT11 0BQ), *b* 1944; *ed* Sherborne: *m* 1st, 1967, Marlene Kathleen, da of late Herbert Edward Peet, and widow of Lt-Cmdr Earle Peter Weavind; 2ndly, 1991, Brenda Janet Goddard, and has issue living (by 1st *m*), Rachel Katherine Louise, *b* 1972. —— Jane Louise Valerie, *b* 1946; JP W Sussex 1994: *m* 1st, 1969 (*m diss* 19—), Charles Tatton Sykes, son of Rodney Tatton Sykes; 2ndly, 1989, Peter Clementson, FRICS, of Rose Cottage, Acre St, W Wittering, Chichester, W Sussex, son of late Charles Hereward Clementson, and has issue living (by 1st *m*), Oliver Tatton, *b* 1974, — Nicholas Tatton, *b* 1977.

PREDECESSORS – (1) CHARLES DUNCOMBE, *cr Baron Feversham* (peerage of United Kingdom) 1826; *d* 1841; *s* by his son (2) WILLIAM, 2nd Baron, *b* 1798; sat as MP for Yorkshire 1826-30, and for N Riding of York (*C*) 1832-41: *m* 1823, Lady Louisa Stewart, da of 5th Earl of Galloway; *d* 1867; *s* by his son (3) WILLIAM, 3rd Baron, *b* 1829; MP for E Retford (*C*) 1852-7, and for N Riding of York 1859-67; *cr Viscount Helmsley* and *Earl of Feversham* (peerage of United Kingdom) 1868: *m* 1851, Mabel Violet, who *d* 1915, da of the Rt Hon Sir James Graham, 2nd Bt, GCB, PC, of Netherby; *d* 1915; *s* by his grandson (4) CHARLES WILLIAM REGINALD (son of late William Reginald, Viscount Helmsley, el son of 1st Earl), 2nd Earl, *b* 1879; Lieut-Col King's Roy Rifle Corps; MP for Yorkshire, W Riding, Thirsk and Malton Div (*C*) 1906-15: *m* 1904, Lady Marjorie Blanche Eva Greville, da of 5th Earl of Warwick; *ka* 1916; *s* by his el son (5) CHARLES WILLIAM SLINGSBY, 3rd Earl; *b* 1906; Lt-Col 13th/18th Hussars and Hon Col Queen's Own Yorkshire Yeo 1962-3; a Lord-in-Waiting to HM 1934-6, Parl Sec Min of Agriculture and Dep Min of Fisheries 1936-9: *m* 1936, Lady Anne Dorothy Wood, MBE, who *d* 1995, first woman to be appointed to Cttee of Masters of Foxhounds Assocn, da of 1st Earl of Halifax; *d* 1963 when the Earldom of Feversham and Viscountcy of Helmsley became ext, and the Barony devolved upon (6) (CHARLES ANTONY) PETER (only son of late Lt-Col Antony John Duncombe-Anderson, TD, eldest son of William Arthur Duncombe-Anderson, OBE, JP, yr son of late Capt Frederick William Duncombe, 3rd son of Hon Arthur Duncombe, 4th son of 1st Baron), 6th Baron and present peer.

FFRENCH, BARON (ffrench) (Baron I 1798, Bt I 1779)

ROBUCK JOHN PETER CHARLES MARIO FFRENCH, 8th Baron, and 9th Baronet: *b* 14 March 1956; *s* 1986; *ed* Ampleforth, and Blackrock, co Dublin: *m* 1987, Dörthe Marie-Louise, da of Capt Wilhelm Schauer, of Zurich, Switzerland, and has issue.

I had rather die than be dishonoured

Arms – Ermine, a chevron sable. **Crest** – A dolphin embowed proper. **Supporters** – *Dexter*, a falcon gules, armed, membered, belled, and wings inverted or; *sinister*, an unicorn gules, armed, unguled, crined, and tufted or, and in its mouth a rose branch thereon, two red roses proper. *Seat* – Castle ffrench, Ballinasloe, co Galway.

DAUGHTER LIVING

Hon Tara Elise Sofia Eleonora, *b* 1993.

SISTERS LIVING

Hon Rose Sophia Iris Mary, *b* 1957: *m* 1989, Dr Albert Alois Fuchs, only son of late Albert Alois Fuchs, of Pocking, Bavaria, and has issue living, Julia Katherina Sonia Mariele, *b* 1992.

Hon Clare Katherine Grace Mary, *b* 1958: *m* 1989, Alexander Timothy Joynson, yr son of William, R. H. Joynson, of Hyam, Malmesbury, Wilts, and has issue living, Peter William, *b* 1994, — Katherine Honor, *b* 1996.

UNCLE LIVING (*Brother of 7th Baron*)

John Charles Mary Joseph Francis (Stockbridge, Mass, USA), *b* 1928: *m* 1963, Sara-Primm, da of James A. Turner, of Stockbridge, Mass, USA, and has issue living, Johanna Felicitas, *b* 1964, — Teodora Crispina, *b* 1965, — Dorcas Sofia, *b* 1967.

AUNTS LIVING (*Sisters of 7th Baron*)

Freida Dora Katherine Mary Josephine, *b* 1916: *m* 1946, Hans Vajda, and has issue living.

Katherine Mary Margaret Frances Josephine, *b* 1917: *m* 1935, Lieut Christopher Valerio Edward Paul Banon, RN, and has had issue, Christopher Benedict Edward Patrick Fitzsimon (Carrig, Mount William Rd, Lancefield 3435, Victoria, Australia), *b* 1943, — Susan Anne Katherine, *b* 1940, *d* 1980, — Camilla Mary Rose (25 Pakenham St, Blackburn, Victoria, Australia), *b* 1947, — Clemency Mary Katherine, *b* 1957. *Residence* – Carrig, Mount William Rd, Lancefield 3435, Victoria, Australia.

Ellen Frances Anna Maria Josephine, *b* 1918: *m* 1946, Thomas Anderson Courtenay Agnew. *Residence* – Cregmore, Ardrahan, co Galway.

WIDOW LIVING OF SEVENTH BARON

KATHERINE SONIA (*Sonia, Baroness ffrench*), da of late Maj Digby Coddington Cayley, late King's Own Borderers (*see* Cayley, Bt, colls): *m* 1954, the 7th Baron ffrench, who *d* 1986. *Residence* – Gordon, Berwickshire.

PREDECESSORS – (1) CHARLES ffrench; *cr* a *Baronet* 1779; *d* 1784; his widow, Rose, was in 1798 *cr* by patent *Baroness ffrench*, of Castle ffrench, co Galway (peerage of Ireland), with remainder to the heirs male of her body, by her husband Sir Charles ffrench, Bt; she *d* 1805; *s* by her son (2) THOMAS, 2nd Baron, who had in 1784 *s* his father as 2nd Bt; *d* 1814; *s* by his son (3) CHARLES AUSTIN, 3rd Baron, *b* 1786: *m* 1809, Maria, el da of John Browne, of Moyne, co Galway; *d* 1860; *s* by his son (4) THOMAS, 4th Baron, *b* 1810: *m* 1851, Mary Anne, who *d* 1906, da and heiress of Richard Thompson, of Stansty Hall, Wrexham; *d* 1892; *s* by his brother (5) MARTIN JOSEPH, 5th Baron, *b* 1813; Resident Magistrate for co Tipperary 1846-82: *m* 1862, Catherine Mary Anne, who *d* 1908, only da of John O'Shaughnessy, of Birchgrove, co Roscommon; *d* 1893; *s* by his el son (6) CHARLES AUSTIN THOMAS ROBERT JOHN JOSEPH, 6th Baron; *b* 1868: *m* 1st, 1892, Mary Margaret, who *d* 1944, el da of Matthew J. Corbally, JP, DL, of Rathbeal Hall, near Swords, co Dublin; 2ndly, 1951, Catherine Elizabeth, who *d* 1960, yst da of Rt Hon Sir Christopher John Nixon, MD, LLD, 1st Bt; *d* 1955; *s* by his nephew (7) PETER MARTIN JOSEPH CHARLES JOHN (el son of late Capt Hon John Martin Valentine ffrench, yr son of 5th Baron) 7th Baron, *b* 1926: *m* 1954, Katherine Sonia, da of late Maj Digby Coddington Cayley, late King's Own Scottish Borderers (*see* Cayley, Bt, colls); *d* 1986; *s* by his only son (8) ROBUCK JOHN PETER CHARLES MARIO, 8th Baron and present peer.

FIELDHOUSE, BARONY OF (Fieldhouse) (Extinct 1992)

SON LIVING OF LIFE BARON

Hon Mark Elliott James, *b* 1955.

DAUGHTERS LIVING OF LIFE BARON

Hon Amanda Elaine, *b* 1959: *m* 1990, Robert John Chalmers, son of John Chalmers, of Remuera, Auckland, NZ, and has issue living, Jonathan James Elliott, *b* 1996. *Residence* – 335 Bank St, S Melbourne, Victoria 3205, Australia.

Hon Sarah Lucinda, *b* 1962: *m* 1987, Christopher le Maitre, son of Anthony J. le Maitre, of 4 Starle Close, Canterbury, Kent, and has issue living, Tom Elliott, *b* 1996. *Residence* – Bushy Cottage, Pusey, nr Faringdon, Oxon SN7 8QE.

WIDOW LIVING OF LIFE BARON

MARGARET ELLEN (*Baroness Fieldhouse*), da of late David Dorrington Cull: *m* 1953, Adm of the Fleet Baron Fieldhouse, GCB, GBE (Life Baron), who *d* 1992.

Fiennes, family name of Baron Saye and Sele.

FIFE, DUKE OF (Carnegie) (Duke UK 1900, Bt S 1663)

JAMES GEORGE ALEXANDER BANNERMAN CARNEGIE, 3rd Duke; *b* 23 Sept 1929; *s* his aunt as Duke of Fife 1959, and his father as 12th Earl of Southesk and 9th Baronet 1992; *ed* Gordonstoun, and RAC Cirencester; Nat Service, Scots Gds (Malayan Campaign) 1948-50; a Senior Liveryman of Clothworkers' Co, and Freeman of City of London; Pres Amateur Boxing Assocn 1959-73, Vice-Patron 1973-94, Vice-Patron of Braemar Royal Highland Soc, and Vice-Pres of British Olympic Assoc; Ship's Pres HMS *Fife* 1967-87: *m* 11 Sept 1956 (*m diss* 1966), Hon Caroline Cicely Dewar, elder da of 3rd Baron Forteviot, and has issue.

Arms – Quarterly, 1st grand quarter, or, a lion rampant gules, armed and langued azure, *Dukedom of Fife*; 2nd grand quarter, counter quartered, 1st and 4th gules, three lions passant guardant in pale or, *England*, 2nd, or, a lion rampant within a double tressure flory counter-flory gules. *Scotland*, 3rd, azure a harp or, stringed argent, *Ireland*; differenced by a label of five points argent, the points charged with two thistles between three crosses of St George gules, *Princess Royal, Duchess of Fife, el da of King Edward VII*; 3rd grand quarter, counter-quartered, 1st and 4th, vert, a fess dancettée ermine between a hart's head cabossed in chief and two escallops in base or, *Duff of Braco*; 2nd and 3rd, gules, three skeans paleways argent hafted and pommelled or, surmounted of as many wolves' heads couped of the third, *Skene of that Ilk*; 4th grand quarter, gules, a banner displayed argent charged with a canton azure, a saltire of the second *Bannerman of Elsick*; over all an inescutcheon ensigned of an Earl's coronet, argent, an eagle displayed azure, armed, beaked, and membered gules, on its breast an antique covered cup or, *Carnegie*. **Crest** – *Centre*, a thunderbolt proper, winged or, *Carnegie*; *dexter*, a knight denoting the ancient MacDuff armed at all points on a horse in full speed, in his dexter hand a sword erected all proper, his jupon argent, on his sinister arm a shield or charged with a lion rampant gules, the visor of his helmet shut, over which, on a wreath of his liveries with a long mantling flowing therefrom behind him and ending in a tassel of the fourth, the doubling of the third is set a lion rampant issuing out of the wreath of the third and fourth, the caparisons of the horse gules, fimbriated or and thereon six shields of the last, each charged with a lion rampant of the fourth, *Dukedom of Fife*; *sinister*, a man in armour issuing from the loins and wearing a tabard emblazoned of the arms, argent on a fess between three boars' heads erased gules three mascles or, sustaining with his dexter hand a banner developed argent having a canton azure charged with a saltire of the first, *Ethel, Countess of Southesk*. **Supporters** – *Dexter*, a lion rampant guardant gules, langued azure, charged with a label of five points argent, the points charged with two thistles between three crosses of St George gules; *Sinister*, a talbot argent collared gules, the collar charged with a label of three points argent.

Seat – Kinnaird Castle, Brechin, Angus DD9 6TZ. *Residence* – Elsick House, Stonehaven, Kincardineshire AB39 3NT. *Club* – Turf.

SON LIVING

DAVID CHARLES (styled *Earl of Macduff* 1961-92, since when *Earl of Southesk*), *b* 3 March 1961; *ed* Eton, Pembroke Coll, Camb (MA 1988), RAC Cirencester, and Edinburgh Univ (MBA 1990); MICAS 1996; Clothworkers' Co, and Freeman City of London 1987: *m* 16 July 1987, Caroline Ann, only da of Martin Bunting, and has issue:—

SONS LIVING — Charles Duff (*Lord Carnegie*), *b* 1 July 1989, — Hon George William, *b* 23 March 1991, — Hon Hugh Alexander, *b* 10 June 1993.

Seat – Kinnaird Castle, Brechin, Angus DD9 6TZ.

DAUGHTER LIVING

Lady Alexandra Clare, *b* 20 June 1959; *ed* Heathfield; Member Royal Geographical Soc, St Moritz Tobogganing Club, and Cavalry and Guards Club.

WIDOWS LIVING OF SONS OF TENTH EARL OF SOUTHESK

Cynthia Averil, TD, eldest da of late Brig Harold Vincent Spencer Charrington, DSO, MC, and formerly wife of Capt Alexander Hugh Gurney: *m* 1969, as his 2nd wife, Cmdr Hon Alexander Bannerman Carnegie, RN, who *d* 1989. *Residence* – West Court, Crondall, Farnham, Surrey.

Claudia Katharine Angela, da of late Hon Lord Blackburn (*see* E Strathmore, 1951 Edn): *m* 1935, Maj Hon James Duthac Carnegie, TD, who *d* 1996, and has issue (see colls, infra).

COLLATERAL BRANCHES LIVING *(Male line in remainder to the Earldom of Southesk)*

Issue of late Cmdr Hon Alexander Bannerman Carnegie, RN, 2nd son of 10th Earl of Southesk, *b* 1894, *d* 1989: *m* 1st, 1919, Susan Ottilia, who *d* 1968, da of late Maj Ernest Rodakowski (*see* E Southesk, 1952 Edn); 2ndly, 1969, Mrs Cynthia Averil Gurney, TD, (ante), eldest da of late Brig Harold Vincent Spencer Charrington, DSO, MC, and formerly wife of Capt Alexander Hugh Gurney:—
(By 1st *m*) Raymond Alexander, *b* 1920; *ed* Eton; late Maj Scots Gds, 1939-45 War (thrice wounded, despatches); writer: *m* 1st, 1943 (*m diss* 1953), Patricia Elinor Trevor, yst da of Cmdr Sir Hugh Trevor Dawson, 2nd Bt, RN; 2ndly, 1964, Diana Denyse Hay, Countess of Erroll (*in her own right*), who *d* 1978; 3rdly, 1989, Maria Congreve, da of Maj Ian Stafford Alexander (*see* Congreve, Bt, ext), and has issue living (by 1st *m*), Alexandra Susan Anne, *b* 1944: *m* 1969, John Sherman, of 97 Barkston Gdns, SW5 0EU, and has issue living, Charles Alexander Hoyt *b* 1970, Ian Andrew Henry *b* 1972, Peter Anthony Carnegie *b* 1978, — Susan Katharine Maud, *b* 1946: *m* 1st, 1968 (*m diss* 1973), Dudley Gordon de Chair, 5th Royal Inniskilling Dragoon Gds; 2ndly, 1974, Rupert Edward Harding-Newman, 4/7th Royal Dragoon Gds, and has issue living (by 1st *m*), Oliver Dudley Raikes *b* 1970, Natasha Alexandra *b* 1971: *m* 1997, William Bertram Ramsay (*see* Ramsay, Bt, colls, *cr* 1806), (by 2nd *m*) Rupert Alexander *b* 1976, Sophia Katharine Louise *b* 1979, — (by 2nd *m*) Hon Jocelyn Jacek Alexander Bannerman (Craggish, Comrie, Perthshire PH6 2JT), *b* 1966; *ed* Glenalmond: *m* 1990, Susie Mhairi, only da of Thomas Mitchell Hastie Butler, of Eastmillhill, Crimond, and has had issue, Merlin Thomas Alexander Bannerman *b* 1991, Maximilian Archibald Josslyn *b* 1995, Finn Kenneth Redvers *b* 1997, Cecilia Diana Catriona Pearl *b* 1993, *d* 1994. *Residence* – Mosstown of Lonmay, by Fraserburgh, Aberdeenshire.

Issue of late Maj James Duthac Carnegie, TD, 3rd and yst son of 10th Earl of Southesk, *b* 1910, *d* 1996: *m* 1935, Claudia Katharine Angela (ante), da of late Hon Lord Blackburn (*see* E Strathmore, 1951 Edn):—
Robin Andrew Duthac (Old Stone Cottage, Barford St Michael, Oxon OX15 0RQ), *b* 1937; *ed* Eton; late Capt Queen's Dragoon Gds: *m* 1st, 1962 (*m diss* 1969), Hon (Selina) Polly Dawson Eccles, da of 1st Viscount Eccles, KCVO, PC; 2ndly, 1970 (*m diss* 1979), Mrs Jennifer Louise Puxley, yr da of George H. Robins, MBE, of Devonshire, Bermuda; 3rdly, 1980 (*m diss* 1992), Avice Rosemary, da of Dr Richard Montagu Littledale, of Luckhurst, Pluckley, Kent, and has issue living (by 1st *m*), Andrew James, *b* 1963, — (by 2nd *m*), Simon Duthac, *b* 1971; *ed* Eton, and Bristol Univ (BA); FCA, — Tessa Lucinda, *b* 1972.

Granddaughters of late Rt Hon Sir Lancelot Douglas Carnegie, GCVO, KCMG, 2nd son of *de jure* 9th Earl of Southesk:—
Issue of late James Murray Carnegie, Capt RA, *b* 1909, *d* 1985: *m* 1939, Diana Winifred Mary, who *d* 1998, da of late Henry Arthur Renshaw (*see* E Leitrim, 1965 Edn):—
Susan Diana, *b* 1943: *m* 1982, James Alexander McKenzie, of 6 Corfe Mews, Caversham Park Village, Reading. —— Charlotte Marion, *b* 1954: *m* 1983, Richard Kenneth Purkis, of Chiswell House, Marsh Green, Edenbridge, Kent, and has issue living, Annabel Diana, *b* 1986, — Rosalind Marion, *b* 1988. —— Sophie Winifred (Derecroft, Five Fields Lane, Four Elms, Kent TN8 6NA), *b* (twin) 1954: *m* 1986 (*m diss* 1992), John Powell Fenton, and has issue living, James Horatio, *b* 1985, — Archie Powell, *b* 1987, — Rose Eleanor Millie, *b* 1990.

Grandsons of late Maj Hon Robert Francis Carnegie (infra):—
Issue of late Robert Murray Carnegie, *b* 1917, *d* 1954, from injuries received in an aeroplane accident: *m* 1949, Pauline Frances, who *d* 1954, da of Capt Francis H. Farmer, of Fairseat, Kent:—
Ian Francis (45 Church St, Staines, Middx TW18 4EN), *b* 1949; *ed* Wellington Coll. —— Alastair Robert (13 Hawley St, Trawden, Colne, Lincs BB8 8BY), *b* 1951; *ed* Wellington Coll: *m* 1976, Joanna D., da of Gerry Enderby-Smith, and has issue living, Helena Mary, *b* 1982.

Issue of late Major Hon Robert Francis Carnegie, 3rd son of *de jure* 9th Earl of Southesk, *b* 1869, *d* 1947: *m* 1913, Violet Mabel, who *d* 1980, da of late Philip Affleck Fraser, of Reelig, Inverness-shire:—
John Fraser, DFC (O Cabeco, Estrada da Serra, 7300 Portalegre, Portugal), *b* 1922; *ed* Prince of Wales Sch, Nairobi; late Flight-Lieut RAF; European War 1941-45 (DFC): *m* 1955, Gunhild Aline Avalon, da of Cmdr Arthur Avalon Mackinnon, OBE, RN (ret), 36th Chief of Clan Fingon, and has issue, †James Robert *b* 1956; *ed* Trin Coll, Glenalmond; *d* 1976, — Susan Mary, *b* 1957: *m* 1st, 1980 (*m diss* 1987), Mark Julian Lloyd Nicholson, son of late George Raymond Tibbitt, and of Mrs Hugo Romer Nicholson, of Topps Farm, Braemore, Hants (*see* Agnew, Bt, *cr* 1895, colls, 1970 Edn); 2ndly, 1988, as his 2nd wife, Timothy Robertson Bruce, of The Old Rectory, Combs, Stowmarket, Suffolk, adopted son of late Capt Hon John Bernard Bruce, RN (*see* E Elgin, colls), and has issue living (by 1st *m*), Rosalie Sheonagh *b* 1983.

Grandson of late George David Howard Fullerton-Carnegie (infra):—
Issue of late Maj George Travers Fullerton-Carnegie, *b* 1921, *d* 1975: *m* 1945, Frances May, who *d* 1974, da of late Lt-Col Alexander Sydney Duggan, MBE:—
(George) Christopher Howard FULLERTON-CARNEGIE, *b* 1946; *ed* La Clerière, Switzerland, and Lausanne Univ: *m* 1988, Cynthia, eldest da of Donald Hildreth, and of late Mrs Josefina Amado, and has issue living, Kirsten Frances, *b* 1995.

Grandson of late Edward Hugo Wakefield Fullerton-Carnegie, OBE, yst son of late Maj-Gen George Fullerton-Carnegie, elder son of George Fullerton-Carnegie, eldest son of John Carnegie (who assumed the additional surname of Fullerton upon his *m* 1796 to Mary Strachan Fullerton), eldest son of George Carnegie, brother of 3rd Bt and *de jure* 6th Earl of Southesk:—
Issue of late George David Howard Fullerton-Carnegie, MC, *b* 1894, *d* 1937: *m* 1920, Marian Margery (who *d* 1980, having *m* 2ndly, 1946, Staffan John Söderblom, sometime Swedish Amb to China), da of late Rev R. L. Lacey, of Castlepark House, Exmouth:—
†David Howard FULLERTON-CARNEGIE, *b* 1926; *d* 1999.

PREDECESSORS – **(1)** WILLIAM Duff, MP for Banffshire 1727-34; *cr Baron Braco*, of Kilbryde, co Cavan (peerage of Ireland) 1735, and *Viscount Macduff*, and *Earl Fife* (peerage of Ireland) 1759; *d* 1763; *s* by his el son **(2)** JAMES, 2nd Earl; *cr Baron Fife* (peerage of Great Britain) 1790; *d* 1809, when the Barony of Fife expired, and the Irish honours devolved upon his brother **(3)** ALEXANDER, 3rd Earl; *d* 1811; *s* by his son **(4)** JAMES, KT, GCH, 4th Earl; a Maj-Gen in the Spanish Army during the Peninsular War, MP 1818-26, Lord Lieut of co Banff, and a Lord of the Bedchamber; *cr Baron Fife* (peerage of United Kingdom) 1827; *d* 1857, when the Barony of Fife expired, and the Irish honours reverted to his nephew (5) JAMES, KT, 5th Earl, son of Gen Hon Sir Alexander, 2nd son of 3rd Earl; *b* 1814; MP for Banffshire (*L*) 1837-57, Lord-Lieut of co Banff 1856-7; *cr Baron Skene* (peerage of United Kingdom) 1857; *d* 1879; *s* by his son (6) ALEXANDER WILLIAM GEORGE, KG, KT, GCVO, PC, 6th Earl; *b* 1849; *cr Earl of Fife* (peerage of United Kingdom) 1885, *Duke of Fife and Marquess of Macduff*, of co Banff (peerage of United Kingdom) 29 July 1889, and *Earl of Macduff*, of co Banff, and *Duke of Fife* (peerage of United Kingdom) 1900, with remainder to the heirs male of his body by his marriage with HRH Princess Louise, and in default of such issue (1) to their el da (*Princess* Alexandra) and her heirs male, (2) in default of such issue to their yr da (*Princess* Maud) and her heirs male, and (3) in default of such issue to each of the after-born daus by HRH Princess Louise and the heirs male of the body and respective bodies of such daus severally and successively, one after another, as they shall be in seniority of age and priority of birth; Lord-Lieut and Custos Rotulorum of co London; Lord-Lieut of Elginshire 1871-1901; MP for Elgin and Nairn (*L*) 1874-9; Capt and Gold Stick of Corps of Gentlemen-at-Arms 1880-81; acted as Lord High Constable at Coronations of King Edward VII and King George V; had Royal Victorian Chain: *m* 27 July 1889, HRH Princess Louise Victoria Alexandra Dagmar (*the Princess Royal*), who *d* 1931, el da of King Edward VII (*see* ROYAL FAMILY); *d* 1912, when the Irish Honours (Barony of Braco, *cr* 1735, and Viscountcy of Macduff and Earldom of Fife, *cr* 1759) became dormant or ext, and the Barony of Skene 1857, Earldom of Fife, *cr* 1885, and Dukedom of Fife and Marquessate of Macduff, *cr* 1889, became ext, while the peerages *cr* 1900 devolved under the special remainder upon his el da (7) HH Princess ALEXANDRA VICTORIA ALBERTA EDWINA LOUISE, RRC; *b* 1891; a GCStJ; appointed Col-in-Ch RAPC 1939; acted as a Counsellor of State during HM's absence abroad 1939, 1943, and 1944: *m* 1913, Maj-Gen HRH Prince Arthur Frederick Patrick Albert of Connaught, KG, PC, KT, GCMG, GCVO, who *d* 1938, only son of HRH the 1st Duke of Connaught and Strathearn; *d* 1959; *s* by her nephew (8) JAMES GEORGE ALEXANDER BANNERMAN Carnegie (*Lord Carnegie*) (only son of 11th Earl of Southesk and HH late Princess Maud Alexandra Victoria Georgina Bertha, yr da of 1st Duke), 3rd Duke, and present peer; also Earl of Macduff, Earl of Southesk, Lord Carnegie of Kinnaird and Leuchars, and Baron Balinhard.

*(1) *Rt Hon Sir* DAVID Carnegie, an Extraordinary Lord of Session of High Sheriff of co Forfar, was *cr Lord Carnegie of Kinnaird* (peerage of Scotland) 1616, and *Earl of Southesk* and *Lord Carnegie of Kinnaird and Leuchars* (peerage of Scotland) 1633, with remainder to heirs male; *d* 1658; *s* by his son (2) JAMES, 2nd Earl; High Sheriff of co Fafar; one of the Commrs chosen to sit in the Parliament of England 1652; *d* 1669; *s* by his son (3) ROBERT, 3rd Earl; High Sheriff of co Forfar; *d* 1688; *s* by his son (4) CHARLES, 4th Earl; High Sheriff of co Forfar; did not go to Court or Parliament after the Revolution; *d* 1699; *s* by his son (5) JAMES, 5th Earl; engaged in the Rebellion of 1715 (honours attainted by Act of Parliament and estates forfeited); *d* 1729; *s* in representation of family by (6) *Sir* JAMES Carnegie, MP, 3rd Bt (see** infra); *s* by his son (7) *Sir* DAVID, MP, 4th Bt; *d* 1805; *s* by his son (8) *Sir* JAMES, MP, 5th Bt; *b* 1799: *m* 1825, Charlotte, da of Rev Daniel Lysons, of Hempsted Court, Gloucester, *d* 1849; *s* by his son (9) *Sir* JAMES, 6th Bt; *b* 1827; confirmed in Earldom as 9th Earl (together with the minor honours) and attainder reversed 1855, and *cr Baron Balinhard*, of Farnell, co Forfar (peerage of United Kingdom) 1860; Lord-Lieut of Kincardineshire 1849-56: *m* 1st, 1849, Lady Catherine Hamilton Noel, who *d* 1855, da of 1st Earl of Gainsborough; 2ndly, 1860, Lady Susan Catherine Mary Murray, who *d* 1915, el da of 6th Earl of Dunmore; *d* 1905; *s* by his el son (10) CHARLES NOEL, 10th Earl; *b* 1854: *m* 1891, Ethel Mary Elizabeth, who *d* 1947, only da of Sir Alexander Bannerman, 9th Bt; *d* 1941; *s* by his el son (11) CHARLES ALEXANDER, KCVO, *b* 1893; Major Scots Gds, DL Kincardineshire and Angus: *m* 1st, 12 Nov 1923, HH Princess Maud Alexandra Victoria Georgina Bertha Maud (acted as Councellor of State 1943), who *d* 14 Dec 1945, yr da of HRH late Princess Louise (*The Princess Royal*), and 1st Duke of Fife (*see* ROYAL FAMILY and ante); 2ndly, 1952, Evelyn Julia, who *d* (30 Aug) 1992, elder da of late Lt-Col Arthur Peere Williams-Freeman, DSO, OBE, and widow of Maj Ion Edward FitzGerald Campbell, Duke of Cornwall's LI (*see* Campbell, Bt, *cr* 1815); *d* (16 Feb) 1992; *s* by his only son (12) JAMES GEORGE ALEXANDER BANNERMAN, 3rd Duke of Fife and 12th Earl of Southesk (ante).

**(1) *Hon* ALEXANDER Carnegie, 4th son of 1st Earl of Southesk, *s* by his son (2) DAVID, *cr* a *Baronet* 1663; *s* by his son (3) JOHN, 2nd Bt; *d* 1729; *s* by his son (4) *Sir* JAMES, 3rd Bt, who *s* the 5th Earl as head of the family (see ante).

FINGALL, EARLDOM OF (Plunkett) (Extinct 1984)

WIDOW LIVING OF TWELFTH EARL

CLAIR HILDA (*Countess of Fingall*), da of late Henry Robert Salmon, of Ballarat, Victoria, Australia, and widow of Frank Richardson, of Geelong, Victoria: *m* 1966, as his 2nd wife, the 12th Earl of Fingall, MC, who *d* 1984, when the title became ext. *Residence* – The Common, Dunsany, co Meath.

FINLAY, VISCOUNTCY OF (Finlay) (Extinct 1945)

DAUGHTER LIVING OF SECOND VISCOUNT

Hon Rosalind Mary (*Hon Lady Hayes*), *b* 1914: *m* 1939, Vice-Adm Sir John Osler Chattock Hayes, KCB, OBE, who *d* 1998, and issue living, Colin John Finlay (Durhams Farmhouse, Butchers Hill, Ickleton, Saffron Walden, Essex CB10 1SR), *b* 1943: *m* 1969, Rosemary Lucie, da of late Rev Canon Herbert Naunton Bates, of Blaxhall, Woodbridge, Suffolk, and has issue living, Alexander Finlay *b* 1971, Oliver Naunton John *b* 1984, Philippa Lucie *b* 1977, — Malcolm Lionel FitzRoy, *b* 1951, — Griselda Mary, *b* 1954: *m* 1989, David Dow, of Edinburgh, and has issue living, James Finlay *b* 1992, Alison Rosalind *b* 1990. *Residence* – Wemyss House, Nigg, by Tain, Ross and Cromarty IV19 1QW.

FINSBERG, BARONY OF (Finsberg) (Extinct 1996)

WIDOW LIVING OF LIFE BARON

Mrs (Yvonne) Elizabeth Sarch (*Baroness Finsberg*), da of late Albert Wright, of Strabane, co Donegal, and formerly wife of Michael Sarch: *m* 1990, as his 2nd wife, Baron Finsberg, MBE (Life Baron), who *d* 1996. *Residence* – ......

FISHER, BARON (Fisher) (Baron UK 1909)

JOHN VAVASSEUR FISHER, DSC, 3rd Baron; *b* 24 July 1921; *s* 1955; *ed* Stowe, and Trin Coll, Camb (BA); sometime Lieut RNVR; 1941-45 War (DSC); JP and DL of Norfolk; *m* 1st, 1949 (*m diss* 1969), Elizabeth Ann Penelope, da of late Maj Herbert Holt, MC, of Nassau, Bahamas; 2ndly, 1970, Hon Rosamund Ann Clifford, da of 12th Baron Clifford of Chudleigh, and formerly wife of late Geoffrey Forrester Fairbairn, and has issue by 1st *m*.

Arms – Argent, in chief two demi-lions rampant erased gules, and in base the stern of an ancient battleship showing three lanterns proper. Crest – A dexter hand in mail armour couped at the wrist grasping the head of a trident erect all proper. Supporters – On either side a sailor of the Royal Navy supporting in the exterior hand an anchor cabled, that to the dexter in bend sinister and that to the sinister in bend dexter, all proper.
Residence – Marklye, Rushlake Green, Heathfield, Sussex.

SONS LIVING (*By 1st marriage*)

Hon PATRICK VAVASSEUR, *b* 14 June 1953; High Sheriff Suffolk 1998: *m* 1977, Lady Karen Jean Carnegie, el da of 13th Earl of Northesk, and has issue living, John Carnegie Vavasseur, *b* 1979, — Benjamin Carnegie Vavasseur, *b* 1986, — Robin Carnegie Vavasseur, *b* 1996, — Juliet Elizabeth, *b* 1978, — Penelope Mary-Jean, *b* 1982, — Suzannah Jane, *b* 1984, — Liberty Jean, *b* (twin) 1996. *Residence* – Kilverstone Hall, Thetford, Norfolk IP24 2RL.
Hon Benjamin Vavasseur, *b* 1958: *m* 1985, Pamela Margaret, only da of A. Cooper, of Tolcarne, Rough Close, Staffordshire, and has issue living, Peter Vavasseur, *b* 1986, — Rose Kathleen, *b* 1988.

DAUGHTERS LIVING (*By 1st marriage*)

Hon Frances Alice, *b* 1951: *m* 1981, Angus J. White, son of late Dr R. A. White, of Mile Ash, Tower Hill, Horsham, Sussex, and has issue living, Thomas Holt, *b* 1983, — Sally, *b* 1985. *Residence* – Cooks Farm, Nuthurst, nr Horsham, Sussex.
Hon Bridget Ann, *b* 1956: *m* 1982, Dr Bruce Stuart Irlam Montgomery, son of Dr S. R. Montgomery, of Telegraph Cottage, Blackdown, nr Haslemere, Surrey, and has issue living, Patrick Christopherson Ross, *b* 1987, — Caroline Jane, *b* 1984, — Katherine Frances, *b* 1985. *Residence* – Chaundler's Farm, Dippenhall St, Crondall, Hants GU10 5NX.

SISTER LIVING

Hon Barbara, *b* 1925: *m* 1961, Leslie Charles Croft Buswell, and has issue living, Gerald John Croft, *b* 1965, — Pamela Gwendolyn, *b* 1968. *Residences* – Flat 6, Les Arches, Le Mont Felard, St Lawrence, Jersey, CI; Normandie Farm, Firgrove, Cape 7110, S Africa.

PREDECESSORS – (1) Adm of the Fleet Sir JOHN ARBUTHNOT Fisher, GCB, OM, GCVO, LLD, son of Capt William Fisher, 78th Highlanders; *b* 1841; Adm of the Fleet; Director of Naval Ordnance 1887-91, Adm Sup of Portsmouth Dockyard 1891-2, a Lord of the Admiralty and Controller of the Navy 1892-7, Com-in-Ch on N American and W Indies Station 1897-9, and of Mediterranean Fleet 1899-1902, Second Lord of the Admiralty 1902-3, Com-in-Ch at Portsmouth 1903-4, Principal Naval ADC to HM 1904-11, First Sea Lord of the Admiralty 1904-10, and again First Sea Lord of the Admiralty 1914-15; *cr Baron Fisher*, of Kilverstone, co Norfolk (peerage of United Kingdom) 1909: *m* 1866, Frances Katharine Josepha, who *d* 1918, only da of late Rev Thomas Delves-Broughton; *d* 1920; *s* by his only son (2) CECIL, 2nd Baron; *b*

1868; assumed by Roy licence 1909 the additional name of Vavasseur: *m* 1910, Jane, who *d* 1955, da of Randal Morgan, of Chestnut Hill, Philadelphia, USA, *d* 1955; *s* by his only son **(3)** JOHN VAVASSEUR, 3rd Baron and present peer.

FISHER OF CAMDEN, BARONY OF (Fisher) (Extinct 1979)

DAUGHTER LIVING OF LIFE BARON

Hon Marilyn Ruth, *b* 1940; BA: *m* 1960, Mervyn Taylor, solicitor, of 4 Springfield Rd, Templeogue, Dublin.

FISHER OF LAMBETH, BARONY OF (Fisher) (Extinct 1972)

SONS LIVING OF LIFE BARON

Hon Sir Henry Arthur Pears, *b* 1918; *ed* Marlborough, and Ch Ch, Oxford (MA); is Fellow of All Souls Coll, Oxford; Bar Inner Temple 1947, and a QC 1960; Recorder of Canterbury (1962-67); Chm of Bar Council 1966-68; a Judge of High Court of Justice (Queen's Bench Div) 1968-70; late Pres of Wolfson Coll, Oxford; a dir Thomas Tilling Ltd, and Equity and Law Life Assurance Soc Ltd; formerly Lt-Col R Leics Regt; Burma 1944-45 (despatches); Knt 1968: *m* 1948, Felicity, da of late Eric Sutton, of 15 Cheyne Place, SW3, and has issue. *Residence* – Garden End, Marlborough, Wilts.

Hon Geoffrey Robert Chevallier, *b* 1926; *ed* Repton, and at Emmanuel Coll, Camb (BA 1947, MB and BChir 1949); D (Obst) RCOG 1952; Surg Lieut RN: *m* 1961, Jill Audrey, el da of J. H. Cooper, and has issue. *Residence* – 3 Wendover Drive, New Malden, Surrey KT3 6RN.

Hon Richard Temple, *b* 1930; *ed* St Edward's Sch, Oxford, and King's Coll, Camb (Choral Scholar, MA); Hon Maj TA Gen List, late 16th/5th Queen's R Lancers; Assist Master and Housemaster at Repton 1953-69, Headmaster of Bilton Grange Prep Sch 1969-92; Chm Inc Assoc of Preparatory Schs 1987: *m* 1969, Clare Margaret, el da of J. Lewen Le Fanu, of Newton House, Repton, and has issue. *Residence* – Crossways, 73 Overslade Lane, Rugby, Warwicks CV22 6EE.

WIDOWS LIVING OF SONS OF LIFE BARON

Ann Gilmour (139 Kermode St, North Adelaide 5006, Australia), da of late Ian Scott Hammond, of Chidikamwadzi, Umvukwes, Zimbabwe: *m* 1st, 1952, Hon Charles Douglas Fisher, who *d* 1978; 2ndly, 1983, Prof Basil S. Hetzel, Chief of Division of Human Nutrition, CSIRO, Adelaide, S Australia.

Diana Beresford (18 Holdsworth St, Woollahra, NSW 2025, Australia), da of C. Beresford Davis: *m* 1959, Hon Humphrey Richmond Fisher, who *d* 1996.

FISHER OF REDNAL, BARONESS (Fisher) (Life Baroness 1974)

DORIS MARY GERTRUDE FISHER, da of late Frederick James Satchwell, BEM; *b* 13 Sept 1919; *ed* Tinker's Farm Girls' Sch, Fircroft Coll, and Bournville Day Continuation Coll; a JP for Birmingham; a City Councillor, Birmingham 1952-74; Nat Pres of Co-operative Guild 1961-62; Crown Representative of Gen Med Council since 1975; a Member of Warrington New Town Development Corpn since 1975, and of New Towns Staff Commn since 1976; Pres Birmingham Royal Inst for the Blind since 1987, and British Fluoridation Soc since 1994; Guardian Birmingham Assay Office 1982-89; Member Hallmarking Council since 1989; MP for Ladywood Div of Birmingham (*Lab*) 1970-74; Member of European Parl, Strasbourg 1975-81; Hon Dr Univ of Central England 1998; *cr Baroness Fisher of Rednal*, of Rednal in City of Birmingham (Life Baroness) 1974: *m* 1939, Joseph Fisher, and has issue.
Residence – 60 Jacoby Place, Priory Rd, Birmingham B5 7UW.

DAUGHTERS LIVING

Hon Pauline Mary, *b* 1940: *m* 1961, Michael James Platt, of Little Acre, Ridings Way, Cublington, Leighton Buzzard, Beds.
Hon Veronica Mary, *b* 1945: *m* 1968, John Adrian Pickering, 8 Marlborough Av, Bromsgrove, Worcs, and has issue.

Fisherwick, Baron, title of Marquess of Donegall on Roll of HL.

FISKE, BARONY OF (Fiske) (Extinct 1974)

SON LIVING OF LIFE BARON (*By 1st marriage*)

Hon Giles Geoffrey, *b* 1935.

DAUGHTER LIVING OF LIFE BARON (*By 1st marriage*)

Hon Rosemary *b* 1931: *m* 19—, A. Holbrow, of Worcester.

WIDOW LIVING OF LIFE BARON

JOSEPHINE (*Baroness Fiske*), da of Alan Coppin, JP, of Hong Kong: *m* 1955, as his 2nd wife, Baron Fiske (Life Baron), who *d* 1975.

FITT, BARON (Fitt) (Life Baron 1983)

GERARD FITT, son of George Patrick Fitt; *b* 9 April 1926; *ed* Christian Brothers' Sch, Belfast; Merchant Navy 1941-53; Councillor Belfast Corpn 1958-81 (Alderman); Member (SDLP) N Belfast, N Ireland Assembly 1973-75, and NI Constitutional Convention 1975-76; Dep Ch Exec, NI Exec, 1974; co-founder and Leader, Social Democratic and Labour Party, 1970-79; MP for W Div Belfast (*Lab*) 1966-83 (Independent Socialist 1979-83); *cr Baron Fitt*, of Bell's Hill, co Down (Life Baron) 1983: *m* 1947, Susan Gertrude (Anne), who *d* 1996, da of — Doherty, and has issue.
Address – c/o House of Lords, SW1.

DAUGHTERS LIVING

Hon (Susan) Joan, *b* 19—: *m* 1975, Vincent Leo Hanna, broadcaster, who *d* 1997, and has issue, two das.
Hon Eileen, *b* 19—.
Hon Patsy, *b* 19—.
Hon Betty, *b* 19—.
Hon Geraldine, *b* 19—.

FITZALAN OF DERWENT, VISCOUNTCY OF (Fitzalan-Howard) (Extinct 1962)

DAUGHTER LIVING OF SECOND VISCOUNT

Hon Alathea Gwendolen Alys Mary, *b* 1923; Dame of Honour and Devotion, Sovereign Mil Order of Malta: *m* 1953, as his 2nd wife, Hon Edward Frederick Ward, of 21b Ave du Temple, Lausanne, Switzerland (*see* E Dudley, 1985 Edn), who *d* 1987.

FitzClarence, family name of Earl of Munster.

FitzGerald, family name of Duke of Leinster.

FitzHarris, Viscount; son of Earl of Malmesbury.

Fitzherbert, family name of Baron Stafford.

Fitzmaurice, Mercer Nairne Petty-, family name of Marquess of Lansdowne.

FitzRoy, family name of Duke of Grafton.

FITZWALTER, BARON (Plumptre) (Baron E 1295)

I will guard

FITZWALTER BROOK PLUMPTRE, 21st Baron; 15 Jan 1914; *s* (on termination of abeyance) 1953; *ed* Diocesan Coll, Cape Town, and Jesus Coll, Camb; Capt The Buffs (Reserve), a JP for Kent, and a Gov of King's Sch, Canterbury; European War 1939-45 in NW Europe and India; *m* 1951, Margaret Melesina, yr da of Herbert William Deedes, JP (B Ashtown, colls), and has issue.

Arms – Argent, a chevron between two mullets pierced in chief, and an annulet in base sable, a crescent sable for difference. Crest – A phoenix or, out of flames proper. Badge – An estoile or.
Seat – Goodnestone Park, Canterbury.

SONS LIVING

Hon JULIAN BROOK, *b* 18 Oct-1952; *ed* Radley, and Wye Coll, London Univ: *m* 1988, (Alison) Sally, only da of late I. M. T. Quiney, and has issue living, Edward Brook, *b* 26 April 1989, — Tom Alexander, *b* 1991, — Max Eustace Ian, *b* 1993.

Hon Henry Bridges (229 Birrell St, Bondi, Sydney, NSW, Australia), *b* 1954 *m* 1981, Susie, only da of F. T. Payne, of Waverley Station, Scone, NSW, Australia, and has issue living, Sam Anthony Bridges, *b* 1982, — Camilla, *b* 1984.

Hon (Wyndham) George, *b* 1956; *ed* Radley, and Jesus Coll, Camb: *m* 1984, Alexandra Elizabeth, da of Prince Michael Cantacuzene, Count Speransky, and of Mrs James Edwards, and has issue living, Wyndham James Alexander, *b* 1986, — Piers Harry Constantine, *b* 1987, — Hermione Amy Katherina, *b* 1991.

Hon William Edward, *b* 1959; *ed* Milton Abbey: *m* 1991, Joanna, yr da of William Dargue, of Los Gigantes, Tenerife, and has issue living, Jeremy William, *b* 1992.

Hon Francis Charles, *b* 1963; *ed* St Edmund's Sch, Canterbury: *m* 1999, Laura J., only da of Richard Price, of Ealing.

SISTERS LIVING

Judith Patricia (24 Raleigh Court, Lower Street, Sherborne, Dorset DT9 3EQ), *b* 1910.

Elizabeth Mary, *b* 1912: *m* 1941, Rev Philip Vivian Rogers Pennant, TD, MA; formerly Capt RWF, of 2 Manor Close, Bradford Abbas, Sherborne, Dorset DT9 6RN, and has issue living, Thomas George Edmund, *b* 1947; *ed* Wrekin, and Trin Coll, Camb: *m* 1979, Eva Gertrud Elisabeth, elder da of Dr Heinz Esser, of D5093 Burscheid Am Jungholzkamp, W Germany, and has issue living, Christina Agnes Katharina *b* 1981, — Philip Pearson (5 Archery Rd, Leamington Spa, Warws CV31 3PT), *b* 1952: *m* 1997, Juliet Elizabeth Randall, — Stephen Owen Falconer (19 Fossil Rd, Lewisham SE.13 7DE), *b* 1956: *m* 1985, Jean Madeleine, da of Rev Rene Tassell, of 12 Gardens Walk, Upton-upon-Severn, Worcs WR8 0LL, and has issue living, Douglas Hunter *b* 1987, Elizabeth Madeleine *b* 1985, Florence Maria *b* 1991, — Philippa Berain Elizabeth Plumptre, *b* 1942: *m* 1962, Bryan Henry Farr, of Worksop Manor, Worksop, Notts S80 3DG, and has issue living, Henry John Philip *b* 1966, Rosalinde Mary *b* 1963, Susannah Margaret *b* 1965, — Sarah Fariana Mary Agnes, *b* 1944: *m* 1st, 1966 (*m diss* 1984), Robert Iain Bescoby Jenkins; 2ndly, 1984, Maj Michael Owen Girdlestone, RA, of The Wharf House, Cropredy, Banbury, Oxon OX17 1PG, and has issue living (by 1st *m*), Robert Brook Pennant *b* 1970, Philip David Alexander *b* 1971, Katie Serena Margaret *b* 1977, — Helen Michèle, *b* 1949: *m* 1986, Jay Hilton Brewer, of Pedlars Cottage, Worthing Rd, Rustington, W Sussex BN16 3PS, son of Joseph Brewer, and has issue living, Rosie Margaretta *b* 1988.

COLLATERAL BRANCHES LIVING

Issue of late Maj Peter Bridges Plumptre, MBE, yr brother of 21st Baron, *b* 1916, *d* 1995: *m* 1944, Maude Helen Mary (Beechwood, Heathfield, Tavistock, S Devon), da of late Geoffrey Henry Baird, of Goodnestone, Kent:—
Timothy George, *b* 1945: *m* 1975, Christine Hamilton, and has issue living, Peter Hamilton, *b* 1980, — Tamsin Mary, *b* 1978. —— Jeremy Peter, *b* 1947: *m* 1985, Carmen Nozal Gonzalez, and has issue living, Samuel, *b* 1989, — Andreas, *b* 1992. —— Michael John, *b* 1955: *m* 1997, Janet Price, and has issue living, Jeremy Charles, *b* 1998. —— Rosalin Helen, *b* 1952: *m* 1970, David Alan Bowler, and has issue living, Nathan, *b* 1972, — Lucy, *b* 1971: *m* 1997, Jamie Maddever.

Issue of late Frederica Anne Plumptre, yst sister of 21st Baron, *b* 1919, *d* 1995: *m* 1942, Anthony Durnford Gaymer, FRIBA, late Maj RA, who *d* 1985:—
Nigel Anthony Plumptre GAYMER (Windrush, Flimwell, Sussex), *b* 1944; FCA: *m* 1969, Kathryn Helen Adams, and has issue living, Adam Timothy, *b* 1973, — Kirstin Anne, *b* 1976. —— Felicity Anne Plumptre, *b* 1950: *m* 1972, John Edward Parker, of 4590 Sumner Place, Victoria, BC, Canada V8N 3V7, and has issue living, Geoffrey James, *b* 1973: *m* 1998, Margaret Shiona Herron and has issue living, Jack Anthony *b* 1999, — Anthony William, *b* 1974: *m* 1999, Cindy Leann Todd, — Jonathan George, *b* 1982, — Olivia Felicity Anne, *b* 1976, — Victoria Rose, *b* 1980.

Grandchildren of late Margaretta Agnes Wright, eldest sister of 20th Baron:—
Issue of late Edward Fitzwalter Wright, *b* 1902, *d* 1957: *m* 1927, Jane Fairie Wilson, who *d* 1989, da of late Thomas Chalmers McGuffie:—
John Leslie Fitzwalter WRIGHT, *b* 1934: *ed* Winchester, and at Ch Ch, Oxford; late 2nd Lieut Sherwood Foresters: *m* 1974, Susan Annette, da of Maj-Gen Allan Elton Younger, DSO, OBE, of The Manor House, Twyford, Winchester, and has issue living, Francis Gideon Fitzwalter, *b* 1975, — David Nathanael Beresford, *b* 1979, — James Emanuel Shakespeare, *b* 1981, — John Joseph Camplyon, *b* 1981, — Jemimah Alianore, *b* 1977. *Residence* – Kirby House, Kirby Bedon, Norwich NR14 7DZ. —— †Margaretta Jane, *b* 1928; assumed surname of Langlands 1977: *m* 1949 (*m diss* 1965), Cmdr (Robert) Ian Langlands Pearse, RN, and *d* 1984, leaving issue, Robert Simon Hugh LANGLANDS (155 Watermoor Rd, Cirencester, Glos GL7 1LF), *b* 1950: *m* 1975, Jane Isobel, da of late Raymond Timothy Porter, of Te Awamutu, NZ, and has issue living, Timothy George *b* 1977, Rupert Hugh Chalmers *b* 1988, Joanna Jane Margaretta *b* 1980, — Adam Philip LANGLANDS (Pennyford Cottage, Burrington, Umberleigh, N Devon EX37 9LN), *b* 1955, — Dominic Walter LANG-

LANDS PEARSE (Holwell Downs Farm, Burford, Oxford OX8 4JX), *b* 1959: *m* 1st, 1986, France Symons, who *d* 1989; 2ndly, 1990, Sarah, da of Sir William Gordon Gordon Cumming, 6th Bt, and has issue living (by 2nd *m*), Ned Roualyn *b* 1993, Kate Margaretta *b* 1994. —— †Jennifer Marion, *b* 1930: *m* 1952, as his 1st wife, Lt-Cmdr Sir John Muir Drinkwater, RN (ret), QC, and *d* 1990, leaving issue, Jonathan Dominick St Clair (Hawthorn Cottage, Swerford, Chipping Norton, Oxon OX7 4BH), *b* 1956: *m* 1984, Philippa Anne, da of Anthony van Beugen Bik, of Busbridge Farmhouse, Godalming, Surrey, and has issue living, Charles Alexander John *b* 1991, William Oscar James *b* 1994, Harriet Frances Jessanda *b* 1989, —— Jane Fairrie, *b* 1954: *m* 1977, Timothy John Comyn, of Ickleton House, Westcot, Wantage, Oxon OX12 9QD, and has issue living, James Edward Daniel *b* 1982, Edward John Fitzwalter *b* 1989, Cressida Rose Katharine *b* 1985, — †Joanna Elizabeth, *b* 1958; *d* 1995. —— Juliet Caroline Leslie, *b* 1961: *m* 1992, Jeffrey George Puckett, of Cross Lanes House, Purton Stoke, Swindon, Wilts SN5 9JN, and has issue living, Melissa Jennifer Lillian *b* 1994, Augusta Joanna Caroline *b* 1996, — Jessanda Katherine Jemima, *b* 1964: *m* 1991, Richard Granville Farrant, of Rose Cottage Farm, Leigh Rd, Norwood Hill, Horley, Surrey. *Residence* – Meysey Hampton Manor, Cirencester. —— Caroline Leslie, *b* 1932. *Residence* – Hill Top Cottage, Shutford, Banbury, Oxon OX15 6PL.

        Issue of late Marion Wright, who *d* 1974, having *m* 1920, 7th Viscount Hawarden, who *d* 1958:—
See V Hawarden.

        Issue of late Margaretta Wright, who *d* 1977, having *m* 1918, Arthur Philip Coote, who *d* 1954:—
See Coote, Bt, colls.

        Issue of late Selina Fanny Plumptre, 2nd sister of 20th Baron, who *d* 1949, having *m* 1897, Lionel
        Sherbrooke Osmaston, who *d* 1969:—
†Robert Lionel OSMASTON, MB, BCh, *b* 1903; *ed* Camb Univ (BA 1924, MB, BCh 1932); MRCS England and LRCP London 1927: *m* 1945, Dorothy (11 Lower Stoke, Limpley Stoke, nr Bath BA3 6HT), da of Albert Edward Ward, and *d* 1994, leaving issue, Margaret Elizabeth, *b* 1946: *m* 1st, 1968 (*m diss* 1985), John Richard Bradley, BDS, LDS, RCS; 2ndly, 1987, William Birkmyre Sutherland McIvor, of 42 Belsay, Toothill, Swindon, Wilts SN5 8HB, and has issue living, (by 1st *m*) Robert John *b* 1979, Nicholas James *b* 1982, — Dorothy June, *b* 1947: *m* 1st 19— (*m diss* 19—), Peter Pickering; 2ndly, 19—, Mervyn Richard Hoy, of 43 King's Rd, Canton, Cardiff CF1 9DA, and has issue living (by 1st *m*), Anthony Charles Peter *b* 1975, David Robert *b* 1981, (by 2nd *m*), Rosemary Georgina *b* 1988. —— †Gwendolen Selina, *b* 1905: *m* 1935, Thomas Gerald Elwin Nash, who *d* 1963, and *d* 1989, leaving issue, Stephen Thomas (Forge Cottage, Goodnestone, nr Canterbury, Kent), *b* 1942. —— Marion Margaretta, *b* 1915: *m* 1st, 1941, Capt David Harold Archer, MC, Roy W Kent Regt, who was *ka* in Tunisia 1943; 2ndly, 1973, Lt Cdr Frank Williams, RN, of Wingletang, Old Farm Rd, Hampton, Middx and has issue living (by 2nd *m*), Sally Elizabeth, *b* 1954: *m* 1983, Stuart Alan Bull, and has issue living, James Daniel *b* 1986, Nicholas Bateman *b* 1988, Sam Frank *b* 1991, Adam Geoffrey *b* 1993.

        Issue of late Elisabeth Eleanor Plumptre, yst sister of 20th Baron, who *d* 1953, having *m* 1902, Maurice
        Beresford Wright, OBE, MD, who *d* 1951:—
Marjorie Prunella, *b* 1912: *m* 1939, Charlie Stuart Grunsell, CBE, FRCVS, and has issue living, Robin Nigel Stuart (17 Lowman Rd, N7), *b* 1946: *m* 1968, Angela Boulton, and has issue living, Jonah Charles *b* 1977, Leila *b* 1973, — Elspeth Ann Grant, *b* 1940: *m* 1965, Edward Godfrey Cantrell, MB, MRCP, of Waterside Cottage, South Baddesley Rd, Lymington, Hants SO41 5SD, and has a son and da, Matthew Ross (6 Beechdale Walk, Calmore, Southampton SO40 2GJ), *b* 1968: *m* 1997, Korinne Simmons, Tamsin *b* 1970: *m* 1st, 1992 (*m diss* 1996), Danny Byrne; 2ndly, 1998, Gavin Marc Woods, of 24 Solent Close, Lymington, Hants SO41 3ST, and has issue living, (by 1st *m*) Thomas Edward George *b* 1994, Emily May *b* 1992, — Susanna (11 Lowe Lane, Wolverley, Kidderminster, Worcs DY11 5QR), *b* 1943. *Residence* – Greenleaves, Mead Lane, Sandford, nr Bristol BS19 5RG.

        Grandchildren of late Elisabeth Eleanor Wright (ante):—
        Issue of late Nigel Wright, *b* 1908, *d* 1989: *m* 1948, Patricia Kidd (who *m* 2ndly, 1994, William Henry George
        Bond, of 5 Cowdray Court, Midhurst, W Sussex GU29 9UA):—
Andrew Firman WRIGHT (Ashleigh, 14 Ashfield Drive, Macclesfield, Cheshire SK10 3DQ), *b* 1953: MIBiol, PhD: *m* 1977, Susan Bowlas, and has issue living, Alan Nigel, *b* 1986, — Joanna, *b* 1983. —— Susan Jane, *b* 1951: *m* 1974, Robert Andrew Allison, of Mill House, Nutbourne, Pulborough, W Sussex RH20 2HE, and has issue living, Elizabeth Sarah, *b* 1980, — Caroline Jane, *b* 1983.

PREDECESSORS – (1) Sir ROBERT FITZWALTER, *b* 1247; Constable of Bere Castle, co Merioneth and of Hadleigh Castle, Essex; Capt and Keeper of the Peace in Essex; summoned to Parliament 1295-1325: *m* 1st, Doverguille, who *d* 1284, da and co-heir of Sir John de Burgh; 2ndly, 1289, Alianore, da of Robert de Ferrers, 6th Earl of Derby (*cr* 1138); 3rdly, 1308, Alice, widow of Sir Warren de l'Isle; *d* 1325; *s* by his son by his 2nd *m* (2) ROBERT, 2nd Baron: *m* Joan da of Thomas Lord Multon; *d* 1328; *s* by his son (3) JOHN, 3rd Baron; summoned to Parliament 1340-60: *m* Alianore, da of Henry, Lord Percy; *d* 1361; *s* by his son (4) WALTER, 4th Baron, *b* 1345; Adm of the Fleet; summoned to Parliament 1369-85: *m* 1st, Alianore, da of Thomas, Lord Dagworth; 2ndly, 1385, Philippa, who *d* 1431, da of John, Lord Mohun; *d* 1386; *s* by his son by his 1st *m* (5) WALTER, 5th Baron, *b* 1368; summoned to Parliament 1390-1404: *m* Joan, da of John, Lord Devereux, of Dinton, Bucks; *d* 1406; *s* by his el son (6) HUMPHREY, 6th Baron, *b* 1398; *d* 1415; *s* by his brother (7) WALTER, 7th Baron, *b* 1400; Master of the King's Hart Hounds and Capt of Vire; summoned to Parliament 1429-30: *m* Elizabeth, da of Sir John Chideock, and widow of William Massy; *d* 1431; *s* by his only child (8) ELIZABETH, Baroness FitzWalter: *m* 1st, of John Radcliffe; 2ndly, 1466, John, Lord Dinham; *d* 1485; *s* by her son (9) JOHN Radcliffe, 9th Baron, *b* 1451; Steward of the King's Household; summoned to Parliament in his mother's Barony 1485-95; attainted of high treason 1495: *m* 1st, Anne, sister of Richard Whetehill, of Calais; 2ndly, Margaret; beheaded 1496; *s* by his son by his 2nd *m* (10) ROBERT, KG, 10th Baron; obtained reversal of attainder by Act of Parliament 1509; summoned to Parliament 1511-23; *cr Viscount FitzWalter* 1525, and *Earl of Sussex* 1529: *m* 1st, Elizabeth, da of Henry Stafford, 2nd Duke of Buckingham; 2ndly, Margaret, da of Thomas Stanley, 2nd Earl of Derby; 3rdly, 1536, Mary, da of Sir John Arundell, of Lanherne, Cornwall; *d* 1542; *s* by his son (11) HENRY, KG, 2nd Earl, *b* 1506: *m* 1st, 1524, Elizabeth, who *d* 1537, da of Thomas, 2nd Duke of Norfolk; 2ndly, 1539, Anne (whom he divorced), da of Sir Philip Calthorpe; *d* 1556; *s* by his el son (12) THOMAS, KG, 3rd Earl, *b* 1525; summoned in his father's Barony 1553: *m* 1st, 1553, Elizabeth, who *d* 1554, da of 1st Earl of Southampton; 2ndly, 1555, Frances, da of Sir William Sydney; *d* 1583; *s* by his brother (13) HENRY, KG, 4th Earl, *b* 1530: *m* 1549, Honora, da of Anthony Pound; *d* 1593; *s* by his only child (14) ROBERT KG, 5th Earl, *b* 1560; Earl Marshal Oct to Dec 1597 and Oct to Dec 1601: *m* 1st, 1599, Bridget, who *d* 1622, da of Sir Charles Morrison; 2ndly, 1623, Frances, da of Hercules Mentas, and widow of Edward Shute; *dsp* legitimate 1629, when the Viscountcy of FitzWalter and Earldom of Sussex (both of which titles became extinct in 1643) passed to his cousin and heir-male Edward Radcliffe, while the Barony of FitzWalter devolved upon the heir-general (15) Sir HENRY Mildmay (descendant of Lady Frances Mildmay, only da of 2nd Earl of Sussex), *de jure* 15th Baron, *b* 1585; claimed Barony 1641 and 1645 (no order made to the petition): *m* Elizabeth, da of Thomas Darcy; *d* 1654; *s* by his grandson **(16)** HENRY, *de jure* 16th Baron; claimed the Barony 1660; *d* 1661; *s* by his brother **(17)** BENJAMIN, 17th Baron, *b* 1646; petitioned for the Barony 1667, and was summoned to House of Lords 1669-70: *m* 1669, Catherine, da of William, 3rd Viscount Fairfax of Emiley; *d* 1679; *s* by his son **(18)** CHARLES, 18th Baron, *b* 1670: *m* 1693, Elizabeth da of Hon Charles Bertie; *d* 1727; *s* by his brother **(19)** BENJAMIN, 19th Baron, *b* 1672; Commr of Essex 1720-28; *cr Viscount Harwich*, co Essex, and *Earl FitzWalter* 1735; Treasurer of the Household 1737-55, and Lord-Lieut of Essex 1741-56: *m* 1724, Frederica, da of the 3rd Duke of Schomberg and Duke of Leinster, and widow of Robert Darcy, Earl of Holderness; *d* 1756, when the Earldom and Viscountcy became ext, while the Barony fell into abeyance among the das of Mary, only sister of the 16th and 17th barons (ante) and so remained until 1924 when (after petition to the House of Lords) the abeyance was determined in favour of **(20)** HENRY FITZWALTER Plumptre, 20th Baron (son of late John Bridges Plumptre, and grandson of Eleanor, wife of Rev Henry Western Plumptre, and da of Sir Brook William Bridges, 4th Bt) (a descendant of Mary, only sister of 16th and 17th Barons), whose el son, Sir Brook William Bridges, 5th Bt, having claimed the Barony of FitzWalter in 1842 as a co-heir, was *cr* Baron FitzWalter by letters patent 1868, but *dsp* 1875, *b* 1860: *m* 1st, 1892, Maude Dora Gertrude, who *d* 1893, da of late Capt Thomas Carpendale Baird (Dorset Regt), of Flatfield, co Ayr; 2ndly, 1908, Emily Harriet Jemima, who *d* 1951, el da of late Capt Thomas Carpendale Baird (ante); *dsp* 1932, when the Barony again fell into abeyance and so remained until 1953, when the abeyance was terminated (after petition to HM the Queen) in favour of **(21)** FITZWALTER BROOK Plumptre (son of late George Beresford Pumptre, yr brother of 20th Baron), 21st Baron and present peer.

FITZWILLIAM, EARLDOM (Wentworth Fitzwilliam) (Extinct 1979)

DAUGHTER LIVING OF EIGHTH EARL

Lady (Anne) Juliet Dorothea Maud, *b* 1935; *ed* St Hilda's Coll, Oxford (MA); a Co Director, and a former Co Councillor of W Suffolk: *m* 1st, 1960 (*m diss* 1972), as his 2nd wife, 6th Marquess of Bristol, who *d* 1985; 2ndly, 1974, as his 4th wife, Capt Somerset Struben de Chair, late RHG, who *d* 1995, son of late Admiral Sir Dudley Rawson Stratford de Chair, KCB, KCMG, MVO; 3rdly, 1997, Dr Christopher Tadgell, and has had issue (by 1st *m*), *Lord* (Frederick William Charles) Nicholas Wentworth Hervey, *b* 1961; *ed* Eton, and Yale Univ, USA; *d* 1998, — (by 2nd *m*) Helena Anne Beatrix Wentworth Fitzwilliam, *b* 1977. *Residence* - Bourne Park, nr Canterbury, Kent.

SISTER LIVING OF EIGHTH EARL

Lady (Marjorie) Joan Mary, *b* 1900: *m* 1st, 1925 (*m diss* 1949), Major Grismond Picton Philipps, CVO (Knt 1953), late Gren Gds, who *d* 1967; 2ndly, 1949, Lt-Col William Wallace Smith Cuninghame of Caprington, DSO, JP, DL, late Life Gds, who *d* 1959, and has issue living, (by 1st *m*) Griffith William Grismond (Cwmgwili, Bronwydd Arms, Carmarthen), *b* 1935; *ed* Eton; High Sheriff Carmarthenshire 1972: *m* 1964, Ingrid Götilda, da of Med Dr G. von Sydow, of Gothenburg, Sweden, and has issue living, John George Grismond *b* 1965, Marianne Sioned *b* 1967, Charlotte Ingrid *b* 1969, Ebba Serena *b* 1971, Eva Götilda Joan *b* 1979. *Club* - English-Speaking Union.

FLATHER, BARONESS (Flather) (Life Baroness 1990)

SHREELA FLATHER, da of late Rai Bahadur Aftab Rai, of New Delhi; *b* 19—; *ed* Univ Coll, London (LLB); DL Berks 1994; Bar Inner Temple 1962; JP Berks 1971; infant teacher ILEA 1965-67, teacher of English as a second language 1968-78; Member Cttee of Inquiry into Education of Children from Ethnic Minority Groups (Swann Cttee) 1979-85, Commn for Racial Equality 1980-86, Police Complaints Bd 1982-85, Lord Chancellor's Legal Aid Cttee 1985-88; UK Delegate to Economic and Social Cttee, European Community, 1987-90; Pres Cambs Chilterns and Thames Rent Assessment Panel since 1983, The League of Friends of Broadmoor Hosp since 1991, and Community Council for Berks since 1991; Vice-Pres The Assocn of District Councils since 1990, and Commonwealth Countries League since 1990; Vice-Chm The Refugee Council (Chm UK Policy Group) since 1991; Dir Meridian Broadcasting (MAI) since 1991, and The Thames Valley Enterprise (TEC) since 1990; Trustee The Hillingdon Hosp Trust since 1990; Member LWT Programme Advisory Bd since 1990, Servite Houses Cttee of Management since 1987, and The Carnegie Inquiry into the Third Age since 1991; past member of many national and local social and ethnic cttees; Councillor Royal Borough of Windsor and Maidenhead 1976-91 (first ethnic minority woman councillor in UK), Dep-Mayor 1985-86, Mayor 1986-87 (first Asian woman to hold this office); *cr Baroness Flather*, of Windsor and Maidenhead, co Berks (Life Baroness) 1990: *m* 19—, Gary Denis Flather, OBE, QC, and has issue.

Address – House of Lords, SW1A 0PW. *Club* – Oriental.

SONS LIVING

Hon Paul, *b* 1954.
Hon Marcus, *b* 1957.

FLETCHER, BARONY OF (Fletcher) (Extinct 1990)

SONS LIVING OF LIFE BARON

Rev the Hon David Clare Molyneux, *b* 1932; *ed* Repton, and Worcester Coll, Oxford; ordained deacon 1958, priest 1959; Scripture Union staff worker 1962-86; Rector of St Ebbe's Oxford 1986-88: *m* 1970, Susan Charlotte, da of late Alan Stockdale Langford. *Residence* – 51 Charlbury Rd, Oxford OX2 6UX.

Rev the Hon Jonathan James Molyneux (Emmanuel Parsonage, 8 Sheep Walk Mews, SW19 4QL), *b* 1942: *ed* Repton, and Hertford Coll, Oxford; ordained deacon 1968, priest 1969; incumbent of Emmanuel, Wimbledon SW19, since 1982.

DAUGHTER LIVING OF LIFE BARON

Hon Elizabeth Jane Molyneux, *b* 1938: *m* 1962, David Blair Wilkinson, of Charnwood Lodge, Repton, Derbys DE65 6FN, and has issue.

WIDOW LIVING OF LIFE BARON

Bessie Winifred (*Baroness Fletcher*), da of late James Butt, of Enfield: *m* 1929, Baron Fletcher, PC (Life Baron), who *d* 1990.

Fletcher, Aubrey, family name of Baroness Braye.

FLOREY, BARONY OF (Florey) (Extinct 1968)

SON LIVING OF LIFE BARON

Hon Charles du Vé (Ninewells Hospital and Medical Sch, Dundee, DD1 9SY), *b* 1934; *ed* Camb Univ (BA, MD, BChir); MPH, Yale Univ, USA, FFCM, FRCPEd; Prof Dept of Epidemiology and Public Health, Ninewells Hospital, Dundee: *m* 1966, Susan Hopkins, and has issue.

DAUGHTER LIVING OF LIFE BARON

Hon Paquita Mary Joanna, *b* 1929: *m* 1955, John McMichael, of 12 Craigleith Gdns, Edinburgh, EH4 3JW, and has had issue.

Flower, family name of Viscount Ashbrook.

FLOWERS, BARON (Flowers) (Life Baron 1979)

BRIAN HILTON FLOWERS, FRS, only son of late Rev Harold J. Flowers, of Swansea; *b* 13 Sept 1924; *ed* Bishop Gore Gram Sch, Gonville and Caius Coll, Camb (MA; Hon Fell) and Birmingham Univ (DSc); Hon DSc Sussex, Wales, Manchester, Leicester, Liverpool and Bristol, Hon DEng Nova Scotia, MA Oxon, Hon DSc Oxon, Hon ScD Dublin; Rutherford Medal and Prize IPPS (1963), Chalmers Medal, Chalmers Univ of Technol, Sweden (1980); Physicist, Head of Theoretical Physics Div at Atomic Energy Research Establishment, Harwell, 1952-58, Prof of Theoretical Physics Manchester Univ 1958-61, Langworthy Prof of Physics 1961-72; Chm Science Research Council 1967-73, Pres Inst of Physics 1972-74, Roy Commn on Environmental Pollution 1973-76, and Standing Commn on Energy and Environment 1978-81; Rector Imp Coll of Science & Technology 1973-85; Pres of European Science Foundation 1974-80; Chm of London Univ Working Party on Future of Medical and Dental Teaching Resources 1979-80; Man Trustee Nuffield Fndn since 1982 and Chm since 1987, Chm Cttee of Vice Chancellors and Principals 1983-85; Vice-Chancellor of London Univ since 1985, Founding Member Exec Council of Academia Europaea 1988; FInstP, Hon FCGI, Hon MRIA, Hon FIEE, Officier de la Légion d'Honneur, Senior Fell Roy Coll of Art; *cr* Kt 1969, and *Baron Flowers*, of Queen's Gate, in the City of Westminster (Life Baron) 1979: *m* 1951, Mary Frances, el da of late Sir Leonard Frederick Behrens, CBE.
Address – c/o The House of Lords, SW1A 0PW.

FOLEY, BARON (Foley) (Baron GB 1776)

That I may do good

ADRIAN GERALD FOLEY, 8th Baron; *b* 9 Aug 1923; *s* 1927; is a composer and pianist: *m* 1st, 1958 (*m diss* 1971), Patricia (DE MEEK), da of Joseph Zoellner III, of Pasadena, California, USA; 2ndly, 1972, Ghislaine, only da of Cornelius Dresselhuys, of The Hague, Holland, formerly wife of (i) Maj Denis James Alexander, Irish Guards (later 6th Earl of Caledon), and (ii) 4th Baron Ashcombe, and has issue by 1st *m*.

𝔄rms – Argent, a fesse engrailed, between three cinquefoils, and the whole within a bordure sable. 𝔒rest – A lion rampant argent, supporting between the fore paws a shield of the arms of *Foley*. 𝔖upporters – Two lions argent, semée of cinquefoils sable.
Residence – c/o Marbella Club, Marbella, Malaga, Spain. *Club* – White's.

SON LIVING (*By 1st marriage*)

Hon THOMAS HENRY, *b* 1 April 1961.

DAUGHTER LIVING (*By 1st marriage*)

Hon Alexandra Mary FOLEY, *b* 1960; resumed her maiden name 1989, and again 1994: *m* 1st, 1987 (*m diss* 1989), (Somerset) Carlo de Chair, 3rd surv son of late Somerset Struben de Chair, of St Osyth Priory, Essex; 2ndly, 1991 (*m diss* 1994), Janos Klamar. *Residence* – Apt 19C 357 East 57th St, New York, NY 10022, USA.

COLLATERAL BRANCH LIVING

Grandchildren of late Paul Henry Foley, only son of Henry John Wentworth Hodgetts-Foley, great-grandson of 1st Baron:—
Issue of late Henry Thomas Hamilton Foley, MBE, *b* 1905, *d* 1959: *m* 1936, Helen Constance Margaret, who *d* 1985, CStJ, el da of Sir Robert Barclay Pearson:—
Andrew Thomas (Stoke Edith House, Stoke Edith, Hereford; *Club* – Boodle's) *b* 1937; *ed* Eton; late Capt Rifle Bde: *m* 1st, 1968 (*m diss* 1995), Gillian, da of William Carleton Brown, of Over Alderley, Ches; 2ndly, 1995, Mrs Melanie Jacqueline Westall-Reece, da of Lawrence Michael Reuben Janes, and formerly wife of Eric Dyer, and has issue living (by 1st *m*), Rupert Thomas, *b* 1970; *ed* Harrow, and Exeter and Camb Univs, — Ian Richard *b* 1973; *ed* Harrow, and Bristol Univ, — (by 2nd *m*) Emily, *b* 1995. —— Sir John Paul, KCB, OBE, MC (*Club* - Boodle's), *b* 1939; *ed* Bradfield; Lt-Gen Rifle Bde; MC 1976, OBE 1979, CB 1991, KCB 1994: *m* 1972, Ann Rosamund, only da of John William Humphries, of

Coval Court, Sunningdale, Berks, and has issue living, Annabel Frances Helen, *b* 1973, — Joanna Beatrice, *b* 1976. —— Anne Victoria Helen, *b* 1943: *m* 1980, Hugh Nigel Henshaw, of 3 Fernshaw Close, SW10, son of late Harold Henshaw, of Rottingdean, Sussex, and has issue living, Thomas Spencer Edward, *b* 1983, — Katharine Louise Emily, *b* 1981.

PREDECESSORS – Thomas Foley, 2nd and last Baron Foley; *cr* 1712; *d* 1766, and his estates passed to his cousin (1) THOMAS Foley; *cr Baron Foley*, of Kidderminster (peerage of Great Britain) 1776; *d* 1777; *s* by his son (2) THOMAS, 2nd Baron; *d* 1793; *s* by his son (3) THOMAS, 3rd Baron; Lord-Lieut of Worcestershire; *d* 1833; *s* by his son (4) THOMAS HENRY, PC, *b* 1808; MP for Worcestershire W (*L*) 1830-3; Capt of Corps of Gentlemen at Arms: *m* 1849, Lady Mary Charlotte Howard, who *d* 1897, da of 13th Duke of Norfolk; *d* 1869; *s* by his son (5) HENRY THOMAS, 5th Baron, *b* 1850: *m* 1889, Evelyn Vaughan, who *d* 1968, da of Arthur Radford, JP, of Smalley, Derbyshire, and Bradfield Hall, Berks; *d* 1905; *s* by his brother (6) FITZALAN CHARLES JOHN, 6th Baron; *b* 1852; *d* 1918; *s* by his cousin (7) GERALD HENRY (son of late Henry St George Foley, grandson of 3rd son of 3rd Baron), 7th Baron; *b* 1898: *m* 1922, Minoru, who *d* 1968, da of late Harry Greenstone, mine-owner, of Johannesburg, S Africa, *d* 1927; *s* by his son (8) ADRIAN GERALD, 8th Baron and present peer.

Foljambe, family name of Earl of Liverpool.

Folkestone, Viscount; son of Earl of Radnor.

FOOKES, BARONESS (Fookes) (Life Baroness 1997)

JANET EVELYN FOOKES, DBE, da of late Lewis Aylmer Fookes, of St Leonards; *b* 21 Feb 1936; *ed* Hastings and St Leonards Ladies' Coll, Hastings High Sch for Girls, and Royal Holloway Coll, Univ of London (BA 1957); Teacher 1958-70; Chm Education Cttee, Hastings County Borough Cncl 1967-70 (Memb 1960-61 and 1963-70); MP for Merton and Morden (C) 1970-74, and for Plymouth Drake 1974-97; Chm Education, Arts and Home Office Sub-Cttee of Expenditure Cttee 1975-79, and Parliamentary Animal Welfare Group 1985-92; Vice-Chm All Party Mental Health Group 1985-92; Member Home Affairs Select Cttee 1984-92, and Commonwealth War Graves Commn 1987-97; Dep Speaker and Second Dep Chm of Ways and Means 1992-97; Memb Cncl RSPCA 1973-92 (Chm 1979-81); *cr* DBE 1989, and *Baroness Fookes*, of Plymouth, co Devon (Life Baroness) 1997.

Arms – Sable four towers in cross their bases conjoined argent between four fuchsias in saltire stamens outwards or. **Supporters** – On either side a cat statant erect sable gorged with a naval crown attached thereto a chain reflexed over the back or.
Address – c/o House of Lords, Westminster, SW1A 0PW.

FOOT, BARON (Foot) (Life Baron 1967)

JOHN MACKINTOSH FOOT, son of late Rt Hon Isaac Foot; *b* 17 Feb 1909; *ed* Bembridge Sch, and Balliol Coll, Oxford (BA); Solicitor 1934; 1939-45 War as Maj RASC (GSO 111, 43rd Div and GSO 11 12th Corps, despatches); *cr Baron Foot*, of Buckland Monachorum, co Devon (Life Baron) 1967: *m* 1936, Anne Bailey, da of Clifford Bailey Farr, MD, of Bryn Mawr, Pa, USA, and has issue.

ẞrms – Or, on a chevron engrailed sable between three lions' gambs erect and erased gules, three wheels or. Crest – Perching on a tower sable, supported by two lions' gambs erect gules, a Cornish chough proper. Supporters – *Dexter*, a buck, and *sinister* a Dartmoor pony, each gorged with a wreath of yew proper, and supporting between the legs a sword erect sheathed or, the whole upon a compartment of rock, in the middle thereof a pit proper.
Residence – Yew Tree, Crapstone, Yelverton, Devon.

SON LIVING

For law and liberty

Hon John Winslow, *b* 1939; *ed* Sidcot Sch, and Philadelphia Coll of Art, USA. *Residence* – Knaven Hill Farm, Alderminster, Stratford upon Avon, Warwicks Glos CV37 8PQ.

DAUGHTER LIVING

Hon Katherine Elliott (36 Albert Park Place, Montpelier, Bristol), *b* 1937: *m* 1st, 1955, David Stavely Gordon; 2ndly, 19—, David Illingworth, who *d* 1976, and has issue by 1st and 2nd *m*.

Forbes, Viscount; son of Earl of Granard.

FORBES, LORD (Forbes) (Lord S 1445)

NIGEL IVAN FORBES, KBE, 22nd Lord and Premier Lord of Scotland; *b* 19 Feb 1918; *s* 1953; *ed* Harrow, and RMC; a Representative Peer for Scotland 1955-63; Maj Gren Gds (Reserve); JP and DL for Aberdeenshire; Board Member Aberdeen and Dist Milk Marketing Board 1962-72, Member of Board Sports Council for Scotland 1966-71; Chm of River Don Dist Board, 1960-73; Dep Chm of Tennent Caledonian Breweries, Ltd, 1964-74; Chm of Nat Playing Fields Assocn (Scottish Branch) 1965-80, Chm Rowlawn Ltd 1975-98, Pres Scottish Scout Council 1970-88; Dir Grampian Television plc 1960-88, Blenheim Travel Ltd 1981-88; Adj Gen Guards 1941-43, Staff Coll, a Dist Councillor for Alford 1955-58, a Member of Inter-Parl Union Delegation to Denmark 1956, to Hungary 1965 and to Ethiopia 1971, Pres Roy Highland and Agric Soc of Scotland 1958-59, and a Member Commonwealth Parl Asscn Delegation to Canada 1961 and of Parl Deleg to Pakistan 1962, Mil Assist to High Commr for Palestine 1947-48, Min of State, Scottish Office 1958-59, and a Board Member Scottish Cttee Nature, Conservancy 1962-65; 1939-45 War (wounded): KBE (Civil) 1960: *m* 1942, Hon Rosemary Katharine Hamilton-Russell, only da of 9th Viscount Boyne, and has issue.

Arms – Azure, three bears' heads couped argent, muzzled gules. **Crest** – A stag's head attired with ten tynes proper. **Supporters** – Two bloodhounds argent, collared gules.
Seat – Castle Forbes, Alford, Aberdeenshire. *Residence* – Balforbes, Alford, Aberdeenshire AB33 8DR. *Club* – Army and Navy.

SONS LIVING

Hon MALCOLM NIGEL (*Master of Forbes*) (Castle Forbes, Alford, Aberdeenshire AB33 8BL), *b* 6 May 1946: *ed* Eton, and Aberdeen Univ; DL Aberdeenshire 1996: *m* 1st, 1969 (*m diss* 1982), Carole Jennifer Andrée, da of late Norman Stanley Whitehead, of Aberdeen; 2ndly, 1988, Mrs Jennifer Mary Gribbon, da of late Ian Peter Whittington, of Tunbridge Wells, and formerly wife of Antony Gribbon, and has issue living (by 1st *m*), Neil Malcolm Ross, *b* 10 March 1970, — Joanne Carole, *b* 1972.

Hon Jonathan Andrew (East Cevidley, Alford, Aberdeenshire AB33 8BH), *b* 1947: *ed* Eton; Capt Grenadier Guards: *m* 1981, Hon Nichola Frances Hawke, da of 10th Baron Hawke, and has issue living, James Frederick Nicholas, *b* 1987, — Camilla Rose, *b* 1983, — Annabella Jane, *b* 1985.

DAUGHTER LIVING

Hon Gillian Rosemary, *b* 1949: *m* 1969, Alexander Neil Foster (*see* E Perth, colls, 1985 Edn), of Church Farmhouse, Blakesley, Towcester, Northants, and has issue living, Michael Alexander, *b* 1973, — Lucia Katharine, *b* 1970: *m* 1996, Matthew G. P. Lamb, son of Maj Gilbert Lamb.

COLLATERAL BRANCHES LIVING

Granddaughter of late Capt Hon Walter Robert Drummond Forbes, 7th son of 18th Lord:—
Issue of late Sir (Victor) Courtenay Walter Forbes, KCMG, *b* 1889, *d* 1958: *m* 1st, 1916 (*m diss* 1949), Luia, da of late Hon Sir Henry Herbert Juta; 2ndly, 1950, Mary, who *d* 1972, da of Francis George Olivieri, and widow of Walter Carter Bizley:—
(By 1st *m*) Sara Elizabeth Ninita, *b* 1917: *m* 1938, Hugh Gyle-Thompson, who *d* 1972, and has issue living, David Courtenay Gladstone, *b* 1943; *ed* Charterhouse, and Ch Ch Oxford: *m* 1970, Penelope Fearnley, and has issue living, Camilla Kate *b* 1974, — Elizabeth Helen Donita, *b* 1939: *m* 1965, George Oliver Papps, of USA, and has issue living, Gillian Sara *b* 1967, Luia Elizabeth *b* 1970, — Sara Anne Robina, *b* 1941: *m* 1969, Christopher Watson, and has issue living, Timothy Hugh James *b* 1970, Angus Christopher Hugo *b* 1972.

Grandsons of late Hon Montagu Ormond Forbes, 8th son of 18th Lord:—
Issue of late Col Courtenay Fergus Ochoncar Grey Forbes, late Coldm Gds, *b* 1898, *d* 1971: *m* 1st, 1924 (*m diss* 1928), Gundrede Mary, yr da of late Capt Graham Owen Robert Wynne (*see* B Killanin, 1957 Edn); 2ndly, 1929, Mary Shelagh, who *d* 1932, da of late Col Arthur Llewellyn, Som LI; 3rdly, 1932, (*m diss* 1954), Dorothea Garnier Staveley, who *d* 1997, da of His Honour late Henry Staveley Staveley-Hill, TD, 4thly, 1954, Emilie de Kosenko, who *d* 1981, da of late Mrs Edward Brooks of New York, and widow of 5th Baron Monteagle of Brandon:—
(By 1st *m*) Fergus Patrick (Atlanta, Georgia, USA), *b* 1925; *ed* Eton; 1939-45 War Lieut Coldstream Gds (wounded): *m* 1st, 1950 (*m diss* 1967), Margaret Elizabeth, twin da of John Percy Wayte, of Bloxham, Banbury, Oxon; 2ndly, 1967, Jeannette Fendryck, of Baltimore, USA, and has issue living (by 1st *m*), Christopher Michael Fergus (Christophe), *b* 1955; *ed* Eton, and Ch Ch, Oxford: *m* 1991, Fanny Marie-France Bénédicte, eldest da of Bertrand Bernard Marie Joseph Toulemonde, of Valenciennes, and has issue living, Graham Clovis *b* 1993, Christabel Bridget *b* 1991, — Grania Elizabeth, *b* 1950: *m* 1st, 1980 (*m diss* 1986), Patrick Blake; 2ndly, 1988, Mark Graham Porter, and has issue living (by 1st *m*), Christian Edward Patrick *b* 1981, Matthew Richard Martin *b* 1984, (by 2nd *m*), George Julius Robert Douglas *b* 1989, — Moira Isobel (Isabella), *b* 1957: *m* 1990, William Matthew Underhill, and has issue living, Celia Elizabeth Tabitha *b* 1992, Hester Charity Clare *b* 1994, — (by 2nd *m*), James Michael, *b* 1974: *m* 1999, Janet Suzanne, da of Charles K. Henderson, of Atlanta, Georgia, USA. —— (By 3rd *m*) John Alistair Ponsonby (All Saints House, nr Axminster, Devonshire EX13 7LR; Boodle's Club), *b* 1937: late Capt Coldm Gds: *m* 1965, Mary Dorothea, da of Sir William Macnamara Goodenough, 1st Bt, and has issue living, James William Courtenay, *b* 1970, — Sophie Louisa Dorothea, *b* 1968.

Granddaughter of late Col Robert Ochoncar Hawkins Forbes, eldest son of Hon Robert Forbes, 6th son of 17th Lord:—
Issue of late Robert Ochoncar Forbes, *b* 1859, *d* 1913: *m* 1898, Juliana Olga, who *d* 1954, da of Major John Nevinson, formerly 4th Hussars:—
Rosalie Jessie Olga (Flat 1, 20 Lansdowne Rd, W11 3LL), *b* 1904: *m* 1938, Thomas Percival Durant Beighton, who *d* 1971.

Granddaughter of late Rev Malcolm Forbes, eldest son of late Maj Frederick Murray Hay Forbes, 2nd son of Hon Robert Forbes (ante):—
Issue of late Maj Malcolm Hay Ochoncar Forbes, *b* 1891, *d* 1973: *m* 1st, 1921, Edith Maud, who *d* 1962, only da of G. A. MacMillan; 2ndly, 1966, Mrs Helen Roslyn Dickson, who *d* 1970, da of A. C. Graham:—
(By 1st *m*) Helen Mary Hay, *b* 1922: *m* 1945, Fl-Lt Terence Dudley Thompson, RAAF, and has issue living, Ian Forbes, *b* 1951, — Pamela Forbes, *b* 1947, — Jane Forbes, *b* 1948, — Georgina Helen Forbes, *b* 1968.

Grandchildren of late Maj Robert Inglis Forbes, eldest son of Col Henry Twisden Forbes, 3rd son of Hon Robert Forbes (ante):—
Issue of late William Robert Townsend Forbes, *b* 1893, *d* 1967: *m* 1925, Evelyn, who *d* 1989, da of late Very Rev Preb H. Erskine-Hill, DD, of Much Dewchurch, Hereford:—
Ian Robert Patrick (93 Steyne Rd, Southbourne, Hants), *b* 1926: *m* 1953 (*m diss* 1971), Patricia Heginbotham, of Brighton. —— William Michael (21 Rosenau Cres, SW11), *b* 1934; Cdr RN: *m* 1st, 1957 (*m diss* 1976), Wendy Ann Birch of Southsea; 2ndly, 1994, Janette Ann Nieder, and has issue living, (by 1st *m*) David Charles, *b* 1959, — Simon Robert, *b* 1964,

— Jeremy Andrew, *b* 1966, — Anne Lesley, *b* 1960; *ed* Bristol Univ (MD). ——— *Rev* Patrick (18 Francis Rd, Hinxworth, Herts SG7 5HL), *b* 1938; writer and broadcaster: *m* 1962, Annette Margaret Miller, of Upper Norwood, SE, and has issue living, Stephen Robert, *b* 1967.

Issue of late Kenneth Herbert Forbes, *b* 1899, *d* 1981: *m* 1st, 1929 (*m diss* 1938), Zara Muriel, da of late Walter Currie; 2ndly, 1947, (Dorothy) Joan (Orchard Cottage, Coopers Hill Lane, Englefield Green, Surrey), da of late Alfred Percival Folkard:—
(By 2nd *m*) Colin Kenneth, *b* 1956. *Residence* – 46 Addison Gdns, W14. ——— (By 1st *m*) Susan, *b* 1933: *m* 1958, Iain Stuart Bain, FSA, of New Cottage, Newnham, Baldock, Herts, and has issue living, Christina Mary, *b* 1961: *m* 1993, Alasdair Anderson, — Catriona Frances, *b* 1964.

Granddaugher of late Col Henry Twisden Forbes (ante):—
Issue of late Herbert Russell Forbes, *b* 1863, *d* 1920: *m* 1896, Amy Ella, who *d* 1935, da of late William Duncan Scott, of Graylands, Chiswick: —
Marjorie Alice, *b* 1900: *m* 1920, John Taylor Porritt, who *d* 1976, of Great Green House, Cockfield, Bury St Edmunds, Suffolk, and has issue living, Joan April, *b* 1921: *m* 19—, — Yates, — Gillian, *b* 1927: *m* 19—, — Lindsey-Renton (PO Box 747, Olifantsfontein 1665, S Africa), and has issue, two das.

Granddaughters of late Charles Twisden Forbes, 3rd son of late Col Henry Twisden Forbes (ante):—
Issue of late Archibald Herbert D'Esterre Forbes, MC, *b* 1899, *d* 1956: *m* 1924, Emily Flora, who *d* 1991, da of late S. K. Keyes, of The Dene, Dartford:—
Isla Hamiton, *b* 1926: *m* 1948, Rev Philip Paul Stanley Brownless, of The Hornpipe, Oak Meadow, Birdham, Chichester, W Sussex, and has issue living, Benjamin Stanley, *b* 1956, — Alison Kilworth, *b* 1950; *ed* Bristol Univ: *m* 1973, Alan Geoffrey Browne, MICE, and has issue living, Radley Alan Forbes *b* 1978, Carola Jody Merchant *b* 1981. ——— Rona Kilworth, *b* 1928: *m* 1952, Raymond Frank Abraham Hunter, MC, of RR1 Lawrencetown, Nova Scotia, Canada B0S 1M0, and has issue living, Charles William Forbes, *b* 1955: *m* 1976, Christine Mairi Parker, and has issue living, Robyn *b* 1981, Chantal *b* 1984, — Jolyon Nigel Forbes, *b* 1958: *m* 1983, Maura Cameron, and has issue living, Matthew *b* 1988, (Raymond) Alexander *b* 1991, Charles *b* 1995, Sarah *b* 1986, Emily Jean *b* 1993, — Mark Raymond Forbes, *b* 1960: *m* 1985, Pauline Irvin, and has issue living, Abby *b* 1990, — William John Forbes, *b* 1965: *m* 1988, Rebecca Houtsma, and has issue living, Piers *b* 1996, Tegan Anneke *b* 1992, (Rona) Katherine *b* 1994. *Residence* – RR1, Lawrencetown, Nova Scotia, Canada B0S 1M0.

Granddaughter of late Francis Sutherland Courtenay Forbes, 2nd son of late Col Walter Ernest Forbes, 4th son of Hon Robert Forbes (ante):—
Issue of late Lt-Cdr Haydon Marriott Sutherland Forbes, DSC, RN, *b* 1897, *d* 1927: *m* 19—, Cecily, da of Capt Armitage, RN:—
Pamela Patricia, *b* 1925.

Granddaughters of late Ernest Colebroke Forbes, yst son of late Col Walter Ernest Forbes (ante):—
Issue of late Atholl Courtenay Forbes, *b* 1892, *d* 1952: *m* 1926, Veronica Elizabeth (who *d* 1966, having *m* 2ndly, 1939, L. A. C. Houston, who *d* 1992), da of Arthur Willis, of Gisbourne, NZ:—
Pamela Jane, *b* 1929; formerly a Sister Tutor, QARNNS: *m* 1958, Richard Bostock, and has issue living, John Edward, *b* 1960: *m* 1986, Katherine Helen Dandy, — David Forbes, *b* 1962: *m* 1990, Yujin Chung, and has issue living, Richard Daejin *b* 1990, — Julia Elizabeth, *b* 1965: *m* 1993, Kevin David Kinsella, and has issue living, Samuel John *b* 1994, Joseph David *b* 1997.

Issue of late Ernest Twisden Forbes, *b* 1902, *d* 1966: *m* 1932, Mavis Amy, who *d* 1973, da of Edward Ingham of Melbourne:—
Barbara Beatrice, *b* 1934: *m* 1963, Hubert Andrew Thebo, BS (10815 Gainsborough Rd, Potomac, Maryland 20854, USA), and has issue living, Christine Forbes, *b* 1967.

Grandchildren of late Bertie St John Ochoncar Forbes, only son of late Arthur St Quintin Forbes, 7th son of late Hon Robert Forbes (ante):—
Issue of late Maj Bertie St John Ochoncar Forbes, *b* 1918, *d* 1998: *m* 1942, Anne Moore Crozer, who *d* 1997:—
Graham Richard, *b* 1946: *m* 1971, Anne Catherine Haigh, of Edinburgh, and has issue living, Callum Richard, *b* 1972; BA, — Murray Douglas, *b* 1974; BA. *Residence* – 4 Lothians View, Rosyth, Fife KY11 2UY. ——— Gillian Margaret, *b* 1951.

Descendants of William Forbes (4th in descent from Hon Duncan Forbes, 2nd son of 2nd Lord), who was *cr* a *Baronet* 1626:
See Stuart-Forbes, Bt.

Descendants of William Forbes (5th in descent from Hon Sir Patrick Forbes, 3rd son of 2nd Lord), who was *cr* a *Baronet* 1630:
See L Sempill and Forbes, Bt, *cr* 1630.

(1) *Sir* ALEXANDER de Forbes, of that Ilk, feudal baron of Forbes; *cr Lord Forbes* (peerage of Scotland) about 1445; *d* 1448; *s* by his son (2) JAMES, 2nd Lord; *d* 1460; *s* by his son (3) WILLIAM, 3rd Lord; *s* by his el son (4) ALEXANDER, 4th Lord; *s* by his brother (5) ARTHUR, 5th Lord; *d* 1493; *s* by his brother (6) JOHN, 6th Lord; *d* 1547; *s* by his son (7) WILLIAM, 7th Lord; *d* 1593; *s* by his son (8) JOHN, 8th Lord; *d* (June) 1606; *s* by his son (by 2nd *m*) (9) ARTHUR, 9th Lord; *d* 1641; *s* by his son (10) ALEXANDER, 10th Lord; *d* 1672; *s* by his son (11) WILLIAM, 11th Lord; *d* 1691; *s* by his son (12) WILLIAM, PC, 12th Lord; *d* 1716; *s* by his el son (13) WILLIAM, 13th Lord; *d* 1730; *s* by his son (14) FRANCIS, 14th Lord; *d* a minor 1734; *s* by his uncle (15) JAMES, 15th Lord; *d* 1761; *s* by his son (16) JAMES 16th Lord, *d* 1804; *s* by his son (17) JAMES OCHONCAR, 17th Lord; Gen in the Army, Repres Peer, and High Commr to Gen Assembly, Ch of

Scotland; *d* 1843; *s* by his son **(18)** WALTER, 18th Lord, *b* 1798; served at Waterloo: *m* 1st 1825, Horatia, who *d* 1862, da of Sir John Gregory Shaw, Bt; 2ndly 1864, Louisa, who *d* 1921, da of late James Ormond; *d* 1868; *s* by his son **(19)** HORACE COURTENAY, 19th Lord, *b* 1829; Repres Peer 1874-1906; *d* 1914; *s* by his brother **(20)** ATHOLL MONSON, 20th Lord; *b* 1841: *m* 1876, Margaret Alice, who *d* 1943, da of Sir William Hammer Dick-Cunnygham, 8th Bt; *d* 1916; *s* by his son **(21)** ATHOLL LAURENCE CUNYNGHAM, 21st Lord; *b* 1882; Maj Gren Gds; Representative Peer 1917-24: *m* 1914, Lady Mabel Anson, who *d* 1972, da of the 3rd Earl of Lichfield; *d* 1953; *s* by his son **(22)** NIGEL IVAN, 22nd Lord, and present peer.

Forbes, family name of Earl of Granard.

*FORESTER, BARON (Weld-Forester) (Baron UK 1821)

Always the same

(GEORGE CECIL) BROOKE WELD-FORESTER, 8th Baron; *b* 20 Feb 1938; *s* 1977; *ed* Eton, and Roy Agric Coll, Cirencester; patron of three livings; DL Shropshire 1995; Dir Linley Farms since 1974, and Sipolilo Estates since 1977, Broseley Hospital Trust Co, Callkilo, Telford Drive, and Bridgnorth Home Care Co-operative; Chm the Lady Forester Trust; Pres Shropshire Cricket League, Midland Flyfisher's Assocn, The Greenwood Trust since 1990; formerly Chm Shropshire CLA, Shropshire Tree Council, and Regional Advisory Cttee of the Forestry Commn, Shopshire W Midlands Show 1997, The Shrewsbury Flower Show 1981: *m* 1967, Hon Catherine Elizabeth Lyttelton, High Sheriff Shropshire 1997, da of 10th Viscount Cobham, and has issue.

Arms – Quarterly: 1st and 4th quarterly, per fesse indented argent and sable, in the 1st and 4th quarters, a bugle horn of the 2nd, *Forester*; 2nd and 3rd azure, a fesse nebulée between three crescents ermine, and in the centre chief point across crosslet fitchée or, *Weld*. **Crests** – 1st, a talbot passant argent, collared sable, and line reflexed or; 2nd, a wyvern sable, guttée, collared, and lined and wings elevated or, on the wing an escallop of the first. **Supporters** – Two talbots argent, collared sable, lined or, and pendant from the collar a bugle horn of the second.
Residences – Willey Park, Broseley, Shropshire; Bassett, Banket, Zimbabwe.

SON LIVING

Hon CHARLES RICHARD GEORGE, *b* 8 July 1975.

DAUGHTERS LIVING

Hon Selina Lucy, *b* 1968: *m* 1998, Ian W. Graham, son of Michael Graham, of Raffingora, Zimbabwe.
Hon Alice Sophie, *b* 1969.
Hon Alexandra Elizabeth (Sasha), *b* 1973.

SISTERS LIVING

Hon Christine Helena, *b* 1932: *m* 1st, 1951 (*m diss* 1981), 7th Baron Bolton; 2ndly, 1985, Philip David Miles, of Hinton Hall, Lea Cross, Shrewsbury SY5 8JA, son of late Maj Walter Harold Miles, MBE (*see* Greenwell, Bt), and has issue (by 1st *m*) (*see* B Bolton).
Hon (Mary Angela) Fiona (*Hon Lady Barttelot*) *b* 1944; CStJ 1998: *m* 1969, Col Sir Brian Walter de Stopham Barttelot, 5th Bt, OBE, DL, and has issue. *Residence* – Stopham Park, Pulborough, W Sussex RH20 1DY.

COLLATERAL BRANCHES LIVING

Grandchildren of late Hon Charles Cecil Orlando Weld-Forester, 2nd son of 5th Baron:—
Issue of late Lieut-Com Wolstan Beaumont Charles Weld-Forester, CBE, RN, *b* 1899, *d* 1961: *m* 1932, Anne Grace Christian, who *d* 1987, da of late Capt William Augustus Stirling-Home-Drummond-Moray (B Kensington):—

Wolstan William, *b* 1941. —— Beatrice Nicola Grace, *b* 1933: *m* 1955 (*m diss* 1977), 6th Marquess of Bute, who *d* 1993.
Residence – Tylers Barn, Wood Norton Rd, Stibbard, Norfolk NR21 0EX.

Grandchildren of late Maj Hon Edric Alfred Cecil Weld-Forester, CVO (infra):—
Issue of late Charles Robert Cecil Weld-Forester, Capt Rifle Bde, *b* 1919, *d* 1988: *m* 1st, 1940 (*m diss* 1947),
Lady Moyra Rosamond Butler, who *d* 1959, da of 4th Marquess of Ormonde; 2ndly, 1948 (*m diss* 1962), Venetia
Dawn, el da of Lt-Col Sir (Ernest) Edward de Winton Wills, 4th Bt (*cr* 1904); 3rdly, 1963, Delia, who *d* 1992,
formerly wife of late Robin Alan Keith, and yr da of late Lt-Col Guy Andrew Heinekey Buxton:—
(By 2nd *m*) Anthony Edward (Old Manse, Gartmore, By Stirling FK8 3RP), *b* 1954; *ed* Harrow, Magdalen Coll, Oxford,
and RMA Sandhurst: *m* 1979, Joanna Mary, yst da of late Eric Cyprian Perry Whiteley, TD, and has issue living, Henry
James, *b* 1981, — Alfred Charles, *b* 1983, — Jocelyn Victoria, *b* 1986, — Clementine Ruth Katey, *b* 1989. —— Mary
Sylvia (1179 NW Rockwood Lane, Bend, Oregon 97701, USA), *b* 1957: *m* 1986 (*m diss* 1997), Bradley Steven Boyd, son
of Robert Boyd, of Woodside, Calif, USA, and has issue living, Alexandra Marisa, *b* 1987, — Jennifer Louise, *b* 1991.

Issue of late Maj Hon Edric Alfred Cecil Weld-Forester, CVO, 6th son of 5th Baron, *b* 1880, *d* 1963: *m*
1916, Lady Victoria Alexandrina, who *d* 1966, da of 1st Marquess of Lincolnshire, and widow of Nigel
Walter Henry Legge-Bourke (*see* E Dartmouth):—
Mary Cecilia Georgina (*Hon Mrs W. Nicholas S. L. H. Villiers*), *b* 1917: *m* 1939, Major Hon (William) Nicholas Somers
Laurence Hyde Villiers, Grenadier Guards (*see* E Clarendon). —— Elizabeth Rosalind, *b* 1923: *m* 1942, Major Francis
Holdsworth Hunt, ERD, late Coldm Gds, of Mayfield House, Hungerford Hill, Lambourn, Berks, and has issue living,
Charles Edric Holdsworth (The Kettle House, High St, Chipping Campden, Glos GL55 6HN), *b* 1943; Capt Coldm Gds:
m 1968, Sarah Mary, who *d* 1997, da of Maj Anthony Peter Howarth Greenly (*see* Gibson, Bt, *cr* 1926, 1995 Edn), and
has issue living, Guy Edric Holdsworth *b* 1970, Edward Charles Holdsworth *b* 1972, Sacha Victoria Holdsworth *b* 1975,
— Elizabeth, *b* 1947: *m* 1st, 1969 (*m diss* 1980), Maj Conway John Edward Seymour, Gren Gds (*see* M Hertford, colls);
2ndly, 1980, as his 2nd wife, Maj A. Francis Gradidge, late 17/21st Lancers, of Old Brewery Cottage, Netheravon, Wilts
(*see* Steel, Bt, 1976 Edn), and has issue (by 1st *m*) (*see* M Hertford, colls).

Granddaughters of late Rev Hon Orlando St Maur Weld-Forester, 2nd son of 4th Baron:—
Issue of late John Orlando Weld-Forester, *b* 1913, *d* 1995: *m* 1938, Lydia Gertrude (25 Toms Close, Chard, Som
TA20 2HD), yr da of late Rev Stephen Harold Wingfield Digby, Canon of Salisbury, and of Mombasa, Kenya:—
Priscilla Mary, *b* 1939: *m* 1974, Neville Henry Prendergast Vereker, of The Old Rectory, E Anstey, Tiverton, Devon EX16
9JP, and has issue (*see* V Gort, colls). —— Elizabeth, *b* 1941: *m* 1962, John Jeremy Inskip Hawkins, of Inmarsh House,
Inmarsh Lane, Seend, Melksham, Wilts SN12 6RX, and has issue living, *Rev* John Edward Inskipp (St Johns Vicarage,
Vicarage Rd, NW4 3PX), *b* 1963: *m* 1986, Rev Emma Woodhead, who *d* 1990, — Bruce James Orlando (250 Rte des
Clausonnes, 06410 Biot, France), *b* 1965: *m* 1993, Fabienne Tamborini, and has issue living, Jade Marie *b* 1994, —
Veronica Caroline, *b* 1967: *m* 1995, Howard Bowles, of 69 Castle Rd, Isleworth, Middlesex TW7 6QR, and has issue
living, Oliver Ray *b* 1998, — Sarah Elizabeth, *b* 1969: *m* 1991 (*m diss* 1997), Jonathan Mark Levesley, of 67 Walsingham
Close, Hatfield, Herts. —— (Dorothy) Katharine, *b* 1944: *m* 1967, John Wyndham Simson, of Emley Farm, Bowlhead
Green, nr Godalming, Surrey GU8 6NW, and has issue living, Christopher Adhémar, *b* 1969: *m* 1997, Rosalind Judith
Anne Taylor, — Henrietta Katharine, *b* 1971, — Penelope Anne, *b* 1974, — Philippa Lydia Rosamond, *b* 1977.
—— Caroline Lydia, *b* 1948: *m* 1st, 1970 (*m diss* 1992), Frank John Montague Wakefield; 2ndly, 1995, David Alexander
Fisher, of The Old Rectory North, Codford St Mary, nr Warminster, Wilts BA12 0PJ, and has issue living (by 1st *m*),
Nicholas John Alexander, *b* 1978, — Anna Charlotte, *b* 1972, — Holly Christina, *b* 1974. —— Rosamund Eleanor FOREST-
ER (37 Balfern St, SW11 3EL), *b* 1950; has resumed her maiden name: *m* 1971 (*m diss* 1978), Raymond James Edmonds.

PREDECESSORS – (1) CECIL Weld-Forester, *b* 1767; assumed by Roy licence 1811, the additional surname of Weld; *cr*
Baron Forester, of Willey Park, co Salop (peerage of United Kingdom) 1821: *m* 1800, Lady Katherine Mary Manners, da
of 4th Duke of Rutland; *d* 1828; *s* by his el son (2) JOHN GEORGE WELD, PC, 2nd Baron; MP or Wenlock 1826-8, and
Capt of Corps of Gentlemen at Arms 1841-6; *d* 1874; *s* by his brother (3) GEORGE CECIL WELD, PC, 3rd Baron; was
Comptroller of HM Queen Victoria's Household 1852 and 1858-9; sat as MP for Wenlock (C) 1828-74; *d* 14 Feb 1886; *s*
by his brother (4) *Rev* ORLANDO WATKIN WELD, 4th Baron, *b* 1813; Canon Residentiary and Preb of York: *m* 1st, 1840,
Sophia Elizabeth, who *d* 1872, da of Richard Norman; 2ndly, 1875, Emma Maria, who *d* 1898, el da of late William
Tollemache; *d* 1894; *s* by his el son (5) CECIL THEODORE WELD, 5th Baron, *b* 1842; MP for Wenlock (C) 1874-85: *m* 1866,
Emma Georgina who *d* 1922, da of Sir Willoughby Wolstan Dixie, 8th Bt; *d* 1917; *s* by his el son (6) GEORGE CECIL
BEAUMONT WELD, 6th Baron, *b* 1867; Capt Roy Horse Guards; Mayor of Wenlock 1920-21 and 1921-22: *m* 1896, Christine
Isabel, who *d* 1948, da of late Lieut-Col Duncan Henry Caithness Reay Davidson: *d* 1932: *s* by his son (7) CECIL GEORGE
WILFRED, 7th Baron; *b* 1899; ADC to Gov Gen of Union of S Africa 1924-27, and Mayor of Wenlock 1936, and 1916; *m*
1931, Marie Louise Priscilla (DStJ), who *d* 1988, da of Sir Herbert Charles Perrott, 6th Bt, CH, CB (ext); *d* 1977, *s* by
his only son (8) (GEORGE CECIL) BROOKE, 8th Baron and present peer.

*This nobleman has in his possession a licence of the time of Henry VIII, giving to John Forester of Watling St,
Shropshire, the privilege of wearing his hat in the Royal presence.

Formartine, Viscount; grandson of Marquess of Aberdeen.

FORRES, BARON (Williamson) (Baron UK 1922, Bt UK 1909)

Little is made larger by little

ALASTAIR STEPHEN GRANT WILLIAMSON, 4th Baron, and 4th Baronet; *b* 16 May 1946; *s* 1978; *ed* Eton; Chm Agriscot Ppty Ltd, Dir Jaga Trading Ppty Ltd; Australian Rep for Tattersalls Ltd, Newmarket: *m* 1969, Margaret Ann, da of late George John Mallam, of Mullumbimby, NSW, and has issue.

Arms – Argent, a saltire wavy between a mullet in chief and another in base and as many boars' heads couped in the flanks sable. **Crest** – A garb or. **Supporters** – (as recorded at Lyon Office), – On either side a condor proper.
Address – c/o Messrs Clark, Oliver, Dewar and Webster, Brothock-bank House, Arbroath, Angus. *Residence* – 4 Arthur St, Edgecliff, Sydney, NSW, Australia. *Clubs* – Brooks's; Australian Jockey; Tattersalls (Sydney); Sydney Turf.

SONS LIVING

Hon GEORGE ARCHIBALD, *b* 16 Aug 1972.
Hon Guthrie John, *b* 1975.

SISTERS LIVING

Hon Juliet Anne, *b* 1949: *m* 1972, Nigel John Eldon Bankes, of Home Farm House, Williamscot, Banbury, Oxon, and has issue living, William Nigel Wynne, *b* 1974, — Louisa Juliet, *b* 1977, — Fiona Gillian, *b* 1981.
Hon Astrid Signe, *b* 1951: *m* 1976, Peter Karl Dobree Bell, of 15/3rd St, Abbotsford, Johannesburg, S Africa, and has issue living, Hugh John, *b* 1982, — Lucy Claire, *b* 1984.

AUNT LIVING (*daughter of 2nd Baron*)

Hon Jean Mary, *b* 1919: *m* 1941, Wing-Com William James Maitland Longmore, CBE (Maitland, Bt, colls), who *d* 1988, and has issue living, Virginia Marjorie, *b* 1945: *m* 1973, Henry D. N. B. Candy, of Kingstone Warren, Wantage, Berks, and has issue living, Emma Juliet *b* 1974, Sophie Bridget *b* 1978, — Carolyn Mary, *b* 1946: *m* 1st, 1966 (*m diss* 1976), Michael E. Denison; 2ndly, 1981, Michael Desmond Poland, MFH (*see* B Stafford, colls), of Lower Preshaw House, Upham, Southampton, and has issue living (by 1st *m*), James Edward *b* 1968, Lucinda Mary *b* 1971, — Jennifer Maitland, *b* 1953: *m* 1975, Maj Patrick J. R. Snowball, 4/7th R Dragoon Gds, of Ash House, Shalden, Alton, Hants GU34 4EB, and has issue living, Robert Joseph Arthur *b* 1981, Thomas Edward James *b* 1984, Edward William George *b* 1990. *Residence* – Cross Lane Cottage, Bishops Waltham, Hants SO3 1FL.

MOTHER LIVING

Gillian Anne Maclean, el da of late Maj John MacLean Grant, RA: *m* 1st, 1945 (*m diss* 1967), the 3rd Baron, who *d* 1978; 2ndly, 1968, Miles Herman de Zoete, who *d* 1987, of Easter Blinkbonny, Haddington, E Lothian.

COLLATERAL BRANCHES LIVING

Issue of late Capt Hon Gerald Hayne Guthrie Williamson, yr son of 1st Baron, *b* 1893, *d* 1966: *m* 1917, Christian Alicia Hersey, who *d* 1958, da of late Edmund Batten Forbes (Stuart-Forbes, Bt, colls):—
Hersey Caroline Ann (Barr, Minard, by Inveraray, Argyll PA32 8YB), *b* 1920; Jun Cdr ATS, served Middle East 1942-44 (despatches), and Italy 1944-45 (despatches): *m* 1st, 1943, Oliver Breakwell, who was *ka* in N Africa 1943; 2ndly, 1945 (*m diss* 1973), Maj Donald Struan Robertson, SG, who *d* 1991, only surviving son of Rt Hon Sir Malcolm Arnold Robertson, GCMG, KBE, and has had issue (by 2nd *m*), Melville Alexander Struan, *b* 1946; *ed* Eton; *dunm* 1969, — Christian Sarah Hersey, *b* 1948: *m* 1984, Pierre Henri René Daviron, of 92 Greenhaven Rd, Rye, NY 10580, USA, and has issue living, Olivier Melville Raoul *b* 1985, Juliette Isabelle Christian *b* 1987, — Alexandra Charlotte, *b* 1952: *m* 1980, James Chandos Blair, and has issue living, Hamish Chandos *b* 1982, Charlotte Rose *b* 1985, — Lucinda Margaret Ann, *b* 1960: *m* 1983, Stephen Dominic Patrick Mahony, of Broadclose House, Babcary, Som TA11 7ED, and has issue living, Dermot Edward Struan *b* 1988, Caroline Mary Hersey *b* 1987. —— Jane Christian Forbes, *b* 1931.

Grandchildren of late Capt Hon Gerald Hayne Guthrie Williamson (ante):—
Issue of late Alexander Fergus Forbes Williamson, *b* 1919, *d* 1987: *m* 1943, Sabina Ann (Tigh-na-Coille, Kincraig, by Kingussie, Inverness-shire PH21 1QD), only da of late Col Sir Dermot McMorrough Kavanagh, GCVO:—
James David Alexander (Alvie, Kincraig, by Kingussie, Inverness-shire), *b* 1947; *ed* Gordonstoun, Univ of New Brunswick, and Aberdeen Univ; BSc, PhD: *m* 1976, Lynette Robyn, only da of James Stewart, of Feilding, NZ, and has issue living, Ruaraidh James Stewart, *b* 1976, — Joanna Mary, *b* 1980, — Catherine Ngaire, *b* 1985. —— Dermot Fergus, *b* 1950; *ed* Eton, and Dundee Univ: *m* 1987, Yu Yu Su, of Beijing, China, and has issue living, Paula Jiao-Jiao, *b* 1988, Emma Tian-Tian *b* 1989. —— Caroline Ann, *b* 1945: *m* 1968, Capt Colin MacGregor, RN, of The Dairy House, Corton Denham, nr Sherborne, and has issue living, James Patrick *b* 1972: *m* 1998, Kerri Leigh-Ann Watson, — Katherine Helen, *b* 1970. —— Rolline Charlotte, *b* 1956: *m* 1989, Robert Edward Jerome Frewen, of Park Hall, Healaugh, Richmond, N Yorks, and has issue (*see* V Selby).

Issue of late David Archibald Forbes Williamson, MC *b* 1922, *d* 1980: *m* 1953, Elizabeth Wilbur (33 Fifth Av, San Francisco, Calif, USA), da of Roy Case, of Seattle, USA:—
(David) Stephen Charles, *b* 1958: *m* 19—, Susan, da of —. —— Alexander Fergus Case, *b* 1960. —— Charlotte Mary, *b* 1955.

PREDECESSORS – (1) *Rt Hon* ARCHIBALD WILLIAMSON, PC, el son of late Stephen Williamson (MP for St Andrews Dist 1880-85, and Kilmarnock Dist 1886-85), of Copley, Thornton Hough, Cheshire, and Glenogil, Forfar; *b* 1860; a partner in Balfour, Williamson & Co, and Chm of Lobitos Oilfields, and of Central Argentine Railway, and other cos; Parliamentary Financial Sec to War Office 1919-21; MP for Elginshire and Nairnshire (*l*) Jan 1906 to Nov 1918 and for Moray and Nairn Dec 1918 to June 1922; *cr* a *Baronet* 1909, PC 1918, and *Baron Forres*, of Glenogil, co Forfar (peerage of United Kingdom) 1922: *m* 1st, 1887, Caroline Maria, who *d* 1911, da of late James Charles Hayne; 2ndly, 1912, Hon Agnes Freda, OBE, who *d* 1942, da of 1st Baron Herschell; *d* 1931; *s* by his el son (2) STEPHEN KENNETH GUTHRIE, 2nd Baron; *b* 1888; Chm of Lobitos Oilfields, and Anglo-Ecuadorian Oilfields; Director of Office Machinery, Board of Trade 1942-45: *m* 1918, Jessica, who *d* 1972, da of late William Alfred Harford, JP, of Petty France, Badminton, Gloucestershire; *d* 1954; *s* by his el son (3) JOHN ARCHIBALD HARFORD, 3rd Baron, *b* 1922; Pres Roy Forest Agric Assocn, Windsor 1963-64; 1939-45 War in Middle East, Sicily, Italy and Normandy (despatches); ADC to Cdr 6th (British) Armoured Div 1944-45: *m* 1st, 1945 (*m diss* 1967), Gillian Ann Maclean, da of Maj John Maclean Grant, RA; 2ndly, 1969 (*m diss* 1974), (Cecily) Josephine, da of Maj Sir Alexander Penrose Gordon-Cumming, 5th Bt, MC, and widow of the 2nd Earl of Woolton; *d* 1978; *s* by his only son (4) ALASTAIR STEPHEN GRANT, 4th Baron and present peer.

FORSTER OF HARRABY, BARONY OF (Forster) (Extinct 1972)

DAUGHTER LIVING OF FIRST BARON

Hon Pamela FORSTER, *b* 1921; resumed her maiden surname of Forster: *m* 1948 (*m diss* 1951), Peter Hitcham Palmer.

FORTE, BARON (Forte) (Life Baron 1982)

CHARLES FORTE, son of Rocco (Giovanni) Forte, of Casalatticio, Italy; *b* 26 Nov 1908; *ed* Alloa Academy, Dumfries Coll, and Mamiani, Rome; Hon DUniv Strathclyde 1992; Fellow and Member Exec Cttee, Catering Inst since 1949; Member Small Consultative Advisory Cttee to Min of Food since 1946; Member of Council of Brit Tourist Authority and of Lond Tourist Bd; Hon Consul Gen for Republic of San Marino; FBIM; *cr Baron Forte*, of Ripley, co Surrey (Life Baron) 1982: *m* 1943, Irene Mary, da of Giovanni Chierico, of Venice, and has issue.

Arms – Argent four pallets gules over all a bend argent fimbriated azure and on a chief azure three mullets of six points gyronny of twelve or and argent. **Crest** – Out of the battlements of a tower azure a bunch of grapes between two ears of corn proper. **Supporters** – *Dexter*, A pheasant proper. *Sinister*, A salmon proper. **Motto** – Fortis ut jus.
Address – c/o House of Lords, SW1A 0PW. *Clubs* – Carlton, Caledonian.

SON LIVING

Hon Sir Rocco John Vincent, *b* 1945, *ed* Downside, and Pembroke Coll, Oxford (MA); Chm RF Hotels Ltd since 1996; Chm Forte (formerly Trusthouse Forte) plc 1992-96 (Chief Exec 1983-92); FMICA, ACA; Ktd 1995: *m* 1986, Aliai, yr da of Prof Giovanni Ricci, of Rome, and has issue living, Charles, *b* 1991, — Lydia Irene, *b* 1987, — Irene, *b* 1988. *Address* – Savannah House, 11 Charles II St, SW1Y 4QU. *Clubs* – Garrick, Turf.

DAUGHTERS LIVING

Hon Olga, CBE, *b* 1947; CBE (Civil) 1990: *m* 1st, 1966, Marchese Alessandro Polizzi di Sorrentino, who was *k* in a motor accident; 2ndly, 1993, as his 3rd wife, Hon William Hartley Hume Shawcross, elder son of Baron Shawcross, GBE, PC (Life Baron), and has issue living (by 1st *m*), Alexandra, *b* 1971, — Charlotte, *b* 1974. *Residence* – 3 Clarendon Close, W2.

Hon Marie Louise, *b* 1950: *m* 1975, Robert Alexander Burness, and has issue living, Georgina Gerda, *b* 1976: *m* 1998, Kenneth Closs, — Julia Irene, *b* 1978. *Residence* – 4 Clarendon Close, W2.

Hon Irene, *b* 1956: *m* 1977, John J. Danilovich, and has issue living, John Charles Amadeus, *b* 1981, — Alexander Gregory, *b* 1993, — Alice Irene Angelica, *b* 1985. *Residence* – 37 Carlyle Sq, SW3.

Hon Giancarla, *b* 1959: *m* 1981, Michael Ulic Anthony Alen-Buckley, and has issue living, Luke Charles Ulic Locke, *b* 1987, — Portia, *b* 1991. *Residence* – 4 Lansdowne Rd, W11.

Hon Portia, *b* 1964.

FORTESCUE, EARL (Fortescue) (Earl GB 1789)

A strong shield is the salvation of leaders

CHARLES HUGH RICHARD FORTESCUE, 8th Earl; *b* 10 May 1951; *s* 1993; *ed* Eton: *m* 1974, Julia, eldest da of Air Commodore John Adam Sowrey, and has issue.

Arms – Azure, a bend engrailed argent, plain cottised or. **Crest** – An heraldic tiger statant argent, armed, maned, and tufted or. **Supporters** – Two greyhounds argent, ducally gorged and lined gules.
Address – House of Lords, SW1.

DAUGHTERS LIVING

Lady Alice Penelope, *b* 1978.
Lady Kate Eleanor, *b* 1979.
Lady Lucy Beatrice, *b* 1983.

SISTER LIVING

Lady Celia Anne, *b* 1957: *m* 1988 (*m diss* 1998), David Alastair Adams, yst son of Dr Michael Shirley Adams, of Alton House, Seaview, I of Wight, and has issue living, Charles Michael Richard, *b* 1992, — Georgina Penelope Anne, *b* 1990. *Residence* – Semley House, Semley, Shaftesbury, Dorset SP7 9AU.

HALF-SISTERS LIVING

Lady Laura Margaret, *b* 1962: *m* 1995, Simon David Auldjo Jamieson, and has issue (*see* D Norfolk). *Residence* – Yarrow House, N Elmham, Dereham, Norfolk NR20 5LD.

Lady Sarah Jane, *b* 1963: *m* 1995, Francis D. S. Chapman, eldest son of Michael Chapman, of Thorington House, Stoke-by-Nayland, Suffolk, and has issue living, Lydia Rose Margaret, *b* 1998.

UNCLE LIVING (*Son of 6th Earl by 1st m*)

Hon MARTIN DENZIL, *b* 5 Jan 1924; *ed* Eton; Lieut RN (Emergency List): *m* 1st, 1954, Prudence Louisa, who *d* 1992, da of Sir Charles Samuel Rowley, 6th Bt, TD (*cr* 1786); 2ndly, 1994, Caroline, da of late William Henry Lovell, MC, Gren Gds, and widow of Lt-Cmdr W. H. P. Loftie, DSC, of Bowerbank House, Pooley Bridge, Cumbria, and has issue living (by 1st *m*), John Andrew Francis (12 Ursula St, SW11), *b* 1955; *ed* Eton: *m* 1990, Phoebe Anne Cecilia, da of late Rev John Eustace Burridge, of Ham Vicarage, Surrey, and has issue living, Thomas Edmund Horatio *b* 1993, Hugh Augustus Francis *b* 1995, — Anthony William (Ryall's Lodge, Gussage St Michael, Wimborne, Dorset), *b* 1962; *ed* Eton: *m* 1992, Emma Davina, da of Peter Lambert, of Holly Tree Farm, Fearby, nr Masham, N Yorks, and has issue living, William George *b* 1994, — Katharine, *b* 1956: *m* 1995, Robert A. M. Whitaker, of 105 Albert Palace Mansions, Lurline Gdns, SW11, only son of late Evald Mattievich Whitaker, and has issue living, Eleanor Mary *b* 1998, — Georgina Elizabeth, *b* 1958: *m* 1982, Nicholas Hilary Stuart Armour, HM Diplo Ser, son of late Brig William Stanley Gibson Armour, of Brandsby, York, and has issue living, Emily Frances *b* 1985, Sophie Elizabeth *b* 1987. *Residence* – Wincombe Park, Shaftesbury, Dorset SP7 9AB.

HALF-UNCLE LIVING (*Son of 6th Earl by 2nd m*)

Hon Seymour Henry (22 Clarendon St, SW1V 4RF), *b* 1942; *ed* Eton, Trin Coll, Camb (MA), and London Graduate Sch of Business Studies (MSc); Ch Executive, Health Education Authority since 1996: *m* 1st, 1966 (*m diss* 1990), Julia, da of late Sir John Arthur Pilcher, GCMG; 2ndly, 1990, Jennifer Ann, da of Frank Simon, of Wrexham, and has issue living (by 1st *m*), James Adrian, *b* 1978; *ed* Stowe, and Exeter Univ, — Marissa Clare, *b* 1973; *ed* Westminster, Worcester Coll, Oxford, and Courtauld Inst, — (by 2nd *m*) Alexandra Kate, *b* 1991.

AUNT LIVING (*daughter of 6th Earl by 1st m*)

Lady Bridget Ellinor, *b* 1927: *m* 1952, Wing-Com Gordon Leonard Sinclair, DFC, and has issue living, Alan Gordon William (The White House, Adstock, nr Buckingham MK18 2JN), *b* 1956; *ed* Eton: Capt Coldstream Gds: *m* 1983, Fiona B., el da of Maj A. M. MacEwan, and has issue living, Thomas *b* 1985, Archie *b* 1988, Geordie *b* 1993, — Robert Alistair, *b* 1965; *ed* Eton, — (Caroline) Fiona *b* 1958: *m* 1982, Julian Raymond Eric Smith, of Balcombe House, W Sussex RH17 6PB, and has issue (*see* Burrell, Bt), — Joanna Rosalind, *b* 1963: *m* 1992, Mark P. R. Rimell, of 11 Louvaine Rd, SW11 2AQ, elder son of Philip Rimell, of SW1, and has issue living, Benjamin Charles Philip *b* 1994, Amelia *b* 1996. *Residence* – Fairwood House, Great Durnford, Salisbury, Wilts SP4 6BD.

DAUGHTERS LIVING OF FIFTH EARL

Lady Margaret FORTESCUE, *b* 1923; resumed 1966 the surname of Fortescue: *m* 1948 (*m diss* 1968), Bernard van Cutsem, who *d* 1975, and has issue living, Eleanor (*Countess of Arran*), *b* 1949; DL Devon 1998: *m* 1974, 9th Earl of Arran, — Rosamund Isabelle, *b* 1952: *m* 1975, Thomas William Fellowes, son of Sir William Albemarle Fellowes, KCVO (*see* V Hampden, colls). *Residence* – The Garden House, Filleigh, Barnstaple, N Devon.

Lady Elizabeth Joan, *b* 1926: *m* 1946, Major William Lloyd (John) Baxendale, Coldstream Guards, DL, JP, who *d* 1982, and has issue living, David Hugh, *b* 1952: *m* 1977, Jacqueline Loveday, da of late John William Hext, of Trelaske, Lewannick, Cornwall, and has issue living, Guy Jonathan *b* 1980, Thomas Lloyd *b* 1983, — Peter Anthony, *b* 1955, — Lucinda Margaret, *b* 1958: *m* 1st, 1983 (*m diss* 1986), Jonathan Edward McCalmont Harington (*see* Harington, Bt, colls); 2ndly, 1992, Nicolas James Goland Crosthwaite, yr son of Major Ivor Crosthwaite, DSO, and of Mrs John Vincent Sheffield, and has issue living (by 2nd *m*), Louis Charles John *b* 1994, Rose Elizabeth France *b* 1992. *Residence* – Hailwell House, Framfield, Uckfield, E Sussex.

WIDOW LIVING OF SEVENTH EARL

CAROLYN MARY (*Carolyn, Countess Fortescue*), da of late Maj Clement Walter Rowland Hill (*see* V Hill, colls), and formerly wife of Edward Lockwood: *m* 1989, as his 3rd wife, the 7th Earl Fortescue, who *d* 1993. *Residence* – The Old Rectory, Bradoc, Lostwithiel, Cornwall PL22 0RN.

COLLATERAL BRANCHES LIVING

Grandchildren of late Capt Hon Arthur Grenville Fortescue, 4th son of 3rd Earl:—
Issue of late Capt Grenville Fortescue, Rifle Brig (Prince Consort's Own), *b* 1887, *ka* 1915: *m* 1912, Adelaide (who *d* 1977, having *m* 2ndly, 1930, Brigadier Robin Leslie Hutchins, MC, who *d* 1973), el da of late Henry Jephson, of 4 Cornwall Gardens, SW (Crampton, Bt):—
Arthur Henry Grenville, MBE, MC (Goddards, Furley, Axminster, Devon EX13 7TR), *b* 1913; *ed* Winchester, and Ch Ch, Oxford; Brig late Coldstream Guards; 1939-45 War (wounded, despatches, MC, MBE); MBE (Mil) 1946: *m* 1946, Rosita Anne, da of late John Charles Campbell, VC, DSO, MC, and has issue living, Nicholas Cecil John (8 Trouville Rd, SW4 8QL), *b* 1953: *m* 1985, Tessa Jane, yr da of Sir (Thomas) David Ainsworth, 4th Bt, and has issue living, Rosie Olivia *b* 1990, Lily Sarah *b* (twin) 1990. —— Diana FORTESCUE, *b* 1915; resumed her maiden name 1947: *m* 1945 (*m diss* 1947), Lieut-Col Charles Murray Floyd, OBE, RE, who *d* 1971 (*see* Floyd, Bt, colls). *Residence* – Mill Meadow, Burley, Ringwood, Hants.

Granddaughters of Brig Arthur Henry Grenville Fortescue, MBE, MC (ante):—
Issue of late Mark Charles Grenville Fortescue, *b* 1947; *d* 1982: *m* 1971, Virginia Rose (Church House, Steeple Ashton, nr Trowbridge, Wilts), formerly wife of Richard Wilfrid Beavoir Berens, and yst da of late Anthony William Fabio Caccia-Birch, MC:—
Sabina Thérèse, *b* 1973. —— Clarissa Rose Frances, *b* 1975.

Grandchildren of late John Bevill Fortescue, yst son of late Hon George Matthew Fortescue, MP, 2nd son of 1st Earl:—
Issue of late Lt Col John Grenville Fortescue, *b* 1896; *d* 1969: *m* 1917, Daphne Marjorie, who *d* 1962, da of late Hon Algernon Henry Bourke (E Mayo, colls):—
John Desmond Grenville (The Stewardry, Boconnoc, Lostwithiel, Cornwall), *b* 1919; *ed* Eton; Coldstream Guards; a DL and JP; High Sheriff of Cornwall 1966-67; 1939-45 War: *m* 1st, 1942, Nina, who *d* 1976, da of late E. Kendall-Lane of Sask, Canada; 2ndly, 1988, Angela Dorothy, widow of T. C. Keigwin, and has issue living (by 1st *m*), Anthony Desmond Grenville (The White House, Queenwood, Broughton, Stockbridge, Hants SO20 8DF), *b* 1946; *ed* Eton: *m* 1977, Elizabeth Ann Evered, da of late Maj Campbell Evered Poole, and has issue living, Clare Elizabeth *b* 1981, Sarah Alexandra *b* 1984, — Anne Desnia, *b* 1948: *m* 1970, Capt Iain Anthony Mackie, 15/19 Hus, and has issue living, Hamish Anthony *b* 1973, Alastair Desmond *b* 1977, Archibald Iain *b* 1979. —— Rosemary Sylvia, *b* 1920: *m* 1944, Douglas Frederick Thomas White, of The Manor, Berwick Bassett, Swindon, Wilts, and has issue living, John Frederick Fortescue (Overtown Manor, Wroughton, Swindon, Wilts), *b* 1946: *m* 1972, Rosemary Kathleen, da of Maj Edward Palmer, of Fernvale, Northam, N Devon, and has issue living, Douglas John *b* 1985, Nancy Ruth *b* 1976, Jessica Rosemary *b* 1979, — David Grenville (The Old Farm House, Berwick Bassett, Swindon, Wilts), *b* 1948: *m* 1970, Diana Penelope, da of Peter Werden Wilson, of The Manor, Clyffe Pypard, Wilts, and has issue living, Edward John Grenville *b* 1973, Lucia Genevieve Rosemary *b* 1977, Anastasia Sophie *b* 1985, — April Rosemary, *b* 1950: *m* 1971, Robert Edward Simpson, of 4 Belgrave Cres, Edinburgh EH4 3AQ, and has issue living, Charles Robert *b* 1980, Nichola Rosemary *b* 1971, Rachel Elizabeth *b* 1974, Emma Louise *b* 1976. —— June Diana, *b* 1924: *m* 1952, Derek Alistair Bigham, of Chalkstone House, Broad Hinton, Swindon, Wilts SN4 9PA, and has issue living, Diana Susan, *b* 1954: *m* 1985, William Brandon Grundy, and has issue living, David Matthew *b* 1988, — Julia Rosemary, *b* 1959: *m* 1988, Anthony Peregrine Dudley Berendt (*see* E Harrowby).

(In remainder to Barony of Fortescue only)

Grandchildren of late William Archer IRVINE-FORTESCUE, son of late Archer Irvine-Fortescue, son of Rev William Fortescue, LLB, 2nd son of Capt Hon Matthew Fortescue, 2nd son of 2nd Baron:—
Issue of late Col Archer Irvine-Fortescue, DSO, *b* 1880; *d* 1959: *m* 1916, Ruth Olive, who *d* 1971, da of late Henry Boddington, JP of Pownall Hall, Wilmslow, Cheshire:—
James William, *b* 1917; *ed* Edinburgh Acad, and Aberdeen Univ (MA honours 1937); CA 1948; 1939-45 War as Maj and Staff Paymaster RAPC; a member of Kincardine Co Council 1952-8 and 1964-73, a JP and DL for Kincardineshire; FSA Scot 1981: *m* 1953, Margaret Guise, da of late Lt-Col G. D. Yates, of Todhillwood, Canonbie, Dumfriesshire, and has issue living, Grenville Archer, *b* 1954; *ed* Fettes; Maj Highlanders: *m* 1985, Virginia, da of Patrick William Townsend, of The Dower House, Gisburn, nr Clitheroe, Lancs, and has issue living, Alexander Thomas *b* 1987, Simon Archer *b* 1988, Edmund William *b* 1995, Juliet *b* 1991, — Henry Boswell, *b* 1958; *ed* St Andrew's Univ (MA 1982): *m* 1989, Hazel J., 2nd da of Ernest Wood, — James Robert (Nordashødga 55, 5046 Radal, Norway), *b* 1960; *ed* Aberdeen and Imperial Coll London (BSc); MIMM: *m* 1990, Wendy Jayne, da of S. A. W. Milne, of King's Gate, Aberdeen, and has issue living,

Camilla Jane *b* 1994, Sophia Rose *b* 1998, — Rachel Sarah, *b* 1956. *Residence* – Kingcausie, Maryculter, Aberdeen AB12 5FR. —— Agnes Virginia FORTESCUE (Village au Brun, N Dame de Cenilly, 50210 France), *b* 1922; Mus Bac, Cape Town; LRAM: *m* 1st, 1944, Donald Spencer Nuttall, Lieut RA, who was *ka* in Burma 1945; 2ndly, 1949 (*m diss* 1964), Jerzy Wladislaw Jaholkowski; 3rdly, 1973 (*m diss* 1986), Eric Lee Attwell.

Issue of late Rev John Faithful Irvine-Fortescue, *b* 1883, *d* 1957: *m* 1917, Anne, who *d* 1976, da of late J. Brockhurst Souter, of Newhaven:—
Hugh William (Fernlea, Broompark, Kelso, Roxburghshire TD5 7SN), *b* 1930; *ed* Glasgow Acad, and Glasgow Univ (BSc 1961); MIEE 1968, Chartered Engr: *m* 1967, Patricia Anne Elizabeth, da of late F. J. Dudgeon, of Kingsknowe, Edinburgh, and has issue living, John Hugh, *b* 1968, — Caroline Anne Patricia, *b* 1971; BSc Univ Coll London 1992, MB BS Royal Free Hosp 1995, — Katherine Helen Isobel, *b* 1974; *ed* Norwich Univ (BA 1996): *m* 1997, Benjamin James Whitlock, of 14c Rothesay Rd, Bedford MK40 3PN. —— Edith Caroline, *b* 1921; *ed* Glasgow Univ (MA 1942). *Residence* – 5 Seton Place, Edinburgh 9.

Issue of late Lt-Col William Grenville Irvine-Fortescue, MC (and bar), RE, *b* 1897, *d* 1980: *m* 1st, 1921 (*m diss* 1929), Joan Evelyn Mary, da of Henry Sydney Powell, of Pocklington, Yorkshire; 2ndly, 1941, Sheila, who *d* 1985, da of Dr W. Bennett Jones, of Liverpool:—
(By 1st *m*) Henry (Xalet Henri, Auvinia, S Julia de Loria, Andorra), *b* 1922; *ed* Cheltenham; Maj (ret) R Tank Regt; European War 1941-45, Korea 1953, Malaya 1955, Cyprus 1957: *m* 1st, 1951, Bridget Unity, who *d* 1981, da of late Col Edmund Portman Awdry, MC, TD, DL, of Chippenham, Wilts; 2ndly, 1983 (*m diss* 1987), Anne van Gruisen, and has issue living (by 1st *m*), Alexander Ramsay (Chernocke House, St Cross Rd, Winchester SO23 9QP), *b* 1952; *ed* Wellington Coll, King's Coll, London (BSc Eng), and Univ of Cape Town (MBA): *m* 1980, Kathryn, da of late Paul Randles, of Natal, S Africa, and has issue living, Mark Paul *b* 1980, Nicholas Alexander *b* 1983, James Ramsay *b* 1987, — Ian Henry (PO Box 5758 Halfway House, 1685 S Africa), *b* 1954; *ed* Wellington Coll, and Keele Univ (BA): *m* 1986, Vanessa Louise, da of Maj John Grey Haswell, of Johannesburg, and has had issue, †Logan McWatt *b* 1988; *d* 1990, Drummond McLeod *b* 1990, Brittany Avalon *b* 1991, Romney Foy *b* 1993, Francesca Unity *b* 1995, — Victoria Awdry, *b* 1957: *m* 1982, Graham Herbert Tibbot, of 7 Delph Lane, Delph, Saddleworth, nr Oldham OL3 5HX, and has issue living, Graham Henry *b* 1985, Bridget Elizabeth *b* 1986, Sarah Hannah *b* 1990, Martha Victoria *b* 1993. —— (By 2nd *m*) William Archer (Wingham House, Canterbury Rd, Wingham, Canterbury, Kent CT3 1BH), *b* 1945; *ed* Wellington Coll, and Wadham Coll, Oxford (MA): *m* 1979, Clare, da of Bernard Ungerson, CBE. —— (By 1st *m*) Valerie Faith (54c Ashgrove Rd, Aberdeen AB2 5AD), *b* 1925. —— (By 2nd *m*) Margaret Ann, *b* 1944; *ed* Aberdeen Univ (MA): *m* 1979, Richard John Jacob, of 2 Christchurch Rd, Norwich NR2 2AD, and has issue living, Mark Robert, *b* 1980, — Peter Richard, *b* 1984.

PREDECESSORS – **(1)** *Sir* HUGH Fortescue; summoned to Parliament 1721 in right of his maternal grandmother, as 14th *Baron Clinton* (peerage of England), and *cr Baron Fortescue* of Castle Hill, co Devon, with remainder to his half-brother Matthew, and *Earl of Clinton* (peerage of Great Britain) 1746; was a Lord of the Bedchamber; *dsp* 1751, when the earldom expired, the Barony of Clinton fell into abeyance, and the Barony of Fortescue passed to his half-brother **(2)** MATTHEW, 2nd Baron; *b* 1719; *d* 1785; *s* by his son **(3)** HUGH, DCL, 3rd Baron; *cr Viscount Ebrington and Earl Fortescue* (peerage of Great Britain) 1789; *d* 1841; *s* by his son **(4)** HUGH, KG, 2nd Earl, *b* 1783; summoned to House of Lords in his father's Barony of Fortescue 1839, Lord-Lieut of Ireland 1839-41: *m* 1st, 1817, Lady Susan Ryder, who *d* 1827, da of 1st Earl of Harrowby; 2ndly, 1841, Elizabeth, da of Piers Geale, and widow of Sir Marcus Somerville, 4th Bt, MP; *d* 1861; *s* by his son **(5)** HUGH, 3rd Earl, *b* 1818; summoned to House of Peers in his father's Barony of Fortescue 1859; sat as MP for Plymouth (*L*) 1841-52, and for Marylebone 1854-9; a Lord of the Treasury, 1846-7, and Sec to Poor Law Board 1847-51; *m* 1847, Georgiana August Charlotte Caroline, who *d* 1866, el da of late Right Hon George Lionel Dawson-Damer; *d* 1905; *s* by his son **(6)** HUGH, KCB, 4th Earl, *b* 1854; Lord-Lieut of Devonshire 1904-28; MP for Tiverton (*L*) 1881-5, and for W, or Tavistock, Div of Devonshire 1885-92: *m* 1886, Hon Emily Ormsby-Gore, CBE, who *d* 1929 (an Extra Lady of the Bedchamber to Queen Mary), da of 2nd Baron Harlech; *d* 1932; *s* by his son **(7)** HUGH WILLIAM, KG, CB, OBE, MC, PC, 5th Earl; *b* 1888; was Col Comdt Hon Artillery Co 1935-41, Capt of the Hon Corps of Gentlemen-at-Arms April to July 1945, and 1951-8, Lord-in-Waiting to HM 1936-45, and Ch Opposition Whip in House of Lords 1945-51: *m* 1917, Hon Margaret Helen Beaumont, CBE, who *d* 1958, da of 1st Viscount Allendale; *d* 1958, *s* by his brother **(8)** DENZIL GEORGE, MC, TD, 6th Earl; *b* 1893; Lt-Col 96th (R Devon Yeo) Regt 1935-41 and 1st Heavy Regt RA 1942-44: *m* 1st, 1920 (*m diss* 1941), Marjorie Ellinor, OBE, who *d* 1964, da of late Col Charles William Trotter, CB (B Hamilton of Dalzell); 2ndly 1941, Hon Sybil Mary Hardinge, who *d* 1985, da of 3rd Viscount Hardinge; *d* 1977; *s* by his el son **(9)** RICHARD ARCHIBALD, 7th Earl, *b* 1922; Capt Coldstream Guards: *m* 1st, 1949, Penelope Jane, who *d* 1959, yr da of late Robert Evelyn Henderson (*see* Clerke, Bt, 1980 Edn); 2ndly, 1961 (*m diss* 1987), Margaret Anne, da of Charles Michael Stratton, of Hall Farm, Evenley, Northants (*see* E Perth, colls, 1985 Edn); 3rdly, 1989, Mrs Carolyn Mary Lockwood, da of late Maj Clement Walter Rowland Hill (*see* V Hill, colls); *d* 1993; *s* by his only son **(10)** CHARLES HUGH RICHARD, 8th Earl and present peer; also Viscount Ebrington, and Baron Fortescue.

FORTEVIOT, BARON (Dewar) (Baron UK 1917, Bt UK 1907)

JOHN JAMES EVELYN DEWAR, 4th Baron, and 4th Baronet; *b* 5 April 1938; *s* 1993; *ed* Eton: *m* 1963, Lady Elisabeth Jeronima Waldegrave, 3rd da of 12th Earl Waldegrave, and has issue.

ᴀrms – Or, on a pale vert the crozier of St Fillan proper, on a chief engrailed gules a holy lamb passant reguardant, staff and cross argent with the banner of St Andrew proper, between two stalks of barley slipped also proper. ᴄrest – A cock proper. ᴓupporters – (as recorded at Lyon Office), — *Dexter*, the figure of St Fillan holding in his exterior hand his crozier proper; *sinister*, an eagle, wings erected proper.
Seat – Dupplin Castle, Perth. *Residence* – Aberdalgie House, nr Perth. *Clubs* – Boodle's, The Royal Perth Golfing Soc, County & City.

SON LIVING

Hon ALEXANDER JOHN EDWARD, *b* 4 March 1971; *ed* Eton, and Newcastle Univ: *m* 1997, Donryn, eldest da of Graham Clement, of Cape Town, S Africa.

DAUGHTERS LIVING

Hon Mary Emma Jeronima, *b* 1965: *m* 1988, Hon Adam Humphrey Drummond, eldest son of Baroness Strange, and has issue (see that title). *Residence* – The Mains of Megginch, Errol, Perth PH2 7RN.

Hon Miranda Phoebe, *b* 1968.

Hon Henrietta Cynthia, *b* 1970.

BROTHER LIVING

Hon Simon Thomas (Terling Park, Moree, NSW 2400, Australia), *b* 1941: *m* 1st, 1970, (*m diss* 1973), Helen Elizabeth, da of W. N. Bassett, of Karoola Park, Roma, Qld; 2ndly, 1979, Jennifer Alexandra, da of late John Edward St J. Hedge, of Avoca Beach, NSW, and has issue living (by 2nd *m*), Fiona Mary, *b* 1980, — Alexandra Jean, *b* 1982, — Mary Caroline, *b* 1984.

SISTERS LIVING

Hon Caroline Cicely (*Hon Lady Worsley*), *b* 1934: *m* 1st, 1956 (*m diss* 1966), 3rd Duke of Fife; 2ndly, 1980, as his 2nd wife, Gen Sir Richard Edward Worsley, GCB, OBE, and has issue (by 1st *m*) (*see* D Fife).

Hon Penelope Cynthia, *b* 1935: *m* 1959 (*m diss* 1978), Norman Frank Paul Butler, and has had issue, Paul, *b* 1960; *d* 1988, — Sean, *b* 1963, — Tracey Penelope, *b* 1961. *Residence* – 73 Duchess Drive, Newmarket, Suffolk.

PREDECESSORS – (1) JOHN ALEXANDER Dewar, son of late John Dewar, distiller, of Perth; *b* 1856; Chm of John Dewar and Sons (Limited); a Director of Buchanan-Dewar (Limited), and of Distillers Co (Limited); twice Lord Provost of Perth; MP for Inverness-shire (L) 1900-1916; *cr* a *Baronet* 1907, and *Baron Forteviot*, of Dupplin, Perthshire (peerage of United Kingdom) 1917: *m* 1st, 1884, Johann, who *d* 1899, da of William Tod, of Gospetry, Kinross-shire; 2ndly, 1905, Margaret Elizabeth, who *d* 1940, el da of late Henry Holland; *d* 1929; *s* by his el son (2) JOHN, 2nd Baron, *b* 1885; Lieut-Col and Brevet Col late 6th/7th Batn Black Watch (TA) Chm of Distillers Co Ltd, and Brigadier Roy Co of Archers (King's Body Guard for Scotland); Lord Provost of Perth, 1922-5; European War 1914-19 (MC): *m* 1st, 1919, Marjory Winton Isobel, ARRC, who *d* 1945, 2nd da of late Lieut-Col Sir Charles Henry Brabazon Heaton-Ellis, CBE, of Wyddiall Hall, Herts; 2ndly, 1946, Muriel Cecil Harriotte, who *d* 1975, da of late Lt-Col Sir Charles Henry Brabazon Heaton-Ellis, CBE, and widow of (i) Richard Charles Graves-Sawle (Graves-Sawle, Bt), and (ii) Major Alwyn Lionel Compton Cavendish (D Devonshire, colls); *d* 1947; *s* by his half-brother (3) (HENRY) EVELYN ALEXANDER, MBE, 3rd Baron; *b* 1906; Chm John Dewar & Sons Ltd; JP and DL Perthshire; 1939-45 War as Maj The Black Watch: *m* 1933, Cynthia Monica, who *d* 1986, el da of late Piers Cecil Le Gendre Starkie (*see* de Hoghton, Bt, 1972-73 Edn); *d* 1993; *s* by his elder son (4) JOHN JAMES EVELYN, 4th Baron and present peer.

Foxford, Baron, title of Earl of Limerick on Roll of HL.

FRANCIS-WILLIAMS, BARONY OF (Williams) (Extinct 1970)

SON LIVING OF LIFE BARON

Hon John Melville, QC, *b* 1931; *ed* St Christopher Sch, Letchworth, and St John's Coll, Camb, Bar Inner Temple 1955, QC 1977: *m* 1955, Jean Margaret, da of Harold Lucas, of Huddersfield, and has issue. *Residence* – Deers Hill, Abinger Hammer, Dorking, Surrey. *Chambers* – 15 Old Square, Lincoln's Inn, WC2.

DAUGHTER LIVING OF LIFE BARON

(Hon) Elizabeth Frances (does not use courtesy title), *b* 19—: *m* 1963, George Alexander Thomson, of 27 Haverfield Gdns, Kew, Richmond, Surrey, and has issue.

Frankland, family name of Baron Zouche.

FRANKS, BARONY OF (Franks) (Extinct 1992)

DAUGHTER LIVING OF LIFE BARON

Hon Alison Elizabeth, *b* 1945: *m* 1973, Stanley Harris Wright, of 6 Holly Place, Holly Walk, Hampstead, NW3.

Fraser, family name of Lord Lovat.

Fraser, family name of Lady Saltoun.

Fraser, family name of Baron Strathalmond.

FRASER OF ALLANDER, BARONY OF (Fraser) (Disclaimed 1966, Extinct 1987)

DAUGHTERS LIVING OF (DISCLAIMED) SECOND BARON *(By 1st marriage)*

Hon Patricia Lydia, *b* 1963.
Hon Belinda Ann, *b* 1964: *m* 1994, J. Mark Hanson, son of Sir John Gilbert Hanson, KCMG, CBE.
Hon Caroline Emily, *b* 1966: *m* 1997, Dean Stone.

DAUGHTER LIVING OF FIRST BARON

Hon Ann Lewis, *b* 1932.

FRASER OF CARMYLLIE, BARON (Fraser) (Life Baron 1989)

PETER LOVAT FRASER, PC, son of Rev George Robson Fraser, of Correnie, Edinburgh; *b* 29 May 1945; *ed* Loretto, Gonville and Caius Coll, Camb, and Edinburgh Univ; QC 1982, Hon Bencher Lincoln's Inn 1989; Advocate since 1969, Visiting Prof of Law, Dundee Univ, since 1985, Standing Junior Counsel (Scotland) to FCO 1979, PPS to Rt Hon George Younger, Sec of State for Scotland, 1981-82, Solicitor-Gen for Scotland 1982-89, Lord Advocate, Min of State Scottish Office 1989-92, Min of State Scottish Office 1992-95, Min of State Dept of Trade and Industry 1995-97; MP Angus South (*C*) 1979-83, and Angus East (*C*) 1983-87; PC 1989; *cr Baron Fraser of Carmyllie*, of Carmyllie in the District Angus (Life Baron) 1989: *m* 1969, Fiona, da of Hugh Murray Mair, of Lanark, and has issue.
Residence – Slade House, Carmyllie, by Arbroath, Angus.

SON LIVING

Hon James Murray, *b* 1974.

DAUGHTERS LIVING

Hon Jane Helen Anne, *b* 1972.
Hon Catriona Elizabeth, *b* 1981.

FRASER OF KILMORACK, BARONY OF (Fraser) (Extinct 1996)

SON LIVING OF LIFE BARON

Hon Angus Simon James, *b* 1945; *ed* Fettes Coll, Selwyn Coll Camb (MA), and INSEAD (MBA); Non-exec Dir Chloride Group PLC, Non-exec Dir Davies Laing & Dick Ltd, Chm Ag-Gene Ltd, Non-exec Dir Kent Technology Transfer Centre, and Non-exec Dir The Singapore Para Rubber Estates PLC: *m* 1970, Jennifer Ann, da of Colin McKean Craig, FRCS, and has issue.

WIDOW LIVING OF LIFE BARON

ELIZABETH CHLOË (*Baroness Fraser of Kilmorack*), eldest da of late Brig Cyril Alexander Fraser Drummond, OBE: *m* 1944, Baron Fraser of Kilmorack, CBE (Life Baron), late Major RA, who *d* 1996. *Residence* – 18 Drayton Court, SW10 9RH.

FRASER OF LONSDALE, BARONY OF (Fraser) (Extinct 1974)

DAUGHTER LIVING OF LIFE BARON

Hon Margaret Joan, *b* 1920: *m* 1939, Arthur Edward McDonald, and has issue.

FRASER OF TULLYBELTON, BARONY OF (Fraser) (Extinct 1989)

SON LIVING OF LIFE BARON

Hon (Alexander) Andrew Macdonell, *b* 1946; *ed* Eton, and St John's Coll, Oxford (MA): *m* 1982 (*m diss* 1985), Sarah Joanna, da of Henry Jones, of Kitsbury Orchard, Oddington, Moreton-in-Marsh, Glos, and has issue living, Bertie *b* 1984. *Clubs* – Brooks's, Leander.

WIDOW LIVING OF LIFE BARON

MARY URSULA CYNTHIA GWENDOLEN (*Baroness Fraser of Tullybelton*), da of Col Ian Harrison Macdonell, DSO, late Highland LI: *m* 1943, Baron Fraser of Tullybelton, PC (Life Baron), who was *k* in a motor accident 1989. *Residence* – Le Clauzel, 24620 Marquay, France.

FREEMAN, BARON (Freeman) (Life Baron 1997)

ROGER NORMAN FREEMAN, son of Norman James Freeman, CBE; *b* 27 May 1942; *ed* Whitgift Sch, and Balliol Coll, Oxford (MA 1970); Pres Oxford Univ Conservative Assoc 1964; Man Dir Bow Publications 1968 (former Memb Cncl and Treasurer, Bow Group); joined Lehman Bros US 1969, Man Dir 1972-83; MP for Kettering (C) 1983-97; Parliamentary Under-Sec of State Armed Forces, MOD 1986-88, and Dept of Health 1988-90; Min of State for Public Transport, Dept of Transport 1990-94, and for Defence Procurement, MOD 1994-95; Chancellor of the Duchy of Lancaster and Cabinet Min for the Public Service 1995-97; Partner, Coopers & Lybrand, Chartered Accountants, 1997-98; Consultant Price Waterhouse Coopers since 1999; Chm Thomson-CSF (UK) Holdings Ltd since 1999; Founder Memb Hundred Group of UK CA Fin Dirs; FCA 1978; *cr* PC 1993, and *Baron Freeman*, of Dingley, co Northants (Life Baron) 1997: *m* 1969, Jennifer Margaret, da of Malcolm Woodward Watson, of Sale, Cheshire, and has issue.

Arms – Argent on a pale cotised sable a pale argent thereon three roses gules barbed and seeded or over all two bars wavy gemel counterchanged. **Crest** – A badger sejant erect proper supporting with the forepaws a pair of dividing compasses points downwards or. **Supporters** – On either side a springer spaniel sable muzzled and bibbed argent gorged with a plain collar attached thereto a chain flexed over the back or.
Address – c/o House of Lords, Westminster, SW1A 0PW. *Clubs* – Carlton, Kennel.

SON LIVING

Hon Edmund Malcolm Roger, *b* 1978; *ed* Harrow, and Manchester Univ.

DAUGHTER LIVING

Hon Olivia Margaret Jennifer, *b* 1986; *ed* Cheltenham Ladies Coll.

Freke, Evans, family name of Baron Carbery.

Fremantle, family name of Baron Cottesloe.

French, family name of Baron de Freyne.

FREYBERG, BARON (Freyberg) (Baron UK 1951)
(Name pronounced Fryburg)

VALERIAN BERNARD FREYBERG, 3rd Baron; *b* 15 Dec 1970; *s* 1993; *ed* Eton, and Camberwell Coll of Art; Sculptor.

𝔄rms – Or, on a chief sable four mullets of the field. 𝔈rest – A demi lion gules holding between the paws an eagle displayed sable. 𝔖upporters – On either side a salamander proper. *Residence* – Munstead House, Godalming, Surrey GU8 4AR.

SISTERS LIVING

Hon Annabel Pauline, *b* 1961.
Hon Venetia Rose, *b* 1963: *m* 1991, Robert Phillips, son of late John Phillips.
Hon Christina Marie-Gabriel, *b* 1967.

WIDOW LIVING OF SECOND BARON

IVRY PERRONELLE KATHARINE (*Baroness Freyberg*), only da of late Cyril Harrower Guild, of Aspall Hall, nr Debenham, Suffolk: *m* 1960, Col the 2nd Baron Freyberg, OBE, MC, who *d* 1993. *Residence* – Munstead House, Godalming, Surrey GU8 4AR.

PREDECESSORS – (1) *Sir* BERNARD CYRIL Freyberg, VC, GCMG, KCB, KBE, DSO, son of J. Freyberg, of Wellington, New Zealand; *b* 1889; Lt-Gen late Grenadier Guards and Manchester Regt; GOC, New Zealand Expeditionary Force 1939-45, and Gov-Gen and C-in-C of New Zealand 1946-52, and Dep Constable and Lt-Gov of Windsor Castle 1953-63; *cr Baron Freyberg*, of Wellington, New Zealand, and of Munstead, co Surrey (peerage of UK) 1951: *m* 1922, Dame Barbara, GBE, who *d* 1973, da of Sir Herbert Jekyll, KCMG, and widow of Hon Francis Walter Stafford MacLaren, MP (B Aberconway); *d* 1963; *s* by his only son (2) PAUL RICHARD, OBE, MC, 2nd Baron, *b* 1923; Col late Gren Guards, served Greece and W Desert 1940-42, N Africa and Italy 1942-45, Palestine 1947-48, Cyprus 1956-58, and Cameroons 1961, AAG HQ London Dist 1962-65, Col Gen Staff to Dir Territorials, Volunteers & Cadets 1971-75; author of *Bernard Freyberg, VC: Soldier of Two Nations* 1991: *m* 1960, Ivry Perronelle Katharine, only da of late Cyril Harrower Guild, of Aspall Hall, nr Debenham, Suffolk; *d* 1993; *s* by his only son (3) VALERIAN BERNARD, 3rd Baron and present peer.

FULTON, BARONY OF (Fulton) (Extinct 1986)

SONS LIVING OF LIFE BARON

Hon (Kenneth Angus) Oliver, *b* 1941; *ed* Eton, Balliol Coll, Oxford (BA) and Univ of California.

Hon Alan Scott, *b* 1946; *ed* Eton and Balliol Coll, Oxford: *m* 1983, (Herminie) Jane, da of Geoffrey J. Bulman, of Pool House, Harpenden, and has issue.

Hon Duncan John Rowntree, *b* 1949; *ed* Eton and Balliol Coll, Oxford.

DAUGHTER LIVING OF LIFE BARON

Hon Charity Marion Annie, *b* 1951.

WIDOW LIVING OF LIFE BARON

JACQUELINE (*Baroness Fulton*) (Brook House, Thornton-le-Dale, N Yorks), da of Kenneth Edward Towler Wilkinson, of York: *m* 1939, Baron Fulton (Life Baron), who *d* 1986.

FURNIVALL, BARONY OF (Dent) (Baron E 1295) (Abeyant 1968)

MARY FRANCES KATHERINE DENT, BARONESS FURNIVALL, *d* 1968, when the Barony fell into abeyance between her two daughters.

DAUGHTERS LIVING OF MARY FRANCES KATHERINE DENT, BARONESS FURNIVALL (19th holder of Barony) (*Co-heiresses to the Barony*)

Hon ROSAMOND MARY (Sister Ancilla, OSB, of St Mildred's Abbey, Minster, Ramsgate), *b* 3 June 1933.

Hon PATRICIA MARY (Trotwood, 11 Gresham Rd, Limpsfield, Oxted, Surrey), *b* 4 April 1935: *m* 1st, 1956 (*m diss* 1963), Capt Thomas Hornsby, late Durham LI, who *d* 1967; 2ndly, 1970, Roger Thomas John Bence, and has issue living, (by 1st *m*), Francis Walton Petre, *b* 1958, — Clare Mary Petre, *b* 1957: *m* 1984, Robert Ralph Harbord, of Grey Gables, High St, Longborough, Moreton-in-Marsh, Glos GL56 0QE, and has issue (*see* B Suffield, colls), — (by 2nd *m*) Richard William Petre, *b* 1976, — Katharine Rosamond Petre, *b* 1971: *m* 1998, Philip Haydn-Slater, of 76A Elsham Rd, W14 8HH.

GAGE, VISCOUNT (Gage) (Sits as Baron GB 1790) (Viscount I 1720, Bt E 1622)

Courage without fear

(HENRY) NICOLAS GAGE, 8th Viscount, and 15th Baronet; *b* 9 April 1934; *s* 1993; *ed* Eton, and Ch Ch, Oxford; 2nd Lieut late Coldstream Gds; DL E Sussex 1998: *m* 1974, Lady Diana Adrienne Beatty, da of 2nd Earl Beatty, and has issue.

𝔄rms – Quarterly: 1st and 4th, per saltire argent and azure, a saltire gules, *Gage*; 2nd and 3rd azure, a sun in splendour or, *St Clere*. 𝔠rest – A ram statant argent, armed and unguled or. 𝔖upporters – Two greyhounds of a light brown colour, proper, gorged with plain collars, adorned on their upper edges with fleurs-de-lis or.

Seat – Firle Place, Lewes, E Sussex. *Residence* – The Cottage, Charwelton, Daventry, Northants.

SONS LIVING

Hon HENRY WILLIAM, *b* 25 June 1975.

Hon David Benedict, *b* 1977.

SISTER LIVING

Hon Camilla Jane (*Hon Lady Cazalet*), *b* 1937; Dir Lumley Cazalet Ltd since 1967, Trustee Glyndebourne Arts Trust since 1978, and Member Royal National Theatre Board 1991-97: *m* 1965, Sir Edward Stephen Cazalet, DL (Hon Mr Justice Cazalet), and has issue living, David Benedict, *b* 1967, — Henry Pelham, *b* 1969, — Lara Imogen Leonora, *b* 1973. *Residences* – 58 Seymour Walk, SW10 9NF; Shaw Farm, Plumpton Green, nr Lewes, E Sussex BN7 3DG.

WIDOW LIVING OF SEVENTH VISCOUNT

DEIRDRE MELINA JANE (*Deirdre, Viscountess Gage*), da of late Thomas James Simmons: *m* 1990, as his 2nd wife, the 7th Viscount Gage, who *d* 1993.

COLLATERAL BRANCHES LIVING

Grandchildren (by 2nd *m*) of late John Fitzhardinge Berkeley Gage (infra):—
Issue of late John Grenville Berkeley Gage, *b* 1933, *d* 1983: *m* 1961, Pauline (Hadley Wood Golf Club, Barnet, Herts), da of Antony Paul Pape:—
Ælla Rupert Fitzhardinge Berkeley, *b* 1966: *m* 1995, Liza Rhian, da of David John Greatrex, of Anglesey, N Wales, and has issue living, Amelia Beatrice Grace, *b* 1997. —— Cassandra Griselda Louise, *b* 1961; *d* 1992. —— Emma Leonora Falaise, *b* 1963: *m* 1994, James Patrick Francis Stableford, elder son of late David Gordon Stableford, of Cowes, I of Wight, and has issue living, Millicent Louise, *b* 1994, — Freya Rose, *b* 1997.

Grandchildren of late Lt-Col Ælla Molyneux Berkeley Gage, son of late Lt-Gen Hon Edward Thomas Gage, CB (infra): –
Issue of late John Fitzhardinge Berkeley Gage, *b* 1901, *d* 1967: *m* 1st, 1923 (*m diss* 1927), Beth Olivia, who *d* 1948, adopted da of late Brig-Gen Ronald Maclachlan, Rifle Bde; 2ndly, 1931 (*m diss* 1937), Griselda Margaret, who *d* 1992, yr da of late Rear-Adm Sir Godfrey Marshall Paine, KCB, MVO; 3rdly, 19—, Jenny Elvira (15 Rodger's Rd, Gibraltar), da of —:—
(By 2nd *m*) Thomas Ælla Godfrey (Hamiltons, Withypool, Minehead, Somerset) *b* 1935; *ed* Eton: *m* 1st, 1960 (*m diss* 1982), Dorothy Isobel Margaret, da of John Baxter Wylie; 2ndly, 1983, Ina Merete, da of Johan Frederik Utke Meincke, of Denmark, and has issue living (by 1st *m*), Andrew Thomas Berkeley, *b* 1961: *m* 1st, 1987 (*m diss* 1992), Angela Denise, da of Donald Graham Frame; 2ndly, 1997, Susan, da of late Peter Bowes McDonald, of Carmunnock, Lanarks, and has issue living (by 2nd *m*), Rebecca Gordon *b* 1997, — John Duncan Godfrey, *b* 1962, — Caroline Margaret, *b* 1966, — Amber Camilla, *b* 1969: *m* 1997, George Dennis Stucley, elder son of Sir Hugh George Coplestone Bampfylde Stucley, 6th Bt. —— Malcolm Edward Fitzhardinge (278 Seafront, Hayling Island, Hants PO11 0AZ), *b* 1936; late RHG; *ed* Eton: *m* 1971, Vanessa Smith, who *d* 1984. —— Dawn Falaise, *b* 1932: *m* 1st, 1952 (*m diss* 1963), John Kershaw Sanders; 2ndly, 1963, Capt John Pym Loughnan, RN, and has issue living (by 1st *m*), John James Godfrey, *b* 1953, — Guy Dominic Robson (Efranoros 12, 116-35 Athens, Greece), *b* 1955, — Hugo Thomas Kershaw, *b* 1957.

Grandsons of late Sir Berkeley Everard Foley Gage, KCMG (infra):—
Issue of late Anthony St Clere Berkeley Gage, *b* 1931, *d* 1984: *m* 1965, Virginia Mary, da of Denis H. Ferens, of Bilver, Ipplepen, S Devon:—
Benjamin Francis, *b* 1969. —— Gregory Bernard, *b* 1971. —— Oliver, *b* 1973.

Grandson of late Brig-Gen Moreton Foley Gage, DSO (infra):—
Issue of late Sir Berkeley Everard Foley Gage, KCMG, sometime HM Amb to Thailand, *b* 1904, *d* 1994: *m* 1st, 1931 (*m diss* 1954), Hedwig Maria Gertrud Eva, da of Carl von Chappuis, of Liegnitz, Silesia; 2ndly, 1954, Mrs Lillian Riggs Miller (*Lady Gage*), da of Vladimir Vukmirovich:—
(By 1st *m*) Ulick Charles Christopher, *b* 1938; *ed* Eton, and St John's Coll, Camb (BA); late 2nd Lieut 12th Lancers; ARIBA, ARIAA: *m* 1964, Helen Mary Janet, da of Air Vice-Marshal Evelyn Michael Thomas Howell, CBE, and has issue living, Marius Berkeley, *b* 1966, — Ulicia Mary, *b* 1965. *Residence* – 19 Bruce St, Stanmore, NSW 2048, Australia.

Grandchildren of late Lieut-Gen Hon Edward Thomas Gage, CB, 3rd son of 4th Viscount:—
Issue of late Brig-Gen Moreton Foley Gage, DSO, late 5th Dragoon Guards, *b* 1873, *d* 1953: *m* 1st 1902, Anne Massie, who *d* 1915, el da of William Everard Strong, of New York City, USA; 2ndly, 1916, Frances, who *d* 1955, da of Senator Henry P. Lippitt, of Providence, Rhode Island, USA:—
(By 1st *m*) Edward Fitzhardinge Peyton, *b* 1906; *ed* Eton, and Ch Ch, Oxford (BA); formerly Maj Coldm Gds; High Sheriff Shropshire 1963: *m* 1931, Thailia Westcott, da of Stephen Caldwell Millett, and has issue living, Robert Westcott Moreton (50 Pimlico Rd, SW1W 8LP), *b* 1934; *ed* Eton, and Ch Ch, Oxford; late Lt Life Gds: *m* 1st, 1964 (*m diss* 1978), Maria Teresa Francisca, da of late Don Emilio Maria Diaz-Caneja; 2ndly, 1990, Elisabeth Nicola Maria, da of Benjamin Hubert Dowson, and has had issue (by 1st *m*), †Henry St Clere Rokewood *b* 1966; *d* 1996, in Madrid, Dolores Isabella *b* 1965, — Anne Caroline Thalia (*Hon Mrs Robin A. Baring*), *b* 1931; *ed* St Hilda's Coll, Oxford (MA): *m* 1960, Hon Robin Alexander Baring (*see* B Ashburton), — Elizabeth Estling (20 Albemarle St, W1), *b* 1937: *m* 1st, 1957 (*m diss* 1965), David Vernon Russell; 2ndly, 1970, David Bruce Douglas Lowe; 3rdly, 1974, Richard Perkins. *Residence* – Château de Combecave, 82190 Bourg de Visa, Tarn et Garonne, France. —— (By 2nd *m*) Quentin Henry Moreton, *b* 1920; *ed* Eton, and Ch Ch, Oxford; formerly Maj Gren Gds, 1939-45 War (wounded): *m* 1949, Hazel Swinton, da of Col George Archibald Swinton Home, DSO, OBE, late 5th Dragoon Gds, and has issue living, Jonathan Moreton, *b* 1954: *m* 1994, Anna C., da of late Stanley Hobson, of Hadlow, Kent, and has issue living, Edward Moreton Quentin *b* 1996, Lavinia *b* 1999, — Deborah Pamela, *b* 1950. *Residence* – Pelham Cottage, Church Lane, Hellingly, E Sussex BN27 4HA. —— Dorothy Louise, *b* 1917: *m* 1941, Maj Anthony George Akers-Douglas, late 13th/18th Hussars (*see* V Chilston, colls), who *d* 1991. *Residence* – 23 Mytten Close, Cuckfield, W Sussex RH17 5LN.

PREDECESSORS – **(1)** THOMAS Gage: *cr a Baronet* 1622; *d* 1633; *s* by his son **(2)** *Sir* THOMAS, 2nd Bt; *d* 1655; *s* by his el son **(3)** *Sir* THOMAS, 3rd Bt; *d unmarried* 1660; *s* by his brother **(4)** *Sir* JOHN, 4th Bt; *s* by his el son **(5)** *Sir* JOHN, 5th Bt; *d* 1700; *s* by his brother **(6)** *Sir* THOMAS, 6th Bt; *d* 1713; *s* by his brother **(7)** *Sir* WILLIAM, KCB, 7th Bt, MP for Seaford; *d unmarried* 1744; *s* by his cousin **(8)** THOMAS, 8th Bt el son of Joseph, 4th son of 2nd Bt; MP for Tewkesbury,

Verderer of the Forest of Dean and Steward of the Household to Frederick, Prince of Wales; *cr* prior to his succession to the baronetcy *Baron Gage*, of Castlebar, and *Viscount Gage* (peerage of Ireland) 1720; *d* 1754; *s* by his son **(9)** WILLIAM HALL, 2nd Viscount; *cr Baron Gage*, of Firle, co Sussex (peerage of Great Britain) 1780, and *Baron Gage*, of High Meadow, co Gloucester (peerage of Great Britain) 1790, and with remainder to his nephew, heir presumptive to the peerage of 1720 and to the baronetcy; *d* 1791, when the Barony of Gage, of Firle became extinct, and the peerages of 1720 and 1790 devolved upon his nephew **(10)** HENRY, 3rd Viscount, el son of Gen Hon Thomas, 2nd son of 1st Viscount; a Major-Gen in the Army; *d* 1808, *s* by his son **(11)** HENRY HALL, 4th Viscount; *d* 1877; *s* by his grandson **(12)** HENRY CHARLES (son of Hon Henry Edward Hall Gage (el son of 4th Viscount), and Sophia Selina, who *d* 1886, da of Sir Charles Knightley, 2nd Bt), 5th Viscount, *b* 1854: *m* 1894, Leila Georgina, who *d* 1916, da of Rev Frederick Peel; *d* 1912; *s* by his only son **(13)** HENRY RAINALD, KCVO, 6th Viscount, *b* 1895; Vice-Lieut for Sussex 1957-70; Chm and Patron Nat Federation of Housing Socs; a Lord-in-Waiting to HM 1924-29 and 1931-39: *m* 1st, 1931, Hon Alexandra Imogen Clair Grenfell, who *d* 1969, da of 1st Baron Desborough (ext) (*see* Bs Lucas of Crudwell); 2ndly, 1971, Diana, who *d* 1992, da of late Col Rt Hon Lord Richard Frederick Cavendish, CB, CMG (*see* D Devonshire, colls), formerly wife of Robert John Graham Boothby (afterwards Baron Boothby), and widow of Lt-Col Hon Ian Douglas-Campbell-Gray (*see* L Gray); *d* 1982; *s* by his el son **(14)** GEORGE JOHN ST CLERE, 7th Viscount; *b* 1932: *m* 1st, 1971 (*m diss* 1975), Valerie Ann, da of Joseph E. Dutch, of Horam, Sussex; 2ndly, 1990, Deirdre Melina Jane, da of late Thomas James Simmons; *d* 1993; *s* by his brother **(15)** HENRY NICOLAS, 8th Viscount and present peer; also Baron Gage.

GAINFORD, BARON (Pease) (Baron UK 1917)

JOSEPH EDWARD PEASE, 3rd Baron; *b* 25 Dec 1921; *s* 1971; *ed* Eton, and Gordonstoun; FRGS; MSST; 1939-45 War as Sgt RAF: *m* 1953 Margaret Theophila Radcliffe, da of late Henry Edmund Guise Tyndale, of Winchester Coll, and has issue.

Peace and hope

Arms – Per fesse azure and gules, a fesse nebuly ermine between two lambs passant in chief argent, and in base upon a mount proper a dove rising argent, holding in the beak a pea stalk, the blossom and pods proper. Crest – Upon the capital of an Ionic column a dove rising, holding in the beak a pea stalk as in the arms. Supporters – On either side a Barbary wild sheep ram guardant or.
Residence – 1 Dedmere Court, Marlow, Bucks SL7 1PL.

DAUGHTERS LIVING

Hon Joanna Ruth Miriam, *b* 1959.
Hon Virginia Claire Margaret, *b* 1960.

BROTHERS LIVING

Hon GEORGE, *b* 20 April 1926; *ed* Eton; ARIBA; MRTPI; ARIAS; 1939-45 War in RNVR: *m* 1958, Flora Daphne, da of late Dr N. A. Dyce-Sharp, and has issue living, Adrian Christopher, *b* 1960, — Matthew Edward, *b* 1962: *m* 1991, Barbara, yr da of E. R. John Griffiths, of Aachen, Germany, and has issue living, Felix George *b* 1992, Clara Jutta *b* 1995, Verity Flora *b* 1997, — Olivia Daphne, *b* 1958; MA (Oxon): *m* 1984, Dr Stephen Roy Langford, PhD, elder son of Roy Langford, of St Peter Port, Guernsey, and has issue living, Rachel Veronica *b* 1988, Esther Rebecca *b* 1992, — Samantha Rachel, *b* 1965: *m* 1996, Peter Baker, of Marondera, Zimbabwe, and has issue living, Nicola *b* 1996, Sasha *b* 1998. *Residence* – Naemoor Gardens, Rumbling Bridge, Kinross KY13 0PY.
(*Hon*) John Michael (does not use courtesy title) (No 5 Chalet, Tayvallich, Lochgilphead, Argyll PA31 8PW), *b* 1930; *ed* Gordonstoun: *m* 1962 (*m diss* 1997), Catherine Margaret, da of Duncan F. Shaw, and has issue living, David Michael, *b* 1964, — Andrew Joseph, *b* 1967, — Daniel John *b* 1973.

PREDECESSORS – **(1)** *Rt Hon* JOSEPH ALBERT Pease, second son of Sir Joseph Whitwell Pease, 1st Bt (*cr* 1882); *b* 1860; appointed Junior Liberal Whip 1897, a Junior Lord of the Treasury Dec 1905, Parliamentary (Patronage) Sec to the Treasury and Ch Liberal Whip May 1908, Chancellor of Duchy of Lancaster (with a seat in the Cabinet) Feb 1910, Pres of Board of Education Oct 1911, and a Member of Committee of Science Council 1915; was Postmaster-Gen Jan to Dec 1916, Chm of British Broadcasting Co 1922-6, and Dep Chm 1926-31; MP for Northumberland, Tyneside Div (L) 1892-1900, for Essex, N, or Saffron Walden, Div May 1901 to Jan 1910, and for Rotherham Div of S Part of W Riding of Yorkshire March 1910 to Dec 1916; *cr Baron Gainford*, of Headlam, co Durham (peerage of United Kingdom) 1917: *m* 1886, Ethel, who *d* 1941, only da of Lieut-Gen Sir Henry Marshman Havelock-Allan, 1st Bt, GCB, VC, MP; *d* 1943; *s* by his son **(2)** JOSEPH, TD, 2nd Baron, *b* 1889: *m* 1921, Veronica Margaret, who *d* 1995, da of Sir George John William Noble, 2nd Bt (*cr* 1902); *d* 1971; *s* by his el son **(3)** Joseph Edward, 3rd Baron and present peer.

GAINSBOROUGH, EARL OF (Noel) (Earl UK 1841, Bt GB 1781)

ANTHONY GERARD EDWARD NOEL, 5th Earl, and 7th Baronet; *b* 24 Oct 1923; *s* 1927; *ed* Worth, Sussex, and Georgetown, Maryland, USA; is patron of two livings (but being a Roman Catholic cannot present), JP Leics 1974 (formerly Rutland 1957), a Bailiff Grand Cross of Sovereign Order of Malta (Pres of British Assocn 1968-74) and KStJ; Chm of Rutland co Council 1970-73: *m* 1947, Mary, da of late Hon John Joseph Stourton, TD (*see* B Mowbray, colls), and has issue.

Arms – Or, fretty gules, and a canton ermine. Crest – A buck at gaze argent, attired or. Supporters – On either side a bull argent, armed and unguled proper, gorged with a naval crown azure, therefrom a chain reflexed over the back gold, pendent from the crown an escutcheon, also azure, charged with an anchor erect, encircled by a wreath of laurel or. *Residence* – Horn House, Exton, Oakham, Rutland LE15 7QU. *Clubs* – Brooks's, Bembridge Sailing, Royal Yacht Sqdn.

All well, or nothing

SONS LIVING

ANTHONY BAPTIST (*Viscount Campden*) *b* 16 Jan 1950; *ed* Ampleforth, and RAC, Cirencester: *m* 1972, Charlotte, LVO, el da of Col Thomas Foley Churchill Winnington, MBE (*see* Winnington, Bt) and has issue:—
SON LIVING— *Hon* Henry Robert Anthony, *b* 1 July 1977.

Seat – Exton Park, Oakham, Rutland LE15 8AN. *Town Residence* – 105 Earl's Court Rd, W8.

Hon Gerard Edward Joseph (10 Porchester Terrace, W2; Timewell House, Morebath, Tiverton, Devon EX16 9BY), *b* 1955; *ed* Ampleforth, and London Univ: *m* 1985, Charlotte, yr (twin) da of Sir William Stratford Dugdale, 2nd Bt, CBE, MC, and has issue living, Reginald, *b* 1987, — Belinda Mary, *b* 1986, — Lettice, *b* 1989.

Hon Thomas (24 Lennox Gdns, SW1), *b* 1958; *ed* Ampleforth, and RAC, Cirencester.

Hon Edward Andrew (16 Stratford Rd, W8 6QD), *b* 1960; *ed* Ampleforth, and British Inst, Paris: *m* 1st, 1990 (*m diss* 1994), Lavinia Jane, only da of late Cmdr George Edward Bingham, of Grenville House, Droxford, Hants; 2ndly, 1997, Sarah Kate, yr da of late David George Warre Yeats Brown, of Wangford, Suffolk (*see* B Auckland, colls).

DAUGHTERS LIVING

Lady Juliana Mary Alice (*Juliana, Countess of Liverpool*) (Turville Barns, East Leach, Glos GL7 3QB), *b* 1949: *m* 1970 (*m diss* 1994), 5th Earl of Liverpool, and has issue (see that title).

Lady Maria, *b* 1951: *m* 1971, Robert Pridden, of Fort Henry House, Exton, Oakham, Leics, and has issue living, Benedict John Anthony, *b* 1973, — Lucy, *b* 1976.

Lady Celestria Magdalen Mary (Marsh Hall, Orleton, Ludlow, Shropshire SY8 4HY), *b* 1954; *ed* St Mary's, Ascot, and St Hilda's Coll, Oxford; writer, Social Ed *Harpers & Queen* 1992-98: *m* 1990, Timothy M. Hales, son of late S. W. M. Hales, MC, and of late Mrs C. G. des Salles d'Epinoix, and has issue living, Catherine Rose Mary, *b* 1990.

BROTHER LIVING

Hon Gerard Eyre Wriothesley, *b* 1926; *ed* Georgetown, Washington DC, USA, and Exeter Coll, Oxford; Bar Inner Temple 1952; Editor of *Catholic Herald* 1971-76, and since 1981: *m* 1958, Adèle Julie Patricia, only da of Maj Bonville Were, and Mrs M. J. Were, OBE, and has issue living, Philip Arthur Nicholas, *b* 1959, — Robert John Baptist, *b* 1962; Bluemantle Pursuivant, Coll of Arms since 1993, — Elizabeth Mary Alice, *b* 1967; *ed* St Mary's, Ascot, and Manchester Coll, Oxford: *m* 1996, Henry John Pitman, eldest son of Lt-Col Hugh Pitman, and of Mrs Andrew Parker Bowles, and has issue living, Luke Nicholas *b* 1999. *Residence* – Westington Mill, Chipping Campden, Glos. *Office* – Herald House, Lamb's Passage, EC1Y 8TQ.

SISTER LIVING

Lady Maureen Thérèse Josephine, *b* 1917: *m* 1st, 1944, the 15th Baron Dormer, who *d* 1975; 2ndly, 1982, as his 2nd wife, Peregrine Edward Launcelot Fellowes, who *d* 1999. *Residence* – The Court, Chipping Campden, Glos.

COLLATERAL BRANCHES LIVING

Grandsons of late Col Hon Charles Hubert Francis Noel, OBE (*infra*):—
Issue of late Col Archibald Charles William Noel, MC, *b* 1914, *d* 1997: *m* 1st, 1945, Bridget Mary, who *d* 1976, only da of late Brig William Albany Fetherstonhaugh, CB, CBE, DSO (*see* Cayley, Bt, colls, 1955 Edn); 2ndly, 1977, Andrée Marie (10 Felden St, SW6), eldest da of Pierre Duchen, of Bayonne:—
(By 1st *m*) Charles William (97 Harbord St, SW6 6PN), *b* 1948; *ed* Ampleforth, and Trin Coll, Camb: *m* 1985, Diane Margaret, only da of Gerald A. de Freitas, of 63 Onslow Gdns, SW7, and has issue living, Alexander Charles Fitzwilliam, *b* 1989, — Elizabeth Bridget Maggie, *b* 1986. —— Edward Albany (26 King's Court, Hamlet Gdns, W6), *b* 1956; *ed* Stanbridge Earls Sch.

Issue of late Col Hon Charles Hubert Francis Noel, OBE, son of 3rd Earl, *b* 1885; *d* 1947: *m* 1912,

May, who *d* 1964, el da of late Brig-Gen Archibald Campbell Douglas Dick, CB, CMG, of Pitkerro, Angus:—
Douglas Robert George (25 Broomhouse Rd, SW6 3QU), *b* 1924; *ed* Oratory Sch; Maj Cold Gds (ret); Italy 1943-45: *m* 1949, Eleanor Susan Jane, da of late Brig George Edward Younghusband, CBE, and has issue living, James Douglas George (74 Kingston Rd, Oxford OX2 6RJ), *b* 1950; *ed* Downside, and London and Oxford Univs; BA, Cert Ed, — William Edward Douglas (Ipsden House, Ipsden, Wallingford, Oxon OX10 6AJ), *b* 1953; *ed* Downside: *m* 1st, 1975 (*m diss* 1982 and annulled 1984), his 4th cousin, Victoria Mary, da of George Oswald Younghusband, of Bessborough House, Nenagh, Ballymacky, co Tipperary; 2ndly, 1993, Mrs Juliet Catherine Hayward, eldest da of Col Arthur Harold Newmarch Reade, LVO, Queens Own Hussars (ret), of Old Post House, Ipsden, Wallingford, Oxon, and has issue living (by 1st *m*), Arthur Douglas *b* 1977; *ed* Downside, Teresa Sybil *b* 1976; *ed* St Mary's, Shaftesbury, d'Overbroeck's Coll, Oxford, and Newcastle Univ, — Caroline Mary Jane, *b* 1956; *ed* St Mary's, Ascot, and Bristol Univ: *m* 1987, Charles Anthony Wentzel, of 81 Balham Park Rd, SW12 8EB, son of John Brunette Wentzel, of Johannesburg, and has issue living, Philippa Mary *b* 1991.

Grandchildren of late Lt-Col Edward William Charles Noel, CIE, DSO, eldest son of late Lt-Col Hon Edward Noel (infra):—
Issue of late Denys Edward Noel, *b* 1925, *d* 1978: *m* 1947, Petronelle Moore (Weavers Cottage, Coombe St, Lyme Regis, Dorset), only da of C. Austin Bostock, of the Hermitage, Newnham, Cambridge:—
Julian Roden Bostock (9 Wigton Place, SE11 4AN), *b* 1949: *m* 1982, Susanna Elisabeth, da of Benjamin Bentley Dodd, of Eel Pie Island, Twickenham, Middx. —— Laura Frances, *b* 1951: *m* 1979, Peter Clement Coe, of 33 Courthope Rd, NW3, and has issue living, Toby Richard, *b* 1983, — Lucy Josephine, *b* 1985, — Jennifer Mary, *b* 1988.

Granddaughter of late Lt-Col Hon Edward Noel, 2nd son of 2nd Earl:—
Issue of late Capt John Baptist Lucius Noel, *b* 1890, *d* 1989; Official Photographer on Mount Everest Expeditions 1922 and 1924; assumed addl forename of John by deed poll 1908: *m* 1st, 1915, Sybil, who *d* 1939, da of J. Graham; 2ndly, 1941, Mary Sullivan, who *d* 1984:—
(By 2nd *m*) Sandra Ruth Catherine, *b* 1943. *Residence* – 6 Barrow Hill Place, Ashford, Kent TN23 1NE.

Grandchildren of late Major Gerard Thomas Noel, eldest son of Hon Henry Lewis Noel (infra):—
Issue of late William Henry Middleton Noel, *b* 1898, *d* 1954: *m* 1934, Jacqueline Naomi, who *d* 1984, yr da of R. Bendall, of Ofcolaco, N Transvaal:—
Gerard Roland, *b* 1936: *m* 1975, Lina, da of E. Micayabas, of Malaybalay, Philippines, and has issue living, John William Bakun, *b* 1981. —— Michael John, *b* 1944: *m* 1973, Amanda Jane, only da of late Wing-Cdr A. B. Corfe, RAF, and has issue living, William Gerard, *b* 1975, — Richard Roland, *b* 1979, — Andrew Corfe, *b* 1982. —— Christopher William (Wild Hawk Farm, Ofcolaco, NE Transvaal, S Africa), *b* 1947: *m* 1971, Rhoda, only da of H. Allen, of Trichardt, E Transvaal, and has issue living, Gillian Frances, *b* 1973, — Catherine Elizabeth, *b* 1976. —— Wilfrid Byron (Wild Hawk Farm, Ofcolaco, NE Transvaal, S Africa), *b* 1949: *m* 1975, Patricia Maud, 2nd da of W. D. J. Van Niekerk, of Johannesburg, and has issue living, Colin Byron, *b* 1980, — Gerard Vernon, *b* 1985, — Penelope Jacqueline, *b* 1976, — Susan Liane, *b* 1977. —— Margaret Celestria, *b* 1939: *m* 1963, Hugh Boswell Brown, of Crake Valley Farm, PO Box 3025, Mutare, Zimbabwe, and has issue living, Robert Jason (Chicago, Illinois, USA), *b* 1969: *m* 1999, Helen Ildi Revi, — Catherine Ann, *b* 1964: *m* 1987, Gary Mark Mair Davidson, of Harare, Zimbabwe, and has issue living, Emma Jacqueline *b* 1997, — Joan Cécile, *b* 1965: *m* 1988, Michael Charles Daly, of Santiago, Chile, and has issue living, Nicholas Charles *b* 1989, — Nicola Noel, *b* 1971: *m* 1994, Stephen Richard, of Cape Town, S Africa, and has issue living, Anthony Richard *b* 1994, Jessica Anne 1996.

Grandchildren of late Hon Henry Lewis Noel, 3rd son of 1st Earl:—
Issue of late Hugh Middleton Noel, *b* 1862, *d* 1956: *m* 1901, Helen Winnefred, who *d* 1956, da of Robert Gibbs, of 32 St Augustine's Rd, Bedford:—
Leland Hugh Wriothesley, *b* 1906; is a Landscape Artist: *m* 1941, Barbara Jean, el da of A. H. Meier, of Chico, Calif, USA, and has issue living, William Hugh (1414 Monroe St, Santa Rosa, Calif, USA), *b* 1950, — Pamela Le NOEL-MACMATH (1724 Terrace Way, Santa Rosa, Calif 95404, USA), *b* 1948: *m* 1984 (*m diss* 1993), Lucas MacMath, and has issue living, Bryce Wolcott *b* 1990, Eston Meier *b* (twin) 1990, Talia Noel *b* 1987. *Residence* – 1421, McDonald Av, Santa Rosa, Calif, USA. —— Diana Catharine (1526, Shoreline Drive, Santa Barbara, Calif, USA), *b* 1914: *m* 1942, Hollis H. Parker, Sgt AA Artillery, who *d* 1948, and has issue living, Geoffrey Hollis, *b* 1944; USA Coast Guard: *m* 1965, Patricia Edwards, and has issue living, Geoffrey Hollis jr *b* 1967, Matthew Donovan *b* 1976, Michelle Diana *b* 1969, — Stephen Hugh Anderson, *b* 1946; *ed* Hawaii Univ, and Cal State Coll, Long Beach.

Grandchildren of late Henry Hamlyn Noel, 3rd son of Hon Henry Lewis Noel (ante):—
Issue of late Major Edward Francis Hamlyn Noel, MRCVS, Indian Army, *b* 1899, *d* 1953: *m* 1926, Doris Marie, who *d* 1983, da of Albert Claude Verrières, CIE:—
Gerard John Hamlyn (Squirrels Hall, Stratford St Mary, Suffolk), *b* 1930; *ed* Wellington Coll; Capt (ret) RE: *m* 1963, Gillian Ralphia, only da of late W. T. B. Head, of Frinton-on-Sea, Essex, and has issue living, Richard Gerard Hamlyn, *b* 1965, — Victoria Gillian Emilia, *b* 1969: *m* 1998, Stephen John Kunzer, son of Paul Kunzer, of Durham. —— Penelope Noel, BD, *b* 1934: *m* 1962, Rev Colin Scott Jee, of 16 Stokes End, Haddenham, Aylesbury, Bucks HP17 8DX, and has issue living, Rev Jonathan Noel (7 Rosemary Way, Hinckley, Leics), *b* 1963: *m* 1989, Juliet Elizabeth, eldest da of Rev John Dudley Morris, of Handcross, W Sussex, and has issue living, Thomas Peter *b* 1991, Daniel James *b* 1993, Timothy David *b* 1996, Rachel Clare *b* (twin) 1993, — Mary Penelope, *b* 1965: *m* 1989, Rev Andrew Malcolm Rimmer, of The Vicarage, 87 Perseus Place, Waterlooville, Hants PO7 8AW, and has issue living, James Edward *b* 1993, Christopher David *b* 1995, Rebecca Mary *b* 1991. —— Lyn Noel (1 Holmes Cottages, Letchmore Heath, Watford, Herts WD2 8EN), *b* 1947: *m* 1968 (*m diss* 1991), Ian Thomas Kennedy, and has issue living, Gordon Noel, *b* 1971: *m* 1998, Tracey Louise, eldest da of D. Lloyd, of Fradley, Lichfield, Staffs, — James Edward (1 Back St, St Cross, Winchester SO23 9SB), *b* 1972; Dr: *m* 1997, Emma Alexandra Elizabeth, eldest da of P. Holmes, of Maresfield, Sussex, — Emilia Jayne, *b* 1980.

(In remainder to Barony of Barham, and to the Baronetcy)

Descendants of late Sir Gerard Noel Noel, 2nd Bt (father of 1st Earl of Gainsborough), by his wife Diana, in her own right, Baroness Barham:—

Granddaughter of late Adm of the Fleet Sir Gerard Henry Uctred Noel, GCB, KCMG, son of late Rev Augustus William Noel, son of late Capt Hon Frederic Noel, RN, 6th son of Diana Baroness Barham:—
Issue of late Francis Arthur Gerard Noel, OBE, *b* 1880, *d* 1955: *m* 1913, Evelyn, who *d* 1988, da of late Benjamin Bond Cabbell, of Cromer Hall, Norfolk:—
Susan Rachel, *b* 1918. *Residence* – Roundways, Holt, Norfolk NR25 6BN.

Granddaughters of late Lt-Col Maurice Waldegrave Noel, AFC (infra):—
Issue of late Peter Maurice William Noel, *b* 1922, *d* 1984: *m* 1946 (*m diss* 19—), Patricia Margaret, yst da of A. C. W. Hill, of Mosman, Sydney, NSW, Australia:—
Diana Margaret NOEL (22 Wudgong St, Mosman, Sydney, NSW 2088, Australia), *b* 1947: *m* 1980, Baron François Maurice Seymour Faverôt de Kerbrech, and has issue living, Chloë Elizabeth Noel, *b* 1980. —— Susan Elizabeth Gay, *b* 1951.

Grandson of late Col William Frederick Noel Noel, el son of Col Edward Andrew Noel, el son of Rev Francis James Noel, 7th son of Sir Gerard Noel Noel, 2nd Bt and Diana Baroness Barham (ante):—
Issue of late Lieut-Col Maurice Waldegrave Noel, AFC, The King's (Liverpool) Regt, *b* 1888, *d* 1958: *m* 1920, Elisabeth Christine Edith, who *d* 1981, el da of late Charles Gairdner, Rangoon, and Tower of Lethendy, Perthshire:—
Robert Gerard Charles, *b* 1928; *ed* Malvern: late Lt RM (invalided); Stockbroker; FIPR, MSI, OLJ: *m* 1961 (*m diss* 1988), Gillian Margaret Halse.

Grandchildren of late Com Montague Wroithesley Noel (infra):—
Issue of late Capt Henry Methuen Noel Noel, *b* 1927, *d* 1998: *m* 1963, Helen Elizabeth Anne, who *d* 1992, da of late Sir William Oliphant Hutchison, of Cholmondeley Lodge, Richmond, Surrey:—
Robert Montague (21 Donne Place, SW3 2NG), *b* 1964; BSc, ARICS: *m* 1992, Sophie M. J., da of Jean-Marie Bourdaire, of Paris. —— William Gerard (Walters Art Gallery, 600 N Charles St, Baltimore, MD 21201-5185, USA), *b* 1965; PhD, MA (Cantab). —— Emma Margery (27a Queen's Mews, W2), *b* 1969.

Grandchildren of late Adm Francis Charles Methuen Noel, 3rd son of Col Edward Andrew Noel (ante):—
Issue of late Com Montague Wriothesley Noel, *b* 1892, *ka* 1941: *m* 1926, Christabel Florence Arthur, who *d* 1965, da of late Rev Henry Startin, V of Horrabridge, Devon:—
Gerard Lionel Gordon (twin) (The Manor, Rockbeare, Exeter, Devon), *b* 1927; *ed* Marlborough Coll, and Trin Hall, Camb (MA); late RE; FRICS: *m* 1965, Caroline Patricia, da of Brig Eric Llewellyn Griffith Griffith-Williams, CBE, DSO, MC, DL, of Rockbeare Manor, Exeter, Devon, and has issue living, Andrew Francis Methuen, *b* 1966, — Thomas Charles Eric, *b* 1970, — Delia Christabel Mary, *b* 1967, — Matilda Theresa Caroline, *b* 1972, — Amy Margaret, *b* 1979. *Club* – Royal Ocean Racing. —— Montague Geoffrey Bickersteth (Monastery House, Little Crawley, Newport Pagnell, Bucks), *b* 1931; *ed* Marlborough Coll, and Trin Hall, Camb (BA), MRCS, LRCP, FFARCS; late Lt R Signals: *m* (Jan) 1958, Audrey Mavis, da of Allen Metcalf, of Wingerworth, Chesterfield, Derbys, and has issue living, David Charles, *b* 1963, — Peter, *b* 1966, — Michael (twin), *b* 1966, — Jennifer Anne, *b* (Dec) 1958. —— Celestria Wilmot Rosalie, *b* 1935: *m* (Jan) 1960, David Jeffrey Bell, of 6 Meadow Close, Tring, Herts HP23 5BT, and has issue living, Charles Montague Jeffrey, *b* 1974, — Caroline Barbara Penelope, *b* (Dec) 1960: *m* 1987, Jeremy Wilfred Duncombe, of Berkhamsted, Herts, and has issue living, Jeffrey Charles William *b* 1988, Elizabeth Alice Rachael *b* 1989, — Joanna Elizabeth Glencairn *b* 1962; has issue living, Alec Henry *b* 1994, — Alice Christabel Ann, *b* 1967: *m* 1993, Stavros Stangos, of Athens, and has issue living, Asteris *b* 1993, Ariadne *b* 1995, — Christina Mary Noel, *b* 1968.

Granddaughters of late Gambier Baptist Edward Noel (infra):—
Issue of late Rear-Adm Gambier John Byng Noel, CB, *b* 1914, *d* 1995: *m* 1936, Joan (Woodpeckers, Haslemere, Surrey), da of late Percy Herbert Stevens:—
Caroline Byng, *b* 1936: *m* 1st, 1973, Ivor Eagling, who *d* 1979; 2ndly, 1982, William Cairns, MBE. —— Penelope Byng, *b* 1939: *m* 1st, 1960 (*m diss* 1967), Anthony Henry John Rawlinson (later 5th Bt); 2ndly, 1967 (*m diss* 1984), Count Axel Du Monceau de Bergendal. —— Virginia Byng, *b* 1943: *m* 1967, Prof Michael Stanley Tite, and has issue living, Sarah, *b* 1970, — Alice, *b* 1972. —— Vanessa Jane, *b* (twin) 1943: *m* 1970 (*m diss* 1986), Tom McClure. *Residence* – 24 The Meadows, Guildford, Surrey GU2 5DT.

Granddaughter of late Capt Robert Lascelles Gambier Noel, RN, 4th son of Col Edward Andrew Noel (ante):—
Issue of late Gambier Baptist Edward Noel, *b* 1888, *d* 1957: *m* 1st, 1914 (*m diss* 1922), Beatrice Eva Tytler, who *d* 1966, da of late Rear-Adm John Clarke Byng (V Torrington, colls); 2ndly, 1924 (*m diss* 1931), Rosalie Sibyl, da of Major S. S. Flower, late Northumberland Fusiliers, and formerly wife of Capt W. L. Aplin Harrison, MC:—
(By 1st *m*) Beatrice Louisa Frances, *b* 1915; formerly Section Officer WAAF: *m* 1943, Capt William Falcon Skelton, RN, who *d* 1966, only son of Engineer Vice-Adm Sir Reginald William Skelton, KCB, CBE, DSO, and has issue living, Peter, *b* 1950; D Phil: *m* 1994, Vanessa Hawkes (*née* Bull), — Sally, *b* 1944: *m* 1969, Marcel Wagner, and has issue living, Dameon *b* 1972, Cosima *b* 1970: *m* 1993, John Piggott, and has issue living, Suilven PIGGOTT-WAGNER *b* 199—, — Judy, *b* 1946; MA, BLitt (Oxon). *Residence* – Boughton Cottage, Green Lane, Henley-on-Thames, Oxon RG9 1LR.

Grandchildren of late Capt John Andrew Vernald Noel, 3rd son of late Capt Robert Lascelles Gambier Noel, RN (ante):—
Issue of late Prof Anthony Robert Alistair Noel, *b* 1927, *d* 1984: *m* 1958, Marthina Cornelia Rousseau (4 The Park, Gardens, Cape Town 8001, S Africa), of Roodepoort, Transvaal:—
Darwin John Robert, *b* 1958: *m* 1996, Mrs Rita Joy Patricia Crozet, da of late James Taylor Holroyd. *Residence* – 33 Kingfisher Drive, Yateley, Hants GU46 6NP.

Issue of late John Edward Barham Noel, *b* 1929; *d* 1954: *m* 1952, Grace Vera (who *m* 2ndly, 1966, Anthony Maurice Thomas, of The Cabin, 31 Castle St, IoW PO32 6RD), yst da of A. Paul, of Herne Hill, SE:—
Jacqueline Susan (Flat 4, 68 Arthur Rd, Shirley, Southampton S015 5DU), *b* 1953: *m* 1972 (*m diss* 1983), Victor Clive Hayton, and has had issue, Thor David Fewlass, *b* 1974, — Jodi William, *b* 1976, *d* 1985.

Granddaughter of late Eugene Frederic Noel, yst son of late Rev Hon Baptist Wriothesley Noel, 10th son of Diana, Baroness Barham:—

Issue of late Evan Baillie Noel, *b* 1879, *d* 1928: *m* 1906, Marjorie, who *d* 1955, da of late R. Deane Sweeting, MD, Bar-at-law, Senior Med Inspector HM Local Govt Board:—

Susan Diana Barham, *b* 1912: *m* 1940, Prof Geoffrey Frederic Powell, DSO, Solicitor and late Sq-Ldr RAFVR, who *d* 1982. *Residence* – 9 Barons Keep, Gliddon Rd, W14 9AT.

PREDECESSORS – (1) *Rt Hon Sir* CHARLES Middleton, PC, Adm of the Red, MP for Rochester and First Lord of the Admiralty, etc; *cr a Baronet* 1781 with remainder to his son-in-law, Gerard Noel Edwards (who in 1798 assumed the surname of Noel), nephew of Henry Noel, 6th Earl of Gainsborough (*cr* 1682), 9th Viscount Campden (*cr* 1628), and 8th Baron Noel (*cr* 1617); *cr Baron Barham* (peerage of United Kingdom) 1805, with remainder to his da Diana, wife of Gerard Noel Noel, Esq (ante); *d* 1813; *s* in baronetcy by his son-in-law (ante), and in barony by his da. (2) DIANA; *d* 1823; *s* by her el son (3) CHARLES, 3rd Baron; *s* to his father's baronetcy 1838, and *cr Baron Noel, Viscount Campden, and Earl of Gainsborough* (peerage of United Kingdom) 1841; *d* 1866; *s* by his el son (4) CHARLES GEORGE, 2nd Earl, *b* 1818; Lord-Lieut of Rutland: *m* 1841, Lady Ida Harriet Augusta, who *d* 1867, da of 16th Earl of Erroll; *d* 1881; *s* by his son (5) CHARLES WILLIAM FRANCIS, 3rd Earl, *b* 1850: *m* 1st, 1876, Augusta Mary Catherine, who *d* 1877, da of late Robert Berkeley, of Spetchley Park, Worcester; 2ndly, 1880, Mary Elizabeth, who *d* 1937, da of late James Arthur Dease, of Turbotston, co Westmeath; *d* 1926; *s* by his son (6) ARTHUR EDWARD JOSEPH, OBE, 4th Earl, *b* 1884; Private Chamberlain to Pope Benedict XV and Pope Pius XI; an Hon Attache in Norway and Sweden 1908-12, and at Washington, USA 1913-14: *m* 1915, Alice Mary, who *d* 1970, da of Edward Eyre, of Gloucester House, Park Lane, W1; *d* 1927; *s* by his son (7) ANTHONY GERARD EDWARD, 5th Earl and present peer; also Viscount Campden, Baron Barham, and Baron Noel.

GAITSKELL, BARONY OF (Gaitskell) (Extinct 1989)

SON LIVING OF LIFE BARONESS (*By 1st marriage*)

Hon Raymond FROST, *b* 1924; *ed* Oundle, and Worcester Coll, Oxford, Dir, Econ Development Inst at World Bank: *m* 1958, June Virginia Johnston, da of late Ing Eduardo Gonzalez Rodriquez del Rey, and has issue, one son and one da.

DAUGHTERS LIVING OF LIFE BARONESS (*By 2nd marriage*)

Hon Julia, *b* 1939; *ed* Somerville Coll, Oxford: *m* 1969, George Peter McNeal, of 18 Frognal Gdns, Hampstead, NW3, and has issue, two sons.
Hon Cressida (18 Frognal Gdns, Hampstead, NW3), *b* 1942; *ed* Somerville Coll, Oxford (MA), and LSE (MSc): *m* 1964, Gordon Joshua Wasserman, Assist Undersecretary of State, Home Office, and has issue, two das.

Galbraith, family name of Baron Strathclyde.

GALLACHER, BARON (Gallacher) (Life Baron 1983)

JOHN GALLACHER, son of late William Gallacher, of Alexandria, Dumbartonshire; *b* 7 May 1920; *ed* St Patrick's, Dumbarton, and the Co-operative Coll, Loughborough (Chartered Sec); Pres Enfield Highway Co-operative Soc 1954-68, Parly Sec to Co-operative Union and a Dir Retail Consortium Ltd 1974-83, sometime Pres Inst of Meat; Corporal RAF, served in Coastal Cmd and 2nd Tactical Air Force; *cr Baron Gallacher*, of Enfield, in Greater London (Life Baron) 1983: *m* 1947, Freda Vivian, da of late Alfred Chittenden, of Maidstone, Kent, and has issue.
Address – c/o House of Lords, SW1A 0PW.

SON LIVING

Hon Robert John, *b* 1955; *ed* Broxbourne Sch, Herts.

GALLOWAY, EARL OF (Stewart) (Earl S 1623, Bt S 1627 and 1687)

Valour strengths from a wound

RANDOLPH KEITH REGINALD STEWART, 13th Earl, and 12th Baronet of Corsewell, and 10th of Burray; *b* 14 Oct 1928; *s* 1978; *ed* Harrow: *m* 1975, Mrs Lily May Budge, yst da of late Andrew Miller, of Duns, Berwickshire.

Arms – Or, a fesse checky argent and azure, surmounted of a bend engrailed gules, within a double tressure flory counterflory of the last. Crest – A pelican in nest, vulning herself argent, winged or. Supporters – *Dexter*, a savage man, wreathed about the head and middle with laurel, and holding in the right hand a club resting on the shoulder, all proper; *sinister*, a lion gules.
Residence – 6 Abercrombie Rd, Castle Douglas, Kirkcudbrightshire DG7 1AY.

SISTER LIVING

Lady Antonia Marian Amy Isabel, *b* 1925: *m* 1946, Sir (Charles) Mark Dalrymple, 3rd Bt, who *d* 1971, when the title became ext. *Residence* – Garden Cottage, Newhailes, Musselburgh, Midlothian.

COLLATERAL BRANCHES LIVING

Grandchildren of late Lt-Col Walter Robert Stewart, DSO, MC, only surv son of late Maj-Gen Hon Alexander Stewart, 3rd son of 9th Earl:—
Issue of late Maj Alexander David Stewart, MBE, TD, *b* 1914, *d* 1985: *m* 1948, Daphne Marion (North Green, Kelsale, Saxmundham, Suffolk), widow of Clyde Euan Miles Graham, Flying Officer, RAF (*see* Peel, E, colls, 1956 Edn), and only da of Sir Reginald Bonsor, 2nd Bt:—
ANDREW CLYDE (9 Lennox Gdns Mews, SW1; Cumloden, Newton Stewart, Kirkcudbrightshire), *b* 13 March 1949; *ed* Eton: *m* 1977, Sara, only da of Brig Patrick Pollock, and has issue living, Alexander Patrick, *b* 1980, — Tania Jane, *b* 1979, — Zoe Inez, *b* 1983. —— (David) Mark (The Old Hall, Reedham, Norwich, Norfolk NR13 3TZ), *b* 1960: *m* 1987, Victoria Georgina, 2nd da of late Brig Thomas Geoffrey Henry Jackson (*see* Jackson, Bt, *cr* 1869, colls), and has issue living, Samuel Mark, *b* 1990, — Harry Alexander, *b* 1992, — Jack, *b* 1999, — Chloe Rose, *b* 1994. —— (Rosemary) Zara, *b* 1952: *m* 1977, G. Ian Fleming, and has issue living, Alistair James, *b* 1982.

Issue of late Capt Ian Michael Stewart, *b* 1917, *d* 1973: *m* 1941 (*m diss* 1952), Peggy Spencer, who *d* 1957, twin da of Spencer Thornton:—
Alastair Grenfell (Highfield House, Nunnington, York), *b* 1944: *m* 1973, Sarah Monica Scott, and has issue living, James Henry, *b* 1975, — Victoria Rose, *b* 1977. — Carolyn Mary, *b* 1942: *m* 1963, Alec Charles Hinchcliff Bond, of Stud Farmhouse, Thenford, Banbury, Oxon, and has issue living, William David Hinchcliff, *b* 1970: *m* 1998, Carolyn Hill.

Granddaughters of late Rev James Stewart, 2nd son of Hon Montgomery Granville John Stewart, MP, 6th son of 7th Earl:—
Issue of late Horatio George Willoughby Stewart, *b* 1877, *d* 1943: *m* 1929, Beatrice Maud, who *d* 1984, da of late James Bedson:—
Flora Margaret, *b* 1930: *m* 1951, Richard Arthur Revell, who *d* 1986, of 16 Bellencroft Gdns, Merry Hill, Wolverhampton, and has issue living, Nicholas Stewart (7 Graspin Lane, Weston Favell, Northampton NN3 3BU), *b* 1952: *m* 1981, Rosemary Jean, yst da of George Stephen Bradley, and has issue living, Matthew James *b* 1983, Stewart George *b* 1985, Melanie Louise *b* 1987, — Clare Victoria, *b* 1956: *m* 1982, Stephen John Brown, and has issue living, Benjamin Jack *b* 1993, — Jennifer Mary, *b* 1968. —— Daphne Isabel (11 Drambuie Court, Kippa-ring, Queensland 4021, Australia), *b* 1932: *m* 1956, Neville Tasker, who *d* 1997, and has issue living, Sheryl Ann, *b* 1959, — Melanie Jane, *b* 1963.

Granddaughter of late Col Charles Edward Stewart, CB, CMG, CIE, son of late Algernon Stewart, yr son of late Hon Edward Richard Stewart, 7th son of 7th Earl:—
Issue of late Lieut-Col Algernon Bingham Anstruther Stewart, DSO, *b* 1869, *d* 1916: *m* 1911, Edith Evelyn (who *m* 2ndly, 1922, Henry de Grey Lennox (D Richmond, colls), and *d* 1932), da of late Sir Arthur Pendarves Vivian, KCB (B Swansea, colls):—
Barbara Jean, *b* (twin) 1915: *m* 1939, Maj George De Pree, King's Roy Rifle Corps, who *d* 1992, and has issue living, Andrew Hugo Stewart (Oakhill House, Tai Happe Rd, RD9, Hastings, N Island, NZ), *b* 1946: *m* 1972, Victoria, only da of David Neilson, of Catton Hall, Burton-on-Trent, and has issue living, Emma *b* 1975, Alice *b* 1978, Olivia *b* 1984, — Jane Mary, *b* 1940: *m* 1961, Giles William Pitman, of Heath House, Patmore Heath, Albury, Ware, Herts, and has issue living, George Eustace *b* 1963: *m* 1996, Elizabeth A., da of Jean Eicher, of Luxemburg, John Struan *b* 1969: *m* 1993, Laura Louise Vintcent (and has issue living, Max *b* 1997), Kate Jane *b* 1965: *m* 1992 Mark Christopher Dalton (and has issue living, Jim Munro *b* 1998, Hester Elizabeth *b* 1994, Nelly Jane *b* 1996), — Rachel Anne, *b* 1950: *m* 1970, James Edward Cory Liddell, of Cottonworth House, Fullerton, Andover, Hants, and has issue (*see* B Ravensworth, colls). *Residence* – 3 Fullerton Manor, Andover, Hants SP11 7LA.

Grandson of late Charles Patrick Stewart, son of late Lt-Col Hon James Henry Keith Stewart, CB, MP, 8th son of 7th Earl:—
Issue of late Charles Nigel Stewart, *b* 1864, *d* 1915: *m* 1895, Edith Mabel, da of late Julius Miller, MD, MRCS:—
Herbert Nigel, *b* 1896; believed to have emigrated to USA.

Grandchildren of late Lt-Col John Stewart, DSO, only son of late John Leveson Douglas Stewart (*b* 1842), grandson of late Leveson Douglas Stewart (*b* 1786), 2nd son of Adm Hon Keith Stewart, 3rd son of 6th Earl:—
Issue of late Lt-Col Keith Ian Douglas Stewart, OBE, *b* 1904, *d* 1990: *m* 1st, 1930, Helena Lucie, who was *k* by enemy action 1940, da of Edward Ashton St Hill, of 7 Queensborough Terr, W2; 2ndly, 1940, Philippa North, who *d* 1966, eldest da of late Robert Nairn, FRCS, of Hastings, NZ; 3rdly, 1967, Frances Auckland Louise Bogue, who *d* 1974, da of late Francis Joseph Hieronymous-Jones; 4thly, 1977, Joan Mary (Stable Steps, Lower St, Merriott, Som), da of late Alban J. H. Francis, of St Peter's, Weston-super-Mare, and widow of Maj Philip Clarke, MC, Royal Warws Regt:—
(By 1st *m*) John Edward Hamish Keith (100 St Andrew's Av, Melbourne, Vic, Australia), *b* 1935; *ed* Lodge Sch, Barbados. —— Jennifer Mary Hamilton, *b* 1931: *m* 1st, 1952 (*m diss* 1962), John Innes Wood; 2ndly, 1963 (*m diss* 1976), Ian Bishop, FRCS; 3rdly, 1977, Dennis Hart, who *d* 1982; 4thly, 1984, David Livingstone, CBE, of 4 Miller's Court, Chiswick Mall, W4 2PF, and has issue living (by 1st *m*), James Keith Innes (Wayland Farm, Tedburn St Mary, Exeter), *b* 1956: *m* 1980, Sally-Anne, da of Dennis Walter Nurding, of Leydene Cottage, Rosers Cross, Heathfield, E Sussex, and has issue living, Matt James Innes *b* 1984, Charlotte Elizabeth Innes *b* 1982, Elizabeth Genevieve Innes *b* 1985, Jessica Katherine Innes *b* 1990, — Jonathan Charles Innes (East Court Farmhouse, Stype, Hungerford, Berks), *b* 1959: *m* 1990, Georgina Jane, only da of late Michael Boileau Henderson, of Park House, Easthorpe, Malton, N Yorks, and has issue living, John Henry Innes *b* 1991, Charles Keith Innes *b* 1992, — Susan Deborah, *b* 1955: *m* 1980, Richard Drybrough Wade, of Adolph Tidemands Vei 11, 4023 Stavanger, Norway, and has issue living, Victoria Katherine *b* 1982, Francesca *b* 1984, — (by 2nd *m*) Louise, *b* 1964: *m* 1990, John Robert Gordon Hunter, of 53 Clapham Common West Side, SW4 9AS, and has issue living, Frederick Robert John *b* 1991, Rory Ian James *b* 1993, Isabel Jennifer *b* 1995.

Grandchildren of late Leveson Douglas Stewart (*b* 1844), eldest son of late George Stewart (*b* 1814), 2nd son of late Leveson Douglas Stewart (*b* 1786) (ante):—
Issue of late Keith Stewart, Canadian Expeditionary Force, *b* 1877, *d* 1947: *m* 1919, Margaret, da of late Nicholas Fox, of Dublin:—
Allan Galloway (1712 Kingslake Blvd, Naples, Florida 33962, USA), *b* 1928: *m* 1st, 1949 (*m diss* 1968), Vivian Waldon; 2ndly, 1969, Marie Marcelle Denise Morand, and has issue living (by 1st *m*), Brian Keith (Toronto, Ontario, Canada), *b* 1952, — Gail Janice, *b* 1951: *m* 1st, 1970 (*m diss* 1976), André Lafreniere; 2ndly, 1976, Kerry Hillier, and has issue living (by 1st *m*), Michael *b* 1970, (by 2nd *m*) David *b* 1978, Sean *b* 1980, Amanda *b* 1982.

Issue of late Randolph Douglas Stewart, late 7th King's Liverpool Regt, *b* 1884, *d* 1961: *m* 1916, Emily Elizabeth Fullagher, who *d* 1976:—
Randolph Douglas (3 Forest Lawn, Liverpool L12 5JA), *b* 1920: *m* 1947, Mabel Thompson, who *d* 1994, and has issue living, Ann, *b* 1947: *m* 1969, Michael Victor Guinney, and has issue living, Mark Stewart *b* 1971, Carl Stewart *b* 1975, — Eileen, *b* 1950: *m* 1974, Peter D. Lawrence, of 1 Gateacre Park Drive, Liverpool L25 1PA, and has issue living, Adam Harvey *b* 1979, Sara Elizabeth *b* 1976. —— †Alexander M., *b* 1924: *m* 1950 (*m diss* 1963), Marion G. Baker, and *d* 1994, leaving issue, Charles Anthony, *b* 1952: *m* 1973 (*m diss* 1984), Nonda Anne Route, and has issue living, Michelle Katrina *b* 1974, Kathrine Jane *b* 1975, and further issue (by Johnann Christine), Stephanie Melissa *b* 1987. —— Catherine Emily, *b* 1917: *m* 1939, Albert Marrion, of 74 Caesars Close, Castlefields, Runcorn, Cheshire, and has issue living, Norma, *b* 1940: *m* 1959, Gordon Colin Tinsley, of 11 Eskdale Close, Beechwood West, Runcorn, Cheshire WA7 2QX, and has issue living, Mark Stewart *b* 1968: *m* 1996, Marian Bernardette Clarke, — Pauline, *b* 1946: *m* 1967, Anthony Joseph Wakefield, of 21 Eskdale Close, Runcorn, Cheshire WA7 2QX, and has issue living, Andrew Anthony *b* 1967, Stewart Joseph *b* 1971: *m* 1995, Sarah Twambley (and has issue living, Abigail *b* 1999). —— Jean, *b* 1934: *m* 1954, Stanley R. Davies, of 104 Barons Hey, Cantrill Farm, Liverpool L28 0QE, and has issue living, Julie *b* 1959: *m* 1981, John Wishman, of 4 Springfield Way, W Derby, Liverpool 12, and has issue living, Michael John *b* 1984, James David *b* 1988, Sarah Jean *b* 1985.

Grandchildren of late Thomas Corrie Stewart, coffee planter in Natal, 2nd son of late George Stewart (*b* 1814) (ante):—
Issue of late George Henry Stewart, *b* 1873, *d* 1931: *m* 19—, Agnes Robina Jessie, who *d* 1949, da of late Lewis Storm, of Scotland:—
Keith (Flat 105, Glendower Place, 99 Linksfield Rd, Edenvale 1609, S Africa), *b* 1915: *m* 1st, 19—, Kathleen Kruger, who *d* 1975; 2ndly, 1977, Mrs Elsie Smith, da of late Enos Ashworth, and widow of Leslie George Smith, and has issue living (by 1st *m*), Malcolm Keith (Unit 58 Greenfields, Harris Rd, Edenglen 1609, S Africa), *b* 1948: *m* 1971 (*m diss* 1980), Joan Carrick, and has issue living, Craig *b* 1972, Neville Keith *b* 1977, Jacqueline *b* 1974, — Audrey, *b* 1951: *m* 1972, Ernest Arthur Atkins, of 28 Utrecht Rd, Gerdview, Primrose, Germiston 1401, S Africa, and has issue living, Chad *b* 1976, Natalie *b* 1973.

Issue of late Leveson Douglas Stewart, *b* 1880, *d* 1946: *m* 19—, Margaret Walker Wilson, who *d* 1975:—
George Bruce (PO Box 716, Hillcrest 3650, Natal), *b* 1923: *m* 1st, 1950, Catherine Aspinall, who *d* 1985; 2ndly, 1986, Shelagh Irene, da of late Albert Sydney Croft, and has two adopted children, John Keith, *b* 1950, — Marie Lynne, *b* 1952.

Issue of late Cecil Francis Stewart, *b* 18—, *d* 1940: *m* 19—, Ethel Alexandria Marshall:—
William Thomas, *b* 19—. —— Vera Alexandria, *b* 19—. —— Joan, *b* 19—. —— Dorothy, *b* 1923.

PREDECESSORS – (1) *Sir* ALEXANDER Stewart, KB, PC (descended from Sir William Stewart, of Jedworth — second son of Sir Alexander Stewart of Darnley and one of the leading men of Scotland during the reigns of his kinsmen, the two first Stewart Kings — whose son Sir John Stewart, *m* Marion, da of Sir Walter Stewart, of Dalswinton); *cr Lord Garlies* (peerage of Scotland) 1607, with remainder to the heirs male of his body succeeding to the estates of Garlies, and *Earl of Galloway* (peerage of Scotland) 1623, with remainder to his heirs male bearing the name and arms of Stewart; *d* 1649; *s* by his son (2) JAMES, 2nd Earl, who in 1627 had been *cr* a *Baronet* (of Corsewell); for his loyalty to the Royal cause in 1654 was fined £4,000 by Cromwell; *d* 1671; *s* by his el son (3) ALEXANDER, 3rd Earl; *s* by his brother (4) ALEXANDER, 4th Earl; *d* unmarried 1694; *s* by his brother (5) JAMES, PC, 5th Earl; an able statesman *temp* Queen

Anne; *d* 1746; *s* by his son (6) ALEXANDER, 6th Earl; a Lord of Police; served heir male as 4th Bt to Sir Archibald Stewart, 2nd Bt (*cr* 1687, of Burray, with remainder to heirs male whatsoever); *d* 1773; *s* by his el son (7) JOHN, KT, 7th Earl; MP for Morpeth, etc, a Lord of the Bedchamber to George III and a Representative Peer 1774-96; *cr Baron Stewart of Garlies* (peerage of Great Britain) 1796; *d* 1806; by his son (8) GEORGE, KT, 8th Earl; an Adm, MP for Cockermouth, etc, and a Lord of the Admiralty; *d* 1834; *s* by his son (9) RANDOLPH, 9th Earl, *b* 1800; MP for Cockermouth 1826-31; Lord-Lieut of co Kirkcudbright 1828-45 and of co Wigtown 1828-51: *m* 1833, Lady Harriet Blanche, who *d* 1885, da of 6th Duke of Beaufort; *d* 1873; *s* by his son (10) ALAN PLANTAGENET, KT, 10th Earl: *b* 1835; MP for Wigtownshire 1868-78; Lord High Commr to Gen Assembly for Ch of Scotland 1876-7: *m* 1872, Lady Mary Arabella Arthur, who *d* 1903, da of 2nd Marquess of Salisbury; *d* 1901; *s* by his brother (11) RANDOLPH HENRY, 11th Earl; *b* 1836; Crimean Campaign 1855, and Indian Mutiny Campaign 1857-9: *m* 1891, Amy Mary Pauline, who *d* 1942, da of late Anthony John Cliffe, of Belle Vue, co Wexford; *d* 1920; *s* by his son (12) RANDOLPH ALGERNON RONALD, 12th Earl, *b* 1892; Lt Col and Hon Col KOSB; JP and Lord-Lieut, Stewartry of Kirkcudbright 1932-75; 1914-18 War; Grand Master Mason of Scotland 1945-49: *m* 1924, Philippa Fendall, who *d* 1974, yr da of late Jacob Wendell, of New York; *d* 1978; *s* by his son (13) RANDOLPH KEITH REGINALD, 13th Earl and present peer; also Lord Garlies, and Baron Stewart of Garlies.

GALPERN, BARONY OF (Galpern) (Extinct 1993)

SON LIVING OF LIFE BARON

Hon Maurice Lionel, *b* 1945: *m* 1971, Karen Ellen, el da of Jay Honickman, of Hyfan Court, Downsview, Ontario, Canada.

DAUGHTER LIVING OF LIFE BARON

Hon Virginia, *b* 1941: *m* 1968 (*m diss* 19—), Alan John Stewart.

WIDOW LIVING OF LIFE BARON

ALICE CAMPBELL, JP (*Baroness Galpern*), da of late Thomas Stewart: *m* 1940, Baron Galpern (Life Baron), who *d* 1993.

GALWAY, VISCOUNT (Monckton-Arundell) (Viscount I 1727)
(Title pronounced "Gaulway") (Name pronounced "Munkton-Arundell")

To extend my fame by deeds

GEORGE RUPERT MONCKTON-ARUNDELL, CD, 12th Viscount, *b* 13 Oct 1922; *s* 1980; Lt-Cdr RCN (ret): *m* 1944, Fiona Margaret, da of late Capt Percival Walter de Putron Taylor, of Sooke, BC, Canada, and has issue.

Arms – Quarterly: 1st and 4th sable, six swallows, three, two, and one, argent, *Arundell*; 2nd and 3rd sable, on a chevron between three martlets or, as many mullets of the field, *Monckton*. **Crest** – 1st, on a chapeau azure, turned up ermine, a swallow argent; 2nd, a martlet or. **Supporters** – Two unicorns ermine, crined, armed and unguled, and each gorged with an Eastern coronet or.
Residence – 787 Berkshire Drive, London, Ontario N6J 3S5, Canada.

SON LIVING

Hon (JOHN) PHILIP, *b* 8 April 1952, *ed* Univ of W Ontario (MA); Manager Scepter Corp, Toronto: *m* 1980 (*m diss* 1992), Deborah Kathleen, da of A. Bruce Holmes, of Ottawa, Canada; has issue living (by Tracey Jean, da of George Montegu Black III), Geoffrey Taylor Black MONCKTON, *b* 1996, — Gillian Elizabeth Black MONCKTON, *b* 1998. *Residence* – 387 Castlefield Av, Toronto, Ont, Canada M5N 1L4.

DAUGHTERS LIVING

Hon Sheelagh Margaret, *b* 1945: *m* 1967, William Arthur Herd, of 726 Galloway Cres, London, Ontario, Canada N6J 2Y7, and has issue living, John David Fyfe Monckton, *b* 1981, — Meghan Alexandra Monckton, *b* 1977.

Hon (Fiona) Marilyn, *b* 1947: *m* 1974, Robert Wilford Shank, BS, CPA, MSc in Taxation, of 9770 SW Buckskin Terr, Beaverton, Oregon 97005, USA, and has issue living, Kevin William, *b* 1976, — Adriane Leigh, *b* 1978.

Hon Rachel Jean MONCKTON, *b* 1957; has resumed her maiden name: *m* 1978 (*m diss* 1989), Ronald John Pressey, and has issue living, Michael John, *b* 1980, — Christopher Ellis, *b* 1981. *Residence* – 44A Byron Av East, London, Ontario N6C 1C5, Canada.

SISTER LIVING

Sylvia Margaret, *b* 1921: *m* 1947, Thomas Bruce Wilson, late Lt-Cdr, RCN, of 1815, W 30th Av, Vancouver, BC, Canada, and has issue living, Patrick John, *b* 1957, — Kathleen Elizabeth, *b* 1948: *m* 1st, 1969 (*m diss* 1979), Roland R. Stéphan; 2ndly, 1985, Henry Nichols Ervin (II), — Rosemary Jean, *b* 1949: *m* 1971 (*m diss* 1979), Niels Bols; 2ndly; 1984, Edgar A. Hendee.

DAUGHTER LIVING OF ELEVENTH VISCOUNT

Hon Rose Wynsome, *b* 1937.

DAUGHTER LIVING OF NINTH VISCOUNT

Hon Charlotte Anne, *b* 1955: *m* 1st, 1983 (*m diss* 1987), Guy Martin James Morrison, only son of M. J. F. Morrison, of West Tytherley, Wilts; 2ndly, 1995, James Reginald Townshend (*see* Rowley, Bt, *cr* 1786), and has issue living (by 1st *m*), Simon George Strangways, *b* 1984, — (by 2nd *m*) (*see* Rowley, Bt, *cr* 1786). *Residence* – Melbury House, Dorchester, Dorset DT2 0LF.

DAUGHTERS LIVING OF EIGHTH VISCOUNT

Hon Mary Victoria, *b* 1924: *m* 1st, 1947 (*m diss* 1972), Maj David Henry Fetherstonhaugh, Coldm Gds, who *d* 1994; 2ndly, 1974, Maj Robert Patricius Chaworth-Musters, who *d* 1992, of Felley Priory, Jacksdale, Notts, and has issue living (by 1st *m*), Hugh Simon (Faenol Bach, Bodelwyddan, Abergele, Clwyd), *b* 1949; *ed* Eton: *m* 1971, Louise, adopted da of late Hon (Richard) Hanning Philipps (*see* B Milford, colls), and has issue living, Edward Dickon Hanning *b* 1981, Fergus Hugh *b* 1990, Sophie Lucia *b* 1973, Alice Maria *b* 1975, — Henry George, *b* 1954: *ed* Eton: *m* 1st, 1978, Nicola, only child of late Lt-Col Peter Payne-Gallwey, DSO (*see* Frankland-Payne-Gallwey, Bt colls); 2ndly, 1996, Davina, da of Duncan James MacLeod, CBE, of Kilwinning, Ayrshire, and has issue living (by 1st *m*), Jack David James *b* 1987, Hector Albert Timothy *b* 1990, (by 2nd *m*), Archibald Henry MacLeod *b* 1998, — Victoria Bronwen, *b* 1951.

Hon Isabel Cynthia (*Baroness King of Wartnaby*), *b* 1926: *m* 1970, Baron King of Wartnaby (Life Baron), of Wartnaby, Melton Mowbray, Leics.

COLLATERAL BRANCHES LIVING

Grandchildren of late Francis Monckton, el son of late Gen Henry Monckton, 4th son of Hon Edward Monckton (infra):—
Issue of late Maj Reginald Francis Percy Monckton, TD, *b* 1896, *d* 1975: *m* 1931, Sheila, JP, who *d* 1999, da of late Henry Gervas Stobart, of Thornton-le-Dale, Pickering:—
Alan Stobart (Stretton Hall, Stafford ST19 9LQ), *b* 1934; FRICS; High Sheriff Staffs 1975, DL 1988; a Bridge Life Master, a Dir of Penk, Ltd, Penk Holdings, Ltd: *m* 1961, Joanna Mary, High Sheriff Staffs 1995, el da of late George Carlos Bird, of Appleton, Abingdon, Berks, and has had issue, Piers Alastair Carlos, *b* 1962: *m* 1988, Georgiana Margaret Elizabeth, only da of Julian Michael Edmund Byng (*see* E Strafford, 1985 Edn), and has had issue, Oliver George Carlos *b* 1993, Isobel Mary Elizabeth *b* 1989 *d* 1991, Emily Louise *b* 1991, — †Simon Francis Carlos, *b* 1967, *d* 1969, — Toby Philip Carlos, *b* 1970, — Davina Claire, *b* 1964: *m* 1987, Gerard John Mytton Downes, of Herrington House, Whiteparish, Salisbury SP5 2RD, and has issue living, Rupert John Mytton *b* 1989, Hugh William Charles *b* 1991, — Sophie Louise (twin), *b* 1967. —— Daphne Alice Cavil, *b* 1937: *m* 1958, Nigel John Lincoln Estlick, Maj RM, of Kent House, Amesbury, Wilts, and has issue living, Robin Monckton, *b* 1968, — Caroline Rosemary, *b* 1962: *m* 1991, Lajos Kalman, and has issue living, Katherine Isabelle *b* 1998, — Marian Heather, *b* 1965: *m* 1992, Rupert Richard Torquil Boswall, and has issue living, Robert William Jolyon *b* 1998, Phoebe Delano Alice *b* 1995.

Grandchildren of late Lieut-Col Edward Philip Monckton, el son of Edward Henry Cradock Monckton, el son of Philip Monckton, 5th son of Hon Edward Monckton, 5th son of 1st Viscount:—
Issue of late Philip Tunnard Monckton, *b* 1870, *d* 1928: *m* 1901, Agnes Carr, who *d* 1956, da of Maxwell Smith, of Darjeeling, India:—
Philip Anthony, *b* 1913; *ed* Sherborne; formerly Pilot Officer RAF Vol Reserve; transferred to REME 1941. —— Sybil Carr, *b* 1902; *m* 1st, 1927 (*m diss* 1949), Ronald Charles Keith Smith; 2ndly, 1955, Capt George Vincent Lardner-Clarke, late King's Regt, who *d* 1966. —— Mary Philippa, *b* 1912: *m* 1st, 1934 (*m diss* 1947), William Michael Gambier Sandwith, Sup of Police, Kenya; 2ndly, 1948, Walter John Smail, and has issue living, (by 1st *m*) Caroline Ann, *b* 1938: *m* 1960, Alan Pickering (c/o Barclays Bank, DCO, Box 88, Mombasa, Kenya), and has issue living, Robert Alan *b* 1964, Tania Mary *b* 1962. *Residence* –

Grandson of late Lt-Col William Parry Monckton, 3rd son of Edward Henry Cradock Monckton (ante):—
Issue of late Ivor Parry Monckton, *b* 1892, *d* 1978: *m* 1921, Olive, da of William Bassett:—
Dennahouse Parry (10 Daniells Walk, Lymington, Hants SO41 3PN), *b* 1930; *ed* Sherborne; Maj RCT: *m* 1966, Mary Elizabeth Doreen, da of James Carson.

Grandchildren of late Hugh Monckton, yst son of late Edward Henry Cradock Monckton (ante):—
Issue of late Hugh Claud Monckton, *b* 1881, *d* 1970: *m* 1st, 1910, Emily Sophia Ray (Dapsie), who *d* 1945, da of E. C. Gibson; 2ndly, 1946, Helen Atherton, who *d* 1974, da of late P. A. Morris, of Sydney, NSW:—
(By 1st *m*) Basil Robert (11 Meadowview Drive, Palm Meadows, Carrara, Qld 4211, Australia), *b* 1917; *ed* NZ Univ (BE); ME Adelaide: MIC; MIEAust; Civil Engineer: *m* 1943, Audrey Constance, da of Arthur Charles Tribe, of Auckland, NZ, and has issue living, Robert Parry (38 Ashburton Av, Turramurra, Sydney, NSW 2074), *b* 1948; *ed* Flinders Univ, Adelaide (BSc), Aust National Univ (BSc Hons, PhD): *m* 1975, Joy Mary, da of late Frank Whitelam of Leicester, and has issue living, Christopher Parry *b* 1977, Timothy Alan *b* 1980, — David Christopher (59 Longueval St, Moorooka, Brisbane, Qld 4105), *b* 1951; *ed* Canberra Coll of Advanced Education (Bach of Applied Science), and Australian Nat Univ (BEc): *m* 1986, Katrina Angela, da of Mario Basile, of 52 Tonks St, Moorooka, Brisbane, Qld, and has issue living, Georgina Elizabeth *b* 1987, Harriette Susan *b* 1994, — Peter Charles (77 Wood St, Manly, NSW 2095), *b* 1955; *ed* Canberra Coll of Advanced Educn, and Sydney Univ (B Arch Hons 1982); AMIA: *m* 1983, Diana (BA Des), da of George Marsh, of Sydney. —— Philip (now known as Christopher Philip Monckton JAY) (Dove Cottage, 49 High St, Chard, Som TA20 1QL), *b* 1921 (Fiji); unofficially adopted in NZ; assumed names of Christopher Philip Jay by deed poll 1949; *ed* Berkhamsted Sch, and Loughborough Coll: *m* 1944, Joan Cynthia, da of late A. T. Hayes, of Birkenhead, and has issue living, Nigel Philip William JAY (Berkley, Tancreds Rd, RD2, Christchurch, NZ), *b* 1945: *m* 1969 (*m diss* 1992), Josanne Elizabeth, da of late I. K. Martin, of Wellington, NZ, and has issue living, Christopher Keir *b* 1972, Simon Philip *b* 1974, Larissa Elizabeth *b* 1976, — Timothy Christopher JAY (6 Woodstock Rd, Taunton, Som TA1 1CJ), *b* 1948: *m* 1975, Gillian Frances, da of L. Thake, of Lincoln, and has issue living, Alistair Michael *b* 1980, Catherine Elizabeth *b* 1978. —— †Hugh Noel Campbell *b* 1923: *ed* NZ Univ (BE); MICE, MNZIE, MRCI, ANZIA; Architect and Engineer: *m* 1950, Elizabeth Rubi Young (46 Woods Av, Matua, Tauranga, NZ), da of Arthur Boswell, of Takapuna, NZ, and *d* 1991, leaving issue, Hugh Geoffrey *b* 1954; BE; B Arch, ANZIA: *m* 1977, Helen Eileen, da of Leslie Dassler, and has issue living, Catherine Jane *b* 1990, — Roger John *b* 1958; BE, — Elizabeth Anne *b* 1953; BA. —— Sybil Dorothy (Unit 11/252 Mainroad, Regents Landing, Maroochydore, Qld 4558, Australia), *b* 1916; resumed the surname of Canard 1962: *m* 1st 1940, Ernest Herbert Canard, P/O RAF, *k* on active service in S Africa 1942; 2ndly, 1957 (*m diss* 1962), Nils A. A. H. Gyllenberg; 3rdly, 1966, Frederick Alma Gearing, who *d* 1991, and has issue living (by 1st *m*), Hugh Jason Paul (21 Tui Glen Rd, Atawhai, Nelson, NZ), *b* 1942; *ed* Rutherford Coll of Tech (IHVE), Newcastle upon Tyne: *m* 1968, Elizabeth Frances Wildridge, and has issue living, Jamie Duncan *b* 1971, Dougal Stephen *b* 1972.

Issue of late Eric Parry Monckton, *b* 1883, *d* 1953: *m* 1917, Wilhelmina (Minna), who *d* 1979, da of late H. W. Erhard, of Sydney, NS Wales:—
James Hugh (121 Jenkins Rd, Carlingsford, NSW 2118, Australia), *b* 1921: *m* 1981, Edith Joan, da of Albert Ernest Wearne, of Bingara, NSW. —— Joan Harriette (14 Jackson St, Balgowlah, NSW, Australia), *b* 1918: *m* 1940, Jack Anderson Stackpool, who *d* 1971, and has issue living, Michael John (7 Oyama Av, Manly, NSW 2095, Australia), *b* 1946; ACIV, QRV, AREI: *m* 1980, Lyndall Rosemary, da of Ian George Hudson, of Dural, and has issue living, Miles Ian *b* 1983, Hugh Jack Monckton *b* 1987, Isobel Claire *b* 1985, — Susan Jane (73 Wyndora Av, Harbord, NSW 2096), *b* 1947: *m* 1969 (*m diss* 1985), Stephen Charles Bowden, and has issue living, Peter Karl *b* 1974: *m* 1993, Candice Pippa Lawson (and has issue living, Conner Samuel James *b* 1996), Timothy Robert *b* 1977.

Grandsons of Henry Grant Monckton, son of Henry Monckton, son of William Monckton, 8th son of Hon Edward Monckton (ante):—
Issue of Maj Frederick Hardy Monckton, *b* 1892, *d* 1981: *m* 1941, Frances, who *d* 1967, da of Paul Ryan, of Dublin:—
Henry William (19 Queens Gate Drive, Birstall, Leicester), *b* 1945; BA Camb; MICE: *m* 1976, Angela Mary, da of Thomas Spencer, of 33 Bath St, Leek, Staffs. —— Michael Frederick (30 Sedgebrook, Liden, Swindon, Wilts SN3 6EY), *b* 1947; *ed* Manchester Univ (BSc); MICE.

Granddaughters of late Rev James Frederick Monckton, eldest son of late Frederick Edward Monckton, son of late William Monckton, 8th son of Hon Edward Monckton (ante):—
Issue of late James Frederick Edward Monckton, *b* 1892, *d* 1985: *m* 1917, Dorothy Verrinder, who *d* 1975, 2nd da of late George Willson, of Upper Sydenham, SE:—
Georgiana Elspeth, *b* 1917: *m* 1st, 1938, Capt Peter Wilkinson Swift, Green Howards, who was *ka* 1942; 2ndly, 1946, Godfrey Walter Thrift, Green Howards, of 9 Doods Park Rd, Reigate, Surrey RH2 0PZ, and has issue living (by 1st *m*), Patricia Elspeth, *b* 1940: ARCM: *m* 1962, Robin William Langford Gritton, ARCM, ARCO, of Heath Farm, Reigate Heath, Surrey RH2 8QP, and has issue living, Peter William *b* 1963; *ed* Clare Coll, Camb (MA); LRAM, Susan Mary *b* 1965; *ed* St Hilda's Coll, Oxford (MA), Lucy Belinda *b* 1970, — (by 2nd *m*) Peter Walter Monckton, *b* 1949; Lloyds Broker. —— Patricia Penn, *b* 1920: *m* 1942, Richard James Ellis, BE, late RAN, of Sinnington, 1 Burgess St, Armidale, NSW 2350, and has issue living, Peter Francis Monckton, *b* 1947: BSc Forestry, Dip Ed: *m* 1978, Rosalie Turner, and has issue living, Martyn Giles *b* 1979, Jacinta Frances *b* 1982, — Michael Richard Penn, *b* 1952: BSc Forestry, Dip Ed: *m* 1982, Elizabeth Giles, and has issue living, Lucy *b* 1982, Emma *b* 1984, — Timothy Willson, *b* 1961: *m* 1984, Rebecca Newland, and has issue living, Michael *b* 1985, Hannah *b* 1989, — Susan Patricia, *b* 1943: *m* 1970, Geoffrey John Lawson, school master, and has issue living, Patrick Geoffrey *b* 1980, Josephine Emily *b* 1972, — Jennifer Ann, *b* 1949: *m* 1978, Richard Roderick Donaldson, farmer, of Cornhill, Puddledock Rd, Armidale, NSW 2350, and has issue living, Warwick John *b* 1979, Christopher Richard *b* 1980, Rachel Patricia *b* 1982, — Winifred Jill, *b* 1958: *m* 1979, Laimonis Kavalieris, MMath, PhD (Australian Nat Univ), and has issue living, Andis *b* 1989, Aleksis *b* 1992. —— Jean Mary, *b* 1927: *m* 1948, Edward Richard Taylor, AM, BE, FIE Aust, of 18A Morella Av, Mosman, NSW, and has issue living, James Edward Monckton (33 Ellery Parade, Seaforth, NSW, Australia), *b* 1949; BE, MIE Aust: *m* 1973, Anne Alison, da of Prof D. G. Stalley, of Manly, NSW, and has issue living, Daniel James Monckton *b* 1977, Peter Edward Richard *b* 1982, Philippa Alice *b* 1980, — Richard John (Marketing Co, 8/31 South St, Double Bay, NSW, Australia), *b* 1955: *m* 1982, Yasmin, da of Steven Nagy, — David Matthew, *b* (twin) 1955; BLArcht, MBEnv (Consv): *m* 1987, Rebecca Monica Grace Lynch, and has issue living, Richard Oliver Lynch *b* 1993, Nicholas Matthew *b* 1995, Genevieve Marguerite *b* (twin) 1993, — Catherine Elizabeth Monckton, *b* 1949 (*m diss* 1983), Donald Ross Kennedy, BSc, and has issue living, Rebecca Jean *b* 1974, Catriona Anne *b* 1977.

Issue of late Lt-Col Gordon Cecil Monckton, *b* 1902, *d* 1989: *m* 1st, 1928 (*m diss* 1948), Mary Catherine, da of late Hugh McCaffrey, of Clones, co Monaghan; 2ndly, 1948, Thérèse (47 Old Wokingham Rd, Crowthorne, Berks RG11 6SS), da of Stephen Minarovic, of Loimersdorf, Marchfield, Austria:—
(By 1st *m*) Elizabeth Ann, *b* 1930: *m* 1962, Martin Rosoff, PhD, of 15 Wellesley Av, Yonkers, NY 10705, USA, and has issue living, David Brian, *b* 1965. —— (By 2nd *m*) James Edward (Poynings, Cookoo Corner, Urchfont, nr Devizes, Wilts SN10 4RA), *b* 1951; *ed* Trin Coll of Music (LTCL): *m* 1971, Jacqueline Ann, only da of N. Conner, and has issue living, Timothy Norman, *b* 1975, — Matthew Gordon, *b* 1976, — Jenna Florence Theresia, *b* 1979. —— Evelyn Stephanie, *b* 1948: *m* 1972, David John Penman, and has issue living, Philip David Spencer, *b* 1977, — Emma Charlotte, *b* 1980. —— Valentine Penn (PO Box 916, Wahroonga, NSW 2076, Australia), *b* 1950; *ed* Univ of SA: *m* 1976 (*m diss*

1997), Robert James Leach, (PO Box 916, Wahroonga, NSW 2076, Australia) and has issue living, Benjamin James, *b* 1983, — Emily Alice Penn, *b* 1986. —— Helen Marina, *b* 1953: *m* 1985, Peter Engzler, of Lot 11 Bulgar Rd, Wallaby Joe Flats, via Wingham, NSW 2429, Australia, and has issue living, Rebeka Freda, *b* 1986, — Sarah Thérèse, *b* 1987.

Grandchildren of late Walter Hilary Monckton, 2nd son of late Frederick Edward Monckton (ante):—
Issue of late Hilary James Monckton, *b* 1889, *d* 1969: *m* 1915, Ruby Rose, who *d* 1982, da of late John Crisp, of Cooma, NSW:—
Walter John Bruce (1 Cromwell St, Cooma, NSW 2630), *b* 1918: *m* 1st, 1942, Betty Allen, who *d* 1974, da of late C. W. Keele, of Bellevue Hill, Sydney, NSW: 2ndly, 1975, Susan Jane, da of Ian Antony Litchfield, of Matong, Cooma, NSW, and has issue living (by 1st *m*) Robin Anne, *b* 1944: *m* 1969, Martin Pitt, of 4/2 Kent Rd, Rose Bay, and has issue living, Angus Andrew *b* 1972, Lucinda *b* 1971, — Rosemary Joan, *b* 1946: *m* 1971, Geoffrey William James Stevens, of 59 Ocean St, Woollahra, NSW, who *d* 1984, and has issue living, James Walter Monckton *b* 1979, Alexandra *b* 1975, Sophie *b* 1977, Jessica Clayre *b* 1981, — Frances Anne, *b* 1951: *m* 1980, Nigel Geoffrey Howard Pilcher, of Edgecliff, NSW, and has issue living, James Howard Monckton *b* 1983, Henry Nigel Monckton *b* 1985. —— Jean Winifred (The Kopje, 2 Cromwell St, Cooma, NSW), *b* 1916: *m* 1940, Maj Charles Cuthbert Wolfe, R Aust Engineers who *d* 1969, and has issue living, Edwin Charles Monckton (58 Henwood Av, Wagga Wagga, NSW 2650, Australia), *b* 1941: *m* 1969, Sally Elaine, da of W. G. Cowley, of Armidale, and has issue living, Matthew Charles *b* 1974: *m* 19—, Renetta Louise, da of Bruce Hackett, of Bathurst, NSW, Benjamin James *b* 1976, Samuel Luke *b* 1978, Sarah Jane *b* 1972: *m* 1998, Robert Dunn Wardman, — Peter Hilary, *b* 1943, — Elizabeth Jean, *b* 1955: *m* 1978, Charles Ian Antony Litchfield, of Muniong, Cooma, NSW, and has issue living, Stephen Charles Owen *b* 1979, Eleanor Jean *b* 1981.

Issue of late Basil Bruce Monckton, *b* 1894, *d* 1976: *m* 1st, 1929 (*m diss* 1949), Edna, da of E. N. R. McMillan, of Rockdale, NSW; 2ndly, 1949, Violet Lillian (8/822 Military Rd, Mosman, NSW), da of P. S. O'Donnell, of Mosman, NSW:—
(By 1st *m*), Margaret Heather, *b* 1930: *m* 1952, Keith Willoughby Payne, architect, of 18c Kirkoswald Av, Mosman, NSW, and has issue living, Geoffrey William, *b* 1953: *m* 1990, Margaret Mary, da of Geoffrey Hough, of Blakehurst, NSW, — David Bruce, *b* 1956: *m* 1987, Clare Patricia, da of Prof J.E. Morton, of Auckland, NZ, and has issue living, Matthew John *b* 1989, Samuel David *b* 1991, — Robyn Louise, *b* 1959: *m* 1984, Peter Randolph Smith, of 60 Nathan Terr, Yeerongpilly, Qld, and has issue living, Timothy Ian *b* 1990, Karen Rose *b* 1988, Sheila Margaret *b* 1993.

Grandsons of late Frederick Edward Monckton (ante):—
Issue of late Cecil Charles Fisk Monckton, *b* 1867, *d* 1954: *m* 1902, Dorothy Tatham, who *d* 1976, yr da of late Walter Tatham Hughes, ISO, of 12 Somerset Place, Bath:—
†Edward Walter, OBE, RN, *b* 1903; Lieut-Com and acting Com; OBE (Mil) 1944: *m* 1932, Margaret Frances, da of late Brig-Gen Frederick Walter Radcliffe, CMG, CIE, CBE, of Whitecroft, Buxton Rd, Weymouth, and *d* 1999, leaving issue, Christopher John Edward (Tuscanny Ledvarigid, Blackwell St, Dingwall, Inverness-shire), *b* 1942; *ed* Gordonstoun: *m* 1st, 1965 (*m diss* 1976), Judith Benson, of Bournemouth; 2ndly, 1977, Anne Ide, of Guildford, Surrey, and has issue living (by 1st *m*), Oliver Edward Walter *b* 1974, Emily Joanna *b* 1966, Heather Mary *b* 1970, (by 2nd *m*) Lawrence Christopher Darwin *b* 1977, — Hugh Francis (Tillytoghills House, Fettercairn, Kincardineshire), *b* 1948; *ed* Gordonstoun; Master Mariner; MNI, MRIN: *m* 1948, Nila Elizabeth, da of John Snazell, of Taunton, and has issue living, Helen Margaret *b* 1985. *Residence* – 42, Ottoline Drive, Troon, Ayrshire. —— Charles Tatham (Dorville, La Route Orange, St Brelade, Jersey), *b* 1913; late Capt 4th/7th R Dragoon Gds: *m* 1946, Ruth Elizabeth Blandy, and has issue living, Timothy James (Flat 7, John Forbes House, Pitville Crescent, Cheltenham, Glos GL52 2QZ), *b* 1947; MRAC, CBiol, MIBiol: *m* 1971, Mary, da of late John Mcleod, of Blackburn, MIEE, and has issue living, Daniel James *b* 1975; BA, John Henry *b* 1979, Antonia Mary *b* 1980, — Richard Charles, *b* 1960, — Felicity Ruth Monckton (Gouden Regenhof 25, 3434 T J Nieuwegein, The Netherlands), *b* 1949; has resumed her maiden name: *m* 1981 (*m diss* 1995), Robert Bastiaan Beydals, and has issue living, Alexander Herman *b* 1986, Sebastiaan Charles *b* 1988.

PREDECESSORS – **(1)** John Monckton, MP for Clitheroe 1722-33, and for Pontefract 1734-51, A Commr of Revenue in Ireland 1734-47, and Surveyor Gen of Woods and Forests in England and Wales 1748-51; *cr Baron Killard*, of co Clare, and *Viscount Galway* (peerage of Ireland) 1727; *d* 1751; *s* by his son **(2)** William, 2nd Viscount; MP for Pontefract and Thirsk, and Receiver of Crown Rents, etc; assumed by Roy licence 1769 the additional surname of Arundell; *d* 1772; *s* by his el son **(3)** Henry William, 3rd Viscount; sat as MP for Pontefract; *d* 1774; *s* by his brother **(4)** Robert Monckton Arundell, PC, KB; MP for York, Pontefract, and Thirsk in several Parliaments; *d* 1810; *s* by his son **(5)** William George, 5th Viscount; discontinued the surname of Arundell by Roy licence 1826, and obtained permission for each successive holders of the title and his el son to use the surnames of Monckton-Arundell, while the younger branches of the family should use the surname of Monckton only; *d* 1834; *s* by his son **(6)** George Edward Arundell, 6th Viscount, *b* 1805; MP for E Retford (*C*) 1847-76, and a Lord-in-Waiting to HM Queen Victoria 1852: *m* 1838, Henrietta Eliza, da of Robert Pemberton Milnes, Esq, and sister of 1st Baron Houghton; *d* 1876: *s* by his son **(7)** George Edmund Milnes, CB 7th Viscount, *b* 1844; was ADC to Queen Victoria 1897-1901, to King Edward VII. 1901-10 and to King George V 1910-20, and was Lord High Steward of Retford; sat as MP for Nottinghamshire North (*C*) 1872-85; *cr Baron Monckton*, of Serlby, co Nottingham (peerage of United Kingdom) 1887: *m* 1879, Vere, who *d* 1921, only da of late Ellis Gosling, of Busbridge Hall, Godalming; *d* 1931; *s* by his son **(8)** Vere Arundel, GCMG, DSO, OBE, PC, 8th Viscount, *b* 1882; Lieut-Col late Life Guards; was Gov-Gen and Com-in-Ch of New Zealand 1935-41: European War 1914-19 (DSO, OBE): *m* 1922, Hon Lucia Emily Margaret White, who *d* 1983, da of 3rd Baron Annaly; *d* 1943; *s* by his only son **(9)** Simon George Robert 9th Viscount, *b* 1929: *m* 1953, Lady Teresa Jane Fox-Strangways (who *d* 1989, having *m* 2ndly, 1972, (Richard) Mark Walter Agnew (*see* Agnew, Bt, *cr 1895, colls)*, who *d* 1998), da of 7th Earl of Ilchester; *d* 1971, when the UK Barony of Monckton (*cr* 1887) became ext; *s* in his other peerages by his kinsman **(10)** William Arundell, who adopted the additional surname of Arundell by Roy Licence on succession for himself and for all successive holders of the title (el son of William Henry Monckton, el son of Hon Edmund Gambier Monckton, 4th son of 5th Viscount), 10th Viscount; *b* 1894; Lt 2nd Bn, R Jersey Ll (Militia): *m* 1939, Joan, who *d* 1973, only child of Maj G. A. Williams, S Staffs Regt, of Purbrook, Hants; *d* 1977; *s* by hs brother **(11)** Edmund Savile, 11th Viscount, *b* 1900; Solicitor: *m* 1927, Kathleen Joyce, who *d* 1975, da of James Musgrave (Musgrave, Bt, *cr* 1782); *d* 1980; *s* by his kinsman **(12)** George Rupert (only surv son (his elder brother, John Philip Monckton, F/O, RCAF, *b* 1919, served in World War II, and was *ka* 1943) of Philip Marmaduke Monckton, only son of Marmaduke John Monckton, 3rd son of Hon Edmund Gambier Monckton, 4th son of 5th Viscount), 12th Viscount, and present peer; also Baron Killard.

GARDINER, BARONY OF (Gardiner) (Extinct 1990)

DAUGHTER LIVING OF LIFE BARON (By 1st marriage)

Hon Carol, b 1929.

GARDNER, BARONY OF (Gardner) (Dormant 1883)

COLLATERAL BRANCHES LIVING

Grandchildren of late Alan Legge Gardner (styled 5th Baron Gardner), only son of late Alan Hyde Gardner (styled 4th Baron Gardner), son of late Stewart William Gardner, son of Rear-Adm Hon Francis ffarington Gardner, 2nd son of 1st Baron:—
Issue of late Alan William Gardner (styled 6th Baron Gardner), b 1908, d 1975: m 1938, Ethel Lydia, who d 1972, da of late James Valentine Gardner, Zamindar of Village Fatehpore, Dist Etah, UP:—
JULIAN JAMES (claims the title) (Village Fatehpur, PO Soron, Dist: Etah, Uttar Pradesh, India), b 2 June 1942: m 1966, Ella, da of Philip Samuel, and has issue living, Ashley Rodney (St Peter's Sch, Mazegaon Rd, Bombay 400010), b 10 Nov 1968, — Christabel Berryl, b 1967: m 1989, David Andrew Luke, and has issue living, Rowan Robin b 1992, — Iona Valerie, b 1971. —— †Archibald Horace, b 1945: m 1976, Ena Hendricks, and d 1993, leaving issue, Adrian Arnold, b 1978, — Ainsley, Edmond, b 1981. —— Dennis Stuart (Swedish Alliance Mission, Nandurbar, Dist Dhule, MS, India), b 1947: m 1984, Kiran, da of Narindernath Khunghar, and has issue living, Denise Ethel, b 1985, — Karin Jane, b 1986. —— Basil Connel (St Peter's Sch, Mazegaon Rd, Bombay 400010), b 1957: m 1991, Lynda, da of Royston Henderson, and has issue living, Alan Stewart, b 19—. —— Barbara Christiana, b 1939: m 1982, Charles Leopold Gardner, and has issue living, Dawn Eileen, b 1983. —— Norma Mary, b 1959: m 1979, Lincoln Solomon, and has issue living, Kevin, b 1989.

Grandchildren of late Charles van Straubenzee Gardner (infra):—
Issue of late Henry Gardner, b 1911, d 1964: m 1941, Emma, who d 19—, da of Harry Gardner:—
David Francis, b 1945: m 19—, — and has issue living, a son, b ca 1978. —— Charles Straubenzee, b 1951. —— Baldwin, b 1955. —— Evelyn, b 1948.

Grandchildren of late Edward Gardner, 2nd son of late Stewart William Gardner (ante):—
Issue of late Charles van Straubenzee Gardner, b 1883, d 1951: m 1900, his cousin Ellen, who d 1952, da of late William Rickards Gardner (ante):—
Edward Kingston (c/o Abdul Wahid, Building No 4442, Nasirabad, Rajasthan, India), b 1917: m 1946, Mary Cicelia, da of G.A. De Silva, and has issue living, Frederick Anthony, b 1946, — Terrance Lewis, b 1952: m 1980, Maryander, da of James Singh, and has issue living, Dorothy b 1980, Elvina Cicelia b 1981, Agnes Gloria b 1984, — Jennet Cicelia, b 1949: m 1972, Abdul Wahid, and has issue living, Aniz b 1974, Hilda b 1976, Shelly Ann b 1978, Mary Rose b 1980. —— Francis Robert, b 1920: m 1953, Irene Martin, and has issue living, George Washington, b 1954. —— Cherry Martha, b 1913: m 1935, Alfred Samuel Tupper, who d 1953, and has issue living, Albert Jasbir Samuel, b 1936, — Arthur Alexander, b 1942, — Ezekiel Habib, b 1948, — Rexey, b 1951, — Margaret Shirin, b 1938, — Maybelle Iris, b 1940. —— Ruby Maggie b 1915: m 1943, James Gideon, and has issue living, a son, b 1944, — a son, b 19—, — a da, b 19—, — a da, b 19—, — a da, b 19—, — a da, b 19—. —— Marjory Julia, b 1925: m 1947, Kenneth Charles Johnson. Residence –

Issue of late Benjamin Gardner, b 1889, d 1937: m 1914, Sophia Shiko, who d 1936:—
Daniel, b 1919: m 1946, Irene Coal, and has had issue, †Noel, b 1946; dunm 19—, — Ivan, b 1949: m 1976, Millicent Joseph, and has issue living, Brian b 1979, Jennifer b 1980, Sherril b 1983. — Mervin, b 1930. —— Lionel Benjamin, b 1934: m 1960, Celestina Singh, and has issue living, Malcolm, b 1962: m 1988, Sangeeta Singh, and has issue living, Alice, b 1990, — Bobby, b 1963: m 1987, Venceta James, and has issue living, Rocky b 1988, Rubeena b 1990, Sandra b 1991, — Joyce, b 1964. —— Caroline, b 1915: m 1940, Rene David, and has issue living, three sons and three das. —— Margaret Ruby, b 1917: m 1936, Linnaeus Arrance Alfred Gardner, son of Alfred Gardner, and has had issue, Albert, b 1938: m 1st, 19—, Lynda Wright; 2ndly, 19—, Yvonne, da of William Gardner, of Kanpur, and has issue living, (by 1st m), Ian b 19—, (by 2nd m) two sons, — Melvyn Wilfred, b 1941: m 19—, Quintella, da of William Gardner, — David (Mickey), b 1945; dunm 19—, — Princeton, b 1947: m 19—, an Iranian lady, and has issue living, a da b 19—, — Elizabeth Faith, b 1938: m 1960, Francis —, and has issue living, Sandra b 19—, — Marian, b 1941: m 19—, Hubert Star, and has issue living, three sons. —— Queenie, b 1921: m 1941, Augustine Paul, and has issue living, Noel, b 1943, — George, b 1945, — Eugene, b 1947, — Joyce, b 1949. —— Hazel, b 1926: m 19—, Mendes, and has issue living,

Alvina, *b* 19—: *m* 19—, Robert Gardner (*see* B Gardner, colls, 1985 Edn), and has issue living, Ashley *b* 19—, Desiree *b* 19—. —— Ouida (Vida) Shirley, *b* 1936: *m* 1952, Leslie Clifford Gardner (infra).

Grandchildren of late George Gardner, only son of late Tandy Gardner, 3rd son of late Stewart William Gardner (ante):—
Issue of late Stewart Gardner, *b* 1897, *d* 1965: *m* 19—, Elizabeth Scott:—
Donald, *b* 19—. —— Norman, *b* 19—. —— Florence (Naini Tal, India), *b* 1926: *m* 19—, — Mackie Hoffland, and has issue living, Robert, *b* 19—: *m* 19—, Sarah Pant, and has issue living, David *b* 19—, Malcolm *b* 19—, — Glenda, *b* 19—: *m* 19—, — Leblond.

Issue of late John Gardner, *b* 1898, *d* 1955: *m* 1918, Clara Callow:—
John (Cloverdale, W Australia), *b* 1926; Lt-Col: *m* 1951, Valerie Jeffroy, and has issue living, John (Attadale, W Australia), *b* 1956: *m* 1980, Eleanor Snowdon, and has issue living, Joshua *b* 1981, Natasha *b* 1981, Alicia *b* 1983, — Deborah, *b* 1953: *m* 19—, Dino Elpitelli, of Bull Creek, W Australia, and has issue living, Daniel *b* 1982, Melissa *b* 1979. —— Phyllis (Nilgiri Hills, India), *b* 1920: *m* 19—, Charles T. O. A. Wright, and has issue living, Dierdre (Bangalore, India), *b* 1953: *m* 1981 (*m diss* 19—), P. Khanna, and has issue living, Harshini Helen *b* 1984, Tejangini Tania *b* 1987. —— Jean, *b* 1923: *m* 1947, Terence Healey, and has issue living, Shirley (Balcatta, W Australia), *b* 1951: *m* 1978, Tony Lizza, and has issue living, Oriano *b* 1984, Jean *b* 1982, — Eleanor (Auckland, NZ), *b* 1956: *m* 1980, Glen Boyce, and has issue living, John *b* 1985, Greer *b* 1987.

Issue of late Leopold Gardner, *b* 1899, *d* 1968: *m* 1930, Charlotte Gardner:—
Rockwell (India), *b* 1931: *m* 1956, Adelaide Edwards, and has issue living, Neville, *b* 1957: *m* 19—, Vivian Edwards, and has issue living, Kieron *b* 19—, Ramona *b* 19—, — Andrew, *b* 19—: *m* 19—, Anuradha Sharma, and has issue living, Anuska *b* 19—, — Roxanne, *b* 19—: *m* 1959, Phillip Chen, and has issue living, Daniel *b* 19—, Nicholas *b* 19—, Ashley *b* 19—, — Charlotte, *b* 1962: *m* 19—, Pravin Mukhia (20 Chowrasta, The Mall, Darjeeling 734101, WB, India), and has issue living, Alana *b* 19—, Nihar *b* 19—, — Anne *b* 1960: *m* 19—, Suresh Vaidya, and has issue living, Vijay *b* 19—, Sophie *b* 19—, — Ida, *b* 1945: *m* 19—, Pradeep Bhandari, and has issue living, Vinay *b* 19—, Vineeta *b* 19—, Sarita *b* 19—. —— Nelson (19 Loris Way, Kardinya, W Australia 6163), *b* 1932: *m* 1958, Dorothea Blewitt, and has issue living, Lynette, *b* 1959: *m* 1987 (*m diss* 19—), Laurence Rea, and has issue living, Benjamin Lewis *b* 1998, — Claudette, *b* 1962: *m* 1985, Stephen Linden, and has issue living, Kelly *b* 1987, Allan *b* 1990. —— Jefferson (St Paul's School, Darjeeling, India), *b* 1937: *m* 1964, Ruth Downes, and has issue living, Glenn, *b* 1965: *m* 19—, Joyce Abraham, and has issue living, Sean *b* 1990, — Aprille, *b* 1967. —— Noreen Mabel, *b* 1934: *m* 1st, 1953, George Mitchell, who *d* 19—; 2ndly, 19—, Rolly Phillips, and *d* 1994, leaving issue (by 1st *m*), Brian, *b* 19—, — Kevin, *b* 19—, — Jenny, *b* 19—, — (by 2nd *m*), Wendy, *b* 19—. —— Ida, *b* 1945.

Issue of late Cyril Gardner, *b* 1902, *d* 1988: *m* 1st, 19—, Mavis — —; 2ndly, 19—, Dolly—:—
(By 1st *m*) Ivan (Sydney, NSW, Australia), *b* 1926: *m* 19—, Joan Gawke, and has issue living, Jeremy, *b* 19—: *m* 19—, Lisa ......, — Susan, *b* 19—, — Gillian, *b* 19—. —— Reginald, *b* 1928. —— Gertrude, *b* 19—: *m* 19—, — Hernandez, and has issue living, Marcel, *b* 19—, — Max, *b* 19—. —— Dagma (Delhi, India), *b* 1937.

Issue of late (Louis) Gerald Gardner, *b* 1904, *d* 1943: *m* 1st, 1930, Muriel Gladys Jahans, who *d* 1932; 2ndly, 1935, Myrtle Sheppard (who *m* 2ndly, 1944, Joseph Simpson):—
(By 1st *m*) Maureen, *b* 1930: *m* 1954, Mervyn Raphael of British Columbia, Canada, and has issue living, Stephen, *b* 1955: *m* 19—, Mary McDougal, and has issue living, Jonathon *b* 1982, Elizabeth *b* 1985, — Christine, *b* 1959, — Pauline, *b* 1966: *m* 19—, Graham Keech. —— (By 2nd *m*) Gerald (Ajmer, India), *b* 1936. —— Yvonne, *b* 1937: *m* 19—, Alec Pape, of London, and has issue living, Michael, *b* 19—.

Grandchildren of late Wellington Gardner (infra):—
Issue of late Richard Gardner, *b* 1919, *d* 1984: *m* 1945, Daisy Margaret, who *d* 1991, da of late Benjamin Gardner (ante):—
Kendrick Navil, *b* 1946: *m* 1973, Enit, da of — Scott, of Kanpur, UP, and has issue living, George Washington, *b* 1974, — Christina, *b* 1975. —— Reginald Wellington, *b* 1950: *m* 1975, Joyce, da of David Shakuntala, of Delhi, and has issue living, Anish, *b* 1976, — Allan Hyde, *b* 1979. —— Edgar Terance (Rosary Church School, Raidio Colony, Nirankari Colony, Delhi 9), *b* 1953: *m* 1981, Vinorika, da of Arthur Ruskin, of Fategarh, UP, and has issue living, Basil Richard, *b* 1984, — Adie Navil, *b* 1990. —— Samson, *b* 19—. —— Beryl Dorothy, *b* 1955: *m* 19—, Morris James, of Gaziabad, UP. —— Elsa Linit, *b* 19—: *m* 19—, King Suberoi, of Delhi.

Grandson of late William Rickards Gardner 4th, son of Stewart William Gardner (ante):—
Issue of late Wellington Gardner, *b* 1881, *d* 19—: *m* 1916, Dorothy, da of Edward Gardner (ante):—
Leslie Clifford, *b* 1926: *m* 1952, Ouida (Vida) Shirley, da of late Benjamin Gardner (ante), and has issue living, Derek *b* 1960, — Dulcie Vida, *b* 1953: *m* 19—, Hector Solomon, of Bareilly, UP, — Ordi Flosy, *b* 1955, — Philomena *b* 1957.

Grandchildren of Major Charles Phillips Gardner (infra):—
Issue of late Lt-Cmdr David William Hyde Gardner, RN, *b* 1913, *d* 1975: *m* 1st, 1936 (*m diss* 1957), Edith Margaret, da of William Henry Wroth; 2ndly, 1958, Susanne Willeter (Lilac Cottage, Waldley, nr Doveridge, Derby), da of John L. Bagshaw, of The Manor House, Uttoxeter, Staffs:—
(By 1st *m*) Alan David Hyde (Bucks, Hyde Lane, Danbury, Essex), *b* 1939: *m* 1973, Penelope Nelson, and has issue living, Edward Morrice Hyde, *b* 1974, — Nicholas George Hyde, *b* 1977, — Jane Rosamund, *b* (twin) 1977. —— John Henry Wroth (Au Bourg, St Astier, Duras, Dordogne, France), *b* 1946: *m* 1973, Tessa Alexandra, da of Capt D. Mallinson, OBE, RN (ret), and has issue living, Thomas Edward Wroth, *b* 1974, — Daniel John Wroth, *b* 1975, — William Henry Wroth, *b* 1978. —— Gillian Margaret (2 Herbert Mansions, 35 Sloane St, SW1X 9LP), *b* 1941: *m* 1962 (*m diss* 1995), John Seager Green, and has issue living, Charles Edward Seager, *b* 1964: *m* 1993, Rosalind Elisabeth Attale, and has issue living, William Toby Seager *b* 1997, Anna Elisabeth Seager *b* 1995, — Joanna Hermione Seager, *b* 1962: *m* 1988, George Gavin Dalrymple Bacon, and has issue living, Thomas Dalrymple *b* 1996, Eliza Ming Rosamund *b* 1998. —— (By 2nd *m*) Wiliam Patrick Hyde, *b* 1960. —— James Francis ffarington, *b* 1962.

Grandchildren of late Capt Alan Hyde Gardner, RN, yst son of Rear-Adm Francis ffarington Gardner (ante):—
Issue of late Major Charles Phillips Gardner, b 1883, d 1932: m 1st, 1910, Dorothy Margaret, who d 1921, 2nd da of William Mullock, formerly of Llantarnam, Monmouth; 2ndly, 1924, Constance Eileen, who d 1975, da of late Major Charles Hay Cox, W Yorkshire Regt:—
(By 1st m) Rosamund Dorothy (PO Box 592, Ranchos de Taos, New Mexico 87557, USA), b 1915. —— (By 2nd m) Susannah Caroline Hyde (Dowager Viscountess Hawarden), b 1928: m 1957, 8th Viscount Hawarden, who d 1991. Residence – The Chicken House, Canterbury Rd, Wingham, nr Canterbury, Kent CT3 1BB.

Grandchildren of late Capt Herbert Calthorpe Gardner, son of late Gen Hon William Henry Gardner, 3rd son of 1st Baron:—
Issue of late Herbert Prescott Gardner, b 1854, d 1938: m 1906, Ethel Mary, who d 1954, da of late Henry Crouch:—
Alan Henry, b 1914: m 1942, Gemma Elizabeth, da of late E. K. McCord, of Coonambula, Eidsvold, Queensland, and has issue living, Alan Peter Prescott (Townsend Rd, Ocean View, Queensland 4521), b 1944: m 1972, Page, da of John M. Neill, of St Lucia, Brisbane, and has issue living, Alice Adrienne b 1974, Susan Patricia b 1977, — Shane McCord (11 Station Rd, Berry, NSW 2535, Australia), b 1946: m 1976 (m diss 19—), Judith da of T. B. Adams of Rainworth, Brisbane, and has issue living, Jacob Adams b 1978, Patrick Alan b 1982, Sarah Louise b 1980, Jessie b 1986, — Mark McCord, b 1954: m 1976, Cathryn Louise, da of Dr Graham Anderson, of Ascot, Brisbane, and has issue living, Gemma Joan b 1979, Mardi Cathryn b 1982, Tilly Anderson b 1984. Residence – The Residence, Norman Pde, Clayfield, Queensland 4011. —— Olivera Graham, b 1911: m 1939, Jack Christian Richards, who was k in a motor accident 1969, and has issue living, Roger Gardner, b 1940: m 1966, Annabel Gee, of Launceston, Tasmania, and has issue living, Josephine b 1968, Frances b 1969, Nikki b 1976, — Alan Gardner, b 1941: m 1969, Sylvia Rasdell, and has issue living, Timothy b 1971, Stephan b 1973, Jennifer b 1975, — Hew Gardner, b 1946: m 1969, Diana Dennis, and has issue living, James Christian b 1971, Matthew Charles b 1978, Rosemary b 1974, — Susanna, b 1944: m 1969, Jean-Michel Allaz, of Geneva, and has issue living, Natalie Claire b 1970, Catherine Helen b 1972. —— Helen Prescott, b 1912: m 1939, Lt-Col James Peile Love, who d 1999, and has issue living, Antony James (48 Miles St, Wooloowin, Brisbane, Qld), b 1946: m 1971, Margot Elizabeth, da of J. G. Moore, of Aspley, Brisbane, Qld, and has issue living, Nicholas James b 1973, Christopher James b 1977, — Judith Prescott, b 1940: m 1962, Dr John Noble, of High View Court, Prince Henry Heights, Toowoomba, Qld 4350, and has issue living, Andrew James b 1963, Cameron Charles b 1968, Louise Annabelle b 1965, — Rosalind Prescott, b 1943: m 1970 (m diss 1983), Michael Ian Minchin, of 103 Waterworks Rd, Dynnyrne, Hobart, Tasmania, and has issue living, Anna Prescott b 1971. Residence – 109 Virginia Av, Hawthorne, Brisbane, Qld.

PREDECESSORS – (1) ALAN Gardner, Adm of the Blue, and Maj-Gen Marine Forces; successively MP for Plymouth and Westminster; was cr a Baronet 1794, Baron Gardner, of Uttoxeter (peerage of Ireland) 1800; and Baron Gardner, of Uttoxeter, co Stafford (peerage of United Kingdom) 1806; d 1809; s by his son (2) ALAN HYDE, KCB, 2nd Baron; was an Adm; gazetted a Viscount 30 Sept 1815, and d 27 Dec following, before the patent had passed the Great Seal; s by his son (3) ALAN LEGGE, 3rd Baron; was a Lord-in-Waiting 1832-41; d 1883, since when the title has remained dormant.

GARDNER OF PARKES (Gardner) (Life Baroness 1981)

(RACHEL) TRIXIE ANNE GARDNER, JP, da of late John Joseph Gregory McGirr; b 17 July 1927; ed Monte Sant Angelo Coll, and Sydney Univ; Dental Surgeon; Member Westminster City Council 1968-78 and GLC, Havering 1970-73, and Enfield Southgate 1977-86; JP (N Westminster, Inner London 1971); British Chm European Union of Women 1978-82; Nat Women's Vice-Chm Conservative Party 1978-82; Gov Nat Heart Hospital 1974-90, UK Rep on UN Status of Women Commn 1982-88; Dir London Electricity Board 1984-89, and Woolwich Building Soc 1988-93; Vice-Chm NE Thames Regional Health Authority 1990-94; Chm PLAN Int (UK) since 1990, and Chm Royal Free Hampstead NHS Trust 1994-98; cr Baroness Gardner of Parkes, of Southgate, Greater London, and of Parkes in the State of New South Wales and Commonwealth of Australia (Life Baroness) 1981: m 1956, Kevin Anthony Gardner, Lord Mayor of City of Westminster 1987-88, son of George Gardner, of Sydney, and has issue.

𝕬rms – Per fess azure and vert in chief a representation of the constellation of the Southern Cross argent issuing in base a sun in splendour or all within a bordure indented gold. Supporters – Dexter, a kangaroo or gorged with a crown palisado vert grasping in the sinister forepaw a branch of Tudor roses slipped and leaved proper; sinister, a lion or gorged with a crown palisado vert grasping in the dexter forepaw a branch of wattle slipped and leaved proper, the compartment comprising a grassy mount growing therefrom two waratah flowers slipped and leaved proper.
Address – House of Lords, SW1.

DAUGHTERS LIVING

Hon Sarah Louise, *b* 1960: *m* 1991, Timothy M. Joiner, eldest son of Hugh Joiner, of Gustard Wood, Wheathampstead, Herts.
Hon Rachel Trixie, *b* 1961; MB BS London 1984: *m* 1988, Dr Alvan John Pope, son of Kenneth Pope, of the Old Rectory, Chastleton, Oxon, and has issue living, Christopher, *b* 1991, — Philip, *b* 1997, — Victoria, *b* 1993, — Katy, *b* 1995. *Residence* – 20 Bark Place, W2 4AR.
Hon Joanna Mary, *b* 1964.

GAREL-JONES, BARON (Garel-Jones) (Life Baron 1997)

(WILLIAM ARMAND THOMAS) TRISTAN GAREL-JONES, PC, son of Bernard Garel-Jones, of Madrid, Spain; *b* 28 Feb 1941; *ed* King's Sch, Canterbury, and Madrid Univ; MP for Watford (C) 1979-97; Assist Govt Whip 1982-83; a Lord Commr of the Treasury 1983-86; Vice-Chamberlain of HM Household 1986-87; Comptroller 1987-89, and Treasurer (Dep Chief Whip) 1989-90; Min of State for Europe, FCO 1990-93; *cr* PC 1992, and *Baron Garel-Jones*, of Watford, co Herts (Life Baron) 1997: *m* 1966, Catalina, da of Mariano Garrigues, of Madrid, and has issue.
Address – c/o House of Lords, Westminster, SW1A 0PW. *Club* – Beefsteak.

SONS LIVING

Hon Julian, *b* 1966; *ed* Westminster: *m* 1993, Ana Phillips, and has issue living, Sam, *b* 1994, — Louis, *b* (twin) 1994, — Jack, *b* 1998, — Ella, *b* 1996.
Hon Inigo, *b* 1967; *ed* Westminster.
Hon Ivan, *b* 1969; *ed* Westminster: *m* 1999, Kate, only da of Arthur Briscoe, of Caversham, Reading.
Hon Sebastian, *b* 1970; *ed* Eton.

DAUGHTER LIVING

Hon Victoria, *b* 1981; *ed* St Mary's, Ascot.

Garmoyle, Viscount; son of Earl Cairns.

GARNER, BARONY OF (Garner) (Extinct 1983)

SONS LIVING OF LIFE BARON

Hon Christopher John Saville, *b* 1939: *m* 1962, Janet, only da of Maj Harold Vaughan Rees, of Winnersh, Wokingham, Berks, and has issue.
Hon Joseph Jonathan, *b* 1940: *m* 1969, Brigitte, da of Louis Pittet, of Sens, France, and has issue.

DAUGHTER LIVING OF LIFE BARON

Hon Helena Geneva, *b* 1947: *m* 1981, Iain Morrison.

Garnock, Viscount; son of Earl of Lindsay.

GARNSWORTHY, BARONY OF (Garnsworthy) (Extinct 1974)

SON LIVING OF LIFE BARON (by 2nd marriage)

Hon Charles Edyvean, b 1974.

WIDOW LIVING OF LIFE BARON

SUE (Baroness Garnsworthy), da of Harold Taylor, and formerly wife of Michael Farley: m 1973, as his 2nd wife, Baron Garnsworthy, OBE (Life Baron), who d 1974.

GARVAGH, BARON (Canning) (Baron I 1818)

NE CEDE MALIS   SED CONTRA

Yield not to misfortunes, but oppose them

(ALEXANDER LEOPOLD IVOR) GEORGE CANNING, 5th Baron; b 6 Oct 1920; s 1956; ed Eton, and Ch Ch Oxford; MBIM; formerly Member of Court of Painter Stainers; Fellow of Inst of Dirs, a Member Inst of Exports; formerly Chm and Managing Dir of The Lord Garvagh and Assos, Ltd, Consultants, London, and Indep Chartering, Ltd, of Camco Machinery, Ltd, of Intersal Commodities, Ltd, and Anglo Brazilian Investments, Ltd, a Dir of AODC (UK), Ltd, Campden Research & Sales, Ltd, The Lord Garvagh & Partners, Ltd, Stonehaven Tankers, Ltd, and Seaways (London), Ltd, Conslt Ptnr Schtumel Towning WI & Ptnrs; Accredited Rep Trade Industry, The Cayman Is 1981; 1939-45 War, Guides Cav, and Capt Indian Army in Burma (despatches): m 1st, 1947 (m diss 1973), Edith Christine, da of late Jack Cooper, of Little Bridley, Worplesdon; 2ndly, 1974, Cynthia, da of late Eric Ernest Falk Pretty, CMG, and has issue by 1st m.

Arms – Quarterly of six: 1st and 6th argent, three Moors' heads, couped in profile, proper, wreathed round the temples, argent and azure, Canning: 2nd gules, three spears' heads palewise in fesse argent, Salmon; 3rd gules, a goat salient or Marshall; 4th argent, three bendlets azure, within a bordure gules. Newburg; 5th, per pale argent and sable, a fesse nebulée, between three griffins' heads erased, all counterchanged, and within a bordure engrailed also counterchanged, of the field, Spencer. Crest – 1st a demi-lion rampant argent, charged with three trefoils vert, holding in the dexter paw an arrow, pheoned and flighted proper, shaft or: 2nd a demi-lion rampant, holding in the dexter paw a battle-axe; 3rd a demi-griffin segreant. Supporters – Dexter, a griffin reguardant, wings elevated and expanded azure, guttée d'or; sinister, an eagle reguardant, wings elevated and expanded sable.
Residence – Half Moon House, Cumberland St, Woodbridge, Suffolk IP12 4AQ.

SON LIVING (By 1st marriage)

Hon SPENCER GEORGE STRATFORD DE REDCLIFFE, b 12 Feb 1953: m 1979, Julia Margery Morison, elder da of Col F.C.E. Bye, of Loddiswell, Devon, and has issue living, Stratford George Edward de Redcliffe, b 7 Feb 1990, — Cordelia Louise Morison, b 1985, — Florence, b 1988. Residence - 1 Church Street, Little Bedwyn, Marlborough, Wilts.

DAUGHTERS LIVING (By 1st marriage)

Hon (Christine) Alexandra, b 1949: m 1971 (m diss 1987), Louis David Lawrence, and has issue living, Stafford, b 1973, — Lucas, b 1976.

Hon Louise Eleanor Alice, *b* 1951: *m* 1975, Mark Lawrence, of Croft House, All Cannings, Devizes, Wilts, and has issue living, Jack Canning, *b* 1982, — Rufus Powell, *b* 1986.

SISTERS LIVING

Hon (Dora) Valerie Patricia, *b* 1919: *m* 1st, 1942, Philip Anthony Wellesley Colley, Lieut RA, who was *ka* 1944; 2ndly, 1950, Peter Sutcliffe, who *d* 1991, and has issue living, (by 1st *m*) Angela, *b* 1942: *m* 1973, David Campbell Anderson, of 14 Lauriston Rd, Wimbledon SW19 4TQ, and has issue living, James *b* 1978, — Elizabeth Jane (*posthumous*), *b* 1945; *ed* St Mary's Ascot: *m* 1966, Peter John Wilson, of Claxby Manor, Claxby, Lincs LN13 0HJ, and has issue living, Camilla Jane *b* 1969, Sarah Louise *b* 1970, Henrietta Mary *b* 1973, Claire Alexandra *b* 1977, — (by 2nd *m*) James (Hemingby House, Hemingby, Lincs LN9 5QF), *b* 1953; *ed* Stowe: *m* 1st, 1980 (*m diss* 1984), Carol Leslie, only da of late Capt C. P. Pratt, of West End, Hants, and of Nigeria; 2ndly, 1988, Susan Diana, da of John Beaumont, of The Manor House, Mill Lane, Legbourne, Louth, Lincs, and formerly wife of Geoffrey Sharp, and has issue living (by 1st *m*), Hannah *b* 1983, (by 2nd *m*) William *b* 1989. *Residence* – 28 Ashford Rd, Tenterden, Kent TN30 6QU.

Hon Daphne Rose, *b* 1922: *m* 1950, Bancroft Svenningson, and has issue living, Victor Stratford de Redcliffe, *b* 1954, — Jennifer, *b* 1955, — Andrea, *b* 1960.

PREDECESSORS – (**1**) GEORGE Canning, FRS, Lord-Lieut of co Londonderry; *cr Baron Garvagh*, of Garvagh, co Londonderry (peerage of Ireland) 1818; *d* 1840; *s* by his son (**2**) CHARLES HENRY SPENCER GEORGE, 2nd Baron, *b* 1826; Capt 10th Hussars: *m* 1851, Cecilia Susannah, who *d* 1898, da of John Ruggles-Brise, of Spains Hall, Brentwood; *d* 1871; *s* by his son (**3**) CHARLES JOHN SPENCER GEORGE, 3rd Baron; *b* 1852: *m* 1877, Florence Alice, MBE, who *d* 1926, da of Baron Joseph de Bretton, of Copenhagen; *d* 1915; *s* by his son (**4**) LEOPOLD ERNEST STRATFORD GEORGE, 4th Baron; *b* 1878: *m* 1st 1906 (*m diss* 1909), Caroline Grace Elizabeth, only da of Charles Ernest Rube; 2ndly, 1919, Gladys Dora May, who *d* 1982, da of Bayley Parker, of Edgbaston, and widow of Lieut-Col D. M. Dimmer, VC, *d* 1956; *s* by his son (**5**) (ALEXANDER LEOPOLD IVOR) GEORGE, 5th Baron and present peer.

GEDDES, BARON (Geddes) (Baron UK 1942)

Strive to hold fast to the greater things

EUAN MICHAEL ROSS GEDDES, 3rd Baron; *b* 3 Sept 1937; *s* 1975; *ed* Rugby, Gonville and Caius Coll, Camb (MA), and Harvard Business Sch; Lt-Cdr RNR (ret): *m* 1st, 1966, Gillian, who *d* 1995, da of William Arthur Butler, of Henley-on-Thames, Oxon; 2ndly, 1996, Mrs Susan M. Hunter, and has issue by 1st *m*.

Arms – Azure three geds naiant or, on a chief engrailed of the last as many boars' heads couped sable, armed argent, langued gules. **Crest** – A demi-pike hauriant environed of the circlet of a Lord Baron's coronet all proper. **Supporters** – On a compartment semée of seapinks, two geds proper.
Clubs – Brooks's, The Hong Kong.

SON LIVING (*By 1st marriage*)

Hon JAMES GEORGE NEIL, *b* 10 Sept 1969.

DAUGHTER LIVING (*By 1st marriage*)

Hon (Margaret) Clair, *b* 1967: *m* 1997, Richard Leslie Mathews, and has had issue, Frederik Batian Lloyd, *b* 1997, *d* 1998. *Address* – Box 24302, Nairobi, Kenya.

SISTER LIVING

Hon Margaret Ross, *b* 1934; *ed* Benenden; is a Member of Asso of Occupational Therapists: *m* 1961, Ralph Emilius Quintus van Koetsveld, and has issue living, Michael William, *b* 1963, — Antony Guy Hans, *b* 1964, — Christopher Dirk, *b* 1969. *Residence* – Northacre, Shackleford, Surrey GU8 6AX.

WIDOWS LIVING OF SONS OF FIRST BARON

HSH Altgräfin Marie-Anne Helena Emanuela (55 Chelsea Sq, SW3 6LH), da of HSH the 6th Prince (Franz Joseph) zu Salm-Reifferscheidt, Krautheim und Dyck: *m* 1964, as his 2nd wife, Col Hon Alexander Campbell Geddes, OBE, MC, TD, who *d* 1972; 2ndly, 1978, Prof Dr Otto Georg von Simson, of Berlin, who *d* 1993, and has issue (by 1st *m*) (see colls, infra).

Diana Elizabeth (Carrickeens, Moyard, co Galway), da of Brig Charles Copley Swift, OBE, MC: *m* 1944, Hon John Reay Campbell Geddes, TD, who *d* 1978, and has issue (see colls, infra).

Gerda (Kirkton of Coull, Coull, Aboyne, Aberdeenshire AB34 4TS), da of late Gerdt Meyer Bruun, of Bergen, Norway: *m* 1948, Major the Hon David Campbell Geddes, TD, PhD, who *d* 1995, and has issue (see colls, infra).

COLLATERAL BRANCHES LIVING

Issue of late Col Hon Alexander Campbell Geddes, OBE, MC, TD, 2nd son of 1st Baron, *b* 1910, *d* 1972: *m* 1st 1934 (*m diss* 1964), Margaret Kathleen, da of late Sir Charles (Stewart) Addis, KCMG;

2ndly, 1964, HSH Altgräfin Marie-Anne Helena Emanuela (who *m* 2ndly, 1978, Prof Dr Otto Georg von Simson, who *d* 1993) (ante), da of HSH the 6th Prince (Franz Joseph) zu Salm-Reifferscheidt, Krautheim und Dyck:—

(By 1st *m*) Andrew Campbell (*His Honour Judge Geddes*) (The Old Vicarage, Minster Lovell, Oxon), *b* 1943; Bar Inner Temple 1972, Circuit Judge, Midland and Oxford Circuit 1994: *m* 1st, 1974 (*m diss* 1983), Jacqueline, 2nd da of Emil Tan-Bunzel; 2ndly, 1985, Bridget Charlotte Helen, formerly wife of John Warren-Swettenham, and da of Lt-Col Christopher White Bowring, of Whelprigg, Casterton, Carnforth, Cumbria, and has issue living (by 1st wife), Nicholas Campbell, *b* 1975, — Dominic Oliver Campbell, *b* 1978, — (by 2nd wife), Leo Patrick, *b* 1981, — Katharine Arabella Campbell, *b* 1986. —— Alexander James Campbell (29 Hugo Rd, N19), *b* 1948: *m* 1971, Vivien, only da of F. H. Salter, of 55 Danycoed Rd, Cyncoed, Cardiff, and has issue living, Christopher Edward Frederick, *b* 1983, Emily Claire Kateryna, *b* 1984. —— Margaret Campbell, *b* 1937: *m* 1960, Peter Gross, and has four sons and two das, James Jonathan Geddes, *b* 1964, — Michael Carl, *b* 1968, — Daniel Paul Geddes, *b* 1970, — Adam John Geddes, *b* 1972, — Sarah Anne, *b* 1967, — Carla Elizabeth, *b* 1969. —— Christina Helen Campbell *b* 1939; MB, ChB, FFRadT: *m* 1965, Roy Kenneth Horrell, of 14 Linkoping Rd, Rondebosch 7700, Cape, S Africa, and has issue living, Jasper Mark Geddes, *b* 1968, — Hamish Harry Geddes, *b* 1970, — Eliza-Jane Geddes, *b* 1966, — Emma Clare Geddes, *b* 1972. —— Jean Campbell, *b* 1940: *m* 1963, Christopher Lubbock Verity, of Boundary House, Brimpton Common, Berks, and has issue living Richard Christopher Geddes, *b* 1965, — Jonathan William Geddes, *b* 1967. —— Caroline Anne Campbell, *b* 1947: *m* 1970, David Kelly, of 8 Crooms Hill, Greenwich, SE10, and has issue living, Nathaniel David, *b* 1982, — Alexandra Mary, *b* 1972, Tabitha May, *b* 1976, — Lucy Anna Margaret, *b* 1979, — Jemima Joanna, *b* 1985. —— Diana Elizabeth Campbell (twin), *b* 1947. —— (By 2nd *m*) Stephen George (55 Chelsea Sq, SW3 6LH), *b* 1969. —— Camilla Joanna Isabella (55 Chelsea Sq, SW3 6LH), *b* 1966.

Issue of late Maj Hon John Reay Campbell Geddes, TD, 3rd son of 1st Baron, *b* 1915, *d* 1978: *m* 1944, Diana Elizabeth (ante), da of Brig Charles Copley Swift, OBE, MC, RE:—

Hugh John Reay (20 Gatcombe Rd, N19), *b* 1945: *m* 1972, Harriet Diana Christabel, da of late Sqdn Ldr Hon John Francis McLaren, RAF (*see* B Aberconway, colls), and has issue living, Luke John McLaren, *b* 1974, — Sam Duncan McLaren, *b* 1975.

Issue of late Major the Hon David Campbell Geddes, TD, PhD, yst son of 1st Baron, *b* 1917, *d* 1995: *m* 1948, Gerda (ante), da of late Gerdt Meyer Bruun, of Bergen, Norway:—

Jane, *b* 1950; *ed* New Hall, Camb (BA), and London Univ (PhD): *m* 1979, Peter Watt, of Kirklands of Coull, Coull, Aboyne, Aberdeenshire AB34 4TS, and has issue living, Henry George, *b* 1980, — David Peter, *b* 1983. —— Harriet, *b* 1953; *ed* New Hall, Camb (BA): *m* 1st, 1976 (*m diss* 1977), Jonathan Allen; 2ndly, 1982, Hugh Devlin, of 20 Windmill Rd, Saintfield, co Down BT24 7DX, and has issue living (by 2nd *m*), Thomas Halcro, *b* 1984, — James Alexander, *b* 1985, — Patrick David, *b* 1988.

PREDECESSORS – (1) *Rt Hon Sir* AUCKLAND CAMPBELL GEDDES, GCMG, KCB, TD, MD, second son of late Acland Campbell Geddes, of Edinburgh: *b* 1879; sometime Professor of Anatomy at Roy Coll of Surgs, Ireland, and at McGill Univ, Montreal: S African War 1901-2, European War 1914-18 on Staff at Gen Headquarters, France (Brevet Lieut-Col, Hon Brig Gen); was Director of Recruiting, War Office 1916-17 (with rank of Brig-Gen), Min of National Ser 1917-18, Pres of Local Govt Board 1918-19, Min of Reconstruction Jan to May 1919, Pres Board of Trade 1919-20 (with a seat in the Cabinet), Ambassador Extraor, and Plen to Washington 1920-24, and Commr for Civil Defence for S-E Region 1939-41, and for N-W Region 1941-2; sat as MP for N, of Basingstoke, Div of Hampshire (*U*) 1917-18, and for Basingstoke Div thereof 1918-20; *cr Baron Geddes*, of Rolvenden, co Kent, (peerage of UK) 1942: *m* 1906, Isabella Gamble, who *d* 1962, da of late William A. Ross, of Staten Island, New York; *d* 1954; *s* by his el son (2) ROSS CAMPBELL, KBE, 2nd Baron, *b* 1907; Pres of Chamber of Shipping of UK 1968: *m* 1931, Enid Mary, who *d* 1999, da of Clarence Howell Butler; *d* 1975; *s* by his yr son (3) EUAN MICHAEL ROSS, 3rd Baron and present peer.

GEDDES OF EPSOM, BARONY OF (Geddes) (Extinct 1983)

DAUGHTER LIVING OF LIFE BARON

Hon Pamela Margaret GEDDES TAYLOR (The Heathers, Bridge Close, Horam, E Sussex TN21 0HJ), *b* 1925: *m* 1957 (*m diss* 1966), Louis Patrick Taylor.

George, Lloyd, family name of Viscount Tenby.

GEORGE-BROWN, BARONY OF (George-Brown) (Extinct 1985)

DAUGHTERS LIVING OF LIFE BARON

Hon Frieda Mary, *b* 1938: *m* 1964, Brian Warman.
Hon Patricia Janet, *b* 1942: *m* 1967, Derek Knowles.

George, see Earl Lloyd George of Dwyfor.

GERAINT, BARON (Howells) (Life Baron 1992)

GERAINT WYN HOWELLS, son of late David John Howells, of Brynglas, Ponterwyd, Cardiganshire; *b* 15 April 1925; *ed* Ardwyn Gram Sch, Aberystwyth; Farmer; CC Cardiganshire 1952-74; Chm Welsh Liberal Party 1972-74, Pres 1974-78, Leader 1979-86; Vice-Chm British Wool Marketing Board 1971-83, Chm Wool Producers of Wales Ltd 1977-87; Liberal Spokesman on Wales 1985-87, Alliance Spokesman on Welsh Affairs 1987, Liberal Spokesman on Agric 1987-89, Liberal Democrat Spokesman on Agric 1989-92; Extra Lord in Waiting to HM since 1998; Sec Ponterwyd Eisteddfod; MP (*L* 1974-88, *Lib Dem* 1988-92) Cardigan 1974-83, and Ceredigion and Pembroke N 1983-92; FRAgS; Life Member, Farmers Union of Wales; *cr Baron Geraint*, of Ponterwyd, co Dyfed (Life Baron) 1992: *m* 1957, Mary Olwen Hughes, da of Margaret Ann Griffiths, of Tregaron, Dyfed, and has issue.
Residence – Glennydd, Ponterwyd, Ceredigion, Dyfed.

DAUGHTERS LIVING

Hon Gaenor Wyn, *b* 1960.
Hon Mari Wyn, *b* 1964.

GERARD, BARON (Gerard) (Baron UK 1876, Bt E 1611)

In God is my hope

ANTHONY ROBERT HUGO GERARD, 5th Baron, and 17th Baronet; *b* 3 Dec 1949; *s* 1992; *ed* Harvard: *m* 1976 (*m diss* 1997), Kathleen, eldest da of Dr Bernard Ryan, of New York, and has issue.

Arms – Argent, a saltire gules. Crest – 1st, a monkey statant proper, environed round the loins and chained argent; 2nd, a lion rampant ermine, ducally crowned or and charged on the shoulder with a saltire couped gules. Supporters – On either side a lion ermine, ducally crowned or, with a collar gemell, and supporting a tilting spear proper.
Address – PO Box 2308, E Hampton, New York, NY 11937, USA.

SONS LIVING

Hon RUPERT BERNARD CHARLES, *b* 17 Dec 1981.
Hon John Frederick William, *b* 1986.

BROTHER LIVING

Peter Charles Rupert, *b* 1951: *m* 1973, Sophie Christine, eldest da of Irénée Du Pont May, of Delaware, USA. *Residence* – 1824 Circle Rd, Baltimore, Maryland 21204, USA.

SISTER LIVING OF FOURTH BARON

Hon Heloise Katherine Marie, *b* 1911; is a nun.

COLLATERAL BRANCH LIVING

Grandchildren of late Lt-Col Charles Robert Tolver Michael Gerard, DSO, OBE, only son of Capt Hon Robert Joseph Gerard-Dicconson (who assumed the additional surname and arms of Dicconson by Roy Licence 1896), 2nd son of 1st Baron:—
Issue of late (Robert) Guy Standish Gerard, *b* 1921, *d* 1980: *m* 1st, 1948 (*m diss* 1964), Barbara, da of Leonard J. Stone, of Merivale, Constant Spring, Jamaica; 2ndly, 1964, Ursula, who *d* 1993, da of late Andrew Mackenzie, of Vancouver, and formerly wife of John Cogswell, of Panama:—
(By 1st *m*) Susan Roberta Caroline, *b* 1951: *m* 1st, 1971 (*m diss* 1984), Andrew Nigel Wendover Beeson; 2ndly, 1984, Lucien Lee Bowman, jr, of Ellman House, Glynde, nr Lewes, Sussex, and has issue living (by 1st *m*), James Gerard, *b* 1976, — Susanna Caroline, *b* 1973, — (by 2nd *m*) (Richard) Frederick Gerard *b* 1988, Lisa Ashley Annabel Helena *b* 1985. —— Diana Sarah, *b* 1952: *m* 1991, Michael Macfarlane Irwin, of 2620 Monte Vista Av, El Cerrito, Calif 94530, USA.

PREDECESSORS – (1) Sir THOMAS Gerard, Knt; *cr* a *Baronet* 1611; the £1,000 he paid for the dignity was returned to him in consideration of the sufferings of his father in the cause of Mary, Queen of Scots; *s* by his son (2) Sir THOMAS, 2nd Bt; *s* by his son (3) Sir WILLIAM, 3rd Bt, a zealous royalist who expended a large estate in the cause of Charles I; *s* by his son (4) Sir WILLIAM, 4th Bt; *s* by hs el son (5) Sir WILLIAM, 5th Bt; *d* 1721; *s* by his el son (6) Sir WILLIAM, 6th Bt; *d* 1732; *s* by his brother (7) Sir WILLIAM, 7th Bt; *d* a minor 1740; *s* by his brother (8) Sir THOMAS, 8th Bt; *d* 1780; *s* by his brother (9) Sir ROBERT, 9th Bt; *d* 1784; *s* by his el son (10) Sir ROBERT, 10th Bt; *d* a minor 1791; *s* by his brother (11) Sir WILLIAM, 11th Bt; *d* 1826; *s* by his nephew (12) JOHN, 12th Bt, el son of John, 3rd son of 9th Bt, by Elizabeth, da of Edward Ferrers, of Baddesley Clinton, co Warwick; *dsp* 1854; *s* by his brother (13) ROBERT TOLVER, 13th; *cr* Baron Gerard (peerage of United Kingdom) 1876: *m* 1849, Harriet, who *d* 1888, da of late Edward Clifton, of Lytham Hall, Lancashire; *d* 1887; *s* by his son (14) WILLIAM CANSFIELD, DSO, 2nd Baron; *b* 1851: *m* 1877, Mary Emmeline Laura, who *d* 1918, da of late Henry Beilby Milner, of West Retford; *d* 1902; *s* by his son (15) FREDERIC JOHN, MC, 3rd Baron; *b* 1883; European War 1914-17 as Capt Roy Horse Guards (twice wounded, MC): *m* 1906, his cousin, Mary Frances Emma, who *d* 1954, da of late Sir Martin Le Marchant Hadsley Gosselin, GCVO, KCMG, CB; *d* 1953; *s* by his only son (16) ROBERT WILLIAM FREDERICK ALWYN, 4th Baron; *b* 1918; *dunm* 1992; *s* by his kinsman (17) ANTHONY ROBERT HUGO (elder son of late Maj Rupert Charles Frederick Gerard, MBE, grandson of late Capt Hon Robert Joseph Gerard-Dicconson, 2nd son of 1st Baron), 5th Baron and present peer.

Gibbs, family name of Baron Aldenham.

Gibbs, family name of Baron Wraxall.

GIBSON, BARON (Gibson) (Life Baron 1975)

(RICHARD) PATRICK TALLENTYRE GIBSON, son of Thornely Carbutt Gibson; *b* 5 Feb 1916; *ed* Eton, and Magdalen Coll, Oxford (MA, Hon Fellow 1977); 1939-45 War as Maj, with Middx Yeo; N Africa 1940-41, POW 1941-43, Special Ops Exec 1943-45, Political Intelligence FO 1945-46; Chm, S Pearson & Son Ltd 1978-83, and of Pearson Longman Ltd 1967-78; Chm of Advisory Council of Victoria and Albert Museum 1970-74, of Arts Council of Gt Britain 1972-77, and of Financial Times Ltd 1975-78; Vice-Chm Westminster Press 1953-78; Chm National Trust 1977-87, Pres S of England Agric Soc for 1987; Member board Roy Opera House 1977-87, and Trustee of Glyndebourne Festival Opera 1965-72 and 1977-86; *cr Baron Gibson*, of Penn's Rocks, co E Sussex (Life Baron) 1975: *m* 1945, (Elizabeth) Dione, da of late Hon (Bernard) Clive Pearson (*see* V Cowdray, colls), and has issue.

Arms – Per pale azure and argent, three acorns slipped and leaved in fesse between as many storks rising all counter-charged. Crest – a stork rising argent between two acorns slipped and leaved and holding in the beak an acorn slipped all proper. Supporters – two nightingales, each holding in the beak a scroll of music proper.
Residences – Penn's Rocks, Groombridge, Sussex; 4 Swan Walk, SW3 4JJ. *Clubs* – Garrick, Brooks's.

SONS LIVING

Hon Hugh Marcus Thornely (The Fold, Parwich, Ashbourne, Derbys DE6 1QL; Reform Club), *b* 1946; *ed* Eton, and Magdalen Coll, Oxford (BA); DL Derbys 19—: *m* 1967, Hon Frances Towneley Strachey, da of late Hon (Thomas) Anthony Edward Towneley Strachey (*see* B O'Hagan), and has issue living, Jasper Tallentyre, *b* 1975, — Effie Dione, *b* 1970, — Amelia Mary, *b* 1973.

Hon Clive Patrick (Monmouth House, Hyde Park Gate, SW7 5DJ; Brooks's Club), *b* 1948; *ed* Eton, and Magdalen Coll Oxford (BA): *m* 1974, Anne Marie Jeanne, da of late Comte Jacques de Chauvigny de Blot, and formerly wife of David Patrick Metcalfe (*see* B Ravensdale, colls), and has issue living, Patrick Clive, *b* 1975, — Beatrice Dione Elizabeth, *b* 1978.

Hon William Knatchbull (46 Victoria Rd, W8 5RQ; Garrick Club), *b* 1951; *ed* Eton, and Magdalen Oxford (BA): *m* 1988, Lori Frances, only da of Herbert Mintz, of Miami, Fla, USA, and has issue living, Matthew Charles, *b* 1990, — Sarah Claire, *b* 1992.

Hon Piers Nathaniel (25 Sumner Place, SW7 3NT), *b* 1956; *ed* Eton, and Magdalen Coll, Oxford (BA): *m* 1981, Melanie Jane Stella, el da of Jack Walters, OBE, of 53 Le Donatello, 13 Avenue des Papalins, Fontvielle 9800, Monaco, and has issue living, Harry Maximilian, *b* 1988, — Theodore Charles, *b* 1991, — Lucy Lavinia, *b* 1986, — Martha Camilla, *b* 1996.

Gibson, family name of Baron Ashbourne.

GIBSON-WATT, BARON (Gibson-Watt) (Life Baron 1979)

JAMES DAVID GIBSON-WATT, MC, PC, el son of late Maj James Miller Gibson-Watt, JP, DL, of Doldowlod, Llandrindod Wells; *b* 1918; *ed* Eton, and Trin Coll, Camb (BA); 1939-45 War, as Maj Welsh Gds in N Africa, and Italy (MC and bar (twice)); a JP and a DL for Radnorshire; PPS to Parl Under-Sec of State, War Office 1957, and to Chancellor of the Exchequer 1962-64, Assist Govt Whip 1957-59, a Lord Commr of the Treasury 1959-61, Chm of Livestock Export Council 1962-74, and Min of State Welsh Office 1970-74; a Forestry Commr 1976-85, and Chm Timber Growers UK 1987-92 (Pres 1992-97); Chm of Council on Tribunals 1980-86; FRAgS; MP for Hereford (*C*) 1956-74; *cr* PC 1974, and *Baron Gibson-Watt*, of The Wye, in the District of Radnor (Life Baron) 1979: *m* 1942, Diana, da of late Sir Charles Hambro, KBE, MC, and has issue.
Residence – Doldowlod, Llandrindod Wells, Powys. *Clubs* – Boodle's and Pratt's.

SONS LIVING

Hon David Julian, *b* 1946; *ed* Eton, and Trin Coll, Camb *m* 1st 1970 (*m diss* 1978), Patricia Hope, el da of Sir Lenox Hewitt, OBE, of Red Hill, Canberra, Australia; 2ndly, 1983, Marie-Thérèse, widow of Anton Wallich-Clifford, and da of Michael McQuade, of Newarthill, Lanarkshire.

Hon Robin (Gelli-Garn, Llanyre, Llandrindod Wells, Powys), *b* 1949; *ed* Eton; High Sheriff Powys 1981, DL 1997: *m* 1971, Marcia Susan, el da of Sir Roger Hugh Cary, 2nd Bt, and has issue living, Anthony David, *b* 1975, — Edward Ricardo, *b* 1978: *m* 1998, Alexandra P. N., elder da of Michael Steele of Templecombe, Som, and has issue living, Mathilda Rose *b* 1999, — Guy Charles, *b* 1982, — Phoebe Charlotte, *b* 1980.

DAUGHTERS LIVING

Hon Claerwen, *b* 1952: *m* 1st, 1970 (*m diss* 1979), Enrique Rene Ulvert, son of Marcel J. Ulvert-Portocarrero, sometime Nicaraguan Ambassador in London; 2ndly, 1980, (John) James Randal Green (*see* B Bicester) and has issue living (by 1st *m*), Marcel David Joaquin, *b* 1971, — Charles Nicholas, *b* 1972, — (by 2nd *m*) (*see* B Bicester). *Residence* – Foxboro' Hall, Melton, nr Woodbridge, Suffolk IP12 1ND.

Hon Sian Diana (*Baroness Biddulph*), *b* 1962: *m* 1993, 5th Baron Biddulph, of Makerstoun, Kelso, Roxburghshire, and has issue (see that title).

Gifford, family name of Earl of Halsbury.

GIFFORD, BARON (Gifford) (Baron UK 1824)
(Name and Title pronounced "Jifford")

Not without God's assistance

ANTHONY MAURICE GIFFORD, 6th Baron; *b* 1 May 1940; *s* 1961; *ed* Winchester, and King's Coll, Camb; Bar Middle Temple 1962, QC 1982; Senior Partner Gifford, Haughton & Thompson, Attorneys-at-Law since 1991: *m* 1st, 1965 (*m diss* 1988), Katherine Anne, da of Dr Max Mundy, of 75 Bedford Gdns, W8; 2ndly, 1988, Elean Roslyn, da of Bishop David Thomas, of Kingston, Jamaica, and has issue by 1st and 2nd *m*.

Arms – Azure, a chevron between three stirrups, with leathers or, within a bordure engrailed argent, pelletée. Crest – A panther's head couped at the neck and affrontée, between two branches of oak proper. Supporters – *Dexter*, a bay horse proper charged on the shoulder with a portcullis or; *sinister*, a greyhound, argent, charged on the body with three ermine spots.
Residences – 67 Lancaster Rd, N4; 71 Duke St, Kingston, Jamaica.

SON LIVING (*By 1st marriage*)

Hon THOMAS ADAM, *b* 1 Dec 1967.

DAUGHTERS LIVING (*By 1st marriage*)

Hon Polly Anna, *b* 1969.

(*By 2nd marriage*)

Hon Sheba Chanel, *b* 1992.

PREDECESSORS – (1) *Rt Hon Sir* ROBERT Gifford, PC; appointed Solicitor-Gen 1817, Attorney-Gen 1819, and Lord Ch Justice of Common Pleas Jan 1824; *cr Baron Gifford*, of St Leonard's Devon (peerage of United Kingdom) 1824, and was afterward Master of the Rolls and Dep Speaker of the House of Lords; *d* 1826; *s* by his son (2) ROBERT FRANCIS, 2nd Baron, *b* 1817: *m* 1845, Frederica Charlotte, who *d* 1920, el da of 1st Baron Fitz-Hardinge; *d* 1872; *s* by his son (3) EDRIC FREDERICK, VC, 3rd Baron, *b* 1849; served with Ashanti Expedition, 1873-4 (medal with clasp, VC), and in Zulu War 1879 (medal with clasp): on Staff of Sir Garnet Wolseley, Gov of Natal 1874 and 1879-80; Colonial Sec for W Australia, and MLC 1880-3, and Colonial Sec at Gibraltar 1883-8: *m* 1880, Sophie Catherine, who *d* 1947, da of late Gen John Alfred Street, CB: *d* 1911; *s* by his brother (4) EDGAR BERKELEY, 4th Baron, *b* 1857: *m* 1st, 1879, Mary, who *d* 1913, da of John Osborne, QC, and widow of Thomas Booth, of West Ashby Manor, Horncastle; 2ndly, 1918, Anne Maud, who *d* 1956, da of late Col Aitchison, Scots Fusilier Guards, of Drummore, Musselburgh; *d* 1937; *s* by his nephew (5) CHARLES MAURICE ELTON (son of late Hon Maurice Raymond Gifford, CMG, 4th son of 2nd Baron), 5th Baron; *b* 1899; Chm of Challis & Benson, Ltd; late Com RN and Flight Lieut RAF; ADC to Gov of NS Wales 1930-35: *m* 1939, (Ellice) Margaret, who *d* 1990, da of late Arthur Wigram Allen, of Merioola, Woollahra, Sydney, NS Wales; *d* 1961; *s* by his only son (6) ANTHONY MAURICE, 6th Baron and present peer.

GILBERT, BARON (Gilbert) (Life Baron 1997)

JOHN WILLIAM GILBERT, PC, only son of Stanley Gilbert, of London; *b* 5 April 1927; *ed* Merchant Taylors', St John's Coll, Oxford, and New York Univ (PhD 1968); Hon LLD Wake Forest (S Carolina) 1983; Chartered Accountant (Canada); MP for Dudley (*Lab*) 1970-74 and Dudley East 1974-97; Opposition Front Bench Spokesman on Treasury Affairs 1972-74; Financial Sec to the Treasury 1974-75; Min for Transport, DOE 1975-76; Min of State, MOD 1976-79; Memb various Select Cttees; Chm PLP Defence Group 1981-83; Vice-Chm Lab Finance and Industry Group 1983-91; Min of State for Defence Procurement since 1997; Memb Cttee on Intelligence and Security 1994-97; FRGS; *cr* PC 1978, and *Baron Gilbert*, of Dudley, co W Midlands (Life Baron) 1997: *m* 1st, 1950 (*m diss* 1954), Hon Hilary Josephine Kenworthy, who *d* 1988, da of 10th Baron Strabolgi; 2ndly, 1963, Jean Olive, elder da of late Capt William Milne Ross Skinner, The Rifle Bde, of 36 Abbotsbury House, W14, and has issue by 1st *m*.

Address – c/o House of Lords, Westminster, SW1A 0PW. *Club* – Reform.

DAUGHTERS LIVING (*By 1st marriage*)

Hon Caroline, *b* 1951: *m* 1st, 19—, ... Le Bas; 2ndly, 1998, Nicolas Rogerson, son of late Hugh Rogerson.
Hon Amanda, *b* 1952.

Gilbey, family name of Baron Vaux of Harrowden.

Gillford, Lord; son of Earl of Clanwilliam.

GILLMORE OF THAMESFIELD, BARONY OF (Gillmore) (Life Baron 1996) (Extinct 1999)

DAVID HOWE GILLMORE, GCMG, son of AV-M Alan David Gillmore, CB, CBE, of Swallowfield, Berks; *b* 16 Aug 1934; *ed* Trent Coll, and King's Coll, Cambridge (MA 19—); served in RAF 1953-55; with Reuters 1958-60, and Polypapier SA, Paris 1960-65; schoolmaster ILEA 1965-69; HM Diplo Ser FCO 1970-72, First Sec, British Embassy, Moscow 1972-75, Counsellor, British Delegation to MBFR Talks, Vienna 1975-78, Head of Defence Dept, FCO 1979-81, Assist Under Sec of State, FCO 1981-83, British High Commissioner to Malaysia 1983-86, Dep Under-Sec of State, FCO 1986-90, Visiting Fell Harvard Univ 1990-91, Permanent Under-Sec of State, FCO and Head of HM Diplo Ser 1991-94 (ret); Company Director, Chm The Art and Antique Dealers' Assoc; Gov of Birkbeck Coll, London and The Ditchley Foundation; *cr* CMG 1982, KCMG 1990, GCMG 1994, and *Baron Gillmore of Thamesfield*, of Putney in the London Borough of Wandsworth (Life Baron) 1996: *m* 1964, Lucile, da of late Jean Morin, of Paris, and *d* 20 March 1999, leaving issue.

SONS LIVING

Dr the Hon Julian, *b* 1967; *ed* Millfield, and Guy's and St Thomas's Medical Sch.
Hon Paul, *b* 1970; *ed* Millfield.

GILMOUR OF CRAIGMILLAR, BARON (Gilmour) (Life Baron 1992, Bt UK 1926)

Not the pen, but custom

NIL PENNA SED USUS

IAN HEDWORTH JOHN LITTLE GILMOUR, PC, *Life Baron*, and 3rd *Baronet*; *b* 8 July 1926; *s* to Baronetcy 1977; *ed* Eton, and Balliol Coll, Oxford; Bar Inner Temple 1952; late Lieut Gren Gds; Editor *The Spectator* 1954-59; an Under-Sec Min of Defence 1970-71, Min of State for Defence Procurement Min of Defence 1971-72, Min of State for Defence 1972-74, and Sec of State for Defence 1974; Chm Conservative Research Dept 1974-75; Lord Privy Seal 1979-81; author of *The Body Politic, Inside Right: A Study of Conservatism, Britain Can Work, Riot, Risings and Revolution, Dancing with Dogma* and *Whatever Happened To The Tories?* ; MP Central Norfolk (*C*) 1962-74, and Chesham and Amersham 1974-92; *cr* PC 1973, and *Baron Gilmour of Craigmillar*, of Craigmillar in the District of the City of Edinburgh (Life Baron) 1992: *m* 1951, Lady Caroline Margaret Montagu Douglas Scott, da of 8th Duke of Buccleuch and Queensberry, and has issue.

𝕬rms – Quarterly, 1st and 4th, azure, three writing pens argent, *Gilmour*, 2nd and 3rd, sable, on a saltire argent a crescent gules, *Little*. Crest - A dexter hand holding a scroll of paper within a garland of laurel proper.
Residence – The Ferry House, Old Isleworth, Middx TW7 6BD. *Clubs* – White's, Pratt's.

SONS LIVING *(in remainder to baronetcy only)*

Hon DAVID ROBERT, *b* 14 Nov 1952; *ed* Eton, and Balliol Coll, Oxford; author of *Lebanon: The Fractured Country, The Transformation of Spain from Franco to the Constitutional Monarchy, The Hungry Generations, Cities of Spain, The Last Leopard: A Life of Giuseppe di Lampedusa, Curzon*, etc: *m* 1975, Sarah Anne, da of Michael Hilary George Bradstock (*see* V Hawarden, colls), and has issue living, Alexander Ian Michael, *b* 19 Feb 1980, — Rachel Anne Caroline, *b* 1977, — Katharine Victoria Mary, *b* 1984, — Laura Elizabeth Rose, *b* 1985. *Residence* - 27 Ann St, Edinburgh EH4 1PL.

Hon Oliver John, *b* 1953; *ed* Eton, Hertford Coll, Oxford, and Akademie Für Musik, Vienna: *m* 1981 (*m diss* 1985), Hon Kathrine (Katya) Grenfell, 2nd da of 2nd Baron St Just, and has issue living, Marco Oliver, *b* 1988, — Natalia Clare, *b* 1981. *Residence* –

Hon Christopher Simon, *b* 1956; *ed* Eton, and Univ of E Anglia: *m* 1992, Mardi C., only da of J. L. Haynes, of Louisa Beach, Queensland, Australia, and has issue living, Leonora Rose Bonnie, *b* 1993, — Gabriella Holly, *b* 1994. *Residence* – 41A Chester Sq, SW1W 9HT.

Hon Andrew James, *b* 1964; *ed* Eton, and Balliol Coll, Oxford: *m* 1991, Emma B., only da of Christopher Williams, of Alrewas Hayes, Staffs, and has issue living, Archie John Ludo, *b* 1993, — Xan, *b* 1996. *Residence* - 139 West 19th St, Apt 7NE, New York, NY 10011, USA.

DAUGHTER LIVING

Hon Jane Victoria, *b* 1959; *ed* St Paul's, and St Hugh's Coll, Oxford: *m* 1986, Hon Peter John Pleydell-Bouverie, yr son of 8th Earl of Radnor, and has issue (see that title). *Residences* – 38 Queensdale Rd, W11 4SA; New Court Farmhouse, Downton, nr Salisbury, Wilts.

HALF-BROTHER LIVING

Alexander Clement, CVO, *b* 1931; *ed* Eton; CVO 1990: *m* 1st, 1954 (*m diss* 1983), Barbara Marie-Louise, el da of late Hon Denis Gomer Berry, TD (*see* V Kemsley); 2ndly, 1983, Susan Janet, el da of late Capt Voltelin James Howard Van der Byl, DSC, RN (ret), and formerly wife of (i) Alwyn Richard Dudley Smith, and (ii) 2nd Baron Chetwode, and has issue living (by 1st *m*), Rory Calvyn, *b* 1958, — Christian Alexander, *b* 1970: *m* 1992, Alexandra Ruth, yst da of Rev C. R. Wolsey, of Frimley, Surrey, — Lucinda Roberte, *b* 1956: *m* 1st, 1981 (*m diss* 1989), Robert Crofts Williams Llewellyn; 2ndly, 1989, Adrian G. Burns, and has issue (by 1st *m*) (*see* Llewellyn, Bt, *cr* 1922), (by 2nd *m*) Jamie *b* 1991. *Residence* – 1 Christopher Mews, Penzance St, W11 4QZ. *Club* – White's.

PREDECESSORS – The 1st baronet, Sir Robert Gordon Gilmour, CB, CVO, DSO (son of Henry Wolrige-Gordon, of Esslemont and Hallhead, Aberdeenshire), assumed the surname of Gilmour on succession to the estates of his great uncle, Walter James Little Gilmour. He was a Brig-Gen Capt of King's Body Guard for Scotland (Royal Company of Archers), and Gentleman Usher of the Green Rod (Order of the Thistle). He *d* 1939, and was *s* by his son, Sir John Little Gilmour, 2nd Bt, *b* 1899; a Stockbroker: *m* 1st, 1922 (*m diss* 1929), Hon Victoria Laura Cadogan, OBE, TD, who *d* 1991, da of late Henry Arthur, Viscount Chelsea; 2ndly, 1930, Lady Mary Cecilia Rhodesia Hamilton, who *d* 1984, da of 3rd Duke of Abercorn; *d* 1977; *s* by his elder son, Sir Ian Hedworth John Little Gilmour, PC (*Baron Gilmour of Craigmillar*), 3rd and present baronet.

GISBOROUGH, BARON (Chaloner) (Baron UK 1917)

*Frugality is the left hand of fortune,
and diligence the right*

THOMAS RICHARD JOHN LONG CHALONER, 3rd Baron; *b* 1 July 1927; *s* 1951; *ed* Eton; late Lt 16th/15th Lancers and Capt Northumberland Hussars; Lt-Col Green Howards Territorials 1967-69; Hon Col Cleveland Cadet Force 1982-92; Co Councillor for N Riding of Yorks 1964-74, and of Cleveland 1974-77, Lord-Lieut Cleveland 1981-97, since when N Yorks; JP; KStJ; *m* 1960, Shane, el da of late Sidney A. Newton (*see* Newton, Bt, colls, *cr* 1924), and has issue.

Arms – Sable, a chevron between three cherubims or. Crest – A demi sea-wolf or. Supporters – On either side a kneeling angel, wings elevated, inverted and endorsed, each ensigned on the head with a cross, all or.
Residences – Gisborough House, Guisborough, Cleveland TS14 6PT; 37 Bury Walk, SW3. *Club* – White's.

SONS LIVING

Hon (THOMAS) PEREGRINE LONG, *b* 17 Jan 1961: *m* 1992, Karen E., only da of Alan Thomas, and of Mrs Wendy Ogiela, of Cape Town, S Africa. *Address* – Falcons Nest, PO 13015, Stellenbosch 7600, S Africa.
Hon (Robert) Toby Long, *b* 1966.

SISTER LIVING

Hon (Angela) Mary (Geranium Cottage, Ditchling, Sussex), *b* 1925: *m* 1946 (*m diss* 1973), Roderick Edward Faure Walker, late Maj Coldstream Guards, and has had issue, Rupert Roderick (Woodhill, Danbury, Essex CM3 4AN), *b* 1947; *ed* Eton and Bristol Univ (BSc): *m* 1975, Sally Anne Vivienne, MB, B Chir, da of Lt-Cmdr Francis John Sidebotham, RN, of List House, Long Melford, Suffolk, and has issue living, Nicholas Alexander *b* 1978, Julia Frances *b* 1980, Joanna Phoebe *b* 1984, — James Edward Bruce (88 Greenwood Rd, Hackney, E8 1NE) *b* 1948; *ed* Eton, St Martins Sch of Art, and Royal Coll of Art: *m* 1st 1973 (*m diss* 1979), Caryn Lois, da of Dr Robert Becker, of 1701, York Av, New York, USA; 2ndly, 1981, Vivien Margaret, da of Donald Frank Knight, of 122 Southam Rd, Hall Green, Birmingham, and has issue living, (by 2nd *m*) Edward James *b* 1989, Josephine Valerie Mary *b* 1986, Duclie May *b* 1991, — Camilla Mary, *b* 1953: *m* 1973, Timothy J. P. Coghlan, of Weedon Lodge Cottage, Everdon, nr Daventry, Northants NN11 3BQ, son of late A. F. Coghlan, of Ludwell Grange, Horsted Keynes, Sussex, and *d* 1981, leaving issue, Christopher Austin *b* 1980; *ed* Kings Coll, London, Alice Mary *b* 1979; *ed* Trinity Coll, Dublin.

COLLATERAL BRANCH LIVING

Issue of late Capt Richard Godolphin Hume Chaloner, Wilshire Regt, el son of 1st Baron, *b* 1883, *k* abroad during European War 1917: *m* 1914, Evelyn Maud, JP, who *d* 1973 (she *m* 2ndly, 1918, Lieut-Col John Clement Wolstan Francis, 15/19th Hussars (ret)), yr da of A. Benyon, of Ashe, Windsor:—
Diana Margaret Bruce: *m* 1948, Ian Melville Wright, who *d* 1971.

PREDECESSORS – (1) RICHARD GODOLPHIN WALMESLEY Chaloner, second son of late Richard Penruddocke Long, MP, of Rood Ashton, Wilts: *b* 1856; assumed by Roy licence 1888 the surname of Chaloner in lieu of his patronymic (under the will of his material grand-uncle, Adm Thomas Chaloner, CB, who inherited the Gisborough Estates through his mother, who was a descendant, through her grandmother, Margaret Bruce of Kennet, of Robert de Brus, Lord of Skelton, who founded Gisborough Priory 1119); Afghan War 1879-80, S Africa 1900; MP for W or Westbury Div of Wilts (C) 1895-1900, and for Abercromby Div of Liverpool 1910-17; *cr Baron Gisborough*, of Cleveland, Yorkshire (peerage of UK) 1917: *m* 1882, Margaret Brocklesby, who *d* 1941, el da of late Rev Weston Brocklesby Davis, V of Ramsbury, Wilts; *d* 1938; *s* by his second but only surviving son (2) THOMAS WESTON PEEL LONG, TD, 2nd Baron, *b* 1889; Maj (ret) Green Howards (TA) and Fl-Lt (Hon Capt) RAF; 1914-18 War in RFC and RAF; 1939-45 War as Fl-Lt RAFVR: *m* 1923, Esther Isabella Madeleine, who *d* 1970, da of late Charles Oswin Hall, of Eddlethorpe Hall, Malton, Yorks; *d* 1951; *s* by his son (3) THOMAS RICHARD JOHN LONG, 3rd Baron, and present peer.

GLADWIN OF CLEE, BARON (Gladwin) (Life Baron 1994)

DEREK OLIVER GLADWIN, CBE, son of Albert Victor Gladwin; *b* 6 June 1930; *ed* Wintringham Gram Sch, Grimsby, Ruskin Coll, Oxford, and LSE; Railway Clerk and Fish Dock worker, Grimsby 1946-52; District and National Officer 1956-70, Regional Secretary (Southern Region) General and Municipal Workers' Union (GMB) 1970-90; Memb of TUC General Council 1986-88; Chm Labour Party Conference Arrangements Cttee 1973-90; Non-Executive Board Memb, The Post Office 1972-94; Non-Executive Dir, British Aerospace Board 1977-91; Chm Governing Cncl, Ruskin Coll, Oxford 1979-99; Visiting Fellow, Nuffield Coll, Oxford 1978-86; Member of Cncl, Industrial Soc since 1968;

Memb Employment Appeal Tribunal; Memb Armed Forces Pay Review Body; Pres Holiday Care Service; Memb of Cncl, Ditchley Foundation; JP Surrey 1969; *cr* CBE 1979, and *Baron Gladwin of Clee*, of Great Grimsby, co Humberside (Life Baron) 1994: *m* 1956, Ruth Ann, da of Herbert Pinion, of Clee Rd, Grimsby, and has issue.
Residence – 2 Friar's Rise, Woking, Surrey GU22 7JL.

SON LIVING

Hon James, *b* 1957; *ed* Winston Churchill Sch, Woking, Epsom Coll of Art, and Goldsmith Coll, London.

GLADWYN, BARON (Jebb) (Baron UK 1960)

MILES ALVERY GLADWYN JEBB, 2nd Baron; *b* 3 March 1930; *s* 1996; *ed* Eton, and Magdalen Coll, Oxford (MA); Senior Management with British Airways until 1983; author of *The Thames Valley Heritage Walk* 1980, *A Guide to the South Downs Way* 1984, *Walkers* 1986, *A Guide to the Thames Path* 1988, *East Anglia* 1990, *A Guide to the Colleges of Oxford* 1992, and *Suffolk* 1995.

Arms – Quarterly vert and or, in the first quarter a falcon argent with bells of the second, and in the last quarter a lure of the third. **Crest** – A lure fessewise argent, and thereon a falcon rising proper with bells or. **Supporters** – *Dexter*, a brown bear proper; *sinister*, a unicorn argent, charged on the shoulder with a patriarchal cross bottony gules.
Residence – E1 Albany, Piccadilly, W1. *Clubs* – Brooks's, Beefsteak.

SISTERS LIVING

Hon Vanessa Mary (*Baroness Thomas of Swynnerton*), *b* 1931; *ed* St Hugh's Coll, Oxford (MA): *m* 1962, Baron Thomas of Swynnerton (Life Baron), of 29 Ladbroke Grove, W11, and has issue.
Hon Stella Candida, *b* 1933: *m* 1959, Baron Joël de Rosnay, Dir Cité des Sciences, Paris, and scientific writer and lecturer, and has issue living, Alexis Marc Louis Joël, *b* 1967: *m* 1994, Charlotte Champion, — (Vanessa) Tatiana Louise, *b* 1961: *m* 1987, Nicholas Jolly, — Cecilia Fiona Louise, *b* 1963: *m* 1995, Cedric de Vaucleroy. *Residence* – 146 rue de l'Université, Paris VII, France.

By hope and work

PREDECESSOR – (1) (HUBERT MILES) GLADWYN Jebb, GCMG, GCVO, CB, son of late Sydney Jebb, of Firbeck Hall, Rotherham, Yorks; *b* 1900; Diplo Scr 1924, Foreign Office 1935-40 (Private Sec to Parly Under Sec of State 1929-31 and to Permanent Under-Sec of State 1937-40), Foreign Policy Adviser to Min of Economic Warfare 1940, etc; Acting Sec-Gen UN 1946, Assist Under-Sec of State and UN Adviser May 1946, UK Representative on Permanent Commn of Brussels Treaty with rank of Ambassador March 1948, Dep Under Sec of State Dec 1948, Permanent Representative of UK to UN 1950-54, Ambassador to France 1954-60; author; *cr Baron Gladwyn*, of Bramfield, co Suffolk (peerage of UK) 1960: *m* 1929, Cynthia, who *d* 1990, da of Sir Saxton William Armstrong Noble, 3rd Bt (*cr* 1902); *d* 1996; *s* by his only son (2) MILES ALVERY GLADWYN, 2nd Baron and present peer.

Glamis, Lord; son of Earl of Strathmore and Kinghorne.

Glamorgan, Earl of; grandson of Duke of Beaufort.

Glandine, Viscount; son of Earl of Norbury.

GLANUSK, BARON (Bailey) (Baron UK 1899, Bt UK 1852)

Liberty

CHRISTOPHER RUSSELL BAILEY, TD, 5th Baron, and 6th Baronet; *b* 18 March 1942; *s* 1997; *ed* Eton, and Clare Coll, Camb (BA); Computer Systems Engr; with English Electric 1964-66, Ferranti 1966-78; Product Marketing Manager, Bestobell Mobrey Ltd 1978-83; Sales Engr (Defence Systems) STC Telecommunications Ltd 1984-86; Gen Manager Autocar 1986-97, Wolfram Research 1997-98; Lieut 7th Bn Cheshire Regt (TA) 1964-67, Capt 94 (Berks Yeo) Signals Sqdn (TA) 1967-78, Capt 80 (Cheshire Yeo) Signals Sqdn (TA) 1978-80, Major HQ11 Signals Bde (TA) 1980-83; TD 1977: *m* 1974, Frances Elizabeth, da of Air Ch Marshal Sir Douglas Charles Lowe, GCB, DFC, AFC, and has issue.

Arms – Argent, between two bars, three annulets in fesse gules between as many martlets of the last. Crest – A griffin sejant argent, semée of annulets gules. Supporters – *Dexter*, a collier proper; *sinister*, a smith proper.
Address – 51 Chertsey Rd, Chobham, Surrey GU24 8PD.

SON LIVING

Hon CHARLES HENRY, *b* 12 Aug 1976; *ed* Eton, and Balliol Coll, Oxford (M Math 1998).

DAUGHTER LIVING

Hon Rosemary Elizabeth, *b* 1979; *ed* Wycombe Abbey, and Balliol Coll, Oxford.

SISTER LIVING

Hon Susan Mary, *b* 1944: *m* 1970, Peter Mansel Lloyd James, MB BS, FRCS, of 104 Pottergate, Norwich, Norfolk, and has issue living, David Lloyd, *b* 1971, — Richard Lloyd, *b* 1976, — Caspar Lloyd, *b* 1980, — Victoria Mary, *b* 1974.

AUNTS LIVING (*Sisters of 4th Baron*) (*Raised to the rank of a Baron's daughters* 1948)

Hon Shirley Joan (27 Headbourne Worthy House, Winchester, Hants SO23 7JG), *b* 1912: *m* 1946, George Dupin Drayson, who *d* 1969, and has issue living, Charles Dupin (Glebe House, Selham, Petworth, W Sussex GU28 0PW), *b* 1947; *ed* Marlborough; Man Dir Firmenich UK Ltd: *m* 1974, Rosemary Ann, da of late Capt D. P. Evans, RN, and has issue living, Timothy William Dupin *b* 1983; *ed* Marlborough, Louise Claire *b* 1978; *ed* Bedales, and Glasgow Sch of Art, Caroline Gail *b* 1980; *ed* Bedales.

Hon Elspeth Lorraine (*Hon Lady Musson*), *b* 1915: *m* 1939, Gen Sir Geoffrey Randolph Dixon Musson, GCB, CBE, DSO, late KSLI (ret), and has had issue, Peter Geoffrey Dixon, *b* 1946; *ed* Wellington Coll, — Penelope Anne, *b* 1941: *m* 1962, Capt William Richard Dudgeon, late The Black Watch, of Ribblesdale House, Stainforth, Yorks BD24 9PH, and *d* 1981, leaving issue, Angus Geoffrey Peter, *b* 1963: *m* 1988, Juliet Ann, da of George Anthony Turnbull (and has issue living, Charles William George *b* 1992, Kitty Penelope Ann *b* 1991), Deborah Elspeth *b* 1968. *Residence* – Barn Cottage, Hurstbourne Tarrant, Andover, Hants.

DAUGHTER LIVING OF THIRD BARON

Hon (Elizabeth) Shân Josephine, LVO, *b* 1943; Lady-in-Waiting to HRH The Princess Royal since 1978; High Sheriff Powys 1992, Lord-Lieut since 1998; LVO 1988: *m* 1964, William Nigel Henry Legge-Bourke, DL, of Penmyarth, Glanusk Park, Crickhowell, Powys NP8 1LP, and has issue (*see* E Dartmouth, colls).

WIDOW LIVING OF THIRD BARON

MARGARET ELDRYDD (*Dowager Viscountess De L'Isle*), da of late Maj-Gen Thomas Herbert Shoubridge, CB, CMG, DSO; High Sheriff Powys 1977: *m* 1st, 1942, as his 2nd wife, the 3rd Baron, who *d* 1948; 2ndly, 1966, as his 2nd wife, 1st Viscount De L'Isle, VC, KG, GCMG, GCVO, PC, who *d* 1991. *Residence* – Glanusk Park, Crickhowell, Powys NP8 1LP.

COLLATERAL BRANCHES LIVING

Grandchildren of Capt Hon John Lancelot Bailey (infra):—
Issue of late Joseph Ferdinand Carey Bailey, *b* 1907, *d* 1984: *m* 1st, 1935 (*m diss* 1946), Alice Cecilia Anne, da of Oswald Magniac, DL, of Nursling, Hants; 2ndly, 1948, Evelyn Marie, da of Robert P. B. Blauveldt, LLB, of Yarmouth, Nova Scotia:—
(By 1st *m*) Lancelot Oswald (11 rue de Béarn, Paris 75003, France), *b* 1936: *m* 1959, Armelle Françoise, da of Jean François Le Roux, of Candé, Maine-et-Loire, France, and has issue living, Antoine Lancelot Gwenaél, *b* 1965. —— Vernon Joseph Russell (43 Prospect St, Montreal, Quebec, Canada H3Z 1W5), *b* 1937: *m* 1968, Melanie Frances Moore, and has issue living, Julian Joseph Russell, *b* 1977, — Sebastian Philip de Magniac, *b* 1979, — Rachel Marjorie, *b* 1969: *m* 19—, Trenholm, and has issue living, Acacia *b* 1996, — Priscilla Anne, *b* 1971: *m* 1994, Jeffrey Walter Stairs. —— Cynthia Mary, *b* 1940: *m* 1963, Patrick Joseph Moran, and has issue living, Malachi Joseph, *b* 1965, — Roisin, *b* 1968, — Garett, *b* 1969, — Fiona Mary, *b* 1964. —— (By 2nd *m*) Herbert Van Courtlandt, *b* 1952: *m* 1989, Kirsteen Susan, da of Alexander Keith Boyle (*see* Kennaway, Bt), and has issue living, Luke Alexander, *b* 1991, — Charlotte Evelyn, *b* 1990. —— Josephine Blauveldt, *b* 1949: *m* 1977, Teddy Dyer, and has issue living, Christopher Teddy, *b* 1979, — Patrick Nicholas Blauveldt, *b* 1982. —— Deborah Evelyn, *b* 1950: *m* 1980, Michael Collison, and has issue living, Andrew, *b* 1981, — Matthew, *b* 1983, — Daniel, *b* 1987, — Jessica, *b* 1992.

Issue of late Capt Hon John Lancelot Bailey, 5th son of 1st Baron, *b* 1878, *d* 1918: *m* 1903, Vivien Dora, who *d* 1938, da of late Ferdinand G. Carey, of Guernsey, and Frogmore, Ceylon:—
Marjorie Vivienne, *b* 1910: *m* 1930, Oliver Fowell Lancaster (*see* Buxton, Bt, colls, 1940 Edn). *Residence* – Daniel Zorrilla 5276, Colon, Montevideo, Uruguay.

Granddaughter of late Richard Crawshay Bailey, son of late Joseph Bailey, el son of 1st baronet:—
Issue of late Rev Canon Charles Henry Bailey, MC, *b* 1882, *d* 1971: *m* 1915, Ethel, who *d* 1962, da of late George Millward:—
Mabel Anna, *b* 1920: *m* 1947, Maj Ronald Patrick Ward, MC, The Border Regt, who *d* 1996, of Ivall's Farm Cottage, Bentworth, Alton, Hants, and has issue living, Charles Patrick, *b* 1949: *m* 1983, Linda Brown, and has issue living, Rebecca Anne *b* 1983, Henrietta Elizabeth *b* 1985, Charlotte Deborah *b* 1986, — Susan, *b* 1948: *m* 1970, John Grosvenor Phillips, and has issue living, Charles Edward *b* 1973, George William *b* 1976, — Deborah Rose, *b* 1957.

Granddaughters of late John Arthur Crawshay Bailey, only son of late Capt John Crawshay Bailey, RN, 3rd son of 1st baronet:—
Issue of late John Henry Bailey, *b* 1889, *d* 1966: *m* 1913, Ruby, who *d* 1972, da of Edward Giles:—
Margaret Elizabeth (PO Box 795, Oliver, BC V0H 1TO, Canada), *b* 1915: *m* 1939, Derrick Thomas Ashworth Douglas, who *d* 1975, and has issue living, Derrick John (158 Aurora Place, 21252 Township Rd 530, Ardrossan, Alberta, Canada T8G 2C4), *b* 1947. *m* 1st, 1969 (*m diss* 1976), Penelope Elizabeth, da of Rudi Krause, of Elmira, Ont; 2ndly, 1978, Marilyn Winnifred, da of late Morley John Edward Bushell, and has issue living (by 1st *m*), Lee Christian *b* 1971, Todd Matthew *b* 1973, — David Henry (twin) (80 Collings Av, Bradford, Ont, Canada L3Z 1S4), *b* 1947: Sergeant RCMP: *m* 1970, Charlotte, da of late Stefan Johannson, of Gimli, Manitoba, and has issue living, Stefan Nathan *b* 1971, Brendan Wyatt *b* 1981, Jill Elizabeth *b* 1974, — Judy Ann, *b* 1941: *m* 1971, Herbert Flax, of PO Box 699, Boyle, Alberta, Canada T0A 0M0, and has issue living, Timothy Aaron *b* 1974, Joanna Susan *b* 1972. —— Barbara, *b* 1927: *m* 1945, Capt Ernest Ronald Matthewson, of 30 Chapel Meadow, Tring, Herts, and has issue living, Michael Derek (18 Haynes Mead, Berkhamsted, Herts), *b* 1946: *m* 1970, Barbara Mary Saunders, and has issue living, Toby *b* 1974, Kirsty *b* 1976.

PREDECESSORS – (1) JOSEPH BAILEY, yr son of John Bailey, of Wakefield; sat successively as MP for Worcester City and Breconshire; *cr* a *Baronet* 1852: *m* 1st, 1810, Maria, who *d* 1827, da of Joseph Latham; 2ndly, 1830, Mary Anne, who *d* 1874, da of late John Thomas Hendry Hopper, ot Witton Castle, co Durham; *d* 1858, *s* by his grandson (2) JOSEPH RUSSELL (son of late Joseph Bailey, MP, el son of 1st Bt), 2nd Bt, *b* 1840; *cr* *Baron Glanusk*, of Glanusk Park, co Brecknock (peerage of United Kingdom) 1899; MP for Herefordshire (C) 1865-85, and for Hereford, 1886-92; was Lord-Lieut of Breconshire: *m* 1861, Mary Ann Jane, who *d* 1935, da of Henry Lucas, MD, of Glan-yr-Afon; *d* 1906; *s* by his son (3) JOSEPH HENRY RUSSELL, CB, CBE, DSO, 2nd Baron, *b* 1864; Lord-Lieut of Breconshire 1905-28: *m* 1890, Editha Elma, CBE, who *d* 1938, da of late Major Warden Sergison; *d* 1928; *s* by his son (4) WILFRED RUSSELL, DSO, 3rd Baron; *b* 1891, Lord-Lieut of Breconshire; late Grenadier and Welsh Guards; European War 1914-19 (DSO): *m* 1st, 1919 (*m diss* 1939), Victoria Mary Enid Anne, da of late Lieut-Col Frank Dugdale, CVO; 2ndly, 1942, Margaret Eldrydd (who *m* 2ndly, 1966, 1st Viscount De L'Isle, VC, KG, GCMG, GCVO, PC, who *d* 1991), da of late Maj-Gen Thomas Herbert Shoubridge, CB, CMG, DSO; *d* 1948; *s* by his cousin (5) DAVID RUSSELL (son of late Hon Herbert Crawshay Bailey, 4th son of 1st Baron), 4th Baron, *b* 1917; Lt Cmdr RN; Man Dir Wandel & Goltermann (UK) Ltd 1966-82, Chm W&G Instruments Ltd 1982-87: *m* 1941, Lorna Dorothy, who *d* (25 June) 1997, only da of late Capt E. C. H. N. Andrews, MBE, RA; *d* (28 June) 1997; *s* by his only son (6) CHRISTOPHER RUSSELL, 5th Baron and present peer.

GLASGOW, EARL OF (Boyle) (Earl S 1703)

The Lord will provide

PATRICK ROBIN ARCHIBALD BOYLE, 10th Earl; *b* 30 July 1939; *s* 1984; *ed* Eton, and Sorbonne; Sub-Lt RNR; sometime Television Documentary Producer and Dir: *m* 1975, Isabel Mary, adopted da of late George Douglas James, and has issue.

𝕬rms – Quarterly: 1st and 4th or, an eagle with two heads displayed gules, armed and beaked azure; a coat of augmentation for the earldom of *Glasgow;* 2nd and 3rd per bend embattled argent and gules, *Boyle:* over all an escutcheon or, charged with three stags' horns gules, for the paternal coat of *Boyle of Kelburn.* 𝕮rest – An eagle with two heads displayed per pale embattled gules and argent. 𝕾upporters – *Dexter,* a savage, wreathed round the temples and loins, and holding in the dexter hand a branch of laurel all proper: *sinister,* a lion per pale embattled argent and gules.
Seat – Kelburn, Fairlie, Ayrshire.

SON LIVING

Hon DAVID MICHAEL DOUGLAS (does not use courtesy title of Viscount of Kelburn), *b* 15 Oct 1978.

DAUGHTER LIVING

Lady Alice Dorothy, *b* 1981.

SISTERS LIVING AND DECEASED

Lady Sarah Dorothea, *b* 1941: *m* 1962, John Edward Baily, of Arletts, Church Rd, Eversley, Hants (*see* E Haddington colls, 1980 Edn), and has had issue, Michael, *b* 1963; *d* 1985, — Peter, *b* 1967, — Tanya Jane, *b* 1965: *m* 1994, Julian D. Martin, son of Russell S. Martin, of Blackburn, Vic, Australia, — Polly Anne, *b* 1972.

Lady Nichola Jane Eleanora (Minervina), *b* 1946: *m* 1976, Thomas G. Carter, and *d* 1997, leaving issue, Matthew, *b* 1978, — Ella Frances Lyle, *b* 1986.

AUNT LIVING (*Daughter of 8th Earl*)

Lady Margaret Dorothea, *b* 1920: *m* 1st, 1944 (*m diss* 1962), Capt Oliver Payan Dawnay, CVO, Coldstream Gds, who *d* 1988 (*see* V Downe, colls); 2ndly, 1973, Peter Douglas Miller Stirling-Aird of Kippendavie, TD, of Kippendavie Lodge, Dunblane, Perthshire FK15 0HR, and 9 Lansdowne Rd, W11 3AG.

MOTHER LIVING

Dorothea, only da of Col Sir Archibald Moir Park Lyle, 2nd Bt, MC: *m* 1937 (*m diss* 1962), Rear-Adm David William Maurice, Viscount Kelburn, CB, DSC, later 9th Earl of Glasgow, who *d* 1984. *Residences –* Marwell House, Owslesbury, nr Winchester, Hants; Albany, Piccadilly, W1.

COLLATERAL BRANCHES LIVING

Grandsons of late Capt Hon James Boyle, 3rd son of 7th Earl:—
Issue of late Lieut-Col Patrick John Salvin Boyle, Roy Scots Fusiliers, *b* 1910, *ka* 1944: *m* 1938, Mary Elizabeth, OBE (who *d* 1996, having *m* 2ndly, 1948, Lieut-Col Charles Murray Floyd, OBE, RE (*see* Floyd, Bt, colls), who *d* 1971), only child of Robert Fleetwood Fuller, of Great Chalfield, Melksham:—
Andrew Robert James (Fairhaven, Northend, Bath BA1 8ES), *b* 1939; *ed* Eton: *m* 1971, Julia, da of N. W. Gardener of Boxted Farm, Hemel Hempstead, Herts, and has issue living, James William, *b* 1973, — Olivia Mary, *b* 1975. —— Simon Hugh Patrick (Penpergwm Lodge, Abergavenny, Gwent), *b* 1941; *ed* Eton; High Sheriff Gwent 1993: *m* 1970, Catriona, da of W. G. Gordon, DFC, of Lude, Blair Atholl, Perths, and has issue living, Alice Catriona Jane, *b* 1972, — Mary Helen Fenella, *b* 1974, — Susannah Elizabeth, *b* 1977, — Christian Laura Frances, *b* 1982. —— David Thomas Alan (Fairstead Hall, Terling, Chelmsford, Essex), *b* 1943; *ed* Eton, and Trin Coll, Camb; JP Essex: *m* 1969, Angela Rose, da of George Frederick Pinney, CBE (*see* Lacy, Bt, 1980 Edn), and has issue living, Robert John, *b* 1970; *ed* Eton, — Edward George, *b* 1972; *ed* Eton, — Patrick Thomas, *b* 1974, — Katherine Griselda Eveline, *b* 1982.

Issue of late Hon Alan Reginald Boyle, AFC, 5th son of 7th Earl, *b* 1886, *d* 1958: *m* 1916, Isabel Julia, who *d* 1977, da of late Edmund Charles Pendleton Hull, JP, of Park Gate House, Ham Common, Richmond, Surrey:—
Jean Isabel, *b* 1919: *m* 1st, 1941 (*m diss* 1976), Bartholomew Guy Ellison; 2ndly, 1980, Iain Robert Cullen Baillie, and has issue living (by 1st *m*), Caroline Anne, *b* 1942: *m* 1967, Rev John Antony Hobbs, of May Cottage, Alice Bright Lane, Crowborough, Sussex, TN6 3SQ, and has issue living, Jonathan Noel Alan *b* 1970: *m* 1997, Bethan Bartram-Whatley, Francesca Agnes *b* 1968: *m* 1992, Rev Adrian Youings (and has issue living, Rebecca Isabel *b* 1997), Rosanna Natasha *b* 1972: *m* 1998, Christopher Davis, — Joanna Fenella, *b* 1945.

(In remainder to Scottish peerages only)

Granddaughters of late Col Patrick David Boyle, el son of late Vice-Adm Alexander Boyle, 2nd son of late Rt Hon David Boyle, Lord Justice-Gen of Scotland, 4th son of late Rev Hon Patrick Boyle, 4th son of 2nd Earl:—
  Issue of late Col Cecil Alexander Boyle, CIE, DSO, *b* 1888, *d* 1941: *m* 1923, Gladys (Dulcie), who *d* 1976, da of late Lt-Col Robert Arthur Edward Benn, CIE:—
Mary Grizel, *b* 1924; 1939-45 War with WAAF: *m* 1947, Lt-Col James Berkeley Sackville Hamilton, RE (ret), of Acklam Grange, Acklam, Malton, Yorks, YO17 9RG, and has issue (*see* V Boyne, colls). —— Patricia (Le Moulin de Quatre Carres, 47150 Monflanquin, France), *b* 1929: a State Registered Nurse: *m* 1955 (*m diss* 1980), Lt-Col Jonathan Robert Alford, RE, who *d* 1986, and has issue living, Michael Robert Patrick, *b* 1958, — Caroline Jane, *b* 1956, — Melissa Anne, *b* 1960, — Victoria Susan, *b* 1963.

Granddaughters of late Alexander Boyle, yst son of Vice-Adm Alexander Boyle (ante):—
  Issue of late Alister Patrick Boyle, *b* 1905, *d* 1973: *m* 1st 1932, Rosa Howard, who *d* 1933, da of Howard Tripp, of S Canterbury, NZ; 2ndly, 1936, Lois Morton (48 Cox St, Christchurch 8001, NZ), da of late C. M. Ollivier:—
(By 1st *m*) Jennifer Frances, *b* 1933: *m* 1965 (*m diss* 1989), Ian Coutts, and has issue living, Hester Frances, *b* 1967, — Rosa Emily, *b* 1969. —— (By 2nd *m*) Mary Montgomerie (9 Andover St, Christchurch 1, NZ), *b* 1937: *m* 1964, Laurence George Holder, who *d* 1974, and has issue living, Patrick George, *b* 1966, — Bridget Mary, *b* 1967, — Alexandra Browning, *b* 1969, — Sara Annabel, *b* 1972. —— Alexandra Montgomerie (Canal House, 120 Lisson Grove, NW8 8LB), *b* 1943: *m* 1988, Douglas Cruden Stephen, who *d* 1991.

Grandsons of late Henry David Boyle, el son of John Boyle, 3rd son of Rt Hon David Boyle (ante):—
  Issue of late David Hugh Montgomerie Boyle, CMG, *b* 1883, *d* 1970: *m* 1916, Laura Grant, who *d* 1971, da of late James Tennant, of Fairlieburne, Fairlie:—
Alasdair David Forbes (50 Castlebay Court, Largs, Ayrshire KA30 8DP), *b* 1919; *ed* Wellington Coll, and RMC; Maj (ret) Argyll and Sutherland Highlanders; MBIM; Sec of Scottish Business Sch; 1939-45 War (wounded, despatches): *m* 1st, 1945 (*m diss* 1958), Elizabeth Winifred, da of late Cdr H. R. Kelway-Bamber, RN; 2ndly, 1958, Mrs Doris Louise Clayton, da of Victor Eaton Usherwood, of Tunbridge Wells, and has had issue, (by 1st *m*) Rory David Alasdair (Firs Cottage, College Grove, Malvern, Worcs WR14 3HP), *b* 1951: *m* 1977, (Althea) Victoria, yr da of late Maj Derek Leslie Lloyd, MC (*see* V Chetwynd, colls, 1995 Edn), and has issue living, Jamie Edward Rory *b* 1978, Harriet Elizabeth Victoria *b* 1980, — Henrietta Elizabeth Flora *b* 1948: *m* 1968, Hon James Malcolm Rollo, and *d* 1998, leaving issue (*see* L Rollo), — (and a da from 2nd *m*) Camilla Josephine Brenda Louise, *b* 1964. —— Ranald Hugh Montgomerie, DSC (The Wooden House, Fairlie, Ayrshire; 906 Beatty House, Dolphin Sq, SW1), *b* 1921; *ed* Wellington Coll, and Exeter Coll, Oxford; late Sudan Govt Ser, HMOCS Kenya; HM Dip Ser; Hambros Bank; a Member of Queen's Body Guard for Scotland (Royal Company of Archers); 1939-45 War as Lt RNVR (wounded, DSC): *m* 1957, Norma, yst da of late Alexander Gray and has issue living, Fergus David (Downcraig Ferry, Millport, I of Cumbrae, Scotland KA28 0AA), *b* 1958, — Alexander Ranald, *b* 1959: *m* 1999, Maria E, only da of Florin Cucoș, of London, — Patrick Mungo, *b* 1961: *m* 1997, Jane, elder da of late David Brierley, — John Quentin, *b* 1964: *m* 1997, Diana M., elder da of James Young, of Edinburgh, and of Mrs Harry Denholm, of Arnprior, Stirlingshire, — Hamish William, *b* 1970, — Laura Grizel, *b* 1963: *m* 1993, Deane C. B. Pennick, elder son of Lt-Col Peter Pennick, and has issue living, Thomas Ranald Bowman *b* 1995, Anastasia Laura *b* 1994, Sophie Beatrice *b* 1997, — Beatrice Elizabeth, *b* 1966: *m* 1994, Richard B. Bath, yr son of Alistair Bath, of Caversham, Berks, and has issue living, Oliver *b* 1997, Ailsa *b* 1999.

Granddaughter of late William Henry David Boyle, son of late Col William Boyle, CB, 4th son of late Rt Hon David Boyle (ante):—
  Issue of late George Frederic Boyle, *b* 1893, *d* 1929: *m* 1920 (*m diss* 1929), Mary Jeffrey (who *d* 1954, having *m* 2ndly, 1929, Douglas Charles Beaumont, MD, MRCP, of Claywood Sway, Hants), da of Sir Peter Jeffrey Mackie, 1st Bt:—
Eleanor Mary, *b* 1921: *m* 1st, 1945 (*m diss* 1962), Capt Hon Arthur Cameron Corbett, Ayrshire Yeo (later 3rd Baron Rowallan), who *d* 1993; 2ndly, 1963, Col (Richard) Derek Cardiff, late Scots Gds, and has issue living (by 1st *m*) (*see* B Rowallan), — (by 2nd *m*) David Richard George, *b* 1964: *m* 1992, Eleanora, da of Dr H. Kessler, of Vienna, Austria. *Residence* – Flat 1, 13 Embankment Gds, SW3 4LW.

Issue, if any, of Robert Fremoult Boyle (*b* 1887), son of late Charles Fremoult Boyle, of Winnipeg, Manitoba, Canada, NW Mounted Police 1876-80, eldest son of late Capt Robert Boyle, RA (infra).

Granddaughter of late Cdr Edward Louis Dalrymple Boyle, CMG, RN, 3rd son of Capt Robert Boyle, RA, 7th son of Rt Hon David Boyle (ante):—
  Issue of late Lt-Col (Edward) Patrick Ogilvie Boyle, MVO, Royal Scots Fus, *b* 1893, *d* 1966: *m* 1934, Audrey (who *d* 1998, having *m* 2ndly, 1970, Maj Clarence J. Henry, who *d* 1973), da of late Lt-Col Audley Willis:—
Jennifer Mary, *b* 1934.

PREDECESSORS – (1) DAVID BOYLE, MP for Buteshire 1689-99; *cr* Lord Boyle, of Kelburn, Stewartown, Cumbrae, Largs and Dalry (peerage of Scotland) 1699, and *Lord Boyle, Viscount of Kelburn* and *Earl of Glasgow* (peerage of Scotland) 1703, with remainder to his heirs male whatsoever; Lord High Commr to Gen Assembly for Ch of Scotland 1706-10, a Representative Peer 1707-08, and Lord Registrar of Scotland 1708-14; *d* 1733; *s* by his son (2) JOHN, 2nd Earl; *d* 1740; *s* by his son (3) JOHN, 3rd Earl; was Lord High Commr to Ch of Scotland 1764-72; *d* 1775; *s* by his son (4) GEORGE, GCH, 4th Earl, *b* 1766; Lord-Lieut of Renfrewshire, and a Representative Peer; *cr Baron Fairlie*, co Renfrew (peerage of United Kingdom) 1815: *m* 1st, 1788, Lady Augusta Hay, da of 14th Earl of Erroll; 2ndly, 1824, Julia, da of the Rt Hon Sir John Sinclair, 1st Bt; *d* 1843; *s* by his 2nd son (5) JAMES, 5th Earl; a Capt RN, and Lord Lieut and Sheriff of Renfrewshire; assumed, 1822, by Roy licence the additional surname of Car; *d* 1869; *s* by his half-brother (6) GEORGE FREDERICK, 6th Earl, *b* 1825; MP for Buteshire (C) 1865, and subsequently Lord Clerk Register of Scotland: *m* 1856, Montagu, who *d* 1931, da of 3rd Baron Abercromby; *d* 1890, when the Barony of Ross became extinct, and the Scottish Peerages devolved upon his cousin (7) DAVID, GCMG (son of Patrick Boyle, of Shewalton, co Ayr, and el great-grandson of Hon Patrick Boyle, 3rd son of 2nd Earl), 7th Earl, *b* 1833; Capt RN; served in White Sea during Russian War 1854, and in China 1857; was Gov of New Zealand 1892-7; *cr Baron Fairlie*, of Fairlie, co Ayr (peerage of United Kingdom) 1897: *m* 1873, Dorothea Elizabeth Thomasina, who *d* 1923, da of Sir Edward Hunter-Blair, 4th Bt; *d* 1915; *s* by his el son (8) PATRICK JAMES, DSO, 8th Earl, *b* 1874; Capt RN; Convener of Ayr Co Council 1947-58: *m* 1906, Hyacinthe

Mary, who *d* 1977, da of late William A. Bell, of Pendell Court, Bletchingley; *d* 1963; *s* by his el son **(9)** DAVID WILLIAM MAURICE, CB, DSC, 9th Earl; *b* 1910; Rear-Adm; Capt of the Fleet, Home Fleet 1957-59; Commodore RN Barracks, Portsmouth 1959-61; Flag-Offr, Malta 1961-63; 1939-45 war in Atlantic, Arctic, and Far East; present at destruction of *Bismarck*; Mem Royal Co of Archers (Queen's Body Guard for Scotland): *m* 1st, 1937 (*m diss* 1962), Dorothea, only da of Col Sir Archibald Moir Park Lyle, 2nd Bt, MC; 2ndly, 1962, Hon Ursula Vanda Maud, who *d* 1984, da of 4th Baron Vivian, and formerly wife of Maj Sir William Fane Wrixon Beecher, 5th Bt, MC; *d* 1984; *s* by his only son **(10)** PATRICK ROBIN ARCHIBALD, 10th Earl, and present peer; also Viscount of Kelburn, Lord Boyle and Baron Fairlie.

GLENAMARA, BARON (Short) (Life Baron 1977)

EDWARD WATSON SHORT, CH, PC, son of Charles Short, of Warcop, Westmorland; *b* 17 Dec 1912; *ed* Bede Coll, Durham Univ (LLB); 1939-45 War as Capt DLI; Opposition Assist Whip 1955-61, Dep Ch Opposition Whip 1962-64, Parl Sec to Treasury and Govt Ch Whip 1964-66, Postmaster Gen 1966-68, Sec of State for Education and Science 1968-70, Dep Leader of Labour Party 1972-76, and Lord Pres of the Council and Leader of House of Commons 1974-76; MP for Central Newcastle upon Tyne (*L*) 1951-76; Chm of Cable and Wireless Ltd, 1976-80; Chancellor, Univ of Northumbria since 1984; Hon DCL Durham, DCL Newcastle, DLitt Northumbria, DUniv Open; author of *The Infantry Instructor*, *The Story of Durham Light Infantry*, *Education in a Changing World*, *Birth to Five; I Knew My Place* and *Whip to Wilson*; *cr* PC 1964, CH 1976, and *Baron Glenamara*, of Glenridding in co Cumbria (Life Baron) 1977: *m* 1941, Jennie, da of Thomas Sewell, of Newcastle upon Tyne, and has issue.
Residences – 21 Priory Gdns, Corbridge, Northumberland NE45 5HZ.

SON LIVING

Hon Michael Christian (Holly House, Whickham, Tyne and Wear), *b* 1943: *m* 1968, Ann, da of Joseph Gibbon, of Whickham, Tyne and Wear.

DAUGHTER LIVING

Hon Jane Bronwen, *b* 1945: *m* 1970, James Weir Fraser, and has issue. *Residence* – 62 Martis Av, Ramsey, NJ 07446, USA.

Glenapp, Viscount; son of Earl of Inchcape.

GLENARTHUR, BARON (Arthur) (Baron UK 1918, Bt UK 1903)

Do and hope

FAC ET SPERA

SIMON MARK ARTHUR, 4th Baron, and 4th Baronet; *b* 7 Oct 1944; *s* 1976; *ed* Eton; commn'd 10th R Hussars (PWO) 1963, ret as Maj 1975; joined R Hussars TA 1976-80; DL Aberdeenshire 1988; Brig Queen's Body Guard for Scotland (Royal Company of Archers), Capt British Airways Helicopters Ltd 1976-82; a Lord in Waiting (Gvt Whip) to HM 1982-83; Parly Under-Sec of State, Dept of Health & Social Security 1983-85, Home Office 1985-86, Min of State Scottish Office 1986-87, Min of State, Foreign & Commonwealth Affairs 1987-89; Dir Aberdeen & Texas Corporate Finance Ltd 1977-82; Senior Executive Hanson plc 1989-96; Chm St Mary's NHS Trust 1991-98, British Helicopter Advisory Board since 1992, European Helicopter Assocn since 1996, International Fedn of Helicopter Assocns since 1996; Dir Lewis Group plc 1993-94, Millennium Chemicals Inc since 1996, Dep Chm Hanson Pacific Ltd 1993-98; MCIT 1979, FRAeS 1992; Pres National Council for Civil Protection since 1991; *m* 1969, Susan, da of late Cdr Hubert Wyndham Barry, RN (ret) (*see* Barry, Bt, colls), and has issue.

Arms – Sable, an escarbuncle or, within an orle of besants. **Crest** – On a rock a pelican in her piety proper. **Supporters** – (as recorded at Lyon Office), — *Dexter*, a bay horse proper; *sinister*, a lion rampant gules.
Address – Northbrae Farmhouse, Crathes, Banchory, Kincardineshire AB31 6JQ. *Clubs* – Cavalry and Guards, Pratt's, White's.

SON LIVING

Hon EDWARD ALEXANDER, *b* 9 April 1973; *ed* Eton.

DAUGHTER LIVING

Hon Emily Victoria, *b* 1975.

BROTHER LIVING

Hon Matthew Richard (Bingfield East Quarter, Hallington, Newcastle upon Tyne), *b* 1948; *ed* Eton, and RAC Cirencester: *m* 1974, Veronica Rosemary, yr da of Capt Michael Hall, Royal Scots Greys, of the Bridge, Kilternan, co Dublin (*see* B Basing, 1980 Edn), and has issue living, Matthew Frederick Michael, *b* 1981, — Jessica Mary, *b* 1979.

SISTER LIVING

Hon Victoria, *b* 1946: *m* 1976, Hugh Richard Mervyn Vernon, of Stairaird, Mauchline, Ayrshire (*see* B Lyveden, colls)

PREDECESSORS – **(1)** *Sir* MATTHEW Arthur, LLD, el son of late James Arthur, of Carlung, Ayrshire, and Barshaw, Renfrewshire, by Jane, da of Thomas Glen, of Thornhill, Renfrewshire; *b* 1852; Chm of Arthur and Co (Limited), of Glasgow, and of Lochgelly Iron and Coal Co (Limited), and a Member of Roy Co of Archers (King's Body Guard for Scotland); Chm of Glasgow and S-W Railway Co 1920-22; *cr* a *Baronet* 1903, and *Baron Glenarthur*, of Carlung, Ayrshire (peerage of United Kingdom) 1918: *m* 1876, Janet Stevenson Bennett, OBE, who *d* 1946, yr da of late Alexander Bennett McGrigor, LLD of Cairnoch, Stirlingshire; *d* 1928; *s* by his son **(2)** (JAMES) CECIL, 2nd Baron; *b* 1883: *m* 1907, Evelyn, who *d* 1959, el da of late Henry March-Phillipps, of Tiverton, N Devon; *d* 1942; *s* by his son **(3)** MATTHEW, OBE, 3rd Baron *b* 1909: *m* 1st, 1931 (*m diss* 1939), Audrey da of late George Crompton Lees Milne (B Glanusk, colls); 2ndly, 1939, Margaret Risk, who *d* 1993, only da of late Capt Henry James Howie, of Stairaird, Mauchline; *d* 1976; *s* by his el son **(4)** SIMON MARK, 4th Baron and present peer.

GLENAVY, BARONY OF (Campbell) (Extinct 1984)

DAUGHTER LIVING OF THIRD BARON

Hon Brigid Margaret, *b* 1948: *m* 19—, — Reilly, of 2535 Panorama Dr, N Vancouver, BC, Canada.

Glencairn, Earldom of (Cunningham) (Earl S 1488 Dormant 1796) See Cuninghame Bt (NS 1672) of Corsehill.

GLENCONNER, BARON (Tennant) (Baron UK 1911, Bt UK 1885)

God will fill the sails

COLIN CHRISTOPHER PAGET TENNANT, 3rd Baron and 4th Baronet; *b* 1 Dec 1926; *s* 1983; *ed* Eton, and New Coll, Oxford; formerly Lieut IG: *m* 1956, Lady Anne Veronica Coke, LVO, da of 5th Earl of Leicester, and has had issue.

Arms – Argent, two crescents in fesse sable, on a chief gules a boar's head couped of the first; a bordure company of the second and first. **Crest** – A mast with a sail hoisted proper. **Supporters** – *Dexter*, a stag proper, gorged with a mural crown or; *sinister*, a tiger also proper, gorged with a crown palissado also or; each charged on the shoulder with a thistle, leaved and slipped, gold.
Residence – Beau Estate, Soufriere, St Lucia, W Indies.

SONS LIVING AND DECEASED

†*Hon* Charles Edward Pevensey, *b* 1957; *ed* Clifton, and Frencham Heights: *m* 1993, Sheilagh (30 Fountainhall Rd, Edinburgh EH9 2LW), da of Matthew Raymond Walker Scott, of Peebles, and *d* 1996, leaving issue, CODY CHARLES EDWARD, *b* 2 Feb 1994.
†*Hon* Henry Lovell, *b* 1960: *m* 1983, Teresa Mary (The Glen, Innerleithen, Peeblesshire), yst da of John McRae Cormack, AFC (*see* B Davies), and *d* 1990, leaving issue, Euan Lovell, *b* 1983.
Hon Christopher Cary, *b* 1967; *ed* Stanbridge Earls: *m* 1996, Anastasia, da of Dimitrios Papadakos, of Athens, and has issue living, (Anne) Bella Veroniki, *b* 1996.

DAUGHTERS LIVING

Hon (Flora) May Pamela, *b* 1970.
Hon Amy Jasmine Elizabeth (twin), *b* 1970.

HALF-BROTHER LIVING

Hon Tobias William (Shaws, Newcastleton, Roxburghshire), *b* 1941: *m* 1963, Lady Emma Cavendish, el da of 11th Duke of Devonshire, and has issue living, Edward Tobias, *b* 1967. — Isabel (23 Stadium St, SW10), *b* 1964: *m* 1997, Piers Hill, son of late Simon Hill, and of Mrs Glen Joel, — Stella, *b* 1970; has issue living (by David Lasnet), Marcel LASNET *b* 1998.

HALF-SISTERS LIVING

Hon Emma Christina TENNANT (141 Elgin Crescent, W11), *b* 1937: *ed* St Paul's Girls' Sch; FRSL; the novelist Emma Tennant, author of *The Bad Sister, Wild Nights, Woman Beware Woman, Strangers*, etc; founder editor of *Bananas*, Literary Newspaper; *m* 1st 1957 (*m diss* 1962), Sebastian Yorke (*see* E Hardwicke, colls); 2ndly, 1963 (*m diss* 19—), Christopher John Penrice Booker, author and journalist; 3rdly, 1968 (*m diss* 1973), Alexander Claud Cockburn (*see* Arbuthnot, Bt, colls, *cr* 1829, 1990 Edn), and has issue living, (by 1st *m*) (*see* E Hardwicke, colls), — (by 3rd *m*) Daisy

Alice, *b* 1969, — (by late Michael Dempsey) Rose Hippolyta, *b* 1973. *Address* – c/o Peters, Fraser & Dunlop, The Chambers, Chelsea Harbour, SW10.

Hon Catherine Elizabeth (*Hon Lady Palmer*), *b* 1947: *m* 1976, Sir (Charles) Mark Palmer, 5th Bt (*cr* 1886), of Mill Hill Farm, Sherborne, Northleach, Glos.

WIDOW LIVING OF SON OF FIRST BARON

Shelagh Anne, da of Maj Sean Rainey, and of Mrs Marion Wrottesley: *m* 1963, as his 3rd wife, Hon David Pax Tennant, who *d* 1968.

WIDOW LIVING OF SON OF SECOND BARON

Elizabeth Marya, da of James Dales, of W Vancouver, BC, Canada, and formerly wife of Ian Romer, of Hawkley, Hants: *m* 2ndly, 1962, as his 2nd wife, Hon James Grey Herbert Tennant, who *d* 1992; 3rdly, 1994, Philip Edwards. *Residence* – 37 Cadogan Place, SW1.

WIDOW LIVING OF SECOND BARON

ELIZABETH (*Elizabeth, Baroness Glenconner*), da of late Lt-Col Evelyn George Harcourt Powell, Gren Gds, of 31 Hillgate Place, W8: *m* 1935, as his 2nd wife, the 2nd Baron Glenconner, who *d* 1983. *Residence* – Rovinia, Liapades, Corfu, Greece.

COLLATERAL BRANCHES LIVING

Issue of late Hon James Grey Herbert Tennant, 2nd son of 2nd Baron, *b* 1929, *d* 1992: *m* 1st, 1955 (*m diss* 1962), Emily Fawaz, da of George Licos; 2ndly, 1962, Elizabeth Marya (ante) (who *m* 3rdly, 1994, Philip Edwards), da of James Dales, of W Vancouver, BC, Canada, and formerly wife of Ian Romer, of Hawkley, Hants:—
(By 1st *m*) Alexander David Gabriel, *b* 1957.

Issue of late Hon David Pax Tennant, 2nd son of 1st Baron, *b* 1902, *d* 1968: *m* 1st, 1928 (*m diss* 1937), Hermione Youlanda Ruby Clinton (Hermione Baddeley the actress), who *d* 1986, da of William Herman Clinton Baddeley; 2ndly, 1938 (*m diss* 1953), Virginia Penelope, da of late Alan Parsons, of The Baas, Broxbourne, Herts; 3rdly, 1963, Shelagh Anne (ante), da of Maj Sean Rainey:—
(By 1st *m*) David Edward Wyndham (Pyt Cottage, Tisbury, Wilts SP3 6NY. *Clubs* – White's and Brooks's), *b* 1930; *ed* Eton: *m* 1964 (*m diss* 1973), Margaret Rachel, da of late Hon Sir Ernest Stowell Scott, KCMG, MVO (*see* E Eldon, colls), and has issue living, Aubone Christopher, *b* 1969; *ed* Eton, and Durham Univ; Capt Scots Guards, — Ivan, *b* 1970; *ed* Stowe, — Laura Hermione, *b* 1967; *ed* St Paul's Girls' Sch, and Jesus Coll, Camb: *m* 1995, Ian J. Irvine, eldest son of Alastair Irvine, of Aberdeen. —— Pauline Laetitia (*Pauline, Lady Rumbold*), *b* 1929: *m* 1st, 1946 (*m diss* 1953), Capt Julian Alfred Lane-Fox Pitt-Rivers, late R Dragoons (*see* By Forster, 1980 Edn); 2ndly, 1954 (*m diss* 1970), Euan Douglas Graham (*see* D Montrose, colls); 3rdly, 1974, Sir (Horace) Anthony (Claude) Rumbold, 10th Bt, KCMG, KCVO, CB, who *d* 1983, of Hatch Cottage, Cokers Frome, Dorchester, Dorset. —— (By 2nd *m*) Annabel Georgiana Skye (Georgia) (Job's Mill, Warminster, Wilts), *b* 1941; has issue (by Paul Stephen McNaney), Ella May, *b* 1984. —— Sabrina Viola (Josie TENNANT), *b* 1943 (relinquished the forenames of Sabrina Viola and assumed that of Josie by deed poll; has reverted to her maiden surname): *m* 1963 (*m diss* 1977), Jonathan Gathorne-Hardy, and has issue (*see* E Cranbrook, colls).

(In remainder to Baronetcy only)

Grandsons of late Francis John Tennant, 5th son of 1st baronet:—
Issue of late Group Capt John Edward Tennant, DSO, MC, RAF Vol Reserve, *b* 1890, *d* on active ser 1941: *m* 1st, 1918 (*m diss* 1925), Georgina Helen, da of Gen Sir George Macaulay Kirkpatrick, KCB, KCSI; 2ndly, 1926, Victoria Maud Veronica, MBE, who *d* 1967, da of Sir Robert (Robin) George Vivian Duff, 2nd Bt (*cr* 1911):—
(By 1st *m*) *Sir* Iain Mark, KT, *b* 1919; *ed* Eton, and Magdalene Coll, Camb; late Capt Scots Guards; a JP (1961) DL (1954) and Lord Lieut Morayshire (now Grampian Region) 1963-94; Chm Gordonstoun Schools Ltd 1956-72, and Grampian TV 1967-89; Crown Estate Commr 1970-90; Dir of the Clydesdale Bank 1968-89 and the Abbey Nat Bldg Soc 1981-89; Lord High Commr to Gen Assembly of Church of Scotland 1987 and 1988; a Member of Queen's Body Guard for Scotland (Roy Co of Archers); 1939-45 War; KT 1986: *m* 1946, Lady Margaret Helen Isla Marion Ogilvy, da of 12th Earl of Airlie, and has issue living, Mark Edward (Innes House, Elgin, Moray), *b* 1947; late Scots Gds; Man Dir (Scotland) Chase Manhatten Bank, Dir Quality Street Ltd: *m* 1971, Hermione Rosamond, da of Lt Col Maurice W. Howe, OBE, and has issue living, Edward Iain *b* 1983, Miranda Hermione Rosamond *b* 1974, Clementine Margaret Georgina *b* 1977, — Christopher John, *b* 1950; a Page of Honour to HM The Queen 1964-66: *m* 1994, Mrs Andrea Lewis, yst da of Donald Payne, — Emma Margaret *b* 1954: *m* 1979, Angus Geoffrey Bruce Ismay Cheape, late Scots Guards, of Middleton Fossoway, Kinross, 2nd son of (Hugh) Bruce Ismay Cheape, TD, of South Lodge, Craignure, Isle of Mull, and has issue living, Henry Bruce Iain Ismay *b* 1980. *Residence* – Lochnabo House, Elgin, Morayshire. —— (By 2nd *m*) Andrew Duff (Muiresk House, Turriff, Aberdeenshire AB53 4HD; White's Club), *b* 1928; *ed* Eton; late Scots Gds: *m* 1953 (*m diss* 1967), Lucinda Evelyn, only da of Arthur Walter James (*see* B Northbourne, colls), and has issue living, Ann Charlotte, *b* 1956. —— Hugh Rinnes Duff (4 Lecky St, SW7), *b* 1932; *ed* Eton; formerly Lt Scots Gds.

Grandchildren of late Rt Hon Harold John Tennant (infra):—
Issue of late Maj John Tennant, TD, *b* 1899, *d* 1967: *m* 1st, 1929 (*m diss* 1939), Hon Antonia Mary Roby Benson, who *d* 1982, da of 1st Baron Charnwood; 2ndly, 1948, Rosemary Irene, da of Sir Alfred Theodore Hennessy, KBE:—

(By 1st *m*) *Sir* Anthony John, *b* 1930; *ed* Eton, and Trin Coll, Camb (BA); late Lt Scots Guards; Chm Guinness plc 1989-92, Chm Christie's 1993-96; *cr* Knt Bach 1992: *m* 1954, Rosemary Violet, el da of Lt-Col Henry Charles Minshull Stockdale (*see* B Faringdon, 1976 Edn), and has issue living, Christopher Sebastian, *b* 1955; *ed* Eton and St Andrew's Univ (MA): *m* 1987, Sally Jennifer, 3rd da of Jack Berner, of 80 Church Rd, Wimbledon, and has issue living, Francesca Rose Antonia *b* 1992, Harriet Daisy *b* 1993, — Patrick Charles, *b* 1958; *ed* Eton, Trin Coll, Camb (MA), and Univ of Pennsylvania (MBA, MA): *m* 1986, Meredith Maye, el da of Jerome Shively, of Churt, Surrey, and has issue living, Barnaby *b* 1994, Oliver *b* (twin) 1994, Jemima Jennifer *b* 1990. —— Mark Iain (Royal Courts of Justice, Strand, WC2A 2LL; 30 Abbey Gdns, NW8 9AT; Balfluig Castle, by Alford, Aberdeenshire; Brooks's Club), *b* 1932; *ed* Eton, and New Coll, Oxford (MA); Bar. Inner Temple 1958, Master of the Bench 1982, Master of the Supreme Court, Queen's Bench Div 1988; Chm Royal Orchestral Soc for Amateur Musicians since 1989; Baron of Balfluig: *m* 1965, Lady Harriot Pleydell-Bouverie, da of 7th Earl of Radnor, and has issue living, Lysander Philip Roby (204 Iverson Rd, NW6 2HL), *b* 1968; *ed* Eton (Musical Exhibitioner 1982), and New Coll, Oxford, — Sophia Roby, *b* 1967; *ed* Magdalen Coll, Oxford (MA). —— (By 2nd *m*) Ivo Simon (70 Waterford Rd, SW6), *b* 1955; *ed* Harrow: *m* 1985, Carole V., da of Maj C.P. Martel, of Richmond, N Yorks, and has issue living, Thomas Simon Alfred, *b* 1991, — Rory James, *b* 1999, — Camilla Rose, *b* 1987. —— Aurea Maryrose (62 Kingswood Rd, Tadworth, Surrey KT20 5EQ), *b* 1949.

Issue of late Archibald Tennant, *b* 1907, *d* 1955: *m* 1947, Diana Primrose (GIBBS) (12 Victoria Sq, SW1), da of late Percy Cuthbert Quilter (*see* Quilter, Bt, colls):—
Veronica Clare, *b* 1950: *m* 1981, Julius von Mengershausen Lister, of 365 Wimbledon Park Rd, SW19, and has issue living, Marina Helen Clare von Mengershausen, *b* 1982. —— Pamela Mary Diana, *b* 1953: *m* 1979, Charles Adam Laurie Sebag-Montefiore of 21 Hazlewell Rd, SW15, and has issue living (*see* Magnus-Allcroft, Bt).

Issue of late Rt Hon Harold John Tennant, 6th son of 1st baronet, *b* 1865, *d* 1935: *m* 1st, 1889, Helen Elizabeth, who *d* 1892, da of Major Gordon Duff, of Drummuir, Banffshire; 2ndly, 1896, May Edith, CH, JP, who *d* 1946, da of late George Whitley Abraham, of Rathgar, co Dublin:—
(By 2nd *m*) Peter, *b* 1913; *ed* Eton, and Trin Coll, Camb (BA 1934, MA 1951): *m* 1938, Valerie, who *d* 1999, da of late John S. Nettlefold, of The Manor House, Bampton, Oxfordshire, and has issue living, Alison Valerie, *b* 1939: *m* 1962, Roger Leon Burnley, of 23 Marchmont Crescent, Edinburgh EH9 1HQ, and has issue living, Julian Lee *b* 1969, Andrea Adwoa *b* 1968, — Fiona, *b* 1940: *m* 1964, Neil Graham Douglas Snow, of Moor End, Invertrossachs, Callander, Perthshire, and has issue living, Justin Douglas Tennant *b* 1965, Jonathan Peter *b* 1968, Catriona Louisa *b* 1967, Kirsten Fiona *b* 1970, — Sheila, *b* 1946: *m* 1970, Edward Findlay Burnett, of Rhynaclach, Port of Menteith, Kippen, Perthshire, and has issue living, Joseph Andrew *b* 1976, Helen Sheila *b* 1978. *Residence* – Laurel Bank, Ancaster Rd, Callander, Perthshire.

PREDECESSORS – (1) CHARLES Tennant, son of John Tennant, DL, JP, of St Rollox. Lanark, a descendant of John Tennant of Blairston, Ayrshire (temp 1635-1728), by his wife Jean McTaggart (temp 1669-1723); *b* 1823; MP for Glasgow (L) 1879-80, and for Peebles and Selkirkshire 1880-86; *cr* a *Baronet* 1885: *m* 1st, 1849, Emma, who *d* 1895, da of Richard Winsloe; 2ndly, 1898, Marguerite Agaranthe, who *d* 1943, having *m* 2ndly, 1907, Major Geoffrey Lubbock, who *d* 1932, da of late Col Charles Miles, of Burtonhill, Malmesbury; *d* 1906; *s* by his fourth son **(2)** EDWARD PRIAULX, 2nd Bt, *b* 1859; Lord-Lieut of Peeblesshire; MP for Salisbury (L) Jan 1906 to Jan 1910; Lord High Commr to Gen Assembly for Church of Scotland 1911, 1912, 1913, and 1914: *cr Baron Glenconner*, of Glen, co Peebles (peerage of United Kingdom) 1911: *m* 1895, Pamela Geneviève Adelaide (who *d* 1928, having *m* 2ndly, 1922, the 1st Viscount Grey of Fallodon), da of late Hon Percy Scawen Wyndham; *d* 1920; *s* by his second son **(3)** CHRISTOPHER GREY, 2nd Baron, *b* 1899: *m* 1st, 1925 (*m diss* 1935), Pamela Winifred, who *d* 1989, da of Sir Richard Arthur Surtees Paget, 2nd Bt (*cr* 1886); 2ndly, 1935, Elizabeth, da of late Lt-Col Evelyn George Harcourt Powell, of 31 Hillgate Place, W8; *d* 1983; *s* by his eldest son **(4)** COLIN CHRISTOPHER PAGET, 3rd Baron and present peer.

GLENDEVON, BARON (Hope) (Baron UK 1964)

JULIAN JOHN SOMERSET HOPE, 2nd Baron; *b* 6 March 1950; *s* 1996; *ed* Eton, and Ch Ch, Oxford; Operatic Producer.

Arms – Azure, on a chevron or between three bezants as many bay-leaves paleways vert. **Crest** – A broken sphere surmounted of a rainbow proper issuant from two bay-leaves slipped vert on either side of the sphere. **Supporters** – Two female figures denoting Hope, their hair dressed sable and braided vert, garnished or, richly vested Argent garnished of vert, and sustaining bendways in their exterior hands light lifeboat anchors with long shafts azure garnished with chains or, and over their exterior shoulders garlands of white lilies proper.
Address – c/o House of Lords, SW1.

BROTHER LIVING

Hon JONATHAN CHARLES, *b* 23 April 1952; *ed* Eton. *Residence* – 20 Roland Gdns, SW7.

My hope is not broken

PREDECESSOR – (1) JOHN ADRIAN Hope, PC, yr (twin) son of 2nd Marquess of Linlithgow; *b* 1912; Capt and temp Maj Scots Gds (Res); Joint Parl Under-Sec of State for Foreign Affairs 1954-56, Parl Under-Sec of State for Commonwealth Relations 1956-57, Joint Parl Under-Sec for Scotland 1957-59, and Min of Works 1959-62; ERD 1988; MP for N Div of Midlothian and Peebles (C) 1945-50, and for Pentlands Div of Edinburgh 1950-64; *cr* PC 1959, and *Baron Glendevon*, of Midhope, co Linlithgow (peerage of UK) 1964: *m* 1948, Elizabeth, who *d* 1998, da of late William Somerset Maugham, CH, the celebrated writer, and formerly wife of Vincent Paravicini; *d* 1996; *s* by his elder son **(2)** JULIAN JOHN SOMERSET, 2nd Baron and present peer.

GLENDYNE, BARON (Nivison) (Baron UK 1922, Bt UK 1914)

The end proves actions

ROBERT NIVISON, 3rd Baron, and 3rd Baronet; *b* 27 Oct 1926; *s* 1967; *ed* Harrow; late Lt Grenadier Guards; 1939-45 War: *m* 1953, Elizabeth, yr da of late Sir Stephen Cecil Armitage, CBE, of Hawksworth Manor, Notts, and has issue.

𝔄rms – Per chevron or and azure, in chief two eagles displayed of the second and in base an eagle rising of the first. 𝔠rest – Upon the battlements of a tower a wolf passsant sable, gorged with a collar and with line reflexed over the back or. 𝔖upporters – On either side a wolf sable, gorged with a collar with line reflexed over the back or, and charged on the shoulder with a saltire couped argent.
Residence – Craigeassie, by Forfar, Angus DD8 3SE. *Club* – City of London.

SON LIVING

Hon JOHN, *b* 18 Aug, 1960.

DAUGHTERS LIVING

Hon Linda, *b* 1954: *m* 1976, Dr Nikolaus Graf Hartig, of Heuberggasse 9, A-1170 Vienna, Austria, and has issue living, Thomas, *b* 1982, — Alexandra, *b* 1980.
Hon Sarah Jane Moira, *b* 1957: *m* 1979, Ian Dreverman, of 2A Water St, Wahroonga, NSW 2076, Australia, and has issue living, James, *b* 1984, — Jeremy, *b* 1988, — a son, *b* 1990, — Melissa, *b* 1982.

SISTER LIVING

Hon Gillian Wightman, *b* 1931: *m* 1953, Maj-Gen Peter Raymond Leuchars, CBE, late Welsh Guards, and has issue living, Christopher John Raymond, *b* 1956. *Residence* – 5 Chelsea Sq, SW3.

PREDECESSORS – (1) ROBERT Nivison, son of John Nivison, of Sanquhar, Dumfriesshire; *b* 1849; senior partner of R. Nivison and Co; *cr* a *Baronet* 1914, and *Baron Glendyne*, of Sanquhar, co Dumfries (peerage of United Kingdom) 1922: *m* 1877, Jane, who *d* 1918, da of John Wightman, of Sanquhar, Dumfriesshire; *d* 1930; *s* by his son (2) JOHN, 2nd Baron, *b* 1878; senior partner of R. Nivison & Co: *m* 1920, Ivy May, who *d* 1971, da of late J. Rose, of Bournemouth; *d* 1967; *s* by his son (3) ROBERT, 3rd Baron, and present peer.

GLENKINGLAS, BARONY OF (Noble) (Extinct 1984)

DAUGHTERS LIVING OF LIFE BARON

Hon Catharine Gina Amita, *b* 1943: *m* 1st, 1964, Peter Conrad Hamilton Vey; 2ndly, 1989, Denzil Robert Onslow How (*see* E Onslow, colls, 1995 Edn), and has had issue (by 1st *m*).
Hon Marya Anne, *b* 1944: *m* 1969, Peter Egerton-Warburton, of Mulberry House, Bentworth, Hants, and has issue (*see* Grey-Egerton, Bt, colls).
Hon Anastasia Diana, *b* 1948: *m* 1967, Jonathan Sinclair Delap, of Little Armsworth, Alresford, Hants, and has issue living, James Robert Onslow, *b* 1969, — Michael Jonathan Sinclair, *b* 1972.
Hon Rebecca Juliet (*Viscountess Dungarvan*), *b* 1950: *m* 1973, John Richard, Viscount Dungarvan, Lt Cdr RN (ret), of Lickford House, Petworth, Sussex, son of 14th Earl of Cork and Orrery, DSC, and has issue (*see* E Cork and Orrory).

WIDOW LIVING OF LIFE BARON

ANNE (*Baroness Glenkinglas*) (7 Egerton Gdns, SW3 2BP), da of Sir Neville Arthur Pearson, 2nd Bt (cr 1916): *m* 1940, Baron Glenkinglas, PC (Life Baron), who *d* 1984.

Glenlivet, see Lord Strathavon and Glenlivet.

GLENTANAR, BARONY OF (Coats) (Extinct 1971)

DAUGHTER LIVING OF SECOND BARON

Hon (Margaret) Jean Dagbjørt, *b* 1928: *m* 1950 (*m diss* 1974), Hon James Michael Edward Bruce (*see* E Elgin and Kincardine). *Residence* – Juniper, 9 Golf Place, Aboyne, Aberdeenshire AB34 5GA.

GLENTORAN, BARON (Dixon) (Baron UK 1939, Bt UK 1903)

By fidelity and constancy

(THOMAS) ROBIN VALERIAN DIXON, CBE, 3rd Baron and 4th Baronet; *b* 21 April 1935; *s* 1995; *ed* Eton; late Major Grenadier Gds; DL co Antrim 1979; Olympic Gold Medal (Bobsleigh) 1964; Man Dir Redland of N Ireland 1972-97; MBE (Civil) 1969, CBE (Civil) 1992: *m* 1st, 1959 (*m diss* 1975), Rona Alice Gabrielle, only child of late Capt George Cecil Colville, CBE, RN (*see* V Colville of Culross, colls); 2ndly, 1979, (*m diss* 1988), Alwyn Gillian, da of Hubert A. Mason, of Grove Lodge, Donaghadee, co Down; 3rdly, 1990, Mrs Margaret Anne Murphy (*née* Rainey), and has issue by 1st *m*.

Arms – Or, on a chevron vair three billets of the first, on a chief crenellé gules a tower proper between two fleurs-de-lis or. **Crest** – A demi-lion rampant azure, charged on the shoulder with a cross patonce surrounded by a civic crown or. **Supporters** – Two war horses argent, unguled or, caparisoned proper, the shabraque sable, broidered of the second.
Residence – Drumadarragh House, Ballyclare, co Antrim. *Clubs* – Carlton, Kildare Street (Dublin), University (Dublin).

SONS LIVING (*By 1st marriage*)

Hon DANIEL GEORGE, *b* 26 July 1959; *ed* Gordonstoun: *m* 1983, Leslie Hope, da of Julian Hope Brooke, and has issue living, Anthony Thomas, *b* 19 June 1987, — Marcus Hope, *b* 1989. *Residence* – The White Cottage, Dummer, nr Basingstoke, Hants RG25 2AD.

Hon Andrew Wynne Valerian, *b* 1961; *ed* Dean Close Sch; commm'd Gren Gds 1980: *m* 1991, Karen Elizabeth, MBE, three-day eventer, only da of late Hugh Charles Straker, of Gaucin, Spain, and has issue living, Rory Hugh Thomas, *b* 1999. *Residence* – Wycliffe Grange, Wycliffe, nr Barnard Castle, co Durham. *Club* – Cavalry and Guards'.

Hon Patrick Anthony, *b* 1963; *ed* Gordonstoun, and Dean Close Sch: *m* 1988, Catharine Margaret, yr da of Theo Willy, of S Petherton, Som, and has issue living, Alice Gabrielle, *b* 1995. *Residence* – Windwhistle, Tildarg Rd, Ballyclare, co Antrim.

BROTHER LIVING

Hon Peter Herbert, *b* 1948; *ed* Eton: *m* 1975, Jane Blanch, da of late Eric Sturdee Cutler, of St Martins, Yattendon, Newbury, Berks, and has issue living, Louise Vyvyan Mary, *b* 1977, — Rose Erika Clare, *b* 1980. *Residence* – The Old Rectory, Yattendon, Berks RG18 0UR.

SISTER LIVING

Hon Clare Rosalind, *b* 1937: *m* 1965 (*m diss* 1977), Rudolph Ion Joseph Agnew (*see* Campbell, Bt, *cr* 1815, colls, 1995 Edn), and has issue living, James Ion Daniel (Shafts House, W Meon, Hants), *b* 1968: *m* 1992, Sarah Kathleen, only da of Peter Newman, of Frensham, Surrey, and has issue living, Henry Andrew Charles *b* 1995, Eliza Newman Clare *b* 1999, — Charlotte Diana Pamela Geraldine (5 Cobbold St, W12 9LA), *b* 1970. *Residence* – 29 Felden St, SW6.

AUNTS LIVING *(Daughters of 1st Baron)*

Hon Angela Ierne Evelyn, *b* 1907: *m* 1st, 1929, Lieut-Com (E) Peter Ross, RN, who was *ka* 1940 (*see* B de Ros); 2ndly, 1943, Lieut-Col Trevor L. Horn, 16th/5th Lancers, who *d* 1966, and has issue living (by 1st *m*) (*see* B de Ros), — (by 2nd *m*) June Victoria Langdale, *b* 1946. *Residence* – Luckington Court, Chippenham, Wilts.

Hon Patricia Clare, *b* 1919: *m* 1940, Lieut-Com Adam McLeod Mackinnon, RN, Fleet Air Arm, and has issue living, Michael Bingham, *b* 1941; *ed* Wellington Coll, — Ian Dixon (9200 Cherry Creek South Drive No. 21, Denver, Colorado 80231, USA), *b* 1944; *ed* Wellington Coll: *m* 1973, Peggy Louisa Gay, of Salinas, California, — Diana Patricia, *b* 1950: *m* 1978, Richard A. B. Lynes, of Penn House, Bannerleigh Rd, Bristol, and has issue living, Thomas Adam Bradley *b* 1982, Peter Richard Bradley *b* 1986, — Teresa Claire, *b* 1955: *m* 1993, Raymond Crossen, of 13 Essex Rise, Warfield, Bracknell, Berks RG12 6XG, — Zara Lavinia, *b* 1959: *m* 1985, William D. Brogden, of 10 Hazells Lane, Shrivenham, Swindon, Wilts SN6 8DS, and has issue living, James William *b* 1992, Jennifer Clare *b* 1990. *Residence* – 76 Chisbury Close, Forest Park, Bracknell, Berks RG12 3TX.

PREDECESSORS – (1) *Rt Hon* DANIEL DIXON, MP, son of late Thomas Dixon, of Larne, co Antrim, *b* 1844; was High Sheriff of co Down 1896, MP for N Belfast (*C*) 1905-07, Mayor of Belfast 1892, and Lord Mayor 1893, 1901-3, 1905-6, and 1906-7; *cr* a *Baronet* 1903: *m* 1st, 1867, Lizzie, who *d* 1868, da of late James Agnew, of Belfast; 2ndly, 1870, Annie, who *d* 1918, da of James Shaw, of Belfast; *d* 1907, *s* by his el son (2) *Sir* THOMAS JAMES, 2nd Bt, *b* 1868; High Sheriff co Antrim 1912, and of co Down 1913, HM's Lieut for Co of City of Belfast, and a Member of Senate of N Ireland 1924-50: *m* 1906, *Dame* Edith Stewart, DBE, da of late Stewart Clark, of Dundas Castle, Linlithgowshire; *d* (May) 1950; *s* by his brother (3) *Rt Hon* HERBERT, PC, OBE, 3rd Bt; *b* 1880; High Sheriff of co Kildare 1916; Capt 6th Inniskilling Dragoons; S Africa 1899-1902, European War 1914-19 with Remounts; Ch Whip of Unionist Party in Parliament of N Ireland, and Parliamentary Sec to Min of Finance 1921-42, and Min of Agriculture 1942-3; sat as MP for Pottinger Div of Belfast (*U*) 1918 to 1922, and for Belfast, E Div 1922 to 1930; also elected for Belfast, E Div in Parliament of N Ireland 1921 and 1925, and for Bloomfield Div of Belfast 1929, 1945 and 1949; *cr Baron Glentoran*, of Ballyalloly, co Down (peerage of United Kingdom) 1939: *m* 1905, Hon Emily Ina Florence Bingham, who *d* 1957, da of 5th Baron Clanmorris, *d* (July) 1950; *s* by his son (4) DANIEL STEWART THOMAS BINGHAM, KBE, 2nd Baron, *b* 1912; Lt-Col Grenadier Gds and Hon Col 6th Bn RUR (TA); Lord Lieut for Co of City of Belfast, Member of House of Commons, NI (*U*) 1950-61, Parl Sec Min of Commerce, NI 1952-53, and Min of Commerce 1953-61, Min in Senate 1961-64 (Speaker of Senate 1964-72), PC (NI) 1953: *m* 1933, Lady Diana Wellesley, who *d* 1984, da of 3rd Earl Cowley; *d* 1995; *s* by his elder son (5) THOMAS ROBIN VALERIAN, 3rd Baron and present peer; also 4th baronet.

Glentworth, Viscount; son of Earl of Limerick.

Gloucester, Duke of, see Royal Family.

Glyn, family name of Baron Wolverton.

GODBER, BARONY OF (Godber) (Extinct 1976)

DAUGHTERS LIVING OF FIRST BARON

Hon Joyce Violet, *b* 1917: *m* 1938, Andrew Agnew, and has issue living, Heather Elizabeth, *b* 1940: *m* 1966, Dr Charles John Roderick Lewis, of Old Rectory, Bodiam, Robertsbridge, Sussex, and has issue living, Henry Roderick Andrew (Churchfield Cottage, Dennington, Suffolk) *b* 1968: *m* 1995, Kate Elizabeth, da of Barry V. Hitchcock (and has issue living, Charles Andrew David *b* 1997), Richard John *b* 1972, — Susan Joyce, *b* 1942: *m* 1966, David Gwynder Lewis, of 57 Victoria Rd, W8 5RH, and has issue living, George David Gwynder *b* 1972, Alexandra Joy Gwynder *b* 1969, — Sally

Caroline, *b* 1949: *m* 1983, Tom William Mahony Jaine, of Allaleigh House, Blackawton, S. Devon, and has issue living, Matilda Aileen *b* 1985, Frances Belle Violet *b* 1987. *Residence* – Sweethaws Farm, Crowborough, Sussex.

Hon Daphne Joan, *b* 1923: *m* 1942, Archibald Ian Scott Debenham, DFC, and has issue living, Michael George Scott (Homefield, Tandridge Lane, Lingfield, Surrey), *b* 1943: *m* 1st, 1966 (*m diss* 1980), Janine Elizabeth, da of Anthony L. Davies, of Crockham Hill, Edenbridge, Kent; 2ndly, 1981, Roberta, da of Luigi Courir, of Genova, Italy, and has issue living (by 1st *m*), Sarah Elizabeth *b* 1968, Anna Caroline *b* 1970, Tessa Kate *b* 1974, — Peter Frederick Scott (30 Ladbroke Grove, W8 11BQ), *b* 1957: *m* 1983, Sarah, da of A. J. Webster, of Claverley, Shropshire, and has issue living, Hannah Rose *b* 1989, Letitia Jane *b* 1991, — Jane Scott (Briars Orchard, Limpsfield Chart, Oxted, Surrey), *b* 1945: *m* 1st, 1966 (*m diss* 1979), Hamish John Benson Skinner; 2ndly, 1979, Geoffrey Dove, and has issue living (by 1st *m*), Paul Andrew *b* 1968, Hugh Antony *b* 1972, Lucy Jane *b* 1969, — Marye Scott, *b* 1954: *m* 1986, David Warren, of 40 Pursers Cross Rd, SW6. *Residence* – Bowerland Farm, Bowerland Lane, Lingfield, Surrey, RH7 6DF.

GODBER OF WILLINGTON, BARONY OF (Godber) (Extinct 1980)

SONS LIVING OF LIFE BARON

Hon Richard Thomas (Hall Farm, Little Linford, Bucks), *b* 1938; DL Bucks 1993: *m* 1962, Candida, da of late Albert Edward Parrish, and has issue.
Hon Andrew Robin (Folly Barn, Folly Lane, Claxton, Norwich NR14 7AX), *b* 1943: *m* 1969, Genevieve, da of late Kenneth Parrish, and has issue.

GODDARD, BARONY OF (Goddard) (Extinct 1971)

DAUGHTER LIVING OF LIFE BARON

Hon (Janet) Margaret (*Hon Lady Sachs*), *b* 1909: *m* 1934, Rt Hon Sir Eric Sachs, MBE, who *d* 1979, and has issue living, Richard Edwin Goddard, *b* 1935; *ed* Shrewsbury, and Ch Ch Oxford (MA), — Katharine Frances Goddard (*Lady Harman*), *b* 1939: *m* 1st, 1965, George Pulay, who *d* 1981; 2ndly, 1987, Sir Jeremiah LeRoy Harman, and has issue living (by 1st *m*), Jessica Mary *b* 1966, Laura Katharine *b* 1968: *m* 1994, Gary N. Gibbon, son of Robert Gibbon, of Paphos, Cyprus. *Residence* – Antioch House West, Rotten Row, Lewes, E Sussex BN7 1TN.

Godley, family name of Baron Kilbracken.

GOFF OF CHIEVELEY, BARON (Goff) (Life Baron 1986)

ROBERT LIONEL ARCHIBALD GOFF, PC, DCL, son of late Lt-Col Lionel Trevor Goff, RA, of Queen's House, Monk Sherborne, Basingstoke; *b* 12 Nov 1926; *ed* Eton, and New Coll, Oxford (MA 1953, DCL 1971), Hon DLitt City 1977, Reading 1990, Hon LLD Buckingham 1990, London 1990, and Bristol 1995; served in Scots Guards 1945-48; Bar Inner Temple 1951, Bencher 1975, QC 1967; Fellow and Tutor, Lincoln Coll, Oxford 1951-55; High Steward Oxford Univ since 1990, Hon Fell Lincoln Coll, New Coll, Oxford, and American Coll of Trial Lawyers 1997; FBA 1987; practiced at bar 1956-75, a Recorder 1974-75, Judge of High Court of Justice (Queen's Bench Div) 1975-82, a

Lord Justice of Appeal 1982-85, a Lord of Appeal in Ordinary 1986-98; Chm Council of Legal Educn 1976-82, Board of Studies 1970-76, Common Professional Examination Bd 1976-78; Hon Prof of Legal Ethics, Univ of Birmingham, 1980-81; Pres Bentham Club, Univ Coll London 1987; Pres Holdsworth Club, Birmingham Univ 1990; Maccabean Lectr, British Acad, 1983, Lionel Cohen Memorial Lectr Jerusalem 1987, Cassel Lectr, Stockholm 1995; Chm British Inst of Internat and Comparative Law since 1986, Chm Court of London Univ 1986-91, Pres Chartered Inst of Arbitrators 1986-91; Member Gen Council of the Bar 1971-74, Senate of Inns of Court and Bar 1974-82 (Chm Law Reform and Procedure Cttee 1974-76); *cr* Kt 1975, PC 1982, and *Baron Goff of Chieveley*, of Chieveley, co Berks (Life Baron) 1986: *m* 1953, Sarah, elder da of Capt Gerald Roger Cousins, DSC, RN, of Child Okeford, Dorset, and has issue (with one son dec'd).

𝕬rms – Az a chevron between two fleurs-de-lis in chief and a lion rampant in base or. 𝕮rest – A squirrel sejant proper. 𝕸otto – fier sans tache.
Address – House of Lords, SW1.

SON LIVING

Hon Robert Thomas Alexander, *b* 1966: *m* 1996, Catherine L., only da of Peter Cregeen, of Hawkley, Hants, and has issue living, Edward Robert Thomas, *b* 1998.

DAUGHTERS LIVING

Hon Katharine Isobel, *b* 1959.
Dr the Hon Juliet Mary Constance, *b* 1961: *m* 1990, Seán D. Jackson, only son of David Jackson, of Armscote House, Stratford-upon-Avon, Warwicks, and has issue living, William David, *b* 1995, — Rupert Timothy, *b* 1998, — Anna Katharine, *b* 1992.

GOODHART, BARON (Goodhart) (Life Baron 1997)

WILLIAM HOWARD GOODHART, 2nd son of late Prof Arthur Lehman Goodhart, KBE (Hon), QC; *b* 18 Jan 1933; *ed* Eton, Trinity Coll, Camb, and Harvard Law Sch; Bar, Lincoln's Inn, 1957, Bencher 1986; QC 1979; Chm Exec Cttee Justice (British Section of Internat Commn of Jurists) 1988-94 (Vice-Chm 1978-88); Memb Council of Legal Education 1986-92, and Internat Commn of Jurists since 1993 (Exec Cttee since 1995); Memb Lib Dem Policy Cttee 1988-97; Memb Cttee on Standards in Public Life since 1997; House of Lords Select Cttees on European Communities and on Delegated Powers since 1998; Chm Cambridge Univ Court of Discipline since 1992; *cr* Kt 1989, and *Baron Goodhart*, of Youlbury, co Oxford (Life Baron) 1997: *m* 1966, Hon Celia McClare Herbert, da of 2nd Baron Hemingford, and has issue.
Residences – 11 Clarence Terrace, NW1 4RD; Youlbury House, Boars Hill, Oxford OX1 5HH.

SON LIVING

Hon Benjamin Herbert, *b* 1972.

DAUGHTERS LIVING

Hon Annabel Frances, *b* 1967: *m* 1995, James Dallas, son of Duncan Dallas, of Leeds, and has issue living, Josephine Juliet, *b* 1997.
Hon Laura Christabel, *b* 1970: *m* 1999, William E. K. Watts, son of Jeffrey Watts, of Windsor, Berks.

GOOLD, BARONY OF (Goold) (Extinct 1997)

SONS LIVING OF LIFE BARON

Hon Michael Kirkland, *b* 1966: *m* 1994, Giannina P., yst da of Teobaldo Moy, of Selsidro, Lima, Peru.
Hon (James) David, *b* 1968.

DAUGHTER LIVING OF LIFE BARON

Hon Anna Jane, *b* 1972: *m* 1995, Stuart McFadyen, yr son of George McFadyen.

Gordon, family name of Marquess of Aberdeen.

Gordon, family name of Marquess of Huntly.

Gordon, Duke of, see Duke of Richmond and Gordon.

GORDON OF STRATHBLANE, BARON (Gordon) (Life Baron 1997)

JAMES STUART GORDON, CBE, son of late James Edward Gordon, of Glasgow; *b* 17 May 1936; *ed* St Aloysius' Coll, Glasgow Univ (MA 1958); DLitt Glasgow Caledonian Univ 1994; DUniv Glasgow 1998; Political Editor, STV 1965-73; Man Dir, Radio Clyde 1973-96; Chm Scottish Radio Holdings plc since 1996 (Chief Exec 1991-96); Chm Commercial Radio Companies Assoc 1994-97; Memb BP Scottish Advisory Board; Dir Clydeport plc 1992-98, Johnston Press plc, and The AIM Tst plc; Memb Scottish Development Agency 1981-90, and Court of Glasgow Univ 1984-97; Chm Scottish Tourist Board 1998, and Advisory Group on Listed Sporting Events 1997-98; Memb Cttee of Inquiry into Teachers' Pay and Conditions 1986; Memb Cttee to Review Funding of the BBC 1999; Trustee, Nat Galleries of Scotland; *cr* CBE 1984, and *Baron Gordon of Strathblane*, of Deil's Craig in Stirling (Life Baron) 1997: *m* 1971, Margaret Anne, da of late Andrew Kirkwood Stevenson, of Glasgow, and has issue.
Residence – Deil's Craig, Strathblane, Glasgow G63 9ET. *Clubs* – New (Edinburgh) Glasgow Art, Prestwick Golf, Buchanan Castle Golf.

SONS LIVING

Hon Michael Stevenson, *b* 1974.
Hon Christopher James, *b* 1976.

DAUGHTER LIVING

Hon Sarah Jane, *b* 1972.

GORDON-WALKER, BARONY OF (Gordon Walker) (Extinct 1980)

SONS LIVING OF LIFE BARON

Hon Alan Rudolf, *b* 1946; *ed* Wellington Coll and Ch Ch, Oxford (MA); publishing consultant: *m* 1976, Louise Frances Amy, el da of Gen Sir Charles Henry Pepys Harington, GCB, CBE, DSO, MC, and has issue. *Residence* – 2 Umbria St, SW15 5DP.

Hon Robin Chrestien, (twin), *b* 1946; *ed* Wellington Coll and E Anglia Univ (BA); Press Offr, Financial Services Authority: *m* 1st, 1974 (*m diss* 1985), June Patricia, da of Patrick Barr, of Eversholt, Beds; 2ndly, 1987, Magally, da of Gilberto Flores, of Valencia, Venezuela, and has issue by 1st and 2nd *m*. *Residence* – 16 Hexham Rd, SE27 9ED.

DAUGHTERS LIVING OF LIFE BARON

Hon Judith Margaret, *b* 1936; *ed* N London Collegiate Sch, Lady Margaret Hall, Oxford (MA), and Univ Coll, London, (BA, PhD); Lecturer in Psychology, Birkbeck Coll, Univ of London, 1966-76, since when Prof of Psychology, Open Univ: *m* 1st, 1957 (*m diss* 1975), Graham Carleton Greene, CBE, son of late Sir (Hugh) Carleton Green, KCMG, OBE; 2ndly 1981, Prof Norman William Dawson Gowar. *Residence* – 3 Canonbury Lane, N1.

Hon Caroline, *b* 1937: *ed* Cheltenham Ladies' Coll, and Lady Margaret Hall, Oxford (MA); formerly Lay Minister, Chaplaincy of Aquitaine, formerly Head of Food and Sciences Unit, Nat Economic Development Office: *m* 1960, David Brierley, of Old Farm, Harthall Lane, King's Langley, Herts, and has issue. *Residence* – La Vicille Ferme, St Germain des Belves, Belves, Dordogne 24170, France.

Hon Ann Marguerite GORDON-WALKER (1230 University Bay Drive, Madison, Wisconsin 53705, USA), *b* 1944; *ed* N London Collegiate Sch, Queen's Coll, Dundee, Univ of St Andrews (BSc), and Oxford Univ (D Phil); Administrator, Biophysics Laboratory, Univ of Wisconsin-Madison, USA; has resumed maiden name: *m* 1968 (*m diss* 1983), Laurence Andrew Ball, and has issue.

WIDOW LIVING OF LIFE BARON

AUDREY MURIEL (*Baroness Gordon-Walker*) (Flat 105 Frobisher House, Dolphin Sq, SW1V 3JJ), da of Norman Andrew Rudolf, of Hopewell, Jamaica: *m* 1934, Rt Hon Lord Gordon-Walker, CH (Life Baron), who *d* 1980.

Gore, family name of Earl of Arran.

Gore, Ormsby, family name of Baron Harlech.

Gore-Booth, Barony of (Gore-Booth) (Extinct 1984) (see Gore-Booth, Bt)

GORELL, BARON (Barnes) (Baron UK 1909)

You may break, you shall not bend me

TIMOTHY JOHN RADCLIFFE BARNES, 4th Baron; *b* 2 Aug 1927; *s* 1963; *ed* Groton (USA), Eton, and New Coll, Oxford, Bar Inner Temple 1951, formerly Lieut Rifle Bde; an Exec, Royal Dutch and Shell Group 1959-84: *m* 1954, Joan Marion, yr da of late John Edmund Collins, MC, of Sway, Hants, and has two adopted das.

ᴀrms – Azure, two lions passant guardant ermine each holding in the dexter paw a sprig of oak slipped or, between three annulets in pale argent. Crest – In front of a cubit arm in armour, the hand grasping a broken sword all proper, the wrist encircled by a wreath of oak or, five annulets interlaced and fesseways argent. Supporters – On either side, a ram proper charged on the shoulder with two annulets interlaced azure. *Residence* – 4 Roehampton Gate, SW15.

ADOPTED DAUGHTERS LIVING

Susan Elizabeth Gorell, *b* 1958: *m* 1985 (*m diss* 1995), Robin H. A. Clark, elder son of J. A. Clark, and has issue living, Kyle Hendrik Gorell, *b* 1988. *Residence* – 63 High St, Arundel, W Sussex.
Jennifer Gorell, *b* 1960: *m* 1986, David James Michael Dally, elder son of B. J. M. Dally, and has issue living, Thomas, *b* 1992, — Samuel, *b* 1992 (triplet), — Megan Elizabeth, *b* 1991, — Kate, *b* 1992 (triplet). *Residence* – 72 Grove Av, Hanwell, W7 3SE.

BROTHER LIVING

Hon RONALD ALEXANDER HENRY, *b* 28 June 1931; *ed* Harrow, and New Coll, Oxford; formerly Lieut Roy Fusiliers, seconded King's African Rifles Capt Roy Northumberland Fus (TA); former Public Relations Officer P & O—Orient Lines; formerly Senior Partner of Stockton & Barnes, Estate Agents: *m* 1957, Gillian Picton, yst da of late Picton Hughes-Jones, of Henstridge, Somerset, and has issue living, John Picton Gorell, *b* 1959, — Elizabeth Gail, *b* 1961. *Residence* – Fernbank, Mingoose, Mount Hawke, nr Truro, Cornwall.

PREDECESSORS – (1) *Rt Hon Sir* JOHN GORELL Barnes, PC (Knt), el son of late Henry Barnes, of Liverpool; *b* 1848; a Judge of the Probate, Divorce, and Admiralty Div of the High Court of Justice 1892-1905, and Pres thereof 1905-9; *cr Baron Gorell*, of Brampton, co Derby (peerage of United Kingdom) 1909: *m* 1881, Mary Humpston, who *d* 1918, da of late Thomas Mitchell, of West Arthurlie; *d* 1913; *s* by his el son (2) HENRY GORELL, DSO, 2nd Baron, *b* 1882; Major RFA (F); *ka* 1917; *s* by his brother (3) RONALD GORELL, CBE, MC, 3rd Baron; *b* 1884; Under-Sec of State for Air and Vice-Pres of Air Council 1921-2, Editor of *Cornhill Magazine* 1933-9; Chm of Prime Min's Cttees on Carlton House Terr 1933-40, and on Regents Park Terr 1946-7; Founder Royal Army Educn Corps: *m* 1922, Maud Elizabeth Furse, who *d* 1954, da of late Alexander Nelson Radcliffe, of 45 Kensington Sq, W8; *d* 1963; *s* by his el son (4) TIMOTHY JOHN RADCLIFFE, 4th Baron and present peer.

Gormanston, Baron, title of Viscount Gormanston on Roll of HL.

GORMANSTON, VISCOUNT (Preston) (Viscount I 1478, Baron I 1365-70) Sits as Baron (UK 1868)

SANS GIS TACHE

Without stain

JENICO NICHOLAS DUDLEY PRESTON, 17th Viscount, and Premier Viscount of Ireland; *b* 19 Nov 1939; *s* 1940: *m* 1st, 1974, Eva Land- zianowski, who *d* 1984; 2ndly, 1997, Mrs Lucy Arabella Grenfell, elder da of Edward Charles Morice Fox, and of Tracy Clare Compton Reed (*see* E Dudley, colls, 1980 Edn), and has issue by 1st *m*.

𝕬rms – Or, on a chief sable, three crescents of the first. Crest – On a chapeau gules turned up ermine, a fox passant proper. Supporters – *Dexter*, a fox proper; *sinister* a lion rampant proper, armed and langued gules. *Residence* – Dalmeny House, 9 Thurloe Place, SW7 2RY.

SONS LIVING (*By 1st marriage*)

Hon JENICO FRANCIS TARA, *b* 30 April 1974.
Hon William Luke, *b* 1976.

COLLATERAL BRANCHES LIVING

Issue of late Hon Robert Francis Hubert Preston, 2nd son of 15th Viscount, *b* 1915, *d* (7 Jan) 1992; assumed by deed poll 1947 the additional surname of Shaw which he subsequently relinquished: *m* 1st, 1941 (*m diss* 1955), Jean Helen, only child of late Capt Charles Henry Shaw, 15th Hus, of Bourton Hall, Rugby, Warwicks; 2ndly, 1970, Mrs Daphne Helen Anne Bradish-Ellames, who *d* (9 Dec) 1992, only da of late Col Robert Hanbury Brudenell-Bruce, DSO (*see* M Ailesbury, colls):—
(By 1st *m*) Jennifer Anne SHAW PRESTON, *b* 1946: *m* 1977, István Siklóssy von Pernesz, and has issue living, Georgina Isabella Maria, *b* 1977, — Stephanie Victoria Maria, *b* 1980. *Residence* – 390 Ave de Tervuren, B-1150, Brussels.

Grandchildren of late Lt-Col Hon Richard Martin Peter Preston, DSO (infra):—
Issue of late Lt-Cmdr Christopher Edward Martin Preston, OBE, DSC, RN, *b* 1918, *d* 1992: *m* 1949, Joy Celeste Agatha, who *d* 1989, da of late Maj Hugh Davidson, IA:—
Philip Martin Jenico (52 Foxgrove Av, Kingsthorpe, Northampton), *b* 1950; *ed* Downside: *m* 1983, Anita Cayas-Peña, and has issue living, Edmund Philip Joseph, *b* 1984, — Mark Christopher Jacob, *b* 1988. —— Stephen Richard Hugh, *b* 1952; *ed* Downside. —— †Matthew Christopher Edward, *b* 1955; *d* 1993. —— Anthony Thomas Patrick, *b* 1964. —— Camilla Mary Lucy, *b* 1959: *m* 1994, Anthony Charles de Winton, elder son of Michael Geoffrey de Winton, CBE, of Stalbridge, Dorset, and has issue living, Henry Christopher Michael, *b* 1995, — Michael Anthony Robert, *b* 1997.

Issue of late Lt-Col Hon Richard Martin Peter Preston, DSO, 2nd son of 14th Viscount, *b* 1884, *d* 1965: *m* 1st, 1908, Belle, who *d* 1936, da of late Frederick Harcourt Hamblin; 2ndly, 1943, Edith Sheilah, who *d* 1951, da of late Reginald de Crecy Steel, of Walton-on-Thames, and widow of Lt-Cdr John Hay Forbes, DSO, RN (*see* Stuart-Forbes, Bt colls):—
(By 1st *m*) Ismay Elizabeth, *b* 1912: *m* 1942, Denzil Robert Clarke, of Puffins, who *d* 1986, 8 South Drive, Wokingham, Berks, and has issue living, Michael Richard Neil, *b* 1946: *m* 1973, Francine Van Schepdael, and has issue living, Geraldine Anne Danielle *b* 1973, Muriel Louise Elizabeth *b* 1978, — Jennifer Robérta Anne, *b* 1944: *m* 1968, Simon Anthony Aldridge, of Gt Bowsers, Little Walden, Saffron Walden, and has issue living, Victoria Helmore Elizabeth *b* 1969, — Francesca Elizabeth Anne, *b* 1951: *m* 1976, David Anselm Bull, of 33 Alwyne Rd, SW19 7AB, and has issue living, Edward Anselm Anthony *b* 1981, James Frederick Simon *b* 1983, Alice Elizabeth *b* 1978, Georgina Victoria *b* 1988, Elizabeth Mary *b* 1990. —— Diana Mary Bruce (Old Sun House, Riseley, Berks), *b* 1914: *m* 1939, John Francis Colledge, who *d* 1954, and has issue living, Simon John (The Well Cottage, Mattingley, Basingstoke), *b* 1940: *m* 1966, Robina Elizabeth Anne, da of late H. L. Light, of Whitewater Cottage, Mattingley, Basingstoke, and has issue living, Timothy Andrew John *b* 1967, Patrick Richard *b* 1968, Henry Charles Valentine *b* 1972, Anna Elizabeth *b* 1980, — Robert Patrick Francis (Keeper's Cottage, North St, Drayton, Langport, Somerset TA10 0LF), *b* 1950; *ed* Downside: *m* 1974, Dena, da of late D. Jones, of Southport, Lancs, and has issue living, James Edward Daniel *b* 1978, Matthew William John *b* 1981, Kate Elizabeth Jane *b* 1976, — Sarah Virginia Mary, *b* 1942, — Judith Cecilia Anne, *b* 1953: *m* 1974, James Calderbank, and has issue living, William Michael *b* 1975, Charles Rufus *b* 1982, Rachel Claire Joanna *b* 1978, Rosie Diana *b* 1990. —— Ursula Anne Marie, *b* 1923: *m* 1952, Cdr Charles Sheridan Moseley, RN, who *d* 1993, of Kilmaloda House, Timoleague, co Cork, and has issue living, Dominic Richard Sheridan, *b* 1955: *m* 1987, Kathryn Fiona, da of late John McLean, and has issue living, James William Sheridan *b* 1988, Edward John Wallace *b* 1990, Charlotte Elizabeth Anne *b* 1992, Emily Kathryn Louise *b* 1994, — Christopher John Wallace, *b* 1957: *m* 1989, Loretta Genevieve, da of Alexander Millar-Brown, of Spain, and has issue living, Isobel Mary Anne *b* 1995, — Justin Robert Patrick, *b* 1962: *m* 1994, Mary Teresa, da of late James Kavanagh, of Dublin, and has issue living, Laura Anne *b* 1996, — Virginia Clare Diana, *b* 1954: *m* 1987, Anthony Cyril McGough, son of late John McGough, of Manchester, and has issue living, John Sheridan *b* 1991, Edmund Joseph *b* 1994, Dominic Peter *b* 1996, Lucy Margaret Anne *b* 1988, Francesca Mary *b* 1989, — Lucy Elizabeth Anne, *b* 1960; Sister Teresa of the Holy Child, Carmelite Convent, Notting Hill, W8.

Issue of late Capt Hon Hubert Anthony John Preston, MC, 3rd son of 14th Viscount, *b* 1885, *d* 1940: *m* (Jan) 1917, Mary, who *d* 1971, da of late Rt Hon William Kenny, a Judge of High Court in Ireland, and widow of R. S. Pringle, Queen's Regt:—
Georgina Ismay Mary, *b* 1919: *m* 1948, Alfred Stanley Head. *Residence* – Hardimans Cottage, High Street, Queen Camel, Yeovil, Somerset BA22 7NE.

Grandsons of late Capt Hon Charles Preston, 5th son of 12th Viscount:—
Issue of late Charles Arthur Preston, *b* 1857, *d* 1924: *m* 1889, Miriam, who *d* 1936, da of late Hon Charles Alleyne, formerly MP for Quebec, and a ME:—
Arthur, *b* 1902: *m* 1928, Marion Blair, da of late John Dean, and has issue living, Richard Dean, *b* 1929. —— Hubert Philip, *b* 1905: *m* 1938, Marie Hester, da of Michale Joseph Aberne, QC, and has issue living, Anthony Ernest Michael, *b*

1938, — Ronald Thomas Edward, *b* 1940, — Andrea Margaret, *b* 1941, — Michelle Joan Adrienne, *b* 1944, — Ruth Jocelyn Vickie, — *b* 1945, — Louise Marie Isabel, *b* 1946. ⸺ Oswald, *b* 1907.

PREDECESSORS – (**1**) *Sir* Robert de Preston (knighted in the field by Lionel, Duke of Clarence, 1361), Lord of Preston in Lancashire, and sometime Lord High Chancellor of Ireland: *m* Margaret, only da of Walter de Bermingham, of Kells; *cr Lord Gormanston* (peerage of Ireland) about 1365-70; *s* by his son (**2**) CHRISTOPHER: *m* Elizabeth, da of William Laundres, Lord of the Barony of Naas; *s* by his son (**3**) CHRISTOPHER; *s* by his son (**4**) *Sir* ROBERT Preston, *Knt*, Dep to Sir John Dynham, Lord Chancellor of Ireland, and during his minority to Richard, Duke of York, Dep of Ireland; *cr Viscount Gormanston* (peerage of Ireland) 1478; sat in the Parliaments of 1490 and 1493; *d* 1503; *s* by his son (**5**) WILLIAM, 2nd Viscount; Dep to Lord Treasurer of Ireland 1493, and Lord Justice of Ireland 1525; *s* by his son (**6**) JENICO, 3rd Viscount; sat in Parliament 1559; *d* 1560; *s* by his son (**7**) CHRISTOPHER, 4th Viscount; sat in Parliament 1580; *d* 1599; *s* by his son (**8**) JENICO, 5th Viscount; sat in Parliament 1613; *s* by his son (**9**) NICHOLAS, 6th Viscount; *s* by his el son (**10**) JENICO, 7th Viscount; for his adherence to James II was indicted for high treason and outlawed 1691; *s* by his brother (**11**) JENICO, 8th Viscount *de jure*; *s* by his brother (**12**) ANTHONY, 9th Viscount *de jure*; *s* by his son (**13**) JENICO, 12th Viscount; having successfully instituted proceedings for the removal of the outlawry of Jenico, 7th Viscount, was summoned to take his seat in the Irish House of Peers 1800; *d* 1860; *s* by his son (**16**) EDWARD ANTHONY JOHN, 13th Viscount, *b* 1796; High Sheriff of Dublin 1845; *cr Baron Gormanston*, co Meath (peerage of United Kingdom) 1868: *m* 1836, Lucretia, da of late William Charles Jerningham, next brother of 8th Baron Stafford, *d* 1876; *s* by his son (**17**) JENICO WILLIAM JOSEPH, GCMG 14th Viscount, *b* 1837; Chamberlain to Lord-Lieut of Ireland (Duke of Abercorn, KG) 1866-8, Gov and Com-in-Ch of Leeward Islands 1885-7, of British Guiana 1887-93, and Gov of Tasmania 1893-1900: *m* 1st, 1861, Hon Ismay Louisa Ursula Bellew, who *d* 1875, da of 1st Baron Bellew; 2ndly, 1878, Georgina, who *d* 1932, da of late Peter Connellan, of Coolmore, Kilkenny; *d* 1907; *s* by his el son (**18**) JENICO EDWARD JOSEPH, 15th Viscount, *b* 1879: *m* 1911, Eileen (who *d* 1964, having *m* 2ndly, 1934, John Black Atkins), da of late Lt-Gen Rt Hon Sir William Francis Butler, GCB; *d* 1925; *s* by his son (**19**) JENICO WILLIAM RICHARD, 16th Viscount, *b* 1914; acting Capt KOYLI: *m* 1939, Pamela (who *d* 1975, having *m* 2ndly, 1943, Maurice Bernard O'Connor, who *d* 1961), da of late Capt Edward Dudley Hanly (*see* E Denbigh, 1973-74 Edn); *ka* 1940; *s* by his son (**20**) JENICO NICHOLAS DUDLEY, 17th Viscount and present peer; also Baron Gormanston (peerage of Ireland 1365-70, and of UK 1868).

GORMLEY, BARONY OF (Gormley) (Extinct 1993)

SON LIVING OF LIFE BARON

Hon Francis Edward, *b* 1938: *m* 1961, Barbara, da of John Garner.

DAUGHTER LIVING

Hon Winifred, *b* 1940: *m* 1960, Arthur Evans.

WIDOW LIVING OF LIFE BARON

SARAH ELLEN (*Baroness Gormley*), da of Levi Mather, of Ashton-in-Makerfield: *m* 1937, Baron Gormley, OBE (Life Baron), who *d* 1993.

GORONWY-ROBERTS, BARONY OF (Roberts) (Extinct 1981)

SON LIVING OF LIFE BARON

Hon Owen Dafydd, *b* 1946: *m* 1st, 1979, Milana Majka Bartonova, el da of Dr M. M. Jelinek, of London; 2ndly, 1987, Sharon Jennifer, da of Terence Taylor, of Duncan, BC, Canada.

DAUGHTER LIVING OF LIFE BARON

Hon Ann Elisabeth, *b* 1947. *Residence* – Plas Newydd, Pwllheli, Gwynedd.

WIDOW LIVING OF LIFE BARON

MARIAN ANN (*Baroness Goronwy-Roberts*) (Plas Newydd, Pwllheli, Gwynedd), yr da of David Evans, of Tresalem, Aberdare: *m* 1942, Baron Goronwy-Roberts, PC (Life Baron), who *d* 1981.

GORT, VISCOUNT (Vereker) (Viscount I 1816)

Truth conquers

FOLEY ROBERT STANDISH PRENDERGAST VEREKER, 9th Viscount; *b* 24 Oct 1951; *s* 1995; *ed* Harrow; Gallery Owner: *m* 1st, 1979 (*m diss* 1987), Julie Denise, only da of D. W. Jones, of Ballasalla, I of Man; 2ndly, 1991, Sharon Lyn, da of Arnold Quayle, of Douglas, I of Man, and has issue by 2nd *m*.

𝔄rms – Quarterly: 1st and 4th azure, on a chevron or, a chaplet vert, *Vereker*; 2nd and 3rd gules, a saltire vairy or and azure, *Prendergast*. 𝔠rest – Out of mural crown gules, a stag's head proper. 𝔖upporters – *Dexter*, a lion proper; *sinister*, an heraldic antelope proper, each gorged with a plain collar gules, rimmed and chained or, chain reflexed over the back.
Residence – The Coach House, Arbory St, Castletown, Isle of Man.

SON LIVING (*By 2nd marriage*)

Hon ROBERT FOLEY PRENDERGAST, *b* 5 April 1993.

DAUGHTER LIVING (*By 2nd marriage*)

Hon Catherine Mary, *b* 1997.

BROTHER LIVING

Hon Nicholas Leopold Prendergast, *b* 1954; *ed* Harrow: *m* 1985, Nicola Frances, yst da of Michael William Pitt.

SISTER LIVING

Hon Elizabeth Jane VEREKER, *b* 1948; has resumed her maiden name: *m* 1988, Michael L. Marshall, son of late A. E. Marshall, of Baldrine, I of Man; has issue living, Jason Colin VEREKER, *b* 1974, — Sarah Jayne VEREKER, *b* 1976. *Residences* – Fruit Lawn House, Abbeyleix, co Laois; Green Hurst, Grove Mount, Ramsey, I of Man.

WIDOW LIVING OF EIGHTH VISCOUNT

BETTINE MARY MACKENZIE (*Dowager Viscountess Gort*), da of late Godfrey Green, of Douglas, I of Man, and formerly wife of Arthur Henry Jarand: *m* 1946, the 8th Viscount Gort, who *d* 1995. *Residence* – Westwood, The Crofts, Castletown, I of Man.

COLLATERAL BRANCHES LIVING

Grandchildren of late Capt Hon Foley Charles Prendergast Vereker RN, 2nd son of 4th Viscount:—
Issue of late Standish Henry Prendergast Vereker, DCM, *b* 1878, *d* 1953: *m* 1908, Eleanor Elizabeth, who *d* 1957, el da of late Henry Bott, OBE, MRCS, of Washenden Manor, Biddenden, Kent:—
Daphne Eleanor, *b* 1910: *m* 1933, Com Sydney Arthur Moorhouse Else, OBE, RN (ret), who *d* 1979, and has issue living, Patrick Arthur Henry (Hector's House, Denmark St, Diss, Norfolk IP22 3LF), *b* 1934: *m* 1965, Jane Ann Ickringill, and has issue living, Henry Patrick Arthur *b* 1979, Sarah-Jane *b* 1966, Sophia Frances *b* 1969: *m* 1994, Andrew Hamilton (and has issue living, Holly Anna *b* 1996), — Nigel Christopher John (17 The Avenue, Hambrook, Chichester, Sussex ME9 8LB), *b* 1939: *m* 1972 (*m diss* 1994), Sandra Whittaker, and has issue living, Lisa Catherine *b* 1975, Fiona Jane *b* 1976; BA, — Oliver Francis (The Hollies, Oad St, Borden, Sittingbourne, Kent ME9 8LB), *b* 1948; MB, BS: *m* 1972, Elizabeth Holman, and has issue living, Timothy Stephen *b* 1974, Christopher John *b* 1976, — Marion Elizabeth, *b* 1940: *m* 1963, Lt-Cdr Peter Russell Gordon-Smith, RN (ret), of Bex Mill, Bex Lane, Heyshott, Midhurst, W Sussex, and has issue living, Russell Guy Morris (Compton Village Stores, Compton, Chichester, W Sussex) *b* 1964: *m* 1989 (*m diss* 1998), Fiona Rutland, David Mark *b* 1968, Louise Ann *b* 1966: *m* 1992, Michael Craig Duffy, of Waxway Farm, East Hill, Ottery St Mary, E Devon (and has issue living, Matthew Peter Michael *b* 1993, Marcus *b* 1995). *Residence* – 139 Brook Gdns, Emsworth, Hants PO10 7LL.

Issue of late Maurice Charles Prendergast Vereker, MC, *b* 1884, *d* 1963: *m* 1928, Winifred Joan, who *d* 1982, da of late Alberic Arthur Twisleton-Wykeham-Fiennes (*see* B Saye and Sele, colls):—
Charles John Prendergast, CBE (Lynn Cottage, Birdingbury, Rugby), *b* 1935; Lt RA (TA); MIPM, MBIM; a JP and Co Councillor of Warwicks, DL Warwicks 1993; Chm Warwicks County Council 1982-84; CBE (Civil) 1995: *m* 1975, Jennifer Lesley Ellaby, and has issue living, Richard John Prendergast, *b* 1978, — Nicholas Charles Prendergast, *b* 1982, — Elizabeth Margaret, *b* 1976. —— Jeffrey Maurice Prendergast (The Post House, Bridge St, Fenny Compton, Leamington Spa, Warwicks), *b* 1940; FRICS: *m* 1972, Denzil Farnsworth, SRN, and has issue living, Edward Foley Prendergast, *b* 1973, — Charlotte Louise, *b* 1974. —— Margaret Joan, *b* 1929. —— Brenda Rosemary, *b* 1931; SRN: *m* 1965, Harold

James Mills, Capt RA, of Glebe House, Bentworth, Alton, Hants, and has issue living, Catherine Joanna, *b* 1967; BSc; ACA: *m* 1994, James Paul Loweth, and has issue living, Annabelle Cayte *b* 1998.

Granddaughter of late Lt-Col John Cayzer Medlicott Vereker, MC (infra):—
Issue of late Lieut John Herbert Radcliffe Medlicott Vereker, RN, *b* 1914, *k* on active ser 1941: *m* 1939, Betty Eleanor Grace (who *m* 2ndly, 1945, Capt Maurice Milton Jones, US Air Force, of Jackson, Mississippi, USA), only child of Charles Edward Shepherd, of Trerice Manor, St Newlyn East, Cornwall:—
Joscelyn, *b* 1940: *m* 1963, Ralph Lancelot Johnston, of Thorpes Gardens, St James, Barbados, W Indies, son of Stanley Everton Lancelot Johnston, and has issue living, Amanda Louise, *b* 1964, — Tracy Kristina, *b* 1967.

Grandchildren of late Major John Medlicott Vereker (infra):—
Issue of late Lt-Col John Cayzer Medlicott Vereker, MC, *b* 1895, who *d* 1962: *m* 1914, Dulce Flores Elder, who *d* 1973, only child of Alexander Randle Skene Radcliffe, formerly of Dilston, Kentville, Nova Scotia:—
Dulciebella Joy BUSWELL (Aldersnapp Cottage, Petersfield, Hants), *b* 1917; assumed surname of Buswell by deed poll 19—: *m* 1st, 1935 (*m diss* 1946), Capt Hender Charles Molesworth St Aubyn (*see* Molesworth-St Aubyn, Bt), who *d* 1986; 2ndly, 1948, Wing-Cdr Harold Frederick Gurney Fry, RAF, who *d* 1978, and has issue living, (by 1st *m*) (*see* Molesworth-St Aubyn, Bt), — (by 2nd *m*) Elizabeth Gurney, *b* 1950: *m* 1st, 1969 (*m diss* 1974), Colin Maurice Sampson; 2ndly, 1975, Colin Roy Wooltorton, and has issue living (by 2nd *m*), George Peter Christopher *b* 1975. —— Shelagh-Moureen (Barton Cottage, Rosebery Rd, W Runton, Cromer), *b* 1925; late WRNAS: *m* 1947 (*m diss* 1971), Hugh Bellasis Martin, MBE, and has issue living, Clive Patrick, *b* 1955; *ed* Harrow, and Wadham Coll, Oxford (BA): *m* 1986, Caroline Anne Freedman, and has issue living, Thomas Christopher *b* 1987, Luke Nicholas *b* 1990, — Corinna Frances Avril *b* 1948; *ed* St Margaret's Sch, Bushey, Homerton Coll, and Newnham Coll Camb: (BEd): *m* 19—, Philip Charles Creasy, MA, of The Head's House, Heath School, Colchester, and has issue living, Mathew Henry *b* 1974, Stella Judith *b* 1977.

Issue of late Capt Stanley Lloyd Medlicott Vereker, OBE, RN, *b* 1899, *d* 1967: *m* 1925, Elaine Irene, who *d* 1982, da of late John Henry Edwards, of 54 Portland Place, W1:—
(John) Stanley Herbert Medlicott (La Garinie, Larroque, Castelnau de Montmiral 81140, France), *b* 1927; *ed* Rugby, and Trin Hall, Camb: *m* 1st, 1954 (*m diss* 1976), Valerie Ann Virginia, who *d* 19—, da of William James Threlfall, CIE, of Skoons, Bembridge, I of W; 2ndly, 1980, Mary St Joan Howard, yr da of Bertram Eric Edmonds (*see* E Carlisle, colls, 1980 Edn), widow of James Ewing Kennaway, and formerly wife of Brian C. Kennaway Cummins, and has had issue (by 1st *m*), †Simon Lloyd William Medlicott, *b* 1955; *d* 1995, in Chile, — Rupert David Peregrine Medlicott (Dunsby Hall, Dunsby, Bourne, Lincs), *b* 1957: *m* 1986, Philippa J., da of J.C. Geoffrey Stocks, of W Bagborough, Som, and has issue living, Freddie *b* 1990, Jack *b* 1992, — Hugo Dominic Charles Medlicott *b* 1961: *m* 1983 (*m diss* 1990), Atalanta, da of late John Cowan. —— David William Leslie Edwards (Holton House, Burwash, Sussex), *b* 1930; *ed* Eton, and Trin Hall, Camb (MA); Lt-Cdr RNVR (ret): *m* 1965, Jane Elizabeth, da of Alan Campbell Gairdner, FRCS, of Branscombe, Whimple, Devon, and has issue living, William David Lloyd Medlicott, *b* 1966, — Henry Alan Charles Medlicott (Ashbeer House, Elworthy, Lydeard St Lawrence, Taunton, Som), *b* 1969: *m* 1995, Anna Lois, da of Jeremy Carr, of Quedley Copse, Flimwell, Sussex.

Issue of late Cdr Charles William Medlicott Vereker, RN, *b* 1903, *d* 1995: *m* 1937, Marjorie Hughes, who *d* 1984, da of William Hughes Whatley:—
Peter William Medlicott (c/o FCO, King Charles St, SW1), *b* 1939; *ed* Marlborough, Trin Coll, Camb (MA), and Harvard Univ (Henry Fellow); HM Diplomatic Ser, Counsellor and Consul-Gen HM Embassy Bangkok 1983-86, Dep Permanent Rep UK Mission at Geneva 1987-90, Head Arms Control Dept FCO 1991-93, Chm Directing Staff Royal Coll of Defence Studies 1994-95, HM Amb to OECD Paris since 1995: *m* 1967, Susan Elizabeth, da of late Maj-Gen Antony John Dyball, CBE, MC, and has issue living, Connel Charles Medlicott, *b* 1971, — Toby John Medlicott, *b* 1973, — Rory James Medlicott, *b* 1981. —— *Sir* John Michael Medlicott, KBE, CB, *b* 1944; *ed* Marlborough, and Keele Univ; with Min of Overseas Development 1967, World Bank 1970-72, Private Sec to Min for Overseas Development 1976-78, PM's Office 1980-83, Prin Finance Offr Overseas Development Admin 1983-88, Dep Sec Dept of Educn and Science 1988-94, since when Permanent Sec Overseas Development Admin; CB 1992, KBE (Civil) 1999: *m* 1971, Judith, da of Hobart Rowen, of Washington, DC, and has issue living, Andrew Shane Medlicott, *b* 1975, — Jennifer Gail, *b* 1973. —— Corinna Mary, *b* 1938: *m* 1961, Col John Tadman, Royal Anglian Regt, of West End Mill, Donhead St Andrew, Shaftesbury, Dorset, and has issue living, Miles William Vereker, *b* 1966, — Carey Joanna, *b* 1962, — Fenella Jane, *b* 1964.

Issue of late Denis Medlicott Vereker, *b* 1906, *d* 1976: *m* 1927 (*m diss* 1942), Marjory Mary, da of Julius A. Fryer, formerly of Port Elizabeth, S Africa:—
Moyra Maureen, *b* 1928: *m* 1st, 1962 (*m diss* 1971), Rodney Graham Smit, CA (S Africa), ACIS; 2ndly, 1976, Roy William Digby, MB, ChB, of Traralgon, Vic, Aust.

Granddaughter of late Hon John Prendergast Vereker, 3rd son of 3rd Viscount:—
Issue of late Major John Medlicott Vereker, *b* 1863, *d* 1940: *m* 1892 (*m diss* 1913), Mary Agnes, who *d* 1930, el da of Sir Charles William Cayzer, 1st Bt, of Gartmore, Perthshire:—
Kathleen Sybil (76 Woodside Av, Cowie's Hill, Durban, S Africa), *b* 1904: *m* 1931, Cdr Michael George Marriott, RN, who *d* 1978, and has issue living, Jeremy Edward Alan (Carnamah, W Aust), *b* 1937; Lt RN: *m* 1963, Teresa Katherine, da of Malcolm Francis Ogilvie-Forbes, of Boyndlie, Aberdeenshire, and has issue living, Benedict Michael Andrew *b* 1963, Peter Malcolm *b* 1966, Felicity Anne *b* 1969, — Bridget Mary, *b* 1934: *m* 1956, Julius Horowitz, of 8 Kernick Av, Melrose North, Johannesburg, S Africa, and has issue living, Adam Mark *b* 1957, Ivan Brandon *b* 1961, Seth William (twin) *b* 1961, Ben Robert *b* 1964, Robyn Ester *b* 1956, Yael Tayce *b* 1959.

Grandchildren of late Hon Henry Prendergast Vereker, LLD, 4th son of 3rd Viscount:—
Issue of late Lieut-Col Charles Granville Vereker, *b* 1869, *d* 1947: *m* 1st, 1895, Adeline Eleanor, who *d* 1930, da of late Maj-Gen Thomas Porter Berthon, RA; 2ndly, 1931, Leila Frances Helena (who *d* 1993, having *m* 2ndly, 1973, Robert Hugh Pardoe, of Bridge House, Bibury, Cirencester), da of late Florian Gustavus Bosanquet:—
(By 2nd *m*) Neville Henry Prendergast (The Old Rectory, E Anstey, Tiverton, Devon EX16 9JP), *b* 1934; FRICS: *m* 1974, Priscilla Mary, el da of John Orlando Weld-Forester (*see* B Forester, colls), and has issue living, John Charles Prendergast, *b* 1975, — Richard Neville Forester, *b* 1977. —— Louise Katherine (Flat N, 78/80 Holland Rd, W14), *b* 1933: *m* 1953 (*m diss* 1961), Geoffrey Whitaker Gotch, and has issue living, Peter Charles Thomas, *b* 1955; *ed*

Birmingham Univ (BSc), and Aston Univ, Birmingham (DipSH); HM Inspector of Factories, Health & Safety Executive 1979-91, since when Group Health & Safety Adviser Babtie Group: *m* 1982, Deborah Jane Ward, and has issue living, Liam Paul *b* 1984, Gemma Jane *b* 1982.

Issue of late Cdr Henry Gosset Vereker, RN, *b* 1871, *d* 1916: *m* 1903, Kate Beatrice, who *d* 1915, el da of late Frank Herbert—

†Charles Henry, *b* 1913; *ed* Lincoln Coll, Oxford (MA, DPhil); Prof of Political Theory and Insts, Durham Univ 1966, Emeritus Prof since 1973; Patron Buckingham Univ 1984; Hon D Litt 1985: *m* 1942, Patricia, JP, da of late S. G. K. Kastelian, MD, and *d* 1996, leaving issue, Julian Charles Prendergast, MBE (Tythe House, Odstock, Salisbury), *b* 1945; MBE 1995: *m* 1968 (*m diss* 1993), Elizabeth Glascott Wise, and has issue living, Annabel Louise *b* 1974, — Katherine Elizabeth, *b* 1949: *m* 1972, Edward John Watson Gieve, of 211 Highbury Quadrant, N5, and has issue living, Daniel Vereker *b* 1980, Matthew Vereker *b* 1982, — Deirdre Patricia, *b* 1954.

PREDECESSORS – (1) *Sir* Thomas Prendergast, a Brig-Gen in the Army, and MP for Monaghan 1703; *cr a Baronet* 1699; killed at Malplaquet 1709; *s* by his son (2) *Sir* Thomas, PC, 2nd Bt; was MP for Chichester and Clonmel, and Postmaster-Gen of Ireland; *dsp* 1760 before the patent creating him Viscount Clonmel had been completed; the baronetcy having expired the estates passed to his nephew (3) John Smyth, 2nd son of Elizabeth (2nd da of 1st Bt), by Charles Smyth, MP for Limerick 1731-76; successively MP for Carlow and Limerick; assumed the surname of Prendergast in lieu of Smyth 1760, and the additional surname of Smyth 1785; *cr Baron Kiltarton* (peerage of Ireland) 1810 with remainder to his nephew Charles, son of his sister Juliana, by her marriage with Thomas Vereker, and *Viscount Gort* (peerage of Ireland) 1816, with similar limitation; *d* 1817; *s* by his nephew (ante) (4) Charles Vereker, PC, 2nd Viscount; MP for Limerick 1790-1817, and afterwards a Representative Peer; *d* 1842; *s* by his son (5) John Prendergast, 3rd Viscount, *b* 1790; successively MP for Limerick and a Representative Peer: *m* 1st, 1814, Hon Maria O'Grady, who *d* 1854, da of 1st Viscount Guillamore; 2ndly, 1861, Elizabeth Mary, who *d* 1880, da of John Jones, and widow of George Tudor, MP for Barnstaple; *d* 1865; *s* by his son (6) Standish Prendergast, 4th Viscount, *b* 1819: *m* 1847, Hon Caroline Harriet Gage, who *d* 1888, da of 4th Viscount Gage, *d* 1900; *s* by his el son (7) John Gage Prendergast, 5th Viscount, *b* 1849: *m* 1885, Eleanor, who *d* 1933, da of late R. Surtees, of Hamsterley Hall, co Durham; *d* 1902; *s* by his el son (8) John Standish Surtees Prendergast, VC, GCB, CBE, DSO, MVO, MC, 6th Viscount *b* 1886; Field Marshal; CIGS 1937-9; European War 1914-18 (four times wounded, MC, DSO with two bars, VC), European War 1939-40 as Com-in-Ch, British Expeditionary Force in France (GCB, Grand Cross of Legion of Honour); Inspector-Gen to Forces for Training 1940-41, Gov and Com-in-Ch, Gibraltar 1941-2, and Malta 1942-4, and High Commr and Com-in-Ch Palestine, and High Commr for Transjordan 1944-5: *cr Viscount Gort*, of Hamsterley, co Durham (peerage of United Kingdom) 1946: *m* 1911 (*m diss* 1925), his cousin, Corinna Katherine, who *d* 1940, da of late Capt George Medlicott Vereker; *d* 1946, when the United Kingdom Viscountcy became ext and the Irish Viscountcy and Barony passed to his brother (9) Standish Robert Gage Prendergast, MC, 7th Viscount; *b* 1888; 1914-18 war as Lt RHA; High Sheriff of Co Durham 1934: *m* 1921, Bessy, who *d* 1972, da of late Aubone Alfred Surtees, of Dinsdale Manor, Co Durham; *d* 1975; *s* by his kinsman (10) Colin Leopold Prendergast (only son of Cdr Leopold George Prendergast Vereker, 2nd son of Capt Hon Foley Charles Prendergast Vereker, 2nd son of 4th Viscount), 8th Viscount, *b* 1916; Lt Cdr RNVR; Member House of Keys, Isle of Man Govt: *m* 1946, Bettine Mary Mackenzie, da of late Godfrey Green, of Douglas, and formerly wife of Arthur Henry Jarand; *d* 1995; *s* by his elder son (11) Foley Robert Standish Prendergast, 9th Viscount and present peer also Baron Kiltarton.

GOSCHEN, VISCOUNT (Goschen) (Viscount UK 1900)

Giles John Harry Goschen, 4th Viscount; *b* 16 Nov 1965; *s* 1977; a Lord in Waiting to HM 1992-94, Parly Under Sec of State, Dept of Transport 1994-97: *m* 1991, Sarah, yr da of late A. G. Horsnail, of Westbury-on-Trym, Bristol.

Arms – Argent, a heart fired and transfixed with an arrow bendwise point upwards gules, in chief two anchors erect sable. **Crest** – On an arrow fessewise, a dove wings endorsed all proper. **Supporters** – *Dexter*, a sailor; *sinister*, a private of the Royal Marines, both proper, each holding in the exterior hand a flagstaff of the last, therefrom flowing a banner argent, charged with a pale gules thereon an anchor cabled and erect or.
Residence – Hilton House, Crowthorne, Berks RG11 6AH.

SISTER LIVING

Hon Caroline Elizabeth, *b* 1963: *m* 1991, William E. J. Grant, eldor oon of Sir (Matthew) Alistair Grant, of Campden Hill Sq, W8, and has issue living, John Alexander, *b* 1992.

WIDOW LIVING OF THIRD VISCOUNT

Alvin (*Alvin, Viscountess Goschen*) (Hilton House, Crowthorne, Berks RG11 6AH), yr of da of late H. England, of Durban, Natal: *m* 1955, as his 2nd wife, the 3rd Viscount Goschen, who *d* 1977.

PREDECESSORS – (1) *Rt Hon* George Joachim Goschen, son of late William Henry Goschen, of Austin Friars, EC, and Templeton House, Roehampton; *b* 1831; sometime a partner in firm of Fruhling and Goschen, of Austin Friars, a

Director of the Bank of England, and Chm of Lloyd's; Vice-Press of Board of Trade 1865-6, Chancellor of Duchy of
Lancaster (with a seat in the Cabinet) 1866, Pres of Poor Law Board 1868-71, First Lord of the Admirality 1871-4, Envoy
Extraor and Min Plen to Constantinople on a Special Mission 1880-81, and Ecclesiastical Commr for England 1882-5,
Chancellor of the Exchequer Jan 1887 to Aug 1892, and again First Lord of the Admirality 1895-1900: MP for City of
London (L) 1863-80, for Ripon 1880-85, for E Div of Edinburgh Borough 1885-6, and for St George Hanover Square (C)
Feb 1887 to Nov 1900; cr PC 1865, and Viscount Goschen, of Hawkhurst, co Kent (peerage of United Kingdom) 1900: m
1857, Lucy, who d 1898, da of late John Dalley; d 1907; s by his son (2) Rt Hon GEORGE JOACHIM, GCSI, GCIE, CBE,
VD, 2nd Viscount, b 1866; Private Sec to Gov of NS Wales (Earl of Jersey) 1890-92; sometime a partner in the firm of
Goschens and Cunliffe, of 12 Austin Friars, EC and Chm of Med Research Council; Lieut-Col and Hon Col (Lieut-Col
Cmdg 1914-18) a Batn Buffs (E Kent Regt); sat as MP for N, or E Grinstead Div of Sussex (C) 1895-1906; appointed a
Member of Roy Chmmn on King's Bench 1912, and Joint Parliamentary Sec (unpaid) Board of Agriculture 1918; was
Controller Labour Div, Food Production Depart 1918-19; Gov of Madras 1924-29 (acted as Viceroy and Gov-Gen of India
June to Oct 1929): m 1893, Lady Margaret Evelyn Gathorne-Hardy, CI, who d 1943, da of 1st Earl of Cranbrook; d 1952;
s by his nephew (3) JOHN ALEXANDER, KBE (son of late Hon Sir William Henry Goschen, KBE, 2nd son of 1st Viscount),
3rd Viscount, b 1906; Col Gren Gds: British Mil Mission to Greece 1945-47; Assist Ch Whip, House of Lords 1962-64;
Capt Yeomen of the Guard and Dep Ch Whip 1970-71: m 1st, 1934 (m diss 1949), Hilda Violet Ursula, da of late Col Hon
St Leger Henry Jervis, DSO (V St Vincent, colls); 2ndly, 1955, Alvin, yr da of H. England, of Durban, Natal; d 1977; s by
his son (4) GILES JOHN HARRY, 4th Viscount and present peer.

GOSFORD, EARL OF (Acheson) Sits as BARON WORLINGHAM (UK 1835) (Earl I 1806, Bt NS 1628)

VIGILANTIBUS

To the watchful

CHARLES DAVID NICHOLAS ALEXANDER JOHN SPARROW
ACHESON, 7th Earl and 13th Baronet; b 13 July 1942; s
1966; ed Harrow, at Byam Shaw Sch of Drawing and
Painting, and Roy Acad Schs: m 1983, Lynnette Redmond, of Sydney, Australia.

Arms – Argent, an eagle with two heads displayed sable, beaked
and membered or; on a chief vert two mullets of the third. Crest –
A cock gules, standing on a trumpet or. Supporters – Two leopards
proper, collared and chained or, the sinister reguardant.
Seat – Gosford Castle, Markethill, co Armagh. Address – c/o House
of Lords, SW1.

SISTERS LIVING AND DECEASED

Lady (Francesca Georgina) Caroline, b 1940: m 1967, David Wallace
Fleming, who d (Dec) 1991, and d (Aug) 1991, leaving issue,
Alexander Montagu Acheson (Zaca Ranch, PO Box 147, Los Olivos,
California 93441, USA), b 1968.
(Lady) Isabella Augusta (does not use courtesy title), b 1950: m
1979, Tevita T. Maka, and has issue living, Charles Nicholas, b
1980, — Toby Manu, b 1985, — James Alipate, b 1989. Address –
PO Box 1234, Nuku A'Lofa, Tonga, S Pacific.

UNCLE LIVING (Son of 5th Earl)

Hon PATRICK BERNARD VICTOR MONTAGU, b 4 Feb 1915; ed Harrow,
Trin Coll, Camb (BA 1937), and Harvard Univ (MBA 1939): m
1946, Judith, da of Earle P. Gillette, of Minneapolis, Minnesota,
USA, and of Mrs F. B. Bate, of Waterford, Virginia, USA, and has
issue living, Nicholas Hope Carter, b 1947: m 1983, Patricia, da of
James Beckford, of Jacksonville Beach, Florida, USA, and has issue
living, Eric James Patrick b 1988, Kelly Lauren b 1987, — Christ-
opher, b 1950: m 1977, Sheryl, da of Carl Benson, of Columbus,
Georgia, USA, and has issue living, Kendall Bate (a son) b 1984,
Karen Erica b 1982, — John Alexander Simon, b 1957: m 1st, 1982
(m diss 1985), Cara, da of Ernest Kulik, of Purcellville, Virginia,
USA; 2ndly, 1988, Lisa Kimberly Bickerstaff, da of Carl Benson, of Columbus, Georgia, USA, and has issue living (by
2nd m), Katherine Genevieve b 1988, Emma Mary Camilla b 1991, — Alexandra Sarah Camilla, b 1962, — Caroline Mary
Patricia (twin), b 1962. Residence – Box 71, Waterford, Va 22190, USA.

AUNT LIVING (Daughter of 5th Earl)

Lady Mary Virginia Shirley, b 1919: m 1941, Fernando Corcuera, who d 1978, and has had issue, Juan Fernando Pedro, b
1948: m 1971, Paloma Gonzalez, and has issue living, Fernando b 1971, Carmen b 1974, Camila b 1979, — Jaime Marcos
Pedro, b 1955: m 1983, HI & RH Archduchess Myriam Adelhaid Hugoline Omnes Sancti Marcus d'Aviano Melchiora of
Austria, 3rd da of HI & RH Archduke Felix of Austria, and has issue living, Karl Sebastian b 1984, Pedro Johannes b
1985, Felipe b 1987, Andres b 1988, — Fernanda Mary, b 1942: m 1967 (m diss 1973), Manuel Valles, and d 1992, leaving
issue, Fernanda b 1967, — Monica Ana, b 1944: m 1970, Harry Troop, and has issue living, Ana Monica b 1971, Isabel
Gabriela b 1972, Maria b 1976, — Marisol Manuela, b 1946: m 1977 (m diss 1983), Luis Padilla, and has issue living,
Jimena b 1977, Natalia b 1979. Residence – Hidalgo 14, San Angel, Mexico DF 01000, Mexico.

MOTHER LIVING

Francesca Augusta Maria (56 Heathfield Rd, W3 8EJ), da of Francesco Cagiati, of Rome: *m* 1935 (*m diss* 1960), as his 1st wife, the 6th Earl of Gosford, who *d* 1966.

WIDOW LIVING OF SIXTH EARL

CYNTHIA MARGARET (*Dowager Countess of Gosford*), da of late Capt Henry Cave West, MC, RHA, and widow of Maj James Pringle Delius, 13th/18th R Hussars: *m* 1960, as his 2nd wife, the 6th Earl of Gosford, who *d* 1966.

COLLATERAL BRANCH LIVING

Issue of late Capt Hon Patrick George Edward Cavendish Acheson, DSO, MVO, RN, yr son of 4th Earl, *b* 1883, *d* 1957: *m* 1915, Norah, who *d* 1970, da of Alfred Jones, formerly of Halifax, Nova Scotia;—
Blanche Theodosia, *b* (twin) 1923: *m* 1950, Com Oliver Russell Moore, RN (ret), and has issue living, Susan Theodosia, *b* 1952: *m* 1990, Christopher Aston Maltin, and has issue living, Arthur Patrick Aston *b* 1991, Alice Mary Theodosia *b* 1992, — Victoria Caroline, *b* 1954: *m* 1989, Nichola, da of co-heir of Sir Robert Hannay, 1st Bt; 2ndly, 1659, Hon Margaret Francis William Orlando Bridgeman-Sutton, and has issue living, Charles Frederick Orlando *b* 1994, Katharine Althea Acheson *b* 1992, — Patricia Alexandra, *b* 1956: *m* 1985, David Philip Dowling Styles, and has issue living, Oliver Michael Dowling *b* 1987, Henry David Dowling *b* 1989. *Residence* – Dash Hayes, Kington Magna, Gillingham, Dorset.

PREDECESSORS – (1) Sir ARCHIBALD Acheson of Edinburgh, later of Market Hill, Clonekearney, co Armagh, successively Solicitor-Gen for Scotland, a Senator of Justice (with title of Lord Glencairnie), an Extraor Lord Session, and Sec of State for Scotland; *cr* a *Baronet* (of Nova Scotia) 1628 with remainder to his heirs male whatsoever: *m* 1st, c 1610, Agnes Vernor; 2ndly, 1622, Margaret, da and heir of Hon Sir John Hamilton (D Abercorn); *d* 1634; *s* by his el son (2) Sir PATRICK, 2nd Bt (son of 1st *m*): *m* 1634, Martha, da and heir of William Moore: *d* 1638; *s* by his half-brother (3) Sir GEORGE, 3rd Bt; *b* 1629: *m* 1st, 1654, Nichola, da of co-heir of Sir Robert Hannay, 1st Bt; 2ndly, 1659, Hon Margaret Caulfeild, da of 2nd Baron Charlemont; *d* 1685; *s* by his son (4) Sir NICHOLAS, 4th Bt (son of 1st *m*); MP for co Armagh 1695: *m* 1686, Anne, da of Thomas Taylor, of Kells; *d* 1701; *s* by his son (5) Sir ARTHUR, 5th Bt; *b* 1688: *m* 1715, Anne, da and heir of Rt Hon Philip Savage; *d* 1749; *s* by his son (6) Sir ARCHIBALD, PC; *b* 1718; successively MP for Dublin Univ, and Enniskillen; *cr Baron Gosford*, of Market Hill, co Armagh (peerage of Ireland) 1776, and *Viscount Gosford* (peerage of Ireland) 1785: *m* 1740, Mary da of John Richardson, of Rich Hill, co Armagh; *d* 1790: *s* by his son (7) ARTHUR, 2nd Viscount; *b* c 1742, MP for Old Leighlin 1783-90; *cr Earl of Gosford* (peerage of Ireland) 1806: *m* 1774, Millicent, da of Lt-Gen Edward Pole, *d* 1807; *s* by his son (8) ARCHIBALD, GCB, 2nd Earl; *b* 1776; Gov of Canada; *cr Baron Worlingham* (peerage of UK) 1835; *m* 1805, Mary, da of Robert Sparrow of Worlingham Hall, Suffolk; *d* 1849; *s* by his (9) ARCHIBALD, KP, 3rd Earl; *b* 1806; who in 1847 had been *cr Baron Acheson of Clancairny*, co Armagh (peerage of UK): *m* 1832, Lady Theodosia Brabazon, who *d* 1876, da of 10th Earl of Meath; *d* 1864; *s* by his son (10) ARCHIBALD BRABAZON SPARROW, KP, 4th Earl; *b* 1841; Lord of the Bedchamber to HRH the Prince of Wales 1886-1901, and Vice-Chamberlain of the Household to HM Queen Alexandra 1901-22; bore Queen Consort's Ivory Rod at Coronation of King Edward VII 1902: *m* 1876, Lady Louisa Augusta Beatrice Montagu, DBE, who *d* 1944, 2nd da of 7th Duke of Manchester, KP; *d* 1922; *s* by his son (11) ARCHIBALD CHARLES MONTAGU BRABAZON, MC, 5th Earl; *b* 1877; Col Coldstream Gds; S Africa 1899-1902, 1914-18 War (MC): *m* 1st, 1910 (*m diss* 1928), Mildred, who *d* 1965, da of John Ridgely Carter, of Balt, USA, American Min to the Balkans; 2ndly, 1928, Beatrice Claflin, who *d* 1967, formerly wife of Robert P. Breese, of New York; *d* 1954; *s* by his el son (12) ARCHIBALD ALEXANDER JOHN STANLEY, OBE, 6th Earl, *b* 1911; a Lord in Waiting to HM 1957-58: *m* 1st, 1935 (*m diss* 1960), Francesca Augusta Maria, da of Francesco Cagiati, of Rome; *d* 1966; *s* by 1960, Cynthia Margaret, da of Capt Henry Cave West, MC, RHA, and widow of Maj James Pringle Delius; *d* 1966; *s* by his only son (13) CHARLES DAVID NICHOLAS ALEXANDER JOHN SPARROW, 7th Earl and present peer; also Viscount and Baron Gosford, Baron Worlingham and Baron Acheson of Clancairny.

GOUDIE, BARONESS (Goudie) (Life Baroness 1998)

MARY TERESA GOUDIE, da of Martin Brick; *b* 2 Sept 1946; *ed* Our Lady of the Visitation Sch, Greenford, and Our Lady of St Anselm Sch, Hayes; Memb Brent Council 1971-78; Assist Dir Brent People's Housing Assoc 1980-97; Organiser and Sec Labour and Solidarity Campaign 1980-84; Dir Hansard Soc 1985-89; Dir The House Magazine 1989-90, Dir of Public Affairs, WWF 1990-95; Independent Public Affairs Consultant since 1995; *cr Baroness Goudie*, of Roundwood in the London Borough of Brent (Life Baroness) 1998: *m* 1969, James Goudie, QC, son of late William Cooper Goudie, of Fife, and has issue.
Residence – 53 Lancaster Grove, NW3 4HB. *Club* – Reform.

SONS LIVING

Hon William Martin Philip, *b* 1973.
Hon Alexander Julian Cooper, *b* 1997.

GOUGH, VISCOUNT (Gough) (Viscount UK 1849, Bt UK 1842)
(Name and Title pronounced "Goff")

SHANE HUGH MARYON GOUGH, 5th Viscount and 5th Baronet; *b* 26 Aug 1941; *s* 1951; *ed* Winchester; late Lt Irish Gds; Member Queen's Body Guard for Scotland (Royal Company of Archers); Mem Exec Cttee, Standing Council of the Baronetage; local Dir Central London Bd Roy Insurance (UK) Ltd; Trustee Gardner's Trust for the Blind, and Schizophrenia Research; Member Exec Council RNIB, and Scottish Lifeboat Council RNLI; FRGS.

Arms – Quarterly; 1st and 4th gules, on a mount vert a lion passant guardant or, supporting with his dexter paw the Union flag flowing to the sinister proper, over the same, in chief, the words "China," "India," in letters of gold; 2nd and 3rd azure, on a fesse argent, between three boars' heads, couped or, a lion passant gules; in the centre chief point, pendent from a riband argent, fimbriated azure, a representation of the badge of the Spanish order of Charles III proper, and on a chief, a representation of the east wall of the fortress of Tarifa, with a breach between two turrets, the dexter turret surmounted by the British flag flying, all proper. Crests – 1st, a boar's head couped or, motto over "Goojerat" (of augmentation); 2nd, on a mural crown argent, a lion passant guardant or, holding in the dexter paw two flag staves in bend sinister proper, the one being the Union flag of Great Britain and Ireland surmounting the other, the staff thereof broken, with a triangular banner flowing therefrom to represent a Chinese flag, having thereon a dragon, and in an escroll above the word "China"; 3rd a dexter arm embowed, in facings of 87th Regiment (gules, faced vert), the hand grasping the colour of the said Regiment displayed, and a representation of a French eagle reversed and depressed, the staff broken proper, in an escroll above the word "Barossa." Supporters – Dexter, a lion reguardant or, gorged with an Eastern crown gules, the rim inscribed with the world "Punjab" in letters of gold, with chain reflexed over the back, also gold; *sinister*, a Chinese dragon or, gorged with a mural crown sable, enscribed with the word "China," and chained gold.
Residences – Keppoch House, Strathpeffer, Ross-shire IV14 9AD; 17 Stanhope Gdns, SW7 5RQ. *Clubs* – Pratt's, White's.

PREDECESSORS – (1) Field-Marshal Rt Hon Sir HUGH Gough, KP, GCB, GCSI, PC; *b* 1779; an eminent Mil Com who achieved brilliant victories in India, and subjugated and annexed the Punjab to the British Dominions: *cr* a *Baronet* 1842, *Baron Gough*, of Chinkangfoo, in China and of Maharajpore and the Sutlej, in the East Indies (peerage of United Kingdom) 1846, and *Viscount Gough of Goojerat*, in the Punjaub, and of the City of Limerick (peerage of United Kingdom) 1849 (title later abbreviated to *Viscount Gough*); thrice thanked by Parliament and awarded a pension of £2,000 a-year for three lives: *m* 1807, Frances Maria, da of Gen Edward Stephens, RA; *d* 1869; *s* by his son (2) GEORGE STEPHENS, 2nd Viscount, *b* 1815; Capt Grenadier Guards: *m* 1st, 1840, Sarah Elizabeth, who *d* 1841, da of late Wray Palliser, of Comragh, Waterford; 2ndly, 1846, Jane, who *d* 1892. da of late George Arbuthnot, of Elderslie, Surrey; *d* 1895; *s* by his el son (3) HUGH, KCVO, 3rd Viscount; *b* 1849; Min Resident at Dresden and Coburg, and Chargé d'Affaires at Court of Waldeck 1901-07: *m* 1889, Lady Georgiana Frances Henrietta Pakenham, who *d* 1943, da of 4th Earl of Longford; *d* 1919; *s* by his son (4) HUGH WILLIAM, MC, 4th Viscount; *b* 1892; Lieut Col Irish Guards; European War 1914-18 (MC): *m* 1935, Margaretta Elizabeth, who *d* 1977, da of Sir Spencer Pocklington Maryon Maryon-Wilson, 11th Bt; *d* 1951; *s* by his son (5) SHANE HUGH MARYON, 5th Viscount, and present peer; also Baron Gough.

GOULD OF POTTERNEWTON, BARONESS (Gould) (Life Baroness 1993)

JOYCE BRENDA GOULD, da of Solomon Joseph Manson; *b* 29 Oct 1932; *ed* Roundhay High Sch for Girls, and Bradford Technical Coll; Dispensing Chemist 1952-65, Assist Regional Organiser and Women's Officer Yorks Labour Party 1969-75, Assist National Agent and Ch Women's Officer 1975-85, Dir of Organisation 1985-93; Exec Member Women's National Commn, Sec National Joint Cttee of Working Women's Organisations, Sec Yorks National Council of Civil Liberties, Cttee Member Campaign Against Racial Discrimination, Exec Member Joint Cttee Against Racism, Member Home Office Cttee on Electoral Matters; Vice-Pres Socialist Internat Women, etc; author of numerous pamphlets on feminism, socialism and sexism, etc; a Baroness in Waiting (Govt Whip) to HM May-Dec 1997; *cr Baroness Gould of Potternewton*, of Leeds, co W Yorks (Life Baroness) 1993: *m* 1953, Kevin Gould, and has issue.
Address – 1/5 Foulser Rd, SW17 8UE.

DAUGHTER LIVING

Hon Jeannette, *b* 1953.

Gower, Leveson-, family name of Earl Granville.

GOWRIE, EARL OF (Ruthven) (Earl UK 1945) (Name pronounced "Rivven")

ALEXANDER PATRICK GREYSTEIL RUTHVEN, PC, 2nd Earl; *b* 26 Nov 1939; *s* to Earldom of Gowrie 1955, and to Barony of Ruthven of Gowrie 1956; in remainder to Lordship of Ruthven of Freeland (*see* E Carlisle); *ed* Eton, at Balliol Coll, Oxford, and Harvard Univ, USA; officially recognised in the name of Ruthven by Warrant of Lord Lyon King of Arms 1957; a Lord-in-Waiting to HM 1972-74; formerly lecturer at State Univ of New York, Univ Coll, London, and Harvard Univ; Conservative Whip 1971-72 and a Lord in Waiting 1972-74; Oppn Spokesman Economic Affrs 1974-79; a Min of State, Dept of Employment 1979-81, N Ireland Office 1981-83; Min for the Arts 1983-85, since when Provost Royal Coll of Art; Chm Sotheby's UK 1987-93; Chm Arts Council 1994-98; PC 1983: *m* 1st, 1962 (*m diss* 1974), Xandra, yr da of Col Robert Albert Glanville Bingley, CVO, DSO, OBE; 2ndly, 1974, Countess Adelheid, yst da of late Fritz-Dietlof, Graf von der Schulenburg, and has issue by 1st *m*.

𝕬rms – Paly of six, argent and gules 𝕮rest – A ram's head couped sable armd or. 𝕾upporters – Two goats sable, armed, unguled and ducally gorged or, with chains also or reflexed over the back. *Residence* – 34 King St, Covent Gdn, WC2.

SON LIVING (By 1st marriage)

PATRICK LEO BRER (*Viscount Ruthven of Canberra*), *b* 4 Feb 1964: *m* 1990, Julie Goldsmith, and has issue living, *Hon* Heathcote Patrick Cornelius Hore, *b* 28 May 1990.

BROTHER LIVING

Malise Walter Maitland Knox Hore RUTHVEN (c/o Chatto & Windus, 30 Bedford Sq, WC2), *b* 1942; *ed* Eton, and Trin Coll, Camb; author of *Islam in the World* (1984), *The Divine Supermarket* (1989), etc: *m* 1967, Ianthe, da of late Lt-Cmdr (Robert) Hugh Hodgkinson, DSC, RN, Headmaster Milton Abbey 1955-69, and has issue living, Chloe, *b* 1969, — Oonagh Orlanda, *b* 1970.

MOTHER LIVING

Pamela Margaret, da of the Rev A. H. Fletcher, of 87, Cadogan Gdns, SW1; was an Extra Woman of the Bedchamber of HM the Queen 1948-51; in 1945 was granted rank and precedence of wife of the el son of an Earl during her widowhood: *m* 1st, 1938, Major Hon (Alexander Harding) Patrick Hore Ruthven, only son of 1st Earl, who *d* of wounds received in action in Libya 1942; 2ndly, 1952, as his 2nd wife, Major (George) Derek Cooper, OBE, MC, The Life Guards.

WIDOW LIVING OF SECOND BARON RUTHVEN OF GOWRIE

JUDITH GORDON (Denbigh, Foreland Rd, Bembridge, Isle of Wight), yr da of late Bertie E. Bell, of Guernsey: *m* 1st, 1953, as his 2nd wife, the 2nd Baron Ruthven of Gowrie (and 10th Lord Ruthven of Freeland), who *d* 1956; 2ndly, 1965, Maj Digby Robert Peel, MC, RA, who *d* 1971.

PREDECESSORS – (1) *Brig-Gen Rt Hon Sir* ALEXANDER GORE ARKWRIGHT Hore Ruthven, VC, GCMG, CB, DSO, PC, 2nd son of 9th Lord Ruthven of Freeland; *b* 1872; Col and Hon Brig-Gen Welsh Guards; Sudan 1898 (despatches, VC), White Nile 1900 (despatches thrice), Somaliland 1903-04, European War 1914-19 in Gallipoli and France (severely wounded, despatches five times, DSO with Bar, French and Belgian Croix de Guerre, CMG, CB); Gov of S Australia 1928-34, Gov of N S Wales 1935-6, and Gov-Gen and Com-in-Ch of Commonwealth of Australia 1936-44; Lieut-Gov and Dep Constable of Windsor Castle 1945-53; *cr Baron Gowrie*, of Canberra in the Commonwealth of Australia, and of Dirleton, co E Lothian (peerage of United Kingdom) 1935, and *Viscount Ruthven of Canberra*, of Dirleton, co E Lothian and *Earl of Gowrie* (peerage of United Kingdom) 1945: *m* 1908, Zara Eileen, who *d* 1965, da of late John Pollok (B Clanmorris); *d* 1955; *s* by his grandson (2) ALEXANDER PATRICK GREYSTEIL (el son of late Maj Hon (Alexander Harding) Patrick Hore Ruthven, only son of 1st Earl), 2nd Earl and present peer; also Viscount Ruthven of Canberra, Baron Gowrie, and Baron Ruthven of Gowrie (*see infra*).

(1) WALTER JAMES RUTHVEN, 9th Lord Ruthven of Freeland (peerage of Scotland) *cr* 1651 (*see* E Carlisle), was *cr Baron Ruthven of Gowrie* (peerage of United Kingdom) 1919: *m* 1869, Lady Caroline Annesley Gore, who *d* 1914, da of 4th Earl

of Arran; *d* 1921; *s* by his el son **(2)** WALTER PATRICK, CB, CMG, DSO, 2nd Baron, *b* 1870; Maj-Gen late Scots Guards; commanded Bangalore Brig 1920-24, and London Dist 1924-8, and was Lieut-Gov of Guernsey 1929-34: *m* 1st, 1895, Jean Leslie, who *d* 1952, da of late Norman George Lampson (Lampson Bt, colls); 2ndly, 1953, Judith Gordon (who *m* 2ndly, 1965, Maj Digby Robert Peel, MC, RA, who *d* 1971), da of late Bertie E. Bell, of Guernsey; *d* 1956; *s* in the Barony of Ruthven of Gowrie (peerage of United Kingdom) by his great-nephew, ALEXANDER PATRICK GREYSTEIL, 3rd Baron, and 2nd Earl of Gowrie (ante).

GRADE, BARONY OF (Grade) (Extinct 1998)

ADOPTED SON OF LIFE BARON

Paul Nicholas, *b* 1952: *m* 1st, 19— (*m diss* 19—), Lisa Pearce; 2ndly, 1986, Beverly Hill, and has issue living (by 1st *m*), Daniel, *b* 1978, — Georgina Elizabeth Frances, *b* 1980.

WIDOW LIVING OF LIFE BARON

KATHLEEN SHEILA (*Baroness Grade*), da of John Moody: *m* 1942, Baron Grade (Life Baron), who *d* 1998. *Address* – c/o The Grade Co, 34 Grosvenor St, W1X 9FG.

GRAFTON, DUKE OF (FitzRoy) (Duke E 1675)

The ornament and recompense of virtue

HUGH DENIS CHARLES FITZROY, KG, 11th Duke; *b* 3 April 1919; *s* 1970; *ed* Eton and Magdalene Coll, Camb; Hon DCL Univ of E Anglia 1990, Hon FRIBA, FSA; late Capt Gren Gds; Hon Air Cdr 2623 (E Anglian) RAAF Regt Sqdn since 1982; ADC to Viceroy of India 1943-47; patron of four livings, and Hereditary Ranger of Whittlebury Forest; DL Suffolk 1973; Member Historic Buildings Council for England 1953-84, Historic Buildings Advisory Cttee and Churches and Cathedrals Cttee English Heritage since 1984; National Trust: Member Exec Cttee, Chm E Anglia Regional Cttee 1966-81, and Member Properties Cttee 1981-94; Member Royal Fine Art Commn 1971-94; Chm Cathedrals Advisory Commn 1981-91, and Architectural Heritage Fund 1976-94, Chm of Trustees Historic Churches Preservation Trust 1980-97, and Sir John Soane's Museum 1975-97 (Life Trustee 1962); Vice Chm of Trustees National Portrait Gallery 1967-92, Trustee Tradescant Trust, Buildings at Risk, Pres Soc for the Protection of Ancient Buildings since 1989, International Students House since 1972, British Soc of Master Glass Painters, E Anglia Tourist Board 1973-93, Suffolk Preservation Soc 1957-96, Chm of Trustees Suffolk Historic Churches Trust 1973-97; KG 1976: *m* 1946, (Ann) Fortune, GCVO (Mistress of the Robes to HM The Queen), only da of late Capt (Evan Cadogan) Eric Smith, and has issue.

Arms – The royal arms of Charles II, viz Quarterly: 1st and 4th, France and England quarterly; 2nd, Scotland; 3rd, Ireland: the whole debruised by a baton sinister-compony of six pieces, argent and azure. **Crest** – On a chapeau gules, turned up ermine, a lion statant guardant or, ducally crowned azure, and gorged with a collar counter-compony argent and of the 4th. **Supporters** – *Dexter*, a lion guardant or, ducally crowned azure; *sinister*, a greyhound argent; each gorged with a collar counter-compony argent and azure.
Seat – Euston Hall, Thetford, Norfolk, IP24 2QW. *Club* – Boodle's.

SONS LIVING

JAMES OLIVER CHARLES (*Earl of Euston*) (6 Vicarage Gdns, W8 4AH; The Racing Stables, Euston, Thetford, Norfolk), *b* 13 Dec 1947; *ed* Eton, and Magdalene Coll, Camb (MA); FCA; a Page of Honour to HM 1962-63; Assist Dir J. Henry Schroder Wagg & Co 1973-82, Exec Dir Enskilda Securities 1982-87, Dir Jamestown Investments Ltd 1987, Dir Central Capital Holdings 1988, and Capel-Cure Myers Capital Management 1988: *m* 1972, Lady Clare Amabel Margaret Kerr, 3rd da of 12th Marquess of Lothian, KCVO, and has issue:—

SON LIVING— HENRY OLIVER CHARLES (*Viscount Ipswich*), *b* 6 April 1978.

DAUGHTERS LIVING—*Lady* Louise Helen Mary, *b* 1973, — *Lady* Emily Clare, *b* 1974, — *Lady* Charlotte Rose, *b* 1983, — *Lady* Isobel Anne, *b* 1985.

Lord Charles Patrick Hugh, *b* 1957; *ed* Eton, and Magdalene Coll, Camb (BA); Dir Fine Art Courses Ltd; author of *Italy, a Grand Tour for the Modern Traveller* (1991), etc: *m* 1988, Diana M., da of late Hubert Miller-Stirling, of Cape Town, S Africa, and has issue living, Nicholas Augustus Charles, *b* 1991, — George James Hugh, *b* 1993. *Residence* – The Old Rectory, Grafton Regis, Towcester, Northants NN12 7SS.

DAUGHTERS LIVING

Lady Henrietta Fortune Doreen, *b* 1949: *m* 1979, Edward G. P. St George, and has issue living, Henry Edward Hugh, *b* 1983, — Katherine Helen Cecilia, *b* 1984. *Residence* – 1 Chester Sq, SW1W 9HH; PO Box F2666, Freeport, Grand Bahama Is, Bahamas.

Lady Virginia Mary Elizabeth, *b* 1954: *m* 1st, 1980 (*m diss* 1987), Lord Ralph William Francis Joseph Kerr, yr son of 12th Marquess of Lothian, KCVO; 2ndly, 1995, Roger Babington Hill, elder son of late Cmdr Harold Babington Hill, of E Chiltington, Sussex. *Residence* – Higher Bootham House, Brampford Speke, Exeter EX5 5HR.

Lady (Olivia) Rose Mildred, *b* 1963: *m* 1995, (John) Guy Elmhirst Monson, and has issue (*see* B Monson). *Residence* – 19 Grafton Sq, SW4 0DA.

HALF-BROTHER LIVING

Lord Edward Anthony Charles, *b* 1928; *ed* Eton; late Capt Coldm Gds; a DL Norfolk 1986; High Sheriff 1987; Chm and Managing Dir Ross Poultry Ltd 1969-75, Dir Ross Breeders Ltd, Nat Poultry Breeders (S Africa) Ltd, Ross Poultry New Zealand Ltd, Dep Chm Bd of Management of Eastern Region of TSB; Dir Trustcard Ltd, Chm Caledonian Cartridge Co Ltd, Chm Norfolk Playing Fields Assoc, and on Council, Norfolk Naturalists Trust, Member of Council Royal Norfolk Agric Assocn; Chm of Governors of Wymondham Coll since 1993: *m* 1956, Veronica Mary, da of Maj Robert Francis Ruttledge, of Cloonee, Ballinrobe, co Mayo, and has issue living, Michael Robert Charles, *b* 1958: *m* 1987, Cornelia A., yr da of Peter Garnett, of Quakers' Orchard, Peaslake, Surrey, and has issue living, Edwin *b* 1992, Olivia Lucy *b* 1989, — Joanna Lucy, *b* 1957: *m* 1982, Martin John Kershaw, and has issue (*see* E Lindsey and Abingdon, colls), — Shauna Anne, *b* 1963: *m* 1989, Adam L. J. Seccombe, yr son of J. A. (Alec) Seccombe, of Pique House, Stockcross, Newbury, Berks, and has issue living, Freddie *b* 1992, Dominick Jasper *b* 1994, Sam *b* 1998. *Residence* – Norton House, Norwich, NR14 6RY. *Club* – Norfolk (Norwich).

SISTER LIVING

Lady Anne Mildred Ismay, *b* 1920: *m* 1947, Maj Colin Dalziel Mackenzie, MBE, MC, DL, late Seaforth Highlanders, Vice Lord Lieut of Lochaber, Inverness, and Badenoch and Strathspey since 1986, and has issue living, Philip Austin George (Glenkyllachy, Tomatin, Inverness-shire IV13 7YA), *b* 1949; *ed* Eton, and Magdalen Coll, Oxford (BA); FCA, MICFor: *m* 1976, (Katherine) Emma, da of late John Anthony Francis Binny (*see* Muir Bt, colls), and has issue living, Lucy *b* 1976, Sabrina *b* 1978, Doune *b* 1980, Isla *b* 1986, Bettine *b* 1991, — Caroline Doreen (5 Danyrallt, Llaneglwys, Builth Wells, Powys LD2 3BJ), *b* 1952, — Laura Patience Kathleen, *b* 1954; BA (Oxon); ALI: *m* 1980, (Ian) Michael Osborne, of The Old Manse, Tyninghame, Dunbar, E Lothian, 2nd son of Maj Gerald Michael Osborne, MC, TD, of Balmadies, Guthrie, Angus, and has issue living, Julian *b* 1982, Oliver *b* 1985, — Harriet Anne, *b* 1958; BA: *m* 1989, Thomas St Andrew Warde-Aldam, of Red Hemmels, Riding Mill, Northumberland NE44 6AB, yr son of Maj David Julian Warde-Aldam, of Healey Hall, Northumberland, and has issue living, Zoe *b* 1992, Zephirine *b* 1996, Zinnia *b* 1997. *Residence* – Farr, Inverness-shire. *Clubs* – Turf, Pratt's, New (Edinburgh).

SISTER LIVING OF NINTH DUKE (*Raised to the rank of a Duke's daughter* 1961)

(*In remainder to the Barony of Arlington, cr 1672, and the Earldom of Arlington cr 1672*)

Lady Mary Rose (*posthumous*), *b* 1918; *m* 1945 (*m diss* 1951), Francis Trelawny Williams, late Lieut RRRC, who *d* 1977 (Salusbury-Trelawny, Bt), and has issue living, Linda Jane Auriol, *b* 1947. *Residence* – The Green, Oddington, Moreton-in-Marsh, Glos.

COLLATERAL BRANCHES LIVING

Issue of late Lord John Percy Samuel FitzRoy, brother of 10th Duke, *b* 1899, *d* 1945: *m* 1929, Kathleen Ruthar Mary (who *m* 2ndly, 1946, Leonard Thomas Carr, and *d* 1967), da of late Rev Arthur Willoughby Rokeby, of Clifton Manor, Shefford, Bedfordshire:—

Ismay Diana, *b* 1933. *Residence* – Moat Cottage, Burnham Rd, Althorne, Southminster, Essex.

Grandson of late Harold Charles Cavendish FitzRoy, only son of late Maj Cavendish Charles FitzRoy, elder son of late Lt-Col Rt Hon Lord Charles FitzRoy, MP, 2nd son of 4th Duke:—

Issue of late Charles Cavendish FitzRoy, *b* 1900, *d* 1960: *m* 1st, 1926, Simone Andrée, who *d* 1957, da of Jules Hennebert; 2ndly, 1957, Nora Bardsley, of 57 Harrow View, Harrow, Middlesex:—

(By 1st *m*) Kenneth Cavendish, *b* 1928: *m* 1st, 1952 (*m diss* 1970), Pamela Mary, da of Leslie Dodson; 2ndly, 1980, Patricia Juliet, who *d* 1989, da of Hugo de Schanschieff; 3rdly, 1992, Sally Anne, da of Malcolm Fullerton Laing, and has issue living (by 1st *m*), Ian Charles Cavendish (Scarletts, Furnace Lane, Cowden, Kent), *b* 1954, — Susan Pamela, *b* 1955: *m* 1997, Philip Whall, of 101 Herne Hill Rd, SE24 0AD, — Rosemary Alison, *b* 1964: *m* 1997, Christopher Robinson, of 54 Fengates Rd, Redhill, Surrey, and has issue living, Patrick Christopher FitzRoy *b* 1999. *Residence –* Oaken Gates, Tompsets Bank, Forest Row, E Sussex RH18 5BG.

Granddaughter of late Sir Almeric William FitzRoy, KCB, KCVO, el son of Francis Horatio FitzRoy (infra):—

Issue of late Nigel Horatio Trevor FitzRoy, *b* 1889, *d* 1953: *m* 1st, 1917 (*m diss* 1928), Constance who *d* 1974, only da of late Capt Robert Henry Paul, RN, of The Highlands, Banbury; 2ndly, 1936, Diana Frances FITZROY-YATES, who *d* 1995, having *m* 2ndly, 1958, William Edward Yates, who *d* 1964, el da of late Brig-Arthur Francis Gore Pery-Knox-Gore, DSO (*see* E Limerick, colls):—

(By 2nd *m*) Susanna Diana Georgina, *b* 1937: *m* 1st, 1964 (*m diss* 1966), William Anthony Coleridge; 2ndly, 1967, George Henry Peter-Hoblyn (*see* Philipson-Stow, Bt, 1985 Edn), of Maizey Manor Farm, Ogbourne St Andrew, Marlborough, Wilts, and has issue living (by 2nd *m*), John FitzRoy, *b* 1968: *m* 1993, Isabel Hayes, and has issue living, Harry George FitzRoy *b* 1994, — Emma Frances, *b* 1970: *m* 1999, Maj Mark James Alexander Cann, late Queen's Royal Lancers, son of Maj John Cann, of Ascot, Berks.

Grandchildren of late Cyril Duncombe FitzRoy, yr son of late Francis Horatio FitzRoy, only son of late Adm Lord William FitzRoy, KCB, 5th son of 3rd Duke:—

Issue of late Charles Francis Mark FitzRoy, *b* 1909, *d* 1994: *m* 1936, Baroness Irmgard (North Lodge, Crimonmogate, Lonmay, Aberdeenshire), eldest da of late Baron Rudolf von Dincklage, of Hanover:—

Felix Rudolf (26 Cairnhill Gdns, St Andrews, Fife KY16 8QX), *b* 1938: MSc, PhD (Heidelberg): *m* 1976, Renate Brüninghaus, and has issue living, James Francis Stuart, *b* 1986, — Olga Henrietta, *b* 1982. —— Christina Margaret, *b* 1944; BSc: *m* 1974, Ali Kemál Caba, of Izmir, Turkey.

Descendants of late Lieut-Gen Charles FitzRoy (2nd son of Lord Augustus FitzRoy, 2nd son of 2nd Duke), who was *cr Baron Southampton* 1780 (see that title).

PREDECESSORS – **(1)** HENRY CHARLES FitzRoy, KG, 2nd natural son of King Charles II, by Barbara Villiers, Duchess of Cleveland; *cr Baron of Sudbury, Viscount Ipswich,* and *Earl of Euston* (peerage of England) 1672, and *Duke of Grafton* (peerage of England) 1675: *m* 1682, Isabella, in her own right Countess of Arlington, who in 1685 had *s* by special remainder her father, Henry Bennet, who had been *cr Baron Arlington* of Arlington, Middlesex (peerage of England) 1665, with special remainder, failing issue male, to the heirs of his body, and *Baron Arlington,* of Arlington, Middlesex, *Viscount Thetford,* and *Earl of Arlington* (peerage of England) 1672 with like special remainder, and in default of heirs of his body, with a further remainder to his brother, Sir John Bennet, KB, and the heirs male of his body; was Lord High Constable at Coronation of James II, and in 1685 commanded part of HM's forces at the landing of the Duke of Monmouth; was afterwards one of the first to desert his royal master for the Prince of Orange, in which cause he was wounded in storming the City of Cork, and *d* within a fortnight afterwards, 9th Oct 1690; *s* by his son **(2)** CHARLES, KG, 2nd Duke, who in 1723 *s* to his mother's peerages (ante): *m* 1713, Henrietta, sister of 2nd Duke of Beaufort; *d* 1757; *s* by his grandson **(3)** AUGUSTUS HENRY, KG, 3rd Duke; a Sec of State 1765, 1st Lord of the Treasury 1766, and Lord Privy Seal 1771: *m* 1st, 1756 (*m diss* 1769), Hon Anne Liddell, da of Henry, Baron Ravensworth (ext 1784); 2ndly, 1769, Elizabeth, da of Very Rev Sir Richard Wrottesley, 7th Bt; *d* 1811; *s* by his el son **(4)** GEORGE HENRY, KG, 4th Duke; Lord-Lieut of Suffolk: *m* 1784, Lady Charlotte Maria, da of 2nd Earl Waldegrave; *d* 1844; *s* by his son **(5)** HENRY, 5th Duke; sometime MP for Thetford: *m* 1812, Mary Caroline, da of late Adm Hon Sir George Berkeley, GCB (E Berkeley); *d* 1863; *s* by his el son **(6)** WILLIAM HENRY, 6th Duke; *b* 1819; MP for Thetford (*L*) 1847-63: *m* 1858, Hon Marie Louisa Anne, who *d* 1928, da of 3rd Baron Ashburton; *dsp* 21 May 1882; *s* by his brother **(7)** AUGUSTUS CHARLES LENNOX, KG, CB, 7th Duke, *b* 1821, a Gen in the Army; Crimean Campaign 1854 (medal with three clasps, Sardinian and Turkish medals, and 5th class Medjidie); an Equerry to Queen Victoria 1849-82, and an Hon Equerry to Queen Victoria 1882-1901, to King Edward VII 1901-10, and to King George V 1910-18: *m* 1847, Anna, who *d* 1857, da of James Balfour, of Whittinghame Hall, Berwick; *d* 1918; *s* by his son **(8)** ALFRED WILLIAM MAITLAND, 8th Duke; *b* 1850: *m* 1st, 1875, Margaret Rose, who *d* 1913, da of Eric Carrington Smith, of Ashfold, Sussex; 2ndly, 1916, Susanna Mary, who *d* 1961, da of Sir Mark John MacTaggart-Stewart, 1st Bt, and widow of 17th Baron Borthwick; *d* 1930; *s* by his grandson **(9)** JOHN CHARLES WILLIAM (son of William Henry Alfred, Viscount Ipswich), 9th Duke: *d* 1936, when the Barony of Arlington (*cr* 1672), and the Viscountcy of Thetford and the Earldom of Arlington (*cr* 1672) fell into abeyance between the sisters of the 9th Duke (*see* Bs Arlington); *s* in the Dukedom by his kinsman **(10)** CHARLES ALFRED EUSTON (son of late Rev Lord Charles Edward Fitz-Roy, 4th son of 7th Duke), 10th Duke, *b* 1892: *m* 1st, 1918, Lady Doreen Maria Josepha Sydney Buxton, who *d* 1923, da of 1st Earl Buxton; 2ndly, 1924, Lucy Eleanor, who *d* 1943, da of Sir George Stapylton Barnes, KCB, KCSI (Buxton, By *cr* 1840, colls); 3rdly, 1944, Rita Emily, who *d* 1970, da of late John Ralph Stockley Carr-Ellison, and widow of Lt-Cdr John Thurburn Currie, RN; *d* 1970; *s* by his el son **(11)** HUGH DENIS CHARLES, 11th Duke, and present peer; also Earl of Euston, Viscount Ipswich, and Baron Sudbury.

Graham, family name of Duke of Montrose.

Graham, Marquess of; son of Duke of Montrose.

GRAHAM OF EDMONTON, BARON (Graham) (Life Baron 1983)

(THOMAS) EDWARD GRAHAM, PC, son of Thomas Edward Graham, of Newcastle-upon-Tyne; *b* 26 March 1925; *ed* elementary sch, Workers' Educational Assocn Co-operative Coll, and Open Univ (BA); Member and Leader Enfield Council 1961-68; Nat Sec Co-operative Party 1967-74; PPS to Min of State, Dept of Prices and Consumer Protection 1974-76; a Lord Commr of HM Treasury 1976-79; Opposition Spokesman on Environment 1980-83; MP for Enfield, Edmonton (*Lab*) 1974-83; *cr Baron Graham of Edmonton*, of Edmonton, in Greater London (Life Baron) 1983, and PC 1998: *m* 1950, Margaret, da of Frederick Golding, of Dagenham, Essex, and has issue.
Residence – 2 Clerks Pierce, Loughton, Essex 1G10 1NR.

SONS LIVING

Hon Martin Nicholas, *b* 1957.
Hon Ian Stuart, *b* 1959.

Granard, Baron, title of Earl of Granard on Roll of HL.

GRANARD, EARL OF (Forbes) Sits as BARON (UK 1806) (Earl I 1684; Bt S 1628)

PETER ARTHUR EDWARD HASTINGS FORBES, 10th Earl, and 11th Baronet; *b* 15 March 1957; *s* 1992; *ed* Eton: *m* 1980, Nora Ann (Noreen), da of Robert Mitchell, of Upper Main St, Portarlington, co Leix, and has issue.

𝕬rms – Azure, three bears' heads couped at the neck argent, muzzled gules. 𝕮rest – A bear statant argent, guttée de sang, and muzzled gules. 𝕾upporters – *Dexter*, an unicorn erminois, armed, maned, tufted, and unguled or; *sinister*, a dragon wings elevated ermine.
Seat – Castle Forbes, Newtown Forbes, co Longford. *Residence* – Strathallan Cliff, Strathallan Rd, Onchan, Isle of Man.

SONS LIVING

JONATHAN PETER HASTINGS (*Viscount Forbes*), *b* 24 Dec 1981.
Hon David Robert Hastings, *b* 1084.
Hon Edward Hastings, *b* 1989.

DAUGHTER LIVING

Lady Lisa Ann, *b* 1986.

SISTERS LIVING

The incitement to glory is the firebrand of the mind

Susan, *b* 1948.
Patricia Moira, *b* 1950.
Caroline Mary, *b* 1954: *m* 1st, 1975 (*m diss* 19—), Dominick Charles Hamilton, yr son of Capt Hubert Charles Paulet

(Paul) Hamilton, of Moyne, Durrow, co Leix; 2ndly, 1983 (*m diss* 1998), Robert John George Dillon-Mahon, and has issue (by 2nd *m*) (*see* Mahon, Bt). *Residence* – Sainte Helene, Quartier Meaulx, 83830 Claviers, Callas, Var, France.

DAUGHTERS LIVING OF NINTH EARL

Lady Moira Beatrice, *b* 1951: *m* 1st, 1971 (*m diss* 1975), HH Prince Charles Antoine Marie Lamoral de Ligne de la Trémoïlle; 2ndly, 1978, José Guerrico, and has issue living (by 2nd *m*), Killian Arthur, *b* 1987, — Shannon Moira Kiara Beatrice, *b* 1983. *Residence* – 5 Avenue Princesse Alice, Monte Carlo.

Lady Georgina Anne, *b* 1952. *Residences* – 11 rue Louis de Savoie, Morges, Switzerland; Castle Forbes, Newtown Forbes, co Longford.

DAUGHTER LIVING OF EIGHTH EARL

Lady Moira Mary, *b* 1910: *m* 1st, 1934 (*m diss* under French civil law 1936), Count Louis de Brantes; 2ndly, 1942 (*m diss* 19—), Count Rossi di Montelera. *Residence* – 16 Chemin des Mouettes, 1007 Lausanne, Switzerland.

MOTHER LIVING

Joan, 3rd da of A. Edward Smith, of Sherlockstown House, Sallins, co Kildare: *m* 1947, Hon John Forbes, yr son of 8th Earl of Granard, who *d* 1982. *Residence* – Perigord II, 6 rue des Lacets St Leon, Monte Carlo, Monaco.

COLLATERAL BRANCHES LIVING

Issue of late Col Hon Donald Alexander Forbes, DSO, MVO, 4th son of 7th Earl, *b* 1880, *d* 1938: *m* 1918, Mary Doreen, who *d* 1987, da of late Andrew Sherlock Lawson (*see* V Mountgarret, 1943 Edn):—
Penelope (*Lady Sitwell*), *b* 1923: *m* 1952, Sir Sacheverell Reresby Sitwell, 7th Bt. *Residences* – 4 Southwick Place, W2 2TN; Renishaw Hall, Derbyshire.

Grandchildren of late Lt-Col George Francis Reginald Forbes, eldest son of late Col Hon William Francis Forbes, yr brother of 7th Earl:—
Issue of late Lt-Col (Walter) Arthur Hastings Forbes, *b* 1905, *d* 1987: *m* 1946, Joan Margaret, who *d* 1995, formerly wife of late Maj Robert Malise Keith Murray (*see* Murray of Ochtertyre, 1970 Edn), and elder da of late Maj Hugh Kettles-Roy, of Nairobi, Kenya:—
Peter Patrick Spencer, *b* 1949; *ed* Milton Abbey, RMA Sandhurst, and Manchester Univ: *m* 1981, Victoria Anne, da of Harry Tudor Bigge, of Lower Lease, Saunton, Braunton, N Devon, and has issue living, Arthur Edward Patrick, *b* 1987, — George Harry Hastings, *b* (twin) 1987, — Katherine Anne, *b* 1983, — Serena Victoria, *b* 1985. *Residence* – The Old Rectory, Farnham, Blandford Forum, Dorset DT11 8DE. —— Rolleen Anne, *b* 1947: *m* 1974, James Christopher Barclay, and has issue living, Robert James, *b* 1977, — Georgina Anne, *b* 1978. *Residence* – Rivers Hall, Waldringfield, Woodbridge, Suffolk.

PREDECESSORS – (1) *Sir* ARTHUR Forbes, Knt, great-great-grandson of the Hon Patrick, 3rd son of 2nd Lord Forbes; *cr* a *Baronet* 1628; obtained grants of land in co Longford; killed in a duel 1632; *s* by his son (2) *Rt Hon Sir* ARTHUR, PC, 2nd Bt; Lt-Gen in the Army; MP for Mullingar 1661; having served under Montrose for the Royal Cause in Scotland, was after the Restoration appointed Marshal of the Army in Ireland, and constituted one of the Lords Justices 1671 and 1673; raised in 1684 the 18th Royal Irish Regt; *cr Baron Clanehugh* and *Viscount Granard* (peerage of Ireland) 1675, and *Earl of Granard* (peerage of Ireland) 1684; *d* 1696; *s* by his son (3) ARTHUR, 2nd Earl; was deprived of his command of the 18th Royal Irish Regt and imprisoned in the Tower; *d* 1734; *s* by his son (4) GEORGE, 3rd Earl; an eminent Adm; Ambassador to Court of Muscovy; called to House of Peers as Lord Forbes in lifetime of his father; *d* 1765; *s* by his son (5) GEORGE, 4th Earl; a Lt-Gen in the Army; *d* 1769; *s* by his son (6) GEORGE, 5th Earl; *d* 1780; *s* by his son (7) GEORGE, 6th Earl; a Gen in the Army, and Clerk of the Crown and Hanaper in Ireland; *cr Baron Granard*, of Castle Donington, co Leicester (peerage of United Kingdom) 1806; *d* 1837; *s* by his grandson (8) GEORGE ARTHUR HASTINGS, KP, 7th Earl (son of Major-Gen George, Viscount Forbes, el son of 6th Earl, by Frances Mary, VA, da of late William Territt, Esq, LLD, of Chilton Hall, Suffolk), *b* 1836; was Lord-Lieut of co Leitrim 1856-72: *m* 1st, 1858, Jane Colclough, who *d* 1872, da of Hamilton Knox Grogan-Morgan, Esq, of Johnstown Castle, Wexford; 2ndly, 1873, Hon Frances Mary, who *d* 1920, da of 12th Baron Petre; *d* 1889; *s* by his el son (9) BERNARD ARTHUR WILLIAM PATRICK HASTINGS, PC, KP, GCVO, 8th Earl; *b* 1874; Lieut-Col 8th Batn City of London Regt, Lieut-Col Reserve of Officers (Scots Guards), Vice-Adm of Province of Connaught, and a Dep Speaker of House of Lords; a Lord-in-Waiting to King Edward VII 1905, Master of the Horse to King Edward VII 1905-10, and to King George V 1910-15; Assist Postmaster-Gen 1906-9, and again Master of the horse 1924-36; a Member of Senate, S Ireland June 1921, and of Irish Free State Dec 1922 to Dec 1934; HM's Comptroller at Ascot 1936-45: *m* 1909, Beatrice, OBE, who *d* 1972, da of late Ogden Mills, of East 69th Street, New York, and Staatsburg, Dutchess Co, New York; *d* 1948; *s* by his el son (10) ARTHUR PATRICK HASTINGS, AFC, 9th Earl; *b* 1915; Air Commodore RAF Vol Reserve, European War 1939-45 (despatches, AFC, Cdr of Legion of Honour, Officer of American Legion of Merit, 4th Class Order of George I of Greece, French Croix de Guerre, Polish Cross of Valour): *m* 1949, Marie Madeleine Eugène, who *d* 1990, yst da of late Jean Maurel, of Millau, Aveyron, and formerly wife of late Prince Humbert de Faucigny Lucinge; *d* 1992; *s* by his nephew (11) PETER ARTHUR EDWARD HASTINGS (only son of late Hon John Forbes, yr son of 8th Earl), 10th Earl and present peer; also Viscount Granard, Baron Clanehugh, and Baron Granard.

Granby, Marquess of; son of Duke of Rutland.

Grant of Grant, family name of Baron Strathspey.

Grant, Ogilvie-, family name of Earl of Seafield.

GRANTCHESTER, BARON (Suenson-Taylor) (Baron UK 1953)

PEACE AND HOLY QUIET

CHRISTOPHER JOHN SUENSON-TAYLOR, 3rd Baron; *b* 8 April 1951; *s* 1995; *ed* Winchester, and London Sch of Economics (BSc); Dairy Farmer and Cattle Breeder: *m* 1973, Jacqueline, da of Dr Leo Jaffé, and has issue.

Arms – Quarterly, 1st and 4th sable, on a fesse engrailed between in chief a fleur-de-lys between two annulets or, and in base as many like annulets a lion passant of the field, *Taylor*; 2nd and 3rd gules, in chief two swans rousant proper each crowned with an antique crown or, and in base barry wavy of six argent and azure, *Suenson*. Crests – 1st, issuant from a crown palisado or an unicorn's head sable and armed and charged on the neck with an annulet of gold and holding in the mouth an acorn leaved and slipped proper, *Taylor*, 2nd, issuant from a coronet composed of eight roses gules seeded argent set upon a rim or, a swan rousant proper crowned with an antique crown gold, *Suenson*. Supporters – *Dexter*, an unicorn sable armed, and crined or, gorged with a collar argent, thereon a fesse wavy azure; *sinister*, a lion or, gorged with a collar of four hearts gules.
Residence – Lower House Farm, Back Coole Lane, Audlem, Crewe, Cheshire.

SONS LIVING

Hon JESSE DAVID, *b* 6 June 1977.
Hon Adam Joel, *b* 1987.

DAUGHTERS LIVING

Hon Holly Rachel, *b* 1975.
Hon Hannah Robin, *b* 1984.

BROTHERS LIVING

Hon Jeremy Kenneth (twin) *b* 1951; *ed* Winchester: *m* 19—, Lindsay Anne Kirby, and has issue living, Daniel, *b* 1983, — Rowan, *b* 1974, — Laurel, *b* 1979, — Zoë, *b* 1982. *Residence* – Church Farm, Chew Stoke, Chew Magna, Bristol.
Hon James Gunnar, *b* 1955; *ed* Eton, and Kingston Univ (BA); Co Dir: *m* 1981, Gillian Susan, yr da of Peter Ayling, of Worcester Park, Surrey, and has issue living, Andrew James, *b* 1985, — Jonathan Gunnar, *b* 1991, — Katherine Joyce, *b* 1988. *Residence* – Birches Over, Wood Lane, St George's Hill, Weybridge, Surrey KT13 0JU.

SISTERS LIVING

Hon Janet Elizabeth Gudrun, *b* 1949; *ed* Cheltenham Ladies Coll, and St Hilda's Coll, Oxford (MA); Conservator of paintings: *m* 1973 (*m diss* 1995), Gerald Edgar Grimstone, of 103 Home Park Rd, SW19, and has issue living, Toby Stephen Gunnar, *b* 1975, — Jenny Elizabeth May, *b* 1979, — Anna Rose Yvonne, *b* 1982.

Hon Deborah Katherine Louise, *b* 1957; *ed* Cheltenham Ladies Coll: *m* 1977, Michael Paul Jones, and has issue living, Christopher Michael, *b* 1987, — Elizabeth Lily, *b* 1992.

Hon Kirsten Victoria Mary, *b* 1961; *ed* Cheltenham Ladies Coll, Godolphin and Latymer, Liverpool Univ (BA), and London Univ (BSc): *m* 1988, Keith Lobban.

AUNT LIVING (*Daughter of 1st Baron*)

Hon Monica Esmé Ebba, *b* 1926; *ed* Queen's Coll, London and Newnham Coll, Camb (MA): *m* 1951 (*m diss* 1965), Graeme Spotswood Parish, and has had issue, Andrew Graeme Spotswood, *b* 1954; *ed* Westminster; *d* in an accident 1973, — Alexandra Francesca Spotswood, *b* 1953: *m* 1987, Nicholas Burnell, and has issue living, Joss Elliott Crystal (a son) *b* 1987, Brittany Leah *b* 1991.

WIDOW LIVING OF SECOND BARON

BETTY (*Dowager Baroness Grantchester*), elder da of late Sir John Moores, CBE: *m* 1947, the 2nd Baron Grantchester, CBE, QC, who *d* 1995. *Residence* – The Gate House, Coombe Wood Rd, Kingston Hill, Surrey.

PREDECESSORS – **(1)** *Sir* ALFRED JESSE Suenson-Taylor, OBE, son of late Alfred George Taylor, of Stowford, Sutton, Surrey; *b* 1893; Chm of London and Manchester Assurance Co 1953-61; Past Pres of London Liberal Party and joint Hon Treas of Liberal Party Organisation; initiated unofficial meetings of EFTA Parliamentarians at Strasbourg; Delegate to Assemblies Council of Europe and W European Union 1957-66; *cr Baron Grantchester*, of Knightsbridge, in City of Westminster (peerage of UK) 1953: *m* 1920, Mara Henrietta (Mamie), who *d* 1976, da of late Albert Suenson, of Copenhagen; *d* 1976; *s* by his son **(2)** KENNETH BENT, CBE, QC, 2nd Baron, *b* 1921; Bar Middle Temple, Recorder of the Crown Courts, Dep Chm in House of Lords: *m* 1947, Betty, elder da of late Sir John Moores, CBE; *d* 1995; *s* by his elder son **(3)** CHRISTOPHER JOHN, 3rd Baron, and present peer.

GRANTLEY, BARON (Norton) (Baron GB 1782)

I follow a long line of ancestry

RICHARD WILLIAM BRINSLEY NORTON, 8th Baron; *b* 30 Jan 1956; *s* 1995; *ed* Ampleforth, and New Coll, Oxford; Pres of Oxford Union 1976; Knt of Honour and Devotion of Sov Mil Order of Malta; a Councillor of Royal Borough of Kensington and Chelsea 1982-86; Merchant Banker.

Arms – Azure, a maunch ermine, surmounted by a bend gules. **Crest** – A Moor's head affrontée, couped at the shoulders proper, wreathed round the temples with laurel, and round the neck a torse, argent and azure. **Supporters** – *Dexter*, a lion, and *sinister*, a griffin, both argent and ducally gorged or, and pendent from the coronets, by a red ribbon, a shield of the arms of *Norton*.
Residence – 8 Halsey St, SW3. *Clubs* – White's, Pratt's.

BROTHER LIVING

Hon FRANCIS JOHN HILARY (12 Amberley Court, Overton Rd, SW9), *b* 28 Sept 1960.

AUNT LIVING (*Daughter of 6th Baron*)

Hon Sarah Katherine Elinor (42 Melton Court, Old Brompton Rd, SW7 3JH), *b* 1920: *m* 1st, 1945 (*m diss* 1953), 3rd Viscount Astor, who *d* 1966; 2ndly, 1953 (*m diss* 1965), Maj Thomas Michael Baring, Derbyshire Yeo (*see* B Northbrook, colls).

WIDOW LIVING OF SEVENTH BARON

Lady DEIRDRE FREDA MARY HARE (*Baroness Grantley*), da of 5th Earl of Listowel: *m* 1955, 7th Baron Grantley, MC, who *d* 1995. *Residences* – Markenfield Hall, Ripon, N Yorks; 2 Warwick Sq, SW1.

PREDECESSORS – **(1)** *Sir* FLETCHER Norton, KB, PC; MP for Appleby 1754-61, and for Wigan 1761-82, Solicitor-Gen 1761, Attorney-Gen 1763 and Speaker of the House of Commons 1769-82; *cr Lord Grantley, Baron of Markenfield*, co York (peerage of United Kingdom) 1782: *m* 1741, Grace, da of Sir William Chapple; *d* 1789; *s* by his son **(2)** WILLIAM, 2nd Baron; *d* 1822; *s* by his nephew **(3)** FLETCHER, 3rd Baron, son of Hon Fletcher, 2nd son of 1st Baron; present at Quatre Bras and Waterloo: *m* 1825, Charlotte, da of Sir William Beechey, the artist; *dsp* 1875; *s* by his nephew **(4)** THOMAS BRINSLEY, 4th Baron, 2nd son of Hon George Chapple Norton, brother of 3rd Baron; *b* 1831: *m* 1854, Maria Chiara Eliza, who *d* 1892, da of Signor Federigo; *d* 1877; *s* by his son **(5)** JOHN RICHARD BRINSLEY, 5th Baron; *b* 1855: *m* 1st, 1879, Katharine, who *d* 1897, da of late William Henry McVickar, of USA; 2ndly, 1899, Alice, who *d* 1942, natural da of 7th Viscount Ranelagh; *d* 1943; *s* by his son **(6)** RICHARD HENRY BRINSLEY, 6th Baron; *b* 1892; *m* 1919, Jean Mary, who *d* 1945, da of Sir David Alexander Kinloch, CB, MVO, 11th Bt; *d* 1954; *s* by his only son **(7)** JOHN RICHARD BRINSLEY, MC, 7th Baron, *b* 1923; Member of Lloyd's; 1939-45 War in Italy as Capt Gren Gds: *m* 1955, Lady Deirdre Freda Mary Hare, da of 5th Earl of Listowel; *d* 1995; *s* by his elder son **(8)** RICHARD WILLIAM BRINSLEY, 8th Baron and present peer.

GRANVILLE, EARL (Leveson-Gower) (Earl UK 1833)
(Name pronounced "Looson-Gore")

You may break, but you will not bend me

GRANVILLE GEORGE FERGUS LEVESON-GOWER, 6th Earl; *b* 10 Sept 1959; *s* 1996; *ed* Eton; Page of Honour to HM The Queen 1973-74: *m* 1997, Anne, only da of Bernard Topping, of Lanark, and has issue.

Arms – Quarterly: 1st and 4th, barry of eight, argent and gules, a cross flory sable, *Gower*; 2nd azure, three laurel leaves or, *Leveson*; 3rd gules, three clarions or, *Granville*; in the centre a crescent for difference. **Crest** – A wolf passant argent, collared and lined or. **Supporters** – Two wolves argent, plain collared, and line reflexed over the back gold, and charged on the shoulder with an escutcheon gules thereon a clarion or.
Residence – Callernish, Lochmaddy, Isle of North Uist, Western Isles.

DAUGHTER LIVING

Lady Rose Alice, *b* 1998.

BROTHER LIVING

Hon NIALL JAMES, *b* 24 Aug 1963: *m* 1996, Amanda, twin da of Derrick J. Blaxell, of Antingham, Norfolk. *Residence* –

SISTER LIVING

Lady Marcia Rose Aileen, *b* 1961: *m* 1986, Jonathan Charles Bulmer, yst son of late Edward Charles Bulmer, and has issue living, James Alexander Howard, *b* 1992, — Hector Charles Marcus, *b* 1993, — Hesper Rose Constance, *b* 1990, — Lara Christabel May, *b* 1995. *Residence* – Amhuinnsuidhe Castle, Isle of Harris.

AUNT LIVING *(Daughter of 4th Earl)*

Lady Mary Cecilia, *b* 1917: *m* 1956, Samuel Wittewronge Clayton, son of late Brig-Gen Sir Gilbert Falkingham Clayton, KCMG, KBE, CB, and has issue living, Gilbert Falkingham, *b* 1958; a Page of Honour to HM Queen Elizabeth The Queen Mother 1973-74: *m* 1994, Rosalind N., da of late Francis Mullen, and of Mrs Nancy Shawcross, — Rose Cecilia, *b* 1960: *m* 1993, William W. Stancer, son of J. A. Stancer, of Old Rectory, Wick Rissington, Glos. *Residence* – 4 Cumberland Lodge, Windsor Great Park, Berks.

WIDOW LIVING OF FIFTH EARL

DOON AILEEN (*Dowager Countess Granville*), da of late Flight-Lieut Hon Brinsley Sheridan Bushe Plunket, RAF Vol Reserve (*see* B Plunket): *m* 1958, Maj the 5th Earl Granville, MC, who *d* 1996. *Residence* – Callernish, Lochmaddy, Isle of North Uist, Western Isles.

PREDECESSORS – **(1)** *Lord* GRANVILLE Leveson-Gower, GCB, PC, yst son of 1st Marquess of Stafford (*see* D Sutherland); *b* 1773; was sometime Sec at War, and successively Ambassador to Russia, Holland and France, *cr Viscount Granville* (peerage of United Kingdom) 1815, and *Baron Leveson*, of Stone, co Stafford, and *Earl Granville* (peerage of United Kingdom) 1833: *m* 1809, Lady Henrietta Elizabeth Cavendish, who *d* 1862, da of 5th Duke of Devonshire; *d* 1846; *s* by his son **(2)** GRANVILLE GEORGE, KG, PC, 2nd Earl; *b* 1815; MP for Morpeth (*L*) 1837-40, and for Lichfield 1841-6; was Under-Sec for Foreign Affairs 1840-41, Vice-Pres of Board of Trade 1848-51, Sec of State for Foreign Affairs 1851-2, 1870-74, and 1880-85, Lord Pres of Council 1852-4, 1855-8, and 1859-66, Chancellor of Duchy of Lancaster 1854-5, Ambassador Extraor to Russia at coronation of Alexander II, 1856, and Sec of State for the Colonies 1868-70 and 1886; sometime Constable of Dover Castle, and Lord Warden of the Cinque Ports: *m* 1st, 1840, Marie Louise Pelline, who *d*

1860, da of Emeric Joseph, Duc de Dalberg, and widow of Sir Ferdinand Richard Edward Acton, 7th Bt; 2ndly, 1865, Castalia Rosalind, who *d* 1938, da of Walter Campbell, of Islay; *d* 1891; *s* by his el son (3) GRANVILLE GEORGE, GCMG, GCVO, PC, 3rd Earl, *b* 1872; a Lord-in-Waiting to Queen Victoria 1895-1905, to King Edward VII, 1905-10, and to King George V 1910-15, Envoy Extraor and Min Plen to Greece 1917-21, to Denmark 1921-6, and to the Netherlands 1926-8, and Ambassador Extraor and Plen to Belgium and Luxembourg 1928-33: *m* 1900, Nina Ayesha, who *d* 1955, da of late Walter Baring; *d* 1939; *s* by his brother (4) WILLIAM SPENCER, KG, KCVO, CB, DSO, 4th Earl; *b* 1880; Vice-Adm; Ch of Staff and Maintenance Capt the Nore 1924-27, and Rear-Adm Comdg Coast of Scotland 1931-33; Lieut-Gov of Isle of Man 1937-45, and Gov of N Ireland 1945-52; 1914-18 War (DSO): *m* 1916, Lady Rose Constance Bowes-Lyon, GCVO, LLD, who *d* 1967, da of 14th Earl of Strathmore; *d* 1953; *s* by his son (5) GRANVILLE JAMES, MC, 5th Earl; *b* 1918, Maj Coldm Gds (Supplementary Reserve), 1939-45 War in Tunisia and Italy (twice wounded, despatches, MC); DL Inverness-shire 1974, Vice Lord Lieut Islands Area, Western Isles 1976-83, Lord Lieut 1983-93, Pres Navy League 1953-66: *m* 1958, Doon Aileen, da of late Flight-Lieut Hon Brinsley Sheridan Bushe Plunket, RAF Vol Reserve (*see* B Plunket); *d* 1996; *s* by his elder son (6) GRANVILLE GEORGE FERGUS, 6th Earl and present peer; also Viscount Granville, and Baron Leveson.

GRANVILLE OF EYE, BARONY OF (Granville) (Extinct 1998)

DAUGHTER LIVING OF LIFE BARON

Hon Linda Elizabeth Mary, *b* 1949: *m* 19—, Emmanuel Gounalakis.

WIDOW LIVING OF LIFE BARON

ELIZABETH (*Baroness Granville of Eye*), da of late Rev William Cecil Hunter, British Mission Sch, India: *m* 1943, Baron Granville of Eye (Life Baron), who *d* 1998. *Residence* – 112 Charlton Lane, Cheltenham.

GRANVILLE-WEST, BARONY OF (West) (Extinct 1984)

SON LIVING OF LIFE BARON

Hon Gerald Hugh Granville, *b* 1942: *m* 1969, Barbara, da of Arthur Strath, of Ellwood Dene, Kilndown, Cranbrook, Kent, and has issue.

DAUGHTER LIVING OF LIFE BARON

Hon Vera Lesley Meryl, *b* 1937: *m* 1959, William Smith, of Hollycroft, Sunnybank Rd, Griffthstown Mon, and has issue.

WIDOW LIVING OF LIFE BARON

VERA (*Baroness Granville-West*), JP, da of J. Hopkins, of Pontypool: *m* 1937, Baron Granville-West (Life Baron), who *d* 1984.

GRAVES, BARON (Graves) (Baron I 1794)

EVELYN PAGET GRAVES, 9th Baron; *b* 17 May 1926; *s* 1994: *m* 1957, Marjorie Ann, OAM, da of late Dr Sidney Ernest Holder, of Wallingford, Berks, and has had issue.

Arms – Gules, an eagle, displayed or ducally crowned argent, on a canton of the last an anchor proper. **Crest** – A demi-eagle, displayed and erased or, encircled round the body and below the wings by a ducal coronet argent. **Supporters** – Two royal vultures, wings close proper.
Residence – Woodlands, 405 Mole Creek Rd, Deloraine, 7304 Tasmania.

The eagle does not catch flies

SONS LIVING AND DECEASED

Hon TIMOTHY EVELYN, *b* 27 March 1960.
†*Hon* Simon Paget, *b* 1963; *d* 1997.

DAUGHTERS LIVING

Hon Wendy Susan, *b* 1958.
Hon Philippa Ann, *b* 1962.

SISTER LIVING

Diana Wellesley, *b* 1934: *m* 1st, 1956 (*m diss* 1974), Edgar Mark Wolfhagen; 2ndly, 1974, Guy Paul Emile Peltzer, of Ravensworth, Langford, 7301 Tasmania, and has issue living (by 1st *m*), Julian Mark, *b* 1957, — Martin Charles, *b* 1959, — Philip Gerret Wellesley, *b* 1963, — Quentin Evelyn, *b* 1969.

COLLATERAL BRANCHES LIVING

Granddaughters of late Capt Hon Adolphus Edward Paget Graves (brother of 5th Baron), 5th son of Hon Henry Richard Graves, 3rd son of 2nd Baron:—
Issue of late Lt-Cmdr Vernon North Graves, DSC, RN *b* 1911, *d* 1960: *m* 1947, Elizabeth Constance (90 Stockton Lane, York YO3 0BS), da of late Capt Robert Francis Uniacke Penrose FitzGerald, RN:—
Janice Iona Penrose (18 Market Place, Kirkbymoorside, York YO6 6DA), *b* 1947: *m* 1st, 1968 (*m diss* 1974), Stephen Van Simons; 2ndly, 1980, Christopher Bernard Rose, and has issue living (by 1st *m*), Isobel Jane, *b* 1972, — (by 2nd *m*) Thomas George, *b* 1981. —— Sarah Frances Paget (90 Stockton Lanc, York YO3 0BS), *b* 1950: *m* 1979, Iannis Tamvakis, and has issue living, Ewan Ferenc GRAVES-TAMVAKIS, *b* 1975, — Charlotte Elizabeth GRAVES-TAMVAKIS, *b* (twin) 1975.

Granddaughter of late Capt Hon Adolphus Edward Paget Graves, 4th son of 2nd Baron:—
Issue of late Cyril Edward Cuthbert Hare Graves, *b* 1860, *d* 1946: *m* 1916, Constance Katherine, who *d* 1951, da of late François Chrysostom Mouflet, of Leamington:—
Mary Caroline Margot, *b* 1919: *m* 1942: *m* 1942 (*m diss* 1964), Albert Arthur Puddick, who *d* 1994, and *d* 1995, leaving issue, Robert Arthur Graves, *b* 1944; *ed* Cranleigh: *m* 1st, 1967 (*m diss* 1990), Jane Margaret Ferrand; 2ndly, 1991, Melanie Anne, da of Richard Alastair Stuart-Hunt, and has issue living (by 1st *m*), Simon Nicholas Graves *b* 1969, Julian Urling Graves *b* 1970, (by 2nd *m*) Charles Oscar Graves *b* 1993, — David Stewart Graves, *b* 1946; *ed* Cranleigh: *m* 1972, Sarah Elizabeth, da of Antony Lamb, and has issue living, Michael Antony Graves *b* 1974, Annabel Sarah *b* 1977, — Christopher Nicholas Graves, *b* 1952; *ed* Cranleigh: *m* 1992, Selena Ann, da of John Thomas Hobbs, and has issue living, Sophie Arabella Graves *b* 1995.

PREDECESSORS – **(1)** THOMAS GRAVES, 2nd son of late Rear-Adm Thomas Graves, of Thanckes, Cornwall; *b* 1725; Adm of the White; was second in command under Lord Howe at great Naval Victory of June 1st, 1794 (*cr* Baron and granted pension of £1,000 per annum): *m* 1771, Elizabeth, who *d* 1827, da of late William Peere Williams, of Cadhay, Devon; *cr Lord Graves, Baron of Gravesend,* co Londonderry (peerage of Ireland) 1794: *d* 1802; *s* by his son **(2)** THOMAS NORTH, 2nd Baron; MP; a Lord of the Bedchamber and Comptroller of the Household to HRH the Duke of Cumberland: *m* 1803, Lady Mary Paget, who *d* 1835, yst da of 1st Earl of Uxbridge, and sister of 1st Marquess of Anglesey, KG, *d* 1830, *s* by his son **(3)** WILLIAM THOMAS, 3rd Baron, *b* 1804: *m* 1st, 1829, Sophie Therese, who *d* 1833, da of Gen Berthier, and widow of Gen Count Bruyere; 2ndly, Louise Adèle Malene, who *d* 1877; *d* 1870; *s* by his son **(4)** CLARENCE EDWARD, *b* 1847: *m* 1870, Katherine Frederica, who *d* 1926, da of Sir Thomas Wilham Clinton Murdoch, KCMG; *d* 1904; *s* by his cousin **(5)** HENRY CYRIL PERCY (son of late Hon Henry Richard Graves, 3rd son of 2nd Baron), 5th Baron, *b* 1847: *m* 1870, Elizabeth Ellen, who *d* 1914, yst da of late Henry Craven, of Wickham Hall, Kent; *d* 1914; *s* by his son **(6)** CLARENCE PERCY RIVERS, 6th Baron, *b* 1871: *m* 1903, his cousin, Mary Ada Isabel, who *d* 1962, da of late Edward Corbett Parker; *d* 1937; *s* by his cousin **(7)** HENRY ALGERNON CLAUDE (son of late Claude Thomas Graves, son of late Hon Henry Richard Graves, 3rd son of 2nd Baron), 7th Baron *b* 1877: *m* 1909 (*m diss* 1922), Vera Blanche Neville, who *d* 1953, da of late Alfred Neville Shepp: *d* 1963: *s* by his son **(8)** PETER GEORGE WELLESLEY, 8th Baron, *b* 1911: Actor: *m* 1960, Winifred Ruby (actress as Vanessa Lee), who *d* 1992, da of Alfred Moule, and widow of Warde Morgan; *d* 1994; *s* by his kinsman **(9)** EVELYN PAGET (only son of late Alwyn Montague Graves, 2nd son of Capt Hon Adolphus Edward Paget Graves (brother of 5th Baron), 5th son of Hon Henry Richard Graves, 3rd son of 2nd Baron), 9th Baron and present peer.

GRAY, LORD (Campbell-Gray) (Lord S 1445)

ANGUS DIARMID IAN CAMPBELL-GRAY, 22nd Lord; *b* 3 July 1931; *s* 1946; *ed* Eton: *m* 1st, 1959, Patricia Margaret, who *d* 1987, only da of late Capt Philip Sylvester Alexander, 8th Hussars (*see* E Caledon, colls, 1985 Edn); 2ndly, 1994, Cecilia Wilfrida, elder da of late John Robert Dimsdale (grandson of 7th Baron Dimsdale), and widow of Paul Williams, and has issue by 1st *m*.

Arms – Gules a lion rampant within a bordure engrailed argent, over all a label of two points or, each point charged gyronny of eight or and sable. Crest – An anchor in pole or. Supporters – Two lions guardant gules charged with a label as in the arms.
Residence – Airds Bay, Taynuilt, Argyll. *Clubs* – Carlton, MCC.

SON LIVING (*By 1st marriage*)

Hon ANDREW GODFREY DIARMID STUART (*Master of Gray*), *b* 3 Sept 1964: *m* 1993, Hon Lucy Elton, yst da of 2nd Baron Elton, and has issue living, Alexander Godfrey Edward Diarmid, *b* 7 Oct 1996. *Residence* – Airds Bay House, Taynuilt, Argyll PA35 1JR.

DAUGHTERS LIVING (*By 1st marriage*)

Hon Lucinda Margaret, *b* 1961.
Hon Iona Doreen, *b* 1962.
Hon (Cethlyn) Isobell, *b* 1969.

WIDOW LIVING OF BROTHER OF TWENTYSECOND LORD

Wendy Helen Katharine, yr da of late William Herbert Dunlop, of Doonside, Ayrshire: *m* 1963, Hon Cailain Douglas Campbell-Gray, who *d* 1994, having been raised to the rank of a Baron's son 1950, yr brother of 22nd Lord, and has issue (see colls, infra). *Residence* – Fanamor, Taynuilt, Argyll PA35 1HR.

COLLATERAL BRANCHES LIVING

Issue of late Hon Cailain Douglas Campbell-Gray, yr brother of 22nd Lord, *b* 1934, *d* 1994: *m* 1963, Wendy Helen Katharine (ante), yr da of late William Herbert Dunlop, of Doonside, Ayrshire:—
James Douglas, *b* 1966. *Residence* – 12 Wetherby Gdns, SW5. ——— Charlotte Anne, *b* 1968: *m* 1995, Charles T. F. White, son of Harvey White, of London. *Residence* – 29 Montefiore St, SW8 3TL.

Issue of late Hon Fiona Faith Campbell-Gray, sister of 22nd Lord, *b* 1933, *d* 1991: *m* 1955, Maj (Ronald Hugh) Desmond Fabling, 14 PWO The Scinde Horse (IA), and 1st Royal Dragoons (ret), who *d* 1974:—
Victoria Theresa FABLING, *b* 1958; has resumed her maiden name: *m* 1993 (*m diss* 1995), Nicolas A. Shugar, elder son of Alan Shugar, of Manor Park, Bristol. *Residence* – 1644 Mission Hill Rd, Westbank, BC, Canada V4T 2M4. ——— Fenella Mary, *b* 1963: *m* 1992 Stephen Barker. *Residence* – 7 Hanover Av, Feltham, Middx TW13 4JR.

Issue of late Christine Anne Campbell-Gray, sister of 22nd Lord, *b* 1938, *d* 1987: *m* 1960, Lt-Col Brian Joseph Lockhart, Blues and Royals, of Dower House, Maugersbury, Cotswold, Glos:—
Crispin Alexander LOCKHART, *b* 1967; Maj Blues and Royals: *m* 1997, Lucy Ellen, da of John Richard Conway Lloyd, of Argent Manor, Stutton, Suffolk (*see* E Westmeath, colls), and has issue living, Oliver Brian, *b* 1999. ——— Edward Angus LOCKHART (adopted son), *b* 1966. ——— Serena Emily (*Hon Mrs Nicholas Jopling*) (adopted da), *b* 1965: *m* 1st, 1989 (*m diss* 1992), Patrick James, Lord Gillford, only son of 7th Earl of Clanwilliam; 2ndly, 1996, Hon Nicholas M. F. Jopling, eldest son of Baron Jopling, PC (Life Baron), and has issue (by 1st *m*) (*see* E Clanwilliam). *Residence* – 53 Richborne Terrace, SW8 1AT.

Issue of late Hon Thora Zelma Grace Gray, da of Eveleen, Lady Gray, *b* 1875, *d* 1966: *m* 1911, Edward Lorne Frederic Clough-Taylor (D Argyll), who *d* 1947:—
Cara Prunella (19 Sherbrooke Rd, SW6), *b* 1919.

Descendants of late Hon Archibald Stuart, 2nd son of late Hon Jean Gray (el da of 11th Lord), who *m* 1763, 9th Earl of Moray (see that title).

PREDECESSORS – (1) ANDREW, son of Sir Andrew Gray; successively Ambassador to England, Master of the Household to King James II, and a Warden of the Marches; *cr Lord Gray* (peerage of Scotland), 1444-5, according to Exchequer Rolls; *s* by his grandson (2) ANDREW, 2nd Lord; a Justiciary of Scotland; *s* by his son (3) PATRICK, 3rd Lord; *d* 1541; *s* by his nephew (4) PATRICK (son of Gilbert Gray, 2nd son of 2nd Lord); *d* 1584; *s* by his son (5) PATRICK, 5th Lord, *b* 1538; a Lord of Session; *d* 1609; *s* by his son (6) PATRICK, 6th Lord, *b* 1584; *d* 1611; *s* by his son (7) ANDREW, 7th Lord; obtained a new patent with remainder to William Gray, husband of his only da Anne, and his heirs male, and failing which to Sir William Gray, of Pittendrum, father of William Gray (ante), and his heirs male whatsoever; *s* by his grandson **(8)** PATRICK, 8th Lord, son of Anne and William Gray (ante); resigned his honours Feb 1707, and in the same month obtained a new patent with the former precedency with remainder to John Gray, of Crichie, husband of his da Marjory, and the heirs of their bodies, and failing which to the el heir female without division; in virtue of this patent **(9)** JOHN GRAY (ante) became 9th Lord, even during the lifetime of Patrick, 8th Lord; John *d* 1724; *s* by his son **(10)** JOHN, 10th Lord; *d* 1738; *s* by his son **(11)** JOHN, 11th Lord; *d* 1782; *s* by his third son **(12)** CHARLES, 12th Lord; was Capt 1st Dragoon Guards; *d* unmarried 1786; *s* by his brother **(13)** WILLIAM JOHN, 13th Lord; *d* unmarried 1807; *s* by his brother **(14)** FRANCIS, 14th Lord; was Postmaster Gen of Scotland; *d* 1842; *s* by his son **(15)** JOHN, 15th Lord; a Representative Peer; *dsp* 1867; *s* by his sister **(16)** MADELINA; *d* unmarried 1869; *s* by her niece **(17)** MARGARET, da of Hon Margaret, 2nd da of 14th Lord, and wife of Hon David Henry Murray, son of 3rd Earl of Mansfield; *d* 1878; *s* by her cousin **(18)** GEORGE PHILIP, 14th Earl of Moray (heir male of Hon Jean el da of 11th Lord Gray ante); *b* 1816; *d* 1895; when the Earldom of Moray and the Baronies of Doune, St Colme, and Stuart passed to his cousin, Edmund Archibald (*see* E Moray), and the Lordship of Gray was adjudged by the Committee for Privileges of the House of Lords to **(19)** EVELEEN, da of late Lady Jane Pounden, da of 10th Earl of Moray, *b* 1841: *m* 1863, James Maclaren Smith, who *d* 1900, having received Royal licence 1897 to assume for himself and wife the additional surname and arms of Gray, and for his issue to assume the surname of Gray in lieu of their patronymic with the arms of Gray only; *d* 1918; *s* by her son **(20)** JAMES MACLAREN STUART, 20th Lord, *b* 1864; *d* 1919; *s* by his sister **(21)** ETHEL EVELEEN, *b* 1866: *m* 1888, Henry Tufnell Campbell, who *d* 1945, having assumed by Roy licence 1920, the additional surname of Gray, son of John Thomas Campbell and Lady Anne Katherine, da of 8th Earl of Lindsay; *d* 1946; *s* by her grandson **(22)** ANGUS DIARMID IAN (son of late Major Hon Lindsay Stuart Campbell-Gray, MC (*Master of Gray*) el son of Ethel Eveleen, Lady Gray), 22nd Lord and present peer.

Gray, Anstruther-, family name of Baron Kilmany.

GRAY OF CONTIN, BARON (Gray) (Life Baron 1983)

HAMISH JAMES HECTOR NORTHEY GRAY, PC, son of late James Northey Gray, of Inverness, who *d* 1979; *b* 28 June 1927; *ed* Inverness R Acad; Assist Gvt Whip 1971-73; a Lord Commr HM Treasury 1973-74; an Opposition Whip 1974-75, Opposition Spokesman on Energy 1975-79, Min of State, Dept of Energy 1979-83; Min of State for Scotland 1983-86; MP for Ross and Cromarty (*C*) 1970-83; DL Inverness-shire 1989, and Lord Lieut since 1996; served in Queen's Own Cameron Highlanders 1945-48; Dir Family and other Cos 1950-70; *cr* PC 1982, and *Baron Gray of Contin*, of Contin, in the District of Ross and Cromarty (Life Baron) 1983: *m* 1953, Judith Waite, da of Noel M. Brydon, MBE, MICE, and has issue.
Residence – Achneim House, Flichity, Inverness-shire IV2 6XE.

SONS LIVING

Hon (James Northey) David, *b* 1955; *ed* Fettes, and Bristol Univ; Head Master Pocklington Sch since 1992: *m* 1978, Lynda Jane Harlow, and has issue living, James Stuart, *b* 1991, — Fiona Sally, *b* 1984, — Julie Harlow, *b* (twin) 1984. *Residence* – Pocklington School, West Green, Pocklington, York.

Hon Peter L., *b* 1959; *ed* Fettes, and Bristol Univ (LLB); Bar and Advocate at Scottish Bar: *m* 1985, Bridget Mary Willcox, and has issue living, Thomas Lachlan, *b* 1994, — Ishbel Mary, *b* 1989, — Madelene Elisabeth, *b* 1992.

DAUGHTER LIVING

Hon Sally Brydon, *b* 1957. *m* 1984, James S. Brown, FRCS, yst son of Stephen W. R. Brown, of Blantyre, Malawi, and has issue living, Angus, *b* 1986, — Duncan James, *b* 1987, — Hamish Stephen, *b* 1989.

Greaves, family name of Countess of Dysart.

Greenall, family name of Baron Daresbury.

GREENE OF HARROW WEALD, BARON (Greene) (Life Baron 1974)

SIDNEY FRANCIS GREENE, CBE, son of Frank James Greene, of London; *b* 12 Feb 1910; Gen Sec NUR 1957-74; Chm of TUC 1969-70; a Dir of Bank of England since 1970; *cr* CBE (Civil) 1966, Knt 1970, and *Baron Greene of Harrow Weald*, of Harrow, Greater London, (Life Baron) 1947: *m* 1936, Masel Elizabeth Carter, and has issue, three das.

Residence – 26 Kynaston Wood, Boxtree Rd, Harrow Weald, Middx.

GREENHILL, BARON (Greenhill) (Baron UK 1950)

MALCOLM GREENHILL, 3rd Baron; *b* 5 May 1924; *s* 1989; *ed* Kelvinside Acad, Glasgow, and Glasgow Univ (BSc); a Chartered Patent Agent; a Member of UK Scientific Mission to Washington, USA, 1950-51, with UK Atomic Energy Authority 1954-73, and with Min of Defence 1973-89.

DAUGHTERS LIVING OF SECOND BARON

Hon Catherine Elizabeth, *b* 1948: *m* 1978, Kenneth Youngren, of 1485 Parkway Blvd, Coquitlam, BC, Canada V3E 3B4.
Hon Sheila Anne, *b* 1951: *m* 1979, Robert Davidson, of 10336 Villa Av, Edmonton, Alberta, Canada T5N 3T9.

WIDOW LIVING OF SECOND BARON

MARGARET JEAN (*Baroness Greenhill*), da of Thomas Newlands, of Hamilton, Ontario, Canada: *m* 1946, the 2nd Baron, MD, DPH, who *d* 1989. *Residence* – 10223 137th St, Edmonton, Alberta, Canada T5N 2G8.

PREDECESSORS – (1) ERNEST Greenhill, OBE, LLD, son of late Maurice Greenhill; *b* 1887; Councillor, Glasgow Corpn 1932; *cr Baron Greenhill*, of Townhead in the City of Glasgow (peerage of UK) 1950: *m* 1914, Ida, who *d* 1985, da of late Mark Goodman; *d* 1967; *s* by his el son (2) STANLEY, MD, DPH, 2nd Baron, *b* 1917, FRSM, FRCP (C), Lecturer in Medicine Alberta Univ, Prof Emeritus 1984: *m* 1946, Margaret Jean, da of Thomas Newlands, of Hamilton, Ontario, Canada; *d* 1989; *s* by his brother (3) MALCOLM, 3rd Baron and present peer.

GREENHILL OF HARROW, BARON (Greenhill) (Life Baron 1974)

DENIS ARTHUR GREENHILL, GCMG, OBE, son of late James Greenhill, of Ashfields, Loughton, Essex; *b* 7 Nov 1913; *ed* Bishop's Stortford Coll, and Ch Ch Oxford (MA) (Hon Student 1977); apprentice London NE Railway 1935-39; entered FO 1946, 1st Sec Sofia 1947-49, and at Washington, DC 1949-52, FO 1952-53, Counsellor to UK Delegation to NATO, Paris 1955-56, and to Office of Commr-Gen for SE Asia, Singapore 1956-58, FO 1958-59, Counsellor Washington 1959-62, and Min there 1962-64, Assist Under-Sec FO 1964-66, Dep Under-Sec 1966-69, and Permanent Under-Sec of State FCO, and Head of Diplo Ser 1969-73; Pres of Roy Soc for Asian Affairs and of Anglo-Finnish Soc; Chm of Governing Body of Sch of Oriental and African Studies since 1978, of Kings Coll Hosp Med Sch Council 1978-83; Dep Chm of BUPA since 1978; Dir of Clerical, Medical and General Life Assurance 1973, of Hawker Siddeley Group 1974, of S. G. Warburg and Co Ltd 1974, and The Wellcome Foundation Ltd 1974; Member of Security Commission 1974-82, Trustee of Rayne Foundation; Grand Cross, Order of the Finnish Lion 1984; 1939-45 War as Col RE in Middle East, N Africa, Italy, India and SE Asia (despatches twice, OBE); *cr* OBE (Mil) 1941, CMG 1960, KCMG 1967, GCMG 1972, and *Baron Greenhill of Harrow*, of Roy Borough of Kensington and Chelsea (Life Baron) 1974: *m* 1941, Angela, da of late William Leitch McCulloch, and has had issue.

Arms – Vert, two barrulets ermine, in chief a lion passant or, a bordure argent. **Crest** – a demi-griffin gules, semée of mullets gold, holding between the claws a mullet also gold. **Supporters** – On either side a Griffin gules semy of mullets or, langued and armed azure.
Residence – 25 Hamilton House, Vicarage Gate, W8 4HL. *Club* – Travellers'.

SONS LIVING AND DECEASED

(*Hon*) Nigel Denis St George (does not use courtesy title), *b* 1942.
Hon Robin James, *b* 1945: *m* 1970 (*m diss* 1975), Elizabeth, da of Sir Eric Roll (later Baron Roll of Ipsden) (Life Baron), KCMG, CB, and *d* 1986.

Greenock, Lord; son of Earl Cathcart.

GREENWAY, BARON (Greenway) (Baron UK 1927, Bt 1919)

Industry and honour

AMBROSE CHARLES DREXEL GREENWAY, 4th Baron, and 4th Baronet; *b* 21 May 1941; *s* 1975; *ed* Winchester; marine photographer and author: *m* 1985, Mrs Rosalynne Schenk, of Bickleigh, Tiverton, Devon, da of Lt-Col Peter Geoffrey Fradgley, of Upcott Manor, Rackenford, N Devon.

𝔄rms – Per pale ermine and ermines, on a chief azure a crescent between two covered cups or. 𝔠rest – A griffin's head, or, erased gules, holding in the beak an anchor sable. 𝔖upporters – On either side a griffin sable, beak and claws or, holding in the beak an anchor and charged on the shoulder with a covered cupgold. *Address* – c/o House of Lords, SW1. *Club* – House of Lords Yacht.

BROTHERS LIVING

Hon MERVYN STEPHEN KELVYNGE (605 Howard House, Dolphin Sq, SW1V 3PG; *Clubs* – MCC, Turf), *b* 19 Aug 1942; *ed* Winchester; FCA, Freeman of City of Lond, Liveryman Vintners Co; Stockbroker; has issue living, Philippa Mary, *b* 1980.
Hon Nigel Paul, *b* 1944; *ed* Winchester: *m* 1979, Gabrielle, el da of late Walter Jean Duchardt, of Obenheim, Alsace, and has issue living, Nicholas Walter Paul, *b* 1988, — Philippe, *b* 1991.

WIDOW LIVING OF THIRD BARON

CORDELIA MARY (*Cordelia, Baroness Greenway*) (703 Collingwood House, Dolphin, Sq, SW1), da of late Maj Humphrey Campbell Stephen, JP, of High Mead, Dormansland, Surrey; Freeman City of London 1978, Liveryman Glovers' Co: *m* 1939, the 3rd Baron Greenway, who *d* 1975.

COLLATERAL BRANCH LIVING

Issue of late Hon Atheling Kelvynge Brooking Greenway, yr son of 2nd Baron, *b* 1921, *d* 1970: *m* 1944 (*m diss* 1962), Stella Alice, da of William Joseph Jennings, of Salisbury, Rhodesia (now Harare, Zimbabwe):—
Neil Kelvynge Brooking (PO Box 374, Harare, Zimbabwe), *b* 1945: *m* 1970, Flora, da of Lindsay Glegg, of Harare, Zimbabwe, and has issue living, Timothy Kelvynge, *b* 1976, — Ashleigh Stella, *b* 1973: *m* 1997, Andrew Barry Crocker, — Teresa Gay, *b* 1974, — Joanne Cordelia, *b* 1977.

PREDECESSORS – (1) CHARLES Greenway, son of John David Greenway, of Taunton, Somerset; *b* 1857: a merchant and banker; snr partner in firm of Shaw Wallace & Co, India and Ceylon, and R. G. Shaw & Co, London; Pres and one of the founders of Anglo-Persian Oil Co Ltd; *cr* a *Baronet* 1919, and *Baron Greenway*, of Stanbridge Earls, co Southampton (peerage of United Kingdom) 1927: *m* 1883, Mabel, who *d* 1940, da of Edwin Augustine Tower; *d* 1934; *s* by his son (2) CHARLES KELVYNGE, 2nd Baron, *b* 1888; Capt Indian Army: *m* 1916, Eileen Constance, who *d* 1963, da of late Maj-Gen Sir Harry Triscott Brooking, KCB, KCSI, KCMG; *d* 1963; *s* by his el son (3) CHARLES PAUL, 3rd Baron; *b* 1917; Maj Parachute Regt: *m* 1939, Cordelia Mary, da of late Maj Humfrey Campbell Stephen, JP, of High Mead, Dormansland, Surrey; *d* 1975; *s* by his el son (4) AMBROSE CHARLES DREXEL, 4th Baron, and present peer.

GREENWOOD, VISCOUNT (Greenwood) (Viscount UK 1937, Bt UK 1915)

MICHAEL GEORGE HAMAR GREENWOOD, 3rd Viscount, and 3rd Baronet; *b* 5 May 1923; *s* 1998; *ed* Eton, and Ch Ch, Oxford; served World War II with Royal Corps of Signals; formerly an Actor.

Arms – Gules, on a chevron ermine between three saltires as many portcullises or. Crest – A demi-lion per fesse gules and sable resting the sinister paw on a portcullis or. Supporters – On either side a lion rampant per fesse gules and sable supporting a staff or, flowing therefrom a banner argent, that on the dexter charged with a rose gules, barbed and seeded proper, and that on the sinister charged with a maple leaf also proper.
Residence – 63 Portsea Hall, Portsea Place, W2 2BY.

SISTER LIVING

Hon Angela Margo Hamar, *b* 1912: *m* 1937, Edward Dudley Delevingne, who *d* 1974, and has had issue, Edward Hamar (Lime Tree Cottage, Dorking, Surrey), *b* 1939: *m* 1982, Fiona, da of Donald Cameron, and has issue living, Katherine *b* 1985, — Charles Hamar (Paddock House, Spencer Park, SW18), *b* 1949: *m* 1983, Pandora Anne, el da of Sir Jocelyn Edward Greville Stevens (*see* Sheffield, Bt), and has issue living, Chloe Jane *b* 1984, Poppy Angela *b* 1986, Cara Jocelyn *b* 1992, — (Anne) Venetia, *b* 1938: *m* 1985, Edward Lavender, and *d* 1987, — (Elizabeth) Caroline Felicia, *b* 1953: *m* 1978, Thomas G. Elek, son of late Dr Imre Elek, of Millom, Cumbria, and has issue living, Charles Thomas Hamar *b* 1986, George Dudley Hamar *b* 1990, Edwina Mary Angela *b* 1980, Flora Tamsin Elizabeth *b* 1982. *Residence* – 22 Ovington St, SW3.

PREDECESSORS – (1) (THOMAS) HAMAR Greenwood, PC, KC, BA, son of John Hamar Greenwood, Bar-at-law, Grays Inn; *b* 1870; Under-Sec of State for Home Depart Jan 1919, an Additional Under-Sec of State for Foreign Depart, Additional Parliamentary Sec to Board of Trade, and Sec to Depart of Overseas Trade July 1919; was last Ch Sec for Ireland (with a seat in the Cabinet) and Chancellor of the Order of St Patrick April 1920 to Oct 1922; sat as MP for York (*L*) 1906-10 for Sunderland 1910-22, and for E Div of Walthamstow (*C*) 1929-4; *cr a Baronet* 1915, *Baron Greenwood*, of Llanbister, co Radnor (peerage of United Kingdom) 1929, and *Viscount Greenwood*, of Holbourne, co London (peerage of United Kingdom) 1937: *m* 1911, *Dame* Margery, DBE, who *d* 1968, da of late Rev Walter Spencer, of Fownhope Court, Herefordshire; *d* 1948; *s* by his el son (2) DAVID HENRY HAMAR, 2nd Viscount; *b* 1914; *d* 1998; *s* by his brother (3), MICHAEL GEORGE HAMAR, 3rd Viscount and present peer; also Baron Greenwood.

GREENWOOD OF ROSSENDALE, BARONY OF (Greenwood) (Extinct 1982)

DAUGHTERS LIVING OF LIFE BARON

Hon Susanna Catherine Crawshay GREENWOOD, *b* 1943; has resumed her maiden name: *m* 1970 (*m diss* 1991), Christopher Gardiner, and has issue living, Thomas Keir, *b* 1982, — Anna Kathryn, *b* 1980.
Dr the Hon Dinah Karen Crawshay (42 Cheverton Rd, N19), *b* 1946; PhD: *m* 1970, David Murray, and has issue living, Bruno *b* 1974, — Leo, *b* 1976, — Fergus, *b* 1978.

GREGSON, BARON, (Gregson) (Life Baron 1975)

JOHN GREGSON, son of John Gregson; *b* 29 Jan 1924; Engineer; AMCT; CBIM; Non-Exec Dir Fairey Group plc, and a Part Time Member of British Steel Board 1976-94; Pres of Defence Manufacturers Assocn; Member Nat Rivers Authority 1992-95; DL Greater Manchester 1979; *cr Baron Gregson*, of Stockport in Greater Manchester (Life Baron) 1975.
Address – 12 Rosemont Rd, Richmond-upon-Thames, Surrey TW10 6QL.

GRENFELL, BARON (Grenfell) (Baron UK 1902)

Honest duty

JULIAN PASCOE FRANCIS ST LEGER GRENFELL, 3rd Baron; *b* 23 May 1935; *s* 1976; *ed* Eton, and King's Coll, Camb (BA); Capt Queen's Westminsters (KRRC) (TA); Ch of Information and Public Affairs for World Bank in Europe 1970, Dep Dir European Office, World Bank, 1973, Special Representative of World Bank to United Nations 1974-81, Sr Adviser External Affairs 1983-90, since when Head of External Affairs in Europe: *m* 1st, 1961, Loretta Maria Olga Hildegarde, da of Alfredo Reali, of Il Cupolino, Florence, Italy; 2ndly, 1970, Gabrielle, only da of Dr Ernst Raab, of Berlin; 3rdly, 1987, Mrs Elizabeth Porter, da of Buford Scott, of Richmond, Va, USA; 4thly, 1993, Mrs Dagmar Langbehn Debreil, da of late Dr Carl Langbehn, of Berlin, and has issue by 1st and 2nd *m*.

Arms – Gules, on a fesse between three organ rests or, a mural crown of the first. Crest – On the battlements of a tower gules, a griffin passant or, holding in the beak a sprig of laurel. Supporters – *Dexter*, An Egyptian cavalryman; *sinister*, an Egyptian infantryman. *Residence* – 18 rue de Bourgogne, 75007 Paris, France.

DAUGHTERS LIVING (*By 1st marriage*)

Hon Isabella Sarah Frances, *b* 1966: *m* 1995, Luigi Pianini Mazzucchetti, of Rimini, Italy.

(*By 2nd marriage*)

Hon Katharina Elizabeth Anne, *b* 1973: *m* 1997, Patrick H. O'Connor, son of Thomas O'Connor, of Florida, USA.
Hon Vanessa Julia Claire, *b* 1976.

SISTER LIVING

Hon Caroline Sarah Aline, *b* 1933: *m* 1965, Zbyszek (Zbigniew) Leon Mieczkowski, Capt (ret) Polish Army, of Rose Cottage, Henley Park, Henley-on-Thames, and has issue living, Stefan Pascoe St Leger, *b* 1967; Capt RGJ: *m* 1996, Jocelyn M. S., elder da of Arthur Kee, of Stranorlar, co Donegal, — Helena Elizabeth Caroline, *b* 1970.

HALF-SISTER LIVING

Hon Aline Mary, *b* 1950.

WIDOW LIVING OF SON OF FIRST BARON

Eleanor Dorothy Alice, only da of Sir (John) Francis William James, of Tamar Bank, Saltash, Cornwall: *m* 1st, 1933, Major Hon Arthur Bernard John Grenfell, who was *ka* 1942; 2ndly, 1944, Capt Brian Herbert Malyon, 10th Hussars, and has issue living (by 1st *m*) (see colls, infra). *Residences* – Chapmansford, Hurstbourne Priors, Whitchurch, Hants GR28 7RR; Middle Combe, Huntsham, Tiverton, Devon.

MOTHER LIVING

Elizabeth Sarah Polk (Betty) (28 Melton Court, Old Brompton Rd, SW7), da of late Capt Hon Alfred Thomas Shaughnessy (*see* B Shaughnessy, colls): resumed the surname of Stafford 1976 until re-marriage: *m* 1st, 1932 (*m diss* 1946), the 2nd Baron Grenfell, who *d* 1976; 2ndly, 1946, Maj Berkeley Buckingham Howard Stafford, KRRC, who *d* 1966; 3rdly, 1969 (*m diss* 1976), Trevor Walton King; 4thly, 1983, Com (Arnold) Derek Arthur Lawson, of Passenham Manor, Stony Stratford, Bucks, who *d* 1984.

COLLATERAL BRANCH LIVING

Issue of late Major Hon Arthur Bernard John Grenfell, 2nd son of 1st Baron, *b* 1908, *ka* 1942: *m* 1933, Eleanor Dorothy Alice (ante) (who *m* 2ndly, 1944, Capt Brian Herbert Malyon, 10th Hussars), only da of Sir (John) Francis William James, of Tamar Bank, Saltash, Cornwall:—
FRANCIS PASCOE JOHN (Lenton House, Lenton, Grantham, Lincs), *b* 28 Feb 1938; *ed* Eton, and Ch Ch, Oxford: *m* 1977, Elizabeth Katharine, da of Hugh Kenyon (*see* Thompson Bt (*cr* 1890)). ⸺ †John St Leger, *b* 1940: *m* 1965, Pauline Mary Walton (Cwm Merwydd, Horeb, Llandyssul, Dyfed SA44 4J2), and *d* 1995, leaving issue, Richard Arthur St Leger, *b* 1966: *m* 1995, Sally Marie Halstead, and has issue living, James St Leger *b* 30 March 1996, — Julian Francis John, *b*

1971, — Sarah Marion, *b* 1968, — Sophie Elizabeth, *b* 1975. ━━━ Margaret, *b* 1935: *m* 1960, Capt Simon Trevor Smail, 11th Hussars of Melcombe Newton Farm, Melcombe Bingham, Dorchester, Dorset (*see* Heathcoat-Amory, Bt, colls).

PREDECESSORS – (1) *Field Marshal Rt Hon Sir* FRANCIS WALLACE Grenfell, GCB, GCMG, PC, son of late P. St L. Grenfell, of Maesteg, Glamorgan; *b* 1841; entered 60th Rifles 1859, and became Field-Marshal 1908; raised 1st Brig Egyptian Army 1883; served in Expedition to Griqualand W 1875, in Kaffir Campaign 1878, in Zulu Campaign 1879 (several times mentioned in despatches, medal with clasp), in Egyptian Expedition 1882, present at battle of Tel-el-Kebir, as AAG, Head Quarters (medal with clasp), in Nile Expedition 1884 (3rd class Medjidie, bronze star), and in command of Frontier Field Force, Egypt 1885, a Div at action of Ginnis 1886, of Anglo-Egyptian Expedition at action of Gamaiza, Suakin 1888, and of Anglo-Egyptian Div at action of Toski 1889; an ADC to HM Queen Victoria 1882-9, Sirdar of Egyptian Army 1885-92, DAG for Auxiliary Forces at Headquarters 1892-4, Inspector-Gen of Auxiliary Forces and of Recruiting 1894-7, in command of Army of Occupation in Egypt 1897-8 (specially thanked by both Houses of Parliament), and Gov of Malta, and in command of Troops there 1898-1902, in command of 4th Army Corps 1902-4, and Gen Officer Cmdg-in-Ch the Forces in Ireland 1904-8; *cr Baron Grenfell*, of Kilvey, co Glamorgan (peerage of United Kingdom) 1902: *m* 1st, 1887, Evelyn, who *d* 1899, da of late Gen R. Blucher Wood, CB; 2ndly, 1903, Hon Margaret Aline who *d* 1911, only da of late Lewis Ashurst Majendie, MP (E Crawford); *d* 1925; *s* by his el son (2) PASCOE CHRISTIAN VICTOR FRANCIS, CBE, TD, 2nd Baron; *b* 1905; Dep Speaker, House of Lords and Chm of Cttees 1963-76: *m* 1st, 1932 (*m diss* 1946), Elizabeth Sarah Polk, da of late Capt Hon Alfred Thomas Shaughnessy (B Shaughnessy, colls); 2ndly, 1946, Irene Lilian, who *d* 1993, da of Harry Augustus George Cartwright, of Buenos Aires, Argentina; *d* 1976; *s* by his only son (3) JULIAN PASCOE FRANCIS ST LEGER, 3rd Baron and present peer.

Grenfell, surname of Barony of St Just.

Grenville, Freeman-, family name of Lady Kinloss.

GRETTON, BARON (Gretton) (Baron UK 1944)

STEADFAST

JOHN LYSANDER GRETTON, 4th Baron; *b* 17 April 1975; *s* 1989; *ed* Shrewsbury, and RAC.

𝕬rms – Quarterly, per fesse indented or and gules, in the second quarter an anchor in bend sinister of the first, in the third an antique lamp also, or, fired proper. 𝕮rest – An arm embowed proper. vested above the elbow argent, holding in the hand a torch erect fired, a sickel in bend sinister both also proper. 𝕾upporters – *Dexter*, a bull sable; *sinister*, a chestnut horse proper, each gorged with a chain pendent therefrom an anchor or.
Residence – Stapleford Farms, Holygate Farm, Stapleford, Melton Mowbray, Leics LE14 2XQ.

SISTER LIVING

Hon Sarah Margaret, *b* 1971: *m* 1999, John Simon Biddulph (*see* B Biddulph, colls).

AUNTS LIVING (*daughters of 2nd Baron*)

Hon Mary Ann Maud Sigrid (Manor House, Stapleford, Melton Mowbray, Leics), *b* 1939; breeder and internat judge of Arabian horses: *m* 1986, Thomas Henry Wragg, son of T. L. Wragg, of Hinckley, Leics.
Hon Elizabeth Margaret, *b* 1945: *m* 1968, Christopher Mark Meynell, of Bergh Apton Hall, Norwich, Norfolk (*see* E Halifax, colls).

WIDOW LIVING OF SECOND BARON

ANNA HELENA MARGARET (*Margaret, Baroness Gretton*), el da of late Capt Henrik Loeffler, of 51 Grosvenor Sq, W1: *m* 1930, the 2nd Baron Gretton, OBE, who *d* 1982. *Residence* – The Old Rectory, Ufford, Stamford.

WIDOW LIVING OF THIRD BARON

JENNIFER ANN (*Baroness Gretton*), only da of late Edmund Sandford Moore, of York (*see* B Grey of Codnor, colls): *m* 1970, the 3rd Baron Gretton, who *d* 1989. *Residence* – Stapleford Farms, Holygate Farm, Stapleford, Melton Mowbray, Leics LE14 2XQ.

PREDECESSORS – (1) *Rt Hon* JOHN Gretton, PC, CBE, VD, TD, son of late John Gretton, of Bladon, Burton-on-Trent; *b* 1867; Chm of Bass, Ratcliff & Gretton, Ltd, brewers, of Burton-on-Trent 1908-45; Lieut-Col and Hon Col 6th Batn Prince of Wales's (N Staffs Regt); sat as MP for S Derbyshire (C) 1895-1906, for Rutland 1907-18, and for Burton Div of Staffordshire 1918-43: *cr Baron Gretton* of Stapleford, co Leicester (peerage of United Kingdom) 1944; *m* 1900, Hon Maud Helen Eveleigh-de-Moleyns, who *d* 1934, da of 4th Baron Ventry; *d* 1947; *s* by his son (2) JOHN FREDERIC; OBE, 2nd Baron, MP for Staffordshire, Burton Div (C) 1943-45: *m* 1930, (Anna Helena) Margaret, el da of late Capt Henrik Loeffler, of 51 Grosvenor Sq, W1; *d* 1982; *s* by his elder son (3) JOHN HENRICK, 3rd Baron; *b* 1941; DL Leics: *m* 1970, Jennifer, only da of late Edmund Sandford Moore, of York (*see* B Grey of Codnor, colls); *d* 1989; *s* by his only son (4) JOHN LYSANDER, 4th Baron and present peer.

Greville, family name of Earl of Warwick.

GREY, EARL (Grey) (Earl UK 1806, Bt GB 1746)

VOULOIR SERVIR
DE BON   LE ROY

To serve the king with good will

RICHARD FLEMING GEORGE CHARLES GREY, 6th Earl, and 7th Baronet; *b* 5 March 1939; *s* 1963; *ed* Hounslow Coll and Hammersmith Coll of Building; Pres of Cost and Exec Accountants Assoc since 1978; Chm Roper Catering Events Ltd, London Cremation Co plc, Academy Beverage Co Ltd; Dir The Countess Grey Collection Ltd; Pres The Cremation Soc of GB, and Lonsdale Internat Sporting Club: *m* 1st, 1966 (*m diss* 1974), Margaret Ann, el da of Henry Bradford, of Ashburton, Devon; 2ndly, 1974, Stephanie Caroline, only da of Donald Gaskell-Brown, of Newton Ferrers, Plymouth, and formerly wife of Surg-Cdr Neil Leicester Denham, RN.

ᴬrms – Gules, a lion rampant, within a bordure engrailed, argent, in dexter chief point a mullet of the last. Ꞓrest – A scaling ladder or, hooked and pointed sable. Ꞩupporters – *Dexter*, a lion guardant purpure, ducally crowned or; *sinister*, a tiger guardant, proper. *Address* – c/o House of Lords, SW1.

BROTHER LIVING

PHILIP KENT, *b* 11 May 1940; Master Mariner, licensed Trin House Sea Pilot (Corpn of Hull, Trin House); Officer RFA Ser: *m* 1968, Ann Catherine, yst da of Cecil Applegate, of Shute Farm, South Milton, Kingsbridge, Devon, and has issue living, Alexander Edward, *b* 20 Dec 1968, — Vanessa Catherine, *b* 1975.

HALF UNCLE LIVING

Rodney York DE CHARMOY GREY, *b* 1921; *ed* Queen's Univ, Kingston, Ontario (BA), and Toronto (MA), and London (PhD) Univs; added the name of de Charmoy before Grey 1970; Assistant Dep Min Depart of Finance, Ottawa, Canada; 1939-45 War with RCAF: *m* 1st, 1945 (*m diss* 1952), Margaret Eileen, da of Colin Hawley, of Bristol; 2ndly, 1952 (*m diss* 1970), Roslyn, da of Max Marcus, of Rothesay, New Brunswick, Canada; 3rdly, 1970, Cozette, da of Louis Roger Guy d'Emmerez de Charmoy, and has issue living, (by 1st *m*) Christopher John (10 Lilac Grove, Luston, nr Leominster, Herefords HR6 0EF), *b* 1946: *m* 1971, Susan Jane, only da of late Arthur Brooks, of Bristol, and has issue living, Duncan Colin *b* 1974, Katherine Jane *b* 1976, Helen Claire *b* 1980, — David York (Rookwood, Church Lane, Goodworth Clatford, Andover, Hants SP11 7HL), *b* 1947: *m* 1st, 1973 (*m diss* 1989), Mary Kathleen, da of late Philip Reilly, of Southall, Middx; 2ndly, 1995, Jacqueline Lesley, da of Harold Roxburgh Hutchings, of Southampton, and has issue living (by 1st *m*), Michael Colin *b* 1982, Louise Ellen *b* 1979, — (by 2nd *m*) Simon Alexander (14 Rue Cloche Perce, 4ème cour, 75004 Paris), *b* 1958, — Marcus Edward (31 Kelly St, NW1), *b* 1960: *m* 1994, Zara Louise, da of John Connor, of Brigg, Lincs. *Residence* – South of France.

DAUGHTER LIVING OF FIFTH EARL

Lady Mary Cecil (*Lady Mary Howick*), *b* 1907: *m* 1935, 1st Baron Howick of Glendale, who *d* 1973. *Residence* – Howick, Alnwick, Northumberland.

STEP-GRANDMOTHER LIVING

Gladys Helen, da of ...... Complin: *m* 1919 (*m diss* 1927), as his 2nd wife, George Archibald Grey, who *d* 1952. Resides in a nursing home in Calgary, Alberta, Canada.

COLLATERAL BRANCHES LIVING

Descendants of late Capt Hon Sir George Grey, KCB, RN (3rd son of 1st Earl), who was *cr* a *Baronet* 1814:—
See Grey, Bt, *cr* 1814.

Grandchildren of late Frederick William Grey, eldest son of late Col Leopold John Herbert Grey, CSI, only son of late Leopold James Henry Grey, 3rd son of late Rt Rev Hon Edward Grey, Bishop of Hereford, 5th son of 1st Earl:—
Issue of late Frederick Arthur Herbert Grey, *b* 1895, *d* 1973: *m* 1919, Adelaide Suchan, who *d* 1949:—
Frederick, *b* 1921. —— Beverly, *b* 1924: *m* 19—, Lou Kennedy, of 8100 Bleriot St, Los Angeles, CA 90045, USA.

Issue of late Robert Maxwell Grey, *b* 1903, *d* 1993: *m* 1928, May Dawn, who *d* 1982, da of Joseph George Washington Brand:—
Barbara Anne (620 South 2nd St, Nederland, Texas 77627, USA), *b* 1934: *m* 1st, 1951 (*m diss* 1963), Truman Derwood Anderson; 2ndly, 19—, ... Wickler, and has issue living (by 1st *m*), Truman Derwod (Jr), *b* 1951, — Elizabeth Ann, *b* 1953, — Rebecca Anne, *b* 1956. —— Jane Ellen, *b* 1940: *m* 1959, Harold Caleb Whitney, Jr, of 622 South 10½ St, Nederland, Texas 77627, USA, and has issue living, Robert Maxwell, *b* 1962, — Katherine Marie, *b* 1961. —— Joyce Elaine, *b* (twin) 1940: *m* 1962, Charles Frederick Theriot, USAF, of PO Box 1227, Dolan Springs, Arizona, USA, and has issue living, Charles Frederick (Jr) (4128 Herblinda Lane, Las Vegas, Nevada 89030, USA), *b* 1970, — Angelique Elaine, *b* 1963: *m* 19—, William Dean Campbell (PO Box 32865, Laughlin, Nevada 89029, USA), and has issue living, Austin Duncan *b* 1993.

Issue of late Leopold John Grey, *b* 1905, *d* 1968: *m* 1929, Ruth Aleen, da of Charles Christian Elmiger:—
Ronald John (PO Box 1184, Corrales, NM 87048, USA; 10501 La Grima de Oro (Apt 306), Albuquerque, NM 87111, USA), *b* 1930; served with US Army in Korean War 1951-53: *m* 1953, Nell Hope, only da of John Fletcher Adams, of Port Charlotte, Florida, USA, and has issue living, Kenneth Alan (21796 Lake Vista Drive, Lake Forest, CA 92630, USA), *b* 1962, — Julia Lynn, *b* 1959: *m* 1983, Douglas Harlow, of 455 Katydid St, Sumter, S Caroline 29154, USA, and has issue living, Margaret Lynn *b* 1992, Adrienne Ruth *b* 1994. —— Joel Edward (PO Box 937, Meadow Vista, CA 95722, USA), *b* 1944; late US Army Res Med Corps: *m* 1968, Kathryn Lee, da of late Paul Fralic, of Van Nuys, Calif, and has issue living, Adam Brady, *b* 1973, — Lauren Emily, *b* 1977.

Grandchildren of late Col Leopold John Herbert Grey, CSI (ante):—
Issue of late Frederick William Grey, *b* 1873, *d* 1950: *m* 1st, 1892 (*m diss* 1917), Agnes Annie, who *d* 1938, da of Peter Gow, MP, and Sheriff of Wellington Co, Ontario, Canada; 2ndly, 1919, Mary Harriet, elder da of Edward Moissant, of Santa Amelia, San Salvador:—
(By 1st *m*) Henry James, *b* 1906: *m* 1930, Alice Mary, da of Alphonse Joseph Samson, and has issue living, Doris Arlene, *b* 1932: *m* 1952, Louis Frederick Repucci, and has issue living, Louis Frederick *b* 1953, Arlene Doris *b* 1954, — Harriet Alice, *b* 1940: *m* 1957, John Ford, and has issue living, Kenneth John *b* 1957, Laurence Robert *b* 1959, Jill Elaine *b* 1960, Janice Carole *b* 19—. —— (By 2nd *m*) Mary Catherine, *b* 1923: *m* 1943, Capt Archibald Bauer MacDonald, USNR (ret), and has issue living, Bruce Grey, *b* 1946, — James Douglas, *b* 1948, — John Mark, *b* 1950, — Craig William, *b* 1962, — Ellen Mary, *b* 1952.

Issue of late Lt-Col Arthur James Herbert Grey, *b* 1880, *d* 1960: *m* 1st, 1911 (*m diss* 1924), Cecile Ruth, da of late François Pogeceniq, Lt Italian Army; 2ndly, 1925, Anna (125, 8403-142 St, Edmonton, Alberta, Canada) (who *m* 4thly, 1963, Cyril Denzil Branch, Bar-at-law, who *d* 1976; *m* 5thly, (Jan) 1978, Clarence V. Frayn, of Edmonton, who *d* (Aug) 1978), da of Axel Vennersten, Grand Marshal to Court of Sweden, and formerly wife of (1) Gosta Otto Rudolf Axelson von Schoultz, and (2) Per Hugo Huitfeldt:—
(By 2nd *m*) *Rev* Axel Robert Henry, *b* 1933, *ed* Wellington Coll, St Andrew's Coll, S Africa, and St Paul's Theological Coll, S Africa (LTh 1958): *m* 1954, Zenith Catherine, da of James Gallagher, and has issue living, Paul, *b* 1958: *m* 1978, Bernadine Veronica, da of Ralph George Seewalt.

Grandson of late William Francis Hungerford Grey, 2nd son of late Sir William Grey, KCSI, 4th son of late Rt Rev Hon Edward Grey, Bishop of Hereford (ante):—
Issue of late Capt William Archibald Swinton Grey, *b* 1883, *d* 1942: *m* 1919, Kathleen Elsie, who *d* 1949, da of W. Paulson, of Mountsorrel, Leicestershire:—
William Ronald (Salisbury Cottage, 13 Robinson Rd, Kenilworth, Cape Town, S Africa), *b* 1920: *m* 1945, Florence Margaret, da of John Martin, and has issue living, David Swinton (6 Cyprian Court, Sophia St, Orangezicht, Cape Town), *b* 1946: *m* 1975, Joy Bowen, and has issue living, Alistair James Egbert *b* 1978, — Margaret Anne, *b* 1949: *m* 19—, Alan Stewart, of 122 Ladies Mile Rd, Bergvliet 7800, RSA, — Jennifer Frances, *b* 1951: *m* 19— (*m diss* 19—), Simon Sutton, and has issue living, Warrick *b* 19—.

Grandchildren of late Dr Francis Temple Grey (infra):—
Issue of late Egerton Francis Grey, Capt Queen's Own Cameron Highlanders, *b* 1930, *d* 1993: *m* 1961, Elizabeth Mary, da of late Peter Blackburn, of Roshven, Lochail:—
Simon Temple, *b* 1962: *m* 1995, Holly Jane, da of Dr James Halliday Cochrane, of Troutbeck, Windermere, Cumbria, and has issue living, Hamish Egerton, *b* 1996, — Pollyanna, *b* 1998. —— John Egerton, *b* 1966: *m* 1990, Joanne Mary, da of William McAskill, of 3 Broom Drive, Inverness, and has issue living, Angus John, *b* 1992, — Charles Egerton, *b* 1996, — Jennifer Ishbel, *b* 1993. —— Frances Mary, *b* 1963. —— Jane Elizabeth Catherine, *b* 1965: *m* 1988, Peter Gregory Isaacson, and has issue living, John Alexander, *b* 1992, — Sophie Claire, *b* 1990.

Grandchildren of late Col Arthur Grey, CIE, eldest son of late Lt-Col Francis Douglas Grey, 7th son of late Rt Rev Hon Edward Grey, Bishop of Hereford (ante):—
Issue of late Francis Temple Grey, MB, ChM, MRCP, Bar-at-law, *b* 1886, *d* 1941: *m* 1928, Eglantine Ellice, who *d* 1989, da of late Major Edward Charles Ellice, DSO:—
Robin Douglas, QC (Dun Cottage, The Marsh, Hungerford, Berks), *b* 1931; *ed* Eastbourne Coll, and King's Coll, London (LLB); Bar Gray's Inn 1957; Recorder 1979, QC 1979: *m* 1st, 1968 (*m diss* 1972), Gillian, da of late Maj Esme Austin Reeves Porch; 2ndly, 1972, Mrs Berenice Anna Adams, da of Denis Wheatley, of 9 Nightingale Cres, W. Horsley; 3rdly, 1993, Mrs Annick Regnault, da of late Henri Kerbiriou, and of Lady Winskill, of Henley, Oxon, and has issue living (by 2nd *m*), Louise Katherine, *b* 1973, — and has adopted his 2nd wife's son, Julian Alexander Grey, *b* 1970. —— John Edward (Ballachulish House, Argyll), *b* 1932; *ed* Epsom Coll: *m* 1965, Elizabeth Anne, only da of late Lt-Col Francis Patrick St Maur Sheil, DSO, and has had issue, †Patrick John, *b* 1966; *ed* Keil Sch, and Stirling Univ (BSc); *k* in a climbing accident on Ben Nevis 1993, — Seumas Edward, *b* 1971; *ed* Merchiston Castle Sch, and Aberdeen Univ, — Ian Michael, *b* 1974; *ed* Merchiston Castle Sch, — Claire Alexandra, *b* 1967. —— Alan Arthur (12 Hough St, Deane, Bolton, Lancs BL3 4LX), *b* 1934; *ed* Epsom Coll, and Univ of Newcastle upon Tyne (BSc): *m* 1966 (*m diss* 1985), Jocelyn Elizabeth, da of John Anthony Cooper, of The Old Croft of Tighphuirst, Glencoe, Argyll (Eden, Bt, colls), and has issue living, Melanie Jane, *b* 1967, — Rebecca Frances, *b* 1968, — Iona Marau, *b* 1972, — Lorna Johane, *b* 1978. —— Harry George (1 Lantana St, Warrego, nr Tennant Creek, Northern Territory 5760, Australia), *b* 1937; *ed* Allhallows Sch. —— †Alexander *b* 1939; *ed* Eastbourne Coll, and Oxford Univ, (MA): *m* 1966 (*m diss* 1992), Eleanor, da of Leonard White, and *d* 1993, leaving issue, Thomas (75 Elms Crescent, SW4 8QF), *b* 1972, — Anna, *b* 1967, — Lucy, *b* 1969. —— Elisabeth Adair (22 Ingrams St, Forest Hill Garden, New York, NY 11375, USA), *b* 1929; *ed* Bryn Mawr Coll, Pennsylvania (BA 1950). —— Joane Eglantine, *b* 1935; *ed* Edinburgh Unv (MA 1961): *m* 1956, Michael Mervyn Whitmore, BSc, MRCVS, who *d* 1959, and has issue living, James Temple, *b* 1958, — William Rupert, *b* 1959: *m* 1984, Kim Milward, and has issue living, Thomas *b* 1985, Jerry (a da) *b* 1990.

Issue of late Sir Paul Francis Grey, KCMG, *b* 1908, *d* 1990: *m* 1936, Agnes Mary (*Lady Grey*) (Holmwood House, Elstead, Godalming, Surrey), da of late Richard Shireburn Weld-Blundell (*see* By Fauconberg and Conyers, colls):—
Nicholas Richard (West Mill, Wherwell, Hants), *b* 1937; *ed* Ampleforth, and Ch Ch Oxford; Dir Wells for India (charity): *m* 1964, Mary Cecilia, da of late Frederick Hugh Hughes, and has issue living, Stephen Hugh Francis, *b* 1968; *ed* Wadham Coll, Oxford (MA); journalist, — Benedict Justin, *b* 1971; *ed* Lincoln Coll, Oxford (MA); social worker: *m* 1993, Sara Filby, and has issue living, Jonathan Richard *b* 1998, — Clare Philomena, *b* 1965; *ed* Ch Ch, Oxford (MA, DPhil); Assoc Prof of Chemistry, Stonybrook Univ, USA: *m* 1993, Dan Raleigh, — Eleanor Mary Grace, *b* 1966; *ed* Merton Coll, Oxford (MA); Bar Gray's Inn 1990. —— Richard Charles Edward (The Old Farmhouse, Elstead, Godalming, Surrey), *b* 1939; *ed* Ampleforth, and Ch Ch Oxford: *m* 1964, Hilary Marguerite Térèse, 4th da of Sq/Ldr Malcolm Ogilvie Forbes, of Esseborne Manor, Hurstbourne Tarrant, Andover, Hants, and has issue living, Demitri Malcolm Paul, *b* 1965, — Malcolm Dominic Antony, *b* 1967, — Eloise Teresa Mary, *b* 1968, — Annabel Lucy, *b* 1971, — Saskia Bernadette, *b* 1973. —— Timothy, *b* 1943; *ed* Ampleforth.

Issue of late Arthur Christopher Grey, BM, BCh, *b* 1911, *d* 1982: *m* 1st, 1941, Diana Marjorie, who *d* 1971, da of Rupert Sackville Gwynne, JP, MP (*see* V Ridley); 2ndly, 1973, Diana, JP, High Sheriff of Isle of Wight (1984) (The White House, Bembridge, Isle of Wight) (who *m* 3rdly, 1984, as his 2nd wife, Rt Rev Edward James Keymer Roberts, formerly Bishop of Ely), da of Ewen Cameron Bruce, DSO, MC, and widow of Anthony Seymour Bellville:—
(By 1st *m*) Rupert Christopher (Hampshire Farm Cottage, S Harting, Petersfield, Hants), *b* 1946; *ed* Wellington Coll, and Univ Coll, London (LLB); solicitor 1976; Roy Humane Soc Vellum Award 1963: *m* 1977, Audrey Janet, da of Donald Vaughan Sinclair, MRCVS, of Southwood Hall, Thirsk, Yorks, and has issue living, Katherine Diana, *b* 1981, — Carmody Theresa Sinclair, *b* 1983, — Rosemary Audrey Sinclair, *b* 1986. —— Jonathan (Fyning Copse, Rogate, Petersfield, Hants GU31 5GH), *b* 1951; *ed* Wellington Coll, and Architectural Assocn (AA Dip 1977): *m* 1978, Rebecca Hall, da of Libby Turner, of Australia, and has issue living, Harry *b* 1984, — Felix, *b* 1987, — Augusta, *b* 1990. —— Stephen (7 Cunningham St, Maraville, NSW, Australia), *b* 1954; *ed* Wellington Coll, and Brunel Univ (BA). —— Edward Christopher (Love Cottage, 20 Chapel St, Petersfield, Hants GU32 3DZ), *b* 1956; *ed* Wellington Coll, and Imperial Coll, London (BSc): *m* 19—, Sonhilde, da of Chauncey Kelley-Patterson, and has issue living, Rowan Tagore, *b* 1992.

Issue of late Maj Martin Grey, *b* 1913, *d* 1975: *m* 1943, Wendy Ursula (East End House, Ditchling, Sussex), da of Charles Creasy Wray:—
David Anthony (East End Cottage, Ditchling, Sussex), *b* 1946; *ed* Allhallows Sch; Chartered Architect; Dip Arch: *m* 1975, Pamela Joan, da of John George Baxter, and has issue living, Thomas Charles, *b* 1979; *ed* Ardingly Coll, — Charles Edward, *b* 1981. —— Priscilla Jane, *b* 1949: *m* 1974, David John Dyer Lewis.

Grandchildren of late Egerton Spenser Grey, CB, son of late Lt-Col Francis Douglas Grey (ante):—
Issue of late Nigel Francis Egerton Grey, *b* 1891, *d* 1974: *m* 1st, 1921 (*m diss* 1949), Eileen Sybil Lyttleton, who *d* 1960, da of late Francis Ludlow Holt; 2ndly, 1949, Mary Rose (THESIGER), who *d* 1962, da of late Hon Guy Laurence Charteris (E Wemyss and March); 3rdly, 1970, Marion, who *d* 1971, da of late Cdr Robert Tennant-Park, OBE, RNR, and widow of Anthony Alfred Harmsworth Marlowe, QC:—
(By 1st *m*) Ann (Pale Green Cottage, Helions Bumpstead, nr Haverhill, Suffolk), *b* 1922: *m* 1955, Pierre Staheyeff, who *d* 1987, and has issue living, Nicholas Peter, *b* 1957: *m* 1st, 1988 (*m diss* 1990), Antoinette Fionna Stagnetto; 2ndly, 1993, Christine Elisabeth, da of William Reiter, of Geneva, Switzerland, — Michael Peter, *b* 1961: *m* 1989, Rosemary, da of Hugh Stafford, OBE, of Wells, Som. —— (By 2nd *m*) Francis John, *b* 1951: *m* 1979, Frances-Jane Cutler, da of Cdr George Wayne Harper, Jr, USN (ret), of The Old Farm, Upper St Jacques, St Peter Port, Guernsey, CI, and has issue living, Telesfora, *b* 1983, — Mary Rose, *b* 1986. *Residence* – 22 Sherborne Rd, Sherborne, nr Cheltenham, Glos GL54 3DR.

Issue of late Cdr Aubrey Arthur Douglas Grey, RN, *b* 1894, *d* 1979: *m* 1928, Joan Fabian, who *d* 1975, da of C. H. Dickinson:—

Aubrey Jeremy Spenser (The Old Coach House, 4 Beech Av, Worcester WR3 8PZ), *b* 1929; late R Hampshire Regt and 2nd Bn The Parachute Regt; ret as Capt; late Maj Lancs Fus (TA): *m* 1958, Jennifer M., da of V. J. Keyte, of Lime Cottage, Beaudesert Park, Minchinhampton, Glos, and has issue living, Charles Spenser (Grimelundsvien 7D, Slemdal, Oslo, Norway), *b* 1959: *m* 1988, Berit, da of Ivar Stokke, of Oslo, Norway, and has issue living, James Axel *b* 1990, Edward Ivar *b* (twin) 1990, William Ole *b* 1997, — James Aubrey (Flat 23, Rusholme Grove, Dulwich, SE19), *b* 1961, — Annabel Clare, *b* 1963: *m* 1993, James R. Chester Walsh, of The Old Smithy, Northend, Henley-on-Thames, Oxon, only son of Richard James Chester Walsh, of Letchworth, Herts, and has issue living, Jack Richard *b* 1996, Emma Clare *b* 1995. —— †Timothy Bryan Richard, *b* 1931: *m* 1st, 1955 (*m diss* 1959), Pamela Anne, da of Col Denys Fitzgerald Murphy, MC; 2ndly, 1960, Gillian A. (The Courtyard, Kirkby Lonsdale, Cumbria), da of E. R. Hillman, of 14 Marshallswick Lane, St Albans, and *d* 1992, leaving issue (by 2nd *m*), Richard Nicholas Aubrey, *b* 1961, — Susannah Emma Jane, *b* 1963: *m* 1993, Maj Martin J. Price, RM, and has issue living, James *b* 1998. —— Michael Francis Adair (Somerset West, CP, S Africa), *b* 1940: *m* 1975, Elizabeth, who *d* 1987, da of late Ivor Lean, QC, of Isle of Man.

Issue of late John Grey, *b* 1899, *d* 1979: *m* 1926, Nancy Augusta, who *d* 1984, da of Vivian Nickalls, of The High House, Newbury, Berks:—

John Egerton, CB (51 St Peter's Rd, W Mersea, Colchester, Essex CO5 8LL), *b* 1929; Bar Inner Temple 1954; Clerk Assistant, House of Lords 1974-88; CB 1981: *m* 1961, his cousin, Patricia, da of late Col Walter Francis Hanna, MC, RE (E Grey, colls, 1976 Edn.), and has two adopted sons, George Christopher, *b* 1961: *m* 1996, Kathryn, da of late Donald Oat, of USA, and has issue living, Theodore Raphael Thomas *b* 1997, — Thomas John, *b* 1963.

PREDECESSORS – (1) *Rt Hon Sir* CHARLES Grey, KB, 4th son of Sir Henry Grey, 1st Bt (infra), *b* 1729; Gen, wounded at Minden 1759; C-in-C W Indies 1793, reducing Martinique, St Lucia and Quadeloupe; Gov of Guernsey 1797-1807; *cr Baron Grey of Howick*, Northumberland (peerage of UK 1801), and *Viscount Howick* and *Earl Grey* (peerage of UK) 1806: *m* 1762, Elizabeth, who *d* 1822, da of George Grey, of Southwick, co Durham; *d* 1807; *s* by his 2nd son (2) CHARLES *KG*, 2nd Earl; *b* 1764; *s* his uncle *Sir* Henry Grey as 3rd Bt 1808 (see *infra); First Lord of the Admiralty 1806, Foreign Sec 1806-7, and First Lord of the Treasury 1830-4: *m* 1794, Hon Mary Elizabeth Ponsonby, who *d* 1861, da of 1st Baron Ponsonby; *d* 1845; *s* by his son (3) *Rt Hon* HENRY GEORGE, KG, GCMG, 3rd Earl, *b* 1802; MP for Winchilsea (*L*) 1826-30, for Higham Ferrers 1831, for Northumberland 1831-3, for N Northumberland 1833-41, and for Sunderland 1841-5; Lord-Lieut of Northumberland 1847-77; Under-Sec for Colonies 1830-33, for Home Depart 1834, and Sec of state for War 1835-9, and for Colonies 1846-52: *m* 1832, Maria, who *d* 1879, da of Sir Joseph Copley, 3rd Bt; *d* 1894; *s* by his nephew (4) *Rt Hon* ALBERT HENRY GEORGE, GCB, GCMG, GCVO (son of late Gen Hon Charles Grey, MP, 2nd son of 2nd Earl), 4th Earl; *b* 1851; Administrator of Rhodesia 1894-7; Lord-Lieut of Northumberland 1899-1904, and Chancellor of Order of St Michael and St George 1916-17; MP for Northumberland S 1880-85, and for Tyneside Div of Northumberland 1885-6; Gov-Gen of Canada 1904-11: *m* 1877, Alice, who *d* 1944, da of late Robert Stayner Holford; *d* 1917; *s* by his son (5) CHARLES ROBERT, 5th Earl, *b* 1879; Lt 1st Life Guards, Maj in the Army, and Hon Col Comdt, Northumberland Vol Regt: *m* 1906, Lady Mabel Laura Georgiana Palmer, CBE, who *d* 1958, da of 2nd Earl of Selborne; *d* 1963; *s* by his kinsman (6) RICHARD FLEMING GEORGE CHARLES (el son of late Albert Harry George Campbell Grey, el son of late George Archibald Grey, only son of late Francis William Grey, 5th son of late Adm Hon George Grey, 4th son of 2nd Earl), 6th Earl and present peer; also Viscount Howick, and Baron Grey of Howick.

*(1) *Sir* HENRY Grey, of Howick, Northumberland, descendant of an ancient family in that Co, 8th in descent from Sir Thomas Grey of Heton, el brother of Sir John Grey, KG, who received the Anglo-Norman Earldom of Tankerville 1419, and 5th in descent from Sir Edward Grey, of Howick, uncle of 1st Baron Grey of Warke (*cr* 1623, ext on death of 4th Baron 1706), *cr* a Baronet 1746: *m* 1720, Hannah, who *d* 1764, da of Thomas Wood, of Falloden; *d* 1749; *s* by his el son (2) *Sir* HENRY, 2nd Bt, *b* 1727; MP for Northumberland 1754-68; *d* unm 1808; *s* by his nephew (3) CHARLES, 2nd Earl Grey (ante).

GREY DE RUTHYN, BARONY OF (Baron E 1324) (Abeyant 1963)

JOHN LANCELOT WYKEHAM BUTLER-BOWDON, BARON GREY DE RUTHYN, *d* 1963, when the Barony fell into abeyance between the descendants of his four great aunts.

COLLATERAL BRANCHES LIVING (*Representatives of the daughters of Barbara, Baroness Grey de Ruthyn, wife of 2nd Marquess of Hastings, are co-heirs of this Barony*)

Descendants of late Lady Edith Maud Rawdon-Hastings (eldest da of Barbara, Baroness Grey de Ruthyn, by her 1st husband, 2nd Marquess of Hastings), who *s* her brother as *Countess of Loudoun* (see that title).

Descendants of late May Evelyn Bertha Emily (elder da of Lady Victoria Mary Louisa KIRWAN, 3rd da of Barbara, Baroness Grey de Ruthyn, by her 1st husband, 2nd Marquess of Hastings): *m* 1895, Count Louis Lubienski Bodenham, JP, DL, of Rotherwas, Hereford, and Bullingham Manor, Hereford:—

Grandchildren of late Count Stanislas Lubienski Bodenham, yr son of late Count Louis Lubienski Bodenham (ante):—

Issue of late Count Charles Henry Lubienski Bodenham, *b* 1935, *d* 1987: *m* 1964, Lia (79 Mortlake Rd, Kew, Richmond, Surrey TW9 4AA), da of late Giuseppe Zappala, of Via R. Zandonai 85, Rome:—
Count Paul, *b* 1965; co-heir to Barony of Grey de Ruthyn. —— *Countess* Elizabeth, *b* 1972. —— *Countess* Monica, *b* (twin) 1972.

Descendants of late Lady Frances Augusta Constance Rawdon-Hastings (4th da of Barbara, Baroness Grey de Ruthyn, by her 1st husband, 2nd Marquess of Hastings): *m* 1863, 4th Earl of Romney, who *d* 1905 (see that title).

Descendants of late Hon Barbara Yelverton (only da of Barbara, Baroness Grey de Ruthyn, by her 2nd husband, Adm Sir Hastings Reginald Henry Yelverton, GCB); *m* 1872, 2nd Baron Churston, who *d* 1910 (see that title).

Issue of late Hon Joan Barbara Yarde-Buller, eldest da of 2nd Baron Churston, *b* 1908, *d* 1997: *m* 1st, 1927 (*m diss* 1936), W/Cdr Thomas Loel Evelyn Bulkeley Guinness, OBE, Auxiliary Air Force (Res), who *d* 1988 (*see* B Audilaun, 1944 Edn); 2ndly, 1936 (*m diss* 1949), Aly Khan, who *d* in a motor accident 1960, son of HH late Rt Hon the Aga Khan, GCSI, GCIE, GCVO; 3rdly, 1986, 2nd Viscount Camrose, who *d* 1995:—
(By 1st *m*) †Patrick Benjamin (Tara) GUINNESS, *b* 1931; *ed* Eton: *m* 1955, Countess Dolores Maria Agatha Wilhelmine Luisa, da of Count Franz Egon von Fürstenberg, and *d* in a motor accident 1965, leaving issue, Loel (Ave de Rumine 37, 1005 Lausanne, Switzerland), *b* 1957, — Alexandra, *b* 1956: *m* 1979, Count Foulques de Quatrebarbes, and has issue living, Foulques Patrick *b* 1981, Laétitia *b* 1983, Aurelia *b* 1984, Olivia *b* 1985, — Victoria (Villa Marguns, PO Box 297, 7500 St Mortiz, Switzerland), *b* 1960: *m* 1984, Philippe Niarchos, eldest son of late Stavros Niarchos, and has issue living, Stavros *b* 1985, Theo *b* 1991, Eugenie *b* 1986, Electra *b* 1995. —— (By 2nd *m*) HH *Prince* Karim (*HH the Aga Khan*) (Aiglemont, 60270 Gouvieux, France), *b* 1936; *ed* Le Rosey, and at Harvard Univ; *s* his grandfather as 4th Aga Khan 1957; is spiritual leader and Imam of Ismaili Muslims all over the world; received personal title of Highness from HM 1957: *m* 1st, 1969 (*m diss* 1995), Sarah Frances, only da of Lt-Col Arthur Edward Croker Poole, of 95 Eaton Sq, SW1, and formerly wife of Lord James Charles Crichton-Stuart (*see* M Bute); 2ndly, 1998, Gabriele Renate, da of Helmut Friedhelm Homey, adopted da of Bodo Thyssen, and formerly wife of Karl Emich, 8th Prince of Leiningen (*see* ROYAL FAMILY), and has issue living (by 1st *m*) *Prince* Rahim, *b* 1971, — *Prince* Hussain, *b* 1974, — *Princess* Zahra, *b* 1970; *ed* Le Rosey, and Harvard Univ: *m* 1997, J. Mark Boyden, only son of John Boyden, of Cheselbourne, Dorset. —— *Prince* Amyn Mohamed AGA KHAN (276 Route de Lausanne, 1292 Chambesy, Geneva, Switzerland; 69 rue de Lille, 75007 Paris), *b* 1937; *ed* Le Rosey, and at Harvard Univ.

GREY OF CODNOR, BARON (Cornwall-Legh) (Baron E 1397)

RICHARD HENRY CORNWALL-LEGH, 6th Baron; *b* 14 May 1936; *s* 1996; *ed* Stowe; High Sheriff Cheshire 1993, DL 1995; late RN; Member British Ski Team 1959-61 (Capt 1960-61): *m* 1974, Joanna Storm, 7th and yst da of Maj Sir Kenelm Henry Ernest Cayley, 10th Bt, and has issue.

Arms – Quarterly; 1st argent a lion rampant gules, *Legh*; 2nd ermine a lion rampant gules crowned or a bordure engrailed sable bezanty, *Cornwall*; 3rd per pale azure and vert on a fesse dancetté between three mural crowns or a crescent gules between two torteaux, *Walker*; 4th barry of six argent and azure, *Grey*. **Crest** – A demi-lion rampant gules collared or and charged for distinction on the shoulder with an ermine spot or. **Supporters** – On either side a demi-lion rampant gules crowned charged on the shoulder with an ermine spot and conjoined with the wings and tail of a wyvern erect or.
Seat – High Legh, nr Knutsford, Cheshire. *Residence* – High Legh House, nr Knutsford, Cheshire WA16 0QR. *Clubs* – Boodle's, MCC.

SONS LIVING

Hon RICHARD STEPHEN CAYLEY, *b* 24 March 1976; *ed* Shrewsbury, and Nottingham Univ.
Hon Kenelm Michael, *b* 1978; *ed* Shrewsbury, and Brookes Univ, Oxford.
Hon George Henry, *b* 1982; *ed* Shrewsbury.

DAUGHTER LIVING

Hon Caroline Philadelphia, *b* 1983; *ed* Downe House.

SISTERS LIVING

Hon Rosemary, *b* 1932: *m* 1959 (*m diss* 1993), Maj Hugh Charles Desmond Laing, late Scots Guards, only son of late Capt Hugh Desmond Bertram Laing, of 16A Prince's Gate Mews, SW7, and has an adopted da, Camilla Catherine Harvey, *b* 1964. *Residence* – 5 Ditchfield Lane, High Legh, Knutsford, Cheshire WA16 0QN.

Hon Julia Margaret, *b* 1939: *m* 1978, Max Prola, DPhil (Psych), of New York, only child of late Joseph Prola, formerly of Aglie, Italy. *Residence* – The Croft, High Legh, Knutsford, Cheshire WA16 0QN.

COLLATERAL BRANCHES LIVING (*all in remainder*)

Issue of late Evelyn Henry Shuldham Cornwall-Legh, yr brother of 5th Baron, *b* 1905, *d* 1975; assumed by deed poll 1926 the surname of Cornwall-Legh in lieu of Walker: *m* 1946, Olga Frieda (Mill House, High Legh, Knutsford, Cheshire WA16 6LS), elder da of Heinrich Bodmer, of Zurich, Switzerland:—
Barbara Katharine, *b* 1947: *m* 1st, 1969 (*m diss* 1973), John James Stewart Farmer; 2ndly, 1978, Giles Heathcote Whittome, and has issue living (by 1st *m*), Katharine Frederica, *b* 1971: *m* 1997, Richard Allen, of 7 Westgate Terr, Long Melford, Suffolk CO10 9DS. *Residence* – 37 Brook Green, W6 7BL.

Grandchildren of late Rev Arthur Edmund Legh Walker, son of late Charles Walker, by his wife Gertrude Mary Cornwall, eldest da of late Rev Henry Cornwall Legh, Rector of Welsh Hampton, Shropshire, great-grandson of late George Legh, of High Legh, Cheshire (who *m* Anna Maria, only da and heiress of Francis Cornwall, 16th and last Baron of Burford, through whom the family inherited the representation of the Barony of Grey of Codnor):—
Issue of late Rev Edward Charles Cornwall Walker, *b* 1918, *d* 1999: *m* 1946, Jean Drummond (Jubilee Cottage, Gt Amwell, Ware, Herts), only da of late Rev Andrew Drummond Harcus, OBE, DD, of Crediton Hill, NW6:—
Charles Legh Cornwall WALKER (Barters Farmhouse, Chapmanslade, Westbury, Wilts), *b* 1947; *ed* Denstone Coll, and Oaklands Coll, St Albans: *m* 1979, Diana, da of Rev Philip Reginald Wilton Tidmarsh, of Dilton Marsh, Wilts, and has issue living, Andrew Philip, *b* 1982; *ed* Dauntsey's Sch, — Anna Clair, *b* 1985. —— †Drummond Harcus, *b* and *d* 1952. —— Drummond Alban Cornwall WALKER (Zypressenstrasse 26, 33699 Bielefeld, Germany), *b* 1959; *ed* Haileybury, and Trin Coll of Music: *m* 1987, Diana Carol, da of Nelson Amos, of Michigan, USA, and has issue living, James Drummond Cornwall, *b* 1996, — Catherine Carol Cornwall, *b* 1991. —— Clair Cornwall, *b* 1950: *m* 1971, Maj Nigel Craig Fairley, late Royal Signals, of Clark's Cottage, 61 The Green, Christian Malford, Wilts, son of late Maj John Craig Fairley, and has issue living, Duncan Craig, *b* 1973; *ed* Haileybury, and City Univ (BSc 1995): *m* 1999, Rebecca Louise, eldest da of Cmdr Richard Kim O'Neill, RN, — Alastair Murray, *b* 1975; *ed* Haileybury, and Portsmouth Univ (BA 1998). —— Mary Cornwall, *b* 1961: *m* 1987, Richard David Eliot Haines, of 40 Alexandra Rd, Ash, Aldershot, Hants, 3rd son of Harry Haines, of Churt, Surrey, and has issue living, George Arthur, *b* 1989, — Holly Nicola, *b* 1988.

Descendants of late Frances Elinor Cornwall, 3rd da of late Rev Henry Cornwall Legh (ante): *m* 1869, as his 2nd wife, George Henry Brooks, of Doctors' Commons, London, and of Windsor:—

Grandsons of late Edmund Hatfield Leslie Cornwall Brooks (infra):—
Issue of late John Edmund Hatfield Brooks, *b* 1909, *d* 1966: *m* 1945, Honoria, who *d* 1998, da of late Aloysius O'Donnell, of co Limerick:—
(John) Nicholas Hatfield BROOKS, *b* 1946. —— †Edmund Hugh Cornwall BROOKS, *b* 1949: *m* 1st, 1980 (*m diss* 1987), Barbara, da of Peter Freckingham, of Ab Kettleby, Leics; 2ndly, 1988, Sally Ann (4 All Saints Close, Asfordby, nr Melton Mowbray, Leics), da of John Taylor, of Leicester, and was *k* in a motor accident 1990, leaving issue, John Edmund Cornwall, *b* (*posthumous*) 1990.

Granddaughter of late Mrs Frances Elinor Cornwall Brooks (ante):—
Issue of late Edmund Hatfield Leslie Cornwall Brooks, *b* 1874, *d* 1934: *m* 1907, Constance Sara, who *d* 1948, da of late Thomas Cook, of Wellingborough, Northants:—
Constance Theodora (Hassingham House, Hingham, Norfolk), *b* 1911: *m* 1932, Edward Stanley Corner, who *d* 1984, and has issue living, Greta Madeline, *b* 1933: *m* 1961, John Allen, of Manor Farm, Barnham Broom, Norwich, and has issue living, Andrew William *b* 1963, David Edward *b* 1965, — Catherine Jill, *b* 1937: *m* 1964, Nigel Armstrong, who *d* 1996, of 3 Squires Court, Main St, Bretforton, Evesham, Worcs WR11 5QD, and has issue living, Iain *b* 1965, Timothy *b* 1969, Amanda *b* 1966.

Grandchildren of late Edmund Hatfield Leslie Cornwall Brooks (ante):—
Issue of late Katharine Madeline Cornwall Brooks, *b* 1917, *d* 1989: *m* 1942, James Lionel Herbert Cloutte, who *d* 1982:—
Colin David CLOUTTE (93 Wetherill St, Goole, Humberside DN14 6EE), *b* 1944. —— Penelope Jane (40a Huddleston Rd, Tufnell Park, N7 0AG), *b* 1946; has issue living, Dora Sara CLOUTTICK, *b* 1983. —— Hilary Juliet, *b* 1950: *m* 1968, Nigel Forde, poet and radio presenter, of The Gate House, Burnby Lane, Pocklington, York YO4 2UL, and has issue living, Victoria Louise, *b* 1968: *m* 1994, Robert Wicks, of 32 Park Grove, York YO3 7LG, eldest son of David Wicks, of Moat Farm, Middlewood Green, Stowmarket, Suffolk, — (Sarah) Tamsin, *b* 1973: *m* 1996, Julian L. Nicol, only son of late Maurice Nicol, of Meolo, Ches.

Grandchildren of late Cecil Thomas Edgar Brooks, 3rd and yst son of late Mrs Frances Elinor Cornwall Brooks (ante):—
Issue of late Cecil Geoffrey Theodore Brooks, *b* 1907, *d* 1980: *m* 1st, 1932 (*m diss* 1945), Jeanne, who *d* 1998, da of Higham Phillipson, of Yorks; 2ndly, 1946 (*m diss* 1967), Winifred Mary (Anne), da of late Frederick Augustin Coupe, of Banwell, Som, and formerly of Preston, Lancs; 3rdly, 1977, Mrs Eileen Bell, who *d* 1982:—
(By 1st *m*) Michaela Theodora Diane, *b* 1934: *m* 1954, Richard Edridge, who *d* 19—, of The Thatched House, 267 Hillbury Rd, Warlingham, Surrey CT3 9TL, and has issue living, Richard Tilden Hurley, *b* 1960, — Annalisa, *b* 1963: *m* 1985, Martin Parrott, of Caterham, Surrey, and has issue living, Kira *b* 1987, — Katarina, *b* 1969. —— Wendy Angela Suzanne BROOKS (205 52 Aspland St, Nambour, Qld 4560, Australia), *b* 1936; has resumed her maiden name: *m* 1960 (*m diss* 19—), Stanley Eduard Hoffman, and has issue living, Dahl Wendell Eduard, *b* 1961, — Bradney Stan Theodore, *b* 1964, — Kyla Jeanell Alicia, *b* 1963: *m* 1st, 1981 (*m diss* 1984), John L. Horvath; 2ndly, 1988 (*m diss* 1991), Mark Douglas

Summers; 3rdly, 1992, Craig Ronald Frost, and has issue living (by 3rd *m*), Taylem James *b* 1992, Danien Ronald *b* 1995, Kadin Craig *b* 1997. —— (By 2nd *m*) Angela Valerie Alicia, *b* 1945: *m* 1963, Ronald Carl Frank, of 383 St Vincent Rd, Nudgee, Qld 4014, Australia, and has issue living, Karl Geoffrey, *b* 1968: *m* 19—, Lara-Lea Herbert, and has issue living, Kristian Jacob *b* 1997, — Bethany Anne, *b* 1973. —— Jennifer Anne Christine, *b* 1949: *m* 1974, Francis Martin Balkwill, and has issue living, Michael Peter, *b* 1976, — Sarah Louise, *b* 1977.

Issue of late Desborough Sutherland George Brooks, *b* 1913, *d* 1990: *m* 1st, 1937, Molly, who *d* 1969, da of late Thomas Edwin Morgan, surveyor, of Lincoln's Inn Fields, and of 80 Bridge Lane, NW11; 2ndly, 1970, Mrs Patricia Dulcie Morgan (*née* Spicer) (21 Northway, NW11 6PB), widow of Donald Morgan, son of late Thomas Edwin Morgan (ante):—
(By 1st *m*) Christopher Desborough Colin BROOKS, *b* 1938; *ed* Univ Coll Sch, Emmanuel Coll, Camb (MA), and St Thomas's Hosp (MB, BChir), LRCP, MRCS: *m* 1979 (*m diss* 1990), Mrs Linda Foster, of Chattanooga, Tenn, USA, and has issue living, Amanda, *b* 1981. —— Jonathan Henry BROOKS (21 Northway, NW11), *b* 1948; *ed* Univ Coll Sch, Emmanuel Coll, Camb, and St Thomas's Hosp; FRCS, MRCOG: *m* 1974, Janet Ruth, da of Walter Leggott, of Burtoft, Lincs, and has issue living, George Morgan, *b* 1980, — Jack Christopher, *b* 1987, — Tabitha Molly, *b* 1983, — Henrietta Jane, *b* 1985.

Granddaughters of late Angela Mary Eveline Brooks, only da of late Mrs Frances Elinor Cornwall Brooks (ante): *m* 1895, Sandford Ffolliott Pierpoint Moore:—
Issue of late Edmund Sandford Moore, *b* 1905, *d* 1980: *m* 1931, Emily Joan, who *d* 1994, da of Francis Cherucca Wheeler, of St Ives, Cornwall:—
Jennifer Ann (*Baroness Gretton*), *b* 1943: *m* 1970, 3rd Baron Gretton, who *d* 1989, and has issue. *Residence* – Stapleford Farms, Holygate Farm, Stapleford, Melton Mowbray, Leics LE14 2XQ.

Issue of late Joyce Mary Theodora Moore, *b* 1907, *d* 1981: *m* 1939, John Guise Malpas:—
Felicity, *b* 1939: *m* 1963, David Isaac. *Residence* – 8 Durnsford Way, Cranleigh, Surrey GU6 7LN.

Grandchildren of late Sir Philip Henry Grey-Egerton, 12th Bt, grandson of late Sir Philip de Malpas Grey-Egerton, 10th Bt, FRS, by his wife Anna Elizabeth, sister of late Rev Henry Cornwall Legh (ante):—
Issue of late Cecely Alice Grey, MBE, *b* 1893, *d* 1981: *m* 1918, Lt-Col Denys Edward Prideaux-Brune, DSO, who *d* 1952:—
Philip Egerton Edmund PRIDEAUX-BRUNE (Plumber Farmhouse, Sturminster Newton, Dorset), *b* 1921; *ed* Harrow; late Warrant Officer RAF: *m* 1944, Pamela Maud, yr da of late Capt George Norman Ferrers-Guy, Worcs Regt (*see* B Avebury, 1965 Edn), and has issue living, Richard John Ferrers, *b* 1946; *ed* Harrow, — Denys Edmund Charles, *b* 1947; *ed* Harrow, — George Brian Philip, *b* 1948, — Timothy Rowland Edward, *b* 1953, — Philippa Anne Madeleine, *b* 1961: *m* 1985, Mark Railing, of 73 Winchendon Rd, SW6 5DH, and has issue living, Maximilian John Prideaux *b* 1987, Philip James *b* 1989, Alexander Peter *b* 1990. —— Rowland Denys Charles PRIDEAUX-BRUNE (500 Dorchester Rd, San Matao, Calif, USA), *b* 1925; *ed* Eton, Calif Inst of Technology, and Magdalene Coll, Camb (MA); Capt The Rifle Bde 1943-47: *m* 1957, Genevieve Poett, da of late Richard Ashe McLaren, of San Mateo, Calif, and has issue living, Cynthia Mary Dean, *b* 1958, — Diana Evelyn, *b* 1960. —— †Cynthia Mary Denise, *b* 1919; JP: *m* 1941, Brian Alexis Fenwick Stephens, MRCS, LRCP, of Tollgate House, Wing, Bucks, and *d* 1995, leaving issue, Nicholas Edward Egerton (Grafton Lodge, Montford Bridge, Shropshire), *b* 1946; *ed* Charterhouse: *m* 1970, Avril Rose, yr da of Lt-Col Morgan Henry Birch-Reynardson, of Le Carriers, St Mary, Jersey, CI, and has issue living, Samantha Jane *b* 1975, Clare Diana *b* 1978, — Hugo Offley Prideaux, *b* 1956; *ed* Charterhouse, — Cecely Isobel Rich, *b* 1958.

Descendants of late Harriot Cornwall Legh, yr sister of late Rev Henry Cornwall Legh (ante): *m* 1838, Capt Herbert Taylor, 85th LI.

PREDECESSORS – HENRY de GREY, of Codnor, co Derby, Grays Thurrock, Essex, and Aylesford and Hoo, Kent, of the Great House of Grey (*see* GEC's Complete Peerage vol VII), was twice summoned for mil serv in the reign of King Edward I, served in Gascony 1295 and 1297, and was summoned to Parliament 1299-1308 by writs directed *Henrico de Grey*; *d* 1308; *s* by his son RICHARD, *b* ca 1281-2, summoned to Parliament 1309-35, pardoned for any part taken against the Despencers 1321, Steward of Gascony 1324, Constable of Nottingham Castle 1325-30, granted the custody of the manor of Overstone, co Northants: *m* Joan, da of Robert, Lord FitzPayn; *d* 1335; *s* by his son, JOHN, summoned to Parliament 1335-92, a distinguished soldier, served in Scotland, Flanders and France, with King Edward III at Crécy, the siege of Calais, etc, Keeper of Rochester Castle, excused from attendance at parliaments, councils, etc, in consideration of his long mil serv 1371: *m* 1st, Eleanor; 2ndly, Alice, da of Sir Warin de Lisle, of Kingston Lisle; *d* 1392; *s* by his grandson (1) *RICHARD, KG, 1st Baron (son of Sir Henry de Grey by his wife, Joan, da of Thomas, Lord Berkeley), *b* ca 1371, summoned to Parliament 1393-1416, served King Richard II in France, Adm of the Fleet from the mouth of the Thames to the North 1401, granted lands in Wales and recommended by Parliament for reward for services against the Welsh rebels 1406, Constable of Nottingham Castle and Master Forester of Sherwood 1407, constantly employed upon confidential missions to the courts of France and Scotland: *m* before 1378, Elizabeth, yr da and co-heiress of Ralph, Lord Bassett of Sapcote; *d* 1418; *s* by his son (2) JOHN, 2nd Baron, *b* in or before 1396; summoned to Parliament 1420-29, Lieut in Ireland 1427 until his death *sp* 1430; *s* by his brother (3) HENRY, 3rd Baron, summoned to Parliament 1430-41: *m* before 1434, Margaret (who *m* 2ndly, Sir Richard Vere, yr son of 12th Earl of Oxford, and *d* 1464), da of Sir Henry Percy, of Atholl; *d* 1444; *s* by his son (4) HENRY, 4th Baron, *b* ca 1435; summoned to Parliament 1459-95, served Queen Margaret at Battle of St Albans 1460, obtained from King Edward IV a licence to practise the transmutation of metals, being answerable to the King for any profit made, given a 40 year grant of lands in Ireland, attended the Coronation of King Richard III, who granted him various manors or lordships in Rutland and Suffolk; *dspl* 1496, when the barony fell into abeyance between his three aunts, the issue of the 1st Baron: (i) Lucy, wife of Sir Roland Lenthall, (ii) Eleanor, wife of Sir Thomas Newport, and (iii) Elizabeth, wife of Sir John Zouche, and so continued until 1989, when the abeyance was terminated (after petition to HM King George V), in favour of (5) CHARLES LEGH SHULDHAM Cornwall-Legh, CBE, senior representative of Lady Lenthall, 5th Baron, *b* 1903; assumed the surname of Cornwall-Legh in lieu of Walker by deed poll (upon the *s* of his father to the High Legh estates), enrolled at the College of Arms, 1926; 1939-45 War with AAF and RAF; High Sheriff, DL and CC Cheshire, Chm New Cheshire CC and Cheshire Police Authority: *m* 1930, Dorothy Catherine Whitson, who *d* 1993, elder da of late John Whitson Scott, of Seal, Sevenoaks, Kent; *d* 1996; *s* by his only son (6) RICHARD HENRY, 6th Baron and present peer; also senior rep in the illegitimate line of Richard, King of the Romans, 2nd son of John, King of England.

*The Committee for Privileges found that the existence of a barony by writ "can only be established by proof of a Royal Writ summoning some ancestor of the claimant to attend a Parliament followed by an actual sitting of such ancestor in the Parliament to which he was summoned." The first three holders of the title, as enumerated in GEC's Complete Peerage, are therefore not shown as such in the above article.

GREY OF NAUNTON, BARON (Grey) (Life Baron 1968)

RALPH FRANCIS ALNWICK GREY, GCMG, GCVO, OBE, son of late Francis Arthur Grey; b 15 April 1910; ed Wellington Coll, NZ, Auckland Univ Coll (LLB), and Pembroke Coll, Camb; Hon LLD, Belfast and Nat Univ of Ireland; Hon D Litt, and Hon DSc, New Univ of Ulster; Bar and Solicitor NZ 1932; a GCStJ (Kt Cdr of the Commandery of Ards 1968-77, Bailiff of Egle 1975-87, Chancellor 1987-88), Lord Prior of Order of St John 1988-91; entered Admin Ser, Nigeria 1937; Assist Financial Sec 1948-52, Development Sec 1952-53, Sec to Gov-Gen and Council of Mins 1954, Ch Sec of Federation 1955-57; and Dep Gov-Gen 1957-59; Gov and C-in-C British Guiana 1959-64, Gov of Bahamas 1964-68, of Turks and Caicos Islands 1965-68, and Gov of N Ireland 1968-73, Dep Chm of Commonwealth Development Corpn 1973-79, Chm 1979-80; Grand Pres, Royal Over Seas League since 1993 (Chm 1976-81, Pres 1981-93); Britain-Nigeria Assoc 1983-89; Overseas Service Pensioners' Assoc since 1983; Chancellor of The New Univ of Ulster 1980-84; Chancellor of The Univ of Ulster since 1984; Hon Bencher Inn of Court, N Ireland; Hon Freeman of Belfast, Lisburn and London; cr OBE (Civil) 1951, CMG 1955, KCVO 1956, KCMG 1959, GCMG 1964, Baron Grey of Naunton, of Naunton, co Gloucester (Life Baron) 1968, and GCVO 1973: m 1944, Esme Mae (CStJ), who d 1996, da of late Albert Victor Kerry Burcher, of Remuera, Auckland, NZ, and widow of PO Kenneth Kirkcaldie, RAFVR, and has issue.

Arms – Bendy argent and azure two lions' faces in pale, issuing from either flank of the shield a cross formy flory dimidiated gules. Crest – A sheathed sword erect gules garnished hilt and pommel or, each quillon ending in a kiwi's head erased gold the scabbard supported by two lions' gambs erased gules winged azure semy of bees volant or. Supporters – Dexter, a lion or, sinister, a crested crane proper, each gorged with an ancient crown flowing therefrom a mantle gules lined vair.
Residence – Overbrook, Naunton, Glos, GL4 5AX. Club – Travellers'.

SONS LIVING

Hon Jolyon Kenneth Alnwick (Upper Swell Farm, Stow on the Wold, Cheltenham, Glos GL54 1EW), b 1946; ed Marlborough, and Pembroke Coll, Camb (MA); Bar Inner Temple, 1968: m 1971, Sarah Jane, da of late Lt-Col Samuel Brian Digby Hood, TD (see V Hood, colls), and has issue living, Tobias Alnwick, b 1973, — Matthew Samuel, b 1976.
Hon Jeremy Francis Alnwick, b 1949; ed Marlborough, and Roy Agric Coll, Cirencester; Lt-Col King's Royal Hussars (ret); Bursar Rendcomb Coll: m 1973, Susan Elizabeth Louise, da of Duncan Richard Fraser, CBE, of Nairobi, Kenya, and has issue living, Barnaby Nicholas Alnwick, b 1976, — Sebastian Jonathan Alnwick, b 1979.

DAUGHTER LIVING

Hon Amanda Mary Alnwick, b 1951; ed St Mary's Sch, Calne, and Bedford Coll, Univ. of London (BA (Hons)): m 1st, 1975 (m diss 1988), José das Neves; 2ndly, 1991, Phillip Clapham, and has issue living (by 2nd m), Mark Ralph, b 1992, — Christopher Jim, b 1995. Residence – Twin Oaks, Sherry River, Wakefield, Nelson, NZ.

GRIDLEY, BARON (Gridley) (Baron UK 1955)

RICHARD DAVID ARNOLD GRIDLEY, 3rd Baron; *b* 22 Aug 1956; *s* 1996; *ed* Monkton Combe, Portsmouth Polytechnic and Brighton Univ (BA); Project Manager in Construction Industry 1979-91, Lecturer in Business and Information Technology, South Downs Coll, since 1994; Hon Patron of Case for the Wild Internat since 1996: *m* 1st, 1979 (*m diss* 1983), Amanda Jane, da of late Ian Mackenzie, of Felixstowe, formerly of Ceylon; 2ndly 1983, Mrs Suzanne Elizabeth Ripper (*née* Hughes), and has issue by 2nd wife.

𝕬rms – Gules three bendlets enhanced and in base a portcullis chained or. 𝕮rest – A wyvern azure semee of lozenges or, resting the dexter claw on a grid iron gules. 𝕾upporters – *Dexter*, a wyvern azure semee of lozenges or: *sinister*, a lion gules semee of grid irons gold. *Residence* – 79 Purbrook Gdns, Purbrook, Waterlooville, Hants PO7 5LE.

SON LIVING (*By 2nd wife*)

Hon Carl Richard, *b* 1981.

DAUGHTER LIVING (*By 2nd wife*)

Hon Danielle Lauren, *b* 1983.

SISTERS LIVING

Hon Susan Lesley, *b* 1950: *m* 1st, 1975 (*m diss* 1982), John Philip Bruce Scott; 2ndly, 1983, Andrew Kinderbee Woods, of 127 Sound Beach Av, Old Greenwich, CT 06870, USA, and has issue living (by 1st *m*), Edward Harry Gridley, *b* 1977, — Carrie Elizabeth Anne, *b* 1979.

Hon Alison Elizabeth Vivienne (81 Finsbury Park Rd, N4 2JY), *b* 1953: *m* 1975 (*m diss* 1978), Michael John Hall.

Hon Vivienne Nicola, *b* 1955; BSc: *m* 1978, John Calvert Harvey, of 1 Place des Freres Tissandier, 78290 Croissy sur Seine, France, and has issue living, William Marc Gridley, *b* 1986, — Hannah Louise, *b* 1983.

AUNT LIVING (*Daughter of 1st Baron*)

Hon Geraldine, *b* 1918: *m* 1939, Lt-Col Norman John Lascelles Field, OBE, Roy Fusiliers, and has issue living, Richard Clive, *b* 1947; *ed* Oakham: *m* 1976, Susan Rosemary Hunter, 2nd da of late Peter Hunter Pearson, of E Sussex, and has issue living, James Peter *b* 1978, Christopher Guy *b* 1981, — Anne Jacqueline, *b* 1942: *m* 1967, Anthony Edward Vicars-Miles, and has issue living, Sarah Elizabeth *b* 1969, Katherine Juliet *b* 1972.

WIDOW LIVING OF SECOND BARON

(EDNA) LESLEY (*Lesley, Baroness Gridley*), eldest da of late Leslie Richard Wheen, of Shanghai: *m* 1948, the 2nd Baron Gridley, who *d* 1996. *Residence* – Coneygore, Stoke Trister, Wincanton, Som BA9 9PG.

COLLATERAL BRANCH LIVING

Issue of late Eric Howard Gridley, yr son of late Sir Arnold Babb Gridley, KBE (later 1st Baron Gridley), *b* 1911, *dvp* 1946: *m* 1936, Florence Sybil, who *d* 1979, da of Charles Darnell Bacon, of Loftus, N Yorks:—

PETER ARNOLD CHARLES, *b* 5 April 1940; *ed* Nautical Coll, Pangbourne: *m* 1966, Padmani Marie, da of late Maj P. D. Pelpola, MBE, of Gampola, Sri Lanka. *Residence* – Bigmore Cottage, Bigmore Lane, Stokenchurch, Bucks HP14 3UP. —— Howard Eric, *b* 1945; *ed* Fettes, Glasgow Univ (BSc), Selwyn Coll, Camb (Dip Agric Sci), and Wolfson Coll, Camb (PhD 1980): *m* 1994, Shoonah Eileen, da of James Leyburn Murphy, of Lisley, co Armagh. *Address* – CIAT, PO Box 6247, Kampala, Uganda.

PREDECESSORS – (1) Sir ARNOLD BABB Gridley, KBE, son of Edward Gridley of Abbey Dore, Herefordshire; *b* 1878; a consulting Engineer; MP for Stockport (C) 1935-50, and Stockport S 1950-55; *cr Baron Gridley* of Stockport, co Palatine of Chester (peerage of UK) 1955: *m* 1905, Mabel, who *d* 1955, da of Oliver Hudson, of Fakenham, *d* 1965; *s* by his el son (2) ARNOLD HUDSON, 2nd Baron, *b* 1906; Colonial Ser, Malaya 1928; interned by Japanese in Changi Gaol, Malaya 1941-45; Acting Dep Controller, Fedn of Malaya 1956-57; Member of Council and Exec Cttee of HM Overseas Ser Pensioners' Assocn; Govt Trustee Far East (POW and Internee) Fund; Political Adviser to People's Trust for Endangered Species; Knt 1957: *m* 1948, (Edna) Lesley, eldest da of late Leslie Richard Wheen, of Shanghai; *d* 1996; *s* by his only son (3) RICHARD DAVID ARNOLD, 3rd Baron and present peer.

GRIFFITHS, BARON (Griffiths) (Life Baron 1985)

(WILLIAM) HUGH GRIFFITHS, MC, PC, *b* 26 Sept 1923, only son of late Sir Hugh Ernest Griffiths, CBE (*d* 1961), by his wife, Doris Eirene, da of W. H. James; *ed* Charterhouse, and St John's Coll, Camb (MA); Pres MCC; Bar Inner Temple 1949, QC 1964, a Judge of High Court of Justice (Queen's Bench Div) 1970-80, and National Industrial Relations Court 1973-74; Member Advisory Council on Penal Reform 1967-70, Chm Tribunal of Inquiry on Ronan Point 1968, Vice-Chm Parole Bd 1976-77, Member Chancellor's Law Reform Cttee since 1976, Pres Senate of Inns of Court and the Bar 1982; a Lord Justice of Appeal 1980-85, a Lord of Appeal in Ordinary 1985-93; Chm Security Comm 1985-92; 1939-45 War as Capt Welsh Gds; MC 1944, *cr* Kt 1971, PC 1980, and *Baron Griffiths*, of Govilon, co Gwent (Life Baron) 1985: *m* 1949, Evelyn, da of Col K. A. Krefting, and has issue.

Address – c/o House of Lords, SW1. *Clubs* – Garrick, MCC, Royal & Ancient, St Andrews, Sunningdale Golf.

SON LIVING

Hon David Hugh, *b* 1958; *ed* Eton, and Magdalene Coll, Camb: *m* 1983, Henrietta, da of David Hall, and of Mrs Julian Wellesley, and has issue living, Thomas, *b* 1984, — Eloise, *b* 1986, — Jessica, *b* 1988.

DAUGHTERS LIVING

Hon Anne Serena, *b* 1951: *m* 1976 (*m diss* 1998), Peter William Urquhart, son of late Maj-Gen Ronald Walton Urquhart, CB, DSO, DL, and has issue living, James, *b* 1980, — Katherine, *b* 1978, — Flora, *b* 1981, — Serena, *b* 1984.

Hon Carolyn Jane, *b* 1952: *m* 1st, 1974 (*m diss* 1984), Justin Bygott-Webb; 2ndly, 1986, Douglas Christopher Patrick McDougall, son of late Patrick McDougall, and has issue living (by 1st *m*), Mark William, *b* 1976, — Samuel John, *b* 1978, — (by 2nd *m*) Fiona Maria, *b* 1987, — Mary Helen, *b* 1990.

Hon Emma Elizabeth, *b* 1964: *m* 1991, Duncan H. R. Matthews, son of M. Matthews, and of Mrs N. J. Hunter, and has issue living, George, *b* 1994.

GRIFFITHS OF FFORESTFACH, BARON (Griffiths) (Life Baron 1991)

BRIAN GRIFFITHS, son of Ivor Winston Griffiths; *b* 27 Dec 1941; *ed* Dynevor Gram Sch, and London Sch of Economics (BSc, MSc); Assist Lecturer in Economics, LSE, 1965-68, Lecturer in Economics 1968-76, Prof of Banking and Internat Finance, City Univ, 1977-85, Dir Centre for Banking and Internat Finance 1977-82, Dean Business Sch, City Univ, 1982-85, Visiting Prof Rochester Univ, USA, 1972-73, Prof of Ethics, Gresham Coll, 1984-87; Head of Prime Minister's Policy Unit (Rt Hon Margaret Thatcher) 1985-90; Dir Bank of England 1984-86; author; *cr Baron Griffiths of Fforestfach*, of Fforestfach, co W Glamorgan (Life Baron) 1991: *m* 1965, Rachel Jane, da of Howard Jones, and has issue.

Address – House of Lords, SW1. *Club* – Garrick.

SON LIVING

Hon James Brian, *b* 1970.

DAUGHTERS LIVING

Hon Aeronwen Jane, *b* 1968.
Hon Owenna Mary Ruth, *b* 1973.

GRIMOND, BARONY OF (Grimond) (Extinct 1993)

SONS LIVING OF LIFE BARON

Hon John Jasper, *b* 1946; *ed* Eton, Balliol Coll, Oxford, and Harvard Univ (Nieman Fell); Foreign Ed *The Economist*: *m* 1973, Kate, el da of late Lt-Col Peter Fleming, OBE, of Nettlebed, Henley-on-Thames, Oxon, and has issue living, Mary Jessie, *b* 1976, — Rose Clementine, *b* 1979, — Georgia Celia, *b* 1983.

Hon (Thomas) Magnus, *b* 1959; *ed* Stromness Acad, and Edinburgh Univ: *m* 1991, Laura Veldes, da of Rt Hon Sir Timothy Hugh Francis Raison, MP (*see* Cunard, Bt, 1976 Edn), and has issue living, Lucy Clare Laura, *b* 1994.

DAUGHTER LIVING OF LIFE BARON

Hon Grizelda Jane, *b* 1942; *ed* St Paul's Girls' Sch, and St Hugh's Coll, Oxford.

Grimston, family name of Earl of Verulam.

Grimston, Viscount; son of Earl of Verulam.

GRIMSTON OF WESTBURY, BARON (Grimston) (Baron UK 1964, Bt UK 1952)

Moderate things are stable

ROBERT WALTER SIGISMUND GRIMSTON, 2nd Baron, and 2nd Baronet; *b* 14 June 1925; *s* 1979; *ed* Eton; formerly Lt Scots Gds, NW Europe 1944-45; Liveryman of Gold and Silver Wyre Drawers' Co; Chm Grays Inn Underwriting Agency Ltd 1970-88; Dir of Hinton Hill and Coles 1962-83; Dir Stewart & Grays Inn Underwriting Agency Ltd 1970-90: *m* 1949, Hon June Mary Ponsonby, da of 5th Baron de Mauley, and has issue.

Arms – Quarterly: 1st and 4th argent, on a fesse sable, three rowels of six points or pierced gules; in the dexter chief an ermine spot sable, *Grimston*; 2nd sable, a fesse dancettée between two leopards' faces or, *Luckyn*; 3rd argent, three bugle horns sable, stringed gules, *Forrester*. **Crest** – A stag's head erased proper, attired or. **Supporters** – *Dexter*, a stag reguardant proper attired or; *sinister*, a horse reguardant argent.
Address – The Old Rectory, Westwell, nr Burford, Oxon. *Clubs* – Boodle's, and City of London.

SONS LIVING

Hon ROBERT JOHN SYLVESTER, *b* 30 April 1951; *ed* Eton, and Reading Univ (BSc); CA 1984; late Capt R Hus (PWO): *m* 1984, Emily Margaret, da of Maj John Evelyn Shirley, of Isle of Man (*see* E Ferrers, colls), and has issue living, Charlotte Elgiva, *b* 1991, — Philippa Margaret, *b* 1995. *Residence* – Elm Farm, Sibford Ferris, Banbury, Oxon OX15 5AA.

Hon (Gerald) Charles Walter (c/o Midland Bank, 69 Pall Mall, SW1; *Clubs* – Boodle's, and City of London), *b* 1953; *ed* Eton, and Exeter Univ (BA); late Maj Scots Gds (served N Ireland and S Atlantic Campaign 1982); Dir Grimston Holdings and Subsidiary Cos, J O Hambro Conning Grimston Ltd, and Woodcote Grove Estates Ltd: *m* 1980, Katherine Evelyn, da of Maj Rupert Berkeley Kettle, DL, of Piper's Hill, Bishop's Itchington, Leamington Spa, Warwicks, and has issue living, Edward Charles Luckyn, *b* 1985, — Alexander Rupert Ponsonby, *b* 1989, — Lucy Katherine Elgiva, *b* 1982.

DAUGHTER LIVING

Hon Georgiana Mary, *b* 1961: *m* 1992, Robin Pike, of 18 Edna St, SW11 3DP, yst son of late Thomas Pike, and has issue living, Jack Augustus Thomas, *b* 1994, — Patrick Belisarius Robert, *b* 1996, — William Aurelius Hubert, *b* 1998.

BROTHERS LIVING

Hon (Cecil) Antony Sylvester (Wellingham Vane, nr Lewes, Sussex BN8 5SN; Naval and Military Club, MCC), *b* 1927; *ed* Eton, and Camb Univ (MA): FRICS, FRSA; late Coldm Gds: *m* 1958 (*m diss* 1995), Dawn Monica Ann, da of Guy Janson, of Fair Hall, Southover, Lewes, and has issue living, Guy Antony Edward, *b* 1963: *m* 1992, Alison Jane, da of John Pile, of Middle Farm, Lewes, and has issue living, Daniel Luke *b* 1997, — John Lionel Charles, *b* 1968.

Hon Michael John Harbottle, *b* 1932; *ed* Eton; *m* 1st, 1957 (*m diss* 1978), Julia Mary, da of Sir George Albu, 2nd Bt; 2ndly, 1982, Denise Angove, and has issue living (by 1st *m*), Simon Harbottle, *b* 1960, — Giles Villiers, *b* 1961, — Katherine Flavia, *b* 1962, — Sybilla Jane, *b* 1966.

SISTERS LIVING

Hon Rosemary Sybella Violet, *b* 1929: *m* 1st, 1953 (*m diss* 1964), (Charles) Edward Underdown, who *d* 1989; 2ndly, 1984, Antony Herbert David Rowse, son of late Herbert James Rowse. *Residence* – 75B Flood St, SW3.

Hon Ella Zia, *b* 1937: *m* 1972, Humphrey K. Humphreys, who *d* 1984, and has issue living, Catherine Sybella, *b* 1977. *Residence* – Ferne Park Cottage, Berwick St John, Shaftesbury, Dorset.

PREDECESSOR – (1) *Sir* ROBERT VILLIERS Grimston, el son of Rev Canon Hon Robert Grimston (*see* E Verulam, colls), *b* 1897, Treas of HM Household 1939-42, Assist Postmaster-Gen 1942-45, Parl Sec to Min of Supply May-July 1945, Member of UK Delegation to Gen Assembly of UN 1960, Dep Chm of Ways and Means, House of Commons 1962-64, Pres of Urban Dist Councils Assocn 1949-71; MP for Westbury Div of Wilts (*C*) 1931-64; *cr* a *Baronet* 1952, and *Baron Grimston of Westbury*, of Westbury, co Wilts (peerage of UK) 1964: *m* 1923, Sibyl Rose, who *d* 1977, da of Sir Sigmund Neumann, 1st Bt, *d* 1979; *s* by his el son (2) ROBERT WALTER SIGISMUND, 2nd Baron and present peer; also 2nd Baronet.

GRIMTHORPE, BARON (Beckett) (Baron UK 1886, Bt UK 1813)

To benefit the State

CHRISTOPHER JOHN BECKETT, OBE, 4th Baron and 8th Baronet; *b* 16 Sept 1915; *s* 1963; *ed* Eton; patron of two livings; Brig (ret) late 9th Queen's R Lancers; Col Comdg 9th Queen's R Lancers 1955-58; Col 9th/12th Lancers (PWO) since 1973; Brig R Armoured Corps, HQ, Western Command 1961-64, and Dep-Cdr Malta and Libya 1964-67; ADC to HM 1964-68; DL N Yorks; OBE (Mil) 1958: *m* 1954, Lady Elizabeth Lumley, DCVO; a Lady of the Bedchamber to HM Queen Elizabeth The Queen Mother 1973; da of 11th Earl of Scarbrough, and has issue.

Arms – Gules, a fesse between three boars' head couped erminois. **Crest** – A boar's head couped of pierced by a cross patée fitchée erect gules. **Supporters** – Two sangliers erminois, each gorged with a collar and pendant therefrom an escutcheon gules charged with a cross patée fitchée or.
Seat – Westow Hall, York. *Club* – Cavalry.

SONS LIVING

Hon EDWARD JOHN, *b* 20 Nov 1954: *m* 1992, Mrs Carey Elizabeth McEwen, yr da of Robin Graham, of Stretton on Fosse, Glos, and has issue living, Harry Maximillian, *b* 28 April 1993. *Residence* – Hurstcroft, Fordham, Ely, Cambs.

Hon Ralph Daniel, *b* 1957: *m* 1987, Susanna W., elder da of Colin Townsend-Rose, and has issue living, Frederick John, *b* 1990, — Thomas Ralph, *b* 1992, — Katharine Flora, *b* 1997. *Residence* – 126 Farm Lane, SW6.

DAUGHTER LIVING

Hon Harriet Lucy, *b* 1961: *m* 1985, Capt (Richard) Mark Smyly, 16th/5th Queen's R Lancers (*see* By Buckland, 1980 Edn), and has issue living, Hugo Richard Seymour, *b* 1990, — George William Dennis, *b* 1992. *Residence* – The Old Glebe House, Sparsholt, Wantage, Oxon OX12 9PU.

BROTHER DECEASED

†*Hon* Oliver Ralph, *b* 1918; *ed* Eton; FRSA: *m* 1944, Hélène Agnes, who *d* (15 Feb) 1999, formerly wife of Richard Tasker-Evans, da of late Constantine Fessas, and *d* (22 May) 1999, leaving issue, Sarah Christine, *b* 1946; artist: *m* 1966 (*m diss* 1977), Jonathan Crook, and has issue living, John Henry *b* 1967, Tara Leonie *b* 1968, Sarah Aline (twin) *b* 1968, — Juliet Mary (2, 42 Upper Tooting Park, SW17), *b* 1949; actress.

HALF-BROTHER LIVING

Hon William Ernest, *b* 1945; *ed* Eton; 2nd Lt 9th/12th R Lancers: *m* 1968, Virginia Helen, only da of late Michael Clark Hutchison, of Wellcroft End, Bucklebury, Berks, and has issue living, Ralph Michael, *b* 1971, — Serena Angela Anne, *b* 1974. *Residence* – 21 Queen's Gate Place, SW7.

SISTER DECEASED

Hon Lucy Clare, *b* 1926: *m* 1957, Wilson Peregrine Nicholas Crewdson (*see* Bacon, Bt, 1995 Edn), and *d* 1999, leaving issue, Giles Wilson Mervyn, *b* 1959; Lieut 9th/12th R Lancers: *m* 1st, 1990 (*m diss* 1993), Hon Aurelia Margaret Amherst Cecil, only da of 4th Baron Amherst of Hackney; 2ndly, 1999, Frances Mary, 3rd da of Charles Kenneth Roylance Nunneley (*see* B Wrenbury, colls), — Diana Constance Mary (twin), *b* 1959: *m* 1980, Christopher J. M. Langley, yr son of late Lt-Col James Langley, of The Old Rectory, Alderton, Woodbridge, Suffolk, and has issue living, Venetia Margaret Clare *b* 1983, Edwina Chantal Elizabeth *b* 1985, Rose Katharine Lucy *b* 1988, — Virginia Clare, *b* 1964: *m* 1991, Giles J. G. Appleton, who *d* 1996, only son of late G/Capt James Appleton. *Residence* – Oak House, Otley, nr Ipswich, Suffolk.

COLLATERAL BRANCH LIVING   (*In special remainder*)

Issue of late Hon (William) Gervase Beckett (2nd son of late William, Beckett-Denison, and brother of 2nd Baron), who was *cr* a *Baronet* 1921:—
See Beckett, Bt, cr 1921.

PREDECESSORS – (1) Sir JOHN Beckett, of Leeds and Somerby Park, Lincs, *b* 1743; *cr* a *Baronet* 1813: *m* 1774, Mary, who *d* 1833, da of Christopher Wilson, Bishop of London; *d* 1826; *s* by his el son (2) JOHN, PC, MP, FRS, 2nd Bt; *b* 1775; MP for Cockermouth (C) 1820-21, Haslemere 1826-32, and Leeds 1835-7; Judge-Advocate-Gen: *m* 1817, Lady Anne Lowther, who *d* 1871, da of 1st Earl of Lonsdale; *dsp* 1847; *s* by his brother (3) THOMAS, 3rd Bt; *b* 1779; *m* 1829, his cousin Caroline, who *d* 1878, da of Joseph Beckett, of Barnsley: *d* 1872; *s* by his brother (4) EDMUND, 4th Bt; *b* 1787; MP for W Riding of York (C) 1841-59; assumed the name and arms of Denison by Roy licence 1816, and resumed his patronymic on succeeding to the Baronetcy: *m* 1814, Maria, who *d* 1874, da of William Beverley, and great-niece and heir of Anne Smithson, wife of Sir Thomas Denison, Justice of King's Bench 1742; *d* 1874; *s* by his el son (5) EDMUND, LLD, KC, 5th Bt; *b* 1816; resumed surname of Beckett in lieu of Denison 1874; Vicar-Gen and Chancellor of York; *cr Baron Grimthorpe*, of Grimthorpe, co York (peerage of UK) 1886, with remainder to the issue male of his father: *m* 1845, Fanny Catharine, who *d* 1901, da of late Right Rev John Lonsdale, DD, Lord Bishop of Lichfield; *d* 1905; *s* under special remainder by his nephew (6) ERNEST WILLIAM 2nd Baron (son of late William Beckett, MP, brother of 1st Baron), *b* 1856; MP for Whitby Div of NR of York (C) 1885-1905; partner in banking firm of Beckett & Co, of Leeds: *m* 1883, Lucy Tracy, who *d* 1891, da of late William P. Lee, of New York; *d* 1917; *s* by his son (7) RALPH WILLIAM ERNEST, TD, 3rd Baron; *b* 1891; Lt-Col (Cmdg 1936-40) Yorkshire Hussars TA, and partner in banking firm of Beckett & Co, of Leeds; PPS to Under Sec of State for War 1919-21: *m* 1st, 1914 (*m diss* 1945), Mary Alice, who *d* 1962, da of Col Mervyn Henry Archdale, 12th Lancers; 2ndly, 1945, Angela, who *d* 1992, da of late Edward Hubert Courage, of Kirkby Fleetham Hall, Bedale, Yorks, and formerly wife of late Cdr David Cecil Lycett Green, RN (*see* Green, Bt, colls); *d* 1963; *s* by his el son (8) CHRISTOPHER JOHN, 4th Baron and present peer.

Grinstead, Baron, title of Earl of Enniskillen on Roll of HL.

Grosvenor, family name of Baron Ebury.

Grosvenor, family name of Duke of Westminster.

Grosvenor, Earl; son of Duke of Westminster.

Guernsey, Baron; son of Earl of Aylesford.

GUEST, BARONY OF (Guest) (Extinct 1984)

SONS LIVING OF LIFE BARON (By 1st marriage)

Hon (Christopher) John Graham (19 Cheyne Row, SW3 5HW), *b* 1929; *ed* Eton, and Clare Coll, Camb: *m* 1960, Myrna, da of late I. Dukes, of Chicago, USA, and has issue living, Christopher, *b* 1967, — Amanda, *b* 1964. *Club* – Chelsea Arts.

(By 2nd marriage)

Hon David William Graham, *b* 1943; *ed* Charterhouse and Clare Coll, Camb (BA; CA): *m* 1992, Dr Jane L. Polglase, da of late E. B. J. Polglase, and has issue living, Lucie Olivia Anne, *b* 1998.

Hon Simon Edward Graham, WS (40 Hope Terrace, Edinburgh, EH9 2AR; Hon Co of Edinburgh Golfers), *b* 1949; *ed* Charterhouse and Dundee Univ (LLB); Solicitor and WS Edinburgh: *m* 1977, Fiona, da of late Robert Wilson Taylor Lamont, of Kilmarnock, and issue living, Michael Simon Lamont, *b* 1980, — Joanna Katie, *b* 1978.

Hon Andrew Beaumont Graham (2 Coltbridge Terrace, Edinburgh EH12 5AE), *b* 1951; *ed* Charterhouse, St Andrew's Univ (MA), and Edinburgh Univ: *m* 1980, Elizabeth, only da of late Alan Cuthbert, and has issue living, David John, *b* 1981, — Catherine Charlotte, *b* 1983.

DAUGHTER LIVING OF LIFE BARON (By 2nd marriage)

Hon (Elizabeth) Jane Graham, *b* 1945; *ed* Univ of Delaware, USA (BS, MS): *m* 1968, George Willing Pepper, of 128 Springton Lake Rd, Media, Pa 19063, USA. *Club* – Union League, Philadelphia.

Guest, family name of Viscount Wimborne.

Guest, see Baron Haden Guest.

Guetesbock, family name of Baron Berkeley.

GUILFORD, EARL OF (North) (Earl GB 1752)

PIERS EDWARD BROWNLOW NORTH, 10th Earl; *b* 9 March 1971; *s* 1999; is patron of two livings: *m* 1994, Michèle C., da of late Gilbert Desvaux de Marigny, of Curepipe, Mauritius, and of Mrs Eric Story, of Durban, S Africa.

𝕬rms – Azure, a lion passant or, between three fleurs-de-lis argent. 𝕮rest – A dragon's head erased sable, ducally gorged and chained or. 𝖲upporters – Two mastiffs proper.
Residence – Waldershare Park, Dover.

With courage and fidelity

AUNTS LIVING (*Sisters of 9th Earl*) (*Raised to the rank of an Earl's daughters 1950*)

Lady Barbara Joan, *b* 1928; OStJ: *m* 1951, Maj Hon Sir Clive Bossom, 2nd Bt, and has issue (see that title). *Residence* – 97 Cadogan Lane, SW1X 9DU.

Lady Angela Mary, *b* 1931: *m* 1955, Peter John Henry Whiteley, of 10 Henning St, SW11 3DR, and has issue living, Simon William Alastair, *b* 1958: *m* 1988, Winifred, yst da of Alex Wu, CBE, of Hong-Kong, — Justin Henry Francis, *b* 1964: *m* 1988, Juliette Margaret, only da of Philip Nicholas Charles Howard (*see* Houldsworth, Bt), and has issue living, Harry Thomas Edward *b* 1989, Charlie Hamish Reginald *b* 1992, Tom *b* 1995, — Emma Louise, *b* 1959: *m* 1993, Henry Campbell Bellingham, MP (*see* Bellingham, Bt, colls).

GREAT UNCLE LIVING (*Son of 8th Earl*)

Hon Charles Evelyn, *b* 1918; *ed* Eton, and London Univ (BSc 1939); European War, 1939-45 as Flight-Lieut RAF: *m* 1st, 1942 (*m diss* 1957), Maureen O'Callaghan, da of Major F. C. B. Baldwin, of Malmo, Park Avenue, Gillingham; 2ndly, 1959, Joan Aston, who *d* 1998, da of Major F. B. Booker, and has issue living, (by 1st *m*) Peter David (10 Uppingham Gdns, Caversham Park Village, Reading, Berks RG4 6SP), *b* 1943; *ed* Dover Coll: *m* 1967 (*m diss* 1984) Jennifer Elizabeth, da of Dr Frank Bernard Anstey, of Bampton, Devon, and has issue living, Amanda Louise *b* 1969, Rebecca Claire *b* 1972, — Susan Caroline, *b* 1947: *m* 1st, 1968 (*m diss* 1981), Peter Richard Jacob; 2ndly, 1983, Dr Timothy John Sharp, of 15 Clanwilliam Rd, Deal, Kent CT14 7BX, and has issue living (by 1st *m*), Lisa-Jane *b* 1968: *m* 1990, Michael Roberts, Sarah Lynne *b* 1970, (by 2nd *m*), Charles Eadgar *b* 1984, Emily Frances *b* 1979, Phoebe Elizabeth Halley *b* 1985. *Residence* – Shepherd's Cottage, Waldershare Park, Dover CT15 5BB.

WIDOW LIVING OF SON OF EIGHTH EARL

Wendy Alexandra, yst da of Francis Robert Peters: *m* 1961, as his 4th wife, Hon John Montagu William North, 2nd son of 8th Earl of Guilford, who *d* 1987. *Residence* – 2 La Brecque Phillippe, Alderney, CI GY9 3TJ.

COLLATERAL BRANCHES LIVING

Issue of late Hon John Montagu William North, 2nd son of 8th Earl, *b* 1905, *d* 1987: *m* 1st, 1927 (*m diss* 1939), Muriel Norton, who *d* 1989, yr da of Sir William Norton Hicking, 1st Bt (*see* North, Bt); 2ndly, 1939 (*m diss* 1949), Marion Dyer, who *d* 1986, yst da of Frank Erving Chase, of Boston, Mass, USA; 3rdly, 1951 (*m diss* 1960), Polly, da of Dick Peabody, of USA; 4thly, 1961, Wendy Alexandra (ante), yst da of Francis Robert Peters:—
(By 1st *m*) *Sir* (William) Jonathan Frederick, 2nd Bt, *b* 1931; *s* his maternal grandfather 1947 (*see* Baronetage). —— Georgiana Mary, *b* 1928: *m* 1960, Esmond Unwin Butler, CM, CVO, Sec to Gov-Gen of Canada, who *d* 1989, and has issue living, Mark William, *b* 1961, — Clare Martine, *b* 1963. *Residence* – 149 Rideau Terrace, Ottawa, Ontario, Canada. —— (By 3rd *m*) Serena Laura Peabody, *b* 1951: *m* 1976, Charles Meredith Hastings Colchester, son of late Rev Halsey Sparrowe Colchester, CMG, OBE, and has issue living, Alexander North Peabody, *b* 1981, — Benjamin Medhurst Pawson, *b* 1983, — Zachary Wheatland Maynard, *b* 1988, — Tamara Sarah Sparrowe, *b* 1985, — (Chloë) Talitha Jacob, *b* 1991, — Zoë Tatiana Francesca, *b* 1995. *Residence* – 59 Mayford Rd, SW12 8SE.

Issue of late Hon Morton William North, brother of 7th Earl, *b* 1852, *d* 1895: *m* 1879, Hylda Hylton, who *d* 1902, da of late Capt Hylton Jolliffe (B Hylton, colls):—
Roger, *b* 1888: *m* 1912, Alice Amy Le Gros. *Residence* –

Granddaughters of late Frederic Dudley North, CMG, elder son of late Charles Augustus North, elder son of late Brownlow North, only son of late Rev Charles Augustus North, brother of 6th Earl:—
Issue of late (Hon) Charles Frederic John North, *b* 1887, *d* 1979; Member Legislative Assembly for Claremont (Speaker 1947-53): *m* 1916, Bessie, da of William Saddington, of Cheshire:—

Muriel Elvia Joan, *b* 1917: *m* 1942, Roy Wilson Parr. —— Mary Rachael June, *b* 1930: *m* 1st, 1955 (*m diss* 1966), Gareth Murray Denny; 2ndly, 1967, Thomas Nolan Cassidy, and has issue living (by 1st *m*), David North Murray, *b* 1958, — Julie Elizabeth, *b* 1961.

Issue of late George Eustace Dudley North, *b* 1893, *d* 1960: *m* 1920, Florence Ethel Yeo, of Mount Street, Perth, W Australia:—
Mary Elizabeth, *b* 1925; former concert pianist: *m* 1948, Geoffrey Norris Russell, who *d* 19—, and has issue living, John Norris Grant, *b* 1951; *ed* Harrow, and Trin Coll, Dublin, — Francis Guilford, *b* 1953; *ed* Harrow; musician: *m* 1980, Manon Regina, el da of late James Mackay Henry Millington-Drake (*see* E Inchcape, 1980 Edn), — Philip Brownlow, *b* 1959. *Residence* – Dunkathel, Glanmire, co Cork.

Descendants, if any, of late Brownlow John Frederic North (*b* 1883), elder son of late Brownlow Hamilton North (*b* 1854) (infra).

Granddaughters of late Brownlow Hamilton North (*b* 1854), of The Knoll Estate, Coonoor, Nilgiri Hills, S India, only son of late Brownlow John Jarvis North (*b* 1831), 2nd son of late Brownlow North (ante):—
Issue of late George Guilford Dudley North, *b* 1884, *d* (April) 1937: *m* 1st, 19—, — , who *d* 19—; 2ndly, 1921, Jane Berkeley (who *d* 1977, having *m* 2ndly, (Oct) 1937, Austin Benedict Caston, of Garakhpur, UP, India), da of Charles Nathaniel Gregg:—
(By 2nd *m*) Patricia Grace Eileen, *b* 1922: *m* 1944, Jackson Samuel Askey, of 7710 Fitzpatrick Drive, Liverpool, NY 13088, USA, and has issue. —— Barbara Violet, *b* 1931: *m* 1957, James Edward Semple, of 8201 Golden Bear Loop, Port Richey, Florida 34668, USA, and has issue living, Cathy Barbara, *b* 1958: *m* 1982, Stephen Andrew Dock, and has issue living, James Matthew *b* 1987, Melissa Jean *b* 1985, Carolyn Jane *b* 1991, — Jane Alice, *b* 1962: *m* 1988, Delano Bookings Trott.

PREDECESSORS – **(1)** *Sir* EDWARD North, an eminent lawyer, MP for Cambridgeshire 1541-2, Lord-Lieut of Cambridgeshire, and one of the executors of Henry VIII; summoned to Parliament as *Baron North*, of Kirtling, co Cambridge (peerage of England) 1554; *d* 1564; *s* by his son **(2)** *Rt Hon* ROGER, KB, 2nd Baron, Ambassador to France and Treasurer of Queen Elizabeth's Household; *d* 1600; *s* by his grandson **(3)** DUDLEY, 3rd Baron; *d* 1666; *s* by his son **(4)** DUDLEY, KB, 4th Baron; *d* 1677: *s* by his son **(5)** CHARLES, 5th Baron; summoned to Parliament during his father's lifetime as *Baron Grey*, of Rolleston, co Stafford (peerage of England) 1673; *d* 1690; *s* by his son **(6)** WILLIAM, 6th Baron North and 2nd Baron Grey; *dsp* 1734, when the Barony of Grey expired and the Barony of North devolved upon his cousin **(7)** FRANCIS, 7th Baron North, who had in 1729 *s* as 3rd *Baron Guilford*, of Guildford, co Surrey (peerage of England, *cr* 1683), a peerage that had been conferred upon Hon Sir Francis, Lord Ch Justice of the Common Pleas, 2nd son of 4th Baron North; *cr Earl of Guilford* (peerage of Great Britain) 1752; *d* 1790; *s* by his el son **(8)** *Rt Hon* FREDERICK, KG, 2nd Earl; an eminent statesman who (when Lord North) held high official positions 1759-83, and was Prime Minister 1778-81; *d* 1792; *s* by his son **(9)** GEORGE AUGUSTUS, 3rd Earl; *d* 1802, when the Barony of North became abeyant (*see* B North), and the earldom devolved upon his brother **(10)** FRANCIS, 4th Earl; *dsp* 1817; *s* by his brother **(11)** FREDERICK, 5th Earl; *dsp* 1827: *s* by his cousin **(12)** *Rev* Francis, 6th Earl; *d* 1861; *s* by his grandson **(13)** DUDLEY FRANCIS (el son of late Dudley, Lord North, el son of 6th Earl), 7th Earl, *b* 1851: *m* 1874, Georgiana, who *d* 1931, da of Sir George Chetwynd, 3rd Bt; *d* 1885: *s* by his son **(14)** FREDERICK GEORGE, TD, 8th Earl, *b* 1876; Lieut-Col Roy E Kent Yeo: *m* 1901, Mary Violet, who *d* 1947, el da of late William Hargrave Pawson; *d* 1949; *s* by his grandson **(15)** EDWARD FRANCIS (only son of late Francis George, Lord North, el son of 8th Earl), 9th Earl, *b* 1933; DL Kent: *m* 1956, (Osyth) Vere Napier, who *d* 1992, da of Cyril Napier Leeston, of Trottiscliffe, W Malling, Kent; *d* 1999; *s* by his only son **(16)** PIERS EDWARD BROWNLOW, 10th Earl and present peer; also Baron Guilford.

Guinness, family name of Earl of Iveagh.

Guinness, family name of Baron Moyne.

Gully, family name of Viscount Selby.

Gummer, family name of Baron Chadlington.

Gurdon, family name of Baron Cranworth.

Gwynedd, Viscount, son of Earl Lloyd George of Dwyfor.

HABGOOD, BARON (Habgood) (Life Baron 1995)

Rt Rev and *Rt Hon* JOHN STAPYLTON HABGOOD, PC, son of late Arthur Henry Habgood, DSO, MB, BCh, by his wife Vera, da of late Edward Chetwynd-Stapylton (*see* V Chetwynd, colls, 1968 Edn); *b* 23 June 1927; *ed* Eton, King's Coll, Camb (BA 1948, MA 1951, PhD 1952, Fell 1952), and Cuddesdon Theological Coll, Oxford; Hon DD Durham 1975, Camb 1984, Aberdeen 1988, Huron 1990, Hull 1991, Oxford 1996, Manchester 1996, York 1996, Hon Fell King's Coll, Camb 1986; former demonstrator in pharmacology, Cambridge; deacon 1954, priest 1955; Curate of St Mary Abbots with St George's London 1954-56; Vice Principal of Westcott House, Cambridge 1956-62; Rector of St John's, Jedburgh 1962-67; Principal of Queen's Coll, Birmingham 1967-73; Hon Canon of Birmingham Cathedral 1971-73; Bishop of Durham 1973-83; Archbishop of York 1983-95; author of *Religion and Science* 1964, *A Working Faith* 1980, *Church and Nation in a Secular Age* 1983, *Confessions of a Conservative Liberal* 1988, *Making Sense* 1993, *Faith and Uncertainty* 1997, *Being a Person* 1998, *Varieties of Unbelief* 1999; *cr* PC 1983, and *Baron Habgood*, of Calverton, co Bucks (Life Baron) 1995: *m* 1961, Rosalie Mary Anne, elder da of Edward Lansdown Boston, of Deeside, Neston, Chester, and has issue.

𝕬rms – Per pale azure and gules a cross ermine floretty or between in dexter chief and sinister base a key in pale wards outwards and in sinister chief and dexter base a lion's head erased also or that in chief langued azure and that in base langued gules. 𝕸otto – Per Aspera Virtus.
Residence – 18 The Mount, Malton, N Yorkshire YO17 7ND. *Club* – Athenaeum.

SONS LIVING

Hon Francis John Stapylton, *b* 1964; *ed* Repton: *m* 1990, Nicolette Campbell, and has issue, Elliott, *b* 1993, — Sebastian, *b* 1995.
Hon Adrian George Chetwynd, *b* 1971; *ed* Repton.

DAUGHTERS LIVING

Hon Laura Caroline, *b* 1963; *ed* Wycombe Abbey: *m* 1997, Dr Virgilio Calderon Joya, of Honduras.
Hon Ruth Barbara, *b* 1967; *ed* The Mount, York: *m* 1991, Mark Kenyon-Slade, and has issue living, Lawrence, *b* 1997.

HACKING, BARON (Hacking) (Baron UK 1945, Bt UK 1938)

DOUGLAS DAVID HACKING, 3rd Baron, and 3rd Baronet; *b* 17 April 1938; *s* 1971; *ed* Charterhouse, and Clare Coll, Camb (MA); Bar Middle Temple 1963-76; Bar State of New York, USA 1975; with Simpson, Thatcher & Bartlett, New York City 1975-76; Solicitor of Supreme Court of England and Wales 1977; with Lovell, White & King, London and New York City 1976-79, with Richards Butler since 1981; Pres of Assocn of Lancastrians in London 1971-72; Freeman Merchant Taylors' Co, and City of London; Lt RNR (ret): *m* 1st, 1965, Rosemary Anne, el da of late Frank Penrose Forrest, FRCSE, of Lytchett Matravers, Dorset; 2ndly, 1982, Tessa Margaret, MB, MRCP, FRCA, da of Roland Hunt, CMG, of Whitchurch Hill, Reading, and has issue by 1st and 2nd *m*.

𝕬rms – Argent, on a chevron azure between three roses gules barbed and seeded proper, two birds bolts of the field, feathered or. 𝕮rest – In front of an oak tree eradicated, two axes in saltire all proper. 𝕾upporters – On either side a griffin gules, on the shoulder an escutcheon argent charged with a blue-bottle (Cyanus), stalked and leaved proper.
Residence – 27 West Square, SE11 4SP.

SONS LIVING *(By 1st marriage)*

Dr the Hon DOUGLAS FRANCIS, *b* 8 Aug 1968.
Hon Daniel Robert, *b* 1972.

(By 2nd marriage)

Hon Alexander Roland Harry, *b* 1984.
Hon (Maxwell David) Leo, *b* 1987.
Hon Christian Eric George, *b* 1989.

DAUGHTER LIVING *(By 1st marriage)*

Dr the Hon Belinda Anne, *b* 1966: *m* 1998, Simon C. Holden, yr son of Maj C. B. Holden, CBE, of Woking, Surrey.

BROTHER LIVING

Hon (Leslie) Bruce (Burchetts, Moushill Common, Milford, Surrey), *b* 1940; *ed* Eton; Member of Court of Assistants, Haberdashers' Co, and City of London: *m* 1967, Hon Fiona Margaret Noel-Paton, yst da of Baron Ferrier (Life Baron), and has issue living, Matthew Bruce, *b* 1969, — Joanna, *b* 1972.

SISTERS LIVING

Hon Sandra Daphne, *b* 1950: *m* 1972, Damon Patrick de Laszlo, of A2 Albany, Piccadilly, W1V 9RD, and Pelham Place, Newton Valence, nr Alton, Hants GU34 3NQ *(see* V Greenwood, 1980 Edn), and has issue living, Robert Damon, *b* 1977, — William Patrick, *b* 1979, — Lucy Deborah, *b* 1975.
Hon Carina Gillian, *b* 1956: *m* 1981, Jean Jacobus du Preez, of 8 Winters Wynd, Newlands 7700, Cape Province, S Africa.

AUNT LIVING *(Daughter of 1st Baron)*

Hon Elizabeth Margery *(Hon Lady Waller)*, *b* 1916; is a JP (Hants); *m* 1936, Rt Hon Sir George Stanley Waller, OBE, who *d* 1999, and has issue living, *Rt Hon Sir* (George) Mark *(Rt Hon Lord Justice Waller)*, *b* 1940, LLB; Bar Gray's Inn, 1964; QC 1979, Recorder 1986, Judge of High Court of Justice, Queen's Bench Div 1989-96, since when a Lord Justice of Appeal; *cr* Kt 1989, PC 1996: *m* 1967, Rachel Elizabeth, da of His Honour Christopher Beaumont, MBE, of Minskip Lodge, Boroughbridge, N Yorks, and has had issue, Charles James *b* 1968, *d* 1997, Richard *b* 1969: *m* 1997, Katie T., da of Stephen Walduck, Philip *b* 1973: *m* 1998, Mary V. M., eldest da of Dr Peter William Monckton Copeman, of Spencer Park, London, — James Irvin (136 Brighton Av, Ottawa, Ont, Canada K1S OT4), *b* 1944; Prof of Criminology, Ottawa Univ: *m* 1st, 1966, Myriam, da of Prof Pierre de Bie, of 2 Chaussée de Namur, Blanden, Belgium; 2ndly, 1983, Susan Gwen, da of Byron Chester Tanner, of 11309 University Av, Edmonton, Alberta, and has issue living, (by 1st *m*) Ann-Virginie *b* 1968: *m* 1995, Samuel Landon, Marie-Katherine *b* 1970, (by 2nd *m*), James Byron Tanner *b* 1984, Mark Patrick Byron Tanner *b* 1986, — Elizabeth Tessa, *b* 1937; Prof of Neuropathology, Harvard Univ: *m* 1959, Prof John Hedley-Whyte, of 355 Fairhaven Rd, Concord, Mass 01742 4406, USA. *Residence* – Hatchway, Hatch Lane, Kingsley Green, Haslemere, Surrey GU27 3LT.

Evangeline Grace, da of Percy Burtsal Shearing, of S Africa: *m* 1950, as his 2nd wife, Maj the Hon Edgar Bolton Hacking, MBE, TD, MRCS, LRCP, who *d* 1998, and has issue (infra). *Residence* – Leeming, Alice Rd, Claremont, Cape, S Africa.

COLLATERAL BRANCH LIVING

Issue of late Maj the Hon Edgar Bolton Hacking, MBE, TD, MRCS, LRCP, yr son of 1st Baron, *b* 1912, *d* 1998: *m* 1st, 1943 (*m diss* 1950), Winifred Mary, da of late John Christie Kelly, of S Africa; 2ndly, 1950, Evangeline Grace (ante), da of Percy Burtsal Shearing, of S Africa:—
(By 1st *m*) (Elizabeth) Anne (Dundarach Poultry Farm, PO Box 7077, Noorder Paarl 7623, S Africa), *b* 1944. —— Susan Margaret, *b* 1946. —— (By 2nd *m*) Douglas Percival Bolton, *b* 1955: *m* 1984, Mary, yr da of late Cyril Puttergill, of Indwe, Cape Prov. —— Geoffrey Edgar Bolton (12 Neave St, Claremont, Cape, 7700 S Africa), *b* 1958: *m* 1983, Elizabeth, only da of late Edward Hiles, of Somerset West, Cape Prov. —— Margery Ethel, *b* 1952: *m* 1973, George du Plessis, son of late V. de Plessis of Cape Town.

PREDECESSORS – (1) DOUGLAS HEWITT Hacking, OBE, PC, son of Joshua Hacking, JP, of Clayton-le-Moors, Lancs, *b* 1884; Financial Sec to War Office and a Member of Army Council 1934-35, and Under-Sec of State for Dominions 1935-36; founded Travel Assoc of Great Britain and Ireland 1928; Chm of Conservative Party 1936-42; MP for Chorley (*U*) 1918 to 1945; *cr a Baronet* 1938, and *Baron Hacking*, of Chorley, co Lancaster (peerage of UK) 1945: *m* 1909, Margery Allen, who *d* 1984, aged 97, el da of H. H. Bolton, JP, of Newchurch-in-Rossendale; *d* 1950; *s* by his el son (2) DOUGLAS ERIC, 2nd Baron, *b* 1910; Chm of Council Trust Houses 1965-70 and Trust Houses Forte Hotel and Catering Group 1970-71; 1939-45 War as Maj RA: *m* 1936, Daphne Violet, who *d* 1998, el da of late Robert Leslie Finnis, of Kensington, W, *d* 1971; *s* by his el son (3) DOUGLAS DAVID, 3rd Baron and present peer; also 3rd baronet.

HADDINGTON, EARL OF (Baillie-Hamilton) (Earl S 1619)

I undertake and persevere   *Virtue is greater than splendour*

JOHN GEORGE BAILLIE-HAMILTON, 13th Earl; *b* 21 Dec 1941; *s* 1986; *ed* Ampleforth: *m* 1st, 1975 (*m diss* 1981), Prudence Elizabeth, da of Andrew Rutherford Hayles, of Bowerchalke, Wilts; 2ndly, 1984, (Susan) Jane Antonia, da of John Heyworth, of Bradwell Grove, Burford, Oxon (*see* By Tweedmouth, 1995 Edn), and has issue by 2nd *m*.

Arms – Quarterly: 1st and 4th grand quarters, 1st and 4th gules, on a chevron between three cinquefoils argent, a buckle azure, between two ermine spots, all within a bordure or, charged with eight thistles vert, *Hamilton of Byres*; 2nd and 3rd argent, a fesse wavy between three roses gules barbed and seeded proper, *Melrose*; 2nd and 3rd grand quarters sable, the sun in his glory betwixt nine stars, three, two, three, and one, argent, *Baillie of Jerviswoode*. **Crests** – 1st, two dexter hands issuing out of clouds, conjoined fessewise and holding betwixt them a branch of laurel erect, all proper; 2nd, a crescent or. **Supporters** – Two talbots argent, plain collared gules.
Seat – Mellerstain, Gordon, Berwicks TD3 6LG.

SON LIVING (*By 2nd marriage*)

Hon GEORGE EDMUND BALDRED (*Lord Binning*), *b* 27 Dec 1985.

DAUGHTERS LIVING (*By 2nd marriage*)

Lady Susan Moyra, *b* 1988.
Lady Isobel Joan, *b* 1990.

SISTER LIVING

Lady Mary, *b* 1934: *m* 1st, 1954 (*m diss* 1965), (John) Adrian Bailey, elder son of late Ronald Graham Bailey, of 7 Lansdowne Crescent, W11; 2ndly, 1965, David Russell, son of Brig Hugh Edward Russell, DSO, and has issue living (by 1st *m*), (William) Anthony, *b* 1957: *m* 1993, Anne C., yr da of Mark Ueland, of Philadelphia, Penn, USA, and has issue living, Geordie Dominic Maximilian *b* 1998, Cecilia Sarah *b* 1995, — Philip Graham, *b* 1959: *m* 1990, Georgina A., da of G. M. C. White, and of Mrs Barbara Makins, — Arabella Sarah Lucy (*Viscountess Chandos*), *b* 1955: *m* 1985, 3rd Viscount Chandos, — (by 2nd *m*) Jason Dominic, *b* 1966: *m* 1996, J. Sybille, elder da of Christopher Gray, of Higginsbrook, co Meath, and has issue living, Natasha Sarah *b* 1997, — Mariana, *b* 1968. *Residence* – Combe Manor, Newbury, Berks.

COLLATERAL BRANCHES LIVING

Grandchildren of late Rev Thomas George Baillie, son of Rev Hon John Baillie, brother of 10th Earl:—
Issue of late Richard George HAMILTON-BAILLIE, b 1869, d 1945: m 1915, Maud Gertrude, who d 1952, only da of late Edward Hadley, Bar-at-Law:—
John Robert Edward, MC, b 1919; ed Camb Univ (MA); Brig (ret) late RE, MICE; 1939-45 War (MC): m 1947, Lettice Mary, da of late C. E. Pumphrey, of Belsay, Northumberland, and has issue living, Thomas Richard (Cavalry and Guards' Club), b 1948; ed Winchester, London Univ (BA), and Oxford Univ; Lt-Col R Green Jackets: m 1975, Marina J. A. S., da of late General Dr Ferdinand von Senger und Etterlin, of Riedern Am Wald, Uhlingen-Birkendorf, Germany, and has issue living, Isobel Ebba b 1979, Daisy Ernestine b 1982, Cecily Marina b 1985, — Benjamin Robert, b 1955: m 1988, Jennifer A., da of late Leslie Hill, of Pinner, Middx, and has issue living, Laurence Benjamin b 1990, Agnes Laetitia b 1992, — Griselda Mary, b 1950; Trustee Royal Academy since 1990: m 1985, William Walter Raleigh Kerr, eldest son of Lord John Andrew Christopher Kerr, and has issue (see M Lothian), — Katherine Maud, b 1957. *Residence* – Rectory House, Stanford-in-the-Vale, Faringdon, Oxon.

Issue of late Charles Jarviswoode Baillie, b 1882, d 1973: m 1915, Dora Lizzie Dunn-Smith, who d 1973:—
Barbara, b 1915: m 1945, Maurice W. Brown, and has issue living, Laurence Charles, b 1955, — Robin Alison, b 1947: m 1968, Kenneth le Drew, and has issue living, Christopher b 1969, — Priscilla Ann, b 1952: m 1973, Allan P. Roe, and has issue living, Corey Christopher b 1977, Jess Patrice b 1974, Gillian Martha b 1975. *Residence* – RR2 Albers Rd, Lumby, BC, Canada V0E 2G0.

Grandchildren of late Charles Jarviswoode Baillie (ante):—
Issue of late Robert Alastair Baillie, b 1919, d 1984: m 1945, Elizabeth Amy (Suite 15, 980 Gilford St, Esher Court, Vancouver, BC, Canada V6G 2N7), da of Alexi Chernoff, of Tiflis, Russia, and of Kelowna, BC:—
Dexter Robert, b 1958: m 19— (m diss 1999), Kristin Grace, da of Ross Bradford, of Warwick, Australia. *Address* – Box 945, Whistler, BC, Canada V0N 1B0. — Eve Sylvia, b 1946: m 1968, John Edward Sample, and has issue living, Barton Kirby, b 1976; has issue (by Cora-Lea Puchmayr), Taylor Kellie b 1998. — Sarah Nicole, b 1971. *Residence* – 5815 Gilpin St, Burnaby, BC, Canada V5G 2J1. — Angeline Cecelia, b 1950: m 1974, Roy Albert Derrick, only son of Rex Raphael Derrick, of Penticton, BC, and has issue living, Kyle Edward b 1987, — Shannon Hillary, b 1980, — Colleen Elizabeth, b 1984. *Residence* – 3623 Selinger Crescent, Regina, Saskatchewan, Canada S4V 2H7.

Granddaughter of Rev Hon John Baillie, brother of 10th Earl (ante):—
Issue of late Rev Thomas George Baillie, b 1842, d 1917: m 1st, 1867, Ellen Isabella, who d 1909, da of Richard Gregson, of Sydney, NSW; 2ndly, 1911, Violet Amy Kate, who d 1961, da of F. W. Dunn:—
(By 2nd m) Violet Georgina Eila, b 1912: m 1931, Albert Ranney Chewett, who d 1965. *Residence* – Reveley Lodge, 88 Elstree Rd, Bushey Heath, Herts WD2 3QY.

Granddaughter (by 1st m) of late George Leslie Baillie-Hamilton, sometime Capt 13th Bn Royal Scots (Lothian Regt) (infra):—
Issue of late George Leslie Baillie-Hamilton, b 1909, d 1968: m 1947, Mrs Millicent Margaret Lambert, who d 1989, da of late Edmund Sopp, and formerly wife of George Ernest Lambert:—
Ann, b 1947: m 1966, James William Maxwell Sheridan, of 995 Forest Rd, E17 4BP, and has issue living, Paul Maxwell, b 1966; has issue living (by Deborah Suzanne Budd), Jarrod James b 1990, Kylie Jade b 1988, — Trevor William, b 1967, — Gavin Robert, b 1976, — Samantha Ann, b 1969.

Grandchildren of late Rev George James Baillie-Hamilton, only son of late Capt Peregrine Charles Baillie-Hamilton, elder son of late Charles John Baillie-Hamilton, MP, 2nd son of late Ven Charles Baillie-Hamilton, 2nd son of Hon George Baillie, brother of 7th Earl:—
Issue of late George Leslie Baillie-Hamilton, sometime Capt 13th Bn Royal Scots (Lothian Regt), b 1877, d 1931: m 1st, 1906, Florence Maud Robinson, who d 1912; 2ndly, 1919, Katherine Ida Sopp (otherwise Pennicard), who d 1943:—
(By 2nd m) David Lincoln, b 1922: m 1956, Mrs Maud Mary Philipps, da of late Samuel George Augustus Schwenke, and widow of Ralph Philipps. — Ella Faith, b 1919: m 1939, Harry Dan Thomas Turner, and has had issue, two sons and one da. — Jean Elizabeth, b 1920: m 1943, Reginald H. Walker, and has issue living, two sons and two das.

Grandsons of late John BUCHANAN-BAILLIE-HAMILTON, 6th son of late Ven Charles Baillie-Hamilton (ante):—
Issue of late John Edmondstone BUCHANAN-BAILLIE-HAMILTON, b 1874, d 1957: m 1925, Bridget Everett, who d 1971, da of John E. Baker, formerly of Cambridge:—
John Neil, b 1926; ed Winchester; Capt (ret) late Black Watch: m 1st, 1955, Hon Caroline Barbara Coupar Barrie, who d 1978, da of 1st Baron Abertay; 2ndly, 1981, Mrs Gillian M. Macdonald, formerly wife of Roderick Macdonald, of Turvey, Beds, and has issue living (by 1st m), John Michael (The Gart, Callander, Perthshire), b 1958; ed Oxford Univ (MA): m 1994, Dr Paula Frances, 2nd da of John Hickman, of London, and has issue living, Angus John Buchanan b 1996, Bruce Charles Buchanan b 1997, — Alexander Neil b 1963; Capt The Black Watch; Equerry to HRH The Duke of York 1990-92. *Residence* = Cambusmore, Callander, Perthshire. James Angus, b 1927; late Lt RN; High Sheriff of Glos (1984); is a farmer: m 1954, Prudence, only da of Cdr Wenman Humfry Wykeham-Musgrave, RN (ret) (E Grey, colls), of Wheelwrights, Barnsley, Cirencester, Gloucestershire, and has issue living, Charles Wenman, b 1957: m 1996, Mrs Sandy J. Righton, yst da of J. E. C. Richford, of Stratford-upon-Avon, and has issue living, Sophie Elizabeth b 1998, — Simon James, b 1963, — Jane, b 1955; MB BS: m 1979, Alastair James Dickson, of West Kennacott, Newton Tracey, Barnstaple, N Devon, and has issue living, James b 1982, Claire Louise b 1984, — Sally, b 1961: m 1987, James Hippisley Kidner, son of Dr Patrick Gerald Kidner, of Manaton, Devon. *Residence* – South Farm, Shipton Oliffe, nr Cheltenham, Gloucestershire. — Alexander, b 1932; ed Glenalmond, and Aberdeen Univ (MB and ChB); Diploma of Industrial Medicine, London 1959: m 1964, Mrs Lilia Julia Mary Eaton, da of late Alan Peter, of St Lucia, W Indies, and has issue living, Fiona Mary, b 1966, — Alexandra Helen, b 1969. *Residence* – Knowle Croft, Shoppenhangers, Maidenhead, Berks.

PREDECESSORS – (1) *Sir* THOMAS Hamilton, successively a Lord of Session (as Lord Drumcairn), a Commr to treat of a Union with England, Lord Clerk Register of Scotland, Sec of State, Pres of Court of Session, and Keeper of the

Privy Seal; *cr Lord Binning* (peerage of Scotland) 1613, *Earl of Melrose*, and *Lord Byres and Binning* (peerage of Scotland) 1619; the title of Melrose was changed in 1627, and he was *cr Earl of Haddington* (peerage of Scotland) with precedence of 1619 and limitation to his heirs male bearing the name of Hamilton; *d* 1637, leaving one of the largest fortunes of his time; *s* by his son **(2)** THOMAS, 2nd Earl, a zealous Covenanter; was killed by an explosion at the Castle of Dunglas, of which he was Gov, 1640; *s* by his el son **(3)** THOMAS, 3rd Earl; *dsp* 1645; *s* by his brother **(4)** JOHN, 4th Earl; *d* 1669; *s* by his son **(5)** CHARLES, 5th Earl; *m* 1674, Lady Margaret Leslie, da of 1st Duke of Rothes, who on the death of her father became in her own right by charter Countess of Rothes; in 1689 was granted a patent confirming the terms of the *m* contract, by which the Earldom of Rothes was to descent to the el son, and the Earldom of Haddington and Lordship of Binning were to revert to the 2nd son; the Countess *d* 1702, and was *s* by her el son (*see* Rothes); the Earl *d* 1681, and was *s* by his 2nd son **(6)** THOMAS, 6th Earl; obtained a charter of the Earldom, and appointed Hereditary Keeper of Holyrood Palace; a Representative Peer 1716-35; *d* 1735; *s* by his grandson **(7)** THOMAS, 7th Earl; el son of Charles, Lord Binning; *d* 1794; *s* by his son **(8)** CHARLES, 8th Earl; a Representative Peer, and Lord-Lieut of Haddingtonshire; *d* 1828; *s* by his son **(9)** THOMAS, KT, PC, 9th Earl; Lord-Lieut of Ireland 1833-4; *cr Baron Melrose*, of Tyninghame (peerage of United Kingdom) 1827; in 1843 resigned the office of Hereditary Keeper of Holyrood Palace for the consideration of £40,000; *d* 1858, when the Barony of Melrose became extinct, and the Scottish honours devolved upon his cousin **(10)** GEORGE, 10th Earl, son of George Baillie, nephew of 7th Earl; *b* 1802; was a Lord-in-Waiting to HM 1867-8, a Representative Peer, and High Commr to Gen Assembly of Ch of Scotland; assumed by Roy licence 1859 the additional surname of Hamilton to that of Baillie, which had been assumed in lieu of Hamilton by his grandfather: *m* 1824, Georgina, da of the Ven Robert Markham, Archdeacon of York; *d* 1870; *s* by his son **(11)** GEORGE, KT, 11th Earl; *b* 1827; Vice-Lieut of co Berwick 1873-1917, and Lord-Lieut of co Haddington 1896-1917; assumed by Roy licence, 1858, the additional surname of Arden after that of Baillie-Hamilton: *m* 1854, Helen Catherine, who *d* 1889, da of Sir John Warrender, 5th Bt; *d* 1917; *s* by his grandson **(12)** GEORGE, KT, MC, TD (son of late Brig-Gen George, Lord Binning, CB, MVO, el son of 11th Earl), 12th Earl, *b* 1984, a Representative Peer for Scotland 1922-63, Capt Scots Greys (Res), Maj 19th (Lothians and Border Horse) Armoured Car Co (TA) and Res of Officers, Lt Queen's Body Guard for Scotland (Royal Company of Archers), Lord Lieut of Berwickshire 1952-69; 1914-18 War in France and Belgium (wounded, MC), 1939-45 War, W/Cdr RAFVR 1941-45; bore the Queen's Ivory Rod at Coronation of King George VI: *m* 1923, Sarah, who *d* 1995, yst da of late George William Cook, of Westmount, Montreal; *d* 1986; *s* by his only son **(13)** JOHN GEORGE, 13th Earl and present peer; also Lord Binning, and Lord Byres and Binning.

Haddo, Earl of; son of Marquess of Aberdeen.

HADEN-GUEST, BARON (Haden-Guest) (Baron UK 1950)

CHRISTOPHER HADEN-GUEST, 5th Baron; *b* 5 Feb 1948; *s* 1996; *ed* The Stockbridge Sch, and New York Univ; Film Dir, Writer, Musician and Actor (as Christopher Guest): *m* 1984, Jamie Lee Curtis, actress, da of Tony Curtis (né Bernard Schwartz), actor, and of Janet Leigh (née Jeanette Helen Morrison), actress, and has an adopted son and da.

𝕬rms – Sable, two flaunches or, three Welsh triple harps in fess counterchanged. 𝕮rest – A caladrius displayed sable, beaked, legged and charged on the breast with a sun in splendour gold. 𝕾upporters – *Dexter*, a leopard sable semy of roundels and grasping in the interior paw a quill gold; *sinister*, a leopard or semy of roundels and grasping in the interior paw a quill sable.
Addresses – 10866 Wilshire Blvd, Suite 1100, Los Angeles, CA 90024, USA; HC-64 Box 8018, Ketchum, Idaho 83349, USA.

SON LIVING

Thomas, *b* 1996.

DAUGHTER LIVING

Anne, *b* 1986.

BROTHER LIVING

Hon NICHOLAS, *b* 5 May 1951; *ed* New Sch for Social Research (BA), American Coll, Paris, Stella Adler Inst, and Herbert Berghof Studio; actor: *m* 1st, 1980 (*m diss* 1989), Jill Ellen Demby; 2ndly, 1989, Mrs Pamela Ann Rack, da of late Lieut Joseph G. Seamon, US Navy, of Akron, Ohio, and has issue living (by 1st *m*), Julia, *b* 1988, — (by 2nd *m*) Elizabeth Ann, *b* 1990. *Address* – PO Box 1069, Burbank, CA 91507, USA.

HALF BROTHER LIVING

Hon Anthony, *b* 1937; *ed* Gordonstoun, and St John's Coll, Camb; Journalist. *Residence* – Garden Apt, 67 East 80th St, New York, NY 10021, USA.

SISTER LIVING

Hon Elissa, *b* 1953; writer: *m* 1981, Nicholas Carey Smith, son of Corlies Morgan Smith, and has issue living, Nathanael Haden, *b* 1988, — Gena Haden, *b* 1984. *Residence* – 287 31st Avenue, San Francisco, CA 94121, USA.

DAUGHTER LIVING OF SECOND BARON

Hon Hadley, *b* 1949; *ed* City Univ of New York (BA 1977). *Residence* – 1301 Milvia Street, Berkeley, CA 94709, USA.

WIDOW LIVING OF THIRD BARON

MARJORIE DOUGLAS (*Marjorie, Baroness Haden-Guest*), da of late Dr Douglas Kennard: *m* 1951, as his 3rd wife, the 3rd Baron Haden-Guest, who *d* 1987. *Residence* – 3 Chemin des Crêts-de-Champel, 1206 Geneva, Switzerland.

WIDOW LIVING OF FOURTH BARON

JEAN PAULINE (*Jean, Baroness Haden-Guest*), da of late Dr Albert George Hindes, of 190 Waverly Place, New York, NY: *m* 1945, as his 2nd wife, the 4th Baron Haden-Guest, who *d* 1996. *Residence* – 198 Old Stone Highway, East Hampton, NY 11937, USA.

PREDECESSORS – (1) LESLIE HADEN Haden-Guest, MC, MRCS, LRCP, son of late Alexander Haden-Guest, Surg and Physician of Manchester; *b* 1877; a Lord-in-Waiting to HM Feb to Oct 1951; sat as MP for N Div of Southwark (*Lab*) 1923-7, and for N Div of Islington 1937-50; *cr Baron Haden-Guest*, of Saling, co Essex (peerage of United Kingdom) 1950: *m* 1st, 1898 (*m diss* 1909), Edith, who *d* 1944, da of Max Low, of London; 2ndly, 1910, Muriel Carmel, who *d* 1943, da of late Col Albert Edward Williamson Goldsmid, MVO; 3rdly 1944, Edith Edgar, who *d* 1977, da of late George Macqueen, of Montrose; *d* 1960; *s* by his el son (2) STEPHEN HADEN, 2nd Baron *b* 1902; editor and translator: *m* 1st, 1948 (*m diss* 1954), Barbara Ann, da of James Harvey Pinson, of W Virginia, USA; 2ndly, 1968, Dorothy, who *d* 1994, da of Thomas Roseberry Good, late of Princeton, New Jersey; *d* 1974; *s* by his brother (3) RICHARD HADEN, 3rd Baron, *b* 1904: *m* 1st, 1926 (*m diss* 1934), Hilda, da of late Dr Thomas Russell-Cruise; 2ndly, 1934, Olive Maria, da of late Anders Gotfrid Nilsson; 3rdly, 1951, Marjorie Douglas, da of late Dr Douglas Kennard; *d* 1987; *s* by his half-brother (4) PETER HADEN, 4th Baron, *b* 1913; Dancer (as Peter Michael) 1935-41; United Nations Official 1946-72; 1939-45 War as Lieut RCNVR

(SB): *m* 1st, 1939 (*m diss* 1945), Mrs Elizabeth Louise Ruth Coker, eldest da of late Paul Wolpert, of Konnigsberg; 2ndly, 1945, Jean Pauline, da of late Dr Albert George Hindes, of 190 Waverly Place, New York, NY; *d* 1996; *s* by his 2nd son (5) CHRISTOPHER, 5th Baron and present peer.

HAIG, EARL (Haig) (Earl UK 1919)

GEORGE ALEXANDER EUGENE DOUGLAS HAIG, OBE, 2nd Earl (*30th Laird of Bemersyde*); *b* 15 March 1918: *s* 1928; *ed* Stowe, and Ch Ch Oxford (MA); Capt Roy Scots Greys; Hon Maj on disbandment of HG 1958; is a Member of Queen's Body Guard for Scotland (Roy Co of Archers), a DL for Roxburghshire (Vice-Lt Berwicks 1967-70); Assoc Royal Scottish Academy 1988; Pres Scottish Craft Centre 1950-75, Chm SE Scotland Disablement Advisory Cttee 1960-73, a Mem of Scottish Arts Council 1969-75, and Pres of Earl Haig Fund (Scotland) 1980-86, Pres of Officers' Assocn (Scottish Cttee) 1987-96 (Chm 1977-87), Chm Bd of Trustees of Scottish National War Memorial 1983-96; a Trustee of National Galleries of Scotland 1962-72; FRSA; KStJ; Chm of R British Legion, Scotland 1962-65, and Pres 1980-86; 1939-45 War (prisoner); was a Train Bearer at Coronation of King George VI; OBE (Civil) 1966: *m* 1st, 1956 (*m diss* 1981), Adrienne Thérèse, da of Derrick Morley, of Quaives, Wickhambreaux, Kent; 2ndly, 1981, Donna Gerolama Lopez y Royo, and has issue by 1st *m*.

Arms – Azure, a saltire between a mullet in chief and another in base, a decrescent and an increscent in the flanks argent. Crest – A rock proper. Supporters – *Dexter*, a bay horse caparisoned thereon mounted a Private of the 7th (Queen's Own) Hussars, habited, armed and accoutred; *sinister* a bay horse, caparisoned, thereon mounted a Lancer of the 17th (Duke of Cambridge's Own) Lancers habited, armed and accoutred all proper.
Seat – Bemersyde, Melrose, Roxburghshire. *Clubs* – Cavalry, New.

SON LIVING (*By 1st marriage*)

ALEXANDER DOUGLAS DERRICK (*Viscount Dawick*), *b* 30 June 1961; *ed* Stowe.

DAUGHTERS LIVING (*By 1st marriage*)

Lady (Adrienne) Rainà, *b* 1958.
Lady (Elizabeth) Vivienne Thérèse, *b* 1959.

SISTER LIVING

Lady Irene Violet Freesia Janet Augusta (*Irene, Baroness Astor of Hever*), *b* 1919; CStJ; an hon Life Member Commonwealth Press Union (1985): *m* 1945, 2nd Baron Astor of Hever, who *d* 1984. *Residences* – 11 Lyall St, SW1X 8DH; Holly Tree House, French St, Westerham, Kent TN16 1PW.

PREDECESSORS – (1) *Field Marshal Sir* DOUGLAS Haig, KT, GCB, OM, GCVO, KCIE, son of late John Haig, of Cameronbridge, Fife, *b* 1861; Nile Expedition 1898, present at battles of Atbara and Khartoum (despatches, Egyptian medal with two clasps, Brevet Major), in S Africa 1899-1902 on the Staff, present at battles of Elandslaagte, operations around Colesberg, relief of Kimberley, and battles of Paardeberg and Belfast, and in command of Mounted Columns with rank of Col (despatches twice, Brevet Lieut-Col and Col, CB), European War 1914-18, first in command of 1st Army Corps, secondly of 1st Army, and thirdly of British Expeditionary Force in France and Flanders (despatches thrice, promoted Gen, Grand Officer Legion of Honour, GCB, GCVO, Field-Marshal, KT, Obilitch medal, Croix de Guerre, Italian Order of St Maurice and St Lazarus, 4th class of Russian Order of St George, and of Michael the Brave of Roumania, Serbian Order of Karageorge with Swords, Order of Tower and Sword of Portugal, Medaille, American Cross of Honour, Grand Cordon of Japanese Order of the Rising Sun with Paulowina, and 1st class Order of Chia Ho of China, Gold Medal of La Solidaridad of Panama, American DSM, thanked by Parliament, *cr* Earl, granted £100,000, presented by people of British Empire with house and fishings of Bemersyde); attached to Egyptian Army 1897-8; appointed an Extra ADC to HM 1902, Inspector-Gen of Cav in India 1903, Director of Mil Training at Head Quarters 1906, Director of Staff Duties there 1907 Ch of Staff in India and a Member of Council of Gov-Gen of India 1909, an ADC Gen to HM 1914, Gen Officer Comdg-in-Ch, Aldershot 1912, and Gen Officer Comdg-in-Ch, Great Britain 1919; *cr* Earl Haig, Viscount

Dawick, and *Baron Haig*, of Bemersyde, co Berwick (peerage of United Kingdom) 1919: *m* 1905, Hon Dorothy Maud Vivian (a DGStJ), who *d* 1939, da of 3rd Baron Vivian; *d* 1928; *s* by his son (2) GEORGE ALEXANDER EUGENE DOUGLAS, 2nd Earl and present peer; also Viscount Dawick, and Baron Haig.

Hailsham, Viscountcy of, see Baron Hailsham of St Marylebone.

HAILSHAM OF ST MARYLEBONE, BARON (Hogg) (Viscount UK 1929, disclaimed 1963, Life Baron 1970)

QUINTIN MCGAREL HOGG, KG, CH, PC, FRS; *b* 9 Oct 1907; *s* as 2nd Viscount Hailsham 16 Aug 1950; *ed* Eton, and Ch Ch Oxford (MA, Hon Student); Hon DCL Oxford; FRS; Fellow of All Souls Coll, Oxford 1931-38, and since 1962; Bar Lincoln's Inn 1932, QC 1953, and Bencher 1956; Hon LLD Camb; 1939-45 War as Maj Rifle Bde (TA) (wounded); Joint Under-Sec of State for Air April to July 1945, First Lord of the Admiralty 1956-57, Min of Educ Jan to Sept 1957, Dep Leader of House of Lords 1957-60, Lord Pres of the Council 1957-59, and again 1960-64, Lord Privy Seal 1959-60, Leader of House of Lords 1960-63, Min & Sec of State for Education and Science 1959-64, Lord High Chancellor 1970-74, and 1979-87; elected R of Glasgow Univ 1959, Chancellor Buckingham Univ 1983-91; MP for Oxford City (*C*) 1938-58, and for St Marylebone 1963-70; PC 1956; disclaimed his peerage for life 20 Nov 1963; *cr Baron Hailsham of St Marylebone*, of Herstmonceux, co Sussex (Life Baron) 1970, CH 1974, and KG 1988: *m* 1st, 1931 (*m diss* 1943), Natalie Antoinette, who *d* 1987, da of late Alan Sullivan, of Sheerland House, Pluckley, Kent; 2ndly, 1944, Mary Evelyn, who *d* 1978, only child of Richard Martin, of 46 Wynnstay Gdns, W8; 3rdly, 1986, Deirdre Margaret, who *d* 1998, elder da of late Capt Peter Shannon, and of Mrs Margaret Briscoe, and has issue by 2nd *m*.

Arms – Argent, three boars' heads erased azure, langued gules, between two flaunches azure each charged with a crescent of the field. **Crest** – Out of an eastern crown argent, an oak-tree fructed proper, and pendent therefrom an escutcheon azure, charged with a dexter arm embowed in armour, the hand grasping an arrow in bend sinister, the point downwards, also proper. **Supporters** – On either side a ram argent armed and unguled or, gorged with a baron's coronet, the *dexter* supporting a representation of the Lord High Chancellor's mace, and the *sinister*, a representation of the Lord High Chancellor's purse, with the initials of Her Majesty Queen Elizabeth II, proper.

SONS LIVING *(By 2nd marriage)*

Rt Hon DOUGLAS MARTIN, MP, *b* 5 Feb 1945; *ha* to Viscountcy of Hailsham; *ed* Eton, and Ch Ch, Oxford; Bar Lincoln's Inn 1968; QC 1990; MP for Grantham (*C*) since 1979; Assist Govt Whip 1983-84, Parly Under-Sec Home Office 1986-89, Min of State DTI (Min for Industry) 1989-90, Min of State Dept of Foreign and Commonwealth Affairs 1990-95, Min of Agriculture, Fisheries and Food 1995-97; PC 1992: *m* 1968, Hon Sarah Elizabeth Mary (*Baroness Hogg*) (*cr* a Life Baroness 1995), yr da of Baron Boyd-Carpenter, PC (Life Baron), and has issue living, *Hon* Quintin John Neil Martin, *b* 1973, — *Hon* Charlotte Mary, *b* 1970.

Hon James Richard Martin, *b* 1951; *ed* Eton, and Ch Ch Oxford; late Capt Gren Gds. *m* 1987, D. Clare, yr da of Maurice Raffael, of Wimbledon, and has issue living, Thomas Neil, *b* 1991, — Domini Alexandra, *b* 1989.

DAUGHTERS LIVING *(By 2nd marriage)*

Hon Dame Mary Claire (*Hon Mrs Justice Hogg*), DBE, *b* 1947; *ed* St Paul's Girls' Sch; Bar Lincoln's Inn 1968; (Bencher 1995), Bar Northern Ireland 1993; QC 1989; Assist Recorder 1986-90, Recorder 1990-95, since when a Judge of High Court of Justice (Family Div); *cr* DBE 1995: *m* 1987, Eric Koops, eldest son of Leendart Koops, of Hellingly, Sussex, and has issue living, William Quintin Eric, *b* 1991, — Katharine Mary, *b* 1989.

Hon Frances Evelyn, *b* 1949; *ed* St Paul's Girls' Sch, and Homerton Coll, Cambridge; JP: *m* 1970, Richard Quintin Hoare, DL Hants 1997, son of late Quintin Vincent Hoare, and has issue living, Alexander Richard Quintin, *b* 1973, — Charles

Martin Richard, *b* 1976, — Elizabeth Mary Frances, *b* 1978. *Residence* – Tangier House, Wootton St Lawrence, Basingstoke, Hants RG23 8PH.

Hon Katharine Amelia, *b* 1962; *ed* Roedean, and St Peter's Coll, Oxford: *m* 1993, Richard A. Collins, son of C. A. Collins, of Penarth, S Glam, and has issue living, Rollo Francis Richard, *b* 1998, — Evelyn Frances, *b* 1996.

PREDECESSORS – **(1)** *Rt Hon Sir* DOUGLAS McGAREL HOGG, PC, son of Quintin Hogg (*see* Hogg Bt, *cr* 1846, colls); *b* 1872; Bar Lincoln's Inn, 1902, a KC 1917, and a Bencher 1920; Attorney-Gen to HRH the Prince of Wales and a Member of Council of Duchy of Cornwall 1920-22, Attorney-Gen (with a seat in the Cabinet) 1924-28, Lord High Chancellor 1928-29 (acted as Prime Min 1928), and Leader of Opposition in House of Lords June to Aug 1931; appointed Sec of State for War (National Govt) and Leader of the House of Lords 1931, and again Lord High Chancellor 1935; Lord President of the Council March to Oct 1938; Recorder of Kingston-upon-Thames 1924-28; sat as MP for St Marylebone (*U*) 1922-28; *cr Baron Hailsham*, of Hailsham, co Sussex (peerage of United Kingdom) 1928, and *Viscount Hailsham*, of Hailsham, co Sussex (peerage of United Kingdom) 1929: *m* 1st, 1905, Elizabeth, who *d* 1925, da of late Judge James Trimble Brown, of Nashville, Tennesee, USA, and widow of Hon Archibald John Majoribanks; 2ndly, 1929, Mildred Margaret, who *d* 1964, da of late Rev Edward Parker Dew, R and Patron of Breamore, Hants, and widow of Hon Alfred Clive Lawrence (B Trevethin & Oaksey); *d* 1950; *s* by his el son **(2)** QUINTIN McGAREL, 2nd Viscount, until he disclaimed his peerages 1963; *cr Baron Hailsham of St Marylebone* (Life Baron) 1970.

HAIRE OF WHITEABBEY, BARONY OF (Haire) (Extinct 1966)

SONS LIVING OF LIFE BARON

Hon Michael John Kemeny, *b* 1945; *ed* St Paul's Sch, Univ Coll, London, and Pennsylvania Univ.
Hon Christopher Peter, *b* 1951; *ed* Holland Park Sch.

WIDOW LIVING OF LIFE BARON

SUZANNE ELIZABETH (*Baroness Haire of Whiteabbey*); da of Dr Eugene Kemeny, of Hatvan: *m* 1939, Baron Haire of Whiteabbey (Life Baron), who *d* 1966.

HALE, BARONY OF (Hale) (Extinct 1985)

SON LIVING OF LIFE BARON

Hon Ian William Percy, *b* 1930. *Residence* – The Grove, Swannington, Leics. LE67 8QN.

DAUGHTER LIVING OF LIFE BARON

Hon Dorothy Lesley, *b* 1927. *Residence* – The Grove, Swannington, Leics. LE67 8QN.

HALIFAX, EARL OF (Wood) (Viscount UK 1866, Baron UK 1925, Earl UK 1944, Bt GB 1784)

CHARLES EDWARD PETER NEIL WOOD, 3rd Earl and 7th Baronet, *b* 14 March 1944; *s* 1980; *ed* Eton, and Ch Ch, Oxford; Vice Lord Lieut of East Riding of Yorks since 1996; DL co Humberside 1983; High Steward York Minster since 1988; KStJ: *m* 1976, Camilla, da of late Charles Frank Johnston Younger, DSO, TD, of Gledswood, Melrose, Roxburghshire, and formerly wife of Richard Eustace Parker Bowles (*see* E Macclesfield, colls), and has issue.

Arms – 1st and 4th azure, three naked savages ambulant in fesse proper, in the dexter hand of each a shield argent, charged with a cross gules, and in the sinister a club resting on the shoulder also proper, on a canton ermine three lozenges conjoined in fesse sable; 2nd and 3rd palybendy or and azure, a canton ermine. **Crest** – A savage as in the arms, the shield sable charged with a griffin's head erased argent. **Supporters** – On either side a griffin sable, gorged with a collar and pendant therefrom a portcullis or.
Seat – Garrowby, York YO4 1QD. *Clubs* – Pratt's, White's.

SON LIVING

JAMES CHARLES (*Lord Irwin*), *b* 24 Aug 1977; *ed* Eton.

DAUGHTER LIVING

Lady Joanna Victoria, *b* 1980.

SISTERS LIVING

Lady Caroline Victoria, *b* 1937: *m* 1st, 1958 (*m diss* 1970), Randle Joseph Feilden, son of Maj-Gen Sir Randle Guy Feilden, KCVO, CB, CBE (*see* V Hampden, colls); 2ndly, 1970, John Gosling. *Residence* – The Claw, Brushford, Dulverton, Somerset.

Lady Susan Diana, *b* 1938: *m* 1959, Brigadier Ian Darsie Watson, CBE, TD, and has issue living, David Charles Darsie, *b* 1960, — Richard Ian, *b* 1962: *m* 1990, Henrietta, only da of Antony Butterwick, of Pinkneys Green, Berks, and has issue living, William *b* 1995, Isabella *b* 1993, Eliza *b* (twin) 1995. *Residence* – Bossall Hall, Bossall, York, YO6 7NT.

UNCLE LIVING (Son of 1st Earl)

Rt Hon Richard Frederick, PC (*Baron Holderness*), *b* 1920; *cr* Baron Holderness 1979 (see that title).

COLLATERAL BRANCHES LIVING (*In remainder to Viscountcy and Baronetcy only*)

Grandsons of late Col Hugo MEYNELL, MC (infra):—
Issue of late Nicholas Edward Hugo Meynell, *b* 1937, *d* 1988: *m* 1966 (*m diss* 1987), Hon Alexandra Rachel Mary Catherine Angelica Lampson, da of 2nd Baron Killearn:—
Hugo Graham Nicholas, *b* 1970: *m* 1998, Natasha O. St C., yr da of late Timothy King. —— Alexander Frederick Miles, *b* 1972.

Grandchildren of late Lieut-Col Francis Hugo Lindley MEYNELL, DSO (infra):—
Issue of late Col Hugo MEYNELL, MC, *b* 1909, *d* 1960: *m* 1936, Dorothy Jean, who *d* 1993, da of Sir Edward Henry Goschen, 2nd Bt:—
David Christian Francis (Horsebrook Hall, Horsebrook Lane, Brewood, Stafford ST19 9LP), *b* 1940: *m* 1962, Susan Lesley, da of George Garfield-Jones, of The Mount, Shrewsbury, and has issue living, Charles Christian George, *b* 1964; Capt The Life Guards: *m* 1992, Elizabeth Zoe, yst da of Dr Patrick Lawrence, of The Mill House, Iffley, Oxford, and has issue living, Cosmo Frederick Charles *b* 1995, — Edward David Lindley, *b* 1971, — Melissa Alexandra Elizabeth Susanna, *b* 1968: *m* 1994, Edward Wilson Bennett Williams, of Tewes Farmhouse, Little Sampford, Saffron Walden, Essex CB10 2QQ, eldest son of Robert Williams, of Mayden Croft Manor, Gosmore, Hitchin, Herts, and has issue living, George Frederick Bennett *b* 1999. —— Frederick James (Oaklands Cottage, E Lytherley, nr Salisbury, Wilts), *b* 1944: *m* 1st, 1969 (*m diss* 1973), Charmian Joy, da of Maj Harcourt Michael Scudamore Gold, MC (*see* By of Trent); 2ndly, 1975, Mary Anne, da of Trevor Leslie Harris, and has issue living (by 2nd *m*) Sophie Louise, *b* 1980, — Lucinda Mary, *b* 1983. —— (Karen) Elizabeth Mary (*Hon Mrs George C. D. Jeffreys*), *b* 1947: *m* 1967, Capt Hon George Christian Darell Jeffreys, of Manor Farm Barn, Alkerton, Banbury, Oxon OX15 6NL (*see* B Jeffreys). —— Alexandra Dorothy Jean (*Baroness Tollemache*), *b* 1949: *m* 1970, 5th Baron Tollemache, of Helmingham Hall, Stowmarket, Suffolk.

Grandchildren of late Hon Frederick George Lindley MEYNELL (who assumed by R Licence for himself and his issue the surname and arms of Meynell in lieu of his patronymic), 4th son of 1st Viscount:—
Issue of late Lieut-Col Francis Hugo Lindley Meynell, DSO, *b* 1880, *d* 1941: *m* 1907, Lady Dorothy Legge, OBE, who *d* 1974, da of 6th Earl of Dartmouth:—

Rev Canon Mark (2 Double St, Framlingham, Suffolk), *b* 1914; *ed* Eton, and Ch Ch, Oxford; Canon Theologian Emeritus of Coventry: *m* 1940, Diana Mary, da of Col Sir Charles Edward Ponsonby, TD, 1st Bt, and has issue living, Christopher Mark (Bergh Apton Hall, Norwich, Norfolk), *b* 1941: *m* 1968, Hon Elizabeth Margaret Gretton, twin da of 2nd Baron Gretton, and has issue living, *Rev* Mark John Henrik *b* 1970: *m* 1997, Rachel J. B., elder da of Graham Carr, of Makindye Hill, Kampala, Uganda, Guy Francis *b* 1973, — *Rev* Andrew Francis (The Rectory, Mill Lane, Monks Risborough, Bucks HP27 9JE), *b* 1943: *m* 1971, Caroline Anne, da of late Rt Hon Sir John Gardiner Sumner Hobson, OBE, TD, QC, MP, and has issue living, Aidan Jonathan Charles *b* 1974, Francesca Clare *b* 1976, — Peter John, *b* 1947: *m* 1973, Judith, da of late Rt Hon Sir (Harry) Neil Marten, of Swalcliffe House, nr Banbury, Oxon, and has issue living, Marten Charles *b* 1977, Anna Louise *b* 1979, Clea Diana *b* 1982, — Anna Mary Barbara, *b* 1960: *m* 1986, Louis Thomas de Soissons, of Ivy Farm, Witton, nr North Walsham, Norfolk NR28 9TT, eldest son of Brian de Soissons, of Swafield Hall, Norwich, Norfolk, and has issue living, Alexander Thomas *b* 1988, Hugo Charles *b* 1991, Guy Louis *b* 1996.

Issue of late Sir Everard Charles Lindley MEYNELL, OBE, MC, *b* 1885, *d* 1956: *m* 1914, Rose, who *d* 1975, da of late Lionel Bulteel, of Yewden Manor, Henley-on-Thames, Oxon:—
†Francis Everard, MBE, *b* 1917; *ed* Eton; Lt-Cdr RN (ret); MBE (Mil) 1962: *m* 1956, Janet Penelope, da of late Engineer-Rear-Adm Albert Kingsley Dibley, CB, and *d* 1996, leaving issue, Rosemary Janet, *b* 1960: *m* 1984, George Walter Bishop, eldest son of Frank Bishop, of Sunningdale Farm, Nottingham Rd, Natal 3280, and has issue living, Charles Andrew Meynell *b* 1986, Sarah Rose *b* 1989, Mary Janet *b* 1992, — Elizabeth Anne, *b* 1961: *m* 1984, Dr Derek Montague Brink, son of late Dr Johannes Brink and has issue living, Nicholas Francis Meynell *b* 1990, Jonathan James Meynell *b* 1992, Derek Anthony Meynell *b* 1994, Peter Andrew Meynell *b* 1997, — Anne Penelope, *b* 1964: *m* 1987, Capt Anthony David Blumer, Royal Australian Regt, yr son of Dr John Blumer, of Sydney, Australia, and has issue living, Natasha Anne *b* 1993, Emma Katherine *b* 1995, Lara Janet *b* 1997. *Residence* – Valbona, 13 Spilhaus Av, Hohenort, Constantia, Cape Province 7800, S Africa. —— Clare, *b* 1932: *m* 1956, John Marsham Hallward, of 1745 Cedar Avenue, PH4, Montreal, Quebec, Canada H3G 1A7 (*see* By Atholstan, 1976 Edn), and has issue living, Peter Marsham, *b* 1968, — Christopher Graham, *b* 1973, — Jennifer Rose, *b* 1963, — Julia Anne, *b* 1965, — Mary Clare, *b* 1966, — Katherine Rosemary, *b* 1972. —— Mary, *b* 1935: *m* 1974, Robert Leonard Clother, of Martlets, Rodmell, Lewes, Sussex BN7 3HF.

Issue of late Capt Charles Wilfrid Lindley MEYNELL, RN, *b* 1890, *d* 1976: *m* 1917, Ida Beatrice, who *d* 1977, da of late Rt Hon Ernest George Pretyman, MP (E Bradford):—
Richard Walter (Berry Hall, Honingham, Norfolk, NR9 5AX), *b* 1923; FCA; 1939-45 War: *m* 1950, Countess Ilse Teresa, da of Lt-Gen Count Theodor von Sponeck, and has issue living, Anthony Charles (Old Hall Farm Cottages, North Tuddenham, Norfolk), *b* 1952; *ed* Eton: *m* 1983, his cousin, Mrs Julia Akel, da of John Kift Winter by his wife Rachel, da of late Lt-Col Francis Hugo Lindley Meynell, DSO (*see* 1995 Edn), and has issue living, Wilfrid *b* 1986, Rachel *b* 1984, — Charles Humphrey, *b* 1954; *ed* Eton, — Patricia Rose, *b* 1960: *m* 1986, Sharad Jain, son of Prof S. P. Jain, of Anandlok, New Delhi. —— Beatrice Mary (12A Long St, Devizes, Wilts), *b* 1918: *m* 1945, Maj John Whitcombe, RA, who *d* 1985, and has issue living, Sarah Rose, *b* 1946: *m* 1973, Rev Barry Thorley, and has issue living, Thomas Edward *b* 1984, — Clarissa Beatrice, *b* 1949: *m* 1969, Robert Anthony Gosling, of Pulham Cottage, Wetherden, Stowmarket (*see* B Ampthill, colls, 1995 Edn), and has issue living, Richard Bennet *b* 1972; *ed* Eton, Camb Univ: *m* 1998, Nicola Jane Robb, Charlotte Arabella Ida *b* 1974.

PREDECESSORS – **(1)** FRANCIS Wood, 2nd son of late Francis Wood, JP, DL, of Barnsley; *b* 1728; *cr a Baronet* 1784, with remainder to his el brother, the Rev Henry, DD, V of Halifax, and failing him to the sons of his younger brother, Charles, of Bowling Hall; *m* 1779, Elizabeth, who *d* 1796, da and heiress of Anthony Ewer, of The Lea, and Bushey Hall, Herts; *d* 1795; *s* by his nephew **(2)** *Sir* FRANCIS LINDLEY, 2nd Bt (son of Charles (ante)); *b* 1771; High Sheriff of Yorkshire 1814-15: *m* 1798, Anne, who *d* 1841, da of Samuel Buck, Recorder of Leeds; *d* 1846; *s* by his son **(3)** CHARLES, GCB, PC, 3rd Bt; *b* 1800; was Chancellor of the Exchequer 1846-52, Pres of Board of Control 1852-5, First Lord of the Admiralty 1855-8, Sec of State for India 1859-66, and Lord Privy Seal 1870-74; sat as MP for Grimsby (*L*) 1826-31, for Wareham 1831-2, for Halifax 1832-65, and for Ripon 1865-6: *cr Viscount Halifax*, of Monk Bretton, co York (peerage of United Kingdom) 1866: *m* 1829, Lady Mary Grey, CI, who *d* 1884, da of 2nd Earl Grey: *d* 1885; *s* by his el son **(4)** CHARLES LINDLEY, *b* 1839; Pres of English Church Union 1869-1919 and 1931-33: *m* 1869, Lady Agnes Elizabeth Courtenay, who *d* 1919, only da of 11th Earl of Devon; *d* 1934; *s* by his only surviving son **(5)** EDWARD FREDERICK LINDLEY, KG, OM, GCSI, GCMG, GCIE, TD, PC, 1st Earl, *b* 1881; formerly Lieut-Col Yorkshire Dragoons Yeo (Hon Col 1935-60); sometime Chm Med Research Council; was Assist Sec Min of National Ser 1917-18, and a British Delegate of League of Nations Assembly 1923; appointed Under-Sec of State for the Colonies 1921; Pres of Board of Education 1922-4, Min of Agriculture and Fisheries 1924-5, Pres of Board of Education (in National Govt) 1932-5, Sec of State for War June to Nov 1935, Lord Privy Seal 1935-7, Leader of the House of Lords 1935-8, Lord Pres of the Council 1937-8, Sec of State for Foreign Affairs 1938 to 1940 (also again Leader of the House of Lords Oct to Dec 1940), and Ambassador Extraor and Plen at Washington 1941-6; a Vice-Pres E India Asso 1931; was Viceroy and Gov-Gen of India 1926-31; elected Chancellor of Oxford Univ 1933, and of Sheffield Univ 1947; appointed Chancellor of Order of the Garter 1943, Chm of Gen Advisory Council of British Broadcasting Corporation 1947 and Grand Master of Order of St Michael and St George 1957; became High Steward of Westminster 1947; bore St Edward's Staff at Coronation of King George VI; sat as MP for Yorkshire, W Riding, E Part, Ripon Div (*C*) 1910-18, and for Ripon Div of W Riding of Yorkshire 1918-25; *cr Baron Irwin*, of Kirby Underdale, co York (peerage of United Kingdom) 1925, and *Earl of Halifax* (peerage of United Kingdom) 1944: *m* 1909, Lady Dorothy Evelyn Augusta Onslow, CI, DCVO, LLD, who *d* 1976, yr da of 4th Earl of Onslow; *d* 1959; *s* by his el son **(6)** CHARLES INGRAM COURTENAY 2nd Earl, *b* 1912; Lord-Lt for E Riding of Yorks, 1968-74, and for Humberside 1974-80; Chm of E Riding of Yorks Co Council 1968-80; High Steward of York Minster 1970-80; Jt Master Middleton Foxhounds 1946-80, Senior Steward Jockey Club 1950-51 and 1958-59; MP for York (*C*) 1937-45: *m* 1936, Ruth Alice Hannah Mary, who *d* 1989, da of late Capt Rt Hon Neil James Archibald Primrose, MC, MP (*see* E Rosebery, colls); *d* 1980; *s* by his only son **(7)** CHARLES EDWARD PETER NEIL, 3rd Earl and present peer, also Viscount Halifax and Baron Irwin.

HALL, VISCOUNTCY OF (Hall) (Extinct 1985)

DAUGHTERS LIVING OF SECOND VISCOUNT (*By 1st marriage*)

Hon Lena Margaret, *b* 1950: *m* 1985, Frederick Neagle, eldest son of late William Neagle.
Hon Georgina Anne, *b* 1953.

WIDOW LIVING OF SECOND VISCOUNT

MARIE-COLETTE (*Viscountess Hall*), da of late Col Henri Bach: *m* 1974, as his 3rd wife, the 2nd Viscount Hall, who *d* 1985.
Residence – Solvain, 41210 St Viatre, Loir et Cher, France.

Hall, family name of Baron Lockwood.

Hall, see Barony of King-Hall.

HALSBURY, EARL OF (Giffard) (Earl UK 1898)
(Title pronounced "Haulsbury")

Form no vile wish

NE·VILE·VELIS

JOHN ANTHONY HARDINGE GIFFARD, 3rd Earl; *b* 4 June 1908; *s* 1943; *ed* Eton; BSc, DTech, FIEE, FICE, FEng, FRS; first Chancellor of Brunel Univ 1966-98: *m* 1st, 1930 (*m diss* 1936), Ismay Catherine, who *d* 1989, da of late Lt-Col Lord Ninian Edward Crichton-Stuart (*see* M Bute, colls, 1985 Edn); 2ndly, 1936, Elizabeth Adeline Faith, who *d* 1983, da of late Maj Harry Crewe Godley, DSO (E Annesley, colls), and has issue by 1st and 2nd *m*.

Arms – Sable, three lozenges conjoined in fesse ermine. Supporters – Two swans ermine, beaked and legged gules, each having pendant from the neck by a ribbon of the last a shield charged as the arms.
Residence – 4 Campden House, 29 Sheffield Terrace, W8 7NE.

SON LIVING (*By 1st marriage*)

ADAM EDWARD (does not use courtesy title), *b* 3 June 1934: *ed* Stowe, Jesus Coll, Camb (MA 1961), and Open Univ (BSc 1995); late 2nd Lt Seaforth Highlanders: *m* 1st, 1963, Mrs Ellen Huxley, da of late Brynjolf Hovde; 2ndly, 1976, Joanna Elizabeth, da of Frederick Harry Cole, and has issue living (by 2nd *m*), Sarah Cole, *b* 1976, — Emma Cole, *b* 1978. *Address* – New Mills, Snapper, Barnstaple, N Devon EX32 7JZ.

DAUGHTERS LIVING (*By 2nd marriage*)

Lady (Elizabeth) Caroline (Elinor Evelyn), *b* 1939: *m* 1968 (*m diss* 1992), Rodney John Derek Blois, and has issue (*see* Blois, Bt). *Residence* – 23 Maxwell Rd, SW6.
Lady Clare Rohais Antonia Elizabeth, *b* 1944: *m* 1964, Col Oliver John Martin Lindsay, CBE, FRHistS, MICFM, Gren Gds, and has issue (*see* Lindsay, Bt). *Address* – c/o Child & Co, 1 Fleet St, EC4Y 1BD.

PREDECESSORS – (1) *Rt Hon Sir* HARDINGE STANLEY Giffard PC, son of late Stanley Lees Giffard, LLD; *b* 1823; was Solictor-Gen 1875-80, and Lord High Chancellor of England June 1885 to Jan 1886, July 1886 to Aug 1892, and June 1895 to Dec 1905; MP for Launceston (*C*) 1877-85, Constable of Launceston Castle 1883-1919; *cr* Knt 1875, PC 1885, *Baron Halsbury*, of Halsbury, co Devon (peerage of United Kingdom) 1885, and *Viscount Tiverton*, of Tiverton, co Devon and *Earl of Halsbury*, in co Devon (peerage of United Kingdom) 1898: *m* 1st, 1852, Caroline, who *d* 1873, da of W. C. Humphreys, of Wood Green, Middlesex; 2ndly, 1874, Wilhelmina, who *d* 1927, da of late Henry Woodfall; *d* 1921; *s* by his son (2) HARDINGE GOULBURN, KC, 2nd Earl, *b* 1880; was Recorder of Carmarthen 1923-35: *m* 1907, Esmé, who *d* 1973, da of late James Stewart Wallace; *d* 1943; *s* by his son (3) JOHN ANTHONY HARDINGE, 3rd Earl and present peer; also Viscount Tiverton, and Baron Halsbury.

HAMBLEDEN, VISCOUNT (Smith) (Viscount UK 1891)

DEO NON FORTUNA FRETUS

Relying on God, not on fortune

WILLIAM HERBERT SMITH, 4th Viscount; *b* 2 April 1930; *s* 1948; *ed* Eton: *m* 1st, 1955 (*m diss* 1988), Maria Carmela Attolico di Adelfia, da of late Count Bernardo Attolico, of 15 Via Porta Latina, Rome, Italy; 2ndly, 1988, Mrs Lesley Watson, and has issue by 1st *m*.

Arms – Argent, on a chevron azure between three oak leaves vert, each charged with an acorn or as many leopards' faces jessant-de-lis of the field. **Crest** – A cubit arm erect habited azure, cuffed and charged with three mascles in chevron argent holding in the hand proper three branches of oak vert, fructed or. **Supporters** – *Dexter*, a sea-lion vert langued gules semée of escallops and gorged with a collar or, pendant therefrom by a gold chain a portcullis of the third; *sinister*, a wyvern gules, langued azure, semée of mullets or, and gorged with a gold chain, therefrom pendant a portcullis of the third.
Address – The Estate Office, Hambleden, Henley-on-Thames, Oxon.

SONS LIVING (*By 1st marriage*)

Hon (WILLIAM) HENRY BERNARD (The Manor House, Hambleden, Henley-on-Thames, Oxon; 109 Eccleston Mews, SW1), *b* 18 Nov 1955: *m* 1983, Sara Suzanne, da of Joseph F. Anlauf, of Palos Verdes Estates, Calif, USA, and has issue living, Sara Marie Celeste, *b* 1986, — Alexandra Patricia, *b* 1989.
Hon Bernardo James, *b* 1957.
Hon Alexander David, *b* 1959.
Hon Nicolas Robin Bartolemeo, *b* 1960: *m* 1992, Yumi Iwasaki, of Japan, and has issue living, Taro, *b* 1993, — Kenji, *b* 1996.
Hon Lorenzo Patrick Harold, *b* 1962.

BROTHERS LIVING

Hon Richard Edward, *b* 1937: *m* 1973, Christine Hickey, and has issue living, Christopher Richard, *b* 1975.
Hon Philip Reginald, *b* 1945, *ed* Eton; Maj (ret) R Green Jackets (despatches); High Sheriff Glos 1992: *m* 1973, Mary, yst da of late John Roberts, of Bottom Farm, Checkendon, Oxon, and has issue living, Thomas William, *b* 1976, — James Edmund Philip, *b* 1983, — Clare Elizabeth, *b* 1974, — Emily, *b* 1980. *Residence* – Campden House, Chipping Campden, Glos.

SISTERS LIVING

Hon Laura Caroline Beatrice, *b* 1931: *m* 1953, Michael Charles Brand, Lieut Coldstream Guards (*see* V Hampden, colls). *Residence* – 6 Howley Place, W2.
Hon Katherine Patricia, *b* 1933: *m* 1st, 1961, Ivan Moffat; 2ndly, 1973, Peter Robert Gascoigne Townend, and has issue living (by 1st *m*), Jonathan David, *b* 1964: *m* 1986, Carmel J. B., 2nd da of L. M. Sawle, of Perth, W Australia, — Patrick Nicholas, *b* 1968. *Residence* – 122 Hurlingham Rd, SW6.

WIDOW LIVING OF SON OF SECOND VISCOUNT.

Lady Helen Pleydell-Bouverie, OBE (King's Copse House, Bucklebury, Berks); OBE (Civil) 1946; DL R County of Berks; da of 6th Earl of Radnor: *m* 1931, Maj Hon David John Smith, CBE, who *d* 1976, and has issue (see colls infra).

COLLATERAL BRANCH LIVING

Issue of late Maj Hon David John Smith, CBE, yst son of 2nd Viscount, *b* 1907, *d* 1976: *m* 1931, Lady Helen Pleydell-Bouverie, OBE (ante), da of 6th Earl of Radnor:—
Julian David (6 The Hermitage, Barnes SW13), *b* 1932: *m* 1966, Eleanor, da of late John Eustace Blyth, MBE, of Ham Common, Surrey, and has issue living, Dickon Julian Henry, *b* 1972, — Alexandra Esther Helen, *b* 1969. —— Antony Frederick (Bouverie, PO Box 155, Mount Barker, W Australia), *b* 1937; *ed* Eton: *m* 1962, Alison Priscilla, da of late Lt-Col John Clark Pyper, OBE, IMS (ret) of Westbury, Tasmania, and has issue living, James Antony David, *b* 1962, — Philip John, *b* 1964, — Harriet Frances, *b* 1967, — Helen Sarah, *b* 1969. —— Peter Henry (Leighton House, Good-

manham, York YO4 3HX), *b* 1939: *m* 1967, Scilla Ann, el da of late Peter Ward Bennett, of Dene House, Little Dene, nr Glynde, Sussex, and has issue living, Charles Henry, *b* 1968, — Clare Scilla, *b* 1971, — Catherine Ann, *b* 1975. —— David Michael (Cwm Gwengad, Aberscit, Powys LD3 9NR), *b* 1947: *m* 1st, 1970 (*m diss* 1992), Caroline, da of R. H. Ardill, of Casa la Briana, Barattano, San Terenziano PG, Italy; 2ndly, 1992, Dr Clare Stephenson; 3rdly, 1998, Mrs Samantha Usborne, and has issue living (by 1st *m*), Jack Robert, *b* 1977, — Rachel Charlotte, *b* 1973. —— Esther Joanna, *b* 1934; *dunm* 1992.

PREDECESSORS – (1) EMILY Smith, el da of late Frederick Dawes Danvers, of the Duchy of Lancaster; *b* 1828; *cr Viscountess Hambleden*, of Hambleden, Bucks (peerage of United Kingdom) 1891, with remainder to the heirs male of her body by the 2nd *m*: *m* 1st, 1854, Benjamin Auber Leach, who *d* 1855; 2ndly, 1858, Rt Hon William Henry Smith, PC (MP for Westminster (*C*) 1868-85, and for Strand 1885-91), who *d* 1891, First Lord of the Admiralty, First Lord of the Treasury, Lord Warden of the Cinque Ports, and Leader of the House of Commons; *d* 1913; *s* by her son (2) WILLIAM FREDERICK DANVERS, 2nd Viscount, *b* 1868; senior partner in the firm of W. H. Smith and Son, of Strand House, Portugal Street, WC; European War 1914-17 (despatches); sat as MP for Strand (*C*) Oct 1891 to Jan 1910: *m* 1894, Lady Esther Caroline Georgiana Gore, who *d* 1955, da of 5th Earl of Arran; *d* 1928; *s* by his son (3) WILLIAM HENRY, 3rd Viscount; *b* 1903; Chm of W. H. Smith & Son, Ltd, of Strand House, Portugal Street, WC: *m* 1928, Lady Patricia Herbert, GCVO, who *d* 1994, da of 15th Earl of Pembroke; *d* 1948; *s* by his son (4) WILLIAM HERBERT, 4th Viscount and present peer.

HAMBRO, BARON (Hambro) (Life Baron 1994)

CHARLES ERIC ALEXANDER HAMBRO, son of late Col Sir Charles Jocelyn Hambro, KBE, MC, of Dixton Manor, Glos; *b* 24 July 1930; *ed* Eton; Coldstream Gds 1949-51; joined Hambros Bank Ltd 1952, Man Dir 1957, Dep Chm 1965, Chm 1972-83, Chm Hambros plc 1983-97; Non-Exec Dir Guardian Royal Exchange Assurance plc 1968 (Dep Chm 1974-88, since when Chm), Peninsular & Oriental Steam Navigation Co since 1987, etc; Trustee British Museum 1984-94; *cr Baron Hambro*, of Dixton and Dumbleton, co Glos (Life Baron) 1994: *m* 1st, 1954 (*m diss* 1976), Rose Evelyn, elder da of Lt-Col Sir Richard Charles Geers Cotterell, 5th Bt, CBE, TD; 2ndly, 1976, Mrs Cherry Felicity Twiss, 2nd da of late Sir John Huggins, GCMG, MC, and has issue by 1st *m*.

Arms – ......
Residence – Dixton Manor, Gotherington, Cheltenham, Glos GL52 4RB. *Clubs* – MCC, White's.

SONS LIVING (By 1st marriage)

Hon Charles Edward, *b* 1959; *ed* Eton; late Coldstream Gds; *m* 1986, Nicole J., only da of Dr James A. Nicholas, of 22 Cayuga Rd, Scarsdale, New York, and has issue living, Charles James, *b* 1991, — Christiana Elizabeth, *b* 1988, — Tatiana Katherine, *b* 1989, — Marina Kimberly, *b* 1995. *Residence* – 23 Kensington Gate, W8.
Hon Alexander Robert, *b* 1962; *ed* Eton, and Trin Coll, Camb: *m* 1994, Harriet, yst da of David Ward Jones, of London, and has issue living, Benjamin Jake, *b* 1996, — Samuel David, *b* 1999, — Jemima Rose, *b* 1997.

DAUGHTER LIVING (By 1st marriage)

Hon Clare Evelyn, *b* 1957: *m* 1989, Eivind Rabben, only son of Knut Rabben, of Oslo, Norway, and has issue living, Edward Olav, *b* 1992, — Alexander Haakon, *b* 1994.

Hamilton, Marquess of; son of Duke of Abercorn.

Hamilton, family name of Duke of Abercorn.

Hamilton, family name of Lord Belhaven.

Hamilton, family name of Baroness Dudley.

Hamilton, family name of Baron Holm Patrick.

Hamilton, Baillie-, family name of Earl of Haddington.

Hamilton, Douglas-, family name of Baron Selkirk of Douglas.

HAMILTON AND BRANDON, DUKE OF (Douglas-Hamilton) (Duke S 1643 and GB 1711)

Never behind

ANGUS ALAN DOUGLAS DOUGLAS-HAMILTON, 15th Duke of Hamilton, 12th Duke of Brandon, and Premier Peer of Scotland; *b* 13 Sept 1938; *s* 1973; *ed* Eton, and Balliol Coll, Oxford (MA); CEng, MIMechE, FBIS; is Hereditary Keeper of Palace of Holyrood House; Fl Lt RAF (ret); test pilot Scottish Aviation 1970-72; KStJ and Prior for Scotland of Order of St John 1975-83; Member of The Queen's Body Guard for Scotland (Royal Company of Archers); Hon Air Commodore No 2 MHU RAAF 1982-93: *m* 1st, 1972 (*m diss* 1987), Sarah Jane, who *d* 1994, da of Sir Walter Scott, 4th Bt (*cr* 1907); 2ndly, 1988 (*m diss* 1995), Mrs Jillian Hulton (*née* Robertson); 3rdly, 1998, Mrs Kay Carmichael, and has issue by 1st *m*.

Arms – Quarterly: 1st and 4th grand quarter counter-quartered, 1st and 4th gules, three cinque foils ermine, *Hamilton*; 2nd and 3rd argent, a lymphad with the sails furled proper; flagged gules, *Arran*; 2nd and 3rd, grand quarters, argent, a man's heart gules, ensigned with an imperial crown proper, on a chief azure, three mullets of the first, *Douglas*. Crests – 1st, on a ducal coronet an oak tree, fructed and penetrated transversely in the main stem by a frame saw proper, the frame or, *Hamilton*; 2nd, on a chapeau gules turned up ermine, a salamander in flames proper, *Douglas*. Supporters – Two antelopes argent, armed, unguled, ducally gorged and chained or.
Seat – Lennoxlove, Haddington, E Lothian. *Residence* – Archerfield Home Farm, Haddington, E Lothian.

SONS LIVING (By 1st marriage)

ALEXANDER DOUGLAS (*Marquess of Douglas and Clydesdale*), *b* 31 March 1978.
Lord John William, *b* 1979.

DAUGHTERS LIVING (By 1st marriage)

Lady Eleanor, *b* 1973.
Lady Anne, *b* 1976: *m* 1998, John Arthur McClure.

BROTHERS LIVING AND DECEASED

Rt Hon Lord James Alexander (*Baron Selkirk of Douglas*), QC, *b* 1942; *s* his uncle as 11th Earl of Selkirk 1994, until he disclaimed his peerages for life; *cr* Baron Selkirk of Douglas (Life Baron) 1997 (see that title).

†*Lord* Hugh Malcolm, *b* 1946; *ed* Eton: *m* 1st, 1971 (*m diss* and annulled 1990), June Mary Curtis; 2ndly, 1994, Sheilagh (*infra*), da of Thomas Ellis, FSA Scot, of 17 Great Stuart St, Edinburgh, and *d* 1995, leaving issue (by 1st *m*), Brendan Thomas, *b* 1974, — Catherine Bride, *b* 1976.

Lord Patrick George, *b* 1950: *m* 1989, Cecilia F. M., elder da of Capt T. G. Usher, of Crossford, Fife, and has issue living, Isabel Rose, *b* 1991. *Residence* – Westfield House, Haddington, E Lothian EH41 4HQ.

Lord David Stephen, *b* 1952; *ed* Eton.

WIDOWS LIVING OF SONS OF THIRTEENTH DUKE

Natalie, CBE, da of Maj Nathaniel Brackett Wales, of New York, and Boston, USA, and widow of Edward Bragg Paine, of New York, USA: *m* 1953, as his 2nd wife, Lord Malcolm Avondale Douglas-Hamilton, OBE, DFC, who *d* 1964 (see colls, infra).

Ann Prunella, da of late Capt Edward Hugh Bagot Stack, Indian Army: *m* 1st, 1938, Squadron-Leader Lord David Douglas-Hamilton, RAF Vol Reserve, who was *k* on flying operations 1944; 2ndly, 1950, Alfred G Albers, who *d* 1951; 3rdly, 1964, Brian St Quentin Power, and has issue living, (by 1st *m*) (see colls, infra). *Residence* – 14 Gertrude St, SW10.

WIDOW LIVING OF SON OF FOURTEENTH DUKE

Sheilagh, da of Thomas Ellis, FSA Scot, of 17 Great Stuart St, Edinburgh: *m* 1994, as his 2nd wife, Lord Hugh Malcolm Douglas-Hamilton, who *d* 1995. *Residences* – Begbie Farmhouse, Haddington, E Lothian; 17 Great Stuart St, Edinburgh.

WIDOW LIVING OF FOURTEENTH DUKE

Lady ELIZABETH IVY PERCY (*Dowager Duchess of Hamilton and Brandon*), OBE, DL (North Port, Lennoxlove, Haddington, E Lothian EH41 4HH), da of 8th Duke of Northumberland, KG, CBE, MVO, LLD: *m* 1937, the 14th Duke of Hamilton, KT, PC, GCVO, AFC, who *d* 1973.

COLLATERAL BRANCHES LIVING

Issue of late Lord Malcolm Avondale Douglas-Hamilton, OBE, DFC, 3rd son of 13th Duke, *b* 1909, *d* 1964: *m* 1st, 1931 (*m diss* 1952), (Clodagh) Pamela, only child of late Lt-Col Hon Malcolm Bowes-Lyon, CBE (*see* E Strathmore, colls); 2ndly, 1953, Natalie, CBE (ante), da of Maj Nathaniel Brackett Wales, of New York, and Boston, USA, and widow of Edward Bragg Paine, of New York:—
(By 1st *m*) Alasdair Malcolm (Lessudden, St Boswells, Roxburghshire TD6 0BH), *b* 1939; *ed* Gordonstoun, and Edinburgh Univ: *m* 1965, Angela Kathleen, 2nd da of James Molony Longley, of W Knoyle, Wilts, and has issue living, Angus Gavin, *b* 1968: *m* 1995, Justine L., only da of Leon Levene, of Clifton, Bristol, and has issue living, Siana *b* 1997, — Geordie Fergus, *b* 1969, — Fenella Mairi, *b* 1966: *m* 1994, H. Igor Zevenbergen, and has issue living, Caspar Charles *b* 1991, Tamara Georgia *b* 1996, — Tessa Catherine, *b* 1980. —— Diana Mairi (Friarshawmuir, Midlem, Selkirk TD7 4PZ), *b* 1932; *ed* North Foreland Lodge, Edinburgh Coll of Art and Bristol Polytechnic: *m* 1955 (*m diss* 1973), Gavin William Younger, and has issue living, Douglas Henry, *b* 1956: *m* 1979, Alison Susan, 2nd da of Guy Urwick Goodbody, and has issue living, Harry Neil *b* 1981, Samuel Guy *b* 1984, Nicholas William *b* 1986, — Hugh Patrick, *b* 1958: *m* 1986, Sophie Helen, eldest da of Felix Benjamin Engel, and has issue living, Joshua Hugh Gaskell *b* 1988, Dominic William *b* 1990, Peter Finn *b* 1992, Benedict Gavin *b* 1995, — Malcolm James, *b* 1959: *m* 1989, Sophie Anne Martha, 2nd da of Michael Dowse, and has issue living, Anna Cecilia *b* 1994, Eliza Victoria *b* 1997, — Robert William, *b* 1964: *m* 1994, Elizabeth, eldest da of Thomas Smeaton, — Alexandra Katharine Anna *b* 1963: *m* 1991, Simon James Milne, and has issue living, Geordie Alexander Maitland *b* 1995, Lorne Ian Johnston. —— Fiona Margaret, *b* 1935; *ed* North Foreland Lodge, Edinburgh Univ and West London Inst: *m* 1973, Jeremy Blackstone Wise, who *d* 1990.

Issue of late Squadron-Leader Lord David Douglas-Hamilton, RAF Vol Reserve, 4th son of 13th Duke, *b* 1912, *k* on flying operations 1944: *m* 1938, Ann Prunella (ante) (who *m* 2ndly, 1950, Alfred G. Albers, who *d* 1951; 3rdly, 1964, Brian St Quentin Power), da of late Capt Edward Hugh Bagot Stack, Indian Army:—
Diarmaid Hugh (729 Cabot St, Beverly, Mass 01915, USA), *b* 1940; *ed* Gordonstoun, Balliol Coll, Oxford, and Harvard Univ: *m* 1st, 1967 (*m diss* 1982), Margaret Barlow, only da of Dr William Matthew Hambrecht, of Lakeville, Conn, USA; 2ndly, 1983, Margaret Murray, el da of Duncan McGlashan Spencer, of New York, and Dublin, New Hampshire. —— Iain, OBE (Lake Naivasha, Kenya), *b* 1942; *ed* Gordonstoun and Oriel Coll, Oxford; OBE (Civil) 1993: *m* 1971, Oria,

2nd da of Lt-Col Mario Rocco, of Dominio di Doriano, Naivasha, Kenya, and has issue living, Saba Iassa, *b* 1970; *ed* St Andrews Univ, — Dudu Mara, *b* 1971; *ed* Cape Town Univ.

Grandchildren of late Algernon Percy Douglas-Hamilton, 2nd son of Col Francis Seymour Douglas-Hamilton, RA, uncle of 13th Duke:—

Issue of late Percy Seymour Douglas-Hamilton, *b* 1875, *d* 1940: *m* 1st, 1901, Edith Annie Hamilton, who *d* 1927, el da of Sir Frederick Wills, 1st Bt; 2ndly, 1929, Barbara Margherita (who *d* 1975 having *m* 2ndly, 1946, David George Arbuthnot (Arbuthnot, Bt, colls)), da of Francis Chiappini, JP, of Wynberg, Cape Province, S Africa:—
(By 2nd *m*) John Percy, *b* 1930: *m* 1st, 1955 (*m diss* 1980), June Mary Clifton Michler, of Rondesbosch, Cape Province, S Africa; 2ndly, 1980, Delia Rose Davies, *neé* Bilbrough, and has issue living (by 1st *m*), John Gavin, *b* 1957, — Tessa Jeanne, *b* 1958: *m* 1990, Peter Gordon Fraser-Grant, son of Gordon Vels Fraser-Grant, and has issue living, Matthew Peter *b* 1991, Chelsea Leigh *b* 1994, — Debra Anne, *b* 1960: *m* 1986 (*m diss* 1995), Christopher John Growstra, son of Johannes Growstra, and has issue living, David Jonathan *b* 1986, Jacqueline Louise *b* 1983, — Diane Barbara, *b* (twin) 1960: *m* 19—, Lawrence James Thackwray, son of late James Vicary Thackwray, and has issue living, Nicolas John *b* 1984, Daniel James *b* 1987. *Residence* – Hillcrest, Forest Av, Bishopscourt, Cape, S Africa. ⸺ Diana Barbara, *b* 1932: *m* 1954, Ian Emslie Austin, of Klein Constantia, Constantia, Cape Prov, S Africa, who *d* 1973, and has issue living, Christopher James (6 Rose Way, Constantia 7800, South Africa), *b* 1955: *m* 1984, Tessa, da of late Kees Scholte, and has issue living, Michael James *b* 1991, Nicola Diana *b* 1989, — Philip Ian, *b* 1959: *m* 1990, Sharon Winnifred Dundas-Starr, da of Derek Starr, of Pietermaritzburg, Natal, and has issue living, Ian Matthew *b* 1991, Mark Philip *b* 1993, — David Douglas, *b* 1961: *m* 1985 (*m diss* 1998), Rozanne Elizabeth, da of Stephen Jaques Malan, of Johannesburg, and has issue living, Anthony Michael *b* 1993, Stephanie Diana *b* 1996, — Gillian Barbara, *b* 1957: *m* 1983, Gert Jeremias van Niekerk, and has issue living, Andre *b* 1985, Linda Diana *b* 1988.

Grandchildren of late Aubrey Reginald Douglas-Hamilton, 3rd son of late Algernon Percy Douglas Hamilton (ante):—

Issue of late Herbert Eustace Seymour Douglas Hamilton, *b* 1886, *d* 1963: *m* 1912, Ruth, who *d* 1974, da of late Cuthbert Harrison:—
Cecil Seymour (Apt 304, 2020 Bellwood Ave, Burnaby, BC, Canada V5B 4P8), *b* 1916; Fl Lt RCAF (ret): *m* 1943, Ada Louise, da of late Orie Donily, and has an adopted da, Catherine Gail, *b* 1941: *m* 1960 (*m diss* 1978), Norman James Felton, and has issue living, Susan Darlene *b* 1961, Marilyn Jean *b* 1962: *m* 1982, Tony Macdonald (and has issue living, Ryan James *b* 1986, Rachel Catherine *b* 1988).

Issue of late Claud Archibald Aubrey Douglas-Hamilton, MBE, *b* 1889, *d* 1961: *m* 1915, Evelyn Addison, who *d* 1975, only da of late Thomas Addison Chater, of 51 Addison Avenue, Kensington, W, and Chesham Bois, Bucks:—
Evelyn Daphne (49 Chatsworth Court, Pembroke Rd, W8 6DH), *b* 1916: *m* 1st, 1940, Rev Jack Rawlins, Chap to the Forces, who *d* 1946; 2ndly, 1956, Hedley Boardman, MB, ChB, DPH, who *d* 1998, and has issue living (by 1st *m*), *Prof* Sir Michael David (29 The Grove, Gosforth, Newcastle upon Tyne; Shoreston House, Shoreston, nr Seahouses, Northumberland), *b* 1941; BSc London; MD, BS, FRCP, FRCPE: *m* 1963, Elizabeth Cadbury, JP, LGSM, only da of Edmund Henry Hambly, MB, BS, FRCS, and has issue living, Victoria Jane *b* 1964: *m* 1988, Andrew George Franks, of West House, Winston, Darlington, co Durham (and has issue living, Laura Elizabeth Sarah *b* 1992, Annabel Jean *b* 1994), Lucy Sarah *b* 1965; *ed* Brighton Univ (BA): *m* 1989, Paul Robert Holmes, of 109 Elstree Rd, Bushy Heath, Herts WD2 3AN (and has issue living, Emily Anna Elizabeth *b* 1993, Charlotte Francesca *b* 1995), Susannah Clara *b* 1972; *ed* Leeds Met Univ (B Ed) — Christopher John (8 Glen Hill Lane, Wilton, Connecticut 06897, USA; Windfall Cottage, E Prawle, nr Kingsbridge, Devon), *b* 1945; BSc London; MIM; LRSC; US Publisher, Stockton Press div, Nature America Inc: *m* 1969, Mary Joan, BSc, only da of Donovan William Goodchild, and has issue living, Jeremy Mark *b* 1974; MB BS Leeds, Sarah Elizabeth *b* 1972; *ed* Coventry Univ (BA): *m* 1998, Nicholas Knapp, of 19 Arthur Rd, St Albans, Herts, Penelope Jane *b* 1977; *ed* Guildford Sch of Acting.

PREDECESSORS – **(1)** JAMES, KG, PC, 3rd Marquess of Hamilton, and 2nd Earl of Cambridge, Gentleman of the Bedchamber, Master of the Horse, etc, *cr Lord Aven and Innerdale, Earl of Arran and Cambridge, Marquess of Clydesdale,* and *Duke of Hamilton* (peerage of Scotland) 1643, with remainder to the heirs male of his body, 2nd in default to his brother William, Earl of Lanark, and his male issue, and in default thereof to his own el da, Anne, and her issue male; appointed Hereditary Keeper of the Palace of Holyrood; commanded the Army raised in Scotland for the relief of Charles I, and being defeated at Preston he surrendered and was beheaded on 9 March 1649; *s* by his brother **(2)** WILLIAM, 2nd Duke, who had in 1639 been *cr Lord Machansire and Polmont,* and *Earl of Lanark* (peerage of Scotland); killed at the battle of Worcester 1651, when his own honours expired and the Dukedom descended to his niece **(3)** ANNE, wife of William, KG, 1st Earl of Selkirk (ante), who in 1660 was *cr* Duke of Hamilton for life: the Duchess surrendered her honours in favour of her el son **(4)** JAMES, KG, KT, 4th Duke, who in 1698 received a novodamus of the titles of Lord *Aven, Polmont, Machansire, and Innerdale, Earl of Arran, Lanark,* and *Cambridge, Marquess of Clydesdale* and *Duke of Hamilton* (peerage of Scotland) with precedence of 1643, and in 1711 was *cr Baron Dutton* and *Duke of Brandon* (peerage of GB); upon applying for his seat in the House of Peers, the House decided that after the union no peer for Scotland could be *cr* a peer of England: killed in a duel 1712; *s* by his son **(5)** JAMES, KT, 5th Duke of Hamilton and 2nd of Brandon; a Lord of the Bedchamber; *d* 1743; *s* by his el son **(6)** JAMES, KT, 6th Duke of Hamilton and 3rd of Brandon; *d* 1758; *s* by his son **(7)** JAMES GEORGE, 7th Duke of Hamilton and 4th of Brandon, *s* to the Marquessate of Douglas and Earldom of Angus (see infra *)* 1761; *d* unmarried 1769; *s* by his brother **(8)** DOUGLAS, 8th Duke of Hamilton and 5th of Brandon; was summoned to House of Lords as Duke of Brandon; *dsp* 1799; *s* by his uncle **(9)** ARCHIBALD, 9th Duke of Hamilton and 6th of Brandon; MP for Lancashire 1768-72; *d* 1819; *s* by his son **(10)** ALEXANDER, KG, PC, 10th Duke of Hamilton and 7th of Brandon; Ambassador to St Petersburg; MP for Lancashire 1802; summoned to House of Lords in his father's Barony of Dutton 1806; Lord-Lieut of Lanarkshire; *d* 1852; *s* by his son **(11)** WILLIAM ALEXANDER ARCHIBALD, 11th Duke of Hamilton and 8th of Brandon; *b* 1811; was Lord-Lieut of Lanarkshire: *m* 1843, Princess Mary of Baden, da of Charles Louis Frederick, late reigning Grand Duke of Baden, and cousin of HIM Napoleon III; *d* 1863, *s* by his son **(12)** WILLIAM ALEXANDER LOUIS STEPHEN, KT, 12th Duke of Hamilton and 9th Duke of Brandon; *b* 1845; granted Dukedom of Chatellerault by Imperial decree Napoleon III, dated 20 April 1864 (*see* D Abercorn), and *s* to the Earldom of Selkirk under special remainder 1886: *m* 1873, Lady Mary Louise Elizabeth Montagu, OBE, who *d* 1934, da of 7th Duke of Manchester; *d* 1895; *s* by his cousin **(13)** ALFRED DOUGLAS (great-grandson of Adm Charles Powell Douglas-Hamilton, 2nd son of Lord Anne Douglas-Hamilton, 3rd son of 4th Duke), 13th Duke, *b* 1862: *m* 1901, Nina Mary Benita, who *d* 1951, da of late Major Robert Poore; *d* 1940; when he was *s* in the Earldom of Selkirk (under the terms of special destination) by his second son Lord (George) Nigel Douglas-Hamilton, and in the Dukedom and other peerages by his el son **(14)** DOUGLAS, KT, GCVO, AFC, PC, 14th Duke, *b* 1903; Ch Pilot Mount Everest Flight Expedition 1933; Lord High Commr to Gen Assembly of Church of Scotland, 1953-55 and 1958; Lord Steward of the Household 1940-64; Chancellor of St Andrews Univ 1948-73: MP for E Renfrewshire (C) 1930-40: *m* 1937, Lady Elizabeth Ivy Percy, da of 8th Duke of Northumberland; *d* 1973; *s* by his el son **(15)** ANGUS ALAN DOUGLAS, 15th Duke and present peer: also Duke of Brandon, Marquess of Douglas, Marquess of Clydesdale, Earl of Angus, Earl of Arran, Lanark, and Cambridge, Lord Abernethy and Jedburgh Forest, Lord Aven and Innerdale, Lord Machansire and Polmont, and Baron Dutton.

*William Douglas, *cr* Earl of Douglas (peerage of Scotland) 1358 (title attainted 1455): *m* 3rdly, Lady Margaret Stewart (da of Thomas, 2nd Earl of Angus, and on the decease of her brother the 3rd Earl), Countess of Angus in her own right, and had issue (1) GEORGE, who in 1389 obtained a grant of his mother's earldom and became *Earl of Angus* (peerage of Scotland): *m* Princess Mary, da of Robert III, by whom he was granted charters of considerable lands; *d* 1402; *s* by his son (2) WILLIAM, 2nd Earl; *d* 1437; *s* by his son (3) JAMES, 3rd Earl; betrothed to Princess Jean, 3rd da of James I (of Scotland), but *d* 1446, before the marriage took place; *s* by his uncle (4) GEORGE, 4th Earl, 2nd son of 1st Earl; received a grant of the forfeited Lordship of Douglas 1457; when Henry VI took refuge in Scotland, the Earl offered the King substantial aid and was promised an English dukedom; *s* by his son (5) ARCHIBALD, PC, 5th Earl; styled the "Great Earl" and "Bell the Cat;" a powerful noble who was High Chancellor of Scotland 1493-8; *d* 1514; *s* by his grandson (6) ARCHIBALD, 6th Earl: *m* Princess Margaret of England, Queen Dowager of James IV of Scotland; *d* before Jan 22nd, 1557; *s* by his nephew (7) DAVID, 7th Earl; *d* June 1557; *s* by his son (8) ARCHIBALD, 8th Earl, who in 1585 *s* his uncle as 5th Earl of Morton (peerage of Scotland, *cr* 1458); *d* 1588; when the Earldom of Morton devolved on Sir William Douglas, of Lochleven, though there were other representatives in a more direct line; *s* in Earldom of Angus by his kinsman (9) WILLIAM, KB, 9th Earl, descendant of Sir William, 2nd son of 5th Earl; obtained in 1591 from James VI a charter confirming to himself and his heirs male the ancient privileges of the Douglas family, viz "The first vote in Parliament or Council; to be the king's Hereditary Lieutenant; to have the leading of the van of the army in the day of battle; and to carry the crown of coronations"; *d* 1591: *s* by his son (10) WILLIAM, 10th Earl; obtained a charter in 1602 under the great seal confirming the charter granted to his father (ante); *d* 1611; *s* by his son (11) WILLIAM, 11th Earl; *cr* Lord Abernethy and Jedburgh Forest and *Marquess of Douglas* (peerage of Scotland) 1633; *m* 1st, Margaret Hamilton, da of 1st Baron Paisley and sister to 1st Earl of Abercorn; 2ndly, Lady Mary Gordon, da of 1st Marquess of Huntly; had with other issue by 1st *m* Archibald, *cr* 1651 *Lord Bothwell and Hartside*, and *Earl of Ormond*, with remainder to the heirs male of his 2nd *m*; William, *cr Lord Daer and Shortcleuch*, and *Earl of Selkirk* (peerage of Scotland) 1646, which peerages he resigned into the King's hands, who in 1688 re-conferred them with precedency of 1646 on his 3rd and yr sons primogeniturely provided that, if any of their representatives succeeded to the Dukedom of Hamilton, *cr* 1648, the Earldom should pass to the then Duke's next brother, and with further remainder to his Grace's other heirs male; he *m* Anne, in her own right, Duchess of Hamilton (see ante), and was himself created *Duke of Hamilton* for life; *d* 1660; *s* by his grandson (12) JAMES, 2nd Marquess, who had in 1655 *s* his father (ante) as 2nd Earl of Ormond; *d* 1700; *s* by his son (13) ARCHIBALD, 3rd Marquess; *cr Lord Douglas of Bonkill, Viscount of Jedburgh Forest, Marquess of Angus and Abernethy*, and *Duke of Douglas* (peerage of Scotland) 1703, all of which honours expired at his death in 1761, when the Marquessate of Douglas devolved upon James George, 7th Duke of Hamilton (see ante), and the Duke of Douglas's nephew, Archibald Stewart, was returned heir of line to the Duke of Douglas. The Duke of Hamilton disputed the return on the ground of Mr Stewart's birth being surreptitious, the Scottish Courts decided in favour of the Duke, but in 1769 the House of Lords reversed the Scottish judgement and awarded the estates to Mr Stewart, who assumed the name of Douglas. He was *cr Lord Douglas*, of Douglas Castle (peerage of Scotland) 1790 (ext 1857) (*see* E Home).

HAMILTON OF DALZELL, BARON (Hamilton) (Baron UK 1886)
(Title pronounced "Hamilton of Dee-el")

Who will oppose

JAMES LESLIE HAMILTON, 4th Baron; *b* 11 Feb 1938; *s* 1990; *ed* Eton; late Coldstream Guards; Member London Stock Exchange 1967-80; Dir Rowton Hotels plc 1978-84; Gov Queen Elizabeth's Foundation for the Disabled (Chm since 1989); DL Surrey 1993: *m* 1967, (Ann Anastasia) Corinna (Helena), High Sheriff Surrey 1995, DL 1996, yr da of late Sir Pierson John Dixon, GCMG, CB, and has issue.

Arms – Gules, an annulet or between three cinquefoils pierced ermine. **Crest** – An antelope proper, attired and hoofed or. **Supporters** – *Dexter*, an antelope proper, ducally gorged and chained, the chain reflexed over the back or; *sinister*, a wild man proper, wreathed about the temples and loins with laurel, and holding over the sinister shoulder a club or.
Residences – Stockton House, Norton Shifnal, Shropshire; Betchworth House, Betchworth, Surrey RH3 7RE.

SONS LIVING

Hon GAVIN GOULBURN, *b* 8 Oct 1968; *ed* Eton, and Buckingham Univ (BSc): *m* 1997, Harriet, yr da of Thomas Roskill, of Brockhampton, Herefords.
Hon Robert Pierson, *b* 1971; *ed* Eton.
Hon John Duff, *b* (twin) 1971, *ed* Eton.
Hon Benjamin James, *b* 1974; a Page of Honour to HM 1986-88.

BROTHER LIVING

Rt Hon Sir Archibald Gavin, MP (House of Commons, SW1), *b* 1941; *ed* Eton; late Coldm Gds; Cllr R Borough of Kensington and Chelsea 1968-71; contested Dagenham (*C*) Feb and Oct 1974, MP for Epsom and Ewell (*C*) since 1978; Assist Govt Whip 1982-84, Lord Commr to HM Treasury 1984-86, Parliamentary Under-Sec for Defence Procurement 1986-87, PPS to Rt Hon Margaret Thatcher, PM, 1987-88, Min of State for the Armed Forces 1988-93; Chm 1922 Cttee since 1997; PC 1991; Ktd 1994: *m* 1968, Anne Catharine, da of late Com Trevylyan Napier, DSC, RN, and has issue living, Laura Katharine, *b* 1969, — Iona Janet, *b* 1971, — Alice Rose Alethea, *b* 1974.

SISTER LIVING

Hon Janet, *b* 1936: *m* 1960, Richard Sackville Lane Fox (By Bingley), and has issue living, Andrew Ward Jackson, *b* 1969, — Harriot, *b* 1966. *Residence* – Kingsley Mill, Black Torrington, Beaworthy, Devon.

PREDECESSORS – **(1)** JOHN GLENCAIRN CARTER Hamilton, son of late A. J. Hamilton of Dalzell; *b* 1829; a Lord-in-Waiting to HM Queen Victoria 1892-4; MP for Falkirk Burgh (*L*) 1857-9, for S Lanarkshire 1868-74 and 1880-85 and for Lanarkshire, S Div 1885-6; *cr Baron Hamilton of Dalzell* co Lanark (peerage of United Kingdom) 1886: *m* 1864, Lady Emily Eleanor, who *d* 1882, 4th da of 10th Earl of Leven and Melville; *d* 1900; *s* by his el surviving son **(2)** GAVIN GEORGE, KT, CVO, MC, 2nd Baron; *b* 1872: Major (ret) Scots Guards; Lord-in-Waiting to HM King Edward VII 1905-10, and to HM King George V 1910-11: *m* 1912, Sybil Mary, who *d* 1933, da of late Lieut-Gen Sir Frederick Marshall, KCMG; *d* 1952; *s* by his nephew **(3)** JOHN D'HENIN, GCVO, MC (son of late Major Hon Leslie d'Henin Hamilton, MVO, Coldstream Guards, 3rd son of 1st Baron), 3rd Baron, *b* 1911; Lord Lieut Surrey 1973-86, Chm Surrey Co Agricultural Exec Cttee 1957-68, a Lord-in-Waiting to HM Queewn Elizabeth II 1968-81: *m* 1935, Rosemary Olive, who *d* 1993, da of late Maj Hon Sir John Spencer Coke, KCVO (*see* E Leicester, colls); *d* 1990; *s* by his elder son **(4)** JAMES LESLIE, 4th Baron and present peer.

HAMLYN, BARON (Hamlyn) (Life Baron 1998)

PAUL BERTRAND HAMLYN, CBE, 2nd son of late Prof Richard Hamburger; *b* 12 Feb 1926; *ed* St Christopher's Sch, Letchworth; Hon DLitt Keele Univ 1988, Warwick Univ 1991; founded publishing firm of Paul Hamlyn Ltd 1950, and Hamlyn Publishing Group 1968, Chm since 1986; Founder and Chm Octopus Publishing Group since 1971; Co-Founder and Co-Chm Conran Octopus since 1983; Dir Reed Book Publishing Ltd since 1971, Reed International plc since 1987, Reed Elsevier plc since 1993, Michelin House Development Ltd since 1985, Bibendum Restaurant Ltd since 1986, Brandchart Ltd since 1987, Château de Bagnols Ltd since 1988, Michelin House Investment Co Ltd since 1989, Book Club Associates (Chm) since 1993, and other cos; Founder The Paul Hamlyn Foundation 1972 (for support of the arts, education and book publishing projects in UK and continental Europe as well as projects in the Third World); Chancellor Thames Valley Univ since 1993; RSA Albert Medal 1993; *cr* CBE 1993, and *Baron Hamlyn*, of Edgeworth, co Glos (Life Baron) 1998: *m* 1st, 1952 (*m diss* 1969), Eileen Margaret (Bobbie), da of Col Richard Watson; 2ndly, 1970, Mrs Helen Guest, and has issue by 1st *m*, one son and one da.
Address – 18 Queen Anne's Gate, SW1H 9AA.

HAMNETT, BARONY OF (Hamnett) (Extinct 1980)

DAUGHTER LIVING OF LIFE BARON

Hon Sheila, *b* 1933: *m* 1962, Eric Layland, of 31 Sevenoaks Av, Heaton Moor, Stockport, Ches.

Hamond, Harbord-, family name of Baron Suffield.

HAMPDEN, VISCOUNT (Brand) (Viscount UK 1884)
(Title pronounced "Hamden")

ANTHONY DAVID BRAND, 6th Viscount; *b* 7 May 1937; *s* 1975; *ed* Eton; DL E Sussex 1986: *m* 1st, 1969 (*m diss* 1988), Caroline Fiona, da of late Capt Claud Proby (*see* Proby, Bt, colls); 2ndly, 1993, Mrs Sara (Sally) Snow, yst da of late Col Sir Charles Jocelyn Hambro, KBE, MC, of Dixton Manor, Glos, and widow of Peter Wallace Snow, and has issue by 1st *m*.

Arms – Azure, two swords in saltire points, upwards argent, pommels and hilts or, between three escallops of the last. Crest – Out of a crown vallory or, a leopard's head argent, semée of escallops and gorged with a gemel gules.
Residence – Glynde Place, Glynde, Lewes, Sussex.

SONS LIVING (By 1st marriage)

Hon FRANCIS ANTHONY, *b* 17 Sept 1970.
Hon Jonathan Claud David Humphrey, *b* 1975.

DAUGHTER LIVING (By 1st marriage)

Hon Saracha Mary, *b* 1973.

SISTERS LIVING

Hon Jean Margaret, *b* 1938: *m* 1976, Robert John Hodgson (*see* Lacon, Bt, colls). *Residence* – 2 St Hilda's Rd, SW13 9JQ.
Hon Philippa Mary Imogen (*Hon Mrs Chetwode*), *b* 1942: *m* 1961, Hon Christopher Roger Chetwode, of Hill House, Cheriton, Alresford, Hants (*see* B Chetwode)

AUNTS LIVING (Daughters of 3rd Viscount)

Hon Barbara Constance, *b* 1907: *m* 1934, Ronald Harry Higham, who *d* 1966, and has issue living, Robin David, *b* 1939: *m* 1978, Janet Emily, yst da of late Michael Edward Gibb, of Forge House, Taynton, Oxon, and has issue living, Jessica Barbara *b* 1982, Edwina *b* 1987, — Caroline (*Hon Mrs Victor Grosvenor*), *b* 1936: *m* 1959, Hon Robert Victor Grosvenor, who *d* 1993, of Bennets Grafton, Oxon (*see* B Ebury). *Residence* – 6, 212 Old Brompton Rd, SW5.
Hon Monica Dorothy, *b* 1914: *m* 1933, D'Arcy Lambton, who *d* 1938 (*see* E Durham, colls). *Residence* – Saxon House, Shottisham, Woodbridge, Suffolk.

DAUGHTERS LIVING OF FOURTH VISCOUNT

See Bs Dacre.

WIDOW LIVING OF FIFTH VISCOUNT

Hon IMOGEN ALICE RHYS (*Imogen, Viscountess Hampden*) (Old School, Glynde, Lewes, Sussex), da of 7th Baron Dynevor: *m* 1936, the 5th Viscount Hampden, who *d* 1975.

COLLATERAL BRANCHES LIVING

(In remainder to Barony of Dacre only)

Issue of late Hon Joan Louisa Brand, eldest da of 3rd Viscount, *b* 1904, *d* 1996: *m* 1925, Sir Basil Samuel Hill-Wood, 2nd Bt, who *d* 1954:—
See Hill-Wood, Bt.

Issue of late Hon Elizabeth Margaret Brand, 3rd da of 3rd Viscount, *b* 1911, *d* 1994: *m* 1935, Cecil Chadwick Lomax, formerly Maj 9th Lancers, who *d* 1988:—
Fiona Valerie, *b* 1936: *m* 1957, Simon Hildebrand Melville Bradley, who *d* 1998, and has issue living, David Charles, *b* 1960, — Mark William, *b* 1904. *m* 1993, Emily, da of Anthony Skinner, of Devon, — Sarah Elizabeth (*Hon Mrs Paul Chetwynd-Talbot*), *b* 1961: *m* 1982, Hon Paul Alexander Anthony Bueno Chetwynd-Talbot, yr son of 21st Earl of Shrewsbury and Waterford. —— Dinah Patricia, *b* 1946: *m* 1977, Pascal Voisin, of 12 Ave du Cap de Nice, 06300 Nice, France, and has issue living, Thomas Gregoire, *b* 1979, — Blaise Noël, *b* 1982, — Camille Aimée, *b* 1977. —— Camilla Elizabeth COSTELLO (44 Octavia St, SW11), *b* 1948; assumed surname of Costello in lieu of her patronymic by deed poll 1980; has issue living (by Kevin Costello), Jack Alexis Lomax COSTELLO, *b* 1984, — Kate Lucille Lomax COSTELLO, *b* 1980.

Issue of late Adm Hon Sir Hubert George Brand, GCB, KCMG, KCVO, 2nd son of 2nd Viscount, *b* 1870, *d* 1955: *m* 1914, Norah Conyngham, who *d* 1924, da of late Rt Hon Sir (William) Conyngham Greene, KCB, Ambassador Extraor and Min Plen to Japan:—

Elizabeth Norah, *b* 1915: *m* 1940, Major John Edward Seymour, Gren Gds, who *d* 1972 (*see* M Hertford, colls). *Residence* – Edgedell Cottage, Martyr Worthy, Winchester.

Grandchildren of late Hon Robert Henry Brand, 4th son of 2nd Viscount, who was *cr Baron Brand* 1946 (extinct 1963):—
Issue of late Hon Virginia Brand, *b* 1918, *d* 1995: *m* 1st, 1939, John Metcalfe Polk, who *d* 1948; 2ndly, 1949, Sir Edward William Spencer Ford, GCVO, KCB, ERD (Canal House, 23 Blomfield Rd, W9 1AD) (*see* E Shrewsbury, colls, 1957 Edn):—
(By 1st *m*) John Robert POLK, *b* 1942: *m* 1969, Benedetta Maryons, da of David Grose, of 49 Elystan St, SW3, and has issue living, James Metcalfe, *b* 1973, — Laura Elizabeth, *b* 1971, — Alice Victoria, *b* 1981. —— Robert Brand POLK (5 Albany Rd, Toorak, Melbourne, Vic 3142, Australia), *b* 1944: *m* 1979, Elizabeth Wells, only da of Alfred Lyndon Gibson, of Melbourne, Vic, and has issue living, Edward John, *b* 1980, — Henry Brand, *b* 1982, — Thomas Robert, *b* 1984. —— (By 2nd *m*) Richard George FORD (56 Seymour Walk, SW10 9NF), *b* 1951; Page of Honour to HM 1964-66: *m* 1986, Elisa Ann, only da of late Michael Jeremy Kindersley Belmont (*see* Tate, Bt, colls, 1995 Edn), and has issue living, Jack, *b* 1989, — Katherine Ann, *b* 1987, — Rose Virginia, *b* 1990. —— David Lionel FORD, *b* 1952: *m* 1990, Margaret (Jubby), da of Richard Reid Ingrams (*see* Reid, Bt, *cr* 1897, 1995 Edn), and has issue living, Samuel Christopher Valentine, *b* 1992, — Phoebe May, *b* 1991, — Lily Dinah, *b* 1996.

Issue of late Hon Dinah Brand, *b* 1920, *d* 1998: *m* 1st, 1943 (*m diss* 1950), Lyttleton Fox, late Cmdr USNR; 2ndly, 1953, Christopher Charles Cyprian Bridge, who *d* 1993:-
(By 1st *m*) James Lyttleton FOX, *b* 1945; *ed* Eton; author of *White Mischief, The Langhorne Sisters*, etc: *m* 1970, Valérie Mariane, da of Alain Lalonde, of 15 Rue de l'Universite, Paris VIII, and has issue living, Thomas Lyttleton, *b* 1971. —— Phyllis Langhorne, *b* 1944. —— (By 2nd *m*) Charles Robert BRIDGE (The Old Vicarage, Firle, nr Lewes, E Sussex), *b* 1956; *ed* Harrow: *m* 1980, Arabella Jane, da of David Bradstock, of Longbottom, Andover, Hants, and has issue living, Oliver James Cyprian, *b* 1983, — Thomas Augustus William, *b* 1987, — Lucy Dinah, *b* 1982. —— Joanna, *b* 1954: *m* 1986, Graeme J. E. Jenkins, of Philipston House, Winterborne Clenston, nr Blandford Forum, Dorset DT11 0NR, and has issue living, Martha Nancy, *b* 1989, — Isabella Dinah, *b* 1991.

Issue of late Brig-Gen Hon Roger Brand, CMG, DSO, 5th son of 2nd Viscount, *b* 1880, *d* 1945: *m* 1913, Muriel Hectorina Lilian, who *d* 1988, da of Henry Boyle Montgomery:—
Patricia Helen Winifred, *b* 1926: *m* 1st, 1950 (*m diss* 1957), John Ralph Lubbock (*see* B Avebury, colls); 2ndly, 1957, Pierre Micheletto. *Residence* – Avenue du Temple 17, Lausanne, Switzerland.

Grandchildren of late Hon Margaret Brand, Mrs Algernon Francis Holford Ferguson, eldest da of 2nd Viscount:—
Issue of late Col Andrew Henry FERGUSON, Life Guards, *b* 1899, *d* 1966: *m* 1927, Marian Louise (who *d* 1996, having *m* 2ndly, 1968, Air Marshal Sir Thomas Walker Elmhirst, KBE, CB, AFC, who *d* 1982), da of late Lt-Col Lord Herbert Andrew Montagu Douglas Scott, CMG, DSO (*see* D Buccleuch, colls):—
Ronald Ivor FERGUSON (Dummer Down House, Dummer, Basingstoke), *b* 1931; *ed* Eton; Maj Life Guards: *m* 1st, 1956 (*m diss* 1974), Susan Mary (who was *k* in a motor accident 1998, in Argentina, having *m* 2ndly, 1975, Hector Barrantes, who *d* 1990, of Argentina), da of late FitzHerbert Wright (*see* V Powerscourt, 1990 Edn); 2ndly, 1976, Susan Rosemary, da of Frederick Deptford, and has issue living (by 1st *m*), Jane Louise, *b* 1957: *m* 1st, 1976 (*m diss* 1991), William (Alex) Makim, of Australia; 2ndly, 1994, Rainer Hans Luedecke, and has issue living (by 1st *m*), Seamus *b* 1981, Ayesha *b* 1986, — Sarah Margaret (*Duchess of York*) (Sunninghill Park, Ascot, Berkshire SL5 7TH), *b* 15 Oct 1959: *m* 23 July 1986 (*m diss* 30 May 1996), HRH The Prince Andrew Albert Christian Edward, Duke of York, CVO, ADC, 2nd son of HM Queen Elizabeth II, and has issue (*see* ROYAL FAMILY), — (by 2nd *m*) Andrew Frederick John, *b* 1978, — Alice Victoria, *b* 1980, — Eliza, *b* 1986.

Issue of late Margaret Susan Ferguson, *b* 1906, *d* 1939: *m* 1931, as his 1st wife, Lt-Col Frederick Edwin Barton Wignall, Life Guards, who *d* 1956 (*see* Tate, Bt, colls, 1956 Edn):—
Ann Margaret, *b* 1932: *m* 1968, as his 3rd wife, James William Hay Verner, who *d* 1995, and has issue living, two sons.

Issue of late Jane Charlotte Ferguson, *b* 1912, *d* (26 Feb) 1986: *m* 1934, Capt Sir William Albemarle Fellowes, KCVO, who *d* (6 April) 1986:—
Rt Hon Sir Robert FELLOWES, GCB, GCVO, QSO *b* 1941; Assist Private Sec to HM 1977-85, Dep Private Sec 1985-90, Private Sec 1990-99; Vice-Chm Barclay's Private Bank Ltd since 1999; LVO 1982, CB 1987, KCVO 1989, PC 1990, KCB 1991, GCVO 1996, GCB 1998, QSO 1999; *cr Baron Fellowes*, of Shotesham, co Norfolk (Life Baron) 1999; *ed* Eton: *m* 1978, Lady (Cynthia) Jane Spencer, 2nd da of 8th Earl Spencer, LVO, DL, and has issue living, Alexander Robert, *b* 1983, — Laura Jane, *b* 1980, — Eleanor Ruth, *b* 1985. —— Thomas William (The Old Rectory, Barking, Ipswich, Suffolk IP6 8HH), *b* 1945; *ed* Eton: *m* 1st, 1968 (*m diss* 1972), Caroline Moira, da of Capt Richard Ker, MC, DL (*see* E Suffolk and Berkshire, colls); 2ndly, 1975, Rosamund Isabelle, da of late Bernard van Cutsem (*see* E Fortescue), and has issue living (by 2nd *m*), Catherine Margaret Jane, *b* 1977, — Mary Eleanor, *b* 1978. —— Susan Mary, *b* 1936: *m* 1960, Michael Cole, of Poplar Farm, Marlesford, Suffolk, and has issue living, Henry Michael, *b* 1968, — Matthew Benjamin, *b* 1970, — Clare Jane, *b* 1963, — Sarah Marguerite, *b* 1964. —— Rachel, *b* 1939; JP: *m* 1959, Joseph Gilfred Studholme, and has issue (*see* Studholme, Bt).

Grandchildren of late Hon Dorothy Louisa Brand, Mrs Percy Henry Guy Feilden, yst da of 2nd Viscount:—
Issue of late Maj-Gen Sir Randle Guy Feilden, KVCO, CB, CBE, *b* 1904, *d* 1981: *m* 1929, Mary Joyce (Cot Farm, Minster Lovell, Oxon OX5 5RS), da of Sir John Frecheville Ramsden, 6th Bt:—
Randle Joseph FEILDEN (Home Farm, Cokethorpe, nr Witney, Oxon), *b* 1931; *ed* Eton: *m* 1st, 1958 (*m diss* 1970), Lady Caroline Victoria Wood, el da of 2nd Earl of Halifax; 2ndly, 19—, Mary Francesca, formerly wife of John Valentine Gosling, and eldest da of late G/Capt Henry William Pearson-Rogers, CBE, JP, of Tostock, Suffolk, and has had issue (by 1st *m*), Randle Charles Roderick, *b* 1961, — †Virginia Mary, *b* 1959: *d* 1994, following a ski-ing accident in France, — Fiona Caroline, *b* 1965: *m* 1991, James D. E. Bryant, son of J. M. Bryant, of Whaplode, Lincs, and has issue living, Thomas James *b* 1997, Sarah Elizabeth *b* 1993, Rebecca Katherine *b* 1995. —— Andrew James (The Old Manor House, Minster Lovell, Oxon), *b* 1941; *ed* Eton: *m* 1977, Rowena Jane, LVO, da of late Lt-Col Hon Peter Esmé Brassey (*see* B Brassey of Apethorpe, colls), and has issue living, James William Guy, *b* 1980, — Emma Jane, *b* 1979.

Issue of late Maj Cecil Henry Feilden, b 1907, d 1983: m 1st, 1941, Olivia Constance Leonora, who d 1975, da of late Lt-Col Hon Guy Victor Baring (B Ashburton, colls); 2ndly, 1976, Tessa Eirene (Manor Farm, Bramdean, Alresford, Hants), da of late Denis Griffiths, of Orlingbury Hall, Northants:—
(By 1st m) Victoria Rose (Bramdean House, Alresford, Hants SO24 0JU), b 1942: m 1971, Gerald Hugo Cropper Wakefield, and has issue (see Wakefield, Bt). —— Mary Henrietta (10 Gertrude St, SW10 0JN), b 1944: m 1998, as his 2nd wife, Nicholas Bache Barlow Davie-Thornhill (see Barlow, Bt, cr 1907, 1976 Edn).

Issue of late Dorothy Priscilla Feilden, b 1909, d 1983: m 1941, Lt-Col John Wilson Seton Galbraith, 11th Hussars:—
Jonathan Charles GALBRAITH (Hetland Hill, Carrutherstown, Dumfriesshire), b 1942. —— (Arthur) Guy (Newbold Revel, Haddington, E Lothian EH41 4HE), b 1947: m 1975, Sarah Jane, da of late Maj Robert Philip Henry Elwes, MBE, MC, of Congham House, King's Lynn, Norfolk (see E Annandale and Hartfell), and has issue living, Rowena Mary, b 1978, — Alice Katherine, b 1980. —— Joanna Katherine, b 1943: m 1967, Capt John William Nelson Mitchell, of Foxwood, Parkgate, Dumfries, and has issue living, Mark Alastair Nelson, b 1969, — Katrina Mary, b 1972, — Miranda Janet, b 1973.

(Male line in remainder to Viscountcy)

Grandsons of late Rear Adm Hon Thomas Seymour Brand, 2nd son of 1st Viscount:—
Issue of late Phoebe Brand, b 1893 d (17 Aug) 1972: m 1914, Lt-Col Edward Anthony Fielden, MC, 10th Hussars, who d (26 Aug) 1972:—
David Edward FIELDEN (PO Kilifi, via Mombasa, Kenya), b 1915; ed Eton; 1939-45 War with E African Forces: m 1942, Kathleen, who d 1998, da of Thomas Grant, of Silverbridge, co Down, and widow of Robert Sturge Ball, and has issue living, Joshua Anthony (283 Bowen Terrace, New Farm, Brisbane, Qld 4005, Australia), b 1944; ed Queens' Coll, Camb (BA), — Sarah Brand, b 1947: m 1971, as his 2nd wife, Antony Martin Donald Seth-Smith, late Kenya Regt, of Half-a-Hill, PO Box 24818, Nairobi, Kenya, and has issue living, Tana b 1977. —— †Philip Brand FIELDEN, MC, b 1919; ed Eton, and Magdalen Coll, Oxford; Lt-Col Royal Dragoons (ret); 1939-45 War (MC): m 1955, Caroline Mary (Manor Farm House, Adlestrop, Moreton-in-Marsh, Glos GL56 0YW), yr da of late Sir John Henry Burder, of Swinbrook Manor, Burford, Oxon, and d 1998, leaving issue, Mark Philip, b 1956, — Nicola, b 1957: m 1986, Terence Edward Stratton, of Lower Farm, Gt Wolford, Shipston-on-Stour, Warwicks, and has issue living, Edward Albert b 1988, George Frederick b 1991. —— John Anthony FIELDEN (Court of Hill, Ludlow, Shropshire), b 1921; ed Eton; 1939-45 War as Lieut (E) RNVR: m 1953, Helen Mary, 2nd da of late Charles Wakefield Christie-Miller, of Swyncombe House, Henley-on-Thames, and has issue living, Samuel John, b 1956, — Lucy Anne, b 1954: m 1993, David William Aspin, of 65 Eaton Sq, SW1, son of G. C. Aspin, of Hythe, Kent.

Grandchildren of late Maj Hon Charles Brand, 4th son of 1st Viscount:—
Issue of late Lieut-Col John Charles Brand, DSO, MC, b 1885, d 1929: m 1916, Lady Rosabelle Millicent, who d 1956, da of 5th Earl of Rosslyn, and widow of David Cecil Bingham (see E Lucan, colls):—
Michael Charles BRAND, b 1925; European War 1943-5 as Lieut Coldstream Guards (wounded): m 1953, Hon Laura Caroline Beatrice Smith, da of 3rd Viscount Hambleden, and has issue living, Charles David William, b 1954: m 1st, 1985, Kirsten Margaret, da of late John Baillie Hamilton Leckie, of Gerrards Cross, Bucks; 2ndly, 1992, Hon Virginia Leslie Bonham Carter, 2nd da of Baron Bonham-Carter (Life Baron), and has issue living (by 2nd m), Henry Joshua Mark b 1995, Violet Laura b 1992, — Charlotte Katharine, b 1961: m 1997, R. Gordon Ring, 2nd son of Brian Ring, of Bloomsbury, WC1, and has issue living, Sophia Patricia b 1999, — Rosabelle Patricia, b 1965: m 1995, Robert Batt, son of late Christopher Batt, of E Beckham, Norfolk, and has issue living, Laura Edwina b 1997, Isobel Beatrice b 1999. *Residence* – 6 Howley Place, W2. —— Patience, b 1922: m 1945 (m diss 1955), Capt Ian Alexander Henderson, late R Horse Guards, who d 1968 (see B Faringdon, colls). *Residence* – Oxleaze Farm, Uffington, Berks.

Issue of late Ruth Brand, b 1882, d 1967: m 1911, 2nd Baron Monk Bretton, who d 1933 (see that title).

Grandchildren of late Evelyn Brand (m 1916, Sir James Crerar, KCSI, CIE, ICS), yst da of late Maj Hon Charles Brand (ante):—
Issue of late David James Crerar, late Fl Lieut RAFVR, b 1922, d 1974: m 1949, Eileen Ismay, who d 1974, eldest da of Henry Francis Chester Walsh, OBE, of Williamstown House, Castlebellingham, co Louth:—
Peter John CRERAR (Rathdaniel, Cellon, co Louth), b 1955: m 1982, Patricia Anne, da of John Alexander Kennedy, of 33 The Peninsula, Yamba, NSW, Australia, and has issue living, James Henry Alexander, b 1988, — Marnie Eileen, b 1984, — Eileen, b 1991. —— Rory James CRERAR (21 Springfield Rd, Templeogue, Dublin), b 1958: m 1983, Margaret Mary, da of late Thomas Paul Marsh, of Glebe House, Stackallen, Navan, co Meath, and has issue living, David James, b 1987, — Carla Catherine, b 1988. —— Jonathan David CRERAR, b 1963. —— Catherine, b 1953: m 1978, Edward Anthony Boland.

Issue of late Elizabeth Jean Crerar, b 1918, d 1981: m 1946, Sir Hugh Evelyn Lockhart-Mummery, KCVO, who d 1988:—
Christopher John LOCKHART-MUMMERY (78 Lansdowne Rd, W11 2LS), b 1947; ed Stowe, and Trin Coll, Camb (BA); Bar Inner Temple 1971, QC 1986, Recorder of the Crown Court, Bencher Inner Temple: m 1st, 1971 (m diss 1992), Hon (Elizabeth) Rosamund Elles, da of Neil Moncrieff Elles, by his wife Baroness Elles; 2ndly, 1993, Mrs (Mary) Lou Putley, and has issue living (by 1st m), Edward, b 1975, — Clare, b 1973, — Alice, b 1980.

PREDECESSORS – (1) Hon HENRY BOUVERIE WILLIAM BRAND, GCB, PC, 2nd son of 21st Baron Dacre, b 1814; Speaker of House of Commons 1872-84; cr Viscount Hampden, of Glynde, co Sussex 1884 (peerage of UK); s his elder brother as 23rd Baron Dacre 1890: m 1838, Eliza, da of Gen Robert Ellice; d 1892; s by his el son (2) HENRY ROBERT, GCMG, 2nd Viscount, b 1841; Gov of NSW 1895-99: m 1st, 1864, Victoria, who d 1865, da of M Jean Sylvain Van de Weyer; 2ndly, 1868, Susan Henrietta, who d 1909, da of late Lord George Henry Cavendish, MP (D Devonshire); d 1906; s by his el son (3) THOMAS WALTER, GCVO, KCB, CMG, 3rd Viscount; b 1869; a Lord in Waiting to HM 1924-36: m 1899, Lady Katharine Mary Montagu-Douglas-Scott, who d 1951, da of 6th Duke of Buccleuch; d 1958; s by his el son (4) THOMAS HENRY, CMG, 4th Viscount, b 1900: m 1923, Leila Emily, who d 1996, da of late Lt-Col Frank Evelyn Seely (Seely, Bt, colls), d 1965, when the Barony of Dacre fell into abeyance (see Bs Dacre); s in the Viscountcy by his brother (5) DAVID

FRANCIS, 5th Viscount; *b* 1902: *m* 1936, Hon Imogen Alice Rhys, da of 7th Baron Dynevor; *d* 1975; *s* by his son **(6)** ANTHONY DAVID, 6th Viscount and present peer.

Hampden, Hobart-, family name of Earl of Buckinghamshire.

HAMPTON, BARON (Pakington) (Baron UK 1874, Bt UK 1846)
(Name pronounced "Packington")

Valour equals strength

RICHARD HUMPHREY RUSSELL PAKINGTON, 6th Baron, and 6th Baronet; *b* 25 May 1925; *s* 1974; *ed* Eton, and Balliol Coll, Oxford; served RNVR 1944-47: *m* 1958, Jane Elizabeth Farquharson, da of late Thomas Frank Arnott, OBE, TD, MB, ChB, and has issue.

𝕬rms – Per chevron sable and argent, in chief three mullets pierced or, in base as many garbs gules. 𝕮rest – A demi-hare azure charged on the shoulder with a quatrefoil argent. 𝕾upporters – *Dexter*, an elephant or, charged on the shoulder with a mullet pierced sable; *sinister*, a talbot argent, charged as the dexter.

SON LIVING

Hon JOHN HUMPHREY ARNOTT, *b* 24 Dec 1964; *ed* Shrewsbury, and Exeter Coll of Art and Design (BA): *m* 1996, Siena E. E., yr da of Remo Caldato, of Rome.

DAUGHTERS LIVING

Hon Catharine Mary Grace, *b* 1960; *ed* Bristol Univ.
Hon Sarah Jane Auriol, *b* 1961; *ed* Bedford Coll, London (BA).

SISTERS LIVING

Hon Hilary Evelyn Spicer, *b* 1914: *m* 1938, David John Vaughan Bevan, TD, BA, who *d* 1986, of Kingsland, Bledington, Oxford, OX7 6UX, and has issue living, Timothy David Vaughan (c/o Lloyds Bank, 36 Cheriton High St, Folkestone, Kent CT19 4EH), *b* 1939; Brig Li: *m* 1st, 1964 (*m diss* 1988), Jill, el da of Leslie Murrell, of Harpford, nr Sidmouth, Devon; 2ndly, 1988, Penelope Edyth, da of Douglas Lavers, of Kohimarama, Auckland, NZ, and has issue living (by 1st *m*), Simon David Vaughan *b* 1970, Charlotte Hilary Vaughan *b* 1968, — Nicholas Vaughan, *b* 1942; Headmaster Shiplake Coll, Henley-on-Thames, Oxon: *m* 1st, 1967 (*m diss* 1977), Penelope Jane, da of Col D. H. Tildesley, of Tettenhall Court, Tettenhall, Staffs; 2ndly, 1978, Ann Marie, el da of John Timothy O'Connor, of Leongatha, Vic, Aust, and has issue living, (by 1st *m*) Edward Duder Vaughan *b* 1971, Katherine Jane Vaughan *b* 1969, (by 2nd *m*) Oliver David *b* 1979, Emily Grace *b* 1982, — Richard Vaughan (1145 17th Av E, Seattle, USA), *b* 1943: *m* 1st, 1972 (*m diss* 1980), Christine, el da of late B. G. Harte, of Bromley Kent; 2ndly, 1991, Lesley Burvill-Holmes, and has issue living (by 2nd *m*), Nicholas *b* 1992, — Jennifer Jill Vaughan, *b* 1946: *m* 1975, Gerald Leslie Hayward, and has issue living, James Fulton *b* 1979, Thomas Seaborne *b* 1980, — Margaret Hilary Vaughan, *b* 1953: *m* 1987, Aidan John Kelly, and has issue living, David John *b* 1988, Peter Richard *b* 1990.
Hon Anne, *b* 1919; *ed* Somerville Coll, Oxford.
Hon Auriol Mary Grace, *b* 1922; SRN, SCM.

PREDECESSORS

PREDECESSORS – **(1)** JOHN SOMERSET Russell, GCB, PC, son of late William Russell, of Powick, by Elizabeth, el da of Sir Herbert Perrott Pakington, 7th Bt; *b* 1799; *s* in 1830 to the estates of his uncle Sir John Pakington, 8th and last Bt, and assumed the surname of Pakington in lieu of his patronymic; sat as MP for Droitwich (*C*) 1837-74; Sec of State for Colonies 1852, First Lord of the Admiralty 1858-9 and 1866-7, Sec of State for War 1867-8, and First Civil Ser Commr 1876-80; *cr a Baronet* 1846, and *Baron Hampton*, of Hampton Lovett and of Westwood, co Worcester (peerage of United Kingdom) 1874: *m* 1st, 1822, Mary, who *d* 1843, da of Moreton Aglionby Slaney; 2ndly, 1844, Augusta Anne, who *d* 1848, da of late Rt Rev George Murray, DD, Bishop of Rochester; 3rdly, 1851, Augusta, da of Thomas Champion de Crespigny, and widow of Col Henry Davies, MP of Elmley Park, Worcester; *d* April 1880; *s* by his son **(2)** JOHN SLANEY, 2nd Baron, *b* 1826: *m* 1849, Lady Diana Boyle, who *d* 1877, da of 4th Earl of Glasgow; *d* 1893; *s* by his half-brother **(3)** HERBERT PERROTT MURRAY, 3rd Baron, *b* 1848: *m* 1877, Evelyn Nina Frances, who *d* 1904, da of Sir George Baker, 3rd Bt; *d* 1906; *s* by his son **(4)** HERBERT STUART CBE, DSO, 4th Baron, *b* 1883: *m* 1883; Maj Worcestershire Yeo, *d* 1962; *s* by his brother **(5)** HUMPHREY ARTHUR, OBE, FRIBA, 5th Baron, *b* 1888; Cdr RN: *m* 1913, Grace Dykes, who *d* 1959, da of Rt Hon Sir Albert Spicer, 1st Bt; *d* 1974; *s* by his son **(6)** RICHARD HUMPHREY RUSSELL, 6th Baron and present peer.

HAMWEE, BARONESS (Hamwee) (Life Baroness 1991)

SALLY RACHEL HAMWEE, da of late Alec Hamwee, by his wife Dorothy (*née* Saunders); *b* 12 Jan 1947; *ed* Manchester High Sch for Girls, and Girton Coll, Camb (MA); Solicitor; formerly Councillor London Borough of Richmond upon Thames, Chm London Planning Advisory Cttee, and Vice-Chm and Pres ALDC (Liberal Democrat Councillors' Assocn); *cr Baroness Hamwee*, of Richmond upon Thames, in the London Borough of Richmond upon Thames (Life Baroness) 1991.
Residence – 101a Mortlake High St, SW14 8HQ.

Handcock, family name of Baron Castlemaine.

HANKEY, BARON (Hankey) (Baron UK 1939)

DONALD ROBIN ALERS HANKEY, 3rd Baron; *b* 12 June 1938; *s* 1996; *ed* Rugby, and Univ Coll, London (Dip Arch), RIBA: *m* 1st, 1963 (*m diss* 1974), Margaretha, yr da of Cand-Jur H. Thorndahl, of Copenhagen; 2ndly, 1974 (*m diss* 1994), Eileen Désirée, yr da of late Maj-Gen Stuart Hedley Molesworth Battye, CB, of Fensacre House, Ascot, Berks; 3rdly, 1994, June, da of late Dr Leonard Taboroff, and has issue by 2nd *m*.

Arms – Per pale azure and gules, a wolf salient erminos vulned on the shoulder of the second, a bordure wavy of the third. Crest – A wolf's head erased at the neck erminois, gorged with a collar wavy azure. Supporters – *Dexter*, a fallow deer resting the sinister hind foot proper on a millrind sable; *sinister*, an alpine chamois resting the dexter hind foot proper on a like millrind.
Residence – 8 Sunset Rd, SE5 8EA.

DAUGHTERS LIVING (*By 2nd marriage*)

Hon Fiona Bevyl, *b* 1975.
Hon Beatrice Eileen, *b* 1978.

BROTHER LIVING

Hon ALEXANDER MAURICE ALERS, *b* 18 Aug 1947; *ed* Rugby, Trin Coll, Camb, and Mass Inst of Technology (PhD): *m* 1970 (*m diss* 1990), Deborah, da of late Myron Benson, of Newton, Mass, USA. *Residence* – Hethe House, Cowden, Edenbrige, Kent TN8 7DZ.

SISTERS LIVING

Hon Juliet Alers, *b* 1931: *m* 1957, Peter John Wrensted Alchin, of Parkstone, Clenches Farm Rd, Sevenoaks, and has issue living, Gordon David, *b* 1961, — Vanessa Frances, *b* 1962, — Chloe Sylvia, *b* 1965.
Hon Adele Bevyl Alers, *b* 1933: *m* 1964 (*m diss* 1987), Dr Erik Emil Anggård, of Stockholm, Sweden, and has issue living, Jon Mikael, *b* 1967, — Eola Anni, *b* 1965, — Irene Malin Adele, *b* 1970. *Residence* – Banergatan 77, 115 53 Stockholm, Sweden.

UNCLES LIVING (*sons of 1st Baron*)

Hon Christopher Alers, OBE (New Cottage, French Street, nr Westerham, Kent), *b* 1911; *ed* Rugby, Oxford (BA honours in History 1932, MA 1947), and London (BSc Eng honours 1939) Univs; Prin Min of Overseas Development 1964-72; 1939-45 War s Major RM; OBE (Civil) 1958: *m* 1st, 1945 (*m diss* 1957), Prudence May, da of late Keith Brodribb, of Frodsley, Tasmania; 2ndly, 1958, Helen Christine, yr da of late A. J. Cassavetti, of Puckshott, Oxted Surrey, and has issue living, (by 2nd *m*) Rupert Christopher Alers, *b* 1960: *m* 1st, 1984 (*m diss* 1990), Jane Elizabeth, eldest da of late

Ian Bruce and of Mrs Alan Pote, of The Priory, Rothwell, Northants; 2ndly, 1999, Maria Jane, eldest da of late Stanislas Muszynski, — (by 1st *m*) Felicity Laura Alers, *b* 1947: *m* 1969, Henry R. C. Edgell, of Dennistoun, Bothwell, Tasmania 7030, son of Geoffrey Edgell, CBE, and has issue living, Thomas *b* 1971, Edward *b* 1981, Chloe *b* 1975.

Hon Henry Arthur Alers, CMG, CVO (Llandaff Barn, 11 Thames St, Eynsham, Witney, Oxon; United Univ Club), *b* 1914; *ed* Rugby, and New Coll, Oxford; Ambassador to Panama 1966-69; Under Sec, FCO 1969-74; CVO 1959, CMG 1960: *m* 1941, Vronwy Mary, who *d* 1998, only da of late Rev Thomas F. Fisher, and has issue living, Christopher Ceri Alers (Route du Gros Chene, Argonay, 74000 France), *b* 1944: *m* 1st, 1970, Eleanor, only da of C. J. C. Beckett, of Danemore House, S Godstone, Surrey; 2ndly, 1980, Annick, only da of Robert Perrucon, of Annecy, and has issue living (by 2nd *m*), Jonathan Ceri Alers *b* 1980, Jason Henry Alers *b* 1989, Deborah Marie Alers *b* 1982, — Maurice Peregrine Alers (The Green, Northmoor, Oxon), *b* 1945: *m* 1970, Juliet, da of Antony Ross Moore, CMG, and has issue living, Antony Thomas *b* 1977, David Henry *b* 1988, Rose Vronwy *b* 1975, — Peter John Alers (Le Lassy, 73410 St German-la-Chambotte, France), *b* 1951: *m* 1981, Margaret Catharine, only da of John D. Walker, of 9 Wilbraham Pl, SW1, and has issue living, Robert *b* 198-, William Walker Alers *b* 1991, Katharine Claire Alers *b* 1987, — Veronica Vronwy Alers, *b* 1957: *m* 1980, Sqdn Ldr (ret) Timothy C. M. Newman, RAF, of Wester Golford, Moyness, Nairn, elder son of late W/ Cdr A. T. Newman, of Honeycritch Cottage, Froxfield, Hants, and has issue living, Thomas Robert Minôt *b* 1990, Elena Vronwy Margaret *b* 1987.

AUNT LIVING *(daughter of 1st Baron)*

Hon Ursula Helen Alers (*Hon Lady Benn*), *b* 1909: *m* 1929, Sir John Andrews Benn, 3rd Bt, Surrey, who *d* 1984. *Residence* – 15 The Waldrons, Oast Rd, Hurst Green, Oxted, Surrey RH8 9DY.

WIDOW LIVING OF SECOND BARON

(ALINE) STEPHANIE PAULET LANGLEY (*Stephanie, Baroness Hankey*), da of late Brig Percy Paulet King, and of late Mrs Kenneth Ford, of W Wittering: *m* 1992, as his 3rd wife, the 2nd Baron Hankey, KCMG, KCVO, who *d* 1996. *Residence* – Hethe House, Cowden, Edenbridge, Kent TN8 7DZ.

PREDECESSORS – **(1)** *Sir* MAURICE PASCAL ALERS Hankey, GCB, GCMG, GCVO, PC, FRS, LLD son of late Robert Alers Hankey of Warcowie, S Australia and Brighton (whose grandfather, William Alers, of City of London, was authorized to assume the surname of Hankey in addition to Alers and to bear the arms of Hankey only with difference by Roy Licence 1815); *b* 1877; Col RMA; Sec, War Cabinet 1916-7, and Imperial War Cabinet 1917-18, British Sec to Peace Conference 1919, Sec to Cabinet 1920-38, Sec to Imperial Conferences 1921, 1923, 1926, 1930, and 1937, Sec-Gen Hague Conference 1929-30, London Naval Conference 1930, and Lausanne Reparation Conference 1932, Clerk to PC 1923-38; Min without Portfolio in War Cabinet 1939-40; Chancellor of Duchy of Lancaster 1940-41, Paymaster-Gen 1941-2, and Chm of Techincal Personnel Cttee 1941-52; *cr Baron Hankey*, of The Chart, Surrey (peerage of UK), and a PC 1939: *m* 1903, Adeline, who *d* 1979, da of late Abraham de Smidt, Surveyor-Gen of Cape Colony; *d* 1963; *s* by his el son **(2)** ROBERT MAURICE ALERS, KCMG, KCVO, 2nd Baron, *b* 1905; HM Ambassador to Sweden 1954-60, UK Delegate to Organization for European Economic Co-operation, Paris 1960, and to Organization for Economic Co-operation and Development 1961-65, Vice-Pres European Inst of Business Admin, Fontainbleau 1960-82, etc; Pres Anglo-Swedish Soc 1970-78; Grand Cross of Order of North Star of Sweden: *m* 1st, 1930, Frances Bevyl, who *d* 1957, da of late Walter Erskine Stuart-Menteth (Stuart-Menteth, Bt, colls); 2ndly, 1962, Joanna Riddall, who *d* 1991, da of late Rev James Johnstone Wright; 3rdly, 1992, Mrs (Aline) Stephanie Paulet Langley, da of late Brig Percy Paulet King, and late Mrs Kenneth Ford, of W Wittering; *d* 1996; *s* by his elder son **(3)** DONALD ROBIN ALERS, and present peer.

HANNINGFIELD, BARON (White) (Life Baron 1998)

PAUL EDWARD WINSTON WHITE, son of Edward Ernest William White, of West Hanningfield, Essex; *b* 16 Sept 1940; *ed* King Edward VI Gram Sch, Chelmsford; Chm Chelmsford Young Farmers 1962; Memb Chelmsford Conservative Party Executive 1962; Memb Nat Executive, NFU 1965; Chm Stock Area of Essex Conservative Party 1968-75; Councillor, Essex CC 1970; held various positions including Chm of Education 1973-98; Leader of Essex CC since 1998; Conservative Leader, Assoc of County Councils 1995-97; Chm Conservative Party Eastern Area Local Govt Advisory Cttee 1995-98; Pres Assembly of European Regions Sub-Commission; Memb Council of Essex Univ; Governor Brentwood Sch; DL Essex 1991; *cr Baron Hanningfield*, of Chelmsford, co Essex (Life Baron) 1998. *Residence* – Pippins Place, Helmons Lane, W Hanningfield, Chelmsford, Essex CM2 8UW.

HANSON, BARON (Hanson) (Life Baron 1983)

JAMES EDWARD HANSON, son of late Robert Hanson, CBE, of Huddersfield, Yorks, by his wife Louisa Anne (Cis) *née* Rodgers; *b* 20 Jan 1922; Hon LLD Leeds 1984; Hon DBA Huddersfield 1991; Hon Fell of St Peter's Coll, Oxford 1996; Hon Fell of Royal Coll of Radiologists 1998; FRSA; CI Mgt; War Service 1939-46; Chm Hanson plc 1965-97, since when Chm Emeritus; Dir Hanson Transport Group Ltd (Chm 1965-96); Freeman of City of London 1964; Liveryman Worshipful Co of Saddlers 1964; Member of Court of Patrons, Royal Coll of Surgeons of England 1991;Trustee Hanson Fellowship of Surgery, Oxford Univ; Fell Cancer Research Campaign; *cr* Kt 1976, and *Baron Hanson*, of Edgerton, co West Yorkshire (Life Baron) 1983: *m* 1959, Geraldine Kaelin, and has issue.

Arms – Vert in fess point a rose argent barbed and seeded proper between six like roses three and three in pale. **Crest** – On a wreath or and vert a demi chestnut horse proper charged on the shoulder with a rose argent barbed seeded slipped and leaved proper. **Supporters** – *Dexter*, a bulldog in trian aspect with a Viking helmet of the seventh century gilded and verde antico on his head proper, and *sinister*, an American bald eagle also proper.

Motto – Prima Peto.
Residence – 1 Grosvenor Place, SW1X 7JH. *Club* – Brooks's, Huddersfield Borough, The Brook (NY), Toronto.

SONS LIVING

Hon Robert William (White's Club), *b* 1960; *ed* Eton, and St Peter's Coll, Oxford.
(*Hon*) (John) Brook (does not use courtesy title) (Brooks's Club), *b* 1964; *ed* Pangbourne.

HANWORTH, VISCOUNT (Pollock) (Viscount UK 1936, Bt UK 1922)

Boldly and strenuously

(DAVID) STEPHEN GEOFFREY POLLOCK, 3rd Viscount, and 3rd Baronet; *b* 16 Feb 1946; *s* 1996; *ed* Wellington Coll, Guildford Tech Coll and Sussex Univ; PhD Amsterdam Univ; Reader in Econometrics, London Univ: *m* 1968, Elizabeth, da of Lawrence Vambe, MBE, of Harare, Zimbabwe, and has issue.

Arms – Azure, three fleurs-de-lis within a bordure engrailed or, on a chief ermine two portcullises of the second. **Crest** – A boar passant quarterly or and vert, pierced through the sinister shoulder with an arrow proper. **Supporters** – (hereditary), — On either side a bear or, muzzled, collared, and chain sable.
Residence – 12 Gladsmuir Rd, N19.

DAUGHTERS LIVING

Hon (Abigail Cecily) Shona, *b* 1971.
Hon Charlotte Anne Catherine, *b* 1973.

BROTHER LIVING

Hon (RICHARD) CHARLES STANDISH, TD, *b* 6 Feb 1951; *ed* Wellington Coll, and Trin Coll, Camb; Maj Royal Yeo (T&AVR); TD 1986: *m* 1982, Annette Louise, da of Peter Lockhart, late of Daisy Cottage, Studham, Common Lane, nr Dunstable, Beds, and has issue living, Harold William Charles, *b* 1988, — Frederick Thomas Charles, *b* (twin) 1988. *Residence* – Brook House, North End, Gt Dunmow, Essex CM6 3PQ.

SISTER LIVING

Hon Gillian Isolda Josephine, *b* 1944: *m* 1963 (*m diss* 1990), Timothy von Weber Sarson, and has issue living, Cosmo Anthony Harold, *b* 1971, — David Alexander, *b* 1977, — Emma Isolda, *b* 1964: *m* 1984, Hugh Davies, only son of late Lt-Col R. M. W. Davies, MC, of Tyn Rhos, Golan, Garn Dolbenmaen, Caernarvonshire, and has issue living, Bryn Michael Timothy *b* 1987, Holly Isolda Wyn *b* 1989, — Ellen Georgina Hester Maria, *b* 1975. *Residence* – 8 Gatcombe Rd, N19 4PT.

WIDOW LIVING OF SECOND VISCOUNT

(ISOLDA) ROSAMOND (*Rosamond, Viscountess Hanworth*), yr da of late Geoffrey Parker (*see* E Macclesfield, colls): *m* 1940, Lt-Col 2nd Viscount Hanworth, who *d* 1996. *Residence* – Quoin Cottage, Shamley Green, Guildford, Surrey.

PREDECESSORS – (1) *Rt Hon Sir* ERNEST MURRAY Pollock, KBE, PC, son of late George Frederick Pollock (Pollock, Bt colls): *b* 1861; was Solicitor-Gen 1919-22, and Master of the Rolls 1923-35; MP for Warwick and Leamington (C) 1910-18, and for Warwick and Leamington Div of Warwickshire 1918-23; *cr a Baronet* 1922, *Baron Hanworth* of Hanworth, co Middlesex (peerage of United Kingdom) 1926, and *Viscount Hanworth*, of Hanworth, co Middlesex (peerage of United Kingdom) 1936: *m* 1887, Laura Helen, who *d* 1954, el da of Sir Thomas Salt, 1st Bt (*cr* 1899); *d* 1936; *s* by his grandson (2) DAVID BERTRAM (only son of late Capt Charles Thomas Anderdon Pollock) (only son of 1st Viscount), *ka* 1918, 2nd Viscount; *b* 1916, Bar Inner Temple 1958; Lt-Col RE; CEng, MIMechE, FIEE, FIQA, FRPS; author of books on colour photography: *m* 1940, (Isolda) Rosamond, yr da of late Geoffrey Parker (*see* E Macclesfield, colls); *d* 1996; *s* by his elder son (3) (DAVID) STEPHEN GEOFFREY, 3rd Viscount and present peer, also Baron Hanworth.

HARBERTON, VISCOUNT (Pomeroy) (Viscount I 1791)

Virtutis fortuna comes

Fortune is the companion of valour

THOMAS DE VAUTORT POMEROY, 10th Viscount; *b* 19 Oct 1910; *s* 1980; *ed* Eton; Lt-Col (ret) RAOC; formerly Lieut Welsh Guards: *m* 1st, 1939 (*m diss* 1946), Nancy Ellen, only da of late C. A. Penoyer, of San Francisco; 2ndly, 1950, Pauline Stafford, who *d* 1971, da of late Wilfred Sydney Baker, of Stoke, Plymouth; 3rdly, 1978, Wilhelmine (Vilma), da of Heinrich Wahl, and widow of Sir Alfred Butt, 1st Bt.

Arms – Or, a lion rampant gules, armed and langued azure, holding between the fore paws an apple proper. Crest – A lion rampant as in the arms. Supporters – Two wolves, the *dexter* proper, the *sinister* argent; both collared and chained or.
Club - Cavalry and Guards'.

SISTER LIVING

Hon Rosamond Mary (The Cottage in Swains Lane, Bembridge, Isle of Wight; Bembridge Sailing Club) (twin), *b* 1916; 1944-45 War in France and Germany with ATS.

WIDOW LIVING OF SON OF EIGHTH VISCOUNT

(Winifred) Anne, 2nd da of late Sir Arthur Colegate, MP, of Hill Grove, Bembridge, I of Wight (*see* Worsley, Bt, 1955 Edn): *m* 1953, Maj Hon Robert William Pomeroy, who *d* 1997, and has issue (see colls, infra). *Residence* – Rockfield House, Nunney, nr Frome, Som BA11 4NP.

COLLATERAL BRANCHES LIVING

Issue of late Maj Hon Robert William Pomeroy, yst son of 8th Viscount, *b* 1916, *d* 1997: *m* 1953, (Winifred) Anne (ante), 2nd da of late Sir Arthur Colegate, MP, of Hill Grove, Bembridge, I of Wight (*see* Worsley, Bt, 1955 Edn):—
HENRY ROBERT (Rockfield Stables, Nunney, Frome, Som BA11 4NP), *b* 23 April 1958: *m* 1990, Caroline Mary, da of Jeremy Grindle, of Viking Cottage, Bosham, W Sussex, and has issue living, Patrick Christopher, *b* 10 May 1995, — Hugh William, *b* 1997. —— Richard Arthur, *b* 1960: *m* 1987, Helena Claire, 2nd da of Andrew Watt Drysdale, of Pitcombe Farm House, Bruton, Som (*see* Newman, Bt, *cr* 1836, 1980 Edn), and has issue living, Tallulah, *b* 1992, — Xanthe, *b* 1995.

Granddaughter of late John Arthur Pomeroy (infra):—
Issue of late Major Francis Knox Pomeroy, *b* 1876, *d* 1962: *m* 1906, Helen, who *d* 1955, da of Arthur Cinnamond, formerly of St Helens, Belfast:—
Helen Mary Ursula, *b* 1909; late Junior Com ATS: *m* 1943, Archibald Richard Sanford Hodgson, DSC, late Lt-Cdr RNVR, who *d* 1990, and has issue living, Nicholas Pomeroy Sanford (The Old Rectory, Odstock, nr Salisbury, Wilts), *b* 1945; *ed* Eton: *m* 1974, Melissa, yr da of Donald B. Prouty, of 32 Foster St, Littleton, Mass, USA, and has issue living, Christopher Prouty Sanford *b* 1980, Geoffrey Peter Sanford *b* 1986, Alexandra Louise Pomeroy *b* 1978, Olivia Cinnamond *b* 1983, — Helen Rose Sanford, *b* 1947: *m* 1979, Capt Ian Cameron de Sales La Terrière, of Dunalastair, Perthshire, and has issue living, Hugh William *b* 1982, Robert Duncan *b* 1984, — Ursula Virginia Sanford, *b* 1952.

Grandchildren of late Maj Francis Knox Pomeroy, 4th son of late John Arthur Pomeroy, elder son of Rev Hon Arthur William Pomeroy, 2nd son of 4th Viscount:—

Issue of late Cmdr Arthur John Cinnamond Pomeroy, VRD, RNVR, *b* 1907, *d* 1995: *m* 1962, Rowena Mary Vesey (39 River Rd, Cantley, PQ, Canada J8V 2Z7), da of late Vice-Adm Reginald Vesey Holt, CB, DSO, MVO:—
†Hugh Reginald Arthur, *b* 1963; *d* as the result of an accident 1986. —— John Francis Vesey, *b* 1965; has issue living (by Lee Ann Hoar), Carrington John, *b* 1993, — Alexandra Mary Lee, *b* 1995.

Issue of late (Jocelyn Francis) Brian Pomeroy, *b* 1912, *d* 1991: *m* 1940, Lucy Margaret, who *d* 1993, da of Robert Hayne, of Osmington, Weymouth:—
Thomas (Springbottom House, Osmington Mills, Weymouth, Dorset DT3 6HL), *b* 1941; *ed* Eton, and Trin Coll, Camb (MA): *m* 1967, Belinda Jane, da of late Maj-Gen John Sheffield, CB, CBE, of 11 Pitt St, W8, and has issue living, Helen Emily Jane, *b* 1971, — Rosalind Lucy, *b* 1973, — Laura Patience, *b* (twin) 1973. —— Simon Robert Valentine (The Old Vicarage, Winscombe, Som), *b* 1943; *ed* Eton, and Keble Coll, Oxford (MA); FCA: *m* 1972, Ursula Jean, yr da of late John Stephen Barclay, and has issue living, Patricia Margaret (Daisy), *b* 1974, — Elizabeth Frances Mary, *b* 1976, — Catherine Harriet, *b* 1981. —— (Frances) Louise (*Lady Heathcoat-Amory*), *b* 1947: *m* 1972, Sir Ian Heathcoat-Amory, 6th Bt, of Calverleigh Court, Tiverton, Devon, and has issue (see that title).

Grandsons of late George Pomeroy Arthur COLLEY (infra):—
Issue of late George Dudley Pomeroy COLLEY, *b* 1911, *d* 1959: *m* 1947, Ann Patricia (The Mill House, Kilmatead, Clondalkin, co Dublin), da of late William Burns:—
Finlay FitzGeorge COLLEY, *b* 1948. —— Anthony William Pomeroy COLLEY (64 Pembroke Rd, Dublin 4), *b* 1951: *m* 1973, Mary, da of Hugh Kelly, and has issue living, Dudley Hugh Pomeroy, *b* 1975, — Jeffrey Andrew Pomeroy, *b* 1978, — Amy Alexandra Pomeroy, *b* 1984.

Granddaughters of late Henry FitzGeorge COLLEY, son of late Hon George Francis COLLEY (who assumed the name of Colley in lieu of his patronymic 1830), 3rd son of 4th Viscount:—
Issue of late George Pomeroy Arthur COLLEY, *b* 1866, *d* 1933: *m* 1909, Edith Maude Olivia, who *d* 1975, el da of late Col Henry Thomas Finlay, DL (V Bangor, colls):—
Veronica Maud Pomeroy (23 Whitebarn Rd, Churchtown, Dublin 14), *b* 1913: *m* 1st, 1935 (*m diss* 1968), Maj Jeffry Arden Patrick Lefroy, MBE, Yorkshire Dragoons, who *d* 1985; 2ndly, 1972, Lt-Col Derrick Arthur Hall-Dare, OBE, who *d* 1985, and has issue living, (by 1st *m*) Jeffry George (Carrigglas Manor, Longford, Ireland), *b* 1936; Maj (ret) late R Irish Rangers: *m* 1964, Teresa Margaret, da of Henry Alwyn White, DL, of Orange Hill, Tanderagee, co Armagh, and has issue living, Jeffry Peter Langlois *b* 1965, Edward Christian Perceval *b* 1967, — Laetitia Mary (40 Ailesbury Lawn, Dundrum, Dublin, 16), *b* 1937. —— Valerie Edith Pomeroy, *b* 1915: *m* 1947, William Patrick Hone, MC, who *d* 1976, and has issue living, Christopher Patrick George, *b* 1949: *m* 1981, Mary Josephine, da of Raymond Jennings, of Riversdale House, Craughwell, co Galway, and has issue living, Timothy Patrick Raymond *b* 1995. *Residence* – Kilmatead, Clondalkin, co Dublin. —— Rosemary Pomeroy *b* 1916: *m* 1947, Henry Nicholas Crocker, who *d* 1982, and has issue living, Henry Alistair Nicholas (22 Freeland Place, Bristol), *b* 1949: *m* 1975, Christina, da of William McMillan, of 70 Eckford St, Glasgow, and has issue living, Ursula Margaret Rosemary *b* 1985, Roberta Harriet *b* 1988, — Rodric John (138 Marlborough Av, Hull), *b* 1954: *m* 1980, Irena, da of Dr Jerzy Kurowski, of Hull, and has issue living, Alexandra Ruth *b* 1981, — Virginia Helen, *b* 1948: *m* 1971, Sqdn Ldr James Edward Malcolm Mustard, RAF (ret), of The Butts, Middle Woodford, Salisbury, Wilts, and has issue living, James Edmond Alexander *b* 1974, Eleanor Clare *b* 1981. *Residence* – 3 Redcliffe Close, Redcliffe Bay, Portishead, Bristol.

Issue of late Rev William Wingfield COLLEY, *b* 1868, *d* 1947: *m* 1915, Helen Isabel who *d* 1974, da of late Rev Duncan John Brownlow:—
Esmé Florence Helen, *b* 1920. *Residence* – Carbery, 12 Albany Court, Ballybrack, co Dublin.

PREDECESSORS – (1) ARTHUR Pomeroy, son of late Rev John Pomeroy; *b* 1723; was MP for co Kildare 1761-83; *cr Baron Harberton* of Carbery (peerage of Ireland) 1783, and *Viscount Harberton* (peerage of Ireland) 1791: *m* 1747, Mary, da of Henry Colley, of Castle Carbery, co Kildare; *d* 1798; *s* by his el son (2) HENRY, 2nd Viscount; *b* 1749: *m* 1778, Mary, who *d* 1823, da of Nicholas Grady, of Grange, co Limerick; *d* 1829; *s* by his brother (3) ARTHUR JAMES, 3rd Viscount, *b* 1753: *m* 1800, Elizabeth, who *d* 1862, da of Thomas Kinsley; *d* 1832; *s* by his brother (4) *Rev* JOHN, 4th Viscount; *b* 1758; Preb of St Patrick's Cathedral, Dublin 1783-1822: *m* 1785, Esther, who *d* 1840, da of James Spencer; *d* 1833; *s* by his son (5) JOHN JAMES, 5th Viscount; *b* 1790: *m* 1822, Caroline, who *d* 1886, da of Rev Sir John Robinson, 1st Bt (*cr* 1819); *d* 1862; *s* by his son (6) JAMES SPENCER, 6th Viscount; *b* 1836: *m* 1861, Florence Wallace, who *d* 1911, da of William Wallace Legge, DL, of Malone House, co Antrim; *d* 1912; *s* by his el son (7) ERNEST ARTHUR GEORGE, 7th Viscount; *b* 1867; sometime Lieut 20th Hussars and Capt Roy Dublin Fusiliers; S Africa 1900 (Queen's medal): *m* 1932, Fairlie, who *d* 1945, da of late Col Charles D'Oyly Harmar, of Ramridge, Andover; *d* 1944; *s* by his brother (8) RALPH LEGGE, OBE, 8th Viscount; *b* 1869; Major Reserve of Officers (Dragoon Guards); S African War 1899-1902 (severely wounded) 1914-18 War: *m* 1907, Mary Katherine, who *d* 1971, da of Arthur Leatham, formerly of Smallfield Place, Surrey; *d* 1956; *s* by his son (9) HENRY RALPH MARTYN, 9th Viscount, *d* 1980; *s* by his brother (10) THOMAS DE VAUTORT, 10th Viscount and present peer; also Baron Harberton.

HARCOURT, VISCOUNTCY OF (Harcourt) (Extinct 1979)

DAUGHTERS LIVING OF SECOND VISCOUNT

Hon (Elizabeth) Ann, *b* 1932: *m* 1954, Crispin Gascoigne (The Manor House, Stanton Harcourt, Oxon), only son of late Maj-Gen Sir Julian Alvery Gascoigne, KCMG, KCVO, CB, DSO (*see* Newman Bt, *cr* 1836, 1980 Edn), and has issue living, William Harcourt Crisp, *b* 1955: *m* 1980, Susan Alexandra, da of Aubrey Greville Williams, of Maypole Farmhouse, E Grimstead, Salisbury, Wilts, and has issue living, Julian Aubrey Harcourt *b* 1984, Frederick William *b* 1986, Ralph

Edward *b* 1989, Lily Ann *b* 1995, — Elizabeth Laura, *b* 1958: *m* 1986, Peter Nicholas Offord, eldest son of late L. R. Offord, of Winchmore Hill, N21, and has issue living, Nicholas Alvery Harcourt *b* 1990, Venetia Vernon *b* 1988, Cecily Katherine *b* 1992, — Mary Ann, *b* 1961: *m* 1986, Matthew Charles Louis Crosby, only son of Dr Jack Lionel Crosby, of Stanhope, co Durham, and has issue living, Miles William Southe *b* 1989, George Crispin Ivo *b* 1992, Flora Mary Alice *b* 1995.

Hon Penelope Mary, *b* 1933: *m* 1954, Capt Anthony David Motion, late 9th Queen's Roy Lancers, of Buckland, Irishtown, Northam, W Australia 6401, and has issue living, Stephen Anthony, *b* 1967, — and an adopted da, Georgina, *bapt* 1965.

HARDIE, BARON (Hardie) (Life Baron 1997)

ANDREW RUTHERFORD HARDIE, son of Andrew Rutherford Hardie, of Ashley Terrace, Alloa; *b* 8 Jan 1946; *ed* St Modan's High Sch, Stirling, and Edinburgh Univ (MA 19—, LLB 19—); Admitted Solicitor 1971; Memb Faculty of Advocates 1973; Advocate Depute 1979-83; Standing Jr Counsel, City of Edinburgh DC 1983-85 (Sr Counsel 1987-96); QC (Scot) 1985; Dean, Faculty of Advocates 1994-97 (Treasurer 1989-94); Lord Advocate since 1997; Convener, Children in Scotland 1994-96; Hon Pres The Muir Soc since 1994; *cr* PC 1997, and *Baron Hardie*, of Blackford in the city of Edinburgh (Life Baron) 1997: *m* 1971, Catherine Storrar, da of David Currie Elgin, of Crescent Wood Rd, SE26, and has issue.

Residence – 4 Oswald Rd, Edinburgh EH9 2HF. *Clubs* – Caledonian (Edinburgh), Murrayfield Golf (Edinburgh).

SONS LIVING

Hon Ewan, *b* 1975.
Hon Niall, *b* 1981.

DAUGHTER LIVING

Hon Ruth, *b* 1977.

HARDING OF PETHERTON, BARON (Harding) (Baron UK 1958)

JOHN CHARLES HARDING, 2nd Baron; *b* 12 Feb 1928; *s* 1989; *ed* Marlborough, and Worcester Coll, Oxford; Maj (ret) 11th Hussars: *m* 1966, Harriet, da of late Maj-Gen James Francis Hare, CB, DSO, and has issue.

𝕬rms – Argent on a bend azure between two lions passant guardant gules as many kukris in saltire proper between two martlets or. 𝕮rest – Out of a mural crown gules a cubit arm in armour the hand gauntleted grasping a Field Marshal's baton in bend sinister proper. 𝕾upporters – *Dexter*, a Private of 1st Life Guards of early nineteenth century; *sinister*, a Somerset Light Infantryman of the late eighteenth century; both habited and accoutred proper.
Residence – Myrtle Cottage, Lamyatt, nr Shepton Mallet, Somerset BA4 6NP.

SONS LIVING

Hon WILLIAM ALLAN JOHN, *b* 5 July 1969.
Hon David Richard John, *b* 1978.

DAUGHTER LIVING

Hon Diana Mary, *b* 1967: *m* 1995, John D. Penrose, son of late David Penrose, of Drinkstone, Suffolk.

PREDECESSOR – (1) *Field Marshal* ALLAN FRANCIS (JOHN) Harding, GCB, CBE, DSO, MC, son of late Francis E. Harding, of Compton Way, S Petherton, Som, *b* 1896; Field Marshal late Somerset LI, ADC Gen to HM King George VI 1950, and HM The Queen 1952-53; Hon Col N Somerset Yeo, Col 6th Queen Elizabeth's Own Gurkha Rifles 1951-61, Somerset LI 1953-59, SCLI 1959-60, and Life Guards 1957-64; GOC-in-C S Cmnd 1947-49, C-in-C Far East Land Forces 1949-51, and BAOR 1951-52, CIGS 1952-55, Gov and C-in-C of Cyprus 1955-57, Gold Stick to HM 1957-64; *cr Baron Harding of Petherton*, of Nether Compton, co Dorset (peerage of UK) 1958: *m* 1927, Mary Gertrude Mabel, who *d* 1983, da of late Joseph Wilson Rooke, JP, of Knutsford, Cheshire; *d* 1989; *s* by his only son (2) JOHN CHARLES, 2nd Baron, and present peer.

HARDING-DAVIES, BARONY OF (Harding-Davies)

SON LIVING (*Raised to the rank of a Baron's son* 1980)

Hon Francis William Harding DAVIES, *b* 1946; *ed* Windlesham House Sch, Nautical Coll Pangbourne, and Strasbourg Univ; Pres ATV Music Gp, Canada, 1982-85, Pres TMP (The Music Publisher) since 1986: *m* 1972, Lynda Margaret Mae Squires, and has issue.

DAUGHTER LIVING (*Raised to the rank of a Baron's daughter* 1980)

Hon Rosamond Ann, *b* 1943: *m* 1968, Charles Marten Metherell.

HARDINGE, VISCOUNT (Hardinge) (Viscount UK 1846, Bt UK 1801)
(Name and Title pronounced "Harding")

MENS·ÆQUA·REBUS·IN·ARDUIS

An equal mind in difficulties

CHARLES HENRY NICHOLAS HARDINGE, 6th Viscount and 8th Baronet; *b* 25 Aug 1956; *s* 1984; *ed* Upper Canada Coll, Trin Coll Sch, and McGill Univ; *s* his kinsman, Sir Robert Arnold Hardinge, 7th Bt, in his baronetcy, 1986: *m* 1985, Mrs Julie Therese Sillett, eldest da of Keith Sillett, of Sydney, Australia, and has issue.

Arms – Gules, on a chevron argent, fimbriated or, three escallops sable. Crest – A mitre gules, charged with a chevron, as in the arms. Supporters – On either side a lion proper, that on the dexter murally crowned, supporting a flag flowing to the dexter or, and that on the sinister crowned with an Eastern crown, supporting a flag flowing to the sinister or.
Residence – 12 Streathbourne Rd, SW17.

DAUGHTERS LIVING

Hon Emilie Charlotte, *b* 1986. —— *Hon* Olivia Margaux, *b* 1989.

BROTHERS LIVING

Hon ANDREW HARTLAND, *b* 7 Jan 1960; *ed* The Gow Sch, and Trin Coll Sch: *m* 1990, Sophia Mary, only da of Capt (William) David (Armstrong) Bagnell, of East Worldham House, Alton, Hants (*see* E Wilton, 1953 Edn), and has issue living, Thomas Henry de Montarville, *b* 19 June 1993, — Jamie, *b* 1996. *Residence* – 20 Niton St, SW6 6NJ.
Hon Maximillian Evelyn, *b* 1969.

HALF-SISTER LIVING

Hon Georgia Victoria, *b* 1984.

AUNTS LIVING (*Daughters of 4th Viscount*)

Hon Carolyn Mary Wynyard, *b* 1932: *m* 1954, John Arthington Worsley (RR2, Uxbridge, Ont, Canada) (*see* Worsley, Bt).
Hon Gay, *b* 1938: *m* 1963, Pierre Raymond, of Stage Coach Rd, Brome, Prov Quebec, Canada, and has issue living, a son, *b* 1965.

MOTHER LIVING

Zoe Ann, da of Hartland de Montarville Molson, OBE, of Montreal, Senator of Canada: *m* 1st, 1955 (*m diss* 1982), as his 1st wife, the 5th Viscount Hardinge, who *d* 1984; 2ndly, 1983, Christopher Mark Henry Murray, of La Glinette, St Aubin, Jersey, CI (*see* Jerningham, Bt (ext), 1955 Edn).

WIDOW LIVING OF FIFTH VISCOUNT

Baroness FLORENCE ELISABETH VON OPPENHEIM, da of late Baron Harold von Oppenheim, of Cologne: *m* 1st, 1982, as his 2nd wife, the 5th Viscount Hardinge, who *d* 1984; 2ndly, 1993, Martin Graham Shelley, son of late John Shelley, of St Boswells, Roxburghshire.

COLLATERAL BRANCHES LIVING

Issue of late Rt Hon Charles Hardinge, KG, GCB, GCSI, GCMG, GCIE, GCVO, ISO, 2nd son of 2nd
Viscount, who was *cr Baron Hardinge of Penshurst* 1910 (see that title).

Granddaughter of late Gen Hon Sir Arthur Edward Hardinge, KCB, CIE, son of 1st Viscount:—
Issue of late Rt Hon Sir Arthur Henry Hardinge, GCMG, KCB, *b* 1859, *d* 1933: *m* 1899, Alexandra Mina, who *d*
1949, da of late Maj-Gen Sir Arthur Edward Augustus Ellis, GCVO, CSI (B Howard de Walden, colls):—
Mary Pamela, *b* 1907; Bar Inner Temple 1940.

(In remainder to baronetcy only)

Grandchildren of late Bradford Hardinge, son of late Maj-Gen Richard Hardinge, brother of 2nd
baronet:—
Issue of late George Nicholas Hardinge, *b* 1865, *d* 1943: *m* 1923, Lady Lilian Frances Graham-Toler, who *d* 1974,
sister of 5th Earl of Norbury:—
Nicholas William (Lock Cottage, Bear St, Nayland, Essex), *b* 1928; *ed* Radley: *m* 1973, Mrs Anne Curtis, who *d* 1998, da
of late Lt-Col Walter Thomas Delamain. —— Phyllis Lilian (Rose Cottage, Bramdean Common, Alresford, Hants), *b*
1925.

PREDECESSORS – (1) *Field Marshal Rt Hon Sir* HENRY Hardinge, GCB, PC, son of Rev Henry Hardinge, R of
Stanhope, whose heirs male are in special remainder to the Baronetcy (*cr* 1801); *b* 1785; entered the Army at an early
age and was present at all engagements throughout the Peninsular War; became Field-Marshal 1855; sat as MP for
Launceston (*C*) 1826-41; was Clerk of the Ordnance 1823, Sec at War 1828, Ch Sec of Ireland 1830 and 1834, again Sec
at War 1841, Gov-Gen of India 1844-8, Master-Gen of the Ordnance 1852, and Gen Com in Ch 1852-6; *cr Viscount Hard-
inge* (peerage of United Kingdom) 1846; twice thanked by Parliament for his military and civil services, and awarded a
pension of £3,000 a year for three lives: *m* 1821, Lady Emily Jane Stewart, who *d* 1865, da of 1st Marquess of
Londonderry, KG, and widow of John James; *d* 1856; *s* by his son (2) CHARLES STEWART, 2nd Viscount, *b* 1822; MP for
Downpatrick 1851-6: *m* 1856, Lady Lavinia Bingham, who *d* 1864, da of 3rd Earl of Lucan; *d* 1894; *s* by his el son (3)
HENRY CHARLES, CB, 3rd Viscount; *b* 1857; Capt Rifle Brig: *m* 1891, Mary Frances (who *d* 1954, having *m* 2ndly, 1928, as
his 3rd wife, the 3rd Marquess of Abergavenny), da of late Hon Ralph Pelham Nevill; *d* 1924; *s* by his son (4) CARYL
NICHOLAS CHARLES, 4th Viscount, *b* 1905; Maj 7th Hus, an ADC to Gov-Gen of Canada 1926-28, and Mil Assist to AG to
Forces 1941-45; MBE (Mil) 1946: *m* 1928, Margaret Elizabeth Arnot, who *d* 1993, da of late Hugh Fleming, of Wynyards,
Rockcliffe, Ottawa; *d* 1979; *s* by his only son (5) HENRY NICHOLAS PAUL, 5th Viscount, *b* 1929; Lieut 7th Hus; Snr Vice-
Pres World Corporate Banking, R Bank of Canada: *m* 1st, 1955 (*m diss* 1982), Zoe Ann, da of Hartland de Montarville
Molson, OBE, of Montreal, Senator of Canada; 2ndly, 1982, Baroness Florence Elisabeth (who *m* 2ndly, 1993, Martin
Graham Shelley), da of late Baron Harold von Oppenheim, of Cologne; *d* 1984; *s* by his eldest son (6) CHARLES HENRY
NICHOLAS, 6th Viscount and present peer.

HARDINGE OF PENSHURST, BARON (Hardinge) (Baron UK 1910)
(Name and Title pronounced "Harding")

JULIAN ALEXANDER HARDINGE, 4th Baron; *b* 23 Aug 1945; *s*
1997; *ed* Eton, and Trin Coll, Camb; Page of Honour to HM
1959-62: *m* 1972 (*m diss* 1993), Anthea June, da of Harold
Mills West, of Martlesham, Suffolk, and has issue.

𝕬rms – Gules, on a chevron argent fimbriated or three escallops sable; a
chief wavy argent, thereon the representation of a French frigate wholly
dismasted, towed towards the dexter by an English frigate in a shattered
state. 𝕮rest – 1st, a dexter hand couped in naval uniform grasping a
sword, surmounting a Dutch and French flag in saltire, on the former
inscribed "Atalanta," on the latter "Piedmontaise," the sword passing
through a wreath of laurel near the point and a little below through one of
cypress, all proper; 2nd, a mitre gules, thereon a chevron argent
fimbriated or charged with three escallops sable. 𝔖upporters – *Dexter*, a
bear proper; *sinister*, a Bengal tiger proper.
Residence – 115 Broomhill Drive, Glasgow G11 7NA.

DAUGHTERS LIVING

Hon Frances Melanie, *b* 1973.
Hon Sophie Jane, *b* 1974.

BROTHERS LIVING

Hon HUGH FRANCIS, *b* 9 April 1948; *ed* Eton. *Residence* – Albion Villa,
Church End, Over, Cambridge CB4 5NH.
Hon Edward Frederick, *b* 1958; *ed* Gordonstoun. *Residence* – 29 The
Springs, Hertford SG13 7DR.

For King and Country

HALF BROTHER LIVING

Hon Charles Alexander, *b* 1967; *ed* Eastbourne, and Bradford Univ (B Eng). *Residence* – Pfaffenweiler Strasse 5, 78052 VS-Rietheim, Germany.

ADOPTIVE STEP-BROTHER LIVING

Dane Anthony TREZISE-HARDINGE, *b* 1957; *ed* Gordonstoun.

AUNT LIVING (*Daughter of 2nd Baron*)

Hon Winifred Mary (*Hon Lady Murray*), *b* 1923; late WRNS: *m* 1943, Maj Sir John Antony Jerningham Murray, CBE, late Grenadier Guards (*see* Jerningham, Bt, ext, 1955 Edn), and has issue living, (George) Alexander John (Woodmancote Manor, Cirencester, Glos), *b* 1947; *ed* Eton; City Ed, Sunday Telegraph, since 19—: *m* 1975 (*m diss* 19—), Caroline, da of John Miller, and has issue living, Alastair John *b* 1982, Laura Cecilia *b* 1979. *Residence* – Woodmancote Manor, Cottage, Cirencester, Glos.

WIDOW LIVING OF THIRD BARON

MARGARET (*Baroness Hardinge of Penshurst*), da of William Thomas Jerrum, of Hastings, Sussex, and formerly wife of Derek Trezise: *m* 1966, as his 2nd wife, the 3rd Baron Hardinge of Penshurst, who *d* 1997. *Residence* – Bracken Hill, 10 Penland Rd, Bexhill-on-Sea, Sussex.

PREDECESSORS – (1) *Rt Hon* CHARLES HARDINGE, KG, GCB, GCSI, GCMG, GCIE, GCVO, ISO, 2nd son of 2nd Viscount Hardinge, *b* 1858; was an Assist Under-Sec of State for Foreign Affairs 1903-4, Ambassador at St Petersburg 1904-6, Permanent Under-Sec of State for Foreign Affairs 1906-10, Viceroy of India 1910-16, again Permanent Under-Sec of State for Foreign Affairs 1916-20, and Ambassador Extraor and Plen in Paris 1920-23; *cr Baron Hardinge of Penshurst,* co Kent (peerage of United Kingdom) 1910: *m* 1890, Hon Winifred Sturt, CI, who *d* 1914, da of 1st Baron Alington; *d* 1944; *s* by his second and only surviving son (2) ALEXANDER HENRY LOUIS, GCB, GCVO, MC, PC, 2nd Baron, *b* 1894; Major Grenadier Guards (ret); was an ADC to Viceroy and Gov-Gen of India 1915-16; an Equerry in Ord and an Assist Private Sec to HM 1920-36 (Assist Keeper of HM's Privy Purse 1935-6), and an Extra Equerry to HM 1936-60, Private Sec to King Edward VIII 1936, and to King George VI 1936-43; European War 1914-18 (wounded, MC); a Gov of St Bartholomew's Hospital, and King's Sch, Canterbury: *m* 1921, Helen Mary, who *d* 1979, da of late Lord Edward Herbert Gascoyne-Cecil, KCMG, DSO (M Salisbury, colls); *d* 1960; *s* by his only son (3) GEORGE EDWARD CHARLES, 3rd Baron, *b* 1921; Lt-Cmdr RN; a Train Bearer at Coronation of King George VI; Publisher with Collins, Longman and Macmillan; author of several crime novels (under the name of George Milner): *m* 1st, 1944 (*m diss* 1962), Janet Christine Goschen, who *d* 1970, da of late Lt-Col Francis Cecil Campbell Balfour, CIE, CBE, MC (*see* E Balfour, colls, 1970 Edn); 2ndly, 1966, Mrs Margaret Trezise, da of William Thomas Jerrum, and formerly wife of Derek Trezise; *d* 1997; *s* by his eldest son (4) JULIAN ALEXANDER, 4th Baron and present peer.

HARDWICKE, EARL OF (Yorke) (Earl GB 1754)

Neither covet nor fear

JOSEPH PHILIP SEBASTIAN YORKE, 10th Earl; *b* 3 Feb 1971; *s* 1974; *ed* Marlborough; Founder and Dir Siamoto Scooters UK 1998.

Arms – Argent, a saltire azure charged with a bezant. **Crest** – A lion's head erased proper, gorged with a plain collar gules, charged on the collar with a bezant. **Supporters** – *Dexter*, a lion guardant or, gorged with a plain collar gules, the collar charged with a bezant; *sinister*, a stag proper, attired or, and collared as the lion.
Residence – Baron's Court, W6.

SISTER LIVING (*Raised to the rank of an Earl's daughter* 1977)

Lady Jemima Rose, *b* 1969.

AUNTS LIVING (*Daughters of 9th Earl*)

Lady Amabel Mary Maud, *b* 1935: *m* 1955, Hon Patrick Lindsay, who *d* 1986, and has issue (*see* E Crawford).
Lady Victoria Mary Verenia Braganza (36 Elms Rd, SW4), *b* 1947: *m* 1976 (*m diss* 1998), Nigel Waymouth, and has issue living, Louis Alexander Philip, *b* 1978, — Adam Django Joseph, *b* 1981.
Lady Rose Mary Sydney *b* 1951: *m* 1st, 19- (*m diss* 19-), Kenneth Delbray; 2ndly, 1981 (*m diss* 1985), Herbert Richard

Vaughan, who *d* 1987; 3rdly, 1990, Tony Turner; has issue living (by David Thompson), Katharine Sarah Tahlita Valour THOMPSON, *b* 1985.

WIDOW LIVING OF NINTH EARL

ENID MUNNICK (*Countess of Hardwicke*), da of Pieter Grunwald, of S Africa, formerly wife of Roy Boulting: *m* 1970, as his 2nd wife, the 9th Earl of Hardwicke, who *d* 1974. Resides in Paris.

COLLATERAL BRANCHES LIVING

Grandsons of late Hon Claud John Yorke, 3rd son of 7th Earl:—
Issue of late David John Napier Edward Yorke, *b* 1919, *d* 1997: *m* 1st, 1950, Anne Margaret, who *d* 1984, yr da of late Denis George Mackail (*see* Burne-Jones, Bt (ext), 1953 Edn); 2ndly, 1990, Mrs June Rose Charlotte Rachel Fyfe (27 Dragon St, Petersfield, Hants GU31 4JN), only da of late Daniel Walter Thomas Gurney, MC (*see* Troubridge, Bt, 1976 Edn), and widow of Robert Duncan Fyfe:—
(By 1st *m*) CHARLES EDWARD (Flat 4, 3 Vicarage Gate, W8 4HH), *b* 18 March 1951; *ed* Eton, and Ruskin Sch of Drawing and Fine Art, Oxford; caricaturist. —— James Alexander (64 Peterborough Rd, SW6 3EB), *b* 1954; *ed* Eton, Balliol Coll, Oxford (BA 1977), and Birkbeck Coll, London Univ (BA 1983): *m* 1986, Primrose Alexandra Mary, only da of late Brig Harold William Kitson, CBE, of Morecombelake, W Dorset, and has issue living, Philip Prospero Alexander, *b* 1987, —— Henry Cosimo Frederick, *b* 1991.

Grandsons of late Vincent Wodehouse Yorke, 2nd son of late John Reginald Yorke, son of late Joseph Yorke, el bro of late Capt James Charles Yorke (*b* 1816) (infra):—
Issue of late Maj Gerald Joseph Yorke, *b* 1901 *d* 1983: *m* 1937, Angela Vivien, who *d* 1988, el da of late Maj-Gen Sir John Duncan, KCB, CMG, CVO, DSO:—
John Sarne (Forthampton Court, Glos), *b* 1938; *ed* Eton, and Trin Coll, Camb; ACA (1965): *m* 1st, 1967, Jean Victoria, who *d* 1989, yr da of Anthony Reynolds, of Sintra, Portugal; 2ndly, 1992, C. Julia, da of late Herbert M. Allen, and has issue living (by 1st *m*), Anabel, *b* 1971, — Sara, *b* 1974. —— Vincent James (The Stalls, Bushley, Glos), *b* 1942; *ed* Eton, and Slade Sch of Art, Univ Coll, Lond: *m* 1970, Francine Caroline, da of late F. W. Barker, of Hythe, and has issue living, Griselda Rose, *b* 1973, — Hester Mary, *b* 1974, — Sophie Catherine, *b* 1977. —— Michael Piers (31 Downside Crescent, NW3), *b* 1944; *ed* Eton, Edin Univ, and London Univ: *m* 1972, Valerie Margaret, da of H. Peter B. Cox, of Chislehurst, Kent, and has issue living, Marcus *b* 1983, — Jessica *b* 1980.

Issue of late Henry Vincent Yorke, *b* 1905, *d* 1973: *m* 1929, Hon Adelaide Mary Biddulph, who *d* 1985, da of 2nd Baron Biddulph:—
Sebastian (Rock Cottage, Lockton, nr Pickering, Yorks YO18 7PZ), *b* 1934; *ed* Eton, and Trin Coll, Oxford: *m* 1st, 1957 (*m diss* 1962), Hon Emma Christina Tennant, da of 2nd Baron Glenconner; 2ndly, 1969 (*m diss* 19—), Evelien Barrau; 3rdly, 1993, Margaret Alison, da of Thomas Hick, of Hove, Sussex, and has issue living (by 1st *m*), Matthew Henry, *b* 1958; has issue living (by Sabina Todaro), Thomas Wodehouse *b* 1993, Liberty *b* 19—.

Grandchildren of late Capt James Hamilton Langdon Yorke, MC (infra):—
Issue of late James John Simon Yorke, DSC, RN *b* 1912, *d* 1963: *m* 1938, Bridget Essex (Constant, Nevern, Newport, Pembrokeshire), da of Adm Sir Alban Thomas Buckley Curteis, KCB:—
James Hamilton Simon, MBE (2831 S Columbus St, Arlington, Virginia 22206, USA), *b* 1939; *ed* Wellington Coll; Lt-Cdr RN (ret); MBE (Mil) 1990: *m* 1st 1966, (*m diss* 1984), Elizabeth Ann, da of Col John Leeper Anketell Macafee, CBE, of Grove House, Bredhurst, Kent; 2ndly, 1989, Jean Anne, da of C. Richard Louis, of Trenton, Michigan, USA, and has issue living (by 1st *m*), Simon Anketell Hamilton, *b* 1967, — Patrick James Langdon, *b* 1968, — Rebecca Mary Amabel, *b* 1970, — Amabel Lucy Elizabeth, *b* 1972. —— Nicholas Roger (Lower Fishguard, Dyfed) *b* 1944; *ed* Wellington Coll; agric engineer: *m* 1st, 1969 (*m diss* 1976), Kathleen Prentice, da of Kent Sanger; 2ndly, 1977 (*m diss* 1989), Carole Crossman, yst da of late Eldon F. le Poer Power, of Ashfield, Beauparc, co Meath, and has issue living (by 2nd *m*), Philip David Emerson, *b* 1983, — Louisa Harriet, *b* 1979. —— Philippa Mary Essex, *b* 1947: *m* 1968, Roger Morrall, of Lower Boddington, Daventry, Northants, and has issue living, Thomas Simon Neil, *b* 1978, — Bridget Essex, *b* 1973.

Granddaughter of late James Charles Yorke (*b* 1847), eldest son of late Capt James Charles Yorke (*b* 1816), yr son of late Joseph Yorke, elder son of late Rt Rev Hon James Yorke, Bishop of Ely, 5th son of 1st Earl:—
Issue of late Capt James Hamilton Langdon Yorke, MC, *b* 1884, *ka* 1917: *m* 1910, Violet Mary, who *d* 1963, da of late James Edmund Vincent, Chancellor of Diocese of Bangor:—
Susannah Mary, *b* 1915: *m* 1st, 1934, Major Gerald Hartas FitzGerald, IMS, who *d* 1937; 2ndly, 1938, Allan Forbes Malcolmson, and has issue living (by 1st *m*), Anne Sara, *b* 1935: *m* 1959, Richard Michael Johnstone Eastham, of Dolau Dwrbach, Scleddau, Fishguard, Pembrokeshire, and has issue living, Cedric Gerald *b* 1960, Jane Francesca *b* 1962, — (by 2nd *m*) Jean Sheila, *b* 1942: *m* 1971, Peter Robjant, of 32 Hilperdon Rd, Trowbridge, Wilts, and has issue living, David Allan *b* 1973, Mary Anna Susan *b* 1975.

Grandchildren of late Hon Mr Justice (Robert Langdon) Yorke, 2nd son of late James Charles Yorke (*b* 1847) (ante):—
Issue of late Maj Patrick Langdon Yorke, Royal Corps of Signals, *b* 1916, *d* of wounds received in action in NW Europe 1945: *m* 1939, Pamela Mary (who *m* 2ndly, 1950, Robert Michael Clive, of The Spinney, Spinney Drive, Gt Shelford, Cambridge), da of late James John S. McD. Dow, of Helensburgh, and has issue living, Andrew Patrick, *b* 1982, — Robert Anthony (Silver Birches, Bashurst Hill, Itchingfield, W Sussex), *b* 1944; *ed* Marlborough, and Clare Coll, Camb (MA): *m* 1975, Morag, da of late John S. McD. Dow, of Helensburgh, and has issue living, Andrew Patrick, *b* 1982, — Sarah Catherine, *b* 1978. —— Caroline Ann *b* 1941: *m* 1969, Peter Roy Chamberlain, of 60 Rock Rd, Cambridge, and has issue living, Juliet Catherine, *b* 1970, — Rachel Claire, *b* 1972.

Grandchildren of late James Charles Yorke (*b* 1847) (ante):—

Issue of late Cdr Joseph Hugh Langdon Yorke, RN, *b* 1888, *d* 1936: *m* 1916, Ursula Mary Vere, who *d* 1959, da of late Col Robert Oliver Lloyd, CB (formerly RE), of Treffgarne Hall, Pembrokeshire:—
Josephine Mary, *b* 1917: *m* 1st, 1945, Maurice Newton, who *d* 1949; 2ndly, 1959, Luis Nicolin y Martinez Del Campo. *Address* – Bolivar 8, 402 Mexico City 1 DF, Mexico. —— April Ursula, *b* 1919; is a Carmelite Nun.

Issue of late Worthington Langdon Yorke, *b* 1901, *d* 1983: *m* 1934, Irene Rebecca, who *d* 1992, da of George O. Britney, of Manyberries, Alberta, Canada:—
Frederick Alton, *b* 1935: *m* 1st, 1961 (*m diss* 19—), Connie Roberts; 2ndly, 1991, Clara Mercier, who *d* 1998, and has issue living (by 1st *m*), Bruce Langdon, *b* 1963. —— Katherine Anne, *b* 1937: *m* 1959, Walter William Yakimets, of 4803 Lansdowne Drive, Edmonton, Alberta, Canada T6H 4K8, and has issue living, Walter John, *b* 1961: *m* 1991, Joan Marie Mills, and has issue living, Beth Britney *b* 1994, Sarah Marie *b* 1996, — Stephen George, *b* 1963: *m* 1986, Marilyn Joan Mitchell, and has issue living, James Mitchell *b* 1995, Megan Joan *b* 1992, — Neil Edward, *b* 1969: *m* 1996, Brenda Diane Card, and has issue living, Braehm Daniel *b* 1997, Chantel Kathlin *b* 1998, — Dawn-Marie Rebecca, *b* 1967: *m* 1996, Mark Herbert Lotz, and has issue living, David Walter *b* 1998. —— Dianne Marie, *b* 1945: *m* 1965, Walter Herman Henry Petersen, and has issue living, Kevin John, *b* 1966, — Gary Michael, *b* 1968, — Brian Langdon Benjamin, *b* 1971.

Issue of late Capt Philip Cecil Langdon Yorke, OBE, RN, *b* 1903, *d* 1970: *m* 1st, 1936, Elsie Margaret, who *d* 1945, da of late F. Davis, of Barnwood, Glos; 2ndly, 1946 (*m diss* 1960), Violet Helen, da of C. Ormonde Trew, of Little Rough, Hindhead; 3rdly, 1961, Rose, who *d* 1966, da of A. Rubinstein, of London:—
(By 2nd *m*) Clare Amabel, *b* 1948: *m* 1969, Jonathan Robert Barclay, of The Old Vicarage, Stoke Holy Cross, Norwich NR14 8AB, and has issue (*see* Barclay, Bt).

Grandchildren of late Reginald Somers Yorke, 2nd son of Capt James Charles Yorke (*b* 1816) (ante):—
Issue of late Reginald Henry Crofton Yorke, *b* 1897, *d* (accidentally drowned) 1947: *m* 1927, Gwendolen Maude, da of late Frank Watkinson:—
John Reginald (9 Mornington Rd, Chingford, E4), *b* 1928; *ed* Bradfield, and King's Coll, Camb: *m* 1959, Catherine Stewart, da of late Frank William Borthwick, of West Ham, and has issue living, Margaret Helen, *b* 1967, — Jennifer Frances, *b* 1970. —— Elizabeth Mary, *b* 1930.

Grandchildren of late Algernon Joseph Yorke, yst son of Capt James Charles Yorke (ante):—
Issue of late Lt-Col Simon Algernon Yorke, *b* 1889, *d* 1977: *m* 1920, Annie Paton, da of late J. P. Fyfe, JP, of Craigielea, Greenock:—
Joseph Algernon, *b* 1922: *m* 1945, Mary Robertson, da of Alexander Brown, of Dunshelt, Fife, and has issue living, Marianne Alexandra, *b* 1946, — Josephine Mary Bunty, *b* 1948. Resides in Canada.

Issue of late Harold Branson Yorke, *b* 1890, *d* 1949: *m* 1920, Stella Catherine, who *d* 1968, da of late Rear-Adm Henry Compton Aitchison, of Shrubs Hill, Lyndhurst:—
Therése, *b* 1925: *m* 1963, as his 2nd wife, Michael Charles Stirling Halford. *Residence* – 6 Old Farm Rd, Nether Stowey, Bridgwater, Som. —— Joan Felicity, *b* 1933: *m* 1957, Count Mario Bizzarri, and has issue living, Flaminia Stella Giovanna Maria, *b* 1958: *m* 1990, Mario di Pilla, of Via Babini 28, Rome, — Alessandra Luisa Teresa Cristina Maria, *b* 1959: *m* 1993, Ben Heijmen, of Groenehilledijk 404A, Rotterdam, Holland, — Paola Maria Augusta Audreina Giovanna, *b* 1960, — Giovanna, *b* 1963, — Carla, *b* 1966. *Residence* – Via Galla e Sidami 49, Rome 00199. —— Christine Anne, *b* 1935: *m* 1958, Alan Neville White, and has issue living, Richard Neville, *b* 1964: *m* 1996, Helen Bernadette O'Connor, — Margaret Lesley, *b* 1959: *m* 1991 (*m diss* 1994), Peter Bowden, — Helen Mary, *b* 1960: *m* 1990, Dr David Halpin. *Residence* – Primrose Lodge, Duddleswell, Uckfield, E Sussex.

Grandson of Lt-Col Philip Charles Yorke, el son of Rev Charles Issac Yorke, 2nd son of Rev Philip Yorke, 2nd son of the Rt Rev Hon James Yorke, 5th son of 1st Earl:—
Issue of late Major Henry Reginald Yorke, MC, *b* 1874, *d* 1944: *m* 1903, Beatrix Victoire, who *d* 1960, da of Capt Lynch-Staunton, formerly 14th Hussars:—
Philip (3 Crowsbury Close, Emsworth, Hants, PO10 7TS) *b* 1905; *ed* Harrow: *m* 1945, Elsie May Heasman.

Grandchildren of late Brig Philip Gerard Yorke, DSO (infra):—
Issue of late Lt-Col Arthur Philip Denys Yorke, MC, *b* 1915, *d* 1971: *m* 1957, Mary Elizabeth (who *m* 2ndly, 1983, Jeffrey Michelmore), da of John Henry Glasbrook, of Childe Okeford Manor, Blandford:—
Michael Philip, *b* 1959. —— Nicholas Simon, *b* 1961: *m* 1991, Esther Victoria, only da of late Barry Desmond Watkins, of Prince of Wales Mansions, SW11, and has issue living, Robert Maximilian Philip, *b* 1991, — Georgina, *b* 1995. —— Delia Mary, *b* 1964.

Granddaughter of Lt-Col Philip Charles Yorke (ante):—
Issue of late Brig Philip Gerard Yorke, DSO, *b* 1882, *d* 1968: *m* 1914, Beryl Emelia, who *d* 1982, da of late Brig-Gen Arthur Henry Croker Phillpotts, formerly RHA (Brady, Bt):—
Amabel Marion, *b* 1924: *m* 1963, Brig Robert Michael Carr, MBE, DFC, formerly RA, of Nethercote, Church Lane, Mollsfont, Romsey, Hants SO51 0LL, and has an adopted son and da, Peter Robert, *b* 1965, — Philippa Amabel, *b* 1966.

PREDECESSORS – (1) *Sir* PHILIP Yorke, having been Solicitor-Gen and Attorney-Gen, was in 1733 appointed Lord Ch Justice of the King's Bench and *cr Baron Hardwicke*, of Hardwicke, co Gloucester (peerage of Great Britain); one of the Lords Justices for Administering the Govt during the King's absences; promoted to be Lord High Chancellor 1737, and *cr Viscount Royston* and *Earl of Hardwicke* (peerage of Great Britain) 1754; resigned the Great Seal 1756; *d* 1764; *s* by his son (2) PHILIP, 2nd Earl: *m* 1740, Lady Jemima Campbell (only da of 3rd Earl of Breadalbane), and afterwards in her own right Baroness Lucas of Crudwell (*cr* 1663), and Marchioness de Grey (*cr* 1740, extinct); the Marchioness *d* 1779 when the Marquessate expired, and the Barony of Lucas of Crudwell devolved upon her da Amabel; the Earl *d* 1796 without male issue; *s* by his nephew (3) PHILIP, KG, 3rd Earl, el son of Hon Charles, 2nd son of 1st Earl, who had been appointed Lord High Chancellor, and *d* 1770 before the patent conferring upon him the title of Baron Morden was completed; was Viceroy of Ireland 1801-6; *d* without surviving male issue 1834; *s* by his nephew (4) CHARLES PHILIP, PC,

4th Earl, son of Vice-Adm Sir Joseph Sydney, KCB, MP, 3rd son of Hon Charles (ante); *b* 1779; was a Vice-Adm; sat as MP for Reigate (C) 1831, and for Cambridgeshire 1831-4; Lord-Lieut of Cambridgeshire, Postmaster-Gen 1852, Lord Privy Seal 1858-9, and sometime a Lord-in-Waiting to HM Queen Victoria: *m* 1833, Hon Susan, who *d* 1886, da of 1st Baron Ravensworth; *d* 1873; *s* by his son (5) CHARLES PHILIP, 5th Earl, *b* 1836; Comptroller of the Household 1866-8, and Master of the Buckhounds 1874-8; MP for Cambridgeshire (C) 1865-73: *m* 1863, Lady Sophie Georgiana Robertine, who *d* 1923, da of 1st Earl Cowley; *d* 1897; *s* by his son (6) ALBERT EDWARD PHILIP HENRY, 6th Earl; *b* 1867; Under Sec of State for India 1900-1902, Under Sec of State for War 1902-3, and again Under Sec of State for India 1903-4; *d* 1904; *s* by his uncle (7) JOHN MANNERS, 7th Earl; *b* 1840; Capt RN: *m* 1869, Edith, who *d* 1930, da of late Alexander Oswald, of Auchencruive, Scotland; *d* 1909; *s* by his el son (8) CHARLES ALEXANDER, 8th Earl; *b* 1869: *m* 1st, 1911 (*m diss* 1927), Ellen, CBE, who *d* 1968, da of late James Russell, of Auckland, NZ; 2ndly, 1930, Mary Radley, who *d* 1938 (having *m* 2ndly, 1938, W. E. L. Jennings, Dist Officer of Dedza, Nyasaland), da of Edward Robert Twist, of Liverpool; *d* 1936; *s* by his nephew (9) PHILIP GRANTHAM (son of late Hon Alfred Ernest Frederick Yorke, 2nd son of 7th Earl), 9th Earl; *b* 1906; late Lt LG; 1939-45 War with City of London Yeo, and as Maj SAS: *m* 1st, 1934, Sarah Katharine, who *d* 1965, da of the Rt Hon Sir Francis Oswald Lindley, GCMG, CB, CBE; 2ndly, 1970, Enid Munnick, of S Africa, formerly wife of Roy Boulting; *d* 1974; *s* by his grandson, JOSEPH PHILIP SEBASTIAN (only son of late Philip Simon Prospero Rupert Lindley, Viscount Royston, only son of 9th Earl: *m* 1968, Virginia Anne, who *d* 1988, da of Geoffrey Lyon, of Hambledon, Surrey), 10th Earl and present peer; also Viscount Royston, and Baron Hardwicke.

HARDY OF WATH, BARON (Hardy) (Life Baron 1997)

PETER HARDY, son of Lawrence Hardy, of Wath-upon-Dearne; *b* 17 July 1931; *ed* Wath-upon-Dearne Gram Sch, Westminster Coll, London, Univ of Sheffield and Univ of Leeds; MP for Rother Valley (Lab) 1970-83, and for Wentworth 1983-97; PPS to Sec of State for the Environment 1974-76, and to Foreign Sec 1976-79; former leader of Labour Delegation to Council of Europe, Western European Union and CSCE Assemblies 1983-97; Chm Council of Europe Environment Cttee 1986-90; Vice-Chm Socialist Group Council of Europe 1983-96; Chm Energy Cttee PLP 1974-92; Hon Sec All-Party Group for Energy Studies 1992-97; Vice-Chm All Party Conservation Cttee 1973-97; Memb Central Exec Council NSPCC 1986-94; DL S Yorks 1997; Patron Yorkshire Wildlife Trust; author of *A Lifetime of Badgers* (1975); *cr Baron Hardy of Wath*, of Wath-upon-Dearne, co S Yorks (Life Baron) 1997: *m* 1954, Margaret Anne, da of Clarence Ernest Brookes, of Canada, and has had issue (1 son dec'd).

Arms – Sable between ten piles wavy argent issuing from the flanks three lady's slipper orchids in pale or. **Crest** – A badger sejant erect proper supporting a miner's safety lamp or. **Supporters** – On either side a greyhound sable winged or.
Residence – 53 Sandygate, Wath-upon-Dearne, Rotherham, S Yorks S63 7LU.

ADOPTED SONS LIVING

Christopher, *b* 1971.
Simon, *b* 1977.

Hardy, Gathorne-, family name of Earl of Cranbrook.

Hare, family name of Viscount Blakenham.

Hare, family name of Earl of Listowel.

HAREWOOD, EARL OF (Lascelles) (Earl UK 1812)
(Title pronounced "Harwood")

IN · SOLO · DEO · SALUS

Salvation in God alone

GEORGE HENRY HUBERT LASCELLES, KBE, 7th Earl; *b* 7 Feb 1923; *s* 1947; *ed* Eton, and King's Coll, Camb (BA); Hon LLD Leeds 1959, Aberdeen 1966, and Bradford 1983; Hon Dr Music, Hull 1962, D Univ York 1982, Hon RAM 1983, Janáček Medal 1978; Capt late Grenadier Guards; was Editor of magazine *Opera* 1950-53, a Dir of R Opera House, Covent Garden 1951-53, and 1969-72, Admin Executive thereof 1953-60, Artistic Dir of Edinburgh Festival 1961-65, Chancellor of York Univ 1963-67; Dir of Leeds Festival 1958-74; and Artistic Adviser of New Philharmonia Orchestra 1966-76; Man Dir of Sadler's Wells Opera (now English Nat Opera) 1972-85 (Chm 1986-96); Pres British Board of Film Classification (formerly Censors) 1985-97; Artistic Dir Adelaide Festival 1988; Artistic Adviser Buxton Festival 1993-98; Pres English Football Assn 1963-72; Pres of Leeds United AFC; a Train Bearer at Coronation of King George VI; an ADC to Gov-Gen of Canada 1945-46; acted as a Counsellor of State during HM King George VI's absence abroad 1947, and during HM Queen Elizabeth II's absence abroad 1953-54 and 1956; 1939-45 War in Italy (wounded, prisoner); KBE (1986): *m* 1st, 1949 (*m diss* 1967), Maria Donata Nanetta Paulina Gustava Erwina Wilhelmina (Marion), former pianist, da of late Erwin Stein, of Melbury Rd, W14 and formerly of Vienna; 2ndly, 1967, Patricia Elizabeth, former violinist, only da of Charles Tuckwell, of Sydney, Aust, and formerly wife of late Athol Shmith, and has issue by 1st and 2nd *m*.

Arms – Sable, a cross patonce within a bordure or. Crest – A bear's head couped at the neck ermine, muzzled gules, buckled or, and gorged with a collar of the second, rimmed and studded gold. Supporters – Two bears ermine; each muzzled gules, buckled or, gorged with a collar of the second, rimmed and studded, and with a chain reflexed over the back gold; pendant from the collar an estucheon sable, charged with a cross patonce or.
Seat – Harewood House, Leeds, LS17 9LG.

SONS LIVING (*By 1st wife*)

DAVID HENRY GEORGE (*Viscount Lascelles*) (Moor House, Harewood, Leeds LS17 9LG), *b* 21 Oct 1950; *ed* Westminster; Pres Leeds Young Musicians: *m* 1st, 12 Feb 1979 (*m diss* 1989), Margaret Rosalind, da of Edgar Frank Messenger; 2ndly, 11 March 1990, Diane Jane, da of John Prince Howse, and has issue:—

    SONS LIVING (*by 1st wife*)— *Hon* Benjamin George, *b* 19 Sept 1978, — *Hon* ALEXANDER EDGAR, *b* 13 May 1980, — *Hon* Edward David, *b* 19 Nov 1982.
    DAUGHTER LIVING (*by 1st wife*)— *Hon* Emily Tsering, *b* 23 Nov 1975.

Hon James Edward, *b* 5 Oct 1953; *ed* Westminster: *m* 1st, 4 April 1973 (*m diss* 1985), Fredericka Ann, da of Prof Alfred Duhrrson, of Deya, Majorca; 2ndly, 4 May 1985, Lori (Shadow), da of John Robert Lee, of Seligman, Arizona, USA, and formerly wife of John Porter; 3rdly, 30 Jan 1999, Joy Elias-Rilwan, of Pimlico, SW1, and has issue living, (by 1st *m*) Rowan Nash, *b* 6 Nov 1977, — Sophie Amber, *b* 1 Oct 1973, — (by 2nd *wife*) Tewa Ziyan Robert George (a son), *b* 8 June 1985, — Tanit (a da), *b* 1 July 1981.

(*Hon*) (Robert) Jeremy Hugh (does not use courtesy title), *b* 14 Feb 1955; *ed* Westminster: *m* 4 July 1981, Julie, da of Robert Baylis, of Mildenham Mill, Claines, nr Worcester, and has issue living, Thomas Robert, *b* 7 Sept 1982; *ed* Latymer Upper Sch, — Ellen Mary, *b* 17 Dec 1984, — Amy Rose, *b* 26 June 1986.

(By 2nd wife)

Hon Mark Hubert, *b* 5 July 1964; *ed* Bryanston: *m* 1992, Andrea Kershaw, and has issue living, Charlotte Patricia, *b* 24 Jan 1996, — Imogen Mary, *b* 3 Jan 1998.

WIDOW LIVING OF SON OF SIXTH EARL

Elizabeth Evelyn, only da of late Brig Sydney Collingwood, CMG, CBE, MC, of The Croft, Dedham, Essex: *m* 17 Nov 1978, as his 2nd wife, Hon Gerald David Lascelles, who *d* 27 Feb 1998, and has issue (see colls, infra). *Residence* – Les Croux, Monbazillac, 24240 Sigoules, France.

COLLATERAL BRANCHES LIVING

Issue of late Hon Gerald David Lascelles, yr son of 6th Earl, *b* 21 Aug 1924, *d* 27 Feb 1998: *m* 1st, 15 July 1952 (*m diss* 1978), Angela Estree, da of late Charles Stanley Dowding; 2ndly, 17 Nov 1978, Elizabeth Evelyn (ante), only da of late Brig Sydney Collingwood, CMG, CBE, MC, of The Croft, Dedham, Essex:—
(By 1st wife) Henry Ulick, *b* 19 May 1953: *m* 25 Aug 1979 (*m diss* 1999), Alexandra Clare Ruth, da of Charles Peter Morton, and has issue living, Maximillian John Gerald, *b* 19 Dec 1991. —— (By 2nd wife) Martin David, *b* 9 Feb 1962: *m* 1999, Charmaine Christine, da of Evansio Russell Eccleston, of Kingston, Jamaica; has issue living (by Carol Anne Douet), Georgina Elizabeth DOUET-LASCELLES, *b* 22 Dec 1988.

Granddaughters of late Com Hon Frederick Canning Lascelles, 2nd son of 4th Earl:—
Issue of late Rt Hon Sir Alan Frederick Lascelles GCB, GCVO, CMG, MC, *b* 1887; *d* 1981: *m* 1920, Hon Joan Frances Vere Thesiger, who *d* 1971, da of 1st Viscount Chelmsford.
Lavinia Joan, *b* 1923: *m* 1st, 1946 (*m diss* 1960), Maj Edward Westland Renton, The Black Watch; 2ndly, 1962 (*m diss* 1964), Gavin Maxwell, author, who *d* 1969 (Maxwell, Bt, *cr* 1681); 3rdly, 1969, Cdr David Kyrle Hankinson, RN, of 12A Barkston Gdns, SW5, and has issue living (by 1st *m*), Nicholas John, *b* 1946: *m* 1st, 1975 (*m diss* 1993), Caroline Mary, da of Kennedy Mayo Harrow, of Auckland, NZ; 2ndly, 1993, Valerie Dunphy, and has issue living (by 1st *m*), Alan Edward Mayo *b* 1976, Joshua Nicholas *b* 1992, Zoë Eleanor *b* 1979, (by 2nd *m*), Catriona Mairead Beth *b* 1994, Aisling Barbara *b* 1996, — Simon Anthony (13 Stonehill Rd, SW14), *b* 1948: *m* 1977, Amanda Jane, da of David Schrire, of Cape Town, S Africa, and has issue living, Julia Esther *b* 1979, Claudia Jessamine *b* 1981. —— Caroline Mary (*Hon Mrs David H. Erskine*), *b* 1928: *m* 1st, 1949, 2nd Viscount Chandos, who *d* 1980; 2ndly, 1985, as his 2nd wife, Hon David Hervey Erskine, of Felsham House, Felsham, Bury St Edmunds, Suffolk, brother of 13th Earl of Mar and Kellie.

Granddaughters of late Hon George Edwin Lascelles, 3rd son of 3rd Earl:—
Issue of late Hon Sir Alfred (George) Lascelles, *b* 1857, *d* 1952: *m* 1911, Isabel Carteret, who *d* 1965, da of late Francis John Thynne (M Bath, colls):—
Ursula, *b* 1914: *m* 1946, Alan George Ross Ormiston, and has issue living, James Christopher Ross, *b* 1949; *ed* Eton, and Worcester Coll, Oxford, — Lavinia Anne Ross (*Baroness Rathcreedan*), *b* 1952: *m* 1978, 3rd Baron Rathcreedan. *Residence* – Coln Orchard, Arlington, Bibury, Glos. —— Kathleen Louisa Isabel, *b* 1916: *m* 1940 (*m diss* 1953), Brigadier Robert Hugh Bellamy, CBE, DSO, late DCLI, who *d* 1972, and has issue living, Martin Hugh (Tumbling Fields, Blackawton, Totnes, Devon TQ9 7BG), *b* 1946; *ed* Stowe: *m* 1979, Elizabeth Burton, and has issue living, Oliver Robert John *b* 1984, Victoria Louise *b* 1981, — Vivien Patricia, *b* 1943: *m* 1967, Anthony John Wyndham Owston, who *d* 1992 (*see* Bromley, Bt, colls, 1995 Edn), and has issue living, Gavin Anthony *b* 1970, Vanessa Rosemary *b* 1968. *Residence* – Manor Cottage, Coln St Aldwyns, Cirencester.

Grandchildren of late Evelyn Herbert Lascelles (infra):—
Issue of late John Edward Lascelles, *b* 1923, *d* 1975: *m* 1946, Isabelle Christine Graham Maxwell, of Gordonvale, N Qld:—
David John, *b* 1948: *m* 1986 (*m diss* 1989). —— Peter James (The Counthouse, Wheal Kitty, St Agnes, Cornwall), *b* 1952: *m* 1981, Mary Louise O'Donovan, of Bega, NSW, Australia, and has issue living, Sean Henry, *b* 1981, — Brennan James Maxwell, *b* 1985, — Marcus Peter, *b* 1990. —— Stephen Charles (11 Tipuana Drive, Capalaba, Qld 4157, Australia), *b* 1954: *m* 1991, Theresa Louise Waller, of Brisbane. —— Isabelle Diana, *b* 1957: *m* 19—, Rodney Phillip Spillane, of Brisbane.

Grandson of late Edward George Lascelles, son of Hon George Edwin Lascelles (ante):—
Issue of late Evelyn Herbert Lascelles, *b* 1893, *d* 1982: *m* 1923, Colleen Una, who *d* 1986, da of John Taylor, of Rockwood Station, Qld:—
Geoffrey George (164 Esplanade, Pt Vernon, Hervey Bay, Qld 4655 Australia), *b* 1927; 1939-45 in RAN: *m* 1951, Gwen Martin, of Yandina, Qld, and has issue living, Scott (60 Battye Av, Beverley Park, Sydney, NSW), *b* 1952: *m* 1981, Lynne Jennifer Boultwood, of Earlwood, Sydney, NSW, and has issue living, Robert Scott *b* 1986, Elinor *b* 1983, — Kent (2 Caffyn Place, Garran, Canberra, ACT 2605), *b* 1954; Lt Cdr RAN: *m* 1st, 1975 (*m diss* 1980), Ann Marie Ludwigsen, of Bellevue Park, Southport; 2ndly, 1985, Vicki Ann Harris, of Wagga Wagga, NSW, and has issue living, (by 1st *m*) Tamara *b* 1975, (by 2nd *m*) Ashleigh Mary *b* 1988, Georgia Erin *b* 1994, — Fiona Jane, *b* 1962: *m* 1991, Paul Longworth, of Farnworth, Bolton, Lancs, and has issue living, Jack Lascelles *b* 1993, Cara Lascelles *b* 1996.

Grandchildren of late Lieut-Col Henry Arthur Lascelles, MVO, 4th son of Rt Hon William Saunders Sebright Lascelles MP, 3rd son of 2nd Earl:—
Issue of late Edward Charles Ponsonby Lascelles, OBE, *b* 1884, *d* 1956: *m* 1911, Leila Winifred Leonor (a DGStJ), who *d* 1979, da of late Sir Vincent Kennett-Barrington:—
(Henry) Anthony, CB, CBE, DSO, *b* 1912; *ed* Winchester, and Oriel Coll, Oxford (BA); Maj-Gen (ret) late RTR; Maj-Gen, Gen Staff, HQ Far East Land Forces 1964-66; Dir-Gen of Winston Churchill Trust 1967-80; Pres Brit Water Ski Federation since 1980; 1939-45 War in Middle East and Italy (despatches twice, DSO, OBE); DSO and OBE (Mil) 1945, CBE (Mil) 1962, CB (Mil) 1967: *m* 1941, Ethne Hyde Ussher, da of late Norman Charles. *Residence* – Manor Farm

Cottage, Hedgerley Green, Bucks. —— Alice Leila *b* 1914; *ed* London Univ (BSc Economics 1936). *Residence* – The Plough, Redford, Midhurst, Sussex.

Issue of late Henry Francis Lascelles, *b* 1886, *d* 1937: *m* 1918, Rose Caroline Georgiana, who *d* 1976, da of late Col Frederick Arthur Aylmer (B Aylmer, colls):—
Oliver, MBE, DSC, *b* 1921, Cdr RN; 1939-45 War (DSC); MBE (Mil) 1950: *m* 1963, Pamela Margaret Enid, da of late Robert Whillis, and has issue living, Harriet Caroline, *b* 1964: *m* 1989, Anthony William Vaughan Fairbank, and has issue (*see* V Chetwynd, colls). — Nicola Jane, *b* 1966: *m* 1996, Roderick J. H. McL. Corrie, yr son of Hugh Corrie, of Wineham, W Sussex. *Residence* – Manor Farm House, Hinton Waldrist, Oxon SN7 8RN.

Issue of late Sir Francis William Lascelles, KCB, MC, *b* 1890, *d* 1979: *m* 1924, Esmée Marion, who *d* 1995, da of late Charles Arthur Bury, of Downings, Salins, co Kildare:—
(Charles) Brian (Bank House, Glenfarg, Perthshire), *b* 1926: *m* 1st, 1953, Elizabeth Mary, who *d* 1978, only da of late Lt-Cdr Geoffrey Seymour Grenfell, RN; 2ndly, 1986, Margaret Anne, yst da of late Alec Maskell Mitchell, of Ferry Reach, Bermuda (*see* B Kinross, 1990 Edn), and formerly wife of Ronald Patrick Thorburn, FRICS, and has issue living (by 1st *m*), Charles Riversdale, *b* 1954: *m* 19— (*m diss* 19—), ..., of USA , — James Dominic (11 Lymington Rd, NW6 1HX), *b* 1956: *m* 1984, Diana Elizabeth, da of late James Okolo, of Lagos, Nigeria, and has issue living, James Theodore Grenfell *b* 1988, Lucy Elizabeth *b* 1985, — Tobias Francis, *b* 1965. —— †(Henry) Giles Francis *b* 1931: *m* 1957, Caroline Venetia, da of late Esmond Charles Baring, OBE (*see* B Ashburton, colls), and *d* 1998, leaving issue, Hugo Giles, *b* 1958: *m* 1986, Joanna Catherine, yr da of Maj Christopher Roland Philipson, of Lofts Hall, Essex (*see* By Woolavington, 1985 Edn), and has issue living, Henry *b* 1994, Rose *b* 1988, Camilla *b* 1991, — Peregrine Simon, *b* 1962, — Sophie Caroline, *b* 1958 (twin): *m* 1983 (*m diss* 1992), Lord (Richard) Bruce Dundas, yst son of 3rd Marquess of Zetland, and has issue (see that title).

Grandson of late Lieut-Col George Reginald Lascelles, CVO, OBE, 2nd son of late Col Walter Richard Lascelles, eldest son of late Hon Arthur Lascelles, 5th son of 2nd Earl:—
Issue of late Lieut-Col John Norman Pulteney Lascelles, *b* 1898, *d* on active ser 1939: *m* 1932, Elizabeth Katharine Joan, who *d* 1986, da of late Lieut-Col Lord Robert William Orlando Manners, CMG, DSO (*see* D Rutland, colls):—
Rupert John Orlando, *b* 1935; late Coldstream Guards: *m* 1st, 1963 (*m diss* 1988), Jeanne Gordon, da of Norman Gordon Farquharson, of Bryanston, Johannesburg; 2ndly, 1990, Hon Mrs Susan Geraldine Uniacke, only da of 20th Baron Willoughby de Broke, and has issue living (by 1st *m*), Robert Norman, *b* 1965, — Frances Sarah Elizabeth, *b* 1970.

PREDECESSORS – (1) EDWARD Lascelles, heir at law of Edwin Lascelles, 1st and last Baron Harewood, of Harewood Castle, co York, having sat as MP for Northallerton in several Parliaments was *cr Baron Harewood*, of Harewood, co York (peerage of Great Britain) 1796, and *Viscount Lascelles* and *Earl of Harewood* (peerage of United Kingdom) 1812; *d* 1820; *s* by his son (2) HENRY, 2nd Earl; Lord-Lieut of W Riding of York; *d* 1841; *s* by his son (3) HENRY, 3rd Earl; *b* 1797; Lord-Lieut of W Riding of York: *m* 1823, Lady Louisa Thynne, da of 2nd Marquess of Bath; *d* 1857; *s* by his son (4) HENRY THYNNE, 4th Earl, *b* 1824: *m* 1st, 1845, Lady Elizabeth Joan De Burgh, who *d* 1854, da of 1st Marquess of Clanricarde; 2ndly, 1858, Diana Elizabeth Matilda, who *d* 1904, da of John George Smythe, of Heath Hall, Wakefield; *d* 1892; *s* by his el son (5) HENY ULICK, GCVO, 5th Earl, *b* 1846; Lord, Lieut of W Riding of Yorkshire 1904-27; sometime an ADC to King George V: *m* 1881, Lady Florence Katherine Bridgeman, who *d* 1943, da of 3rd Earl of Bradford; *d* 1929; *s* by his el son (6) HENRY GEORGE CHARLES, KG, GCVO, DSO, TD, 6th Earl, *b* 1882; a Personal ADC to HM; Lord-Lieut of W Riding of Yorkshire 1927-47; Chancellor of Sheffield Univ 1944; European War 1914-19 with Grenadier Guards (DSO): *m* 28 Feb 1922, HRH Princess (Victoria Alexandra Alice) Mary (*The Princess Royal*), CI, GCVO, GBE, RRC, TD, CD, who *d* 28 March 1965, only da of HM King George V (*see* ROYAL FAMILY); *d* 1947; *s* by his son (7) GEORGE HENRY HUBERT, 7th Earl and present peer; also Viscount Lascelles, and Baron Harewood.

HARLECH, BARON (Ormsby Gore) (Baron UK 1876)

FRANCIS DAVID ORMSBY GORE, 6th Baron; *b* 13 March 1954; *s* 1985: *m* 1986 (*m diss* 1998), Amanda Jane, da of Alan Thomas Grieve, of Stoke Lodge, Ludlow, Shropshire, and has issue.

Arms – Quarterly: 1st and 4th gules, a fesse between three cross-crosslets fitchée or, *Gore*; 2nd and 3rd gules, a bend between six cross-crosslets or, *Ormsby*. **Crest** – 1st, an heraldic tiger rampant argent; 2nd, a dexter arm embowed in armour proper, holding in the hand a man's leg also in armour, couped at the thigh. **Supporters** – *Dexter*, an heraldic tiger argent, maned and tufted sable, ducally gorged or; *sinister*, a lion or.
Residence – The Mount, Race Course Rd, Oswestry, Shropshire SY10 7PH.

SON LIVING

Hon JASSET DAVID CODY, *b* 1 July 1986.

DAUGHTER LIVING

Under this sign thou shalt conquer

Hon Tallulah Sylvia, *b* 1988.

SISTERS LIVING

Hon Jane Teresa Denyse, *b* 1942: *m* 1966 (*m diss* 1984), Michael Sean O'Dare Rainey, son of Maj Sean Rainey, and Mrs Marion Wrottesley, and has issue living, Saffron (son), *b* 1967, — Gawaine O'Dare, *b* 1971, — Rose Soley, *b* 1969, — Ramona Alba, *b* 1973. *Residence* – Brogyntyn Home Farm, Oswestry, Salop.

Hon Victoria Mary, *b* 1946: *m* 1972, Julian Richard Leslie Lloyd (*see* V Chetwynd, colls, 1995 edn), and has issue living, Lester Guy Julian, *b* 1982, — Poppy Zita Aline, *b* 1972, — Zita Crystal Rosemary, *b* 1974. *Residence* – The Glebe, Leixlip, co Kildare.

HALF-SISTER LIVING

Hon Pandora Beatrice, *b* 1972.

UNCLE LIVING (*Son of 4th Baron*)

Hon John Julian, *b* 1925; *ed* Eton, and New Coll, Oxford; late Capt Coldstream Guards.

AUNTS LIVING (*Daughters of 4th Baron*)

Hon Mary Hermione (*Hon Lady Mayall*), *b* 1914: *m* 1st, 1936 (*m diss* 1946), Capt Robin Francis Campbell, CBE, DSO, who *d* 1985, only son of late Rt Hon Sir Ronald Hugh Campbell, GCMG; 2ndly, 1947, Sir (Alexander) Lees Mayall, KCVO, CMG, who *d* 1992, and has issue living, (by 1st *m*) Gerard Francis Campbell (491 Fulham Rd, SW6), *b* 1937: *m* 1964, Theodora Elizabeth, da of Col Sir Roderick (Napoleon) Brinckman, 5th Bt, and has issue living, Tarquin *b* 1966, Caspar *b* 1967, — Charles, *b* 1939: *m* 1963, Philippa, da of J. C. H. Le B. Croke, and has issue living, Phineas *b* 1965, Orlando *b* 1967, — (by 2nd *m*) Robert George Lees (13 St Mark's Place, W10), *b* 1954: *ed* Eton: *m* 1992, Maria, 5th da of late B. N. White-Spunner, of Lower Swell, Glos, — Cordelia Isobel, *b* 1948: *m* 1969 (*m diss* 19—), John Nelson Summerscale, son of Sir John Percival Summerscale, KBE, and has issue living, Aaron Piers *b* 1969, Gideon *b* 1970, — Alexandra Beatrice, *b* 1949: *m* 1st, 1971 (*m diss* 1978), John Culme-Seymour; 2ndly, 1992, Dominic Paul Morland, 2nd son of late Sir Oscar Charles Morland, GBE, KCMG. *Residence* – Sturford Mead, Warminster, Wilts.

Hon Dame Katharine Margaret Alice (*Viscountess Macmillan of Ovenden*), DBE, *b* 1921; DBE (Civil) 1974: *m* 1942, Maurice Victor, Viscount Macmillan of Ovenden, who *d* 1984, only son of 1st Earl of Stockton, and has issue (*see* E Stockton). *Residence* – 9 Warwick Sq, SW1.

Hon Elizabeth Jane, *b* 1929: *m* 1962, Hon William Simon Pease (*see* B Wardington). *Residences* – 29 Upper Addison Gdns, W14 8AJ; Lepe House, Exbury, Southampton.

WIDOW LIVING OF FIFTH BARON

PAMELA (*Pamela, Baroness Harlech*), only da of late Ralph Frederick Colin, of New York City: *m* 1969, as his 2nd wife, the 5th Baron Harlech, KCMG, PC, who *d* as the result of a motor accident 1985.

PREDECESSORS – William Gore (*see* E Arran, colls); MP for Leitrim, for Carnarvon Borough, and for N Shropshire: *m* 1815, Mary Jane, da and heiress of Owen Ormsby, whose name he assumed; *d* 1860 leaving issue **(1)** JOHN RALPH ORMSBY-GORE, MP for Carnarvonshire (*C*) 1837-41, and for N Salop 1859-75; a Groom-in-Waiting to HM 1841-59; *cr Baron Harlech*, of Harlech, co Merioneth (peerage of United Kingdom) 1876, with remainder to his brother: *m* 1844, Sarah, who *d* 1898, da and co-heir of Sir John Tyssen Tyrell, 2nd Bt; *d* 1876; *s* by his brother **(2)** WILLIAM RICHARD, 2nd Baron, *b* 1819; Lieut of co Leitrim; MP for Sligo (*C*) 1841-52, and for co Leitrim 1858-76: *m* 1850, Lady Emily Charlotte, who *d* 1892, da of late Adm Sir George Francis Seymour, GCB; *d* 1904; *s* by his el surviving son **(3)** RALPH CHARLES, 3rd Baron, *b* 1855; appointed Lieut of co Leitrim 1904, and Lord-Lieut of Merionethshire and Constable of Harlech Castle 1927; MP for Shropshire W, or Oswestry Div (*C*) 1901-4: *m* 1881, Lady Margaret Ethel Gordon, who *d* 1950, da of 10th Marquess of Huntly; *d* 1938; *s* by his son **(4)** WILLIAM GEORGE ARTHUR, KG, GCMG, PC, 4th Baron; *b* 1885; MP for Denbigh Dist (*C*) 1910-18, and Stafford 1918-38; Under-Sec of State for Colonies 1922-24, Postmaster-Gen Sept to Nov 1931, First Commr of Works 1931-36, and Sec of State for the Colonies 1936-38, High Commr for Bechuanaland, Basutoland and Swaziland, and High Commr in Union of S Africa 1941-44, Lord Lt of Merionethshire 1938-57, Constable of Harlech Castle 1938-64, and Caernarvon Castle 1945-63, Pro-Chancellor of Univ of Wales 1945-56: *m* 1913, Lady Beatrice Edith Mildred Gascoyne-Cecil, DCVO, da of 4th Marquess of Salisbury; *d* 1964; *s* by his yr son **(5)** WILLIAM DAVID, KCMG, PC, 5th Baron, *b* 1918; Maj RA (TA); DL for Salop; Min of State for Foreign Affairs 1957-61; Ambassador to USA 1961-65, and Dep Leader of Opposition House of Lords 1966-67; Chm Harlech TV 1967-85; Pres British Board of Film Censors; MP for Oswestry Div of Salop (*U*) 1950-61; PC 1957, KCMG 1961: *m* 1st, 1940, Sylvia, who was *k* in a motor accident 1967, da of late Hugh Lloyd Thomas, CMG, CVO (*see* Bellew, B, colls, 1967 Edn); 2ndly, 1969, Pamela, only da of Ralph F. Colin, of New York City, and *d* as the result of a motor accident 1985, when he was *s* by his only surv son (his elder son, Hon Julian Hugh, *b* 1940, *d* 1974) **(6)** FRANCIS DAVID, 6th Baron and present peer.

HARMAR-NICHOLLS, BARON (Harmar-Nicholls) (Life Baron 1974, Bt UK 1960)

HARMAR HARMAR-NICHOLLS, *Life Baron*, and 1st *Baronet*, son of Charles Edward Craddock Nicholls, of Walsall, Staffs; *b* 1 Nov 1912; assumed by deed poll the surname of Harmar-Nicholls in lieu of his patronymic; *ed* Queen Mary's Gram Sch, Walsall; 1939-45 War as Lt RE in India and Burma; a Dir of J & H Nicholls (Paints) Ltd, of Nicholls and Hennessy Group Ltd, of Radio Luxembourg (London) Ltd, of Cannon Insurance, Ltd, Chm Malvern Festival Theatre Trust; an Underwriter of Lloyd's and a JP for Staffs; PPS to Assist Postmaster-Gen 1951-55, Parl Sec Min of Agric Fisheries and Food 1955-57, and to Min of Works 1957-60; MP for Peterborough Div of Northants (*C*) 1950-74; elected rep to European Assembly 1979; *cr* a Baronet, of Darlaston, co Stafford (UK) 1960 and *Baron Harmar-Nicholls*, of Peterborough, Cambridgeshire: *m* 1940, Dorothy Elsie, el da of James Edwards, of Tipton, Staffs, and has issue.

Arms – Per pale and per chevron gules and sable, two arrows with broad heads pilewise, the shafts argent, the feathers and heads or overall a chevron engrailed gold. **Crest** – Gules and sable two keys in saltire wards upwards argent supporting a Davey lamp proper, all tied about with a Stafford knot, the strands gules and sable, the tassels also gules. *Residence* – Abbeylands, Weston, Stafford. *Clubs* – Constitutional, St Stephen's, Unionist City and Counties (Peterborough).

DAUGHTERS LIVING

Hon Judith Ann, *b* 1941: *m* 1973, Alan Aspden.
Hon Susan Frances Nicholls, *b* 1943; actress (as Susan Nicholls): *m* 1993, Mark Eden, actor.

HARMSWORTH, BARON (Harmsworth) (Baron UK 1939)

He does well who works diligently

THOMAS HAROLD RAYMOND HARMSWORTH, 3rd Baron; *b* 20 July 1939; *s* 1990; *ed* Eton, and Ch Ch, Oxford; 2nd Lieut RHG: *m* 1971, Patricia Palmer, da of late Michael Palmer Horsley, of Waltham House, Brough, N Humberside, and has issue.

Arms – Azure, two rolls of paper in saltire or, banded in the centre gules, between two bees volant in pale and as many trefoils in fesse of the second. **Crest** – A cubit arm erect, the hand holding a roll of paper fessewise proper between two ostrich feathers or. **Supporters** – On either side a deep sea fisherman proper. *Residence* – The Old Rectory, Stoke Abbott, Beaminster, Dorset DT8 3JT.

SONS LIVING

Hon DOMINIC MICHAEL ERIC, *b* 18 Sept 1973; *ed* Eton.
Hon Timothy Thomas John, *b* 1979.

DAUGHTERS LIVING

Hon Philomena Hélène Olivia, *b* 1975.
Hon Abigail Patricia Thérèse, *b* 1977.
Hon Pollyanna Mary Clare, *b* 1981.

SISTER LIVING

Madeleine Thérèse Margaret, *b* 1941; *ed* Poles Convent, and Somerville Coll, Oxford; journalist. *Residence* – 15 Sudeley St, Islington, N1.

DAUGHTER LIVING OF SECOND BARON

Hon Margaret Askew Alexander, *b* 1928; painter and sculptor: *m* 1st, 1949, Wendell Holmes McCulloch, son of late Wendell McCulloch, of Bowling Green, Kentucky, USA; 2ndly, 1960, Frank Gibson Phillips, son of late Henry Gibson Phillips, of Windmill Hill, Alton, Hants, and has issue living (by 1st *m*), Kevin Desmond Harmsworth (Lime Lodge, Egham, Surrey), *b* 1950; *ed* Harrow, — (by Fredi Re'em), Dan Eric Harmsworth McCULLOCH (369 Montezuma Av, Suite No.110, Santa Fé, NM 87501, USA), *b* 1951; *ed* Bedales; interior designer, photographer, underwater marine videographer and fine art print publisher: *m* 1st, 1978 (*m diss* 1983), Donna Maria Santoro; 2ndly, 1992, Yana Halouzka, and has issue living (by 1st *m*), Francesca Prembindu *b* 1978, (by 2nd *m*) Angelo Halouzka *b* 1993, Inanna Halouzka *b* 1995. *Residences* – 15 Square de Chantillon, Paris 75014, France; Lime Lodge, Egham, Surrey.

PREDECESSORS – (1) CECIL BISSHOPP Harmsworth, 3rd son of late Alfred Harmsworth, Bar-at-Law (see also V North-cliffe (ext) and V Rothermere); *b* 1869; was Parliamentary Private Sec (unpaid) to Pres of Board of Agriculture and Fish-eries (Rt Hon W Runciman, MP) 1911-15; Parliamentary Under-Sec of State, Home Depart 1915-19, and for Foreign Affairs 1919-22; in Prime Min's Secretariat 1917-19; sat as MP for Worcestershire Mid, of Droitwich Div (*L*) 1906-10, for S, or Luton Div of Bedfordshire 1911-18, and for Luton Div thereof 1918-22; *cr Baron Harmsworth*, of Egham, co Surrey (peerage of UK) 1939: *m* 1897, Emilie Alberta, who *d* 1942, da of William Hamilton Maffett, Bar-at-Law, formerly of St Helena, Finglas, co Dublin; *d* 1948; *s* by his el son **(2)** CECIL DESMOND BERNARD, 2nd Baron, *b* 1903; painter, Chm Dr Johnson's House Trust: *m* 1926, Dorothy Alexander, who *d* 1990, da of late Hon Joseph Charles Heinlein (sometime a State Senator), of Bridgeport, Ohio, USA; *d* 1990; *s* by his nephew **(3)** THOMAS HAROLD RAYMOND (son of late Hon Eric Beauchamp Northcliffe Harmsworth, yst son of 1st Baron, by his 1st wife, Hélène Marie, who *d* 1962, elder da of Col Jules-Raymond Dehove, of Paris), 3rd Baron and present peer.

Harmsworth, family name of Viscount Rothermere.

HARRINGTON, EARL OF (Stanhope) (Earl GB 1742)

From God and the king

WILLIAM HENRY LEICESTER STANHOPE, 11th Earl; *b* 24 Aug 1922; *s* 1929 to the Earldom of Harrington, Viscountcy of Petersham and Barony of Harrington; and 1967 to Viscountcy of Stanhope of Mahon and Barony of Stanhope of Elvaston; *ed* Eton; Capt 15th/ 19th King's R Hussars: *m* 1st, 1942 (*m diss* 1946), Eileen, only da of Sir John Foley Grey, 8th Bt (*see* Lambert, Bt); 2ndly, 1947 (*m diss* 1962), Anne Theodora, only da of late Maj Richard Arenbourg Blennerhassett Chute; 3rdly, 1964, Priscilla Margarete, da of late Hon Archibald Edward Cubitt (*see* B Ashcombe, colls), and has had issue by 1st, 2nd and 3rd *m*.

ᶁrms – Quarterly; ermine and gules. Crest – A tower azure, a demi-lion rampant issuant from the battlements or, in the paws a bomb fired proper. Supporters – *Dexter*, a talbot guardant argent, guttée de poix; *sinister*, a wolf erminois; each gorged with a chaplet of oak proper.
Residence – The Glen, Ballingarry, co Limerick.

SONS LIVING (*By 1st marriage*)

CHARLES HENRY LEICESTER (*Viscount Petersham*), *b* 20 July 1945; *ed* Aysgarth, and Eton: *m* 1st, 1966, Virginia Alleyne Freeman, da of late Capt Harry Free-man Jackson, of Cool-na-Grena, co Cork; 2ndly, 1984, Anita Robsahm, formerly wife of 21st Earl of Suffolk, and da of late Robin Robsahm Fuglesang, of Lay-cock, Wilts, and has issue:—

SON LIVING (*By 1st m*)— *Hon* William Henry Leicester, *b* 14 Oct 1967; *ed* Aysgarth, and Aiglon Coll.

DAUGHTER LIVING (*By 1st m*)— *Hon* Serena Alleyne (*Viscountess Linley*), *b* 1970: *m* 1993, David Albert Charles, Viscount Linley, only son of 1st Earl of Snowdon, and of HRH The Princess Margaret, Countess of Snowdon.

(*By 2nd marriage*)

Hon Steven Francis Lincoln (Dooneen Stud, Patrickswell, co Limerick), *b* 1951: *m* 1978, Maureen Elizabeth Irvine, da of Maj Harold William Cole, of Poundbury, Dorchester, Dorset, and has issue living, Ben, *b* 1978, — Tara, *b* 1979.

(*By 3rd marriage*)

Hon John Fitzroy, *b* 1965.

DAUGHTERS LIVING AND DECEASED (*By 1st marriage*)

Lady Jane, *b* 1942: *m* 1965, Anthony Cameron, son of Clifford Cameron, of Dowth Hall, Drogheda, co Meath, and was *k* in a motor accident 1974, leaving issue, James William, *b* 1967, — Henrietta Jane, *b* 1970.
Lady Avena Margaret Clare, *b* 1944: *m* 1969 (*m diss* 1993), Adrian James Maxwell, only son of Maj James Kennedy Maxwell, MC, of Buckby Folly House, E Haddon, Northants, and has issue living, Sacha Jane, *b* 1974, — Kerry Alice, *b* 1978. *Residence* – Beechwood House, Cullen, co Tipperary.

(By 2nd marriage)

Lady Trina Maria, *b* 1947.
Lady Sarah Sue (twin), *b* 1951: *m* 1970, Robert John Barry, and has issue living, Mark James, *b* 1972, — Tristan James, *b* 1975, — Guy William (twin), *b* 1975.

(By 3rd marriage)

Lady Isabella Rachel (*Countess Cawdor*), *b* 1966: *m* 1994, 7th Earl Cawdor, and has issue (see that title). *Residence –* Cawdor Castle, Nairn.

COLLATERAL BRANCHES LIVING

        Granddaughter of late Aubrey Charles Stanhope (infra):—
        Issue of late Lt-Col Aubrey Charles Stanhope, DFC, USAF, *b* 1920, *d* 1994: *m* 1941, Muriel Grace, da of late William Anderson Lauther, of Truro, Nova Scotia:—
Paulette Beatrice, *b* 1946: *m* 1968, her 1st cousin once removed, Gilbert Mark Rollo, and has issue (*see* L Rollo, colls).

        Grandchildren of late Russell Charles Stanhope (*b* 1866) (infra):—
        Issue of late Aubrey Charles Stanhope, *b* 1895, *d* 1953: *m* 1st, 1919, Paulette Bordier du Raincy, of France, who *d* 1922; 2ndly, 19—, An American Lady; 3rdly, 1931, Evelyn Wadsworth, who *d* 1981:—
(By 1st *m*) Marie Annick (1606 Golf View Drive, Urbana, Illinois, USA), *b* 1921: *m* 1953, Lt-Col Richard Davis, USAF, who *d* 1977. —— (By 2nd *m*) Jonathan, *b* 19—. —— Christian (a da), *b* 19—. —— (By 3rd *m*) Noel, *b* 1946 *m* 19—, Karen Davis, who *d* ca 1986, and has issue living, Elizabeth, *b* ca 1972.

        Issue of late Leicester de Maclot Stanhope, *b* 1901, *d* 1978: *m* 1930, Rose Mary Farnham, of New York:—
Leicester (3633 Tangier Terr, Sarasota, Florida, USA) *b* 1932: *m* 1955, Priscilla Carrington Young, of Conn, USA, and has issue living, Leicester de Maclot, *b* 1957, — Russell Charles, *b* 1958, — Margot, *b* 1960, — Jennifer, *b* 1961. —— Philip (Hidden Harbor Rd, Sarasota, Florida, 33578, USA), *b* 1939: *m* 19—, Bonnie —, and has issue living, Philip, *b* 1973, — Sean, *b* 1980, — Justin, *b* 1982. —— Nina (Delray Beach, Florida 33444, USA), *b* 1931: *m* 19—.

        Grandchildren of late Russell Charles Stanhope, son of late Hon Sir Francis Charles Stanhope, KCH, 5th son of 3rd Earl:—
        Issue of late Russell Charles Stanhope, *b* 1866, *d* 1945: *m* 1894, Augustine Madeleine Thompson, of USA, who *d* 1916:—
Russell Charles (575 Hollow Tree Ridge Rd, Darien, Conn, 06820, USA), *b* 1899: *m* 1934, Jean Kennedy, of New York, and has issue living, Michelle, *b* 1945: *m* 1976, Dr Frank Converse Sparks, and has issue living, Kristin *b* 1978, Ashley *b* 1980, Nicole *b* 1983, — Celeste, *b* 1947: *m* 1964, John Nicholas Pierce, and has issue living, Michela Stanhope *b* 1965, Elizabeth *b* 1971. —— Violet Augustina *b* 1912: *m* 1936, Major Robert Duncan Rollo, Suffolk Regt (*see* L Rollo, colls), who *d* 1986.

PREDECESSORS – (1) *Rt Hon* WILLIAM Stanhope (son of John Stanhope of Elvaston, Derbys); grandson of Sir John Stanhope of Elvaston, yr half-brother of 1st Earl of Chesterfield, (infra) *b* about 1683; Ambassador to Spain 1721-27 and 1729-30, Prin Sec of State 1738-42, Lord Pres of Council 1742-45 and Lord Lt of Ireland 1746-50; in consideration of his services for negotiating Treaty of Seville, *cr Baron Harrington*, of Harrington, co Northampton (peerage of GB) 1730, and *Viscount Petersham* and *Earl of Harrington* (peerage of GB) 1742: *m* 1718, Anne, who *d* 1719, da and heir of Col Edward Griffith; *d* 1756; *s* by his son (2) WILLIAM, 2nd Earl; *b* 1719; Gen: *m* 1746, Lady Caroline FitzRoy, who *d* 1784, da of 2nd Duke of Grafton; *d* 1799; *s* by his son (3) CHARLES, GCH, 3rd Earl; *b* 1753; Gen and Col 1st Life Guards; Gov and Constable of Windsor Castle 1812-29: *m* 1779, Jane, who *d* 1824, da and co-heir of Sir John Fleming, 1st Bt of Brompton Park, Middlesex; *d* 1829; *s* by his el son (4) CHARLES, 4th Earl; *b* 1780; Col: *m* 1831, Maria (actress), who *d* 1867, da of Samuel Foote; *d* 1851; *s* by his brother (5) LEICESTER FITZGERALD CHARLES, 5th Earl; *b* 1784; Col: *m* 1831, Elizabeth Williams, who *d* 1898, da and heir of William Green, of Trelawney, Jamaica; *d* 1862; *s* by his son (6) SEYMOUR SYDNEY HYDE, 6th Earl; *b* 1845; *d* 1866; *s* by his cousin (7) CHARLES WYNDHAM, 7th Earl; son of Very Rev Hon FitzRoy Henry Richard, 4th son of 3rd Earl; *b* 1809: *m* 1839, Elizabeth Still, who *d* 1912, da of Robert Lucas de Pearsall; *d* 1881; *s* by his son (8) CHARLES AUGUSTUS, 8th Earl, *b* 1844: *m* 1869, Hon Eva Elizabeth Carington, who *d* 1919, da of 2nd Baron Carrington; *d* 1917; *s* by his brother (9) DUDLEY HENRY EDEN, 9th Earl; *b* 1859: *m* 1883, Kathleen, who *d* 1948, da of J. Carter Wood, of Weybourne Hall, Weybourne, Norfolk; *d* 1928; *s* by his son (10) CHARLES JOSEPH LEICESTER, MC, 10th Earl, *b* 1887; Bt Maj 15th Hussars: *m* 1919, Margaret Trelawney (Susan), who *d* 1952 (having *m* 2ndly, 1934, Luke Theodore Lillingston of Ulverscroft, Leics, and 3rdly, 1949, Maj Stephen C Johnston), da of Maj H. H. D. Seaton, formerly Remount Ser, *d* 1929; *s* by his son (11) WILLIAM HENRY LEICESTER, 11th Earl, and present peer; also Viscount Stanhope of Mahon, Viscount Petersham, Baron Stanhope of Elvaston (see infra*) and Baron Harrington.
*(1) JAMES Stanhope, el son of Hon Alexander Stanhope, yst son of 1st Earl of Chesterfield; *b* 1673; Lt Gen; C-in-C of British Forces in Spain 1708-10 (effected capture of port of Mahon, Minorca 1708 and gained victories of Almenara and Saragossa 1710); Sec of State 1714-17 and 1718-21, 1st Lord of the Treasury and Chancellor of the Exchequer 1717-18, *cr Baron Stanhope of Elvaston*, co Derby, and *Viscount Stanhope of Mahon*, in island of Minorca (peerage of GB) 1717, with remainder to the descendants in the male line of his kinsman, John Stanhope of Elvaston (ante), (whose son William was *cr* Earl of Harrington); *cr Earl Stanhope* 1718d (peerage of GB) with remainder to heirs male of his body: *m* 1713, Lucy, who *d* 1723, da of Thomas Pitt of Blandford; *d* 1721; *s* by his el son (2) PHILIP, 2nd Earl; *b* 1714; FRS: *m* 1745, Grisel, who *d* 1811, da of Charles Hamilton, Lord Binning, el son of 6th Earl of Haddington; *d* 1786; *s* by his 2nd son (3) CHARLES, 3rd Earl, *b* 1753, FRS; perfected process of stereotyping and experimented with fire-proof buildings, steam vessels and calculating machines: *m* 1st, 1774, Lady Hester Pitt, who *d* 1780, da of 1st Earl of Chatham; 2ndly, 1781, Louisa, who *d* 1829, da and heir of Hon Henry Grenville (E Temple); *d* 1816; *s* by his el son (4) PHILIP HENRY, 4th Earl, *b* 1782; FRS; Keeper of the Records, Bermingham Tower, Dublin Castle 1805-55: *m* 1803, Hon Catherine Lucy Smith, who *d* 1843, da of 1st Baron Carrington; *d* 1855; *s* by his el son (5) PHILIP HENRY, 5th Earl; *b* 1805, FRS; Under Sec for Foreign Affairs 1834-35; historian; founder and 1st Chm of National Portrait Gallery: *m* 1834, Emily Harriet, who *d* 1874, da of Gen Sir Edward Kerrison, GCH, KCB, 1st Bt; *d* 1875; *s* by his el son (6) ARTHUR PHILIP, 6th Earl; *b* 1838; a Lord of the Treasury 1874-75: *m* 1869, Evelyn Henrietta, who *d* 1923, only da of Richard Pennefather, of Knockevan, co

Tipperary; *d* 1905; *s* by his el son **(7)** JAMES RICHARD, KG, DSO, MC, PC, 7th Earl; *b* 1880; Civil Lord of the Admiralty 1924-29, Parl and Financial Sec to the Admiralty and Civil Lord 1931, Parl Under Sec of State for War and Vice-Pres of Army Council 1931-34, Parl Under Sec of State for Foreign Affairs 1934-36, 1st Commr of Works 1936-37, Pres of Board of Education 1937-38, 1st Lord of Admiralty 1938-39, and Lord Pres of Council 1939-40; *s* his kinsman, Edward Henry Scudamore-Stanhope, as 13th Earl of Chesterfield and 13th Baron Stanhope of Shelford 1952 (but did not apply for writ of summons): *m* 1921, Lady Eileen Agatha Browne, who *d* 1940, da of 6th Marquess of Sligo; *d* 1967, when the Earldoms of Chesterfield and Stanhope, and the Barony of Stanhope of Shelford became ext, and the Viscountcy of Stanhope of Mahon and the Barony of Stanhope of Elvaston devolved upon the 11th Earl of Harrington (*ante*), who thereupon became the representative of the Stanhope family.

HARRIS, BARON (Harris) (Baron UK 1815)

ANTHONY HARRIS, 8th Baron; *b* 8 March 1942; *s* 1996; *ed* Eastbourne Coll: *m* 1966, Anstice, da of Alfred Winter, of Westcliffe-on-Sea, Essex, and has issue.

Arms – Vert, on a chevron embattled erminois, between three hedgehogs or, as many bombs sable, fired proper; on a chief of augmentation, a representation of the gates and fortress of Seringapatam, the drawbridge let down, and the Union flag of Great Britain and Ireland hoisted above the standard of Tippoo Sahib, all proper. Crest – On a mural crown or, a royal tiger passant guardant vert, striped or, spotted of the first, pierced in the breast with an arrow of the last, vulned gules, and charged on the forehead with the Persian character implying "Hyder", and crowned with an Eastern coronet both of the first. Supporters – *Dexter*, a grenadier in uniform of 73rd Foot, supporting with the exterior hand a flag staff, thereon hoisted the Union Flag of Great Britain and Ireland flying towards the dexter over the standard of Tippoo Sultan; and below the same tricoloured flag of the French Republic depressed and furled all proper; *sinister*, a Sepoy of the Madras Establishment of the East India Company, supporting with the exterior hand a flag staff thereon hoisted the flag of the said Company, flying over that of Tippoo Sultan towards the sinister; and below same the tricoloured flag of the French Republic as in the dexter.
Seat – Belmont Park, Faversham, Kent. *Residence* – 1 Linkenholt Mansions, Stamford Brook Av, W6.

DAUGHTERS LIVING

Hon Isabel, *b* 1973.
Hon Laura, *b* 1976.

SISTER LIVING

Hon Amanda, *b* 1953: *m* 1974 (*m diss* 1984), Jeremy Mainwaring, and has issue living, Guy, *b* 1975, — Max, *b* 1985, — Rosie, *b* 1980. *Residence* – 55 Clissold Crescent, Stoke Newington Green, N16.

COLLATERAL BRANCHES LIVING

Grandchildren of late George Lucian Taylor Harris, eldest son of late George Anstruther Harris, 2nd son of Hon Michael Thomas Harris, 2nd son of 1st Baron:—
Issue of late George Temple James Harris, *b* 1876, *d* 1929: *m* 1910, Eva, who *d* 1942, having *m* 2ndly, 1933, Randle North Kenyon, who *d* 1968 (*see* B Kenyon, colls), da of late Lt-Col Henry Green Wilkinson (*see* B Bateman, 1923 Edn):—
ANTONY JOHN TEMPLE, OBE (Hawthorns, Park Place, Wickham, Hants), *b* 5 Aug 1915; Cdr RN (ret); OBE (Mil) 1963: *m* 1940, Doris, only child of late Frank Dufford Drake, of Winter Park, Florida, USA, and has issue living, Michael George Temple (c/o Naval Sec, Victory Building, HM Naval Base, Portsmouth PO1 3LS), *b* 1941; *ed* Nautical Coll Pangbourne; Rear Adm RN: *m* 1970, Caroline Sandra Pietre Katrina, da of late Group Capt Patrick George Chichester, OBE (*see* Chichester, Bt, colls), and has issue living, Tamsin Caroline Temple *b* 1971, Rebecca Eva Temple *b* 1973, Emily Vesta Temple *b* 1979, — John Frank Temple (24 Manor Close, Wickham, Fareham, Hants PO17 5BZ), *b* 1944; *ed* Sherborne: *m* 1972, Sandra Dobson, da of late Charles Stones, of Bishop Auckland, co Durham. —— June Rosemary Temple (4 Dale Av, Hassocks, W Sussex BN6 8LW), *b* 1928.

Granddaughter of late Col Charles John Birch Harris, 3rd son of late George Anstruther Harris (*ante*):—
Issue of late Hugh Anstruther Harris, *b* 1882, *d* 1951: *m* 1922, Ada Miller, who *d* 1966:—
Nina Denise, *b* 1924: *m* 1946, Donald R. Miller, and has issue living, Michael Jeffrey, *b* 1947, — Gary Lee, *b* 1949, — Jeffrey Hugh, *b* 1952, — Wendy Louise, *b* 1954, — Julie Diane *b* 1962.

Grandchildren of Hermann Gundert Harris, 7th son of late George Anstruther Harris (*ante*):—
Issue of late Eric Townsend Harris, *b* 1902, *b* 1979: *m* 1st, 1920 (*m diss* 1927), Marjorie Peggy, da of late Charles Vokes, of Winnipeg; 2ndly, 1946, Helen, da of late Howard Francis Bidwell, of Boston, Mass, USA:—
(By 1st *m*) Joan Patricia, *b* 1922. —— Elizabeth Anne, *b* 1926. —— (By 2nd *m*) Patricia Anne, *b* 1950.

Issue of late George Rutherford Harris, *b* 1903, *d* 1983: *m* 1927, Olive Alexandria Hall, who *d* 1986:—
Gerald Rutherford (1245 Pacific Drive, Delta, BC, Canada V4M 2K2), *b* 1928: *m* 1955, Vernette Harris, and has issue
living, Scott, *b* 1960, — Shelley Ann, *b* 1957. —— Alfred James (5315 156th Av, Edmonton, Alberta, Canada T5Y 2T3), *b*
1942; RCM Police: *m* 1965, Alexandra Konopelka, and has issue living, Dwayne Stephen, *b* 1966, — Suzanne Marie, *b*
1967. —— Lucille Olive Iona, *b* 1930: *m* 1951, William A. Spaidal, of 1044 Charland Av, Coquitlam, BC, Canada V3K
3K9, and has issue living, Richard Arnold, *b* 1952: *m* 1979 (*m diss* 1993), Sandra Jeanine Hough, and has issue living,
Shane Arnold *b* 1980, Kelly Anne *b* 1983, — William Randall, *b* 1957: *m* 1977 (*m diss* 1982), Alison Jean Perry, and has
issue living, Ryan Randall *b* 1979, Jessica Jean *b* 1977, — Robert Matthew, *b* 1968, — Linda Lucille, *b* 1963: *m* 1987,
Kenneth Norman Palk, and has issue living, Matthew Tyler *b* 1987, Joseph Patrick *b* 1991. —— Violet Joyce, *b* 1935: *m*
1959, Donald Watkins, of 612 Vermouth Av, Mississauga, Ontario, Canada L5A 2C2, and has issue living, Norman
Douglas, *b* 1963, — Steven Patrick, *b* 1964: *m* 1989, Shawna Dorothy Cuttress, and has issue living, Michael David *b*
1992, Kaitlyn Amber *b* 1989.

Grandchildren of late Alfred Herschell Harris, 8th son of late George Anstruther Harris (ante):-
Issue of late Christopher Money Harris, *b* 1907, *d* 1997: *m* 1935, Ruth Cunliffe, da of late George Harwood, MP,
of Bolton:-
Robert Julian Brownlow (Flat 4, 24 Pembridge Villas, W11 3EL; *Club* – Brooks's), *b* 1943: *m* 1971 (*m diss* 1976), Lady
Camilla Dorothy Godolphin Osborne, da of 11th Duke of Leeds, and has issue living, Emily Kate Godolphin, *b* 1972.
—— Phoebe Georgina, *b* 1950: *m* 1970, Guy Rudolf Bentinck, of Erth Barton, Saltash, Cornwall PL12 4QY, and has issue
living, Caspar William, *b* 1973, — Chloe Rose, *b* 1978.

PREDECESSORS – (1) *Sir* GEORGE Harris, GCB, a Gen in the Army and Col 73rd Regt was Com in Ch at siege and
capture of Seringapatam and conquest of Mysore 1799; *cr Baron Harris*, of Seringapatam and Mysore, E Indies, and of
Belmont, co Kent (peerage of United Kingdom) 1815; *d* 1829; *s* by his son (2) WILLIAM GEORGE, KCH, CB, 2nd Baron, a
Lt-Gen in the Army and Col 73rd Foot; *d* 1845; *s* by his son (3) GEORGE FRANCIS ROBERT, GCSI, 3rd Baron; *b* 1810; was
Gov of Trinidad 1846-54, and of Madras 1854-9, a Lord in Waiting to HM Queen Victoria 1860-3, and Chamberlain to
Princess of Wales 1863-71; *m* 1850, Sarah, who *d* 1853, da of Ven George Cummins, Archdeacon of Trinidad; *d* 1872; *s*
by his son (4) GEORGE ROBERT CANNING, GCSI, GCIE, CB, 4th Baron, *b* 1852; Under-Sec for India 1885-6, Under-Sec for
War 1886-9, Gov of Bombay 1890-95, a Lord-in-Waiting to Queen Victoria 1895-1900, Vice-Lieut of Kent 1914-15; bore
Queen Consort's Sceptre with Dove at Coronation of King Edward VII: *m* 1874, Hon Lucy Ada Jervis, CI, who *d* 1930, da
of 3rd Viscount St Vincent, *d* 1932; *s* by his son (5) GEORGE ST VINCENT, CBE, MC, 5th Baron, *b* 1889; Capt Yeo; served
World War I (wounded, despatches); Chm Kent Police Authority; JP, Vice-Lieut (1944-72) and Co Commr for Kent; a
Gov King's Sch, Canterbury; St John's Ambulance Brig 1940-45: *m* 1918, Dorothy Mary, who *d* 1981, da of Rev John
William Crookes, formerly V of Borden, Sittingbourne; *d* 1984; *s* by his only son (6) GEORGE ROBERT JOHN, 6th Baron, *b*
1920; Capt RA; *dunm* 1995; *s* by his kinsman (7) DEREK MARSHALL (great great grandson of Hon Michael Thomas Harris,
2nd son of 1st Baron), 7th Baron; *b* 1916; Maj Duke of Wellington's Regt: *m* 1st, 1938 (*m diss* 1968), Laura Cecilia, who
d 1995, da of late Maj Edward Thomas William McCausland, Indian Army; 2ndly, 1987, Mrs Pauline Elisabeth Skinner,
who *d* 1997, da of Ernest Giles, of Menston-in-Wharfdale, Yorks, and previously wife of Martyn Skinner; *d* 1996, *s* by his
only son (8) ANTHONY 8th Baron and present peer.

Harris, family name of Earl of Malmesbury.

HARRIS OF GREENWICH, BARON (Harris) (Life Baron 1974)

JOHN HENRY HARRIS, PC, son of Alfred George Harris; *b* 5 April 1930; *ed* Pinner Gram Sch, Middx;
Personal Assist to Leader of the Opposition 1959-62; Dir of Publicity, Labour Party 1962-64, Special
Assist to Foreign Sec 1964-66, to Home Sec 1966-67, and to Chancellor of the Exchequer 1967-70,
and a Min of State, Home Office 1974-79; Chm Parole Board for England and Wales 1979-82; a
Political Correspondent with *The Economist* 1970-74; *cr Baron Harris of Greenwich*, of Greenwich in
Greater London (Life Baron) 1974, and PC 1998: *m* 1st, 1952 (*m diss* 1982), Patricia Margaret, da of
George Neuby Alstrom; 2ndly, 1983, Angela Smith, and has issue by 1st *m*.
Address – c/o House of Lords, SW1. *Clubs* – Reform, MCC.

SON LIVING (*By 1st marriage*)

Hon Francis Oliver Alstrom, *b* 1961.

DAUGHTER LIVING (*By 1st marriage*)

Hon Deborah Jane Alstrom, *b* 1958.

HARRIS OF HARINGEY, BARON (Harris) (Life Baron 1998)

(JONATHAN) TOBY HARRIS, son of late Prof Harry Harris, FRS, of Pennsylvania, USA; *b* 11 Oct 1953; *ed* Haberdashers' Aske's Sch, and Trin Coll, Camb (BA 1975); with Economics Division of Bank of England 1975-79; joined Electricity Consumers' Council 1979, Dep Dir 1983-86; Dir Assoc of Community Health Councils for England and Wales 1987-98; Councillor, Haringey BC (Lab) since 1978, Chm Social Services Cttee 1982-87, Leader 1987-99; Chm Assoc of London Authorities 1993-95 (Chm Social Services Cttee 1984-88, Dep Chm 1990-93); Chm Assoc of London Govt since 1995, Labour Group LGA since 1996, Community Safety Panel LGA 1997-98 and Social Exclusion Panel LGA since 1998; Dep Chm AMA 1991-96 (Chm Social Services Cttee 1986-93); Chm LBTC Training for Care 1986-94; Memb Cttee of the Regions of the Euro Union since 1994; Chm Local Govt Anti-Poverty Unit 1994-96; Jt Chm London Pride Partnership since 1995 and London Waste Action since 1997; Chm English National Stadium Trust since 1997; Chm, Memb or Trustee of many other organisations; author; FRSA 1993; *cr Baron Harris of Haringey*, of Hornsey in the London Borough of Haringey (Life Baron) 1998: *m* 1979, Ann Sarah, da of late Stephen Austen Herbert, of Wells, Som, and has issue.

𝕬rms – ......
Address – c/o House of Lords, Westminster, SW1A 0PW.

SONS LIVING

Hon James Philip, *b* 1981; *ed* William Ellis Sch.
Hon Matthew Anthony, *b* 1984; *ed* Highgate Wood Sch.

HARRIS OF HIGH CROSS, BARON (Harris) (Life Baron 1979)

RALPH HARRIS, *b* 10 Dec 1924; *ed* Tottenham Grammar Sch, and Queens' Coll, Camb (MA); Lecturer in Polit Economy St Andrews Univ 1949-56; Leader-writer *Glasgow Herald* 1956; Gen Dir Inst of Economic Affairs 1957-87, Chm 1987-89, and Founder Pres since 1992; Chm FOREST since 1987; Independent Nat Dir Times Newspaper Holdings since 1991; *cr Baron Harris of High Cross*, of Tottenham, Greater London (Life Baron) 1979: *m* 1949, Jose Pauline, da of late Roger Frederick Jeffery, and has had issue.
Residence – 5 Cattley Close, Wood St, Barnet, Herts EN5 4SN.

SONS DECEASED

Hon Simon Ralph, *b* 1953; *d* 1979.
Hon Julian Paul, *b* 1956; *d* 1992.

DAUGHTER LIVING

Hon Angela Caroline, *b* 1951: *m* 1977, Roland Triponel, of 1 rue E. Lesueur, 76130 Mont St Aignan, France, and has issue.

HARRIS OF PECKHAM, BARON (Harris) (Life Baron 1995)

PHILIP CHARLES HARRIS, son of Charles William Harris, MC, of Peckham, *b* 15 Sept 1942; *ed* Streatham Gram Sch; Hon Fell Oriel Coll, Oxford 1989; Chm Harris Queensway plc 1964-88 (Chief Executive 1987), since when of Harris Ventures Ltd, Carpetright plc, and C. W. Harris Properties Ltd; Dir Harveys Holdings plc since 1986; non-exec Dir of Great Universal Stores plc since 1986, Fisons plc 1986-94, and Molyneux Estates plc 1990-95, Memb of British Showjumping Assoc and Court of Patrons RGOG; Chm of Guy's and Lewisham NHS Trust 1991-93; Vice Chm Lewisham Hosp NHS Trust since 1993; Hambro Businessman of the Year 1983; *cr* Knt 1985, and *Baron Harris of Peckham*, of Peckham in the London Borough of Southwark (Life Baron), 1995: *m* 1960, Pauline Norma, da of late Bertie William Chumley, and has issue.

Arms –
Address – Harris Ventures Ltd, Philip Harris House, 1A Spur Rd, Orpington, Kent BR6 0QR.

SONS LIVING

Hon Charles William, *b* 1963; *ed* Grenville Coll, Bideford, Devon.
Hon Peter Alexander, *b* 1963; *ed* Millfield.
Hon Martin James, *b* 1969; *ed* Millfield.

DAUGHTER LIVING

Hon Susan Louise, *b* 1961; *ed* Springfield Park, Horsham: *m* 19—, Sadler, son of ...... Sadler, of ...... *Residence* – ....

HARROWBY, EARL OF (Ryder) (Earl UK 1809)

The promise made to the ashes of my forefathers has been kept

DUDLEY DANVERS GRANVILLE COUTTS RYDER, TD, 7th Earl; *b* 20 Dec 1922; *s* 1987; *ed* Eton; served 1939-45 War 59 Inf Div (wounded), 5 Para Bde in N-W Europe, India and Java (political officer) 56 Armoured Div, 1941-45, Lt-Col RA OC 254 (City of London) Field Regt RA (TA) 1962-65; a Dep Chm National Westminster Bank plc 1971-87 (Dir 1968), Chm International Westminster Bank 1977-87 and Chm National Westminster Investment Bank 1986-87; Dep Chm Coutts & Co 1970-89 (Man Dir 1949); Chm Dowty Gp plc 1986-91; Powell Duffryn Group 1976-86 (Chm 1981-86); Trustee of Psychiatry Research Trust since 1982, etc; Hon Fell Roy Coll of Psychiatrists 1983; Hon Treas Staffordshire Soc 1947-51 (Pres 1957-59), Exec Ctte of London Area Conservative Assocn 1949-50, Kensington Borough Council 1950-65, Family Welfare Assocn 1951-65, and S Kensington Conservative Assocn 1953-56; Manager of Fulham and Kensington Hospital Gp 1953-56, etc; Bd of Govs Roy and Maudsley (Postgraduate Teaching) Hospitals 1955-73 (Chm 1965-73), also Univ of Keele 1956-68; Lord Chancellor's Advisory Investment Ctte for Court of Protection 1965-77, etc: *m* 1949, Jeanette Rosalthé, who *d* 1997, da of late Capt Peter Johnston-Saint, and has issue.

Arms – Azure, three crescents or, each charged with an ermine spot sable. Crest – Out of a mural coronet a dragon's head argent, charged on the neck with an ermine spot sable. Supporters – Two griffins, wings elevated, argent, each charged on the shoulder with an ermine spot sable, gorged with a plain collar azure, thereon three crescents or, and affixed thereto a chain reflexed over the back, of the last.

Seats – Sandon Hall, Stafford; Burnt Norton, Chipping Campden, Glos. *Town Residence* – Apartment 20, Albert Bridge House, 127 Albert Bridge Rd, SW11 4PL.

SON LIVING

DUDLEY ADRIAN CONROY (*Viscount Sandon*), *b* 18 March 1951; *ed* Eton, Univ of Newcastle-upon-Tyne, and Magdalene Coll, Camb (MA); Executive Dir Compton Street Securities Ltd since 1988; Governor John Archer Sch, Wandsworth 1968-88; FRICS: *m* 1st, 1977, Sarah Nichola Hobhouse, who *d* 1994, only da of Capt Anthony Denys Phillpotts Payne, of Carraway Barn, Carraway Lane, Marnhull, Dorset; 2ndly, 1998, Mrs Caroline J. Coram James, da of Geoffrey Markes, and has issue by 1st *m*. *Residence* – Burnt Norton, Chipping Campden, Glos GL55 6PR.

SONS LIVING (*by 1st marriage*)— *Hon* Dudley Anthony Hugo Coventry, *b* 5 Sept 1981, — *Hon* Frederick Whitmore Dudley, *b* 1984, — *Hon* Henry Mansell Dudley, *b* 1985.
DAUGHTER LIVING (*by 1st marriage*)— *Hon* Emily Georgina Hobhouse, *b* 1992.

DAUGHTER LIVING

Lady Rosalthé Frances, *b* 1954: *m* 1976, Francis Richard Seton Rundall, yr son of late Frank Lionel Montagu Rundall, TD, of Stoneleigh House, Longborough, Glos, and has issue living, (Francis) Thomas Mansell, *b* 1981, — Mark Dudley Ridgway, *b* 1982, — John William Nathaniel, *b* 1987. *Residence* – Manor Farm, Aston Subedge, Chipping Campden, Glos.

BROTHER LIVING

Hon John Stuart Terrick Dudley, *b* 1924; *ed* Eton; formerly Warrant Officer Pilot, RAF, European War 1942-45 (wounded): *m* 1946, Dorothy Ethel, da of J. T. Swallow, of Mansfield, and has issue living, John Robert, *b* 1947: *m* 1970, Rosemary Rita Tester, and has issue living, Claire Jane *b* 1970, Sara Helena Louise *b* 1973, — David Anthony, *b* 1951: *m* 1973, Judith Jean Sinclair, of Sydney, NSW, and has issue living, John David Dudley *b* 1979, Jessica Judith Jean *b* 1983. *Residence* – Horley, Surrey.

SISTER LIVING

Lady Frances Virginia Susan, *b* 1926; *ed* St Hugh's Coll, Oxford: *m* 1949, Frank Ernest Berendt, and has issue living, Anthony Peregrine Dudley (56 Lancaster Rd, W11), *b* 1957; *ed* Ampleforth, and Worcester Coll, Oxford: *m* 1988, Julia Rosemary, only da of Derek Alistair Bigham (*see* E Fortescue, colls), and has issue living, Hermione Helena *b* 1995, Ottilie Frances *b* 1998, — Susan Venetia, *b* 1952: *m* 1977, Paul Joseph Williams, of Walnut Tree House, 20 Lower Teddington Rd, Hampton Wick, Middlesex, and has issue living, Christopher James Dudley *b* 1980, Gavin Dominic *b* 1986, Paul Gerard Quentin *b* 1988, Hew Anthony John *b* 1990, Emma Louise *b* 1977, Joanna Frances *b* 1981, Helena Lucy *b* 1983. *Residence* – 34 The Marlowes, Boundary Rd, NW8 6NA.

COLLATERAL BRANCHES LIVING

Grandchildren of late Hon Archibald Dudley Ryder (infra):—
Issue of late Richard Dudley Ryder, OBE, *b* 1904, *d* 1987: *m* 1945, Pamela Gerturde, who *d* 1982, da of late Aubrey Hammick Ford, of Wortham, Crowborough, Sussex:—
Victoria, *b* 1948: *m* 1976, Simon J. C. Connell, of Riverside Cottage, Beaminster, Dorset.

Issue of late Douglas Dudley Ryder, JP, *b* 1905, *d* 1984: *m* 1931, Sheilah Moore (16 St John Garden, Cassia Drive, Port Elizabeth, S Africa), da of S. H. Gillesie, of Carrick Cradock, S Africa:—
Hugh Donald Dudley (44 Princes Rd, Claremont, Cape Town, S Africa), *b* 1936: *m* 1st, 1963 (*m diss* 1969), Pamela Joan, da of S. O. Butow, of East London, Cape Province; 2ndly, 1969, Maria, da of Max Pitterman, of Bielefeld, W Germany, and has issue living (by 2nd *m*), Axel Dudley, *b* 1970, — Douglas Dudley, *b* 1971. —— Atholl Graham Dudley (50 Stella Londt Drive, Port Elizabeth, Cape, S Africa), *b* 1938: *m* 1964, Irène, da of J. J. van Duuren, of Port Elizabeth, and has issue living, Gary Dudley, *b* 1966, — Peter Dudley, *b* 1968, — Jennifer Rosemary, *b* 1979.

Issue of late Hon Archibald Dudley Ryder, 2nd son of 4th Earl, *b* 1867, *d* 1950: *m* 1898, Eleanor Frederica, who *d* 1958, el da of Edward R. Fisher-Rowe (E Ravensworth):—
Atholl Dudley (502-95 Fiddler's Green Rd, London, Ontario, Canada N6H 4TI), *b* 1909: *m* 1940, Kathleen, yst da of late Robert Pearson, of London, Ontario, and has issue living, Lawrence Dudley (Box 209, 421 Green St, Port Elgin, Ontario, Canada N0H 2CO) (adopted son), *b* 1949: *m* 1st, 1973 (*m diss* 1981), —; 2ndly, 1984, Kathryn Elspeth, da of late Warren Shular, of Southampton, Ont, and has issue living (by 1st *m*), Leigh Janice *b* 1977, — Peter Douglas Dudley (10 Matthew Dr, Guelph, Ont, Canada N1H 7L7), *b* 1952: *m* 1976, Michelle, da of Derek Foreman, of London, Ont, and has issue living, Andrew Douglas Dudley *b* 1985, James Richard Dudley (twin) *b* 1985, Sarah Michelle *b* 1982, Jennifer Elizabeth *b* 1984. —— †Peter Hugh Dudley, MBE, *b* 1913; Hon Lt-Col late R Armoured Corps; sometime in Political Intell Dept, Foreign Office; MBE (Civil) 1944: *m* 1940, Susannah Sarah (Ardmore, 21 Riverbank Rd, Ramsey, I of Man), da of late Geoffrey Francis Bowes-Lyon (*see* E Strathmore, colls), and *d* 1993, leaving issue, Adrian Dudley, *b* 1941; BA (Econ): *m* 1976, Katrina Olga, da of Dr Socrates Christie, PhD, and has issue living, Peter Socrates Dudley *b* 1984, Lara Erasmia *b* 1982, Tanya Serena *b* 1989. — Bruce Dudley (Crix, Hatfield Peverel, Chelmsford, Essex CM3 2EU), *b* 1942: *m* 1969, Charlotte Olivia, da of Mark Frederick Strutt, MC, TD (*see* B Rayleigh, colls), and has issue living, Mark Reedham Dudley *b* 1970, Oliver Hugh Dudley *b* 1974, Leonora Mary Charlotte *b* 1978, — Sandra Anne, *b* 1954: *m* 1978, Dimitris Pepelasis, of Palaion Patron Germanou, Davaki, Philothei, Athens, and has issue living, Diamandis *b* 1979, Alexander *b* 1984

Grandchildren of late Maj Henry Dudley Ryder, MC (infra):—
Issue of late Edward Dorrien Dudley Ryder, b 1924, d 1984: m 1948, Valerie Nina (22 St Mary Abbot's Terrace, W14 8NX), only da of late James Beecroft Soames, of Kenya:—
Nicholas Henry Dudley, b 1960: m 1995, Marina Natascha Beatrice, da of late Richmond Chartres Sturdy, and of Mrs Caroline Lowe, of Chadlington, Oxon, and has issue living, India Nina Dudley, b 1997. —— Jennifer Davina, b 1949: m 1st, 1971, Charles Berkeley Johnston Dingwall (see V Galway, colls, 1985 Edn); 2ndly, 1990, George William Pilkington, of Sanfoin House, Wash Common, Newbury, Berks RG14 6PP, and has issue living (by 1st m), Sophie, b 1972, — Anthea Lucy, b 1977, — Amelia Sarah, b 1978. —— Vanessa, b 1951: m 1976, Paul F. Irvine Cole, of Whatcombe, Wantage, Oxon OX12 9NW, and has issue living, Alexander James, b 1977, — Oliver Nicholas, b 1980, — Mark Edward, b 1986.

Granddaughters of late Hon Edward Alan Dudley Ryder, 3rd son of 4th Earl:—
Issue of late Major Henry Dudley Ryder, MC, b 1894; d 1958: m 1918, Dorothy Marion, da of Sidney Streatfeild:—
Maud Marion, b 1919. Residence – Dean Cottage, Horsted Lane, Sharpthorne, Sussex. —— Dorothy Joan, b 1921: m 1951, Alan Williams Horton, and has issue living, James McAfee b 1954: m 1976, Nancy, da of Roger Eastman, of Hanover, NH, USA, and has issue living, Oliver McAfee b 1989, Jenna Beth b 1985, — Edward Alan Douglas, b 1957: m 1991, Zoë Jane, el da of Ian Wilkinson, of Esher, Surrey, and has issue living, Lily Azella b 1992, Eliza Joan b 1994, — Carol Ryder, b 1952. Address – RR1, Box 1424, Randolph, New Hampshire 03570, USA.

Issue of late Major Hon Robert Nathaniel Dudley Ryder, 4th son of 4th Earl, b 1882, ka 1917: m 1908, Beryl (who d 1970, having m 2ndly, 1945, Lt-Col William Baring Du Pre, DL, JP, who d 1946), da of Charles Angas, of Lindsay Park, Angaston, S Australia:—
Rosemary Beryl (Lady Loehnis), b (twin) m 1929, Com Sir Clive Loehnis, KCMG, RN (ret), who d 1992, and has issue living, Anthony David, CMG (11 Cranleigh, 139 Ladbroke Rd, W11 3PX), b 1936; CMG 1988: m 1965, Jennifer Forsyth, da of late Sir Donald Forsyth Anderson (see Llewellyn Bt, cr 1922), and has issue living, Dominic Anthony b 1967, Alexander Garrett b 1969, Barnaby David b 1971, — Serena Jane (Baroness Remnant) (Bear Ash, Hare Hatch, Reading, Berks, RG10 9XR), b 1932: m 1953, 3rd Baron Remnant. Residence – 12 Eaton Place, SW1.

Grandchildren of late Capt Cyril John Ryder, 2nd son of late Dudley Henry Ryder, son of late Hon Granville Dudley Ryder, MP, 2nd son of 1st Earl:—
Issue of late Maj Dudley Claud Douglas Ryder, JP, b 1901, d 1986: m 1st, 1927 (m diss 1938), Nancy Edith, who d 1985, da of E. M. Baker, late Federated Malay States Civil Ser; 2ndly, 1938, Vera Mary, who d 1980, da of Sir Herbert Frederick Cook, 3rd Bt, and formerly wife of George Mervyn Anstey Hamilton-Fletcher:—
(By 1st m) James Calcraft Dudley (Rempstone Hall, Corfe Castle, Dorset), b 1934; ed Sherborne, and RAC Cirencester; late 2nd Lt King's Own Regt: m 1st, 1966 (m diss 1979), Sarah Victoria, only da of late Michael Guy Bircham, of Reepham, Norfolk; 2ndly, 1984, Georgina Susan, only da of Edward George Adrian Farnham, of Quorn House, Quorn, Leics, and formerly wife of Charles Howard Cole, and has issue living (by 1st m), Lara Caroline Dudley (Hon Mrs Mervyn R. Manningham-Buller), b 1968: m 1996, Hon Mervyn Reginald Manningham-Buller, yr son of 2nd Viscount Dilhorne, — Melanie Isobel, b 1971: m 1993, Nicholas S. Moriarty, eldest son of Maj M. N. S. Moriarty, of Briantspuddle, Dorset, and has issue living, Jack Nicholas Sean b 1994, Sam Alexander b 1996, — Emma Katherine, b 1974. —— Benjamin Guy Dudley (twin) (The Old Farmhouse, Rempstone, Corfe Castle, Dorset), b 1934; ed Sherborne: m 1960, Philippa Mary, da of Alan Maitland Cunningham, of Compton House, Wareham, Dorset, and has issue living, Douglas Alan Dudley, b 1963: m 1988, Rosemary Victoria Clara Rhys-Davies, — Guy, b 1968, — Vanessa Frances, b 1965. —— Gabriel Nancy (Lady Coghill), b 1928: m 1958, Sir Egerton James Nevill Tobias (Toby) Coghill, 8th Bt. —— Jenifer Cherry, b 1929: m 1953, Jeremy Charles Browne, of Higher Houghton, Blandford, Dorset, and has issue living, Simon Jeremy, b 1957, — Katherine Richenda, b 1956, — Sarah Caroline, b 1960, — Emily Charlotte, b 1965. —— Jacqueline Iris b 1930: m 1957 (m diss 1969), Thomas Ralph Winser, and has had issue, Hugh James, b 1958; d 1992, — Polly Joan, b 1959, — Tamsin Jacqueline, b 1962. —— (By 2nd m) Richard Hood Jack Dudley, b 1940; ed Sherborne, Pembroke Coll, Camb (MA, PhD), Columbia Univ, New York, and Edin Univ (Dip Clinical Psych 1967); Chm Soc for Prevention of Cruelty to Animals 1977-79: m 1974, Audrey Jane, da of Frank Rae Arthur Smith, of Chesham Bois, Bucks, and has issue living, Henry Arthur Woden Calcraft Dudley, b 1981, — Emily Nancy Charlotte, b 1978.

Grandson of late William Henry Ryder, 3rd son of late Dudley Henry Ryder (ante):—
Issue of late Cdr Frederick Granville Dudley Ryder, RNVR, b 1905, d 1970: m 1st, 1929 (m diss 1934), Gillian Eleanor, da of C. H. B. Quennell; 2ndly, 1939, Muriel Eleanor, who d 1975, da of William S. Corby, of Wash, USA:—
(By 1st m) Richard Peter Guy Dudley (Hardway House, 3411 Poinciana Av, Miami, Florida, USA), b (Dec) 1929: m 1955, Angela Jiovanna, da of Morris M. Melotti, of Johnstown, Pa, USA, and has issue living, Christopher Frederick Dudley, b 1959, — Mark Campbell Dudley, b 1963.

Granddaughters of late Rev Algernon Charles Dudley Ryder (infra):—
Issue of late Major Algernon Frederick Roland Dudley Ryder, MC, b 1891, d 1957: m 1921, Olive, who d 1973, da of John Baillie, of Montreal:—
Dione Frances, b 1924: m 1954, (Claud Andrew) James Graham-Watson, and has issue living, Frederick Paul, b 1957: m 1987, Catherine Irene, elder da of Reginald Rimington Wilson, of Sussex and of W Riding of Yorks, and has issue living, Rory William b 1990, Angus James b 1991, Thomas Henry b 1993, Archie George b 1999, Isobel Serena b 1996, — Iona Mary, b 1955, — Sanda Susan, b 1959: m 1986, James Irvine Hinchliffe Friend, of Winnington Grange, Market Drayton, Shropshire TF9 4DW, son of Irvine Friend, of Mucklestone Old Rectory, Market Drayton, Shropshire, and has had issue, Harry James Hinchliffe b and d 1988, Alexander James Hinchliffe b 1989, Nicholas Andrew Irvine b 1995, Georgina Mary Flavia b 1991, Louisa Dione Frederica b and d 1992. Residence – Falconers, Shipley, Horsham, Sussex. —— Charis Elizabeth, b 1930.

Granddaughter of late Rev Algernon Charles Dudley Ryder, 4th son of Hon Frederick Dudley Ryder, 3rd son of 1st Earl:—
Issue of late Lt-Col Hugh Granville Leveson Dudley Ryder, TD, b 1900, d 1983: m 1st, 1926, Diana Vivian, who d 1951, el da of Sir Paul Augustine Makins, 2nd Bt; 2ndly, 1955, Patricia Geraldine (66 Whitelands House, Cheltenham Terrace, SW3), da of late Gerald Macleay Browne, OBE, and widow of Maj (Basil Arthur) John Peto, King's Drag Gds (see Peto, Bt, colls, cr 1927):—

(By 1st *m*) Jane Christine (Haylands, Martyr Worthy, Winchester), *b* 1927: *m* 1955, Denzil Walter Hugh Ffennell, who *d* 1977, and has issue living, Simon, *b* 1956: *m* 1986, Lucinda, elder da of Lt Cdr Christopher John Ringrose-Voase, MBE, RN, of Alnaby House, Upham, Southampton, and has issue living, Jessica *b* 1989, Georgina *b* 1992, — Diana Elizabeth, *b* 1963.

Granddaughter of late Lieut-Col Spencer Charles Dudley Ryder, BSC, son of late Rt Rev Hon Henry Ryder, Bishop of Lichfield and Coventry, 3rd son of 1st Baron Harrowby:—
Issue of late Lieut-Col Wilfred Ironside Ryder, *b* 1866, *d* 1948: *m* 1901, Tempé Rosa Ridehalgh, who *d* 1942, da of late Maj-Gen James Edmund Bacon Parsons, of The Gables, Southbourne-on-Sea, Hants:—
Margery Julia, *b* 1904: *m* 1934 (*m diss* 1948), Capt Charles Oliver Meeres, late RA.

Grandchildren of late Col Charles Henry Dudley Ryder, CB, CIE, DSO, 7th and yst son of late Lieut-Col Spencer Charles Dudley Ryder, BSC (ante):—
Issue of late Major Lisle Charles Dudley Ryder, Roy Norfolk Regt, *b* 1902, *ka* France 1940: *m* 1938, Enid Helen Constance, who *d* 1977, only child of late Maj Robert Ralston-Patrick, of Trearne, Ayrshire:—
Ralston Patrick Dudley, *b* 1939; *ed* Harrow. *Residence* – 357 Boston Rd, Ontario, NY 14519, USA.

Issue of late Major Ernle Terrick Dudley Ryder, Indian Army, *b* 1906, *ka* off Sumatra 1942: *m* 1936, Daphne Joan Pillans, only child of late John Greig, of Rosewood, Ascot, Berks:—
Elizabeth Jean *b* 1938: *m* 1959, James John Vernon, MA, of Briarwood, East End, Lymington, Hants, and has issue living, James Michael, *b* 1960: *m* 1994, Mhairi Patricia, eldest da of Maj John Nisbet, of South Lodge, Blackadder, nr Duns, Berwickshire, — Peter John, *b* 1963: *m* 1988, Patricia Jean, da of J. C. N. Nicol, and has issue living, Kate Elizabeth *b* 1992, Philippa Vernon *b* 1994, — William Ernle Hardy, *b* 1965: *m* 1988, Emma Mary, yst da of Sir John Barry Salusbury-Trelawny, 13th Bt, and has issue living, Thomas Lisle Trelawny *b* 1997, James Wolfenden Trelawny (Jago) *b* 1999, Elizabeth Laetitia Trelawny *b* 1996, — Julia Elizabeth, *b* 1961: *m* 1992, Jonathan Denton, elder son of late John Denton, and has issue living, Douglas James *b* 1994, Edward *b* 1996. ——Anthea Daphne, *b* 1940: *m* 1968 (*m diss* 1974), Donald Leroy Brown, and has issue living, Andrew Kevin, *b* 1972. *Residence* – 357 Boston Rd, Ontario, NY 14519, USA.

Issue of late Capt Robert Edward Dudley Ryder, VC, RN, cmd'd Naval Forces in attack on St Nazaire 1942, *b* 1908, *d* 1986: *m* 1941, (Constance) Hilaré Myfanwy, who *d* 1982, da of Rev Lumley Cecil Green-Wilkinson (*see* Edwards, Bt, *cr* 1907, 1949 Edn):—
Rev Canon Lisle Robert Dudley (1 Holywell Hill, Henwick Rd, Worcester), *b* 1943; *ed* Selwyn Coll, Camb (MA); Diploma in Pastoral Studies, Univ of Birmingham; Hon Canon Worcester Cathedral 1989: *m* 1977, Olivia Elvira, da of Col Roland Stephen Langton, MVO, MC, of Dial House, Peppard Common, Oxon, and has issue living, Philip Robert Dudley, *b* 1982, — Harriet Elvira, *b* 1980. ——Susan Myfanwy Prudence, *b* 1944: *m* 1965, Martin Graves Bates, of 17 Queen's Gate Place, SW7, and has issue (*see* Bates, Bt, *cr* 1880, colls).

PREDECESSORS – Sir Dudley Ryder, Knt (great grandson of Robert Ryder, of Wisbech) Lord Ch Justice of the King's Bench 1754-6, was offered a peerage by the King on 24 May 1756, but *d* the following day, before the patent was completed; *s* by his son (**1**) NATHANIEL, MP for Tiverton; *cr Baron Harrowby*, of Harrowby, co Lincoln (peerage of Great Britain) 1776; *d* 1803; *s* by his son (**2**) DUDLEY, PC, 2nd Baron; *b* 1762; *cr Viscount Sandon* and *Earl of Harrowby* (peerage of United Kingdom) 1809; was successively Sec of State for Foreign Affairs and Lord Pres of the Council; *d* 1847; *s* by his son (**3**) DUDLEY, KG, DCL, 2nd Earl; *b* 1798; sat as MP for Tiverton (*C*) 1819-31, and for Liverpool 1831-47, was Chancellor of Duchy of Lancaster 1854-5, and Lord Privy Seal 1855-7: *m* 1823, Lady Frances Stuart, da of 1st Marquess of Bute; *d* 1882; *s* by his son (**4**) DUDLEY FRANCIS STUART, PC, 3rd Earl, *b* 1831; MP for Lichfield (*C*) 1856-9, and for Liverpool 1868-82; was Vice-Pres of Committee of Council on Education 1874-8, Pres of Board of Trade 1878-80, and Lord Privy Seal 1885-6: *m* 1861, Lady Mary Frances Cecil, who *d* 1917, da of 2nd Marquess of Exeter; *d* 1900; *s* by his brother (**5**) HENRY DUDLEY, 4th Earl, *b* 1836: *m* 1859, Susan Juliana Maria Hamilton, who *d* 1913, da of late Villiers Dent, of Barton Court, Lymington; *d* 1900; *s* by his el son (**6**) JOHN HERBERT DUDLEY, 5th Earl; *b* 1864; Lord High Steward of Newcastle under Lyme; Lord-Lieut of Staffordshire 1927-48; MP for Gravesend (*C*) 1898-1900: *m* 1887, Hon Dame Mabel Smith, DBE, who *d* 1956, da of Emily, Viscountess Hambleden; *d* 1956; *s* by his son (**7**) DUDLEY, 6th Earl, *b* 1892; author of *Geography of Everyday Things*, and *England at Worship*; PPS to Sec of State for Air 1922-23, a Memb of Commn on Historical Manuscripts 1935-66; MP for Salop, Shrewsbury Div (*C*) 1922-23 and 1924-29: *m* 1922, Lady Helena Blanche Coventry, who *d* 1974, da of late George William, Viscount Deerhurst (*see* E Coventry, 1973-74 Edn); *d* 1987; *s* by his el son (**8**) DUDLEY DANVERS GRANVILLE COUTTS, 7th Earl and present peer; also Viscount Sandon and Baron Harrowby.

HART OF SOUTH LANARK, BARONY OF (Hart) (Extinct 1991)

SONS LIVING OF LIFE BARONESS

Hon Richard Oliver, *b* 1949; *ed* Tiffin's Sch, and King's Coll, Camb: *m* 1985, Dr Ailsa Jane, da of John Allan Auchnie, of Hong Kong, and has issue living, June Judith Auchnie, *b* 1993.
Hon Stephen Cobbett, *b* 1952; *ed* Tiffin's Sch, and King's Coll Camb: *m* 19—, —, and has issue living, Daniel Hart MAYER *b* 1984, — Anna MAYER, *b* 1986.

Hartington, Marquess of; son of Duke of Devonshire.

Hartismere, Baron, title of Baron Henniker on Roll of HL.

HARTWELL, BARON (Berry) (Viscount UK 1941, disclaimed 1995, Life Baron 1968, Bt UK 1921)

(WILLIAM) MICHAEL BERRY, MBE, TD, *Life Baron*, and 3rd *Baronet*, 2nd son of 1st Viscount Camrose; *b* 18 May 1911; *s* as 3rd Viscount Camrose 15 Feb 1995, disclaimed his hereditary peerages for life 9 March 1995; *ed* Eton, and Ch Ch Oxford (MA); Editor *Sunday Mail*, Glasgow 1934-35, Managing Editor *Financial Times* 1937-39, Chm Amalgamated Press Ltd 1954-59, Chm and Editor-in-Chief *The Daily Telegraph* and *Sunday Telegraph* (ret 1987); 2nd Lieut 11th (City of London Yeo) Light Anti-Aircraft Regt RA (TA) 1938, Maj 1940, Lt-Col Gen Staff 1944; 1939-45 War (despatches twice, MBE); *cr* MBE (Mil) 1945, and *Baron Hartwell*, of Peterborough Court, City of London (Life Baron) 1968: *m* 1936, Lady Pamela Margaret Elizabeth Smith, who *d* 1982, yr da of 1st Earl of Birkenhead, and has issue.

𝖆rms – Argent, three bars gules, over all a pile ermine. 𝕮rest – A griffin sejant reguardant sable, collared or. 𝖲upporters – *Dexter*, a stag and *Sinister* a wolf proper, both collared or, and standing on a compartment with a well between paving to the dexter and grass to the sinister proper.
Residences – Oving House, Whitchurch, nr Aylesbury; 18 Cowley St, SW1. *Clubs* – White's, Beefsteak, Royal Yacht Squadron.

SONS LIVING

Hon Adrian Michael (11 Cottesmore Gdns, W8), *b* 1937; *ed* Eton, and Ch Ch, Oxford: *m* 1967, Marina Beatrice, da of Cyrus Sulzberger, of 2 ter Avenue de Ségur, Paris, and has issue living, Jonathan William, *b* 1970: *m* 1996, Aurélie E. C., da of Jean-Pierre Molin, of Paris, and has issue living, Olivia Grace *b* 1998, — Jessica Margaret, *b* 1968.

Hon Nicholas William, *b* 1942; *ed* Eton, and Ch Ch, Oxford: *m* 1977, Evelyn, da of late Jacques Prouvost, and has issue living, William Alexander, *b* 1978, — Alexander, *b* 1981.

DAUGHTERS LIVING

Hon Harriet Mary Margaret, *b* 1944: *m* 1981, Martin Cullen, of 117 Cheyne Walk, SW10, son of Martin Cullen, of Buenos Aires, and has issue living, Miguel *b* 1982, — Domingo *b* 1983.

Hon Eleanor Agnes, *b* 1950.

HARVEY OF PRESTBURY, BARONY OF (Harvey) (Extinct 1994)

SON LIVING OF LIFE BARON (By 1st marriage)

Hon Guy Alan Vere, *b* 1947: *m* 1977, Margaret C. B., da of Lewis Robertson, of The Blair, Blairlogie, Stirling.

ADOPTED DAUGHTERS LIVING OF LIFE BARON

Charmaine, *b* 1966: *m* 1991, Paul Gilbert Cox, eldest son of Gilbert Cox, of Canada.
Rowena, *b* 1968.
Petra, *b* 1973.

WIDOW LIVING OF LIFE BARON

CAROL (*Baroness Harvey of Prestbury*), da of late Austin Cassar-Torreggiani: *m* 1978, as his 3rd wife, Baron Harvey of Prestbury, CBE, who *d* 1994. *Residence* – Rocklands, Les Vardes, St Peter Port, Guernsey, CI.

HARVEY OF TASBURGH, BARON (Harvey) (Baron UK 1954, Bt UK 1868)

PETER CHARLES OLIVER HARVEY, 2nd Baron and 5th Baronet; *b* 28 Jan 1921; *s* 1968; *ed* Eton and Trin Coll, Camb; 1939-45 War with RA in N Africa and Italy: *m* 1957, Penelope Anne, who *d* 1995, yr da of late Lt-Col Sir William Vivian Makins, 3rd Bt, and has issue.

𝖆rms – Erminois, on a chief indented gules between two crescents argent, a representation of the gold medal presented to Sir Robert John Harvey, by command of HRH the Prince Regent, for his services at the battle of Orthes, pendent from a riband gules, fimbriated azure, beneath it the word *Orthes*; a canton ermine charged with a representation of the insignia of a Knight of the Royal Portuguese order of the Tower and Sword, pendent from a riband azure. 𝕮rest – Out of a mural crown or, above a dexter cubit arm erect, proper, a crescent argent between two branches of laurel also proper. 𝖘upporters – *Dexter*, a lion or; *sinister*, a cock or.
Residence – Crownick Woods, Restronguet, Mylor, Falmouth, Cornwall.
Club – Brooks's.

DAUGHTERS LIVING

Hon Juliet Annora Christine, *b* 1958: *m* 1996, Richard T. Lee, son of Prof T. A. Lee, of Tuscaloosa, Alabama, USA, and has issue living, Erin Penelope, *b* 1997.
Hon Miranda Jean HARVEY, *b* 1960; has resumed her maiden name: *m* 1987 (*m diss* 19—), Timothy H. Smithies, 2nd son of R. W. Smithies, of Harrow-on-the-Hill, Middx.

COLLATERAL BRANCH LIVING

Issue of late Hon John Wynn Harvey, yr son of 1st Baron, *b* 1923, *d* 1989: *m* 1950, Elena Maria-Teresa (Coed-y-Maen, Meifod, Powys; 7(a) Friese Green House, Chelsea Manor St, SW3), yr da of late Giambattista, Marchese Curtopassi:—
CHARLES JOHN GIUSEPPE, *b* 4 Feb 1951; *ed* Eton: *m* 1979, Margaret (Maggie), da of Cecil Walter Brown, and has issue living, John, *b* 1993, — Elena, *b* 1982, — Nina, *b* 1985, — Stephanie, *b* 1989. *Residence* – 162 East Dulwich Grove, SE22.
—— Robert Lambart, *b* 1953; *ed* Eton, and Ch Ch, Oxford; MP SW Clwyd (C) 1983-87; Memb House of Commons Foreign Affairs Cttee 1984-87: *m* 1981, Jane Louisa, eldest da of E. Alan Roper, of The Manor, S Brent, Devon, and has issue living, Oliver John Edward Giuseppe, *b* 1988. —— Antonella Sophia Gabriella Maria, *b* 1957: *m* 1988, Al-Sharif Abdullah bin Al-Hussein, and has issue living, Abdulillah, *b* 1992, — Hassein, *b* 1994, — Badia (a da), *b* 1990.

PREDECESSORS

– (1) ROBERT JOHN Harvey, el son of late Gen Sir Robert John Harvey, KCB, of Mousehold House, Norwich; *b* 1817; MP for Thetford 1865-8; *cr* a Baronet 1868: *m* 1845, Lady Henrietta Augusta Lambart, who *d* 1874, sister of 8th Earl of Cavan; *d* 1870; *s* by his son (2) CHARLES, 2nd Bt; *b* 1849; Col 4th Batn Norfolk Regt and a JP: *m* 1st, 1870, Jane Ann, who *d* 1891, da of Benjamin Green, of Newcastle; 2ndly, 1893, Mary Anne Edith, who *d* 1929, da of G. F. Cooke, of Holmewood, Norwich; *d* 1928; *s* by his son (3) CHARLES ROBERT LAMBART EDWARD, 3rd Bt; *b* 1871: *m* 1st, 1891, Jessie, who *d* 1913, da of late E. Turnbull, of Smedley, Lancashire; 2ndly, 1921, Lydia, who *d* 19—, da of Alexis

Konshine, of Petrograd, Russia; *d* 1954; *s* by his half-brother (**4**) OLIVER CHARLES, GCMG, GCVO, CB, 4th Bt, *b* 1893; *cr Baron Harvey of Tasburgh*, of Tasburgh, co Norfolk (peerage of UK) 1954; Dep Under-Sec of State, Foreign Office 1946-48; Ambassador to France 1948-54: *m* 1920, Maud Annora, who *d* 1970, da of late Arthur Watkin Williams-Wynn (Williams-Wynn, Bt, colls); *d* 1968; *s* by his son (**5**) PETER CHARLES OLIVER, 2nd Baron and present peer.

HARVINGTON, BARONY OF (Grant-Ferris) (Extinct 1997)

SON LIVING OF LIFE BARON

Rev Hon (Henry Michael) Piers, OSB (Monastery of Our Lady of Mount Grace, 18 North End, Osmotherley, Northallerton, N Yorks DL6 3BB), *b* 1933; *ed* Ampleforth; late Irish Guards; Monk of St Benedict at Ampleforth Abbey; Assist Priest Workington 1977-89, Leyland 1989-93, Brindle 1993-98, since when Osmotherley.

DAUGHTER LIVING OF LIFE BARON

Hon Greta Sheira Bernadette (*Hon Lady Brinckman*), *b* 1937: *m* 1st, 1956, John Frederick Edward Trehearne; 2ndly, 1970, Christopher Mark Henry Murray (*see* Jerningham, Bt (ext), 1955 Edn); 3rdly, 1983, as his 2nd wife, Sir (Theodore George) Roderick Brinckman, 6th Bt, and has issue (by 1st *m*) Edward Piers Grant, *b* 1963, — Lucinda Elizabeth Scarlett, *b* 1957: *m* 1st, 1984 (*m diss* 1986), 3rd Baron Banbury of Southam; 2ndly, 1990, (John) Patrick Wrigley, of Delbury Hall, Craven Arms, Shropshire (*see* Brocklebank, Bt, 1985 Edn), and has issue living (by 2nd *m*), Jack Hamish *b* 1991, Kate Victoria *b* 1992, — (Petrina) Jane, *b* 1959: *m* 1990, Roderick Arthur Scott, of Harsford Manor, Wisborough Green, Billingshurst, W Sussex RH14 0BD (*see* B Colgrain, colls, 1995 Edn), and has issue living, Sebastian Angus Edward *b* 1993, Hannah Augusta *b* 1991, Augusta Fiona Sheira *b* 1996. *Residence* – Hazleton Manor, Cirencester, Glos.

HASKEL, BARON (Haskel) (Life Baron 1993)

SIMON HASKEL, son of late Isaac Haskel, of ......; *b* 8 Oct 1934; *ed* Sedbergh, and Salford Coll of Advanced Technology (now Salford Univ); joined Perrotts Ltd 1961; Chm Perrotts Group plc and associated companies since 1973; Vice-Chm Institute for Jewish Policy Research since 1993; Chm Thames Concerts Society 1982-90; Memb Select Cttee Science and Technology 1994-97; Co-Chm House of Lords Parliamentary Manufacturing and Industry Group; Opposition Spokesman on Trade and Industry 1994-97; Opposition Whip 1994-97; a Lord in Waiting to HM 1997-98; Chm Labour Finance and Industry Group, Labour Party 1990-96; National Service Commn with RA 1959; *cr Baron Haskel*, of Higher Broughton, co Greater Manchester (Life Baron) 1993: *m* 1962, Carole, da of Wilbur Lewis, of New York, USA, and has issue.
Address – House of Lords, SW1A 0PW. *Clubs* – Reform, Tandem.

SON LIVING

Hon Jonathan Edward, *b* 1964; *ed* ....

DAUGHTER LIVING

Hon Lisa Frances, *b* 1967; *ed* ....

HASKINS, BARON (Haskins) (Life Baron 1998)

CHRISTOPHER ROBIN HASKINS, son of Robin Haskins, of Wicklow; *b* 30 May 1937; *ed* Trinity Coll, Dublin (BA 1959); with Ford Motor Co, Dagenham 1960-62; joined Northern Foods (formerly Northern Dairies) 1962, Chm since 1986; Chm Express Dairies since 1998; Chm Better Regulation Task Force since 1997; Memb Hampel Cttee on Corporate Governance 1996-97, UK Round Table on Sustainable Development 1994-98; Memb CBI President's Cttee since 1996, DEMOS since 1993, Civil Liberties Trust since 1997, and Legal Assistance Trust since 1998; *cr Baron Haskins*, of Skidby

in the County of the E Riding of Yorkshire (Life Baron) 1998: *m* 1959, Gilda, da of Alec Horsley, of Hessle, E Yorks, and has issue.
Residence – Quarryside Farm, Main St, Skidby, nr Cottingham, E Yorks HU16 5TG.

SONS LIVING

Hon Paul, *b* 1961; *ed* S Hunsley Comprehensive Sch, and Bishop Burton Agricultural Coll: *m* 1987, Jeanette Horn, and has issue living, Gary, *b* 1993, — Ryan, *b* 1994.
Hon Daniel, *b* 1962; *ed* S Hunsley Comprehensive Sch, and Trin Coll, Dublin: *m* 1999, Jessica North.
Hon David, *b* 1966; *ed* Cottingham Sch; has issue (by Joanne Burton), Megan *b* 1999.

DAUGHTERS LIVING

Hon Gina, *b* 1964; *ed* Cottingham Sch, and Corpus Christi Coll, Oxford: *m* 1992, Stephen Hocking, and has issue living, Aidan, *b* 1991, — Jack, *b* 1993, — Isabel, *b* 1995.
Hon Kate, *b* 1967; *ed* Cottingham Sch, and Sunderland Univ.

HASLAM, BARON (Haslam) (Life Baron 1990)

ROBERT HASLAM, son of late Percy Haslam; *b* 4 Feb 1923; *ed* Bolton Sch, and Birmingham Univ (BSc); Hon DTech Brunel Univ 1987, Hon DEng Birmingham Univ 1987; Dep-Chm ICI plc 1980-83, Chm Tate and Lyle plc 1983-86, British Steel Corpn 1983-86, British Coal 1986-90, Bechtel Ltd since 1991, and Wasserstein Perella & Co Internat Ltd since 1991; Dir Bank of England 1985-93; Advisory Dir Unilever plc 1985-93; Hon FIMinE; *cr* Knt 1985, and *Baron Haslam*, of Bolton, Greater Manchester (Life Baron) 1990: *m* 1st, 1947, Joyce, who *d* 1995, da of late Frederick Quinn; 2ndly, 1996, Elizabeth, da of late William Norman Pitt, of Hampton, Middx, and widow of Hon Michael David Sieff, CBE (*see* By Sieff), and has issue by 1st *m*.
Address – House of Lords, SW1A 0PW. *Office* - Wasserstein Perella & Co Internat Ltd, 10-11 Park Place, SW1A 1LP.

SONS LIVING (By 1st marriage)

Hon Roger J., *b* 1948; *ed* Westminster, and Dundee Univ (BSc): *m* 1972, Astrid, da of Kristian Rognøy, of Omsheim, 5470 Rosendal, Norway, and has issue living, Sara Caroline Rognøy, *b* 1974, — Roberta Louise Rognøy, *b* 1980.
Hon Nigel R., *b* 1952; *ed* Westminster, and Birmingham Univ (BA): *m* 1988, Alison Vanessa, da of Alec Raymond Gourd Knight, of Chy Meor, Newquay, Cornwall, and has issue living, James Robert Alexander, *b* 1990, — Sophie Antonia, *b* 1988. *Residence* – 17 Blithfield St, W8 6RH.

HASTINGS, BARON (Astley) (Baron E 1290, Bt E 1660)

EDWARD DELAVAL HENRY ASTLEY, 22nd Baron, and 12th Baronet; *b* 14 April 1912; *s* 1956; *ed* Eton; is Major Coldstream Guards (Reserve), and patron of seven livings; a Lord-in-Waiting to HM 1961-62, and Joint Parl Sec to Min of Housing and Local Government 1962-64; Grand Officer of Order of Merit of Italy: *m* 1954, Catherine (Cecilia) Rosaline Ratcliffe (COATS), yr da of late Capt Harold Virgo Hinton, and has issue.

Arms – Quarterly: 1st azure, a cinquefoil pierced ermine, within a bordure engrailed or, *Astley*; 2nd argent, a lion rampant gules, ducally crowned or, *Constable of Melton*; 3rd gules, two lions passant argent, *Le Strange*; 4th or, a maunch gules, *Hastings*. Crest – Out of a ducal coronet or, a plume of five feathers argent. Supporters – On either side a lion gules, ducally crowned, and gorged with a plain collar or, pendant therefrom an escutcheon of the arms of *Hastings*.
Tenacious of justice
Seat – Seaton Delaval Hall, Whitley Bay, Northumberland NE26 4QR. *Clubs* – Brooks's, Army and Navy, Northern Counties, and Norfolk.

SONS LIVING

Hon DELAVAL THOMAS HAROLD, *b* 25 April 1960; *ed* Radley and Hatfield Coll, Durham: *m* 1987, Veronica M., elder da of Richard A. Smart, of Elizabeth Crescent, Queen's Park, Chester, and has issue living, Jacob Addison, *b* 5 Sept 1991, — Molly, *b* 1993, — Caitlin, *b* 1996. *Residence* – 39 Colville Gdns, W11.

Hon Justin Edward, *b* 1968. *Residence* – Thornage Hall, Holt, Norfolk.

DAUGHTER LIVING

Hon Harriet Marguerite, *b* 1958. *Residence* – Arusha, Tanzania.

SISTERS LIVING

Hon Helen Elizabeth Delaval, *b* 1907: *m* 1st, 1930 (*m diss* 1940), Ian Bulloch; 2ndly, 1941, George Field, who *d* 1941; 3rdly, 1948, John David Haw, who *d* 1982, and has issue living (by 1st *m*), Donald Ian (11 Montclair Av, Woodvale, Perth, W Australia 6026), *b* 1931: *m* 1956, Joyce Illman, and has issue living, Nevill (Harare, Zimbabwe) *b* 1959: *m* 1987, Daria Garizio, Donald *b* 1961, Elinor (Constantia, Cape Prov, S Africa) *b* 1957: *m* 1983 (*m diss* 1993), Andrejz Misiewicz, — James Angus, *b* 1935: *m* 1st, 1956 (*m diss* 1960), Penelope Burrows; 2ndly, 1961, Margaret Conley, of NSW, and has issue living (by 1st *m*), Anthea *b* 1957: *m* 19—, Rohan Vos (PO Box 511, Constantia, Cape Prov 7848, S Africa) (and has issue living, Shaun *b* 1976, Brenda *b* 1978, Bianca *b* 1984, Tiffany 1986), Janet *b* 1958: *m* 1984, Alan Wale (and has issue living, Craig *b* 1987, Keith *b* 1988), (by 2nd *m*) Simon *b* 1961: *m* 1986 (*m diss* 1997), Sonia Linkston (and has issue living, Melissa *b* 1989, Kirsty *b* 1994), Keith *b* 1964, — Alasdair George (60 Corbel St, Shelley, Perth, W Australia 6155), *b* 1938: *m* 1963, Marion Mill, and has issue living, Samantha *b* 1966, Pepita *b* 1969, Jaye *b* 1970. *Residence* – Windermere Estate, 158 Bibra Drive, Bibra Lake, W Australia 6163.

Hon Jean, *b* 1917; formerly in WRNS: *m* 1945, Lieut-Com Mark Napier, RN, who *d* 1962, and has issue (*see* L Napier and Ettrick, colls). *Residence* – 12 Grassmere Close, Felpham, Bognor Regis, Sussex.

WIDOW LIVING OF SON OF TWENTY-FIRST BARON

Lady Joan Patricia Quirk, da of 1st Earl Wavell: *m* 1st, 1943, Maj Hon Simon Nevill Astley who *d* 1946; 2ndly, 1948, Harry Alastair Gordon, who *d* 1965; 3rdly, 1973, Maj Donald Struan Robertson, SG, who *d* 1993, and has issue living (by 1st *m*) (see colls, infra). *Residence* – Swallowfield House, Spanish Green, Stratfield Turgis, Hook, Hants RG27 0AD.

COLLATERAL BRANCHES LIVING *(All of whom are in remainder to the Barony of Hastings.)*

Issue of late Maj Hon Simon Nevill Astley, 2nd son of 21st Baron, *b* 1919, *d* 1946: *m* 1943, Lady Joan Patricia Quirk (ante) (she *m* 2ndly, 1948, Maj Harry Alastair Gordon, Gordon Highlanders, who *d* 1965, and 3rdly, 1973, Maj Donald Struan Robertson, SG, who *d* 1993, of Winkfield Plain Farm, Winkfield, Windsor, Berks, son of late Rt Hon Sir Malcolm Arnold Robertson, GCMG, KBE), da of 1st Earl Wavell:—
Diana Jane, *b* 1943: *m* 1975, Robert I. W. Kellie, of The King's, Oxlynch, Stonehouse, Glos GL10 3DE, and has issue living, Rupert Simon Chamier, *b* 1977, — Toby Alastair Struan, *h* 1984, — Tara Margaret Joan, *b* 1980.

Issue of late Hon Armyne Margaret Astley, 2nd da of 21st Baron, *b* 1909, *d* 1979: *m* 1933, William George Broadbent Schofield, who *d* 1987:—
Armyne Morar Helen (*Lady Stirling*), *b* 1934: *m* 1959, Sir Angus Duncan Aeneas Stirling, of 25 Ladbroke Grove, W11, and has issue (*see* E Dunmore). —— Marigold Elizabeth, *b* 1937: *m* 1962, Capt John Anthony Cromek Warrington, The Green Howards, of Low Burton Hall, Masham, N Yorks HG4 4DQ, and has issue living, George Simon Cromek, *b* 1964, — Patrick William Cromek, *b* 1966: *m* 1990, Jane Alice Patience, da of Joseph Andrew Christopher Hoare, of Hartridge Manor Farm, Cranbrook, Kent (*see* E Antrim, 1990 Edn), and has issue living, Ferdinand Joseph *b* 1996, Christopher Sheridan Cromek *b* 1998, Flora Lucy Christina *b* 1991, Eleanor *b* 1993, — Olivia Sarah (*Hon Mrs Ralph C. Assheton*), *b* 1963: *m* 1996, Hon Ralph Christopher Assheton, elder son of 2nd Baron Clitheroe, and has issue (see that title). —— Cicely Rose, *b* 1941: *m* 1972, Harold Irvin Golden, of 12311 Marine St, Los Angeles, Calif, USA.

Grandchildren of late Capt Hon (Charles) Melton Astley, yst son of 20th Baron:—
Issue of late Maj George Delaval Astley, Royal Fus, *b* 1915, *d* 1993: *m* 1st, 1942 (*m diss* 1946), Hope Shuttleworth, yr da of late Lt-Col Francis Holden Shuttleworth Rendall, DSO, Duke of Cornwall's LI; 2ndly, 1949, Diana Christian, who *d* 1996, only da of late Brig-Gen Robert Hugh Hare, CB, CMG, DSO, MVO:—
(By 2nd *m*) (Delaval) Hugh (170 Arundel Av, Toronto, Canada M4K 3A9), *b* 1950; *ed* Aiglon Coll, Switzerland: *m* 1976, Penelope, da of Charles Henry Underwood, and has issue living, Christopher Delaval, *b* 1976, — Caroline Zoë, *b* 1975. —— (Caroline) Susan, *b* 1951; resumed her maiden name until remarriage: *m* 1st, 1974 (*m diss* 1984), Charles Philip Barrington Woollett; 2ndly, 1992, James Stymeist, of Crossroads, Stratford, Prince Edward Island, Canada, and has issue living (by 2nd *m*), Alexandra Diana, *b* 1992.

Issue of late Hon Hester Winifred Astley, da of 20th Baron, *b* 1899, *d* 1980: *m* 1923, Alan Houghton Brodrick, who *d* 1973:—
John Alan St John BRODRICK, *b* 1924. *Residence* – 33 Chesil Court, Chelsea Manor St, SW3.

Grandson of late Hubert Delaval Astley, son of Lt-Col Francis L'Estrange Astley, brother of 16th Baron:—

Issue of late Col Philip Reginald Astley, CBE, MC, *b* 1896, *d* 1958: *m* 1st, 1931 (*m diss* 1940), Edith Madeleine (the actress Madeleine Carroll), who *d* 1987, da of late John Carroll; 2ndly, 1949, Penelope Joan McKerrow, OBE (15/161 Fulham Rd, SW3 6SN), da of late Trevor Bright of Freshford, Bath:—
(By 2nd *m*) Richard Jacob (6 Meadow View, Water Eaton Rd, Oxford OX2 7QS), *b* 1950; *ed* Eton; BA, London: *m* 1974, Rosanna, el da of late Sir (John) Anthony Quayle, CBE, the actor, and has issue living, Thomas Jacob, *b* 1975, — Harry Richard, *b* 1977, — Jenny Miranda, *b* 1980.

PREDECESSORS – This ancient family descends from Sir Thomas Astley, who fell at the battle of Evesham 1265 with Simon de Montfort, Earl of Leicester, *temp* Henry III. *Sir* Isaac Astley, *cr* a Bt 1641 (nephew of Jacob, 1st Baron Astley of Reading, Commander of King Charles I's Infantry at the battle of Naseby, *cr* 1644, ext 1668); *d* without issue 1659, when the Baronetcy expired, and his estates passed to his nephew **(1)** *Sir* JACOB Astley (son of Edward Astley, by his wife (and cousin), Elizabeth, da of Jacob, 1st Baron Astley of Reading), 40 years MP for Norfolk; *cr* a *Baronet* 1660; *d* 1729; *s* by his son **(2)** *Sir* PHILIP, 2nd Bt; *d* 1739; *s* by his son **(3)** *Sir* JACOB, 3rd Bt; *d* 1760; *s* by his son **(4)** *Sir* EDWARD, 4th Bt; 24 years MP for Norfolk; *d* 1802; *s* by his son **(5)** *Sir* JACOB HENRY, 5th Bt; 20 years MP for Norfolk; *d* 1817; *s* by his son **(6)** *Sir* JACOB, 6th Bt; summoned to Parliament by writ and became 16th Baron Hastings 1841, the abeyance (see *infra) having been terminated in his favour; *d* 1859; *s* by his el son **(7)** JACOB HENRY DELAVAL, 17th Baron; *d* 1871; *s* by his brother **(8)** *Rev* DELAVAL LOFTUS, 18th Baron; *b* 1825: *m* 1848, Hon Frances Diana Manners Sutton, da of 1st Viscount Canterbury; *d* 1872; *s* by his el son **(9)** BERNARD EDWARD DELAVAL, 19th Baron; *b* 1855; *d* 1875; *s* by his brother **(10)** GEORGE MANNERS, 20th Baron; *b* 1857: *m* 1880, Hon Elizabeth Evelyn Harbord, who *d* 1957, da of 5th Baron Suffield; *d* 1904; *s* by his son **(11)** ALBERT EDWARD DELAVAL, 21st Baron; *b* 1882; Lieut-Col late 7th Hussars; High Steward of Norwich Cathedral; bore one of the Golden Spurs at Coronations of King George VI and Queen Elizabeth II: *m* 1907, Lady Marguerite Helen Nevill, who *d* 1975, da of 3rd Marquess of Abergavenny; *d* 1956; *s* by his son **(12)** EDWARD DELAVAL HENRY, 22nd Baron and present peer.

*(1) *Sir* JOHN Hastings, who in right of his mother and by tenure of the Castle of Bergavenny was Baron Bergavenny, was summoned to Parliament as *Baron Hastings* 1290-1313; assisted in the Scottish Wars of Edward I, and received in 1273 from the King a grant of the whole co of Menteth, with the Isles and also all the manors and lands of Alan; 6th Earl of Menteth, then declared a rebel; was seneschal of Aquitaine, and in 1290 a competitor for the Crown of Scotland: *m* 1st, 1275, Isabel de Valence, who *d* 1305, da of William, Earl of Pembroke; 2ndly, 13-, Isabella Despencer, da of 1st Earl of Winchester; *d* 1313; *s* by his son **(2)** JOHN, 2nd Baron; summoned to Parliament 1313-25; served in the Scottish Wars of Edward II, and was sometime Gov of Kenilworth Castle: *m* 13-, Juliana (who *m* 2ndly, 1326, Sir Thomas Blount, and 3rdly, 1327, William, Lord Clinton, and *d* 1367), da of Sir Thomas Leybourne; *d* 1325; *s* by his son **(3)** LAURENCE, 3rd Baron; *b* 1320; *cr Earl of Pembroke* (peerage of England) 1339; served with valour in the French Wars of Edward III: *m* 1328, Agnes Mortimer (who *m* 2ndly, 13-, John Hakelut, and *d* 1368), da of 1st Earl of March; *d* 1348; *s* by his son **(4)** JOHN, KG, 2nd Earl; *b* 1347; was sent as Lieut into Aquitaine with a fleet of ships, but no sooner had he got his vessels within the harbour of La Rochelle than he was suddenly attacked by the Spanish fleet, and having suffered a signal defeat was taken prisoner and detained four years in captivity: *m* 1st, 1359, Margaret, who *d* 1361, da of Edward III; 2ndly, 1363, Anne, who *d* 1384, da of Walter, 1st Lord Manny; *d* 1375; *s* by his son **(5)** JOHN, 3rd Earl; *b* 1372: *m* 1st, 1380 (*m diss* 1383), Elizabeth, da of John of Gaunt, Duke of Lancaster; 2ndly, 13-, Philippa Mortimer (who *m* 2ndly, 13-, Richard FitzAlan, 15th Earl of Arundel, and 3rdly, 1399, Thomas Poynings, 5th Lord St John of Basing, and *d* 1401), da of the 3rd Earl of March; *d* 1389, when 17 years of age, from a wound received in tilting, from the lance of Sir John St John, when the earldom became ext and he was *s* in the barony (according to the decision of the House of Lords 1841) by his kinsman **(6)** *Sir* JOHN, *de jure* 6th Baron (el son of Sir Hugh Hastings, son of 1st Baron), *b* 1328, *d* 1393; *s* by his great-nephew **(7)** *Sir* HUGH (son of Sir Hugh Hastings, of Elsing, Norfolk, and of Fenwick, co York, and grandson of Sir Hugh Hastings, brother of *de jure* 6th Baron, *b* 1376): *m* 13- Constance (who *m* 2ndly, 14-, Sir John Sutton, of Dudley, Staffs), da of Walter Blount, of Barton Blount, Derbyshire; *d* 1396; *s* by his brother **(8)** *Sir* EDWARD, *de jure* 8th Baron, *b* 1382; unsuccessfully claimed to carry the Second Sword before the King at Henry IV's Coronation, and to carry Great Gilt Spurs, and to perform the office of Ch Napperer: *m* 1st, 14-, Muriel, da of Sir John de Dinham, of Hartland, Devon: 2ndly, 14-, Margery (who *m* 2ndly, 14-, John Wyndham, of Felbridge, Norfolk, and *d* 1456), da of Sir Robert Clifton, of Bokenham, Norfolk; *d* 1438; *s* by his son **(9)** JOHN, *de jure* 9th Baron, *b* 1412; Constable of Norwich Castle and Gaol 1441: *m* 1434, Anne, who *d* 1471, da of Thomas Morley, Lord Morley; *d* 1477; *s* by his son **(10)** *Sir* HUGH, *de jure* 10th Baron, *b* 1447; Sheriff of Yorkshire 1479-80: *m* 1455, Anne, da of Sir William Gascoigne, of Gawthorpe, Yorkshire; *d* 1488; *s* by his son **(11)** *Sir* JOHN, *de jure* 11th Baron, *b* 1466: *m* 1st, 14-, Isabel, who *d* 1495, da and heir of Sir Ralph Babthorpe, of Babthorpe, Yorkshire; 2ndly, 14-, Katherine, da of Sir John Aske, of Aughton Yorkshire; *d* 1504; *s* by his brother **(12)** *Sir* GEORGE, *de jure* 12th Baron; *b* 1474: *m* 1493, Joan, da and co-heir of Roger Brabazon, of Eastwell, Leicestershire; *d* 1511; *s* by his son **(13)** JOHN, *de jure* 13th Baron, *b* 1498; *d* 1514; *s* by his brother **(14)** *Sir* HUGH, *de jure* 14th Baron, *b* 1505: *m* 1523, Katherine (who *m* 2ndly, 1554, Thomas Gawdy, Serjeant-at-Law, and *d* 1558), da of Robert L'Estrange, of Winfarthing, Norfolk; *d* 1540; *s* by his son **(15)** JOHN *de jure* 15th Baron, *b* 1530; *d* unmarried 1542, when the Barony fell into abeyance between his sisters (i) Anne, wife of William Browne, of Elsing, Norfolk, and (ii) Elizabeth, wife of Hamon L'Estrange of Hunstanton, Norfolk, and so remained until 1841, when the House of Lords reported that the co-heirs were Frances Berney, widow of the Rev Richard Browne, Henry L'Estrange Styleman le Strange, of Hunstanton, co Norfolk, and Sir Jacob Astley, 6th Bt, whereupon the abeyance was terminated in favour of the last-named, who was 9th in descent from Elizabeth L'Estrange (ante).

Hastings, Abney-, family name of the Countess of Loudoun.

HATCH OF LUSBY, BARONY OF (Hatch) (Extinct 1992)

SONS LIVING OF LIFE BARON (by 1st marriage)

Hon Barrie, *b* 19—: *m* and has issue.
Hon Stewart, *b* 19—: *m* and has issue.

WIDOW LIVING OF LIFE BARON

EVA (*Baroness Hatch of Lusby*), da of —, of Greece, and formerly wife of A. Cyril Grant, of Richmond, Surrey: *m* 19—, as his 5th wife, Baron Hatch of Lusby (Life Baron), who *d* 1992. *Residence* – 28 The Vale, Swainsthorpe, Norwich, Norfolk NR14 8PL.

HATHERTON, BARON (Littleton) (Baron UK 1835)

One God, and one king

EDWARD CHARLES LITTLETON, 8th Baron, *b* 24 May 1950; *s* 1985; Agronomist: *m* 1974, Hilda María, da of Rodolfo Robert, of San José, Costa Rica, and has issue.

Arms – Argent, a chevron between three escallops sable. **Crest** – A stag's head cabossed sable, attired or; between the attires a bugle horn of the first, garnished and pendant from two annulets conjoined gold. **Supporters** – *Dexter*, a stag proper, plain collared or, and suspended therefrom an escutcheon argent, charged with a bugle stringed sable; *sinister*, a lion gules, ducally gorged, and suspended from the coronet an escutcheon, charged as in the dexter.
Address – PO Box 1341-2150 Moravia, Costa Rica.

SON LIVING

Hon THOMAS EDWARD, *b* 7 March 1977.

DAUGHTERS LIVING

Hon Melissa Anne, *b* 1975.
Hon Valerie Anne, *b* 1981.

SISTERS LIVING

Aileen Pamela Hyacinthe LITTLETON, *b* 1941: *m* 1963, Roberto Padilla Odor, and has issue living, Roberto, *b* 1964, — Andreas, *b* 1968, — Mervyn, *b* 1971, — Luciana, *b* 1964. *Address* – PO Box 3358-1000, San Jose, Costa Rica.
Cynthia Ann LITTLETON, *b* 1943: *m* 1964, Giovanni Sosto Peralta, and has issue living, Giovanni, *b* 1967, — Eugenio, *b* 1971, — Carlo, *b* 1972, — Alexandra Eugenia, *b* 1968. *Address* – PO Box 546-1007, San Jose, Costa Rica.

DAUGHTER LIVING OF SEVENTH BARON

Hon Hyacinthe Ann, *b* 1934; LLB Newcastle; Solicitor 1978: *m* 1954, Patrick Peterken, of Claypool Farm, Hutton Henry, Castle Eden, co Durham, and has issue living, Patrick James Littleton, *b* 1957, — Nicholas John Littleton, *b* 1960, — Frances Josephine, *b* 1962: *m* 1994, Justin M. A. Boyd, son of Brig Compton Boyd, of Gt Eversden, Cambs.

SONS LIVING OF SIXTH BARON (By 2nd wife)

Hon Richard Brownlow (Foresters Lodge, Nether Alderley, Macclesfield, Cheshire), *b* 1949: *m* 1st, 1975 (*m diss* 19—), Shirley Margaret Adamson; 2ndly, 1992, Linda Hoyland, and has issue living (by 1st *m*), Ian Brownlow, *b* 1981, — Kirsty Emma, *b* 1985.
Hon Jonathan Lloyd, *b* (twin) 1949: *m* 1970, Maxine Elizabeth, who *d* 1995, da of Alistair Brough Mills, of Mynderley, High Park, All Stretton, Shropshire, and has issue living, Alexander John Walhouse, *b* 1970, — Jonathan Maxwell, *b* 1982, — Rosalind Elizabeth, *b* 1972, — Melissa Mary, *b* 1975.

DAUGHTERS LIVING OF SIXTH BARON

(By 1st wife)

Hon Moonyeen Merriel (9 Church Lane, Witney, Oxon OX8 6LB), *b* 1933.

(*By 2nd wife*)

Hon Modwena Louise, *b* 1947: *m* 1st, 1968 (*m diss* 1974), Edward Willison; 2ndly, 1978, Peter Fleming Orchard, and has issue living (by 1st *m*), Trecia, *b* 1969, — Rachel, *b* 1971.

DAUGHTERS LIVING OF FIFTH BARON

Hon Joanna Ida Louisa, *b* 1926: *m* 1948, Robert Westby Perceval, of Pillaton Old Hall, Penkridge, Stafford, and has issue living, Antony Robin Walhouse Westby LITTLETON (Old Walls, Hannington, Basingstoke, Hants), *b* 1950; *ed* Eton; adopted by Royal Licence 1971 the surname of Littleton: *m* 1980, Hon Aileen Mary Fitzherbert, eldest da of 14th Baron Stafford, and has issue living, Thomas Alastair Westby *b* 1986, Katrina Mary *b* 1983, Rosanna Sophie *b* 1989, — Sara Jane Modwena, *b* 1954: *m* 1981, Richard Burnaby Kennedy Dyott, FRICS, of Freeford Manor, Lichfield, Staffs, only son of late William Boyd Kennedy Shaw, OBE, by his wife Eleanor, yr da of late Richard Archibald Dyott, of Freeford Manor (*see* M Anglesey, colls, 1960 Edn), and has issue living, William Richard Perceval *b* 1987, Caroline Eleanor Frances *b* 1985, — Diana Mary, *b* 1959: *m* 1980, Peter Henry Burden, of Gwynfe House, Sutton St Nicholas, Hereford, son of Paul Burden, of Burnham, Bucks, and has issue living, Edward Hugh *b* 1986, Archibald Robert *b* 1990, Alice Titania *b* 1988.

Hon Jane Anne Caroline, *b* 1929: *m* 1967, Rev Charles Piachaud Wright, of Meadowsweet Lodge, Uppingham, Rutland, Leics.

DAUGHTER LIVING OF FOURTH BARON

Hon Hester Mary Modwena (Pitt Manor Cottage, Winchester), *b* 1912; 1939-45 with WTS/FANY.

MOTHER LIVING

Margaret Ann, da of Frank Sheehy, of Canada: *m* 1940, Mervyn Cecil Littleton, only son of late Lt-Col Hon Charles Christopher Josceline Littleton, DSO, who *d* 1970. *Address* – PO Box 1341-2150, Moravia, Costa Rica.

WIDOW LIVING OF SIXTH BARON

MARY ALICE (*Mary, Baroness Hatherton*), Capt (ret) QAIMNS; da of John Roberts, of Ruthin, Denbighshire: *m* 1955, as his 2nd wife, the 6th Baron Hatherton, who *d* 1973.

COLLATERAL BRANCHES LIVING

Granddaughters of late Maj Hon William Hugh Littleton (infra):—
Issue of late John William Littleton, *b* 1924, *d* 1992: *m* 1956, Hilda Ruth (The Bridges, 92 King's Av, Christchurch, Hants), only da of J. Pardy, of Christchurch, Hants:—
Deborah Jayne, *b* 1960: *m* 1981 (*m diss* 1993), Thomas Collins, only son of Thomas Collins, of Grimsby, Humberside, and has issue living, Steven Andrew, *b* 1981. —— Susan Jennifer, *b* 1965.

Issue of late Major Hon William Hugh Littleton, 4th son of 3rd Baron, *b* 1882, *d* 1956: *m* 1920, Lilian, who *d* 1954, da of Charles E. Davis, of Clifton, Bristol:—
Margaret Hyacinthe, *b* 1921; 1939-45 War in VAD: *m* 1948, Edward Roderick Dew, CBE, who *d* 1997. *Residence* – Highdown, Bridge Reeve, Chulmleigh, N Devon.

Grandchildren of late Rear-Adm Hon Algernon Charles Littleton, 2nd son of 2nd Baron:—
Issue of late Capt Algernon Edward Percy Littleton, *b* 1881, *d* 1943: *m* 1912, Violet Agnes Lætitia, who *d* 1973, da of Sir John William Salusbury-Trelawny, 11th Bt:—
Robert Jocelyn Henry, DFC, *b* 1915; *ed* Malvern; Flight-Lt RAF; 1939-45 War (DFC): *m* 1946, Wendy, da of late S. Stevens, and has issue living, Susan Elaine, *b* 1952, — Zoë Annette, *b* 1955.

Issue of late Lt-Col Josceline William Littleton, MC, ED, *b* 1886, *d* 1969: *m* 1920, Annie McKerrell, who *d* 1961, da of Lt-Col Arthur George Wolley-Dod:—
Margaret Anne (1345, W Tulare Av, Visalia, Cal 93277), *b* 1921: *m* 1st, 1943 (*m diss* 1948), Fl-Lt Alfred John Smitz, DFC, RAF; 2ndly, 1948 (*m diss* 1963), Robert Leech; 3rdly, 1967 (*m diss* 1974), Arthur Dale Harder, and has issue living (by 1st *m*) Peter Gerard Littleton (96 Hollyburn Rd, Calgary, Alberta, Canada T2V 3HI), *b* 1944; a Constable, Royal Canadian Mounted Police: *m* 1965, Carol Thew, of Richmond Hill, Ont, and has issue living, Stephen Douglas *b* 1975, Leigh-Ann Kimberly *b* 1971, — (by 2nd *m*) Robert Timothy, *b* 1961, — Marta Anne, *b* 1951: *m* 1969, Kerry Wayne King, of 130 East Cedar, Exeter, Calif 93221, USA, — Josceline Henrietta, *b* 1952: *m* 1st, 1971 (*m diss* 1976), Mark S. Wingo; 2ndly, 1979, Philip Lon Bower, who *d* 1981; 3rdly, 1984, John Douglas Koopman, and has issue living (by 1st *m*), Jason Marcus *b* 1973, (by —) Aisha Christine Gaut *b* 1977, (by 2nd *m*) Delaney Brie *b* 1981.

Issue of late Com Richard Charles Arthur Littleton, RN (ret), *b* 1888, *d* 1945: *m* 1934, Lucy Veronica, who *d* 1979, da of Rev Robert Cecil Salmon, R of Chiddingstone, Kent:—
Marilyn Eve (Chibbett, Exford, Minehead, Som), *b* 1937.

Issue of late Capt Cecil Francis Henry Littleton, *b* 1890, *d* of wounds received during European War 1917: *m* 1913, Brenda (who *d* 1972, having *m* 2ndly, 1919, Arthur Alexander Baillie, and 3rdly, 1922 (*m diss* 1934), Alwyne R. M. Scrase-Dickins, who *d* 1983), da of late George Southby Hewitt, of 26A North Audley St, W1:— Diana, *b* 1915: *m* 1948 (*m diss* 1960), Henry Stephen Earley. *Residence* – 27 Parkside, Cuddesdon, Oxford OX44 9EZ.

PREDECESSORS – *Sir* Edward Littleton, 4th and last Bt, of Pillaton, *cr* 1627, devised his estates to his grand-nephew **(1)** EDWARD JOHN Walhouse, PC (MP for Staffordshire 1812-35), who thereupon assumed the surname of Littleton in lieu of his patronymic; *b* 1791; was Ch Sec for Ireland 1834, and Lord-Lieut of Staffordshire 1854-62; *cr Baron Hatherton*, of Hatherton, co Stafford, 1835: *m* 1st, 1812, Hyacinthe Mary, natural da of 1st Marquess Wellesley; 2ndly, 1852, Caroline Anne, who *d* 1897, da of Richard Hurt, of Worksworth, and widow of Edward Davies Davonport, of Capesthorne, Cheshire; *d* 1863; *s* by his son **(2)** EDWARD RICHARD, CB, 2nd Baron, *b* 1815; sat as MP for Walsall (*L*) 1847-52, and for S Staffordshire 1853-7: *m* 1841, Lady Margaret Percy, who *d* 1897, da of 5th Duke of Northumberland; *d* 1888; *s* by his el son **(3)** EDWARD GEORGE PERCY, CMG, 3rd Baron, *b* 1842; was Sec and Mil Sec to Earl of Dufferin (Gov-Gen of Canada) 1875-8, Mil Sec to Marquess of Lorne 1878-9, and an Hon Commr in Lunacy 1890-98: *m* 1867, Charlotte Louisa, who *d* 1923, da of Sir Charles Robert Rowley, 4th Bt; *d* 1930; *s* by his el son **(4)** EDWARD CHARLES ROWLEY, 4th Baron; *b* 1868; formerly Lieut 3rd Batn N Staffordshire Regt; in Ser of Raja of Sarawak 1890-96: *m* 1897, Hester Edith, who *d* 1947, da of late Thomas Tarrant Hoskins, MD, JP, of Tasmania; *d* 1944; *s* by his el son **(5)** EDWARD THOMAS WALHOUSE, 5th Baron, *b* 1900; Lt Cdr RN: *m* 1st, 1925 (*m diss* 1951), Ida Guendolen, who *d* 1969, da of Robin Legge; 2ndly, Kathleen May, who *d* 1983, da of Clarence Ernest Orlando Whitechurch, and formerly wife of Maj Oscar Westendarp; *d* 1969; *s* by his brother, **(6)** JOHN WALTER STUART, 6th Baron; *b* 1906: *m* 1st, 1932, Nora Evelyn, who *d* 1955, da of R. C. Smith, of Edgbaston; 2ndly, 1955, Mary Alice, Capt (ret) QUAIMNS, da of John soberts, of Ruthin, Denbighshire; *d* 1973; *s* by his brother **(7)** THOMAS CHARLES TASMAN, TD, 7th Baron, *b* 1907; Capt RA (TA): *m* 1933, Ann Scott, who *d* 1994, only da of late Lt-Cdr Thomas MacLeod, RN; *d* 1985; *s* by his kinsman **(8)** EDWARD CHARLES (only son of late Mervyn Cecil Littleton, only son (by 1st *m*) of Lt-Col Hon Charles Christopher Josceline Littleton, DSO, 3rd son of 3rd Baron), 8th Baron and present peer.

HATTERSLEY, BARON (Hattersley) (Life Baron 1997)

ROY SYDNEY GEORGE HATTERSLEY, PC, son of late Frederick Roy Hattersley, of Sheffield, and Enid Hattersley (Lord Mayor of Sheffield 1981-82); *b* 28 Dec 1932; *ed* Sheffield City Gram Sch, and Hull Univ (BSc (Econ) 19—); joined Labour Party 1949; Memb Sheffield City Cncl 1957-65; MP for Birmingham Sparkbrook (Lab) 1964-97; PPS to Min of Pensions and Nat Insurance 1964-67; Jt Parliamentary Sec of State for Employment and Productivity 1967-69; Min of Defence for Admin 1969-70; Opposition Spokesman on Defence 1972, and Education and Science 1972-74; Min of State, FCO 1974-76; Sec of State for Prices and Consumer Protection 1976-79; Chief Opposition Spokesman on Environment 1979-80, Home Affairs 1981-83, Treasury and Economic Affairs 1983-87, and Home Affairs 1987-97; Dep Leader, Labour Party 1983-92; journalist and author; Columnist of the Year, What the Papers Say (Granada TV) 1982; *cr* PC 1975, and *Baron Hattersley*, of Sparkbrook, co W Midlands (Life Baron) 1997: *m* 1956, Edith Mary (Molly), da of Michael Loughran.

Address – c/o House of Lords, Westminster, SW1A 0PW. *Clubs* – Reform, Garrick, Pratt's.

Hatton, Finch, family name of Earl of Winchilsea.

HAVERS, BARONY OF (Havers) (Extinct 1992)

SONS LIVING OF LIFE BARON

Hon Philip, QC, *b* 1950; *ed* Eton, and Corpus Christi Coll, Camb; barrister-at-law; QC 1995; Recorder SE Circuit since 1997: *m* 1976, Patricia Frances, da of Sidney Alexander Searle, of Tideways, Old Bosham, Chichester, and has issue living, Daniel Alexander, *b* 1981, Holly Linnell, *b* 1978. *Club* – Garrick.

Hon Nigel, *b* 1951; actor: *m* 1st, 1974 (*m diss* 1989), Carolyn Gillian, da of Vincent Cox; 2ndly, 1989, Mrs Polly Bloomfield, da of late Hugh Williams, and has issue living (by 1st *m*), Katharine, *b* 1977. *Residence* – 125 Gloucester Rd, SW7.

WIDOW LIVING OF LIFE BARON

CAROL ELIZABETH, da of Stuart Lay, of London: *m* 1st, 1949, Baron Havers, PC, QC (Life Baron), who *d* 1992; 2ndly, 1993, Charles Frederick Hughesdon, AFC, of Leckhampstead House, Leckhampstead, nr Reading, Berks RG16 8QH.

HAWARDEN, VISCOUNT (Maude) (Viscount I 1793, Bt I 1705)
(Name pronounced "Haywarden")

Safe by manliness

(ROBERT) CONNAN WYNDHAM LESLIE MAUDE, 9th Viscount, and 11th Baronet; *b* 23 May 1961; *s* 1991; *ed* St Edmund's Sch, Canterbury, and RAC Cirencester: *m* 1995, Judith Anne, yst da of John Bates, of Upton Wood, Shepherdswell, Kent, and has issue.

Arms – Quarterly: 1st and 4th azure, a lion rampant argent, *Maude*; 2nd and 3rd argent, three bars gemelles sable, over all a lion rampant gules, charged on the shoulder with a cross-crosslet fitchée or. **Crest** – A lion's jamb erased erect proper, grasping a sprig of oak leaves slipped vert. **Supporters** – Two lions gules, each charged on the shoulder with a cross-crosslet fitchée or.
Seat – Wingham Court, nr Canterbury. *Residence* – Great Bossington Farm House, Adisham, Canterbury, Kent CT3 3LN.

SON LIVING

Hon VARIAN JOHN CONNAN EUSTACE, *b* 1 Sept 1997.

BROTHER LIVING

Hon Thomas Patrick Cornwallis, *b* 1964; *ed* Rudolph Steiner Sch, nr Canterbury, and Hadlow Agric Coll: *m* 1998, Christine Lydia, da of Henry Stowe. *Residence* – Cedar Lodge, Wingham Court, nr Canterbury, Kent.

SISTER LIVING

Hon Sophia-Rose Eileen, *b* 1959: *m* 1982, Timothy Michael Steel, only son of Anthony Steel, of Rock House Farm, Lower Froyle, Alton, Hants, and has issue living, Anthony Nicholas Robert, *b* 1988, — Isabella Ann Augusta, *b* 1984, — Emily Susannah Letitia, *b* 1992, — Oriel Sophia Rosamund, *b* 1995. *Residence* – Norton Court, Teynham, Sittingbourne, Kent ME9 9JU.

UNCLE LIVING (*son of 7th Viscount*)

Hon Henry Cornwallis, *b* 1928; *ed* Marlborough, and Worcester Coll, Oxford (BA 1953, MA 1957); co-patron of five livings; High Sheriff Kent 1989; 1939-45 War with Queen's R Regt, and as Sergeant Educational Corps: *m* 1964, Elizabeth Georgina, only da of David McNaught Lockie, of Grasse, France, and has issue living, Francis Hugh Cornwallis, *b* 1966; *ed* Eton, and Clare Coll, Camb (BA 1988, MA 1992); RIBA: *m* 1994, Caroline, only da of Lt-Cdr Donald Aish, of Dorchester, Dorset, — Anthony Eustace David, *b* 1972; *ed* Winchester, and Collingwood Coll, Durham (BA 1993), — Elizabeth Arabella Marion, *b* 1967; *ed* Benenden: *m* 1993, Andrei Majidian, eldest son of Jalil Majidian, of Sari, Iran, — Diana Caroline Alice, *b* 1971; *ed* West Heath. *Residence* – Sparrow Court, Kingsdown, Deal, Kent CT14 8DP.

AUNT LIVING (*daughter of 7th Viscount*)

Hon Helen Margaretta, *b* 1921: *m* 1947 (Walter) Peter Baxter, who *d* 1977, and has issue living, Charles Peter, *b* 1950; *ed* Marlborough: *m* 1974, Nicola Caroline, 2nd da of late Maj N. S. John, of Warminster, Wilts, — Joanna Rosamond, *b* 1948: *m* 1970, Michael George Patrick Falkiner, of Downclose Stud, N Perrott, Crewkerne, Som (*see* Falkiner, Bt), — Margaretta Helena, *b* 1954: *m* 1983, John Giles Mansfield, son of Cyril Peter Mansfield, of Kiambu, Kenya, — Victoria Marion, *b* 1956: *m* 1st, 1977 (*m diss* 1985), Brian John Blundy; 2ndly, 1986, William Stephen Cadman, of Woodhouse Cross, Gillingham, Dorset. *Residence* – Stourbridge House, Milton-on-Stour, Gillingham, Dorset.

WIDOW LIVING OF EIGHTH VISCOUNT

SUSANNAH CAROLINE HYDE (*Dowager Viscountess Hawarden*), da of late Maj Charles Phillips Gardner (*see* By Gardner, colls): *m* 1957, the 8th Viscount Hawarden, who *d* 1991. *Residence* – Old Chicken House, Wingham Court, Canterbury, Kent CT3 1BB.

COLLATERAL BRANCHES LIVING

Grandchildren of late Cdr Eustace Downman Maude, RN, 2nd son of late Lt-Col Sir George Ashley Maude, KCB, 2nd son of late Rev Hon John Charles Maude, 5th son of 1st Viscount:—
  Issue of late George Ashley Maude, *b* 1889, *d* 1973: *m* 1921, Ruth, who *d* 1984, da of Cdr M. Updegraff, US Navy:—
George Ashley (10137, W Saanich Rd, Sidney, BC, Canada), *b* 1925: *m* 1952, Nancy Mary, da of John Ingvard Reitan, and has issue living, Anthony John Ashley, *b* 1954: *m* 1st, 1978 (*m diss* 1980), Gale Victoria, da of Lt-Cdr Sydney Dalton Bryant, RCN; 2ndly, 1982, Sharyl, da of William Edward Rusk, and has an adopted son, David Andrew *b* 19—, — Christopher George, *b* 1957: *m* 1982, Pamela May, da of Leonard Lang, and has issue living, Curtiss John Ashley *b* 1984, Glenn Douglas George *b* 1989, — David Philip, *b* 1964. —— Alison Beauclerk, *b* 1923.

Granddaughters of late Lt-Col Aubrey Maurice Maude, 4th son of late Lt-Col Sir George Ashley Maude, KCB (ante):—

Issue of late Brig Christian George Maude, DSO, OBE, MC, *b* 1884, *d* 1971: *m* 1st, 1920 (*m diss* 1930), Hon Patience Kemp, who *d* 1935, da of 1st Baron Rochdale; 2ndly, 1931, Hester Joan, who *d* 1993, da of late Charles Augustus Egerton, of Mountfield Court, Robertsbridge, Sussex:—
(By 2nd *m*) Gillian Mabelle Beauclerk, *b* 1932: *m* 1st, 1960, Maj Estcourt Richard Cresswell, MC, MA 15th/19th King's R Hussars, who *d* 1983; 2ndly, 1984, John Anthony David Lord, son of late Lt-Col John Arthur Lord, of Saintbury Close, Broadway, Worcs. *Residence* – Four Wells, Lower Slaughter, Cheltenham, Glos. —— Priscilla Douglas, *b* 1934: *m* 1962, Michael Frederick Tremain Maude (infra). —— Elizabeth Joan, *b* 1940: *m* 1st, 1967, Capt Christopher Evelyn Twiston-Davies, late 4th/7th R Dragoon Gds, who *d* 1980, son of late Sir Leonard Twiston-Davies, KBE, of Rockfield Park, Monmouth; 2ndly, (June) 1992, Malcolm Allinson Anson, who *d* (Aug) 1992, son of late Sir (George) Wilfrid Anson, MBE, MC, of West Hay, Wrington, Bristol, and has issue living (by 1st *m*), William Ashley Christopher, *b* 1969; *ed* Radley, and RAC Cirencester, — Benjamin James, *b* 1971; *ed* Radley, and St Andrews Univ. *Residence* – Drax House, Tilshead, Salisbury, Wilts.

Granddaughter of late Brig Christian George Maude, DSO, OBE, MC (ante):—
Issue of late Capt Peter George Egerton Maude, *b* 1926, *k* in the Manchester air accident 1957: *m* 1952, Olivia Elizabeth (who *m* 2ndly, 1961, Brig Hugh Marlborough Hale Ley, CBE, DL, of The Dower House, Burrow, via Carnforth, Lancs, LA6 2RJ), el da of Lt-Col Hugh O. Wright, of Melling, Carnforth, Lancs:—
Sarah Patience, *b* 1954.

Grandson of late Christopher Hugh Maude, 3rd son of late Maurice Ceely Maude, 3rd son of Rev Hon John Charles Maude, 5th son of 1st Viscount:—
Issue of late Capt Maurice Christopher Maude, KRRC, *b* 1925, *d* 1997: *m* 1st, 1954 (*m diss* 1963), Venetia, da of William Patterson Doyle, of Kuwait, 2ndly, 1967 (*m diss* 19—), Susan Frances, da of George Lepper, of Blacknest, Alton, Hants:—
(By 2nd *m*) Christopher George, *b* 1969; Nat Hunt jockey: *m* 199—, Clare Catherine (Dolly), da of Edward Pegna, of Wick St, Gloucester, and has issue living, William George, *b* 1997. *Residence* – The Old Post Office, Snowshill, Broadway, Worcs.

Grandchildren of Lt-Gen Sir Frederick Stanley Maude, KCB, CMG, DSO, son of Gen Sir Frederick Francis Maude, VC, GCB, 4th son of Rev Hon John Charles Maude (ante):—
Issue of late Brig Edward Frederick Maude, OBE, *b* 1897, *d* 1984: *m* 1929, Sylvia, who *d* 1987, da of Robert Brewster, of New York, USA:—
Michael Frederick Tremain (Manor Farm, W Overton, Marlborough, Wiltshire SN8 4ER), *b* 1935: *m* 1962, Priscilla Douglas, da of late Brig Christian George Maude, DSO, OBE, MC (ante), and has issue living, Rupert Frederick, *b* 1965: *m* 1997, Silvia, yr da of Alejandro Lacorcel Ruiz, of Murcia, Spain, — Andrew Tremain, *b* 1967, — Alexandra, *b* 1963: *m* 1993, Maj James Nicholas John Gray, late 3rd Queen's Dragoon Gds, son of Col Nicholas Gray, RA, of Yalding, Kent, and has issue living, Maximillian Oliver Arthur *b* 1997, — Victoria, *b* 1970. —— Eileen FOSTER (621 Pleasant St, Boulder, Colorado 80302, USA), *b* 1931; assumed by deed poll the surname of Foster 1959 for herself and her issue: *m* 1954, Lloyd George, who *d* 1974, and has issue living, Lloyd Edward, *b* 1955: *m* 1994, Tina McCammack, and has issue living, Joshua Robin *b* 1995, — Robert Douglas, *b* 1957: *m* 1981, Virginia Huffman, and has issue living, Robert David *b* 1981, Jennifer *b* 1985, — Ronald Wayne, *b* 1957: *m* 1987, Audrey Poage, and has issue living, Richard *b* 1986, Renée *b* 1987, — Michael Daniel, *b* 1959: *m* 1984, Christine Oberholzer, and has issue living, Daniel George *b* 1987, Laura Elizabeth *b* 1986, — Laura Ellen, *b* 1956: *m* 1982, John Grace, and has issue living, Matthew Eric *b* 1984, Jeremy Colin *b* 1986. —— Barbara (52 Cornwall Gdns, SW7 4BG), *b* 1932: *m* 1958 (*m diss* 1988), William Clarkson Marshall, and has issue living, Thomas Alan, *b* 1963, — Cynthia, *b* 1959.

Granddaughter of late Cyril Francis Maude, actor-manager, eldest son of Capt Charles Henry Maude, 2nd son of Capt Hon Francis Maude, RN, 6th son of 1st Viscount:—
Issue of late His Honour Judge John Cyril Maude, QC, *b* 1901, *d* 1986: *m* 1st, 1927 (*m diss* 1954), Rosamund Willing, da of Dr T. Morris Murray, of 21 Marlborough St, Boston, USA; 2ndly, 1955, Maureen Constance (BUCHANAN), who *d* 1998, da of late Hon Arthur Ernest Guinness (*see* E Iveagh, colls, 1995 Edn), and widow of 4th Marquess of Dufferin and Ava:—
(By 1st *m*) Anne Murray, *b* 1929: *m* 1950, Michael Hilary George Bradstock, of Whitefold, Clunas, Nairn IV12 5UT, and has issue living, James Michael Murray, *b* 1951, — Rupert John (The Old Rectory, West Woodhay, Newbury, Berks RG20 0BL), *b* 1958: *m* 1987, Anna L., yr da of Maj John Riley, of Trinity Manor, Jersey, CI, and has issue living, James Rupert *b* 1993, Camilla Rose *b* 1996, — Alastair George (14 Dawson Place, W2 4TJ), *b* 1961: *m* 1994, Helen Katharine, da of Michael Shaw-Stewart (*see* Shaw-Stewart, Bt, colls), and has issue living, Isabella Mary Stewart *b* 1998, — Sarah Anne (*Hon Mrs David R. Gilmour*), *b* 1954: *m* 1975, Hon David Robert Gilmour, of 27 Ann St, Edinburgh EH4 1PL, eldest son of Baron Gilmour of Craigmillar, PC (Life Baron), and has issue (see that title).

Grandchildren of late Alwyn Julian Maude, 4th son of late Capt Charles Henry Maude (ante):—
Issue of late Dr Dudley Jack Maude, *b* 1897, *d* 1988: *m* 1925, Marcia, da of late John Williamson, solicitor, of Sydney, NSW:—
John Alwyn (Lynton, 618 Argyle St, Moss Vale, NSW 2577, Australia), *b* 1930: *m* 1955, Susan Theresa Gidley, da of George Gidley King, of Sydney, NSW, and has issue living, John Philip Cornwallis, *b* 1959: *m* 1986 (*m diss* 1991), Helen Tatt, and has issue living, Angela *b* 1989, — Lisa Margaret, *b* 1960: *m* 1984, Martin James Bryant, and has issue living, Maximillian Quentin Hugh *b* 1985, Oscar Charles Rowsell *b* 1987, Leopold George Roy *b* 1989, — Jessica Mary, *b* 1970. —— Jacqueline Mary, *b* 1927: *m* 1956, Llewellyn Daniel Wheeler, Surg, of 124 Ruthven St, Bondi Junction, NSW 2022, and has issue living, Andrew John, *b* 1957: *m* 1st, 1982 (*m diss* 1989), Louise Flna, da of Denis V. Hansen, of Carlingbah, NSW; 2ndly, 1991, Anne Margaret, da of John Verschuer, and has issue living (by 2nd *m*), Georgiana Rhiannon *b* 1992, — Daniel Julian, *b* 1959: *m* 1982, Michele Anne, da of L. Bruce Harper, of Pacific Hill, Dubbo, NSW, and has issue living, Rachel Ellen *b* 1989, Fallon Elizabeth *b* 1990, — Frances Llewellyn Maude, *b* 1961: *m* 1988, Andrew Philip Dudman, and has issue living, Phillip John *b* 1995, Alastair James *b* 1997.

Grandchildren of late Capt Charles Henry Maude (ante):—
Issue of late Maurice Douglas Maude, *b* 1868, *d* 1953: *m* 1906, Zima Irene Lily, who *d* 1952, da of John Godfrey Koch, FSL, formerly Assit Sup of Surveys, Perak, Malaya:—
Valerie Blanche, *b* 1908: *m* 1939, John Chichester Longhurst, who *d* 1957. —— Cicely, *b* 1918: *m* 1948, Roland Cumberbatch, MB, of Middle Farm House, Sutton, Ditcheat, Shepton-Mallet, Somerset, and has issue living, Toby John, *b* 1949, — Judith Mary, 1952, — Hyacinth Anne, *b* 1954.

Issue of late Major Ralph Walter Maude, DSO, *b* 1873, *d* 1922: *m* 1905 (*m diss* 1915), Alice, only da of Noël Hereford Thomson, of Dinan, France:—

†*Rev* (Ralph) Henry Evelyn, *b* 1909; *ed* St Peter's Hall, Oxford (MA): *m* 1933, Marjorie Cecilia Emily, who *d* 1998, da of late Rev Philip Harold Rogers, and *d* 1999, leaving issue, Roger Philip (School Cottage, School Lane, Ockham, nr Ripley, Surrey), *b* 1937: *m* 1972, Penelope Joy, da of late Christopher Rowe, Solicitor, and has issue living, Peter Timothy Daniel *b* 1975, Polly Emma Frances *b* 1978, — (Rachel) Anne, *b* 1934: *m* 1964, John Donald Cullum, of 17 Gloucester Tops Rd, Gloucester, NSW 2422, Australia, and has issue living, Simon Richard *b* 1967: *m* 1994, Kalina Yacef (and has issue living, Nathan David *b* 1998), Joanna Margaret *b* 1969.

PREDECESSORS – **(1)** ROBERT Maude, MP for Gowran 1703, St Canice 1715, and Bangor 1729, was *cr* a *Baronet* 1705; *d* 1750; *s* by his el son **(2)** *Sir* THOMAS, 2nd Bt, MP for co Tipperary 1761; *cr Baron de Montalt*, of Hawarden, co Tipperary (peerage of Ireland) 1776; *d* 1777, when the barony expired and the baronetcy devolved upon his brother **(3)** *Sir* CORNWALLIS, 3rd Bt, MP for Roscommon; *cr Baron de Montalt*, of Hawarden, co Tipperary (peerage of Ireland) 1785, and *Viscount Hawarden* (peerage of Ireland) 1793; *d* 1808; *s* by his el son **(4)** THOMAS RALPH, 2nd Viscount; *d* 1807, without issue; *s* by his half-brother **(5)** CORNWALLIS, 3rd Viscount; *b* 1780; *m* 1811, Jane, who *d* 1852, da of Patrick Crawford Bruce, of Taplow Lodge, Bucks; *d* 1856; *s* by his son **(6)** CORNWALLIS, 4th Viscount; *b* 1817; a Lord-in-Waiting to Queen Victoria 1866-8 and 1874-80; *cr Earl de Montalt*, of Dundrum, co Tipperary (peerage of United Kingdom) 1886: *m* 1845, Clementina, who *d* 1865, el da and co-heir of late Adm Hon Charles Elphinstone-Fleeming; *d* 1905, when the Earldom of De Montalt became ext, and he was *s* in the other honours by his cousin **(7)** ROBERT HENRY (son of late Very Rev Hon Robert William Henry Maude, Dean of Clogher, 2nd son of 1st Viscount), 5th Viscount, *b* 1842: *m* 1881, Caroline, who *d* 1930, da of late Major Arthur Ogle; *d* 1908; *s* by his son **(8)** ROBERT CORNWALLIS, 6th Viscount, *b* 1890; Lieut Coldstream Guards; *ka* 1914; *s* by his cousin **(9)** EUSTACE WYNDHAM (son of late Ludlow Eustace Maude, son of late Very Rev Hon Robert William Henry Maude, 2nd son of 1st Viscount), 7th Viscount; *b* 1877; Major (ret) Queen's Roy Regt: *m* 1920, Marion, who *d* 1974, da of late Albert Leslie Wright (B Fitzwalter); *d* 1958; *s* by his el son **(10)** ROBERT LESLIE EUSTACE, 8th Viscount, *b* 1926; European War 1945 in Coldstream Guards (invalided): *m* 1957, Susannah Caroline Hyde, da of late Maj Charles Phillips Gardner (*see* By Gardner, colls); *d* 1991; *s* by his elder son **(11)** (ROBERT) CONNAN WYNDHAM LESLIE, 9th Viscount and present peer; also Baron de Montalt.

HAWKE, BARON (Hawke) (Baron GB 1776)

EDWARD GEORGE HAWKE, TD, 11th Baron; *b* 25 Jan 1950; *s* 1992; *ed* Eton; 1st Bn Coldstream Gds 1970-73, The Queen's Own Yeo 1973-93; Hon Col Cheshire Yeo since 1998; FRICS: *m* 1993, Bronwen M., da of William T. James, BVMS, MRCVS, and has issue.

𝔄rms – Argent, a chevron erminois, between three pilgrims' staves purpure. 𝔠rest – A hawk rising ermine, belled, and charged on the breast with a fleur-de-lis or. 𝔖upporters – *Dexter*, a figure of Neptune, his mantle vert, edged argent, crowned with an eastern crown or, his dexter arm erect and holding in the act of striking, a trident sable, point downwards silver, and resting his left foot on a dolphin proper; *sinister*, a sea horse or, holding between the fore fins a banner argent, the staff broken sable.

SON LIVING

Hon WILLIAM MARTIN THEODORE, *b* 23 June 1995.

DAUGHTER LIVING

Hon Alice Julia, *b* 1999.

SISTERS LIVING AND DECEASED

Hon Nichola Frances, *b* 1949: *m* 1981, Hon Jonathan Andrew Forbes, and has issue (*see* L Forbes). *Residence* – East Cevidley, Alford, Aberdeenshire AB33 8BH.

Hon Vanessa Nathalie Mary, *b* 1957: *m* 1985, (Peter) Adam William Brodie, yst son of late Maj-Gen Thomas Brodie, CB, CBE, DSO, of Green Ball, Crawley Ridge, Camberley, Surrey, and has issue living, Nathalie Jane, *b* 1986, — Elizabeth Sarah, *b* 1989. *Residence* – Brook Farm, Eglwys Cross, Whitchurch, Shropshire SY13 2JT.

Hon Julia Georgette, *b* 1960; missing presumed drowned, 1997, Galapagos Is.

HALF-SISTERS LIVING

Hon Sarah Elizabeth Jane, *b* 1935: *m* 1957, John Norris Fennell, elder son of late Col Harold Percival Fennell, and has issue living, Adrian Martin Alexander (Van Hall Laan 34, 1412 CT Naarden, The Netherlands), *b* 1963: *m* 1990, Anna Meriel, da of William John Gowing, of Buxton, Norfolk, and has issue living, Alexander Theo Felix *b* 1993, — Olivia Louise (*Hon Mrs Martin Hunt*), *b* 1961: *m* 1993, Hon Martin John Hunt, yr son of Baron Hunt of Tanworth, GCB (Life Baron). *Residence* – 31 Summers St, Lostwithiel, Cornwall PL22 0DH.

Hon Catherine Mary, *b* 1940: *m* 1963, Charles Groves Darville Brook, MD, FRCP, yst son of late Air Vice-Marshal William Arthur Darville Brook, CB, CBE, and has issue living, Charlotte Griselda Mary, *b* 1965: *m* 1995, Peter D. Nissenbaum, son of Roger Nissenbaum, of Ottawa, Canada, and has issue living, Jonah Charles *b* 1997, — Henrietta Diana Darville, *b* 1968: *m* 1994, James W. B. Bainbridge, son of late John Bainbridge, of Ash, Kent, and has issue living, Annabel Catherine *b* 1998. *Residence* – 7 The Hermitage, Richmond, Surrey.

DAUGHTERS LIVING OF NINTH BARON

Hon Caroline Ina Maud, *b* 1937; Bar Middle Temple 1959: *m* 1960, John Francis Easton, Bar-at-law, and has issue living, Nicholas John, *b* 1961, — Ina Frances, *b* 1964: *m* 1988, Vincent L. Nelson, son of S. A. Nelson of Black River, Mandeville, Jamaica, and has issue living, Oliver John *b* 1989, Edward Simeon *b* 1994, Saffron *b* 1992. *Residence* – The Old Hall, Barley, nr Royston, Herts.

Hon Annabel, *b* 1940: *m* 1961, (Nicholas) Adam Ridley, and has issue living, Caspar Hawke Michael, *b* 1967: *m* 1997, Rebecca M., elder da of Paul Dallyn, of Gillingham, Dorset, and has issue living, Sophie Mary *b* 1998, — Celia Kirstin, *b* 1964: *m* 1991, Nicholas John Willis, yr son of Dr Peter Willis, of Stillington, Yorks, and has issue living, Jack Michael *b* 1997, — Harriet Clare, *b* 1970. *Residence* – 29 Richmond Hill, Richmond, Surrey.

Hon Cecilia Anne (*Hon Lady Scott*), *b* 1943: *m* 1st, 1963 (*m diss* 1971), Peter Hannay Bailey Tapsell, MP (later Sir Peter Tapsell); 2ndly, 1979, Rt Hon Sir Nicholas Paul Scott, KBE, JP, MP, and has had issue (by 1st *m*) James Hawke, *b* 1966, *d* 1985, — (by 2nd *m*) Patrick Martin Iain, *b* 1982, — Amber Teresa, *b* 1987.

Hon Lavinia Mary, JP, *b* 1945: *m* 1965, Maj Nicholas Maclean Verity Maclean-Bristol, OBE, DL, of Breacachadh Castle, Isle of Coll, Argyll, and has issue living, Charles Bladen, *b* 1967; KOSB (ret): *m* 1997, Kim E., da of R. S. Rowland, of Tatsfield, Surrey, — Alexander Stanhope, *b* 1970: *m* 1998, Seonaid, da of Ian Lochhead, of Malta, — Lauchlan Neil, *b* 1974.

Hon Rowena Margaret, *b* 1948; a Lady in Waiting to HRH Princess Michael of Kent: *m* 1st, 1971, Philip William Leatham (*see* By Buckland, 1976, Edn); 2ndly, 1990, William T. Sanders, of Hankerton Priory, nr Malmesbury, Wilts SN16 9JZ, and has issue living (by 1st *m*), Patrick Hawke, *b* 1974, — Frederick Bladen, *b* 1981, — Arabella Rose, *b* 1976.

Hon Prunella Jane Alice *b* 1951: *m* 1976, Albert Hendrik Servatius, of Van Alkemadelaan 354, 2597 As Den Haag, Netherlands, and has issue living, Timothy, *b* 1979, — Julian, *b* 1982.

Hon Olivia Mary, *b* 1955: *m* 1983, Timothy John Pethybridge, of 64 Hendham Rd, SW17 7DQ, only son of J. H. Pethybridge, of Barn Park, Bodmin, Cornwall, and has issue living, Henry John Hawke, *b* 1989, — Mary-Rose Olivia, *b* 1985, — Flora Louise, *b* 1987.

WIDOW LIVING OF NINTH BARON

INA MARY FAURE (*Dowager Baroness Hawke*), da of late Henry Faure Walker, of Highley Manor, Balcombe, Sussex: *m* 1934, the 9th Baron Hawke, who *d* 1985. *Residence* – Faygate Place, Faygate, Sussex.

WIDOW LIVING OF TENTH BARON

GEORGETTE MARGARET (*Georgette, Baroness Hawke*), da of late George S. Davidson, of 73 Eaton Sq, SW1: *m* 1947, as his 2nd wife, the 10th Baron Hawke, who *d* 1992. *Residence* – Old Mill House, Cuddington, Northwich, Cheshire CW8 2TA.

PREDECESSORS – (1) *Adm Sir* EDWARD HAWKE, KCB, son of late Edward Hawke, Bar-at-law, of Lincoln's Inn; *b* 1710; a celebrated Naval commander; signally defeated the French off Bellisle 1759 (thanked by Parliament, rewarded with a pension of 2,000 a year); was First Lord of the Admiralty 1766-71; *cr Baron Hawke*, of Towton, co York (peerage of Great Britain), 1776: *d* 1781; *s* by his son (2) MARTIN BLADEN, LLD, 2nd Baron; *d* 1805; *s* by his son (3) EDWARD, 3rd Baron; assumed the additional surname of Harvey; *d* 1824; *s* by his el son (4) EDWARD WILLIAM, 4th Baron; *d* 1867; *s* by his brother (5) STANHOPE, 5th Baron; *d* unmarried 1870; *s* by his cousin (6) *Rev* EDWARD HENRY JULIUS, 6th Baron, son of late Hon Martin Bladen Edward, 2nd son of 2nd Baron, by Hannah, da of Thomas Nisbet, of Mersington, *b* 1815; *m* 1857, Jane, who *d* 1915, da of late Henry Dowker, of Laysthorpe, York; *d* 1887; *s* by his son (7) MARTIN BLADEN, 7th Baron, *b* 1860: *m* 1916, Maude, who *d* 1936, da of late William Peacock Edwards, JP, and widow of Arthur Graham Cross; *d* 1938; *s* by his brother (8) EDWARD JULIAN, 8th Baron; *b* 1873: *m* 1900, Frances Alice, who *d* 1959, da of late Col John Randal Wilmer, Indian Army; *d* 1939; *s* by his son (9) BLADEN WILMER, 9th Baron, *b* 1901; a Lord-in-Waiting to HM 1953-57 and a Church Commr 1958-74: *m* 1934, Ina Mary Faure, da of late Henry Faure Walker, of Highley Manor, Balcombe, Sussex; *d* 1985; *s* by his brother (10) (JULIAN STANHOPE) THEODORE, 10th Baron; *b* 1904; S/Ldr Auxiliary Air Force: *m* 1st, 1933 (*m diss* 1946), Angela Margaret Griselda, who *d* 1984, da of late Capt Edmund William Bury; 2ndly, 1947, Georgette Margaret, da of late George S. Davidson, of 73 Eaton Sq, SW1; *d* 1992; *s* by his only son (11) EDWARD GEORGE, 11th Baron and present peer.

Hawkesbury, Viscount; son of Earl of Liverpool.

Hay, family name of Earl of Erroll.

Hay, family name of Earl of Kinnoull.

Hay, family name of Marquess of Tweeddale.

HAYHOE, BARON (Hayhoe) (Life Baron 1992)

BERNARD JOHN (BARNEY) HAYHOE, PC, son of late Frank Stanley Hayhoe; *b* 8 Aug 1925; *ed* Borough Poly; Conservative Research Dept (Head of Research Section) 1965-70, PPS to Lord Pres and Leader of House of Commons 1972-74, Opposition Spokesman on Employment 1974-79, Parly Under Sec of State for Defence (Army) 1979-81; Min of State for Civil Service 1981, Treasury 1981-85, and Health 1985-86; Gov Birkbeck Coll 1976-79; Chm The Hansard Soc 1990-94; MP Heston and Isleworth (*C*) 1970-74, Hounslow, Brentford and Isleworth 1974-92; *cr* PC 1985, Kt Bach 1987, and *Baron Hayhoe*, of Isleworth in the London Borough of Hounslow (Life Baron) 1992: *m* 1962, Ann Gascoigne, da of late Bernard W. Thornton, and has issue.

Residence – 20 Wool Rd, SW20 0HW. *Club* – Garrick.

SONS LIVING

Hon Crispin Bernard Gascoigne, *b* 1963.
Hon Dominic Adam Scott, *b* 1965.

DAUGHTER LIVING

Hon Sarah Anne Sherwood, *b* 1967.

HAYMAN, BARONESS (Hayman) (Life Baroness 1995)

HELENE VALERIE HAYMAN, da of late Maurice Middleweek, of Wolverhampton; *b* 26 March 1949; *ed* Wolverhampton Girls' High Sch, and Newnham Coll, Camb (MA 1971); Pres of Cambridge Union 1969; worked with Shelter, Nat Campaign for the Homeless, and Camden Social Services Dept; MP for Welwyn and Hatfield (*Lab*) 1974-79; Vice-Chm Bloomsbury Health Authority 1988-90, Bloomsbury and Islington Health Authority 1991-92, Chm Whittington Hospital NHS Trust 1992-97; Parly Under Sec of State Dept of Environment and Transport 1997-98, since when Under Sec of State Health Dept; *cr Baroness Hayman*, of Dartmouth Park, in the London Borough of Camden (Life Baroness) 1995: *m* 1974, Martin Hayman, son of late Ronald Hayman, of Cadgwith, Cornwall, and has issue.

Address – c/o House of Lords, SW1A 0PW.

Hon Ben, *b* 1976; *ed* William Ellis Sch.
Hon Joseph, *b* 1980; *ed* William Ellis Sch.
Hon Jacob, *b* 1982; *ed* William Ellis Sch.
Hon David, *b* 1985; *ed* William Ellis, Sch.

HAYTER, BARON (Chubb) (Baron UK 1927, Bt UK 1900)

Safe by being cautious

GEORGE CHARLES HAYTER CHUBB, KCVO, CBE, 3rd Baron, and 3rd Baronet; *b* 25 April 1911; *s* 1967; *ed* Leys Sch, and Trin Coll, Camb (MA); Chm of Chubb & Son's Lock & Safe Co Ltd; CBE (Civil) 1976, KCVO 1977: *m* 1940, Elizabeth Anne, MBE, only da of late Thomas Arthur Rumbold (*see* Rumbold, Bt, colls), and has issue.

Arms – Quarterly: 1st and 4th azure, a cross erminois between in first and fourth quarters a bezant and in second and third quarters a rose or, *Chubb*, 2nd and 3rd azure, a chevron between two bulls' heads couped in chief, and in base an escallop all or, *Hayter*. Crest – In front of a demi lion rampant azure supporting between the paws a bezant charged with a rose gules, a key fesswise wards upwards or. Supporters – On either side a lion azure, holding in the mouth a rose gules, barbed seeded, leaved and slipped proper, and charged on the shoulder with a key pale-wise wards downwards and to the dexter or
Residence – Ashtead House, Ashtead, Surrey.

SONS LIVING

Hon GEORGE WILLIAM MICHAEL (Rookery Cottage, Monk Sherborne, Hants RG26 5HS), *b* 9 Oct 1943; *ed* Marlborough and Nottingham Univ (BSc): *m* 1983, Waltraud, yr da of J. Flackl, of Sydney, Australia, and has issue living, Thomas Frederik Flackl, *b* 23 July 1986.

Hon John Andrew (Manor Farm House, Warborough, Oxon), *b* 1946; *ed* Marlborough and Southampton Univ; FCA: *m* 1975, Sandy, only da of late Alfred E. Brereton, of London, and has issue living, Alfred, *b* 1977, — Georgia, *b* 1978.

Hon Charles Henry Thomas (32 Park Town, Oxford OX2 6SJ), *b* 1949; *ed* Marlborough, and King's Coll, Camb (MA 1974); MB BS (Barts 1978), MRCGP: *m* 1979, (Ann) Nicola, MB BS, da of late Charles William Stewart French Manning, FRCS, of Moor Lane House, Sarratt, Herts, and has issue living, (Mark) Henry, *b* 1980, — Jack Charles, *b* 1985, — Josephine Anne, *b* 1983, — Alice Christine, *b* 1989.

DAUGHTER LIVING

Hon Sarah, *b* 1941: *m* 1963, Rev David Humphrey Clark, and has issue living, Andrew David, *b* 1964, — Alison Tamsen, *b* 1967, — and two adopted children, Simon William, *b* 1968, — Katherine Mary, *b* 1970.

WIDOW LIVING OF SON OF SECOND BARON

Veronica, da of William Clifton, of Shanghai: *m* 1939, Cmdr Hon David William Early Chubb, RN, who *d* 1993, and has issue (see colls, infra). *Residence* – St Mary's Cottage, Broughton, Hants.

COLLATERAL BRANCH LIVING

Issue of late Cmdr Hon David William Early Chubb, RN, yr son of 2nd Baron, *b* 1914, *d* 1993: *m* 1939, Veronica (ante), da of William Clifton, of Shanghai:—
Jeremy David Knyvett, *b* 1941; *ed* Sherborne: *m* 1978, Mrs Valerie Anne Evans, yst da of H. J. Wightman, and has issue living, Patrick David, *b* 1980, — Andrew Harry, *b* 1982.

PREDECESSORS – GEORGE HAYTER Chubb, 2nd son of late John Chubb; *b* 1848; a lock and safe manufacturer: *m* 1870, Sarah Vanner, who *d* 1940, da of late Charles Early, JP, of Witney, Oxon: *cr* a Baronet 1900, and *Baron Hayter*, of Chislehurst, co Kent (peerage of United Kingdom) 1927; *d* 1946; *s* by his son (2) CHARLES ARCHIBALD, 2nd Baron, *b* 1871; Managing Dir of Chubb & Sons Lock & Safe Co Ltd: *m* 1st, 1898, Mary, who *d* 1948, el da of John F. Haworth, JP, of Manchester; 2ndly, 1949, Margaret Alison, who *d* 1986, da of J. G. Pickard, of Leicester; *d* 1967; *s* by his el son (3) GEORGE CHARLES HAYTER, 3rd Baron and present peer.

HAZLERIGG, BARON (Hazlerigg) (Baron UK 1945, Bt E 1622)

For our altars and our hearths

ARTHUR GREY HAZLERIGG, MC, 2nd Baron, and 14th Baronet; *b* 24 Feb 1910; *s* 1949; *ed* Eton, and Trin Coll, Camb (BA 1932); is a Major RA (TA), and a JP and DL; European War 1939-45 (MC): *m* 1945, Patricia, who *d* 1972, da of late John Pullar of Durban, Natal and has issue.

Arms – Argent, a chevron sable between three hazel leaves vert. Crest – Issuant from a cap of maintenance gules turned up ermine a Scot's head and shoulders couped proper. Supporters – *Dexter*, a Cromwellian Soldier holding in his exterior hand a sword point downwards; *sinister*, a Coldstream Guardsman of the seventeenth century supporting with his exterior hand by the muzzle a musket all proper.
Seat – Noseley Hall, Billesdon, Leicester LE7 9EH. *Clubs* – Army and Navy, MCC.

SON LIVING

Hon ARTHUR GREY, *b* 5 May 1951: *m* 1986 (*m diss* 1998), Laura, eldest da of Sir William Stratford Dugdale, 2nd Bt, CBE, MC, and has issue living, Arthur William Grey, *b* 13 May 1987, — Eliza Patricia, *b* 1989, — Amelia Frances, *b* (twin) 1989, — Viola Camilla Alice, *b* 1993. *Residence* – Noseley Hall, Billesdon, Leics LE7 9EH.

DAUGHTERS LIVING

Hon Angela Christine, *b* 1946: *m* 1969, Timothy Effingham MacDowel, of 22 Murrayfield Gdns, Edinburgh EH12 6DF, and has issue living, Benjamin St George, *b* 1970, — Richard Arthur *b* 1973.
Hon Priscilla Frances, *b* 1952: *m* 1975, Hon Richard Arthur Louis Dillon, and has issue (*see* V Dillon).

WIDOW LIVING OF SON OF FIRST BARON

Anne Frances Roden, eldest da of late Capt Roden Henry Victor Buxton, CBE, RN (*see* Buxton, Bt, colls), and formerly wife of Henry Winterstein Gillespie, MD: *m* 1979, as his 3rd wife, Maj the Hon Thomas Heron Hazlerigg, who *d* 1998. *Residence* – Caflida, Klosters, Switzerland.

COLLATERAL BRANCHES LIVING

Issue of late Maj the Hon Thomas Heron Hazlerigg, 2nd son of 1st Baron, *b* 1914, *d* 1998: *m* 1st, 1942 (*m diss* 1956), Audrey Cecil, who *d* in a motor accident 1994, da of late Maj Cecil Robert Bates, DSO, MC (*see* Bates, Bt, *cr* 1880); 2ndly, 1957 (*m diss* 1974), Mrs Doussa Cayzer, who *d* 1997, da of Fahmy Bey Wissa, of Remleh, Egypt; 3rdly, 1979, Mrs Anne Frances Roden Gillespie (ante), eldest da of late Capt Roden Henry Victor Buxton, CBE, RN (*see* Buxton, Bt, colls):—
(By 1st *m*) Rupert Heron (94 Elms Rd, SW4), *b* 1943; *ed* Eton: *m* 1979, Caroline, eldest da of John Burkinshaw Fitzwilliams, and formerly wife of John Hugh Chetwynd (*see* V Chetwynd, colls), and has issue living, Cecilia, *b* 1980, — Alexandra, *b* 1983. —— Simon Martival TD (128 Castelnau, SW13 9ET), *b* 1945; *ed* Eton; Maj (TA) 15th/19th The King's Royal Hussars: *m* 1984, Caroline Margaret Mary, yr da of late Edward Ahlberg, OBE, and has issue living, Antonia Margot, *b* 1985, — Alice Olivia, *b* 1987.

Issue of late Maj the Hon Robert Maynard Hazlerigg, yst son of 1st Baron, *b* 1916, *d* 1997: *m* 1942, Rose, who *d* 19—, da of Charles Cox:—
Rosemary, *b* 1942: *m* 1965, Malcolm Connell, of 18 Kenilworth Av, Wimbledon, SW19 7LW, and has issue living, Emma, *b* 1972. —— Gillian, *b* 1946: *m* 1974, Maurice Bradley, of 9 Church St, Northboro, Peterborough, and has issue living, Robert William, *b* 1987, — Jessica Mary, *b* 1988.

(*In remainder to Baronetcy only*)

Grandson of late Lt-Col Thomas Hazlerigg, DSO, 2nd (but elder surv) son of late Maj-Gen Thomas Maynard Hazlerigg (infra):—
Issue of late Lt-Col Arthur William Hazlerigg, *b* 1904, *d* 1987: *m* 1st, 1935 (*m diss* 1946), Marjorie Dorothea, da of late Col George Frederick Brown Turner, DSO, of Blackheath, SE3; 2ndly, 1947, Jane, who *d* 1977, da of late David Wilson, OBE:—
(By 1st *m*) Arthur Robert, *b* 1936; *ed* Leys Sch, and Coll of Estate Management (BSc), FRICS: Capt RHA (ret): *m* 1963, Janet Christine Hermione, only da of late Edward Simpson Anderson, MBE, of Elgin, and has issue living, Catrina Louise, *b* 1964: *m* 1992, Lars Jaeger, son of Mrs L. Ager-Harris, of Caversham, Reading, and has issue living, Charlotte Louise *b* 1996. *Residence* – Paddock Lodge, Whitchurch-on-Thames, Pangbourne, Reading, Berks RG8 7EX.

Grandchildren of late Capt Greville Hazlerigg, yst son of late Maj-Gen Thomas Maynard Hazlerigg, 2nd son of 12th Bt:—
Issue of late Capt Arthur Greville Maynard Hazlerigg, *b* 1910, *d* 1990: *m* 1941, Nancy (Downside, North St, Mere, Wilts BA12 6AZ), da of late Capt John Alexander Ingles, RN:—

(Arthur) Patrick (30 West St, Bere Regis, Dorset), *b* 1943; *ed* Milton Abbey; Maj RA (ret 1994): *m* 1973, Susan Elizabeth, da of Lt-Cmdr Patrick Kenneth Truckle, RN, and has issue living, Arthur Philip Greville, *b* 1978, — Harriet Jane, *b* 1976. —— Diana Elizabeth, *b* 1947: *m* 1971, Col Anthony Michael Thomas Moody, Royal Irish Rangers, elder son of late Maj Thomas Moody, of Omagh, co Tyrone, and has issue living, Victoria Natalie, *b* 1973, — Alexandria Jane, *b* 1976. —— Sheelagh Marion, *b* 1951: *m* 1985, Cmdr Andrew D. Bell, RN, of Firenze, Chetcombe Rd, Mere, Wilts BA12 6AZ, son of C. D. T. Bell, of Westerham, Kent, and has issue living, Georgina Hazlerigg, *b* 1986, — Natasha Hazlerigg, *b* 1988.

Granddaughter of late Rev William Greville Hazlerigg, 4th son of 12th Bt:—
Issue of late Roger Greville Hazlerigg, *b* 1877, *d* 1952: *m* 1919, Esther Rosamond, who *d* 1976, da of Lacey Nussey Everett, of Rushmere Lodge, Pool, nr Leeds:—
Jean Mary, *b* 1921: *m* 1947, Major Kenneth Leonard Perrin. *Residence* – The Old Rectory, Great Comberton, nr Pershore, Worcestershire.

Grandson of late Allen Martival Hazlerigg, yst son of 12th Baronet:—
Issue of late Martival Grey Hazlerigg, *b* 1884, *d* 1971: *m* 1925, Marian (Flat 1, Craddock Court, Forest Green Nailsworth, Glos), da of late Michael Ray:—
Martival Spencer Woolf (33 Belvedere Mews, St Mary's, Chalford, Stroud, Glos GL6 8PF), *b* 1927: *m* 1947, Kitty, da of late William Johnson Bowhill, of Carhampton, Som, and has issue living, Marilyn Kay, *b* 1952: BScEng: *m* 1976, Roger Huckerby, BScEng, of 31 Bowes Rd, Walton-on-Thames KT12 3HT, — Martine Grey, *b* 1957: *m* 1977 (*m diss* 1991), Raymond Anthony Dawson, MScEng.

Grandchildren (by 1st *m*) of late Grey Hazlerigg, OBE (infra):—
Issue of late Herbert William Grey Hazlerigg, *b* 1910, *d* 1991: *m* 1937, Gladys Margaret (37 Barrhill Av, Brighton BN1 8UE), da of David Alan Knighton, of Ealing:—
Alexander David Grey, *b* 1939; BSc, PhD: *m* 1961, Rosemary, el da of Leslie Clarence Ottewill, and has issue living, David Grey, *b* 1967; *ed* Camb Univ (BSc, PhD), — Andrew Alexander, *b* 1969; BA. *Residence* – Glanclywedog, Staylittle, Llanbrynmair, Powys SY19 7BU. —— Alan Peter Maynard, *b* 1941; BSc. —— Arthur Richard Thomas, *b* 1945; Lt-Col Royal Logistic Corps: *m* 1st, 1967 (*m diss* 1979), Lesley —; 2ndly, 1980, Elaine Elizabeth, da of John Machey Reed, and has issue living (by 1st *m*), Nichola Michelle, *b* 1973. — (by 2nd *m*) Charles Rupert Edward, *b* 1984, — Antonia Rebecca Alexandrina, *b* 1983, — Alexandra Machey Elizabeth, *b* 1986. —— Margaret Julia, *b* 1946: *m* 1967, John David Gilbert, BSc, PhD, and has issue living, Christopher Peter, *b* 1973, — Susan Ruth, *b* 1971; RGN.

Grandchildren of late Rev Grey Hazlerigg, 3rd son of 11th baronet:—
Issue of late Grey Hazlerigg, OBE, *b* 1879, *d* 1948. *m* 1st, 1908 (*m diss* 1924), Sarah Dorothy, who *d* 1965, da of late Herbert Bakewell Whetstone, JP, formerly of Ilketshall Hall, Bungay, Suffolk; 2ndly, 1933, Fannie, who *d* 1949, widow of Frederick Hardy, late of Staunton Hall, Notts:—
(By 1st *m*) Alexander Maynard, *b* 1914; *ed* Lewes County Sch; entered Colonial Civil Ser 1935; appointed Sub-Inspector of Constabulary, Trinidad 1937. —— Dorothy Mary Louise, *b* 1912.

Granddaughter of late Arthur Hesilrige, Lieut 59th Regt, son of late Rev Charles Maynard Hesilrige, brother of 11th baronet:—
Issue of late Arthur George Maynard Hesilrige, Editor of *Debrett* 1887-1935, *b* (*posthumous*) 1863, *d* 1953: *m* 1889, Amy Florence, who *d* 1947, da of late M. S. Myers, of Thorney Hedge, High Rd Chiswick, W4:—
Violet Maynard, *b* 1900: *m* 1943, Maj George Reginald Jackson, RASC, late Reserve of Officers, who *d* 1954. *Residence* – 6 Sunstar Lane, Polegate, Sussex.

Grandson of late Thomas Greville Hesilrige, son of late Rev Charles Maynard Hesilrige (ante):—
Issue of late Thomas Greville Hesilrige, *b* 1878, *d* 1955: *m* 1st, 1901, Florence Elizabeth, who *d* 1919, da of Edwin Henry Griffiths, formerly of Mount Pleasant, Shrewsbury; 2ndly, 1921, Gertrude May, who *d* 1985, da of William Downs, formerly of Uplands, Coventry:—
(By 2nd *m*) Roger Greville, *b* 1932: *m* 1957 (*m diss* 1976), Barbara Shirley, da of Henry Edward Daniel, of 80 Manor Estate, Wolston, nr Coventry, and has issue living, Charles Greville, *b* 1958: *m* 1985, Elizabeth June Davies, and has issue living, Rebecca Lynne *b* 1987. *Residence* – 168 Rugby Rd, Binley Woods, Coventry.

PREDECESSORS – (1) THOMAS Hesilrige, son of late Thomas Hesilrige, of Noseley Hall, Leicestershie; *b* 1564; MP for Leicestershire 1614 and 1624-5 (Sheriff 1612-13; *cr* a *Baronet*, 1622: *m* 16—, Frances, who *d* 1638, da of late Sir William Gorges, of Alderton; *d* 1629); *s* by his son (2) ARTHUR, 2nd Bt; *b* 16—; MP for Leicestersire 1640-45 and for Leicester 1654-9; sometime Gov of Newcastle, during Civil War, in which he rendered signal Sers, was Col in Parliamentary Army Comdg a Regt of Cuirassiers (known as the Lobsters): *m* 1st 1625, Frances, who *d* 1632, da of late Thomas Elmes; 2ndly, 16—, Dorothy, who *d* 1650, da of late Fulke Greville, and sister of 2nd Baron Brooke (*cr* 1620); *d* (whilst a prisoner in Tower of London) 1660; *s* by his el son (3) THOMAS, 3rd Bt; *b* 1625: *m* 1664, Elizabeth, who *d* 1673, da of late George Fenwick, of Brunton Hall, Northumberland; *d* 1680; *s* by his only son (4) THOMAS, 4th Bt; *b* 1664; MP for Leicestershire 1690-95 (Sheriff 1686-7); *d* 1700; *s* by his uncle (5) ROBERT (only surviving son of 2nd Bt), 5th Bt; *b* 1640: *m* 1664, Bridget, who *d* 1697, da of late Sir Samuel Rolle, of Heanton, Devon; *d* 1713; *s* by his son (6) ROBERT, 6th Baronet; *b* 1668; Sheriff of Leicestersire 1715-16: *m* 1696, Hon Dorothy Maynard, who *d* 1740, da of 3rd Baron Maynard (*cr* 1721); *s* by his only son (7) ARTHUR, 7th Bt; *b* 17—: *m* 1725, Hannah Sturges, who *d* 1765; *d* 1763; *s* by his son (8) ROBERT, 8th Bt; *b* 17—: *m* 17—, Sarah, who *d* 17—, da of late Nathaniel Waller, of Roxburgh, New England, USA; *d* 17—; *s* by his son (9) ARTHUR, 9th Bt; *b* 17—; sometime in HEICS; *m* 1st, 17—, Elizabeth Charnaud, of Smyrna, who *d* 1797; 2ndly, 17—, Charlotte Elizabeth, who *d* 1817 (having *m* 2ndly, 1805, Capt Henry William Wilkinson), da of Capt F. E. S. Grey; *d* 1805; *s* by his uncle (10) THOMAS MAYNARD (3rd son of 7th Bt), 10th Bt; *b* 17—: *m* 1st, 1805, Mary, who *d* 1809, da of late Edmund Tyrrell, of Gipping Hall, Suffolk; 2ndly, 1811, Hon Letitia Wodehouse, who *d* 1864 (having *m* 2ndly, 1842, Frederick Fielding, Bar-at-Law), da of 1st Baron Wodehouse; *d* 1817; *s* by his nephew (11) ARTHUR GREY (el son of Col Grey Hesilrige, 5th son of 7th Bt), 11th Bt; *b* 17—; assumed by Roy licence 1818 the surname of Hazlerigg in lieu of his patronymic: *m* 1811, Henrietta Anne, who *d* 1868, da of late John Bourne, of Stanch Hall, Hants; *d* 1819; *s* by his el son (12) ARTHUR GREY, 12th Bt; *b* 1812; Sheriff of Leicestershire 1837: *m* 1835, Elizabeth, who *d* 1883, da of late Charles Allen Phillips, of St Bride's Hill, Pembrokeshire; *d* 1890; *s* by his grandson (13) ARTHUR GREY (only son of Lieut-Col Arthur Grey Hazlerigg, el son of 12th Bt), 13th Bt; *b* 1878; was Lord Lieut and Custos Rotulorum for Leicestershire (High Sheriff 1909); *cr Baron Hazlerigg*, of Noseley, co Leicester (peerage of United Kingdom) 1945: *m*

1903, Dorothy Rachel, who *d* 1972, el da of late John Henry Buxton, JP, DL, of Easneye, Ware; *d* 1949; *s* by his son **(14)** ARTHUR GREY, 2nd Baron and present peer.

HEAD, VISCOUNT (Head) (Viscount UK 1960)

RICHARD ANTONY HEAD, 2nd Viscount; *b* 27 Feb 1937; *s* 1983; *ed* Eton, and RMA Sandhurst; late Capt Life Gds; racehorse trainer 1968-83; farmer: *m* 1974, Alicia Brigid, el da of Julian John William Salmond, of The Old Manor House, Didmarton, Badminton, Avon (*see* B Lucas of Crudwell, colls), and has issue.

Arms – Sable a chevron argent between two unicorns' heads couped in chief, and in base as many arrows in saltire and filed by a ducal crown or. **Crest** – A unicorn's head couped sable armed and crined or, between two arrows erect, points downward of the last. **Supporters** – On either side a Staffordshire terrier sable gorged with a dog collar or.
Residence – Throope Manor, Bishopstone, Salisbury. *Club* – White's.

SONS LIVING

Hon HENRY JULIAN, *b* 30 March 1980.
Hon George Richard, *b* 1982.

DAUGHTER LIVING

Hon Sarah Georgiana, *b* 1984.

BROTHER LIVING

Hon Simon Andrew, *b* 1944; *ed* Eton, Ch Ch, Oxford, and Berkeley Univ, Cal, USA; assist ed *Far East Economic Review*, Hong Kong, 1966-67, correspondent *Financial Times*, SE Asia, 1970-72, New York correspondent, *New Statesman*, 1970-76, a contributor on foreign affairs to New York *Review of Books* since 1973; contested S Dorset Div for SDP-Liberal Alliance, 1983. *Residence* – 155 Cranmer Court, Sloane Av, SW3.

SISTER LIVING

Hon Teresa Mary, *b* 1938: *m* 1972 (*m diss* 1983), Richard Deacon Haddon, and has had issue, Edward Antony Deacon, *b* 1973, — Joseph Richard, *b* 1974; *d* 1994, in an accident, — Alice Mary, *b* (twin) 1974. *Residence* – The Granary, Fawler, Oxford OX7 3AH.

PREDECESSOR – ANTONY HENRY Head, GCMG, CBE, MC, PC, son of Geoffrey Head, of 51 South St, W1; *b* 1906; Brig Life Gds, Assist Sec Cttee of Imperial Defence 1940-41, GSO2, Guards Armoured Div 1942, Ch Mil Planner (Combined Operations) 1942-43, and Representative (Brig) with Directors of Plans for Amphibious Operations 1943-46; Sec of State for War Oct 1951-Oct 1956, Min of Defence Oct 1956-Jan 1957; High Commr for UK in Fed of Nigeria 1960-63, High Commr for UK in Fed of Malaysia 1963-66; MP for Carshalton Div of Surrey (C) 1945-60; *cr Viscount Head*, of Throope, co Wilts (peerage of UK) 1960: *m* 1935, Lady Dorothea Louise Ashley-Cooper, who *d* 1987, da of 9th Earl of Shaftesbury; *d* 1983; *s* by his el son **(2)** RICHARD ANTONY, 2nd Viscount and present peer.

HEADFORT, MARQUESS OF (Taylour) Sits as BARON KENLIS (UK 1831) (Marquess I 1800, Bt I 1704)
(Name pronounced 'Taylor')

He attains whatever he seeks

THOMAS GEOFFREY CHARLES MICHAEL TAYLOUR, 6th Marquess, and 9th Baronet; *b* 20 Jan 1932; *s* 1960; *ed* Stowe, and Christ's Coll, Camb (MA); FRICS, FIArb; holds Commercial Pilots' Licence; Freeman of Guild of Air Pilots and Air Navigators; late 2nd Lt Life Guards, and acting PO RAFVR: *m* 1st, 1958 (*m diss* 1969), Hon Elizabeth Angela Veronica Rose Nall-Cain, da of 2nd Baron Brocket; 2ndly, 1972, Virginia, da of late Mr Justice Nable, of Manila, and has issue by 1st *m*.

Arms – Quarterly: 1st and 4th ermine, on a chief gules a fleur-de-lys between two boars' heads couped and erect or: 2nd vert, a Pegasus courant, wings endorsed ermine, a chief or a crescent for difference, *Quin*; 3rd argent, two bendlets gules, on a chief azure a lion passant of the first. Crest – A naked arm couped at the shoulder embowed, holding an arrow proper. Supporters – *Dexter*, a lion guardant or; *sinister*, a leopard guardant proper, both collared and chained argent.
Residence – 1558 Carissa St, Dasmarinas Village M.M., Philippines; Ellerslie, Crosby, IoM. *Clubs* – Cavalry and Guards', Kildare Street and University, RAF Reserve, Lansdowne, Manila Yacht, Manila Polo, House of Lord's Yacht, Aberdeen Boat, Hong Kong Club, Foreign Correspondents', Royal Hong Kong Jockey, Hong Kong Aviation, Little Ship Club.

SON LIVING (*By 1st marriage*)

THOMAS MICHAEL RONALD CHRISTOPHER (*Earl of Bective*), *b* 10 Feb 1959: *m* 1987, Susan Jane, elder da of late C. Anthony Vandervell, of Horseshoe Hill House, Burnham, Bucks, and has issue. *Residence* – 1 Cadogan St, SW3 2PP.
    SONS LIVING—THOMAS RUPERT CHARLES CHRISTOPHER (*Baron Kenlis*), *b* 18 June 1989, — Hon Henry James Anthony Christopher, *b* 1991.
    DAUGHTERS LIVING—*Lady* Natasha Jane Rosanagh, *b* 1997, — *Lady* Alexandra, *b* 1998.

DAUGHTERS LIVING (*By 1st marriage*)

Lady Rosanagh Elizabeth Angela Mary, *b* 1961: *m* 1983, Andrew Congreve Dent, of Newbarn Farm, Ditchley Park, Chipping Norton, Oxon, eldest son of Robin Dent, of Olivers, Painswick, Glos, and has issue living, Michael, *b* 1989, — Iona Katherine, *b* 1991.
Lady Olivia Sheelin Davina Anne, *b* 1963: *m* 1986, David Charles Henry Waddy, of Milburn, Cheviot, 2RD Canterbury, NZ, elder son of late Ian Waddy, of 495 Durham St, Christchurch 1, NZ, and has issue living, George Patrick David, *b* 1998, — Veronica Elizabeth Mary, *b* 1993, — Davina Claudia Rose, *b* 1996.

SISTER LIVING

Lady Olivia Elsie June, *b* 1929: *m* 1955, Victor Echevarri Waldron, and has issue living, Sarah Rose Echevarri, *b* 1956: *m* 1983, Peter Allen Sweeny, of 364 President St, Brooklyn, NY 11231, USA, and has issue living, Miles Taylour *b* 1991, Petrea Rose Echevarri *b* 1989, — Virginia Elizabeth Echevarri, *b* 1957: *m* 1st, 1979 (*m diss* 1989), Anil Kumar Varma, who *d* 1990, only son of late Omi and Devki Varma; 2ndly, 1991, Mark D. R. Clifford-Holmes, of PO Box 113, Constantia, Cape Town 7848, S Africa, yr son of Hugo Holmes, of Totnes, Devon, and has issue living (by 1st *m*), Jai Kumar (a son) *b* 1986, Lauren Devika Olivia *b* 1985, (by 2nd *m*), David Geoffrey *b* 1995. *Residence* – Idleigh Cottage, nr Meopham, Kent.

COLLATERAL BRANCHES LIVING (*in remainder to Earldom of Bective only*)

Descendants of late Hon Clotworthy TAYLOR (4th son of 1st Earl of Bective), who was *cr Baron Langford* 1800 (see that title).

Grandson of late Capt Basil Reginald Hamilton TAYLOUR, RN, yr son of Col Rt Hon Thomas Edward Taylor, MP, son of late Rev Hon Henry Edward Taylor, 5th son of 1st Earl:—
    Issue of late Basil Richard Henry Osgood TAYLOUR, *b* 1904, *d* 1969: *m* 1935, Gwendoline Edith Marion, who *d* 1975, da of His Honour late William Evans:—
(Douglas) Terence William Lenthall TAYLOUR (Drumman House, Milltownpass, co Westmeath), *b* 1939: *m* 1964, Marjorie Rosalind, da of Rev Robert Bowie Thompson, and has issue living, Edward Terence, *b* 1966: *m* 1993, Jennifer Anne, da of Bruce Taylor, of Southampton, and has issue living, Zachary Thomas Henry *b* 1997, Chloe Louise *b* 1995, — Kenlis Jean, *b* 1965: *m* 1988, Holger Hans Bruno Sircoulomb, son of Adi Sircoulomb, of SW Africa, and has issue living, Tatjana Leigh *b* 1999, — Gwendoline May, *b* 1983.

PREDECESSORS – (1) Rt Hon THOMAS Taylor, son of late Thomas Taylor, of Kells, co Meath; *b* 1662; sometime MP for Kells; *cr a Baronet* 1704: *m* 1682, Anne, who *d* 1710, da of Sir Robert Cotton, 1st Bt; *d* 1736; *s* by his son (2) *Sir*

THOMAS, PC, 2nd Bt, *b* 1686; MP for Kells 1711; *s* by his son **(3)** *Sir* THOMAS, KP, PC, 3rd Bt, *b* 1724; MP for Kells 1747; *cr Baron Headfort*, of Headfort, co Meath (peerage of Ireland) 1760, *Viscount Headfort* (peerage of Ireland) 1762, and *Earl of Bective* (peerage of Ireland) 1766; *d* 1795; *s* by his son **(4)** THOMAS, KP, 2nd Earl, *b* 1757; a Lord of the Bedchamber; assumed the surname of Taylour in lieu of his patronymic; *cr Marquess of Headfort* (peerage of Ireland) 1800; *d* 1829; *s* by his son **(5)** THOMAS, KP, PC, 2nd Marquess: *b* 1787; was a Lord-in-Waiting to HM Queen Victoria 1837-41, and Lord-Lieut of Cavan; *cr Baron Kenlis*, of Kenlis, co Meath (peerage of United Kingdom), 1831: *m* 1st, 1822, Olivia, who *d* 1834, el da of Sir John Stevenson; *d* 1870; *s* by his son **(6)** THOMAS, KP, PC, 3rd Marquess, *b* 1822; MP for Westmorland (C) 1854-70; Lord-Lieut of Co Meath: *m* 1st, 1842, Amelia, who *d* 1864, only da of late W. Thompson, MP, of Underley Hall, Westmoreland; 2ndly, 1875, Emily Constantia, who *d* 1926, da of late Rev Lord John Thynne, DD, and widow of Capt Eustace John Wilson-Patten: *d* 1894; *s* by his yr son **(7)** GEOFFREY THOMAS, 4th Marquess, *b* 1878; a Senator of Irish Free State 1928-8: *m* 1901, Rose, who *d* 1958, da of Charles Boote; *d* 1943; *s* by his el son **(8)** TERENCE GEOFFREY THOMAS, TD, 5th Marquess: *b* 1902; Capt Warwick Yeo (TA); was ADC to Gov of S Australia 1939-40: *m* 1928, Elsie Florence, who *d* 1972, da of James Partridge Tucker, of Devon, and widow of Sir Rupert Turner Havelock Clarke, 2nd Bt (*cr* 1882); *d* 1960; *s* by his only son **(9)** THOMAS GEOFFREY CHARLES MICHAEL, 6th Marquess and present peer; also Earl of Bective, Viscount Headfort, Baron Headfort, and Baron Kenlis.

HEADLEY, BARONY OF (Allanson-Winn) (Extinct 1994)

DAUGHTERS LIVING OF SEVENTH AND LAST BARON

Hon Pamela Jean, *b* 1928: *m* 1948, Ivan Beshoff, and has issue living, David Rowland, *b* 1950.

Hon Janet Diana, *b* 1932: *m* 1st, 1955 (*m diss* 1969), Antony John Vlassopulos, Bar-at-Law; 2ndly, 1975, David Walter Webb, of Springs, Rookery Drive, Westcott, Surrey, and has issue living (by 1st *m*), Christopher John Antony (8040 NW 15th Manor Plantation, Florida, USA), *b* 1958, — Mark Charles Antony, *b* 1959.

Hon Susan Ethel, *b* 1936.

WIDOW LIVING OF SON OF FIFTH BARON

Ruth, da of late Cecil Orpin, of Strand House, Youghal, co Cork, and formerly wife of Harry Stuart Pearson: *m* 1938, Hon Owain Gwynedd Allanson-Winn, who *d* 1993. *Residence* – PO Box 4340, George East, S Africa.

HEALEY, BARON (Healey) (Life Baron 1992)

DENIS WINSTON HEALEY, CH, MBE, PC, son of late William Healey, of Keighley, Yorks; *b* 30 Aug 1917; *ed* Bradford Gram Sch, and Balliol Coll, Oxford (MA); Hon Fellow Balliol Coll 1980, Hon DLitt Bradford 1983, Hon LLD Sussex 1989; 1939-45 War as Maj RE in N Africa and Italy (despatches, MBE); Sec Internat Dept Labour Party 1945-52, Member Parl Cttee Labour Party 1959-64 and 1970-74, Sec of State for Defence 1964-70, Chancellor of the Exchequer 1974-79, Dep-Leader Labour Party 1981-83; Freeman City of Leeds 1991; Grand Cross Order (W Germany) 1979; author; MP SE Div of Leeds (*Lab*) 1952-55, and E Div of Leeds 1955-92; MBE (Mil) 1945, PC 1964, CH 1979, and *Baron Healey*, of Riddlesden, co W Yorks (Life Baron) 1992: *m* 1945, Edna May, da of Edward Edmunds, of Coleford, Glos, and has issue.

Residence – Pingles Place, Alfriston, E Sussex.

SON LIVING

Hon Timothy Blair, *b* 1949; *ed* Highgate, and Balliol Coll, Oxford: *m* 1972, Joanna Margerison, da of Ralph Broehl, and has issue living, Charles Edward, *b* 1984, — Susanna Jade, *b* 1979.

DAUGHTERS LIVING

Hon Jenifer Clare, *b* 1948; *ed* Camden Sch for Girls, and Froebel Educational Inst, Roehampton: *m* 1971, Derek Copsey, and has issue living, Thomas, *b* 1975, — Kate, *b* 1978.

Hon Cressida, *b* 1954; *ed* Camden Sch for Girls.

HELSBY, BARONY OF (Helsby) (Extinct 1978)

SON LIVING OF LIFE BARON

Hon Nigel Charles (Abbots Wood, The Street, Salcott-cum-Virley, Maldon, Essex, CM9 8HW), *b* 1941: *m* 1969, Sylvia Rosena, da of Ronald Brown, of Burnham-on-Crouch, and has issue.

DAUGHTER LIVING OF LIFE BARON

Hon Margaret Wilmett, *b* 1939: *m* 1st, 1960, (John Frederick) Keith St Pier, of Chadhurst Farm, Coldharbour Lane, Dorking, Surrey; 2ndly, 1976, Brian Davey of 7 Brook Rd, Thornton Heath, Surrey CR7 7RD.

WIDOW LIVING OF LIFE BARON

WILMETT MARY (Logmore Farm, Dorking, Surrey), da of late W. G. Maddison, of Durham: *m* 1st, 1938, Baron Helsby, GCB, KBE (Life Baron), who *d* 1978; 2ndly, 1983, R. K. Hines.

HEMINGFORD, BARON (Herbert) (Baron UK 1943)

DENNIS NICHOLAS HERBERT, 3rd Baron; *b* 25 July 1934; *s* 1982; *ed* Oundle, and Clare Coll, Camb (MA); known professionally as Nicholas Herbert; with Reuters 1956-61; assistant Washington correspondent, The Times 1961-65; Middle East correspondent 1966-68; Dep Features Editor 1968-70; Editor, Cambridge Evening News 1970-74; Editorial Director, Westminster Press 1974-92, Dep Chief Executive 1992-95; Pres Guild of British Newspaper Editors 1980-81; Pres Media Soc 1982; Member British Exec, Internat Press Inst 1974-95, Hon Sec Assocn of British Editors 1985-95, Member E Anglian Regional Cttee Nat Trust since 1983 (Chm since 1990), Gov Bell Educational Trust 1986-90; Pres Huntingdonshire Family History Soc since 1985; Fell of Royal Soc for the Encouragement of Arts, Manufactures and Commerce (RSA) since 1989: *m* 1958, Jennifer Mary Toresen, OBE, DL Cambs 1996, da of late Frederick William Bailey, of 42 Kent Rd, Harrogate, and has issue.
Residence – The Old Rectory, Hemingford Abbots, Huntingdon, Cambs. *Clubs* – Royal Commonwealth Soc, Civil Service.

SON LIVING

Hon CHRISTOPHER DENNIS CHARLES, *b* 4 July 1973; *ed* Oundle, and Victoria Univ, Manchester (BA).

DAUGHTERS LIVING

Hon Elizabeth Frances Toresen, *b* 1963; *ed* Durham Univ (BA): *m* 1994, John Nigel Evered Witt, elder son of late Nigel Witt, of Farnham, Surrey, and has issue living, Harry John Evered, *b* 1997, — Alice Toresen Isabelle, *b* 1996.
Hon Caroline Mary Louise, *b* 1964; *ed* Liverpool Poly (BEd); has issue living, Thomas Elliot HERBERT-MAYNARD, *b* 1995, — Osar James HERBERT-MAYNARD, *b* 1997, — Jessica Louise HERBERT-MAYNARD, *b* 1993.
Hon Alice Christine Emma, *b* 1968: *m* 1992, Christopher McManus, son of Ira McManus, of Florham Park, NJ, USA, and has issue living, James Nicholas, *b* 1994, — Jeremy Bailey, *b* 1998.

SISTERS LIVING

Hon Celia McClare (*Baroness Goodhart*), *b* 1939; *ed* St Hilda's Coll, Oxford (MA); Chm Exec Cttee Oxford Soc since 1990: *m* 1966, Baron Goodhart, QC (Life Baron), of 11 Clarence Terrace, NW1 4RD, and has issue.
Hon Catherine Grevile, *b* 1942: *m* 1962, Harry Traherne Moggridge, OBE, and has issue living, Geoffrey Dillwyn, *b* 1967, — Lawrence Weston, *b* 1970, — Harriet Fearne, *b* 1965: *m* 1992, Dr Nicholas John Lawrence, and has issue living, Joseph Lawrence Moggridge *b* 1993, Henry William Lawrence Moggridge *b* 1995.

UNCLE LIVING (*Son of 1st Baron*)

Hon Oliver Hayley Dennis *b* 1919; *ed* Oundle, and Wadham Coll, Oxford; formerly Major Queen's Roy Regt, attached Indian Army: *m* 1976 (*m* annulled 1983), Rosemary Muriel, da of Rev Canon Roland Bate.

COLLATERAL BRANCH LIVING

Issue of late Lt-Col Hon Valentine Henry Okes Herbert, RA, 2nd son of 1st Baron; *b* 1905; *d* 1983: *m* 1st, 1931, Winifred Mabel, who *d* 1955, da of late Sir Herbert Grayhurst Pearson; 2ndly, 1956, Janet, who *d* 1982, da of late Rev Gerrard Edmund Wigram (*see* Wigram, Bt colls):—
(By 1st *m*) Timothy William Okes, *b* 1936; *ed* Oundle; Maj RWF: *m* 1977, Erica Anne Jackson, *née* Odell. —— Rosemary Ann, *b* 1932: *m* 1957, William George Rhyll Turner, Duke of Edinburgh's Roy Regt, and has issue living, Valerie Jane, *b* 1958, — Penelope May, *b* 1960, — Susan Diana, *b* 1964. —— Sylvia Valentine, *b* 1948: *m* 1st, 1978, P. Jeremy B. Sayce, who *d* 1980; 2ndly, 1983, J. Robin K. Peile, and has issue living (by 1st *m*), Emily Valentine, *b* 1978, — (by 2nd *m*) Maxwell Herbert, *b* 1984.

PREDECESSORS – (1) *Rt Hon Sir* DENNIS HENRY Herbert, KBE, el son of late Rev Henry Herbert, R of Hemingford Abbots, Huntingdon; *b* 1869; was Dep Chm of Ways and Means in House of Commons 1928-9 and Chm of Ways and Means and Dep Speaker 1931-43; sat as MP for Watford Div of Herts (*U*) 1918-43; *cr Baron Hemingford,* of Watford, co Hertford (peerage of United Kingdom) 1943: *m* 1903, Mary Graeme, who *d* 1966, da of late Valentine Graeme Bell, CMG; *d* 1947; *s* by his son (2) DENNIS GEORGE RUDDOCK, 2nd Baron, *b* 1904; Lord Lieut of Huntingdon and Peterborough 1968-74, Lieut for Cambs 1974-5; Head Master of King's Coll, Budo, Uganda 1939-47, Rector of Achimota Training Coll, Gold Coast 1948-51, Chm of Africa Bureau 1952-63: *m* 1932, Elizabeth McClare, who *d* 1979, da of late Col John McClare Clark, TD, of Haltwhistle, Northumberland; *d* 1982; *s* by his son (3) DENNIS NICHOLAS, 3rd Baron and present peer.

HEMPHILL, BARON (Martyn-Hemphill) (Baron UK 1906)

Steadily and fearlessly

PETER PATRICK FITZROY MARTYN MARTYN-HEMPHILL, 5th Baron; *b* 5 Sept 1928; *s* 1957; *ed* Downside, and Brasenose Coll, Oxford (MA); assumed by deed poll 1959 the additional surname of Martyn: *m* 1952, Olivia Anne, el da of Major Robert Francis Ruttledge, MC, of Cloonee, Ballinrobe, co Mayo, and has issue.

Arms – Or, on a fesse gules between two chevronels and three stars, as many trefoils slipped of the field. **Crest** – A Boar passant gules charged with a chevron and a portcullis or. **Supporters** – On either side an Irish wolfhound gorged with a plain collar or. *Residence* – Dunkellin, Kiltulla, co Galway. *Clubs* – Irish Cruising, White's.

SON LIVING

Hon CHARLES ANDREW MARTYN, *b* 8 Oct 1954; *ed* Downside, and St Benet's Hall, Oxford (BA); Dir Morgan Grenfell Asset Management: *m* 1985, Sarah J. F., eldest da of Richard Edward Walter Lumley, of Roundwood, Windlesham, Surrey, and has issue living, Richard Patrick Lumley, *b* 17 May 1990, — Oliver Francis Robert, *b* 1998, — Clarissa Mary, *b* 1986, — Amelia Rose, *b* 1988, — Marina Olivia Astrid, *b* 1992. *Residence* – 78 Streathbourne Rd, SW17 8QY. *Club* – White's.

DAUGHTERS LIVING

Hon Angela Mary Martyn, *b* 1953: *m* 1982, Robert Edwin Cookson (*see* V Falmouth, colls, 1990 Edn), and has issue living, Edward Peter, *b* 1988, — Serena Louise, *b* 1986. *Residence* – Manor Farm, Upper Slaughter, Cheltenham, Glos.
Hon Mary Anne, *b* 1958.

PREDECESSORS – (1) CHARLES HARE Hemphill, PC, son of late John Hemphill, of Cashel, and Rathkenny, co Tipperary; *b* 1821; MP for N Div of Tyrone co (*L*)1895-1965; Solicitor-Gen, for Ireland 1892-5; *cr Baron Hemphill,* of Rathkenny and of Cashel, co Tipperary (peerage of United Kingdom) 1906: *m* 1849, Augusta Mary, who *d* 1899, da of late Major Hon Sir Francis Charles Stanhope, KCH; *d* 1908; *s* by his el son (2) STANHOPE CHARLES JOHN, 2nd Baron, *b* 1853: sometime Crown Prosecutor for co Wicklow: *m* 1913, Hon May Clarke Mary Nisbet Hamilton, who *d* 1970, da of Lord Belhaven and Stenton; *d* 1919; *s* by his brother (3) FITZROY, 3rd Baron, *b* 1860; Dep Chm of London Co Council 1907-8, Mary, who *d* 1958, da of late Andrew Martyn, of Spiddal, co Galway; *d* 1930; *s* by his son (4) MARTYN CHARLES ANDREWS, 4th Baron; *b* 1901; Bar King's Inns, Dublin and Middle Temple: *m* 1927 (*m diss* in Reno, USA 1945), Emily, who *d* 1990, da of F. Irving Sears, of Webster, Massacusetts, USA; *d* 1957; *s* by his only son (5) PETER PATRICK FITZROY MARTYN, 5th Baron and present peer.

Henderson, family name of Baron Faringdon.

Henderson, family name of Baron Rowley.

HENDERSON OF BROMPTON, BARON (Henderson) (Life Baron 1984)

PETER GORDON HENDERSON, KCB, son of James Alexander Leo Henderson, of London; *b* 16 Sept 1922; *ed* Stowe, and Magdalen Coll, Oxford; served with Scots Guards 1942-44; Clerk, House of Lords 1954-60; seconded to HM Treasury as Sec to Leader and Chief Whip, House of Lords 1960-63; Reading Clerk and Clerk of Public Bills 1964-74; Clerk Assistant 1974; Clerk of the Parliaments 1974-83; Member Cttee on Preparation of Legislation 1973-74; *cr* KCB 1975, and *Baron Henderson of Brompton*, of Brompton in the Royal Borough of Kensington and Chelsea and of Brough, co Cumbria (Life Baron) 1984: *m* 1950, Susan Mary, da of Richard Charles Gordon Dartford, of Swallowfield Park, Berks, and has issue.

Residences – 16 Pelham Street, SW7 2NG; Helbeck Cottage, Brough, Kirkby Stephen, Cumbria CA17 4DD.

SONS LIVING

Hon Launcelot Dinadan James, QC (17 Carlisle Rd, NW6 6TL), *b* 1951; *ed* Westminster, and Balliol Coll, Oxford; QC 1995: *m* 1989, Elaine Elizabeth, elder da of Kenneth Frank Webb, of Dringhouses, York, and has issue living, Peter George Galahad, *b* 1990, — Arthur Frank Gabriel, *b* 1994, — Matilda Jane, *b* 1992.
Rt Rev the Hon Richard Crosbie Aitken, *b* 1957; *ed* Westminster, and Magdalen Coll, Oxford (MA, DPhil 1984); Ordained Deacon 1986, Priest 1987; Preb of Cork 1995-98, Dean of Ross 1995-98, since when Bishop of Tuam, Killala and Achonry: *m* 1985, Anita Julia, da of Antony Gerald Stroud Whiting, and has issue living, one son and two das. *Residence* – Bishop's House, Knockglas, Crossmolina, co Mayo.

DAUGHTERS LIVING

Hon Lucy Jess, *b* 1954: *m* 1980, Paul Benedict Askew.
Hon Mary Sophia, *b* 1965: *m* 1994, Robert Cumming.

HENLEY, BARON (Eden) Sits as BARON NORTHINGTON (UK 1885) (Baron I 1799)

OLIVER MICHAEL ROBERT EDEN, 8th Baron; *b* 22 Nov 1953; *s* 1977; *ed* Clifton, and Durham Univ; Bar Middle Temple, 1977; a Lord in Waiting 1989; Pres Cumbria Assocn of Local Councils 1981-89, Chm Penrith & Border Conservative Assocn 1987-89, Cumbria County Council 1986-89; Under Sec of State, Dept of Social Security 1989-93, Parly Under Sec of State, Dept of Employment 1993-94, Min of Defence 1994-95, Min of State, Dept for Educn and Employment 1995-97, Principal Opposition Sokesman on Home Affairs 1997-98, Opposition Ch Whip, House of Lords since 1998: *m* 1984, Caroline Patricia, JP, da of late A. G. Sharp, of Mackney, Oxon, and has issue.

Arms – Quarterly: 1st and 4th gules, on a chevron argent, between three garbs or, banded vert, as many escallops sable, *Eden*; 2nd and 3rd azure, a lion rampant argent, ducally crowned or, within a bordure of the second, charged with eight torteaux, *Henley*. Crest – A dexter arm in armour couped at the shoulder proper, and grasping a garb or. Supporters – *Dexter*, a lion argent, semée of torteaux, ducally crowned or having a plain collar or the last rimmed azure, on the collar three escallops sable, and pendent therefrom a shield gold, charged with an eagle displayed with two heads sable; *sinister*, a stag argent, semée of torteaux, attired or, and gorged with a plain collar of the last rimmed azure, and charged with three escallops sable, pendant therefrom an escutcheon also or, charged with an eagle displayed with one head also sable.

If there be prudence

SI SIT PRVDENTIA

Residence – Scaleby Castle, Carlisle. *Clubs* – Brooks's, Pratt's.

SONS LIVING

Hon JOHN MICHAEL OLIVER, *b* 30 June 1988.
Hon Patrick Francis, *b* 1993.
Hon Edward Andrew, *b* 1996.

DAUGHTER LIVING

Hon Elizabeth Caroline, *b* 1991.

BROTHER LIVING

Hon Andrew Francis (88 Seymour St, W2 2JJ), *b* 1955: *m* 1997, Liann, da of Robert Bartlett, of New Jersey, USA, — Mrs Patricia Vasbinder, of New Hampshire, USA, and has issue living, Rebecca Marjorie, *b* 1998.

HALF-SISTER LIVING

Hon Victoria Catherine Elizabeth, *b* 1944: *m* 1965, Hon John Hedworth Jolliffe, son of 4th Baron Hylton.

SISTERS LIVING

Hon Ursula Nancy, *b* 1950: *m* 1978, William Thomas, and has issue, Philip Stephen William, *b* 1982, — Jessica Nadine, *b* 1978.
Hon Ingaret Barbara (37 Fairholme Rd, W14), *b* 1951.
Hon Rose Griselda (Granary House, The Square, Ramsbury, Wilts SN8 2PE), *b* 1957: *m* 1st, 1976 (*m diss* 1979), Stuart Ballin; 2ndly, 1984 (*m diss* 1991), Hon Christopher James Bellew, yr son of 7th Baron Bellew; 3rdly, 1993, Laurence Emerson Foulds, yr son of Emerson Foulds, of Guildford, Surrey.

UNCLE LIVING *(Son of 6th Baron)*

Hon Roger Quentin Eden, *b* 1922; *ed* Rugby; MRAeS; formerly F/O RAFVR: *m* 1st, 1946, Carys Wynne, who *d* 1990, da of late I. H. D. Davies, of Camwy, Penrhyndeudraeth, Gwynedd; 2ndly, 1994, Barbara Daphne, da of late J. F. W. Singleton, of Glasgow and Calcutta, and has issue living (by 1st *m*), Morton Roger (59 Grove Close, Thulston, Derbys), *b* 1949; *ed* Rugby, and St Cuthbert's Soc, Durham: *m* 1975, Sally L., da of late W. H. Brittain, of Redcar, Cleveland, and has issue living, William Morton *b* 1985, — Elvyn Alexander (7 Radcliffe Rd, N21), *b* 1954; *ed* Shiplake Coll: *m* 1982, Claudia Marli, da of late Sid Colin, of 52 Church Path, W4, and has issue living, Dorcas Claudia *b* 1983, Emma Alexandra *b* 1983 (twin), Gudrun Dorothy *b* 1989, — Carol Rosamund, *b* 1947, — Jane Rebecca (Askerton Castle, Brampton, Cumbria CA8 2BD), *b* 1956: *m* 1983 (*m diss* 1997), William Nicholas Russell Kellock, and has issue living, Howard Nicholas *b* 1985, Christopher Charles *b* 1989, Siân Louise *b* 1987, Clara Carys *b* 1992. *Residence* – 29A, Hamilton Terrace, NW8 9RE.

AUNTS LIVING *(Daughters of 6th Baron)*

Hon Barbara Dorothy, *b* 1915: *m* 1938, Peter Calvocoressi, and has issue living, Paul Peter, *b* 1939; *ed* Eton, — David Sebastian (11a Bathwick St, Bath, Avon BA2 6NX), *b* 1941; *ed* Eton: *m* 1971 (*m diss* 1992), Dzagbe Cudjoe, of Accra, Ghana, and has issue living, Nuku Vanonyi *b* 1974, Nuname Ankaret *b* 1976, Nujoji Peter *b* 1977. *Residence* – 1 Queen's Parade, Bath, Avon BA1 2NJ.
Hon Griselda Rosalind, *b* 1917: *m* 1939 (*m diss* 1964), John Buckman, late Squdn Ldr RAFVR, and has issue living, Christopher Simon (7 Chestnut Close, Amersham, Bucks HP6 6EQ), *b* 1940: *m* 1970, Gwenola, da of Comte de Kersaintgilly of Poizay les Ormes, France, and has issue living, Andrew Pierre *b* 1972, Sophie Rosalind *b* 1978, — (Jennifer) Susan, *b* 1944: *m* 1963, John Jellis Ashby, of Limes Farm, Watford Rd, Crick, Northants, and has issue living, Jeremy Robert *b* 1964, Sarah Charlotte *b* 1966. *Residence* – Limes Farm, Watford Rd, Crick, Northants.
Hon Nancy Clare, *b* 1918: *m* 1941, Edmund Ernest Wynne, Lt Reconnaissance Corps, and has issue living, Robert Edmund (676A Lytham Rd, Blackpool FY4 1RG), *b* 1956: *m* 1988, Gaynor, da of Eric Williams, of Sunny Bank Av, Newton with Scales, nr Preston, and has issue living, James Robert *b* 1989, Anna Gaynor *b* 1991, Maria Nancy Hazel *b* 1994, — Rosalind Clare (2172 E Holladay St, Tucson, Arizona 85706, USA), *b* 1942: *m* 1965 (*m diss* 1989), David Gow, and has issue living, Donovan Fergus *b* 1970, Caitlin Fiona *b* 1972, — Deborah Dorothy (8 Eirinis, Makri Nea, Attiki, Greece), *b* 1944: *m* 1968, Michael Stagonakis, — Clare Catherine, *b* 1946: *m* 1969, Colin Smith, of 50 Broom Park, Teddington, Middx, and has issue living, Christian *b* 1971, Eleanor Charlotte *b* 1975, — Marilyn Anne, *b* 1947: *m* 1967, Stephen Padgett, of 587 Lytham Rd, Blackpool, and has issue living, Christopher Stephen *b* 1969, Richard Anthony *b* 1970, — Alexandra Mary, *b* 1953: *m* 1st, 1980 (*m diss* 1984), Eric Scott, who *d* 1997; 2ndly, 1985, Peter Gauthier, of 52 Westgate Rd, Lytham St Anne's, Lancs, and has issue living, Alexander Peter *b* 1990, Harriet Louise *b* 1985, Juliet Elizabeth *b* 1988, Gabrielle Nancy *b* 1995.

MOTHER LIVING

Nancy Mary (10 Abbey St, Cerne Abbas, Dorchester, Dorset DT2 7JQ), only da of late Stanley Walton of The Hill, Gilsland, Carlisle: *m* 1949 (*m diss* 1975), as his 2nd wife, the 7th Baron Henley, who *d* 1977.

COLLATERAL BRANCHES LIVING

Issue of late Brig-Gen Hon Anthony Morton HENLEY, CMG, DSO, 3rd son of 3rd Baron, b 1873, d 1925: m 1906, Hon Sylvia Laura Stanley, OBE, who d 1980, da of 4th Baron Sheffield (see B Stanley of Alderley):—
Juliet Olive, b 1917: m 1944 (m diss 1965), John Stuart Daniel, QC, Bar-at-law, who d 1977, and has issue living, Laura, b 1947. Residence – 20 Fitzroy Gdns, SE19.

Grandsons of late Capt Charles Beauclerk HENLEY, Royal Indian Navy (infra):—
Issue of late Cdr Robert Stephen HENLEY, OBE, DSC, RN, b 1917, d 1991: m 1940, Noreen (Eden Lodge, Liss, Hants GU33 6JQ), only da of late Eric Hudson:—
(Robert Anthony) Nigel (Boldre Bridge House, Boldre, Lymington, Hants S041 8PA), b 1942: m 1st, 1968 (m diss 1986), Celia, only da of Leslie Ford; 2ndly, 1988, Anne Louise, only da of James Beadle, of Great Missenden, Bucks, and has issue living, (by 1st m) Robert Alexander, b 1973, — Deborah Lucie b 1971, — Victoria Elizabeth, b 1978, — (by 2nd m) Richard James, b 1989, — Joanna Katharine, b 1992. —— Timothy David (Palings, Warboys Rd, Kingston Hill, Surrey KT2 7LS), b 1945: m 1972, Jane Hughes, da of late John Fisher, of Chiswick Staithe, W4, and has issue living, Sarah Margaret, b 1975, — Rachel Katherine, b 1978. —— (Christopher) Basil Patrick (55 Napier Av, SW6 3PS), b 1953. —— Jonathan Paul Sebastian (Finches Cottage, Langley, nr Liss, Hants GU33 7JL), b 1956: m 1st, 1980 (m diss 1986), Caroline Fiona, yr da of D.D.A. Beattie, of Aston Mead, Windsor, Berks; 2ndly, 1987, Rowena Jane, da of Lionel David Cowan, of Cobham, Surrey, and has issue living (by 2nd m), James William, b 1989, — Clare Olivia b 1991, — Katherine Alexandra, b 1993.

Grandchildren of late Rev Hon Robert HENLEY, 2nd son of 2nd Baron:—
Issue of late Capt Charles Beauclerk HENLEY, Royal Indian Navy, b 1869, d 1945: m 1910, Nellie Barbara, who d 1961, da of late E. F. Stranack:—
David Beauclerk (9 Chalfont Court, Lansdowne Rd, Worthing, W Sussex BN11 4NA), b 1923: m 1951, Eileen Fuller. —— Elizabeth Barbara, b 1911. Residence – 9 Wynne's Park Cottages, Brookhouse Rd, Denbigh, Clwyd LL16 4YB.

Grandchildren of late Lt William Gaven Eden, RN, el son of late Rev Arthur Eden, eldest surv son of late Rev William Eden (infra):—
Issue of late Cecil Eden, b 1876, d 1963: m 1914, Inez Gilmour (Estancia Santa Inez, 2609- Marie Teresa, Argentina), da of William Orr:—
Cecil Gilmour Orr (Estancia Santa Inez, 2609- Maria Teresa, Prov Santa Fé, Argentina), b 1921: m 1953, Anne Mabel, da of George Bridger, and has issue living, Robert Gilmour, b 1954, — David Arthur, b 1961, — Joanna Inez. b 1957, — Margaret Alice (twin), b 1961. —— Constance Edna, b 1924: m 1956, Geoffrey Arthur Lees, of St George's College Preparatory Sch, 1978- Quilmes, Argentina, and has issue living, John Arthur, b 1960, — Elizabeth Inez, b 1958.

Grandchildren of late Robert Charles Eden, yst son of late Rev Hon William Eden, 2nd son of 1st Baron:—
Issue of late Morton Edward Eden, b 1867, d 1914: m 1894, Marie Elizabeth, who d 1900, da of late James Stewart, of Dansville, New York, USA:—
Robert Henley Stuart, b 1896.

Issue of late Reginald Yelverton Eden, b 1871, d 1949: m 18—, Sophie, da of T. Hart, USA:—
Anne Louise: m 19—, Lurelle Van Arsdale Guild, and has issue living, Cynthia Eden, b 1938. —— Beatrice Elizabeth, b 1902.

PREDECESSORS – (1) MORTON Eden, 8th son of Sir Robert Eden, 3rd Bt (see Eden of Winton, B); Min at Vienna and Madrid; cr Baron Henley, of Chardstock (peerage of Ireland) 1799; d 1830: m 1783, Lady Elizabeth Henley, who d 1821, yst da of 1st Earl of Northington, Lord Chancellor, and sister and co-heir of the 2nd Earl; s by his son (2) ROBERT Henley, 2nd Baron; b 1789; was a Master in Chancery; assumed by Roy licence 1831 the surname of Henley in lieu of his patronymic: m 1823, Harriet, who d 1869, da of Sir Robert Peel, 1st Bt; d 1841; s by his son (3) ANTHONY HENLEY, 3rd Baron, b 1825; MP for Northampton (L) 1859-74; cr Baron Northington, of Watford, co Northampton (peerage of UK) 1885: m 1st, 1846, Julia Emily Augusta, who d 1862, da of late Very Rev John Peel, DDD, Dean of Worcester; 2ndly, 1870, Clara Campbell Lucy, who d 1922, da of late Joseph H. S. Jekyll; d 1898; s by his el son (4) FREDERIC, 4th Baron, b 1849: m 1900, Augusta Frederica, who d 1905, da of late Herbert Langham; d 1923; s by his brother (5) ANTHONY ERNEST, 5th Baron, b 1858: m 1st, 1882, Georgina Caroline Mary, who d 1888, da of late Lieut-Col Richard Michael Williams; 2ndly, 1889, Emmeline Stuart, who d 1933, da of late George (Gammie) Maitland, of Shotover Park, Oxon; d 1925; s by his half-brother (6) FRANCIS ROBERT, 6th Baron, b 1877; Chm of Northants Co Council 1945-9; assumed by deed poll (enrolled at College of Arms) 1925, the surname of Eden in lieu of Henley: m 1913, Lady Dorothy Georgiana Howard, who d 1968, da of 9th Earl of Carlisle; d 1962; s by his son (7) MICHAEL FRANCIS, 7th Baron, b 1914; Member of Council of Country Landowners' Association; Chm of Council for Protection of Rural England: m 1st, 1943 (m diss 1947), Elizabeth, who d 1995, da of Sir Arthur Lawrence Hobhouse (see Jackson, Bt, cr 1869, colls, 1965 Edn); 2ndly, 1949 (m diss 1975), Nancy Mary, only da of Stanley Walton, of The Hill, Gilsland, Carlisle; d 1977; s by his el son (8) OLIVER MICHAEL ROBERT, 8th Baron and present peer; also Baron Northington.

Hennessy, family name of Baron Windlesham.

HENNIKER, BARON (Henniker-Major) Sits as BARON HARTISMERE (UK 1866) (Baron I 1800, Bt GB 1765)

JOHN PATRICK EDWARD CHANDOS HENNIKER-MAJOR, KCMG, CVO, MC, 8th Baron and 9th Baronet; *b* 19 Feb 1916; *s* 1980; *ed* Stowe, and Trin Coll, Camb (MA); a DL of Suffolk 1988; Maj (ret) Rifle Bde; Head of FO Personnel Dept 1953-60; Ambassador to Jordan 1960-62, and Denmark 1962-66; Dir-Gen of British Council 1968-72, Dir of Wates Foundation 1972-78; 1939-45 War (wounded, MC); CMG 1956, CVO 1960, KCMG 1965: *m* 1st 1946, Margaret Osla, who *d* 1974, da of late James William Benning, of Montreal; 2ndly 1976, Mrs Julia Marshall Poland, el da of George M. Mason, of Kew, and has issue, by 1st *m* .

Arms – Quarterly: 1st and 4th azure, three Corinthian columns, two and one palewise, or each having on the capital a golden ball, *Major*; 2nd and 3rd or, on a chevron gules, between two crescents in chief and an escallop in base azure, three estoiles argent, *Henniker*. Crests – 1st a dexter arm embowed, habited azure, cuffed argent, and charged on the elbow with a plate; the hand proper, holding a baton or; 2nd, and escallop, or, charged with an estoile gules. Supporters – *Dexter*, a stag argent, attired and unguled or, gorged with a chaplet of oak proper, fructed gold, and pendent therefrom an escutcheon azure, charged with the crest of Henniker; *sinister*, an otter argent, gorged with

God the greater support

a ducal coronet or, and pendent therefrom an escutcheon of the arms of Major.
Residence – The Red House, Thornham Magna, Eye, Suffolk. *Club* – Special Forces.

SONS LIVING *(By 1st marriage)*

Hon MARK IAN PHILIP CHANDOS (Thornham Hall, Thornham Magna, Eye, Suffolk), *b* 29 Sept 1947; *ed* Eton, and Trin Coll, Camb (MA); LLM (London); FCI Arb; MRAeS; Solicitor: *m* 1973 (*m diss* 1996), Mrs Lesley Antoinette Masterton-Smith, da of Wing Cdr G. W. Foskett, of Fernvale, Qld, Australia, and has issue living, Frederick John Chandos, *b* 31 March 1983, — Edward George Major, *b* 1985, — Jessica Sarah, *b* 1977, — Josephine Helen, *b* 1979, — Harriet Laura, *b* 1981.
Hon Charles John Giles, *b* 1949; *ed* Stowe: *m* 1980, Mrs Sally D. M. Kemp, el da of Donald Newby, of Halesworth, Suffolk, and has issue living, Thomas Charles John, *b* 1982, — Osla Mary, *b* 1981, — Ruth Felicity, *b* 1985. *Residence* – Great Chilton Farm, nr Ferry Hill, co Durham DL17 0JY.

DAUGHTER LIVING *(By 1st marriage)*

Hon Jane Elizabeth, *b* 1954: *m* 1st, 1979 (*m diss* 1993), Richard John Grenville Spring, son of late Herbert Spring, of 2 Regency Park, Kenilworth, Cape Town; 2ndly, 1997, Richard D. Szpiro, son of late George Szpiro, and has issue living (by 1st *m*), Frederick John Otway, *b* 1987, — Sophia Romilly Alexandra, *b* 1983. *Residence* – 124 Cambridge St, SW1V 4QF.

BROTHER LIVING

Hon Richard Arthur Otway (13 Market Cross Place, Aldeburgh, Suffolk), *b* 1917; *ed* Stowe and Magdalene Coll, Camb (BA); admitted a Solicitor 1948; Lieut (ret) RA; 1939-45 War (prisoner): *m* 1946, Nancy Pauline, da of late Sir John Armitage Stainton, KCB, KBE, QC (B Forteviot), and has issue living, David Richard (Westbourne House, 37 Northside, Hutton Rudby, nr Yarm, Cleveland), *b* 1949: *m* 1973, Valerie Ann, el da of Francis Martin Lanigen-O'Keeffe, MD, of 10 Priory Rd, Kenilworth, Warwicks, and has issue living, Anna Natalie *b* 1976, Fiona Louise *b* 1978, — John Alexander (Harewell House, Stourton, nr Shipston-on-Stour, Warwicks CV36 5HG), *b* 1952: *m* 1976, Mary Mathiesen, and has issue living, George Richard *b* 1985, Charlotte Alice *b* 1979, Rose Clementine *b* 1982, — Susan Rose, *b* 1947: *m* 1976, Peter John Croft.

COLLATERAL BRANCHES LIVING

Grandsons of late Capt Frederick Henniker, yst son of Rear-Adm Hon Maj Jacob Henniker, brothr of 3rd Baron:—
Issue of Charles Henry Henniker, *b* 1880, *d* 1966: *m* 1914, Dorothy Albinia Cecil, who *d* 1959, da of late Rev Cecil Locke:—
Charles John Chandos (107 Chemin de Croix Vercors, 38250 Lans en Vercors, France), *b* 1916; *ed* Univ of BC (BApSc), and Washington (PhD) Univs: *m* 1954, Magdeleine Adèle, da of Albert Caton, chartered accountant, of Marseilles, France, and has issue living, Hélène Dorothy, *b* 1957: *m* 1983, Baron Pierre de Prittwitz, of 7 rue du Pandore, F-69740 Genas, France, and has issue living, Gregory Charles *b* 1983, Igor Antoine *b* 1993, Fiona Natacha *b* 1988, — Eve Alice, *b* 1962.

Issue of late Capt Augustus Major Henniker, *b* 1884, *d* 1957: *m* 1910, Dorothy Roche, who *d* 1956, da of Lieut-Col Roche Rahilly, formerly RAMC:—
Anthony Trecothic Major (8 Evans Av, Allestree, Derby), *b* 1912; European War 1939-40 in France as Pilot Officer RAF: *m* 1950, Ann Elizabeth Gwinnell, who *d* 1993, el da of Lt-Col G. C. G. Grey, OBE, late RA, and has issue living, Christopher Anthony Major (29 Rusthall Av, Bedford Park, W4), *b* 1952; *ed* Bedford Sch, and Manchester Univ (LLB); Sol 1978: *m* 1979, Bernadette, da of F. J. Ball, of Wallington, Surrey, and has issue living, Charles Edwin Major *b* 1984, James Christopher Major *b* 1986, Rosanna Josephine Major *b* 1989.

Descendants of late Lieut-Gen Hon Sir Brydges Trecothic Henniker (yst son of 1st Baron) who was *cr* a *Baronet* 1813:—

See Henniker, Bt.

PREDECESSORS – (1) JOHN Major, MP for Scarborough 1761, and senior Elder Brother of the Trinity House 1741-81, was *cr* a *Baronet* 1765, with remainder to John Henniker, husband of his da Anne; *d* 1781; *s* by his son-in-law (2) JOHN Henniker, 2nd Bt, successively MP for Sudbury and Dover; *cr Baron Henniker*, of Stratford-upon-Slaney, co Wicklow (peerage of Ireland) 1800; *d* 1803; *s* by his son (3) JOHN, 2nd Baron; MP 1777-1802; assumed the surname of Major by Roy licence 1792: *dsp* 1821; *s* by his nephew (4) JOHN MINET, 3rd Baron, son of Hon Major Henniker, 2nd son of 1st Baron; assumed the additional surname of Major by Roy licence 1822; *d* 1832; *s* by his son (5) JOHN, 4th Baron; sat as MP for E. Suffolk 1832-47 and 1856-66; *cr Baron Hartismere*, of Hartismere, co Suffolk (peerage of United Kingdom) 1866: *m* 1837, Anna, who *d* 1889, da of Lieut-Gen Sir Edward Kerrison, GCH, KCB, 1st Bt *(ext)*; *d* 1870; *s* by his son (6) JOHN MAJOR, 5th Baron; *b* 1842; MP for E Suffolk (C) 1866-70; a Lord-in-Waiting to Queen Victoria 1877-80, 1885-6, 1886-92, and July to Nov 1895, and Lieut-Gov of Isle of Man 1895-1902: *m* 1864, Lady Alice Mary, who *d* 1892, da of 3rd Earl of Desart; *d* 1902; *s* by his el surviving son (7) CHARLES HENRY CHANDOS, 6th Baron; *b* 1872; Col Rifle Brig; *d* 1956; *s* by his brother (8) JOHN ERNEST DE GREY, 7th Baron, *b* 1883; Page of Honour to Queen Victoria 1895-99; European War as Staff-Lieut, and in RAF (Croix de Guerre); *m* 1914, Molly, who *d* 1953, da of late Sir Robert William Burnet, KCVO, MD; *d* 1980; *s* by his el son (9) JOHN PATRICK EDWARD CHANDOS, 8th Baron and present peer; also Baron Hartismere.

Herbert, Lord; son of Earl of Pembroke and Montgomery.

Herbert, family name of Earl of Carnarvon.

Herbert, family name of Baron Hemingford.

Herbert, family name of Earl of Pembroke.

Herbert, family name of Earl of Powis.

Herbert, surname of Barony of Tangley.

HEREFORD, VISCOUNT (Devereux) (Viscount E. 1550, Bt E 1611)
(Name pronounced 'Deverooks')

ROBERT MILO LEICESTER DEVEREUX, 18th Viscount, Premier Viscount of England, and 15th Baronet; *b* 4 Nov 1932; *s* 1952; *ed* Eton; OStJ: *m* 1969 (*m diss* 1982), Susan Mary, only child of Maj Maurice Godley, of Ide Hill, Sevenoaks, Kent and has issue.

ᴁrms – Argent, a fesse gules, in chief three torteaux. Crest – Out of a ducal coronet or, a talbot's head argent, eared gules. Supporters – *Dexter*, a talbot argent, eared gules, ducally gorged of the last; *sinister*, a reindeer gules, attired, gorged with a ducal coronet, and lined or. Second Motto – *Basis virtutum constantia* (Firmness the basis of virtue).
Address – c/o House of Lords, SW1A 0PW.

SONS LIVING

Hon (CHARLES) ROBIN DE BOHUN, *b* 11 Aug 1975.
Hon Edward Mark de Breteuil *b* 1977.

SISTER LIVING

(Raised to rank of a Viscount's daughter 1953)

Hon Diana Bridget, *b* 1931: *m* 1967, Col Samuel Charles Casamajor Gaussen, Welsh Guards, of 60 Alder Lodge, Stevenage Rd, SW7, and Nutbeam, Duntisbourne Leer, Cirencester, Glos, and has issue living, Robert Casamajor, *b* 1968, — Mariana Diana, *b* 1971.

COLLATERAL BRANCHES LIVING

Envy is the attendant of virtue

Grandchildren of late Humphrey Bourchier Devereux, eldest son of late Hon Henry de Bohun Devereux (infra):—
Issue of late Rupert Montague Devereux, *b* 1907, *d* 1974: *m* 1940, Joan Ursula, who *d* 1983, da of D. W. Thomas:—
(Blanche) Rosemary, *b* 1943: *m* 1966, Harvey Nausbaum, of 61 Chichester Drive, Arundel, Qld 4214, Australia, and has issue living, Aaron, *b* 1972, — Sarah Rosemary, *b* 1974. —— Susan Ursula, *b* 1947: *m* 1967, Terrence Adrian Currie, of 125 Koutu Rd, Rotorua, NZ, and has issue living, Simon Zane, *b* 1967: *m* 1997, Rosemary King, — Bridget Susan, *b* 1971.

Issue of late George Makgill de Bohun Devereux, *b* 1909, *d* 1976: *m* 1937, Olga Christian (3 Mays Rd, Onehunga, Auckland, SE5, NZ), da of late Karl S. Larsen, of Auckland, NZ:—
Colin de Bohun, *b* 1941: *m* 1st, 1964, (*m diss* 1976), Helen Ann, da of K. Buchanan, of Takanini, NZ; 2ndly, 1976, Carole Ann, da of J. Parkes, of Dannevirke, NZ, and has issue living (by 2nd *m*), Justin de Bohun, *b* 1976. —— Dorothy Wyn, *b* 1938: *m* 1958, Graham Leaning, of 3 Mays Rd, Onehunga Auckland, SE5, NZ, and has issue living, Karl Stuart, *b* 1964, — Christine Ann, *b* 1961. —— Marilyn Joan, *b* 1948: *m* 1971, Robert Leslie Hessey, of 28 Littlejohn St, Hillsborough, Auckland, NZ, and has issue living, Steven James, *b* 1977, — Rachel Ann, *b* 1975.

Grandchildren of late Hon Henry de Bohun Devereux, 2nd son of 15th Viscount:—
Issue of late Godfrey Vaughan Devereux, *b* 1893, *d* 1976: *m* 1925, Ellen, who *d* 1986, da of late John Black, of Keri Keri, Bay of Islands, NZ:—
Robin Geoffrey (76 Colman Av, Upper Riccarton, Christchurch, NZ), *b* 1927: Capt RNZAC: *m* 1953, Glennis Fyfe, da of T. F. Kerr, and has issue living, Susan Lee, *b* 1956: *m* 1981, R. Noel Strez, of 49 Sayers Cres, Christchurch, NZ, and has issue living, Simon Geoffrey *b* 1986, Kirsten Anna *b* 1983, — Vicki Anne, *b* 1959: *m* 1982, James Bennie, of 46 Woodard Terrace, Christchurch, NZ. —— David de Bohun (432 Fraser St, Tauranga, NZ), *b* 1928: *m* 1951, Roberta Barbara, da of late F. G. R. Souness, and has issue living, Malcolm Fergus (129 Deep Creek Rd, Torbay, Auckland, NZ), *b* 1952; F/Lt RNZAF: *m* 1975 (*m diss* 1995), Barbara, da of R. Irwin, of Pukekohe, NZ, and has issue living, Mark Robert *b* 1978, Ross Timothy *b* 1980, — Wendy Anne, *b* 1956: *m* 1st, 1978 (*m diss* 1989), John Roy Donaldson; 2ndly, 1990, Ashley Richard Philip, of 3 Endeavour Ave, Tauranga, NZ, and has issue living (by 1st *m*), Matthew James *b* 1988, Melissa Joy *b* 1983, Sarah Marie *b* 1985. —— Francis Richard (Tangowahine, RD2, Dargaville, NZ), *b* 1937: *m* 1st, 1978 (*m diss* 1984), Linda Jane, da of late Edward James Branson, of Tanyard Farm; 2ndly, 1998, Tracy Lee, da of Norman Smith, of Tangowahine, NZ, and has issue living (by 1st *m*), Richard John, *b* 1982. —— Jennifer Mary, *b* 1933: *m* 1959, Lt-Col George Scott Finlayson, RNZ Corps of Sigs, and has issue living, George Robert, *b* 1960: *m* 1991, Michelle Judith, da of A. R. McLennan, — James Scott, *b* 1963, — Helen Mary, *b* 1966, — Judith Anne, *b* 1970.

Grandchildren of late Walter de Laci Devereux, only son of late Rear-Adm Hon Walter Bourchier Devereux, 3rd son of 14th Viscount:—
Issue of late Lt-Col Robert de Bohun Devereux, MBE, *b* 1897; *d* 1981: *m* 1925, Enid Marion, who *d* 1976, da of late Gen Sir Henry Bulkley Burlton Watkis, KCB:—
Robert Humphrey Bourchier (Woolbeding Cottage, Bepton, nr Midhurst, W Sussex), *b* 1930; *ed* Marlborough, and Exeter Coll, Oxford: *m* 1954, Barbara, who *d* 1989, only da of Norman Heywood, of Ealing, W5, and has issue living, Robert Harold Ferrers (5 Ladbroke Terrace, W11), *b* 1955; *ed* Marlborough, and Downing Coll, Camb: *m* 1983, Vanessa, da of Edward James Branson, of Tanyard Farm, Shamley Green, Guildford, Surrey, and has issue living, Noah Edward de Bohun *b* 1987, Louis Robert de Laci *b* 1991, — Godfrey Edmund de Bohun, *b* 1956; *ed* Marlborough: *m* 1982, Barbara, da of late William Accousti, of Connecticut, USA, and has issue living, Arum *b* 1983, — Henrietta Marion Clare, *b* 1960. —— Marion Blanche, *b* 1927: *m* 1958, Rev Timothy Knowles Hollis, and has issue living, Timothy John Walter, *b* 1968: *m* 1991, Michaela Francis, and has issue living, Ryan Arthur *b* 1991, Rebecca Anne *b* 1993, — Jennifer Marion, *b* 1961, — Lucy Anne, *b* 1962.

PREDECESSORS - (1) WALTER Devereux, KG; in 1500 s his father as 10th *Baron Ferrers*, of Chartley (peerage of England, *cr* 1299, see E Ferrers); *cr Viscount Hereford* (peerage of England) 1550; distinguished himself in the French Wars of Henry VIII; was Justice of S Wales 1524; *d* 1558; s by his grandson (2) WALTER, KG, 2nd Viscount, son of Sir Richard, 2nd son of 1st Viscount; s 1570, in right of his gt-grandmother, as 8th *Baron Bourchier* (peerage of England, *cr* 1342, see * infra); *cr Earl of Essex* (peerage of England) 1572; was Field-Marshal of the Forces sent to suppress the Rebellion of the Earls of Northumberland and Westmorland; was also Earl Marshal of Ireland; *d* 1576; s by his son (3) ROBERT, KG, PC, 2nd Earl; was Lord Lieut of Ireland and Earl Marshal of England; well known in history as the unfortunate favourite of Queen Elizabeth; was Master of the Horse, Earl Marshal of England, Lord Dep of Ireland, and Chancellor of Cambridge Univ; having conspired against the Queen he made a fruitless effort at insurrection, was taken prisoner, convicted of high treason, and beheaded on Tower Hill 25 Feb 1601; s by his son (4) ROBERT, KG, who in 1603 was restored in blood and became 3rd Earl; was attached to the Royal cause until 1642, when he accepted a commission in the Parliament army and afterwards distinguished himself as a Parliamentary Generalissimo; *d* 1646; interred with national obsequies in Westminster Abbey, the two Houses of Parliament attending the funeral; at his death the Earldom of Essex expired, the Barony of Ferrers became abeyant (abeyance terminated 1677, see E Ferrers), the Barony of Bourchier became abeyant (and still remains so), and the Viscountcy of Hereford devolved upon his kinsman (5) WALTER, 5th Viscount, son of Sir Edward Devereux (*cr Baronet* 1611 and *d* 1622), who was 4th son of 1st Viscount; s by his son (6) LEICESTER, 6th Viscount; *d* 1676; s by his el son (7) LEICESTER, 7th Viscount, *d* aged 9 years 1683; s by his brother (8) EDWARD, 8th Viscount; *dsp* 1700; s by his kinsman (9) PRICE, 9th Viscount, great-grandson of Sir George, Knt, (ante); *d* 1760; s by his el son (12) EDWARD, 12th Viscount; *dsp* 1783; s by his son (15) *Rev* ROBERT, 15th Viscount; *b* 1809; was an Hon Canon of Durham: *m* 1841, Emma Jemima, who *d* 1870 (having *m* 2ndly, 1857, Lieut-Col John Ireland-Blackburne), da of George Ravenscroft; *d* 1855; s by his son (16) ROBERT, 16th Viscount; *b* 1843: *m* 1863, Hon Mary Anna Moran, who *d* 1924, da of 1st Baron Tredegar; *d* 1830; s by his son (17) ROBERT CHARLES, 17th Viscount; *b* 1865; was Capt 1st (Breconshire) Vol Batn S Wales and Borderers, and Chm of Breconshire Quarter Sessions 1907-27: *m* 1892, Ethel Mildred, who *d* 1945, da of late John Shaw, of Welburn Hall, Kirkby Moorside; *d* 1952; s by his grandson (18) ROBERT MILO LEICESTER (only son of late Hon Robert Godfrey de Bohun Devereux, only son of 17th Viscount), 18th Viscount and present peer.

*(1) ROBERT de Bourchier, sometime Lord Chancellor of England, afterwards distinguished himself at Crecy; summoned to English Parliament as *Baron Bourchier* 1342-9; *d* 1349; s by his son (2) JOHN, KG, 2nd Baron; summoned to Parliament 1381-99; was engaged for many years in the French Wars of Edward III and Richard II, and was sometime Ch Gov of Flanders; *d* 1400; s by his son (3) BARTHOLOMEW, 3rd Baron; summoned to Parliament 1400-9; *d* 1409; s by his only da (4) ELIZABETH; she *m* 1st, Sir Hugh Stafford, KB, and 2ndly, Sir Lewis Robsart, KG, each of whom on his marriage assumed the dignity of Lord Bourchier, but was only summoned to Parliament in his own name; *d* without issue 1432; s by her cousin (5) HENRY, 5th Baron, grandson of William, 2nd son of 1st Baron, and son of William Bourchier, 1st Count of Eu, in Normandy, by Anne, heiress of Thomas of Woodstock, Duke of Gloucester (yst son of Edward III), and his wife Allianore de Bohun, el co-heir of the last Earl of Hereford, Essex, and Northampton; he previously s his father as 2nd Count of Eu, in Normandy title created by Henry V; summoned to Parliament as 'Count of Ewe' 1435, and as Viscount Bourchier 1446, and constituted Lord Treasurer of England 1455; subsequently espoused the interests of the Earls of March and Warwick, and was, on the accession of Edward IV, re-invested with Lord Treasure-ship, and shared largely in the confiscated estates of the attained Earls of Warwick and Wiltsire and Lord Roos; *cr Earl of Essex* (peerage of England) 1461; *d* 1483; s by his grandson (6) HENRY, 2nd Earl; had a principal command at the Battle of Blackheath; at the famous tournament held by Henry VIII, on 19-20 May, 1516, he answered all comers; accompanied HM to France, and assisted at the pagentry in the King's interview with Francis I upon the Field of the Cloth of Gold; *d* 1539, when the Earldom of Essex and the Viscountcy of Bourchier expired, and the Barony of Bourchier devolved upon his only da (7) ANNE, Lady Parr; *d* 1570, but her issue being illegitimated (by Act of Parliament 5th of Edward VI), the Barony passed to (8) WALTER Devereux, 2nd Viscount Hereford (ante).

HERRIES OF TERREGLES, LADY (Cowdrey) (Lordship S 1490)

ANNE ELIZABETH FITZALAN-HOWARD, el da of 16th Duke of Norfolk; *b* 12 June 1938; s 1975: *m* 1985, Baron Cowdrey of Tonbridge, CBE (Life Baron).

𝔄rms – Not exemplified at time of going to press.
Seat – Angmering Park, Littlehampton, W Sussex.

SISTERS LIVING

See D Norfolk, of whom *Lady* MARY KATHARINE MUMFORD is *hp*.

COLLATERAL BRANCHES LIVING

Issue of late Hon Angela Mary Constable-Maxwell, yr da of 11th Lord, *b* 1877, *d* 1965: *m* 1904, 16th Earl of Perth, who *d* 1951:—
See E Perth.

Grandchildren of late Hon Joseph CONSTABLE-MAXWELL- SCOTT, 3rd son of 10th Lord:—
Issue of late Maj-Gen Sir Walter Joseph Constable-Maxwell-Scott, Bt, CB, DSO, who was *cr* a *Baronet* 1932:—
See Constable-Maxwell-Scott, Bt (*cr* 1932) (ext).

Issue of late Rear-Adm Malcolm Joseph Raphael Constable-Maxwell-Scott, DSO, RN, *b* 1883, *d* 1943: *m* 1918, Fearga Victoria Mary, who *d* 1969, da of late Rt Hon Sir Nicholas Roderick O'Connor, GCB, GCMG (M Linlithgow colls):—
See Constable-Maxwell-Scott, Bt (*cr* 1642).

Issue of late Herbert Francis Joseph Constable-Maxwell-Scott, *b* 1891, *d* 1962: *m* 1924, Eileen Josephine, who *d* 1974, da of late Henry Smail, of Donhead Lodge, Wimbledon, SW:—
Simon Malcolm (Foss House, Strensall, York), *b* 1939: *m* 1962, Moyna, da of S. Y. Gore, of Calcutta, India, and has issue living, Amanda Mary, *b* 1962: *m* 1987, Charles John Kay, son of Dr John Anthony Kay, of Alne, York, — Fiona Anne, *b* 1964, — Joanna Jane, *b* 1965. ——— David Darragh (56 Hazlewell Rd, SW15 6LR), *b* 1944: *m* 1969, H. Isabel, da of Leonard Caplan, QC, of 1 Pump Court, Temple, EC4, and has issue living, James Herbert, *b* 1971, — Charles Leonard, *b* 1975. ——— Aurea Mary Josephine, *b* 1926: *m* 1947, Peter Humphrey Williams, who *d* 1987, and has had issue, Michael Humphrey (657 Carlaw Av, Toronto, Ontario, Canada M4K 3K6), *b* 1948: *m* 1983, Anne Catherine, da of late Edgar James Thomas, and has issue living, Jake Peter Thomas *b* 1988, — Ian Maxwell, *b* 1951: *m* 19—, Mary Jo —, and has issue living, Christopher *b* 19—, Trevor *b* 19—, Kathleen *b* 19—, — David Andrew, *b* 1955, — †Deborah Mary, *b* 1950; accidentally drowned 1956, — Elizabeth Anne, *b* 1953: *m* 1975, Jan Joseph Rzyzora, of Box 889, Knowlton, Prov Quebec, Canada J0E 1VO, and has issue living, Matthew Scott *b* 1981, Simon Peter *b* 1982, Deborah Katherine *b* 1976, Andrea Jan *b* 1978, — Sheila Mary, *b* 1956: *m* 1985, Andries Johannes Stephanus van der Merwe, and has issue living, Pamela Jo *b* 1987, Stephanie Ann *b* 1990, Megan Elizabeth *b* 1993, — Joanna Susan (848 Goodwin Rd, Mississauga, Ontario, Canada L5G 4JT), *b* 1958, — †Pamela Jane, *b* 1961; *d* 1976. ——— Susan Mary (2 Westfield House, West Cross, Tanterden, Kent TN30 6JL), *b* 1931. ——— Mary Monica (St Mary's House, St George's Retreat, Burgess Hill, Sussex), *b* 1945.

Issue of late Mary Josephine Constable-Maxwell-Scott, *b* 1876, *d* 1922: *m* 1897, Alexander Augustus Dalglish:—
James Campbell DALGLISH, *b* 1898, whose grandson is Mr John Dalglish, of Pomeroy, Goulburn, NSW, Australia.

Grandchildren (by 2nd *m*) of late Hon Bernard CONSTABLE MAXWELL, 4th son of 10th Lord (infra):—
Issue of late Capt Ian Simon Joseph Constable-Maxwell, *b* 1891, *d* 1975: *m* 1937, Janette Louisa, who *d* 1944, elder da of Lt-Col Wilfrid Ricardo, DSO, of Hook Hall, Surrey:—
Jeannette Alice Norah (12 Chelsea Embankment, SW3), *b* 1942.

Issue of late Wing Com Gerald Joseph Constable-Maxwell, MC, DFC, AFC, *b* 1895, *d* 1959: *m* 1920, Caroline Burns, who *d* 1984, da of George Alexander Carden, of New York:—
Peter George (8 The Studio, Priory Grove, SW8 2PH; Les Moureaux, Neuffons, 33580 Monsegur, France; Cavalry and Guards' Club), *b* 1944; *ed* Ampleforth, and New Coll, Oxford; Lieut Gren Gds; Kt of Sovereign Mil Order of Malta: *m* 1973, Virginia Ann, da of Lt-Col John Ewart, and has issue living, Benedict Gerald John, *b* 1976, — Laura Katherine, *b* 1974, — Eleanor Margaret, *b* 1977, — Elizabeth Marsha, *b* 1983. ——— Anne Mary Teresa (*Duchess of Norfolk*), CBE, *b* 1927; Founder and Co-Chm Help the Hospices; CBE (Civil) 1992: *m* 1949, 17th Duke of Norfolk, and has issue. *Residences* - Arundel Castle, Sussex; Carlton Towers, Goole, Humberside; Bacres House, Hambleden, Henley-on-Thames, Oxon. ——— (Veronica) Diana Margaret, *b* 1930: *m* 1960, Timothy Lawrie Boyd Wilson, Scots Gds (Reserve), of Ardelve, Kyle of Lochalsh, Ross-shire, and California, USA, and has issue living, William Lawrie Joseph, *b* 1963, — Lucy Mary Carolyn, *b* 1961: *m* 1993, Mark Stephen German, of 113 Jasper Rd, Beaconsfield, Quebec, Canada H9W 5R7, and has issue living, Lawrie Kai *b* 1997, — Magdalen Margaret, *b* 1966. ——— Carolyn Mary Rose, *b* 1938: *m* 1960, Maj Count Charles John de Salis, DL, Scots Gds (Reserve), of Yarlington House, Wincanton, Som, and Bondo Promontagno, Grisons, Switzerland, and has issue living, Isabel Oriane Clare, *b* 1961; MA, MB BS, MSc: *m* 1992, Dr Hugh J. Herzig (*see* Buxton, Bt, colls), and has issue living, Wilfred Leo Charles *b* 1995, Patrick Merlin Christopher *b* 1999, Jessica Angelica Carrie *b* 1993, — Frances Mary Josephine, *b* 1963: *m* 1988, Michael W. R. Dobson, yr son of late Sir Denis William Dobson, KCB, OBE, QC, of 50 Egerton Cres, SW3, and has issue living, Olivia Carolyn Romsey *b* 1998, — Julia Mary Blanche, *b* 1968: *m* 1996, T. Luke C. Piper, eldest son of late Edward Piper, of The Old Laundry, Marston Bigot, Frome, Som, — Theresa Mary Bridget, *b* 1970. ——— Rosemary Isabel, *b* 1941: *m* 1965, Antony Craven Chambers, Gren Gds, of The Lake House, Alresford, Hants, and has issue living, Dominic Peter Craven (Houseboat Trafalgar, 106 Cheyne Walk, SW10 0DG), *b* 1966: *m* 1992, Nicola Marina Merry, yst da of Maj Hon Edward Renfric Arundell (*see* B Talbot of Malahide), — Sebastian George Craven (Park Farm House, Corsley, nr Warminster, Wilts), *b* 1967: *m* 1989, Maria Mercedes, only da of John Frederick Scrope (*see* Sykes, Bt, *cr* 1783, 1990 Edn), and has issue living, Alfred Chad *b* 1990, John Moses *b* 1996, Mungo Swithin *b* 1998, Martha Carmen, *b* 1992, — Edmund Mungo Craven, *b* 1977, — Antonia Mary Craven, *b* 1974, — Alexandra Bridget Craven, *b* 1979.

Issue of late Maj David TURVILLE-CONSTABLE-MAXWELL, TD, RA; assumed the additional surname of Turville before his patronymic 1960, *b* 1904, *d* 1985: *m* 1930, Mary Alethea Elizabeth Evelyn, who *d* 1995, 2nd da of late Lt-Col Oswald Henry Philip Turville-Petre (*see* B Petre, colls, 1995 Edn):—
Robert John TURVILLE-CONSTABLE-MAXWELL (Bosworth Hall, Husbands Bosworth, Lutterworth, Liecs LE17 6LZ; Cavalry and Guards' Club), *b* 1933; *ed* Ampleforth; late Lieut Gren Gds; High Sheriff Leics 1991-92; DL Leics 1994; assumed the additional surname of Turville before his patronymic 1960: *m* 1960, Susan Mary, only da of late Capt Stephen Francis Gaisford-St Lawrence, RN (*see* Mostyn, Bt, colls, 1985 Edn), and has issue living, Anthony Nicholas, *b* 1961; *ed* Ampleforth, — Stephen Bernard, *b* 1963; *ed* Ampleforth: *m* 1992, Louise Anne, only da of Alan Crossland, of Twichells, Wychnor, nr Burton on Trent, Staffs, and has issue living, Thomas William, *b* 1998, Olivia Sarah *b* 1995, Kate Sophie *b* 1996, — Alice Marion, *b* 1969. ——— Christopher (Kit) Thomas Bernard TURVILLE-CONSTABLE-MAXWELL (La Silonniere, 37240 Ciran, Indre et Loire, France; Cavalry and Guards' Club), *b* 1940; *ed* Ampleforth; late Lieut Scots Gds; FRGS; assumed the additional surname of Turville before his patronymic 1960: *m* 1963, Lavinia Moira, only da of late Hubert Arthur George Howard (*see* E Carlisle, colls), and has issue living, Simon Hubert, *b* 1965, — Gavin Herries, *b* 1967. ——— †Mary Belinda, *b* 1931: *m* 1951 (*m diss* 1976), 9th Earl of Carrick, who *d* 1992, and *d* 1993, leaving issue. ——— Jennifer Mary, *b* 1937: *m* 1970, Christopher David Newton, TD, JP, of Manor Park, Ripe, Lewes, E Sussex BN8 6AW, and has issue living, James Nicholas Turville, *b* 1971; *ed* Eton, — Lucinda Rosalinde Mary, *b* 1975. ——— Marcia Helen (Château de Cheseaux, 1033 Vaud, Switzerland), *b* 1947: *m* 1st, 1968, Capt Sir (Joseph Benedict) Everard Henry Radcliffe, 6th Bt, MC, who *d* 1975; 2ndly, 1988, Howard Montagu Stuart Tanner.

Issue of late Lt-Col Andrew Bernard Constable Maxwell, MBE, MC, Scots Gds (Res), *b* 1906, *d* 1990: *m* 1949, Militza, da of Mark Kerkes, of USA:—
Andreina Philomena, *b* 1950.

Issue of late Hon Bernard CONSTABLE MAXWELL, 4th son of 10th Lord, *b* 1848, *d* 1938: *m* 1st, 1881, Mathilda, who *d* 1882, da of late Alfred D. Jessup, of Philadelphia; 2ndly, 1890, Hon Alice Charlotte Fraser, who *d* 1958, da of 15th Lord Lovat:—
(By 2nd *m*) Michael Hugh CONSTABLE MAXWELL, DSO, DFC (Theobalds House, Old Park Ride, Waltham Cross, Herts EN7 5HX; Newton House, Kirkhill, Inverness-shire IV5 7PU; RAF, New (Edinburgh), White's and Highland Brigade Clubs), *b* 1917; *ed* Ampleforth, and Hertford Coll, Oxford (BA 1939, MA 1943); Wing-Cdr RAF (ret); a Member of Queen's Body Guard for Scotland (Royal Company of Archers), and Knt of Sovereign Mil Order of Malta; commn'd 4th Bn Queen's Own Cameron Highlanders (TA) 1935, transferred to RAF 1939, Battle of Britain 1940 (DFC 1943, DSO 1944), Netherlands E Indies 1944-45 (despatches): *m* 1962, Susan Joan, da of late W. Trevor Davies, of Glanrhiw, Oakdale, Gwent, and has issue living, Hugh Peter (34 Rumbold Rd, SW6 2HX; White's and Brooks's Clubs), *b* 1963; *ed* Ampleforth, and Digby Stuart Coll, Roehampton (BSc 1985): *m* 1994, Anna Maria, eldest da of Giuseppe Cruciata, of Alcamo, Sicily, and has issue living, Julian Edward *b* 1997, — Thomas Bernard (Ash Mount, Husthwaite, York), *b* 1966; *ed* Ampleforth, and Heythrop Coll, Lond Univ: *m* 1992, Alice Ellinor Mary, only da of Jonathan Julian Cotterell (*see* B Camoys), and has issue living, Timothy James *b* 1998, Helena Mary *b* 1993, Theresa Maria *b* 1995. ── Ursula Marcia Mary, *b* 1911: *m* 1960, Chalmers Davidson, FRCP. *Residence* – Farlie House, Beauly, Inverness-shire.

Grandchildren (by 2nd *m*) of late Hon Bernard Constable Maxwell (ante)—
Issue of late Mary Philomena Constable Maxwell, *b* 1893, *d* 1953: *m* 1926, Maj Anthony Buxton, who *d* 1953:—
See Buxton, Bt, colls.

Issue of late Winifride Mary Ethelreda Constable Maxwell, *b* 1898, *d* 1994: *m* 1923, Capt Ronald Arthur Charteris Foster, late Rifle Bde, who *d* 1977:—
David Philip FOSTER, *b* 1924; *ed* Ampleforth, and Trin Coll, Camb (BA); Capt RE (ret); ARIAS: *m* 1969, Margaret Helen, eldest da of late Ian Gordon Lindsay, OBE (*see* B Loch, 1973-74 Edn), and has issue living, Ronald Ian, *b* 1972; BEng, — Peter John, *b* 1976, — Elizabeth Mary, *b* 1970; *ed* Aberdeen Univ (BEng); PhD. *Residence* – Wyndford Farm, Broxburn, W Lothian EH52 6NW. ── Giles Anthony FOSTER, *b* 1927; *ed* Ampleforth, and RAC Cirencester; late Lt Rifle Bde.

Issue of late Joan Constable Maxwell, *b* 1901, *d* 1991: *m* 1930, Lt-Col Hon Henry George Orlando Bridgeman, DSO, MC, who *d* 1972:—
See E Bradford, colls.

Grandchildren of late Mary Anne Constable Maxwell, yst da of 10th Lord: *m* 1884, her cousin, Edmund Constable-Maxwell-Stuart (infra).

Granddaughter of late Capt Francis Joseph CONSTABLE-MAXWELL-STUART (infra):—
Issue of late Capt Peter D'Arcy John Joseph Constable-Maxwell-Stuart, IA, *b* 1922, *d* 1990: *m* 1956, Flora (Traquair House, Innerleithen, Peeblesshire), da of Sir Alexander Morris Carr-Saunders, KBE:—
Catherine Margaret Mary, *b* 1964: *m* 1995, John Patrick Grey, who *d* 1998, and has issue living, Isabella Stuart, *b* 1997. *Residence* – Traquair House, Innerleithen, Peeblesshire.

Grandchildren of late Edmund CONSTABLE-MAXWELL-STUART, 4th son of late Hon Henry Constable-Maxwell-Stuart, brother of 10th Lord:—
Issue of late Capt Francis Joseph Constable-Maxwell-Stuart, *b* 1886, *d* 1962: *m* 1917, Dorothy Mary, who *d* 1975, da of late J. D'Arcy Hartley, of Billesdon Coplow, Leics:—
Michael Joseph Edmund (Baitlaws, Lamington, Lanarks), *b* 1932: *m* 1970, Kirsty, el da of late Capt H. K. Salvesen, of Inveralmond, Edinburgh, and has issue living, Justin, *b* 1973, — Laura Mary, *b* 1971. ── Madeleine Mary Josephine, *b* 1918: *m* 1946, John Sherbrooke, of Churchen Green, East Morden, Wareham, Dorset, and has issue living, Simon (Bolney, Salisbury Rd, Blandford, Dorset DT11 7SP), *b* 1947: *m* 1977, Miranda, da of Michael McCrea, of Tweedbank, Kelso, Roxburghshire, and has issue living, Archie John *b* 1980, Benedict *b* 1984, Luke *b* 1986, Edmund *b* 1993, Rosanna *b* 1982, — Hugh (Middle Farm, Taston, Oxford OX7 3JL), *b* 1948: *m* 1974, Nicola Mary Hamilton, yr da of Anthony Andrew Francis Tabor (*see* B Dulverton, colls), and has issue living, Harry *b* 1977, Tom *b* 1979, — Alexander, *b* 1957, — Elizabeth, *b* 1959. ── †Joan Margaret Mary, *b* 1920: *m* 1943, Charles Erik Paterson, who *d* 1983, and *d* 1987, leaving issue, David Francis Joseph (15B, 6 Po Shan Rd, Hong Kong; 30 Walpole St, SW3), *b* 1944; *ed* Stonyhurst, and Oriel Coll, Oxford: *m* 1983, Jayne, da of late T. Y. Tung, of Hong Kong, — Michael Charles Joseph (73 Hendham Rd, SW17 7DH), *b* 1948; *ed* Stonyhurst, and Oriel Coll, Oxford: *m* 1987, Marguerite, da of Vice Adm Sir Iwan Raikes, KCB, CBE, DSC, DL, of Aberyscir Court, Brecon, and has issue living, David *b* 1990, Hermione *b* 1987, Sophia *b* (twin) 1990, — Caroline Mary Madeleine, *b* 1945: *m* 1975, Edward Pearce Serocold, of 1 Morella Rd, SW12, son of late Lt-Col Walter Pearce Serocold, DSO, TD, of Ridge House, Highclere, Berks, and has issue living, Charles *b* 1976, Mark *b* 1979, Henry *b* 1985, Georgina *b* 1978.

Issue of late William Joseph Peter Constable-Maxwell-Stuart, *b* 1895, *d* 1964: *m* 1st, 1932, Ruth Patricia Craven, who *d* 1952, da of late Charles Craven Sykes, of 15 Oval Rd, Regent's Park, NW; 2ndly, 1955, Anne Christine, da of late Peter John Williamson, of 42 East Claremont St, Edinburgh:—
(By 2nd *m*) Joseph Peter, *b* (Jan) 1956: *m* 1988, Deirdre, yr da of John O'Neil, of Struthers Crescent, E Kilbride, and has issue living, Laurence, *b* 1990, — Rebecca, *b* 1989. ── Julian Francis, *b* (Dec) 1956.

Issue of late Marcia Mary Gertrude Constable-Maxwell-Stuart, *b* 1888, *d* 1956: *m* 1920, Douglas Christopher Leng, who *d* 1930:—
Christopher Anthony William LENG, OBE (Juniper Bank, Walkerburn, Peeblesshire), *b* 1922; *ed* Downside, and Hertford Coll, Oxford (BA 1947, MA 1947); European War 1939-45 as Capt 27th Lancers in Middle East, and in Italy (despatches) and Burma; Dep Lord Lieut of Peeblesshire since 1983; OBE (Civil) 1987: *m* 1953, Patricia, da of W. Edmund Lillywhite, of Pilgrims, Chilham, Kent, and has issue living, Malcolm Simon Christopher (West Bold, Walkerburn, Peeblesshire), *b* 1959: *m* 1990, Fiona C., elder da of P. A. M. Murray, of Painswick Lodge, Painswick, Glos, and has issue living, Christopher Marmaduke Patrick *b* 1995, Barclay Malcolm Dominic *b* 1997, Marmion Douglas William *b* 1998, Demelza Fiona *b* 1993, — Rupert William (13 St Steven's Place, Edinburgh), *b* 1961: *m* 1991, Helen R., da of late H. A. Nicholson, of Balnald, Kirkmichael, — Fiona Anne, *b* 1954: *m* 1988, as his 2nd wife, Nicholas Charles Gilmour Marshall, and has issue (*see* Gilmour, Bt, *cr* 1897, colls), — Teresa Madeleine, *b* 1955. ── David Joseph Timothy LENG (134 Norwich Rd,

Fakenham, Norfolk NR21 8LF), *b* 1924; *ed* Downside, and New Coll, Oxford (BA 1948); European War 1940-45, as Capt 4th Batn Gren Gds: *m* 1951, Dorothy Lucie, who *d* 1967, da of late C. Seymour, of Folkstone, and has issue living, Felicity Mary, *b* 1952: *m* 19—, George Whitman (of USA), of 37 Rue de la Bucherie, 75005 Paris, and has issue living, Sylvia *b* 1979, — Leonara Rosemary, *b* 1956.

Granddaughter of late Hon Henry CONSTABLE-MAXWELL-STUART (ante):—
    Issue of late Henry Joseph Constable-Maxwell-Stuart, *b* 1861, *d* 1932: *m* 1908, Florence, who *d* 1956, da of William Wickham, of Chestnut Grove, Boston Spa, Yorks:—
Clare Mary, *b* 1914: *m* 1938, S/Ldr James Patrick Cafferkey, RAF (ret), who *d* 1978, and has issue living, Patrick Charles, *b* 1941: *m* 1998, Elizabeth Ann, yr da of George Courtney Palmer, of Sydney, Australia. *Residence* – 4 Apple Garth, Easingwold, York YO6 3LZ.

PREDECESSORS – (1) HERBERT Herries, was summoned to Parliament of Scotland as *Lord Herries of Terregles* 1490; *s* by his son (2) ANDREW, 2nd Lord; *d* 1513; *s* by his son (3) WILLIAM, 3rd Lord; *s* by his el da (4) AGNES: *m* Sir John Maxwell, 2nd son of 5th Lord Maxwell (*cr* 1440), who became *jure uxoris* Lord Herries of Terregles; *d* 1582; *s* by his son (5) WILLIAM, 5th Lord, *d* 1603; *s* by his son (6) JOHN Maxwell, 6th Lord; *d* 1631; *s* by his son (7) JOHN, 7th Lord: who in 1667 *s* by special remainder his kinsman as 3rd Nithsdale (the 1st Earl, Robert, 9th Baron Maxwell, was *cr Lord Maxwell, Eskdale and Carlyle*, and *Earl of Nithsdale*, with remainder to his heirs male, and precedence of 1581); *s* by his son (8) ROBERT, 4th Earl; *d* 1685; *s* by his son (9) WILLIAM, 5th Earl; celebrated for effecting his escape from the Tower of London the night before his execution, through the agency of his wife; peerages attainted; *d* 1744, leaving a son WILLIAM (6th Earl but for the attainder); *d* 1776, leaving a da WINIFRED (who but for the attainder would have inherited the Lordship): *m* William Haggerston-Constable (2nd son of Sir Carnaby Haggerston, 3rd Bt); *d* 1801; her son MARMADUKE WILLIAM Constable-Maxwell; *d* 1819; *s* by his son (10) WILLIAM, who became 10th Lord by decision of House of Lords 1858 (the descendants of the 5th Earl of Nithsdale having been restored in blood by Act of Parliament 1848); *b* 1804: *m* 1835, Marcia, who *d* 1883, da of Hon Sir Edward Marmaduke Joseph Vavasour, 1st Bt, *d* 1876; *s* by his son (11) MARMADUKE FRANCIS, 11th Lord; *b* 1837; Lord-Lieut of Kirkcudbrightshire and of E Riding of York; *cr Baron Herries*, of Carlaverock Castle, co Dumfries (peerage of UK) 1884: *m* 1875, Hon Angela Mary Charlotte Fitzalan-Howard, who *d* 1919, da of 1st Baron Howard of Glossop; *d* 1908, when the UK Barony became ext and the Scottish Lordship devolved upon his el da (12) GWENDOLEN MARY, *b* 1877: *m* 1904, 15th Duke of Norfolk, who *d* 1917; *d* 1945; *s* by her only son (13) BERNARD MARMADUKE, KG, GCVO, GBE, TD, PC, 13th Lord, who had *s* as 16th Duke of Norfolk 1917; see that title; *b* 1908, *d* 1975, *s* by his el da (14) ANNE ELIZABETH, present peeress.

HERSCHELL, BARON (Herschell) (Baron UK 1886)

Quickly

ROGNVALD RICHARD FARRER HERSCHELL, 3rd Baron; *b* 13 Sept 1923; *s* 1929; *ed* Eton; a Page of Honour to HM 1935-40; was a Train Bearer at Coronation of King George VI; Capt Coldstream Guards, served 1942-47; has Coronation medal (1937): *m* 1948, Lady Heather Margaret Mary Legge, da of 8th Earl of Dartmouth, and has issue.

𝔄rms – Per fesse azure and sable, in fesse a fasces proper between three stags' heads couped or. ℭrest – On a mount vert a stag proper, gorged with a collar gemel azure, and supporting with its dexter fore-foot a fasces in bend or. 𝔖upporters – On either side a stag proper, collared azure, standing on a fasces or.
Residence – Westfield House, Ardington, Wantage, Oxon OX12 8PN.

DAUGHTER LIVING

Hon Arabella Jane, *b* 1955: *m* 1984, Maj-Gen John Panton Kiszely, late SG, son of Dr John Kiszely, of Whitefield, Totland Bay, IoW, and has issue living, Alastair, *b* 1986, — Mathew, *b* 1987, — Andrew, *b* 1990.

PREDECESSORS – (1) FARRER HERSCHELL, GCB, PC, son of late Rev Ridley Herschell; *b* 1837; Recorder of Carlisle 1873-80, Solicitor-Gen 1880-85, and Lord High Chancellor Feb to July 1886 and Aug 1892 to June 1895; MP for Durham (peerage of United Kingdom) 1886: *m* 1876, Agnes Adela, da of Edward Leigh Kindersley, of Clyffe, Dorset; *d* 1899; *s* by his only son (2) RICHARD FARRER, GCVO, 2nd Baron; *b* 1878; Private Sec to Lord-Lieut of Ireland (Earl of Aberdeen) Dec 1905 to Aug 1907, and a Lord-in-Waiting to King Edward VII 1907-10, and to King George V 1910-19, and 1924-29; *m* 1919, Annie Vera Violet, who *d* 1961, da of Sir Arthur Thomas Bennett Nicolson, 10th Bt; *d* 1929; *s* by his son (3) ROGNVALD RICHARD FARRER, 3rd Baron, and present peer.

HERTFORD, MARQUESS OF (Seymour) (Marquess GB 1793)
(Title pronounced "Harford" and name "Seamer")

By faith and love

HENRY JOCELYN SEYMOUR, 9th Marquess; *b* 6 July 1958; *s* 1997; *ed* Harrow, and RAC Cirencester; patron of three livings: *m* 1990, Beatriz, da of Jorge Karam, of Copacabana, Rio de Janeiro, Brazil, and has issue.

Arms – Quarterly: 1st and 4th sable, on a bend cotised argent, a rose gules between two annulets of the first, *Conway*; 2nd and 3rd quarterly, 1st and 4th or, a pile gules, charged with three lions of England between six fleurs-de-lis azure; 2nd and 3rd gules, two wings conjoined in lure or, *Seymour*. **Crest** – 1st, the bust of a Moor in profile couped at the shoulders proper and wreathed about the temples argent and azure, *Conway*; 2nd, out of a ducal coronet a demi-phœnix in flames, *Seymour*. **Supporters** – Two Blackamoors proper, wreathed about the temples or and sable, habited in a short garment or, adorned about their waists and shoulders with green and red feathers and buskins gold; each resting his exterior hand on an antique shield azure, adorned gold; that of the *dexter* supporter charged with the sun in splendour, and that of the *sinister* with a crescent.
Seat – Ragley Hall, Alcester, Warwickshire B49 5NJ.

SONS LIVING

WILLIAM FRANCIS (*Earl of Yarmouth*), *b* 2 Nov 1993.
Lord Edward George, *b* 1995.

DAUGHTERS LIVING

Lady Gabriella Helen, *b* 1992.
Lady Antonia Louisa, *b* 1998.

SISTERS LIVING

Lady Carolyn Mary, *b* 1960.
Lady Diana Helen SEYMOUR, *b* 1963; resumed her maiden name by deed poll 1995: *m* 1992 (*m diss* 1994), Timothy Verdon.
Lady Anne Katherine, *b* 1966.

WIDOW LIVING OF EIGHTH MARQUESS

Countess (PAMELA THERESE) LOUISE DE CARAMAN CHIMAY (*Dowager Marchioness of Hertford*), only da of late Lt-Col Prince Alphonse de Chimay, TD (*see* D Abercorn, colls, 1985 Edn): *m* 1956, the 8th Marquess of Hertford, who *d* 1997. *Residence* – The Garden House, Alcester, Warwicks B49 5NH.

COLLATERAL BRANCHES LIVING

Grandsons of late Cmdr Lord George Frederick Seymour, RN, 4th son of 6th Marquess:—
Issue of late Squadron Leader Paul de Grey Horatio Seymour, RAF, *b* 1911, *ka* 1942: *m* 1937, Hilary Mary (who *d* 1998, having *m* 2ndly, 1948, Ian Hamilton Barrett, who *d* 1985), da of late Douglas Crickmay, OBE:—
Andrew Conway Paul, *b* 1939; *ed* Stowe; A/Cdre RAF 1963-93: *m* 1964, June Ann, da of Frederick Gardner, and has issue living, Elizabeth Jane, *b* 1972: *m* 1997, Nicholas B. S. Fresson, yr son of James Fresson, of Mayfield, Sussex.

Issue of late Lieut-Col George Victor Seymour, MC, Roy Scots Fusiliers, *b* 1912, *d* 1953: *m* 1946, Mrs Hilda Elizabeth Kemp, who *d* 1986, da of late Harold Lionel Phillips (*see* Phillips, Bt, *cr* 1912):—
Nicholas George Mark (*posthumous*), *b* 1953: *m* 1978 (*m diss* 1981), Nicola Clare, da of Walter William Burgoyne Chalwin (*see* O'Brien, Bt). *Residence* – 15 Cargill Rd, SW18 3ED.

Grandson of late Col Lord Albert Charles Seymour, 2nd son of 5th Marquess:—
Issue of late Lieut-Col Charles Hugh Napier Seymour, DSO, *b* 1874, *d* 1933: *m* 1905, Mary Adelaide, who *d* 1977, da of William Morton Philips (E Courtown, colls):—
William Napier (Park House, Shaftesbury, Dorset), *b* 1914; *ed* Eton; Major (ret) Scots Guards; Palestine 1936, Burma 1941-42 (despatches), Palestine 1946, Malaya 1948: *m* 1945, Rachel Mary, da of late Capt Angus V. Hambro, of Milton Abbas, Dorset, and has issue living, Carolyn Sarah, *b* 1946: *m* 1967, Simon Thomas Cecil Hanbury, late Life Gds, who *d* 1997, of La Mortola, 18030 Ventimigia, Italy, and has issue living, Jonathan Cecil *b* 1977, Serena Mary *b* 1970, Melissa Jane *b* 1971, — Sarah Jane, *b* 1947: *m* 1974, Richard David O'Mahony Page, of Grange Con, co Wicklow, and has issue living, Dermot Michael *b* 1976, Patricia Hannah *b* 1978, Arabella Jennifer *b* 1980, — Arabella Mary, *b* 1952: *m* 1973, Christopher Julian Elwes, of The Old Rectory, Checkendon, Oxon, and has issue living, Rupert William *b* 1975, James Rex *b* 1983, Charlotte Vanda *b* (twin) 1983.

Grandchildren of late Rev Lord Victor Alexander Seymour, 4th son of 5th Marquess:—

Issue of late Major Conway Hugh Seymour, MC, *b* 1886, *d* 1931: *m* 1916, Kathleen Louisa, who *d* 1950, da of Lieut-Col Francis John Paul Butler, of Wyck Hill, Gloucestershire:—
Adrian John Conway, *b* 1918; *ed* Radley, and Ch Ch, Oxford (MA); Col (ret) Scots Guards; Lt-Col Comdg Scots Guards 1962-64; 1939-45 War (despatches): *m* 1953, Elizabeth Ann, da of Lieut-Gen Sir Edwin Otway Herbert, KBE, CB, DSO, and has had issue, Virginia Kathleen, *b* 1955: *m* 1983, Alexander Theodore Terence Rottenburg, of 14 Sugden Rd, SW11, and has issue living, William Alexander Seymour *b* 1986, Charlotte Elizabeth Virginia *b* 1988, — Angela Mary, *b* 1957; *d* 1979. *Residence* – Wantsley Farm, Broadwindsor, Dorset. —— Francis Hugh, *b* 1922; *ed* Radley: *m* 1951, Helen Elizabeth, who *d* 1986, da of Rev Canon David J. Cornish, of Port Dover, Ont, Canada, and has issue living, William Thomas (3279 Sedgewick Drive, Victoria, BC, Canada V9C 3K6), *b* 1955: *m* 1984, Cindy Linda Marie, da of Christian Murray, of Chicoutimi, Quebec, and has issue living, Gillian Nathalie Elizabeth *b* 1987, Hilary Roseline *b* 1990, — Margaret Louise SEYMOUR (7341 123rd St, Surrey, BC, Canada V3W 9V2), *b* 1953; has resumed her maiden name: *m* 1986, George William Boldick, of Surrey, BC, Canada. *Residence* – 404 West Crescent Rd (Box 105), Qualicum Beach, British Columbia, Canada V9K 1S7.

Issue of late Cdr William John Seymour, RN, *b* 1900, *d* 1967: *m* 1930, Wilma, who *d* 1987, da of late W. J. T. Clarke, of Wimmarleigh, Toorak, Vic, Aust:—
Conway William Hugh (43 Officers Parade, Condobolin, NSW 2877, Australia), *b* 1934: *m* 1959, Susan Evizel, da of R. R. McKay, of Coonabarabran, NSW, and has issue living, Conway Ronald Hugh, *b* 1962, — Kristin Susan, *b* 1960, — Jane Evizel, *b* 1965. —— Sarah Gardenia, *b* 1939.

Grandchildren of late Hugh Francis Seymour, son of late Hugh Horatio Seymour, son of late Lt-Col Hugh Henry Seymour, MP, 2nd son of late Adm Lord Hugh Seymour, 5th son of 1st Marquess:—
Issue of late Sir Horace James Seymour, GCMG, CVO, *b* 1885, *d* 1978: *m* 1917, Violet Amy, who *d* 1996, da of Thomas Edward Erskine (*see* E Buchan, colls):—
Hugh Francis (Luccombe Mill, Bratton, Westbury, Wilts), *b* 1926: *m* 1954, Mary Elizabeth, da of T. H. Roberts, of Pucklechurch House, nr Bristol, and has issue living, (Hugh) James (67 Eaton Terr, SW1W 8TN), *b* 1956: *m* 1st, 1986, Felicity Anne, who *d* 1993, da of P. H. Webber, of Jincox Farm, Oxted, Surrey; 2ndly, 1996, Anya Susannah, da of Michael Hindmarch, of Riffhams, Danbury, Essex, and has issue living (by 1st *m*), Hugo Frederick James *b* 1988, Rupert Alexander Erskine *b* 1992, Octavia Claire Camac *b* 1990, — Julian, *b* 1961, — Francis Benedict, *b* 1966, — Charlotte, *b* 1957, — Sarah Catherine, *b* 1962. —— Virginia (The Old Bakery, Kimpton, Andover, Hants), *b* 1919: *m* 1st, 1945, as his 2nd wife, Sir Ivo Herbert Evelyn Joseph Stourton, CMG, OBE, who *d* 1985; 2ndly, 1986, William Hilary Young, CMG, and has issue (by 1st *m*) (*see* B Mowbray, colls). —— Joan (97 Forbes Rd, Orange, NSW, Australia), *b* 1920: *m* 1945, Flight-Lt Clive Gordon Thompson, DFC, RAAF, who *d* 1969, and has issue living, Anthony Seymour, *b* 1946, — Nicholas Austen, *b* 1948, — Jeremy, *b* 1950.

Grandchildren of late Frederick Charles William Seymour, 5th son of late Adm Lord Hugh Seymour (*ante*):—
Issue of late Horace Alfred Damer Seymour, CB, *b* 1843, *d* 1902 (having been nominated, but not invested, a KCB): *m* 1880, Elizabeth Mary (raised to the rank of a Knight's Widow 1902), who *d* 1950, da of late Col Frederick Romilly:—
Leopold Robert, *b* 1888; sometime in Depart of Pensions and National Health, Canada; 1914-18 War as Pte 31st Bn Canadian Force (wounded): *m* 1914, Mary Elizabeth, who *d* 1955, da of late Thomas Frayer. *Residence* – 1716, 5A Street, SW, Calgary, Alberta, Canada. —— Margaret Lily Winifred, *b* 1891: *m* 1916, Maj Cecil Francis Aleck Walker, MC, Grenadier Guards, who *d* 1925.

Grandchildren of late Lt-Col Leopold Richard Seymour, 2nd son of late Rt Hon Sir George Hamilton Seymour, GCB, GCH, el son of Lord George Seymour, MP, 7th son of 1st Marquess:—
Issue of late Richard Sturgis Seymour, MVO, *b* 1875, *d* 1959: *m* 1911, Lady Victoria Alexandrina Mabel, who *d* 1969, da of late Rev Lord Charles Edward FitzRoy (D Grafton):—
Leopold (Leo) Richard, *b* 1912; late Capt Grenadier Guards; High Sheriff of Herts 1964: *m* 1940, Sheila, who *d* 1999, da of Lt-Col Charles Butler, and has issue living, Hugh Leopold (Home Farm, Stobo, Peebles), *b* 1943: *m* 1st, 1971 (*m diss* 1978), Emma Mary, da of Robert Alistair Henderson (*see* Lowther, Bt, *cr* 1824, colls); 2ndly, 1979, Camilla Madelaine Gerard, yr da of Col William Henry Gerard Leigh (*see* Leslie, Bt, *cr* 1625); 3rdly, 1998, Hon Georgina Frances Baillie, 3rd da of 3rd Baron Burton, and has issue living (by 2nd *m*), Molly Rose *b* 1983, — Charles Richard, *b* 1955: *m* 1994, Henrietta Margaret Cynthia, da of Gerald Arthur Hohler (*see* Stucley, Bt), and has issue living, a son *b* 1997, — Anthea Rosemary (*Hon Mrs David E. H. Bigham*), *b* 1941: *m* 1965, Hon David Edward Hugh Bigham, of Hurston Place, Pulborough, W Sussex (*see* V Mersey), — Sarah Victoria Frances, *b* 1952: *m* 1979, William Jay Ducas, of 194 Village Av, Dedham, Mass, USA, son of late Robert Ducas, and Mrs Jean Weir Ducas, of Quaker Hill, Pawling, NY, and has issue living, Benjamin Colin *b* 1981, Patrick Leopold *b* 1983, William Alexander *b* 1988, — Lavinia Sheila, *b* 1954: *m* 1977, John Norman Gerard Leigh (*see* Leslie, Bt, *cr* 1625). *Residence* – 2 Pembroke Gdns, W8. *Club* – Brooks's. —— †George FitzRoy, *b* 1923; *ed* Winchester; Lord of the Manor of Thrumpton, a JP and DL of Notts (High Sheriff 1966), and patron of one living; 1939-45 War with KRRC (invalided): *m* 1946, Hon Rosemary Nest Scott-Ellis, da of 8th Baron Howard de Walden, and *d* 1994, leaving issue, Thomas Oliver, *b* 1952: *ed* Radley: *m* 1989, Sallie Ward, da of Henry P. Coolidge, of Lincoln, Mass, USA, and has issue living, Edward Alexander *b* 1992, William Russell Coolidge *b* 1994, Charlotte Emily *b* 1990, — Miranda (The Garden Flat, 53 Belsize Park Gardens, NW3), *b* 1948: *m* 1st, 1972 (*m diss* 1986), Andrew Annandale Sinclair; 2ndly, 1989, Anthony John Gottlieb, son of Felix Gottlieb, of London, and has issue living (by 1st *m*), Merlin George *b* 1973. *Residences* – Thrumpton Hall, Notts; 38 Molyneux St, W1. —— Alexandra Victoria, *b* 1914: *m* 1939, Capt Samuel Edmund Gurney, TD, who *d* 1990, of Heggatt Farm House, Horstead, Norfolk, son of late Sir Eustace Gurney, and has had issue, Timothy Samuel, *b* 1940; *ed* Radley, and Magdalene Coll, Camb; *k* in a motor accident 1962, — Richard Eustace Thomas (Heggatt Hall, Horstead, Norfolk), *b* 1943; *ed* Radley, and RAC Cirencester: *m* 1977, Margaret Elizabeth Diana, da of Stephen William Agnew (*see* Agnew, Bt, *cr* 1895), and has issue living, Henry Robert Timothy *b* 1980, Oliver Samuel *b* 1983, Isabel Margaret *b* 1979, Richenda Victoria Amelia *b* 1986, — Jane Mary Alexandra (White House Farm, Rackheath, Norfolk NR13 6LB), *b* 1948: *m* 1970, Simon Warren Macfarlane, son of late William Keith Macfarlane, of Lymington, Hants, and has issue living, Thomas Edward Hastings *b* 1972, Louisa Alexandra *b* 1974, Alice Victoria *b* 1979.

Grandsons of late Maj Sir Edward Seymour, KCVO, DSO, OBE, 3rd son of late Lt-Col Leopold Richard Seymour (*ante*):—
Issue of late Maj John Edward Seymour, *b* 1915, *d* 1972: *m* 1940, Elizabeth Norah (Edgedell Cottage, Martyr Worthy, Winchester), only child of late Adm Hon Sir Hubert George Brand, GCB, KCMG, KCVO (*see* V Hampden, colls):—

Conway John Edward, b 1941; Lt-Col Gren Gds, ret 1992: m 1st, 1969 (m diss 1980), Elizabeth, da of Maj Francis Holds-worth Hunt, late Coldm Gds (see B Forester, colls); 2ndly, 1981, Diana Elizabeth, da of late Michael Gibb, of Forge House, Taynton, Oxon, and formerly wife of Hon Trevor Garro Trefgarne (see Trefgarne, B), and has issue living (by 1st m), Harry Edward, b 1971, — Arabella Elizabeth, b 1974, — (by 2nd m), Emily Diana, b 1982. ——Richard Hubert (Dell House, Chilland Lane, Martyr Worthy, Winchester, Hants SO21 1EB), b 1947: m 1982, Amanda Claire, yr da of Ian McAuslan Hardie, of 15 and 16 Admirals Court, Hamble, Hants, and has issue living, James Richard Edward, b 1985, — Sarah Kathleen, b 1987.

Grandchildren of late Lt-Col Leopold Richard Seymour (ante):—
Issue of late Maj Beauchamp Seymour, b 1878, d 1965: m 1928, Eva Douglas, who d 1949, da of late Rev Herbert Brown, R of St Lawrence, Southminster, Essex:—
Julian Conway (Waterdale House, E Knoyle, Salisbury, Wilts), b 1934; ed Eton: m 1st, 1958, Alexandra, only da of Douglas MacLeod, of The Mill House, Stratton, Dorchester; 2ndly, 1971, Lavinia Margaret, el da of Sir William Law-rence, 4th Bt, and has issue living (by 1st m), Leopold Conway, b 1959; Lieut RN, — Mark Hamilton (5 Culverden Rd, SW12), b 1960; Lieut RN: m 1989, Louise C, eldest da of late W. T. Whittingham, — (by 2nd m) Harry William, b 1974, — Camilla Jane, b 1973. ——Jane Mary Naomi (3 Forge Close, Benson, Oxon OX10 6EX), b 1929: m 1954 (m diss 1976), Maj Desmond Eric Renforth Scarr, 14th/20th King's Hussars, and has issue living, Edward Desmond Renforth, b 1958, — Susan Renforth, b 1956: m 1989 (m diss 1994), Richard Hamill, son of late Francis Hamill, and has issue living, Matthew Desmond Fergal b 1990, — Sarah Anne Renforth, b 1960: m 1997, Richard F. Berry, yr son of David Berry, of Cadham, Fife. ——Anne Victoria (twin), b 1929: m 1951, Maj Henry Robert Mansel Porter, MBE, 60th Rifles, Palestine 1946-48 (MBE, despatches), High Sheriff Worcs 1970, of Brockham, Birlingham, Pershore, Worcs, and has issue living, Henry Christopher Mansel, b 1953; ed Wellington, Manchester Univ (BA), and Perugia Univ; editor Illustrated London News 1987-89: m 1990, Elizabeth Mary Elliot, and has issue living, Miranda Victoria Elliot b 1985, Charlotte Mary Clementine Elliot b 1988, — Michael Beauchamp Mansel (South House, The Green, Adderbury, Oxon), b 1954; ed Well-ington Coll, Exeter Univ (BA), and London Business Sch (MSc): m 1989, Elizabeth A. P., da of late Maj George Had-shar, KHS, of Woburn Sands, Beds, and has an adopted son, Oliver George Mansel b 1996.

Grandchildren of late Brig-Gen Archibald George Seymour, DSO, MVO, eldest son of late George Evelyn Seymour, 4th son of late Rt Hon Sir George Hamilton Seymour, GCB, GCH (ante):—
Issue of late Lt-Col (Evelyn) Roger Seymour, OBE, TD, RA, b 1908, d 1987: m 1936, Rosemary Evelyn (Sakins, Roydon, Essex), da of late Maj Horace John Flower, DSO, MC, 60th Rifles:—
(Archibald) John (Longfields, Ledburn, Leighton Buzzard, Beds LU7 0QB), b 1937; ed Eton; served with 10th Hussars 1957-58: m 1961, (Lavinia Mary) Louise, 2nd da of late Christopher York, DL, of South Park, Long Marston, York, and has issue living, Charlotte Louise, b 1963, — Susanna Clare, b 1966: m 1993, James E. Fletcher, yr son of G. E. Fletcher, of Stourton, Staffs, and has issue living, George b 1995, Rosa Louisa b 1998, — Melinda Nell, b 1969. ——Julian Roger (37 Surrey Lane, SW11 3PA), b 1945; ed Eton: m 1984, Diana Daniels, and has issue living, Archie Christopher, b 1989, — Rose Elizabeth, b 1987.

Issue of late Maj Christopher George Seymour, b 1913, d 1983: m 1940, Honor (Pamplins, Bentley, Farnham, Surrey), da of late Capt Cecil Leatham, of Redbourn House, Wentworth:—
(Christopher) Mark, b 1942; ed Eton, and RNC Dartmouth: m 1968, Carol Daphne, yr da of Peter Pitman, formerly of Muirfield Wood, Gullane, E Lothian, and has issue living, Thomas Mark Middleton, b 1972, — Peter Christopher James, b 1977, — Katharine Louise, b 1970. Residence – Thorntree, Arnprior, Stirlingshire. ——Penelope Jane, b 1944: m 1st, 1966 (m diss 1974), (Robert Alexander) Neon Reynolds; 2ndly, 1979 (m diss 19—), Neil James Kennedy, and has issue living (by 1st m), Alexander Seymour, b 1969, — (by 2nd m) Patrick, b 1978, — Lisa, b 1979.

Grandchildren of late George Evelyn Seymour, 4th son of late Rt Hon Sir George Hamilton Seymour, GCB, GCH (ante):—
Issue of late Lieut-Col Sir Reginald Henry Seymour, KCVO, b 1878; d 1938: m 1st, 1922, Winifred Boyd-Rochfort, who d 1925, da of late John Bathurst Akroyd; 2ndly, 1930, Lady Katharine Hamilton, DCVO, who d 1985, da of 3rd Duke of Abercorn:—
(By 1st m) George Raymond, CVO, b 1923; is Major King's Roy Rifle Corps; High Sheriff Berks 1989, DL 1992; appointed a Page of Honour to HM King George V 1935, an Extra Equerry to HM Queen Elizabeth the Queen Mother 1956, and an Equerry to HM Queen Elizabeth the Queen Mother since 1984; was a Train Bearer at Coronation of King George VI; Assist Private Sec and Equerry to HM Queen Elizabeth the Queen Mother since 1993; LVO 1972, CVO 1990: m 1957, Hon Mary Quenelda Ismay, da of 1st Baron Ismay, and widow of Robert Mervyn Fitz Finnis, and has issue living, Katharine Margaret Lucy (Hon Mrs John Harbord-Hamond), b 1959: m 1983, Hon John Edward Richard Harbord-Hamond, 2nd son of 11th Baron Suffield. Residences – The Old Vicarage, Bucklebury, Reading, Berks; Appletrees, Swains Rd, Bembridge, Isle of Wight. Club – Boodles. ——(By 2nd m) Henry Charles (The Dower House, West Wycombe, Bucks) b 1936; ed Eton; was a Page of Honour to HM King George VI 1949-52, and to HM Queen Elizabeth II 1952-53: m 1st, 1960 (m diss 1965), Yolande, da of Richard Murray, of Banhoek, Stellenbosch, S Africa; 2ndly, 1966 (m diss 19—), Alexandra Mary Hilda, da of Maj Sir Victor Basil John Seely, 4th Bt, and has had issue (by 2nd m), †Conway Seely Reginald, b 1968; d 1980. ——Mary Virginia, OBE, b 1932; OBE (Civil) 1995.

PREDECESSORS – (1) Rt Hon FRANCIS Seymour, PC, 4th son of the Rt Hon Sir Edward Seymour, PC, 4th Bt (cr 1611) (see D Somerset); b 1697; at the death of his el brother, s to the estates of his cousin, Edward, 1st and last Earl of Conway; MP for Bramber 1701-02 and Gov of Carrickfergus 1728-32; assumed the additional surname of Conway; cr Lord Conway, Baron Conway of Ragley, co Warwick (peerage of England) 1703, and Baron Conway of Killultagh, co Antrim (peerage of Ireland) 1712: m 1st, 1703, Lady Mary Hyde, who d 1708, da of 1st Earl of Rochester, 2ndly, 1716, Charlotte, who d 1733, da ot John Shorter of Bybrook, Kent; d 1732: s by his son (2) FRANCIS, KG, 2nd Baron, b 1718; was successively Lord-Lieut of co Warwick, Viceroy of Ireland, Master of the Horse, and Vice-Chamberlain of the Household; cr Viscount Beauchamp and Earl of Hertford (peerage of Great Britain) 1750, and Earl of Yarmouth and Marquess of Hertford (peerage of Great Britain) 1793: m 1741, Lady Isabella FitzRoy, who d 1782, yst da of 2nd Duke of Grafton; d 1794; s by his son (3) FRANCIS, KG, PC, 2nd Marquess; b 1743; was successively Lord Chamberlain of the Household, Lord-Lieut of co Warwick, and Gov of Antrim; assumed by Roy licence the additional surname of Ingram: m 1768, Hon Alice Elizabeth Windsor, who d 1772, da of 2nd Viscount Windsor; 2ndly, 1776, Hon Isabella Anne Ingram Shepherd, who d 1836, da of 9th Viscount Irvine; d 1822; s by his son (4) FRANCIS CHARLES, KG, PC, 3rd Marquess; b 1777; Warden of the Stannaries and Ch Steward and Vice-Adm of the Duchy of Cornwall: m 1798, Maria Emily Fagniani, who d 1856; d 1842; s by his son (5) RICHARD, KG, 4th Marquess; b 1800; d 1870; MP for co Antrim (C) 1822-6; s by his cousin (6) FRANCIS HUGH GEORGE, GCB, PC (son of late Adm of the Fleet Sir George Francis Seymour, GCB, GCH, el son of Adm Lord Hugh Seymour, 5th son of 1st Marquess), 5th Marquess; b 1812; was a Gen in the Army, and Lord Chamberlain of the Household 1874-9: m 1839, Lady Emily Murray, who d 1902, da of 3rd Earl of Mansfield; d 1884; s by his son (7)

HUGH DE GREY, CB, PC, 6th Marquess; *b* 1843; Lord-Lieut of Warwickshire; Comptroller of Queen Victoria's Household 1879-80: *m* 1868, Hon Mary Hood, who *d* 1909, da of 1st Viscount Bridport; *d* 1912; *s* by his el son **(8)** GEORGE FRANCIS ALEXANDER, 7th Marquess; *b* 1871: *m* 1903 (*m diss* 1908), Alice Cornelia, da of late William Thaw, of Pittsburg, USA; *d* 1940; *s* by his nephew **(9)** HUGH EDWARD CONWAY (son of late Brig-Gen Lord Henry Charles Seymour, DSO, 2nd son of 6th Marquess), 8th Marquess; *b* 1930; DL Warwicks 1959; Memb Historic Houses Cttee British Tourist Authority, Pres W Midlands Tourist Board; opened Ragley Hall to the public 1958: *m* 1956, Countess Pamela Therese Louise de Cara-man Chimay, only da of late Lt-Col Prince Alphonse de Chimay, TD (*see* D Abercorn, colls, 1985 Edn); *d* 1997; *s* by his only son **(10)** HENRY JOCELYN, 9th Marquess and present peer; also Earl of Hertford, Earl of Yarmouth, Viscount Beauchamp, Lord Conway, Baron Conway of Ragley, and Baron Conway of Killultagh.

Hervey, family name of Marquess of Bristol.

HESKETH, BARON (Fermor-Hesketh) (Baron UK 1935, Bt GB 1761)

Now and always

THOMAS ALEXANDER FERMOR-HESKETH, KBE, 3rd Baron, and 10th Baronet; *b* 28 Oct 1950; *s* 1955; *ed* Ampleforth; Lord in Waiting 1986-89, Under Sec at DoE 1989-90, Min of State Dept of Trade and Industry 1990-92, Capt, Gentlemen at Arms (Chief Whip) 1992-97; KBE (Civil) 1997: *m* 1977, Hon Claire Georgina Watson, el da of 3rd Baron Manton, and has issue.

Arms – 1st and 4th, argent, on a bend sable three garbs or, *Hesketh*; 2nd and 3rd, argent, a fesse sable between three lions' heads erased gules, *Fermor*. **Crests** – A garb or banded azure; 2nd, out of a ducal coronet or, a cock's head gules, combed and wattled or. **Supporters** – On either side a griffin or, gorged with a collar gules, thereon a fleur-de-lis gold, and charged on the shoulders with a rose also gules barbed and seeded proper.
Seat – Easton Neston, Towcester, Northants.

SON LIVING

Hon FREDERICK HATTON, *b* 13 Oct 1988.

DAUGHTERS LIVING

Hon Flora Mary, *b* 1981.
Hon Sophia Christian, *b* 1984.

BROTHERS LIVING AND DECEASED

†*Hon* Robert, *b* 1951; *ed* Ampleforth: *m* 1979, Jeanne, da of Patrick McDowell, of co Clare, and *d* in a motor accident 1997, San Francisco, Calif, leaving issue, Blaise Isambard Robert, *b* 1987.
Hon John, *b* 1953; *ed* Ampleforth: *m* 1st, 1980, Anna, only da of Hamish Wallace, of Old Corrimony, Glen Urquhart, Inverness; 2ndly, 1986, Helena Marian, only da of Robert Hunt, of Petropolis, Brazil, and has issue living (by 2nd *m*), Alice Mary Louisa, *b* 1987. *Residence* – 53 Old Church St, SW3 5BS.

WIDOW LIVING OF SECOND BARON

CHRISTIAN MARY (*Dowager Baroness Hesketh*), OBE, only da of Sir John Helias Finnie McEwen, 1st Bt, DL, JP; Hon LLD Leicester Univ 1982; DL Northants; High Sheriff 1981; OBE 1984: *m* 1949, the 2nd Baron Hesketh, who *d* 1955. *Residences* – Pomfret Lodge, Towcester, Northants; 20a Tregunter Rd, SW10.

PREDECESSORS – **(1)** THOMAS Hesketh, el surviving son of late Thomas Hesketh, of Rufford, Lancashire, whose family had been settled in Lancashire since the 13th century (a Robert Hesketh being knighted by Henry VIII, and a Thomas by Queen Elizabeth I); *cr* a *Baronet* 1761, with special remainder, failing heirs male of his body, to his brother, Robert: *m* Harriett, who *d* 1807, da of Ashley Cowper; *d* 1778; *s* (under special remainder) by his brother **(2)** ROBERT, 2nd Bt; *b* 1729; obtained permission 1792, to assume the surname and arms of his maternal great-grandfather, Sir William Juxon, Bt; *m* 1748, Sarah, who *d* 1792, da of late William Plumbe, of Wavertree, Lancashire; *d* 1796; *s* by his grandson **(3)** THOMAS DALRYMPLE, 3rd Bt; *b* 1777: *m* 1798, Sophia, who *d* 1817, da of late Rev Nathaniel Hinde; *d* 1842; *s* by his el son **(4)** THOMAS HENRY, 4th Bt; *b* 1799: *m* 1824, Annette Maria, who *d* 1879, el da of Robert Bomford, of Rabinstown House, Meath; *d* 1843; *s* by his son **(5)** THOMAS GEORGE, 5th Bt; *b* 1825; MP for Preston (*C*); assumed by Roy licence 1867 for himself, and his 2nd son (later 7th Bt) the surname of Fermor before Hesketh and the arms of Fermor and Hesketh quarterly: *m* 1846, Lady Anna Maria Arabella Fermor, who inherited Easton Neston and who *d* 1870, sister and heiress of George 5th and last Earl of Pomfret (ext); *d* 1872; *s* by his el son **(6)** THOMAS HENRY, 6th Bt; *b* 1847; *d* 1876; *s* by his brother **(7)** THOMAS GEORGE, 7th Bt; *b* 1849: *m* 1880, Florence Emily, who *d* 1924, da of William Sharon; *d* 1924; *s* by his only surviving son **(8)** THOMAS, 8th Bt; *b* 1881; MP for Enfield Div of Middlesex (*C*) 1922-23; *cr Baron Hesketh*, of Hesketh, co Palatine of Lancaster (peerage of United Kingdom) 1935: *m* 1909, Florence Louise, who *d* 1956, da of late John Witherspoon Breckinridge, of San Francisco, USA; *d* 1944; *s* by his el surviving son **(9)** FREDERICK, 2nd Baron; *b* 1916; Major Scots Guards and DL Northants: *m* 1949, Christian Mary, OBE, only da of Sir John Helias Finnie McEwen, 1st Bt, DL, JP, LLD; *d* 1955; *s* by his el son **(10)** THOMAS ALEXANDER, 3rd Baron and present peer.

Hewitt, family name of Viscount Lifford.

HEWLETT, BARONY OF (Hewlett) (Extinct 1979)

SONS LIVING OF LIFE BARON

Hon Thomas Anthony, *b* 1952; *ed* Oundle, and Magdalene Coll, Camb (MA); Proprietor Portland Gallery since 1985: *m* 1980, Jane Elizabeth, da of Brian A. Dawson, of Aldeburgh, Suffolk, and has issue living, Harry, *b* 1986, — Charles, *b* (twin) 1986, — Emily, *b* 1983, — Georgina, *b* 1984. *Residence* – Kyson House, Woodbridge, Suffolk.

Hon (John) Richard, *b* 1955; *ed* Oundle, and Bath Acad of Art: *m* 1982, Rachel, younger da of late Peter Kay, of Weston-super-Mare, Avon, and has issue living, George Clyde William, *b* 1985, — Polly Elizabeth, *b* 1983. *Residence* – 21 Galveston Rd, SW15.

HEYCOCK, BARONY OF (Heycock) (Extinct 1990)

SON LIVING OF LIFE BARON

Hon Clayton Rees (6 Tanygroes Place, Taibach, Port Talbot, W Glam); *b* 1941; *ed* Univ of Wales (MSc), and Leicester Univ (MA); formerly Sec and Ch Exec Welsh Joint Education Cttee: *m* 1964, Lynda Williams, and has issue living, Alyson Sian, *b* 1970, — Rebecca Louise, *b* 1973.

HEYTESBURY, BARON (Holmes à Court) (Baron UK 1828, Bt GB 1795)

GRANDESCUNT · AUCTA · LABORE

Increased by labour, they grow large

FRANCIS WILLIAM HOLMES À COURT, 6th Baron, and 7th Baronet; *b* 8 Nov 1931; *s* 1971; *ed* Bryanston, and Pembroke Coll, Camb (BA): *m* 1962, Alison J., el da of Michael Graham Balfour, CBE, of 5B, Prince Arthur Rd, NW3, and has issue.

ᴀrms – Quarterly: 1st and 4th, barry wavy of six, or and azure; on a canton gules, a lion of England, *Holmes*; 2nd and 3rd per fesse or and paly of six erminois and azure, in chief an eagle displayed sable, beaked and membered gules, charged on the body with two chevronels argent, *à Court*. Crests – 1st, out of a naval crown or, an arm embowed in armour, the hand proper, grasping a trident azure, headed or; 2nd, an eagle displayed sable, charged on the body with two chevronels or, and holding in the beak a lily slipped proper. Supporters – Two eagles, wings elevated and displayed sable, beaked and membered gules, each holding in the beak a lily slipped proper.
Residence – Manor House, Tarrant Keyneston, Dorset.

SON LIVING

Hon JAMES WILLIAM, *b* 30 July 1967: *m* 1995, Polly Jane, da of A. G. Kendrick, of Norfolk, Virginia, USA.

DAUGHTER LIVING

Hon Sarah Camilla, *b* 1965: *m* 1989, James T. C. Dobell, twin son of Mrs Jenny Dobell, of London EC2, and has issue living, Edward, *b* 1993, — Arthur, *b* 1996. *Residence* – 73 Montagu Mansions, W1H 1LG.

COLLATERAL BRANCHES LIVING

Grandchildren of late Peter Worsley Holmes à Court, yr son of late Hon Henry Worsley Holmes à Court, brother of 3rd and 4th Barons:—
Issue of late (Michael) Robert (Hamilton) Holmes à Court, *b* 1937, *d* 1990: *m* 1966, Janet Lee, BSc (Heytesbury Pty Ltd, 140 St George's Terrace, Perth, W Australia 6000), da of late F. H. Ranford of Perth, W Australia:—
Peter Michael Hamilton, *b* 1968; *ed* Middlebury Coll, Vermont, USA (BA), and Pembroke Coll, Oxford (MA): *m* 1995, Divonne, da of Richard Jarecki, of Las Vegas, USA. —— Simon Antony, *b* 1972; *ed* Dartmore Coll, USA (BA): *m* 1997, Katrina, da of Erich Otto Herwart, Baron von Möller-Harteneck, of Hatzfeld, Romania. —— Paul William (37 Craig Rd, Donvale, Victoria 3111, S Australia), *b* 1973; *ed* Middlebury Coll, USA (BA), and Univ of Western Australia. —— Catherine Elizabeth, *b* 1969; *ed* Univ of W Australia (BA), Merton Coll, Oxford (BA), and Lond Univ; has issue living (by Rob Mather), Emma Bern HOLMES À COURT-MATHER, *b* 1999.

Grandchildren of late Hon Charles George Holmes a Court, 4th son of 2nd Baron:—
Issue of late Capt Reginald Ashe Holmes à Court, MC, *b* 1879, *d* 1973: *m* 1911, Gwladys Mary Eyre, who *d* 1971, da of Henry Ralfe, Bar-at-law, of Tasmania:—
Ruth Vaughan Ashe (Heatherdown, Brock Hill, Bere Regis, Dorset), *b* 1915; 1939-45 War as Jr Cdr ATS: *m* 1944, Maj-Gen George Peregrine Walsh, CB, CBE, DSO, who *d* 1972, and has issue living, David Peregrine (Claypits Farm, Winfrith Newburgh, Dorchester, Dorset), *b* 1949; *ed* Sherborne, and Fitzwilliam Coll, Camb (MA): commn'd 1st The Queen's Dragoon Gds 1968: *m* 1980, Harriet Glen, of Sydney, NSW, and has issue living, Simon Glen Ashe *b* 1991, — Jonathan à Court Peregrine (Broadmayne House, Broadmayne, Dorchester, Dorset), *b* 1950; *ed* Sherborne; commn'd 16th/5th Queen's Royal Lancers 1972: *m* 1977, Diana Susan, da of late William Ernest Jones, and has issue living, Charles Peregrine *b* 1980, Thomas William Peregrine *b* 1983, Rebecca Jane à Court *b* 1979, — Anne à Court Peregrine, *b* 1952: *m* 1976, Maj T. A. Colquhoun, of Heatherdown, Brock Hill, Bere Regis, Dorset, and has issue living, Alastair George *b* 1979, Emma Louise *b* 1980.

Issue of late Lieut-Col Alan Worsley Holmes à Court, MD, *b* 1887, *d* 1957, *d* 1957: *m* 1913, Eileen who *d* 1971, da of Arthur Rouse, of Sydney, NS Wales:—
Peter (5 Wolsely Rd, Mosman 2088, NSW, Aust), *b* 1925; *ed* Sydney Univ (BEng); late RAAF: *m* 1950, Margaret Browne, da of Col Eric Campbell, DSO, of Billaboola, Young, NSW, and has issue living, Alan William, *b* 1953; *ed* Sydney Univ (BEng): *m* 1977, Jane Purnell, of Sydney, NSW, and has issue living, Nicholas William *b* 1981, Timothy Charles *b* 1983, — Campbell Worsley, *b* 1958, — Penelope, *b* 1951: *m* 1977, E. A. Notter, and has issue living, Stephanie Juliet *b* 1980, Harriet Andrea *b* 1982, — Juliet Helen, *b* 1955. —— Pamela, *b* 1921: *m* 1945, Mark Russell Glasson, RAAF, and has issue living, David Alan Russell (Jimenbuen, Dalgety, NSW, Australia), *b* 1949: *m* 1976, Jane Barton Heap, and has issue living, Jonathan Russell *b* 1979, Sarah Russell *b* 1977, — Anne Russell, *b* 1946: *m* 1968, William Howard Pendrill Charles, of Rockybah, Nimmitabel, NSW, and has issue living, Andrew Mark Pendrill *b* 1973, Sally Pendrill *b* 1971, — Jillian Russell, *b* 1951: *m* 1980, Adam Richard Granger Johnson, Barrister-at-law, of 129 Queen St, Woollahra, NSW, and has issue living, William Mark Granger *b* 1987.

Grandchildren of late Capt William Alexander Russell Holmes à Court (infra):—
Issue of late William Charles Holmes à Court, *b* 1918, *d* 1967: *m* 1st, 1943 (*m diss* 1946), Joan Patricia, only da of J. Lindsay Ellis, of Sutton, Surrey; 2ndly, 1946, Elisabeth Anne (7 920 Croydon Av, Winnipeg, Manitoba, Canada R3M 0Y5), yr da of Eric Tayleur, of Winnipeg, Canada:—
(By 2nd *m*) William Walter, *b* 1948: *m* 1975 (*m diss* 1981), Catherine Anne Bannister. —— Phillip John, *b* 1960: *m* 1988, Deborah Anne Haachman, and has issue living, Eric Robert, *b* 1992. —— Mark Richard, *b* 1995. —— †Eric Robert, *b* 1963; *d* 1985. —— Margaret Anne, *b* 1951: *m* 1973, Ronald Chevrefils, of Box 571, Pine Falls, Manitoba, Canada, and

has issue living, Lawrence, *b* 1980, — Kevin, *b* 1983. —— Deborah Mary, *b* 1953: *m* 1976, Francis Richard Nogier, of 134 Forester Rd, Saskatoon, Sask, and has issue living, William Charles Heathcote, *b* 1973, — Margaret Elisabeth, *b* 1978, — Stacy Annette, *b* 1979, — Melissa Lee Anne, *b* 1982. —— Barbara Jane, *b* 1955: *m* 1980, A. Ross Russell, of 4605 Moreuilwood Dr SW, Calgary, Alberta, Canada TST 5NI, and has issue living, Christopher, *b* 1982, — Nicholas, *b* 1984.

Grandchildren of late Hon Arthur Wyndham Holmes à Court, 6th son of 2nd Baron:—
Issue of late Capt William Alexander Russell Holmes à Court, Canadian Mil, *b* 1878, *d* 1942: *m* 1916, Priscilla (who *d* 1955, having *m* 2ndly, 1954, Reginald Victor Miles), da of Charles Grey, of Bosham, Sussex:—
Priscilla Anne, *b* 1917: *m* 1948, Herbert Samuel McCloy, and has issue living, Samuel Boyd (RR1, Prince Albert, Saskatchewan, Canada), *b* 1952: *m* 1976, Elaine Joyce, da of Raymond Smith, of Holbein, Saskatchewan, and has issue living, Jaret Kyle *b* 1983, — Russell Alexander (Box 421, Prince Albert, Saskatchewan, Canada S6V 7R7), *b* 1954: *m* 1st, 1973 (*m diss* 1980), Elaine June, da of Albert Aalbers, of Prince Albert, Saskatchewan; 2ndly, 1987 (*m diss* 1998), Janet Muriel Crosland, and has issue living (by 1st *m*), Jason Albert *b* 1974 (who has issue living (by Carrie Mitchell), Brayden Alexander *b* 1998), (by 2nd *m*), Shane Alexander *b* 1988, Bethany Jane *b* 1990, — James Andrew, *b* 1959: *m* 1978, Sherri Dawn, da of Peter Dyck, of Prince Albert, Saskatchewan, and has issue living, Benjamin John *b* 1978, Ryan James *b* 1981, Kristin Dawn *b* (twin) 1981, — Constance Gail, *b* 1961: *m* 1980, Kent Mark Walters, of RR1, Prince Albert, Saskatchewan, Canada, and has issue living, Matthew Adam *b* 1983, Brock Carl *b* 1987, Amy Monelle *b* 1989. *Address –* RR1, Prince Albert, Saskatchewan, Canada S6V 5P8.

Issue of late Thomas Edward Holmes à Court, *b* 1879, *d* 1943: *m* 1918, Violet Constance, da of Templeton Blackwell, of Poona, India:—
Constance Ann Berkeley, *b* 1924.

Grandchildren of Leonard William Daly Holmes à Court, MBE, 4th and yst son of late Hon Arthur Wyndham Holmes à Court (ante):—
Issue of late Robert Douglas Hardtman Holmes à Court, *b* 1913, *d* 1983: *m* 1941, Sheila Gwendolyn (101 Montana Vista, Aliwal Rd, Kenilworth 7700, S Africa), da of Hugo Hauffman Gibbon, of Trinidad:—
Robert Leonard (104 Forest Lodge, Main Rd, Rondebosch 7700, S Africa), *b* 1946; *ed* Haileybury, and Univ of Cape Town (MSc Elec Eng). —— Sheila Lou, *b* 1942: *m* 1964, Nigel Gordon Armstrong, of The Bungalow, Ellwood Green, Ellwood, nr Coleford, Glos GL16 7NB.

PREDECESSORS – (1) WILLIAM PIERCE ASHE à COURT, MP for Heytesbury 1781-1806, and Col in the Army; *cr* a *Baronet* 1795; *d* 1817; *s* by his son (2) *Sir* WILLIAM, GCB, PC, 2nd Bt; *b* 1779; MP for Dorchester 1812-14; *cr Baron Heytesbury,* of Heytesbury, co White (peerage of United Kingdom) 1828; was Ambassador to St Petersburg 1828-32, and Viceroy of Ireland 1844-6: *m* 1808, Maria Rebecca, da of Hon William Henry Bouverie (E Radnor), *d* 1860; *s* by his son (3) WILLIAM HENRY ASHE, 2nd Baron, *b* 1809; MP for Isle of Wight (*C*) 1837-47; assumed the additional surname of Holmes, on his marriage, 1833, with Elizabeth, who *d* 1874, da of late Sir Leonard Worsley Holmes, Bt; *d* 1891; *s* by his grandson (4) WILLIAM FREDERICK (son of late Hon William Leonard Holmes à Court Beadon), *b* 1862: *m* 1887, Margaret Anna, who *d* 1920, da of late J. N. Harman, of Tadmarton, Oxford; *d* 1903; *s* by his brother (5) LEONARD, 4th Baron, *b* 1863; Major (ret) Wiltshire Regt, and Col late Special Reserve: *m* 1896, Sybil Mary, who *d* 1937, da of late Capt Frank B. Morris, Bengal Army; *d* 1949; *s* by his son (6) WILLIAM LEONARD FRANK, 5th Baron, *b* 1906: *m* 1926, Beryl, who *d* 1968, yst da of Albert Edward Bredin Crawford, DCL, LLD, of Aston Clinton House, Bucks; *d* 1971; *s* by his son (7) FRANCIS WILLIAM, 6th Baron and present peer.

Hibbert, Holland-, family name of Viscount Knutsford.

Hicks, Joynson-, family name of Viscount Brentford.

HIGGINS, BARON (Higgins) (Life Baron 1997)

TERENCE LANGLEY HIGGINS, KBE, PC, son of late Reginald Higgins, of Dulwich; *b* 18 Jan 1928; *ed* Alleyn's Sch, Dulwich, Gonville and Caius Coll, Camb (MA 1962), and Yale Univ, USA; NZ Shipping Co 1948-55; Lecturer in Economic Principals, Yale Univ 1958-59; Economist, Unilever 1959-64; MP for Worthing (C) 1964-97; Min of State, Treasury 1970-72; Financial Sec to Treasury 1972-74; Opposition Spokesman on Treasury and Economic Affairs 1966-70 and 1974, and on Trade 1974-76; Chm Conservative Parliamentary Sports Cttee 1979-81, Conservative Parliamentary Transport Cttee 1979-90, House of Commons Liaison Cttee 1983-97, Treasury and Civil Service Select Cttee 1983-91 (Memb 1980-91), and Public Accounts Cmmn 1996-97 (Memb 1983-97); Opposition Spokesman on Social Security (House of Lords) since 1998; Memb Cncl, Institute of Advanced Motorists 1982-97; Govr of Dulwich Coll 1978-96 and Alleyn's Sch, Dulwich since 1995; Memb Cncl, NIESR since 1989, and Policy Studies Inst 1988-95; Trustee, Industrial and Parliamentary Trust 1987-91; Dir Warne Wright Group 1976-84, Lex Service Group 1980-92, and First Choice Holidays plc (formerly Owners Abroad Group plc) 1991-97; Memb British Olympic Athletics Team 1948 and 1952; Pres Cambridge Union Soc 1958; DL W Sussex 1988; cr PC 1979, KBE 1993, and *Baron Higgins*, of Worthing, co W Sussex (Life Baron) 1997: *m* 1961, Rosalyn, DBE, QC, a Judge of the Internat Court of Justice, da of Lewis Cohen, of London, and has issue.

Address – c/o House of Lords, Westminster, SW1A 0PW.

SON LIVING

Hon Daniel Matthew Langley, *b* 1970.

DAUGHTER LIVING

Hon Madeleine Rachel Langley, *b* 1968: *m* 1993, Douglas James Campbell.

HILL, VISCOUNT (Clegg-Hill) (Viscount UK 1842, Bt GB 1727)

Forward

ANTONY ROWLAND CLEGG-HILL, 8th Viscount, and 10th Baronet; *b* 19 March 1931; *s* 1974; *ed* Kelly Coll and RMA; late Capt RA; has freedom of Shrewsbury: *m* 1st, 1963; (*m diss* 1976), Juanita Phyllis, da of John W Pertwee, of White Gates, Cross Oak Lane, Salfords, Surrey; 2ndly, 1989, Elizabeth Harriett, da of Ronald Offer, of Salisbury, Wilts.

Arms – Quarterly: 1st and 4th, ermine, a fesse sable, charged with a castle, triple towered argent, *Hill*; 2nd and 3rd, per pale sable and azure a cross-crosslet crossed between two acorns in bend dexter, and as many fleurs-de-lys in bend sinister argent, *Clegg*. **Crest** – 1st, a tower argent, issuant from the battlements a wreath of laurel, all proper, *Hill*; 2nd, in front of two branches of oak in saltire, fructed proper, a cross-crosslet crossed or, *Clegg*. **Supporters** – *Dexter*, a lion argent, murally crowned or and gorged with a wreath of oak fructed proper: *sinister*, a horse argent, bridled and saddled, and gorged with a mural crown gules.

Address – c/o House of Lords, SW1.

WIDOW LIVING OF SON OF SIXTH VISCOUNT

Alice Dorothy, da of late Rear-Adm Cuthbert Godfrey Chapman, MVO (B Newborough): *m* 1938, Major Hon Frederick Raymond Clegg-Hill, King's Shropshire LI, who was *ka* in Germany 1945, and has issue living (see colls, infra). *Residence* – The Old Forge, Stone in Oxney, nr Tenterden, Kent.

WIDOW LIVING OF SEVENTH VISCOUNT

CATHERINE MARY (MOLLY) (*Molly, Viscountess Hill*), da of Dr Rowland Venables Lloyd-Williams of Malford, Denbigh: *m* 1942, as his 2nd wife, the 7th Viscount Hill, who *d* 1974.

COLLATERAL BRANCHES LIVING

Issue of late Major Hon Frederick Raymond Clegg-Hill, King's Shropshire LI, 2nd son of 6th Viscount, *b* 1909, *ka* in Germany 1945: *m* 1938, Alice Dorothy (ante), da of late Rear-Adm Cuthbert Godfrey Chapman, MVO (B Newborough):—
PETER DAVID RAYMOND CHARLES, *b* 17 Oct 1945 (*posthumous*): *m* 1973, Sharon Ruth Deane, of Kaikohe, NZ, and has issue living, Paul Andrew Raymond, *b* 4 May 1979, — Michael Charles David, *b* 1988, — Catherine Anne, *b* 1974, — Jennifer Louise, *b* 1976, — Susan Dorothy, *b* 1980, — Rachel Emma, *b* 1984, — Melissa Jane, *b* 1986.

Issue of late Capt Hon Gerald Spencer Clegg-Hill, JP, 5th son of 3rd Viscount, *b* 1879, *d* 1930: *m* 1907, Dorothy, who *d* 1978, da of Rev Sir George Boughey, 5th Bt:—
Anne Selina Elizabeth (Aqualate Hall, Newport, Shropshire TF10 9DB), *b* 1915: *m* 1st, 1940 (*m diss* 1947), Edward Hanbury Carington David Lloyd-Davies; 2ndly, 1947, Janusz Maria Stanislaw Eugeniusz Juhre, late 2nd Lt Polish Army, of Lwow, Poland, and has issue living (by 2nd *m*), Tadeusz Maria Gerald Alexander (Aqualate Hall, Newport, Shropshire), *b* 1951, — Maria Jadwiga Teresa, *b* 1948: *m* 1973, Andrew Maryniák, of 181 Pitshanger Lane, W5 1RQ, and has issue living, Richard *b* 1977, Martin *b* 1980, Stefan *b* 1982, Joanna *b* 1974, — Jadwiga Maria Teresa Celina, *b* 1949: *m* 1972, Richard Saller, of 92 Grove Av, W7 3ES , and has issue living, Michael *b* 1976, Andrew *b* (twin) 1976, Jan Fryderyk *b* 1983, Teresa *b* 1974, Monika *b* 1990, — Anna Zofia Maria (18 Parkcroft Rd, Westbridgeford, Nottingham NG2 6FN), *b* 1954: *m* 1974 (*m diss* 1991), Dr George Behnke, and has issue living, Wojciech *b* 1983, Margaret *b* 1980, Katheryn *b* 1981.

(In remainder to Barony and Baronetcy)

Grandchildren of late John Hill (1840-1928), eldest son of late Rev John Hill (1802-1891) (infra):—
Issue of late John Kenyon Hill, *b* 1869, *d* 1945: *m* 1906, Mary Ruby, da of Frank Watkins, of Parklands, Nairobi, Kenya:—
Mary Sybil (30B Conway Rd, Leamington Spa, Warwicks CV32 5PA), *b* 1909; missionary in Ethiopia: *m* 1935 (*m diss* 1947), Sqdn-Ldr Colin Alexander MacKenzie, RAFVR, and has issue living, Ewen Rowland Francis (PO Box 269, Graskop 1270, Mpumalanga, S Africa), *b* 1936; *ed* Reading Univ (BA): *m* 19—, Margot Christina Dunnet, of NZ, and has issue living, Rowland Charles *b* 1966, Leeann *b* 1968: *m* 1996, Jeremy Roots, of 100 Bellenden Rd, SE15. —— Muriel Rachel (Tantoni, PO Box 63, Kilifi, Kenya), *b* 1911: *m* 1935, John Wilson Lichfield Harris, who *d* 19—, and has issue living, Charles John (Longonot Farm, PO Box 86, Naivasha, Kenya), *b* 1935: *m* 1961, Rosemary Thian, and has issue living, Simon John Charles *b* 1965: *m* 19—, Katrinika Croze (and has issue living, Katya *b* 19—), Georgina Moir *b* 1962: *m* 1st, 19— (*m diss* 19—); 2ndly, 1991, (Gerald Anthony) Peregrine Pole-Carew (and has issue (by 2nd *m*) (*see* Pole, Bt, colls, *cr* 1628)), — David Richard Kenyon, *b* 1941: *m* 1972 (*m diss* 19—), Josephine Martin, and has issue living, John *b* 1974, — Mary Victoria, (PO Box 309, Kilifi, Kenya), *b* 1940: *m* 1964, Jeremy Needham-Clark, and has issue living, Giles *b* 19—, Hugo *b* 19—

Issue of late Frederick Rowland Hill, *b* 1870, *d* 1947: *m* 1910, Theodora Ann, who *d* 1961, da of late Rev R. H. Quick:—
Rev Preb Richard Hebert, *b* 1911; *ed* Wrekin Coll; Preb Emeritus of Hereford Cathedral, and a Freeman of Shrewsbury; 1939-45 War: *m* 1945, Suzanne, da of late Dr Horace Gooch, of Ragleth House, Church Stretton, and has issue living, Frederick Peter Gooch (Springbank, Well Lane, Little Witley, Worcester WR6 6LN), *b* 1946; *ed* Worksop Coll, and Grey Coll, Durham; admitted a sol 1972; Freeman of Shrewsbury: *m* 1975, Diana Mary, da of Richard Ekin, and has issue living, Matthew Anthony *b* 1982, Mary Elizabeth *b* 1976, — Richard Stephen (The Old Vicarage, Cockshutt, Ellesmere, Shropshire SY12 0JQ), *b* 1949; *ed* Worksop Coll, and Sheffield Poly (BSc); FRICS; Freeman of Shrewsbury: *m* 1976, Susan, da of Ronald Wren, of NZ, and has issue living, Nicholas Anthony Owen *b* 1979, Jeremy David Rhydian *b* 1981. *Residence* – 4 Old School, Henley Rd, Ludlow, Shropshire SY8 1RA.

Grandsons of late Frederick Rowland Hill (ante):—
Issue of late Rev Canon Rowland Edward Hill, *b* 1913; *d* 1981, Elizabeth, who *d* 1981, da of late Roland Maddison Vaisey, of Tring, Herts:—
David Rowland (9 Relugas Rd, Edinburgh EH9 2NE), *b* 1940; *ed* Glenalmond, and Keble Coll, Oxford (MA), Dip Ed, BA, MSc, Inst for Applied Language Studies, Edinburgh Univ; Freeman of Shrewsbury: *m* 1st, 1969 (*m diss* 1984), Sonya, da of Stuart McClusky; 2ndly, 1984, Janet Elizabeth, da of Harold John Powell, and has issue living (by 1st *m*), Charlotte Ruth, *b* 1973, — (by 2nd *m*) Christopher Rowland, *b* 1989, — Katharine Martha, *b* 1987. —— Nigel John (32 Colebrooke Av, Ealing W13 8JY), *b* 1943; *ed* Glenalmond, and Univ Coll, Durham (BA); Ch Inspector Met Police (ret); Freeman of Shrewsbury: *m* 1968, Gillian Mary, yr da of late Ian Heath Stock, MC, and has issue living, Oliver Rowland Vaisey (77 Brookfield Rd, W4 1DF), *b* 1972; *ed* Latymer Upper, and Reading Univ (BA): *m* 1998, Annabel Clare, yr da of Richard William Nweth Payne, of Warlingham, Surrey, — Clarissa Mary, *b* 1969; *ed* Notting Hill & Ealing High Sch, and Girton Coll, Camb (MA): *m* 1991, Daniel Haydn Withers Poulson, of 125 West Hill Rd, SW18 5IIN (and has issue living, Noah Michael Haydn *b* 1997), — Rosanna Seymour, *b* 1978; *ed* Notting Hill & Ealing High Sch, and Van Mildert Coll, Durham. —— James Geoffrey (The Priory, 11 Friars Lane, Lanark ML11 9EL), *b* 1948; *ed* Glenalmond, Univ Coll, Durham (BA), and Birmingham Univ (MB, ChB); Freeman of Shrewsbury: *m* 1974, Eileen Frances Rachel, da of late Charles Rodney Webster, WS, of Edinburgh, and has issue living, Katriona Helen, *b* 1976; *ed* Park Sch, and Aberdeen Univ, — Anna Elizabeth *b* 1979, — Sara Frances, *b* 1983, — Nicola Margaret, *b* 1985. —— Andrew Vaisey (17 Cockle Crescent, Clovelly, Cape Province 7975, S Africa), *b* 1950; *ed* Shrewsbury, and Univ Coll, Durham (BA), Freeman of Shrewsbury: *m* 1st, 1974 (*m diss* 1990), Zaria Caroline Annabel, da of late Maj Joseph Theodore Knowles, Wilts Regt; 2ndly, 1991, Shirley Joan Marais (*née* Stofberg), and has issue living (by 1st *m*), Jonathan Rowland Vaisey, *b* 1980; *ed* Cheltenham, — Rowena Jane Imogen, *b* 1977; *ed* Cheltenham Ladies' Coll, and Sussex Univ (BA).

Granddaughters (by 2nd *m*) of late Sir Clement Lloyd Hill, KCB, KCMG, MP (1845-1913), 3rd son of late Rev John Hill (1802-1891), next brother of 2nd Viscount:—
Issue of late Maj Clement Walter Rowland Hill, Queen's Own Cameron Highlanders, *b* 1909, *d* 1997: *m* 1st, 1935 (*m diss* 1941), Violet, who *d* 1988, eldest da of Charles Phillimore, of The Old Farm, Swinbrook, Oxon; 2ndly, 1947, Elizabeth Theresa, who *d* 1970, 3rd da of late Capt Jersey J. J. de Knoop, of Calveley Hall, Cheshire, and formerly wife of John Henry Hambro, CMG; 3rdly, 1971, Kathleen, who *d* 1982, da of Frank Dickle, of Truro, Nova Scotia, and widow of Norman Walduck:—
(By 1st *m*) Carolyn Mary (*Carolyn, Countess Fortescue*), *b* 1937: *m* 1st, 1968 (*m diss* 1983), Edward C. Lockwood; 2ndly, 1989, as his 3rd wife, 7th Earl Fortescue, who *d* 1993, and has issue living (by 1st *m*), Richard Rowland, *b* 1971, — Louisa Elizabeth, *b* 1969. *Residence* – The Old Rectory, Bradoc, Lostwithiel, Cornwall PL22 0RN. —— Joanna Clementine, *b* 1939: *m* 1965, Charles C. Bastin, and has issue living, Alexander Charles, *b* 1969, — Nicholas Rowland, *b* 1970. *Residences* – Rutland Lodge, 83 Albert Bridge Rd, SW11 4PH; and Larroque, 47370 Tournon d'Agenais, France.

Grandchildren of late Henry Alan Hill, eldest son of Henry Philip Hill, yr son of Lt-Col Richard Frederick Hill, 3rd son of Col John Hill (ante):—
Issue of late Henry James Hill, *b* 1921, *d* 1985: *m* 1953, Ina Rosemary Philpott, of El Refugio, 2852 E Carbo, Entre Rios, Argentina:—

Henry John (Urquiza 78, 2840 Gualeguay, Entre Rios, Argentina), *b* 1962: *m* 1993, Susana N. Jodor, and has issue living, Sofia, *b* 1995, — Victoria, *b* 1997. — Virginia Rosemary, *b* 1954: *m* 1975, Ronald Joffre Bain, of Urquiza 78, 2840 Gualeguay, Entre Rios, Argentina, and has issue living, Joffre Enrique, *b* 1978, — Alan, *b* 1980, — Karen Ivonne, *b* 1976. — Margaret Ina, *b* 1956: *m* 1980, Christian Dougall, of Chacra Alcala, Flaubert 950, 1661 Bella Vista, Prov Buenos Aires, Argentina, and has issue living, James Alexander, *b* 1982, — Lorraine, *b* 1983, — Jennifer Ina, *b* 1989, — Melanie, *b* 1995. — Christine Marion (Santa Fe 410 - 11'H', (1641) Acassuso, Buenos Aires, Argentina), *b* 1959.

Grandson of late Henry Philip Hill, yr son of Lt-Col Richard Frederick Hill, 3rd son of Col John Hill (ante):—
Issue of late Rowland Philip Hill, *b* 1888, *d* 1979: *m* 1912, Ruth, who *d* 1976, da of C. H. Stott:—
†Brian Henry Rowland, *b* 1917; *ed* Christ's Coll, Christchurch, NZ, and Otago Univ (MB, ChB); DDM Sydney; Middle East 1945 with Roy NZ Med Corps: *m* 1945, Marjorie Virginia (11 Milton Terrace, Napier, NZ), da of Capt Euan Dickson, DSC, DFC, of Auckland, NZ, and *d* 1998, leaving issue, Heathcote Hamish Rowland (The Ivy Longhouse, Bath Rd, Chippenham, Wilts SN15 2AE), *b* 1949; assumed forename of Hamish in lieu of Henry by deed poll; artist, — Simon Philip (7 Thompson Rd, Napier, NZ), *b* 1951, — Angela Francesca, *b* 1946: *m* 1977, Kim Campbell of 61 Spencer St, Remuera, Auckland 5, NZ, and has issue living, Benjamin *b* 1980, Tristan *b* 19—.

(In remainder to Baronetcy)

Grandsons of Robert Hill, son of Capt Alfred Edward Hill, 2nd son of Sir Robert Chambré Hill, CB, 4th son of 3rd baronet:—
Issue of late Alfred Brabant Hill, *b* 1896, *d* 1979: *m* 1933, Frances, who *d* 1986, da of Edward Pooley:—
John Richard, *b* 1935; *ed* British Columbia Univ (BSc), and McGill Univ (PhD). — Peter Robert (1840 Nigel Court, Vienna, Va 22182, USA), *b* 1937; *ed* British Columbia Univ (BA, Sc): *m* 1st, 1968, Mary Lynn, who *d* 1993, da of late Keller Smith; 2ndly, 1994, Mrs Joyce Ann Ralston, da of late Robert E. Prowty, and has issue living (by 1st *m*), Peter Brabant, *b* 1970, — Charles Edward Keller, *b* 1980, — Molly Cochran, *b* 1972.

Grandson of late Henry Daniel Hill, 3rd son of late Robert Greene Hill (*b* 1801), son of late Rev Robert Wilbraham Bromhall Hill, el son of late Rev Robert Hill, 4th son of 1st baronet:—
Issue of late Roger Wilbraham Hill, *b* 1883, *d* 1962: *m* 1912, Mary Ann, who *d* 1971, da of James Sadler, of Acton, Chester:—
Gerald Roger (Hough Gates, Hough, Crewe CW2 5JG), *b* 1921; *m* 1953, Jane Elizabeth, JP, da of Frank Haighton, of Elm House, Nantwich, and has issue living, Gerald Robert Wilbraham, *b* 1958, — Elizabeth Mary *b* 1955; PhD.

Grandchildren of late John Francis Hill (infra):—
Issue of late Alaric Bryan Hill, *b* 1921, *d* 1992: *m* 1948, Elizabeth Margaret Allen, who *d* 1994:—
Dallas John (PO Box 283, Kokstad, Natal 4700, S Africa), *b* 1950: *m* 1975 (*m diss* 1994), Bronwyn Lucie Van Der Leeuw, and has issue living, Christopher John, *b* 1975, — Rowland John, *b* 1978, — Dallas Joseph, *b* 1989. — Carol Elizabeth, *b* 1953: *m* 1974, Gordon Redvers Bell, of 12 Gibson Close, Singleton Heights, NSW 2330, Australia, and Box 278, Singleton, NSW 2330, Australia, and has issue living, Julian Redvers, *b* 1978, — Cherié Elizabeth, *b* 1974.

Granddaughter of late Francis Robert Wilbraham Hill, 5th and yst son of late Robert Greene Hill (*b* 1801) (ante):—
Issue of late John Francis Hill, *b* 1882, *d* 1948: *m* 1916, Natalie Ivy, who *d* 1967, da of Thomas Payne St James (*see* V Hill, colls, 1937 Edn):—
Vivette Natalie, *b* 1925: *m* 1949, Johan Heinrich Moll, BSc, FMIMechE, and has issue living, Victor Derek (Box 1309 Oranjemund, 9000 Namibia), *b* 1954: *m* 1984, Patricia Du Randt, — Coleen Yvonne MOLL, *b* 1951, BSocSc, B Com; has resumed her maiden name: *m* 1975 (*m diss* 1983), Roger Charles Peplow, MSc, of Durban, Natal, S Africa. *Residence* – 15 Straker Av, Gun Hill, Harare, Zimbabwe.

Grandchildren of late Lt-Gen George Mytton Hill, yr son of late Richard Hill, 5th son of late Rev Robert Hill (ante):—
Issue of late Maj Arthur Rowland Hill, *b* 1880, *ka* 1915: *m* 1908, Kathleen, da of late C. James Todd:—
Alison Kathleen, *b* 1911: *m* 1934, Henry Seaward Morley, MD, FRCP, who *d* 1961, and has issue living, John Henry, *b* 1936; *ed* Wellington Coll, and Downing Coll, Camb (MA): *m* 1963, Felicity Faith Beryl, el da of John Peile, of Grindleford, Sheffield, and has issue living, Rupert Oliver Henry *b* 1965, Benjamin William Mervyn *b* 1969, — Timothy Rowland, *b* 1939; *ed* Wellington Coll, and Downing Coll, Camb (MA); MB, BCh, FRCS, LRCP: *m* 1966, Mary Elspeth Holborn, da of Noel Frederick Adeney, FRCS, of Bournemouth, and has issue living, David Mark Rowland *b* 1969; *ed* London Univ (BA), Nicola Susie Gray *b* 1968; *ed* Leeds Univ (BSc): *m* 1993, Andrew Philip Martello Gray (and has issue living, James Angus Martello *b* 1996, Sophie Rowan Holborn *b* 1999). *Residence* – Fife House, 16A Heath Drive, Walton-on-the-Hill, Tadworth, Surrey KT20 7QQ.

Issue of late Cdr George Mytton Hill, RN, *b* 1883, *d* 1935: *m* 1919, Olive Odell, who *d* 1966, da of W. Millar, of Eskbank:—
Doreen Odell, *b* 1920: *m* 1950, Maj Hector McNeill Tytler Reith, RA (ret), and has issue living, Douglas McNeill Mytton, *b* 1953, *ed* St George's Sch, Tonbridge, and Webber Douglas Acad of Dramatic Art.

Issue of late Harold Brian Cunningham Hill, FRGS, *b* 1887, *d* 1980: *m* 1920, Elsie, who *d* 1971, da of J. Jeppe, JP, Consul-Gen for Greece and for Roumania, and Senior Roy Danish Consul in S Africa:—
Noel Brian (Balneath Manor Farm, S Chailey, nr Lewes, E Sussex BN8 4AP), *b* 1926; *ed* Eastbourne Coll: *m* 1958, Gladys Rosa, da of late Sidney George West, OBE, and has issue living, Nicola Anne, *b* 1959; *ed* Moira House, and Warwick Univ (BA): *m* 1985, Paul Jonathan Woodley, of Broad Oak, Copthorne, E Sussex, and has issue living, Christopher Benjamin *b* 1989, Daisy Anne *b* 1991, — Philippa Jane, *b* 1962, — and an adopted da, Jill Adrienne, *b* 1953; *ed* Moira House, and Sussex Univ (BA). — †Julian, *b* 1932; *ed* Eastbourne Coll; served as Lieut 1st Bn 22nd (Cheshire) Regt in Egypt 1953-54; Man Dir Julian Hill Ltd, and Scanhill Ltd; Freeman of City of London; FBIM; MInstM; FIOD: *m* 1956, Ruth Monica (Huntsland Cottage, Huntsland Lane, Crawley Down, Sussex RH10 4HB), yst da of late Paul Sekvens

Toll, of 10 Villagatan, Stockholm, and *d* 1999, leaving issue, Rowland Paul (16 Ashley Mansions, Vauxhall Bridge Rd, SW1V 1BS), *b* 1956; *ed* Eastbourne Coll; ACA, — Michael Mytton (La Ruelle, 16 rue Basse, 62770 Le Fresnoy, Pas de Calais, France), *b* 1960; *ed* Eastbourne Coll, W Surrey Coll of Art & Design (BA), and Duncan of Jordanstone Coll of Art, Dundee (MA): *m* 1990, Priscilla, yst da of Frank Morgan, and has issue living, Christopher Robert *b* 1993, Joshua Julian *b* 1996, — Anne-Louise, *b* 1963; *ed* Moira House, St Claire's Hall, Oxford, and Edinburgh Univ (MA): *m* 1996, Paul Hottinger, of 5 Linzee Rd, Crouch End, N8 7RG, and has issue living, Rory Alexander *b* 1997.

Issue of late Reginald Herbert Hill, *b* 1889, *d* 1978: *m* 1st, 1914, Elizabeth Wallace, da of late A. S. Coubrough, JP, of Blanefield, Stirlingshire; 2ndly, 1931, Gertrude, da of J. Perry, of Tavistock, Devon:—
(By 1st *m*), Kathleen Agnes, *b* 1916: *m* 1946, George Elden Burrell, of 2760 Burdick Av, Victoria, BC, Canada V8R 3L9, and has issue living, Robin Elden Adair (2797 Musgrave St, Victoria, BC, Canada V8R 5Y7), *b* 1951: *m* 1st, 1982, Katharine Regina, da of Colin D. McCullough, of Victoria, BC; 2ndly, 1996, Geraldine Mary Phillips, and has issue living (by 1st *m*), Patrick McCullough *b* 1986, Jamison Alexander *b* 1990, — Keith Edgar (4596 Teviot Place, N Vancouver, BC, Canada V7K 4M5), *b* 1953: *m* 1981, Leslie Jean, da of Ian C. Colquhoun, of Vancouver, BC, and has issue living, Scott Thomas *b* 1983, Ross Edward *b* 1990, — Wendy Evelyn (2585 Cavendish Av, Victoria, BC, Canada V8R 2G5), *b* 1948: *m* 1st, 1969 (*m diss* 1983), Bruce Ronald McConnan; 2ndly, 1984 (*m diss* 1990), David Marley, and has issue living (by 1st *m*), Brock Stewart *b* 1976, Kelly Evelyn *b* 1973. —— Winifred Evelyn, *b* 1920: *m* 1945, Charles M. Humphrys, of 3613 Nico Wynd Drive, Surrey, BC V2A 2W3, Canada, and has issue living, Daphne Mary, *b* 1947: *m* 1968, Douglas James Lovick, of 3126 W 37th Av, Vancouver, BC, Canada V6N 2V2, and has issue living, Heidi Marie *b* 1970, Cynthia Evelyn *b* 1973, Anna Marjory *b* 1983, — Sheila Elizabeth, *b* 1947: *m* 1969, Brian Paul Jagger, of 5961 Adera St, Vancouver, BC, Canada V6M 3J3 and has issue living, Brigham Humphry *b* 1976, Ryan Selwyn *b* 1978, Christina Catherine *b* 1974, Stephanie Elizabeth *b* 1980, — Brenda Ann, *b* 1953: *m* 1974, David William Haskett, of 120 Silver Springs Green, NW Calgary, Alberta, Canada T3B 3Y9, and has issue living, Kevin *b* 1983, Kathryn Jane *b* 1982, Kelly Evelyn *b* 1988, — Nancy Maureen (3555 W 24th, Vancouver, BC, Canada V6S 1L5), *b* 1958: *m* 1st, 1981, Douglas Alan Leard; 2ndly, 1996, Andrew Martin, and has issue living (by 1st *m*), James Douglas *b* 1984, Kerry Alana *b* 1986. —— (By 2nd *m*) (Arthur) Brian Montague (2545 Rolling Hills Court, Alamo, Cal 94507, USA), *b* 1932: *m* 1960, Brenda Margaret, da of W. A. Murray of Bebington, Ches, and has an adopted son, George Mytton, *b* 1969.

PREDECESSORS – *Sir* Richard Hill, PC, an eminent statesman and diplomatist; *d* unmarried, and devised his Hawkstone estates to his nephew **(1)** ROWLAND Hill, who in consideration of his uncle's important sers was *cr* a *Baronet* 1727, with remainder to his cousins Samuel Hill, of Shenstone, Thomas Hill, of Tern, whose el son was *cr* Baron Berwick, and to Rowland Hill, brother of Thomas (ante); sat as MP for Lichfield 1734; *d* 1783; *s* by his el son **(2)** *Sir* RICHARD, 2nd Bt, MP for co Salop 1780-1802; *d* unmarried 1809; *s* by his brother **(3)** *Sir* JOHN, 3rd Bt, MP for Shrewsbury 1784-1802; his 2nd son Rowland, GCB, a distinguished Gen and Com in Ch 1828-42, was *cr Baron Hill*, of Almarez and of Hawkestone, co Salop (peerage of United Kingdom) 1814, and *Viscount Hill* (peerage of United Kingdom) 1842, with remainder in each instance to the issue of his el brother John; Sir John *d* 1824, and was *s* by his grandson **(4)** ROWLAND, 4th Bt, son of John (ante); in 1842 *s* his uncle (ante) as 2nd Viscount Hill; *b* 1800; was MP for Shropshire 1821-32 and for N Shropshire (C) 1832-42, and Lord Lieut of Salop: *m* 1831, Anne, only child of Joseph Clegg, of Peplow Hall, Salop, and sole heir of Arthur Clegg; *d* 1875; *s* by his son **(5)** ROWLAND CLEGG, 3rd Viscount, *b* 1833; MP for N Shropshire (C) 1857-65; assumed in 1875 the additional surname of Clegg: *m* 1st, 1855, Mary, who *d* 1874, da of William Madax; 2ndly, 1875, Hon Isabella Elizabeth Wynn, who *d* 1898, da of 3rd Baron Newborough; *d* 1895; *s* by his el son **(6)** ROWLAND RICHARD, 4th Viscount, *b* 1863; was Master of Spectacle Makers' Co: *m* 1890, Aunie Edith, who *d* 1937, da of late William Irwin, of Tandrago, co Sligo; *d* 1923; *s* by his brother **(7)** FRANCIS WILLIAM, 5th Viscount, *b* 1866: *m* 1905, Caroline Anna, who *d* 1941, da of late Capt Frank Corbett, of Greenfield, Presteigne, Radnorshire; *d* 1924; *s* by his grandson **(8)** CHARLES ROWLAND, DSO, 6th Viscount, *b* 1876; Lieut-Col late Roy Welch Fusiliers: *m* 1st, 1903, Mildred, who *d* 1936, da of Thomas Bulteel; 2ndly, 1936, Berthe Maria Emilie, who *d* 1959, da of late A. Schmidt-Immer, of Strasbourg, Alsace-Lorraine; *d* 1957; *s* by his son **(9)** GERALD ROWLAND, 7th Viscount, *b* 1904: *m* 1st, 1930 (*m diss* 1942), Elisabeth Flora, who *d* 1967, da of Brig-Gen George Nowell Thomas Smyth-Osbourne, CB, CMG, DSO, DL, of Ash, Iddlesleigh, N Devon; 2ndly, 1942, Catherine Mary (Molly), da of Dr Rowland Venables Lloyd-Williams, of Maiford, Denbigh; *d* 1974; *s* by his el son **(10)** ANTONY ROWLAND, 8th Viscount and present peer; also Baron Hill.

Hill, family name of Marquess of Downshire.

HILL OF LUTON, BARONY OF (Hill) (Extinct 1989)

SONS LIVING OF LIFE BARON

Hon Robert (33 Meadow View, Dunvant, Swansea, W Glamorgan), *b* 1938; *ed* Epsom, and Harper Adams Agricultural Coll: *m* 1960, Ann, da of E. Williamson, of Southampton, and has issue.
Hon John (48 Sheehan St, Pearce, ACT 2607, Australia), *b* 1945; *ed* Epsom, and Camb Univ: *m* 1974, Dawn, da of I. Lance, of Sydney, NSW, Australia and has issue.

DAUGHTERS LIVING OF LIFE BARON

(Hon) Jennifer (does not use courtesy title), *b* 1933: *m* 1st, 1960 (*m diss* 1973), Robert Duncan Barnaby Leicester, MB; 2ndly, 1975, Thomas Trenerry, of 8/6 Bells Rd, Dundas, NSW 2117, Australia, and has issue (by 1st *m*).

Hon Elizabeth, *b* 1935: *m* 1964, David Maxwell Morris, of 9 St Leonards Rd, Exeter, and has issue.

Hon Susan, *b* 1936: *m* 1958, David Ritchie Fairbairn, of 11 Oak Way, West Common, Harpenden, Herts, and has issue.

Hill, Clegg-, family name of Viscount Hill.

HILL-NORTON, BARON (Hill-Norton) (Life Baron 1979)

·TRY·HARDER·

PETER JOHN HILL-NORTON, GCB, son of Capt Martin John Norton; *b* 8 Feb 1915; *ed* RN Colls Dartmouth and Greenwich; Adm of the Fleet; Com-in-Ch UK Forces in Far East 1969-70; First Sea Lord 1970-71; Chief of the Defence Staff 1971-74; Chm NATO Military Cttee 1974-77; *cr* CB (Mil) 1964, KCB (Mil) 1967, GCB (Mil) 1970 and *Baron Hill-Norton*, of South Nutfield, co Surrey (Life Baron) 1979: *m* 1936, Margaret Eileen, da of Carl Adolph Linstow, and has issue.

Arms – On a bend gules between in chief a terrestrial sphere proper and in base three cannon balls sable within an annulet azure four anchors or. **Crest** – Out of a naval crown or on a mount vert a springbok trippant proper. **Supporters** – On either side a hippocampus holding in the tail an anchor proper.
Residence – Cass Cottage, Hyde, Fordingbridge. *Clubs* – Army and Navy, Royal Navy of 1765.

SON LIVING

Hon Sir Nicholas John, KCB, *b* 1939; Vice Adm RN; KCB (Mil) 1991: *m* 1966, (Ann) Jennifer, da of Vice-Adm Dennis Mason, CB, CVO, and has issue living, Simon Nicholas Sebastian, *b* 1967: *m* 1997, Tamara L., elder da of Lt Cmdr Nicko Franks, of Little Mockbeggar, Kent, — Peter Tom, *b* 1975, — Claudia Genevieve Jane, *b* 1969: *m* 1994, Thomas M. Bradby, and has issue living, Jack Humphrey *b* 1996, Louisa *b* 1997.

DAUGHTER LIVING

Hon Carla Ann, *b* 1943: *m* 1st, 1966, Christopher Thomas Jowett; 2ndly, 1974, Graeme McLintock, of Slate Cottage, Elsted, nr Midhurst, W Sussex GU29 0JZ, and has had issue (by 1st *m*), Benjamin, *b* 1967, — James, *b* 1969, *d* 1991.

HILLINGDON, BARONY OF (Mills) (Extinct 1982)

DAUGHTERS LIVING OF FIFTH BARON

Hon Sarah Patricia, *b* 1933: *m* 1955, Maj Jonathan Michael Henry Balcon, TD, Inns of Court and City Yeo, of The Grey House, Seal, Sevenoaks, Kent, and has issue living, Deborah Louisa Kate, *b* 1956: *m* 1st, 1978 (*m diss* 1996), Timothy Jackson Wilson; 2ndly, 1997, Stephen John Richards, of Rivermead Court, SW6, and has issue living (by 1st *m*), Alexander Edward Jackson *b* 1982, Oliver Patrick Henry *b* 1985, — Sarah Clair, *b* 1957: *m* 1987, Julian James Neuburger, only son of Henry Neuburger, of Locrano, Switzerland, and has issue living, James Michael *b* 1991, Lucy *b* 1989, — Henrietta Beatrice Jane, *b* 1960: *m* 1985, Maj Timothy Hugh Breitmeyer, Gren Gds, and has issue (*see* Abertay, By).

Hon Jenefer, *b* 1935: *m* 1962, His Honour Joseph Dean, of The Hall, West Brabourne, Kent, and has issue living, Ptolemy Hugo, *b* 1967, — Antigone Lucy, *b* 1963: *m* 1997, John Anthony Leonard, and has issue living, Ivo Joseph Tressidder *b* 1999, — Tacita Charlotte, *b* 1965.

DAUGHTERS LIVING OF FOURTH BARON

Hon Victoria Elizabeth *b* 1948: *m* 1st, 1971 (*m diss* 1979), Anthony Roff; 2ndly, 1981, D. G. R. Cruickshank, of 15 Elder St, E1, and has issue living (by 1st *m*), Nandi Rita, *b* 1972, — Alice Diana, *b* 1974, — (by 2nd *m*) Isabel Mary Rose, *b* 1981.

Hon Jessica Anne, *b* 1957: *m* 1991, Benjamin Henry Gaskell, and has issue (*see* B Bagot, colls).

Hon Catherine Gray, *b* 1963.

DAUGHTER LIVING OF THIRD BARON.

Hon Ursula Sibyl (Wakefield Cottage, Wembworthy, nr Chulmleigh, Devon), *b* 1918.

WIDOW LIVING OF FOURTH BARON

PHOEBE MAXWELL (*Baroness Hillingdon*), da of late Capt Mervyn James Hamilton, of Cornacassa, Monaghan (V Bangor, colls), and formerly wife of (i) Lt-Cdr John Sholto Fitzpatrick Cooke, CBE, RNVR, and (ii) John Cooper; *m* 1978, as his 2nd wife, the 4th Baron Hillingdon, who *d* 1978. *Residence* – Shalom Hall, Layer Breton, Colchester, Essex.

Hillsborough, Earl of; son of Marquess of Downshire.

HILTON OF EGGARDON, BARONESS (Hilton) (Life Baroness 1991)

JENNIFER HILTON, da of late John Robert Hilton, CMG, of London; *b* 1936; *ed* Bedales Sch, and Manchester Univ (MA); Police Officer, Metropolitan Police Ser 1956-90 (Cdr 1984-90); *cr Baroness Hilton of Eggardon*, of Eggardon, co Dorset (Life Baroness) 1991.

Arms – Azure, between two bees in fess and volant upwards and outwards proper, growing from a grassy mount in base and protected by palings about its trunk an oak tree also proper and fructed gold. **Supporters** – *Dexter*, on a grassy mount growing therefrom two dog roses proper, a crested newt statant erect vert holding by its inner forefoot a tipstaff proper; *sinister*, on a grassy mount growing therefrom two dog roses proper, a griffin statant erect argent, armed, winged and tail tufted or, grasping in its inner foreclaw a serpent entwined about the foreleg also proper.

Address – c/o Barclays Bank plc, 1 The Causeway, Teddington, Middx.

Hinchingbrooke, Viscount; son of Earl of Sandwich.

HINDLIP, BARON (Allsopp) (Baron UK 1886, Bt UK 1880)

Hasten slowly

CHARLES HENRY ALLSOPP, 6th Baron, and 6th Baronet; *b* 5 Aug 1940; *s* 1993; *ed* Eton; late Lieut Coldstream Gds; Chm Christie Manson & Wood 1970, Dep Chm 1985, Chm 1986: *m* 1968, Fiona Victoria Jean Atherley, only child of late Hon William Johnston McGowan (*see* B McGowan, colls), and has issue.

𝕬rms – Sable, three pheons in chevron or, between as many doves rising argent, each holding in the beak a wheat-ear or. 𝕮rest – A plover, holding in beak a wheat-ear or, standing on a pheon also gold. 𝕾upporters – Two fox-hounds, each gorged with a pair of couples proper.
Residences – The Cedar House, Inkpen, Berks; 55 Campden Hill Rd, W8. *Clubs* – White's, Pratt's.

SON LIVING

Hon HENRY WILLIAM, *b* 8 June 1973.

DAUGHTERS LIVING

Hon Kirstie Mary, *b* 1971.
Hon Sophia Atherley, *b* 1980.
Hon Natasha Fiona, *b* 1986.

BROTHER LIVING

Hon John Peter, *b* 1942; *ed* Eton: *m* 1976, Daryl, 3rd da of Leonard Shawzin, of Huisinbois, Constantia, CP, South Africa, and has issue living, James Leonard, *b* 1978, — Kathryn Sarah, *b* 1981, — Camilla Rose, *b* 1990.

SISTER LIVING

Hon Sarah Cecily, *b* 1944: *m* 1967, Hugh Robert Myddelton, of 139, Holland Park Av, W11, and has issue (*see* M Lansdowne).

AUNTS LIVING (*Daughters of 3rd Baron*)

Hon Diana Joan (*Hon Lady Hardy*), *b* 1908: *m* 1930, Lieut-Col Sir Rupert John Hardy, 4th Bt, Life Guards, who *d* 1997, and has issue. *Residence* – Gullivers Lodge, Guilsborough, Northampton NN6 8RB.
Hon Nancy Marion, *b* 1910: *m* 1936, Peter Geoffrey Brooke, and has issue living, Michael Peter, *b* 1937; Maj 16th/15th Lancers: *m* 1970, Susan Rhona Martin, yr da of A. W. Peacop, of Blue Hills, Finchampstead, Berks. *Residence* – Dial House, Chilmark, Wilts.

DAUGHTERS LIVING OF FOURTH BARON

Hon Penelope Jane, *b* 1940: *m* 1965, Theodore Demetrius Velissaropoulos. *Residence* – Taxilis 75, Athens 15771, Greece.
Hon Elizabeth Tulla, *b* 1942. *Residence* – 40 Bloomfield Terr, SW1W 8PQ

WIDOW LIVING OF FIFTH BARON

CECILY VALENTINE JANE (*Dowager Baroness Hindlip*), only da of late Lt-Col Malcolm Borwick, DSO, of Haselbech Hill, Northampton: *m* 1939, Maj the 5th Baron Hindlip, who *d* 1993. *Residence* – Tytherton House, E Tytherton, Chippenham, Wilts.

COLLATERAL BRANCHES LIVING

Grandchildren of late Lt-Col Hon Ranulph Allsopp, 4th son of 1st Baron:—
Issue of late Samuel Ranulph Allsopp, CBE, *b* 1899, *d* 1975: *m* 1923, Hon Norah Hyacinthe Littleton, who *d* 1997, da of 4th Baron Hatherton:—
Michael Edward Ranulph (Little Coxwell Grove, Faringdon, Oxon; White's and Pratt's Clubs), *b* 1930; *ed* Eton: *m* 1953, Patricia, da of late Geoffrey H. Berners of Little Coxwell Grove, Faringdon, Oxon, and has issue living, Frances Jane Berners, *b* 1955: *m* 1st, 1975 (*m diss* 1980), Dermot Michael Claud Chichester (*see* M Donegall); 2ndly, 1984, Maj David John Basil Woodd, 14th/20th King's Hus, of The Homestead, Little Coxwell, Faringdon, Oxon, elder son of late Col Basil Bethune Neville Woodd, of Kingsgate, Rolvenden, Kent, and has issue living (by 2nd *m*), Matilda Elizabeth *b* 1990, Tabitha Ann *b* 1991, — Carolyn Anne Berners, *b* 1957, — Davina Hyacinthe Berners (*Lady Powell*), *b* 1960: *m* 1987, as his 2nd wife, Sir Nicholas Folliott Douglas Powell, 4th Bt, and has issue, — Jessica Elizabeth Berners (*Hon Mrs Edward Leigh-Pemberton*), *b* (twin) 1960: *m* 1984, Hon Edward Douglas Leigh-Pemberton, of Longcot House, Longcot, Faringdon, Oxon, 3rd son of Baron Kingsdown, PC (Life Baron), and has issue. —— David Samuel, *b* 1933; *ed* Eton: *m* 1st, 1960 (*m diss* 1966), Tan Doris May, da of Frederick J Arnold, of Turbary Rd, Parkstone, Dorset; 2ndly, 1972, Sally, da of late

V. H. Thirkell, of High Tilt Farm, Cranbrook, Kent, and has issue living (by 2nd *m*), James Samuel, *b* 1972, — Melanie Angela, *b* 1977. —— Juliet Modwena, *b* 1925; formerly WRNS: *m* 1952, Samuel Arthur Scott (*see* Scott, Bt *cr* 1962). —— Charmian Hyacinthe (Sycamore House, Tissington, Ashbourne, Derby), *b* 1926: *m* 1962, Rev David Henry FitzHerbert, who *d* 1976 (*see* FitzHerbert, Bt).

Issue of late Capt John Ranulph Allsopp, *b* 1908, *ka* in N Africa 1943: *m* 1934, Audrey Carteret Priaulx (who *d* 1960, having *m* 2ndly, 1944, Oliver Van Oss, who *d* 1992), da of late Major E. G. Fellows, of Barberry Cottage, Cheapside, Ascot:—

†Mark Ranulph, *b* 1938; *ed* Eton: *m* 1960, Tania Anna (Portishead House, The Walls, Mistley, Colchester, Essex), da of late Capt John Eustace-Smith, of Thrunton, Whittingham, Northumberland, and *d* 1996, leaving issue, Jonathan Ranulph, *b* 1962, — Richard Mark (1 Batoum Gdns, W6), *b* 1963: *m* 1990, Alexandra Dominica, da of Maj John Grosch, of Stoke-by-Nayland, Suffolk, and has issue living, Milo Johnnie Mark *b* 1996, Matilda May Cornelia *b* 1993, — Charles Samuel, *b* 1970; *ed* Eton, and RMA Sandhurst, — Arabella Sarah Georgianna, *b* 1972. —— Peter William (Mill Barn, Mill Lane, Bramley, Surrey), *b* 1940; *ed* Eton: *m* 1962, Pepita, da of Lt-Cmdr Peter E. Mason, DSC, of Auburn, Bramshott Court, Liphook, Hants, and has issue living, Amanda Caroline, *b* 1964: *m* 1988, John Howard Perry, of Spring Cottage, Moushill Lane, Milford, Surrey, only son of H. A. Perry, of Bradpole, Bridport, Dorset, and has issue living, Joshua Sam *b* 1996, Isabella Rose *b* 1999, — Sophie Victoria, *b* 1967; has issue living (by James Coope), Marshall Edward *b* 1996, — Katherine Pepita, *b* 1970: *m* 1993, Timothy Scott Ireland, of Kogarah, NSW, Australia, 2nd son of Donald Ireland, of North Rocks, Sydney, NSW, and has issue living, Benjamin James *b* 1995, Jack Edward *b* 1998.

PREDECESSORS – (1) *Sir* HENRY Allsopp, 3rd son of late Samuel Allsopp, of Burton-on-Trent *b* 1811; sat as MP for E Worcestershire (*C*) 1874-80; *cr* a *Baronet* 1880, and *Baron Hindlip*, of Hindlip, co Worcester and of Alsop-en-le-Dale, co Derby (peerage of United Kingdom) 1886: *m* 1839, Elizabeth, who *d* 1906, da of William Tongue, of Comberforf Hall, Tamworth; *d* 1887; *s* by his son (2) SAMUEL CHARLES, 2nd Baron; *b* 1842; MP for E Staffordshire (*C*) 1873-80, and for Taunton 188207: *m* 1868, Georgiana Millicent, who *d* 1939, da of late Charles Rowland Palmer-Morewood, of Alfreton, Derbyshire; *d* 1897; *s* by his son (3) CHARLES, OBE, 3rd Baron, *b* 1877; S Africa 1900, European War 1914-18 (despatches, twice, OBE, Legion of Honour); Junior Unionist Whip in House of Lords 1907-14; *m* 1904, Agatha Lillian, who *d* 1963, da of late John Charles Thynne (M Bath, colls), *d* 1931; *s* by his el son (4) CHARLES SAMUEL VICTOR, 4th Baron, *b* 1906: *m* 1st, 1932 (*m diss* 1934), Bridget, da of late Harold Nickols; 2ndly, 1939, Hansina Cecilia Elfrida (Tulla), who *d* 1988, da of late Frederick William Harris; *d* 1966; *s* by his brother (6) HENRY RICHARD, 5th Baron, *b* 1912; Maj Coldstream Gds, American Bronze Star Medal; a JP and DL for Wilts: *m* 1939, Cecily Valentine Jane, da of late Lt-Col Malcolm Borwick, DSO, of Haselbech Hill, Northampton; *d* 1993; *s* by his elder son (7) CHARLES HENRY, 6th Baron and present peer.

HINTON OF BANKSIDE, BARONY OF (Hinton) (Extinct 1983)

DAUGHTER LIVING OF LIFE BARON

Hon Susan Mary, *b* 1932: *m* 1957: Arthur Charles Mole, of 2 Second Av, Charmandean, Worthing, Sussex, BN14 9NX, son of late Sir Charles Johns Mole, KBE, MVO, and has issue, two sons, the elder of whom, Christopher C., *b* 1960: *m* 1986, Carolyn J., elder da of S. E. Deboo, of Telham, Battle, Sussex.

HIRSHFIELD, BARONY OF (Hirshfield) (Extinct 1993)

WIDOW LIVING OF LIFE BARON

BRONIA (*Baroness Hirshfield*), da of Joseph Eisen: *m* 1951, Baron Hirshfield, who *d* 1993. *Residence* – 44 Imperial Court, Prince Albert Rd, NW8 7PT.

HIRST, BARONY OF (Hirst) (Extinct 1943)

GRANDDAUGHTER OF FIRST BARON

Issue of late Harold Hugh Hirst (Lt 21st Manchester Regt, attached RE Signals), son of 1st Baron, *b* 1893, *d* 1919: *m* 1917, Carol Iris, MBE (by whom he had an only son, Hugh Harold Hirst, Pilot Officer RAFVR, *b* 1919, *k* 1941, while on operational duties), da of late Lewis Lindon, of Sussex Sq, W; she *m* 2ndly, 1926, Maurice Theodore Alexander Dreyfus, and *d* 1966:—

Hon Pamela Muriel Dorine, MBE (Peartrees, Dormansland, Surrey RH7 6QY) *b* 1918: late Junior Com ATS; raised to rank of a Baron's daughter 1943; a member of Godstone RDC 1955-74 (Chm 1969-72) and of Tandridge Council 1974-75; Hon Alderman of Tandridge District Council; Chm of Lingfield Parish Council 1957-69; MBE (civil) 1983: *m* 1st, 1940 (*m diss* 1947), Capt Arthur George Bevington Colyer, RA; 2ndly, 1949, Roy Edward Goodale, who *d* 1969, and has issue living (by 2nd *m*), Hugh Roy (H. R. Goodale Ltd, Edenbridge, Kent), *b* 1953: *m* 1985, Colette Mansuy, and has issue living, Hugo *b* 1991, Marianne *b* 1986.

HIVES, BARON (Hives) (Baron UK 1950)

MATTHEW PETER HIVES, 3rd Baron; *b* 25 May 1971; *s* 1997.

Arms – Or on a chevron sable, three bee hives of the field. **Crest** – In front of a sun in splendour or, an eagle rising proper. **Supporters** – *Dexter*, the figure of a mechanic proper overalls azure, holding in the exterior hand a micrometer; *sinister*, the figure of a draughtsman proper coat argent holding under the exterior arm a set square and a T square also proper.

Residence – Harmer Garry, Harmer Green Lane, Welwyn, Herts.

SISTERS LIVING

Julie Laura, *b* 1957: *m* 1st, 1979, Thomas J. Macnab, who *d* 1988, only son of late J. Campbell Macnab, of Troon, Ayrshire; 2ndly, 1990, Dr Anthony Reed, son of late Dr E. S. Reed, MBE, of Shalford, Surrey, and has issue living (by 1st *m*), Robert Thomas Peter Campbell, *b* 1982, — Camilla Laura, *b* 1984, — (by 2nd *m*), Frederick Anthony Spencer, *b* 1992, — Clementine Florence, *b* 1991. *Residence* – The Old Rectory, Walkern Rd, Benington, Herts.

Lisa Joanna, *b* 1963; has issue living, Oscar, *b* 1992, — Alice, *b* 1993.

Sophie Josephine, *b* 1964.

UNCLES LIVING (*sons of 1st Baron*)

Hon MICHAEL BRUCE, *b* 12 March 1926; *ed* Repton: *m* 1951, Janet Rosemary, da of late W. E. Gee, of Lynngarth, Duffield, Derby, and has issue living, Robert George (The Meadows, Church Lane, Barrow Upon Trent, Derby), *b* 4 March 1953: *m* 1975, Annabelle Vickers, and has issue living, William Duncan *b* 23 Feb 1977, Jeremy Robert *b* 1982, Thomas Francis *b* 1985, Victoria Jane *b* 1980, — Paul Michael, *b* 1963: *m* 1987, Ellen, da of J. M. Kaufman, of 33 Fifth Av, New York City, NY, — Jillian Sarah, *b* 1955: *m* 1988, Kevin Titterton. *Residence* – Fairfield, The Pastures, Duffield, Derbys.

Hon David Benjamin, *b* 1931; *ed* Repton; Gp Capt RAF: *m* 1954, Shirley, da of late Harold Walker, of Cumberhill House, Duffield, Derby, and has had issue, Nigel Ian Edward, *b* 1960: *m* 1983, Helen Louise, da of W. N. K. Rowley, of Derby, and *d* 1997, leaving issue, Lawrence Ernest William *b* 1987, Imogen Jean *b* 1990, — Sally Margaret, *b* 1955: *m* 1978, Malcolm Howard Lambie, and has issue living, Peter Benjamin *b* 1984, William Ian *b* 1985, Hannah Louise *b* 1989, — (Sandra) Dawn, *b* 1958: *m* 1990, Col Jack M. W. Stenhouse, OBE, MVO, The Gordon Highrs, elder son of Lt-Col D. R. Stenhouse, MBE, of East Sheen, SW14, and has issue living, Catriona Rose *b* 1991, Elizabeth Maitland *b* 1993. *Residence* – Cumberhill House, Duffield, Derbys DE56 4HA.

AUNTS LIVING (*Daughters of 1st Baron*)

Hon Joan Mary, *b* 1917: *m* 1939, Adrian Gee, and has issue living, Wendy Elizabeth, *b* 1943; *m* 1963, Thomas Neville, of Beech Tree House, Audlem, Cheshire, and has issue living, Alexander William *b* 1965, Sally Anne *b* 1968, — Jane Anne, *b* 1945: *m* 1967, John Hodgson Berry, of Bunystone Cottage, Bunnison Lane, Colston Bassett, Notts, and has issue living, Duncan Gee *b* 1968, Nicholas Gee *b* 1970. *Residence* – 9 Chestnut Close, Duffield, Derbys DE6 4HD.

Hon Ruth Margaret, *b* 1922: *m* 1941, Joseph Graham Riley, and has issue living, Michael Edward, *b* 1947, — John Andrew (twin), *b* 1947, — David Ernest, *b* 1951.

Hon Philippa Ann, *b* 1928: *m* 1978, His Honour Judge Alexander John Henderson Morrison, of Eastwood Drive, Littleover, Derby.

MOTHER LIVING

Dinah (Harmer Garry, Harmer Green Lane, Welwyn, Herts), da of F. Wilson-North, of Walcott, Norfolk: *m* 1956, Hon Peter Anthony Hives, who *d* 1974, and has issue living (see colls, infra).

WIDOW LIVING OF SECOND BARON

GLADYS MARY (*Baroness Hives*), da of Alfred Seals: *m* 1972, as his 2nd wife, 2nd Baron Hives, CBE, who *d* 1997. *Residence* – 3 John Port Close, Etwall, Derby DE65 6NW.

PREDECESSORS – **(1)** ERNEST WALTER HIVES, CH, MBE, son of John Hives, of Reading; *b* 1886; Chm and Managing Dir of Rolls-Royce Ltd; *cr Baron Hives*, of Duffield, co Derby (peerage of UK) 1950: *m* 1913, Gertrude Ethel, who *d* 1961, da of John Warwick, of Derby; *d* 1965; *s* by his el son **(2)** JOHN WARWICK, CBE, 2nd Baron, *b* 1913; a farmer; raised a herd of pedigree British Fresian dairy cattle at Bendalls, Milton, Derbys, where his prize bull, Bendalls Adema, established a record as the second most prolific bull in history: *m* 1st, 1937, Olwen Protheroe Llewellin, who *d* 1972; 2ndly, 1972, Gladys Mary, da of Alfred Seals; *d* 1997; *s* by his nephew **(3)** MATTHEW PETER (only son of late Hon Peter Anthony Hives, Lt RNVR, third son of 1st Baron), 3rd Baron and present peer.

HOBHOUSE OF WOODBOROUGH, BARON (Hobhouse) (Life Baron 1998)

JOHN STEWART HOBHOUSE, PC, 2nd son of late Sir John Richard Hobhouse, MC, of Glebe Court, W Monkton, Taunton, Som; *b* 31 Jan 1932; *ed* Eton, and Ch Ch Oxford (BCL 1958, MA 1958); Bar Inner Temple 1955; practised at Commercial Bar until 1982; QC 1973; Judge of the High Court of Justice (Queen's Bench Div and Commercial Court) 1982-93; Lord Justice of Appeal 1993-98, since when a Lord of Appeal in Ordinary; Chm Council of Legal Education 1986-89; *cr* Kt 1982, PC 1993, and *Baron Hobhouse of Woodborough*, of Woodborough, co Wilts (Life Baron) 1998: *m* 1959, Susannah Sybil Caroline, only da of late Sir (John) Ashton Wentworth Roskill, QC (*see* Dilke, Bt, 1931 Edn), and has issue.

Arms – ......
Address – c/o House of Lords, Westminster, SW1A 0PW.

SONS LIVING

Hon William, *b* 1963.
Hon Sebastian, *b* 1964.

DAUGHTER LIVING

Hon Charlotte, *b* 1961: *m* 19—, Edward Farquharson.

HOBSON, BARONY OF (Hobson) (Extinct 1966)

DAUGHTER LIVING OF LIFE BARON

Hon Marian Elizabeth, *b* 1941; *ed* Newnham Coll, Camb (MA, PhD): *m* 1968, Michel Jeanneret, MA, Dr ès L, and has issue. *Residence* – 21 Church Lane, Trumpington, Cambridge CB2 2LA.

Hodge, Hermon-, family name of Baron Wyfold.

HOFFMANN, BARON (Hoffmann) (Life Baron 1995)

LEONARD HUBERT HOFFMANN, PC, son of B. W. Hoffmann, of S Africa; *b* 8 May 1934; *ed* S African Coll Sch, Cape Town, Univ of Cape Town (BA 19—), and The Queen's Coll, Oxford (Rhodes Scholar, MA 19—, BCL 19—, Vinerian Law Scholar, Hon Fell 1992); Hon DCL City Univ 1992; Advocate of Supreme Court of S Africa 1958-60, Bar, Gray's Inn 1964, Bencher 1984; QC 1977; Judge, Courts of Appeal, Jersey and Guernsey 1980-85; Judge of High Court of Justice, Chancery Div 1988-92, Lord Justice of Appeal 1992-95, since when a Lord of Appeal in Ordinary; *cr* Kt 1985, PC 1992, and Baron Hoffmann, of Chedworth, co Glos (Life Baron) 1995: *m* 1957, Gillian Lorna, da of ...... Sterner, of ......, and has issue, two das.
Residence – Surrey Lodge, 23 Keats Grove, NW3 2RS.

HOGG, BARONESS (Hogg) (Life Baroness 1995)

SARAH ELIZABETH MARY HOGG, yr da of late Baron Boyd-Carpenter, PC (Life Baron); *b* 14 May 1946; *ed* St Mary's Convent, Ascot, and Lady Margaret Hall, Oxford; Hon MA Open Univ 1987, Hon DLitt Loughborough Univ 1992; Master of the Bench, Lincoln's Inn 1995; Economics Editor, Sunday Times 1981-82 and The Times 1983-86; Assistant Editor, Business and Finance Editor, The Independent 1986-89; Economics Editor, The Daily Telegraph and Sunday Telegraph 1989-90; Head of Policy Unit, 10 Downing St with rank of second permanent sec 1990-95; *cr Baroness Hogg*, of Kettlethorpe, co Lincs (Life Baroness) 1995: *m* 1968, Rt Hon Douglas Martin Hogg, MP, eldest son of Baron Hailsham of St Marylebone, KG, CH, PC, FRS (Life Baron), and has issue.
Address – c/o House of Lords, SW1A 0PW.

SON LIVING

Hon Quintin John Neil Martin, *b* 1973.

DAUGHTER LIVING

Hon Charlotte Mary, *b* 1970.

Hogg, family name of Baron Hailsham of St Marylebone.

HOGG OF CUMBERNAULD, BARON (Hogg) (Life Baron 1997)

NORMAN HOGG, son of late Norman Hogg, CBE; *b* 12 March 1938; *ed* Causewayend Sch, Aberdeen, and Ruthrieston Secondary Sch, Aberdeen; Dist Offr, Nat and Local Govt Officers Assoc 1967-69; Memb Transport Users' Consultative Cttee for Scotland 1977-79; Non-Exec Dir Kelvin Central Buses Ltd 1990-96; MP for E Dunbartonshire (*Lab*) 1979-83, and for Cumbernauld and Kilsyth 1983-97; Memb Select Cttee for Scottish Affairs 1979-82, and Public Accounts 1991-92; Scottish Labour Whip 1982-83; Lab Dep Chief Whip 1983-87; Opposition Front Bench Spokesman for Scottish Affairs 1987-88; Memb Chm's Panel 1969-97; Chm Labour Friends of Israel 1993-97; Lord High Commr to the General Assembly of the Church of Scotland 1998; *cr Baron Hogg of Cumbernauld*, of Cumbernauld in N Lanarkshire (Life Baron) 1997: *m* 1964, Elizabeth McCall, da of John Christie.
Address – c/o House of Lords, Westminster, SW1A 0PW.

HOLDERNESS, BARON (Wood) (Life Baron 1979)

RICHARD FREDERICK WOOD, PC, yr son of 1st Earl of Halifax; *b* 5 Oct 1920; *ed* Eton and New Coll, Oxford; Hon LLD Sheffield 1963; Hon LLD Leeds 1978; Hon LLD Hull 1982; late Lt KRRC; Hon Col Queen's Roy Rifles 1962-67, Hon Col 4th (vol) Bn R Green Jackets, T & AVR 1967-89; Parl Sec to Min of Pensions and Nat Insurance 1955-58, and to Min of Labour 1958-59; Min of Power 1959-63 and Min of Pensions and Nat Insurance 1963-64, and Min of Overseas Development 1970-74; Chm Disablement Services Authority 1987-91; Regional Dir Lloyd's Bank (Yorks and Humberside) 1981-90; 1939-45 War in Middle East (severely wounded); MP for Bridlington Div of E Riding of Yorks (*C*) 1950-79; a DL for E Riding 1967; PC 1959; *cr Baron Holderness*, of Bishop Wilton, co Humberside (Life Baron) 1979; *m* 1947, Diana, only da of late Col Edward Orlando Kellett, DSO, MP, and has issue.

Arms – 1st and 4th azure, three naked savages ambulant in fesse proper in the dexter hand of each a shield argent, charged with a cross gules and in the sinister a club resting on the shoulder also proper, on a canton ermine three lozenges conjoined in fesse sable, *Wood*; 2nd, or, three torteaux gules and differenced with a lable axure, *Courtenay*; 3rd, or, a lion rampant azure. In the centre a mullet gules. Crest – A savage as in the arms, the shield sable charged with a griffin's head erased argent. Supporters – *Dexter*, an officer of the Kings Royal Rifle Corps circa 1904. *Sinister*, a boar sable armed unguled and bristled or, gorged with a collar argent thereon Cornish cloughs proper and pendant therefrom a cinquefoil argent resting the inner rear leg upon an anchor bendwise gold.
Residence – Flat Top House, Bishop Wilton, York.

SON LIVING

Hon Edward Orlando Charles, *b* 1951: *m* 1st, 1977 (*m diss* 19—), Joanna Harriet, elder da of John Pinches, MC, of Parliament Piece, Ramsbury, Wilts; 2ndly, 1993, Katherine M., yst da of Brig Denis Leonard Ormerod, CBE, of Kirkbank House, High Halden, Kent, and has issue living (by 1st *m*), Leonora Sarah Clare, *b* 1982, — (by 2nd *m*) Georgia Emily Rosanna, *b* 1995, — a da, *b* 1998.

DAUGHTER LIVING

Hon Emma Myrtle Mary Anne (*Hon Lady Brooksbank*), *b* 1949: *m* 1970, Capt Sir (Edward) Nicholas Brooksbank, 3rd Bt.
Residence – Ryton Grange, Malton, N Yorks.

HOLLENDEN, BARON (Hope-Morley) (Baron UK 1912)

Tenacious of purpose

IAN HAMPDEN HOPE-MORLEY, 4th Baron; *b* 23 Oct 1946; *s* 1999; *ed* Eton: *m* 1st, 1972 (*m diss* 1985), Beatrice Saulnier, da of Baron Pierre d'Anchald, of Paris; 2ndly, 1988, Caroline N., only da of Kim Ash, of Johannesburg, and has issue by 1st and 2nd *m*.

Arms – Argent, a leopard's face jessant-de-lis sable between three griffins heads erased gules. **Crest** – A demi-griffin argent, wings elevated ermine, holding between the claws a leopard's face jessant-de-lis as in the arms. **Supporters** – On either side a stag proper, chained around the neck and suspended therefrom an anchor or.
Seat – Hall Place, Leigh, Tonbridge, Kent. *Address* – c/o Estate Office, Gt Hampden, Gt Missenden, Bucks HP1 6RE. *Club* – Brooks's.

SONS LIVING (*By 1st marriage*)

Hon EDWARD, *b* 9 April 1981.

(*By 2nd marriage*)

Hon Alastair Kim, *b* 1990.
Hon Henry Gordon, *b* 1993.

DAUGHTER LIVING (*By 1st marriage*)

Hon Juliette, *b* 1974.

BROTHERS LIVING

Hon Robin Gordon, *b* 1949; *ed* Brickwall, Northiam. *Residence* – Flat 2, 159 Ebury St, SW1.
Hon Andrew James Sundt, *b* 1952; *ed* Eton: *m* 1993, Jennifer, only da of Henry Uvedale Antrobus Lambert, of Lowton, Som.

AUNTS LIVING (*Sisters of 3rd Baron*) (*Raised to the rank of a Baron's daughters* 1979)

Hon Ann Rosemary Hope (*Hon Lady Newman*) (Blackpool House, Dartmouth, S Devon TQ6 0RG), *b* 1916; 1939-45 War as Junior Comdt ATS: *m* 1946, Sir Ralph Alured Newman, 5th Bt, who *d* 1968, and has issue living (see that title).
Hon Stella Hope, *b* 1919; 1939-45 War as 2nd Officer WRNS: *m* 1950, Neville Whiteoak Robinson, of 107 Old Church St, SW3, and has issue living, Anthony David Whiteoak, *b* 1953: *m* 1982, Claire Milligan, and has issue living, Michael Humphrey Whiteoak *b* 1988, — Brian Robert Whiteoak, *b* 1956: *m* 1988, Jayne Connelly, — Julia Mary, *b* 1954.
Hon Lorna Margaret Dorothy (*Hon Lady Hanley*) *b* 1929; JP: *m* 1957, Sir Michael Bowen Hanley, KCB, and has issue living, Peter Michael, *b* 1968: *m* 1998, Fanny Mari-Torres, — Sarah Margaret, *b* 1967: *m* 1st 1992 (*m diss* 1997), Simon L. H. Ash, yst son of late Michael Ash, of Trowbridge, Wilts; 2ndly, 1998, Robert Frederick Pittman, and has issue living, (by 2nd *m*) Emily Rachael *b* 1998.

DAUGHTER LIVING OF SECOND BARON

Hon (Mary) Joan Fenella Hope, *b* 1915: *m* 1st, 1941 (*m diss* 1965), David Babington Smith, who *d* 1989, son of late Sir Henry Babington Smith, GBE, CH, KCB, CSI (E Elgin); 2ndly, 1966, Geoffrey John, who *d* 1996, of Glanton, Alnwick, Northumberland, and has issue living (by 1st *m*), Catherine, *b* 1952: *m* 1979, Maj John McMorrough Carr-Ellison, el son of Sir Ralph Harry Carr-Ellison, TD, of Hedgeley Hall, Powburn, Northumberland (Buxton, Bt, colls), and has issue living, Thomas Ralph *b* 1987, Harry John *b* 1991, Lucy Emma *b* 1986, Hannah Mary *b* 1989.

WIDOW LIVING OF SECOND BARON

VIOLET NORRIS (*Anne, Baroness Hollenden*) (Valley Farm, Duntisbourne Hill, nr Cirencester) da of Alfred Leverton, of Glapthorn, Peterborough, and widow of Dr Frank Dutch Howitt, CVO, MD, FRCP: *m* 2ndly, 1963, as his 3rd wife, the 2nd Baron Hollenden, who *d* 1977.

WIDOW LIVING OF THIRD BARON

SONJA (*Sonja, Baroness Hollenden*), da of late Thorolf Sundt, of Bergen, Norway: *m* 1945, the 3rd Baron Hollenden, who *d* 1999. *Residence* – Hall Place, Leigh, Tonbridge, Kent.

PREDECESSORS – (1) SAMUEL HOPE Morley, el son of late Samuel Morely, JP, DL (MP for Nottingham 1865-6, and for Bristol 1868-85), by his wife, Rebekah Maria, da of Samuel Hope, of Liverpool; *b* 1845; a partner in the firm of I. and R. Morley, of Wood Street, EC; was a Gov of the Bank of England 1903-5; *cr Baron Hollenden*, of Leigh, Kent (peerage of United Kingdom) 1912: *m* 1884, Laura Marianne, who *d* 1945, da of late Rev G. Royds Birch; *d* 1929; *s* by his son (2) GEOFFREY HOPE Hope-Morley, 2nd Baron; JP for Kent; High Sheriff of co London 1917; Prime Warden of Fishmongers' Co 1938-39; assumed by deed poll (enrolled at College of Arms) 1923 the additional surname of Hope: *m* 1st, 1914 (*m diss* 1928), Hon Mary Sidney Katherine Almina Gardner, who *d* 1982, da of 1st Baron Burghclere; 2ndly, 1929, Muriel Ivy, who *d* 1962, yst da of Sir John Evelyn Gladstone, 4th Bt; 3rdly, 1963, Violet Norris, da of Alfred Leverton, of Glapthorn, Peterborough, and widow of Frank Dutch Howitt, CVO, MD, FRCP; *d* 1977; *s* by his nephew (3) GORDON HOPE HOPE-MORLEY (only son of late Capt Hon Claude Hope Hope-Morley, yr son of 1st Baron), 3rd Baron, *b* 1914; Maj Black Watch; 1939-45 War; Alderman City of London: *m* 1945, Sonja, da of late Thorolf Sundt, of Bergen, Norway; *d* 1999; *s* by his eldest son (4) IAN HAMPDEN, 4th Baron and present peer.

HOLLICK, BARON (Hollick) (Life Baron 1991)

CLIVE RICHARD HOLLICK, son of Leslie George Hollick, of Southampton; *b* 20 May 1945; *ed* Taunton's Sch, Southampton, and Nottingham Univ (BA); joined Hambros Bank Ltd 1968, Dir since 1973; Chief Exec MAI plc since 1974 (formerly Mills & Allen Internat plc); Chm Shepperton Studios Ltd 1976-84, and Garban Ltd (USA) since 1983; Dir Logica plc since 1987, Avenir Havas Media SA since 1989, and Satellite Information Systems Ltd since 1990; Founding Trustee Inst for Public Policy Research since 1988, Member Nat Bus Co Ltd since 1984; *cr Baron Hollick*, of Notting Hill, Royal Borough of Kensington and Chelsea (Life Baron) 1991: *m* 1977, Susan Mary Woodford, da of HE P. L. U. Cross, of Trinidad and Tobago, and has issue.

Residence – 14 Kensington Park Gdns, W11. *Club* – Royal Automobile.

DAUGHTERS LIVING

Hon Caroline Daniela, *b* 1975.
Hon Georgina Louise, *b* 1979.
Hon Abigail Miranda, *b* 1981.

HOLLIS OF HEIGHAM, BARONESS (Hollis) (Life Baroness 1990)

PATRICIA LESLEY HOLLIS, PC, da of (Harry) Lesley George Wells, of Norwich; *b* 24 May 1941: *ed* Plympton Gram Sch, Plymouth, Coll, Camb (BA 1962, MA 1965), Univ of California, Berkeley, Columbia Univ, NY, and Nuffield Coll, Oxford (DPhil 1968); FRHistS; DL Norfolk 1994; Harkness Fellow 1962-64, Nuffield Scholar 1964-67, Reader in Modern History, E Anglia Univ since 1967, Senior Fellow, also Dean of English and American Studies 1988-90; Councillor Norwich City Council 1968-91 (Leader 1983-88), and Norfolk CC 1981-85; Member E Anglia Economic Planning Council 1975-79, Govt Cmmn on Housing 1975-77, Regional Health Authority 1979-83, Press Council 1989-91, BBC Regional Advisory Cttee, Commr English Heritage 1988-91, Under-Sec of State Social Security since 1998; author of *The Pauper Press* 1970, *Class and Class Conflict 1815-50* 1973, *Pressure from Without* 1974, *Women in Public 1850-1900* 1979, *Ladies Elect: Women in English Local Government 1865-1914* 1987, *Jennie Lee, A Life* 1997; *cr Baroness Hollis of Heigham*, of Heigham, City of Norwich (Life Baroness) 1990, and PC 1999: *m* 1965, Prof (James) Martin Hollis, FBA, who *d* 1998, and has issue.

Residence – 30 Park Lane, Norwich.

SONS LIVING

Hon Simon, *b* 1969.
Hon Matthew, *b* 1971.

HOLM PATRICK, BARON (Hamilton) (Baron UK 1897)

The same as from the beginning

QUALIS AB INCEPTO

HANS JAMES DAVID HAMILTON, 4th Baron; *b* 15 March 1955; *s* 1991; *ed* Harrow: *m* 1984, Mrs Gill Francesca Anne du Feu, eldest da of late Sqdn Ldr Kenneth James (Toby) Harding, DFC, RAF, of Binisafua, Minorca, and has issue.

𝔞rms – Gules, three cinquefoils ermine, a mullet argent for difference; on a chief or, a heart gules. 𝔠rest – A demi-antelope argent, hoofed and armed or, holding a heart gules, and charged on the shoulder with a mullet of the last. 𝔖upporters – *Dexter*, an antelope argent gorged with a collar flory counterflory or, pendent therefrom an escutcheon ermine charged with a heart gules; *sinister*, a lion gules gorged with a collar flory counterflory or, pendent therefrom an escutcheon ermine, charged with a heart of the first.
Residence – 67 Vicarage Rd, St Agnes, Cornwall TR5 0JH.

SON LIVING

Hon James Hans Stephen, *b* 1982.

BROTHERS LIVING

Hon ION HENRY JAMES (The Steward's Lodge, Ballinlough, Clonmellon, co Westmeath), *b* 12 June 1956; *ed* Harrow.
Hon Evelyn William James, *b* 1961; *ed* Rannoch: *m* 1990, Nicola Jane Fullerton, and has issue living, Ross Andrew James, *b* 1990.

AUNT LIVING (*Daughter of 2nd Baron*)

Hon Caroline, *b* 1926: *m* 1951, Maj John Henry Hamilton Bonham, and has issue living, Oliver John Hans (Camino la Fuente, Los Dominicos, Las Condes, Santiago, Chile), *b* 1954; *ed* St Columba's, Trin Coll, Dublin (BA), and Dalhousie Univ, Halifax, Nova Scotia (MSc): *m* 1979, Ann, da of Michael Proulx, of Gainsborough, Lincs, and has issue living, Michael John *b* 1985, Patricia *b* 1981, Elizabeth *b* 1983, — Francis Richard Hamilton (40 The Fairway, South Ruislip, Middx HA4 0R7), *b* 1956; *ed* St Columba's, and Trin Coll, Dublin (BA, MSc): *m* 1983, Christine, da of George Hunter, of Blackrock, co Dublin, and has issue living, Kate *b* 1990, — John Arthur Norris, *b* 1961; *ed* St Columba's: *m* 1990, Amanda, da of David Potterton, of Dunboyne, co Meath, and has issue living, Richard David *b* 1993, Andrew James *b* 1996. *Residence* – Trumroe, Castlepollard, co Westmeath.

PREDECESSORS – (1) ION TRANT Hamilton, PC, son of late James Hans Hamilton, MP for co Dublin 1841-63; *b* 1839; Lord-Lieut and Custos Rotulorum of co Dublin; MP for Dublin co (C) 1863-85; *cr Baron Holm Patrick*, of HolmPatrick, co Dublin (peerage of United Kingdom), 1897: *m* 1877, Lady Victoria Alexandrina Wellesley, who *d* 1933, sister of 3rd and 4th Dukes of Wellington; *d* 1898; *s* by his only son (2) HANS WELLESLEY, DSO, MC, 2nd Baron; *b* 1886; late Capt 16th Lancers and Bde Maj; 1914-18 War (MC, DSO): *m* 1925, Lady Edina Dorothy Hope, who *d* 1964, da of 4th Marquess Conyngham; *d* 1942; *s* by his only son (3) JAMES HANS, 3rd Baron; *b* 1928; late Lieut 16/5th Lancers; Keeper of the Matchbook at the Irish Turf Club, Sec Kenyan Jockey Club: *m* 1954, Anne Loys Roche, who *d* 1998, only da of Cdr Ernest Padwick Brass, RN (ret), of Haroldston House, Haverfordwest, Pembrokeshire; *d* 1991; *s* by his eldest son (4) HANS JAMES DAVID, 4th Baron and present peer.

HOLME OF CHELTENHAM, BARON (Holme) (Life Baron 1990)

RICHARD GORDON HOLME, CBE, son of late Jack Richard Holme; *b* 27 May 1936; *ed* Royal Masonic Sch, and St John's Coll, Oxford (MA); Chm Constitutional Reform Centre since 1984, Chm Threadneedle Publishing Group since 1988; Vice-Chm Liberal Party Exec 1966-67, Pres Liberal Party 1980-81, Dir Campaign for Electoral Reform 1976-85, Sec Parly Democracy Trust since 1977; Chm Dod's Publishing and Research since 1988, Black Box Publishing since 1988, and Hollis Directories since 1988; commn'd 10th Gurkha Rifles, Malaya, 1954-56 *cr* CBE (Civil) 1983, and *Baron Holme of Cheltenham*, of Cheltenham, co Glos (Life Baron) 1990: *m* 1958, Kay Mary, da of Vincent Powell, and has issue.
Clubs — Reform, Brooks's.

SONS LIVING

Hon Richard Vincent, *b* 1966: *m* 1992, Caroline Elizabeth, da of Michael Holman, of Hazlemere, Bucks.
Hon John Gordon, *b* (twin) 1966.

Hon Nicola Ann, *b* 1959.
Hon Penelope Jane, *b* 1962; *m* 1992, Roger Timothy Kirman, son of Peter Kirman, of Wimbledon, SW20.

HOME, EARL OF (Douglas-Home) (Earl S 1605)
(Name pronounced "Hume")

DAVID ALEXANDER COSPATRICK DOUGLAS-HOME, CVO, CBE, 15th Earl; *b* 20 Nov 1943; *s* 1995; *ed* Eton, and Ch Ch Oxford; Chm Coutts & Co since 1999; Gov Commonwealth Inst since 1988; CBE (Civil) 1991, CVO 1997: *m* 1972, Jane Margaret, da of late Col John Francis Williams-Wynne, CBE, DSO (*see* Williams-Wynn, Bt, colls), and has issue.

Arms – Quarterly: 1st and 4th grand quarters counter quartered, 1st and 4th grand quartered, 1st and 4th vert, a lion rampant argent, armed and langued gules, *Home*; 2nd and 3rd argent, three popinjays vert, beaked and membered gules, *Pepdie*; over all an escutcheon or, charged with an orle azure, *Landale*; 2nd and 3rd grand quarters counter-quartered, 1st azure, a lion rampant argent, armed and langued gules, crowned with an imperial crown or, *Lordship of Galloway*; 2nd or, a lion rampant gules, armed and langued azure, debruised of a ribbon sable, *Abernethy*; 3rd argent, three piles gules, *Lordship of Brechin*; 4th or, a fesse checky azure and argent, surmounted of a bend sable, charged with three buckles of the field, *Stewart of Bonkhill*; over all on an escutcheon argent, a man's heart, ensigned with an imperial crown proper, and a chief azure, charged with three mullets of the field, *Douglas*. **Crests** – 1st, on a cap of maintenance proper, a lion's head erased argent, *Home*; 2nd, on a cap of maintenance proper, a salamander vert, encircled with flames of fire proper. **Supporters** – Two lions argent, armed and langued gules.

Seats — The Hirsel, Coldstream, Berwickshire TD12 4LR; Castlemains, Douglas, Lanarkshire ML11 0RN. *Town Residence* – 99 Dovehouse St, SW3 6JZ.

SON LIVING

MICHAEL DAVID ALEXANDER (*Lord Dunglass*), *b* 30 Nov 1987; Page of Honour to HM since 1998.

DAUGHTERS LIVING

Lady Iona Katherine, *b* 1980; *ed* Charterhouse.
Lady Mary Elizabeth, *b* 1982.

SISTERS LIVING

Lady (Lavinia) Caroline, *b* 1937; a Woman of the Bedchamber to HM Queen Elizabeth the Queen Mother 1963-65; a Lady in Waiting to HRH the Duchess of Kent 1966-67; Trustee Nat Museum of Antiquities of Scotland 1982-86; DL Berwickshire 1982; FSA Scot. *Residence* – Heaton Mill House, Cornhill-on-Tweed, Northumberland TD12 4XQ.

Lady Meriel Kathleen, *b* 1939: *m* 1964, Adrian Marten George Darby, Fellow Keble Coll, Oxford, and has issue living, Matthew George, *b* 1967; *ed* Eton, and Edinburgh Univ, — Catherine Monica, *b* 1964; *ed* Oxford High Sch, Marlborough, and Bristol Univ. *Residence* – Kemerton Court, Tewkesbury, Glos GL20 7HY.

Lady Diana Lucy, *b* 1940: *m* 1963 (*m diss* 1976), James Archibald Wolfe Murray, and has issue (*see* Murray, Bt, *cr* 1628, colls). *Residence* – 97 Wandsworth Bridge Rd, SW6 2TD.

UNCLE LIVING (*son of 13th Earl*)

Hon Edward Charles, *b* 1920; *ed* Eton; 2nd Lieut RA; 1939-45 War (wounded, prisoner): *m* 1946, Nancy Rose, only da of late Sir Thomas Dalrymple Straker-Smith, of Carham Hall, Cornhill-on-Tweed, and has issue living, Simon (70 Cloncurry St, SW6 6DU), *b* 1947; *ed* Eton: *m* 1971, Sally, da of late Sqdn-Ldr Bertram Beard, and has issue living, Edward *b* 1980, Joanna *b* 1973, Louisa *b* 1976, — Andrew (The Lees, Coldstream, Berwickshire TD12 4LF), *b* 1950; *ed* Eton: *m* 1980, Jane, da of late Maurice Oliver Pease, and has had issue, Richard *b* 1983, Nicholas *b* 1985, †Freddie *b* 1989, *d* 1990, — Mark (25 India St, Edinburgh EH3 6HE), *b* 1951; *ed* Eton: *m* 1976, Colette, da of ...... O'Reilly, of ......, and has issue living, Rory *b* 1981, Rebecca *b* 1978. *Residence* – Westnewton, Kirknewton, Wooler, Northumberland.

WIDOWS LIVING OF SONS OF THIRTEENTH EARL

Felicity Betty, da of late Maj Aubrey Thomas Jonsson, and formerly wife of Hon Victor Patrick Hamilton Wills (*see* B Dulverton): *m* 1966, as his 3rd wife, Maj Hon Henry Montagu Douglas-Home, MBE, who *d* 1980, and has issue (see colls infra). *Residence* – Old Greenlaw, Berwickshire TD10 6UP.

Rachel Leila (*Baroness Dacre*) (in her own right): *m* 1951, Hon William Douglas-Home, who *d* 1992, and has issue (*see* Bs Dacre). *Residence* – Derry House, Kilmeston, nr Alresford, Hants.

COLLATERAL BRANCHES LIVING

Grandsons of late Maj Hon Henry Montagu Douglas-Home, MBE (infra):—
Issue of late Capt (Cecil) Robin Douglas-Home, *b* 1932, *d* 1968: *m* 1959 (*m diss* 1965), Sandra Clare (who *m* 2ndly, 19—, Nigel Grandfield, who *d* 1998, and 3rdly, 1975, Rt Hon Michael Howard, QC, MP, Home Sec 1993-97), yr da of late W/Cmdr Saville Paul, MRCS, LRCP, of High Chimneys, Windlesham, Surrey:—
(Alexander) Sholto, *b* 1962; *ed* Bradfield, and Warwick Univ; advertising manager BT plc since 1995: *m* 1992, Alexandra Jane, yr da of Benjamin Miller, of 42 Pembroke Rd, W8, and has issue living, Louis Robin, *b* 1999.

Issue of late Charles Cospatrick Douglas-Home, *b* 1937, *d* 1985; editor of *The Times* 1982-85: *m* 1966, Jessica Violet (who *m* 2ndly, 1993, Rodney Leach), da of late Maj John Nevile Wake Gwynne, RA (*see* Morrison-Bell, Bt, *cr* 1923, ext):—
Tara John, *b* 1969; *ed* Eton, and UEA: *m* 1999, Jonkvrouwe Francine A., yr da of Jonkheer Alexander Beelaerts van Blokland, of The Hague. —— Luke Cospatrick, *b* 1971; *ed* Eton, and Edinburgh Univ.

Issue of late Maj Hon Henry Montagu Douglas-Home, MBE, 2nd son of 13th Earl, *b* 1907, *d* 1980: *m* 1st, 1931 (*m diss* 1947), Lady (Alexandra) Margaret Elizabeth Spencer, who *d* 1996, da of 6th Earl Spencer; 2ndly, 1947, Vera Bugge, who *d* 1963, da of late Carl Herman Jensen, of Oslo, Norway, and formerly wife of Ivan Johansen; 3rdly, 1966, Felicity Betty (ante) da of late Maj Aubrey Thomas Jonsson, and formerly wife of Hon Victor Patrick Hamilton Wills (*see* B Dulverton):—
(By 1st *m*) Fiona Margaret (*Lady Fraser*), *b* 1936; resumed her maiden name until remarriage: *m* 1st, 1962 (*m diss* 1981), Gregory Martin; 2ndly, 1993, as his 2nd wife, Sir Ian James Fraser, CBE, MC (*see* L Lovat, colls), of South Haddon, Skilgate, Som, and has issue living (by 1st *m*), Kezia Alexandra Lilian, *b* 1970. — Lydia Georgiana Bridget, *b* 1975. —— (By 2nd *m*) George Erik Montagu, *b* 1948; *ed* Blanerne Sch, Berwicks. —— (By 3rd *m*) Peregrine Montagu (Old Greenlaw, Berwickshire TD10 6UP), *b* 1967.

Issue of late Hon William Douglas-Home, playwright, 3rd son of 13th Earl, *b* 1912, *d* 1992: *m* 1951, Rachel Leila (*Baroness Dacre*) (in her own right) (ante):—
See Bs Dacre.

PREDECESSORS – (1) *Sir* ALEXANDER Home, of Home, Berwickshire, Baron of Douglass, (el son of Sir Alexander Home) *k* at Battle of Verneuil 1424: Ambassador to England 1459; *cr Lord Home* (peerage of Scotland) 1473; *m* 1st, before 1424, Marion, da and heir of John Lauder; 2ndly, before 1467, Margaret, da of Alexander Montgomerie, Master of Montgomerie; *d* 1491; *s* by his grandson (2) ALEXANDER, 2nd Lord (son of Alexander Home), and Agnes, da of Sir Adam Hepburn of Hailes: *m* 1st, Isabel Douglas (annulled on grounds of consanguinity 1476); 2ndly, before March 1493, Nichola (who *d* 1527/28 having *m* 2ndly, Sir Alexander Ramsay of Dalhousie), da of George Ker of Samuelston, Haddington; *d* 1506; *s* by his son (3) ALEXANDER, 3rd Lord, commanded the van with the 4th Earl of Huntly at Flodden, and was one of the few surviving commanders of that battle; afterwards embraced the English interest in opposition to the Regent Albany; whilst visiting the Court in 1516 was taken prisoner, and after a hasty trial was executed, and his titles and estates declared forfeit; these were restored in 1522 to his brother (4) GEORGE, 4th Lord: *m* 1531, Mariot Halyburton, who *d* about 1563, da and co-heir of the 5th Lord Dirletun; killed in a skirmish at Fauside two days before battle of Pinkie 1547; *s* by his son (5) ALEXANDER, 5th Lord; supported Mary Queen of Scots; convicted of treason 1573 and his title and estates forfeited: *m* 1st, Margaret, da of Sir Walter Kerr; 2ndly, Agnes (who *m* 3rdly, Sir Thomas Lyon, Master of Glamis), da of 4th Lord Gray, and widow of Sir Robert Logan of Restalrig; *s* by his son (by 2nd wife) (6) ALEXANDER, 6th Lord; *b* about 1566; *cr Lord Dunglass* and *Earl of Home* (peerage of Scotland) 1605 with remainder to his heirs male whatsoever: *m* 1st, 1586, Christian, da of 6th Earl of Morton, and a widow of Laurence, Master of Oliphant; 2ndly, before June 1607, Mary Sutton, who *d* 1645, da of 9th Baron Dudley; *d* 1619; *s* by his son (by 2nd wife) (7) JAMES, 2nd Earl; *b* about 1607: *m* 1st, 1622, Hon Katherine Cary, da of 1st Viscount Falkland; 2ndly, Lady Grace Fane, da of 1st Earl of Westmorland; *dsp* 1633; *s* by his kinsman (8) JAMES, 3rd Earl, only son of Sir James Home of Whitrig (by Lady Anna * el dau and co-heir of George Home, 1st Earl of Dunbar and 1st Lord Home (or Hume) of Berwick), el son of Sir John Home of Cowdenknows, great grandson of Mungo Home, el son of John yr brother of 2nd Lord: *m* 1640, Lady Jean Douglas, who *d* 1694, da of 7th Earl of Morton; *d* 1666; *s* by his el son (9) ALEXANDER, 4th Earl: *m* 1671, Lady Anne Sackville, who *d* 1672, da of 5th Earl of Dorset; *d* 1674; *s* by his brother (10) JAMES, 5th Earl: *m* Lady Anne Ramsay, da of 2nd Earl of Dalhousie; *d* 1687; *s* by his brother (11) CHARLES, 6th Earl: *m* about 1680, Anne, da of Sir William Purves of Purves, Bt; *d* 1706; *s* by his son (12) ALEXANDER, 7th Earl; imprisoned in Edinburgh Castle 1715-16 on suspicion of being involved in Jacobite rising: *m* Lady Anne Kerr (who *d* 1727, having *m* 2ndly, Henry Ogle), da of 2nd Marquess of Lothian; *d* 1720; *s* by his el son (13) WILLIAM, 8th Earl; Lt-Gen; Gov of Gibraltar 1757-61: *m* 1742, Elizabeth, who *d* 1784, da and heir of William Gibbons, and widow of James Lawes; *d* 1761; *s* by his brother (14) *Rev* ALEXANDER, 9th Earl: *m* 1st, Hon Primrose Elphinstone, who *d* 1759, da of 9th Lord Elphinstone; 2ndly, Marion, who *d* 1765, da of his uncle Hon James Home; 3rdly, 1768, Abigail Browne, who *d* 1814, da and co-heir of John Ramey, of Yarmouth; *d* 1786; *s* by his son (15) ALEXANDER, 10th Earl; assumed by Royal Licence the addition surname of Ramey 1814: *m* 1798, Lady Elizabeth Scott, who *d* 1837, da of 3rd Duke of Buccleuch; *d* 1841; *s* by his son (16) COSPATRICK ALEXANDER, 11th Earl; *b* 1799; Under-Sec for Foreign Affairs 1828-30, a Representative Peer 1842-74, Lt-Gen of Royal Co of Archers, and Keeper of the Great Seal of Scotland; on death of his mother 1877 took the additional surname of Douglas of Douglas under deed of entail of Douglas estates; *cr Baron Douglas*, of Douglas, co Lanark (peerage of United Kingdom), 1875: *m* 1832, Hon Lucy Elizabeth, who *d* 1877, el da of 2nd and last Baron Montagu of Boughton; by Jane Margaret, da of Archibald Douglas (formerly Stewart) 1st Baron Douglas of Douglas (*cr* 1790, ext 1857); *d* 1881; *s* by his son (17) CHARLES ALEXANDER, KT, 12th Earl, *b* 1834: *m* 1870, Maria, who *d* 1919, da of late Capt Charles Conrad Grey, RN; *d* 1918; *s* by his son (18) CHARLES COSPATRICK ARCHIBALD, KT, TD, 13th Earl; Brig of King's Body Guard for Scotland (Roy Co of Archers): *m* 1902, Lady Lilian Lambton, who *d* 1966, da of 4th Earl of Durham; *d* 1951; *s* by his son (19) ALEXANDER FREDERICK, KT, PC, 14th Earl; *b* 1903; Maj Lanark Yeo (TA Res), Brig Royal Company of

Archers (Queen's Body Guard for Scotland), DL Lanarks; MP Lanark Div of Lanarkshire (C) 1931-45 and 1950-51, and for Kinross and W Perth Div of Pertshire and Kinross-shire 1963-74; Sec of State for Commonwealth Relations April 1955-July 1960 (also Lord Pres of the Council Jan 1957-Sept 1960), Sec of State for Foreign Affairs July 1960-Oct 1963, Prime Min and First Lord of the Treasury 1963-64, Leader of the Opposition 1964-65, Sec of State for Foreign and Commonwealth Affairs 1970-74; Pres MCC 1966, NATO Council 1974, and Peace Through NATO 1985; Chancellor of Order of the Thistle; bore Sword of Scotland at Coronation of Queen Elizabeth II; disclaimed his peerages for life 23 Oct 1963, and was *cr Baron Home of the Hirsel*, of Coldstream, co Berwick (Life Baron) 1974: *m* 1936, Elizabeth Hester, who *d* 1990, da of late Very Rev Cyril Argentine Alington, DD, Dean of Durham (*see* V Cobham, 1958 Edn); *d* 1995, when the life barony became ext, and he was *s* in the earldom and minor honours by his only son **(20)** DAVID ALEXANDER COSPATRICK, 15th Earl and present peer; also Lord Home, Lord Dunglass, and Baron Douglas.

*The Lordship of Home (or Hume) of Berwick, *cr* by patent 1604 upon George Home, High Treasurer of Scotland (who in 1605 was cr Earl of Dunbar), with remainder to his heirs for ever, is held to have descended to the Earls of Home through Lady Anna Home. Whether this was an English Barony, as thought by Dugdale, or a Scottish Lordship, which is thought more likely in view of the remainder, is uncertain.

Home, Douglas-, family name of Earl of Home.

HOOD, VISCOUNT (Hood) (Viscount GB 1796, Bt GB 1778)

With favourable winds

ALEXANDER LAMBERT HOOD, 7th Viscount, and 7th Baronet; *b* 11 March 1914; *s* 1981; *ed* Trin Coll, Camb (MA), and at Harvard (MBA); Lt-Cdr RNVR; former Dir Continental & Industrial Trust plc, Tanks Investment plc, George Wimpey plc, and of other cos: *m* 1957, Diana Maud, CVO, el da of late Hon George William Lyttelton (*see* V Cobham, colls) and has issue.

Arms – Azure, a frette argent, on a chief or three crescents sable. **Crest** – A Cornish chough sable, in front of an anchor in bend sinister or. **Supporters** – *Dexter*, a merman, holding in the right hand a trident; *sinister*, a mermaid, holding in the left hand a look-glass. **Residences** – Loders Court, Bridport, Dorset; 67 Chelsea Sq, SW3. **Club** – Brooks's.

SONS LIVING

Hon HENRY LYTTELTON ALEXANDER (4 Alexander St, W2 5NT), *b* 16 March 1958: *m* 1991, Flora Susan, yr da of Cdr Michael Bernard Casement, OBE, RN (*see* Greenwell, Bt), and has issue living, Archibald Lyttelton Samuel, *b* 16 May 1993, — Atticus Michael Alexander, *b* 1995, — Willoughby, *b* 1998, — Edith, *b* (twin) 1998.
Hon John Samuel (72 Thurleigh Rd, SW12), *b* 1959: *m* 1982, Melissa Anne, 2nd da of Kerry D. Bell, of 221 Burns Bay Rd, Lane Cove, New South Wales 2066, Australia, and has issue living, Christian Alexander, *b* 1989, — Samuel Francis Wheeler, *b* 1991, — Gemma Kathryn, *b* 1986.
Hon James Francis Touzalin (4 Phene St, SW3), *b* 1962.

COLLATERAL BRANCHES LIVING

Granddaughters of Lt-Col Hon Neville Albert Hood, CMG, DSO, RGA (infra):—
Issue of late Peter Neville Hood, *b* 1913, *d* 1969: *m* 1936, Nancy Warrington, who *d* 1968, da of late Tristram W. Haward, JP, of Abbey Lands, Alnwick, Northumberland:—
Sally Penelope, *b* 1937: *m* 1959, Edward Martin Amphlett Thompson, of The Bolt Hole, Six Ashes, Bridgnorth, Shropshire (E Coventry, colls), and has issue living, Stephen Peter, *b* 1960, — Mary Jane, *b* 1963, — Sarah Ann, *b* 1965, — Rosemary Claire, *b* 1969. —— Anna Rosemary (220 Marlborough Rd, Oxford OX1 4LT), *b* 1940: *m* 1968 (*m diss* 1974), Peter Christopher Glazebrook, and has issue living, Anthony Peter, *b* 1970. — Daniel George, *b* 1978. —— (Eveline) Jane Venetia, *b* 1957: *m* 1996, Simon Bushell, of Brookside, Luxborough, Som, and has issue living, Katherine, *b* 1992.

Issue of late Lieut-Col Hon Neville Albert Hood, CMG, DSO, RGA, 4th son of 4th Viscount, *b* 1872, *d* 1948: *m* 1908, Eveline Mary, who *d* 1967, da of late Herman Usticke Broad (who subsequently assumed the surname of Pender), of Tresilian, Falmouth:—
Eveline Suzanne, *b* 1917: *m* 1945, as his 2nd wife, Henry Arthur Frederick Hohler, CMG (V Gort), and has issue living, Katherine Elizabeth, *b* 1948: *m* 1972, Christopher Ernest Nelson Harries, and has issue living, Eleanor Annabel *b* 1972, Emma Susan *b* 1975, — (Edith) Mabel, *b* 1952: *m* 1984, Stephen D. McLeod, elder son of G. R. McLeod, of Bethesda,

Maryland, USA, and has issue living, Robert Charles *b* 1986, Franklin Henry *b* 1990, Susan Leighann *b* 1988. *Address* – 7835 Berkshire Lane, Gloucester, Virginia 23061, USA.

Grandson of late Col Hon Francis George Hood, yst son of 4th Viscount:—
Issue of late Francis Basil Hood, *b* 1905, *d* 1986: *m* 1934, Catherine Anna, da of late Hon Sir Richard McBride, KCMG, KC, Premier of British Columbia 1903-16:—
John Francis Alexander (4533 46B St, Delta, BC, Canada V4K 2N2), *b* 1935: *m* 1963, Barbara Anne, da of late Cyril Turner, of Vic, BC, and has issue living, Valerie Anne, *b* 1966, — Christine Frances, *b* 1971.

Grandsons of late Hon Albert Hood, 2nd son of 3rd Viscount:—
Issue of late Capt Albert Oscar Hood, Irish Guards, *b* 1870, *d* 1952: *m* 1912, Theresa Emily Margery, who *d* 1970, da of late Col Hon Everard Charles Digby (B Digby colls):—
John Oscar Everard, *b* 1913; *ed* Eton, and Worcester Coll, Oxford; Middle East 1940-45 with Sudan Defence Forces (despatches): *m* 1953, Winifred Mary Milne. *Residence* – Longpré, Gorey, Jersey.

Issue of late Capt Alexander Frank Hood, *b* 1874, *d* 1923: *m* 1905, Gladys Ursula, who *d* 1968, 3rd da of late Edward C. Youell, of Galatz, Roumania:—
John Michael Alexander (11 Shiremore Hill, Marriott, Somerset TA16 5PH), *b* 1918.

Issue of late Robert Valentine Hood, *b* 1876, *d* 1942: *m* 1917, Mignon, who *d* 1973, da of late John E Cooke:—
Robin Julian Patrick (50 Pont St Mews, SW1), *b* 1919; *ed* Eton.

Grandchildren of late Capt Alexander Frank Hood (ante):—
Issue of late Lt-Col Samuel Brian Digby Hood, TD, *b* 1910, *d* 1988: *m* 1937, Myrtle Baron, who *d* 1982, niece and adopted da of Sir Louis Bernhard Baron, 1st Bt (ext):—
Alexander Robert, *b* 1945; *ed* Eton; late Rifle Bde: *m* 1967, Ann Marie, da of John O'Donovan, of Greenwich, and has issue living, Samuel, *b* 1967, — Padraig, *b* 1971, — Jane, *b* 1969, — Sarah, *b* 1972. *Residence* – Greys Green Farm, Rotherfield Greys, Henley-on-Thames, Oxon RG9 4QG. —— Sarah Jane (twin) (*Hon Mrs Jolyon Grey*), *b* 1945: *m* 1971, Hon Jolyon Kenneth Alnwick Grey (*see* B Grey of Naunton). *Residence* – Upper Swell Farm, Stow-on-the-Wold, Cheltenham, Glos GL54 1EW.

Grandson of late Hon Alexander Frederick GREGORY (who assumed by Roy licence in 1910 the surname of Gregory in lieu of his patronymic, and the arms of Gregory quarterly with his family arms), 3rd son of 3rd Viscount:—
Issue of late Major Charles Hugh GREGORY-HOOD, The Buffs (ret), *b* 1877, *d* 1951 (having assumed by deed poll 1927 (enrolled at College of Arms) the additional surname of Gregory): *m* 1911, Dorothy, who *d* 1983, da of late Hon Marshall Jones Brooks (*see* B Crawshaw, colls):—
Alexander Marshall Horace, OBE, MC, *b* 1915; *ed* Winchester; Col (ret) late Grenadier Guards; MBE (Mil) 1954, OBE (Mil) 1959; European War 1939-45 (despatches, wounded, MC and Bar): *m* 1943 (*m diss* 1949), Diana, who *d* 1987, da of Major Sir John Little Gilmour, 2nd Bt (*see* Gilmour, Bt, *cr* 1929, 1985 Edn), and has issue living, Peter Charles Freeman (73 Cambridge St, SW1) *b* 1943; Diplo Ser: *m* 1966, Camilla, da of Richard Anthony Bethell (*see* E Radnor), and has issue living, Clare *b* 1968, Carolyn Jane *b* 1970, Lucy *b* 1973, — Jane, *b* 1946: *m* 1965, Brian A. FitzGerald, of Sherfield Mill, Sherfield English, Romsey, Hants SO51 6FN, and has had issue, Richard Derek *b* 1967, *d* 1997, James Mark *b* 1973, Sarah Jane *b* 1968. *Residence* – Loxley Hall, Warwick.

Descendants of late Hon Samuel Hood (2nd son of 2nd Viscount), and grand-nephew of Sir Alexander Hood, MP (brother of 1st Viscount), who was *cr Baron Bridport* (peerage of Ireland) 1794, *Baron Bridport* (peerage of Great Britain) 1796, and *Viscount Bridport* (peerage of Great Britain) 1800, and whom he *s* (under special remainder) in the Irish Barony (*see* V Bridport).

PREDECESSORS – (1) *Adm Sir* SAMUEL Hood, GCB, a celebrated Naval Com; *cr* a Baronet 1778, *Baron Hood*, of Catherington, co Hants (peerage of Ireland) 1782, and *Viscount Hood* (peerage of Great Britain) 1796; his wife Susannah, who *d* 1806, da of Edward Linzee, of Portsmouth, was *cr Baroness Hood*, of Catherington, co Hants (peerage of Great Britain) 1795; *d* 1816; *s* by his son (2) HENRY, 2nd Viscount, who had in 1806 *s* his mother as 2nd Baron Hood (*cr* 1795); *d* 1837; *s* by his grandson (3) SAMUEL, 3rd Viscount; *b* 1808; assumed the additional name of Tibbits by Roy licence 1840: *m* 1837, Mary Isabella, da and heiress of Richard John Tibbits, of Barton Seagrave; *d* 1846; *s* by his son (4) FRANCIS WHEELER, 4th Viscount; *b* 1838: *m* 1865, Edith Lydia Drummond, who *d* 1911, da of Arthur W. Ward, of Calverley, Tunbridge Wells; *d* 1907; *s* by his el son (5) GROSVENOR ARTHUR ALEXANDER, OBE, 5th Viscount; *b* 1868; some-time Major Grenadier Guards and Lieut-Col comdg 7th Batn London Regt: *m* 1st, 1911, Jane Primrose, who *d* 1919, da of Col Hon Richard Southwell George Stapleton-Cotton: 2ndly, 1928, his cousin, Marguerite (Margot) Jenny, who *d* 1966, da of Hon Albert Hood; *d* 1933; *s* by his nephew (6) SAMUEL, GCMG (son of late Rear-Adm Hon Sir Horace Lambert Alexander Hood, KCB, MVO, DSO, 3rd son of 4th Viscount), 6th Viscount; *b* 1910; Assist Private Sec to Sec of State for India 1936-39, Private Sec to Min of Information 1939-41; 1st Sec Madrid 1947-48; Counsellor at British Embassy, Paris 1948-51, and Min at British Embassy, Washington, USA 1958-62; Dep Under-Sec Foreign Office 1962-69; *dunm* 1981; *s* by his brother (7) ALEXANDER LAMBERT, 7th Viscount and present peer; also Baron Hood.

Hood, family name of Viscount Bridport.

HOOPER, BARONESS (Hooper) (Life Baroness 1985)

GLORIA HOOPER, da of Frederick Hooper, *b* 25 May 1939; *ed* Southampton Univ (BA); admitted Solicitor 1973; ptnr Taylor & Humber (now Taylor Joynson Garret) 1974-85; Member European Parliament (C) Liverpool 1979-84, Baroness-in-Waiting 1985-87, Under-Sec for Education 1987-88, Under-Sec for Energy 1988-89, Under-Sec for Health 1989-92; *cr Baroness Hooper*, of Liverpool and of St James's in the City of Westminster (Life Baroness) 1985.
Address – c/o House of Lords, SW1A 0PW.

HOOSON, BARON (Hooson) (Life Baron 1979)

(HUGH) EMLYN HOOSON, QC, son of late Hugh Hooson, of Colomendy, Denbigh; *b* 26 March 1925; *ed* Denbigh Gram Sch, and Univ Coll of Wales; Bar Gray's Inn 1949, QC 1960, Bencher 1968; Dep Chm Merioneth Quarter Sessions 1960-67, Chm 1967-71, Dep Chm Flint Quarter Sessions 1960-71; Recorder of Merthyr Tydfil 1971, of Swansea 1971; a Recorder of Crown Court from 1972; Treas Gray's Inn 1986; MP for Montgomeryshire (L) 1962-79; Leader Welsh Liberal Party 1966-79, Leader Wales and Chester Circuit 1971-74, a Vice-Pres of Peace through NATO 1985; *cr Baron Hooson*, of Montgomery, co Powys (Life Baron) 1979; *m* 1950, Shirley Margaret Wynne, da of late Sir George Hamer, CBE, of Summerfield, Llanidloes, Powys, and has issue living, two das.
Address – 3 Gray's Inn Sq, Gray's Inn, WC1R 5AH.

Hope, family name of Baron Glendevon.

Hope, family name of Marquess of Linlithgow.

Hope, family name of Baron Rankeillour.

HOPE OF CRAIGHEAD, BARON (Hope) (Life Baron 1995)

(JAMES ARTHUR) DAVID HOPE, PC, son of late Lt-Col Arthur Henry Cecil Hope, OBE, TD, WS (see M Linlithgow, colls); b 27 June 1938; ed Edinburgh Acad, Rugby, St John's Coll, Camb (BA 1962, MA 1978, Hon Fell 1985), and Edinburgh Univ (LLB 1965, Hon LLD 1985); late Lieut Seaforth Highlanders; Advocate 1965, Advocate-Depute 1978-82, Dean of Faculty of Advocates 1986-89, a Lord of Session with the title of Lord Hope, Lord Justice-Gen and Lord Pres of the Court of Session 1989-96; a Lord of Appeal in Ordinary since 1996; Chancellor, Strathclyde Univ since 1998; cr PC 1989, and Baron Hope of Craighead, of Bamff in the District of Perth and Kinross (Life Baron) 1995: m 1966, (Katharine) Mary, da of late William Mark Kerr, WS, of Edinburgh, and has issue.

Arms – Azure on a chevron or between three bezants a bay leaf between two quill pens vert. Crest – A broken terrestrial sphere proper charged with an anchor gules surmounted by a rainbow proper. Supporters – Two blackfaced rams proper. Motto – Spes non est fracta (My hope is not broken).
Residence – 34 India St, Edinburgh EH3 6HB.

SONS LIVING

Hon William Thomas Arthur, b 1969; ed Edinburgh Acad, George Watson's Coll, Univ of Victoria, BC (BA 1994), and Napier Univ (PgDip 1997).
Hon James David Louis (2 Streatley Buildings, Streatley Place, Hampstead, NW3 1HR), b (twin) 1969; ed Edinburgh Acad, Christ's Coll, Camb (BA 1991), and Edinburgh Univ (LLB 1993): m 19—, Maria-Pia Midenbäck.

DAUGHTER LIVING

Hon Lucy Charlotte Mary, b 1971; ed St George's Sch for Girls, St Andrews Univ (BSc Hons 1993), and Edinburgh Univ (LLB 1995).

Hopetoun, Earl of; son of Marquess of Linlithgow.

Hopkinson, family name of Baron Colyton.

Hopwood, family name of Baron Southborough.

HORDER, BARONY OF (Horder) (Extinct)

DAUGHTER LIVING OF FIRST BARON

Hon Dorothea Joy, *b* 1905: *m* 1930, Edward Revill Cullinan, CBE, MD, FRCP, who *d* 1965, and has issue living, Edward Horder (62 Camden Mews, NW1), *b* 1931; ARIBA: *m* 1961, Rosalind Sylvia, yst da of late V. M. Yeates, and has issue living, Thomas Edward *b* 1965, Emma *b* 1962, Kate *b* 1963, — Timothy Revill, *b* 1932: *m* 1956, Helen Veronica, yst da of Brig Edmund James Paton-Walsh, and has issue living, Paul *b* 1957, Dominic *b* 1960, Charlotte *b* 1959, Harriet *b* 1962, — Paul (in religion Thomas) Anthony, OSB *b* 1935, — Susan Joy, *b* 1937: *m* 1st, 1959 (*m diss* 1978), John Murray Owen; 2ndly, 1981, Michael Houlihan, and has issue living (by 1st *m*), Clare Joy *b* 1960, Joanna *b* 1961, Philippa *b* 1963, Lucy *b* 1965. *Residence* – 10 Camden Mews, NW1.

HOTHAM, BARON (Hotham) (Baron I 1797, Bt E 1622)
(Name pronounced Hutham")

For my country

PRO · PATRIA

LEAD ON

HENRY DURAND HOTHAM, 8th Baron, and 18th Baronet; *b* 3 May 1940; *s* 1967; *ed* Eton; late Lt Grenadier Guards; patron of one living; ADC to Gov of Tasmania 1963-66; DL Humberside 1981: *m* 1972, Alexandra Mary, 2nd da of late Maj Andrew Charles Stirling Home Drummond Moray, and has issue.

Arms – Barry of ten argent and azure, on a canton or, a Cornish chough proper. **Crest** – Out of waves of the sea a demi-man naked, holding a sword erect proper, and having on the left arm a shield of the arms of Hotham. **Supporters** – Two sailors habited proper, and resting their exterior hands on a cutlass point downwards.
Seats – Dalton Hall, Dalton Holme, Beverley, Yorks; Scorborough Hall, Driffield, Yorks.

SONS LIVING

Hon WILLIAM BEAUMONT, *b* 13 Oct 1972
Hon George Andrew, *b* 1974; *ed* Harrow.

DAUGHTER LIVING

Hon Elizabeth Henrietta Alexandra, *b* 1976.

BROTHERS LIVING

Hon Peter William, *b* 1944; *ed* Eton, and Ch Ch, Oxford (BA): *m* 1978, Deborah S., da of late G. Macdonald-Brown, of Rose Cottage, Campsall, Doncaster, and has issue living, Charles Peter, *b* 1982, — Caroline Susan, *b* 1979.
Hon Nicholas Charles Frederick, *b* 1947; *ed* Eton: *m* 1974, Jane Brydon, of Thirley Beck Farm, Harwood Dale, Scarborough, Yorks, and has issue living, David Charles, *b* 1976, — Catherine Frances, *b* 1978.

WIDOWS LIVING OF BROTHERS OF SEVENTH BARON

Margaret (Plas Newydd, Glascoed, Abergele, N Wales), yr da of Col Sir Robert William Herbert Watkin Williams-Wynn, 9th Bt, KCB, DSO, TD: *m* 1934, Maj Hon Peter Hotham, late KOYLI, who *d* 1991 (having been raised to the rank of a Baron's son 1924), and has issue (see colls, infra).
Aileen (31 Brynmaer Rd, SW11), da of late Capt Harry Coates, Durham LI: *m* 1st, 1939, Lieut-Com Hon John David Hotham, DSC, RN, who *d* 1962 (having been raised to the rank of a Baron's son 1924); 2ndly, 1969, Cdr Colin Hugh Smith, RN, who *d* 1975, and has issue living by 1st *m* (see colls, infra).

COLLATERAL BRANCHES LIVING

Issue of late Maj Hon Peter Hotham, late KOYLI, brother of 7th Baron, *b* 1904, *d* 1991; *m* 1934, Margaret (ante), yr da of Col Sir Robert William Herbert Watkin Williams-Wynn, 9th Bt, KCB, DSO, TD:—
Edward Durand, *b* 1944; *ed* Stowe; late Lieut 15th/19th King's Royal Hussars; *m* 1982, Susan Elisabeth, da of late Noel Tilley, of Stokke, Marlborough, Wilts. —— Caroline Alathea, *b* 1937: *m* 1959, Col Harry Llewellyn Davies, RA, who *d* 1981, and has issue living, Catherine Margaret, *b* 1962, — Thora Lucinda, *b* 1965. —— Mary Elizabeth, *b* 1940: *m* 1964, Lt-Col Peter Harman, 14th/20th King's Hussars, and has issue living, Andrew Charles, *b* 1967, — Nicola Jane, *b* 1969.

Issue of late Lieut-Com Hon John David Hotham, DSC, RN, brother of 7th Baron, *b* 1911, *d* 1962: *m* 1939, Aileen (ante) (she *m* 2ndly, 1969, Cdr Colin Hugh Smith, RN), who *d* 1975, da of late Capt Harry Coates, Durham LI:—
Martin Patrick (The Old Rectory, Drinkstone, Bury St Edmunds, Suffolk), *b* 1941; *ed* Stowe: *m* 1965, Erica Antoinette, twin da of late Lt-Col Brian Maxwell Strang, of Maes Heulyn, Denbigh, and has had issue, Charles Beaumont David, *b*

1969, — Henry Ralph, b 1974; d 1986. — Sophia Henrietta, b 1967, — Amelia Oriana Philadelphia, b 1971. —— Henrietta Elizabeth, b 1944: m 1967, Maj Philip A. J. Wright, late Gren Gds, Dep Assistant Serjeant-at-Arms, House of Commons, son of late Sir Andrew Barkworth Wright, KCMG, CBE, MC, and has issue living, Romayne Louise, b 1972, — Melanie Clare, b 1974. —— Georgina Rose, b 1947: m 1971, Lt-Col John V. E. F. O'Connell, Gren Gds (c/o Barclays Bank, 19 Fleet St, EC4), and has issue living, James Alexander, b 1973, — Simon David Sebastian, b 1974, — Emily Mary Frances, b 1976.

Grandchildren of late Adm of Fleet Sir Charles Frederick Hotham, GCB, GCVO, el son of late Capt John Hotham, 4th son of Lt-Col George Hotham, el son of Gen George Hotham, brother of 1st Baron:—
Issue of late John Beaumont Hotham, b 1874, d 1924: m 1905, Gladys Mary, who d 1972, 2nd da of late Col John Gerald Wilson, CB, of Cliffe Hall, Yorkshire (B Inchiquin, colls):—
John David Durand, b 1917; ed Eton, and New Coll, Oxford; formerly Lieut Roy Armoured Corps (TA): m 1954, Marianne Becker, who d 1996, of Vienna. Residence – Milne Graden, Coldstream, Berwickshire. —— Anne (Baroness Howard of Penrith), b 1913: m 1st, 1934, Anthony Gardner Bazley, who d 1937 (see Bazley, Bt, colls); 2ndly, 1944, 2nd Baron Howard of Penrith. Residence – Dean Farm, Coln St Aldwyns, Gloucestershire.

Grandson of late Capt John Hotham (ante):—
Issue of late George Hotham, b 1856, d 1948: m 1896, Louisa Hildegarde Neumeister, who d 1958, of Le Mar, Plymouth Co, Iowa, USA:—
George Edward, b 1906.

Grandchildren of late Capt William Charles Hotham, son of late Rev Edwin Hotham (infra):—
Issue of late Lieut-Col John Clarence Hotham, b 1882, d 1959: m 1909, Margaret Emily Anne, who d 1952, el da of Horace Wilmer, formerly of Church House, Brede, Sussex:—
Diana, b 1918: m 1948, John Calkin Whately-Smith, and has issue living, David John, b 1949: m 1982, Penny Stone, and has issue living, Alastair Charles b 1986, Jessica Clare b 1984, — Jeremy William, b 1956: m 1988, Kathrin Norah Murray Prior, and has issue living, Jonathan b 1990, — Susan Jane, b 1950: m 1973, Oswald Eberhardt, of Schlosshotel, Rosenegg, Fieberbrunn, Tyrol, Austria, and has issue living, Andreas b 1980, Elisabeth b 1978, Kathrin b (twin) 1978, — Charlotte Anne, b 1952: m 1978, David Richard Charles Agnew, and has issue (see Agnew, Bt, cr 1895, colls). Residence – Thatchover, Knole, Langport, Som.

Issue of late Com William Montagu Hotham, Roy Canadian Navy, b 1884, d 1951: m 1905, Margaret Broune:—
Ronald St Vincent Carew, b 1911; ed St Michael's Sch, Victoria: m 1936, Muriel Eva Maria Sheather. —— Alan Geoffrey (1130, Channel Drive, Santa Barbara, California, USA), b 1921; ed Brentwood Sch, and at British Columbia Univ (BASc); 1939-45 War in Research Branch, RCAF: m 1951, Kathleen Cramer-Coxhead, and has issue living, Peter Alan, b 1952, — Daryl, b 1953, — Lisa, b 1955.

Grandsons of late Rev Edwin Hotham, el son of late Adm Sir William Hotham, GCB, 2nd son of late Gen George Hotham (ante):—
Issue of late Montagu Conyers Hotham, b 1850, d 1931: m 1883, Francisca Rosa Pizarro:—
Edwin, b 1887. —— George, b 1899: m 1932, Adriana Maria Franco, and has issue living, Charles Edward, b 1934, — Richard Alan, b 1936.

PREDECESSORS – **(1)** Sir JOHN Hotham, Knt; Gov of Hull, temp Charles I; cr a Baronet 1622; he and his el son being discovered in correspondence with the Royalists were tried by Court Martial at Guildhall, sentenced to death and beheaded on Tower Hill 1645; s by his grandson **(2)** Sir JOHN, 2nd Bt; d 1689; s by his son **(3)** Sir JOHN, 3rd Bt; d 1691; s by his cousin **(4)** Sir CHARLES, 4th Bt; MP for Beverley; s by his son **(5)** Sir CHARLES, 5th Bt; MP for Beverley, and a Groom of the Bedchamber; d 1737; s by his son **(6)** Sir CHARLES, 6th Bt; a Groom of the Bedchamber; d 1767; s by his uncle **(7)** Sir BEAUMONT, 7th Bt; d 1771 s by his el son **(8)** Sir CHARLES Hotham-Thompson, KB, 8th Bt; assumed the additional surname of Thompson; d 1794; s by his brother **(9)** Rt Rev Sir JOHN Hotham, 9th Bt, Lord Bishop of Clogher; d 1795; s by his son **(10)** Sir CHARLES, 10th Bt; s by his uncle **(11)** WILLIAM, 11th Bt, 3rd son of 7th Bt; a distinguished Adm; cr Baron Hotham, of South Dalton (peerage of Ireland) 1797, with remainder to the heirs male of his father; d unmarried 1813; s by his brother **(12)** BEAUMONT, KB, 2nd Baron; a Baron of the Court of Exchequer; d 1814; s by his grandson **(13)** BEAUMONT, 3rd Baron; a Gen in the Army; served at Waterloo; MP for Leominster 1820-41, and for E Riding of York 1841-68; d unmarried 1870; s by his nephew **(14)** CHARLES, 4th Baron, son of Rear-Adm George Frederick (brother of 3rd Baron), by Lady Susan Maria O'Bryen, el da and co-heir of 2nd Marquess of Thomond; served with 18th Foot in Crimean Campaign 1855 (wounded); d unmarried 1872; s by his brother **(15)** JOHN, 5th Baron; b 1838; d unmarried 1907; s by his cousin **(16)** FREDERICK WILLIAM, 6th Baron (son of late Rev William Francis Hotham, son of 2nd Baron), b 1863: m 1902, Benita, who d 1954, da of late Thomas Sanders, of Sanders Park, Charleville, co Cork; d 1923; s by his cousin **(17)** HENRY FREDERICK, CBE, (el son of late Capt Henry Hotham, son of late Rev Frederick Harry Hotham, son of 3rd son of 2nd Baron), 7th Baron, b 1899; Maj Grenadier Guards; Hon Col 440th LAA; m 1937, Lady Letitia Sibell Winifred Cecil, who d 1992, da of 5th Marquess of Exeter; d 1967; s by his 3rd son **(18)** HENRY DURAND, 8th Baron and present peer.

HOTHFIELD, BARON (Tufton) (Baron UK 1881, Bt UK 1851)

ANTHONY CHARLES SACKVILLE TUFTON, 6th Baron, and 7th Baronet; *b* 21 Oct 1939; *s* 1991; *ed* Eton, and Magdalene Coll, Camb (MA); C Eng, MICE: *m* 1975, Lucinda Marjorie, da of Capt Timothy John Gurney (*see* de Bathe, Bt, ext), and formerly wife of Capt Graham Morison Vere Nicoll (*see* Madden, Bt), and has issue.

𝔄rms – Sable, an eagle displayed ermine, within a bordure wavy or. 𝔠rest – A sea lion sejant argent, debruised by a bendlet wavy sable. 𝔖upporters – On either side an eagle ermine, gorged with a collar gules pendent therefrom an escutcheon of the arms of Tufton.
Residence – Drybeck Hall, Appleby-in-Westmorland, Cumbria CA16 4TF.

The bird flies to its own

SON LIVING

Hon WILLIAM SACKVILLE, *b* 14 Nov 1977; *ed* Eton.

DAUGHTER LIVING

Hon Emma, *b* 1976.

BROTHER LIVING

Hon Nicholas William Sackville, *b* 1946; *ed* Eton, and RAC Cirencester: *m* 1978, Meriel, da of Maj William Acworth, and has issue living, Richard Charles, *b* 1980; *ed* Eton, — Henry George, *b* 1983; *ed* Eton. *Residence* – The Red House, Barkway, nr Royston, Herts.

SISTER LIVING

Hon Jennifer Margaret, *b* 1937: *m* 1965, Edward Robert Raikes, yr son of late Julian Henry Raikes, and has issue living, Jason Alexander, *b* 1966; *ed* Stowe, and Exeter Univ: *m* 1992, Emma, da of Peter Budgen, and has issue living, Thomas William *b* 1994, Alexander Caspian *b* 1997, Henry Pendragon *b* 1998, — Benedick Arthur, *b* 1969; *ed* Eton, and LSE, — Stella Mary Evelyn, *b* 1972. *Residence* – Parsonage Oasts, Yalding, Kent.

UNCLE LIVING (*brother of 5th Baron*)

Francis Charles Sackville, VRD (Church Farm House, Clothall, nr Baldock, Herts SG7 6RG), *b* 1913; *ed* Eton, and Trin Coll, Oxford (MA); Lt-Cdr (ret) RNVR; a Knight of Order of Dannebrog of Denmark: *m* 1942, Eileen Joyce Clara, who *d* 1985, da of Sir Edward Henry Goschen, 2nd Bt (*cr* 1916), and has issue living, Edward Philip Sackville (70 Perrymead St, SW6), *b* 1948; *ed* Eton, and Magdalene Coll, Camb (MA), — Mary Josephine, *b* 1943: *m* 1979, John Yorkston Paxton, of Church Farm House, Upwood, nr Ramsay, Cambs, and has issue living, John Edward Sackville, *b* 1985, Charles Thomas *b* 1988.

AUNT LIVING (*sister of 5th Baron*)

Susan Stella, *b* 1908: *m* 1936, Col Thomas Alexander Hamilton Coltman, OBE, DL, RA, who *d* 1998, of Laigh Aldons, Girvan, Ayrshire KA26 0TB, and has issue living, Timothy Charles (Skellingthorpe Hall, nr Lincoln LN6 5UU), *b* 1939; *ed* Eton, and Trin Coll, Camb (BA): *m* 1st, 1964, Joanna Mary, who *d* 1986, only da of John Richard Bergne-Coupland, of Skellingthorpe Hall, nr Lincoln; 2ndly, 1989, Anne Clare, da of Rt Rev Kenneth Riches, and has issue living (by 1st *m*), Sarah Elizabeth *b* 1966, Mary Jane *b* 1968, — David Alexander (Haystoun House, Peebles EH45 9JG), *b* 1942; *ed* Eton, and Edinburgh Univ: *m* 1972, Hon Mary Cecilia, 3rd da of 1st Viscount Whitelaw, and has issue living, Susannah Mary Lavinia *b* 1987.

COLLATERAL BRANCH LIVING

Granddaughter of late Alfred Charles Tufton, brother of 1st Baron:—
Issue of late Alfred Guy Tufton, *b* 1889, *d* 1968: *m* 1916, Marjorie Neville, who *d* 1979, da of late Frederick Charles Thompson, of 40 Porchester Sq, W2:—
Barbara Marjorie, *b* 1920.

PREDECESSORS – (1) RICHARD Tufton, *b* at Verdun, France, 1813; *s* by devise to the estates of his reputed natural father Henry, 11th and last Earl of Thanet; naturalized, with his family, 1849; *cr* a *Baronet* 1851: *m* 1843, Adelaide Amelie Lacour; *d* 1871; *s* by his son (2) Sir HENRY JAMES, 2nd Bt, *b* 1844; *s* as 2nd *Baronet* 1871, and *cr Baron Hothfield*, of Hothfield, co Kent (peerage of United Kingdom) 1881; Lord-Lieut. of Westmorland 1881-1926, Vice-Admiral of Coast of Cumberland and Westmorland 1883-1926, and a Lord-in-Waiting to Queen Victoria 1886: *m* 1872, Alice Harriet Argyll, who *d* 1914, da of late Rev William James Stracey-Clitherow; *d* 1926; *s* by his son (3) JOHN SACKVILLE RICHARD, DSO, 2nd Baron, *b* 1873; Lieut 1st Life Guards, and Major Roy Sussex Regt; Mayor of Appleby 1937-44; S Africa 1901-2, European War 1915-18 (DSO): *m* 1st, 1896, Lady Ierne Louisa Arundel Hastings, who *d* 1935, da of 13th Earl of Huntingdon;

2ndly, 1935, Sybil Augusta, who *d* 1950, da of John Sant; *d* 1952; *s* by his son (4) HENRY HASTINGS SACKVILLE THANET, 3rd Baron, *b* 1897; Lieut 15th/19th Hussars; appointed Assist Director of Public Relations, Home Forces 1942: *m* 1918, Dorothy, who *d* 1981, el da of late William George Raphael, of 9 Connaught Place, W2; *d* 1961; *s* by his cousin (5) THOMAS SACKVILLE (only son of late Hon Sackville Philip Tufton, 2nd son of 1st Baron), 4th Baron, *b* 1916; *dunm* 1986; *s* by his cousin (6) GEORGE WILLIAM ANTHONY (elder son of late Hon Charles Henry Tufton, CMG, 3rd son of 1st Baron), 5th Baron, *b* 1904; Lt-Col RA (TA), DL Herts: *m* 1936, Evelyn Margarette, who *d* 1989, eldest da of late Eustace Mordaunt (*see* Mordaunt, Bt, 1990 Edn); *d* 1991; *s* by his elder son (7) ANTHONY CHARLES SACKVILLE, 6th Baron and present peer.

HOUGHTON OF SOWERBY, BARONY OF (Houghton) (Extinct 1996)

WIDOW LIVING OF LIFE BARON

VERA (*Baroness Houghton of Sowerby*), CBE, da of John Travis, of Southall, Middx: *m* 1939, Baron Houghton of Sowerby, CH, PC (Life Baron), who *d* 1996. *Residences* – 110 Marsham Court, SW1; Becks Cottage, White Hill Lane, Bletchingley, Surrey.

Howard, family name of Earl of Carlisle.

Howard, family name of Earl of Effingham.

Howard, family name of Baron Strathcona.

Howard, family name of Earl of Suffolk.

Howard, Fitzalan, family name of Duke of Norfolk.

HOWARD DE WALDEN AND SEAFORD, BARON (Scott-Ellis) (Baron E 1597 and UK 1826)

Light in darkness

Not by whom, but in what manner

†JOHN OSMAEL SCOTT-ELLIS, 9th Baron Howard de Walden, and 5th Baron Seaford; *b* 27 Nov 1912; *s* 1946; *ed* Eton, and Magdalene Coll, Camb (BA 1934); is Major Westminster Dragoons (TA): *m* 1st, 1934, Countess Irene Harrach, who *d* 1975, yst da of Count Hans Albrecht Harrach; 2ndly, 1978, Gillian Magaret, only da of Cyril Francis Stuart Buckley, and formerly wife of 17th Viscount Mountgarret, and has issue by 1st *m*. Lord Howard de Walden *d* 9th July 1999.

Arms – Quarterly: 1st and 4th crminois, a cross sable, charged with five crescents argent, *Ellis*; 2nd and 3rd or, on a bend azure a star betwixt two crescents of the field, in chief a crescent gules, all within a bordure engrailed of the last, *Scott*. Crests – 1st, on a mount vert, a goat's head erased argent, *Ellis*; 2nd, a dexter hand issuing out of the wreath holding an annulet or in which is set a carbuncle proper, *Scott*. Supporters – Two lions argent, each charged on the neck with three trefoils slipped vert, within a collar gules.
Residences – Avington Manor, Hungerford, Berks RG17 0UL; Flat K, 90 Eaton Sq, SW1W 9AG. *Clubs* – Turf, White's, Jockey.

DAUGHTERS LIVING *(By 1st marriage) (Co-heiresses to the Barony of Howard de Walden)*

Hon (MARY) HAZEL CARIDWEN, *b* 12 Aug 1935: *m* 1957, Count Joseph Czernin, and has issue living, Peter John Joseph, *b* 1966: *m* 1994, Lucinda S., yr da of Richard Wright, of Gt Wilbraham, Cambs, and has issue living, Audrey *b* 1997, — Charlotte Mary Sidonia, *b* 1958: *m* 1986, Neil A. Girkins, son of Gerard Girkins, of Bordeaux, France, and has issue living, Benedict James Seward *b* 1992, Maximilian George Seward *b* 1995, Emily Alexandra Mary *b* 1991, — Henrietta Mary Rosario, *b* 1960: *m* 1985, C. Alistair Currey, eldest son of Charles Currey, of Bosham, Sussex, and has issue living, Camilla Rose Francesca *b* 1986, Alice Catarina Mary *b* 1988, Louisa Henrietta Anne *b* 1990, Rosanna Mariella Claire *b* 1992, Isabelle Quinta Marina *b* 1996, — Alexandra Mary Romana, *b* 1961: *m* 1992, David Mark Noël Kelly, and has issue (see D Norfolk), — Philippa Mary Loretta, *b* 1963: *m* 1998, Alexander W. R. Mitchell, son of Rear Adm Geoffrey Charles Mitchell, CB, of 10 Nelson Close, Stockbridge, Hants, — Isabelle Mary Benedicta, *b* 1967: *m* 1999, Mark N.S. Burnell, elder son of Peter Charles Desborough Burnell, of Northumberland. *Residences* – 47 Queens Gate Gdns, SW7 5ND; White Oak House, Highclere, Newbury, Berks RG20 9RJ.

Hon (BLANCHE) SUSAN FIONODBHAR, *b* 6 Oct 1937: *m* 1961, Capt David William Sinclair Buchan of Auchmacoy (E Caithness), and has issue living, (John) Charles Augustus David, yr of Auchmacoy, *b* 1963: *m* 1998, Sharon, da of late Capt George McArthur, of Holt, Norfolk, — James Alexander Stephen, *b* 1964, — Thomas Richard Sinclair, *b* 1966, — Robert Edward William, *b* 1968, — Sophia Jane Elizabeth, *b* 1962: *m* 1991, David William Hamilton Ruck, son of Dr Colin Ruck, of Crowborough, Sussex, and has issue living, Matilda Rose Athena *b* 1994, Cordelia Mary Augusta *b* 1996, Louisa Grace Olivia *b* 1998. *Residences* – Auchmacoy House, Ellon, Aberdeenshire AB41 8RB; 30 Chipstead St, SW6 3SS.

Hon JESSICA JANE VRONWY, *b* 6 Aug 1941: *m* 1966, Adrian Tancred White (see Lawson-Tancred, Bt, colls, 1980 Edn), and has issue living, Nicholas John Sebastian, *b* 1967: *m* 1997, Cristina V., yr da of Dottore Gaetano Caltagirone, of Rome, Simon James Alexander, *b* 1968, — Richard Dominic Edward, *b* 1970, — Michael Philip Alistair, *b* 1977. *Residence* – Farnborough Downs Farm, Wantage, Oxon OX12 8NW.

Hon CAMILLA ANNE BRONWEN, *b* 1 April 1947: *m* 1971, Guy Acloque, and has issue living, Alexander John Sebastian, *b* 1978, — Henrietta Mary Rose, *b* 1979, — Laura Isabella Helen, *b* 1979 (twin). *Residence* – Alderley Grange, Wotton-under-Edge, Glos, GL12 7QT.

SISTERS LIVING

Hon Bronwen Mary (twin), *b* 1912: *m* 1933, Hon James Louis Lindsay (see E Crawford), who *d* 1997. *Residence* – Sutton Manor, Sutton Scotney, nr Winchester, Hants SO21 3JX.

Hon Margaret Irène Gaenor, *b* 1919: *m* 1938, Richard Frank Heathcoat-Amory (see Heathcoat-Amory, Bt, colls), who *d* 1957. *Residence* – Hele Manor, Exebridge, Dulverton, Somerset TA22 9RN.

Hon Rosemary Nest, *b* 1922: *m* 1946, George FitzRoy Seymour (see M Hertford, colls), who *d* 1994. *Residences* – Thrumpton Hall, Notts; 1st Floor Flat North, 25 Wimpole St, W1.

COLLATERAL BRANCHES LIVING

Grandchildren of late Henry Guysulf Bertram Ellis (infra):—
Issue of late Maj William Felton Ellis, *b* 1912, *d* 1978: *m* 1940, Edwina, who *d* 1977, da of late Maj R. E. Bond, Indian Army:—
COLIN HUMPHREY FELTON ELLIS (Bush Farm, West Knoyle, Warminster, Wilts BA12 6AE), *b* 19 April 1946; *ed* Sherborne, *hp* to Barony of Seaford: *m* 1st, 1971 (*m diss* 1992) Susan Magill; 2ndly, 1993, Penelope Mary Bastin, and has issue living (by 1st *m*), Benjamin Felton Thomas, *b* 1976, — Humphrey Henry Guysulf, *b* 1983, — Harriet Fay, *b* 1973, — Charlotte Susan, *b* 1975. —— Jill Kathleen, *b* 1944: *m* 1968, Rev Jeremy Dudgeon Anderson, of The Croft, Church Rd, Crowborough, E Sussex TN6 1ED, and has issue living, William Maurice, *b* 1973, — Kathleen Fleur, *b* 1971.

Granddaughters of late Rev Hon William Charles Ellis, 2nd son of 6th Baron:—
Issue of late Henry Guysulf Bertram Ellis, *b* 1875; *d* 1947: *m* 1911, Kathleen Roberta, who *d* 1940, only da of William Charles Mitchell, formerly of Marmount, co Down:—

Henrietta Roberta Elizabeth, *b* 1911: *m* 1943, Thomas Stewart Lewis Russell, and has issue living, David Guysulf, *b* 1944, — Peter Stuart, *b* 1948, — Michael Roland, *b* 1950. *Residence* – 44 Churchside, Vigo Village, Meopham, Kent. —— Catherine Rosemary (Court House, West Milton, Bridport, Dorset DT6 3SH), *b* 1918: *m* 1945, Douglas Alexander Clarke-Smith, who *d* 1959, and has issue living, Humphrey Douglas Bevis, *b* 1948: *m* 1975, Christine Quy, and has issue living, Benedict *b* 1978, Orlando *b* 1980, — Lucinda Mary, *b* 1946, *m* 1977, Nigel Henzell-Thomas, of Town Mill House, Whitchurch, Hants RG28 7LZ, and has issue living, Lucy *b* 1978, — Susan, *b* 1950: *m* 1973, Joseph Santolini, of The Stables, Milton Court, Alfriston, E Sussex RG26 5RT, and has issue living, Lindsay *b* 1979.

(In remainder to the Barony of Howard de Walden only)

Issue of late Hon Elisabeth Gwendolen Scott-Ellis, 2nd da of 8th Baron, *b* 1914, *d* 1976: *m* 1st, 1935, Lt-Cdr Count Serge Orloff-Davidoff, RNVR, who was *k* in a motor accident 1945; 2ndly, 1959, Bernard Wheeler Robinson, DSc, who *d* 1997:—
(By 1st *m*) Tatiana, *b* 1936: *m* 1972, William John Whitworth Mallinson, MB, MRCP, and has issue living, Thecla, *b* 1973. Mrs Mallinson also has issue, Sophie Orloff-Davidoff, *b* 1963. *Residence* – 67 Camberwell Grove, SE5 8JE. —— Marina (*Viscountess Bury*), *b* 1937; ARIBA, AADip: *m* 1964, as his 2nd wife, Lt-Col Derek William Charles, Viscount Bury, late 13th/18th Hussars, who *d* 1968, eldest son of 9th Earl of Albemarle. *Residence* – Hurst Barns Farm, East Chiltington, Lewes, E Sussex BN7 3QU.

Issue of late Hon (Essylt) Priscilla Scott-Ellis, 3rd da of 8th Baron, *b* 1916, *d* 1983: *m* 1st, 1945 (*m diss* 1972), Jose Luis de Vilallonga y Cabeza de Vaca, Marques de Castellvell (Grandee of Spain); 2ndly, 19—, Ian Hanson, who *d* 19—:—
(By 1st *m*) Juan Alfonso DE VILALLONGA, *b* 1946: *m* 1981, Michèle, da of late Capt Charles Gaston Meyer, and has issue living, Maria Atalanta, *b* 1986. *Residence* – 03500 Verneuil en Bourbonnais, St Pourçain-sur-Sioule, France. —— Susanna Carmen Margarita Beatriz, *b* 1947: *m* 1975, Gregory John Foster, and has issue living, Adam Kevin Salvador, *b* 1978. *Residence* – 68 Ventry St, Alexandra, NZ.

Grandchildren of late Hon Evelyn Henry Ellis, 5th son of 6th Baron:—
Issue of late Mary Ellis, OBE, *b* 1888, *d* 1971: *m* 1916, Maj Denis Granville Coskey Critchley Salmonson, MC, RSF, who *d* 1943:—
†John Albert Myles Critchley Salmonson, *b* 1916; Maj 12th R Lancers: *m* 1946, Joan, who *d* 1995, da of Col Robert Henry Haseldine, DSO, OBE, and *d* 1998, leaving issue, Denis Patrick Antony (The Glebe House, Dunsyre, Carnwath, Lanarks), *b* 1953; *ed* Downside; Capt Coldm Gds: *m* 1976, Angela Jane, da of Brig Hon (Henry Ernest) Christopher Willoughby (*see* B Middleton), and has issue living, John Henry Guy *b* 1986, Katherine Adini Mary *b* 1979, Isabella Caroline *b* 1981, — Mary Clare, *b* 1947: *m* 1989, Henry John Scrope (*see* E Mexborough, 1972-73 Edn), of Brandsby, York, and has issue living, William John A. *b* 1991, — Antonia Isabella Mary, *b* 1949: *m* 1973, Christopher William Courtenay Tregoning, of The Old Vicarage, Chrishall, Royston, Herts, 3rd son of late Col John L. Tregoning, MBE, and has issue living, Harold John William *b* 1976, Daniel Christopher Leonard *b* 1977, Thomas Anthony Cecil *b* 1982, — Henrietta Margaret Mary *b* 1959: *m* 1985, Jacques Baudouin, of 431 rue des Auges, Grandfresnoy, France, only son of late Lt-Col Roger Baudouin (Chevalier de la Legion d'Honneur), of 35 rue Vauvenargues, Paris, and has issue living, Alexandre John *b* 1986, Maxime Roger *b* 1987, Luke Jacques *b* 1990, Timothy Joseph *b* 1994. —— Peter Evelyn George CRITCHLEY, OBE (Dormans, Combe St Nicholas, Chard, Somerset), *b* 1919; served 1939-45 War as Sqdn-Ldr RAF (fighter pilot); adopted the surname of Critchley by deed poll 1954; OBE (Civil) 1975: *m* 1948, Grace, da of Col J. L. Oliver, and has issue living, Michael Shaun, *b* 1952, — Kim Hardinge, *b* 1954, — Peter Granville Kerr, *b* 1957, — Mark Nicholas, *b* 1959. —— Denise Irene Mary, *b* 1918.

PREDECESSORS – (1) *Sir* THOMAS HOWARD, KG, PC, el son of 4th Duke of Norfolk by his 2nd *m* to Margaret, da and heiress of Thomas KG, 1st and last Baron Audley of Walden summoned to Parliament of England as *Baron Howard of Walden* 1597, and *cr Earl of Suffolk* (peerage of England) 1603 (see E Suffolk); *d* 1626; *s* by his son (2) THEOPHILUS, KG, PC, 2nd Earl; *d* 1640; *s* by his son (3) JAMES, KB 3rd Earl; *d* without male issue, when the earldom devolved upon his brother, and the barony became abeyant between his daus Essex and Elizabeth; in 1784 the abeyance was terminated in favour of the descendant of Essex (4) *Field Marshal Sir* JOHN GRIFFIN Whitwell-Griffin, KB, 4th Baron; *cr Baron Braybrooke* (peerage of Great Britain) 1788; twice *m*, but *dsp* 1797, when the Barony of Braybrooke devolved in terms of the remainder upon his kinsman (see B Braybrooke), and the Barony of Howard of Walden reverted to the heir male of Elizabeth (ante) (5) Right Rev FREDERICK AUGUSTUS Hervey, 4th Earl of Bristol (see M Bristol); *d* 1803; when the earldom passed to his 2nd son, and the Barony of Howard of Walden reverted to his great-grandson (6) CHARLES AUGUSTUS, GCB, 6th Baron, grandson of John Augustus, Lord Hervey, whose da Elizabeth Catherine Caroline *m* Charles Rose Ellis, who *d* 1845 having been *cr Baron Seaford*, of Seaford, co Sussex (peerage of United Kingdom) 1826; *b* 1799; was Min Plen at Stockholm 1832-3, at Lisbon 1833-46, and at Brussels 1846-68: *m* 1828, Lady Lucy Cavendish-Bentinck, da of 4th Duke of Portland; *d* 1868; *s* by his son (7) FREDERICK GEORGE, 7th Baron Howard de Walden, and 3rd Baron Seaford, *b* 1830: *m* 1876 (*m diss* 1893), Blanche, who *d* 1911, having *m* 2ndly 1903, (2nd Baron Ludlow), da of late William Holden, of Palace House, Lancashire; *d* 1899; *s* by his son (8) THOMAS EVELYN, 8th Baron Howard de Walden and 4th Baron Seaford, *b* 1880; Hon Col Westminster Dragoons, and Pres of Queen Charlotte's Hospital; assumed by Roy licence 1917 the additional surname and arms of Scott: *m* 1912, Margherita, CBE, who *d* 1974, da of late Charles Van Raalte, of Brownsea Island, Dorset; *d* 1946; *s* by his son (9) JOHN OSMAEL, 9th Baron and present peer; also Baron Seaford.

Howard of Effingham, Baron; son of Earl of Effingham.

HOWARD OF HENDERSKELFE, BARONY OF (Howard) (Extinct 1984) (see E Carlisle, colls)

HOWARD OF PENRITH, BARON (Howard) (Baron UK 1930)

FRANCIS PHILIP HOWARD, 2nd Baron: *b* 5 Oct 1905; *s* 1939; *ed* Downside, and Trin Coll, Camb (BA); Bar Middle Temple 1931; Capt RA; 1939-43 War: *m* 1944, Anne, da of late John Beaumont Hotham (*see* B Hotham, colls), and widow of Anthony Gardner Bazley (*see* Bazley, Bt, colls), and has issue.

Virtue alone is unconquerable

Arms – Quarterly, 1st, gules, a bend between six cross-crosslets fitchée argent; on the bend an escutcheon or, charged with a demi-lion rampant, pierced through the mouth with an arrow, within a double tressure flory counterflory all gules, *Howard*; 2nd, gules three lions passant guardant in pale or, and in chief a label of three points argent, *Brotherton*; 3rd, checky or and azure, *Warren*; 4th, gules, a lion rampant or, *Fitzalan*. **Crests** – 1st, issuant from a ducal coronet or, a pair of wings gules, each charged with a bend between six cross-crosslets fitchée argent; 2nd, on a chapeau gules, turned up ermine, a lion statant guardant with tail extended or, ducally gorged argent; 3rd, on a mount vert a horse passant argent, holding in the mouth a slip of oak fructed proper. **Supporters** – *Dexter*, a lion argent: *sinister*, a horse argent, holding in the mouth a sprig of oak fructed proper; each charged on the shoulder with an escutcheon barry of six argent and azure, three chaplets gules.
Residence – Dean Farm, Hatherop, Gloucestershire.

SONS LIVING

Hon PHILIP ESME (45 Erpingham Rd, SW15 1BQ), *b* 1st May 1945; *ed* Ampleforth, and Ch Ch Oxford: *m* 1969, Sarah, da of late Barclay Walker, and has issue living, Thomas Philip, *b* 1974, — Michael Barclay, *b* 1984, — Natasha Mary, *b* 1970, — Laura Isabella, *b* 1976.

Hon Michael Edmund, *b* 1947; *ed* Ampleforth.

Hon David Francis, *b* 1949; *ed* Ampleforth: *m* 1981, Diana, da of late John S. Radway, and formerly wife of Timothy L. B. Davis, and has issue living, Rachel Anne, *b* 1982, — Alice Isabella, *b* 1983, — Olivia Charlotte, *b* 1986, — Frances Elizabeth, *b* 1988, — Charlotte Grace, *b* 1993. *Residence* – Glebe House, Ulcombe, nr Maidstone, Kent ME16 1DN.

Hon William John, *b* 1953: *m* 1981, Alexandra Josephine, da of Maurice Graham, and has issue living, Miranda Catherine, *b* 1982, — Elizabeth Clara, *b* 1984.

BROTHER LIVING

Hon Edmund Bernard Carlo, CMG, MVO, *b* 1909; *ed* Downside, and New Coll, Oxford (BA); Bar Middle Temple 1934; Capt KRRC 1939-45 War; 2nd Sec (Information) Rome 1947-51, and in Foreign Office 1951-53, 1st Sec Madrid 1953-57, Head of Chancery Bogota 1957-59, Consul-Gen, San Marino and Consul Florence, 1960-61, Counsellor Rome 1961-65, and Consul-Gen Genoa 1965-69, MVO (4th class) 1961, CMG 1969: *m* 1936, Cécile, da of Charles Geoffroy-Dechaume, of Valmondois, France, and has issue living, Esme Francis (57 Westcroft Sq, W6 0TA), *b* 1938, *ed* Downside, and New Coll, Oxford (BA): *m* 1st, 1963 (*m diss* 1973), Tessa Longhurst, da of late Maj Kenneth Evan Meredith, Dorset Regt; 2ndly, 1979, Diane Marie Kačić, of St Louis, Missouri, USA, and has issue living (by 1st *m*), Dominic William *b* 1964: *m* 1993, Belinda Sarah, yr da of Anthony Cassidy, of Albury, Surrey (and has issue living, Eleanor Louise Tessa *b* 1997), Stephen Anthony *b* 1966: *m* 1994, Emma L., da of Adrian Platt, of W Horsley, Surrey (and has issue living, Florence Elizabeth Mary *b* 1998), Elizabeth Anne *b* 1965: *m* 1995, Benedict H. Dunhill, son of John Dunhill, of Newton Ferrers, S Devon (and has issue living, Henry Robert Alfred *b* 1999, Camilla Cécile Alice *b* 1997), (by 2nd *m*) Edmund Philip *b* 1980, Katherine Lelia *b* 1984, — John Edmund (4 Ivy Cross, Shaftesbury, Dorset) *b* 1940; *ed* Downside, and New Coll, Oxford (BA): *m* 1971, Gloria Cano, of Medellin, Colombia, and has had issue, Alejandro *b* 1973, *d* 1994, Edmund Francis *b* 1985, Patricia Anita *b* 1972, Caterina *b* 1977, — Anthony Richard (48 Batoum Gdns, W6 7QD), *b* 1017; *ed* Downside, and Guildhall Sch of Music and Drama (GGSM): *m* 1978, Anstice Bridget, 2nd da of Maj Martin Antony Gibbs, of Sheldon Manor, Chippenham, Wilts (*see* Hamilton-Dalrymple, Bt), and has two children, Geoffrey John Bernard *b* 1986, Cecily Mary Margaret *b* 1983, — Katherine Isabella, *b* 1952: *m* 1977, Rev Christopher Woods, of Holy Trinity Vicarage, Traverse St, Parr Mount, St Helen's Merseyside, and has issue living, Francis *b* 1981, Thomas *b* 1983, Isabella *b* 1977, Madeline *b* 1979, Lydia *b* 1989. *Residence* – Jerome Cottage, Marlow Common, Bucks SL7 2QR.

WIDOW LIVING OF SON OF FIRST BARON

Adèle le Bourgeois (Bushby House, Greystoke, Penrith, Cumberland), da of late Reese Denny Alsop, of New York City, USA; *m* 1937, Lt-Col Hon Henry Anthony Camillo Howard CMG, Coldm Gds, who *d* 1977, yst son of 1st Baron, and has issue living (see colls, infra).

COLLATERAL BRANCH LIVING

Issue of late Lt-Col Hon Henry Anthony Camillo Howard, CMG, yst son of 1st Baron, *b* 1913, *d* 1977: *m* 1937, Adèle le Bourgeois (ante), da of late Reese Denny Alsop, of New York City, USA:—
Mary Rosalind, *b* 1938, *m* 1961, Ian Harlowe Lowe, of Newton Reigny, Penrith, Cumbria, and has issue living, Esme Charles Harlowe (White's Club), *b* 1962; *ed* Ampleforth; late Coldstream Gds: *m* 1990, Carlotta L. M., elder da of Gian Carlo Guglielmino, of Chester Sq, SW1, and has issue living, Philip Charles Harlowe *b* 1994, Cosima Anne Julia *b* 1992. —— Susan Isabella, *b* 1940; Canoness of St Augustine; *d* 1963. —— Joan Dacre (Greystoke Castle, Greystoke, Penrith, Cumbria CA11 0TG), *b* 1946, *m* 1st, 1966 (*m diss* 1979), William Lacey; 2ndly, 1980, Gordon W. Richards, who *d* 1998, of Old Rectory, Greystoke, Penrith, Cumbria, and has issue living (by 1st *m*), William John, *b* 1967: *m* 1993, Claire Baker, and has issue living, William James *b* 1998, — Anne Marie, *b* 1972. —— Adèle Cristina Sophia (*Hon Mrs Timothy J. Palmer*), *b* 1952: *m* 1984, Hon Timothy John Palmer, of West Woodyates Manor, Salisbury, Wilts, brother of 11th Baron Lucas of Crudwell, and has issue (*see* B Lucas of Crudwell). —— Charlotte Fell, *b* 1953: *m* 1985, Ian Mintrim.

PREDECESSOR – (1) ESME WILLIAM Howard, GCB, GCMG, CVO, 4th son of late Henry Howard, MP, of Greystoke, Cumberland (D Norfolk, colls); *b* 1863; was Envoy Extraor and Min Plen to Swiss Confederation 1911-13, and to Sweden 1913-19, and Ambassador Extraor and Plen to Spain 1919-23, and to Washington 1923-30; *cr Baron Howard of Penrith*, of Gowbarrow, co Cumberland (peerage of United Kingdom) 1930: *m* 1898, Lady Maria Isabella Giovanna Teresa Gioacchina Giustiniani-Bandini, who *d* 1963, da of 8th Earl of Newburgh; *d* 1939; *s* by his 2nd but el surviving son (2) FRANCIS PHILIP, 2nd Baron and present peer.

HOWE, EARL (Curzon) (Earl UK 1821)

FREDERICK RICHARD PENN CURZON, 7th Earl; *b* 29 Jan 1951; *s* 1984; *ed* Rugby, and Ch Ch Oxford (MA); a Lord-in-Waiting to HM 1991-92; Govt Spokesman on Employment and Transport 1991-92, Parly Sec, Ministry of Agriculture, Fisheries and Food 1992-95, Under Sec of State Defence Dept 1995-97: *m* 1983, Elizabeth Helen, DL Bucks 1995, elder da of Capt Burleigh Edward St Lawrence Stuart (*see* E Castle Stewart, colls), and has issue.

𝔄rms – Quarterly: 1st and 4th or, a fesse between three wolves' heads couped sable, *Howe*; 2nd and 3rd argent, on a bend sable, three popinjays or, collared gules, *Curzon*. 𝔠rests – 1st, out of a ducal coronet or, a plume of five ostrich feathers azure, *Howe*; 2nd, a popinjay wings displayed and inverted or, collared gules, *Curzon*. 𝔖upporters – On either side a Cornish chough proper, around the neck a plain gold chain.
Residence – Penn House, Amersham, Bucks HP7 0PS.

SON LIVING

THOMAS (*Viscount Curzon*), *b* 22 Oct 1994.

DAUGHTERS LIVING

Lady Anna Elizabeth, *b* 1987.
Lady Flora Grace, *b* 1989.
Lady Lucinda Rose, *b* 1991.

SISTER LIVING (*raised to the rank of an Earl's daughter* 1985)

Lady Emma Charlotte, *b* 1953.

DAUGHTERS LIVING OF SIXTH EARL (*By 1st marriage*)

Lady (Priscilla) Mary Rose, *b* 1940: *m* 1962, Charles William Lyle Keen, of The Old Rectory, Duntisbourne Rous, Glos, and has issue living, William Walter Maurice, *b* 1970, — Laura Mary Catherine (*Hon Mrs Nicholas D. Beatty*), *b* 1963: *m* 1990, Hon Nicholas Duncan Beatty, yr son of 2nd Earl Beatty, and has issue (see that title), — Eleanor Margaret, *b* 1965, — Alice Priscilla Lyle, *b* 1966; Poet in Residence, Dartington Hall, Devon 1996-97: *m* 1994, Peter C. P. Oswald, eldest son of Peter David Hamilton Oswald, of Fliskmillan, Fife, and has issue living, Joseph Michaelmas, *b* 1996.
Lady Jennifer Jane, *b* 1941: *m* 1962, Alan Joseph Ponté, and has issue living, David Joseph Marcus Blundell, *b* 1964, — Gideon Léo FitzRoy, *b* 1965, — Joshua Albert Coriat *b* 1970, — Luke Antony Archibald, *b* 1974, — (Rebecca) Kate Priscilla Clara, *b* 1967: *m* 1995, David H. Kirton, son of Roger Kirton. *Residence* – 35 Usborne Mews, SW8.

(By 2nd marriage)

Lady Mary Gaye Georgiana Lorna, *b* 1947: *m* 1st, 1971 (*m diss* 1976), (Kevin) Esmond (Peter) Cooper-Key (*see* V Rothermere), who *d* 1985; 2ndly, 1977 (*m diss* 1987), John Austen Anstruther-Gough-Calthorpe (*see* Anstruther-Gough-Calthorpe, Bt); 3rdly, 1988 (*m diss* 1994), Jeffrey Bonas; 4thly, 1996, Christopher Shaw, and has issue living (by 1st *m*) (*see* V Rothermere), — (by 2nd *m*) (*see* Anstruther-Gough-Calthorpe, Bt), — (by 3rd *m*) Cressida, *b* 1989. *Residence* – Hinton Ampner House, Alresford, Hants SO24 0LA.

Lady Charlotte Elizabeth Anne, *b* 1948: *m* 1988, (John) Barry Dinan, former Capt Irish Guards, and has issue living, Richard Assheton Dermot, *b* 1986. *Residence* – Chalkpit House, Knotty Green, Beaconsfield, Bucks HP9 2TY.

DAUGHTERS LIVING OF FIFTH EARL *(By 2nd and 3rd marriages)*

Lady Frances Esmé, *b* 1939: *m* 1st, 1962, Derek Alan Whiting; 2ndly, 1976, Harold Denman (*see* B Denman) and has issue living (by 1st *m*), Alexander, *b* 1967, — Frances, *b* 1965, — (by 2nd *m*) (*see* B Denman).

Lady Sarah Marguerite, *b* 1945: *m* 1st, 1966, Piers Raymond Courage, who *d* 1970; 2ndly, 1972, John Victor Aspinall, of 1 Lyall St, SW1, and has issue living (by 1st *m*) Jason Piers, *b* 1967, — Amos Edward Sebastian, *b* 1969, — (by 2nd *m*) Bassa Wulfhere, *b* 1972.

WIDOW LIVING OF FIFTH EARL

Sybil Boyter, only child of late Capt Francis Johnson, of Palmeira Sq, Hove, and formerly wife of late Maj Ernest Duncombe Shafto: *m* 2ndly, 1944, as his third wife, the 5th Earl Howe, who *d* 1964; 3rdly, 1972, Graham Goodson, who *d* 1988.

COLLATERAL BRANCHES LIVING

Grandchildren of late Charles Ernest Basset Lothian Curzon, only son of late Maj Ernest Charles Penn Curzon, eldest son of late Col Hon Ernest George Curzon, 6th son of 1st Earl:—
Issue of late Capt James Quintin Penn Curzon, Gordon Highlanders, *b* 1923, *d* 1985: *m* 1st, 1966 (*m diss* 1980), Jennifer Anne, da of late Percy Douglas Harrison, of Southsea; 2ndly, 1980, Mary Ann Vere Ogilvy (who *m* 3rdly, 1987, Maj John David Makgill-Crichton-Maitland; *see* E Lauderdale, colls), only da of late Maj Charles Herbert Harberton Eales, MC (*see* Ogilvy, Bt, colls), and formerly wife of Charles Pepler Norton:—
(By 1st *m*) (Charles) Mark Penn, *b* 1967. —— Camilla Mary, *b* 1969: *m* 1997, Simon J. Chambers, son of J. S. W. Chambers, of Perth, Australia.

Granddaughter of late Major Ernest Charles Penn Curzon, son of late Col Hon Ernest George Curzon (ante):—
Issue of late Charles Ernest Basset Lothian Curzon, *b* 1885, *d* 1952: *m* 1917, Geraldine Fosbery, who *d* 1962, da of Sir James Mills, KCMG:—
Mary Eleanora Basset, *b* 1920: *m* 1941, Maj James Malcolm Hay of Seaton, Gordon Highlanders (*see* M Tweeddale, colls), who *d* 1987. *Residence* – Edinglassie, Huntly, Aberdeenshire.

Grandchildren of late Adm Hon Sir Assheton Gore Curzon-Howe, GCVO, KCB, CMG, 9th son of 1st Earl:—
Issue of late Capt Leicester Charles Assheton St John Curzon-Howe, MVO, RN, *b* 1894, *d* on active ser 1941: *m* 1923, Marguerite Graham, who *d* 1977, da of A. Allan Mackenzie of Montreal:—
Anne Rita, *b* 1923; late WRNS: *m* 1st, 1955, as his 2nd wife, 19th Baron Teynham, who *d* 1972; 2ndly, 1975, Dr Ian Edwards, who *d* 1988. *Residence* – Inwood House, Holly Hill Lane, Sarisbury Green, Southampton SO3 6AH.

Issue of late Lieut-Col Assheton Penn Curzon-Howe-Herrick, RA, *b* 1898, *d* 1959, having assumed by Roy licence 1946, the additional surname and arms of Herrick: *m* 1930, Joan Henrietta, OBE (The Hermitage, Thornton Watlass, Ripon N Yorks), da of late James Windsor Lewis, of 67 Cadogan Place, SW1:—
Assheton Montagu Windsor (Le Chastanet, Collonges, Corrèze, France), *b* 1939. —— Marigold Mary, *b* 1934; SRN: *m* 1982, Patrick Benjamin Walker, and *d* 1983.

PREDECESSORS – **(1)** Assheton Curzon, 2nd son of Sir Nathaniel Curzon, 4th Bt (*see* B Scarsdale); MP for Clitheroe 1754-77 and 1790-4; *cr Baron Curzon*, of Penn, co Bucks (peerage of Great Britain) 1794, and *Viscount Curzon* (peerage of United Kingdom) 1802; his only son, Assheton, MP, *d* 1797, having *m* Sophia Charlotte, who in 1799 on the death of her father, Richard, KG, 1st and last Earl Howe (*cr* 1788 *Baron Howe*, of Langar, co Notts peerage of Great Britain, with remainder to his das), became Baroness Howe; **(2-3)** Assheton had by his marriage to the Baroness one son Richard William Penn, PC, GCH, who in 1820 *s* his grandfather as 2nd Viscount and Baron Curzon, and in 1836 *s* his mother as 3rd Baron Howe; assumed the additional name of Howe by Roy licence 1821; *cr Earl Howe* (peerage of United Kingdom) 1821; was Lord Chamberlain to Queen Adelaide: *m* 1st, 1820, Harriet Georgiana, who *d* 1836, da of 6th Earl of Cardigan; 2ndly, 1845, Anne who *d* 1877, da of late Adm Sir John Gore; *d* 1870; *s* by his son **(4)** George Augustus Frederick Louis, 2nd Earl; *b* 1821; sat as MP for S Leicestershire (*C*) 1857-70; *d* 1876; *s* by his brother **(5)** Richard William Penn, GCVO, CB, 3rd Earl, *b* 1822; a Gen in the Army; Mil Sec to Com-in-Ch in India 1854, and sometime ADC to HRH the Duke of Cambridge: *m* 1858, Isabella Katherine, who *d* 1922, da of late Maj-Gen Hon George Anson; *d* 1900; *s* by his el son **(6)** Richard George Penn, GCVO, 4th Earl, *b* 1861; Treasurer of Queen Victoria's Household 1896-1900, a Lord-in-Waiting to Queen Victoria Oct 1900 to Jan 1901, and to King Edward VII Jan 1901 to Sept 1903, and Lord Chamberlain to late Queen Alexandra Sept 1903 to Nov 1925; MP for S, or Wycombe, Div of Bucks (*C*) 1885-1900; received Roy Victorian Chain 1925: *m* 1st, 1883, Lady Georgiana Elizabeth Spencer Churchill, who *d* 1906, da of 7th Duke of Marlborough; 2ndly, 1919, Florence (Flora), who *d* 1925, da of John H. Davis, of 24 Washington Square, New York, and widow of 2nd Marquess of Dufferin and Ava; 3rdly, 1927, Lorna Katherine, who *d* 1961, da of Major Ernest Charles Penn Curzon, and widow of Capt Quintin Dick, DL; *d* 1929; *s* by his son **(7)** Francis Richard Henry Penn, CBE,

VD, PC, 5th Earl, *b* 1884; Chm of Roy National Life-Boat Instn: *m* 1st, 1907 (*m diss* 1937), his cousin Mary, who *d* 1962, da of Col Hon Montagu Curzon, 8th son of 1st Earl Howe; 2ndly, 1937 (*m diss* 1943), Joyce Mary McLean, da of Charles McLean Jack, of Johannesburg; 3rdly, 1944, Sybil Boyter (who *m* 3rdly 1972 Graham Goodson), da of Capt Francis Johnson, of Edinburgh, and formerly wife of late Maj Ernest Duncombe Shafto; *d* 1964; *s* by his only son (**8**) EDWARD RICHARD ASSHETON PENN, CBE, 6th Earl *b* 1908; Pres British Automobile Racing Club and Inst of Road Safety Officers: *m* 1st, 1935 (*m diss* 1943), Priscilla Crystal Frances Blundell, only da of Sir (William Ernest George) Archibald Weigall, 1st Bt, KCMG; 2ndly, 1946, Grace Lilian, OStJ, who *d* 1985, da of Stephen Frederick Wakeling, of Durban, S Africa, and formerly wife of Capt A. N. Barker; *d* 1984; *s* by his kinsman (**9**) FREDERICK RICHARD PENN (only son (by 2nd *m*) of Cdr Chambré George William Penn Curzon, RN (ret), son of Hon Frederick Graham Curzon, 2nd son of 3rd Earl), 7th Earl and present peer; also Viscount Curzon, Baron Curzon, and Baron Howe.

HOWE OF ABERAVON, BARON (Howe) (Life Baron 1992)

(RICHARD EDWARD) GEOFFREY HOWE, CH, PC, elder son of late Benjamin Edward Howe, of Port Talbot, Glam; *b* 20 Dec 1926; *ed* Winchester, and Trin Hall, Camb (MA, LLB, Hon Fellow 1992); Hon LLD Wales 1988; Bar Middle Temple 1952, Member Gen Council of the Bar 1957-61, QC 1965, Bencher 1969, Member Exec Cttee "Justice" 1963-70, Dep-Chm Glamorgan Quarter Sessions 1966-70, Solicitor- Gen 1970-72, Min for Trade and Consumer Affairs 1972-74, Chancellor of the Exchequer and Lord Commr of the Treasury 1979-83, Chm IMF Policy-Making Interim Cttee 1982-83, Sec of State Foreign and Commonwealth Affairs 1983-July 1989, Leader of the Commons and Lord Pres of the Council July 1989-Nov 1990, Dept PM July 1989-Nov 1990; Member of Council Surrey Univ since 1970, Patron Enterprise Europe since 1990, Pres GB-China Centre since 1992, etc; non-exec Dir Glaxo plc and BICC plc 1991-97, Special Advisor to Jones, Day, Reavis & Pogue, Member Internat Advisory Councils of J. P. Morgan & Co, Inst for Internat Studies Stanford Univ, and Bertelsmann Foundation Bonn; Memb European Advisory Councils of The Carlyle Group and Fiji Bank; Visitor to Sch of Oriental and African Studies London Univ since 1991; Member Exec Cttee The Pilgrims since 1998; Grand Cross Order of Merit Germany 1992; served 1945-48 as Lieut Royal Signals and E African Signals; MP Bebington (C) 1964-66, Reigate 1970-74, and E Surrey 1974-92; *cr* Kt Bach 1970, PC 1972, *Baron Howe of Aberavon*, of Tandridge, co Surrey (Life Baron) 1992, and CH 1996: *m* 1953, Elspeth Rosamund Morton, CBE, JP, da of late Philip Morton Shand, and has issue.

Arms – ......
Address – c/o House of Lords, SW1A 0PW.

SON LIVING

Hon Alexander Edward Thomson, *b* 1959; *ed* Marlborough, and York Univ.

DAUGHTERS LIVING

Hon Caroline, *b* 1955: *m* 19— (*m diss* 19—), — Thornton, and has issue living, Christopher, *b* 1980.
Hon Amanda, *b* (twin) 1959: *m* 19—, S. F. Glanvill, and has issue living, James, *b* 1989.

HOWELL, BARONY OF (Howell) (Extinct 1998)

SONS LIVING OF LIFE BARON

Hon Andrew, *b* 1957: *m* 1986, Ceridwen, da of—

Hon Michael, *b* 1959: *m* 1992, Elizabeth, da of—

DAUGHTER LIVING OF LIFE BARON

Hon Kathryn, *b* 1962: *m* 1983 (*m diss* 19—), Michael Molloy.

WIDOW LIVING OF LIFE BARON

BRENDA MARJORIE (*Baroness Howell*), da of Stephen Willson: *m* 1955, Baron Howell, PC (Life Baron), who *d* 1998. *Residence* – 33 Moor Green Lane, Moseley, Birmingham B13 8NE.

HOWELL OF GUILDFORD, BARON (Howell) (Life Baron 1997)

DAVID ARTHUR RUSSELL HOWELL, PC, son of late Col Arthur Howard Eckford Howell, DSO, TD (*see* Bowater, Bt, *cr* 1939, 1985 Edn); *b* 18 Jan 1936; *ed* Eton, and King's Coll, Camb (MA 19—); worked in Economic Section of Treasury 1959-60; Leader Writer, Daily Telegraph 1960-64; Chm Bow Group 1961-62; Editor of Crossbow 1962-64; Dir Conservative Political Centre 1964-66; MP (C) Guildford 1966-97; Lord Commissioner of the Treasury 1970-71; Parliamentary Sec, Civil Service Dept 1970-72; Parliamentary Under-Sec for Employment 1971-72, and for N Ireland March-Nov 1972; Min of State, N Ireland 1972-74, and for Energy 1974; Sec of State for Energy 1979-81, and for Transport 1981-83; Chm House of Commons Foreign Affairs Cttee 1987-97; Chm UK Japan 2000 Group; Monks Investment Trust and John Laing (Investment), Singapore plc; Memb International Advisory Board, Swiss Bank Corporation 1988-97; Advisory Dir Warburg Dillon Read since 1997; Liveryman, Worshipful Co of Clothworkers; 2nd Lieut Coldstream Guards 1954-56; *cr* PC 1979, and *Baron Howell of Guildford*, of Penton Mewsey, co Hants (Life Baron) 1997: *m* 1967, (Cary) Davina, da of late Maj David Wallace, and has issue.

𝕬rms – Not exemplified at time of going to press.
Address – House of Lords, SW1A 0PW. *Club* – Buck's.

SON LIVING

Hon Toby David, *b* 1975: *ed* ....

DAUGHTERS LIVING

Hon Frances Victoria, *b* 1969: *m* 1998, George Gideon Oliver Osborne, eldest son of Sir Peter George Osborne, 17th Bt.
Hon Kate Davina, *b* 1970: *m* 1991, Paul Bain, son of K. J. Bain.

Howells, family name of Baron Geraint.

HOWICK OF GLENDALE, BARON (Baring) (Baron UK 1960)

CHARLES EVELYN BARING, 2nd Baron; *b* 30 Dec 1937; *s* 1973; *ed* Eton, and New Coll, Oxford; Dir of Baring Brothers & Co Ltd 1969-82; Member of Exec Cttee Nat Art Collections Fund: *m* 1964, Clare Nicolette, yr da of Col Cyril Darby, MC, of Kemerton Court, Tewkesbury, Glos, and has issue.

Arms – Azure, a fesse or, in chief a bear's head proper muzzled and ringed or, differenced by an eastern crown azure. **Crest** – A mullet erminois between two wings argent. **Supporters** – *Dexter*, a tiger guardant proper gorged with an Eastern crown or; *Sinister*, a lion guardant purpure crowned with a ducal coronet or, and gorged with an eastern crown or.
Residence – Howick, Alnwick, Northumberland NE66 3LB.

SON LIVING

Hon DAVID EVELYN CHARLES, *b* 26 March 1975.

DAUGHTERS LIVING

To serve the King with goodwill

Hon Rachel Monica, *b* 1967: *m* 1989, Capt (George Charles) Nicholas Lane Fox, The Blues and Royals (*see* B Bingley, ext, 1980 Edn), and has issue living, George Sackville, *b* 1992, — Frederick Evelyn, *b* 1994, — Charles Edward, *b* 1996, — Harry, *b* 1998, — Sophie Grey, *b* 1991. *Residence* – Bramham Park, Wetherby, W Yorks LS23 6ND.

Hon Jessica Mary Clare, *b* 1969: *m* 1995, Marcus J. A. Laithwaite, eldest son of Paul Laithwaite, of Deeside House, Chester, and has issue living, Hugo Charles Richard *b* 1998. *Residence* – 51 Masboro Rd, W14 0LU.

Hon Alice Olivia, *b* 1971.

SISTERS LIVING

Hon Katherine Mary Alice (*Hon Lady Wakefield*), *b* 1936: *m* 1974, as his 3rd wife, Sir (Edward) Humphry Tyrrell Wakefield, 2nd Bt.

Hon Elizabeth Beatrice, *b* 1940: *m* 1962, Capt Nicholas Albany Gibbs, who *d* 1984, and has issue living, Andrew Lionel John, *b* 1966: *m* 1999, Alexandra Tembe, eldest da of Garry Wilson, of Magaliesburg, S Africa, — Mary Camilla, *b* 1964, — Eliza Jane, *b* 1968: *m* 1994, William Browne-Swinburne, of The Old School, Capheaton, Newcastle-upon-Tyne, son of John Browne-Swinburne, of Capheaton, and has issue living, Jessica *b* 1996, Lucy *b* 1997. *Residence* – 54 Stokenchurch St, SW6 3TR.

WIDOW LIVING OF FIRST BARON

Lady MARY CECIL GREY (*Lady Mary Howick*) (Howick, Alnwick, Northumberland NE66 3LB), da of 5th Earl Grey: *m* 1935, the 1st Baron Howick of Glendale, who *d* 1973.

PREDECESSOR – (1) *Hon Sir* EVELYN Baring, KG, GCMG, KCVO, yst of 1st Earl of Cromer, *b* 1903; Gov of S Rhodesia 1942-44, UK High Commr in Union of S Africa, and for Basutoland, Bechuanaland and Swaziland 1944-51, and Gov of Kenya 1952-59; *cr Baron Howick of Glendale*, of Howick, co Northumberland 1960: *m* 1935, Lady Mary Cecil Grey, da of 5th Earl Grey; *d* 1973; *s* by his son (2) CHARLES EVELYN, 2nd Baron, and present peer.

HOWIE OF TROON, BARON (Howie) (Life Baron 1978)

WILLIAM HOWIE, el son of Peter Howie of Troon; *b* 2 March 1924; *ed* Marr Coll, Troon, and Royal Tech Coll, Glasgow (BSc); Hon DSc City Univ 1992, Hon DL Strathclyde Univ 1994; Civil Engineer, publisher and journalist; FICE; Assistant Whip 1964-66; Lord Commr of the Treasury 1966-67, Comptroller HM Household 1967-68 and a Vice-Chm Parl Labour Party 1968-70: MP for Luton (*Lab*) 1963-70; Member of Council Instn of Civil Engineers 1964-67, and of Gov Body, Imperial Coll of Science and Technology 1965-67, and of Gov Council, City Univ 1968-91; Pro-Chancellor City Univ 1984-91; Member of Cttee of Inquiry into the Engineering Profession 1977-80; *cr Baron Howie of Troon*, of Troon, Kyle and Carrick (Life Baron) 1978: *m* 1951, Mairi Margaret, da of late John Sanderson, of Troon.
Residence – 34 Temple Fortune Lane, NW11 7UL.

SONS LIVING

Hon Angus, *b* 1963.
Hon Alexander Robin, *b* 1965.

DAUGHTERS LIVING

Hon Annabel Martha, *b* 1956: *m* 1979, — Gibb.
Hon Alisoun Mary Kyle, *b* 1959: *m* 1991, ... Batterham.

Howland, Baron; grandson of Duke of Bedford.

HOY, BARONY OF (Hoy) (Extinct 1976)

SON LIVING OF LIFE BARON

Hon Ian Richard, *b* 1945; *ed* George Heriot's Sch, Edinburgh; Member City of Edinburgh Dist Council since 1988.

HOYLE, BARON (Hoyle) (Life Baron 1997)

(ERIC) DOUGLAS HARVEY HOYLE, son of late William Hoyle, of Adlington, Lancs; *b* 17 Feb 1930; *ed* Adlington Sch, and Horwich and Bolton Technical Colls; Engineering Apprentice, British Rail, Horwich 1946-51; Sales Engineer, AEI, Manchester 1951-53; Sales Engineer and Marketing Executive, Charles Weston Ltd, Salford 1951-74; JP 1958; Memb Manchester Regional Hosp Board 1968-74 and NW Regional Health Authority 1974-75; MP (*Lab*) for Nelson and Colne 1974-79 and for Warrington 1981-97; Chm Parliamentary Labour Party since 1991; Memb of Shadow Cabinet 1992-97; Memb House of Commons Trade and Industry Select Cttee 1985-92; a Lord-in-Waiting to HM (Govt Whip) since 1998; *cr Baron Hoyle*, of Warrington, co Cheshire (Life Baron) 1997: *m* 1953, Pauline, who *d* 1991, da of William Spencer, of Blackrod, Lancs, and has issue.
Address – 30 Ashfield Rd, Anderton, nr Chorley, Lancs PR6 9PN.

SON LIVING

Hon Lindsay, *b* 19—, *ed* Adlington County Sch, and Lords Coll, Bolton: *m* 1993, Catherine, da of John Maxwell Swindley.

Hubbard, family name of Baron Addington.

HUDSON, VISCOUNTCY OF (Hudson) (Extinct 1963)

DAUGHTER LIVING OF SECOND VISCOUNT

Hon Annabel Jocelyne (8 Moncorvo Close, SW7), *b* 1952: *m* 1970, (Anthony) Juan Garton, and has issue living, Anthony William, *b* 1974, — Angela Maria Annabel, *b* 1972, — Annabel Katherine Madeline Maria, *b* 1982, — Annabel Rose Maria Francesca, *b* 1984.

Huggins, family name of Viscount Malvern.

Hughes, family name of Baron Cledwyn of Penrhos.

HUGHES, BARON (Hughes) (Life Baron 1961)

WILLIAM HUGHES, CBE, PC, son of late Joseph Hughes; *b* 22 Jan 1911; *ed* Balfour Street Sch, Dundee, and at Dundee Technical Coll; Hon LLD St Andrews 1960; Chm Roy Commn on Legal Sers in Scotland 1976-80, and E Kilbride Development Corpn 1975-82; Pres Scottish Fedn of Housing Assocns; Delegate to Council of Europe and Western European Union 1976-87; a DL for co of City of Dundee, and a Chevalier of Legion of Honour; formerly a Member of Dundee Town Council (Lord Provost and Lord-Lt of co of City of Dundee 1954-60); Chm of E Regional Hosp Board (Scotland) 1948-60 and a Member of Court of St Andrews Univ 1954-63 and of Council of Queen's Coll, Dundee 1954-63, Chm of Glenrothes Development Corporation 1960-64, and a Member of N Scotland Hydro-Electric Board 1956-64; a Parl Under-Sec of State, Scottish Office 1964-69, and Min of State, Scottish Office 1969-70, and 1974-75; ARP Controller, Dundee, 1939-43, India, Borneo and Burma 1944-46 as Capt RAOC; *cr* OBE (Civil) 1942, CBE (Civil) 1956, *Baron Hughes*, of Hawkhill, co of City of Dundee (Life Baron) 1961, and PC 1970: *m* 1951, Christian Clacher, who *d* 1994, da of late James Gordon, and has issue.
Residence – The Stables, Ross, Comrie, Perthshire PH6 2JU.

DAUGHTERS LIVING

Hon Christian Alison, *b* 1952; *ed* Strathclyde Univ (BSc): *m* 1973, Allan Cameron Cassels Henry, of Tigh-an-Lios, Ross, Comrie, Perthshire, and has issue, two sons and two das.
Hon Janet Margaret (Alltan, by Tulloes, Forfar), *b* 1956; *ed* Edinburgh Univ (BSc).

HUGHES OF WOODSIDE, BARON (Hughes) (Life Baron 1997)

ROBERT HUGHES, son of Mitchell Hughes, of Pittenweem, Fifeshire; *b* 3 Jan 1932; *ed* Robert Gordon's Coll, Aberdeen, Benoni High Sch, Transvaal, and Pietermaritzburg Technical Coll, Natal;

engineering apprentice in S Africa; Chief Draughtsman, C. F. Wilson & Co (1932) Ltd, Aberdeen until 1970; MP for Aberdeen North (*Lab*) 1970-97; Memb Standing Cttee on Immigration Bill 1971, Scottish Affairs Select Cttee 1971 and 1992-97; Parliamentary Under-Sec of State, Scottish Office 1974-75; Jnr Opposition Spokesman 1981-83, and Principal Opposition Spokesman on Agriculture 1983-84, and Transport 1985-88; Memb Shadow Cabinet 1985-88; Chm Aberdeen City Labour Party 1961-69, Anti-Apartheid Movement 1976-94, Action for Southern Africa (successor to AAM) since 1994, and Aberdeen CND (Founder Memb); Memb AEU since 1952, Gen Medical Cncl 1976-79, and Scottish Poverty Action Group; *cr Baron Hughes of Woodside*, of Woodside in the City of Aberdeen (Life Baron) 1997: *m* 1957, Ina Margaret, da of Andrew Miller, of Mey, Caithness, and has issue.

Address – c/o House of Lords, Westminster, SW1A 0PW.

SONS LIVING

Hon Michael, *b* 1962.
Hon John, *b* 1964.

DAUGHTERS LIVING

Hon Jenny, *b* 1958.
Hon Mary, *b* 1960.
Hon Joanne Margaret, *b* 1967.

Hunsdon of Hunsdon, Baron, see Baron Aldenham.

HUNT, BARONY OF (Hunt) (Extinct 1998)

WIDOW LIVING OF LIFE BARON

Joy (*Baroness Hunt*), da of late Dr Mowbray-Green: *m* 1936, Brig the Baron Hunt, KG, CBE, DSO, who *d* 1998. *Residence* – Highway Cottage, Aston, Henley-on-Thames, Oxon.

HUNT OF FAWLEY, BARONY OF (Hunt) (Extinct 1987)

SONS LIVING OF LIFE BARON

Dr the Hon Jonathan Philip Henderson, *b* 1947; *ed* Charterhouse, and Pembroke Coll, Oxford (MA, BM, BCh): *m* 1977, Monika, only da of Dr Herbert Kuhlmann, of Schloss Urstein, Salzburg, Austria, and has issue, three das. *Residence* – 29 South Terrace, SW7 2TB.
Dr the Hon Christopher Godfrey Evill (twin) *b* 1947; MB, BS London; MRCS Eng; LRCP London; DObst, RCOG: *m* 1979, Carol McDermott, of Toronto, Ontario, Canada, and has issue, two das. *Residence* – 4642 West 15th Av, Vancouver, BC V6R 3B6, Canada.

DAUGHTERS LIVING OF LIFE BARON

Hon Rosemary, *b* 1943; *ed* St Andrews Univ (MA): *m* 1974, Dr Clive Malcolm Senior, BA, PhD, of 20 Derby St, Swanbourne, Perth, W Australia, and has issue, one son and one da.
Hon Gillian Mary, *b* 1951: *m* 1972, Paul Andrew Richards, MA, of Arborfield, Wantage, Oxon, and has issue, three sons and one da.

HUNT OF KINGS HEATH, BARON (Hunt) (Life Baron 1997)

PHILIP ALEXANDER HUNT, OBE, son of Rev Philip Lacey Winter Hunt, of Oxford; *b* 19 May 1949; *ed* City of Oxford High Sch, Oxford Sch, and Leeds Univ (BA 19—); Catering Assist, Mount Newman, Western Australia 1971-72; Work Study Offr, Oxford Regional Hospital Board 1972-74; Hospital Administrator, Nuffield Orthopaedic Centre 1974-75; Sec, Edgware/Hendon Community Health Centre 1975-78; Assist Sec, Nat Assoc of Health Authorities (NAHA) 1978-79, Assist Dir 1979-84, Dir 1984-90; Dir Nat Assoc of Health Authorities and Trusts (NAHAT) since 1990; Memb Cncl, Assoc for Public Health 1992-94, since when Co-Chm; Memb Oxford City Council 1973-79, Oxford Area Health Authority 1975-77, and other bodies; a Lord in Waiting to HM (Govt Whip) since 1998; MHSM; *cr* OBE 1993, and *Baron Hunt of Kings Heath*, of Birmingham, W Midlands (Life Baron) 1997: *m* 1st, 1974 (*m diss* 19—), Helen C. Munro; 2ndly, 1988, Selina Ruth Helen, da of Prof John David Stewart, of Birmingham, and has issue by 1st and 2nd *m*.
Residence – 31 Ashfield Av, Kings Heath, Birmingham B14 7AT.

SONS LIVING (By 2nd marriage)

Hon Jacob, *b* 1988.
Hon Benjamin, *b* 1992.
Hon Joshua, *b* 1995.

DAUGHTERS LIVING (By 1st marriage)

Hon Phillipa, *b* 1975.

(By 2nd marriage)

Hon Esther, *b* 1990.

HUNT OF TANWORTH, BARON (Hunt) (Life Baron 1980)

JOHN JOSEPH BENEDICT HUNT, GCB, son of late Maj Arthur L. Hunt, MC; *b* 23 Oct 1919; *ed* Downside, and Magdalene Coll, Camb (MA); Hon Fellow 1977; Lieut RNVR 1940-46; entered Dominions Office 1946; 2nd Sec UK High Commr's Office, Ceylon 1948-50, 1st Sec UK High Commr's Office, Canada 1953-56; Pte Sec to Sec of Cabinet 1956-58, and to Permanent Sec to Treas and Head of Civil Ser 1957-58; Assist Sec, Commonwealth Relations Office 1958-60, Cabinet Office 1960-62, and HM Treas 1962-65, and Under Sec HM Treas 1965-68; 1st Civil Ser Commr 1968-71, Dep Sec HM Treas 1971-72, and 2nd Permanent Sec, Cabinet Office 1972-73, and Sec of the Cabinet 1973-79; Chm Banque Nationale de Paris plc 1980-97; Chm Prudential Corpn plc 1985-90, and Dir IBM (UK) Ltd 1980-90; Advisory Dir Unilever 1980-90; Chm Ditchley Foundation 1983-91; Chm European Policy Forum 1992-98; Pres Local Govt Assoc since 1997; *cr* CB (Civil) 1968, KCB (Civil) 1973, GCB (Civil) 1977, and *Baron Hunt of Tanworth*, of Stratford-upon-Avon (Life Baron) 1980: *m* 1st, 1941, Hon Magdalen Mary Robinson, who *d* 1971, da of 1st Baron Robinson (ext); 2ndly, 1973, Madeleine Frances, da of late Sir William Hume, CMG, FRCP, and widow of Sir John Charles, KCB, FRCP, and has had issue by 1st *m*.
Residence – 8 Wool Rd, SW20 0HW.

SONS LIVING (By 1st marriage)

Hon Michael Anthony, *b* 1942: *m* 1st, 1963 (*m diss* 1986), Rosemary Ann, only da of late Col Theodore Ernle Longridge, OBE, of Marylands, Lynch Rd, Farnham, Surrey; 2ndly, 1986 (*m diss* 1997), Jennee Lynn, da of G. Thomas Baker, of Reno, Nevada, USA; 3rdly, 1997, Kim Marie, da of David Kirk, of Toronto, Canada, and has issue living (by 1st *m*) Mary

Louise, *b* 1967, — Frances Kate, *b* 1969, — Mary Clare, *b* 1977, — (by 2nd *m*) James Theodore Oakes, *b* 1985, — Justin Michael, *b* 1986, — Joanna Marie, *b* 1987. *Residence* – 1407 Clipperton Av, Henderson, Nevada 89014, USA.

Hon Martin John, *b* 1962; *ed* Worth: *m* 1993, Olivia Louise, only da of John Norris Fennell (*see* B Hawke), and has issue living, Theodore Martin Benedict, *b* 1998, — Georgemma (Georgie) Charlotte Olivia, *b* 1996.

DAUGHTER DECEASED (*By 1st marriage*)

Hon Charlotte Mary Magdalen, *b* 1947: *m* 1976, Dr Herbert Gill, of 22230 Drums Court, Woodland Hills, California 91364, USA, son of Jack Gill, of California, USA, and *d* 1995, leaving issue, Julia Magdalen, *b* 1980.

HUNT OF WIRRAL, BARON (Hunt) (Life Baron 1997)

DAVID JAMES FLETCHER HUNT, MBE, PC, son of late Alan Nathaniel Hunt, OBE; *b* 21 May 1942; *ed* Liverpool Coll, Montpellier Univ, Bristol Univ, and Guildford Coll of Law; Solicitor; partner Stanley Wasbrough & Co 1965-77, and Beachcroft Stanleys since 1977 (Senior partner since 1996); PPS to Trade Sec 1979-81 and to Defence Sec 1981; Junior Conservative Whip 1981-83; a Lord Commr of the Treasury (Govt Whip) 1983-84; Vice-Chm of the Conservative Party 1983-85; Parliamentary Under-Sec of State, Dept of Energy 1984-87; Treasurer of HM Household (Dept Govt Chief Whip) 1987-89; Minister for Local Govt and Inner Cities 1989-90; Sec of State for Wales 1990-93; Sec of State for Employment 1993-94; Chancellor of the Duchy of Lancaster (with responsibility for Science and the Citizens' Charter) 1994-95; Pres Tory Reform Group since 1991; MP for Wirral (*C*) 1976-83 and for Wirral W 1983-97; *cr* MBE 1973, PC 1990, and *Baron Hunt of Wirral*, of Wirral, co Merseyside (Life Baron) 1997: *m* 1973, Patricia Margery, da of Roger Orchard, and has issue, two sons and two das.

Address – Beachcroft Stanleys, 20 Furnival St, EC4A 1BN.

HUNTER OF NEWINGTON, BARONY OF (Hunter) (Extinct 1994)

SONS LIVING OF LIFE BARON

Dr the Hon Robert Douglas (2 Lindsay Av, Cheadle Hulme, Cheshire SK8 7BQ), *b* 1945: *m* 1969, Marion Mackenzie.
Dr the Hon Alan Marshall (31 Hillcrest Av, Nether Poppleton, York YO2 6L0), *b* 1946: *m* 1971, Elizabeth Goodall.
Hon Ian Thorburn (27 Affleck Gdns, Monikie, by Dundee), *b* 1951: *m* 1974, Angela Hill.

DAUGHTER LIVING OF LIFE BARON

Hon Gillian Margaret, *b* 1948: *m* 1973, Dr Malcolm Greig Edward, of 82 Lordswood Rd, Harborne, Birmingham B17 9BY.

WIDOW LIVING OF LIFE BARON

KATHLEEN MARGARET (*Baroness Hunter of Newington*), da of James Wilkie Douglas: *m* 1940, Baron Hunter of Newington, MBE, FRCP (Life Baron), who *d* 1994. *Residence* – 3 Oakdene Drive, Barnt Green, Birmingham 45 8LQ.

HUNTINGDON, EARL OF (Hastings-Bass) (Earl E 1529)

Victory is in truth

WILLIAM EDWARD ROBIN HOOD HASTINGS-BASS, 16th Earl; *b* 30 Jan 1948; *s* 1990; *ed* Winchester, and Trin Coll, Camb; Trainer to HM at W Ilsley Stables 1989-98: *m* 1989, Susan Mary Gavin, da of late John Jellicoe Pelham Francis Warner (son of late Sir Pelham Warner, MBE).

Arms – Argent, a maunch sable. Crest – A bull's head erased sable, armed and ducally gorged or. Supporters – Two man tigers (or lions guardant with human faces) or, the faces proper.
Residence – Hodcott House, W Ilsley, nr Newbury, Berks.

BROTHERS LIVING (*Raised to the rank of an Earl's sons*, 1992)

Hon SIMON AUBREY ROBIN HOOD, *b* 2 May 1950; *ed* Winchester, and Trin Coll, Camb. *Residence* – Coronation House, Newmarket, Suffolk.
Hon John Peter Robin Hood, *b* 1954; *ed* Winchester, and Trin Coll, Camb: *m* 1982, Sophie, only da of Peter Ewald Scarisbrick, of 11 Chester Terr, NW1, and has issue living, Alice Victoria Mary, *b* 1983, — Lily Frances Mary, *b* 1986. *Residence* – Ashmansworth Manor, Newbury, Berks.

SISTER LIVING (*Raised to the rank of an Earl's daughter*, 1992)

Lady Emma Alice Mary, *b* 1949: *m* 1969, Ian Anthony Balding, LVO (Trainer to HM), son of late Gerald Balding, of Weyhill House, Andover, Hants, and has issue living, Andrew Matthews, *b* 1972, — Clare Victoria, *b* 1971. *Residence* – Park House, Kingsclere, Newbury, Berks.

DAUGHTERS LIVING OF FIFTEENTH EARL (*By 1st marriage*)

Lady Moorea, MBE, *b* 1928: Under Warden Guild of Freemen of City of London 1998; JP; MBE (Civil) 1999: *m* 1st, 1957 (*m diss* 1966), Woodrow Lyle Wyatt (later Baron Wyatt of Weeford) (Life Baron), who *d* 1997; 2ndly, 1967, Brinsley Black, and has issue living (by 1st *m*) (*see* B Wyatt of Weeford), — (by 2nd *m*) Octavius Orlando Irvine Casati, *b* 1968. *Residence* – 17 Lansdowne Walk, W11.

(*By 2nd marriage*)

Lady Selina Shirley HASTINGS (c/o Rogers, Coleridge & White, 20 Powis Mews, W11 1JN), *b* 1945; writer.
Lady (Caroline) Harriet, *b* 1946: *m* 1970, Hon Charles Edward Ernest Shackleton, who *d* 1979, only son of late Baron Shackleton, KG, OBE, PC (Life Baron); has issue living, David Charles, *b* 1986, — Emma Jane Miranda, *b* 1985.

MOTHER LIVING

Priscilla Victoria, da of Capt Sir Malcolm Bullock, 1st Bt, MBE (ext): *m* 1947, Capt Peter Robin Hood Hastings-Bass, who *d* 1964, having assumed by deed poll the additional surname of Bass 1954. *Residence* – Wells Head House, Kingsclere, Newbury, Berks.

COLLATERAL BRANCHES LIVING

Granddaughter of late Capt Hon Osmond William Toone Westenra Hastings, 2nd son of 13th Earl:—
Issue of late Lt-Col Robin Hood William Stewart Hastings, DSO, OBE, MC, *b* 1917, *d* 1990: *m* 1950, Jean Suzanne, who *d* 1995, da of late Henry Palethorpe, of Stone Manor, Chaddesley Corbett, Worcs, and formerly wife of John Ronald Christopher Holbech:—
Lucinda Ileene, *b* 1955: *m* 1983, Michael Thomas Waterhouse (*see* D Marlborough, 1990 Edn), and has issue living, Robin Hood E. T., *b* 1987, — Marcus Charles, *b* 1990. *Residence* – Middleton Hall, Bakewell, Derbys.

Issue of late Hon Aubrey Craven Theophilus Robin Hood Hastings, 3rd son of 13th Earl, *b* 1878, *d* 1929: *m* 1907, Winifred, who *d* 1977, da of T. Forsyth-Forrest, formerly of The Querns, Cirencester:—
Joan, *b* 1917: *m* 1st, 1942, Thomas Frank Bartlett; 2ndly 1948, Kenneth Porter, who *d* 1986, of 141 Skunks Misery Rd, Locust Valley, NY 11560, USA, and has issue living (by 2nd *m*), Steven Kenneth (17 Birch Hill Rd, Loudonville, NY 12211, USA), *b* 1951: *m* 1977, Melinda Smith, and has issue living, Whitney Kemp *b* 1979, Steven Lawrence *b* 1981, — Grant Aubrey, *b* (twin) 1951: *m* 1976, Christina French, and has issue living, Christina Chrysler *b* 1982.

Grandchildren of late Hans Francis Hastings, eldest son of late Vice-Adm Hon George Fowler Hastings, CB, 2nd son of 11th Earl:—
Issue of late George Godolphin Hastings, *b* 1905, *d* 1981: *m* 1932, Marjorie Harris:—
Warren Francis *b* 1938: *m* 1st, 1963, Heather Jean, da of late Collins Watson Gordon, of 2 Ashley Parade, Fairlight, NSW; 2ndly, 1968 (*m diss* 1976), Elaine Adams; 3rdly, 1976, Elisabeth Kay Vine-Hall, and has issue living (by 3rd *m*), Adam Francis, *b* 1977, — Emma Louise, *b* 1979. —— Edyth Leonie, *b* 1933: *m* 1956 (*m diss* 19—), Ross Ekins, and has issue living, David Ross, *b* 19—, — Russell John, *b* 19—, — Linda Margaret, *b* 19—.

Granddaughters of late Adm Alexander Plantagenet Hastings, CB, 2nd son of late Capt Hon Edward Plantagenet Robin Hood Hastings, 3rd son of 11th Earl:—

Issue of late Capt Edward George Godolphin Hastings, CBE, RN, *b* 1887, *d* 1973: *m* 1922, Hon Grisell Annabella Gem Cochrane-Baillie, who *d* 1985, da of 2nd Baron Lamington:—

(Sheila) Felicity Phoebe, *b* 1925: *m* 1954, John Humphrey Scrimgeour, TD, of Huntick Farm, Lytchett Matravers, Dorset, and has issue living, Alexander John Humphrey, *b* 1957: *m* 1993, Sarah Beatrix, only da of late John Horatio (Rae) Gordon Shephard, — Benjamin Victor Shedden, *b* 1960: *m* 1988, Christian Clare, yst da of Maj Sir Hamish Stewart Forbes, 7th Bt, MBE, MC, and has issue living, Charlie Atlas *b* 1995, India Rose *b* 1993, — Sally Belinda, *b* 1955: *m* 1987, Graham Lewis Mitchell, of Golden Grove Estate, Tobago, only son of Mrs E. W. Hill, of Dukes Kiln, Gerrards Cross, Bucks, and has issue living, James Alexander *b* 1995, Olivia Rose *b* 1994. —— Bridget Anne, *b* 1928: *m* 1955, Patrick Stephens Leigh, and has issue living, William Patrick, *b* 1956; *ed* Eton, and Ch Ch Oxford: *m* 1987, Nancy Oliveira, da of João Lavinsky, of Bahia, Brazil, and has issue living, Natasha Maria *b* 1988, — Edward Harold, *b* 1960; *ed* Eton: *m* 1988, Blanca Daphne, da of Paul Wansbrough, and has issue living, Benjamin Patricio *b* 1989, Dominic Pablo *b* 1991, Cosmo James *b* 1996, — Belinda Grisell, *b* 1958; has issue living, Eppie Irene *b* 1988, — Annabella Hylda, *b* 1968. *Residence* – Ragged Lands, Glynde, nr Lewes, Sussex BN8 6RP.

Grandson of late Henry John Churchill Hastings, yst son of late Rev Hon Richard Godolphin Hastings, 4th son of 11th Earl:—

Issue of late Henry Theophilus James Hastings, *b* 1910, *d* 1977: *m* 1941, Muriel Hyde, who *d* 1977, da of Walter Turner, of Athol Place, Banket, Rhodesia:—

David Walter Theophilus (Robin Hood Estate, Box 54, Shamva, Zimbabwe), *b* 1947: *m* 1971, Margaret Netta Allyson, da of Douglas Andrew Wilkinson, of Umvukwes, Rhodesia, and has issue living, Ian David, *b* 1975, — Kate Rosemary, *b* 1973.

PREDECESSORS – (1) *Sir* WILLIAM de Hastings, Knt (descent deduced from Robert de Hastings, Dispensator to William the Conqueror); *cr Baron Hastings*, of Ashby de la Zouch (peerage of England) 1461; as Master of the Mints at London and Calais introduced the "Noble," a gold coinage of the value of 8s. 4d.; was Ambassador in France and Lord Chamberlain; subsequently fell a victim to the Protector, Gloucester (Richard III), and was beheaded at the Tower 1483; *s* by his son (2) EDWARD, KB 2nd Baron, who in 1482 had been summoned to Parliament of England in right of his wife as *Baron Hungerford*, she having obtained the reversal of the attainder of her father and grandfather in the baronies of Hungerford (*cr* 1462), Botreaux (*cr* 1368), and De Moleyns (*cr* 1347); *d* 1507; *s* by his son (3) GEORGE, 3rd Baron; attended Henry VIII 1513 at taking of Terouenne and Tournay; *cr Earl of Huntingdon* (peerage of England) 1529; *d* 1544; *s* by his el son (4) FRANCIS, KG, PC, 2nd Earl; was Lt-Gen and Com-in-Ch of the Army 1549, Lord-Lieut of Rutland, Leicester, and Warwick, and Master of the Queen's Hart Hounds: *m* 1532, Katherine, who *d* 1576, da and co-heiress of Henry Pole, Lord Montague, and grandda of Margaret, Countess of Salisbury (da and sole heiress of George, Duke of Clarence, brother of King Edward IV); *d* 1560; *s* by his son (5) HENRY, KG, 3rd Earl; *d* 1595; *s* by his brother (6) GEORGE, 4th Earl; *d* 1605; *s* by his grandson (7) HENRY, 5th Earl; *d* 1643; *s* by his son (8) FERDINANDO, 6th Earl; *d* 1655; *s* by his son (9) THEOPHILUS, 7th Earl; *d* 1701; *s* by his el son (10) GEORGE, 8th Earl; carried the sceptre at Coronation of Queen Anne 1702; *d* 1705, *s* by his half-brother (11) THEOPHILUS, 9th Earl; carried the Sword of State at Coronation of George II; *d* 1746 *s* by his son (12) FRANCIS, 10th Earl; carried the Sword of State at Coronation of George III; *d* 1789, when the Baronies of Hastings, Botreaux, and De Moleyns devolved upon his eldest sister, Elizabeth, wife of 1st Earl Moira (see E Loudoun), and the Earldom became dormant, although it was assumed by the lineal descendant of the 2nd Earl, Rev Theophilus Henry Hastings, el uncle of (13) HANS FRANCIS, *b* 1779, who took his seat as 11th Earl 1819; was Gov of Dominica: *m* 1st, 1803, Frances, who *d* (March) 1820, da of Rev Richard Chaloner, R of Great Marlow, Bucks; 2ndly (Sept) 1820 Eliza Mary, who *d* 1846 (having *m* 2ndly, 1838, Col Sir Thomas Noel Harris, KH), da of Joseph Bettesworth, of Ryde, Isle of Wight, and widow of Alexander Thistelthwayte; *d* 1828; *s* by his son (14) FRANCIS THEOPHILUS HENRY, 12th Earl: *m* 1835, Elizabeth Anne, who *d* 1857, da of Richard Power, MP; *d* 1875; *s* by his son (15) FRANCIS POWER PLANTAGENET, 13th Earl, *b* 1841: *m* 1867, Mary Anne Wilmot, who *d* 1894, da of Hon John Craven Westenra, MP; *d* 1885; *s* by his son (16) WARNER FRANCIS JOHN PLANTAGENET, 14th Earl, *b* 1868: *m* 1892, Maud Margaret, who *d* 1953, da of late Sir Samuel Wilson, of 10 Grosvenor Square, W; *d* 1939; *s* by his son (17) FRANCIS JOHN CLARENCE WESTENRA PLANTAGENET, 15th Earl, *b* 1901, an artist (pupil of Diego Rivera, Mexican mural painter). Prof Sch of Arts & Crafts, Camberwell, and Central Sch of Arts and Crafts, London, chm Cttee of Soc of Mural Painters 1951-58, and Pres of Solent Protection Soc 1958-68, Parl Sec to Min of Agriculture and Fisheries 1945-50, author: *m* 1st, 1925 (*m diss* 1943), Maria Cristina, who *d* 1953, da of the Marchese Casati, of Palazzo Barberini, Rome; 2ndly, 1944, Margaret (the writer Margaret Lane), who *d* 1994, only child of late Harry George Lane, of Vernham Dean, Andover, and formerly wife of Bryan Wallace (son of late Edgar Wallace, author); *d* 1990; *s* by his cousin (18) WILLIAM EDWARD ROBIN HOOD, eldest son of late Capt Peter Robin Hood Hastings-Bass (who assumed by deed poll the additional surname of Bass 1954) (only son of late Hon Aubrey Craven Theophilus Robin Hood Hastings, 3rd son of 13th Earl), 16th Earl and present peer.

HUNTINGFIELD, BARON (Vanneck) (Baron I 1796, Bt GB 1751)

Just and loyal

JOSHUA CHARLES VANNECK, 7th Baron, and 9th Baronet; *b* 10 Aug 1954; *s* 1994; *ed* Eton, and Magdalene Coll, Camb (MA); 2nd Lieut Scots Dragoon Gds: *m* 1982, Arabella Mary, eldest da of late Maj Alastair Hugh Joseph Fraser, MC, of Moniack Castle, Kirkhill, Inverness-shire (*see* L Lovat, colls), and has issue.

Arms – Argent, three bugle horns, two and one, gules, stringed or, and in the fesse point a torteau. Crest – A bugle horn gules, between two wings elevated argent, tipped or. Supporters – Two greyhounds ermine, each gorged with a collar paly of six, gules and or, and chained gold.
Residence – 1 Clanricarde Mansions, Clanricarde Gdns, W2.

SONS LIVING

Hon GERARD CHARLES ALASTAIR, *b* 12 March 1985.
Hon John Errington, *b* 1988.
Hon Richard Fraser, *b* 1990.
Hon David Guise, *b* (twin) 1990.

DAUGHTER LIVING

Hon Vanessa Clare, *b* 1983.

SISTERS LIVING AND DECEASED

Hon Sara Anne, *b* 1944: *m* 1966 (*m diss* 1976), as his 1st wife, Marcus Hugh Crofton Binney, and *d* 1979.
Hon Christina Louise, *b* 1946: *m* 1967, Anthony Darell-Brown, R Green Jackets, and has issue living, Mark Philip Anthony, *b* 1969, — Henry Robert, *b* 1971: *m* 1998, Lindsey P., da of David Webster, of Micheldean, and of Mrs Patricia Ashton, of Stonehouse, Glos, — Juliet Cordelia Diana, *b* 1973. *Residence* – The Old Rectory, Witnesham, Ipswich, Suffolk.
Hon Katharine Grace (twin), *b* 1954; BA: *m* 1976, Nicholas John Bacon, of Church Gate Barn, Colston Bassett, Notts NG12 3FP, and has issue living, Sara Elizabeth, *b* 1980, — Frances Louise, *b* 1983, — Charlotte Helena, *b* 1991.

UNCLE LIVING (*son of 5th Baron*)

Hon Sir Peter Beckford Rutgers, GBE, CB, AFC, AE, *b* 1922; *ed* Geelong Gram Sch, Aust, Stowe, Trin Coll, Camb (MA), and at Harvard Univ, USA; Hon DSc, City Univ TEng (CEI); late Lt (P) RN; 601 Sqdn RAuxAF 1950-57, Hon Air Commodore RAuxAF; OC No 3619 (Suffolk) Fighter Control Unit RAuxAF 1959-61; Inspector, RAuxAF 1962-73; Hon Inspector-Gen RAuxAF 1974-83; Hon Air Commodore No 1 MHU RAuxAF; ADC to HM 1963-73; a Gentleman Usher to HM 1967-79, and Alderman of City of London 1969-79 (a Sheriff 1974-75); Lord Mayor of London 1978-79; elected rep to European Assembly 1979-89; High Sheriff of Suffolk 1974; KJStJ; a DL Gtr London; 1939-45 War in RN; OBE (Mil) 1963, CB (Mil) 1973, GBE (Civil) 1977: *m* 1st, 1943 (*m diss* 1984), Cordelia, da of Capt Reginald Hugh Errington, RN (ret) (*see* E Dartmouth, colls, 1980 Edn); 2ndly, 1984, Mrs Elizabeth Lechmere Forbes, formerly wife of Spencer Malcolm Edward Forbes (*see* Stuart-Forbes, Bt, colls), and da of late Sandys Stuart Macaskie, of Lustleigh, S Devon, and has issue living (by 1st *m*), Charlotte Susan (*Baroness Stevenson of Coddenham*), *b* 1947: *m* 1972, Baron Stevenson of Coddenham (Life Baron), CBE, of 32 Catherine Place, SW1E 6HL, and has issue living, Alexander *b* 1974, John Heneage *b* 1978, Charles Dennistoun *b* 1980, William Beckford James *b* 1984. *Residences* – 2/10 Brompton Square, SW3; Red House, Sudbourne, Woodbridge, Suffolk IP12 2AT. *Clubs* – White's, Pratt's, Royal Yacht Squadron and Royal London Yacht.

AUNTS LIVING (*daughters of 5th Baron*)

Hon Sara Carola, *b* 1913: *m* 1936, David Arthur Peel, MC, T/Major Irish Guards, who was *ka* in NW Europe 1944 (*see* E Peel, colls). *Residence* – Huntingfield Hall, Halesworth, Suffolk, IP19 0QA.
Hon Anne Margaret Theodosia, *b* 1918: *m* 1940 (*m diss* 1984), Peter Moro, CBE, FRIBA, who *d* 1998, and has issue living, Frances, *b* 1945: *m* 1st, 1966 (*m diss* 1979), John Barnes; 2ndly, 1987, Michael Edward Thomas Molloy, of 61 Annandale Rd, SE10, and has issue living (by 1st *m*), Samuel *b* 1968, Jessie *b* 1972, — Alice, *b* 1948: *m* 1978, Jacek Lech Basista, of 23 Culverden Park, Tunbridge Wells, Kent TN4 9QT, and has issue living, Tom *b* 1984, Rose Zofia *b* 1991, — Dinah, *b* 1960.

WIDOW LIVING OF SIXTH BARON

JANETTA LOIS (*Dowager Baroness Huntingfield*), da of Capt Reginald Hugh Errington, RN (*see* E Dartmouth, colls, 1980 Edn): *m* 1941, the 6th Baron Huntingfield, who *d* 1994. *Residence* – 53 Barron's Way, Comberton, Cambs CB3 7EQ.

COLLATERAL BRANCHES LIVING

Issue of late Hon Andrew Nicolas Armstrong Vanneck, MC, 3rd son of Hon William Arcedeckne Vanneck, 2nd son of 3rd Baron, *b* 1890, *d* 1965: *m* 1st , 1930 (*m diss* 1933), Louise, who *d* 1970, da of

Henry Clews, of The Chateau of La Napoule, France, AM; 2ndly, 1939, Britta Ingeborg Nilsdotter, who d 1998, only da of Count Nils Gustaf Bonde, of Stockholm, Sweden:—
(By 2nd m) William Bonde (31 Pymble Av, Pymble, NSW 2073, Australia), b 1943: m 1971, Jane Blanton, and has issue living, Mark Alexander Blanton, b 1979, — Nina Sara, b 1975. —— Margita, b 1940: m 1961, David Michael Wheeler, of Broadlands, La Hougue Bie, Grouville, Jersey, CI, and has issue living, Andrew Michael, b 1963, — James Nicholas, b 1966.

Grandchildren of late John Torrance Vanneck, grandson of late Hon Tompson Vanneck, 3rd son of 1st Baron:—
Issue of late John Vanneck, b 1906, d 1974: m 1930, Barbara, who d 1994, da of Frank Bailey:—
†John Bailey, b 1938: m 1st, 1965 (m diss 1981), Isabelle Adele Knipe; 2ndly, 1985, Cynthia Laney (1100 Park Av, New York, NY 10128, USA), and d 1998, leaving issue (by 1st m), F. Bailey, b 1970: m 1999, Neely Mallory Rapp, — Alexandra Knipe, b 1965: m 1991, Charles Capel Smith, jr, and has issue living, Gordon Hartel b 1995, Torrance Capel b 1998, — Cynthia Gordon, b 1967. —— William Prentice (217 West Indies Rd, Palm Beach, Florida 33480, USA), b 1941: m 1st, 1962 (m diss 1990), Nancy Buck; 2ndly, 1990 (m diss 1998), Rebecca Heffington; 3rdly, 1999, Ann Maria Lilja, and has issue living (by 1st m), John Lanphear, b 1963: m 1999, Kimberly Thompson Kane, — Richard Prentice, b 1966: m 1991, Karen Elizabeth Bugniazet, and has issue living, Lindsay Bailey b 1992, William James b 1994, — Christine Walker, b (twin) 1963: m 1st, 1992 (m diss 1994), Robert Thomas Owen; 2ndly, 1999, J. Mark Thompson, and has issue living (by 1st m), Sarah Ann b 1992, — Sandra Brookman, b 1967. —— Marion Louise (720 Milton Rd, Rye, NY 10580, USA), b 1937: m 1959 (m diss 1989), Raymond Robert Konopka, and has had issue, Raymond Robert, b 1961; d 1993, — Lee Bailey, b 1963: m 1987, Ann Smith, and has issue living, Christopher Walter b 1988, Grace Ann b 1991, Kelsey Barbara b 1994, — Steven Bailey, b 1966: m 1992 (m diss 1997), Megan Cassidy, — Suzanne Louise, b 1959: m 1983, Bryan M. Fitzpatrick, and has issue living, Bryan Michael II b 1986, Bryce Galvin b 1989, Ashley Louise b 1985, Morgan Bailey (a da) b 1988. —— Barbara Anne (Kelleher Rd, Dorset, Vermont, USA), b 1946: m 1968 (m diss 1976), James S. May, and has issue living, Wendy Bailey, b 1968, — Tanya Sheridan, b 1973.

PREDECESSORS – (1) JOSHUA Vanneck, an eminent London banker; cr a Baronet 1751; d 1777; s by his el son (2) Sir Gerard, MP, 2nd Bt; d unmarried 1791, s by his brother (3) Sir JOSHUA, 3rd Bt, MP for Dunwich; cr Baron Huntingfield, of Heveningham Hall (peerage of Ireland) 1796; d 1816; s by his el son (4) JOSHUA, 2nd Baron; b 1778: m 1st 1810, Catherine, da of Chaloner Arcedeckne, of Glevering Hall, co Suffolk; 2ndly, 1817, Lucy Anne, who d 1889, da of Sir Charles Blois, Bt; d 1844: s by his son (5) CHARLES ANDREW, 3rd Baron, b 1818: m 1839, Louisa, who d 1898, da of late Andrew Arcedeckne, of Glevering Hall, Suffolk; d 1897; s by his el son (6) JOSHUA CHARLES, 4th Baron; b 1842; d 1915; s by his nephew (7) WILLIAM CHARLES ARCEDECKNE, KCMG (son of Hon William Arcedeckne Vanneck, 2nd son of 3rd Baron), 5th Baron, 1883; MP for Eye Div, E Suffolk (C) 1923-29; Gov of Vic, Aust 1934-39; m 1st, 1912, Margaret Eleanor (CStJ), who d 1943, only da of late Judge Ernest Crosby, of New York; 2ndly, 1944, Muriel May Georgina, who d 1953, da of late Col Jemmet Duke, 17th Lancers, and widow of 1st Baron Eltisley; d 1969; s by his el son (8) GERARD CHARLES ARCEDECKNE, 6th Baron, b 1915; UN Secretariat 1946-75; 1939-45 War as Fl Sgt RAFVR: m 1941, Janetta Lois, da of Capt Reginald Hugh Errington, RN (see E Dartmouth, colls, 1980 Edn); d 1994; s by his only son (9) JOSHUA CHARLES, 7th Baron and present peer.

HUNTLY, MARQUESS OF (Gordon) (Marquess S 1599)

Abiding

By courage, not by stratagem

GRANVILLE CHARLES GOMER GORDON, 13th Marquess, and Premier Marquess of Scotland; b 4 Feb 1944; s 1987; ed Gordonstoun; Member Council Nat Trust for Scotland 1977-80, Nat Cttee Scottish Georgian Soc 1976-81 Patron, Inst of Commercial Management since 1982, Pres Inst of Financial Accountants since 1990, Chm Freecall Ltd, and Cock o' the North Liqueur Co Ltd, Dir Ampton Investments since 1988: m 1st, 1972 (m diss 1990), Jane Elizabeth Angela, da of late Lt-Col Alistair Monteith Gibb, R Wilts Yco (see V Cowdray, 1980 Edn); 2ndly, 1991, Mrs Catheryn Millbourn, da of Gay Kindersley (see B Kindersley, colls), and has issue by 1st and 2nd m.

Arms – Quarterly: 1st azure, three boars' heads couped or, Gordon; 2nd or, three lions' heads erased gules, langued azure, Badenoch; 3rd or, three crescents within a double tressure flory counter-flory gules, Seton; 4th azure, three fraises argent, Frazer. **Crest** – Issuing from a ducal coronet or, a hart's head and neck affrontée proper, attired with ten tynes of the first. **Supporters** – Two deer-hounds argent, each gorged with a collar gules, the collars charged with three buckles or. Seat – Aboyne Castle, Aberdeenshire.

SON LIVING (By 1st marriage)

ALISTAIR GRANVILLE (Earl of Aboyne), b 26 July 1973; ed Harrow.

DAUGHTERS LIVING (By 1st marriage)

Lady Amy Jane, b 1975.
Lady Lucy Yoskyl, b 1979.

(By 2nd marriage)

Lady Rose Marie-Louise, *b* 1993.

SISTER LIVING

Lady (Pamela) Lemina, *b* 1941: *m* 1970, Hon Ian Henry Calthorpe Lawson Johnston, of Coldstone House, Logie Cold-stone, Aboyne, Aberdeenshire AB34 5NP (*see* B Luke).

WIDOWS LIVING OF BROTHERS OF TWELFTH MARQUESS

Pamela (Hethersett, Littleworth Cross, Seale, Farnham, Surrey), da of Alexander Herriot Bowhill, CBE, of Inchmarlo, Banchory, Kincardineshire: *m* 1947, Maj Lord Adam Granville Gordon, KCVO, MBE, RA, who *d* 1984, and has issue (see colls, infra).

Baroness Joana Alexandra, 2nd da of Ion Bujoiu, and formerly wife of (i) Prince Serban Ghica, and (ii) Chevalier de Stuers: *m* 1949, as his 2nd wife, Maj Lord Roderic Armyne Gordon, MBE, TD, who *d* 1996.

Bridget (The Old Rectory, Stockbridge, Hants), da of late Gerald Bryan Ingham, and formerly wife of Maj Alexander Hutchison, of Fife: *m* 1962, as his 2nd wife, Lt-Col Lord Douglas Claude Alexander Gordon, DSO, who *d* 1994, and has issue (see colls, infra).

WIDOW LIVING OF TWELFTH MARQUESS

ELIZABETH HAWORTH (*Dowager Marchioness of Huntly*), da of late Lt-Cdr Frederick Haworth Leigh, RD, RNR: *m* 1977, as his 2nd wife, the 12th Marquess of Huntly, who *d* 1987. *Residence* – Hollybrook, Ewhurst Rd, Cranleigh, Surrey.

COLLATERAL BRANCHES LIVING

Issue of late Maj Lord Adam Granville Gordon, KCVO, MBE, RA, brother of 12th Marquess (raised to the rank of a Marquess's son 1937), *b* 1909, *d* 1984: *m* 1947, Pamela (ante), da of Alexander Herriot Bowhill, CBE, of Inchmarlo, Banchory, Kincardineshire:—

Adam Alexander (Heatheryleys, by Glenfarg, Perthshire), *b* 1948; *ed* Eton; Member Queen's Body Guard for Scotland (Royal Company of Archers): *m* 1979, Jennifer Susan, el da of Col William George McHardy, CVO, MBE, MC, of Woodend House, Banchory, Kincardineshire, and has issue living, Alexander Charles Adam, *b* 1989, — Joanna Mary, *b* 1986. —— Douglas Herriot, *b* 1951; a Page of Honour to HM 1965-67; Member Queen's Body Guard for Scotland (Royal Company of Archers): *m* 1978, Susan Jennifer, da of Anthony White, of 46 Aubrey Walk, W8, and has issue living, James Adam Anthony, *b* 1991, — Alexandra Anne, *b* 1979, — Katherine Louisa, *b* 1981, — Isabella Clare, *b* 1985. *Residence* – 24 Juer St, SW11 4RF.

Issue of late Maj Lord Roderic Armyne Gordon, MBE, TD, brother of 12th Marquess (raised to the rank of a Marquess's son 1937), *b* 1914, *d* 1996: *m* 1st, 1937 (*m diss* 1949), Anne, who *d* 1997, yr da of late Lt-Col Hon Sir Osbert Eustace Vesey, KCVO, CMG, CBE (*see* V De Vesci, colls); 2ndly, 1949, Baroness Joana Alexandra, 2nd da of Ion Bujoiu, and formerly wife of (i) Prince Serban Ghica, and (ii) Chevalier de Stuers:—

(By 1st *m*) David Esme Douglas, *b* 1937; *ed* Sherborne: *m* 1st, 1959 (*m diss* 1962), Audrey Diana, da of E. Dermot Carey, of Knutsford, Cheshire; 2ndly, 1962, Valerie Elizabeth, da of Henry Charles Guy Owen; 3rdly, 1979, Anne, da of Per Thor Brockdorff-Knutzon, of Copenhagen, and has issue (by 2nd *m*), Samantha, *b* 1962. —— Angus Lindsay Eustace, *b* 1941; *ed* Nautical Coll, Pangbourne, and Bloxham Sch: *m* 1966, Diana Mary, da of Robert C. Pawlyn, of Windsmont, Mevagissey, Cornwall, and formerly wife of Graham Clive Crockford.

Issue of late Lt-Col Lord Douglas Claude Alexander Gordon, DSO, brother of 12th Marquess (raised to the rank of a Marquess's son 1937), *b* 1916, *d* 1994: *m* 1st, 1940 (*m diss* 1961), Suzanne, da of late Lt-Col Arthur Houssemayne du Boulay, DSO; 2ndly, 1962, Bridget (ante), da of late Gerald Bryan Ingham, and formerly wife of Maj Alexander Hutchison, of Fife:—

(By 1st *m*) Andrew Granville Douglas (Elm Lodge, 230 Petersham Rd, Richmond, Surrey TW10 7AL), *b* 1942; *ed* Eton; a Page of Honour to HM 1957-60: *m* 1st, 1963 (*m diss* 1969), Gillian Thorne; 2ndly, 1976, Brigitte, da of Herbert Marx, and has issue living (by 1st *m*), David, *b* 1963, — Jamie, *b* 1965, — (by 2nd *m*) Glen, *b* 1984, — Kitty, *b* 1980. —— Douglas George (Geordie) Alexander (25 Coleherne Mews, SW10 9DZ; Whitehouse of Dunira, Comrie, Perthshire), *b* 1947; *ed* Gordonstoun; Member Queen's Body Guard for Scotland (Royal Company of Archers): *m* 1975, Celina d'Orey, da of Peter Landsberg, CBE, of Rio de Janeiro, Brazil, and has issue living, Thomas Peter Douglas, *b* 1979, — James Alexander Douglas, *b* 1984, — Georgina Violet, *b* 1976. —— Jane Elizabeth (*Lady Robert Mercer Nairne*), *b* 1950: *m* 1972, Lord Robert Harold Mercer Nairne, of Kinclaven Church House, Kinclaven, by Stanley, Perthshire, and of 10105 SE 25th Bellevue, Washington 98004, USA, yr son of 8th Marquess of Lansdowne, and has issue (*see* M Lansdowne). —— (By 2nd *m*) Sarah Alexandra, *b* 1963.

PREDECESSORS – Sir Adam Gordon, Knt, of Huntly, being slain at the battle of Homildon 1402, was *s* in his estates by his da (1) ELIZABETH, wife of Alexander Seton, who in conjunction with her husband obtained in 1408 from Robert, Duke of Albany, a charter of the lands of Gordon, etc, with remainder to their joint heirs; *s* by their son (2) ALEXANDER Seton; *cr Earl of Huntly* (peerage of Scotland) 1445; employed in various negotiations to the Court of England 1451-8; defeated the Earl of Crawford then in rebellion at Brechin 1452; *s* by his son (3) GEORGE, 2nd Earl; *d* 1470; *s* by his son (4) ALEXANDER, PC, 3rd Earl; commanded with Lord Home the left wing of the Scottish Army at Flodden Field; was one of the Council of Regency 1517; *s* by his grandson (5) GEORGE, 4th Earl; constituted Lord Chancellor of Scotland 1546; *ka* 1562; his body was afterwards produced in Parliament and in 1563 an Act of Attainder was passed whereby all his honours became forfeited; *s* by his son (6) GEORGE, 5th Earl; condemned to death for high treason in 1563; was subsequently pardoned, and in 1565 was constituted Lord Chancellor of Scotland; procured a reversal of his father's attainder 1567; *d* 1576; *s* by his son **(7)** GEORGE, 6th Earl; engaged in a treasonable correspondence with Court of Spain 1588, erected the standard of rebellion in the North 1589, and surrendered to James VI; tried and found guilty of treason, but was released shortly afterwards on the occasion of the King's marriage; in 1593 his honours were forfeited for complicity in the Spanish and Jesuit Conspiracy; in conjunction with the Earl of Errol defeated the Royal Army at Strathaven 1594; in 1597 his honours were restored; *cr Marquess of Huntly, Earl of Enzie, and Lord Gordon of Badenoch* (peerage of Scotland) 1599; *d* 1636; *s* by his son **(7)** GEORGE, 2nd Marquess, who in 1611 had received a charter of the Lordship of Badenoch and in 1632 had been *cr Viscount Aboyne* with special remainder to his second son; was a zealous adherent of Charles I, and in consequence was beheaded and his honours attainted in 1649; *s* by his son **(8)** LEWIS, 3rd Marquess; in 1651 was granted by the King remission of the attainder of 1649; *s* by his son **(9)** GEORGE, 4th Marquess; in 1661 the attainder of 1649 (which had been remitted by the King in 1651) was reversed by Act of Parliament; *cr Duke of Gordon, Marquess of Huntly, Earl of Huntly and Enzie, Viscount of Inverness, Lord Badenoch, Lochaber, Strathavon, Balmore, Auchindoun, Garthie, and Kincardine* (peerage of Scotland) 1684; *d* 1716; *s* by his son **(10)** ALEXANDER, 2nd Duke; an earnest partisan of the Chevalier St George, 1715; *d* 1728; *s* by his son **(11)** COSMO GEORGE, KT, 3rd Duke; a Representative Peer; *d* 1752; *s* by his son **(12)** ALEXANDER, KT, 4th Duke; *cr Baron Gordon of Huntly and Earl of Norwich* (peerage of Great Britain) 1784; inherited (through his grandmother) the Barony of Mordaunt of Turvey (*cr* 1532), and possibly that of Beauchamp of Bletsoe (*cr* 1363); *d* 1827; *s* by his son **(13)** GEORGE, GCB, 5th Duke; a Gen in the Army, etc; *d* 1836, when the Dukedom of Gordon (and its accompanying titles, *cr* 1684), the Earldom of Norwich, and the Barony of Gordon of Huntly became ext, the Baronies of Mordaunt of Turvey and Beauchamp of Bletsoe became abeyant, and he was *s* in the Marquessate (*cr* 1599) by his kinsman (who also claimed the Earldom of Enzie and the Lordship of Gordon of Badenoch, but whose claim to the Marquessate only was allowed) **(14)** GEORGE, KT, 9th Marquess (see note * infra); a Representative Peer 1796-1807; *d* 1853; *s* by his son **(15)** CHARLES, 10th Marquess; *b* 1792; MP for East Grinstead: *m* 1st, 1826, Elizabeth Henrietta, who *d* 1839, da of 1st Marquess of Conyngham; 2ndly, 1844, Maria Antoinette, who *d* 1893, da of the Rev Peter William Pegus, and his wife Susannah Elizabeth, Countess Dowager of Lindsey; *d* 1863; *s* by his son **(16)** CHARLES, PC, 11th Marquess, *b* 1847; was a Lord-in-Waiting to HM Queen Victoria 1870-73, and Capt of Hon Corps of Gentlemen-at-Arms 1881: *m* 1st, 1869, Amy, who *d* 1920, da of Sir William Cunliffe Brooks, 1st and last Bt; 2ndly, 1922, Charlotte Isabella, who *d* 1939, da of late John H. Fallon, and widow of James Macdonald, of Cincinatti, Ohio, USA; *d* 1937; *s* by his great-nephew **(17)** DOUGLAS CHARLES LINDSEY, son of late Lieut-Col (Granville Cecil) Douglas Gordon, CVO, DSO (son of late Granville Armyne Gordon, 6th son of 10th Marquess), 12th Marquess, *b* 1908; Lieut Gordon Highlanders: *m* 1st, 1941 (*m diss* 1965), Hon (Mary) Pamela Berry, who *d* 1998, da of 1st Viscount Kemsley; 2ndly, 1977, Elizabeth Haworth, da of late Lt-Cdr F. H. Leigh, RD, RNR; *d* 1987; *s* by his only son **(18)** GRANVILLE CHARLES GOMER, 13th Marquess and present peer; also Earl of Aboyne, Lord Gordon of Strathavon and Glenlivet, and Baron Meldrum.

*(1) *Lord* CHARLES Gordon, 4th son of 2nd Marquess; *cr Earl of Aboyne*, and Lord Gordon of Strathavon and Glenlivet (peerage of Scotland) 1660; *d* 1681; *s* by his son **(2)** CHARLES, 2nd Earl; *d* 1702; *s* by his son **(3)** JOHN, 3rd Earl; *d* 1732; *s* by his son **(4)** CHARLES, 4th Earl; *d* 1794; *s* by his son **(5)** GEORGE, 5th Earl; *cr Baron Meldrum*, of Morven, co Aberdeen (peerage of United Kingdom) 1815: *s* his kinsman as 9th Marquess of Huntly (ante).

HURD, BARONY OF (Hurd) (Extinct 1966)

SONS LIVING OF LIFE BARON

Right Hon Douglas Richard, CH, CBE (*Baron Hurd of Westwell*) *b* 1930; *cr* Baron Hurd of Westwell (Life Baron) 1997 (see that title).
Hon Stephen Anthony (Glebe House, Mildenhall, Marlborough, Wilts SN8 2LU), *b* 1933; *ed* Winchester, and Magdalene Coll, Camb; JP Wilts 1969: *m* 1973, Pepita Lilian, yr da of late Lt-Col Walter George Hingston, OBE, of The Old Vicarage, Ramsbury, Marlborough, and has issue living, William Robert, *b* 1976, — Christopher Francis Walter, *b* 1977.

HURD OF WESTWELL, BARON (Hurd) (Life Baron 1997)

DOUGLAS RICHARD HURD, CH, CBE, PC, eldest son of late Baron Hurd (Life Baron); *b* 8 March 1930; *ed* Eton, and Trinity Coll, Camb (BA 1952, MA 1957); in Diplomatic Service 1952-66 (Peking, UK Mission to UN, Rome, and Priv Sec to Permanent Under-Sec, FO); Conservative Research Dept 1966-68 (Head of Foreign Affairs Section 1968); MP (*C*) for Mid Oxon 1974-83, and for Witney 1983-97; Priv Sec to Rt Hon Edward Heath as Leader of the Opposition 1968-70; Political Sec to Prime Minister 1970-74; Opposition Spokesman on Foreign Affairs (with special responsibility for EEC) 1976-79; Min of State, FCO 1979-83, and Home Office 1983-84; Sec of State for N Ireland 1984-85; Home Secretary 1985-89; Sec of State for Foreign and Commonwealth Affairs 1989-95; Chm British Invisibles since 1996; Dep Chm Coutts & Co since 1998; Chm Prison Reform Trust since 1997; Fellow, Nuffield Coll, Oxford; Fellow of Eton Coll 1981-96; *cr* CBE 1974, PC 1982, CH 1996, and *Baron Hurd of Westwell*, of Westwell, co Oxon (Life Baron) 1997: *m* 1st, 1960 (*m diss* 1982), Tatiana Elizabeth Michelle, only da of (Arthur Charles) Benedict Eyre, MBE, of Bury, Sussex;

2ndly, 1982, Judy J......, 2nd da of Sidney Smart, of Oak Ash, Chaddleworth, Berks, and has issue by 1st and 2nd *m*.

Address – House of Lords, SW1A 0PW. *Clubs* – Beefsteak, Travellers', Pratt's.

SONS LIVING (*By 1st marriage*)

Hon Nicholas Richard, *b* 1962; *ed* ......: *m* 1988, Kim, elder da of Ray Richards, of Hartley Court, Reading, and has issue living, Maximillian, *b* 1991, — Gus, *b* 1993, — Katie Mae, *b* 1996, — Florence Amy, *b* (twin) 1996.

Hon Thomas Robert Benedict, *b* 1964; *ed* ......: *m* 1994, Catherine Siân, da of Dr Daniel Roland Aubrey, of Mattingley, Hants, and has issue living, Benedict Roland Julian, *b* 1996, — Sebastian Harry Bartholomew Aubrey, *b* 1998, — Lara Lilly Tatiana Juliet, *b* 1997.

Hon Alexander Paul Anthony, *b* 1969; *ed* ....

(*By 2nd marriage*)

Hon Philip Arthur, *b* 1983; *ed* ....

DAUGHTER LIVING (*By 2nd marriage*)

Hon Jessica Stephanie, *b* 1985.

HUSSEY OF NORTH BRADLEY, BARON (Hussey) (Life Baron 1996)

MARMADUKE JAMES HUSSEY, son of late Eric Robert James Hussey, CMG; *b* 29 Aug 1923; *ed* Rugby, and Trinity Coll, Oxford (MA, Hon Fellow 1989); joined Associated Newspapers Ltd 1949, Dir 1964, Man Dir Harmsworth Publications 1967-70, Man Dir and Chief Exec Times Newspapers Ltd 1971-80; Dir Thomson Organisation 1971-80, Times Newspapers Ltd 1982-86, Colonial Mutual Group (British Board) 1982-96, MK Electric Group 1982-88, William Collins plc 1985-89; Chm Ruffer Investment Management Ltd since 1995; Rhodes Trustee 1972-92; Trustee, Royal Academy Trust 1988-96; Chm Royal Marsden NHS Trust 1985-98; Chm Board of Governors of BBC 1986-96; Chm King's Fund London Commn 1991-92 and since 1995; Memb British Council 1982-96; Memb Govt Working Party on Artificial Limbs and Appliance Centres in England 1984-86; Memb Management Cttee of King Edward's Hospital Fund for London since 1987; Pres Iris Fund for Prevention of Blindness since 1998; served in World War II as Lieut Gren Gds 1942-45; *cr Baron Hussey of North Bradley*, of North Bradley, co Wilts (Life Baron) 1996: *m* 1959, Lady Susan Katharine Waldegrave, DCVO, 5th da of 12th Earl Waldegrave, KG, GCVO, TD, and has issue.

𝔄rms – Argent on three bars sable five crowns in cross or. ℭrest – A greyhound sejant sable grasping in the dexter paw a caduceus or. 𝔖upporters – On either side a hind argent unguled and gorged with a collar or pendent therefrom by a string sable a bugle horn or virolled and stringed sable.

Residence – Flat 15, 45-47 Courtfield Rd, SW7 4DB. *Club* – Brooks's.

SON LIVING

Hon James Arthur, *b* 1961; *ed* ......; a Page of Honour to HM 1975-76: *m* 1st, 1988 (*m diss* 1993), Jacqueline, da of Dr (George) Hugh Barrington Baker, of Sutton, Surrey; 2ndly, 1993, Emma, da of John Shelley, of Wimbledon, and has issue living (by 2nd *m*), Arthur Eric, *b* 1995, — Rose Rachel, *b* 1994, — Helena Susan, *b* 1998. *Residence* – ....

DAUGHTER LIVING

Hon Katharine Elizabeth (*Hon Lady Brooke*), *b* 1964: *m* 1989, Sir Francis George Windham Brooke, 4th Bt, and has issue (*see* Brooke, Bt, *cr* 1903).

DEBRETT'S ILLUSTRATED PEERAGE   P 869

Hutchinson, Viscount, title of Earl of Donoughmore on Roll of HL.

HUTCHINSON OF LULLINGTON, BARON (Hutchinson) (Life Baron 1978)

JEREMY NICOLAS HUTCHINSON, QC, only son of late St John Hutchinson, QC, by his wife Mary, only da of late Sir Hugh Shakespear Barnes, KCSI, KCVO, BCS (see Strachey, Bt, 1892 Edn), b 28 March 1915; ed Stowe, and Magdalen Coll, Oxford; Bar, Middle Temple 1939, Bencher 1963; Recorder of Bath 1962-72, and a Recorder of Crown Court 1972-76; a Member of Cttee on Immigration Appeals 1966-68, and Cttee on Identification Procedures 1974-76; Vice-Chairman, Arts Council of Great Britain 1977-79; Chm Trustees, Tate Gallery, 1979-83; RNVR 1939-45 War; cr Baron Hutchinson of Lullington, of Lullington, co East Sussex (Life Baron) 1978; m 1st, 1940 (m diss 1966), Dame Peggy (Edith Margaret Emily) S. Ashcroft, DBE, the actress, who d 1991, da of late William Worsley Ashcroft, of Croydon, and formerly wife of (i) Rupert (later Sir Rupert) Hart-Davis, and (ii) Theodore Komisarjevsky; 2ndly, 1966, Mrs June Osborn, da of late Capt Arthur Edward Capel, CBE (see By Ribblesdale, 1980 Edn), and formerly wife of Franz Osborn, and has issue by 1st m.

Arms – Not exemplified at the College of Arms at time of going to press.
Address – c/o House of Lords, SW1A 0PW. Club – MCC.

SON LIVING (By 1st marriage)

Hon Nicholas St John, b 1946: m 19—, — , and has issue living, March (a da), b 19—.

DAUGHTER LIVING (By 1st marriage)

Hon Eliza, b 1941: m 1974, Pierre Loizeau, and has issue living, Manon, b 19—, — Emily, b 19—.

Hutchinson, Hely-, family name of Earl of Donoughmore.

HUTTON, BARON (Hutton) (Life Baron 1997)

(JAMES) BRIAN EDWARD HUTTON, PC, son of late James Hutton, of Belfast; b 29 June 1931; ed Shrewsbury, Balliol Coll, Oxford (BA 1953, Hon Fell 1988), and Queen's Univ, Belfast (Hon LLD 1992); Bar-at-law NI 1954; Junior Counsel to Attorney-Gen, NI 1969; QC (NI) 1970; Senior Crown Counsel, NI 1973-79; Judge of the High Court of Justice (NI) 1979-88; Lord Chief Justice of NI 1988-97, since when a Lord of Appeal in Ordinary; Memb Joint Law Enforcement Commn 1974; Dep Chm Boundary Commn for NI 1985-88; Pres NI Assoc for Mental Health since 1983; contributor to Modern Law Review; cr Kt 1988, PC 1988, and Baron Hutton, of Bresagh, co Down (Life Baron) 1997: m 1975, Mary Gillian, da of James Murland, of Saintfield, co Down, and has issue.
Address – House of Lords, Westminster, SW1A 0PW.

DAUGHTERS LIVING

Hon Louise, *b* 1976.
Hon Helen, *b* 1978.

Hyde, Lord; son of Earl of Clarendon.

HYLTON, BARON (Jolliffe) (Baron UK 1866, Bt UK 1821)

RAYMOND HERVEY JOLLIFFE, 5th, Baron, and 5th Baronet; *b* 13 June 1932; *s* 1967; *ed* Eton (King's Scholar), and at Trin Coll; Oxford (MA); Hon Dr Soc Sci Southampton; Lt Coldstream Guards (Reserve); DL Som 1975-90; ARICS; Assist Private Sec to Gov-Gen of Canada 1960-62; formerly Chm Catholic Housing Aid Soc, Trustee of Shelter Housing Aid Centre, Chm Nat Fedn of Housing Assocns, Chm Help the Aged Housing Trust, and of Housing Assocns Charitable Trust; currently Chm St Francis and St Sergius Trust re Russia, MICOM re Moldova, Christian Coll for Adult Educn, and Hugh of Witham Foundation; Pres N Ireland Assocn for Care and Resettlement of Offenders: *m* 1966, Joanna Elizabeth, da of late Andrew de Bertodano (*see* E Mexborough, 1948 Edn), and has issue.

Arms – Quarterly: 1st and 4th argent, on a pile vert, three dexter hands proper, *Jolliffe*: 2nd and 3rd argent, two bars azure, *Hylton*. Crest – A cubit arm erect, the hand grasping a scimitar proper, vested vert, cuffed argent, on the sleeve a pile of the last. Supporters – Two lions guardant azure, each charged on the shoulder with three annulets, two and one, or.
Residence – Ammerdown, Radstock, Bath, Som BA3 5SH.

As much as I can

SONS LIVING

Hon WILLIAM HENRY MARTIN, *b* 1 April 1967; *ed* Ampleforth, and RAC Cirencester. *Residence* – 24 Smith Terrace, SW3 4DL.
Hon Andrew Thomas Peter, *b* 1969: *m* 1997, Diana J., yr da of Clifford Teare, of Ramsey, I of Man, and has issue living, Isabel Maria, *b* 1998.
Hon Alexander John Charles Martin, *b* 1973.
Hon John Edward Arthur, *b* 1977.

DAUGHTER LIVING

Hon Emily Sylvia Rose Elizabeth, *b* 1975.

BROTHER LIVING

Hon John Hedworth (Church House, Chesterblade, Shepton Mallet, Som), *b* 1935; *ed* Eton (King's Scholar), and Ch Ch Oxford (BA); High Sheriff Som 1993; a Dir of Bain Dawes plc 1979-89, and of Duckworth Media Ltd since 1997; edited *Raymond Asquith, Life and Letters* (1980), author of *Clive Pearson* (1992), *Woolf at the Door* (1998), and *Glyndebourne, An Operatic Miracle* (1999): *m* 1965, Hon Victoria Catherine Elizabeth Eden, el da of 7th Baron Henley, and has issue living, Hugo Conrad William, *b* 1966: *m* 1999, Rebecca D. J., yr da of Dan Lawrence, of W8, — Robert Francis Raymond, *b* 1968, — Benedict Thomas Aldhelm, *b* 1970.

SISTER LIVING

Hon (Mary) Alice, *b* 1937: *m* 1st, 1959 (*m diss* 1968), John Paget Chancellor (*see* Paget, Bt, *cr* 1886, 1995 Edn); 2ndly, 1969, Hon Richard Archer Alan Windsor-Clive, of Combe, Nettlecombe, Taunton (*see* E Plymouth), and had issue living (by 1st *m*), (John) Edward Horner, *b* 1962, — Isabel Rose, *b* 1959: *m* 1982, John Joseph Boothby, and has issue (*see* Boothby, Bt, colls), — Katharine Sylvia Anthony, *b* 1961: *m* 1989, William Woodard Self, son of Prof Peter Self, of Canberra, Australia, and has issue living, Alexis *b* 1990, — Anna Theodora, *b* 1965; actress: *m* 1995, Nigel Robert Redfern Willoughby, and has issue living (by Jack Scott), Poppy *b* 1987, — (by 2nd *m*) (*see* E Plymouth).

COLLATERAL BRANCHES LIVING

Granddaughters of late Maj Berkeley Gerald Jolliffe (infra):—
Issue of late John Neil Hylton Jolliffe, *b* 1923, *d* 1976: *m* 1957, Eileen Mary (Barratts Farm, Corton Denham, Sherborne, Dorset), da of late Col George Harold Absell Ing, CMG, DSO:—
Sarah, *b* 1960: *m* 1981, Dominic William Michael Nelson, 2nd son of Sir William Vernon Hope Nelson, 3rd Bt, OBE, and has issue (see that title). —— Lucy, *b* 1962: *m* 1992, Samuel Anthony Kellie-Smith, of 59 Cornwall Gdns, SW7 (*see* Chaytor, Bt, colls, 1985 Edn), and has issue living, Calum James, *b* 1994.

Granddaughters of late Capt Hon William Sydney Hylton Jolliffe, 4th son of 1st Baron:—
Issue of late Maj Berkeley Gerald Jolliffe, *b* 1878, *d* 1956: *m* 1919, Mary Viola, who *d* 1984, da of Capt John Douglas Maude Guthrie, of Guthrie Castle, Scotland:—
Cynthia Myra, *b* 1920. —— Eileen Daphne, *b* 1921: *m* 1st, 1946 (*m diss* 1955), Arthur Harold Morse; 2ndly, 1955, Richard Arthur Edwards, of Top of the Hill, Melton Grange, Woodbridge, Ipswich, Suffolk IP12 1EX, and has issue living (by 1st *m*), Simon Arthur Davidson (2 Robert Lodge, 4 Milner St, SW3; Thicket Cottage, Leckhampstead, Newbury, Berks), *b* 1952, — Lavinia May, *b* 1947: *m* 1980, Nicholas Adrian Penrhys-Evans, of Hollow Lane Farm, Badingham, Woodbridge, Suffolk, and has issue living, Toby Fortescue *b* 1985, Zoe Viola *b* 1982, — (by 2nd *m*) Chloë Annabel (*Hon Mrs Maurice Robson*), *b* 1956: *m* 1985, Hon (Erik) Maurice William Robson, and has issue (*see* Bs Robson of Kiddington), — Miranda Bridget, *b* 1961.

PREDECESSORS – (1) WILLIAM GEORGE HYLTON Jolliffe, PC, son of late Rev William John Jolliffe, son of William Jolliffe, MP and his wife Eleanor, da of heir of Sir Richard Hylton Bt of Hayton Castle, Cumberland (by Anne, his wife, sister and co-heir of John Hylton, of Hylton Castle, co Durham); *b* 1800; sat as MP for Petersfield (C) 1830-31 and 1837-66; Under-Sec for Home Depart 1852, and Joint Sec of Treasury 1858-59; *cr a Baronet* 1821, and *Baron Hylton*, of Hylton Castle, co Durham, and of Petersfield, co Southampton (peerage of United Kingdom) 1866, being heir representative of Barony of Hylton or Hilton (*cr* 1295): *m* 1st, 1825, Eleanor, who *d* 1862, da of the Hon Berkeley Paget; 2ndly, 1867, Sophia Penelope, who *d* 1882, da of Sir Robert Sheffield, 4th Bt, and widow of 4th Earl of Ilchester; *d* 1876; *s* by his son (2) HEDWORTH HYLTON, *b* 1829; MP for Wells (C) 1855-68; *m* 1st, 1858, Lady Agnes Mary Georgiana Byng, who *d* 1878, da of 2nd Earl of Strafford; 2ndly, 1879, Anne, who *d* 1917, da of Henry Lambert, of Carnagh, co Wexford, and widow of 3rd Earl of Dunraven and Mount Earl; *d* 1899; *s* by his el son (3) HYLTON GEORGE HYLTON, 3rd Baron, *b* 1862; in Diplo Ser 1888-95; MP for Wells Div of Somerset (C) 1895-99; was Lord-in-Waiting to HM 1915-18, Joint Ch Govt Whip in House of Lords 1916-22, and Capt of Yeomen of the Guard 1918-24: *m* 1896, Lady Alice Adeliza Hervey, who *d* 1962, da and co-heir of 3rd Marquess of Bristol; *d* 1945: *s* by his son (4) WILLIAM GEORGE HERVEY, 4th Baron, *b* 1898; Lt-Col Coldstream Guards; Lord-Lieut of Somerset 1949-67: *m* 1931, Lady Perdita Rose Mary Asquith, who *d* 1996, sister of 2nd Earl of Oxford and Asquith; *d* 1967; *s* by his son (5) RAYMOND HERVEY, 5th Baron and present peer.

HYLTON-FOSTER, BARONESS (Hylton-Foster) (Life Baroness 1965)

AUDREY PELLEW HYLTON-FOSTER, DBE, da of 1st Viscount Ruffside (ext) (*see* Brown, Bt, colls); *b* 19 May 1908; *ed* St George's Ascot, and at Ivy House, Wimbledon, Pres of Co London Branch British Red Cross Soc 1960-73 (Dir of Chelsea Div 1950-60, Pres and Chm London Branch 1960-85, Patron 1984); a Member of National Council 1966-76, Hon Consultant 1984-86; Pres Prevention of Blindness Research Fund 1965-76; Convenor Cross Bench Peers since 1974; sits as an Independent Peer; *cr* DBE 1990, and *Baroness Hylton-Foster*, of City of Westminster (Life Baroness 1965): *m* 1931, Rt Hon Sir Harry Braustyn Hylton Hylton-Foster, QC, MP, Speaker of House of Commons 1959-65, who *d* 1965.
Residence – The Coach House, Tanhurst, Leith Hill, Holmbury St Mary, Dorking, Surrey, RH5 6LQ.

HYNDLEY, VISCOUNTCY OF (Hindley) (Extinct 1963)

DAUGHTER LIVING OF FIRST VISCOUNT

Hon Elizabeth Cairns (Meads Lodge, Rondle Wood, nr Liphook, Hants) *b* 1912.

IDDESLEIGH, EARL OF (Northcote) (Earl UK 1885, Bt E 1641)
(Title pronounced "Idsly") (Name pronounced "Northcut")

The Cross of Christ is my Light

STAFFORD HENRY NORTHCOTE, 4th Earl and 11th Baronet; *b* 14 July 1932; *s* 1970; *ed* Downside; late 2nd Lt Irish Gds; DL Devon 1979, Vice Lord-Lieut since 1999; Dir Devon & Exeter Steeplechases Ltd, Dir Gemini Radio Ltd 1992-98; Chm South West TSB 1980-83; SW Regional Chm England and Wales TSB 1983-88, Dir TSB Group plc 1987-88, United Dominions Trust Ltd 1983-88, and Television South West plc 1982-92; Knt of Honour and Devotion Sovereign Mil Order of Malta: *m* 1955, Maria Luisa (Mima) Alvarez-Builla y Urquijo (Condesa del Real Agrado in Spain, *cr* 1771), OBE, DL Devon 1987, only da of late Don Gonzalo Alvarez-Builla y Alvera, and of late Maria Luisa, Viscountess Exmouth, and has issue.

Arms – Argent, three cross-crosslets in bend sable. Crest – Upon a chapeau gules, turned up ermine a stag trippant argent. Supporters – Two stags proper, and pendant from the neck of each by a gold chain an escutcheon ermine, charged with a fir-cone or.
Seat – Pynes, Exeter, EX5 5EF. *Residence* – Shillands House, Upton Pyne, Exeter, Devon, EX5 5EB. *Club* – Army and Navy.

SON LIVING

JOHN STAFFORD (*Viscount St Cyres*) (Hayne Barton, Newton St Cyres, Devon), *b* 15 Feb 1957; *ed* Downside, and Royal Agric Coll, Cirencester: *m* 1983 (*m diss* 1999), Fiona Caroline Elizabeth, da of Paul Alan Campbell Wakefield, of Barcelona, Spain, and has issue:—

SON LIVING— *Hon* Thomas Stafford, *b* 5 Aug 1985.
DAUGHTER LIVING— *Hon* Elizabeth Rose Adèle, *b* 1989.

DAUGHTER LIVING

Lady Mary Louise, *b* 1959: *m* 1981, Maj Simon Nicholas Fishwick, late 13th/18th Royal Hus, yr son of Clifford Fishwick, of Salisbury House, Monmouth St, Topsham, Devon, and has had issue, James Nicholas, *b* 1983, — Hugh Simon, *b* 1984, *d* 1987, — Lucy Mary, *b* 1988. *Residence* – Lower Woodrow, Brampford Speke, nr Exeter, Devon EX5 5DY.

BROTHER LIVING

Hon Edward Frederic, TD, *b* 1934; *ed* Downside, and Trin Coll, Oxford (MA); Maj Intelligence Corps (T & AVR); Cyprus 1957; Assocn of Inst of Chartered Management Accountants; a Prin Officer HM Treasury 1969-71; FSS: *m* 1963 (*m diss* 1980), Vivien Sheena, da of Col Robert John Augustine Hornby, OBE (*see* Bruce, Bt, colls, *cr* 1628), and has issue living, (Edward) Bede Robert Hornby, *b* 1964; *ed* Wimbledon Coll: *m* 1998, Sarah (Sally) F., yr da of Dr Ian Eminson, of Messingham, Lincs, and has issue living, Harriet Georgina May *b* 1998, — (Alexander) Benet Paul Hornby, *b* 1971: *m* 1998, (Auriol) Davina, elder da of Sir Michael James Harwood Harrison, 2nd Bt (*cr* 1961), — Modwenna Vivien Hornby (*Hon Mrs Thomas Rees-Mogg*), *b* 1968: *m* 1996, Hon Thomas Fletcher Rees-Mogg, elder son of Baron Rees-Mogg (Life Baron). *Residence* – Flat 38, Westmore Court, Carlton Drive, SW15 2BU.

SISTER LIVING

Lady Catherine Cecilia Mary, *b* 1931; is a Religious of the Assumption; teacher and author.

COLLATERAL BRANCHES LIVING

Granddaughter of late Sir Geoffrey Alexander Stafford Northcote, KCMG, only son of late Rev Hon Arthur Francis Northcote, 4th son of 1st Earl:—
Issue of late Major Amyas Henry Stafford Northcote, MC, *b* 1916, *ka* in Burma 1944: *m* 1941, Mollie Gordon Buchanan (who *d* 1990, having *m* 2ndly, 1947, Charles Antony Russell Smallwood, who *d* 1987), da of Major George Buchanan Scott, of Zaria, Horsham:—
Sylvia Rosalind Stafford, *b* 1942: *m* 1968, Antony Cokayne Doulton, of 51 Park Close, Ilchester Place, W14 8NH, and has issue living, Amyas John Stafford, *b* 1977, — Natasha Ophelia Stafford, *b* 1971.

Granddaughter of late Hon Hugh Oliver Northcote, 5th son of 1st Earl:—
Issue of late Hugh Hamilton Stafford Northcote, *b* 1887, *d* 1929: *m* 1925, Josephine, who *d* 1928, da of late Thomas O'Shaughnessy, of Killacolla, Glin, co Limerick:—
Mary Edith (29 Thackeray Court, Elystan Place, SW3 3LB), *b* 1926.

(In remainder to Baronetcy, cr 1641, only)

Grandchildren of late James Alfred Northcote, MBE, 5th son of late Rev Henry Moubray Northcote,
brother of 8th Bt:—
Issue of late Thomas Francis Northcote, *b* 1894, *d* 1977: *m* 1924, Frances Vera, who *d* 1980, da of late Arthur
Hope, of Tumanako, Timaru, NZ:—
Peter Stafford, *b* 1928: *m* 1957, Geraldine Margaret, da of Gerald Murray, of Glenmore, Lake Tekapo, NZ, and has issue
living, Hugh Stafford, *b* 1960, — Michael John, *b* 1962, — Margaret Anne, *b* 1959. —— (George) Arthur (310 Old West
Coast Rd, Christchurch RD6, NZ), *b* 1929: *m* 1960, Julia Elvira Morton Watkins, and has issue living, Charles Moubray,
b 1961: *m* 1984, Ynez Powers, and has issue living, Richard Powers *b* 1985, Anthony Charles *b* 1989, — Cynthia Jane, *b*
1962: *m* 1987 (*m diss* 19—), Andrew Matt Palmer, — Diana Mary, *b* 1964: *m* 1993, Duncan James Priestley.
—— Frances Roma, *b* 1931: *m* 1956, John Endell Wanklyn, of Te Tua, Governors Bay, RD1 Lyttelton, Christchurch, NZ,
and has issue living, David Endell (24a Gamblins Rd, St Martin's, Christchurch, NZ), *b* 1959, — Catherine Frances, *b*
1957: *m* 1982, David John Thacker, of Mount Peel (No 7 RD), Gore, Southland, NZ, and has issue living, Rebecca Jane *b*
1984, Kate Frances *b* 1987, — Jaquetta Jane, *b* 1958: *m* 1982, Andrew Robert Hazledine, of 1 Ballarat Rd, Rangiora, N
Canterbury, NZ, and has issue living, Jenny Frances *b* 1987, Josie Amanda *b* (twin) 1987, Bridget Claire *b* 1990.

Granddaughters of late Cecil Stafford Northcote (infra):—
Issue of late Lewis Stafford Northcote, *b* 1907, *d* 1977: *m* 1935, Esme Geraldine Seignelay, who *d* 1979, da of
late Capt Arthur Robert Seignelay Lyon-Campbell, of Stockhill, Settle, Yorks:—
Sarah Caroline Patricia, *b* 1936: *m* 1962, Capt Patrick Timothy Sheehan, CBE, RN, of St Catherine's, East Hendred,
Wantage, Oxon, and has issue living, Timothy Stafford, *b* 1966, — Clare Anne, *b* 1963: *m* 1994, Thomas Richard Glen
Downes, — Joanna Mary, *b* 1965: *m* 1993, David Charles Carreras, solicitor. —— Jaqueta Seignelay, *b* 1937.

Grandsons of late Capt Lewis Stafford Northcote, only son of late Rev Stafford Charles Northcote, 3rd
son of 7th Bt:—
Issue of late Cecil Stafford Northcote, *b* 1870, *d* 1912: *m* 1906, Ida Sybil Mary, who *d* 1963, da of Capt Joseph
Boulderson:—
Cecil Henry, OBE, *b* (*posthumous*) 1912; *ed* Douai, and Queen's Coll, Oxford (MA); is Headmaster of St Bede's Sch,
Bishton Hall, Staffs, a Co Councillor of Staffs, Chm of Stafford and Stone Conservative Assocn, and of Co Records &
Shugborough & Co Museum Cttee, a Gov of King Edward VI Gram Sch Stafford and Church of England Sch, Colwich,
Staffs; High Sheriff co Staffs (1981), and a Knight of Honour and Devotion of Sovereign Order of Malta; a Rural Dist
Councillor; OBE (Civil) 1982: *m* 1936, Freda, da of late Frederic Williams and has issue living, Amyas Henry Stafford, *b*
1937; *ed* Ampleforth, and Ch Ch, Oxford (MA); a JP of Staffs; a Kt of Honour and Devotion of Sovereign Mil Order of
Malta, — Hugh Cecil Camden (Bishton Hall, Staffs), *b* 1938; *ed* Ampleforth, and Trin Coll, Camb (MA) a Kt of Honour
and Devotion, Sov Mil Order of Malta: *m* 1974, Hilary Jane, yr da of Col R. J. C. Evans, TD, DL, of Cage Hill, Stowc-by-
Chartley, and has issue living, Charles Walter Hugh *b* 1977, Arabella Lucy Mary *b* 1975, Beatrice Eleanor Margaret *b*
1979, Helena Jane Alice *b* 1980, Katherine Sybil Ruth *b* 1983, — Julia Marguerite Mary, *b* 1941; *ed* Assumption, Bury St
Edmunds, and Webber Douglas Sch of Dramatic Art. *Residence* – Bishton Hall, Staffs.

Issue of late Ernest Alfred Stafford Northcote, *b* 1875, *d* 1944: *m* 1900, Sarah Potwin, who *d* 1911, da of late Col
Gilbert Dwight Munson, Judge and Lawyer, Ohio, USA:—
Oliver Stafford, *b* 1906; *ed* Stanford Univ Cal (AB, LLB); Bar Cal, 1933; a member of legal firm of Chandler, Wright,
Tyler & Ward, of Los Angeles, USA, and of American, Californian and Los Angeles Bar Assos, and Lt-Cdr USNR; Lt
USN 1942-45: *m* 1933, Dorothy Lucille, da of James A. Ham, and has issue living, Philip Stafford (2192 Racquet Hill,
Santa Ana, Calif 92705, USA), *b* 1937: *m* 1966, —, da of Henry Reichert, and has issue living, Kent Stafford *b* 1969,
Kristin *b* 1970, — Geoffrey Stafford (twin) (305 Calle Paisano, San Clemente, Calif 92672, USA) *b* 1937: *m* 1964, Sharon
Ann, da of Vachel Conn Foree, Jr, and has issue living, Douglas Stafford *b* 1971, — John Stafford (PO Box 754, Carmel,
Calif 93921, USA), *b* 1940: *m* 1966, Virginia Lee Camden, da of late William Henry Wright, and has issue living, Stafford
Oliver *b* 1975. *Residence* – 830 W Orange Grove Av, Arcadia, Calif 91006, USA.

Grandchildren of late Stafford Henry Northcote (*b* 1872), eldest son of late Stafford Charles Northcote
(*b* 1844), eldest son of Stafford Henry Northcote (*b* 1813), son of Stafford Northcote (*b* 1783), 2nd son
of Henry Northcote, 2nd son of 5th Bt:—
Issue of late Stafford Charles Robert Northcote, *b* 1909, *d* 1977: *m* 1st, 1947, Helen Isabel, who *d* 1965, da of
Herbert Nelson Hawker, of Christchurch, NZ; 2ndly, 1972, Sheila Mary, who *d* 1986, widow of Dr Paul H.
Sandifer:—
(By 1st *m*) Stafford Robert, *b* 1948: *m* 1969, Penelope Anne Tracy, da of (Thomas) Michael Eastham, QC. —— Helena
Ann Stafford (48 Rothsay Rd, Forest Gate, E7), *b* 1951.

Issue of late Geoffrey Stafford Northcote, *b* 1912, *d* 1968: *m* 1938, Rhoda C. Ruth (who *m* 2ndly, 1975, Philip
Williamson), da of late A. McNeill, of Auckland, NZ:—
Robert Stafford (38 Cooper Place, Beaumont, 5066, S Aust), *b* 1939; *ed* Univ of Wellington (MSc), and Univ of Adelaide
(PhD); Prof of Computer Studies, SA Inst of Tech, Adelaide: *m* 1963, Patricia Margaret, da of late Arthur Baillie, of
Adelaide, and has issue living, Roger Stafford, *b* 1966, — Bruce Stephen, *b* 1969, — Michelle Patricia, *b* 1972. —— Alan
McNeill (71 James Cook Drive, Welcome Bay, Tauranga, NZ), *b* 1940; *ed* Univ of Wellington (BCom), ACANZ, ACIS: *m*
1963, Mary Vesey, da of late E. A. Zambra, of Napier, NZ, and has issue living, Peter Bruce, *b* 1964, — Stuart Paul, *b*
1966, — Susan Mary, *b* 1967 —— Geoffrey John (25 Spencer Rd, Mosman, NSW 2088, Australia), *b* 1947; Gen Man.
—— Margaret Moralee (101 Grange Rd, Tauranga, NZ), *b* 1950: *m* 1971 (*m diss* 1994), Wallace Donald Thomson, and
has issue living, Robert Wallace, *b* 1974, — Kathryn Helen, *b* 1977.

Grandchildren of late Cyril Charles Stafford Northcote, 2nd son of late Stafford Charles Northcote (*b*
1844) (ante):—
Issue of late John Wilfrid Cyril Stafford Northcote, *b* 1904, *d* 1970: *m* 1st, 1933 (*m diss* 1937), Mary Caroline, yr
da of late Robert Collier, FRIBA; 2ndly, 1938, Grace Carruthers, da of E. Carruthers Webb, of Mill Hill, Middx;
3rdly, 1952, Janet, el da of Ronald Grose, of Manor Rd, Taunton:—
(By 1st *m*) Jennifer Anne Stafford, *b* 1935: *m* 1955, John Morley, of 18 The Parkway, Leabrook, Adelaide, S Aust, and
has issue living, Robert, *b* 1956, — Jasper, *b* 1959, — David John, *b* 1964, — Amanda Caroline, *b* 1966. —— (By 3rd *m*)

Martin Charles Stafford (30 Madeley Rd, W5 2LH), *b* 1953: *m* 199-, Lucy Patricia, da of late P. A. Willard, and has issue living, Henry Charles, *b* 1992, — Nadia Mary, *b* (twin) 1992. ——— Nigel John Stafford, *b* 1960. ——— Andrew Alexander Stafford, *b* 1964. ——— Gillian Stafford, *b* 1954.

Grandchildren (by 1st *m*) of late Maj Leonard Augustus Stafford Northcote (infra):—
Issue of late Lt-Col Denis Leonard Stafford Northcote, RA, *b* 1904, *d* 1978: *m* 1st, 1929, Sylvia Mary Manners, da of late Col John Manners Smith, VC, CIE, CVO, IA; 2ndly, 1947, Beatrice Margaret, who *d* 1985, da of late Robert Malcolm, of Rawalpindi, India:—
(By 1st wife) William John, *b* 1939. ——— Sylvia Alison, *b* 1930. ——— Veronica Phyllis, *b* 1932. ——— (By 2nd wife) Jaqueta Stafford, *b* 1941: *m* 1968, Michael Robert Philip, of Bank House, Hatherton, Nantwich, Cheshire CW5 7PQ, and of Bollington Grange, Nether Alderley, Cheshire, and has issue living, Nicholas Alexander Michael, *b* 1973; *ed* Wrekin Coll, — Olivia Kate, *b* 1975; *ed* West Chester Coll of Art, and Aberystwith Univ.

Grandchildren of late Stafford Charles Northcote (ante):—
Issue of late Maj Leonard Augustus Stafford Northcote, *b* 1879, *d* 1942: *m* 1st, 1903 (*m diss* 1914), Lilian Cora, da of late J. van Praagh, formerly of 209 Maida Vale, W; 2ndly, 1916, Ida, who *d* 1978, da of 5th Marquis Testaferrata-Olivier du Puget (Maltese Nobility):—
(By 1st *m*) Iris Blanche Stafford, *b* 1909; formerly Fashion Ed (as Iris Ashley) *Daily Mail* (ret 1964): *m* 1st, 1928 (*m diss* 19—), Maurice Ashley Brown, who *d* 1978; 2ndly, 1939, (Stanley) John Knowles, who *d* 19—; 3rdly, 1964, His Honour Desmond Harvey Weight Vowden, QC, who *d* 1990, and has issue living (by 2nd husband), Penelope Ann (2 Clarendon Place, W2 2NP), *b* 1937: *m* 1962, Michael John Wigram, of Madrid, Spain, and has issue living, Lionel Nicholas Richard *b* 1962: *ed* Eton, and Brasenose Coll, Oxford, Benjamin Peter Desmond *b* 1970; *ed* Emanuel Sch, Sophie Denia *b* 1964; *ed* St Paul's Girls' Sch, and Somerville Coll, Oxford: *m* 1995, William Edward Orlando Corke (*see* B Bridges). ——— (By 2nd *m*) (Henry) James STAFFORD NORTHCOTE, *b* 1922; *ed* Downside; served 1939-45 War with Oxfordshire and Buckinghamshire LI, and Intelligence Corps in Europe and SEAC; feature film technician: *m* 1949 (*m diss* 1961), Sheila, actress, da of late Capt John Manahan, of Dublin.

Issue of late Major Arthur Frederick Stafford Northcote, DSO, *b* 1881, *d* 1949: *m* 1st, 1905 (*m diss* 1930), Constance Fanny (who *d* 19—), da of late Col William Henry Salmon, Indian Army (ret); 2ndly, 1930, Dora, who *d* 1932, da of Congreve Jackson, OBE; 3rdly, 1938, Beryl, who *d* 1989, da of late Rev W. H. Weekes, of Devizes:—
(By 2nd *m*) Annette Stafford, *b* 1931: *m* 1st 1952 (*m diss* 1970), Harry Alexander Thomas McPhee; 2ndly, 1971, David Crichton Paterson, who *d* 1993, of 365 E Queen's Rd, N Vancouver, BC, Canada V7N 1G7, and has issue living (by 1st *m*), Roderick Jody, *b* 1965: *m* 1996, Denise Fulton, — Beverly Eve, *b* 1956: *m* 1990, John Alexander Dodd, and has issue living, Jordi Michael *b* 1993, Sarah Elizabeth *b* 1991, — Deborah Jane, *b* 1959, — Judith Leah, *b* 1960, — (by 2nd *m*) John Leslie, *b* 1973.

Grandchildren of Leonard Beauchamp Northcote, yst son of late Stafford Henry Northcote (*b* 1813) (ante):—
Issue of late Henry Peter Northcote, *b* 1891, *d* 1971: *m* 1924, Eileen (Coston, Moreland Drive, Gerrards Cross, Bucks), da of Edwin Charles Irish:—
Edwin Charles Stafford (Hatherly Brake, Wilton Lane, Jordans, Beaconsfield, Bucks), *b* 1926; *ed* Blundell's Sch: *m* 1956 (*m diss* 1974), Angela, da of James Edward Hutton, and has issue living, Ashley James Stafford, *b* 1959, — Belinda Susan, *b* 1965. ——— Anne, *b* 1936: *m* 1959 (*m diss* 1972), Ernst Zumbrunn, of Interlaken, Switzerland, and has issue living, Helene Diana, *b* 1963.

Issue of late Frederick Beauchamp Northcote, *b* 1893, *d* 1937: *m* 1923, Jessie Florence, who *d* 1988, da of William James:—
†Leon Frederick James, *b* 1924; *ed* Swansea Grm Sch; European War with RN 1942-46; in first wave of tank landing craft on Juno beach on D Day 1944: *m* 1951, Valerie May (29 Orchard Rd, Longlevens, Gloucester), da of Victor Thomas George Bennett, of Gloucester, and *d* 1997, leaving issue, Richard Leon Stafford (38 Juniper Close, Towcester, Northants), *b* 1952: *m* 1976, Jeanette May, da of Thomas Rich, of Upton St Leonards, Gloucester, and has issue living, Christopher Thomas Stafford *b* 1985, Jessica Elizabeth *b* 1981, — Susan Elizabeth, *b* 1954: *m* 1st, 19— (*m diss* 1979), — ; 2ndly, 1981, Peter William Dove, of 5 Wren Close, Saint Bridge, Gloucester, and has issue living, (by 1st *m*) Stewart Richard DOVE *b* 1972; legally adopted by his stepfather, David Graham DOVE *b* 1978; legally adopted by his stepfather, (by 2nd *m*) James Peter *b* 1983.

Grandchildren of late Edward Northcote, son of late Gilbert Charles Northcote, 7th son of late Stafford Northcote (*b* 1783) (ante):—
Issue of late Gilbert Charles Northcote, *b* 1903, *d* 1967: *m* 1930, Marguerite Muriel, who *d* 1984, da of Joseph William Nicholas:—
Mildred Reynell, *b* 1931: *m* 1961, Alexander Walter English, of Redbank, Deniliquin, NSW 2710, and has issue living, Alexander Northcote Charles, *b* 1966, — Jean Constance Northcote, *b* 1962, — Marguerite Louise Northcote, *b* 1964: *m* 1987, Kenneth Maxwell Davis, of Pine View, Corowa, NSW, and has issue living, William James *b* 1990, Kimberley Ann *b* 1989, Georgina Louise *b* 1992. ——— Gillian Mary Stafford, *b* 1932: *m* 1954, Mardi Walker, of Rankin Park, PO 142, Holbrook, NSW 2644, and has issue living, Rowena Marius, *b* 1960: *m* 1985, Michael Henry Stubbe, of 2 Poath Rd, Oakleigh, Vic, and has issue living, John Gilbert *b* 1988, Christopher Michael *b* 1990.

Granddaughters of late Horace Northcote, son of late Horace Northcote, son of late Gilbert Charles Northcote (ante):—
Issue of late Ronald Cecil Northcote, OBE, MM, *b* 1895, *d* 1972: *m* 1934, Joan Eileen, who *d* 1992, da of John Everard Grafton Grattan:—
Veronica Stella *b* 1940: *m* 1987, Trevor Claude Long (who *d* 1991, having assumed by deed poll 1988 the surname NORTHCOTE-LONG in lieu of his patronymic). *Residence* – Nimrod, 5 Aspen Close, Woodbridge, Suffolk IP12 1SG.

Issue of late Capt Malcolm Philip Northcote, *b* 1908, *d* 1971: *m* 1st, 1933 (*m diss* 1954), Eileen Natalie Colt

(dec), da of Edward Walter David Colt Williams, MC, Bar-at-law; 2ndly, 1956, Moya Angela, who d 1990, yr da of late William Maidment, of Parrett Lodge, Bridgwater, Som:—
(By 2nd m) Amanda Louise, b 1958: m 1982, Michael Anthony Burling, and has issue living, Philippa Frances, b 1986. Residence – 92 Iffley Rd, W6 0PF. —— Vanessa Jane (twin), b 1958: m 1986, Justin Timothy Donegan, 2nd son of Patrick Terence Nessan Donegan, QC, of Petworth, Sussex, and has issue living, Matthew Justin Philip, b 1992, — Luke Dominic Peter, b 1995, — Chloë Elizabeth, b 1989.

Granddaughter of late Ronald Cecil Northcote, OBE, MM (ante):—
Issue of late Geoffrey Malcolm Northcote, b 1942, d 1981: m 1969 (m diss 1974), Diana Maria, da of late Edmund Maria Hellmer, of Vienna:—
Lara Veronica STEINLECHNER (Stollenstrasse 3A, 6065 Thaur, Tirol, Austria), b 1970; assumed surname of Steinlechner in lieu of her patronymic 1981; has issue living, Yana STEINLECHNER, b 1994.

PREDECESSORS – (1) JOHN NORTHCOTE, MP for Ashburton 1640-48, for Devon 1654-60, and for Barnstaple 1667-76, cr a Baronet 1641; d 1676; s by his son (2) ARTHUR, 2nd Bt; d 1688; s by his son (3) FRANCIS, 3rd Bt; dsp 1709; s by his brother (4) HENRY, MD, 4th Bt; d 1729; s by his son (5) HENRY, 5th Bt, MP for Exeter 1734-43; d 1743; s by his son (6) STAFFORD, 6th Bt; d 1771; s by his son (7) STAFFORD HENRY, 7th Bt; d 1851; s by his grandson (8) STAFFORD HENRY, GCB, DCL, PC, 8th Bt, son of late Henry Stafford Northcote, Esq (el son of 7th Bt); b 1818; was Pres of Board of Trade 1866-7, Sec of State for India 1867-8, Chancellor of the Exchequer 1874-80, First Lord of the Treasury 1885-6, Sec of State for Foreign Affairs 1886-7, and Lord-Lieut of Devonshire; sat as MP for Dudley (C) 1855-7, for Stamford 1858-66, and for N Devon 1866-85; cr Viscount St Cyres, of Newton St Cyres, co Devon, and Earl of Iddesleigh (peerage of United Kingdom) 1885: m 1843, Cecilia Frances, CI, who d 1910, sister of 1st Baron Farrer, d 12 Jan 1887; s by his el son (9) WALTER STAFFORD, CB, 2nd Earl, b 1845; Private Sec to his father 1867-8, and 1874-7, Commr of Inland Revenue 1877-86, Dep Chm thereof 1886-92, and Chm 1892: m 1868, Elizabeth Lucy, who d 1928, da of Sir Harry Stephen Meysey-Thompson, 1st Bt; d 1927; s by his nephew (10) HENRY STAFFORD (yst son of late Rev Hon John Stafford Northcote, 3rd son of 1st Earl), 3rd Earl, b 1901: m 1930, Elizabeth, JP, who d 1991, da of late Frederic Sawrey Archibald Lowndes, of 9 Barton St, Westminster, SW1; d 1970; s by his son (11) STAFFORD HENRY, 4th Earl and present peer; also Viscount St Cyres.

Ikerrin, Viscount; son of Earl of Carrick.

ILCHESTER, EARL OF (Fox-Strangways) (Earl GB 1756)

Deeds without words

MAURICE VIVIAN DE TOUFFREVILLE FOX-STRANGWAYS, 9th Earl; b 1 April 1920; s 1970; ed Kingsbridge Sch; Group Capt RAF (ret); CEng, MRAeS, FINucE (Pres 1982-84), FIMgt, Hon FSE (Pres 1974); Hon Fellow Coll of Preceptors; Co Dir; Pres RAF Assoc (SE Area); Pres Grant-Maintained Schs Foundation; Member House of Lords Select Cttee on Science and Technology 1984-89; Liveryman Guild of Air Pilots and Air Navigators: m 1941, Diana Mary Elizabeth, el da of late George Frederick Simpson, of Cassington, Oxon.

Arms – Quarterly: 1st and 4th sable, two lions passant paly of six argent and gules, Strangways; 2nd and 3rd ermine, on a chevron azure, three foxes' heads erased or, a canton of the 2nd, charged with a fleur-de-lis of the 3rd, Fox. Crest – On a chapeau azure, turned up ermine, a fox sejant or. Supporters – Dexter, a fox ermine, frette or, collared dovetail azure, and the collar charged with three fleurs-de-lis gold; sinister, a fox proper, collared as the dexter.
Residence – Farley Mill, Westerham, Kent. Club – RAF.

BROTHER LIVING

Hon RAYMOND GEORGE (4 Trull Green Drive, Trull, Taunton, Som TA3 7JL), b 11 Nov 1921; ed Exeter Sch, and Seale Hayne Agric Coll; Civil Ser 1949-76 (ret); 1939-45 War in RAF: m 1941, Margaret Vera, da of late James Force, of North Surrey, BC, and has issue living, Robin Maurice (Little Haven, Frankton, nr Rugby, Warwicks CV25 9PL), b 1942; ed Loughborough Coll; in banking: m 1969, Margaret Elizabeth, da of late Geoffrey Miles, of Camberley, Surrey, and has issue living, Simon James b 1972, Charlotte Helen b 1974, — Paul André (c/o 4 Trull Green Drive, Trull, Taunton, Som TA3 7JL), b 1950; ed Loughborough Coll, and Sussex Univ (BSc (hons), MA); Lecturer Brighton Univ.

SISTER LIVING

Lady Jeanne Doreen (Elisabeth), *b* 1931; Founder and Principal Lady Elizabeth Livingstone Modelling School 1983: *m* 1st, 1958 (*m diss* 1969), Peter Skelton, publisher; 2ndly, 1977, John Livingstone, and has one da (from 1st *m*), Caroline, *b* 1962. *Residence* – 72a Fore St, Bovey Tracey, Newton Abbot, Devon.

PREDECESSORS – (1) STEPHEN FOX, MP for Shaftesbury 1726-41; *cr Lord Ilchester*, of Ilchester, co Somerset, *Baron of Woodford Strangways*, co Dorset (peerage of Great Britain) 1741, *Lord Ilchester and Stavordale, Baron of Redlynch*, co Somerset (peerage of Great Britain) 1747, with remainder to the issue male of his brother Henry, and *Earl of Ilchester* (peerage of Great Britain) 1756, with like remainder; assumed the additional surname of Strangways 1758; *d* 1766; *s* by his son (2) HENRY THOMAS, 2nd Earl; *d* 1802; *s* by his son (3) HENRY STEPHEN, DCL, 3rd Earl; Capt of Yeomen of the Guard; *d* without surviving male issue 1858; *s* by his half-brother (4) WILLIAM THOMAS HORNER, 4th Earl; *b* 1795; was Under Sec of State for Foreign Affairs 1835 and Ambassador to German Confederation 1840-9; *dsp* 1865; *s* by his nephew (5) HENRY EDWARD (son of Hon John George Charles, 4th son of 2nd Earl, by Amelia, who *d* 1886, sister of 1st Baron Tweedmouth), 5th Earl; *b* 1847; Capt of HM Queen Victoria's Corps of Gentlemen-at-Arms 1873-4, and Lord-Lieut of Dorsetshire: *m* 1872, Lady Mary Eleanor Anne Dawson, who *d* 1935, only da of 1st Earl of Dartrey; *d* 1905; *s* by his son (6) GILES STEPHEN HOLLAND, GBE, 6th Earl; *b* 1874; Chm of Trustees of National Portrait Gallery, a Trustee of British Museum, Chm of Roy Commn on Historical Documents (England), and a FSA; Pres of Roy Literary Fund 1940-50: *m* 1902, Lady Helen Mary Theresa Vane-Tempest-Stewart, who *d* 1956, da of 6th Marquess of Londonderry; *d* 1959; *s* by his el son (7) EDWARD HENRY CHARLES JAMES, 7th Earl; *b* 1905: *m* 1931, Helen Elizabeth, who *d* 1970, da of late Capt the Hon Cyril Augustus Ward, MVO (E Dudley); *d* 1964; *s* by his kinsman (8) WALTER ANGELO (el son of Maurice Walter Fox-Strangways, 2nd son of Col Walter Fox-Strangways, great-grandson of Rev Hon Charles Fox-Strangways, 3rd son of 1st Earl), 8th Earl, *b* 1887: *m* 1916, Laure Georgine Emilie, who *d* 1970, da of late Evanghelos Georgios Mazaraki, Treasurer, Suez Canal Co; *d* 1970; *s* by his el son (9) MAURICE VIVIAN DE TOUFFREVILLE, 9th Earl and present peer; also Baron Ilchester, Baron Strangways, and Baron Ilchester and Stavordale.

ILIFFE, BARON (Iliffe) (Baron UK 1933)

Live, that you may live

ROBERT PETER RICHARD ILIFFE, 3rd Baron; *b* 22 Nov 1944; *s* 1996; *ed* Eton, and Ch Ch, Oxford; High Sheriff Warwicks 1983; Chm Yattendon Estates Ltd; Chm Yattendon Investment Trust plc (parent company of Marina Developments Ltd, Cambridge Newspapers Ltd, The Burton Daily Mail Ltd, Herts and Essex Newspapers Ltd, Staffordshire Newsletter Ltd); Scottish Provincial Press Ltd; former Chm Birmingham Post and Mail Ltd and Coventry Newspapers Ltd; Member of Council Royal Agric Soc of England since 1972, Chm of Council 1994-98: *m* 1966, Rosemary Anne, twin da of late Cmdr Arthur Grey Skipwith, RN (*see* Skipwith, colls), and has issue.

Arms – Sable, a lion rampant double-queued between four crosses pattée flory or. **Crest** – In front of a demi-lion rampant double-queued sable, collared or, three crosses as in the arms. **Supporters** – *Dexter*, a scribe holding in the exterior hand an open parchment proper; *sinister*, a printer of the time of Caxton holding in the exterior hand in front of his body a composing stick proper.
Seat – Yattendon Park, Yattendon, Berks RG16 0UT. *Clubs* – Boodle's, Royal Yacht Sqdn.

SONS LIVING

Hon EDWARD RICHARD, *b* 13 Sept 1968; *ed* Edinburgh Univ, and South Bank Univ: *m* 19—, Teleri, only da of J. D. P. Evans, of Ystrad-Teilo, Llanthystud, Dyfed, and has issue living, Alys Christina, *b* 1997.
Hon George Langton, *b* 1970.
Hon Thomas Arthur, *b* 1973.

DAUGHTER LIVING

Hon Florence Clare, *b* (twin) 1973: *m* 1999, Richard S. Kipling, son of Harry Kipling, of Lincoln, and of Mrs Barry Banbury, of Welwyn, Herts.

BROTHER LIVING

John David, *b* 1947; *ed* Eton, and Ch Ch, Oxford.

MOTHER LIVING

Christine Marie, da of late Alfred Eaton Baker, MD, of Hastings, Sussex: *m* 1940, Hon (William Henry) Richard Iliffe, who *d* 1959. *Residences* – Church Cottage, Aldworth, Reading, Berks; 11 Evelyn Gdns, SW7 3BE.

WIDOW LIVING OF SECOND BARON

RENÉE MARIE EUGÉNIE (*Renée, Baroness Iliffe*), elder da of René Merandon du Plessis, of Chamarel, Mauritius: *m* 1938, the 2nd Baron Iliffe, who *d* 1996. *Residences* – Basildon Park, Lower Basildon, nr Reading, Berks RG8 9NR; Villa Roquebrune, 6 Avenue Paul Doumer, Roquebrune-Cap Martin, 06190 France.

PREDECESSORS – (1) EDWARD MAUGER Iliffe, GBE, son of late William Isaac Iliffe, JP, of Allesley, near Coventry; *b* 1877; Chm of Guildhall Insurance Co, Ltd, a Director of London Assurance, Pres and Principal Proprietor *Birmingham Post* and *Birmingham Mail*, proprietor of *Coventry Evening Telegraph*, and *Cambridge Daily News*, and a Member of Lloyd's; sometime Chm of Kelly's Directories, Ltd, and of Iliffe & Sons, Dep Chm of Allied Newspapers, Ltd, and part owner of *Daily Telegraph*; Controller of Machine Tool Depart, Min of Munitions 1917-18; Pres of Asso of British Chambers of Commerce 1932-3, and of Govs of Shakespeare Memorial Theatre of Stratford-on-Avon 1933-58, Master of Coach Makers' and Coach Harness Makers' Co 1936, of Stationers' and Newspapermakers' Co 1937, and of Clock-makers' Co 1946; Hon Air-Commodore No 916/7 Squadron RAF 1939-44; Chm of Duke of Gloucester's Red Cross and St John Fifty-Seven Million Fund 1939-45; sat as MP for Warwickshire, Tamworth Div (*U*) 1923-9; *cr Baron Iliffe*, of Yattendon, co Berks (peerage of United Kingdom) 1933: *m* 1902, Charlotte, who *d* 1972, da of Henry Gilding, JP, of Gateacre, near Liverpool; *d* 1960; *s* by his el son (2) EDWARD LANGTON, 2nd Baron, *b* 1908; Vice-Chm *Birmingham Post & Mail Ltd* 1957-74, Dir *Coventry Evening Telegraph*, and Trustee of Shakespeare's Birthplace; 1939-45 War in RAF Vol Res (despatches): *m* 1938, Renée Marie Eugénie, elder da of René Merandon du Plessis; *d* 1996; *s* by his nephew (3) ROBERT PETER RICHARD, elder son of late Hon William Henry Richard Iliffe, yr son of 1st Baron, 3rd Baron and present peer.

IMBERT, BARON (Imbert) (Life Baron 1999)

PETER MICHAEL IMBERT, QPM, son of late William Henry Imbert, of Folkestone; *b* 27 April 1933; *ed* Harvey Gram Sch, Folkestone, Kent; joined Metropolitan Police 1953, Detective Chief Super-intendent until 1976; Assist then Dep Chief Constable, Surrey Constabulary 1976-79; Chief Constable, Thames Valley Police 1979-85, Dep Commr 1985-87, Commr 1987-93; Chm Capital Eye Security Ltd, Retainagroup Ltd; Non-Exec Dir Camelot Group plc, and Securicor plc; Memb Ministerial Advisory Board, Royal Parks; DL Greater London 1994; Lord Lieutenant of Greater London since 1998; awarded QPM 1980; *cr* Kt 1988, and *Baron Imbert*, of New Romney, co Kent (Life Baron) 1999: *m* 1956, Iris Rosina, da of late Christopher Thomas Charles Dove, of London, and has issue.

Arms – Azure between three scallop shells a portcullis flanked by two keys palewise in fess their wards outward argent and in middle chief a dove statant wings also argent.
Address – c/o House of Lords, Westminster, SW1A 0PW.

SON LIVING

Hon Simon, *b* 1958.

DAUGHTERS LIVING

Hon Elaine, *b* 1960.
Hon Sally, *b* 1966.

INCHCAPE, EARL OF (Mackay) (Earl UK 1929)

With a strong hand

MANU · FORTI

KENNETH PETER LYLE MACKAY, 4th Earl; *b* 23 Jan 1943; *s* 1994; *ed* Eton; late Lieut 9/12th Royal Lancers; AIB; Chm The Glenapp Estate Co, Dir Inchcape Family Investments Ltd, Saracen Power plc, Duncan MacNeill (Holdings) Ltd, The Assam Co Ltd, and formerly Dir Gray Mackenzie & Co Ltd, and Inchcape UK Ltd; Master Grocers' Co 1993-94, 5th Warden Shipwrights' Co 1994-95; Pres Inchcape Soc since 1994; Member Queen's Body Guard for Scotland (Royal Company of Archers): *m* 1966, Georgina, da of Sydney Cresswell Nisbet, and has issue.

꽃rms – Per chevron azure and argent in chief two lymphads of the last, and in base a Bengal tiger proper. Crest – A cubit arm holding a falcon proper. Supporters – *Dexter*, a lion rampant gules supporting a pendant argent charged with a saltire also gules; *sinister*, a Bengal tiger proper supporting a like pendant.
Residences – Manor Farm, Clyffe Pypard, nr Swindon, Wilts; 63 Pont St, SW1. *Clubs* – White's, Oriental, New (Edinburgh), Pratt's.

SON LIVING

FERGUS JAMES KENNETH (*Viscount Glenapp*), *b* 9 July 1979.

DAUGHTERS LIVING

Lady Elspeth Pease, *b* 1972, — *Lady* Ailsa Fiona, *b* 1977.

BROTHER LIVING

Hon James Jonathan Thorn (34A Dorset Sq, NW1), *b* 1947; *ed* Eton, and Trin Coll, Camb (MA), *m* 1970, Mary Caroline, el da of Peter Joyce, of Becklands Farm, Whitchurch Canonicorum, Dorset, and has issue living, Aidan James Turner, *b* 1978, — Sophie, *b* 1974.

HALF-BROTHERS LIVING

Hon Shane Lyle, *b* 1973.
Hon Ivan Cholmeley, *b* 1976.

ADOPTIVE BROTHER LIVING

Anthony Kenneth, *b* 1967.

SISTER LIVING

Lady Lucinda Louise MACKAY, *b* 1941; *ed* Edinburgh Univ (MA); has resumed her maiden name: *m* 1983 (*m diss* 1987), David Bogie; late Sheriff of Grampian, Highlands and Islands.

HALF-UNCLE LIVING (*son of 2nd Earl by 2nd marriage*)

Hon Simon Brooke (*Baron Tanlaw*), *b* 1934; *cr Baron Tanlaw* (Life Baron) 1971 (see that title).

HALF-AUNT LIVING (*daughter of 2nd Earl by 2nd marriage*)

Lady Rosemary, *b* 1936: *m* 1957, Francis Martin French, and has had issue, Ewan Alexander Francis, *b* 1959; *d* 198—, — Anna-Louise Rosemary, *b* 1961: *m* 1994, Rupert D. Bruce, son of Ian Bruce, of Dumfries, and has issue living, Laura Elizabeth *b* 1998, — Nicola Catharine, *b* 1967: *m* 1993, Lawrence Charles Reintjes, elder son of Anthony Reintjes, of Preston, Herts, and has issue living, Freddie *b* 199—, Alistair *b* 1997, — Kirsty Elizabeth, *b* 1970. *Residence* – Little Offley, Hitchin, Herts.

MOTHER LIVING

Aline Thorn, da of Sir Richard Arthur Pease, 2nd Bt (*cr* 1920), and widow of Patrick Claude Hannay, FO AAF: *m* 2ndly, 1941 (*m diss* 1954), 3rd Earl of Inchcape, who *d* 1994; 3rdly, 1955 (*m diss* 1968), Thomas Chambers Windsor Roe, who *d* 1988. *Residence* – 23 Rue Pre-du-Marché, Apt 114, Lausanne, Switzerland.

WIDOW LIVING OF SON OF SECOND EARL

Countess Lucie Catinka Christiane Julie, only da of Count Curt Ludwig Haugwitz-Hardenberg-Reventlow, of Brahe-Trolleborg, Korinth, Fyn, Denmark, and previously wife of John Boswell: *m* 1955, as his 3rd wife, Hon Alan John Francis Mackay, who *d* 1999. *Residence* – Enterkine, Annbank, Ayrshire KA6 5AL.

WIDOW LIVING OF THIRD EARL

CAROLINE CHOLMELEY (*Dowager Countess of Inchcape*), el da of Cholmeley Harrison, of Emo Court, co Leix: *m* 1965, as his 2nd wife, the 3rd Earl of Inchcape, who *d* 1994.

COLLATERAL BRANCH LIVING

Issue of late Hon Alan John Francis Mackay, yr son of 2nd Earl (by 1st *m*), *b* 1919, *d* 1999: *m* 1st, 1945 (*m diss* 1947), Janet Mary, who *d* 1978, yst da of Frederick Wallis, of Elvendon Priory, Goring-on-Thames, Oxon; 2ndly, 1948 (*m diss* 1953), Sonia Cecilia Helen, da of late Capt James Richard Tylden, of Milsted Manor, Kent; 3rdly, 1955, Countess Lucie Catinka Christiane Julie (ante), only da of Count Curt Ludwig Haugwitz-Hardenberg-Reventlow, of Brahe-Trolleborg, Korinth, Fyn, Denmark, and previously wife of John Boswell:—

(By 2nd *m*) Siobhan Amanda, *b* 1949: *m* 1973, Christopher O. B. Carver. *Residence* – ……. ——— Kristina Mary, *b* 1951: *m* 1975, Simon M. F. Lamb. *Residence* – …….

PREDECESSORS – (1) JAMES LYLE Mackay, GCSI, GCMG, KCIE, son of late James Mackay, of Arbroath, Forfarshire, by his wife, Deborah Lyle; *b* 1852; four years Pres of Bengal Chamber of Commerce, and a Member of Council of India 1897-1911; a partner in Mackinnon, Mackenzie and Co, of Calcutta, Bombay, Karachi, Colombo, Hong Kong, and Shanghai, of Gray, Dawes and Co, and of Macdonald, Hamilton and Co of Australia, a Director of National Provincial Bank, Ltd, Chm and Managing Director of British India Steam Navigation Co, and P and O Steam Navigation Co, Chm of P & O Banking Corporation, and Vice-Pres of Suez Canal Co; *cr Baron Inchcape*, of Strathnaver, co Sutherland (peerage of United Kingdom) 1911, *Viscount Inchcape*, of Strathnaver, co Sutherland (peerage of United Kingdom) 1924, *Viscount Glenapp*, of Strathnaver, co Sutherland, and *Earl of Inchcape* (peerage of United Kingdom) 1929: *m* 1883, Jane Paterson, who *d* 1937, el da of late James Shanks, of Rosely, Arbroath, Forfarshire; *d* 1932; *s* by his son (2) KENNETH, 2nd Earl; *b* 1887; a partner in Mackinnon, Mackenzie & Co, Pres of P & O Banking Corporation, and a Director of P & O Steam Navigation Co: *m* 1st, 1915 (*m diss* 1931), Frances Caroline Joan (who *d* 1933), da of late Rt Hon John Francis Moriarty, Lord Justice of Appeal; 2ndly, 1933, Leonora Margaret, who *d* 1996 (having *m* 2ndly, 1946, Col Francis Parker Tompkins, US Army, who *d* 1968), el da of HH the late Rajah (Sir Charles Vyner Brooke) of Sarawak, GCMG (V Esher); *d* 1939; *s* by his son (3) KENNETH JAMES WILLIAM, 3rd Earl, *b* 1917; 1939-45 War with 12th Lancers in France, and Maj 27th Lancers in Central Mediterranean; Life Pres Inchcape plc (Exec Chm 1958-82), Chm Inchcape Family Investments Ltd, sometimes Dir BAII, Burmah Oil Co, British Petroleum, and Standard Chartered Bank plc; Pres Royal Soc for India, Pakistan and Ceylon, and Gen Council of British Shipping: *m* 1st, 1941 (*m diss* 1954), Aline Thorn, da of Sir Richard Arthur Pease, 2nd Bt (*cr* 1920), and widow of Patrick Claude Hannay, FO AAF; 2ndly, 1965, Caroline Cholmeley, el da of Cholmeley Harrison, of Emo Court, co Leix; *d* 1994; *s* by his eldest son (3) KENNETH PETER LYLE, 4th Earl and present peer, also Baron Inchcape, Viscount Inchcape, and Viscount Glenapp.

INCHIQUIN, BARON (O'Brien) (Baron I 1543, Bt I 1686)

LAMH·LAIDIR·AN·UACHTAR

VIGVEVR   DE·DESSVS

Strength from above

CONOR MYLES JOHN O'BRIEN, 18th Baron, 10th Baronet, and Chief of the Name; *b* 17 July 1943; *s* 1982; *ed* Eton; late Capt 14th/20th King's Hussars: *m* 1988, Helen O'Farrell, da of Gerald Fitzgerald O'Farrell, of Curry Lodge, Longford, co Longford, and has issue.

Arms – Quarterly: 1st and 4th, gules, three lions passant guardant in pale; per pale or and argent; 2nd, argent, three piles meeting in point issuing from the chief gules; 3rd, or, a pheon azure. **Crest** – Issuing from a cloud an arm embowed, brandishing a sword argent, pommel and hilt or. **Supporters** – Two lions guardant per fesse or and argent.
Residence – Thomond House, Dromoland, co Clare.

DAUGHTERS LIVING

Hon Slaney Alexandra Anne, *b* 1989.
Hon Lucia Josephine Mary, *b* 1991.

SISTER LIVING

Fiona Jane, *b* 1941: *m* 1965, Romano Louis Obert de Thieusies (2nd son of late Vicomte Alain Martel Marie Joseph Ghislain Obert de Thieusies), of 47 Chiddingstone St, SW6 3TQ, and Chateau de Thoricourt, Thoricourt, Hainaut, Belgium, and has issue living, Patrick Conor Alain, *b* 1968, — Isabelle Stephanie, *b* 1966, — Sophie Patricia, *b* 1972.

DAUGHTERS LIVING OF SIXTEENTH BARON

Hon Deirdre Jane Frances, *b* 1924: *m* 1954, Horace Beecher Chapin, MD, who *d* 1992. *Residence* – Mizzentop No 47, Harbour Rd, Warwick WK06, Bermuda.
Hon Grania Rachel, *b* 1928: was Social Sec to British Ambassador to Peru 1958-60, and to British Ambassador to Japan 1954-57 and Spain 1952: *m* 1973, Hugh William Lindsay Weir, of Ballinakella Lodge, Whitegate, co Clare.

MOTHER LIVING

Josephine Reine (5 Blenkarne Rd, SW11 6HZ), da of late Joseph Eugene Bembaron, of The Old House, Westcott, Surrey: *m* 1939, Hon Fionn Myles Maryons O'Brien, who *d* 1977, 3rd son of 15th Baron Inchiquin.

WIDOW LIVING OF SEVENTEENTH BARON

VERA MAUD (*Vera, Baroness Inchiquin*) (Hanway Lodge, Richards Castle, Ludlow, Shropshire), da of late Rev Clifton Samuel Winter: *m* 1945, Maj the 17th Baron, who *d* 1982.

COLLATERAL BRANCHES LIVING

Branches from younger sons of 14th Baron

Issue of Lieut-Col Hon Murrough O'Brien, DSO, MVO, 2nd son of 14th Baron, *b* 1866, *d* 1934: *m* 1906, Marguerite, who *d* 1958, da of William Lewis, of New York:—
MURROUGH RICHARD, *b* 25 May 1910; *ed* Eton, and at Balliol Coll, Oxford; sometime Major Irish Guards; 1939-45 War: *m* 1st, 1942, Irene Clarice (formerly wife of (i) the 10th Marquess of Queensberry, and (ii) Sir James Hamet Dunn, 1st Bt (*cr* 1921), who *d* 1977), da of H. W. Richards, of Regent's Park, NW1; 2ndly, 1952, Joan, da of Charles Pierre Jenkinson, and widow of Capt Woolf Barnato, and has issue living, (by 2nd *m*) Conor John Anthony, *b* 1952; *ed* Eton: *m* 1982, Vivian, yr da of Col Adrian Rouse, of 17 Alexander Sq, SW3, and has issue living, Fionn Murrough *b* 1987, Slaney Victoria *b* 1989, — Melissa Jane *b* 1956: *m* 1st, 1979, Nicholas Simunek, of New York, USA; 2ndly, 19—, Jorge de Paiva Raposo, Manor Farmhouse, Upper Wootton, Basingstoke, Hants, and has issue living (by 2nd *m*), Charles Murrough Jorge *b* 1996, Alessandra Belinda *b* 1991. *Residences* – Shelleys House, Wick Lane, Englefield Green, Surrey TW20 0XE; 34 Connaught Sq, W2. *Club* – White's. —— Edward Cecil, OBE (The Old Barn, 1 Station Rd, Docking, Norfolk PE31 8LS), *b* 1915; *ed* Eton; sometime Capt Irish Gds, and Maj Parachute Regt; OBE (Civil) 1959: *m* 1st, 1943 (*m diss* 1968), Elizabeth Margaret, who *d* 1998, da of late Col Sir Henry William Henry Dyke Acland, 3rd Bt (*cr* 1890), MC, AFC, TD: 2ndly, 1991, Phyllis Elsie Margaret, who *d* 1994, da of Phillip Heber-Jones, and formerly wife of Derek Chudleigh, and has issue living (by 1st *m*), Lucia Jane, *b* 1947: *m* 1973, David Lawrence Gilbert Smith, of 68 Goldington Av, Bedford, and has issue living, Caroline Teresa Slaney *b* 1976, Isabel Helen *b* 1980, — Emily Teresa O'BRIEN (6 Beaufort House, Beaufort St, SW3 5AD), *b* 1952; has resumed her maiden name: *m* 1978 (*m diss* 1998), Stephen Anson, and has issue living, Nicholas Phaedrig Charles *b* 1989.

Granddaughters of late Capt Hon Henry Barnaby O'Brien (*infra*):—

Issue of late Desmond Barnaby O'Brien, b 1926, d 1969: m 1955, Cherry Angela Mary, who d 1992, yr da of late Lt-Col (Frank) James (Wriothesley) Seely (see Seely Bt, colls):—
Karen, b 1956: m 1978, Paul William Cowan, of The Old Farmhouse, Weald, Bampton, Oxon, and has issue living, Jonathan, b 1981, — Lara Frances, b 1979, — Nina Elizabeth, b 1980, — Molly, b 1988. ——— Sara Jane, b 1961: m 1986, Simon Cellan-Jones, of 8 Priory Grove, SW8, and has issue living, Daniel, b 1996, — Kate, b 1988.

Issue of late Capt Hon Henry Barnaby O'Brien, 5th son of 14th Baron, b 1887, d 1969: m 1st, 1925, Lady Helen Baillie-Hamilton, OBE, who d 1959, sister of 12th Earl of Haddington; 2ndly, 1964, Edith Lawrie, who d 1996, widow of T. M. Steele:—
(By 1st m) Michael George, b 1928; late Irish Guards: m 1955, Susan Mary Matilda, da of late Wing-Cdr Robert Cevil Talbot Speir, OBE, RAF, and has issue living, Peter Thomond, b 1961, — John Michael, b 1964, — Gillian Ursula Helen, b 1956, — Rebecca, b 1957.

Branch from 3rd son of 13th Baron

Grandchildren of late Hon William Henry Ernest Robert Turlough O'Brien, 3rd son of 13th Baron:—
Issue of late Turlough George Henry O'Brien, b 1907, d 1976: m 1939 (m diss 1966), Catherine, da of late Dr John Watt Senter, of Edinburgh:—
Patrick Brian (via Marco Aurelio 42, Flat 15, Rome, Italy), b 1943. ——— Diana, b 1941: m 1961, Ronald Anthony Ostwald, of 8 Cholmeley Park, Highgate, N6, and has issue living, Christian Mark Sebastian, b 1962; has issue (by Joanna Lynn Kelly), Samuel Thomas b 1996, Kitty Annabel Kelly b 1993, (by Joanne Lilian Brown), Lewis George b 1997, — Cassie Kate Louise, b 1978.

Branches from younger brothers of 13th Baron

Grandchildren of late William Dermod O'Brien (infra):—
Issue of late Brendan Edward O'Brien, MD, FRCPI, b 1903, d 1984: m 1936, Pamela Kathleen Helen, RHA, Pres of Water Colour Soc of Ireland, who d 1982, only da of Maj H. G. Wilmer, IA:—
Dermod Wilmer (Glenside, Lee Rd, Carrigohane, co Cork), b 1941; ed Dublin Univ (BA, BAI): m 1966, Rosalind, da of Robert G. Service, of Helensburgh, and has issue living, Jeremy William, b 1971, — Lucia Jane, b 1969, — Charlotte Elizabeth, b 1974. ——— Anthony Derek, b 1947; ed Haileybury, and Dublin Univ (BA): m 1974, Najma Madhavjee, and has issue living, Cormac Brendan, b 1979, — Murrough Idries, b 1983, — Zahara Grace, b 1976.

Issue of late Maj David Lucius O'Brien, MRCVS, b 1904, d 1988: m 1st, 1929 (m diss 1946), Mary Katharine Drummond, who d 1987, da of Rt Hon Sir Arthur Drummond Ramsay-Steel-Maitland, 1st Bt (ext); 2ndly, 1954, Shirley (Scottsdale, Tasmania), da of late C. P. Hurford, of Worcester Park, Surrey:—
(By 1st m) Michael David, b 1930. Residence – Addlestead Farm, Headley, Epson, Surrey. ——— Lucia Margaret, b 1932. Residence – 84 Colehill Lane, SW6. ——— (By 2nd m) Tasman David, b 1955: m 1986, Brenda Goodwin, and has issue living, Kirby, b 1986, — Conor Michael, b 1988. Residence – 13 Harrison Close, Whitfield Park, Cairns 4870, N Queensland, Australia. ——— Donough William, b 1956. Address – c/o Daylesford, Victoria, Australia.

Grandchildren of late Edward William O'Brien, JP, DL, of Cahirmoyle, co Limerick, eldest son of William Smith O'Brien, MP, (infra):—
Issue of late William Dermod O'Brien, b 1865, d 1945: m 1902, Mabel Emmeline, who d 1942, da of late Sir Philip Crampton Smyly, MD (B Plunket):—
(Horace) Donough, AM, b 1911; ed Dublin Univ (MB and BCh 1934); FRCSI 1939; FRACS 1958; FACRM; Lt-Col (ret) RAMC; AM 1976: m 1st, 1941 (m diss 1950), Pamela Charlotte, da of Capt Barrington Goodbody; 2ndly, 1950, Lucy Ann Stafford, da of T. E. Stafford O'Brien, and has issue living, (by 2nd m) Bartholemew Brendan (28 Wheaton Rd, Stepney, Adelaide 5069, S Australia), b 1953; RGN, BN, PhD, MRCNA: m 1981, Lauri Therese, da of late James Cadzow, and has issue living, David Nicholas b 1990, Alice Louise b 1986, — Alexander Kennedy, b 1955: m 1985 (m diss 1992), Lynley Keynes, — (by 1st m) Caroline Phyllis Ann, b 1942: m 1982, Arthur James Cox (14409 Brookmead Drive, Germantown, Maryland 20874, USA), son of late J. Cox, of Pulaski, Virgina, USA. ——— Mary Elinor, b 1907; BA: m 1934, Bruce Martin Flegg, ARIBA, late Sqdn-Ldr RAF, and has issue living, Aubrey Martin, b 1938; BA, PhD: m 1966, Jennifer Condell, MLitt, of Dublin, and has issue living, Nigel Patrick Martin b 1970, Eleanor Minta b 1967, — Katharine Elinor, b 1934; ARCM: m 1964, N. Dimitriakopoulos, of Thessaloniki, Greece. Residence – St Nicholas House, Rostrevor Rd, Rathgar, co Dublin. ——— Rosaleen Brigid, b 1909; a Roy Hibernian Academician: m 1936, Andrew Ganly, MA, FFD, RCSI, BDentSc, who d 1982, and has issue living, Eoghan Timothy, b 1938: m 1966, Vera Behan, and has issue living, Brian b 1967, — Helen Phillida, b 1939: m 1963, Henry Brian Smith, MB, and has issue living, Conor Melville b 1967, Desmond Brian b 1978, Kathleen Brigid b 1970. Residence – 5A Laurel Hill, Glenageary Rd, Dun Laoghaire, co Dublin.

Grandchildren of late Very Rev Lucius Henry O'Brien, son of William Smith O'Brien, MP, brother of 13th Baron:—
Issue of late Donough Richard O'Brien, b 1876, d 1938: m 1914, Cecilia Maud, who d 1981, da of Rev Frederick Neville Carus-Wilson, of Glenfield, Bath:—
Geraldine Mary, b 1922: m 1948, David Coote Hely-Hutchinson, who d 1994, and has issue (see E Donoughmore, colls). Residence – Parteenalax, Limerick.

Issue of late Charles Murrough O'Brien, b 1877, d 1939: m 1903, Agnes Purdon, who d 1970, da of James Wilson, formerly of McLeod, Alberta, Canada:—
†Donough Robert Murrough, b 1910: m 1940, Rita Denny, da of late Rev William Musson, of Buckingham, and d 1991, leaving issue, Murrough (230 Hector Rd, RR3, Victoria, BC V8X 3X1), b 1947: m 1968, Patricia Arlene, da of George C. Ellison, of N Vancouver, — Francine Denny O'BRIEN, b 1942; has resumed her maiden name: m 1969 (m diss 1991), Donald Vincent Kissinger, and has issue living, Simon Raven John b 1972, Sarah Tsu Emily O'BRIEN (has assumed the surname of O'Brien) b 1974. ——— Eileen Moira Agnes, b 1912: m 1939, Dan Stephenson Heelas, who d 1985, of 79, 5550 Langley By-Pass, Langley, BC V3A 7Z3, and has issue living, Moira Jessica, b 1942: m 1963, Henry Stephens, of 7902

Glover Rd, RR6 Langley, BC, V3A 4P9, and has issue living, Sheryl Lynn *b* 1963: *m* 1984, Guy Anthony Widiner (and has issue living, Brett Stephen *b* 1990, Dylan Daniel *b* 1994), Yvonne Doreen *b* 1967, — Joan Zenda, *b* 1944: *m* 1973, Lynden Sharman, and has issue living, Paul Richard *b* 1977, Keith Stephenson *b* 1980.

Grandson of late Charles Murrough O'Brien (*b* 1849), son of late William Smith O'Brien MP (ante):—
Issue of late Brian O'Brien, MD, *b* 1872, *d* 1915: *m* 1903, Mary Henrietta, who *d* 1968, da of late Maurice Charles Hime, JP, LLD, BL, of Cluain Fóis, Buncrana, co Donegal:—
Charles Murrough, *b* 1903; *ed* Trin Coll, Dublin (MB and BCh 1928): *m* 1930, Elizabeth Joyce, who *d* 1988, da of late Ven Gerald W. Peacocke, Archdeacon of Kildare, and has issue living, Brian Murrough Fergus (Rathkeale Cottage, Castlematrix, Rathkeale, co Limerick; Reform and Kildare St Clubs), *b* 1931; *ed* Bedford Sch, and at Univ Coll, Oxford (MA); Bar Lincoln's Inn 1955, — David Donough (Jordan House, Newton Lane, Braybrooke, Northants), *b* 1933: *m* 1962, Carole June Walters, and has issue living, Nicholas Charles Donough, *b* 1963: *m* 1993, Mrs Kathryn Ann Hutchins (*neé* Randle), and has issue living, Anastasia Grace Ailne *b* 1993, Seamus Timothy Lucius, *b* 1965.

Grandchildren of late Brian O'Brien, MD (ante):—
Issue of late Brian O'Brien, MD, *b* 1908, *d* 1968: *m* 1938, Dorothea, who *d* 1980, da of John F. A. Simms, of Combermore, Lifford:—
Brian Dermod, *b* 1942; *ed* Univ of Alberta, Edmonton, and Queen's Univ, Kingston (BSc, MD, LMCC); FRCPC 1978, served RCAF Medical Branch 1959-89 (ret as Col): *m* 1962, Barbara Eileen, da of W/Cmdr John F. Brennagh, of Ottawa, Ont, and has issue living, Brian David, *b* 1963: *m* 1990, Susan Anne, da of Francis Martin, of Halifax, and has issue living, Christopher Keaton *b* 1989, Eliot Mary Brennagh *b* 1992, — Patrick John, *b* 1965: *m* 1988, Karen Helen, da of John Lyons, of Calgary, Alberta, — Christopher Michael, *b* 1969: *m* 1994, Sheila Isobel, da of Dr Robert Loughrey, of Brockville, Ontario, — Katherine Jennifer Eileen, *b* 1971. *Residence* – 5863 Macleod Drive, Halifax, NS, Canada B3H 1C6. ▬▬ George Lucius (95 Empress Ave, North York, Ontario, Canada M2N 3T5), *b* 1944; *ed* Queen's Univ, Kingston (MSc), and Dartmouth Coll, New Hampshire (AM, PhD): *m* 1976, Elizabeth Frances, da of Thomas Sharpless Ely, of Rochester, NY, and has issue living, William Thomas, *b* 1982, — Margaret Clare, *b* 1984, — Katherine Elizabeth, *b* 1987. ▬▬ Deirdre O'BRIEN, *b* 1940; *ed* Ottawa Univ (BSc, MHA); Reg N; resumed the surname of O'Brien 19—: *m* 1963 (*m diss* 1975), James Moxley Shearer, BSc, and has issue living, James O'Brien, *b* 1965, — George Brodie, *b* 1969, — Margaret Kathleen, *b* 1967, — Joan Hilary, *b* 1968.

Grandchildren of late Robert Vere O'Brien, yr son of late Hon Robert O'Brien (raised to the rank of a Baron's son by R Licence 1862), brother of 13th Baron:—
Issue of late Hugh Murrough Vere O'Brien, MC, *b* 1887, *d* 1955: *m* 1915, his 2nd cousin, Margaret Ernestine, who *d* 1968, da of late Edward William O'Brien (ante):—
Murrogh Vere, *b* 1919; *ed* Dublin Univ (BAI 1940), and at Roy Sch of Mines, London (ARSM 1947); BSc London 1947; Dir Geological Survey of Ireland 1952-64; Fell Inst of Mining and Metallurgy 1974, and Hon Fell 1987: *m* 1945, Zsuzsánna Eva Szeréna, da of Károly Károlyi, of Budapest, Hungary, and has had issue, Colm Murrogh Vere; *b* 1947; *ed* Dublin Univ; represented Ireland at fencing in Olympic Games Mexico 1968: *d* 1985, in Miami, Florida, — Hugh Stephen Vere (10 Dungar Terr, Dun Laoghaire, co Dublin), *b* 1948; *ed* Univ Coll, Dublin; architect: *m* 1983, Alison Ann Cooke, and has issue living, Robert Murrogh Vere *b* 1991, Donough Patrick Vere *b* 1992, Catherine Lucy Bebhinn *b* 1987, — Sylvia Caroline Piroska, *b* 1946; *ed* Dublin Univ (BA), and Simon Fraser Univ (MSc); botanist: *m* 1971 Julian Douglas Reynolds, Fell and Sr Lecturer in Biology at TCD, of 115 Weirview Drive, Stillorgan, co Dublin, and has issue living, Conor Charles O'Brien *b* 1976, Owen Ralph Douglas *b* 1981, Elinor Florence Dirny *b* 1978, — Iseult Anne, *b* 1952: *m* 1981, Bryan Fergus Murphy, of Thatch House, Adare, co Limerick, and has issue living, Hugh Patrick Fergus *b* 1982, Slany Elizabeth *b* 1985, — Charlotte Elinor, *b* 1962; *ed* Dublin Univ (BA 1984), and Imperial Coll Lond (MSc 1985). *Residences* – Monare, Foynes, co Limerick; 69 The Elms, Mt Merrion Av, Blackrock, Co Dublin. ▬▬ Elinor Vere (62 Carroll House, Lancaster Gate, W2), *b* 1918: *m* 1956, Reginald Wiltshire, who *d* 1968.

Granddaughters of late Edward O'Brien, el son of Rev Hon Henry O'Brien (raised to the rank of a Baron's son by R Licence 1862), yst brother of 13th Baron:—
Issue of late Major Murrough Charles O'Brien, MD, JP, Canadian Army Med Corps, *b* 1868, *d* 1955: *m* 1901, Margaret Eleanor Barber, who *d* 1958:—
Muriel Oclanis, *b* 1904: *m* 1932, Hamilton Stewart McKee.

Issue of late Lieut-Col Aubrey John O'Brien, CIE, CBE, *b* 1870, *d* 1930: *m* 1906, Annie Winifred, who *d* 1936, da of late James D'Arcy, of Kew:—
Moira Winifred Oclanis, *b* 1912: *m* 1st, 1932, John Michael Orpen Barstow, who *d* 1976; 2ndly, 1990, Capt George Baillie Barstow, RN, who *d* 1991, and has issue living (by 1st *m*), Elizabeth Catharine Oclanis, *b* 1933: *m* 1959, Charles Richard Cubitt Bevis, of 15 Abbey Rd, Sheringham, Norfolk, and has issue living, Elizabeth Margaret Moira *b* 1960: *m* 1982, Julian Bryan Stevens (and has issue living, Frederick *b* 1988, Harriet *b* 1985, Olivia *b* 1989), Maria Catharine Oclanis *b* 1962: *m* 1995, Stephen James Ariam McCoy, Alexandra Anne Cecilia *b* 1963: *m* 1986, Steven Andrew Carl White (and has issue living, Henry *b* 1991, Felicity *b* 1989, Imogen *b* 1994), Lucinda Mary Sophia *b* 1965: *m* 1986, Jonathan David Walter Starling (and has issue living, Anna *b* 1986, Sophia *b* 1988), Selena Penelope Beatrice *b* 1969, Xanthe Frances Henrietta *b* 1972, — Anne Moira Olivia (74 Clarence Rd, St Albans, Herts), *b* 1940: *m* 1st, 1965, Derek Landale Christie, who *d* 1974; 2ndly, 1977, Roger Beament, and has issue living, (by 1st *m*) John Michael Landale *b* 1966: *m* 1993, Karen, da of Michael Heaney (and has issue living, Rachel Helen Olivia *b* 1995, Caitlin Francesca Rose *b* 1998), Edward Hugh Landale *b* 1968: *m* 1995, Sarah, da of John McClay (and has issue living, Thomas Edward Hugh *b* 1996), Annabella Moira Orpen *b* 1969, (by 2nd *m*) Emily Catharine Olivia *b* 1978, — Mary Geraldine Sheila, *b* 1943: *m* 1970, Graham McGregor Finch, who *d* 1995, of 38 Sion Hill, Bath, Avon, and has issue living, Henrietta Lucy Anne *b* 1975; *ed* Oxford Univ, Cressida Mary Frances *b* 1979; *ed* Oxford Univ, — Henrietta Penelope, *b* 1945: *m* 1968, Nicholas Frank Killeen Rose, of 23 All Saints Villas Rd, Cheltenham, Glos, and has issue living, Thomas Michael Orpen *b* 1978, Beatrice Caroline Ellen *b* 1974, — Brigid Evelyn Cecilia, *b* 1947: *m* 1973, Charles Michael Brett, of St Margaret's, St Michael's Rd, Winchester, Hants, and has issue living, Aubrey Francis Patrick *b* 1974, Caroline Moira Cecilia *b* 1977. *Residence* – Butt House, Painswick, Glos. ▬▬ Winifred Mary Sheila, *b* 1918; is Sister Sheila, Community of St John Baptist. *Address* – Convent of St John Baptist, Hatch Lane, Windsor, Berks.

Grandchildren of late Lt-Col Aubrey John O'Brien, CIE, CBE (ante):—
Issue of late Maj Turlough Aubrey O'Brien, CBE, RA, *b* 1907, *d* 1997: *m* 1945, Phyllis Mary, who *d* 1986, twin da of late Edward Grosvenor Tew (B Hawke):—

Teige Henry Patrick (10 Fairlawn Grove, W4 5EH), *b* 1949: *m* 1976, Sarah Catherine, da of Henry Wilson, and has issue living, Grania Catherine, *b* 1982, — Finola Clare, *b* 1985. —— (Brian Edward) Nicholas (Hawthorn Cottage, Milford, Surrey GU8 5BH), *b* 1951: *m* 1992, Miranda Penelope Gillian, da of late Maj Jack Warren Pollock, RA (*see* Pollock, Bt, colls). —— Corinna Moira (2 Kingswood Rd, SW19), *b* 1955: *m* 1993, Christopher Edge, son of Bruce Edge.

Issue of late Edward Donough O'Brien, *b* 1909, *d* 1979: *m* 1st, 1936, Sylvia Inchbold, who *d* 1950, da of Court Denny, of 30 Addison Rd, W14; 2ndly, 1952, Leonora Thayne, who *d* 1999, el da of Manning Leonard Railton:—
(By 1st *m*) Donough Antony (66 Clonmel Rd, SW6), *b* 1939: *m* 1st, 1969, Clare, da of Leonard Read; 2ndly, 1980, Philippa, da of Maj-Gen Mervyn Janes, CB, MBE; 3rdly, 1990, Elizabeth, da of Lieut Gen Sir John Guise Cowley, GC, KBE, CB, and has issue living (by 1st *m*) Murrough, *b* 1971, — (by 2nd *m*) Edmond Mahon, *b* 1981. —— Natalie Deirdre Teresa, *b* 1941: *m* 1964, Roger Henry Brough Whittaker, of Cubberley House, Ross-on-Wye, Herefords, son of late Edward Whittaker, of Nairobi, and has two sons and three das, (Edward) Guy, *b* 1974, — Alexander Michael, *b* 1978, — Emily Clare, *b* 1968: *m* 1991, Stewart Malcolm Kennedy, son of late S/Ldr Ewen Kennedy, — Lauren Marie, *b* 1970, — Jessica Jane, *b* 1973. —— Geraldine Moira, *b* 1945: *m* 1968, Rolfe Elholm, of Norway, and *d* 1987, leaving issue, Astri, *b* 1971. —— (By 2nd *m*) Fionn Murrough Manning (Madrid), *b* 1953: *m* 1st, 1973, Carole Ann, da of William Whitlock; 2ndly, 1996, Monica Van Der Eg, and has issue living (by 1st *m*), Zoe, *b* 1973, (by 2nd *m*), Murrough Marinus Edward *b* 1997. —— Lucius Edward (22 Henrick Av, SW12), *b* 1957: *m* 1986, Caroline Veronica Mary, da of Maj Hywel Colwyn Phillips, of Mostyn, Clwyd, and has issue living, Caroline Louisa Maire, *b* 1992, — Olivia Alison Clare, *b* 1993.

Granddaughter of late Lt-Col Henry Eoghan O'Brien, DSO, only son of Murrough John O'Brien, 2nd son of Rev Hon Henry O'Brien (ante):—
Issue of late Lieut-Cmdr Brian Eoghan O'Brien, RN, *b* 1907; *ka* 1940: *m* 1936, Elizabeth (who *m* 2ndly, 1949, P. Dennis, who *d* 1983), da of Stuart Séguin Strahan, MB, BCh, of Hong Kong:—
Olivia Fiona, *b* 1938: *m* 1960, Sebastian Robinson, of 22 Athole Gdns, Glasgow, W2, and has issue living, James Lucius O'Brien, *b* 1962, — Amanda Mary Victoria, *b* 1961: *m* 1983, Martyn D. Smith.

Descendants of late Donough O'Brien (*d* 1797), yr son of Sir Edward O'Brien, 2nd Bt.

PREDECESSORS – Turlogh, King of Munster and principal King of Ireland, had with other issue, Dermot, King of Munster, from whom descended Conor O'Brien, inaugurated King of Thomond 1528; *d* 1540, when his son Donough was set aside, the principality being usurped by his brother **(1)** MURROUGH O'Brien, PC, who surrendered his royalty to Henry VIII, and was *cr* 1543 *Earl of Thomond* (peerage of Ireland), with remainder to his nephew Donough, and *Baron Inchiquin* (peerage of Ireland) to him and the heirs male of his body; *s* in the Barony by his son **(2)** DERMOT, 2nd Baron; *d* 1557; *s* by his son **(3)** MURROUGH, 3rd Baron; *d* 1573; *s* by his son **(4)** MURROUGH, 4th Baron: *d* 1597; *s* by his son **(5)** DERMOT, 5th Baron; *d* 1624; *s* by his son **(6)** MURROUGH, 6th Baron; a military officer of great renown; *cr Earl of Inchiquin* (peerage of Ireland) 1654; *d* 1674; *s* by his son **(7)** WILLIAM, 2nd Earl; Gov of Jamaica; *d* 1691; *s* by his son **(8)** WILLIAM, 3rd Earl; *d* 1719; *s* by his son **(9)** WILLIAM, 4th Earl; *d* 1777; *s* by his nephew and son-in-law **(10)** MURROUGH, KP, 5th Earl son of the Hon James, MP, 3rd son of 3rd Earl; *cr Marquess of Thomond* (peerage of Ireland), with remainder to the issue male of his brother Edward, and *Baron Thomond*, of Taplow, co Bucks (peerage of United Kingdom) 1801; *d* 1808, when the Barony of Thomond expired and the Marquessate and Barony of Inchiquin devolved upon his nephew **(11)** WILLIAM, KP, 2nd Marquess, 3rd son of Hon Edward, 2nd brother of 2nd Earl; a Representative Peer; *cr Baron Tadcaster*, of Tadcaster, co York (peerage of United Kingdom) 1826; *d* 1846, when the barony of Tadcaster expired and the Irish peerages devolved upon his brother **(12)** JAMES, GCH, 3rd Marquess; an Adm; *d* 1855, when all the titles became extinct except the Barony of Inchiquin, which descended to **(13)** LUCIUS O'Brien, 13th Baron and 5th Bart (see note * infra); *b* 1800; sat as MP for co Clare (C) 1826-30 and 1847-52; a Representative Peer, and Lord-Lieut of Clare: *m* 1st, 1837, Mary, who *d* 1849, el da of William Fitzgerald; 2ndly, 1854, Louisa, da of Major James Finucane, of Ennistymon House, Clare; *d* 1872; *s* by his son **(14)** EDWARD DONOUGH, 14th Baron, KP, *b* 1839; a Representative Peer, and Lieut for co Clare: *m* 1st, 1862, Hon Emily Holmes à Court, who *d* 1868, da of 2nd Baron Heytesbury; 2ndly, 1874, Hon Ellen Harriet White, who *d* 1913, da of 2nd Baron Annaly; *d* 1900; *s* by his son **(15)** LUCIUS WILLIAM, 5th Baron; *b* 1864; a Representative Peer for Ireland: *m* 1896, Ethel Jane, who *d* 1940, el da and co-heiress of late Johnston J. Foster, of Moor Park, Ludlow; *d* 1929; *s* by his el son **(16)** DONOUGH EDWARD FOSTER, 16th Baron; *b* 1897; Capt Rifle Bde: *m* 1921, Hon Anne Molyneux Thesiger, who *d* 1973, da of 1st Viscount Chelmsford; *d* 1968; *s* by his brother **(17)** PHAEDRIG LUCIUS AMBROSE, 17th Baron, *b* 1900, Maj Rifle Bde, Colonial Service Geological Survey, 1939-45 War in Somalia, Abyssinia and Madagascar, attached E African Intelligence Corps (wounded, despatches): *m* 1945, Vera Maud, da of late Rev Clifton Samuel Winter; *d* 1982; *s* by his nephew **(18)** CONOR MYLES JOHN, only son of late Hon Fionn Myles Maryons O'Brien, yst son of 15th Baron, 18th Baron and present peer.

* **(1)** DONOUGH O'Brien, PC and MP for co Clare, was *cr* a *Baronet* 1686; *d* 1717; *s* by his grandson **(2)** *Sir* EDWARD, 2nd Bt; was MP for Clare; *d* 1765; *s* by his son **(3)** *Sir* LUCIUS, PC, 3rd Bt, MP for co Clare; *d* 1795; *s* by his son **(4)** *Sir* EDWARD, 4th Bt, MP for Ennis and co Clare; *d* 1837; *s* by his son **(5)** *Sir* LUCIUS, 5th Bt, who *s* as 13th Baron Inchiquin (ante).

INCHYRA, BARON (Millar) (Baron UK 1962)

ROBERT CHARLES RENEKE HOYER MILLAR, 2nd Baron; *b* 4 April 1935; *s* 1989; *ed* Eton, and New Coll, Oxford; Chm NABC since 1994; late Scots Guards; Member Queen's Body Guard for Scotland (Royal Company of Archers): *m* 1961, Fiona Mary, da of late Edmund Charles Reginald Sheffield (*see* Sheffield, Bt, colls), and has issue.

𝕬rms – Quarterly: 1st, or, a cross moline azure and base barry undy gules and vert, on a chief of the third a lozenge of the first between two spur-revels also of the first, *Millar*, 2nd, per bend argent and vert a lion passant gules, *Hoyer*, 3rd Azure, a chevron argent between two spur-revels in chief and a demi-moon reversed or, *van Swinderen*; 4th, azure, a cross argent cantoned between four roses or, *de Marees*. 𝕮rest – A cubit arm, the hand erect and in the act of blessing proper. 𝕾upporters – Two blackcock proper.
Residence – Rookley Manor, King's Somborne, Stockbridge, Hants SO20 6QX. *Clubs* – White's and Pratt's.

SON LIVING

Hon CHRISTIAN JAMES CHARLES HOYER, *b* 12 Aug 1962; *ed* Eton, and Edinburgh Univ: *m* 1992, Caroline J., da of late Robin Swan, of Lower Wield, Hants, and has issue living, Jake, *b* 10 July 1996, — Eleanor Mary, *b* 1994. *Residence* – 29 Caithness Rd, W14 0JA.

DAUGHTERS LIVING

Hon Henrietta Julia Hoyer, *b* 1964: *m* 1988, Carlos Manuel Villanueva Brandt, son of late Manuel Villanueva, of Caracas, Venezuela, and has issue living, Alfredo Henrique, *b* 1993, — Mateo Carlos, *b* 1996. *Residence* – 34 Guildford Rd, SW8 2BX.
Hon Louisa Mary Hoyer, *b* 1968: *m* 1997, Jaime Parladé, son of Francisco Parladé, of Banahavis, Malagá, Spain.

BROTHER LIVING

Hon Alastair James Harold Hoyer, *b* 1936; *ed* Eton; late Scots Guards; Sec Pilgrim Trust 1980-96: *m* 1974, Virginia Margaret Diana, da of late William Perine Macauley, of Ballyward House, Manor Kilbride, co Wicklow (*see* V Camrose, 1995 Edn), and has issue living, Mark Christian Frederick, *b* 1975, — Martha Harriet Alice, *b* 1976. *Residence* – 16 Pembridge Villas, W11.

SISTERS LIVING AND DECEASED

Hon Elizabeth Anne Hoyer, *b* 1933: *m* 1965, William Euan Wallace, who *d* 1977 (*see* E Lytton, 1964 Edn), and *d* 1990.
Hon Annabel Alice Hoyer, LVO, *b* 1943; a Lady in Waiting to HRH Princess Margaret, Countess of Snowdon 1971-75, an Extra Lady in Waiting 1975-92, since when a Lady in Waiting; LVO 1986: *m* 1973, Christopher James Bovill Whitehead, of 5 Vicarage Gdns, W8, and has issue living, Robert William Bovill, *b* 1977, — (Christina) Daisy Elizabeth, *b* 1975.

WIDOW LIVING OF FIRST BARON

ELIZABETH (*Dowager Baroness Inchyra*), da of late Jonkheer Reneke de Marees van Swinderen, sometime Netherlands Min in London: *m* 1931, the 1st Baron Inchyra, GCMG, CVO, who *d* 1989. *Residence* – Inchyra House, Glencarse, Perthshire.

PREDECESSOR – **(1)** FREDERICK ROBERT HOYER Millar, GCMG, CVO, son of late Robert Hoyer Millar; *b* 1900, entered Diplo Ser 1923, 1st Sec at Washington 1939, Min Washington 1948, High Commr German Federal Republic 1953-55, Ambassador 1955-56, and Permanent Under-Sec for Foreign Affairs 1957-61, *cr Baron Inchyra*, of St Madoes, co Perth (peerage of UK 1962): *m* 1931, Elizabeth, da of late Jonkheer Reneke de Marees van Swinderen, formerly Netherlands Min in London; *d* 1989; *s* by his elder son **(2)** ROBERT CHARLES RENEKE HOYER, 2nd Baron and present peer.

INGE, BARON (Inge) (Life Baron 1997)

PETER ANTHONY INGE, GCB, son of late Raymond Albert Inge, of Sevenoaks, Kent; b 5 Aug 1935; ed Wrekin Coll, and RMA Sandhurst; DL N Yorks 1994; Hon DCL Newcastle 1995; commn'd Green Howards 1954; served Hong Kong, Malaya, Germany, Libya and N Ireland; ADC to GOC 4 Div 1960-61; Adjt 1st Green Howards 1963-64; Student Staff Coll 1966; MOD 1967-69; Co Cmdr 1st Green Howards 1969-70; Student JSSC 1971; BM 11th Armoured Brigade 1972; Instructor, Staff Coll 1973-74; CO 1st Green Howards 1974-77; Cmdt Jr Div Staff Coll 1977-79; cmd'd 4th Armoured Brigade 1979-81; Chief of Staff, HQ 1st (BR) Corps 1982-83; GOC NE Dist and Cmdr 2nd Infantry Div 1984-86; DGLP (A) MOD 1986-87; cmd'd 1st (BR) Corps 1987-89; C-in-C BAOR and cmd'd NORTHAG 1989-91; Col Cmdt RMP 1987-92; ADC (Gen) to HM The Queen 1991-94; CGS 1992-94; CDS 1994-97; FM 1994; Constable, HM Tower of London since 1996; Col The Green Howards 1982-94; Col Cmdt APTC; Non-Exec Dir Racal Electronics plc since 1997; Pres Army Benevolent Fund since 1998; Dep Chm Historic Royal Palaces; CIMgt 1993; cr KCB 1988, GCB 1992, and Baron Inge, of Richmond, co N Yorks (Life Baron) 1997: m 1960, Letitia Marion Beryl, yr da of late Trevor Thornton-Berry, of Swinithwaite, N Yorks, and has issue.

Arms – Argent on a cross nowy formy throughout gules the limbs voided vert a rose argent barbed and seeded or. Crest – Issuant from a representation of the White Tower of the Tower of London argent a phoenix or enflamed gules. Supporters – Dexter, a ram or armed unguled and gorged with lozenges conjoined; sinister, a lion or gorged with lozenges conjoined gules each supporting a Field Marshal's baton proper the compartment comprising a limestone rock also proper.
Address – Horseguards SW1A 0PW. Clubs – Army and Navy, MCC, Boodle's, Beefsteak.

DAUGHTERS LIVING

Hon Antonia, b 1962.
Hon Verity, b 1965.

Ingestre, Viscount; son of Earl of Shrewsbury.

INGLEBY, VISCOUNT (Peake) (Viscount UK 1956)

MARTIN RAYMOND PEAKE, 2nd Viscount; *b* 31 May 1926; *s* 1966; *ed* Eton, and Trin Coll, Oxford; Bar Inner Temple 1955; late Lt Coldstream Guards; a Co Councillor of N Riding of Yorks 1964-67: *m* 1952, Susan, who *d* 1996, da of Capt Henderson Russell Landale, of Ewell Manor, W Farleigh, Maidstone, and has had issue.

Arms – Sable three crosses pattee argent within an orle of eight fleurs-de-lys and a bordure or. **Crest** – A heart gules between two wings displayed erminois. **Supporters** – On either side a Black-faced Swaledale ram proper holding in the mouth a rose argent barbed seeded slipped and leaved also proper.
Residences – Snilesworth, Northallerton, N Yorks DL6 3QD; Flat 1, 61 Onslow Sq, SW7.

SON DECEASED

†*Hon* Richard Martin Herbert, *b* 7 Aug 1953; *ed* Eton; *d* 19 July 1975.

DAUGHTERS LIVING

Hon Fiona Catherine, *b* 1955: *m* 1977, (Gavin) Tobias Alexander Winterbottom Horton (formerly Winterbottom), of Whorlton Cottage, Swainby, Northallerton, N Yorkshire DL6 3ER, nephew of late Baron Winterbottom (Life Baron), and has issue living, George William Arthur, *b* 1983; *ed* Eton, — Thomas Henry Ralph, *b* 1985; *ed* Winchester, — Alice Emily Rose, *b* 1978, — Violet Constance Lily, *b* 1980.
Hon Sarah Rachel, *b* 1958: *m* 1982, James Felton Somers Hervey-Bathurst, and has issue (*see* Hervey-Bathurst, Bt).
Hon Henrietta Cecilia Imogen, *b* 1961: *m* 1990, James J. P. McNeile, elder son of Rory J. McNeile, of Nonsuch, Bromham, Wilts, and has issue living, Miles, *b* 1994, — Matilda, *b* 1996.
Hon Katherine Emma Charlotte, *b* 1963: *m* 1996, James S. Freeman, elder son of Dr Brian Freeman, of All Hallows Farm, Wimborne St Giles, Dorset, and has issue living, William Martin Spencer, *b* 1997.

SISTERS LIVING (*Daughters of 1st Viscount*)

Hon Iris Irene Adele, LVO, *b* 1923; Lady-in-Waiting to HRH Princess Margaret 1952-62, and an Extra Lady-in-Waiting 1962-63; LVO 1957: *m* 1963, Capt Oliver Payan Dawnay, CVO, who *d* 1988, of Flat 5, 32 Onslow Sq, SW7, and Wexcombe House, nr Marlborough, Wilts, and has issue (*see* V Downe, colls).
Hon Sonia Mary, *b* 1924; served 1939-45 War in WRNS: *m* 1st, 1946 (*m diss* 1958), Lt David George Montagu Hay, GC, RNR (later 12th Marquess of Tweeddale), who *d* 1979; 2ndly, 1966, Maj Michael William Vernon Hammond-Maude, JP, 5th R Inniskilling Dragoon Gds (ret), who *d* 1998, and has issue (by 1st *m*) (*see* M Tweeddale).
Hon Mary Rose, *b* 1940: *m* 1959, Major Everard John Robert March Phillipps de Lisle, DL, Roy Horse Guards (ret), and has issue living, Charles Andrew Everard, *b* 1960; *ed* Eton, and Worcester Coll, Oxford, — Timothy John (63 College Cross, N1 1PT), *b* 1962; *ed* Eton, and Worcester Coll, Oxford: *m* 1991, Amanda Helen, 2nd da of Clive Julian Stanley Barford, of Pibworth House, Aldworth, Berks (*see* B Ashfield, 1985 Edn), and has issue living, Daniel Barford *b* 1994, Laura *b* 1998, — Mary Rosanna, *b* 1968; *ed* St Hugh's Coll, Oxford. *Residences* – Stockerston Hall, Uppingham, Leics LE15 9JD; 4 Hereford Mansions, Hereford Rd, W2 5BA.

UNCLE LIVING (*Not in remainder*)

Edward Charles, *b* 1911; *ed* Eton, and at Trin Coll, Camb; Bar Inner Temple 1939; formerly Flight-Lieut RAF Vol Reserve; unsuccessfully contested Blaydon Div of Durham (*C*) July 1945, and Cleveland Div of N Riding of Yorkshire Feb 1950: *m* 1935, Baroness Santina Maria, who *d* 1999, da of Baron Alfred von Henikstein, of Salzburg, Austria, and has had issue, †Henry Alfred, *b* 1937; *ed* Ampleforth, and Ch Ch, Oxford; *dunm* 1990, — †Robert Alexander, *b* 1938; *ed* Ampleforth, and Trin Coll, Dublin: *m* 1968, Meriel Elizabeth (96 Campden Hill Rd, W8 7AP), da of William Lyon Bowie, of Dublin, *d* 1994, leaving issue, James Robert William *b* 1978; *ed* Charterhouse, and Bristol Univ, Lucy Meriel *b* 1972; *ed* Charterhouse, and London Univ, — Christopher George (34 Bettridge Rd, SW6 3QD), *b* 1951; *ed* Ampleforth, and Queens' Coll, Camb: *m* 1993, Ann Marie, only da of John O'Rourke, of Chelsea, SW3, — Marianna Clotilde, *b* 1939: *m* 1974, Maj Rupert Charles Langham, R Corps of Signals, of 5 Bournside Rd, Cheltenham, Glos GL51 5AL, and has issue living, Jonathan Charles *b* 1975, Caroline Mary *b* 1976, — Christina Maria, *b* 1949: *m* 1974, Dr Peter Francis Leadlay of 17 Clarendon Rd, Cambridge CB2 2BH, and has issue living, Francesca Catherine *b* 1978, Louisa Clare *b* 1980, Serena Imogen Alice *b* 1985. *Residence* – 6 Westberry Court, Grange Rd, Cambridge CB3 9BG. *Clubs* – Brooks's, Travellers'.

COLLATERAL BRANCH LIVING

(*Not in remainder*)

Issue of late Air-Commodore Sir Harald Peake, brother of 1st Viscount, *b* 1899, *d* 1978: *m* 1st, 1933 (*m diss* 1944), Countess Resy de Baillet-Latour, OBE, who *d* 1994, da of Henri, Count Baillet-Latour, of Brussels; 2ndly, 1952, *Dame* Felicity Hyde, DBE, AE, JP (Court Farm, Tackley, Oxon, OX5 3AQ; Flat 5, 35 Bryanston Sq, W1H 7LP), da of late Col Humphrey Watts, OBE, TD, and widow of John Charles Mackenzie Hanbury, P/O RAF:—

(By 1st *m*) David Alphy Edward Raymond (Sezincote, Moreton-in-Marsh, Glos; 15 Ilchester Place, W14), *b* 1934: *m* 1962, Susanna, da of Lt-Cdr Sir Cyril Hugh Kleinwort, RNVR (*see* Kleinwort, Bt, colls), and has issue living, Edward, *b* 1964, — Katharine Sophie, *b* 1965: *m* 1989, Thomas Assheton, and has issue (*see* B Clitheroe). —— (By 2nd *m*) Andrew Charles, *b* 1956: *m* 1990, Suzette Ray, elder da of Sampson Mitchell, DL, of Woore, Shropshire, and has issue living, Alexander Harald, *b* 1993, — George Sampson, *b* 1997.

PREDECESSOR – (1) OSBERT Peake, PC, son of Maj George Herbert Peake; *b* 1897; Under Sec of State for Home Affairs 1939-44, Financial Sec to Treasury 1944-45, Min of National Insurance 1951-55 (and Pensions 1953-55); MP for N Leeds (*C*) 1929-55, and N-E Leeds May to Dec 1955; *cr Viscount Ingleby*, of Snilesworth, N Riding of York (peerage of UK) 1956: *m* 1922, Lady Joan Rachel de Vere Capell, who *d* 1979, da of 7th Earl of Essex; *d* 1966; *s* by his only son (2) MARTIN RAYMOND, 2nd Viscount and present peer.

INGLEWOOD, BARON (Fletcher-Vane) (Baron UK 1964)

(WILLIAM) RICHARD FLETCHER-VANE, 2nd Baron; *b* 31 July 1951; *s* 1989; *ed* Eton, Trin Coll, Camb (MA), and Cumbria Coll of Agriculture and Forestry; DL Cumbria 1993; Bar Lincoln's Inn 1975; FRICS; Member Lake District Special Planning Board 1984-89, and NW Water Authority 1987-89; MEP Cumbria and Lancs North 1989-94; British Conservative Spokesman Legal Affairs European Parl 1989-94, Dep Whip 1992-94, Ch Whip 1994, Lord in Waiting and Conservative Ch Whip European Parl 1994-95, Capt Queen's Body Guard of Yeomen of The Guard (Dep Ch Whip) Jan-July 1995, Under Sec of State National Heritage 1995-97; *m* 1986, Cressida R., photographer, yst da of late Alan Desmond Frederick Pemberton-Pigott, CMG, of Fawe Park, Keswick, and has issue.

Arms – Azure three sinister gauntlets or. Crest – A dexter hand in armour couped at the wrist proper, holding a sword argent pommel and hilt or. Supporters – On either side a roebuck proper collared and pendent from the collar a pheon argent.
Seat – Hutton-in-the-Forest, Penrith, Cumbria CA11 9TH. *Clubs* – Travellers', Pratt's.

SON LIVING

Hon HENRY WILLIAM FREDERICK, *b* 24 Dec 1990.

DAUGHTERS LIVING

Hon Miranda Mary, *b* 1987.
Hon Rosa Katharine, *b* 1989.

BROTHER LIVING

Hon Christopher John, *b* 1953; *ed* Eton, and Trin Coll, Camb (MA); Bar Inner Temple 1976: *m* 1990, Margaret M., da of late Dr Paul Eisenklam, of London, and has issue living, Francis William Paul, *b* 1992, — Arthur Vladek Jocelyn, *b* 1995, — Olivia Evelyn Mary, *b* 1991. *Residences* – 2 Osborne Villas, Jesmond, Newcastle upon Tyne NE2 1JU; Morton House, Morton, Calthwaite, Penrith, Cumbria CA11 9PZ. *Clubs* – Travellers', Northern Counties (Newcastle upon Tyne).

PREDECESSOR – (1) WILLIAM MORGAN Fletcher-Vane, TD, son of late Col Hon William Lyonel Vane (*see* B Barnard colls), *b* 1909, assumed by deed poll 1931 the surname of Fletcher-Vane in lieu of his patronymic, Joint Parl Sec to Min of Pensions and National Insurance 1958-60, and to Min of Agriculture 1960-62, Leader of UK Delegation to World Food Congress (FAO) Washington 1963, MP for Westmorland (*C*) 1945-64, DL Westmorland, *cr Baron Inglewood*, of Hutton in the Forest, co Cumberland (peerage of UK) 1964: *m* 1949, Mary, who *d* 1982, eldest da of late Maj Sir Richard George Proby, 1st Bt, MC; *d* 1989; *s* by his elder son (2) WILLIAM RICHARD, 2nd Baron and present peer.

Ingrams, family name of Baroness Darcy de Knayth.

INGROW, BARON (Taylor) (Life Baron 1983)

JOHN AKED TAYLOR, OBE, TD, son of late Percy Taylor, of Knowle Spring House, Keighley, by his wife Gladys Broster (who *m* 2ndly, Sir (John) Donald Horsfall, 2nd Bt); *b* 15 Aug 1917; *ed* Shrewsbury; served in 1939-45 War (Major, Duke of Wellington's Regt and Royal Signals); Member Keighley Town Council 1946-67; Mayor 1956; Vice Lord-Lieut West Yorkshire 1976-85, Lord Lieut 1985-92; JP (1949) Borough of Keighley; DL West Yorkshire 1971; TD 1951; *cr* OBE (Civil) 1960, Knt 1972, and *Baron Ingrow*, of Keighley, co W Yorks (Life Baron) 1983: *m* 1949, Barbara Mary, who *d* 1998, da of Percy Wright Stirk, of Crestmead, Keighley, and has issue.

Arms – Vert two chevronels between in chief as many garbs of barley and in base a talbot sejant or holding in the mouth an arrow in bend the head downwards proper. Crest – A demi talbot or holding in the mouth an arrow in bend the head downwards proper. Supporters – *Dexter*, a shire horse arg harnessed and bridled proper; *Sinister*, a lion or head and mane gules gorged with a chaplet of roses arg barbed and seeded proper, the compartment comprising a grassy mount growing therefrom on each side a rose arg barbed, seeded and leaved proper between two sprigs of oak fructed also proper.

·SEMPER·FIDELIS·

Residence – Fieldhead, Keighley, West Yorkshire.

DAUGHTERS LIVING

Hon Anne Elizabeth, *b* 1951: *m* 1975, Charles Jonathan Dent, of Ribston Hall, Wetherby, Yorks, elder son of John Harker Dent.
Hon Diana Mary, *b* 1953: *m* 1979, John Patrick Dent, of Clock Farm, Hunsingore, Yorks, yr son of John Harker Dent.

INMAN, BARONY OF (Inman) (Extinct 1979)

DAUGHTER LIVING OF FIRST BARON

Hon Rosemary, *b* 1933: *m* 1st, 1955 (*m diss* 1982), Nickolas Kollitsis, MD, FRCS; 2ndly, 1982, Dr Raphael Eban, FRCP, FRCR, and has issue living (by 1st *m*), Philip Milton, *b* 1957, — Marina Christallene, *b* 1956, — Alexandra, *b* 1961. *Residence* – 59 Northway, NW11 6PD.

WIDOW LIVING OF SON OF FIRST BARON

Judith, da of Albert George James Gibbins, of Mount Pleasant, Stocklane, Langford, Bristol: *m* 1st, 1966, as his 3rd wife, Hon Philip John Inman, who *d* 1968, only son of 1st Baron; 2ndly, 1970, Jonathan Fitzuryan Rhys Wingfield (*see* V Powerscourt, colls). *Residence* – Fayre Court, Fairford, Glos.

Inskip, family name of Viscount Caldeote.

INVERFORTH, BARON (Weir) (Baron UK 1919)

ANDREW PETER WEIR, 4th Baron; *b* 16 Nov 1966; *s* 1982.

Arms – On a fesse azure, between in chief an escutcheon per bend azure and gules, charged with a bend sinister gules and azure a bend argent, and in base an ancient galley, flags flying to the dexter gules, three mullets of the first. *Crest* – A dexter and sinister hand couped at the wrists proper supporting an ancient galley as in the arms. *Supporters* – On either side a sailor of the Mercantile Marine.

SISTER LIVING

Hon Clarinda Jane, *b* 1968: *m* 1994, Jonathan S. H. A. Kane, son of Douglas Kane.

UNCLE LIVING (*Son of 2nd Baron*)

Hon (JOHN) VINCENT, *b* 8 Feb 1935; *ed* Malvern; late Chm Andrew Weir Group.

WIDOW LIVING OF THIRD BARON

JILL ELIZABETH (*Baroness Inverforth*), da of late John Ward Thornycroft, CBE, of Steyne, Bembridge, I of W: *m* 1966, the 3rd Baron Inverforth, who *d* 1982.

Through labour to honour

PREDECESSORS – (1) *Rt Hon* ANDREW WEIR, PC, *b* 1865; senior partner in the firm of Andrew Weir & Co, shipowners and merchants, Surveyor-Gen of Supply, War Office and a Member of Army Council 1917-19, and Min of Munitions 1919-21; *cr Baron Inverforth*, of Southgate, co Middlesex (peerage of United Kingdom) 1919: *m* 1889, Anne, who *d* 1941, yr da of late Thomas Kay Dowie; *d* 1955; *s* by his only son (2) ANDREW ALEXANDER MORTON, 2nd Baron; *b* 1897: *m* 1929, Iris Beryl, who *d* 1996, da of late Charles Vincent, 4th Bn The Buffs; *d* 1975; *s* by his el son (3) (ANDREW CHARLES) ROY, 3rd Baron, *b* 1932: *m* 1966, Jill Elizabeth, da of late John Ward Thornycroft, CBE; *d* 1982; *s* by his only son (4) ANDREW PETER, 4th Baron and present peer.

Inverurie, Lord; son of Earl of Kintore.

Ipswich, Viscount; grandson of Duke of Grafton.

Irby, family name of Baron Boston.

IRONSIDE, BARON (Ironside) (Baron UK 1941)

EDMUND OSLAC IRONSIDE, 2nd Baron; *b* 21 Sept 1924; *s* 1959; *ed* Tonbridge; Lt (ret) RN; Coronation Medal 1953, Hon FCGI 1987; 1939-45 War: *m* 1950, Audrey Marigold, yst da of late Col Hon Thomas George Breadalbane Morgan-Grenville, DSO, OBE, MC (*see*Ly Kinloss, colls), and has issue.

𝕬rms – Per bend sable and gules, on a bend argent a bendlet wavy azure, in sinister chief a garb or, and in base a lion salient or, and in fess a gauntletted dexter hand grasping a sword paleways argent hilted or. Crest – A dexter gauntletted hand grasping a sword paleways argent hilted and pommelled or. Supporters – Two bull terriers proper.
Residence – Priory House, Old House Lane, Boxted, Colchester, Essex CO4 5RB.

SON LIVING

Hon CHARLES EDMUND GRENVILLE (46 Mayford Rd, SW12 8SN), *b* 1 July 1956: *m* 1985, Hon Elizabeth Mary Law, eldest da of 2nd Baron Coleraine, and has issue living, Frederick Thomas Grenville, *b* 22 April 1991, — Emily Charlotte Olivia, *b* 1988, — Alice Octavia Louise, *b* 1990.

DAUGHTER LIVING

Hon Fiona Georgina, *b* 1954: *m* 1978, Roland Maclean Jack, of The Old Vicarage, Lyford, Wantage, Oxon, and has issue living, Oliver Edmund Maclean, *b* 1983, — Anthea Audrey Charlotte, *b* 1985.

SISTER LIVING

Hon Elspeth Mariot, *b* 1917: *m* 1941, Capt Andrew Gilbert Hendry, Black Watch (Roy Highland Regt), who *d* 1987, and has issue living, Michael Andrew, *b* 1942, *ed* Stanbridge Earls Sch, Romsey, — John Edmund Gordon, *b* 1949: *m* 1979, Gillian Margaret, da of David Young, of Sheilds House, Newtonhill, Kincardineshire, and has issue living, Edmund John Ironside *b* 1988, Johanna Katherine *b* 1981, Sophia Elizabeth Hariot *b* 1984, — David Robert Charles, *b* 1955. *Residence* – 4 Easter Ferrygate, Abbotsford Rd, N Berwick, E Lothian EH39 5DD.

PREDECESSOR – (1) *Field Marshal Sir* (WILLIAM) EDMUND Ironside, GCB, CMG, DSO, Hon LLD, son of late Surg-Maj William Ironside, RHA; *b* 1880; S Africa 1899-1902, special serv 1902-04, European War 1914-19, finally as Chief of Staff Comdg-in-Ch Allied Forces at Archangel, N Russia; Ismid 1920; GOC NW Persia 1920-21, European War 1939-40; was Comdt of Staff Coll 1922-6, 2nd Div, Aldershot 1926-8, and Meerut Dist 1928-31, Lieut Gov of Tower of London 1931-3, appointed QMG of Army in India 1933, Gen Officer Comdg-in-Ch, E Command 1936, ADC-Gen to HM 1937-40; Gov and Com-in-Ch, Gibraltar 1938-39, Inspector-Gen of Overseas Forces July 1939, and Ch of Imperial Gen Staff Sept 1939; Com-in-Ch Home Forces, May to July 1940; Col Comdt RA 1932-47; *cr Baron Ironside*, of Archangel, and of Ironside, co Aberdeen (peerage of United Kingdom) 1941: *m* 1915, Mariot Ysabel, who *d* 1984, da of late Charles Cheyne, ISC; *d* 1959; *s* by his only son (2) EDMUND OSLAC, 2nd Baron and present peer.

IRVINE OF LAIRG, BARON (Irvine) (Life Baron 1987)

ALEXANDER ANDREW MACKAY IRVINE, son of Alexander Irvine, by his wife Margaret Christina, da of late Alexander Macmillan; *b* 23 June 1940: *ed* Inverness Acad, Hutchesons' Boys' Gram Sch, Glasgow, Glasgow Univ (MA, LLB), and Christ's Coll, Camb (BA, LLB); Bar Inner Temple 1967, QC 1978, Bencher 1985; Univ Lecturer LSE 1965-69; a Recorder 1985-88; Dep Judge High Court 1987-97, since when Lord Chancellor; Pres Magistrates Assocn since 1997, Joint-Pres Industry and Parliament Trust since 1997, British-American Parliament Group since 1997, and Inter-Parliamentary Union since 1997; Hon Fellow Christ's Coll, Camb 1996, Hon LLD Glasgow Univ 1997; *cr Baron Irvine of Lairg*, of Lairg, District of Sutherland (Life Baron) 1987: *m* 1st, 19— (*m diss* 1973), Margaret Veitch, of Ayr; 2ndly, 1974, Mrs Alison Mary Dewar, yst da of Dr James Shaw McNair, MD, and has issue by 2nd *m*.
Address – 11 King's Bench Walk, Temple, EC4Y 7EQ. *Club* – Garrick.

SONS LIVING (*By 3rd marriage*)

Hon David, *b* 1974.
Hon Alastair, *b* 1976.

IRVING OF DARTFORD, BARONY OF (Irving) (Extinct 1989)

SON LIVING OF LIFE BARON

Hon Stephen John (25 Princes Av, Dartford, Kent DA2 6NF), *b* 1959; *ed* Dartford Gram Sch: *m* 1984, Lesley Anne, yr da of late (Richard) Neil Herbert, of Wilmington, Kent, and has issue living, James Richard, *b* 1994, — Emily Rebecca, *b* 1990.

DAUGHTER LIVING OF LIFE BARON

Hon Susan Anne, *b* 1946: *m* 1966, John House, only son of late John House, and has issue living, Katharine Anne, *b* 1969, — Victoria Julienne, *b* 1971, — (Alison) Louise, *b* 1973.

WIDOW LIVING OF LIFE BARON

MILDRED (*Baroness Irving of Dartford*), da of Charlton Weedy, of Morpeth, Northumberland: *m* 1942, Baron Irving of Dartford, PC (Life Baron), who *d* 1989. *Residence* – 10 Tynedale Close, Dartford, Kent.

Irwin, Lord; son of Earl of Halifax.

Isaacs, Rufus, family name of Marquess of Reading.

ISLWYN, BARON (Hughes) (Life Baron 1997)

ROYSTON JOHN (ROY) HUGHES, son of late John Hughes, of Pontllanfraith, Mon; *b* 9 June 1925; *ed* Pontllanfraith County Gram Sch, and Ruskin Coll, Oxford; Official, TGWU 1959-66; Memb Coventry City Cncl and Sec, Coventry Borough Labour Party 1962-66; MP for Newport (*Lab*) 1966-83, and for Newport East 1983-97; Front Bench Spokesman on Welsh Affairs 1984-88; Memb Executive, Inter-Parliamentary Union 1987-92 (Treasurer 1990-92); Memb Cncl of Europe and WEU since 1990, Vice-Chm since 1999; Jt Chm All Party Rugby Union Group 1993-97; DL Gwent 1992; *cr* *Baron Islwyn*, of Clasnewydd, co Gwent (Life Baron) 1997: *m* 1957, Florence Marion, da of John Appleyard, of Scarborough, and has issue.

ᾰrms – Per pale gules and sable between two flaunches conjoined to a fess argent thereon two flaunches that on the dexter gules and that on the sinister sable conjoined to a bar per pale gules and sable two round-els argent each ensigned by an ancient crown or and charged with a fleur-de-lis per pale gules and sable. Crest – A demi dragon gules supporting with both feet a miner's safety lamp or. Supporters – On either side a badger sejant erect reguardant proper gorged with an ancient crown or.
Residence – Chapel Field, Chapel, Abergavenny, Gwent NP7 7BT.

Hon Rosemary Eluned, *b* 1958.
Hon Pamela Hilda, *b* 1964.
Hon Meriel Ann, *b* 1966.

ISMAY, BARONY OF (Ismay) (Extinct 1965)

DAUGHTERS LIVING OF FIRST BARON

Hon Susan Katharine (The Bothy, Wormington Grange, Broadway, Worcs) *b* 1922: *m* 1st, 1942 (*m diss* 1946), Maj Neville Ewart Hyde Chance; 2ndly, 1949, Lieut-Col Michael John Evetts, MC, RHF, son of late Lt-Gen Sir John Fullerton Evetts, CB, CBE, MC, and has issue living, (by 1st *m*) Patricia Kathleen, *b* 1942: *m* 1963, David Henry Smyly (*see* By Buckland, 1980 Edn), of Bell Farm, Dorstone, Herefords, and has issue living, Giles Richard Ismay *b* 1966: *m* 1996, Kim, da of late Raymond Crocker, and of Mrs Peter Deal, of Cranham, Essex, Susannah Louise *b* 1964, — (by 2nd *m*) John Hastings (Wormington Grange, nr Broadway, Worcs), *b* 1951: *m* 1980, Mrs Caroline Fiona Jane Tropman, da of David Lucius Shakespeare Vardy, of Abbeylands, Stackhouse, Settle, Yorks, and has issue living, Matthew John *b* 1987, Lucy Katherine *b* 1989, — James Michael Ismay (Ryefield House, Wormington, Broadway, Worcs), *b* 1953: *m* 1986, Peta Jeanette, only da of Ridley Lamb, of Boville Park, Osmotherley, N Yorks, and has issue living, Thomas Ridley Becher *b* 1989, Camilla Alice *b* 1987.

Hon Sarah Field, *b* 1928: *m* 1948 (*m diss* 198-), 3rd Viscount Allendale. *Residences* – Bywell Hall, Stocksfield-on-Tyne, Northumberland; Allenheads Hall, Allenheads, Northumberland.

Hon Mary Quenelda, *b* 1929: *m* 1st, 1952, Robert Mervyn Fitz Finnis, who *d* 1955; 2ndly, 1957, Major George Raymond Seymour, CVO (*see* M Hertford, colls), and has issue living (by 1st *m*) Jane Laura FINNIS, *b* 1953; has resumed her maiden name: *m* 1975 (*m diss* 1995), Peter Butselaar, formerly of Melbourne, Australia, and has issue living, Nicholas Peter *b* 1981, Emily Kate *b* 1978, Vanessa Mary *b* 1987, — Sarah Lavinia, *b* 1955: *m* 1987, Mark C. G. Menzies, yr son of late Michael Menzies, of Oyster Bay, New York, and has issue living, Angus *b* 1989, Harry *b* 1991, Amelia *b* 1993, — (by 2nd *m*) (*see* M Hertford, colls). *Residence* – The Old Vicarage, Bucklebury, nr Reading, Berks.

IVEAGH, EARL OF (Guinness) (Earl UK 1919, Bt UK 1885)
(Title pronounced "Iver", and "Ivy" in Ireland)

My hope is in God

ARTHUR EDWARD RORY GUINNESS, 4th Earl, and 4th Baronet; *b* 10 Aug 1969; *s* 1992.

𝕬rms – Quarterly; 1st and 4th, per saltire gules and azure, a lion rampant, or; on a chief ermine a dexter hand couped at the wrist of the first, *Guinness*; 2nd and 3rd argent, on a fesse between three crescents sable a trefoil slipped or, *Lee*. 𝕮rests – 1st, a boar passant, quarterly or and gules; 2nd, on a pillar argent, encircled by a ducal coronet or, an eagle preying on a bird's leg erased proper. 𝕾upporters – Two stags gules, collared gemmel and attired or, each resting a hind hoof upon an escutcheon vert, charged with a lion rampant or.
Address – Iveagh House, 41 Harrington Gdns, SW7 4JU.

BROTHER LIVING

Hon RORY MICHAEL BENJAMIN, *b* 12 Dec 1974.

SISTERS LIVING

Lady Emma Lavinia, *b* 1963; *ed* Lincoln Coll, Oxford: *m* 1995, James P. Barnard, son of P. Geoffrey Barnard, and has issue living, Benjamin Philip, *b* 1996, — Arthur James, *b* 1998. *Residence* – Parham Park, Pulborough, W Sussex.

Lady Louisa Jane, *b* 1967: *m* 1999, Rupert William Uloth, yst son of Col A. C. Uloth, of Stockbridge, Hants.

AUNT LIVING (*sisters of 3rd Earl*) (*raised to the rank of an Earl's daughter* 1969)

Lady Elizabeth Maria, *b* 1939; JP Berks: *m* 1st, 1960 (*m diss* 1990), David Hugh Lavallin Nugent (*see* Nugent, Bt, *cr* 1795); 2ndly, 1992, as his 2nd wife, (Robert) Martin Mays-Smith. *Residence* – Chaddleworth House, Chaddleworth, Newbury, Berks.

GREAT AUNT LIVING (*daughter of 2nd Earl*)

Lady Patricia Florence Susan (*Patricia, Viscountess Boyd of Merton*), *b* 1918: *m* 1938, 1st Viscount Boyd of Merton, who *d* 1983. *Residence* – Ince Castle, Saltash, Cornwall PL12 4RA.

MOTHER LIVING

Miranda Daphne Jane, da of late Maj (Charles) Michael Smiley, of Castle Fraser, Aberdeenshire (*see* Smiley, Bt, colls): *m* 1963 (*m diss* 1984), the 3rd Earl of Iveagh, who *d* 1992. *Residence* – Wilbury Park, Newton Toney, Wilts SP4 0HS.

COLLATERAL BRANCH LIVING

Descendants of late Rt Hon Walter Edward Guinness, DSO (3rd son of 1st Earl), who was *cr Baron Moyne* 1932 (see that title).

PREDECESSORS – (1) *Sir* EDWARD CECIL Guinness, KP, GCVO, 3rd son of Sir Benjamin Lee Guinness, MP, 1st Bt, by Elizabeth, who *d* 1865, 3rd da of late Edward Guinness, of Dublin; *b* 1847; High Sheriff for Dublin City 1876; *cr* a *Baronet* 1885, *Baron Iveagh*, of Iveagh, co Down (peerage of United Kingdom) 1891, KP 1897, *Viscount Iveagh*, of Iveagh, co Down (peerage of United Kingdom) 1905, GCVO 1910, and *Earl of Iveagh*, and *Viscount Elveden*, of Elveden, co Suffolk (peerage of United Kingdom) 1919: *m* 1873, Adelaide Maria, who *d* 1916, da of late Richard Samuel Guinness, MP for Barnstaple (B Ardilaun, colls); *d* 1927; *s* by his son (2) RUPERT EDWARD CECIL LEE, KG, CB, CMG, 2nd Earl; *b* 1874; Chm of Arthur Guinness, Son & Co 1927-62, Chancellor Dublin Univ 1927-63; MP for Haggerston Div, Shoreditch (*C*) 1908-10, S-E Essex 1912-18, and Southend-on-Sea 1918-27; S Africa 1900 (despatches, medal, CMG): *m* 1903, Lady Gwendolen Florence Mary Onslow, CBE, MP Southend-on-Sea (*C*) 1927-35, Chm Women's Conservative Assocn, and Founder Overseas Training Sch for Women, who *d* 1966, da of 4th Earl of Onslow; *d* 1967; *s* by his grandson (3) ARTHUR FRANCIS BENJAMIN (only son of Maj Arthur Onslow Edward, Viscount Elveden (by his wife, Lady Elizabeth Cecilia Hare, OBE, who *d* 1990, having *m* 2ndly, 1947, (Edward) Rory More O'Ferrall, who *d* 1991, yr da of 4th Earl of Listowel), 2nd son of 2nd Earl), 3rd Earl, *b* 1937; Chm Guinness Group: *m* 1963 (*m diss* 1984), Miranda Daphne Jane, da of late Maj (Charles) Michael Smiley, of Castle Fraser, Aberdeenshire (*see* Smiley, Bt, colls); *d* 1992; *s* by his elder son (4) ARTHUR EDWARD RORY, 4th Earl and present peer; also Viscount Iveagh, Viscount Elveden, and Baron Iveagh.

JACKSON OF BURNLEY, BARONY OF (Jackson) (Extinct 1970)

DAUGHTERS LIVING OF LIFE BARON

Hon Anne Boswall, *b* 1939: *m* 1st, 1967, David Garner Freeston; 2ndly, 1996, Dr William Little, and has issue (by 1st *m*).
Hon Ruth Lesley, *b* 1945: *m* 1970, David John Moffatt, of 191 Myton Rd, Warwick, and has issue.

WIDOW LIVING OF LIFE BARON

MARY ELIZABETH (*Baroness Jackson of Burnley*), da of Dr Robert Oliphant Boswall: *m* 1938, Baron Jackson of Burnley (Life Baron), who *d* 1970. *Residence* – Cherwood House, Buckingham Rd, Bicester, Oxon.

Jackson, family name of Baron Allerton.

JACKSON OF LODSWORTH, BARONY OF (Jackson) (Extinct 1981)

SON LIVING OF LIFE BARONESS

Hon Robert Ward, *b* 1956: *m* 1978, Caroline Benedik, da of late Richardson Peele, of Grey House, Stow-on-the-Wold, Glos.

JACOBS, BARON (Jacobs) (Life Baron 1997)

(DAVID) ANTHONY JACOBS, son of Ridley Jacobs, of ......; *b* — Nov 1931; *ed* Clifton Coll, and London Univ (BCom 19—); FCA; Chm Nig Securities Group 1957-72, Tricoville Group 1961-90 and 1992-94, and British Sch of Motoring 1973-90; Jt Treasurer, Liberal Party 1984-87; Vice-Pres Soc and Lib Dem 1988, Memb Federal Exec, Soc and Lib Dem 1988; *cr* Kt 1988, and *Baron Jacobs*, of Belgravia in the City of Westminster (Life Baron) 1997: *m* 1954, Evelyn Felicity, da of Hildegarde Patchett, of Dresden, Germany, and has issue.

𝕬rms – Or in chief a seven-branched candlestick and in base a wheel both sable on a chief ermine a lion passant gules. 𝕮rest – An artist's palette the thumb hole transfixed by a pomegranate slipped and leaved all proper. 𝕾upporters – On either side a giant anteater statant erect argent armed and gorged with a plain collar attached thereto a chain reflexed over the back or.

Residence – 9 Nottingham Terrace, NW1 4QB. *Clubs* – Coombe Hill Golf, Palm Beach Country (USA).

SON LIVING

Hon Simon Paul, *b* 1960; *ed* ....

DAUGHTER LIVING

Hon Nicola Ann, *b* 1956; *ed* ....

JACOBSON, BARONY OF (Jacobson) (Extinct 1988)

SONS LIVING OF LIFE BARON

Hon Philip (29 Carmalt Gdns, SW15), *b* 1938; Paris correspondent *The Times*: *m* 1967, Ann, da of late Gilbert Mathison.
Hon Colin (48 Parkway, NW1), *b* 1941: *m* 1972, Josephine, da of John William Gates.

DAUGHTER LIVING OF LIFE BARON

Hon Pamela (Witteys Lane, Thorncombe, nr Chard, Som), *b* 1944.

JACQUES, BARONY OF (Jacques) (Extinct 1995)

SONS LIVING OF LIFE BARON

Hon (Cecil) Philip (Golden Gateway Center, 550 Battery St, San Francisco, CA 94111-2327, USA), *b* 1930; BSc (Hons) London: *m* 1st 1960 (*m diss* 1977), Rita Ann Florence Hurford; 2nd 1983, Carrine Royston, *née* Johnson, who *d* 1998, and has issue (by 1st *m*), John Hurford, *b* 1962, — Neil Philip, *b* 1963.
Hon Paul (Pinestead, 1(b) Twentylands Drive, East Leake, Loughborough, Leics), *b* 1932; MB, ChBEd: *m* 1958, Nina Mollie MacKenzie, and has issue.

DAUGHTER LIVING OF LIFE BARON

Hon Anne, *b* 1941.

WIDOW LIVING OF LIFE BARON

VIOLET EVANGELINE MABEL (*Baroness Jacques*), da of late Alfred John Davies: *m* 1989, as his 2nd wife, Baron Jacques (Life baron), who *d* 1995.

JAKOBOVITS, BARON (Jakobovits) (Life Baron 1988)

IMMANUEL JAKOBOVITS, son of Rabbi Julius Jakobovits, of Konigsberg, Germany; *b* 8 Feb 1921; *ed* London Univ, Jews' Coll, London, and Yeshivah Etz Chaim, London; Minister of three London synagogues 1941-49, Chief Rabbi of Ireland 1949-58, Rabbi Fifth Ave Synagogue, New York 1958-67, Chief Rabbi of The United Hebrew Congregations of the British Commonwealth of Nations 1967-91, since when Emeritus Chief Rabbi; author; *cr* Kt 1981, and *Baron Jakobovits*, of Regent's Park in Greater London (Life Baron) 1988: *m* 1949, Amelie, da of Rabbi Elie Munk, of Paris, and has issue.
Address – 44A Albert Rd, NW4 2SJ.

SONS LIVING

Hon Julian, *b* 1950; doctor: *m* 1973, Michelle Tauber, and has issue living, Nechemya, *b* 1974, — David, *b* 1975, — Nathan, *b* 1977, — Elie, *b* 1982, — Jeremy, *b* 1985, — Chaim, *b* 1995, — Penina, *b* 1979, — Tzippora, *b* 1981, — Sima, *b* 1988.
Hon Samuel, *b* 1951; Rabbi: *m* 1973, Ester Gitel Kahana, and has issue living, Yaacov, *b* 1979, — Shraga Feitel, *b* 1975, — Zipora, *b* 1977, — Yehudit, *b* 1988.

DAUGHTERS LIVING

Hon Esther, *b* 1953: *m* 1971, Rabbi Chaim Zundel Pearlman, and has issue living, Yehuda, *b* 1972, — Eliezer, *b* 1974, — Ephraim, *b* 1978, — Eliyohu, *b* 1982, — Daniel, *b* 1985, — Zipporah, *b* 1976, — Adina, *b* 1980, — Sarah, *b* 1988.
Hon Jeanette (Shoshana), *b* 1956: *m* 1977, Norman David Turner, and has issue living, Ezriel, *b* 1978, — Yehuda, *b* 1981, — Elie, *b* 1983, — Yoel, *b* 1995, — Hadassa, *b* 1979, — Ayala, *b* 1987, — Simcha, *b* 1994.
Hon Aviva, *b* 1958: *m* 1978, Dr Joseph Samuel Adler, and has issue living, Pierre, *b* 1979, — Nathan, *b* 1980, — Abraham, *b* 1989, — Tobi, *b* 1992, — Ann, *b* 1982,   Tzippora, *b* 1983, — Gila, *b* 1985, — Miriam, *b* 1994, — Sarah, *b* 1997.
Hon Elisheva, *b* 1966: *m* 1985, Sam Eli Homburger, and has issue living, Meir, *b* 1986, — Pinchos Jacob, *b* 1988, Yehoshua, *b* 1990, — Isaac Aryeh, *b* 1992, — Yoel, *b* 1995, — Avigail Esther, *b* 1987.

James, family name of Baron Northbourne.

JAMES OF HOLLAND PARK, BARONESS (White) (Life Baroness 1991)

PHYLLIS DOROTHY JAMES, OBE, da of late Sydney Victor James; *b* 3 Aug 1920; *ed* Cambridge High Sch for Girls; Assoc Fellow Downing Coll, Camb 1986, Hon DLitt Buckingham 1992, London 1993, Hertfordshire 1994, Glasgow 1995, Durham 1998, and Portsmouth 1999; Hon DUniv Essex 1996; Hon Fell St Hilda's Coll, Oxford 1996; FRSL, FRSA; JP Willesden 1979-82, Inner London 1984; Administrator NHS 1949-68; Principal Police and Criminal Policy Dept, Home Office, 1968-79; novelist, author (as P. D. James) of *Cover Her Face* (1962), *A Mind to Murder* (1963), *Unnatural Causes* (1967), *Shroud for a Nightingale* (1971), *The Maul and the Peartree* (with T. A. Critchley, 1971), *An Unsuitable Job for a Woman* (1972), *The Black Tower* (1975), *Death of an Expert Witness* (1977), *Innocent Blood* (1980), *The Skull Beneath the Skin* (1982), *A Taste for Death* (1986), *Devices and Desires* (1989), *The Children of Men* (1992), *Original Sin* (1994), *A Certain Justice* (1997), and *Time to be in Earnest* (1999); Member BBC Gen Advisory Council 1987-88, Arts Council 1988-92 (Chm Literature Advisory Panel 1988-92), British Council 1988-93 (Literature Advisory Cttee since 1988); Chm Booker Prize Panel of Judges 1987, and Soc of Authors 1984-86 (Pres since 1997); a Gov BBC 1988-93; Member Detection Club; OBE (Civil) 1983, *cr Baroness James of Holland Park*, of Southwold, co Suffolk (Life Baroness) 1991: *m* 1941, Connor Bantry White, who *d* 1964, and has issue.

🛡️rms – Vert, between two oak trees eradicated or a bend sinister wavy argent, thereon another azure charged with a quill pen argent, the quill or, a chief azure issuant thereon a representation of Southwold Lighthouse proper. 🛡️upporters – On either side a tabby cat salient guardant proper wearing a collar vert, edged, buckled and studded or, reposing the exterior paw upon an open book, the pages lettered proper edged or and bound gules each upright on a set of two closed books edged or, their spines outward, one bound vert lying on top of the other azure. *Address* – c/o Greene & Heaton Ltd, 37 Goldhawk Rd, W12 8QQ.

DAUGHTERS LIVING

Hon Clare Bantry, *b* 1942: *m* 1963, Lyn Flook.
Hon Jane Bantry, *b* 1944: *m* 1972, Peter Duncan McLeod.

JAMES OF RUSHOLME, BARONY OF (James) (Extinct 1992)

SON LIVING OF LIFE BARON

Hon Oliver Francis Wintour (Sleightholmedale, Kirkbymoorside, York), *b* 1943; *ed* Winchester, and Balliol Coll, Oxford (MA, BM, BCh): *m* 1965, Rosanna, el da of late Maj Gordon Bentley Foster, of Sleightholme Dale, Fadmoor, York (*see* B Revelstoke, colls), and has issue living, Patrick Esmond, *b* 1967: *m* 1996, Natasha Anne, 2nd da of Duncan Davidson, of Lilburn Tower, Alnwick (*see* D Norfolk, 1990 Edn), — Helen, *b* 1970.

WIDOW LIVING OF LIFE BARON

CORDELIA MARY (*Baroness James of Rusholme*), da of Maj-Gen FitzGerald Wintour, CB, CBE (*see* Foster, Bt (ext), 1980 Edn): *m* 1939, Baron James of Rusholme (Life Baron), who *d* 1992. *Residence* – Penhill Cottage, W Witton, Leyburn, N Yorks.

JANNER, BARONY OF (Janner) (Extinct 1982)

SON LIVING OF LIFE BARON

Hon Greville Ewan, QC, MP (*Baron Janner of Braunstone*); *b* 1928; *cr* Baron Janner of Braunstone (Life Baron) 1997 (see that title).

DAUGHTER LIVING OF LIFE BARON

Hon Ruth Joan Gertrude Rahle (*Baroness Morris of Kenwood*); *b* 1932; *ed* St Paul's Girls' Sch; Solicitor 1956; Chm Dept of Social Security Appeals Tribunal, Pres Habonim Dror, Trustee Rowan Educn Trust, Dir and Trustee Womankind Worldwide, Vice-Pres Women of the Year Luncheon and Assembly: *m* 1958, 2nd Baron Morris of Kenwood. *Residence* – 35 Fitzjohn's Av, NW3 5JY.

JANNER OF BRAUNSTONE, BARON (Janner) (Life Baron 1997)

GREVILLE EWAN JANNER, only son of late Baron Janner (Life Baron); *b* 11 July 1928; *ed* Bishop's Coll Sch, Canada, St Paul's, Trinity Hall, Camb (MA 19—), and Harvard Post Graduate Law Sch; Bar, Middle Temple, 1954; QC 1971; author, journalist and broadcaster; MP for Leicester NW (*Lab*) 1970-74, and for Leicester W 1974-97; Chm Select Cttee on Employment 1992-96; Chm All Party Safety Group; formerly Co-Chm All Party Employment Group; Vice-Chm All Party Cttee for Release of Soviet Jewry; first Chm Holocaust Educational Trust since 1990; Pres Inter-Parliamentary Council Against Anti-Semitism since 1990; Pres Retired Executives Action Clearing House (REACH) since 1980; Vice-Pres World Jewish Congress since 1981; Pres Board of Deputies of British Jews 1979-85; first Pres Commonwealth Jewish Council since 1982; *cr Baron Janner of Braunstone*, of Leicester, co Leics (Life Baron) 1997: *m* 1955, Myra Louise, who *d* 1996, da of Emmanuel Sheink, of Melbourne, Victoria, Australia, and has issue.

𝕬rms – Paly of four vert and gules a pile terminating in a triangle interlaced with a triangle reversed between two piles each terminating in a fleur-de-lis argent. 𝕮rest – A hippopotamus statant gules in the mouth an orchid argent slipped and leaved vert. 𝕾upporters – On either side a rabbit sejant erect argent that on the dexter gorged with a plain collar and holding in the exterior paw a top hat gules and that on the sinister gorged with a plain collar vert and holding in the exterior paw a sword point upwards argent hilt pommel and quillons vert.
Address – c/o House of Lords, Westminster, SW1A 0PW.

SON LIVING

Hon Daniel, *b* 1957; *ed* Univ Coll Sch, Trin Hall, Camb, and Middle Temple: *m* 198—, Caroline, da of ...... Gee, of

DAUGHTER LIVING

Hon Marion, *b* 1959; *ed* S Hampstead High Sch, and Selwyn Coll, Camb.
Hon Laura, *b* 1962; *ed* S Hampstead High Sch, and Trinity Hall, Camb: *m* 1988, David Klausner, and has issue living, Natan, *b* 1994, — Tali, *b* 1991, — Ella Avigail, *b* 1997.

JAUNCEY OF TULLICHETTLE, BARON (Jauncey) (Life Baron 1988)

CHARLES ELIOT JAUNCEY, only child of late Capt John Henry Jauncey, DSO, RN, of Tullichettle, Comrie, Perthshire; b 8 May 1925; ed Radley, Ch Ch Oxford (MA 1953, Hon Student 1990) and Glasgow Univ (LLB 1949); late Sub Lieut RNVR, served European War 1943-46; Advocate Scottish Bar 1949, Standing Jnr Counsel to Admiralty 1954, Kintyre Pursuivant of Arms 1955-71, Hon Sheriff Substitute of Perthshire 1962, QC 1963, Sheriff Principal of Fife and Kinross 1971-74, Judge of the Courts of Appeal of Jersey and Guernsey 1972-79, a Lord of Session in Scotland 1979, a Lord of Appeal in Ordinary 1988-96; Member of Royal Co of Archers (The Queen's Body Guard for Scotland) 1951; Memb Historic Buildings Council for Scotland 1971-92; cr Baron Jauncey of Tullichettle, of Comrie, in the District of Perth and Kinross (Life Baron) 1988: m 1st, 1948 (m diss 1969), Jean, only da of late Adm Sir Angus Edward Malise Bontine Cunninghame Graham, KBE, CB, of Ardoch, Cardross, Dunbartonshire; 2ndly, 1973 (m diss 1977), Elizabeth, widow of Maj John Ballingal, MC, and da of Capt R. H. V. Sivewright, DSC, RN; 3rdly, 1977, (Sarah) Camilla, yst da of late Lt-Col Charles Frederick Cathcart, DSO (see E Cathcart, colls), and has issue by 1st and 3rd m.

𝕬rms – Or, three chevronels engrailed Gules in chief two lions rampant and respectant of the Second. 𝕮rest – An arm embowed in armour Argent, holding in the gauntlet Or a battle-axe in fess, also Argent, the forearm environed of a wreath of laurel Vert. 𝕾upporters – dexter, a lion Gules gorged of a collar Or, charged with a chevronel engrailed Gules; sinister, a buck Proper, attired, collared and chained Or, the collar charged with a chevronel engrailed Gules. 𝕸otto – Virtute Majorum.
Seat – Tullichettle, Comrie, Perthshire. Club – Royal (Perth).

SONS LIVING (By 1st marriage)

Hon James Malise Dundas, b 1949: ed Radley, and Aberdeen Univ (LLB); author of The Albatross Conspiracy 1991, The Mapmaker 1994, The Crystal Keeper 1996: m 1st, 1980 (m diss 1986), Caroline Elizabeth, da of Charles Ede, of The Garden House, Hollington, Newbury, Berks; 2ndly, 1988, Sarah Jacqueline, yr da of late Lt-Col (David Ludovic) Peter Lindsay, DSO (see E Crawford and Balcarres, colls), and has issue living (by 1st m), Sophie Jean Elizabeth, b 1980, — Eleanor Fleur, b 1983, — (by 2nd m) Jake Ludovic Dundas, b 1991, — Anna Maria, b 1989. Residence – Drummond Hall, Stanley, Perthshire PH1 4PL.

Hon Simon Helias, b 1953; ed Radley, and Bristol Univ (BA): m 1979, Aurora, da of Juan de Jesus Castaneda, of Apartado Aereo 33394, Bogota, Colombia, and has issue living, Jeremy Cunninghame, b 1984, — Thomas Charles, b 1987. Residence – Upper Ballunie, Kettins, Coupar Angus, Perthshire PH13 9JS.

DAUGHTERS LIVING (By 1st marriage)

Hon Arabella Bridget Rachel, b 1965: m 1989, James H. B. Maudslay, yr son of late Sir (James) Rennie Maudslay, GCVO, MBE, and has issue living, Angus Charles Rennie, b 1993, — Henry Joseph Dundas, b 1996. Residence – Frightsbridge Farm, Woodchurch, Ashford, Kent TN26 3PR.

(By 3rd marriage)

Hon Cressida Jane, b 1981.

JAY, BARONY OF (Jay) (Extinct 1996)

SONS LIVING OF LIFE BARON (By 1st marriage)

Hon Peter, b 1937; ed Winchester, and Ch Ch Oxford (MA); HM Amb to USA 1977-79; writer, broadcaster and publishing exec; m 1st, 1961 (m diss 1986), Margaret Ann (later Baroness Jay of Paddington, Life Baroness), da of Rt Hon (Leonard) James Callaghan, KG (later Baron Callaghan of Cardiff, Life Baron); 2ndly, 1986, Emma Bettina, da of Peter Kai Thornton, and has issue living (by 1st m) (see Bs Jay of Paddington), — (by 2nd m) Thomas Hastings, b 1987,

— Samuel Arthur Maxwell, *b* 1988, — James William Hagen Thornton, *b* 1992, — (by Jane Tustian) Nicholas James Tustian, *b* 1980. *Residence* – Hensington Farmhouse, Woodstock, Oxon OX20 1LH. *Club* – Garrick.

Hon Martin, *b* 1939; *ed* Winchester, and New Coll, Oxford (BA); industrialist: *m* 1969, Sandra Williams, and has issue living, Adam, *b* 1976, — Claudia, *b* 1971, — Tabitha, *b* 1972. *Residence* – Bishop's Court, Bishop's Sutton, Alresford, Hants.

DAUGHTERS LIVING OF LIFE BARON *(By 1st marriage)*

Hon Helen, *b* 1945; *ed* North London Collegiate, and Sussex Univ (BA): *m* 1st, 1975 (*m diss* 1982), David Kennard; 2ndly, 1986, Rupert Pennant-Rea, and has issue living (by 1st *m*), Amanda, *b* 1976, — Juliet, *b* 1979, — (by 2nd *m*) Edward, *b* 1986.

Hon Catherine, *b* (twin) 1945; *ed* North London Collegiate, and Sussex Univ (BA): *m* 1970, Stewart Boyd, QC, and has issue living, Matthew, *b* 1976, — Rachel, *b* 1972, — Emily, *b* 1973, — Hannah, *b* 1987. *Residences* – 1 Gayton Cres, Hampstead, NW3; Wraxall Manor, Higher Wraxall, Dorchester, Dorset DT2 0HP.

WIDOW LIVING OF LIFE BARON

Mary Lavinia (*Baroness Jay*), da of Hugh Lewis Thomas: *m* 1972, as his 2nd wife, Baron Jay, PC (Life Baron), who *d* 1996. *Residence* – Causeway Cottage, Minster Lovell, Oxon OX8 5RN.

JAY OF PADDINGTON, BARONESS (Adler) (Life Baroness 1992)

Margaret Ann Adler, PC, elder da of Baron Callaghan of Cardiff, KG, PC (Life Baron); *b* 18 Nov 1939; *ed* Blackheath High Sch, and Somerville Coll, Oxford (BA); formerly in Current Affairs and Educn depts of BBC TV; Reporter for *Panorama* 1981-86, Reporter and Producer *This Week* 1986-88, since when a Broadcaster and Presenter for Radio and Television, including *Social History of Medicine, Family Matters, Newsnight*, etc; sometime Member Ealing, Hounslow and Hammersmith Area Health Authority, Member Governing Board Queen Charlotte's Maternity Hosp, and Chelsea Hosp for Women, Member Paddington and N Kensington Dist Health Authority (now Parkside Health Authority) since 1984 (Vice-Chm since 1990), Member Central Rescarch and Devpt Cttee for NHS since 1991, Member Min for Health's AIDS Action Group since 1991, Patron ReAction Trust (part of Help the Aged) since 1991, Council Member The London Lighthouse, and Member Management Board of Positively Women; Founder and Dir Nat AIDS Trust since 1988; Min of State for Health 1997-98, since when Lord Privy Seal, Leader of House of Lords and Min for Women; co-author *Battered- The Story of Child Abuse* (1986); *cr* Baroness Jay of Paddington, of Paddington in the City of Westminster (Life Baroness) 1992, and PC 1998: *m* 1st, 1961 (*m diss* 1986), Peter Jay, son of Rt Hon Douglas Patrick Thomas Jay (later Baron Jay, Life Baron); 2ndly, 1994, as his 3rd wife, Prof Michael William Adler, and has issue by 1st *m*.

Arms – Quarterly vert and azure in the former a portcullis or in the latter a lymphad with an anchor at its prow and masted or the sail set argent and pennants flying gules overall a fess or to the sinister thereof a grassy mount with a hurst of oak trees and issuing therefrom passant to the dexter a wolf proper.

Residences – 44 Blomfield Rd, W9 2PF; Elm Bank, Glandore, co Cork.

SON LIVING *(By 1st marriage)*

Hon Patrick James Peter Jay, *b* 1971; *ed* Winchester, and Sch of Oriental and African Studies, London Univ.

DAUGHTERS LIVING *(By 1st marriage)*

Hon Tamsin Margaret, *b* 1965; *ed* St Paul's Girls' Sch and Bristol Univ: *m* 1989, Simon Anthony Raikes (*see* Hanson, Bt, 1995). *Residence* – 63 St Peter's St, N1 8JR.

Hon Alice Katharine Jay, *b* 1968; *ed* Bedales, and Pembroke Coll, Oxford.

Jebb, family name of Baron Gladwyn.

JEFFREYS, BARON (Jeffreys) (Baron UK 1952)

Every gift from God

CHRISTOPHER HENRY MARK JEFFREYS, 3rd Baron; *b* 22 May 1957; *s* 1986; *ed* Eton: *m* 1985, Anne Elisabeth, da of Antoine Denarie, and of Mrs Derek Harry Johnson, and has issue.

Arms – Ermine a lion rampant sable, and a canton sable. **Crest** – On a wreath ermine and sable a demi-lion or, grasping with the dexter claw a wreath of laurel vert. **Supporters** – On either side a lion regardant sable crowned with an ancient crown or, and charged on the shoulder with two swords in saltire points upwards gold.
Residence – The Corner House, Sewstern, Grantham, Lincs NG23 5RF.
Club – White's.

SON LIVING

Hon ARTHUR MARK HENRY, *b* 18 Feb 1989.

DAUGHTER LIVING

Hon Alice Mary, *b* 1986.

BROTHER LIVING

Hon (Alexander) Charles Darell, *b* 1959; *ed* Harrow: *m* 1991, Sonamara M. A., da of Barry Sainsbury, of London.

SISTERS LIVING

Hon Laura, *b* 1961.
Hon Rose Amanda, *b* 1962: *m* 1993, Dominic C. Prince, elder son of late John Prince, of Chipping Warden, Oxon.

HALF-SISTER LIVING (*Daughter of 2nd Baron by 2nd marriage*)

Hon Sophie Louise, *b* 1972: *m* 1996, as his 2nd wife, Prof Roger Vernon Scruton, son of late John Scruton, of High Wycombe, Bucks, and has issue living, Samuel Andrew, *b* 1998.

UNCLE LIVING (*Brother of 2nd Baron*) (*Raised to rank of a Baron's son 1961*)

Hon George Christian Darell, *b* 1939; *ed* Eton; late Capt Grenadier Guards; Dir of Seccombe Marshall and Campion plc 1976: *m* 1967, Karen Elizabeth Mary, elder da of late Col Hugo Meynell, MC, of Hollybush Park, Burton-on-Trent (*see* E Halifax, colls), and has issue living, Christopher George Hugo, *b* 1984, — Zara Serena, *b* 1972, — Susannah Elizabeth, *b* 1975. *Residence* – Manor Farm Barn, Alkerton, Banbury, Oxon OX15 6NL. *Club* – Boodle's.

MOTHER LIVING

Sarah Annabella, only da of late Maj Henry Claude Lyon Garnett, of Somerton House, Winkfield, Berks: *m* 1st, 1956 (*m diss* 1967), the 2nd Baron Jeffreys, who *d* 1986; 2ndly, 1968 (*m diss* 1998), Alexander Edward Pennant Clarke (*see* Falkiner, Bt, 1963 Edn). *Residence* – Foxhill House, Hawling, Glos.

WIDOW LIVING OF SECOND BARON

SUZANNE, da of James Stead, of Trowswell, Goudhurst, Kent, and formerly wife of — Gilbert: *m* 2ndly, 1981, as his 3rd wife, the 2nd Baron Jeffreys, who *d* 1986; 3rdly, 1990, Geoffrey C. Martin, of Heathfield, Sussex.

PREDECESSORS – (1) *Gen Sir* GEORGE DARELL JEFFREYS, KCB, KCVO, CMG, DL, son of late Rt Hon Arthur Frederick Jeffreys, JP, DL, MP, of Burkham House, Hants; *b* 1878; Col of Grenadier Guards 1952-60; Comdt Guards Depot 1911-14; Nile Expedition 1898, present at battle of Khartoum, S Africa 1900-1902, European War 1914-18 Comdg successively 2nd Batn of his Regt, 58th, 57th, and 1st Guards Brig, and 19th Div; in command of Light Div, Army of the Rhine 1919, and London Dist 1920-24; commanded 43rd (Wessex) Div TA and Wessex Area 1926-30; Gen Officer Comdg-in-Ch S Command, India 1932-36, and ADC Gen to HM 1936-38; Chm of Basingstoke Co Bench 1925-32, and again 1936-52, Hon Col 48th (Hampshire) Anti-Aircraft Regt RA (TA) (now 583rd (Hampshire) Heavy Anti-Aircraft Regt, RA) 1938-48, and Col of Roy Hampshire Regt 1945-48; sat as MP for Petersfield Div of Hampshire (*C*) 1941-51; *cr Baron Jeffreys*, of Burkham, co Southampton (peerage of United Kingdom) 1952; *m* 1905, Dorothy, who *d* 1953, da of John Postle Heseltine, of Walhampton, Lymington, and widow of Viscount Cantelupe, el son of 7th Earl De La Warr; *d* 1960; *s* by his grandson (2) MARK GEORGE CHRISTOPHER (son of late Capt Christoper John Darell Jeffreys, MVO, who was *ka* 1940, by his wife, Lady Rosemary Beatrice Agar, who *d* 1984, da of 4th Earl of Normanton, only son of 1st Baron), 2nd Baron, *b* 1932; Maj Gren Gds: *m* 1st, 1956 (*m diss* 1967), Sarah Annabella, only da of late Maj Henry Claude Lyon Garnett, of Somerton House, Winkfield, Berks; 2ndly, 1967 (*m diss* 1981), Anne-Louise, yr da of His Honour Judge Sir (William) Shirley Worthington-Evans, 2nd Bt (ext); 3rdly, 1981, Mrs Suzanne Gilbert (who *m* 3rdly, 1990, Geoffrey C. Martin, of Heathfield, Sussex), da of James Stead, of Goudhurst, Kent; *d* 1986; *s* by his elder son (3) CHRISTOPHER HENRY MARK, 3rd Baron and present peer.

JEGER, BARONESS (Jeger) (Life Baroness 1979)

LENA MAY JEGER, da of Charles Chivers, of Yorkley, Glos *b* 19 Nov 1915; *ed* Southgate County Sch, Middlesex and Birkbeck Coll, London Univ (BA); Civil Ser, Customs and Excise, Minof Information and Foreign Office 1936-49, Manchester Guardian, London Staff 1951-54 and since 1961; Member St Pancras Borough Council 1945-59, and LCC for Holborn and St Pancras South 1952-55; Member Nat Exec Cttee, Labour Party since 1963, and of Chm's Panel, House of Commons since 1971; UK Rep on Status of Women Commn UN 1967, Member Consultative Assembly of Council of Europe and of W European Union 1969-71; Chm Labour Party 1979-80; MP (*Lab*) for Holborn and St Pancras South 1953-59 and 1964-74, and for Camden, Holborn and St Pancras South 1974-79; *cr Baroness Jeger*, of St Pancras in Greater London (Life Baroness) 1979: *m* 1948, Dr Santo Wayburn Jeger, MP, who *d* 1953.

Residence – 9 Cumberland Terr, Regent's Park, NW1.

JELLICOE, EARL (Jellicoe) (Earl (UK) 1925)

GEORGE PATRICK JOHN RUSHWORTH JELLICOE, KBE, DSO, MC, PC, 2nd Earl; *b* 4 April 1918; *s* 1935; *ed* Winchester, and at Trin Coll, Camb (Exhibitioner); FRS 1990; in Foreign Ser 1947-57; formerly 1st Sec, Washington, DC, and Brussels and Dep Sec-Gen Baghdad Pact; a Lord-in-Waiting to HM Feb to June 1961, Joint Parliamentary Sec, Min of Housing and Local Govt 1961-62, Min of State, Home Office 1962-63, and First Lord of Admiralty 1963-64, and Min of Defence for RN April to Oct 1964, Dep Leader of Opposition, House of Lords 1967-70; Lord Privy Seal, Leader of House of Lords 1970-73, and Min for Civil Ser Dept; Dir Tate & Lyle plc 1973-93 (Chm 1978-83), Chm Davy Corp 1985-90, Booker Tate 1988-91, European Capital 1991-95, and Greece Fund 1988-94; a Dir of S G Warburg & Co Ltd 1964-70 and 1973-88, Smiths Industries 1973-86, Morgan Crucible 1974-1988, and Sotheby's 1973-85; Chm BOTB 1983-86; Review of Prevention of Terrorism Act 1983; Chm East European Trade Council 1986-90, Pres London Chamber of Commerce and Industry 1979-82, Parly and Scientific Cttec 1980-83, Chm MRC 1982-90, Pres British Heart Foundation 1992-95, RGS 1993-97, and SAS

SUI MEMORES MERENDO

Regimental Assocn since 1996; Chm British Advisory Cttee on Pollution of the Sea (ACOPS) 1968-70, Chm Council King's Coll, London 1977-84; Chancellor Southampton Univ 1984-95; a Page of Honour at Coronation of King George VI; 1939-45 War in Middle East as Lt-Col Coldm Gds, I SAS Regt and SBS Regt (wounded, despatches thrice, DSO, MC, Legion of Honour, French Croix de Guerre, Greek Order of Honour); DSO 1942; cr PC 1963, and KBE 1986: m 1st, 1944 (m diss 1966), Patricia Christine, only da of Jeremiah O'Kane, of Vancouver, Canada; 2ndly, 1966, Philippa, da of late Philip Dunne, of Gatley Park, Leominster, and has issue by 1st and 2nd m.

𝕬rms – Argent, three bars wavy azure, over all a whale hauriant sable. 𝕮rest – Out of a crown or, a demi-wolf azure. 𝕾upporters – On either side a sea griffin or.
Residences – Flat 5, 97 Onslow Sq, SW7 3LU; Tidcombe Manor, Tidcombe, nr Marlborough, Wilts SN8 3SL. Club – Brooks's, Special Forces.

SONS LIVING (By 1st marriage)

PATRICK JOHN BERNARD (Viscount Brocas), b 29 Aug 1950; ed Eton: m 1971 (m diss 1981), Geraldine Ann FitzGerald Jackson, and has issue:—

> SONS LIVING - Hon Justin Amadeus, b 1970; ed Eton; has issue living (by Emma Hibbert), Jasmine Coralie JELLICOE, b 1990. —— Viscount Brocas has further issue (by Clare Fisher), Jack JELLICOE, b 1977:—

Residence – 5 South View, Tiverton, Devon EX16 6LX.

Hon Nicholas Charles, b 1953; ed Eton, and York Univ: m 1982, Patricia, da of late Count Arturo Ruiz de Castilla, of Madrid, and Lima, Peru, and has issue living, Zoë Anaya Georgina, b 1988, — Francesca Nicole, b 1992. Residence – 30 Chemin de la Ramière, Preverenges, CH 1028, Switzerland

(By 2nd marriage)

Hon John Philip, b 1966; ed Bryanston. Residence – 4 rue de Son Serre, 05100, Briancon, France.

DAUGHTERS LIVING (By 1st marriage)

Lady Alexandra Patricia Gwendoline, b 1944: m 1970, (Edward) Philip Wilson, and has issue (see Wilson, Bt, cr 1874, colls). Residence – 24 Highbury Place, N5 1QP.
Lady Zara Lison Josephine JELLICOE, b 1948; has retained her maiden name: m 1st, 1983 (m diss 1987), Bruce Gilliam, son of Alvin Bruce Gilliam, of Houston, Texas; 2ndly, 1997, Richard Banghart. Residence – 1991 N Harrison Rd, E Lansing, Michigan, USA.

(By 2nd marriage)

Lady Emma Rose, b 1967. Residence – Manor Cottage, Tidcombe, nr Marlborough, Wilts SN8 3SL.
Lady Daisy, b 1970.

SISTERS LIVING (In special remainder to the Viscountcy only)

Lady Norah Beryl Cayzer, b 1910: m 1935, Major Edward William Rhys Wingfield, King's Roy Rifle Corps (see V Powerscourt, colls), who d 1984. Residence – Salterbridge, Cappoquin, co Waterford.
Lady Prudence Katharine Patton, b 1913; formerly a JP for Co of Kent: m 1936, Francis William Hope Loudon, who d 1985, and has issue living, James Rushworth Hope (Olantigh, Wye, Ashford, Kent), b 1943; ed Eton, and Magdalene Coll, Camb (BA): m 1975, Jane Gavina Fryett, and has issue living, Hugo John Hope b 1978, Alexander Guy Rushworth b 1980, Antonia Louise Cameron b 1977, — Katharine Louise Frederica (Lady Wilkinson), b 1937: m 1964, Sir William Henry Nairn Wilkinson, who d 1996, and has issue living, Matthew Loudon Nairn b 1969, Sophia Louise Prudence b 1971, Alice Laura Gillian b 1974, — Annabella Constance, b 1939: m 1965, Jonathan Scott, CBE, of Lasborough Manor, Tetbury, Glos, and has issue living, Alexander James Jonathan b 1966, Justin William Erskine b 1970, Julia Katharine Selina b 1969. Residence – 92 Bridge St, Wye, nr Ashford, Kent.

COLLATERAL BRANCHES LIVING (In remainder to Viscountcy only)

Issue of late Lady Gwendoline Lucy Constance Rushworth Jellicoe, eldest da of 1st Earl, b 1903, d 1997: m 1935, Col Edward Latham, MC, RHA, who d 1957:—
John Edward Jellicoe, b 1936; ed Eton; late 2nd Lieut RAC: m 1967, Catherine Patricia, only da of Dr Allan William Forsyth Craig, MB, of Greenways, Darlington Place, Bath, and has issue living, Jasper Nicholas Jellicoe, b 1970; ed Radley, and Edinburgh Univ (MA), — Gabrielle Jane, b 1971; ed Cheltenham Ladies' Coll, and Edinburgh Univ (MA), — Rosalind Vaari, b (twin) 1971; ed Cheltenham Ladies' Coll, and Edinburgh Univ (MA), — Rosalind. Residence – Harwood's House, Bledington, Oxon. Club – Cavalry and Guards'. —— Richard Henry Ringrose, b 1943: ed Eton, RNC Dartmouth, and Univ of Paris; late Sub-Lieut RN; MBA Cranfield Inst of Tech; Lieut RNR (ret): m 1968, Virginia Jane, eldest da of late John Herbert Mount (see E Erne, colls), and has issue living, Edward George Ringrose, b 1970; ed Eton, and St Catherine's Coll, Oxford (BA); Capt Coldm Gds, — Harry John Jellicoe, b 1972; ed Milton Abbey, and Guildhall Sch of Music and Drama, — Selina Louise, b 1976, — Emily Rose Jane, b 1979. Residence – Stowting Hill House, Ashford, Kent TN25 6BE. —— Susan Phyllida, b 1938; ed Lady Margaret Hall, Oxford (BA), and Birkbeck Coll, London (PhD): m 1958, Michael Rose, Solicitor, and has issue living, David Jacob Edward, b 1959; ed UCS, and Magdalen Coll, Oxford:

m 1989 (*m diss* 1999), Shyama Perera, and has issue living, Anyusha *b* 1991, Tushara *b* 1994, — Bernard John Max, *b* 1960; *ed* UCS, and National Film Sch: *m* 1988 (*m diss* 1997), Sandra McKibben, and has issue living, Ruby Victoria *b* 1992, — Philip Thomas Solomon, *b* 1963; *ed* UCS, Exter Coll, Oxford, and Liverpool Univ: *m* 1990, Ditta Neumann, and has issue living, Rona Olga Katharina *b* 1996, — Dinah Gwen Lison, *b* 1965; *ed* City of London Sch for Girls, and Magdalen Coll, Oxford; Bar Gray's Inn 1989: *m* 1991, Peter Kessler, and has issue living, Hannah Rose *b* 1997. *Residence* – Heath Winds, Merton Lane, Highgate, N6.

Issue of late Lady Myrtle Grace Brocas Jellicoe, 3rd da of 1st Earl, *b* 1908, *d* 1945: *m* 1932, Lionel Maxwell Joachim Balfour, who *d* 1973.

Christopher John Jellicoe, *b* 1934; *ed* Trin Coll, Camb (BA): *m* 1960, Ann Schuyler Butlin, and has issue living, Maxwell James, *b* 1961, — Juliet Ann, *b* 1963; BSc, MB BS: *m* 1989, Jonathan Bench, and has issue living, Thomas Joshua *b* 1991, Sebastian James *b* 1994, Hugo Jellicoe *b* 1997, — Katherine Susan, *b* 1968: *m* 1996, Harry Michael Charles Morley (*see* Aykroyd, Bt, *cr* 1929). *Residence* – 25 Clausentum Rd, St Cross, Winchester SO23 9QE. ── Karen Myrtle, *b* 1944: *m* 1967, Fabyan Peter Leaf Evans, and has issue living, Nigel Henley Fabyan, *b* 1971, — Alexander Peter Sommerville, *b* 1976, — Jessica Ann, *b* 1973.

PREDECESSOR – (1) Adm *of the Fleet Sir* JOHN RUSHWORTH Jellicoe, GCB, OM, GCVO, son of late Capt John Henry Jellicoe, of Northfield, Ryde, Isle of Wight; *b* 1859; Egyptian War 1882 (medal, bronze star), China 1900, Comdg Naval Brig and as Ch of Staff to Vice-Adm Sir E Seymour during attempt to relieve British Legation at Pekin (severely wounded, CB), European War 1914-16 in command of Grant Fleet, and at battle of Jutland (GCB, GCVO, OM, Order of Leopold of Belgium, French and Belgian Croix de Guerre, Grand Cross of Legion of Honour, Grand Cross of Military Order of Savoy, Japanese Order of the Rising Sun with Paulownia, 3rd class of Russian Order of St George, American DSM, Adm of the Fleet, thanked by Parliament, granted £50,000); commander of HMS "Victoria" when lost off Tripoli June 1893; was Director of Naval Ordnance 1905-7, a Lord of the Admiralty and Controller of the Navy 1908-10, in command of Atlantic Fleet 1910-11, and of 2nd Squadron of Home Fleet 1911-12, Second Sea Lord of the Admiralty 1912-14, Com-in-Ch of Grand Fleet 1914-16, and First Sea Lord of the Admiralty (also Ch of Naval Staff) 1916-17; Pres of British Legion 1928-32; Gov-Gen and Com-in-Ch of New Zealand 1920-24; *cr Viscount Jellicoe*, of Scapa, co Orkney (peerage of United Kingdom) 1917, with remainder to heirs male of his body, and in default of such issue with remainder (1) to his el da and to the heirs male of her body, and (2) to every other da successively in order of seniority of age and priority of birth, and heirs male of their bodies, and *Viscount Brocas*, of Southampton, co Southampton, and *Earl Jellicoe* (peerage of UK) 1925: *m* 1902, Florence Gwendoline, who *d* 1964, da of Sir Charles William Cayzer, 1st Bt (*cr* 1904); *d* 1935; *s* by his son (2) GEORGE PATRICK JOHN RUSHWORTH, 2nd Earl and present peer; also Viscount Jellicoe, and Viscount Brocas.

JENKIN OF RODING, BARON (Jenkin) (Life Baron 1987)

(CHARLES) PATRICK FLEEMING JENKIN, PC, son of late Charles O. F. Jenkin, of Gerrards Cross, Bucks; *b* 7 Sept 1926; *ed* Clifton, and Jesus Coll, Camb; Queen's Own Cameron Highlanders 1945-48; Bar Middle Temple 1952-57; Distillers Co Ltd 1957-70; Front Bench Spokesman on Treasury, Trade and Finance 1965-70; Joint Vice-Chm Conservative Parl Trade and Power Cttee 1966, Financial Sec to Treasury 1970-72, Chief Sec 1972-74, Minister for Energy Jan-March 1974, Shadow Spokesman on Energy 1974-76, and on Social Services 1976-79, Sec of State for Social Services 1979-81, Industry 1981-83, and DoE 1983-85; Chm Friends Provident Life Office 1988-98, Forest Healthcare NHS Trust 1991-97, UK-Japan 2000 Group 1986-90, and Chm Foundation for Science and Technology; Council Memb UK Centre for Economic and Environmental Development; Chm Westfield Coll Trust, Queen Mary and Westfield Coll Public Policy Research Unit Advisory Board 1990-96, Visual Handicap Group 1991-98; Sr Vice-Chm World Congress on Urban Growth and the Environment, Hong Kong 1994; Memb Supervisory Board Achmea (Holdings) BV 1993-98, and Internat Advisory Board Marsh & McLennan Group of Cos Inc 1990-98; Advisor Andersen Consulting Nat Economic Research Assocs Inc, and Sumitomo Trust and Banking Co Ltd, London Branch; Memb of Council of Guide Dogs for the Blind Assocn 1987-97; MP for Wanstead and Woodford (*C*) 1964-87; *cr* PC 1973, and *Baron Jenkin of Roding*, of Wanstead and Woodford in Greater London (Life Baron) 1987: *m* 1952, Alison Monica, eldest da of late Capt Philip Skelton Graham, RN (*see* Christison, Bt, ext), and has issue.

𝕬rms – Argent a lion rampant reguardant sable armed and langued gules within a bordure also sable. 𝕮rest – On a mural crown per pale argent and sable a lion rampant reguardant sable armed and langued gules. 𝕾upporters – *Dexter*, a seal erect on a rock; *Sinister*, a stag erect guardant on a grassy mound all proper.
Address – House of Lords, SW1A 0PW.

SONS LIVING

Rev Hon Charles Alexander Graham, *b* 1954; *ed* Highgate, Univ Coll, London, and Westcott House, Camb; ordained 1984; Team Rector Melton Mowbray since 1994: *m* 1984, Susan, da of Roy Collins, and has issue living, Alexandra Emily, *b* 1989, — Rebecca Charlotte, *b* 1991. *Residence* – Melton Mowbray Rectory, 67 Dalby Rd, Melton Mowbray, Leics LE13 0BQ.

Hon Bernard Christison, *b* 1959; *ed* Highgate, William Ellis Sch, and CCC Camb: *m* 1988, Anne Caroline, elder da of late Hon Charles Richard Strutt (*see* B Rayleigh), and has issue living, Robert Patrick Christison, *b* 1989, — Peter Andrew Graham, *b* 1991. *Residence* – 116 Kennington Rd, SE11 6RE.

DAUGHTERS LIVING

Hon Nicola Mary, *b* 1956; *ed* N London Collegiate Sch, Royal Coll of Music, and Hochschüle für Müsik, Vienna. *Residence* – Top Flat, 16 Handforth Rd, SW9 0LP.

Hon Flora Margaret, *b* 1962; *ed* Felsted, St John's Coll, Durham, and Trin Coll of Music; professional name (singer), Flora Christison: *m* 1990 (*m diss* 1998), Jacoby Michael Thwaites, yst son of Prof Sir Bryan Thwaites. *Residence* – 84B Tyrwhitt Rd, SE4 1QB.

JENKINS OF HILLHEAD (Jenkins) (Life Baron 1987)

ROY HARRIS JENKINS, OM, PC, only son of late Arthur Jenkins, MP, of Greenlands, Pontypool; *b* 11 Nov 1920; *ed* Abersychan Gram Sch, and Balliol Coll, Oxford; Hon DCL Oxford, and honorary degrees from twenty three other Univs; Hon FBA 1993; 1939-45 War with RA; PPS to Sec of State for Commonwealth Relations 1940-50, Min of Aviation 1964-65, Home Sec 1965-67, Chancellor of the Exchequer 1967-70, Dep Leader of Parl Labour Party 1970-72, Home Sec 1974-76; Pres Commn of European Communities 1977-81; Founder Member SDP 1981, Leader SDP 1982-83; Trustee Pilgrim Trust since 1973, Pres Univ of Wales Inst of Science and Technology 1975-81, Chancellor Oxford Univ since 1987, Pres Royal Soc of Literature since 1988; Dir Morgan Grenfell Holdings 1981-82; author of *Mr Attlee, Pursuit of Progress, Mr Balfour's Poodle, Sir Charles Dilke, Asquith, Afternoon on the Potomac, Nine Men of Power, Truman, Baldwin, Twentieth Century Portraits, European Diary 1977-81, A Life at the Centre, Portraits and Miniatures*, etc; MP for Central Div of Southwark (*Lab*) 1948-50, and Stechford Div of Birmingham 1950-76; *cr* PC 1964, OM 1993, and *Baron Jenkins of Hillhead*, of Pontypool, co Gwent (Life Baron) 1987: *m* 1945, Dame (Mary) Jennifer, DBE, da of late Sir Parker Morris, and has issue.

Residences – St Amand's House, E Hendred, Oxon; 2 Kensington Park Gdns, W11 3HB. *Clubs* – Brooks's, Athenaeum, Reform, Pratt's, United Oxford and Cambridge, Beefsteak.

SONS LIVING

Hon Charles Arthur Simon, *b* 1949; *ed* Winchester, and New Coll, Oxford: *m* 1971, Ivana Sertić, and has issue living, Alexandra Dorothea, *b* 1986, — Helena Harriet, *b* 1988. *Residence* – 9 Leppoc Rd, SW4.

Hon Edward Nicholas, *b* 1954; *ed* City of London Sch, and Trin Hall, Camb: *m* 1979, Sally Turner, and has issue living, Fergus Orlando Nicholas, *b* 1986, — Flora Rayne Victoria, *b* 1984. *Residence* – 7 Carthew Villas, W6.

DAUGHTER LIVING

Hon Cynthia Delanie, *b* 1951; *ed* St Paul's Girls' Sch, and St Anne's Coll, Oxford: *m* 1984, John Crosthwait, and has issue living, David Robert Jenkins, *b* 1982, — Hugh Michael Jenkins, *b* 1985, — George Nicholas Jenkins, *b* 1988.

JENKINS OF PUTNEY, BARON (Jenkins) (Life Baron 1981)

HUGH GATER JENKINS, son of Joseph Walter Jenkins; *b* 27 July 1908; *ed* Enfield Gram Sch; Research and Publicity Officer National Union of Bank Employees; Assist Gen Sec British Actors Equity Assocn; London CC 1952-64; Chm Standing Advisory Cttee on Local Authorities and the Theatre

1950-64; Min for the Arts 1974-76; Consultant (formerly Chm) The Theatres Trust, Joint Life Pres since 1995; Pres (formerly Chm) Theatres Advisory Council; Vice-Pres Campaign for Nuclear Disarmament (formerly Chm); Fl-Lt Fighter Command UK and SEAC (Burma) 1941-46; MP for Putney (*Lab*) 1964-79; *cr Baron Jenkins of Putney*, of Wandsworth, Greater London (Life Baron) 1981: *m* 1936, Marie Ethel, who *d* 1989, da of Sqdn-Ldr Ernest Christopher Crosbie; 2ndly, 1991, Helena Maria, who *d* 1994, da of Nicholas Paulidis, architect, of Athens.
Address – c/o House of Lords, SW1.

JERSEY, EARL OF (Child Villiers) (Earl E 1697)
(Name pronounced "Villers")

(George Francis) William Child Villiers, 10th Earl; *b* 5 Feb 1976; *s* 1998; *ed* Canford, and Birmingham Sch of Speech and Drama; Actor.

Arms – Quarterly: 1st and 4th, argent, on a cross gules, five escallops or, *Villiers*; 2nd and 3rd, gules, a chevron engrailed ermine, between three eaglets argent, ducally gorged or, and in the chief point, for distinction, an escallop or, *Child*. **Crests** – 1st, a lion rampant argent, ducally crowned or; 2nd, on a rock proper, an eagle rising argent, ducally gorged or, holding in the beak an adder proper, and charged on the breast, for distinction, with an ermine spot. **Supporters** – Two lions argent, ducally crowned or, and gorged with a plain collar gules, charged with three escallops or.
Residence – 5 Mimosa St, SW6 4DS.

HALF-BROTHER LIVING (*son of George Henry, Viscount Villiers by 3rd marriage*)

Hon Jamie Charles, *b* 31 May 1994.

SISTERS LIVING

Hon Helen Katherine Luisa, *b* 1978.
Hon Luciana Dorothea Sacha, *b* 1981.

The Cross is the test of faith

HALF-SISTER LIVING (*daughter of George Henry, Viscount Villiers by 1st marriage to Verna (now Lady Hanley), 2nd da of late Kenneth A. Stott, of St Mary, Jersey*)

Hon Sophia Georgiana, *b* 1971. *Residence* – 6 Butts Mead, Northwood, Middx HA6 2TL.

AUNT LIVING (*daughter of 9th Earl by 3rd marriage*)

Lady Isabella Bianca Rosa, *b* 1950: *m* 1974, Peter Edward Harrison, and has issue living, Matthew Alexander Charles, *b* 1980; *ed* Winchester, — Alexandra Venetia, *b* 1977. *Residence* – Constantia Manor, Isfield, nr Uckfield, E Sussex TN22 5XU.

HALF-AUNT LIVING (*daughter of 9th Earl by 1st marriage*)

Lady Caroline, *b* 1934: *m* 1st, 1952 (*m diss* 1965), as his 1st wife, Gilbert Edward George Lariston, Viscount Melgund, MBE (later 6th Earl of Minto, OBE); 2ndly, 1969 (*m diss* 1972), as his 2nd wife, Hon John Douglas Stuart, who *d* 1990, yr son of 1st Viscount Stuart of Findhorn, CH, MVO, MC, PC; 3rdly, 1980, as his 2nd wife, Hon James Donald Diarmid Ogilvy, yst son of 12th Earl of Airlie, KT, GCVO, MC, and has issue (by 1st *m*) (*see* E Minto). *Residence* – Sedgebrook Manor, nr Grantham, Lincs NG32 2EU.

GREAT-AUNTS LIVING (*daughters of 8th Earl*)

Lady Joan, *b* 1911: *m* 1933, Lieut David Richard Colville, RNVR (*see* V Colville, colls), who *d* 1986. *Residence* – Hollybush Farm, Stoneyheath, Ramsdell, nr Tadley, Hants RG26 5SL.
Lady Ann, *b* 1916: *m* 1937, Major Alexander Henry Elliot, late RA (*see* E Minto, colls), who *d* 1986. *Residence* – Broadford, Chobham, nr Woking, Surrey GU24 8EF.

MOTHER LIVING

Sacha Jane Hooper, elder da of Peter Hooper Valpy, of Jersey, and formerly wife of Keith Fullerton Lauder: *m* 1974 (*m diss* 1988), as his 2nd wife, George Henry, Viscount Villiers, who *d* (19 March) 1998.

WIDOW LIVING OF SON OF NINTH EARL

Stephanie Louise, da of John Ian Penman, of Scotland: *m* 1st, 1992, as his 3rd wife, George Henry, Viscount Villiers, who *d* (19 March) 1998; 2ndly, (Nov) 1998, Michael Morley. *Residence* – 4 Hunters Meadow, Gt Shefford, Hungerford, Berks RG17 7EQ.

WIDOW LIVING OF NINTH EARL

BIANCA MARIA ADRIANA LUCIANA (*Countess of Jersey*), da of late Enrico Mottironi, of Via Goffredo Casalis, Turin, Italy: *m* 1947, as his 3rd wife, the 9th Earl of Jersey, who *d* (9 Aug) 1998. *Residence* – Radier Manor, Le Chemin du Radier, Grouville, Jersey JE3 4DR, CI.

COLLATERAL BRANCHES LIVING

Issue of late Hon Charles Victor Child Villiers, yr son of 9th Earl, *b* 1952, *d* 1991: *m* 1975 (*m diss* 1989), Brigitte Elisabeth Germaine, da of Robert Jean Rolland Marchand:—
Eleanor Monica, *b* 1979. —— Barbara Béatrice, *b* 1981.

Issue of late Sqn-Ldr Hon (Edward) Mansel Child-Villiers, yr son of 8th Earl, *b* 1913, *d* 1980: *m* 1st, 1934 (*m diss* 1940), Barbara Mary, who *d* 1991, only da of late Capt William John Goulburn Shipdem Frampton, E Lancs Regt, of Newton Hall, Clitheroe; 2ndly, 1946 (*m diss* 1971), Princess Maria Gloria Pignatelli Aragona Cortez, only da of late Prince Antonio Pignatelli Aragona Cortez, Duke of Terranova, of Rome:—
(By 1st *m*) (Edward) John Mansel Hugh Frampton (Stable House, Mystole, Canterbury, Kent CT4 7DB), *b* 1935; *ed* Harrow: *m* 1958, Celia Elinor Vadyn, only da of late Cyril Hall Green, of Ballyvolane House, Castlelyons, co Cork (*see* Blake, Bt, *cr* 1622, colls), and has issue living, Alexander (19 King's Court North, 189 King's Rd, SW3 5EQ), *b* 1961; *ed* Clayesmore: *m* 1988 (*m diss* 1993), Linda-Benedicte, da of Bjørn-Arild Solheim, of Oslo, Norway, and has issue living, Frederick Mansel *b* 1990, — Roderick Anthony (36 Cristowe Rd, SW6 3QE), *b* 1963; *ed* Harrow. —— (By 2nd *m*) (George Anthony) Robert (3 Clos du Macon, La Rue Mahier, St Ouen, Jersey, CI), *b* 1947; *ed* The Oratory Sch, Reading: *m* 1st, 1973 (*m diss* 1989), Margot Vida, 3rd da of late Kenneth A. Stott, of St Mary, Jersey (ante); 2ndly, 1989, Mrs Norah Mary Jennifer Gladwell, yr da of late Edwin Basil Binyon, and has issue living (by 2nd wife), Miranda Kate, *b* 1986. —— Mary Ann CHILD-VILLIERS (Star Broadway, Petite Route des Mielles, St Brelade, Jersey, CI), *b* 1951; has resumed her maiden name: *m* 1971 (*m diss* 1986), Stephen John Beck, and has issue living, Christian Mark Stephen, *b* 1976, — Honor Marie, *b* 1979. —— Maria Consuelo (Lily) (3 Hazelmere Rd, NW6), *b* 1953; has issue living (by Prince Costantino Filippo Maria Ruspoli di Poggio Suasa), Bartolomeo Sebastian, *b* 1976; actor.

Descendants of late Hon Thomas Villiers (2nd son of 2nd Earl of Jersey) who was *cr Earl of Clarendon* 1776 (see that title).

PREDECESSORS – (1) *Sir* OLIVER St John; *cr Viscount Grandison of Limerick* (peerage of Ireland) 1620 with remainder to the male heirs of his niece Barbara, wife of Sir Edward Villiers, el half-brother of George, Duke of Buckingham, the celebrated favourite of James I; *d* 1630; *s* by his el grand-nephew (2) WILLIAM Villiers, 2nd Viscount, el son of Barbara (ante); a zealous partisan of Charles I; *d* of wounds received at battle of Bristol 1643; *s* by his brother (3) JOHN, 3rd Viscount; *dsp*; *s* by his brother (4) GEORGE, 4th Viscount; *d* 1699; *s* by his grandson (5) JOHN, 5th Viscount; *cr Earl Grandison* (peerage of Ireland) 1721; *d* 1766, when the Earldom became ext, and he was *s* in the Viscountcy by his kinsman (6) WILLIAM, 3rd Earl of Jersey (see * infra); *d* 1769; *s* by his son (7) GEORGE BUSSY, 4th Earl; successively a Lord of the Admiralty, Lord Chamberlain of the Household and Master of the Buckhounds; *d* 1805; *s* by his son (8) GEORGE, 5th Earl; *b* 1773; assumed the additional surname of Child by Roy licence 1819, was twice Lord Chamberlain to William IV, and twice Master of the Horse to Queen Victoria: *m* 1804, Sarah Sophia (who inherited Osterley Park, Middx, from her mother 1793), da of 10th Earl of Westmorland; *d* 1859; *s* by his son (9) GEORGE AUGUSTUS FREDERICK, 6th Earl; *b* 1808; successively MP for Honiton, Weymouth, and Cirencester (C): *m* 1841, Julia, da of the Rt Hon Sir Robert Peel, 2nd Bt; *d* 1859; *s* by his son (10) VICTOR ALBERT GEORGE, GCB, GCMG, PC, 7th Earl, *b* 1845; a partner in the banking firm of Child and Co, Fleet Street, EC; a Lord-in-Waiting to HM Queen Victoria 1875-7; Lord-Lieut for Oxfordshire 1887-1915; Paymaster-Gen 1889-90; Gov and Com-in-Ch of NS Wales 1890-93, and Acting Agent-Gen for New South Wales in London 1904-5: *m* 1872, Hon Margaret Elizabeth Leigh, DBE, who *d* 1945, da of 2nd Baron Leigh; *d* 1915; *s* by his el son (11) GEORGE HENRY ROBERT CHILD, 8th Earl, *b* 1873; a partner in the firm of Child and Co, bankers, of Fleet Street, EC; a Lord-in-Waiting to HM Jan to Aug 1919: *m* 1908, Lady Cynthia Almina Constance Mary, who *d* 1947 (having *m* 2ndly, 1925, Com William Rodney Slessor, RNVR, who *d* on active ser 1945), da of 3rd Earl of Kilmorey; *d* 1923: *s* by his son (12) GEORGE FRANCIS, 9th Earl; *b* 1910; Maj RA (TA); gave Osterley Park to the National Trust 1949; Pres World Jersey Cattle Bureau: *m* 1st, 1932 (*m diss* 1937), Patricia Kenneth, da of Kenneth Richards, of Cootamundra, NSW, Australia; 2ndly, 1937 (*m diss* 1946), Virginia, who *d* 1996, da of James Cherrill, of Hollywood, California, USA, and formerly wife of Archibald Alexander Leach (the film actor Cary Grant); 3rdly, 1947, Bianca Maria Adriana Luciana, da of late Enrico Mottironi, of Via Goffredo Casalis, Turin, Italy; *d* 1998; *s* by his grandson (13) (GEORGE FRANCIS) WILLIAM (elder son of late George Henry, *Viscount Villiers*, elder son of 9th Earl), 10th Earl and present peer; also Viscount Villiers of Dartford, Viscount Grandison of Limerick, and Baron Villiers of Hoo.

*Sir Edward Villiers, 5th son of Barbara St John, niece of 1st Viscount Grandison, had with other issue (1) EDWARD, PC, Knt, *cr Baron Villiers of Hoo*, co Kent, and *Viscount Villiers of Dartford*, co Kent (peerage of England) 1691, and *Earl of the Island of Jersey* (peerage of England) 1697; successively Special Ambassador to the Hague, Ambassador to the States Gen and to France, Lord Justice of Ireland, Sec of State, Master of the Horse, Lord Chamberlain of the Household and Knight Marshal; *d* 1711; *s* by his son (2) WILLIAM, 2nd Earl; *d* 1731; *s* by his son (3) WILLIAM, PC, 3rd Earl, who *s* his kinsman as 6th Viscount Grandison (ante).

Jervis, family name of Viscount St Vincent.

JESSEL, BARONY OF (Jessel) (Extinct 1990)

GRANDDAUGHTER LIVING OF SECOND BARON

Issue of late Hon Timothy Edward Jessel, only son of 2nd Baron, *b* 1935, *d* 1969: *m* 1st, 1961 (*m diss* 1965), Janet Calliope, yr da of Maurice Smith, of Bidborough, Kent; 2ndly, 1965, Jill Elizabeth (infra) (who *m* 2ndly, 1977, (Edwin) Donald Gomme), only da of late George Alexander Powell, of Auckland, NZ:—

(By 2nd *m*) Annabel Helen, *b* 1968. *Residence* – 55 Winchendon Rd, SW6.

DAUGHTER LIVING OF SECOND BARON (*By 1st marriage*)

Hon Camilla Edith Mairi Elizabeth JESSEL, *b* 1940; has resumed her maiden name: *m* 1960 (*m* annulled 1972), as his 1st wife, Don Juan Carlos del Prado y Ruspoli, Marques de Caicedo, and has issue living, *Don* Miguel Angel, *b* 1961: *m* 1989, Natalia, da of Nicolas Sartorius, of Spain, and has issue living, Claudia Rebeca Leonor *b* 1992, — *Don* Alfonso Segundo, *b* 1966: *m* 1996, Nicole, eldest da of Comte Geoffroy de Vitry d'Avaucourt, of Montpellier, France. *Residence* – Calle Lope de Vega 29, Madrid Spain.

WIDOW LIVING OF SON OF SECOND BARON

Jill Elizabeth, da of late George Alexander Powell, of Auckland, NZ: *m* 1st, 1965, as his 2nd wife, Hon Timothy Edward Jessel, who *d* 1969; 2ndly, 1977, (Edwin) Donald Gomme, and has issue (by 1st *m*) (ante). *Residence* – Av Edouard Rod 30, 1007 Lausanne, Switzerland.

WIDOW LIVING OF SECOND BARON

JESSICA MARIAN (*Baroness Jessel*), da of late William de Wet, of Somerset East, S Africa, and of Mrs Herbert Taylor, of Rondesbosch, Cape Town, S Africa: *m* 1960, as his 2nd wife, the 2nd Baron Jessel, CBE, who *d* 1990, when the title became extinct. *Residence* – 4 Sloane Terrace Mansions, SW1X 9DG.

Jocelyn, Viscount; son of Earl of Roden.

Jocelyn, family name of Earl of Roden.

JOHN-MACKIE, BARONY OF (Mackie) (Extinct 1994)

SONS LIVING OF LIFE BARON

Hon James Alexander, *b* 1935: *m* 19—, Irene Fullerton.
Hon John Maitland (52 Lucas Lane, Hitchin, Herts), *b* 1944: *m* 1st, 19—, Marion Halliday; 2ndly, 1984, Janet Ann Hart, and has issue living (by 2nd *m*), Louise, *b* 1985.
Hon George Yull (The Bungalow, Harolds Park Farm, Nazeing, Essex), *b* 1949: *m* 1983, Catherine MacLeod.

DAUGHTERS LIVING OF LIFE BARON

Hon Jean Simpson (31 Arbirlot Rd, Arbroath), *b* 1937: *m* 19—, Alexander Fairweather.
Hon Mary Yull, *b* 1940.

WIDOW LIVING OF LIFE BARON

JEANNIE (*Baroness John-Mackie*), da of Robert Milne: *m* 1934, Baron John-Mackie, who *d* 1994. *Residence* – Harold's Park Farm, Nazeing, Essex.

JOHNSTON OF ROCKPORT, BARON (Johnston) (Life Baron 1987)

CHARLES COLLIER JOHNSTON, eldest son of late Capt Charles Moore Johnston, by his late wife Muriel Florence, da of Reuben Mellon; *b* 4 March 1915; *ed* Tonbridge; Maj RA (ret), served in 1939-45 War; TD; Man Dir Standex Internat Ltd (formerly Roehlen-Martin Ltd) 1948-76 (Chm 1951-77), Engravers and Engrs, Chm Standex Holdings since 1986; Chm Macclesfield Constituency Conservative Assocn 1961-65, Hon Treas NW Conservatives and Memb Conservative Bd of Finance 1965-71, Chm NW Area Conservatives 1971-76; a Vice Pres Nat Union of Conservative and Unionist Assocs, Joint Hon Treas Conservative Party 1984-87; *cr* Kt 1973, and *Baron Johnston of Rockport*, of Caversham, co Berks (Life Baron) 1987: *m* 1st, 1939, Audrey Boyes, da of late Edgar Monk; 2ndly, 1981, Mrs Yvonne Shearman, da of late Reginald Marley, and has issue by 1st *m*.
Address – c/o House of Lords, SW1.

SONS LIVING (*By 1st marriage*)

Hon Michael Charles (Court Hay Cottage, Farrington, Blandford Forum, Dorset), *b* 1942.
Hon Timothy Courtenay (22 Nerida Rd, Kareela, NSW 2232, Australia), *b* 1945.

Johnston, Lawson, family name of Baron Luke.

Johnstone, Hope, family name of Earl of Annandale and Hartfell.

Johnstone, Vanden-Bempde-, family name of Baron Derwent.

JOICEY, BARON (Joicey) (Baron UK 1906, Bt UK 1893)

JAMES MICHAEL JOICEY, 5th Baron, and 5th Baronet; *b* 28 June 1953; *s* 1993; *ed* Eton, and Ch Ch, Oxford: *m* 1984, Agnes Harriet Frances Mary, yr da of Rev William Thompson, of Oxnam Manse, Jedburgh, Roxburghshire, and has issue.

Arms – Argent, three lozenges sable within two bendlets invected gules between two miner's picks in bend proper. **Crest** – A demi-man affrontée in armour proper, garnished or, the helmet adorned with three feathers gules, holding in the dexter hand a scimitar of the first, pommel and hilt gold, supporting with the sinister hand an escutcheon argent, charged with three torteaux within two bendlets invected of the second between two fleurs-de-lis sable. **Supporters** – On either side a Shetland pony proper, haltered or.
Seats – Etal Manor, Cornhill-on-Tweed, TD15 4TL; Ford Castle, Berwick-on-Tweed. *Residence* – East Flodden Farmhouse, Milfield, Wooler, Northumberland NE71 6JF.

SONS LIVING

Hon WILLIAM JAMES, *b* 21 May 1990.
Hon Richard Michael, *b* 1993.

DAUGHTERS LIVING

Hon Hannah Elisabeth, *b* 1988.
Hon Claire Vida, *b* 1994.

Every land is a native country to a brave man

BROTHER LIVING

Hon Andrew Hugh, *b* 1955; *ed* Eton, and Ch Ch, Oxford: *m* 1994, Corinne J., eldest da of John Cockburn, of Cockburnspath, Berwickshire, and has issue living, Victoria Marianne, *b* 1997. *Residence* – New Etal, Cornhill-on-Tweed, Northumberland TD12 4XL.

SISTER LIVING

Hon Katherine Jane, *b* 1959: *m* 1984, Thomas Crosbie Dawson (*see* Sutton, Bt, 1985 Edn), and has issue living, Robert Hugo, *b* 1992, — Lucy Charlotte, *b* 1987, — Helen Amanda, *b* 1989. *Residence* – Pawston, Mindrum, Northumberland.

WIDOW LIVING OF FOURTH BARON

ELISABETH MARION (*Elisabeth, Baroness Joicey*), da of late Lt-Col Hon Ian Leslie Melville, TD (*see* E Leven and Melville, colls): *m* 1952, the 4th Baron Joicey, who *d* 1993. *Residence* – Beech House, Etal, Berwick-on-Tweed TD15 2PU.

PREDECESSORS – (1) JAMES Joicey, son of George Joicey, of Newcastle-upon-Tyne; *b* 1846; MP for Durham co, Chester-le-Street Div (*L*) 1885-1905; *cr* a Baronet 1893, and *Baron Joicey* of Chester-le-Street, co Durham (peerage of United Kingdom) 1906: *m* 1st, 1879, Elizabeth Amy, who *d* 1881, da of late Joseph Robinson, JP, of North Shields; 2ndly, 1884, Marguerite Smyles, who *d* 1911, da of late Col Drever, HEICS; *d* 1936; *s* by his el son (2) JAMES ARTHUR, 2nd Baron, *b* 1880; was High Sheriff of co Durham 1910: *m* 1904, Georgina Wharton, who *d* 1952, da of Major Augustus Edward Burdon, formerly of Hartford Hall, Bedlington, Northumberland; *d* 1940; *s* by his brother (3) HUGH EDWARD, 3rd Baron, *b* 1881; High Sheriff of Northumberland 1933: *m* 1921, Lady Joan Katherine Lambton, who *d* 1967, da of 4th Earl of Durham; *d* 1966; *s* by his yr son (4) MICHAEL EDWARD, 4th Baron, *b* 1925; Capt Coldstream Guards; DL Northumberland 1985: *m* 1952, Elisabeth Marion, da of late Lt-Col Hon Ian Leslie Melville, TD (*see* E Leven and Melville, colls); *d* 1993; *s* by his elder son (5) JAMES MICHAEL, 5th Baron and present peer.

Jolliffe, family name of Baron Hylton.

Jones, see Baron Wynne-Jones.

Jones, family name of Baron Maelor.

Jones, Armstrong-, family name of Earl of Snowdon.

Jones, Gwynne, family name of Baron Chalfont.

JOPLING, BARON (Jopling) (Life Baron 1997)

(THOMAS) MICHAEL JOPLING, PC, son of late Mark Bellerby Jopling, of Masham, N Yorks; *b* 10 Dec 1930; *ed* Cheltenham, and King's Coll, Newcastle-upon-Tyne (BSc Agric 1952), Hon DCL Newcastle 1992; Memb Nat Council, NFU 1962-64; MP (*C*) Westmorland 1964-83, and Westmorland and Lonsdale 1983-97; PPS to Min of Agriculture 1970-71, Assist Govt Whip 1971-73, a Lord Commr of The Treasury 1973-74, Opposition Whip 1974, Opposition Spokesman on Agriculture 1974-79, Shadow Min for Agriculture 1975-76, Parly Sec to Treasury and Govt Chief Whip 1979-83, Min of Agriculture, Fisheries and Food 1983-87; Pres EEC Councils of Agriculture and Fishery Ministers 1986; Hon Sec British-American Parliamentary Group since 1987; Leader, UK Delegation OSCE Parliamentary Assembly 1991-97; Memb Foreign Affairs Select Cttee 1987-97; Int Exec Commonwealth Parliamentary Assoc 1988-89 (Memb UK Executive 1974-79 and 1987-97, Vice-Chm 1977-79); Memb of Select Cttee on Sittings of the House of Commons (Chm 1991-92); Pres Auto Cycle Union since 1989; DL Cumbria 1991-97, DL N Yorks 1998; Liveryman of Worshipful Co of Farmers; *cr* PC 1979, and *Baron Jopling*, of Ainderby Quernhow, co N Yorks (Life Baron) 1997: *m* 1958, Gail, da of late Ernest Dickinson, of Harrogate, and has issue.
Residence – Ainderby Hall, Thirsk, N Yorks YO7 4HZ. *Clubs* – Beefsteak, Buck's (Hon Memb), RAC (Hon Memb).

SONS LIVING

Hon Nicholas M. F., *b* 1961; *ed* Eton, and Newcastle Univ: *m* 1st, 1987 (*m diss* 19—), Jayne, da of late Derek Benson, of Bedale, N Yorks; 2ndly, 1996, Serena Emily, adopted da of late Lt-Col Brian Joseph Lockhart (*see* L Gray, colls), and formerly wife of Patrick James, Lord Gillford, and has issue living (by 1st *m*), one son and one da. *Residence* – 53 Richborne Terrace, SW8 1AT.
Hon Jeremy M. N., *b* 1963; *ed* Eton, and Edinburgh Univ: *m* 1997, Sam Taylor-Wood, da of David Taylor, of Ramsgate, Kent, and has issue living, one da.

JOSEPH, BARONY OF (Joseph) (see Joseph, Bt).

JOWITT, EARLDOM OF (Jowitt) (Extinct 1957)

DAUGHTER LIVING OF FIRST EARL

Lady Penelope, *b* 1923: *m* 1943, George Wynn-Williams, FRCS, FRCOG, who *d* 1993, and has issue living, William Jowitt Dafydd (14 Hendham Rd, SW17 7DQ), *b* 1947: *m* 1st, 1975 (*m diss* 1988), Amanda S. B., only da of Col John Childs, of 23 Lennox Gdns, SW3; 2ndly, 1990, Fiona Mary, da of Graham Pilcher, and has issue living (by 1st *m*), William Alexander Taillefer *b* 1978, James Henry Jowitt *b* 1983, — Huw James (Brook House, Philpot Lane, Chobham, Surrey GU24 8HD), *b* 1955; Bar Middle Temple 1977: *m* 1979, Mary L., only da of William Vaughan, of Chobham Farm Cottage, Chobham, Surrey, and has issue living, Harry George *b* 1984, Laura Jane *b* 1982, Lucy Mary *b* 1987, — Lesley-Jane, *b* 1944: *m* 1st, 1965 (*m diss* 1976), William Mortimer Man; 2ndly, 1976 (*m* annulled 1980); 3rdly, 1981, Peter Charles Nicholson, of Mere House, Hamble, Hants, and has issue living (by 1st *m*), David Mortimer *b* 1969: *m* 1994, Hon Stephanie Jane Moore, only da of Baron Moore of Lower Marsh, PC (Life Baron) (and has issue: *see* B Moore of Lower Marsh), Philippa Lesley *b* 1966: *m* 1989 (*m diss* 1991), — (and has issue living, Ben ODGERS *b* 1989), Fiona Lesley *b* 1970. *Residence* – 102 Napier Court, SW6 3XA.

JUDD, BARON (Judd) (Life Baron 1991)

FRANK ASHCROFT JUDD, son of late Charles Wilfred Judd, CBE, of 42 The Crescent, Belmont, Sutton, Surrey; *b* 28 March 1935; *ed* City of London Sch, and LSE (BSc); F/O RAF 1957-59; Gen Sec Internat Voluntary Ser 1960-66; PPS to Min of Housing and Local Govt 1967-70, to Leader of Opposition 1970-72, Joint Opposition Defence Spokesman 1972-74, Parly Under Sec of State for Defence RN 1974-76, Min for Overseas Devpt 1976-77, FCO 1977-79; Assoc Dir Internat Defence & Aid Fund for Southern Africa 1979-80, Dir VSO 1980-85, Chm Internat Council of Voluntary Agencies 1985-90, and Dir Oxfam 1985-91; Council Member Overseas Devpt Inst, Member Governing Body Queen Elizabeth House, Oxford Univ, and Gov LSE since 1982; Member Council for Charitable Support since 1991, Member World Health Organisation Task Force on Health and Development Policies since 1994; Gov Westminster Coll, Oxford; Trustee Portsmouth Cathedral Development Trust, plc; Hon Fellow Portsmouth Univ 1978, Hon DLitt Bradford Univ 1987, FRSA 1988; MP Portsmouth W (*Lab*) 1966-74, and Portsmouth N 1974-79; author; *cr Baron Judd*, of Portsea, co Hants (Life Baron) 1991; *m* 1961, Christine Elizabeth Louise, da of late Frederick Ward Willington, of Kent, and has issue.
Club – Commonwealth Trust.

DAUGHTERS LIVING

Hon Elizabeth, *b* 1967.
Hon Philippa, *b* 1969.

KABERRY OF ADEL, BARONY OF (Kaberry) (Extinct 1991) (see Kaberry, Bt).

KADOORIE, BARONY OF (Kadoorie) (Extinct 1993)

SON LIVING OF LIFE BARON

Hon Michael David *b* 1941; *ed* King George V Sch, Hong Kong, and Le Rosey, Switzerland; Chm The Hong Kong &

Shanghai Hotels Ltd, etc: *m* 1984, Betty, da of Juan E. Tamayo, of Coral Gables, Fla, USA, and has issue living, Philip *b* 1992, — Natalie *b* 1986, — Bettina, *b* 1987. *Residence* – 68 Deep Water Bay Rd, Hong Kong.

DAUGHTER LIVING OF LIFE BARON

Hon Rita Laura, *b* 1940: *m* 1965, Ronald James McAulay, and has issue living, Andrew James Kadoorie, *b* 1967, — Deborah Jane Kadoorie, *b* 1969.

WIDOW LIVING OF LIFE BARON

MURIEL (*Baroness Kadoorie*), da of D. S. Gubbay, of Hong Kong: *m* 1938, Baron Kadoorie, CBE (Life Baron), who *d* 1993. *Residence* – 24 Kadoorie Av, Kowloon, Hong Kong.

KAGAN, BARONY OF (Kagan) (Extinct 1995)

SONS LIVING OF LIFE BARON

Hon Michael George, *b* 1950.
Hon Daniel, *b* 1953.

DAUGHTER LIVING OF LIFE BARON

Hon Ann Eugenia, *b* 1965.

WIDOW LIVING OF LIFE BARON

MARGARET (*Baroness Kagan*), da of George Strom: *m* 1943, Baron Kagan, who *d* 1995.

KALDOR, BARONY OF (Kaldor) (Extinct 1986)

DAUGHTERS LIVING OF LIFE BARON

Hon Katharine Margaret, *b* 1937: *m* 1958, Anthony Hungerford Hoskyns, of 25 Hamilton Gdns, NW8 (*see* Hoskyns, Bt).
Hon Frances Julia, *b* 1940: *m* 1962, Michael John Stewart.
Hon Penelope Jane, *b* 1942: *m* 1964, Robert Charles Milsom, of 2 Adams Rd, Cambridge.
Hon Mary Henrietta, *b* 1946; writer.

Kearley, family name of Viscount Devonport.

Keith, family name of Earl of Kintore.

KEITH OF AVONHOLM, BARONY OF (Keith) (Extinct 1964)

SON LIVING OF LIFE BARON

Hon Henry Shanks (*Baron Keith of Kinkel*), *b* 1922; *cr* Baron Keith of Kinkel (Life Baron) 1976 (see that title).

DAUGHTER LIVING OF LIFE BARON

Hon Elizabeth Hamilton, *b* 1916: *m* 1945, Raymond Alan Lolley, who *d* 1980, and has issue.

KEITH OF CASTLEACRE, BARON (Keith) (Life Baron 1980)

Truth conquers

KENNETH ALEXANDER KEITH, son of late Edward Charles Keith, of Swanton Morley House, Dereham, Norfolk, *b* 30 Aug 1916; *ed* Rugby; 1939-45 War as Lt-Col WG in N Africa and NW Europe (despatches, Croix de Guerre with Silver Star); Chm Hill Samuel Gp Ltd 1970-80, and Rolls Royce Ltd 1972-80; Pres Royal Norfolk Agricultural Assocn 1989, Pres British Standards Inst since 1989, Pres RoSPA since 1989; *cr* Knt 1969, and *Baron Keith of Castleacre*, of Swaffham, co Norfolk (Life Baron) 1980 *m* 1st, 1946 (*m diss* 1958), Lady Ariel Olivia Winifred Baird, da of 1st Viscount Stonehaven, by his wife late Countess of Kintore (in her own right); 2ndly, 1962 (*m diss* 1972), Nancy, who *d* 1990, da of Edward B. Gross, of Monterey, Calif, and formerly wife of (i) Howard Hawks (*d* 1977), film dir, and (ii) Leland Hayward (*d* 1971), of Manhasset, New York; 3rdly, 1973, Marieluz, elder da of late Capt Robert Peel Dennistoun-Webster, DSC, RN, of Hurst Grange, nr Twyford, formerly wife of (i) Adrian Donald Henderson (*see* Faringdon, B, colls), and widow of Col James Robert Hanbury, of Burley-on-the-Hill, Oakham, Rutland, and has issue by 1st *m*.

Arms – Paly of six or and gules, on a chief argent three stags heads caboshed proper. Crest – A garb or supported by two stags respectant proper. Supporters – *Dexter*, A foreman proper, his overall argent charged on the breast pocket with a monogram composed of the letters RR superimposed one above the other, with the word Rolls and beneath the word Royce, all in capital letters gules, the collar azure, holding in his outer hand a worksheet in its folder proper: *Sinister*, a farmer in plus-four suit and cap of brown tweed with heather mixture stockings, and brown boots holding in the crook of his outer arm a shotgun proper.
Residences – 9 Eaton Sq, SW1W 9DB; The Wicken House, Castleacre, Norfolk PE32 2BP. *Clubs* – Pratt's, White's; Links Club (New York).

SON LIVING (*By 1st marriage*)

Hon Alastair James, *b* 1947; *ed* Eton, and Harvard Univ; *m* 1983, Jayne Will, yr da of late Walter C. Teagle, jr, and has issue living, Alexander Teagle, *b* 1984.

DAUGHTER LIVING (*By 1st marriage*)

Hon Camilla Margaret (twin) (*Hon Lady Mackeson*) (Apt 36E, 1365 York Av, New York 10021, USA), *b* 1947: *m* 1968 (*m diss* 1972), Sir Rupert Henry Mackeson, 2nd Bt.

KEITH OF KINKEL, BARON (Keith) (Life Baron 1976)

HENRY SHANKS KEITH, GBE, PC, son of late Baron Keith of Avonholm (Life Baron); *b* 7 Feb 1922; *ed* Edinburgh Acad, Magdalen Coll, Oxford (MA; Hon Fellow 1977) and Edinburgh Univ (LLB); Bar Gray's Inn 1951; Bencher 1976; Advocate Scotland 1950; QC 1962; Standing Jr Council to Dep of Health for Scotland 1957-62; a Member of Scottish Valuation Advisory Council 1959-70 (Chm 1972-76), of Law Reform Cttee for Scotland 1964-70, of Panel of Arbiters under European Fisheries Convention 1964-71, and under Convention on Settlement of Investment Disputes between States and Nationals of other States 1968-71, and of Cttee on Law of Defamation 1971-75; Dep Chm Parl Boundaries Commn for Scotland 1975; Sheriff-Prin of Roxburgh, Berwick and Selkirk 1970-71; 1939-45 War in Scots Gds (despatches); a Lord of Session with title of Lord Keith 1971-76, Lord of Appeal in Ordinary 1976-96; Chm Joint Cttee on Consolidation Bills 1978-80; Chm Cttee on Enforcement Powers of the Revenue Depts 1980-84; *cr Baron Keith of Kinkel,* of Strathtummel in District of Perth and Kinross (Life Baron) 1976, PC 1976, and GBE (Civil) 1997: *m* 1955, Alison Hope Alan, JP, yr da of Alan Brown, and has issue.
Residence – Strathtummel, Pitlochry, Perthshire PH16 5RP.

SONS LIVING

Hon James Alan, *b* 1959: *m* 1987, Eleanor Mary, yr da of Col Michael ffolliott Woodhead, OBE, of 56 Chesilton Rd, SW6, and has issue living, Samuel Henry Michael, *b* 1994, — Flavia, *b* 1991, — Phoebe, *b* 1997.
Hon Thomas Hamilton, *b* 1961; *ed* Magdalen Coll, Oxford; Bar-at-law. *Chambers* – Fountain Court, Temple, EC4Y 9DH.
Hon Hugo George, *b* 1967; *ed* Magdalen Coll, Oxford; Bar-at-Law. *Chambers* – 3 Raymond Buildings, Gray's Inn, WC1R 5BP.
Hon Alexander Lindsay, *b* 1967: *m* 1995, Sally Ann, twin da of B. O'Regan, and has issue living, Ossian Leo Henry, *b* 1998.

DAUGHTER LIVING

Hon Deborah Jane, *b* 1957; *ed* Univs of Edinburgh, London, and E Anglia.

Kelburn, Viscount of; son of Earl of Glasgow.

Kellie, Earl of; Earl of Mar and Kellie.

KELVEDON, BARON (Channon) (Life Baron 1997)

(HENRY) PAUL GUINNESS CHANNON, PC, son of late Sir Henry Channon, MP, of Kelvedon Hall, Brentwood, Essex, by his wife Lady Honor Guinness, da of 2nd Earl of Iveagh; *b* 9 Oct 1935; *ed* Eton, and Ch Ch, Oxford; MP (*C*) Southend W 1959-97; PPS to Minister of Power 1959-60; PPS to Home Secretary 1960-62, and to Foreign Secretary 1963-64; opposition spokesman on Arts and Amenities 1967-70; Parliamentary Sec, Ministry of Housing and Local Government 1970; Parliamentary Under-Sec, DOE 1970-72; Min of State for N Ireland 1972; Min of Housing and Construction, Environment Dept 1972-74; opposition spokesman on Prices and Consumer Protection 1974, and on Environmental Affairs 1974-75; Min of State, Civil Service Dept 1979-81; Min for the Arts 1981-83, and for Trade 1983-86; Sec of State for Trade and Industry 1986-87, and for Transport 1987-89; served with Royal Horse Guards 1954-56, Central and Eastern Europe 1993-97; Liveryman, Worshipful Co of Goldsmiths; Chm British Assoc for Central and Eastern Europe since 1993; *cr* PC

1980, and *Baron Kelvedon*, of Ongar, co Essex (Life Baron) 1997: *m* 1963, Ingrid Olivia Georgia, formerly wife of Hon Jonathan Bryan Guinness (later 3rd Baron Moyne), and da of late Maj Guy Richard Charles Wyndham, MC (*see* B Egremont, colls), and has had issue.

Arms – ......
Residence – c/o Iveagh Trustees Ltd, 41 Harrington Gdns, SW7 4JU.

SON LIVING

Hon Henry, *b* 1970; *ed* ......: *m* 1996, Henrietta, da of late David Towill, and of Mrs Arthur Boyd-Rochfort. *Residence* –

DAUGHTERS LIVING AND DECEASED

Olivia Gwendolen Violet, *b* 1964; *d* 1986.
Hon Georgia Honor Margaretha, *b* 1966: *m* 1997, Antony Geoffrey Fanshawe (*see* Farquhar, Bt).

Kemp, family name of Viscount Rochdale.

KEMSLEY, VISCOUNT (Berry) (Viscount UK 1945, Bt UK 1928)

PERSEVERA ET VINCE

Persevere and conquer

RICHARD GOMER BERRY, 3rd Viscount, and 3rd Baronet; *b* 17 April 1951; *s* 1999; *ed* Eton: *m* 1st, 1981 (*m diss* 1988), Tana-Marie, elder da of Clive William Lester, of Beaulieu, Hants; 2ndly, 1994, Elizabeth Jane, da of Dennis Norman Barker, of Ampthill, Beds, and has issue by 2nd *m*.

Arms – Gules, three bars or, on a pile ermine as many martlets sable. Crest – A griffin sejant sable, collared and chained, the chain reflexed over the back and resting the dexter claw on a catharine wheel or. Supporters – On either side a stag guardant or, gorged with a chaplet of mistletoe proper.
Residence – Church Hill Farm, Church Lane, Brockenhurst, Hants SO42 7UB.

SON LIVING (By 2nd marriage)

Hon LUKE GOMER, *b* 2 Feb 1998.

SISTER LIVING

(Anne) Denise, *b* 1948: *m* 1970, Brian Peter Harvey Orange, and has issue living, Michael Richard, *b* 1973, — Simon George, *b* 1974, — Jonathan Charles, *b* 1976. *Residence* – Fromans House, King's Somborne, Hants.

HALF-SISTERS LIVING AND DECEASED

Barbara Marie-Louise, *b* 1935: *m* 1954 (*m diss* 1983), Alexander Clement Gilmour, and has issue (*see* B Gilmour of Craigmillar). *Residence* – Fox House, Little Coxwell, Faringdon, Oxon. —— Susan Lilian Constance, *b* 1938: *m* 1st, 1963 (*m diss* 1978), Christopher George Francis Harding (later Sir Christopher Harding), 2ndly, 1989, Raymond Muir, and *d* 1989, leaving issue (by 1st *m*), Rupert Christopher, *b* 1965, — Louise Amanda, *b* 1966.

DAUGHTERS LIVING OF SECOND VISCOUNT

Hon Mary Anne, *b* 1934: *m* 1960, Charles Henry van Raalte, of 7 Meadowcourt Rd, Oadby, Leics, and has issue living, Marcus Lionel, *b* 1961, — Kristina Beryl, *b* 1962: *m* 1984, — Ghislaine Sara, *b* 1964.
Hon Pamela Jane Margaret (*Hon Lady Mobbs*), *b* 1937: *m* 1961, Sir Gerald Nigel Mobbs, Lord Lieut Bucks since (Jan) 1997, of Widmer Lodge, Lacey Green, Aylesbury, Bucks, HP17 0RJ, and has issue living, Christopher William, *b* 1965: *m* 1991, Elizabeth Dora, yr da of late Maj J. F. A. Overton, LI, of Hillesden, Bucks, and has issue living, Charles William

John *b* 1997, Lucinda Dora Jane *b* 1992, Georgina Dora Jane *b* 1995, — Virginia Elizabeth, *b* 1968: *m* 1994, Simon P. Astill, eldest son of Paul Astill, of Thurnby, Leics, and has issue living, David Paul *b* 1997, Rebecca Jane *b* 1999, — Penelope Helen (twin), *b* 1968: *m* 1997, Edward J. Powell, son of John Powell, of W Kensington.

Hon Caroline Helen, *b* 1942: *m* 1965, John Peter Houison Craufurd of Craufurdland and Braehead, of Craufurdland Castle, Kilmarnock, Ayrshire, and has issue living, John Alexander, *b* 1966, — Simon Douglas, *b* 1972, — Teresa Eleanor, *b* 1967: *m* 1991, Christopher L. Geall, son of John D. Geall, of Bickley Lodge, No Mans Heath, Cheshire.

Hon Catherine Francis Lilian, *b* 1944: *m* 1969, Richard Douglas Fowler Bream, of Manor Farm, Grace Dieu, Whitwick, Leics, and has issue living, Tamerlane Douglas Fowler, *b* 1971, — Atlanta Mary, *b* 1970.

WIDOW LIVING OF SON OF FIRST VISCOUNT

Sarah Anne (*Hon Lady Berry*) (Fox's Walk, Shurlock Row, Reading, Berks RG10 0PB), da of Raymond Clifford-Turner: *m* 1966, as his 2nd wife, Hon Sir Anthony George Berry, MP, who *d* 1984, and has issue (see colls infra).

WIDOW LIVING OF SECOND VISCOUNT

Lady Hélène Candida Hay (*Dowager Viscountess Kemsley*), da of 11th Marquess of Tweeddale: *m* 1933, the 2nd Viscount Kemsley, who *d* 1999. *Residence* – Field House, Thorpe Lubenham, Market Harborough, Leics LE16 9TR.

COLLATERAL BRANCH LIVING

Issue of late Hon Sir Anthony George Berry, MP, yst son of 1st Viscount, *b* 1925, *d* (*k* in the bomb explosion at the Grand Hotel, Brighton) 1984: *m* 1st, 1954 (*m diss* 1966), Hon Mary Cynthia Burke Roche, da of 4th Baron Fermoy; 2ndly, 1966, Sarah Anne (ante), da of Raymond Clifford-Turner:—
(By 1st *m*) Edward Anthony Morys (103 Stormont Rd, SW11), *b* 1960: *m* 1989, Joanna Clare, yr da of Anthony George Leschallas (*see* E Romney, colls), and has issue living, William Anthony Edward, *b* 1993, — Alice Elisabeth, *b* 1990, — Rose Ophelia, *b* 1992. —— Alexandra Mary, *b* 1955: *m* 1982, Reinhold Bartz. —— Antonia Ruth, *b* 1957: *m* 1990, Mark F. Butterworth, of 3 Lansdowne Crescent, Bath, son of A. K. Butterworth, of Dharamsala, India, and has issue living, Jessica *b* 1990. —— Joanna Cynthia, *b* (twin) 1957. —— (By 2nd *m*) George Raymond Gomer, *b* 1967. —— Sasha Jane, *b* 1969.

PREDECESSORS – (1) (JAMES) GOMER Berry, GBE, son of Alderman John Mathias Berry, JP, of Gwaelodygarth, Merthy Tydfil (V Camrose); *b* 1883; Newspaper proprietor; Chm of Kemsley Newspapers Ltd, and Editor-in-Ch, *Sunday Times*, 1937-59; *cr* a *Baronet* 1928, *Baron Kemsley*, of Farnham Royal, co Bucks (peerage of UK) 1936, and *Viscount Kemsley*, of Dropmore, co Bucks (peerage of UK) 1945, GBE (Civil) 1959: *m* 1st, 1907, Mary Lilian, who *d* 1928, da of late Horace George Holmes, JP, of 8 Brondesbury Park, NW6; 2ndly, 1931, Edith, who *d* 1976, da of E. N. Merandon du Plessis, of Constance, Flacq, Mauritius, formerly wife of Cornelius Willem Dresselhuys; *d* 1968; *s* by his el son (2) (GEOFFREY) LIONEL, 2nd Viscount; *b* 1909; Dep Chm Kemsley Newspapers Ltd 1938-59; Master of Spectacle Makers' Co 1949-51 and 1959-61; Pres Assocn of Independent Hospitals 1976-83; Chm St Andrew's Hosp, Northampton; a Memb of Chapter Gen of OStJ; 1939-45 War as Capt Gren Gds (invalided out 1942); MP for Buckingham (C) 1943-45; High Sheriff and DL Leics; FRSA: *m* 1933, Lady Hélène Candida Hay, da of 11th Marquess of Tweeddale; *d* 1999; *s* by his nephew (3) RICHARD GOMER (only son of late Maj the Hon Denis Gomer Berry, TD, 2nd son of 1st Viscount), 3rd Viscount and present peer; also Baron Kemsley.

KENILWORTH, BARON (Siddeley) (Baron UK 1937)

(JOHN) RANDLE SIDDELEY, 4th Baron; *b* 16 June 1954; *s* 1981; *ed* Northease Manor, West Dean Coll, and London Coll of Furniture; Lord of Manor of Kenilworth: *m* 1st, 1983 (*m diss* 1990), Kim, only da of Danie Serfontein, of Laybourne Cottage, Jesmond Dene Rd, Newcastle upon Tyne; 2ndly, 1991, Mrs Kiki McDonough (*née* Axford), formerly wife of David McDonough, and has issue by 2nd *m*.

Arms – Per chevron or and azure in chief two goats' heads erased and in base a triangular castle with three towers, on a chief of the second two wings conjoined in fesse all counterchanged. **Crest** – Issuant out of the battlements of a tower a goat's head argent armed or in front of a rising sun also issuant gold. **Supporters** – On either side a goat or gorged with a collar azure pendent therefrom by a chain gold and escutcheon chequy of the first and second a chief ermine.
Address – c/o House of Lords, SW1.

By striding

SONS LIVING (by 2nd marriage)

Hon WILLIAM RANDLE, *b* 24 Jan 1992.
Hon Edward Oscar, *b* 1994.

SISTER LIVING

Hon Belinda Jane, *b* 1950: *m* 1st 1971 (*m diss* 1974), Christopher Aston James; *m* 2ndly 1983, David Ian McCarraher, and has issue living (by 2nd *m*), Tara Louise, *b* 1989. *Residence* – Old Manor Farm, Low Ham, Langport, Somerset TA10 9DE.

WIDOW LIVING OF THIRD BARON

JACQUELINE PAULETTE (*Jacqueline, Baroness Kenilworth*) (2 Lexham Walk, W8), da of late Robert Gelpi: *m* 1948, the 3rd Baron Kenilworth, who *d* 1981.

COLLATERAL BRANCH LIVING

Issue of late Hon Ernest Hall Siddeley, 2nd son of 1st Baron, *b* 1895, *d* 1985: *m* 1921, Muriel, who *d* 1988, da of late John R. Quick:—

Audrey Joan, *b* 1922; resumed her maiden name by deed poll 1968: *m* 1st, 1951 (*m diss* 1955), John Main; 2ndly, 1971 (*m diss* 1974), Francis Bermingham. *Residence* – Belmont, Barford Rd, Bloxham, Banbury, Oxon OX15 4EZ.

PREDECESSORS – (1) JOHN DAVENPORT Siddeley, CBE, son of late William Siddeley, of Manchester; *b* 1866; a Motor and Aircraft Engineer; was Chm and Managing Director of Armstrong-Siddeley Motors, Ltd, of Parkside, Coventry, and of Sir W. G. Armstrong-Whitworth Aircraft, Ltd; High Sheriff of Warwickshire 1932; *cr Baron Kenilworth*, of Kenilworth, co Warwick (peerage of United Kingdom) 1937: *m* 1893, Sara Mabel, who *d* 1953, da of late James Goodier, of Macclesfield; *d* 1953; *s* by his el son (2) CYRIL DAVENPORT, CBE, TD, 2nd Baron; *b* 1894; *d* 1971: *m* 1919, Marjorie Tennant, who *d* 1977, da of late Harry Firth, of Dewsbury, Yorks; *s* by his son (3) JOHN DAVENPORT, 3rd Baron, *b* 1924: *m* 1948, Jacqueline Paulette, da of Robert Gelpi; *d* 1981; *s* by his only son (4) (JOHN) RANDLE, 4th Baron and present peer.

Kennedy, family name of Marquess of Ailsa.

Kenlis, Baron, grandson of Marquess of Headfort, and title of Marquess of Headfort on Roll of HL.

KENNEDY OF THE SHAWS, BARONESS (Kennedy) (Life Baroness 1997)

HELENA ANN KENNEDY, da of late Joshua Patrick Kennedy, of Glasgow; *b* 12 May 1950; *ed* Holyrood Secondary Sch, Glasgow, and Council of Legal Education; Hon LLD Strathclyde 1992, Teesside 1993; Keele 1994, Lancaster 1994, Leeds Metropolitan Univ 1995, Bristol 1997, Wolverhampton 1997, Open Univ 1997, Univ of Abertay, Dundee 1997, Tavistock Centre under auspices of Univ of London 1997, and Derby 1998; Hon Fell, Inst of Advanced Legal Studies, London Univ; Bar, Gray's Inn, 1972; Memb Bar Council 1990-93; QC 1991; Memb Cttee, Assoc of Women Barristers since 1991; Nat Board, Women's Legal Defence Fund 1989-91; Council, Howard League for Penal Reform since 1989; CIBA Commn on Child Sexual Abuse 1981-83; Exec Cttee, NCCL 1983-85; Board, Minority Access to Legal Professional Project, Poly of S Bank 1984-85; Chancellor, Oxford Brookes Univ since 1994; Chm Haldane Soc 1983-86, since when Vice-Pres; Charter '88 since 1992; Standing Cttee for Youth Justice, NACRO since 1993; Leader of enquiry into health, environmental and safety aspects of Atomic Weapons Establishment, Aldermaston (report 1993); Patron, Civil Liberties Trust since 1991, Victims Helpline, Clean Break Theatre Co (for ex-prisoners), Fleet Counselling, Prisoners of Conscience, S Essex Rape and Incest Crisis Centre, and Bishops Simeon Trust; Commr BAFTA Enquiry into future of BBC 1990, Hamly Nat Commn on Education since 1991;

Chm London Internat Festival of Theatre 1993; Visiting Lecturer on Criminal Law, BPMF since 1991; Adviser, Mannheim Inst on Criminology, LSE since 1992; Board Memb, City Limits Magazine 1982-84, New Statesman since 1990, Council Magazine since 1990, Hampstead Theatre since 1989; broadcaster and presenter, author; FRSA; *cr Baroness Kennedy of the Shaws*, of Cathcart in the City of Glasgow (Life Baroness) 1997: partner (1978-84), (Roger) Iain Mitchel; *m* 1986, Dr (Iain) Louis Hutchison, son of ...... Hutchison, of ......, and has issue by both.
Address – c/o Hilary Hard, 12 Athelstan Close, Harold Wood, Essex RM3 0QJ.

SONS LIVING *(By former partner)*

Keir MITCHEL, *b* 19—; *ed* ....

(By marriage)

Hon Roland HUTCHISON, *b* 19—; *ed* ....

DAUGHTER LIVING *(By marriage)*

Hon Clio HUTCHISON, *b* 19—; *ed* ....

KENNET, BARON (Young) (Baron UK 1935)

WAYLAND HILTON YOUNG, 2nd Baron; *b* 2 Aug 1923; *s* 1960; *ed* Stowe, and at Trin Coll, Camb; Hon FRIBA; Writer; a Member of British Delegation, Assemblies W European Union and Council of Europe 1962-65, and Chm of UK Cttee for International Co-operation Year 1965;. Parl Sec, Min of Housing and Local Govt 1966-70; Labour Spokesman on Foreign Affairs 1970-74; Chm of Advisory Cttee on Oil Pollution of the Sea 1970-74, and of Council for Protection of Rural England 1971-72, and of Internat Parl Conferences on the Environment 1971-80; Dir of Europe Plus Thirty 1974-76; a Member of European Parliament 1978-79; Chm of the Architecture Club 1983-94; Vice-Pres of Parliamentary and Scientific Cttee 1989-98; SDP Chief Whip in House of Lords 1981-83 and Spokesman on Foreign Affairs and Defence 1981-90; War Ser 1942-45 as Ordinary Seaman and Sub-Lt RNVR; in Foreign Office 1946-47, and 1949-51: *m* 1948, Elizabeth Ann, da of late Capt Bryan Fullerton Adams, DSO, RN, of Cherry Tree, Hacheston, Suffolk, and has issue.

In colle domus.

A house on a hill

Arms – Per fesse sable and argent: in chief two lions rampant-guardant, and in base an anchor erect with a cable, all counterchanged. **Crest** – A demi-unicorn couped ermine, armed, maned, and hoofed or, gorged with a naval crown azure supporting an anchor erect sable.

Residence – The Lacket, Lockeridge, Marlborough, Wilts SN8 4EQ.

SON LIVING

Hon (WILLIAM ALDUS) THOBY, *b* 24 May 1957; *ed* Marlborough, and Sussex Univ: *m* 1987, Hon Josephine Mary Keyes, yr da of 2nd Baron Keyes, and has issue living, Archibald Wayland Keyes, *b* 7 June 1992, — Maud Elizabeth Aurora, *b* 1989. *Address* – 100 Bayswater Rd, W2 3HJ.

DAUGHTERS LIVING

Hon Easter Donatella, *b* 1949; *ed* Keele Univ: *m* 1981, Frank Joffre Russell, and has issue living, Louis Inigo, *b* 1983, — Theo Joffre, *b* 1986, — Alice Ella, *b* 1979.
Hon Emily Tacita, *b* 1951; *ed* Chelsea Sch of Arts, and St Martin Sch of Art; has issue living, Arthur William Phoenix Young Jeffes, *b* 1978.
Hon Mopsa Mary, *b* 1953; *ed* Holland Park Sch: *m* 1981, Richard Douglas English, 28 Warneford Rd, Oxford OX4 1LU, and has issue living, Joseph Edward, *b* 1987, — Thomas Eliot, *b* 1991, — Lilian Mary, *b* 1989.
Hon (Audrey) Louisa, *b* 1959; *ed* Trinity Coll, Camb; has issue living, Isabel Adomakoh YOUNG, *b* 1993.

Hon (Alice Matelda) Zoe, *b* 1969; *ed* Sussex Univ.

PREDECESSOR – (1) EDWARD HILTON Young, GBE, DSO, DSC, PC, yst son of Sir George Young, 3rd Bt (*cr* 1813); *b* 1879; Bar Inner Temple 1904; European War 1914-19 in HMS "Iron Duke" and "Centaur", with British Naval Mission in Serbia, with Naval Guns in Flanders, at Zeebrugge in "Vindictive", and in N Russia in charge of Armoured Train; was Assist Editor *Economist* 1909-10, and City Editor *Morning Post* 1910-14, Parliamentary Private Sec to Pres of Board of Education 1919-21, Financial Sec to the Treasury 1921-22, Ch Liberal Whip 1922-3, Parliamentary Sec to Depart of Overseas Trade (in National Govt) Sept to Nov 1931, and Min of Health 1931-35; a Member of Hague Commn 1922; sat as MP for Norwich (*L*) 1915-22, and 1924-29 (*L*, afterwards *C*), and for Sevenoaks Div of Kent (*C*) 1929-35; *cr Baron Kennet*, of the Dene, co Wilts (peerage of United Kingdom) 1935: *m* 1922, Edith Agnes Kathleen, who *d* 1947, da of late Rev Canon Lloyd Stewart Bruce (Bruce, Bt, *cr* 1804, colls), and widow of Capt Robert Falcon Scott, CVO, RN; *d* 1960; *s* by his only son (2) WAYLAND HILTON, 2nd Baron and present peer.

KENSINGTON, BARON (Edwardes) (Baron I 1776 and UK 1886)

Keep the faith

HUGH IVOR EDWARDES, 8th Baron; *b* 24 Nov 1933; *s* 1981; *ed* Eton: *m* 1961, Juliet Elizabeth Massy, da of late Alexander Massy Anderson, and has issue.

Arms – Quarterly: 1st and 4th ermine, a lion rampant sable, *Edwardes*; 2nd and 3rd gules, a chevron between three crosses bottony or, *Rich*. **Crest** – On a mount vert, a wyvern, wings expanded, argent. **Supporters** – Two reindeer proper, armed and unguled or.
Residence – Friar Tuck, PO Box 549, Mooi River, 3300 Natal, S Africa.

SONS LIVING

Hon WILLIAM OWEN ALEXANDER, *b* 21 July 1964: *m* 1991, Marie Hélène Anne Véronique, eldest da of Jean-Alain Lalouette, of 29 River Walk, Vacoas, Mauritius, and has issue living, William Francis Ivor, *b* 23 March 1993, — Nadia Marie Hilda Massy, *b* 1997.
Hon Hugh Rupert, *b* 1967: *m* 1995, Susan Dawn, yst da of John Nowell, of Munster, Natal, S Africa.

DAUGHTER LIVING

Hon Amanda Louise Massy, *b* 1962: *m* 1984 (*m diss* 1998), Anthony Michael Greene, eldest son of Michael Victor Greene, of Natal, S Africa, and has issue living, James Stuart, *b* 1985, — Stephanie Louise Massy *b* 1987, — Rachel Delia, *b* 1988.

SISTER LIVING (*Raised to the rank of a Baron's daughter* 1982)

Hon Meriel Davina, *b* 1935: *m* (Jan) 1972, David Andrew Long, of Manor Cottage, Puncknowle, Dorchester, Dorset DT29 BP, and has issue living, James Philip, *b* (Dec) 1972, — Harry Simon, *b* 1976.

WIDOW LIVING OF SON OF SIXTH BARON

Elizabeth (Carpenter's Yard, Compton Pauncefoot, Yeovil, Som), yst da of late Robert Alexander Longman Broadley, of Suddon Farm, Wincanton, Som: *m* 1939, Com Hon David Edwardes, DSC, RN, 3rd son of 6th Baron, who *d* 1983, and has issue (see colls infra).

COLLATERAL BRANCHES LIVING

Issue of late Com Hon David Edwardes, DSC, RN, 3rd son of 6th Baron, *b* 1907, *d* 1983: *m* 1939, Elizabeth (ante), yst da of late Robert Alexander Longman Broadley, of Suddon Farm, Wincanton, Som:—
Susan, *b* 1945: *m* 1967, Col Hugh Michael Sandars, The Queen's Own Hussars (Twin Pillars Cottage, Micheldever, Winchester, Hants), and has issue living, Andrew George, *b* 1969, — Claire Catherine, *b* 1972. —— Mary Ann, *b* 1947: *m* 1968, Brig Hugh William Kellow Pye, 9th/12th R Lancers (Prince of Wales's), of Tuxwell Farm, Spaxton, Bridgwater, Somerset TA5 1DF, and has issue living, Robert Alec Kellow, *b* 1970, — Victoria Ann, *b* 1973. —— Louisa Jane, *b* 1950: *m* 1979 (*m diss* 1994), Christopher L. P. Weedon, and has issue living, George David Martin, *b* 1985, — Simon Edward Peter, *b* 1987.

Issue of late Capt Hon George Henry Edwardes, MC, 4th son of 4th Baron, *b* 1877, *d* 1930: *m* 1903, Olive, who *d* 1968, da of late Charles Wyndham Rudolph Kerr (M Lothian, colls):—
George Llewellyn, *b* 1906.

Granddaughter of late Lt-Col Hon Cuthbert Ellison Edwardes, 2nd son of 3rd Baron:—
Issue of late Capt Richard Edwardes, b 1894, d 1967: m 1929, Ada Mary, who d 1979, da of late William R. MacGeorge, of Glasgow:—
Joan Margaret, b 1932: m 1958, John Spencer Clarke, who d 1993, of The Roos, Whitchurch, Hants, and has issue living, Charles Richard Spencer, b 1960: m 1986, Jane Caroline Sargeant, — James Alured, b 1964: m 1997, Bridget Tennent, — Sally Aletta, b 1959: m 1982, Clive Julian Spencer, — Fiona Jane, b 1963.

Grandchildren of late Rev Hon Thomas Edwardes, 6th son of 2nd Baron:—
Issue of late Edward Henry Edwardes, OBE, b 1875, d 1955: m 1907, Eleanor Matilda, who d 1925, da of late Rev William Nuttall (formerly V of Atherton, Manchester), of 58 Park Rd, Southport:—
Barbara, b 1909: m 1939, August Henry Gernaey, of Oakwood House, Birkacre, Chorley, Lancs, and has issue living, Susan Leonie, b 1940, — Joanna, b 1942. — Caroline, b 1945. —— Eleonora, b 1911: m 1942, Joseph Hugh Scott Gardner, who d 1989, and has issue living, Hugh Martin, b 1951, — Sarah, b 1944.

Grandsons of late Edward Henry Edwardes, OBE (ante):—
Issue of late William Edwardes, b 1908, d 1983: m 1st, 1937, Dorothy Robertshaw, only da of Aaron Wedgwood, of Worsley, Lancs; 2ndly, 1943, Joan (Spinneys, Church St, Eccleshall, Stafford), only da of Ernest Topping, of Atherton, Lancs:—
(By 2nd m) David William (41 Redwood Av, Stone, Staffs), b 1944: m 1972, Diana June, yst da of William Eden Morton, of London, and has issue living, Rebecca Evelyn, b 1983, — Gemma Rachael, b 1985.

Issue of late Rev Edward Edwardes, b 1912, d 1973: m 1940, Norah, who d 1991, only da of late J. W. Watson, of Corbridge, Newcastle:—
Antony (1 Priory Close, Newport Pagnell, Bucks MK16 9AQ) b 1942. —— Nigel Kim, b 1948: m 1972, Kay Marjorie, el da of late Samuel Barnes, of Pitt Farm, Whitchurch Canonicorum, Dorset, and has issue living, Guy Kristian, b 1974. *Residence* – Byways, St Mary's Lane, Yawl, Uplyme, Lyme Regis, Dorset DT7 3XH.

PREDECESSORS – (1) WILLIAM Edwardes, MP for Haverfordwest; inherited through his mother on the death of his cousin the 7th Earl of Warwick the estates of the Rich family; *cr Baron Kensington* (peerage of Ireland) 1776; *d* 1801; *s* by his son (2) WILLIAM, 2nd Baron; *b* 1777; MP for Haverfordwest 1801-18; *d* 1852; *s* by his son (3) WILLIAM, 3rd Baron Capt RN and Lord-Lieut of co Pembroke; *m* 1833, Laura Jane, da of Cuthbert Ellison, Esq, of Hepburn, Durham; *d* 1872; *s* by his son (4) WILLIAM, PC, 4th Baron, *b* 1835; Lord-Lieut of co Pembroke; MP for Haverfordwest (L) 1868-85; a Groom-in-Waiting to HM Queen Victoria 1873-4, Comptroller of HM Queen Victoria's Household 1880-85, a Lord-in-Waiting to HM Queen Victoria 1886, and Capt of Yeomen of the Guard 1892-5; *cr Baron Kensington*, of Kensington, co Middlesex (peerage of United Kingdom) 1886; *m* 1867, Grace Elizabeth, who *d* 1910, da of late Robert Johnstone-Douglas, *d* 1896; *s* by his el son (5) WILLIAM, 5th Baron, *b* 1868; Capt 2nd Life Guards; *d* 1900; *s* by his brother (6) HUGH, CMG, DSO, TD, 6th Baron, *b* 1873; Col (ret) TA; S Africa 1900-1901 (DSO), European War 1914-19 (CMG): *m* 1903, Mabel Carlisle, who *d* 1934, da of George Pilkington, of Stoneleigh, Woolton, Lancashire; *d* 1938; *s* by his son (7) WILLIAM, 7th Baron, Lt-Col IA; ADC to Gov of Punjab 1933-35; *d* 1981; *s* by his nephew, (8) HUGH IVOR (s of Hon Capt (Hugh) Owen Edwardes, 2nd son of 6th Baron), 8th Baron and present peer.

KENSWOOD, BARON (Whitfield) (Baron UK 1951)

JOHN MICHAEL HOWARD WHITFIELD, 2nd Baron, *b* 6 April 1930; *s* 1963; *ed* Harrow, at Grenoble Univ, and at Emmanuel Coll, Camb (BA 1952): *m* 1951, Deirdre Anna Louise, da of late Colin Malcolm Methven, and has issue.

Arms – Azure an argosy in full sail pennons flying or, a chief argent thereon a lion passant gules holding in the dexter forepaw a thunderbolt proper. **Crest** – between two wings or, a sprig of oak fructed proper. **Supporters** – *Dexter*, a figure representing St Cecilia habited argent cloaked azure with organ-pipes proper in her exterior hand; *sinister*, a figure representing St Gregory the Great habited argent cloaked gules holding with his exterior arm a papal staff or and holding in the hand a book proper bound sable.

SONS LIVING

Hon MICHAEL CHRISTOPHER, *b* 3 July 1955.
Hon Anthony John, *b* 1957.
Hon Steven James, *b* 1958.
Hon Benjamin Matthew, *b* 1961.

DAUGHTER LIVING

Hon Anna Louise, *b* 1964.

SISTER LIVING

Hon Ann Sophia Madeline, *b* 1928: *m* 1st, 1948, Richard Bethuen Buzzard, BM, BCh, who *d* 1980 (B Monkswell, colls); 2ndly, 19—, — Cabot, of USA, and has issue living, Nicholas John, *b* 1952, — Jacqueline Frances, *b* 1950, — Jennifer Ann, *b* 1954, — Angela Caroline, *b* 1956.

Give me wisdom

PREDECESSOR – (1) ERNEST ALBERT Whitfield, son of John Henry Whitfield, of London; *b* 1887; professional violinist; ret from concert platform 1935; a Gov of BBC 1946-50; Pres, National Federation of Blind 1951-4: *m* 1st, 1920, Sophie Madeline, who *d* 1961, da of Ernest Walters Howard; 2ndly, 1962, Mrs Catherine Chilver-Stainer, who *d* 1992, da of

Frank Luxton, and widow of Charles A. Chilver-Stainer, RIBA; *cr Baron Kenswood*, of St Marylebone, co London (peerage of UK) 1951; *d* 1963; *s* by his only son **(2)** JOHN MICHAEL HOWARD, 2nd Baron and present peer.

Kent, Duke of, see Royal Family.

Kenworthy, family name of Baron Strabolgi.

KENYON, BARON (Tyrell-Kenyon) (Baron GB 1788, Bt GB 1784)

Sustain the Cross with magnanimity

LLOYD TYRELL-KENYON, 6th Baron, and 6th Baronet; *b* 13 July 1947; *s* 1993; *ed* Eton, and Magdalene Coll, Camb (BA); High Sheriff Clwyd 1986; Memb Wrexham Maelor Borough Council 1991-96, Wrexham County Borough Council since 1995, EU Cttee of The Regions 1994-97; patron of one living: *m* 1971, Sally Carolyn, eldest da of Jack Frank Page Matthews, of The Firs, Thurston, Bury St Edmunds, and has issue.

Arms – Quarterly: 1st and 4th sable, a chevron engrailed or, between three crosses-flory argent *Kenyon*; 2nd and 3rd argent, two chevronels azure, within a bordure engrailed gules, *Tyrell*. **Crests** – 1st, a lion sejant proper, resting the dexter fore paw on a cross flory argent; 2nd, a boar's head couped and erect argent, and issuing from the mouth a peacock's tail proper. **Supporters** – On either side a tiger reguardant proper, round the neck a chain or pendent therefrom an escutcheon of the arms of *Tyrell*.
Seat – Gredington, nr Whitchurch, Shropshire SY13 3DH.

SONS LIVING

Hon LLOYD NICHOLAS, *b* 9 April 1972; *ed* Eton, and Manchester Univ.
Hon Alexander Simon, *b* 1975; *ed* Eton.

BROTHERS DECEASED

†*Hon* Richard, *b* 1948; *ed* Eton, and Seale Hayne Coll; *d* 1982 (see colls, infra).
†*Hon* Thomas, *b* 1954; *ed* Tabley House; *d* 1993.

SISTER LIVING

Hon Katherine, *b* 1959: *m* 1985, David Nigel Vardon Churton, MBE, elder son of Col Geoffrey Vardon Churton, MBE, MC, TD, of Manley Cottage, Manley, nr Warrington, Cheshire, and has issue living, Oscar Vardon, *b* 1987, — Rollo Crispin, *b* 1989, — Zara Fleur, *b* 1991.

AUNT LIVING (*Daughter of 4th Baron*)

Hon Sarah Myfida Mary, MBE, *b* 1917; formerly in VAD; MBE (Civil)1952: *m* 1966, Col Desmond Aubrey Robert Bancroft Cooke, late 13/18th Hussars, who *d* 1987.

WIDOW LIVING OF FIFTH BARON

LEILA MARY (*Dowager Baroness Kenyon*), da of late Cmdr John Wyndham Cookson, RN (*see* Colquhoun, Bt, 1963 Edn), and widow of Hugh William Jardine Ethelston Peel, Lieut Welsh Guards (*see* Buchanan-Jardine, Bt, 1945 Edn): *m* 1946, the 5th Baron Kenyon, CBE, who *d* 1993. *Residence* – Redbridge House, Birch Lane, Ellesmere, Shropshire SY12 9AA.

COLLATERAL BRANCHES LIVING

Issue of late Hon Richard Tyrell-Kenyon, 2nd son of 5th Baron, *b* 1948, *d* 1982: *m* 1st, 1970 (*m diss* 1976), Davina Jane, da of David Charles George Jessel (*see* Jessel, Bt); 2ndly, 1980, Janet LINLEY (née Nelson), stepda of Donald Linley, of Denbigh, Clwyd:—
(By 1st *m*) Vanessa Zoë, *b* 1974.

Grandchildren of late Gordon Lloyd Trevor Kenyon, only son of late Rev Hon William Trevor Kenyon, 5th son of 3rd Baron:—
Issue of late Lloyd Gordon Trevor Kenyon, *b* 1911, *d* 1994: *m* 1939, Joyce Alma (31 Frays Av, W Drayton, Middx UB7 7AG), da of late F. J. Parker:—
Roger Lloyd, *b* 1940: *m* 1963, Barry Thomas Gouldstone, who *d* 1998, of 9 Mortimer Close, Mudeford, Christchurch, Dorset, and has issue living, Jeremy Thomas, *b* 1964; BMus (London Univ): *m* 1997, Suzanne Debra, da of J. R. Moss, — Penelope Joan, *b* 1968; *ed* Brighton Univ (BA): *m* 1999, Christian Mark Carman. —— Carol Ann, *b* 1944.

Granddaughter of late Lt-Col Herbert Edward Kenyon, DSO (*infra*):—
Issue of late Kenneth Herbert Kenyon, *b* 1908, *d* 1970: *m* 1934, Barbara Joan, who *d* 1979, da of late J. E. M. Urry, of Homedene, Cranley Gdns, N10:—
Anne Judith (7 Hembury Park, Buckfast, Devon TQ11 0ES), *b* 1939.

Grandchildren of late Maj-Gen Edward Ranulph Kenyon, CB, CMG, 3rd son of late John Robert Kenyon, QC, DCL (*infra*):—
Issue of late Lieut-Col Herbert Edward Kenyon, DSO, *b* 1881, *d* 1958: *m* 1907, Gwendoline Ethel Graham, who *d* 1958, da of late F. G. Ommanney, of Sheen House, Walmer:—
Lloyd Douglas (15 Oxford St, Waimate, S Canterbury, NZ), *b* 1912; *ed* Framlingham Coll, and Waitaki BHS: *m* 1939, Joan, da of late R. Appleby, of Geraldine, New Zealand, and has issue living, Gwendolyn Jane, *b* 1942: *m* 1964, Trevor William Payton, of 274 Pine Hill Rd, Pine Hill, Dunedin, NZ, and has issue living, Grant Michael *b* 1974, Kim Maree *b* 1966: *m* 1991, Miran Kremesec, Jill Michelle *b* 1967, Raeleen Jan *b* 1971, — Sally Mavourneen, *b* 1944: *m* 1966, David George Drayton, of 102 Huntsbury Av, Christchurch 2, NZ, and has issue living, Tania May *b* 1970, Leanne Mavourneen *b* 1971: *m* 1997, Jared Gray. —— John Frederick, OBE, MC, *b* 1921; *ed* Marlborough; Col (ret) RA and Gen Staff, Mil Asst to C in C Far East Land Forces 1962-64, and Defence, Naval and Mil Attaché, Belgium and Luxembourg 1971-73; County Co Shropshire 1977-85; a Freeman of Shrewsbury (Grand Master) and of the City of London; a Liveryman of the Farmers' Co; President of the Assocn of Freemen in England and Wales 1981-91; SE Asia 1943-45 (MC); OBE (Mil) 1970; Officer of Order of Leopold of Belgium 1989: *m* 1st, 1947 (*m diss* 1960), Jean Molyneux, who *d* 1997, da of late Howard Godfrey, MC; 2ndly, 1960, Mrs Margaret Bowker Franks, who *d* 1997, da of late Mrs C. C. B. Remington, of Wadham, Horsell, Surrey; 3rdly, 1982, Mrs Janet Mary Jackson (née Maddicott), of Dainton Cross, Ipplepen, Devon, and has issue living, (by 1st *m*) John Robert (28 Radyr Court Close, Radyr Court Rd, Llandaff, Cardiff CF5 2QG), *b* 1948; *ed* St Edward's Sch, Oxford, and Southampton Univ (BA); ALA, FSA, FRHistS: *m* 1973, Christine Ann, da of Mrs E. M. Green, of Lightcliffe, Yorks, and has issue living, Philippa Mary *b* 1974, Joanna Louise Charlotte *b* 1978, — Richard Howard Trevor (The Coppice, Tararua Drive, RD8, Masterton, NZ), *b* 1951; *ed* St Edward's Sch, Oxford, and Harper Adams Agric Coll: *m* 1977, Mrs Carol Jackson, da of C. F. May, of Blenheim, NZ, and has issue living, Wendy Jean *b* 1977. *Residence* – Pradoe, Oswestry, Shropshire SY11 4ER. *Club* – Farmers. —— Margaret Gwendoline (65 Clark St, Wolcott, Conn, USA 06716) *b* 1918; 1939-45 War with VAD (Defence and War Medals): *m* 1945, Stanley Steven Baranoski, 1st/Sgt (ret) US Marines, who *d* 1979, and has issue living, Robert Steven, *b* 1947; 1st/Sgt US Marines; Okinawa and Viet Nam: *m* 1971, Kyoko Nakama, and has issue living, Stanley Steven *b* 1972, Margaret Gwendoline *b* 1971, — Michael John, *b* 1948; *ed* Massachusetts Coll of Arts (BFA in Architecture): *m* 1978, Diane Lynn Fasciano, — David Stanley, *b* 1953: *m* 1972, Alana Sue Jones, and has issue living, Jeremy David *b* 1973, — Peter Kenyon, *b* 1955, — Richard Lloyd, *b* 1957: *m* 1981, Nereida Otero, — Kenneth Owen, *b* 1963: *m* 1985, Janice Marie Pease, and has issue living, Brittany Marie *b* 1989, — Gwendoline Mary, *b* 1949, — Heather Joy, *b* 1956; *ed* Univ of Connecticut Agric Sch: *m* 1981, Terri Lim. —— Irene Patricia, *b* 1923, late WAAF (War medal): *m* 1953, Keith Louis Kerr, of 6 Ancrum St, Roxburgh, Central Otago, NZ, and has issue living, Graham Keith, *b* 1954; *ed* Waitaki BHS, Oamaru, NZ, — Patricia Louise, *b* 1956: *m* 1st, 1976 (*m diss* 1988), Ian Leslie Reeves; 2ndly, 1989, Kenneth MacKenzie, of Otapiri, Southland, NZ, and has issue living (by 1st *m*), Joshua Mark *b* 1979, Jamie Matthew *b* 1980, (by 2nd *m*) Jenna Kelland Louise *b* 1992.

Grandsons of late Eustace Alban Kenyon, son of late John Robert Kenyon, QC, DCL (*infra*):—
Issue of late Lieut-Col William Patrick Kenyon, MC, late RWF, *b* 1898, *d* 1992: *m* 1928, Joan Mary, who *d* 19—, yr da of late Allan Edward Batchelor (*see* Makins, Bt, 1951 Edn):—
Martin Robert (70 Stockwell Park Rd, SW9; *Club* – Travellers'), *b* 1929; *ed* Eton, and Corpus Christi Coll, Oxford; late 2nd Lieut RWF; Exec Sec Overseas Students' Trust since 1962: *m* 1975, Mary Anne, da of Lt-Cdr Patrick Henry James Southby, RN (ret) (*see* Southby, Bt), and has issue living, Eliza Hope, *b* 1976, — Nina Joan, *b* 1977. —— (Eustace Allan) Michael, *b* 1931; *ed* St Edward's Sch, Oxford; late Lieut RWF; a Farmer, Manager Nicolton Orchards, Suffolk: *m* 1977, Susanna, da of late Maj Arthur H. Pearson, of Hillside, Bayford Hill, Wincanton. —— Thomas David (Toby), *b* 1932; *ed* Wellington Coll, and RMA Sandhurst; Maj RWF; served Malaya 1954 (wounded), and Cyprus 1958.

Issue of late Rowland Lloyd Kenyon, *b* 1901; *d* 1959: *m* 1936 (*m diss* 1950), Gwendoline Doris Dorman (who *m* 2ndly, 1954 (*m diss* 1969), Maj Leslie Dunn, Coldm Gds and E Surrey Regt (ret)):—
Peter Rowland (Lady Whincups, Rendham, Saxmundham, Suffolk), *b* 1937; late RAF; market gardener: *m* 1962, Wilma, da of Ludwig Pranger of Pöttsching (Burgenland), Siedlung, 16, Austria, and has issue living, Rupert Peter, *b* 1968, — Berenice Sofia, *b* 1964, — Rebecca Louise, *b* 1966. —— Robert Nicholas Andrew (2/5 Franks Grove, Kew, Vic 3101, Aust), *b* 1939; formerly in RE.

Granddaughter of late Maj-Gen Lionel Richard Kenyon, CB, son of late John Robert Kenyon, QC, DCL, 3rd son of late Hon Thomas Kenyon, 3rd son of 1st Baron :—
Issue of late Major Harold Anthony Kenyon, MC, b 1897, d 1934: m 1931, Iris Veronica Margaret, (who m 2ndly), 1936, as his 2nd wife Maj-Gen Mervyn Savile Wheatley, CB, CBE, who d 1979, da of late Lt-Col M. McL. Corbyn, of Little Grange, Woodbridge, Suffolk:—
Elisabeth Veronica, b 1931: m 1953 (m diss 1974), Robert Arthur David Shutes, and has issue living, Anthony David, b 1955; ed Wellington Coll, and Univ Coll, London (BSc); CEng, MIMM (1982): m 1983, Lucille Alison Hunter, and has issue living, Frederick Thomas Kenyon b 1991, Phillippa Fern Kenyon b 1988, Henrietta Iris Kenyon b 1994, — Caroline Ann Veronica (21 College Hill, Bargate Wood, Godalming, Surrey), b 1954: m 1976 (m diss 1990), John Dalziel Riddell, and has issue living, Oliver John b 1978, Benjamin James b 1980, Daniel Robert b 1981. Residence – Ford Cottage, Send, nr Guildford, Surrey.

Grandchildren (by 1st m) of late Maj Robert Orlando Rodolph Kenyon-Slaney (infra):—
Issue of late Robert Ivan Kenyon-Slaney, b 1926, d 1984: m 1964, Meriel Rose (who m 2ndly, 1985, Peter Maurice Afia, of 7 Douro Place, W8 5PH, and Hatton Grange, Shifnal, Shropshire TF11 9HS), da of late Capt Joseph Gurney Fowell Buxton (see Buxton, Bt, colls):—
Rupert David, b 1965; ed Eton, and Univ of East Anglia (BA). ——Thomas Alexander, b 1966; ed Eton, and European Univ, Versailles; late Lieut Gren Gds. —— Natasha Vivien, b 1969; ed Wycombe Abbey, and Royal Holloway and Bedford New Coll, Univ of London (BA): m 1998, Barnabas Martin Henry Branston, late Capt Welsh Guards, yr son of Martin Branston of Battersea.

Grandchildren of late Col Rt Hon William Slaney Kenyon-Slaney, MP, eldest son of Col William Kenyon-Slaney, 5th son of Hon Thomas Kenyon (ante):—
Issue of late Maj Robert Orlando Rodolph Kenyon-Slaney, b 1892, d 1965: m 1st, 1917 (m diss 1930), Lady Mary Cecilia Rhodesia Hamilton, who d 1984, da of 3rd Duke of Abercorn; 2ndly, 1931, Nesta, who d 1947, da of Sir George Ferdinand Forestier-Walker, 3rd Bt (cr 1835):—
(By 1st m) Ursula Jane, b 1920: m 1st, 1940 (m diss 1946), Lt-Col David Ludovic Peter Lindsay, DSO, Irish Gds, who d 1971 (see E Crawford, colls); 2ndly, 1946, as his 2nd wife (m diss 1950), Group Capt Hon (John William) Maxwell Aitken, DSO, DFC (later Sir Maxwell Aitken, 2nd Bt), who d 1985 (see B Beaverbrook); 3rdly, 1951, Robert Edward John Compton (see M Northampton, colls), of Newby Hall, Ripon, Yorks. —— (By 2nd m) William Simon Rodolph (Chyknell, Bridgnorth, Shropshire), b 1932; ed Eton; late Lt Gren Gds; FRICS; JP; KStJ; County Councillor 1977-85; High Sheriff 1979, DL 1986, Vice Lord-Lieut (Shrops) 1996: m 1960, Mary Helena, el da of late Lt-Col Hon Henry George Orlando Bridgeman, DSO, MC (see E Bradford, colls), and has issue living, Henry James Rodolph, b 1961; ed Eton, and Southampton Univ (BSc): m 1995, Laura Anne, yr da of Capt Derek O'Reilly, of Broad Chalk, Wilts, and has issue living, Miles Christian Rodolph b 1997, Laetitia Mary Grace b 1998, — Andrew William Orlando, b 1965; ed Cranleigh, Shrewsbury, Reading Univ (BSc), and Cranfield Univ (MBA), — Francis Alan, b 1966; ed Eton, and Reading Univ (BSc): m 1997, Fenella Jane, elder da of James Nicholas Headlam (see E Verulam, colls).

Grandchildren of late Percy Robert Kenyon-Slaney, 6th and yst son of late Col William Kenyon-Slaney (ante):—
Issue of late Gerald William Kenyon-Slaney, OBE, b 1899, d 1953: m 1928, (Barbara) Nannette, who d 1995, da of late Rev Granville Gore Skipwith (see Skipwith, Bt, colls):—
Orlando Michael Philip, b 1929; ed Winchester and at Ch Ch, Oxford (BA 1953): m 1960, Philippa Margaret, da of Sir Thomas Claude Harris Lea, 3rd Bt, and has issue living, Jeremy Francis Gerald, b 1966; ed Bethany Sch, — Philip Thomas Christopher, b 1969; ed Marlborough. Residence – Bachelors Cottage, High Halden, Ashford, Kent. —— Gerald Timothy Granville (c/o Bachelors Cottage, High Halden, Ashford, Kent), b 1937; ed Bradfield Coll; late Grenadier Guards. —— Thomasina Angela Jane, b 1933: m 1st, 1954 (m diss 1968), Maj Thomas David Ogilvy Codner, late Coldstream Guards; 2ndly, 1982, William Albert Tarling of 12 Bettridge Rd, SW6, and has issue living (by 1st m), Vivien Ogilvy, b 1957: m 1988, Aziz Laghzaoui, of 5 Norham Gdns, Oxford, and has issue living, Otto b 1990, Kenza May b 1992, Talia b 1994, — Clare Jane, b 1959: m 1993, Marcus Emerson.

Granddaughters of late Charles Robert Kenyon, el son of late Rev Charles Orlando Kenyon, 6th son of late Hon Thomas Kenyon (ante):—
Issue of late Charles Orlando Kenyon, b 1886, d 1973: m 1st, 1915, Marguerite Laura, who d 1948, da of Alexander Kealman, of Santos, Brazil; 2ndly, 1950, Sarah (Santos, Brazil), da of:—
(By 1st m) Dorothy Beatrice, b 1917; 1939-45 War with WAAF (Defence Medal): m 1946, Donald Stanford Egremont, and has issue living, Christopher Andrew, b 1948: m 1st, 1975 (m diss 1986), Annabel Heather, da of Malcolm Proverbs, and of Mrs James Ward; 2ndly, 1989, Jacqueline Sarah, eldest da of late Capt Peter Bateman, of Cheselbourne, Dorset, and has issue living (by 1st m), Christopher William b 1983, James Donald b 1985, (by 2nd m) Thomas Joshua b 1993, Lucinda Rebecca b 1990, Hannah Mary b (twin) 1993, — Donald Alexander, b 1955. —— Elizabeth Matilda, b 1920: m 1st, 1942 (m diss 1945); 2ndly, 1947, Robert E. Dennison, of 865 Riomar Dr, Vero Beach, Florida 32963, USA, and has issue living (by 2nd m), Robert Kenyon, b 1948, — William Alexander (24 West Delaware Av, Pennington, NJ 08534, USA), b 1951: m 1976, Tara, da of Pamela Brotherton, of Earlswood House, Pitton, Salisbury, Wilts, and has issue living, William Oliver b 1984, Edwina Elizabeth Kenyon b 1987, — John Keasbey, b 1958. —— (By 2nd m) Sylvia Elena, b 1952.

PREDECESSORS – (1) Sir LLOYD Kenyon, KB; Ch Justice of Chester 1780, Attorney-Gen 1782, Master of the Rolls 1784, and Lord Ch Justice of England 1788; cr a Baronet 1784, and Lord Kenyon, Baron of Gredington, co Flint (peerage of Great Britain) 1788; d 1802; s by his son (2) GEORGE, 2nd Baron; d 1855; s by his son (3) LLOYD, 3rd Baron; b 1805; d 1869; s by his grandson (4) LLOYD (son of late Hon Lloyd, el son of 3rd Baron), 4th Baron, b 1864; Lord-Lieut of Denbighshire, and Registrar of Priory of Order of St John for Wales; a Lord-in-Waiting to Queen Victoria and King Edward VII 1900-1905, and to King George V 1916-18; assumed by Roy licence 1912 the additional surname of Tyrell: m 1916, Gwladys Julia, who d 1965, da of late Col Henry Richard Lloyd Howard, CB; d 1927; s by his only son (5) LLOYD, CBE, 5th Baron; b 1917, Capt RA (TA), JP and DL Flintshire, Dir Lloyds Bank 1962-85, Pres Univ Coll, N Wales 1947-82, Ch Commr Boy Scouts for Wales 1948-66, Member Standing Commn on Museums and Art Galleries 1953-60, Gov Welbeck Coll 1952, Trustee Nat Portrait Gallery 1953-87 (Chm 1966), Member Royal Commn on Historical MSS since 1966: m 1946, Leila Mary PEEL, da of late Cmdr John Wyndham Cookson, RN (see Colquhoun, Bt, 1963 Edn), and widow of Hugh William Jardine Ethelston Peel, Lieut Welsh Guards (see Buchanan-Jardine, Bt, 1945 Edn); d 1993; s by his eldest son (6) LLOYD, 6th Baron and present peer.

Keppel, family name of Earl of Albemarle.

Ker, Innes, family name of the Duke of Roxburghe.

Kerr, family name of the Marquess of Lothian.

Kerr, family name of Baron Teviot.

KERSHAW, BARON (Kershaw) (Baron UK 1947)

EDWARD JOHN KERSHAW, JP, 4th Baron; *b* 12 May 1936; *s* 1962; *ed* Selhurst Gram Sch, Croydon; RAF 1955-57; Chartered Accountant 1964; JP 1982: *m* 1963, Rosalind Lilian, da of late Ian Strachan Rutherford, of 16 Castlegate, Richmond, and has issue.
Residence – 38 High View, Hempsted, Glos.

SON LIVING

Hon JOHN CHARLES EDWARD, *b* 23 Dec 1971.

DAUGHTERS LIVING

Hon Victoria Anne, *b* 1964: *m* 1989, Ian C. Harvey-Piper, son of C. D. Harvey-Piper, of Wimbledon, SW19. *Residence* – 6 Ripley Rd, Hampton, Middx TW12 2JH.
Hon Isobel Mary, *b* 1967: *m* 1993, Robert A. Slater, son of J. F. Slater, of Derby. *Residence* – 17 Rossignol Gdns, off Nightingale Rd, Carshalton, Surrey SM5 2ED.

SISTER LIVING

Hon Patricia Margaret, *b* 1943: *m* 1968, David Anniss Pickett, BSc, BMus, and has issue living, Caroline Mary, *b* 1969, — Rachel Elizabeth, *b* 1972.

UNCLE LIVING (*Son of the 1st Baron*)

Hon Peter John, *b* 1924; *ed* Queen Elizabeth's Sch, Barnet, and at King's Coll, London (BSc, 1948) FEng, FICE; Sub-Lieut RNVR 1945-46: *m* 1948, Brenda Margaret, who *d* 1999, da of late James Austin Smith, of Brighton, and has issue living, Michael James, *b* 1951. *Residence* – 22 Orchard Rise, Richmond, Surrey, TW10 5BX.

WIDOWS LIVING OF SECOND AND THIRD BARONS

CISSIE BURNESS (*Cissie, Baroness Kershaw*), da of Charles E. Smythe, of Friern Barnet: *m* 1933, the 2nd Baron Kershaw, who *d* (July) 1961. *Residence* – 29 St Ann's Rd, Newquay, Cornwall.

KATHARINE DOROTHEA (*Katharine, Baroness Kershaw*), da of Charles H. Staines, of Clapham, SW: *m* 1935, the 3rd Baron Kershaw, who *d* 1962. *Residence* – 3 Windmill Court, Northern Crescent, E Wittering, W Sussex PO20 8RJ.

COLLATERAL BRANCH LIVING

Issue of late Hon Donald Arthur Kershaw, 3rd son of 1st Baron, *b* 1915, *d* 1991: *m* 1942, Barbara Edith, who *d* 1986, only child of Lt-Col Cecil Graham Ford, of Richmond:—
Ian Graham Frederick, *b* 1948. *Residence* – 22 Priory Gdns, Old Basing, Hants RG24 7DS. ——— Mark Nigel, *b* 1951. *Residence* – 19 Beechnut Lane, Solihull, West Midlands B91 2NN.

PREDECESSORS – (1) FRED KERSHAW, OBE, son of John Joseph Kershaw, of Prestwich, Lancashire; *b* 1881; a Dep Speaker House of Lords, a Gov of Westminster Hospital, Chm of Gordon Hospital, and of Marie Curie Memorial Foundation, a Co Director, Vice-Pres of Workers' Temperance League, and Founder Member of Manor House Hospital; a Lord-in-Waiting to HM King George VI 1949-51; *cr Baron Kershaw*, of Prestwich, co Palatine of Lancaster (peerage of United Kingdom) 1947: *m* 1903, Frances Edith, who *d* 1960, da of James Thomas Wigmore, of Hereford; *d* (Feb) 1961; *s* by his el son (2) HERBERT, 2nd Baron; *b* 1904; European War and Far East 1939-45 as Sub Lieut RNVR: *m* 1933, Cissie Burness, da of Charles E. Smythe, of Friern Barnet; *d* (July) 1961; *s* by his brother (3) EDWARD AUBREY, 3rd Baron; *b* 1906: *m* 1935, Katharine Dorothea, da of Charles H. Staines, of Clapham, SW; *d* 1962; *s* by his son (4) EDWARD JOHN, 4th Baron and present peer.

KEYES, BARON (Keyes) (Baron UK 1943, Bt UK 1919)

Acquired by virtue

ROGER GEORGE BOWLBY KEYES, 2nd Baron and 2nd Baronet, *b* 14 March 1919; *s* 1945; Lieut RN (ret 1949); European War 1939-45 in N Sea and Mediterranean: *m* 1947, Grizelda Mary, who *d* 1993, da of late Lieut-Col William Vere Packe, DSO, and has issue.

𝕬rms – Per chevron gules and sable, three keys or, the wards of the two in chief facing each other, and of the one in base to the sinister, on a canton argent a lion rampant of the first. 𝕮rest – An open hand couped at the wrist proper, holding between the forefinger and thumb a key or. 𝕾upporters – (hereditary), — *Dexter*, a sailor of the Royal Navy in blue working rig proper, supporting in the exterior hand a staff argent ensigned with a naval crown or, and flying the banner of Saint George also proper; *sinister*, a Royal Marine in field service dress, armed and equipped for trench raiding, all proper.
Residence – St George's Lodge, Malling Rd, Teston, Kent ME18 5AU. *Clubs* – Anglo-Belgian, House of Lords Yacht.

SONS LIVING

(*Hon*) CHARLES WILLIAM PACKE (does not use courtesy title), *b* 8 Dec 1951; *ed* Eton: *m* 1st, 1978, Sadiye Yasmin, da of Mahir Coskun, of Istanbul; 2ndly, 1984, Sally, da of Thomas Jackson, and has issue living (by 2nd *m*), Anna Merula, *b* 1985.

Hon Leopold Roger John, *b* 1956; *ed* Eton: *m* 1988 (*m diss* 19—), Jane Elizabeth, only da of Trevor B. Owen, CBE, of Meadow Cottage, Carswell Marsh, Oxon.

Hon Adrian Christopher Noel, *b* 1962; *ed* Lancing. Resides in Spain.

DAUGHTERS LIVING

Virginia Mary Clementine (does not use courtesy title), *b* 1950; *ed* Sherborne, and Sheffield Univ: *m* 1972, Rev Roger Martyn Crompton, of The Vicarage, Church St, Golcar, Huddersfield HD7 4PX, and has issue living, Heather Rose Mary, *b* 1976, — Bryony Judith, *b* 1978, — Rowan Elizabeth, *b* 1981, — Holly Susannah, *b* 1983.

Hon Josephine Mary, *b* 1958; *ed* Benenden, and Newnham Coll, Camb: *m* 1987, Hon (William Aldus) Thoby Young, only son of 2nd Baron Kennet, and has issue.

PREDECESSOR – (**1**) *Sir* Roger John Brownlow Keyes, GCB, KCVO, DSO, DCL, LLD, son of late Gen Sir Charles Patton Keyes, GCB; *b* 1872; entered RN 1885, and became Adm of the Fleet 1930; E Africa 1890, China 1900, European War 1914-19 as Commodore Submarines, subsequently as Ch of Staff, E Mediterranean Squadron, Capt and Rear-Adm Grand Fleet, Director of Plans at Admiralty, and Acting Vice-Adm Comdg Dover Patrol (despatches, CMG, DSO, Com Legion of Honour, KCB, KCVO, thanked by War Cabinet, Belgian and French Crois de Guerre Grand Cordon of Order of Leopold of Belgium, Grand Officer Legion of Honour, Com of Order of St Maurice and St Lazarus of Italy, American DSM, thanked by Parliament, *cr* Baronet, granted £10,000 for blocking the sea-ward end of Bruges ship canal, sole exit for ocean-going U-Boats based at Bruges, at Zeebrugge 23 April 1918); a Lord of the Admiralty and Dep-Ch of Naval Staff, Admiralty 1921-5; commanded Mediterranean Fleet 1925-8; Com-in-Ch Portsmouth 1929-31; Hon Col Comdt, Portsmouth Div, RM 1932-42; 1st Ch of Combined Operations 1940-41; Special Liason Officer to King of the Belgians May 1940; sat as MP for N Div of Portsmouth (*C*) 1934-43; *cr* a *Baronet* 1919, and *Baron Keyes*, of Zeebrugge, and of Dover, co Kent 1943: *m* 1906, Eva Mary Salvin, who *d* 1973, da of late Edward Salvin Bowlby, DL, of Gilston Park, Herts, and Knoydart, Inverness-shire (his el son, Lt-Col Geoffrey Charles Tasker, VC, MC, Croix de Guerre, Roy Scots Greys (*b* 1917) was killed leading his (11th) Commando attempt to capture General Rommel at Sidi Rafa, Libya 1941, for which he was awarded a posthumous VC); *d* 1945; *s* by his only surviving son (**2**) Roger George Bowlby, 2nd Baron and present peer.

<h2 style="text-align:center">KILBRACKEN, BARON (Godley) (Baron UK 1909)</h2>

John Raymond Godley, DSC, 3rd Baron; *b* 17 Oct 1920; *s* 1950; *ed* Eton, and Balliol Coll, Oxford (BA and MA 1948); is an Author and Journalist; European War 1940-45 in RNVR (Air Branch), Lieut-Com (A) 1945 (DSC): *m* 1st, 1943 (*m diss* 1949), Penelope Anne, yst da of late Rear-Adm Sir Cecil Nugent Reyne, KBE; 2ndly, 1981 (*m diss* 1989), Susan Lee, da of late Norman Heazlewood, of Melbourne, Australia, and has issue by 1st and 2nd *m*.

Arms – Argent, three unicorns' heads erased sable, horned gules, two and one, and three trefoils slipped vert, one and two. **Crest** – A unicorn's head erased argent, horned gules, charged with three trefoils slipped vert. **Supporters** – *Dexter*, a griffin sable charged with four stars argent in cross; *sinister*, a lion argent, charged with four roses gules in cross. *Seat* – Killegar, co Leitrim (postal address: Killegar, Cavan).

<h3 style="text-align:center">SONS LIVING (By 1st marriage)</h3>

Hon Christopher John (Four Firs, Marley Lane, Haslemere, Surrey), *b* 1 Jan 1945; *ed* Rugby, and Reading Univ (BSc Agric 1967); Agriculturalist: *m* 1969, Gillian Christine, da of late Lt-Cdr S. W. Birse, OBE, DSC, RN (ret), of Alverstoke, Hants, and has issue living, James John, *b* 1972, — Louisa Laheen, *b* 1974.

<h3 style="text-align:center">(By 2nd marriage)</h3>

Hon Seán Garech, *b* 1981.

<h3 style="text-align:center">BROTHER LIVING</h3>

Prof the Hon Wynne Alexander Hugh (Jasmine House, The Green, Cavendish, Sudbury, Suffolk CO10 8BB) *b* 1926; *ed* Rugby, and at New Coll, Oxford (BA 1947); Fellow of King's Coll, Camb and Prof of Applied Economics: *m* 1955, Mrs Kathleen Eleanora (Kitty) Freud, da of late Sir Jacob Epstein, KBE, and formerly wife of Lucian Freud, and has issue living, Eve Katharine, *b* 1967.

PREDECESSORS – (**1**) *Sir* John Arthur Godley, GCB, only son of late John Robert Godley, of Killegar; *b* 1847; Commr of Inland Revenue 1882-3, and Permanent Under-Sec for India 1883-1909; *cr Baron Kilbracken*, of Killegar, co Leitrim (peerage of United Kingdom) 1909: *m* 1871, Hon Sarah James, who *d* 1921, da of 1st Baron Northbourne; *d* 1932; *s* by his elder and only surv son (**2**) Hugh John, CB, KC, 2nd Baron; *b* 1877; Assist Parliamentary Counsel to the Treasury 1917-22, and Counsel to Chm of Committees, House of Lords 1922-44: *m* 1st, 1919 (*m diss* 1936), Elizabeth Helen Monteith, who *d* 1958, da of Vereker Monteith Hamilton, and widow of W/Cdr N. F. Usborne, RNAS; 2ndly, 1936, Rhoda Leonora, who *d* 1948, da of Percy Taylor; *d* 1950; *s* by his elder son (**3**) John Raymond, 3rd Baron and present peer.

KILBRANDON, BARONY OF (Shaw) (Extinct 1989)

SONS LIVING OF LIFE BARON

Hon Patrick James (Leitir, Lochawe, Dalmally, Argyll), *b* 1938: *m* 1964, Elisabeth Grace Melfort Gibson, and has issue living, Donald Patrick, *b* 1967, — Shuna Caroline, *b* 1965, — Heather Grace, *b* 1971, — Eilidh Elisabeth, *b* 1973.
Hon Michael Frank (Kilbrandon House, Balvicar, by Oban, Argyll) *b* 1944: *m* 1978, Catherine Ballantine, and has issue living, Torquil James Brandon, *b* 1981, — Tamara Caroline, *b* 1980.

DAUGHTERS LIVING OF LIFE BARON

Hon Teresa Caroline Glencairn (PO Box Rongai, Kenya) *b* 1940: *m* 1969, Christopher D. A. Orme-Smith, and has issue living, Andrew, *b* 1974, — Philippa, *b* 1969: *m* 1990, Robin J. E. Witt, of 7 Church St, Nunney, nr Frome, Som, eldest son of Michael Witt, of Whatley, Som, — Nicola, *b* 1971: *m* 1993, James F. D. Hutchings, eldest son of Maj Edgar Hutchings, of Withypool, Som.
Hon Mary Anna, *b* 1946: *m* 1971, Thomas Horatio Congreve Shephard, and has issue (*see* Congreve, Bt, ext). *Residence* – Claigan Farmhouse, Dunvegan, Isle of Skye.
Hon Elizabeth Cecilia, *b* 1948: *m* 1984, Jean-Marc Peysson, and has issue living, Jean-Christophe, *b* 1986, — Claire Elizabeth, *b* 1991. *Residence* – La Maison Neuve, 03210 Autry Issards, Allier, France.

WIDOW LIVING OF LIFE BARON

RUTH CAROLINE (*Baroness Kilbrandon*), da of Frank Morrison Seafield Grant, of Knockie, Inverness: *m* 1937, Baron Kilbrandon, PC (Life Baron), who *d* 1989. *Residence* – Kilbrandon House, Balvicar, by Oban, Argyll PA34 4RA.

Kildare, Marquess of; son of Duke of Leinster.

KILLANIN, BARON (Morris) (Baron UK 1900, Bt UK 1885)

SI·DEUS·NOBISCUM·QUIS·CONTRA·NOS

If God be with us, who is against us?

(GEORGE) REDMOND FITZPATRICK MORRIS, 4th Baron, and 4th Baronet; *b* 26 Jan 1947; *s* 1999; *ed* Gonzaga Coll, Dublin, Ampleforth, and Trin Coll, Dublin: *m* 1972, Pauline, only da of Geoffrey Horton, of The Lawns, Cabinteely, co Dublin, and has issue.

Arms – Ermine, a fesse indented sable, in base a lion rampant of the last armed and langued gules. Crest – On a fasces fessewise proper, a lion's head erased argent, guttë de sang. Supporters – Two lions gules, each gorged with a chain or, pendant therefrom an escutcheon ermine charged with a sword erect proper, pommel and hilt gold and standing on a fasces also proper.
Seat – St Annins, Spiddal, co Galway. *Residence* – Doughty Cottage, Richmond Hill, Richmond, Surrey TW10 6RN.

SON LIVING

Hon LUKE MICHAEL GEOFFREY, *b* 22 July 1975.

DAUGHTER LIVING

Hon Olivia Rose Elizabeth, *b* 1974.

BROTHERS LIVING

Hon Michael Francis Leo (Everard's Grange, Fethard, co Tipperary), *b* 1951; *ed* St Conleth's Coll, Dublin and Ampleforth: *m* 1979, Susanna Clark, and has issue living, James Michael, *b* 1983, — Christopher Michael, *b* 1985.

Hon John Martin (5 Rus-in-Urbe, Lower Glengeary Rd, Dun Laoghaire, co Dublin), *b* 1951 (twin); *ed* St Conleth's Coll, Dublin, and Ampleforth: *m* 1972, Thelma, da of Mrs Mansfield, of Monkstown, co Dublin, and has issue living, Roderic Michael, *b* 1976, — Michael-John, *b* 1979.

SISTER LIVING

Hon (Monica) Deborah, *b* 1950: *m* 1970, William Campbell Rough Bryden, Associate Dir National Theatre, since 1975, and has issue living, Dillon Michael George, *b* 1972, — Mary Kate, *b* 1975. *Residence* – 3 Orchard Cottage, Clifton Rd, Kingston upon Thames, Surrey.

WIDOW LIVING OF THIRD BARON

MARY SHEILA CATHCART, MBE (*Dowager Baroness Killanin*), da of Rev Canon Douglas Dunlop, of Oughterard, co Galway: *m* 1945, Maj the 3rd Baron Killanin, MBE, TD, who *d* 1999. *Residence* – St Annins, Spiddal, co Galway; 9 Lower Mount Pleasant Av, Dublin 5.

PREDECESSORS – (1) *Rt Hon* MICHAEL Morris, PC, son of late Martin Morris, JP, of Spiddal, co Galway; *b* 1827; MP for Galway (LC) 1865-7; Recorder of Galway 1857-65; Solicitor-Gen for Ireland 1866, Attorney-Gen 1866-7, Justice of common Pleas for Ireland 1867-76, Lord Ch Justice thereof 1876-87, Lord Ch Justice of Ireland 1887-9, an a Lord of Appeal in Ordinary 1889-1900: *cr* a *Baronet* 1885, *Baron Morris* (life peerage), of Spiddal, co Galway 1889, and *Baron Killanin*, of Galway, co Galway (peerage of United Kingdom) 1900: *m* 1860, Anna, who *d* 1906, da of late Hon H. G. Hughes, a Baron of the Exchequer in Ireland; *d* 1901, when the Barony of Morris, being a Life Peerage, expired, and he was *s* in the Barony of Killanin by his el son (2) MARTIN HENRY FITZPATRICK, PC, 2nd Baron, *b* 1867: Member of Senate of Roy Univ of Ireland 1904-9, Gov of Univ Coll, Galway 1909-22; MP for Galway (C) 1900-1; Lieut and Custos Rotulorum for co Galway; *d* 1927; *s* by his nephew (3) MICHAEL, MBE, TD (son of late Lieut-Col Hon George Henry Morris, yr son of 1st Baron), 3rd Baron, *b* 1914; Pres Olympic Council of Ireland 1950-73 (Hon Pres 1981), Memb Internat Olympic Cttee 1952 (Pres 1972-80, Hon Life Pres 1980); Chm Irish Nat Heritage Council; Memb Nat Monuments Advisory Council of Ireland (Chm 1960-65); Memb Irish Nat Hunt Steeplechase, and Irish Turf Club (Steward); Chm Dublin Theatre Festival 1960-70; Pres Irish Club, London 1947-65; author, war correspondent *Daily Mail*, political correspondent *Sunday Dispatch*; film producer; Maj KRRC, served NW Europe 1944-45; received many foreign orders and decorations: *m* 1945, Mary Sheila Cathcart, MBE, da of Rev Canon Douglas Dunlop, of Oughterard, co Galway; *d* 1999; *s* by his eldest son (4) (GEORGE) REDMOND FITZPATRICK, 4th Baron and present peer.

KILLEARN, BARON (Lampson) (Baron UK 1943, Bt UK 1866)

Persevere and conquer

VICTOR MILES GEORGE ALDOUS LAMPSON, 3rd Baron, and 4th Baronet; *b* 9 Sept 1941; *s* 1996; *ed* Eton; formerly Capt Scots Guards: *m* 1971, Melita Armaryllis Pamela Astrid, 2nd da of Rear-Adm Sir Morgan Charles Morgan-Giles, DSO, OBE, GM, DL, and has issue.

Arms – Per saltire argent and gules, two gryphons' heads in fesse and as many escarbuncles in pale counterchanged. **Crest** – A gryphon's head erased gules, charged with an escarbuncle argent, between two wings paly of four, argent and gules. **Supporters** – *Dexter*, a camel proper with head stall and rope reflexed over the back gules; *sinister*, a Chinese dragon also proper.
Residence – Little Sodbury Manor, Little Sodbury, Chipping Sodbury, S Glos BS37 6QA. *Clubs* – White's, Pratt's, City of London.

SONS LIVING

Hon MILES HENRY MORGAN, *b* 10 Dec 1977; *ed* Eton.
Hon Alexander Victor William, *b* 1984.

DAUGHTERS LIVING

Hon Pamela Camilla Roxana, *b* 1973.
Hon Miranda Penelope Amber, *b* 1975.

SISTERS LIVING

Hon Jacquetta Jean Frederica, *b* 1943: *m* 1964 (*m diss* 1990), 10th Earl of St Germans. *Residence* – Innisfree, nr Polzeath, Wadebridge, N Cornwall PL27 6UF.

Hon Roxana Rose Catherine Naila, *b* 1945: *m* 1966, Ian Cowper Ross, and has issue living, Atticus Matthew Cowper, *b* 1968; *ed* Eton, — Milo Joseph Charles, *b* 1970; *ed* in Los Angeles, Calif, — Leopold Lincoln Fitzgerald, *b* 1980; *ed* Holland Park Comprehensive, — Holly Zahava Josephine, *b* 1971, — Mia Vanilla Catherine, *b* 1973, — Liberty Lettuce Lark, *b* 1978. *Residence* – 16 Kelfield Gdns, W10 6LS.

DAUGHTERS LIVING OF SECOND BARON

Hon Alexandra Rachel Mary Catherine Angelica (Black Horse House, E Knoyle, Wilts SP3 6AL), *b* 1947; JP Staffs 1971: *m* 1st, 1966 (*m diss* 1987), Nicholas Edward Hugo Meynell (*see* E Halifax, colls), who *d* 1988; 2ndly, 1997, (Antony) Julian Gibbs.
Hon Nadine Marisa (*Hon Lady Bonsor*), *b* 1948; JP Beds 1972: *m* 1969, Sir Nicholas Cosmo Bonsor, 4th Bt, MP, of Liscombe Park, Leighton Buzzard, Beds.

DAUGHTER LIVING OF THIRD BARONET

Sophia Curtis (Mill House Farm, Brightling, Sussex), *b* 1935: *m* 1955, Ronald J. Milwidsky, BSc(Eng), AMIEE, who *d* 1966, and has issue living, Peter Julian, *b* 1960, — Caroline Natasha, *b* 1956, — Sarah Janet, *b* 1962.

WIDOW LIVING OF FIRST BARON

JACQUELINE ALDINE LESLIE (*Dowager Baroness Killearn*) (23 Harley St, W1N 1DA; Haremere Hall, Etchingham, Sussex); da of late Marchese Senator Aldo Castellani, KCMG, FRCP, FACP, DSc, MD; a CStJ: *m* 1934, as his 2nd wife, the 1st Baron Killearn, who *d* 1964.

WIDOW LIVING OF SECOND BARON

NADINE MARIE CATHRYN (*Nadine, Baroness Killearn*), only da of late Vice-Adm Cecil Horace Pilcher, DSO: *m* 1946, the 2nd Baron Killearn, who *d* 1996. *Residence* – 58 Melton Court, Old Brompton Rd, SW7 3JJ.

PREDECESSORS – **(1)** *Rt Hon Sir* MILES WEDDERBURN Lampson, GCMG, CB, MVO, 2nd son of late Norman George Lampson, yst son of 1st Bt (infra), *b* 1880; Min to China 1926-33, High Commr for Egypt and the Sudan 1933-36, Ambassador to Egypt and High Commr for Sudan 1936-46 and Special Commr in S-E Asia 1946-48; *cr Baron Killearn*, of Killearn, co Stirling (peerage of UK) 1943: *m* 1st, 1912, Rachel Mary Hele, who *d* 1930, da of William Wilton Phipps; 2ndly, 1934, Jacqueline Aldine Leslie, da of late Marchese Senator Aldo Castellani, KCMG, FRCP, FACP, DSc, MD; *d* 1964; *s* by his el son **(2)** GRAHAM CURTIS, 2nd Baron; *b* 1919; Major Scots Guards (US Bronze Star): *m* 1946, Nadine Marie Cathryn, only da of late Vice-Adm Cecil Horace Pilcher, DSO; *d* 1996; *s* by his half-brother **(3)** VICTOR MILES GEORGE ALDOUS, 3rd Baron and present peer.
*****(1)** *Sir* CURTIS MIRANDA Lampson (yst son of William Lampson, of New Haven, Vermont, USA); *b* 1806, naturalized British subject 1848; Dep Chm Atlantic Telegraph Co 1865, which Co laid the first Atlantic telegraph cable, for which sers he was *cr a Baronet* 1866; Founder of C M Lampson & Co: *m* 1827, Jane Walter, who *d* 1891, da of Gibbs Sibley, of Sutton, Mass, USA; *d* 1885; *s* by his el son **(2)** Sir GEORGE CURTIS, 2nd Bt, *b* 1833: *m* 1887, Sophia, who *d* 1926, yst da of Manuel Van Gelderen; *d* 1899; *s* by his only son **(3)** *Sir* CURTIS GEORGE, 3rd Bt; *b* 1890; FRGS; explorer in Central and W Africa, author and journalist: *m* 1920, Maud Lawton, who *d* 1960, da of Alfred Wrigley, of Manchester; *d* 1971; *s* by his cousin, 2nd Baron Killearn (ante).

KILMAINE, BARON (Browne) (Baron I 1789, Bt NS 1636)

Follow right

JOHN DAVID HENRY BROWNE, 7th Baron, and 13th Baronet, *b* 2 April 1948; *s* 1978; *ed* Eton; a Dir of Fusion (Bickenhill) Ltd 1969-98, and of Whale Tankers Ltd: *m* 1982, Linda, yr da of Dennis Robinson, of East Terrace, Budleigh Salterton, and has issue.

Arms – Sable, in bend three lions passant between two double cotises argent. **Crest** – An eagle displayed vert. **Supporters** – Two lions reguardant argent, ducally crowned, plain collared and chained or.

SON LIVING

Hon JOHN FRANCIS SANDFORD, *b* 4 April 1983.

DAUGHTER LIVING

Hon Alice, *b* 1985.

SISTERS LIVING

Hon Carola, *b* 1932: *m* 1960, John Michael Carlyon Lowry Hudson, and has issue living, John Carlyon, *b* 1961: *m* 1989, Fiona J., yr da of G. F. White, of Dunedin, NZ, and has issue living, Tristrem Carlyon Francis *b* 1993, Piera J. *b* 1996, — Thomas Christopher, *b* 1963: *m* 1997, Joanne Susan, yr da of A. B. Robinson, of Mt Palm, NZ, — Phyllida, *b* 1966: *m* 1996, Stuart Barrie Gibson, and has issue living, Hannah Carola *b* 1998. *Residence* – Gwavas Station, Tikokino, Hawkes Bay, NZ.

Hon Phyllida, *b* 1935: *m* 1959, John Edward Previté, QC, Circuit Judge, and has issue living, Andrew Capper, *b* 1961: *m* 1992, Antonia Hamilton, yr da of E. W. Davis, of SW3, and has issue living, Edward Jolyon Capper *b* 1994, Robert Angus Capper *b* 1996, Fergus Harold Capper *b* 1997, — Matthew John, *b* 1963: *m* 1992, Elizabeth S., elder da of A. J. Pull, of Headley, Hants, and has issue living, Thomas Anthony John *b* 1995, Grace Alexandra *b* 1993, Annabel Victoria *b* 1998. *Residence* – The Wilderness, Hampton Wick, Kingston upon Thames, Surrey.

<h3 style="text-align:center">WIDOW LIVING OF SIXTH BARON</h3>

WILHELMINA PHYLLIS (*Dowager Baroness Kilmaine*) (The Red Cottage, High Street, Brasted, Kent), only da of late Scott Arnott, of Tanners, Brasted, Kent: *m* 1930, Lt-Col the 6th Baron Kilmaine, CBE, who *d* 1978.

COLLATERAL BRANCHES LIVING

Grandson of late Frederick Howe Browne, yst son of late George Richard Browne, son of late Hon Richard Howe Browne, 5th son of 2nd Baron:—
Issue of late Noel Francis HOWE BROWNE, *b* 1884, *d* 1943: *m* 1919, Jessie Selwyn Tudhope:—
Peter Kilmaine (Morningside Farm, PO Box 692, Rustenburg, Transvaal), *b* 1920; late Capt King's African Rifles: *m* 1948, Grace Dorothy Robson, of Nakuru, Kenya, and has issue living, Margaret Jess, *b* 1950, — Joan Selwyn, *b* 1951.

Grandchildren of Capt Aubrey Caulfeild Browne (infra):—
Issue of late Cecil John Osborne Caulfeild BROWNE, *b* 1892, *d* 1983: *m* 1st, 1923, Gladys Isobel Mason, who *d* 1962; 2ndly, 1965, Mrs Madeline Constance Ferguson (15 Caroma Av, Kyeemagh, N Brighton, NSW, Australia):—
(By 1st *m*) *Rev* Aubrey Robert Caulfeild (St Anthony's Vicarage, 2a Carden Rd, SE15 3UD), *b* 1931; *ed* Newington Coll, Sydney, and Moore Coll, Sydney (ThL); Regional Manager, United Soc for Propagation of the Gospel.

Issue of late Edward James CAULFEILD BROWNE, MBE, *b* 1903, *d* 1984: *m* 1st, 1925 (*m diss* 1941), Eileen, da of Jack O'Hearn, of Ireland; 2ndly, 1942, Mary Winifred, who *d* 1987, da of George Albert Green:—
(By 1st *m*) †Reginald M., *b* 1928: *m* 1st, 1954 (*m diss* 1961), Valerie Therese Hogan; 2ndly, 1965 (*m diss* 1991), Margaret Kathleen Glennon, and *d* 1998, leaving issue, (by 1st *m*) Loretta Sandra *b* 1955, — Yolanda Therese, *b* 1956, — (by 2nd *m*) Mark, *b* 1966, — Helen Luise, *b* 1973. —— Noreen, *b* 1926: *m* 19—, — Sharp. —— (By 2nd *m*) Nigel George, *b* 1947: *m* 1st, 1968 (*m diss* 1973), Susan Mary Green; 2ndly, 1974 (*m diss* 1983), Jill Christine Masters; 3rdly, 1984, Jane Elizabeth Skinner, and has issue living, (by 1st *m*) Sharon Ann, *b* 1970, — (by 2nd *m*) James Alexander, *b* 1976, — Sophie Victoria, *b* 1978, — Lucy Alexandra, *b* 1980, — (by 3rd *m*) Matthew John, *b* 1987. —— Robin James, *b* 1949: *m* 1970 (*m diss* 1978), Annette Heavey; 2ndly, 1979, Denise Dodd, and has issue living, (by 1st *m*) Edward Patrick, *b* 1972, — Christopher Robert, *b* 1974, — (by 2nd *m*) Jason Robin, *b* 1987. —— Dawn Rosemary, *b* 1943: *m* 19—, Robert Edward Collins, and has issue living, Mark Robert, *b* 1973, — Amanda Jane, *b* 1972.

Grandchildren of late Rev William James Caulfeild Browne, son of late Rev James Caulfeild Browne, DCL, son of late Hon George Browne, 3rd son of 1st Baron:—
Issue of late Capt Aubrey Caulfeild Browne, *b* 1860, *d* 1953: *m* 1st, 1888, Caroline Mitchell, who *d* 1893; 2ndly, 1894, Ida B. Graham, who *d* 1942:—
(By 2nd *m*) Norah, *b* 1896. —— Kathleen, *b* 1898.

Issue of late James Cecil Caulfeild Browne, *b* 1862, *d* 1917: *m* 1887, Elsie M., who *d* 19—, da of late G. Manning, British Consul at San Salvador:—
Edwin Caulfeild, *b* 1895. —— Cecily Caulfeild, *b* 1891: *m* 1908, Henry Snell.

Issue of late Harold John Caulfeild Browne, *b* 1864, *d* 1953: *m* 1916, Margaret Delamere Booth, who *d* 1971, da of Maj James Booth Clarkson:—
Edith Margaret, *b* 1919: *m* 1955, Thomas Henry Standish Goodlake, who *d* 1989, and has two adopted sons, John Stephen, *b* 1959, — Christopher James, *b* 1964. *Residence* – 1336 W King Edward Av, Vancouver, BC V6H-1Z9, Canada.

(In remainder to Baronetcy only)

Descendants of John Browne, MP, of Westport, co Mayo (grandson of Col John Browne, 2nd son of 1st baronet), who was *cr Earl of Altamont* 1771 (*see* M Sligo).

Descendants of John Browne, only son of Peter Browne, el son of Dominick Browne, 3rd son of 1st baronet:—

Grandchildren of late Maj Dominick Sidney Browne, JP, DL (ante):—
Issue of late Brig Dominick Andrew Sidney Browne, CBE, *b* 1904; *d* 1982: *m* 1930, Iris Kathleen, who *d* 1977, da of late Gerald Henry Deane, of Littleton House, Winchester, Hants:—
Peter Dominick, MBE, *b* 1949; Lt-Col R Green Jackets (ret 1990); MBE (Mil) 1984: *m* 1974, Sally Jane, el da John Eric Marrett, MRCS, LRCP, of Clare House, Howe Green, Sandon, Essex, and has issue living, Henry Dominick, *b* 1989, — Eleanor Jane, *b* 1987. *Residence* – Ludwell Farm, Glympton, Woodstock, Oxon OX20 1AZ. —— Fiona Naomi, *b* 1935: *m* 1956, Cdr Hugh Douglas Younger Faulkner, CVO, RN, of Currie Lee, Crichton, nr Pathhead, Midlothian EH37 5XD, and has issue living, Christopher Gerald (6 Rosemount Rd, W Ealing, W13 0HJ), *b* 1958: *m* 1987 (*m diss* 1999), Ming F., da of late Mark Veevers-Carter, and of Mrs John Blower, and has issue living, Clarence Dominick Hugh *b* 1992, Olivia *b* 1990, — Anthony Dominick Hugh, *b* 1961: *m* 1990, Joanne Kay, da of Edgar Denton, and has issue living, Samuel

Anthony *b* 1992. —— Anne Patricia, *b* 1944: *m* 1st, 1967, David J. Forcey; 2ndly, 1978, Robin John Hay, of Stoke Cottage, Fullards Av, Taunton, Som TA1 3DE, and has issue living (by 1st *m*), Annabelle Jane, *b* 1971, — (by 2nd *m*) Alexander Robin, *b* 1980.

PREDECESSORS – **(1)** JOHN Browne, el son of Josias Browne, of The Neale; *cr a Baronet* 1636; *d* 1670; *s* by his son **(2)** *Sir* GEORGE, 2nd Bt; *d* 1698; *s* by his son **(3)** *Sir* JOHN, 3rd Bt; *d* 1711; *s* by his el son **(4)** *Sir* GEORGE, 4th Bt; *dsp* 1737; *s* by his brother **(5)** *Sir* JOHN, 5th Bt; *d* 1762; *s* by his el son **(6)** *Sir* GEORGE, 6th Bt; *d* 1765; *s* by his brother **(7)** *Sir* JOHN, MP; 7th Bt; *cr Baron Kilmaine*, of The Neale, co Mayo (peerage of Ireland) 1789; *d* 1794; *s* by his el son **(8)** JAMES CAULFEILD, 2nd Baron; *d* 1825; *s* by his el son **(9)** JOHN CAVENDISH, 3rd Baron; *b* 1794; a Representative Peer; *m* 2ndly, 1839, Mary, da of Hon Charles Ewan Law, MP (B Ellenborough); *d* 1873; *s* by his son **(10)** FRANCIS WILLIAM, 4th Baron, *b* 1843; a Representative Peer for Ireland: *m* 1877, Alice Emily, who *d* 1925, da of Col Deane Shute; *d* 1907; *s* by his only son **(11)** JOHN EDWARD DEANE, 5th Baron, *b* 1878; a Representative Peer for Ireland: *m* 1901, Lady Aline Kennedy, who *d* 1957, da of 3rd Marquess of Ailsa; *d* 1946; *s* by his son **(12)** JOHN FRANCIS ARCHIBALD, CBE, 6th Baron; *b* 1902, High Steward of Harwich; 1939-45 War as Lt-Col RASC; Sec to Oxford Soc 1933-40 (Chm 1949-73), to Pilgrim Trust 1945-67, and to Dulverton Trust 1953-66; a Trustee of Historic Churches Preservation Trust: *m* 1930, Wilhelmina Phyllis, only da of Scott Arnott, of Tanners, Brasted, Kent; *d* 1978; *s* by his son **(13)** JOHN DAVID HENRY, 7th Baron and present peer.

KILMANY, BARONY OF (Anstruther-Gray) (Life Baron 1966, Bt UK 1956) (Extinct 1985)
(see Anstruther of that Ilk, Bt, colls)

KILMARNOCK, BARON (Boyd) (Baron UK 1831)

I trust

ALASTAIR IVOR GILBERT BOYD, 7th Baron; *b* 11 May 1927; *s* 1975; *ed* Bradfield, and King's Coll, Camb; Lt late IG; Chief of Clan Boyd; Page to Lord High Constable of Scotland at Coronation of HM King George VI; author of *Sabbatical Year* 1958, *The Road from Ronda* 1969, *The Companion Guide to Madrid and Central Spain* 1974, *The Essence of Catalonia* 1988, *The Sierras of the South* 1992, etc; Palestine 1947-48: *m* 1st, 1954 (*m diss* 1969), Diana Mary Grant, who *d* 1975, only da of D. Grant Gibson; 2ndly, 1977, Hilary Ann, yr da of Leonard Sidney Bardwell, and formerly wife of Kingsley Amis (later Sir Kingsley Amis, CBE), and has issue by 2nd wife.

Arms – Quarterly: 1st azure a fesse chequy argent and gules, *Boyd*; 2nd argent three inescutcheons gules, *Hay*; 3rd argent three gillyflowers with a double tressure flory counter flory vert, *Livingston*; 4th sable a bend between six billets or, *Callendar*. **Crest** – A dexter hand erect in pale having the two outer fingers bowed inwards. **Supporters** – Two squirrels proper.
Residence – ...... *Club* – Pratt's.

SON LIVING (by 2nd wife)

Hon James Charles Edward, *b* 1972.

BROTHER LIVING

Hon ROBIN JORDAN, *b* 6 June 1941; *ed* Eton, and at Keble Coll, Oxford (MA); MB BS, LRCP, MRCS, DCH; Page to Lord High Constable of Scotland at Coronation of HM Queen Elizabeth II 1953. *Residence* –

HALF-BROTHERS LIVING

Hon Jonathan Aubrey Lewis, *b* 1956: *m* 1982, Annette Madeleine, el da of Joseph Constantine, FRICS, of 3 Cottesmore Gdns, W8, and has issue living, Edward Gilbert C., *b* 1989, — Arthur William, *b* 1994. *Residence* – ....
Hon Timothy Ian, *b* 1959: *m* 1988, Lucy Teresa Emily, yr da of Michael Gray, and has issue living, Daisy, *b* 1988. *Residence* – Flat 2, 23 Ladbroke Cres, W11 1PS.

SISTERS LIVING AND DECEASED (*in remainder to Earldom of Erroll*)

†*Hon* Laura Alice, *b* 1934: *m* 1962, (Robert) Anthony Hyman, and *d* 1999, leaving issue (*see* E Erroll, colls).
Hon Caroline Juliet, *b* 1939: *m* 1969, Alan Bloss.

PREDECESSORS – (1) WILLIAM GEORGE HAY, KT, GCH, PC, 18th Earl of Erroll; *b* 1801; was Lord Steward of the Household, Master of the Staghounds, and Lord-Lieut of Aberdeenshire; *cr Baron Kilmarnock* of Kilmarnock, co Ayr (peerage of United Kingdom) 1831: *m* 1820, Lady Elizabeth Fitzclarence, who *d* 1856, nat da of King William IV; *d* 1846; *s* by his son (2) WILLIAM HENRY, 19th Earl, *b* 1823; Maj (ret) Rifle Brig; Crimea 1854-55: *m* 1848, Eliza Amelia, VA, who *d* 1916, da of late Gen Hon Sir Charles Gore, GCB; *d* 1891; *s* by his son (3) CHARLES GORE, KT, CB, LLD, 20th Earl, *b* 1852; Hon Maj-Gen in the Army; a Lord-in-Waiting to King Edward VII, 1903-5: *m* 1875, Mary Caroline, who *d* 1934, da of late Edmund L'Estrange, of Tynte Lodge, co Leitrim; *d* 1927; *s* by his son (4) VICTOR ALEXANDER SERELD, KCMG, 21st Earl, *b* 1876; acted as Chargé d'Affaires at Berlin 1919-21; was British High Commr of Rhineland Commn 1921-28: *m* 1900, Mary Lucy Victoria, who *d* 1957, only da of Sir Allan Russell Mackenzie, 2nd Bt (*cr* 1890); *d* 1928; *s* by his son (5) JOSSLYN VICTOR, 22nd Earl; *b* 1901: *m* 1923 (*m diss* 1930), Lady (Myra) Idina (Gordon) Sackville, who *d* 1957, da of 8th Earl De La Warr; 2ndly, 1930, Edith Mildred Mary (RAMSAY-HILL), who *d* 1939, da of late R. W. Maude, of Cleveland, Yorks; *d* 1941, when the Earldom of Erroll devolved upon his only da, and he was *s* in the Barony of Kilmarnock by his brother (6) GILBERT ALLAN ROWLAND, MBE, TD, 6th Baron, *b* 1903; deputised for Lord High Constable of Scotland at Coronation of HM Queen Elizabeth II 1953; assumed for himself and issue by Warrant of Lord Lyon King of Arms 1941, the surname of Boyd in lieu of that of Hay: *m* 1st, 1926, (*m diss* 1955), Hon Rosemary Sibell Guest, who *d* 1971, da of 1st Viscount Wimborne; 2ndly, 1955, Denise Aubrey Doreen, who *d* 1989, only da of late Maj Lewis Coker (*see* M Donegall, colls, 1985 Edn); *d* 1975; *s* by his el son (7) ALASTAIR IVOR GILBERT, 7th Baron and present peer.

KILMOREY, EARL OF (Needham) (Earl I 1822)
(Title pronounced "Kilmurry")

NUNC AUT NUNQUAM

Now, or never

RICHARD FRANCIS NEEDHAM, PC, 6th Earl (*Rt Hon Sir Richard Needham*) (does not use his peerage); *b* 29 Jan 1942; *s* 1977; *ed* Eton; did not use courtesy title of Viscount Newry and Morne 1969-77; Hereditary Abbot of the Exempt Jurisdiction of Newry and Mourne; Member Public Accounts Cttee 1982-83, PPS to Rt Hon James Prior 1983-84, and to Rt Hon Patrick Jenkin 1984-85; an Under-Sec of State, N Ireland Office, 1985-92, Min of Trade, Dept of Trade and Industry 1992-95; Dir GEC plc 1995-97, Maggitt plc since 1997, MICE plc since 1998, Dyson Appliances Ltd since 1995; Founder Memb Anglo-Japanese 2000 Group, and Anglo-Korean Forum for the Future; Chm Gleneagles UK Ltd since 1995; author of *Honourable Member* (1983), and *Battling For Peace* 1998; MP for Chippenham (*C*) 1979-83, and for Wiltshire North (*C*) 1983-97; PC 1994, *cr* Kt Bach 1997: *m* 1965, Sigrid Juliane Thiessen-Gairdner, only da of late Ernst Thiessen, of Hamburg, and of Mrs John Gairdner, and has issue.

𝕬rms – Argent, a bend azure, between two bucks heads cabossed sable. 𝕮rest – A demi phœnix proper. 𝕾upporters – *Dexter*, a bay horse, mane and tail sable *sinister*, a stag proper.
Seat – Mourne Park, Newry, co Down. *Clubs* – Pratt's; Beefsteak.

SONS LIVING

ROBERT FRANCIS JOHN (*Viscount Newry and Morne*), *b* 30 May 1966; *ed* Eton, Lady Margaret Hall, Oxford, and Imperial Coll, London (MBA): *m* 1991, Laura Mary, only da of Michael Tregaskis, of Cosham, Hants, and has issue living, *Hon* Thomas Francis Michael, *b* 25 Sept 1998, — *Hon* Julia Helen Mary, *b* 1997.
Hon Andrew Francis, *b* 1969; *ed* Eton, and Edinburgh Univ: *m* 1997, Lindsay J., da of Lance Stephenson, of Thompson, Norfolk.

DAUGHTER LIVING

Lady Christina Clare, *b* 1977.

BROTHERS LIVING

Hon Christopher David, *b* 1948; *ed* Milton Abbey: *m* 1974, Marina, el da of Rodi Malvezzi, of Milan, and has issue living, Francis, *b* 1982, — Armyne, *b* 1978. *Residence* – 63 Foro Buonaparte, Milan, Italy.

Hon (Patrick) Jonathan, *b* 1951: *m* 1st, 1979 (*m diss* 1993), Jane, 2nd da of Geoffrey Hinbest, of Winterbourne, Bristol; 2ndly, 1997, Karen, eldest da of Ken Barnes, of St James's Sq, Bath. *Residence* – 9 Vale View Terrace, Batheaston, Bath BA1 7RH.

AUNT LIVING *(Raised to the rank of an Earl's daughter 1962)*

Lady Mary Esther Constance, *b* 1918: *m* 1949, Com Anthony Boyce Combe, RN (ret), who *d* 1990, and has issue living, David Boyce, *b* 1952: *m* 1985 (*m diss* 1991), Fiona Helen, da of Derek C. Thomson, of Invereighty House, Forfar, and has issue living, James Anthony Derek *b* 1987, Alexander *b* 1988, Annabel *b* 1989, — Peter, *b* 1955; S/Ldr RAAF: *m* 1982, Colleen Margaret, da of Thomas Thompson, of 15 Nathan St, Deakin, ACT, Australia, and has issue living, Martin Peter *b* 1989, Thomas Anthony *b* (twin) 1989, Sarah Ellen *b* 1984, Siobhan Romaine *b* 1985, — John (Bagamoyo, Malcolm Rd, Borrowdale, Harare, Zimbabwe), *b* (twin) 1955: *m* 1976, Mary Geraldine, da of late Lt-Col Duncan Frederick Basil Rhodes, of Cheshire, and formerly wife of Nello Howard Davies, and has issue living, Shay Rebecca *b* 1977, — Anne Romaine, *b* 1950: *m* 1985, Douglas Jardine, eldest son of Col N. Jardine, of Port Alfred, Cape, S Africa, and has issue living, Robert Gourley *b* 1987, Anthony Boyce *b* 1987. *Residence* – Grove Cottage, South Creake, Fakenham, Norfolk.

WIDOW LIVING OF BROTHER OF FIFTH EARL

Janet Beatrice Winifred (*Hon Mrs Peter Needham*) (The Old Manor House, Helmsley, York), yst da of late Capt George Taylor Ramsden, MP, of Bramham, Yorks: *m* 1951, Maj Hon Arthur Edward Peter Needham, who was raised to the rank of an Earl's son 1962, and *d* 1979.

WIDOW LIVING OF FIFTH EARL

HELEN BRIDGET (*Countess of Kilmorey*), da of Sir Lionel Lawson Faudel Faudel-Phillips, 3rd Bt; resumed her former style 1990: *m* 1st, 1941, the 5th Earl of Kilmorey, who *d* 1977; 2ndly, 1978 (*m diss* 1990), Harold William Elliott. *Residence* – 8 The Dormers, Highworth, Swindon, Wilts.

COLLATERAL BRANCHES LIVING

Grandchildren of Maj Hon Francis Edward Needham, MVO, 2nd son of 3rd Earl:—
Issue of late Maj Hon Arthur Edward Peter Needham (raised to the rank of an Earl's son 1962), *b* 1921, *d* 1979: *m* 1951, Janet Beatrice Winifred (ante), yst da of late Capt George Taylor Ramsden, MP, of Bramham, Yorks:—
Robert (Robin) Arthur John, *b* 1953: *m* 1981, Lucy Potter, only da of Capt Howard Bucknell III, USN (ret), of East Hampton, NY, USA, and has issue living, Nathaniel Peter, *b* 1984, — Robert Bucknell, *b* 1985, — Sonali Anna, *b* 1989, — Rupali Sarah, *b* (twin) 1989. *Residence* – The Old Manor House, Helmsley, York. ——— Thomas Francis, *b* 1959: has issue living (by Caroline Stockbridge), Finn Barnaby NEEDHAM, *b* 1992, — Florence Lily Stockbridge, *b* 1995. ——— Jane Diana, *b* 1955: *m* 1975 (*m diss* 1993), John Bell, of The Hall, Thirsk, N Yorks (*see* M Ailsa, 1969 Edn), and has issue living, Daisy *b* 1984, — Lettice, *b* 1987, — Zillah, *b* 1990.

Granddaughter of late Francis Henry Needham, 3rd son of Hon Francis Henry Needham (infra):—
Issue of late Francis Charles Needham, *b* 1889, *d* 1958: *m* 1922, Violet, who *d* 1963, da of William Kaye Parker:—
Thyra Frances (G6/182 Dornoch Terr, Highgate Hill, Brisbane, Qld, Australia), *b* 1923.

Grandsons of late Alfred Edwin Needham, 3rd son of late Hon Francis Henry Needham, 3rd son of 2nd Earl:—
Issue of late Francis Jack Needham, *b* 1892; *d* 1974: *m* 1926 Mary Clare, who *d* 1979, da of late Patrick Alban O'Sullivan of Brisbane:—
Patrick Francis Jack (93 Haigh Av, Belrose, NSW 2085, Australia), *b* 1927: *m* 1955, Margaret Anne, el da of Hilton John Daley, of Monavale Station, Hughenden, Qld, and has issue living, Robert Francis Jack (57 Stone Parade, Davidson, NSW 2085, Australia), *b* 1956: *m* 1981, Kathleen Anne, only da of John O'Connor, of Dubbo, NSW, and has issue living, Andrew Francis Jack *b* 1983, Christopher Robert *b* 1985, Thomas John *b* 1988, Jack Patrick Dominic *b* 1991, — John Edward (99 Sir Thomas Mitchell Drive, Davidson, NSW 2085, Australia), *b* 1963: *m* 1987, Jennifer Gay Doreen, da of Graham Napier, of Bilgola Plateau, NSW, and has issue living, Clare Jennifer *b* 1993, Elise Johanna *b* 1995, — Patrick Thomas (19 Bowen Close, Cherry Brook, NSW 2126, Australia), *b* (twin) 1963: *m* 1987, Michelle Anne, da of Louis Samuel Harris, of Normanhurst, NSW, and has issue living, Benjamin Edward *b* 1994, Nicholas Harry *b* 1996, — Mary Margaret, *b* 1958: *m* 1980, Anthony Francis Walsh, of 14 Sandy Beach Rd, Korora, NSW 2450, Australia, and has issue living, Michael Francis *b* 1983, Simon Anthony *b* 1985, Daniel Robert *b* 1987, Robert Christopher *b* 1993, — Judith Anne, *b* 1960: *m* 1978, Brian Lindsay Kerr, of 79 Chester St, Teneriffe, Queensland 4005, Australia, and has issue living, Sandra Kate *b* 1978, Danielle Jan *b* 1980, Judith Louise *b* 1987, Jacqueline Margaret *b* 1989, Olivia Anne *b* 1992, — Patricia Clare, *b* 1973. ——— Robert Cust (40 Palm Av, Ascot, Brisbane, Qld), *b* 1928: *m* 1958, Annette Mary Beiers, el da of Michael Patrick O'Rourke, of 104 Reeve St, Clayfield, Brisbane, and has issue living, Robert Michael, *b* 1963: *m* 1996, Susan Eileen, da of Donald Francis James McDonald, — Michael Francis Jack, *b* 1967, — Morna Irene, *b* 1959: *m* 1982, John Henry Allen, of Woodville St, Clayfield, Brisbane, and has issue living, Douglas Henry *b* 1990, Prudence Anne *b* 1986, Isobelle Susan *b* 1988, — Susan Clare, *b* 1961: *m* 1990, Patrick John Russo, of 3 Hammond St, Brighton, Vic, and has issue living, Robert Patrick *b* 1991, Isabella Clare *b* 1993, Charlotte Anne *b* 1995, Olivia Susan *b* 1996, — Lucy Ann, *b* 1969. ——— Thomas Edwin (Narrien Court, Samford, Qld 4520, Australia), *b* 1931: *m* 1964, Julia Elizabeth, da of William O. Moore, of Shadyside, Longreach, Qld, and has issue living, Deborah Clare, *b* 1970, — Natalie Barbara, *b*

1972. —— Edward Laurence (Christian Brothers, 4 Thames St, Balmain, NSW 2041, Australia), *b* 1936; assumed by deed poll 1981 the forename of Laurence in lieu of Francis.

Grandchildren of late Frederick William Needham (infra):—
Issue of late Capt James Owen Needham, *b* 1897, *d* 1975: *m* 1929, Marjorie Hylda (13 Voltaire, Kew, Surrey), da of late Charles George Lumley Cator (Blois, Bt):—
Christopher James Blois (Snode Hill House, Beech, Alton, Hants), *b* 1931: *m* 1955, Nicola Anne, only da of late Capt Robert Coles, and has issue living, Henrietta Aeddan, *b* 1957: *m* 1979, Russell Baylis, only son of J. R. Baylis, of Rose Cottage, Great Comberton, Worcs, and has issue living, Camilla Annabelle *b* 1981, Harriet Alicia *b* 1983, Emily Charlotte *b* 1985, Araminta Rose *b* 1988, — Alicia Claire, *b* 1959: *m* 1988, Henry Vane Eden (*see* B Auckland), — (Camilla) Romaine, *b* 1961: *m* 1986, Nicholas R. I. Foot, eldest son of Dennis Foot, and has issue living, Alexander James Frederick *b* 1987, Tarquin Nicholas Needham *b* 1996. —— David John Manners (Pine Lodge, Cokes Lane, Chalfont St Giles, Bucks), *b* 1934: *m* 1965, Evelyn Elizabeth (who assumed by deed poll 1965, for herself and her issue the surname of Palmers-Needham), da of Theodore L. Palmers, Consul Gen for Nicaragua in London, and has issue living, Katherine Elizabeth Theodora, *b* 1970. —— Patricia Deline, *b* 1942: *m* 1st, 1968 (*m diss* 1982), John Michael Singer; 2ndly, 1984, Cdr William Jonathan Richard Pennefather, RN, of Westmark House, Westmark, Sheet, Petersfield, Hants GU31 5AT, and has issue living (by 1st *m*), Jeremy James, *b* 1974, — Caroline Emma Louise, *b* 1969, — Serena Claire, *b* 1972.

Granddaughter of late Hon Francis Henry Needham (ante):—
Issue of late Frederick William Needham, *b* 1861, *d* 1928: *m* 1886, Geraldine, who *d* 1946, da of Edmund Arthur Paget, of Thorpe Satchville Hall, Melton Mowbray:—
Audrey Deline, *b* 1895: *m* 1918, Capt Adrian Dura Stoop, MC, TA (ret), who *d* 1957, and has issue living, James Richard, *b* 1920; Sqdn-Ldr RAF (ret), — Michael, MC, *b* 1922; *ed* Univ Coll, Oxford; Maj (ret) Gren Gds; 1939-45 War (MC): *m* 1st, 1948 (*m diss* 19—), Micheline, da of Baron de Posson, of 56 Rue Gachard, Brussels; 2ndly, 19— (*m diss* 19—), Mrs Diana Buchanan; 3rdly, 1959, Beverley Ann, da of Herbert Roberts, of Glangwa, Caernarvon, and has issue living, (by 1st *m*) Adrian Gaston *b* 1949, Caroline *b* 1950. *Residence* – Half-Tiles, 5 Meadow Lane, Hartley Wintney, Hants.

PREDECESSORS – **(1)** *Sir* ROBERT Needham, KB, one of the Council of the Pres of Wales; *cr Viscount Kilmorey* (peerage of Ireland) 1625; *d* 1625; *s* by his el son **(2)** ROBERT, 2nd Viscount; *d* 1653; *s* by his son **(3)** Robert, 3rd Viscount; *dsp* 1657; *s* by his half-brother **(4)** CHARLES, 4th Viscount; *d* 1660; *s* by his el son **(5)** ROBERT, 5th Viscount; *b* 1655; *d* 1668; *s* by his brother **(6)** THOMAS, 6th Viscount; *d* 1687; *s* by his son **(7)** ROBERT, 7th Viscount; *d* 1710; *s* by his el son **(8)** ROBERT, 8th Viscount; *d* 1716; *s* by his brother **(9)** THOMAS, 9th Viscount; *dsp* 1768; *s* by his brother **(10)** JOHN, 10th Viscount; a Col in the Army; *d* 1791; *s* by his el surviving son **(11)** ROBERT, 11th Viscount; *d* 1818; *s* by his brother **(12)** FRANCIS, 12th Viscount; a Gen in the Army; *cr Viscount Newry and Morne* and *Earl of Kilmorey* (peerage of Ireland) 1822; *d* 1832; *s* by his son **(13)** FRANCIS JACK, 2nd Earl; MP for Newry 1818-26: *m* 1st, 1814, Jane, who *d* 1867, da of George Gun Cuninghame, of Mount Kennedy, co Wicklow; 2ndly, 1867, Martha, who *d* 1907, da of John Foster, of Lenham, Kent; *d* 1880; *s* by his grandson **(14)** FRANCIS CHARLES, KP (el son of Francis Jack (Viscount Newry and Morne), MP for Newry 1941-51, by Anne Amelia, da of Gen Hon Sir Charles Colville, GCB (B Colville)), 3rd Earl; *b* 1842; a Representative Peer; MP for Newry (*C*) 1871-4: *m* 1881, Ellen Constance, who *d* 1920, da of late Edward Holmes Baldock, MP for Shrewsbury; *d* 1915; *s* by his el son **(15)** FRANCIS CHARLES ADELBERT HENRY, OBE, VRD, PC, 4th Earl; *b* 1883; Capt 1st Life Guards, Capt Comdg Ulster Div RNVR, Lieut for co Down, and High Sheriff 1913; Vice-Adm of Ulster 1937-61: *m* 1920, Lady Norah Frances Hastings, who *d* 1985, da of 14th Earl of Huntingdon; *d* 1961; *s* by his nephew **(16)** FRANCIS JACK RICHARD PATRICK (son of late Major Hon Francis Edward Needham, MVO, 2nd son of 3rd Earl), 5th Earl; *b* 1915; Maj Gren Gds: *m* 1941, Helen Bridget (who *m* 2ndly, 1978, Harold William Elliott), da of Sir Lionel Lawson Faudel Faudel-Phillips, 3rd Bt; *d* 1977; *s* by his el son **(17)** RICHARD FRANCIS, 6th Earl and present peer; also Viscount Kilmorey, and Viscount Newry and Morne, but does not use his peerages.

KILMUIR, EARLDOM OF (Fyfe) (Extinct 1967)

DAUGHTERS LIVING OF FIRST EARL

Lady Pamela Maxwell, *b* 1928; a JP of Inner London: *m* 1st, 1950, Clive Wigram, Bar-at-law, who *d* 1956; 2ndly, 1957, Courtenay Thomas Gardner Blackmore, who *d* 1992, and has issue living, (by 1st *m*) Caroline, *b* 1952: *m* 1983, A. Jonathan D. Pearson, and has issue living, John William *b* 1986, Hannah Jane *b* 1988, — (by 2nd *m*) Thomas David Maxwell Fyfe (1 The Coachyard, Chiddingstone Castle, Chiddingstone, Kent TN8 7AD), *b* 1960: *m* 1985, Susan Eleanor, yr da of late Senhouse Martindale Casson, of Bury St Edmunds, Suffolk, and has issue living, Lily Casson *b* 1996, — Katharine Fanny (now known as Kate FYFE), *b* 1958: *m* 1984 (*m diss* 1996), J. W. Partridge, only son of Bryan Partridge, of Hastings, Sussex, — Victoria Jane, *b* 1965: *m* 1997, Andrew Geraint Morgan, of 89 Putney Bridge Rd, SW15, and has issue living, Megan Courtenay *b* 1998. *Residence* – 24 Seaforth Lodge, SW13 9LE.

Lady Miranda Maxwell, *b* 1938: *m* 1960, Michael Ormiston Cormack, who *d* 1993, and has issue living, David Ormiston, *b* 1964: *m* 1st, 1984 (*m diss* 19—), Helen, yr da of Keith Jarvis, of Sevenoaks, Kent; 2ndly, 1995, Michelle, da of David Dowek, of Sutton, Surrey, and has issue living (by 2nd *m*), Mia *b* 1996, — Alistair Kilmuir, *b* 1970, — Helen Madeleine, *b* 1963: *m* 1995, Stephen Martin Peter Kelly, son of Kevin Kelly, and has issue living, Imogen Ann *b* 1996. *Residence* – 17 Pontoise Close, Sevenoaks, Kent.

KILPATRICK OF KINCRAIG, BARON (Kilpatrick) (Life Baron 1996)

ROBERT KILPATRICK, CBE, son of late Robert Kilpatrick, of Coaltown of Wemyss, Fife; *b* 29 July 1926; *ed* Buckhaven High Sch, and Edinburgh Univ (MB ChB 1949, MD 1960), Hon DUniv Edinburgh 1987, Hon LLD Dundee 1992, Hon DSc Hull 1994, Hon DSc Leicester 1994, Hon LLD Sheffield 1995, Hon FRCS 1995, Hon FRCP (Dublin) 1995, FRCSE 1996, Hon FRCPE 1963; Lecturer, Sheffield Univ 1955-66, Prof of Clinical Pharmacology and Therapeutics 1966-75, Dean of Faculty of Medicine 1970-73; Dean of Faculty of Medicine, Leicester Univ 1975-89, Prof and Head of Dept of Clinical Pharmacology and Therapeutics 1975-83, Prof of Medicine 1984-89; Pres of Gen Medical Council 1989-95; *cr* CBE 1979, Kt 1986, and *Baron Kilpatrick of Kincraig*, of Dysart, in the District of Kirkcaldy (Life Baron) 1996: *m* 1950, Elizabeth Gibson Page, da of Alexander Sharp Forbes, of East Wemyss, Fife, and has issue.

Arms – Per chevron sable and or in chief a plate charged with a saltire gules accompanied by two swans respectant with wings expanded proper and in base in a sea undy azure and argent a three masted ship sable sails proper and flagged of Scotland. Crest – A swan's head neck erased proper holding in the beak a veronica flower slipped proper.
Residence – 12 Wester Coates Gdns, Edinburgh EH12 5LT. *Clubs* – Reform, Royal and Ancient.

SONS LIVING

Hon Neil, *b* 1956; *ed* King Edward VII Sch, Sheffield, and Edinburgh Univ.
Hon John, *b* 1959; *ed* King Edward VII Sch, Sheffield, and Birmingham Univ.

DAUGHTER LIVING

Hon Katherine, *b* 1951; *ed* Girls' High Sch, Sheffield, and Edinburgh Univ: *m* 1973, Alan Marshall, son of William Marshall, of Edinburgh.

Kilwarlin, Viscount; grandson of Marquess of Downshire.

KIMBALL, BARON (Kimball) (Life Baron 1985)

MARCUS RICHARD KIMBALL, son of late Maj Lawrence Kimball, Leics Yeo, of Alderholt Park, Fordingbridge, Hants, by his 1st wife, late Kathleen Joan, only surv da of Richard Henry Ratcliff, of Stanford Hall, Loughborough, Leics; *b* 18 Oct 1928; *ed* Eton, and Trin Coll, Camb; Lieut Leics Yeo (TA) 1947, Capt 1952, Maj 1955; MP for Gainsborough Div of Lincs (*C*) 1956-83, CC Rutland 1955-62, and a DL Leics since 1984; Privy Council Rep, Council of RCVS, 1969-82 (Hon ARCVS 1982); External Member Council Lloyd's 1982-89; Chm British Field Sports Soc 1966-82; *cr* Knt 1981, and *Baron Kimball,* of Easton, co Leics (Life Baron) 1985: *m* 1956, June Mary, only da of Montagu John Fenwick, JP, of Great Stukeley Hall, Huntingdon (*see* D Manchester, colls, 1942 Edn), and has issue.

Arms – Arg, a pale gu, charged with a lion rampant of the field, on a chief sa a bezant between two crescents or. Crest – In front of two arrows points downwards saltirewise gu, a bull's head erased sa, armed or, ducally crowned also gu, between two branches of laurel fructed ppr. Supporters – On either side a wild turkey proper.
Residence – Great Easton Manor, Market Harborough, Leics LE16 8TB.
Clubs – White's, Pratt's.

DAUGHTERS LIVING

Hon (Sarah) Marcia, *b* 1958: *m* 1982, David Alexander Somerset Gibbs, 2nd son of Patrick Somerset Gibbs, of Hazeley House, Mortimer, Reading, and has issue living, James Patrick, *b* 1983, — Emily Rose, *b* 1985, — Alexandra Harriet, *b* 1989. *Residence* – Kentmere House, Castor, Peterborough, Cambs PE5 7BU.

Hon Sophie Henrietta, *b* 1960: *m* 1982, Reuben Thomas Coppin Straker, 4th and yst son of late Hugh Charles Straker, of Gaucin, Spain, and has issue living, Edward Marcus Reuben, *b* 1991, — Camilla Sophie, *b* 1985, — Lucy Charlotte, *b* 1988. *Residence* – Stonecroft, Fourstones, Hexham, Northumberland NE47 5AX.

KIMBERLEY, EARL OF (Wodehouse) (Earl UK 1866, Bt E 1611)
(Name pronounced "Woodhouse")

Strike hard

JOHN WODEHOUSE, 4th Earl and 11th Baronet; *b* 12 May 1924; *s* 1941; *ed* Eton and Magdalene Coll, Camb; Lt Gren Gds 1942-45, Guards Armoured Div 1943-45; Vice-Pres of World Council on Alcoholism; Chm of Nat Council on Alcoholism since 1982; former Liberal Spokesman on Aerospace, Defence and Voluntary Community Services; Hon Sec House of Lords All Party Defence Study Group since 1978, Pres since 1992, Chm Foreign Affairs Cttee, Monday Club, 1979-83, Air League Council since 1981, British Maritime League Council since 1977, Member Royal United Services Inst since 1976, Int Inst for Strategic Studies, etc; Associate Royal Aeronautical Soc since 1977; UK Delegate to N Atlantic Assembly 1981-93: *m* 1st, 1945 (*m diss* 1948), Diana Evelyn only da of late Lt-Col Hon Sir Piers Walter Legh, GCVO, CMG, CIE, OBE (*see* B Newton, colls); 2ndly, 1949 (*m diss* 1952), Carmel June, who *d* 1992, formerly wife of Derek Dunnett, and 3rd da of late Michael Joseph Maguire, of Melbourne, Aust; 3rdly, 1953 (*m diss* 1960), Cynthia Abdy, who *d* 1999, formerly wife of Charles Gustav Westendarp, and yr da of Eric Abdy Collins, FRCS, MRCP, of The Chantrey, Saxmundham, Suffolk; 4thly, 1961 (*m diss* 1965), Margaret, da of Albert Simons; 5thly, 1970 (*m diss* 1982), Gillian, da of Col Norman Ireland-Smith, and formerly wife of John Raw; 6thly, 1982, Sarah Jane Hope, eldest da of late Lt-Col Christopher D'Arcy Preston Consett, DSO, MC, and has issue by 2nd, 3rd and 4th *m*.

Arms – Sable, a chevron or, gutté de sang between three cinquefoils ermine. Crest – A dexter arm couped below the elbow, vested argent, and grasping a club or. Supporters – Two wild men, wreathed about the loins, and holding in the exterior hand a club, raised in the attitude of striking, sable.

Residence – Hailstone House, Cricklade, Swindon, Wilts SN6 6JP. *Clubs* – White's, MCC, Naval and Military, House of Lords Yacht.

SONS LIVING *(By 2nd marriage)*

JOHN ARMINE *(Lord Wodehouse)* (Kingswood, Henley Rd, Medmenham, Marlow, Bucks SL7 2EU), *b* 15 Jan 1951; *ed* Eton, and Univ of E Anglia (MSc); CEng 1993; systems programmer with Glaxo Group Research Ltd (now Glaxo Wellcome) from 1979 (joined as research chemist in 1974); Assoc Fellow British Interplanetary Soc since 1981, Fellow 1984; Chm of UK Info Users GP 1981-83; Member British Computer Soc 1988; FRSA: *m* 1973, Rev the Hon Carol Lylie Palmer, el da of 3rd Baron Palmer, and has issue:—

> SON LIVING—*Hon* David Simon John, *b* 10 Oct 1978.
>
> DAUGHTER LIVING—*Hon* Katherine Frances, *b* 1976.

(By 3rd marriage)

Hon Edward Abdy (12 Queensgate Place Mews, SW7 5BQ), *b* 1954; *ed* Eton: *m* 1st, 1980 (*m diss* 1983), Pandora JEF-FREYS, eldest da of Mrs W. J. Germing, of Castlenau, Barnes; 2ndly, 1988, Sarah Katherine, da of Richard Allen, of Ranskill, Retford, Notts, and of Mrs Patrick Dean, of E Mere, Lincoln.
Hon Henry Wyndham (33 Stone Banks, Walton-on-Thames, Surrey KT12 2QE), *b* 1956; *ed* Millfield: *m* 1st, 1979 (*m diss* 1988), Sarah M., only da of J. A. Fleming, of Hampton, Middx; 2ndly, 1992, Elizabeth Ellen, da of Edmund Parkin, and has issue living (by 1st *m*), Thomas Henry John, *b* 1981, — Clare Margaret, *b* 1980.

(By 4th marriage)

Hon Charles James, *b* 1963: *m* 1997, Angela Mary, da of Michael Horner, of Hampton Hill, Middx.

COLLATERAL BRANCHES LIVING

> Grandchildren of late Arthur Wodehouse (1813-1893), of Hamilton, Ont, Canada, 4th son of late Rev Hon William Wodehouse, 4th son of 1st Baron. Although documentary evidence of his *m* to Eliza Fleet Perkins (*d* 1916, aged 96) has not yet been found, this line is represented by:—
Herbert (1a Roanoke Place, Hamilton, Ont, Canada L8S 3P4), *b* 1916. —— Robert A. (1001-1201 Northshore Blvd, Burlington, Ont, Canada L7S 1Z5), *b* 1919. —— Roy (34 Toynbee Trail, Scarboro, Ont, Canada M1E 1E9), *b* 1928. —— Marie (Mrs Tinsley) (437 Indian Rd, Burlington, Ont, Canada L7T 3T5), *b* 1926.

(In remainder to Baronetcy only)

> Granddaughters of late Rev Philip John Wodehouse, el son of Col Philip Wodehouse, el son of Rev Philip Wodehouse, 2nd son of 5th Bt, and brother of 1st Baron:—
Issue of late Capt Philip George Wodehouse, DSO, RN, *b* 1883, *d* 1973: *m* 1st, 1915 (*m diss* 1928), Beaujolais Theresa Constance, who *d* 1986, only da of late Arthur George Ridout, of Condercum, Benwell, Northumberland; 2ndly, 1928, Alice Margaret (Ebor House, Park Lane, Barnstaple, N Devon), da of late William Rowe:—
(By 1st *m*) Beaujolois Inez, *b* 1919: *m* 1942, Capt Hubert Gordon Compton Cavendish, RASC, who *d* 1993, of Bosvathick, Constantine, Falmouth, Cornwall (*see* D Devonshire, colls). —— Valencia, *b* 1920; served 1939-45 War in ATS. *Residence* – Cliff Cottage, Point, Devoran, Truro, Cornwall TR3 6NQ.

> Grandsons of late Rev Frederic Armine Wodehouse, 3rd son of late Col Philip Wodehouse (ante):—
Issue of late Vice-Adm Norman Atherton Wodehouse, CB, RN, *b* 1887, *ka* 1941: *m* 1923, Theodosia Frances, who *d* 1966, da of late Com Edward Louis Dalrymple Boyle, CMG, RN, and widow of Capt Douglas William Swire, Shropshire Yeo (*see* E Glasgow, colls):—
Rev Armine Boyle (103 Orient Palace, 1 rue de la Republique, 06500 Menton, France), *b* 1924; *ed* Radley; 1939-45 War with Gren Gds: *m* 1st, 1952, Diana Helen Arabella, who *d* 1990, only da of late Charles Sidney Bowen Wentworth-Stanley, CBE (*see* Brocklebank, Bt, colls, 1948 Edn); 2ndly, 1997, Mrs Vera Robinson, and has issue living (by 1st *m*), Armine Mark Robin (Villa Concordia, Ave de Lattre de Tassigny, 06360 St Laurent d'Eze, France), *b* 1960; *ed* Radley, and Downing Coll, Camb: *m* 1986, Yoma Irene Mandra, da of J. B. Jackson, of Monte Carlo and has issue living, Sarah Casmen Diane *b* 1989, Nikki Robyn Alba *b* 1995, — Julia Katherine, *b* 1955: *m* 1981, William John Hunt, of 43 Hamilton Terr, NW8 9RG, son of late W. E. Hunt, and has issue living, Oliver William *b* 1988, Miranda Katherine *b* 1984, Arabella Katrina *b* 1985, — Victoria Frances, *b* 1957: *m* 1979, Evan John Thatcher, of Peel Forest, Geraldine, S Canterbury, NZ, and has issue living, Hamish John *b* 1981, David Michael *b* 1983, Benjamin Samuel *b* 1993, Lucinda Katherine *b* 1980. —— Charles Norman Boyle, *b* 1927: *m* 1953, Joyce Marie Williamson, da of late John Dobson, MC, and has issue living, Dominic Charles John, *b* 1968, — Fiona Clare, *b* 1958, — Charlotte Thea Fleur, *b* 1962. *m* 1991, Phillip M. Bubb, eldel son of M.A.T. Bubb, of Measham, Burton-on-Trent. *Residence* – 23 Altenburg Gdns, SW11 1JH.

> Grandchildren of late Henry Ernest Wodehouse, CMG, 5th son of late Col Philip Wodehouse (ante):—
Issue of late Ernest Armine Wodehouse, *b* 1879, *d* 1936: *m* 1919, Helen, da of late Patrick Harnett:—
Patrick Armine, *b* 1920; *ed* Cheltenham, and Imperial Coll of Science and Technology; BSc; ACGI, MIEE; Consultant Eng; Fl-Lt RAuxAF (ret); *m* 1947, Joyce Lilian, da of Charles Champion, and has issue living, Nigel Armine, *b* 1948.

> Issue of late Richard Lancelot Deane Wodehouse, *b* 1892, *d* 1940: *m* 1st, 1925, Katherine, who *d* 1932, da of W Wallace Cook, OBE; 2ndly, 1934, Winifred Baker, who *d* 1979, da of Brig-Gen William Baker-Brown, CB, and widow of Robert Arthur Williams:—

(By 1st *m*) Ann Elizabeth, *b* 1930: *m* 1953, Lt-Col Richard Gerald Higgins, RA, of 11/12 Red Lion St, Kings Sutton, nr Banbury, Oxon OX17 3RH, and has issue living, Andrew Richard (Holloway House, Hornton, nr Banbury, Oxon OX15 6DB), *b* 1954: *m* 1982, Alison Margaret, da of Col Anthony Gilks, of The Grange, Braunston, Rutland, and has issue living, Peter Anthony *b* 1989, James Patrick *b* 1991, — Michael James (6 Hobury St, SW10 0JD), *b* 1956: *m* 1985, Kim Maria Stevens, elder da of Col N. Flower, of 47 York Rd, Camberley, Surrey, and has issue living, Josias (Joss) Wode-house *b* 1994, Ella May Frances *b* 1996, — John Deane (71 Bute Gdns, W6 7DX), *b* 1962: *m* 1988, Rosemary Jane Cecilia, da of F. J. D. Boot, of 2 Charnwood Way, Woodborough, Notts NG14 6EW, and has issue living, Livia Harriet *b* 1994, Isobel Victoria *b* 1996. —— Katharine Jane Armine, *b* 1932: *m* 1955, Graeme Roper Wallace, who *d* 1999, of The Old Smithy, Culver St, Newent, Glos GL18 1JE, and has issue living, Ross Matthew Walker (13 Weare Close, Fortuneswell, Portland, Dorset DT5 1JP), *b* 1956, — Neil Richard Deane (White House Court, Westwell, Ashford, Kent TN25 4LQ), *b* 1958: *m* 1992, Anya Margaret Gray, da of late Scott Ralph Izat, of The Old Rectory, Forncett St Peter, Norwich, and has issue living, Florence Armine Mary *b* 1995, Freya Grace Lewarne *b* 1997, Cecilia Elizabeth Worcester *b* 1998, — Constance Armine Louise, *b* 1960: *m* 1993, Richard William Smith, of Delf Cottage, 9-13 Delf Hill, Rastrick, Brighouse, W Yorks HD6 3NL, and has issue living, Angus William Wallace *b* 1994, Duncan Robert Wodehouse *b* 1997.

Grandchildren of late James Hay Wodehouse (*b* 1861), elder son of late Maj James Hay Wodehouse (*b* 1824), 2nd son of late Ven Charles Nourse Wodehouse, 2nd son of late Rev Philip Wodehouse (ante):—
Issue of late James Archibald Hay Wodehouse, *b* 1895, *d* 1973: *m* 1st, 1916, Florence, who *d* 1937, da of Edward Boyd: 2ndly, 1938, Elizabeth K., da of William K. Buchanan:—
(By 1st *m*) Mildred Pauahi Hay, *b* 1916: *m* 1942, Capt Asa Alan Clark III, US Navy, of 46-416 Hulupala Place, Kaneohe, Hawaii 96744, and has issue living, Asa Alan (IV) (134 E 93rd St, 3B, NY, USA), *b* 1944: Col US Army (ret): *m* 1968, Margie Slocum, and has had issue, Matthew Shannon *b* 1968: *d* 1988, Christopher *b* 1972, — Jeffrey Wodehouse (Rt 1, Box 190, Manton, California 96059, USA), *b* 1947, — Bruce Shannon (54-112 Kealalani Place, Hauula, Hawaii 96717), *b* 1953: *m* 1991, Diane Kelly. —— (By 2nd *m*) James Hay, *b* 1946. —— (Florence) Elizabeth Hay, *b* 1939: *m* 1963, George Warren Freeland, of 439 Front St, Lahaina, Maui, Hawaii 96761, and has issue living, George Warren, *b* 1965, — Kimberley Kaiulani, *b* 1967; has issue living, Nohea Edward FREELAND *b* 1993, — Denby Elizabeth Hay, *b* 1971.

Grandchildren of late Guy Armine Wodehouse (*b* 1863), 2nd son of late Maj James Hay Wodehouse (*b* 1824) (ante):—
Issue of late Everard Hay Wodehouse, *b* 1895, *d* 1970: *m* 1st, 1927 (*m* annulled 1934), Dorothy Eileen, da of J. G. Cameron, of Santiago, Chile; 2ndly, 1937, Winifred Mary, who *d* 1978, da of Reginald Ashton, of Lima, Peru:—
(By 2nd *m*) Richard Everard, *b* 1949: *m* 1979, Mary Jean, da of William Warren Johnson, of Elkton, Oregon, and has issue living, Carissa Renée, *b* 1982, — Paloma Carin, *b* 1988. *Residence* – 628 Pacific View Drive, San Diego, California 92108, USA. —— Diana Elaine, *b* 1939: *m* 1964, Donald Ralph Strong, and has issue living, Everard George, *b* 1968, — Miriam Ruth, *b* 1966. *Residence* – 1700 W 106th St, Chicago, Illinois 60643, USA. —— (Marilyn) Joanna, *b* 1943: *m* 1964, Garvin Olaf Muri, and has issue living, Michelle Ingrid, *b* 1967, — Jenelle, *b* 1970. *Residence* – 934 31st St, Bismark, N Dakota 58501, USA.

Issue of late James Millie Wodehouse, *b* 1896, *d* 1971: *m* 1930, Helen Mary Edith, who *d* 1994, elder da of Sir John Murray, 12th Bt (*cr* 1628):—
Margaret Lily Ann, *b* 1947. *Residence* – Casilla 7, Vallenar, Chile.

Grandchildren of late Kenneth Charles Wodehouse, yst son of late Maj James Hay Wodehouse (*b* 1824) (ante):—
Issue of late John Hay Wodehouse, *b* 1917, *d* 1993: *m* 1st, 1941, Maria Francisca Garrido, who *d* 1945; 2ndly, 1947 (*m diss* 1959), Carmen Meza Valdés; 3rdly, 1960, Jeanette Wackenhut:—
(By 1st *m*) Cyprian Gerard (6 Whittier Place, Apt 15H, Boston, Mass 02114, USA), *b* 1941; has issue living, Lisa Sharon, *b* 1982. —— (By 2nd *m*) Kenneth John (1166 Carrollton Av, Metairie, Louisiana 70005, USA; 337 39h St, New Orleans, Louisiana 70124, USA), *b* 1957: *m* 1987, Lisa Marie, da of Paul T. White, and has issue living, Evan John, *b* 1989, — Craig Alen, *b* 1993. —— (By 3rd *m*) Roderick Dhu, *b* 1965: *m* 1994, Isabel Margarita Bravo, and has issue living, Philip, *b* 1997. —— Sharon Elizabeth, *b* 1962: *m* 1991, Rodrigo Fontecilla, and has issue living, Maximiliano *b* 1993.

Grandchildren of late Rear-Admiral Capel Wodehouse, yr son of late Rev Nathaniel Francis Wodehouse, son of late Thomas Wodehouse, 3rd son of 5th Bt, and brother of 1st Baron:—
Issue of late Brigadier Edmond Wodehouse, CBE, *b* 1894, *d* 1959: *m* 1935, Persis (who *m* 2ndly, 1980, Lt-Col Robert Michael FitzHugh, of The Brow, Overton, Wrexham, Clwyd), only da of Plumer Rooper, of Min-yr-Afon, Overton Bridge, Wrexham:—
Armine John (c/o Lloyds Bank, 6 Pall Mall, SW1), *b* 1936; *ed* Winchester; Maj Roy Welch Fusiliers: *m* 1965, Louise Kynaston, da of Mark Kynaston Mainwaring (Rankin Bt), of Oteley, Ellesmere, and has issue living, Edmond Armine, *b* 1968, — Rosemary Louise, *b* 1966, — Rowena Carolyn, *b* 1971. —— Hugh Capel (50 Doneraile St, SW6 6EP), *b* 1945; *ed* Winchester, and Wadham Coll, Oxford: *m* 19—, Mrs Anthea M. Courtauld, da of R. H. Priestley, of Oakley, Hants, and has issue living, Katie Rose, *b* 1983. —— Rachel Mary (Down House, Soberton, Hants), *b* 1938: *m* 1965, Robert Charles Copeman, and has issue living, James Robert, *b* 1966, — Charlotte Anne, *b* 1968. —— Carolyn Persis, *b* 1943: *m* 1968, Michael Cemlyn-Jones, of Avenido Dias Da Silva 185/1, 3000 Coimbra, Portugal, and has issue living, Tara Persis, *b* 1970, — Jessica Melfis, *b* 1973.

PREDECESSORS – (1) *Sir* PHILIP Wodehouse, son of late Sir Roger Wodehouse, MP, *b* 15—; was MP for Castle Rising 1586-7; *cr* a *Baronet* 1611: *m* 1582, Grizell, who *d* 1635, da of William Yelverton, of Rougham, Norfolk, and widow of Hamon L'Estrange, of Hunstanton, Norfolk; *d* 1623; *s* by his son (2) *Sir* THOMAS, 2nd Bt; MP for Thetford 1640-53; *d* 1658; *s* by his son (3) *Sir* PHILIP, 3rd Bt; *b* 1608: MP in Restoration Parliament; *d* 1681; *s* by his grandson (4) *Sir* JOHN, 4th Bt; *b* 1669, MP for Norfolk; *d* 1754; *s* by his son (5) *Sir* ARMINE, 5th Bt; *b* 1714; MP for Norfolk 1737-67; *d* 1777; *s* by his son (6) *Sir* JOHN, 6th Bt; *b* 1741; MP for Norfolk 1784-97; *cr Baron Wodehouse*, of Kimberley, Norfolk (peerage of Great Britain) 1797; *d* 1834; *s* by his son (7) JOHN, 2nd Baron; *b* 1771; MP for Great Bedwyn 1802-6, and Marlborough 1820-26, and Lord-Lieut of Norfolk, etc; *d* 1846; *s* by his grandson (8) JOHN, KG, PC (son of Hon Henry, el son of 2nd Baron, by Anne, da of Theophilus Thornhaugh Gurdon, of Letton, Norfolk), 3rd Baron; *b* 1826; Under-Sec for Foreign Affairs 1852-6 and 1859-61, Envoy to Russia 1856-8, Special Envoy to Copenhagen 1863, Under-Sec for India 1864, Lord-Lieut of Ireland 1864-6, Lord Privy Seal 1868-70, Sec of State for Colonies 1870 and 1880-82, Chancellor of Duchy of Lancaster 1882-3, Sec of State for India 1882-5 and Jan to July 1886, Sec of State for India and Lord Pres of the Council

Aug 1892 to March 1894, and Sec of State for Foreign Affairs March 1894 to June 1895; *cr Earl of Kimberley* (peerage of United Kingdom) 1866: *m* 1847, Lady Florence FitzGibbon, CI, who *d* 1895, el da of 3rd and last Earl of Clare (*ext*); *d* 1902; *s* by his son (9) JOHN, 2nd Earl, *b* 1848: *m* 1875, Isabel Geraldine, who *d* 1927, da of Sir Henry Josias Stracey, 5th Bt; *d* 1932; *s* by his son (10) JOHN, CBE, MC, 3rd Earl; *b* 1883; MP for Norfolk, Mid Div (*L*) 1906-10: *m* 1922, Frances Margaret, who *d* 1950, da of late Lieut-Col Leonard Howard Lloyd Irby; *d* as a result of enemy action 1941; *s* by his only son (11) JOHN, 4th Earl and present peer; also Baron Wodehouse.

Kimbolton, Lord; grandson of Duke of Manchester.

KINDERSLEY, BARON (Kindersley) (Baron UK 1941)

With God's assistance

ROBERT HUGH MOLESWORTH KINDERSLEY, 3rd Baron, *b* 18 Aug 1929; *s* 1976; *ed* Eton, Trin Coll, Oxford, and Harvard Business Sch, USA; Lt Scots Gds in Malaya 1948-49; Chm Commonwealth Development Corpn 1980-89, a Dir of Lazard Brothers & Co Ltd 1960-90, a Dir of Sun Alliance & London Insurance Gp, and Maersk Co Ltd: *m* 1st, 1954 (*m diss* 1989), Venice Marigold (Rosie), da of late Capt Lord (Arthur) Francis Henry Hill, The Greys (Reserve) (*see* M Downshire); 2ndly, 1989, Patricia Margaret, only da of late Brig Hugh Ronald Norman, DSO, of Lower St Clere, Kemsing, Kent, and formerly wife of Henry Colum Crichton-Stuart (*see* M Bute, colls), and has had issue by 1st *m*.

𝕬rms – Per bend gules and azure, a lion rampant argent, within an orle of cross crosslets and fleurs-de-lis alternately or. 𝕮rest – In front of a hawthorn tree proper, charged with an escutcheon azure, thereon a lion rampant argent a greyhound sejant also argent. 𝕾upporters – *Dexter*, a greyhound argent, gorged with a collar azure, charged with three cross crosslets or; *sinister*, a lion argent, gorged with a collar gules, charged as the dexter; each standing on a branch of hawthorn proper.
Residence – West Green Farm, Shipbourne, Kent TN11 9PU.

SONS LIVING (By 1st marriage)

Hon RUPERT JOHN MOLESWORTH (83 Hutchison Av, Elliot Lake, Ont, Canada P5A 1W7), *b* 11 March 1955; *ed* Eton: *m* 1975, Sarah Anne, da of late John D. Warde, and has issue living, Frederick Hugh Molesworth, *b* 9 Jan 1987, — Rebecca, *b* 1985.
Hon Dickon Michael (64 Chestnut Grove, SW12 8JJ), *b* 1962: *m* 1991, Victoria S., eldest da of T. J. Coles, of Saltwood, Brasted Chart, Kent and has issue living, Bertie, *b* 1995, — Harry, *b* 1998, — Phoebe, *b* 1993.

GRANDDAUGHTER LIVING

Issue of late Hon Hugh Francis Kindersley, 2nd son of 3rd Baron, *b* 1956, *d* 1991: *m* 1987 (*m diss* 1990), (Evelyn) Rosamond, eldest da of (Robert Jestyn) Gwent Forestier-Walker (*see* Forestier-Walker, Bt, colls):—
Rosanna, *b* 1987.

DAUGHTER LIVING (By 1st marriage)

Hon Anna Lucy, *b* 1965.

SISTER LIVING

Hon Patricia Nassau (*Hon Lady Crookenden*), *b* 1922: *m* 1948, Lt-Gen Sir Napier Crookenden KCB, DSO, OBE, late Cheshire Regt, and has issue living, James Napier *b* 1949: *m* 1974, Claire Ella Thorne, and has issue living, Benjamin Napier Lane *b* 1978, Lucinda Nan Annaliese *b* 1975, — Charles Stephen Napier, *b* 1957: *m* 1998, Michelle Lynn, da of Joseph Ott, of Pittsburg, Penn, USA, — Elizabeth Jane, *b* 1950: *m* 1st, 1970 (*m diss* 1980), Sam G. S. Hughes, of

Toronto; 2ndly, 1980, Thomas Charles Wilson, of The Old Rectory, Upper Clatford, nr Andover, Hants, and has issue living (by 1st *m*), Geoffrey Samuel *b* 1977, (by 2nd *m*), James Thomas *b* 1984, Tobina Kate *b* 1981, — Catherine Nancy, *b* 1958: *m* 1993, Martin Clive Jamieson, son of W/Cdr H. C. Jamieson, of Barrington, Cambs, and has issue living, Henry Guy *b* 1994, Isobel Sophie *b* 1996. *Residence* – Twin Firs, Four Elms, Edenbridge, Kent.

AUNT LIVING (*Daughter of 1st Baron*)

Hon Elizabeth Joan, *b* 1911: *m* 1930, Major Hon James Perrott Philipps, TD (*see* B Milford). *Residence* – Dalham Hall, Newmarket, Suffolk.

COLLATERAL BRANCH LIVING

Issue of late Capt Hon Philip Leyland Kindersley, 4th and yst son of 1st Baron, *b* 1907, *d* 1995: *m* 1st, 1929 (*m diss* 1936), Oonagh, who *d* 1995, da of late Hon (Arthur) Ernest Guinness (*see* E Iveagh, colls); 2ndly, 1936, (Violet) Valerie, who *d* 1997, da of late Lt-Col Hon (Edward) Gerald Fleming French, DSO (*see* E Ypres, ext), and formerly wife of 4th Baron Brougham and Vaux:—
(By 1st *m*) Gay (College Farm, E Garston, Hungerford, Berks RG17 7EU; Turf Club), *b* 1930; *ed* Eton: *m* 1st, 1956 (*m diss* 1976), Margaret Diana, only da of Hugh Wakefield; 2ndly, 1976, Philippa Harper, and has issue living (by 1st *m*), Robin, *b* 1956; *ed* Eton, — Kim, *b* 1960; *ed* Eton, — Catheryn (*Marchioness of Huntly*), *b* 1958: *m* 1st, 1980, Robert Lennon Millbourn, son of late Cecil Millbourn, of 1 Eaton Place, SW1; 2ndly, 1991, as his 2nd wife, 13th Marquess of Huntly, of Aboyne Castle, Aberdeenshire, and has issue living (by 1st *m*), Tara Vanessa *b* 1981, (by 2nd *m*) (*see* M Huntly), — Tania, *b* 1967, — (by 2nd *m*), Rory, *b* 1977; *ed* Harrow, — Oliver, *b* 1980; *ed* Harrow. —— (By 2nd *m*) Christian Philip (11 St Maur Rd, SW6 4DR; *Clubs* – White's, City of London, MCC), *b* 1950: *m* 1st, 1973 (*m diss* 1991), Hilary Luise, da of late David Radcliffe Guard, of Ryders Wells House, Lewes, Sussex; 2ndly, 1992, Lara Hepburn, da of Frederick George Pohl, of Constantia, Cape Town, and has issue living (by 1st *m*), Alexander, *b* 1982, — Vanessa, *b* 1980, — Davina, *b* 1986, — (by 2nd *m*), Rosanna, *b* 1995, — Isabelle, *b* 1999. —— Nicolette Leila, *b* 1939: *m* 1963, Robert Nicholas Philipson-Stow, and has issue (*see* Philipson-Stow, Bt, colls). —— Virginia Alexandra de l'Etang (*Hon Mrs Peregrine J. W. Fairfax*), *b* 1943: *m* 1965, Hon Peregrine John Wishart Fairfax, and has issue (*see* L Fairfax of Cameron).

PREDECESSORS – (1) *Sir* ROBERT MOLESWORTH Kindersley, GBE, son of late Capt Edward Nassau Molesworth Kindersley, of Sherborne, Dorset; *b* 1871; was a Director of Bank of England 1916-46, Pres of National Savings Committee 1920-46 (first Chm 1916-20), High Sheriff of Sussex 1928-9, and Prime Warden of Fishmongers Co 1933-4; *cr Baron Kindersley*, of West Hoathly, co Sussex (peerage of United Kingdom) 1941: *m* 1896, Gladys Margaret, who *d* 1968, da of late Maj-Gen J. P. Beadle, RE, of 6 Queen's Gate Gdns, SW; *d* 1954; *s* by his son (2) HUGH KENYON MOLESWORTH, CBE, MC, 2nd Baron, *b* 1899; Man Dir of Lazard Brothers & Co Ltd 1927-64 (Chm 1953-64); Chm of Rolls-Royce Ltd 1956-68; Gov of the Royal Exchange Assurance 1955-69; 1914-18 War; 1939-45 War as Brig Scots Gds (wounded): *m* 1921, Nancy Farnsworth, who *d* 1977, da of late Dr Geoffrey Boyd, of Toronto, Canada; *d* 1976; *s* by his son (3) ROBERT HUGH MOLESWORTH, 3rd Baron and present peer.

King, see Baron Maybray-King.

King, family name of Earl of Lovelace.

KING OF WARTNABY, BARON (King) (Life Baron 1983)

JOHN LEONARD KING, yr son of Albert John King, by his wife Kathleen; b Aug 1918; Chm Babcock International plc (formerly Babcock & Wilcox) since 1972; Chm British Airways since 1981-92, since when Pres; Chm other cos; Chm Alexandra Rose Day since 1980; MFH Badsworth Foxhounds 1944-58; MFH Duke of Rutland's Foxhounds (Belvoir) 1958-72; FBIM; Cmdr Royal Order of the Polar Star (Sweden) 1983; cr Knt 1979, and Baron King of Wartnaby, of Wartnaby, co Leics (Life Baron) 1983: m 1st, 1941, Lorna Kathleen, who d 1969, da of Arthur Sykes, of Clandon; 2ndly, 1970, Hon Isabel Cynthia Monckton, yst da of 8th Viscount Galway, and has issue by 1st m.

Arms – Or five piles two reversed vert each charged with an acorn slipped or. Crest – An otter sejant vert holding in the dexter paw a sceptre or. Supporters – On either side two horses reguardant sable unguled or in the mouth of each a sprig of oak vert fructed gold.
Residences – Wartnaby, Melton Mowbray, Leics LE14 3HY; 15 Eaton Sq, SW1. Clubs – White's, Brook (New York).

SONS LIVING (By 1st marriage)

Hon Richard John Rodney, b 1943; ed Le Rosey: m 1985, Monika, da of Erich Boehm, of Boca Raton, Florida, USA, and has issue living, John-Erich b 1986. Residence – 7612 Covey Chase, Charlotte, North Carolina, NC 28210, USA.

Hon Philip James Stephen, b 1950; ed Harrow: m 1989, Caroline, da of E. G. A. Hillesley, of Gillingham, Kent, and has issue living, Charlotte Kathleen Rachel, b 1990, — Philippa Anne Lorna, b 1991. Residence – 77 Stanhope Mews East, SW7.

Hon (John) Rupert Charles, b 1950 (twin); ed Harrow: m 1986, Cherry M., only da of R. B. Jessop, OBE, of Ingoldsby, Lincs, and has issue living, Philip James Bateman, b 1988. Residence – Garden Cottage, Wartnaby, Melton Mowbray, Leics.

DAUGHTER LIVING (By 1st marriage)

Hon Rachel Mary Frances, b 1945, m 1st, 1968 (m diss 1974), Michael Gibson; 2ndly 1980 (m diss 1985), Guy Henry René Bondonneau, of Paris; 3rdly, 1987, Melvyn Marckus. Residence – 25 Waterford Rd, SW6 2DJ.

KING-HALL, BARONY OF (King-Hall) (Extinct 1966)

DAUGHTERS LIVING OF LIFE BARON

Hon Edith Jean Ann (11 North Side, Clapham Common, SW4 0RF), b 1920.
Hon (Frances Susan) Adrianna (Old Barn, Northdown Rd, Woldingham, Caterham, Surrey CR3 7BD), b 1927.
Hon Jane (SE7 Javea, Alicante, Spain) KING-HALL, b 1930; has resumed maiden name: m 1951 (m diss 19—), Yves Barraud, of Les Saules, Les Cullayes, Vaud, Switzerland.

Kinghorne, Earl of, see Earl of Strathmore and Kinghorne.

KINGSALE, BARON (de Courcy) (Baron I about 1340, precedence 1397)

JOHN DE COURCY, 30th Baron, and Premier Baron of Ireland; *b* 27 Jan 1941; *s* 1969; *ed* Stowe; 2nd Lt IG.

Arms – Argent, three eagles, displayed gules, ducally crowned or. **Crest** – Out of a ducal coronet or, an eagle displayed with two heads argent. **Supporters** – Two unicorns azure, armed unguled, crined and tufted, gorged with collars adorned with crosses pattée and fleurs-de-lis, and chained, all gold.
Addresses – 15 Dallimore Mead, Nunney, Frome, Somerset BA11 4NB; 1st Floor Macarthur Chambers, 201 Edward St, Brisbane, Queensland 4000, Australia. *Club* – Cavalry and Guards'

Truth conquers all things

SISTER LIVING

Dione May, *b* 1937: *m* 1965 (*m diss* 1976), David Kemp Daffin, and has issue living, Miles Irl de Courcy, *b* 1969. — Thomas Chester de Courcy, *b* 1971.
Residence – Cadbury Court Cottage, N Cadbury, Yeovil, Som BA22 7DR.

AUNT LIVING (*Daughter of 29th Baron*) (*By 1st marriage*)

Hon Bridget Doreen, *b* 1915: *m* 1st, 1938 (*m diss* 1951), Rev George Ian Falconer Thomson, who *d* 1987; 2ndly, 19—, Stephen Watson, and has issue living, (by 1st *m*), Margaret Doreen Rosemary (Emma), *b* 1940, — (by 2nd *m*), a son *b* 19—. *Residence* – Parsonage Farm, E Sutton, Maidstone, Kent.

(*By 2nd marriage*)

Hon Diana Ruth, *b* 1951.

COLLATERAL BRANCHES LIVING

Granddaughter of late Hon Robert Charles Sinclair de Courcy, 4th son of 27th Baron:—
Issue of late Group-Capt John Arthur Gerald de Courcy, MC, RAF, *b* 1894, *d* on active service 1940: *m* 1917, Anna Felicia, who *d* 1952, da of late Hon George Wright, a Judge of High Court of Justice, Ireland (Barrington, Bt):—
Suzanne, *b* 1923: *m* 1948, Edward James Bryant, and has issue living, Edward de Courcy (29 Wingate Rd, W6), *b* 1951; *ed* Rugby, and Magdalene Coll, Camb (MA); Bar Middle Temple 1976: *m* 1982, Frances, eldest da of Dr Guy Newton, of Oxford, — David de Courcy, *b* 1954; *ed* Rugby.

Grandson of late Col Nevinson Willoughby de Courcy, CB, 2nd son of late Capt Nevinson de Courcy, RN, son of Adm Hon Michael de Courcy, 3rd son of 20th Baron:—
Issue of late Nevinson William de Courcy, *b* 1869, *d* 1919: *m* 1919, Matilda Hetty Grace, who *d* 1967, da of late John B. Russell, of Auckland, NZ:—
†Nevinson Russell, *b* (*posthumous*) 1920: *m* 1954, Nora Lydia, who *d* 1994, da of James Arnold Plint, of Great Crosby, Lancs, and *d* 1999, leaving issue, NEVINSON MARK, *b* 11 May 1958. — Katherine Grace, *b* 1955: *m* 1979, Gregory Lawrence Smith, and has issue living, Robert Russell Maunganui *b* 1987, Henrietta Lydia de Courcy *b* 1984. *Residence* – 15 Market Rd, Remuera, Auckland 5, NZ.

Granddaughter of late Rupert John Nevinson de Courcy, son of John Sinclair Bremer de Courcy, 3rd son of Capt Nevinson de Courcy, RN (ante):—
Issue of late Nevinson Egerton de Courcy, *b* 1885, *d* 1979: *m* 1923, Dorothy Mary, who *d* 1979, da of John Bernard Carroll:—
Angela Mary, *b* 1927: *m* 1951, Ian McDonald Wright, of The Rosary, Lock Island, Marlow-on-Thames, Bucks SL7 1QE, and has issue living, Teresa Dorothy de Courcy, *b* 1955: *m* 1988, Jeremy Paul Ryall, of Penlan, Llanigon, Hay-on-Wye, Herefs HR3 5QP, and has issue living, Benjamin Charles *b* 1992, Max Joseph *b* 1993, Poppy Alexandra *b* 1990, — Isobel Eileen, *b* 1958: *m* 1985, Geoffrey Thomas Martin, of 9 Annie King Lane, Dover, Mass 02030, USA, and has issue living, James Peter de Courcy *b* 1990, Alexander Nevinson *b* 1993, Laura de Courcy *b* 1987.

Grandchildren of late Walter Stephen de Courcy, son of late Stephen de Courcy, son of Patrick de Courcy, great grandson of David de Courcy, 2nd son of James de Courcy, eldest son of Hon James de Courcy, 3rd son of 10th Baron (according to a pedigree recorded at the Office of the Chief Herald of Ireland):—
Issue of late John Frederick Manuel de Courcy, *b* 1901, *d* 1974: *m* 1941, Norah de Courcy, eldest da of late Dr R. P. Beatty, of Swindon House, Swindon, Wilts:—
Mary Kathleen, *b* 1947: *m* 1967, David Allen Carse.

Issue of late Kenneth Hugh de Courcy, *b* 1909, *d* 1999: *m* 1950 (*m diss* 1973), Rosemary Catherine, only da of late Cmdr Henry Leslie Spofforth Baker, OBE, RN, of Carrowduff House, Ballymacurly, co Roscommon:—
Joseph Kenneth Charles (Blacklains Farm, Birdlip, Glos), *b* 1955; *ed* Radley, and Oriel Coll, Oxford: *m* 1987, Jayne P. Potter, of Midhurst, W Sussex, and has issue living, Patrick Miles Hugh, *b* 1993, — Rachel Frances, *b* 1987, — Alice Olivia, *b* 1990. — Richard Henry Stephen, *b* 1960; *ed* Radley. —— Rosemary Minnie Frances, *b* 1951; *ed* Girton Coll, Camb: *m* 1979, Anthony J. V. Cheetham, of Paxford Manor, nr Chipping Campden, Glos, yr son of Sir Nicolas

Cheetham, KCMG, and has issue living, Emma Rosemary, *b* 1981, — Rebecca Sophie, *b* 1983. —— Catherine Sarah, *b* 1952: *m* 1989, Charles Edward Martin Benson, of Fen Farm, Wavendon, Milton Keynes, Bucks MK17 8AA, elder son of Edward Douglas Benson.

PREDECESSORS – The origin and early descent of this Peerage is obscure. In 1489, when eleven Irish barons were summoned to Greenwich, this Barony ranked after Athenry and before Gormanston. *The Complete Peerage* considers that Miles de Courcy, *b* about 1286, may have become *Lord Courcy of Kinsale* about 1340, but adds a footnote "it is more probable that the family acquired peerage rank 50 years later." In 1397, William de Courcy received a licence, as *Dominus et Baro de Courcy*, to buy a ship in England and sail it to France. Precedence of the Barony in the Peerage of Ireland had been given from this date. A list of Peers present at the Irish Parliament 1490 includes *Dominus de Kinsale*, but until the 17th century, *Lord Courcy, of Ringrone and Kinsale* was the style more usually adopted. Patrick de Courcy, whose parentage is uncertain, but who was most probably a descendant or close relative of Sir John de Courcy, Baron by tenure of Kingsale prior to 1205: *m* a da of Miles de Cogan; *d* before 1261. His son, Miles *d c* 1290. His son John was killed 1291. His el son **(1)** MILES, 1st Baron, *b c* 1286; Sheriff of Cork 1329-32: *m* 13—: Joan; *d* before 1344; *s* by his son **(2)** MILES, 2nd Baron, *d* unm 1372; *s* by his kinsman **(3)** JOHN, 3rd Baron, (perhaps son of Edmund de Courcy, whose lineage is uncertain); *d c* 1390; *s* by his son **(4)** WILLIAM, 4th Baron: *m* Margaret Peinnel (who had Robes of the Garter 1399); *d c* 1400; *s* by **(5)** NICHOLAS, 5th Baron, *d c* 1410; *s* by **(6)** PATRICK, 6th Baron, *d c* 1499; *s* by his el son **(7)** NICHOLAS, 7th Baron: *m* Mary, da of More O'Mahony; *d c* 1475; *s* by his el son **(8)** JAMES, 8th Baron: *m* Ellena Roche, da of David, Baron of Fermoy; *d* 1499; *s* by his only surviving son **(9)** EDMUND, 9th Baron, *d c* 1505; *s* by his uncle **(10)** DAVID, 10th Baron (2nd son of 7th Baron): *m* Joan, da of Edmund Roche; *d c* 1520; *s* by his el son **(11)** JOHN, 11th Baron: *m* Sarah, da of Donogh MacCarthy, of Dowallagh; *d* 1535; *s* by his only son **(12)** GERALD, 12th Baron; commanded an Irish Regt at siege of Boulogne; knighted on the field 1567: *m* Ellen, da of Cormac MacDonagh McCarthy of Carbery; *d* 1599; *s* by his kinsman **(13)** JOHN, 13th Baron (son of Edmund Oge de Courcy, grandson of 10th Baron); fought against Spaniards at Siege of Kinsale 1601; was a Gentleman of the Bedchamber to King James I: *m* 1st, Catherine, da of William Cogan; 2ndly, Mary, da of Cormac O'Cruly, of Carbery, co Cork; *d* 1628; *s* by his el son **(14)** GERALD, 14th Baron: *m* 16—, Elene, da of Sir John FitzGerald, of Dromana, co Waterford; *d* 1642; *s* by his brother **(15)** PATRICK, 15th Baron: *m* 16—, Mary, who *d* 1678, da of Sir John Fitzgerald (ante); *dc* 1663; *s* by his son **(16)** JOHN, 16th Baron: *m* 16—, Ellen, da of Charles MacCarthy Reagh; *d* 1667; *s* by his el son **(17)** PATRICK, 17th Baron, *b* 1660; *d* 1669; *s* by his brother **(18)** ALMERICUS, 18th Baron; outlawed 1691 for his adhesion to the fortunes of James II, but which outlawry was removed 1692: *m* 1698, Anne, da of Robert Dring, of Isleworth, Middlesex; *d* 1719; *s* by his cousin **(19)** GERALD, 19th Baron (son of Col Hon Miles de Courcy, 3rd son of 15th Baron), *b* 1700; PC Ireland 1744; *m* 1725, Margaretta, who *d* 1750, da of John Essington, of Grossington Hall, Glos; *d* 1759; *s* by his kinsman **(20)** JOHN, 20th Baron (son of Miles de Courcy, of Newport, Rhode Island, N America, 2nd son of Anthony de Courcy, of Bandon, co Cork, only son of Hon David de Courcy, yst son of 13th Baron); confirmed in the Baronies of Kingsale and Ringrone 1761, and their descent in the male line: *m* 1746, Martha, who *d* 1803, da of Rev William Heron, of Dorchester, Dorset; *d* 1776; *s* by his son **(21)** JOHN, 21st Baron: *m* 1763, Susanna, who *d* 1819, da of Conway Blennerhassett, of Castle Conway, co Kerry; *d* 1822; *s* by his son **(22)** *Rev* THOMAS, 22nd Baron, *b* 1774; *d* 1832; *s* by his nephew **(23)** JOHN STAPLETON, 23rd Baron (son of Capt Hon Michael de Courcy, RN, 3rd son of 21st Baron), *b* 1805: *m* 1825, Sarah, who *d* 1883, da of Joseph Chadder, of Portlemouth, Devon; *d* 1847; *s* by his son **(24)** JOHN CONSTANTINE, 24th Baron, *b* 1827; Capt E Devon Mil: *m* 1855, Adelaide, who *d* 1885, da of Joseph Proctor Brown-Westhead, of Lea Castle, Worcs; *d* 1865; *s* by his brother **(25)** MICHAEL CONRAD, 25th Baron, *b* 1828; *d* 1874; *s* by his cousin **(26)** JOHN FITZROY, 26th Baron (el son of Lieut-Col Hon Gerald de Courcy, 4th son of 21st Baron), *b* 1821; Maj in Turkish Contingent during Crimean War 1854-5, and Col in Federal Army during American Civil War: *m* 1864, Elia Elizabeth, who *d* 1893, da of C. de François de Ponchalon, of Alençon, France, and widow of C. de Bosque de Beaumont, of Airel, Manche; *d* 1890; *s* by his cousin **(27)** MICHAEL WILLIAM, 27th Baron (el son of Rev Michael de Courcy, DD, son of Adm Hon Michael de Courcy, 3rd son of 20th Baron), *b* 1822: *m* 1st, 1852, Esther Eleanor, who *d* 1864, da of Thomas Williams, of Dublin; 2ndly, 1874, Jessie Maud, who *d* 1902, da of Rev Edward Polwhele, sometime R of Fillaton; *d* 1895; *s* by his el son **(28)** MICHAEL CONSTANTINE, 28th Baron, *b* 1855: *m* 1880, Emily Frances Anne, who *d* 1926, da of late William Sinclair de Courcy, brother of 27th Baron Kingsale, *d* 1931; *s* by his son **(29)** MICHAEL WILLIAM ROBERT, DSO, 29th Baron, *b* 1882: *m* 1st, 1906, Constance Mary Rancé, who *d* 1946, da of late Maj-Gen Sir Tom Percy Woodhouse, KCMG, CB; 2ndly, 1947 (*m diss* 1957), Ruth, only child of Herbert Thomas Holmes, OBE; *d* 1969; *s* by his grandson **(30)**, JOHN (only surviving son of Lieut-Col Hon Michael John Rancé de Courcy, RN, only surviving son of 29th Baron, *b* 1907, *k* on active ser 1940, who *m* 1st, 1929 (*m diss* 1933), Glory Elizabeth, da of Eng-Cdr Alfred Claremont Evans, RN (ret); 2ndly, 1936, Joan, who *d* 1967, da of Robert Reid, JP, of Moor Park, nr Harrogate), *b* (*posthumous*) 1941, 30th Baron and present Peer; also Baron of Ringrone.

Kingsborough, Viscount; son of Earl of Kingston.

KINGSDOWN, BARON (Leigh-Pemberton) (Life Baron 1993)

ROBERT (ROBIN) LEIGH-PEMBERTON, KG, PC, eldest son of late Capt Robert Douglas Leigh-Pemberton, MBE, MC, of Torry Hill, Kent (*see* Frankland-Payne-Gallwey, Bt, 1985 Edn); *b* 5 Jan 1927; *ed* Eton, RMC, and Trin Coll, Oxford (MA 1953, Hon Fellow 1984); late Lieut Gren Guards, Hon Col Kent and County of London Sharpshooters Yeo Sqdn, 265 (KCLY) Signal Sqdn (V), 5 (Vol) Bn The Queen's Regt, Pres SE TAVR Assocn and Kent SSAFA; Bar Inner Temple 1954, London and SE Circuit 1954-60, Hon Bencher 1983; Dir Birmid Qualcast 1966-83 (Dep-Chm 1970, Chm 1975-77), University Life Assurance Soc 1967-78, Redland Ltd 1972-83 and 1993-98, and Equitable Life Assurance Soc 1979-83, Chm National Westminster Bank 1977-83 (Dir 1972-83, Dep-Chm 1974), and Cttee of London Clearing Bankers 1982-83, Gov Bank of England 1983-93; Dir Glaxo plc, Hambros plc, and Foreign and Colonial Investment Trust 1993-98; JP Kent 1961-75, CC 1961-77, DL 1970, Vice Lord-Lieut 1972-82, since when Lord-Lieut; Trustee Emeritus Royal Academy of Arts Trust, Trustee Kent CCC, Kent County Playing Fields Assocn, Kent County Agric Soc, etc, Chm Canterbury Cathedral Trust, Seneschal of Canterbury Cathedral, Pres Royal Agric Soc of England 1989-90, Pro-Chancellor Kent Univ 1977-83, Member RSA; FCIB; Hon DCL Kent 1983, Hon DLitt City of London 1988, Loughborough 1989, and City Poly 1990; KStJ; *cr* PC 1987, KG 1994, and *Baron Kingsdown*, of Pemberton, co Lancs (Life Baron) 1993: *m* 1953, Rosemary Davina, OBE, only da of late Lt-Col David Walter Arthur William Forbes, MC, Coldstream Guards, of Callendar House, Falkirk (*see* B Faringdon, colls, 1980 Edn), and has had issue.

Arms – Quarterly, 1st and 4th, Ermine an estoile or between three buckets sable, hoops and handles gold (*Pemberton*), 2nd and 3rd, Gules a cross engrailed argent between four lozenges ermine (*Leigh*). **Crests** – 1, A dragon's head ermine erased gules ducally gorged or and transfixed by an arrow fessways proper (*Pemberton*), 2, A demi-lion rampant gules charged on each shoulder with an ermine spot and holding between the paws a lozenge argent thereon a rose gules barbed and seeded proper (*Leigh*). **Supporters** – *Dexter*, a wyvern ermine ducally gorged or and charged on the shoulder with an estoile gules; *sinister*, a lion gules charged on the shoulder with a lozenge argent thereon an ermine spot gules. **Residence** – Torry Hill, Sittingbourne, Kent. **Club** – Brooks's, Cavalry and Guards'.

SONS LIVING AND DECEASED

Hon John David, *b* 1955; *ed* Eton, and Magdalen Coll, Oxford: *m* 1st, 1980, Rosamond P., 4th da of Oliver Richard Jessel, of Sponden House, Sandhurst, Cranbrook, Kent; 2ndly, 1985, Kathryn Felice, da of Martin Robert Lampard, of Theberton House, Theberton, Suffolk, and has issue living (by 2nd *m*), Arthur Evelyn, *b* 1989, — Robert Eustace Walter, *b* 1991, — Maude Alexandra Frances, *b* 1995. *Residence* – Yokes Court, Frinstead, Sittingbourne, Kent.

Hon James Henry, *b* 1956; *ed* Eton, and ChCh, Oxford: *m* 1985, Catarina Elizabeth, da of John Cowan, of New Coll, Oxford, and of Mrs Karin Stielow, of Hamburg, and has issue living, Sophia Loveday, *b* 1985, — Lucinda Rose, *b* 1987, — Letitia Jane, *b* 1989. *Residence* – The Old Rectory, Milstead, Sittingbourne, Kent ME9 0AS.

Hon Edward Douglas, *b* 1959; *ed* Eton, and RAC Cirencester: *m* 1984, Jessica Elizabeth Berners, yr twin da of Michael Edward Ranulph Allsopp (*see* B Hindlip, colls), and has issue living, David Geoffrey Berners, *b* 1988, — Ranulph Berners, *b* 1989, — Patrick Berners, *b* 1991. *Residence* – Longcot House, Longcot, Faringdon, Oxon SN7 7TF.

†Thomas Robert Arnold, *b* 1961; *ed* Eton, St Edmund Hall, Oxford; *k* in a motor accident in Zimbabwe 1993.

Hon William Francis, *b* 1964; *ed* Eton, and Jesus Coll, Oxford.

KINGSLAND, BARON (Prout) (Life Baron 1994)

CHRISTOPHER JAMES PROUT, PC, TD, QC, son of late Frank Yabsley Prout, MC; *b* 1 Jan 1942; *ed* Sevenoaks, Manchester Univ (BA 1963), and The Queen's Coll, Oxford (BPhil 1966, DPhil 1968); DL Shropshire 1997; TA Offr (Major) OU OTC 1966-74, 16th/5th The Queen's Royal Lancers 1974-82, 3rd Armoured Div 1982-88, since when RARO; Bar, Middle Temple 1972, Bencher 1996, QC 1988; ESU Fell, Columbia Univ, New York 1963-64; Staff Memb Internat Bank for Reconstruction and Development (UN), Washington, DC 1966-69; Leverhulme Fell and Lecturer in Law, Sussex Univ 1969-79; MEP Shropshire and Stafford (C) 1979-94; Dep Whip, Euro Democratic Group (EDG) 1979-82, Chief Whip 1983-87, Chm Parliamentary Cttee on Legal Affairs 1987, leader of Conservative MEPs in European Parliament 1987-94, Chm and Leader of EDG 1987-92, Vice-Chm EPP Parliamentary Group 1992-94; Shadow Lord Chancellor since 1997; TD 1987; awarded La Grand Medaille de la Ville de Paris 1988; *cr* Knt 1990, PC 1994, and *Baron Kingsland*, of Shrewsbury, co Shropshire (Life Baron) 1994.

Arms – Paly of six gules and vert an eagle displayed or charged on the breast with a leopard's face gules. Crest – Rising from a grassy mound proper a demi-horse sable gorged with a wreath argent and sable with four tails two argent two sable supporting with the forelegs a lance argent flying therefrom a forked pennon per fess gules and argent. Supporters – *Dexter*, a sea-horse per fess argent and vert gorged with a mural crown vert pendent therefrom a gunstone charged with an acorn slipped and leaved all within a bordure or; *sinister*, a sea-lion per fess gules and vert gorged with a naval crown or pendent therefrom a like gunstone charged with an acorn slipped and leaved all within a bordure or the compartment comprising a grassy mount growing therefrom penny royal plants flowered and leaved all proper. Motto – Patria Rex Meus.
Address – 4 Breams Buildings, Temple, EC4. *Clubs* – Pratt's, Beefsteak, Royal Ocean Racing, Royal Yacht Squadron.

KINGS NORTON, BARONY OF (Roxbee Cox) (Extinct 1997)

SONS LIVING OF LIFE BARON (*by 1st marriage*)

Hon Christopher Withers, *b* 1928: *m* 1955, Rosemary, da of late Frederick Day Ardagh, and has issue, two sons.
Hon Jeremy William, *b* 1932: *m* 1962, Anne, da of late Albert Moore Linton, and has issue, one son and one da.

WIDOW LIVING OF LIFE BARON

JOAN RUTH (*Baroness Kings Norton*), da of late William George Pack, of Torquay, Devon, and formerly wife of K. A. Pascoe: *m* 1982, as his 2nd wife, Baron Kings Norton (Life Baron), who *d* 1997. *Residence* – Westcote House, Chipping Campden, Glos GL55 6AG.

KINGSTON, EARL OF (King-Tenison) (Earl I 1768, Bt I 1682)

Heaven is our highest hope

BARCLAY ROBERT EDWIN KING-TENISON, 11th Earl, and 15th Baronet; *b* 23 Sept 1943; *s* 1948; *ed* Winchester; late Lt R Scots Greys: *m* 1st, 1965 (*m diss* 1974), Patricia Mary, da of late E. C. Killip, of Beoley Lodge, Uttoxeter, Staffs; 2ndly, 1974 (*m diss* 1979), Victoria, only da of D. C. Edmonds of Northwood, Middlesex; 3rdly, 1990, Corleen Jennifer Rathbone, and has issue by 1st *m*.

Arms – Quarterly: 1st and 4th gules, on a bend engrailed or, between two leopards' faces of the last, jessant-de-lis-azure, three crosses-crosslet sable, *Tenison*, 2nd and 3rd gules, two lions rampant combatant; supporting a dexter hand, couped at the wrist and erect all argent, *King*. Crests – 1st, a leopard's face as in the arms in front of a crozier and a cross-crosslet fitchée in saltire sable, *Tenison*; 2nd, out of a five-leaved ducal coronet or a dexter hand erect, the third and fourth fingers turned down proper, *King*. Supporters – Two lions, per fesse argent and gules ducally crowned of the last.
Address –

SON LIVING (*By 1st marriage*)

ROBERT CHARLES HENRY (*Viscount Kingsborough*), *b* 20 March 1969.

DAUGHTER LIVING (*By 1st marriage*)

Lady Maria Lisette, *b* 1970.

SISTER LIVING

Lady Kara Virginia Louisa, *b* 1938: *m* 1964 (*m diss* 1974), Anthony John Conroy Hawks, MB, BS, DCH, and has issue living, Honor Louise, *b* 1966.

COLLATERAL BRANCHES LIVING

Grandson of late Sir Charles Anthony King-Harman, KCMG, yst son of late Hon Lawrence Harman King-Harman, 2nd son of 1st Viscount Lorton, and brother of 6th Earl of Kingston:—
Issue of late Capt Robert Douglas King-Harman, DSO, DSC and bar, RN, *b* 1891, *d* 1978: *m* 1st, 1916 (*m diss* 1926), Lilly, who *d* 1966, da of late Alexander Moffatt, Sheriff-Substitute of Arnotdale, Falkirk; 2ndly, 1927, Bessie Lilian Bull, who *d* 1974, da of late William James Davis, of Junee Reefs, NSW; 3rdly, 1975, Eva Mary, who *d* 1987, da of late Archdale Stuart Palmer:—
(By 1st *m*) Anthony Lawrence, OBE (Ouse Manor, Sharnbrook, Beds, MK44 1PG; Anglo-Belgian Club), *b* 1918; *ed* Wellington Coll; Col late RA; 1939-45 War (despatches); OBE (Civil) 1983; OStJ 1987; DL Beds 1987: *m* 1944, Jeanette Stella Dunkerley, and has issue living, Anthony William (60a Ladbroke Grove, W11 2PB), *b* 1946; *ed* Wellington Coll, and RMAS; Col late RA: *m* 1991, Mrs Judith Serena Buxton, da of John Richard Rumsey, and formerly wife of Robert Hugh Buxton (*see* Buxton, Bt, colls), — Michael Charles, *b* 1947; *ed* Wellington Coll, William and Mary, and Univ of Virginia; Dir of Hunt Deltel and Co, Seychelles; has issue (by Barbara Elizabeth, da of Kenneth Veasey Lightfoot, of 23 Matangi St, Christchurch 4, NZ), Charles *b* 1988, Jasper *b* 1992, Alizé *b* (triplet) 1988, Bibette *b* (triplet) 1988.

Granddaughters of late Col John Robert King, 2nd son of Capt John Wingfield King (infra):—
Issue of late Capt Robert Guy Cyril King, Roy Australian Artillery, *b* 1877, *d* 1940: *m* 1st, 1905, Albertina Millicent, da of Philip Steele, of Melbourne; 2ndly, 1919, Mary Catherine, da of John Robert Russell, of Brackly:—
(By 1st *m*) Millicent Francklyn (22 Millicent Av, Toorak, Australia 3142), *b* 1907: *m* 1st, 1928, Archibald Jennings Ironside, who *d* 1941; 2ndly, 1942, William Bethel Thompson, Sqdn Ldr RAAF, who *d* 1945, and has issue living, (by 1st *m*) Margaret Joan Francklyn, *b* 1929, — Philip Norman Jennings, *b* 1931: *m* 1960, Dorothy Rosemary Joy, da of Alan Bell, of Melbourne, and has issue living, Andrew Philip *b* 1962, Alan Francklyn *b* 1964.

Issue of late Lt-Col John Francklyn King, RAOC, *b* 1882, *d* 19—: *m* (Jan) 1914, Mary Elspeth, da of Edwin Hellard:—
Phyllis Mary, *b* (Nov) 1914. *Residence* – 21 Chapman Terrace, Kingscote, S Australia 5223.

Grandchildren of Gerald Fitzgerald King, 5th son of Capt John Wingfield King, eldest son of Lt-Gen Hon Sir Henry King, KCB, 3rd son of 2nd Earl:—
Issue of late Wingfield Charles Gerald King, *b* 1886, *d* 1972: *m* 1st, 1912, Annabel Mae Brown, who *d* 1914; 2ndly, 1915, Lena Mae Stewart, who *d* 1934; 3rdly, Mamie Green Slusser, who *d* 1990, of Augusta, Georgia, USA:—
(By 2nd *m*) (John Charles) Alwyn (Hallowes) (121 South Hanover St, Carlisle, Pennsylvania 17013, USA), *b* 1920; *ed* McGill Univ (BEng), Columbia Univ, New York (MSc), and Stuttgart Technical Univ (DSc); Col US Army (ret); 1939-45 War in Pacific and NW Europe: *m* 1st, 1942, Mary Parker, da of Herbert Daniel Casey, of Ozark, Alabama, USA; 2ndly, 1952, Grace Margaret Stanley, who *d* 1988; 3rdly, 1995, Bonnie Jean, da of William Harry Thain, and has issue living, (by 1st *m*) Judy Marilyn, *b* 1943, — (by 2nd *m*) Carolyn Joan, *b* 1957. —— Elizabeth Avarina Joan, *b* 1926: *m* 1952, Duane Caldwell, of 827 Pioneer Drive, N Tonawanda, New York, USA and has issue living, Stewart Duane Sandes, *b* 1953: *m* 1982, Johanna Grace Howard, and has issue living, Mary Rebecca Christine *b* 1985, Kathleen Avarina Suzanne *b*

1989, — Deborah Grace, *b* 1955; has issue living, Megan Avarina-Mae CALDWELL, *b* 1978: *m* 1999, Todd Anthony Sholtz (and has issue living, Conner Anthony Stewart *b* 1998), — Gail Heather, *b* 1963: *m* 1982 (*m diss* 1998), David Spencer Barone, jr, and has issue living, David Spencer (III) *b* 1986, Lisa Ann *b* 1985, Christina Marie *b* 1988, Amanda Lee *b* 1994.

Issue of late John Wingfield King, *b* 1891, *d* 1975: *m* 1916, Alice Mary Prefontaine, who *d* 1974:—
Gerald Rene Wingfield (C-10 Harding Rd, RR1, Powell River, BC, Canada), *b* 1924; Sqdn Ldr RCAF; Maj (ret) Canadian Armed Forces (War Medal 1939-45), two medals; Airways Inspector, Min of Transport (ret): *m* 1st, 1958 (*m diss* 1972), Sonia Lanjin, of Yugoslavia; 2ndly, 1987, Grace Marion Sayce.

Grandchildren of late Capt John Wingfield King (ante):—
Issue of late Percy Wingfield King, *b* 1868, *d* 1930: *m* 18—, Mary Cecelia Foley:—
†James Fitzgerald, *b* 1911: *m* 19—, and *d* 1976, leaving issue, James, *b* 19—, — John, *b* 19—, — Eileen, *b* 19—.
— Ena, *b* 1901: *m* 19—. —— Mary, *b* 1903: *m* 19— —— Ida, *b* 1907: *m* 19—.

Granddaughters of late Percy Wingfield King (ante):—
Issue of late John Wingfield King, *b* 1899, *d* 1963: *m* 1st, 1922, Margaret Fraser, who *d* 1941, da of late Isaac Van Cleef, of New Jersey, USA, 2ndly, 1944, Alice, who *d* 1989, da of late John Malone, of Philadelphia, Pa, USA:—
(By 1st *m*) Jean Margaret, *b* 1923: *m* 1944, Raymond A. Connelly, and has issue living, Robert (26 Longwood Rd, Austin, Texas 78737, USA), *b* 1948: *m* 1st, 1969, Jacqueline Marie Schlickenmaier; 2ndly, 1982, Jane Heffington, and has issue living (by 1st *m*), Shane Jason *b* 1974, Stacy Michael *b* (twin) 1974, Heather Janelle *b* 1972, — Carol, *b* 1945: *m* 1st, 1963, D. R. Robles; 2ndly, 1973, George Michael Belanger, of 6359 Christie Lane, Roanoke, Virginia 24018, USA, and has issue living (by 1st *m*), Kateri Jean Louise *b* 1965: *m* 1988, Michael Joles, of 904 E 4th St S, Ladysmith, Wisconsin 54848-2212, USA (and has issue living, Sydney Elaine *b* 1991), (by 2nd *m*) Victoria Elizabeth Caroline *b* 1977. —— (By 2nd *m*) Patricia Barry, *b* 1950. *Residence* – 35 Plum St, Vincentown, NJ 08088, USA.

Granddaughters of late Col Edward Richard King, son of late Lieut Gen Hon Sir Henry King, KCB (ante):—
Issue (by 2nd *m*) of late Lieut-Col Robert Ambrose Cecil King, *b* 1852, *d* 1897: *m* 1st, 1884, Bessie, who *d* 1892, da of late Rev J. Mecredy, DD, R of Killalan, and widow of Major J. L. Bell, RA; 2ndly, 1893, Lilian Walters, da of Rochfort Davies, formerly ICS:—
Eileen Mary Fridiswede, *b* 1894. —— Sybil Doreen, *b* 1896.

PREDECESSORS – (**1**) ROBERT King, PC, MP for co Roscommon (yr brother of John King, of Kingston, co Dublin, who was *cr* Baron Kingston 1660, and which title became *ext* 1761); *cr* a *Baronet* 1682; *d* 1708; *s* by his el son (**2**) *Sir* John, 2nd Bt, MP for co Roscommon; *dsp* 1720; *s* by his brother (**3**) *Sir* HENRY, PC, 3rd Bt; MP for co Roscommon; *m* 1722, Isabella Wingfield, sister of 1st Viscount Powerscourt; *d* 1740; *s* by his el son (**4**) *Sir* ROBERT, 4th Bt; *cr Baron Kingsborough* (peerage of Ireland) 1748; *d* unmarried 1755 when the barony expired, and the baronetcy devolved upon his brother (**5**) *Sir* EDWARD, 5th Bt; *cr Baron Kingston of Rockingham*, co Roscommon (peerage of Ireland) 1764, *Viscount Kingston of Kingsborough*, co Sligo (peerage of Ireland) 1766, and *Earl of Kingston* (peerage of Ireland) 1768; *d* 1797; *s* by his son (**6**) ROBERT, 2nd Earl; was MP for co Cork; his 2nd son, Robert Edward, a Gen in the Army, and Lord-Lieut of Roscommon, was *cr Baron Erris*, of Boyle, co Roscommon (peerage of Ireland) 1800, and *Viscount Lorton*, of Boyle, co Roscommon (peerage of Ireland) 1806; the Earl *d* 1799; *s* by his son (**7**) GEORGE, 3rd Earl: *cr Baron Kingston of Mitchelstown*, co Cork (peerage of United Kingdom) 1821; *d* 1838; *s* by his el surviving son (**8**) ROBERT HENRY, 4th Earl; *d* 1867; *s* by his brother (**9**) JAMES, 5th Earl: *m* 1860, Anne, da of Matthew Brinkley, of Parsonstown, Meath; *dsp* 1869 when the Barony of Kingston of Mitchelstown expired, and the Irish peerages reverted to his cousin (**10**) ROBERT, 6th Earl, who had in 1854 *s* his father as 2nd Viscount Lorton; *b* 1804: *m* 18298, Anne, da of Sir Robert Newcomen Gore-Booth, Bt; *d* 1869; *s* by his el son (**11**) ROBERT EDWARD, 7th Earl; *d* 1871; *s* by his brother (**12**) HENRY ERNEST NEWCOMEN, 8th Earl, *b* 1848; Lord-Lieut of co Roscommon, and a Representative Peer for Ireland; assumed by Roy licence 1883, the additional surname of Tenison: *m* 1872, Florence Margaret Christine, who *d* 1907, da of late Col Edward Tenison, of Kilronan Castle; *d* 1896; *s* by his only son (**13**) HENRY EDWYN, 9th Earl, *b* 1874; a Representative Peer for Ireland; sometime Capt Irish Guards; S Africa 1900-02, 1914-18 War (wounded): *m* 1897, Ethel Lisette, who *d* 1949, yst da of Sir Andrew Barclay Walker, 1st Bt (*cr* 1886); *d* 1946; *s* by his only son (**14**) ROBERT HENRY ETHELBERT, 10th Earl, *b* 1897; sometime Lieut Roy Scots Greys: *m* 1st, 1937 (*m diss* 1947), Gwyneth (Joan), who *d* 1987, da of William Howard Evans, of Tenby, Pembrokeshire; 2ndly, 1947, Jean Sinclair, who *d* 1983 (having *m* 2ndly, 1953, Cecil Geoffrey Monson who *d* 1974), da of late James L. Alexander, of Orkney and Aberdeen; *d* 1948; *s* by his only son (**15**) BARCLAY ROBERT EDWIN, 11th Earl and present peer; also Viscount Kingston of Kingsborough, Viscount Lorton, Baron Kingston of Rockingham, and Baron Erris.

KINLOSS, LADY (Freeman-Grenville) (Lordship S 1602)

For God, country and friends

(BEATRICE) MARY GRENVILLE FREEMAN-GRENVILLE, *b* 1922; *s* 1944; assumption with her husband of the surname of Freeman-Grenville recognised by decree of Lord Lyon King of Arms 1950: *m* 1950, Greville Stewart Parker Freeman, DPhil, MA, BLitt (Oxon), FSA, FRAS, Capt late Roy Berks Regt, Kt of the Holy Sepulchre of Jerusalem, Papal Cross *Pro Ecclesia et Pontifice* (for services on Pope John Paul II's visit to York 1982), and has issue.

ᴀrms – Quarterly, 1st vert, on a cross argent five torteaux, *Grenville*; 2nd, paly of six argent and or, a lion rampant reguardant sable, armed and langued gules, charged with a cross-crosslet of the second, between four quatrefoils of the third, *Morgan*; 3rd, or, a pile gules, *Chandos*; 4th per fess azure and vair-ancient, three fusils in chief, a bordure or for difference, *Freeman*; over all, an escutcheon ensigned with the coronet of a Lord-Baron in the Peerage of Scotland for her Lordship of Kinloss, quarterly 1st and 4th, or, a saltire gules, on a chief of the last three crescents of the first, *Bruce*; 2nd and 3rd, argent, two open crowns in fesse gules and a martlet in base azure, on a chief of the last a mullet of the field, *Kinloss*. ᴄrest – On a chapeau gules furred, ermine a lion passant, tail extended gules, armed and langued azure, supporting with his dexter forepaw a shield emblazoned with the arms of Kinloss, vizt, argent, two open crowns in fess gules, and a martlet in base azure, on a chief of the last a mullet of the field. ꙅupporters – Two savages wreathed about the middle and temples with laurel, supporting in their exterior hands banners floating inwards, that on the dexter having a staff of these liveries or and azure and surmounted of an abbot's mitre, of the ensigns armorial of the abbot of Kinloss, vizt, azure, semée of fleur-de-lys or, an inescutcheon parted per pale, the dexter bendy of six or and azure within a bordure gules, sinister, argent, two open crowns in fesse gules and a martlet in base azure, on a chief of the last a mullet of the field; that on the sinister with a staff of these liveries gules and or, and ensigned with a Baroness's coronet, of the ensigns armorial of Bruce of Kinloss, vizt, or, a saltire gules, on a chief of the last three crescents of the first.
Residence – North View House, Sheriff Hutton, York YO60 6ST. *Club* – Civil Service.

SON LIVING

Hon BEVIL DAVID STEWART CHANDOS (*Master of Kinloss*), *b* 20 June 1953.

DAUGHTERS LIVING

Hon Teresa Mary Nugent, *b* 1957.
Hon Hester Josephine Anne, *b* 1960: *m* 1984, Peter Haworth, yr son of A. F. C. P. Haworth, of Malton, York, and has issue living, Joseph Anthony, *b* 1985, — David Arnold, *b* 1987, — Christopher John, *b* 1989. *Residence* – Newstead Grange, Thirsk Rd, Easingwold, York YO6 3NH.

SISTER LIVING (*Raised to the rank of a Baron's daughter* 1947)

Hon Caroline Jane Grenville, *b* 1931: *m* 1958, Gordon Glynne-Walton, FRGS, FRMetSoc, FRAS, FGS, late Duke of Wellington's Regt, and has issue living, Charlotte Elizabeth Sophia Caroline Louise, *b* 1961; MBA (Bradford), BA (Leeds Metropolitan Univ), Diplom Betriebswirt (Bremen), Post Graduate Certificate of Education (Leeds): *m* 1990, Paul Stephen Fox, yst son of J. M. Fox, of Clifton, W Yorkshire, and has issue living, Luis John Gordon Temple Grenville, *b* 1997. *Residence* – West Bank House, W Haddlesey, Selby, N Yorks YO8 8PZ.

COLLATERAL BRANCHES LIVING

Grandchildren of late Lt-Col Hon Thomas George Breadalbane Morgan-Grenville, DSO, OBE, MC (infra):—
Issue of late Pamela Mary Ruth, *b* 1919, *d* 1989: *m* 1944, Capt Alec David Charles Francis, late WG, of The Grange, Malmesbury, Wilts, who *d* 1993:—
Nigel Charles Audley FRANCIS, *b* 1949: *m* 1990, Julia Anne Grayson. —— Priscilla Annabelle, *b* 1947: *m* 1969, Frederick Hugh Philip Hamilton Wills, Capt late 11th Hus, and has issue (*see* B Dulverton, colls).

Issue of late Lt-Col Hon Thomas George Breadalbane MORGAN-GRENVILLE, DSO, OBE, MC, 3rd son of Mary, Lady Kinloss, *b* 1891, *d* 1965: *m* 1916, Georgina May St John, who *d* 1973, da of late Albert St John Murphy, of The Island House, Little Island, co Cork:—
Cynthia Avril, *b* 1921: *m* 1948, Christopher Michael Aliaga-Kelly, who *d* 1999, of Chancery House, Rakehanger, Hill Brow, Liss, Hants, and has issue living, Peter Edward Grenville, *b* 1956: *m* 1979, Eileen S. Lenihan, of Claregalway, co Galway, and has issue living, Benjamin Peter Mark *b* 1983, Isabel Katherine *b* 1985, — Veronica Ann Cynthia, *b* 1950: *m* 1978, John P. V. Bevan, QC, of 2 Harcourt Bldgs, Temple, EC4Y 9DB, and has issue living, Henry Thomas Vaughan *b* 1981, Charlotte Emily Vaughan *b* 1985. —— Audrey Marigold (*Baroness Ironside*), *b* 1931: *m* 1950, 2nd Baron Ironside, of Priory House, Boxted, Colchester, Essex CO4 5RB.

Grandchildren of late Capt Hon Robert William Morgan-Grenville (infra):—
Issue of late Robert Grenville Plantagenet Morgan-Grenville, *b* 1916, *d* 1993: *m* 1944, Mabel, who *d* 1985, da of
Charles Osborne Ellis, of Birmingham:—
Richard Harvey MORGAN-GRENVILLE (67 Chartwell Drive, Durban, S Africa), *b* 1947; *ed* Millfield: *m* 1st, 1969 (*m diss*
19—), Diana Jane, da of Ralph Chambler, of 29 Osprey Av, Birdwell, Barnsley, Yorks; 2ndly, 1982, Valerie de Marigny,
and has issue living (by 1st *m*), Robert Ralph, *b* 1974, — Richard John, *b* 1977, — Georgina Jane, *b* 1975.
—— †Caroline Irene, *b* 1949: *m* 1st, 1972 (*m diss* 1976), Edward James Windham-Bellord (*see* Bowyer-Smyth, Bt, colls);
2ndly, 1977, Robert Denman, and *d* 1979, leaving issue (by 1st *m*) (*see* Bowyer-Smyth, Bt, colls).

Issue of late John Richard Bine Morgan-Grenville, *b* 1927, *d* 1994: *m* 1955, Joan Margaret (Upperton House, Pet-
worth, W Sussex), 2nd da of Air Ch Marshal Sir Wilfred Rhodes Freeman, 1st Bt, GCB, DSO, MC:—
Roger Temple MORGAN-GRENVILLE (Park Cottage, Upperton, W Sussex GU28 9BL), *b* 1959: *m* 1993, Caroline Mary, da of
David Michael Summerhayes, CMG, of Harting, W Sussex, and has issue living, Tom, *b* 1995. —— Joanna Jane, *b* 1957:
m 1991, Cdr John C. L. Wotton, RN, of Tichborne Cottage, Tichborne, Alresford, Hants SO23 0NA, son of Lt-Col Gordon
Wotton, of Old Burleadon, Hants, and has issue living, Laura Elizabeth, *b* 1993, — Iona, *b* 1995.

Issue of late Capt Hon Robert William Morgan-Grenville, 4th son of Mary, Lady Kinloss, *b* 1892, *d*
1988: *m* 1st, 1915, Irene Alice Gertrude, who *d* 1916, da of Sir Robert Grenville Harvey, 2nd Bt; 2ndly,
1922, Elizabeth Hope Bine, who *d* 1969, da of Sir Charles Bine Renshaw, 1st Bt, and widow of Maj
Francis William Lindley Gull (Gull, Bt):—
(By 2nd *m*) Gerard Wyndham MORGAN-GRENVILLE (Milton Mill, W Milton, Bridport, Dorset), *b* 1931; *ed* Eton; late Capt
Rifle Bde: *m* 1st, 1955 (*m diss* 1981), Virginia Anne, eldest da of late Maj (Basil Arthur) John Peto, King's Drag Gds (*see*
Peto, Bt, *cr* 1927, colls); 2ndly, 1981 (*m diss* 1989), Mrs Fern Diana Roberts, who *d* 1993, 2nd da of Capt E.R.S. Jackson,
RN, and formerly wife of Tim Roberts; 3rdly, 1990, Margaret Mary Doyle, and has issue living (by 1st *m*), Hugo Gerard
(The Red House, Mendham, nr Harleston, Suffolk IP20 0JD), *b* 1958: *m* 1992, Sophie eldest da of William Andrewes, of
Ludlow, Shropshire, and has issue living, Hector William *b* 1995, Oscar Constantine *b* 1997, — George Septimus, *b* 1964:
m 1997, Mrs Caroline A. M. Style, da of Anthony Sparrow, of Abinger Hammer, Surrey, and formerly wife of John
Richard Style (*see* Style, Bt, colls), — Laura Isabel Hester, *b* 1961: *m* 1984, Major Euan Glen Kelway-Bamber, SG, The
Tout, Penterry, St Arvans, Chepstow, Gwent (*see* D Devonshire, colls, 1980 Edn), and has issue living, Hamish Euan *b*
1998, Rose Olivia *b* 1987, Selina Anne *b* 1989.

Issue of late Hon Harry Nugent Morgan-Grenville, OBE, 5th son of Mary, Lady Kinloss, *b* 1896, *d* 1979:
m 1921, Mary Alice Oliphant, who *d* 1981, da of late Capt Hon Edward Oliphant Murray (*see* L Elibank,
colls):—
David Bevil MORGAN-GRENVILLE (Tamarack Farm, Sutton, Quebec, Canada), *b* 1928: *m* 1951, Nancy, who *d* 1994, el da of
late Prof Seymour Guy Martin, of Washington, DC, and has issue living, Geoffrey (310 Pine Av, Oakville, Ontario,
Canada), *b* 1956: *m* 1981, Julia Louise Newcomb, — Andrew (1243 Laurel St, Apt D, Menlo Park, Calif, USA), *b* 1967: *m*
1992, Jennifer Howard, — Sarah, *b* 1953: *m* 1981, Prof Steven Antler, of 534 Stratford St, Chicago, Illinois, USA.
—— Rosalind Mary, *b* 1933: *m* 1st, 1955 (*m diss* 1975), Maj Phillip Ivor Caleb, DFC, AFM, late USAF; 2ndly, 1976, John
Frederick Weston, of 336 Grove Court, Elkhart, Ind 46514-3060, USA, and has issue living (by 1st *m*), Caroline Mary, *b*
1956, — Penelope Frances, *b* 1963. —— Elizabeth Caroline (Moor Hill Cottage, Fovant, Salisbury, Wilts), *b* 1944: *m*
1969 (*m diss* 1981), John Kendrick Williams, CEng, MICE, and has issue living, Victoria Caroline Kendrick, *b* 1971, —
Rachael Mary Kendrick (twin), *b* 1971.

Grandsons of late Lt-Col Richard Sydney Grenville Close-Smith, OBE (infra):—
Issue of late Robert Richard Close-Smith, *b* 1936, *d* 1992: *m* 1960, Ena Mary (Ashmore Farm, Water Stratford,
Buckingham), da of Edwin Rooks, of Quinton:—
Charles Robert CLOSE-SMITH, *b* 1961: *m* 1995, Kelli A., yst da of Robert Andrew, of Atlanta, Georgia, USA.
—— Christopher Paul, *b* 1962: *m* 1989, Charlotte Nina, da of Dr William Lloyd Brace, of Woodford Green, Essex, and
has issue living, James Robert, *b* 1996, — Isobel Charlotte, (b (twin) 1996. —— Henry Richard Christian, *b* 1965.

Grandchildren of late Hon Caroline Mary Elizabeth Grenville Close-Smith (infra):—
Issue of late Lt-Col Richard Sydney Grenville Close-Smith, OBE, *b* 1910, *d* 1973: *m* 1st, 1935 (*m diss* 1954),
Baroness Florence von Ompteda, da of late Robert, Baron von Ompteda; 2ndly, 1954, (Josephine) Judith (Steart
Hill Lodge, Little Horwood, Milton Keynes, Bucks), da of Vincent Wood Mullins, and widow of Michael Bruce
Urquhart Dewar, of Stagenhoe Park, Hitchin:—
(By 1st *m*) Venice Mary Grenville, *b* 1938: *m* 1959, John Duncan Maitland Gordon-Colebrooke, of 2 Minshull Close,
Moreton Rd, Buckingham, and has issue living, James Richard Maitland, *b* 1961: *m* 1988, Wendy Jane, da of Mrs D.
Stokes, of Grenville Rd, Buckingham, — Jeremy Patrick Grenville, *b* 1963, — John Angus Childerstone, *b* 1967.

Issue of late Charles Nugent Close-Smith, TD, *b* 1911, *d* 1988: *m* 1946, (Elizabeth Emily) Vivien (The
Heymersh, Britford, Salisbury, Wilts), da of late Maj William Augustus Cecil Kinsman, DSO, OBE, late Royal
Inniskilling Fus (ret):—
Thomas William CLOSE-SMITH, *ed* Eton: *m* 1st, 1973, Lillian Moira Weston, twin da of John Weston Adamson, of Oldstead
Hall, Coxwold, York; 2ndly, 1979, Rachel M., yst da of L. D. Earp, of Priory Farmhouse, Wilmington, Sussex, and has
issue living (by 2nd *m*), James Grenville, *b* 1982, — Nicola Jane, *b* 1980, — Sophie Mary, *b* 1986. —— Anthony
Grenville, *b* 1950; *ed* Eton, and Liverpool Univ: *m* 19—, Sara, eldest da of David Breton, of 12 Thurloe Sq, SW7, and has
issue living, a da, *b* 1988. —— Edward Vivian, *b* 1951; *ed* Eton: *m* 1983, Sarah Felicity, eldest da of William Daniel
Dane, of 11 Biltmore Estates, Phoenix, Arizona, USA, and has issue living, Charles William, *b* 1987, — Samantha Vivien,
b 1984, — Caroline, *b* 1985, — Lucy, *b* 1994.

Grandson of Mary, Lady Kinloss:—
Issue of late Hon Caroline Mary Elizabeth Grenville Morgan-Grenville, *b* 1886, *d* 1972: *m* 1909, Maj Thomas
Close-Smith, who *d* 1946:—
Henry Temple CLOSE-SMITH (The Old Vicarage, Messing, Colchester, Essex), *b* 1918; assumed the additional surname of
Close; late Welsh Gds: *m* 1948, Cicely Margaret Wingfield, yr da of late Rev Eustace Hill, and has issue living, Richard
Henry, *b* 1951, — Caroline Mary, *b* 1954: *m* 1981, Jonathan Lawrence Compton, of Birch Holt, Layer Marney,

Colchester, Essex, 2nd son of A. J. A. Compton, of Petersham, Surrey, and has issue living, Edmund Alfred Henry *b* 1990, Emily Glen May *b* 1984, Rosalind Eleanor Caroline *b* 1986.

Descendants of late Lady Anne Eliza Mary, da of 2nd Duke of Buckingham and Chandos, *b* 1820, *d* 1879: *m* 1846, William Henry Powell Gore-Langton, MP, who *d* 1873 (*see* E Temple of Stowe).

PREDECESSORS – (1) *Rt Hon Sir* EDWARD Bruce, a Lord of Session 1597-1603, accompanied King James to England on his accession 1603, was naturalized that year, and appointed Master of the Rolls for life; received charter of Kinloss with title of *Lord Kinloss* (peerage of Scotland) 1602, with remainder to his heirs and assigns and *cr Lord Bruce of Kinloss* (peerage of Scotland) 1604, with remainder to his heirs male whatsoever, and later (1608) with remainder to heirs male of the body, failing whom to heirs and assigns *d* 1610; *s* by his el son (2) EDWARD, KG 2nd Lord; killed in a duel 1613; *s* by his brother (3) THOMAS, 3rd Lord; *cr Earl of Elgin* (peerage of Scotland) 1633, with remainder to heirs male whatever bearing the name and arms of Bruce, and *Baron Bruce*, of Whorlton, co York (peerage of England) 1640, (4—6) in which title the Lordship of Kinloss was merged until the death of the 6th Earl of Elgin in 1746, when it devolved (in accordance with the subsequent decision of the House of Lords) on (7) JAMES, 3rd Duke of Chandos, as *de jure* 7th Lord Kinloss; at his death his da (8) ANNA ELIZA (Duchess of Buckingham and Chandos) became *de jure* Lady Kinloss, and her son (9) RICHARD PLANTAGENET (Duke of Buckingham and Chandos) *de jure* 9th Lord Kinloss; in 1868 his son (10) RICHARD PLANTAGENET CAMPBELL Temple-Nugent-Brydges-Chandos-Grenville, GCSI, CIE, PC, DCL, 3rd Duke of Buckingham and Chandos (*see* V Cobham), established his right to the title as 10th Lord Kinloss, *b* 1823; Chm of Committees and Dep Speaker in House of Lords: *m* 1st, 1851, Caroline, who *d* 1874, da of Robert Harvey, of Langley Park, Bucks; 2ndly, 1885, Alice Anne, who *d* 1931, el da of Sir Graham Graham-Montgomery, 3rd Bt; *d* 1889; *s* by his el da (11) MARY Morgan, *b* 1852: *m* 1884, Luis Ferdinand Harry Courthope Morgan, of Biddlesden Park, Bucks, who *d* 1896 (having assumed by Roy licence the additional surname and arms of Grenville 1890): *d* 1944; *s* by her grand-daughter (12) BEATRICE MARY GRENVILLE, el da of late Rev Hon Luis Chandos Francis Temple Morgan-Grenville (*Master of Kinloss*), 2nd and el surviving son of Mary, Lady Kinloss, present holder of the title.

KINNAIRD, LORD (Kinnaird) (Dormant or Extinct 1997)

DAUGHTERS LIVING OF THIRTEENTH LORD

Hon Caroline, *b* 1949: *m* 1st, 1970 (*m diss* 1986), Christopher Wigan (*see* B Faringdon, colls, 1995 Edn); 2ndly, 1986, James Douglas Best, and has had issue (by 1st *m*), George Rowan, *b* 1977; *d* 1998, in Goa, India, — Leila Willow, *b* 1974: *m* 1997, Henry P. Hope-Frost, — (by 2nd *m*) Samuel Douglas, *b* 1987, — Arthur Jack, *b* 1989. *Residence* – Rossie Priory, Inchture, Perthshire PH14 9SG.

Hon Anna, *b* 1952: *m* 1988 (*m diss* 19—), Edward Henry Liddell, and has issue (*see* B Ravensworth, colls). *Residence* – Heneford Mill, Chetnoble, Sherborne, Dorset DT9 6PE.

Hon Susan, *b* 1956: *m* 1987, Francis Rupert Chad Lea (*see* Lea, Bt).

Hon Mary Clare, *b* 1960: *m* 1988, Jonn C. Staib, only son of late Edward Staib, of Las Palmas, Canary Is, and of the Dowager Countess of Dundonald, and has issue living, James Alexander Christian, *b* 1990, — Annabel Mary, *b* 1992. *Residence* – Speeds Farm, Lamyatt, Somerset.

DAUGHTER LIVING OF TWELFTH LORD

Hon Madeline Elisabeth, *b* 1908: *m* 1929, Rt Rev Hugh Rowlands Gough, CMG, OBE, TD, DD, Archbishop of Sydney and Primate of Australia 1959-66, who *d* 1997, and has issue living, Lucy (*Baroness Swansea*), *b* 1931: *m* 1st, 1959 (*m diss* 1971), Harold Mervyn Temple-Richards (*see* Temple, Bt, colls, 1990 Edn); 2ndly, 1983, as his 2nd wife, 4th Baron Swansea, and has a da (from 1st *m*), Olivia Merielle Lucy *b* 1964: *m* 1991, Timothy C. Heywood, elder son of Christopher Heywood, Berwickshire, SW20. *Residence* – 17 Cheyne Gdns, SW3.

WIDOW LIVING OF THIRTEENTH LORD

DIANA MARGARET ELIZABETH (*Lady Kinnaird*), yr da of late Robert Shuckburgh Copeman, of Roydon Hall, Diss, Norfolk: *m* 1940, as his 2nd wife, the 13th Lord Kinnaird, who *d* 1997. *Residences* – The Garden House, Rossie Estate, Inchture, Perthshire PH14 9SG.

KINNOULL, EARL OF (Hay) (Earl S 1633)

Renew your courage

ARTHUR WILLIAM GEORGE PATRICK HAY, 15th Earl; *b* 26 March 1935; *s* 1938; *ed* Eton; FRICS; a Member of Agricultural Valuers' Assocn; a Member, Queen's Body Guard for Scotland (Royal Company of Archers) since 1965; Pres of National Council on Inland Transport 1964-76, Junior Conservative Whip, House of Lords 1966-68; Pres of Scottish Clans Assocn 1970; Vice-Pres of Nat Assocn of Parish Councils 1971-83; a Dir of Property Owners' Building Soc 1972 (Chm 1979); Snr Partner, Langley-Taylor Chartered Surveyors; Mem British Delegation, Council of Europe 1983; Council Mem, R Nat Mission to Deep Sea Fishermen 1978: *m* 1961, Gay Ann, elder da of Sir Denys Colquhoun Flowerdew Lowson, 1st Bt, and has issue.

Arms – Quarterly: 1st and 4th grand quarters counterquartered, 1st and 4th azure, an unicorn salient argent, armed, maned, and unguled or, within a bordure of the last, charged with eight half thistles vert, and as many half roses gules joined together per pale as a coat of augmentation, *Kinnoull*; 2nd and 3rd argent, three escutcheons two and one gules, *Hay*; 2nd and 3rd grand quarters counterquartered 1st and 4th or, three bars wavy gules, surmounted of a scimitar in pale argent, *Drummond*; 2nd and 3rd or, a lion's head erased within a double tressure flory counterflory gules, a coat of augmentation, *Strathallan.* Crest – A countryman, couped at the knees, vested grey, his waistcoat gules and bonnet azure, bearing on his right shoulder an ox yoke proper. Supporters – Two countrymen habited as in the crest, the *dexter* holding over his shoulder the coulter, and the *sinister* the paddle of a plough proper.
Residences – 15 Carlyle Sq, SW3; Pier House, Seaview, Isle of Wight. *Clubs* – Lansdowne, Turf, Pratt's, White's, and MCC.

SON LIVING

CHARLES WILLIAM HARLEY (*Viscount Dupplin*), *b* 20 Dec 1962, *ed* Eton, and Ch Ch Oxford; Bar Middle Temple 1990; Atholl Highlander. *Residences* – 59 Scarsdale Villas, W8; Pitkindie House, Abernyte, Perthshire. *Clubs* – White's, Turf, MCC.

DAUGHTERS LIVING

Lady Melissa Ann, *b* 1964.
Lady Iona Charlotte, *b* 1967: *m* 1997, Charles T. M. Ind, eldest son of Dr John Ind, of Chelsea, SW3.
Lady Atalanta Rose, *b* 1974.

SISTERS LIVING

Lady Venetia Constance Kathleen Luz, *b* 1929: *m* 1953, Maj Joseph Trevor Davies, who *d* 1992, and has issue living, Nicola Jane, *b* 1957, — Sally May, *b* 1960: *m* 1992, A. Mark Fairbanks Smith, of 10 Milton Mansions, Queen's Club Gdns, W14 9RP, and has issue living, Charles Joseph *b* 1994, Hetty Alexandra *b* 1997. *Residence* – 14 Old School Court, Grimston Gdns, Folkestone, Kent CT20 2UA.
Lady June Anne (*Baroness Onslow of Woking*), *b* 1932: *m* 1955, Baron Onslow of Woking, KCMG, PC (Life Baron), and has issue. *Residence* – Highbuilding, Fernhurst, Sussex.

GREAT-AUNT LIVING (*Daughter of 13th Earl*)

Lady Elizabeth Blanche Mary, *b* 1903: *m* 1st, 1925 (*m diss* 1935), Peter Stanley Chappell; 2ndly, 1935 (*m diss* 1945), Douglas William Ernest Gordon, who *d* 1951; 3rdly, 1945, William H. S. Dent, MC, and has issue living, (by 1st *m*) Michael Stanley Fitzroy (760 Grover Av, Coquitlam, New Westminster, BC, Canada), *b* 1926: *m* 1952, Eileen Day, of Vancouver, Canada

COLLATERAL BRANCHES LIVING

Descendants of late Capt Edward William Auriol Drummond-Hay, son of late Very Rev Edward Auriol Hay-Drummond, DD, Dean of Bocking, brother of 10th Earl:—

Granddaughers of late Rev Frederic Drummond-Hay, elder son of late Sir Edward Hay Drummond-Hay, elder son of late Capt Edward William Auriol Drummond-Hay (ante):—
Issue of late Robert Drummond-Hay, *b* 1870, *d* 1907: *m* 1895, Gertrude Agatha, who *d* 1924, da of Thomas Forbutt:—

Barbara May Gertrude, b 1904: m 1938, Peter Drummond-Hay, of New Wing, Nerina Gdns, Recreation Rd, Fish Hoek 7975, CP, S Africa, son of James Chapman Drummond-Hay, and has issue living, Peter James Robert, b 1939, — Anthony John Blackwood, b 1940, — Errol David Joseph, b 1944, — Christopher Ian, b 1945. — Michael Kevin, b 1946, — Fiona Mary, b 1942. —— Veronica Florence Muriel Aileen, b 1907: m 1926, Alfred Camacho, who d 1964, and has issue living, Margaret Mary, b 1928, — Sheila Mary, b 1930.

Grandchildren of late Robert Drummond-Hay (b 1870) (ante):—

Issue of late Ernest Patrick Hay, b 1900, d 1988; discontinued use of surname Drummond: m 1930, Elsie May Baldwin, who d 1973, formerly of Leytonstone, London:—
Kenneth John HAY, b 1932: m 1951, Rita Edith, da of late Fred Barton, of Wembley, Middx, and has issue living, Roberta Elaine, b 1956: m 1978 (m diss 1984), Martin William Long, and has issue living, Christopher Ross LONG b 1981, and further issue (by John Covill, of Fern Lea, Natland Green, Kendal, Cumbria), Sam COVILL b 1988. Residence - 18 Esthwaite Av, Heron Hill, Kendal, Cumbria LA9 7NN. —— Shirley Patricia, b 1935: m 1954, Peter William Johnson, and has issue living, Garry Daniel, b 1955: m 1981, Maureen, da of Kevin O'Shea, and has issue living, James Christopher b 1982, Sarah Jane b 1984, — Aileen Denise, b 1959. Residence - 41 Buderim Pines Drive, Buderim, Queensland 4556, Australia.

Issue of late Geoffrey Francis Drummond-Hay, b 1898, d 1992: m 1936, Margaret Fenlon, who d 1959:—

Peter (Grange Garden, Flowers Hill, Pangbourne, Berks) b 1943: m 1st, 1966 (m diss 1972), Carolyn Macdonald, of Wichita, Kansas, USA; 2ndly, 1972, Celia Humphris, and has issue living (by 1st m), Samantha, b 1966, — (by 2nd m) Luke, b 1974. —— Alison, b 1946: m 1968, Keith Wills, of Les Virboulain, Mondonbleau, Loir et Cher, France, and has issue living, Alexander, b 1972, — Jake, b 1974.

Grandchildren of late Sir Robert Hay-Drummond-Hay, CMG, son of late Rt Hon Sir John Hay Drummond-Hay, GCMG, KCB, yr son of late Capt Edward William Auriol Drummond-Hay (ante):—

Issue of late Edward William Hay-Drummond-Hay, b 1877, d 1941: m 1904, Margaret Alice, who d 1954, da of late E. W. Meade-Waldo, of Stonewall Park, and Hever Castle, Kent:—
John Waldo Edward HAY-DRUMMOND-HAY, TD, b 1906; ed Marlborough, and at Trin Coll Camb; Major (ret), Queen's Own Roy W Kent Regt (TA), and attached Indian Army: m 1st, 1937, Anne Rachel, who d 1975, da of W. T. Prideaux, of Elderslie, Ockley; 2ndly, 1976, Mrs Jennifer Roosen, who d 1989, da of Bostock-Wilson, and has issue living (by 1st m), Robert Prideaux (Barrow Hill Cottage, 25 Mixbury, Brackley, Northants NN13 5RR), b 1941; ed Eton: m 1965, Sally Catherine, da of Ian Redfern, of Winchester, and has issue living, (Robert) Simon (Fawler Mill, nr Charlbury, Oxon) b 1967: m 1991, Julia E., da of John Roberts, of Cowbridge, S Glamorgan (and has issue living, Edward John b 1994, Auriol Sophia b 1996), Katherine Louise b 1973, Caroline Sarah b 1974, — Peter Charles Hay DRUMMOND-HAY (86 Rowayton Av, Rowayton, Connecticut 06853, USA; Le Pestou, Castelsagrat, France), b 1948; ed Eton, and Trin Coll, Camb; assumed 1975 the surname of Drummond Hay in place of Hay-Drummond-Hay and the christian name of Hay: m 1975, Lady Bettina Mary Lindsay, da of the 29th Earl of Crawford, and 12th Earl of Balcarres, KT, and has issue living, Thomas Auriol Leo b 1989, Tamsin Rachel b 1977, Alice Ruth b 1980, Lily Iona b 1983, — Auriol Marion, b 1946: m 1st, 1968 (m diss 1994), Donald Alvin Hessemer; 2ndly, 1995, Jeffrey Kennedy Mann, of Kentallen Farm, 212 Highway 213, Calera, Alabama 35040, USA. Residence - The Oaks, Swainham Lane, St Leonards-on-Sea, E Sussex TN38 8ED.

Issue of late Cecil Lawrence Hay-Drummond-Hay, b 1882, d 1952: m 1st, 1911 (m diss 1924), Jessie, who d 1961, yr twin da of late Lawrence Munro; 2ndly 1925, Doris Rachel, who d 1971, da of late Dudley Hill, of Christchurch, NZ:—

(By 2nd m) Annette Alistair, b 1927: m 1948 (m diss 1977), David Stanford, and has issue living, Matthew Bedell, b 1951, — Jonathan David, b 1953, — Giles Timothy, b 1961, — Anna Bethell, b 1949, — Charlotte Sylvia b 1963.

Grandchildren of Humphry Ringler Drummond-Hay, eldest son of late Charles Drummond-Hay (b 1856), eldest son of late Col Thomas Robert Hay Drummond-Hay, 3rd son of late Capt Edward William Auriol Drummond-Hay (ante):—

Issue of late George Thomson Drummond-Hay, b 1916, d 1983: m 1st, 1939 (m diss 1949), Elizabeth Barbara Fraser, of Regina; 2ndly, 1949 (m diss 1960), Mrs Adrienne Ruth Russell, da of John William Southin, of Vancouver, BC; 3rdly, 1964, Mrs Shirlee Montgomery, da of Harry J. Gibbons, of Sioux City, Iowa, USA:—
(By 1st m) Elizabeth Sandra, b 1945. —— (By 2nd m) Eric Thomson (10 Trumbull Court, Novato, California 94947, USA), b 1951: m 1981, Mary Elizabeth, da of Sherwin Ray Murry, and has issue living, Charles Thomson, b 1987, — Anne Elizabeth, b 1985. —— Charles Webster (4616 SE Roethe 78, Milwaukie, Oregon, 97267 USA), b 1952. —— Leslie Katherine, b 1954.

Grandchildren of late Harold Sanford Drummond-Hay (infra):—

Issue of late Charles Robert Drummond-Hay, late Fl-Lt RCAF, b 1917, d 1966: m 1940, Ina Mary, da of late George H. Disbrow, of Vancouver:—
Humphrey Blake, b 1945. —— Brian Maxwell, b 1947. —— Lee Sanford, b 1950. —— Jane Macpherson, b 1953: m 1990, David Alexander Saba, of 3005 West 29th St, Vancouver, BC, Canada V6L 1Y5, son of late Clarence Saba, of Vancouver, BC, Canada.

Granddaughter of late Charles Drummond-Hay (b 1856) (ante):—

Issue of late Harold Sanford Drummond-Hay, b 1890, d 1951: m 1915, Effie Caldwell, who d 1964, da of late Robert Adamson, of Winnipeg:—
Jeanette (Jean) Audrey, b 1919.

Grandchildren of late Sir Francis Ringler Drummond-Hay, 5th son of late Capt Edward William Auriol Drummond-Hay (ante):—

Issue of late Francis Edward Drummond-Hay, MVO, b 1868, d 1943: m 1895, Eveline Austey, MBE, who d 1963, da of late Rev Edmund Thomas Bennett, formerly R of Littleton, Winchester, of Castle Roe, co Londonderry:—
Claude Francis, b 1898; ed Cheltenham Coll; 1915-18 War in Salonika and France as Capt Black Watch (R Highlanders): m 1st, 1921, (m diss 1928), Gladys Grant; 2ndly, 1933, Ellenor, da of late G. Carlin, of Cleadon Meadows, Cleadon, Durham; 3rdly, 1957, Mrs Gladys Beatrice Robinson, of Babbacombe Cliffs, Torquay, and has issue living, (by 2nd m)

John Francis (44 Inanda Rd, Hillcrest, Natal), *b* 1938: *m* 1961, Beverley Ann, da of Francis Howes, of Hillcrest, Natal, and has issue living, Sean Francis *b* 1962, Deborah Joan *b* 1963, — Jeffrey Derrick Edward, *b* 1943, — Joan, *b* 1935.

Issue of late Frederick William Drummond-Hay, *b* 1870, *d* 1923: *m* 1st, 1894, Ellen Marion, who *d* 1896, da of late Major Charles Johnson Anthony Deane, Indian Army; 2ndly, 1905, Louise Agnes Burke, who *d* 1920, da of Denis Comerford, of co Tipperary:—
(By 2nd *m*) Rita O'Brien, *b* 1906: *m* 1932 (*m diss* 1954), Arthur Harly Whitcomb, and has issue living, Cheyne, *b* 1933, — Brenda, *b* 1935.

PREDECESSORS – (1) *Sir* GEORGE HAY, KB; was successively a Gentleman of the Bedchamber, and Clerk Register of Scotland, and Lord High Chancellor of Scotland 1622-34; *cr Viscount Dupplin* and *Lord Hay of Kinfauns* (peerage of Scotland) 1627, with remainder to the heirs male of his body, and *Earl of Kinnoull, Viscount Dupplin,* and *Lord Hay of Kinfauns* with remainder to his heirs male (peerage of Scotland) 1633; *d* 1634; *s* by his son (2) GEORGE, PC, 2nd Earl; Capt of Yeomen of the Guard; *d* 1644; *s* by his el son (3) GEORGE, 3rd Earl, of whom "The Scots Peerage," published 1908, says "is not given by the Peerage writers, but there is undoubted evidence for his existence"; *d* about 1650; *s* by his brother (4) WILLIAM, 4th Earl; became in 1660 proprietor of the Island of Barbados, and in 1661 disposed of it to Charles II; during the Civil Wars was taken by the Republicans and committed to Edinburgh Castle whence he escaped 1654, and in Nov of that year was made prisoner by the English; *d* 1677; *s* by his el son (5) GEORGE, 5th Earl; *d* 1687; *s* by his brother (6) WILLIAM, 6th Earl; *d* 1709; after resignation received a re-grant of his honours in 1704, with remainder to his kinsman Thomas, Viscount Dupplin, and heirs male of his body, whom failing to his heirs of tailzie and provision; *s* by the said (7) THOMAS, 7th Earl, great-grandson of Peter Hay, yr brother of 1st Earl; MP for Perthshire 1693-7; had been *cr Viscount Dupplin* (peerage of Scotland) 1697 with remainder to heirs male of his body, whom failing to his heirs of entail; imprisoned in Edinburgh Castle 1715 on breaking out of rebellion; *d* 1719; *s* by his son (8) GEORGE HENRY, 8th Earl, who had in 1711 been *cr Baron Hay,* of Pedwardine, co Hereford (peerage of Great Britain) *d* 1758; *s* by his son (9) THOMAS, 9th Earl; *dsp* 1787; *s* by his nephew (10) ROBERT HAY-DRUMMOND, PC, 10th Earl, son of the Most Rev the Hon Robert Hay-Drummond, Archbishop of York, 2nd son of 8th Earl; assumed for himself the additional surname of Drummond; was Lord Lyon King of Arms; *d* 1804; *s* by his el son (11) THOMAS ROBERT, 11th Earl; *b* 1785; was Lord-Lieut of Perthshire, and Lyon King of Arms: *m* 1824, Louisa Burton, who *d* 1885, da of Adm Sir Charles Rowley, GCB, 1st Bt; *d* 1866; *s* by his el son (12) GEORGE, 12th Earl, *b* 1827: *m* 1848, Lady Emily Blanche Charlotte Somerset, who *d* 1895, da of 7th Duke of Beaufort, KG; *d* 1897; *s* by his el surviving son (13) ARCHIBALD FITZROY GEORGE, 13th Earl; *b* 1855; served with late Baker Pasha, as Ch of his Staff during Campaign on Red Sea: *m* 1st, 1879 (judicially separated 1885), Josephine Maria, who *d* 1900, da of late John Hawke, solicitor, of Burlington Gardens, W; 2ndly, 1903, Florence Mary, who *d* 1941 (having *m* 2ndly, 1919, Major John Joseph Berington, RMA), da of late Edward Tierney Gilchrist Darell; *d* 1916; *s* by his grandson (14) GEORGE HARLEY (only surviving son of late Capt Edmund Alfred Rollo George, Viscount Dupplin, el son of 13th Earl), 14th Earl, *b* 1902: *m* 1st, 1923 (*m diss* 1927), Enid Margaret Hamlyn, only child of Major Ernest Gaddesden Fellows; 2ndly, 1928, Mary Ethel Isobel, who *d* 1938, da of late Ferdinand Richard Holmes Meyrick, MD, of 59 Kensington Court, W8; *d* 1938; *s* by his 3rd but only surviving son (15) ARTHUR WILLIAM GEORGE PATRICK, 15th Earl, and present peer; also Viscount Dupplin, Lord Hay of Kinfauns, and Baron Hay of Pedwardine.

Kinrara, Earl of March and; son of Duke of Richmond.

KINROSS, BARON (Balfour) (Baron UK 1902)

Nothing rashly

CHRISTOPHER PATRICK BALFOUR, 5th Baron, *b* 1 Oct 1949; *s* 1985; *ed* Eton, St Andrew's Univ, and Edinburgh Univ (LLB); WS: *m* 1974, Susan Jane, da of Ian Robert Pitman, WS, and has issue.

𝕬rms – Ermine, on a chevron sable between in chief two torteaux and in base an open book, an otter's head proper. 𝕮rest – On a rock a mermaid holding in the dexter hand an otter's head erased, and in the sinister a swan's head erased, all proper. 𝕾upporters – On either side an otter proper, charged on the shoulder with two swords saltirewise, also proper. *Residence* – 11 Belford Pl, Edinburgh.

SONS LIVING

Hon ALAN IAN, *b* 4 April 1978.
Hon Derek Andrew, *b* 1981.

HALF SISTER LIVING (*daughter of 4th Baron by 1st m*)

Hon Ariadne Maria (2 Halesden Rd, Heaton Chapel, Stockport, Cheshire), *b* 1939: *m* 1961 (*m diss* 1990), Richard Elliot

Nicholson, yr son of late Robert Watson Nicholson, of Newcastle-upon-Tyne, and has issue living, Robert David, *b* 1964, — Matthew Charles, *b* 1968, — Edward Alan, *b* 1971, — Camilla Jane, *b* 1962.

AUNT LIVING (daughter of 2nd Baron)

Hon Ursula Nina, *b* 1914: *m* 1939, Col Christopher James York Dallmeyer, DSO and bar, WS, Lothian and Border Horse Yeo, who *d* 1996, and has issue living, Gavin Richard James (Craigiewood, N Kessock, by Inverness IV1 1XG), *b* 1942: *m* 1970, Araminta Morgan and has issue living, Thomas Charles *b* 1979, Flora Jane *b* 1975, — Andrew Victor (2 Rosevale Terrace, Edinburgh 6), *b* 1945: *m* 1969, Vivienne Dixon, and has issue living, Tobias *b* 1973, Amy Jane Eleanor *b* 1985, — James, *b* 1948: *m* 1978, Margherita Elizabeth Dimambro, — Rosemary Nina *b* 1940: *m* 1962, Rev Paul Roderick Nicolson, of The Vicarage, Turville, nr Henley-on-Thames, Oxon, and *d* 1995, leaving issue, Roderick John *b* 1962, Hugo James *b* 1965, Thomas Paul *b* 1966, Claire Katherine *b* 1968, Kristina Belle *b* 1975. *Residence* – Green Corner, Tyninghame, Dunbar, E Lothian.

WIDOW LIVING OF FOURTH BARON

RUTH BEVERLEY *(Dowager Baroness Kinross)*, da of late William Henry Mill, SSC, of Edinburgh, and formerly wife of Kenneth William Bruce Middleton, Sheriff of Lothian and Borders at Edinburgh and Haddington: *m* 1972, as his 3rd wife, the 4th Baron Kinross, OBE, TD, who *d* 1985. *Residence* – 58 India St, Edinburgh.

COLLATERAL BRANCH LIVING

Issue of late Hon Harry Robert Chichester Balfour, 4th son of 1st Baron, *b* 1882, *d* 1964: *m* 1921, Dorothy Constance, who *d* 1963, da of late Henry Goulburn Willoughby Chetwynd (V Chetwynd, colls):—
Anthony John Chetwynd, CBE (Cymbeline, Ellesborough Rd, Wendover, Bucks; Leander Club), *b* 1926; *ed* Eton, and at King's Coll, Camb (MA, MB, BChir); Consultant in Pathology, RAF Med Branch; FRCPath; Air Commodore (ret) RAF; CBE (Mil) 1987: *m* 1958, Judith Ann Margaret, yr da of Leslie Field Anderson, of Pines Av, Worthing, and has issue living, Peter John Torquil, *b* 1959; BSc, MB, ChB (Birmingham): *m* 1st, 1985 (*m diss* 1987), Nicola Jane, da of David Charles Yarwood, of Mount Sorel, Leics; 2ndly, 1994 (*m diss* 1996), Patricia, da of Jerome Dawson, of Orangefield Gdns, Belfast, — Harry Luke Chetwynd, *b* 1963, — Helena Clare, *b* 1961; SRN: *m* 1989, John Trevor Eades, of Wimbledon, and has issue living, Louis John Frederick *b* 1991, Jack Edward Luke *b* 1993, David Harry Robert *b* 1995. —— Hilary Joan Gwendolen (1 The Maisonettes, Icknield Rd, Goring-on-Thames, nr Reading, Berks), *b* 1924.

PREDECESSORS – (1) JOHN BLAIR Balfour, son of Rev P. Balfour, Min of Clackmannan; Solicitor-Gen for Scotland April 1880 to Aug 1881, and Lord-Advocate Aug 1881 to June 1885, Feb to July 1886, and Aug 1892 to June 1895; MP for Clackmannan and Kinross-shire (*L*) Nov, 1880 to Nov 1899, when he became Lord Justice-General for Scotland (with judicial title of *Lord Blair Balfour*); *cr* a PC 1883, and *Baron Kinross*, of Glasclune, co Haddington (peerage of United Kingdom) 1902: *m* 1st, 1869, Lilias Oswald, who *d* 1872, da of late Hon Lord Mackenzie, a Lord of Session; 2ndly, 1877, Hon Marianne Eliza, who *d* 1913, da of 1st Baron Moncreiff: *d* 1905; *s* by his el son (2) PATRICK, KC, 2nd Baron; *b* 1870; a Brigadier, Roy Co of Archers (King's Body Guard for Scotland); Sheriff of Dumfries and Galloway, 1927-39: *m* 1903, Caroline Elsie, who *d* 1969, da of late Arthur Henry Johnstone-Douglas (M Queensberry); *d* 1939; *s* by his son (3) JOHN PATRICK DOUGLAS, 3rd Baron, *b* 1904; Author and Journalist; Sqdn-Ldr RAFVR: *m* 1938 (*m diss* 1942), Angela Mary, da of late Capt George Culme-Seymour (Culme-Seymour, Bt, colls); *d* 1976; *s* by his brother (4) DAVID ANDREW, OBE, TD, 4th Baron, *b* 1906; Col RA (TA); a Member of Queen's Body Guard for Scotland (R Co of Archers); Hon Col 27th (Lowland) Field Regt, City of Edinburgh Artillery; a DL for City of Edinburgh; Chm British Legion, Scotland, 1965-68; Vice-Chm RA Council for Scotland; 1939-45 War in UK and Burma: *m* 1st, 1936 (*m diss* 1941), Araminta, da of late Lt-Col Willoughby Ewart Peel, DSO (*see* Hunter-Blair, colls, 1966 Edn); 2ndly, 1948, Helen Anne, who *d* 1969, da of late Alan Welwood Hog, of Edinburgh, and formerly wife of Lt-Col Patrick Cassan Perfect; 3rdly, 1972, Ruth Beverley, da of late William Henry Mill, of Edinburgh; *d* 1985; *s* by his only son (5) CHRISTOPHER PATRICK, 5th Baron and present peer.

KINTORE, EARL OF (Keith) (Earl S 1677)

MICHAEL CANNING WILLIAM JOHN KEITH, 13th Earl and 4th Baronet; *b* 22 Feb 1939; *s* 1989; *ed* Eton, and RMA Sandhurst; late Lieut Coldstream Guards: *m* 1972, Mary, only da of late Sqdn Ldr Elisha Gaddis Plum, of Rumson, NJ, USA, and has issue.

Arms – Quarterly; 1st and 4th, argent on a chief, gules three pallets or, *Keith*; 2nd, azure, a falcon displayed between three mullets argent, on his breast a man's heart gules, *Falconer of Halkerton*; 3rd, per pale engrailed gules and or, a boar passant counterchanged, *Baird of Ury*; over all, on an inescutcheon gules, a sceptre and sword in saltire with an Imperial Crown between the upper corners all proper, within an orle of eight thistles slipped near the head or, ensigned with an Earl's coronet (*being the Coat of Augmentation granted to John, 1st Earl of Kintore, for his services in the preservation of the Regalia of Scotland*). **Crests** – *Dexter*, a noble lady from the middle richly attired, holding in her right hand a garland proper (*Crest of Augmentation for Earldom of Kintore*); *Sinister*, a roebuck's head proper, attired or, *Keith*. **Supporters** – Two men in complete armour proper, each holding a spear gules banded argent, in posture of sentinels.
Seat – Keith Hall, Inverurie, Aberdeenshire.

SON LIVING

JAMES WILLIAM FALCONER (*Lord Inverurie, Master of Kintore*), *b* 15 April 1976; *ed* Gordonstoun.

DAUGHTER LIVING

Lady Iona Delia Mary Gaddis, *b* 1978.

BROTHER LIVING

Hon Alexander David BAIRD, *b* 1946; *ed* Tabley House. *Residence* – 3 Osterley Crescent, Isleworth, Middx.

SISTER LIVING

Lady Diana Elizabeth Virginia Sydney, *b* 1937: *m* 1957, John Francis Holman, OBE, of Rickarton House, Stonehaven, Kincardineshire, and 6 St Luke's St, SW3 3RS (*see* By Trent, 1985 Edn), and has issue living, Richard Ian HOLMAN-BAIRD, (Glenton House, Rickarton, Stonehaven, Kincardineshire AB39 3TD), *b* 1958: *m* 1st, 1985, Saragh, who *d* 1987, only da of late Maj Robert Wood, of Sycamore House, Glassonby, Penrith, Cumbria; 2ndly, 1996, Polly Sophia, da of late Angus Thomson, of Ansdell Terr, Kensington, W8, and has issue living, (by 1st *m*) Louise Saragh *b* 1986, (by 2nd *m*), Angus John *b* 1997, Amelia Jo *b* 1998, — Edward Alexander, *b* 1960, — Georgina Mary, *b* 1962: *m* 1989, Charles Stirrup, eldest son of John Stirrup, of Simon's Town, S Africa, and has issue living, William John *b* 1992, Timothy Charles *b* 1994, Isabelle Diana *b* 1997, — Emma Charlotte, *b* 1966: *m* 1990, Ben Charles Cole, elder son of Anthony Brian Cole of Staplecross, Sussex, and has issue living, Patrick James *b* 1994, Sophie Charlotte *b* 1992.

AUNTS LIVING (*daughters of (Ethel) Sydney, Countess of Kintore*)

Lady Ariel Olivia Winifred, CVO, *b* 1916; appointed Lady-in-Waiting to HRH Princess Alice, Countess of Athlone 1940: *m* 1946 (*m diss* 1958), Sir Kenneth Alexander Keith, late Lt-Col WG (later Baron Keith of Castleacre), and has issue (see that title). *Residence* – 16 Melton Court, Old Brompton Rd, SW7 3JQ.
Lady (Hilda) Ava Fiona Nancy, *b* 1919: *m* 1945, Lt-Col Ronald Fulton Lucas Chance, MC, King's Roy Rifle Corps, who *d* 1996, and has issue living, Nicholas John Lucas (Caulcott House, Caulcott, Oxon OX6 3NE), *b* 1946; JP N Oxford 1985: *m* 1975, Anne Heather Gard, only da of late Maj J. E. V. Rice, of Exhurst Manor, Staplehurst, Kent, and has issue living, Alexander *b* 1978, Hugo *b* 1980, Sophia *b* 1984, — Louise Annette *b* 1950: *m* 1976, Edward Alexander Goschen, son of Maj Sir Edward Christian Goschen, 3rd Bt, DSO, and has issue living (*see* Goschen, Bt). *Residence* – 2 Abbot's Gdns, Malmesbury, Wilts SN16 9HY.

WIDOW LIVING OF TWELFTH EARL

DELIA (*Delia, Countess of Kintore*), da of late William Lewis Brownlow Loyd, of Upper House, Shamley Green, Guildford (*see* B Brabourne, 1967 Edn): *m* 1935, the 12th Earl of Kintore, who *d* 1989. *Residence* – 16 Garden Wood, Inchmarlo, Banchory, Kincardineshire AB3 4AW.

COLLATERAL BRANCHES LIVING

Issue of late Sqdn-Ldr Hon (Robert Alexander) Greville BAIRD, RAF, 2nd son of 1st Viscount Stonehaven and (Ethel) Sydney, Countess of Kintore, *b* 1910, *ka* 1943: *m* 1939, Dorviegelda Malvina, who *d* 1997, having *m* 2ndly, 1947, Sqdn-Ldr Algernon Ivan Sladen, DSO, who *d* 1976, late RAF (E Dunmore), da of Alexander Ronald MacGregor (*see* MacGregor, Bt, *cr* 1795):—

†Alaisdair Aulin John, *b* 1942, lost at sea 1962. —— Ceanan Donald (Coxmoor Farm, Crondall, Farnham, Surrey GU10 5RT), *b* (*posthumous*) 1943: *m* 1973, Janet Mary, da of Donald R. Scott, and has issue living, Hamish Duncan, *b* 1975, — Amanda Louisa, *b* 1977. —— Rinalda Malvina, *b* 1940: *m* 1963, Col David Henry Sandford Leslie Maitland-Titterton, late 9th/12th R Lancers, of Rimes Gigot, Rhymes Lane, Baughurst, Basingstoke (*see* E Lauderdale, colls, 1985 Edn), and has issue living, Rupert Seymour Aulin Leslie, *b* 1965: *m* 1995, Sarah Louise, da of Anthony Mason, of Wickham, Hants, and has issue living, Toby Cleland Leslie *b* 1997, — Shân Gelda Jane, *b* 1967: *m* 1994, (Timothy) Giles Redpath, only son of Trevor Redpath, of Headbourne Worthy Grange, Winchester, and has issue living, Lily Jemima *b* 1996, Imogen Nella *b* 1998.

Granddaughters of late Lady Blanche Catherine Keith-Falconer (who *m* 1883, Col Granville Roland Francis Smith, CVO, CB), da of the 8th Earl of Kintore:—
Issue of late Granville Keith-Falconer Smith, *b* 1886, *d* 1914: *m* 1910, Lady Kathleen Clements, who *d* 1975, having *m* 2ndly, 1919, Cdr Ronald Granville Studd, DSO, RN, who *d* 1956 (Studd, Bt), da of the 4th Earl of Leitrim:—
Rosemary Winifred, *b* 1912. *Residence* – Thatchers, Princes Risborough, Bucks. —— Merial Kathleen, *b* 1914. *Residence* – Postboys, Stoke by Nayland, Colchester, Essex.

Grandchildren of late Rev Roland Audley Smith, 2nd son of late Lady Blanche Catherine Smith (ante):—
Issue of late Granville Roland Smith, *b* 1919, *d* 1984: *m* 1st, 1944, Aimée Rosemary Patricia, who *d* 1963, only da of late George Henry Preston Moore-Browne, of Port Stewart Castle, co Derry, and formerly wife of Dr John Forbes; 2ndly, 1965, Margaret Clare (40 Raynham St, Hertford, Herts), da of Daniel Coonan, of Tenterfield, NSW:—
(By 1st *m*) Rachael Margaret Pleasance ROLAND SMITH, *b* 1944, *Residence* – 15 Flaghill Cottages, Great Bentley, Colchester, Essex.

Issue of late Samuel Erskine Roland Smith, *b* 1924, *d* 1963: *m* 1948, Margaret Anne, who *d* 1990, el da of Brig John Eric Chippindall, CBE, MC, of 11 The Royal Cres, Bath:—
Amanda Jane ROLAND SMITH, *b* 1951; has retained her maiden name: *m* 1986, Stephen Ireland, of Forest Grove House, 3 Weston Av, Mount Hooton Rd, Nottingham, and has issue living, Emma Jane, *b* 1986. —— Vanessa Anne, *b* 1955: *m* 1980, Frederick Norris, who *d* 1993, of 9 Queen's Acre, Newnham, Glos GL14 1DJ, and has issue living, Samantha Mary, *b* 1978.

Issue of late Marion Blanche Smith, *b* 1915, *d* 1989: *m* 1952, Cdr Michael Peer-Groves, RN, who *d* 1988:—
William Keith PEER-GROVES (15 Church St, Buntingford, Herts), *b* 1954. —— Michael Roland PEER-GROVES, *b* 1957: *m* 1991, Linda Wurster, of Long Island, NY, USA, and has issue living, Emily Louisa, *b* 1997.

Granddaughters of late Lady Blanche Catherine Smith (ante):—
Issue of late Lt-Gen Sir Arthur Francis Smith, KCB, KBE, DSO, MC, *b* 1890, *d* 1977: *m* 1918, Hon Monica Victoria Crossley, who *d* 1990, da of 1st Baron Somerleyton:—
Auriol Blanche, *b* 1919: *m* 1944, Maj Michael Warren Ingram, late Gren Gds, of The Manor House, S Cerney, Cirencester (*see* Ingram, Bt). —— Susan Monica, *b* 1921: *m* 1943, Capt Thomas Gillespie Browne, late RE, who *d* 1997, of 12 Walpole Court, Puddletown, Dorset DT2 8TJ, and has issue living, Jennifer Anne, *b* 1944: *m* 1st, 1965 (*m diss* 1975), John Patrick Michael Hugh Evelyn; 2ndly, 1978, Robert Alexander Neon Reynolds, of Close Hill, Bridestowe, Okehampton, Devon, and has issue living (by 1st *m*), Peter John *b* 1970, (by 2nd *m*) Susanna Clare *b* 1979, — Hilary Jane, *b* 1945: *m* 1965, Julian Alexander Ludovic James, of Craigforth, Chapel Greer, Leven, Fife, and has issue living, Christopher Mark William *b* 1967, David Hugh Geoffrey *b* 1969, Andrew Michael Richard *b* 1976, — Monica Jean, *b* 1949: *m* 1st, 1970 (*m diss* 1981), David Robin Millais James-Duff; 2ndly, 1986, Michael Anthony Spalding Gould Stewart, of Fernfield, Crinan, Argyllshire, and has issue living (by 1st *m*), Rory Thomas *b* 1978, Fiona Louise *b* 1971, Tania Robin *b* 1973, Nicola Mary *b* 1980.

Grandchildren of late Lt-Gen Sir Arthur Francis Smith, KCB, KBE, DSO, MC (ante):—
Issue of late Hazel Charlotte Smith, *b* 1924, *d* 1981: *m* 1943, Maj Peter Gordon Rowley, RA, who *d* 1987:—
David Gordon ROWLEY, *b* 1946; *ed* Bryanston. —— Wendy Drusilla, *b* 1950. —— Hazel Jane, *b* 1959.

PREDECESSORS – (1) *Hon Sir* JOHN Keith, 3rd son of William, 6th Earl Marischal, *cr Lord Keith of Inverurie and Keith Hall*, and *Earl of Kintore* (peerage of Scotland) 1677 with remainder to the heirs male of his body; in 1694 he resigned his honours and had a regrant of the titles and estates to him and the heirs male of his body, whom failing to the heirs male of his brother George, Earl Marischal, whom failing to the heirs-general of his own body; appointed 1660 hereditary Knight-Marischal of Scotland in consideration of his loyalty in preserving the regalia of Scotland from the hands of Cromwell; *d* 1714; *s* by his son (2) WILLIAM, 2nd Earl; being engaged in the rebellion of 1715 lost the office of Knight-Marischal; *d* 1718; *s* by his el son (3) JOHN, 3rd Earl; appointed Knight-Marischal; *dsp* 1758; *s* by his brother (4) WILLIAM, 4th Earl; *d* 1761, when the estates devolved upon George, 10th Earl Marischal (title attainted 1715), and the peerage remained dormant until his decease 1778, when it passed to his kinsman (5) ANTHONY ADRIAN Falconer, 5th Earl, who in 1776 *s* as 7th *Lord Falconer of Halkerton* (see that title); *d* 1804; *s* by his son (6) WILLIAM, 6th Earl; *d* 1812; *s* by his son (7) ANTHONY ADRIAN, 7th Earl; *cr Baron Kintore*, of Kintore, co Aberdeen (peerage of United Kingdom) 1838; *d* 1844; *s* by his son (8) FRANCIS ALEXANDER, 8th Earl; *b* 1828; Lord-Lieut of co Kincardine 1856-64, and of co Aberdeen 1864-80: *m* 1851, Louisa Madeleine, who *d* 1916, da of Francis Hawkins, Esq; *d* 1880; *s* by his son (9) ALGERNON HAWKINS THOMOND, KT, GCMG, PC, 9th Earl; *b* 1852; a Lord-in-Waiting to Queen Victoria 1885-6, Capt of the Yeomen of the Guard 1886-9, Gov of S Australia 1889-95, again a Lord-in-Waiting to Queen Victoria 1895-1901, and to King Edward VII 1901-5; a Dep Speaker House of Lords 1915, and a Member of Select Committee on Peerages in abeyance 1925: *m* 1873, Lady Sydney Charlotte Montagu, who *d* 1932, da of 6th Duke of Manchester; *d* 1930; *s* by his son (10) ARTHUR GEORGE, 10th Earl, *b* 1879; officially recognised by the name of Keith by Warrant of Lord Lyon King of Arms 1956: *m* 1937, Helena, who *d* 1971, da of Eugene Zimmerman of Cincinnati, USA, and formerly wife of 9th Duke of Manchester; *d* 1966, when the Barony of Kintore (peerage of UK) became ext, the Lordship of Falconer of Halkerton became dormant (see that title), and the Earldom of Kintore and the Lordship of Keith of Inverurie and Keith Hall devolved on his sister (11) ETHEL SYDNEY, Countess of Kintore, *b* 1874: *m* 1905, the 1st Viscount Stonehaven, who *d* 1941; *d* 1974, *s* by her el son (12) JAMES IAN, 12th Earl, *b* 1908, changed his name and arms from Baird to Keith by Interlocutor Lyon Court 28 June 1967, Vice-Lieut Kincardineshire, served 1939-45 War as Maj RM: *m* 1935, Delia, da of late William Lewis Brownlow Loyd, of Upper House, Shamley Green, Guildford (*see* Brabourne, 1967 Edn); *d* 1989; *s* by his elder son (13) MICHAEL CANNING WILLIAM JOHN, 13th Earl and present peer; also Viscount Stonehaven, Baron Stonehaven, and Lord Keith of Inverurie and Keith Hall (see infra).

*(1) Sir ALEXANDER Baird, GBE, son of late John Baird, of Urie; Lord-Lieut of Kincardineshire 1889-1918; *cr* a *Baronet* 1897: *m* 1873, Hon Annette Maria, who *d* 1884, da of 1st Baron Haldon; *d* 1920; *s* by his el son **(2)** *Rt Hon Sir* JOHN LAWRENCE, GCMG, DSO, PC, 2nd Bt, *b* 1874; European War 1914-15 (despatches, DSO); appointed Parliamentary Private Sec to the Leader of the Opposition in the House of Commons (Rt Hon A. Bonar Law, MP) 1911, Parliamentary Representative of Air Board 1916, Parliamentary Under-Sec of State to Air Min 1918, and Joint Parliamentary Sec to Min of Munitions 1919 (but declined); was Parliamentary Under-Sec of State, Home Depart 1919-22, First Commr of Works (also Min of Transport) 1922-4, Gov-Gen and Com-in-Ch of Commonwealth of Australia 1925-30, and Chm of Conservative Party 1931-6; sat as MP for Warwickshire, Rugby Div (*C*) 1910-22, and for Ayr 1922-5; *cr Baron Stonehaven*, of Ury, co Kincardine (peerage of United Kingdom) 1925, and *Viscount Stonehaven*, of Ury, co Kincardine (peerage of United Kingdom) 1938: *m* 1905, Lady Ethel Sydney Keith-Falconer (who *d* 1974, having *s* as Countess of Kintore 1966) da of 9th Earl of Kintorc; *d* 1941, *s* by his el son **(3)** (JAMES) IAN, 2nd Viscount (see ante).

KIRKHILL, BARON (Smith) (Life Baron 1975)

JOHN FARQUHARSON SMITH, son of Alexander Findlay Smith; *b* 7 May 1930; *ed* Robert Gordon's Colls, Aberdeen; Hon LLD Aberdeen; Lord Provost of Aberdeen 1971-75, Min of State, Scottish Office 1975-79; Delegate to Parliamentary Assembly of COE and WEU 1981-87; Chm Cttee on Legal Affairs and Human Rights of the COE 1991-95; *cr Baron Kirkhill*, in District of City of Aberdeen (Life Baron) 1975: *m* 1965, Frances Mary Walker Reid.
Residence – 3 Rubislaw Den North, Aberdeen.

Kirkwall, Viscount; son of Earl of Orkney.

KIRKWOOD, BARON (Kirkwood) (Baron UK 1951)

DAVID HARVIE KIRKWOOD, 3rd Baron; *b* 24 Nov 1931; *s* 1970; *ed* Rugby, and Trin Hall, Camb (MA, PhD); CEng: *m* 1965, Judith Rosalie, da of late John Hunt, of Leeds, and has issue.

Arms – Argent, two chevronels round-embattled on their upper edges sable between two oak-sprigs slipped and fructed proper in chief and a cog-wheel azure in base. Crest – The bow of a ship afrontée proper. Supporters – *Dexter*, an Ayrshire bull; *sinister*, a Clydesdale stallion, both proper, the latter harnessed or.
Residence – 56 Endcliffe Hall Av, Sheffield.

DAUGHTERS LIVING

Hon Ruth Emily, *b* 1966.
Hon Anne Judith, *b* 1969.
Hon Lucy Jennifer, *b* 1972.

BROTHER LIVING

Hon JAMES STUART (The Cearne, Kent Hatch, Crockham Hill, Edenbridge, Kent), *b* 19 June 1937; *ed* Rugby, and at Trin Hall, Camb (MA); FRICS: *m* 1965, Alexandra Mary, da of late Alec Dyson, of Holt, Norfolk, and has issue living, Kate Victoria, *b* 1966, —

Georgina Grace, *b* 1969.

WIDOW LIVING OF SECOND BARON

EILEEN GRACE (*Eileen, Baroness Kirkwood*) da of late Thomas Henry Boalch, of Pill, Bristol: *m* 1931, the 2nd Baron Kirkwood, who *d* 1970.

COLLATERAL BRANCHES LIVING

Issue of late John Kirkwood, eldest son of 1st Baron, *b* 1900, *d* 1942: *m* 1932, Ellen Florence, who *d* 1976, da of late Thomas Peter Haggar, of Witham, Essex:—
Jean (288 Warwick Rd, Solihull, W. Midlands), *b* 1935.

Issue of late Robert Smith Kirkwood, 2nd son of 1st Baron, *b* 1901, *d* 1950: *m* 1927, Annie Kerr, who *d* 1963, da of John Marshall, of Shettleston, Glasgow:—
Agnes Young (11 Chesterfield Court, Glasgow, W2), *b* 1930. —— Elizabeth Smith, *b* 1937.

Issue of late Hon James Smith Kirkwood, 4th and yst son of 1st Baron, *b* 1912, *d* 1983: *m* 1944, Mary Helen, who *d* 1970, da of James Marshall, of Elgin:—
David, *b* 1945. —— James Marshall Smith, *b* 1954. —— Elizabeth Joan, *b* 1947, *d* 19—.

PREDECESSORS – (1) *Rt Hon* DAVID Kirkwood, PC, son of late John Kirkwood, of Parkhead, Glasgow; *b* 1872; was Chm of David Kirkwood and Sons, Ltd, of 9 Woodside Place, Glasgow; sat as MP for Dumbarton Burghs (*Lab*) 1922-50, and for E Div of Dunbartonshire 1950-51; *cr Baron Kirkwood*, of Bearsden, co Dunbarton (peerage of United Kingdom) 1951: *m* 1899, Elizabeth, who *d* 1956, da of Robert Smith, of Parkhead, Glasgow; *d* 1955; *s* by his 3rd (but el surviving) son (2) DAVID, 2nd Baron; *b* 1903: *m* 1931, Eileen Grace, da of late Thomas Henry Boalch, of Pill, Bristol; *d* 1970; *s* by his el son (3) DAVID HARVIE, 3rd Baron and present peer.

KISSIN, BARONY OF (Kissin) (Extinct 1997)

SON LIVING OF LIFE BARON

Hon Robert David (34 Cadogan Place, SW1X 9RX), *b* 1947: *m* 1976, Lesley Chapman, and has issue living, Alexander Jonathan Toby, *b* 1985, — Samantha Rose, *b* 1984.

DAUGHTER LIVING OF LIFE BARON

Hon Evelyn Anne, *b* 1944: *m* 1972, Jack Donald Singer, MD, FAAPaed, of 45 Campden Hill Court, Campden Hill Rd, W8 7HU, and has issue, Jeremy, *b* 1974, — Juliet, *b* 1978.

WIDOW LIVING OF LIFE BARON

RUTH DEBORAH (*Baroness Kissin*), da of Siegmund Samuel: *m* 1935, Baron Kissin (Life Baron), who *d* 1997. *Residence* – 17 Av de l'Annonciade, Monte Carlo, Monaco.

KITCHENER OF KHARTOUM AND OF BROOME, EARL (Kitchener) (Earl UK 1914)

HENRY HERBERT KITCHENER, TD, 3rd Earl; *b* 24 Feb 1919; *s* 1937; *ed* Winchester, and at Trin Coll, Camb; a Page of Honour at Coronation of King George VI; a DL for Cheshire; Maj (ret) R Signals (TA).

𝔄rms – Gules, between three bustards close proper a chevron azure, cotised argent. 𝔠rest – A stag's head couped, the neck transfixed by an arrow proper between the attires a horseshoe or. 𝔖upporters – *Dexter*, a camel proper, bridle trappings and line pendent reflexed over the back gules, gored with a collar or suspended therefrom an escutcheon paly bendy azure and ermine, a canton of the last charged with a portcullis gold; *sinister*, a gnu proper gorged with a collar or suspended therefrom an escutcheon ermine charged with a chevron engrailed vert thereon four horseshoes or.
Residence – Westergate Wood, Eastergate, Chichester, W Sussex PO20 6SB. *Club* – Brooks's.

SISTER LIVING (*Raised to the rank of an Earl's daughter* 1938)

Lady Kenya Eleanor, *b* 1923; late 3rd Officer WRNS; BA, MCSP, SRP; Chartered Physiotherapist in private practice since 1971: *m* 1947, as his 2nd wife, John Stewart Tatton-Brown, who *d* 1971, and has issue living, Margaret Caroline, *b* 1950: *m* 1984, A. John Aaronson, son of A. W. Aaronson, of Hornsey, — (Adela) Charlotte, *b* 1951: *m* 1982, Patrick B. Appleby, yr son of late Kenneth Appleby, and has issue living, Charles *b* 1983, Benjamin *b* 1985, James Michael *b* 1988, — Augusta Kenya, *b* 1955: *m* 1976, James D. P. Saunders, of PO Box 149, Jerramungup, 6337 W Australia, and has issue living, Duncan John *b* 1977, Peter Eden *b* 1979. *Residence* – Westergate Wood, Eastergate, Chichester, Sussex PO20 6SB.

WIDOW LIVING OF BROTHER OF THIRD EARL (*who was raised to the rank of an Earl's son* 1938)

Ursula Hope (Croylands, Old Salisbury Lane, Romsey, Hants SO51 0GD), da of late Capt Cyril Montagu Luck, CMG, DSO, Roy Indian Navy, and RN: *m* 1959, Hon Charles Eaton Kitchener, who *d* 1982, and has issue (infra).

COLLATERAL BRANCH LIVING

Issue of late Hon Charles Eaton Kitchener, yr son of Capt Henry Franklin Chevallier, *Viscount Broome*, RN, only son of 2nd Earl, *b* 1920; *d* 1982: *m* 1959, Ursula Hope Luck (ante):—
Emma Joy, *b* 1963: *m* 1990, Julian Alexander Kitchener-Fellowes (previously Fellowes), who assumed by deed poll 1998 the additional surname of Kitchener before that of his patronymic, yst son of late Peregrine Edward Launcelot Fellowes, of The Court, Chipping Campden, Glos, and has issue living, Peregrine Charles Morant Kitchener, *b* 1991. *Residence* – 15 Moore St, SW3 2QN.

Granddaughters of Lt-Gen Sir Frederick Walter Kitchener, KCB, yr brother of 1st Earl (*in special remainder*) (infra):—
Issue of late Major Henry Hamilton Kitchener, *b* 1890, *d* 1984: *m* 1st, 1916, Winifred Esther Everest, who *d* 1959, el da of Hon A. W. Bluck; 2ndly, 1961, Mrs Gwynneth Champion, who *d* 1983:—
(By 1st *m*) Winifred Jean, *b* 1917: *m* 1954, Lieut Peter John Hall, RN, of Oakfield House, Spreyton, Crediton, Devon EX17 5AL, and has issue living, Christopher Peter, *b* 1955: *m* 1981, Sarah Jane Downs, and has issue living, James Henry *b* 1985, Robert Hamilton *b* 1987, George Howard *b* 1990. —— Eleanor Elizabeth Madge (86 Waller Crcs, Camp bell, ACT 2601, Australia), *b* 1920: *m* 1947, Louis Norman Cornhill, who *d* 1971, and has issue living, Peter Robert, *b* 1949, — Robert Louis Henry, *b* 1953.

PREDECESSORS – (1) *Field Marshal Rt Hon Sir* HORATIO HERBERT Kitchener, KG, KP, GCB, OM, GCSI, GCMG, GCIE, second son of late Lieut-Col Henry Horatio Kitchener (13th Dragoons), of Cossington, Leicester; *b* 1850; served in Soudan Campaign 1883-5, being DAA and QMG 1884-5 (despatches frequently, medal with clasp, 3rd class Osmanieh), in command of troops at action of Handoub 1888 (severely wounded, 2nd class Medjidie), a Brig of Soudanese troops at action of Gemaizah, Suakin, 1888 (despatches, clasp). Mounted troops at action of Toski on the Nile 1889 (despatches, clasp, CB), Dongola Expedition 1896 (despatches, Grand Cordon Osmanieh, promoted Maj-Gen), Nile Expedition 1897 (despatches) and 1898 (despatches), and Soudan Campaign 1898, present at battle of Omdurman, recapture of Khartoum, and subsequent expedition to Fashoda (Khedive's medal with five clasps, peerage, GCB, specially thanked by both Houses of Parliament, granted £30,000), and in S Africa 1899-1902 first as Ch-of-the-Staff (despatches twice, GCMG), and subsequently as Com-in-Ch (thanked by Parliament, promoted Gen, cr Viscount, granted £50,000), and acted as High Commr of S Africa, and Administrator of Transvaal and of Orange River Colony 1901; employed on Palestine Survey 1874-8, and on Cyprus Survey 1878-9 (awarded Livingstone gold medal 1915); Director of Survey, Cyprus 1880-82, Vice-Consul in Anatolia 1879-80, in command of Egyptian Cavalry 1882-4, HM Queen Victoria's Commr for delimitation of territory of Sultan of Zanzibar 1885, Gov of Suakin 1886-8 (2nd class Medjidie), ADC to HM Queen Victoria 1888-96, and AG and 2nd in command of Egyptian Army, as well as Inspector-Gen of Police 1888-92 (2nd class Osmanieh), Sirdar of Egyptian Army 1892-99 (1st class Medjidie and Osmanieh), Gov-Gen of the Soudan 1899, and Com-in-Ch in India and a Member of Viceroy's Council 1902-9, Agent and Consul-Gen in Egypt 1911-14, and Sec of State for War 1914-16 (forming during European War "Kitchener's Army"); *cr Baron Kitchener of Khartoum*, and of Aspall, co Suffolk (peerage of United Kingdom) 1898, and *Viscount Kitchener of Khartoum*, and of the Vaal, Colony of the Transvaal, and of Aspall, co Suffolk (peerage of United Kingdom) 1902, with remainder to the heirs male of his body, and in default of such issue with remainder (i) to his first daughter and the heirs male of her body, (ii) to his other daughters and the heirs male of their bodies (infra), and (iii) in default of such issue, with remainder to his elder brother, Henry Elliott Chevallier Kitchener, and the heirs male of his body, and (iv) with remainder to his yr brother, Frederick Walter Kitchener, and the heirs male of his body, and *Earl Kitchener of Khartoum and of Broome, Viscount Broome*, of Broome, co Kent, and *Baron Denton*, of Denton, co Kent (peerage of United Kingdom) 1914 with similar special remainders to the above-mentioned; *d* on active ser 1916 when the Barony *cr* 1898 became ext and he was *s* (under the special remainder) in the other peerages by his el brother (2) HENRY ELLIOTT CHEVALLIER, 2nd Earl; *b* 1846; Col (ret); formerly Lieut-Col Duke of Cornwall's LI; France 1870 (medal), Burma 1891 (despatches, medal with clasp), Manipur Expedition 1891 (despatches, clasp), European War 1914-17 (1914 star, two medals, Croix de Guerre); was DAAG, Jamaica 1893-8; sometime Col Comdg W India Regt Depôt: *m* 1877, Eleanor Fanny, who *d* 1897, only child of late Lieut-Col Franklin Lushington, CB; *d* 1937; *s* by his grandson (3) HENRY HERBERT (son of late Capt Henry Franklin Chevallier, Viscount Broome, only son of 2nd Earl), 3rd Earl and present peer; also Viscount Kitchener of Khartoum, Viscount Broome, and Baron Denton.

Kitson, family name of Baron Airedale.

Knatchbull, family name of Baron Brabourne.

Knatchbull, family name of Countess Mountbatten of Burma.

Knebworth, Viscount; son of Earl of Lytton.

KNIGHT OF COLLINGTREE, BARONESS (Knight) (Life Baroness 1997)

INTEGRITY

(JOAN CHRISTABEL) JILL KNIGHT, DBE, da of late A. E. Christie, of Bristol; *b* 9 July 1927; *ed* Fairfield Sch, Bristol, and King Edward Gram Sch, Birmingham; Memb Northampton County Borough Cncl 1956-66; MP for Birmingham, Edgbaston (*C*) 1966-97; Memb Parliamentary Select Cttee on Race Relations and Immigration 1969-72, Council of Europe 1977-78, WEU 1977-78, Select Cttee for Home Affairs 1980-83 and 1992-97, and Standards and Privileges Select Cttee 1993-97; Chm Lords and Commons All-Party Child and Family Protection Group 1978-97, Conservative Back Bench Health and Social Services Cttee 1982-97, and Inter Parliamentary Union 1994-97; Pres W Midlands Conservative Political Centre 1980-83; Vice-Pres

𝕬rms – Argent an oak tree eradicated azure fructed or within a mascle azure thereon four needles in lozenge argent
each enfiled and entwined by a thread or the ends thereof knotted in chief and in base. 𝕾upporters – On either side a
lynx azure gorged with a plain collar attached thereto a chain reflexed over the back.
Address – c/o House of Lords, Westminster, SW1A 0PW.

SONS LIVING

Hon Andrew, *b* 1950; *ed* Northampton Gram Sch, and Royal Coll of Music.
Hon Roger, *b* 1953; *ed* Northampton Gram Sch.

Knightley, Finch-, family name of Earl of Aylesford.

KNIGHTS, BARON (Knights) (Life Baron 1987)

PHILIP DOUGLAS KNIGHTS, CBE, QPM, son of late Thomas James Knights, of Ottershaw, Surrey; *b* 3
Oct 1920; *ed* King's Sch, Grantham, and Police Staff Coll; DL W Midlands 1985; Sergt Lincs
Constabulary 1946, Home Office 1946-50, Inspector Lincs Constabulary 1953, Supt 1955, Chief Supt
1957, Assist Chief Constable Birmingham City Police 1959, Home Office and Dep Comdt Police
Coll 1962-66, Dep Chief Constable Birmingham City Police 1970, Chief Constable Sheffield and
Rotherham Constabulary 1972-74, S Yorks Police 1974-75, and W Midlands Police 1975-85; Pres
Assocn of Chief Police Offiers 1978-79, Trustee Police Foundation since 1979, Member Advisory
Council Cambridge Inst of Criminology since 1986, Member of Council Aston Univ since 1985;
served 1939-45 War in RAF; CBIM, QPM (1964), OBE (1971), CBE (1976), Knt 1980, *cr Baron
Knights*, of Edgbaston, co W Midlands (Life Baron) 1987: *m* 1945, Jean, da of late James Henry
Burman.
Address – c/o House of Lords, SW1A 0PW.

KNOLLYS, VISCOUNT (Knollys) (Viscount UK 1911)
(Name and Title pronounced "Noles")

In every way prepared

DAVID FRANCIS DUDLEY KNOLLYS, 3rd Viscount; *b* 12 June 1931; *s*
1966; *ed* Eton; late 2nd Lt Scots Guards: *m* 1959, Hon Sheelin
Virginia Maxwell, da of late Lt-Col Hon Somerset Arthur Maxwell,
MP (*see* B Farnham), and has issue.

𝕬rms – Per pale gules and argent a chevron counterchanged and charged with
three roses also counterchanged barbed and seeded proper. 𝕮rest – Between
two crosses moline per pale azure and or fimbriated counterchanged an elephant
statant argent. 𝕾upporters – On either side an Heraldic Antelope the dexter
argent and sinister or both tufted, horned and unguled sable and charged on the
shoulder with a cross as in the Crest.
Residence – The Bailiff's House, Bramerton Hall Farm, Norwich, Norfolk NR14
7DN. *Club* – White's.

SONS LIVING

Hon PATRICK NICHOLAS MARK, *b* 11 March 1962; *ed* Wymondham Coll, Norfolk,
and RMA Sandhurst; commn'd Scots Guards 1982 (ret 1988): *m* 1998, Mrs Sarah
W. Wright, only da of Michael Petch, of Chobham, Surrey.
Hon Christopher Edward, *b* 1964; *ed* Exeter Univ (BA); commn'd Scots Guards 1987: *m* 1997, Sarah, da of late Edmund
St John Gwynne, and of Mrs William Merton, and has issue living, Edmund, *b* 1998.

IN·UTRUMQUE·PARATUS

Hon Michael James George, *b* 1968; *ed* Wymondham Coll, Norfolk, and RMA Sandhurst; commn'd Scots Guards 1989.

DAUGHTER LIVING

Hon Clarinda Susan, *b* 1960: *m* 1988, Andrew M. B. Snowball, yr son of late Brig Edward Joseph Dove Snowball, OBE, of Ballochneck, Thornhill, Perthshire, and has issue living, Alexander Charles Edward, *b* 1995, — Emma Sheelin, *b* 1992. *Residence* – Glebe House, Glass, Huntly, Aberdeenshire AB54 4XH.

SISTER LIVING

Hon Ardyne Mary, *b* 1929: *m* 1958, Ronald James Owen, of Paradise Wood, Upper Hartfield, Sussex, and has two das, Sandra Mary, *b* 1963, — Rachel Elizabeth, *b* 1965.

PREDECESSORS – **(1)** *Rt Hon Sir* FRANCIS Knollys, GCB, GCVO, KCMG, ISO, second son of late Gen Rt Hon Sir William Thomas Knollys, KCB, PC; *b* 1837; a Gentleman Usher Quarterly Waiter to Queen Victoria 1868-1901, Groom-in-Waiting to the Prince of Wales 1886-1901, and Private Sec to Prince of Wales 1870-1901, and to King Edward VII 1901-10, Joint Private Sec to King George V 1910-13, and a Lord-in-Waiting to Queen Alexandra 1910-24; *cr Baron Knollys*, of Caversham, co Oxford (peerage of UK) 1902, and *Viscount Knollys*, of Caversham, co Oxford (peerage of UK) 1911: *m* 1887, Hon Ardyn, who *d* 1922, who *d* 1987, da of Sir Henry Thomas Tyrwhitt, 3rd Bt; *d* 1924, *s* by his son **(2)** EDWARD GEORGE WILLIAM TYRWHITT, GCMG, MBE, DFC, 2nd Viscount, *b* 1895; Gov of Bermuda 1941-43, Chm of BOAC 1943-47, of Vickers Ltd 1956-62, and of Northern and Employers Assurance Co 1954-66: *m* 1928, Margaret Mary Josephine, who *d* 1987, da of Sir Stuart Auchinloss Coats, 2nd Bt; *d* 1966, *s* by his son **(3)** DAVID FRANCIS DUDLEY, 3rd Viscount, and present peer; also Baron Knollys.

Knox, family name of Earl of Ranfurly.

KNUTSFORD, VISCOUNT (Holland-Hibbert) (Viscount UK 1895, Bt UK 1853)

MICHAEL HOLLAND-HIBBERT, 6th Viscount, and 7th Baronet, *b* 27 Dec 1926: *s* 1986; *ed* Eton, and Trin Coll, Camb; late Capt Welsh Gds; DL Devon 1977, High Sheriff 1977-78; a Dir Barclays Bank, Exeter 1956-86, Member Nat Trust Exec Cttee and Council 1965-86, and Finance Cttee 1986-99: *m* 1951, Hon Sheila Constance Portman, da of 5th Viscount Portman, and has issue.

𝔄rms – Quarterly, 1st and 4th ermine, on a bend nebuly sable three crescents argent, in the sinister chief point a cross bottonée fitchée of the second, *Hibbert*; 2nd and 3rd per pale argent and azure, semée-de-is, a lion rampant guardant all counterchanged, the whole debruised by a bendlet engrailed gules, *Holland*. 𝔠rests – 1st, in front of a dexter cubit arm erect proper, vested azure, cuff ermine, holding in the hand a crescent argent a demi catherine wheel also argent, *Hibbert*; 2nd, out of a crown vallery or, a demi-lion guardant per bend argent and azure, debruised by a bendlet engrailed counterchanged, and holding in the dexter paw a fleur-de-lis of the second, *Holland*. 𝔖upporters – Two lions guardant argent gutée de larmes, each charged on the body with two fleur-de-lis in fesse between bars-geme engrailed azure.
Residence – Broadclyst House, Exeter, Devon EX5 3EW.

Look backwards, look around, look forwards

RESPICE ASPICE PROSPICE

SONS LIVING

Hon HENRY THURSTAN, *b* 6 April 1959; *ed* Eton, RMA, and RAC Cirencester; Lieut Coldm Gds 1979-83; Dir Lane Fox (Residential) Ltd: *m* 1988, Katherine, da of Sir John Bruce Woollacott Ropner, 2nd Bt (*cr* 1952), and has issue living, Thomas Arthur, *b* 15 Dec 1992, — Rosanna (Rosie) Sarah, *b* 1990, — Isabel Katherine, *b* 1995. *Residence* – Munden, Watford, Herts WD2 7PZ.

Hon James Edward, *b* 1967; *ed* Eton.

DAUGHTER LIVING

Hon Lucy Katherine, *b* 1956: *m* 1979, Mark Charles Liddell, yr son of late Peter John Liddell, DSC, of Moorhouse Hall, Warwick-on-Eden, Carlisle, and has issue living, James Peter, *b* 1987, — Katherine Alexandra, *b* 1983, — Sophie Charlotte, *b* 1990. *Residence* – Cumrew House, Cumrew, Carlisle.

SISTERS LIVING

Lavinia, *b* 1919; served 1939-45 War as Jun Com ATS: *m* 1953, Maj Peter John Orde, 15th/19th King's Roy Hussars (ret), son of Sir Percy Lancelot Orde, CIE, and has two adopted children, Justin Robert, *b* 1957; *ed* Stowe, and RMA Sandhurst, — Clarissa Mary, *b* 1958: *m* 1989, Andrew Windsor Latchmore, of The Old School House, Weeton, nr Leeds, N Yorks LS17 0AW, son of late Arthur John Craig Latchmore, MBE, FRCS, of Linton, Wetherby, Yorks, and has issue living, Max Andrew *b* 1993, Chlöe Roseanna *b* 1991. *Residence* – Watling House, Watling St, Corbridge, Northumberland.

Delia Mary, *b* 1922; served 1939-45 War as 3rd Officer WRNS: *m* 1946, Lt-Col William McGhie Cunningham, LVO, OBE, MC, late 11th Hussars, who *d* 1992, elder son of James Scott Cunningham, of Auchendarroch, Wishaw, Lanarkshire, and has issue living, Jeremy James (86 Hamilton Rd, Oxford OX2 2QA), *b* 1948; *ed* Eton, and Pembroke Coll, Oxford: *m* 1974, Eiko, da of Kenji Kouchi, of Tokyo, and has issue living, Julian Kenji *b* 1977, Alexander Shuji *b* 1988, Fiona Izumi *b* 1979, — Mark William, *b* 1950; *ed* Eton, and New Coll, Oxford: *m* 1996, Isolde, da of late Dr Johan Rauscher, of Tübingen, Germany, — Lavinia Mary, *b* 1952: *m* 1978, Bryan Denzil Winch, of Park House, Bordean, Petersfield, Hants GU32 1ET, son of David Clark Brook Winch, of Old Bosham, W Sussex, and has issue living, Robin Mark *b* 1983, Toby David *b* 1988, Tanya Katherine *b* 1980. *Residence* – Southfield Farm, Wigginton, Banbury, Oxon.

COLLATERAL BRANCHES LIVING

(In remainder to the Baronetcy only)

Grandchildren of Capt Michael James Holland, MC (*infra*):—
Issue of late Antony Francis Holland, MC, *b* 1913, *d* 1982: *m* 1946, Ann (Lullings, Balcombe, Sussex), da of Henry Faure Walker, of Highley Manor, Sussex:—
Thurstan James, *b* 1948; *ed* Eton, and Nottingham Univ: *m* 1987, Elizabeth Joan Serena, 2nd da of late Alistair Philip Cobbold, of Holbrook Lodge, Ipswich, Suffolk (*see* M Abergavenny, colls, 1958 Edn), and has issue living, Frederick Thurstan Alistair *b* 1991. *Residence* – Old Lullings, Balcombe, Sussex RH17 6QY. —— Anthea, *b* 1947: *m* 1973, John St Andrew Warde, of Squerryes Court, Westerham, Kent TN16 1SJ, and has issue living, Charles Antony, *b* 1974, — Henry John, *b* 1976, — Ann Charlotte, *b* 1982. —— Arabella Ann, *b* 1956.

Grandchildren of late Rev Francis James Holland, brother of 1st Viscount:—
Issue of late Capt Michael James Holland, MC, *b* 1870, *d* 1956: *m* 1911, Marion Ada Flora, who *d* 1969, da of late H. J. T. Broadwood, of Lyne, Horsham, Sussex:—
David Cuthbert Lyall, CB, *b* 1915; *ed* Eton, and at Trin Coll, Camb; late Roy Sussex Regt; Librarian, House of Commons 1967-76; CB (Civil) 1976: *m* 1949, Rosemary, da of David Llewellyn Griffiths, OBE, and has had issue, *Rev* Matthew Francis, *b* 1952; *ed* Eton, LSE, and Queen's Coll, Birmingham: *m* 1979, Jayne Emerson, and has issue living, Joseph John *b* 1988, Bridget Mary *b* 1984, Caitlin Frances *b* 1986, — †Peter Gwinnell, *b* 1954; *d* 1983, — Lucinda Jane, *b* (twin) 1954: *m* 1977, Paul Carpenter, and has issue living, William James *b* 1978. *Residence* – The Barn, Milton St, Polegate, E Sussex. *Club* – Athenaeum.

PREDECESSORS – (1) HENRY Holland; *b* 1788; Physician in Ordinary to HM Queen Victoria 1850-73, and to HRH the Prince Consort 1840-61, was *cr* a *Baronet* 1853: *m* 1st, 1822, Margaret Emma, who *d* 1830, da of James Caldwell of Linley Wood, co Stafford; 2ndly, 1834, Saba, who *d* 1866, da of Rev Sydney Smith, Canon of St Paul's; *d* 1873; *s* by his el son (2) HENRY THURSTAN, GCMG, PC, 2nd baronet; *b* 1825; Legal Adviser to Colonial Office 1867-70, Assist Under-Sec there 1870-74, Financial Sec to Treasury 1885, Vice-Pres of Committee of Council on Education Sept 1885 to Jan 1886, and July 1886 to Jan 1887, and Sec of State for Colonies Jan 1887 to Aug 1892; MP for Midhurst (C) 1874-85, and for Hampstead 1885-8; *cr* PC 1885, GCMG 1886, *Baron Knutsford*, of Knutsford, Cheshire (peerage of United Kingdom) 1888, and *Viscount Knutsford*, of Knutsford, Cheshire (peerage of United Kingdom) 1895: *m* 1st, 1852, Elizabeth Margaret, who *d* 1855, da of Nathaniel Hibbert, of Munden, Watford, Herts; 2ndly, 1858, Margaret Jean (a Lady of Justice of Order of St John of Jerusalem in England), who *d* 1906, el da of Sir Charles Edward Trevelyan, KCB, 1st Bt; *d* 1914; *s* by his el son (2) SYDNEY GEORGE, 2nd Viscount, *b* 19 March 1855; many years Chm of London Hospital: *m* 1883, Lady Mary Ashburnham, who *d* 1947, da of 4th Earl of Ashburnham; *d* 1931; *s* by his twin brother (3) ARTHUR HENRY Holland-Hibbert, 3rd Viscount, *b* (twin) 19 March 1855; High Sheriff of Herts 1891; assumed by Roy licence 1876, the additional surname and arms of Hibbert: *m* 1884, Ellen, who *d* 1949, el da of Sir Wilfrid Lawson, 2nd Bt (*cr* 1831); *d* 1935; *s* by his el son (4) THURSTAN, 4th Viscount; *b* 1888: *m* 1912, Viola Mary, who *d* 1964, da of late Thomas Meadows Clutterbuck, of Putteridge Bury, Herts, and Micklefield Hall, Rickmansworth, Herts; *d* 1976; *s* by his son (5) JULIAN THURSTAN, CBE, 5th Viscount, *b* 1920; Lt Coldm Gds; JP for Herts; served 1939-45 War (wounded); *d* 1986; *s* by his cousin (6) MICHAEL (son of Hon Wilfrid Holland-Hibbert, 2nd son of 3rd Viscount), 6th Viscount and present peer; also Baron Knutsford.

Kynynmound, Elliot Murray , family name of Earl of Minto.

Lade, Milles-, surname of Earldom of Sondes.

LAING OF DUNPHAIL, BARON (Laing) (Life Baron 1991)

HECTOR LAING, son of Hector Laing, of Edinburgh, by his late wife, Margaret Norris, da of Sir Alexander Grant, 1st Bt (ext 1947); *b* 12 May 1923; *ed* Loretto, and Jesus Coll, Camb; Hon DUniv Stirling and Heriot Watt; FRSE 1989; served European War 1939-45 as Capt Scots Guards 1942-47 (American Bronze Star, despatches 1944); joined McVitie & Price 1947 (Chm 1963), Dir United Biscuits 1953 (Man Dir 1964, Chm United Biscuits (Holdings) plc, 1972-90), Chm Food and Drink Industries Council 1977-79, Scottish Business in the Community 1982-90, City and Industrial Liaison Council 1985-94, and Business in the Community 1987-91; Dir Bank of England 1973-91 and Exxon Corpn Inc 1984-94; Gov Wycombe Abbey 1981-94; Pres Project Trident 1992-94; Treas Conservative Party 1988-93, Chm Trustees The Lambeth Fund 1983, and Joint Chm The Per Cent Club 1986-90; Trustee Royal Botanic Gardens, Kew Foundation, 1990; *cr* Knt 1978, and *Baron Laing of Dunphail*, of Dunphail, District of Moray (Life Baron) 1991: *m* 1950, Marian Clare, da of Maj-Gen Sir John Emilius Laurie, 6th Bt, CBE, DSO, and has issue.

Arms – Per pale Or and Gules, a chief counterchanged. **Crest** – a dexter cubit arm issuant cuffed as in the Arms grasping a dagger Proper hilted and pommelled Or all paleways. **Supporters** – two Pekinese dogs guardant Proper. *Residence* – High Meadows, Windsor Rd, Gerrards Cross, Bucks SL9 8ST. *Club* – White's.

SONS LIVING

Hon Mark Hector, *b* 1951; *ed* Eton, and Selwyn Coll, Camb: *m* 1980, Susanna Anson, da of John Anson Crawford, of Chatton Lodge, 108 Hepburn Gdns, St Andrews, Fife, and has issue living, Hector Grant, *b* 1988, — Kathryn Rose, *b* 1983, — Georgina Clare, *b* 1985. *Residence* – The White House, Totley Wells, by Winchburg, W Lothian EH52 6QJ.

Hon Robert John, *b* 1953; *ed* Eton, and Selwyn Coll, Camb: *m* 1992, Mrs Fiona M. Nunneley, da of late Freddy Grant, of Church House, Washington, Sussex. *Residence* – Humbie House, Humbie, E Lothian EH36 5PB.

Hon Anthony Rupert, *b* 1955; *ed* Eton: *m* 1985, Fiona, yr da of John Brooke-Hunt, of Bairnkine Lodge, Jedburgh, Roxburghshire, and has issue living, Rupert Andrew, *b* 1986, — Christopher Hector, *b* 1988, — Rebecca Claire, *b* 1990. *Residence* – 14 Saxe Coburg Place, Edinburgh EH3 5BR.

Lamb, family name of Baron Rochester.

Lambart, family name of Earl of Cavan.

LAMBERT, VISCOUNT (Lambert) (Viscount UK 1945)

THE GOOD EARTH PROVIDES

MICHAEL JOHN LAMBERT, 3rd Viscount; *b* 29 Sept 1912; *s* 1989: *m* 1939, Florence Dolores, da of late Nicholas Lechmere Cunningham Macaskie, QC, and has issue.

Arms – Azure, a chevron or fretty of the first between, in chief two garbs and in base a fleece of the second. Crest – Issuant from a mount vert an apple tree fructed proper. Supporters – On either side of a Cornish chough proper collared or.
Residence – Casanuova di Barontoli, 53010 S Rocco a Pilli, Siena, Italy.

DAUGHTERS LIVING

Hon Sophia Jane, *b* 1943.
Hon Caelia Anne Georgiana, *b* 1946: *m* 1971 (*m diss* 1985), Emmanuel Irismir Pereira, and has issue living, Joaquim Michael, *b* 1975, — Antonia Catarina, *b* 1972. *Residence* – 60 Bolingbroke Rd, W14.
Hon Flavia Mary, *b* 1949. *Residence* – 9 Alwyne Rd, Canonbury, N1.

DAUGHTER LIVING OF SECOND VISCOUNT

Hon Louise Barbara (*Hon Lady Gibbings*), *b* 1944: *m* 1975, Sir Peter Walter Gibbings, and has issue living, Dominic George Lambert, *b* 1976.

PREDECESSORS – (1) *Rt Hon* GEORGE Lambert, son of late George Lambert; *b* 1866; Capt 3rd Batn Devonshire Regt; Civil Lord of the Admiralty 1905-15; was a County Councillor for Devonshire 1889-1912, and a County Alderman 1912-52; sat as MP for N, or S Molton, Div; of Devonshire (*L*) 1891-1918, and for S Molton Div of Devon 1918-24, and 1929-45; *cr* Viscount Lambert, of South Molton, co Devon (peerage of United Kingdom) 1945: *m* 1904, Barbara, who *d* 1963, da of late George Stavers, of Morpeth; *d* 1958; *s* by his el son (2) GEORGE, TD, 2nd Viscount, *b* 1909, Lt-Col TA, served 1939-45 War, Chm Devon and Exeter Savings Bank 1959-70, Pres National Federation of Young Farmers' Clubs 1968-70, DL Devon 1969, MP for S Molton Div of Devon (*L*) 1945-50 and for Torrington Div of Devon (*Nat L* and *C*) 1950-58: *m* 1939, Patricia Mary, who *d* 1991, da of late Joseph Francis Quinn, of London; *d* 1989 (his only son, Hon George Lambert, *b* 1941, Capt RHG, *d* 1970); *s* by his brother (3) MICHAEL JOHN, 3rd Viscount and present peer.

Lambton, Viscount, see Earldom of Durham.

LAMBURY, BARONY OF (Lord) (Extinct 1967)

DAUGHTER LIVING OF FIRST BARON

Hon Joan Marquerite, *b* 1927: *m* 1st, 1951 (*m diss* 1965), Miles Lucas Breeden; 2ndly, 1966, Angus James Macdonald, and has issue living, (by 1st *m*) Guy Charles, *b* 1953, — Gail Amanda, *b* 1956.

LAMING BARON (Laming) (Life Baron 1998)

(WILLIAM) HERBERT LAMING, CBE, son of William Angus Laming, of Newcastle upon Tyne; *b* 19 July 1936; *ed* Durham Univ (D Soc Sci 1960); DL Herts 1999; Probation Offr, Nottingham Probation Service 1961-68; Assist Chief Probation Offr, Nottingham City and County Probation Service 1968-

71; Dep Dir then Dir, Herts CC Social Services 1971-91; Chief Inspector, Social Services Inspectorate, Dept of Health 1991-98; Pres Assoc of Directors of Social Services 1982-83; *cr* CBE 1985, Kt 1996, and *Baron Laming*, of Tewin, co Herts (Life Baron) 1998: *m* 1962, Aileen Margaret, da of Harry Pollard, of Birmingham.

Residence – 1 Firs Walk, Tewin Wood, Welwyn, Herts AL6 0NY.

LAMONT OF LERWICK, BARON (Lamont) (Life Baron 1998)

NORMAN STEWART HUGHSON LAMONT, PC, son of late Daniel Lamont, of Lerwick, Shetland; *b* 8 May 1942; *ed* Loretto, and Fitzwilliam Coll, Camb (BA 19—); MP for Kingston-upon-Thames (*C*) 1972-97; PPS to Minister for Arts 1974; Opposition Spokesman on Consumer Affairs 1975-76, and on Industry 1976-79; Under-Sec of State, Dept of Energy 1979-81; Minister of State, Dept of Trade and Industry 1981-85; Minister for Defence Procurement, Ministry of Defence 1985-86; Financial Sec to the Treasury 1986-89; Chief Sec to the Treasury 1989-90; Chancellor of the Exchequer 1990-93; Non-exec Dir N. M. Rothschild & Sons Ltd 1993-95; Dir Balli plc since 1995; Chm E European Food Fund and Dir various investment trusts since 1995; Adviser to the Roumanian Govt since 1997; *cr* PC 1986, and *Baron Lamont of Lerwick*, of Lerwick in the Shetland Islands (Life Baron) 1998: *m* 1971, Alice Rosemary, da of Lt-Col Peter White, of . . . . . ., and has issue.

Address – c/o House of Lords, Westminster, SW1A 0PW. *Club* – Garrick.

SON LIVING

Hon . . . . . ., *b* 19—; *ed* . . . .

DAUGHTER LIVING

Hon . . . . . ., *b* 19—; *ed* . . . .

Lampson, family name of Baron Killearn.

LANE, BARON (Lane) (Life Baron 1979)

GEOFFREY DAWSON LANE, PC, AFC, son of late Percy Albert Lane of Lincoln; *b* 17 July 1918; *ed* Shrewsbury, and Trin Coll, Camb; Bar Gray's Inn 1946, and QC 1962; a Judge of High Court of Justice (Queen's Bench Div) 1966-74; a Lord Justice of Appeal 1974-79, a Lord of Appeal in Ordinary 1979-80, Lord Ch Justice of England 1980-92; 1939-45 War Sqdn-Ldr RAF; AFC (1943); *cr* Knt 1966, PC 1974, and *Baron Lane*, of St Ippollitts, co Hertfordshire (Life Baron) 1979: *m* 1944, Jan, da of Donald Macdonald, and has issue.

Address – c/o Messrs Child & Co, 1 Fleet St, EC4.

SON LIVING

Hon Richard, *b* 1948.

LANE OF HORSELL, BARON (Lane) (Life Baron 1990)

PETER STEWART LANE, son of late Leonard George Lane; *b* 29 Jan 1925; *ed* Sherborne; Sub-Lieut RNVR 1943-46; JP Surrey since 1976; FCA, Senior Partner BDO Binder Hamlyn, Chartered Accountants, 1979-92, Chm Brent International 1985-95, and Attwoods plc 1994, Dep Chm More O'Ferrall 1985-97; Gov Nuffield Nursing Homes Trust 1985-92, Chm 1992-96; Chm Exec Cttee Nat Union of Conservative Assocns 1986-91; Freeman City of London; cr Knt 1984, and *Baron Lane of Horsell*, of Woking, co Surrey (Life Baron) 1990: *m* 1951, Doris Florence, who *d* 1969, da of late Robert Simpson Botsford, and has issue.

𝕬rms – Per pale and per chevron azure and or counterchanged, on a chevron gules three leopard's heads or langued azure all between as many mullets of six points also counterchanged and pierced of the field. 𝕮rest – A demi-lion azure, head and mane or, charged on the body with pierced mullets each of six points also or and supporting by both forepaws a branch of oak fructed of five acorns gold. 𝕾upporters – *Dexter,* A male griffin regardant argent its head, neck, mane and forelegs or rayed also or beaked argent and holding in the beak a double warded key bow downwards gold; *sinister-* A strawberry roan horse proper maned and hooved or its head elevated and regardant holding in its jaws a double warded key bow downwards gold, the compartment comprising a grassy mount raised on each side and growing therefrom two springs of oak each fructed of an acorn gold.
Address – c/o House of Lords, SW1. *Clubs* – Boodle's, MCC, Beefsteak.

DAUGHTERS LIVING

Hon Rosalie (*Baroness Trefgarne*), *b* 1946: *m* 1968, 2nd Baron Trefgarne, and has issue. *Address* – c/o National Westminster Bank, Woking, Surrey.
Hon Alexandra, *b* 1956: *m* 1978, Rev Jeremy Peter Cresswell, and has issue living, Caroline Ruth Anastasia, *b* 1981, — Lucinda Miriam Charlotte, *b* 1983, — Alice Mary Clementine, *b* 1987. *Address* – c/o Lloyds Bank, Woking, Surrey.

LANESBOROUGH, EARLDOM OF (Butler) (Extinct 1998)

DAUGHTERS LIVING AND DECEASED OF NINTH EARL (*By 1st marriage*)

Hon Georgina Ione, *b* 1941; *d* 1947.
(*Lady*) Denyne Gillian Patricia (does not use courtesy title), *b* 1945; Canadian citizen since 1970. *Residence* – 12294 Imperial Drive, Richmond, BC, Canada V7E 6J6.

WIDOW LIVING OF NINTH EARL

PATRICIA JULIA (*Countess of Lanesborough*), da of late Frederick William Meston, MC: *m* 1995, as his 2nd wife, Major the 9th Earl of Lanesborough, TD, who *d* 1998. *Residence* – Allerly, Gattonside, Melrose, Roxburghshire TD6 9LT.

COLLATERAL BRANCHES LIVING

Granddaughters of late Capt Hon Francis Almeric Butler (infra):—
Issue of late Cdr Terence Brinsley John Danvers Butler, RN, *b* 1913, *d* 1987: *m* 1st, 1937 (*m diss* 1947), Hermione, only child of late Cdr T. C. H. Williams, RN; 2ndly, 1947 (*m diss* 1970), Beryl, da of late George Trotter, and formerly wife of Frederick Kennedy Axten; 3rdly, 1972, Mrs Jacqueline Balmer, da of late Winthrop Greene, of Washington, DC:—
(By 1st *m*) Valentine Gay, *b* 1939: *m* 1st, 1964 (*m diss* 1973), Arthur Clyde Nicholson, of Ponder, Texas, USA; 2ndly, 1975, Desmond Waterstone, of 3 Greenfield Manor, Greenfield Park, Donnybrook, Dublin 4, son of John Waterstone, of Caterham, Surrey, and has issue living (by 1st *m*), Felicity, *b* 1969, — (by 2nd *m*) Simon John, *b* 1975, — Harry Desmond, *b* 1978. —— (By 2nd *m*) (Clemency Anne) Susan (Birstwith House, Birstwith, Harrogate, N Yorks), *b* 1949; MA Oxon, LRPS: *m* 1974, John Behrens, son of late Col William Edward Boaz Behrens, of Swinton Grange, Malton, N Yorks, and has issue living, Timothy Edward John, *b* 1978, — Georgina Emily Caroline, *b* 1976. —— Charlotte Gabrielle, *b* 1951: *m* 1983, Marek Skuratowitcz, of Poland, and has issue living, Sophia Lara, *b* 1986. —— Perryn Joanna, *b* 1953: *m* 1984, Robert Hughes, and has issue living, Felix, *b* 1988, — Ramsey, *b* 1989. —— Teresa Jane, *b* 1959; MSc; *d* 1989.

Issue of late Capt Hon Francis Almeric Butler, 3rd son of 6th Earl, *b* 1872, *d* 1925: *m* 1902, Madeline Sarah, who *d* 1961, da of late Richard Birkett Gibbs;—
Maida Daughne Laurel, *b* 1906: *m* 1928, Com Christopher Bryan Stracey Clitherow, DSC, RN, who *d* 1977 (*see* Stracey, Bt, colls).

LANG OF MONKTON, BARON (Lang) (Life Baron 1997)

IAN BRUCE LANG, PC, son of late James Fulton Lang, DSC; *b* 27 June 1940; *ed* Lathallan Sch, Kincardineshire, Rugby, and Sidney Sussex Coll, Camb (BA 1962); MP for Galloway (*C*) 1979-83, and for Galloway and Upper Nithsdale 1983-97; Assist Govt Whip 1981-83; a Lord Commr of the Treasury 1983-86; Parliamentary Under-Sec of State, Dept of Employment 1986, and Scottish Office 1986-87; Min of State, Scottish Office 1987-90; Sec of State for Scotland 1990-95; Pres Board of Trade (Sec of State for Trade and Industry) 1995-97; Vice-Chm Scottish Conservative Party 1983-86; Tstee West of Scotland Tstee Savings Bank 1974-81; Memb Royal Company of Archers (Queen's Body Guard for Scotland) 1974; Chm Murray Ventures plc since 1998; Dep Chm European Telecom plc since 1997; Dir General Accident plc, Marsh C. McLennan Companies Inc (US), Second Scottish Nat Trust plc, Lithgows Ltd; Gov of Rugby Sch; OStJ 1974; *cr* PC 1990, and *Baron Lang of Monkton*, of Merrick and the Rhinns of Kells in Dumfries and Galloway (Life Baron) 1997: *m* 1971, Sandra Caroline, da of late John Alastair Montgomerie, DSC, of Kilmacolm, Renfrewshire, and Sorn, Ayrshire, and has issue.

Arms – Tierced per fess vert azure and vert two thistle stalks slipped and leaved fessways and conjoined at the bases argent at the centre point between two acorns slipped and leaved or in chief a three-masted sailing ship sails furled in base or and at the honour point a fleu-de-lis of the last. **Crest** – A stock dove holding in the beak an olive branch slipped and leaved proper. **Address** – c/o House of Lords, Westminster, SW1A 0PW. *Clubs* – Western (Glasgow), Prestwick Golf, Pratt's.

DAUGHTERS LIVING

Hon Venetia Jane, *b* 1971; *ed* St Mary's Sch, Ascot, and Edinburgh Univ (BA).
Hon Lucy Caroline, *b* 1973; *ed* St Mary's Sch, Ascot, and Bristol Univ (BSc).

LANGFORD, BARON (Rowley-Conwy) (Baron I 1800)

With faith and love

GEOFFREY ALEXANDER ROWLEY-CONWY, OBE, 9th Baron; *b* 8 March 1912; *s* 1953; *ed* Marlborough, and RMA Woolwich; Constable of Rhuddlan Castle, and Lord of the Manor of Rhuddlan; DL co Clwyd; Freeman City of London; commn'd RA 1932, served 1939-45 War, Singapore (Maj RA, evaded capture) and Burma (Arakan, Kohimà) (Lt-Col Indian Mountain Artillery) 1941-45 (OBE); Staff Coll, Quetta 1945, Berlin Air Lift 1948-49, GSO I 42 Inf Div TA 1949-52 (ret 1957), Hon Col 470 Regt RA TA 1961-67, since when Hon Col; OBE (Mil) 1943: *m* 1st, 1939 (*m diss* 1956), Ruth St John, who *d* 1991, da of late Albert St John Murphy, of the Island House, Little Island, co Cork; 2ndly, 1957, Grete, who *d* 1973, da of late Col E. T. C. von Freiesleben, Danish Army, of Strandvej 104, Snekkersten, Denmark; 3rdly, 1975, Susan, da of C. H. C. Denham, of Wrexham, and has issue by 2nd and 3rd wives.

Arms – Quarterly: 1st and 4th, sable on a bend argent cotised ermine a rose gules barbed and seeded proper between two annulets of the first, *Conwy*; 2nd and 3rd, or on a bend cotised gules three crescents argent, *Rowley*. **Crests** – 1st, a moor's head couped at the shoulders sable wreathed about the temples and

Residence – Bodrhyddan, Rhuddlan, Clwyd. *Club* – Army and Navy.

SONS LIVING (By 2nd wife)

Dr the Hon Peter Alexander (17 St John's Rd, Neville's Cross, Durham), *b* 1951; *ed* Marlborough, and Magdalene Coll, Camb (MA, PhD Archaeology); Lecturer, Durham Univ: *m* 1979, Deborah Jane, only da of Col John H. G. Stevens, late RE, of All Hallows Cottage, Middle St, Brockham, Dorking, and has issue living, Gabrielle Catrin, *b* 1984, — Eleanor, *b* 1986.

Hon John Seymour (66 Fentiman Rd, SW8), *b* 1955, *ed* Marlborough, Magdalene Coll,Camb (BA) and Oriel Coll, Oxford (MSc): *m* 1983, Emma Josephine, da of Maj Peter Brown, of Longworth, Oxon, and has issue living, William Geoffrey Peter, *b* 1988, — Huw Grenville *b* 1993, — Katherine Grete Clare, *b* 1985.

Hon OWAIN GRENVILLE (Stonehouse, Bodrhyddan, Rhuddlan, Denbighshire LL18 5SB), *b* 27 Dec 1958; *ed* Marlborough, and RAC Cirencester: *m* 1986 (*m diss* 1993), Joanna, da of Jack Featherstone, of Cae Siôn, Trefnant, Clwyd, and has issue living, Thomas Alexander, *b* 20 March 1987, — Madeleine Guinevere, *b* 1988.

(By 3rd wife)

Hon Christopher Geoffrey Hugh, *b* 1978.

DAUGHTER LIVING (By 3rd wife)

Hon Charlotte Susan Gabrielle, *b* 1980.

SISTER LIVING (Raised to the rank of a Baron's daughter 1955)

Hon Rose Marian, *b* 1915: *m* 1938, Ralph Becher Skinner, who *d* 1994, and has issue living, David Rafe (28 Natal St, Bellvue East 2198, S Africa), *b* 1939: *m* 1981, Shirley, da of late Francis James Fulton Starrett, — Meriel Ann, *b* 1941: *m* 1963, Jasper M. Garnham, of Harewood Lodge, Bulstrode Way, Gerrards Cross, Bucks, — Rosalind Hope (83 Links Way, Croxley Green, Rickmansworth Herts), *b* 1942. *Residence* – The Fold, Cwm, Dyserth, Clwyd.

PREDECESSORS – (1) *Hon* CLOTWORTHY Taylour, 4th son of 1st Earl of Bective assumed the surname of Rowley, and was *cr Baron Langford*, of Summerhill, co Meath (peerage of Ireland) 1800; *d* 1825; *s* by his son (2) HERCULES LANGFORD, 2nd Baron; *d* 1839; *s* by his son (3) CLOTWORTHY WELLINGTON WILLIAM ROBERT, 3rd Baron; *b* 1824: *m* 1846, Louisa Augusta, da of late Col Edward Michael Conolly, MP; *d* 1854; *s* by his son (4) HERCULES EDWARD ROWLEY, KCVO, 4th Baron, *b* 1848; State Steward to Viceroy of Ireland 1886-92, and Comptroller of the Household to Lord-Lieut of Ireland 1895:1902: *m* 1st, 1889, Georgina Mary, who *d* 1901, da of Sir Richard Sutton, 4th Bt; 2ndly, 1915, Margaret Antonia, who *d* 1976, da of late Rev William Mitchell-Carruthers, of Kingham Hill, Kingham, Oxon; *d* 1919; *s* by his son (5) JOHN HERCULES WILLIAM, 5th Baron: *b* 1894; *d* 1922; *s* by his uncle (6) WILLIAM CHAMBRE, 6th Baron, *b* 1849: *m* 1889, Hon Mabel Maud Leigh, who *d* 1966, da of 1st Baron Newton; *d* 1931; *s* by his nephew (7) CLOTWORTHY WELLINGTON THOMAS EDWARD (son of late Hon Randolfe Thomas Randolfe Thomas Rowley, 3rd son of 3rd Baron), 7th Baron; *b* 1885: *m* 1922, Florence Eileen O'Donovan, who *d* 1989, da of Isaac Shiel, of Dublin; *d* 1952; *s* by his kinsman (8) ARTHUR SHOLTO LANGFORD, CMG (son of late Col Hon Hercules Langford Boyle Rowley, 2nd son of 2nd Baron), 8th Baron; *b* 1870; HM's Consul-Gen at Barcelona 1917-23, at Antwerp 1923-30, and Paris 1930-32: *m* 1st, 1908, Margareta Ines, who *d* 1928, da of Hugh R. F. Jameson, of Iquique, Chile; 2ndly, 1929, Maude Alice, who *d* 1958, da of late Henri Lelacheur, of Guernsey; *d* 1953; *s* by his kinsman (9) GEOFFREY ALEXANDER (only son of late Maj Geoffrey Seymour Rowley-Conwy (*ka* Gallipoli 1915) (by his wife, Bertha Gabrielle, who *d* 1984, da of Lt Alexander Cochran, RN, of Ashkirk, Selkirkshire), 3rd son of late Capt Conwy Grenville Hercules Rowley-Conwy, only son of late Hon Richard Thomas Rowley, 2nd son of 1st Baron), 9th Baron and present peer.

Langton, Temple-Gore-, family name of Earl Temple.

LANSDOWNE, MARQUESS OF (Mercer Nairne Petty-Fitzmaurice) (Marquess GB 1784)

By courage, not words

†GEORGE JOHN CHARLES MERCER NAIRNE PETTY-FITZMAURICE, PC, 8th Marquess; *b* 27 Nov 1912; *s* 1944; *ed* Eton, and Ch Ch, Oxford; is a Member of Queen's Body Guard for Scotland (R Company of Archers), a Patron of two livings; a DL for Wilts 1952-73; 1939-45 War as Capt Scots Greys and Maj with French Free Forces (Legion of Honour, Croix de Guerre); appointed Private Sec to HM's Ambassador in Paris 1944; a Lord-in-Waiting to HM 1957-58, Joint Parl Under Sec of State for Foreign Affairs 1958-62, and Min of State for Colonial Affairs 1962-74; assumption of additional surnames of Petty-Fitzmaurice recognized by decree of Lord Lyon 1947; PC 1964: *m* 1st, 1938, Barbara, who *d* 1965, da of Harold Stuart Chase, of Santa Barbara, Calif, USA; 2ndly, 1969 (*m diss* 1978), Hon Selina Polly Dawson Eccles, da of 1st Viscount Eccles, and formerly wife of Robin Andrew Duthac Carnegie (*see* E Southesk); 3rdly, 1978, Gillian Anna, who *d* 1982, da of Alured Morgan; 4thly, 1995, Penelope Eve, da of late Cdr George Francis Norton Bradford, RN, and widow of Hon John Astor (*see* B Astor of Hever, colls), and has issue by 1st *m*.

The 8th Marquess of Lansdowne *d* 25 Aug 1999.

Arms – Quarterly: 1st and 4th, ermine, on a bend azure, a magnetic needle pointing to the polar star or, *Petty;* 2nd and 3rd, argent, a saltire gules, and a chief ermine, *Fitzmaurice.* **Crests** – 1st a bee-hive beset with bees, volante, all proper; 2nd, a sagittary passant proper. **Supporters** – On either side a pegasus ermine, winged, and unguled or, each charged on the shoulder with a fleur-de-lis azure.
Residence – Meikleour House, Perthshire. *Clubs* – Turf, New (Edinburgh).

SONS LIVING (*By 1st marriage*)

CHARLES MAURICE (*Earl of Shelburne*), *b* 21 Feb 1941; *ed* Eton; late Kenya Regt, R Wilts Yeo and R Wessex Yeo; DL Wilts 1991; a Page of Honour to HM 1956-57; Pres Wiltshire Playing Fields Assocn 1965-74; Chm Calne and Chippenham RDC 1972-73; Co Councillor of Wilts since 1970-85; Chm N Wilts Dist Council 1973-76, since when Pres Wiltshire Assocn of Boys and Youth Clubs; Member of S-W Economic Planning Council 1972-77; Chm Population and Settlement Cttee (SWEPC) 1972-77; Parly Candidate for Coventry NE 1977-79; Member Historic Buildings and Monuments Commn 1983-89; Pres N Wilts Conservative Assocn 1986-90, and Historic Houses Assocn 1988-93; Member of Council of Duchy of Cornwall since 1990: *m* 1st, 1965 (*m diss* 1987), Lady Frances Helen Mary Eliot, da of 9th Earl of St Germans; 2ndly, 1987, Fiona Mary, da of Donald Merritt, and has issue by 1st *m*:—

> SONS LIVING (*by 1st marriage*) — Simon Henry George (*Viscount Calne and Calstone*), *b* 24 Nov 1970. —— *Hon* William Nicholas Charles, *b* 1973.
>
> DAUGHTERS LIVING (*by 1st marriage*) — *Lady* Arabella Helen Mary, *b* 1966: *m* 1993, Rupert W. H. Unwin, yr son of Martin I. H. Unwin, of Shipton Moyne, Glos, and has issue living, Abrahm Arthur George, *b* 1996. — Gala Ellen Theodora, *b* 1998. — *Lady* Rachel Barbara Violet, *b* 1968: *m* 1991, James William Richard Spickernell, and has issue (*see* E Leicester, colls).

Residence – Bowood House, Calne, Wilts. *Clubs* – Brooks's, Turf.

Lord Robert Harold MERCER NAIRNE (Kinclaven Church House, Kinclaven, by Stanley, Perthshire PH1 4QW), *b* 1947; *ed* Gordonstoun, Univ of Kent (BA), and Univ of Washington Graduate Sch of Business (MBA, PhD); FBIM: *m* 1972, Jane Elizabeth, el da of late Lt-Col Lord Douglas Claude Alexander Gordon, DSO (*see* M Huntly, colls), and has issue living, Samuel George, *b* 1976, — Joseph Douglas, *b* 1980, — Emily Jane, *b* 1974.

DAUGHTERS LIVING AND DECEASED (*By 1st marriage*)

Lady Caroline Margaret, *b* 1939; *d* 1956.
Lady Georgina Elizabeth FITZMAURICE, *b* 1950; has resumed her maiden name: *m* 1st, 1974 (*m diss* 1980), Guy Hamilton; 2ndly, 1981, Robert Eric Miller, and has issue living (by 1st *m*), Josiah Stirling, *b* 1975, — Emma Carissa, *b* 1977.

SISTER LIVING (*Raised to the rank of a Marquess's daughter* 1946)

Lady Mary Margaret Elizabeth, *b* 1910: *m* 1931, Lt-Col Ririd Myddelton, CVO, Coldstream Gds, who *d* 1988, and has issue living, David Foulk (New Hall, Wrexham), *b* 1932; late Coldstream Gds; High Sheriff of Clwyd 1980: *m* 1st, 1965 (*m diss* 1968), Anne, only da of late Charles Brotherton, of Kirkham Abbey, York; 2ndly, 1970, Christine Serena Cherry, da of Arthur Malcolm Morris, OBE, Depart of External Affairs, Canberra, Aust, and has issue living, (by 1st *m*), Guy Charles *b* 1966: *m* 1995, Emma Frances, da of Col Arthur David Bentley Brooks (*see* By Rushcliffe) (and has issue living, Edward Arthur George *b* 1999), (by 2nd *m*) Mark Ririd *b* 1973, Sian Moyra *b* 1971: *m* 1997, Mark James Arthur Hickmott, son of David William Ralph Hickmott, of Plymouth, Devon, — Hugh Robert (139 Holland Park Av, W11), *b* 1938, late Coldstream Gds: *m* 1967, Hon Sarah Cecily Allsopp, da of 5th Baron Hindlip, and has issue living, Alexander Ririd Henry *b* 1969, Claerwen Georgina Margaret *b* 1972: *m* 1996, John H. S. Maclean, elder son of Rev Kenneth Maclean, of Bicton, Shrops, — Fiona Violet (*Lady Aird*), GVO *b* 1934; appointed a Lady-in-Waiting to HRH Princess Margaret 1960, LVO 1980: *m* 1963, Capt Sir Alastair Sturgis Aird, GCVO, Capt 9th Lancers (*see* Aird, Bt, colls). *Residence* – Chirk Castle, nr Wrexham, N Wales.

DAUGHTER LIVING OF SIXTH MARQUESS

Lady Elizabeth Mary, *b* 1927: *m* 1950, Major Charles William Lambton, Coldstream Guards (ret) (*see* E Durham, colls).
Residence – The Old Rectory, Calstone, Calne, Wilts.

COLLATERAL BRANCH LIVING

Descendants of late Hon Thomas FitzMaurice (son of 1st Earl of Shelburne and brother of 1st Marquess of Lansdowne), who *m* 1777, Mary, *Countess of Orkney* (in her own right) (*see* E Orkney).

PREDECESSORS – **(1)** THOMAS FitzMaurice; *cr Baron of Kerry and Lixnaw* (peerage of Ireland); *d* 1280; *s* by his son **(2)** MAURICE, 2nd Baron; sat in Parliament at Dublin 1295; *d* 1303; *s* by his son **(3)** NICHOLAS, 3rd Baron; *s* by his son **(4)** MAURICE, 4th Baron; having a dispute with Desmond Oge MacCarthy, killed that chief on the bench before the Judge of Assize at Tralee in 1325, for which he was tried and attainted by the Parliament of Dublin, but was not put to death; his lands were, however, forfeited, but restored after his decease in 1339 to his brother and successor **(5)** JOHN, 5th Baron; summoned to Parliament 1375; *s* by his son **(6)** MAURICE, 6th Baron; *d* 1398; *s* by his son **(7)** PATRICK, 7th Baron; *d* 1410; *s* by his son **(8)** EDMUND, 8th Baron; *d* 1469; *s* by his son **(9)** EDMUND, 9th Baron; *d* 1489; *s* by his son **(10)** EDMUND, 10th Baron; resigned his estates to his el son and became a lay brother of the Order of St Francis in the Friary of Ardfert; *d* 1954; *s* by his son **(11)** EDMOND, 11th Baron; *cr Baron Odorney*, of co Kerry, and *Viscount Kilmaule* (peerage of Ireland) 1537; *d* without male issue 1541, when the Barony of Odorney and Viscountcy became extinct, and the Barony of Kerry devolved upon his brother **(12)** PATRICK, 12th Baron; *d* 1547; *s* by his el son **(13)** THOMAS, 13th Baron; *d* a minor 1549; *s* by his brother **(14)** EDMUND, 14th Baron; *d* 1549; *s* by his uncle **(15)** GERALD, 15th Baron; *d* 1550; *s* by his brother **(16)** THOMAS, 16th Baron; served many years in the military service of Emperors of Germany; *d* 1590; *s* by his son **(17)** PATRICK, 17th Baron; brought up at Court of Queen Elizabeth, but was in rebellion against HM after his succession to title; *d* 1600; *s* by his son **(18)** THOMAS, 18th Baron; surrendered his estates to James I, who in 1604 granted him a free pardon, and in 1612, by patent, confirmed his estates to him and his heirs and assigns for ever; *d* 1630; *s* by his el son **(19)** PATRICK, 19th Baron; took his seat in Parliament 1634, and removed to England 1641; *d* 1660; *s* by his el son **(20)** WILLIAM FITZMAURICE, 20th Baron; *d* 1697; *s* by his son **(21)** *Rt Hon* THOMAS, 21st Baron; *cr Viscount Clan Maurice* and *Earl of Kerry* (peerage of Ireland) 1722; *d* 1741; *s* by his son **(22)** WILLIAM, PC, 2nd Earl; Gov of Ross Castle, Col of Coldstream Guards, and Custos Rotulorum of co Kerry; *d* 1747; *s* by his son **(23)** FRANCIS THOMAS, 3rd Earl; *dsp* 1818; *s* by his cousin **(24)** HENRY Petty-FitzMaurice, KG, PC, 3rd *Marquess of Lansdowne* (see * infra); a distinguished statesman; Lord Lieut of Wilts, MP for Camelford Chancellor of the Exchequer 1806-7, Lord Pres of the Council 1830-4 and 1846-52, and a member of the Cabinet without office 1852-8; *d* 1863; *s* by his son **(25)** HENRY, KG, 4th Marquess; *b* 1816; sat as MP for Calne (*L*) 1847-56; was a Lord of the Treasury 1847, and Under-Sec for Foreign Affairs 1856-8; summoned to Parliament in his father's Barony of Wycombe: *m* 1843, Emily Jane Mercer Elphinstone de Flahault, who *d* 1895, in her own right Lady Nairne (infra): *d* 1866; *s* by his son **(26)** HENRY CHARLES KEITH, KG, GCSI, GCMG, GCIE, who *s* as 9th Lord Nairne 1895, 5th Marquess, *b* 1845; a Commr of Exchequer of Great Britain, and of Treasury of Ireland 1868-72, Under-Sec of State for War 1872-4, Under-Sec for India 1880, Gov-Gen of Canada and Com-in-Ch of Prince Edward Island 1883-8, Viceroy of India 1888-94, Sec of State for War 1895-1900, and Sec of State for Foreign Affairs 1900-1905, and Min (without portfolio) May 1915 to Dec 1916; Lord-Lieut of Wilts 1896-1820; Chancellor or Order of St Michael and St George 1917-20; had Roy Victorian Chain; bore Royal Standard at Coronation of King George V 1911: *m* 1869, Lady Maud Evelyn Hamilton, VA, CI, GBE, CH, who *d* 1932, da of 1st Duke of Abercorn, KB; *d* 1927; *s* by his son **(27)** HENRY WILLIAM EDMOND, DSO, MVO, 6th Marquess, *b* 1872; MP for W Div of Derbyshire (*U*) 1908-18; sometime a Senator of Irish Free State: *m* 1904, Elizabeth Caroline (who *d* 1964, having *m* 2ndly, 1940, Lord Colum Edmund Crichton-Stuart), da of Sir Edward Stanley Hope, KCG; *d* 1936; *s* by his son **(28)** CHARLES HOPE, 7th Marquess *b* 1917; Capt Roy Wilts Yeo (TA); *ka* Italy 20 Aug 1944, when he was *s* in the Lordship of Nairne by his el sister, Lady Katherine Evelyn Constance Bigham (Viscountess Mersey), and in all the other peerages by his cousin **(29)** GEORGE JOHN CHARLES MERCER (only son of late Major Lord Charles George Francis MERCER NAIRNE, MVO, 2nd son of 5th Marquess) 8th Marquess and present peer; also Earl of Wycombe, Viscount Calne and Calstone, Lord Wycombe, Baron of Chipping Wycombe, Earl of Kerry, Earl of Shelburne, Viscount ClanMaurice and FitzMaurice, Baron of Kerry and Lixnaw, and Baron Dunkerron.

*(1) *Hon* JOHN FitzMaurice, PC, 2nd son of 1st Earl of Kerry (ante) inherited the estates of his maternal uncle Henry, 1st and last Earl of Shelburne (*cr* 1719) whose surname of Petty he assumed; was sole Gov of co Kerry, and MP for Chipping Wycombe; *cr Baron Dunkeron* and *Viscount FitzMaurice* (peerage of Ireland) 1751, *Earl of Shelburne* (peerage of Ireland) 1753, and *Baron Wycombe*, of Chipping Wycombe, co Bucks (peerage of Great Britain) 1760; *d* 1761; *s* by his son **(2)** WILLIAM, KG, PC, 2nd Earl; MP for Chipping Wycombe 1763, a Lord of Trade, a Major-Gen in the Army, ADC to HM 1760, a Principal Sec of State 1766, and Prime Minister and First Lord of the Treasury 1782; *cr Viscount Calne and Calstone, Earl of Wycombe*, and *Marquess of Lansdowne* (peerage of Great Britain) 1784; *d* 1805; *s* by his son **(3)** JOHN HENRY, 2nd Marquess; MP for Chipping Wycombe 1786-90; *dsp* 1809; *s* by his half-brother **(4)** HENRY, 3rd Marquess (see ante).

Lascelles, Viscount; son of Earl of Harewood.

Lascelles, family name of Earl of Harewood.

LATHAM, BARON (Latham) (Baron UK 1942)

It is good to try

DOMINIC CHARLES LATHAM, 2nd Baron; *b* 20 Sept 1954; *s* 1970; *ed* NSW Univ (BE Civil 1977, Hons I, MEngSc 1981); Civil Engr with Electricity Commn of NSW 1979-88; Structural Engr with Rankine & Hill Consulting Engrs 1988-91; Sr Structural Engr, Gerard Barry Assocs 1992; Social Dancing Teacher since 1993.

𝕬rms – Per fesse gules and chequy or and sable a fesse barry wavy argent and azure in chief a seax fessewise point to the sinister cutting edge upwards proper pomel and hilt of the second ensigned with a Saxon crown also of the second. 𝕮rest – Two spurs one in bend the other in bend sinister rowels upwards or straps sable with buckles gold. 𝕾upporters – On either side a horse sable charged on the shoulder with a plate and gorged with a mural coronet with chain reflexed over the back or.
Address – PO Box 355, Kensington, NSW 2033, Australia.

BROTHER LIVING

ANTHONY MICHAEL (twin), *b* 20 Sept 1954: *m* 19—, Margot. Resides in Queensland, Australia.

AUNTS LIVING (*Daughters of 1st Baron*)

Hon Barbara Wendy (Maia), *b* 1920; 1942-44 War as 1st class Aircraftwoman WAAF: *m* 1st, 1941 (*m diss* 1945), Capt Denis Charles Wildish, RASC; 2ndly, 1946 (*m diss* 1951), Peter Anthony Charles Kurt Bruckmann, late Capt E Surrey Regt; 3rdly, 1966, Malcolm Blundell Cole-Fontayn, solicitor, and has issue living, (by 2nd *m*) Karin Francesca, *b* 1948: *m* 1973, John Cornelius Fitzgerald.

Hon Jean Helen *b* 1921; WRNS 1940-45: *m* 1st 1945 (*m diss* 1961), Sqdn-Ldr Wilfred Ronald Gellatly, RNZAF; 2ndly, 1970, James Oswald Dykes, and has issue living, (by 1st *m*), Paul Latham *b* 1946: *m* 1969, Patricia Edith, da of late John Richardson Halliday, and has issue living, Neil Paul *b* 1973, Elizabeth *b* 1975.

Hon Diana Dorothy, *b* 1925: *m* 19—, Barringer.

PREDECESSOR – (1) CHARLES Latham, son of late George Latham, of Norwich; *b* 1888, Leader of LCC 1940-47, Chm of London Transport Exec 1947-53; Chm of Finance Cttee of Metropolitan Water Board 1957-65; Lord Lieut of Middx 1945-56; *cr Baron Latham*, of Hendon, co Middx (peerage of UK) 1942: *m* 1st, 1913 (*m diss* 1957) Maya Helen, who *d* 1978, da of Louis George Allman, of Hendon; 2ndly, 1957, Sylvia May, who *d* 1985, da of Alexander Newmark, of London, and widow of Alexander Kennard; *d* 1970; *s* by his grandson (2) DOMINIC CHARLES (el twin son of Hon Francis Charles Allman Latham, who *d* 1959, having *m* 1951, as his 3rd wife, Gabrielle Monica, who *d* 1987, da of Dr S. M. O'Riordan), 2nd Baron and present peer.

LATYMER, BARON (Money-Coutts) (Baron E 1431-2)

To be, not to seem

HUGO NEVILL MONEY-COUTTS, 8th Baron; *b* 1 March 1926; *s* 1987; *ed* Eton: *m* 1st, 1951 (*m diss* 1965), Hon Penelope Ann Clare, yr da of late Thomas Addis Emmet, and of Baroness Emmet of Amberley (Life Baroness, ext 1980); 2ndly, 1965, Jinty Ann, 2nd da of late Peter George Calvert (*see* B Ashcombe, 1963 Edn), and has issue by both *m*.

𝕬rms – Quarterly: 1st and 4th, a stag's head erased gules, between the attires a pheon azure, all within a bordure embattled of the last, charged with four buckles or, *Coutts*; 2nd and 3rd or, on a pile azure ten besants, four, three, two, and one, on a chief ermine a lion passant of the second, *Money*. 𝕮rests – 1st, a man from the middle upwards, shooting an arrow from a bow, all proper, *Coutts*; 2nd, a besant between two wings azure, each semée-de-lis, or, *Money*. 𝕾upporters – On either side a griffin or.
Residence – Vivero Hortus, Santa Maria, Mallorca.

SONS LIVING (*By 1st marriage*)

Hon CRISPIN JAMES ALAN NEVILL, *b* 8 March 1955; *ed* Eton, and Keble Coll, Oxford: *m* 1st, 1978 (*m diss* 1995), Hon Lucy Rose Deedes, yst da of Baron Deedes (Life Baron); 2ndly, 1995, Mrs Shaunagh Anne Henrietta Heneage, da of George Silver Oliver Annesley Colthurst (*see* Colthurst, Bt), and has issue living (by 1st *m*), Drummond William Thomas, *b* 11 May 1986, — Sophia Patience, *b* 1985, — Evelyn Rose, *b* 1988. *Address* – c/o Coutts & Co, 440 Strand, WC2R 0QS.

Hon Giles Thomas Nevill, *b* 1957; *ed* Eton, and Oriel Coll, Oxford.

(By 2nd marriage)

Hon Henry Eugene, *b* 1967; *ed* Eton.

DAUGHTERS LIVING *(By 1st marriage)*

Hon Clare Louise, *b* 1952; *ed* Cobham Hall: *m* 1979, John Edmunds, son of John Edmunds, of Quinton, Glos. *Residence* – Buscott Farm, Ashcott, Bridgwater, Som.

(By 2nd marriage)

Hon Vera Dulcie Harriet, *b* 1972; *ed* Bryanston.
Hon Fanny Clara Maria, *b* 1973; *ed* Bryanston.

SISTERS LIVING

Hon Joanna Harriet Nevill, *b* 1928: *m* 1951, Pierre Langlais, and has issue living, Eric, *b* 1952, — Nicole, *b* 1953, — Louise, *b* 1954, — Odette, *b* 1961, — Jacqueline, *b* 1962. *Residence* – PO Box 113, N Hartland, Vermont 05052, USA.

Hon Susan Margaret Nevill, *b* 1933: *m* 1st 1956 (*m diss* 1965), Michael John Turner, QC (*cr* Kt Bach 1985) (*see* By Schuster, 1980 Edn); 2ndly, 1965, Ian A. K. Dipple, of Nether Walstead, Lindfield, Sussex RH16 2QJ, and has issue living (by 1st *m*), Mark Christopher (The Old Black Swan, 41 High St South, Stewkley, Leighton Buzzard, Beds LU7 0HP), *b* 1959; *ed* Radley: *m* 1985, Michèle, da of late Dirk Trevor Spencer, of Isle of Man, and has issue living, Daniel Thomas *b* 1985, Sarah Ellen *b* 1988, Jessica Louise Mary *b* 1991, — Louise Margaret Ruth, *b* 1960: *m* 1993, Michael H. Crouch, of Stepaside Cottage, Aldingbourne, Chichester, W Sussex PO20 6UB, son of late Henry Crouch, of Walton-on-Thames, Surrey, — (by 2nd *m*) Alexandra Margaret, *b* 1967, — Joanna Shannon, *b* 1968.

COLLATERAL BRANCHES LIVING

Issue of late Lieut-Col Hon Alexander Burdett Money-Coutts, OBE, 2nd son of 6th Baron, *b* 1902, *d* 1994: *m* 1930, Mary Elspeth, who *d* 1990, da of Sir Reginald Arthur Hobhouse, 5th Bt:—
Sir David Burdett, KCVO (Magpie House, Peppard Common, Henley-on-Thames, Oxon RG9 5JG), *b* 1931; *ed* Eton, and New Coll, Oxford; late Capt Royal Gloucestershire Hussars; Chm Coutts & Co 1976-93, Chm M & G Group plc 1991-97; KCVO 1991: *m* 1958, Helen Penelope June Utten, da of late Cdr Killingworth Richard Utten Todd, Royal Indian Navy (*see* E Morton, colls, 1948 Edn), and has issue living, Benjamin Burdett (Overbury Court, Old Odiham Rd, Alton, Hants GU34 4BX), *b* 1961: *m* 1987, Patricia Anne, eldest da of Dr Carl Trepagnier, of Houston, Texas, and has issue living, Christopher Burdett *b* 1990, Zachary Alexander *b* 1994, Cecily Anne *b* 1992, — Harriet St Bride, *b* 1959: *m* 1st, 1979 (*m diss* 1985), Charles Spencer Chetwode Ram, yst son of late Maj Henry Stopford Chetwode Ram, RE: 2ndly, 1985 (*m diss* 1999), Martin Neil Pottinger, yr son of late Peter Henry Jameson Pottinger, of Corstorphine, Edinburgh, and has issue living (by 2nd *m*), William Jameson, *b* 1985, Thomas George *b* 1989, Robin David *b* 1990, Flora St Bride *b* 1987, — Laura Isabella, *b* 1965: *m* 1987, P. Jamie Corrie, of Foxley, Peppard Common, Henley-on-Thames, Oxon RG9 5LB, elder son of late Peter Corrie, of Corner House, Peppard Common, Henley-on-Thames, Oxon, and has issue living, Joshua Richard *b* 1992, Lucinda Mary *b* 1994.

Issue of late Maj Hon Godfrey Burdett Money-Coutts, 3rd son of 6th Baron, *b* 1905, *d* 1979: *m* 1931, Anne Cecilia, who *d* 1969, da of late Hon Wilfred James (B Northbourne, colls):—
Julia Jane *b* 1933; assumed the surname of St John Aubin 1968 until remarriage: *m* 1st, 1951 (*m diss* 1968), Capt Richard John Fisher Turner, RN; 2ndly, 1991, Christopher Thomasson, of Somerton Castle, Boothby Graffoe, Lincoln LN5 0LL, and has issue living (by 1st *m*), Antony Robin Fisher, *b* 1952: *m* 1973, Barbara Maeve, da of Harry Stokes, of Guildford, Surrey, and has issue living, Barnaby Adam Fisher *b* 1978, Adam Benedict Fisher *b* 1982, — Simon John Fisher, *b* 1954, — James Michael Fisher, *b* 1956: *m* 1983, Linda Richardson.

Issue of late Hon Mercy Burdett Money-Coutts, only da of 6th Baron, *b* 1910, *d* 1993: *m* 1947, Michael Seiradhakis, of 19 Odos Seirenon, Byronas, Athens 162 31:—
John Hugh SEIRADHAKIS (Ethnikis Symfiliosis 39, GR 57019, Perea, Greece), *b* 1948: *m* 1978 (*m diss* 1999), Benedicta Teppe, and has issue living, Michael, *b* 1981, — Elena, *b* 1979. —— Sophia Hester SEIRADHAKI (Photimari, Kea, 830 02 Greece), *b* 1949; has continued to use her maiden name since 1978: *m* 1st, 1974 (*m diss* 1978), George Pinderis; 2ndly, 1985, Charalambos Papoutsakis.

Issue of late Hon Clara Burdett Money-Coutts, el da of 5th Baron, *b* 1877, *d* 1969: *m* 1905, Rev Melville Watson Patterson, Fellow and Sr Tutor, Trin Coll, Oxford, who *d* 1944:—
Rosamund Margaret (Brackley Fields Retirement Home, Halse Rd, Brackley, Northants), *b* 1905: *m* 1934, Selwyn Duruz, who *d* 1976. —— Joan Elisabeth (2 College House, High St, Brackley, Northants NN13 7NR), *b* 1908: *m* 1st, 1931 (*m diss* 1937), Sebastian Max Alexander Myer Clement Salaman, who *d* 1976; 2ndly, 1947, Raymond Coxon, IG, who *d* 1983, and has issue living, (by 1st *m*) Clement Francis (5 Second Av, Mortlake, SW14 8QF), *b* 1932: *m* 1961, Juliet Nicholson, — Frederick Nicholas Paul (Flat 6, 62 Elm Park Gdns, SW10), *b* 1936; *ed* Radley, and Trin Coll, Oxford: *m* 1st, 1960 (*m diss* 1974), Elisabeth Cecily, da of Francis Sclater, of Bunces Farm, Newick, Uckfield, Sussex; 2ndly, 1983, Lyndsay Margaret, da of James Meiklejohn, of Wise Lane, Mill Hill, and has issue living (by 1st *m*), Sophia *b* 1963, Charlotte *b* 1966, (by 2nd *m*) Rose Clementine *b* 1983, Phoebe Joy *b* 1987. —— Lindsay Marion, *b* 1916: *m* 1939, Humphry Gilbert

Bohun Lynch, of 19 Eastfield Court, Church St, Faringdon, Oxon SN7 8SL, and has issue living, Francis Nicholas (Hadley, Wootton Rivers, Marlborough, Wilts), *b* 1944; *ed* Merton Coll, Oxford: *m* 1st, 1965 (*m diss* 1974), Amanda Underwood; 2ndly, 1983, Susan, da of Eric Wright, of Hawaii, USA, and has issue living (by 2nd *m*), Hugh Arthur *b* 1991 , — Alison Harriet, *b* 1955.

Grandchildren of late Hon Joan Burdett Nixon (infra):—
Issue of late Arundel James Nixon, *b* 1907, *d* 1949: *m* 1st, 1930 (*m diss* 1940), Edna Duffy; 2ndly, 1941, Paloma Margaret (who *m* 2ndly, 1951, Geoffrey Thomas Luke, of Victoria, Australia, and *d* 1980), da of David Maccreesh, of USA:—
(By 1st *m*) Peter NIXON, *b* 1934. *Residence* – Australia. —— (By 2nd *m*) David Guy NIXON-LUKE, *b* 1945: *m* 1970, Charryce Laleen Yolanna, yst da of Montague Neville Lea, of 188 Rocky Point Rd, Kogarah, NSW, Australia, and has issue living, Guy Jaeger Evans Arundel, *b* 1976, — Jordan Geoffrey Bradshaw, *b* 1982, — Reece David Valmont, *b* 1986. *Residence* – 22 Lambert Rd, Toorak, Victoria 3142, Australia. —— Nikki, *b* 1942: *m* 1961 (*m diss* 1982), Robert William Martin, and has issue living, James Patrick, *b* 1965, — Sarah Jane, *b* 1963. *Residence* – 96 Bendigo St, E Richmond, Victoria, Australia.

Issue of late Hon Joan Burdett Money-Coutts, 3rd da of 5th Baron, *b* 1882, *d* 1968: *m* 1905 (*m diss* 1941), Lt-Col James Arundel Nixon, DSO, formerly King's Own (R Lancaster) Regt, who *d* 1950:—
Guy John NIXON (47 Mount Row, St Peter Port, Guernsey GY1 1NU), *b* 1909; *ed* Eton, and Pembroke Coll, Camb (BA); AIB: *m* 1933, Barbara Helen, who *d* 1991, yr da of late Francis William Whitbourn Morgan; 2ndly, 1992, Mrs Michelle James, da of late James Frederick Carey, of Guernsey, and has issue living (by 1st *m*), Sara, *b* 1933: *m* 1959, John Gordon Mathias of Sanson's Cottage, Leysbourne, Chipping Campden, Glos GL55 6AD, and has issue living, Jeremy (5 St David's Sq, E14 3WA) *b* 1963: *m* 1992, Jane, da of Jacques Marie Joseph Plujol, of Chazé sur Argos, France (and has issue living, Henry Jean Jacques *b* 1999), Penelope, *b* 1960.

Granddaughters of Hon Margaret Burdett Still (infra):—
Issue of late Robert Still, *b* 1910, *d* 1971: *m* 1944, Elizabeth Eleanor (Bucklebury Lodge, Bucklebury, nr Reading, Berks RG7 6PB), da of S. K. Westman, FRCS, of Harley St, W1:—
Susan, *b* 1945: *m* 1965, R. C. R. Chesters, of Winchester, and has issue living, William, *b* 1971, — Celia, *b* 1973. —— Anthea, *b* 1947: *m* 1974, Michael Dillon, of Oxford, and has issue living, Simon, *b* 1975, — Timothy, *b* 1983, — David, *b* 1985, — Ruth, *b* 1977. —— Katharine, *b* 1949: *m* 1971, Peter Hyde, of Hove, and has issue living, Robert, *b* 1972, — David, *b* 1981, — Jonathan, *b* 1990, — Elizabeth, *b* 1983. —— Claudia, *b* 1954: *m* 1977 (*m diss* 1987), Lucian W. N. Camp, of Hampstead, London.

Issue of late Hon Margaret Burdett Money-Coutts, yst da of 5th Baron, *b* 1886, *d* 1948: *m* 1907, Major Francis Churchill Still, solicitor, of 5 New Sq, Lincoln's Inn, WC2, who *d* 1937:—
Ursula Margaret, *b* 1913: *m* 1935, Archibald Walter Bury, who *d* 1998. Resides in Australia.

PREDECESSORS – **(1)** Sir GEORGE Nevill, 5th son of 1st Earl of Westmorland; summoned to Parliament by writ as *Baron Latymer* 1431-2: *m* Elizabeth, da of 5th Earl of Warwick; *d* 1469; *s* by his grandson **(2)** RICHARD, *b* 1468 summoned to Parliament 1492-1529: *m* 1490, Anne, da of Sir Humphrey Stafford, of Grafton and Blatherwycke; *d* 1530; *s* by his son **(3)** JOHN, *b* 1493; summoned to Parliament 1533-4 and 1541-2: *m* 1st, 1518, Elizabeth, da of Sir Richard Musgrave, of Hartland; 2ndly, Dorothy, who *d* 1526-27, da of Sir George Vere; 3rdly Katharine (who subsequently *m* King Henry VIII), da of Sir Thoms Parr, of Kendal and widow of Edward, Lord Burgh; *d* 1543; *s* by his only son by 2nd *m* **(4)** JOHN; summoned to Parliament 1543-80: *m* Lucy, da of 2nd Earl of Worcester; *d* 1577, when the Barony fell into abeyance between his four das and co-heirs; in July 1912, the Committee for Privileges of the House of Lords reported (other co-heirs not appearing) that a claim to the Barony had been made out by **(5)** FRANCIS THOMAS Money-Coutts, 5th Baron, only son of late Rev James Drummond Money, by Clara Maria, who *d* 1899 (having assumed by Roy licence 1880, for herself and son, the additional surname of Coutts), 4th da of Sir Francis Burdett, 5th Bt (*cr* 1618-19); *b* 1852; proved his claim to the Barony before the Committee for Privileges of the House of Lords July 1912 (claiming through Frances, el da of Lucy (who *m* Sir William Cornwallis), 3rd da of 4th Baron), and the abeyance was determined in his favour Dec 1912; assumed by Roy licence 1914, the additional surname and arms of Nevill in lieu of that of Money and after that of Coutts: *m* 1875, Edith Ellen, who *d* 1942, da of Charles Churchill, of Weybridge Park, Surrey; *d* 1923; *s* by his son **(6)** HUGH BURDETT Money-Coutts, TD, 6th Baron; *b* 1876; sometime Capt N. Devon Hussars Yeo; European War 1915-17 in Gallipoli and Egypt; *m* 1900, Hester Frances, who *d* 1961, da of late Maj-Gen John Cecil Russell, CVO; *d* 1949; *s* by his son **(7)** THOMAS BURDETT, 7th Baron, *b* 1901; Chm London Cttee of Ottoman Bank and of Investment Trust Corpn Ltd, Dir Coutts and Co and of Nat Prov Bank, Vice-Chm Middlesex Hosp: *m* 1925, Patience Margaret, who *d* 1982, da of late William Courtenay-Thompson; *d* 1987; *s* by his only son **(8)** HUGO NEVILL, 8th Baron and present peer.

LAUDERDALE, EARL OF (Maitland) (Earl S 1624, Bt S 1680)

By wisdom and courage

PATRICK FRANCIS MAITLAND, 17th Earl, and 13th Baronet; *b* 17 March 1911; *s* 1968; *ed* Lancing, and Brasenose Coll, Oxford (BA); Hereditary Bearer of National Flag of Scotland by decrees of Lord Lyon King of Arms 1790 and 1952; recognised by Lord Lyon as Chief of Clan Maitland 1968; Editor of *The Fleet Street Letter Service*, and *The Whitehall Letter* 1945-58; Pres of Church Union 1959-62; MP for Lanark (*C*) 1951-59; a Member of Coll of Guardians of Nat Shrine of Our Lady of Walsingham 1949-65, since when Guardian Emeritus; Founder of Expanding Commonwealth Group of House of Commons (Chm 1955-61); Chm Sub-Cttee F (Energy, Transport Research) of House of Lords Select Cttee on EEC 1974-79: *m* 1936, Stanka, da of Prof Milivoye Losanitch, of Belgrade, and has issue.

Arms – Or, a lion rampant gules couped at all his joints of the field, within the Royal tressure azure, in a dexter canton argent a saltire azure, surmounted of an inescutcheon or, charged with a lion rampant within a double tressure flory counterflory gules, behind the shield on staffs in saltire proper two representations of the Sovereign's National Flag of Scotland (Cross of St Andrew), fringed or, ropes and tassels of the last (Insignia of Office of Bearer for the Sovereign of the Sovereign's National Flag of Scotland). **Crest** – A lion sejant affrontee gules, ducally crowned proper, in his dexter paw a sword of the last, hilted and pommelled or, and in his sinister a fleur-de-lis azure. **Supporters** – Two eagles proper.
Residence – 12 St Vincent St, Edinburgh.

SONS LIVING

IAN (*Viscount Maitland, Master of Lauderdale*) (150 Tachbrook St, SW1V 2NE), *b* 4 Nov 1937; *ed* Radley, and Brasenose Coll, Oxford (MA); Lt RNR: *m* 1963, Ann Paule, da of Geoffrey Clark, of 511 Hood House, Dolphin Sq, SW1, and has issue:—

> SON LIVING—*Hon* John Douglas (*Master of Maitland*), *b* 1965; *ed* Radley, and Van Mildert Coll, Durham (BSc). *Residence* – 2 Claverley Grove, N3 2DG.

> DAUGHTER LIVING—*Hon* Sarah Caroline, *b* 1964; *ed* St Paul's Girls' Sch, and Trevelyan Coll, Durham (BA): *m* 1988, Stuart G. Parks, son of late K. Parks, of Wargrave, Berks, and has issue living, Thomas George Maitland, *b* 1995, — Hugh Charles Maitland, *b* 1997. *Residence* – The Old Vicarage, Church Close, E Hagbourne, Oxon OX11 9LP.

Rev the Hon Sydney Milivoye Patrick (14 Kersland St, Glasgow G12 8BL), *b* 1951; *ed* Eton, Edinburgh University (BSc) and Strathclyde University (Dip TP); ordained Priest in Scottish Episcopal Church 1987: *m* 1974, (Dorothy) Eileen, da of A. R. Bedell of The Knowe, Chapleton, Strathaven, Lanarkshire.

DAUGHTERS LIVING

Lady (Helen) Olga, *b* 1944: *m* 1969, Robin William Patrick Hamilton Hay, of 21 Cloudesley St, N1, and has issue living, Alastair Patrick Hamilton, *b* 1972, — Fergus William Hamilton *b* 1981, — Camilla Charlotte Hamilton, *b* 1975.
Lady Caroline Charlotte Militsa (12 St Vincent St, Edinburgh), *b* 1946.

GRANDDAUGHTERS LIVING OF FIFTEENTH EARL (*Raised to the rank of an Earl's daughters* 1953)

Issue of late Ivor Colin James (*Viscount Maitland*) Lieut RAC (TA), only son of 15th Earl, *b* 1915, *ka* 1943: *m* 1936, Helena Ruth (infra), yr da of Sir Herbert Charles Perrott, 6th Bt (ext), CH, CB:—
Lady Mary Helena (*Lady Mary Biddulph*) *b* 1938; a Tweed Commr: *m* 1958, 4th Baron Biddulph, who *d* 1988. *Residence* – Greatridgehall, Makerstoun, Kelso, Roxburghshire TD5 7PD. —— *Lady* Anne Priscilla, *b* 1940: *m* 1968, John Joseph Eyston, of Mapledurham House, Reading (*see* E Mexborough, 1985 Edn), and has issue living, Edward Thomas Ivor, *b* 1969: *m* 1997, Alexandra L., da of Frederick Grounds, of March, Cambs, and has issue living, Agatha Martha Dorothy *b* 1997, — Katharine Agnes Mary, *b* 1970, — Mary Amicia Helena, *b* 1972. —— *Lady* Elizabeth Sylvia *b* (*posthumous*) 1943. *Residence* – 11 Boundary Close, Woodstock, Oxon OX20 1LR.

WIDOW LIVING OF SON OF FIFTEENTH EARL

Helena Ruth (*Helena, Viscountess Maitland*), yr da of Sir Herbert Charles Perrott, 6th Bt (ext), CH, CB; is an OStJ: *m* 1936, Ivor Colin James, Viscount Maitland, Lieut RAC (TA), who was *ka* 1943, only son of 15th Earl, and has issue living (ante). *Residences* – Flat E, 34 Cadogan Sq, SW1; Park House, Makerstoun, Kelso, Roxburghshire, TD5 7PA.

COLLATERAL BRANCHES LIVING

Descendants of late Gen Hon Sir Alexander Maitland (5th son of 6th Earl), who was *cr* a *Baronet* 1818:—

See Maitland, Bt.

Descendants of Capt Hon Frederick Lewis Maitland, RN, of Rankeilour, 6th son of 6th Earl, *b* 1730, *d* 1786: *m* 1767, Margaret, who *d* 1825, da of James Dick of Rankeilour (heir of line of Makgill of Rankeilour), son of Rev William Dick, of Cupar, by his wife, Isabel, yr da of David Makgill of Rankeilour, *de jure* 3rd Viscount of Oxfuird, and had issue, Charles Maitland of Rankeilour, sometime 17th Dragoons, *b* 1769, *d* 1820: *m* 1794, Mary, who *d* 1824, da of David Johnston of Lathrisk:—

Granddaughter of Maj Charles Julian Maitland-Makgill-Crichton (*b* 1880) (infra):—
Issue of late Maj Douglas Maitland-Makgill-Crichton, *b* 1909, *d* 1968: *m* 1936, Sybil Frederica Coore, who *d* 1992, da of late Frederick Lechmere Paton, JP (B Ashtown, colls):—
Veronica Ann, *b* 1938: *m* 1978, Ian Joicey Dickinson, who *d* 1996, of The Manor House, Riding Mill, Northumberland.

Grandson of late Maj Douglas Maitland-Makgill-Crichton (ante):—
Issue of late Charles Maitland Makgill Crichton of that Ilk; recognised by Lord Lyon as Chief of Clan Crichton 1980; *b* 1942, *d* 1992: *m* 1971, Isla Susan (Monzie Castle, Crieff, Perthshire), da of late Matthew Frederick Gloag, of Bonhard, Perthshire:—
David, *b* 1972; heir of line of 1st Viscount Frendraught.

Granddaughters of late David Maitland-Makgill-Crichton (*b* 1854), son of late Charles Julian Maitland-Makgill-Crichton, eldest son of late David Maitland-Makgill-Crichton (*b* 1801) (infra):—
Issue of late Major Charles Julian Maitland-Makgill-Crichton, Gordon Highlanders, *b* 1880, *ka* 1915: *m* 1902, Sybil Twynihoe, who *d* 1984 (aged 105), da of late Twynihoe William Erle, a Master of Supreme Court, of Bramshott Grange, Liphook, Hants:—
Rosemary Julian (37 Clareville Grove, SW7) *b* 1915: *m* 1940, James Herbert Lonsdale Musker, Fl Lt RAFVR, formerly 7th Hussars, who *d* 1966, and has issue living, Juliet Alexandra Sarah, *b* 1941: *m* 1965, William Edward Barry, of 12 Kensington Park Mews, W11, and Malthouse Farmhouse, Manningford Abbotts, Pewsey, Wilts, and has issue (*see* Barry, Bt, colls).

Issue of late Lt-Cdr James Henry Maitland-Makgill-Crichton, RN (ret), *b* 1885, *d* 1948: *m* 1908, Emily Christina, who *d* 1972, yr da of late Hugh Weir-MacColl, of Appin, Argyll, and The Woods, Newlands, Cape Province,S Africa:—
Alice Mary Emily, *b* 1914: *m* 1937, Vernon Charles Chambers, of Iverna Court, Kensington, W8, who *d* 1983, and has issue living, Virginia, *b* 1942: *m* 1968, George Digby MacDougall Dodd, who *d* 1987, and has issue living, Tamsin Serena Georgina *b* 1971, Julian Crichton *b* 1973, — Vanessa, *b* 1946: *m* 1977, James Alan Fleischmann, MD, MRCP (UK), MRCGP, CPE, DCH, DRCOG, of Portland House, Rt 1, 217A, Caledonia, Minnesota 55921, USA, and has issue living, James Maitland *b* 1985, Diana Maitland *b* 1982. *Residence* – Portland House, Rt 1 217A Caledonia, Minnesota 55921, USA.

Granddaughters of late Cdr Coventry Makgill-Crichton-Maitland, RN, eldest son of late Maj-Gen David Makgill-Crichton-Maitland (*b* 1841) (infra):—
Issue of late Col Henry David Makgill-Crichton-Maitland, OBE, *b* 1904, *d* 1970: *m* 1st, 1930 (*m diss* 1949), Barbara Ellen, who *d* 1994, da of Brig-Gen Sir George Ayscough Armytage, 7th Bt, CMG, DSO; 2ndly, 1949, Audrey Estelle Ljuflng (who *d* 1994, having *m* 3rdly, 1982, Maurice J. C. Allom, of Dene Park, Tonbridge, Kent), da of Henry John Hyde-Johnson, and widow of Lt Peter Thorp Eckersley, RNVR, MP:—
(By 1st *m*) Judith Elizabeth, *b* 1933: *m* 1965, Anthony John Houssemayne du Boulay, of Langford Farm, Sydling St Nicholas, Dorchester, Dorset. —— Sarah, *b* 1936: *m* 1st, 1958, Count Alessandro Monneret de Villard; 2ndly, 1984, Francesco Boscu, of Via Monti 11, Varallo, Pombia, Italy, and has issue living (by 1st *m*), Raffaella, *b* 1961, — Xenia, *b* 1965, — Tatiana, *b* 1970.

Grandsons of late Maj-Gen David Makgill-Crichton-Maitland (*b* 1841), (changed the sequence of his surnames 1884), 2nd son of late David Maitland-Makgill-Crichton (*b* 1801), 2nd son of late Capt Charles Maitland, el son of the Hon Frederick Lewis Maitland RN (ante):—
Issue of late Col Mark Edward Makgill-Crichton-Maitland, CVO, DSO, *b* 1882, *d* 1972: *m* 1924, Patience Irene Fleetwood, who *d* 1974, da of Sir John Michael Fleetwood Fuller, 1st Bt, KCMG:—
John David (Daluaine, Rhynie, Huntly, Aberdeenshire AB54 4WA), *b* 1925; *ed* Eton; Maj (ret) Gren Gds; Lord Lieut of Renfrewshire 1980-94: *m* 1st, 1954, Jean Patricia, who *d* 1985, da of late Maj-Gen Sir Michael O'Moore Creagh, KBE, MC (McGrigor, Bt); 2ndly, 1987, Mary Ann Vere, widow of Capt James Quintin Penn Curzon (*see* E Howe, colls), formerly wife of Charles Pepler Norton, and only da of late Maj Charles Herbert Harberton Eales, MC (*see* Ogilvy, Bt, colls), and has issue living (by 1st *m*), Mark Archibald (44 Cloncurry St, SW6), *b* 1955; *ed* Eton: *m* 1987, Mrs Judith I. G. Mainwaring, elder da of late H. G. Turner, of Mapperly Park, Nottingham, and has issue living, Archie David *b* 1988, Nicholas Hugh *b* 1990. — Mary Elizabeth, *b* 1962: *m* 1993, Roy North, of Woolmer Cottage Stables, Brinkley, Newmarket, Suffolk CB8 0SW, son of K. North, of Horncastle, Lincs, and has issue living, Frederick David George *b* 1995, Benjamin Edward Mark *b* 1997. —— Mark Michael (2 Grosvenor Cres, Edinburgh, EH12 5EP), *b* 1928; Maj (ret) Gordon Highlanders.

Grandchildren of late Andrew Coventry Maitland-Makgill-Crichton, yst son of late David Maitland-Makgill-Crichton (*b* 1801) (ante):—
Issue of late Lieut-Col David Edward Maitland-Makgill-Crichton, Queen's Own Cameron Highlanders, *b* 1879, *d* 1952: *m* 1909, Phyllis, who *d* 1982, da of late Claude Arthur Cuthbert, formerly of Bryn Garth, Much Dewchurch, Herefordshire (Rankin, Bt):—
Edward, OBE (211 Braid Rd, Edinburgh EH10 6HT), *b* 1916; *ed* Bedford Sch and RMC; Maj-Gen late Cameron Highlanders; GOC 51st Highland Div 1966-68; ret 1968; Middle East 1940-44 (wounded, despatches), NW Europe 1944-45 (MBE); MBE (Mil) 1945, OBE (Mil) 1948: *m* 1951, Sheila Hibbins, and has issue living, David Edward, *b* 1952; *ed* Bedford Sch; Maj Queen's Own Highlanders: *m* 1979, Sheena Anne, da of Alexander Dougal Callander, of Coldon, Stirlingshire, and has issue living, Andrew Alexander *b* 1986, Amanda Claire *b* 1984, — (Andrew) James, *b* 1953; *ed* Bedford Sch, and RMA; Lt-Col The Gordon Highlanders: *m* 1977, Karen Gail, da of Derick Charles Smith, of Copperhill,

Sutton Valence, Kent, and has issue living, William Roderick *b* 1979, Edward Thomas *b* 1982, Thomas James *b* 1986, Eila Victoria *b* 1990, — Charles William, *b* 1961; *ed* Strathallan Sch, and RMA . —— Katherine Grizel, *b* 1930: *m* 1954, Russell Barton, MB, MRCP, DPM, FRCPsych (London), FRCP (C), MD, NY, of 2322, Clover St, Rochester, NY 14618, USA, and has issue living, Karen Elizabeth, *b* 1956; *ed* Vassar Coll (BA), Univ of Toronto (MA), and George Mason Univ (MBA): *m* 1998, Alan Curtis Wald, son of late Curtis Wald, of Des Moines, Iowa, USA, — Sarah Muriel, *b* 1958; *ed* Univ of Toronto (BA), Albany Law Sch (JD), and Tulane Law Sch (LLM): *m* 1988, Edward Ross, and has issue living, Daniel Russell Bernard *b* 1989, Caroline Sarah Katherine *b* 1993.

Issue of late John Denys Maitland-Makgill-Crichton, *b* 1897, *d* 1931: *m* 1930, Denise (who *m* 2ndly, 1932 (*m diss* 1943), Douglas S. Fraser, and *d* 1984, having resumed her former name of Maitland-Makgill-Crichton), da of J. H. Crosby:—
†Michael John, *b* 1931; *ed* Rhodes Univ (BA 1952), at Witwatersrand (LLB 1954), and Oriel Coll, Oxford: *m* 1958, Euphemia Daphne Joan Hopkins (Candy Cottage, PO Box 177, Rivonia 2128, Johannesburg, S Africa), and *d* 1998, leaving issue, Anthony John (34 Waterbuck Crescent, River Club Estate, Sandton 2146, Johannesburg, S Africa), *b* 1960; *ed* Univ of Witwatersrand (BA 1982, LLB 1984); Solicitor, Notary Public and Conveyancer, — Philippa Anne, *b* 1965; has retained her maiden name: *m* 1988, Laurence Charles Grubb, of 24 Sycamore Av, River Club, Sandton 2146, Johannesburg, S Africa, and has issue living, Georgina Frances Crichton *b* 1999.

Grandchildren of late Frederick Lewis Maitland, only surv son of late Rear-Adm Lewis Maitland, of Lindores, Fife, 5th son of late Charles Maitland of Rankeilour, sometime 17th Light Dragoons (*b* 1769) (ante):—
Issue of late Surg-Lieut-Cmdr David Randolph Maitland, VRD, RNVR, *b* 1902, *d* (April) 1995: *m* 1930, Barbara Mary Carnegie (Hatton Hill, Newburgh, Fife), da of late Edward Henry Wemyss, of Kirkton, Fife:—
†David Lewis, *b* 1932: *m* 1st, 1961, Anna Mary Smith, who *d* 1968, ward of J. de R. Kent, of Valewood, Haslemere, Surrey; 2ndly, 1969, Jenifer Mary, da of W. O. Davis, of Isle of Soay, Inverness-shire, and *d* (May) 1995, leaving issue (by 1st *m*), Lewis Randolph, *b* 1962, — Niall David, *b* (twin) 1962, — Angus Charles, *b* 1964, — (by 2nd *m*), Sarah Mary, *b* 1971. —— Henry Christopher (Grange of Lindores, Newburgh, Fife), *b* 1935; *ed* Trin Coll, Glenalmond: *m* 1968, Charlotte Mary Ross, da of Roe Tod, of 17 South Oswald Rd, Edinburgh, and widow of Lt W. Harvey, RN, and has issue living, Christopher Ross, *b* 1969, — Gavin Edward, *b* 1976, — Barbara Anne, *b* 1972, — Mary Flora Muriel, *b* (twin) 1976. — Mary, *b* 1939: *m* 1962, Peter Lauritz Wang, of Lawhead Loch, W Calder, Midlothian EH55 8LW, and has issue living, Mark Sigurd Maitland (25 Calder Rd, Bellsquarry, W Lothian EH54 9AA), *b* 1963: *m* 1993, Jayne Chantry, and has issue living, Markus Edward *b* 1994, Magnus Henry *b* 1996, — Patrick David (Rudaki Prospect 83, Penjikent, Tajikistan 735500), *b* 1965; MA Oxon: *m* 1994, Carol Scott, and has issue living, Lawrence Scott *b* 1996, — Robert Magnus (Woodside, Pitcairlie, Newburgh, Cupar, Fife KY14 6EU), *b* 1969: *m* 1998, Dorothy Jean, da of K. M. Fraser, of Pitcairlie Estate, Newbrugh, Fife.

Granddaughters of late Andrew Agnew Maitland-Heriot (latterly Heriot-Maitland), el son of late Frederick Maitland-Heriot (*b* 1818), el son of late James Maitland-Heriot of Ramornie, 2nd son of Capt Hon Frederick Lewis Maitland, RN (ante), 6th son of 6th Earl:—
Issue of late Frederick Lewis Heriot-Maitland, *b* 1889, *d* 1953: *m* 1919, Mabel Mary, who *d* 1962, da of late James Keenan, of Rosario, Argentina:—
Pamela Gertrude, *b* 1921: *m* 1940, Major Christopher Evelyn Boothby, RM, who *d* 1991 (*see* Boothby Bt, colls). *Residence* – 26 Cwrt Deri, Heol-y-Felin, Rhiwbina, Cardiff CF4 6JB. —— Jean Ursula (82 Beaufort Mansions, Beaufort St, SW3 5AF), *b* 1923; 1941-45 with WRNS: *m* 1st, 1944 (*m diss* 1952), Capt Alan Seaforth Cox; 2ndly, 1955, John G. Adams, who *d* 1978, and has issue living, (by 1st *m*) Andrew Frederick Seaforth (8 Morpeth Mansions, Morpeth Terr, SW1), *b* 1945: *m* 1st, 1964 (*m diss* 1976), Carol Ilott; 2ndly, 1978, Tricia Harley, and has issue living (by 1st *m*), Oliver *b* 1967, Emma *b* 1964, Zoe *b* 1969, (by 2nd *m*) Toby *b* 1974, Charlie *b* 1982, — (by 2nd *m*) Sebastian Thomas Maitland, *b* 1961.

Grandchildren of late Frederick Maitland-Heriot, 2nd son of late Frederick Maitland-Heriot (*b* 1818) (ante):—
Issue of late Frank de Courcy Maitland-Heriot, *b* 1882, *d* 1957: *m* 1st (Jan) 1912, Marguerita Mary, who *d* 1935, da of George Logan, MD, of Cressfield, Ecclefechan, Dumfriesshire; 2ndly, 1939, Marion Mercer Moore, of Greystone, Los Cocos, Sierras de Cordoba, Argentina:—
(By 1st *m*) Jean, *b* 1915: *m* 1935, Henry Ranald, Martin, OBE, who *d* 1979, and has issue living, Ian Duncan (PO Box 546, Asunción, Paraguay), *b* 1937: *m* 1961, June Hope Castleton, and has issue living, Angus Ian *b* 1973, Patrick Duncan Ian *b* 1975, Virginia Jean *b* 1963, Anthea Lorraine *b* 1966, Andrea June *b* 1968, — Norman (Estancia Chica, Radial Conchillas, Dept Colonia, Uraguay), *b* 1941: *m* 1965, Jacqueline Ann Booth, and has issue living, Ian Ranald Calvert *b* 1966, Alastair Reginald *b* 1968, Nicholas Andrew *b* 1970, Anthony Norman *b* 1974, — Donald de Courcy (Box 9, Valencia, Venezuela), *b* 1943: *m* 1969, Elizabeth Mary Christie, of Montevideo, and has issue living, Angus Donald *b* 1973, Kenneth James *b* 1976, Veronica Ann *b* 1971, Fiona Jean *b* 1976, — Adrian Ranald, *b* 1953. *Residence* – Guardizabal 1619, Montevideo, Uruguay.

Issue of late (Charles) Adrian Maitland-Heriot, DSC, *b* 1886, *d* 1950: *m* 1919, Dorothy Mary, who *d* 1979, da of A. Egerton-Savory, of Eastbourne:—
Audrey Enid, *b* 1921, 1939-45 War in WAAF: *m* 1972, John Rogerson, of 95 Ridgmount Gdns, WC1E 7AZ.

Issue of late George Vivian Maitland-Heriot, *b* 1891, *d* 1972: *m* 1919, Marjorie Kathleen, who *d* 1983, da of Edward J. Silcock, MICE, of Roundhay, Leeds:—
†Torrance, *b* 1920; *ed* Lancing; 1939-45 War with RAF (wounded): *m* 1947, Elda Carmen, who *d* 1963, da of John Stevenson Pearson, of Adrogue, Argentina, and *d* 1999, leaving issue, Edward John (Dorrego 486, 1846 José Mármol, Argentina), *b* 1950: *m* 1981, Leonor María, da of Hector A. Durando, of José Mármol, Argentina. —— Frederick Euan, *b* 1924; 1939-45 War with Fleet Air Arm: *m* 1954, Vera Margaret, yst da of late Gavin Greig Watson. —— †Nigel Hugh, *b* 1926; 1939-45 War in Far East with RAC: *m* 1953, Beryl Francis, who *d* 1989, eldest da of John Robert Anderson, and *d* 1991, leaving issue, Christopher John (Rancho Alegre, Yei-Pora, Concordia, Entre Rios, Argentina), *b* 1955: *m* 1980, Maria Elena Cristina Cocco, and has issue living, Leonardo Nicolas *b* 1984, Pablo Alexander *b* 1986, Veronica Natalia *b* 1982, — Elizabeth Vivian, *b* 1959: *m* 1993, Ernesto Bernardo Sarli, of Dr Chabrillon 50, 3200 Concordia, Entre Rios, Argentina. —— Clare Antoinette, *b* 1922; 1939-45 War with WAAF: *m* 1980, Oscar Cividiño, who *d* 1998.

Issue of late Ralph Lionel Maitland-Heriot, MC, *b* 1895, *d* 1935: *m* 1927, Moira (who *d* 1985, having *m* 2ndly, 1938, George Scott), da of Harry Hugh Jefferies, of Fisherton, Argentina:—
Ralph Desmond, *b* 1930: *m* 1955, Anneslie Atkinson, and has issue living, Richard Patrick, *b* 1956, — Timothy James, *b* 1958, — Rosalind Elizabeth, *b* 1962. —— Pamela Avril (9 Grasmere Av, SW15), *b* 1928: *m* 1952, Anthony Benjamin Oliveira, FRCS, who *d* 1983, and has issue living, *Prof* David Benjamin Graeme (62 Coombe Lane West, Kingston, Surrey KT2 7BY), *b* 1955; *ed* Stowe, and Camb Univ; FRCP, PhD: *m* 1984, Patricia Margaret, da of G/Capt John Edward Ffrancon Williams, CBE, and has issue living, Benjamin Anthony *b* 1985, Samuel John *b* 1987, Amelia Sophie *b* 1988, — Lynette Moira, *b* 1957: *m* 1992, Sqdn-Ldr Jonathan P. Q. Reid, of Stable Lodge, Middleton Stoney, Oxon, son of Sir John Reid.

Issue of late Lt-Col Gerald Ian Maitland-Heriot, MC, ED, *b* 1898, *d* 1987: *m* 1931, Paula Elsie Barbara (8 Barhill Crescent, Dalbeattie, Kirkcudbrightshire), da of late Cuthbert Henry Gordon, of Bihar, India:—
Celia, *b* 1934: *m* 1961, Robert Edmund Scott Hanbury, of Drumstinchall, Dalbeattie, Kirkcudbrightshire, and has issue living, Roland William Edmund (63 Highlands Heath, Portsmouth Rd, Putney, SW15), *b* 1964; *ed* Eton: *m* 1993, Heather Gail, da of Douglas Adams, of Dunmurry, co Antrim, — Melanie Rhona, *b* 1967: *m* 1993, P. Mark Parry, of Banks Lodge, Drumstinchall, Dalbeattie, Kirkcudbrightshire, son of late Cmdr Myles Parry, RN, of Upper Clatford, Hants, and has issue living, Christina Rose *b* 1998.

Grandchildren of late Cdr William Maitland Dougall, son of late Adm William Heriot Maitland Dougall, 2nd son of late James Maitland-Heriot of Ramornie (*b* 1774) (ante):—
Issue of late Col Wilmot Edward Maitland Dougall, DSO, MC, *b* 1890, *d* 1972: *m* 1st, 1930, Mary Louisa, who *d* 1959, da of Capt Arthur Schreiber, of Brook's Hall, Ipswich; 2ndly, 1960, Hilda, widow of Lt-Col J. R. H. Baddeley:—
(By 1st *m*) Colin (Dowhill, Kelty, Fife), *b* 1933; Lt-Cdr RN: *m* 1964, Philippa Blackstone, da of Cdr G. H. Wise, RN, of Titchfield, Hants, and has a son, Frederick Andrew, *b* 1973. —— Eve Diana (The Priest's House, Sutton Montis Yeovil, Som), *b* 1936: *m* 1st, 1959 (*m diss* 1977), her 3rd cousin, Maj Arthur John French, R Irish Rangers (*see* E Lauderdale, colls, 1954 edn); 2ndly, 1977 (*m diss* 1993), Desmond Saville Hunter, TD, and has issue living (by 1st *m*), Miles Arthur Maitland (70A Middle St, Brighton BN1 1AL), *b* 1961; *ed* Wellington Coll: *m* 1991, Mrs Anne Rosemary Maurice, elder da of Sir Charles Boscawen Frederick, 10th Bt, and has issue living, Raphael Maitland *b* 1994, Naomi Hilda *b* 1992, Matilda Joan Mary *b* 1999, — Dominick George Maitland, *b* 1970, — Amelia Mary Katherine, *b* 1963.

Grandchildren of late Brig-Gen James Dalgleish Heriot-Maitland, CMG, DSO, elder son of late Maj-Gen Sir James Makgill Heriot-Maitland, KCB, yst son of James Maitland-Heriot of Ramornie (*b* 1774) (ante):—
Issue of late Richard Ogilvy Heriot Maitland, JP, DL, *b* 1913, *d* 1972: *m* 1935, Patricia (Woodlands Lodge, Errol, Perthshire), el da of late Lt-Col Cecil Bevis:—
Lewis Dalgleish, TD (Errol Park, Errol, Perthshire), *b* 1943: *m* 1976, Prudence Jane, da of John Richard Bertram Norris, of Canberra, Aust, and has issue living, James Richard *b* 1978, — Lucia Jane, *b* 1981, — Eliza Mary, *b* 1983, — Kirsty Lorne, *b* 1985. —— Patrick Richard (Fossoway Lodge, Kinross), *b* 1947: *m* 1978, Marilyn Lois, da of Russell Grant, of St Petersburg, Florida, USA, and has issue living, Charles Patrick, *b* 1980, — Katherine Louise, *b* 1983, — Sophie Joanna, *b* 1985, — Alexandra Clare, *b* 1989. —— Mary Lorne, *b* 1945.

Grandson of Lt-Gen John Maitland, yst son of John Maitland, only son of Hon Patrick Maitland, 7th son of 6th Earl:—
Issue of late Patrick Lauderdale Maitland, *b* 1862, *d* 1939: *m* 1904: Julia Elizabeth, who *d* 1953, da of late George May, of Cleveland, Ohio, USA:—
Lawrence Lauderdale, *b* 1905; *ed* Ackworth Sch, and Sheffield Univ; Major (ret) late Gordon Highlanders, and an Engineer. *Residence* – 24 Coopersfield, Debenham, Stowmarket, Suffolk IP14 6QR.

PREDECESSORS – (1) *Sir* JOHN Maitland, Knt, Keeper of the Privy Seal 1567, and a Lord of Session 1568-70, when his office was forfeited for his adhesion to the Queen's party; appointed a Lord of Session 1581, constituted a Sec of State for life 1584, and Keeper of the Great Seal of Scotland for life with title of Vice Chancellor 1586; *cr Lord Maitland of Thirlestane* (peerage of Scotland) 1590; *d* 1595; *s* by his son (2) JOHN, 2nd Lord; was a Lord of Session or Pres of the Council; *cr Viscount of Lauderdale* (peerage of Scotland) 1616, with remainder to his heirs male and successors in the Lordship of Thirlestane, and *Lord Thirlestane and Boltoun, Viscount Maitland*, and *Earl of Lauderdale* (peerage of Scotland), 1624 with remainder to his heirs male bearing the name and arms of Maitland; *d* 1645; *s* by his el son (3) JOHN, 2nd Earl, KG, PC, a zealous partizan of Charles II and one of the historic personages of his time; was a Commr appointed by the Church of Scotland to meet the assembly of Divines at Westminster 1643, and was several times employed as a Parliament Commr; taken prisoner at battle of Worcester 1651 and was confined in the Tower until 1660; for his fidelity to the king he was made Sec of State, Pres of the Council, Heritable High Sheriff of co Edinburgh, an Extraordinary Lord of Session, First Commr of the Treasury, Lord High Commr to the Parliament, and Gov of Edinburgh Castle; *cr Marquess of March* and *Duke of Lauderdale* (peerage of Scotland) 1672, and *Baron Petersham* and *Earl of Guilford* (peerage of England) 1674; *d* 1682, when all the peerages conferred upon himself became extinct and the other honours reverted to his brother (4) CHARLES, 3rd Earl; was Gen of the Mint, and Dep Treasurer and a Judge of the Court of Session; *d* 1691; *s* by his el son (5) RICHARD, KB, PC, 4th Earl; was Gen of the Mint, and Lord Justice Gen 1681-4; outlawed 1694 for his adhesion to the cause of James II; *dsp* 1695; *s* by his brother (6) JOHN, 5th Earl; *cr a Baronet* of Nova Scotia 1680; MP for co Edinburgh 1685; a Lord of Session with title of Lord Ravelrig 1689-1710; *d* 1710; *s* by his son (7) CHARLES, 6th Earl, a Representative Peer, Master of the Mint, and Lord-Lieut of co Edinburgh; *d* 1744; *s* by his son (8) JAMES, 8th Earl; *cr Baron Lauderdale*, of Thirlestane, co Berwick (peerage of United Kingdom) 1806; *d* 1839; *s* by his el son (10) JAMES, 9th Earl; MP for Appleby 1820-31, and Lord-Lieut of co Berwick; *d* unmarried 1860; *s* by his brother (11) ANTHONY, GCB, KCMG, 10th Earl; an Adm of the Red; *d* 1863, when the English barony expired, and the other peerages devolved upon his cousin (12) THOMAS, GCB, 11th Earl, son of Gen Hon William Mordaunt Maitland, 3rd son of 7th Earl; a Representative Peer, and Adm of the Fleet, etc; *d* 1878; *s* by his kinsman (13) CHARLES, 12th Earl, who *d* Aug 1884; *s* by his kinsman (14) FREDERICK HENRY (son of late Gen Frederick Colthurst Maitland, son of late Patrick Maitland, 2nd son of Col Hon Richard Maitland, 4th son of 6th Earl), 13th Earl, *b* 1840; established his claim to the title before Committee for Privileges of the House of Lords, July 1885; Lord-Lieut of Berwickshire 1889-1901; for 31 years a Representative Peer for Scotland; *m* 1st, 1864, Charlotte Sarah, who *d* 1879, da of the late Lieut-Col Sleigh (77th Regt); 2ndly, 1883, Ada Twyford, who *d* 1931, da of late Rev Henry Trail Simpson, R of Adel, York; *d* 1924; *s* by his son (15) FREDERICK COLIN, OBE, 14th Earl, *b* 1868; a Representative Peer for Scotland, one of HM's Hon Corps of Gentlemen-of-Arms, and Ensign Roy Co of Archers (King's Body Guard for Scotland): *m* 1890, Gwendoline Lucy, who *d* 1929, da of late Judge R. Vaughan Williams, of Bodlonfa, Flintshire; *d* 1931; *s* by his son (16) IAN COLIN, 15th Earl; *b* 1891; a Member of Queen's Body Guard for Scotland (Roy Co of Archers); was ADC to Viceroy of Ireland 1915-16 and

1918: *m* 1912, Ethel Mary, who *d* 1970, da of James Jardine Bell-Irving, of Makerstoun House, Kelso; *d* 1953; *s* by his cousin **(17)** *Rev* ALFRED SYDNEY FREDERICK (son of late Rev Hon Sydney George William Maitland, 2nd son of 13th Earl), 16th Earl, *b* 1904: *m* 1st, 1938, Norah Mary, who *d* 1938, da of late William Henry La Touche; 2ndly, 1940, Irene Alice May, who *d* 1995, da of late Rev C. P. Shipton, of Halsham, Yorks; *d* 1968; *s* by his brother **(18)** PATRICK FRANCIS, 17th Earl and present peer; also Viscount of Lauderdale, Viscount Maitland, Lord Maitland of Thirlestane, and Lord Thirlestane and Boltoun.

Law, family name of Baron Coleraine.

Law, family name of Baron Ellenborough.

LAWRENCE, BARON (Lawrence) (Baron UK 1869, Bt UK 1858)

DAVID JOHN DOWNER LAWRENCE, 5th Baron and 5th Baronet; *b* 4 Sept 1937; *s* 1968; *ed* Bradfield.

Arms – Ermine, on a cross raguly gules an Eastern crown or; a chief azure, thereon two swords in saltire proper, pommels and hilts gold, between as many leopards' faces argent. **Crest** – Out of an Eastern crown or, a cubit arm entwined by a wreath of laurel and holding a dagger all proper. **Supporters** – *Dexter*, an officer of the Guide Cavalry (Irregulars), of the Pathan tribe, in the province of Peshawar, habited and accoutred proper; *sinister*, an officer of the Sikh Irregular Cavalry, also habited and accoutred proper. *Address* – 2 Gray's Inn Sq, WC1.

AUNT LIVING *(Daughter of 3rd Baron)*

Hon Nona Georgette, *b* 1922; Dame of S Gregory 1997: *m* 1945, W/Cdr Vincent George Byrne, RAF, who *d* 1978, and has had issue, Nicholas John Joseph, *b* 1946: *m* 1968, Catherine Penelope (Wincombe Cottage, Donhead St Mary, Shaftesbury, Dorset), da of Douglas Smith, and *d* 1994, leaving issue, Kirstie Mary Kate *b* 1969: *m* 1997, Tim Burgess, Tara Mary Fiona *b* 1971, Fiona Georgina Mary *b* 1976, — James Vincent (Hawkyard House, Chipping Norton, Oxon), *b* 1950; MD, FRCS, FRCR: *m* 1975, Juliet Elizabeth Anson, da of John Bailey, and has issue living, Thomas Vincent Lawrence *b* 1979, George Henry St Clare *b* 1981, Henry Charles Mogeridge *b* 1985, Rowena Catherine Anson *b* 1977, — (Vincent) Patrick (17 Birchland Av, SW12), *b* 1952: *m* 1989, Mary Gabriel, 2nd da of Sir James Napier Finnie McEwen, 2nd Bt, and has issue living, Elliot James *b* 1991, John Joseph *b* 1995, Rosanna Clare *b* 1993, — Dominic Lawrence (Truthan Manor, Truthan, Truro, Cornwall), *b* 1959; MD, MRCOG: *m* 1990, Susan Amanda, BSc, MRCOG, da of Capt Richard Bates, RN, of Winchester, and has issue living, Nicholas Michael *b* 1994, Charles Louis Vincent *b* 1996, Katharine Letitia *b* 1992, — Rory Shaun (Wildwood, Coombe, Kingston, Surrey), *b* 1961: *m* 1988, Andrea Carina, da of Peter Riediker, of Zurich, Switzerland, and has issue living, Edward Alexander *b* 1990, Christian Rory *b* 1992, Jessica Katherine *b* 1989, Melanie Anne *b* 1995, — Teresa Marie, *b* 1947: *m* 1968, Robin Herbert Wickham, of Maynards Farm, Matfield, Tonbridge, Kent, and has issue living, Simon James Wykeham *b* 1969, Patrick David Wykeham *b* 1972, — Clare Mary Anne, *b* 1955: *m* 1981, Tass Whittaker, of Mayfield House, Rogate, Hants GU31 5HN, and has issue living, Lara Nona Jane *b* 1983, Amy Marie Clare *b* 1986, Eleanor Charlotte *b* 1988, — Fiona Rosaleen Mary, *b* 1957: *m* 1983, Robert J. Rolls, of 41 Doneraile St, SW6, and has issue living, Giles Thomas Alexander *b* 1984, Annabel India Sarah *b* 1986, Sophie Amelia Lucy *b* 1988. *Residence* – 45 King George Gdns, Chichester, Sussex PO19 4LB.

PREDECESSORS – **(1)** *Rt Hon Sir* JOHN LAIRD MAIR LAWRENCE, GCB, BCSI, PC, DCL LLD, 5th son of late Lieut-Col Alexander Lawrence, Gov of Upton Castle, Kent, *b* 1811; entered Bengal Civil Ser 1828, and having held numerous minor positions became Commr of the Jullunder Doab 1846, and was subsequently Member of Board of Administration for the Punjab 1849-52, Chief Commr of the Punjab 1852-8, First Lt-Govr of that province 1858-9, Viceroy of India 1864-8, and chm of London School Board 1870-3; *cr* a *Baronet* 1858, and *Baron Lawrence*, of the Punjab and of Grateley, co Southampton 1869; *m* 1841, Harriette Katherine, CI, who *d* 1917, da of Rev Richard Hamilton; *d* 1879; *s* by his son **(2)** JOHN HAMILTON, 2nd Baron, *b* 1846; Lord-in-Waiting to Queen Victoria 1895-1901, and to King Edward VII 1901-5: *m* 1872, Mary Caroline Douglas, who *d* 1938, only da of late Richard Campbell of Auchinbreck and Glencarradle, Argyllshire; *d* 1913; *s* by his son **(3)** ALEXANDER GRAHAM, 3rd Baron, *b* 1878: *m* 1st, 1907, Dorothy Helen, CBE, who *d* 1935, da of late Anthony Pemberton Hobson, many years Inspector-Gen of Police, St Vincent, W Indies; 2ndly, 1935,

Jessie, who *d* 1936, da of late Col Byron Gordon Daniels, US Army, and widow of William Frederic Lawrence, of Cowesfield House, Wilts; 3rdly, 1938, Catherine Louisa, who *d* 1965, da of late Charles Fernihough, and widow of William Burnet Craigie; *d* (June) 1947; *s* by his son (4) JOHN ANTHONY EDWARD, 4th Baron, *b* 1908: *m* 1st, 1936 (*m diss* 1947), Margaret Jean, who *d* 1977, da of Arthur Downer, of Rotherfield, Kent; 2ndly, 1948, Joan Alice Mildred (who *d* 1995, having *m* 2ndly, 1969, John Eddison, who *d* 1989), da of Maj Arthur John Lewer, OBE, of Norwood Green, Middx; *d* 1968; *s* by his son (5) DAVIS JOHN DOWNER, 5th Baron and present peer.

Lawrence, family name of Baron Oaksey.

LAWSON, BARONY OF (Lawson) (Extinct 1965)

DAUGHTERS LIVING OF FIRST AND LAST BARON

Hon Irene, *b* 1909: *m* 1935, Charles Frederick Campbell Lawson, and has issue living, Ruth Ellison, *b* 1936, — Elizabeth Graham, *b* 1943, — Elaine Campbell, *b* 1944.
Hon Edna, *b* 1912: *m* 19—, D. Brown, and has issue living, David, *b* 1945.
Hon Alma, *b* 1920.

Lawson, family name of Baron Burnham.

LAWSON OF BLABY, BARON (Lawson) (Life Baron 1992)

NIGEL LAWSON, PC, only son of late Ralph Lawson; *b* 11 March 1932; *ed* Westminster, and Ch Ch, Oxford (BA 1954); Fellow Nuffield Coll, Oxford 1972-73; editorial staff *Financial Times* 1956-60, City Ed *Sunday Telegraph* 1961-63, Ed *The Spectator* 1966-70; Special Assist to PM (Sir Alec Douglas-Home) 1963-64, and Special Political Adviser Conservative HQ 1973-74; Financial Sec to the Treasury 1979-81, Energy Sec 1981-83, Chancellor of the Exchequer 1983-Oct 1989 (resigned); Dir Barclays Bank since 1990, Dir GPA Group 1990-93, Chm Central Europe Trust since 1990; Sub-Lieut RNVR 1954-56; MP Blaby (*C*) 1974-92; *cr* PC 1981, and *Baron Lawson of Blaby*, of Newnham, co Northants (Life Baron) 1992; *m* 1st, 1955 (*m diss* 1980), Vanessa Mary Addison, who *d* 1985, 2nd da of late Felix Addison Salmon, of Ham Common Surrey; 2ndly, 1980, Thérèse Mary, da of late Henry Charles Maclear Bate, of Putney, London, and has had issue by 1st and 2nd wives.
Address – c/o House of Lords, SW1A 0PW. *Clubs* – Garrick, Pratt's.

SONS LIVING (*by 1st wife*)

Hon Dominic Ralph Campden, *b* 1956; *ed* Westminster, and Ch Ch, Oxford; Ed *The Spectator* 1990-95, since when Ed *The Sunday Telegraph*; author: *m* 1st, 1982, Jane Fiona, da of David Christopher Wastell Whytehead, of W Dulwich, SE21; 2ndly, 1991, Hon Rosamond Mary Monckton, only da of 2nd Viscount Monckton of Brenchley, CB, OBE, MC, and has issue living (by 2nd *m*), Savannah Vanessa Lucia, *b* 1992, — Domenica Marianna Tertia, *b* 1995. *Clubs* – Academy, MCC.

(by 2nd wife)

Hon Thomas Nigel Maclear, *b* 1976; *ed* Eton.

DAUGHTERS LIVING AND DECEASED *(by 1st wife)*

Hon Nigella Lucy, *b* 1960; *ed* Godolphin & Latymer, and Lady Margaret Hall, Oxford; journalist and broadcaster: *m* 1992, John Diamond, and has issue living, Bruno Paul Nigel, *b* 1996, — Cosima Thomasina, *b* 1993.
Hon Thomasina Posy, *b* 1961: *m* 1985, Ivan Hill, and *d* 1993.
Hon Horatia Holly, *b* 1966: *m* 1997, Hon (Charles) Inigo Gladwyn Thomas, elder son of Baron Thomas of Swynnerton (Life Baron).

(by 2nd wife)

Hon Emily Hero, *b* 1981.

LAYTON, BARON (Layton) (Baron UK 1947)

GEOFFREY MICHAEL LAYTON, 3rd Baron; *b* 18 July 1947; *s* 1989; *ed* St Paul's Sch, Stanford Univ, and Univ of Southern Calif: *m* 1st, 1969 (*m diss* 1970), Viviane, da of François Cracco, of Louvain, Belgium; 2ndly, 1989, Caroline Jane, da of William Thomas Mason, of Fairford, Glos, and formerly wife of Adm Spyros Soulis, of Athens.

SISTER LIVING

Hon Deanna Christine, *b* 1938: MB, BS, MRCS, LRCP: *m* 1964, Melvin Calverley Jennings, MB, FRCS, Barn Ridge, 18 High Trees Rd, Reigate, Surrey RH2 7EJ, and has issue living, Andrew Melvin, *b* 1965: *m* 1998, Anne C., yr da of Graham Barber, of Lyminge, Kent, — Simon, *b* 1967, — Robert, *b* 1970.

UNCLES LIVING *(sons of 1st Baron)*

Hon DAVID, MBE (18 Grove Terrace, Highgate Rd, NW5), *b* 5 July 1914; *ed* Gresham's Sch, Holt, and Trin Coll, Camb; MBE (Mil) 1946: *m* 1st, 1939 (*m diss* 1972), Elizabeth, da of Rev Robert Millar Gray; 2ndly, 1972, Joy Parkinson, and has issue living (by 1st *m*), Jonathan Francis, *b* 1942: *m* 1971, Julia Goodwin, and has issue living, Jeremy *b* 1978, Robert *b* 1982, Jessica *b* 1974, — Mark Oliver, *b* 1944, — Hilary Ruth, *b* 1947.
Hon Christopher Walter, *b* 1929; *ed* Oundle, and King's Coll, Camb: *m* 1st, 1952 (*m diss* 1957) Annaliese Margaret, da of Joachim von Thadden, of Hanover; 2ndly, 1961, Margaret Ann, da of Leslie Moon, of Molesey, Surrey, and has had issue (by 1st *m*), John Stephen, *b* 1955, — Diana, *b* 1953, — (by 2nd *m*) Eleanor Rachel, *b* 1963; *d* 1985, — Sarah Jean *b* 1964, — Lesley Claire, *b* 1971. *Residence* – Grimstone Mews, Jordan Lane, Horrabridge, nr Yelverton, Devon PL20 7QY.

AUNTS LIVING *(daughters of 1st Baron)*

Hon Jean Mary, *b* 1916: *m* 1944, Paul Eisler, who *d* 1966, and has issue living, John, *b* 1946: *m* 1977, Eva Tlustá, of Prague, and has issue living, Martin *b* 1977, Mark *b* 1980, — Ivan, *b* 1948: *m* 1971, Zuzana Tibenska, of Bratislava, Slovakia, and has issue living, Philip *b* 1973, Lucinka *b* 1976. *Residence* – Syskon Cottage, 2 Millfield Lane, N6 6JD.
Hon Olive Shirley, *b* 1918: *m* 1943, Peter Gellhorn, conductor, and has issue living, Martin Oliver, *b* 1945: *m* 1969 (*m diss* 1976), Susanna Elizabeth, da of Thomas Howard Beauchamp Gladstone, MB, BS, of Ilkeston, Derbys, and has issue living, Catherine *b* 1969, — Philip Nicholas, *b* 1951, — Mary Ann, *b* 1959, — Barbara Dorothea, *b* 1960. *Residence* – 33 Leinster Av, SW14 7JW.
Hon Elizabeth Ruth Frances, *b* 1923: *m* 1944 (*m diss* 1965), Bobbie Pegna, and has issue living, Robin, *b* 1945: *m* 1968, Catherine Bridge Gray, da of John Henderson, of Greenwood, Frant, Sussex, and has issue living, Jonathan *b* 1982, Catherine *b* 1973, Alice *b* 1976, — Christopher John, *b* 1956, — Shirley, *b* 1951. *Residence* – 2 Farmington, Cheltenham, Glos GL54 3NQ.

PREDECESSORS – (1) WALTER THOMAS LAYTON, CH, CBE, son of Alfred John Layton, of Woking, Surrey; *b* 1884; Editor, *The Economist* 1922-38, and Chm 1944-63, Chm News Chronicle Ltd 1930-50, and Star Newspaper Co Ltd 1936-50; Head of Joint War Production Staff and Ch Adviser on Programmes and Planning Min of Production 1942-43, and Vice-Pres of Assembly of Council of Europe 1949-57; *cr Baron Layton*, of Danehill, co Sussex (peerage of UK) 1947: *m* 1910, Eleanor Dorothea, who *d* 1959, da of Francis Beresford Plumtre Osmaston, of Stoneshill, Limpsfield, Surrey: *d* 1966; *s* by his el son (2) MICHAEL JOHN, 2nd Baron, *b* 1912; Dir Wolff Steel Holdings Ltd 1977-83, and *The Economist* Newspaper

Ltd 1973-85; Head Internat Relations Dept of British Iron and Steel Fedn 1948-55, etc: *m* 1938, Dorothy Rose, who *d* 1994, da of Albert Luther Cross, of Rugby; *d* 1989; *s* by his only son **(3)** GEOFFREY MICHAEL, 3rd Baron and present peer.

LEATHERLAND, BARONY OF (Leatherland) (Extinct 1992)

SON LIVING OF LIFE BARON

Hon John Charles (4 Manor Way, Chingford, E4), *b* 1929; *ed* Brentwood; *m* 1954, Esther Stella Steckman, and has issue.

DAUGHTER LIVING OF LIFE BARON

Hon Irene Mary (19 The Greens Close, Loughton, Essex), *b* 1923: *m* 1961 (*m diss* 1977), Douglas Richards, and has issue.

LEATHERS, VISCOUNT (Leathers) (Viscount UK 1954)

While I breathe I serve

CHRISTOPHER GRAEME LEATHERS, 3rd Viscount; *b* 31 Aug 1941; *s* 1996; *ed* Rugby, and Open Univ (BA); JP: *m* 1964, Maria Philomena, yr da of late Michael Merriman, of Charlestown, co Mayo, and has issue.

𝕬rms – Azure, a lymphad, sails set or, flags flying to the dexter gules, on a chief of the second three lozenges sable. 𝕮rest – A lozenge sable in front of two anchors in saltire or. 𝕾upporters – *Dexter*, a sea-lion; *sinister*, a sea horse argent gorged with a collar of lozenges conjoined sable.
Residence – Lime Cottage, High St, Burwash, Etchingham, E Sussex TN19 7EL.

SON LIVING

Hon JAMES FREDERICK, *b* 27 May 1969; *ed* Rugby, and Corpus Christi Coll, Camb.

DAUGHTER LIVING

Hon Melissa Maria, *b* 1966: *m* 1994, Timothy James Wesley, and has issue living, Thomas Patrick, *b* 1996.

BROTHER LIVING

Hon Jeremy Baxter, *b* 1946: *m* 1969, Fiona Lesley, el da of late G. S. Pitt, of Rowbarns Manor, E Horsley, Surrey, and has issue living, Luke Alexander, *b* 1974, — Tara Charlotte, *b* 1972, — Fern Griselda, *b* 1979.

SISTERS LIVING

Hon Anne Catherine, *b* 1944: *m* 1977, Arthur Sydney Centner, of Suite 159, Post Net X18, 7701 Rondesbosch, South Africa, and has issue living, Lucy Emma, *b* 1977.
Hon Deborah Elspeth, *b* 1947: *m* 1st, 1966 (*m diss* 1970), Thomas Richard Chadbon; 2ndly, 1980, Richard William Pitt, of 6 Bassingham Rd, SW18 3AG, yst son of late G. S. Pitt (ante), and has issue living (by 1st *m*), Dominic Thomas, *b* 1966, — Nicholas Richard, *b* 1968, — (by 2nd *m*), Isabelle, *b* 1981.

UNCLE LIVING (son of 1st Viscount)

Hon Leslie John (14 Seymour Place, Odiham, Hants RG29 1AY), *b* 1911; *ed* Brighton Coll; admitted a Solicitor 1935; is Maj late RA, Staff Coll Camberley: *m* 1937, Elizabeth Stella, only da of Thomas Stanley Nash, of Haywards Heath, and has issue living, Michael John Nash (Oldhams, Fox Hill, Petworth, W Sussex GU28 9NU), *b* 1938: *m* 1962, Shelley Matthews, da of late Keith Marten, of Gedgrave Hall, Orford, Suffolk, and has issue living, Simon Michael John *b* 1964, Sean Patrick James *b* 1966, Richard Anthony *b* 1968, Benjamin Matthew *b* 1971, Nicholas Paul Tarquin *b* 1974, — David Frederick James (14 Holmead Rd, SW6 2JG), *b* 1942; FCA: *m* 1968, Amanda Elizabeth Ann Vyvyan, da of Lt-Col Arthur Vyvyan Denton, of Dial House, Lower Bourne, Farnham (*see* Strickland Constable, Bt, colls), and has issue living, Jonathan James *b* 1974, Andrew Thomas *b* 1975, — Rosemary Elizabeth, *b* 1945: *m* 1972, Winfried F. W. Bischoff, of 28 Bloomfield Terr, SW1W 8PQ, son of Paul Helmut Bischoff, of Johannesburg and Dusseldorf, and has issue living, Christopher William *b* 1973, Charles Francis *b* 1975.

AUNT LIVING (daughter of 1st Viscount)

Hon Audrey Mary, *b* 1915: *m* 1938, Edward Noel Evans, who *d* 1964, and has had issue, Richard Edward Craig, *b* 1945: *m* 1973 (*m diss* 1998), Jillian Sonia, yr da of late H. W. Reid, of The Manse, Royston, Herts, and has issue living, Charles Noel Edward *b* 1975, Hilary Jane *b* 1977, Melissa Kate *b* 1981, — Peter James, *b* 1946: *m* 1979, Lynne, da of James Irving Cosgrove, and widow of Desmond Hawe, and *d* 1988, leaving issue, Katie Samantha *b* 1982, Jessica Jane *b* 1984, — Jacqueline Mary, *b* 1940: *m* 1st, 1961 (*m diss* 1969), Barrington Hugh Lawes; 2ndly, 1969, Michael Hind, and has issue living, (by 1st *m*) Nicholas Hugh *b* 1962: *m* 1987, Julie, da of Sir Noel Edward Vivian Short, MBE, MC, Suzanna Jane *b* 1964, (by 2nd *m*) Sally Louise *b* 1970. *Residence* – 29 Crittles Court, Townlands Rd, Wadhurst, E Sussex TN5 6BY.

WIDOW LIVING OF SECOND VISCOUNT

LORNA MAY (*Dowager Viscountess Leathers*), MCSP, Vice-Pres Mission to Seamen, Memb Gardeners' Co, and Metropolitan Public Gardens Assocn, da of late A. K. Marshall, and widow of Arthur A. C. Barnett: *m* 1983, as his 2nd wife, the 2nd Viscount Leathers, who *d* 1996. *Residence* – Huntsmore, Shackleford, Surrey GU8 6AN. *Club* – RAC.

PREDECESSORS – **(1)** FREDERICK JAMES Leathers, CH, PC, son of Robert Leathers, of Stowmarket, Suffolk; *b* 1883; Min of War Transport 1941-45, and Sec of State for Co-ordination of Transport Fuel and Power 1951-53; *cr Baron Leathers* of Purfleet, co Essex (Peerage of UK) 1941, and *Viscount Leathers*, of Purfleet, co Essex (Peerage of UK) 1954: *m* 1907, Emily Ethel, who *d* 1971, da of late Henry Baxter, of Southend; *d* 1965; *s* by his el son **(2)** FREDERICK ALAN, 2nd Viscount, *b* 1908; Chm Wm Cory & Sons, Ltd: *m* 1st, 1940 (*m diss* 1983), Elspeth Graeme, who *d* 1985, da of late Sir Thomas Alexander Stewart, KCSI, KCIE; 2ndly, 1983, Lorna May, da of late A. K. Marshall, and widow of Arthur A. C. Barnett; *d* 1996; *s* by his elder son **(3)** CHRISTOPHER GRAEME, 3rd Viscount and present peer; also Baron Leathers.

Leconfield, Baron, see Baron Egremont.

LEE OF NEWTON, BARONY OF (Lee) (Extinct 1984)

DAUGHTER LIVING OF LIFE BARON

Hon Pamela Margaret, *b* 1945: *m* 1965, Rodney Flint, of The Willows, Church Drive, Newton-le-Willows, Merseyside, WA12 9SR.

WIDOW LIVING OF LIFE BARON

AMELIA (*Baroness Lee of Newton*) (52 Ashton Rd, Newton-le-Willows, Merseyside EA12 0AE), da of William Shay: *m* 1938, Baron Lee of Newton, PC (Life Baron), who *d* 1984.

LEEDS, DUKEDOM OF (Osborne) (Extinct 1964)

DAUGHTER LIVING OF ELEVENTH DUKE

Lady Camilla Dorothy Godolphin, *b* 1950: *m* 1st, 1971 (*m diss* 1976), Robert Julian Brownlow Harris (*see* B Harris, colls); 2ndly, 1977, Nigel Richard Patton Dempster, and has issue living (by 1st *m* — *see* B Harris, colls), — (by 2nd *m*) Louisa Beatrix, *b* 1979.

WIDOW LIVING OF ELEVENTH DUKE

CAROLINE FLEUR (*Dowager Lady Hobart*) yr da of late Col Henry Monckton Vatcher, MC, of Valeran, St Brelade's Jersey: *m* 1st, 1955, as his 3rd wife, the 11th Duke of Leeds, who *d* 1963; 2ndly, 1968 (*m diss* 1975), Peter Hendrik Peregrine Hoos (*see* B Brownlow); 3rdly, 1975, as his 2nd wife, Lt-Cdr Sir Robert Hampden Hobart, 3rd Bt, who *d* 1988. *Residence* – Flat 14, 42 Egerton Gdns, SW3 2BZ.

Legge, family name of Earl of Dartmouth.

Legh, family name of Baron Newton.

Legh, Cornwall-, family name of Baron Grey of Codnor.

LEICESTER, EARL OF (Coke) (Earl UK 1837)
(Name pronounced "Cook")

He is prudent who is patient

EDWARD DOUGLAS COKE, 7th Earl; *b* 6 May 1936; *s* 1994; *ed* St Andrew's Coll, Grahamstown, Cape Province; Pres Historic Houses Assocn since 1998: *m* 1st, 1962 (*m diss* 1985), Valeria Phyllis, eldest da of late Leonard A. Potter, of Berkhamsted, Herts; 2ndly, 1986, Mrs Sarah de Chair, da of Noel Henry Boys Forde, of Wells-next-the-Sea, Norfolk, and formerly wife of Colin Graham Ramsey de Chair, and has issue by 1st *m*.

Arms – Per line gules and azure, three eagles displayed argent. Crest – On a chapeau azure, turned up ermine, an ostrich argent, holding in its mouth a horse-shoe. Supporters – On either side an ostrich argent, that on the *dexter* gorged with a ducal coronet per pale gules and azure, line reflexed over the back of the first; that on the *sinister* gorged with a like coronet, per pale azure and gules, and line reflexed over the back azure.
Seat – Holkham Hall, Wells, Norfolk. *Club* – Brooks's, White's, Farmers'.

SONS LIVING (*By 1st marriage*)

THOMAS EDWARD (*Viscount Coke*), *b* 6 July 1965; *ed* Eton, and Manchester Univ (BA); sometime Page of Honour to HM, and Equerry to HRH The Duke of Kent 1991-93: *m* 1996, Polly M., yst da of (Thomas) David Whately, MC, of Pensbury House, Shaftesbury, Dorset, and has issue living, *Hon* Hermione Belinda, *b* 1998. *Club* – Cavalry and Guards', White's.
Hon Rupert Henry John, *b* 1975.

DAUGHTER LIVING (*By 1st marriage*)

Lady Laura-Jane Elizabeth, *b* 1968: *m* 1993, Jonathan Paul, elder son of Alastair Paul, of Edinburgh, and of Mrs Jonathan Woollatt, of Honiton, Devon, and has issue living, Barnaby Edward Oliver, *b* 1999.

BROTHER LIVING

Hon (Wenman) John (Peterstone Priory Farm, Holkham, Wells-next-the-Sea, Norfolk NR23 1RR), *b* 1940: *m* 1969, Carolyn Mary, el da of late D. D. Steuart Redler, of Cape Town, S Africa, and has issue living, Anthony Stuart, *b* 1969, — Richard Oliver, *b* 1975, — Rosalind Elizabeth, *b* 1971.

SISTER LIVING

Lady Almary Bridget, *b* 1938: *m* 1963, Peter Ivens-Ferraz, of Splashy Fen, PO Box 186, Underberg, Natal 4590, S Africa, and has issue living, Robyn Ann, *b* 1964, — Bronwen Mary, *b* 1965, — Penelope Kate, *b* 1967, — Caitlin Tessa, *b* 1970.

DAUGHTERS LIVING OF FIFTH EARL

Lady Anne Veronica (*Baroness Glenconner*), LVO, *b* 1932; Train Bearer to HM The Queen at the Coronation, 1953, an Extra Lady-in-Waiting to HRH The Princess Margaret, Countess of Snowdon, since 1971; Pres Nat Assocn for Maternal and Child Welfare 1985, Pres SOS 1979-83; LVO 1991: *m* 1956, 3rd Baron Glenconner. *Residences* – Flat 2, 19 Holland Park, W11; East End Farm, Burnham Thorpe, King's Lynn, Norfolk PE31 8HW; Beau Estate, Soufriere, St Lucia, WI.
Lady Carey Elizabeth, *b* 1934: *m* 1960, Bryan Ronald Basset, CBE (*see* E Dartmouth). *Residence* – Quarles, Wells-next-Sea, Norfolk NR23 1RY.
Lady Sarah Marion, *b* 1944: *m* 1970, Maj David Finlayson Wylie Hill Walter, late Scots Gds, and has issue living, Nicholas Robert, *b* 1972, — James George, *b* 1975, *Residence* – The Garden House, Balthayock, by Perth.

DAUGHTER LIVING OF FOURTH EARL

Lady Silvia Beatrice (The Manor House, Burnham Thorpe, Kings Lynn), *b* 1909; is a JP: *m* 1932, Capt Simon Harvey Combe, MC, Irish Guards, who *d* 1965, and has issue living, Robin Harvey (Bayfield Hall, Holt, Norfolk), *b* 1934; Lt RN: *m* 1960, Olga, da of R. J. Wise, of Bridgend, Glam, and has issue living, Roger Mark Harvey *b* 1960, Simon James (4 Brandlehow Rd, SW15 2ED) *b* 1962: *m* 1992, Elizabeth A., da of John Knight, of Spratton, Northampton, Carey Romaine *b* 1964, Silvia *b* 1967, — Rowena Marion, *b* 1935: *m* 1963 (*m diss* 1983), Jocelyn Rupert Rowland Geoffrey Feilding (*see* E Denbigh, colls).

COLLATERAL BRANCHES LIVING

Issue of late Maj Hon Richard Coke, Scots Gds, 3rd son of 2nd Earl, b 1876, d 1964: m 1st, 1907 (m diss 1927), Hon Doreen O'Brien, who d 1960, da of 14th Baron Inchiquin; 2ndly, 1932, Elizabeth Vera Catherine Alice, who d 1988, da of late Louis-Leopold M. B. de Beaumont (see B O'Hagan, 1973-74 Edn):—

(By 1st m) Richard Lovel, DSO, MC, ERD (Weasenham Hall, King's Lynn, Norfolk), b 1918; ed Stowe, and RAC Cirencester; 1939-45 War as Maj Scots Gds in Italy (MC, DSO); DSO 1945; ERD 1992; DL 1977 and High Sheriff Norfolk 1981: m 1951, Molly, who d 1997, yr da of W. T. Fletcher, of Dorchester, and has had issue, Richard Townshend, b 1954, — Edward Justin b 1961: m 1996, Susannah Elizabeth Olivia, only da of Lt-Col Paul Long, of Assington Green, Suffolk, — Diana Caroline, b 1953: m 1975, 20th Earl of Caithness, and d 1994, leaving issue (see E Caithness). ——— Hersey (Waterloo Cottage, Gayton, King's Lynn, Norfolk), b 1915: m 1946, Lt-Col Peter William Marsham, MBE, Gren Gds (ret), who d 1970 (see E Romney, colls). ——— Bridget Doreen (Dowager Baroness Rathcavan) (Killala Lodge, Killala, co Mayo), b 1924: m 1st, 1943 (m diss 1952), Capt Thomas Richard Edwards-Moss, who d 1974 (see Edwards-Moss Bt, colls); 2ndly, 1953, 2nd Baron Rathcaven, who d 1994. ——— (By 2nd m) Henry Francis (5A Rocks Lane, Barnes, SW13 0DB), b 1938: m 1st, 1966 (m diss 1971), Marie Christina Rosalind, da of Robert McCrone, of Pitliver, by Dunfermline, Fife; 2ndly, 1976 (m diss 1993), Margaret Victoria Louise, da of Patrick Brodie, of Horley, Surrey; 3rdly, 1999, Mrs Caroline Sheila Hodges, da of Maj David Victor Bonsor, MC (see Bonsor, Bt), and has issue living (by 1st m), Nicola Katherine, b 1967, — Sarah Victoria Dayas, b 1971, — (by 2nd m) Georgina Sarah Brodie, b 1979, — Camilla Anne Brodie, b 1980. ——— (Mildred Jeanne) Carolyn (41 Christchurch Hill, Hampstead, NW3 1LA), b 1934: m 1966 (m diss 1971), David Stephen Harms, and has issue living, Hera b 1956: m 1991, Derek Dale Peterson, eldest son of Dale Gunnar Peterson, of Belleview, Florida, USA, and has issue living, Jacob Gunnar b 1994, Jacklyn Elise b 1997, — Jane Mary, b 1968. ——— (Elizabeth) Charmian, b 1935: m 1960, Richard Francis Spickernell (see Boothby, Bt, colls, 1970 Edn), of Bincknoll House, Wootton Bassett, Wilts, and has issue living, Godfrey John Wenman, b 1962, — James William Richard, b 1965: m 1991, Lady Rachel Barbara Violet Petty-Fitzmaurice, yr da of Charles Maurice, Earl of Shelburne (see M Lansdowne), and has issue living, Benjamin Thomas Richard b 1994, Frederick Charles William b 1996, Olivia Alice Georgie b 1999.

Grandchildren of late Maj Hon Sir John Spencer Coke, KCVO, Scots Gds, 5th son of 2nd Earl:—
Issue of late Lt-Col Gerald Edward Coke, CBE, b 1907, d 1990: m 1939, Patricia, who d 1995, da of late Rt Hon Sir Alexander George Montagu Cadogan, GCMG, KCB (see E Cadogan, colls):—
John Alexander (Bury Court, Bentley, Hants), b 1946; ed Eton: m 1980 (m diss 1987), Karen Johnson. ——— David Edward (The Old Hall, Jervaulx, Ripon, N Yorks), b 1951; ed Eton, and Univs of E Anglia and Manchester: m 1973, Karen Phillips, and has issue living, Michael Alexander, b 1979, — Charis Hester, b 1975. ——— Lavinia Mary, b 1944: m 1967, Peter Raymond Wilson, of Vale Court, Colerne, Chippenham, Wilts, and has issue living, Nicholas Peter, b 1971; ed Eton, and Univ of the West of England: m 1998, Hannah Corcut, — Andrew Michael, b 1974; ed Eton, and Bristol Univ, — Miranda Mary, b 1969: m 1993, Colin Acheson-Gray, and has issue living, Lucy Elizabeth b 1996, Emily Mary b 1998.

Issue of late Capt Hon Reginald Coke, DSO, 8th son of 2nd Earl, b 1883, d 1969: m 1924, Katharine, who d 1977, da of late Hon Edward Alan Dudley Ryder (see E Harrowby, colls, 1976 Edn):—
Mary Margaret (76 Abercrombie St, SW11 2JD) b 1925. ——— Katharine Vera, b 1927: m 1951, Peter John Cator, of The Barns, Condicote, Cheltenham, Glos GL54 1ES (B Mostyn, colls), and has issue living, Charles Henry (5 Halsey St, SW3 2QH), b 1952; ed Eton, and Bristol Univ; Dep Chm Christie, Manson & Woods Ltd, — Caroline Sarah, b 1954: m 1985, Piers H. de la Force, of 48 Ellison Rd, SW16 5BY, yr son of late Martin de la Force, of Montevideo, Uruguay, and late Mrs Falaise de la Force, of 3 Herbert Cres, SW1, and has issue living, James Edward b 1987, Alexandra Eloise b 1989.

Grandchildren of late Hon Henry John Coke, 3rd son of 1st Earl:—
Issue of late Reginald Grey Coke, b 1864, d 1930: m 1st, 1887 (m diss 1888), Elizabeth Wilson; 2ndly, 1892 (m diss 1908), Phylis Susan, who d 1939, da of late Francis William Bott, of Somersal, Derby; 3rdly, 1909, Galia, who d 1947, da of Michael Hambourg, formerly of 2 Clifton Gardens, W.:—
(By 3rd m) Henry, b 1912: m 1934, Joyce, da of Gerald E. Rattigan, has issue living, Basil, b 1935. ——— Stella, b 1910: m 1931, John Michael Ryan, of 43 Westminster Court, St Stephens Hill, St Albans, Herts, and has issue living.

PREDECESSORS – (1) THOMAS WILLIAM Coke, son of late Wenman Coke (formerly Roberts); b 1754; many years MP for co Norfolk; cr Viscount Coke and Earl of Leicester (peerage of United Kingdom) 1837: m 1st, 1775, Jane, who d 1800, da of James Dutton; 2ndly, 1822, Lady Anne Amelia Keppel, who d 1884 (having m 2ndly, 1843, Rt Hon Edward Ellice, MP), da of 4th Earl of Albemarle; d 1842; s by his son (2) THOMAS WILLIAM, KG, 2nd Earl; b 1822; Lord-Lieut of Norfolk 1846-1906; sometime a Member of Council of Duchy of Cornwall and Keeper of the Privy Seal: m 1st, 1843, Juliana, who d 1870, da of late Samuel Charles Whitbread, of Southill, Beds; 2ndly, 1875, Hon Georgiana Caroline Cavendish, who d 1937, el da of 2nd Baron Chesham; d 1909; s by his el son (3) THOMAS WILLIAM, GCVO, CMG, 3rd Earl; b 1848; sometime Col 2nd Batn Scots Guards; Egypt 1882, Suakin 1885, S Africa 1901-2 (CMG); Lord-Lieut of Norfolk 1906-29: m 1879, Hon Dame Alice White, DBE, who d 1936, da of 2nd Baron Annaly; d 1941; s by his el son (4) THOMAS WILLIAM, 4th Earl; b 1880; Lord-Lieut of Norfolk 1944-49: m 1905, Marion Gertrude, who d 1955, da of late Col Hon Walter Rodolph Trefusis, CB; d 1949; s by his son (5) THOMAS WILLIAM EDWARD, MVO, 5th Earl; b 1908; an Equerry to HRH The Duke of York 1934-36, an Extra Equerry to HM King George VI 1936-52, and to HM Queen Elizabeth II 1952-76: m 1931, Lady Elizabeth Mary Yorke, DCVO, who d 1985, da of 8th Earl of Hardwicke; d 1976; s by his cousin (6) ANTHONY LOUIS LOVEL (son of late Hon Arthur George Coke, 2nd son of 3rd Earl), 6th Earl, b 1909; 1939-45 War in RAF: m 1st, 1934 (m diss 1947), Moyra Joan, who d 1987, da of late Douglas Crossley; 2ndly, 1947, Vera, who d 1984, da of Herbert William Haigh, of Durham; 3rdly, 1985, Elizabeth Hope Smith, who d 1998, da of Clifford Arthur Johnstone, of Kiswani, Addo, CP, S Africa, and d 1994, in S Africa; s by his elder son (7) EDWARD DOUGLAS, 7th Earl and present peer; also Viscount Coke.

LEIGH, BARON (Leigh) (Baron UK 1839)

All comes from God

JOHN PIERS LEIGH, 5th Baron; *b* 11 Sept 1935; *s* 1979; *ed* Eton, Oxford, and London Univ: *m* 1st, 1957 (*m diss* 1974), Cecilia Poppy, yst da of late Robert Cecil Jackson, of Redlynch, Wilts; 2ndly, 1976 (*m diss* 1982), Susan, yst da of John Reginald Cleave, of Whitnash, Leamington Spa; 3rdly, 1982 (*m diss* 1998), Lea, only da of Col Harry Noël Havelock Wild, and formerly wife of Lt-Col Brian Gustavus Hamilton-Russell (*see* V Boyne), and has issue by 1st and 2nd *m*.

Arms – Gules, a cross engrailed argent and in the first quarter a lozenge argent. Crest – An unicorn's head erased, armed and crined or. Supporters – On either side an unicorn, armed, maned, tufted and unguled or, gorged with a ducal coronet gules, pendant therefrom an escutcheon charged with the arms of *Brydges*, viz argent, a cross sable, thereon a leopard's face or. *Address* – c/o House of Lords, SW1.

SONS LIVING (*By 1st marriage*)

Hon CHRISTOPHER DUDLEY PIERS, *b* 20 Oct 1960; *ed* Eton, and RAC Cirencester: *m* 1990, Sophy-Ann, da of Richard Burrows, MBE, of The Old Hall, Groby, Leics, and has issue living, Rupert Dudley, *b* 21 Feb 1994, — Lucy Alexandra, *b* 1995. *Residence* – Fern Farm, Adlestrop, Moreton-in-Marsh, Glos GL56 0YL.

(*by 2nd marriage*)

Hon Piers Henry John, *b* 1979.

DAUGHTER LIVING (*By 1st marriage*)

Hon Camilla Anne, *b* 1962.

BROTHERS LIVING

Hon William Rupert, *b* 1938; *ed* Eton, RMA Sandhurst and RAC Cirencester; late Lt 11th Hussars: *m* 1965, Priscilla Elizabeth, yr da of late Lt-Cdr Edward Francis Patrick Cooper, RN (ret), of Markree Castle, co Sligo (*see* B Castlemaine, colls, 1967 Edn), and has had issue, James Rupert, *b* 1967, — Edward William, *b* 1968, — †Richard Thomas, *b* 1974; *d* 1978, — Francis Dudley, *b* 1982. *Residence* – Ranaghan, Collooney, co Sligo.

Hon Benjamin Chandos, *b* 1942; *ed* Eton; late Lt 11th Hussars: *m* 1979, Jennifer Vivian, da of late Capt Peter Winser, and formerly wife of Hon Richard Henry Strutt (*see* B Belper), and has issue living, Samantha Jane Hazel, *b* 1980. *Residence* – Little Rissington House, Little Rissington, Cheltenham, Glos GL54 2NB.

Hon Michael James, *b* 1945; *ed* Eton, and Keble Coll, Oxford: *m* 1972 (*m diss* 1980), Cherry Rosalind, da of late David Long-Price. Resides in Australia.

PREDECESSORS – (1) CHANDOS Leigh, son of late James Henry Leigh, *b* 1791; gained favourable reputation as a poet; *cr Baron Leigh*, of Stoneleigh, co Warwick (peerage of United Kingdom) 1839: *m* 1819, Margarette, who *d* 1860, da of late Rev William Shippen Wiles, of Astrop House, Northamptonshire, *d* 1850; *s* by his son (2) *Rt Hon* WILLIAM HENRY, LLD, 2nd Baron; *b* 1824; Lord-Lieut and a High Steward of Sutton Coldfield *m* 1848, Lady Caroline Amelia Grosvenor who *d* 1906, da of 2nd Marquess of Westminster; *d* 1905; *s* by his son (3) FRANCIS DUDLEY, 3rd Baron; Lord-Lieut of co Warwick: *m* 1st, 1890, Frances Hélène Forbes, who *d* 1909, da of late Hon N. M. Beckwith, of New York; 2ndly, 1923, Marie, who *d* 1949, da of late Alexander Campbell, of New York; *d* 1938; *s* by his nephew (4) RUPERT WILLIAM DUDLEY, TD, DL (only son of late Major Hon Rupert Leigh, 3rd son of 2nd Baron), 4th Baron, *b* 1908; High Steward of Sutton Coldfield; Lt-Col 1st Roy Glos Hussars: *m* 1931, Anne, who *d* 1977, da of late Ellis Hicks Beach (*see* E St Aldwyn, colls); *d* 1979; *s* by his el son (5) JOHN PIERS, 5th Baron and present peer.

LEIGHTON OF ST MELLONS, BARON (Seager) (Baron UK 1962, Bt UK 1952)

By Courage and Faith

ROBERT WILLIAM HENRY LEIGHTON SEAGER, 3rd Baron and 3rd Baronet; *b* 28 Sept 1955; *s* 1998: *m* 1978, Wendy Elizabeth, da of Herbert John Hopwood, of Cardiff, and has issue.

𝕬rms – Azure a cross moline between in bend dexter two lymphads and in bend sinister as many mullets all argent. 𝕮rest – Between two wings azure each charged with a mullet a cross moline argent. 𝕾upporters – *Dexter*, a sea-horse (hippocampus) azure; *sinister*, a dragon segreant gules.

DAUGHTER LIVING

Hon Emma Elizabeth Leighton, *b* 1980.

BROTHER LIVING

Hon SIMON JOHN LEIGHTON, *b* 25 Jan 1957: *m* 1982, Gillian A. Rawlinson, and has issue living, Louise Tracey Leighton, *b* 1983, — Kim Angela Leighton, *b* 1983, — Hayley Marie Leighton, *b* 1987.

SISTER LIVING

Hon Carole Mary Leighton, *b* 1958: *m* 1991, Donald K. Perring, and has issue living, Donna Elizabeth, *b* 1993.

UNCLE LIVING (*son of 1st Baron*)

Hon Douglas Leighton (Leighton House, 5929 Hudson, Vancouver BC, Canada), *b* 1925: *m* 1960, Gillian Claire, da of Leonard Warwick Greenwood, of Pound Piece, Astley, Stourport, Worcs, and has issue living, Nicola Claire Leighton, *b* 1961, — Wendy Elizabeth Leighton, *b* 1963, — Michelle Leighton, *b* 1967.

AUNTS LIVING (*daughters of 1st Baron*)

Hon Thelma Margaret Leighton, *b* 1923: *m* 1st, 1951 (*m diss* 1981), Michael Edmonds; 2ndly, 1983, Joseph Evan Lloyd, and has issue living (by 1st *m*), Christopher Leighton, *b* 1958: *m* 1992, Diane, da of William Burnell, — Susan Leighton, *b* 1952: *m* 1971, Timothy Vicary, and has issue living, Joanna Claire *b* 1980, Alice Megan *b* 1985, — Jane Leighton, *b* 1954: *m* 1984, John Nelson.

Hon Zoë Leighton, *b* 1928: *m* 1st, 1955, Malcolm James Peniston, of The Fishermans, King St, Emsworth, Hants, who *d* 1981; 2ndly, 1984, Alan Carnegie Stewart, of Westwood, Hardgate, Castle Douglas, Kirkcudbrightshire DG7 3LD, and has issue living (by 1st *m*), Douglas James *b* 1959: *m* 1990, Lyana, da of Peter Hodgson, of Tiverton, Cheshire, and has issue living, Charlotte Eloise *b* 1991, Arabella Leighton *b* 1993, — Angela Clare, *b* 1956: *m* 1982, Jeremy J. Adams, — Rosemary Leighton, *b* 1964: *m* 1996, Simon O'Hea, elder son of Jerome O'Hea, OBE, of Chichester, W Sussex.

PREDECESSORS – **(1)** *Sir* (GEORGE) LEIGHTON SEAGER, CBE (son of Sir William Henry Seager, of Lynwood, Cardiff, founder of the firm of W. H. Seager & Co, shipowners and managers, and ships' suppliers); *b* 1896; an underwriting member of Lloyd's, Pres of Cardiff Chamber of Commerce 1934-35, and of Council of Shipping 1944; High Sheriff of Monmouthshire 1938-39 and Vice-Lieut 1957-63; *cr* a Knt 1938, a *Baronet* 1952 and *Baron Leighton of St Mellons*, of St Mellons, co Monmouth 1962: *m* 1921, Marjorie, who *d* 1992, da of William Henry Gimson, of Breconshire, *d* 1963; *s* by his son **(2)** JOHN LEIGHTON, 2nd Baron, *b* 1922: *m* 1st, 1953, Elizabeth Rosita, who *d* 1979, only da of late Henry Hopgood; 2ndly, 1982 (*m diss* 1994), Ruth Elizabeth, widow of John Hopwood; *d* 1998; *s* by his elder son **(3)** ROBERT WILLIAM HENRY LEIGHTON, 3rd Baron and present peer.

LEINSTER, DUKE OF (FitzGerald) Sits as VISCOUNT (GB 1747) (Duke I 1766)
(Title pronounced "Linster")

GERALD FITZGERALD, 8th Duke and Premier Duke, Marquess, and Earl of Ireland; *b* 27 May 1914; *s* 1976; *ed* Eton, and RMC; late Maj 5th R Inniskilling Dragoon Gds; 1939-45 War (wounded): *m* 1st, 1936 (*m diss* 1946), Joane, el da of late Maj Arthur MacMurrough Kavanagh, MC (Buxton, Bt, colls); 2ndly, 1946, Anne, yr da of late Lt-Col Philip Eustace Smith, MC, and has issue by 1st and 2nd *m*.

𝔄rms – Argent, a saltire gules. 𝔠rest – A monkey statant proper, environed round the loins and chained or. 𝔖upporters – Two monkeys proper environed round the loins and chained or. *Residence* – Kilkea House, Wilcote Lane, Ramsden, Oxon OX7 3BA.

SONS LIVING (By 2nd marriage)

MAURICE (*Marquess of Kildare*) (Courtyard House, Oakley Park, Frilford Heath, Oxon OX13 6QW), *b* 7 April 1948; *ed* Millfield: *m* 1972, Fiona Mary Francesca, da of late Harry Hollick, of Long Barn, Sutton Courtenay, Oxon, and has had issue:—
 SON DECEASED — †Thomas (*Earl of Offaly*), *b* 12 Jan 1974; *d* in a motor accident in Ireland 9 May 1997.
 DAUGHTERS LIVING — *Lady* Francesca Emily Purcell, *b* 1976, — *Lady* Pollyanna Louisa Clementine, *b* 1982.

Lord John, 1952; *ed* Millfield, and RMA Sandhurst; late Capt 5th R Inniskilling Dragoon Gds: *m* 1982, Barbara, el da of late Andreas Zindel, of St Moritz, Switzerland, and has issue living, Edward, *b* 1988, — Hermione, *b* 1985.

Crom to Victory

DAUGHTERS LIVING (By 1st marriage)

Lady Rosemary Ann FITZGERALD (Beggars Roost, Lilstock, nr Bridgwater, Som TA5 1SU), *b* 1939; *ed* Lady Margaret Hall, Oxford; has resumed the surname of FitzGerald: *m* 1963 (*m diss* 1967), Mark Killigrew Wait.

Lady Nesta, *b* 1942: *m* 1977, Philip Charles Seppings Tirard, who *d* 1993, of Coolnabrune, Borris, co Carlow, Eire, and has issue living, Siobhan Eleanor, *b* 1978, — Eithne, *b* 1982.

COLLATERAL BRANCHES LIVING

Grandchildren of late Lord Charles FitzGerald, 5th son of 4th Duke:—
 Issue of late Rupert Augustus FitzGerald, *b* 1900, *d* 1969: *m* 1st, 1924 (*m diss* 1932), Irene, da of J. Jennings, of Melbourne, Vic, Aust; 2ndly, 1936, Ivy, who *d* 1945, da of late J. Simmons, of Melbourne, Aust—
(By 1st *m*) Peter Charles, *b* 1925; 1939-45 War with AMF: *m* 1950, June, da of W. Murray, of East St Kilda, Vic, Aust, and has issue living, Stephen Peter, *b* 1953, — Lynette Pamela, *b* 1951. —— (By 2nd *m*) Elizabeth Mary, *b* 1937: *m* 1958, Ronald Smith, of 24 Ireland Av, Doncaster East, Vic, Aust, and has issue living, Gary Ronald, *b* 1960, — Amanda Elizabeth, *b* 1962.

Issue of late Lord Henry FitzGerald, 7th son of 4th Duke, *b* 1863, *d* 1955: *m* 1891, Inez, who *d* 1967, da of late Cdr William John Casberd-Boteler, RN, of Eastry, Kent:—
Denis Henry, DSO, OBE, *b* 1911; *ed* Eton; was ADC to Gen Officer Comdg N Ireland Dist 1938-39, and GSO, Headquarters Guards Armoured Div 1941-42, Instructor at Staff Coll, Camberley 1942-43, and GSO at Headquarters 30th Corps 1944, AQMG, War Office 1949-50, and Headquarters, London Dist 1950-51, Col Comdg Irish Guards 1951-52, Brigadier Comdg 4th Guards Brig 1953-55, Imperial Defence Coll 1956, and Director of Plans (War Office) 1957-58; European War 1939-45 in Norway and N-W Europe (DSO), Palestine 1947; DSO, 1945, OBE (Mil) 1951. *Residence* – Glenshelane House, Cappoquin, co Waterford.

PREDECESSORS – (1) GERALD FitzGerald; *cr Baron of Offaly*, co Kildare, before 1203; *d* about 1203; *s* by his son (2) MAURICE, 2nd Baron; Lord Ch Justice of Ireland; introduced into Ireland 1216 the Order of the Franciscans, and in 1229 the Order of the Dominicans, built in 1231 the Franciscan Abbey of Youghal, where he *d* 1267; *s* by his son (3) MAURICE, 3rd Baron; was Ch Gov of Ireland; *d* 1277, *s* by his son (4) GERALD, 4th Baron; founded the Franciscan Order at Clane 1271; *d* 1287; *s* by his cousin (5) MAURICE, 5th Baron; *dsp*; *s* by his cousin (6) JOHN, 6th Baron; a valiant soldier who assisted Edward I in his Scottish campaigns 1296, 1299, and 1301, and afterwards dispersed the rebels in Munster, and opposed Robert Bruce who had entered the N of Ireland with 6,000 men, *cr Earl of Kildare* (peerage of Ireland) 1316; there is a tradition that the Earl while an infant was asleep at Woodstock Castle, near Athy, when an alarm of fire was raised; in the confusion the child was forgotten, and on the servants returning to search for him they found the room in which he had lain to be in ruins; soon after, hearing a strange noise in one of the towers, they looked up and saw an ape, which was usually kept chained, carefully holding the child in his arms; he afterwards in gratitude for his preservation adopted a monkey for his crest; *d* 1316; *s* by his son (7) THOMAS, 2nd Earl; was three times Lord Justice of Ireland; *d* 1328; *s* by his son (8) RICHARD, 3rd Earl; *d* 1329; *s* by his brother (9) MAURICE, KB, 4th Earl; present at siege of Calais; *d* 1390; *s* by his son (10) GERALD, 5th Earl; was Lord Dep to Thomas, Duke of Gloucester, Lord-Lieut of Ireland; *d* 1410; *s* by his brother (11) JOHN, 6th Earl; strengthened and enlarged the Castle of Maynooth; *d* 1427: *s* by his son (12) THOMAS, 7th Earl; was Lord Dep of Ireland 1454-9, and Lord Chancellor of Ireland

1468; being involved with the Earl of Desmond he was attainted, but subsequently pardoned, released, restored in blood by Act of Parliament, and appointed Lord Justice of Ireland 1471; *d* 1477; *s* by his son (13) GERALD, KG, 8th Earl; Lord Dep and Lord Justice of Ireland for thirty-three years, an eminent military commander who invaded Ulster, took numerous castles, and in 1504 obtained a complete victory over the Irish chiefs of Connaught; *d* 1513; *s* by his son (14) GERALD, 9th Earl; Lord Dep of Ireland, was deprived of his high office, and with his five half-brothers was committed to the Tower and sentenced to be executed as a traitor; *d* a prisoner 1534; *s* by his son (15) THOMAS, 10th Earl; having heard that his father was to be beheaded he threw off all allegiance to the English crown; he eventually surrendered on the promise of receiving a full pardon; this promise was violated by Henry VIII, and in 1537 he, together with his five uncles, was hanged, drawn and quartered at Tyburn, and his honours were attainted; *s* by his half-brother (16) GERALD, 11th Earl; was *ed* Rome by his kinsman Cardinal Pole, and subsequently became Master of the Horse to Cosmo de Medici, Duke of Florence, returned to England after the death of Henry VIII and received Knighthood from Edward VI, and a regrant of all the Irish family estates, and Queen Mary restored to him all his ancestral honours; *d* 1585; *s* by his son (17) HENRY, 12th Earl; *d* 1597; *s* by his brother (18) WILLIAM, 13th Earl; lost at sea 1599; *s* by his cousin (19) GERALD, 14th Earl; *d* 1612; *s* by his son (20) GERALD, 15th Earl; *d* 1620; *s* by his cousin (21) GEORGE, 16th Earl; *d* 1655; *s* by his son (22) WENTWORTH, 17th Earl; *d* 1664; *s* by his son (23) JOHN, 18th Earl; *dsp* 1707; *s* by his cousin (24) ROBERT, 19th Earl; an eminent statesman; *d* 1744; *s* by his son (25) JAMES, 20th Earl; Master-Gen of the Ordnance in Ireland; *cr* Viscount Leinster (peerage of Great Britain) 1747, *Earl of Offaly* and *Marquess of Kildare* (peerage of Ireland) 1761, and *Duke of Leinster* (peerage of Ireland) 1766; *d* 1773; *s* by his son (26) WILLIAM ROBERT, KP, 2nd Duke; *d* 1804; *s* by his son (27) AUGUSTUS FREDERICK, PC, 3rd Duke; *b* 1791; HM Lieut of co Kildare: *m* 1818, Charlotte Augusta Stanhope, da of 3rd Earl of Harrington; *d* 1874; *s* by his son (28) CHARLES WILLIAM, PC, 4th Duke; *b* 1819; sat as MP for Kildare 1847-52; *cr* (in the lifetime of his father) *Baron Kildare* (peerage of United Kingdom) 1870: *m* 1847, Lady Caroline Sutherland Leveson-Gower, da of 2nd Duke of Sutherland; *d* 1887; *s* by his son (29) GERALD, PC, 5th Duke, *b* 1851; HM Lieut of co Kildare: *m* 1884, Lady Hermione Whilhelmina Duncombe, who *d* 1895, da of 1st Earl of Feversham; *d* 1893; *s* by his el son (30) MAURICE, 6th Duke, *b* 1887; *d* 1922; *s* by his brother (31) EDWARD, 7th Duke*; *b* 1892; *m* 1st, 1913 (*m diss* 1930), May (May Etheridge, the stage soubrette), who *d* 1935, da of late Jesse Etheridge; 2ndly, 1932 (*m diss* 1946), Agnes Rafaella, who *d* 1993, da of Robert Davidson Kennedy, and formerly wife of late Clare Van Neck; 3rdly, 1946, Jessie, who *d* 1960, da of late Alfred John Smither, and formerly wife of (1) 3rd Baron Churston and (2) Theodore Wessel; 4thly 1965, Vivien Irene, who *d* 1992, da of late Thomas Albert Felton, of London, and formerly wife of George William Conner; *d* 1976; *s* by his son (32) Gerald, 8th Duke and present peer; also Marquess of Kildare, Earl of Kildare, Earl and Baron of Offaly, Viscount Leinster, and Baron Kildare.

*The 7th Duke also left recognised issue (by Yvonne Denison Percy, who *d* 1973, having assumed the surname of FitzGerald by deed poll 1952, eldest da of late Col Percy John Probyn, DSO, RAMC), Adrian Dighton Desmond FITZGERALD (2 Trevarrian Mews, Trevarrian, Mawgan Porth, Newquay, Cornwall), *b* 1952: *m* 1st, 1972 (*m diss* 1975), Colleen Teresa, da of Gordon James Cross, of Foxhole, St Austell; 2ndly, 1982 (*m diss* 1992), Mrs Linda Jane Harris, da of Charles James Clark, of London, and has issue living (by 1st *m*), Kirsty, *b* 1973: *m* 1993, Andrew Simon Keetch.

Leith, family name of Baron Burgh.

Lennox, Duke of, see Duke of Richmond and Gordon.

Lennox, Gordon, family name of Duke of Richmond and Gordon.

LEONARD, BARONY OF (Leonard) (Extinct 1983)

SON LIVING OF LIFE BARON

Hon Derek John, *b* 1956; *ed* Harrow, and Aberystwyth Univ (LLB); ptnr Leonard & Kalim, Solicitors. *Address* – 777/9 High Rd, Leytonstone, E11.

DAUGHTER LIVING OF LIFE BARON

Hon Elizabeth Margaret, *b* 1946; *ed* Univ of Wales (LLB): *m* 1963, Michael Harwood of The Hague, Netherlands.

WIDOW LIVING OF LIFE BARON

GLENYS EVELYN (*Baroness Leonard*), da of Ernest Kenny: *m* 1945, Baron Leonard, OBE (Life Baron), who *d* 1983. *Residence* – 19 Queen Anne Sq, Cardiff CF1 3ED.

Le Poer, Baron; grandson of Marquess of Waterford.

Leslie, family name of Earl of Rothes.

LESTER OF HERNE HILL, BARON (Lester) (Life Baron 1993)

ANTHONY PAUL LESTER, QC, son of late Harry Lester, of London; *b* 3 July 1936; *ed* City of London Sch, Trin Coll, Camb (BA), and Harvard Law Sch (LLM); 2nd Lieut RA 1955-57; Bar Lincoln's Inn 1963, QC 1975, Bencher 1985, NI Bar 1984, and Irish Bar 1983, Recorder SE Circuit 1987; Special Advisor to Home Sec 1974-76, and Standing Commn on Human Rights in NI 1975-77; formerly Chm Board of Govs James Allen's Girls' Sch, Gov Westminster Sch, Chm Interights (Internat Centre for Legal Protection of Human Rights), Co-Chair Board of European Roma Rights Center, Member Board Salzburg Seminar, formerly Chm Runnymede Trust; Hon Visiting Prof of Law Univ Coll London; ACIArb; author and contributor to learned journals; *cr Baron Lester of Herne Hill*, of Herne Hill, in the London Borough of Southwark (Life Baron) 1993: *m* 1971, Catherine Elizabeth Debora, da of late Michael Morris Wassey, of London, and has issue.
Chambers – Blackstone Chambers, Blackstone House, Temple, EC4Y 9BW. *Club* – Garrick.

SON LIVING

Hon Gideon, *b* 1972.

DAUGHTER LIVING

Hon Maya, *b* 1974.

LESTOR OF ECCLES, BARONY OF (Lestor) (Life Baroness 1997)

(Extinct 1998)

JOAN LESTOR, da of late Charles Lestor; *b* 13 Nov 1931; *ed* William Morris Secondary Sch, Walthamstow, and London Univ; Teacher 1952-59; ran own Kindergarten 1959-68; Memb LCC 1962-64; Parliamentary Under-Sec of State, Dept of Education and Science 1969-70, and FCO 1974-75; Memb Labour Party NEC 1967-82 (Chm 1977-78); Chm International Cttee of Labour Party 1978-97; Opposition Front Bench Spokesperson on Women's Rights and Welfare 1981, Aid and Development 1987-89, Children, Juvenile Offenders and Race 1989-93, Children and Family 1993-94, and Overseas Development 1994-96; MP (*Lab*) for Eton and Slough 1966-83, and for Eccles 1987-97; *cr Baroness Lestor of Eccles*, of Tooting Bec in the London Borough of Wandsworth (Life Baroness) 1997; had an adopted son and an adopted da. Baroness Lestor of Eccles *d* 27 March 1998.

LEVEN and MELVILLE, EARL OF (Leslie Melville) (Earl S 1641 and 1690)

*For King and country
Heaven at last*

ALEXANDER ROBERT LESLIE MELVILLE, 14th Earl of Leven and 13th Earl of Melville; *b* 13 May 1924; *s* 1947; *ed* Eton; Capt (ret) Coldstream Guards, served NW Europe (wounded), ADC to Gov-Gen of NZ 1951-52; DL Nairn 1961; Lord Lieut for Nairn since 1969, Chm Nairn CC 1970-74; Chm of Governors Gordonstoun Sch 1971-89; Pres British Ski Federation 1981-85, and Hon Pres Scottish Nat Ski Council: *m* 1953, Susan, da of Lieut-Col Ronald Steuart-Menzies of Menzies, of Arndilly House, Craigellachie, Banffshire, and has issue.

Arms – Quarterly: 1st, azure, a thistle slipped proper, ensigned with an Imperial Crown or, a coat of augmentation to the arms of *Leslie*; 2nd, gules, three crescents within a bordure argent, charged with eight roses of the first, *Melville*; 3rd argent, a fesse gules, *Melville of Raith*; 4th, argent, on a bend azure, three buckles or, *Leslie*. Crests – 1st,a demi-chevalier in complete armour, holding in his right hand a dagger point downwards proper, pommel and hilt or, *Leslie*; 2nd, a ratchhound's head erased proper, collared gules, *Melville*. Supporters – *Dexter*, a knight in complete armour, holding in his dexter hand the banner of Scotland, all proper, *Leslie*; *sinister*, a ratchhound proper, collared gules, *Melville*.
Residence – Raith, Old Spey Bridge, Grantown-on-Spey, Morayshire PH26 3NQ. *Club* – New (Edinburgh).

SONS LIVING

DAVID ALEXANDER (*Lord Balgonie*), *b* 26 Jan 1954; *ed* Eton: *m* 1981, Julia Clare, yr da of Col Ian Ranald Critchley, OBE, The Black Watch, of Greenden, by Brechin, Angus (*see* V Arthbuthnott, 1980 Edn), and has issue living, Alexander Ian, *b* 29 Nov 1984, — Louisa Clare, *b* 1987. *Residence* – Glenferness House, Nairn IV12 5UP.
Hon Archibald Ronald, *b* 1957; *ed* Gordonstoun; Lt Queen's Own Highlanders: *m* 1987, Julia Mary Greville, yr da of Basil Fox, of 32 Pembroke Gdns, W8, and has issue living, Alice Catherine, *b* 1990, — Camilla Jane, *b* 1992, — Joanna, *b* 1994. *Residence* – Orwell House, Manse Rd, Milnathort, Kinross-shire KY13 7LN.

DAUGHTER LIVING

Lady Jane Catherine, *b* 1956: *m* 1977, Philip Mark Gurney Hudson, of Southcott Lodge, Pewsey, Wilts, and has issue living, Katherine, *b* 1983, — Susanna, *b* 1986.

BROTHER LIVING

Hon Alan Duncan, *b* 1928; *ed* Eton; Capt (ret) Rifle Bde: *m* 1997, Sally, widow of M. J. Haywood, of Fettes Farmhouse, Muir of Ord, Ross-shire. *Residence* – South Cantray, Croy, Inverness IV2 5PW.

SISTER LIVING

Lady Jean Elizabeth, *b* 1921. *Residence* – Flat 24, Homesmith House, Evesham, Worcs WR11 4EH.

WIDOWS LIVING OF SONS OF THIRTEENTH EARL

Diana Mary, yr da of late Brig Sir Henry Walter Houldsworth, KBE, DSO, MC, TD (*see* E Morton, colls, 1980 Edn): *m* 1955, Maj Hon George David Leslie Melville, 2nd (twin) son of 13th Earl, who *d* 1997, and has issue (see colls, infra). *Residence* – Inneshewen, Aboyne, Aberdeenshire AB34 5BH.

Ruth, only da of late Dr John Duckworth, DSc, FRSE: *m* 1962, Hon Ronald Joscelyn Leslie Melville, 3rd son of 13th Earl, who *d* 1987, and has issue (see colls, infra). *Residence* – Little Deuchar, Fern, Forfar, Angus DD8 3RA.

COLLATERAL BRANCHES LIVING

Issue of late Maj Hon George David Leslie Melville, 2nd (twin) son of 13th Earl, *b* 1924, *d* 1997: *m* 1955, Diana Mary (ante), yr da of late Brig Sir Henry Walter Houldsworth, KBE, DSO, MC, TD (*see* E Morton, colls, 1980 Edn):—

James Hugh, *b* 1960: *m* 1987, Clare Jean, 2nd da of Lt-Col Robert Henry Heywood-Lonsdale (*see* L Rollo), and has issue living, John (Jack) Alastair, *b* 1991, — George William, *b* 1993, — Rosanna Clare, *b* 1995. *Residence* – Berryhill House, Grange of Lindores, Newburgh, Fife KY14 6HZ. —— Annabel Clare, *b* 1956: *m* 1979, Nigel R. Savory, son of John Savory, of Bridge Cottage, Thorpland, Fakenham, Norfolk. *Residence* – Thorpland Hall, Fakenham, Norfolk NR21 0HD.

Issue of late Hon Ronald Joscelyn Leslie Melville, 3rd son of 13th Earl, *b* 1926, *d* 1987: *m* 1962, Ruth (ante), only da of late Dr John Duckworth, DSc, FRSE:—

†Andrew John, *b* and *d* 1964. —— Roderick Justice, *b* 1965. —— Robert Jeffrey, *b* 1967. —— Angus Jack, *b* 1968. —— Rosamond Joscelyn, *b* 1962: *m* 1986 (*m diss* 1991), Christopher Pogson, only son of Lt Cmdr Tony Pogson, of Durley, Surrey.

Issue of late Hon David William Leslie Melville, MBE, 3rd son of 11th Earl, *b* 1892, *d* 1938: *m* 1st, 1914 (*m diss* 1928), Susanna Elizabeth Johanna, da of Francis Sleigh, of Cape Town, S Africa; 2ndly, 1929, Eleanor Mary, who *d* 1974, having *m* 2ndly, 1939, Capt Arthur Miller, who *d* on active ser 1942, da of Arthur John Abrahall, formerly of Shustoke, near Coleshill, Warwickshire:—

(By 2nd *m*) Gillian Mary (Flat 503 San Jose, 51 Olivia Rd, Berea 2198, Johannesburg, S Africa), *b* 1930: *m* 1st, 1950 (*m diss* 19—), Peter Riley; 2ndly, 19—, Martin Dowling, and has issue living (by 2nd *m*), David, *b* 19—, — Eleanor, *b* 19—.

Grandchildren of late Lt-Col Hon Ian Leslie Melville, TD (infra):—
Issue of late Maj Michael Ian Leslie-Melville, TD, *b* 1918, *d* 1997: *m* 1943, Cynthia, who *d* 1986, eldest da of late Sir Charles Jocelyn Hambro, KBE, MC:—

(Ian) Hamish, *b* 1944; *ed* Eton, and Ch Ch, Oxford (MA); Member of Queen's Body Guard for Scotland (Royal Company of Archers): *m* 1968, Lady Elizabeth Compton, yr da of 6th Marquess of Northampton, and has issue living, James Ian, *b* 1969: *m* 1997, Emma J., yr da of Geoffrey Thorp, of Guildford, Surrey, and has issue living, Rory Ian *b* 1998, — Henry Bingham, *b* 1975. *Residence* – Lochluichart, by Garve, Ross-shire. *Clubs* – Turf, New (Edinburgh). —— Pamela, *b* 1947. *Residence* – 11 Queen's Rd, Windsor, Berks SL4 3BQ. —— Fiona Evelyn, *b* 1950; ARCM: *m* 1973, James Campbell David Brodie, yr son of late Maj David James Brodie of Lethen, and has issue living, Alexander John, *b* 1974, — Charlotte Sophia, *b* 1976, — Anna Louise, *b* 1979. *Residence* – Aikbank, Farleton, Carnforth, Lancs LA6 1PD.

Issue of late Lt-Col Hon Ian Leslie Melville, TD, yst son of 11th Earl, *b* 1894, *d* 1967: *m* 1915, Charlotte Isabel, who *d* 1968, da of late Maj William Stirling, of Fairburn, Ross-shire:—

Elisabeth Marion (*Elisabeth, Baroness Joicey*), *b* 1928: *m* 1952, 4th Baron Joicey, who *d* 1993. *Residence* – Beech House, Etal, Berwick-on-Tweed.

Granddaughters of late Galfrid John Leslie Melville, only son of late Capt Hon Norman Leslie Melville, 4th son of 9th Earl:—
Issue of late Norman Victor Leslie Melville, *b* 1896, *d* 1974: *m* 1918, Dorothea, who *d* 1982, da of late Walter Stead:—

Joan Frances Ruth (The Close, Fairford, Glos), *b* 1922: *m* 1st, 1941 (*m diss* 1954), Norman Henry Gibbs, DPh, who *d* 1990; 2ndly, 1955, Richard John Marshall Amphlett, who *d* 1978, and has issue living (by 1st *m*), Kathleen Vanessa, *b* 1942: *m* 1965, Peter John Quarrell, of Vyners Cottage, Long Compton, Shipston-on-Stour, Warwicks, and has issue living, Rachel Emma Louise *b* 1968, Philippa Kathryn *b* 1970, — Judith Rowena, *b* 1946: *m* 1st, 1967 (*m diss* 19—), William Rupert Brent Pelly (*see* Pelly, Bt, colls); 2ndly, 1987, Roger W. Young, of Priors Court, Aylton, Herefords, and has issue (by 1st *m*) (*see* Pelly, Bt, colls). —— Anne, *b* 1929: *m* 1953 (*m diss* 1977), Matthew Joseph McDermott. *Residence* – Kitebrook House, nr Moreton-in-Marsh, Glos.

Granddaughters of late Rev Frederick Abel Leslie Melville, 5th son of late Hon Alexander Leslie Melville, yst son of 7th Earl:—
Issue of late Malcolm Alexander Leslie Melville, *b* 1882, *d* 1946: *m* 1924, Ruth Ellen, who *d* 1982, having *m* 2ndly, 1951, Arthur Ernest Mallett, who *d* 1960, da of James Dowker, of Mount Tolmie, Victoria, BC:—

Eleanor Constance, *b* 1926; *m* 1953, David William Metcalfe, and has issue living, Margaret Rose, *b* 1955: *m* 1979, Albert Lawson Munday, — Sandra Gail, *b* 1957: *m* 1976, Bruce Douglas Crowe, and has issue living, Andrew Jackson, *b* 1989, — Heather May, *b* 1965. *Residence* – 640 Fernhill Rd, Victoria, British Columbia. —— Margaret Wardlaw (1833, West 37th Av, Vancouver V6M 1N3, British Columbia), *b* 1928.

PREDECESSORS – (1) *Sir* Robert Melville, KB, PC, was twice Ambassador to England, Hereditary Keeper of Linlithgow Palace Vice-Chancellor and Treasurer depute, and an Extraordinary Lord of Session with title of Lord Murdocarnie 1594-1601; *cr Lord Melville of Monymaill* (peerage of Scotland), 1616, with remainder to heirs male of his brother John; *d* 1621, *s* by his son (2) Robert, PC, KB, 2nd Lord; an Extraordinary Lord of Session as Lord Burntisland 1601-8; in 1628 obtained a new charter of the lordship with remainders to his heirs general bearing the name of Melville; *d* 1635; *s* by his cousin (3) John, 3rd Lord, son of John (ante), brother of 1st Lord; *d* 1643; *s* by his son (4) George, 4th Lord; being involved in the rebellion of the Duke of Monmouth he was attainted by Act of Parliament 1685;

he escaped to Holland, from whence in 1688 he returned to England with the Prince of Orange (William III); in the following year the attainder was rescinded, and in 1690 he was *cr Lord Raith, Monymaill and Balwearie, Viscount Kirkaldie* and *Earl of Melville* (peerage of Scotland) 1690; Sec of State 1690-1, High Commr to Parliament 1690, Keeper of the Privy Seal 1691-6, and Pres of the Council 1696: *m* Lady Catherine Leslie, da of 2nd Earl of Leven; *d* 1707; *s* by his son (5) DAVID, PC, 2nd Earl, who had in 1682 *s* as 3rd of Leven (see note * infra); was Gov of Edinburgh Castle, Gen of the Ordnance, Lieut-Gen and Com in Ch in Scotland, a Commr of the Union, and a Representative Peer; *d* 1728; *s* by his grandson (6) DAVID, 4th Earl of Leven and 3rd Earl of Melville; *d* a minor 1729; *s* by his uncle (7) ALEXANDER, 5th and 4th Earl; was a Lord of Session, a Representative Peer 1747, and High Commr to Church of Scotland 1741-3; *d* 1745; *s* by his son (8) DAVID, 6th and 5th Earl; High Commr to Gen Assembly 1783-1801; *d* 1802; *s* by his son (9) ALEXANDER, 7th and 6th Earl; *d* 1820; *s* by his el son (10) DAVID, 8th and 7th Earl; a Rear-Adm, Comptroller of the Customs in Scotland, and a Representative Peer; *d* 1860; *s* by his brother (11) JOHN THORNTON, 9th and 8th Earl; *b* 1786; a Representative Peer: *m* 1st, 1812, Harriet, who *d* 1832, da of Samuel Thornton, MP, of Albury park and Clapham; 2ndly, 1834, Sophia, who *d* 1887, da of Henry Thornton, of Battersea, Surrey; *d* 1876; *s* by his son (12) ALEXANDER, 10th and 9th Earl, *b* 1817; a Representative Peer; *d* 1889; *s* by his half-brother (13) RONALD RUTHVEN, PC, KT, 11th and 10th Earl, *b* 1835; a Representative Peer and Lord Keeper of the Privy Seal of Scotland; Lord High Commr to Gen Assembly of Church of Scotland 1898, 1899, 1900, 1901, 1902, 1903, 1904, and 1905: *m* 1885, Hon Emma Selina, who *d* 1941, da of 2nd Viscount Portman; *d* 1906; *s* by his el son (14) JOHN DAVID, 12th and 11th Earl, *b* 1886; a Representative Peer; *d* 1913; *s* by his brother (15) ARCHIBALD ALEXANDER, 13th and 12th Earl, *b* 1890; a Representative Peer, Lieut-Col and Brevet-Col (retired) Lovat Scouts, and Lord Lieut of Nairnshire: *m* 1918, Lady Rosamond Sylvia Diana Mary Foljambe, who *d* 1974, da of 1st Earl of Liverpool (*cr* 1905); *d* 1947; *s* by his son (16) ALEXANDER ROBERT, 14th and 13th Earl and present peer; also Viscount Kirkaldie, Lord Melville of Monymail, Lord Balgonie, and Lord Raith, Monymaill and Balwearie.

*(1) *Sir* ALEXANDER Leslie, having served with distinction in the Swedish Army, in which service he attained the rank of Field-Marshal in 1638, took command of the Covenanters' Army and defeated the King's troops in various engagements; at the treaty of peace signed at Ripon 1641 the King *cr* him *Lord Balgonie* and *Earl of Leven* (peerage of Scotland) 1641, with remainder to his heirs whatsoever; he subsequently joined the Parliamentary Army with 21,000 men, and defeated the Royalists at Marston Moor 1644, but after the execution of the King he served against the Parliamentarians and joined in the cause of the Restoration; he was in 1651 surprised and taken prisoner by Gen Monk, and incarcerated in the Tower, from whence he was released at the intercession of Christina, Queen of Sweden; *d* 1661; *s* by his grandson (2) ALEXANDER, 2nd Earl; who obtained in 1665 a charter with remainder to (i) the heirs male of his body, (ii) the heirs female of his body, (iii) the 2nd son of John, 6th Earl of Rothes, (iv) the heirs male of George, 4th Lord Melville (ante), (v) the 2nd son of David, 2nd Earl of Wemys, (vi) his own heirsmale whatsoever, and (vii) to his heirs and assignees whatsoever; *d* without male issue 1663; *s* by his el da (3) MARGARET; *dsp* 1674; *s* by her sister (4) KATHERINE; *d* 1682; *s* by her kinsman (5) DAVID, 3rd Earl (see 2nd Earl of Melville (ante)), the three first remainders having failed.

LEVENE OF PORTSOKEN, BARON (Levene) (Life Baron 1997)

PETER KEITH LEVENE, KBE, son of late Maurice Pierre Levene, of Chelsea; *b* 8 Dec 1941; *ed* City of London Sch, and Manchester Univ (BA (Econ) 19—); JP City of London 1984; Chm United Scientific Holdings plc 1982-85 (Man Dir 1968-85); Chm Defence Manufacturers Assoc 1984-85; Personal Adviser to Sec of State for Defence 1984; Chief of Defence Procurement, MOD 1985-91; Dir UK Nat Armaments 1988-91; Chm IEPG (Euro) Nat Armaments Dirs 1989-90; Special Adviser to Sec of State for the Environment 1991-92; Special Adviser to President of Board of Trade 1992-95; Efficiency Adviser to the Prime Minister 1992-97; Senior Adviser Morgan Stanley and Co Ltd since 1996; Dep Chm Wasserstein Perella & Co Ltd 1991-95; Chm Docklands Light Railway 1991-94; Chm and Chief Exec Canary Wharf Ltd 1993-96; Gov City of London Sch for Girls 1984-85, City of London Sch since 1985, and Sir John Cass Primary Sch 1985-93 (Dep Chm); Vice-Pres City of London Red Cross; Memb Court of HAC; Chm London Homes for the Elderly 1990-93; Hon Col Cmdt RLC since 1993 (RCT 1991-93); Common Cncllr Ward of Candlewick 1983-84; Alderman Ward of Portsoken since 1984; Sheriff, City of London 1995-96; Lord Mayor of London 1998-99; Master of Worshipful Co of Carmen 1992-93; *cr* KBE 1989, and *Baron Levene of Portsoken*, of Portsoken in the City of London (Life Baron) 1997: *m* 1966, Wendy Ann, da of Frederick Fraiman, of London, and has issue.

Arms – Per pale gules and azure between three swords palewise in fess the outer two with their points downwards all three argent their hilts pommels and quillons or two towers also argent masoned proper in front of the portal of each tower a cart wheel gules and on a chief per pale azure and gules a boar's head couped or langued gules tusked argent between two loving cups of silver all proper. **Crest** – A mail gauntlet clenched argent in front of two vine branches in saltire leaved and fructed all proper. **Supporters** – *Dexter*, a scorpion or the stinger azure; *sinister*, a scorpion or, the stinger gules. **Address** – House of Lords, Westminster SW1A 0PW. **Clubs** – Guildhall, City Livery, RAC.

SONS LIVING

Hon John, b 1968.
Hon Timothy, b 1973.

DAUGHTER LIVING

Hon Nicole Juliette, b 1969: m 1996, Matthew Daniel Walsh, son of David Walsh, of St John's Wood, NW8.

LEVER, BARONY OF (Lever) (Extinct 1977)

SON LIVING OF LIFE BARON

Hon Bernard Lewis (45 Hardman St, Manchester M3 3HA), b 1951; ed Clifton, and Queen's Coll, Oxon, Bar Middle Temple 1975: m 1985, Anne Helen, only da of Patrick Chandler Gordon Ballingall, MBE, of Seaford, E Sussex, and has issue.

DAUGHTER LIVING OF LIFE BARON

Hon June A, b 1940; ed Chelteham Ladies' Coll: m 1962, Emanuel S. Rosen, MD, FRCS, FRPS, of 18A Torkington Rd, Wilmslow, Cheshire SK9 2AE, and has issue.

WIDOW LIVING OF LIFE BARON

RAY ROSALIA (Baroness Lever) (9 Plowley Close, Didsbury, Manchester, M20 2DB), only child of Dr Leon Levene of Leicester; JP for Manchester: m 1939, Baron Lever (Life Baron), who d 1977.

Lever, family name of Viscount Leverhulme.

LEVER OF MANCHESTER, BARONY OF (Lever) (Extinct 1995)

DAUGHTERS LIVING OF LIFE BARON (By 2nd marriage)

Hon Judith, b 1947.

(By 3rd marriage)

Hon Annabelle P. F., b 1962.
Hon Isabelle A. N., b 1964: m 1988, Dr Antony Laurent, elder son of late Jacques Condou, and of Mme Jacques Bertheau, of Nanteau-sur-Essonne, France, and has issue living, Lily, b 1993, — Cordelia, b 1995.
Hon Donatella Arabelle Yasmine, b 1966.

Mrs DIANA ZILKHA (*Baroness Lever of Manchester*), da of late Saleh Bashi, of Geneva, and formerly wife of Selim Zilkha: *m* 1962, as his 3rd wife, Baron Lever of Manchester, PC, who *d* 1995.

LEVERHULME, VISCOUNT (Lever) (Viscount UK 1922, Bt UK 1911)
(Title pronounced "Leverhume")

I scorn to change or fear

PHILIP WILLIAM BRYCE LEVER, KG, TD, 3rd Viscount, and 3rd Baronet; *b* 1 July 1915; *s* 1949; *ed* Eton, and Trin Coll, Camb; Hon Col (Cheshire Yeo Sqdn) The Queen's Own Yeo, RAC, TAVR since 1972. Advisory Dir of Unilever, Ltd, a JP and a KStJ; Lord-Lieut of Cheshire 1949-90; Steward of Jockey Club 1973-76; Chancellor Liverpool Univ 1980-93, Hon LLD 1967, Hon FRCS 1970, KG 1988: *m* 1937, Margaret Ann, who *d* 1973, only child of John Moon, of Tiverton, Devon, and has issue.

Arms – Quarterly, 1st and 4th, per pale argent and barry of eight or and azure, two bendlets sable, the upper one engrailed; 2nd and 3rd, per chevron or and gules, in chief two chaplets of roses and in base a lion's head all counterchanged. **Crest** – A trumpet fessewise, thereon a cock proper, charged on the breast with a rose as in the arms. **Supporters** – On either side an elephant or, the dexter charged on the shoulder with a rose gules and the sinister with a chaplet of roses also gules.
Residences – Thornton Manor, Thornton Hough, Wirral, Cheshire L63 1JB; Badanloch, Kinbrace, Sutherland; Flat 6, Kingston House East, Princes Gate, SW7 1LJ. *Clubs* – Boodle's, Jockey.

DAUGHTERS LIVING

Hon Susan Elizabeth Moon *b* 1938: *m* 1957 (*m diss* 1973), (Hercules) Michael Roland Pakenham (*see* E Longford, colls). *Residence* – Dibbinsdale Lodge, Bromborough, Wirral, Cheshire.

Hon Victoria Marion Ann, *b* 1945: *m* 1st, 1966 (*m diss* 1973), John Richard Walter Reginald Carew Pole (later Sir Richard Carew Pole, 13th Bt); 2ndly, 1975, Robert Gordon Lennox Apsion; 3rdly, 1990, Brig Peter Tower, of 8 Mulberry Walk, SW3, and has issue living (by 2nd *m*), Philip Gordon William, *b* 1976, — Robert George Neville, *b* 1978, — Alexandra Victoria, *b* 1983.

Hon Margaret Jane, *b* 1947: *m* 1966, Algernon Eustace Hugh Heber-Percy, of Hodnet Hall, Market Drayton, Shropshire (*see* D Northumberland, colls).

PREDECESSORS – (1) WILLIAM HESKETH Lever, son of the late James Lever, of Bolton, Lancashire; *b* 1851; founder of Port Sunlight, and Chm of Lever Bros (Limited); High Sheriff of Lancashire 1917-18; MP for Wirral Div of Cheshire (*L*) Jan 1906 to Dec 1909; *cr* a Baronet 1911, *Baron Leverhulme*, of Bolton-le-Moors, co Palatine of Lancaster (peerage of United Kingdom) 1917, and *Viscount Leverhulme*, of The Western Isles, in the cos of Inverness and Ross and Cromarty (peerage of United Kingdom) 1922: *m* 1874, Elizabeth Ellen, who *d* 1913, da of Crompton Hulme, of Bolton; *d* 1925; *s* by his son (2) WILLIAM HULME, 2nd, Viscount, *b* 1888; Gov of Lever Bros, and of Unilever Ltd; High Sheriff of Cheshire 1923; Pres of London Chamber of Commerce 1931-4, of Institution of Chemical Engineers 1932-4, of Roy Warrant Holders' Asso 1933, and of So of Chemical Industry 1936-8; was Pro-Chancellor Liverpool Univ 1932-6; Charter Mayor of Bebington 1937 (first Hon Freeman 1945): *m* 1st, 1912 (*m diss* 1936), Marion Beatrice, who *d* 1987, having *m* 2ndly, 1937, Wing-Cdr Selden Herbert Lond, DSO, MC (*d* 1952), da of late Bryce Smith, of Whalley and Manchester; 2ndly, 1937, Winifred Agnes (LEE MORRIS), who *d* 1966, yr da of Lt-Col Lloyd, of Brentwood, Bidston, Cheshire; *d* 1949; *s* by his son (3) PHILIP WILLIAM BRYCE, 3rd Viscount and present peer; also Baron Leverhulme.

LEVY, BARON (Levy) (Life Baron 1997)

MICHAEL ABRAHAM LEVY, son of Samuel Levy, of London; *b* 11 July 1944; *ed* Fleetwood Primary Sch, and Hackney Downs Gram Sch; FCA 1966; with Lubbock Fine (Chartered Accountants) 1961-66; Principal, M. Levy & Co 1966-69; Partner, Wagner Prager Levy & Partners 1969-73; Chm Magnet Group of Cos 1973-88 and D. & J. Securities Ltd 1988-92; Vice-Chm Phonographic Performance Ltd 1979-84 and British Phonographic Industry Ltd 1984-87; Chm British Music Industry Awards Cttee 1992-95, M. & G. Records 1992-97 and Chase Music Ltd since 1992; Patron, British Music Industry Awards since 1995; Nat Campaign Chm Jt Israel Appeal 1982-85 (Hon Vice-Pres since 1994); Chm Jewish Care 1991-97 (Pres since 1998) and Jewish Care Community Foundation since 1995; Vice-Chm Central Council for Jewish Community Services since 1994; Chm Chief Rabbinate Awards for Excellence since 1992 and Foundation for Education since 1993; Memb Jewish Agency World Board of Governors 1990-95 (World Chm Youth Aliyah Cttee 1991-95), Keren Hayesod World Board of Trustees 1991-95, World Commn on Israel-Diaspora Relations since 1995 and Internat Board of Governors, Peres Center for Peace since 1997; Hon Pres Community Ser Vols since 1998; Govr Jewish Free School 1990-95 (Hon Pres since 1995); Memb Advisory Cncl to the Foreign Policy Centre since 1997; Memb FCO Panel 2000 since 1998; B'nai B'rith First Lodge Award 1994; Scopus Award (Hebrew Univ) 1998; *cr Baron Levy*, of Mill Hill in the London Borough of Barnet (Life Baron) 1997: *m* 1967, Gilda, da of Benjamin Altbach, of London, and has issue.

Arms – Per pale argent and sable five bars counterchanged over all three trumpets bells upwards and a chief engrailed of two arches or. **Crest** – A dove argent beaked and legged gules the dexter wing expanded inverted and supporting a harp or in the beak a sprig of olive or. **Supporters** – On either side a dove contourny and supporting with the wings addorsed and inverted argent beaked and legged gules in the beak a sprig of olive or.
Residence – Chase House, Nan Clarks Lane, NW7 4HH.

SON LIVING

Hon Daniel Edward, *b* 1968; *ed* Haberdashers' Aske's Sch for Boys, and Camb Univ (MA 1990).

DAUGHTER LIVING

Hon Juliet Bella, *b* 1970; *ed* Haberdashers' Aske's Sch for Girls, and Manchester Univ (BSc 1993).

LEWIN, BARONY OF (Lewin) (Extinct 1999)

SONS LIVING OF LIFE BARON

Hon Timothy Charles Thornton, *b* 1947: *m* 1972, Carolyn Thain.
Hon Jonathan James, *b* 1959: *m* 1990, Madeline Marsh.

DAUGHTER LIVING OF LIFE BARON

Hon Susan, *b* 1949: *m* 1969, Peter Roe, and has issue living, Cosmo, *b* 1972, — Emily, *b* 1975, — Jessica, *b* 1982.

WIDOW LIVING OF LIFE BARON

JANE (*Baroness Lewin*), da of late Rev Charles James Branch Evans: *m* 1944, Adm of the Fleet Baron Lewin, KG, GCB, MVO, DSC (Life Baron), who *d* 1999.

LEWIS OF NEWNHAM, BARON (Lewis) (Life Baron 1989)

JACK LEWIS, son of Robert Lewis of Askham; *b* 13 Feb 1928; *ed* Barrow Gram Sch, London Univ (BSc, DSc), Nottingham Univ (PhD), Manchester Univ (MSc), and Camb Univ (MA, ScD); Hon DUniv Rennes 1980, Open 1982, and Kingston 1993, Hon DSc E Anglia 1983, Nottingham 1983, Keele 1984, Waterloo (Canada) 1988, Birmingham 1988, Leicester 1988, Manchester 1990, Wales 1990, Sheffield 1992, Cranfield Inst of Technology, 1993, Edinburgh 1994, Bath 1995, Durham 1996 and Hong Kong 1998, Hon Fell UCL 1990, UMIST 1990 and Univ of Central Lancs 1993; FRS, FRIC, FRSA; lecturer and reader UCL 1957-61, Prof of Chemistry Manchester Univ 1961-67, UCL 1967-70, and Camb Univ since 1970; Warden Robinson Coll, Camb since 1975; Chm Royal Commn on Environmental Pollution 1985-92, and Dept of Educn and Science Visiting Cttee to Cranfield Inst 1982-92, Pres Royal Soc of Chemistry 1986-88, Hon Fell 1998; member of various Science Research Council Cttees, etc; *cr* Kt 1982, *Baron Lewis of Newnham*, of Newnham, co Cambs (Life Baron) 1989, Chevalier l'Ordre des Palmes Académiques 1993, and Cmdr Cross of the Order of Merit (Poland) 1996: *m* 1951, Elfreida Mabel, da of Frank Alfred Lamb, of Manchester, and has issue.
Residence – Warden's Lodge, 4 Sylvester Rd, Cambridge. *Club* – Oxford & Cambridge.

SON LIVING

Hon Ian Peter, *b* 1958; *ed* Leys Sch: *m* 1982 (*m diss* 1991), Ann Carlton, and has issue living, Adam Rajiv, *b* 1987, — Leela Sarah, *b* 1984.

DAUGHTER LIVING

Hon Penelope Jane, *b* 1956: *m* 1982, Howard Allaker Chase, and has issue living, George Howard, *b* 1984, — Charlotte Elizabeth, *b* 1986.

LICHFIELD, EARL OF (Anson) (Earl UK 1831)

THOMAS PATRICK JOHN ANSON, 5th Earl; *b* 25 April 1939; *s* 1960; *ed* Harrow, and RMA Sandhurst; late Lt Gren Gds; DL Staffs 1996; photographer; FBIPP; FRPS: *m* 1975 (*m diss* 1986), Lady Leonora Mary Grosvenor, elder da of 5th Duke of Westminster, and has issue.

Arms – Quarterly: 1st, argent, three bends engrailed and in the sinister chief point a crescent gules, *Anson*; 2nd, ermine, three cats-a-mountain passant guardant, in pale sable, *Adams*; 3rd, azure, three salmon naiant in pale, per pale or and argent, *Sambrooke*; 4th, sable, a bend or, between three spears' heads argent, *Carrier*. **Crest** – 1st, out of a ducal coronet or, a spear head proper; 2nd, a greyhound's head erased ermines, gorged with a collar, double gemelle or. **Supporters** – *Dexter*, a sea-horse; *sinister*, a lion guardant, both proper and each gorged with a collar double gemelle or.
Residences – Shugborough Hall, Stafford ST17 0XB; 86 Holland Park, W11 3RZ. *Studio* — 133 Oxford Gdns, W10 6NE.

SON LIVING

THOMAS WILLIAM ROBERT HUGH (*Viscount Anson*), *b* 19 July 1978.

DAUGHTERS LIVING

Lady Rose Meriel Margaret, *b* 1976.
Lady Eloise Anne Elizabeth, *b* 1981.

SISTER LIVING (*Raised to the rank of an Earl's daughter* 1961)

Lady Elizabeth Georgiana, *b* 1941; founder Party Planners 1960, trading as Lady Elizabeth Anson: *m* 1972, as his 2nd wife, Sir Geoffrey Adam Shakerley, 6th Bt. *Residence* – 56 Ladbroke Grove, W11 2PB.

NIL + DESPERANDUM

Despair of nothing

AUNT LIVING (*Daughter of 4th Earl*)

Lady Betty Marjorie, *b* 1917: *m* 1944, Col Thomas Foley Churchill Winnington, MBE, Grenadier Guards, who *d* 1999, and has issue (*see* Winnington, Bt). *Residence* – 182 Rivermead Court, Ranelagh Gdns, SW6 3SG.

COLLATERAL BRANCHES LIVING

Grandchildren of late Capt Hon Rupert Anson (infra):—
Issue of late Geoffrey Rupert Anson, *b* 1929, *d* 1997: *m* 1957, Verna Grace Hall (2000 Jonathan Drive, Martinsburg, W Virginia 25401, USA):—
George Rupert (Lilies, High St, Weedon, nr Aylesbury, Bucks HP22 4NS), *b* 1960: *m* 1987, Kirsty Jane, da of A. S. D. Day, of Billesdon, Leics, and has issue living, Douglas Rupert, *b* 1992, — Peter Francis, *b* 1997, — Josceline Elizabeth, *b* 1989. —— Christopher Leonard, *b* 1963. —— †Edward Peter, *b* 1965; *d* 1982. —— Jennifer Marion, *b* 1961.

Issue of late Capt Hon Rupert Anson, yst son of 3rd Earl, *b* 1889, *d* 1966: *m* 1919, Marion Emma Ruthven, who *d* 1965, da of James Halliday, of Harrow-on-the-Hill:—
Thomas Peter (Radstone Manor, Brackley, Northants NN13 5PZ), *b* 1933: Col Queen's R Irish Hussars: *m* 1964, Judith Hilary, da of late Capt John Nicholl Kennard, RN, and has issue living, Henry James (27 Mablethorpe Rd, SW6 6AQ), *b* 1967: *m* 1992, Joanna C., da of D. R. Lamb, of W Littleton, Bath, and has issue living, Archie Augustus *b* 1996, — Patrick John (25 Dordrecht Rd, W3 7TE), *b* 1969: *m* 1998, Kate E., yr da of A. J. Agnew, of Merryfields, West St, Corfe Castle, Dorset. —— Anne Rosemary (c/o Coutts & Co, 440 Strand, WC2R 0GS), *b* 1924: *m* 1946 (*m diss* 1974), Capt Paul Coombe, and has issue living, Geoffrey Paul (Dianalaan 7, Amstelveen, Holland), *b* 1951: *m* 1998, Lucas Bernardus Maria Lubbers, — Michael Anthony (PO Box 171, Milsons Point, NSW 1565, Australia), *b* 1955: *m* 1st, 1975, Karen Elizabeth O'Hara, who *d* 1990; 2ndly, 1992, Karin Penny South, and has issue living (by 1st wife), Benjamin Michael *b* 1982, (by 2nd wife) Lucy Romy *b* 1992, Alice Christina *b* 1999, — Diana Mary, *b* 1947: *m* 1st, 1967 (*m diss* 1986), Timothy Gaines; 2ndly, 1987 (*m diss* 1989), Jess Mount; 3rdly, 1990, Richard Stewart, 633 SE Kane St, Roseburg, Oregon 97470, USA, and has issue living (by 1st *m*), David Allan *b* 1970, Daniel Anson *b* 1972, Devon Ashley *b* 1974. —— Felicity Marion (Shepherds, Ansty, Dorchester, Dorset), *b* 1927: *m* 1952, John Arbon Woodhouse, who *d* 1986, and has issue living, Mark John Michael (Cherrington Farm Cottage, N Cheriton, Templecombe, Som BA8 0AP), *b* 1955: *m* 1979, Teresa Jane, only da of Michael Kennedy Merriam, of Stowell House, Sherborne, Dorset (*see* M Ailsa, 1985 Edn), — Andrew Harold Rupert, *b* 1957, — Clare Marian, *b* 1965.

Granddaughters of late Lt-Col Hon Sir George Augustus Anson, KCB, CBE, MVO, 2nd son of 2nd Earl:—
Issue of Claud Ronald Anson, *b* 1895, *d* 1965: *m* 1st, 1915, Frederica Heath, who *d* 1941, da of late Frederic James Harrison, of Maer Hall, Staffs; 2ndly, 1944, Mrs Lilian Gallia Meiklejohn, da of late David George Davies, of New York; 3rdly, 1949, Mrs Noreen Stella Cross, da of late H. G. Barlow:—
(By 1st *m*) Mary (Weston Meres, Maer, Newcastle, Staffs, and Lyons Hill, Minterne Magna, Dorchester, Dorset), *b* 1918: *m* 1940 (*m diss* 1960), Lt-Col John Anthony Dene, Duke of Cornwall's LI, and has issue living, John Michael, *b* 1946, — David Frederick, *b* 1948, — Margaret Katharine, *b* 1942: *m* 1st, 1962 (*m diss* 1976), Michael Charles Power; 2ndly, 1977, Patrick Bernard Lucas, of Chalknewton House, Maiden Newton, Dorchester, Dorset, and has issue living (by 1st *m*), Anthony George Bertram *b* 1968, Katharine Mary *b* 1965, Erica Margaret *b* 1967. —— Joan (Enton Wood, Godalming, Surrey), *b* 1919: *m* 1945, Maj J. C. Lee, Roy Netherlands Army, who *d* 1963.

Grandchildren of late Hon Claud Anson, 5th son of 2nd Earl:—
Issue of late Anthony John Anson, *b* 1904, *d* 1981: *m* 1926, Rosalind Désirée, who *d* 1985, only da of Rear-Adm Sir Robert Keith Arbuthnot, 4th Bt, KCB, MVO:—
John Anthony Robert (30 Tibbets Close, SW19), *b* 1927: MRCS, LRCP: *m* 1st, 1962, (Fiona) Brook, MB BS, who *d* 1987, da of late Colin Frederick George Wills; 2ndly, 1989, (Angela) Jane Millican, and has had issue (by 1st *m*), Martin Anthony Wills, *b* 1963, — Annabel Frances Rosalind, *b* 1967, *d* 1988. —— Colin Shane (18 Ripplevale Grove, N1), *b* 1931; *ed* Stowe, and Slade Sch of Fine Art. —— Sarah Rose, *b* 1944: *m* 1969, Capt Robin Gifford Kerr, RN, of 3 Lansdown Place East, Bath, and has issue living, Bryony Charlotte, *b* 1972, — Julia Emily, *b* 1974.

Issue of late Maj Hugo Edward Anson, *b* 1908, *d* 1991: *m* 1st, 1935 (*m diss* 1946), Elizabeth, who *d* 1997, eldest da of late Capt Sir Harold George Campbell, GCVO, DSO, RN (ret) (*see* E Leven and Melville, colls, 1946 Edn); 2ndly, 1946, Duchessa Annina Badoglio, who *d* 1991, da of Marchese Silj, of Rome, and widow of Duca Paolo Badoglio:—
(By 1st *m*) Michael (Windrush Hill, Hawling, Cheltenham, Glos), *b* 1937; *ed* Stowe, and Edinburgh Univ; a Page of Honour to HM 1950-53: *m* 1963, Claire-Elizabeth Seymour, da of late Lt-Col Frederick Arthur Morris, of St Katherine's, Cradley, Malvern, Worcs, and has issue living, Alexandra Albinia *b* 1965: *m* 1992, Marcus A. Hodge, of Whitehouse Lodge, 31 Whitehouse Rd, Oxford, elder son of Spencer Hodge, of Roquebrune, France, and has issue living, Clara Albinia *b* 1997, — Josephine Emma, *b* 1968: *m* 1996, Alastair John Graham-Campbell, son of Ronald Niall Graham-Campbell, of Pitlochry, Perthshire, — Catherine Elizabeth, *b* 1971. —— (By 2nd *m*) Bernard Anthony (Villa Silj, via di Santa Cornelia Kml, 008891 Prima Porta, Rome), *b* 1948: *ed* Harrow, and Trin Coll, Dublin: *m* 1st, 1975 (*m diss* 1984), Anna, da of John Cooper; 2ndly, 1984, Eleanora, da of Carlo Monini, and has issue living (by 2nd *m*), Edoardo, *b* 1991. —— Andrea Vittorio (203 Prince St, New York, NY 10012, USA), *b* 1951; *ed* Harrow.

Grandchildren of late Hon Francis Anson, 6th son of 2nd Earl:—
Issue of late Wing-Com Henry Adelbert Anson, RAF, *b* 1895, *d* 1955: *m* 1st, 1927 (*m diss* 1930), Hilda Suzanne, da of S. Carson Allen, of 39 Circus Rd, St John's Wood, NW8; 2ndly, 1930, Muriel Irene, who *d* 1996, da of Edgar Cecil Smith:—
(By 1st *m*) David Richard, *b* 1929. Resides in Australia. —— (By 2nd *m*) Vanessa Irene (*Lady Hannam*), *b* 1940: *m* 1st, 1962, John Edward Robert Wauchope; 2ndly, 1983, Sir John Gordon Hannam, MP, of 85 Bromfelde Rd, SW4 6PP, and has issue living (by 1st *m*) Andrew Charles Anson, *b* 1974; *ed* Exeter Sch, and Trin Coll of Music, — Arabella Jane, *b* 1963: *m* 1986, G. H. C. P. (Harry) Huddart, of 61 Frewin Rd, SW18 3LR, only son of Edward William Huddart, of Littlecourt, Derriford, Plymouth, and has issue living, Joseph Edward Anson *b* 1989, Johnny William *b* 1995, Georgiana Rose *b* 1986, Augusta Louisa *b* (twin) 1989, Flora Vanessa Elizabeth *b* 1990, — Lucy Anne Margaret, *b* 1965: *m* 1st, 1987 (*m diss* 1989), James F. D. Rolls; 2ndly, 1995 (*m diss* 1997), Julien Lachicotte McCall, Jr; 3rdly, 1998, Charles Oliver O'Donnell, of 13 West Eaton Place, SW1X 8LT, son of Columbus O'Donnell, of Oxton Lodge, Oxton, Notts, and of Mrs Sibilla Clark, of Lyford Cay, Nassau, Bahamas, and has issue living (by 3rd *m*), Columbus Ivar Charles Kames *b* 1998, — Alexandra Gladys, *b* 1968: *m* 1998, Nicholas Clive William Meinard Lester, of 6 Worfield St, SW11 4RD, only son of Clive Lester, of Beaulieu, Hants, and has issue living, Anna-Scarlet *b* 1998.

Grandchildren of late Maj William Alfred Anson (infra):—
Issue of late Francis Richard Anson, *b* 1926, *d* 1989: *m* 1st, 1948 (*m diss* 1960), Ann, da of Sir John Lionel Arm-
ytage, 8th Bt; 2ndly, 1960 (*m diss* 1983), Bridgett Ann, only da of Dudley Gerald Greenhough, of 25 Aldford
House, Park Lane, W1; 3rdly, 1984, Elisabeth Gildroy (11 Anley Rd, W14), da of late Edward Philip Shaw, of
Commoners, Englefield Green, Surrey, and formerly wife of late Oliver Simon Willis Fleming;—
(By 1st *m*) Anthony Francis (Pigeon House, Pigeon Lane, Hanmer, Whitchurch, Shropshire), *b* 1951; *ed* Harrow: *m* 1985,
Sally C., da of Col Geoffrey Vardon Churton, MBE, MC, TD, and has issue living, Patrick Francis, *b* 1996, — Caroline
Myra, *b* 1990. —— Amanda Jane, *b* 1950: *m* 1982, Jeremy D. P. Pratt, of 63 Colehill Lane, SW6 5EF, son of David Pratt,
of The Old Rectory, Shottisham, Woodbridge, Suffolk. —— (By 2nd *m*) Juliet May, *b* 1961. —— Emma Louise, *b* 1963:
m 1988, Dr Alan Hargreaves, son of Eric Hargreaves, of Durban, S Africa.

Grandson of late Hon Francis Anson, 6th son of 2nd Earl:—
Issue of late Major William Alfred Anson, *b* 1897, *d* 1952: *m* 1919 Dorothy Helme, who *d* 1988, da of late
Richard Mashiter, of 22 Princes Gate, SW, and Hillend, Glamorgan:—
Edward William, *b* 1929; *ed* Harrow.

Issue of late Capt Hon William Anson, 7th son of 2nd Earl, *b* 1872, *d* 1926: *m* 1917, Louisa Goddard,
who *d* 1952, da of Frederick De Voe Van Wagenen, of Fulton, New York:—
Edith, *b* 1921: *m* 1st, 1943, Capt Alfred Ryland Howard, who was *ka* in Normandy 1944; 2ndly, 1947, Lieut-Col Ford Mill-
spaugh Boulware, and has issue living (by 1st *m*), Alfred Ryland (III) (114 Park Hill, San Antonio, Texas 78212, USA), *b*
1944: *m* 1985, Pamela, only da of Hugh A. Fitzsimons, of San Pedro Ranch, Carrizo Springs, Texas, and of Mrs William
Negley, of San Antonio, Texas, and has issue living, Anson Boulware *b* 1987, Laura Isabel *b* 1989, Louisa Carrigan *b*
1992. *Residence* – 1104 Montecito Dr, San Angelo, Texas 76901, USA.

PREDECESSORS – **(1)** Thomas Anson; MP for Lichfield 1789-1806 (great nephew of Adm George Anson, who circum-
navigated the world 1740, and was *cr Lord Anson, Baron of Soberton*, co Southampton 1747); *cr Baron Soberton*, co South-
ampton, and *Viscount Anson* (peerage of United Kingdom) 1806; *d* 1818; *s* by his son **(2)** Thomas William, PC, 2nd
Viscount; *b* 1795; *cr Earl of Lichfield* (peerage of United Kingdom) 1831; Master of the Buckhounds 1830-34, and
Postmaster-Gen 1835-41: *m* 1819, Louisa Barbara Catherine, who *d* 1879, da of Nathaniel Phillips, of Slebech Hall, co
Pembroke; *d* 1854; *s* by his son **(3)** Thomas George, 2nd Earl, *b* 1825; MP for Lichfield 1847-54, and Lord-Lieut of
Staffordshire 1863-71; *m* 1855, Lady Harriet Georgiana Louisa Hamilton, who *d* 1913, el da of 1st Duke of Abercorn, KG;
d 1892; *s* by his el son **(4)** Thomas Francis, 3rd Earl, *b* 1856: *m* 1878, Lady Mildred Coke, who *d* 1941, da of 2nd Earl of
Leicester; *d* 1918; *s* by his son **(5)** Thomas Edward, 4th Earl; *b* 1883; Capt London Regt; ADC and Acting Master of the
Horse to Lord-Lieut of Ireland (Earl of Aberdeen 1906-10); Lord High Steward of Borough of Stafford 1933: *m* 1st, 1911,
Evelyn Maud, who *d* 1945, da of late Col Edward George Keppel, MVO; 2ndly, 1949, Violet Margaret (Philips), who *d*
1988, da of late Henry Dawson Dawson-Greene, JP, of Slyne, and Whittington Hall, Lancashire; *d* 1960; *s* by his grand-
son **(6)** Thomas Patrick John (son of late Lt-Col Thomas William Arnold, Viscount Anson (by his 1st wife, Anne Ferelith
Fennella, who *d* 1980, da of Hon John Herbert Bowes-Lyon, 2nd son of 14th Earl of Strathmore and Kinghorne), el son
of 4th Earl), 5th Earl and present peer; also Viscount Anson, and Baron Soberton.

Liddell, family name of Baron Ravensworth.

LIFFORD, VISCOUNT (Hewitt) (Viscount I 1781)

BE JUST AND FEAR NOT

(EDWARD) JAMES WINGFIELD HEWITT, 9th Viscount; *b* 27 Jan 1949; *s* 1987; Member London Stock Exchange; Dir Rathbones plc, City of Winchester Investments plc, WCIMS plc and Town Pages plc: *m* 1976, Alison Mary, da of Robert Law, of Turnpike House, Withersfield, Suffolk, and has issue.

𝕬rms – Gules, a chevron engrailed, between three owls argent. 𝕮rest – On a stump of a tree, with one branch growing thereon, an owl proper. 𝕾upporters – *Dexter*, a vulture, proper, wings inverted, gorged with a plain collar sable, thereon three bezants; *sinister*, a griffin, proper, wings elevated, gorged as the dexter.
Residence – Field House, Hursley, nr Winchester, Hants. *Clubs* – Boodle's, Pratt's.

SON LIVING

Hon (JAMES) THOMAS WINGFIELD, *b* 29 Sept 1979.

DAUGHTERS LIVING

Hon Annabel Louise, *b* 1978.
Hon Alice Mary, *b* 1990.

SISTERS LIVING

(*Hon*) Lydia Mary (does not use courtesy title) (Quedley Farm, Flimwell, Wadhurst, E Sussex), *b* 1938: *m* 1965 (*m diss* 1983), Michael Christopher Swann, el son of Sir Anthony Charles Christopher Swann, 3rd Bt, CMG, OBE.
Hon Belinda Anne, *b* 1939: *m* 1963, Rev Piers Eliot de Dutton Warburton, of Rowan Cottage, Station Rd, Chilbolton, Stockbridge, Hants SO20 6AL and has issue living, Piers Richards Grove, *b* 1964, — Elizabeth Jane, *b* 1967.
Hon Flora Elizabeth (73 Sycamore Av, Chandlers Ford, Hants), *b* 1947: *m* 1965 (*m diss* 1975), Edward Bell Henderson, and has issue living, Samantha Elizabeth, *b* 1967: *m* 1994, Nicholas C. Gibbon, yr son of W. A. Gibbon, of Salisbury, — Victoria Amanda, *b* 1971.

WIDOW LIVING OF EIGHTH VISCOUNT

ALISON MARY PATRICIA (*Mary Viscountess Lifford*), 2nd da of late Thomas Wingrave Ashton, of The Cottage, Hursley, nr Winchester: *m* 1935, the 8th Viscount Lifford, who *d* 1987. *Residence* – The Barn, Hursley, Winchester, Hants.

COLLATERAL BRANCHES LIVING

Grandsons of late James Francis Katharinus Hewitt, 3rd son of late Rev Hon James John Pratt Hewitt, 2nd son of 2nd Viscount:—
Issue of late John Stanley Hewitt, *b* 1875, *d* 1937: *m* 1909, Avice Alureda, who *d* 1939, da of late Rev Arthur Langdale Langdale-Smith, R of Holton, Wheatley, Oxon:—
Terence John Lifford, *b* 1911; European War 1940-45 as Act Capt Gurkha Rifles, Liaison Offr 2/9 Gurkhas (pow 3½ years, Siam-Burma rlwy): *m* 1946, Rowena Edith Mabel, 2nd da of late Ernest Taylor England, of 26 Field Park, Newbridge, Monmouthshire, and has issue living, Anthea Avice Yvonne, *b* 1947: *m* 1970, Richard Geoffrey Horsford Kemp, of Slaymaker, Holton, Oxon. *Residence* – Holton Cottage, Holton, Oxon. —— Theodore Denis, *b* 1918; 1940-45 War as Lt and acting Capt Gurkha Rifles.

Issue of late Cdr Brian Lifford Hewitt, OBE, RN, *b* 1881, *d* 1962: *m* 1914, Roie (11 Ely Av, Remuera, Auckland, NZ), da of late Alfred Nathan, of Wickford, Auckland, New Zealand:—
†Michael James Alfred Lifford, *b* 1916: *m* 1947, Sybil Grace (724 Gladstone Rd, Gisborne, New Zealand), yst da of late William Arthur Izard (E Eglinton and Winton, colls), and *d* 1993, leaving issue, Peter Lifford (3 Kawau St, One Tree Hill, Auckland, NZ), *b* 1948: *m* 1983, Mary, da of J. A. Parkinson, and has issue living, Christopher *b* 1984, Ellen *b* 1986, — Anthony James, *b* 1951: *m* 1978, Susan Elizabeth, da of Lt Col M. J. J. Rolt, of Byfleet, Surrey, and has issue living, Oliver Michael James *b* 1985, Victoria Louise *b* 1980, Emily Kate *b* 1982, — Rosemary Ruth, *b* 1949: *m* 1975, Geoffrey Martin Brodie, of 31 Carlton Mill Rd, Merivale, NZ, and has issue living, Thomas Nathan *b* 1982, Timothy Paul *b* 1984, Caroline *b* 1977, Amy *b* 1979, — Elizabeth Grace *b* 1956: *m* 1990, Kevin Francis Bradley, of 36 Fancourt St, Meadowbank, Auckland, NZ, and has issue living, Hamish Michael Patrick *b* 1992, Olivier Roie *b* 1993. —— Patrick Francis (31 Dell Av, Remuera, Auckland, NZ), *b* 1921: *m* 1st, 1944 (*m diss* 1954), Mary, da of Trevor N. Holmden, of Remuera, Auckland, NZ; 2ndly, 1954, Judith, da of late John Hellaby, of 5 Ridings Rd, Remuera, Auckland, NZ, and has issue living (by 1st *m*) Brian James Lifford (56 Birchmans Grove, via Bungendore, NSW 2621, Australia) *b* 1945; Lt-Col NZ and Australian Armies, served Vietnam 1969-70; memb Commonwealth Monitoring Force in Zimbabwe-Rhodesia 1979-80; Management Consultant, Canberra, Australia: *m* 1st, 1972 (*m diss* 1984), Erin Margaret, eldest da of Keith Charles Walshe, of Te Anau, NZ; 2ndly, 1984, Julie Margaret-Anne, eldest da of Maurice James Beuth, of Ashburton, NZ, and has issue living, (by 1st *m*) Richard James Lifford *b* 1975: *m* 1999, Jane Louise, da of Richard C. Shenfield, of Beaumaris, Victoria, Australia, Rebecca Roie Cecilia *b* 1978, (by 2nd *m*) Danielle Margaret *b* 1985, Antonia Julie *b* 1987.

Grandchildren of late John Edward Hewitt, eldest son of late Capt James Dudley Ryder Hewitt, RN (infra):—

Issue of late William Robert Riddiford Hewitt, *b* 1903, *d* 1976: *m* 1930, Nancy Charlotte Ellen, who *d* 1988, el da of Sydney Arthur Robert Mair, of Wharekuru, NZ:—

†Ian Robert *b* 1931: *m* 1955, Jean Hamilton (479 College St, Palmerston North, NZ), da of Henry Nicholas Johnson, MD, of Invercargill, NZ, and *d* 1992, leaving issue, Robert Johnson (53 Hawthorne St, Papanui, Christchurch, NZ), *b* 1962: *m* 1992, Margot Joan, da of Ian Hanmer Atkinson, of Hanmer Springs, NZ, and has issue living, William Ian Atkinson *b* 1994, — Louise Johnson, *b* 1958: *m* 1983, Malcolm Lawrence Sincock, of Omaha Beach Rd, RD6, Warworth, Auckland, NZ, and has issue living, James Robert *b* 1986, Matthew Thomas *b* 1990, Tara Jane *b* 1985, — Mary-Anne Johnson (10 Endeavour St, Nelson, NZ), *b* 1959: *m* 1984 (legally separated), Christopher William Gates, and has issue living, Rebecca Mary *b* 1989, Stephanie Louise *b* 1991, Philippa Jean *b* 1995. —— Peter David (Balfour Farm, RD4, Pahiatua, NZ), *b* 1937: *m* 1963, Heather Jean, da of Robert Allen Donald, of Papatahi, Featherston, NZ, and has issue living, James Donald (RD2 Waipukurau, NZ), *b* 1965: *m* 1991, Susan Jean, da of David Petersen, of Waipukurau, NZ, and has issue living, Hamish William *b* 1996, Anna Charlotte *b* 1994, — Peter John (Mironui, RD1, Pahiatua, NZ), *b* 1967: *m* 1998, Jody Lee, da of Perry Jones, of Marton, NZ, and has issue living, Lucy Georgia *b* 1998, — Timothy David (Balfour Farm, RD4, Pahiatua, NZ), *b* 1968: *m* 1995, Nicola Jane, da of Geoffrey Dunn, of Waipukurau, NZ, and has issue living, George Geoffrey *b* 1996, Edward Alexander *b* (twin) 1996, Hugo Oliver *b* 1999, — Teena Anne, *b* 1964: *m* 1994, Stephen Scoular Richards, of The Point, Darfield, Canterbury, NZ, and has issue living, James Francis *b* 1996, Sophie Claire *b* 1998. —— Judith Anne, *b* 1936: *m* 1965, John Henry Armstrong, of 212a Waiwhetu Rd, Lower Hutt, NZ, and has issue living, Jane Margaret, *b* 1966: *m* 1994, Paul Andrew Hanson, and has issue living, James William *b* 1998, — Kate Amanda, *b* 1969, — Nicola Anne, *b* 1972.

Granddaughters of late Capt James Dudley Ryder Hewitt, RN (infra):—

Issue of late Lt-Col Dudley Riddiford Hewitt, CIE, *b* 1877, *d* 1971: *m* 1913, Marjorie Middlemas, who *d* 1954, yr da of late William Fleming Inglis, of Shanghai:—

Dorothy Mary Riddiford, *b* 1914: *m* 1948, Capt William James Lysley, 11th Hussars, who *d* 19—, and has issue living, Rachel Marjorie Sarah Anne, *b* 1949: *m* 1979, Michael Norman Scott-Ruddock, and has issue living, Alexander James Scott *b* 1984, Camilla Dorothy Scott *b* 1982. *Residence* – Flint House, Gt Barton, Bury St Edmunds, Suffolk IP31 2SW.

Issue of late Charles Gervais Hewitt, *b* 1885, *d* 1970: *m* 1911, Elsie Mary, who *d* 1974, el da of Herbert Pryce, of Rangitawa, Halcombe, NZ:—

Cushla Mary (81 Cologne St, Martinborough, Wairarapa, NZ), *b* 1916. —— Ruth Lifford (81 Cologne St, Martinborough, Wairarapa, NZ), *b* 1918.

Grandchildren of James Francis Daniel Hewitt (infra):—

Issue of late Richard Walter Hewitt, *b* 1909, *d* 1974: *m* 1951, Joan Millicent (35 Kitchener St, Masterton, NZ), el da of Thomas Edward Holdgate, of Timaru, NZ:—

Timothy James (Taratanui, Ponatahi, Carterton, Wellington, NZ), *b* 1954: *m* 1978, Judith Clair, da of Trevor Simson, of Waverley, NZ, and has issue living, Richard James, *b* 1979, — Thomas Cameron, *b* 1987, — Catherine Jane, *b* 1981. —— Mary Ellen, *b* 1952: *m* 1975, David Carleton Hadfield, of Lindale, Main Rd, Paraparaumu, Wellington, NZ, eldest son of Barry Hadfield, of Lindale, Paraparaumu, NZ, and has issue living, Richard Henry, *b* 1979, — Samuel Mark, *b* 1984, — Melissa Maisie, *b* 1976.

Granddaughter of late Capt James Dudley Ryder Hewitt, RN, 6th son of Rev Hon James John Pratt Hewitt (ante):—

Issue of late James Francis Daniel Hewitt, *b* 1881, *d* 1963: *m* 1st, 1908, Ellen Westbury, who *d* 1938, da of R. S. Abraham, of Palmerston North, New Zealand; 2ndly, 1942, May Evelyn, da of E. J. Wright, of Kerikeri, New Zealand:—

(By 1st m) June Lifford, *b* 1910: *m* 1934, Robert Oswald Young of 14 Matenga St, Waikanae, NZ, and has issue living, Robin Slingsby, *b* 1935, — Simon Vivian Riddiford, *b* 1936, — James Francis, *b* 1940, — Thomas Lifford, *b* 1951, — Ellen Jennifer, *b* 1938.

PREDECESSORS – (1) JAMES Hewitt, PC, was a Justice of the King's Bench in England 1766-8, and Lord Chancellor of Ireland 1768-82; *cr Baron Lifford*, of Lifford, co Donegal (peerage of Ireland) 1768, and *Viscount Lifford* (peerage of Ireland) 1781; *d* 1789; *s* by his son **(2)** JAMES, DD, 2nd Viscount; was Dean of Armagh; *d* 1830; *s* by his son **(3)** JAMES, 3rd Viscount; *b* 1783; *m* 1809, Hon Mary Anne Maude, who *d* 1877, da of 1st Viscount Hawarden; *d* 1855; *s* by his son **(4)** JAMES, 4th Viscount, *b* 1811: was a Representative Peer: *m* 1st, 1835, Lady Mary Acheson, who *d* 1850, el da of 2nd Earl of Gosford; 2ndly, 1851, Lydia Lucy, who *d* 1919, el da of Rev John Digby Wingfield Digby, V of Coleshill, and widow of Charles Purdon-Coote; *d* 1887; *s* by his el son **(5)** JAMES WILFRID, 5th Viscount; *b* 1837; *m* 1867, Annie Frances, who *d* 1927, el da of late Sir Arthur Hodgson, KCMG, of Clopton House, Stratford-on-Avon; *d* 1913; *s* by his brother **(6)** ARCHIBALD ROBERT, 6th Viscount, *b* 1844; Capt RN: *m* 1878, Helen Blanche, who *d* 1942, only da of late Charles S. Geach; *d* 1925; *s* by his son **(7)** EVELYN JAMES, DSO, 7th Viscount; *b* 1880; Lieut-Col (ret) Dorsetshire Regt; S Africa 1902, European War 1914-18 (DSO and Bar): *m* 1919, Charlotte Rankine, who *d* 1954, da of late Sir Robert Maule, and widow of Capt Edgar Walker; *d* 1954; *s* by his cousin **(8)** ALAN WILLIAM WINGFIELD (son of late Hon George Wyldbore Hewitt, 7th son of 4th Viscount), 8th Viscount, *b* 1900; Lieut Hants Regt: *m* 1935, Alison Mary Patricia, 2nd da of late Thomas Wingrave Ashton, of The Cottage, Hursley, nr Winchester; *d* 1987; *s* by his only son **(9)** (EDWARD) JAMES WINGFIELD, 9th Viscount and present peer; also Baron Lifford.

LILFORD, BARON (Powys) (Baron GB 1797)
(Name pronounced "Poe-is")

GEORGE VERNON POWYS, 7th Baron; *b* 8 Jan 1931; *s* 1949; *ed* Stonyhurst: *m* 1st, 1954, Mrs Eve Bird; 2ndly, 1957 (*m diss* 1958), Anuta, only da of L. F. Merritt, of Johannesburg, S Africa; 3rdly, 1958 (*m diss* 1961), Norma Yvonne, only da of V. Shell, of Johannesburg, S Africa; 4thly, 1961 (*m diss* 1969), Mrs Muriel Spottiswoode; 5thly, 1969 (*m diss* 1991), Margaret, da of A. Penman, of Roslin, Midlothian; 6thly, 1995, Mrs Pamela St Helier Adams (*née* Weait), and has issue living by 4th and 5th *m*.

To maintain acquired possessions

Arms – Or, a bear's jamb erased in bend dexter, between two cross crosslets fitchée in bend sinister, gules. **Crest** – A lion's jamb couped and erect gules, holding a staff headed with a fleur-de-lis, also erect or. **Supporters** – *Dexter*, a reaper habited in a loose shirt, leather breeches loose at the knees, white stockings, and black hat and shoes; in his hat ears of corn, in his right hand a reaping-hook, and at his feet a garb, all proper; *sinister*, a man in the uniform of the Northamptonshire Yeomanry Cavalry, viz a green long coat, ornamented on the cuffs and button-holes with gold lace, yellow waistcoat and breeches, and black top boots; a black stock; a round hat; adorned with a white feather in front and a green one behind, the sword-belt inscribed with the letter NY and the exterior hand resting on his sword sheathed and point downwards.
Seat – Bank Hall, Bretherton, Preston, Lancs. *Residence* – Le Grand Câtelet, St John, Jersey CI.

SON LIVING (By 5th marriage)

Hon MARK VERNON, *b* 16 Nov 1975.

DAUGHTERS LIVING (By 4th marriage)

Hon Clare Lynette, *b* 1962.
Hon Emma-Jane, *b* 1964.

(By 5th marriage)

Hon Sarah Margaret, *b* 1971.
Hon Hannah Victoria, *b* 1974.

SISTERS LIVING

Hilary Betty (73 Woodside Village, Nortonway, Rondebosch 7701, S Africa), *b* 1929: *m* 1950, Philip Donald Millar, who *d* 1967, and has issue living, Christopher, *b* 1961: *m* 1989, Tracey Lynn Boddington, and has issue living, Guy Philip *b* 1992, Rhys Christopher *b* 1998, Andrea Leigh *b* 1995, — Philippa Ann, *b* 1958: *m* 1989, Paul Edward Roisen Sater, of Hong Kong.
Beryl Irene, *b* 1932.

COLLATERAL BRANCHES LIVING

Grandson of late Henry Littleton Powys, 4th son of late Robert Horace Powys, 2nd son of 2nd Baron:—
Issue of late Frank Lilford Powys, *b* 1902, *d* 1972: *m* 1929, Gertrude Frances Elizabeth, who *d* 19—, da of G. G. F. Meyer:—
Robert Charles Lilford (PO Box 2138, Port Alfred 6170, Cape, S Africa), *b* 1930: *m* 1st, 1957 (*m diss* 1972), Charlotte Webb; 2ndly, 1973, Janet Wightwick.

Grandson of late Wilfred Owen Powys, 5th son of late Robert Horace Powys (ante):—
Issue of late Horace Victor Powys, *b* 1907, *d* 1956: *m* 1928, Olive Maude Peets, of Durban, S Africa:—
Michael John (03 Jan Smuts Av, Winston Park, Gillitts 3610, Kwazulu Natal), *b* 1934: *m* 1957, Lynette Bernice Hodges, of Durban, Natal, and has had issue, Victor Michael (PO Box 783, Gillitts 3603, Kwazulu Natal), *b* 1961: *m* 1986, Yvonne Joan McCort, and has issue living, Matthew Paul *b* 1996, Victoria Amy *b* 1993, Sarah Lynn *b* 1998, — †Andrew John, *b* 1970; *k* in a motor accident 1985, — †Paul Michael, *b* 1974; *k* in a motor accident 1985, — Susan Lynn (6 Chase Place, Westville 361, Kwazulu Natal), *b* 1958: *m* 1978, Peter Gary Bahrs, and has issue living, Justin Peter *b* 1983, Jacqueline Susan *b* 1979, Nicola Susan *b* 1981, Megan Lynn *b* 1986.

Grandchildren of late Richard Atherton Norman Powys, 2nd son of Rev Hon Atherton Legh Powys, 4th son of 2nd Baron:—
Issue of late Atherton Richard Norman Powys, *b* 1888, *d* 1976: *m* 1st, 1915, Elsie Dyus, who *d* 1957, da of late Frederick Robert Mattingly; 2ndly, 1957, Edith, who *d* 1977, da of John Smart, of Edinburgh:—
(By 1st *m*) John Frederick Atherton, *b* 1916. —— Richard Atherton Legh, *b* 1923: *m* 1962, Ann Patricia Blanchard, and has issue living, Anthony Richard Atherton, *b* 1963, — David John Atherton, *b* 1965, — Christopher James Atherton, *b*

1967, — Michael Paul Atherton, *b* 1970, — Nicholas, *b* 1971. —— Mary Elizabeth Anne, *b* 1921. —— (By 2nd *m*) Ian Atherton (97 Robin Hood Lane, Kingston Vale, SW15 3QR), *b* 1930; *ed* Haileybury, and RMA Sandhurst: *m* 1955, Beryl Mary, da of late Percy Hirst Lomax, of Bolton, and has issue living, Richard Ian Lomax, *b* 1955, — Andrew John, *b* 1961.

Grandsons of late Thomas Charles Leycester Powys-Keck, el son of late Thomas Bancho Powys-Keck (infra):—
Issue of late Thomas Leycester POWYS-KECK, *b* 1919, *d* 1959: *m* 1949, Joyce (Clarence Drive, Littlehampton, Sussex), da of Albert Hills, of Worthing, Sussex:—
Thomas Charles Leycester, *b* 1951: *m* 1st, 1979 (*m diss* 1983), Judith Harris; 2ndly, 1985, Evelyn K. Dobner, and has issue living (by 1st *m*), Leycester Charles, *b* 1981, — (by 2nd *m*), Christian Rhys, *b* 1992, — Jacqueline Lauren, *b* 1989. —— Piers Anthony Leycester (12 Meadow Way, Ferring, Worthing, W Sussex BN12 5LD), *b* 1954: *m* 1982 (*m diss* 1995), Pauline Ann Short, and has issue living, Thomas Anthony Leycester, *b* 1988, — Emma Leigh, *b* 1983, — Danielle Kelly, *b* 1985.

Granddaughter of late Thomas Bancho Powys-Keck, son of late Maj Hon Henry Littleton Powys-Keck, 5th son of 2nd Baron:—
Issue of late Capt Horatio James POWYS, King's Roy Rifle Corps, *b* 1873, *d* 1952, having resumed in 1930 for himself only the family name of Powys only in lieu of Powys-Keck: *m* 1902, Edith Mary POWYS-KECK, who *d* 1971, da of Alexander Harvey, of St John's, Newfoundland:—
Gwladys Maïta Joan, *b* 1911; has discontinued the use of the christian name of Margarita, and is known as Maïta: *m* 1933 (*m diss* 1959), David Fenwick, who *d* 1982, and has issue living, Anthony Benedict Xavier (Sholebroke, Towcester, Northants), *b* 1934; *ed* Ampleforth: *m* 1958, Susan Deirdre, yr da of Lt-Col Peter Heber-Percy, OBE (*see* D Northumberland, colls), and has issue living, Alexius John Benedict (15 Glazbury Rd, W14), *b* 1959: *m* 1st, 1984 (*m diss* 1988), Briony Gretel, elder da of Bruce Gyngell, of Sydney, Australia; 2ndly, 1990, Lady Sophia Anne Crichton-Stuart, only surv da of 6th Marquess of Bute (and has issue living (by 2nd *m*), Georgia Jessie *b* 1990), Celestria Chantal Arabella *b* 1963: *m* 1987, James Boyd Alexander-Sinclair, of Blackpitts House, Whittlebury, Northants, elder son of Maj-Gen David Boyd Alexander-Sinclair, CB (and has issue living, Archie Benedict Boyd *b* 1988, Maxim Boyd *b* 1994, Stroma Georgina *b* 1990), — Charles Xtopher Sebastian, LVO (Higham Place, Higham, Stoke by Nayland, Suffolk CO7 6JT), *b* 1946; *ed* Ampleforth; Maj Gren Gds; Adjt 1973-75; Equerry to HRH The Duke of Edinburgh 1975-77; LVO 1977: *m* 1997, Mrs Sara Elizabeth Nickerson, da of late Col John Howlett Jewson, MC, of Mergate Hall, Norwich, and widow of David George Francois Nickerson (*see* Walker, Bt, *cr* 1868, colls), — Timothy Dominic Ignatius (Rue du Mont 1, 5650 Biesmes-la-Colonoise, Belgium), *b* 1947 *ed* Ampleforth: *m* 1971, Jeanne Marie Julienne, only da of Joseph Marechal, of Bastogne, Belgium, — Justin Francis Quintus, QC (Geldeston Hall, Geldeston, Norfolk), *b* 1949; *ed* Ampleforth, and Clare Coll, Camb; Maj Gren Gds; Adjt 1977-79; Equerry to HRH The Duke of Edinburgh 1979-81; Bar Inner Temple 1980, QC 1993: *m* 1975, Marcia Mary, el da of late Archibald Dunn, of Overbury Hall, Hadleigh, Suffolk (*see* Astley, Bt), and has issue living, Hubert George Francis *b* 1990, Corisande Mary *b* 1983, Rosamond Xanthe *b* 1985, Madeleine Isobel *b* 1988, — Sebastian Edmund Stephen (Puslynch, Yealmpton, Plymouth, Devon), *b* 1953; *ed* Ampleforth, — Serena Mary (Hope Cottage, Gerrards Cross, Bucks), *b* 1944. *Residence* – Oratory Lodge, Brompton Rd, SW7 2RW.

PREDECESSORS – (1) THOMAS Powys, MP for Northamptonshire 1774-97; *cr Baron Lilford* of Lilford, co Northampton (peerage of Great Britain) 1797; *d* 1800; *s* by his son (2) THOMAS 2nd Baron; *d* 1825; *s* by his son (3) THOMAS ATHERTON, 3rd Baron; was a Lord-in-Waiting to HM Queen Victoria: *m* 1830, Hon Mary Elizabeth Fox, da of 3rd Baron Holland; *d* 1861, *s* by his son (4) THOMAS LITTLETON, 4th Baron, *b* 1833: *m* 1st, 1859, Emma Elizabeth, who *d* 1884, da of Robert William Brandling, of Low Gosforth, Northumberland; 2ndly, 1885, Clementina Georgiana, who *d* 1929, da of late Ker Baillie-Hamilton, CB; *d* 1896; *s* by his el surviving son (5) JOHN, 5th Baron, *b* 1863: *m* 1894, Milly Louisa, who *d* 1940, da of late George William Culme Soltau-Symons, of Chaddlewood, Plympton: *d* 1945; *s* by his brother (6) STEPHEN, 6th Baron, *b* 1869; *d* 1949; *s* by his kinsman (7) GEORGE VERNON (son of late Robert Horace Powys, only son of late Robert Vernon Powys, 2nd son of late Hon Robert Vernon Powys, 2nd son of 2nd Baron), 7th Baron and present peer.

LIMERICK, EARL OF (Pery) Sits as BARON FOXFORD (UK 1815) (Earl I 1803)

By courage, not by craft

PATRICK EDMUND PERY, 6th Earl, KBE, *b* 12 April 1930; *s* 1967; *ed* Eton, and New Coll, Oxford (MA); DL W Sussex 1988; late Maj City of London Yeo (TA), Hon Col 71st Yeo Signal Regt (Vol); CA; Dir Kleinwort Benson Ltd 1967-87 (Vice-Chm 1983-85, Dep-Chm 1985-87), Dir Kleinwort Benson Group 1982-90, Parly Under Sec of State for Trade 1972-74, Chm British Overseas Trade Board 1979-83 (Board Memb 1975-91), Vice-Pres Assoc of British Chambers of Commerce since 1977 (Pres 1974-77), Chm Cttee for Middle East Trade 1975-79 (Vice-Chm 1968-75), Chm British Invisibles 1984-91 (Board Memb 1983-91); Pres Inst of Export 1983-95, Dir Kleinwort Benson Australian Income Fund Inc since 1986, Chm Pirelli UK plc since 1989, Dep Chm Henderson plc since 1998, Chm AMP Asset Management plc 1992-98, Chm of Trustees City Parochial Foundation 1992-96 (Trustee since 1971), Chm De La Rue plc 1993-97 (Dir since 1983), Pres Canning House 1994-97; Chm Court of Govs London Guildhall Univ (formerly City of London Polytechnic) since 1984; Chm Cttee of Univ Chairmen 1995-97; Chm Britain-Australia Soc since 1997; Pres Anglo-Swiss Soc since 1984; Pres S of England Agric Soc since 1993; DL W Sussex 1998; Master, Company of World Traders 1991; *cr* KBE (Civil) 1983: *m* 1961, Sylvia Rosalind, CBE, Chm Council of British Red Cross Soc (since 1985), el da of late Brig Maurice Stanley Lush, CB, CBE, MC, and has issue.

᭙rms – Quarterly: gules and or, on a bend argent three lions passant sable. Crest – A fawn's head erased proper. Supporters – *Dexter*, a lion ermine; *sinister*, a fawn proper, ducally collared and chained or.
Residences – Chiddinglye, West Hoathly, East Grinstead, W Sussex RH19 4QT; 30 Victoria Rd, W8 5RG.

SONS LIVING

EDMUND CHRISTOPHER (*Viscount Glentworth*), *b* 10 Feb 1963; *ed* Eton, New Coll, Oxford, and Pushkin Inst, Moscow; Bar Middle Temple 1987; HM Diplomatic Ser 1987-92; Freshfields Solicitors 1993-94, Milbank Tweed, Solicitors 1994-96, since when Deutsche Bank: *m* 1990, Emily K., only da of Michael Gavin Lynam Thomas, of Worcester, and has issue:—
SONS LIVING — *Hon* Felix Edmund, *b* 16 Nov 1991, — *Hon* Ivo Patrick, *b* 1993.
Residence – 30 Victoria Rd, W8 5RG.
Hon Adrian Patrick, *b* 1967; *ed* Eton, RMA Sandhurst, and RMCS Shrivenham (GCGI 1994); Capt Light Dragoons: *m* 1997, Suzanne E., da of District Judge Peter Wartnaby, of Leek Wootton, Warwicks.

DAUGHTER LIVING

Lady Alison Dora, *b* 1964.

BROTHER LIVING

Hon Michael Henry Colquhoun (Ardtur, Appin, Argyll), *b* 1937; *ed* Eton, and New Coll, Oxford (BA 1960); late Lt Inns of Court and City Yeo; formerly Man Dir, Sifam Ltd; Dir London Life Assoc: *m* 1963, Jennifer Mary, el da of J. A. Stuart-Williams, of Causeway House, Braughing, Herts, and has issue living, Marcus Alexander Kemal, *b* 1965, — Fergus Anthony Colquhoun, *b* 1967: *m* 1997, Emma C., da of Dr John Rhind-Tutt, of Wargrave, Berks, — Pervaneh Frances, *b* 1969, — Azelle Fiona, *b* 1971.

SISTER LIVING

Lady Anne Patricia, *b* 1928; *ed* North Foreland Lodge, and St Hugh's Coll, Oxford (MA, DPhil); Sr Research Fellow at Imperial Coll London, author of *Spectrophysics* 1974, 1988, 1999, and of many papers published in scientific journals: *m* 1959, Lt-Col Sir Peter Francis Thorne, KCVO, CBE, ERD, former Serjeant at Arms of House of Commons, yst son of late Gen Sir (Augustus Francis) Andrew (Nicol) Thorne, KCB, CMG, DSO, DL, and has issue living, Andrew Henry, *b* 1965: *m* 1994, Sarah, eldest da of Trevor Fanconi, of Sticklepath, Devon, — Bridget Iolanthe, *b* 1961: *m* 1995, Peter T. Sychta, son of late Dr Stanislav Sychta, and has issue living, Helen Olivia *b* 1998, — Meriel Patricia, *b* 1963: *m* 1998, Philip J. H. Stinson, elder son of Robert Stinson, of Englefield Green, Surrey, and has issue living, Thomas Francis Hunter *b* 1999, — Janet Melinda, *b* 1968. *Residence* – Chiddinglye Farmhouse, W Hoathly, E Grinstead, Sussex.

COLLATERAL BRANCHES LIVING

Grandson of late Hon Edmond Aubrey Templar Pery (Sub-Lt RN), 3rd son of 2nd Earl:—
Issue of late Harry Reddall de Vere Pery, *b* 1877, *d* 1937: *m* 1907, Bertha, who *d* 1936, da of John Edward Fouscha:—
Lyndon de Vere (20 Wyandra Cres, Port Macquarie, NSW 2444, Australia), *b* 1914: *m* 1934, Eileen May, da of Henry Ernest Reid, and has issue living, Barry Lyndon de Vere (9/120 Ramsgate Rd, Ramsgate, NSW 2217, Australia), *b* 1935, — Carol Ann, *b* 1940: *m* 19—, James Fletcher, of 45 Bibby St, Carlton, NSW 2218, Australia.

Grandchildren of Edmond Arthur Gore PERY-KNOX-GORE, el son of Edmond Henry Cokayne PERY-KNOX-GORE (infra):—
Issue of late Maj Edmond Myles PERY-KNOX-GORE, *b* 1904, *d* 1965: *m* 1st, 1929 (*m diss* 1948), Gundrede Mary, da of late Capt Graham Owen Robert Wynne (*see* B Killanin, 1957 Edn); 2ndly, 1948, Ingrid Margaret Mary (Coolcronan Cottage, Ballina, co Mayo), da of late Henry MacDermot, KC, of 19 Fitzwilliam Sq, Dublin, and widow of Capt Francis Holdsworth ffrench-Davis, RASC (*see* B Mowbray, colls):—
(By 1st *m*) Simon (12 Eastbrook Rd, SE3), *b* 1927: *m* 1961, Moira, da of Thomas Jariath Egan, of The Rise, Sevenoaks, Kent, and has issue living, Myles, *b* 1970, — Caroline, *b* 1962, — Katherine Lucy, *b* 1964, — Siobhan, *b* 1966: *m* 19—, Steven Way, and has issue living, Edward Seain *b* 1993. —— (By 2nd *m*) Mark (173 Orwell Rd, Rathgar, Dublin 6), *b* 1955: *m* 1986, Ann, da of Patrick Mallon, of Ambrosetown House, Duncormic, co Wexford. —— Sarah, *b* 1950.

Grandchildren of late Edmond Henry Cokayne PERY-KNOX-GORE, el son of Hon Edmond Sexten Pery, 4th son of 1st Earl:—
Issue of late Brigadier Arthur Francis Gore PERY-KNOX-GORE, CB, DSO, late RASC, *b* 1880, *d* 1954: *m* 1909, Evangeline, who *d* 1967, da of late Capt John William St John Hughes (Hughes, Bt, *cr* 1773, colls):—
Mary Agnes (*Lady Barrowclough*), *b* 1923: *m* 1949, Sir Anthony Richard Barrowclough, QC, and has issue living, Richard Edmond (Pyncombe Farm, Wiveliscombe, Som), *b* 1953: *m* 1978, Laura Selina Madeline, only da of Prof Sir (Albert) Raymond Maillard Carr (*see* Strickland-Constable, Bt, colls), and has issue living, Milo Edmond *b* 1984, Conrad Oliver *b* 1986, a son *b* 1990, Sibell Augusta *b* 1982, — Claire Cecilia, *b* 1956: *m* 1982, Nicholas Welham Paul, of 5 King's Rd, Richmond, Surrey, and has issue living, Matthew Edmond Welham *b* 1994, Flora Valentine *b* 1985, Phoebe Henrietta *b* 1986, Dominica Rose *b* 1989. *Residence* – The Old Vicarage, Winsford, Minehead, Som.

Issue of late Major Aubrey Edmond Pery-Knox-Gore, OBE, *b* 1883, *d* 1960: *m* 1916, Monica, who *d* 1973, da of Capt John Strachan Bridges (E Courtown):—
Cullen, *b* 1917: *m* 1st, 1942, Barbara, who *d* at sea 1942 as a result of enemy action, only da of G. L. Stuart, of Dalkeith, Bramhall, Cheshire; 2ndly, 1948, Priscilla Wendy, da of J. S. Corr, of Johannesburg, S Africa, and has issue living (by 2nd *m*), Janet Barbara, *b* 1950, — Dianna Wendy, *b* 1951. —— David Edmond Strachan, *b* 1920; is Lt RNVR; 1940-45 War (despatches): *m* 1948, Molly, da of late A. Daly, of Pretoria, S Africa, and widow of Maj Frank Robertson, S African Air Force.

PREDECESSORS – (1) *Right Rev* WILLIAM CECIL Pery (yr brother of Edmond Sexten Pery, *cr Viscount Pery* 1785, ext 1800), successively Bishop of Killala and Limerick; *cr Baron Glentworth*, of Mallow (peerage of Ireland) 1790; *d* 1794; *s* by his son (2) EDMOND HENRY, 2nd Baron; MP for Limerick City 1785-94; *cr Viscount Limerick* (peerage of Ireland), 1800, *Earl of Limerick* (peerage of Ireland) 1803, and *Baron Foxford*, of Stackpole Court, co Limerick (peerage of United Kingdom) 1815; *d* 1844; *s* by his grandson (3) WILLIAM HENRY TENNISON, 2nd Earl; *b* 1812: *m* 1st, 1838, Susannah, da of William Sheaffe, of Cornwall; 2ndly, 1842, Margaret Jane, da of Capt Nicholas Horsley, 96th Regt; *d* 1866; *s* by his son (4) WILLIAM HALE JOHN CHARLES, KP, PC, 3rd Earl; *b* 1840; a Lord-in-Waiting to HM Queen Victoria 1886-9, and Capt of the Yeomen of the Guard 1889-92 and 1895-6: *m* 1st, 1862, Caroline Maria, who *d* 1877, da of late Rev Henry Gray; 2ndly, 1877, Isabella, who *d* 1927, da of late Chevalier James Colquhoun; *d* 1896; *s* by his el son (5) WILLIAM HENRY EDMOND DE VERE SHEAFFE, 4th Earl; *b* 1863: *m* 1890, May Imelda Josephine, CBE, who *d* 1943, da of late Joseph Burke Irwin, formerly Resident Magistrate, of Stelleen House, Drogheda; *d* 1929; *s* by his half-brother (6) EDMUND COLQUHOUN, GBE, CH, KCB, DSO, TD, 5th Earl; *b* 1888; Brevet Col RHA (TA) and Comdg 11th Bde; Pres of Med, Research Council 1952-60, and Council of T & AFA 1954-56: *m* 1926, Angela Olivia, GBE, CH, who *d* 1981, da of Lt-Col Sir Henry Trotter, KCMG, CB, *d* 1967; *s* by his el son (7) PATRICK EDMUND, 6th Earl and present peer; also Viscount Limerick, Baron Glentworth, and Baron Foxford.

LINCOLN, EARL OF (Fiennes-Clinton) (Earl E 1572)

EDWARD HORACE FIENNES-CLINTON, 18th Earl; *b* 23 Feb 1913; *s* 1988 (although he has not yet established his right to the Peerage): *m* 1st, 1940, Leila Ruth, who *d* 1947, da of late John James Millen, of Kalgoorlie, W Australia; 2ndly, 1953, Linda Alice, da of Charles Cred, and widow of James O'Brien, of Kalgoorlie, W Australia, and has had issue by 1st *m*.

Arms – Argent six cross crosslets fitchy sable three two and one on a chief azure two mullets or pierced gules. **Crest** – Out of a coronet gules a plume of five ostrich feathers argent banded with a line laid chevronwise and knotted azure. **Supporters** – Two greyhounds argent collared and line gules. **Motto** – Loyaulte n'a Honte.
Residence – Flat 45, Elanora Villas, 37 Hastie St, Bunbury, W Australia 6230.

SON DECEASED (*By 1st marriage*)

†(*Hon*) Edward Gordon, *b* 7 Feb 1943: *m* 1970, Julia, da of William Howson, of 10 Waltham Rd, Armadale, Perth, and *d* 12 Jan 1999, leaving issue, ROBERT EDWARD (PO Box 955, Mandurah, Western Australia 6210, Australia), *b* 1972, — William Roy, *b* 1980, — Marian Dawn, *b* 1973. *Residence* – 16 Tucky St, Pinjarra, W Australia 6208.

DAUGHTER LIVING (*By 1st marriage*)

(*Lady*) Patricia Ruth, *b* 1941: *m* 1959 (*m diss* 1970), Alexander George Stuart Elrick, who *d* 1979, and has issue living, Nicholas James, *b* 1959: *m* 1st, 1979 (*m diss* 1992), Rosa Audino; 2ndly, 19—, Monique Veronica Gardner (*née* Truman), and has issue living (by 1st *m*), Steven John *b* 1980, Peter James *b* 1981, — David Wayne, *b* 1961, — Warren Stuart, *b* 1962, — Leilani Yvonne, *b* 1974. *Residence* – Lot 27 West Rd, Bullsbrook, W Australia 6084.

COLLATERAL BRANCHES LIVING

Grandsons of late Henry Fiennes-Clinton, only son of late Clement Walter Fiennes-Clinton, 3rd son of Rev Henry Fiennes-Clinton, only son of Clinton James Fynes-Clinton, MP, 2nd son of Rev Charles Fynes-Clinton (*infra*):—
Issue of late Henry Bernard Fiennes-Clinton, *b* 1929, *d* 1990: *m* 1961 (*m diss* 1980), Carol Priscilla, da of James Greig, of Toronto:—
Gregory Edward (1749 Victoria Park Av, Flat 401, Scarborough, Ontario, Canada M1R 1S2), *b* 1970: *m* 1994, Sharon, da of Guardsman Cornelius Alpheus Quammie, of Toronto. —— Richard James (27 Pintail Crescent, North York, Ontario, Canada M3A 2Y6), *b* 1972.

Grandchildren of late Rev Charles Edward Fynes-Clinton, eldest son of late Rev Osbert Fynes-Clinton,

3rd son of late Rev Charles John Fynes-Clinton, 3rd son of late Rev Charles Fynes-Clinton, lineal representative of Hon Sir Henry Fynes-Clinton, 3rd son of 2nd Earl of Lincoln:—

Issue of late Hugh Arthur Fynes-Clinton, *b* 1913, *d* 1991: *m* 1945, Pauline Ruth Ashton Dold (20 Oakwood Park, Forest Row, E Sussex):—

Oliver John (Trees, Priory Rd, Forest Row, E Sussex), *b* 1948; *ed* Cape Town Univ (BA): *m* 1978, Christine Elisabeth Brittaine, and has issue living, Francis Bernard Peter, *b* 1979, — Laura Emily, *b* 1984. —— Rozanne Jean, *b* 1946.

Grandsons of late Osbert Henry Fynes-Clinton, 2nd son of late Rev Osbert Fynes-Clinton (ante):—

Issue of late David Osbert Fynes-Clinton, *b* 1909, *d* 1978: *m* 1st 1933 (*m diss* 1947), Laure Léoncie Mathilde Reyne, only da of late Pierre Felix Suquet; 2ndly, 1947 (*m diss* 1958), Betty Annie, who *d* 1989, da of late Arthur C. Lawrence, of Iquique, Chile:—

(By 2nd *m*) Michael Peter (32 Hamilton Rd, St Albans, Herts AL1 4PZ), *b* 1949: *m* 1st, 1973 (*m diss* 1978), Paula Valerie Neuss, who *d* 1988; 2ndly, 1989, Annette Barbara, da of Colin Arthur Pugh-Williams, of Christchurch, NZ.

Issue of late Robert Fynes-Clinton, *b* 1879, *d* 1962: *m* 1907, Margaret Emma, who *d* 1949, yr da of late Rev Stephen Philipps, DD, of Heacham, Norfolk:—

Pelham (1 Gerrard Rd, West Kirby, Wirral), *b* 1910; *ed* Radley: *m* 1937, Joan Elizabeth, who *d* 1984, da of Alfred Chaplin, of West Kirby, and has issue living, Margaret Julia, *b* 1949.

Grandson of late Rev Canon Geoffrey Fynes-Clinton, 6th son of Rev Charles John Fynes-Clinton (ante):—

Issue of late Geoffrey De Berdt Granger Fynes-Clinton, *b* 1878, *d* 1922: *m* 1903, Maybelle, who *d* 1971, da of late John Finamore Edwardes:—

Philip Nevill (James Ommaney Village, 146 Capitol Drive, Jindalee, Queensland 4074), *b* 1908: *m* 1931, Isobel Maud Wilks, and has had issue, Geoffrey William Norreys, *b* 1932; *ed* Queensland Univ (BA, LLB), *m* 1957, Joyce Kathleen Lynch (9 Ormond St, Ascot, Queensland), and *d* 1987, leaving issue, Stephen Philip *b* 1960; *ed* Queensland Univ, Matthew James *b* 1963: *m* 1988, Jane Williams, Timothy Pelham *b* 1965, Emma Mary *b* 1968, — Arthur Nevill (Pantheon St, Jindalee, Queensland 4074), *b* 1934; *ed* Queensland Univ (BA): *m* 1956, Jacqueline Baker, and has issue living, Jamie *b* 1957: *m* 1987, Elizabeth Jean Morgan (and has issue living, Ben Thomas *b* 1988), Alan *b* 1958, Neil *b* 1962.

PREDECESSORS – **(1)** EDWARD, KG, PC, 9th Baron Clinton (*see* B Clinton), successively Lord High Adm, Gov of Boulogne, a Lord of the Bedchamber, Gov of the Tower, and Com in Ch of the fleet and forces sent against France and Scotland; was *cr Earl of Lincoln* (peerage of England) 1572; *d* 1585; *s* by his son **(2)** HENRY, KB, PC, 2nd Earl; *d* 1616; *s* by his son **(3)** THOMAS, 3rd Earl; *d* 1619; *s* by his son **(4)** THEOPHILUS, KB, 4th Earl; was a staunch Royalist, and performed the office of Carver at the Coronation of Charles II; *d* 1667; *s* by his grandson **(5)** EDWARD, 5th Earl; *dsp* 1692, when the Barony of Clinton became abeyant (*see* B Clinton), and the earldom reverted to his cousin **(6)** FRANCIS FIENNES, KB, 6th Earl, grandson of Sir Edward, 2nd son of 2nd Earl; *d* 1693; *s* by his son **(7)** HENRY, KG, 7th Earl, *b* 1684; was unsuccessively a Gentleman of the Bedchamber to Prince George of Denmark, Master of the Horse to Prince of Wales, Paymaster-Gen, Constable of the Tower, and Cofferer of the Household: *m* 1717, Lucy, who *d* 1736, da of 1st Baron Pelham, and sister of Thomas, 1st Duke of Newcastle; *d* 1728; *s* by his el son **(8)** GEORGE, 8th Earl, *b* 1717; *d* 1730; *s* by his brother **(9)** HENRY FYNES, KG, PC, 9th Earl, *b* 1720; was a Gentleman of the Bedchamber, Lord-Lieut of Cambridge, High Steward of Westminster, and Comptroller of the Customs of Port of London: *m* 1744, his cousin, Catherine, who *d* 1760, da and heiress of Right Hon Henry Pelham, and in 1768, inherited the Dukedom of Newcastle, on the death of his maternal, and the countess's paternal uncle, Thomas Pelham Holles, who in 1756 had been *cr Duke of Newcastle-under-Lyme* (peerage of Great Britain), with special remainder to Henry, 9th Earl of Lincoln; assumed the additional surname of Pelham by Roy licence; *d* 1794; *s* by his son **(10)** THOMAS, 3rd Duke, *b* 1752; Maj-Gen in the Army and Col 17th Light Dragoons: *m* 1782, Lady Anna Maria Stanhope, who *d* 1834 (having *m* 2ndly, 1800, Gen Sir Charles Gregan Craufurd, GCB, who *d* 1821); *d* 1795; *s* by his son **(11)** HENRY PELHAM, KG, 4th Duke, *b* 1785; Lord-Lieut of co Nottingham, *m* 1807, Georgiana Elizabeth, da of Edward Miller Mundy, of Shipley, Derbyshire: *d* 1851; *s* by his son **(12)** HENRY PELHAM, KG, 5th Duke, *b* 1811; was Sec of State for the Colonies 1852-4 and 1859-64, Ch Sec for Ireland, Sec of State for War, Lord Warden of the Stanneries, and successively MP for S Notts, and the Falkirk Burghs: *m* 1832 (*m diss* 1850), Lady Susan Harriet Catherine Hamilton Douglas-Hamilton, who *d* 1889 (having *m* 2ndly, 1860, M. Opdebeck, of Brussels); *d* 1864; *s* by his son **(13)** HENRY PELHAM ALEXANDER, 6th Duke; *b* 1834: *m* 1861, Henrietta Adela, who *d* 1913, da of late Henry Thomas Hope; *d* 1879; *s* by his son **(14)** HENRY PELHAM ARCHIBALD DOUGLAS, 7th Duke, *b* 1864: *m* 1889, Kathleen Florence May, OBE, who *d* 1955, da of late Major Henry Augustus Candy; *d* 1928; *s* by his brother **(15)** HENRY FRANCIS HOPE, 8th Duke; *b* 1866; assumed by Roy licence 1887 the additional surname of Hope: *m* 1894 (*m diss* 1902), Mary Augusta (an actress), who *d* 1938, da of William Yohe; 2ndly, 1904, Olive Muriel, who *d* 1912, da of late George Horatio Thompson, banker, of Melbourne, and formerly wife of Richard Owen; *d* 1941; *s* by his son **(16)** HENRY EDWARD HUGH, OBE, 9th Duke, *b* 1907; Sqdn-Ldr and Acting Wing-Com Auxiliary Air Force: *m* 1st, 1931 (*m diss* 1940), Eugenia Van Voorhees, who *d* 1968, adopted da of David Banks, of Park Av, New York; 2ndly, 1946 (*m diss* 1959), Lady (Mary) Diana Montagu-Stuart-Wortley-Mackenzie, who *d* 1997, da of 3rd Earl of Wharncliffe; 3rdly, 1959 (*m diss* 19—), Mrs Sally Ann Wemyss Hope, formerly wife of Fikret Jemal, and elder da of Brig John Henry Anstice, DSO, of Kyrenia, Cyprus; *d* (4 Nov) 1988; *s* by his kinsman **(17)** EDWARD CHARLES (elder but only surv son of late Capt Guy Edward Pelham-Clinton, MC, yr son of late Henry William Pelham-Clinton, 2nd son of late Lord Charles Pelham-Clinton, 2nd son of 4th Duke), 10th Duke, *b* 1920; lepidopterist, Dep Keeper Royal Scottish Museum, Edinburgh; served 1939-45 War as Capt RA (despatches); *dunm* (25 Dec) 1988, when the Dukedom of Newcastle became ext, and the Earldom of Lincoln passed to his distant kinsman **(18)** EDWARD HORACE (grandson of late Charles Edward Fiennes-Clinton, grandson of late Rev Charles Fynes-Clinton, lineal representative of Hon Sir Henry Fynes-Clinton, 3rd son of 2nd Earl), 18th Earl and present peer.

LINDGREN, BARONY OF (Lindgren) (Extinct 1971)

SON LIVING OF LIFE BARON

Hon Graham Alastair, *b* 1928: *m* 1953, Gwendolyne Mary, who *d* 1991, da of late Arthur Miller. *Residence* – 43 Westly Wood, Welwyn Garden City, Herts AL7 1QN.

LINDSAY, EARL OF (Lindesay-Bethune) (Earl S 1633)
(Name pronounced "Beeton")

I love

JE·AYME

LIVE BUT DREID

JAMES RANDOLPH LINDESAY-BETHUNE, 16th Earl; *b* 19 Nov 1955; *s* 1989; *ed* Eton, Edinburgh Univ (MA), and California Univ, Davis; a Lord in Waiting to HM Jan-July 1995, Under Sec of State Scottish Office 1995-97; Chm Assured British Meat Ltd (ABM) since 1997, Scottish Salmon Growers Assocn Ltd (SSGA) 1997-98, RSPB Scotland since 1998, and Scottish Aquaculture since 1998: *m* 1982, Diana Mary, elder da of Maj Nigel Donald Peter Chamberlayne-Macdonald, OBE, LVO (*see* Bosville-Macdonald, Bt), and has issue.

𝕬rms – Quarterly, 1st and 4th gules, fesse checky argent and azure, in chief three mullets of the second; 2nd and 3rd, counter quartered, 1st and 4th azure, a fess between three lozenges or; 2nd and 3rd argent, on a chevron sable an otter's head erased of the first, all within a bordure embattled gold. 𝕮rest – A swan with wings expanded proper. 𝕾upporters – Two griffins gules, armed and beaked or.
Residence – Lahill, Upper Largo, Fife KY8 6JE. *Club* – New (Edinburgh).

SONS LIVING

WILLIAM JAMES (*Viscount Garnock*), *b* 30 Dec 1990.
Hon David Nigel, *b* 1993.

DAUGHTERS LIVING

Lady Frances Mary, *b* 1986.
Lady Alexandra Penelope, *b* 1988.
Lady Charlotte Diana, *b* (twin) 1993.

SISTER LIVING

Lady Caroline Janet, *b* 1957: *m* 1981, Sir George Richard Bourchier Wrey, 15th Bt, and has issue. *Residences* – Hollamoor Farm, Tawstock, Barnstaple, N Devon; 60 The Chase, SW4.

UNCLE LIVING (*son of 14th Earl*)

Hon John Martin (Muircambus, Elie, Leven, Fife KY9 1HD), *b* 1929; *ed* Eton, and Trin Hall, Camb; formerly Lieut Scots Gds: *m* 1st, 1953 (*m diss* 1976), Enriqueta Mary Jeanne, only da of Peter Koch de Gooreynd (*see* M Queensberry, colls, 1990 Edn); 2ndly, 1977, Jean Maxwell, da of Brig Eric Brickman, and formerly wife of Stephen John Younger, and has issue living (by 1st *m*), Nicholas John (89 East Sheen Av, East Sheen, SW14 8AX), *b* 1956: *m* 1977, Maria Teresa, da of Luis Prats, of 2467 Singalong St, Manila, and has issue living, Andrew Nicholas *b* 1979, Henry William *b* 1983, Dominic Luis *b* 1985, — Jonathan Patrick, *b* 1959: *m* 1st, 1989 (*m diss* 1995), Heike, da of Rolf Christ; 2ndly, 1996, Wilhelmina, da of late Archibald Jamieson Thomson and has issue living (by 1st *m*), Kevin Patrick *b* 1989, (by 2nd *m*), Jonathan Daniel *b* 1999, — Simon Charles, *b* 1962: *m* 1990, Melissa Jane, only da of Roderick Webb, of Ditchling, Sussex, — Sally Alexandra Jane, *b* 1954: *m* 1977, Peter Breeden, of Woodside House, Freshford, Bath BA3 6EJ, and has issue living, Alexander Peter *b* 1979, Jamie George *b* 1981, Benjamin Jonathan *b* 1985, Rosie Alexandra Charlotte *b* 1987.

AUNT LIVING (*daughter of 14th Earl*)

Lady Mary Bethune, *b* 1935: *m* 1956, Capt Owen Buckingham Varney, late Scots Gds and has issue living, Mark Lindesay Buckingham, *b* 1958; Capt late Scots Gds: *m* 1987, Katie J., yr da of Eric Bean, of Leckhamstead Thicket, Newbury, Berks, and has issue living, Alexander Edward Lindesay *b* 1991, Joscelyn James Buckingham *b* 1993, Dominic Mark William *b* 1996, — Guy Nicholas Buckingham, *b* 1962; Capt late Scots Gds: *m* 1992, Louise D., elder da of Peter

Owen, of Whitelands Farm, Ashington, Sussex, and has issue living, Nicholas James Lindesay b 1994, Edward Hugh Buckingham b 1996, Harry William Bethune b 1998, — Georgina Mary Bethune, b 1960: m 1984, Christopher Neil Hunter Gordon, yst son of late Maj Patrick Hunter Gordon, CBE, MC, DL, JP, of Ballindoun House, Beauly, Inverness-shire, and has issue living, Sam William b 1988, Ivan Patrick b 1989, Ione Mary b 1992, Hebe Elizabeth b 1996. *Residence* – Hill House, Dedham, nr Colchester, Essex CO7 6EA.

MOTHER LIVING

Hon Mary Clare Douglas Scott Montagu, yst da of 2nd Baron Montagu of Beaulieu: m 1st, 1953 (m diss 1968), David Bethune, Viscount Garnock (later 15th Earl of Lindsay), who d 1989; 2ndly, 1979, Timothy Charles Austin Horn. *Residence* – Chapel House, Builth Wells, Powys.

WIDOW LIVING OF FIFTEENTH EARL

PENELOPE GEORGINA (*Penelope, Countess of Lindsay*), da of late Anthony Crommelin Crossley, MP (*see* Crossley, Bt, colls), and formerly wife of Maj Henry Ronald Burn Callander, MC: m 1969, as his 2nd wife, the 15th Earl of Lindsay, who d 1989. *Residence* – Lindsay Lodge, Combermere, Whitchurch, Shropshire SY13 4AJ.

PREDECESSORS – (1) *Sir* William Lindsay, a celebrated knight, 4th son of David 6th Lord Crawford, obtained the Barony of the Byres by charter 1366 on the resignation of his elder brother Sir Alexander of Glenesk, from whom descends the present Earl of Crawford and Balcarres: m Christian, da of Sir William More, of Abercorn; s by his son (2) Sir William, 2nd of the Byres (and Lord of Abercorn); s by his son (3) *Sir* JOHN, Justiciary of Scotland N of the Forth 1457; cr *Lord Lindsay of the Byres* (peerage of Scotland) 1445; s by his el son (4) DAVID, 2nd Lord; noted in history as having presented the "great grey horse" to James III on the eve of the battle of Sauchieburn 1488; dsp 1492; s by his brother (5) JOHN, 3rd Lord, surnamed "John out with the Sword"; d without male issue 1497; s by his brother (6) PATRICK, 4th Lord; a celebrated advocate; had a grant of the Sheriffdom of Fife to himself, his son and grandson; d 1526; s by his grandson (7) JOHN, 5th Lord; one of the four nobles to whom the charge of the infant Queen Mary was committed in 1542, and whose mediation between the Lords of the Congregation and the Regent, Mary of Guise, led to the pacification of 1559; d 1563; s by his son (8) PATRICK, 6th Lord; an ardent Reformer and Lord of the Congregation; remembered for his share in the murder of Rizzio, the deposition of Queen Mary, and his challenge to Bothwell at Carbery Hill; appointed hereditary bailie of the regality of the Archbishopric of St Andrews; s by his son (9) JAMES, 7th Lord; d 1601; s by his el son (10) JOHN, 8th Lord; d 1609; s by his brother (11) ROBERT, 9th Lord; s by his son (12) JOHN, 10th Lord; cr *Lord Parbroath* and *Earl of Lindsay* (peerage of Scotland) 1633, with remainder to his heirs male, and being described in the patent as "one of the most ancient of the Scottish nobility, and the first in the rank of the greater Barons and Lords of Parliament"; Ludovic, 16th Earl of Crawford, having no children resigned in 1642 the Earldom of Crawford into the hands of Charles I for a re-grant in favour of John, Earl of Lindsay, and the heirs male of his body, and failing which with remainder to Earl Ludovic's collateral heirs male; sentence of forfeiture having been passed on Earl Ludovic by Parliament in rebellion 1644 John, 10th Lord Lindsay was during Earl Ludovic's lifetime (he d 1652), put in possession of the dignity as 17th *Earl of Crawford* (peerage of Scotland, cr 1398), and he and his five next successors each assumed the style of "Earl of Crawford-Lindsay"; he was one of the leading spirits of the Covenant, High Treasurer of Scotland 1644, and President of the Parliament 1645; opposed the surrender of Charles I to the English 1647, and joined the engagement for the King's rescue 1648; taken prisoner by Cromwell 1651, and confined in the Tower and Windsor until the Restoration 1660, when he was reconstituted Treasurer-President of Parliament and Extraordinary Lord of Session; retired into private life 1663; d 1676; s by his son (13) WILLIAM, 18th Earl of Crawford, 2nd Earl of Lindsay, and 11th Lord Lindsay; known as "great and good Earl of Crawford": an ardent Presbyterian; concurred in the Revolution of 1688; was President of the Council 1689; d 1698; s by his son (14) JOHN, 19th and 3rd Earl and 12th Lord; a celebrated military comander; was the first officer to command the Black Watch (Royal Highlanders, then known as "Lord Crawford-Lindsay's Highlanders"); d 1749, from the effects of a wound received at the battle of Krotska in 1738; s by his kinsman (16) GEORGE, 21st and 5th Earl, and 14th Lord, who had in 1738, s as 4th *Viscount Garnock* (see * infra); d 1778; s by his son (17) GEORGE, 22nd Earl of Crawford, 6th Earl of Lindsay, 5th Viscount Garnock, and 15th Lord Lindsay; a Maj-Gen in the Army; d 1808, when the Earldom of Crawford devolved upon Alexander, 6th Earl of Balcarres as heir male of Ludovic, 16th Earl of Crawford (see E Crawford and Balcarres) and the Earldom of Lindsay and minor honours reverted to his kinsman (18) DAVID, de jure 7th Earl of Lindsay, 6th Viscount Garnock, and 16th Lord Lindsay (the descendant of David, brother of 5th Lord Lindsay); was a Sergeant in the Perths Militia; several noblemen offered money to enable him to establish his claim to the peerage, and the Duke of York offered him a commission if his claim succeeded; d 1809; s by his kinsman (19) PATRICK, KB, de jure 8th Earl, 7th Viscount, and 17th Lord; a distinguished Gen: dsp 1839; s by his kinsman (20) HENRY Lindsay-Bethune, de jure 9th Earl, 8th Viscount, and 18th Lord, the heir male of William, 2nd son of 4th Lord Lindsay; b 1787; served with remarkable distinction as Commander of the Persian forces against Russian 1804-19, and against the rebel Zulli Sultan 1834-6; cr a Bt 1836, at the request of the Shah; assumed the additional surname of Bethune 1816; m 1822, Coutts, who d 1877, da of John Trotter, of Dyrham Park; d 1851; s by his son (21) JOHN TROTTER, 10th Earl, 9th Viscount, and 19th Lord, b 1827; s as 2nd Bart 1857, and established his right to the Earldom of Lindsay and minor honours 1878: m 1858, Jeanne Eudoxie Marie, who d 1897, da of Mons Jacques Victor Duval, of Bordeaux; d 1894, when the Baronetcy became extinct, and he was succeeded in the other titles by his cousin (22) DAVID CLARK Lindsay (son of late David Aytone Lindesay, a descendant of 4th Lord), 11th Earl, b 1832; assumed (without official authority) the surname and arms of Bethune in lieu of those of Lindesay: m 1866, Emily Marian, who d 1920, da of late Robert Crosse, of Doctors' Commons, and widow of Capt Edmund Charles Barnes (of HM's late St Helena Regt); d 1917; s by his son (23) REGINALD BETHUNE Lindesay-Bethune, 12th Earl, b 1867; was a Representative Peer for Scotland 1917-39; matriculated the Arms and additional surname of Lindesay 1918: m 1892, Beatrice Mary, who d 1944, da of late John Shaw, of Welburn Hall, Kirbymoorside, Yorkshire; d 1939; s by his brother (24) ARCHIBALD LIONEL, 13th Earl, b 1872: m 1900, Ethel, who d 1942, da of W. A. Tucker, of 47 Bay State Rd, Boston, USA; d 1943; s by his son (25) WILLIAM TUCKER, 14th Earl, b 1901; Maj Scots Gds, Hon Col Fife and Forfar Yeo, Scottish Horse; a Member Queen's Body Guard for Scotland (R Company of Archers); a Representative Peer 1947-59; Pres Shipwrecked and Mariners R Benevolent Soc: m 1925, Marjory, who d 1988, da of late Arthur Graham Cross; d 1985; s by his elder son (26) DAVID BETHUNE, 15th Earl b 1926, Vice-Chm (Canada) British Overseas Trade Bd, N America, Dir Internat Harvester, Carpets Internat plc, Bank of Montreal, Festiniog Railway Co, etc, FRSA: m 1st, 1953 (m diss 1968), Hon Mary Clare Douglas Scott Montagu, yst da of 2nd Baron Montagu of Beaulieu; 2ndly 1969, Mrs Penelope Georgina CALLANDER, da of late Anthony Crommelin Crossley, MP (see Crossley, Bt); d 1989; s by his only son (27) JAMES RANDOLPH, 16th Earl and present peer; also Viscount Garnock, Lord Parbroath, Lord Kilbirnie, Kingsburn and Drumry, and Lord Lindsay of the Byres.

*(1) JOHN Lindsay, son of Patrick, 2nd son of 1st Earl of Lindsay; cr *Lord Kilbirnie, Kingsburn, and Drumry,* and *Viscount Garnock* (peerage of Scotland) 1703; d 1709; s by his son (2) PATRICK, 2nd Viscount; d 1735; s by his el son (3) JOHN, 3rd Viscount; dsp 1738; s by his brother (4) GEORGE, 4th Viscount s as 21st Earl of Crawford (ante).

Lindsay, family name of Earl of Crawford.

LINDSAY OF BIRKER, BARON (Lindsay) (Baron UK 1945)

JAMES FRANCIS LINDSAY, 3rd Baron; *b* 29 Jan 1945; *s* 1994; *ed* Geelong Gram Sch and Keele Univ; joined Australian Dept of Foreign Affairs 1972; Dep High Commr, Islamabad, Pakistan 1993-96, since when Dep High Commr, Nairobi, Kenya: *m* 1969 (*m diss* 1983), Mary Rose, da of W. G. Thomas, of Cwmbran, Mon.
Address – Box 39341, Nairobi, Kenya.

SISTERS LIVING AND DECEASED

Hon Erica Susan, *b* 1942; *d* 1993.
Hon Mary Muriel, *b* 1951: *m* 1976, Kenneth Kyle Abbott, Jr, and has issue living, Thomas Lindsay, *b* 1978, — Michael William, *b* 1985.

AUNT LIVING (*Daughter of 1st Baron*)

Hon (Anna) Drusilla (*Hon Lady Scott*), *b* 1911: *m* 1937, Sir Ian Dixon Scott, KCMG, KCVO, CIE, and has issue living, Peter John Lindsay, *b* 1948: *m* 1976, Susan Dobson, — (Mary) Pauline, *b* 1939: *m* 1971, Samih Sadek, — Rachel Erica, *b* 1940: *m* 1960, David Britton, — Ann Catherine, *b* 1942: *m* 1975, Jack Shepherd, — Monica Margaret, *b* 1947: *m* 1975, Ian Lanman. *Residence* – Ash House, Alde Lane, Aldeburgh, Suffolk IP15 5DZ.

WIDOW LIVING OF SON OF FIRST BARON

Erica, da of Maj Eric Thirkell-Cooper: *m* 1961, as his 3rd wife, Maj the Hon Thomas Martin Lindsay, MBE, who *d* 1995. *Residence* – 8 Avenue de Pinsons, 1410 Waterloo, Belgium.

WIDOW LIVING OF SECOND BARON (*By 1st marriage*)

HSIAO LI (*Dowager Baroness Lindsay of Birker*), da of Col Li Wen Chi, Chinese Army, of Lishih, Shansi, China: *m* 1941, the 2nd Baron Lindsay of Birker, who *d* 1994. *Residence* – Apt 1, Building 17, Fangguyuan, Beijing, China.

COLLATERAL BRANCH LIVING

Issue of late Maj the Hon Thomas Martin Lindsay, MBE, yr son of 1st Baron, *b* 1915, *d* 1995: *m* 1st, 1939 (*m diss* 1951), Denise Theresa, da of Gerald Albert Vaughan; 2ndly, 1951 (*m diss* 1961), Felicitas, da of Dr Martin Lange; 3rdly, 1961, Erica (ante), da of Maj Eric Thirkell-Cooper:—
(By 1st *m*) ALEXANDER SEBASTIAN, *b* 27 May 1940. —— Thomas Martin, *b* 1942. —— Teresa, *b* 1945. —— (By 2nd *m*) Stuart Martin, *b* 1951. —— Alexander Gordon, *b* 1952. —— (By 3rd *m*) Benjamin Martin, *b* 1962. —— Robert William, *b* 1967.

PREDECESSORS – (1) ALEXANDER DUNLOP Lindsay, CBE, LLD, son of late Rev T. M. Lindsay, DD, Principal of United Free Church Coll, Glasgow; *b* 1879; Fellow and Classical Tutor, Balliol Coll 1906, Jowett Lecturer in Philosophy 1910, and Professor of Moral Philosophy, Glasgow Univ 1922; Master of Balliol Coll, Oxford 1924-49, Vice-Chancellor of Oxford Univ 1935-38, and Principal of Univ Coll, N Staffs 1949-52; *cr Baron Lindsay of Birker*, of Low Ground, co Cumberland (peerage of United Kingdom) 1945: *m* 1907, Erica Violet, who *d* 1962, da of F. Storr; *d* 1952; *s* by his el son (2) MICHAEL FRANCIS MORRIS, 2nd Baron; *b* 1909; Prof of Far Eastern Studies, American Univ, Washington, DC 1959-74: *m* 1941, Hsiao Li, da of Col Li Wen Chi, Chinese Army; *d* 1994; *s* by his only son (3) JAMES FRANCIS, 3rd Baron and present peer.

LINDSEY AND ABINGDON, EARL OF (Bertie) (Earl E 1626 and 1682)
(Name pronounced "Barty")

Valour is stronger than a battering ram

RICHARD HENRY RUPERT BERTIE, 14th Earl of Lindsey and 9th Earl of Abingdon, *b* 28 June 1931; *s* 1963; *ed* Ampleforth; late Lt Royal Norfolk Regt; High Steward of Abingdon since 1963: *m* 1957, Norah Elizabeth Farquhar-Oliver, 2nd da of late Mark Oliver, OBE (*see* Farquhar, Bt, colls, 1980 Edn), and has issue.

ᴀrms – Argent, three battering rams fessewise in pale proper headed, armed and garnished azure. Crest – A Saracen's head affrontée, couped at the shoulders proper, ducally crowned or, and charged on the chest with a fret azure. Supporters – *Dexter*, a friar habited in russet grey, with a crutch and rosary, all proper; *sinister*, a savage proper wreathed about the temples and waist with oak leaves vert; each charged on the breast with a fret azure.
Residences – Gilmilnscroft House, Sorn, Mauchline, Ayrshire KA5 6ND; 3 Westgate Terrace, SW10 9BT. *Clubs* – Pratt's, Turf, White's.

SONS LIVING

HENRY MARK WILLOUGHBY (*Lord Norreys*), *b* 6 June 1958; *ed* Eton, and Edinburgh Univ; Kt of Honour and Devotion of Sovereign Mil Order of Malta, Kt of Justice of Sacred Mil Constantinian Order of St George, Kt of Order of Ss Maurice and Lazarus: *m* 1989, Lucinda Sol, 2nd da of Christopher Stewart Moorsom, and of María del Pilar Sánchez y Betancourt, Mrs Bayard Osborn, and has issue:—

SONS LIVING— *Hon* Willoughby Henry Constantine St Maur, *b* 15 Jan 1996, — *Hon* James Frederick Christopher Ninian, *b* 1997.
Residence – Alameda de la Alcaldesa 1, Urb La Virginia, 29600 Marbella (Málaga), Spain. *Clubs* – Pratt's, Puffin's (Edinburgh).

Hon Alexander Michael Richard, *b* 1970; *ed* Eton, and The Queen's Coll, Oxford (BA 1992): *m* 1998, Catherine Davina, only da of late Prof Gordon Campbell Cameron, of Cambridge Univ. *Residence* – 17 Noel Rd, N1 8HQ.

DAUGHTER LIVING

Lady Annabel Frances Rose, *b* 1969; *ed* St Mary's, Ascot, and Edinburgh Univ (MA 1991). *Residence* – 3 Westgate Terrace, SW10 9BT.

STEP MOTHER LIVING

Lilian Isabel, elder da of late Charles Edward Joseph Cary-Elwes, of Staithe House, Beccles, Suffolk, and widow of Lt-Cdr Francis Dayrell Montague Crackanthorpe, RN: *m* 1949, as his 2nd wife, Lt-Col Hon Arthur Michael Bertie, DSO, MC, who *d* 1957.

COLLATERAL BRANCHES LIVING

Issue of late Lt-Cdr Hon James Willoughby Bertie, RN, 3rd son of 7th Earl of Abingdon, *b* 1901, *d* 1966: *m* 1928, Lady Jean Crichton-Stuart, who *d* 1995, da of 4th Marquess of Bute:—
His Most Eminent Highness Frà Andrew Willoughby Ninian (Palazzo Malta, via Condotti 68, 00187 Rome, Italy) *b* 1929; Lt Scots Guards (SR), Prince and Grand Master of Sovereign Mil Order of Malta since 1988 (*Arms* - Quarterly: 1st and 4th, gules a cross argent, *Order of Malta*; 2nd and 3rd, argent three battering rams fessewise in pale proper armed and garnished azure, *Bertie*). —— (Charles) Peregrine Albemarle (Frilsham Manor, Hermitage, Newbury, Berks RG18 9UZ), *b* 1932; Capt late Scots Guards, and a Kt Grand Cross of Honour and Devotion in Obedience of Sovereign Mil Order of Malta, Kt Cdr Order of St Gregory, Cdr of Merit with Swords Order of Pro Merito Melitensi; Member Queen's Body Guard for Scotland (Royal Company of Archers); High Sheriff Berks 1986; KStJ: *m* 1960, Susan Griselda Ann Lyon, el da of Maj John Lycett Wills, Life Guards (ret) (*see* Wills, Bt, *cr* 1904), and has issue living, David Montagu Albemarle, *b* 1963: *m* 1994, Catherine Cecily, only da of Anthony Feilden Mason-Hornby, of Dalton Hall, nr Carnforth, Cumbria (*see* Wigan, Bt, colls, 1980 Edn), and has issue living, Charlotte Iona Rose *b* 1995, Lucy Victoria Isabella *b* 1998, — Caroline Georgina Rose, *b* 1965: *m* 1991, Andrew L. Carrington, son of Capt Norman Carrington, of Saxonmead, Haywards Heath, Sussex, and has issue living, Charles Alexander Francis *b* 1996, Georgia Elizabeth Jean *b* 1994.

(In remainder to Barony of Norreys of Rycote only)

Granddaughters of late Lady Mary Caroline Bertie, da of 7th Earl of Abingdon, *b* 1859, *d* 1938: *m* 1879, 1st Viscount Fitz Alan of Derwent, who *d* 1947 (extinct 1962) (see that title).

Grandsons of late Lady Alice Josephine Bertie (Lady Josephine Reynties), da of 7th Earl of Abingdon:—
Issue of late Priscilla Cecilia Maria, CBE, *b* 1899, *d* 1991: *m* 1st, 1921 (*m diss* 1929), Alexander Koch de Gooreynd, who *d* 1985, having assumed by deed poll 1923 the surname of Worsthorne in lieu of de Gooreynd; 2ndly, 1933, 1st Baron Norman, who *d* 1950:—

(By 1st *m*) *Sir* Simon Peter Edmund Cosmo William TOWNELEY, KCVO (Dyneley Hall, Burnley, Lancs), *b* 1921; Lieut KRRC; JP Lancs 1956, Co Councillor 1961-64, High Sheriff 1971-72, Lord Lieut 1976-96; Member of Council of Duchy of Lancaster 1986-96; Trustee British Museum 1988-93; hon Col Duke of Lancaster's Own Yeo 1979-88; assumed by deed poll 1945 the additional surname of Towneley before his patronymic, and, by Royal Licence 1955, the arms of Towneley, and relinquished by deed poll 1955 the surname of Worsthorne; KStJ, KCSG, KCVO 1994: *m* 1955, Mary, da of late Cuthbert Fitzherbert, and has issue living, Peregrine Henry, *b* 1962: *m* 1998, Sarah T., da of William MacLeod, of Texas, and of Mrs Nicholas Marriner, of N Yorks, — Alice Mary, *b* 1956: *m* 1984, Michael O'Neill, only son of W/Cmdr H. F. O'Neill, DFC, RAF (ret), and has issue living, Oswald *b* 1987, Matilda Mary *b* 1986, Eleanor Elizabeth *b* 1989, Frideswide Cecilia *b* 1990, — Charlotte Mary, *b* 1957; *ed* Royal Northern Coll of Music: *m* 1986, Arthur Edmund French, and has issue (*see* B de Freyne, colls), — Katharine Mary, *b* 1958: *m* 1985, William Marr Couper Grant, WS, yr son of Douglas Marr Kelso Grant, of Drumellan House, Maybole, Ayrshire, and has issue living, Cosmo Douglas *b* 1991, Clementine Priscilla *b* 1986, Eliza Mary *b* 1989, — Victoria Mary, *b* 1964: *m* 1992, Edward Bowen-Jones, eldest son of Adrian Bowen-Jones, and has issue living, Rowland Edward *b* 1996, Benjamin Adrian *b* 1998, — Cosima Cecilia, *b* 1967, — Frances Teresa, *b* 1969: *m* 1997, Daniel A. Scoular, only son of Mrs Leslie Phillips, and stepson of Leslie Phillips. —— *Sir* Peregrine Gerard WORSTHORNE (The Old Rectory, Hedgerley, Bucks SL2 3UY), *b* 1923; Lieut Oxford and Bucks LI attached GHQ Liaison Regt (Phantom) 1939-45 War; Knt 1991: *m* 1st, 1950, Mrs Claudia Baynham, who *d* 1990, da of Victor Bertrand de Colasse, of 43 Ave Ernest Rayer, Paris; 2ndly, 1991, Lady Lucinda Lambton, eldest da of Antony Claud Frederick Lambton (6th Earl of Durham until he disclaimed his title 1970), and has issue living (by 1st *m*), Dominique Elizabeth Priscilla, *b* 1952: *m* 1978, Jonathan Busill Maynard Keeling, of Whichford Pottery, Whichford, Shipston-on-Stour, Warwicks CV36 5PG, son of Robert Keeling, of Hembury Knoll, Hook Heath Rd, Woking, Surrey, and has issue living, Adam Busill Worsthorne *b* 1980, Thomas Karol *b* 1982, Maia Claudia Priscilla *b* 1985, Theodora Sophia Mary *b* 1988, Columba David *b* 1991.

Issue of late Lady Gwendeline Theresa Mary Bertie, da of 7th Earl of Abingdon, *b* 1885, *d* 1941: *m* 1908, Maj John Strange Spencer-Churchill, DSO, who *d* 1947 (*see* D Marlborough, colls).

Issue of late Lady Elizabeth Constance Mary (Betty) Bertie, OBE, da of 7th Earl of Abingdon, *b* 1895, *d* 1987: *m* 1st 1914, Maj Sigismund William Joseph Trafford, Rifle Bde (Prince Consort's Own), who *d* 1953; 2ndly, 1956, Col Henry Antrobus Cartwright, CMG, MC, who *d* 1957:—
(By 1st *m*) Edward Willoughby TRAFFORD, *b* 1924; *ed* Harrow, and Downside; late Scots Guards; Knight of Honour and Devotion of Sovereign Mil Order of Malta: *m* 1952, June Imelda, only da of Richard Joseph Anthony Harding, of Echo Valley, Springbook, Queensland, and has issue living, Michael Francis (Manor Farm, Rackheath, Norwich, Norfolk), *b* 1953; *ed* Downside, — Bernard Edward (8 Duchess Court, Mudgeeraba, Queensland 4213, Australia), *b* 1955; *ed* Downside: *m* 1980, Corinne Jean, da of Alan Furnell, of Bryn Collen, Llandover, Gwent, and has issue living, Edward Alexander *b* 1981, Charles Henry *b* 1983, — Andrew Martin, *b* 1960: *m* 1990, Karen Ann Mary, da of Robert Alexander McEwen, of Canberra, Australia, — Amanda Gabrielle Mary, *b* 1959: *m* 1st, 1984, Mark Edmond Garthwaite; 2ndly, 1993, Stephen Hardcastle (Fred) Agnew (*see* Agnew, Bt, *cr* 1895), and has issue living (by 1st *m*), Alice Sophie Elizabeth *b* 1987, (by 2nd *m*) (*see* Agnew, Bt, *cr* 1895). *Residence* – Broad House, Wroxham, Norfolk. —— Helen Mary, *b* 1915: *m* 1936, Capt Peter Evelyn Fanshawe, CBE, DSC, RN (*see* E Erne, colls, 1948 Edn), who *d* 1994, of 12 Lincoln Av, Wimbledon, SW19 5JT, and has issue living, Richard Henry William (Rafters, Waldron, Heathfield, E Sussex TN21 0QY), *b* 1939; *ed* Ampleforth, and RNC Dartmouth: *m* 1966, Hon Maura Clare Evans-Freke, da of 11th Baron Carbery, and has issue living, Louisa Mary Constance *b* 1987, — Veronica Evelyn, *b* 1947: *m* 1977, Maj Charles Napier St Pierre Bunbury, MBE, The Duke of Wellington's Regt (*see* Bunbury, Bt, colls). —— Sophie Mary (*Baroness Lyell*), *b* 1916: *m* 1938, 2nd Baron Lyell, VC, who was *ka* 1943. *Residence* – Kinnordy, Kirriemuir, Angus. —— Diana Rosemary, *b* 1920: *m* 1st, 1951, John Reford; 2ndly, 1977, Col L. M. Collins, who *d* 1984. *Residence* – 15 St Petersburgh Mews, W2.

(In remainder to the Earldoms and Barony)

Grandchildren of late Rev Hon Alberic Edward Bertie, 3rd son of 6th Earl of Abingdon:—
Issue of late Lieut-Com Aubrey Charles Bertie, RN, *b* 1882, *d* 1944: *m* 1916, Jeanne, da of M. A. Vissers:—
Albert Arnaud (Maison du Coin, Route du Coin, St Brelade, Jersey CI), *b* 1919: *m* 1950, Joan, da of A. E. Sidery, and has issue living, John Peregrine *b* 1952: *m* 1st, 1972 (*m diss* 1977), Mary, da of Cedric Rosenvinge; 2ndly, 1986, Belinda, da of Timothy Orpe Adkin, and has issue living (by 1st *m*), Caroline Emma *b* 1973, (by 2nd *m*) Georgina Anne *b* 1990, Harriet Olivia *b* 1992, Sabrina Dawn *b* 1993, — Peter Mark, *b* 1959; *ed* Pembroke Coll, Camb (MA): *m* 1993, Karen, da of Raymond Anthony Hewitt. —— Christine Caroline, *b* 1917.

Issue of late Schomberg Montagu Bertie, *b* 1888; *d* 1937: *m* 1922, Edith Mary (who *m* 2ndly, 1941, Harry August Anders, and *d* 1982), da of John England:—
Caroline Edith (30 Hickory St, S Fremantle, W Australia 6162), *b* 1923: *m* 1952, Gordon Ernest Ross, who *d* 1971, and has issue living, Alan Gordon Schomberg *b* 1955, — Dagmar Caroline Edith, *b* 1953, — Hilary, *b* 1960. —— Rose Patricia, *b* 1926; *ed* Queensland Univ (MSc Agr): *m* 1951, Harold Edwin Kleinschmidt, of 45 Kersley Rd, Kenmore, Brisbane, Queensland, and has issue living, Christopher Montagu, *b* 1963: *m* 1991, Tammy Joan, eldest da of Henry Vincent Neller, — Felicity Rose, *b* 1965: *m* 1989, Raymond Andrew Hembrow, and has issue living, Elise Robyn *b* 1994, — Elise Caroline, *b* 1970: *m* 1994, Gordon Robert Smith.

Issue of late Capt Alberic Willoughby Bertie, MC, *b* 1891, *d* 1969: *m* 1922, Maria Flore who *d* 1925, da of Philippe Reinhort:—
Marie Lucette: *m* 1943, Capt Ronald Frank Kershaw, late 60th Rifles, of Cobwood House, Wootton Hill, nr Newbury, Berks RG15 9TW, and has issue living, Martin John (Brights Farm, Christian Malford, Chippenham, Wilts SN15 4DA), *b* 1954: *m* 1982, Joanna Lucy, el da of Lord Edward Anthony Charles FitzRoy (*see* D Grafton), and has issue living, Simon Edward *b* 1985, William Ronald *b* 1987, David Robert *b* 1990, Louisa *b* 1992, — Clarissa Mary, *b* 1944: *m* 1970, Capt Peter Malcolm Roe, The Royal Hussars (PWO), of Clench Farm House, nr Marlborough, Wilts, and has issue living, Jeremy Malcolm Ninian *b* 1973, Christopher John Edward *b* 1975, Nicholas James Buxton *b* 1982, — Serena Jane (*Lady Graham*), *b* 1948: *m* 1975, Sir James Fergus Surtees Graham, 7th Bt, of Kirkandrews Tower, Longtown, Cumbria, and has issue (*see* Graham Bt, *cr* 1783), — Gabrielle Lavinia, *b* 1951: *m* 1975, Christopher James Hodgson, of Souldern Court, nr Bicester, Oxon, and has issue living, Henry James *b* 1977, Clare Lucy *b* 1979, Sarah Rebecca *b* 1982, Camilla Rose *b* 1984.

Issue of late Lavinia May Bertie, *b* 1887, *d* 1978: *m* 1921, Theodore Stephen Hubbard, who *d* 1934:—

Theodore Bernard Peregrine HUBBARD (The Flat, Horsecroft Hall, Horsecroft Rd, Bury St Edmunds, Suffolk IP29 5NY), *b* 1923; Lt-Cdr (ret) RN; 1939-45 War: *m* 1952, Lady Miriam Fitzalan Howard, who *d* as the result of an accident 1996, sister of 17th Duke of Norfolk, and has issue living, Martin Peregrine Thomas, *b* 1954; *ed* Ampleforth, — Theodore Bernard Peter (143 Studdridge St, SW6 3T1), *b* 1959; *ed* —Coll, Camb (MA): *m* 1985, Penelope D., eldest da of Alan Thomas Street, of Ollerton Hall, Knutsford, Cheshire, and has issue living, Francesca *b* 1989, Kinvara *b* 1992, — Mary-Miranda Josephine, *b* (Jan) 1956: *m* 1974, Roger John Pratt, of 32 High St, Haddenham, Ely, Cambs, and has issue living, Alexander Roger Martin *b* 1978, James Malcolm *b* 1980, Matthew Charles *b* 1982, — Lucinda Mary Lavinia, *b* (Dec) 1956; *ed* Leeds Univ (BSc), Liverpool Univ (MSc), and Queen's Univ, Belfast (PhD): *m* 1988, Richard Patrick Blakiston Houston (see Blakiston, Bt, colls), — Vanessa Mary Theresa, *b* 1958: *m* 1st, 1980 (*m diss* 1987), David St Vincent Llewellyn (see Llewellyn, Bt, *cr* 1922); 2ndly, 1987, as his 2nd wife, John Austen Anstruther-Gough-Calthorpe (see Anstruther-Gough-Calthorpe, Bt). ——†Thomas Francis HUBBARD, *b* 1925; *ed* Wadham Coll, Oxford (BA 1949); Sub-Lieut (ret) RN; 1939-45 War: *m* 1954, Melise Marie (160 rue de Grenelle, Paris 75007), eldest da of late Marquis de Merindol, of 34 Gordon Place, W8, and *d* 1998, leaving issue, John Francis, *b* 1955, — Mark Fernand, *b* 1957, — Richard Peter, *b* 1959.

        Granddaughter of late Capt Frederic Arthur Bertie, 5th son of late Rev Hon Frederic Bertie, 5th son of 4th Earl of Abingdon:—
        Issue of late Margaret Grace Bertie, *b* 1883, *d* 1978: *m* 1914, Lt-Col Hugh Cleivion Jagger, OBE, RAVC (TA), who *d* 1931:—
Margaret Rosemary Helen, *b* 1922; formerly in WRNS: *m* 1950, Drayton Alfred Wiltshire, and has issue living, Richard Drayton, *b* 1951, — Robin Cleivion, *b* 1956: *m* 1986, Catherine Eva FitzSimon, and has issue living, Rupert Charles *b* 1993.

PREDECESSORS – (1) ROBERT Bertie, KG, 12th Baron Willoughby de Eresby (for his predecessor see that family); was Gov of Berwick and Lord High Adm of England; established his claim in right of his mother to the hereditary office of Lord Great Chamberlain of England; *cr Earl of Lindsey* (peerage of England) 1626; *k* at battle of Edgehill when in command of a division of the King's army 1642; *s* by his son (2) MONTAGU, KG, PC, 2nd Earl; surrendered himself a prisoner at Edgehill, in order to attend upon his mortally wounded father; subsequently fought at both battles of Newbury, and at Naseby, etc; was a Lord of the Bedchamber to Charles I, and Lord-Lieut of Oxfordshire; his el son by his 2nd marriage was *cr Earl of Abingdon; d* 1666; *s* by his el son (3) ROBERT, 3rd Earl; *d* 1701; *s* by his son (4) ROBERT, PC, 4th Earl; summoned to Parliament in his father's lifetime as Baron Willoughby de Eresby; was Lord Lieut of co Lincoln and one of the Lords Justices before the arrival of George I; *cr Marquess of Lindsey* (peerage of Great Britain) 1706, and *Duke of Ancaster and Kesteven* (peerage of Great Britain) 1715; *d* 1723; *s* by his son (5) PEREGRINE, PC, 2nd Duke; summoned to Parliament in his father's Barony of Willoughby de Eresby; was Lord-Lieut of Lincolnshire and Lord Warden of all HM's parks, chasse, forests, etc, North of the Trent; *d* 1742; *s* by his son (6) PEREGRINE, 3rd Duke; was a Gen in the Army, Master of the Horse, and Recorder of Lincoln; officiated as Lord Great Chamberlain at the Coronation of George III; *d* 1778; *s* by his son (7) ROBERT, 4th Duke; *d* unmarried 1779, when the Barony of Willoughby de Eresby became abeyant between his sister, Priscilla (afterwards Baroness Willoughby de Eresby) and Georgiana (Marchioness of Cholmondeley), the Lord Great Chamberlainship devolved jointly upon those ladies, and the dukedom reverted to his uncle (8) BROWNLOW, 5th Duke; *d* without male issue 1809, when the dukedom and marquessate became extinct, and the earldom devolved upon his kinsman (9) ALBEMARLE, 9th Earl, great-grandson of Hon Charles Bertie, of Uffington, 5th son of 2nd Earl: *b* 1744; was a Gen in the Army, Col 89th Regt, Gov of Blackness Castle, and sometime MP for Stamford: *m* 1809, Charlotte Susannah Elizabeth, da of Very Rev Charles P. Layard, Dean of Bristol; *d* 1818; *s* by his el son (10) GEORGE AUGUSTUS FREDERICK ALBEMARLE 10th Earl; *d* unmarried 1877; *s* by his brother (11) MONTAGU PEREGRINE, 11th Earl *b* 1815: *m* 1854, Felicia Elizabeth, who *d* 1927, da of late Rev John Earle Welby; *d* 1899; *s* by his only son (12) MONTAGU PEREGRINE ALBEMARLE, 12th Earl, *b* 1861: *m* 1890, Millicent, who *d* 1931, el da of J. C. Cox, formerly of Craig Cruich, Sydney, NS Wales; *d* 1938; *s* by his kinsman (13) MONTAGU HENRY EDMUND CECIL, 13th Earl (who had *s* as 8th Earl of Abingdon 1928) (see * infra); succession recognized 1951; *b* 1887; Capt Gren Gds; High Steward of Abingdon: *m* 1928, Elizabeth Valetta, who *d* 1978, da of late Maj-Gen Hon Edward James Montagu-Stuart-Wortley, CB, CMG, DSO (E Wharncliffe, colls); *d* 1963; *s* by his cousin (14) RICHARD HENRY RUPERT (son of late Lt-Col Hon Arthur Michael Bertie, DSO, MC, 2nd son of 7th Earl of Abingdon), 14th Earl of Lindsey, 9th Earl of Abingdon, and present peer, also Baron Norreys of Rycote.

*(1) Sir HENRY NORRIS, KB, Ambassador to France, was summoned to Parliament 1572-97; *d* 1600; *s* by his grandson (2) FRANCIS, 2nd Baron; *cr Viscount Thame* and *Earl of Berkshire* (peerage of England) 1620, and *d* the same year without male issue when the Viscountcy and Earldom became extinct; his only da had issue, one da, who *m* as his second wife the 2nd Earl of Lindsey, by whom she had (3) JAMES BERTIE, summoned to Parliament of England 1675 as *Baron Norreys of Rycote* (with Precedence of 1572), and *cr Earl of Abingdon* (peerage of England) 1682; was Lord-Lieut of Oxfordshire 1674-97; *d* 1699; *s* by his son (4) MONTAGU, 2nd Earl; assumed by Roy licence 1687 the additional surname of Venables; *d* 1743; *s* by his nephew (5) WILLOUGHBY, 3rd Earl, el son of Hon James, 2nd son of 1st Earl; *d* 1760; *s* by his el son (6) WILLOUGHBY, 4th Earl; *d* 1799; *s* by his son (7) MONTAGU, DCL, 5th Earl, *b* 1784; was Lord-Lieut of Berkshire, and officiated as cup-bearer at the coronation of George IV; *d* 16 Oct 1854; *s* by his el son (8) MONTAGU, DCL, 6th Earl, *b* 1808; sat as MP for Oxfordshire 1830 and 1832-52, and for Abingdon (LC) 1852-54; was Lord-Lieut of Berks 1855-81: *m* 1835, Elizabeth Lavinia, who *d* 1858, da of late George Granville Vernon-Harcourt, MP, of Nuneham Park, Oxfordshire; *d* 1884; *s* by his el son (9) MONTAGU ARTHUR, 7th Earl; *b* 1836; High Steward of Abingdon: *m* 1st, 1858, Caroline Theresa, who *d* 1873, da of late Charles Towneley, of Towneley, Lancs; 2ndly, 1883, Gwendeline Mary, who *d* 1942, da of late Lt-Gen Hon Sir James Charlemagne Dormer, KCB; *d* 1928; *s* by his grandson (10) MONTAGU HENRY EDMUND CECIL (son of late Capt Montagu Charles Francis, Lord Norreys, el son of 7th Earl), who *s* as 13th Earl of Lindsey 1938 (succession recognised 1951), 8th Earl.

LINKLATER OF BUTTERSTONE, BARONESS (Linklater) (Life Baroness 1997)

VERONICA LINKLATER, da of Lt-Col (Archibald) Michael Lyle, OBE, of Riemore Lodge, Dunkeld, Perthshire (see Lyle, Bt); *b* 15 April 1943; *ed* Cranbourne Chase Sch, Sussex Univ, and London Univ (Dip Soc); Child Care Offr, London Borough of Tower Hamlets 1967-68; Co-founder Visitors'

Centre, Pentonville Prison 1971-77; Govr of three Islington Schs 1970-85; Prison Reform Trust Project, Winchester Prison 1981-82; Co-Founder, Administrator, Cnslt, then Trustee, The Butler Trust Prison Service Annual Award Scheme since 1983; JP Inner London 1985-88; Co-ordinator then Trustee and Vice-Chm, The Pushkin Prizes (Scotland) since 1989; Memb Children's Panel, Edinburgh South 1989-97; Pres Soc of Friends of Dunkeld Cathedral since 1989; Memb Cttee, The Gulliver Award for the Performing Arts in Scotland 1990-96; Founder and Executive Chm The New Sch, Butterstone since 1991; Trustee, Esmée Fairbairn Charitable Trust since 1991, and The Young Musicians' Trust 1993-97; Patron, The Sutherland Trust since 1993; Dir The Maggie Keswick-Jencks Cancer Caring Centres Trust since 1997; *cr Baroness Linklater of Butterstone*, of Riemore in Perth and Kinross (Life Baroness) 1997: *m* 1967, Magnus Duncan Linklater, son of Eric Robert Linklater, CBE, TD, of The Mains of Haddo, Tarves, Aberdeenshire, and has issue.
Residence – 5 Drummond Place, Edinburgh EH3 6PH.

SONS LIVING

Hon Alexander Ragnar, *b* 1968.
Hon Saul Archibald Robert, *b* 1970.

DAUGHTER LIVING

Hon Freya Elizabeth Erica, *b* 1975.

Linley, Viscount; son of Earl of Snowdon.

LINLITHGOW, MARQUESS OF (Hope) (Marquess UK 1902, Bt NS 1698)

But my hope is not broken

AT · SPES · NON · FRACTA

ADRIAN JOHN CHARLES HOPE, 4th Marquess and 12th Baronet; *b* 1 July 1946; *s* 1987; *ed* Eton: *m* 1st, 1968 (*m diss* 1978), Anne Pamela, eldest da of Arthur Edmund Leveson, of Hall Place, Ropley, Hants; 2ndly, 1980 (*m diss* 1997), Peta Carol, da of Charles Victor Ormonde Binding, of Congresbury, Somerset; 3rdly, 1997, Auriol Veronica, yr da of late Capt Graham Lawrie Mackeson-Sandbach, of Caerllo, Llangernyw, Abergele, Denbighshire, and formerly wife of Sir John Bruce Woollacott Ropner, 2nd Bt (*cr* 1952), and has issue by 1st and 2nd *m*.

Arms – Azure, on a chevron or, between three bezants, a laurel leaf vert.
Crest – A broken terrestrial globe, surmounted by a rain-bow proper.
Supporters – Two female figures representing "Hope" habited in loose garments and with hair dishevelled, each resting the exterior hand on an anchor all proper.
Seat – Hopetoun House, South Queensferry, W Lothian. *Town Residence* – 123 Beaufort St, SW3.

SONS LIVING (By 1st marriage)

ANDREW VICTOR ARTHUR CHARLES (*Earl of Hopetoun*), *b* 22 May 1969; *ed* Eton, and Exeter Coll, Oxford; a Page of Honour to HM Queen Elizabeth the Queen Mother 1984-86: *m* 1993, Skye Laurette, elder da of Maj Bristow Charles Bovill, 5th Royal Inniskilling Dragoon Gds, of Shipston-on-Stour, Warwicks (*see* Leigh, Bt, 1985 Edn), and has issue:—

DAUGHTERS LIVING - *Lady* Olivia Rose, *b* 1997, — *Lady* Georgina Anne, *b* 1998.
Lord Alexander John Adrian, *b* 1971.

(By 2nd marriage)

Lord Robert Charles Robin Adrian, *b* 1984.

DAUGHTER LIVING *(By 2nd marriage)*

Lady Louisa Vivienne, *b* 1981.

SISTER LIVING

Lady (Mary) Sarah Jane, *b* 1940: *m* 1967 (*m diss* 1978), Michael Gordon Learoyd, yr son of late Philip Halkett Brooke Learoyd, of Pryonnos, Britwell Salome, Watlington, Oxon, and has issue living, Jeremy Anthony Gordon, *b* 1971; *ed* Milton Abbey. *Residence* – East Lodge, Hopetoun, South Queensferry, W Lothian.

AUNT LIVING *(Daughter of 2nd Marquess)*

Lady Anne Adeline, *b* 1914: *m* 1939, Lt-Com Patrick Henry James Southby, RN (*see* Southby, Bt). *Address* – Robins Mill, Overbury, Tewkesbury, Glos.

COLLATERAL BRANCHES LIVING

Branch from yr son of 2nd Marquess

Issue of late Rt Hon Lord John Adrian Hope (*Baron Glendevon*), yr (twin) son of 2nd Marquess, *b* 1912, *d* 1996; *cr* Baron Glendevon 1964:—
See that title.

(In remainder to the Earldom of Hopetoun)

Branches from younger sons of 4th Earl of Hopetoun

Granddaughters of late John George Frederick Hope-Wallace, el son of Lt-Col Hon James Hope-Wallace, MP, 2nd son of 4th Earl of Hopetoun:—
Issue of late James Hope-Wallace, Lt Northumberland Fusiliers, *b* 1872, *ka* 1917: *m* 1909, Hon Ursula Mary Addington, who *d* 1962, da of 4th Viscount Sidmouth:—
Ruth, *b* 1911: *m* 1937, Capt Eric Cairns, Roy Northumberland Fusiliers, and has issue living, Jane, *b* 1939: *m* 1965, Peter Butcher, of Crooks Farm, Gilsland, Carlisle, Cumbria, and has issue living, David James Peter *b* 1967, — Clare, *b* 1947: *m* 1985, Michael Jeffery Steinberg, of 1216 Cornell Av, Berkeley, CA 94706, USA. *Residence* – Hallbank Head, Featherstone, Haltwhistle, Northumberland.

Issue of late Charles Nugent Hope-Wallace, MBE, *b* 1877; *d* 1953: *m* 1905, Mabel, who *d* 1970, da of late Col Allan Chaplin, formerly Madras Army:—
Dorothy Jacqueline, CBE, *b* 1909; *ed* Lady Margaret Hall, Oxford (BA); Under-Sec, Nat Assistance Board 1958-64, and Min of Housing and Local Govt 1965-69; ret 1969; a Commonwealth Fellow 1952-53; CBE (Civil) 1958. *Residence* – 17 Ashley Court, Morpeth Terrace, SW1P 1EN.

Grandson of late James Louis Alexander Hope, 2nd son of late Lt-Col Hon James Hope-Wallace, MP (ante):—
Issue of late Capt Laurence Nugent Hope, *b* 1890, *d* 1973: *m* 1st, 1919, Hilda Mary, who *d* 1938, only da of late Michael Joseph Hunter, JP, of Stoke Hall, Derbys; 2ndly, 1941, Constance Elizabeth Shell, who *d* 1996:—
(By 1st *m*) John Nugent (The Power House, Whitney-on-Wye, Herefords), *b* 1924; *ed* Eton, and Magdalene Coll, Camb: *m* 1st, 1953, Polly, el da of late Gen Sir Hugh Charles Stockwell, GCB, KBE, DSO; 2ndly, 1986, Mrs Penelope Berengaria Walker, el da of late Lawrence George Durrell, FRSL, the writer, and has issue living (by 1st *m*), Augustine Jason Nugent, *b* 1961: *m* 1991, Maureen Patricia, da of late Douglas Hymers, of Seattle, USA, and has issue living, John Gabriel *b* 1992, Annie Eloise *b* 1996.

Grandson of late Sir Charles Dunbar Hope-Dunbar, 6th Bt (who proved his claim to the Baronetcy of Dunbar of Baldoon 1916); grandson of late Hon Charles Hope, 3rd son of 4th Earl of Hopetoun:—
See Hope-Dunbar, Bt.

Granddaughter of late Capt Hon Louis Hope, 7th son of 4th Earl of Hopetoun:—
Issue of late Herbert George Hope, MBE, *b* 1875, *d* 1956: *m* 1920, May Winifred, who *d* 1960, da of late Lt-Col F. F. Sheppee, RA, and widow of John Harley:—
Isabel Susan, *b* 1922: *m* 1955, Peter Haviland Hiley, son of late Col Sir (Ernest) Haviland Hiley, KBE, and has issue living, William John Haviland (Ashley Hill House, Clarendon, Salisbury SP5 3HA), *b* 1960; *ed* Eton, and Bristol Univ: *m* 1993, Camilla Jane, elder of Charles Edward Weatherby, of Mixbury Lodge Farm, Brackley, Northants (*see* Ley, Bt), and has issue living, Harry Haviland *b* 1998, Tara Elizabeth *b* 1995. *Residence* – 7 St John's St, Chichester, Sussex PO19 1UR.

Branch from 4th son of 2nd Earl of Hopetoun

Grandchildren of late Capt George Everard Hope of Luffness, MC, only son of late Henry Walter Hope of Luffness, 2nd son of late George William Hope of Luffness, MP, 2nd son of late Gen Hon Sir Alexander Hope, GCB, 4th son of 2nd Earl of Hopetoun:—
Issue of late Col Archibald John George Hope of Luffness, MBE, RA, *b* 1912, *d* 1987: *m* 1937, Mary Pilar Elizabeth, who *d* 1989, yr da of late Brig-Gen Alister Fraser Gordon, CMG, DSO (*see* B Stafford, colls, 1969 Edn):—
George Archibald HOPE OF LUFFNESS (Luffness, Aberlady, E Lothian EH32 0QB), *b* 1938; *ed* Eton, and Edinburgh Univ; late Gren Gds and Royal Scots (TA); Kt of Honour and Devotion, Sov Mil Order of Malta; CA: *m* 1996, Anna Maria Willemina Jacoba, da of late Frederick Wilhelm Fabius, and of Mrs Anna Maria Wilhelmina Jacoba Labouchere Crommelin, of Zeist, Utrecht, The Netherlands, and widow of Jean Gaspart Haitsma Mulier, of Zeist, Utrecht, The Netherlands, and of Garsdon Manor, Chippenham, Wilts. ——— Margaret Mary Lucy, *b* 1940: *m* 1978, Richard Simon Baillie, of Allanbank, Lauder, Berwickshire TD2 6RW, elder son of Capt Alexander Maciej Gucewicz-Baillie, of Hendersyde, Kelso, Roxburghshire, and has issue living, Alexander Simon, *b* 1982, — Edward George, *b* 1985. ——— Mary Catherine Elizabeth, *b* 1943: *m* 1989, Bey Yalçin Adar, of Istanbul, Turkey. ——— Elizabeth Caroline (6 Rede Place, W2 4TU), *b* 1948: *m* 1984 (*m diss* 1998), James Patrick Scott, son of Munro Mackenzie Scott, of Cakemuir, Tynehead, Midlothian, and has issue living, James William Hope, *b* 1988, — Catriona Mary, *b* 1984. ——— Cecilia Mary, *b* 1952; *ed* St Andrew's Univ (MA): *m* 1987, Christopher Peter Latilla-Campbell, of Lochton, Abernyte, Perthshire PH14 9TA, elder son of Peter Latilla-Campbell, of Bulawayo, and of Mrs Merrick Burrell.

Granddaughter of late Maj John Alexander Henry Hope, only son of late Sir Edward Stanley Hope, KCB, 5th son of late George William Hope of Luffness, MP (ante):—
Issue of late Maj Edward James Hope, MC, *b* 1911, *d* 1989: *m* 1st, 1937 (*m diss* 1950), Enid, who *d* 1988, da of late Robert Gunther, of Parkwood, Englefield Green; 2ndly, 1952, Winifred Gwendolyne Marie (Ibstock Close, Little Tew, Oxon), el da of late Maj John Byng Paget:—
(By 1st *m*) Sarah Elizabeth (Avendale, 6 Nags Head Lane, Avening, Glos), *b* 1942: *m* 1964 (*m diss* 1987), Benjamin L. C. Wordsworth, and has issue living, Marcia, *b* 1965: *m* 1993, Mark Walton, of Christchurch, NZ, and has issue living, George Wordsworth *b* 1997, Sophie Wordsworth *b* 1994, — Lucy, *b* (twin) 1965: *m* 1992, Kostka Garcia Miñaur de la Rica, and has issue living, Lucas Dylan *b* 1992, Theo Gregory *b* 1995, Joe Patrick *b* 1996, — Rebecca, *b* 1967: *m* 1st, 1989 (*m diss* 1996), Julian A. Lloyd; 2ndly, 1996, Jason Peter Moore, and has issue living (by 1st *m*), Oscar Benjamin Wordsworth *b* 1989, (by 2nd *m*) Flora Wordsworth *b* 1997, Imogen Wordsworth *b* (twin) 1997.

Descendants of late Rt Hon James Fitzalan HOPE (*Baron Rankeillour*); *cr Baron Rankeillour* 1932, son of James Robert Hope-Scott, QC, 3rd son of Gen Hon Sir Alexander Hope, GCB (ante) (see that title).

Branch from 2nd son of 1st Earl of Hopetoun

Grandchildren of late Charles Douglas Hope (infra):—
Issue of late Major Adrian Alexander Hope, Transvaal Scottish, *b* 1897; *ka* in Italy 1945: *m* 1926, Eleanor (35 Leisure Gdns, Knysna 6570, S Africa), da of Lieut-Col George Ritchie Thomson, CMG, MB:—
William Adrian (9 Montagu St, Knysna 6570, S Africa), *b* 1927; *ed* Michaelhouse, Natal, at Witwatersrand Univ (BA), and at Trin Coll, Oxford (MA); an Advocate of Johannesburg, S Africa, and of Salisbury, Rhodesia; published *A Digest of Rhodesian Mining Law* 1965; 1939-45 War with S African Artillery in Italy: *m* 1960, Hazel, da of Adelbert Johnstone, of Gwelo, Rhodesia, and has issue living, Adrian Charles, *b* 1962, — James Graham, *b* 1970. — Patricia Anne, *b* 1961, — Sarah Jane, *b* 1964. ——— Anne Eleanor (407 Thayer Av, Silverspring, Md 20910, USA), *b* 1930, BA Rhodes Univ; Diploma in Education, Oxford.

Issue of late James Hope, *b* 1899, *d* 1970: *m* 1937, Doreen (1 Protea Flats, Protea Av, Fish Hoek, Cape 7975, S Africa), da of Prof Armstrong:—
Christopher James (273 Burton Rd, Oakville, Ontario L6K 2K7, Canada), *b* 1938: *m* 19—, Erica —, and has issue living, Thomas, *b* 19—. ——— Alastair Frederick (5 Malleson Rd, Mowbray, Cape, S Africa), *b* 1941: *m* 1963, Mary Elizabeth, da of Arthur Cecil Bilbrough, of Carmunnock, Somerset West, S Africa, and has issue living, Charles Andrew, *b* 1966, — Paul James, *b* 1968, — Bridget Moira, *b* 1964. ——— Angela Ruth Alice, *b* 1939: *m* 19— (*m diss* 19—), Warwick Manning, and has issue living, Joanne, *b* 19—.

Issue of Henry Francis Hope, *b* 1900, *d* 1971: *m* 1930, Aileen Elinor, who *d* 1993, da of late William Falkiner Harnett, CBE;—
Gillian Margaret, *b* 1933: *m* 1955, Neville Price Boyce, of 23 Ashwold Rd, Saxonwold, Johannesburg, and has issue living, Richard Henry Price, *b* 1957, — Diana Mary, *b* 1959. — Margaret Louise, *b* 1961. ——— Rosemary Patricia, *b* 1936: *m* 1963, Guy Everingham Hitchings, of Spring Bank, Speldhurst, Kent, and has issue living, Charles Robin, *b* 1967, — Mark Alexander, *b* 1969, — Andrew Hope, *b* 1971, — Alice Elizabeth, *b* 1965: *m* 1994, Michael Andrew Bennett, of 2 Dudley Rd, Wimbledon, SW19, and has issue living, William George *b* 1998.

Issue of late Charles Christopher Hope, *b* 1902, *d* 1963: *m* 1937, Una Mainguy, who *d* 1989, da of late W. P. Le Feuvre, MD, of Kenilworth, Cape Town:—
Charles Richard Christopher (Royal Canadian Yacht Club, and Royal Commonwealth Society), *b* 1938; *ed* Downside and Toronto Univ (BA): *m* 1970, Mary Lou da of John Francis Fitzpatrick of 178 King St, Saint John, New Brunswick, and has issue living, Mary Mainguy, *b* 1971, — Tiffany Anne Granton, *b* 1972.

Granddaughter of late Lieut-Col William Hope, VC, el son of late Rt Hon John Hope (Lord Justice Clerk of Scotland) el son of late Rt Hon Charles Hope (Lord Justice-Gen of Scotland), el son of late John Hope (*b* 1739), 2nd son of late Hon Charles Hope-Vere, 2nd son of 1st Earl of Hopetoun:—
Issue of late Charles Douglas Hope, *b* 1867, *d* 1947: *m* 1896, Alice Mary, who *d* 1947, da of Hon A. Wilmot (Papal Count, Papal Chamberlain), MLC, of Cape Colony:—

Patricia Anne (2642 Ottawa Av, W Vancouver, BC, Canada), b 1908: m 1937, Capt Sebastian F. Newdigate, DSC, RNR, who d 1954, and has issue living, Anne Charlotte, b 1938: m 1960, Humphrey Edward Waldock, of 3638 Osler St, Vancouver 9, BC, Canada, son of late Sir (Claud) Humphrey (Meredith) Waldock, CMG, OBE, QC, and has issue living, Harold Sebastian b 1961, Henry Bernard b 1962, Thomas Edward b 1965: m 1988, Jane Little, Mary Beatrice b 1969, Alice Patricia b 1973, Susan Katherine Margaret b 1977, — Lilah Mary Amphelis (Sister Mary Lucy) (Carmelite Monastery, PO Box 6, Kew, Vic 3101, Aust), b 1940.

Grandson of late Adm Sir George Price Webley Hope, KCB, KCMG, 2nd son of late Rear-Adm Charles Webley Hope (infra):—
Issue of late Brig Maurice Webley Hope, DSO, b 1901, d 1986: m 1943, Pamela, who d 1998, da of late J. K. Osborne, of NSW:—
David George Osborne, b 1944; ed Winchester, and Balliol Coll, Oxford: m 1970, Jane Lesley, da of Edward Ellis, of Durham, and has issue living, Joseph Cornelius Ellis, b 1971.

Grandchildren of late Rear-Adm Charles Webley Hope, only son of Rear-Adm Charles Webley Hope, 2nd son of the Rt Hon Charles Hope (Lord Justice-Gen of Scotland) (ante):—
Issue of late Lt-Col William Henry Webley Hope, CMG, b 1871, d 1919: m 1900, Florence, who d 1918, da of late Charles Walter Hill, of Clapham, Sussex:—
James Webley, OBE (SA4 Kenilworth Gdns, Bowral, NSW 2576; Australia (Sydney) Club), b 1903; Lt-Col (ret) S Wales Borderers; Waziristan 1937 (despatches), Burma 1945 (despatches, OBE); OBE (Mil) 1946: m 1st, 1928, Harriet Mary, who d 1931, da of late Henry Louis King, DL, JP, of Ballylin, Ferbane, King's co (V Bangor, colls); 2ndly, 1934, Veda Annie, who d 1986, da of late Dr Alfred Walter Campbell, of Sydney, Aust, and has issue living, (by 2nd m) Gillian Florence, b 1935: m 1961, Col George Mark Chirnside, late 13th/18th Hus, of Stone Cottage, Beer Hackett, Sherborne, Dorset.

Issue of the late Col Adrian Victor Webley Hope, CIE, b 1873, d 1960: m 1920, Ethel Mary, who d 1938, da of late J. S. Middleton, of Cadamaney, Mysore:—
Margaret Isobel, b 1921: m 1st, 1943 (m diss 1949), James Veitch Telfer; 2ndly, 1950, Squadron-Leader James Geoffrey Cutcliffe Hepburn, DFC, and has issue living, (by 1st m) Alison, b 1944; BA Oxon; PhD London: m 1970, Terence Parry Jones, and has issue living, William George Parry b 1976, Sally Louise Parry b 1974, — Kate, b 1947; MA Roy Coll of Art; has issue living, Usha Junge b 1978, — (by 2nd m) Harriet Rose, b 1965; BA Oxon; ACA. Residence - 68 Parliament Hill, Hampstead, NW3.

Issue of late Adm Herbert Willes Webley Hope, CB, CVO, DSO, RN, b 1878, d 1968: m 1905, Katherine Maria Antoinette, who d 1966, da of late Rev Francis Kewley:—
Ellen Katherine Webley, b 1907: m 1st, 1929 (m diss 1937), David William Heneker, formerly Lt-Col RASC, son of late Lt-Gen Sir William Charles Giffard Heneker, KCB, KCMG, DSO; 2ndly, 1941, Lt-Col Charles Vaughan King, OBE, Devonshire Regt, of 8 New Court, Sutton Manor, Sutton Scotney, Winchester, Hants, and has issue living (by 1st m), Peter David Grenfell (Parc Helyg, Llechryd, Cardigan, Dyfed SA43 2NJ), b 1931; ed Wellington Coll, and Brasenose Coll, Oxford: m 1954, Josephine Anne, eldest da of Lt-Col James William Lewis-Bowen, of Boncath, Dyfed, and has issue living, David Marius b 1958, Sam Gerald William b 1961, Nicholas Charles Adrian b 1963, Piers Herbert b 1964, Simon Thomas b 1965, — (by 2nd m) Adrian Charles Richard, b 1944.

Granddaughters of late Lieut-Col William Henry Webley Hope, CMG, 3rd son of Rear-Adm Charles Webley Hope (ante):—
Issue of late Lt-Cdr Charles Webley Hope, RN, b 1902; d on active ser: m 1933, Harriott Barbara, who d 1970, da of late Lt-Col R. G. E. Locke, DL, JP, of Hartlip House, Hartlip, Kent:—
Mary, b 1934. ——— Janet, b 1937: m 1960, Richard Wilson Froggatt, of Stonecross Farm, Wadhurst, Sussex, and has issue living, Ian Wilson, b 1962, — Peter Webley, b 1964: m 1990, Michele Hobday, and has issue living, Hayley Louise b 1990, — Nigel Thomas, b 1966, — Eric Charles (twin), b 1966, — Jenny Patricia (twin), b 1962: m 1987, Simon John Pickhaver, and has issue living, Joanna Ruth b 1990, Sarah Elizabeth b 1992, — Alison Clare (twin), b 1964.

Grandsons of late Adrian James Robert Hope, CIE, only son of late Charles William Hope, eldest son of late James Hope, 3rd son of late Rt Hon Charles Hope (Lord Justice-Gen of Scotland) (ante):—
Issue of late Charles Adrian Hope, b 1918, d 1986: m 1951, Susan Elizabeth Rona Kruse (23 Ann St, Edinburgh EH4 1PL):—
Adrian Kruse Anthony (The Old Smithy, Stobo, Borders EH45 8NX), b 1953; ed Edinburgh Acad, and Sheffield and Edinburgh Colls of Art; designer and silversmith: m 1977, Linda Caroline Lewin, and has issue living, Adam Poyntz, b 1981, — Thomas Joseph, b 1994, — Claire Evelyn, b 1984. ——— James William Drever (10 Brondesbury Park Mansions, NW6), b 1957; ed Edinburgh Acad, Bristol Univ and Bristol Old Vic Theatre Sch; actor.

Grandchildren of late James Arthur Hope, WS, only son of late David Boyle Hope, 2nd son of late James Hope, WS (ante):—
Issue of late Lt-Col Arthur Henry Cecil Hope, OBE, TD, WS, b 1896, d 1986: m 1937, Muriel Ann Neilson Collie (8A Randolph Cliff, Edinburgh EH3 7TZ):—
James Arthur David, PC (Baron Hope of Craighead), b 1938; cr Baron Hope of Craighead (Life Baron) 1995 (see that title). ——— John William Lewis (12B Moray Place, Edinburgh EH3 6DT), b 1940; ed Edinburgh Acad, and St Andrews Univ (MA): m 1974, Hazel late Goh Mei Ling, da of Goh Siew Hiong, of Kuching, Sarawak, Borneo, and has issue living, Charles Arthur Robertson, b 1976; ed Edinburgh Acad, and UMIST (BEng), — Thomas John Alexander, b 1978; ed Edinburgh Acad, — Geraldine Katherine Ann, b 1982. ——— Alexander Robertson Boyle (Croftinloan Sch, Pitlochry, Perthshire), b 1947; ed Edinburgh Acad, Rugby, and Durham Univ (BA). ——— Elspeth Mary Neilson (7 Irvine Place, Aberdeen), b (twin) 1947: m 1969 (m diss 1994), Dolf Andries Mogendorff, and has issue living, Andrew Michael Alexander, b 1972, — Richard Arthur John, b 1974, — David Martin James, b 1978, — Robin Paul Neilson, b 1980. ——— Angela Muriel Evelyn (812 Linkleas Av, Victoria, BC, Canada V8S 5C3), b 1948; SRN: m 1976 (m diss 1995), Brian Richard Anscombe, and has issue living, Philip Hayward, b 1979, — Jaqueline Hope, b 1981.

Issue of late Lt-Col James Louis Hope, TD, WS, b 1906, d 1995: m 1939, Kathleen Colquhoun Sconce:—

Charles Louis (Woodside, Ockham Rd North, W Horsley, Surrey), *b* 1940; *ed* Edinburgh Acad, Rugby, and Magdalene Coll, Camb (MA); CEng, MIEE: *m* 1963, Susan Jane Elizabeth McDowall, and has issue living, Joanna Mary, *b* 1968, — Fiona Jane, *b* 1972. —— Michael Edmund (The Hermitage, Evershot, Dorchester DT2 0PQ), *b* 1943; *ed* Edinburgh Acad, Rugby, Trin Coll, Dublin (BA), and St Andrews Univ (MA).

Descendants of Vice-Adm Sir William Johnstone-Hope, GCB, 3rd son of John Hope (*b* 1739), 2nd son of Hon Charles Hope-Vere, 2nd son of 1st Earl of Hopetoun:—
See E Annandale and Hartfell.

Grandchildren of late Charles Hope (*b* 1845) yr son of Maj-Gen Frederick Hope, 2nd son of Capt Charles Hope, RN, 4th son of Hon Charles Hope-Vere (ante):—
Issue of late Charles Henry Sawyer Hope, *b* 1880, *d* 1964: *m* 1913, Olive Lois, who *d* 1954, da of late Arthur Francis Godwin, of 16 Hans Place SW1:—
Jaqueline (42 Telegraph Lane East, Norwich), *b* 1914; a State Registered Physiotherapist, Supt Physiotherapist Univ Coll Hosp West Indies 1953-55, Norfolk and Norwich Hospital 1950-53 and 1955-73; MCSP; 1939-45 War with Naval VAD. —— Anne Vere, *b* 1918; 1939-45 War with ATS, as architectural draughtswoman; *d* 1996.

Issue of late George Leonard Nelson Hope, *b* 1884, *d* 1973: *m* 1908 Honoria Mary Victoria, who *d* 1968, yst da of late John Giffard Riddell, of Swinburne Castle and Felton Park, Northumberland:—
†*Sir* (Charles) Peter, KCMG, TD, *b* 1912; *ed* Oratory Sch and London (BSc), and Camb Univs; 1939-45 War as Lt-Col RA; HM Foreign Ser 1946 as 1st Sec Paris; Assist Head of UN Dept; FO 1950, Counsellor, Bonn 1953, Head of News Dept, FO 1956, HM Min, Madrid 1959, HM Consul-Gen for Texas and New Mexico 1963, Alternate British Repres to UN 1965-68, and Ambassador to Mexico 1968-72; Grand Cross Order of Aztec Eagle of Mexico; TD 1946, KStJ 1984; CMG 1957, KCMG 1972: *m* 1936, Hazel Mary (*Lady Hope*) (Guillard's Oak House, Midhurst, W Sussex), da of late G. L. Turner, and *d* 1999, having had issue, (Charles) Jeremy (Netherhill, Awbridge, Romsey, Hants SO51 0HG), *b* 1937, *ed* Downside; late Gren Gds; *m* 1961, Judith Ann, da of late H. T. Pearce, and has issue living, Dominic Mark *b* 1963, Jonathon Paul *b* 1965, — Adrian Philip, *b* 1942; *ed* Downside, and Trin Coll, Camb, — †Richard Andrew, *b* 1947; *ed* Downside, and St Thomas Univ, Houston, Texas; *d* 1994.

PREDECESSORS – (**1**)*Sir* CHARLES Hope, KT, grandson of late Sir James Hope, KB, 6th son of Sir Thomas Hope, 1st Bt (*cr* 1628); *cr Lord Hope, Viscount Aithrie* and *Earl of Hopetoun* (peerage of Scotland) 1703, with remainder to heirs male and female of his body; *d* 1742; *s* by his son (**2**) JOHN, 2nd Earl, in whom the *Baronetcy* (*cr* NS 1698) of Kirkliston; became vested on the death of the 3rd Bt 1783; Lord High Commr to Gen Assembly of Church of Scotland; *d* 1781; *s* by his son (**3**) JAMES, 3rd Earl; Lord-Lieut of co Linlithgow, and a Representative Peer 1784-94; in 1792 *s* to the estates of his grand-uncle, George, 3rd Marquess of Annandale (title dormant), and assumed the additional surname of Johnstone; *cr Baron Hopetoun*, of Hopetoun (peerage of United Kingdom) 1809, with remainder to the heirs male of his father; *d* 1817; *s* by his half-brother (**4**) JOHN, GCB, 4th Earl; Col of 42nd Regt, a distinguished Gen in the Peninsula; *cr Baron Niddry*, of Niddry Castle, co Linlithgow (peerage of United Kingdom) 1814, with remainder to the male issue of his father; *d* 1823; *s* by his son (**5**) JOHN, 5th Earl; Lord-Lieut of co Linlithgow; *d* 1843; *s* by his son (**6**) JOHN ALEXANDER, 6th Earl; *b* 1831; Lord-Lieut of co Linlithgow: *m* 1860, Ethelred Anne, who *d* 1884, da of Charles Thomas Samuel Birch-Reynardson, of Holywell Hall, near Stamford; *d* 1873; *s* by his son (**7**) JOHN ADRIAN LOUIS, KT, GCMG, GCVO, PC, 7th Earl; *b* 1860; a Lord-in-Waiting to Queen Victoria 1885-6 and 1886-9, Lord High Commr of Gen Assembly of Church of Scotland 1887-9, Gov of Victoria 1889-95, Paymaster-Gen 1895-8, Lord Chamberlain of Queen Victoria's Household 1898-1900, first Gov-Gen of the Commonwealth of Australia 1900-1902, and Sec for Scotland and Keeper of the Great Seal of Scotland, with a seat in the Cabinet Feb to Dec 1905; *cr Marquess of Linlithgow*, co Linlithgow or West Lothian (peerage of United Kingdom) 1902: *m* 1886, Hon Hersey Alice Eveleigh-de Moleyns, who *d* 1937, da of 4th Baron Ventry; *d* 1908; *s* by his son (**8**) *Rt Hon* VICTOR ALEXANDER JOHN, KG, KT, GCSI, GCIE, OBE, TD, 2nd Marquess; *b* 1887; Civil Lord of the Admiralty 1922-24, Viceroy and Gov-Gen of India 1936-43, and Lord High Commr to Gen Assembly of Church of Scotland 1944-45; Chancellor of Edinburgh Univ 1944: Lord-Lieut of W Lothian, Capt King's Body Guard for Scotland (Roy Co of Archers), Chm Midland Bank 1945-52, and a PC, *m* 1911, Doreen Maud, CI, who *d* 1965, yr da of Rt Hon Sir Frederick George Milner, 7th Bt; *d* 1952; *s* by his son (**9**) CHARLES WILLIAM FREDERICK, TD, MC, 3rd Marquess, *b* 1912 (twin), Capt Lothians and Border Horse, RAC (TA), Lieut Scots Guards (Reserve), Lord Lieut W Lothian, 1939-43 War (prisoner): *m* 1st, 1939, Vivien, who *d* 1963, da of Capt Robert Orlando Rodolph Kenyon-Slaney (B Kenyon, colls); 2ndly, 1965, Judith, who *d* 1991, da of late Stanley Matthew Lawson, of Cincinnati, USA, widow of Lt-Col Esmond Charles Baring, OBE (*see* B Ashburton, colls), and formerly wife of John Symonds Radway; *d* 1987; *s* by his only son (by 1st *m*), (**10**) ADRIAN JOHN CHARLES, 4th Marquess and present peer; also Earl of Hopetoun, Viscount Aithrie, Lord Hope, Baron Hopetoun, and Baron Niddry.

LISBURNE, EARL OF (Vaughan) (Earl I 1776)

I will not return unavenged

JOHN DAVID MALET VAUGHAN, 8th Earl; *b* 1 Sept 1918; *s* 1965; *ed* Eton, and Magdalen Coll, Oxford (MA); Bar Inner Temple 1948; patron of one living; 1939-45 War as Capt Welsh Guards: *m* 1943, Mary Shelagh, da of late T. A. Macauley, of Montreal, Canada, and has issue.

Arms – Sable, a chevron between three fleurs-de-lis argent. **Crest** – An arm embowed in armour, the hand holding a sword, point to the sinister, all proper. **Supporters** – *Dexter*, a dragon reguardant, armed and langued or, collared sable and chained gold, the collar charged with three fleurs-de-lis argent; *sinister*, a unicorn reguardant argent, the mane, horn and hoofs or, collared and chained as the other. *Residence* – The Manor House, Hopton Wafers, Kidderminster, Worcs DY14 2NA.

SONS LIVING

DAVID JOHN FRANCIS MALET (*Viscount Vaughan*) *b* 15 June 1945; *ed* Ampleforth: *m* 1973, Jennifer Jane, only da of late James Desiré John William Fraser Campbell, of Glengarry, Inverness-shire, and has issue:—

SON LIVING—*Hon* Digby Dylan, *b* 1973.

DAUGHTER LIVING   *Hon* Lucy Bronwyn, *b* 1971.

Hon Michael John Wilmot Malet, *b* 1948; *ed* Ampleforth, and New Coll, Oxford (MA): *m* 1978, Hon Lucinda Mary Louise Baring, da of 7th Baron Ashburton, and has issue living, Edward Wilmot Malet, *b* 1998, — Emma Rose Nightingale, *b* 1993, — Sophie Louise Malet, *b* 1994. *Residences* – 44 Tite St, SW3; Itchen Stoke House, Alresford, Hants SO24 0QU.

Hon John Edward Malet, *b* 1952; *ed* Ampleforth, and RAC Cirencester: *m* 1st, 1977 (*m diss* 1983), Catharine Euphan, only da of J. P. Waterer, of Coombe Bissett, Salisbury; 2ndly, 1989, Sandra Caroline, formerly wife of Michael Charles Craufurd Cooper, and da of Lt-Col Brian Harold Thomson, DL, of Kemback House, by Cupar, Fife, and has issue living (by 2nd *m*), Henry John Augustus, *b* 1990. *Residence* – 6 Broomwood Rd, SW11 6HT.

SISTERS LIVING

Lady Honor Morvyth Malet, *b* 1919; a JP for Cardiganshire: *m* 1943, Maj William Herbert Rhidian Llewellyn, MC, Welsh Gds, of 4 St Omer Rd, Guildford, Surrey GU1 2DB (*see* Llewellyn, Bt, *cr* 1922).

Lady Auriel Rosemary Malet, *b* 1923. *Residence* – Haute Folie de Breux, par Tillières sur Avre, 27570 Eure, France

COLLATERAL BRANCH LIVING

Grandson of late Edmund Mallet Vaughan, son of late Hon William Mallet Vaughan, 4th son of 3rd Earl:—

Issue of late Major Eugène Napoléon Ernest Mallet Vaughan, DSO, *b* 1878, *d* 1934: *m* 1914, Hilda Winifred, who *d* 1972, el da of late Neville Hanbury Mander, of Penn Wolverhampton:—

Edmund Bernard Mallet (The Bath Farm, Codsall Wood, Wolverhampton) *b* 1920; Maj (ret) late Gren Gds: *m* 1950, Jean, only da of late Col John Walton Nelson, of Sevenoaks, Kent, and has issue living, David John, *b* 1953: *m* 1st, 1990 (*m diss* 1997), Lynette Luckett; 2ndly, 1998, Janet Burley, — Michael Edmund, *b* 1957: *m* 1988, Rowena Jane, da of John Pettit, of Roselawn, Freshford, Bath, and has issue living, Tess Anne *b* 1996, — Diana Mary (62 Yeldham Rd, W6 8JG) *b* (twin), 1953.

PREDECESSORS – (1)JOHN Vaughan, MP for Cardiganshire in several Parliaments; *cr Baron Fethard*, of Feathered, co Tipperary, and *Viscount Lisburne* (peerage of Ireland) 1695: *d* 1720; *s* by his el son (2) JOHN, 2nd Viscount; *d* 1741; *s* by hs brother (3) WILMOT, 3rd Viscount; *d* 1766; *s* by his son (4) WILMOT, 4th Viscount; was MP for Cardiganshire 1755-61 and 1768-96, Lord-Lieut of Cardiganshire, a Lord of Trade 1768, and a Lord of the Admiralty 1770-82; *cr Earl of Lisburne* (peerage of Ireland) 1776; *d* 1800; *s* by his el son (5) WILMOT, 2nd Earl; *d* 1820; *s* by his half-brother (6) JOHN, 3rd Earl; Col in the Army; *d* 1831; *s* by his 2nd son (7) ERNEST AUGUSTUS, 4th Earl; *b* 1800: *m* 1st, 1835, Mary, who *d* 1851, da of Sir Lawrence Palk, 2nd Bt; 2ndly, 1853, Hon Elizabeth Augusta Harriett, who *d* 1883 (formerly a Maid of Honour to HM Queen Adelaide), da of Col Hugh Henry Mitchell: *d* 1873; *s* by his son (8) ERNEST AUGUSTUS MALLET, 5th Earl, *b* 1836: *m* 1st, 1858, Laura Gertrude, who *d* 1865, da of Edwyn Burnaby, of Baggrave Hall, Leicester; 2ndly, Alice Dalton, who *d* 1933 (having *m* 2ndly, 1889, as his 2nd wife, 3rd Earl Amherst, who *d* 1910; 3rdly, 1914, HSH Prince Jean Sapieha-Kodenski), da of late Edmund Probyn, of Huntley Manor, near Gloucester; *d* 1888; *s* by his son (9) ERNEST GEORGE HENRY ARTHUR, 6th Earl; *b* 1862: *m* 1888, Evelyn, who *d* 1931, da of late Edmund Probyn, of Huntley Manor and Longhope, Gloucester; *d* 1899; *s* by his son (10) ERNEST EDMUND HENRY MALET, 7th Earl; *b* 1892; Lord-Lieut for Cardiganshire 1923-56 (Sheriff 1923): *m* 1st, 1914, Regina, who *d* 1944, da of late Don Julio Bittencourt, Attaché to Chilean Legation in London; 2ndly, 1961, Audrey Maureen Leslie, who *d* 1978, yst da of late James Meakin, of Westwood Manor, Staffs, and widow of Hon Robert Godfrey de Bohun Devereux (V Hereford); *d* 1965; *s* by his son (11) JOHN DAVID MALET, 8th Earl and present peer; also Viscount Lisburne, and Baron Fethard.

LISLE, BARON (Lysaght) (Baron I 1758)
(Title pronounced "Lyle") (Name pronounced "Lycett")

Wars! horrid wars!

PATRICK JAMES LYSAGHT, 8th Baron; *b* 1 May 1931; *s* 1997; *ed* Shrewsbury: *m* 1957 (*m diss* 1979), Mary Louise, 2nd da of late Lt-Col Geoffrey Reginald Devereux Shaw, of Scottow Hall, Norfolk (*see* Durrant, Bt, 1960 Edn), and formerly wife of Euan Guy Shaw-Stewart (later 10th Bt), and has issue.

Arms – Argent, three spears erect gules, on a chief azure, a lion passant guardant or. Crest – A dexter arm embowed in armour, the hand holding a sword proper. Supporters – Two lions or.
Residence – 30 Springhurst House, Greenham, Newbury, Berks RG14 7UD.

SONS LIVING

Hon (JOHN) NICHOLAS GEOFFREY, *b* 20 May 1960; *ed* Lingfield. *Residence* – 50 The Fairstead, Scottow, Norwich, Norfolk NR10 5AQ.

Hon David James, *b* 1963; *ed* East Anglia Univ (BSc): *m* 1989, Rebecca, da of Russell Charles Abbott, of Norwich, and has issue living, George, *b* 1997, — Matilda, *b* 1995. *Residence* – Wayside Cottage, Ingham, Norfolk NR12 9TQ.

DAUGHTER LIVING

Hon Mary-Jane, *b* 1959: *m* 1986, Paul Stephen Roberts, and has issue living, Lucy, *b* 1988. *Residence* – Carpenters Town, Castle Pollard, Mullingar, co Westmeath.

BROTHER LIVING

Dermot Edward (Crews Court, Upton Bishop, Herefords), *b* 1935; *ed* Dauntseys; late 2nd Lieut 8th King's Royal Irish Hussars: *m* 1961, Tessa Susan, only da of late Capt Terence Hugh Back, CBE, RN, of Blaisdon House, nr Longhope, Glos, and has issue living, Cornelius James Terence (16A Dunraven Rd, W12), *b* 1965; *ed* Eton; racing correspondent, — Georgina Mary, *b* 1966; *ed* Exeter Univ (BA 1988).

HALF-SISTERS LIVING

Deirdre Elizabeth, *b* 1954: *m* 1991, Ian Granville Ward, and has issue living, Amy, *b* 1993, — Pippa, *b* 1996. *Residence* – 12 Birch Close, Undy Magor, Monmouthshire NP6 3LW.

Phillipa Jane, *b* 1955; late Flt-Lt PMRAFNS: *m* 1982, Paul McMahon, late Maj RCT, and has issue living, Samuel James, *b* 1985, — Jack, *b* 1988.

STEPMOTHER LIVING

Vyrna, da of John Evan Jones, of Pontypool: *m* 1952, as his 2nd wife, Horace James William Lysaght, who *d* 1977, yr brother of 7th Baron Lisle. *Residence* – 12 St John's Gdns, Chepstow, Monmouthshire.

COLLATERAL BRANCHES LIVING

Issue of late George Henry Lysaght, yst brother of 7th Baron (ante), *b* 1911, *d* 1985: *m* 1935, Pauline Ann, elder da of Patrick J. Dillon, of The Grove, Girley, Kells, co Meath:—
Horace George (Abbeycourt, Kinsale, co Cork), *b* 1936: *m* 1961, Anne Phyllis, da of late David Daly, of Cork, and has issue living, Stephen Henry, *b* 1963, — John Gareth *b* 1965, — Susan Anne, *b* 1962, — Jennifer Mary, *b* 1967. —— Lawrence George (Killestry, Killaloe, co Clare), *b* 1937; LRCPI, LRCSI. —— John Patrick George (Vancouver, BC, Canada), *b* 1939. —— Pauline Anne, *b* 1942.

Grandchildren of late Rev John Arthur Constantine Lysaght (infra):—
Issue of late John Charles Fettiplace Lysaght, *b* 1909, *d* 1976: *m* 1939, Phyllis Jean, who *d* 1976, da of late T. H. Massey, of Newcastle, NSW:—
John Daniel Blandy (PO Box 100 Austinmer, NSW 2515, Australia), *b* 1943: *m* 1976, Pauline McCormack, da of late Paul Patrick McCormack, and has issue living, Georgia, *b* 1981, — Philippa, *b* 1983, — and an adopted stepson, Scott, *b* 1969. —— Nicholas Richard Fettiplace (21 Brookside Av, Kelmscott, W Australia 6111), *b* 1946: *m* 1980, Maria Emelyn, da of late Lamberto Madla, and has issue living, Michael Charles Fettiplace, *b* 1983, — Kristian Robert Vaughan, *b* 1984, — Primrose May Louise, *b* 1985. —— Primrose Mary, *b* 1940: *m* 1st, 1963 (*m diss* 1981), Jørgen Andersen; 2ndly, 1988, Ian Ross Sully, of 7 Laurel St, Willoughby, NSW 2068, Australia, and has issue living (by 1st *m*), Kristian Charles, *b* 1967, — Timothy Jørgen, *b* 1971. —— Sarah Louise (92 Dover St, Hawthorne, Queensland 4171, Australia), *b* 1953; has issue living, James Charles LYSAGHT, *b* 1984.

Issue of late Nicholas Henry Lyster Lysaght, TD, DL, *b* 1911, *d* 1977: *m* 1950, Gillian Mary (6 Hafod Gdns, Ponthir, Newport, Gwent; Naval and Military Club), da of R. F. Huggett, of Risca, Gwent:—
Mary Susan, *b* 1952: *m* 1988, John Wallace Lanning, son of Maj E. C. Lanning, MBE, FSA, of S Godstone, Surrey, and has issue living, Sophie Alexandra Rose, *b* 1991, — Gemma Katherine Amy, *b* 1994. —— Philippa Jane, *b* 1954: *m* 1985,

Nicholas M. S. Dale-Harris, eldest son of T. I. Dale-Harris, of Milson Rd, W14, and Mrs Allday, of Tretire, Herefordshire, and has issue living, Lucy Annabel, *b* 1986, — Polly Louise, *b* 1988, — Chloe Alexandra, *b* 1989. —— Elizabeth Anne, *b* 1961: *m* 1986, Wayne Vernon Lysaght-Mason (formerly Mason), of Walnut Tree Cottage, 112 Chester Rd, Hazel Grove, Stockport, Cheshire SK7 6HE, 2nd son of late B. A. Mason, of Walsgrave, Coventry, and has issue living, Charlotte Jennifer, *b* 1991, — Abigail Frances, *b* 1992.

Issue of late W/Cdr Philip Michael Vaughan Lysaght, Auxiliary Air Force, *b* 1914; *ka* 1943: *m* 1941, Christine, who *d* 1968, having *m* 2ndly, 1948, Cdr C. G. Procter, RN (ret) (RR9, Wood Lake, Columbus 47201, Indiana, USA), da of late W. Mackenzie Edwards, of Inverness:—
Diana Mary Philippa, *b* 1943: *m* 1962, Graham Edward Frank Snell, of 2B Moor Park Rd, SW6, and has issue living, Matthew Michael Charles, *b* 1965, — Louise Jane, *b* 1969.

Grandchildren of late Rev Hon Henry Lysaght, 4th son of 5th Baron:—
Issue of late Rev John Arthur Constantine Lysaght, *b* 1876, *d* 1950: *m* 1902, Mary Nicholl, who *d* 1967, da of Adam Fettiplace Blandy, of The Warren, Abingdon:—
Christopher David Blandy, *b* 1919. —— Winifred Joyce, *b* 1903.

PREDECESSORS – (1) JOHN Lysaght, MP for Charleville 1727; *cr Baron Lisle*, of Mount North, co Cork (peerage of Ireland) 1758; *d* 1781; *s* by his son (2) JOHN, 2nd Baron; *d* 1798; *s* by his el son (3) JOHN, 3rd Baron; *dsp* 1834; *s* by his brother (4) GEORGE, 4th Baron, *b* 1783: *m* 1st, 1810, Elizabeth, who *d* 1815, da of Samuel Knight; 2ndly, 1816, Elizabeth Anne, who *d* 1825, da of John Davy Foulkes; 3rdly, 1836, Elizabeth, who *d* 1855, da of John Church; *d* 1868; *s* by his son (5) JOHN ARTHUR, 5th Baron; *b* 1811: *m* 1837, Henrietta Anne, sister of his stepmother, who *d* 1860, da of late John Church; *d* 1898; *s* by his el son (6) GEORGE WILLIAM JAMES, 6th Baron; *b* 1840: served throughout Maori War 1864-5; *m* 1868, Amy Emily, who *d* 1918, da of late Ayliffe Langford, of St Heliers, Jersey, and Ventnor, Isle of Wight; *d* 1919; *s* by hs grandson (7) JOHN NICHOLAS HORACE (son of late Hon Horace George Lysaght, only son of 6th Baron), 7th Baron; *b* 1903; Founder Member Irish Peers Assocn; served in Home Guard in 1939-45 war: *m* 1st, 1928 (*m diss* 1939), Vivienne, who *d* 1948, da of Rev M. Brew; 2ndly, 1939, Marie Helen, who *d* 1999, da of late Adolph D. Purgold, of Parkgate, Cheshire; *d* 1997; *s* by his nephew (8) PATRICK JAMES (elder son late Horace James William Lysaght, 2nd son of late Hon Horace George Lysaght, only son of 6th Baron), 8th Baron and present peer.

Lister, Cunliffe-, family name of Earl of Swinton.

LISTOWEL, EARL OF (Hare) Sits as BARON HARE (UK 1869) (Earl I 1822)

I hate whatever is profane

FRANCIS MICHAEL HARE, 6th Earl; *b* 28 June 1964; *s* 1997; *ed* Westminster, and London Univ.

Arms – Gules, two bars and a chief indented or. **Crest** – A demi-lion rampant argent, ducally gorged or. **Supporters** – Two dragons, ermine. *Residence* – 10 Downshire Hill, NW3.

BROTHER LIVING

Hon TIMOTHY PATRICK, *b* 23 Feb 1966.

SISTER LIVING

Lady Diana, *b* 1965: *m* 1990, Timothy John Voss, yst son of Douglas J. Voss, of Adelaide, Australia, and has issue living, Billy Douglas, *b* 1998.

HALF SISTERS LIVING (*Daughter of 5th Earl by 1st marriage*)

Lady Deirdre Freda Mary (*Baroness Grantley*), *b* 1935; *ed* Lady Margaret Hall, Oxford: *m* 1955, 7th Baron Grantley, who *d* 1995. *Residences* – Markenfield Hall, Ripon, N Yorkshire; 53 Lower Belgrave St, SW1.

(*Daughter of 5th Earl by 2nd marriage*)

Lady Fiona Eve Akua, *b* 1960: *m* 1987, Christopher Geordie Douglas Mackintosh, son of Charles Mackintosh, of Calgary, Alberta, Canada, and has issue living, Billy Douglas, *b* 1990, — Emma Frances, *b* 1988, — Zoë Beatrice, *b* 1992. *Residence* – 133 Sunnyside Av, Ottawa, Ontario, Canada K1S 0R2.

AUNT LIVING (*Daughter of 4th Earl*)

Lady (Ethel) Patricia (*Lady Patricia Milnes-Coates*), *b* 1912: *m* 1st, 1936, Lt-Col Charles Thomas Milnes Gaskell, Coldm Gds, who was *k* in an aeroplane accident on active ser 1943 (E Ranfurly); 2ndly, 1945, Lt-Col Sir Robert Edward James Clive Milnes-Coates, 3rd Bt, DSO, Coldm Gds, who *d* 1982, and has issue living, (by 1st *m*) James (Montpelier Plantation, Nevis, W Indies), *b* 1937; *ed* Eton, and Queens' Coll, Camb: *m* 1982, Celia Elizabeth Voelcker, of Montpelier, Nevis, West Indies, and has issue living, Charles Paul *b* 1983, Anna Elizabeth *b* 1985, — Andrew (3 St James Rd, Tunbridge Wells, Kent), *b* 1939; *ed* Eton, and Trin Coll, Dublin, — Tom (Rome, Italy), *b* 1942; *ed* Eton, and McGill Univ, — (by 2nd *m*) (*see* Milnes-Coates, Bt). *Residence* – Moor House Farm, Helperby, York.

WIDOW LIVING OF SON OF FOURTH EARL

Jill Peggotty, yr da of late (Frank William) Gordon North, of Pinner, Middx: *m* 1945, Maj Hon Alan Victor Hare, MC, who *d* 1995, and has issue (see colls, infra). *Residence* – 53 Rutland Gate, SW7.

WIDOW LIVING OF FIFTH EARL

PAMELA MOLLY (*Countess of Listowel*), da of late Francis Day, of Croydon, Surrey, and formerly wife of John Alexander Read: *m* 1963, as his 3rd wife, the 5th Earl of Listowel, GCMG, PC, who *d* 1997. *Residence* – 10 Downshire Hill, NW3.

COLLATERAL BRANCHES LIVING

Issue of late Rt Hon John Hugh Hare, OBE, PC (*Viscount Blakenham*), 3rd son of 4th Earl:—
See Blakenham, V.

Issue of late Maj Hon Alan Victor Hare, MC, 4th and yst son of 4th Earl, *b* 1919, *d* 1995: *m* 1945, Jill Peggotty (ante), yr da of late (Frank William) Gordon North, of Pinner, Middx:—
(Alan Simon) Mercury (11 Denbigh St, SW1), *b* 1948; *ed* Eton: *m* 1988, Hon (Alexandra) Elizabeth Charmian Amery, yst da of Baron Amery of Lustleigh, PC (Life Baron), and has issue living, Alice Alexandra, *b* 1989, — Florence Freda, *b* 1993. —— Marcia Persephone (*Viscountess Blakenham*), *b* 1946: *m* 1965, her cousin, 2nd Viscount Blakenham, and has issue (see that title).

Granddaughters of late Capt Harry Vivian Hare (infra):—
Issue of late Capt Richard George Windham Hare, OBE, RN, *b* 1910, *d* 1995: *m* 1937, Doreen Chetwode, who *d* 1993, da of late Rev Nixon Chetwode Ram:—
(Rosemary) Vivien, *b* 1939: *m* 1961, Roger Philip Laurence Chetwode Clarke, of 207 Monroe Drive, Williamsville, NY 14221, USA, and has issue living, Dominic Windham, *b* 1963, —— Cleone Rachel Vivien, *b* 1964. —— Caroline Veronica, *b* 1941: *m* 1968, Richard Baden Bradley, late Capt Royal Fus, of 14 Moore St, SW3 2QN, and has issue living, Robert Edward Baden, *b* 1969, — Virginia Clare Baden, *b* 1970, — Victoria Elizabeth Baden, *b* 1973. —— (Shelagh) Virginia, *b* (twin) 1941: *m* 1964 (*m diss* 1983), James Alan Edward Morshead, and has issue living, Charmian Juliet, *b* 1966, — Veronica Anne, *b* 1969, — Caroline Violet, *b* 1971: *m* 1997, Philip R. Henson, yst son of Richard Henson, of Braceby Lincs.

Granddaughter of late Rear-Adm Hon Richard Hare, 2nd son of 2nd Earl:—
Issue of late Capt Harry Vivian Hare, *b* 1881, *ka* 1914: *m* 1908, Ellen Louisa Marie, who *d* 1968, da of Sir Edward Hudson Hudson-Kinahan, 1st Bt:—
Emily Lavender, *b* 1912: *m* 1st, 1935, Tom E. Montgomery, who *d* of wounds received at Arnhem 1944; 2ndly, 1948, Ronald Paul Lancaster Rose, who *d* 1977 (*see* Rose, Bt *cr* 1874, colls), and has issue living (by 1st *m*), Thomas Carey *b* 1937, — Dawn Vivian *b* 1936: *m* 1963, David Connington, of Warden's Lodge, Kingston, Ilminster, Som, and has issue living, Sarah Rose *b* 1964, Lucy Clare *b* 1966.

Granddaughters of late Hon Henry Hare, 4th son of 2nd Earl:—
Issue of late Capt Percy Richard Hare, TD, *b* 1870, *d* 1937: *m* 1903, Matilda Gertrude, who *d* 1972, da of late Henry F. Tiarks, of Foxbury, Chislehurst:—
Victoria Katherine, *b* 1914: *m* 1961, as his 2nd wife, Maj George Seton Wills, Roy Wilts Yeo, who *d* 1979 (*see* Wills Bt, *cr* 1904). *Residence* – Eastridge, Ramsbury, nr Marlborough, Wilts. —— Lilah Mary, *b* 1915: *m* 1st, 1935 (*m diss* 1946), Maj George Seton Wills, Roy Wilts Yeo, who *d* 1979 (ante); 2ndly, 1946, as his 2nd wife, Col Nigel Victor Stopford Sackville, CBE, TD, who *d* 1972 (*see* E Courtown, colls). *Residence* – West Farm House, Collingbourne Ducis, nr Marlborough, Wilts SN8 3DZ.

Grandchildren of late Brig-Gen Robert William Hare, CMG, DSO (infra):—
Issue of late Lt-Col Robert Gerald Dillon Hare, late Royal Norfolk Regt, *b* 1910, *d* 1997: *m* 1951, Evelyn Nora, who *d* 1994, da of late Thomas Pratt, of Teddington, Middx:—
Anthony Gerald (3 Roseneath Av, Winchmore Hill, N21 3NE), *b* 1956. —— Carolyn Elizabeth, *b* 1952: *m* 1990, Martin Douglas Noble, of Nab Cottage, 19 Alexandra Av, Hayling Island, Hants PO11 9AL, and has issue living, Lucy Robin Elizabeth, *b* 1990, — Elizabeth Rose Eleanor, *b* 1993.

Granddaughters of late Robert Dillon Hare, son of late Hon Robert Hare, brother of 2nd Earl:—
Issue of late Brig-Gen Robert William Hare, CMG, DSO, late Norfolk Regt, *b* 1872, *d* 1953: *m* 1908, Helen Mary, who *d* 1972, da of late Lt-Col Guy Newcomen Atkinson, JP (E Kingston, colls):—

Elizabeth (*Elizabeth, Lady Shakespeare*) *b* 1914; Freeman of City of London 1974; Section Officer WAAF 1940-45 (despatches, Bronze Star of USA): *m* 1952, as his 2nd wife, Rt Hon Sir Geoffrey Hithersay Shakespeare, 1st Bt, who *d* 1980. *Residence* – 36 Clare Park, Crondall, nr Farnham, Surrey GU10 5DT. —— Nancy Violet (*Lady Temple*), *b* 1915: *m* 1942, Sir John Meredith Temple, who *d* 1994, and has issue living, Guy, *b* 1946: *m* 1972, Philomena Henrietta Baynes, of Seal, Sevenoaks, Kent, and has issue living, Christina Philomena Nancy *b* 1973, — Diana, *b* 1943: *m* 1965, Robert McConnell, of The Priests House, Puddington, Wirral L64 5SS, and has issue living, Frederick Bruce *b* 1970, Anne Helen *b* 1968. *Residence* – Picton Gorse, Chester.

PREDECESSORS – (1) WILLIAM Hare, el son of late Richard Hare; MP for Cork City 1790-7, and for Athy 1798-1800; *cr Baron Ennismore*, co Kerry (peerage of Ireland) 1800, *Viscount Ennismore and Listowel* (peerage Ireland) 1816, and *Earl of Listowel* (peerage of Ireland) 1822: *m* 1st, 1772, Mary, who *d* 1810, only da of late Henry Wrixon, of Ballygiblin, co Cork; 2ndly, 1812, Anne, who *d* 1859, da of late John Latham, of Meldrum, co Tipperary; *d* 1837; *s* by his grandson (2) WILLIAM, KP (son of late Richard, Viscount Ennismore, el son of 1st Earl), 2nd Earl; *b* 1801; was Vice-Adm of Munster: *m* 1831, Maria Augusta, who *d* 1871, da of Vice-Adm William Windham, of Felbrigge Hall, and widow of George Thomas Wyndham, of Cromer Hall, Norfolk: *d* 1856; *s* by his son (3) WILLIAM, KP, 3rd Earl; *b* 1833; *cr Baron Hare* (peerage of United Kingdom) 1869; a Lord-in-Waiting to Queen Victoria in 1880: *m* 1865, Lady Ernestine Mary Brudenell-Bruce, who *d* 1936, da of 3rd Marquess of Ailesbury: *d* 1924; *s* by his el son (4) RICHARD GRANVILLE, 4th Earl, *b* 1866; sometime in Life Guards: *m* 1904, Hon Freda Vanden-Bempde-Johnstone, who *d* 1968, da of 2nd Baron Derwent; *d* 1931; *s* by his el son (5) WILLIAM FRANCIS, GCMG, PC, 5th Earl, *b* 1906; Postmaster-Gen 1945-47, Sec of State for India 1947-48, Min of State for Colonial Affairs 1948-50, Parl Sec to Min of Agriculture and Fisheries 1950-51, and Gov-Gen and Cmdr-in-Ch of Ghana 1957-60: *m* 1st, 1933 (*m diss* 1945), Judith, only da of Raoul de Marffy-Mantuano, of Budapest, Hungary; 2ndly, 1958 (*m diss* 1963), Stephanie Sandra Yvonne, da of Samuel Wise, of Toronto, Canada, and formerly wife of Hugh Currie; 3rdly, 1963, Pamela Molly, da of late Francis Day, of Croydon, Surrey, and formerly wife of John Alexander Read; *d* 1997; *s* by his elder son (6) FRANCIS MICHAEL, 6th Earl and present peer; also Viscount Ennismore and Listowel, Baron Ennismore, and Baron Hare.

Littleton, family name of Baron Hatherton.

LIVERPOOL, EARL OF (Foljambe) (Earl UK 1905)
(Name pronounced "Fulljum")

Be steadfast

EDWARD PETER BERTRAM SAVILE FOLJAMBE, 5th Earl; *b* 14 Nov 1944; *s* 1969; *ed* Shrewsbury: *m* 1st, 1970 (*m diss* 1994), Lady Juliana Mary Alice Noel, eldest da of 5th Earl of Gainsborough; 2ndly, 1995, Marie-Ange, da of Comte Géraud Michel de Pierredon, of Château de la Roche, Gençay, France, and has issue by 1st *m*.

Arms – Sable, a bend between six escallops or, and as an honourable augmentation (granted Aug 1906) on the bend in chief, on an escutcheon vert a key surmounted by a baton in saltire or. Crest – 1st (of honourable augmentation granted Aug 1906), on a chapeau gules turned up ermine a lion rampant of the first, charged on the shoulder with a besant, thereon an eagle displayed sable, and resting the dexter hind paw on a plate charged with a bend azure, thereon three garbs or, and surmounted by an escutcheon argent charged with an eagle displayed also sable, charged on the breast with a fleur-de-lis also or, the lion crowned gold and supporting with the fore paws a man-of-war's church pennant proper; 2nd, a seaweed rock proper, thereon a sea-lion sejant azure resting the *dexter* paw on an escutcheon per fesse wavy argent and azure, in chief a cormorant sable, beaked and legged gules, holding in the beak a branch of sea-weed, called laver, inverted vert (*Liverpool*), and in base a hawk, wings elevated and addorsed argent (*Hawkesbury*); 3rd a man's leg unarmed, couped at the thigh, quarterly or and sable spurred gold. Supporters – On either side a griffin, wings elevated or, beaked, membered, ducally gorged, and on the wing three fleurs-de-lis one and two all azure, that on the *dexter* side charged on the breast with a torteau thereon a cross-crosslet fitchée argent (the badge of *Howard*), and that on the *sinister* with a pellet thereon a stag's head cabossed also argent (*Cavendish*).

Residence – Scofton Farm House, Osberton, nr Worksop, Notts S81 0UE. *Clubs* – Turf, Pratt's.

SONS LIVING (By 1st marriage)

LUKE MARMADUKE PETER SAVILE (*Viscount Hawkesbury*), *b* 25 March 1972.
Hon Ralph Edward Anthony Savile, *b* 1974.

SISTER LIVING (*Raised to the rank of an Earl's daughter* 1970)

Lady Jane Rosamond Mary, *b* 1943; *ed* Durham Univ (BA); SRN 1982. *Residence* – Kilvington Hall, Thirsk, N Yorks.

AUNT LIVING

Ursula Susan Annette Mary, *b* 1916: *m* 1939, Maj Stephen Carrington Smith, TD, of Dawnedge, Aspley Guise, Beds, and has issue living, Maj Nigel Antony Carrington (Redwings, Orchard Close, Brancaster Staithe, Kings Lynn, Norfolk), *b* 1943: *m* 1980, Jane Elizabeth Lee, and has issue living, Guy Savile *b* 1983, Miles Stephen *b* 1985, Sarah Jane *b* 1982, Diana Mary *b* 1989, — Angela Selina Carrington, *b* 1948: *m* 1971, John Bunker, of Woburn Lane, Aspley Guise, Bucks MK17 8JH, and has issue living, Nicholas James *b* 1977, Alice Louise *b* 1974.

PREDECESSORS – (1) *Sir* CHARLES Jenkinson, 7th Bt, el son of Col Charles Jenkinson (who was 2nd in command of the Blues at Dettingen, and commanded them at Fontenoy, 3rd son of Sir Robert Jenkinson, 2nd Bt), *b* 1729, held many high offices of State, and was *cr Baron Hawkesbury*, of co Gloucester (peerage of Great Britain) 1786, and *Earl of Liverpool* 1796; *d* 1808; *s* by his el son (2) ROBERT BANKS, KG, 2nd Earl, *b* 1770; called to the House of Lords 1803, in the lifetime of his father; Prime Min and First Lord of the Treasury 1812-27; *dsp* 1828; *s* by his half-brother (3) CHARLES CECIL COPE, GCB, 3rd Earl, *b* 1784; Lord Steward 1841-6: *m* 1810, Julia Evelyn Medley, who *d* 1814, only child of Sir George Shuckburgh-Evelyn, 6th Bt; *d* 1851, when the peerages became ext and the baronetcy reverted to his cousin; the *Barony of Hawkesbury* was revived 1893, and the *Earldom of Liverpool* 1905 in the person of his grandson and principal heir (4) CECIL GEORGE SAVILE Foljambe, PC, el son of late George Savile Foljambe, of Osberton, Notts, and Aldwarke, Yorks, by his 2nd wife, Selina Charlotte, 2nd da and co heiress (el leaving issue) of 3rd Earl of Liverpool (*cr* 1796, *ext*), and 3rd Baron Hawkesbury (*cr* 1786, *ext*), and widow of William Charles, Viscount Milton; *b* 1846; a Lord-in-Waiting to Queen Victoria 1894-5, and Lord Steward of King Edward VII's Household 1905-7; MP for N Nottinghamshire (*L*) 1880-85, and for Notts, Mansfield Div 1885-92; *cr Baron Hawkesbury*, of Haselbech, co Northampton, and of Ollerton, Sherwood Forest, co Nottingham (peerage of United Kingdom) 1893, and *Viscount Hawkesbury*, of Kirkham, co York, and of Mansfield, co Nottingham, and *Earl of Liverpool* (peerage of United Kingdom) 1905; PC 1906: *m* 1st, 1869, Louisa Blanche, who *d* 1871, el da of late Frederick John Howard, of Compton Place, Sussex (E Carlisle, colls); 2ndly, 1877, Susan Louisa, who *d* 1917, el da of late Lieut-Col William Henry Frederick Cavendish, of West Stoke, Sussex, and 47 Cromwell Houses, SW, 2nd cousin both paternally and maternally of his 1st wife; *d* 1907; *s* by his el son (5) ARTHUR WILLIAM DE BRITO SAVILE, GCB, GCMG, GBE, MVO, PC, 2nd Earl, *b* 1870; was State Steward and Chamberlain to Lord-Lieut of Ireland 1906-8, Comptroller of HM's Household 1909-12, Gov of New Zealand 1912-17, and First Gov-Gen of the Dominion of New Zealand 1917-20: *m* 1897, Hon Annette Louise Monck, GBE, who *d* 1948, only da of 5th Viscount Monck; *d* 1941; *s* by his half-brother (6) GERALD WILLIAM FREDERICK SAVILE, DSO, 3rd Earl *b* 1878; Lieut-Col King's Roy Rifle Corps; S Africa 1899-1902; 1914-18 War as OC 21st Bn: *m* 1909, Constance Isabelle, who *d* 1976, only da of John Holden, of Nuttall Temple, Notts; *d* 1962; *s* by his brother (7) ROBERT ANTHONY EDWARD ST ANDREW SAVILE, 4th Earl; *b* 1887; *d* 1969; *s* by his great-nephew (8) EDWARD PETER BERTRAM SAVILE (grandson of Maj Hon Bertram Marmaduke Osbert Savile Foljambe, MC, 6th son of 1st Earl), 5th Earl and present peer; also Viscount Hawkesbury, and Baron Hawkesbury.

LLEWELYN-DAVIES, BARONY OF (Llewelyn Davies) (Extinct 1981)

DAUGHTERS LIVING OF LIFE BARON

Hon Melissa, *b* 1945; documentary film maker: *m* 1974, Christopher Desmond Curling (*see* Bonham, Bt, 1990 Edn), of 3 Richmond Crescent, N1, and has issue living, Richard William Samuel, *b* 1983, — Allegra Rose Elizabeth, *b* 1979.
Hon Harriet Lydia Rose, *b* 1955; has issue living (by Christopher John Holmes, CBE), Cub LLEWELYN-DAVIES, *b* 1991, — Sara LLEWELYN-DAVIES, *b* 1996.
Hon Rebecca, *b* 1957: *m* 1983, Hon Daniel William Rea, of 4 Queensgate Villas, Victoria Park Rd, E9, 2nd son of 3rd Baron Rea, and has issue living (*see* Rea, B).

LLEWELYN-DAVIES OF HASTOE, BARONY OF (Llewelyn-Davies) (Extinct 1997)

DAUGHTERS LIVING OF LIFE BARONESS

See preceeding article.

LLOYD, BARONY OF (Lloyd) (Extinct 1985)

DAUGHTERS LIVING OF SECOND BARON

Hon Davina Margaret, *b* 1943. *Residence* – 11 Morpeth Mansions, Morpeth Terrace, SW1.
Hon Laura Blanche Bridget, *b* 1960. *Residence* – 4 Patience Rd, SW11.

WIDOW LIVING OF SECOND BARON

Lady VICTORIA JEAN MARJORIE MABELL OGILVY (*Baroness Lloyd*), da of 12th Earl of Airlie: *m* 1942, the 2nd Baron Lloyd, MBE, DL, who *d* 1985.

LLOYD GEORGE OF DWYFOR, EARL (Lloyd George) (Earl UK 1945)

OWEN LLOYD GEORGE, 3rd Earl; *b* 28 April 1924; *s* 1968; *ed* Oundle; an underwriting member of Lloyd's; carried the Sword at Investiture of HRH the Prince of Wales, Caernarvon Castle 1969; a Member of Historic Buildings Council for Wales 1971-94, and of Court, Nat Museum of Wales, 1978-89; 1939-45 War as Capt Welsh Guards; DL Dyfed: *m* 1949 (*m diss* 1982), Ruth Margaret, only da of late Richard Coit, of 18 Thurloe Sq, SW7; 2ndly, 1982, (Cecily) Josephine, el da of Maj Sir Alexander Penrose Gordon Cumming, MC, 5th Bt, widow of 2nd Earl of Woolton, and formerly wife of 3rd Baron Forres, and has issue by 1st *m*.

Arms – Azure over water barry wavy in base a bridge of one arch proper, on a chief argent a portcullis sable between two daffodils stalked and leaved also proper. *Crest* - A demi-dragon gules holding between the claws a portcullis sable. *Supporters* – *Dexter*, a dragon or; *sinister*, an eagle wings addorsed or; each gorged with a collar vert.
Residences – Ffynone, Boncath, Pembrokeshire SA37 0HQ; 47 Burton Court, Franklin's Row, SW3 4SZ. *Clubs* – White's, Pratt's.

SONS LIVING (*By 1st marriage*)

DAVID RICHARD OWEN (*Viscount Gwynedd*) (Cobblers, The Old Hill, Wherwell, nr Andover, Hants SP11 7JB), *b* 22 Jan 1951; *ed* Eton: *m* 1985, Pamela Alexandra, only da of late Alexander Kleyff, and has issue:—
    SONS LIVING   *Hon* William Alexander, *b* 16 May 1986, — *Hon* Frederick Owen, *b* 1987.
Hon Robert John Daniel (23 Shek O, Big Wave Bay Rd, Hong Kong; 9 St Alban's Grove, W8), *b* 1952; *ed* Eton (King's Scholar), and Univ Coll, Oxford; Chm Lloyd George Mgmnt Ltd (Hong Kong); author of *A Guide to Asian Stock Markets* (1989), and *The East West Pendulum* (1991): *m* 1st, 1978 (*m diss* 1991), Kim, only da of Carl Fischer, of New York City; 2ndly, 1992, Donna Jean, only da of John Archbold Hufty, of Palm Beach, Florida, and has issue living (by 1st *m*), Richard Joseph, *b* 1983, — Alice Margaret, *b* 1987, — (by 2nd *m*) Alexander Gwilym, *b* 1994, — Nicholas, *b* 1998, — Robert Owen, *b* 1999, — Julia Frances, *b* 1993.

DAUGHTER LIVING (*By 1st marriage*)

Lady Julia Margaret Violet, *b* 1068: *m* 1984, Simon Erroll Prior-Palmer (*see* Linlithgow, M, 1995 Edn), and has issue living, George Erroll Owen, *b* 1988, — Arthur Frederick Victor, *b* 1991, — Harold John Alfred, *b* 1998, — Lara Ruth Hope, *b* 1994.

SISTER LIVING

Lady Valerie Davidia, *b* 1918: *m* 1940, Sir Goronwy Hopkin Daniel, KCVO, CB, DPhil, and has issue living, David Llewelyn (31 Westway, Petts Wood, Kent), *b* 1950: *m* 1977, Mary Helen, da of A Kent Maytham, of Glen Druid, Cabinteely, co Dublin, and has issue living, Owen Maytham *b* 1982, Katharine Megan *b* 1984, — Anne Margaret, *b* 1944: *m* 1977, Bernard Thomas Harrison, of 29 St Stephen's Rd, Ealing W13, and has issue living, Florence Ceridwen Dorothy *b* 1977, Eleanor Mary Gwyneth *b* 1979, — Gwyneth Roberta, *b* 1946: *m* 1971, Avi Shlaim, of 8 Chalfont Rd, Oxford, and has issue living, Tamar Megan *b* 1980.

COLLATERAL BRANCH LIVING

Issue of late Rt Hon Gwilym Lloyd George, TD (*Viscount Tenby*), yr son of 1st Earl Lloyd George of Dwyfor, *b* 1894, *d* 1971; *cr* Viscount Tenby 1957:—
See that title.

PREDECESSORS – *Rt Hon* DAVID Lloyd George, OM, son of late William George, of Bulford, Pembrokeshire; *b* 1863; Hon DCL Oxford 1908 and Durham 1919, Hon LLD Wales 1908, Glasgow 1917, Edinburgh 1918, Cambridge 1920, and Birmingham 1921, Hon DLitt Sheffield 1919, Hon Fellow Jesus Coll, Oxford 1910; admitted Solicitor 1884; sometime a partner in the legal firm of Lloyd George and George, of Criccieth; a JP, DL, and County Alderman for Caernarvonshire (Chm of Quarter Sessions 1929-38), Prior and Chancellor of the Priory for Wales of Order of St John of Jerusalem, a KGStJ, and a Freeman of many towns; appointed Pres of the Board of Trade Dec 1905, Chancellor of the Exchequer April 1908, Min of Munitions May 1915 (also a Member of Cabinet War Council), and Sec of State for War and Member of Army Council July 1916; was Prime Minister and First Lord of the Treasury Dec 1916 to Oct 1922; elected Lord Rector of Edinburgh Univ 1920; Sessional Chm of Parliamentary Liberal Party 1924-31; appointed Constable of Caernarvon Castle 1908; Ch British Representative at Paris Peace Conference 1919 (1914-15 star, War and Victory medals, Grand Cordon of Legion of Honour, and Italian Order of St Maurice and St Lazarus); sat as MP for Caernarvon Dist (*L*) April 1890 to Dec 1944; *cr Viscount Gwynedd*, of Dwyfor, co Caernarvon, and *Earl Lloyd George of Dwyfor* (peerage of United Kingdom) 1945: *m* 1st, 1888, *Dame* Margaret, GBE, LLD, JP, who *d* 1941, da of Richard Owen, of Mynydd Ednyfed, Criccieth; 2ndly, 1943, Frances Louise, CBE, who *d* 1972, da of John Stevenson, of Wallington, Surrey; *d* 1945; *s* by his el son (2) RICHARD, 2nd Earl, *b* 1889: *m* 1st, 1917 (*m diss* 1933), Roberta Ida Freeman, who *d* 1966, da of Sir Robert McAlpine, 1st Bt; 2ndly, 1935, Winifred Emily, who *d* 1982, da of late Thomas William Peedle, and formerly wife of Henry Michael Calve; *d* 1968; *s* by his son (3) OWEN, 3rd Earl and present peer; also Viscount Gwynedd.

LLOYD OF BERWICK, BARON (Lloyd) (Life Baron 1993)

ANTHONY JOHN LESLIE LLOYD, PC, son of Edward John Boydell Loyd, of Little Bucksteep, Dallington, Sussex; *b* 9 May 1929; *ed* Eton, and Trin Coll, Camb; late Coldstream Gds; DL E Sussex 1983; Bar Inner Temple 1955, QC 1967, Attorney-Gen to HRH The Prince of Wales 1969-77, Judge of High Court of Justice (Queen's Bench Div) 1978-84, Lord Justice of Appeal 1984-93, a Lord of Appeal in Ordinary 1993-98; former Memb Top Salaries Review Body, Chm Civil Ser Security Appeals Panel 1982-95, Security Commn since 1992; Memb Parole Board 1983-84; Chm Glyndebourne Arts Trust 1975-92; Dir RAM 1979-95; Vice-Pres Corpn of Sons of the Clergy since 1996; Reader Inner Temple 1998, Treasurer 1999; Upper Warden Salters' Co 1999, Master 2000; *cr* Knt 1978, PC 1984, and *Baron Lloyd of Berwick*, of Ludlay, co E Sussex (Life Baron) 1993: *m* 1960, Jane Helen Violet, High Sheriff of E Sussex 1994, da of Cornelius William Shelford, of Chailey Place, nr Lewes, Sussex.

Arms – Per fess gules and or a pale per fess and a fess per fess, in chief an escallop between two hedgehogs and in base a hedgehog between two escallops all counterchanged. Crest – A hedgehog gules spined or holding in its dexter claw an ostrich plume erect proper.
Residences – Ludlay, Berwick, E Sussex; 68 Strand-on-the-Green, Chiswick W4 3PF.
Club – Brooks's.

LLOYD OF HAMPSTEAD, BARONY OF (Lloyd) (Extinct 1992)

DAUGHTERS LIVING OF LIFE BARON

Hon Naomi Katharine, *b* 1946: *m* 1967, Peter Campbell Hodges, of 52 Park Rd, Kingston, Surrey KT2 6AU, and has issue.
Hon Corinne Deborah (14 Locarno Av, Kallista, Melbourne, Victoria 3791, Australia), *b* 1951; MA: *m* 1st, 1971 (*m diss* 1977), Dr Michael Newman, MB, BCh; 2ndly, 1990, Hugh Henderson, MBA.

LLOYD OF HIGHBURY, BARONESS (Lloyd) (Life Baroness 1996)

JUNE KATHLEEN LLOYD, DBE, da of late Arthur Cresswell Lloyd, MBE; *b* 1 Jan 1928; *ed* Royal Sch, Bath, Bristol Univ (MB ChB 1951, MD 1965), and Durham Univ (DPH 1958), FRCP London 1969 (MRCP 1954), FRCPE 1990, FRCGP 1990, Hon DSc Bristol 1991, Birmingham 1993; Senior Lecturer, Inst of Child Health, London 1965-69, Reader 1969-74, Professor 1974-75; Professor, St George's Med Sch 1975-85; Nuffield Professor of Child Health, London Univ 1985-92; Scientific Adviser, Assoc of Medical Research Charities 1992-96; Chm Gene Therapy Advisory Cttee 1992-96; *cr* DBE 1990, and *Baroness Lloyd of Highbury*, of Highbury, in the London Borough of Islington (Life Baroness) 1996.
Residence – 37 Allingham St, N1 8NX.

LLOYD OF KILGERRAN, BARONY OF (Lloyd) (Extinct 1991)

DAUGHTERS LIVING OF LIFE BARON

Hon Elizabeth Mary Gerran, *b* 1944; JP SW London since 1989; Hon LLD 1998: *m* 1968, Daniel Gerard Robins, QC, BSc, LLB, who *d* 1989, of 66 Church Rd, Wimbledon, SW19, and has issue living, Charlotte Jane Gerran, *b* 1971, — Sophie Elizabeth Gerran, *b* 1974, — Anneli Mary Gerran, *b* 1976.
Hon Catherine Gerran, *b* 1947: *m* 1972, Philip Gwynfryn Edwards, of 2 Woodhill House, Kentish Lane, Essendon, Herts AL9 6JY, and has issue living, Thomas Gerran, *b* 1982, — Rosalind Gerran, *b* 1975, — Bryony Gerran, *b* 1976, — Felicity Gerran, *b* 1980.

WIDOW LIVING OF LIFE BARON

PHYLLIS MARY (*Baroness Lloyd of Kilgerran*), da of late Ronald Shepherd, JP, of Chilworth, Hants: *m* 1940, Baron Lloyd of Kilgerran, CBE, QC (Life Baron), who *d* 1991. *Residence* – 15 Haymeads Drive, Esher, Surrey.

Lloyd, see Baron Geoffrey-Lloyd.

LLOYD-WEBBER, BARON (Lloyd Webber) (Life Baron 1997)

ANDREW LLOYD WEBBER, son of late William Southcombe Lloyd Webber, CBE; *b* 22 March 1948; *ed* Westminster, Magdalen Coll, Oxford, and Royal Coll of Music (FRCM 1988); Composer; musicals include *Joseph and the Amazing Technicolor Dreamcoat* (1968, revived 1973 and 1991) *Jesus Christ Superstar* (1970), *Evita* (1976, stage version 1978), *Cats* (1981), *Starlight Express* (1984), *The Phantom of the Opera* (1986), and *Sunset Boulevard* (1993); also many film scores and orchestral works; recipient of many awards and honours, including FRCM 1992; *cr* Kt 1992, and *Baron Lloyd-Webber*, of Sydmonton, co Hants (Life Baron) 1997: *m* 1st, 1971 (*m diss* 1983), Sarah Jane Tudor, da of ...... Hugill, of ......; 2ndly, 1984 (*m diss* 1990), Sarah Brightman (actress and singer), da of late Grenville Geoffrey Brightman, of Bournemouth; 3rdly, 1991, Madeleine Astrid, 2nd da of Brig Adam Brampton Douglas Gurdon, CBE, of Burgh House, Woodbridge, Suffolk, and has issue by 1st and 3rd *m*.
Address – c/o The Really Useful Group Ltd, 22 Tower St, WC2H 9NS.

SONS LIVING (*By 1st marriage*)

Hon Nicholas, *b* 1979; *ed* ....

(*By 3rd marriage*)

Hon Alastair Adam, *b* 1992.
Hon William Richard, *b* 1993.

DAUGHTER LIVING (*By 1st marriage*)

Hon Imogen, *b* 1977.

LOCH, BARONY OF (Loch) (Extinct 1991)

DAUGHTER LIVING OF FOURTH BARON (*by 1st marriage*)

Hon Sara Nan, *b* 1949. *Residence* – The Old House, The Close, Blandford, Dorset DT11 7HA.

DAUGHTER LIVING OF THIRD BARON (*by 4th marriage*)

Hon Allegra Helen, *b* 1982.

DAUGHTER LIVING OF SECOND BARON

Hon Helen, MBE, *b* 1919; MBE (Civil) 1987; DL Perthshire 1980, JP 1976: *m* 1947, (George) Ronald Service, who *d* 1961, and has issue living, James Ronald, *b* 1948: *m* 1976, Mrs Gabrielle Armitage, da of late Philip Lloyd, of Thornton Hough, Wirral, Cheshire. *Residence* – Kinfauns House, Kinfauns, by Perth.

WIDOW LIVING OF THIRD BARON

SYLVIA BARBARA, da of Alexander Gordon Beauchamp Cameron, of Delmahoy, Midlothian, and formerly wife of Christopher Beauchamp-Wilson; *m* 2ndly, 1975, as his 4th wife, Maj the 3rd Baron Loch, who *d* 1982; 3rdly, 1984, Richard G.P. Hawkins. *Residence* – ....

WIDOW LIVING OF FOURTH BARON

DAVINA JULIA (*Baroness Loch*), da of late FitzHerbert Wright, of Collihole Farm, Chagford, Devon (*see* V Powerscourt, 1990 Edn), and formerly wife of Sir Richard Boughey, 10th Bt: *m* 1979, as his 2nd wife, Maj the 4th Baron Loch, MC, who *d* 1991, when the title became extinct. *Residences* – The Cobbles, Shillingstone, Blandford Forum, Dorset DT11 0SF; Lochluichart by Garve, Ross-shire IV23 2PZ.

LOCKWOOD, BARONESS (Hall) (Life Baroness 1978)

BETTY LOCKWOOD, da of Arthur Lockwood; *b* 22nd Jan 1924; *ed* Eastborough Council Sch, Dewsbury, and Ruskin Coll, Oxford; a DL for W Yorks (1987); Ch Woman Officer, Labour Party 1967-75, Chm Equal Opportunities Comm 1975-83; since when Pres Birkbeck Coll, London Univ; Pro-Chancellor of Univ of Bradford since 1987, and Chm of Council since 1992; Member of Council

Advertising Standards Authority since 1983, and Leeds Development Corpn since 1988; *cr Baroness Lockwood*, of Dewsbury, co W Yorks (Life Baroness) 1978: *m* 1978, Lt-Col Cedric Hall, who *d* 1988.
Residence – 6 Sycamore Dr, Addingham, Ilkley, W Yorks LS29 0NY.

Loder, family name of Baron Wakehurst.

LOFTHOUSE OF PONTEFRACT, BARON (Lofthouse) (Life Baron 1997)

GEOFFREY LOFTHOUSE, son of late Ernest Lofthouse, of Featherstone, Leeds; *b* 18 Dec 1925; *ed* Featherstone Primary and Secondary Schs, Whitwood Technical Coll, and Leeds Univ; Manpower Office, NCB 1964-70; Personnel Manager, NCB, Fryston 1970-78; MP (*Lab*) for Pontefract and Castleford 1978-97; Memb Select Cttee on Energy, First Dep Chm of Ways and Means (Dep Speaker of the House) 1992-97; Councillor, Pontefract Borough District Council 1962-74 (Leader 1969-74); Councillor, Wakefield Metropolitan District Council 1974-79 (first Chm); JP Pontefract 1970; FIPM 1984; *cr* Kt 1995, and *Baron Lofthouse of Pontefract*, of Pontefract, co W Yorkshire (Life Baron) 1997: *m* 1946, Sarah, who *d* 1985, da of Joesh Thomas Onions, of Pontefract and has issue.

Arms – Azure on a pale between and conjoined to two grilles throughout or the whole surmounted by three chevronels argent over all on a pale sable three ellipses palewise. **Crest** – A canary or holding in the dexter foot a miner's lamp sable glazed proper. **Supporters** – On either side a mole sejant erect holding in the mouth a rose argent barbed seeded slipped and leaved or.
Residence – 67 Carleton Crest, Pontefract, W Yorks WF8 2QR.

DAUGHTER LIVING

Hon Lynne, *b* 1952; *ed* Pontefract Girls' High Sch, and Northern Coll of Educn: *m* 1989, Tim Lindley, son of Desmond Lindley, of Thornhill, and has issue living, two children.

Loftus, Viscount; son of Marquess of Ely.

LONDESBOROUGH, BARON (Denison) (Baron UK 1850)

ADVERSA VIRTUTE REPELLO

I repel adversity with courage

RICHARD JOHN DENISON, 9th Baron; *b* 2 July 1959; *s* 1968; *ed* Wellington and Exeter Univ: *m* 1987, Rikki, da of J. E. Morris, of Bayswater, London, and has issue.

𝕬rms – Quarterly: 1st and 4th ermine, a bend azure, cotised sable, between an unicorn's fitchée in base gules, *Denison;* 2nd and 3rd argent, a shake fork between three mullets one and two sable, *Conyngham.* 𝕮rest – 1st, issuant from clouds a dexter arm in bend proper, vested gules, cuffed ermine, and charged with a covered cup or, pointing with the fore finger to an estoile radiated gold, *Denison;* 2nd, an unicorn's head erased argent, armed and maned or, *Conyngham.* 𝕾upporters – *Dexter*, a horse argent, maned, unguled, and charged on the shoulder with an eagle displayed or, with a crescent sable for difference; *sinister*, a stag argent, attired, unguled, and charged on the shoulder with a griffin's head erased or, with a crescent sable for difference.
Residence – Edw Cottage, Aberedw, Powys.

SON LIVING

Hon JAMES (JACK) FREDERICK, *b* 4 June 1990.

DAUGHTER LIVING

Hon Laura Rose, *b* 1992.

COLLATERAL BRANCH LIVING

Granddaughter of late Hon Henry Charles Denison, 3rd son of 1st Baron:—

Issue of late Commodore Edward Conyngham Denison, MVO, RN, *b* 1888, *d* 1960: *m* 1919, Maira Amy Brabazon, who *d* 1994, da of late Lt-Col Sir Charles Henry Brabazon Heaton-Ellis, CBE, of Wyddiall Hall, Buntingford, Herts:—

Sonia Myrtle, *b* 1921: *m* 1st, 1940, Major Edgard FitzGerald Heathcoat-Amory, Royal Devon Yeo, who was *ka* in Normandy 1944 (*see* Heathcoat-Amory, Bt, colls); 2ndly, 1947, Brigadier Roderick Heathcoat-Amory, MC, The Royals (*see* Heathcoat-Amory, Bt, colls), who *d* 1998. *Residence* – Allington Grange, Chippenham, Wilts SN14 6LW.

PREDECESSORS – **(1)** *Lord* ALBERT Conyngham, KCH, FRS, 2nd surviving son of Henry, 1st Marquess Conyngham, by Elizabeth, da of Joseph Denison of Denbies, co Surrey; *b* 1805; was Vice-Adm of Yorkshire; assumed the surname of Denison by Roy licence 1849: *cr Baron Londesborough*, of Londesborough, co York (peerage of United Kingdom) 1850: *m* 1st, 1833, Henrietta Maria, who *d* 1841, da of 1st Baron Forester; 2ndly, 1847, Ursula Lucy Grace (who *d* 1883, having *m* 2ndly, Rt Hon Lord Otho Augustus Fitzgerald, PC, MP, who *d* 1882 (D Leinster)), da of Rear-Adm Hon Charles Bridgeman (E Bradford); *d* 1860; *s* by his son **(2)** WILLIAM HENRY FORESTER, 2nd Baron, *b* 1834; MP for Beverley (*L*) 1857-9 and for Scarborough 1859-60; *cr Viscount Raincliffe*, of Raincliffe, co York, and *Earl of Londesborough* (peerage of United Kingdom) 1887: *m* 1863, Lady Edith Frances Wilhelmine Somerset, who *d* 1915, da of 7th Duke of Beaufort; *d* 1900: *s* by his son **(3)** WILLIAM FRANCES HENRY, KCVO, 2nd Earl, *b* 1864; *m* 1887, Lady Grace Augusta Fane, who *d* 1933, da of 12th Earl of Westmorland; *d* 1917; *s* by his son **(4)** GEORGE FRANCIS WILLIAM HENRY, 3rd Earl, *b* 1892; *d* 1920; *s* by his brother **(5)** HUGO WILLIAM CECIL, 4th Earl, *b* 1894: *m* 1935, Marigold Rosemary Joyce (who *d* 1976, having *m* 2ndly, 1948 (*m diss* 1954), Zygmund de Łubicz-Bakanowski), da of late Edgar Lubbock, LLB (B Avebury, colls); *d* 1937, when the Earldom and Viscountcy became ext, and the Barony passed to his kinsman **(6)** ERNEST WILLIAM, MBE (son of late Rear-Adm Hon Albert Denison Somerville Denison, 2nd son of 1st Baron), 6th Baron; *b* 1876; Capt RN; MBE (Civil) 1946: *m* 1905, Sybil May, who *d* 1963, da of late Capt H. T. Anley, of The First, Binstead, Isle of Wight; *d* 1963; *s* by his cousin **(7)** CONYNGHAM CHARLES, DSO, RN (only son of Cdr Hon Conyngham Albert Denison, RN, 4th son of 1st Baron), 7th Baron, *b* 1885; Cdr RN: *m* 1st, 1912 (*m diss* 1925), Vera, da of late Francis Hugh Baxendale; 2ndly, 1926, Mabel, who *d* 1951, da of Matthew George Megaw; 3rdly, 1952, Jocelyn Helen, who *d* 1998, da of late Lt-Cdr Hugh Duppa Collins, RN; *d* 1967; *s* by his cousin **(8)** JOHN ALBERT LISTER, TD (only son of Hon Harold Albert Denison, 5th son of 1st Baron). 8th Baron; *b* 1901: *m* 1st 1949 (*m diss* 1953), Lesley Maxwell Gordon, OBE, da of late Lt-Col Herbert Forbes Churchill, OBE, and widow of Lt-Col J. H. Wooldridge, Indian Army; 2ndly, 1957, (Elizabeth) Ann, who *d* 1994, da of late Edward Little Sale, ICS, and formerly wife of late Thomas Chambers Windsor Roe; *d* 1968; *s* by his son **(9)** RICHARD JOHN, 9th Baron and present peer.

LONDONDERRY, MARQUESS OF (Vane-Tempest-Stewart) Sits as EARL VANE (UK 1823)
(Marquess I 1816)

The dragon's crest is to be feared

ALEXANDER CHARLES ROBERT VANE-TEMPEST-STEWART, 9th Marquess; *b* 7 Sept 1937; *s* 1955; *ed* Eton: *m* 1st, 1958 (*m diss* 1971), Nicolette Elaine Katherine, who *d* 1993, only da of late Michael Harrison, of Netherhampton House, Netherhampton, Wilts, and 33 Chesham Place, SW1; 2ndly, 1972 (*m diss* 1989), Doreen Patricia Wells, and has issue by 1st and 2nd *m*.

Arms – Quarterly: 1st and 4th or, a bend counter compony argent and azure, between two lions rampant, gules, *Stewart*; 2nd argent, a bend engrailed, between six martlets, three and three, sable, *Tempest*; 3rd azure, three sinister gauntlets, *Vane*. **Crest** – 1st, a dragon statant or, *Stewart*; 2nd, a griffin's head erased, per pale argent and sable, beaked gules, *Tempest*; 3rd, a dexter cubit arm in armour, the hand in a gauntlet proper grasping a sword also proper, pommel and hilt or, *Vane*. **Supporters** – *Dexter*, a Moor, wreathed about the temples argent and azure, holding in the exterior hand a shield of the last, garnished or, charged with the sun in splendour gold; *sinister*, a lion or, collared argent, the collar charged with three mullets sable.

SONS LIVING (*By 2nd marriage*)

FREDERICK AUBREY (*Viscount Castlereagh*), *b* 6 Sept 1972.
Lord Reginald Alexander, *b* 1977.

DAUGHTERS LIVING (*By 1st marriage*)

Lady Sophia Frances Anne, *b* 1959: *m* 1987, Jonathan Mark Pilkington, yst son of Ronald Charles Leslie Pilkington, of Hill House, Stanstead Abbots, Herts, and has issue living, Hermione Alice, *b* 1989, — Allegra Rose, *b* 1991.
*Lady Cosima Maria Gabriella (*Lady Cosima Somerset*), *b* 1961: *m* 1st, 1982 (*m diss* 1986), Cosmo Joseph Fry, son of Jeremy Fry, of Bath; 2ndly, 1990, Lord John Robert Somerset, yst son of 11th Duke of Beaufort, and has issue (by 2nd *m*) (see that title).

SISTERS LIVING

Lady Jane Antonia Frances (*Baroness Rayne*), *b* 1932: *m* 1965, as his 2nd wife, Baron Rayne (Life Baron), of 33 Robert Adam St, W1M 5AH, and has issue (see that title).
Lady Annabel, *b* 1934: *m* 1st, 1954 (*m diss* 1975), Marcus Oswald Hornby Lecky Birley, son of late Sir Oswald Hornby Lecky Birley, MC; 2ndly, 1978, Sir James Michael Goldsmith, MEP, who *d* 1997, and has had issue (by 1st husband), Rupert Oswald Robin, *b* 1955; missing, presumed drowned at sea, Lomé, W Africa, 1986, — Robin Marcus, *b* 1958, — India Jane Romaine, *b* 1961: *m* 1st, 1981 (*m diss* 1988), Jonathan Halsey Luke Colchester, son of late Rev Halsey Sparrowe Colchester, CMG, OBE; 2ndly, 1993, Francis Bruce Pike, son of Esmund Francis Victor Wallace Pike, — (by 2nd husband) Zacharias Frank, *b* 1975: *m* 1999, Shcherazade Ventura Bentley, da of John Bentley, and Vivianc Ventura, — Benjamin James, *b* 1980; *ed* Eton, — Jemima Marcelle, *b* 1974: *m* 1995, Imran Khan, and has issue living, Sulaiman Isa *b* 1996, Kasim *b* 1999. *Residence* – Ormeley Lodge, Ham Common, Surrey.

AUNT LIVING (*Daughter of 7th Marquess*)

Lady Mairi Elizabeth (*Lady Mairi Bury*), *b* 1921; JP co Down; Patron British Red Cross Soc N Ireland, Liveryman Guild of Air Pilots and Air Navigators, Fellow Royal Philatelic Soc: *m* 1940 (*m diss* 1958), as his 1st wife, Lt-Col Derek William Charles, Viscount Bury, late 13th/18th Hussars, who *d* 1968, el son of 9th Earl of Albemarle. *Residence* – Mount Stewart, Newtownards, co Down.

COLLATERAL BRANCHES LIVING

Grandson of late Maj Francis Adolphus Vane-Tempest, only son of late Lord Adolphus Frederick Charles William Vane-Tempest, 3rd son of 3rd Marquess:—
Adopted son of late Francis Charles Joseph Vane-Tempest, *b* 1911, *d* 1994: *m* 1st, 1931 (*m annulled* 1935), Pamela Mary, who *d* 1953, 2nd da of late Maj Edwin Philip Abel Smith, of Great Kimble House, Princes Risborough, Bucks; 2ndly, 1936 (*m diss* 1952), Penelope Joan, da of Edmund Henry Bevan, JP (*see* B Grantley, 1942 Edn):—
Richard Conyers VANE-TEMPEST, *b* 1941; *ed* Downside, and Lond Hosp Med Coll (MB BS), LRCP, MRCS, DObst RCOG; Fell Australasian Coll for Emergency Medicine; Emergency Physician at John Hunter Hosp, NSW: *m* 1st, 1964 (*m diss* 1969), Carol Susanne Connal; 2ndly, 1970 (*m diss* 1996), Mary Rose McLoughlin, and has issue living (by 1st *m*), Jane, *b* 1966, — Clare, *b* 1967, — (by 2nd *m*), Kate, *b* 1973, — Elspeth, *b* 1984. *Address* – PO Box 165, Newcastle, NSW 2300, Australia.

---

*In April 1998 Lady Cosima Somerset published an article in the *Daily Telegraph*, in which she declared that her father was the late Capt (Cecil) Robin Douglas-Home (*see* E Home, colls). At the time of going to press, however, she is still legally the daughter of the Marquess of Londonderry.

Grandson of late Charles Henry Vane-Tempest, son of late Lord Ernest M'Donnell Vane-Tempest, 4th son of 3rd Marquess:—

Issue of late Ernest Charles William Vane-Tempest, DSC, *b* 1894, *d* 1957: *m* 1st, 1918 (*m diss* 1933), Aline Mary Loftus, who *d* 1967, da of late Loftus St George (St George, Bt, colls); 2ndly, 1933, Anne Elizabeth, who *d* 1968, da of Capt Evan Humphreys, of Borth-y-gest, Portmadoc, Caernarvonshire:—

(By 1st *m*) Charles Stewart M'Donnell, MBE, *b* 1921; *ed* Haileybury; 1939-45 War with RAF; MBE (Civil) 1996: *m* 1st, 1948 (*m diss* 1956), Diana Constance, da of late Maj Kenneth Arthur Seth-Smith; 2ndly, 1957, Maija-Liisa, da of Col Erkki Elias Puomi, and has issue living, (by 1st *m*) (Charles) Stewart Martin St George (Lower House Farm, The Endway, Steeple Bumpstead, Suffolk CB9 7DW), *b* 1950; *ed* Stowe: *m* 1st, 1972 (*m diss* 1976), Pamela Elizabeth, da of M. Jenkin; 2ndly, 1977, Jillian Barbara, da of Dr John Evelyn Bulow, of Bondi, 34 Shirley Av, Cheam, Surrey, and has issue living (by 2nd *m*), Christopher James Stewart *b* 1978, James Alexander Stewart *b* 1981, — Aline Elizabeth Stewart, *b* 1952: *m* 1984, Philip John Lester Nash, son of Lancelot Lester Nash, of Veronica Cottage, Thruxton, Hants, and has issue living, Jonathan Guy Randell *b* 1988, Camilla Judith *b* 1986, — (by 2nd *m*) Charles Erkki William, *b* 1958: *m* 1981, Stina Maria Veronica, da of Per-Erik Törnblom, of Virkby, Finland, and has issue living, Charles Petter *b* 1990, — Donald John Ernest, *b* 1961: *m* 1985, Pirkko Maritta, da of Vaino Salminen, of Alastaro, Finland, and has issue living, Thomas Christopher *b* 1986, Maria Elizabeth *b* 1989, — Harold Michael St George, *b* 1962: *m* 1987, Merja Anneli, da of Teuvo Karinkanta, of Vantaa, Finland, and has issue living, John Michael *b* 1990, Timothy Alexander *b* 1992, — Mary-Anne Elizabeth (twin), *b* 1962. *Residence* – Kiveliöntie 14, 02340 Esbo, Finland.

PREDECESSORS – (1) ROBERT Stewart, MP for co Down 1770-89; *cr Baron Londonderry* (peerage of Ireland) 1789, *Viscount Castlereagh* (peerage of Ireland) 1795, *Earl of Londonderry* (peerage of Ireland) 1796, and *Marquess of Londonderry* (peerage of Ireland) 1816; *d* 1821; *s* by his el son (2) ROBERT, KG, 2nd Marquess; a distinguished statesman; *dsp* 1822; *s* by his half-brother (3) CHARLES WILLIAM, KG, GCB, GCH, 3rd Marquess, who had in 1814 been *cr Baron Stewart*, of Stewart's Court and Ballylawn, co Donegal (peerage of United Kingdom); *b* 1778; a distinguished general and diplomatist, Lord-Lieut of co Durham, Custos Rotulorum of cos Londonderry and Down, and Col 2nd Life Guards; *cr Viscount Seaham* and *Earl Vane* (peerage of United Kingdom) 1823, with remainder to the male issue of his 2nd marriage; *d* 1854, when the Viscountcy of Seaham and Earldom of Vane passed to his 2nd son George Henry (infra), and the marquessate and minor honours devolved upon his el son (4) FREDERICK WILLIAM, KP, PC, 4th Marquess; MP for co Down 1831-52; *dsp* 1872; *s* by his half-brother (5) GEORGE HENRY ROBERT CHARLES WILLIAM, KP, LLD, 5th Marquess who had in 1854 *s* his father as 2nd Earl Vane: assumed in 1851 the additional surname of Tempest; sat as MP for N Durham (C) 1847-54; was Lord-Lieut of Durham: *m* 1846, Mary Cornelia, only da of Sir John Edwards, 1st Bt (*ext*); *d* 6 Nov 1884; *s* by his son (6) CHARLES STEWART, KG, GCVO, CB, PC, 6th Marquess, *b* 1852; Postmaster-Gen 1900, first Pres of Board of Education 1902, also Lord Pres of the Council 1903, Pres of Committee on Education in Scotland 1905, Lord-Lieut of Ireland 1886-9, and Lord-Lieut of co of City of Belfast 1900-1903; assumed by Roy licence 1885 the additional and principal surname of Stewart: *m* 1875, Lady Theresa Susey Helen, who *d* 1919, el da of 19th Earl of Shrewsbury; *d* 1915; *s* by his son (7) CHARLES STEWART HENRY, KG, MVO, TD, PC, 7th Marquess; *b* 1878; Major and Brevet Lieut-Col late Life Guards; Lord-Lieut of co Durham; was Finance Member of Air Council 1919, Under-Sec of State for Air and Vice-Pres of Air Council 1920-21, first Min of Education in Ulster Parliament 1921-6, a Member of Senate of N Ireland 1921-9 (Leader 1921-6), First Commr of Works (England) 1928-9, and (in National Govt) Aug to Nov 1931, Sec of State for Air 1931-5, and Lord Privy Seal and Leader of House of Lords June to Nov 1935; appointed Chancellor of Queen's Univ, Belfast 1923, and of Durham Univ 1930; sat as MP for Maidstone (C) 1906-15: *m* 1899, Dame Edith Helen Chaplin, DBE, who *d* 1959, da of 1st Viscount Chaplin; *d* 1949; *s* by his son (8) EDWARD CHARLES STEWART ROBERT, 8th Marquess; *b* 1902; Hon Col 12th Batn (Cadet) Durham LI; Hon Attaché, British Embassy, Rome 1924-5; sat as MP for co Down (C) 1931-45; *m* 1931, Romaine, who *d* 1951, da of Major Boyce Combe, of Great Holt, Dockenfield, Surrey; *d* 1955; *s* by his son (9) ALEXANDER CHARLES ROBERT, 9th Marquess, and present peer; also Earl of Londonderry, Earl Vane, Viscount Castlereagh, Viscount Seaham, Baron Londonderry, and Baron Stewart.

LONG, VISCOUNT (Long) (Viscount UK 1921)

RICHARD GERARD LONG, CBE, 4th Viscount; *b* 30 Jan 1929; *s* 1967; *ed* Harrow; late Wilts Regt; a Lord in Waiting to HM 1979-97; Vice-Pres Wilts Roy British Legion, and Bath Light Operatic Club; Pres Bath & Wilts Gliding Club; CBE (Civil) 1993: *m* 1st, 1957 (*m diss* 1984), Margaret Frances, da of late Ninian B. Frazer; 2ndly, 1984 (*m diss* 1990), Mrs Catherine Patricia Elizabeth Mier Woolf, da of Charles Terrence Miles-Ede, of South Africa; 3rdly 1990, Helen Millar Wright Fleming-Gibbons, and has had issue by 1st *m*.

Arms – Sable, within two flaunches and semée of cross-crosslets or, a lion rampant argent. **Crest** – A lion's head argent, erased or, holding in the mouth a dexter hand erased gules. **Supporters** – On either side a lion argent, holding a flag-staff erect proper, flowing therefrom a pennon sable, that on the dexter charged with a portcullis chained and that on the sinister with a fetterlock or.

Pious, though valiant

SON LIVING (*By 1st marriage*)

Hon JAMES RICHARD, *b* 31 Dec 1960.

DAUGHTERS LIVING AND DECEASED (*By 1st marriage*)

Hon Sarah Victoria, *b* 1958: *m* 1990, George G. C. Littler, elder son of George Clegg Littler, and of Mrs Frithjof Meidell-Anderson, and has issue living, Alexander George Richard Clegg, *b* 1996. *Residence* – 20 Oakley Gdns, London SW3 5QG.

Hon Charlotte Helen, *b* 1965; actress; *d* 1984 in a motor accident.

BROTHER LIVING

Hon John Hume, *b* 1930; *ed* Harrow; late Black Watch, BSA Police Rhodesia 1951: *m* 1st, 1957 (*m diss* 1969), Averil Juliet, only da of Henry Stobart, of Salisbury, Rhodesia; 2ndly, 1994, Anne R., da of late Capt H. L. Taunton, of St Lawrence, Jersey, CI, and has issue living (by 1st *m*), Bridget Gwendolyn, *b* 1963.

SISTER LIVING

Hon Noreen, *b* 1921: *m* 1947, Capt John Cairns Bartholomew, Roy Wilts Yeo, and has issue living, Charles John Eric (The Mill House, Bulkington, Devizes, Wilts SN10 1SP), *b* 1951; DL Wilts 1996: *m* 1979, Rosemary Anne, da of Rev Canon V. H. Julien, of The Rectory, Hamilton, Melbourne, Vic, Australia, and has issue living, Toby John *b* 1986, Camilla *b* 1984, — William W., *b* 1956: *m* 1982, Carolyn J. W., el da of Barry Pride, of Knock House, Stone-in-Oxley, Kent, and has issue living, Jack William *b* 1989, Sophie Virginia *b* 1990, — Susan, *b* 1949: *m* 19—, — Bruce. *Residence* – Poulshot Court, Poulshot, Devizes, Wilts.

DAUGHTER LIVING OF SECOND VISCOUNT

Hon (Antoinette) Sara (Frances Sibell), *b* 1934: *m* 1954 (*m diss* 1984), Hon Charles Andrew Morrison, MP (later Hon Sir Charles Morrison) (*see* B Margadale). *Residences* – 45 Westminster Gdns, SW1; Upper Farm, Milton Lilbourne, Pewsey, Wilts.

PREDECESSORS – (1) *Rt Hon* WALTER HUME Long, son of late Richard Penruddock Long, MP; *b* 1854; Parliamentary Sec to Local Govt Board Aug 1886 to June 1892, a Member of Roy Commn on Agricultural Depression 1893, Pres of Board of Agriculture (with a seat in the Cabinet) July 1895 to Nov 1900, Pres of Local Govt Board (with a seat in the Cabinet) Nov 1900 to March 1905, Ch Sec for Ireland (with a seat in the Cabinet) March to Dec 1905 and Lord-Lieut of Wilts 1920-24; appointed again Pres of Local Govt Board May 1915, Sec of State for the Colonies in National Min Dec 1916, and First Lord of the Admirality Jan 1917 (resigned Feb 1921); MP for N Wilts (C) April 1880 to Nov 1886, for Wilts, E, or Devizes, Div Nov 1885 to June 1892 for Liverpool, W Derby Div Jan 1893 to Sept 1900, for Bristol, S Div Oct 1900 to Jan 1906, for Dublin co, S Dublin Div Jan 1906 to Jan 1910, for Strand 1910-18, and for St George's Div of Westminster 1918 to May 1921; *cr Viscount Long*, of Wraxall, co Wilts (peerage of United Kingdom) 1921: *m* 1878, Lady Dorothy Blanche Boyle, who *d* 1938, da of 9th Earl of Cork and Orrery; *d* 1924; *s* by his grandson (2) WALTER FRANCIS DAVID (son of late Brig-Gen Walter Long, CMG, DSO, who was *ka* 1917), 2nd Viscount, *b* 1911; Major Coldstream Guards: *m* 1933 (*m diss* 1943), Frances Laura, who *d* 1990, da of Hon Guy Lawrence Charteris (E Wemyss and March); *ka* 1944; *s* by his uncle (3) (RICHARD) ERIC (ONSLOW), TD (2nd son of 1st Viscount), 3rd Viscount, *b* 1892; a JP for Wilts 1923-67, and a DL 1946-67; MP for Wilts Westbury Div (C) 1927-31: *m* 1916, Gwendolyne Hague, who *d* 1959, da of late Thomas Reginald Hague Cook (Elliot, Bt); *d* 1967; *s* by his el son (4) RICHARD GERARD, 4th Viscount and present peer.

LONGFORD, EARL OF (Pakenham) Sits as BARON PAKENHAM (UK 1945) (Earl I 1785)

Glory is the shadow of virtue

FRANCIS AUNGIER PAKENHAM, KG, PC, b 5 Dec 1905; cr *Baron Pakenham*, of Cowley, City of Oxford (peerage of UK) 1945, PC 1948, KG 1971, and s as 7th Earl 1961; ed Eton, and New Coll, Oxford (BA 1928, MA 1934); was a Lord-in-Waiting to HM Oct 1945 to Oct 1946, Parliamentary Under-Sec of State for War Oct 1946 to April 1947, Chancellor of Duchy of Lancaster April 1947 to May 1948, Min of Civil Aviation May 1948 to May 1951, First Lord of the Admiralty May to Oct 1951 and Lord Privy Seal 1964-65, Sec of State for the Colonies 1965-66, again Lord Privy Seal 1966-68; Chm of Nat Youth Employment Council 1968-71, and of Sidgwick & Jackson 1970-80, author: m 1931, Elizabeth, CBE, MA, writer, da of Nathaniel Bishop Harman, FRCS, of 108 Harley St, W1, and has had issue.

Arms – Quarterly: 1st quarterly or and gules, in the first quarter an eagle displayed vert *Pakenham*; 2nd argent, a bend dancette sable, between two plain cottises azure, the bend charged with three fleurs-de-lis argent, each cottise charged with three bezants, *Cuffe*; 3rd ermine, a griffin segreant azure, *Aungier*; 4th per bend embattled argent and gules, *Boyle*. Crest – Out of a mural coronet or, a demi-eagle displayed gules. Supporters – *Dexter*, a lion azure, charged on the shoulder with a carbuncle or; *sinister*, a griffin azure, wings, elevated ermine, beaked and clawed or.
Residences – Bernhurst, Hurst Green, Sussex; 18 Chesil Court, Chelsea Manor St, SW3.

SONS LIVING

THOMAS FRANK DERMOT (does not use courtesy title) b 14 Aug 1933; ed Ampleforth, and Magdalen Coll, Oxford; writer, author of *The Scramble for Africa* (1992), etc: m 1964, Valerie Susan, yst da of late Maj Ronald Guthrie McNair Scott, of Huish House, Old Basing, nr Basingstoke, Hants (*see* V Camrose, 1995 Edn), and has issue living, Edward Melchior, b 1970, — Frederick Augustus, b 1971, — (Anna) Maria, b 1965: m 1997, Bogislav M. Winner, elder son of Prof Dr Matthias Winner, of Rome, — Eliza, b 1966: m 1993, Alexander James Chisholm, and has issue (*see* B Windlesham). *Residence* – Tullynally, Castlepollard, co Westmeath.

Hon Patrick Maurice b 1937; ed Ampleforth, and Magdalen Coll, Oxford; Bar Inner Temple 1962: m 1968 (m diss 19—), Mary Elizabeth, el da of Maj H. A. J. Plummer, of Winchester, and has issue living, Richard, b 1969, — Guy, b 1970: m 1996, Kia Louise, da of Michael Page, and of Mrs Marilyn Woodgate, — Harry Michael, b 1972. *Residence* – 24 Chesil Court, Chelsea Manor St, SW3.

Hon Michael Aidan, CMG (23 Sutherland Pl, W2; 3052 P St, Washington DC, USA), b 1943; ed Ampleforth, Trin Coll, Camb, and Rice Univ, Texas, USA; CMG 1993: m 1980, Meta (Mimi) Landreth, el da of William Conway Doak, of Philadelphia, USA, and formerly wife of — Lavine, and has issue living, Alexandra Clio, b 1981, — Clio Isabelle Blaise, b 1985.

Hon Kevin John Toussaint, b 1947: ed Ampleforth, New Coll, Oxford, and St Antony's, Oxford: m 1st, 1972 (m diss 1984), Ruth Lesley, da of Leslie Douglas Colbeck Jackson; 2ndly, 19—, Mrs Clare CHATEL, elder da of John Edward Melvill Hoare, of Montague House, Holton St Peter, Halesworth, Suffolk, and has issue living (by 1st wife), Thomas John Chamberlain, b 1977, — Catherine Ruth, b 1975, — (by 2nd wife), Benjamin John, b 1983, — Dominic Balthazar, b 1989, — Hermione Clare, b 1984.

DAUGHTERS LIVING AND DECEASED

Lady Antonia, b 1932; ed Oxford Univ (MA 1969), writer: m 1st 1956, (m diss 1977), Rt Hon Sir Hugh Charles Patrick Joseph Fraser, MBE, MP, who d 1984 (*see* L Lovat); 2ndly, 1980, Harold Pinter, CBE, playwright.

(*Lady*) Judith Elizabeth (does not use courtesy title) (32 Ladbroke Grove, W11 3BQ), b 1940; ed Oxford Univ (BA 1961): m 1963 (m diss 1982), Alexander John Kazantzis, and has issue living, Arthur Constantine, b 1967, — Miranda Elizabeth, b 1964.

Lady Rachel Mary, b 1942; ed London Univ (BA); writer: m 1967, Kevin Billington, of The Court House, Poyntington, Dorset, and has issue living, Nathaniel Kevin, b 1970, — Caspar Leo, b 1979, — Catherine Rose, b 1973, — Chloe Margaret, b 1976.
Lady Catherine Rose, b 1946; k in a motor accident 1969.

SISTERS LIVING

Lady Mary Katharine, b 1907; writer: m 1939, Major Meysey George Dallas Clive, Grenadier Guards, who was ka 1943, and has had issue, George Meysey, b 1940; ed Eton, and Ch Ch Oxford; d 1999, — Alice Mary (*Viscountess Boyd of Merton*), b 1942; High Sheriff Cornwall 1987, DL 1995: m 1962, 2nd Viscount Boyd of Merton, of 9 Warwick Sq, SW1, and Ince Castle, Saltash, Cornwall. *Residence* – Whitfield, Allensmore, Herefordshire.

Lady Violet Georgiana, b 1912; writer: m 1934, Anthony Dymoke Powell, CH, CBE, and has issue living, Tristram Roger Dymoke (3 Stockwell Park Cres, SW9 0DQ), b 1940: m 1968, Virginia Beatrice, da of late Archibald Julian Lucas (*see* B Grenfell, 1980 Edn), and has issue living, Archibald Thomas Llywelyn b 1970, Georgia b 1969, — John Marmion Anthony (137 Kennington Park Rd, SE11), b 1946. *Residence* – The Chantry, nr Frome, Som.

COLLATERAL BRANCHES LIVING

Grandson of late Col Hercules Arthur Pakenham, CMG, elder son of late Lieut-Gen Thomas Henry Pakenham, CB, 3rd son of late Lieut-Gen Hon Sir Hercules Robert Pakenham, KCB, 3rd son of 2nd Baron:—
Issue of late Major Hercules Dermot Wilfrid Pakenham, *b* 1901, *d* of wounds received in action 1940: *m* 1927, Hetty Margaret (who *m* 2ndly, 1950 (*m diss* 1959), Lieut-Col Richard Walter Byng Pembroke, OBE, late Coldstream Guards (*see* V Torrington, colls, 1969 Edn)), da of late Capt Roland Stuart Hebeler, The Queen's Roy Regt:—
(Hercules) Michael Roland, *b* 1935: *ed* Eton: *m* 1st, 1957 (*m diss* 1973), Hon Susan Elizabeth Moon Lever, da of 3rd Viscount Leverhulme, KG; 2ndly, 1973 (*m diss* 1982), Margaret, da of Charles William Fisher, of Wold Cottage, Upham, Hants; 3rdly, 1984 (*m diss* 1994), Fiona Jane, da of Gordon Barrie Peters, of Tiphams End, nr Dorking, Surrey, and has issue living (by 2nd *m*), Rebecca Kate, *b* 1977, — and two children (by 1st *m*), Dermot Philip Michael, *b* 1961: *m* 1988, Johanna, elder da of Dr Ian Perry, of The Old Farm House, Grateley, Hants, and has issue living, Arthur *b* 1992, Emma *b* 1989, Alice *b* (twin) 1989, Claire Alexandra (Anna) *b* 1990, — Caroline Susan Margaret, *b* 1963: *m* 1990, A. Henry M. Wilson, yst son of late John Wilson, of Ovington Gdns, SW3, and has issue living, Alexander James Kirkland *b* 1991, Madelaine Rose Kirkland *b* 1993. *Residence –* Lomer Cottage, Warnford, Southampton SO32 3LJ.

Granddaughter of late Lieut-Col William Wingfield Verner Pakenham, Indian Army, son of late William Sandford Pakenham (infra):—
Issue of late William Henry Verner Pakenham, *b* 1885, *d* 1956: *m* 1905, Alice, who *d* 1966, da of Charles Smith, of Fulwood Park, Liverpool:—
Frances Josephine, *b* 1919: *m* 1946, Eric Douglas Rowlands, of 2 Acorn Grove, Scholes, Holmfirth, Huddersfield, and has issue living, William Verner Pakenham (5 Highfield Rd, Highburton, Huddersfield, W Yorks HD8 0RQ), *b* 1947; BSc; LIM: *m* 1974, Ann, only da of late John Tyas, of Skelmanthorpe, Yorks, and has issue living, Richard William *b* 1976, Victoria Nicola *b* 1977, — Cynthia Jane Olive, *b* 1951; BSc: *m* 1974, Andrew Fisher, who *d* 1981, of 299 Shenley Fields Rd, Selly Oak, Birmingham 29, and has issue living, Daniel Andrew *b* 1976, Emily Jane *b* 1978, Sarah Elizabeth *b* (twin) 1978.

Granddaughter of late Frederick Edward Sandford Pakenham, 2nd son of late William Sandford Pakenham (infra):—
Issue of late Michael Ceely Sandford Pakenham, *b* 1903, *d* 1978: *m* 1st, 1933 (*m diss* 1948), Aline Mary Loftus, who *d* 1967, da of late Loftus St George (St George, Bt colls), and formerly wife of Ernest Charles William Vane-Tempest, DSC (*see* M Londonderry, colls); 2ndly, 1948, Patricia, who *d* 1986, da of late Capt William Harvey Murray, of Mill House, Boyton, Essex:—
(By 1st *m*) Aline Marguerite Constance Sandford, *b* 1934: *m* 1959, Keith William Boyd, of 137 Rouse St, Tenterfield, NSW, Australia, and has issue living, William Michael Sandford, *b* 1964, — Jane Maria Loftus, *b* 1960, — Christina Theresa, *b* 1961.

Grandson of late Robert Sandford Pakenham, 5th son of late William Sandford Pakenham (infra):—
Issue of late Robert Wingfield Pakenham, *b* 1912, *d* 1998: *m* 1941, Alice Gwendoline, who *d* 1982, 2nd da of late T. H. James, of Haverford West, Pembs:—
Clive Sykes (31 Barton Gdns, Sherborne, Dorset), *b* 1947: *m* 1973, Jane, yst da of H. J. Antell, of Sherborne, and has issue living, Daniel Nicholas, *b* 1973, — Adam Geoffrey, *b* 1978.

Grandsons of late Hamilton Richard Pakenham, MB, BCh (infra):—
Issue of late Richard Hercules Wingfield Pakenham, CBE, *b* 1906, *d* 1993: *m* 1947, Eileen Isolde (Apt 20, Flete, Ermington, Ivybridge, Devon PL2 9NZ), elder da of late Oscar Faber, CBE, DCL, DSc:—
John Hubert (Tor Down House, Belstone, Okehampton, Devon EX20 1QY), *b* 1951: *m* 1991, Maureen Denise, da of late W/Cmdr Patrick Woolley, RAF, of Flete, Ermington, Devon. —— Richard Arthur (adopted son), *b* 1949.

Grandson of late William Sandford Pakenham, 3rd son of late Very Rev Hon Henry Pakenham, 5th son of 2nd Baron:—
Issue of late Hamilton Richard Pakenham, MB, BCh, *b* 1867, *d* 1957; Church Missionary Soc, Fukien Prov, S China: *m* 1900, Emily Willis, who *d* 1975, da of late Thomas Stringer, of Merrion Hall, Dublin:—
Henry Desmond Verner, CBE, *b* 1911; *ed* Monkton Combe, and St John's Coll, Oxford (scholar); British Dep High Commr, Sydney, NSW 1968-71; CBE (Civil) 1964: *m* 1st, 1946 (*m diss* 1960), Crystal Elizabeth, da of late Lt-Col Edward York Brooksbank (*see* Brooksbank, Bt); 2ndly, 1963, Venetia, da of William Paterson Doyle, and formerly wife of Maurice Christopher Maude, and has issue living (by 1st *m*), Anthony Edward (53 Blomfontein Av, W12 7BJ), *b* 1952; *ed* Eton, and Ch Ch, Oxford, — Pandora Clare, *b* 1948: *m* 1969, Matthieu Millet, of 8 rue de Champagne, 92600 Asnières, France, and has issue living, Alexandre François *b* 1974, Thomas *b* 1990, Sophie Emilie *b* 1976, Catherine *b* 1981, — (by 2nd *m*) Mark Edmund, *b* 1965, — Sarah Catherine, *b* 1966. *Residence –* The Mill House, Prentice St, Lavenham, Sudbury, Suffolk.

Granddaughters of late Thomas Compton Pakenham, MC (infra):—
Issue of late Compton Christopher Pakenham, *b* 1921, *d* 1995: *m* 1947, Dorothy Rebecca Cullingford, who *d* 1984:—
Diane (Box 192, Harwood, Missouri 64750, USA), *b* 1949: *m* 1980, John Pennington, and has issue living, Lucas Christopher, *b* 1989, — Catherine Elisabeth, *b* 1993. —— Monica, *b* 1954. —— Jennifer (4 Cavesson Drive, Smithville, NJ 08201, USA), *b* (twin) 1954: *m* 1983, Gary Sandy Sawhill, and has issue living, Cody Pakenham (a son), *b* 1987, — Sloan Pakenham (a da), *b* 1984.

Grandchildren of late Gustavus Conolly Pakenham, 2nd son of late Capt George Dent Pakenham (infra):—
Issue of late Thomas Compton Pakenham, MC, *b* 1893, *d* 1957: *m* 1st, 1915 (*m diss* 1920), Phyllis Mona, da of Col William Price, RE; 2ndly, 1921, Alma Clark; 3rdly, 1925, Sara, who *d* 1976, da of Charles Manning Furman, of Clemson, S Carolina, USA:—

(By 1st *m*) Simona Vere, *b* 1916: *m* 1st, 1938, Noel Paterson Durnford Iliff, who *d* 1984; 2ndly, 1984, Kenneth William Bruce Middleton, who *d* 1994, and has issue living (by 1st *m*), David Anthony (Green Willows, Station Rd, Woodmancote, Cheltenham, Glos GL52 4HN), *b* 1939: *m* 1966, Celia Winifred Foot, and has had issue, Stephanie Brigid Laura *b* 1968, *d* 1998, Alison Deborah Caroline *b* 1970. *Residence* – Cobbler's Cottage, Ledwell, Chipping Norton, Oxon OX7 7AN. —— (By 3rd *m*) Edward Michael, *b* 1932; editor *New York Daily News*. —— Joan Compton, *b* 1932: *m* 19—, — Breiter.

Grandsons of late Frederick Edward Pakenham (infra):—
Issue of late Thomas Hume Pakenham *b* 1907, *d* 1965: *m* 1st, 1928 (*m diss* 1945), Margaret Olwen da of late Capt Thomas Corrance, of Ervin, Wigtownshire; 2ndly, 1946, Isabella Nimmo, da of Archie Cowie, of Airdrie, Lanarkshire:—
(By 1st *m*) Thomas David Corrance (1100 Normandy Cres, Ottawa, Ont K2C 0L8, Canada), *b* 1929: *m* 1951, Edith McDerby, and has issue living, Thomas McDerby (1024 Arrowhead Place, Ottawa, Ont K1C 2S4, Canada), *b* 1961: *m* 1987, Maura Ann, da of William Tubridy, of Toronto, and has issue living, Kathryn Tubridy *b* 1993, — James Arthur, *b* 1962, — Teresa Christine PAKENHAM, *b* 1959; has resumed her maiden name: *m* 1977 (*m diss* 1984), Michael Sabourin, and has two adopted das, Angela Sarah Christine PAKENHAM *b* 1976, Candace Debra Elaine PAKENHAM *b* 1984, — Jocelyn Patricia, *b* 1955: *m* 1975, Warren Reade, of SS3 Site 9 Comp 87, Prince George, BC V2N 2S7, Canada, and has issue living, Jennifer Alison Ella *b* 1979, Kathryn Ann Dorothy *b* 1981, — Edith Lorraine PAKENHAM, *b* 1958; has resumed her maiden name: *m* 19— (*m diss* 19—), Donald Bond, and has issue living, Shaun Donald Pakenham *b* 1980, Daniel Scott *b* 1983, — Maria Aline, *b* 1965. —— John Edwin, *b* 1930: *m* 1st, 1954 (*m diss* 1959), Wendy Cox; 2ndly, 1962, Gaylynn Evon, da of Weir Powellson Armstrong, and has issue living, (by 1st *m*) Cheryl Olwen, *b* 1955, — (by 2nd *m*) Sean Thomas, *b* 1963, — Edward Austin Westmoreland, *b* 1967, — Naja Chrisanna, *b* 1968.

Grandchildren of late Capt George Dent Pakenham, only son of late Thomas Pakenham, 2nd son of late Adm Hon Sir Thomas Pakenham, GCB, yst son of 1st Baron Longford and Elizabeth Countess of Longford:—
Issue of late Frederick Edward Pakenham, *b* 1869, *d* 1923: *m* 1906, Nancy Jane, da of Charles Youmans, formerly of Hazleton, British Columbia:—
†Arthur Godfrey, *b* 1910: *m* 1st, 1938 (*m diss* 1950), Wanda Hatcher; 2ndly, 1951, Rose Marie, da of Anton Eberle, and *d* 1993, leaving issue, (by 2nd *m*) Patricia Eve, *b* 1956. *Residence* – 1210 NE 124th Street, Seattle, Washington 98125, USA. —— William Christopher (The Rosedale Retirement Centre, RR1 Brockville, Ontario, Canada K6V 5T1), *b* 1922: *m* 1st, 1943 (*m diss* 1954), Mona May Morris; 2ndly, 1955, Marjorie Jane, who *d* 1978, da of late Duncan Ried Wilson, of Montrose, Scotland, and has issue living, (by 1st *m*) Frederick Edward (1286 Brockmount Place, Brockville, Ont, Canada K6V 5Z7), *b* 1944: *m* 1971, Theresa Marie Fleury, da of Rheal Laurier, and has issue living, Christopher James *b* 1975, John Laurier *b* 1978, Matthew Edward *b* 1984, — (by 2nd *m*) Ronald Arthur (145 Dana St, Brockville, Ont, Canada K6V 6X1), *b* 1957: *m* 1984, Mary Ellen, da of Clifford Stanley Ross, and has issue living, Kurt William Frederick *b* 1984, — Donna Marie, *b* 1959: *m* 1987, John Walton MacLeod, and has issue living, Jennifer Marjorie *b* 1993. —— Norma Muriel Doreen, *b* 1913: *m* 1938, Donald Holmes, and has issue living. *Residence* – 220 196th St SE No 67, Bothell, Washington 98012, USA.

Grandsons of late William Law Pakenham, el son of Wellington Montagu Pakenham (infra):—
Issue of Capt the late Rev Thomas Arthur Charles Pakenham, RN, *b* 1900, *d* 1981: *m* 1925, Clara Talbot, who *d* 1985, da of late William Middleton, of Monks Pond, Lymington:—
William Thomas Talbot (Croft Mews, Botley, Hants), *b* 1926; Capt RN; 1944-45 War: *m* 1957, Antonia Mary, da of late Capt Antony Coleby, RN, of Hapton House, Hambledon, Hants, and has issue living, Robin Thomas Cliff, *b* 1963: *m* 1994, Mrs Susan Mary Graham, elder da of late Frederick Henry Timson, of Keyworth, Notts, and has issue living, Benjamin Thomas William *b* 1997, — John Neville, *b* 1964, — Katherine Clara, *b* 1960. —— *Rev* Stephen Walter (Chattis Hill Mews, Spitfire Lane, Stockbridge, Hants SO20 7JS), *b* 1929; *ed* Cambridge Univ (MA); Lt RN (ret); V of Donnington and Apuldram 1964-75, V of Durrington 1975-81, V of St Mary Bourne and Woodcott 1981-88; 1968 record singlehanded crossing of Atlantic in 21 days, 15 hrs and 7 mins in a 32ft ketch: *m* 1957, Elizabeth Ann, only da of late Rt Rev Kenneth Edward Norman Lamplugh, Suffragan Bishop of Southampton, and has issue living, Jonathan Hugh Rust, *b* 1958: *m* 1985, Nina Diana, da of late Lawrence Woodhouse Mason, of Winchester, and has issue living, George Lawrence *b* 1987, Timothy James *b* 1990, Henry Francis Benjamin *b* 1997, — Marcus Charles, *b* 1960: *m* 1991, Lisa A. M., da of Bengt Delaryd, of Repulse Bay, Hong Kong, — Olivia Judith Clare, *b* 1963: *m* 1992, Mark Elton, eldest son of Ronald George Johnson, and has issue living, Samuel Luke Pakenham *b* 1996, Bethany Charlotte Pakenham *b* 1993.

Grandchildren of late Com Arthur McClellan Pakenham, RD, RNR (infra):—
Issue of late Peter Hugh Percy Holwell Pakenham, *b* 1913; *d* 1982: *m* 1st 1939, Nancy, who *d* 1966, da of Herbert George Alexander, of Woodlands, Westonbirt, Glos; 2ndly, 1973, Ailsa Jean (The Red Cottage, Roode Ashton, Trowbridge, Wilts), widow of Kenneth George Marsh, of Potticks House, Bradford on Avon, Wilts:—
(By 1st *m*) Jeremy Edwin Montagu (The Old Manor, Rudge, Frome, Somerset), *b* 1948: *m* 1974, Caroline, da of late Albert Maurice Redman, of Wonham House, Bampton, Devon, and has issue living, James Edwin Holwell, *b* 1977, — Edward Charles Montagu, *b* 1980, — Victoria Louise, *b* 1984. —— Susan Daphne, *b* 1942: *m* 1965, Brig George Gerald Blakey, of Farrington House, Farrington, Dorset, and has issue living, Lucinda Jane, *b* 1967: *m* 1993, Hugo John Vaux, 2nd son of Maj John Vaux, of Moulton Manor, Moulton, N Yorks, and has issue living, Fergus Peter *b* 1996, Ellie Louise *b* 1998.

Grandson of late Wellington Montagu Pakenham, 2nd son of late Adm John Pakenham, 4th son of late Adm Hon Sir Thomas Pakenham, GCB (ante):—
Issue of late Com Arthur McClellan Pakenham, RD, RNR, *b* 1876, *d* 1948: *m* 1st, 1910, Ethel Louise, who *d* 1934, da of late R. A. W. Holwell; 2ndly, 1938, Katharine Joan (who *m* 2ndly 19—), da of Sidney A. Horstman, of Fair Lawn, Bath:—
(By 1st *m*) Patrick Christopher Montagu Holwell, *b* 1922; formerly Capt Roy Signals; Burma 1942-45 (despatches twice). *Residence* – 2 Ave de Budé, Geneva 1202, Switzerland.

Grandchildren of late Maj Charles Pakenham, 4th son of late Rev Robert Pakenham, DD, 6th son of late Adm Hon Sir Thomas Pakenham, GCB (ante):—
Issue of late Col George de la Poer Beresford Pakenham, CMG, CBE, DSO, *b* 1875, *d* 1960: *m* 1st 1905, Emilie Elsie, who *d* 1921, da of late William Fowler, of Broadlands, Liverpool; 2ndly, 1923, Marie Marthe Amalie, who *d* 1968, widow of Capt Jacques Henri Joucia, French Army:—

(By 1st *m*) Raymond Beresford, *b* 1907; *ed* Haileybury; Lt-Col (ret) Border Regt and acting Group Capt RAF: *m* 1st, 1930 (*m diss* 1934), Sheila Barbara Kathleen, da of late Joseph Masoon (Price, Bt, *cr* 1815, colls); 2ndly, 1934 (*m diss* 1937), Sophie Patricia, da of late Capt R. D. Pollock, of Teign-na-Mara, Bangor, co Down; 3rdly, 1948, Catherine Lillian Elizabeth, da of late H. Smith, of Salisbury.

Issue of late Capt Hewitt John Havelock Pakenham, *b* 1880, *d* 1978: *m* 1st, 1906, Claire May, who *d* 1944, only da of late Edmond Berdoe-Wilkinson, of Eashing, Godalming; 2ndly, 1946, Molly, who *d* 1976, el da of late William Henry Cook, of The Old Cross Houyse, Heretford, and widow of Capt Oswell Jones, Roy West Kent Regt:—
(By 1st *m*) †Arthur John Edmond, *b* 1907; Maj Queen's R Regt (W Surrey) TA (Reserve); Burma 1942-45: *m* 1st 1932 (*m diss* 1948), Sarah, da of late Capt Rowland Alston, late Coldm Gds, formerly of Odell Castle, Beds; 2ndly, 1952, Heidi, el da of late Emil Wegmann, of Frauenfeld, Switzerland, and *d* 1996, leaving issue, (by 2nd *m*) Timothy James Robert (26 New Rd, Chiscldon, Wilts SN4 0LU), *b* 1961: *m* 1989, Kim, da of John Gibson, of Bayston Hill, Shropshire, and has issue living, Sophie *b* 1993, Hannah *b* 1995, — Christine Catherine (29 Eastlands Close, Oxted, Surrey RH8 0EY), *b* 1953: *m* 1980 (*m diss* 1989), Nigel Buckler Cooper, and has issue living, Robert John *b* 1987. *Residence* – 29 Eastlands Close, Oxted, Surrey RH8 0EY. —— Cynthia Marion Blanche (The Hollies, 3A Compton Way, Olivers Battery, Winchester, Hants), *b* 1909: *m* 1st, 1935 (*m diss* 1947), Capt Alexander Glazebrook Acton Pierce, RA; 2ndly, 1947, Guy Fothergill Batho, MBE, who *d* 1992, and has issue living (by 2nd *m*), William Nicholas Pakenham, *b* 1948; *ed* Canford Sch, and RNC Dartmouth; Capt RN: *m* 1973, Jennifer, da of W. R. Best, of Embleton, Northumberland, and has issue living, William Guy Pakenham *b* 1980, Julia Elizabeth *b* 1978.

PREDECESSORS – (**1**) THOMAS Pakenham, MP for Longford Borough; *cr Baron Longford* (peerage of Ireland) 1756; he *d* 1776, and his widow was *cr Countess of Longford* (peerage of Ireland) 1785; she *d* 1794; he was *s* by his el son (**2**) EDWARD MICHAEL, PC, 2nd Baron; MP for co Longford 1765; *d* 1792; *s* by his son (**3**) THOMAS, 3rd Baron, who became in 1794, on the death of his grandmother, 2nd Earl of Longford; *cr Baron Longford*, of co Southampton 1821; *b* 1774: *m* 1817, Lady Georgiana Emma Charlotte Lygon, da of 1st Earl Beauchamp; *d* 1835; *s* by his el son (**4**) EDWARD MICHAEL, 3rd Earl; was Capt 2nd Life Guards; *d* unmarried 1860; *s* by his brother (**5**) WILLIAM LYGON, GCB, 4th Earl; *b* 1819; was Col 1st and 2nd Btns Northumberland Fusiliers: *m* 1862, Hon Selina Rice-Trevor, who *d* 1918, da of 4th Baron Dinevor; *d* 1887; *s* by his son (**6**) THOMAS, KP, MVO, 5th Earl, 1864; Col Life Guards; Lieut and Custos Rotulorum for co Longford 1887-1915: *m* 1899, Lady Mary Julia Child Villiers, who *d* 1933, da of 7th Earl of Jersey; *ka* at Dardanelles while Brig-Gen 2nd S Midland Mounted Brig, 1915; *s* by his el son (**7**) EDWARD ARTHUR HENRY, 6th Earl, *b* 1902; a Senator of Eire 1946-8: *m* 1925, Christine Patty, who *d* 1980, da of late Richard Trew, of Cheddar, Somerset; *d* 1961; *s* by his brother (**8**) FRANCIS AUNGIER, 7th Earl and present peer; also Baron Longford (peerage of Ireland), Baron Silchester, and Baron Pakenham.

LONSDALE, EARL OF (Lowther) (Earl UK 1807, Bt GB 1764)

The office shows the man

JAMES HUGH WILLIAM LOWTHER, 7th Earl and 8th Baronet; *b* 3 Nov 1922; *s* 1953; *ed* Eton; 1939-45 War in RAC and as Capt E Riding Yeo (despatches): *m* 1st, 1945 (*m diss* 1954), Tuppina Cecily, who *d* 1984, da of late Capt Geoffrey Henry Bennet; 2ndly, 1954 (*m diss* 1962), Hon Jennifer Lowther, da of late Maj Hon Christopher William Lowther (*see* V Ullswater); 3rdly, 1963, Nancy Ruth (STEPHENSON), da of late Thomas Cobbs, of Pacific Palisades, Cal, USA; 4thly, 1975, Caroline Sheila, yst da of Sir Gerald Gordon Ley, TD, 3rd Bt, and has issue by 1st, 2nd, 3rd and 4th *m*.

Arms – Or, six annulets, three, two, and one sable. **Crest** – A dragon passant argent. **Supporters** – Two horses argent, gorged with wreaths of laurel vert.
Residences – Askham Hall, Penrith, Cumbria CA10 2PF. *Club* – Brooks's.

SONS LIVING (*By 1st marriage*)

HUGH CLAYTON (*Viscount Lowther*) (Towcett House, Newby, Penrith), *b* 27 May 1949: *m* 1st, 1971, Pamela Colleen Middleton; 2ndly, 1986, Angela Mary, da of Capt Peter Wyatt, of Dartmouth, Devon.

(*By 2nd marriage*)

Hon William James, *b* 1957.

(*By 3rd marriage*)

Hon James Nicholas, *b* 1964: *m* 199—, Vanessa, da of Alan Catchpole, of Broke Hall, Nacton, Suffolk, and of Mrs Ronald Foster Pegg, of The Coach House, Grundisburgh, Suffolk, and has issue living, Matilda Grace, *b* 1995, — Ishbel Cecily, *b* 1997.

DEBRETT'S ILLUSTRATED PEERAGE

(By 4th marriage)

Hon Charles Alexander James, *b* 1978.

DAUGHTERS LIVING *(By 1st marriage)*

Lady Jane Helen Harbord, *b* 1947: *m* 1st, 1969, Gary Hunter Wooten, of Calif, USA; 2ndly, 1978, Robert Charles Benson, eldest son of late Lt-Cdr Nicholas Robin Benson, of Aycote House, Rendcomb, Cirencester, Glos (*see* D Rutland, 1971 Edn), and has issue living (by 2nd *m*), Laura Jane, *b* 1980, — Sophie Camilla, *b* 1984. *Residence* – Glebe House, Lowther, Penrith, Cumbria.

(By 2nd marriage)

Lady Miranda, *b* 1955; resumed maiden name by deed poll 1983-86: *m* 1st, 1978, Martin Dunne; 2ndly, 1986, Ian Cronshaw; 3rdly, 19—, Michael Glen, and has issue living (by 2nd *m*), Samantha, *b* 1986, — (by 3rd *m*) Sarah, *b* 1992.
Lady Caroline, *b* 1959: *m* 1st, 1978 (*m diss* 19—), Guy P. T. Forrester; 2ndly, 1982, Stephen Christopher Ernest Hunt; 3rdly, 1987, Charles John Patrick Lawson, only son of Col Sir John Charles Arthur Digby Lawson, 3rd Bt (*cr* 1900), DSO, MC, and has issue living (by 2nd *m*), George Stephen, *b* 1982, — (by 3rd *m*) (*see* Lawson, Bt, *cr* 1900). *Residence* – Heckwood, Sampford Spiney, Yelverton, Devon PL20 6L9.

(By 4th marriage)

Lady Marie-Louisa Kate, *b* 1976.

WIDOW LIVING OF BROTHER OF SEVENTH EARL

Lavinia (Whitbysteads, Askham, Penrith, Cumbria), only child of late Thomas H. Joyce, of San Francisco, Cal, USA: *m* 1958, Capt Hon Anthony George Lowther, MBE, who *d* 1981, and has issue (see colls, infra).

WIDOW LIVING OF SON OF SIXTH EARL

Susan Ann FoÀ, da of Capt Leonard Stephen Smallwood, of Jersey: *m* 1977, as his 2nd wife, Hon Timothy Lancelot Edward Lowther, who *d* 1984, and has issue (see colls, infra). *Residence* – Ivystone House, Rue De La Croix, St Clements, Jersey, Channel Is JE2 6LQ.

COLLATERAL BRANCHES LIVING

Issue of late Capt Hon Anthony George Lowther, MBE, yr brother of 7th Earl (raised to the rank of an Earl's son 1954), *b* 1925, *d* 1981: *m* 1958, Lavinia (ante), only child of late Thomas H. Joyce, of San Francisco, USA:—
Thomas Scott Anthony, *b* 1966: *m* 1997, Victoria M., da of (Thomas) David Whately, MC, of Pensbury House, Shaftesbury, Dorset, and has issue living, a son, *b* 1998. —— Camilla Ann, *b* 1959. —— Arabella Mary, *b* 1962. —— Sarah Lavinia, *b* 1964: *m* 1990, Steven G. Husband, 2nd son of George William Husband, of Billingham, Cleveland.

Issue of late Hon Timothy Lancelot Edward Lowther, yr son (by 2nd *m*) of 6th Earl, *b* 1925, *d* 1984: *m* 1st, 1966 (*m diss* 1976), Margaret Elizabeth, elder da of late John Herring, MC, of 50 Harley St, W1, and formerly wife of Baron Giovanni Testaferrata-Abela: 2ndly, 1977, Susan Ann FoÀ (ante), da of Capt Leonard Stephen Smallwood, of Jersey:—
(By 2nd *m*) Melinda Clare, *b* 1978.

Descendants of late Rt Hon Sir James William Lowther, GCB (son of late Hon William Lowther, brother of 3rd Earl), who was *cr Viscount Ullswater* 1921 (see that title).

(In remainder to Viscountcy only)

Descendants of late John Lowther, MP (brother of 1st Earl), who was *cr a Baronet* 1824:—
See Lowther, Bt, *cr* 1824.

PREDECESSORS – (1) *Sir* JOHN Lowther, MP for Westmorland 1660-75; 30th Knight of the family in almost direct succession; *cr a Baronet* 1640; *d* 1675; and was's by his grandson (2) *Sir* JOHN, PC, 2nd Bt, MP for Westmorland 1680-96; was Vice-Chamberlain of the Household, First Lord Commr of the Treasury, and Lord-Lieut of Westmorland and Cumberland; *cr Baron Lowther* and *Viscount Lonsdale* (peerage of England) 1696; *d* 1700; *s* by his son (3) RICHARD, 2nd Viscount; *d* 1713; *s* by his brother (4) HENRY, who *dsp* 1750, when the peerages became extinct, and the baronetcy devolved upon (5) *Sir* JAMES, MP, 5th Bt, grandson of Richard, 2nd son of 1st Bt; *cr Baron Lowther, Baron Kendal, Baron Burgh, Viscount Lowther,* and *Earl of Lonsdale* (peerage of Great Britain) 1784, and *Baron Lowther* and *Viscount Lowther* (peerage of Great Britain) 1797, with remainder to the heirs male of his cousin, Rev Sir William Lowther, Bt, of

Swillington (cr 1764); dsp 1802; s in the honours of 1797 by his kinsman (6) Sir WILLIAM KG, 2nd Viscount; cr Earl of Lonsdale 1807; d 1844; s by his el son (7) WILLIAM, PC, 2nd Earl; b 1787; Lord of the Admiralty 1809, a Commr for Indian Affairs 1810-18, a Lord of the Treasury 1813-27, Ch Commr of Woods and Forests 1828-30, Vice Pres of Board of Trade and Treasurer of the Navy 1834-5, and Lord Pres of the Council 1852; d 1872; s by his nephew (8) HENRY, 3rd Earl; b 1818; sometime MP for W Cumberland, Capt 1st Life Guards Col Cumberland and Westmorland Yeo Cav, and Lord-Lieut and Custos Rotulorum of Westmorland and Cumberland: m 1852, Emily Susan, who d 1917, da of St George Francis Caulfeild, of Donamon; d 1876; s by his el son (9) ST. GEORGE HENRY, 4th Earl; b 1855; d 8 Feb 1882; s by his brother (10) HUGH CECIL, KG, GCVO, TD, 5th Earl; b 1857; Lord-Lieut and Custos Rotulorum of Cumberland, and Chm of Quarter Sessions for Westmorland; Mayor of Whitehaven 1894 and 1895: m 1878, Lady Grace Cicelie Gordon, CBE, who d 1941, da of 10th Marquess of Huntly; d 1944; s by his brother (11) LANCELOT EDWARD, OBE, 6th Earl, b 1867; European War 1914-19 as Capt 3rd Batn Border Regt, and Gen Staff (OBE): m 1st, 1889, Sophia Gwendoline Alice, who d 1921, el da of Sir Robert Sheffield, 5th Bt; 2ndly, 1923, Sybil Beatrix, who d 1966, da of late Maj-Gen Edward Feetham, CB, CMG; d 1953; s by his grandson (12) JAMES HUGH WILLIAM (son of late Anthony Edward, Viscount Lowther, el son of 6th Earl), 7th Earl and present peer; also Viscount Lowther and Baron Lowther.

Lopes, family name of Baron Roborough.

Lorne, Marquess of; son of Duke of Argyll.

LOTHIAN, MARQUESS OF (Kerr) (Marquess S 1701)
(Name pronounced "Karr")

Late, but in earnest

SERO SED SERIO

PETER FRANCIS WALTER KERR, KCVO, 12th Marquess; b 8 Sept 1922; s 1940, ed Ampleforth Coll, and Ch Ch, Oxford; FRSA; Lt Scots Guards, a Member of Queen's Body Guard for Scotland (Royal Company of Archers), DL Roxburghshire 1962, Comdt, Roxburgh, Selkirk and Berwickshire Special Constabulary, and a Knight of Sovereign Order of Malta; Joint Parl Sec to Min of Health, April to Oct 1964; Lord-in-Waiting to HM 1962-64, and again 1972-73; an Under-Sec, Foreign and Commonwealth Office 1970-72; Lord Warden of the Stannaries and Keeper of the Privy Seal of Duke of Cornwall 1977-83; cr KCVO 1983: m 1943, Antonella, OBE, da of late Maj-Gen Sir Foster Reuss Newland, KCMG, CB, and has issue.

Arms – Quarterly: 1st and 4th azure, a sun in splendour or, Lothian; 2nd and 3rd gules, on a chevron argent three mullets of the field, Kerr. Crest – 1st, a sun in splendour or; 2nd, a stag's head erased proper. Supporters – Dexter, an angel proper, verted azure, surcoat vert, winged and crined cr; sinister, an unicorn argent armed, unguled, manned, and tufted or.
Seat – Ferniehirst Castle, Jedburgh, Roxburghshire; Town Residence - 177 Cranmer Court, Whitehead's Grove, SW3 3HF. Clubs – Boodle's, New (Edinburgh).

SONS LIVING

MICHAEL ANDREW FOSTER JUDE (Rt Hon Earl of Ancram), MP, b 7 July 1945; ed Ampleforth, and Ch Ch, Oxford (MA, LLB); Advocate Edinburgh 1970, QC 1996; Member Queen's Body Guard for Scotland (Royal Company of Archers); DL Roxburgh, Ettrick and Lauderdale 1990; Member Select Cttee on Energy 1979-83; Chm Conservative Party in Scotland 1980-83; Under Sec of State, Scottish Office, 1983-87, and N Ireland Office 1993-94, Min of State for N Ireland 1994-97, Dep Party Chm Conservative Party June-Oct 1998, since when Chm; MP for Berwickshire and E Lothian (C) Feb to Oct 1974, for Edinburgh South 1979-June 1987, and for Devizes since 1992; PC 1996: m 1975, Lady (Theresa) Jane Fitzalan-Howard, da of 16th Duke of Norfolk, and has issue:—

DAUGHTERS LIVING — Lady Clare Therese, b 1979, — Lady Mary Cecil, b 1981.

Clubs – Pratt's, Beefsteak.

Lord Ralph William Francis Joseph (20 Upper Cheyne Row, SW3; Melbourne Hall, Melbourne, Derby DE7 1EN), b 1957; ed Ampleforth; Member Queen's Body Guard for Scotland (Royal Company of Archers): m 1st, 1980 (m diss 1987), Lady Virginia Mary Elizabeth FitzRoy, 2nd da of 11th Duke of Grafton; 2ndly, 1988, Marie-Claire, yr da of (Michael) Donald Gordon Black, MC, of Edenwood, Cupar, Fife, and has issue living (by 2nd m), John Walter Donald Peter, b 8 Aug 1988, — Frederic James Michael Ralph, b 1989, — Francis Andrew William George, b 1991, — Amabel Mary Antonella, b 1995, — Minna Alice Priscilla Elizabeth, b 1998.

DAUGHTERS LIVING

Lady Mary Marianella Anne, *b* 1944; BA (Open Univ): *m* 1970, Charles von Westenholz, of Little Blakesware, Widford, Ware, Herts, and has issue living, Alexander Peter Frederik, *b* 1971, — Mark Henry Cosimo, *b* 1973, — Nicholas Anthony Philip, *b* 1975.

Lady Cecil Nennella Therese *b* 1948; BA (London Univ): *m* 1974, Donald Angus Cameron of Lochiel yr, elder son of Sir Donald Hamish Cameron of Lochiel (*see* D Montrose, 1976 Edn), and has issue (*see* E Cranbrook, colls). *Residences* – Achnacarry, Spean Bridge, Inverness-shire; 26 The Little Boltons, SW10.

Lady Clare Amabel Margaret (*Countess of Euston*), *b* 1951; *ed* London Univ (BA, MA): *m* 1972, James Oliver Charles, Earl of Euston, son of 11th Duke of Grafton, and has issue (see that title). *Residences* – The Racing Stables, Euston, Thetford, Norfolk; 6 Vicarage Gdns, W8.

Lady Elizabeth Marian Frances (*Countess of Dalkeith*), *b* 1954; *ed* LSE (BSc) Chm Scottish Ballet 1990-95; Trustee, Nat Museums of Scotland 1991-99: *m* 1981, Richard Walter John, Earl of Dalkeith, son of 9th Duke of Buccleuch, and has issue (see that title). *Residences* – Dabton, Thornhill, Dumfriesshire; 24 Lansdowne Rd, W11 3LL.

BROTHER LIVING *(Raised to the rank of a Marquess's son 1941)*

Lord John Andrew Christopher, *b* 1927; *ed* Ampleforth, and Ch Ch, Oxford; late Capt Scots Guards: *m* 1949, Isabel Marion, da of Sir Hugh Gurney, KCMG, MVO (E Southesk, colls), and has issue living, William Walter Raleigh (The Dower House, Melbourne Derby), *b* 1950: *m* 1985, Griselda Mary, elder da of Brig John Robert Edward Hamilton-Baillie, MC (*see* E Haddington, colls), and has issue living, Robert John Edward *b* 1987, Walter William Raleigh *b* 1992, Cordelia Isabel Marie *b* 1988, — David John, *b* 1952: *m* 1980, Carol Prior, and has issue living, John Andrew David *b* 1981, Andrew Christopher *b* 1984, — Andrew Peter Hugh (29 The Green, Steventon, Oxon), *b* 1955, — Marion Isabel, *b* 1960: *m* 1987, Simon David May, of 17 Campion Way, Witham, Chelmsford, Essex, elder son of C. J. May, of 1 The Rushes, Marlow, Bucks, and has issue living, Susannah Isabel Catherine *b* 1990, Rebecca Isabel Laura *b* 1994, — Catherine Richenda Margaret, *b* 1965: *m* 1st, 1991, Alan McCallie, yst son of J. McCallie, of 23 Birnham Av, Banana Point, NSW; 2ndly, 19—, Darren Williams, and has issue living (by 1st *m*), Beau James *b* 1991, (by 2nd *m*) Isabel Richenda Eileen *b* 1996, Matthew Ross *b* 1991. *Residence* – Holly Bank, Wootton, Woodstock, Oxford.

COLLATERAL BRANCHES LIVING

Grandchildren of late Capt Henry Francis Hobart Kerr (infra):—
Issue of late Lt-Col Francis Robert Newsam Kerr, OBE, MC, The Royal Scots, *b* 1916, *d* 1995: *m* 1941, Anne Frederica (The Coach House, Howden, Jedburgh, Roxburghshire), yr da of late William Edmundstoun Kitson, of Blanerne House, Edrom, Berwicks:—
Henry Mark William (Gate Lodge, Dysertmore, Mullinavat, co Kilkenny), *b* 1946; *ed* Ampleforth: *m* 1982, Pamela Christine, da of late Alfred Edward Noel Delafield, of 59 Howard Rd, Plymstock, Plymouth, Devon. —— David Anthony Francis (Howden, Jedburgh, Roxburghshire), *b* 1953: *m* 1975, Julia Veronica, da of late William James Bertram, and has issue living, Sarah Anne, *b* 1978, — Jane Elizabeth, *b* 1980. —— Susan Mary KERR, *b* 1952; has retained her maiden name: *m* 1981, Andrew Robert King, of 30 Ebsworth St, Mount Lawley, Perth, W Australia 6050, and has issue living, Rory Francis, *b* 1985.

Granddaughters of late Francis Ernest Kerr, 3rd and yst son of Rev Lord Henry Francis Charles Kerr, 2nd son of 6th Marquess:—
Issue of late Capt Henry Francis Hobart Kerr, *b* 1878, *d* 1972: *m* 1915, Gertrude Mary, who *d* 1969, da of James Anthony:—
Monica Mary Cecil, *b* 1917: *m* 1939, Gp Capt William George Devas, CBE, DFC, AFC, RAF (ret), and has issue living, Christopher William Kerr (Wadmill Farm, Stour Row, Shaftesbury, Dorset SP7 0QB), *b* 1944; JP 1992: *m* 1st, 1970 (*m diss* 1983), Hon Penelope Anne, da of Baron O'Neill of The Maine (Life Baron); 2ndly, 1994, Veronica Susan, da of Lt-Col Eric Surtees Scott, MBE (*see* E Eldon, colls), and widow of Michael Conway Phayre-Mudge, and has issue living (by 1st *m*), William Thomas *b* 1975, — John Robin Ambrose (24 Sydenham Rd, Cotham, Bristol BS6 5SJ), *b* 1947; AA Dip, RIBA, Ordre des Architectes Français: *m* 1970, Rachel Geraldine, da of late Capt Gerald Seymour Tuck, DSO, RN, and has issue living, Frédéric Seymour *b* 1978, Claire-Noëlle *b* 1976. *Residence* – 3 Cavendish St, Chichester, W Sussex PO19 3BS. —— Anne Margaret D'Arcy, *b* 1923: *m* 1948, Christopher Scott of Gala (who *d* 1997, having assumed the surname of Scott in lieu of his patronymic 1940), only son of late Philip Beaumont Frere, MC, and has had issue, John Philip Henry Schomberg (The Kirk House, Bowden, by Melrose), *b* 1952: *m* 1977, Jaqueline Dawn, el da of Colin Rae, MC, of Little Weston House, Little Weston, Som, and has issue living, Alexander Hugh Frere *b* 1982, James Julian Frere *b* 1985, — Dominic Christopher Hugh (Netherbarns Farm House, Netherbarns Farm, by Galashiels), *b* 1955: *m* 1984, Melanie Lydia, elder da of late Craven Nicholas Charrington, of Bures Manor, Reigate, Surrey, and has issue living, Joseph Christopher Frere *b* 1997, Samara Olga Frere *b* 1985, Isabella Zinaida Frere *b* 1986, Anastasia Amelia Frere *b* 1989, Sasha Scarlett Frere *b* 1991, — Julian Sebastian Frere, *b* 1956: *m* 1982, Alexandra Hough, and *d* 1984, — Rupert Benjamin Bartle Frere (2 Whitehorse St, W1), *b* 1958: *m* 1997, Hon Mary Rachel Douglas-Scott-Montagu, only da of 3rd Baron Montagu of Beaulieu, — Sebastian Simon Frere, *b* 1961. *Residence* – Hollybush, Galashiels.

Grandchildren of late Charles Wyndham Rodolph Kerr, el son of Lt-Col Lord Charles Lennox Kerr, 4th son (el by 2nd *m*) of 6th Marquess:—
Issue of late Charles Iain Kerr (*Baron Teviot*), DSO, MC, *b* 1874, *d* 1968 (see that title).

Issue of late Major Basil Kerr, DSC, *b* 1879, *d* 1957: *m* (Feb) 1912, Winifred Katharine, who *d* 1974, da of late George Blezard (V Chetwynd):—
Diana Katharine (*Lady Clowes*), MBE, *b* 1916; MBE (Civil) 1977: *m* 1941, Col Sir Henry Nelson Clowes, KCVO, DSO, OBE, late Scots Gds (V Hatherton, colls), who *d* 1993, and has issue living, Andrew Henry, *b* 1942; late Capt Scots Gds; Equerry to HRH the Duke of Gloucester 1966-68: *m* 1968, Georgiana Elizabeth, da of Capt Richard Edward Osborne Cavendish (*see* D Devonshire, colls), and has issue living, Richard (Dickon) William Andrew *b* 1971, Emma Georgiana *b* 1974. *Residence* – 235 Cranmer Court, SW3. —— Elizabeth, *b* 1919: *m* 1946, Lt-Col George Demetriadi, MBE, TD, US Bronze Star, late R Welsh Fus, who *d* 1991. *Residence* – 17 Cheyne Gdns, SW3.

Grandchildren of late Arthur Herbert Kerr, elder son of late Adm Lord Frederic Herbert Kerr (infra):—
Issue of late Com Mark Peregrine Charles Kerr, RN, *b* 1891, *d* 1951: *m* 1918, Mary Catherine, who *d* 1982, da of late Henry Offley Wakeman (*see* Wakeman, Bt, colls):—
Frederic Mark, DFM, *b* 1919; *ed* Canford; 1939-45 War as WO RAFVR (prisoner): *m* 1st, 1947 (*m diss* 1952), Iris Margaret (URQUHART), da of late William Palk Tully; 2ndly, 1952, June, da of Capt Lancelot Gerrard Laurence, and has issue living, (by 2nd *m*) Peregrine Gerrard Mark (Charlton Cottage, Flax Bourton, Bristol), *b* 1955: *m* 1988, Susan Jane, da of Dennis Tucker, of Pound Farm, Cumnor, Oxford, — Christian Anthony Mark, *b* 1960. —— (Mark) David (4/5 Russell Garth Cottage, Eynsford, Dartford, Kent), *b* 1921; *ed* Canford, and Keble Coll, Oxford (BA); late F/O RAFVR; 1939-45 War (despatches): *m* 1959, Diana Law, da of late Arthur Fawcett, of Newmarket. —— John Anthony (East Membury Farm, Membury, E Devon), *b* 1926; *ed* Radley. —— Andrew Philip (Rectory Cottage, Church End, Standlake, Oxon OX8 7SG) *b* 1933; *ed* Radley; has issue (by Jytte Klamer, of Copenhagen), Jonah Piggott KERR, *b* 1976, — Martha KERR, *b* 1973. —— Elizabeth Mary, *b* 1928: *m* 1957, Walter Michael Woodin, of Oak Tree Cottage, Appleton, Abingdon, Oxon, and has issue living, Mark Chandler, *b* 1966: *m* 1990, Joanna, da of Dr Ray Franklin, of 31 Chawley Lane, Cumnor, Oxford, — Elizabeth Mary Anne, *b* 1960: *m* 1982, Robert Patrick Frank Florey, of Rectory Farm, Northmoor, nr Oxford, son of Patrick Florey, of Northmoor, nr Oxford, and has issue living, James Edward Robert *b* 1985, Samuel Michael Thomas *b* 1987.

Granddaughter of late Adm Lord Frederic Herbert Kerr, 6th and yst son of 6th Marquess:—
Issue of late Adm Mark Edward Frederic Kerr, CB, MVO, *b* 1864, *d* 1944: *m* 1906, Rose Margaret, OBE, who *d* 1944, da of late Wilfred Gough, Royal Dragoons:—
Luise Rosemary, *b* 1908. *Residences* – 26 Upper Strand St, Sandwich, Kent; 19 Draycott Av, SW3.

Granddaughters of late Frederic Walter Kerr, DSO, yst son of late Adm Lord Frederic Herbert Kerr (ante):—
Issue of late Ronald William Kerr, *b* 1906, *d* 1972: *m* 1939, Barbara Helen (Barnacarry, Kilninver, Oban, Argyll), da of C. J. Crawford, of Wayside, St Andrews:—
Patricia Margaret, *b* 1940: *m* 1965, Robert James Wakeford, of The Hatch, Staverton, Daventry, Northants, and has issue living, Mark Robert, *b* 1966: *m* 1993, (Julie) Belinda Stannage, and has issue living, Lucy Georgina *b* 1996, Emma Charlotte *b* 1998, — James Richard, *b* 1968, — Ian Frederick, *b* 1974. —— Angela Helen, *b* 1942: *m* 1971, John James Goddard, of 20 Hackthorne Rd, Cashmere, Christchurch, NZ, and has had issue, Nicholas James, *b* 1975; *d* 1995, — Penelope Helen, *b* 1978. —— Elizabeth Daphne, *b* 1949: *m* 1975, Charles Colclough Butterworth, who *d* 1988, and *d* 1997, leaving issue, Tom William, *b* 1978, — Janet Helen, *b* 1980.

Descendants of late Vice-Adm Lord Mark Robert Kerr (3rd son of 5th Marquess), who *m* 1799, Charlotte, *Countess of Antrim* in her own right (see that title).

Grandsons of late Capt William Walter Raleigh Kerr, grandson of Lt-Col Lord Robert Kerr, 4th son of 5th Marquess:—
Issue of late Lt-Col Sir (Louis William) Howard Kerr, KCVO, CMG, OBE, late Equerry to HRH the Duke of Gloucester, *b* 1894, *d* 1977: *m* 1928, Christina Stephanie Mary, who *d* 1986, da of late Arthur Ram, of Ramsfort, co Wexford:—
Henry Howard Philip Sackville Casamayor Ram (13 Westbourne Gdns, Hove, Sussex), *b* 1932. —— Andrew Robert Stephen Casamayor (Ninian House, Glasserton, nr Whithorn, Wigtownshire), *b* 1936: *m* 1988, Jacqueline Ellen Andre, da of late Frederick John Bryan, CA, of Vancouver, Canada. —— Julian James Casamayor (53 Belper Rd, Derby), *b* 1941; BA (Hons) Open 1998: *m* 1966, Glenys Ann, da of Rev Thomas Hugh Roberts, of Grantham, Lincs, and has issue living, Andrew James, *b* 1967; *ed* Manchester Univ (LLB): *m* 1997, Jane, da of David Wilkinson, of Prestatyn, — Philip Hugh, *b* 1971; *ed* Manchester Univ (MA), — Robert Michael, *b* 1974.

(Not in remainder to the Marquessate)

Grandchildren of late Lt-Col Alexander Nairne Kerr, MC, 10th of Abbotrule, son of late Col John Mac-Gregor Kerr (infra):—
Issue of late Capt John Kinloch Kerr, 11th of Abbotrule (matriculated arms at Lyon Court 1975), *b* 1924, *d* 1994: *m* 1951, Jane Barbara (Pond House, Frocester, Stonehouse, Glos), yst da of Montgomery Du Bois Ferguson, OBE, MD, of York:—
James Alexander KERR OF ABBOTRULE (Stamford Hall, Ettington, Stratford-on-Avon, Warwicks CV37 7PA), *b* 1952; 12th of Abbotrule; late Capt Coldm Gds: *m* 1984, Alice Rosamond, yr da of Beresford Norman Gibbs, DL, of The Willow Tree, Crudwell, Malmesbury, Wilts, and has issue living, John Montgomery, *b* 1989; yr of Abbotrule, — Henrietta Cecily, *b* 1992. —— Andrew Nigel (Poplar Gate Lodge, Stanley Downton, Stonehouse, Glos GL10 3QX), *b* 1953; late Capt 17/21st Lancers, and Royal Gloucestershire Hus: *m* 1979, Frances Columbel, only da of late Maj Robin Leach, of Greengates, Pirbright, Surrey, and has issue living, Alexander Robert, *b* 1985, — Laura Columbel, *b* 1981, — Lucy Rose, *b* 1982. —— Rosemary Ann, *b* 1955: *m* 1980, Roger Edward Wilson, of Parks Farm, Winchcombe, Cheltenham, Glos GL54 5BX, 2nd son of Kenneth Wilson, JP, DL, of Sudeley Lodge, Winchcombe, Cheltenham, and has issue living, Charles Kenneth, *b* 1982, — Henry John, *b* 1984, — Rupert Thomas Edward, *b* 1988. —— Georgina Eve, *b* 1960: *m* 1982, Rodney Hill Style, of Knowle Farmhouse, North Newington, Oxon OX15 6AN, and has issue (*see* Style, Bt, colls).

Granddaughter of late Col John MacGregor Kerr, son of late Col Alexander Boyd Kerr, grandson of late Patrick Kerr, 6th of Abbotrule, great-grandson of Hon Charles Kerr, 2nd of Abbotrule, yst son of 1st Earl of Lothian:—
Issue of late Lt-Col Evan Sinclair Kerr, late The Queen's Own Royal W Kent Regt, *b* 1894, *d* 1990: *m* 1925, Marian Catherine, who *d* 1970, da of late Ven Archdeacon Thomas Karl Sopwith, of Canterbury:—
Janetta Marian, *b* 1927: *m* 1949, Louis Philip Miéville, of Sandhill Farmhouse, Rogate, Petersfield, Hants GU31 5HU and has issue living, Marian Susan Julia, *b* 1951: *m* 1977, Guy Wyndham Stocker, and has issue living, Guy Philip William *b* 1981, Louisa Marian *b* 1978, — Sara Jane, *b* 1955: *m* 1992, William Bruce Woodhead, and has issue living, Anna Jane *b* 1992, Alys Mary *b* 1994.

PREDECESSORS – **(1)** MARK KER (el son of Mark Ker of Cessford, Commendator or Abbot of Newbottle), an Extraordinary Lord of Session, and Master of Requests, had the Abbey of Newbottle including the Baronies of Newbottle and Prestongrange erected into a barony with title of *Baron* 1587; was *cr Lord Newbottle* (peerage of Scotland) with remainder to his heirs male and assignees 1591; a Commr for holding the Parliament 1597; *cr Earl of Lothian* (peerage of Scotland) with remainder to heirs male of his body 1606; *d* 1609; *s* by his el son **(2)** ROBERT, 2nd Earl; Master of Requests 1606; not having male issue obtained permission from Crown to transfer titles and estates to el da; *d* 1624, when the earldom was assumed by his next brother William, who, however, was interdicted from using it by the Lords of Council 1632, and the titles were confirmed to his niece **(3)** ANNE, Countess of Lothian, who *m* Sir William Kerr, Knt, of Ancram branch of the Kerrs of Ferniehurst and a zealous convenanter (engaged in all actions of Scottish Army from commencement of differences between King and Parliament till 1643), el son of Robert Kerr, who in 1633 was *cr Lord Kerr*, of Nisbet, Longnewton and Dolphinstoun, and *Earl of Ancram* (peerage of Scotland), with remainder to the issue male of his 2nd marriage, and in default of those to his heirs male whatsoever; Sir William, was *cr Lord Newbottle*, and *Earl of Lothian* (peerage of Scotland) 1631: *d* 1675; *s* by his el son **(4)** ROBERT, PC, 4th Earl; received in 1678 a patent of the Earldom with original precedence; *s* by his kinsman Charles, 2nd Earl of Ancram, who *dsp*, in Earldom of Ancram and minor honours; was Justice Gen and in 1692 High Commr to Gen Assembly to Church of Scotland; *cr Lord Ker*, of Newbottle, Oxnam, Jedburgh, Dolphinstoun, and Nisbet, *Viscount of Briene, Earl of Ancram*, and *Marquess of Lothian* (peerage of Scotland) 1701, with remainder to heirs of entail succeeding to his estate in all times to come: *d* 1703; *s* by his son **(5)** WILLIAM, KT, 2nd Marquess, who had in 1692 *s* by special remainder his kinsman as 4th *Lord Jedburgh* (peerage of Scotland) *cr* 1622; was a Representative Peer, Col 7th Dragoons, and a Lieut-Gen; *d* 1722; *s* by his son **(6)** WILLIAM, KT, 3rd Marquess; was a Representative Peer 1731-60, Lord Clerk Register 1739-56, and Lord High Commr to Gen Assembly 1732-8; *d* 1767; *s* by his son **(7)** WILLIAM HENRY, KT, 4th Marquess; a Gen in the Army; sat as MP for Richmond 1747-60, and was afterwards a Representative Peer: *m* 1735, Caroline, who *d* 1778, da of 3rd Earl of Holderness; *d* 1775; *s* by his son **(8)** WILLIAM JOHN, KT, 5th Marquess; a Gen in the Army, Col 1st Life Guards, and a Representative Peer 1778-84; *d* 1815; *s* by his son **(9)** WILLIAM, KT, 6th Marquess, *b* 1763; Lord-Lieut of Midlothian and co Roxburgh; *cr Baron Ker*, of Kersheugh, co Roxburgh (peerage of United Kingdom) 1821: *m* 1st, 1793, Henrietta, who *d* 1805, da of 2nd Earl of Buckinghamshire; 2ndly, 1806, Harriet, who *d* 1833, da of 3rd Duke of Buccleuch and Queensberry; *d* 1824; *s* by his el son **(10)** JOHN WILLIAM ROBERT, 7th Marquess; *b* 1794; Lord-Lieut of co Roxburgh: *m* 1831, Lady Cecil Chetwynd Talbot, da of 2nd Earl Talbot; *d* 1841; *s* by his el son **(11)** WILLIAM SCHOMBERG ROBERT, 8th Marquess, *b* 1832: *m* 1857, Lady Constance Harriet Mahonesa Talbot, who *d* 1901, da of 18th Earl of Shrewsbury; *dsp* 1870; *s* by his brother **(12)** SCHOMBERG HENRY, 9th Marquess; *b* 1833; sometime in Diplo Ser; Sec for Scotland, Keeper of Great Seal of Scotland, and Vice-Pres of Scottish Education Depart 1887-92; Capt-Gen of Roy Co of Archers and Gold Stick of Scotland, Lord Keeper of Privy Seal of Scotland, and Pres of So of Antiquaries of Scotland: *m* 1865, Lady Victoria Alexandrina Montagu-Douglas-Scott, who *d* 1938, da of 5th Duke of Buccleuch, KG; *d* 1900; *s* by his only surviving son **(13)** ROBERT SCHOMBERG, 10th Marquess; *b* 1874; *d* 1930; *s* by his cousin **(14)** PHILIP HENRY, KT, CH, PC (son of late Maj-Gen Lord Ralph Drury Kerr, KCB, 3rd son of 7th Marquess), 11th Marquess; *b* 1882; Sec to Prime Min 1917-21, and to Rhodes Trust 1925-39, Chancellor of Duchy of Lancaster Aug to Nov 1931, Under-Sec of State for India Nov 1931 to Sept 1932, and Ambassador Extraor, and Plen at Washington 1939-40; *d* 1940; *s* by his kinsman **(15)** PETER FRANCIS WALTER (son of late Capt Andrew William Kerr, RN, grandson of 7th Marquess), 12th Marquess and present peer; also Earl of Ancram, Earl of Lothian, Viscount of Briene, Lord Newbottle, Lord Jedburgh, Lord Kerr (*cr* 1633), Lord Ker (*cr* 1701), and Baron Ker (*cr* 1821).

LOUDOUN, COUNTESS OF (Abney-Hastings) (Lordship S 1601 and 1633. Earldom S 1633)

BARBARA HUDDLESTON ABNEY-HASTINGS, *Countess of Loudoun*; *b* 3 July 1919; *s* 1960; assumed (with her husband) by deed poll 1955 the surname of Abney-Hastings in lieu of that of Griffiths; Hereditary Gov of Repton Sch, and Etwall Hospital; is a co-heiress (with her sister, nephew and nieces) to the Baronies of Botreaux, Stanley (*cr* 1456) and Hastings (*cr* 1461): *m* 1st, 1939 (*m diss* 1945), Capt Walter Strickland Lord; 2ndly, 1945, Capt Gilbert Frederick Greenwood, who *d* 1951; 3rdly, 1954, Peter Griffiths, who assumed the surname of Abney-Hastings in lieu of his patronymic by deed poll, 1955, and has issue by 1st, 2nd, and 3rd *m*.

𝕬rms – Quarterly; 1st and 4th argent, a maunch sable, *Hastings*; 2nd and 3rd or, on a chief gules, a demi-lion issuant argent, *Abney*. 𝕾upporters – *Dexter*, a man in armour, plumed on the head with three feathers gules, and holding with the right hand a spear in bend proper; *sinister*, a lady richly apparelled plumed on the head with three feathers argent, and holding in the left hand a letter of challenge.
Residence – Mount Walk, Ashby-de-la-Zouch, Leics.

SONS LIVING (*By 1st marriage*)

MICHAEL EDWARD ABNEY-HASTINGS (*Lord Mauchline*) (74 Coreen St, Jerilderie, NSW 2716, Australia), *b* 22 July 1942; *ed* Ampleforth; assumed by deed poll 1946 the surname of Abney-Hastings in lieu of his patronymic: *m* 1969, Noelene Margaret, da of W. J. McCormick, of Barham, NSW, and has issue:—

SONS LIVING—*Hon* SIMON MICHAEL, *b* 1974, — *Hon* Marcus William, *b* 1981.

DAUGHTERS LIVING—*Hon* Amanda Louise, *b* 1969, — *Hon* Lisa Maree, *b* 1971, — *Hon* Rebecca Lee (twin), *b* 1974.

(By 2nd marriage)

Hon Frederick James ABNEY-HASTINGS, *b* 1949.

DAUGHTERS LIVING *(By 2nd marriage)*

Lady Selina Mary, *b* 1946: *m* 1967, William Newman, and has issue living, Christopher James Loudoun, *b* 1972, — Selina Anne, *b* 1968. *Residence* – Old Place, Ansty, W Sussex.

(By 3rd marriage)

Lady Margaret Maude, *b* 1956: *m* 1977, Brian Peter Ludlow, and has issue living, Thomas William, *b* 1983, — Peter Arthur, *b* 1987, — Kathleen Rose, *b* 1981, — Iona Clare (twin), *b* 1981, — Alice Selina, *b* 1985, — Joy Elizabeth, *b* 1990.
Lady Mary Joy, *b* 1957: *m* 1982, David John Flowers, and has issue living, Clare Hannah, *b* 1987.
Lady Clare Louise ABNEY-HASTINGS, *b* 1958.

SISTER LIVING *co-heiress to the Baronies of Botreaux, Stanley (cr 1456) and Hastings (cr 1461)*

Lady Edith Huddleston, *b* 1925: *m* 1947, Major David Kenneth Maclaren, and has issue living Norman Angus, *b* 1948, — Roderick John (Ardvullin, Ardgour, by Fort William, Inverness-shire) *b* 1950: *m* 1st, 1981 (*m diss* 1993), Victoria Helen Elizabeth Glaysher; 2ndly, 1993, Kirsty Rowena Amabel, yr da of Sir Charles Edward McGrigor, 5th Bt, and formerly wife of David Norman G. Barraclough, and has issue living (by 1st *m*), Christopher Rory James *b* 1988, (by 2nd *m*) Catriona Mary Edith *b* 1993. *Residence* – Church Cottage, Port Sonachan, by Dalmally, Argyll.

COLLATERAL BRANCHES LIVING *also in remainder to the Baronies of Botreaux, Stanley (cr 1456), and Hastings (cr 1461)*

Grandchildren of late Edith Maud, Countess of Loudoun, 13th holder of the peerage:—
Issue of late Lady Jean Huddleston Campbell of Loudoun (*s* to the estate by deed of gift from her mother, and assumed the surname of Campbell), *b* 1920, *d* 1981: *m* 1st, 1940 (*m diss* 1949), Edgar Wright Wakefield; 2ndly, 1954 (*m diss* 1964), Capt Arthur Alexander Hubble, Queen's Bays:—
(By 1st *m*) Sheena, *b* 1941; co-heiress to Baronies of Botreaux, Stanley and Hastings: *m* 1968, Donald Russell Williams, of New York City, USA, and has issue living, Amanda Sara Edith, *b* 1970. *Residence* – 3210 Northbutton Wood Lane, Tucson, Arizona 85712, USA. ——— (By 2nd *m*) Flora Ann Madeleine, *b* 1957; co-heiress to Baronies of Botreaux, Stanley and Hastings: *m* 1975 (*m diss* 1992), John Robert Kerr, and has issue living, John Campbell, *b* 1980, — Britt Jean, *b* 1975, — Emma Jennifer, *b* 1977. *Residence* – Peelhill Farm, Drumclog, Lanarks ML10 6RQ.

Issue of late Lady Fiona Huddleston Abney-Hastings, *b* 1923, *d* 1990: *m* 1940, Capt Robert Conroy-Robertson, who *d* 1995, having assumed by deed poll 1944 the surname of de Fresnes, in lieu of his patronymic, having *s* his maternal grandfather as 12th Baron de Fresnes (*cr* France 1642):—
(Christopher) Ian (Elm Tree House, High Halden, Ashford, Kent), *b* 1942; co-heir to Baronies of Botreaux, Stanley and Hastings; *ed* Ampleforth, and Glasgow Sch of Art: *m* 1st, 1969 (*m diss* 1971), Elvira Maria, da of W/Cdr Marcel Pustelniak; 2ndly, 1973, Angela Margaret, da of Lt-Col Denys Ainsworth Yates, and has issue living (by 1st *m*), Robert Marcel, *b* 1970, — (by 2nd *m*) Rawdon Alexander Denys, *b* 1974, — Nicola Margaret, *b* 1975. ——— Nigel Diarmid (8839 Broadway St, Chilliwack, BC, Canada), *b* 1944; *ed* Ampleforth: *m* 1965, Dolores Emelyn, da of Isidore Douglas Grinder, of Clinton, BC, Canada, and has issue living, Robert Aaron Bryan, *b* 1969, — Christel Rose Helen, *b* 1966: *m* 1993, Michael John Fisher, and has issue living, Adrian Isidore Robert *b* 1991, — Iona Elisabeth Louise, *b* 1968. ——— Paulyn Armand, *b* 1949; *ed* Ampleforth: *m* 1973 (*m diss* 19—), Kaija, da of Dr Franf, of Finland, and has issue living, Ida Piri Pulikukka Fiona, *b* 1974. ——— Vivian Robert James George, *b* 1960; *ed* Merchiston Castle Sch, Edinburgh: *m* 1988, Jill, da of Peter Hendrie, of Edinburgh, and has issue living, Peter James *b* 1989, Joseph Robert *b* 1990. ——— (Iona Mary) Nicole, *b* 1957: *m* 1982, Timothy John Kerr Kirkwood, of Culfoichmore, Advie, Grantown on Spey, Morayshire, and has issue living, Toby John, *b* 1989, — Arthur George, *b* 1992, — Harriet Mary, *b* 1984, — Matilda Alice, *b* 1986, — Jemima Jane, *b* 1987, — Phoebe Maud, *b* 1990, — Augusta Fiona, *b* 1994.

Issue of late Hon Lelgarde de Clare Elizabeth Rawdon Hastings, only da of 1st Viscount St Davids, by his 2nd wife Elizabeth Frances, Baroness Strange of Knokin, Hungerford and de Moleyns (yr sister of Edith Maud, Countess of Loudoun), *b* 1918, *d* 1984: *m* 1950 (*m diss* 1967), Colin Charles Evans:—
See V St Davids.

Granddaughters of late Gilbert Theophilus Clifton, 3rd Baron Donington, brother of 11th Earl of Loudoun:—
Issue of late Hon Margaret Selina Flora Maud, *b* 1895, *d* 1975: *m* 1917, Sir Edward Orde MacTaggart-Stewart, 2nd Bt, late Capt Gren Gds, who *d* 1948:—
See MacTaggart-Stewart, Bt (ext).

Issue of late Hon Irene Mary Egidia, *b* 1898, *d* 1961: *m* 1927, Lt-Col Richard St Barbe Emmott, MFH, late 6th Gurkha Rifles, who *d* as the result of a hunting accident 1949:—
Patricia Egidia Hastings, *b* 1929: *m* 1950, Lt-Col Stafford Nugent Floyer-Acland, CBE, King's Own Yorkshire LI, who *d* 1994, and has issue (*see* Acland, Bt, *cr* 1678, colls). *Residence* – The Dairy House, W Stafford, Dorchester, Dorset. ——— Moira Anne St Barbe, *b* 1931: *m* 1st, 1953 (*m diss* 1965), Capt David Anderson Vetch, Queen's Royal Irish Hus; 2ndly, 1980, Lt-Col Alec Dow, who *d* 1987, of 1 Parkway, Ruishton, Taunton, Som TA3 5JX, and has issue living (by 1st

m), James William Anderson (47 New North Rd, South Park, Reigate, Surrey RH2 8LZ), *b* 1958: *m* 1978, Patricia Eileen, da of Daniel Haste, of 59 Hatch Gdns, Tadworth, Surrey, and has issue living, Rachel Anne *b* 1980, Amanda Jane *b* 1982, — Belinda Louise ANNAKIN, *b* 1956 assumed surname of Annakin 1978; has issue living (by Ian James McKee), Aniella Caitlin Emmott MCKEE *b* 1993. —— Bridget Griselda Kemble, *b* 1934: *m* 1955, John Anthony Copley, JP, DL, and has issue living, Robert Anthony (Park Farm, Gt Barrington, Glos), *b* 1960: *m* 1986, Diana Mary, yst da of Charles Talbot Rhys Wingfield (*see* V Powerscourt, colls), and has issue living, Jack Anthony Talbot *b* 1989, Alice Florence Hastings *b* 1992, — Jane Belinda, *b* 1957: *m* 1985, John David Beaton, of Wester Balchrystie, by Colinsburgh, Fife, and has issue living, Camilla Jane Moira *b* 1987, Emily *b* 1989. *Residence* – Winter Field Farm, Melbury Abbas, Dorset.

Descendants of late Lady Victoria Mary Louisa Kirwan, 3rd da of 2nd Marquess of Hastings and 7th Earl of Loudoun (*see* By Grey de Ruthyn).

Descendants of late Lady Frances Augusta Constance Muir, yst da of 2nd Marquess of Hastings and 7th Earl of Loudoun, and wife of 4th Earl of Romney (see that title).

PREDECESSORS – (**1**) *Sir* HUGH Campbell of Loudoun, co Ayr, PC; *cr Lord Campbell of Loudoun* (peerage of Scotland) 1601; *d* 1622; *s* by his grand-da (**2**) MARGARET (el da of George, Master of Loudoun): *m* c 1620, Sir John Campbell of Lawers (descended from Campbell of Glenorchy), who was *cr Earl of Loudoun* and *Lord Tarrinzean and Mauchline* (peerage of Scot) 1633, with remainder to his heirs male, but, since he opposed the crown, the patent was superseded until 1641, when it was issued with original precedence; Lord Chancellor of Scotland 1641-1660 and 1st Commr of the Treasury, 1641-44; *d* 1662; *s* by his son (**3**) JAMES, 2nd Earl: *m* 1666, Lady Margaret Montgomerie, da of 7th Earl of Eglinton; *d* 1684; *s* by his son (**4**) HUGH, KT, PC, 3rd Earl; resigned his titles 1707, and obtained a new patent with remainder to heirs male of his body, heirs gen of 1st Earl and heirs male whatsoever of 1st Earl; Lord Keeper of Scotland 1708-13: *m* 1700, Lady Margaret Dalrymple who *d* 1779, da of 1st Earl of Stair; *d* 1731; *s* by his son (**5**) JOHN, 4th Earl; *b* 1705, Gen; *d* unm 1782; *s* by his cousin (**6**) JAMES, Mure-Campbell, 5th Earl (son of Hon Sir James Campbell, 3rd son of 2nd Earl); Maj-Gen *m* 1777, Flora, who *d* 1780, da of John MacLeod of Raasay; *d* 1786; *s* by his only da (**7**) FLORA, Countess of Loudoun; *b* 1780: *m* 1804, Francis Rawdon-Hastings, 2nd Earl of Moira,* who was *cr Marquess of Hastings* 1816 and *d* 1826; she *d* 1840, and was *s* by her only surv son (**8**) GEORGE AUGUSTUS FRANCIS, 7th Earl (and 2nd Marquess of Hastings); *b* 1808: *m* 1831, Barbara, Baroness Grey de Ruthyn, who *d* 1858, (having *m* 2ndly, 1845, Adm Sir Hastings Reginald Yelverton, GCB); *d* 1884; *s* by his el son (**9**) PAULYN REGINALD SERLOE, 8th Earl (and 3rd Marquess); *b* 1832; *d* unm 1851; *s* by his brother (**10**) HENRY WEYSFORD CHARLES PLANTAGENET, 9th Earl (and 4th Marquess); *b* 1842; *s* his mother 1858 as *Baron Grey de Ruthyn: m* 1864, Lady Florence Cecilia Paget, who *d* 1907 (having *m* 2ndly, 1870, Sir George Chetwynd, 4th Bt); *d* 1868, when the Marquessate of Hastings and subsidiary peerages became ext (except the English Baronies mentioned below), and the Scottish peerages devolved upon his el sister (**11**) EDITH MAUD; *b* 1833: *m* 1853, Charles Frederick Clifton, who assumed 1859 by Act of Parl the surname of Abney-Hastings, was *cr Baron Donington* 1880, and *d* 1895; she *d* 1874; *s* by her son (**12**) CHARLES EDWARD HASTINGS, 11th Earl; *b* 1855; assumed 1887 by Roy licence the name of Rawdon-Hastings; bore one of the gold spurs at Coronation 1902 and 1911: *m* 1880, Hon Alice Mary Elizabeth Fitzalan-Howard, who *d* 1915, da of 1st Baron Howard of Glossop; *d* 1920, when the Barony of Donington passed to his 2nd brother, and the Scottish peerages to his niece, (**13**) EDITH MAUD, Countess of Loudoun (el da of Hon Paulyn Francis Cuthbert Rawdon-Hastings); *b* 1883: *m* 1916 (*m diss* 1947), Capt Reginald Mowbray Chichester Huddleston: they assumed by Roy licence 1918 the surname of Abney-Hastings; *d* 1960; *s* by her el da (**14**) BARBARA HUDDLESTON, present peeress, also Lady Campbell of Loudoun, and Lady Tarrinzean and Mauchline.

*The 1st Marquess of Hastings, *s* in 1808 to the Baronies of Botreaux (*cr* 1368), Hungerford (*cr* 1426), Moleyns (*cr* 1445), and Hastings (*cr* 1461). They fell into abeyance 1868 between the sisters of the 4th Marquess of Hastings, but were called out in 1871 in favour of Edith Maud Countess of Loudoun (*b* 1833). They again fell into abeyance in 1920 between Edith Maud Countess of Loudoun (*b* 1883) and her sisters. In 1921 the baronies of Botreaux, Stanley (*cr* 1456), and Hastings were called out of abeyance in favour of the Countess of Loudoun, but on her death in 1960 they again fell into abeyance between her daughters, of whom the el is the Countess of Loudoun.

Loughborough, Lord; son of Earl of Rosslyn.

LOUTH, BARON (Plunkett) (Baron I 1541)

OTWAY MICHAEL JAMES OLIVER PLUNKETT, 16th Baron; *b* 19 Aug 1929; *s* 1950; *ed* Downside: *m* 1951, Angela Patricia, da of W. Cullinane, of St Helier, Jersey, and has issue.

𝕬rms – Sable, a bend, and in the sinister chief a tower argent. 𝕮rest – A horse passant argent. 𝕾upporters – *Dexter*, a pegasus, wings inverted, per fesse, or and argent; *sinister*, an antelope argent, armed, unguled, plain collared and chained or.
Residence – Les Sercles, 8 La Grande Pièce, St Peter, Jersey.

Hasten slowly

SONS LIVING

Hon JONATHAN OLIVER (Les Sercles, La Grande Pièce, St Peter, Jersey), *b* 4 Nov 1952; *ed* de la Salle Coll, Jersey, Hautlieu Sch, Jersey, and Hull Univ (BSc); AMIEE: *m* 1981, Jennifer, da of Norman Oliver Hodgetts, of Weston-super-Mare, and has issue living, Matthew Oliver, *b* 22 Dec 1982, — Agatha Elizabeth, *b* 1985.

Hon Otway Jeremy Oliver, *b* 1954: *m* 1st, 1971 (*m diss* 1982), Ruth Levine; 2ndly, 1983, Alice Veronica Tierney, and has issue living (by 1st *m*), Oliver, *b* 1972, — Benjamin Otway, *b* 1974.

Hon Timothy James Oliver (17 South Riding, Bricket Wood, St Albans, Herts AL2 3NG), *b* 1956; *ed* de la Salle Coll, Jersey: *m* 1984, Julie Anne Cook, and has issue living, Joseph Timothy Oliver, *b* 1989, — Sophie Louise, *b* 1987, — Emma Jane, *b* 1991, — Stephanie Anne, *b* 1993.

DAUGHTERS LIVING

Hon Olivia Jane, *b* 1953: *m* 1974 (*m diss* 1982), Trevor Billingsley, and has issue living, James Michael *b* 1975, — Nicola Jane, *b* 1977.

Hon Stephanie Patricia (Forest Farm, Forest Lane, Hanbury, Worcs B60 4HP), *b* 1963.

WIDOW LIVING OF SON OF FOURTEENTH BARON

Gwendoline Mary, da of E. A. Cowling, of Torquay: *m* (Feb) 1936, Hon Randal Patrick Ralph Oliver Plunkett, who *d* (July) 1936. *Residence* –

COLLATERAL BRANCHES LIVING

Issue (if any) of late Harry Edward Plunkett, el son of late Hon Edward Sydney Plunkett (infra), *b* 1848, *d* 1906: *m* 1877, Marianne, da of George Smith, of Dalkey, co Dublin.

Grandsons of late Charles Seale Plunkett, Lieut 95th Regt, son of late Major Hon Edward Sydney Plunkett, 5th son of 11th Baron:—
Issue of late Sydney Wilmott Plunkett, *b* 1877, *d* 1955: *m* 1904, Elizabeth Josephine, who *d* 1960, da of John Patrick Higgins, of Rathmines, Dublin:—
Charles Seale (180 Perth Street West, Hull), *b* 1908; 1939-45 War (despatches): *m* 1934, Julia Elizabeth, da of Walter Brown, of Hull, and has issue living, Merrick Shawe (51 Woodlands Rd, Willerby, Hull), *b* 1934: *m* 1956, Eileen, da of T. Armstrong, of Leeds, and has issue living, Patrick Allan *b* 1958; *ed* Hull Gram Sch, and Bretton Hall Coll (BEd), Glenn Charles *b* 1966, Angela *b* 1963. —— Norman Dawson (Brand Hill House, Brand Hill Rd, Hampstead, NW5), *b* 1910; *ed* Bishop Wordsworth's Sch, Salisbury, Muresk Agricultural Coll, W Aust, and Sch of Mines and Metallurgy, W Aust (BA, BSc); Founder of Norden Youth Club. —— †Randal Otway, *b* 1914; 1939-45 War: *m* 1935, Sylvia May, da of E. Rutherford, of Hull, and *d* 1998, leaving issue, Anthony Patrick (29 Davenport Av, Hessle, N Humberside HU13 0RL), *b* 1939; *ed* Hull Gram Sch: *m* 1969, Ann Elisabeth Bennett, and has issue living, Matthew Patrick *b* 1972, Simon James *b* 1975, — Eve, *b* 1935: *m* 1958, Philip John Turner of 974 Anlaby Rd, Hull, E Yorks HU4 6AT, and has issue living, Mark Stephen *b* 1959: *m* 1994, Francesca, da of K. E. Dodd, of Welwyn, Herts (and has issue living, Harvey George *b* 1997), Nicholas Matthew *b* 1960. —— Oliver Penson, *b* 1917: *m* 1947, Jean Elizabeth, da of H. Hewson, of Hull, and has issue living, Sean Patrick (14 Burghley Rd, St Andrews, Bristol BS6 5BN), *b* 1948; *ed* Hull Gram Sch, and Ealing Tech Coll: *m* 1985, Antonia Susan, da of Florian Brann, of London, and has issue living, Leo Joseph *b* 1988, Caitlin Martha *b* 1986. *Residence* – 4 Hartoft Rd, Hull, Yorks HU5 4LB.

Grandchildren of late Matthew Penson Plunkett, 4th son of Merrick Shawe Plunkett, 2nd son of Hon Matthew Plunkett, 2nd son of 10th Baron:—
Issue of late Sydney Penson Plunkett, *b* 1903, *d* 1976: *m* 1928 (*m diss* 1955), Helen Margaret, only da of H. A. Pattullo, MB, of Kelsall, Cheshire:—
Anthony Penson (Abbey View, Dunkeswell Abbey, Honiton, Devon EX14 0RP), *b* 1931: *m* 1956, Anne Malkin White, of Harpenden, Herts, and has issue living, Timothy Penson, *b* 1959: *m* 1st, 1982 (*m diss* 1991), Carol Anne Parr; 2ndly, 1994, Jane Ann Nurden, and has issue living (by 1st *m*), Mark Penson *b* 1989, — Andrew Christopher, *b* 1961: *m* 1985 (*m diss* 1996), Christine Anne Meysner, and has issue living, James Matthew Oliver *b* 1989, Harry Thomas Joseph *b* 1993. —— Jean Margaret, *b* 1929: *m* 1955, John Travers Clark, and has issue living, Charles James Travers, *b* 1961: *m* 1988, Maura Teresa Lynch, and has issue living, Adam Sén *b* 1996, Suzanne *b* 1998, — Caroline Travers, *b* 1957: *m* 1985, Sqdn Ldr Clive Wood, and has issue living, Benjamin Richard *b* 1987, Rosemary Helen *b* 1989, — Bridget Travers, *b* 1959: *m* 1981, Richard Pilling, and has issue living, Christopher *b* 1990, Katherine Anne *b* 1987.

PREDECESSORS – **(1)** *Sir* OLIVER Plunkett, Knt; *cr Baron Louth* (peerage of Ireland) 1541; *s* by his son **(2)** THOMAS, 2nd Baron; *d* 1571; *s* by his el son **(3)** PATRICK, 3rd Baron; was slain 1575 in endeavouring to recover cattle that had been stolen from him; *s* by his brother **(4)** OLIVER, 4th Baron; *d* 1607; *s* by his son **(5)** MATTHEW, 5th Baron; *d* 1629; *s* by his son **(6)** OLIVER, 6th Baron; joined the Royalists 1639, and served at the siege of Drogheda; appointed Col-Gen of all the forces to be raised in co Louth; outlawed 1642; *d* 1679; *s* by his son **(7)** MATTHEW, PC, 7th Baron; was restored to his estates after the Restoration, and appointed Lord Lieut of co Louth; attached himself to the cause of James II, and was exiled 1689; *d* 1689; *s* by his son **(8)** OLIVER, 8th Baron, who however was not permitted to take his seat in consequence of his father's outlawry not having been reversed; *d* 1707; *s* by his son **(9)** MATTHEW, 9th Baron; *d* 1754; *s* by his son **(10)** OLIVER, 10th Baron; *d* 1763; *s* by his son **(11)** THOMAS OLIVER, 11th Baron; procured a reversal of the outlawry, and was restored to his ancestral honour 1798; *d* 1823; *s* by his son **(12)** THOMAS OLIVER, 12th Baron; *b* 1809; *d* 1849; *s* by his son **(13)** RANDAL PERCY OTWAY, 13th Baron, *b* 1832: *m* 1st, 1867, Anna Maria McGeough, who *d* 1868, da of late Walter McGeough Bond, of Drumsill and the Argory, co Armagh; 2ndly, 1877, Elizabeth Lily, who *d* 1916, da of late John Black of Ceylon; *d* 1883; *s* by his son **(14)** RANDAL PILGRIM RALPH, 14th Baron, *b* 1868: *m* 1st 1890 (*m diss* 1912), Eugénie de Miarritze, who *d* 1952, da of late Capt Edmund Hooke Wilson Bellairs, HM's Vice-Consul at Biarritz, France; 2ndly, 1913, Dorothy Lettice, who *d* 1923, da of late Col Thomas Lewis Hampton-Lewis, of Henllys, Anglesey; 3rdly, 1926, Marie Ethel, who *d* 1941, da of late Charles Read, solicitor, of Hampstead, NW, and widow of Sir John Prichard-Jones, 1st Bt; *d* 1941; *s* by his son **(15)** OTWAY RANDAL PERCY OLIVER, 15th Baron, *b* 1892: *m* 1927, Ethel Molly, who *d* 1992, da of Walter John Gallichen, of Jersey: *d* 1950; *s* by his son **(16)** OTWAY MICHAEL JAMES OLIVER, 16th Baron and present peer.

LOVAT, LORD (Fraser) (Lord S 1458-64, Baron UK 1837)
(Title pronounced "Luvvut")

I am ready

SIMON FRASER, 16th (*de facto*) Lord and 18th but for the attainder; *b* 13 Feb 1977; *s* 1995; *ed* Harrow, and Edinburgh Univ; 25th Ch of Clan Fraser; Col-in-Ch 78th Fraser Highlanders (Canada) 1997.

Arms – Quarterly: 1st and 4th azure, three cinquefoils argent; 2nd and 3rd argent, three antique crowns gules. **Crest** – A buck's head erased, proper. **Supporters** – Two bucks, proper.
Residence – Beaufort Lodge, Beauly, Inverness-shire.

BROTHER LIVING

JACK (*Master of Lovat*), *b* 22 Aug 1984.

SISTERS LIVING

Violet, *b* 1972.
Honor, *b* 1973.

UNCLES LIVING (*Sons of 15th Lord*)

Hon Kim Maurice, *b* 1946; *ed* Ampleforth; late Lieut Scots Gds: *m* 1975, Joanna Katherine, da of Maj Geoffrey Edward Ford North, MC (*see* B Walsingham), and has issue living, Thomas Oswald Mungo, *b* 1976; *ed* Eton, — Joseph Oscar Edward, *b* 1978; *ed* Eton, — Maximilian Alexander Kim, *b* 1981. *Residences* – Kirkton House, Bunchrew, Inverness-shire; Wedhampton House, Devizes, Wilts SN10 3QE.

Hon Hugh Alastair Joseph, *b* 1947; *ed* Ampleforth, and Ch Ch, Oxford: *m* 1976, Drusilla Jane, da of J. Alastair Montgomerie, of Gilmilnscroft Mains, Sorn, Ayrshire, and has issue living, Raoul Alastair Joseph, *b* 1980; *ed* Ampleforth, — Poppy Augusta, *b* 1979, — Eloise Hermione, *b* 1986. *Residence* – Balblair House, Beauly, Inverness-shire IV4 7AZ.

AUNTS LIVING (*Daughters of 15th Lord*)

Hon Fiona Mary, *b* 1941: *m* 1982, Robin Richard Allen. *Address* – PO Box 6655, Dubai, United Arab Emirates.
Hon Annabel Térèse (Tessa), *b* 1942: *m* 1st, 1964 (*m diss* 1978), 14th Lord Reay; 2ndly, 1985, Henry Neville Lindley Keswick, eldest son of late Sir William Johnston Keswick, of Glenkiln, Shawhead, Dumfries (*see* B Lindley, 1950 Edn), and has issue (by 1st *m*) (*see* L Reay). *Residence* – 6 Smith Sq, SW1P 3HT.

GREAT AUNT LIVING (*Daughter of 14th Lord*)

Hon Veronica Nell (*Hon Lady Maclean of Dunconnel*), *b* 1920: *m* 1st, 1940, Lieut Alan Phipps, RN, who was *ka* Leros 1943 (*see* M Normanby, colls), 2ndly, 1946, Brigadier Sir Fitzroy Hew Royle Maclean of Dunconnel, 1st Bt (*cr* 1957), KT, CBE, who *d* 1996, and has issue living, (by 1st *m*) (*see* M Normanby, colls), — (by 2nd *m*) (*see* Maclean, Bt), *cr* 1957. *Residence* – Strachur House, Argyll.

WIDOW LIVING OF SON OF FIFTEENTH LORD

Lady Charlotte Anne Greville (*Lady Charlotte Fraser*), only da of 8th Earl of Warwick: *m* 1979, Hon Andrew Roy

Matthew Fraser, who was *k* in a hunting accident in E Africa (15 March) 1994, and has issue (see colls, infra). *Residence* – 1 Petyt Place, Old Church St, SW3 5DJ.

MOTHER LIVING

Virginia, da of David Grose, of Cranmer Court, London SW3: *m* 1st, 1972, Hon Simon Augustine Fraser, Master of Lovat, who *d* (26 March) 1994; 2ndly, 1998, Frank Robert Johnson, editor *The Spectator*. *Residences* – Beaufort Lodge, Beauly, Inverness-shire; 31 St Leonard's Terr, SW3 4QG.

WIDOW LIVING OF FIFTEENTH LORD

ROSAMOND (*Lady Lovat*), only da of Maj Sir Henry John Delves Broughton, 11th Bt: *m* 1938, Brig the 15th Lord Lovat, DSO, MC, TD, who *d* 1995. *Residence* – Balblair House, Beauly, Inverness-shire

COLLATERAL BRANCHES LIVING

Issue of late Hon Andrew Roy Matthew Fraser, yst son of 15th Lord, *b* 1952, *k* in a hunting accident in E Africa (15 March) 1994: *m* 1979, Lady Charlotte Anne Greville (ante), only da of 8th Earl of Warwick:—
Daisy Rosamond, *b* 1985. —— Laura Alfreda, *b* 1987.

Issue of late Rt Hon Sir Hugh Charles Patrick Joseph Fraser, MBE, MP, yr son of 14th Lord, *b* 1918, *d* 1984: *m* 1956 (*m diss* 1977), Lady Antonia Pakenham, da of 7th Earl of Longford:—
Benjamin Hugh (North Lodge, Pylewell Park, Lymington, Hants), *b* 1961: *m* 1991, Hon Lucy Elspeth Roper-Curzon, 3rd da of 20th Baron Teynham, and has issue living, Thomas Roper, *b* 1992, — William Melville, *b* 1995, — Hugh Douglas, *b* 1996, — Eliza Wedderburn, *b* 1993, — Phoebe Montagu, *b* 1998. —— Damian Stafford, *b* 1964: *m* 1992, Paloma Porraz del Amo, da of Don Alfredo Porraz Ortiz de la Huerta, of Mexico City, and has issue living, Ana Sofia, *b* 1996, — Oriana Paloma, *b* 1998. —— Orlando Gregory, *b* 1967. —— Rebecca Rose, *b* 1957; writer and journalist: *m* 1988, Edward Hamilton Fitzgerald, QC, of 42 Melrose Gdns, W6, yr son of late Carroll Fitzgerald, and has issue living, Blanche Catharine, *b* 1990, — Atalanta Rose, *b* 1992, — Honor Antonia, *b* 1995. —— Flora Elizabeth, *b* 1958; *ed* St Paul's Girls' Sch, and Wadham Coll, Oxford; writer: *m* 1st, 1980 (*m diss* 1992), Robert James Powell-Jones, barrister, who *d* 1998, son of John Ernest Powell-Jones, CMG; 2ndly, 1997, Peter Soros, elder son of Paul Soros, of New York, USA, and has issue living (by 1st *m*), Stella Elizabeth, *b* 1987, — (by 2nd *m*), Simon Tivadar, *b* 1998, — Thomas Hugh, *b* 1999. —— Natasha Antonia, *b* 1963; writer and journalist: *m* 1997, Jean-Pierre Cavassoni, of 14 Rue de Castiglione, 75001 Paris, son of Giovanni Cavassoni.

Grandchildren of late Maj Hon Alastair Thomas Joseph Fraser, DSO (infra):—
Issue of late Maj Alastair Hugh Joseph Fraser, MC, Lovat Scouts: *m* 1950, Philippa Margaret (Moniack Castle, Kirkhill, Inverness-shire), da of late Sir Anselm William Edward Guise, 6th Bt:—
Alastair James (Petit Moniack, CH-1873 Val d'Illiez, VS, Switzerland), *b* 1951; *ed* Ampleforth: *m* 1981, Elizabeth von Wartburg, and has issue living, Victoria Alexandre, *b* 1982, — and an adopted son, Philip, *b* 1985, — and an adopted da, Anne-Sophie, *b* 1983. —— Roderick Joseph (Berwicks Farm House, Hatfield Peverel, Chelmsford, Essex), *b* 1953; *ed* Ampleforth: *m* 1981, Mary Jean, yr da of late Hon Charles Richard Strutt (*see* B Rayleigh, colls), and has issue living, Charles Alastair, *b* 1982, — Harry Edward, *b* 1984, — Caroline Mary, *b* 1988, — Georgina, *b* 1990. —— Christopher (Kit) James (Moniack Castle, Kirkhill, Inverness-shire), *b* 1954; *ed* Ampleforth: *m* 1983, Sarah Louise, only da of J. H. Gladwin, of Bishops Stortford, Herts, and has issue living, Sandy John, *b* 1988, — Calum Aonghas, *b* 1993, — Angelica Ishbel, *b* 1987, — Vita Simone, *b* 1990. —— (Peter) Anselm (Myreside Grange, Gifford, E Lothian), *b* 1957; *ed* Ampleforth: *m* 1981, Antonia Hope, da of Lt-Col Thomas Holroyd Gibbon, OBE, of The Field House, Sutton, W Sussex, and has issue living, James Anselm, *b* 1986, — Thomas Alastair, *b* 1987. —— Arabella Mary (*Baroness Huntingfield*), *b* 1959: *m* 1982, 7th Baron Huntingfield, and has issue (see that title). —— Sophia Margaret, *b* 1964: *m* 1992, Robin Yates.

Issue of late Maj Hon Alastair Thomas Joseph Fraser, DSO, Lovat Scouts, yst son of 13th Lord, *b* 1877, *d* 1949: *m* 1915, Lady Sibyl Grimston, who *d* 1968, da of 3rd Earl of Verulam:—
Sir Ian James, CBE, MC (South Haddon, Skilgate, Som), *b* 1923; *ed* Ampleforth, and Magdalen Coll, Oxford; Capt Scots Guards (ret); Chm Rolls-Royce Motors Ltd 1971-80, and Chm Lazard Bros & Co Ltd 1980-85; 1939-45 War (MC); *cr* CBE (Civil) 1972, Kt 1986: *m* 1st, 1958, Evelyn Elizabeth Anne, who *d* 1984, yr da of late Allaster Edward George Grant, MC, late Capt 9th Lancers (*see* E Carnarvon, colls); 2ndly, 1993, Mrs Fiona Margaret Douglas-Home, da of late Maj Hon Henry Montagu Douglas-Home, MBE (*see* B Home of the Hirsel, colls), and formerly wife of Gregory Martin, and has issue living (by 1st *m*), Alexander Charles Evelyn, *b* 1962, — James Hector Ian, *b* 1963, — Consuelo Catherine Sibyl, *b* 1959: *m* 1989, Guy William Anthony Barker, only son of Kenneth W. Barker, of Cadogan Gdns, SW, and has issue living, Inigo Julian Clare *b* 1993, Theodora *b* 1990. — Domenica Margaret Anne, *b* 1960: *m* 1989, Philip Martin Dunne, elder son of Sir Thomas Raymond Dunne, KCVO, of Gatley Park, Leominster, Herefords, and has issue living, Thomas Hugo Rendel *b* 1995, Edward Cosmo John *b* 1998, Evelyn Anne *b* 1990, Matilda Rose *b* 1992. —— †Roderick Andrew Fraser, *b* 1927; *ed* Ampleforth; late Lieut Scots Guards: *m* 1958, Ethel Mary (who *m* 2ndly, 1969, Edward Eyre, of The Field House, Gt Durnford, Salisbury, Wilts (*see* B Acton, 1995 Edn)), da of late Cdr Charles H. Drage, RN (ret), of 38 Sheffield Terrace, W8, and *d* 1964, leaving issue, Anthony Henry Joseph (Flat 4, Wilmington House, Highbury Crescent, N5; Keepers House, Deene Rd, nr Corby, Northants NN17 3AB), *b* 1959; *ed* Ampleforth, and Downing Coll, Camb; Capt Scots Guards: *m* 1994, Hon Fiona Mary Biddulph, only da of 4th Baron Biddulph, and has issue living, Rory Ivor Charles *b* 1996, Marina Hesper Madeleine *b* 1999, — Archibald Ian Charles (45 Chiddingstone St, SW6 3TQ), *b* 1960; *ed* Ampleforth, and Magdalen Coll, Oxford: *m* 1997, (Rosalind) Henrietta, 2nd da of (Robert) Martin Mays-Smith, of Chaddleworth House, Chaddleworth, Berks, — Thomas William Gerard, *b* 1964: *m* 1989 (*m diss* 1994), Emma Louise, da of Ronald Russell Hobbs, of Harrogate, N Yorks, and Mrs Andrew Wilson, of Canford Park, Poole, Dorset, — Eleanor Clare, *b* 1961: *m* 1993, Viscount Olivier Tanguy Antoine Marie-Ghislain de Rosmorduc, of 38 rue Henri Pensis, L-2322 Luxembourg, son of late Viscount Tanguy de Rosmorduc, of Château de Pencran, F-29800, Pencran, France, and has issue living, Marguerite *b* 1994, Sophie *b* (twin) 1994. —— Simon Joseph (38 Clarendon Rd, W11), *b* 1929; *ed* Ampleforth, and Magdalen Coll, Oxford: *m* 1956, Elspeth Jane, da of H. S. Mackintosh, of 37 Cheyne Court, SW6, and

has issue living, Rupert James (Bruiach House, Kittarlity, Inverness-shire), *b* 1958: *m* 1987, Anne Elizabeth, da of J. H. Kingston, of Gresham, Woldingham, Surrey, and has issue living, Simon Peter James *b* 1993, Lucy Miranda Jean *b* 1989, Alice Felicity Jane 1991, — Cordelia Jane, *b* 1959: *m* 1986, Arthur I. Trueger, of 50 Laurel St, San Francisco, Calif, USA, and has issue living, Alastair William James *b* 1987, Hugh Robin Charles *b* 1988, Ruari Simon Paul *b* 1990, Ian Julian Joseph *b* 1992, Archie Rupert Leo *b* 1996, — Katharine Julia, *b* 1961: *m* 1990, Mark D. R. Rowan, of Kerswell Priory, Broadhembury, nr Cullompton, Devon EX15 2EA, yr son of late Sir Thomas Leslie Rowan, KCB, CVO, and has issue living, Thomas Simon Leacroft *b* 1992, Alexander Charles Hugh *b* 1994, Hugh Jonathan Ranulph *b* 1996, — Olivia Mary Juliet, *b* 1965: *m* 1991, William Benedict Hamilton-Dalrymple, yst son of Sir Hew Fleetwood Hamilton-Dalrymple, 10th Bt, KCVO, and has issue (*see that title*), — Perdita Rachel Josephine, *b* 1967: *m* 1995, Davide G. Taliente, of Kittisford House, Kittisford, Wellington, Som TA21 0SA, yst son of Commendatore Ugo Taliente, and has issue living, Theodora Giovanna *b* 1997, — Helena Jane, *b* 1972. —— Frances Mary, *b* 1916: *m* 1948, Lt-Col Humphrey Joseph Giles Weld, MC, The Queen's Bays (ret), who *d* 1998, of Chideock Manor, Dorset, and has issue living, Charles Humphrey Joseph, *b* 1949: *m* 1991, Georgina Helen, 2nd da of Sir Francis John Vernon Hereward Dashwood, 11th Bt (*cr* 1707) and has issue living, Frederick Humphrey Joseph *b* 1994, Thomas Giles *b* 1996, Katharine Frances *b* 1995, Eliza Victoria *b* (twin) 1996, — Gabrielle Mary Frances, *b* 1950: *m* 1980, Amyas Michael George Martelli, of Wooth Manor, Bridport, Dorset, and has issue living, Frederick Amyas *b* 1984, Bartholomew Michael Augustus *b* 1989, Anna-Rose *b* 1983, — Lucinda Mary Rose, *b* 1952: *m* 1977, Tomas Alastair Christie, of Kellas House, by Elgin, Moray, and has issue living, Alexander Tomas *b* 1980, Robert Sylvester *b* 1981, Ewen Humphrey *b* 1988, Isabella Frances Mary *b* 1984, Georgina Mary Rose *b* 1986, — Candida Mary Sibyl, *b* 1956: *m* 1980, Sebastian Anthony Arbuthnot-Leslie, of Warthill, Aberdeenshire, and has issue living, William Anthony *b* 1982, John Alexander *b* 1989, Sofia Louisa *b* 1984, Rose Eleanor *b* 1987, Portia Elizabeth *b* 1990.

PREDECESSORS – (1) HUGH Fraser, one of the hostages for the ransom of James I 1424 was by that monarch granted the Barony of Kinnell, and is sometimes known as Lord Lovat: *d* 1440; *s* by his son (2) THOMAS; *d* 1450; *s* by his son (3) HUGH; *cr* a Lord of Parliament as *Lord Lovat or Lord Fraser of Lovat* 1458-64; *s* by his son (4) THOMAS, 2nd Lord; *s* by his son (5) HUGH, 3rd Lord; having resigned his estates, they were incorporated into a Barony, and granted 1539 with remainder to his heirs male whatsoever, failing whom to his heirs whatsoever; *s* by his (6) ALEXANDER, 4th Lord; *d* 1557; *s* by his son (7) HUGH, 5th Lord, *d* 1576; *s* by his son (8) SIMON, 6th Lord; *s* by his son (9) HUGH, 7th Lord; *d* 1646; *s* by his grandson (10) HUGH, 8th Lord; *d* 1672; *s* by his son (11) HUGH, 9th Lord; *d* 1696; *s* by his great-uncle (12) THOMAS, 10th Lord, 3rd son of 7th Lord; *d* 1696; *s* by his son (13) SIMON, 11th Lord; was outlawed in 1701 for having seized the widow of the 9th Lord, getting the marriage ceremony performed, and forcibly consummating the nuptials; returned in 1715 on the breaking out of Rebellion, and supported the Govt, for which his outlawry was reversed; in 1745 joined the Pretender, who appointed him Gen of the Highlands, and *cr* him Duke of Fraser; was arrested 1746, and being found guilty of treason was beheaded on Tower Hill, 9 April 1747, his honours and estates being forfeited; his el son (14) SIMON; obtained a full pardon and subsequently distinguished himself as a British Gen; *d* 1782; *s* by his brother (15) ARCHIBALD CAMPBELL; Col in the Army; *dsp* 1815; his kinsman (16) THOMAS ALEXANDER, heir male of Thomas, 2nd son of 4th Lord; *b* 1802; Lieut and Sheriff Principal of co Inverness; *cr Baron Lovat*, of Lovat, co Inverness (peerage of United Kingdom) 1837; in 1854 obtained the reversal of the 11th Lord's attainder, and in 1857 established his right to be 12th Lord Lovat (peerage of Scotland): *m* 1823, Hon Charlotte Georgina Jerningham, da of 7th Baron Stafford; *d* 1875; *s* by his son (17) SIMON, 13th Lord; *b* 1828; Lord-Lieut of Inverness: *m* 1866, Alice, who *d* 1938, da of Thomas Weld Blundell, of Ince Blundell Hall, near Liverpool; *d* 1887; *s* by his son (18) SIMON JOSEPH, KT, GCVO, KCMG, CB, DSO, TD, 14th Lord; *b* 1871; Hon Maj-Gen (ret) TA; S Africa 1900-02, as Capt Lovat Scouts (which he raised), 1914-18 War, Comdg Highland Mounted Bde, and as a Dir of Forestry; Chm Forestry Commn 1919-27, and Under-Sec of State for Dominion Affairs Dec 1926 to Dec 1928: *m* 1910, Hon Laura Lister, who *d* 1965, da of 4th Baron Ribblesdale (ext); *d* 1933; *s* by his son (19) SIMON CHRISTOPHER JOSEPH, DSO, MC, TD, 15th Lord; *b* 1911; Brig Army Commandos, Scots Gds and Lovat Scouts (TA); Joint Under-Sec of State for Foreign Affairs May-July 1945; 1939-45 War at operations in Norway, at Dieppe and in Normandy (wounded, Legion of Honour, Croix de Guerre, etc): *m* 1938, Rosamond, only da of Maj Sir Henry John Delves Broughton, 11th Bt; *d* 1995; *s* his by grandson (20) SIMON (elder son of late Hon Simon Augustine Fraser, Master of Lovat), 16th Lord and present peer.

Lovel and Holland, Baron, title of Earl of Egmont on Roll of HL.

LOVELACE EARL OF (King) (Earl UK 1838)

Labour itself is a pleasure

PETER AXEL WILLIAM LOCKE KING, 5th Earl; *b* 26 Nov 1951; *s* 1964; *ed* privately: *m* 1st, 1980 (*m diss* 1989), Kirsteen Oihrig, da of Calum Kennedy, of Leethland House, Leethland, Renfrewshire; 2ndly, 1994, Kathleen Anne Rose, da of Lem Smolders, of Milouka, Langwarrin, Australia.

Arms – Sable, three spear heads argent, imbrued proper, on a chief or as many battleaxes azure. **Crest** – A cubit arm vested azure, charged with three ermine spots in fesse or, cuffed argent, grasping in the hand proper, the broken shaft of a spear in bend sinister sable, the butt argent. **Supporters** – Two mastiffs reguardant of a black colour with white belly and nose, collared gules.
Residence – Torridon House, Torridon, Ross-shire.

PREDECESSORS – (1) *Sir* PETER King, Knt, PC; MP for Beeralston 1700-14; was successively Recorder of London, Ch Justice of the Common Pleas, and 1725-33 Lord High Chancellor; *cr Lord King, Baron of Ockham,* co Surrey, 1725; *d* 1734; *s* by his el son (2) JOHN, 2nd Baron; was Out Ranger of Windsor Forest; *dsp* 1740; *s* by his brother (3) PETER, 3rd Baron; *d* unmarried 1754; *s* by his son (6) PETER, 6th Baron; *d* 1793; *s* by his son (7) PETER, 7th Baron; *b* 1776; *m* 1804, Lady Hester Fortescue, da of 1st Earl Fortescue; *d* 1833; *s* by his son (8) WILLIAM, 8th Baron, *b* 1805; *cr Viscount Ockham and Earl of Lovelace* (peerage of United Kingdom) 1838; Lord-Lieut of Surrey; assumed for himself and issue by Roy licence 1860, the additional surname and arms of Noel: *m* 1st, 1835, Augusta Ada, who *d* 1852, only da of 6th Baron Byron (the poet); 2ndly, 1865, Jane Crawford, who *d* 1908, widow of Edward Jenkins, BCS; *d* 1893; *s* by his 2nd son (9) RALPH GORDON NOEL Milbanke, 2nd Earl, *b* 1839; assumed by Roy licence 1861 the surname of Milbanke in lieu of Noel; in 1862; *s* as 13th Baron Wentworth (*see* E Lytton): *m* 1st, 1869, Fannie, who *d* 1878, 3rd da of late Rev George Heriot, of Fellow Hills, Berwick; 2ndly, 1880, Mary Caroline, who *d* 1941, el da of late Rt Hon James Stuart-Wortley; *d* 1906, when the Barony of Wentworth passed to his only child Ada Mary, while in the other honours he was *s* by his half-brother (10) LIONEL FORTESCUE, DSO, 3rd Earl, *b* 1865; European War 1915-19 as Major Northumberland Fusiliers, and Staff-Capt; in 1895 received for himself only, Roy licence to continue to use the additional surname and arms of Noel, but resumed by Roy licence 1908 the surname and arms of King only for himself and issue: *m* 1895, Lady Edith Anson, who *d* 1932, da of 2nd Earl of Lichfield; *d* 1929; *s* by his son (11) PETER MALCOLM, 4th Earl, *b* 1905: *m* 1st, 1939, Doris Evison, who *d* 1940; 2ndly, 1951, Manon Lis, who *d* 1990, da of Axel Sigurd Transo of Copenhagen, Denmark, and widow of Baron Carl Frederick von Blixen Finecke; *d* 1964; *s* by his only son (12) PETER AXEL WILLIAM LOCKE, 5th Earl and present peer; also Viscount Ockham, and Lord King, Baron of Ockham.

LOVELL-DAVIS, BARON (Lovell-Davis) (Life Baron 1974)

PETER LOVELL LOVELL-DAVIS, son of late William Lovell Davis, *b* 8 July 1924; *ed* Christ's Coll, Finchley, King Edward VI Sch, Stratford-on-Avon, and Jesus Coll, Oxford (MA); 1939-45 War as Fl Lt, RAF; Man Dir of Davis & Harrison Ltd 1971-73, and of Central Press Features Ltd 1952-71; a Member of Press Gallery of House of Commons 1951-71; Chm of The Features Syndicate Ltd 1972-74; a Dir of other Printing Publishing and Newspaper Cos; a Lord in Waiting to HM 1974-75; Parl Under-Sec of State for Energy 1975-76; Member of Board Commonwealth Development Corpn 1978-84; Vice-Pres of Youth Hotels Assocn since 1977; Trustee of Academic Centre of Whittington Hosp, Highgate, since 1980; Chm Lee Cooper Licensing Services Ltd 1983-90, and Pettifer Morrow & Assocs Ltd 1986-99; Member Islington Health Authority 1982-85; *cr Baron Lovell-Davis, of Highgate, in Greater London (Life Baron) 1974: m* 1950, Jean, da of late Peter Foster Graham, and has issue.
Residence – 80 North Rd, Highgate, N6 4AA.

SON LIVING

Hon Stephen Lovell, *b* 1955.

DAUGHTER LIVING

Hon Catherine Ruth, *b* 1958.

Low, family name of Baron Aldington.

LOWRY, BARONY OF (Lowry) (Extinct 1999)

DAUGHTERS LIVING (By 1st marriage)

Hon Sheila Mary, *b* 1950: *m* 1974, Jonathan Austyn Corrall, of 5 Beaconsfield Rd, St Albans, Herts.
Hon Anne Lynd, *b* 1952: *m* 1980, Neville McCoubrey, QGM, and has issue, one son and two das.
Hon Margaret Ina, *b* 1956.

WIDOW LIVING OF LIFE BARON

BARBARA ADAMSON (*Baroness Lowry*), QC, da of late Albert Parker, CBE, of Northwood, Middx, and widow of John Thornton Calvert, CBE: *m* 1994, as his 2nd wife, Baron Lowry (Life Baron), PC, who *d* 1999. *Residence* – White House, Crossgar, co Down.

Lowther, Viscount; son of Earl of Lonsdale.

Lowther, family name of Earl of Lonsdale.

Lowther, family name of Viscount Ullswater.

Lubbock, family name of Baron Avebury.

LUCAN, EARL OF (Bingham) Sits as BARON BINGHAM (UK 1934) (Earl I 1795, Baron UK 1934, Bt S 1634)

Christ is my hope

RICHARD JOHN BINGHAM, 7th Earl, 3rd Baron (UK), and 13th Baronet; *b* 18 Dec 1934; *s* 1964; *ed* Eton; Lt Coldstream Guards (Reserve); Patron of one living: *m* 1963, Veronica Mary (*Countess of Lucan*), 3rd da (el by 2nd *m*) of late Maj Charles Moorhouse Duncan, MC, and has issue. (The 7th Earl has been missing since 8 Nov 1974).

Arms – Azure a bend plain cottised between six crosses patee or. Crest – On a mount vert a falcon rising proper, armed, membered, and belled or. Supporters – Two wolves azure, plain collared and chained or.

SON LIVING

*GEORGE CHARLES (*Lord Bingham*), *b* 21 Sept 1967; *ed* Eton, and Trin Hall, Camb.

DAUGHTERS LIVING

Lady Frances, *b* 1964; *ed* St Swithun's, Winchester, and Bristol Univ.
Lady Camilla, *b* 1970; *ed* St Swithun's, Winchester, and Balliol Coll, Oxford: *m* 1998, Michael G. Bloch, QC, son of John Bloch, of Petersfield, Hants.

BROTHER LIVING

Hon Hugh (6 Gledhow Gdns, SW5), *b* 1939; *ed* Charterhouse, and Hertford Coll, Oxford.

SISTERS LIVING

Lady Jane, *b* 1932; *ed* Badminton Sch, Bristol; MB and BS London 1957: *m* 1960, James D. Griffin, and has issue living, Nicholas Driscoll, *b* 1962, — John Christopher *b* 1963, — Benjamin Dawson, *b* 1966, — Kaitilin Bingham, *b* 1961. *Residence* – 444 East 66th St, New York, NY 10021, USA.
Lady Sarah, *b* 1936; *ed* Badminton Sch, Bristol: *m* 1958, Rev Canon William Gilbert Gibbs, and has issue living, Oliver John, *b* 1961: *m* 1993, Isabelle J. R., da of Lt-Col John Halford, of Paris, — Marcia Kaitilin, *b* 1959: *m* 1986, Lt-Col Charles H. C. Lynch-Staunton, LI, yr son of Maj A. C. Lynch-Staunton, of The Coach House, Nunney, Somerset, and has issue living, George Henry *b* 1988, Nicholas John *b* 1989, Patrick Charles *b* 1993, — Selina Helen, *b* 1964: *m* 1989, Abdullah (Apo) Akinci, son of late A. O. Akinci, of Umraniye, Istanbul, and has issue living, Mustafa Noah *b* 1990, Lütfiye (a da) *b* 1992, Hatice Sara *b* 1997, Ayse Filiz *b* 1999, — Madeleine Susannah, *b* 1965. *Residence* – The Old Coach House, Winwick Manor, Winwick, Northampton NN6 7PD.

WIDOW LIVING OF SON OF FIFTH EARL

Dorothea, yr da of late Rev John Kyrle Chatfield, BD, LLB: *m* 1942, Maj Hon John Edward Bingham, TD, who *d* 1992, and has issue (see colls, infra). *Residence* – Nicholls, Udimore, Rye, E Sussex.

COLLATERAL BRANCHES LIVING

Issue of late Maj Hon John Edward Bingham, TD, yr son of 5th Earl, *b* 1904, *d* 1992: *m* 1942, Dorothea (ante), yr da of late Rev John Kyrle Chatfield, BD, LLB:—
Nicholas Charles (Court Lodge Oast, Udimore, Rye, E Sussex TN31 6BB), *b* 1943; *ed* Eton, and INSEAD (Fontainebleau) (MBA): *m* 1976, Catherine Violet, eldest da of late Maj Nigel Stuart Hunter, and has issue living, Charles Nigel, *b* 1979, — Alexandra Romina, *b* 1977. —— Peter John (Lambsland Farm, Rolvenden, Kent TN17 4PX), *b* 1945; *ed* Eton, and RNC Dartmouth: *m* 1971, Penella, only da of late Dr E. C. Herten-Greaven, of Buenos Aires, and has issue living, Philip Charles, *b* 1974, — Richard Patrick, *b* 1978. —— David Julian (31 Crescent Grove, SW4 7AF), *b* 1951; *ed* Eton, and Trin Coll, Camb (MA); FRICS.

Grandson of late Maj-Gen Hon Sir Cecil Edward Bingham, GCVO, KCMG, CB, 2nd son of 4th Earl:—
Issue of late Lt-Col Ralph Charles Bingham, CVO, DSO, *b* 1885, *d* 1977: *m* 1913, Dorothy Louisa, who *d* 1967, da of late Edward Roger Murray Pratt (B Dunleath):—
John Nigel (Stone House, Brimpton, Reading), *b* 1915; *ed* Eton, and Trin Coll, Camb (BA); Capt Coldm Gds (Reserve); 1939-45 War: *m* 1943, Elisabeth Rosamund, da of late Maj Sir Algernon Thomas Peyton, 7th Bt, and has issue living, Lavinia Frances, *b* 1949: *m* 1975, Robert David Barbour, of Baglake Farm, Litton Cheney, Dorchester, Dorset, only son of late Brig David Charles Barbour, OBE, of Shortheath House, Sulhamstead, Reading, and has issue living, Henry George *b* 1979, Alexandra Frances *b* 1981, — Veronica Annabel, *b* 1952: *m* 1988, Raymond John Williams, of Gardener's Cottage, Stone House, Brimpton, Reading, eldest son of Howard John Williams, of 21 Pilgrims Lane, Bugbrook, Northants, and has issue living, Anna Grace Joan *b* 1994.

---

*The High Court of Justice, Chancery Division, having ruled on 11 December 1992 that the 7th Earl of Lucan was sworn to have died on or after 8 November 1974, Lord Bingham has applied for a writ of summons to Parliament in the UK Barony of Bingham.

PREDECESSORS – (1) HENRY Bingham; *cr* a *Baronet* 1634; *s* by his son (2) *Sir* GEORGE, 2nd Bt; *s* by his el son (3) *Sir* HENRY, 3rd Bt; *dsp*; *s* by his half-brother (4) *Sir* GEORGE, 4th Bt; *s* by his son (5) *Sir* JOHN, 5th Bt, MP for and Gov of co Mayo; *d* 1749; *s* by his el son (6) *Sir* JOHN, 6th Bt, MP for co Mayo; *d* unmarried 1752; *s* by his brother (7)*Sir* CHARLES, 7th Bt, MP for co Mayo; *cr Baron Lucan*, of Castlebar (peerage of Ireland) 1776, and *Earl of Lucan* (peerage of Ireland) 1795; *d* 1799; *s* by his son (8) RICHARD, 2nd Earl; *b* 1764; a Representative Peer: *m* 1794, Lady Elizabeth Belasyse, da and co-heir of Henry, 2nd Earl Fauconberg, and the divorced wife of Bernard Edward, 12th Duke of Norfolk; *d* 1839; *s* by his son (9) GEORGE CHARLES, GCB, 3rd Earl, *b* 1800; was Field Marshal in the Army: *m* 1829, Lady Anne Brudenell, who *d* 1877, da of 6th Earl of Cardigan; *d* 1888; *s* by his el son (10) GEORGE, KP, 4th Earl, *b* 1830; a Representative Peer; bore Sceptre with Dove at Coronation of King Edward VII; sat as MP for Mayo (LC) 1865-74; Lieut and Custos Rotulorum of co Mayo, and Vice-Adm of the Province of Connaught: *m* 1859, Lady Cecilia Catherine Gordon-Lennox, who *d* 1910, da of the 5th Duke of Richmond, KG, *d* 1914; *s* by his el son (11) GEORGE CHARLES, GCVO, KBE, CB, TD, PC, 5th Earl, *b* 1860; Hon Brig-Gen, a Lord-in-Waiting to HM 1920-24, and 1924-9, and Capt of Hon Corps of Gentlemen-at-Arms 1929 and 1931-40; Capt of Yeomen of Guard 1950-51; Parl Under-Sec of State for Commonwealth Relations June to Oct 1951, and Ch Opposition Whip, House of Lords 1954-64: *m* 1929, Kaitilin Elizabeth Anne, who *d* 1985, da of late Capt Hon Edward Stanley Dawson, RN (E Dartrey, colls); *d* 1964; *s* by his el son (13) RICHARD JOHN, 7th Earl; also Baron Lucan, and Baron Bingham.

LUCAS OF CHILWORTH, BARON (Lucas) (Baron UK 1946)

MICHAEL WILLIAM GEORGE LUCAS, 2nd Baron, *b* 26 April 1926; *s* 1967; *ed* Peter Symond's Sch, Winchester, and Luton Tech Coll; late RTR; TEng (CEI); FIMI, FInst TA; Pres League of Safe Drivers 1976-80, Inst of Transport Admin 1980-83, UK delegate N Atlantic Assembly 1981-83 and since 1988, Member RAC Public Policy Cttee 1981-83 and since 1989, Member House of Lords Select Cttee Science & Technology 1980-83, a Lord in Waiting to HM 1983, Parliamentary Under-Sec of State, Dept of Trade and Industry, 1984-87; Vice Pres RoSPA since 1980, and Institute of the Motor Industry since 1992: *m* 1955 (*m diss* 1990), Anne-Marie, only da of Ronald William Buck, of Southampton, and has issue.

Arms – Per fesse wavy or and azure, in chief between two annulets a rose gules barbed and seeded proper, and in base two bars wavy argent surmounted by a bull's head caboshed sable. **Crest** – A representation of Apollo affronte or. **Supporters** – *Dexter*, a lion or; *sinister*, a Russian bear sable, each resting the interior paw upon an annulet therein a rose gules barbed and seeded proper. *Address* – c/o House of Lords, SW1. *Club* – RAC.

SONS LIVING

Hon SIMON WILLIAM, *b* 6 Feb 1957; *ed* Leicester Univ (BSc): *m* 1993, Fiona, yr da of Thomas Mackintosh, of Vancouver, BC, Canada, and has issue living, John Ronald Muir, *b* 1995.

Hon Timothy Michael, *b* 1959; *ed* Lancing, and Surrey Univ (BSc). *Residence* – 23 Common Lane, Weybridge, Surrey.

DAUGHTER LIVING

Hon Rachel Ann, *b* 1963: *m* 1991, Howard J. Wilder, elder son of John R. Wilder, of Eastleigh, Hants, and has issue living, a da, *b* 1993.

BROTHER LIVING

Hon Ivor Thomas Mark, CMG, *b* 1927; *ed* St Edward's Sch, Oxford, and Trin Coll, Oxford (BA 1951, MA 1956); late RA; Diplo Ser 1951-84; CMG 1980: *m* 1954, Christine Mallorie, el da of late Com Arthur Mallorie Coleman, OBE, DSC, RN (ret), of 44 Dartmouth Row, SE10, and has issue living, Mark Haselden, *b* 1955: *m* 1983, Melinda Jane, yr da of Sir Alastair Frederick Down, OBE, MC, of Sherborne, Dorset, and has issue living, Nicholas Alastair James *b* 1988, Georgina Sophie *b* 1986, Laura Evelyn *b* 1990, Eleanor Grace *b* 1994, — Crispin Mallorie, *b* 1958: *m* 1993, Heather Patricia, elder da of William Boyd, of Aldeburgh, Suffolk, and has issue living, William Mallorie *b* 1996, Katherine Emily *b* 1998, — (Adrian) George, *b* 1963: *m* 1997, Elisabeth Tate, eldest da of Charles Schmitz, of Bethesda, Maryland, USA, and of Mrs Augustus Putnam, of New York City.

SISTERS LIVING

Hon Nadia, *b* 1923: *m* 1944 (*m diss* 1980), Flight Lieut Hamish Selkirk, DFC, RAF, and has had issue, Christopher Rattray Lucas, *b* 1949. — Alastair Hamish Lawson, *b* (twin) 1949; *d* 1982, — Lindsay Alexandra, 1945: *m* 1st, 1965 (*m diss* 1970), Alan Stuart-Hutcheson; 2ndly, 1979, as his 3rd wife, David Jacobs, radio and television broadcaster, and has issue living (by 1st *m*), Guy James *b* 1966.

Hon Tatiana Sonia, *b* 1933: *m* 1964, Kenneth Bradford, of Nashdom, 13 Woodlands Rd, Surbiton, Surrey, son of Arthur Bradford, of Beckenham, Kent, and has issue living, Adam George, *b* 1966: *m* 1992, Caroline Louise, eldest da of R. John Dorrell, of Surbiton, Surrey, — Justin Nicholas, *b* 1967: *m* 1993, Anne Caroline Younger, da of Mrs S. Horwood, of Claygate, Surrey.

PREDECESSOR – (1) GEORGE WILLIAM Lucas, son of Percy William Lucas, of Oxford; *b* 1896; a Lord-in-Waiting to HM 1948-49, Capt of Yeomen of the Guard 1949-50, and Parl Sec to Min of Transport 1950-51; *cr Baron Lucas of Chilworth*, of Chilworth, co, Southampton (peerage of UK) 1946: *m* 1917, Sonia, who *d* 1979, da of Marcus Finkelstein, of Libau, Latvia; *d* 1967; *s* by his el son (2) MICHAEL WILLIAM GEORGE, 2nd Baron and present peer.

LUCAS OF CRUDWELL, BARON, AND DINGWALL, LORD (Palmer) (Lordship S 1609 and Barony E 1663)

RALPH MATTHEW PALMER, 11th Baron Lucas of Crudwell and 8th Lord Dingwall; *b* 7 June 1951; *s* 1991; *ed* Eton, and Balliol Coll, Oxford; a Lord in Waiting to HM 1994-97: *m* 1st, 1978 (*m diss* 1995), Clarissa Marie, da of George Vivian Lockett, TD, of Stratford Hills, Stratford St Mary, Colchester; 2ndly, 1995, Amanda Atha, and has issue by 1st *m*.

Arms – Argent, two bars sable, charged with three trefoils slipped of the field; in chief a greyhound courant of the second, collared or. **Crest** – A mount vert, thereon a greyhound sejant sable, collared or, charged on the shoulder with a trefoil slipped argent. **Supporters** – On either side a wyvern with wings erect or.
Residence – 18 Wilton Place, SW1X 8RL.

SON LIVING (*By 1st marriage*)

Hon LEWIS EDWARD, *b* 7 Dec 1987.

DAUGHTER LIVING (*By 1st marriage*)

Hon Hannah Rachel Elise, *b* 1984.

BROTHER LIVING

Hon Timothy John, *b* 1953; *ed* Eton, and Balliol Coll, Oxford: *m* 1984, Adèle Cristina Sophia, 4th da of late Lt-Col Hon Henry Anthony Camillo Howard, CMG (*see* B Howard of Penrith, colls), and has issue living, Henry Jocelyn, *b* 1987, — Robert Dominic, *b* 1993, — Nan Cristina, *b* 1985, — Isabella Spring, *b* 1989. *Residence* – West Woodyates Manor, Salisbury, Wilts.

SISTER LIVING

Hon Anthea Amabel, *b* 1956; assumed by deed poll 1963 the additional christian name of Amabel; *ed* Westfield Coll, London.

COLLATERAL BRANCHES LIVING

(*In remainder to Lordship of Dingwall and Baronies of Butler and Lucas of Crudwell*)

Issue of late Hon Rachel Cooper, yr da of Nan Ino, Baroness Lucas of Crudwell, *b* 1921, *d* 1976: *m* 1948, Maj Hon Spencer Douglas Loch, MC (later 4th Baron Loch), who *d* 1991:—
Hon Sara Nan LOCH, *b* 1949. *Residence* – The Old House, The Close, Blandford, Dorset DT11 7HA.

Grandson of late Ethel Anne Priscilla Fane, only da of Hon Julian Henry Charles Fane (4th son of 11th Earl of Westmorland) by his wife Lady Adine Eliza Anne Cowper, sister of 7th Earl Cowper: *m* 1887, 1st Baron Desborough:—
Issue of late Hon Monica Margaret Grenfell, *b* 1893, *d* 1973: *m* 1924, as his 2nd wife, Marshal of the RAF Sir John Maitland Salmond, GCB, CMG, CVO, DSO, who *d* 1968:—
Julian John William SALMOND, *b* 1926: *m* 1950, Brigid Louise, da of late FitzHerbert Wright (*see* V Powerscourt, 1990 Edn), and has issue living, David John Julian, *b* 1969, — Alicia Brigid (*Viscountess Head*), *b* 1951: *m* 1974, 2nd Viscount Head, of Throope Manor, Bishopstone, Salisbury, — Georgiana Monica, *b* 1952: *m* 19—, ... Roberts, and has issue living, Miran (a son), *b* 19—, — Venetia Anne, *b* 1957: *m* 1984, David John Morrison, of 21 Albert Bridge Rd, SW11 (*see* B Margadale). *Residence* – Old Manor House, Didmarton, Badminton, Avon.

Grandchildren of late Hon Monica Margaret Grenfell (Hon Lady Salmond) (ante):—
Issue of late Rosemary Laura Salmond, *b* 1928, *d* 1991: *m* 1947 (*m diss* 1974), 3rd Baron Ravensdale (see that title).

Grandchildren of late Ethel Anne Priscilla Fane (Baroness Desborough) (ante):—
Issue of late Hon Alexandra Imogen Clare Grenfell, *b* 1905, *d* 1969: *m* 1931, 6th Viscount Gage, who *d* 1982 (see that title).

Descendants of late Lady Amabel Cowper, sister of 7th Earl Cowper: *m* 1873, Adm of the Fleet Lord Walter Talbot Kerr, GCB (*see* M Lothian).

(In remainder to Barony of Lucas of Crudwell only)

Descendants of late Mary Evelyn Compton Vyner (assumed by Royal Licence 1915 the additional surname and arms of Vyner), da of Robert Charles de Grey Vyner, son of Lady Mary Gertrude de Grey, da of 2nd Earl Grey: *m* 1886, Capt Lord Alwyne Frederick Compton, DSO, son of 4th Marquess of Northampton (see that title).

Descendants (by 1st *m*) of late Violet Aline Vyner, yr da of Robert Charles de Grey Vyner (ante): *m* 1st, 1890 (*m diss* 1902), 5th Earl of Rosslyn; 2ndly, 1903, Lt-Col Charles Jarrott, OBE (*see* E Rosslyn).

PREDECESSORS – *LORDSHIP OF DINGWALL — **(1)** Sir RICHARD Preston, KB; *cr Lord Dingwall* (peerage of Scotland) 1609, with remainder to his heirs whatsoever; *s* by his da **(2)** ELIZABETH, wife of James, 12th Earl of Ormonde, *cr* Duke of Ormonde (*see* M Ormonde) her el son who predeceased his father, was summoned by writ to English Parliament, as *Baron Butler*, of Moore Park, 1666; she *d* 1684; *s* by her grandson **(3)** JAMES, KG, 2nd Duke of Ormonde and 3rd Lord Dingwall, who had in 1680 *s* as 2nd Baron Butler; was attainted of high treason and deprived of all his honours 1715, and the Lordship of Dingwall and the Barony of Butler remained dormant till 1871, when the attainder was removed and the titles reverted to **(4)** FRANCIS THOMAS de Grey, 7th Earl Cowper, as heir of Henrietta, Countess Grantham,. 2nd da of 1st Baron Butler, whose 2nd da, Lady Henrietta, *m* 2nd Earl Cowper; *b* 1834; Lord-Lieut of Bedfordshire; Viceroy of Ireland 1880-82: *m* 1870, Lady Katrine Cecilia Compton, who *d* 1913, da of 4th Marquess of Northampton; *d* 1905, when the Barony of Butler fell into abeyance, and the Lordship of Dingwall and Barony Lucas of Crudwell passed to his nephew **(5)** AUBERON THOMAS Herbert (son of late Hon Auberon Edward William Molyneux Herbert, by Lady Florence Amabel, who *d* 1886, el sister of 7th Earl Cowper), 5th Lord Dingwall, and 8th Baron Lucas of Crudwell (right confirmed by Committee for Privileges of House of Lords 1907), *b* 1876; Parliamentary Under-Sec of State for War and a Member of Army Council 1908-11, when he became Under-Sec of State for the Colonies; appointed Parliamentary Sec of Board of Agriculture and Fisheries Oct 1911, and Pres thereof 1914; served during 1914-18 War in RFC; *ka* 1916; *s* by his sister **(6)** NAN INO; *b* 1880; *m* 1917, Col Howard Lister Cooper, late RAF, who *d* 1972; *d* 1958; *s* by her elder da **(7)** ANNE ROSEMARY; *b* 1919: *m* 1950, Maj Hon Robert Jocelyn Palmer, MC, late Coldstream Guards, who *d* (30 Nov) 1991, 3rd son of 3rd Earl of Selborne; *d* (31 Dec) 1991; *s* by her elder son **(8)** RALPH MATTHEW, 8th and present Lord Dingwall, also 11th Baron Lucas of Crudwell.

BARONY OF LUCAS — **(1)** MARY, only child of Sir John Lucas, Knt (*cr* Baron Lucas of Shenfield), was *cr Baroness Lucas of Crudwell* (peerage of England) 1663, with remainder to her heirs male by Anthony Grey, 11th Earl of Kent, and failing which to her heirs female without division; *d* 1702; *s* by her el son **(2)** HENRY GREY, 2nd Baron Lucas and 12th Earl of Kent; *cr Viscount Goderich, Earl of Harold*, and *Marquess of Kent* (peerage of Great Britain) 1706, *Duke of Kent* (peerage of Great Britain) 1710, and *Marquess Grey* (peerage of Great Britain) 1740, with remainder to his grand-da, Lady Jemima Campbell, da of 3rd Earl of Breadalbane; *d* 1740, when the peerages of 1706 and 1710 became extinct, *s* in the Barony of Lucas and Marquessate of Grey by his grand-da **(3)** JEMIMA (ante): *m* Philip, 2nd Earl of Hardwicke; *d* without male issue 1797; *s* in Barony of Lucas of Crudwell by her da **(4)** AMABEL GREY; *cr Countess de Grey* (peerage of United Kingdom) 1816, with remainder to her sister, Mary Jemima, wife of 2nd Baron Grantham, and her heirs male (M Ripon); *d* 1833; *s* by her nephew **(5)** THOMAS PHILIP, 2nd Earl, 5th Baron Lucas of Crudwell, and 3rd Baron Grantham; *d* 1859, without male issue; *s* in Barony of Lucas of Crudwell by his da **(6)** ANNE FLORENCE: *m* 1833, George Augustus, 6th Earl Cowper; *d* 1880; *s* by her son **(7)** FRANCIS THOMAS DE GREY, 7th Earl Cowper, 7th Baron Lucas of Crudwell, and 4th Lord Dingwall* (ante).

LUDFORD, BARONESS (Ludford) (Life Baroness 1997)

SARAH ANN LUDFORD, da of ...... Ludford, of ......; *b* 14 March 1951; *ed* Portsmouth High Sch, LSE (BSc Econ 19—, MSc Econ 19—), and Inns of Court Sch of Law; Bar, Gray's Inn, 1979; with European Commn 1979-85; European Adviser, Lloyd's of London 1985-87; Vice-Pres, Corporate External Affairs, American Express Europe 1987-90; Memb Islington LBC (Lib Dem) since 1991; Memb Lib Dem Federal Policy Cttee since 1990 (Vice-Chm since 1992); Vice-Chm London Lib Dems 1990-94; Memb Management Board, European Movement, UK; *cr Baroness Ludford*, of Clerkenwell in the London Borough of Islington (Life Baroness) 1997.
Residence – 70 St Peters St, N1 8JS.

LUKE, BARON (Lawson Johnston) (Baron UK 1929)

Never unprepared

ARTHUR CHARLES ST JOHN LAWSON JOHNSTON, 3rd Baron; *b* 13 Jan 1933; *s* 1996; *ed* Eton, and Trin Coll, Camb (BA); Co Councillor Beds 1965-70 (Chm Staffing Cttee 1967-70), High Sheriff Beds 1969-70, DL 1989; Pres Nat Assocn of Warehouse-keepers 1962-78, Member Court of Corpn of Sons of the Clergy since 1980, Member Court Drapers' Co since 1993 (Jr Warden 1993); Cdr St John Ambulance Bde, Beds 1985-90 (Commr 1972-85); a Conservative Whip and Front Bench Opposition Spokesman in the House of Lords since 1997; Art Dealer; KStJ: *m* 1st, 1959 (*m diss* 1971), Silvia Maria, yr da of Don Honorio Roigt, former Argentine Ambassador at The Hague; 2ndly, 1971, Sarah Louise, da of late Richard Hearne, OBE, and has issue by 1st and 2nd *m*.

Arms – Argent, on a saltire sable between four daggers points downwards gules, the sun in his splendour or, on a chief of the third three cushions of the fourth. **Crest** – A spur between two wings or. **Supporters** – *Dexter*, a heron; *sinister*, a flamingo; both proper. *Residence* – Odell Manor, Odell, Bedfordshire, MK43 7BB.

SONS LIVING (*By 1st marriage*)

Hon (IAN) JAMES ST JOHN, *b* 3 Oct 1963; *ed* Eton: *m* 1998, Rowena Jane, yst da of John Aldington, of Powys.

(*By 2nd marriage*)

Hon Rupert Arthur, *b* 1972; *ed* Shiplake Coll.

DAUGHTERS LIVING (*By 1st marriage*)

Hon Rachel Honoria, *b* 1960: *m* 1984, Antony William Parrack, eldest son of late Kenneth Parrack, and has issue living, Archie St John Beach, *b* 1989, — Felix Honorio Beach, *b* 1991, — Betsy Dorothy Mary, *b* 1998. *Residence* – Cambridge House, 53 Wandle Rd, SW17.
Hon Sophia Charlotte, *b* 1966: *m* 1995, Charles Reggie Kirk, son of Major J. O. Kirk (*see* E Fingall, 1973-74 Edn), and has issue living, Mamie Honoria, *b* 1997, — Genevieve (Evie) Grace, *b* 1999. *Residence* – Ashfield House, Sawley, Ripon, N Yorks HG4 3ED.

BROTHERS LIVING

Hon (Ian) Henry Calthorpe, *b* 1938; *ed* Harrow; late Lieut 5th Beds Regt (TA): *m* 1970, Lady (Pamela) Lemina Gordon, da of 12th Marquess of Huntly, and has issue living, Percy FitzRoy, *b* 1971; *ed* Harrow, — Henrietta Lemina, *b* 1973. *Residence* – Coldstone House, Logie Coldstone, Aboyne, Aberdeenshire AB34 5NP. *Club* – Royal Northern, Aberdeen.
Hon (George) Andrew, *b* 1944; *ed* Eton: *m* 1968, Sylvia Josephine Ruth, eldest da of Michael Richard Lloyd Haynes (*see* Shelley, Bt, colls), and has issue living, Justin, *b* 1971; *ed* Rannoch, — Giles Spencer, *b* 1974; *ed* Gordonstoun: *m* 1999, Demelza, yr da of Maj John Harvey, of Halston, Shropshire, — Daniel George, *b* 1978; *ed* Gordonstoun, — Tania Georgiana, *b* 1977. *Residence* – Inverernan House, Strathdon, Aberdeenshire AB36 8YA.
Hon Philip Richard, *b* 1950; *ed* Eton: *m* 1977, Saskia Moyne, eldest da of Terence George Andrews, MBE, and has issue living, Harry, *b* 1979, — Edward, *b* (twin) 1979, — Samuel, *b* 1982, — Saskia Rose, *b* 1985. *Residence* – 307 Woodstock Rd, Oxford OX2 7NY. *Clubs* – ....

SISTER LIVING

Hon Caroline Jean, *b* 1935: *m* 1958, James Bristow, and has issue living, Timothy Dominic Ian James (Hermeston Hall, Oldcotes, Notts), *b* 1959; *ed* Bedford, Exeter Univ, and Cranfield Sch of Management: *m* 1984 (*m diss* 1992), Annabel Judith Dorrell, yr da of David Palmer, of The Old Vicarage, Biddenham, Beds, and has issue living, Arthur Timothy James *b* 1986, Lily Annabel Mary *b* 1989, — George Edward FitzRoy (Stonelands, School Lane, Lodsworth, Petworth, W Sussex GU28 9DH), *b* 1961, *ed* Bedford: *m* 1987, Juliet J., only da of Paul Knocker, of Parnham, Dorset, and has issue living, Edward George *b* 1990, Fergus James Paul *b* 1994, Lucinda Joy *b* 1988, — Barnaby James St John, *b* 1966; *ed* Bedford: *m* 1996, Nathalie Y., eldest da of late Michael Curtin, of Commugny, Switzerland, — Melissa Caroline, *b* 1963: *m* 1994, Mathew Thurlow Laws, of East Lodge, Long Lane, Wrington, Som, only son of Charles Laws, of Winford, Som, and has issue living, James Thurlow *b* 1997, Isabella Grania Melissa *b* 1995, Lara Fiona *b* 1996. *Residence* – Penmorfa, Seaview, Isle of Wight PO34 5HE.

UNCLE LIVING (*son of 1st Baron*)

Hon Hugh de Beauchamp, TD, *b* 1914; *ed* Eton, Chillon Coll, and Corpus Christi Coll, Camb (MA); late Capt 5th Batn Bedfordshire Regt (TA Reserve); with Bovril 1935-71 (Chm 1971), Chm Pitman Ltd 1973-81 and Tribune Investment

Trust Ltd 1950-86; Chm of Cttees United Soc for Christian Literature 1949-82; High Sheriff Beds 1961-62, DL 1964; author of *Argentina Revisited*: *m* 1946, Audrey Warren, da of late Col Frederick Warren Pearl, of 20 Lowndes Sq, SW1, and has issue living, Primrose Pearl, *b* 1948: *m* 1975, Martin Arthur Hudson, of 62 Wilton Av, W4 2HY, and has issue living, Hugh James *b* 1977; *ed* Eton, Mark Oliver *b* 1978; *ed* St Paul's Sch, Ian Alexander *b* 1979; *ed* Eton, Christopher Martin *b* 1981; *ed* Eton, — Juliet Amy, *b* 1950: *m* 1975, Simon Crocker, of 62 Battledean Rd, Highbury, N5, and has issue living, Barnaby William de Beauchamp *b* 1976; *ed* Marlborough, Amy *b* 1979, — Marguerite Laura (10 Foxford Close, W Hunsbury, Northampton NN4 9UH), *b* 1952: *m* 1977, Timothy John Clark, who *d* 1994 and has issue living, Jamie Duncan *b* 1979; *ed* Roade Sch, Thomas Edward *b* 1986, Anna Camilla *b* 1981, Jessica Roddie *b* 1984. *Residence* – Woodleys Farm House, Melchbourne, Beds MK44 1AG.

AUNT LIVING *(daughter of 1st Baron)*

Hon (Laura) Pearl, OBE, *b* 1916; Joint MFH Oakley 1938-40; JP Beds 1941-84 (Chm 1978-84); County Pres St John Ambulance Brig 1971-90, and a DStJ; DL, High Sheriff Beds 1985; OBE (Civil) 1946. *Residence* – Woodleys Stud House, Melchbourne, Beds MK44 1AO.

WIDOW LIVING OF SECOND BARON

BARBARA (*Barbara, Baroness Luke*), da of Sir FitzRoy Hamilton Anstruther-Gough-Calthorpe, 1st Bt: *m* 1932, Lt-Col the 2nd Baron Luke, KCVO, who *d* 1996. *Residence* – Orchard Cottage, Odell, Beds.

PREDECESSORS – (1) GEORGE Lawson Johnston, KBE, 2nd son of John Lawson Johnston, of Kingswood, Kent, *b* 1873; a Director of Lloyds Bank, Ltd, and Bovril Ltd, and Lord-Lieut, Co Councillor, and a JP for Bedfordshire (High Sheriff 1924); *cr Baron Luke*, of Pavenham, co Bedford (peerage of United Kingdom) 1929: *m* 1902, Hon Edith Laura St John, who *d* 1941, da of 16th Baron St John of Bletso; *d* 1943; *s* by his el son (2) IAN ST JOHN, KCVO, 2nd Baron, *b* 1905; Chm Bovril Ltd 1943-70, Chm Electrolux Ltd 1963-68, Chm National Playing Fields Assocn 1950-75; Pres Advertising Assocn 1955-58; sometime Dir Lloyds Bank and IBM; Member Internat Olympic Cttee 1951-88; Hon Col 5th Bn Bedfordshire and Hertfordshire Regt 1947-62; Master of Foxhounds Oakley Hunt; JP and DL Beds; Master Drapers' Co 1962-63: *m* 1932, Barbara, da of Sir FitzRoy Hamilton Anstruther-Gough-Calthorpe, 1st Bt; *d* 1996; *s* by his eldest son (3) ARTHUR CHARLES ST JOHN, 3rd Baron and present peer.

Lumley, Viscount; son of Earl of Scarbrough.

Lumley, family name of Earl of Scarbrough.

LYELL, BARON (Lyell) (Baron UK 1914, Bt UK 1894)

To the brave,not to the dastardly

CHARLES LYELL, 3rd Baron, and 3rd Baronet; *b* 27 March 1939; *s* 1943; *ed* Eton, and Ch Ch Oxford; late 2nd Lt Scots Gds; DL Angus; CA; a Lord in Waiting to HM 1979-84, since when an Under Sec of State for N Ireland.

Arms – Or, a cross parted and fretty azure between four crosses patée gules, all within a bordure of the last. **Crest** – Upon a rock a dexter cubit arm erect in armour proper, charged with a cross parted and fretty gules, the hand grasping a sword in bend sinister also proper. **Supporters** – Not yet recorded at College at Arms.
Seat – Kinnordy, Kirriemuir, Angus. *Town Residence* – 20 Petersham Mews, SW7. *Clubs* – Turf, White's.

WIDOW LIVING OF SECOND BARON

SOPHIE MARY (*Baroness Lyell*), da of late Major Sigismund William Joseph Trafford (*see* E Lindsey and Abingdon, colls): *m* 1938, the 2nd Baron, VC, who was *ka* 1943. *Residences* – Kinnordy, Kirriemuir, Angus; 20 Petersham Mews, SW7.

PREDECESSORS – (1) LEONARD Lyell, el son of late Lieut-Col Henry Lyell, and nephew and heir of Sir Charles Lyell, 1st Bt (*cr* 1864) (ext); *b* 1850; MP for Orkney and Shetland (*L*) 1885-1900; *cr* a Baronet 1894, and *Baron Lyell*, of Kinnordy, co Forfar (peerage of United Kingdom) 1914: *m* 1874, Mary, who *d* 1929, da of late Rev John Mayne Stirling; *d* 1926; *s* by his grandson (2) CHARLES ANTONY, VC (son of late Major Hon Charles Henry Lyell, only son of 1st Baron), 2nd Baron; *b* 1913; Capt Scots Guards; European War 1939-43 (VC): *m* 1938, Sophie Mary, da of late Major Sigismund William Joseph Trafford (*see* E Lindsey and Abingdon, colls); *ka* 1943; *s* by his only son (3) CHARLES, 3rd Baron and present peer.

Lymington, Viscount; son of Earl of Portsmouth.

Lyon, Bowes, family name of Earl of Strathmore and Kinghorne.

LYONS OF BRIGHTON, BARONY OF (Lyons) (Extinct 1978)

SONS LIVING OF LIFE BARON

Hon Rodney Mair (102 Pennsylvania Rd, Exeter EX4 6DQ), *b* 1941; *ed* St Paul's, and Magdalen Coll, Oxford (BA, post-grad Cert Ed); Principal of Taunton's Coll, Southampton 1989-97: *m* 1963, Cory Frances, da of Dr William Owen Hassall, of the Manor House, Wheatley, Oxford, and has issue, one son and one da.
Hon William (69 Perryn Rd, W3 7LS), *b* 1945; Writer, Story Ed, and Storyliner *EastEnders*, etc; Winner Writers' Guild of GB Award for Educational Drama 1977: *m* 1st, 1963 (*m diss* 19—), Petra Deanna, da of William Tibble; 2ndly, 1986, Gillian Mary, da of Alfred Tullett, and has issue living (by 1st *m*), Kevin Oliver, *b* 1964, — Teena Fern, *b* 1967, — (by 2nd *m*) Braham William Ash, *b* 1990, — Natasha Beatrice Holly, *b* 1987.

DAUGHTER LIVING OF LIFE BARON

Hon Deborah, *b* 1965.

Lysaght, family name of Baron Lisle.

Lyttelton, family name of Viscount Chandos.

Lyttelton, family name of Viscount Cobham.

LYTTON, EARL OF (Lytton) (Earl UK 1880, Bt UK 1838)

This is the work of valour

JOHN PETER MICHAEL SCAWEN LYTTON, 5th Earl and 6th Baronet; *b* 7 June 1950; *s* 1985; *ed* Downside, and Reading Univ; FRICS; sole proprietor John Lytton & Co, Chartered Surveyors, since 1988; Chm Leasehold Enfranchisement Advisory Service since 1994; Pres Newstead Abbey Byron Society; Pres Horsham Chamber of Trade and Commerce since 1995: *m* 1980, Ursula, da of Anton Komoly, of Vienna, Austria, and has issue.

Arms – Quarterly: 1st and 4th, ermine on a chief dancettée azure, two ducal coronets or, a canton argent, charged with a rose gules, *Lytton*; 2nd and 3rd gules, on a chevron argent, between three eaglets reguardant or, as many cinquefoils sable, *Bulwer*. Crests – 1st a griffin's head erased ermine, eared and maned or; 2nd, a bittern in flags, all proper; 3rd, an eagle, reguardant argent, holding in the beak a branch of laurel vert. Supporters – Two angles proper, each holding an easter crown or.

Residence – Newbuildings Place, Shipley, Horsham, W Sussex RH13 7JQ.

SONS LIVING

PHILIP ANTHONY SCAWEN (*Viscount Knebworth*), *b* 7 March 1989, — *Hon* Wilfrid Thomas Scawen, *b* 1992.

DAUGHTER LIVING

Lady Katrina Mary Noel, *b* 1985.

BROTHER LIVING

Hon (Thomas) Roland Cyril Lawrence, *b* 1954; *ed* Downside. *Residence* – Bratton Court Farm, Minehead, Somerset.

SISTERS LIVING

Lady Caroline Mary Noel, *b* 1947; *ed* Birmingham Univ, and Sir John Cass Sch of Art; silversmith.
Lady Lucy Mary Frances, *b* 1957; hydrogeologist.
Lady Sarah Teresa Mary, *b* 1959: *m* 1984, P. David Nash Solly, yst son of late Lt-Col R. J. N. Solly, and has issue living, Benedict Nash, *b* 1995, — Isabelle Kate, *b* 1992.

HALF-AUNT LIVING (*Daughter of 3rd Earl by 2nd wife*)

Lady Madeleine Elizabeth (4 rue des Hauts-Tillets, 92310 Sèvres, France), *b* 1921; dancer, choreographer and teacher; has issue living, Eleanore LYTTON, *b* 1957; lyricist.

DAUGHTER LIVING OF SECOND EARL

Lady (Margaret) Hermione (Millicent) (*Lady Hermione Cobbold*), *b* 1905: *m* 1930, 1st Baron Cobbold, who *d* 1987. *Residence* – Stables Cottage, Knebworth, Herts.

WIDOW LIVING OF FOURTH EARL

CLARISSA MARY (*Dowager Countess of Lytton*), da of late Brig-Gen Cyril Eustace Palmer, CB, CMG, DSO (Blakiston, Bt, colls): *m* 1946, the 4th Earl, who *d* 1985. *Residence* – Garden Wing, Newbuildings Place, Shipley, nr Horsham, W Sussex RH13 7JQ.

PREDECESSORS – (1) *Rt Hon Sir* EDWARD GEORGE EARLE Bulwer-Lytton, GCMG, PC, DCL, LLD; *b* 1803; a distinguished poet, novelist, orator, and statesman; MP for St Ives 1831, for Lincoln (*L*) 1832-41, and for Hertfordshire 1852-66; was Sec of State for the Colonies 1858-9, and Lord Rector of Glasgow Univ 1856-8; author of numerous popular novels, of well-known poems and dramas, and of essays on general literature and politics; assumed the additional surname of Lytton 1844; *cr* a *Baronet* 1838, and *Baron Lytton*, of Knebworth, co Herts (peerage of United Kingdom) 1866: *m* 1827, Rosina Doyle, who *d* 1822, da of Francis Massey Wheeler, *d* 1873; *s* by his son (2) EDWARD ROBERT LYTTON, GCB, GCSI, CIE, PC, 2nd Baron; *b* 1831; a distinguished diplomatist and poet, Minister at Lisbon 1874-6, Viceroy and Gov-Gen of India 1876-80, and Ambassador at Paris 1887-91; Lord Rector of Glasgow Univ 1887-90; *cr Earl of Lytton*, of co Derby, and *Viscount Knebworth*, of co Herts, 1880: *m* 1864, Edith, VA, CI, who *d* 1936, da of late Hon Edward Ernest Villiers; *d* 1891; *s* by his son (3) VICTOR ALEXANDER GEORGE ROBERT, KG, GCSI, GCIE, PC, 2nd Earl; *b* 1876; appointed a Civil Lord of the Admiralty 1916, additional Parliamentary Sec to Admiralty 1917, British Commr for Propaganda in France 1918, Dep First Lord of the Admiralty 1918, again Civil Lord of the Admiralty 1919, and Under-Sec of State for India 1920; was Gov of Bengal 1922-7 (acted as Viceroy of India and Gov-Gen April to Aug 1925): *m* 1902, Pamela Frances Audrey, CI, who *d* 1971, da of late Sir Trevor John Chichele Chichele-Plowden, KCSI; *d* 1947; *s* by his brother (4) NEVILLE STEPHEN, OBE, 3rd Earl; *b* 1879; a Portrait and Landscape Painter: *m* 1st, 1899 (*m diss* 1923), Judith Anne Dorothea (*Baroness Wentworth* in her own right), who *d* 1957; 2ndly, 1924, Rosa Alexandrine Fortel, who *d* 1980, of St Rambert-en-Burgey, Ain, France; *d* 1951: *s* by his son (5) NOEL ANTHONY SCAWEN, OBE, 4th Earl; *b* 1900; Lt-Col Rifle Bde; assumed by deed poll 1925 the additional surname of Milbanke after that of Lytton; discontinued by deed poll 1951 the use of this additional surname: *m* 1946, Clarissa Mary, da of late Brig-Gen Cyril Eustace Palmer, CB, CMG, DSO (Blakiston, Bt, colls); *d* 1985; *s* by his son (6) JOHN PETER MICHAEL SCAWEN, 5th Earl and present peer; also Viscount Knebworth, Baron Wentworth (see * infra), and Baron Lytton.

*(1) *Rt Hon Sir* THOMAS Wentworth, PC, summoned to English Parliament as *Baron Wentworth*, 1529-48; was Lord Chamberlain of the Household; *d* 1551; *s* by his son (2) THOMAS, 2nd Baron; *d* 1584; *s* by his son (3) HENRY, 3rd Baron; *d* 1593; *s* by his son (4) THOMAS, 4th Baron; *cr Earl of Cleveland*, co York (peerage of England) 1625; *d* 1667; *s* by his son (5) THOMAS, 5th Baron; *b* 1613; was summoned in his father's Barony of Wentworth 1640; *dvp* 1664, who was *s* by his da (6) HENRIETTA; *s* by her aunt (7) ANNE, wife of 2nd Baron Lovelace; *d* 1697; *s* by her grandda (8) MARTHA, who was confirmed in the Barony 1702: *d* 1745; *s* by her kinsman (9) *Sir* EDWARD Noel, 6th Bt, heir of Hon Margaret Noel, da of Anne, Baroness Wentworth (ante), who became 9th Baron; *cr Viscount Wentworth* (peerage of England) 1762; *d* 1774; *s* by his son (10) THOMAS, LLD, 2nd Viscount; as a Lord of the Bedchamber; *dsp* 1815, when the viscountcy became extinct, and the barony became abeyant and remained so until 1856, when it was terminated in favour of (11) ANNE ISABELLA, widow of George Gordon, 6th Baron Byron, who in 1822 assumed by Roy licence the additional surname of Noel, *d* 1860; *s* by her grandson (12) BYRON NOEL King-Noel (Viscount Ockham), el son of Hon Augusta Ada, da of Anne Isabella, Baroness Wentworth and Byron (ante) by her mariage with William, 1st Earl of Lovelace; *d* unmarried 1862; *s* by his brother (13) RALPH GORDON, 13th Baron; *b* 1839; assumed by Roy licence 1861 the surname of Milbanke in lieu of Noel in 1893; *s* as 2nd Earl of Lovelace (see that title): *m* 1st, 1869, Fannie, who *d* 1878, 3rd da of late Rev George Heriot, of Fellow Hills, Berwick; 2ndly, 1880, Mary Caroline, el da of late Right Hon James Stuart-Wortley; *d* 1906, when the Earldom of Lovelace, Viscountcy of Ockham, and Barony of King devolved upon his half-brother Lionel Fortescue King-Noel, while he was *s* in the Barony of Wentworth by his ony child (14) ADA MARY *b* 1871; *d* 1917; *s* by her aunt (15) ANNE ISABELLA (da of 1st Earl of Lovelace), *b* 1837: *m* 1869, Wilfrid Scawen Blunt, who *d* 1922, of Crabbet Park, Crawley, Sussex; *d* 1917; *s* by her da (16) JUDITH ANNE DOROTHEA, *b* 1873; assumed by deed poll 1904 the surname of Blunt-Lytton: *m* 1899 (*m diss* 1923), Maj Hon Neville Stephen Bulwer-Lytton, OBE, who *d* 1951, afterwards 3rd Earl of Lytton; *d* 1957; *s* by her son (17) NOEL ANTHONY, OBE, who *s* as 4th Earl of Lytton 1951 (ante), and 17th Baron Wentworth.

LYVEDEN, BARON (Vernon) (Baron UK 1859)

Vernon always flourishes

RONALD CECIL VERNON, 6th Baron; *b* 10 April 1915; *s* 1973: *m* 1938, Queenie Constance, da of Howard Ardern, and has issue.

Arms – Quarterly: 1st and 4th argent, a fret sable, *Vernon*; 2nd and 3rd gules, three bars gemelles argent a chevron ermine, on a chief of the second three blackamoors' heads proper; a canton of the field, charged with a battle axe or, all within a bordure counter compony of the second and azure, *Smith*. **Crests** – *Dexter* (Vernon) 1st, a boar's head erased sable, ducally gorged or; 2nd, *Sinister* (Smith) a cubit arm erect, in armour proper, charged with a battle-axe sable, the hand grasping two wreaths of laurel, pendant on either side, also proper. **Supporters** – *Dexter*, a boar sable, ducally gorged, and suspended therefrom by a chain an escutcheon or, charged with a rose gules slipped proper; *sinister*, a wyvern vert, plain collared, and suspended therefrom by a chain an escutcheon or, charged with a rose, slipped, proper.
Residence – 20 Farmer St, Te Aroha, NZ.

SONS LIVING

Hon JACK LESLIE (17 Carlton St, Te Aroha, NZ), *b* 10 Nov 1938: *m* 1961, Lynette June, da of William Herbert Lilley, and has issue living, Colin Ronald, *b* 3 Feb 1967, — Wendy Caroline, *b* 1962, — Karen Marie, *b* 1964.
Hon Robert Howard (2175 Avenue Rd Apt 106, Toronto, Ontario, Canada), *b* 1942: *m* 1968, Louise Smith, and has issue living, Russell Sydney *b* 1969: *m* 1995, Kathryn Johnston, and has issue living Mitchell Robert Allan, *b* 19—.
Hon Grant (40 Emma St, Te Aroha, NZ), *b* 1952: *m* 1992, Karen Teresa Margaret Green, and has issue living, Daniel Grant James, *b* 1993.

SISTER LIVING

Hon Maureen Dawn, *b* 1926: *m* 1946, Noel Surrell, who *d* 1995, of 49A Huka Falls Rd, Taupo, NZ, and has issue living, Andrew Gray (49A Huka Falls Rd, Taupo, NZ), *b* 1952: *m* 1970, Rowena Anne Doel, and has issue living, Jason Carey *b* 1971, Carlene *b* 1974.

COLLATERAL BRANCHES LIVING

Granddaughters of late Cecil Sydney Archibald Vernon, 2nd son of late Hon Greville Richard Vernon (infra):—
Issue of late John Lyveden Vernon, *b* 1895; *d* 1970: *m* 1922, Catherine Mary Draffin, who *d* 1970:—
Bettina Mary Paulinus NAIR (81 Charles St, Westshore, Napier, NZ), *b* 1926: *m* 1950 (*m diss* 1977), Archibald Reid McLeay, and has issue living, Eain Dougald John, *b* 1953: *m* 1977, Jennifer Raye Thomsen, and has issue living, Devin Eain *b* 1983, Holley Jennifer *b* 1981, Casey Leah *b* 1986, — Jane Imelda, *b* 1951 (and has issue living, Amber Lea *b* 1977), — Leah Paule (twin), *b* 1951: *m* 1974, Ralph John Johansson, of Bucklands Beach, Auckland, NZ, — Victoria Catherine Ethel (twin), *b* 1953: *m* 1974 (*m diss* 1977), Lee Nicholas Fatouros, and has issue living, Marley Reid *b* 1980. —— Jillyan Imelda, *b* 1935: *m* 1955, Charles Woolnough Locke, of 55 Pacific Parade, Whangaparaoa Peninsula, Hibiscus Coast 1463, NZ, and has issue living, Gregory Charles Woolnough, *b* 1957, — Antoinette Marie, *b* 1956: *m* 1977, William Sylvester Stuart, of 12 Cameron St, Sydney, Australia, and has issue living, William Gregory Charles *b* 1978, Kellie Ann Imelda *b* 1979, — Katherine Hélène, *b* 1961: *m* 1987, Olivier Michel Jean Wardecki, of Ferme de Vaufron, Vezelay, France, and has issue living, Ava Alice WARDECKI-LOCKE *b* 1996.

Grandson of late Capt Eustace Vernon, 4th son of late Hon Greville Richard Vernon (infra):—
Issue of late Greville Rupert Eustace Vernon, *b* 1899, *d* 1967: *m* 1925, Francisca, who *d* 1997, da of John Henry Little:—
Greville Richard Eustace (2/16 Diana Court, Riverside, Tasmania 7250, Australia) *b* 1926; BSc TTC: *m* 1953, Nancy Grace Haslam, and has issue living, Jane Suzanne, *b* 1957: *m* 1978, Laurence James Rogers, of 17 Tanner Drive, Legana, Tasmania, and has issue living, Jonathan Alexander *b* 1986, Kate Frances *b* 1984.

Grandsons of late Greville Rupert Eustace Vernon (ante):—
Issue of late Robert Harcourt Vernon, *b* 1929, *d* 1987: *m* 1954, Isobel Jennifer Miller (2 Kenyon St, Launceston, Tasmania):—
Robert Courtenay John (44 Richardson Cres, Burnie, Tasmania, Australia), *b* 1955: *m* 1982, Vicki Maree Davis, and has issue living, Robert Andrew, *b* 1983, — Christopher Richard, *b* 1986. —— Hugh Gowran, *b* 1957. —— David Stewart Lyveden, *b* 1958: *m* 1982, Meredith Caroline Reeve, and has issue living, Stephanie Caroline, *b* 1985, — Rebecca Isobel, *b* 1988, — Georgina Amy, *b* 1991.

Grandchildren of late Robert Rupert Charles Vernon (infra):—
Issue of late Maj Mervyn Sydney Bobus Vernon, MVO, late Gren Guards, *b* 1912, *d* 1991: *m* 1937, Lady Violet Mary Baring, who *d* 1978, yr da of 2nd Earl of Cromer:—
Greville Edward Mervyn (Newington House, Kingscote, Glos), *b* 1944; *ed* Eton: *m* 1969, Fiona Dawn Cory, da of Lt-Col William Handley Ferguson, of Ozleworth Park, Wooton-under-Edge, Glos (*see* Cory, Bt, 1985 Edn), and has issue living, James Fitzpatrick Greville, *b* 1971, — Zara Caroline, *b* 1973, — Sasha Elizabeth, *b* 1979. —— (Hugh) Richard Mervyn (Stairaird, Mauchline, Ayrshire), *b* 1947: *ed* Eton, DL Ayrshire and Arran: *m* 1976, Hon Victoria Arthur, da of 3rd Baron Glenarthur, and has issue living, Andrew Robert Richard *b* 1979; *ed* Eton, — Catherine Victoria, *b* 1977, — Emma Mary,

b 1983. —— Veronica Elizabeth, *b* 1938: *m* 1968, as his 3rd wife, (George) Jonathan Hargreaves (*see* V Goschen, 1990 Edn), who *d* 1991, of Glen Cottage, Luckington, Chippenham, Wilts.

Granddaughter of late Hon Greville Richard Vernon, 4th son of 1st Baron:—
        Issue of late Robert Rupert Charles Vernon, DSO, *b* 1872, *d* 1940: *m* 1906, Dorothy Inez Elinor, who *d* 1965, only da of George Benjamin Thorneycroft, of Dunston Hall, Stafford:—
Susan Diana Mary, *b* 1915: *m* 1946, Francis Reitman, MD, who *d* 1955, and has issue living, Robert Vernon Michael (Thiat, Bussière Poitevine 87320, France), *b* 1947; *ed* Radley, — Susan Theresa Maria (The West Wing, Triscombe House, Bishop's Lydeard, Taunton, Som TA4 3HG), *b* 1950, — Roseanna Mary Blanche (*Countess of Stradbroke*) *b* 1953: *m* 1977, 6th Earl of Stradbroke. *Residence* – The West Wing, Triscombe House, Bishop's Lydeard, Taunton, Somerset TA4 3HG.

PREDECESSORS – (1) ROBERT Vernon (son of Robert Percy Smith, of Cheam, Surrey, Judge Advocate Gen in India, MP for City of Lincoln, by his wife, Caroline Maria, 2nd da of Richard Vernon, MP, of Hilton Park, Stafford), PC, MP for Tralee 1829-31 and for Northampton (*L*) 1831-59; was a Lord of the Treasury 1830-4, Sec of Board of Control 1835-9, Under-Sec for the Colonies 1839-41, Sec of War 1852, and Pres of Board of Control 1855-8; assumed for his children in 1846 by Roy licence the surname of Vernon, and in 1859 assumed for himself the surname of Vernon in lieu of his patronymic Smith; *cr Baron Lyveden*, of Lyveden, co Northampton (peerage of United Kingdom) 1859; *b* 1800: *m* 1823, Emma Mary Fitz Patrick who *d* 1882, sister of 1st Baron Castletown; *d* 1873; *s* by his son (2) FITZ-PATRICK HENRY, 2nd Baron, *b* 1824; in Diplo Ser 1846-50: *m* 1st, 1853, Lady Albreda Elizabeth Wentworth-FitzWilliam, who *d* 1891, da of 4th Earl FitzWilliam, KG; 2ndly, 1896, Julia Kate, who *d* 1949, da of Albert Emary, of Harold Rd, Clive Vale, Hastings; *d* 1900; *s* by his nephew (3) COURTENAY ROBERT PERCY (son of late Rev Hon Courtenay John Vernon, 3rd son of 1st Baron), 3rd Baron; *b* 1857, Capt 3rd Bn, Highland LI; Pres British Cttee for study of foreign municipal insts; Prussian Order of the Crown (2nd class); a Purser in the Mercantile Marine; European War 1914-13 as Lieut-Com RNVR; a Member of the Dramatic Profession: *m* 1st, 1890, Fanny Zelie, who *d* 1924, da of late Maj Charles Hill, of Wollaston Hall, nr Wellingborough; 2ndly, 1925, Mrs Ada SPRINGATE (the actress Lynda Martell), who *d* 19—, da of Arthur Hodgkinson, of Accrington, and formerly wife of Richard Springate; *d* 1926: *s* by his son (4) ROBERT FITZ-PATRICK COURTENAY, 4th Baron, *b* 1892: *m* 1949, Doris Violet, who *d* 1985, da of late Henry Francis Coghlan White, previously wife of Cdr J. G. Bower, RN, and widow of Capt Eric Paterson; *d* 1969; *s* by his kinsman (5) SYDNEY MUNROE ARCHIBALD (grandson of Hon Greville Richard Vernon, yst son of 1st Baron), 5th Baron, *b* 1888: *m* 1st, 1912, Ruby, who *d* 1932, da of Robert John Shandley; 2ndly, 1957, Gladys, who *d* 1986, widow of John Cassidy; *d* 1973; *s* by his only son (6) RONALD CECIL, 6th Baron and present peer.

MABANE, BARONY OF (Mabane) (Extinct 1969)

WIDOW LIVING OF FIRST BARON

STELLA JANE (*Baroness Mabane*), da of late Julian Duggan, of Buenos Aires: *m* 1944, the 1st Baron Mabane, who *d* 1969, when the title became extinct. *Residence* –

McALPINE OF MOFFAT, BARONY OF (McAlpine) (Extinct 1990)

SONS AND DAUGHTERS OF LIFE BARON (*see* following article, and McAlpine, Bt)

McALPINE OF WEST GREEN, BARON (McAlpine) (Life Baron 1984)

(ROBERT) ALISTAIR MCALPINE, 2nd son of Baron McAlpine of Moffat (Life Baron) (*see* Baronetage); *b* 14 May 1942; *ed* Stowe; Hon Treasurer 1975-90 (jtly since 1981) and Dep Chm 1979-83, Conservative and Unionist Party; Dir Sir Robert McAlpine Ltd 1963-95; Hon Treasurer European Democratic Union 1978-88; Member Arts Council of Great Britain 1981-82, Chm Arts Council Touring Cttee; Vice-Pres Ashmolean Museum; *cr Baron McAlpine of West Green*, of West Green, co Hants (Life Baron) 1984: *m* 1st, 1964 (*m diss* 1979), Sarah Alexandra, da of late Paul Hillman Baron, of 72 Bryanston Court, George Street, W1; 2ndly, 1980, Romilly Thompson, only da of Alfred Thompson Hobbs, of Knights Farm House, West Green, Hartley Wintney, Hants, and has issue by 1st and 2nd *m*.

🛡️rms – Per chevron vert and or two chevronels one in chief argent the other in base azure. Crest – A cubit arm grasping a chaplet of pine fructed proper. Supporters – *Dexter*, an aborigine girt with a body belt pendent therefrom a lonca-lonca armed with a spear and in his sinister hand a boomerang and extending the other to and behind the head of a kangaroo sejant beside him all proper; *sinister*, a gardener in his working clothes wearing an apron of green baize in his exterior hand a spade and having perched upon the wrist and palm of his other hand a parrot proper.
Clubs – Garrick, Carlton.

DAUGHTERS LIVING (*by 1st marriage*)

Hon (Mary) Jane, *b* 1965: *m* 1987, Simon J. E. du B. Taylor, eldest son of Timothy Taylor, of Meadle, Bucks, and has issue living, Henry, *b* 1995.
Hon Victoria Alice, *b* 1967: *m* 1992, Lionel Digby Sheffield Neave, and has issue (*see* Neave, Bt, colls).

(*By 2nd marriage*)

Hon Skye, *b* 1984.

MacANDREW, BARON (MacAndrew) (Baron UK 1959)

CHRISTOPHER ANTHONY COLIN MACANDREW, 3rd Baron; *b* 16 Feb 1945; *s* 1989; *ed* Malvern: *m* 1975, Sarah Helen, only da of Lt-Col Peter Hendy Brazier, of Nash Court Farmhouse, Marnhull, Dorset, and has issue.
Residence – Hall Farm, Archdeacon Newton, Darlington, co Durham

SON LIVING

Hon OLIVER CHARLES JULIAN, *b* 3 Sept 1983.

DAUGHTERS LIVING

Hon Diana Sarah, *b* 1978.
Hon Tessa Deborah, *b* 1980.

BROTHER LIVING

Hon Nicholas Rupert (The Old Chapel, Greywell, Hook, Hants), *b* 1947; *ed* Eton: *m* 1st, 1975 (*m diss* 1994), Victoria Rose, da of George Patrick Renton, of Paddock Lodge, Isington, Alton, Hants; 2ndly, 1998, Joy Elizabeth Meadows, and has issue living (by 1st *m*), Robin Glen, *b* 1978, — Rose Clare, *b* 1980, — Rachel Emma, *b* 1984.

SISTER LIVING

Hon Deborah Jane *b* 1956: *m* 1979, Lt-Col Mark William Bingham Faulkner, The Royal Dragoon Gds (*see* de Trafford, Bt, colls, 1995 Edn), and has issue living, James William MacAndrew, *b* 1983, — Alexander Charles MacAndrew, *b* 1987, — Patrick Mark MacAndrew, *b* 1992.

AUNT LIVING (*daughter of 1st Baron by 1st marriage*)

Hon Elizabeth Lilian Graham (*Hon Lady Coats*), *b* 1929: *m* 1950, Sir William David Coats, and has issue living, Brian Glen Heywood, *b* 1951; *ed* Eton: *m* 1979, Consuelo, da of Luis Eduardo Marquez, of Carrera 3A, no 18-24, Pereira, Risaralda, Colombia, and has issue living, Andrew William Heywood *b* 1983, Julia Caroline *b* 1981, — Adrian James MacAndrew *b* 1955; *ed* Eton: *m* 1979, Mary Elizabeth, da George Robin Clover, of 3 Wallside, Monkwell Sq, Barbican, EC2, and has issue living, Alistair Thomas Edward *b* 1984, Rachel Olivia Askernish *b* 1982, — Frances Alice *b* 1958: *m* 1982, Michael John Adam Fowle, and has issue living, Jonathan Richard Adam *b* 1986, Alexandra Jane Adam *b* 1985. *Residence* – The Cottage, Symington, Ayrshire.

HALF-AUNT LIVING (*daughter of 1st Baron by 2nd marriage*)

Hon Mary Margaret Hastings, *b* 1942: *m* 1967, Maj-Gen Charles Alexander Ramsay, of Bughtrig, Coldstream, Berwickshire (*see* Ramsay, Bt (*cr* 1806), colls).

PREDECESSORS – (1) CHARLES GLEN MacAndrew, TD, PC, served in European War 1914-19 with Machine Gun Corps, Cmd'd Ayrshire Yeo 1932-36; Dep Speaker and Chm Ways and Means Cttee, House of Commons 1951-59; MP for Kilmarnock Div. of Ayrshire and Bute (C) 1924-29, for Patrick Div of Glasgow 1931-35, and for Bute and N Ayrshire Dir of Ayrshire and Bute 1935-59; *cr* Kt 1935, PC 1952, and *Baron MacAndrew*, of the Firth of Clyde (peerage of United Kingdom) 1959: *m* 1st, 1918 (*m diss* 1938), Lilian Cathleen, who *d* 1978, da of James Prendergast Curran, of St Andrews; 2ndly, 1941, Mona, who *d* 1994, da of James Alexander Ralston Mitchell, of Perceton House, Irvine, Ayrshire; *d* 1979; *s* by his el and only surv son, (2) COLIN NEVIL GLEN, 2nd Baron, *b* 1919, served 1939-45 War with Ayrshire Yeo, sometime Master of Zetland Foxhounds: *m* 1943, Ursula Beatrice, who *d* 1986, yr da of Capt Joseph Steel, of Kirkwood, Lockerbie, Dumfriesshire; *d* 1989; *s* by his elder son (3) CHRISTOPHER ANTHONY COLIN, 3rd Baron and present peer.

McCARTHY, BARON (McCarthy) (Life Baron 1975)

WILLIAM EDWARD JOHN McCARTHY, son of Edward McCarthy; *b* 30 July 1925; *ed* Holloway County Sch., Ruskin Coll, Merton Coll, and Nuffield Coll, Oxford (MA, DPhil); a Fellow of Nuffield Coll; *cr Baron McCarthy*, of Headington in City of Oxford (Life Baron) 1975: *m* 1957, Margaret, da of Percival Godfrey.
Residence – 4 William Orchard Close, Old Headington, Oxford. *Club* – Reform.

MACAULAY OF BRAGAR, BARON (Macaulay) (Life Baron 1989)

DONALD MACAULAY, son of late John Macaulay, shipyard labourer, of Bragar, Isle of Lewis, by his wife, Henrietta (*née* McLean); *b* 14 Nov 1933; *ed* Clydebank High Sch, and Glasgow Univ (MA, LLB); served RASC 1958-60; QC (Scot) 1975; Chm Supreme Court Legal Aid Cttee; Scottish Chm for Abolition of Paybeds for NHS; Founder Memb and former Chm Advocates' Criminal Law Group; Memb Dean's Council of Faculty of Advocates, Memb Faculty of Advocates' Gen Standing Cttee and Governor of Courts' Cttee; *cr Baron Macaulay of Bragar*, of Bragar, co Ross and Cromarty (Life Baron) 1989: *m* 1962, Mary, da of Murdo Morrison, of Bragar, and has issue, two das.
Address – c/o House of Lords, SW1.

MACCLESFIELD, EARL OF (Parker) (Earl GB 1721)

Dare to be wise

RICHARD TIMOTHY GEORGE MANSFIELD PARKER, 9th Earl; *b* 31 May 1943; *s* 1992; *ed* Stowe, and Worcester Coll, Oxford (BA 1965): *m* 1st, 1967 (*m diss* 1985), (Tatiana) Cleone Anne, only da of Maj Craig Wheaton Smith, US Army (*see* Craig, Bt, ext); 2ndly, 1986, Mrs Sandra Hope Mead, da of Sylvio Fiore, of Florida, USA, and previously wife of late Peter Radford Mead, and has issue by 1st *m*.

Arms – Gules, a chevron between three leopards faces or. **Crest** – A leopard's head erased at the neck affrontée, or, ducally gorged gules. **Supporters** – Two leopards reguardant proper, ducally gorged gules.
Seat – Shirburn Castle, Watlington, Oxon OX9 5DL.

DAUGHTERS LIVING (*By 1st marriage*)

Lady Tanya Susan, *b* 1971.
Lady Katharine Ann, *b* 1973.
Lady Marian Jane, *b* (twin) 1973.

BROTHER LIVING

Hon JONATHAN DAVID GEOFFREY, *b* 2 Jan 1945; *ed* Stowe: *m* 1968, Lynne Valerie, yr da of George William Butler, of Middle Barton, Oxon, and has issue living, Timothy George, *b* 23 Aug 1969; *ed* Stowe, — Elizabeth Anne, *b* 1971, — Jessica, *b* 1977. *Residence* – Model Farm, Shirburn, Watlington, Oxford OX9 5DX.

UNCLE LIVING (*son of 7th Earl*)

Hon Jocelyn George Dudley, *b* 1920; *ed* Stowe; European War 1939-45 as Lieut RNVR: *m* 1948, Daphne Irene, 2nd da of late Maj George Cecil Whitaker, of Britwell House, Watlington, Oxon, and has issue living, Robert George, *b* 1955, — Mary Joanna Isabel (Eastfield Farm, Shirburn, Watlington, Oxon), *b* 1951: *m* 1973, Peter Robert Boone, who *d* 1986, son of Maj Ronald Edward Boone, late Parachute Regt. *Residence* – Pyrton Field Farm, Watlington, Oxon.

COLLATERAL BRANCHES LIVING

Granddaughter of late Hon Cecil Thomas Parker, 2nd son of 6th Earl:—
Issue of late Geoffrey Parker, *b* 1880, *d* 1954: *m* 1912, Isolda Mabel Cecil, who *d* 1955, da of Sir Charles William Frederick Craufurd, 4th Bt.—
Isolda Rosamond (*Rosamond, Viscountess Hanworth*), *b* 1918: formerly Senior Cdr Auxilliary Territorial Ser; JP Surrey 1962-88 (Supplementary List), DL 1986; FSA 1970: *m* 1940, 2nd Viscount Hanworth, who *d* 1996. *Residence* – Quoin Cottage, Shamley Green, Guildford, Surrey.

Grandchildren of late Robert Edward Parker (infra):—
Issue of late Capt Robert Kenyon Parker, *b* 1907, *d* 1968: *m* 1st, 1935, Frances Mary, who *d* 1964, da of Robert William Gawthropp, of Little Somerford, Wilts; 2ndly, 1965, Ealga Hester Balgriffin, who *d* 1990, eldest da of late Cyril Joseph Kildare Burnell, MA, of co Dublin:—
(By 1st *m*) Nigel Kenyon (3 Hopetoun Terr, Bucksburn, Aberdeen), *b* 1942: *m* 1964, Joey, da of John Jack, and has issue living, Karen Antonia, *b* 1965, — Lisa Anne, *b* 1969. —— Jennifer Elizabeth, *b* 1938.

Issue of late Alexander Patrick Parker, *b* 1910, *d* 1991: *m* 1st, 1949 (*m diss* 1962), Joan Olive, da of Benjamin Sayer, of Saxingham Thorpe, Nethergate, Norwich; 2ndly, 1965, Helen Mary (Algarsthorpe, Marlingford, Norwich), da of late John Owen Bond, of Eaton Hill, Norwich:—
(By 1st *m*) Patrick Edward Benjamin, *b* 1958. —— Tania Lynn, *b* 1950: *m* 1st, 1970 (*m diss* 1975), Stephen William Widdows; 2ndly, 1978, Thomas Patrick Moore, of 22 The Plantation, Aldburgh, Suffolk, and has issue living (by 1st *m*), Matthew Adam, *b* 1973, — (by 2nd *m*) Thomas Edward Alexander, *b* 1982, — Tiphanie Anne, *b* 1980. —— Alexandra Vanessa PARKER-MILNE (Read Mead, Glastonbury, Som), *b* 1952: *m* 1976 (*m diss* 1986), William Andrew Milne, and has issue living, Charlotte Francesca, *b* 1977, — Jessica Emily, *b* 1980. —— Amanda Rose, *b* 1960: *m* 1988, Rodney William Beckwith, of Algarsthorpe, Marlingford, Norwich.

Grandchildren of late Rev Hon Algernon Robert Parker (infra):—
Issue of late Robert Edward Parker, *b* 1878, *d* 1942: *m* 1904, Emily, who *d* 1951, da of late J. J. Dawson Paul, JP, DL:—
Michael Edward (Oriental Club), *b* 1916; *ed* Eton; 1939-45 War as Lt-Col Norfolk Yeo (RA): *m* 1st, 1940 (*m diss* 1956), Florence Margaret Catto, da of James Catto Duffus, OBE, MC; 2ndly, 1958, Estella Mary, da of H. A. Dalby, of York, and widow of George Hall, of Sheriff Hutton, Yorks, and has issue living (by 1st *m*), Timothy Robert Walter, *b* 1944, — Alexander Michael, *b* 1950, — Elizabeth Susan, *b* 1947. —— Elizabeth Mary, *b* 1914: *m* 1940, Frederick Colin George Preston, and has issue living, Frederick Robert (Toad Hall, Mulbarton, Norwich, Norfolk NR14 8JT), *b* 1947, — Anna Susan, *b* 1943: *m* 1979, Dirk Murray Bouwens, of Ivy Green House, Wymondham, Norfolk, and has issue living, Theodore Frederick Thomas *b* 1981. *Residence* – Paddock Farm, Mulbarton, Norwich.

Issue of late Hugh Algernon Parker, *b* 1879, *d* 1954: *m* 1911, Averil Frances, who *d* 1969, da of late Brownlow Richard Christopher Tower (B Brownlow):—
Camilla Mary, *b* 1916: *m* 1st, 1939, Capt Sir Lionel Francis Phillips, 2nd Bt, who was *ka* in Italy 1944; 2ndly, 1950, John G. Pisani, of 21 Chancellor House, 17 Hyde Park Gate, SW7 5DQ, who *d* 1982, and has issue living (by 1st *m*) (*see* Phillips, Bt). ——— Juliet Leonora (Flat 17, Swallowfield Park, Reading, Berks RG7 1TG), *b* 1920: *m* 1945, John Frederick Cathers McCreery, late RNVR and HM Overseas Civil Ser, who *d* 1993, and has issue living, Crispin Hugh (Holy Island Lighthouse, PO Lamlash, Arran KA27 8LR), *b* 1953, — Sean Frederick (128 Mallinson Rd, SW11 1BJ), *b* 1964: *m* 1997, Alexandra Gay, MVO, elder da of Charles Barry D'Arcy Fearn, FRCS, of Haywards Heath, Sussex.

Grandchildren of late Eustace Bowles (who assumed by Royal licence 1920 the surname of Bowles in lieu of his patronymic, and the arms of Bowles quarterly with those of Parker), 4th son of late Rev Hon Algernon Robert Parker, 3rd son of 6th Earl:—
Issue of late Derek Henry PARKER BOWLES, *b* 1915, *d* 1977: *m* 1939, Dame Ann, DCVO, CBE, who *d* 1987, eldest da of Sir Humphrey Edmund de Trafford, 4th Bt, MC:—
Andrew Henry, OBE, *b* 1939; *ed* Ampleforth, and RMA Sandhurst; Silver Stick in Waiting since 1987; Brig The Blues and Royals 1991 (ret 1994); OBE (Mil) 1983: *m* 1st, 1973 (*m diss* 1995), Camilla Rosemary, da of Maj Bruce Shand, MC (*see* B Ashcombe, 1995 Edn); 2ndly, 1996, Mrs Rosemary Alice Pitman, yst da of Robert Joicey Dickinson, of Howden Close, Corbridge, Northumberland, and formerly wife of Lt-Col (John) Hugh Pitman, The Blues and Royals, and has issue living (by 1st *m*), Thomas Henry Charles, *b* 1974; *ed* Eton, and Worcester Coll, Oxford, — Laura Rose, *b* 1978. ——— Simon Humphrey (17 Scarsdale Villas, W8), *b* 1941; *ed* Eton: *m* 1974, Carolyn, yr da of late Sir (William) Ian Potter, of Del Rio, Elizabeth Bay, Sydney, Australia, and has issue living, Luke Derek Ian, *b* 1978, — Sam William Francis, *b* 1981. ——— Richard Eustace, *b* 1947; *ed* Ampleforth: *m* 1973 (*m diss* 1976), Camilla, da of late Charles Frank Johnston Younger, DSO, TD, of Garrowby, Yorks, and has issue living, Emma Teresa, *b* 1974. ——— Mary Ann (North Lodge Farm, Warfield, Berks), *b* 1945: *m* 1967 (*m diss* 1987), Maj Nicolas Vincent Somerset Paravicini, Life Gds, and has issue living, Charles Vincent Somerset, *b* 1968: *m* 1995, Lucia F., yr da of late Laurence Laurie, of Fulham, SW6, and has issue living, Sophie Mary Elizabeth *b* 1997, Charlotte *b* 1999, — Derek Nicolas Somerset, *b* 1979, — Elizabeth Ann, *b* 1970: *m* 1997, Capt Robert C. S. Hall, The Life Gds, son of Brig Robert Hall, of Manningford Abbots, Wilts.

Grandchildren of late Capt Oliver Ivan Parker, 2nd son of late Hon Francis Parker (infra):—
Issue of late Timothy Oliver Parker, *b* 1924, *d* 1995: *m* 1952, Rosemary, who *d* 1984, da of late Maj John Henry Dent-Brocklehurst, OBE, of Sudeley Castle, Glos (*see* B Trevor, 1968 Edn):—
Oliver John (18 Elia St, N1 8DE), *b* 1953: *m* 1990, Amanda Jane, yr da of late Lt-Col W. D. H. McCardie. ——— Michael Henry (Corsley Mill, Corsley, Warminster, Wilts BA12 7QA), *b* 1955: *m* 1991, Julia Jane Craven, elder da of Nigel Craven Humphreys, of Meadow House, Smannell, Andover, Hants, and has issue living, Thomas Edward, *b* 1992, Amelia Rosemary, *b* 1994, — Lucy Harriet, *b* 1997. ——— Emma Mary, *b* 1964: *m* 1991, James M. Garvin, of 24 St Michael's Rd, SW9 0SN, son of Stephen Garvin, MBE, of Little Bricklehurst, Stonegate, E Sussex, and has issue living, Alexander Stephen, *b* 1995, — Eliza Rose Clare, *b* 1994, — Katharine Lucy, *b* 1998.

Granddaughter of late Hon Francis Parker, 4th son of 6th Earl:—
Issue of late Ivo Murray Parker, *b* 1899, *d* 1957: *m* 1923, Dulcibella, who *d* 1974, da of late Capt Charles William Daubeny, of The Brow, Combe Down, Bath:—
Penelope Joan, *b* 1924: *m* 1946, Arthur John Hughes, MC, TD, DL, who *d* 1984, and has issue living, Max Ivo Arthur (Chaffeymoor House, Bourton, Gillingham, Dorset), *b* 1947; BSc Hons: *m* 1974, Clara Christabel Harries, and has issue living James Ivo Arthur *b* 1976, Emma Penelope *b* 1975, — Jane Philippa, *b* 1948: *m* 1972, Richard I. W. Ware, of The Elms, Little Wymondley, Hitchin, Herts, and has issue living, Christopher Arthur Corry *b* 1972, Samantha *b* 1975, Georgina *b* 1977, Henrietta Daubeny *b* 1979. *Residence* – Vineyards, Welwyn, Herts AL6 9NE.

Grandchildren of late Rev Hon Archibald Parker, 9th son of 6th Earl:—
Issue of late Capt Charles Edward Parker, MC, *b* 1890, *d* 1962: *m* 1915, Hilda Margaret, who *d* 1979, da of Sir John Ralph Starkey, 1st Bt:—
Charles George Archibald (The White House, Nuffield, Oxon), *b* 1924; *ed* Eton, and New Coll, Oxford (MA); 1939-45 War as Capt Rifle Bde; JP and DL Oxon (High Sheriff 1989), Vice Lord-Lieut 1996-99: *m* 1958, Mrs Shirley Follett Rutland, da of Lt-Col Frank Follett Holt, TD, JP, of Corrybrough, Tomatin, Inverness-shire, and adopted her da, Davina Jane, *b* 1954: *m* 1986, John Walter of 6 Elms Rd, SW4 9ER, only son of late John Walter, of Lugano, Switzerland, and of late Mrs Vladimir Daskaloff, of Palma, Mallorca (*see* E Enniskillen, colls, 1990 Edn), and has issue living, John Charles *b* 1987, Edward William *b* 1990.

Issue of late Frederic Archibald Parker, *b* 1894, *d* 1977: *m* 1927, his cousin, Evereld Adela, who *d* 1980, da of late Capt James Randolph Innes-Hopkins, of London, SW:—
Joan Sylvia, *b* 1931: *m* 1956, Theodore Luke Giffard Landon, of Great Bromley House, nr Colchester, and has issue living, Mark Eustace Palmer, *b* 1958; *ed* Downside: *m* 1st, 1983 (*m diss* 1987), Julia Ruth, elder da of John Luddington, of Mill House, Brancaster, Norfolk; 2ndly, 1987, Veronica Claire, only da of late Harvey Jones, of 10 Palace Rd, Llandaff, Cardiff, and has issue living (by 2nd *m*), Samuel *b* 1994, Bethan Emily *b* 1990, — Philip James Aislabie, *b* 1962; *ed* Downside, and Kent Univ (BA), — Benjamin Edward Giffard, *b* 1967; *ed* Worth Coll, Durham Univ (BA), and Keele Univ (MA), — Felicity Juliana Mary, *b* 1960; *ed* New Hall: *m* 1990, Christopher Gerald Payne, and has issue living, Edward Charles Aislabie *b* 1992, — Rohais Elizabeth Jane, *b* 1964; *ed* New Hall, and Warwick Univ (MA): *m* 1992, David Peter Haughton, of Forge View, Lower Rd, Somersham, Ipswich IP8 4PH, and has issue living, William George Rosgill *b* 1994, Anna Sophie Rose *b* 1998.

Grandchildren of late Frederic Archibald Parker (ante):—
Issue of late Archibald Henry Parker, *b* 1928, *d* 1984: *m* 1st, 1951 (*m diss* 1979), Una-Mary, da of late Hugh Power Nepean-Gubbins, of Rumbling Bridge Cottage, Dunkeld, Perthshire; 2ndly, 1979, Comtesse Georgette Contini di Lumezzane da of late William Bryant Backer, of New York:—
(By 1st *m*) Philip Archibald Reginald (Buffy), *b* 1955: *m* 1st, 1981, Kathryn Jane Micaela, da of Dr John Frederick Lewis Aldridge, OBE, of East House, Charlton, Chichester, W Sussex; 2ndly, 1997, Gabrielle L., da of Tom Salter, and has issue living (by 1st *m*), Archie William Charles, *b* 1987, — Lucy Elizabeth Rebecca, *b* 1983, — Amelia Kathryn Louise, *b* 1984, — Charlotte Laura Mary, *b* 1990. *Residence* – Finkley House, Finkley, nr Andover, Hants SP11 6AE. ——— Una-Mary Diana, *b* 1953: *m* 1976, Robert Henry Hobart, and has issue (*see* Hobart, Bt). *Residence* – 12 Brunswick Gardens, W8.

Issue of late Hon Henry Parker, 10th son of 6th Earl, *b* 1860, *d* 1952: *m* 1916, Henrietta Judith, who *d* 1946, da of late Rev Robert Lowbridge Baker (E St Aldwyn):—

Peter Henry, *b* 1918; *ed* Eton, and New Coll, Oxford (MA); Maj (ret) KRRC; JP and DL Oxon (High Sheriff 1973); 1939-45 War: *m* 1953, Susan Rosemary, who *d* 1997, el da of late Maj Mowbray Buller, MC, of Downes, Crediton, Devon (E Portsmouth), and has issue living, Henry Mowbray (Downes, Crediton, Devon), *b* 1957; *ed* Eton, and Exeter Coll, Oxford: *m* 1991, Susan Jane da of John William Alvin, and of Mrs A. Thomson, of 24 Belvedere Park, Edinburgh, and has issue living, Redvers Charles *b* 1992, Stroma Anne *b* 1995, — Belinda Rosemary (*Hon Mrs A. Julian Aylmer*), *b* 1955: *m* 1990, Hon (Anthony) Julian Aylmer, only son of 13th Baron Aylmer, and has issue (*see* B Aylmer). *Residence* – The Hays, Ramsden, Oxon OX7 3BA.

Grandchildren of late Hon Alexander Edward Parker, OBE, 11th son of 6th Earl:—

Issue of late Sidney Alexander Parker, *b* 1899, *d* 1969: *m* 1st 1937, Adelaide Mary, who *d* 1947, da of late Maj Sidney George Everitt, RWF; 2ndly, 1951, June Rosemary, who *d* 1954, da of late Rev Herbert Arthur Woodman, R of Filleigh, N Devon; 3rdly, 1955, Rosemary Moon (Conygree Farm, Aldsworth, Glos), da of late Capt Henry Errington Moon Ord, and widow of Derek Welton:—

(By 1st *m*) David Alexander (Greghams Farm, Fords Water, Axminster, Devon), *b* 1943; *ed* Wellington: *m* 1971, Frances Marie, da of Francis W. Meehan, and has issue living, Christopher Alexander, *b* 1976, — Charles Edward, *b* 1977, — Sarah Adelaide, *b* 1973. —— Anne Mary, *b* 1940: *m* 1961, Paul Georges Emile Clément, of Mas de Valetière, Le Fontanil, 38120 St Egrève, France, and has had issue, Germaine Anne Marie, *b* 1962, — Dominique Jeanne Alice, *b* 1964, — Adelaide, *b* and *d* 1968, — Marie-Jeanne Paule Andrée, *b* 1969, — Alexandra Paule Emmanuelle, *b* 1970. —— Rosemary Elizabeth, *b* 1945: *m* 1st, 1964 (*m diss* 1989), Walter John Dawe Taylor, of Cricket St Thomas, Chard, Som; 2ndly, 1999, Anthony Robert Osborne, of Tilworth House, Hawkchurch, Axminster, Devon EX13 5UB, and has issue living (by 1st *m*), Jeremy John Alexander, *b* 1967, — Celia May Adelaide, *b* 1966: *m* 1993, Alastair Guy White Beor Roberts, of Hampnett Lodge, Northleach, Glos, and has issue living, Bertram Sidney White *b* 1995, Daisy Clare Ogilvy *b* 1996, — Olivia Anne Nicola, *b* 1972.

(In special remainder to Earldom)

Descendants of Elizabeth (da of 1st Earl), who *m* 1720, Sir William Heathcote MP, 1st Bt:—
See Heathcote, Bt (of Hursley).

PREDECESSORS – **(1)** *Sir* THOMAS Parker, Knt; was MP for Derby 1705-8, Ch Justice of Queen's Bench 1710-18, and Lord High Chancellor of Great Britain 1718-25; *cr Baron Parker of Macclesfield*, co Chester (peerage of Great Britain) 1716, *Viscount Parker of Ewelm*, co Oxford, and *Earl of Macclesfield* (peerage of Great Britain) 1721, with remainder (in default male issue) to his da Elizabeth, wife of Sir William Heathcote, 1st Bt, of Hursley Park, and her issue male; the Earl of 1725 was impeached on charges of corruption, and being convicted at the bar of the House of Lords, was, after a trial of twenty-one days, found guilty and sentenced to pay a fine of £30,000; *d* 1732; *s* by his son **(2)** GEORGE, 2nd Earl; was Pres of R Society; *d* 1764; *s* by his son **(3)** THOMAS, 3rd Earl; *d* 1795; *s* by el son **(4)** GEORGE, 4th Earl: was Lord-Lieut of Oxfordshire; *d* 1842; *s* by his brother **(5)** THOMAS, DCL, 5th Earl; *b* 1763: *m* 1st, 1796, a da of Lewis Edwards, of Talgarth, co Merioneth; 2ndly, 1807, Eliza, who *d* 1862, da of William Breton Wolstenholme, of Hollyhill, Sussex; *d* 1850; *s* by his son **(6)** THOMAS AUGUSTUS WOLSTENHOLME, 6th Earl, *b* 1811; MP for Oxfordshire (C) 1837-41; High Steward of Henley and Vice-Lieut of Oxfordshire: *m* 1st, 1839, Henrietta, who *d* 1839, da of Edmund Turnor, of Stoke Rochford, Lincolnshire; 2ndly, 1842, Lady Mary Frances Grosvenor, who *d* 1912, da of 2nd Marquess of Westminster: *d* 1896; *s* by his grandson **(7)** GEORGE LOVEDEN WILLIAM HENRY (son of George Augustus, Viscount Parker, el son of 6th Earl), 7th Earl: *b* 1888; Lord-Lieut of Oxon 1954-63: *m* 1909, Lilian Joanna Vere, who *d* 1974, da of late Maj Charles John Boyle (E Cork, colls); *d* 1975; *s* by his el son **(8)** GEORGE ROGER ALEXANDER THOMAS, 8th Earl; *b* 1914; served European War 1939-45 as Lieut RNVR: *m* 1938, Hon Valerie Mansfield, who *d* 1994, only da of 4th Baron Sandhurst: *d* 1992; *s* by his elder son **(9)** RICHARD TIMOTHY GEORGE MANSFIELD, 9th Earl and present peer; also Viscount and Baron Parker.

McCLUSKEY, BARON (McCluskey) (Life Baron 1976)

JOHN HERBERT MCCLUSKEY, QC, son of Francis John McCluskey, solicitor; *b* 12 June 1929; *ed* St Bede's Coll, Manchester, Holy Cross Acad, Edinburgh, and Edinburgh Univ (MA, LLB); F/O (Sword of Honour) RAF 1953; Advocate Scotland 1955; QC 1967; Sheriff Prin of Dumfries and Galloway 1973-74, Solicitor-Gen for Scotland 1974-79; Senator of the College of Justice in Scotland since 1984; *cr Baron McCluskey*, of Churchhill in District of City of Edinburgh (Life Baron) 1976: *m* 1956, Ruth, da of Aaron Friedland, and has issue.

Residence – 5 Lansdowne Crescent, Edinburgh, EH12 5EQ.

SONS LIVING

Hon John Mark, *b* 1960: *m* 1986, Judith Fernie.
Hon David Francis, *b* 1963: *m* 1989, Katherine Elizabeth Marion Douglas.

DAUGHTER LIVING

Hon Catherine Margaret, *b* 1962.

McCOLL OF DULWICH, BARON (McColl) (Life Baron 1989)

IAN McCOLL, son of late Frederick George McColl, of Dulwich; *b* 6 Jan 1933; *ed* Hutchesons' Gram Sch, Glasgow, St Paul's, London, and London Univ (MB BS 1957); FRCS 1962, FRCSE 1962, MS 1966, FACS 1975; Research Fellow Harvard Med Sch, and Moynihan Fellowship, Assocn of Surgs 1967; Reader in Surgery St Bartholomew's Hosp Med Coll 1967 (Sub Dean 1969); Hon Sec British Soc of Gastroenterology 1970-74, Dir of Surgical Unit, Guy's Hosp, since 1971, Prof of Surgery Univ of London (United Med Schs of Guy's and St Thomas's Hosps) 1971-98, Consultant Surg Guy's Hosp since 1971, Dir of Surgery since 1985, and Consultant Surg Edenbridge Dist Memorial Hosp 1978-91, and Lewisham Hosp 1983-92; Vice-Chm Special Health Authority for Disablement Servs 1987-91; Hon Consultant in Surgery for the Army 1982-98, Chm King's Fund Centre Cttee 1976-86, Medical Advisor to BBC 1976-92, Member of Council of Met Hosp Sunday Fund 1986-89, Gov-at-Large for England, Board of Govs, American Coll of Surgs 1982-88, Chm Govt Working Party on Artificial Limbs, Wheel-chairs and Appliance Centres in England 1984-86, Pres Mildmay Mission Hosp since 1985, Member Council of Royal Coll of Surgeons 1986-94, Pres Soc of Minimally Invasive Gen Surgery 1991-97, Member of Court of Patrons of Royal Coll of Surgeons of England since 1997, Vice-Pres Prince of Wales's Advisory Group on Disability, Dir of Mercy Ships UK, Chm Board of Govs James Allen's Girls' Sch, Vice-Pres British Digestive Foundation, Vice-Pres John Groom's Assocn for Disabled People since 1990, and Gov Dulwich Coll Prep Sch since 1978; author of numerous medical articles, etc; *cr Baron McColl of Dulwich*, of Bermondsey, London Borough of Southwark (Life Baron) 1989: *m* 1960, Dr Jean Lennox, 2nd da of late Arthur James McNair, FRCS, FRCOG, of London, and has issue.

Arms – Azure, a cross or between in the first quarter a leg embowed in armour; in the second quarter a dove volant to the sinister; in the third quarter a fleam, and in the fourth quarter a fish haurient, all argent. **Crest** – A demi-lion rampant or, head and mane gules, gorged with three barrulets wavy argent, flanked by oak branches formed chevronwise as an 'M' leaved argent and fructed or, on an escroll proper. **Supporters** – *dexter*, a dachshund rampant proper; *sinister*, an eagle close also proper armed or and crowned with an ancient crown gold.
Address – House of Lords, SW1A 0PW. *Club* – Royal College of Surgeons.

SON LIVING

Dr the Hon Alastair James, *b* 1961: *m* 1987, Dr Michelle Judd.

DAUGHTERS LIVING

Dr the Hon Caroline Lennox, *b* 1963: *m* 1994, Simon Brook Holmes.
Hon Mary Alison McCOLL (15 Doune Court, Burbage Rd, Dulwich, SE24 9HH), *b* 1966; has resumed her maiden name: *m* 1989, Rory Nicholas Knight.

McCONNELL, BARON (McConnell) (Life Baron 1995)

(ROBERT WILLIAM) BRIAN McCONNELL, PC, son of late Alfred Edward McConnell, 2nd son of Sir Robert John McConnell, 1st Bt; *b* 25 Nov 1922; *ed* Sedbergh, and Queen's Univ, Belfast (BA 1945, LLB 1947); Bar Northern Ireland 1948; MP for S Antrim (U) in Northern Irish Parliament 1951-68, Minister for Home Affairs 1964-66; President of Industrial Court 1968-88; Vice-Chm of European Movement in Northern Ireland 1987-92, President 1992-95; *cr* PC N Ireland 1964, and *Baron McConnell*, of Lisburn, co Antrim (Life Baron) 1995: *m* 1951, Sylvia Elizabeth Joyce, da of late Samuel Agnew, of Belfast, and has issue.

Arms – Per pale azure and gules, to the dexter a ship in full sail proper, to the sinister an arm embowed and couped at the shoulder argent, the hand grasping a trefoil slipped or, on a chief of the fourth, three stags' heads cabossed sable. Crest – A Stag's head erased azure attired and charged on the neck with a bee volat or. *Residence* – 50A Glenavy Rd, Lisburn, co Antrim BT28 3UT.

SONS LIVING

Hon Richard Alfred, *b* 1955; *ed* Sedbergh, and Campbell Coll: *m* 1988, Julie, da of Edward Ellis, of Michigan, USA, and has issue living, Kira, *b* 1994. *Residence* – 642 38th St, Richmond, CA 94805, USA.

Hon Samuel James, *b* 1958; *ed* Campbell Coll: *m* 1985, Christine Molly, da of Smyth McRobert, of Glenavy, co Antrim, and has issue living, Laura Elizabeth, *b* 1987, — Ruth Mary, *b* 1990, — Joanne Christine, *b* 1993. *Residence* – 50 Glenavy Rd, Lisburn, co Antrim BT28 3UT.

DAUGHTER LIVING

Hon Helen Elizabeth, *b* 1964; *ed* Friends' Sch, Lisburn: *m* 1987, Thomas Nelson, son of Thomas Nelson, of Lambeg, Lisburn, and has issue living, Philip, *b* 1989, — Rachel Elizabeth, *b* 1992, — Sarah Jane, *b* 1994.

McCORQUODALE OF NEWTON, BARONY OF (McCorquodale) (Extinct 1971)

DAUGHTER LIVING OF FIRST BARON

Hon Prudence Fiona, *b* 1936: *m* 1962, Carel Maurits Mosselmans, TD, and has issue living, Michael Lodowick Stewart (8 Cedars Rd, SW13), *b* 1962: *m* 1992, Heather E., da of R. Croot, of Gowerton, W Glam, — Julian Frederick Willem, *b* 1964. *Residence* – 15 Chelsea Sq, SW3 6LF.

MacDERMOTT, BARONY OF (MacDermott) (Extinct 1979)

SONS LIVING OF LIFE BARON

Rt Hon Lord Justice John Clarke, *b* 1927; *ed* Campbell Coll, Belfast, at Trin Hall, Camb (BA), and at Queen's Univ, Belfast; Bar Inner Temple and N Ireland 1949: QC, N Ireland 1974; Judge of High Court NI 1973; Lord Justice 1987: *m* 1953, Margaret Helen, da of late Hugh Dales, of Belfast, and has issue living, Helen, *b* 1954, — Anne, *b* 1956, — Janet, *b* 1958, — Gillian, *b* 1959. *Residence* – 6 Tarawood, Holywood, co Down BT18 0HS.

Rev the Hon Robert William Johnston (Glenburnbeg, Broadleas, Ballymore Eustace, co Kildare), *b* 1934: *ed* Campbell Coll, Belfast, Trin Hall, Camb (BA 1955), at New Coll, Edinburgh (BD), at Assembly's Coll, Belfast, and Yale Univ Divinity Sch (STM): *m* 1979, Janet, da of Very Rev Dr T. A. B. Smyth.

Hon Edith Louise, *b* 1930; MB and BCh 1954: *m* 1955, Samuel Barbour Cunningham, of Ballytrim, Killyleagh, co Down, and has issue.

Hon (Lydia) Elizabeth Palmer, *b* 1939; *ed* Wycombe Abbey Sch, and at Belfast Coll of Art: *m* 1964, Capt David McKenzie Chalmers, RAF (ret), of Upland House, Upper Harford, Bourton-on-the-Water, Glos GL54 3BY, and has issue.

MACDONALD, BARON (Macdonald of Macdonald) Baron I 1776

By sea and land

The Heathery Isle

GODFREY JAMES MACDONALD OF MACDONALD, 8th Baron; *b* 28 Nov 1947; *s* 1970; *ed* Eton; Chief of the Name and Arms of Macdonald: *m* 1969, Claire, el da of Commodore Thomas Noel Catlow, CBE, RN, of Gabriel Cottage, Tunstall, via Carnforth, Lancs and has issue.

Arms – Quarterly: 1st argent, a lion rampant gules armed and langued azure; 2nd or, a hand in armour fesseways holding a cross-crosslet fitchée gules; 3rd or, a lymphad, sails furled and oars in action sable, flagged gules; 4th vert, a salmon naiant in fesse proper; over all (as Chief of the Name and Arms of Macdonald), on an inescutcheon en surtout or, an eagle displayed gules, surmounted of a lymphad, sails furled. oars in action sable. Crest – A hand in armour fesseways couped at the elbow proper, holding a cross-crosslet fitchée gules. Supporters – Two leopards proper. *Residence* – Kinloch Lodge, Isle of Skye.

SON LIVING

Hon (GODFREY EVAN) HUGO THOMAS, *b* 24 Feb 1982.

DAUGHTERS LIVING

Hon Alexandra Louisa, *b* 1973: *m* 1993, Magnus Gunn, son of W/Cmdr A. C. Gunn, of Balmyle House, Ballintuim, Bridge of Cally, Perthshire.
Hon Isabella Claire, *b* 1975.
Hon Meriel Iona, *b* 1978.

BROTHER LIVING

Hon Alexander Donald Archibald, *b* 1953; *ed* Eton.

SISTER LIVING

Hon Janet Anne, *b* 1946.

PREDECESSORS – (1) DONALD MacDonald, of Slate; *cr a Baronet* of Nova Scotia 1625, with a special clause of precedency, placing him second of that order in Scotland; *d* 1643; *s* by his son (2) *Sir* JAMES, 2nd Bt; joined the Marquess of Montrose 1645, and sent some of his men to assist Charles II, when he marched into England in 1651: *d* 1678; *s* by his son (3) *Sir* DONALD, 4th Bt; joined the Rebellion of 1715, and was attainted; *d* 1718; *s* by his son (5) *Sir* DONALD, 5th Bt; *d* unmarried 1720; *s* by his uncle (6) *Sir* JAMES, 6th Bt; *d* 1723; *s* by his son (7) *Sir* ALEXANDER, 7th Bt, for whom as "Alexander Macdonald of Macdonald" the family estates were re-erected into a feudal Barony of Macdonald 1727; *d* 1746; *s* by his el son (8) *Sir* JAMES, 8th Bt; *d* unmarried 1766; *s* by his brother (9) *Sir* ALEXANDER, 9th Bt; *cr Baron Macdonald*, of Slate, co Antrim (peerage of Ireland) 1776; *d* 1795; *s* by his el son (10) ALEXANDER WENTWORTH, 2nd Baron; *d* 1824; *s* by his brother (11) GODFREY, 3rd Baron: a Maj-Gen in the Army; assumed in 1814 by R licence the additional surname of Bosville and discontinued it by Roy licence 1824; *m* (in England) 15 Dec 1803, Louisa Maria La Coast, who *d* 1835, ward of Farley Edsir; *d* 1832, when (according to a decree of the Court of Session in June 1910) the Scottish Baronetcy passed *de jure* to Alexander William Bosville (*b* 12 Sept 1800, before the date of his parents' English marriage, but according to the law of Scotland legitimated by this *m*) (see Bosville Macdonald, Bt): *s* in the Irish peerage by his el son (born after the *m*) (12) GODFREY WILLIAM WENTWORTH, 4th Baron; *b* 1809: *m* 1845, Maria Anne, who *d* 1892, da of George Thomas Wyndham, of Cromer Hall, Norfolk; *d* 1863; *s* by his son (13) SOMERLED JAMES BRUDENELL, 5th Baron; *d* 1874; *s* by his brother (14) RONALD ARCHIBALD, 6th Baron, *b* 1853: *m* 1875, Louisa, who *d* 1922, da of Col George William Holmes Ross, of Cromarty; *d* 1947; *s* by his grandson (15) ALEXANDER GODFREY, MBE, TD (son of late Hon Godfrey Evan Hugh Macdonald, who was *ka* 1914, 7th Baron, *b* 1909; Maj Queen's Own Cameron Highlanders); Lord Lieut for Inverness-shire 1952-70: *m* 1945, Anne, who *d* 1988, only da of late Alfred Whitaker; *d* 1970; *s* by his el son (16) GODFREY JAMES, 8th Baron and present peer.

MACDONALD OF GWAENYSGOR, BARON (Macdonald) (Baron UK 1949)

GORDON RAMSAY MACDONALD, 2nd Baron; *b* 16 Oct 1915; *s* 1966; *ed* Upholland Gram Sch, and Manchester Univ (MA); UK Trade Commr in Australia 1947-53, Man Dir Internat Group, Tube Investments Ltd 1953-64, Plessey Ltd 1964-66, and Chm and Ch Exec Hayek Engineering Ltd (UK) 1966-77, since when Economic and Commercial Adviser to various business groups; 1939-45 War in Burma (despatches), Malaya, India and Middle East as Maj RA and a GSO: *m* 1941, Leslie Margaret, da of John Edward Taylor, of Rainford, Lancs, and has issue.
Address – c/o House of Lords, SW1.

DAUGHTERS LIVING

Hon Susan, *b* 1947: *m* 1968 (*m diss* 1991), David Hensley Adair Stride, and has had issue, Toby David Macdonald, *b* 1972, — Jessica Charlotte Macdonald, *b* 1970, *d* 1984.
Hon Helen Margaret, *b* 1950: *m* 1974 (*m diss* 19—), James Edward Richard Prisinzano.
Hon Marylyn Jane, *b* 1951: *m* 1977, Peter Jost, and has issue living, Edward Peter, *b* 1980, — Thomas William, *b* 1983.

SISTER LIVING

Hon Glenys, *b* 1923; a JP for Lancs: *m* 1949, Robert Fullard, BSc, and has issue living, Judith Mary, *b* 1952: *m* 1973, Christopher John Norton Ellis, and has issue living, Richard Gordon *b* 1979, Laura Kate *b* 1981, — Cathryn Elisabeth, *b* 1955: *m* 1978, Michael John Morris, and has issue living, Robert James *b* 1982, Rachel Elisabeth *b* 1984.

WIDOW LIVING OF SON OF FIRST BARON

Maureen Margaret, only da of late David Watson-Allan, of Churston Ferrers, Devon: *m* 1952, Hon Kenneth Lewis Macdonald, yr son of 1st Baron, who *d* 1990. *Residence* – Fir Trees, Frog Lane, Balsall Common, West Midlands CV7 7FP.

COLLATERAL BRANCH LIVING

Issue of late Hon Kenneth Lewis Macdonald, yr son of 1st Baron, *b* 1921, *d* 1990: *m* 1952, Maureen Margaret (ante), only da of late David Watson-Allan, of Churston Ferrers, Devon:—
Sarah Margaret, *b* 1954: *m* 1st, 1974 (*m diss* 1998), David Henry Waldron; 2ndly, 1998 Robert Bertram, and has issue living (by 1st *m*), William David MacDonald, *b* 1980, — Charlotte Sarah, *b* 1978. —— Laura Jane, *b* 1966: *m* 1994, James Edward Reeve, and has issue living, Frederick James, *b* 1996.

PREDECESSOR – (1) *Sir* GORDON Macdonald, KCMG, PC, son of Thomas Macdonald, of Gwaenysgor, Flintshire; *b* 1888; Member Miners' Fedn of Gt Britain 1920-29; Chm of Cttees, House of Commons 1934-41, Gov and C-in-C of Newfoundland 1946-49, and Chm of Commn of Govt of Newfoundland and Dependencies 1946-49, Paymaster-Gen 1949-51; MP for Ince Div of Lancs (*Lab*) 1929-42 (resigned), Controller Min of Fuel and Power 1942-46, Gov BBC, Chm BBC (Wales) 1952-60, Dir Colonial Development Corpn 1952-59; *cr Baron Macdonald of Gwaenysgor*, of Gwaenysgor, co Flint (peerage of UK) 1949: *m* 1913, Mary who *d* 1967, da of William Lewis, of Blaenau Festiniog; *d* 1966; *s* by his el son (2) GORDON RAMSAY, 2nd Baron and present peer.

MACDONALD OF TRADESTON, BARON (Macdonald) (Life Baron 1998)

ANGUS JOHN (GUS) MACDONALD, CBE, son of late Colin Macdonald; *b* 20 Aug 1940; *ed* Allan Glen's Sch, Glasgow; Producer, Presenter and Dir Granada TV 1967-85; Dir of Programmes, Scottish Media Group plc (formerly Scottish Television plc) 1985-90, Man Dir 1990-96, since when Chm; Chm ITV Broadcast Board 1992-94; FRSA, FRTS, author; *cr* CBE 1997, and *Baron Macdonald of Tradeston*, of Tradeston in the City of Glasgow (Life Baron) 1998: *m* 1963, Alice (Theresa), da of ...... McQuaid, and has issue.
Address – Scottish Media Group plc, Cowcaddens, Glasgow G2 3PR. *Clubs* – Groucho, RAC.

DAUGHTERS LIVING

Hon Jean, *b* 1965; *ed* ......
Hon Rowan, *b* 1967; *ed* ......

McDonnell, family name of Earl of Antrim.

McFADZEAN, BARONY OF (McFadzean) (Extinct 1996)

SON LIVING OF LIFE BARON

Hon (Gordon) Barry (17 Yeoman's Row, SW3 2AL), *b* 1937; *ed* Winchester, and Ch Ch, Oxford (MA); FCA: *m* 1st, 1968 (*m diss* 1972), Julia Maxine, da of Max Dillon (now Sir Max Dillon), of Pymble, Sydney, NSW; 2ndly, 1984, Diana Rosemary, yst da of late Sam Waters, of Norfolk, and has issue (by 1st *m*), two das.

DAUGHTER LIVING OF LIFE BARON

Hon Angela Caroline, *b* 1942: *m* 1963, Robin Vyvyan Carter Donald, of Osborne House, Bathampton, Bath, and has issue.

WIDOW LIVING OF LIFE BARON

EILEEN (*Baroness McFadzean*), eldest da of Arthur Gordon, of Blundellsands, Lancs: *m* 1933, Baron McFadzean, KT, who *d* 1996. *Residence* – Osborne House, Bathampton, Bath BA2 6SW.

McFADZEAN OF KELVINSIDE, BARONY OF (McFadzean) (Extinct 1992)

DAUGHTER LIVING OF LIFE BARON (by 1st marriage)

Hon Felicity Carmen Francesca (*Baroness Marsh*), *b* 1946: *m* 1979, Baron Marsh, PC (Life Baron).

WIDOW LIVING OF LIFE BARON

SONJA LIAN HOA NIO (*née* Khung) (*Baroness McFadzean of Kelvinside*), of Indonesia: *m* 1988, as his 2nd wife, Baron McFadzean of Kelvinside (Life Baron), who *d* 1992. *Address* – c/o Lloyds Bank plc, 56 High St, Marlow, Bucks SL7 1AJ.

MACFARLANE OF BEARSDEN, BARON (Macfarlane) (Life Baron 1991)

NORMAN SOMERVILLE MACFARLANE, KT, son of late Daniel Robertson Macfarlane; *b* 5 March 1926; *ed* Glasgow High Sch; commn'd RA 1945, served Palestine 1945-47; founder N. S. Macfarlane & Co 1949, which became Macfarlane Group (Clansman) plc 1973, Chm 1973-98 and Man Dir 1973-90, Hon Life Pres since 1999, Chm United Distillers plc 1987-96, since when Hon Life Pres, United Distillers UK (formerly Arthur Bell Distillers plc) since 1989, American Trust plc 1984-97, and The Fine Art Soc plc 1976-98 (Hon Pres 1998); Jt Chm Guinness 1987-89; Dep Chm Guinness plc 1989-92; Dir Clydesdale Bank plc 1980-96 (Dep Chm 1993-96), Gen Accident, Fire & Life Assurance Corpn plc 1984-96, Edinburgh Fund Managers plc 1980-88; Dir Glasgow Chamber of Commerce 1976-79, Scottish Nat Orchestra 1977-82, Third Eye Centre 1978-81; Pres Stationers' Assoc of GB and Ireland 1965, and Stationers' Co of Glasgow 1968-70; Member Royal Fine Art Commn for Scotland 1980-82, Pres Royal Glasgow Inst of the Fine Arts 1976-87, Gov Glasgow Sch of Art 1976-87, Board Member Scottish Devpt Agency 1979-87, Member of Court Glasgow Univ 1980-88, Dir Scottish Ballet 1975-83 and Vice Chm Scottish Ballet 1983-87, Scottish Patron The Nat Art Collection Fund since 1978, Lord High Commr to Gen Assembly of Church of Scotland 1992, 1993 and 1997, Chm of Govs Glasgow High Sch 1979-92, since when Hon Pres; Memb Court, Univ of Glasgow 1979-87; Regent RCSE 1997; Patron Scottish Licensed Trade Assoc 1992; Chm Glasgow Action 1985-90; Chm Glasgow Development Agency 1990-92; Trustee Nat Heritage Memorial Fund, and Nat Galleries of Scotland; Hon Vice Pres Glasgow Batn Boys' Bde; Underwriting Member of

Lloyd's; Hon FRIAS 1984, Hon LLD Strathclyde 1986, Glasgow 1988, Hon D Univ Glasgow Caledonian Univ 1993, Hon LLD Aberdeen 1995, Hon RSA 1987, Hon RGI 1987, Hon FRCPS Glasgow 1992, Hon DUniv Stirling 1992, Hon Dr *honoris causa* Edinburgh 1992, Hon Fell Glasgow Sch of Art 1993; *cr* Knt 1983, *Baron Macfarlane of Bearsden*, of Bearsden in the District of Bearsden and Milngavie (Life Baron) 1991, and KT 1996: *m* 1953, Marguerite Mary, da of John Johnstone Campbell, of 17 Norwood Drive, Whitecraigs, and has issue.
Residence – 50 Manse Rd, Bearsden, Glasgow G61 3PN. *Club* – New (Edinburgh).

SON LIVING

Hon Hamish, *b* 1961: *m* 1990, Laura Pitt.

DAUGHTERS LIVING

Hon Fiona, *b* 1955: *m* 1982, J. S. M. McNaught.
Hon Gail, *b* 1957: *m* 1992, Lt Simon Allbutt, RN.
Hon Marjorie, *b* 1960: *m* 1991, J. B. (Jack) Roberts, son of J. B. Roberts, of Bearsden, Glasgow.
Hon Marguerite, *b* 1966.

McFARLANE OF LLANDAFF, BARONESS (McFarlane) (Life Baroness 1979)

Prof JEAN KENNEDY MCFARLANE, da of James McFarlane; *b* 1 April, 1926; *ed* Howell's Sch, Llandaff, and Bedford and Birkbeck Colls, Univ of London (MA, BSc (Soc)); Hon DSc (Ulster), Hon DEd (CNAA), Hon DLit (Glamorgan), Hon MD (Liverpool), Hon LLD (Manchester), Hon FRCP, Fell of Birkbeck Coll, FCN (Australia) 1984; SRN, SCM, FRCN 1976; Univ of Manchester; Sen Lecturer in Nursing, Dept of Social and Preventive Medicine 1971-73; Sen Lecturer and Head of Dept of Nursing 1973-74; Prof and Head of Dept of Nursing 1974-1988; Chm English Board for Nursing, Midwifery and Health Visting 1980-83; Member of Commn of Commonwealth War Graves 1983-86 *cr Baroness McFarlane of Llandaff*, of Llandaff, co Glamorgan (Life Baroness) 1979.
Residence – 5 Dovercourt Av, Heaton Mersey, Stockport, Cheshire SK4 3QB.

McGOWAN, BARON (McGowan) (Baron UK 1937)

Union is strength

(HARRY) DUNCAN CORY MCGOWAN, 3rd Baron; *b* 20 July 1938; *s* 1966; *ed* Eton: *m* 1962, Lady Gillian Angela Pepys, da of 7th Earl of Cottenham, and has issue.

𝕬rms – Per saltire argent and azure two lions rampant in pale gules and as many horseshoes in fesse proper. 𝕮rest – A tower or, between two horseshoes proper. 𝕾upporters – *Dexter*, a figure representing St Barbara proper, holding in the exterior hand a tower or; *sinister*, a figure representing St Kentigern proper, holding in the exterior hand his crozier or.
Residences – Highway House, Lower Froyle, Alton, Hants; 12 Stanhope Mews East, SW7. *Club* – Boodle's.

SON LIVING

Hon HARRY JOHN CHARLES, *b* 23 June 1971.

DAUGHTERS LIVING

Hon Emma Louise Angela, *b* 1963: *m* 1987, Guy H. C. Hill, eldest son of R. J. C. Hill, of Croxton Kerrial, Leics, and has issue living, Charles, *b* 1988, — a son, *b* 1997, — Davina, *b* 1991.
Hon Annabel Kate Cory, *b* 1965: *m* 1991, Ashley J. Bealby, yr son of J. Bealby, of Barrowby, Lincs.

BROTHERS LIVING

Hon Dominic James Wilson (Bragborough Hall, Daventry, Northants), *b* 1951: *m* 19—, Brigitta, eldest da of late C. Papadimitriou, of Athens.

Hon Mungo Alexander Cansh (Bragborough Farm, Daventry, Northants), *b* 1956: *m* 1983, Hon (Arabella) Charlotte Eden, yr da of Baron Eden of Winton (Life Baron), and has issue living, James Alexander Cory, *b* 1985, — Laura Charlotte Iona, *b* 1987, — Rose, *b* 1991.

SISTERS LIVING

Hon Moana Elizabeth Jean, *b* 1948: *m* 1978, as his 2nd wife, John David Vaughan Seth-Smith, only son of late Cdr David Keith Seth-Smith, and has issue living, Edward David Harry, *b* 1979, — William Jonathan Cory, *b* 1985. *Residence* – The Old School House, Whilton, Daventry, Northants.

Hon Catriona Carmen Harriet, *b* 1953.

COLLATERAL BRANCH LIVING

Issue of late William Johnston McGowan, TD, yr son of 1st Baron, *b* 1909, *d* 1977: *m* 1946, Helen Myrtle Dorothy, MBE, JP, who *d* 1976, da of late Arthur Atherley, JP, DL, of Landguard Manor, Isle of Wight, and widow of Col Edward Orlando Kellett, DSO, MP:—
Fiona Victoria Jean Atherley (*Baroness Hindlip*), *b* 1947: *m* 1968, 6th Baron Hindlip. *Residences* – The Cedar House, Inkpen, Berks; 55 Campden Hill Rd, W8.

PREDECESSORS – (1) *Sir* HARRY DUNCAN McGowan, KBE, son of late Henry McGowan, of Glasgow, *b* 1874; Hon Pres (Chm 1930-50) of Imperial Chemical Industries Ltd, Pres of So of Chemical Industry 1931, of Institute of Fuel 1934-5, and of British Standards Institution 1947; *cr Baron McGowan*, of Ardeer, co Ayr (peerage of UK) 1937: *m* 1903, Jean Boyle, who *d* 1952, da of late William Young, of Paisley; *d* 1961; *s* by his el son (2) HARRY WILSON, 2nd Baron, *b* 1906: *m* 1937, Carmen, who *d* 1996, da of Sir (James) Herbert Cory, 1st Bt, *cr* 1919; *d* 1966; *s* by his el son (3) (HARRY) DUNCAN CORY, 3rd Baron and present peer.

McGREGOR OF DURRIS, BARONY OF (McGregor) (Extinct 1997)

SONS LIVING OF LIFE BARON

Hon (William) Ross, *b* 1948; *ed* Haberdashers' Aske's Sch: *m* 1981, Ann Holmes, da of Archibald MacGregor, of Fife, and widow of Matthew Johnson, of Edinburgh.

Hon Alistair John, *b* 1950.

Hon Gregor Weate, *b* 1952: *m* 1978, Wendy Elizabeth, da of Sydney Carlisle, of Yorkshire.

WIDOW LIVING OF LIFE BARON

NELLIE (*Baroness McGregor of Durris*), da of Harold Weate, of Manchester: *m* 1944, Prof Baron McGregor of Durris (Life Baron), who *d* 1997. *Residence* – Far End, Wyldes Close, NW11 7JB.

McINTOSH OF HARINGEY, BARON (McIntosh) (Life Baron 1983)

ANDREW ROBERT McINTOSH, son of late Prof Albert William McIntosh, OBE, by his wife Helena Agnes (Jenny) Britton; *b* 30 April 1933; *ed* Haberdashers' Aske's Sch, Royal Gram Sch, High Wycombe, Jesus Coll Oxford (MA), and Ohio State Univ (Fell in Economics 1956-57); Member Hornsey Borough Council 1963-65; Member Haringey Borough Council 1964-68; mem GLC for Tottenham 1973-83 (Leader of the Opposition 1980-81), Dep Leader of the Opposition and Opposition Spokesman on Home Affairs, House of Lords, 1992-97; Chm Market Research Society 1972-73 (Pres 1995-98); Chm Fabian Soc 1985-86; Dep Chm IFF Research Ltd 1988-95 (Man Dir

1965-81, Chm 1981-88); Capt Queen's Body Guard of the Yeomen of the Guard (Dep Ch Whip, House of Lords) since 1997; *cr Baron McIntosh of Haringey*, of Haringey in Greater London (Life Baron) 1983; *m* 1962, Naomi Ellen Sargant, Pro Vice-Chancellor (Student Affairs), Open Univ 1974-78, Prof of Applied Social Research 1978-81, Senior Commissioning Editor, Channel Four Television Co Ltd 1981-88, da of late Thomas Sargant, OBE, JP, and previously wife of Peter Joseph Kelly, and has issue.

Residence – 27 Hurst Av, N6 5TX.

SONS LIVING

Hon Francis Robert, *b* 1962; *ed* Highgate Wood Sch, and London Coll of Furniture.
Hon Philip Henry Sargant, *b* 1964; *ed* Highgate Wood Sch, and Kingston Polytechnic.

Mackay, family name of Earl of Inchcape.

Mackay, family name of Lord Reay.

Mackay, family name of Baron Tanlaw.

MACKAY OF ARDBRECKNISH, BARON (Mackay) (Life Baron 1991)

JOHN JACKSON MACKAY, PC, son of late Jackson Mackay, of Tayvallich, Argyll; *b* 15 Nov 1938; *ed* Glasgow Univ (BSc, Dip Ed); formerly Head of Maths Dept, Oban High Sch; PPS to Sec of State for Scotland (Rt Hon George Younger) 1982, Parly Under Sec of State Scottish Office 1982-87; Chief Exec Scottish Conservative Central Office 1987-90, Chm Sea Fish Industry Authority 1990-93, Lord-in-Waiting (Govt Whip) Oct 1993-Jan 1994, Parly Under Sec of State Dept of Transport (Min for Aviation and Shipping) 1994-July 1995, Min of State Social Security Dept 1995-97; MP Argyll (*C*) 1979-83 and Argyll and Bute 1983-87; Dep Leader of Conservative Opposition, House of Lords since 1998; *cr Baron Mackay of Ardbrecknish*, of Tayvallich, District of Argyll and Bute (Life Baron) 1991, and PC 1996: *m* 1961, Sheena, da of late James Wagner, of Bishopton, Renfrewshire, and has issue.

Residence – Innishail, 51 Springkell Drive, Glasgow G41 4EZ.

SONS LIVING

Hon David Ferguson, *b* 1967.
Hon Colin James, *b* 1969.

DAUGHTER LIVING

Hon Fiona Jackson, *b* 1964.

MACKAY OF CLASHFERN, BARON (Mackay) (Life Baron 1979)

JAMES PETER HYMERS MACKAY, KT, PC, QC, FRSE, son of James MacKay; *b* 2 July 1927; *ed* George Heriot's Sch, Edinburgh, and Edinburgh Univ (MA); BA Camb 1952; LLB Edinburgh 1955; FRSE (1984), Hon Fell Royal Coll of Surgeons (Edin) 1989, Hon Fell Royal Coll of Physicians (Edin) 1989, Hon Fell ICE 1988, Hon Fell Royal Coll of Obstetricians and Gynaecologists 1996; admitted to Faculty of Advocates 1955; Sheriff Prin Renfrew and Argyll 1972-74; Vice-Dean, Faculty of Advocate 1973-76, Dean 1976-79, Lord Advocate 1979-84, Senator College of Justice in Scotland 1984-85; a Lord of Appeal in Ordinary 1985, Lord High Chancellor (Oct) 1987-97; *cr* PC 1979, KT 1997, and *Baron Mackay of Clashfern*, of Eddracchillis in the District of Sutherland (Life Baron) 1979: *m* 1958, Elizabeth Gunn Hymers, and has issue.

Arms – Azure, on a chevron Argent between two bears' heads couped Argent, muzzled Gules in chief and a fleece Argent in base, a roebuck's head erased between two hands grasping daggers, the points turned towards the buck's head all Proper. Crest – a dexter arm, couped at the elbow Proper, the hand grasping a pair of balances Or. Behind the Shield are placed in saltire two great maces ensigned with Imperial Crowns Or and pendent below the Shield by string, nowed, buttoned and tassled, a Purse Gules, embroidered all over with the Royal Arms to denote the Office of Lord High Chancellor. Supporters – *Dexter*, a male figure attired in the Robes of the Lord High Chancellor, *Sinister*, a male figure attired in the Robes of one Her Majesty's Counsel learned in the Law in Scotland Proper.
Address c/o House of Lords, SW1. *Club* – New (Edinburgh).

SON LIVING

Hon James, *b* 1958; *ed* Camb Univ (MA), Edinburgh Univ (MB, ChB); Hon Registrar and Research Fell Dept of Clinical Surg Univ of Edinburgh: *m* 1991, Marion E., da of J. E. McArthur, of Edinburgh, and has issue living, Heather Mairi, *b* 1992, — Catriona Elizabeth, *b* 1994.

DAUGHTERS LIVING

Hon Elizabeth Janet, *b* 1961: *m* 1982, James Campbell, and has issue living, two sons and three das.
Hon Shona Ruth, *b* 1968.

MACKAY OF DRUMADOON, BARON (Mackay) (Life Baron 1995)

DONALD SAGE MACKAY, PC, son of late Rev Donald George Mackintosh Mackay, of Edinburgh; *b* 30 Jan 1946; *ed* George Watson's Boys' Coll, Edinburgh, Univ of Edinburgh (LLB 1966, LLM 1968), and Univ of Virginia, USA (LLM 1969); apprentice Solicitor with Davidson & Syme, CS, Edinburgh 1969-71; Solicitor with Allan McDougall & Co, SSC, Edinburgh 1971-76; Bar Scotland 1976; Advocate-Depute 1982-85; QC (Scot) 1987; Memb of Criminal Injuries Compensation Board 1989-95; Solicitor-Gen for Scotland 1995; Lord Advocate 1995-97; Opposition Spokesman in House of Lords on Constitutional and Legal Affairs since 1997; *cr* PC 1996, and *Baron Mackay of Drumadoon*, of Blackwaterfoot, District of Cunninghame (Life Baron) 1995: *m* 1979, Lesley Ann, da of late Edward Waugh, of Edinburgh, and has issue.
Residence – 39 Hermitage Gdns, Edinburgh EH10 6AZ. *Club* – Western (Glasgow).

SON LIVING

Hon Simon, *b* 1984.

DAUGHTERS LIVING

Hon Caroline, *b* 1980.
Hon Diana, *b* 1982.

MACKENZIE OF FRAMWELLGATE, BARON (Mackenzie) (Life Baron 1998)

BRIAN MACKENZIE, OBE, son of Frederick George Mackenzie, of Catterick; *b* 21 March 1943; *ed* London Univ (LLB 1974), and FBI Academy, Quantico, USA (Graduate); Chief Superintendent of Police, Durham (retired); former Pres Police Superintendents' Association of England and Wales; *cr* OBE 1998, and *Baron Mackenzie of Framwellgate*, of Durham, co Durham (Life Baron) 1998: *m* 1965, Jean, da of James Seed, of Leeds, and has issue.

Arms – Azure a cross voided throughout or the angles thereof enfiling the inner cuff of four handcuffs in saltire argent. Crest – A prairie dog sejant erect azure supporting with the forepaws a truncheon or. Supporters – On either side a great crested newt or semy of roundels azure.
Residence – Peelers, Etherley Close, Newton Hall, Durham City DH1 5XQ. *Club* – Dunelm (Durham).

SONS LIVING

Hon Brian James, *b* 1968; *ed* Framwellgate Moor Comprehensive Sch, and Sheffield City Polytechnic.
Hon Andrew Craig, 1971; *ed* Framwellgate Moor Comprehensive Sch.

Mackenzie, family name of Earl of Cromartie.

MACKENZIE-STUART, BARON (Mackenzie Stuart) (Life Baron 1988)

ALEXANDER JOHN MACKENZIE STUART, only son of late Prof Alexander Mackenzie Stuart, KC, of Aberdeen; *b* 18 Nov 1924; *ed* Fettes, Sidney Sussex Coll, Camb (BA), and Edinburgh Univ (LLB); Hon DUniv Stirling 1973, Hon Fell Sidney Sussex Camb 1977, Hon LLD Exeter 1978, Edinburgh 1978, Glasgow 1981, Aberdeen 1983, Camb 1987, and Birmingham 1988; served RE 1942-47; admitted Faculty of Advocates 1951; QC (Scot) 1963, Hon Bencher Middle Temple 1978, and King's Inn, Dublin 1983; Keeper of Advocates Library 1970-72, Standing Junior Counsel, Scottish Home Dept 1956-57, Inland Revenue in Scotland 1957-63, Sheriff-Prin of Aberdeen, Kincardine and Banff 1971-72, Senator of Coll of Justice in Scotland (as Hon Lord Mackenzie Stuart) 1972, Judge of the Court of Justice, European Communities, Luxembourg 1973-84, Pres 1984-88; Gov Fettes Coll 1962-72; Prix Bech for services to Europe 1989; *cr Baron Mackenzie-Stuart*, of Dean in the District of the

City of Edinburgh (Life Baron) 1988: *m* 1952, Anne Burtholme, da of late John Sidney Lawrence Millar, WS, of Edinburgh, and has issue.

Residences – 7 Randolph Cliff, Edinburgh EH3 7TZ; Le Garidel, Gravieres, 07140 Les Vans, France.

DAUGHTERS LIVING

Hon Amanda Jane, *b* 1954: *m* 1977, Michael George Hay, son of George Ronald Hay, and has issue living, Daisy Elizabeth, *b* 1981, — Marianna Clare, *b* 1985. *Residence* – 3 Blenheim Drive, Oxford.

Hon Katherine Anne, *b* 1956. *Residence* – 99a Grosvenor Av, Highbury, N1.

Hon Laura Margaret, *b* 1961: *m* 1997, Tomek Borkowy, son of Dr Borkowy, of Warsaw. *Residence* – 18 Queensferry St, Edinburgh.

Hon Judith Mary, *b* 1964: *m* 1989, Nicholas David Aspinall, elder son of late Dr Dennis L. Aspinall.

MACKIE OF BENSHIE, BARON (Mackie) (Life Baron 1974)

GEORGE YULL MACKIE, CBE, DSO, DFC, son of late Maitland Mackie, OBE, and brother of Lord John-Mackie (Life Baron); *b* 10 July 1919; *ed* Aberdeen Gram Sch, and Aberdeen Univ; 1939-45 War with Bomber Command RAF (DSO, DFC); Farmer; Chm of Scottish Liberal Party 1965-70 (Vice-Chm 1960-65); MP for Caithness and Sutherland (*L*) 1964-66; former Chm Caithness Glass Ltd; a Member of National and Local Cttees for Scotland, of NFU, and of Scottish Advisory Cttee of British Council; Rector of Dundee Univ 1981-83; *cr* DSO 1944, CBE (Civil) 1971, and *Baron Mackie of Benshie*, of Kirriemuir, co Angus (Life Baron) 1974: *m* 1st, 1944, Lindsay Lyall, who *d* 1985, da of late Alexander Sharp, Advocate, of Aberdeen; 2ndly, 1988, Jacqueline, da of late Col Marcel Rauch, French Air Force, and widow of Andrew Lane, and has issue by 1st *m*.

Residence – Cortachy House, by Kirriemuir, Angus, DD8 5QG. *Clubs* – Garrick, Farmers', Scottish Liberal (Edinburgh), RAF.

DAUGHTERS LIVING (*By 1st marriage*)

Hon Lindsay Mary, *b* 1945: *m* 1982, Alan Rusbridger.

Hon Diana Lyall, *b* 1946: *m* 1968, John Carlyle Hope, of 3 St Bernard Cres, Edinburgh.

Hon Jeannie Felicia, *b* 1953: *m* 1982, David Leigh.

MACKINTOSH OF HALIFAX, VISCOUNT (Mackintosh) (Viscount UK 1957, Bt UK 1935)

JOHN CLIVE MACKINTOSH, 3rd Viscount and 3rd Baronet, *b* 9 Sept 1958; *s* 1980; *ed* The Leys Sch, and Oriel Coll, Oxford, Chartered Accountant, Partner Price Waterhouse Coopers since 1992: *m* 1st, 1982 (*m diss* 1993), Elizabeth, only da of late D. G. Lakin; 2ndly, 1995, Mrs Claire Jane Wishart, yst da of Stanislaw Nowak, and has issue by 1st *m*.

Arms – Or, on a chevron between two lions rampant in chief and a lymphad in base sable, a bezant charged with a representation of the head of St John the Baptist proper, between two hearts of the field. Crest – Upon a rock proper, charged with two roses argent, barbed and seeded, a cat sejant also proper. Supporters – On either side a squirrel proper. suspended from the neck by a cord a purse or.
Address – House of Lords, Westminster, SW1A 0PW.

SONS LIVING (*By 1st marriage*)

Hon THOMAS HAROLD GEORGE, *b* 8 Feb 1985.
Hon George John Frank, *b* 1988.

BROTHER LIVING

Hon Graham Charles, *b* 1964; *ed* The Leys Sch, and Newcastle Univ (BSc); Chartered Surveyor: *m* 1994 (*m diss* 1999), Anjella Ruth, yst da of Bryan Fisher, of Tenbury Wells, Worcs. *Residence* – The Mill House, Cuddesdon, Oxon OX44 9HQ.

HALF-SISTERS LIVING

Hon Diana Mary, *b* 1947.
Hon Elizabeth Constance (*Baroness Astor of Hever*), *b* 1950: *m* 1st, 1972, Timothy Cutting; 2ndly, 1980, Nicolas Chagrin; 3rdly, 1990, as his 2nd wife, 3rd Baron Astor of Hever, and has issue living (by 2nd *m*), Natalya Isabel, *b* 1981, — (by 3rd *m*) (*see* B Astor of Hever).

AUNT LIVING (*Daughter of 1st Viscount*)

Hon Mary, *b* 1927; is a JP for Norfolk: *m* 1949, (Charles) Michael Watt, and has issue living, Charles Jonathan (Narborough House, Stoke Holy Cross, Norwich, Norfolk), *b* 1950: *m* 1974, Catherine Anna Lilley, and has issue living, Charles Henry William *b* 1980, Edward Alastair Donald *b* 1984, Elizabeth Anna *b* 1977, — Henry Donald, *b* 1962: *m* 1992, Tania Elizabeth, only da of Charles Ian Strafford, of Chelmsford, Essex, — Susan Mary, *b* 1953: *m* 1980, Ivan Alexander Shenkman, of 34 Royal Crescent, W11, and has issue living, Maximilian Ivan Michael *b* 1982, Alexander Ivan Marcus *b* 1988, Melissa Alexandra Mary *b* 1984. *Residence* – Wychwood House, Hethersett, nr Norwich, Norfolk, NR9 3AT.

WIDOW LIVING OF SECOND VISCOUNT

GWYNNETH CHARLESWORTH (*Gwynneth, Viscountess Mackintosh of Halifax*) (The Old Hall, Barford, Norwich NR9 4AY), da of late Charles Henry Gledhill: *m* 1956, as his 2nd wife, 2nd Viscount Mackintosh of Halifax, OBE, BEM, who *d* 1980.

PREDECESSORS – (1) *Sir* HAROLD VINCENT Mackintosh, son of John Mackintosh, JP, of Greystones, Halifax; *b* 1891; Chm of John Mackintosh & Sons Ltd, toffee manufacturers, of Halifax; Chm of National Savings Cttee 1943-64, and Pres 1958-64; *cr* a *Baron Mackintosh of Halifax*, of Hethersett, co Norfolk (peerage of UK) 1948, and *Viscount Mackintosh of Halifax*, of Hethersett, co Norfolk (peerage of UK) 1957: *m* 1916, Constance Emily, who *d* 1975, da of Edgar Cooper Stoneham, OBE, of Acton, W3; *d* 1964; *s* by his only son (2) JOHN, OBE, BEM, 2nd Viscount, *b* 1921; Dir John Mackintosh & Son Ltd: *m* 1st, 1946 (*m diss* 1956), Bronda, only da of late Louis John Fibiger, of South Shields, co Durham; 2ndly, 1956, Gwynneth Charlesworth, da of late Charles Henry Gledhill; *d* 1980; *s* by his el son (3) JOHN CLIVE, 3rd Viscount and present peer; also Baron Mackintosh of Halifax.

McLaren, family name of Baron Aberconway.

MacLAURIN OF KNEBWORTH, BARON (MacLaurin) (Life Baron 1996)

IAN CHARTER MacLAURIN, son of late Arthur George MacLaurin, of Esher, Surrey; *b* 30 March 1937; *ed* Malvern; Hon DPhil Stirling (1987), Hon LLD Herts (1995), Hon FCGI (1992), FRSA (1986), FInstM (1987); joined Tesco PLC as first company trainee 1959, Dir 1970, Man Dir 1973, Deputy Chm 1983, Chm 1985-97; Non-Exec Dir Enterprise Oil PLC 1984-90, Guinness PLC 1986, National Westminster Bank PLC since 1990, and Gleneagles Hotels PLC since 1992; Chm UK Sports Council and England and Wales Cricket Board; Pres Inst of Grocery Distribution 1989-92; Govr of Malvern Coll; Memb Save the Children Fund Commerce and Industry Cttee, Stock Exchange Advisory Cttee 1988-91; Chancellor of Univ of Hertfordshire since 1996; DL Herts 1992; Freeman of the City of London 1981, Liveryman of Worshipful Co of Carmen 1982; nat service with RAF Fighter Command 1956-58; *cr* Kt 1989, and *Baron MacLaurin of Knebworth*, of Knebworth, co Herts (Life Baron) 1996: *m* 1960, Ann Margaret, who *d* 1999, da of late Edgar Ralph Collar, of London, and has issue.

𝕬𝖗𝖒𝖘 – ......
Address – Tesco PLC, Tesco House, Delamere Rd, Cheshunt, Herts EN8 9SL. *Club* – MCC.

SON LIVING

Hon Neil Ralph Charter, *b* 1966; *ed* Malvern: *m* 1990, Anna Margaret McKinnon, of Sydney, Australia, and has issue living, James Charter, *b* 1993, — Oliver Charles, *b* 1995.

DAUGHTERS LIVING

Hon Fiona Margaret, *b* 1962: *m* 19— (*m diss* 19—), ... Archer, and has issue living, Frederick Charles Russell, *b* 1993, — Poppy Victoria Margaret, *b* 1991.
Hon Gillian, *b* 1964.

MACLAY, BARON (Maclay) (Baron UK 1922, Bt UK 1914)

JOSEPH PATON MACLAY, 3rd Baron and 3rd Baronet; *b* 11 April 1942; *s* 1969; *ed* Winchester; Man Dir Denholm Maclay Co, Ltd, and a Dir of Milton Shipping Co, Ltd, North of England Protection & Indemnity Assocn and The British Steamship Short Trades Assocn, Man Dir Milton Timber Services Ltd since 1983: *m* 1976, Elizabeth Anne, only da of G. M. Buchanan, of Delamere, Pokataroo, NSW, and has issue.

𝕬𝖗𝖒𝖘 – Or, a lion rampant azure, armed and langued gules, resting its sinister paw on an anchor sable, all within an orle of the second. 𝕮𝖗𝖊𝖘𝖙 – A lymphad sails furled sable, flagged proper. 𝕾𝖚𝖕𝖕𝖔𝖗𝖙𝖊𝖗𝖘 – Two wolves proper, each gorged with a chain, pendant therefrom an escutcheon argent, charged with a salmon on its back holding a ring in its mouth proper.
Residences – Duchal, Kilmacolm, Renfrewshire; Milton, Kilmacolm, Renfrewshire.

SONS LIVING

Hon JOSEPH PATON, *b* 6 March 1977.
Hon Thomas Maxwell, *b* 1981.

DAUGHTER LIVING

Hon Rebecca Delamere, *b* 1979.

BROTHERS LIVING

Hon David Milton (12 Langton St, SW10), *b* 1944; *ed* Winchester: *m* 1968, Valerie, da of late Lt-Cdr J. P. Fyfe, of Kinkell, St Andrews, Fife, and has issue living, Duncan, *b* 1974.

Hon Angus Grenfell (Whitelee, St Boswells, Roxburghshire TD6 0SH), *b* 1945; *ed* Winchester: *m* 1st, 1970, Hon (Elizabeth) Victoria Baillie, who *d* 1986, el da of 3rd Baron Burton; 2ndly, 1990, Jane Elizabeth Angela, da of late Lt-Col Alistair Monteith Gibb, R Wilts Yeo (*see* V Cowdray, 1980 Edn), and formerly wife of 13th Marquess of Huntly, and has issue living (by 1st *m*), Robert Michael, *b* 1972, — Fergus *b* 1981, — Sarah Elizabeth, *b* 1977.

SISTERS LIVING AND DECEASED

Hon Sarah, *b* 1937: *m* 1968, David Richard Hayes, of Factors House, Pityulish, Aviemore, Inverness-shire (*see* Muir, Bt).

Hon Lucy, *b* 1938: *m* 1966, James Ian Alexander Robertson, of Glenside Farm, Plean, Stirlingshire, and *d* 1987, leaving issue, Hugh Sebastian, *b* 1967, — David Ian, *b* 1969, — Dominic James, *b* 1973, — Anna Marcelle, *b* 1971; *d* 1989.

WIDOW LIVING OF SECOND BARON

Nancy Margaret (*Nancy, Baroness Maclay*) (Milton, Kilmacolm, Renfrewshire), da of Robert Coventry Greig, of Hall of Caldwell, Uplawnmoor, Renfrewshire: *m* 1936, the 2nd Baron Maclay, who *d* 1969.

COLLATERAL BRANCHES LIVING

Grandchildren of late Hon Walter Symington Maclay, CB, OBE, MD (infra):—
Issue of late Dr Walter Strang Symington Maclay, *b* 1931, *d* 1987: *m* 1956, Elizabeth Ann (Findings, Hambledon, Surrey GU8 5TS) (who *m* 2ndly, 1991, Thomas Roderick Loxley Waring), eldest da of Willis C. Cooper, of Tintern, Esher Close, Esher, Surrey:—
Andrew Strang, *b* 1958: *m* 1987, Felicity Neal. —— Christopher Willis, *b* 1964: *m* 1988, Louise Nelson. ——Janet Susan, *b* 1960.

Issue of late Hon Walter Symington Maclay, CB, OBE, MD, 4th son of 1st Baron, *b* 1901, *d* 1964: *m* 1928, Dorothy, who *d* 1993, da of late William Lennox, WS:—
John Lennox Sim (12 Stafford Court, Kensington High St, W8 7DJ) *b* 1937; *ed* Winchester, and St John's Coll, Camb (MA). —— Mark Paton (Sladen Green, Binley, Andover, Hants), *b* 1943; *ed* Winchester, and RAC Cirencester; FRICS: *m* 1967, Elizabeth Ruth, da of late Worsfold McClenaghan, of Westfield House, Highclere, Newbury, Berks, and has issue living, James Paton, *b* 1971, — Alasdair Worsfold, *b* 1973, — Caroline Elizabeth, *b* 1976. —— (Shirley) Georgina (Cedar House, Hellidon, Daventry, Northants NN11 6LG), *b* 1933: *m* 1st, 1955 (*m diss* 1974), Robert David Ogden; 2ndly, 1989, Prof Michael Stuart King, and has issue living (by 1st *m*), Robert Nicholas, *b* 1958, — Joseph Jeremy (twin), *b* 1958, — Benjamin Patrick, *b* 1966, — Emma Maclay, *b* 1961.

PREDECESSORS – (1) *Rt Hon* Joseph Paton Maclay, son of late Ebenezer Maclay, of Glasgow; *b* 1857; sometime Chm of Maclay & Macintyre, Ltd, shipowners, of 21 Bothwell Street, Glasgow; Min of Shipping and a Member of War Cabinet 1916-21; *cr* a *Baronet* 1914, and *Baron Maclay*, of Glasgow, co Lanark (peerage of United Kingdom) 1922: *m* 1889, Martha, who *d* 1929, da of William Strang, manufacturer of Glasgow; *d* 1951; *s* by his el surviving son (2) Joseph Paton, KBE, 2nd Baron, *b* 1899; MP for Paisley (L) 1931-45; *m* 1936, Nancy Margaret, da of Robert Coventry Greig, of Hall of Caldwell, Uplawnmoor, Renfrewshire; *d* 1969; *s* by his el son (3) Joseph Paton, 3rd Baron and present peer.

MACLEAN, BARONY OF (Maclean) (Extinct 1990)

SON, DAUGHTER AND WIDOW OF LIFE BARON (*see* Maclean, Bt, *cr* 1631)

McLEAVY, BARONY OF (McLeavy) (Extinct 1976)

SON LIVING OF LIFE BARON

Hon Frank Waring, *b* 1925: *m* 1954, Verena, da of Emil Lüscher, of Unterkulm, Switzerland, and has issue.

WIDOW LIVING OF SON OF LIFE BARON

Janet Elizabeth, da of Harry Ogden: *m* 1958, Hon Douglas John McLeavy, who *d* 1969, and has issue, Mark, *b* 1969, — Ruth, *b* 1964.

MACLEHOSE OF BEOCH, BARON (MacLehose) (Life Baron 1982)

CRAWFORD MURRAY MACLEHOSE, KT, GBE, KCMG, KCVO, son of late Hamish A. MacLehose, of Grange, Culroy, Ayrshire; *b* 16 Oct 1917; *ed* Rugby, and Balliol Coll; a DL of Ayr and Arran; Malayan Civil Ser 1939-46, Foreign Ser 1946-82; acting Consul Hankow 1947-48, acting Consul-Gen 1948-49, and 1st Sec 1949-50, 1st Sec and Consul Prague 1951-54, seconded to Wellington, NZ 1954-56, 1st Sec at Paris 1958-59, Counsellor and Political Advisor, Hong Kong 1959-62, Head of Far Eastern Dept, FO 1963-65, Prin Private Sec to Foreign Sec 1965-67, and Ambassador to Vietnam 1967-69, and to Denmark 1969-71, Gov and C-in-C of Hong Kong 1971-82; Dir Nat Westminster Bank 1983-88, Chm Govs SOAS, London Univ 1985-90 (Hon Fell 1983), Chm Victoria League for Commonwealth Friendship 1983-87, Scottish Trust for the Physically Disabled, and Margaret Blackwood Housing Assocn since 1983; 1939-45 War as Lt RNVR; *cr* MBE (Mil) 1946, CMG 1964, KCMG 1971, KCVO 1975, GBE 1977, KT 1983, and *Baron MacLehose of Beoch*, of Maybole, in the district of Kyle and Carrick, and of Victoria in Hong Kong (Life Baron) 1982: *m* 1947, Margaret Noel, yst da of late Sir (Thomas) Charles Dunlop, TD, of Doonside, Ayrshire, and has issue.

Arms – Argent, on a chevron ensigned at the top with a cross pattée sable, between two escutcheons azure each charged of a mullet of the first in chief and a demi double headed eagle displayed azure beaked sable in base, a book expanded argent. Crest – A dragon's head erased affrontée or, armed and langued gules. Supporters – *dexter*, a Chinese dragon or armed and langued gules gorged of a collar indented sable; *sinister*, a black faced ram proper. Motto – Spe vitae melioris.
Residence – Beoch, Maybole, Ayrshire. *Club* – Athenaeum.

DAUGHTERS LIVING

Hon Elfrida Sandra, *b* 1949: *m* 1971, Martin Amery Wedgwood, of Collalis, Gartocharn, by Alexandria, Dunbartonshire, and has issue.
Hon Sylvia Margaret, *b* (twin) 1949: *m* 1970 Ronald Leighton, Sandeman, of Rosgaradh, West Dhuhill Drive, Helensburgh, Dunbartonshire G84 9AW, and has issue.

MACLEOD OF BORVE, BARONESS (Macleod) (Life Baroness 1971)

EVELYN HESTER MACLEOD, da of late Rev Gervase Vanneck Blois (*see* Blois, Bt, colls), *b* 19 Feb 1915; JP for Middx; a DL of Greater London; first Chm of National Gas Consumers' Council 1972-

77; Chm Nat Assocn of Leagues of Hospital Friends 1976-85 (Pres 1985-89), Pres Nat Assocn of Widows since 1976; Member IBA 1972-77, Parole Bd 1978-82; Gov Queenswood Sch 1977-85; Pres Crisis at Christmas since 1970; *cr Baroness Macleod of Borve*, of Borve, Isle of Lewis (Life Baroness) 1971: *m* 1st, 1937, Mervyn Charles Mason, who was *k* by enemy action 1940; 2ndly, 1941, Rt Hon Iain Norman Macleod, MP, who *d* 1970, and has issue by 2nd *m*.
Residence – Luckings Farm, Coleshill, Amersham, Bucks HP7 0LS.

SON LIVING (*By 2nd marriage*)

Hon Torquil Anthony Ross, *b* 1942; *ed* Harrow: *m* 1967 (*m diss* 1973) (Elizabeth) Meriol, da of late Brig Arthur Pelham Trevor, DSO, and has issue living, Iain Ross, *b* 1970.

DAUGHTER LIVING (*By 2nd marriage*)

Hon Diana Hester, *b* 1944; *m* 1968 David Heimann, of Hertfordshire House, Coleshill, Bucks, and has three sons, Hugo Iain Philip, *b* 1972, — James Iain Philip, *b* 1974, — Charles Gervase Andrew, *b* 1977.

MacLEOD OF FUINARY, BARONY OF (MacLeod) (Extinct 1991)

SONS AND DAUGHTER OF LIFE BARON (*see* MacLeod, Bt, *cr* 1924)

Macmillan, family name of Earl of Stockton.

Macmillan of Ovenden, Viscount; son of Earl of Stockton.

McNAIR, BARON (McNair) (Baron UK 1955)

PERICULUM·IN·MORA

Danger in delay

DUNCAN JAMES McNAIR, 3rd Baron; *b* 26 June 1947; *s* 1989; *ed* Bryanston: *m* 1st, 19—, Kodikaraarachige Perera, of Sri Lanka; 2ndly, 1995, Mrs Hannah Margaret Elizabeth Reese, da of ......, and has issue, by 1st wife.

Arms – Gules, three barrulets wavy argent surmounted of a lion rampant or, armed and langued azure, between two thistleheads stalked and leved paleways of the third. **Crest** – On a wreath of the liveries an ancient ship under full sail, flagged azure, the sail emblazoned of ensigns armorial as on the escutcheon. **Supporters** – Two Bedlington terriers proper.

SON LIVING (*By 1st wife*)

Hon Thomas John, *b* 1972.

DAUGHTERS LIVING (*By 1st wife*)

Charlotte, *b* 1968 (adopted da).
Hon Victoria, *b* (twin) 1972.

BROTHER LIVING

Hon WILLIAM SAMUEL ANGUS, *b* 19th May 1958: *m* 1981 (*m diss* 1990), Emma S. Procter, and has issue living, John Samuel, *b* 1984, — Emily Harriet, 1982.

SISTER LIVING

Hon Josephine Margaret, *b* 1949.

AUNTS LIVING (*daughters of 1st Baron*)

Hon Sheila Margaret Ramsay, *b* 1918: *m* 1946, John Harold Barwell, who *d* 1983, and has issue living, Hugh John (119 Remingford Rd, Cambridge CB2 3BY), *b* 1949: *m* 1973, Glynis Christine Rolfe, and has issue living, Guy Harold *b* 1989, Leigh Ellen *b* 1978, — Alice Marjorie Sheila, *b* 1947; *ed* Somerville Coll, Oxford; DPhil, FRHistS: *m* 1971, Franklyn Kimmel Prochaska, PhD, FRHistS, of 9 Addison Bridge Place, W14 8XP, and has issue living, William Anton Franklin *b* 1982, Elizabeth Harriet *b* 1980, — Lucy Elizabeth (Unison Farm, Round Hill, Virginia, USA), *b* 1951: *m* 1st, 1973 (*m diss* 1978), Lloyd Herman Bernstein; 2ndly, 1990, Mitch Diamond, — Claire Bridget, *b* 1953; *ed* Somerville Coll, Oxford (BA 1975): *m* 1979, Gil Aufray, of 53c Randolph Av, W9, and has issue living, Oliver Daniel *b* 1988. *Residence* – 33 Fulbrooke Rd, Cambridge CB3 9EE.

Hon Elinor Ruth, *b* 1924: *m* 1955, Raymond Hanscomb, and has issue living, Benjamin Douglas *b* 1956: *m* 1993, Sandra Ellis, and has issue living, Isobel Rose *b* 1995, Lucy Jessica *b* 1998, — and two adopted children, George Sebastian, *b* 1965, — Emma Frances Mary, *b* 1963: *m* 1995, Clive Matthew Gawlik, yr son of Jan Gawlik, of Uley, Glos. *Residence* – Powells End, Kempley, Dymock, Glos.

WIDOW LIVING OF SECOND BARON

VERA (*Vera, Baroness McNair*), da of Theodore James Faithfull, MRCVS, of Birmingham: *m* 1941, the 2nd Baron McNair, who *d* 1989. *Residence* – Glyn Teg, Tregynon, Newtown, Powys SY16 3EH.

PREDECESSORS – (1) *Sir* ARNOLD DUNCAN McNAIR, CBE, QC, LLD, FBA, son of late John McNair, of Court Lane, Dulwich Village, SE; *b* 1885; Vice-Chancellor of Liverpool Univ 1937-45; a Judge of Internat Court of Justice 1946-55 (pres. 1952-55); Pres Inst of Internat Law 1959-60; 1st Pres of Court of European Rights at Strasbourg 1959-65; *cr Baron McNair*, of Gleniffer, co Renfrew (peerage UK) 1955: *m* 1912, Marjorie, who *d* 1971, da of late Hon Sir Clement Meacher Bailhache; *d* 1975; *s* by his only son (2) (CLEMENT) JOHN, 2nd Baron, *b* 1915: *m* 1941, Vera, da of Theodore James Faithfull, MRCVS, of Birmingham; *d* 1989; *s* by his elder son (3) DUNCAN JAMES, 3rd Baron and present peer.

McNALLY, BARON (McNally) (Life Baron 1995)

THOMAS (TOM) McNALLY, son of late John Patrick McNally, of Old Swan, Liverpool; *b* 20 Feb 1943; *ed* Coll of St Joseph, Blackpool, and Univ Coll, London (BSc 1966, Fell 1995); Assist Gen Sec of The Fabian Soc 1966-67; Vice-Pres NUS 1966-67; International Sec, Labour Party HQ 1969-74 (researcher 1966-77); MP Stockport South (*Lab* until 1981, SDP thereafter) 1979-83; Head of Public Affairs, Hill and Knowlton (UK) Ltd 1987-93, since when Dir of Public Affairs, Shandwick Consultants Ltd; *cr Baron McNally*, of Blackpool, co Lancs (Life Baron) 1995: *m* 1st, 1970 (*m diss*

1990), Eileen Isobel, da of Thomas Powell, of Dumfries; 2ndly, 1990, Juliet, da of George Lamy Hutchinson, of Swansea, and has issue by 2nd *m*.

SONS LIVING (By 2nd marriage)

Hon John, *b* 1990.
Hon James George, *b* 1993.

DAUGHTER LIVING (By 2nd marriage)

Hon Imogen, *b* 1995.

Macpherson, family name of Baron Strathcarron.

MACPHERSON OF DRUMOCHTER, BARON (Macpherson) (Baron UK 1951)

Touch not this cat but a glove

(JAMES) GORDON MACPHERSON, 2nd Baron; *b* 22 Jan 1924; *s* 1965; *ed* Loretto, and Wells House, Malvern; FRES, FRSA, FZS, a JP for Essex 1961 and Chm of Macpherson, Train & Co, Ltd, Food and Produce Importers and Exporters, and subsidiary and Assoc Cos since 1964, and A. J. Macpherson & Co Ltd, Bankers since 1973; Past Chm of W India Cttee 1973-75; Hon Game Warden for the Sudan since 1974; Member 1001 (nature trust); a Member of London Chamber of Commerce 1958-75; Pres of British Importers Confedn 1972; Dep Chm Brentwood Bench 1972-75; a Trustee of Head Injuries Rehabilitation Trust 1970-75; Freeman of City of London, a Member of Butchers' Co since 1969, Life Managing Gov, Royal Scottish Corporation since 1975, and a Gov of Brentwood Sch 1970-74; Member Northern Meeting, Highland Soc of London (1975); 1939-45 War with RAF: *m* 1st, 1947, (Dorothy) Ruth, who *d* 1974, da of late Rev Henry Coulter, of Bellahouston, Glasgow; 2ndly, 1975, Catherine Bridget, only da of Dr Desmond MacCarthy, of Queens Rd, Brentwood, and has had issue by 1st and 2nd *m*.

Arms – Per fesse or and azure, a lymphad sail furled flags and pennon flying counter-changed between in chief a dexter hand fessewise couped at the wrist grasping a dagger point upwards, and a cross-crosslet fitchée gules, and in base an oak tree eradicated proper fructed or. Crest – A wildcat sejant guardant proper holding a cross-crosslet fitchée gules. Supporters – *Dexter*, a lion gules, gorged with a collar, pendent therefrom an escutcheon or, charged with a garb azure; *sinister*, a bull gules, armed and unguled azure, gorged with a collar pendent therefrom an escutcheon gold charged with a boar's head couped also azure.
Residence – Kyllachy, Tomatin, Inverness-shire. *Clubs* – Boodle's, E India, Devonshire Sports, Public Schools.

SON DECEASED (By 1st marriage)

Hon Thomas, *b* 1951; *d* 1978.

SON LIVING (By 2nd marriage)

Hon JAMES ANTHONY, *b* 27 Feb 1979.

DAUGHTERS LIVING *(By 1st marriage)*

Hon Wendy Shona Coulter, *b* 1950: *m* 1st, 1972 (*m diss* 1980), Brian Anthony Fountain; 2ndly, 1987, Derek Everest, and has issue living, (by 1st *m*) Stewart James Coulter, *b* 1978, — Shona Fountain, *b* 1981, — (by 2nd *m*) Douglas, *b* 1988.

Hon Elizabeth Shirley, *b* 1953: *m* 1st, 1978 (*m diss* 1989), Mark William Ransome; 2ndly, 1990, Robert Frederick Shaw, of 72 Tyorne Av, Park View 2122, Gauteng, Johannesburg, S Africa, and has issue living (by 1st *m*), James Gordon, *b* 1981, — Sarah Emma Ashley, *b* 1984.

(By 2nd marriage)

Hon Jennifer Margaret, *b* 1976.
Hon Anne Alexandra, *b* 1977.

SISTER LIVING

Hon Shona Catherine Greig, *b* 1929: *m* 1952, Donald le Strange Campbell, MC, and has issue living Donald Bruce le Strange *b* 1956: *m* 1982, Kristine, el da of Maj L. H. Nash, of Woodruff, Kingsley Green, Haslemere, Surrey, — Victoria Louise, *b* 1959: *m* 1985, Russell Charles Crockford, son of Charles Crockford, of Donnell, Camberley, Surrey, and has issue living, Alexander Charles *b* 1990.

PREDECESSORS – (1) THOMAS Macpherson, son of James Macpherson, of Muirhead, Chryston, Lanarkshire; *b* 1888; Chm of Macpherson, Train & Co Ltd, Food and Produce Importers and Exporters; MP for Romford (*Lab*) 1945-50; *cr* *Baron Macpherson of Drumochter*, of Gt Warley, co Essex (peerage of UK) 1951: *m* 1920, Lucy, who *d* 1984, da of late Arthur Butcher, of Heybridge Basin, Maldon, Essex; *d* 1965; *s* by his only son (2) JAMES GORDON, 2nd Baron and present peer.

MADDOCK, BARONESS (Maddock) (Life Baroness 1997)

DIANA MARGARET MADDOCK, da of late Reginald Derbyshire, of Wantage; *b* 19 May 1945; *ed* Shenstone Training Coll, and Portsmouth Polytechnic (Cert Ed; Postgraduate Linguistics Dip); ESL Teacher, Extra Mural Dept, Stockholm Univ 1969-72; MP for Christchurch (*Lib Dem*) 1993-97; Lib Dem Spokesperson on housing, the family and women's issues 1974-97; Pres of Liberal Democrats since 1998; Sec All Party Parliamentary Group Homelessness and Housing Need; Vice-Chm All Party Parliamentary Group Electoral Reform; Lib Dem Spokesperson on Housing, House of Lords; Pres Nat Housing Forum; a Vice-Pres Nat Housing Federation; Board Memb Western Challenge Housing Assoc; *cr Baroness Maddock*, of Christchurch, co Dorset (Life Baroness) 1997: *m* 1966, Robert Frank Maddock, son of Oswald Maddock, of Southampton, and has issue.
Address – House of Lords, Westminster, SW1A 0PW. *Club* – National Liberal.

DAUGHTERS LIVING

Hon Becki, *b* 1976.
Hon Anna, *b* 1978.

MAELOR, BARONY OF (Jones) (Extinct 1984)

SON LIVING OF LIFE BARON

Hon James Glynmore, *b* 1929.

DAUGHTER LIVING OF LIFE BARON

Hon Enid Angharad, *b* 1936: *m* 1961, E. Jurkiewicz, of 16 Snowdon Drive, Wrexham.

Maffey, family name of Baron Rugby.

Maidstone, Viscount; son of Earl of Winchilsea and Nottingham.

MAIS, BARONY OF (Mais) (Extinct 1993)

SONS LIVING OF LIFE BARON

Hon Richard Jeremy Ian (79 Seal Hollow Rd, Sevenoaks, Kent. *Club* – AA), *b* 1945; *ed* Stowe; MCIOB; Chm CNC Properties plc: *m* 1972, Janice, el da of Ralph Dean, of 11 The Spinney, Frogmill, Hurley, Berks, and has issue living, Alexander, *b* 1975, — Vanessa, *b* 1977, — Lydia, *b* 1981.

Hon Jonathan Robert Neal (2 Lyric Rd, Barnes, SW13 9PZ), *b* 1954; *ed* Hurstpierpoint: *m* 1st, 1978 (*m diss* 1982), Frances Louise, da of late Robert Mark Barrington Brown; 2ndly, 1990, Gillian Margaret, da of Raymond Hollingworth, and has issue living (by 1st *m*), Joel Robert Barrington, *b* 1979, — Duncan Jonathan Christopher, *b* (twin) 1979.

DAUGHTER LIVING OF LIFE BARON

Hon Angela Clare (McCrossin Cottage, 12400 McCrossin Lane, Potomac, Maryland 20854, USA), *b* 1946; *ed* St Margaret's, Bushey, and House of Citizenship: *m* 1976 (*m diss* 1983), Robert M Beckman.

WIDOW LIVING OF LIFE BARON

Lorna Aline (*Baroness Mais*), da of late Stanley Aspinall Boardman, of Addiscombe, Surrey: *m* 1936, Baron Mais, GBE, ERD, TD (Life Baron), who *d* 1993. *Residence* – The Penthouse, 12A Copperfields, 48 The Avenue, Beckenham, Kent BR3 5ER.

Maitland, Viscount; son of Earl of Lauderdale.

Maitland, family name of Earl of Lauderdale.

Major, Henniker-, family name of Baron Henniker.

Makgill, family name of Viscount of Oxfuird.

Makins, family name of Baron Sherfield.

Malden, Viscount; son of Earl of Essex.

MALLALIEU, BARONESS (Cassel) (Life Baroness 1991)

ANN MALLALIEU, da of late Sir (Joseph Percival) William Mallalieu, of Village Farm, Boarstall, Aylesbury, Bucks; *b* 27 Nov 1945; *ed* Holton Park Girls' Gram Sch, Wheatley, Oxon, and Newnham Coll, Camb (MA, LLM; first woman pres Camb Union Soc; Hon Fell 1993); Bar Inner Temple 1970, Recorder 1985-93, QC 1988; *cr Baroness Mallalieu*, of Studdridge, co Bucks (Life Baroness) 1991: *m* 1979, as his 2nd wife, Timothy Felix Harold Cassel, eldest son of His Honour Sir Harold Felix Cassel, 3rd Bt, and has issue.

𝕬rms – Azure, on a chevron ermine between three fleurs-de-lys argent four bezants, on a chief ermines a rose of the third barbed and seeded proper. 𝕾upporters – *Dexter*, a horse argent; *sinister*, a fox-hound proper both gorged with a torse argent and azure and each statant erect on a field of stubble with a hedgerow that on the dexter having a stile and palings and that on the sinister a gate with palings all in perspective proper.
Chambers - 6 King's Bench Walk, Temple, EC4.

DAUGHTERS LIVING

Hon Bathsheba Anna, *b* 1981.
Hon Cosima Ione Harriet, *b* 1984.

MALMESBURY, EARL OF (Harris) (Earl GB 1800)
(Title pronounced Marmsbury")

I will maintain

To remember my country everywhere

WILLIAM JAMES HARRIS, TD, 6th Earl; *b* 18 Nov 1907; *s* 1950; *ed* Eton, and Trin Coll, Camb (MA); Maj late R Hampshire Regt (TA), Hon Col 65th Signal Regt TA 1959-66 and of 2nd Bn Wessex Vols 1971-74; ARICS; Chm Hants & Isle of Wight T & AF Asscn 1960-68, and of E Wessex TA & VR Assocn 1968-70 (Vice-Pres 1973-78, since when Pres); Chm New Forest 9th Centenary Trust 1977-87, since when Pres; Personal Liaison Officer to Min of Agric for W Cos for SE Region 1959-64; Master of Skinners' Co 1952-53; Chm of Hants Agric Exec Cttee 1959-66; Lord Lt for co Southampton 1973-82, and a DL for Hants since 1983; Vice Pres Mary Rose Trust since 1979; Official Verderer of New Forest 1966-74; Stowaway of The Master Mariners (Southampton District) since 1988; KStJ; JP; a Gold Staff Officer at Coronation of King George VI; has Coronation Medals (1937 and 1953) and Silver Jubilee Medal 1977; TD (two clasps): *m* 1st, 1932, Hon Diana Claudia Patricia Carleton, who *d* 1990, da of 2nd Baron Dorchester; 2ndly, 1991, Margaret Fleetwood, OBE, who *d* 1994, widow of Capt Raymond Alexander Baring (*see* Baring, Bt), and yst da of late Col Robert William Pigott Clarke Campbell-Preston, of Ardchattan Priory, Argyllshire; 3rdly, 1996, Bridget Graham, who *d* 1999, widow of Capt Peter F. Hawkings, and has issue by 1st *m*.

Arms – Azure, a chevron erminois, between three hedgehogs or, on a chief argent, the black eagle of Prussia, crowned with an imperial crown, holding in the claws a sceptre and mound, charged on the breast with the cipher "FR" and on each wing a trefoil slipped, all gold. **Crest** – A hedgehog or, charged on the body with three arrows, one erect and two in saltire, sable, and over them a key barwise azure. **Supporters** – *Dexter*, an eagle, wings expanded and elevated sable, crowned with an imperial crown and charged on the breast with the cipher "FR" and on each wing with a trefoil slipped, all gold; *sinister*, a reindeer proper, attired and hoofed or.
Residence – The Ford, Deptford Lane, Greywell, Hook Hants, RG29 1BA. *Club* – Royal Yacht Squadron (Vice-Commodore 1971-77).

SON LIVING (*By 1st marriage*)

JAMES CARLETON (*Viscount FitzHarris*) (Greywell Hill, Greywell, Hook, Hants, RG29 1DG), *b* 19 June 1946; *ed* Eton, and Queens Coll, Univ of St Andrews; DL Hants 1997: *m* 1969, Sally Ann, yr da of late Sir Richard Newton Rycroft, 7th Bt, and has issue:—

SONS LIVING, — *Hon* James Hugh Carleton, *b* 29 April 1970: *m* 1997, Jemima Nancy Grace, eldest da of Capt Michael Fulford-Dobson, RN, of Cerne Abbey, Dorset, — *Hon* (Charles) Edward, *b* 1972, — *Hon* Guy Richard, *b* 1975.
DAUGHTERS LIVING, — *Hon* Frances Maria *b* 1979, — *Hon* Daisy Catherine *b* 1981.

DAUGHTERS LIVING (*By 1st marriage*)

Lady Sylvia Veronica Anthea, *b* 1934: *m* 1956, John Newcombe Maltby, CBE, who *d* 1998, son of late Air Vice-Marshal Sir Paul Copeland Maltby, KCVO, KBE, CB, DSO, AFC, DL, and has issue living, William John, *b* 1959: *m* 1985, Sarah Catherine, da of Cdr James Ekins, of Old Lime House, Easton, Winchester, Hants, and has issue living, George William de Blaquiere *b* 1989, Alice Diana *b* 1992, Poppy Elizabeth *b* 1994, — Caroline Jane, *b* 1957: *m* 1990, Alexander F. J. Roe, elder son of Frederick Roe, of The Bacchus House, Elsdon, Northumberland, and has issue living, Edward Frederick John *b* 1994, James *b* 1996, Charlotte *b* 1992, — Sophia Louise, *b* 1963: *m* 1995, Alexander Guy Campbell Ross, eldest son of David Ross, of The Little Boltons, SW10, and has issue living, Jasper David Campbell *b* 1996, Natasha Sylvia Campbell *b* (twin) 1996. *Residence* – The Coach House, Greywell Hill, Hook, Hants RG29 1DG.
Lady Nell Carleton, *b* 1937: *m* 1962 (*m diss* 19—), Capt Michael Patrick Radcliffe Boyle, Irish Guards (ret) (*see* E Shannon, colls). *Residence* – The Dower House, Greywell, Hook, Hants.

PREDECESSORS – **(1)** *Rt Hon Sir* JAMES HARRIS, GCB, PC, el son of James Harris, MP, Sec and Comptroller to Queen Charlotte (wife of King George III), *b* 1746; an eminent diplomatist; was Ambassador to Spain 1771, to Berlin 1772, to Russia 1776, to the Hague 1783 and 1788, and to France 1796-7, Lieut Gov of Isle of Wight 1807, and Lord-Lieut of Hants; *cr Baron Malmesbury*, of Malmesbury, co Wilts (peerage of Great Britain) 1788, and *Viscount FitzHarris* and *Earl of Malmesbury* (peerage of Great Britain) 1800; *s* by his el son **(2)** JAMES EDWARD, 2nd Earl, *b* 1778; was MP for Helston 1802, and Gov of the Isle of Wight: *m* 1806, Harriet Susan, who *d* 1815, da of Francis Bateman Dashwood, of Well Vale, Lincolnshire; *d* 1841; *s* by his el son **(3)** JAMES HOWARD, GCB, PC, 3rd Earl, *b* 1807; sat as MP for Wilton (C) 1841; Sec for Foreign Affairs 1852, and 1858-9, and Lord Privy Seal 1866-8, and 1874-6: *m* 1st, 1830, Lady Corisande Emma Bennet, who *d* 1876, da of 5th Earl of Tankerville; 2ndly, 1880, Susan, who *d* 1935 (having *m* 2ndly, 1896, Maj-Gen Sir John Charles Ardagh, KCMG, KCIE, CB, LLD, RE, who *d* 1907), da of late John Hamilton, of Fyne Court, Somerset; *dsp* 1889; *s* by his nephew **(4)** EDWARD JAMES, 4th Earl (el son of late Adm Hon Sir Edward Alfred John Harris, KCB, 2nd son of 2nd Earl), *b* 1842; Lieut-Col (ret) 2nd Batn Roy Irish Rifles: *m* 1870, Sylvia Georgina, who *d* 1934, yr da of late

Alexander Stewart, of Ballyedmond Castle, Rostrevor, co Down; *d* 1899; *s* by his el son **(5)** JAMES EDWARD, 5th Earl, *b* 1872; was Assist Private Sec (unpaid) to Under Sec of State for the Colonies 1901, a Co Councillor for London 1904-5, a Lord-in-Waiting to HM 1922-24, and Chm of Hants Co Council 1927-38: *m* 1905, Hon Dorothy Gough Calthorpe, CBE, who *d* 1972, yst da of 6th Baron Calthorpe; *d* 1950; *s* by his only son **(6)** WILLIAM JAMES, 6th Earl and present peer; also Viscount FitzHarris, and Baron Malmesbury.

Maltravers, Lord; grandson of Duke of Norfolk

MALVERN, VISCOUNT (Huggins) (Viscount UK 1955)

Let us all persevere together

ASHLEY KEVIN GODFREY HUGGINS, 3rd Viscount; *b* 26 Oct 1949; *s* 1978.

Arms – Argent, on a fesse sable between three hearts gules a lion passant guardant or. **Crest** – A lion sejant rampant guardant or the sinister paw resting on a fountain. **Supporters** – *Dexter*, a lion guardant gules grasping in the exterior forepaw a rod of aesculapius proper; *sinister*, a sable antelope guardant proper.
Address – c/o Standard Bank, Cecil Sq, Harare, Zimbabwe.

BROTHER LIVING

Hon Michael Patrick John *b* 1946.

SISTER LIVING

Hon Haoli Elizabeth Jane, *b* 1953.

UNCLE LIVING (*Son of 1st Viscount*)

Hon (MARTIN) JAMES, *b* 13 Jan 1928; *ed* Hilton Coll, Natal; a farmer.

WIDOW LIVING OF SECOND VISCOUNT

PATRICIA MARJORIE (*Viscountess Malvern*), da of Frank Renwick-Bower, of Durban: *m* (Jan) 1949, the 2nd Viscount Malvern, who *d* 1978.

PREDECESSORS – **(1)** *Rt Hon Sir* GODFREY MARTIN Huggins, CH, KCMG, FRCS, son of late Godfrey Huggins; *b* 1883; Prime Min of S Rhodesia 1933-53 and Fedn of Rhodesia and Nyasaland 1953-56; *cr Viscount Malvern*, of Rhodesia and of Bexley, co Kent (peerage of UK) 1955: *m* 1921, Blanche Elizabeth, who *d* 1976, da of late James Slatter, of Pietermaritzburg, Natal; *d* 1971; *s* by his el son **(2)** JOHN GODFREY, 2nd Viscount, *b* 1922; 1939-45 War as Fl/Lt RAF; pilot with a commercial airline in Rhodesia: *m* (Jan) 1949, Patricia Marjorie, da of Frank Renwick-Bower, of Durban; *d* 1978; *s* by his yr son **(3)** ASHLEY KEVIN GODFREY, 3rd Viscount, and present peer.

MANCHESTER, DUKE OF (Montagu) (Duke GB 1719)

By disposing of me, not by changing me

ANGUS CHARLES DROGO MONTAGU, 12th Duke; *b* 9 Oct 1938; *s* 1985; *ed* Gordonstoun: *m* 1st, 1961 (*m diss* 1970), Mary Eveleen, da of Walter Gillespie McClure, of Geelong, Australia; 2ndly, 1971 (*m diss* 1985), Diane Pauline, da of Arthur Plimsaul, of 50 Highmoor Rd, Corfe Mullen, Wimborne, Dorset; 3rdly, 1989, Mrs Ann-Louise Bird, da of Dr Alfred Butler Taylor, of Cawthorne, S Yorks, and has issue by 1st *m*.

Arms – Quarterly: 1st and 4th argent, three lozenges conjoined in fesse gules, within a bordure sable, *Montagu*; 2nd and 3rd or, an eagle displayed vert, beaked and membered gules, *Monthermer*. **Crest** – A griffin's head couped at the neck or, gorged with a plain collar argent, charged with three lozenges gules between two wings sable. **Supporters** – *Dexter*, a heraldic antelope, or, armed, unguled, and tufted argent: a *sinister*, griffin, wings elevated or, collared as in the crest.
Residence – 15 Broad Reach, The Embankment, Bedford MK40 3PB.

SONS LIVING (By 1st marriage)

ALEXANDER CHARLES DAVID DROGO (*Viscount Mandeville*), *b* 11 Dec 1962; *ed* Geelong Church of England Gram Sch; Pres Global Atlantic Investments and Summit Investments, Turks and Caicos Is, BWI: *m* 1992, Wendy Dawn, da of Michael Buford, of Anaheim Hill, Calif, and has issue. *Residence* – 537 Newport Center Drive, Newport Beach, California 92660, USA.

SON LIVING — Alexander Michael Charles David Francis George Edward William Kimble Drogo (*Lord Kimbolton*), *b* 13 May 1993.
DAUGHTER LIVING — *Hon* Ashley Faith Maxine Nell, *b* 1999.

Lord Kimble, *b* 1964.

DAUGHTER LIVING (By 1st marriage)

Lady Emma (PO Box 43, Toorak, Victoria 3142, Australia), *b* 1965.

WIDOW LIVING OF TENTH DUKE

ELIZABETH (*Dowager Duchess of Manchester*) (PO Box 303, Pebble Beach, California 93953, USA; Ca Vendramin, 13 Giudecca, 30123 Venice, Italy), da of Samuel Clyde Fullerton, of Miami, USA, and formerly wife of W. W. Crocker: *m* 1969, as his 2nd wife, the 10th Duke of Manchester, who *d* 1977.

COLLATERAL BRANCHES LIVING

Issue of late Lord Edward Eugene Fernando Montagu, yr son of 9th Duke, *b* 1906, *d* 1954: *m* 1st, 1929 (*m diss* 1937), Norah Macfarlane, da of Albert Edward Potter, of Ontario, Canada; 2ndly, 1937 (*m diss* 1947), Dorothy Vera Peters; 3rdly 1947, Martha Mathews Hatton Bowen, who *d* 1951; 4thly 1953, Roberta (*dec*), da of Mrs Flora Herald Joughin:—
(By 1st *m*) Roderick Edward Drogo, *b* 1930: *m* 1968, Mary Deas.

Grandchildren of late Lt-Cdr Robert Acheson Cromie Montagu, RN, 2nd son (by 1st *m*) of Rt Hon Lord Robert Montagu (infra):—
Issue of late John Michael Cromie Montagu, *b* 1881, *d* 1966; *m* 1907, Libia Maria, who *d* 1979, da of late Senor Martin Montes, of Quilmes, Argentine Republic:—
Robert Alexander (88 Chestnut Rise, Plumstead, SE18 1RL), *b* 1917: *m* 1946, Eileen Teresa, da of John Lamont, and has issue living, Michael Anthony, *b* 1955, — Eileen Patricia, *b* 1947: *m* 1968, Hugh McGarry, of 3 Antrim Gdns, Portrush, co Antrim, and has issue living, Stephen Hugh *b* 1968, Michael Edward Drogo *b* 1983, Shirley Ellen *b* 1969, Alicia Patricia Teresa *b* 1971, Susan Mary Doreen *b* 1975, — Sylvia Valerie Heather, *b* 1949: *m* 1969, Colin Sidney Brooks, of 12 Leckwith Av, Bexleyheath, Kent, and has issue living, Stuart Robert *b* 1971, Steven Alexander *b* 1982, Cheryl Ann *b* 1973, — Cynthia Christine Jeanette, *b* 1949 (twin): *m* 1st, 1967 (*m diss* 1979), David Nicholls; 2ndly, 1979, Victor Pawley, of Portsmouth, Hants, and has issue living (by 1st *m*), Michael David Nicholls *b* 1967 (assumed the surname of PAWLEY by deed poll 1979), Robert Alexander *b* 1972 (assumed the surname of PAWLEY by deed poll 1979), (by 2nd *m*) Rebecca Jane *b* 1974, Dawn Michele (twin) *b* 1974, — Helena May, *b* 1951: *m* 1973, Peter George Suckling, of 21 First Av, Bexleyheath, Kent DA7 5SS, and has issue living, Jayne Ellen *b* 1981, Louise Ann *b* 1984, — Deirdre Veronica, *b* 1959: *m* 1982, Brian Richards, of 132 Sutherland Av, Welling, Kent, and has issue living, Barry Charles Montagu *b* 1984, Alan James Montagu *b* 1986, Michael Anthony Montagu *b* 1988. —— Alicia May JOHNSON MONTAGU (30 Canterbury Court, Station Rd, Dorking, Surrey RH4 1HH), *b* 1919: assumed by deed poll 1963 the surname of Johnson Montagu: *m* 1st, 1941, Fl-Lt Stuart James Lovell, RAF, who was *ka* 1944; 2ndly, 1946 (*m diss* 1963), John Dobney Johnson, PhD, and has issue living, (by 2nd *m*), Adrian Michael Montagu, *b* 1947: *m* 1982, Elizabeth Ann, da of late T. J. O'Shea, of Maesteg, S Wales, — Warwick Martin Montagu, *b* 1950: *m* 1970, Gaye Marina Harding, and has issue living, Robert James *b* 1978, Simon David *b* 1981, Melissa Gaye *b* 1973, Sarah Louise *b* 1975, — Phillip Leicester Montagu (Brook Cottage, Yeovil

Marsh, Som), *b* 1951: *m* 1973, Fiona Madeleine Williams, and has issue living, Rebecca Claire Montagu *b* 1981, — Michèle Veronica Montagu, *b* 1953: *m* 1st, 1973 (*m diss* 1982), Alan Craig Worrell; 2ndly, 1984, David John Robinson.

Issue of late Austin Robert Montagu, *b* 1885, *d* 1958: *m* 1934, Violet Vera, who *d* 1982, da of late Charles William Sandles:—
Henry Robert Sanderson (22 Sandpiper St, Florida Lake, Florida 1709, S Africa), *b* 1935: *m* 1963, Margaret Elizabeth, da of Norman Sinclair Pyper, of Sandpiper St, Florida, and has issue living, Gail, *b* 1968: *m* 1986, John Dugmore, and has issue living, Lloyd John *b* 1986, Robyn Gail *b* 1991, — Janet Frances, *b* 1972: *m* 1993, Craig John Fraser. —— Cyril John Sanderson (101 Melville Av, Ontdekkers Park, Florida 1709, S Africa), *b* 1937: *m* 1966, Annette Mary, da of late Castlyn Barnard, and has issue living, Graeme Peter, *b* 1967, — Christopher John *b* 1968. —— Gerard Philip Sanderson (35 Boeing Drive, Helderkruin ext 1, Roodepoort 1725, S Africa), *b* 1940: *m* 1963, Elizabeth Sinden, da of late John Sinden Jarvis, and has issue living, Matthew Gerard, *b* 1976, — Alison Elizabeth, *b* 1971.

Grandchildren of late Capt Monthermer Stanley Hume Montagu, MC, eldest son (by 2nd *m*) of late Rt Hon Lord Robert Montagu, MP (infra):—
Issue of late Capt Walter Bernard St John Montagu, TD, *b* 1915, *d* (April) 1992: *m* 1948, Doris Jean, who *d* (Jan) 1992, da of late J. Albany Morton, of Culzean, Busby, Lanarks:—
John Charles Monthermer Albany, *b* 1951; *ed* Gordonstoun, and Hull Univ (LLB); late Gren Gds and HAC. —— Elizabeth Anne Kennedy (15 Priory Rd, Cambridge CB5 8HT), *b* 1949: *m* 1971 (*m diss* 1983), Victor Bayntun Hippisley, and has issue living, Antonia Frances Serena Olivia, *b* 1975.

Grandchildren of late Rt Hon Lord Robert Montagu, MP, 2nd son of 6th Duke:—
Issue of late Capt Henry Bernard Montagu, RN, *b* 1872, *d* 1941: *m* 1922, Rosamond, who *d* 1972, da of late Dudley Bowditch Fay, of Boston, USA:—
John Drogo, *b* 1923; MRCS England and LRCP London, 1946; late Surg-Lieut RNVR: *m* 1946, Katharine Mary, da of late Brig-Gen Noble Fleming Jenkins, CMG, CBE, and has issue living, Robert Drogo (7 St Margaret's Close, Barming, Maidstone, Kent), *b* 1947: *m* 1st, 1970 (*m diss* 1985), Glenis Diane Littaur; 2ndly, 1985, Lancy Lim, and has issue living (by 1st *m*) James Drogo *b* 1975, Rachel Bernard *b* 1974, — Christopher Bernard (c/o National Westminster Bank, Covent Garden, WC2E 8NN), *b* 1950; Acting Group Capt RAF: *m* 1975, Christine Elizabeth Peatfield, and has issue living, David William *b* 1976, Thomas Edward *b* 1979, — Rosamond Anne *b* 1953: *m* 1984, Jonathan Chapple, of 30 Barham Rd, Wimbledon, SW20 0ET, and has issue living, Katharine Rose *b* 1984. *Residence* – High Acre, Hunger Hill, East Stour, Gillingham, Dorset SP8 5JR. —— Katharine Anne, *b* 1925; MSc (London 1952), BA (Farnham 1998).

(Not in remainder to Dukedom)

Descendants of late Hon James Montagu, MP, 3rd son of 1st Earl of Manchester:—

Grandsons of late Col Edward Montagu, CBE, 2nd son of late Gen Sir Horace William Montagu, KCB, 3rd son of late Rev George Montagu, 2nd son of late Gerard Montagu, 3rd in descent from late James Montagu, eldest son of late Hon James Montagu, MP (ante):—
Issue of late Capt Charles Edward Montagu, late RE, *b* 1900, *d* 1995: *m* 1928, Rachel Alice, who *d* 1996, da of late W. H. Martin, of Shrublands, Swaffham, Norfolk:—
Michael Drogo, *b* 1929; Maj RA: *m* 1955, Verity Jane, da of late William James Coode, OBE, of Polgooth, St Austell, Cornwall, and has issue living, Richard Lionel James (Jocks Lodge, Geldeston, Norfolk), *b* 1956: *m* 1984, Aileen Amanda, da of Charles Gordon Birchall, of The Close, Norwich, and has issue living, George Charles Drogo *b* 1993, Lucy Elizabeth *b* 1990, — Alan Edward, *b* 1958: *m* 1990, Louise Helen, twin da of A. G. H. Gaden, of Trull, Taunton, Som, and has issue living, Miles Sebastian Roland *b* 1994, Madeleine *b* 1993, — James Robert, *b* 1962. —— Ralph Edward (Old Hall Farm, Ringsfield, Beccles, Suffolk), *b* 1932: *m* 1st, 1963, June Margaret (Lisa), who *d* 1979, only da of late James Wiliam Finlayson, of Vaucluse, Sydney, Australia; 2ndly, 1989, Stephanie Roberta, da of late Patrick Arthur Cattell, of Pallastown, Belgooly, co Cork, and formerly wife of Don Leavy, of Kilbritain, co Cork, and has issue living (by 1st *m*), David Charles, *b* 1965, — Caroline Elizabeth, *b* 1964, — Victoria Jane, *b* 1967: *m* 1993, Julian J. Brown, son of J. E. Brown, of Dauntsey Lock, Wilts, and has issue living, Olivia Liza *b* 1996, — Katharine Fiona, *b* (twin) 1967.

Grandsons of late Maj James Gerard Edgar Drogo Montagu, only son of late Capt Cecil Edgar Montagu, yr son of late Edgar Montagu, 3rd and yst son of late Gerard Montagu (ante):—
Issue of late Lt-Cdr William Gerard Drogo Montagu, RN, *b* 1921, *d* 1991: *m* 1950, Charlotte Delma (7 Shernfold Park, Frant, E Sussex TN3 9DL), only child of late Frank Reitmeyer Calburn, of Effingham Manor, Surrey:—
Charles Edward Drogo, *b* 1952; *ed* Tonbridge Sch, and CCC, Oxford: *m* 1986, Marie-Jocelyne, da of Gabriel Dardenne, of Napier Rd, Tottenham, and has issue living, Edward Harry, *b* 1990, — Robert William, *b* 1997, — Emily Frances, *b* 1993. —— Francis Gerard Drogo (White Lodge, Ropers Lane, Wrington, N Som), *b* (twin) 1952; *ed* Tonbridge Sch, and Pembroke Coll, Camb; Solicitor: *m* 1991, Olivia Mary, da of Dr Patrick John Hardie, MBE, of Elm Cottage, Shipton Moyne, Tetbury, Glos. —— James William Drogo (Culvers, Hartfield, E Sussex), *b* 1954; *ed* Tonbridge Sch: *m* 1979, Charlotte Elizabeth, da of Richard John Goad Crosfield, of May Hill House, Droxford, Hants, and has issue living, Elizabeth Charlotte Ann, *b* 1983, — Sarah Caroline, *b* 1985.

Grandsons of late Capt George Edward Montagu, el son of late Adm John William Montagu, son of late Adm Sir George Montagu, GCB, son of late Adm John William Montagu, MP (infra):—
Issue of late John William Montagu, *b* 1877, *d* 1954: *m* 1913, Violet Irene, who *d* 1970, da of James Shuter, late of Little Park, Newbury:—
(John) Drogo, *b* 1916; *ed* Exeter Sch, and RMC Sandhurst; Lt-Col (ret) Indian Army; Far East 1939-45 (despatches): *m* 1952, Dorothy Boreham, who *d* 1990, yr da of C. E. Chuter, of Brisbane, Australia, and has issue living, Michael Charles Drogo, *b* 1956; Lt-Col ILI: *m* 1984, Caroline Louise Marie, only da of John George Griffiths, of Algarve, Portugal, and has issue living, James Robert Drogo *b* 1985, Frederic Charles *b* 1988, Arthur John *b* 1992, — Nigel Edward, *b* 1958; Lt-Col RE, — Richard John (Cardadoc, Church St, Clun, Shropshire SY7 8JW), *b* 1959; *ed* Pocklington Sch, and RMA Sandhurst; Major LI (ret): *m* 1986, Jane Emma, da of Bruce Pearson, of Guifron Bank, Bettws-y-Crwyn, Shropshire, and has issue living, Edward Drogo *b* 1989, George Ferdinand *b* 1990, — Sally Ann, *b* 1954: *m* 1988, Lt-Col Harold Crispin Hardy Ellison, MBE, RTR, son of His Honour Judge (John Harold) Ellison, of Egham, Surrey, and has issue living, Henry *b*

19—, Robert Hamilton Montagu *b* 1997, Harriet Dorothy Montagu *b* 1992, — Felicity Jane, *b* 1960: *m* 1985, Alan Sutherland Nixon, son of Prof George Sutherland Nixon, of St Andrews, and has issue living, Luke Sutherland *b* 1996, Olivia Chuter *b* 1990. *Residence* – The Officer's House, Freshwater, I of Wight. —— James Edward, *b* 1920; late Capt RA; 1939-45 War: *m* 1946, Joan, da of late J. McPherson, of Fieldway, Barrow-in-Furness, and has issue living, Philip James, *b* 1949: *m* 1971, Jennifer, da of Leonard Lower, of Brighton, and has issue living, Darren James *b* 1971: *m* 1997, Kay, da of Wolf Dietrich Roller, of Edinburgh, Paul Andrew *b* 1974, Rachel Mary *b* 1980, — Robin William, *b* 1953: *m* 1986, Janice, da of John Threlkeld Taylor, of Oldham. *Residence* – 64 Hill Rd, Barrow-in-Furness, Lancashire.

Grandchildren of late John Francis Vaughan Montagu (infra):—
Issue of late John Edward Coley Montagu, *b* 1910, *d* 1983: *m* 1st, 1936 (*m diss* 1955), Flora Elizabeth, who *d* 1981, da of late Col James Robertson-Cumming, of Langrigg, Strathearn, Scotland; 2ndly, 1958, Anne Alice Harriet (47 Pomona Gdns, Hillcrest, Natal, S Africa), da of late Col Donald Rolfe Hunt, of Natal, S Africa:—
(By 1st *m*) John Anthony Francis (3 Kelvin Grove, Beacon Bay, E London, S Africa), *b* 1938: *m* 1966, Denise Catherine, eldest da of late James Peter Dallas, of E London, S Africa, and has issue living, James Anthony John, *b* 1976, — Joanne Catherine, *b* 1969, — Leigh Elizabeth, *b* 1971. —— David Vaughan, *b* 1948: *m* 1976, Victoria Alice, yr da of Allan Cunningham, of 4 Riverside Av, Newquay, Cornwall, and has issue living, Christopher John Allan, *b* 1977, — Laura Anne, *b* 1979. —— Gillian Denise, *b* 1940: *m* 1966, Michael Keyworth Glover, of 35 Esmeralda Cres, Randburg, Transvaal, and has issue living, Mark Keyworth, *b* 1968, — Marguerite Tracey, *b* 1967, — Jennifer Lynn, *b* 1972.

Grandson of late Edward Vaughan Montagu, 2nd son of late John Edward Montagu, eldest son of late John Montagu (*b* 1797) (infra):—
Issue of late John Francis Vaughan Montagu, *b* 1877, *d* 1960: *m* 1909, Ada Mary, who *d* 1957, da of late James Dougal Coley, of Claremont, Cape Town, S Africa:—
Denis Vaughan, *b* 1913: *m* 1st, 1939, Margarieta, who *d* 1981, da of Henry Usher Gradwell, of Bloemfontein, S Africa; 2ndly, 1983, Joan Patricia Chambers. *Residence* – 65 Gold Reef Village, Brakpan, Transvaal, S Africa.

Grandsons of late Frederick George Montagu, 4th son of late John Edward Montagu (ante):—
Issue of late Arthur Drogo Turing Montagu, *b* 1900, *d* 1969: *m* 1934, Dorothy Rittener, el da of Harry Taylor Pitt, of Hill-Top, Woodingdean, Brighton:—
John Drogo (56 Brookdale Av, Pinelands, 7405 S Africa), *b* 1935: *m* 1980, Margaret, 2nd da of late Lt-Cdr John Richard Windle, RNR, of Broadway House, Broadway, Blyth, Northumberland. —— William Pitt (13 Windsor Rd, Oosterzee, 7500 S Africa) *b* 1939: *m* 1966, Elsa, da of late J. A. Fourie, of Eerste River, Cape, and has issue living, Michelle, *b* 1969, — Colleen, *b* 1971, — Wendy (twin) *b* 1971.

Grandchildren of late Lieut-Gen Alfred Worsley Montagu, yr son of late John Montagu (*b* 1797), son of late Lt-Col Edward Montagu, 4th son of late Adm John Montagu, great grandson of late Hon James Montagu, MP, (ante):—
Issue of late Alfred Worsley Montagu, *b* 1860, *d* 191—: *m* 1887, Ruth Lily Wallace, of Stawell, Victoria, Australia:—
Herbert Clive, *b* 1897. —— Ruth Mabel Josephine, *b* 1888. —— Jeffie Ina, *b* 1891. —— Vere Faerie, *b* 1984.

PREDECESSORS – (1) *Sir* HENRY Montagu, PC; MP for London 1604-16, and Recorder of London; appointed Lord Ch Justice of the King's Bench 1615, Lord Treasurer of England 1620, and Lord Privy Seal 1626; *cr Baron Montagu*, of Kimbolton, co Huntingdon, and *Viscount Mandeville* (peerage of England) 1620, and *Earl of Manchester* (peerage of England) 1626; *d* 1642; *s* by his son (2) EDWARD, 2nd Earl, KG, KB, PC, FRS, who had previously been summoned to Parl as *Baron Kimbolton*; was a distinguished Gen in the Parliamentary army, and gained the celebrated victory at Marston Moor; he refused to sanction the execution of Charles I, and retired from Parliament until 1660, when he voted for the restoration of Charles II, and was deputed by the Lords as their speaker to congratulate the King upon his return to his capital; Lord Chamberlain 1660-71, Chancellor of Camb Univ 1660-71, Lord-Lieut of Hunts and Northants; *d* 1671; *s* by his son (3) ROBERT, 3rd Earl; MP for Hunts 1660-71, Lord-Lieut of Hunts *d* 1682; *s* by his son (4) CHARLES, PC, 4th Earl; served at the battle of the Boyne; was Ambassador to Venice 1696, to France 1699, and to Vienna 1707, Principal Sec of State 1701, Lord-Lieut of Hunts, and a Lord of the Bedchamber to George I; *cr Duke of Manchester* (peerage of Great Britain) 1719; *d* 1722; *s* by his el son (5) WILLIAM, KB, 2nd Duke; Capt Yeomen of the Guard 1737-39, Lord-Lieut of Hunts, Lord of the Bedchamber to King George I and King George II *d* 1739; *s* by his brother (6) ROBERT, 3rd Duke; MP for Hunts 1734-39, Lord Chamberlain to Queen Charlotte 1761, Lord-Lieut of Hunts, Lord of the Bedchamber to King George II *d* 1762; *s* by his son (7) GEORGE, PC, 4th Duke; Master of the Horse 1780; Lord Chamberlain 1782-83; Ambassador to France 1783, Lord-Lieut of Hunts, Lord of the Bedchamber to King George III *d* 1788; *s* by his son (8) WILLIAM, 5th Duke; was Gov of Jamaica 1807-27; Postmaster Gen 1827-30; Collector of Customs for Port of London, and Lord-Lieut of Hunts: *m* 1793, Lady Susan Gordon, who *d* 1828, da of 4th Duke of Gordon, KT, FRS; *d* 1843; *s* by his son (9) GEORGE, 6th Duke; a Com RN, MP for Hunts (C) 1826-37: *m* 1st, 1822, Millicent, who *d* 1848, da of Gen R. B. Sparrow, of Brampton Park, Hunts; 2ndly, 1850, Harriet Sydney (who *d* 1907, having *m* 2ndly, 1858, Sir Stevenson Arthur Blackwood, KCB), da of Conway Richard Dobbs, MP, of Castle Dobbs, co Antrim; *d* 1855; *s* by his son (10) WILLIAM DROGO, KP, 7th Duke, *b* 1823; sat as MP for Bewdley (C) 1848-52, and for Huntingdonshire 1852-5; Capt Gren Gds, Col Hunts Mil, a Lord of the Bedchamber to the Prince Consort 1852: *m* 1852, Countess Louise Frederica Augusta, who *d* 1911 (having *m* 2ndly, 1892, 8th Duke of Devonshire), da of Count von Alten, of Hanover; *d* 1890; *s* by his el son (11) GEORGE VICTOR DROGO, 8th Duke, *b* 1853; Capt R Irish Fus; MP for Hunts 1877-80: *m* 1876, Consuela Yznaga, who *d* 1909, da of Senor Antonio Yznaga de Valle, of Louisiana, USA, and Cuba; *d* 1892; *s* by his el son (12) WILLIAM ANGUS DROGO, PC, 9th Duke *b* 1877; Capt Lancs Fus; Capt of Yeomen of the Guard 1906-7: *m* 1st, 1900 (*m diss* 1931), Helena, who *d* 1971, having *m* 2ndly, 1937, 10th Earl of Kintore, da of late Eugene Zimmerman, of Cincinnati, USA; 2nd, 1931, Kathleen, who *d* 1966, da of W. H. Dawes, *d* 1947; *s* by his son (13) ALEXANDER GEORGE FRANCIS DROGO, OBE, 10th Duke, *b* 1902; Cdr RN; ret 1930: *m* 1st, 1927, Nell Vere, who *d* 1966, da of Sidney Vere Stead, of Melbourne; 2ndly, 1969, Elizabeth, da of Samuel Clyde Fullerton, of Miami, USA, and formerly wife of W. W. Crocker; *d* 1977; *s* by his el son (14) SIDNEY ARTHUR ROBIN GEORGE DROGO, 11th Duke, *b* 1929: *m* 1st, 1955 (*m diss* 1978), (Adrienne) Valerie, who *d* 1988, da of late John Kenneth Christie, of Sedgerfield, Cape Prov, S Africa; 2ndly, 1978, Andrea, who *d* 1996, da of Cecil Alexander Joss, of Johnannesburg, and formerly wife of (i) Maj Stuart Whitehead, and (ii) G. J. W. Kent; *d* 1985; *s* by his brother (15) ANGUS CHARLES DROGO, 12th Duke and present peer; also Earl of Manchester, Viscount Mandeville, and Baron Montagu of Kimbolton.

MANCROFT, BARON (Mancroft) (Baron UK 1937, Bt UK 1932)

BENJAMIN LLOYD STORMONT MANCROFT, 3rd Baron; *b* 16 May 1957; *s* 1987; *ed* Eton; MFH; Chm Drug and Alcohol Foundation since 1994; Chm Addiction Recovery Foundation since 1989; Dir Phoenix House Housing Assoc 1989-95 (Vice-Chm 1992-95); Dep Chm British Field Sports Soc 1992-98; Dir Countryside Alliance since 1998; Chm Inter Lotto (UK) Ltd since 1995; MFH, VWH Hunt 1987-89; Patron Osteopathic Centre for Children, Patsy Hardy Trust and Sick Dentists Trust: *m* 1990, Emma L., eldest da of Thomas Peart, of Addison Rd, W8, and has issue.

Arms – Gules, a chevron chequy argent and sable, between in chief two portcullises chained and in base a castle (Farnham) triple towered or, on a chief of the last a lion pasant guardant of the third. **Crest** – In front of a castle (Norwich) with three cupolas, issuant from each a staff proper flying therefrom a banner argent, charged with a cross gules, a sword sheathed also gules, garnished or, pomel and hilt of the last, and a mace gold in salt-ire (ie, a representative of the ancient Crystal Mace and the Sword in the Regalia of the Corporation of the City of Norwich). **Supporters** – On either side a Whiffler of the Corporation of the City of Norwich.
Address – House of Lords, SW1A 0PW.

SONS LIVING

Hon ARTHUR LOUIS STORMONT, *b* 3 May 1995.
Hon Maximilian Michael, *b* 1998.

DAUGHTER LIVING

Hon Georgia Esme, *b* 1993.

SISTERS LIVING

Hon Victoria (*Princess Nicholas von Preussen*), *b* 1952: *m* 1980, HRH Prince (*Frederick*) Nicholas von Preussen, of Maperton House, Wincanton, Som, and has issue (*see* Royal Family).
Hon Jessica Rosetta, *b* 1954: *m* 1983, as his 2nd wife, Simon Clervaux Dickinson (*see* Chaytor, Bt, 1990 Edn), of Wortley House, Wotton-under-Edge, Glos, and has issue living, Milo Clervaux Mancroft, *b* 1989, — Phoebe Victoria, *b* 1984, — Octavia Jessica, *b* 1986.

AUNT LIVING (*Daughter of 1st Baron*)

Hon Rosetta Mancroft SAMUEL, *b* 1918: *m* 1st, 1947, Alfred John Bostock Hill, late Puisne Judge, Malaya, who *d* 1959; 2ndly, 1966, Dr Cai Christian Holm, who *d* 1983. *Residence* – 12 Eaton Place, SW1.

PREDECESSORS – (1) ARTHUR MICHAEL SAMUEL, el son of late Benjamin Samuel, of Norwich; *b* 1872; Parliamentary Under-Sec of State for Foreign Affairs, Parliamentary Sec to Board of Trade, and Minister for Depart of Overseas Trade 1924-7, and Financial Sec to the Treasury 1927-9; Chm of Public Accounts Committee of House of Commons 1930 and 1931; was Lord Mayor of Norwich 1912-13, received Hon Freedom of City of Norwich 1928; sat as MP for Farnham Div of Surrey (*U*) 1918-37: *cr* a *Baronet* 1932, and *Baron Mancroft*, of Mancroft, in City of Norwich (peerage of UK) 1937: *m* 1912, Phoebe, who *d* 1969, 2nd da of late Dr (George) Alfred Chune Fletcher, Med Officer to the Charterhouse, London; *d* 1942; *s* by his son (2) STORMONT MANCROFT, KBE, TD, 2nd Baron, *b* 1914, Bar Inner Temple 1938, Pres London Tourist Board 1963-73, and of St Marylebone Conservative Assocn 1961-67, Lord-in-Waiting to HM 1952-54, Chm Horse-race Totalisator Board 1972-76; etc; served 1939-45 War as Lt-Col RA (TA) (despatches twice, MBE, Croix de Guerre); assumed by deed poll 1925 the surname of Mancroft: *m* 1951, Diana Elizabeth, who *d* 1999, only da of Lt-Col Horace Lloyd, DSO, and formerly wife of Richard St John Quarry; *d* 1987; *s* by his only son (3) BENJAMIN LLOYD STORMONT, 3rd Baron and present peer.

Mandeville, Viscount; son of Duke of Manchester

MANNERS, BARON (Manners) (Baron UK 1807)

In order to accomplish

JOHN ROBERT CECIL MANNERS, 5th Baron; *b* 13 Feb 1923; *s* 1972; *ed* Eton, and Trin Coll, Oxford; Fl-Lt RAFVR: *m* 1949, Jennifer Selena, who *d* 1996, da of late Stephen Ian Fairbairn (*see* Arbuthnot, Bt, colls, 1990 Edn), and has issue.

Arms – Or, two bars azure, a chief quarterly, azure and gules, the 1st and 4th quarters charged with two fleurs-de-lis gold, and the 2nd and 3rd with a lion of England. **Crest** – On a chapeau gules, turned up ermine, a peacock in pride proper. **Supporters** – Two unicorns, argent, armed, unguled, crined, and tufted, or, the *dexter* charged on the shoulder with a cross flory, azure; the *sinister* similarly charged with a portcullis, sable.
Residence – Sabines, Avon, Christchurch, Dorset. *Clubs* – Brooks's, Boodles'.

SON LIVING

Hon JOHN HUGH ROBERT, *b* 5 May 1956; *ed* Eton: *m* 1983, Lanya Mary Patricia, da of late Dr H. E. Heitz, and of Mrs Ian Jackson, of 23 Springfield Rd, NW8, and has issue living, Harriet Frances Mary, *b* 1988, — Catherine Mary Patricia, *b* 1992. *Residence* – North Ripley House, Avon, nr Christchurch, Dorset BH23 8EP. *Club* – Pratt's.

DAUGHTERS LIVING

Hon Venetia Jane, *b* 1950: *m* 1972, Alasdair John Colborne-Malpas, of Keeper's Cottage, Ramsdell, Hants.
Hon Selena Mary, 1952: *m* 1974, Maj Christopher Jeremy George Langlands, 1st The Queen's Drag Gds, of Hartgrove House, Shaftesbury, Dorset, and has issue living, Andrew Charles, *b* 1981, — George William, *b* 1987, — Lucinda Mary, *b* 1977.

BROTHERS LIVING

Hon Richard Neville, *b* 1924; *ed* Eton: *m* 1945, Juliet Mary, da of late Col Sir Edward Hulton Preston, 5th Bt, DSO, MC, and has issue living, Edward Preston (Askania Park, Ourimbah, NSW 2258, Australia; *Club* – The Australian), *b* 1948; *ed* Gresham's Sch, Holt; DUniv Newcastle: *m* 1973, Catherine, da of late Mr Justice (William) Ash, of Turramurra, NSW, and has issue living, Sarah Mary Ash *b* 1981, — Rupert Francis Henry (Box 788, Armidale, NSW 2350, Australia), *b* 1950; *ed* Gresham's Sch, Holt: *m* 1975, Wynn, da of W. Miller, of Sydney, NSW, and has issue living, Stephen Francis *b* 1978, Philip *b* 1980, — (Thomas) Benjamin CABBELL MANNERS (West Wing, Cromer Hall, Cromer, Norfolk), *b* 1954; *ed* Gresham's Sch, Holt: *m* 1981, Diana (Dido) Dorothy Elizabeth, yr da of Maj Anthony Richard Gurney, of Manor Farm, Northrepps, Cromer, Norfolk, and has issue living, Rupert *b* 1990, Hugh *b* 1993, Jessica *b* (twin) 1990, — Christine Margaret Lavender, *b* 1946: *m* 1970, Timothy John Barry Pallister, of The Old Vicarage, Tunstead, nr Wroxham, Norwich, Norfolk NR12 8HT, and has issue living, James Francis Timothy *b* 1971, Richard John *b* 1976, Charlotte Henrietta *b* 1972. *Residence* – South Wing, Cromer Hall, Norfolk.
Hon Thomas Jasper, *b* 1929; *ed* Eton: *m* 1955, Sarah, da of late Brigadier Roger Peake, DSO, OBE, and has issue living, Charles Henry, *b* 1957: *m* 1986, Nichola E., da of late Peter Howard Thompson, of Astley Farm, Bridgnorth, Shropshire, and has issue living, Joseph Peter *b* 1991, Ralph Frederick Sandys *b* 1995, Zoë *b* 1989, Molly Elizabeth *b* 1994, — Arthur Roger, *b* 1959: *m* 1984, Anna C. M., da of Roger Ryland, of 32A Pembroke Sq, W8, and has issue living, Hugo *b* 1989, Olivia *b* 19—, Laura *b* 1996, — Robert Hugh, *b* 1962: *m* 1989, Samantha S., da of Richard Jukes, of Old Rectory, Pattiswick, Braintree, Essex, and has issue living, Archie Thomas *b* 1993, Orlando Douglas *b* 1995, Humphrey Wilmot *b* 1998. *Residence* – The Old Malt House, Ashford Hill, Newbury, Berks. *Clubs* – White's; Pratt's.

SISTER LIVING

Hon Patricia Anne, *b* 1927: *m* 1946, John Bonham Kidston, late Lt Grenadier Guards, who *d* 1968 (Bonham, Bt), and has issue living, Francis George, *b* 1947, — Jonathan James, *b* 1951: *m* 1981, Joanna R., da of late Col Michael Panton, — Virginia Lilian, *b* 1953.

PREDECESSORS – (1) THOMAS Manners-Sutton, PC, 5th son of Lord George Manners Sutton (3rd son of 3rd Duke of Rutland and father of 1st Viscount Canterbury); was Solicitor Gen of England 1802-5, a Baron of the Exchequer in England 1805-7, and Lord Chancellor of Ireland 1807; *cr Baron Manners*, of Foston, co Lincoln (peerage of United Kingdom) 1807; *d* 1842; *s* by his son (2) JOHN THOMAS, 2nd Baron; *b* 1818: *m* 1848, Lydia Sophia, who *d* 1916, da of Vice-Adm William Bateman Dashwood; *d* 1864; *s* by his el son (3) JOHN THOMAS, 3rd Baron; *b* 1852: *m* 1st, 1885, Constance Edwina, who *d* 1920, da of late Col Henry Edward Hamilyn-Fane; 2ndly, 1922, Zoë Virginie, who *d* 1953, da of late Albert Llewellyn Nugent, and widow of Claude Hume Campbell Guinness; *d* 1927; *s* by his son (4) FRANCIS HENRY, MC, 4th Baron; *b* 1897: *m* 1921, Mary Edith, who *d* 1994, da of late Rt Rev Lord William Rupert Ernest Gascoyne-Cecil, DD, 65th Bishop of Exeter (M Salisbury); *d* 1972; *s* by his el son (5) JOHN ROBERT CECIL, 5th Baron, and present peer.

Manners, family name of Duke of Rutland.

MANSFIELD AND MANSFIELD, EARL OF (Murray) (Earl GB 1776 and 1792)

I hope for better things

Friendly to virtue alone

WILLIAM DAVID MUNGO JAMES MURRAY, 8th Earl; *b* 7 July 1930; *s* 1971; *ed* Wellesley House, Eton, and Ch Ch Oxford; Bar Inner Temple 1958; Lt Scots Gds (Reserve); Malaya 1949-50; Hereditary Keeper of Bruce's Castle of Lochmaben; Hon Sheriff of Perthshire 1974; a Co Councillor of Perthshire 1971-75, JP 1975, and DL Perth and Kinross since 1980; a Member of Tay Salmon Fishery Board 1971-79, and a Dir of General Accident Fire & Life Assurance Gp 1972-79 and 1985-98, and other cos; a Member of British Delegation to European Parl 1973-75, an Opposition Front Bench Spokesman in House of Lords 1975-79; Min of State Scottish Office 1979-83, Min of State N Ireland Office 1983-84; Pres of Scottish Assocn of Boys' Clubs 1974-79, Ordinary Dir of Royal Highland & Agric Soc 1976-79, Pres of Scottish Assocn for the Care and Resettlement of Offenders 1974-79, and Chm of Historic Houses Assocn in Scotland 1976-79; Pres of Saint Andrew Soc (Glasgow) 1972-82, Royal Scottish Country Dance Soc since 1977, and Fedn des Assocns de Chasse de l'Europe 1977-79, Hon Pres Scottish Beekeepers' Assocn; First Crown Estate Commissioner 1985-95: *m* 1955, Pamela Joan, (OStJ 1982), da of late Wilfred Neill Foster, CBE, and has issue.

Arms – Quarterly: 1st and 4th, azure, three mullets argent, within a double tressure flory counter flory or, *Murray*; 2nd and 3rd, gules, three crosses patée argent *Barclay*. **Crest** – A buck's head couped proper, between his attires a cross patée argent **Supporters** – Two lions gules, armed or.
Seat – Scone Palace, Perthshire PH2 6BE. *Town Residence* – 16 Thorburn House, Kinnerton St, SW1X 8EX. *Clubs* – Turf, Pratt's, White's, Beefsteak.

SONS LIVING

ALEXANDER DAVID MUNGO (*Viscount Stormont*), *b* 17 Oct 1956; *ed* Eton: *m* 1985, Sophia Mary Veronica, only da of late Philip Biden Derwent Ashbrooke (*see* B Mowbray, colls), of St John, Jersey, and has issue:—

SON LIVING - *Hon* William Philip David Mungo (*Master of Stormont*), *b* 1 Nov 1988.

DAUGHTERS LIVING - *Hon* Isabella Mary Alexandra, *b* 1987, — *Hon* Iona Margaret Sophia, *b* 1992, — *Hon* Louisa Frederica Olivia, *b* 1996.

Clubs – White's, Turf, Pratt's.
Hon James William, *b* 1969.

DAUGHTER LIVING

Lady Georgina Dorothea Mary, *b* 1967: *m* 1998, John L. Bullough, only son of Michael Bullough, of Westmains of Huntingtower, Perth.

SISTERS LIVING

Lady Malvina Dorothea (*Countess of Moray*), *b* 1936: *m* 1964, 20th Earl of Moray, of Doune Park, Doune, Perthshire, and Darnaway Castle, Forres, Morayshire.
Lady Mariota Cecilia, *b* 1945; *m* 1969, Hon (Charles) Malcolm Napier (*see* L Napier and Ettrick), of Bardmony House, Alyth, Perthshire.

COLLATERAL BRANCH LIVING

Issue of late Major Hon Alexander David Murray, brother of 6th Earl, *b* 1871, *d* 1924: *m* 1908, Christian Maule, who *d* 1964, da of Sir James Thomas Stewart-Richardson, 14th Bt:—
†David John, TD, *b* 1919; *ed* Wellington Coll, and at Magdalene Coll, Camb; Maj Seaforth Highlanders; European War 1939-45 in France, Middle East, Italy and Germany: *m* 1961, Joanna (Moy, Forres, Morayshire), da of late Lt J. G. Lincoln, RN, and *d* 1998, leaving issue, Alexander David, *b* 1963; *m* 1987, Susan Jayne, da of Brian Savage, and has issue living, Emma Kate *b* 1988, Adina Louise *b* 1990. — William John David, *b* 1976. —— Margot Louisa (Windyridge, Dunphail, Morayshire) *b* 1910. —— Elizabeth Helen (Ellangowan, 4 Polinard, Comrie, Crieff, Perthshire PH6 2HJ), *b* 1912: *m* 1937 (*m diss* 1945), Lt-Col Charles Richard Wynn Brewis, MC, Welch Regt, who *d* 1967, and has issue living, Simon David Richard Wynn, MBE, *b* 1941; Lt-Col Parachute Regt. —— Christian Anne (Roadside Cottage, Invergeldie, Comrie, Perthshire), *b* 1913; late 3rd Officer WRNS.

PREDECESSORS – (1) *Sir* DAVID Murray, Knt, Cupbearer and Master of the Horse, and Capt of the Guard to James VI of Scotland; accompanied the King to England, and was *cr Lord Scone* (peerage of Scotland) 1605, and *Viscount*

Stormont (peerage of Scotland) 1621, with remainder to Sir Mungo Murray, 4th son of John, 1st Earl of Tullibardine (D Atholl), to John (Earl of Annandale), and to Andrew Murray, who in 1641 was *cr Lord Balvaird* peerage of Scotland &c; *dsp* 1631; *s* by **(2)** *Sir* MUNGO, 2nd Viscount (ante); *dsp* 1642; *s* by **(3)** JAMES 3rd Viscount, who had previously *s* as 2nd *Earl of Annandale*; *dsp* 1658, when the Earldom of Annandale became extinct, and the Lordship of Scone and Viscountcy of Stormont devolved upon **(4)** DAVID, 4th Viscount, who had previously *s* by his father Andrew Murray (ante) as 2nd *Lord Balvaird*; was fined £1,500 by Cromwell's Act of grace and pardon 1654; *d* 1668; *s* by his son **(5)** DAVID, 5th Viscount; opposed the Union, and was called upon to surrender at the breaking out of the Rebellion 1715; *d* 1731; *s* by his son **(6)** DAVID, 6th Viscount; *d* 1748; *s* by his son **(7)** DAVID, KT, PC, 7th Viscount; was Justice Gen of Scotland, Ambassador to Paris and Vienna 1772-8, a Sec of State 1779-82, Pres of the Council, and a Representative Peer 1754-90; *s* his uncle as 2nd *Earl of Mansfield* (see * infra); *d* 1793; *m* 2ndly, 1776, Hon Louisa Cathcart (E Cathcart), who in 1793 *s* her uncle as Countess of Mansfield under patent of 1776, she *d* 1843, and was *s* by her grandson the 4th Earl; *d* 1796; *s* by his son **(8)** WILLIAM, KT, 3rd Earl; *b* 1777; was Lord-Lieut of Clackmannanshire: *m* 1797, Frederica, da of the Most Rev William Markham, Archbishop of York; *d* 1840; *s* by his son **(9)** WILLIAM DAVID, KT, 4th Earl; *b* 1806; MP for Aldborough *(C)* 1830, for Woodstock 1831, for Norwich 1832-7, and for Perthshire 1837-40; a Lord of the Treasury 1834-5, and Lord High Commr of Scottish Gen Assembly 1852, 1858, and 1859; Lord-Lieut and Sheriff Principal of Clackmannan; in 1843 *s* his grandmother (ante) in the Earldom of 1776: *m* 1829, Louisa, who *d* 1837, da of Cuthbert Ellison, of Hebburn, Durham; *d* 1898; *s* by his grandson **(10)** WILLIAM DAVID, PC (son of late William David, Viscount Stormont), 5th Earl; *b* 1860; *s* by his brother **(6)** ALAN DAVID, 6th Earl; *b* 1864; Gentleman Usher of the Green Rod (Order of the Thistle) 1895-1917: *m* 1899, Margaret Helen Mary, who *d* 1933, da of Sir Malcolm MacGregor, 4th Bt: *d* 1935; *s* by his son **(7)** MUNGO DAVID MALCOLM, 7th Earl; *b* 1900; Gov of Edinburgh and E of Scotland Coll of Agric 1925-30; Lord High Commr to Gen Assembly of Ch of Scotland 1961-62; Lord Lieut of Perthshire 1960-71; MP for Perthshire and Kinross 1931-35: *m* 1928, Dorothea Helena, who *d* 1985, da of late Rt Hon Sir Lancelot Douglas Carnegie, GCVO, KCMG (E Southesk, colls); *d* 1971; *s* by his son **(8)** WILLIAM DAVID MUNGO JAMES, 8th Earl and present peer; also Viscount Stormont, Lord Scone, and Lord Balvaird.

*(1) *Hon* WILLIAM Murray, 3rd son of 5th Viscount Stormont; successively Solicitor-Gen Attorney-Gen, and Lord Ch Justice of England; *cr Baron Mansfield*, co Notts (peerage of Great Britain) 1756, and *Earl of Mansfield*, co Nottingham (peerage of Great Britain) 1776, with remainder to his niece Louisa, wife of his nephew David, 7th Viscount Stormont, and *Earl of Mansfield*, co Middlesex (peerage of Great Britain) 1792, with remainder to his nephew David, 7th Viscount Stormont (ante); *dsp* 1793, when the Barony of Mansfield expired, and the Earldom of 1776 devolved upon LOUISA (ante), and the Earldom of 1792 upon his nephew DAVID, 7th Viscount Stormont (ante).

Mansfield, family name of Baron Sandhurst.

MANTON, BARON (Watson) (Baron UK 1922)

JOSEPH RUPERT ERIC ROBERT WATSON, 3rd Baron; *b* 22 Jan 1924; *s* 1968; *ed* Eton; late Capt 7th Hussars, and Life Guards; Sr Steward Jockey Club 1982-85 and former Jockey Club Representative on Horserace Betting Levy Bd 1970-75; DL Humberside 1980: *m* 1951, Mary Elizabeth, da of late Maj Thomas Dennehy Hallinan, of Ashbourne, Glounthaune, co Cork, and has issue.

Arms – Argent, on a chevron azure between four martlets, three in chief and one in base sable, a crescent between two roses of the field. **Crest** – A gryphon passant sable in front of an oak tree proper. **Supporters** – On either side a gryphon per fesse azure and argent, charged on the shoulder with a rose also argent. *Residence* – Houghton Hall, Sancton, York. *Clubs* – White's, Jockey.

SONS LIVING

Hon MILES RONALD MARCUS, *b* 7 May 1958; *ed* Eton; Maj Life Gds: *m* 1984, Elizabeth Adams, eldest da of Julian Russell Story, of Westcott, Surrey, and has issue living, Thomas Nigel Charles David, *b* 19 April 1985, — Ludovic Waldo Rupert, *b* 1989.

Hon Thomas Philip (triplet), *b* 1958; *ed* Eton, and RAC Cirencester; late Lt Queen's Own Hus, Lt Yorks Yeomanry: *m* 1988, Venetia Margaret Cadogan, da of Paul Spicer, of 22 Ovington Gdns, SW3, and has issue living, Alexander Paul Rupert, *b* 1989, — Tara Cadogan, *b* 1993.

DAUGHTERS LIVING

Hon Claire Georgina (*Baroness Hesketh*), *b* 1952: *m* 1977, 3rd Baron Hesketh, KBE, of Easton Neston, Towcester, Northants.

Hon Fiona Caroline Mary, *b* 1953: *m* 1978, Mark Swinfen Cottrell, of Molehill, Paris, Ashton-under-Hill, Evesham, Worcs, son of David Vernon Swynfen Cottrell, of Tewkesbury, Glos, and has issue living, George, b 1993, — Laura Marina, b 1988.

Hon Victoria Monica (triplet), b 1958: m 1993, as his 2nd wife, Anthony Henry (Harry) Westropp, of Wootton Downs Farmhouse, Woodstock, Oxon OX20 1AF, yr son of late Col Lionel Henry Mountifort Westropp, of Wye, Kent, and has issue living, a da, b 1993.

COLLATERAL BRANCHES LIVING

Issue of late Hon Robert Fraser Watson, 2nd son of 1st Baron, b 1900, d 1975: m 1st, 1928, Angela Blanche, who d 1959, da of late Lt-Col George Talbot Lake Denniss, R. Wilts Regt; 2ndly, 1961, Enid Agnes Maud, who d 1993, da of the late Arthur Levita, and formerly wife of Ewen Donald Cameron:—
(By 1st m) Shirley Angela Josephine, b 1932: m 1st, 1958 (m diss 1974), David T Chantler; 2ndly, 1977, John Hines Kennedy, MD (Harvard), of Old Court, Nethergate St, Clare, Suffolk; and 48 Egerton Gdns, SW3, and has issue living (by 1st m), Peter David Robert, b 1963, — Angela Margaret Jennifer, b 1961.

Issue of late Hon Alastair Joseph Watson, 3rd son of 1st Baron, b 1901, d 1955: m 1925, Joan, who d 1988, da of late Capt Philip Wyndham Cobbold (M Abergavenny, colls):—
Michael Oliver, b 1926; ed Stowe; late Capt Life Gds; JP: m 1950, Virginia, da of late Eustace Benyon Hoare (E Coventry), and has issue living, Alastair James, b 1958; ed Stowe; late Capt Life Gds: m 1991, Camilla Jane, da of Maj Christopher Wordsworth, late The Life Gds, and has issue living, Katharine Rachel b 1996, Laura Virginia b 1998, — George William, b 1962; ed Stowe, and Wye Coll London (MSc); Lt RN: m 1997, Alison Beryl Crane, — Amanda Virginia, b 1956: m 1985, Antony Richardson Finley, and has issue living, Harry George b 1987, Thomas Geoffrey b 1989, Toby Michael b 1995. *Residence* – Chillesford Lodge, Sudbourne, Woodbridge, Suffolk. *Club* – Cavalry. —— Andrew Philip, b 1930; ed Eton, and at Magdalene Coll, Camb (BA 1952, MA 1957): m 1957, Annette Mary Helena, da of Gerald Wellington Williams, JP (see D Northumberland, colls, 1985 Edn), and has issue living, Simon Mark, b 1959, — Nicholas Andrew, b 1961, — Jonathan Philip, b 1965, — Hugh Gerald, b 1968. *Residence* – Faldonside, Melrose, Roxburghshire.

PREDECESSORS – (1) JOSEPH Watson, only son of George Watson, of Donisthorpe House, Moor Allerton, Yorkshire; b 1873; Chm of Joseph Watson and Sons (Limited), and of Olympia Agricultural Co (Limited), and a Director of London and North-Western Railway; cr Baron Manton, of Compton Verney, co Warwick (peerage of United Kingdom) 1922: m 1898, Frances Claire, who d 1944, da of Harold Nickols, of Sandford House, Kirkstall, near Leeds, and 2 Seamore Place W: d 1922; s by his el son (2) GEORGE MILES, 2nd Baron, b 1899: m 1st, 1923 (m diss 1936), Alethea Alice Mary Pauline, who d 1979, da of late Lt-Col Philip Joseph Langdale, OBE, JP, DL (B Mowbray, colls); 2ndly, 1938, Leila Joan (who m 3rdly, 1969, as his 3rd wife, 6th Baron Brownlow, and d 1983) da of late Maj Philip Guy Reynolds, DSO, and formerly wife of late John Dane Player; d 1968; s by his only son (3) JOSEPH RUPERT ERIC ROBERT, 3rd Baron and present peer.

MANVERS, EARLDOM (Pierrepont) (Extinct 1955)

DAUGHTER LIVING OF SIXTH EARL

Lady (Frederica) Rozelle (Ridgway), b 1925; 1939-5 War as Leading Wren Stoker WRNS (1943-46), authoress: m 1st, 1953 (m diss 1961), Maj Alexander Montgomerie Greaves Beattie, Coldstream Gds; 2ndly, 1965, Richard Hollinge Raynes, MB, BS, DPH, MFCM. *Residences* – Dolphin's Leap, St Margaret's Bay, Kent CT15 6HP; 88 Narrow St, E14 8BP.

MAR, COUNTESS OF (of Mar) (Earl precedence S 1404)

Think more

MARGARET OF MAR, *Countess of Mar* in her own right (Premier Earldom of Scotland); *b* 19 Sept 1940; *s* 1975; recognised in the surname of "of Mar" by warrant of Lord Lyon 1967, when she abandoned her second christian name of Alison: *m* 1st, 1959 (*m diss* 1976), Edwin Noel Artiss (who was recognised in the surname of "of Mar" by warrant of the Lord Lyon 1969; 1967; 2ndly, 1976 (*m diss* 1981), John Leslie Salton, who was recognised in the surname of "of Mar" by warrant of the Lord Lyon 1976, when he abandoned his christian name of Leslie; 3rdly, 1982, John H. Jenkin, MA, FRCO, LRAM, ARCM, and has issue by 1st *m*.

Arms – Azure, a bend between six cross-crosslets fitchée or. Crest – Upon a chapeau gules faced ermine, two wings each of ten pen feathers, erected and addorsed both blazoned as the shield. Supporters – On either side a griffin argent, armed, beaked and winged or.
Residence – St Michael's Farm, Great Witley, Worcs WR6 6JB.

DAUGHTER LIVING (By 1st marriage)

Lady SUSAN HELEN (*Mistress of Mar*), *b* 31 May 1963: *m* 1989, Bruce Alexander Wyllie, and has issue living, Isabel Alice, *b* 10 Sept 1991, — Frances Alexandra, *b* 1994. *Residence* – Firethorn Farm Cottage, Plough Lane, Ewhurst Green, Cranleigh, Surrey GU6 7SG.

SISTER LIVING

Lady Janet Helen OF MAR, *b* 1946; *ed* St Andrews Univ (MA): *m* 1969, Lt-Cdr Laurence Duncan McDiarmid Anderson, MA, RN, who was recognised in the surname of "of Mar" by warrant of Lord Lyon 1969, and has issue living, Elizabeth, *b* 1970, — Catherine Jane, *b* 1971: *m* 1995, Stuart Kelly, and has issue living, Jack Alexander *b* 1996, Eleanor Louise *b* 1997. *Residence* – 2 Lyndhurst Rd, Maidstone, Kent ME15 7EQ.

COLLATERAL BRANCHES LIVING

Issue of late Lady Margaret Isabel Lane (raised to the rank of an Earl's daughter 1967), sister of 30th Earl, *b* 1921, *d* 1989: *m* 1943, Maj John Bulley Bray Ayre, TD, RA (ret), who *d* 1994:—
Michael Desmonde Erskine AYRE (419 Wilverside Way, Calgary SE, Alberta, Canada T2J 1Z6), *b* 1944; *ed* Sir George Williams' Univ, Montreal (BEng): *m* 1971, Jane Erica, da of Cmdr E. G. Lock, RN, and has issue living, Nicholas Robert Erskine, *b* 1973; *ed* Univ of Calgary (BSc in Geology and Applied and Environmental Geology), — Robin Michael, *b* 1975. — Rosemary Bray (Apt 507, 95 La Rose Ave, Etobicoke, Ontario, Canada M9P 3T2), *b* 1950; *ed* McGill Univ (BA).

Grandchildren of late Maj Seymour Hamilton Maule Cole, VD, eldest son of late Lady Eliza Philadelphia Erskine Goodeve (who *m* 1862, Rev Edward Maule Cole), sister of 27th Earl:—
Issue of late Maj Douglas Seymour Francis Erskine Maule Cole, *b* 1898, *d* 1985: *m* 1st, 1924 (*m diss* 1934), Iris, who *d* 1972, da of late Col G. S. Broome, IA (ret); 2ndly, 1942, Rosa Florence, who *d* 1983, only da of late Lieut Stanley George Bartley, RN:—
(By 1st *m*) Louis Malcolm Erskine MAULE COLE (20 St Catherine's Rd, Crawley, Sussex), *b* 1931: *m* 1955, Kathleen Jarvis, and has issue living, Julia Erskine, *b* 1961: *m* 1984, Timothy John Barber, of 3 Kenmara Close, Three Bridges, Crawley, W Sussex, and has issue living, Matthew James *b* 1989, Philip John *b* 1993, Rachael Eleanor Alice *b* 1991, — Louise Erskine (20 St Catherine's Rd, Crawley, Sussex), *b* 1963; has issue living, Eve Erskine MAULE COLE *b* 1989. —— Iris Erskine, *b* 1929: *m* 1950, Roger Harrison, MPS, of Hippica Internacional, Camino de la Sierra, Churriana, Malaga, Spain, and has issue living, Sally Erskine HARRISON (Hippica Internacional, Camino de la Sierra, Churriana, Malaga, Spain), *b* 1951; has resumed her maiden name: *m* 1st, 1970, Andrew Aitkenhead, who *d* 1971; 2ndly, 1973 (*m diss* 1976), Grenville Stacey; 3rdly, 1978 (*m diss* 1987), Anthony Curtis; 4thly, 1988 (*m diss* 1996), Duncan McLaren, and has issue living (by 3rd *m*), Candice Samantha *b* 1978, — Victoria Erskine, *b* 1956: *m* 1975, Garry Stephen Doherty, of 1 Lilac Grove, Chadderton, Manchester, and has issue living, Lorraine Ann *b* 1982.

Grandchildren of late Mrs Florence Violet Erskine Clive (infra):—
Issue of late John Ivor Erskine Penn Bowen, *b* 1916, *d* 1967: *m* 1939, Kate Molly Faith, who *d* 1990, da of Capt Bernard Arthur Mildmay, IA:—
Hugh Erskine PENN BOWEN (29 Hilltop Crescent, Weeley, Essex), *b* 1945: *m* 1st, 1963 (*m diss* 1983), Marion May Wells; 2ndly, 1989, Mrs Bernadette Evelyn Grace Widlake (*née* Carlsson), and has issue living (by 1st *m*), Mark James, *b* 1964: *m* 1st, 1987 (*m diss* 1992), Susan Aspridge; 2ndly, 1993, Catherine Ann, da of Brian Paul Taylor, — Jason Ivor, *b* 1970: *m* 1st, 1989 (*m diss* 1992), Shirley M. Szafinski; 2ndly, 1994, Mrs Sarah Jane Parker, da of Dieter Heinz McDonald, and has issue living, Holly May *b* 1994. —— Elizabeth Angelo PENN BOWEN (PO Box 129, Urangan, Queensland 4655, Australia), *b* 1947; has resumed her maiden name: *m* 1966 (*m diss* 19—), (David) Peter D. Gregory, and has issue living, David, *b* 19—, Samantha Georgette A., *b* 1967, — Phaedra Simone, *b* 1968. Mrs Penn Bowen also has further issue, Liam, *b* 19—, — Jesse, *b* 19—. —— Halcyon SIMPSON (6 Juno Mews, Colchester, Essex CO2 9PQ), *b* 1949; assumed the surname of Simpson by deed poll 1982: *m* 1st, 1965 (*m diss* 1973), Brian Sidney Mole; 2ndly, 1974 (*m diss* 1981), Andrew David Lee, and has issue living (by 1st *m*), Wendy Lynn, *b* 1965: *m* 1986, Carl Gary Baker, and has issue living James Carl *b* 1988, Holly Sarah *b* 1991.

Grandchildren of late Maj Seymour Hamilton Maule Cole, VD (ante):—
Issue of late Florence Violet Erskine CLIVE, *b* 1893; resumed her former surname of Clive 1948, *d* 1967: *m* 1st, 1911 (*m diss* 1924), Col John Alexander Barclay Penn Bowen, RE (ret); 2ndly, 1925, Maj Henry William Fitzroy Clive, Indian Army, who *d* 1932; 3rdly, 1933 (*m diss* 1944), Frederick James St John Croley:—
(By 1st *m*) Barbara Lilian (55/24 Malvern Rd, Miranda, NSW 2228, Australia), *b* 1918: *m* 1941, Raleigh Cornwallis Amesbury, who *d* 1986, and has issue living Christopher Raleigh Cornwallis (31 Annesley Av, Stanwell Tops, NSW 2508), *b* 1943: *m* 1966, Wendy Lloyd, and has issue living, Richard Anthony *b* 1971, Michelle Ann *b* 1967, Heather Marie *b* 1969, — Bruce Hamilton (1 Poets Glen, Werrington Downs, NSW 2750), *b* 1944: *m* 1st, 1964 (*m diss* 1971), Maureen Patricia Presswell; 2ndly, 1981, Maria Luz Pritchett, and has issue living (by 1st *m*), Joanne Patricia *b* 1966, (by 2nd *m*) Grant Raleigh Ross *b* 1983, Crystal Luzette *b* 1982, — Gary John (92 Beaconsfield Rd, Revesby, NSW 2212), *b* 1949: *m* 1980, Marilyn Watts, and has issue living, Jason Raleigh *b* 1982, Melanie Rae *b* 1985, — Stephen Anthony (8 Eames Av, Baulkham Hills, NSW 2153), *b* 1953: *m* 1982, Jacquelene, da of D. Hunt, of Blaxland, NSW, and has issue living, Caitlin Maree *b* 1987, — Tina Maria, *b* 1959: *m* 1985, Harry Ernest Ivison, of Lot 33 Hume Drive, Helensburgh, NSW 2508, and has issue living, Danielle Barbara *b* 1987. —— (By 2nd *m*) Henry Robert Somerset CLIVE (1-21 Burke St, Concorde West, NSW 2137, Australia), *b* 1926; *ed* Wellington Coll: *m* 1949, —, da of late Mohintri Passi, of Raniganj, W Bengal, and has had issue, Saluchna, *b* 1950, *d* 1952.

Issue of late Crystal Mary Vera Erskine Cole, *b* 1895, *d* 1972: *m* 1915 (*m diss* 1925), Leonard Charles Simpson, who *d* 1958, late Indian State Railways:—
†Robert Seymour Erskine SIMPSON *b* 1917; *ed* Dulwich, served 1939-45 War as Flt-Lieut RAF, Pilot, Atlantic Star: *m* 1945, Ivy May Jackson (33 Woodley Crescent, Melville Heights, W Australia 6156), and *d* 1994, leaving issue, Robert Neil (48 Riverview Terrace, Mount Pleasant, W Australia 6153), *b* 1952; *ed* Dulwich; Air Traffic Controller, Perth, WA: *m* 1978, Catherine Faull, and has issue living, Alicia Catherine Faull *b* 1986, Hannah Jackson Waddy *b* 1987, — Jean Elizabeth, *b* 1947: *m* 1968, Johan Daniel Stub Ravn, of 49 Barbican St, Shelley, W Australia 6155, and has issue living, Johan Daniel Stub *b* 1970, Kristian Robert *b* 1973, Ingrid Kirsten *b* 1974. — Yvonne Lilian (7927 Plantation Lakes Drive, Port St Lucie, Florida 34986, USA), *b* 1919: *m* 1941, Frank Dator, who *d* 1985, and has issue living, William Frank (597 Wyckoff Av, Mahwah, NJ 07430, USA), *b* 1943: *m* 1964, Linda O'Lear, and has issue living, William Frank *b* 1971, Lisa Lynn *b* 1965, Rebecca Ann *b* 1969, — Raymond James (12 S Railroad Av, Mahwah, NJ 07430, USA), *b* 1946: *m* 1967 (*m diss* 1978), Barbara Ann Roosa, and has issue living, Michele Lynn 1967, Erin Ashley *b* 1969, — Darryl (14 Snow Drive, Mahwah, NJ 07430, USA), *b* 1947: *m* 1976 (*m diss* 1993), Thomas John Kopplin, and has issue living, Michael Thomas *b* 1985, Katherine Elisabeth *b* 1981. —— Pamela Bernadene (2 Highgate, King's Lynn, Norfolk PE30 1PS), *b* 1921: *m* 1st, 1940 (*m diss* 1948), Thomas Wallace Greenwood; 2ndly, 1948, Lt-Col Reginald John Isaac, OBF, MC, Intelligence Corps, who *d* 1984, and has issue living, (by 1st *m*) Patricia Frances, *b* 1941; HM Diplo Ser 1962-74; JP W Norfolk 1991: *m* 1981, Peter Knights, of The Old Music House, 5 London Rd, King's Lynn, Norfolk PE30 5PY, — Marilyn Evelyn, *b* 1946, — (by 2nd *m*) James Robert ISAAC-COLE (106 Manns Rd, Narara, NSW 2250, Australia), *b* 1950; *ed* Millfield: *m* 1973, Suzanne Gay Musgrove, of Sydney, NSW, and has issue living, Russell Jason *b* 1984, — Lionel Seymour John (38 Burke St, Capalaba, Qld 4157, Australia), *b* 1954; *ed* Wells Cathedral Sch, Som, and Loughborough Univ (BSc): *m* 1984, Beth Slater, and has issue living, Alexander *b* 1993, Philadelphia Jane *b* 1987, Natasha *b* 1989.

Issue of late Edna Beryl Mavis Erskine Cole, *b* 1896, *d* 1985: *m* 1919, Constantine Demetriadi, MBE, who *d* 1951:—
Michael Anthony DEMETRIADI, OBE, TD (Office Farm House, Mutton Lane, Brandeston, Woodbridge, Suffolk IP13 7AR; Army and Navy Club), *b* 1920; *ed* Radley; Col TAVR; served 1939-45 War as Maj RWF (wounded, despatches twice, Burma Star); Member Territorial Assocn of Lowlands of Scotland 1968-75, and E Anglia 1976-85; Vice Chm Suffolk Cttee; ADC to HM 1974-75; MInst PS, MInst AM; a JP for Dunbartonshire 1973-76; Member Sec of State for Scotland's Advisory Cttee to Lord Lieut on appt of JPs; a cotton expert, with J & P Coats Ltd, Glasgow, 1951-75; Dep Sec Diocese of St Edmundsbury & Ipswich 1979-86; Chm Agricultural Dwelling Houses Advisory Cttee (MAF&F) in Suffolk 1986-91; KJStJ; Commr St John Ambulance Bde, Suffolk, 1979-85, Dir St John Ambulance Assocn, Suffolk since 1986, and Cmdr since 1982, OBE (Civil) 1993: *m* 1948, Nancy Anna, el da of late Ambrose John Rodocanachi, of Rolletts, Darsham, Saxmundham, Suffolk, and has issue living, Peter Michael (8 Homestalls Meadow, Pillerton Priors, Warwicks CV35 0PZ; Army and Navy Club and MCC), *b* 1953; *ed* Radley, and Univ Coll, London (BA); Chm Midland Petrochemical Ltd, Henley-in-Arden; EsqStJ: *m* 1980, France Marie Anne Nicole, eldest da of Judge Bodson, of Av Commandant Lothaire 58, 1040 Brussels, and has issue living, Guy Peter Michael Erskine *b* 1983, James Paul Christian Erskine *b* 1985, Jennifer Anne Nancy *b* 1982, — Philippa Nancy, *b* 1949: *m* 1st, 1975 (*m diss* 1983), Nikos Stamatopoulos; 2ndly, 1986, Jan Doman, of Dostojevske'ho Rad 13, Bratislava 811-09, Slovakia, and has issue living (by 1st *m*) Lucinda Polixeni *b* 1976; *ed* Felixstowe Coll, — Antonia Claire (12A Porchester Square, W2 6AN), *b* 1959; *ed* Wycombe Abbey; editor.

Issue of late Lilian Maude Erskine Cole, *b* 1900, *d* 1965: *m* 1st, 1926 (*m diss* 1933), Cyril Ernest Musgrave Ridsdale, BN Railway, who *d* 1957; 2ndly, 1933, William Louis Charles Gerard Cook, OBE (formerly Indian Imperial Police):—
(By 2nd *m*) David William Erskine Gerard COOK, *b* 1936; *ed* Bedford Sch: *m* 1960, Joanne Elizabeth, da of John Fisher, of Sydney, and has issue living, Jonathan David, *b* 1961, — Jeremy Nicholas, *b* 1963, — Caroline Louise, *b* 1965. *Residence* - Weyburn, 20 Lansdowne Av, Codsall, Staffs WV8 2EN. —— (By 1st *m*) Suzanne June Toy, *b* 1928: *m* 1st, 1951 (*m diss* 1955), David John Lush; 2ndly, 1957, Claude Guy de la Faye d'Entrains Biard, who *d* 1991, and has issue living, (by 1st *m*) Sarah Jane Judith, *b* 1952: *m* 1st, 1974 (*m diss* 1981), Christopher John Dean; 2ndly, 1982, Andrew Quinton Steggall, of Ormond House, Temple St, Brill, Bucks, and has issue living (by 1st *m*), Matthew Christopher *b* 1975, Adam James *b* 1977 (by 2nd *m*) Edward Dicken *b* 1984. *Residence* - Silver Wood, 10 Souller Rd, Thame, Oxon OX9 2EE.

Grandchildren of late Beatrice Madeline Erskine Ferguson (infra):—
Issue of late George Hamilton Ferguson, KPM, *b* 1896, *d* 1970: *m* 1931 (*m diss* 1948), Dorothy Mary Kate Susie Emily Vaughan, da of the late Sir Robert (Vaughan) Gower, KCVO, OBE, MP:—
Robert Maule Gower FERGUSON, *b* 1932; *ed* Harrow. —— Beatrice Margaret, *b* 1933: *m* 1903, (Norman) Carey Booth Creek, of 9433 Ardmore Dr, N Saanich, BC, Canada, son of late F. Norman S. Creek, MBE, MC, and has issue living, Carey Hamish Ferguson, *b* 1964; *ed* Concordia Univ (B Comm), — Benjamin Robert, *b* 1965, — Nicola Robin, *b* 1967: *m* 1989, Edward James Heavener, of Courtenay, BC, son of Raymond Heavener, of Sidney, BC, and has issue living, Jared Robert *b* 1997, Jade Hope *b* 1995, — Kanina Susanna Erskine, *b* 1970. —— Sally Pauline June (c/o Royal Bank of Scotland, Oban, Argyll), *b* 1941: *m* 1968, Lt-Cdr Ian Cochrane, RN (ret), who *d* 1988, and has issue living Frances Sarah Nicola, *b* 1960 (adopted by her stepfather 1968), — Harriet Elizabeth Alexandra *b* 1970, — Emma Catherine Anne *b* 1972.

Issue of late Roland Edward Stuart Ferguson, late RNAS, RAF and IA, *b* 1899, *d* 1976: *m* 1941, Veronica Catherine (Tangs, Shipley Bridge, S Brent, S Devon TQ10 9ED), yr da of Henry Gore Hawker, of Strode, Ermington, Devon):—
Andrew Stuart FERGUSON (Penllyn, Cathedine, Bwlch, Powys), *b* 1948; Ionosphericist and sometime Base Cdr with British Antarctic Survey 1971-74; Nature Conservancy Council since 1979: *m* 1975, Helen Alice, only da of Col P. N. Lodge, RA (ret), of The Manor House, Compton Abdale, Glos, and has issue living, Geoffrey Roland, *b* 1976, — Ian Antony, *b* 1980.
—— Janet Erskine (Cracklewood, Didworthy, S Brent, S Devon), *b* 1946; WRNS 1964-68: *m* 1st, 19— (*m diss* 1977), John Goodwin Fisk, 8th Hussars; 2ndly, 1978, Lt Cdr Adrian John Bomback, MC, RN, who was *k* while on leave by a tree during the storm of 25 Jan 1990, and has issue living (by 1st *m*), Adrian John Stuart Erskine, *b* 1970, — Peter Maule Erskine, *b* 1973.

Issue of late Helen Evelyn Ferguson, *b* 1886, *d* 1962: *m* 1914, Harold Henry Wyndham Newman, who *d* 1963:—
Durnford Frederick Wyndham NEWMAN (c/o National Westminster Bank, PO Box 320, 5 Station Approach, West Byfleet, Surrey KT14 6YJ), *b* 1917; Diploma of Faraday House; CEng, FIEE; Ch Eng, British Airports Authority, Heathrow Airport, London 1972-77; late Sqdn-Ldr RAF; 1939-45 War as Capt RE: *m* 1948, Joan (Jane) Merriel Hollway, and has issue living, James Richard Wyndham (Studlands, 8 The Knoll, Fairmile Park Rd, Cobham, Surrey), *b* 1950; BSc (Hons): *m* 1st, 1975, Ann Caroline Lawrence, who *d* 1984; 2ndly, 1985, Carole Ann Dove, and has issue living, (by 2nd *m*) Thomas Philip Wyndham *b* 1987, James Frederick Wyndham *b* 1991, — Clare Marian Wyndham, *b* 1953: *m* 1982, Robert Tony Alter, of 11145 NW 1st Place, Coral Springs, Florida 33071, USA, and has issue living, Edward Donald *b* 1989, Katharine Dora *b* 1994.

Issue of late Mary Beatrice Erskine Ferguson, *b* 1888, *d* 1970: *m* 1st, 1912, Maj Hubert Symons, RFA, who was *ka* 1918; 2ndly, 1937, Graham Parsons Earwaker, who *d* 1971:—
(By 1st *m*) Jean Erskine (Withycombe, Winsford, Minehead, Somerset), *b* 1916: *m* 1940, Maj Richard Andrew Joscelyne, MC, RTR, who *d* 1992, and has issue living, Andrew Michael Hubert, *b* 1946; Col Gren Gds (ret), — Sarah Anne, *b* 1941: *m* 1963, Anthony Owen Blishen, OBE, HM Diplo Ser, of Ash Barn, Edistone, Hartland, N Devon, and has issue living, James Peter Anthony *b* 1966, Robert Edward Henry *b* 1970, David Francis Andrew *b* 1972, Catherine Annabelle *b* 1964.

Grandchildren of late Mary Beatrice Erskine Earwaker (ante):—
Issue of late Peter Nicholas Symons, *b* 1917, *d* 1951: *m* 1940, Suzanne Penzer Haynes (*Lady Marshall*) (who *m* 2ndly, 1953, Cdr Sir Douglas Marshall, RNVR, who *d* 1976), of Hatt, Saltash, Cornwall:—
Heugh Sherwood SYMONS (Bicton Farm House, Hatt, Saltash, Cornwall) *b* 1949: *m* 1976, Fiona Ann Mitchell, and has issue living, Genevieve Penn, *b* 1979, — Emily Penn, *b* 1980, — Suzanna Penn, *b* 1984. —— Nicola Penn, *b* 1942: *m* 1963, John Philip Coverdale, of Bevere Manor, Bevere, Worcester WR3 7RG, and has issue living, Peter John Penn, *b* 1970, — Philip Anthony Penn *b* 1978, — Anna Frances Mary Penn, *b* 1966: *m* 1990, Andrew Christopher Kennedy Davis, and has issue living, Oliver John Kennedy *b* 1991, Emily Elizabeth Esmé *b* 1998, — Sarah Elizabeth Penn, *b* 1968. —— Celia Mary (Swiftaford Farmhouse, Hatt, Saltash, Cornwall PL12 6PP), *b* 1947: *m* 1973 (*m diss* 1988), Erich Gerhard Rinagl, and has issue living, Marc Gerard Penn, *b* 1979, — Nina Penn, *b* 1983. —— Melanie Anne, *b* (twin) 1947: *m* 1970, Jeremy John Shales, of 70 Princes Rd, Teddington, Middx, and has issue living, Joanna Penn, *b* 1979, — Louise Alexandra Penn, *b* 1980.

Granddaughter of late Lady Eliza Philadelphia Erskine (ante):—
Issue of late Beatrice Madeline Erskine Cole, *b* 1863, *d* 1936: *m* 1884, Henry Tanner Ferguson, MICE, late of Wolleigh, Bovey Tracey, Devon, who *d* 1909:—
Violet Madeline (11 Unsworth Rd, N Ringwood, Victoria 3134, Australia), *b* 1893: *m* 1919 (*m diss* 1926), Philip Eric Bernard, and has issue living, Barbara Nancy (11 Unsworth Rd, N Ringwood, Victoria 3134, Australia), *b* 1920: *m* 1945, Ronald Hyde, MRCS, LRCP, who *d* 1965, and has issue living, Timothy David Erskine *b* 1946; Member Sydney Stock Exchange 1983: *m* 1987, Caroline Noelle Scheidat (and has issue living, Philippa Annabelle Jane *b* 1987), Robin Paul Christopher *b* 1948; a Member of Australian Inst of Export: *m* 1st, 1975 (*m diss* 1979), Margaret Anne Weichelt; 2ndly, 1979, Aoura Sangsingkeo (and has issue living (by 2nd *m*), Andrew Chatvalin *b* 1985, Samantha Darupat *b* 1983), Max Anthony John *b* 1951; *ed* Monash Univ, Victoria (BA): *m* 1983, Carla Lavinia Holding (and has issue living, Rebecca Louise Austen *b* 1984), James Rupert (Allambie, Olympic Way, Wombat, NSW 2587, Australia) *b* 1955: *m* 1988, Stella Moutos (and has issue living, Jeremy Rupert *b* 1989, Stephanie Anne *b* 1987, Bianca Natalie *b* 1991), Lucy Susan Elizabeth *b* (twin) 1955: *m* 1976, Anthony John Lemprière Sheaffe (and has issue living, Jonathan Lemprière *b* 1979, Susan Elizabeth *b* 1980, Alexandra Jane *b* 1984).

Descendants of late Hon Henry David Erskine, 3rd son of 24th Earl (*see* E Mar and Kellie).

Granddaughter of late Mary Margaret Anna ZWILCHENBART-ERSKINE, da of late Rev Hon Thomas Erskine (4th son of 24th Earl), *b* 1829, *d* 1906 (having assumed the additional name of Erskine for herself and son 1884): *m* 1864, as his 2nd wife, Rodolph Zwilchenbart, who *d* 1883:—
Issue of late Gratney Rodolph ZWILCHENBART-ERSKINE, *b* 1871, *d* 1930: *m* 1896, Theodora, who *d* 1958, da of late W. H. Laverton, of Leighton, Westbury, Wilts;—
Helen Mary, *b* 1901: *m* 1928, Brigadier Alec Palmer ffleetwood Churchill, OBE, Indian Army, who *d* 1947, and has issue living, John ffleetwood (Victoria Lodge, Charters Rd, Sunningdale, Berks SL5 9QB), *b* 1934; *ed* Wellington Coll, and Trin Hall, Camb: *m* 1970 (*m diss* 1990), Stephanie, da of H. van den Bergh, of The Hague, Holland, and has issue living, John Edward ffleetwood *b* 1973, Gratia Mary Anne ffleetwood *b* 1975, Juliet Kathleen ffleetwood *b* 1978, — Charles ffleetwood (Spindrift, 31 Irsha St, Appledore, N. Devon EX39 1RZ), *b* 1937; *ed* Wellington Coll, and Jesus Coll, Camb. *Residence* – Fremington Manor Nursing Home, Fremington, N Devon.

PREDECESSORS – According to Lord Hailes the origin of the Earls of Mar is "lost in antiquity" A Mormaer of Mar served at the battle of Clontarf 1014. **(1)** ROTHRI, Mormaer (or Earl) of Mar witnessed foundation charter of Scone 1114-15, and King David I's charter to Dunfermline Abbey 1124-29; *s* by **(2)** MORGUND, who was *s* by **(3)** GILCHRIST, *s* by **(4)** DUNCAN (son of Morgund), who was *s* by his son **(5)** WILLIAM; *s* by his son **(6)** DONALD, father of **(7)** GRATNEY, who *s* about 1297: *m* Christian (1st *Lady of Garioch*), sister of King Robert I of Scotland; *d* before 1305; *s* by his son **(8)** DONALD, Regent of Scotland, *d* 1332; *s* by his son **(9)** THOMAS, Great Chamberlain of Scotland; Lordship of Garioch confirmed 1357; *dsp* 1373/4; *s* by his sister **(10)** MARGARET, Countess of Mar; *d* 1390; *s* by her da (by her 1st husband William, Earl of Douglas) **(11)** ISABEL, Countess of Mar; *d* 1408, having in 1404 granted a life rent in the Earldom to her husband, **(12)** Sir ALEXANDER Stewart, who *d* 1435; *s* by **(13)** ROBERT, 1st Lord Erskine, son of Sir Thomas Erskine, of Alloa and Dun, by his 2nd wife, Janet; returned heir of line of Isabel (ante), and assumed the Earldom; *d* 1452; *s* by his son **(14)** THOMAS, 2nd Lord Erskine (and *de jure* 14th Earl); in 1457 before an Assize of Error the Earldom was found to have devolved upon the Crown, but this was negatived by Queen Mary's restoration and by the ruling of the Court of Session in 1626: he was *s* by his son **(14)** ALEXANDER (*de jure* 15th Earl), who was *s* by his son **(16)** ROBERT (*de jure* 16th Earl); fell at Flodden 1513; *s* by his son **(17)** JOHN (*de jure* 17th Earl) *d* 1555; *s* by his son **(18)** JOHN, 6th Lord Erskine, who was in 1565 *restored* by Queen Mary to the Earldom of Mar and Lordship of Garioch (through Janet, great-granddaughter of Gratney, 7th Earl of Mar (ante)), and of which his ancestor Thomas, 2nd Lord Erskine was declared to have been unjustly dispossessed, and this restoration was confirmed by an Act of Parliament which expressly recognized Robert, 1st Lord Erskine to have been rightfully Earl of Mar, and in the Decreet of Ranking of 1606 (according to the documents then produced) the Earl of Mar was assigned a position conformable to writs of 1393 and 1404: was Regent of Scotland 1571-72; *d* 1572; *s* by his son **(19)** JOHN, KG, 19th Earl; attainted 1584 and restored 1585; was Lord Treasurer of Scotland 1616-30; *cr Lord Cardross* 1610 (with power of nomination); *d* 1634; *s* in the Lordship of Cardross (according to nomination) (*see* E Buchan), and in the Earldom of Mar by his son, **(20)** JOHN, PC, 20th Earl, an Extraordinary Lord of Session 1620-26 and 1628-30; *d* 1654; *s* by his son **(21)** JOHN, 21st Earl; *d* 1668; *s* by his son, **(22)** CHARLES, PC, 22nd Earl; Col Roy Scots Fusiliers, which Regt he raised; *d* 1689; *s* by his son, **(23)** JOHN, KT, PC, 23rd Earl; Sec of State 1706, Keeper of the Signet, and a Representative Peer; having defended the cause of the Stuarts in 1715 his honours were attainted and his estates forfeited; *d* 1732, and the Alloa property was entailed on his da Lady Frances Erskine, who but for the attainder would have been Countess of Mar; *s* by his grandson **(24)** JOHN FRANCIS Erskine, 24th Earl, to whom the Earldom was restored by Act of Parliament 1824 through his mother, Lady Frances, as "grandson and lineal representative" of the attainted Earl; *d* 1825; *s* by his son **(25)** JOHN THOMAS, 25th Earl; *d* 1828; *s* by his son, **(26)** JOHN FRANCIS MILLER, 26th Earl; served at Waterloo; successfully claimed to be 11th *Earl of Kellie* 1835; *dsp* 1866, when the Earldom of Kellie devolved upon his cousin, while he was *s* in the ancient Earldom of Mar by his nephew (the heir-general) **(27)** JOHN FRANCIS ERSKINE Goodeve-Erskine, 27th Earl (son of Lady Frances Jemina (el sister of 26th Earl), by her marriage with William James Goodeve, of Clifton); *b* 1836; assumed by legal authorization 1866 the additional surname of Erskine; for 36 years a Representative Peer for Scotland: succession to heir-general confirmed with precedence of 1404 by the Declaratory Act of Parliament passed in 1885 (Restitution of Mar Act): *m* 1866, Alice Mary Sinclair, who *d* 1924, da of late John Hamilton, of Hilston Park, Monmouthshire; *d* 1930; *s* by his only son, **(28)** JOHN FRANCIS HAMILTON SINCLAIR CUNLIFFE BROOKS FORBES, 28th Earl: *m* 1903, Sibyl May Dominica, who *d* 1958, da of late Robert Heathcote; *d* 1932; *s* by his cousin **(29)** LIONEL WALTER Young, 29th Earl (grandson of Lady Frances Jemima Erskine Young), el sister of 27th Earl, *b* 1891; assumed the additional name of Erskine (registered in Court of Lord Lyon) 1933; *d* 1965; *s* by his kinsman, **(30)** JAMES CLIFTON, 30th Earl (el son of Charles Macdonald Lane), CSI, el son of Alice, who *m* James Horsburgh Lane, da of Lady Frances Jemima Erskine Young (ante); recognised in the surname of "of Mar" by warrant of Lord Lyon 1959: *m* 1st, 1939 (*m diss* 1958), Millicent Mary, who *d* 1993, da of William Salton; 2ndly, 1960, Marjorie Aileen, who *d* 1975, da of late John Reginald Miller, and widow of Maj C. W. S. Grice, Indian Army; *d* 1975; *s* by his el da **(31)** MARGARET, present peeress, and Lady Garioch.

MAR and KELLIE, EARL OF (Erskine) (Earl of Mar S 1565, Earl of Kellie S 1616)

I think more
He adds honour to that of his ancestors

UNIONE · FORTIOR

Strengthened by unity

JAMES THORNE ERSKINE, 14th Earl of Mar, and 16th Earl of Kellie, Premier Viscount of Scotland; *b* 10 March 1949; *s* 1993; *ed* Eton, Moray House Coll of Educn, Edinburgh (Dip Social Work, Dip Youth & Co Work), and at Inverness Coll (Certificate in Building); Hereditary Keeper of Stirling Castle, DL Clackmannan 1991; Page of Honour to HM 1962-63; Social Worker; P/O RAuxAF 1979-82, F/O 1982-86 (2622 Highland Sqdn), Memb RN Aux Ser 1985-89: *m* 1974, Mrs Mary Irene Mooney, yr da of late Dougal McDougal Kirk, of Edinburgh, and formerly wife of Roderick James Mooney.

Arms – Quarterly: 1st and 4th argent, a pale sable, *Erskine*; 2nd and 3rd azure, a bend between six cross crosslets fitchée or, *Mar*: over all, on an escutcheon gules, the royal crown of Scotland proper, within a double tressure flory counterflory or, ensigned with an earl's coronet, *Kellie*; behind the shield are placed in saltire a key, wards outwards or, and a baton gules, garnished or, and ensigned with a castle of the last (the insignia of the office of Hereditary Keeper of the Castle of Stirling). **Crests** – 1st, on a cap of maintenance gules, turned up ermine a dexter hand, holding a skene in pale argent, hilted and pommelled or, over crest "Je pense plus" (I think more); 2nd, on a cap of maintenance gules, turned up ermine a demi-lion rampant guardant gules, armed argent, over crest "Decori decus addit avito" (He adds honour to the honour of his ancestors). **Supporters** – Two griffins gules, armed, beaked, and winged or.
Residence – Erskine House, Kirk Wynd, Clackmannan, FK10 4JF; **Club** – Farmers'.

BROTHERS LIVING

Hon ALEXANDER DAVID (34 Awaba St, Mosman, NSW 2088, Australia), *b* 26 Oct 1952; *ed* Eton, and Pembroke Coll, Camb (BA): *m* 1977, Katherine Shawford, elder da of late Thomas Clark Capel, of Narrabri, NSW (*see* M Bute, colls), and has issue living, Alexander Capel, *b* 1979, — Isabel Katherine, *b* 1982.
Rev the Hon Michael John, *b* 1956; *ed* Eton, and Edinburgh Univ (MA, BD): *m* 1987, Jill, elder da of late Campbell S. Westwood, of 11 Leighton Gdns, Ellon, and has issue living, Euan Stewart, *b* 1992, — Laura Anne, *b* 1990. *Residence* – The Manse, Kilmelfort, Argyllshire.

SISTER LIVING

Lady Fiona, *b* (twin) 1956: *m* 1980, Lt-Col Andrew P. W. Campbell, Argyll and Sutherland Highlanders, yr son of late Wilson Campbell, of Coquet House, Warkworth, Northumberland, and has issue living, Barnabas William Erskine, *b* 1983, — Elizabeth Poppy, *b* 1985, — Rosanna Katherine, *b* 1986.

UNCLES LIVING *(Brothers of 13th Earl of Mar)*

Hon David Hervey, *b* 1924; *ed* Eton, and Trin Coll, Camb (MA); Bar, Inner Temple 1950; late Capt Scots Gds; Co Councillor 1969-85, and a JP and DL for Suffolk; Italy and Palestine 1943-45 (Italy star): *m* 1st, 1953, Jean Violet, who *d* 1983, el da of Lt-Col Archibald Vivian Campbell Douglas, late Scots Gds (*see* de Bunsen, Bt, ext); 2ndly, 1985, Caroline Mary, yr da of late Rt Hon Sir Alan Frederick Lascelles, GCVO, KCB, CMG, MC (*see* E Harewood, colls), and widow of 2nd Viscount Chandos, and has issue living (by 1st *m*), Janet Cicely, *b* 1955: *m* 1980, Gordon Drake Arthur, of High-fields, Smeeton Westerby, Leicester LE8 0LT, elder son of Allan Arthur, MBE, DL, of Mount Maskall, Boreham, Essex, and has issue living, Allan Douglas Erskine *b* 1987, Isobel Jean Douglas *b* 1984, Margaret Frances Ramsay *b* 1989, — Catherine Marjorie, *b* 1958: *m* 1979, Edward Georges Rossdale, son of John Rossdale, of 37 De Vere Gdns, W8, and has issue living, Venetia *b* 1981, Sophie *b* 1982, Caroline *b* 1986, — Mary (Molly) Viola, *b* 1962: *m* 1987, (Edward) Seymour Adams, of 33 Radipole Rd, SW6 5DN, son of Philip Adams, of Havant, Hants, and has issue living, Max Philip Erskine *b* 1992, Ellen Catherine Jean *b* 1990, Rosalind Elizabeth *b* 1994. *Residences* – Felsham House, Felsham, Bury St Edmunds; 17 Clareville Court, Clareville Grove, SW7. *Club* – Brooks's.

Hon Robert William Hervey, *b* 1930; *ed* Eton, and King's Coll, Camb; late 2nd Lieut Scots Gds: *m* 1st, 1955 (*m diss* 1964), Jennifer Shirley, yr da of L. J. Cardew Wood, of Farnham Royal Bucks; 2ndly, 1969 (*m diss* 1975), Annemarie, da of Jean Lattès, of 31 Rue Guinegand, Paris VI; 3rdly, 1977, Belinda Mary Rosalind, da of Raymond Blackburn, of London, and has issue living, (by 2nd *m*) Alistair Robert, *b* 1970, — (by 3rd *m*) Thomas Gerald, *b* 1978, — Felix Benjamin, *b* 1980. *Residence* – 100 Elgin Cres, W11 2JL.

COLLATERAL BRANCHES LIVING

Issue of late Capt Hon Francis Walter Erskine, yr son of 12th Earl, *b* 1899, *d* 1972: *m* 1925, Phyllis, who *d* 1974, da of late John F. Burstall, of Quebec, Canada:—
Rosemary Susan, *b* 1927: *m* 1st, 1947 (*m diss* 1974), Mark Alastair Coats, late Lt Gren Gds; 2ndly, 1974, David Laidlaw, of Grand Rue, 81170, Cordes, France, and has issue living (by 1st *m*), Nicholas James (8 Kempson Rd, SW6), *b* 1952: *m* 1987, Belinda, da of Gordon McKechnie, and has issue living, James Michael *b* 1987, Rosanna Sarah *b* 1990, — Virginia Jane, *b* 1954: *m* 1977, Andrew Nicholas John Hay, of 10 Favart Rd, SW6, son of Sir (Alan) Philip Hay, KCVO, TD (*see* M Hertford, 1973-74 Edn), and has issue living, Timothy George Nicholas *b* 1980, Christopher James Philip *b* 1984, Olivia Margaret Rose *b* 1990.

Issue of late Rt Hon Sir William Augustus Forbes Erskine, GCMG, MVO, Ambassador to Poland 1928-31, 2nd son of 11th Earl, *b* 1871, *d* 1952: *m* 1908, Georgie Viola Eleanor, who *d* 1972, da of late William Humble Dudley Ward (E Dudley, colls):—
†Cynthia Romola, *b* 1910: *m* 1943, Pierre Bressy, former Ambassador, French Diplo Ser, who *d* 1973, and *d* 1997 leaving issue, François Pierre Erskine (L'Enclos, rue Gabrielle Bénier, Bouviers, 78280 Guyancourt, France), *b* 1946: *m* 1975, Monique Vanwelsenaere, and has issue living, Jean Sebastien *b* 1979, — Catherine Marie Charlotte, *b* 1945: *m* 1972, Vicomte Jean-Marie de Bourgoing, of 54 Boulevard de la Tour-Maubourg, Paris VII, and has issue living, Guillaume Pierre Denis *b* 1976, Philippe Marie François *b* 1978, Marguerite Roseline Romola *b* 1975. *Residence* – Alloa, Bargemon, Var 83, France. —— Margaret Elsie Viola, *b* 1913: *m* 1950, Major Denys Ernest Glynn Oglander, who *d* 1977, and has had issue, William Auberon Erskine, *b* 1953, — John Peter Erskine (West Lodge, Nunwell, Brading, IoW), *b* 1957: *m* 1987 (*m diss* 1988), Fiona Stuart, da of Ronald Stuart Brisbane, of 105 Down St, Belgrave, Leicester, and St Vincent, WI, and has issue living, Susanna Anastasia *b* 1987, — Frances Mary Viola OGLANDER, *b* 1951; has retained her maiden name: *m* 1977, Michael Solosy, who *d* 1998, of Hardingshute Farm, Ryde, IoW, and has issue living, Robert John Solosy OGLANDER *b* 1981, — Mary Theresa Catherine Joan, *b* 1955: *m* 1981, Josef Hubbard, and *d* 1982. *Residence* – Nunwell Park, Brading, Isle of Wight.

Issue of late Rev Hon Alexander Penrose Forbes Erskine, 3rd son of 11th Earl, *b* 1881, *d* 1925: *m* 1916, Irene Annette who *d* 1968, having *m* 2ndly, 1930, Rt Rev Frederic Llewellyn Deane (Bishop of Aberdeen and Orkney 1917-43), who *d* 1952, da of late Rt Rev Archibald Ean Campbell, Bishop of Glasgow and Galloway (E Midleton):—
Archibald Walter Forbes, *b* 1918; *ed* Eton, and New Coll, Oxford (BM and BCh 1942, MA 1946): *m* 1958, Joan Mary Thérèse Frances, el da of late John Benedict Heppel, of Bromley, Kent, and has issue living, James Alexander, *b* 1959; MB BS, DA, DTM & H: *m* 1993, Debbie de Lacy-Leacey, — Robert John (41 Park Lane, Sutton Bonington, Leics LE12 5NQ), *b* 1960; MB BS, FRCA: *m* 1990, Dr Gillian Margaret Turner, da of Charles Thomas Turner, and has issue living, Lucy Emmeline *b* 1994, — Benjamin David, *b* 1971. *Residence* – 130 Walm Lane, NW2. —— David Alexander John, TD, *b* 1921; *ed* Eton, and New Coll, Oxford (MA); formerly Capt 5th Bn Queen's Own Cameron Highlanders (TA); 1939-45 War: *m* 1st, 1947 (*m diss* 1969), Margaret Eleanor, da of late Rear-Adm Steuart Arnold Pears, CBE; 2ndly, 1970, Mrs Joan Mary Gilmour, da of Brig James Brindley Bettington, DSO, MC, and has issue living, (by 1st *m*) Robin David (Hill Top, Langley-on-Tyne, Hexham, Northumberland NE47 5LY), *b* 1948; *ed* Eton: *m* 1985 (*m diss* 1997), Belinda Ann, formerly wife of David W. Pulford, and 2nd da of Thomas Aydon Bates, of Langley, Northumberland (*see* Musgrave, Bt, *cr* 1782), and has issue living, Caspar James Pears *b* 1986, Imogen Felicia Anne *b* 1989, — Peter Alexander (Packwood Haugh, Ruyton-XI-Towns, Shrewsbury), *b* 1950: *m* 1976, Charlotte, twin da of late Wing-Cdr Sir (Eric) John Hodsoll, CB, and has issue living, Andrew John Hodsoll *b* 1985, Emily Clare *b* 1978, Harriet Alice *b* 1981, — Alistair John (58 Ravenslea Rd, SW12), *b* 1959: *m* 1987, Fiona Sue Awdry, eldest da of Maurice Lovett-Turner, of Windlesham, Surrey, and has issue living, Oliver Stewart *b* 1989, Edmund Alexander *b* 1993. *Residence* – Les Loriers, Rue Beau Repaire, St Peter Port, Guernsey.

Granddaughter of late Augustus Erskine, el son of late Hon James Augustus Erskine (*infra*):—
Issue of late Capt Bushby Lyons Erskine, *b* 1890, *d* 1919, Lilian, da of Francis William Blenkey, of Beckenham:—
Sheelah Kathleen ERSKINE, *b* 1921; resumed surname of Erskine 19—: *m* 19—, — Tortonese.

Grandchildren of late Hon James Augustus Erskine, brother of 12th Earl of Kellie:—
Issue of late Evelyn Pierrepont Erskine, *b* 1870, *d* 1953: *m* 1897, Amy Maria, who *d* 1959, da of Joseph Hough, grazier, of Collie River, W Australia:—
Charles Seymour (21 Bellevue Terr, Swanbourne, W Australia 6010), *b* 1905: *m* 1928, Mona Roslynn, da of Henry Murphy, of co Cork. —— Gratney Pierrepont (12 Devon Rd, Swanbourne, W Australia 6010), *b* 1911; 1939-45 War with AIF: *m* 1st, 1931 (*m diss* 1935), Elsie Evelyn, da of late I. Nutall, of W Australia; 2ndly, 1940, Beth Rosemary Kenworthy, and has issue living (by 1st *m*), Yvonne Constance (23 Catesby St, City Beach, W Australia PC 6015), *b* 1932, — (by 2nd *m*) Gratney Evelyn (20 Knight St, Wembley Downs, W Australia), *b* 1941: *m* 1967, Elaine Joy Marchant, of Claremont, W Australia, and has issue living, Gregory Bryce *b* 1972, Janine Gaye *b* 1969.

Issue of late Hugh Bushby Johnson (who assumed by Deed Poll 1952 that surname in lieu of his patronymic for himself only), *b* 1872, *d* 1956: *m* 1897, May, who *d* 1950, da of John Valentine, of Bunbury, W Australia:—
John William ERSKINE, *b* 1899: *m* 19—, and has issue living, Hugh Walter Bushby, *b* 19—: *m* 19—, Doris Gwen Crundwell, and has issue living, Christine Maria *b* 1946. —— Esmé Mai Lydia, *b* 1910: *m* 1935, Claude Wentworth Jefferson, late Flt-Lt RAAF, who *d* 1974, and has issue living, Ian David (1/3 Werambri St, Woolwich Sydney, NSW 2110, Australia), *b* 1945: *m* 1968, Kay Leslie, da of John Farren Price, of Sydney, NSW, and has issue living, Kalena Ann *b* 1971, Fiona *b* 1975. *Residence* – 1 Budgdrec St, Norah Head, NSW 2263, Australia.

Grandchildren of late Hugh Bushby Johnson (ante)
Issue of late Kellie Edmund ERSKINE, *b* 1902, *d* 1988: *m* 1924, Annie, who *d* 1975, da of Robert Knox:—
Kellie Knox (4 Palermo Place, Allambie Heights, NSW 2100, Australia), *b* 1931: *m* 1959, Pamela Ann, da of late Alfred Edward Leer, and has issue living, Bryan Andrew, *b* 1966, — Robyn Ann, *b* 1963, — Keryn Maree, *b* 1971.

Issue of James Keith Brodie ERSKINE *b* 1907, *d* 1981: *m* 1949, Mary Douglas (Cobham Av, W Ryde, NSW, Australia), da of Arthur Ernest Savage, of Woolwich, Sydney, NSW:—
Lynette Mary, *b* 1950: *m* 1978, Patrick Philip Duncan, son of Patrick Duncan, of Wellington, NZ, and has issue living, Guy Philip, *b* 1980, — Stacey Mary, *b* 1982. —— Catherine Evelyn, *b* 1953. —— Joanne Margaret, *b* 1960.

PREDECESSORS – (1) *Sir* ROBERT Erskine of Alloa and Dun by his 2nd wife, Janet, da and heir of Sir Edward Keith, of Synton, and widow of Sir David Barclay, of Brechin, a Commr to treat for the release of James I 1421, and one of the hostages for his ransom 1424, sat as *Lord Erskine* in Scottish Parliament 1426; served heir of Isabel, Countess of Mar 1438; *s* by his son (2) THOMAS, 2nd Lord; dispossessed of the Earldom at an Assize of Error 1457; sat in Parliament as Lord Erskine 1467: *m* Janet Douglas; *d* 1493; *s* by his son (3) ALEXANDER, 3rd Lord; guardian of James IV; *d* 1510; *s* by his son (4) ROBERT, 4th Lord; killed at Flodden 1513; *s* by his son (5) JOHN, 5th Lord, guardian of James V; Ambassador to France 1515 to 1535, and an Extraordinary Lord of Session, &c; *d* 1555; *s* by his son (6) JOHN, 6th Lord, was Regent of Scotland 1571, and guardian of James VI, &c; Mary Queen of Scots restored to him the *Earldom of Mar* by charter 1565, though, according to the decision of the Committee of Privileges of the House of Lords in 1875, a new Earldom was created with remainder to heirs male; *d* 1572; *s* by his son (7) JOHN, KG, PC, 2nd Earl; High Treasurer of Scotland 1615-30; attainted 1584, and restored 1585; Ambassador to England 1603; *cr Lord Cardross* (peerage of Scotland) 1610, with the right to assign the Lordship to whomsoever he might elect, which right was confirmed by charter in favour of his 2nd son Henry 1618; *d* 1634; *s* in Lordship of Cardross by his grandson David (*see* E Buchan), and in Earldom by his son (8) JOHN, PC, KB, 3rd Earl; an Extraordinary Lord of Session 1620-6 and 1628-30, &c; *d* 1654; *s* by his son (9) JOHN, 4th Earl; *d* 1668; *s* by his son (10) CHARLES, PC, 5th Earl; was Col Roy Scots Fusiliers 1679-86, which regt he raised; *d* 1689; *s* by his son (11) JOHN, KT, PC, 6th Earl; Sec of State 1706, Keeper of the Signet, and a Representative Peer 1707-13; was attainted by Act of Parliament for having raised the insurrection of 1715; his forfeited estates were purchased by his brother Lord Grange (a Lord of Session) and David Erskine, of Dun, and the Alloa property was entailed on the heirs male of his da Lady Frances Erskine, wife of James Erskine, Lord Grange's son; *d* 1732; *s* by his grandson (12) JOHN FRANCIS, 7th Earl, who in 1824 was restored to the Earldom by Act of Parliament (but the Lordship of Erskine remains forfeit) as grandson and lineal representative of the attainted Earl; *d* 1825; *s* by his son (13) JOHN THOMAS, 8th Earl; *d* 1828; *s* by his son (14) JOHN FRANCIS MILLER, 9th Earl, as an officer in the Guards served at Waterloo; in 1835 successfully claimed to be 11th *Earl of Kellie* see * (infra); *dsp* 1866; *s* in Earldom of Kellie, the Viscountcy of Fentoun, and Lordship of Erskine of Dirleton, and of Dirleton by his cousin (15) WALTER CONINGSBY, CB, 12th Earl of Kellie, Viscount Fentoun and Lord Erskine of Dirleton, 3rd son of Hon Henry David, 3rd son of 7th Earl of Mar; served in India with distinction, both as a military and a political officer; *d* 1872; *s* by his son (16) WALTER HENRY, 13th Earl of Kellie (who in 1875 successfully claimed to be 11th Earl of Mar, *cr* 1565); *b* 1839; was a Representative Peer for Scotland: *m* 1863, Mary Anne, who *d* 1927, da of the late Wiliam Forbes; *d* 1888; *s* by his el son (17) WALTER JOHN FRANCIS, KT, 12th Earl of Mar, and 14th Earl of Kellie; *b* 1865; was Lord-Lieut of Clackmannanshire 1898-1955; appointed Hereditary Keeper of Stirling Castle (with remainder to heirs male) 1923; Lord Clerk Register and Keeper of Signet of Scotland 1936-44, and Chancellor of Order of the Thistle 1933-49: *m* 1892, Lady Susan Violet Ashley, who *d* 1938, da of 8th Earl of Shaftesbury; *d* 1955; *s* by his grandson (18) JOHN FRANCIS HERVEY (el son of late John Francis Ashley, Lord Erskine, GCSI, GCIE, el son of 12th Earl), 13th Earl of Mar, and 15th Earl of Kellie; *b* 1921; Maj Scots Gds and Argyll and Sutherland Highlanders (TA), 1939-45 War (despatches), a Representative Peer for Scotland, Lord Lieut and Vice Convenor Clackmannanshire, and an Elder of Church of Scotland: *m* 1948, Pansy Constance, OBE, who *d* 1996, da of late Gen Sir (Augustus Francis) Andrew Nicol Thorne, KCB, CMG, DSO (*see* B Penrhyn, 1967 Edn); *d* 1993; *s* by his eldest son (19) JAMES THORNE, 14th Earl of Mar, and 16th Earl of Kellie, and present peer; also Viscount Fentoun, Lord Erskine of Dirleton, and Lord Dirleton.

*(1) *Sir* THOMAS Erskine, KG, 4th son of Hon Sir Alexander, 4th son of 5th Lord Erskine; *cr Lord Erskine of Dirleton* (peerage of Scotland) 1604, *Viscount Fentoun* and *Lord Dirleton* (peerage of Scotland) 1606, with remainder to his heirs male whatsoever, and *Earl of Kellie* (peerage of Scotland) 1619, with remainder to his heirs male whatsoever bearing the name of Erskine; *d* 1639; *s* by his grandson (2) THOMAS (son of Alexander, Viscount Fentoun), 2nd Earl; *d* unmarried 1643; *s* by his brother (3) ALEXANDER, 3rd Earl, whose line failed on the death of (4-7) ALEXANDER, 7th Earl; *d* 1797; *s* by his kinsman (8) *Sir* CHARLES Erskin, 8th Earl, descendant of Hon Charles, 3rd son of 1st Earl, who in 1666 and been *cr* a *Baronet*; *d* unmarried 1799; *s* by his uncle (9) THOMAS, 9th Earl: *m* 1771, Anne, who *d* 1829, da of Adam Gordon, of Ardoch, *d* 1828; *s* by his brother (10) METHVEN, 10th Earl: *m* 1781, Joanna, da of Adam Gordon (ante); *d* 1829; *s* by his kinsman (11) JOHN FRANCIS MILLER, 11th Earl, who had previously *s* as 9th Earl of Mar (see ante).

March and Kinrara, Earl of (peerage of England); son of Duke of Richmond.

March, Earl of (peerage of Scotland), see Earl of Wemyss and March.

MARCHAMLEY, BARON (Whiteley) (Baron UK 1908)

LIVE·TO·LIVE

WILLIAM FRANCIS WHITELEY, 4th Baron; b 27 July 1968; s 1994.

Arms – Per fesse dancettée sable and gules, in chief a pale or, theron three bars of the second, in base a fleur-de-lis argent. Crest – A stag's head couped argent, attired or, holding in the mouth a bell gold. Supporters – Dexter, a griffin sejant: sinister, a hawk; both per fesse gules and sable, armed and membered or, each charged on the fesse line with a fleur-de-lis argent.
Address – c/o House of Lords, SW1A 0PW.

WIDOW LIVING OF THIRD BARON

SONIA KATHLEEN (Baroness Marchamley), yr da of Francis Henry Richardson Pedrick, of Yealmpton, S Devon: m 1967, the 3rd Baron Marchamley, who d 1994.

PREDECESSORS – (1) GEORGE Whiteley, PC, el son of late George Whiteley, JP, of Woodlands, Blackburn; b 1855; Parliamentary (Patronage) Sec to the Treasury and Ch Liberal Whip Dec 1905 to June 1908; MP for Stockport (L) Feb 1893 to Sept 1900, and for Pudsey Div of E Part of W Riding of Yorkshire Oct 1900 to June 1908; cr Baron Marchamley, of Hawkstone, co Salop (peerage of United Kingdom) 1908; m 1881, Alice, who d 1913, only child of late William Tattersall, JP, of Quarry Bank, Blackburn, and St Anthony's Milnthorpe; d 1925: s by his (2) WILLIAM TATTERSALL, 2nd Baron; b 1886; High Sheriff, co Southampton 1921; European War 1915-18 as Lieut-Com RNVR, European War 1939-45 as Flight-Lieut RAF: m 1911, Margaret Clara, who d 1974, da of Thomas Scott Johnstone, formerly of Glenmark, Waipara, NZ; d 1949; s by his only son (3) JOHN WILLIAM TATTERSALL, 3rd Baron; b 1922: m 1967, Sonia Kathleen, yr da of Francis Henry Richardson Pedrick; d 1994; s by his only son (4) WILLIAM FRANCIS, 4th Baron and present peer.

MARCHWOOD, VISCOUNT (Penny) (Viscount UK 1945, Bt UK 1933)

Always prepared

DAVID GEORGE STAVELEY PENNY, 3rd Viscount, and 3rd Baronet; *b* 22 May 1936; *s* 1979; *ed* Winchester; late 2nd Lieut RHG; Chm Moët-Hennessy (UK) Ltd and holds other directorships in Moët-Hennessy Group: *m* 1964, Tessa Jane, who *d* 1997, 2nd da of Wilfred Francis Norris, of Glebe Park, Lurgashall, nr Midhurst, Sussex, and has issue.

Arms – Gules, six fleurs-de-lis, three, two, and one or, on a chief engrailed of the second, three roses of the first, barbed and seeded proper. Crest – Issuant from a circlet or, a demi lion gules, collared sable, charged on the shoulder with a rose, and holding in the dexter paw a fleur-de-lis gold. Supporters – *Dexter*, a Malayan tiger proper; *sinister*, a sea lion proper.
Residence – The Filberts, Aston Tirrold, Didcot, Oxon. *Clubs* – White's, MCC.

SONS LIVING

Hon PETER GEORGE WORSLEY, *b* 8 Oct 1965; *ed* Winchester: *m* 1995, Annabel C., yr da of Rex Cooper, of E Bergholt, Suffolk, and has issue living, India Rose, *b* 1997. *Residence* – 44 Elsynge Rd, SW18.
Hon Nicholas Mark Staveley, *b* 1967.
Hon Edward James Frederick, *b* 1970: *m* 1996, Selina M., da of late Frederick Sasse, of Afonwen, Flintshire, and has issue living, Alexander George Robert, *b* 1997.

BROTHER LIVING

Hon Patrick Glyn (29 Chester Row, SW1. *Club* – White's), *b* 1939; *ed* Nautical Coll, Pangbourne; Lieut R. Wilts Yeo 1962-65, late 2nd Lieut RHG: *m* 1st, 1968 (*m diss* 1974), Sue Eleanor Jane, da of late Charles Phipps Brutton, CBE; 2ndly, 1979, Lynn Vanessa Knox, da of John Leslie Wyles, of Wimbledon, and formerly wife of (i) Colin Hart, and (ii) John Birkett Knox, and has issue living (by 1st *m*), Sasha Jane, *b* 1969.

SISTER LIVING

Hon Carol Ann, *b* 1948: *m* 1978, Patrick John Quirk, of 9 Lambourn Rd, SW4 0LX, and has issue living, Tom Michael, *b* 1979, — Toby James, *b* 1983.

PREDECESSORS – (1) (FREDERICK) GEORGE PENNY, KCVO, 2nd son of late Frederick James Penny, of Sydney Cottage, Bitterne, Hants; *b* 1876; a Master Mariner, and Master of Master Mariners' Co 1941-5; Senior Partner of Fraser & Co, Government exchange brokers, of Singapore; was Parliamentary Private Sec to Financial Sec to War Office 1923-4, a Govt Whip 1926-8, a Junior Lord of the Treasury 1928-9 and (in National Govt) Sept to Nov 1931, Vice-Chamberlain of HM's Household 1931-2, Comptroller of HM's Household 1932-5, and Treasurer of HM's Household 1935-7; sat as MP for Kingston-upon-Thames (C) 1922-37; *cr* a *Baronet* 1933, *Baron Marchwood* of Penang and of Marchwood, co Southampton (peerage of United Kingdom) 1937, and *Viscount Marchwood*, of Penang and of Marchwood, co Southampton (peerage of United Kingdom) 1945: *m* 1905, Anne Boyle, who *d* 1957, da of late Sir John Gunn, JP, of St Mellons, Cardiff; *d* 1955; *s* by his only son (2) PETER GEORGE, MBE, 2nd Viscount, *b* 1912; Hon Maj RA 1939-45 War; Dir George Wimpey & Co, Contractors 1960-71: *m* 1935, Pamela, who *d* 1979, only child of John Staveley Colton-Fox, JP, of Todwick Grange, nr Sheffield; *d* 1979; *s* by his el son (3) DAVID GEORGE STAVELEY, 3rd Viscount and present peer; also Baron Marchwood.

MARGADALE, BARON (Morrison) (Baron UK 1964)

JAMES IAN MORRISON, TD, 2nd Baron; *b* 17 July 1930; *s* 1996; *ed* Eton, and RAC Cirencester; Major Royal Wilts Yeo (ret), formerly 2nd Lieut Life Guards; Hon Col Royal Wilts Yeo 1982-89; CC Wilts 1955 and 1973-77, Alderman 1969-74, High Sheriff 1971, DL 1977; Chm Westbury Conservative Assocn 1967-71, Pres 1972-84, Chm Tattersalls Cttee 1969-80, and Wilts CLA 1978-81; Member Queen's Body Guard for Scotland (Royal Company of Archers); TD 1963: *m* 1952, Clare, eldest da of Anthony Lister Barclay, of Broad Oak End, Hertford, and has issue.

Arms – Tierced in pairle azure, sable and gules, in chief a Saracen's head couped affrontée and in base two Saracens' heads addorsed in profile all argent, and at the fess point an inescutcheon parted per pale dexter per bend sinister embattled gules and or, in dexter chief a battle axe paleways argent, and in sinister base, issuant from a base undy azure and argent, a tower sabre, masoned argent, port gules (*Morrison of Islay*) sinister, vert powdered with bezants, a horse rearing on its hind legs argent, langued and hoofed gules (*Lordship of Margadale*). **Crest** – Three Saracens' heads conjoined in one neck one looking to the dexter, one affrontée, and one looking to the sinister all proper. **Supporters** – Two Woodcocks proper.
Residence – Fonthill House, Tisbury, Wilts SP3 5SA. *Estate Offices* - Fonthill Bishop, Salisbury, Wilts SP3 5SH; Bridgend, Islay, Argyll PA44 7PB. *Clubs* – White's, Jockey.

SONS LIVING

Hon ALASTAIR JOHN, *b* 4 April 1958; *ed* Harrow, and RAC Cirencester: *m* 1988, Lady Sophia Louise Sydney Murphy, yr da of 11th Duke of Devonshire, KG, PC, and has issue living, Declan James, *b* 11 July 1993, — Nancy Lorna, *b* 1995. *Address* – Estate Office, Fonthill Bishop, Salisbury, Wilts SP3 5SH.

Hon Hugh, *b* 1960; *ed* Eton, and Ealing Coll (BA): *m* 1986, Jane, da of Bryan Jenks, of Le Schuylkill, Blvd de Suisse, Monte Carlo, and has issue living, Geordie Anthony, *b* 1989, — Amber Belinda, *b* 1993. *Residence* – Sheepdrove House, Lambourn, Berks RG17 7UN.

DAUGHTER LIVING

Hon Fiona Elizabeth (*Viscountess Trenchard*), *b* 1954: *m* 1975, 3rd Viscount Trenchard. *Residence* – Summerdown, East Ilsley, Newbury, Berks RG20 7LB.

BROTHER LIVING

Hon Sir Charles Andrew, *b* 1932; *ed* Eton; Capt Royal Wilts Yeo (ret), 2nd Lieut Life Guards; DL Hereford and Worcester 1995; Vice Chm 1922 Cttee 1974-83, Chm Nat Cttee for Electoral Reform 1985-92, Dir Sothebys 1989-95, Bankers Insurance Co Ltd 1989-93, Chm The Game Conservancy 1987-94, British Trust for Conservation Vols 1972-78 (Pres 1978-82), etc; Council Member Salmon & Trout Assocn since 1966; MP Devizes Div Wilts (C) 1964-92; Knt 1988: *m* 1st, 1954 (*m diss* 1984), Hon (Antoinette) Sara Frances Sibell Long, only da of 2nd Viscount Long; 2ndly, 1984, Mrs Rosalind Elizabeth Ward, da of late Hon Richard Edward Lygon (*see* Earldom of Beauchamp), and has issue living (by 1st *m*), David John (21 Albert Bridge Rd, SW11), *b* 1959; *ed* Eton, and St Benet's Hall, Oxford: *m* 1984, Venetia Anne, 2nd da of Julian John William Salmond (*see* B Lucas of Crudwell, colls), and has issue living, Ivo Charles David *b* 1990, Tara Sibyl Caolila *b* 1988, — Anabel Laura Dorothy, *b* 1955: *m* 1st, 1979 (*m diss* 1984), Michael Harry Stapleton; 2ndly, 1985, David William Arnold Loyd (*see* E Albemarle, colls), and has issue living (by 1st *m*), Harry Edward John *b* 1982, Scarlett Margaret Laura *b* 1980, (by 2nd *m*) (*see* E Albemarle, colls). *Residence* – The Old Rectory, Fonthill Bishop, Salisbury, Wilts SP3 5SF.

SISTER LIVING

Hon Mary Anne, DCVO, *b* 1937: *ed* Heathfield Sch, Ascot; a Woman of the Bedchamber to HM since 1960; DCVO 1982. *Residence* – The Old Rectory, Fonthill Bishop, Salisbury, Wilts SP3 5SF.

PREDECESSOR – (1) JOHN GRANVILLE Morrison, TD, son of late Hugh Morrison, of Fonthill House, Tisbury, Wilts (*see* E Granville, 1934 Edn), *b* 1906; served 1939-45 War with Royal Wilts Yeo in Middle East; Hon Col Royal Wilts Yeo 1960-72, and Royal Yeo 1965-72; Lord Lieut Wilts 1969-81; Chm 1922 Cttee 1955-64; MP Salisbury (C) 1942-64; Pres British Field Sports 1980-85; sometime Master South and West Wilts Foxhounds; *cr Baron Margadale*, of Islay, co Argyll (peerage of UK) 1964: *m* 1928, Hon Margaret Esther Lucie Smith, who *d* 1980, da of 2nd Viscount Hambleden; *d* 1996; *s* by his eldest son (2) JAMES IAN, 2nd Baron and present peer.

MARGESSON, VISCOUNT (Margesson) (Viscount UK 1942)

Loyalty binds me

FRANCIS VERE HAMPDEN MARGESSON, 2nd Viscount; *b* 17 April 1922; *s* 1965; *ed* Eton and Trin Coll, Oxford; Information Officer, British Consulate-General, New York, 1964-70; 1939-45 War as Lt RNVR: *m* 1958, Helena, da of late Heikki Backstrom, of Oulu, Finland, and has issue.

Arms – Sable, a lion pasant guardant argent, a chief engrailed or, thereon between two pallets azure a pale of the last charged with an ostrich feather erect of the second. **Crest** – Upon a coronet composed of four roses set upon a rim or, a lion passant guardant sable, collared gold, and charged with a rose argent, barbed and seeded proper. **Supporters** – On either side a falcon, wings elevated argent, armed and belled or, and charged with a portcullis chained sable.
Residence – Ridgely Manor, Box 254, Stone Ridge, New York 12484, USA.

SON LIVING

Hon RICHARD FRANCIS DAVID, *b* 25 Dec 1960; *ed* St Paul's Sch, New Hampshire, USA, Eton, and Exeter Univ; Maj Coldm Gds: *m* 1990, Wendy Maree, da of James Hazelton, of Kempsey, NSW, Australia, and has issue living, Isabel, *b* 1995. *Club* – Cavalry and Guards'.

DAUGHTERS LIVING

Hon Rhoda France, *b* 1962.
Hon Sarah Helena, 1963.
Hon Jane Henrietta, *b* 1965.

SISTER LIVING (*Daughter of 1st Viscount*)

Hon (Mary) Gay Hobart (*Baroness Charteris of Amisfield*), *b* 1919: *m* 1944, Baron Charteris of Amisfield, GCB, GCVO, OBE, QSO, PC, of 11 Kylestrome House, Cundy St, SW1W 9JT, and Wood Stanway, Cheltenham, Glos GL54 5PG.

PREDECESSOR – (1) HENRY DAVID REGINALD Margesson, MC, PC, el son of Sir Mortimer Reginald Margesson and Lady Isabel Augusta Hobart-Hampden, sister of 7th Earl of Buckinghamshire; *b* 1890; Ch Govt Whip 1931-40, and Sec of State for War 1940-42; MP for Upton Div, W Ham (C) 1922-23, and for Rugby 1924-42; *cr Viscount Margesson*, of Rugby, co Warwick (peerage of UK) 1942: *m* 1916 (*m diss* 1940), Frances, who *d* 1977, da of Francis H Leggett, of New York, *d* 1965; *s* by his only son (2) FRANCIS VERE HAMPDEN, 2nd Viscount and present peer.

MARKS OF BROUGHTON, BARON (Marks) (Baron UK 1961)

SIMON RICHARD MARKS, 3rd Baron; *b* 3 May 1950; *s* 1998; *ed* Eton, and Balliol Coll, Oxford: *m* 1982, Marion, only da of Peter F...... Norton, of the Azores, and has issue.

Arms – Pily argent and azure a pair of scales or **Crest** – A dove wings addorsed argent, beaked and membered gules, gorged with an antique crown, and to the beak a gimmel ring. **Supporters** – On either side a lion or supporting a cornucopia argent the fruit proper, that on the dexter holding aloft with the interior forepaw a red rose slipped and leaved also proper, and that on the sinister two interlaced triangles or.
Address – Michael House, Baker St, W1A 1DN.

SON LIVING

Hon MICHAEL, *b* 13 May 1989.

DAUGHTERS LIVING

Hon Miriam Ann, *b* 1983.
Hon Susannah Elizabeth, *b* 1986.
Hon Rebecca, *b* 1997.

SISTERS LIVING

Hon Naomi Anne, *b* 1952: *m* 1980, Martin Christian Wölffer, and has issue living, Jake Edward, *b* 1998, — Joanna Claire, *b* 1982, — Georgina Chloe, *b* 1985.

Hon Sarah Elizabeth, *b* 1953: *m* 1979 (*m diss* 1989), Nicholai Radomir, and has issue living, Michael Richard, *b* 1981, — Leo Mark, *b* 1985.

AUNT LIVING (*only daughter of 1st Baron*)

Hon Hannah Olive (La Rocabella, 24 Avenue Princesse Grace, Monte Carlo, 98000 Monaco), *b* 1918: *m* 1st, 1941 (*m diss* 1959), Alec Lerner; 2ndly, 1960, Gerald William Harold Marcow, who *d* 1992, and has issue living (by 1st *m*), Joel David, *b* 1942; *ed* Stowe, and McGill Univ, Montreal: *m* 1982, Deborah, da of Colin Travers, of Woking, Surrey, and has issue living, Simon Michael *b* 1986, Miranda Hannah *b* 1983, — Diana Toby, *b* 1947: *m* 1st, 1969, Michael John Glass, who *d* 19—; 2ndly, 19—, ..., — Maureen Ann, *b* 1952: *m* 1983, Terence A. Willson, and has issue living, Simon Zachary *b* 1985, Jessica Sophie Hannah *b* 1989.

MOTHER LIVING

Ann Catherine, da of late Maj Richard James Pinto, MC: *m* 1949 (*m diss* 1958), Michael Marks (later 2nd Baron Marks of Broughton), who *d* 1998.

WIDOW LIVING OF SECOND BARON

MARINA (*Dowager Baroness Marks of Broughton*), da of Demetrios Sacalis, of Athens, and formerly wife of Prof Leslie J. D. Collins: *m* 1994, as his 5th wife, the 2nd Baron Marks of Broughton, who *d* 1998. *Address* – c/o Michael House, 47-67 Baker St, W1.

PREDECESSORS – (1) *Sir* SIMON Marks, son of Michael Marks, of Manchester; *b* 1888; Chm and joint Managing Dir of Marks & Spencer Ltd; *cr Baron, Marks of Broughton*, of Sunningdale, co Berks (peerage of UK) 1961: *m* 1915, Miriam, who *d* 1971, da of Ephraim Sieff; *d* 1964; *s* by his only son (2) MICHAEL, 2nd Baron, *b* 1920: *m* 1st, 1949 (*m diss* 1958), Ann Catherine, da of late Maj Richard James Pinto, MC; 2ndly, 1960 (*m diss* 1965), Helene, da of Gustave Fischer; 3rdly, 1976 (*m diss* 1985), Toshiko Shimura, of Japan; 4thly, 1988, Li Ying Zhang; 5thly, 1994, Mrs Marina Collins, da of Demetrios Sacalis, of Athens; *d* 1998; *s* by his only son (3) SIMON RICHARD, 3rd Baron and present peer.

MARLBOROUGH, DUKE OF (Spencer-Churchill) (Duke England 1702)
(Name pronounced "Maulbro")

JOHN GEORGE VANDERBILT HENRY SPENCER-CHURCHILL, 11th Duke, *b* 13 April 1926; *s* 1972; *ed* Eton; late Capt Life Gds; JP and DL of Oxon: *m* 1st, 1951 (*m diss* 1960), Susan Mary, only da of late Michael Charles St John Hornby (*see* E Dudley, colls, 1985 Edn); 2ndly, 1961 (*m diss* 1971), Athina (Tina), who *d* 1974, da of late Stavros G. Livanos, and formerly wife of late Aristotle Onassis: 3rdly, 1972, (Dagmar) Rosita (Astri Libertas), da of late Count Carl Ludwig Douglas, and has issue by 1st and 3rd *m*.

Arms – Quarterly: 1st and 4th sable, a lion rampant argent; on a canton of the second a cross gules, *Churchill*; 2nd and 3rd quarterly argent and gules; on a bend sable, between two frettes or, three escallops of the first, *Spencer*; over all (as an honourable augmentation), in the centre chief point, on an escutcheon argent, the cross of St George surmounted by another escutcheon azure, charged with three fleurs-de-lis, two and one or. **Crest** – 1st, a lion couchant and guardant argent, supporting a banner gules, charged with a dexter hand couped argent, *Churchill*; 2nd, out of a ducal coronet or, a griffin's head,

Faithful, though unfortunate

expanded, argent, *Spencer*. **Supporters** – Two wyverns, wings elevated, gules.
Seat – Blenheim Palace, Woodstock, Oxon. *Residence* – Lee Place, Charlbury, Oxon.

FIEL·PERO·DESDICHADO

SONS LIVING (*By 1st marriage*)

(CHARLES) JAMES (*Marquess of Blandford*) (Gate Farm, Kiddington, Woodstock, Oxon; 16 Lawrence St, SW3), *b* 24 Nov 1955; *ed* Harrow: *m* 1990, Rebecca Mary, da of Peter Few Brown, and of Mrs John Winnington-Ingram, and has issue:—
SON LIVING - George (*Earl of Sunderland*), *b* 28 July 1992.

(*By 3rd marriage*)

Lord Edward Albert Charles, *b* 1974.

DAUGHTERS LIVING (*By 1st marriage*)

Lady Henrietta Mary SPENCER-CHURCHILL, *b* 1958; has resumed her maiden name: *m* 1980 (*m diss* 1989), Nathan Gelber, son of Aba Gelber, and has issue living, David Aba, *b* 1981, — Maximilian Henry, *b* 1985.

(*By 3rd marriage*)

Lady Alexandra Elizabeth Mary, *b* 1977.

BROTHER LIVING

Lord Charles George William Colin, *b* 1940; *ed* Eton: *m* 1st, 1965 (*m diss* 1968), Gillian, da of Andrew Fuller, of New York City, and Fort Worth, Texas, USA; 2ndly, 1970, Elizabeth Jane, el da of Capt Hon Mark Hugh Wyndham, MC (*see* B Egremont), and has issue living (by 2nd *m*), Rupert John Harold Mark, *b* 1971, — Dominic Albert Charles, *b* 1979, — Alexander David, *b* 1983.

SISTERS LIVING

Lady Sarah Consuelo SPENCER-CHURCHILL, *b* 1921; has resumed her maiden name: *m* 1st, 1943 (*m diss* 1966), Lt Edwin F. Russell, USA Navy; 2ndly, 1966 (*m diss* in Mexico 1967), Guy Burgos, of Santiago, Chile; 3rdly, 1967 (at Philadelphia), Theodorous Roubanis, and has issue living (by 1st *m*), Serena Mary Churchill, *b* 1944: *m* 1st, 1966 (*m diss* in Mexico 1967), R. Stephen Salant; 2ndly, 1968, Neil A. McConnell; 3rdly, 1978, Neil Roxburgh Balfour, of 55 Warwick Sq, SW1V 2AJ, and has issue living (by 2nd *m*), Morgan Alexandra *b* 1973, Lucinda Mary *b* 1975, (by 3rd *m*) Alastair Albert David *b* 1981, Consuelo Lily *b* 1979, — Consuelo Sarah, *b* 1946: *m* 1st, 1968 (*m diss* in Mexico 1969), James Toback; 2ndly 1970, Mark Schulman, of New York City, USA; 3rdly, 19—, B. William Judson, and has issue living (by 2nd *m*), Alexandre *b* 1971, (by 3rd *m*), Nicholas *b* 1976, Ian *b* 1978, — Alexandra Brenda, *b* 1949: *m* 1970, Timothy Biech, of Camp Hill, Penn, USA, — Jacqueline, *b* 1958: *m* 1981, Eugene Williams, and has issue living, Eugene III *b* 1985, Harry *b* 1988, Philip *b* 1989. *Residence* – 13 Hemlock Rd, Essex, CT 06426, USA.

Lady Rosemary Mildred, *b* 1929: *m* 1953, Charles Robert Muir, who *d* 1972, and has issue living, Alexander Pepys, *b* 1954, — Simon Huntly (Angel Farm, Monks Alley, Binfield, Berks), *b* 1959: *m* 1990, Sarah-Jane E., only da of Barry Jenkinson, of Chetton Grange, Bridgnorth, Shropshire, and has issue living, Robin Hugo *b* 1993, Thomas Sebastian *b* 1995, — Mary Arabella, *b* 1962: *m* 1991, J. Timothy Haynes, of 29 Henning St, SW11 3DR, son of late J. H. Haynes, of Fuente del Rempujo, San Enrique de Guadiaro, Spain, and has issue living, Jack Cresswell *b* 1993, Rowley *b* 1996. *Residence* – Orange Hill House, Binfield, Bracknell, Berks.

WIDOW LIVING OF SON OF NINTH DUKE

Betty, da of late J. C. Cunningham, of 27 Culross Street, W1: *m* 1947, Lord Ivor Charles Spencer-Churchill, who *d* 1956, and has issue living (see colls infra).

COLLATERAL BRANCHES LIVING

Issue of late Lord Ivor Charles Spencer-Churchill, yr son of 9th Duke, *b* 1898, *d* 1956: *m* 1947, Betty (ante), da of late J. C. Cunningham, of 27 Culross Street, W1:—
Robert William Charles, *b* 1954; *ed* Eton: *m* 1979, Jeanne M., el da of Etienne Maze, of 47 Victoria Rd, W8 (son of late Paul Maze, DCM, the painter), and has issue living, John Robert I—, *b* 1984, — Ivor Charles E—, *b* 1986.

Grandchildren of late Rt Hon Sir Winston Leonard Spencer Churchill, KG, OM, CH, TD, FRS (infra):—
Issue of late Hon Randolph Frederick Edward Spencer Churchill, MBE, *b* 1911, *d* 1968: *m* 1st, 1939 (*m diss* 1946), Hon Pamela Beryl Digby, who *d* 1997, da of 11th Baron Digby; 2ndly, 1948 (*m diss* 1961), June Hermione, who *d* 1980, da of Col Rex Hamilton Osborne, DSO:—
(By 1st *m*) Winston Spencer CHURCHILL, *b* 1940; *ed* Eton, and Ch Ch, Oxford; author and journalist; MP for Stretford (*C*) 1970-83, MP for Davyhulme (*C*) 1983-97; Member of Executive 1922 Cttee 1979-88, Member of Select Cttee on Defence since 1983; Conservative Party Defence Spokesman 1976-78 and 1982-84: *m* 1st, 1964 (*m diss* 1997), Mary Caroline, da of late Sir Gerard John Regis d'Erlanger, CBE; 2ndly 1997, Mrs Luce Danielson (*née* Engelen), and has issue living (by 1st *m*), Randolph Leonard, *b* 1965; Lieut RN (ret); ACA Investment Banker: *m* 1992, Catherine Z., elder da of Antony Lancaster, of Kensington, and has issue living, Serena Barbara Spencer *b* 1996, Zoe Spencer *b* 1998, — John Gerard Averell, *b* 1975, — Jennie, *b* 1966: *m* 1993, James P. Repard, yr son of Hugo Repard, of Westerton, Sussex, and has issue living, George *b* 1994, Arabella *b* 1996, — Marina, *b* 1967; has issue living, Henry BROUNGER *b* 1998. —— (By 2nd

m) Arabella CHURCHILL (2 St Edmund's Cottages, Bove Town, Glastonbury, Somerset), *b* 1949; Dir The Children's World Charity; Organiser of Theatre and Circus Areas of Glastonbury Festival of Contemporary Performing Arts: *m* 1st, 1972, James J. Barton; 2ndly, 1988, Ian McLeod (juggler, as Haggis McLeod), son of late Harold Leonard Hodges, and has issue living (by 1st *m*), Jake Nicholas, *b* 1973, — (by 2nd *m*) Jessica Jules, *b* 1988.

Grandchildren of late Rt Hon Lord Randolph Henry Spencer Churchill, MP, 3rd son of 7th Duke:—
Issue of late Rt Hon Sir Winston Leonard Spencer Churchill, KG, OM, CH, TD, Prime Minister 1940-45 and 1951-55, *b* 1874, *d* 1965: *m* 1908, Dame Clementine Ogilvy, GBE (*Baroness Spencer-Churchill*), who *d* 1977 (*cr* a Life Baroness 1965), da of late Col Sir Henry Montagu Hozier, KCB (*see* E Airlie, 1925 Edn):—
Hon Mary, DBE (*Baroness Soames*), *b* 1922; formerly Junior Cdr ATS; author; Hon Fell Churchill Coll, Camb; a Gov of Harrow Sch; Chm Royal Nat Theatre Board 1989-95; Chm Winston Churchill Memorial Trust since 1991; Chev de la Légion d'Honneur 1995; MBE (Mil) 1945, DBE (Civil) 1980: *m* 1947, Baron Soames, GCMG, GCVO, CH, CBE, PC, Life Baron, who *d* 1987.

Issue of late Major John Strange Spencer Churchill, DSO, *b* 1880, *d* 1947: *m* 1908, Lady Gwendeline Theresa Mary Bertie, who *d* 1941, da of 7th Earl of Abingdon:—
Henry Winston (Peregrine), *b* 1913; *ed* Harrow, and Camb Univ, Hon Degree Mechanical Science: *m* 1st, 1954, Patricia Ethel Louisa, who *d* 1956, da of late Thomas March; 2ndly, 1957, Yvonne Henriette Marie Jéhannin, of Rennes, France. *Residence* – Fairdown, Vernham Dean, Hants. —— Clarissa (*Countess of Avon*), *b* 1920: *m* 1952, as his 2nd wife, 1st Earl of Avon, who *d* 1977. *Residence* – 32 Bryanston Square, W1H 7LS.

Granddaughter of late Maj John Strange Spencer Churchill, DSO (ante):—
Issue of late John George Spencer Churchill, painter, sculptor and composer, *b* 1909, *d* 1992: *m* 1st, 1934 (*m diss* 1938), Angela Mary, da of late Capt George Culme-Seymour (*see* Culme-Seymour, Bt, colls); 2ndly, 1941 (*m diss* 1952), Mary, only da of late Kenneth Cookson, OBE, of Wynberg, CP, S Africa (*see* Butler, Bt, *cr* 1628, colls, 1980 Edn); 3rdly, 1953, Mrs Kathlyn Maude Muriel Hall Tandy, who *d* 1957, only da of late Maj-Gen Walter Samuel Hall Beddall, CB, OBE; 4thly, 1958 (*m diss* 1972), Anna Gunvor Maria (Lullan), da of Johan Janson, of Kristianstad, Sweden, and widow of Granger Boston:—
(By 1st *m*) Sarah Cornelia (*Baroness Ashburton*), *b* 1935: *m* 1st, 1957, James Colin Crewe (*see* M Crewe, 1948 Edn); 2ndly, 1987, 7th Baron Ashburton, KG, KCVO, and has issue living (by 1st *m*), Peregrine John, *b* 1959, — Emma, *b* 1962: *m* 1993, Nicholas G. S. Vester, and has issue living, Cleo *b* 1995, — Annabel Sophia, *b* 1965; has issue living (by Daniel Richard Butler), Jack Badger BUTLER-CREWE *b* 1994, Molly Megan BUTLER-CREWE *b* 1997. *Residence* – Lake House, Northington, Alresford, Hants.

Descendants of late Lord Francis Almeric Spencer (3rd son of 4th Duke) who was *cr Baron Churchill* 1815 (*see* V Churchill).

Grandchildren of late Sir Charles Gordon Spencer, 4th son of late Rev Charles Vere Spencer (infra):—
Issue of late John Gray Churchill SPENCER BERNARD, MA, MD, FRCS (who assumed the additional name of Bernard by deed poll 1955), *b* 1907, *d* 1977: *m* 1933, Elsie Phyllis, MA (Nether Winchendon House, Aylesbury, Bucks), da of Ferrand Corley, of The Christian Coll, Madras, and of Woodside, Witney:—
Charles Francis Churchill (18 rue Barbette, 75003 Paris, France), *b* 1942; *ed* Marlborough, and Magdalene Coll, Camb: *m* 1974, Rosalyn Anne, da of Maj Patrick Plunkett, of Hazelbury Plucknett, Som (*see* Wheler, Bt, 1985 Edn), and has issue living, Jane Beatrice, *b* 1979, — Sarah Penelope Katharine, *b* 1983, — Elizabeth Joanna *b* 1986. —— Robert Vere (Nether Winchendon House, Aylesbury, Bucks HP18 0DY), *b* 1944; *ed* Marlborough and Trin Coll, Oxford; Bar Inner Temple 1969: *m* 1975, Katharine Margaret, da of Lt-Col Claud Everard Montagu Douglas Scott, MC (*see* D Buccleuch and Queensberry, colls). —— Julia Diana, *b* 1936: *m* 1959, John Simon Baskerville Cadwallader Hopton, of Village Farm House, Boarstall, Aylesbury, Bucks, and has issue living, Richard Henry Cadwallader, *b* 1962, — Edward Charles Adams, *b* 1964, — Isobel Georgiana, *b* 1967. —— Clare Rosemary, *b* 1938: *m* 1963, Rio Tyrell Arthur Hohler, of Chevreloup, 27 Route de Perdreauville, 78950 Gambais, France, elder son of Henry Arthur Frederick Hohler, CMG, and has issue living, Rupert John Frederick, *b* 1972, — Harriet Valentine, *b* 1967, — Camilla Clare, *b* 1968, — Amanda Sophie, *b* 1970.

Issue of late Charles Bernard Spencer, *b* 1909, *d* 1963: *m* 1st, 1936, Nora, who *d* 1947, da of Frederick Gibbs; 2ndly, 1961, Anne Margaret Helen (who *m* 2ndly, 1969, Rock Noel Humphreys, of Bark Barn Cottage, 12 West Dean, Salisbury, Wilts), da of late Alan George Marjoribanks:—
(By 2nd *m*) Piers Bernard, *b* 1963. *Residence* – 36 Alma Sq, St John's Wood, NW8 9QD

Granddaughters of late Rev Charles Vere Spencer, son of Rev Frederick Charles Spencer, son of late John Spencer, MP, el son of late Lord Charles Spencer, MP, 2nd son of 3rd Duke:—
Issue of late Rev Frederick Augustus Morland Spencer, DD, *b* 1878, *d* 1962: *m* 1913, Gertrude, Lucie, MA, who *d* 1970, el da of late George John Burke, MICE, of St Kilda, Melbourne:—
Marion Gertrude (10 Longdown Lane North, Ewell, Epsom, Surrey KT17 3JQ), *b* 1916: *m* 1940 (*m diss* 1971), Kenneth Ninian Hoare, MBE, MA, and has issue living, Gillian Sheila, *b* 1947: *m* 1971, Richard James Kenneth Button (Gulf Stevedoring, PO Box 19860, Jeddah 21445, Saudi Arabia), and has had issue, Daniel Mark *b* 1983 *d* 1987, Sarah Nicola (9 Sympson Close, Abingdon, Oxon OX14 5RB) *b* 1971, Teresa Jane (Flat 602, Duncan House, Dolphin Square, SW1V 3PP) *b* 1974, — Celia Jennifer (10 Longdown Lane North, Ewell, Epsom, Surrey KT17 3JQ), *b* 1952: *m* 1975, Capt Keith Reading, and has issue living, Kyle Gareth *b* 1983, Katrina Louise *b* 1976. —— Geraldine Mildred (70C Currong Flats, Braddon, Australia 2601) *b* 1920; *ed* Sydney Univ, NSW (BA).

Descendants of late John Spencer, MP (son of late Hon John Spencer, MP, 3rd son of 3rd Earl of Sunderland), who was *cr Earl Spencer* 1765 (see that title).

PREDECESSORS – (1) *Right Hon Sir* JOHN CHURCHILL, KG, PC, el son of Sir Winston Churchill; *b* 1650; the most distinguished Gen of his time, was *cr Lord Churchill*, of Eyemouth, co Berwick (peerage of Scotland) 1682, *Baron Churchill of Sandridge* co Hertford (peerage of England) 1685, *Earl of Marlborough* (peerage of England) 1689, *Marquess of Blandford* and Duke of Marlborough (peerage of England) 1702, *Prince of the Holy Roman Empire* 1704 (and to all descendants male and female), and *Prince of Mindelheim* in Suabia 1705; was sometime Ambassador to France from James II, he assisted at the victory of Sedgmoor, and in the Convention Parliament voted in favour of the Prince and Princess of Orange filling the throne; commanded the English troops in the Netherlands 1689; having displeased William III, he was confined for a short time in the Tower; appointed upon the accession of Queen Anne, Capt-Gen of all HM's forces in England; in 1702-3 he reduced Venloo, Stevenswaert, Ruremonde, and Liège; in 1704 won the celebrated victory of Blenheim, and afterwards achieved other victories, notably Ramillies 1706, Oudenard 1708, and Malplaquet 1709; for his victories at and before Blenheim he was awarded by Act of Parliament the royal manor of Woodstock, and a splendid palace was erected by HM's orders; in 1706 an Act was passed settling his honours on his posterity and granting him and each successor in the title a pension of £5,000 a year: *m* 1678, Sarah, who *d* 1744, da and co-heiress of Richard Jennings, of Sandridge, Herts; he had surviving issue Henrietta, wife of Francis, 2nd Earl of Godolphin, and Anne, 2nd wife of Charles Spencer, KG, 3rd Earl of Sunderland (see infra); *d* 1722, when the Scottish Barony of Church-ill of Eyemouth became ext; *s* in his other under the special Act of Parliament by his da (2) HENRIETTA (ante); *d* without surviving male issue 1733; *s* by her nephew (3) CHARLES, KG, 3rd Duke, 2nd son of Anne (ante), who had in 1729 *s* his brother as 5th *Earl of Sunderland* (see*infra); was Lord-Lieut of cos Oxford and Buckingham, and a distinguished military commander; *d* 1758; *s* by his son (4) GEORGE, KG, 4th Duke; Lord Chamberlain of the Household 1762-3, and Lord Privy Seal 1763-5; *d* 1817; *s* by his son (5) GEORGE, 5th Duke; MP for Oxford 1790-96 and for Tregony 1802-6; assumed in 1817 by Roy licence the additional surname of Churchill; called to House of Lords in his father's barony of Spencer 1806; *d* 1840: *s* by his son (6) GEORGE, 6th Duke, *b* 1793; was Lord-Lieut of Oxfordshire; *d* 1857; *s* by his son (7) JOHN WINSTON, KG, DCL, 7th Duke; sat as MP for Woodstock (*C*) 1844-5 and 1847-57; was Lord-Lieut of co Oxford, Lord Pres of the Council 1868, and Viceroy of Ireland 1876-80: *m* 1843, Lady Frances Anne Emily Vane, da of 3rd Marquess of Londonderry; *d* 1883; *s* by his son (8) GEORGE CHARLES, 8th Duke, *b* 1844: *m* 1st, 1869 (*m diss* 1883), Lady Albertha Frances Anne Hamilton, who *d* 1932, da of 1st Duke of Abercorn, KG; 2ndly, 1888, Lillian Warren (who *m* 3rdly 1895, Lord William de la Poer Beresford, VC, KCIE, and *d* 1909), da of Cdr Cicero Price, of US Navy and widow of Louis Hammersley, of New York; *d* 1892, *s* by his only son (9) CHARLES RICHARD JOHN, KG, PC, 9th Duke, *b* 1871; Lord-Lieut of Oxfordshire; Paymaster-Gen 1899-1902; acted as Lord High Steward at Coronation of King Edward VII; Under-Sec of State for Colonies 1903-5, and John Parl Sec (unpaid) to Board of Agriculture 1917-18: *m* 1st, 1895 (*m diss* 1920), Consuelo, who *d* 1964, da of late William Kissam Vanderbilt, of New York; 2ndly, 1921, Gladys Marie, who *d* 1977, da of late Edward Parker Deacon, of Boston, USA; *d* 1934; *s* by his el son (10) JOHN ALBERT EDWARD WILLIAM, 10th Duke, *b* 1897; Lt-Col Life Gds (Reserve); High Steward of Oxford 1937: *m* 1st, 1920, Hon Alexandra Mary Hilda Cadogan, CBE, JP, who *d* 1961, da of late Henry Arthur, Viscount Chelsea (E Cadogan); 2ndly, 1972, Frances Laura, who *d* 1990, da of late Capt Hon Guy Lawrence Charteris (E Wemyss and March, colls), formerly wife of (i) 2nd Viscount Long and (ii) 3rd Earl of Dudley, and widow of Michael Temple Canfield, *d* 1972; *s* by his el son (11) JOHN GEORGE VANDERBILT HENRY, 11th Duke, and present peer; also Marquess of Blandford, Earl of Sunderland, Earl of Marlborough, Baron Spencer, and Baron Churchill of Sandridge, as well as Prince of the Holy Roman Empire, and Prince of Mindelheim in Suabia.

*(1) *Sir* ROBERT Spencer, Knt; *cr Baron Spencer*, of Wormleighton, co Northampton (peerage of England) 1603; *d* 1627; *s* by his son (2) WILLIAM, 2nd Baron; *d* 1636; *s* by his son (3) HENRY, 3rd Baron; *cr Earl of Sunderland* (peerage of England) 1643; killed at Newbury 1643, fighting for the royal cause, *s* by his son (4) ROBERT, KG, 2nd Earl; *d* 1702; *s* by his son (5) CHARLES, KG, 3rd Earl; was a Principal Sec of State to Queen Anne and George I; *d* 1722; *s* by his son (6) ROBERT, 4th Earl; *d* unmarried 1729: *s* by his brother (7) CHARLES KG, 5th Earl, who *s* as 3rd Duke of Marlborough (ante).

MARLESFORD, BARON (Schreiber) (Life Baron 1991)

MARK SHULDHAM SCHREIBER, only son of late John Shuldham Schreiber, DL, of Marlesford Hall, Woodbridge, Suffolk (*see* B Faringdon, 1946 Edn); *ed* Eton, and Trin Coll, Camb (MA); late Lieut Coldstream Guards; DL Suffolk 1991; Fisons Ltd 1957 63, Conservative Research Dept 1963-67, Dir Conservative Public Sector Research Unit 1967-70, Special Advisor HM Govt 1970-74, to Leader of the Opposition 1974-75, Editorial Consultant *The Economist* 1974-91 (Parliamentary Lobby Correspondent); Dir Eastern Electricity plc since 1989; and Times Newspaper Holdings since 1991; Member Countryside Commn 1980-92 and Rural Devpt Commn 1985-93; Chm Council for the Protection of Rural England since 1993; Lord of the Manor of Marlesford and patron of the living; *cr Baron Marlesford*, of Marlesford, co Suffolk (Life Baron) 1991: *m* 1969, Gabriella Federica, da of Conte Teodoro Veglio di Castelletto Uzonne, and has issue.

Arms – Ermine, on a roundel sable between three griffin's heads erased vert a cross engrailed or. **Crest** – A dexter arm in armour the upper arm charged with a roundel sable thereon a cross engrailed or the hand grasping a dagger point downwards proper hilt and pomel or. **Supporters** – Two griffins ermine the aquiline parts vert forelegs or both collared with a ring of cloude radiated proper and each segreant on a grassy mount also ppr.
Seat – Marlesford Hall, Woodbridge, Suffolk IP13 0AU. *Town Residence* 6 Kersley St, SW11 4PR. *Club* – Pratt's.

DAUGHTERS LIVING

Hon Nicola Charlotte, *b* 1971.
Hon Sophie Louisa, *b* 1973.

MARLEY, BARONY OF (Aman) (Extinct 1990)

WIDOW LIVING OF SECOND AND LAST BARON

CATHERINE DOONE (*Baroness Marley*), da of late Frank Angwyn Beal, of L'Eden, Cap d'Ail, France: *m* 1956, as his 2nd wife, 2nd Baron Marley, who *d* 1990. *Residence* – 104 Ebury Mews, SW1.

MARPLES, BARONY OF (Marples) (Extinct 1978)

WIDOW LIVING OF LIFE BARON

RUTH (*Baroness Marples*), da of late F. W. Dobson, JP, FSA, of Nottingham: *m* 1956, as his 2nd wife, Baron Marples, PC (Life Baron), who *d* 1978.

Marquis, family name of Earl of Woolton.

MARSH, BARON (Marsh) (Life Baron 1981)

NON·EST·VIVERE·SED·VALERE·VITA·

RICHARD WILLIAM MARSH, PC, son of William Marsh, of Belvedere Kent; *b* 1928; *ed* Jennings Sch, Swindon, Woolwich Poly and Ruskin Coll, Oxford; Parly Sec Min of Labour 1964-5; jt Parly Sec Min of Technology 1965-66, Min of Power 1966-68, Min of Transport 1968-70; Chm British Railways 1970-75, Chm Newspaper Publishing Assoc 1975-90; Chm British Iron and Steel Consumers Council 1977-83 and Lee Cooper plc since 1982; Dep Chm TVAM Ltd 1981 and Chm 1983; Chm Lopex plc, Laurentian Finance Group plc, and China & Eastern Inv Co Ltd; FCIT; MP for Greenwich (*Lab*) 1959-71; *cr* Kt 1977, and *Baron Marsh*, of Mannington, co Wilts (Life Baron) 1981: *m* 1st, 1950 (*m diss* 1973), Evelyn Mary, da of Frederick Andrews, of Southampton; 2ndly, 1973, Caroline Dutton, who *d* 1975; 3rdly, 1979, Hon Felicity Carmen Francesca McFadzean, da of Baron McFadzean of Kelvinside (Life Baron), and has issue living by 1st *m*.

Arms – Argent four pallets wavy azure on a chevron over all gules a leopard's face between two keys wards upwards and outwards or on a chief gules a double warded key wards upwards between two leopards' faces gold. **Crest** – Upon a mount vert a bear sejant upon its haunches and erect or holding between its forepaws a mitra preciosa gold pannelled vert garnished and lined gules the infulae vert and fringed at their ends gold. **Supporters** – On either side a Japanese crane (Grus japonensis) proper the interior wing and leg of each supporting the shield the whole upon a compartment composed of water barry wavy of four azure and argent between two banks of marshy ground proper sprouting therefrom plants of marsh buckler fern marsh mallow and bulrush all slipped and leaved proper. **Motto** – Non Est Vivere Sed Valere Vita. *Address* – c/o House of Lords, SW1A 0PW.

SONS LIVING (*By 1st marriage*)

Hon Andrew, *b* 1950.
Hon Christopher, *b* 1960.

MARSHALL OF GORING, BARONY OF (Marshall) (Extinct 1996)

SON LIVING OF LIFE BARON

Dr the Hon Jonathan Charles Walter, *b* 1963; *ed* Abingdon Sch, Oxford, and Univ Coll, London (BSc, MD, MRCP): *m* 1997, Esther R., eldest da of Andrew Cinnamond, of Belfast.

DAUGHTER LIVING OF LIFE BARON

Dr the Hon Victoria Ann, *b* 1959; *ed* St Helen's Sch, Abingdon, and Birmingham Univ (BSc), and Reading Univ (PhD); *m* 1984 (*m diss* 1992), Alan Burrill.

WIDOW LIVING OF LIFE BARON

ANN VIVIENNE (*Baroness Marshall of Goring*), da of late Ernest Vivian Sheppard, of Cardiff: *m* 1955, Baron Marshall of Goring, CBE, FRS (Life Baron), who *d* 1996. *Residence* – Bridleway House, Goring-on-Thames, Oxon RG8 0HS.

MARSHALL OF KNIGHTSBRIDGE, BARON (Marshall) (Life Baron 1998)

COLIN MARSH MARSHALL, son of Marsh Edward Leslie Marshall, of Nottingham; *b* 16 Nov 1933; *ed* Univ Coll Sch; Hon DUniv Lancaster 1997; with Orient Steam Navigation Co 1951-58; joined Hertz Corporation 1958, Gen Man (Mexico) 1959-60, Assistant to Pres (NY) 1960, Gen Man (UK) 1961-62, Gen Man (UK, Netherlands and Belgium) 1962-64; Regional Man and Vice-Pres Avis Inc (Europe 1964-66, Europe and Middle East 1966-69, Worlwide 1969-71), Exec Vice-Pres and Chief Operating Offr (NY), Pres 1975, Chief Exec 1976, Co Chm 1979 (following takeover by Norman Simon Inc of which he became Exec Vice-Pres 1979); Dir and Dep Chief Exec Sears Holdings plc 1981-83; Chief Exec British Airways plc 1983-95, Dep Chm 1989-93, since when Chm; Chm Inchcape plc since 1996; Dep Chm British Telecommunications plc since 1996 (Dir since 1995); Chm Siebe plc since 1998; Dir other Cos and organisations; Liveryman Guild of Air Pilots and Air Navigators, Liveryman Worshipful Co of Information Technologists; *cr* Kt 1987, and *Baron Marshall of Knightsbridge*, of Knightsbridge in the City of Westminster (Life Baron) 1998: *m* 1958, Janet Winifred, da of John Cracknell, of Great Henny, Suffolk, and has issue.
Address – Chairman's Office, British Airways plc, Berkeley Square House, Berkeley Square, W1X 6BA *Club* – Queen's.

DAUGHTER LIVING

Hon Anna, *b* 1960; *ed* Benenden, and Girton Coll, Camb: *m* 1996, Simon Birkett, son of Edward Miles Birkett, of co Durham.

MARSHALL OF LEEDS, BARONY OF (Marshall) (Extinct 1990)

DAUGHTERS LIVING OF LIFE BARON

Hon Angela Hermione (The Home Farm, Sand Hutton, York YO41 1JZ), *b* 1944: *m* 1st, 1966 (*m diss* 1979), Myles Spencer Harrison Hartley; 2ndly, 1986, Maj Geoffrey J. Widdows, 15th/19th Royal Hussars, yr son of A/Cdre S. C. Widdows, CB, DFC, of St Peter Port, Guernsey, C1, and has issue living (by 1st *m*), Robert, *b* 1974, — Annabelle, *b* 1967: *m* 1996, Giles C. R. Griffiths, only son of Graham Griffiths, of Warnham, W Sussex, — Alexandra, *b* 1972: *m* 1997, Robin C. Freeman, yr son of Dr Brian Freeman, of Wimborne St Giles, Dorset.

Hon Virginia Mary, *b* 1949: *m* 1971, Nigel James Alexander Learmond, of 52 Marryat Rd, Wimbledon, SW19, and has issue living, Alexander Marshall, *b* 1989, — Marissa Virginia Stuart, *b* 1973.

Marsham, family name of Earl of Romney.

MARTONMERE, BARON (Robinson) (Baron UK 1964)

JOHN STEPHEN ROBINSON, 2nd Baron; *b* 10 July 1963; *s* 1989; *ed* Lakefield Coll Sch, and Senaca Univ.

Arms – Argent a three masted merchant ship of early eighteenth century date, the mainsails furled proper, on a chief azure a portcullis chained between two roses or. **Crest** – A lion's head erased or in the mouth a crescent gules. **Supporters** – *Dexter*, a lion or collared flory counterflory gules; *Sinister*, a stag gules attired and unguled collared flory counterflory or.
Residence – 390 Russell Hill Rd, Toronto, Ontario, Canada M4V 2V2.

BROTHER LIVING

DAVID ALAN, *b* 15 Sept 1965; *ed* Upper Canada Coll, Neuchatel, Switzerland, and Queen's Univ; BA Weston Univ; MBA.

SISTER LIVING

Carolyn Elizabeth, *b* 1969.

AUNT LIVING (*daughter of 1st Baron*)

Hon Loretta Anne, *b* 1939: *m* 1963, Edward Samuel Rogers, and has issue living, Edward Samuel, *b* 1969, — Lisa Anne, *b* 1967, — Melinda Mary, *b* 1971, — Martha Loretta, *b* 1972. *Residence* – 3 Frybrook Rd, Toronto, Canada M4V 1Y7.

MOTHER LIVING

Wendy Patricia, da of late James Cecil Blagden, of Bapchild Court, nr Sittingbourne, Kent: *m* 1959, Hon Richard Anthony Gasque Robinson, only son of 1st Baron, who *dvp* 1979. *Residence* – 390 Russell Hill Rd, Toronto, Ontario, Canada M4V 2V2.

PREDECESSOR – (1) (JOHN) ROLAND Robinson, GBE, KCMG, PC, son of late Roland Walkden Robinson, of Blackpool; *b* 1907, Chm Conservative Commonwealth Affairs Cttee, House of Commons, 1954-64, and of Gen Council of Commonwealth Parliamentary Assocn 1960-61, Gov of Bermuda 1964-72, and MP for Widnes Div of Lancs (*C*) 1931-45, and for S Div of Blackpool 1945-64; *cr Baron Martonmere*, of Blackpool, co Palatine of Lancaster 1964: *m* 1930, Maysie, who *d* (Oct) 1989, da of late Clarence Warren Gasque, and *d* (May) 1989; *s* by his grandson (2) JOHN STEPHEN, elder son of late Hon Richard Anthony Gasque Robinson (only son of 1st Baron), 2nd Baron and present peer.

MASHAM OF ILTON, BARONESS (Cunliffe-Lister) (Life Baroness 1970)
(Title pronounced "Massam")

SUSAN LILIAN PRIMROSE CUNLIFFE-LISTER (*Countess of Swinton*), yr da of late Sir Ronald Norman John Charles Udny Sinclair, 8th Bt (*cr* 1704), *b* 14 April, 1935; *ed* Heathfield, and London Polytechnic; Vice-Chm All-Party Drug Misuse Cttee since 1984, Vice-Chm All-Party Aids Cttee; Member All-Party Penal Affairs Group since 1975, All-Party Children's Group and All-Party Disablement Cttee since 1970; President of N Yorks Red Cross 1963-88, Chartered Soc of Physiotherapy 1975-82, and Papworth and Enham Village Settlements 1973-85; Memb Yorkshire Regional Health Authority 1982-90; President, Vice-President, or Chm of many other associations for the disabled and physically handicapped; Hon Fell of Royal Coll of General Practitioners 1981; Hon MA Open Univ 1981; Hon MA York 1985; Hon Master of Law Leeds 1988; Hon Fell of Bradford and Ilkley Community Coll 1988; Hon DSc Ulster 1990; Hon LLD Univ of Teesside 1993; Hon Freeman of Borough of Harrogate 1989; DL N Yorks 1991; *cr Baroness Masham of Ilton*, of Masham in N Riding, co York (Life Baroness) 1970: *m* 1959, 2nd Earl of Swinton, and has two adopted children (*see* E Swinton).

Arms – Not exemplified at time of going to press.
Residences – Dykes Hill House, Masham, Ripon, Yorks HG4 4NS; 46 Westminster Gdns, Marsham St, SW1.

Mason, family name of Barony of Blackford.

MASON OF BARNSLEY, BARON (Mason) (Life Baron 1987)

ROY MASON, PC, son of late Joseph Mason, of Carlton, nr Barnsley; *b* 18 April 1924; *ed* Carlton and Royston Elementary Schs, and LSE; Min of State, Board of Trade 1964-67, Min of Defence for Equipment 1967-68, Postmaster Gen April-June 1968, Min of Power 1968-69, and Pres of Board of Trade 1960-70; Sec of State for Defence 1974-76, Sec of State for N Ireland 1976-79; MP (*Lab*) for Barnsley 1953-83, and for Barnsley Central 1983-87; *cr* PC 1968, and *Baron Mason of Barnsley*, of Barnsley, S Yorks (Life Baron) 1987: *m* 1945, Marjorie, da of Ernest Sowden, of Royston, W Riding, Yorks, and has issue.
Residence – 12 Victoria Av, Barnsley, S Yorks.

DAUGHTERS LIVING

Hon Susan Ann, *b* 1947: *m* 1969, Allen Duke, and has issue living, Steven Allen, *b* 1975, — Caroline Ann, *b* 1978.

Hon Jill Diane, *b* 1955: *m* 1979, Kevin Charles Edward Martin, and has issue living, Andrew Ian, *b* 1986.

MASSEREENE AND FERRARD, VISCOUNT (Skeffington) Sits as BARON ORIEL (UK 1821) (Viscount I 1660)

Through difficulties to honours

JOHN DAVID CLOTWORTHY WHYTE-MELVILLE FOSTER SKEFFINGTON, 14th Viscount; *b* 3 June 1940; *s* 1992; *ed* Millfield, and Inst Monte Rosa; Gren Gds 1959-61; Stockbroker with M. D. Barnard & Co: *m* 1970, Anne Denise, da of late Norman Rowlandson, and has issue.

Arms – Quarterly: 1st and 4th, argent, three bulls' heads erased sable, armed or, *Skeffington*; 2nd and 3rd azure a chevron between three chaplets, or, *Clotworthy*. Crest – A mermaid with comb and mirror, all proper. Supporters – Two stags sable, attired and unguled or, each gorged with a chaplet of roses argent.
Address – c/o House of Lords, SW1A 0PW. *Residence* – 70 Vauxhall Grove, SW8 1TA. *Clubs* – Turf, Pratt's, House of Lords Yacht.

SONS LIVING

Hon CHARLES JOHN FOSTER CLOTWORTHY WHYTE-MELVILLE, *b* 7 Feb 1973.
Hon Henry William Norman Foster Clotworthy, *b* 1980.

DAUGHTER LIVING

Hon Harriette Denise Margaretta Eileen, *b* 1975.

SISTER LIVING

Hon Oriel Annabelle Diana, *b* 1950: *m* 1st, 1971 (*m diss* 1989), Dominik Luczyc-Wyhowski; 2ndly, 1992, Michael Francis Stratford, and has issue living (by 1st *m*), Sofia Oriel Laura, *b* 1973, — Kassia Annabelle Susan, *b* 1980. *Residence* – Ben More Lodge, Aros, Isle of Mull, Argyll.

WIDOW LIVING OF THIRTEENTH VISCOUNT

ANNABELLE KATHLEEN (*Dowager Viscountess Massereene and Ferrard*), elder da of late Henry David Lewis, of Combwell Priory, Hawkhurst, Kent: *m* 1939, the 13th Viscount Massereene and Ferrard, who *d* 1992. *Residence* – Carpenters, Boughton Aluph, nr Ashford, Kent.

COLLATERAL BRANCHES LIVING   (*In remainder to Viscountcy of Massereene and Barony of Loughneagh only*)

Grandchildren of late Hon Norah Florence Margaretta, Mrs Charles Johnston, eldest da of 11th Viscount:—
Issue of late Algernon George Henry Johnston, *b* 1899, *d* 1948: *m* 1926, Eileen Magdalene, da of — Kearney, of Creagh House, Doneraile, co Cork:—
Anthony James Rex JOHNSTON, *b* 1931. —— Rosemary Margaretta Norah, *b* 1929. —— Gabrielle, *b* 1943.

Issue of late John Edward Arthur Johnston, *b* 1902, *d* 1958: *m* 1933, Grietje, yst da of Jelle Zoethout, of Leeuwarden, Holland:—
†Michael John Anthony JOHNSTON, *b* 1939: *m* 1965, Myrtle Stevens, of Springs, S Africa, and *d* 1965, leaving issue, Craig Alastair, *b* 1964. —— Peter Charles Anthony, *b* 1945: *m* 1967, Deborah Jane, da of John Wilding, of Forest Town, Johannesburg, and has issue living, Christopher John, *b* 1970, — Katharine Ann, *b* 1973, — Susan Margaret, *b* 1974.

Grandchildren of late Hon Ethel Mary Catherine, Mrs Richard Atherton d'Anyers Willis, 2nd da of 11th Viscount:—
Issue of late Maj Charles Rodolph d'Anyers Willis, *b* 1907, *d* 1961: *m* 1936, Ursula (who *m* 2ndly, 1963, Maj E. J. Fitz-Gerald, late Coldstream Guards), only child of late Brig-Gen Sir Robert Harvey Kearsley, KCVO, CMG, DSO (Peto, Bt, *cr* 1855, colls):—
Martin Atherton d'Anyers WILLIS, *b* 1939; *ed* Eton. —— Julian Charles d'Anyers (53 Halford Rd, Durban, S Africa), *b* 1945; *ed* Eton: *m* 1972, Gillian Curtis, el da of Earle Smith, of Pietermaritzburg, and has issue living, Sean d'Anyers, *b* 1974. —— Caroline Ann (2 Sandways Cottage, Bourton, Gillingham, Dorset) *b* 1937: *m* 1st, 1960 (*m diss* 1967), Col Dudley Lancelot Guy Carleton Smith, who *d* 1984; 2ndly, 1967 (*m diss* 1971), Richard Courtenay Thorne, and has issue living (by 2nd *m*), David Courtenay, *b* 1968.

Issue of late Winifred Alice, *b* 1910, *d* 1977: *m* 1934, Lt-Col Count Peter Francis de Salis, Coldstream Gds, who *d* 1982:—
Richard John DE SALIS (Holly Hatch, Owslebury, Winchester, Hants SO21 1LN), *b* 1935; *ed* Downside, and Trin Coll, Camb (BA); Maj RA: *m* 1959, Susan Elizabeth, da of Cdr G. H. Thompson, RN, and has issue living, Peter John Francis, *b* 1964; Capt Royal Glos, Berks and Wilts Regt (TA): *m* 1996, Sue M., da of J. D. Porter, of Eastbourne, Sussex, and has issue living, Emily Elizabeth *b* 1998, — Elizabeth Mary, *b* 1961: *m* 1988, Charles Tyson Richard Hezlet, of Lingcroft House, Plealey, Shrewsbury, Shropshire SY5 0XT, and has issue living, Charles Salis Richard *b* 1990, Edward Salis

William *b* 1992, — Jane Sarah, *b* 1962: *m* 1986, Rudolph Bihr, of Altes Jagdhaus, Unterkniesenberg 45B, 5625 Kallern, Switzerland, and has issue living, August Rudolph Peter *b* 1998, Sophia Violanta *b* 1992, — Anne Frances, *b* 1970. —— Bernard Peter (12 Park Vista, Greenwich, SE10 9LZ), *b* 1936; *ed* Downside, and RNC Dartmouth; Lt-Cdr RN: *m* 1967, Monica Juanita, yst da of Cdr Robert Tatton Bower, RN (*see* Strickland, By), and has issue living, Piers Robert, *b* 1969, — Hugo John, *b* 1971. —— Nicholas George (Church House, Barrow St, Much Wenlock, Shropshire TF13 6EN), *b* 1938; *ed* Downside: *m* 1964, Norma Christine, da of Maj C. H. Dennis, RAMC, of Ashtead, Surrey, and has issue living, Alexander Edward, *b* 1969: *m* 1999, Raquel Rose Taylor, — Christian Henry, *b* 1973: *m* 1997, Lori Lyn, yr da of Vincent Garino, of Medway, Massachusetts, USA. —— James Anthony (Middle Barn, Manor Court, Chadlington, Chipping Norton, Oxon OX7 3LW), *b* 1949; *ed* Downside: *m* 1987, Helen Margaret Guy. —— Thomas Peter (26 Eastwell Close, Paddock Wood, Kent), *b* 1950; *ed* Downside.

Issue of late Hon Constance Harriet Georgiana Skeffington, 3rd da of 11th Viscount, *b* 1877, *d* 1965: *m* 1905, Maj Herbert Rushton Sykes, who *d* 1952:—
†(Arthur) Patrick SYKES, MBE, *b* 1906; *ed* Eton, and Magdalene Coll, Camb (BA 1928); Lt-Col KRRC (ret); served N Africa 1943 (wounded); MBE (Mil) 1945; JP and DL Shropshire, High Sheriff 1961-62: *m* 1st, 1936 (*m diss* 1967), Prudence Margaret, eldest da of late Maj-Gen Donald Elpinston Robertson, CB, DSO; 2ndly, 1968, Katharine Diana Bartlett (Lydham Manor, Bishops Castle, Shropshire), and *d* 1994, leaving issue (by 1st *m*), William, *b* 1939: *m* 1970, Pamela Strickland Skailes, and has issue living, Camilla *b* 1971, Angela *b* 1973, — (Gillian Diana) Juniper, *b* 1937: *m* 1964, Maj (William) John Martin Greener, OBE, DL, of Langebride House, Long Bredy, Dorset DT2 9HU, and has issue living, James *b* 1967, Juliet *b* 1970. —— †Humphrey Hugh, *b* 1907; *ed* Rugby; Maj late 9th Lancers: *m* 1st, 1936 (*m diss* 1948), Grizel Sophie, da of late AV-M Sir Norman Duckworth Kerr MacEwen, CB, CMG, DSO; 2ndly, 1958, Muriel, da of late Col John Charles Hooper, DSO, of Harewell, Faversham, Kent, and Hallyards, Peebles, and *d* 1991, leaving issue (by 1st *m*), Richard, *b* 1940, — Alexander, *b* 1942, — Jane, *b* 1938: *m* 1963, John Deen, and has issue living, Emma Sophie Louise *b* 1964, — Annabelle, *b* 1944. —— Robin George, TD, *b* 1917; *ed* Eton, and Ch Ch, Oxford (MA, BM, BCh, DA, FFARCS); Col late RAMC (TA); HM Hon Surg 1964: *m* 1947, Jean, da of H. Cunningham, of Muirlagganmore, Killin, Perthshire, and has issue living, Edward Colin Richard, *b* 1952, — Gillian, *b* 1950. *Residence* – Greenwood, Shotley Bridge, co Durham.

Grandchildren of late Florence Clementina VERE-LAURIE, Viscountess Massereene and Ferrard (infra):—
Issue of late Lt-Col George Halliburton Foster Peel VERE-LAURIE, *b* 1906, *d* 1981: *m* 1st, 1932 (*m diss* 1968), Caroline Judith, yr da of Edward Francklin, JP, of Gonalston Hall, Notts; 2ndly, 1968 (*m diss* 197-), Bridget Mary, da of F. Arthur Good; 3rdly, 1979, Joyce Mary Letts (The Dower House, Carlton-on-Trent, Newark, Notts):—
(By 1st *m*) George Edward VERE-LAURIE (Carlton Hall, Carlton-on-Trent, Newark, Notts), *b* 1935; *ed* Eton; Lt-Col 9th/12th Lancers; DL Notts 1993: *m* 1st, 1962 (*m diss* 1977), Georgina Nefert, da of Anthony Claud Riall, of Rutland Cottage, Rutland Gdns, SW7; 2ndly, 19—, Barbara Ann Tweed, and has issue living (by 1st *m*), George Anthony, *b* 1963, — Georgina Caroline Sylvia Victoria, *b* 1965: *m* 1990, C. Martin Hale, only son of C. Hale, of Folkestone, Kent, and has issue living, James George *b* 1991, William Edward, *b* 1992, Frederick Clifford *b* 1994. —— (Florence) Mary, *b* 1939; Lord Lieut Hants since 1994: *m* 1960, Capt Christopher Tarleton Feltrim Fagan, late Gren Gds, of Deane Hill House, Deane, Basingstoke, and has had issue, †Christopher Hugh Tarleton Feltrim, *b* 1964; *d* in a motor accident 1987, — James Tarleton Feltrim, *b* 1965: *m* 1995, Mrs Sarah Mary Cotterill Verney, da of Richard Paul Voelcker, of Stanton St Quinton, Wilts, and formerly wife of Harry George Vivian Verney (*see* Verney, Bt, *cr* 1818 colls), and has issue living, Hugh Tarleton Feltrim *b* 1998.

Granddaughter of late Hon Sydney William Foster-Skeffington, 3rd son of 10th Viscount Massereene:—
Issue of late Florence Clementina VERE-LAURIE, *b* 1873, *d* 1978; assumed by deed poll 1915 the additional surname of VERE: *m* 1st, 1905, Lt-Col George Brenton Laurie, R Irish Rifles, who was *ka* 1915; 2ndly, 1940, as his 2nd wife, her cousin, 12th Viscount Massereene and Ferrard (infra), who *d* 1956:—
(By 1st *m*) Eleanor Blanche Helen Margaretta (PO Box 44, 69 Crescent Av, Hudson Heights, Prov Quebec, Canada), *b* 1907; Freeman of City of London: *m* 1932, Andrew Wauchope Johnstone, who *d* 1980, and has issue (*see* Johnstone, Bt, colls).

PREDECESSORS – **(1)** Sir JOHN Clotworthy, *cr Baron Loughneugh* and *Viscount Massereene* (peerage of Ireland) 1660, with remainder to his son-in-law Sir John Skettington, 5th Bt, of Fisherwick and his issue male, and in default thereof to his heirs-general; *d* 1665; *s* by **(2)** Sir JOHN Skeffington (ante) 2nd Viscount; *d* 1695; *s* by his son **(3)** CLOTWORTHY, 3rd Viscount; *d* 1713; *s* by his son **(4)** CLOTWORTHY, 4th Viscount; *d* 1738; *s* by his son **(5)** CLOTWORTHY, 5th Viscount; *cr Earl of Massereene* (peerage of Ireland) 1756; *d* 1757; *s* by his son **(6)** CLOTWORTHY, 2nd Earl; *dsp* 1800; *s* by his brother **(7)** HENRY, 3rd Earl; *d* unmarried 1811; *s* by his brother **(8)** CHICHESTER, 4th Earl; *d* 1816, when the Baronetcy and Earldom expired, and the Barony of Loughneagh and the Viscountcy of Massereene devolved upon his da **(9)** HARRIET wife of Thomas Henry Foster, 2nd Baron *Oriel* and 2nd *Viscount Ferrard* (see **infra*); *d* 1831; *s* by her son **(10)** JOHN, KP, 10th Viscount; *b* 1812; assumed the surname of Skeffington in addition to that of Foster 1843; *m* 1835, Olivia Deane, da of Henry Deane O'Grady, of Lodge, co Limerick, and Stillorgan Castle, Dublin; *d* 1863; *s* by his son **(11)** CLOTWORTHY JOHN EYRE, 11th Viscount; *b* 1842; Lieut co Louth and co and Town of Drogheda *m* 1870, Florence Elizabeth, who *d* 1929, only child of the late Major George John Whyte-Melville; *d* 1905; *s* by his son **(12)** ALGERNON WILLIAM JOHN CLOTWORTHY, DSO, 12th Viscount; *b* 1873; Major N Irish Horse, and 17th Lancers, and Hon Col 188th (Antrim) Heavy Battery RA (TA); S Africa 1900-2 (wounded, despatches twice, DSO), European War 1914-18 (despatches); Lieut for co Antrim 1916-45; first Parliamentary Sec to Prime Min in Ulster Parliament, and a Member of Senate, N Ireland 1921-9: *m* 1st, 1905, Jean Barbara, who *d* 1937, el da of Sir John Stirling Ainsworth, MP, 1st Bt; 2ndly, 1940, his cousin, Florence Clementina Vere, who *d* 1978, da of late Hon Sydney William Foster Skeffington, and widow of Lt-Col George Brenton Laurie; *d* 1956; *s* by his only son **(13)** JOHN CLOTWORTHY TALBOT FOSTER WHYTE-MELVILLE, 13th Viscount, *b* 1914; Lieut Black Watch (Supp Res) 1933-36 and 1939-40 (invalided), served Small Vessels Pool, RN 1944; Freeman City of London, DL co Antrim 1957, Gold Staff Officer at Coronation of Queen Elizabeth II 1953; Whip, Conservative Peers Cttee (IUP) House of Lords 1958-65, Dep-Chm 1965-70; Chm Scottish Clans Assocn of London 1974-76, etc: *m* 1939, Annabelle Kathleen, elder da of late Henry David Lewis, of Combwell Priory, Hawkhurst, Kent; *d* 1992; *s* by his only son **(14)** JOHN DAVID CLOTWORTHY WHYTE-MELVILLE FOSTER, 14th Viscount and present peer; also Baron of Loughneagh, Baron Oriel, of Collon, and Baron Oriel, of Ferrard.

*(1) JOHN FOSTER, PC, MP for many years, and sometime Speaker of the Irish Parliament was *cr Baron Oriel*, of Ferrard, co Louth (peerage of United Kingdom) 1821: *m* 1764, Margaret Amelia, *cr Baroness Oriel*, of Collon (peerage of Ireland) 1790, and *Viscountess Ferrard* (peerage of Ireland) 1797, da of Thomas Burgh, of Birt, co Kildare, she *d* 1831; *s* by her son **(2)** THOMAS HENRY, 2nd Viscount Ferrard (see ante), who had in 1828 *s* his father as 2nd Baron Oriel, and in 1817 has assumed by Roy licence the surname of Skeffington in lieu of Foster.

MASSY, BARON (Massy) (Baron I 1776)

For the liberty of my country

HUGH HAMON JOHN SOMERSET MASSY, 9th Baron; *b* 11 June 1921; *s* 1958; *ed* Clongowes Wood Coll, and Clayesmore Sch; European War 1940-45 as Private RAOC: *m* 1943, Margaret Elizabeth, da of late John Flower, of Barry, co Meath, and has issue.

𝔄rms – Argent, on a chevron between three lozenges sable, a lion passant or. Crest – Out of a ducal coronet or, a bull's head gules, armed sable. Supporters – *Dexter*, a lion; *sinister*, a leopard reguardant; both proper and collared and chained or.
Residence –

SONS LIVING

Hon DAVID HAMON SOMERSET, *b* 4 March 1947; *ed* St George's Coll, Weybridge; serving with Merchant Navy.
Hon John Hugh Somerset, *b* 1950: *m* 1978, Andrea, da of Alan West, of Leicester, and has issue living, Luke John Somerset, *b* 1984.
Hon Graham Ingoldsby Somerset, *b* 1952.
Hon Paul Robert, *b* 1953: *m* 1976, Anne Bridget, da of James McGowan, of Leicester, and has issue living, Kevin James Somerset, *b* 1978, — Colin Hugh Somerset, *b* 1979.

DAUGHTER LIVING

Hon Sheelagh Marie Louise, *b* 1958.

AUNT LIVING (*Daughter of 7th Baron*)

Hon Muriel Olive, *b* 1892.

COLLATERAL BRANCHES LIVING

Granddaughter of late Hugh Hamon John Massy, son of late Hon George William Massy, 2nd son of 3rd Baron:—
Issue of late Rollo Dillon Dunham Massy, *b* 1856, *d* 1934: *m* 1884, Emma Augusta, who *d* 1926, da of James Inman, of Lymington:—
Louisa Bythia, *b* 1887.

Grandchildren of late Rev Xavier Peel Massy, 4th son of Edward Taylor Massy, of Cottesmore, co Pembroke, only son of Hon Edward Massy, of Ballynort, co Limerick, 2nd son of 2nd Baron:—
Issue of late Godfrey Massy, *b* 1879, *d* 1953: *m* 1908, Marianne, who *d* 1951, da of late Ezra Gooderidge, of Goold, Yorkshire:—
Lawrence Xavier Peel (Box 165, Savona, nr Kamloops, BC, Canada), *b* 1909: *m* 1934, Hazel, da of Edwin Hartt, of Thelma, Alberta, and has issue living, Marianne Belle, *b* 1938: *m* 19—, Edward Heidinger.

Issue of late Lieut Lawrence Peel Massy, DSC, RNR, *b* 1883, *d* 1932: *m* 1914, Constance Jean Anne, who *d* 1949, el da of late John James Galletly, solicitor, of Inchdrewer, Colinton, Midlothian, and Kinnaird, Pitlochry:—
Doreen Constance Peel, *b* 1919; late WRNS; LRAM: *m* 1st, 1945 (*m diss* 1956), Conrad Laviolette; 2ndly, 1959, John Woolls, of Maipenrai, Sea Dyke Way, Marshchapel, Lincs, and has issue living (by 1st *m*) Derry Keith, *b* 1951; CPO, RN (ret), — Lorna Doreen (46 Craigieburn Gdns, Maryhill Park, Glasgow), *b* 1946; late WRNS: *m* 1967 (*m diss* 1993), Percival N. Skedgell, Glasgow G20 0NU, and has issue living, Elinor Peel *b* 1971, Lindsey Northcott *b* 1976.

Grandsons of late Lieut Lawrence Peel Massy, DSC, RNR (ante):—
Issue of late Maj Arthur Lawrence John Peel Massy, W Yorks Regt, *b* 1916, *d* 1992: *m* 1943, Margaret Alison, who *d* 1983, da of late Rev Ernest Bell Sharpe, of Purulla, India:—
David Lawrence Peel (1012 Santa Ynez Av, Henderson, Nevada, USA), *b* 1949; Sub Lieut (E) RNR: *m* 1976, Linda, da of Edgar Clanachan, of Holywood, Dumfriesshire, and has issue living, Ian Grant Peel, *b* 1983, — Douglas Edgar Peel, *b* 1985. —— John Eversdon Peel (31 Poplar Rd, Clayton Park, St Andrews, Fife KY16 9YB), *b* 1954.

Grandchildren of late Arthur Wellington Massy, 5th son of Edward Taylor Massy (ante):—
Issue of late Lt-Gen Hugh Royds Stokes Massy, CB, DSO, MC, *b* 1884, *d* 1965, *m* 1912, Maud Ina Nest, who *d* 1960, da of late Col Thomas James Roch, JP, DL, of Llether Pembrokeshire:—
†Hugh Peter Stokes, *b* 1914; *ed* Bradfield Coll; Lt-Col (ret) Roy Tank Regt 1939-45 War (despatches): *m* 1945, Jean H., who *d* 1993, da of late Sqdn Ldr M. G. Kidston, of Kamiti Downs, Kahawa, Kenya, and *d* 1998, leaving issue, Diana Rosamund, *b* 1947: *m* 1973, Lt-Col Philip Eric Scott, 16th/5th Lancers, and has issue living, James *b* 1975, — Pauline Lorraine, *b* 1951: *m* 1980, Richard Malcolm Cyril Scott, of 34 Christchurch Rd, Longham, Wimborne, Dorset, and has issue living, Louise Sarah *b* 1984. —— Mary Nest (Fulmar House, Twyford, Fontmell Magna, Shaftesbury, Dorset), *b* 1915: *m* 1940 (*m diss* 1947), Gerald Wilfred Charles Carter, and has issue living, Miles Richard, *b* 1941, — Jandy, *b* 1943: *m* 1975, Acting Cdr David Andrew Hobbs, MBE, son of A. S. Hobbs, and has issue living, Andrew Arthur Duncan *b* 1978.

Issue of late Brig Charles Walter Massy, CBE, DSO, MC, *b* 1887, *d* 1973: *m* 1st, 1920, Muriel Lorna Bell, who *d* 1958, da of J. A. Hallinan, of Glandalane, Fermoy; 2ndly, 1958, Irene Gillbee, who *d* 1990, da of late Richard Gillbee Thorold (*see* Thorold, Bt, colls), and widow of Clifford Hackney, MRCS:—
(By 1st *m*) Hugh Charles (RR No 1, Box 30, South Woodstock, Vermont 05071, USA), *b* 1921: *m* 1970, Janice, who *d* 1994, da of late Maurice de Kay Thompson, of Boston, Mass, and widow of Grenville Goodwin. —— John Royds, MRCS, LRCP (Hazel Lodge, Hensting Lane, Fishers Pond, Eastleigh, Hants SO50 7HH), *b* 1925; MRCS and LRCP 1960: *m* 1957, Eileen, da of F. Evans, of Thornfield, Hobb Lane, Hedge End, Southampton, and has issue living, David Hugh, *b* 1962, — Peter John (19 Netley Firs Rd, Hedge End, Southampton S03 4AY), *b* 1964: *m* 1987, Jennifer Freeman, and has issue living, Gregory Hugh *b* 1995, Helen Clare *b* 1993, — Anne Sarah, *b* 1959: *m* 1991, Kees de Koning, of Holland, — Clare Muriel, *b* 1960: *m* 1991, Jonathan Brian Evans, of 96 Upton Rd, Sutton, Surrey SM2 5JB, son of T. J. Evans, of Radyr, S Glamorgan, and has issue living, Harriet Frances *b* 1994, Philippa Lucy *b* 1995.

Granddaughter of late Rev George Eyre Massy, Rector of Gumfreston, co Pembroke, 6th and yst son of Edward Taylor Massy (ante):—
Issue of late Capt Villiers Wilfred Peel Massy, *b* 1882, *d* 1932: *m* 1915, Beatrice, who *d* 1952, da of late Carlos Vetter, of 6 Neville Street, SW:—
Bridget Ursula Elaine, *b* 1920: *m* 1948, Leonard Arthur Hammond Riddett, and has issue living, John Villiers (46 Back St, Ashwell, Herts), *b* 1949: *m* 1985, Linda Marie West, of Auckland, NZ, and has issue living, Paul James Massy *b* 1990, Guy Edward West *b* 1992, Leo Patrick Steward *b* 1995, — Patrick Hammond (Box 76, Takaka, NZ), *b* 1951, — Philip Peel (4 Macquarie Terr, Balmain, NSW, Australia), *b* 1957, — Sara Caroline, *b* 1953: *m* 1981, Dominic Kingsley Eason Scott, of 34 St Andrew's Rd, Henley-on-Thames, Oxon, and has issue living, Martha Jane *b* 1983, Jemima Kate *b* 1986. *Residence* – Half Acre, Witheridge Hill, Henley on Thames, Oxon RG9 7PE.

Grandsons of late Hugh Hamon George Massy, only son (by 1st *m*) of Lt-Col George Eyre Massy (infra):—
Issue of late Hugh Hamon de Moleyns Massy, *b* 1895, *d* 1976: *m* 1923, Helen Violet, who *d* 1994, da of late Allen Hamilton Morgan, of Hope Vale, Natal:—
†Hugh Allen Oliver, *b* 1925; *d* 1996. —— Evan (abandoned Christian names of Eyre Pennefather) (60 Maclean St, Umkomaas, Natal 4170), *b* 1930: *m* 1965, Lynette Marion, da of Arthur Stuart Clark, of Tenby, Hilton, Natal, and has issue living, Jennifer Lynne, *b* 1966, — Helen Louise, *b* 1969: *m* 1995, Stuart Young, and has issue living, Keagan Stuart *b* 19—, Darren Sean, *b* 19—.

Grandchildren of late Capt James Eyre Massy (infra):—
Issue of late George Eyre Massy, *b* 1914, *d* 1989: *m* 1950: Marella Margaret Helen, who *d* 1998, da of late James McQueen:—
Timothy James Hamon, *b* 1953: *m* 1983, Karen Maria, da of Gerard McCrea, of Karratha, W Australia, and has issue living, Lauren Elizabeth, *b* 1984. —— Jacqueline Cynthia, *b* 1952. —— Nicola Jane, *b* 1954.

Granddaughter (by 2nd *m*) of Lt-Col George Eyre Massy, eldest son of Hugh Massy, eldest son of Hon George Eyre Massy, 3rd son of 2nd Baron:—
Issue of late Capt James Eyre Massy, *b* 1873, *d* 1952: *m* 1903, May Evelyn, who *d* 1980, da of John Carmichael, JP, of Tracton Park, co Cork:—
Cynthia Evelyn, *b* 1916: *m* 1938, Eric Reade, of Conifers, The Close, Brighton Rd, Sway, Hants SO41 6ED, son of late Arthur Reade, DSO, MC, of Monmouth, and has issue living, Michael Wildin, *b* 1948, — Phylida Anne, *b* 1946.

Grandchildren of late John George Beresford Massy-Beresford, only surv son of late Very Rev John Maunsell Massy-Beresford, 3rd son of late John Massy, 4th son of 2nd Baron:—
Issue of late Brig Tristram Hugh Massy-Beresford, DSO, MC, *b* 1896, *d* 1987: *m* 1927, Helen Lindsay, who *d* 1979, da of late Lindsay Crompton Lawford, of Montreal:—
Michael James (11 Charleville Mansions, Charleville Rd, W14), *b* 1935; *ed* Eton, and Jesus Coll, Camb (BA); Maj RGJ (ret). —— Christopher Kerry (4 Vaughan Av, Stamford Brook, W6), *b* 1939; *ed* Eton, and Ch Ch, Oxford (MA): *m* 1979, Marjory Snow, and has issue living, Helen Emily, *b* 1980. —— Patricia Nell, *b* 1931: *m* 1958, Maj James Otway George Paton, 13th/18th Hus (ret), of Park Corner Farm, Odiham, Hants RG29 1JB, and has issue living, Timothy James (13 Eatonville Rd, SW17 7SH), *b* 1964: *m* 1995, Catherine Jane Strong, — Nicholas George (45 Crowborough Rd, SW17 9QB), *b* (twin) 1968: *m* 1995, Eliza Ann O'Driscoll, and has issue living, Emer Rose *b* 1997, — Penelope Loveday, *b* 1963: *m* 1992, Matthew Alan Fleet, of The Stables, Park Corner, Odiham, Hants RG29 1JB, and has issue living, Emily Charlotte Rose *b* 1996, Molly Elizabeth *b* 1998, — Elizabeth Gwendoline, *b* 1967.

Grandchildren of late Francis Staunton Massy-Dawson, son of late Francis Dennis Massy-Dawson, son of late James Hewitt Massy-Dawson, son of late Hon James Massy-Dawson, 2nd son of 1st Baron:—
Issue of late Capt Francis Evelyn Massy-Dawson, DSO, RN, *b* 1872, *d* 1939: *m* 1st, 1922, Emily Banner Clough, who *d* 1928, da of Lieut-Com Somerset James Somerset-Johnstone, RN, and widow of Capt Herbert Algernon Adam, CBE, RN (Johnstone, Bt colls); 2ndly, 1928, Mary Caroline, who *d* 1950, da of Herbert Taylor, of Holmer, Hereford:—
(By 2nd *m*) Francis Patrick, *b* 1934: *m* 1961, Anne Marie, da of W. H. Heritage, and has issue living, Suzanne, *b* 1963, — Nicola Jane, *b* 1965. —— Rosemarie Julia, *b* 1933: *m* 1961, John William Halse.

Grandson of late William Masscy, son of late Robert George Massey, eldest son of Hon George Massy, 6th and yst son of 1st Baron:—
Issue of late George William Hughes MASSEY, *b* 1864, *d* 1914: *m* 1st, 1889, Edith Margaret, who *d* 1910, da of late John Birroll, of Beechwood, London, Ontario, Canada; 2ndly, 1912, Marion (who *d* 1973, having *m* 2ndly, 1935, Brig Jesse (Jake) Pevensey Duke, DSO, MC, Royal Warwicks Regt), da of late George Bryson Clarke, of Petton Grange, Shropshire:—
(By 2nd *m*) Patrick Godfrey Goolden MASSEY, MC (Arawai House, Liss, Hants), *b* 1913; *ed* Harrow, and RMC Sandhurst; Hodson's Horse IA 1933, served 1939-45 War in India, Iraq, Iran and Burma (despatches, MC 1945), Lt-Col comdg 5/10th Baluch Regt, Comdt HE Gov-Gen's Body Guard 1946, transferred Royal Dragoons, Lt-Col comdg 1947 (ret): *m* 1st, 1941, Bessie Lee, who *d* 1978, da of late William J. Byrne, of Melbourne, Australia; 2ndly, 1978, Aylmer Jean Philippa, da of late Donald Macfarlane, CIE, of Little Hadlow, Sussex, and widow of (i) Capt Brian Eveleigh, 16/5th Lancers (*ka*

1944), and (ii) Maj Philip le Grand Gribble, and has issue living (by 1st *m*), Hamon Patrick Dunham (Pollachar, Isle of S Uist, Outer Hebrides), *b* 1950; *ed* Harrow, and RMA Sandhurst; Col The Blues and Royals, Comdg Household Cavalry Mounted Regt 1992: *m* 1st, 1973 (*m diss* 1987), Caroline, who *d* 1988, da of Lt-Col George Baker, of Dickhurst, Haslemere, Surrey; 2ndly, 1988, Mrs Cathleen Teresa Poole, da of Neil Campbell, of Benbecula, Outer Hebrides, and has issue living (by 1st *m*), Edward Hamon Russell *b* 1976, Eleanore Joan Diana *b* 1977, (by 2nd *m*) Lee Anna Margot *b* 1989, Garda Christina Sylvia *b* 1990, — Peregrine Tatton Eyre (Boldshaves, Woodchurch, Ashford, Kent TN26 3RA), *b* 1952; *ed* Harrow, and Magdalene Coll, Camb (MA); Bar Middle Temple 1975: *m* 1977, Deirdre Mary, eldest da of Commodore Spencer Heneage Drummond, DSC, RN (*see* E Perth, colls), and has issue living, Emma Rachel Lee *b* 1981, Alexandra Clare Louise *b* 1983, Laura Helena Ruth *b* 1986, — William Greville Sale (30 Brodrick Rd, SW17; Old Manor, Beanacre, Melksham, Wilts), *b* 1953; *ed* Harrow, and Hertford Coll, Oxford (MA); Bar Middle Temple 1977; QC 1996: *m* 1978, Cecilia D'Oyly, 2nd da of Daniel Edmund Awdry, TD, DL, of Old Manor, Beanacre, Melksham, Wilts, and has issue living, Patrick William Edmund *b* 1983, Richard Daniel Hugh *b* 1985, Edmund Greville Robert *b* 1990.

PREDECESSORS – **(1)** HUGH Massy, MP For co Limerick in several parliaments, was *cr Baron Massy*, of Duntrileague, co Limerick (peerage of Ireland) 1776; *d* 1788; *s* by his son **(2)** HUGH, 2nd Baron; MP for co Limerick; *d* 1790; *s* by his son **(3)** HUGH, 3rd Baron; *d* 1812; *s* by his son **(4)** HUGH HAMON, 4th Baron; *b* 1793: *m* 1826, Matilda, who *d* 1883, da of Luke White Esq, of Woodlands, co Dublin; *d* 1836; *s* by his el son **(5)** HUGH HAMON INGOLDSBY, 5th Baron: *m* 1855, Isabella, who *d* 1917, da of George MacNisbett; *dsp* 1874; *s* by his brother **(6)** JOHN THOMAS WILLIAM, 6th Baron, *b* 1835; a Representative Peer: *m* 1863, Lady Lucy Maria Butler, who *d* 1896, da of 3rd Earl of Carrick; *d* 1915; *s* by his son **(7)** HUGH SOMERSET JOHN, 7th Baron, *b* 1864: *m* 1886, Ellen Ida Constance, who *d* 1922, da of late Charles William Wise, of Rochester, Cahir, co Tipperary; *d* 1926; *s* by his son **(8)** HUGH HAMON CHARLES GEORGE, 8th Baron, *b* 1894: *m* 1919, Margaret, who *d* 1971 da of late Richard Leonard, of Meadsbrook, Ashbourne, co Limerick, and widow of Dr Moran, of Tara, co Meath; *d* 1958; *s* by his only son **(9)** HUGH HAMON JOHN SOMERSET, 9th Baron, and present peer.

MATTHEWS, BARONY OF (Matthews) (Extinct 1995)

SON LIVING OF LIFE BARON

Hon Ian V., *b* 1962: *m* 1986, Mrs Helen Christina Cooke, da of Francis Norman Jasper, of Trelyn, 10 Croft Way, Frimley, Camberley, Surrey, and has issue living, Emma Victoria, *b* 1989, — Lucy Helen, *b* 1990, — Sarah Rosie Jane, *b* 1993. *Residence* – Waverley Farm, Le Mont Arthur, St Brelade, Jersey, JE3 8AH, CI.

Mauchline, Lord; son of Countess of Loudoun.

Maud, see Baron Redcliffe-Maud.

Maude, family name of Viscount Hawarden.

MAUDE OF STRATFORD-UPON-AVON, BARONY OF (Maude) (Extinct 1993)

SON LIVING OF LIFE BARON

Rt Hon Francis Anthony Aylmer, *b* 1953; *ed* Abingdon Sch, and Corpus Christi Coll, Camb; Barrister-at-law; MP (C) Warwickshire N 1983-92; an Under-Sec of State, Dept of Trade & Industry, 1987-89, Min of State, Foreign and Commonwealth Office 1989-90, Financial Sec HM Treasury 1990-92, Shadow Chancellor of the Exchequer since June 1998; PC 1992: *m* 1984, Christina Jane, yr da of A. Peter Hadfield, of Copthorne, Shewsbury, and has issue living, Henry Peter Angus, *b* 1990, — Alastair Timothy Charles, *b* 1994, — Julia Elizabeth Barbara, *b* 1986, — Cecily Mary Anne, *b* 1988, — Lydia Helen Grace, *b* 1996.

DAUGHTERS LIVING OF LIFE BARON

Hon Elizabeth Jane, *b* 1946, *m* 1973, Peter Brotherton Spurrier, lately York Herald, of 15 Morella Rd, Wandsworth Common, SW12, and has issue living, Benedict John Emlyn, *b* 1979, — Thomas Alan Earnshaw, *b* 1982, — Lucinda, *b* 1985.
Hon Deborah Gervaise, *b* 1948; *ed* Banbury Gram Sch, and Bristol Univ: *m* 1973, Paul David Grenville Hayter, LVO, Chief Clerk House of Lords, of Walnut House, Charlton, Banbury, Oxon, and has issue living, William James Goodenough, *b* 1978, — Giles Angus Danvers, *b* 1981, — Arabella Katherine Maude, *b* 1984.

MAUGHAM, VISCOUNTCY OF (Maugham) (Extinct 1981)

DAUGHTER LIVING OF FIRST VISCOUNT

Hon Diana Julia: *m* 1932, Kenneth Marr-Johnson, who *d* 1986, and has issue living, Frederick James Maugham, *b* 1936; Circuit Judge SE Circuit 1991: *m* 1966, Susan, da of late Maj Richard Philip Hastings Eyre, OBE, of Winsford, Som, and has issue living, Thomas Maugham *b* 1966, Helen Rachel *b* 1969, — (Clifford) Simon Romer (8 Bassett Rd, W10), *b* 1938: *m* 1966, Catharine Mary, da of late Cdr John Smyth, OBE, of Llanbedr, Breconshire, and has issue living, Prosper Henry, *b* 1967: *m* 1997, Annabel M., da of David McEuen, of Sevenoaks, Kent (and has issue living, Molly Ebba *b* 1999), Alexander Merlin, *b* 1971, Diana Romilly *b* 1969, — (John) William (62 Rodenhurst Rd, SW4 8AR) *b* 1945: *m* 1986, Marion Elaine Hamilton, only da of Col J. H. Allford, DSO, of Withersdale, Suffolk. *Residence* – Flat 3, 14 Onslow Sq, SW7.

Maxwell, family name of Baron Farnham.

Maxwell, family name of Baron de Ros.

MAY, BARON (May) (Baron UK 1935, Bt UK 1931)

With God's help work prospers

MICHAEL ST JOHN MAY, 3rd Baron and 3rd Baronet; *b* 26 Sept 1931; *s* 1950; *ed* Wycliffe Coll, and Magdalene Coll, Camb; late Lt Roy Signals: *m* 1st, 1958 (*m diss* 1963), Dorothea Catherine Ann, da of Charles McCarthy, of Boston, USA; 2ndly, 1963, Jillian Mary, only da of late Albert Edward Shipton, of Wroxton Mill, Wroxton, Oxon, and has issue by 2nd *m*.

Arms – Gules, on a chevron between in chief three billets or, and in base an eagle argent, three roses of the field, barbed and seeded proper. Crest – A demi-leopard proper, holding in the dexter paw a bezant and resting the sinister paw on a terrestrial globe also proper. Supporters – *Dexter*, a griffin, and *sinister* a dragon or, each charged on the shoulder with a sprig of mayflower slipped and leaved proper. *Residences* – Gautherns Barn, Sibford Gower, Oxon; 9 Palace Mews, SW6.

SON LIVING (*By 2nd marriage*)

Hon JASPER BERTRAM ST JOHN, *b* 24 Oct 1965; *ed* Harrow.

DAUGHTER LIVING (*By 2nd marriage*)

Hon Miranda Jane, *b* 1968.

SISTER LIVING

Hon June Lisette, *b* 1929; *ed* St Paul's Sch: *m* 1958, Raymond Charles Lisser, and has issue living, Aidan Charles, *b* 1959: *m* 1994, Caroline M., yr da of Allan Wordsworth, of Mayfield, E Sussex. *Residences* – School House, Stanton, Broadway, Worcs; 6H Hyde Park Mansions, NW1.

WIDOW LIVING OF SECOND BARON

ELISABETH, da of George Ricardo Thoms: *m* 1st, 1929, as his second wife, the 2nd Baron, who *d* 1950; 2ndly, 19-, W. H. Hallam. *Residence* – 46 Lyndon Rd, Bramham Mead, Yorks.

COLLATERAL BRANCH LIVING

Issue of late Hon Patrick William May, yr son of 1st Baron, *b* 1911, *d* 1956: *m* 1st, 1934 (*m diss* 1948), Dorothy Patience, da of Francis Du Croz, of Weybridge; 2ndly, 1951, (Audrey) Gillian (JACKSON), who *d* 1989, da of Edward Bagot, of Cross Farm, West Coker, Somerset:—
(By 1st *m*) Caroline, *b* 1934: *m* 1954, Edwin Waldman, of 45 Burleigh St, Waterville, Maine, 04901, USA, and has issue living, Joshua Patrick, *b* 1957, — Noah William, *b* 1962, — Victoria Rose, *b* 1959, — Andrea Karen, *b* 1961. —— Valentine Virginia, *b* 1938: *m* 1963, Malcolm Walker MacLeod, of 70 Belden Hill Rd, Wilton, Conn 06897, USA, and has issue living, Sarah Walker, *b* 1965, — Alexandra Louise, *b* 1968. —— (By 2nd *m*) (Philippa) Jane, *b* 1952: *m* 1987, Anthony Crabtree of Cornwall House, Tenbury Wells, Worcs WR15 8EG, and has issue living, Christopher, *b* 1987, — Melanie, *b* 1988, — Alice, *b* 1990. —— (Elisabeth) Patricia (*posthumous*), *b* 1957; has issue living, Tanya, *b* 1980, — Samantha, *b* 1981.

PREDECESSORS – (1) *Sir* GEORGE ERNEST May, KBE, son of William C. May, of Cheshunt, *b* 1871; many years Sec of Prudential Assurance Co; sometime Manager of American Dollar Securities Committee; appointed Chm of Import Duties Advisory Committee 1932; *cr a Baronet* 1931, and *Baron May*, of Weybridge, co Surrey (peerage of United Kingdom) 1935: *m* 1903, Lily Julia, OBE, who *d* 1955, yr da of G. Strauss; *d* 1946; *s* by his el son (2) JOHN LAWRENCE, 2nd Baron; *b* 1904: *m* 1st, 1925, Cicely Beryl, who *d* 1928, only child of late Ernest Fleming, of Raska, Clarendon Rd, Watford; 2ndly, 1929, Elisabeth, da of George Ricardo Thoms; *d* 1950; *s* by his only son (3) MICHAEL ST JOHN, 3rd Baron and present peer.

MAYBRAY-KING, BARONY OF (Maybray-King) (Extinct 1986)

DAUGHTER LIVING OF LIFE BARON (*By 1st marriage*)

Hon Margaret Eleanor, *b* 1926: a JP of Havant (ret): *m* 1945, Roy Wilson, of 26 Blenheim Rd, Westbury Park, Bristol.

WIDOW LIVING OF LIFE BARON

SHEILA CATHERINE (*Baroness Maybray-King*), da of — Atkinson: *m* 1986, as his 4th wife, Baron Maybray-King, PC (Life Baron), who *d* 1986. *Residence* – 37 Manor Farm Rd, Bitterne Park, Southampton S09 3FQ.

MAYHEW, BARONY OF (Mayhew) (Extinct 1997)

SONS LIVING OF LIFE BARON

Rev the Hon David Francis (Mitford Vicarage, Stable Green, Mitford, Morpeth, Northumberland NE61 3PZ), *b* 31 July 1951; *ed* St Paul's, and Ch Ch Oxford; MA; ordained deacon 1991, priest 1992: *m* 1979, Elizabeth Helen, da of Lt-Col Pusinelli, of Chinagarth, Thornton-le-Dale, N Yorks, and has issue living, Jessica Elizabeth, *b* 1980, — Nicola Helen, *b* 1981, — Hannah Ruth, *b* 1986.

Hon (Christopher) James (Le Passous, Quettreville sur Seinne 50660, France), *b* 1959; *ed* St Paul's, and King's Coll, London (BSc): *m* 1985, Deborah Anne, only da of Mark John Lewis, of New Zealand, and has issue living, Emily Rose, *b* 1989, — Grace, *b* 1994.

DAUGHTERS LIVING OF LIFE BARON

Hon Teresa Ruth, *b* 1953; *ed* Cheltenham Ladies' Coll, and Lady Margaret Hall, Oxford (BA): *m* 1991, Robert Arthur Wyatt Lyle, only son of late Robert David Lyle Lyle (formerly Wyatt), of Bonython, Helston, Cornwall, and has issue living, Christopher Robert David Wyatt, *b* 1992.

Hon Judith Emily Ann, *b* 1955; *ed* Wimbledon High Sch, and Royal Academy of Music; Royal Opera House Orchestra.

WIDOW LIVING OF LIFE BARON

CICELY ELIZABETH (*Baroness Mayhew*), da of George Ludlam: *m* 1949, Baron Mayhew (Life Baron), who *d* 1997. *Residence* – Chaucer's Cottage, 26 Park St, Woodstock, Oxon OX20 1SP.

MAYHEW OF TWYSDEN, BARON (Mayhew) (Life Baron 1997)

PATRICK BARNABAS BURKE MAYHEW, QC, PC, son of late (Alfred) Geoffrey Horace Mayhew, MC, of Sevenoaks Weald, Kent, by his wife Sheila Margaret Burke Roche (*see* B Fermoy, colls, 1959 Edn); *b* 11 Sept 1929; *ed* Tonbridge, and Balliol Coll, Oxford (MA 19—); Bar, Middle Temple, 1956, Bencher 1982; QC 1972; MP (*C*) for Tunbridge Wells 1974-97; Vice-Chm Conservative Home Affairs Cttee and Memb Exec 1922 Cttee 1976-79; Parliamentary Under Sec for Employment 1979-81; Min of State, Home Office 1981-83; Solicitor-Gen 1983-87; Attorney-Gen 1987-92; Sec of State for Northern Ireland 1992-97; Proo Aircy Ncave Tiust since 1997, *cr* Kt 1983, PC 1986, and *Baron Mayhew of Twysden*, of Kilndown, co Kent (Life Baron) 1997: *m* 1963, Jean Elizabeth, OBE, 2nd da of John Gurney, of The Abbey, Walsingham, Norfolk (*see* Ogilvy, Bt, colls, 1995 Edn), and has issue.

Arms – ......
Address – House of Lords, SW1A 0PW. *Clubs* – Pratt's, Beefsteak, Garrick, Tunbridge Wells Constitutional.

SONS LIVING

Hon James Barnabas Burke, *b* 1964; *ed* Tonbridge, Balliol Coll, Oxford, and RMA, Sandhurst.

Hon Henry Edmund Burke, *b* 1965; *ed* Tonbridge, and Bristol Univ.

Hon Tristram Thomas Burke, *b* 1968; *ed* Tonbridge, Edinburgh Univ, and RMA, Sandhurst; Capt Royal Dragoon Gds: *m* 1998, Rebecca K. S., eldest da of late Richard Hobbs, and of Mrs John Morgan, of Northchapel, W Sussex.

Hon Jerome Patrick Burke, *b* 1970; *ed* Tonbridge, and Edinburgh Univ; Bar, Middle Temple, 1996.

MAYO, EARL OF (Bourke) (Earl I 1785)
(Name pronounced "Burke")

Salvation from the Cross

TERENCE PATRICK BOURKE, 10th Earl; *b* 26 Aug 1929; *s* 1962; Lt RN (ret): *m* 1st, 1952 (*m diss* 1987), (Margaret) Jane (Robinson), who *d* 1992, only da of late Gerald Joseph Cuthbert Harrison, DL, of Wetheral, Cumberland; 2ndly, 1987, Sally Anne, only da of F. G. Matthews, of Bampton, Oxon, and has issue by 1st and 2nd *m*.

Arms – Per fesse or and ermine, a cross gules, in the 1st quarter a lion rampant, and in the 2nd a dexter hand erect couped at the wrist, both sable. **Crest** – A cat-a-mountain sejant guardant proper, collared and chained or. **Supporters** – Two Chevaliers in complete armour, each holding in the exterior hand a pole-axe, proper.
Residence – Château d'Arlens, Couloumé Mondebat, 32160 Plaisance-du-Gers, France *Clubs* – RNVR, Galway County.

SONS LIVING (*By 1st marriage*)

CHARLES DIARMUIDH JOHN (*Lord Naas*) (Derryinver, Beach Rd, Clifden, co Galway), *b* 11 June 1953; *ed* Portora Royal Sch, and Queen's Univ, Belfast; Works Manager, MAG Briggs Amasco Ltd, Leeds: *m* 1st, 1975 (*m diss* 1979), Marie Antoinette Cronnelly; 2ndly, 1985, Marie Veronica, da of Francis Mannion, of Clifden, co Galway, and has issue by 1st and 2nd *m*:—

SONS LIVING (by 2nd *m*)— *Hon* Richard Thomas, *b* 7 Dec 1985, — *Hon* Eoin Patrick, *b* 1989.
DAUGHTER LIVING (by 1st *m*)— *Hon* Corinne Mary Jane, *b* 1975.

Hon Patrick Antony, *b* 1955.
Hon Harry Richard, *b* 1960.

(*By 2nd marriage*)

Hon James Edward Maurice, *b* 1986.

SISTER LIVING

Sheelagh Wilmot, *b* 1925: *m* 1955, Frank Merton Trier, of Fairlawn, W Horsley, Surrey, and has issue living, Terence Anthony Merton, *b* 1957, — Ysolde Gwynedd, *b* 1956.

AUNT LIVING (*Daughter of 8th Earl*)

Lady Betty Jocelyn, *b* 1917: *m* 1st, 1943, Capt Ronald Banon, late 60th Rifles, who *d* 1943; 2ndly, 1953, Samuel Clarke, who *d* 1980, and has issue living, (by 2nd *m*) Elizabeth Charlotte, *b* 1955: *m* 1989, Gary J. Pielak, and has issue living, Peter Samuel *b* 1991, Charlotte Isabell *b* 1989, — Jocelyne Margaret, *b* 1957: *m* 1st, 1981 (*m diss* 1988), Michael J. Woodman; 2ndly, 1992, Carl Coert Grobler. *Residence* – 22 Grove St, Oxford OX2 7JT.

STEPMOTHER LIVING

Patricia May, el da of late H. B. Dickinson, MD, FRCS, of Hereford: *m* 1952, as his 2nd wife, Capt Hon Bryan Longley Bourke, RIF, who *d* 1961. *Residence* – Dashells, Dog Village, Broadclyst, Exeter, Devon EX5 3AB.

COLLATERAL BRANCHES LIVING

Grandson of late Maj Hon Edward Roden Bourke, 6th son of 5th Earl:—
Issue of late Col Nigel Edward Jocelyn Bourke, *b* 1886, *d* 1970: *m* 1927, Doris, who *d* 1949, da of Allan Wills, of Aberdeen:—
Josslyn Allan Roden, *b* 1930: *m* 1951, Barbara Alison, da of Wilson Braddock, and has issue living, Alice Grania, *b* 1954, — Deborah Madeline, *b* 1958, — Susan Doris, *b* 1960.

Grandson of late Lt Hubert Edward Madden BOURKE-BORROWES, RN, son of Richard Bourke, son of late Rev Hon George Theobald Bourke, 4th son of 3rd Earl:—
Issue of late Dermot Richard Southwell Bourke-Borrowes, *b* 1884, *d* 1968: *m* 1941, Mrs Elisabeth Burton, who *d* 1999, da of G. F. Burgess, of Hall Garth, Over Kellett, Lancs, and formerly wife of R. N. Burton:—
Kildare Hubert (The Lower House, North Aston, Oxon OX6 4JA; St James's Club), *b* 1942; *ed* Wellington and Magdalen Coll, Camb; JP: *m* 1st 1971 (*m diss* 1983), Pippa Marguerite, who *d* 1992, yr da of late Lt-Col O. S. Steel, of Meriden Court, Chelsea Manor St, SW3; 2ndly, 1984, Sarah Louise, da of late John Robert McCready, of Naro Moru, Kenya, and has issue living (by 1st *m*), Olivia Helene, *b* 1974, — Catherine Hayley, *b* 1977, — (by 2nd *m*) Hubert Alexander Robert, *b* 1985, — Thea Anne, *b* 1986.

Granddaughter of late Maj-Gen Sir George Deane Bourke, KCMG, CB, son of late Lieut-Col Thomas Joseph Deane Bourke, son of late Rev Hon George Theobald Bourke (ante):—
Issue of late Group-Capt Ulick John Deane Bourke, CMG, *b* 1884, *d* 1948: *m* 1917 (*m diss* 1932), Irene, da of Lewis Ashhurst, of Norwich:—
Bridget (Sparrows, North Aston, Oxon), *b* 1920; Bar Lincoln's Inn 1956: *m* 1963, Leigh Edward Parker, who *d* 1973.

PREDECESSORS – This family, formerly of Moneycrower, co Mayo, descends from John Bourke, 4th son of Sir Thomas Bourke, 1397 styled "MacWilliam Eighter", head of Mayo or Lower Connaught branch, as distinct from "MacWilliam Oughter" of Galway or Upper Connaught (*see* M Sligo), whose 2nd son Edmund was ancestor of Viscounts Mayo (*cr* 1627, ext or dormant 1767), and was a branch of the Anglo-Norman family of de Burgh **(1)** *Rt Hon* JOHN Bourke, of Moneycrower, MP, First Commr of Revenue, Ireland 1749-80; *cr Baron Naas*, of Naas, co Kildare 1776, and *Viscount Mayo*, of Moneycrower, co Mayo 1781; and *Earl of Mayo* 1785 (all in Peerage of Ireland): *m* 1726, Mary, who *d* 1774, da of Rt Hon Joseph Deane; *d* 1790; *s* by his el son **(2)** JOHN, 2nd Earl, *b* about 1729; MP: *m* 1764, Lady Margaret Leeson, who *d* 1794, da of 1st Earl of Milltown; *d* 1792; *s* by his brother **(3)** *Most Rev* JOSEPH Deane, DD, 3rd Earl; *b* 1736; Bishop of Leighlin 1772-82, and Archbishop of Tuam 1782-94: *m* 1760, Elizabeth Meade, who *d* 1807, sister of 1st Earl of Clanwilliam; *d* 1794; *s* by his son **(4)** JOHN, GCH, PC, 4th Earl; *b* 1766; a Representative Peer 1816-49: *m* 1792, Arabella (Lady of the Bedchamber to Queen Adelaide), who *d* 1843, da of William Mackworth Praed, of Bitton House, Devon; *d* 1849; *s* by his nephew **(5)** ROBERT (only son of Rt Rev Hon Richard Bourke, Bishop of Waterford and Lismore, 2nd son of 3rd Earl), 5th Earl, *b* 1797; a Representative Peer 1852-67: *m* 1820, Anne Charlotte, who *d* 1867, da of Hon John Jocelyn (E Roden); *d* 1867; *s* by his son **(6)** *Rt Hon* RICHARD SOUTHWELL, KP, GCMG, 6th Earl; *b* 1822; MP for Kildare (*C*) 1847-52, for Coleraine 1852-7, and for Cockermouth 1857-68; Ch Sec for Ireland 1852, 1858, and 1866, and Gov-Gen of India 1868-72, when he was assassinated in the Andaman Islands: *m* 1848, Blanche Julia, CI, VA, who *d* 1918, da of 1st Baron Leconfield; *s* by his el son **(7)** *Rt Hon* DERMOT ROBERT WYNDHAM, KP, 7th Earl, *b* 1851; a Representative Peer for Ireland and Lieut of co Kildare; a Member of Senate of Irish Free State 1922-7: *m* 1885, Geraldine Sarah, who *d* 1944, da of late Hon Gerald Henry Brabazon Ponsonby; *d* 1927; *s* by his cousin **(8)** WALTER LONGLEY (son of late Rev Hon George Wingfield Bourke, 4th son of 5th Earl), 8th Earl; *b* 1859: *m* 1st, 1887, Ethel Kathleen Jane, who *d* 1913, only da of late Capt John Freeman, of Rockfield, Herefordshire; 2ndly, 1916, Margaret Anah, who *d* 1964, da of late Major John Harvey Scott, Indian Army; *d* 1939; *s* by his son **(9)** ULICK HENRY, 9th Earl; *b* 1890; 2nd Lt, King's Roy Rifle Corps; 1914-18 War as Lt, King's African Rifles: *m* 1937, Nöel Jessie Haliburton, who *d* 1993, aged 102, da of late William James Wilson, of High Park, nr Kendal; *d* 1962; *s* by his nephew **(10)** TERENCE PATRICK (only son of late Hon Bryan Longley Bourke, 3rd son of 8th Earl), 10th Earl and present peer; also Viscount Mayo, and Baron Naas.

MEATH, EARL OF (Brabazon) Sits as BARON CHAWORTH (UK 1831) (Earl I 1627)

My life is devoted

JOHN ANTHONY BRABAZON, 15th Earl; *b* 11 May 1941; *s* 1998; *ed* Harrow; a Page of Honour to HM 1956-58; commn'd Gren Gds 1959-62: *m* 1973, Xenia, yr da of Paul Goudime, of Windlesham Park, Surrey, and has issue.

ᴀrms – Gules: on a bend or, three martlets sable. Crest – On a mount vert, a falcon rising or. Supporters – Two wyverns or, collared and chained gules.
Seat – Killruddery, Bray, co Wicklow. *Residence* – Ballinacor, Rathrum, co Wicklow.

SON LIVING

ANTHONY JACQUES (*Lord Ardee*), *b* 30 Jan 1977; *ed* Harrow.

DAUGHTERS LIVING

Lady Corinna Lettice, *b* 1974.
Lady Serena Alexandra, *b* 1979.

BROTHER LIVING

Hon David Geoffrey Normand (North Wing, Killruddery, Bray, co Wicklow), *b* 1948: *m* 1972, Gay Dorothea, yr da of Cdr William (Jock) Whitworth, DSC, RN, of Trudder, co Wicklow (*see* M Ely, 1972-73 Edn), and has had issue, †Geoffrey William *b* 1975; *d* 1998, following an accident, — Celia Antonia, *b* 1973, — Diana Elizabeth, *b* 1981.

SISTERS LIVING

Lady Romayne Aileen, *b* 1943: *m* 1968, Capt Robert Eben Neil Pike, late Gren Gds, of Kidborough House, Danehill, Sussex, and has issue living, Harry Eben, *b* 1974, — Tamsin Lucy, *b* 1972.
Lady Lavinia Anne, *b* 1945: *m* 1969, John Ernest Baron Jobson, of Barnacullia, Kilmacanoge, co Wicklow, and has issue living, James Robert, *b* 1977, — Rebecca Catherine, *b* 1971, — Charlotte Naomi Marya, *b* 1973, — Suzannah Elizabeth, *b* 1976.

AUNT LIVING (*daughter of 13th Earl*)

Lady Meriel Aileen, *b* 1913: *m* 1947, Maj Ernest Gerald Howarth, MBE, who *d* 1967, and has issue living, Sarah Ann HOWARTH (Acacia House, High St, Mistley, Manningtree, Essex CO11 1HD), *b* 1950; resumed her maiden name by statutory declaration 1991: *m* 1st, 1972 (*m diss* 1982), Robert Adam Hughes Smeddle (*see* Hughes, Bt, *cr* 1773, colls); 2ndly, 1987 (*m diss* 1991), Alastair D. M. Ritchie, and has issue living (by 1st *m*) (*see* Hughes, Bt, *cr* 1773, colls), — (Aileen) Jane (66 Houblon Rd, Richmond, Surrey TW10 6DE), *b* 1951: *m* 1977 (*m diss* 1995), Michael D. B. Oram, and has issue living, Francesca Louise *b* 1978, — (Elizabeth) Meriel, *b* 1953: *m* 1979, Patrick Frank Alain White, of Dunster Lodge, 1 Bristol Gdns, SW15 3TG, and has issue living, Sebastian Patrick *b* 1985, Jocelyn Claud Howarth *b* 1987, Dominic Christian *b* 1989, Marina Charlotte *b* 1983, — Penelope Susan, *b* 1958: *m* 1st, 1988, Timothy P. G. Carew, who *d* 1990; 2ndly, 1994, Tom Plant, of 44 St John's Av, Newmarket, Suffolk, and has issue living (by 1st *m*), Frederick Roger Ernest *b* 1989, (by 2nd *m*), Conor David *b* 1996, Catherine Serena *b* 1995. *Residence* – 8 Ferndale Close, Newmarket, Suffolk CB8 7DZ.

WIDOW LIVING OF FOURTEENTH EARL

ELIZABETH MARY (*Elizabeth, Countess of Meath*), da of late Capt Geoffrey Vaux Salvin Bowlby, RHG (*see* V Valentia, 1985 Edn): *m* 1940, Major the 14th Earl of Meath, who *d* 1998. *Residence* – Kilruddery House, Bray, co Wicklow.

COLLATERAL BRANCHES LIVING

Issue of late Lieut-Col Hon Claud Maitland Patrick Brabazon, OBE, 3rd son of 12th Earl, *b* 1874, *d* 1959: *m* 1915, Kathleen, who *d* 1961, da of late Arthur Maitland, of Shudy Camps Park, Cambridgeshire:—
Elizabeth Maitland, *b* 1915: *m* 1942, Lieut-Col Evered Mansfield Poole, RA (ret) (By Ilkeston (ext)), who *d* 1982, and has issue living, Catherin Elizabeth, *b* 1980, James Keith Forrester, of Copper Beeches, Sikeside, Kirklinton, Carlisle CA6 6DR, and has issue living, Jack James Evered *b* 1994, Anne-Marie Catherin *b* 1983, Charlotte Antonia *b* 1986, Alice Elizabeth *b* 1988. *Residence* – Robin Hood Cottage, Standford, Borden GU35 8RA.

(*In special remainder to the Earldom*)

Descendants of late Hon Sir Anthony Brabazon, 3rd son of 1st Baron Ardee:—

Grandsons of Samuel Levinge Brabazon (b 1829), elder son of late Rev James Brabazon, son of late Anthony Brabazon, elder son of late Philip Brabazon (b 1733), great grandson of late Capt James Brabazon, son of late Hon Sir Anthony Brabazon (ante):—
Issue of late Gerald Hugh Brabazon, b 18—, d 19—: m 189—, Eleanor Murphy:—
Clarence Levinge, b 18—. ——— Claude Hugh, b 18—. ——— Edward Alfred, b 18—.

Grandchildren of late Charles James Anthony Brabazon, eldest son of late Anthony Godsell Brabazon (b 1841), yr son of late Rev James Brabazon (ante):—
Issue of late Anthony Godsell Brabazon, b 1899, d 1982: m 1925, Margaret Victoria, only da of late J. A. Gibson, of Sydney, NSW:—
Margaret Ann (1 Boorana St, Jindalee, Brisbane, Qld 4074, Australia), b 1927; FASA, ACIS, JP: m 1974, Rt Rev Ian Wotton Allnutt Shevill, sometime Bishop of Newcastle, NSW, who d 1988.

Issue of late Charles Reginald Brabazon, b 1904, d 1987: m 1940, Minnie Isabel, da of James Lennox Arthur, of Quambetook, Nelia, N Qld:—
Judge Charles James Lennox (48 Tenth Av, St Lucia, Brisbane, Qld, Australia), b 1944; BA, LLM, QC: m 1981, Justice Michelle May, and has issue living, Sarah Margaret, b 1991, — Lucinda Claire, b (triplet) 1991, — Alice Elizabeth, b (triplet) 1991. ——— Richard Anthony, b 1949; ed The Southport Sch: m 1975, Susan Margaret, da of G. Greentree, and has issue living, Timothy Richard, b 1979, — Jennifer Amy, b 1981.

Issue of late Rupert William Brabazon, b 1908, d 1979: m 1952, Margaret Cecil Pender, da of late Edward Pender Phillott, of Colane, Winton, Qld:—
Anthony Edward (39 Guara Grove, Pimpama, Qld 4209, Australia), b 1953: m 1993, Tracy Clarkson. ——— †William Robert, b 1960; d 1982. ——— Wendy Pender (3/11 Sunbrite Av, Mermaid Beach, Qld 4218, Australia), b 1955. ——— Patricia Rain (2/66 Bauer St, Southport, Qld 4215, Australia), b 1957.

Granddaughters of late Rupert Levinge Brabazon (infra):—
Issue of late Rupert Macdonald Brabazon, b 1907, d 1983: m 1934, Moyra Joy, who d 1974, da of Edgar Joyce, of The Overflow, Beaudesert, Qld:—
Barbara Joan, b 1938: m 1963, Kenneth Maddox, of 41 Mabel St, Cunnamulla, Qld 4490, Australia, and has issue living, Kim Anita, b 1965; has issue living, Zachary Wayne b 1990, — Kerryanne, b 1967: m 1993, Mark Edward Andrews. ——— Patricia Elizabeth, b 1940: m 1960, Harold Bergman, of 46 Kooringal Drive, Jindalee, Qld 4074, Australia, and has issue living, Anthony, b 1965, — Thomas b 1966, — Patricia, b 1961, — Colleen, b 1963, — Rosemary, b 1968, — Margaret, b 1970, — Jeanette, b 1972.

Grandchildren of late Anthony Godsell Brabazon (b 1841) (ante):—
Issue of late Charles James Anthony Brabazon, b 1869, d 1944: m 1897, Amy Ruby Victoria, who d 1947, da of William McMillan, of Culparoo, Longreach, Qld:—
Kathleen Patricia (6/9 Norwood St, Toowong, Brisbane, Qld 4066, Australia), b 1903. ——— Eileen Emma, b 1907: m 1929, Bernard Carr Clark, of 2/121 Maloney St, N Rockhampton, Qld 4701, Australia, and has had issue, †Michael George, b 1930; d 1991, — Adam Charles (Bimbadeen, Taroom, Qld 4420), b 1933: m 1954, Dorothy Isabel, da of J. S. B. Milne, of Dalby, Qld, and has issue living, Bruce Robert b 1955: m 1987, Judy Clare, da of J. Bazley, of Brooklands, Ullenhall, Warwicks (and has issue living, Darryl James Carr b 1993, Nicole Hanna Carr b 1991), Ian Charles b 1956, Owen Mark b 1967: m 1991, Helen Marian, da of D. Kimber, of Bowen, Qld (and has issue living, Emily Kate b 1992, Rachael Louise b 1993), Kevin Adam b 1969, Wendy Ann b 1961: m 1981, Rodney Hans Woodrow, of Juandah Plains, Wandoan, Qld 4419 (and has issue living, Rowan Max b 1985, Ryan Wayne b 1990, Megan Rose b 1983, Krystal Lee b 1988), — Robert Anthony (Mutation, Clermont, Qld 4721), b 1936: m 1967, Margot Grant, da of late A. F. G. Cameron, of Brisbane, Qld, and has issue living, Michael Robert b 1969, Ann Laura b 1970.

Issue of late Rupert Levinge Brabazon, b 1871, d 1924: m 1904, Grace Eva, who d 1948, da of late Campbell Livingstone Macdonald, of Bromelton, Beaudesert, Qld:—
Robert Charles, b 1912: m 1950, Geraldine Hope Gordon, da of Robert John Gordon Burrow, and has issue living, Mark Levinge, b 1958; ed Brisbane Boys' Coll; BA, LLB.

Granddaughter of late George Philip Augustus Brabazon (infra):—
Issue of late Cecil George Le Normand Brabazon, b 1887, d 1975: m 1927, Gladys May (183 3rd Av, 700 Chula Vista, Cal 92010, USA), da of Nathan Wyman Downs, of Chula Vista, Cal, USA:—
Cora Jane, b 1934: m 1962, Charles F. Ruhr, of 4750 Washington Av, White Bear Lake, Minnesota 55110, USA, and has had issue, Christopher Patrick, b 1968; d 1995, — Ann Cecilia, b 1965: m 1992, Nicholas Stuart Pifer, of 719 Goodrich Ave, St Paul, Minnesota 55105, USA, and has issue living, Christopher William b 1995.

Granddaughter of late Rev Philip Robert Waller Brabazon, son of late Rev George Brabazon (b 1780), yr son of late Philip Brabazon (b 1733) (ante):—
Issue of late George Philip Augustus Brabazon, b 1845, d 1912: m 1886, Rhoda Jane, who d 1946, da of late Edmond Nugent, MD, FRCSI, of San Diego, California:—
Marian Constance, b 1900: m 1936, Howard Jonathan Edwards, who d 1950. Residence – Cloisters Con Centre, 3680 Reynard Way, San Diego, California, USA.

Grandson of late George Philip Augustus Brabazon (ante):—
Issue of late Montague Philip Le Normand Brabazon, b 1890, d 1967: m 1916, Edwina Meston, da of late George T. Smith, of Alpine, San Diego, Cal, USA:—
Keith Elmer (5738 Willows Rd, Alpine, Cal 92001, USA), b 1917: m 1963, Clara Carolina, da of Rudolph Wenger, of Max, N Dakota, and has had issue, †Lee Monte, b 1964: m 19—, Kathleen Lorraine (5670 Willow Rd, Alpine, Calif 92001, USA), da of Barry Hulahan, of San Diego, Calif, and dsp 1997.

PREDECESSORS – (1) *Rt Hon Sir* EDWARD Brabazon, KT, PC, MP for co Wicklow 1585, and High Sheriff of Staffordshire 1606; *cr Baron Ardee* (peerage of Ireland) 1616; *d* 1625; *s* by his son (2) WILLIAM, KB, 2nd Baron; *cr Earl of Meath* (peerage of Ireland) 1627, with remainder to his brother Anthony; *d* 1675; *s* by his son (3) EDWARD, 2nd Earl; *d* 1675, *s* by his son (4) WILLIAM, 3rd Earl; *d* 1684; *s* by his el son (5) EDWARD, 4th Earl; was Ranger of the Phoenix Park, Dublin; *dsp* 1707; *s* by his brother (6) CHAMBRE, 5th Earl; *d* 1715; *s* by his el son (7) CHAWORTH, 6th Earl; *dsp* 1758; *s* by his brother (8) EDWARD, 7th Earl; *d* 1772; *s* by his son (9) ANTHONY, 8th Earl; *d* 1790; *s* by his el son (10) WILLIAM, 9th Earl; killed in a duel 1797; *s* by his brother (11) JOHN CHAMBRE, KP, 10th Earl; *b* 1772; Lord-Lieut of co Dublin; *cr Baron Chaworth*, of Eaton Hall, co Hereford (peerage of United Kingdom) 1831; *m* 1801, Lady Melosina Adelaide, who *d* 1866, da of 1st Earl of Clanwilliam; *d* 1851; *s* by his son (12) WILLIAM, 11th Earl; *b* 1803; *m* 1873, Harriot, who *d* 1898, da of Sir Richard Brooke, 6th Bt; *d* 1887; *s* by his son (13) REGINALD, KP, GCVO, GBE, PC, 12th Earl, *b* 1841; Founder and Chm of Metropolitan Public Gardens Asso; Chancellor of Roy Univ of Ireland 1902-6: *m* 1868, Lady Mary Jane Maitland, who *d* 1918, only da of 11th Earl of Lauderdale; *d* 1929; *s* by his son (14) REGINALD LE NORMAND, CB, CBE, 13th Earl; *b* 1869; Brig-Gen (ret) late Grenadier and Irish Guards; S Africa 1900-02, European War 1914-19 (CB, CBE): *m* 1908, Lady Aileen May Wyndham Quin, who *d* 1962, da of 4th Earl of Dunraven; *d* 1949; *s* by his son (15) ANTHONY WINDHAM NORMAND, 14th Earl, *b* 1910; Maj late Gren Guards; ADC to Gov of Bengal 1936: *m* 1940, Elizabeth Mary, da of late Capt Geoffrey Vaux Salvin Bowlby; *d* 1998; *s* by his son (16) JOHN ANTHONY, 15th Earl and present peer; also Baron Ardee, and Baron Chaworth.

Medina, Earl of; son of Marquess of Milford Haven.

Medway, Lord; son of Earl of Cranbrook.

MELCHETT, BARON (Mond) (Baron UK 1928, Bt UK 1910)

PETER ROBERT HENRY MOND, 4th Baron, and 4th Baronet; *b* 24 Feb 1948; *s* 1973; *ed* Eton, Pembroke Coll, Camb, and Keele Univ; a Lord in Waiting to HM 1974-75, and Under-Sec of State, Industry 1975-76, Min of State, N Ireland 1976-79; Pres of Ramblers Assoc 1981-84; Chm of Community Industry 1979-85, and the Working Party on Pop Festivals 1975-76; Chm Wildlife Link 1981-86; Chm Greenpeace UK 1986-89; Chm Greenpeace Japan since 1995; Executive Dir Greenpeace UK since 1989.

Arms – Quarterly, 1st and 4th, gules, a demi-lion rampant between in chief a decrescent and an increscent, and in base a crescent, all or; on a chief argent an eagle displayed between two mullets sable, *Mond*; 2nd and 3rd, azure, on a pile between three mullets argent, an eagle displayed sable, *Lowenthal*. **Crest** – A demi-bear holding between the paws a fountain, both proper. **Supporters** – *Dexter*, a Doctor of Science of the University of Oxford, holding in the exterior hand a chemical measure glass; *Sinister*, a labourer, holding in the exterior hand a pick resting on the shoulder all proper.
Address – c/o House of Lords.

SISTERS LIVING

(Hon) Kerena Ann (does not use courtesy title), *b* 1951: *m* 1st, 1980, Richard Moorehead; 2ndly, 1985, Adam Boulton, and has issue living, (by 1st *m*) Lucy, *b* 1981, — (by 2nd *m*) Blaise, *b* 1990, — Hannah, *b* 1987.

(Hon) Pandora Shelley (does not use courtesy title), *b* 1959: *m* 1991, Nicholas Wesolowski, son of late Michael Joseph Wesolowski, of Pelham St, SW3, and has issue living, Ludovic, *b* 1995, — Alexander Jozef, *b* 1997.

AUNT LIVING *(Daughter of 2nd Baron)*

Hon Karis Valerie Violet, *b* 1927: *m* 1st, 1949 *(m diss* 1956), John Hackman Sumner; 2ndly, 1956, Brian Wallace, and has issue living, (by 1st *m*) Justin Mark, *b* 1953, — (by 2nd *m*) Jessica Karis, *b* 1957, — Arabella Katherine, *b* 1959. *Residence* – Greenways, Lambourn, Berks.

WIDOW LIVING OF SON OF SECOND BARON

Yvonne Victoria, only child of T. Douglas Searle, of Cornerways, The Park, Cheltenham: *m* 1st, 1942, Lt Hon Derek John Henry Mond, RNVR, who was *k* on active ser 1945; 2ndly, 1951, Richard Louis Rowe. *Residence* – 4133 Marlowe Av, Montreal H4A 3M3, Canada.

WIDOW LIVING OF THIRD BARON

SONIA ELIZABETH (Flat 20, Millennium House, 132 Grosvenor Rd, SW1V 3JY), da of late Col Roland Harris Graham, RAMC (ret), of The Lodge, Bridge, Kent; novelist and travel writer; Council Member Royal Court Theatre since 1983, and The Royal National Theatre 1983-93: *m* 1st, 1947, the 3rd Baron Melchett, who *d* 1973; 2ndly, 1984, as his 2nd wife, Dr Andrew Annandale Sinclair, author.

PREDECESSORS – (1) *Rt Hon* ALFRED MORITZ Mond, LLD, DSc, FRS, son of late Ludwig Mond, PhD, FRS, of The Poplars, 20 Avenue Rd, St John's Wood, NW, and Winnington Hall, Norwich, by his wife, Frieda, who *d* 1923, da of Adolph Meyer Löwenthal, of Cologne; *b* 1868; first Chm of Imperial Chemical Industries, Ltd, Chm of Mond Nickel Co, and of Amalgamated Anthracite Collieries, Ltd, a Director of Westminster Bank, Ltd, Pres of British Science Guild, Chm of National Federation of Chemical Employers, and of Council of Jewish Agency for Palestine, and Joint Chm of Conference on Industrial Reorganisation and Industrial Relations; was First Commr of Works 1916-21, and Min of Health 1921-2; MP for Chester (*L*) Jan 1906 to Jan 1910, for Swansea, Swansea Town Div (*L*) Jan 1910 to Nov 1918, for W Div thereof (*L*) Dec 1918 to Nov 1923, and for Carmarthenshire, Carmarthen Div (*L*) Aug to Oct 1924, and (*C*) Oct 1924 to June 1928; *cr a Baronet*, of Hartford Hill, Great Budworth, co Chester 1910, and *Baron Melchett*, of Landford, co Southampton (peerage of United Kingdom) 1928: *m* 1894, Violet Florence Mabel, who *d* 1945, DBE, da of late James Henry Goetze; *d* 1930; *s* by his son (2) HENRY LUDWIG, 2nd Baron; *b* 1898; was Vice-Chm of Imperial Chemical Industries Ltd, a Director of International Nickel Co of Canada, Ltd, of Industrial Finance and Investment Corporation, Ltd, and of Palestine Electric Corporation, Ltd, Chm of Palestine Plantations, Ltd, etc, and a Trustee of Ramsay Memorial Fellowship; sat as MP for Isle of Ely (*L*) 1923-4, when he was defeated, and for Liverpool, E Toxteth Div (*C*) 1929-30: *m* 1920, Amy Gwen, who *d* 1982, da of late John Wilson, of Parktown, Johannesburg, S Africa; *d* 1949; *s* by his son (3) JULIAN EDWARD ALFRED, 3rd Baron, *b* 1925; Chm of British Steel Corpn 1967-73, and a Member of NEDC 1969-73: *m* 1947, Sonia Elizabeth, da of late Col Roland Harris Graham, RAMC (ret), of the Lodge, Bridge, Kent; *d* 1973; *s* by his son (4) PETER ROBERT HENRY, 4th Baron and present peer.

Melgund, Viscount; son of Earl of Minto.

MELLISH, BARONY OF (Mellish) (Extinct 1998)

SONS LIVING OF LIFE BARON

Hon Robert (20 Shermanbury Rd, Worthing), *b* ca 1942/43: *m* 19—, Erica.

Hon David (47 Little Heath, SE7), *b* 1944: *m* 1967, Mary Josephine, da of John Patrick Leahy, and has issue living, Daniel David, *b* 1969, — Claire Mary, *b* 1968.

Hon Paul, *b* ca 1952/53.

Hon Stephen (45 Lancing Park, Lancing, Sussex), *b* 1955: *m* 1976, Elizabeth Ann, da of John Henry Skinner, and has issue living, Nicholas, *b* 1986.

WIDOW LIVING OF LIFE BARON

ANNE ELIZABETH (*Baroness Mellish*), da of George Warner: *m* 1938, Baron Mellish, PC (Life Baron), who *d* 1998. *Residence* – 39 Bromley Rd, Catford, SE6.

Melville, see Earl of Leven and Melville.

Melville, Leslie, family name of Earl of Leven and Melville.

MELVILLE, VISCOUNT (Dundas) (Viscount UK 1802)

ROBERT DAVID ROSS DUNDAS, 9th Viscount; *b* 28 May 1937; *s* 1971; *ed* Wellington Coll; Capt (Reserve) Scots Gds; Lieut Ayrshire Yeo; Pres Lasswade Civic Soc, CC and District Councillor, Lasswade, Midlothian: *m* 1982, Fiona Margaret, da of late Roger Kirkpatrick Stilgoe, of Derby House, Stogumber, Taunton, Somerset, and has issue.

Arms – Argent, a lion rampant gules, armed and langued azure, within a bordure of the last charged with three boar's heads couped or, armed proper and langued of the second. **Crest** – A lion's head affrontée gules struggling through an oak-bush proper. **Supporters** – *Dexter*, a leopard regardant proper; *sinister*, a stag proper attired argent.
Residences – Solomons Court, Chalford, Stroud, Glos; 3 Roland Way, SW7. *Clubs* – Cavalry and Guards', Turf, Midlothian County.

SONS LIVING

Hon ROBERT HENRY KIRKPATRICK, *b* 23 April 1984.
Hon James David Brouncker, *b* 1986.

COLLATERAL BRANCHES LIVING

Issue of late Hon Cospatrick Philip Brooke Dundas, 2nd son of 6th Viscount, *b* 1879, *d* 1954: *m* 1913, Isabella, who *d* 1969, da of E. A. W. McKenzie:—
Daphne Roseabella Louise, *b* 1923: *m* 1943, Rankin Hodgin, of Lethbridge, Alberta, Canada.

Issue of late Hon Richard Serle Dundas, 3rd son of 6th Viscount, *b* 1880, *d* 1968: *m* 1st, 1907, Lydia Catherine, who *d* 1922, da of E. A. W. R. McKenzie, of Pelly, Saskatchewan, Canada; 2ndly, 1926, Mathilde Mary who *d* 1979, da of Louis Saxon, of Yorkton, Saskatchewan, Canada:—
(By 1st *m*) Hugh McKenzie (298 Alfred St, Pembroke, Ont, Canada K8A 3A6; *Clubs* – Toronto Royal Canadian Military Institute, and Pembroke Golf and Country), *b* 1910; *ed* Sask Univ (BA); 1939-45 War: *m* 1939, Catherine Sanderson, who *d* 1994, da of late John Wallace, of Edinburgh, and has issue living, Robert Hugh Sanderson (Box 82, Hesperia, CA 92345, USA), *b* 1943; *ed* Sask Univ (BA), Carleton Univ (MA): *m* 1980, Nancy, da of Kenneth Howard Sullivan, of Montreal, — Catherine Marion Wallace (298 Alfred St, Pembroke, Ontario, Canada K8A 3A6), *b* 1948; *ed* Carleton Univ (BA). —— Richard Serle (II) (Box 281, Paradise Hill, Saskatchewan, Canada S0M 2G0), *b* 1911; 1939-45 War: *m* 1942, Marianne Elizabeth, da of late William Hugh Semple, of N Battleford, Sask, Canada, and has issue living, Richard Serle (III), *b* 1948: *m* 1970, Denise Paulette, da of Frank Dechant, of Manning, Alberta, Canada, and has issue living, Richard Serle (IV) *b* 1971, Kelsi Shannon *b* 1974, — Dianne Mary, *b* 1946: *m* 1965, Lyle Merle Winder, of Box 301 Paradise Hill, Saskatchewan, Canada S0M 2G0, and has issue living, Laurie Dianne *b* 1966, — Carolyn Patricia, *b* 1954; *ed* Univ of Regina, Sask (BEd): *m* 1978, Daniel Brian Gervais, of 2302-49th Av, Lloydminster, Sask, Canada S9V 1M1, and has issue living, Aaron Daniel *b* 1983, Danelle Lindsay *b* 1979, Whitney Nicole *b* 1986. —— †Kenneth Brooke, *b* 1913; *ed* Sask Univ (BE Civil); Tech Dir of R & D Domtar Chemicals, Ltd, Montreal: *m* 1942, Dorothy Helen, who *d* 1994, da of late John A. Walters, of Saskatoon, and *d* 1988, leaving issue, Anthony John, *b* 1946; *ed* Queens Univ Ont, (BA), and Duke Univ (MA); *m* 1972, Carol A., da of R. Brunini of Pointe Claire, Quebec, and has issue living, Amy Leana *b* 1978, Kristina *b* 1982, — Peter Melville, *b* 1948; *ed* Univ of Sask (BA): *m* 1973, Mary Ann, da of J. Thorne, of Ottawa, and has issue living, Zachary David *b* 1979, Jennifer Mary *b* 1975, — Christopher Charles, *b* 1950; *ed* Queens Univ (BA) and Univ of California (MBA): *m* 1976, Marie Madeleine Suzanne, da of late Vianney Provencher, of Gentilly, Quebec, and has issue living, Sarah Daisy *b* 1977, Carla *b* 1982, — Dorothy Anne, *b* 1945: *m* 1977 (*m diss* 19—), R. Stephen Becker, of Springfield, Ill, USA. —— †Gerald Alexander, *b* 1916: *m* 1939, Alice Marjorie (who *m* 2ndly, 1996, Douglas Ordinal, of 508-4 Franklyn Court, Dartmouth, Nova Scotia, Canada B3A 2K1), da of Richard M. Lister, of Pelly, Saskatchewan, Canada, and *d* 1966, leaving issue, Richard Melville (62 Lindburgh Crescent, St John's Newfoundland A1N 2E6), *b* 1940; RCMP: *m* 1965, Dorothy Vivian, da of Alex Bursey, of St John's, Newfoundland, and has issue living, Karen Anne *b* 1965, Katherine Dawn *b* 1969, — Gerald James (126 Munroe Place, Regina, Saskatchewan, Canada S4S 4P9), *b* 1959; *ed* Univ of Regina (BA): *m* 1983, Colleen Julie, da of Norman Frank Stepan, of Regina, Sask, and has issue living, Sydney Lauren *b* 1986, Tori Alexandra *b* 1987, Bret Julie *b* 1989, — Pamela Marion, *b* 1942; SRN: *m* 1st, 1965, Anthony Braun, who *d* 1980; 2ndly, 1985, Arthur Dahl, who *d* 1994; 3rdly, 1996, Morris Koschinsky, of 146 Daly Crescent, Brandon, Manitoba, Canada R7A 6W3, and has issue living (by 1st *m*), Leslie Simone *b* 1966, Hilary Louise *b* 1968. —— Robert Montague (5738 Wallace St, Vancouver, BC, Canada), *b* 1920; *ed* Royal Military Coll, Kingston, and BC Univ (BASc, BA,

MA); Lt-Cdr RCNR (ret); 1939-45 War as Lt RCNVR: *m* 1953, Shirley Janet, da of Urwin Finch, of Vancouver, and has had issue, James Urwin, *b* 1954, — †*Fr* Hugh Montague, *b* 1959; Roman Catholic Priest; *d* 1993, — Janet Glencora, *b* 1956; *ed* York House: *m* 1982, Stephen Corbett, of 4640 Duncliffe Rd, Richmond, BC V7E 3N1, Canada, and has issue living, George Miles *b* 1984, Madeline Janet *b* 1987, — Patricia Hope, *b* 1965; *ed* Crofton House. —— Grace Edith Marian, *b* 1918; *ed* Sask Univ (BHSc); *d* 1998. —— (By 2nd *m*) Oenone Judith, *b* 1927: *ed* BC Univ (BA), London Univ (MA); PhD Wisconsin. —— Iris Ann Alayne (Salt Spring Island, BC, Canada), *b* 1928: *m* 1952, Rt Rev Ronald Francis Shepherd, late Bishop of British Columbia, formerly Dean of Montreal, and R of Christ Church Cathedral, and has issue living, Jeremy Michael, *b* 1956, — Christopher Patrick, *b* 1958, — Timothy David, *b* 1962, — Peter Andrew Dundas, *b* 1966, — Mary Mathilde, *b* 1954, — Susan Clare, *b* 1960.

Grandson of late Lieut Hon Kenneth Robert Dundas, RNVR, 4th son of 6th Viscount:—
Issue of late Claud Kenneth Melville Dundas, *b* 1911, *d* 1993: *m* 1939, Janet, who *d* (1 Oct) 1993, da of John Donaldson:—
Kenneth Ninian Melville (West Hill, Gt Rissington, Cheltenham, Glos GL54 2LP), *b* 1943; *ed* Trin Coll, Glenalmond: *m* 1967, Susan Marion, da of late Charles Ian Harper Hunter, of Heswall, Wirral, Merseyside, and has had issue, †Alistair Robert Melville, *b* 1975; *d* 1995. — Samantha Gillian, *b* 1972, — Philippa Marjorie, *b* 1978.

PREDECESSORS – (1) HENRY DUNDAS, PC (4th son of Robert Dundas of Arniston, cadet of Dundas of that Ilk), MP for co Edinburgh 1774-90, and for Edinburgh City 1790-1802; was successively Lord Advocate for Scotland, Sec of State for Home Depart, Pres of India Board of Control, Keeper of Privy Seal of Scotland, Sec of State for War, Treasurer of the Navy, and First Lord of the Admiralty; *cr Baron Dunira*, of co Perth, and *Viscount Melville* (peerage of United Kingdom) 1802; was impeached by the House of Commons in 1805 of malversation whilst treasurer of the Navy, and being tried by his peers was acquitted; *d* 1811; *s* by his son (2) ROBERT, KT, PC, 2nd Viscount; *b* 1771; sat as MP for Hastings and co Edinburgh 1794-1811; was successively Pres of Indian Board of Control, Ch Sec for Ireland, Registrar of Seizins and Lord Privy Seal of Scotland; Gen and Vice-Pres of Royal Co of Archers, an Elder Brother of the Trinity House, etc; assumed for himself the additional surname of Saunders: *m* 1796, Anne, da of Richard Huck Saunders, MD; *d* 1851; *s* by his el son (3) HENRY, GCB, 3rd Viscount; a Gen in the Army, Gov of Edinburgh Castle, Col 60th Rifles, and Vice Pres of Royal Co of Archers; *d* unmarried 1876; *s* by his brother (4) ROBERT, 4th Viscount; *d* unmarried 1886; *s* by his nephew (5) HENRY (son of late Rev Hon Charles Dundas, 4th son of 2nd Viscount, by Louisa Maria, da of Sir William Boothby, 9th Bt), 5th Viscount; *b* 1835: *m* 1891, Hon Violet Marie Louise Cochrane-Baillie, who *d* 1943, da of 1st Baron Lamington; *d* 1904; *s* by his brother (6) CHARLES SAUNDERS, ISO, 6th Viscount, *b* 1843; Consul at Santos 1869-77, for Canary Islands 1877-82, and Stettin 1882-5, and Consul-Gen at Hamburg 1885-97, and at Christiania 1897-1906: *m* 1st, 1872, Grace Selina Marian, who *d* 1919, da of late William Scully, of Rio de Janeiro, and formerly of co Tipperary; 2ndly, 1891, Mary, who *d* 1919, da of late George Hamilton, MD, of Falkirk; 3rdly, 1920, Margaret, who *d* 1961, da of late William James Todd; *d* 1926; *s* by his son (7) HENRY CHARLES CLEMENT, 7th Viscount, *b* 1873; was Vice-Consul at Zanzibar 1897-8, at Dar-es-Salaam 1898-1902, at Galatz 1902-6, and at Algiers 1906-7, and Consul for Bolivia 1907-8, for Tahiti 1908-9, for Bahia 1909, and for Corsica 1909-21: *m* 1899, Agnes Mary Florence, who *d* 1954, da of late Henry Brouncker, of Boveridge Park, Cranborne, Dorset; *d* 1935; *s* by his son (8) HENRY CHARLES PATRIC BROUNCKER, 8th Viscount, *b* 1909, *d* 1971; *s* by his nephew (9) ROBERT DAVID ROSS (only son of late Hon Robert Maldred St John Melville Dundas, yr son of 7th Viscount), 9th Viscount and present peer; also Baron Dunira.

MENUHIN, BARON (Menuhin) (Life Baron 1993) (Extinct 1999)

YEHUDI MENUHIN, OM, KBE, son of late Moshe Menuhin, by his wife, Marutha (*née* Sher), who *d* 1996, aged 100; *b* 22 April 1916, New York, USA; *ed* privately; adopted British nationality 1985; Hon DMus Oxford, Belfast, Leicester, London and Camb; Hon LLD Liverpool, St Andrews, Sussex and Bath; Hon DLit Warwick; FRCM, Snr Fellow Royal Coll of Art, Hon Fellow and Pres Trin Coll of Music, Hon Fellow St Catharine's Coll, Camb; has received many honorary doctorates from overseas univs; Cobbett Medal Musicians' Co 1959, Gold Medal Royal Philharmonic Soc 1962, Mozart Medal 1965, Gold Medal Canadian Music Council 1975, Albert Medal RSA 1981, Una Vita Nella Musica Italy 1983, Brahms Medal Hamburg 1987, Brahms Orden Hamburg 1988, Gold Medal Cordoba Univ 1990, Glenn Gould Prize Canada 1990, Yehudi Menuhin and Luciano Berio Wolf Prize 1991; Violinist and Conductor; initiated annual Music Festivals at Gstaad 1957, Bath 1959 and Windsor 1969; Founded Yehudi Menuhin Sch of Music, Surrey, 1963, Founder and Pres Internat Menuhin Music Acad at Gstaad 1976, Founder Live Music Now 1977; former Pres UK Internat Music Council of UNESCO, Pres and Associate Conductor Royal Philharmonic Orchestra since 1982 and Hallé Orchestra since 1992, Pres European String Teachers' Assocn, Young Musicians' Symphony Orchestra, and Musicians' Internat Mutual Aid Fund; Principal Guest Conductor English String Orchestra since 1988, Founder and Conductor

Asian Youth Orchestra; Jawaharlal Nehru Award for Internat Understanding 1968, Legion of Honour 1986, Cdr de l'Ordre des Arts et des Lettres and Cross of Lorraine (France), Cdr Order of Leopold (Belgium) and Officer of the Crown of Belgium, Kt Cdr and Grand Cross Order of Merit (Germany), Order of Merit of the Republic (Italy), Order of the Phoenix (Greece), and Cdr Order of Orange-Nassau (Netherlands); Freeman Cities of Edinburgh and Bath; Hon Swiss Citizenship 1970; *cr* Hon KBE (Civil) 1965, OM 1987, and *Baron Menuhin*, of Stoke D'Abernon, co Surrey (Life Baron) 1993: *m* 1st, 1938, Nola Ruby, da of late George Nicholas, of Melbourne, Australia; 2ndly, 1947, Diana Rosamond, da of late Gerard L. E. Gould, of Paris and London, and of late Lady Harcourt (Evelyn Suart, the pianist), and *d* 12 March 1999, leaving issue by 1st and 2nd *m*.

ᴀrms – Azure four bendlets between as many violin bridges gold. ᴄrest – Out of an eastern crown or inscribed on either side with a crotchet rest a sharp semi-quaver a flat and a semi-quaver rest sable a pair of cubit arms proper supporting a terrestrial globe the land vert fimbriated or the sea azure. ꙅupporters – On either side a representation of a firebird à la Benois wings elevated and addorsed gules beaked and membered with wings tipped or the tail bleu celeste that to the dexter gorged with a chain or pendant therefrom a hurt fimbriated and charged with a menorah or the candles argent enflamed proper that to the sinister gorged with a like chain pendent therefore a bezant charged with a representation of the gypsy flag mon proper the compartment a grassy mound with bluebells and blue poppies growing therefrom all proper with at the centre thereof a plough gold. ᴍotto – (in Hebrew) — Knowledge, Understanding, Wisdom, Faith, Hope, Charity.

SONS LIVING *(By 1st marriage)*

Hon Krov Nicholas, *b* 1940: *m* 1967, Elizabeth Ann, da of late Herbert Christoffers, and has issue living, Aaron Nicholas, *b* 1982. *Residence* – Mas de la Baleine, 13210 St Remy de Provence, France.

(By 2nd marriage)

Hon Gerard, *b* 1948: *m* 1983 (*m diss* 19—), and has issue living, Maxwell Duncan, *b* 1990. *Address* – PO Box 55, CH-3780, Gstaad, Switzerland.
Hon Jeremy, *b* 1951: *m* 1983 (*m diss* 1991), Hon Brigid Gabriel Forbes-Sempill, yst da of 19th Lord Sempill, and has issue living, Petroc Forbes, *b* 1988, — Nadja Cecilia, *b* 1985.

DAUGHTER LIVING *(By 1st marriage)*

Hon Zamira, *b* 1939: *m* 1st, 1960 (*m diss* 1969), Fou Ts'ong, concert pianist; 2ndly, 1975, Jonathan Charles Mackenzie Benthall, son of late Sir (Arthur) Paul Benthall, KBE, of Benthall Hall, Broseley, Shropshire, and has issue living (by 1st *m*), Lin ᴍᴇɴᴜʜɪɴ (a son), *b* 1964, — (by 2nd *m*), Dominic, *b* 1976, — William, *b* 1981. *Residence* – 212 Hammersmith Grove, W6 7HG.

Mereworth, Baron, title of Baron Oranmore and Browne on Roll of HL.

MERLYN-REES, BARON (Merlyn-Rees) (Life Baron 1992)

ᴍᴇʀʟʏɴ ᴍᴇʀʟʏɴ-ʀᴇᴇꜱ, PC, son of Levi Daniel Rees, of Cilfynydd, S Wales; assumed by deed poll 1992 the surname of Merlyn-Rees in lieu of his patronymic; *b* 18 Dec 1920; *ed* Harrow Weald Gram Sch, Goldsmiths' Coll, London, LSE and London Univ Inst of Educn; Hon DLL Wales Univ; RAF 1941-46 as Sqdn-Ldr; Schoolmaster 1949-60, Economics Lecturer 1962-63; PPS to Chancellor of the Exchequer 1964, Parly Under Sec MOD (Army) 1965-66, (RAF) 1966-68, and Home Office 1968-70, NI Sec 1974-76, and Home Sec 1976-79; Member Franks Cttee on Official Secrets Act 1972, and Franks Cttee on Falklands 1982; Chm S Leeds Groundwork Trust 1987; Pres Video Standards Cncl 1990; Freeman of the City of Leeds 1993; Fell of Goldsmiths' Coll 1984; Hon DL Univ of Leeds 1992; Chancellor of Glamorgan Univ 1994; author; MP S Leeds (*Lab*) 1963-83, and Morley and Leeds S 1983-92; *cr* PC 1974, and *Baron Merlyn-Rees*, of Morley and S Leeds, co W Yorks, and of Cilfynydd, co Mid Glam (Life Baron) 1992: *m* 1949, Colleen Faith, da of Henry F. Cleveley, of Kenton, Middx, and has issue.

Address – c/o House of Lords, SW1.

SONS LIVING

Hon Patrick Merlyn, *b* 1954; Solicitor: *m*, and has issue, one son and one da.
Hon Gareth David, *b* 1956; Barrister-at-law: *m*, and has issue, one son and two das.
Hon Glyn Robert, *b* 1960: *m*, and has issue, one son and one da.

MERRIMAN, BARONY OF (Merriman) (Extinct 1962)

DAUGHTER LIVING OF FIRST BARON

Hon Violet Grace, OBE (c/o Westminster Bank, 195 Earls Court Rd, SW5), *b* 1911; a British Council Officer; OBE (Civil) 1948.

WIDOW LIVING OF FIRST BARON

JANE LAMB (*Baroness Merriman*), da of late James Stormonth, of Belfast: *m* 1953, as his 3rd wife, the 1st Baron, who *d* 1962, when the title became ext. *Address* – Northern Bank Ltd, 9 Donegall Sq North, Belfast.

MERRIVALE, BARON (Duke) (Baron UK 1925)

We conquer by degrees

JACK HENRY EDMOND DUKE, 3rd Baron; *b* 27 Jan 1917; *s* 1951; *ed* Dulwich, in France, and Ecole des Sciences Politiques, Paris; FRSA; Pres Institute of Traffic Administration, of Railway Development Assocn, and Chm of Anglo-Malgasy Soc; (despatches): *m* 1st, 1939 (*m diss* 1974), Colette, da of John Douglas Wise; 2ndly, 1975, Betty, widow of Paul Baron, and has issue by 1st *m*.

Arms – Argent, an anchor fouled sable between three chaplets, all within a bordure engrailed azure. **Crest** – Issuant from a chaplet fessewise argent a demi griffin holding between the claws a fasces erect or. **Supporters** – On either side a griffin or, the *dexter* gorged with a chain sable, pendant therefrom an escutcheon argent charged with a saltire between four castles sable, and the *sinister* gorged with a like chain suspended therefrom an escutcheon per pale gules and sable, charged with a triple towered castle or.
Residence – 16 Brompton Lodge, 9-11 Cromwell Rd, SW7.

SON LIVING (*By 1st marriage*)

Hon DEREK JOHN PHILIP, *b* 16 March 1948: *m* Guillemette ......, and has issue, Thomas, *b* 19—, ...

DAUGHTER LIVING (*By 1st marriage*)

Hon Elizabeth Anne Marie Violet, *b* 1939.

SISTER LIVING

Hon Elizabeth Suzanne, *b* 1921: *m* 1st, 1942 (*m diss* 1953), Capt Jean Pompei, French Air Force; 2ndly, 1955, Jacques Bechmann, banker, who *d* 1985, and has issue living, (by 1st *m*) François (249 rue du Faubourg St Martin, 75010 Paris, France), *b* 1944: *m* 1973 (*m diss* 1992), Elizabeth, da of Christian Dupuy, and has issue living, Antoine *b* 1975, Louis *b* 1977, Philip *b* 1978, Marie *b* 1980, — Nicole POMPEI (7 rue Presle, 75015 Paris, France), *b* 1946; has resumed her maiden name: *m* 1968 (*m diss* 1980), Jean Louis Bouchard, and has issue living, Robert *b* 1971, Alexandra *b* 1969: *m* 1991, Laurent Rousseau, of 10 rue Raynouard, 75016 Paris (and has issue living, Paul *b* 1995, Marie *b* 1993, Anna *b* 1997), — (by 2nd *m*) Pierre, *b* 1957. *Residence* – La Charité, 60500 Chantilly, France.

PREDECESSORS – (1) *Rt Hon Sir* HENRY EDWARD DUKE, son of William Edward Duke, granite merchant, of Merrivale, S Devon; *b* 1855; MP for Plymouth (*C*) 1900-1906, and for Exeter 1910-18, Attorney-Gen and a Member of Council of Duchy of Cornwall 1915, Ch Sec for Ireland 1916-18, a Lord Justice of Appeal 1918-19, and Pres of Probate, Divorce, and Admiralty Div of High Court of Justice 1919-33; *cr Baron Merrivale*, of Walkhampton, co Devon (peerage of United Kingdom) 1925: *m* 1876, Sarah, who *d* 1914, da of late John Shorland; *d* 1939; *s* by his son (2) EDWARD, OBE, 2nd Baron; *b* 1883; Sec to Pres of Probate, Divorce and Admiralty Div of High Court of Justice 1919-33; S Africa 1901 as Lieut, European War 1914-19 as Capt (OBE); *m* 1st, 1912 (*m diss* 1939), Odette, da of Edmond Roger, of Paris; 2ndly, 1939, Meta Therèse, who *d* 1980, da of Hermann Wolczon, of Danzig; *d* 1951; *s* by his son (3) JACK HENRY EDMOND, 3rd Baron and present peer.

MERSEY, VISCOUNT (Bigham) (Viscount UK 1916)

I advance

RICHARD MAURICE CLIVE BIGHAM, 4th Viscount; *b* 8 July 1934; *s* to the Viscountcy 1979, and to the Lordship of Nairne 1995; *ed* Eton, Balliol Coll, Oxford; Hon FRAM (1994); formerly Lieut Irish Guards; Documentary Film Producer: *m* 1961, Joanna Dorothy Corsica Grey, el da of late John Grey Murray, CBE, of Cannon Lodge, Cannon Place, NW3 (*see* B Shuttleworth, 1967 Edn), and has issue.

Arms – Per bend dancettée azure and or, a bend invected between three crosses patée in chief and as many horseshoes in base all counterchanged. **Crest** – A horse per pale or and sable, charged on the body with three horseshoes fesseways counterchanged, and resting the dexter foreleg on a cross patée gules. **Supporters** – On either side a mermaid proper crowned with a naval crown gules, that to the *dexter* supporting with the exterior hand an anchor or, that to the *sinister* an oar argent.
Residence – Bignor Park, Pulborough, W Sussex.

SON LIVING

Hon EDWARD JOHN HALLAM (*Master of Nairne*) (32 Bloemfontein Rd, W12 7BX), *b* 23 May 1966; *ed* Eton, Balliol Coll, Oxford, and Trinity Coll of Music, London: *m* 1994, Claire Louise, da of David Haigh, of Woking, Surrey.

BROTHERS LIVING (*also in remainder to the Lordship of Nairne*)

Hon David Edward Hugh (Hurston Place, Pulborough, W Sussex RH20 2EW; *Club* – Buck's), *b* 1938; *ed* Eton; late Cornet RHG; Dir Tryon Gallery: *m* (Jan) 1965, Anthea Rosemary, el da of Capt Leopold Richard Seymour (*see* M Hertford, colls), and has issue living, Charles Richard Petty, *b* 1967; *ed* Eton, and Edinburgh Univ: *m* 1996, Claire J., da of Col John Worthington, of Wiveliscombe, Som, — Patrick David Hugh, *b* 1969; *ed* Harrow, and Edinburgh Univ, — James Edward Conway, *b* 1973; *ed* Eton, and Edinburgh Univ, — Lucinda Emma, *b* (Nov) 1965.
Hon Andrew Charles (High Mill, Coverham, Middleham, N Yorks DL8 4RN; *Club* – Brooks's), *b* 1941; *ed* Eton, and Worcester Coll, Oxford; late 2nd Lt Irish Gds; Schoolmaster, Aysgarth Sch, Bedale, N Yorks 1968-89, and at Sunningdale Sch, Berks 1989-94.

AUNT LIVING (*daughter of 6th Marquess of Lansdowne*) (*in remainder to the Lordship of Nairne*)

Lady Elizabeth Mary Fitzmaurice, *b* 1927: *m* 1950, Maj Charles William Lambton, Coldm Gds (ret), and has issue (*see* Earldom of Durham). *Residence* – The Old Rectory, Calstone, Calne, Wilts SN1 8PZ.

COLLATERAL BRANCHES LIVING

Issue of late Hon Sir (Frank) Trevor Roger Bigham, KBE, CB, yst son of 1st Viscount, *b* 1876, *d* 1954: *m* 1st, 1901, Frances Leonora, who *d* 1927, da of late John Leonard Tomlin, of Richmond, N Yorks; 2ndly, 1931, Edith Ellen, OBE, who *d* 1985, da of Lieut-Col David Drysdale:—
(By 1st *m*) Celia Margaret Hermione, *b* 1909. *Residence* – 4 Harley Gdns, SW10 9SW.

(*In remainder to the Lordship of Nairne*)

Descendants of late Maj Lord Charles George Francis Mercer-Nairne, MVO, 2nd son of 9th Lord, and 5th Marquess of Lansdowne, *b* 1874, *ka* 1914: *m* 1909, Lady Violet Mary Elliot-Murray-Kynynmound (who *d* 1965, having *m* 2ndly, 1916, 1st Baron Astor of Hever), da of 4th Earl of Minto:—
See M Lansdowne.

Descendants of late Lady Evelyn Emily Mary Fitzmaurice, GCVO, eldest da of 9th Lord, and 5th Marquess of Lansdowne, b 1870, d 1960: m 1892, 9th Duke of Devonshire, KG, who d 1938:—

See D Devonshire.

Descendants of late Lady Beatrix Frances Fitzmaurice, GBE, 2nd da of 9th Lord, and 5th Marquess of Lansdowne, b 1877, d 1953: m 1st, 1897, 6th Marquess of Waterford, KP, who d 1911; 2ndly, 1918, 12th Duke of St Albans, who d 1964:—

(By 1st m) See M Waterford.

Descendants of late Lady Emily Louisa Anne, only da of Emily, Lady Nairne, by her husband the 4th Marquess of Lansdowne, b 1855, d 1939: m 1886, Col Hon Everard Charles Digby, Gren Gds (see B Digby), who d 1915:—

See V Hood, cols.

PREDECESSORS – (1) Rt Hon Sir JOHN CHARLES Bigham, son of late John Bigham, merchant, of Liverpool, b 1840; MP for Liverpool, Exchange Div (LU) 1895-7; a Judge of the High Court of Justice 1897-1909 (also Judge in Bankruptcy 1904-8), and Pres of Probate, Divorce, and Admiralty Div 1909-10; Roy Commr for Revision of Martial Law in S Africa 1902, and Pres of Railway and Canal Commn of United Kingdom 1912, and a Member of Roy Commn of Civil Ser 1915; cr Baron Mersey, of Toxteth, co Palatine of Lancaster (peerage of United Kingdom) 1910, and Viscount Mersey of Toxteth, co Palatine of Lancaster (peerage of United Kingdom) 1916: m 1871, Georgina Sarah, who d 1925, da of John Rogers, of Liverpool; d 1929; s by his el son (2) CHARLES CLIVE, PC, CMG, CBE, 2nd Viscount; b 1872; Lieut-Col late Grenadier Guards, Dep Speaker of House of Lords and Dep Chm of Committees, and Chm of Westminster Territorial Committee; was Hon Attaché in Diplo Ser 1896-1900, ADC to Lord-Lieut of Ireland 1901-2, and Ch Liberal Whip in House of Lords 1944-9; China 1900 (CMG), European War 1914-18 (CBE): m 1904, Mary Gertrude, JP, who d 1973, da of late Horace Alfred Damer Seymour, CB (nominated, but not invested, KCB); d 1956; s by his el son (3) EDWARD CLIVE, 3rd Viscount, b 1906; a DL for W Sussex; 1939-45 War as Capt Irish Gds: m 1933, Lady Katherine Evelyn Constance Petty-Fitzmaurice (Lady Nairne in her own right) (see *infra), who d 1995, el da of the 6th Marquess of Lansdowne; d 1979; s by his el son (4) RICHARD MAURICE CLIVE, 4th Viscount and present peer, also Lord Nairne and Baron Mersey.

*(1) Sir ROBERT Nairne, Knt, a Scottish advocate and a zealous partisan of the house of Stuart; was imprisoned in the Tower of London 1651-61; appointed a Lord of Session 1661, and a Lord of Justiciary 1671; cr Lord Nairne (peerage of Scotland) 1681, with remainder to the husband of his da Margaret and the heirs of their bodies; d 1683; s by his son-in-law (ante) (2) Lord WILLIAM Murray, 2nd Lord, 4th son of 1st Marquess of Atholl; refused to take the oaths of allegiance or his seat in Parliament until after the Revolution; took part in the rebellion of 1715, was taken prisoner at Preston, and after being confined in the Tower was in 1716 attainted of high-treason and sentenced to be executed, which sentence was however respited; d 1725; s by his son (3) JOHN, who had previously been attainted for his connection with the rising of 1715; by Act of Parliament 1738, he was enabled to inherit property and to carry on law-suits; engaged in the insurrection of 1745, and was again attainted, having previously been cr by the Pretender Viscount Stanley and Earl of Nairne; d 1770; s by his son (4) JOHN, 4th Lord, a Lieut-Col in the Army; d 1782; s by his son (5) WILLIAM MURRAY, 5th Lord, who was restored to the family honours by Act of Parliament 1824; d 1830; s by his son (6) WILLIAM, 6th Lord; d unmarried 1837; s by his kinswoman (7) MARGARET, who had in 1823 s her father in the Barony of Keith (peerage of Ireland, cr 1803); b 1788: m 1817, Auguste Charles Joseph, Comte de Flahault-de-la-Billarderie; d 1867, when the Barony of Keith expired, and the Lordship of Nairne devolved upon her el da (8) EMILY JANE, b 1819; established her claim to the title 1874; m 1843, Henry, 4th Marquess of Lansdowne, who d 1866; she d 1895; s by her el son (9-11) HENRY CHARLES KEITH, 5th Marquess of Lansdowne, the Lordship being merged in the Marquessate until 1945, when, on the death of the 7th Marquess, it devolved upon his sister (12) KATHERINE EVELYN CONSTANCE, b 1912: m 1933, 3rd Viscount Mersey, who d 1979, and d 1995; s by her eldest son (13) RICHARD MAURICE CLIVE, 4th Viscount Mersey (ante).

MERTHYR, BARONY OF (Lewis) (Baron UK 1911, Bt UK 1896, disclaimed 1977)

Perseverance

Do thy duty come what may

(Sir) TREVOR OSWIN LEWIS, CBE, DL, b 29 Nov 1935; s as 4th Baron Merthyr and 4th Baronet, 5 April 1977; disclaimed his peerage for life 26 April 1977, and does not use his title of baronet; ed Eton, Magdalen Coll, Oxford, and Magdalene Coll, Camb; Member, Countryside Commn 1973-83, Dep Chm 1980-83, and Chm of Cttee for Wales 1973-80; JP for Pembs 1969-94, DL 1994; CBE (1983): m 1964, Susan Jane, da of Arthur John Birt-Llewellin, of Boulston Manor, Haverfordwest, and has issue.

Arms – Sable, a lion rampant argent, over all a fesse or charged with three bees volant proper. Crest – An eagle displayed azure, charged on the breast with a bee volant or, and holding in the beak a roll of paper argent. Supporters – (borne by Baron Merthyr) On either side a lion rampant sable, charged on the shoulder with a bezant thereon a bee volant proper.
Seat – Hean Castle, Saundersfoot, Pembrokeshire SA69 9AL.

SON LIVING

DAVID TREVOR, b 21 Feb 1977.

DAUGHTERS LIVING

Lucy Delia, b 1967; Lieut RN 1987-94: m 1990, Harvey John Bradnam, only son of John Bradnam, of Craigs Farmhouse, Crossford, by Dunfermline, Fife.

Elizabeth Anne (Honeywell, Grove Rd, Sherston, Malmesbury, Wilts SN16 0NF), b 1970.

Jessamy Jane, b 1972: m 1996, Capt C. Marcus R. Elmhirst, Scots Guards, eldest son of Paul Binder Elmhirst, of Swallow House, Stillingfleet, York, and has issue living, R. Jeremy W., b 1996, — C. Rupert, b 1998.

BROTHERS LIVING

Hon Peter Herbert (The Old Rectory, Chilfrome, Dorchester DT2 0HA), *b* 1937; *ed* Eton; Lt-Col 9th/12th R Lancers (POW): *m* 1974, Caroline Monica, el da of Erik Cadogan, of Wasperton Hill, Barford, Warwick (*see* E Cadogan, colls), and has issue living, Amanda Caroline, *b* 1977.

(Hon) John Frederick (does not use courtesy title) (1 Cedar Hill, Carisbrooke, I of Wight), *b* 1938; *ed* Eton, and St John's Coll, Camb: *m* 1966, Margaret (Gretl), twin da of Lt-Col James William Lewis-Bowen, of Clynfiew, Boncath, Dyfed, and has issue living, Paul William, *b* 1979, — Deborah, *b* 1967, — Sarah, *b* 1968, — Hannah, *b* 1983.

Hon Robin William, OBE (The Cottage, Cresswell Quay, Kilgetty, Pembs), *b* 1941; *ed* Eton, and Magdalen Coll, Oxford; Chm and Man Dir The Magstim Co Ltd; Board Memb Welsh Development Agency (Dep Chm 1995-98); Chm The Nat Trust Cttee for Wales 1994-97; Chm Gen Advisory Council of IBA 1989-90; High Sheriff Dyfed 1987; OBE (Civil) 1988: *m* 1967, Judith Ann, only da of Vincent Charles Arthur Giardelli, MBE, of Llethr, Pendine, Carmarthenshire, and has issue living, Christopher William, *b* 1970: *m* 1997, Julia, only da of Gisilot von Rohr, of Isernhagen, Germany, — Katharine Ann, *b* 1972.

Hon Antony Thomas (The Skreen, Erwood, Builth Wells, Powys LD2 3SJ), *b* 1947; *ed* Eton: *m* 1974, Mary Carola Melton, yr da of Rev Humphrey John Paine, of Fressingfield Vicarage, Diss, Norfolk.

WIDOW LIVING OF THIRD BARON

VIOLET (*Baroness Merthyr*) (Churchton, Saundersfoot, Dyfed, SA69 9BB), da of Brig-Gen Sir Frederick Charlton Meyrick, 2nd Bt, CB, CMG: *m* 1932, the 3rd Baron Merthyr, who *d* 1977.

PREDECESSORS – (1) *Sir* WILLIAM THOMAS Lewis, GCVO, el son of late Thomas William Lewis, of Abercanaid House, Merthyr Tydfil, by Mary Anne, who *d* 1887, da of Watkin John; *b* 1837; was a large employer of labour in connection with Collieries, Iron and Steel Works, Tinplate Works, and other industries in S Wales, Founder (many years Chm) of Monmouthshire and S Wales Coal Asso, of S Wales Sliding Scale Committee (18 Year Chm), and of S Wales Miner's Provident Fund (30 years Chm); *cr a Baronet* 1896, and *Baron Merthyr*, of Senghenydd, co Glamorgan (peerage of United Kingdom) 1911: *m* 1864, Anne, who *d* 1902, el da of William Rees colliery proprietor, of Llettyshenkin, Glamorgan; *d* 1914; *s* by his el son (2) HERBERT CLARK, 2nd Baron, *b* 1866: *m* 1899, Elizabeth Anna, who *d* 1925, el da of late Maj-Gen Richard Short Couchman, formerly MSC, of 117 Victoria St, SW; *d* 1932; *s* by his son (3) WILLIAM BRERETON COUCHMAN, KBE, PC, TD, 3rd Baron; *b* 1901; Lord Chm of Cttees, House of Lords 1957-65, and Dep Speaker, House of Lords 1957-74; a Member of Several Roy Commns; Vice-Pres Nat Marriage Guidance Council (Chm 1951-57), Magistrates Assocn (Chm of Council 1952-70) and Family Planning Assocn; Hon Treas NSPCC 1952-57 and RSPCA 1953-57; Bar-at-law, and Maj Pembroke Heavy Regt RA (TA) (prisoner Hong Kong 1941-45): *m* 1932, Violet, da of Brig-Gen Sir Frederick Charlton Meyrick, 2nd Bt, CB, CMG; *d* 1977; *s* by his el son (4) TREVOR OSWIN, 4th Baron, until he disclaimed his peerage for life.

Merton, Viscount; son of Earl Nelson.

MESTON, BARON (Meston) (Baron UK 1919)

In God is my trust

JAMES MESTON, 3rd Baron; *b* 10 Feb 1950; *s* 1984; *ed* Wellington Coll, St Catharine's Coll, Camb, and Leicester Univ; Bar Middle Temple 1973; Jr Counsel to Queen's Proctor 1992; QC 1996: *m* 1974, Jean Rebecca Anne, yr da of John Carder, of Stud Farm House, Chalvington, Sussex, and has issue living.

Arms – Argent, a palm tree, eradicated proper, on a chief azure, an Eastern crown between two thistles slipped and leaved or. **Crest** – An angel proper, habited argent, holding in the dexter hand an Eastern crown as in the arms. **Supporters** – *Dexter*, a demoiselle crane proper; *sinister*, a stag also proper, charged on the shoulder with a saltire argent.
Chambers - Queen Elizabeth Building, Temple, EC4.

SON LIVING

Hon THOMAS JAMES DOUGALL, *b* 21 Oct 1977; *ed* Eton.

DAUGHTERS LIVING

Hon Laura Anne Rose, *b* 1980.
Hon Elspeth Mary, *b* 1988.

BROTHER LIVING

Hon William Dougall (11 The Green, Mistley, Manningtree, Essex CO11 1EU), *b* 1953; *ed* Wellington Coll: *m* 1982, Elizabeth Mary Agnes, yst da of late Dr Peter Dawes, of Cavendish Mansions, W1, and Mijas, Spain, and has issue living, Dougall William, *b* 1985, — Felix Peter, *b* 1987, — Louise Elizabeth Joan, *b* 1996.

WIDOW LIVING OF SECOND BARON

DIANA MARY CAME (*Diana, Baroness Meston*), only da of late Capt Otto Sigismund Doll, FRIBA, of 16 Upper Cheyne Row, SW3: *m* 1947, the 2nd Baron Meston, who *d* 1984. *Residence* – Staplehurst, High St, Mistley, Manningtree, Essex CO11 1HD.

PREDECESSORS – (1) *Sir* JAMES SCORGIE Meston, KCSI, son of late James Meston, of Aberdeen; *b* 1865; Financial Sec to Govt of India 1906-12, and Lieut-Gov of United Provinces of Agra and Oudh 1912-18; Finance Member of Viceroy's Executive Council 1918-19; Chancellor of Aberdeen Univ 1928; *cr Baron Meston*, of Agra and Dunottar (peerage of United Kingdom) 1919: *m* 1891, Jeanie, CBE (a DStJ), who *d* 1946, only da of late James McDonald; *d* 1943; *s* by his son (2) DOUGALL, 2nd Baron, *b* 1894; Bar Lincoln's Inn, SE Circuit: *m* 1947, Diana Mary Came, only da of Capt Otto Sigismund Doll, FRIBA; *d* 1984; *s* by his el son (3) JAMES, 3rd Baron and present peer.

METHUEN, BARON (Methuen) (Baron UK 1838)

Virtue is the mark of envy

ROBERT ALEXANDER HOLT METHUEN, 7th Baron; *b* 22 July 1931; *s* 1994; *ed* Shrewsbury, and Trin Coll, Camb: *m* 1st, 1958 (*m diss* 1993), Mary Catherine Jane, only da of Ven Charles German Hooper, sometime Archdeacon of Ipswich, of East Green Cottage, Kelsale, Saxmundham, Suffolk; 2ndly, 1994, Margrit Andrea, da of Friedrich Karl Ernst Hadwiger, of Vienna, and has issue by 1st *m*.

Arms – Argent, three wolves' heads erased, proper, borne on the breast of an imperial eagle. **Supporters** – Two fiery lynxes reguardant proper, collared and lined or.
Residence – Knabb Hall, Knabb Lane, nr Matlock, Derbyshire DE4 2FJ.

DAUGHTERS LIVING (By 1st marriage)

Hon Charlotte Mary, *b* 1964. *Residence* – Lotharstrasse 8, 45131 Essen, Germany.
Hon Henrietta Christian (Kittie), *b* 1965: *m* 1990, Robert Llewelyn Jones, who assumed the surname of Methuen-Jones, elder son of D. Ll. Jones, of Reigate, Surrey, and has issue living, Teresa Mary, *b* 1990, — Keziah Lynne, *b* 1992, — Miriam Lucy, *b* 1997. *Residence* – Ravenswood, Gladstone Street, Derby DE23 6PQ.

SISTER LIVING

Hon Elizabeth Penelope, *b* 1928: *m* 1956, Malcolm Henry Alastair Fraser, late RHG, and has issue living, Elizabeth Mary Alexandra, *b* 1957: *m* 1982, Mark Geoffrey Sewell, late Gren Gds, of Dinsdale House, Tysoe, Warwicks CV35 0TX (*see* Williams-Wynn, Bt, colls, 1990 Edn), and has issue living, Emma Lucy Alexandra *b* 1985, Rosanna Mary Alice *b* 1988, Lucinda Charlotte Anne *b* 1993, — Anne Catriona Hamilton, *b* 1961: *m* 1997, J. William B. May Somerville, only son of Michael May Somerville, of Lamerhooe, Devon, and has issue living, Philippa *b* 1998. *Residence* – South Bank House, Lacock Rd, Corsham, Wilts SN13 9HS.

COLLATERAL BRANCHES LIVING

Grandchildren (by 1st *m*) of late Hon Laurence Paul Methuen (infra):—
Issue of late Christopher Paul Mansel Campbell METHUEN-CAMPBELL, *b* 1928, *d* 1998: *m* 1st, 1950 (*m diss* 1973), Oona Cicely, da of late John Dalrymple Winn Treherne (*see* M Sligo); 2ndly, 1975, Mrs Judith Anne Bassett (*née* Crowther), formerly wife of late David Bassett:—
(By 1st *m*) JAMES PAUL ARCHIBALD (Corsham Court, Corsham, Wilts SN13 0BZ), *b* 25 Oct 1952. —— Joanna Olive, *b* 1951: *m* 1977, Edward Ashley Martin, of Oak Tree Farm, Hitcham, Ipswich, Suffolk IP7 7LS. —— Lucinda Sheelah (6 Beaufort Close, Langland, Swansea SA3 4PA), *b* 1959; has issue living, Angus George Archibald CHATFIELD, *b* 1998, — Poppy Evelyn METHUEN CAMPBELL, *b* 1984. —— Catherine Alice Mansel (7 Chapel Hill, Lewes, E Sussex BN7 2BB), *b* 1965; has issue living, Gulliver James METHUEN CAMPBELL, *b* 1985, — Orlando David METHUEN CAMPBELL, *b* 1988, — Alexander Patrick METHUEN CAMPBELL, *b* 1990, — Hamish Paul BENJAMIN, *b* 1998. —— (By 2nd *m*) Thomas Rice Mansel (Penrice Castle, Reynoldston, Swansea SA3 1LN), *b* 1977.

Issue of late Hon Laurence Paul METHUEN, 3rd son of 3rd Baron; *b* 1898; assumed the additional surname of Campbell, which he relinquished by deed poll 1969; *d* 1970: *m* 1st, 1927, Hon Olive Douglas Campbell, who *d* 1949, da of 4th Baron Blythswood (ext); 2ndly, 1950, Lady Maureen Margaret Brabazon, who *d* 1980, da of 13th Earl of Meath:—
(By 1st *m*) David Archibald James (45 Redcliffe Rd, SW10), *b* 1929: *m* 1978, Elizabeth Anne, da of James Fletcher Martin of Egdon Cottage, Swanage, Dorset. —— Diana Evelyn (*Lady McNair-Wilson*), *b* 1932: *m* 1953, Capt Sir Patrick McNair-Wilson, MP, of 5 Kelso Pl, W8, and has issue living, Guy Patrick Adam Campbell, *b* 1968, — Jennifer Jean, *b* 1954, — Arabella Jane Campbell, *b* 1959: *m* 1984, David Nicholas (Nick) Ashley, of Flat 8, 50 Cornwall Gdns, SW7, son of Sir Bernard Albert Ashley, — Patricia Ann Campbell, *b* 1964, — Kate Campbell, *b* 1975. —— Daphne Mary Jean (*Hon Mrs Cecil T. H. Law*), *b* 1935: *m* 1957, Hon Cecil Towry Henry Law (*see* B Ellenborough). —— (By 2nd *m*) Caroline Aileen, *b* 1952; assumed by deed poll 1969 the surname of Methuen in lieu of her patronymic: *m* 1988, Charles Lloyd Fox, of Tredrea, Perranarworthal, Truro, Cornwall TR3 7QE, 2nd son of Philip Hamilton Fox, of Glendurgan, Falmouth, Cornwall, and has issue living, Meriel Sophia, *b* 1990, — Stella Caroline, *b* 1992, — Roselle Viola, *b* 1994.

PREDECESSORS – **(1)** PAUL Methuen, MP for Wiltshire in several parliaments, *cr Baron Methuen* of Corsham, co Wilts (peerage of United Kingdom) 1838; *b* 1779: *m* 1810, Jane Dorothea, da of Sir Henry Paulet St John Mildmay, 3rd Bt; *d* 1849; *s* by his son **(2)** FREDERICK HENRY PAUL, 2nd Baron, *b* 1818; ADC to HM Queen Victoria; was a Lord-in-Waiting to HM Queen Victoria 1859-66, 1868-74, 1880-85, and 1886: *m* 1844, Anna Horatia Caroline, da of Rev John Sanford, of Nynehead, Somerset; *d* 1891; *s* by his el son **(3)** PAUL SANFORD, 3rd Baron, GCB, GCMG, GCVO, LLD, *b* 1845; a Field-Marshal; Ashantee War 1873-4, as AA and QMG in Egyptian Campaign 1882, as Press Censor during Tirah Expedition 1897, in S Africa 1899-1902, in command of 1st Inf Div at battles of Belmont, Enslin, Modder River, and Magersfontein; Mil Sec Ireland 1877, Mil Attaché at Berlin 1877-81, AA and QMG Home Dist 1881-4, DAG Cape of Good Hope 1888-90, in command of Home Dist 1892-7, of E Command 1904-8, and of troops in S Africa 1908-12 (Gov of Natal 1910), and Gov and Com-in-Ch, Malta 1914-19; commanded "Methuen's Horse" in Bechuanaland 1885; was Constable of Tower of London 1920-32: *m* 1st, 1878, Evelyn, who *d* 1879, da of Sir Frederick Hutchinson Hervey-Bathurst, 3rd Bt; 2ndly, 1884, Mary Ethel, CBE, who *d* 1941, da of late William Ayshford Sanford, of Nynehead Court, Somerset; *d* 1932; *s* by his son **(4)** PAUL AYSHFORD, 4th Baron, *b* 1886; FSA, Royal Academician; a Trustee of Nat Gallery, and Tate Gallery 1938-45, and Imperial War Museum 1950-52: *m* 1915, Eleanor Norah, who *d* 1958, da of late William John Hennessy, of Rudgwick, Sussex; *d* 1974; *s* by his brother **(5)** ANTHONY PAUL, 5th Baron; *b* 1891; Chartered Architect, 1914-18 War as Capt Scots Gds: *m* 1920, Grace Durning, who *d* 1972, da of Sir Richard Durning Holt, 1st Bt (*cr* 1935), *d* 1975; *s* by his 2nd son **(6)** ANTHONY JOHN, 6th Baron, *b* 1925; ARICS; Scots Gds and Royal Signals 1943-47; Land Officer, Air Min 1951-62; *d* 1994; *s* by his brother **(7)** ROBERT ALEXANDER HOLT, 7th Baron and present peer.

MEXBOROUGH, EARL OF (Savile) (Earl I 1766)

JOHN CHRISTOPHER GEORGE SAVILE, 8th Earl; *b* 16 May 1931; *s* 1980; *ed* Eton, and Worcester Coll, Oxford; late 2nd Lieut Gren Gds: *m* 1st, 1958 (*m diss* 1972), Lady Elisabeth Hariot Grimston, who *d* 1987, el da of 6th Earl of Verulam; 2ndly, 1972, Catherine Joyce, yst da of James Kenneth Hope, CBE, DL, of West Park, Lanchester, co Durham, and formerly wife of Maj Hon Nicholas Crespigny Laurence Vivian (later 6th Baron Vivian), and has had issue by 1st and 2nd *m*.

Arms – Argent, on a bend sable, three owls of the field. **Crest** – An owl argent. **Supporters** – Two lions proper, collared and chained or. *Seat* – Arden Hall, Hawnby, York; *Town Residence* – 14 Lennox Gdns Mews, SW1. *Clubs* – All England Lawn Tennis, Air Squadron.

SONS LIVING (By 1st marriage)

JOHN ANDREW BRUCE (*Viscount Pollington*), *b* 30 Nov 1959.

(By 2nd marriage)

Hon James Hugh Hope John, *b* 1976.

DAUGHTERS LIVING AND DECEASED (By 1st marriage)

Lady Alethea Frances Clare, *b* 1963; *d* 1994.

(By 2nd marriage)

Lady Lucinda Sarah Catherine, *b* 1973.

BROTHER LIVING

Hon (Charles) Anthony, *b* 1934; *ed* Eton, and Trin Coll, Cambridge; late Lt Grenadier Guards: *m* 1966, Zita Loretta, da of Leslie White, and has issue living, Henry Charles, *b* 1970, — Andrew David, *b* 1973. *Residence* – Youngsbury, Ware, Herts. *Club* – All England Lawn Tennis.

COLLATERAL BRANCH LIVING

Granddaughter of late Rev Hon Philip Yorke Savile, 3rd son of 3rd Earl:—
Issue of late Rev William Hale Savile, *b* 1859, *d* 1925: *m* 1888, Mabel Ann, who *d* 1947, only da of late Maj Count Hippolyt Victor Alexander von Bothmer, a Count of the Holy Roman Empire (naturalized 1857):—
Veronica Yorke Hélène Cecilia, *b* 1902: *m* 1926, Willem Karel Marie de Bruijn van Gouderack, Belgian Consulate Service (ret), who *d* 1984, only son of late Eduard Rudolf Marie de Bruijn. *Residence* – Huis De Werve, Cartier van Disselstraat 64, Breda, Netherlands 4835 KP.

PREDECESSORS – (1) *Sir* JOHN Savile, KB, *b* 1719; MP for Hedon, co York 1747-54; *cr Baron Pollington*, Ireland (peerage of Ireland) 1753, and *Viscount Pollington* and *Earl of Mexborough* (peerage of Ireland) 1766; *d* 1778; *s* by his son (2) JOHN, 2nd Earl; *d* 1830; *s* by his son (3) JOHN, 3rd Earl; *b* 1783; MP for Pontefract: *m* 1807, Lady Anne, who *d* 1870, da of 3rd Earl of Hardwicke; *d* 1860; *s* by his son (4) JOHN CHARLES GEORGE, 4th Earl, *b* 1810; MP for Gatton (C) 1831, and for Pontefract 1835-47: *m* 1st, 1842, Lady Katherine Walpole, who *d* 1854, el da of 3rd Earl of Orford; 2ndly, 1861, Agnes Louisa Elizabeth, who *d* 1898, da of John Raphael; *d* 1899: *s* by his el son (5) JOHN HORACE, 5th Earl, *b* 1843; High Sheriff of Yorkshire 1877: *m* 1st, 1867, Venetia Stanley, who *d* 1900, da of Sir Rowland Stanley Errington, 11th Bt; 2ndly, 1906, Donna Sylvia Cecilia Maria, who *d* 1915, da of the Noble Carlo de Ser Antoni, of Lucca and Naples, and widow of Capt Claude Clerke, CIE; 3rdly, 1916, Anne, who *d* 1943 (having *m* 3rdly, 1920 (*m diss* 1926), as his 2nd wife, Alfred Charlemagne Lambart, who *d* 1943), da of late Rev Andrew Holmes Belcher, of Fasque, Kincardineshire, and formerly wife of George Bainbridge Ritchie; *d* 1916; *s* by his half-brother (6) JOHN HENRY, 6th Earl, *b* 1868; Hon Capt in the Army: *m* 1905, Hon Margaret Eva de Burgh Knatchbull-Hugessen, who *d* 1957, el da of 2nd Baron Brabourne; *d* 1945; *s* by his son (7) JOHN RAPHAEL WENTWORTH, 7th Earl, *b* 1906; ADC to Gov of Bihar 1944-45; Pres York Lawn Tennis Club, and English Billiards Assoc: *m* 1930, Josephine Bertha Emily, who *d* 1992, da of late Capt Andrew Mansel Talbot Fletcher (Winnington, Bt); *d* 1980; *s* by his son (8) JOHN CHRISTOPHER GEORGE, 8th Earl and present peer; also Viscount and Baron Pollington.

MICHELHAM, BARONY OF (Stern) (Extinct 1984)

(Title pronounced "Mitch-lam")

WIDOW LIVING OF SECOND BARON

MARIE-JOSE DUPAS (*Baroness Michelham*): *m* 1980, as his 2nd wife, the 2nd Baron Michelham, who *d* 1984, when the title became ext. Resides in France.

MIDDLETON, BARON (Willoughby) (Baron GB 1711, Bt E 1677)

Truth without fear

(DIGBY) MICHAEL GODFREY JOHN WILLOUGHBY, MC, 12th Baron, and 13th Baronet; *b* 1 May 1921; *s* 1970; *ed* Eton, and Trin Coll, Camb (MA); patron of seven livings; a CC and JP for E Riding and Kingston upon Hull 1964-74, a CC for N Yorks 1974-77, DL of N Yorks; a Member of Yorks & Humberside Economic Planning Council 1968-79; Pres Yorks Agric Soc 1976, and of the Country Landowners Assoc 1981-83; a Member of Nature Conservancy Council 1986-89; a Member of House of Lords Select Cttee on European Communities; Hon Col 2nd Bn Yorks Vol 1976-87; 1939-45 War a Maj Coldm Gds (despatches, MC, Croix de Guerre): *m* 1947, Janet; JP N Yorks; Founding Chm Lloyds External Names Assocn; only da of Gen Sir James Handyside Marshall Cornwall, KCB, CBE, DSO, MC, and has issue.

𝔄rms – Quarterly: 1st and 4th or, fretty azure, *Willoughby of Parham*; 2nd and 3rd or, on two bars gules three water bougets two and one argent, *Willoughby of Middleton*. 𝔄rest – The bust of a man couped at the shoulders and affrontée proper, ducally crowned or. 𝔖upporters – *Dexter*, a pilgrim or grey friar in his habit proper, with his beads, cross, etc, and staff in his right hand, argent; *sinister*, a savage with a club in his exterior hand, wreathed about his temples and middle with laurel all proper; each supporter holding a banner gules fringed, or ensigned with an owl argent, gorged with a ducal coronet collared and chained gold, the owl being the crest of *Willoughby of Middleton*.
Residence – Birdsall House, Malton, N Yorks. *Club* – Boodle's.

SONS LIVING

Hon MICHAEL CHARLES JAMES (North Grimston House, Malton, N Yorks), *b* 14 July 1948; *ed* Eton; late Lt-Coldm Gds and Queens Own Yeomanry: *m* 1974, Hon Lucy Corinna Agneta Sidney, yst da of 1st Viscount De L'Isle, VC, KG, and has issue living, James William Michael, *b* 8 March 1976; *ed* Eton, and Edinburgh Univ, — Charles Edward Henry, *b* 1986, — Charlotte Jacqueline Louise, *b* 1978, — Emma Coralie Sarah, *b* 1981, — Rose Arabella Julia, *b* 1984.

Hon (John) Hugh Francis (4 Westmorland Terr, SW1), *b* 1951; *ed* Eton; late Capt Coldm Gds.

Hon (Thomas Henry) Richard *b* 1955; *ed* Harrow, and Manchester Univ (BSc).

BROTHER LIVING

Hon (Henry Ernest) Christopher, *b* 1932; *ed* Eton and RMA Sandhurst; Brig Coldm Gds, and Brig Defence Attache Ankara: *m* 1st, 1955 (*m diss* 1990), Jean Adini, da of Lt-Col John David Hills, MC (*see* E Cromer); 2ndly, 1990, J. Elizabeth, da of late Robert Philip Sidney Bache, OBE, of Himbleton, Worcs, and has issue living (by 1st *m*), Guy Nesbit John (Gilchristland House, Thornhill, Dumfriesshire DG3 5HN), *b* 1960; *ed* Eton; late Coldstream Gds; Director The HALO Trust: *m* 1990, Fiona K., da of Patrick Stewart-Blacker, of Blairgowrie, Perthshire, and has issue living, James Patrick Hugh *b* 1999, Louisa Ariana Rose *b* 1992, Eritrea Isabella *b* 1996, — Angela Jane, *b* 1956: *m* 1976, Capt Denis Patrick Antony Critchley-Salmonson, Coldm Gds, and has issue (*see* B Howard de Walden, colls), — Caroline Rosemary, *b* 1957. *Residence* – Somerleyton House, White Hart St, E Harling, Norfolk NR16 2NE. *Club* – Norfolk.

SISTERS LIVING

Hon Angela Hermione Ida, *b* 1924: *m* 1947, Lieut-Com Hon Charles Henry Romer Wynn, RN, and has issue (*see* B Newborough). *Residence* – Bunkersland, Withleigh, Tiverton, Devon.

Hon Jean Elizabeth Mary (*Hon Lady Matheson*), *b* 1928; JP: *m* 1952, Major Sir Fergus John Matheson, 7th Bt, Coldstream Guards, and has issue (*see* Matheson, Bt). *Residence* – Hedenham Old Rectory, Bungay, Norfolk.

COLLATERAL BRANCHES LIVING

Issue of late Col Hon Claude Henry Comaraich Willoughby, CVO, 7th son of 8th Baron, b 1862, d 1932: m 1904, Sibyl Louise, who d 1957, da of late Charles James Murray (E Dunmore, colls):—
Mary Bridget (*Lady Howard-Vyse*) (Town Farm Cottage, Langton, Malton, Yorks), b 1910: m 1940, Lt-Gen Sir Edward Dacre Howard-Vyse, KBE, CB, MC, who d 1992, and has issue living, Richard Edward (Town Farm, Langton, Malton, Yorks) b 1941; TD, JP, DL: m 1965, Sally Rosemary, da of Cdr R. R. Whalley, RN, and has issue living, Thomas Norcliffe b 1971, Mary Elizabeth b 1975, Alice Joan Lucy b 1978, — John Cecil (Old Vicarage, Burneston, Bedale, N Yorks DL8 2HP), b 1947; Lt-Col RA: m 1972, Jennifer Anne, el da of Maj-Gen Geoffrey de Egglesfield Collin, MC, of Roecliffe, Boroughbridge, and has issue living, James Edward b 1977, Georgina b 1975, Victoria b 1980, — Elizabeth, b 1945: m 1983, Rev George A. Perera, of St Hilda's Vicarage, 7 Kingsmead Drive, Hunts Cross, Liverpool L25 0NG, elder son of J. K. P. Perera, FRCS, of Blundellsands, Liverpool, and has issue living, Timothy Mark Grant b 1985, Christopher John Kenneth b 1987, Robert b 1989.

Granddaughters of late Capt Hon Alexander Hugh Willoughby, yst son of 8th Baron:—
Issue of late Wing-Com James Alexander Willoughby RAF, b 1890, d 1955: m 1st, 1918 (m diss 1926), Dorothea Marion, da of late Richard Hilton Burbrook, of 7 Buxton Gdns, W; 2ndly, 1926, Jill, who d 1977, yr da of late David Denton, FRCC, of Newport Pagnell, Bucks:—
(By 1st m) Diana Evelyn Mary, b 1919: m 1941, John Erwin Martens, Flt Capt ATA, who d 1984. *Residence* – 1 Tower House, London Rd, Arundel, W Sussex BN18 9BH. —— Susan Clara, b 1922: m 1963, Robert Bellord, Maj IG, who d 1970, and has issue living, Sarah Mary, b 1950: m 1st, 1969 (m diss 1984), Martin Charles Neale Thompson, son of late Lt-Col Sir Edward Hugh Dudley Thompson, MBE, TD, DL, of Culland Hall, Brailsford, Derby; 2ndly, 1986, Richard William Godfrey Astell, of 14 Keswick Rd, SW15 2JN, and has issue living (by 1st m), Rupert Alexander Robert Neale b 1973, Edward Charles Neale b 1974, Miranda Mary b 1971: m 1996, Mark Louis Harvie-Watt, only son of Sir James Harvie-Watt, 2nd Bt. *Residences* – 60 Clarewood Court, Crawford St, W1H 5DF; Shaggs Cottage, E Lulworth, Dorset. —— (By 2nd m) Griselda Mary Honoria, b 1931: m 1955, Lt Paul Julian David Gifford, RN, of Holly Lodge, Weathercock Lane, Woburn Sands, Bucks, and has issue living, Mark Richard Alexander, b 1960, — Nicola Jane, b 1965.

Issue of late Capt Joe Henry Claude Willoughby, RN, b 1892, d 1966: m 1919, Enid Mary, who d 1980, da of Harry J. Clements, of Somerville House, Sutton Coldfield:—
Anne Honoria Mary, b 1920: m 1st, 1940, Sqdn-Ldr P. Campbell Canney, RAF, who was ka 1942; 2ndly, 1944 (m diss 19—), John Dean; 3rdly, 19—, Wayne Etive, and has issue living (by 1st m), Josephine, b 1942.

Granddaughter of late Maj Charles Stuart Percival Willoughby, 3rd son of late Rev Hon Charles James Willoughby (infra):—
Issue of late Maj Geoffrey St Maur Willoughby, Hampshire Regt, b 1881, d 1954: m 1st, 1910, Julia Henrietta Cave, who d 1946, da of Rev Edmund Joseph Francis Johnson (formerly R of Sarsden, Oxon); 2ndly, 1947, Gwyneth Preston, who d 1981, only da of Arthur Henry Willmore, of Oak Ridge, Chandler's Ford, Hants:—
(By 1st m) (Julia) Hermione, b 1913: m 1936, Lt-Com (S) Richard William Chamberlen, RNR, who d 1995. *Residence* – Little Pitt, Wonston, Winchester, Hants SO21 3LR.

Grandchildren of late James Frederick Digby Willoughby, OBE, 7th son of late Rev Hon Charles James Willoughby, 2nd brother of 8th Baron:—
Issue of late Cdr Ronald James Edward Willoughby, RN (ret), b 1884, d 1971: m 1930, Constance Louisa, who d 1977, da of late Rev Nevile Sherbrooke:—
Christopher Ronald (World Bank, 1818 H St NW, Washington, DC 20433, USA), b 1938: m 1972, Marie-Anne, el da of late Emile Normand of Chamalières, Clermont-Ferrand, France. —— Josephine Cicely Alice (45 Templar Rd, Oxford OX2 8LS), b 1931; SRN. —— Nina Mary, b 1933: m 1959, Cdr David Lines, OBE, RN, of Ewens Farm, West Chelborough, Dorchester, Dorset DT2 0PY, and has issue living, Charles Willoughby, b 1960: m 1986, Catherine Campbell, and has issue living, Jonathan Richard b 1992, Jessica Mary b 1987, — Patrick Simon, b 1963, — James Michael, b 1965; Lt-Cmdr RN: m 1995, Christine Haddon, and has issue living, Samuel Toby b 1997, Felix Harry b 1998, — Rupert Martin, b 1969, — Vanessa Jane, b 1961: m 1988, Richard Harold Davison, son of late Eric Davison, and has issue living, Edward Henry b 1990, Harriet Lucy b 1991, Sarah Constance Louisa b 1994, Elizabeth Alice b 1997.

Issue of late Com Archibald Macdonald Willoughby, RN, b 1887, d on active ser 1943: m 1st, 1912 (m diss 1935), Mabel Doris, who d 1956, el da of Sir William Norton Hicking, 1st Bt (North, Bt); 2ndly, 1935, Elizabeth (who d 1981, having m 2ndly, 1951, Capt Charles Devaynes Smyth, who d 1962), da of late Maj-Gen Sir John Hanbury-Williams, GCVO, KCB, CMG:—
(By 1st m) Pamela Mary Norton (Flat 5, 21 Osberton Rd, Oxford), b 1916: m 1952, Rev Ronald Curnow Parkinson, who d 1984. —— Prudence Joan Mabel, b 1918: m 1949, John Alexander Hannay, and has issue living, Jonathan Howard (20 Florence Park, Westbury Park, Bristol BS6 7LP), b 1951: m 1989, Rebecca McGraw, and has issue living, Ella Ruth b 1991, — Philippa Catherine, b 1953: m 1986, David Squire Dixon, of 19/1c Kooringa Rd, Chatswood, NSW 2067, Australia. *Residence* – Hill Cottage, 11-13 The Hill, Gt Walsingham, Norfolk. —— Sheila Katherine, b 1921: m 1952, Cdr Edward Astley-Jones, RN, and has issue living, Hugh Edward Arthur, b 1953, — Hilary Margaret Doris, b 1958. *Residence* – Newlands, Old Bakehouse Lane, Liskeard Rd, Callington, Cornwall PL17 7RA. —— Anne Rosemary, b 1926: m 1956, George Frederick Rothwell, and has issue living, James Peter (8 Jefferies Close, Marlborough, Wilts SN8 1UB), b 1958: m 1985, Elizabeth Eileen, da of W. B. Atkinson, of Ealing, and has issue living, Edward James b 1992, Thomas Henry b 1993, Nicholas George b 1996, Rebecca Elizabeth b 1992, — Gerald Charles (Flat 4, 36 Dorset Sq, NW1 6QN), b 1963, — Charlotte Jane (Flat 4, 9 Belsize Sq, NW3 4HT), b 1964, — Frances Elizabeth (*Baroness Norton*), b 1966: m 1997, as his 2nd wife, 8th Baron Norton. *Residence* – Little Breach, Moulsford, Oxon OX10 9JN.

Issue of late Rev Canon Bernard Digby Willoughby, b 1896, d 1997: m 1944, Ruth (Salruck, Renvyle, co Galway), da of late Walter Browne Barber, of Beacon Hill, Hucknall, Notts:—
Colin James, b 1949; ed Portora Royal Sch: m 1976, Bridget, da of late Brig Philip Henry Cecil Hayward, CBE, of The Old Mill House, Roughton, Norwich, and has issue living, Philip Mark Digby, b 1993. —— Elisabeth Grace, b 1945: m 1964, Thomas Miller Ormsby, of Milford, Cloghan's Hill, Tuam, co Galway, and has issue living, Thomas Anthony Bowen Miller, b 1969: m 1993, Amanda Lex Edgley, — John Charles Croasdaile Miller, b 1971, — Lucy Anne, b 1966: m 1992, Geoffrey Patrick John Tottenham, of Cloragh, Ashford, co Wicklow, — Catherine Isabel, b 1973.

Grandchildren of late Col Herbert Percival Willoughby, RA, eldest son of late Rev Hon Percival George
Willoughby (infra):—
Issue of late Capt John Herbert Willoughby, RE, late RM, *b* 1896, *d* 1975: *m* 1st, 19— (*m diss* 19—), Kate
Emily, da of ...... Roost; 2ndly, 1941, Dorothy Mary, da of late Dr William Hammond Hodgson, of Horsham, W
Sussex:—
(By 2nd *m*) John Nigel (Newstead, 2 Ashleigh Gdns, Headcorn, Kent TN27 9TW), *b* 1942; late Major RM; with Bedge-
bury Sch; FCIS 1993: *m* 1965, Mrs Mette Ellefsen Nybo, da of Ellef Fredrik Ellefsen, of Aalesund, Norway, and has
adopted his stepson, Sigurd Edward, *b* 1963, — and has issue living, John Fredrik Francis, *b* 1967. —— Lois Ann Mary,
b 1943.

Grandchildren of late Rev Nesbit Edward Willoughby, 2nd son of late Rev Hon Percival George
Willoughby, 3rd brother of 8th Baron:—
Issue of late Rear Adm Guy Willoughby, CB, *b* 1902, *d* 1987: *m* 1923, Mary, who *d* 1990, da of James George
Wilcox Aldridge, AMICE:—
Hugh Nesbit (12 Park Court, Park Rd, Stroud, Glos GL5 2HQ), *b* 1925; *ed* Monckton Combe; ARIBA, AADip of
Architectural Assocn; served World War II in RAF, and in RE 1943-47.

Issue of late Surg-Cdr Lawrence Willoughby, RNVR, *b* 1908, *d* 1980: *m* 1st, 1936, Dorothy Hughes, who *d* 1956;
2ndly, 1957, Elizabeth, who *d* 1987, da of late Alexander Sadowski, of Rosko, Poland;—
(By 2nd *m*) Guy Alexander (11823-83rd St, Edmonton, Alberta, Canada), *b* 1958. —— Veronica Anne, *b* (twin) 1958.

PREDECESSORS – (1) FRANCIS Willoughby; *cr Baronet* 1677, with remainder to his only brother; *d* 1688; *s* by his
brother (2) *Sir* THOMAS, 2nd Bt; successively MP for Newark and Nottinghamshire; *cr Baron Middleton*, of Middleton,
co Warwick (peerage of Great Britain) 1711; *d* 1729; *s* by his son (3) FRANCIS, 2nd Baron; *d* 1758; *s* by his el son (4)
FRANCIS, 3rd Baron; *d* unmarried 1774; *s* by his brother (5) THOMAS, 4th Baron; *d* 1781; *s* by his cousin (6) HENRY, 5th
Baron, son Hon Thomas, 2nd son of 1st Baron; *d* 1800; *s* by his son (7) HENRY, 6th Baron; *dsp* 1835; *s* by his cousin (8)
DIGBY, 7th Baron, Capt RN, grandson of late Hon Thomas, 2nd son of 1st Baron; *d* unmarried 1856; *s* by his cousin (9)
HENRY, 8th Baron, great-grandson of late Hon Thomas, 2nd son of 1st Baron; *b* 1817; *m* 1843, Julia Louisa, da of late
Alexander William Bosville, *de jure* 12th Bt, of Thorpe and Gunthwaite, co York; *d* 1877; *s* by his el son (10) DIGBY
WENTWORTH BAYARD, 9th Baron, *b* 1844: *m* 1860, Eliza Maria, who *d* 1922, da of Sir Alexander Penrose Gordon
Cumming, 3rd Bt; *d* 1922; *s* by his brother (11) GODFREY ERNEST PERCIVAL, 10th Baron, *b* 1847; Midshipman RN;
subsequently entered 9th Lancers and retired as Capt; sometime Starter to the Jockey Club: *m* 1881, Ida Eleanora
Constance, who *d* 1924, da of late George W. H. Ross, of Cromarty House, Cromarty; *d* 1924; *s* by his 2nd son (12)
MICHAEL GUY PERCIVAL, KG, MC, TD, 11th Baron; *b* 1887; Chancellor of Hull Univ 1931-70; Lord-Lt for E Riding 1936-68:
m 1920, Angela Florence Alfreda, who *d* 1978, da of late Charles Oswin Hall, of Eddlethorpe Hall, Malton; *d* 1970; *s* by
his el son (13) (DIGBY) MICHAEL GODFREY JOHN, MC, 12th Baron.

MIDLETON VISCOUNT (Brodrick) (Viscount I 1717, Baron GB 1796)

ALAN HENRY BRODRICK, 12th Viscount: *b* 4 Aug 1949: *s*
1988: *ed* St Edmund's Canterbury: *m* 1978, Julia Helen,
da of Michael Pitt, of Lias Cottage, Compton Dundon,
Somerton, Som, and has issue.

Arms – Argent, on a chief vert, two spears' heads of the field,
erect, and embrued gules. **Crest** – Out of a ducal coronet or, a
spear head argent, embrued gules. **Supporters** – Two men in armour, proper, each holding a spear in the exterior hand.
Residence – 2 Burrell's Orchard, Westley, Bury St Edmunds, Suffolk IP33 3TH.

SONS LIVING

Hon ASHLEY RUPERT, *b* 25 Nov 1980.
Hon William Michael, *b* 1982.

DAUGHTER LIVING

Hon Charlotte Helen, *b* 1983.

SISTERS LIVING

Susan Margaret, *b* 1945: *m* 1971, Robert Andrew Swann, of 44
Munster Rd, Teddington, Middx, and has issue living, Benedick
Rupert Christopher, *b* 1976, — Tabitha Mary, *b* 1972, — Jessica
Araminta May, *b* 1978.
Elizabeth Ann, *b* 1947: *m* 1974, Stephen James Kershaw, of 1 West-
bourne Rd, N7 8AR.

WIDOW LIVING OF SON OF FIRST EARL

Margaret Lætitia, only da of late Maj Hon Charles Henry Lyell (*see* B Lyell); was Assist Commercial Sec, British
Embassy, Moscow 1944-45: *m* 1st, 1937, Maj Hon Francis Alan STEWART-MACKENZIE OF SEAFORTH, who was *ka* 1943,
having assumed by declaration 1935 the surname of Stewart-Mackenzie of Seaforth in lieu of his patronymic; 2ndly, 1944,
Charles Henry Pearson Gifford, OBE. *Residence* – 1 Wyndham House, Aldeburgh, Suffolk.

MOTHER LIVING

Alice Elizabeth, da of late George Robertson Roberts, of Maloya, Purley, Surrey: *m* 1941, Alan Rupert Brodrick, who *d* 1972. *Residence* – 104 Fitzjohn's Av, Hampstead, NW3 6NT.

COLLATERAL BRANCHES LIVING

Issue of late His Honour Norman John Lee Brodrick, brother of 11th Viscount, *b* 1912, *d* 1992: *m* 1940, Ruth Severn, who *d* 1998, da of late Sir Stanley Unwin, KCMG:—

His Honour Judge Michael John Lee, *b* 1941; *ed* Charterhouse, and Merton Coll, Oxford (MA); Bar Lincoln's Inn 1965, Western Circuit, elected to Senate of Inns of Court and the Bar 1979, served 1979-82, Recorder 1981-87, Memb Wine Cttee of W Circuit 1982-86, Judicial Memb of Transport Tribunal since 1986, Circuit Judge Western Circuit since 1987, Liaison Judge to SE Hants Magistrates 1989-93, and IoW Magistrates since 1989; Memb Lord Chancellor's Advisory Cttee for Appointment of Magistrates for Portsmouth 1990-93, since when for SE Hants 1993; Memb Cttee of the Council of HM's Circuit Judges since 1991; Counsellor to Dean and Chapter of Winchester Cathedral since 1993: *m* 1969, Valerie Lois, da of Gerald Max Stroud, of Pond House, Rogate, Petersfield, Hants, and has issue living, Robert John Lee (The Garden Flat, 52A Cumberland St, SW1V 4LZ), *b* 1972; *ed* Charterhouse, and Univ of London, R Holloway Coll (BA); Solicitor, — Tessa Elizabeth Camilla, *b* 1975; *ed* Downe House, and King's Coll, London; MCSP. — Christopher David (41 Strowan Rd, Christchurch, NZ), *b* 1953; *ed* Gordonstoun: *m* 1975, Kirsty Margaret, da of late Hon Sir Ian Macarthur, of Christchurch, NZ, and has issue living, Peter Hannay, *b* 1978, — Katherine Ruth, *b* 1980. — Peter Matthew (Hillcroft, Midcross Lane, Chalfont St Peter, Bucks SL9 0LF), *b* 1954; *ed* Charterhouse, and Charing Cross Hosp Medical Sch, Univ of London (MB BS), LRCP, MRCS (Royal Colls), FRCA (Royal Coll of Anaesthetists): *m* 1982 (*m diss* 1993), Melanie Jean, da of Lloyd Forbes, of 8 Challacombe Place, Newton, Swansea, and has an adopted son and da, James Christopher, *b* 1988, — Camila Alice, *b* 1989. — Frances Mary Severn, *b* 1947: *m* 1972, Pedro Prá-Lopez, of 59 Twyford Av, N2, and has issue living, Nicholas Norman Pedro, *b* 1974, — Thomas Severn, *b* 1977.

Granddaughter of late Rev Hon Alan Brodrick, 5th son of 7th Viscount:—

Issue (by 1st *m*) of late Alan Melvill Brodrick, *b* 1868, *d* 1933: *m* 1st, 1898 (*m diss* 1901), Beatrice, da of Henry Ernst Hall, formerly of Unsted Park, Godalming; 2ndly, 1912, Diana, who *d* 1930, widow of Thomas Davey Peacey:—

Beatrice Mary Alleyne, *b* 1899: *m* 1945, Alban Churton Roe, Flying Officer, RAF Vol Reserve. *Residence* –

PREDECESSORS – (1) ALAN Brodrick, Solicitor-Gen for Ireland 1695, Attorney-Gen 1707; MP for Cork 1692-1709, and for Midhurst 1717-22, sometime Speaker of the House of Commons in Ireland, Ch Justice of the King's Bench in Ireland 1709-10, Lord Chancellor of Ireland 1714-28, and a Lord Justice of Ireland 1716-17, 1719, and 1723-4; *cr Baron Brodrick*, of Midleton, co Cork (peerage of Ireland), 1715, and *Viscount Midleton* (peerage of Ireland) 1717; *d* 1728; *s* by his son (2) ALAN, 2nd Viscount; a Commr of English Customs; *d* 1747; *s* by his son (3) GEORGE, 3rd Viscount; MP for Ashburton 1754-61; *d* 1765; *s* by his son (4) GEORGE, 4th Viscount; MP for Whitchurch, Hants 1774-96; *cr Baron Brodrick*, Peper Harow, co Surrey (peerage of Great Britain) 1796, with remainder to the issue male of his father; *d* 1836; *s* by his son (5) GEORGE ALAN, 5th Viscount; *dsp* 1848; *s* by his cousin (6) CHARLES, 6th Viscount, el son of Most Rev Hon Charles, Archbishop of Cashel, 4th son of 3rd Viscount; *d* 1863, *s* by his brother (7) WILLIAM JOHN, 7th Viscount; *b* 1798; was Dean of Exeter and Chaplain to HM Queen Victoria: *m* 1st, 1824, Lady Elizabeth Anne Brudenell, da of 6th Earl of Cardigan, and widow of Hon John Perceval (E Egmont); 2ndly, 1829, Hon Harriet Brodrick, 3rd da of 4th Viscount Midleton; *d* 1870; *s* by his son (8) WILLIAM, 8th Viscount; *b* 1830; Lord High Steward of Kingston 1875-93, and Lord-Lieut of co Surrey 1896-1905; MP for Mid Surrey (C) 1868-70: *m* 1853, Hon Augusta Mary, who *d* 1903, da of 1st Baron Cottesloe; *d* 1907; *s* by his el son (9) WILLIAM ST JOHN FREMANTLE, PC, KP, 9th Viscount; *b* 1856; an Alderman of London County Council 1907-13; was Financial Sec to War Office 1886-92; and Under-Sec of State for War 1895-8, Under-Sec of State for Foreign Affairs 1898-1900, Sec of State for War 1900-03, Sec of State for India 1903-5, and a Member of Irish Convention 1917-18; elected a Member of Senate of S Ireland June 1921; sat as MP for W Div of Surrey (C) 1880-85, and for SW or Guildford Div of Surrey 1885-1906; *cr Viscount Dunsford* of Dunsford, co Surrey, and *Earl of Midleton* (peerage of UK) 1920: *m* 1st, 1880, Lady Hilda Charteris, who *d* 1901, da of 9th Earl of Wemyss and March; 2ndly, 1903, Madeleine Cecilia Carlyle, who *d* 1966, da of late Lt-Col Hon John Constantine Stanley; *d* 1942; *s* by his el son (10) GEORGE ST JOHN, MC, 2nd Earl, *b* 1888: *m* 1st 1917 (*m diss* 1925), Margaret, da of J. Rush, of Cromer; 2ndly, 1925 (*m diss* 1975), Jeanne Guinivere, who *d* 1978, da of Alexander Sinclair, of Dublin, widow of George Jay Gould (of the Banking Family of New York); 3rdly, 1975, Irène Lilian Creese (Rène Ray, the actress), who *d* 1993, and *d* 1979, when the Earldom of Midleton and the Viscountcy of Dunsford became extinct, and the Viscountcy of Midleton and the other peerages devolved upon his kinsman (11) TREVOR LOWTHER (el son of William John Henry Brodrick, OBE, 2nd son of Rev Hon Alan Brodrick, yst son of 7th Viscount), 11th Viscount, *b* 1903: *m* 1940, Sheila Campbell, who *d* 1995, da of late Charles Campbell MacLeod, of Cawthorpe House, Bourne, Lincs; *d* 1988; *s* by his nephew (12) ALAN HENRY (only son of late Alan Rupert Brodrick, yr brother of 11th Viscount), 12th Viscount and present peer; also Baron Brodrick, of Midleton, and Baron Brodrick of Peper Harow.

Midlothian, Earl of, see Earl of Rosebery.

MILFORD, BARON (Philipps) (Baron UK 1939, Bt UK 1919)

Patriotism my motive

HUGO JOHN LAURENCE PHILIPPS, 3rd Baron, and 3rd Baronet; *b* 27 Aug 1929; *s* 1993; *ed* Eton, and King's Coll, Camb; a farmer: *m* 1st, 1951 (*m diss* 1958), Margaret, only da of late Capt Ralph Heathcote, DSO, RN, of Gressingham, Lancs; 2ndly, 1959 (*m diss* 1984), Hon Mary Makins, twin da of 1st Baron Sherfield, GCB, GCMG; 3rdly, 1989, Mrs Felicity Leach, da of late Murray Ballantyne, of Montreal, Canada, and has issue by 1st and 2nd *m*.

Arms – Argent, a lion rampant sable ducally gorged and chained or. Crest – A lion as in the arms. Supporters – On either side a horse, argent charged on the shoulder with three bars wavy azure.
Residence – Llanstephan House, Llanstephan, Brecon, Powys.

SONS LIVING (*By 2nd marriage*)

Hon GUY WOGAN, *b* 25 July 1961; *ed* Eton, and Magdalen Coll, Oxford (MA); Bar Inner Temple 1986: *m* 1st, 1988 (*m diss* 1996), Rebecca, yr da of Nigel Nicolson, MBE, of Sissinghurst Castle, Cranbrook, Kent (*see* B Carnock, colls); 2ndly, 1996, Alice Sherwood, and has issue living (by 2nd *m*), Archie Sherwood, *b* 1997.
Hon Roland Alexander, *b* 1962; *ed* Eton, and Trin Coll, Camb (MA): *m* 1991, Felicity Kate, da of Hilary Harold Rubinstein, of 32 Ladbroke Grove, W11, and has issue living, Nathaniel Alexander, *b* 1996. *Residence* – 231 Westbourne Park Rd, W11 IEB.
Hon Ivo Laurence, *b* 1967; *ed* Eton, and Bristol Univ.

DAUGHTERS LIVING (*By 1st marriage*)

Hon Anna Margaret, *b* 1954: *m* 1975, Hon Christopher Richard James Woodhouse, MB BS, FRCS, and has issue (*see* B Terrington). *Residence* – 14 Crescent Grove, SW4 7AH.

(*By 2nd marriage*)

Hon Katherine Nina, *b* 1964: *m* 1994, Jean-Pierre Elien Frederic Juteau, and has issue living, Alexis Michel Hugo, *b* 1998, — Charlotte Mary Suzanne, *b* 1996. *Residence* – 27 rue Leconte de Lisle, 75016 Paris.

AUNT LIVING (*daughter of 1st Baron*)

Hon Gwenllian, OBE, *b* 1916; formerly Subaltern ATS; is a JP for Radnorshire; a Co Councillor for Radnorshire 1959-64, and High Sheriff 1970-71; OBE (Civil) 1962. *Residence* – The Old Rectory, Boughrood, Llyswen, Brecon.

WIDOW LIVING OF SON OF FIRST BARON

Hon Elizabeth Joan Kindersley (Dalham Hall, Newmarket, Suffolk), da of 1st Baron Kindersley: *m* 1930, Maj Hon James Perrott Philipps, TD, who *d* 1984, and has issue (see colls infra).

WIDOW LIVING OF SECOND BARON

TAMARA (*Dowager Baroness Milford*), da of — Kravetz, of —, and widow of William Rust: *m* 1954, as his 3rd wife, the 2nd Baron Milford, who *d* 1993. *Residence* – Flat 2, 8 Lyndhurst Rd, Hampstead, NW3 5PX.

COLLATERAL BRANCHES LIVING

Issue of late Maj Hon (Richard) Hanning Philipps, MBE, 2nd son of 1st Baron, *b* 1904, *d* 1998: *m* 1930, Lady Marion Violet Dalrymple, who *d* 1995, da of 12th Earl of Stair:—
Jeremy Hew (Picton Castle, Haverfordwest, Pembs), *b* 1931; *ed* Eton; a Member of Lloyd's, and Chm Laurence Philipps & Co Ltd: *m* 1959, Susan, yr da of late Henry Edward Bowden Gundry, of Grange, Honiton, Devon, and has issue living, Clare Marion, *b* 1961, — Nicola, *b* 1964. —— Louise (adopted da), *b* 1946: *m* 1971, Hugh Simon Fetherstonhaugh, and has issue (*see* V Galway).

Issue of late Maj Hon James Perrott Philipps, TD, 3rd son of 1st Baron, *b* 1905, *d* 1984: *m* 1930, Hon Elizabeth Joan Kindersley (ante), da of 1st Baron Kindersley:—

Peter Anthony (Parsonage Farm, Ugley, nr Bishop's Stortford, Herts), *b* 1933; *ed* Eton, and Trin Coll, Camb; Member of London Stock Exchange: *m* 1957 (*m diss* 1981), Susannah Margaret, el da of S. W. Eaton, and has issue living, Charles Edward Laurence, *b* 1959; *ed* Eton: *m* 1984, Fiona, da of late Frank Gordon Land, of Knoll Gate, Nayland, Suffolk, and has issue living, Henry Roland Laurence *b* 1993, Georgina Clare *b* 1990, Emma Louise *b* 1990, — James Anthony Hanning (Garden House, Dalham, Newmarket, Suffolk CB8 8TB), *b* 1961: *m* 1984, Catherine Charlotte, only da of Anthony Gosselin Trower, of Stanstead Bury, Ware, Herts, and has issue living, Henrietta Catherine Elizabeth *b* 1985, Venetia Margaret *b* 1988, — Gavin Piers Alexander, *b* 1963. —— Penelope Doune, *b* 1931: *m* 1950, Capt Anthony Walsham Neville Lake (*see* Walsham, Bt, colls, 1990 Edn), of Higham's Farm, Wimbish, Saffron Walden, Essex, and *d* 1985, leaving issue, David Anthony, *b* 1953, — Simon Neville, *b* 1956, — Mark Philip, *b* 1958. —— Daphne Deirdre (Springfield Maltings, Stogumber, Taunton, Som), *b* 1940: *m* 1963, Robin Hugh Lewes, TD, who *d* 1969, and has issue living, James Hugh (7 Whitmore Rd, Taunton, Som TA2 6DY), *b* 1967: *m* 1998, Emma Milton, and has issue living, Rosie Jennifer *b* 1997, — Katherine Mary, *b* 1968, — Sarah Jane (twin), *b* 1968.

Issue of late Capt Hon William Speke Philipps, CBE, yst son of 1st Baron, *b* 1908, *d* 1975: *m* 1939, Lady Jean Meriel McDonnell, who *d* 1998, da of 7th Earl of Antrim:—

Geoffrey Mark (Slebech Park, Haverfordwest, Pembrokeshire), *b* 1948; *ed* Eton: *m* 1984, Georgina Bridget, only da of Rear-Adm John Gervaise Beresford Cooke, CB, DSC, of Downstead House, Morestead, Winchester, and has issue living, Alexander Gervaise, *b* 1985, — Lara Helen, *b* 1986, — Leonora Isabel Jean, *b* 1989. —— David William, *b* 1952: *m* 1971, Stella Katharine Anne, only da of A. W. Fordham, and has issue living, Frederick William, *b* 1973. —— Georgina Rose, *b* 1942: *m* 1967, David Llewellyn Pryse Lloyd, and has had issue, Huw Llewellyn, *b* 1971, — Jonathan, *b* 1973, — Isabel Rose, *b* 1968; *d* 1989, — Juliet Ann, *b* 1970. —— Theresa Margaret, *b* 1946: *m* 1972, Christopher John Payne, and has issue living, Joseph Vernon William, *b* 1975, — Benjamin Christopher John, *b* 1978, — Harriet Sarah Jean, *b* 1982.

PREDECESSORS – Sir Richard Philipps, 7th Bt (*cr* 1621) (*see* V St Davids); *cr Baron Milford* 1776, which title became ext on his death in 1823, and was revived in favour of (1) LAURENCE RICHARD Philipps, 6th son of Rev Canon Sir James Erasmus Philipps, 12th Bt; *b* 1874; High Sheriff of Hants 1915; a Gov of Univ Coll of Wales and Founder of Paraplegic Hospital in Wales; *cr* a Bt 1919, and *Baron Milford*, of Llanstephan, co Radnor (peerage of UK) 1939: *m* 1901, Ethel Georgina, who *d* 1971, da of late Rev Benjamin Speke, of Jordans, Somerset; *d* 1962; *s* by his el son (2) WOGAN, 2nd Baron; *b* 1902; Memb Internat Brigade, Spanish Civil War; Communist Cllr Cirencester RDC 1946-49; Painter: *m* 1st, 1928 (*m diss* 1944), Rosamond Nina, CBE (the celebrated novelist, Rosamond Lehmann), who *d* 1990, da of late Rudolph Chambers Lehmann, of Fieldhead, Bourne End, Bucks, and formerly wife of Walter Leslie Runciman (later 2nd Viscount Runciman of Doxford); 2ndly, 1944, Maria Cristina, who *d* 1953, da of the Marchese Casati, of Palazzo Barberini, Rome, and formerly wife of 15th Earl of Huntingdon; 3rdly, 1954, Tamara (*née* Kravetz), widow of William Rust, Editor of the *Daily Worker*, *d* 1993; *s* by his only son (3) HUGO JOHN LAURENCE, 3rd Baron and present peer.

MILFORD HAVEN, MARQUESS OF (Mountbatten) (Marquess UK 1917)

GEORGE IVAR LOUIS MOUNTBATTEN, 4th Marquess; *b* 6 June 1961; *s* 1970: *m* 1st, 1989 (*m diss* 1996), Sarah Georgina, elder da of George Alfred Walker, and formerly wife of Andrcas L. Antoniou; 2ndly, 1997, Mrs Clare H. Wentworth-Stanley, yst da of late Anthony N. Steel, of Rock House Farm, Lower Froyle, Hants, and formerly wife of Nicholas Philip Wentworth-Stanley (*see* E Erne, colls, 1995 Edn), and has issue by 1st *m*.

Arms – Quarterly: 1st and 4th azure, a lion rampant double-queued barry of ten argent and gules, armed and langued of the last, crowned or, within a bordure compony of the second and third; 2nd and 3rd argent, two pallets sable, charged on the honour point with an escutcheon of the arms of the late *Princess Alice* (i.e. the Royal arms differenced with a label of three points argent, the centre point charged with a rose gules barbed vert, and each of the other points with an ermine spot sable). **Crests** – 1st, out of a ducal coronet or two horns barry of ten argent and gules, issuing from each three linden leaves vert, and from the outer side of each horn four branches barwise, having three like leaves pendent therefrom of the last, *Hesse*; 2nd, out of a ducal coronet or a plume of four ostrich feathers alternately argent and sable, *Battenberg*. **Supporters** – On either side a lion double-queued and crowned all or.

SON LIVING (*By 1st marriage*)

HENRY (HARRY) DAVID LOUIS (*Earl of Medina*), *b* 19 Oct 1991.

DAUGHTER LIVING (*By 1st marriage*)

Lady Tatiana Helen Georgia, *b* 1990.

BROTHER LIVING

Lord Ivar Alexander Michael, *b* 1963: *m* 1994, Penelope Ann Vere, da of Colin Thompson, of Warminster, Wilts, and Mrs Timothy A. P. Walker, of Chippenham, Wilts, and has issue living, Ella Louise Georgina, *b* 1996, — Alexandra Nada Victoria, *b* 1998. *Residence* – Bridwell Park, Uffculme, Devon EX15 3BU.

WIDOW LIVING OF THIRD MARQUESS

JANET MERCEDES (*Janet, Marchioness of Milford Haven*), only da of late Maj Francis Bryce, OBE: *m* 1960, as his 2nd wife, the 3rd Marquess of Milford Haven, who *d* 1970.

PREDECESSORS – **(1)** LOUIS ALEXANDER Mountbatten, GCB, GCVO, KCMG, son of HGDH late Prince Alexander of Hesse, GCB, by his morganatic *m* to Julie, Princess of Battenberg; *b* 24 May 1854; naturalized 1868 as Prince Louis of Battenberg; Adm of the Fleet; was Naval Adviser to Inspector-Gen of Fortifications 1893-4, Assist Director of Naval Intelligence 1899-1901, Director thereof 1902-5, in Command of second Cruiser Squadron 1905-7, Second in Command of Mediterranean Fleet 1907-8, Com-in-Ch of Atlantic Fleet 1908-10, in Command of 3rd and 4th Divs Home Fleet 1911, Second Sea Lord of the Admiralty 1911-12, and First Sea Lord 1912-14; appointed Hon ADC to Queen Victoria 1896, and Personal Naval ADC to King Edward VII 1901 and to King George V 1910; *cr Viscount Alderney*, co Southampton, *Earl of Medina*, and *Marquess of Milford Haven* (peerage of United Kingdom) 17 July 1917, having by Roy Warrant, 14 July 1917, at HM's request, discontinued the use, style and title of "Serene Highness" and "Prince," and appellation of "Battenberg," and assumed for himself and descendants the surname of Mountbatten: *m* 1884, Victoria Alberta Elizabeth Mathilde Marie, VA, who *d* 1950, el da of HRH the late Grand Duke Ludwig IV of Hesse, KG, by HRH Princess Alice Maud Mary, VA, 2nd da of HM Queen Victoria; *d* 1921; *s* by his el son **(2)** GEORGE LOUIS VICTOR HENRY SERGE, GCVO, 2nd Marquess; *b* 1892; Capt (ret) RN; European War 1914-18, present at battle of Heligoland, Dogger Bank, and Jutland: *m* 1916, Countess Nadejda de Torby, who *d* 1963, yr da of HIH the late Grand Duke Michael Michaelovitch of Russia and late Countess de Torby; *d* 1938; *s* by his only son **(3)** DAVID MICHAEL, OBE, DSC, 3rd Marquess, *b* 1919: *m* 1st, 1950 (*m diss* at El Paso, Mexico 1954, and in England 1960), Romaine Dahlgren, only da of late Vinton Ulric Dahlgren Pierce, and formerly wife of William Simpson; 2ndly, 1960, Janet Mercedes, only da of late Maj Francis Bryce, OBE; *d* 1970; *s* by his el son **(4)** GEORGE IVAR LOUIS, 4th Marquess and present peer; also Earl of Medina, and Viscount Alderney.

Millar, family name of Baron Inchyra.

MILLER OF CHILTHORNE DOMER, BARONESS (Miller) (Life Baroness 1998)

SUSAN ELIZABETH MILLER, da of late Oliver Meddows Taylor; *b* 1 Jan 1954; *ed* Sidcot Sch, and Oxford Poly; publisher with David & Charles, Weidenfeld & Nicholson, and Penguin Books; self employed bookseller in Sherborne and Yeovil; Leader, S Somerset District Council 1996-98 (Cncllr 1991-98); Cncllr, Somerset CC 1997; Chm Somerset Forum 1996; Memb Lib Dems and Women Lib Dems, Greenpeach, and Somerset Wildlife Trust; *cr Baroness Miller of Chilthorne Domer*, of Chilthorne Domer, co Somerset (Life Baroness) 1998: *m* 1980 (*m diss* 1998), John Christopher Miller, and has issue.
Address – c/o House of Lords, SW1A 0PW.

DAUGHTERS LIVING

Hon Charlotte Sarah, *b* 1981.
Hon Madeleine Lucy, *b* 1984.

MILLER OF HENDON, BARONESS (Miller) (Life Baroness 1993)

DOREEN MILLER, MBE, da of Bernard Henry Feldman; *b* 13 June 1933; *ed* LSE; Co Dir; Chm Barnet Family Health Services Authority 1990-94; Crown Agents 1990-94; Member Monopolies & Mergers Commn 1992-93; Treasurer Greater London Area Conservative Assocns 1990-93, Chm 1993-96, and Pres 1996-98; Chm Nat Assocn of Hospital & Community Friends since 1997; JP Brent 1970; Baroness in Waiting to HM 1994-97; MBE (Civil) 1989; *cr Baroness Miller of Hendon, of Gore, in the London Borough of Barnet* (Life Baroness) 1993; *m* 1955, Henry Lewis Miller, son of Ben Miller, and has issue.

Arms – ......
Address – c/o House of Lords, SW1A 0PW. *Clubs* – St Stephen's Constitutional, Reform, Carlton.

SONS LIVING

Hon Michael Steven, *b* 1956.
Hon Paul Howard, *b* 1959: *m* 1992, Sharon Hunt.

Hon David Philip, *b* 1962.

MILLETT, BARON (Millett) (Life Baron 1998)

PETER JULIAN MILLETT, PC, son of late Denis Millett, of London; *b* 23 June 1932; *ed* Harrow, and Trinity Hall, Camb (MA 1955, Hon Fell 1994); Standing Jr Council to BOT and DTI 1967-73; QC 1973; Bencher Lincoln's Inn 1980; Memb Insolvency Law Review Cttee 1977-82; Judge of the High Court of Justice (Chancery Div) 1986-94; a Lord Justice of Appeal 1994-98, since when a Lord of Appeal in Ordinary; *cr* Kt 1986, PC 1994, and *Baron Millett, of St Marylebone in the City of Westminster* (Life Baron) 1998: *m* 1959, Ann Mireille, da of late David Harris, of London, and has had issue.
Residences – 18 Portman Close, W1H 9HJ; 28 Kewhurst Av, Cooden, Sussex.

SONS LIVING AND DECEASED

Hon Richard, *b* 1961; *ed* Harrow, and Trinity Hall, Camb: *m* 1988, Patricia, da of Bernard Spencer, and has issue living, Edward George Denis, *b* 1993, — Alexia Florence, *b* 1991, — Eliza Eve, *b* 1996,
Hon Andrew, *b* 1965; *ed* Harrow, and Trinity Hall, Camb: *m* 1996, Vanessa, da of Prof Norman Frederick Morris, and has issue living, James Hugo, *b* 1998.
Robert, *b* and *d* 1965.

MILLS, VISCOUNT (Mills) (Viscount UK 1962, Bt UK 1953)

CHRISTOPHER PHILIP ROGER MILLS, 3rd Viscount, and 3rd Bt; *b* 20 May 1956; *s* 1988; *ed* Oundle Sch, and London Univ: *m* 1980, Lesley Alison, elder da of Alan Bailey, of Lichfield, Staffs.

Arms – Per chevron azure and argent in chief two millrinds of the last and in base a balance sable. Crest – A bear's gamb erased or, supporting a flint-lock proper. Supporters – On either side a lion or collared and chained azure pendant from the collar an escutcheon of the last charged with a sun in splendour gold.
Residence – 20 Murray Rd, Northwood, Middx HA6 2YJ.

SISTERS LIVING

Hon Felicity Jane, *b* 1947: *m* 1970, Roger B. Pickford, of Heddfan, Ffawyddog, Llangattock, Crickhowell, Powys.
Hon Phillipa Susan, *b* 1950: *m* 1970, Russell Scott Arthurton.

AUNT LIVING (*daughter of 1st Viscount*)

Hon Beatrice Margaret, *b* 1916: *m* 1941, Walter Goodwin Davis, and has issue living, Patrick, *b* 1947, — Andrew, *b* 1950, — Jane, *b* 1957. *Residence* – Chantry House, Sheep St, Stow-on-the-Wold, Glos.

PREDECESSORS – (1) *Rt Hon Sir* PERCY HERBERT Mills, KBE, PC, son of D. Mills, of Stockton-on-Tees; *b* 1890; Min of Power 1957-59; Paymaster-Gen 1959-61; Min without Portfolio 1961-62; Controller-Gen of Machine Tools, Min of Supply 1940-44; *cr* a Baronet 1953, *Baron Mills*, of Studley, co Warwick 1957, and *Viscount Mills*, of Kensington, co London 1963: *m* 1915, Winifred Mary, who *d* 1974, da of George Conaty, of Birmingham; *d* 1968; *s* by his only son (2) ROGER CLINTON, 2nd Viscount, *b* 1919; Bar Inner Temple, Colonial Ser Kenya, Maj RA 1939-45 War: *m* 1945, Joan Dorothy, who *d* 1998, da of James Shirreff, of London; *d* 1988; *s* by his only son (3) CHRISTOPHER PHILIP ROGER, 3rd Viscount, and present peer; also Baron Mills.

Mills, family name of Baron Hillingdon.

MILNE, BARON (Milne) (Baron UK 1933)

Studies make illustrious

GEORGE DOUGLASS MILNE, 2nd Baron; *b* 10 Feb 1909; *s* 1948; *ed* Winchester and New Coll, Oxford; a Member of Inst of Chartered Accountants of Scotland; Master of Grocers' Co 1961-62; Senior Memb of Court 1983-90; a Member of Lambeth Hosp Management Cttee 1947-51; Dep Chm of London and Northern Group 1982-87; TD; 1939-45 War as Maj RA (TA) in Norway and Middle East (despatches, wounded, prisoner): *m* 1940, Cicely, da of late Ronald Leslie, and has issue.

Arms – Or, a cross moline pierced lozengeways of the field between four mullets azure. Crest – A dexter hand holding up an open book proper, leaved or. Supporters – *Dexter*, an officer of the Royal Horse Artillery; *sinister*, an officer of the Greek Evzone Guard, both in full dress uniform.
Residence – 33 Lonsdale Rd, Barnes, SW13 9JP.

SONS LIVING

Hon GEORGE ALEXANDER (188 Broom Rd, Teddington, Middx), *b* 1 April 1941; *ed* Winchester; Livery of Grocers' Co 1971.
Hon Iain Charles Luis (c/o Agrisouth, Talca, Chile), *b* 1949, *ed* Oundle; FCA; Livery of Grocers' Co: *m* 1987, Berta (Ita), da of Enrique Urzua Guerrero, of San Felipe, Chile, and has issue living, Iain Eduardo Alexander, *b* 1990, — Leslie Axel Fernando, *b* 1993.

DAUGHTER LIVING

Hon Ann Geraldine, *b* 1946, Freeman of City of London (1967) and Livery of Grocers' Co 1984: *m* 1969, Ian Frederick Lawrence Straker, of Hever Warren, Hever, Kent, and has issue living, Ross Alexander Lawrence, *b* 1977; *ed* Millfield, — Frances Georgina *b* 1980; *ed* Heathfield, and Bedgebury Park.

PREDECESSOR – **(1)** *FM Sir* GEORGE FRANCIS Milne, GCB, GCMG, DSO, son of late George Milne, of Westwood, Aberdeen; *b* 1866; became Field-Marshal 1928; Nile Expedition 1898, S Africa 1899-1902 (DSO), European War 1914-19 on Staff and as Gen Officer Comdg Salonika Army (KCB, KCMG, GCMG); was Lieut of The Tower 1920-23, Ch of Imperial Gen Staff 1926-33, Master Gunner, St James's Park 1929-46, and Constable of The Tower 1933-8; Grand Pres of British Empire Ser League, Chm Empire Sos War Hospitality Committee, Pres of London Fever Hospital, Chm of Executive Committee of Roy Cancer Hospital, Patron of Salonika Reunion Asso, and Pres of Old Contemptibles' Asso, Army Cadet Asso, Roy Artillery Asso, and Roy Artillery Memorial Asso; bore second sword at Coronation of King George VI; *cr Baron Milne*, of Salonika and of Rubislaw, co Aberdeen (peerage of United Kingdom) 1933: *m* 1905, Claire Marjoribanks, MBE, who *d* 1970, da of Sir John Nisbet Maitland, 5th Bt; *d* 1948; *s* by his son **(2)** GEORGE DOUGLASS, 2nd Baron and present peer.

MILNER OF LEEDS, BARON (Milner) (Baron UK 1951)

(ARTHUR JAMES) MICHAEL MILNER, AE, 2nd Baron; *b* 12 Sept 1923; *s* 1967; *ed* Oundle, and Trin Hall, Camb (MA); Solicitor 1951; consultant in the legal firm of Gregory, Rowcliffe & Milners, of London; Opposition Whip 1971-74; Ft Lt 609 (W Riding) Sqdn RAuxAF 1947-52; 1939-45 War as Fl Lt RAF: *m* 1951, Sheila Margaret, da of late Gerald Hartley, of Leeds, and has had issue.

Arms – Gules on a chevron ermine between in chief two bits or and in base a rose argent barbed and seeded proper a Teazel sable. **Crest** – Perched on a sword with point to the dexter proper and hilt and pomel or an owl also proper, gorged with a collar sable thereon three mullets argent, pendent therefrom a pair of scales and resting on the dexter claw on a portcullis chained or. **Supporters** – On either side an owl proper gorged with a collar sable thereon three mullets argent pendent therefrom a portcullis chained or. *Residence* – 2 The Inner Court, Old Church St, SW3 5BY.

SON LIVING

Hon RICHARD JAMES, *b* 16 May 1959; *ed* Charterhouse, and Surrey Univ (BSc): *m* 1988, Margaret Christine, yst da of Gerald Francis Voisin, of Jersey, CI, and has issue living, Charlotte Emma, *b* 1990, — Nicola Louise Christine, *b* 1992. *Residence* – Roche d'Or, Trinity, Jersey.

DAUGHTERS LIVING AND DECEASED

Hon Geraldine Jane, *b* 1954: *m* 1978, Mark Anthony Fenton, of 3 Darnley Rd, Leeds LS16 5JF, and has issue living, Harry James Oliver, *b* 1982, — Alexander Philip Guy, *b* 1992, — Kate Emma Jane, *b* 1984.

Hon Meredith Ann, *b* 1956, *dunm* 1993.

SISTER LIVING

Hon Shelagh Mary Margaret, *b* 1925: *m* 1948 (*m diss* 1965), Harry Barker Grimshaw, and has issue living, John Sherwood, *b* 1950, — Miranda, *b* 1952. *Residence* – High Barn, Thorner, Yorks.

PREDECESSOR – **(1)** *Rt Hon* JAMES Milner, MC, TD, PC, el son of late James Henry Milner of Leeds; *b* 1889; MP for SE Leeds (Lab) 1929-51; Chm of Ways and Means and Dep Speaker of House of Commons 1943-45, and 1945-51; *cr Baron Milner of Leeds*, of Roundhay, City of Leeds (Peerage of UK) 1951: *m* 1917, Lois Tinsdale, who *d* 1982, da of Thomas Brown, of Roundhay, Leeds; *d* 1967, *s* by his only son **(2)** (ARTHUR JAMES) MICHAEL, 2nd Baron, and present peer.

MILVERTON, BARON (Richards) (Baron UK 1947)

Mind makes the man

Rev FRASER ARTHUR RICHARD RICHARDS, 2nd Baron; *b* 21 July 1930; *s* 1978; *ed* Ridley Coll, Ontario, Clifton Coll, Egerton Agric Coll, Njoro, Kenya, and Bishop's Coll, Cheshunt, Herts; in Roy Signals 1949-50; in Kenya Police 1952-53; made Deacon 1957, ordained Priest 1958, Curate 1957-63, V of Okewood, Surrey 1963-67, Vicar of Christian Malford with Sutton Benger and Tytherton Kellaways 1967-93; Chap to Wilts ACF: *m* 1957, Mary Dorothy, BD, da of late Leslie Fly, of Pulteney St, Bath, and has issue.

Arms – Argent, three lozenges conjoined in fesse gules between two barrulets sable, all within two flaunches of the second, both charged with a spearhead of the field. Crest – A Malay tiger's head erased proper, gorged with a collar lozengy argent and gules. Supporters – On either side a Malay tiger proper, gorged with a collar lozengy argent and gules.
Residence – Riverview, Bath Rd, Manton, Marlborough, Wilts SN8 1PS.

DAUGHTERS LIVING

Hon Susan Mary, *b* 1962: *m* 1991, Robert Adam Brisbane Cross, elder son of Diarmid A. Cross, of Tavistock, Devon, and has issue living, Alice Rose, *b* 1993.
Hon Juliet Elizabeth, *b* 1964: *m* 1992, Maurice Charles Steuart-Corry, yr son of William Steuart-Corry, of Helensburgh, Dunbartonshire, and has issue living, Charles, *b* 1998, — Sophie, *b* 1993, — Emma, *b* (twin) 1993, — Katie, *b* 1996.

BROTHER LIVING

Hon MICHAEL HUGH, *b* 1 Aug 1936; *ed* Ridley Coll, Ont, Clifton Coll, and RMA Sandhurst; Capt (ret) Rifle Bde; Malaya 1957 (despatches); attached R Nigerian Army 1962, and a Member of UN Congo Force 1963-65; Man Dir Philip Morris Nigeria Ltd 1972-77; Dir Africa Carreras Rothmans Ltd 1978-82; Man Dir Murray Sons and Co 1982-87; Personnel Dir Rothmans International Tobacco 1987-93; Man Dir Rothmans of Pall Mall (New Zealand) Ltd 1993-96: *m* 1960, Edna Leonie B., yst da of Col Leo Stevenie, OBE, MC, IA (ret), and has issue living, Arthur Hugh, *b* 10 Jan 1963. *Club* – Cavalry and Guards'.

SISTER LIVING

Hon Diana Benda, *b* 1928; *ed* Havergal Coll, Toronto, Cheltenham Ladies' Coll, at London Univ, and Sorbonne, Paris: *m* 1960, Sq-Ldr Glyn John Clement, RAF, and has issue living, Paul Nicholas Arthur, *b* 1961: *m* 1994, Britt Meyland-Smith, da of Dr Robin Smith-Saville, — Caroline Benda, *b* 1966. *Residence* – The Bell House, Kewstoke Rd, Worle, Weston-super-Mare, Som.

WIDOW LIVING OF FIRST BARON

NOELLE BENDA, CStJ (*Noelle, Baroness Milverton*), da of Charles Basil Whitehead, of Torquay: *m* 1927, the 1st Baron Milverton, who *d* 1978. *Residence* – Flete, Ermington, Ivy Bridge, S Devon.

PREDECESSOR – (1) *Sir* ARTHUR FREDERICK Richards, GCMG, son of late William Richards, of Bristol; *b* 1885; Gov of N Borneo 1930-33, of Gambia 1933-36, and of Fiji (and High Commr of Pacific) 1936-38, Capt-Gen and Gov-in-Ch of Jamaica 1938-43, and Gov of Nigeria 1943-47; *cr* CMG 1933, KCMG 1935, GCMG 1942, and *Baron Milverton*, of Lagos, and of Clifton, in the City of Bristol (Peerage of UK) 1947: *m* 1927, Noelle Benda, CStJ, da of Charles Basil Whitehead, Torquay; *d* 1978; *s* by his el son (2) *Rev* FRASER ARTHUR RICHARD, 2nd Baron and present peer.

Minster, Baron, title of Marquess Conyngham on Roll of HL.

MINTO, EARL OF (Elliot-Murray-Kynynmound) (Earl UK 1813, Bt S 1700)

He needs not the bow

Mildly but firmly

GILBERT EDWARD GEORGE LARISTON ELLIOT-MURRAY-KYNYNMOUND, OBE, 6th Earl, and 9th Baronet; *b* 19 June 1928; *s* 1975; *ed* Eton, and RMA Sandhurst; Capt Scots Gds (Reserve); Brig Queen's Body Guard for Scotland (Royal Company of Archers); JP for Roxburghshire; DL Borders Region, Roxburgh, Ettrick and Lauderdale; Chm Scottish Council on Alcoholism; Member on Borders Regional Council (Hermitage Div) 1974-80; Dep Traffic Commr for Scotland 1975-81; Exec Vice-Pres S Scotland Chamber of Commerce 1978-80, Pres 1980-82; Dir Noel Penny Turbinse Ltd since 1971; 2nd Lieut Scots Gds 1948, served in Malaya 1949-51; ADC to CIGS 1953-55, and to Gov of Cyprus 1955; MBE (Mil) 1955, OBE (Civil) 1986: *m* 1st, 1952 (*m diss* 1965), Lady Caroline Child-Villiers, da of 9th Earl of Jersey; 2ndly, 1965, Mary Elizabeth, who *d* 1983, da of late Peter Ballantine, of Stonehouse Farm, Gladstone, NJ, USA; 3rdly, 1991, Mrs Caroline Jane Larlham, da of Stanley Godfrey, of Ruislip, Middlesex, and formerly wife of Christopher Larlham, and has issue by 1st *m*.

Arms – Quarterly: 1st and 4th grand quarters quarterly, 1st and 4th argent, a hunting horn sable, stringed gules, and on a chief azure, three mullets of the field, *Murray*; 2nd and 3rd azure, a chevron argent, between three fleurs-de-lis or, *Kynynmound*; 2nd and 3rd grand quarters gules, within a bordure vair, a bend engrailed or, thereon a baton azure, *Elliot*, above all a chief of augmentation argent, and thereon a Moor's head sable, being the arms of the island of Corsica. Crest – A dexter arm embowed issuant from clouds, throwing a dart, all proper. Supporters – *Dexter*, an Indian sheep proper; *sinister*, a fawn proper.
Seat – Minto, Hawick, Roxburghshire; *Club* – Puffin's (Edinburgh)

SON LIVING (By 1st marriage)

GILBERT TIMOTHY GEORGE LARISTON (*Viscount Melgund*), *b* 1 Dec 1953; *ed* Eton, and NELP (BSc); ARICS; Lt Scots Gds, Member Queen's Body Guard for Scotland (Royal Company of Archers): *m* 1983, Diana Barbara, yr da of Brian S. L. Trafford (*see* B Taylor of Hadfield), of Tismans, Rudgwick, W Sussex, and has had issue. *Residence* – Upper Ham Farm, Thornhill, Wootton Bassett, Wilts. *Club* – White's.

SONS LIVING AND DECEASED — *Hon* GILBERT FRANCIS, *b* 15 Aug 1984, — †*Hon* Lorne David, *b* and *d* 1986, — *Hon* Michael Timothy, *b* 1987.
DAUGHTER LIVING — *Hon* Clare Patricia, *b* 1991.

DAUGHTER LIVING (By 1st marriage)

Lady Laura, *b* 1956: *m* 1984, John Reginald David Palmer, yr son of William Alexander Palmer, of Bussockwood House, Newbury, Berks, and has issue living, Sam, *b* 1985, — Nicholas, *b* 1987. *Residence* – The New House, Carlton Curlieu, Leics LE8 0PH.

BROTHER LIVING

Hon (George Esmond) Dominic ELLIOT (88 St James's Street, SW1A 1PW; *Clubs* – White's and New (Edinburgh)), *b* 1931; *ed* Eton, and Madrid Univ; formerly Lt Scots Gds: *m* 1st, 1962 (*m diss* 1970), Countess Marianne, da of late Count Thomas Esterhazy; 2ndly, 1983, Jane Caroline, da of Lawrence Reeve, of Sandridge Lodge, Bromham, Wilts, and has had issue (by 1st *m*), †Alexander, *b* 1963; *d* 1985, — Esmond, *b* 1965, — (by 2nd *m*) George William Hugh, *b* 1990, — Violet Elizabeth Marion, *b* 1988.

SISTERS LIVING

Lady Bridget, *b* 1921: *m* 1st, 1944, Lt-Col James Averell Clark, Jun, DFC, USAAF, who *d* 1990; 2ndly, 1954 (*m diss* 1963), Major Henry Claude Lyon Garnett, CBE, who *d* 1990; 3rdly, 1966 (*m diss* 1970), Major (Edward) Peter Godfrey Miller Mundy, MC, who *d* 1981, and has issue living (by 1st *m*), Christopher (Crow Hall Farm, Denver, Norfolk PE38 0DG), *b* 1949: *m* 1986, Alice, only da of late Thomas Auckland Hall, of the Old Hall, Rockland St Mary, Norwich, and has issue living, Thomas Averell *b* 1987, James Auckland *b* 1994, Scarlett Alexandra *b* 1989. *Residence* – The Dower House, Crow Hall Farm, Denver, Norfolk.

Lady Willa, *b* 1924: *m* 1946, Major George David Chetwode, MBE, Coldstream Guards, and has issue (*see* B Chetwode, colls). *Residence* – Swiss Farm House, Upper Slaughter, Cheltenham, Glos GL54 2JP.

COLLATERAL BRANCHES LIVING

Grandson of late Hon Arthur Ralph Douglas Elliot, 2nd son of 3rd Earl:—
Issue of late Capt Hubert William Arthur Elliot, *b* 1891, *d* 1967: *m* 1st, 1919, Mary Hester, who *d* 1945, da of late Hon Sir Langer Meade Loftus Owen, CBE, KC, formerly Ch Judge in Divorce, Supreme Court of NSW; 2ndly, 1955, Mrs Pamela Violet Cathcart, who *d* 1996, da of late Lt-Col Patrick Douglas Stirling, OBE, MC, JP, of Kippendavie, and formerly wife of Lt-Col Charles Frederick Cathcart, DSO (*see* E Cathcart, colls):—
(By 1st *m*) John William Owen (Old House Farm, Cockfield, Bury St Edmunds, Suffolk), *b* 1921; *ed* Eton, and Trin Coll, Camb; Capt late Scots Gds: *m* 1944, Mary Norah, da of late Hon (Godfrey) John Arthur Murray Lyle Mulholland, MC (*see* B Dunleath, colls), and has issue living, Hugh John (1207 Gladstone Place, Alexandria, Virginia, USA), *b* 1946; *ed* Eton, and Gonville and Caius Coll, Camb (MA): *m* 1987, Mary Anna, da of John Portner, of Washington DC, USA, — Timothy David (Hessett, nr Bury St Edmunds, Suffolk) *b* 1952; *ed* Eton, and Bristol Univ: *m* 1975 (*m diss* 1989), Helen Margaret, da of Michael Graham Lacey, of Honycombe House, Weare Giffard, Bideford, N Devon, and has issue living, Robert John *b* 1977, Michael David *b* 1982, Rebecca Frances *b* 1979, — Susan Mary *b* 1948: *ed* Goldsmith's Coll, London Univ (DipEd): *m* 1969, Patrick Gilbert Dominick Toriglioni del Cassero-Nisbett, Gren Gds, of Wood Hall, Little Waldingfield, Suffolk, and has issue living, Dominick Gilbert *b* 1972, Hugo Alexander *b* 1977, Edmond Dudley *b* 1982, Olivia Eleanora *b* 1975.

Granddaughter of late Hugh Samuel Roger Elliot, son of late Hon Hugh Frederick Hislop Elliot, 3rd son of 3rd Earl:—
Issue of late Herbert Hugh Elliot, Pilot Officer RAF, *b* 1909, *k* on active ser 1942: *m* 1939, Kate Marjorie, who *d* 1972, da of late Rev Vernon Iles, of South Marston, Swindon, Wilts:—
Patricia, *b* 1940: *m* 1964, Maj Ieuan Davies, 11th Hussars, who *d* 1998. *Residence* – Fistral, Southway, Windmill, Padstow, Cornwall PL28 8RZ.

Granddaughter of late Rt Hon Sir Henry George Elliot, GCB, 2nd son of 2nd Earl:—
Issue of late Sir Francis Edmund Hugh Elliot, GCMG, GCVO, *b* 1851, *d* 1940: *m* 1881, Henrietta Augusta Mary, who *d* 1938, da of late Rt Hon Sir Francis Clare Ford, PC, GCB, GCMG:—
Dorothy, *b* 1888: *m* 1914, Henry Montesquieu Anthony, CBE, who *d* 1949, and has issue living, Lydia Margaret Elliot, *b* 1918. *Residence* – 14 Princes St, S Exeter.

Grandchildren of late Gilbert Compton Elliot (*infra*):—
Issue of late Maj Alexander Henry Elliot, RA, *b* 1913, *d* 1986: *m* 1937, Lady Ann Child-Villiers (Broadford, Chobham, Surrey), da of 8th Earl of Jersey:—
Gilbert Francis, *b* 1949. —— Victoria Cynthia, *b* 1938: *m* 1960, John Robert Hunter, RN (ret), of Minto, Mount Rankin, Bathurst, NSW 2795, Australia, and has issue living, David John, *b* 1961: *m* 19—, Trish, da of Richard Law, and has issue living, Peter *b* 19—, Jessica Margaret *b* 1996, — James Max, *b* 1963, — Michael Alexander, *b* 1965, — Andrew William, *b* 1976. —— Patricia Joan (Selwood Cottage, Odiham, Hants), *b* 1940: *m* 1964 (*m diss* 1986), David John Curry, RAF, and has issue living, Alexander David Ian, *b* 1974, — Georgina Sophie Gay, *b* 1967.

Granddaughter of late Frederick Boileau Elliot, son of late Adm Hon Sir George Elliot, KCB, MP, 2nd son of 1st Earl:—
Issue of late Gilbert Compton Elliot, *b* 1871, *d* 1931: *m* 1910, Marguerita, who *d* 1955, da of late Henry Barbey, of New York:—
Cynthia Sophie, BEM (c/o Chase Manhatten Bank, Tortola, British Virgin Islands), *b* 1916; whilst herself a prisoner, rendered sers to prisoners in hospitals in Germany during 1939-45 War (BEM): *m* 1st, 1944, 1st Baron Hore-Belisha, who *d* 1957; 2ndly, 1957, Maj Ian Victor Major, DSC, RM (ret), who *d* 1973.

Grandchildren of late Dudley Sinclair Elliot, eldest son of late Capt Charles Sinclair Elliot, RN (*infra*):—
Issue of late Dudley Charles Howard Elliot, *b* 1918, *d* 1990: *m* 1943, Rosalie Yvonne, da of late Francis Walter Vizard, of S Australia:—
Gilbert Dennis (19 Wilga St, Concord West, NSW 2138, Australia), *b* 1947; *ed* NSW Univ: *m* 1973, Jane, da of John Guinane, of NSW, and has issue living, Robert Gilbert Sinclair, *b* 1979, — Gerard Charles Cameron, *b* 1982, — Lenore Elizabeth, *b* 1977. —— Victor Roderick (14 Dune St, Fingal Head, NSW 2487, Australia), *b* 1950. —— Hugh Kent (Honeydew Mountain, 2 Jerry Creek Rd, Langshaw, via Gympie, Queensland 4570, Australia), *b* 1953. —— Roslyn Kristin, *b* 1944: *m* 1966, Ronald Charles Newland, of 1B Oratava Av, W Pennant Hills, NSW 2120, Australia, and has issue.

Grandchildren of late Capt Charles Sinclair Elliot, RN, 3rd and yst son of late Capt Amyand Powney Charles Elliot, 3rd son of late Hon John Edmund Elliot, MP, 3rd son of 1st Earl:—
Issue of late Maj Alban Charles Elliot, MC, AIF, *b* 1892, *d* 1978: *m* 1919, Fanny Compton, who *d* 1974, da of Francis Henry Atherton, of Gympie, Queensland, and of Taunton, Som:—
Charles Atherton (Pathfield, Bells Line of Rd, Bilpin, NSW 2758, Australia), *b* 1921; *ed* Sydney Univ (LLB): 1939-45 War with AIF in New Guinea: *m* 1955, Doris May, da of late William Edward Pritchard, RWF, of Denbigh, N Wales, and has issue living, Timothy Charles, *b* 1960, — Owen Francis, *b* 1963. —— Eileen (79 Gordon St, Manly Vale, NSW 2093, Australia), *b* 1924; served in World War II with AWAS in New Guinea: *m* 1947, Alasdair David Thomson, who *d* 1993, and has issue living, Peter David, *b* 1948, — Ian Charles, *b* 1953, — John Elliot, *b* 1958, — Patricia Eileen, *b* 1951. —— Hilary, *b* 1927; served in World War II with AWAS: *m* 1952, Denys Eric Head, of 6 Greenacres, Crooksbury Rd, Runfold, Farnham, Surrey GU10 1QU, and has issue living, Roger Denys, *b* 1957, — Lynette Ann, *b* 1954, — Gillian Margaret, *b* 1955.

Grandchildren of late Ninian Lowis Elliot, 3rd son (by 1st *m*) of Augustus John Elliot (*infra*):—
Issue of late Lieut-Com Archibald Guthrie Elliot, RN, *b* 1898, *d* 1931: *m* 1929, Evelyn Agnes, who *d* 1965, da of late Alexander Buchanan:—
John Alexander Ninian (Portman's Bridge, Box 6, Gilgil, Kenya), *b* 1930: *m* 1962, Jean Patricia, da of Arthur Willis Winfield Sale, of Pulborough, Sussex. —— Margaret Dolores, *b* (*posthumous*) 1931: *m* 1953, Timothy Romer Matthews,

of 7 Chislehurst Rd, Richmond, Surrey, and has issue living, Sophia Elizabeth b 1955: m 1982, William Gerald Kelly, of The Mall, Ramelton, co Donegal.

Grandchildren of late Archibald Campbell Elliot, 4th son (by 1st m) of Augustus John Elliot (infra):—
Issue of late Lt-Col Augustus John Elliot, IA, b 1901, d 1979: m 1st, 1930 (m diss 1946), Theodora Dorothy, who d 1982, da of late Engr-Cdr T. G. R. Harvey, RIM Bombay (ret); 2ndly, 1946, Ilona (who m 2ndly, 1980, Arthur Douglas Ingrams, who d 1988, of Martins, Furley, Axminster, Devon), da of late Frederic Charles Wilson Bindley, of Eastbourne:—
(By 1st m) Archibald Keith (78 Howard Rd, Queens Park, Bournemouth), b 1932; RAF (ret): m 1957, Pauline Mary, da of late Cecil Edwin Pearman Parker, of Watford, Herts, and has issue living, Ross Ian, b 1958, — Clive Graham, b 1960: m 1993, Helena Mary, da of Denis Martin Prendergast, of co Kerry, and has issue living, Jasmine Portia b 1994. — Angus Ian (Gorse Cottage, 82 Coleshill Rd, Marston Green, Birmingham 37), b 1937: m 1959, Carol Ann, da of William Henry Evans, and has issue living, Mark Keith, b 1960, — Jamie Ian, b 1964. —— Betty Anne, b 1933: m 1956, Capt Jeffrey Edward Power Browning, 8th King's R Irish Hus (ret), of The Grange, Worlingworth, Woodbridge, Suffolk, and has issue living, Charles Richard Power, b 1957: m 1993, Kate Borwick, — Alastair Jeffrey Power, b 1960, — Philippa Anne Campbell, b 1963: m 1994, Timothy John Inskip, — Joanna Elizabeth Newcombe, b 1967.

Grandchildren of late Augustus John Elliot, 4th son of late Hon John Edmund Elliot, MP (ante):—
Issue of late Gilbert Augustus Elliot, b 1873, d 1959: m 1905, Phyllis Baret, who d 1972, da of late Major Edward William Stokes, 4th King's Own Regt, of Ellel Hall Lancaster:—
Gilbert Cecil Ninian b 1907: m 1942, Esther Rosamond, who d 1987, da of late Capt Hugh Alfred Cholmley (see V Hill, colls, 1969 Edn), and has issue living, Gilbert Hugh Cholmley (22 Limewood Close, St Johns, Woking, Surrey), b 1947; ed St Peter's Sch, York: m 1979, Beryl Breakspear, and has issue living, Jonathan b 1983, Rebecca b 1980, — Rowland George Cholmley (2 Old Earswick Village, York), b 1949: m 1986, Ruth Skovgaard, of Bornholm, Denmark, and has issue living, Samuel Gilbert b 1990, Hanna Rosamond b 1988, Marianne Esther b 1995, — Jane, b 1943: m 1st, 1963 (m diss 1985), Maj Iain Alastair McKay, Scots Gds; 2ndly, 1995, David John Ewart, of Court Hill House, Potterne, Devizes, Wilts SN10 5PN, and has issue living (by 1st m), Alastair James Mark b 1963: m 1993, Susan Lee (and has issue living, Peter James b 1997, Eleanor Jane b 1995), Andrew Simon Charles b 1970, Catriona Jane b 1966: m 1995, Phillip Littlehales (and has issue living, Sarah Matilda b 1996, Jemima Jessica b 1999), Arabella Charlotte b 1968, — Lorna (Foxhanger Cottage, Priorsfield Rd, Godalming, Surrey GU7 2RG), b 1945: m 1967 (m diss 1991), John Edward Clive, and has issue living, Simon John David b 1970, Edward Thomas b 1974, Sarah Margarita b 1968. —— Daphne Patricia, b 1917: m 1949, Capt Godfrey Carrington Royle, RA (TA), of Home Farm, Balscote, nr Banbury, Oxon OX15 6JP.

(In remainder to Baronetcy only)

Grandson of late Frederick Augustus Hugh Elliot, CIE, el son of late Edward Francis Elliot, 2nd son of late Rt Hon Hugh Elliot, 2nd son of 3rd baronet:—
Issue of late Lieut-Col Edward Halhed Hugh Elliot, DSO, b 1876, d as a result of enemy action 1944: m 1911, Ethel Winifred, who d 19-, da of late John Fair:—
Frederick John Hugh, b 1914.

PREDECESSORS – (1) GILBERT Elliot, KT, having been under forfeiture 1685-90 as an accessory to the Rebellion of 1679, received Knighthood; was afterwards Clerk to PC, MP for Roxburghshire 1702-7, and a Lord of Session (as Lord Minto); cr a Baronet 1700, with remainder to his heirs male; d 1718; s by his son (2) Sir GILBERT, 2nd Bt; MP for Roxburghshire 1722-7; was a Lord of Session (as Lord Minto) 1726-33, a Lord of Justiciary 1733-63, and Lord Justice Clerk 1763-6, d 1766; s by his son (3) Sir GILBERT, 3rd Bt, MP for co Selkirk 1753-65, and for Roxburghshire 1765-77; was Lord of the Admiralty 1756, Treasurer of the Chamber 1762, Keeper of the Signes in Scotland 1767, and Treasurer of the Navy 1770; d 1777; s by his son (4) Sir GILBERT, 4th Bt; MP for co Roxburgh 1777-84, and for Helston 1790-5; was Viceroy of Corsica 1795-7, Envoy Extraor to Vienna 1799, Pres of Board of Control India 1806, and Gov-Gen of Bengal 1807-13; assumed by Roy licence 1797 the additional surnames of Murray-Kynynmound after that of Elliot; cr Baron Minto, of Minto, co Roxburgh (peerage of Great Britain) 1797, and Viscount Melgund and Earl of Minto (peerage of United Kingdom) 1813; d 1814; s by his son (5) GILBERT, 2nd Earl, GCB, PC; b 1782; was MP for Roxburghshire 1812-14, Ambassador to Berlin 1833-4, First Lord to the Admiralty 1835-41, and Lord Privy Seal 1846-52: m 1806, Mary, who d 1853, da of Patrick Brydone, of Lennel House, Berwick; d 1859; s by his son (6) WILLIAM HUGH, KT, 3rd Earl, b 1814; MP for Hythe (L) 1837-41, for Greenock 1847-52, and for Clackmannanshire 1857-9: m 1844, Emma Eleanor Elizabeth, who d 1882, heiress of Gen Sir Thomas Hislop, Bt (ext); d 1891; s by his el son (7) GILBERT JOHN, KG, GCSI, GCMG, GCIE, PC, 4th Earl; b 1845; was Gov-Gen of Canada 1898-1904, and Viceroy and Gov-Gen of India 1905-10: m 1883, Mary Caroline, CI, who d 1940, da of late Gen Hon Charles Grey; d 1914; s by his el son (8) VICTOR GILBERT LARISTON GARNET, 5th Earl, b 1891; Capt Scots Gds: m 1921, Marion, OBE, who d 1974, da of George William Cook, of Montreal; d 1975; s by his el son (9) GILBERT EDWARD GEORGE LARISTON, 6th Earl and present peer; also Viscount Melgund, and Baron Minto.

MISHCON, BARON (Mishcon) (Life Baron 1978)

VICTOR MISHCON, son of Rabbi Arnold Mishcon; *b* 14 Aug 1915; *ed* City of London Sch; Solicitor 1937; Consultant to Mishcon De Reya, Member of Nat Theatre Board 1965-90, and of South Bank Theatre Board 1977-82; former Chm LCC and various Cttees; former Chm General Purposes Cttee GLC; former Chm Finance Cttee of Lambeth Borough Council; former Member House of Lords European Community Cttee, and of Lords Standing Joint Cttee with Commons on Consolidation of Bills; Vice-Chm Law Society All Parliamentary Gp; Official Opposition Spokesman on Home Affairs and Legal Matters; Member of various Govt Departmental Cttees; Member of Select Cttee of House of Lords on Medical Ethics 1993-94; QC (Hon); Hon LLD Birmingham; Hon Fell of Univ Coll, London; DL for Greater London; Cdr Order of North Star of Sweden and Star of Ethiopia, Star of Jordan (1st class); *cr Baron Mishcon*, of Lambeth, Greater London (Life Baron) 1978: *m* 1976, Joan Estelle, da of Bernard Monty, and has issue by former *m* to Beryl Honor, da of J. E. Posnansky.

Arms – Per pale argent and azure between in chief and in base bar gennel wavy counterchanged a tent per pale azure and argent lined gules. Crest – Upon a wreath argent and azure a lion or and a lamb proper rampant and supporting between them a sword erect gules the pommel resting on a book bound azure edged and garnished gold. Supporters – *Dexter*, a lamb reguardant proper gorged with a collar gules with flames issuing above and below proper; *sinister*, a lion reguardant or gorged with a Saxon crown azure. Motto – Dwell in peace.
Address – House of Lords, Westminster, SW1.

SONS LIVING (By former m)

Hon Peter Arnold, *b* 1946: *m* 1967, Penny Green, and has issue living, Oliver, *b* 1968, — Anna, *b* 1972, — Kate, *b* 1973, — Eliza, *b* 1977.
Hon Russell Orde (Wick Lodge, Englefield Green, Surrey TW20 0HJ), *b* 1948; *ed* City of London Sch: *m* 1975, Marcia Regina Leigh, and has issue living, Joel, *b* 1977, — Portia, *b* 1979—Honor Meg, *b* 1991.

DAUGHTER LIVING (By former m)

Hon Jane Malca, *b* 1950: *m* 1st, 1971 (*m diss* 1979), Anthony Jay; 2ndly, 1990, Edward Landau, and has issue living (by 1st *m*), Adam, *b* 1972, — Lucy, *b* 1974.

MITCHISON, BARONY OF (Mitchison) (Extinct 1970)

SONS LIVING OF LIFE BARON

Hon Denis Anthony, CMG (14 Marlborough Rd, Richmond, Surrey), *b* 1919; *ed* Abbotsholme Sch, and Trin Coll, Camb (MB, ChB), FRCP London, FRCPath; Emeritus Prof of Bacteriology, London Univ; *m* 1st, 1940, Ruth Sylvia, MB, BCh, da of Hubert Gill; 2ndly, 1993, Honora, da of Christopher Carlin, and has issue (by 1st *m*) two sons and two das.
Hon (John) Murdoch (Great Yew, Ormiston, E Lothian EH35 5NJ), *b* 1922; FRS, FRSE; *ed* Winchester, and Trin Coll, Camb (MA, ScD); Prof of Zoology, Edinburgh Univ 1963-88; mem of Roy Commission on Environmental Pollution 1974-79 and the Science Board SRC 1976-79: *m* 1947, Rosalind Mary, da of Edward Murray Wrong, of Toronto, and has issue one son and three das.
Hon Nicholas Avrion (14 Belitha Villas, N1), *b* 1928; FRS; Prof of Zoology, London Univ: *m* 1958, Lorna Margaret, da of Maj-Gen John Simson Stuart Martin, CSI, of Husabost, by Dunvegan, Isle of Skye, and has issue two sons and three das.

DAUGHTERS LIVING OF LIFE BARON

Hon (Sonja) Lois, *b* 19-: *m* 1959, John Godfrey, and has issue two das.
Hon Valentine Harriet Isabella Dione *b* 1930: *m* 1955, Mark Arnold-Forster, DSO, DSC, who *d* 1981, of 11 Kingsbridge Rd, W10, and has issue three sons and two das.

Mitford, family name of Baron Redesdale.

MOLESWORTH, VISCOUNT (Molesworth) (Viscount I 1716)

ROBERT BYSSE KELHAM MOLESWORTH, 12th Viscount; *b* 4 June 1959; *s* 1997; *ed* Cheltenham, and Sussex Univ (BA).

𝕬rms – Gules, an escutcheon vair, within an orle of eight cross-crosslets or. 𝕮rest – A dexter arm embowed in armour proper, holding a cross crosslet or. 𝕾upporters – *Dexter*, a pegasus argent, wings elevated or; *sinister*, a pegasus, wings elevated gules, semée of cross crosslets or.
Residence – Garden Flat, 2 Bishopswood Rd, Highgate, N6.

BROTHER LIVING

Hon WILLIAM JOHN CHARLES, *b* 20 Oct 1960; *ed* Cheltenham, and Trin Coll, Camb (MA); LTCL.

COLLATERAL BRANCHES LIVING

Branch from 8th Viscount

Issue of late Hon Arthur Ernest Parnell Molesworth, 3rd son of 8th Viscount, *b* 1870, *d* 1951: *m* 1910, Nellie Maud, JP, who *d* 1956, da of George W. Banks, formerly of Wellington, New Zealand, and widow of Dr George Watson, of S America:—

†Frank Ernest Bysse, *b* 1911: *m* 1st, 1934 (*m diss* 1940), Phyllis Margaret Patrick, da of late George Wells; 2ndly, 1943 (*m diss* 1957), Joan, JP, da of A. G. Lethbridge, of Thames Valley and Taranaki, NZ; 3rdly, 1961, Nellie Verdun, da of late Edward Hughes, of Hikurangi, NZ; 4th, 1982, Bernice Sheila Polden Bell, 7th da of George Augustus Hawkes, of NZ, and *d* 1998, leaving issue, (by 3rd *m*) Helen Deirdre Velvet, *b* 1962: *m* 1995, Chris O'Donnell, of NZ, and has issue living, Conor *b* 1996, Eamon *b* 1998. Mrs O'Donnell also has issue, Jamie *b* 1981, Alice *b* 1986. *Address* – 30 Chorley Ave, Massey, Auckland 8, NZ. ⸺ Betty Eleanor Gosset, OBE (Los Barrios, Cadiz Province, Andalucia, Spain), *b* 1913; OBE (Civil) 1998: *m* 1948, Frank Geoffrey Harald Allen, late Wing-Cdr RAFVR, who *d* 1985.

Branch from brother of 7th Viscount

Grandson of late Lionel Charles Molesworth, 3rd but only surv son of late Maj Richard Molesworth, eldest son of late Capt Hon Anthony Oliver Molesworth, RA, 3rd brother of 7th Viscount:—
Issue of late Col Roger Bevil Molesworth, RA (ret), *b* 1901, *d* 1974: *m* 1929, Iris, who *d* 1977, da of late Lt-Col Roger Lloyd Kennion, CIE, of Durford Wood, Petersfield:—
Allen Henry Neville (31 Norland Sq, W11 4PU), *b* 1931: *m* 1970, Gail Cheng Kwai, LRAM, ARCM, LGSM, da of I. C. Chan, of 10 Holland Rise, Singapore 10.

Granddaughter of late Col William Molesworth, CIE, CBE, MB, eldest son of late Lt-Col Anthony Oliver Molesworth (infra):—
Issue of late Lieut-Col William Earle Molesworth, MC, *b* 1894, *d* 1955: *m* 1918, Dorothy Loftus, who *d* 1985, da of late Col St George Loftus Steele, CB, of Cheltenham:—
Pamela, *b* 1919: *m* 1950, Robert Anthony Langham, and has issue living, Peter Anthony (Silverdale, Woodmead Rd, Lyme Regis, Dorset), *b* 1953: *m* 1983, Cynthia Maynard, and has issue living, Catherine *b* 1984, — Susan Marie, *b* 1951: *m* 1982, Raymond Purdy, of 100 Upper North St, Brighton, Sussex, and has issue living, Daniel *b* 1982, Lara *b* 1985. *Residence* – 19 Alexandra Rd, Reading, Berks.

Grandchildren living of late Hugh Wilson Molesworth, CBE (infra)—
Issue of late Hugh Mervyn Molesworth, *b* 1907, *d* 1980: *m* 1st, 1934 (*m diss* 1936), Mary Langhorne, yr da of Harry Langhorne Johnson, CBE, of Hurst Copthorne; 2ndly, 1939, Enid Mary, who *d* 1969, da of late John Utrick Roger Grave, AMICE, of Manchester:—
(By 2nd *m*) Roger (Little Jordans, Colgate, Sussex), *b* 1945; *ed* Marlborough: *m* 1974, Pauline Fay, da of Philip Hunt, of Wood Green, N22. ⸺ Donald (Balmoral, Benenden, Kent), *b* 1948; *ed* Embley Park: *m* 1982, Charlotte Rosalie Penelope, da of J. W. K. Cox, of Green Lane Farm, Challock, Kent.

Issue of late Lt-Col Denys Hope Molesworth, MC, RA, *b* 1910, *d* 1989: *m* 1945, Dorothy May, who *d* 1984, yr da of late William C. Johnston, of Calcutta, India:—
Gillian Tessa, *b* 1946: *m* 1972, Juan Planells, of Ibiza, and has issue living, Nicolas Juan, *b* 1973, — Emma Maria, *b* 1976, — Sara Luisa, *b* 1980. ⸺ Jennifer Margaret, *b* 1948: *m* 1984, Farad Azima, of 9 Madingley Rd, Cambridge, and has issue living, Cyrus Alexander, *b* 1985, — Artemis Natasha, *b* 1986.

Grandchildren of late Lieut-Col Anthony Oliver Molesworth, 4th son of late Capt Hon Anthony Oliver Molesworth, RA (ante):—
Issue of late Hugh Wilson Molesworth, CBE, *b* 1870, *d* 1959: *m* 1903, Dora Hanbury, who *d* 1972, only da of late Maj Sir (Robert) Hanbury Brown, KCMG, of Newlands, Crawley Down, Sussex:—
Eileen Rose, *b* 1904: *m* 1931, Lt-Col Basil Woods Ballard, CIE, MBE, Indian Army (Political Ser), and has issue living, Timothy John (Harpsden Grange, Harpsden Way, Henley, Oxon), *b* 1932; *ed* Marlborough, and Sydney Sussex Coll, Camb (MA); FICE: *m* 1964, Helen Mary Christopherson, and has issue living, Patrick Robert *b* 1975, Bridget Anne *b* 1970, Jennifer Clare *b* 1971, — William Richard (Olivers Cottage, Capel St Mary, Suffolk), *b* 1933: *ed* Marlborough, and Coll of Aeronautics, Cranfield (MSc); CEng, MIMechE: *m* 1967, Marianne Jean Elspeth, da of late Lt-Col Hugh Arbuthnott (*see* V Arbuthnott colls), and has issue living, Hugh William *b* 1968; *ed* Aberdeen Univ (MA): *m* 1998, Rebecca Hardisty, Andrew James *b* 1976; *ed* Edinburgh Univ (BSc). *Residence* – Shepherds Oak, Crawley Down, Sussex.

Issue of late Col Francis Crofton Molesworth, late RE, *b* 1880, *d* 1955: *m* 1913, Eileen, who *d* 1951, da of late Lieut-Col Richard Denny (Denny, Bt, colls):—
Richard Denny (25 Naunton Way, Cheltenham, Glos GL53 7BQ) *b* 1919; *m* 1972, Eva Emily Elizabeth Bowler. —— Stephen Lindsay (11 Chetwood Rd, NW5), *b* 1925; 1939-45 War (wounded, despatches); is an ARIBA: *m* 1959, Eve Lovie, and has issue living, Ivan Alexander, *b* 1964, — Anna Cordelia, *b* 1960, — Polly, *b* 1967. —— Beatrix, *b* 1917. *Address* – Chapel Garth, Galphay, Ripon, Yorks.

Grandchildren of late Maj Ernest Kerr Molesworth, 3rd son of late Lt-Col Anthony Oliver Molesworth (ante):—
Issue of late Brownlow David Molesworth, OBE, MRCS, LRCP, *b* 1913, *d* 1986: *m* 1939, Rosemary Katharine, who *d* 1989, da of Lt-Col A. W. Moore, RAMC:—
Patrick David, *b* 1946: *m* 1974, Sheila Doreen Cooling, and has issue living, Peter Patrick, *b* 1983, — Ian David, *b* 1985. —— Anthony Simon, *b* 1955. —— Jenifer Rosemary, *b* 1940: *m* 1960, Peter David Rohde, FRCPsych, FRCP Ed, of 84 Burbage Rd, SE24, and has issue living, Simon Peter, *b* 1962: *m* 1988, Juliette Ann Louise Hinchliff, and has issue living, Florence Rebecca *b* 1992, — Katherine Leslie, *b* 1963: *m* 1991, Paul Simon Bogan, and has issue living, Raphael David *b* 1993. —— Sheila, *b* 1942: *m* 1967, (Charles) Jeremy Harvey, MA, of Obridge House, Obridge Rd, Taunton, Som TA2 7QA, and has issue living, Benjamin David, *b* 1972, — Rachel Claire, *b* 1969, — Joanna Elizabeth, *b* 1970.

Granddaughter of late Rev Anthony Oliver Molesworth, 5th son of Lt-Col Anthony Oliver Molesworth (ante):—
Issue of late Group Capt Anthony Oliver Molesworth, RAF, *b* 1908, *k* on active ser 1944: *m* 1933, Noëlle, who *d* 1999, da of late John Richard Holmes, formerly Pres of District Court, Cyprus:—
Dawn Noëlle, *b* 1934: *m* 1955, Simon Jerrard Findlay Muirhead, of 61, Merton Hall Rd, Wimbledon, SW19 3PR, and has issue living, Anthony Oliver Molesworth (3777 Caribeth Drive, Encino, CA 91436, USA), *b* 1957; *ed* Edinburgh Univ (MA): *m* 1985, Cora Ann, only child of Martin D. Seiler, of Studio City, California, USA, and has issue living, Molly Laura *b* 1991, — Lauriston Philip (409 Nowland Av, Lavington, NSW 2641, Australia), *b* 1959; *ed* Newcastle Univ (BSc): *m* 1984, Katherine Barbara, da of late John Rutty, of Kuantan, Malaya, and has issue living, Dauntie Claire *b* 1989, — Imogen Jane, *b* 1963; *ed* Edinburgh Univ (MA, MSc).

Branch from 4th son of 1st Viscount

Granddaughter of late James Murray Molesworth, 3rd son of late Rev William Nassau Molesworth, LLD, eldest son of late Rev John Edward Nassau Molesworth, DD, el son of late John Molesworth, elder son of late Major Hon Edward Molesworth, 4th son of 1st Viscount:—
Issue of late Robert Murray Nassau Molesworth, *b* 1895, *d* 1976: *m* 1st, 1916 (*m diss* 1925), Lucie Amy Gertrude, who *d* 1971, da of late Edward Lawrence, of Clifton, Bristol; 2ndly, 1926, Nora Madelene, da of William John Connell, of Sparkhill, Birmingham; 3rdly, 1955, Clare, widow of T. W. Price:—
(By 2nd *m*) Emily Patricia, *b* 1927: *m* 19—, — Reid.

Grandchildren of late William Nassau Molesworth, 5th son of late Rev William Nassau Molesworth, LLD (ante):—
Issue of late Major William Nassau Molesworth, MC, Manchester Regt, *b* 1888, *d* 1959: *m* 1917, Hester Winifred, who *d* 1966, da of late Alfred Watkin, of Danebank, Lymm:—
Rev Canon Anthony Edward Nassau (3 Barrow Hill, Stourton Caundle, Sturminster Newton, Dorset DT10 2LD), *b* 1923; *ed* Haileybury, and Pembroke Coll, Camb (MA) and at Coll of Resurrection, Mirfield; Canon of Pro-Cathedral of St Michael, Eshowe, Zululand 1963-68, and of Dioc of Swaziland 1968-71 (Canon Emeritus of Swaziland); Commissary to Bishop of Swaziland 1973, Rector of Charlton Musgrove with Stoke Trister and Cucklington 1984-90: *m* 1969, Susan, SRN, yr da of Prof H. R. B. Fenn, of Weald, Sevenoaks, Kent, and has issue living, Hugh William Nassau, *b* 1972, — Anna Margaret, *b* 1970. —— Gwendolen Clara Nassau (*Lady Lloyd*), *b* 1919; 1939-45 War in WAAF: *m* 1947, Sir (John) Peter (Daniel) Lloyd, who *d* 1996, and has issue living, David William Molesworth (108 Wellington St, Mundingburra, Queensland 4812), *b* 1950: *m* 1977, Deborah Armstrong, who *d* 1994, and has issue living, Carson James *b* 1978, Zoë *b* 1980, — John Peter Anthony (16A Kalamajere Drive, Suffolk Park, NSW 2481), *b* 1956, — Judith Mary (16 Maroona St, E Malvern, Victoria 3145), *b* 1947: *m* 1st, 1968 (*m diss* 1975), Robert Anthony Hyndes; 2ndly, 1977 (*m diss* 1984), John Paul Kent, and has issue living (by 1st *m*), Anthony Peter *b* 1968, — Angela Hester Olwen, *b* 1940: *m* 1st, 1971, John Gipps Knox-Knight, who *d* 1979; 2ndly, 1983, David Robert Langley, of Hawthorn Park, Chanters Lane, Tylden, Victoria 3444, and has issue living (by 1st *m*), Lucy Charlotte *b* 1974, Emily Sarah *b* 1976 (by 2nd *m*), Jessica Penelope *b* 1984, — Penelope, *b* 1953: *m* 1976, Adam Thomson, and *d* 1996, leaving issue, Edward William *b* 1986, Hugh Lloyd *b* 1988, Alice Clara Margaret *b* 1992, — Sarah Jane LLOYD (RSD 999A, Birralee, Tas 7303), *b* 1955; has resumed her maiden name: *m* 1978 (*m diss* 1981), Robert Sheehy, and has issue living, Nicholas *b* 1979. *Residence* – 90 Carrington St, Macedon, Victoria 3440, Australia.

Grandson of late Maj John Davenport Newall Molesworth, MC, Royal Corps of Signals (TA), 3rd and yst son of late Frederick Nassau Molesworth, 2nd son of John Molesworth (*b* 1818), 2nd son of Rev John Edward Nassau Molesworth, DD (ante):—
Issue of late W/Cmdr John Henry Nassau Molesworth, DSO, DFC, AFC, *b* 1913, *d* 1994: *m* 1946, Pamela Joan (Beehive Cottage, Eltisley, St Neots, Cambs PE16 4TH), da of late Frederick William Guildford, of Ramsgate, Kent:—

Peter John Norman (20 Elgin Park, Bristol BS6 6RX), b 1956; ed Oakham Sch, and Newcastle Univ (BSc); late Capt Green Howards; Capt Yorks Vol: m 1990, Julie A., da of Vince Wicks, of Cairns, Australia, and has issue living, John Henry, b 1994, — Frances Jane, b 1992.

Grandchildren of late John Molesworth (b 1858), 3rd son of late John Molesworth (b 1818), 2nd son of late Rev John Edward Nassau Molesworth, DD (ante):—
Issue of late John Molesworth, b 1894, d 1971; m 1927, Dorothy Josephine Mudge (205 Foley St, Junction, Texas, USA):—
John Mudge (PO Box 104, Junction, Texas 76849, USA), b 1928: m 1951, Joanne Hill, of New York, USA, and has issue living, John, b 1952, — Lynn Hill, b 1955, — Cynthia, b 1953. —— Fred (Route 3, Box 437B, Amarillo, Texas 79107, USA), b 1931: m 1962, Ann Spoon, of Memphis, Texas, and has issue living, Fred Vance, b 1963. —— Dorothy Patricia, b 1929: m 1949, William Eugene Craft, of Drawer M, Clarendon, Texas 79226, USA, and has issue living, William Patrick, b 1952, — John Robert, b 1962, — Catherine, b 1950: m 1974, John Throckmorton Keene, of 222 Halcyon, San Antonio, Texas 78209, USA, and has issue living, Kathleen b 1977, — Christine, b 1957.

Granddaughter of late John Molesworth (b 1818) (ante):—
Issue of Lawrence Teesdale Molesworth, b 1864, d 1941: m 1893, Anna Maria Caroline Wallace, who d 1933, da of G. S. Bournes, of Rossport, Belmullet, co Mayo:—
Margaret Patricia Newall, b 1904: m 1st, 1928, Theophilus Jones, who d 1959; 2ndly 1965, Howard John Bettany, who d 1984, and d 1985, leaving issue, (by 1st m) Theophilus Molesworth RHYS JONES (Ash Cottage, Upper Framilode, Glos), b 1929; ed Kelly Coll, Tavistock: m 1964, Jyllian, da of late John de Vic Carey, of Ash Cottage, Upper Framilode, Glos, and has issue living, Cressida Helen b 1971, — Christopher Bournes RHYS-JONES (Homestead Farmhouse, Palmers Green Lane, Brenchley, Kent), b 1931; ed King's Sch, Bruton: m 1961, Mary, da of late C. T. O'Sullivan, and has issue living, David Bournes b 1963: m 1996, Zara L., elder da of late H. S. Freeland, of Beckley, Sussex (and has issue living, Oliver Hugh b 1999), Sophie Helen (HRH the Countess of Wessex) b 20 Jan 1965: m 19 June 1999, HRH The Prince Edward Antony Richard Louis, Earl of Wessex, CVO, yst son of HM Queen Elizabeth II.

Grandchildren of late Reginald Balfour Molesworth, el son of late Cdr George Mill Frederick Molesworth, 4th son of late Rev John Edward Nassau Molesworth, DD (ante):—
Issue of late Rev Gilbert Edmund Nassau Molesworth, b 1895, d 1976: m 1923, Florence Edith Mary (Berrimans, Northam, Bideford, N Devon), da of late Rev Thomas Fisher Maddrell, V of Gulval, Penzance:—
Michael Nassau (Berrimans, Northam, Bideford, N Devon), b 1924; ed King Edward VI Sch, Birmingham, and Sidney Sussex Coll, Camb (MA); late Sub-Lt RNVR; 1939-45 War: m 1951, Heather, who d 1965, da of late Adm Sir Henry Daniel Pridham-Wippell, KCB, CVO, and has issue living, William Martin Nassau, b 1957, — Peter Timothy Nassau, b 1959, — Susan Claire, b 1961. —— John Edmund Nassau (1 Prospect Place, Sandford, Crediton, Devon EX17 4LR), b 1926; ed King's Sch, Bruton, Sidney Sussex, Coll, Camb, at London Univ, at Middle East Centre of Arab Studies, and at St Luke's Coll, Exeter; Fl-Lt RAF (ret): m 1952, Pamela Anne, da of Harold Richard Summers MacMullen, and has issue living, David Reginald Nassau, b 1953; ed Arborfield Coll, Reading, — Carol Anne (10 Northdown Drive, Bideford, N Devon), b 1956, — Elizabeth Stephanie, b 1958: m 1983, Martin C. Rees, of 104 Banbury Rd, Stratford-upon-Avon, Warwicks, and has issue living, David Benjamin b 1985, Harriet Stephanie b 1990, — Hilary, b 1964: m 1986, Benjamin Reed, of 6 Springfield Terrace, East-the-Water, Bideford, N Devon, son of late Fl Lt Arthur James Broomhall Reed, and has issue living, Jacob b 1988, Thomas b 1990, Hugh b 1992, Hannah b 1986. —— Richard Mark Nassau (9 Webb Farm Rd, Monroe, NY, USA 10950), b 1930; ed King Edward VI Sch, Birmingham, and Birmingham Univ (BSc): m 1958, Margaret Elizabeth, da of George Thomas Alexander Hastings, MD, and has issue living, Philip Nassau, b 1960, — Richard Nassau, b 1962, — John Nassau, b 1963, — William Nassau, b 1971, — Jennifer Ann, b 1959, — Elizabeth Mary, b 1975. —— Elizabeth Raphael, b 1934: m 19-, Duncan Urquhart, of Grays Hills, Fairlie, NZ, and has issue living, Mark Alexander, b 1967, — Roger David, b 1970, — Lorna Mary, b 1966, — Joanna, b 1968.

Granddaughters of late Rev Rennell Francis Wynn Molesworth, 5th son of late Rev John Edward Nassau Molesworth, DD (ante):—
Issue of late Rev John Hilton Molesworth, b 1856, d 1921: m 1908, Everilda Hamer, who d 1928, el da of late Rev Canon James Hamer Rawdon (Hon Canon of Manchester), of The Hermitage, Stockton-on-Forest, York:—
Rachel Frances Hilton, b 1912: m 1936, Commodore Neil Alexander Mackinnon, RAN, who d 1991, and has issue living, Peter William Alexander (The Old Fox, Lewknor, Oxon), b 1938, John Hugh Molesworth (28 Nelson St, Woollahra, NSW 2025, Australia), b 1941; BA Oxon, — Fiona Margaret, b 1946: m 1970, Ian Horsley, of Gundillawah, Adelong, NSW 2729, Australia, and has issue living, Pamela Chloë b 1974, Sarah Rachel b 1976. Residence – The Old Fox, Lewknor, Oxon. —— Cecilia Margaret (Lady Mogg), b 1914: m 1939, Gen Sir (Herbert) John Mogg, GCB, CBE, DSO, DL, and has issue living, Brig John Nigel Ballard (Brightwell Park, Brightwell Baldwin, Oxon), b 1940; MA Cantab; DL Oxon 1998; Brig late RGJ: m 1967, Tessa Elizabeth, da of late F. D. Wright, of Brightwell Park, Brightwell Baldwin, Oxon, and has issue living, John Peter Francis b 1969; BA, ACMA: m 1999, Henrietta Annelie, yr da of Terence Flay, of The Old Cottage, W Green, Hants, Richard Julian Charles b 1971; BSc, — Patrick Henry Molesworth, b 1942, — Rev Timothy David RAWDON-MOGG (St Andrew's Vicarage, Shrivenham, nr Swindon, Wilts), b 1945; ed St John's Coll, Durham (BA): m 1981, Rachel Mary, da of late Ven D. I. T. Eastman, of 43 Clay Lane, Beaminster, Dorset, and has issue living, Christopher James David b 1984, John Charles Timothy (twin) b 1984, Alice Mary b 1982. Residence – Church Close, Watlington, Oxon OX9 5QR.

Grandsons of late Rev Ernest Hilton Molesworth, 3rd son of Rev Rennell Francis Wynn Molesworth (ante):—
Issue of late Eric Mackinnon Molesworth, MB, ChB, b 1890, d 1963: m 1916, Ethel A., who d 1984, da of late Issac Clark Griffith:—
Selwyn Hilton, MRCS, LRCP (Trevelen, Cots Hill, Stratton, Bude, Cornwall), b 1917; ed Epsom Coll, and Manchester Univ; MRCS, LRCP; Lt RA: m 1949, Margaret Seymour, BA, da of late Percy Arthur Smith, of Dormar, Westridge, Bridlington, E Yorks, and has had issue, †Christopher Roger, b 1951; ed Lancaster Royal Gram Sch, and Nottingham Univ: m 1976, Annette Caroline (44 Oliver's Battery Rd North, Winchester, Hants), only da of G. C. Holliday, of 206 Rutland Rd, W Bridgeford, Nottingham, and d as the result of a train accident 1988, leaving issue, Steven Richard b 1981, Caroline Patricia b 1980, — William Hugh, b 1952; ed Lancaster R Gram Sch, St Peter's Coll, Oxford, and The Open Univ (BA Hons): m 1977, Angela Jane Walker, only da of Mrs Doreen Smith, of 35 Kennington Rd, Kennington, Oxford, and has issue living, Thomas Edward Alexander b 1978, Benjamin James b 1985, Emma Catherine Seymour b 1981, — Arthur David, b 1956; ed Shebbear Coll, Bristol Univ, and London Univ (MSc): m 1996, Emma Ruth, da of Angus Mackinnon, of Kettering, Northants, and has issue living, Daniel Thomas Mackinnon b 1986, George Edward Mackinnon b 1989, Joshua William Mackinnon b 1993. —— Rev Robert Mackinnon (RD4 Whangarei, NZ), b 1923; ed Oundle, and

Magdalene Coll, Camb (MA); Lt RNVR (ret) and an ARIBA: *m* 1st, 1947 (*m diss* 1967), Ursula, only da of late Alwin Julius Jaeger, of Thalwil-Zürich, Switzerland; 2ndly, 1967, Mary Craig, el da of late Vice-Adm Sir Maxwell Richmond, KBE, CB, DSO, and has issue living (by 2nd *m*) Peter Maxwell, *b* 1974; *ed* Pompallier Coll, and Massey Univ (BSc), — Elizabeth Anna, *b* 1968; *ed* Whangarei Girls' High Sch, and Cent Inst Tech, Wellington, NZ: *m* 1992, Michael Gregan, and has issue living, Aidan Jack *b* 1998, Sian Catherine *b* 1996, — Catherine Julia, *b* 1969; *ed* Whangarei Girls' High Sch; has issue living (by James Andrew McNamara), Jacob James McNAMARA *b* 1994, Lani Nicole McNAMARA *b* 1998. —— David William (37 Lacy Drive, Wimborne Minster, Dorset BH21 1DG), *b* 1930; *ed* King's Sch, Canterbury; Sqdn-Ldr RAF: *m* 1955, Doreen Joyce, da of George Hunter, of Dunelm, Yarborough Cres, Lincoln, and has issue living, Caroline Shona (22 Chemin des Tieulieres, Montpeyroux 34150, France), *b* 1956; *ed* St Helen's Sch, Abingdon, and Univ Coll Hosp (SRN): *m* 1979, David R. B. Martin, and has issue living, Daniel Russell *b* 1982, Anna Catherine *b* 1986, — Melanie Susan, *b* 1958; *ed* St Helen's Sch, Abingdon: *m* 1987, Martin Gerald Wesley Dennis, eldest son of J. G. W. Dennis, of Malaga, Spain, and has issue living, George Wesley *b* 1988, Ralph Wesley *b* 1992, — Diana Louise (23 Gladstone St, Ringstead, Northants NN14 4DE), *b* 1964; *ed* Pipers Sch, High Wycombe, and St Mary's Hosp (RGN, RSCN): *m* 1989, Roy M. Kirby, PhD, eldest son of T. M. Kirby, of Wimborne, Dorset, and has issue living, Jack William Michael *b* 1992, Harold Alfred Molesworth *b* 1995.

Grandson of late Eric Mackinnon Molesworth (ante):—
Issue of late Lieut (E) Richard Charles Victor Molesworth, RN, *b* 1919, *d* on active ser: *m* 1940, Doreen Mary (who *m* 2ndly, 1967, Bruce Page, of 422 Macquarie St, S Hobart, Tasmania), only da of Joseph Greenwood:—
Eric Richard (422 Macquarie St, S Hobart, Tasmania), *b* 1942; *ed* Christ's Hospital, and Southampton Univ; Master Mariner.

Grandchildren of late Rev Rennell Francis Wynn Molesworth (ante):—
Issue of late Theodore Henderson Molesworth, FRCS, *b* 1872, *d* 1955; *m* 1906, Ethel Alexandra, who *d* 1955, da of late Edward Upton, of The Haven, St Margaret's Bay, near Dover:—
Peter Rennell Henderson (61 Sinah Lane, Hayling Island, Hants PO11 0HJ), MRCS, LRCP, *b* 1923; MRCS England and LRCP London 1946: *m* 1953, Rosemary Ann, da of Cdr R. A. Gould, OBE, RN, of Hayling Island, and has issue living, Simon Peter Henderson (19 The Avenue, Hambrook, Chichester, W Sussex PO18 8TZ) *b* 1954: *m* 1975, Joan Lesley Anderson, and has issue living, Alexis Ralph Henderson *b* 1975, Jason Oliver Henderson *b* 1978, — David Rennell Henderson (Bottle Hill, Hemerdon, Plymouth, Devon), *b* 1955; *ed* Dauntsey's Sch: *m* 1984, Debra C. Dixon, and has issue living, Duncan Richard Henderson *b* 1992, Holly Elizabeth *b* 1993, — Nigel Piers Henderson (70 Vale St, Wilston, Queensland 4051, Australia), *b* 1960; MB BS, DCH, MRCGP; *ed* All Hallows, Lyme Regis, and Middlesex Hosp: *m* 1987, Jane Cecilia, da of Oscar Victor Erzetich, of Brisbane, Qld, and has issue living, Nicholas Oscar Henderson *b* 1992, Emma Jane *b* 1995. —— Joan Frances, *b* 1918: *m* 1944, Lancelot Mitchell Shutte, of 1 Sea View Cottages, St Margarets-at-Cliffe, Dover, and has issue living, Susan Frances, *b* 1952: *m* 1st, 1972, Peter Derek Lapage, BSA Police; 2ndly, 1986, J. J. Van Der Walt, of PO Box 248, Gweru, Zimbabwe, and has had issue (by 1st *m*) Sally Frances *b* 1975, (by 2nd *m*) Andrew Mitchell *b* 1990, *d* 1991, — Mary Jane, *b* 1959: *m* 1980, Selwyn Ronald Danielson, of 18 Bredell St, Edenglen Ext 40, Edenvale 1610, Transvaal, S Africa, and has issue living, Kyle Bruce *b* 1982, Megan Nicole *b* 1986.

Issue of late Walter Henderson Molesworth, *b* 1873, *d* 1952: *m* 1910, Theodosia Maud, who *d* 1920, da of John Chapman, formerly of Ramsdale, Hants:—
Ernest Walter (Little Orchard, Hinton St George, Somerset; RAC, Royal Overseas and Golfers', Clubs), *b* 1911; *ed* Dover Coll, and London Univ; 1939-45 War (prisoner of Japanese): *m* 1947, Irene, da of Rev S. F. Whitehead, of Aston Somerville, Glos. —— Richard Nassau, *b* 1913. —— Margery Evelyn, *b* 1918: *m* 1st, 1946, Anthony Orde; 2ndly, 1974, Maj Phineas Arthur Jackson, FCIS, FCII, of 14 Bluecoat Pond, Christs Hospital, Horsham, W Sussex RH13 7NW.

Branch from el son of 7th son of 1st Viscount

Grandchildren of late Arthur Nepean Molesworth (*b* 1856), el son of Arthur Molesworth (*b* 1821), el son of Arthur Nepean Molesworth (*b* 1799), son of Maj Arthur Molesworth, el son of Hon Bysse Molesworth, 7th son of 1st Viscount:—
Issue of late Arthur William Bysse Nepean Molesworth, *b* 1902, *d* 1958: *m* 1922, Ruth Patricia, who *d* 1970, da of late Thomas Gracey, of Moy, co Armagh:—
Guilford Nepean, *b* 1923. *Residence* – 64 Hill Pole, Clawton, Queensland 4019, Australia. —— John Robert, *b* 1930: *m* 1954, Mary, da of Alexander Rodgers, of Montreal, and has issue living, Deborah, *b* 1957, — Kathryn, *b* 1962, — Sandra, *b* 1964. *Residence* – 527 Crumlinside Rd, London, Ontario, Canada. —— Kathleen Violet, *b* 1927. —— Ann, *b* 1928: *m* 1961, Dr Herman Gelber, Scarborough Centenary Hosp, Scarborough, Ont, and has issue living, Sean Roderick (589 Jamaica Court, London, Ontario N6K 1N2, Canada), *b* 1968.

Grandchildren of late Balfour Nepean Molesworth, 2nd son of late Thomas Nepean Molesworth, 2nd son of Arthur Nepean Molesworth (*b* 1799) (ante):—
Issue of late Herbert Nepean Molesworth, *b* 1888, *d* 1978: *m* 1912, Marjorie Kittredge who *d* 1976, da of late W. M. Thompson, of Penetanquishene, Ont, Canada:—
William Herbert (1850, des Chenaux St, Trois-Rivières, Québec, Canada), *b* 1915: *m* 1938, Joan Anne da of late Charles Percival Rudman, of Grand-Mere, Québec, and has issue living, Michael Herbert (101-6th St, Grand-Mere, Québec), *b* 1944: *m* 1982, Sylvie Desbiens, and has issue living, David Alexander Hamilton *b* 1986, Allison Louise *b* 1983, — Patricia Anne, *b* 1942: *m* 1st, 1964 (*m diss* 1978), Clifford Hastings Laurence; 2ndly, 1978, Stephen Alexander Osterman, BSc, DipEd, of 12 Terrasse St, Maurice, Cap-de-la-Madeleine, Québec, and has issue living (by 1st *m*), William Hastings *b* 1966; BA, LLB, Kelly Anne *b* 1965; BCOM, (by 2nd *m*), Michael Alexander *b* 1979, Steven Bradley *b* 1980, Jennifer Joan *b* 1982. —— Robert Nepean (11285 Greenhill Dr, RR2 Ladysmith, BC V0R 2E0, Canada), *b* 1923: *m* 1943, Cecily Elizabeth, da of late Lt-Cdr Cecil Alexander Wade, RN (ret), of Edgeley, Whitchurch, Shropshire, and has issue living, Robert Alexander (7909 Macpherson Drive, Burnaby, BC, Canada, V5J 4P4), *b* 1946: *m* 1973 (*m diss* 19—), Rosalind Anne Stacey, and has issue living, Ryan Jason *b* 1977, Brent Russell *b* 1979, — †Gregory Daniel, *b* 1951: *m* 1st, 1975, Claire Marie Deschambeault; 2ndly, 1985, Terri Kazemir (1375 Manson Crescent, Prince George, BC, Canada V2M 4A4), and *d* 1998, leaving issue Danielle Elizabeth *b* 1988, — Susan Elizabeth, *b* 1944: *m* 1st, 1965 (*m diss* 1970) Robert J. Black; 2ndly, 1970 (*m diss* 1973), Troy Lee Roper II; 3rdly, 1983, Fraser Thomas Sibbald, of 721-19th St, Pacific Grove 93950, Calif, USA, and has issue living (by 2nd *m*) Troy Lee (III) *b* 1971. —— Marjorie Julia Kittredge, *b* 1919: *m* 1948, John MacLeod Ellis, of Ross Ferry Rd, Boulardarie Bras d'Or, Cape Breton, Nova Scotia, Canada, and has issue living, Marnie MacLeod, *b* 1951: *m* 1987, Peter Douglas Adair Crosby, MD, of 68 Chapel Drive, Norwalk, Ohio 44857, USA, and has issue living, Alexander Douglas Judson *b* 1992, William Russel Arthur *b* 1993.

Grandsons of late William Ponsonby Molesworth, yst son of late Thomas Nepean Molesworth (ante):—
Issue of late George Nepean Molesworth, b 1885, d 1958: m 1916, Helen Nelles, who d 1954, da of late Sydney
Bellingham Sykes, of Toronto:—
John Sydney (Oakville, Ontario, Canada), b 1919: m 1946, Barbara Caroline, who d 1998, da of Dr Carswell Marshall
(4616 Route 620, Limekiln Rd, New Brunswick, Canada E6B 1G6), of Leeds, W Yorks, and has issue living, William
Marshall, b 1949: m 1992, Susan Irene Newell, of Kapuskasing, and Ottawa, Ontario, — Hugh Carswell (PO Box 622,
Shelburne, Ontario, Canada L0N 1S0), b 1952: m 1975, Rosemary Druscilla, da of A. Ulch, of Simcoe, Ontario, — James
Colin (310-8th Av West, New Westminster, BC, Canada V3L 1YZ), b 1959: m 1994, Patricia, da of Robert Cameron, and
has issue living, Cameron Marshall b 1998, — Helen Mary, b 1954: m 1985, David Weiser, of 6488 Bay St, W Vancouver,
BC, Canada V7W 2H1. —— David Hugh George (156 Collier St, Toronto, Ontario, Canada), b 1927: m 1952, Ann
DeVeber, who d 1997, da of late Major Alfred Clarence Larter, of Toronto, Canada, and has issue living, Ian DeVeber (4
Sydenham St, Guelph, Ontario, Canada), b 1956, — Tony Nelles (49 Lawlor Av, Toronto, Ontario, Canada), b 1958;
legally assumed the forename of Tony in lieu of Anthony.

Grandson of late Bevil Hugh Molesworth el son of late Rev Hugh Thomas Molesworth (infra):—
Issue of late Hugh Bevil Alec Molesworth, b 1925, d 1960: m 1959, Patricia (who m 2ndly, 1963, Dr Ian Martin,
of 40 Carlyle Rd, E Lindfield, NSW, 2070), da of late Clive Quinton, of Wahroonga, Sydney, NSW:—
Hugh Bevil Clive, b (posthumous) 1960: m 1989, Karen Roberta, da of Irwin David Staller, of Stockton, California, and has
issue living, Maude Clara Felice, b 1994, — Talia Ruby Camille, b 1997. Residence – 176 Parnassus Avenue, San
Francisco, California 94117, USA.

Grandson of late Rev Thomas Molesworth, son of late Thomas William Ponsonby Molesworth, son of
Maj Arthur Molesworth (ante):—
Issue of late Rev Hugh Thomas Molesworth, b 1860, d 1930: m 1889, Alice Marian, who d 1939, da of Edward
Deshon, CMG, sometime Auditor-Gen of Queensland:—
Guilford Bysse, b 1907: m 1931, Catherine Maud, da of late Edward Charles Woodward, of Coorparoo, Queensland, and
has issue living, William Guilford Hugh (39 Newman Av, Camp Hill, Brisbane, Qld 4152), b 1943: m 1968, Helen, da of
John Edward McCaskie, of Coorparoo, Brisbane, Queensland, and has issue living, Mark William b 1975: m 1999, Jane
Elizabeth, da of George Ross Munro, of Montville, Queensland, Peter John b 1979. Residence – 27 Marriott St,
Coorparoo, Brisbane, Queensland 4151, Australia.

Branch from 2nd son of 7th son of 1st Viscount

Grandchildren of late Maj-Gen Hickman Thomas Molesworth, el son of Maj-Gen Arthur Molesworth, el
son of Capt Robert Molesworth, 2nd son of Hon Bysse Molesworth (ante):—
Issue of late Lt-Col Robert Everard Molesworth, b 1861, d 1941: m 1st, 1889, Catherine Isabella, who d 1904, da
of J. Allen; 2ndly 1908, Gladys Eleanor, who d 1976, da of late Louis Otto Law:—
(By 2nd m) Robert Louis, b 1910; formerly Lt Indian Army. —— Marianne Sheila Lindsay, b 1914: m 1935, Thomas
Bogue Alder, and has issue living, Lucinda Ann, b 1936, — Hermione Sarah, b 1941.

Granddaughter of late Rev Thomas Charles Underwood Molesworth, 5th son of Maj-Gen Hickman
Thomas Molesworth (ante):—
Issue of late Lt-Col Richard Cecil Molesworth, b 1898, d 1974: m 1933, Susan, who d 1994, da of Harry Bazeley,
of Bideford, N Devon:—
Gillian Ann, b 1959: m 1959, Dr John Dupré, of 64 Hartson Rd, London, Ont, Canada N6H 3S8, and has issue living,
Matthew, b 1961, — Luke, b 1972, — Louisa, b 1962.

Grandsons of late Col Richard Piggot Molesworth, CMG, 6th son of Maj-Gen Hickman Thomas Moles-
worth (ante):—
Issue of late Maj Ralph Gerard Lindsay Molesworth, b 1910, d 1960: m 1st, 1933 (m diss 19—), Eleanor, el da of
R. G. Rooke; 2ndly, 1948, Valerie St Claire (1 Town Mills, Church St, Dawlish, Devon), da of Charles Francis
Earle:—
(By 1st m) Christopher Ralph, b 1934. Address – Batam Base, McDermott Sea Pte Ltd, Maxwell Rd, PO Box 3034,
Singapore. —— Anthony John Lindsay, MBE; b 1936; Col, MBE (Mil) 1972. —— (By 2nd m) Richard Charles Lindsay,
b 1950; ed Belmont Abbey, and Univ Coll, Wales; LLB (Lond). Residences – 1 Town Mills, Church St, Dawlish, Devon.

Granddaughter of late Maj-Gen Hickman Thomas Molesworth (ante):—
Issue of late Col Herbert Ellicombe Molesworth, CMG, DSO, b 1872, d 1941: m 1914, Eileen Mary, who d 1969,
da of Col Henry Waugh Renny-Tailyour, of Burrowfield, co Forfar (V Powerscourt):—
Phyllis Eileen (Russets, Lowerbourne, Porlock, Som TA24 8PZ), b 1914: m 1956, Cyril Pickard. —— Betty Lindsay
(Russets, Lowerbourne, Porlock, Som TA24 8PZ), b 1919: m 1946, Frederick A. Craswell, and has issue living, Lindsay (a
da) (Huntscott Cottage, Huntscott, Wootton Courtenay, Timberscombe, Som), b 1951.

Grandchildren of Hickman Molesworth (b 1842), el son of Sir Robert Molesworth, son of Hickman
Blayney Molesworth, 2nd son of Capt Robert Molesworth (ante):—
Issue of late Surg-Lt Hickman Walter Lancelot Molesworth, FRCS, b 1892, d 1969: m 1923, Caryl Margaret, who
d 1997, da of Stanley Hoare, of 17 Cornwall Terr, Regent's Park, NW:—
†Robert Stanley Hickman, b 1934; solicitor 1963: m 1965, Ann (23 Pavenham Rd, Carlton, Beds), da of A. Metcalfe-
Gibson, of Greensidehead, Ravenstonedale, Westmorland, and d 1998, leaving issue, William Metcalfe, b 1968, — Philip
Hoare, b 1970, — Catherine Jessie, b 1960. —— Richard Baxter (Little Swifts, Spotted Cow Lane, Buxted, E Sussex
TN22 4UG), b 1939: m 1966, Ann Kathleen Duncan, da of late F. N. H. Pexton, and has issue living, Edward James
Hickman, b 1967, — Rachel Jane, b 1970: m 1996, Gavin R. C. Manger, son of Capt N. I. C. Manger, RN, of Forest Row,
Sussex, — Victoria Bridget, b 1975. —— Bridget Margaret, b 1931: m 1954, John Ormerod Heyworth, of 1 Wesley
Close, Park Lane, Reigate, Surrey RH2 8JS, and has issue living, James Hickman Frederick (14 Clavering Av, Barnes,
SW13 9DY), b 1958: m 1993, Julie Caroline, da of late John Bannister, of Frampton, Lincs, and of Mrs Stephen Read, of
Scrafield, Lincs, and has issue living, George Marshall John b 1995, Thomas James Oliver b 1997, — Peter Lawrence

Ormerod (82 Manchuria Rd, SW11 6AE), *b* 1963: *m* 1994, Susan Kathryn, da of John Gill, of Vessy, Geneva, Switzerland, — Caroline Margaret, *b* 1956.

Grandchildren of late Robert Arthur Molesworth, 2nd son of Sir Robert Molesworth (ante):—
Issue of late John Matheson Molesworth, *b* 1878, *d* 1942: *m* 1906, Elizabeth Flora Frances Hill who *d* 1952, da
of late Edwin M. James, MRCSE:—
Richard William Edwin, *b* 1908: *m* 1937, Dirleen Muriel, da of Leslie Sprague, of Charlemont, Geelong, Australia, and
has issue living, Michael John Leslie (119 Albert St, Windsor, Victoria 3181, Australia), BSc, MSc, *b* 1941: *m* 1st, 1967
(*m diss* 1984), Caroline Carse Hay (BA); 2ndly, 1984, Annette Milton, and has issue living (by 1st *m*), Tamsin Louise *b*
1972, Amanda Frances *b* 1976, Charlotte Marie Louise *b* 1981 (by 2nd *m*) Christopher James Michael *b* 1981, Timothy
Mark Richard *b* 1985, Louise Annette Marie *b* 1988, — Simon Richard, AM (19 Linacre Rd, Hampton, Victoria 3188,
Australia), BA, LLB, *b* 1954; Queen's Counsel; AM 1994; QC 1995: *m* 1983, Rosalind Marie Cochrane (BSc), and has
issue living, Lachlan James Simon *b* 1984, Oliver Simon William *b* 1990, Anika Genevieve Fleur *b* 1987, — Corinne
Dirleen, BA, *b* 1949: *m* 1981, David Ross Fraser (BA), and has issue living, Hamish Ross Molesworth *b* 1985, Edwina
Ross Molesworth *b* 1983. *Residence* – Cowl Cowl, 19 Linacre Rd, Hampton, Victoria 3188, Australia. —— John Robert
Nassau, DFC (Ballark, Morrisons, Elaine, Victoria 3334, Australia), *b* 1910; S/Ldr RAAF, and a Councillor,
Coleraineshire, Victoria; 1939-45 War (DFC): *m* 1940, Sheila Morrell, who *d* 1994, da of Charles Armytage, of The Wild-
erness, Coleraine, Victoria, and has issue living, Robert John Armytage (Lindavale, Morrisons, Elaine, Victoria 3334,
Australia), *b* 1941: *m* 1967, Amanda Grage, and has issue living, Charles John Matheson *b* 1968, Edward Paul *b* 1971,
Peter Robert *b* 1976, Katrina Mary *b* 1974, — John Denis Peter (Ballark, Morrisons, Elaine, Victoria 3334, Australia), *b*
1944: *m* 1st, 1970, Georgina Mary Pierrepoint; 2ndly, 1989, Elizabeth Kathleen Eddy, and has issue living (by 1st *m*),
James Robert Beiri *b* 1975, Emma Pamela Pierrepoint *b* 1972, (by 2nd *m*), Kate Elizabeth *b* 1993, — Morrell Frances
Armytage, *b* 1945: *m* 1967, Michael Guy Earle, and has issue (*see* Earle, Bt, colls), — Jackalyn Armytage, *b* 1949: *m*
1974, Barry Lazarus, of 21 Dwyer St, Sunshine Beach, Qld 4567, Australia, and has issue living, James Albert *b* 1982,
Georgina Armytage *b* 1979. —— †Edwin Noel Waulter (Mittagong, 31 Governor's Drive, Mount Macedon, Victoria 3441,
Australia), *b* 1916; was a Councillor, and former Pres, Ballanshire, Victoria: *m* 1940, Alison Mary, da of late W. A.
Dalrymple, of Glenluce, Gisborne, Victoria, and *d* 1995, leaving issue, William Anthony Hill, *b* 1941: BAgSc: *m* 1973,
Merran Sutherland, and has issue living, Stephen Alexander *b* 1975, Amy Merran Hill *b* 1979, — Richard Matheson, *b*
1948: BAgSc: *m* 1977, Janet Elaine McIntyre, and has had issue, Louise Elizabeth *b* 1980, *k* in an accident 1997,
Katherine Wendy *b* 1982, *k* in an accident 1997. —— Mary Margaret Hill, OAM (Burlendi, Coleraine, Victoria 3315,
Australia) *b* 1922; OAM 1991: *m* 1943, Richard Sladen Hope, who *d* 1981, and has issue living, Christopher Sladen (24
Browning Drive, Templestowe, Victoria 3106, Australia), *b* 1947; MIE, Polar Medal: *m* 1982, Wendy Patricia, da of
Patrick Jones, of Victoria, and has issue living, Richard Francis Sladen *b* 1984, David William *b* 1986, — Roland Moles-
worth (Burlendi, Coleraine, Victoria 3315, Australia), *b* 1949, — Linden Kenney (Wolta Wolta, Bungower Rd, Moorooduc,
Vic), *b* 1954; MB, BS: *m* 1977, Priscilla Jane, da of late Ross Boaden, MSc, of Mount Eliza, Victoria, and has issue living,
Edward Charles Kenney *b* 1984, Emily Jane Kenney *b* 1981.

Grandchildren of late John Matheson Molesworth (ante):—
Issue of late John Bysse Molesworth, *b* 1912, *d* 1977: *m* 1941, Jessie Martha, da of W. Thomas, of Charters
Towers, Queensland:—
David John (5 Spinnaway Close, Port Douglas, Queensland 4871, Australia), *b* 1942: *m* 1965 (*m diss* 1976), Diana Lynette,
da of T. E. Mann, of S Caulfield, Victoria, and has issue living, Nicolas Andrew, *b* 1973. —— Judith Hill, *b* 1946; BA: *m*
1st, 1969 (*m diss* 1981), Roger John Young, BEng; 2ndly, 1981, Peter Fleming Terracall, and has issue living (by 1st *m*),
Tristan Samuel, *b* 1972, — Imogen Matilda, *b* 1974, — (by 2nd *m*) Mikaila Hill, *b* 1981.

PREDECESSORS – (1) ROBERT Molesworth, *b* 1656; *ed* Trin Coll, Dublin (BA); PC, FRS, FSA; Envoy Extraordinary to
Court of Denmark; MP successively for Camelford, Dublin, Swords, Lostwithiel, East Retford and St Michael; Commr of
Trade & Plantations; *cr Baron Philipstown* and *Viscount Molesworth*, of Swords (Peerage of Ireland) 1716: *m* 1676, Hon
Letitia Coote, who *d* 1729, da of Richard, Baron of Colooney (ext) *d* 1725; *s* by his el son (2) JOHN, 2nd Viscount; *b*
1679; Commr of Stamp Office, Commr of Trade & Plantations, Envoy Extraordinary to Grand Duke of Tuscany, Rep of
Genoa and Court of Sardinia; Minister at Florence, Venice and Switzerland: *m* 1718, Mary, who *d* 1766, da of Thomas
Middleton, MP; *dsp* 1726; *s* by his brother (3) RICHARD, 3rd Viscount; *b* 1680; MP for Swords, PC, FRS; ADC to Duke to
Marlborough (whose life he saved) at Ramillies 1706, Officer of Dragoons at Preston (wounded) 1715, Col of Moles-
worth's Foot 1725, Maj-Gen 1735, Brig-Gen 1736, Keeper of the Great Seal of Ireland 1736, Lt-Gen of the Ordnance 1739,
Master-Gen of the Ordnance 1740, Lt-Gen on the Establishment 1742, Gen of Horse 1746, Com in Ch of Forces in Ire-
land 1751 and Field-Marshal 1757; *m* 1st, Jane Lucas, who *d* 1742; 2ndly, 1743, Mary Jenney, who *d* 1763, da of Rev
William Usher, Archdeacon of Clonfert; *d* 1758; *s* by his son (4) RICHARD NASSAU, 4th Viscount; *b* 1748; *ed* Trin Coll,
Dublin; *d* unmarried 1793; *s* by his cousin (5) ROBERT, el son of Capt Hon William, MP for Philipstown, 3rd son of 1st
Viscount, by Anne, da of Robert Adair, MP, of Holybrook, co Wicklow, 5th Viscount; *b* 1729; ADC to Marquess of
Lothian: *m* 1761, Mary Anne, who *d* 1819, da of Israel Alleyne, of Cork; *d* 1813; *s* by his el son (6) WILLIAM JOHN, 6th
Viscount; *b* 1763; Ensign 46th Foot (America) 1780, Lieut 46th Foot (S Devons) 1784, Capt 1794, Major 9th Foot (E Nor-
folk) 1799, Lt-Col of Newfoundland *Fencibles* 1803, appointed Lt-Col 1st Ceylon Regt 1805, Lt-Col of 9th Foot, Brevet-Col
1812, Maj-Gen 1814 and Commandant of Point de Galle, Ceylon; *d* with his wife and family in shipwreck of *Arniston*, off
Cape Agulhas, 1815; *s* by his cousin (7) RICHARD PIGOTT, el son of Richard, Secretary to the Treasury, 3rd son of
William (ante), by Catherine, da of Thomas Cobb, of Twickenham, Middlesex, 7th Vicount; *b* 1786; a Capt in East Indian
Military Service; *d* unmarried 1875; *s* by his nephew (8) *Rev* SAMUEL son of Capt John, RN, 3rd son of Richard (ante), by
Louisa, da of late Rev Dr Tomkyns, 8th Viscount, *b* 1829; *ed* Cheltenham, and St John's Coll, Camb (MA); R of St
Petrock Minor: *m* 1st, 1862, Georgina Charlotte Cecil, who *d* 1879, da of George Bagot Gosset, formerly of 4th Dragoon
Guards; 2ndly, 1883, Agnes, who *d* 1905, da of late Dugald Dove, of Nutshill, Renfrewshire, *d* 1906; *s* by his el son (9)
GEORGE BAGOT, 9th Viscount; *b* 1867; *ed* Wellington; Capt DCLI, served in operations on NW Frontier of India 1897-8
with Tirah Expedition (medal with two clasps) and in Great War 1914-18 as Major, Army Pay Dept: *m* 1894, Nina Alida,
who *d* 1958, da of late Col H. D. Faulkner, 42nd Madras Inf; *d* 1947; *s* by his brother (10) CHARLES RICHARD, 10th
Viscount; *b* 1869; *ed* Cheltenham: *m* 1906, Elizabeth Gladys, who *d* 1974, da of late Edward Martin Langworthy; *d* 1961; *s*
by his el son (11) RICHARD GOSSET, 11th Viscount; *b* 1907; *ed* Elizabeth Coll, and Lancing; served RAF Middle East
1941-44 (invalided); Freeman City of London: *m* 1958, Mrs Anne Florence Womersley, who *d* 1983, da of John Freeman
Cohen, of St James's Court, SW1; *d* 1997; *s* by his el son (12) ROBERT BYSSE KELHAM, 12th Viscount and present peer;
also Baron Philipstown.

MOLLOY, BARON (Molloy) (Life Baron 1981)

WILLIAM JOHN MOLLOY, son of William John Molloy; *b* 26 Oct 1918; *ed* St Thomas, Swansea, and Swansea Coll, Univ of Wales (Hon Fellow); FRGS; Member Transport and General Worker's Union 1936-46; Civil Service Union 1946-52 (Ed Civil Service Review 1949-53); Chm Staff-Side Foreign Office Whitley Council, Germany/Austria Sections, 1950-53; Leader Fulham Borough Council 1959-62 (Member since 1954); formerly Vice-Chm Parl Labour Party Gp for Common Market and European Affairs; Parl Adviser London Trades Council Transport Cttee 1968-70; PPS to Min of Posts and Telecommunication 1969-70; Pres Disabled Drivers Assocn from 1969; Sponsored MP Confederation Health Service Employees 1972; Member European Parl and Council of Europe, WEU 1976-79; Chm Parl Lab Party Social Services Gp 1974; Political Adviser to The Arab League 1981-84, Member Saudi Arabia, Kuwait, Abu Dhabi, Bahrein, Iraq and Dubai Parliamentary Groups; Chm British Tunisian Soc, and Met Area Royal British Legion 1985-93; Nat Vice Pres Royal British Legion since 1994; Hon Life Pres London Univ Soc, Hon Associate British Vetinary Assocn since 1988; served RE 1939-46; MP (*Lab*) Ealing North 1964-79; *cr Baron Molloy*, of Ealing, in Greater London (Life Baron) 1981: *m* 1st, 1946, Eva Lewis, who *d* 1980; 2ndly, 1981 (*m diss* 1987), Doris Paines, and has issue by 1st *m*.

ᎪᏒᎷᎦ – Vert on a rounded mount or an oak tree proper leaved and fructed also or and in base two barrulets wavy argent all within a bordure ermine. **Ꮯᵲᵉᵴᵗ** – Upon rocks thereon oyster shells proper a representation of the Mumbles Lighthouse at Swansea diffusing light from its lantern all proper. **Ꮪᵘᵖᵖᵒᵲᵗᵉᵲᵴ** – *Dexter*, on a grassy mount proper a dragon passant its tail looped gules tongue and claws or; *sinister*, on a like mount a swan wings displayed inverted and addorsed all proper. **Ꮇᵒᵗᵗᵒ** – Justice and Compassion.
Address – House of Lords, SW1.

DAUGHTER LIVING (*By 1st marriage*)

Hon Marion Ann, *b* 1947: *m* 1974, Laurence George Motl, and has issue living, Julia Marion, *b* 1976, — Ann Lillian, *b* 1979. *Residence* – 6225 Idylwood Lane, Edina, Minnesota 55436, USA.

MOLYNEAUX OF KILLEAD, BARON (Molyneaux) (Life Baron 1997)

JAMES HENRY MOLYNEAUX, KBE, PC, son of late William Molyneaux, of Seacash, Killead, co Antrim; *b* 27 Aug 1920; *ed* Aldergrove Sch, co Antrim; MP (Ulster Unionist) for Antrim South 1970-83, and for Lagan Valley 1983-97; Vice-Pres Ulster Unionist Council 1974-79; Leader Ulster Unionist Parliamentary Party 1974-95, and Ulster Unionist Party 1979-95; Memb Antrim CC 1964-73; JP co Antrim 1957-66; served with RAF 1941-46: *cr* PC 1983, KBE 1996, and *Baron Molyneaux of Killead*, of Killead, co Antrim (Life Baron) 1997.

🙠rms – Gyronny of eight or and azure a cross moline between four alder leaves slipped inwards all counterchanged. ℭrest – A wolf statant or holding in the dexter forepaw a flax flower azure slipped and leaved or. ℨupporters – On either side a heraldic tyger reguardant argent gorged with a plain collar attached thereto a chain reflexed over the back or.
Residence – Aldergrove, Crumlin, co Antrim BT29 4AR.

MONCK, VISCOUNT (Monck) Entitled to sit as BARON (UK 1866) (Viscount I 1801)

CHARLES STANLEY MONCK, 7th Viscount; *b* 2 April 1953; *s* 1982; *ed* Eton; does not use the title.

Boldly, faithfully, successfully

🙠rms – Gules, a chevron between three lions, heads erased argent. ℭrest – A dragon passant wings elevated sable. ℨupporters – *Dexter*, a dragon; *sinister*, a lion; both argent, and holding in the fore paw a branch of laurel resting on the shoulder fructed proper.

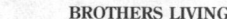

BROTHERS LIVING

Hon GEORGE STANLEY (Yew Tree House, Lea, Malmeslbury, Wilts SN16 9PA), *b* 12 April 1957: *m* 1986, Camilla E.V., 2nd da of late John Naylor, of The Mill House, Bramley, Hants, and has had issue, †Henry, *b* and *d* 1991.
Hon James Stanley, *b* 1961.

WIDOW LIVING OF SIXTH VISCOUNT

BRENDA MILDREDA, da of late George William Adkins, of Bower's Close, Harpenden, Herts: *m* 1st, 1951, as his 2nd wife, the 6th Viscount Monck, OBE, who *d* 1982; 2ndly, 1985, as his 2nd wife, Brig Gerald (Ged) Michael Palmer, MC, who *d* 1991, of Pilgrims Farm, Overton, Hants.

PREDECESSORS – (1) CHARLES STANLEY Monck; *cr* Baron Monck, of Ballytrammon (peerage of Ireland) 1797, and *Viscount Monck* (peerage of Ireland) 1801; *d* 1802; *s* by his el son (2) HENRY STANLEY, 2nd Viscount; *cr Earl of Rathdowne* (peerage of Ireland) 1822; *d* 1848, when the earldom expired and the barony and viscountcy devolved upon his brother (3) CHARLES JOSEPH KELLY, 3rd Viscount; *b* 1791: *m* 1817, Bridget, da of late John Willington, Esq, of Killoskehane, co Tipperary; *d* 1849; *s* by his son (4) CHARLES STANLEY, GCMG, PC, 4th Viscount, *b* 1819; MP for Portsmouth 1852-7; was a Lord of the Treasury 1855-8, Gov-Gen of Canada 1861-7, and of Dominion of Canada 1867-8, Ch Commr in Ireland 1869-81, and Lord-Lieut of co Dublin 1874-92; *cr Baron Monck* (peerage of United Kingdom) 1866: *m* 1844, his cousin, Lady Elizabeth Louise Mary Monck, who *d* 1892, da of 1st Earl of Rathdowne (*ext*); *d* 1894; *s* by his son (5) HENRY POWER CHARLES STANLEY, 5th Viscount; *b* 1849; Vice-Lieut co Wicklow (High Sheriff 1887): *m* 1874, Lady Edith Caroline Sophia Scott, who *d* 1929, da of 3rd Earl of Clonmell; *d* 1927; *s* by his grandson (6) HENRY WYNDHAM STANLEY, OBE, JP, DL (son of late Capt Hon Charles Henry Stanley Monck, who was *ka* 1914, el son of 5th Viscount), 6th Viscount, *b* 1905; Vice-Chm Nat Asso of Boys' Clubs 1938-78: *m* 1st, 1937 (*m diss* 1951), Eva Maria, Baroness Vreto, 2nd da of Professor Zaunmuller-Freudenthaler, of Vienna; 2ndly, 1951, Brenda Mildreda (who *m* 2ndly, 1985, as his 2nd wife, Brig Gerald (Ged) Michael Palmer, MC, who *d* 1991, only da of late George William Adkins, of Bower's Close, Harpenden, Herts; *d* 1982; *s* by his el son (7) CHARLES STANLEY, 7th Viscount and present peer; also Baron Monck.

MONCKTON OF BRENCHLEY, VISCOUNT (Monckton) (Viscount UK 1957)

To spread fame by deeds

GILBERT WALTER RIVERSDALE MONCKTON, CB, OBE, MC, 2nd Viscount; *b* 3 Nov 1915; *s* 1965; *ed* Harrow, and Trin Coll, Camb (MA); FSA; Maj-Gen (ret), late 12th R Lancers, formerly 5th R Inniskilling Dragoon Gds; Col 9th/12th R Lancers 1967-73; Hon Col Kent and Sharpshooters Yeo 1974-79; Dep-Chm Gulf Guarantee Bank; Comdg RAC, 3rd Div 1958-63, Dep Dir of Personnel Admin 1962, Dir of Public Relations, War Office 1960-65, and Ch of Staff, HQ, BAOR 1965-67; Pres Kent Assocn of Boys' Clubs 1965-78, and Inst of Heraldic and Genealogical Studies since 1965, of Kent Archaeological Assocn and of Medway Productivity Assocn 1968-74; County Vice-Chm of Scout Assocn (Kent) 1968-74; a DL of Kent; Pres of British Assocn Order of Malta 1974-83; Pres of Anglo-Belgian Union 1973-83; 1939-45 War (MC); Korea 1951-52; a Liveryman of Broderers' Co (Master 1978-79); Baliff Grand Cross of Obedience Sovereign Mil Order of Malta, and KStJ (Chm of Council or Order of St John for Kent 1969-75); Grand Officer of the Order of Leopold II; Cdr of Order of the Crown of Belgium; Bailiff Grand Cross of Justice Constantinian Order of St George; OBE (Mil) 1956, CB (Mil) 1966: *m* 1950, Marianna Laetitia, Dame of Honour and Devotion Sov Mil Order of Malta; Pres St John's Ambulance for Kent 1973-80, Member of SSAFA Central Council since 1968; High Sheriff of Kent (1981); Freeman City of London 1983; OStJ, da of Cdr Robert Tatton Bower, RN (By Strickland), and has issue.

Arms – Quarterly; 1st and 4th, sable, on a chevron between three martlets or, as many mullets of the field, *Monckton*; 2nd and 3rd, or a chevron gules a chief vair (*St Quintin*). **Crest** – On a wreath sable and or a martlet or. **Supporters** – On either side a horse argent crined and unguled or gorged with a chain gold pendant therefrom an escutcheon sable charged with a rose also argent barbed and seeded proper.
Residence – Runhams Farm, Runham Lane, Harrietsham, Maidstone, Kent, ME17 1NJ. *Clubs* – Brooks's, Cavalry, MCC, Casino Maltese (Valetta).

SONS LIVING

Hon CHRISTOPHER WALTER *b* 14 Feb 1952; *ed* Harrow, Churchill Coll, Camb (MA) and Univ Coll, Cardiff; a DL of Greater London since 1988; OStJ (1973), Kt of Honour and Devotion Sov Mil Order of Malta; a Liveryman of Broderers' Co, leader-writer Yorkshire Post Newspapers, Ltd, Leeds 1975-77; press officer Conservative Central Office 1977-78; Editor, *The Universe* 1979-81; Sec Economic Accounting Study Group, centre for Policy Studies 1980; Man Ed *The Sunday Telegraph Magazine* 1981-82; Member PM's policy unit 1983-86; Assist Ed *Today* 1986-87, Consulting Ed *Evening Standard* 1987-92; Dir Christopher Monckton Ltd since 1987, Dir Beechwood Clothing Co since 1993; Freeman of City of London: *m* 1990, Juliet Mary Anne, yst da of Jorgen Malherbe Jensen, of Doughty St, WC1. *Residence* – Crimonmogate, Fraserburgh, Aberdeenshire AB43 8SE. *Clubs* – Beefsteak, Brooks's, Pratt's.

Hon Timothy David Robert, *b* 1955; *ed* Harrow, and RAC, Cirencester; Kt of Honour and Devotion, Sov Mil Order of Malta: *m* 1984, Jennifer J., 2nd da of Brendan Carmody, of 72 Ashbourne Rd, W5, and formerly of Sydney Australia, and has issue living, Dominic Walter, *b* 1985, — James Timothy, *b* 1988, — William Henry, *b* 1992. *Residence* – 46 Peacock St, Seaforth, Sydney 2092, Australia.

Hon Jonathan Riversdale St Quintin (twin), *b* 1955; *ed* Worth; Monk of the Order of St Benedict, Worth Abbey 1975-89: *m* 1992, Carina Therese, da of Brian Beeson, OBE. *Residence* – 90 Innes Gdns, Putney Heath, SW15 3AD.

Hon Anthony Leopold Colyer, *b* 1960; *ed* Harrow, and Magdalene Coll, Camb (MA), comm'd 9th/12th R Lancers 1982, Capt 1984 (ret 1987); Head British Embassy Office Banja Luka since 1998: *m* 1985, Philippa Susan, yr da of late Gervase Christopher Brinsmade Wingfield (*see* V Powerscourt, colls), and has issue living, Edward Gervase Colyer, *b* 1988, — Camilla Mary, *b* 1989. *Club* – MCC.

DAUGHTER LIVING

Hon Rosamond Mary, *b* 1953; Man Dir Tiffany, London; Freeman of Goldsmith's Co: *m* 1991, as his 2nd wife, Hon Dominic Ralph Campden Lawson, son of Baron Lawson of Blaby, PC (Life Baron), and has issue (*see* B Lawson of Blaby).

SISTER LIVING

Hon Valerie Hamilton (*Senator Hon Lady Goulding*), *b* 1918; Hon LLD, National Univ of Ireland 1968; late Subaltern WRAC (Reserve); Senator of Republic of Ireland; Chm and Man Dir Central Remedial Clinic, Dublin since 1951; Founder Member, Nat Rehabilitation Bd (1955), and Union of Voluntary Organisations for the Handicapped; a Gov St Patrick's Hosp; Member, Management Cttee Mater Hosp, Southern Movement for Peace, etc; Dame of Honour and Devotion, Sov Mil Order of Malta: *m* 1939, Wing Com Sir William Basil Goulding, 3rd Bt, who *d* 1982. *Residence* – Dargle Cottage, Enniskerry, co Wicklow.

PREDECESSOR – (1) *Rt Hon Sir* WALTER TURNER Monckton, GCVO, KCMG, MC, PC, QC, son of Frank William Monckton, of Ightham Warren, Kent; *b* 1891; Attorney-Gen to Duchy Cornwall 1932-47 and 1948-51, Dir-Gen of Min of Information, and an Additional Dep Under-Sec of State for Foreign Affairs 1940, Head of Information Sers Cairo 1941-42, Solicitor Gen 1945, Min of Labour and Nat Ser 1951-55, Min of Defence 1955-56, and Paymaster-Gen 1956-57; MP for Bristol West (C) 1951-57; *cr Viscount Monckton of Brenchley*, of Brenchley, co Kent (peerage of UK) 1957: *m* 1914 (*m diss* 1947), Mary Adelaide Somes, who *d* 1964, da of Sir Thomas Colyer Colyer-Ferguson, 3rd Bt; 2ndly, 1947, Bridget Helen, Lady Ruthven of Freeland (in her own right), who *d* 1982, and formerly wife of 11th Earl of Carlisle; *d* 1965; *s* by his only son (2) GILBERT WALTER RIVERSDALE, CB, OBE, MC, 2nd Viscount and present peer.

MONCREIFF, BARON (Moncreiff) (Baron UK 1873, Bt S 1626 and UK 1871)

HARRY ROBERT WELLWOOD MONCREIFF, 5th Baron and 15th Baronet of Moncreiff, and 5th of Tullibole; *b* 4 Feb 1915; *s* 1942: *ed* Fettes Coll; Hon Lt-Col (retired) RASC Burma 1939-45 (despatches): *m* 1952, Enid Marion Watson, who *d* 1985, only da of Major Henry Watson Locke, of Belmont, Dollar, and has issue.

Arms – Quarterly: 1st and 4th argent, a lion rampant gules, armed and langued azure, a chief ermine; 2nd and 3rd argent, an oak tree issuing out of a well in base proper. **Crest** – A demi-lion rampant, as in the arms. **Supporters** – Two men armed cap-a-pie, holdng in the exterior and a spear resting on the shoulder all proper, the breastplate charged with a crescent gules.
Seat – Tullibole Castle, Kinross-shire.

SON LIVING

Hon RHODERICK HARRY WELLWOOD, *b* 22 March 1954: *m* 1982, Alison Elizabeth Anne, only da of late James Duncan Alastair Ross, of West Mayfield, Dollar, Clackmannanshire, and has issue living, Harry James Wellwood, *b* 12 Aug 1986, — James Gavin Francis, *b* 1988. *Residence* – The Cottage, Tullibole Castle, Crook of Devon, by Kinross, Kinross-shire KY13 7QN.

BROTHER LIVING

On hope

Hon Robert Frederick Arthur (26 Croft St, Galashiels, Selkirk), *b* 1924: *m* 1951, Aileen Margaret Marr, da of Robert Marr Meldrum, LDS, PhD, and has issue living, Richard Gerard Arthur, *b* 1964, — Gillian Nicola Ann, *b* 1954: *m* 1981, Norman Alexander Stewart, and has issue living, Rory Alexander *b* 1989, Rebecca Jane *b* 1986.

SISTERS LIVING

Hon Lilian Vida Lechmere, *b* 1912: *m* 1942, David Robert Young, and has issue living, Robert Arthur Moncreiff, *b* 1944; *ed* Fettes, — Caroline Vida Rosemary, *b* 1951: *m* 19—, James Munro, of 88 Old Edinburgh Rd, Inverness. *Residence* – Tanworth, Fossoway, Kinross-shire.

Hon Nicola Gladys, *b* 1917: *m* 1st, 1940, Capt Frederick W. Gifford, RA, who was *ka* 1943; 2ndly, 1946, Charles John Derek Renny, who *d* 1970, late Lt RNVR, and has issue living, (by 1st *m*) James Alexander Moncreiff (Fernlee, Banff), *b* 1942: *m* 1967, Patricia Dalton, and has issue living, Robert James Moncreiff *b* 1974, Lucinda Felicity Moncreiff *b* 1971, Samantha Louise Moncreiff *b* 1985, — (by 2nd *m*) Nicholas Charles Moncreiff (USA), *b* 1954: *m* 1982, Carol M., da of Neal R. Ashman, of Home House, St Martin's Guernsey, and has issue living, Alicia Nicola Rose *b* 1985, Emily Ellen Miranda *b* 1987, Abigail Eloise Mateldy *b* 1988, Felicity Alice Prudence *b* 1990, — Susan Miranda Fitzherbert, *b* 1950: *m* 1972, Anthony John O'Donnell, MB, BS, of Le Vieux Rouvet, St Saviours, Guernsey, and has issue living, Nicholas John Renny *b* 1975, Alexa Caroline *b* 1973, Abigail Kate *b* 1978, — Prudence Jane Fitzherbert, *b* 1952: *m* 1977, Paul Lynch, of 8 Kinnaird Av, Chiswick, W4, and has issue living, James Patrick Moncreiff *b* 1980, Harry John Renny *b* 1983. *Residence* – Greenways, Montville Rd, St Peter Port, Guernsey.

Hon Pamela Anne, *b* 1927; MB, ChB Edinburgh 1949: *m* 1st, 1951 (*m diss* 1973), Edward James White; 2ndly, 1979, Ernest Frederic Epps, who *d* 1987, of 13 Barntongate Av, Edinburgh EH4 8BQ, and has issue living (by 1st *m*) Nicolas Alan (100 Vanderlip Drive, Palos Verdes, LA, California 90275, USA), *b* 1953: *m* 1984, Louise Anne Scrimgeour; has issue living, Nicolas Alexander *b* 1975, — Douglas Andrew, *b* 1959, — Vivienne Lucy, *b* 1957: *m* 1976, Alan Urquhart, and has issue living, Katrina Lucy *b* 1982, Sheona Anne *b* 1984. The Hon Mrs Epps also has issue, Anne, *b* 1946; legally adopted by her stepfather, Edward James White: *m* 1st, 1970 (*m diss* 19—), John K. Nichol; 2ndly, 1979, Donald McDonald Grant, who *d* 1982; 3rdly, 1990, Alexander George Reilly, of Blaeberry Cottage, Berryhill Farm, Grange-of-Lindores, Fife, and has issue living (by 1st *m*), Susan Pamela *b* 1971.

WIDOW LIVING OF SON OF FOURTH BARON

Catriona Sheila, da of James MacDonald, of Devonshaw House, Dollar: *m* 1955, Hon Donald Graham Fitz-Herbert Moncreiff, who *d* 1993, and has issue (see colls, infra). *Residence* – 26 Dollerie Terrace, Crieff, Perthshire PH7 3EG.

COLLATERAL BRANCHES LIVING

Issue of late Hon Donald Graham Fitz-Herbert Moncreiff, 2nd son of 4th Baron, *b* 1919, *d* 1993: *m* 1955, Catriona Sheila (ante), da of James MacDonald, of Devonshaw House, Dollar:—
Ranald Patrick MacDonald, *b* 1965. —— Barbara Jane (2 Newton Grove, Chiswick, W4 1LB), *b* 1957. —— Frances Catriona Fitz-Herbert, *b* 1959: *m* 1991, Alan O'Hara, and has issue living, Daniel James, *b* 1992, — Liam Donald, *b* 1994. —— Theresa Madeline Fitz-Herbert, *b* 1961: *m* 1987, James Stephen Hanna, and has issue living, Siobhan Rosemary Fitz-Herbert, *b* 1988, — Madeleine Lisa Marie, *b* 1990.

Granddaughter of late Hon James William Moncreiff, 3rd son of 1st Baron:—
Issue of late Edwin Robert Moncreiff, *b* 1877, *d* 1962: *m* 1904, Mary, who *d* 1953, da of late Matthew Montgomerie Bell, WS, of Edinburgh:—
Mary Eileen, *b* 1909: *m* 1st, 1929, Maj John Roy Oakley, Roy Scouts who was *ka* in Palestine 1939; 2ndly, 1939, Capt Charles Philip McLaughlan, architect, and has issue living, (by 2nd *m*) Ian Wellwood, *b* 1940; Maj Scots Guards, — Ann Wellwood, *b* 1944: *m* 1965, David Bryan Godfrey-Faussett, of Keepers Cottage, Bickleigh, Devon EX16 8RA, and has issue living, Katherine Sarah *b* 1971.

Grandchildren of late James Hamilton Moncreiff, yr son of late Hon Francis Jeffrey Moncreiff (infra):—
Issue of late Frederick Henry Wellwood Moncreiff, *b* 1909, *d* 1990: *m* 1939, Gwendolen Alma (Box 98, Haenertsburg, Transvaal, S Africa), da of Patrick Gifford:—
Andrew Malcolm (Crossways House, Vann Rd, Fernhurst, Haslemere, Surrey), *b* 1944; *ed* Pembroke Coll, Camb (MA): *m* 1971, Jennifer Margaret, da of John Chapman, of Johannesburg, and has issue living, Michael Patrick, *b* 1974, — Robert James, *b* 1977. —— Patricia Jane (Box 146, Haenertsburg, Northern Province, 0730 South Africa), *b* 1941.

PREDECESSORS – **(1)** JOHN Moncreiff, MP, *cr* a *Baronet* 1626 (of Moncreiff) with remainder to his heirs male whatsoever; *d* 1650; *s* by his el son **(2)** JOHN, 2nd Bt, who in 1663 sold the Moncreiff estates to his cousin Thomas Moncreiff, who in 1685 was *cr* a *Baronet*; *d* 1675; *s* by his brother **(3)** DAVID, 3rd Bt; *s* by his brother **(4)** JAMES, 4th Bt, at whose decease the direct line of the 1st Bt expired and the baronetcy reverted to the son of Hugh Moncreiff, yst brother of the 1st Bt. **(5)** JOHN, 5th Bt; was an eminent Physician; *d* 1710; *s* by his son **(6)** HUGH, 6th Bt; *d* 1744; *s* by his kinsman, a descendant of Archibald Moncreiff, uncle of 1st Bt **(7)** *Rev* WILLIAM, 7th Bt; *d* 1767; *s* by his son **(8)** *Rev* HENRY, DD; was an eminent Divine of the Church of Scotland; assumed the additional surname of Wellwood; *d* 1827; *s* by his son **(9)** JAMES WELLWOOD, 9th Bt; *b* 1776; was a Lord of Session and Justiciary of Scotland 1829-51: *m* 1808, Ann, who *d* 1843, da of Capt George Robertson, RN; *d* 1851; *s* by his son **(10)** HENRY WELLWOOD, DD, 10th Bt, was an eminent Divine of the Free Church of Scotland; *dsp* 1883; *s* by his brother **(11)** JAMES, PC, LLD, 11th Bt, who had previously been *cr* a *Baronet* (of Tulliebole) 1871, and *Baron Moncreiff*, of Tulliebole, co Kinross (peerage of United Kingdom) 1873; *b* 1811; MP for Leith Dist (*L*) 1851-9, for Edinburgh 1859-68, and for Glasgow and Aberdeen Univs 1868-9; was Dean of Faculty of Advocates for Scotland 1858-69, Solicitor-Gen for Scotland 1850-51, Lord Advocate 1851, 1852-8, 1859-66, and Lord Justice-Clerk 1869-88: *m* 1834, Isabella, who *d* 1881, da of Robert Bell, Sheriff of Berwick and Haddington; *d* 1895; *s* by his el son **(12)** HENRY JAMES, 2nd Baron; *b* 1840; Sheriff of Renfrew and Bute 1881-8, and a Judge of Court of Session, Scotland (with title of *Lord Wellwood*) 1888-1905: *m* 1st, 1866, Susan Wilhelmine, who *d* 1869, 3rd da of Sir William H. Dick-Cunyngham, 8th Bt; 2ndly, 1873, Millicent Julia, who *d* 1881, da of late Col Fryer, of Moulton Paddocks, Newmarket; *d* 1909; *s* by his brother **(13)** *Rev* ROBERT CHICHESTER, 3rd Baron; *b* 1843; V of Tanworth 1885-1913: *m* 1871, Florence Kate, who *d* 1926, da of late Lieut-Col Richard Henry FitzHerbert; *d* 1913; *s* by his son **(14)** JAMES ARTHUR FITZHERBERT, 4th Baron ; *b* 1872: *m* 1906, Lucy Vida, who *d* 1973, da of David Lechmere Anderson, LRCP, of Doncaster; *d* 1942; *s* by his el son **(15)** HARRY ROBERT WELLWOOD, 5th Baron and present peer.

Mond, family name of Baron Melchett.

MONK BRETTON, BARON (Dodson) (Baron UK 1884)

JOHN CHARLES DODSON, 3rd Baron; *b* 17 July 1924; *s* 1933; *ed* Westminster, and New Coll, Oxford: *m* 1958, Zoë Diana, da of Ian Douglas Murray Scott, and has issue.

Arms – Argent, on a fesse raguly plain cotised between six fleurs-de-lis all gules, a sword fesseways point to the dexter proper, pommel and hilt or. **Crest** – Two lion's jambs erased and in saltire gules, entwined by a serpent, head to the dexter proper. **Supporters** – On either side a female figure proper, vested argent, mantle azure, each resting the exterior hand of an antique shield also azure, adorned gold, that on the *dexter* charged with a balance suspended, and that on the *sinister*, with a staff erect entwined by a serpent all or.
Residence – Shelley's Folly, Cooksbridge, nr Lewes, E Sussex BN8 4SU. *Club* – Farmers'.

Successful by favour of Providence

SONS LIVING

Hon CHRISTOPHER MARK, *b* 2 Aug 1958; *ed* Eton, and Univ of S California (MBA): *m* 1988, Karen L., only da of B. J. McKelvain, of Fairfield, Conn, USA, and has issue living, Ben, *b* 1989—James, *b* 1994, — Emma, *b* 1990.

Hon Henry, *b* 1960; *ed* Eton; BSc (1983) Council for Nat Academic Awards; ARICS 1986.

PREDECESSORS – (1) *Rt Hon* JOHN GEORGE Dodson, CB, only son of late Rt Hon Sir John Dodson LLD, MP for Rye 1819-23; *b* 1825; Dep Speaker and Chm of Committees of House of Commons 1865-72, Financial Sec to Treasury 1873-4, Pres of Lord Govt Board 1880-82, 1874-80, *cr Baron Monk Bretton*, of Conyboro and Hurstpierpoint, co Sussex (peerage of United Kingdom) 1884, Florence, da of W. J. Campion, of Danny, Sussex; *d* 1897; *s* by his son (2) JOHN WILLIAM, CB, 2nd Baron; *b* 1869; a JP and DL for E Sussex; Private Sec to Sec of State for Colonies 1900-1903; Chm of London County Council 1929-30: *m* 1911, Ruth, who *d* 1967, da of late Hon Charles Brand; *d* 1933; *s* by his son (3) JOHN CHARLES, 3rd Baron and present peer.

MONKSWELL, BARON (Collier) (Baron UK 1885)

GERARD COLLIER, 5th Baron; *b* 28 Jan 1947; *s* 1984; *ed* George Heriot's Sch, Edinburgh: *m* 1974, Ann Valeria, da of James Collins, of Liverpool, and has issue.

Arms – Argent, on a chevron azure, between in chief two demi-unicorns courant and in base an elephant's head erased gules, three oak branches slipped, leaved and fructed or. **Crest** – A demiman affrontee proper, holding in the dexter hand an oak branch slipped and leaved proper, fructed or, and resting the sinister hand on an escutcheon azure, charged with two keys saltirewise or. **Supporters** – Two Druids vested argent, wreathed about the temples with laurel leaves vert, each resting the exterior hand on an escutcheon azure, charged with a balance suspended or.
Address – c/o House of Lords, SW1.

SONS LIVING

Hon JAMES ADRIAN, *b* 29 March 1977.
Hon Robert William Gerard, *b* 1979.

DAUGHTER LIVING

Hon Laura Jennifer, *b* 1975.

BROTHER LIVING

Neil Adrian José, *b* 1948; *ed* George Heriot's Sch, E Anglia Univ (BSc), and Leicester Univ (Cert Ed): *m* 1st, 1975 (*m diss* 1985), Frances Myra Chapman; 2ndly, 1987, Judith Bosca Brandes, da of late Rico G. Bosca. *Residence* – 1335 Peralta Av, Berkeley, Calif 94702, USA.

HALF-BROTHER LIVING (*Son of disclaimed 4th Baron by 3rd wife*)

Benjamino, *b* 1958: *m* 1984, Clare Maria Murphy, and has issue living, Daniel James William Paulo, *b* 1987, — Seamus, *b* 1989. *Residence* – Church Farm, Batcombe, Shepton Mallet, Som.

HALF-SISTER LIVING (*Daughter of disclaimed 4th Baron by 3rd wife*)

Tiaré Penelope Katherine, *b* 1952. *Residence* – The Clatterway, Bonsall, nr Matlock, Derbys.

UNCLE LIVING (*Brother of disclaimed 4th Baron*)

Perceval Gerard, *b* 1915: *m* 1st, 1940 (*m diss* 1947), Lorraine Walker; 2ndly, 1949, Sheila, who *d* 1975, elder da of late Capt Stuart Mackintosh Macpherson, OBE, RAMC, and formerly wife of S/Ldr Robert Francis Doe, DSO and bar, RAF; 3rdly, 1977, Brenda Mary, da of Nathaniel Victor Fortescue, and formerly wife of Geoffrey Dacre Carpenter, and has issue living (by 1st *m*), Anthony Gerard (W/5 Water Rat, T/O Entrepotdok 55, 1018 AD, Amsterdam, Holland), *b* 1942; *ed* Leicester Univ, — (by 2nd *m*), Gavin (113 Mesa Vista 3, Santa Fe, New Mexico 87501, USA), *b* 1951, — Tessa Jill, *b* 1950: *m* 19—, Stephen Roberts, of 17 Bays Court, Bays Rd, Lymington, Hants SO41 8JB. *Residence* – 27 Ickenham Rd, Ruislip, Middlesex.

AUNT LIVING (*Sister of disclaimed 4th Baron*)

Anna Evangeline, *b* 1918: *m* 1940, Elvin Thorgerson, of 19 Earl St, Cambridge, and has issue living, Storm Elvin, *b* 1944.

WIDOW LIVING OF FOURTH BARON (*who disclaimed the peerage for life* 1964)

NORA SELBY (*Mrs William A. L. Collier*): *m* 1951, as his 3rd wife, the 4th Baron Monkswell, who disclaimed his peerage for life 1964, and who *d* 1984. *Residence* – 6 Corona Rd, Cambridge.

MOTHER LIVING

Helen, da of James Dunbar, of Edinburgh (infra): *m* 1st, 1945 (*m diss* 1950), as his 2nd wife, William Adrian Larry Collier, MB, BCh, later 4th Baron Monkswell (until he disclaimed his peerage for life 1964), who *d* 1984; 2ndly, 1954, Edward Edmund Kemp. *Residence* – 31 Orchard Rd South, Edinburgh EH4 3JA.

COLLATERAL BRANCHES LIVING

Grandchildren of late Hon Gerard Collier, 2nd son of 2nd Baron:—
Issue of late John Bernard Collier, *b* 1920, *d* 1993: *m* 1947, Elsie (12 Argyle Crescent, Portobello, Edinburgh), da of James Dunbar, of Edinburgh (ante):—
Anna Lee, *b* 1948: *m* 19— (*m diss* 19—), Michael Gates, and has issue living, Catherine, *b* 1973. —— Sarah, *b* 1950: *m* 1987, John Bett, of East Lodge, Balbirnie, Markinch, Fife, and has issue living, Leo Mark Sean Collier, *b* 1988. —— The late John Bernard Collier also had issue (by Barbara Oriel Markham), Piers Markham COLLIER (11 Northbank Walk, Didsbury, Manchester), *b* 1947: *m* 1973 (*m diss* 1993), Susan Margaret Robinson, and has issue living, Matthew John Samuel, *b* 1978, — Esme Lorraine, *b* 1976.

Grandson of late Hon John Collier, OBE, 2nd son of 1st Baron:—
Issue of late Sir Laurence Collier, KCMG, *b* 1890, *d* 1976: *m* 1917, Eleanor Emma Antoinette, who *d* 1975, only da of late William Luther Watson, S Lancs Regt:—
William Oswald, *b* 1919; *ed* Bradfield Coll, and Balliol Coll, Oxford; FSA; FRHistS: *m* 1st, 1947 (*m diss* 1957), Hon Muriel Joan Lowry Lamb, da of 1st Baron Rochester; 2ndly, 1958, Ina Mary Grace, da of C. Crowne, of Littlehampton, Sussex, and has issue living (by 1st *m*), Sylvia Antoinette, *b* 1952: *m* 1985, Stephen Kenneth Godfrey, of 33 Observatory Rd, SW14 7QB, — (by 2nd *m*), Jonathan Charles Laurence (3 Sheengate Mansions, 307 Upper Richmond Rd West, SW14 8QS), *b* 1959, — Lucy Eleanor Mary, *b* 1961: *m* 1988, David William Hewitt, of 63 Magdalen Rd, SW18 3NE, — Stella Catherine Juliet (17 Prospect St, Erskineville, Sydney, NSW 2043, Australia), *b* 1965. *Residence* – 34 Berwyn Rd, Richmond, Surrey. *Club* – Athenaeum.

PREDECESSORS – (1) *Rt Hon Sir* ROBERT PORRETT Collier: was Solicitor-Gen 1863-6, and Attorney-Gen 1868-71; MP for Plymouth (*L*) 1852-71, and a Judge of Judicial Committee of Privy Council; 1871-86; *cr Baron Monkswell*, of Monkswell, co Devon (peerage of United Kingdom), 1885; *b* 1817: *m* 1844, Isabella, who *d* 1886, el da of William Rose Rose, of Wolston Heath, Coventry; *d* 27 Oct 1886; *s* by his el son (2) ROBERT, 2nd Baron; *b* 1845; a Lord-in-Waiting to Queen Victoria 1892-5, and Under-Sec of State for War 1895: *m* 1873, Mary Josephine, who *d* 1930, da of late Joseph Alfred Hardcastle, MP: *d* 1909; *s* by his el son (3) ROBERT ALFRED HARDCASTLE, 3rd Baron, *b* 1875; 2nd Sec Foreign office 1905-10: *m* 1908, Ursula Mary, who *d* 1915, da of Col Hugh Gurney Barclay, MVO, of Colney Hall, Norwich (B Magheramorne); 2ndly, 1925, Katherine Edith, who *d* 1985, da of William Shaw Harriss Gastrell, of Rockbeare Grange, nr Exeter; *d* 1964; *s* by his nephew (4) WILLIAM ADRIAN LARRY, MB, BCh, DPH (son of late Hon Gerard Collier, 2nd son of 2nd Baron), 4th Baron, until he disclaimed his peerage 7 April 1964, *b* 1913; adopted additional christian name of Larry 1932; Member of Halstead UDC 1954-67, and Co Councillor Essex 1958-61; Gen Practitioner, District MO Falmouth, Jamaica; 1939-45 War with RAMC in M-W Europe and Middle East: *m* 1st, 1939 (*m diss* 1945), Erika, da of Dr Edward Kellner, of Vienna; 2ndly, 1945 (*m diss* 1950), Helen, da of James Dunbar, of Edinburgh; 3rdly, 1951, Nora Selby; *d* 1984; *s* by his eldest son (5) GERARD, 5th Baron and present peer.

MONRO OF LANGHOLM, BARON (Monro) (Life Baron 1997)

HECTOR SEYMOUR PETER MONRO, AE, PC, son of late Capt Ian Alastair Seymour Hale Monro, Cameron Highlanders (*see* E Lisburne, 1941 Edn); *b* 4 Oct 1922; *ed* Canford, and King's Coll, Camb; MP for Dumfries (*C*) 1964-97; Scottish Conservative Whip 1967-70; Lord Commr of the Treasury 1970-71; Parliamentary Under-Sec, Scottish Office 1971-74; Opposition Spokesman on Scottish Affairs 1974-75, and Sport 1974-79; Parliamentary Under-Sec for the Environment (with special responsibility for sport) 1979-81; Parliamentary Under-Sec of State, Scottish Office 1992-95; Chm Dumfriesshire Unionist Assoc 1958-63; Memb Queen's Body Guard for Scotland (Royal Company of Archers); Dumfries T & AFA 1959-67; NFU Scotland Area Cttee; Hon Air Cdre 2622 (Highland) RAuxAF Regt Sqdn since 1982; Hon Inspector-Gen RAuxF since 1990; Pres Scottish Rugby Union 1976-77, Auto-Cycle Union 1983-90, Nat Small Bore Rifle Assoc 1987-92; Memb Nature Conservancy Council 1982-91; JP Dumfries 1963, DL 1973; served 1939-45 War as Fl Lt RAF, RAuxAF 1946-53; *cr* AE 1953, Kt 1981, PC 1995, and *Baron Monro of Langholm*, of Westerkirk in Dumfries and Galloway (Life Baron) 1997: *m* 1st, 1949, (Elizabeth) Anne, who *d* 1994, da of Maj Harry Welch, of Longstone Hall, Derbyshire; 2ndly, 1994, Mrs Doris Kaestner, of Woodbrook, Baltimore, Maryland, USA, and has issue by 1st *m*.

Arms – Or an eagle's head erased gules holding in its beak a stem of club moss vert, on a chief paly of six or and sable a bend counterchanged. **Crest** – A golden eagle close proper.
Residence – Williamwood, Kirtlebridge, Lockerbie, Dumfries. *Clubs* – RAF, RSAC, MCC, Royal and Ancient.

SONS LIVING (*By 1st marriage*)

Hon Seymour Hector Russell Hale, CBE; *b* 1950; *ed* Glenalmond; Brig late 20th Highlanders; CBE 1996; ADC 1998 *m* 1978, Angela, da of Wing Cdr Barney Sandeman, of Rhu, and has issue living, Harry Seymour Edward, *b* 1979, — Alexander Hector Barney, *b* 1981, — Robert John Ewart, *b* 1983.
Hon Hugh Brisbane Henry Ewart, MBE, *b* 1953, *ed* Glenalmond; Brig late Highland Regt; MBE 1988: *m* 1982, Catriona, da of Rev A. R. Torrie, of Ardgour, and has issue living, Flora Lotus, *b* 1984, — Clare Marion, *b* 1986, — Ailsa Rona, *b* 1990.

MONSELL, VISCOUNTCY (Eyres Monsell) (Extinct 1993)

SISTER LIVING OF SECOND VISCOUNT

Hon Joan Elizabeth, *b* 1912: *m* 1st, 1939 (*m diss* 1947), William John Rayner CBE; 2ndly, 1968, Patrick Michael Leigh Fermor, DSO, OBE, writer. *Residence* – Kardamyli, Messenia, Greece.

MONSLOW, BARONY OF (Monslow) (Extinct 1966)

DAUGHTER LIVING OF LIFE BARON (*By 1st marriage*)

Hon Rosemary, *b* 1921: *m* 1948, William Harold Sparks, who *d* 1985, of 41 Trinity St, Rhostyllen, Wrexham, Clwyd.

WIDOW LIVING OF LIFE BARON

JEAN BAIRD (*Baroness Monslow*) (4 Kirklea Circus, Glasgow), da of Rev Angus Macdonald: *m* 1960, as his 2nd wife, Baron Monslow (Life Baron), who *d* 1966.

MONSON, BARON (Monson) (Baron GB 1728, Bt E 1611)
(Name and Title pronounced "Munson")

Ready for my country

JOHN MONSON, 11th Baron, and 15th Baronet; *b* 3 May 1932; *s* 1958; *ed* Eton, and Trin Coll, Camb (BA 1954): *m* 1955, Emma, da of late Anthony Devas, ARA, and has issue.

𝔄rms – Or, two chevronels gules. ℭrest – A lion rampant proper, supporting a column or. 𝔖upporters – *Dexter*, a lion or; *Sinister*, a griffin wings elevated argent, beaked and membered azure; each gorged with a plain collar azure, charged with three crescents or, and having a line reflexed over the back blue.
Residence – The Manor House, South Carlton, Lincoln.

SONS LIVING

Hon NICHOLAS JOHN, *b* 19 Oct 1955; *ed* Eton: *m* 1981, Hilary, only da of Kenneth Martin, of PO Box 42, Ukunda, Mombasa, Kenya, and has issue living, Alexander John Runan, *b* 1984, — Isabella, *b* 1986. *Residence* – 24 Fentiman Rd, SW8 1LS.
Hon Andrew Anthony John, *b* 1959: *m* 1993, Emily C., yr da of Richard Clement Wheeler-Bennett, of The Mill House, Calstone Wellington, nr Calne, Wilts, and has issue living, Seraphina Lucea Ellen, *b* 1998.
Hon Stephen Alexander John, *b* 1961.

BROTHERS LIVING

Hon Jeremy David Alfonso John, *b* 1934; *ed* Eton, and RMA; Maj Gren Gds (ret 1967); CC Berks 1981-93; High Sheriff Berks 1994-95: *m* 1958, Patricia Mary, yr da of late Maj George Barker, MFH, of Stanlake Park, Twyford, Berks, and has issue living, (John) Guy Elmhirst (19 Grafton Sq, SW4), *b* 1962: *m* 1995, Lady (Olivia) Rose Mildred FitzRoy, yst da of 11th Duke of Grafton, KG, and has issue living, Olivia Effie Fortune *b* 1995, — Antonia Debonnaire, *b* 1959. *Residence* – Keepers Cottage, Scarletts Wood, Hare Hatch, nr Reading, Berks RG10 9TL.
Hon Anthony John, *b* 1944; *ed* Malvern.

SISTER LIVING

Hon Sandra Debonnaire, *b* 1937: *m* 1958 (*m diss* 1971), Maj (William) Garry Patterson, Life Guards, and has issue living, James William John, *b* 1970, — Debonnaire Jane, *b* 1959: *m* 1984, Count Leopold von Bismarck, yst son of late Prince Otto von Bismarck, of Friedrichsruh, W Germany, and has issue living, *Count* Nikolai Leopold Archibald *b* 1986, *Count* Tassilo Valentine Christian *b* 1989, *Count* Caspar Maximilian Otto *b* 1991, *Count* Carl Alexander Sascha Ludwig John *b* 1995, — Juliet Mary, *b* 1963: *m* 1995, Richard J. W. Milliken, son of late Julian Milliken, of Hammer Hill, Abinger, Surrey and has issue living, Tatiana Laura *b* 1998, — Annabel Kate (*Baroness Rayleigh*), *b* 1965: *m* 1991, 6th Baron Rayleigh, of Terling Place, Chelmsford, Essex, and has issue (see that title). *Residence* – 23 Lamont Rd, SW10 0HR.

WIDOW LIVING OF TENTH BARON

BETTIE NORTHRUP, da of late Lieut-Col E. Alexander Powell, of Riverain, Falls Village, Connecticut, USA; *m* 1st, 1931, the 10th Baron Monson, who *d* 1958; 2ndly, 1962, Capt James Arnold Phillips, who *d* 1983. *Residence* – La Corderie, Rue St Pierre, St Peter in the Wood, Guernsey, CI.

COLLATERAL BRANCHES LIVING

Granddaughter of late Rev Hon Evelyn John Monson, 6th son of 6th Baron:—
Issue of late Capt Charles Evelyn John Monson, *b* 1878, *d* 1953: *m* 1924, Mabel Gertrude (Orotara, 123 Yarborough Rd, Lincoln), da of Edwin Benjamin Pritchard, of Lincoln:—
Rachel Anne, *b* 1920.

Grandchildren of late Alfred John Monson, 3rd son of Rev Thomas John Monson (infra):—
Issue of late Philip Evelyn John Monson, DD, PhD, *b* 1887, *d* 1964: *m* 1st, 1920, Doris Murray, who *d* 1942; 2ndly, 1956, Catherine A.—:—
(By 1st *m*) †Philip John, *b* 1928; *d* 1983, California, USA. —— Margaret Enid, *b* 1922.

Grandson of late Rev Thomas John Monson, son of Rev Hon Thomas Monson, 5th son of 2nd Baron:—
Issue of late Henry John Monson, b 1862, d 1930: m 1901, Theodosia Anne Emily, who d 1951, da of Rev
George Howard-Wright, R of Offord D'Arcy, Hunts (B Denman):—
Thomas Debonnaire John (c/o Lawn Hospital, Union Rd, Lincoln), b 1905; ed Haileybury: m 1934 (m diss 1956), Anna
Phillipe Bois Clements.

PREDECESSORS – (1) Sir Thomas Monson, MP for co Lincoln 1597-8, for Castle Rising 1604-11, and for Cricklade
1614; Master of Armoury and Master of Armoury and Master Falconer to James 1; cr Baronet 1611; d 1641; s by his son
(2) Sir John, KB, 2nd Bt; MP for Lincoln City 1660 and 1664-78; d 1683; s by his grandson (3) Sir Henry, 3rd Bt; MP
for Lincoln City 1679-80; dsp 1718; s by his brother (4) Sir William, PC, 4th Bt; d 1727; s by his nephew (5) Sir John,
5th Bt; MP for Lincoln City 1722-8; cr Baron Monson, of Burton, co Lincoln (peerage of Great Britain); was Capt of Band
of Gentlemen Pensioners 1733, and First Commr of Trade and Plantations 1737; d 1748; s by his son (6) John, 2nd
Baron; d 1774; s by his son (7) John, 3rd Baron; d 1806; s by his son (8) John George, 4th Baron; b 1785, d 1809; s by
his son (9) Frederick John, 5th Baron; dsp 1841; s by his cousin (10) William John, 6th Baron; b 1796: m 1828, Eliza,
who d 1863, da of late Edmund Larken, of Bedford Square; London; d 1862; s by his son (11) William John, PC, 7th
Baron; b 1829; MP for Reigate (L) 1858-62, Treasurer of HM Queen Victoria's Household 1874, Capt, of HM's Yeomen
of the Guard 1880-85 and 1886, Master of the Horse 1892-4, and Militia ADC to HM 1886-96; cr Viscount Oxenbridge, of
Burton, co Lincoln (peerage of Great Britain) 1886: m 1869, Hon Maria Adelaide, who d 1897, sister of 1st Earl de
Montalt, and widow of 2nd Earl of Yarborough; d 1898, when the Viscountcy became ext, and he was s in the Barony by
his brother (12) Debonnaire John, CVO, 8th Baron, b 1839; Sergeant-at-Arms to HM Queen Victoria's Household, and
Equerry, Comptroller, and Treasurer to HRH the Duke of Saxe-Coburg and Gotha (Duke of Edinburgh); m 1861,
Augusta Louisa Caroline, who d 1936, da of late Lieut-Col Hon Augustus Ellis; d 1900; s by his son (13) Augustus
Debonnaire John, 9th Baron, b 1868: m 1903, Romaine Madeleine, who d 1943, da of late Gen Roy Stone, of Mendham,
New Jersey, USA, and widow of Lawrence Turnure, of New York, d 1940; s by his son (14) John Rosebery, 10th Baron;
b 1907: Bar Inner Temple 1931, Bettie Northrup (who m 2ndly, 1962, Capt James Arnold Phillips, who d 1983), da of
Lieut-Col E. Alexander Powell, of Journey's End, Chevy Chase, Maryland, USA; d 1958: s by his el son (15) John, 11th
Baron and present peer.

Montagu, family name of Duke of Manchester.

Montagu, family name of Baron Swaythling.

MONTAGU OF BEAULIEU, BARON (Douglas-Scott-Montagu) (Baron UK 1885)
(Title pronounced "Montagu of Bewly")

Let us be judged by our actions

EDWARD JOHN BARRINGTON DOUGLAS-SCOTT-MONTAGU, 3rd Baron; *b* 20 Oct 1926; *s* 1929; *ed* Ridley Coll, St Catharine's, Ontario, Eton, and New Coll, Oxford; Lt Gren Gds 1945-48; Founder Montagu Motor Museum at Beaulieu 1952; Chm Nat Motor Museum Trust since 1972, and English Heritage 1984-92; Pres Museums Assocn 1982-84; Development Commr 1980-84; Founder Pres Historic Houses Assocn 1973-78, and Pres Union of European Historic Houses 1978-81; Pres Southern Tourist Bd, Assocn Brit Transport and Engr Museums and UK Vineyards Assocn; Chancellor Wine Guild of UK; Hon Fellow Museums Assocn; FRSA, FIPR, Hon DTech; Commodore Beaulieu River Sailing Club, Nelson Boat Owners' Club, and Vice Commodore House of Lords Yacht Club; Commodore Royal Southampton Club 1983-86; Hon Fell Inst of Motor Industry, Pres Historic Commercial Vehicle Soc, Disabled Drivers' Motor Club, Fedn of British Historic Vehicle Clubs; Founder British Vehicle Salvage Fedn; Millennium Pres Inst of Journalists; Founder and publisher of *The Veteran and Vintage Magazine* 1956-79, and author of books on Motoring History, and Historic Houses: *m* 1st 1959 (*m diss* 1974), (Elizabeth) Belinda, only da of late Capt Hon John de Bathe Crossley (*see* B Somerleyton, colls); 2ndly, 1974, Fiona Margaret, da of Richard Herbert, and has issue by 1st and 2nd *m*.

Arms – Quarterly of four: 1st and 4th grand quarter, 1st and 4th argent, three lozenges conjoined in fesse gules, within a bordure sable, *Montagu*; 2nd and 3rd or, an eagle displayed vert, beaked and membered gules, *Monthermer*; 2nd grand quarter argent on a bend azure, an estoile or, between two crescents also or, *Scott*; 3rd grand quarterly, 1st and 4th argent, a human heart gules imperially crowned or, on a chief azure three mullets of the field, *Douglas*; 2nd and 3rd azure, a bend between six crosses crosslet fitchée, the whole within a bordure or, charged with a double tressure flory counterflory, *Mar*. **Crests** – 1st, a griffin's head, couped at the neck or, winged and beaked sable; 2nd, a stag trippant proper; 3rd, a human heart gules, imperially crowned or, between two wings of the second. **Supporters** – Two griffins or, winged and beaked sable, each charged on the shoulder with a cap of maintenance azure.
Seat – Palace House, Beaulieu, Hants SO42 7ZN. *Town Residence* – Flat 11, Wyndham House, 24 Bryanston Sq, W1H 7FJ.

SONS LIVING (*By 1st marriage*)

Hon RALPH, *b* 13 March 1961.

(*By 2nd marriage*)

Hon Jonathan Deane, *b* 1975.

DAUGHTER LIVING (*By 1st marriage*)

Hon Mary Rachel, *b* 1964: *m* 1997, Rupert Benjamin Bartle Frere Scott (*see* M Lothian, colls).

SISTERS LIVING

Hon Anne Rachel Pearl (*Hon Lady Chichester*), *b* 1921: *m* 1st, 1946, Maj Howel Joseph Moore-Gwyn, Welsh Guards, who *d* 1947; 2ndly, 1950, Sir (Edward) John Chichester, 11th Bt, and has issue living, (by 1st *m*) David John Howel (7 Phillimore Terr, Allen St, W8), *b* 1947: *m* 1974, Alison Frances, yr da of Clifford G. White, and has issue living, Henry John Howel *b* 1975, George Augustus Joseph *b* 1987, Alice Beatrice Rachel *b* 1978, — (by 2nd *m*) (*see* Chichester, Bt). *Residence* – Battramsley Lodge, Lymington, Hants SO41 8PT.
Hon Caroline Cecily, *b* 1925: *m* 1950 (*m diss* 1987), (George) Grainger Weston, and has issue living, Galvin (6 Paultons St, SW3 5DP), *b* 1951: *m* 1st, 1976 (*m diss* 1979), Lily Lori, da of late Bill Lipscy; 2ndly, 1997, Michelle Louise, yst da of late Sqdn-Ldr David Evans, RAF, of Canford Cliffs, Dorset, and has issue living (by 1st *m*), Garrett (a son) *b* 1977, — Gregg (690 Laurel Lane, New Braunfels, Texas 78130, USA), *b* 1956: *m* 1988, Monique, da of Claude Degagne, of Ottawa, Canada, and has issue living, Charlotte *b* 1995, Isabella Gabrielle *b* 1998, — Graham (112 E Pecan St, Box 6, San Antonio, Texas 78205, USA), *b* 1964: *m* 1995, Elizabeth, da of Elwood Cluck, of San Antonio, Texas, and has issue living, Glenn (a son) *b* 1997, Grant *b* 1998, — Sarah, *b* 1953: *m* 1975, Dr Mark Eidson, of 3001 Old Dennis Rd, Weatherford, Texas 76087, USA, and has issue living, Weston (a son) *b* 1979, Beau (a son) *b* 1982, Barrett (a son) *b* 1985. *Residence* – 985 Allen St, New Braunfels, Texas 78130, USA.
Hon Mary Clare *b* 1928: *m* 1st, 1953 (*m diss* 1968), David Bethune, Viscount Garnock (later 15th Earl of Lindsay), who *d* 1989; 2ndly, 1979, Timothy Charles Austin Horn, of Chapel House, Builth Wells, Powys, and has issue (by 1st *m*) (*see* E Lindsay).

HALF-SISTER LIVING

Hon Elizabeth Susan, *b* 1909: *m* 1962, Col Arthur Noel Claude Varley, CBE, who *d* 1985. *Residence* – The Mill Race, Beaulieu, Hants.

PREDECESSORS – **(1)** HENRY JOHN Douglas-Scott-Montagu, 2nd son of 5th Duke of Buccleuch; *b* 1832; MP for Selkirkshire (*C*) 1861-8, and for S Hampshire 1868-84; sometime Official Verderer of the New Forest; *cr Baron Montagu of Beaulieu* (peerage of United Kingdom) 1885: *m* 1865, Hon Cecily Susan Stuart-Wortley, who *d* 1915, sister of 1st Earl of Wharncliffe; *d* 1905; *s* by his el son **(2)** JOHN WALTER EDWARD, KCIE, CSI, 2nd Baron; *b* 1866; Founder *The Car Illustrated* and Editor, and other publications; a Member of Road Board; acted as a Member of War Aircraft Committee March to April 1916, and was Adviser on Mechanical Transport Ser to Govt of India during European War (Hon Brig-Gen); a Member of Mechanical Warfare Board; MP for Hants, New Forest Div (*C*)1892-1905; CSI 1916, KCIE 1919: *m* 1st, 1889, Lady Cecil Victoria Constance, who *d* 1919, el da of 9th Marquess of Lothian; 2ndly, 1920, (Alice) Pearl (who *d* 1996, aged 101, having *m* 2ndly, 1936, Capt Hon Edward Pleydell-Bouverie, MVO, RN (*see* E Radnor, colls), who *d* 1951), da of late Major Edward Barrington Crake, Rifle Bde; *d* 1929; *s* by his son **(3)** EDWARD JOHN BARRINGTON, 3rd Baron and present peer.

Montague, family name of Baron Amwell.

MONTAGUE OF OXFORD, BARON (Montague) (Life Baron 1997)

MICHAEL JACOB MONTAGUE, CBE, son of late David Elias Montague, of Willesden; *b* 10 March 1932; *ed* High Wycombe Royal Gram Sch, and Magdalen Coll Sch, Oxford; founded Gatehill Beco Ltd 1959, sold company to Valor and became Dep Man Dir 1962, Chm Valor 1965; founded Hospitality Hotels Ltd 1970; non-exec Dir President Entertainments 1985-87, and Pleasurama plc 1987-89; created Yale & Valor plc 1987-92; Pres Hana Maui De Luxe Hotel and Ranch, Hawaii 1990-93; non-exec Dir Jarvis Hotels Ltd since 1990; non-exec Dir Williams Holdings plc (following merger with Yale & Valor plc) 1991-93; non-exec Chm Superframe plc since 1995; non-exec Dir Jarvis Hotels plc since 1990; Chm Cyprus Tourism Advisory Cttee 1969-74, Enquiry into Overseas Trade Organisation 1974, and English Tourist Board 1979-84; Memb Ordnance Survey Advisory Board 1983-85; Pres British Assoc of Industrial Editors 1983-85; Chm Nat Consumer Council 1985-87; Vice-Pres Council of Royal Albert Hall 1985-94; Pres Oxford Brookes Univ Assoc 1990; Chm Board of Henley Festival Ltd 1991-94; Gov Oxford Brookes Univ 1991-96; Memb Select Fundraising Cttee Entertainment Artistes' Benevolent Fund 1991-95; Dir Greater London Enterprise Ltd 1991-92; Memb Millennium Commn until 1997; *cr* CBE 1970, and *Baron Montague of Oxford*, of Oxford, co Oxon (Life Baron) 1997.

𝕬rms – Gules on a fess wavy between two bulls' heads caboshed argent armed or a bull's head caboshed gules armed or. 𝕮rest – A demi yale sable armed tusked unguled and supporting with the hooves a key wards downwards and inwards or. 𝕾upporters – On either side a red crested cardinal reguardant proper in the beak a chrysanthemum.
Residences – Astwood House, 16 Courtfield Rd, SW7 4DD; River Willows, 67 Abingdon Rd, Dorchester-on-Thames, Oxon OX10 9LB.

MONTEAGLE OF BRANDON, BARON (Spring Rice) (Baron UK 1839)

GERALD SPRING RICE, 6th Baron; *b* 5 July 1926; *s* 1946; *ed* Harrow; Capt (retired) Irish Gds; One of HM's Body Guard of Hon Corps of Gentlemen-at-Arms 1978-96; Member London Stock Exchange 1958-76, Lloyds 1978-98: *m* 1949, Anne, da of late Col Guy James Brownlow, DSO, DL, Rifle Brig, of Ballywhite, Portaferry, co Down, and has issue.

𝕬rms – Quarterly; 1st and 4th, quarterly, 1st and 4th, quarterly 1st and 4th, per pale indented argent and gules, 2nd and 3rd, azure, a lion rampant or; 2nd, or, on a chevron sable, between three mascles, as many mullets argent,; 3rd, paly of six argent and azure, a bend sable. 𝕮rest – A leopard's head affrontée, ducally crowned or. 𝕾upporters – Not on record.
Residence – 242A Fulham Rd, SW10. *Clubs* – Cavalry and Guards', Pratt's, Kildare Street and University.

SON LIVING

Faith does not fear

Hon CHARLES JAMES, *b* 24 Feb 1953; *ed* Harrow; Head of English, Holy Family Coll, Walthamstow since 1992: *m* 1987, Mary Teresa Glover, and has issue living, Helena Maire, *b* 1987, — Charlotte Etain, *b* 1988, — Agnes Imogen, *b* 1991, — Thea Teresa, *b* 1995. *Residence* – 26 Malvern Rd, E8 3LP.

DAUGHTERS LIVING

Hon Elinor, *b* 1950: *m* 1974, Myles Clare Elliott, of 41 Ravenscourt Rd, W6, and has issue living, Thomas Emerson, *b* 1977, — Nina Anne, *b* 1980, — Emma Clare, *b* 1983.
Hon Angela (twin) *b* 1950; resumed her maiden name 1982: *m* 1st, 1973 (*m diss* 1982), Christopher Richard Seton Sheppard; 2ndly, 1991, Peter Alan Kirby Ottewill of 24 Marney Rd, SW11 5EP, son of Maj W. K. Ottewill, of Rafford, Moray, and has issue living (by 1st *m*), Catherine Christy Seton, *b* 1976.
Hon Fiona, *b* 1957: *m* 1982, Andrew Louis Garber, of Beech Tree Cottage, Preston Candover, Hampshire RG25 2EJ, yst son of S. Garber, of St John's Wood, NW8, and has issue living, Rose Anne, *b* 1985, — Eliza Kate, *b* 1987, — Alice Finola, *b* 1991.

BROTHER LIVING

Hon Michael, *b* 1935; *ed* Harrow; late Lieut Irish Gds: *m* 1959, Fiona, yr da of late James Edward Kenneth Sprot, of Natal, and has issue living, Jonathan, *b* 1964: *m* 1997, Natalie Lara, elder da of Anthony Rivett Robinson, of Bracknell, Berks, — Kerry (da), *b* 1962. *Residence* – Fosseway House, Nettleton Shrub, Chippenham, Wilts SN14 7NL. *Clubs* – Boodle's, Pratt's, Royal and Ancient Golf and Swinley Forest Golf.

SISTER LIVING

Hon Joan, *b* 1928: *m* 1953, Michael Shears Payne, MC (Harvey, Bt (*cr* 1868) ext), of Scotlands Farm, Cockpole Green, nr Wargrave, Berks RG10 8QP, and has issue living, Ashley Desmond, *b* 1956: *m* 1998, Emma Louise, elder da of late Colin James, of Cotleigh, Devon, — Karina, *b* 1954.

PREDECESSORS – (1) Rt Hon THOMAS Spring Rice; *b* 1790; MP for Limerick 1820-32, Cambridge 1832-9, Under-Sec for Home Depart 1827, Sec of Treasury 1830-4, Sec of State for War and Colonies 1834, Chancellor of the Exchequer 1835-9, and Comptroller Gen of the Exchequer 1835-65; *cr Baron Monteagle of Brandon* co Kerry (peerage of United Kingdom) 1839; *d* 1866; *s* by his grandson (2) THOMAS (el son of late Hon Stephen Edmond Spring Rice, el son of 1st Baron, by Ellen Mary, da of late Serjeant William Frere), 2nd Baron; *b* 1849: *m* 1875, Elizabeth, who *d* 1908, da of late Most Rev Rt Hon Samuel Butcher, DD, 90th Lord Bishop of Meath; *d* 1926; *s* by his son (3) THOMAS AUBREY, CMG, MVO, 3rd Baron, *b* 1886; in Diplo, Ser; *d* 1934; *s* by his uncle (4) FRANCIS (younger son of late Hon Stephen Edmund Spring Rice (ante)); *b* 1852; Cdr (ret) RN: *m* 1st, 1882, Elizabeth Ann, who *d* 1922, da of Sir Peter Fitzgerald, 1st Bt (19th Knight of Kerry); 2ndly, 1935, Julia Emma Isabella, who *d* 1936, da of Sir Peter George FitzGerald, 1st Bt (ante), and widow of Stephen Edward Spring Rice, CB; *d* 1937; *s* by his son (5) CHARLES, 5th Baron, *b* 1887: *m* 1925, Emilie de Kosenko (who *m* 2ndly, 1954, Col Courtenay Fergus Ochoncar Grey Forbes, late Coldstream Guards (*see* L Forbes, colls), and *d* 1981), da of Mrs Edward Brooks, of New York, USA; *d* 1946; *s* by his son (6) GERALD, 6th Baron and present peer.

Montgomerie, Lord; son of Earl of Eglinton and Winton.

Montgomerie, family name of Earl of Eglinton and Winton.

Montgomery, Earl of, see Earl of Pembroke and Montgomery.

MONTGOMERY OF ALAMEIN, VISCOUNT (Montgomery) (Viscount UK 1946)

DAVID BERNARD MONTGOMERY, CBE, 2nd Viscount; *b* 18 Aug 1928; *s* 1976; *ed* Winchester, and Trin Coll, Camb; late Lt RTR; a Councillor R Borough of Kensington and Chelsea 1974-78; Chm of Economic Affairs Cttee, Canning House 1973-75; a Dir, Yardley Internat Ltd 1963-74; Man Dir Terimar Services Ltd since 1974; Chm Baring Puma Fund since 1991; Editorial Adviser Vision Interamericana 1974-94; Dir Korn/Ferry Internat 1977-93, Northern Engr Industries 1981-87; Chm Antofagasta (Chili) & Bolivia Rlwy Co 1980-82, and Hispanic & Luso Brasilian Council 1978-80 (Pres 1987-94); Chm, Brasilian Chamber of Commerce in GB 1980-82, Pres Anglo-Argentine Soc 1977-87, Redgrave Theatre Trust 1978-89, Restaurateurs Assocn of GB 1982-90; Pres Centre for Internat Briefing (Farnham Castle) since 1985; CBE (Civil) 1975; Gran Oficial, Orden Bernardo O'Higgins (Chile) 1989; Gran Oficial, Orden Libertador San Martin (Argentina) 1992; Grande Oficial, Orden Nacional Cruzeiro do Sul (Brazil) 1993; Encomienda, Orden de Isabel la Catolica (Spain) 1993; Commander's Cross, Order of Merit (Germany) 1993; Encomienda, Orden del Aguila Azteca (Mexico) 1994, Cmdr, Order of Leopold II (Belgium) 1997, Gran Cruz, Order of San Carlos (Colombia) 1998, and Gran Oficial, Orden Libertador (Venezuela) 1999: *m* 1st, 1953 (*m diss* 1967), Mary Raymond, yr da of late Sir Charles Connell; 2ndly, 1970, Tessa, da of late Lt-Gen Sir Frederick Arthur Montague Browning, GCVO, KBE, CB, DSO (by his late wife, Dame Daphne du Maurier, DBE), and formerly wife of late Maj Peter P. J. de Zulueta, Welsh Gds, and has issue by 1st *m*.

𝔄rms – Azure, two lions passant guardant between three fleurs-de-lys, two in chief and one in base, and two trefoils in fesse all or. 𝔠rest – Issuant from a crescent argent an arm embowed in armour, the hand grasping a broken tilting spear in bend sinister, the head pendent proper. 𝔖upporters – *Dexter*, a Knight in chain armour and surcoat resting his exterior hand on his sword; *sinister*, a soldier in battle dress all propr.
Residence – 54 Cadogan Square, SW1 0JW. *Clubs* – Canning, Garrick.

SON LIVING (*By 1st marriage*)

Hon HENRY DAVID (Manor House, All Stretton, Shropshire) *b* 2 April 1954: *m* 1980, Caroline J., da of late Richard Odey, of Hotham Hall, York, and has issue living, Alexa Maud, *b* 1984, — Flora Veronica, *b* 1988, — Phoebe Matilda, *b* 1990.

DAUGHTER LIVING (*By 1st marriage*)

Hon Arabella Clare, *b* 1956: *m* 1982, Jeremy Hugh Stuart-Smith, of Pie Corner, Bedmond, Herts, and has had issue (*see* E Verulam, colls).

PREDECESSOR – **(1)** *Field Marshal Sir* BERNARD LAW Montgomery, KG, GCB, DSO, son of late Rt Rev Henry Hutchinson Montgomery, KCMG, DD, Preb of St Paul's and Prelate of Order of St Michael and St George, of New Park, Morville, co Donegal; *b* 1887; GOC-in-C 8th Army 1942-43, GOC Allied Army in UK 1944, and 21st Army Group 1944-45; C-in-C BAOR 1945-46; CIGS 1946-48; Chm of W Europe C-in-C Cttee 1948-51; Dep Supreme Cdr, Allied Powers in Europe 1951-58; *cr Viscount Montgomery of Alamein*, of Hindhead, co Surrey (peerage of UK) 1946: *m* 1927, Elizabeth, who *d* 1937, da of late Robert Thompson Hobart, ICS, and widow of Capt Oswald Armitage Carver; *d* 1976; *s* by his only son (2) DAVID BERNARD, CBE, 2nd Viscount, and present peer.

MONTROSE, DUKE OF (Graham) (Duke S 1707, Bt S 1625)

Forget not

JAMES GRAHAM, 8th Duke, and 12th Baronet; *b* 6 April 1935; *s* 1992; *ed* Loretto; Hereditary Sheriff of co Dunbarton; Member Queen's Body Guard for Scotland (Royal Company of Archers) since 1965, Brig since 1976; Member Council Scottish Nat Farmers' Union 1981-86 and 1987-90; OStJ 1978: *m* 1970, Catherine Elizabeth MacDonnell, yst da of late Capt Norman Andrew Thomson Young, Queen's Own Cameron Highlanders of Canada, of Ottawa, and has issue.

𝔞rms – Quarterly: 1st and 4th or, on a chief sable three escallops of the field, *Graham*; 2nd and 3rd argent, three roses gules, barbed and seeded proper, *Montrose*. ℭrest – An Eagle, wings hovering or, preying on a stork on its back proper. Ꙃupporters – Two storks argent, beaked and membered gules.
Seat – Auchmar, Drymen, Glasgow G63 0AG. *Clubs* – Royal Scottish Pipers' Soc, and Royal Highland Agricultural.

SONS LIVING

JAMES ALEXANDER NORMAN (*Marquess of Graham*), *b* 16 Aug 1973; *ed* Eton, Edinburgh Univ (BSc), and Cape Town Univ (MSc), — *Lord* Ronald John Christopher, *b* 1975; *ed* Eton, and Edinburgh Univ.

DAUGHTER LIVING

Lady Hermione Elizabeth, *b* 1971; Wycombe Abbey, and Magdalen Coll, Oxford.

HALF-BROTHERS LIVING

Lord Donald Alasdair, *b* 1956; *ed* St Andrew's Coll, Grahamstown, St Andrews Univ (BSc), and INSEAD (MBA): *m* 1981, his 2nd cousin, Bride Donalda Elspeth, yst da of Maj Allan John Cameron, of Allangrange, Ross and Cromarty (*see* D Montrose, 1976 Edn), and has had issue, Alasdair John Cameron, *b* 1986, *d* 1988, — Caitriana Mary Alice, *b* 1984, — Violet Elizabeth Helen, *b* 1992, — Jennie Alexandra Cameron, *b* 1993. *Residence* – Nether Tillyrie, Milnathort, Kinross-shire KY13 7RW.

Lord Calum Ian, *b* 1958; *ed* St Andrew's Coll, Grahamstown, Cape Town Univ (BSc), and INSEAD (MBA): *m* 1991, Catherine Beatrice, yst da of John Peter Fraser-Mackenzie (*see* Scott, Bt, *cr* 1913), and has issue living, Iain Angus, *b* 1995, — Euan Douglas, *b* 1996. *Address* – Montrose Estate, Drymen, Glasgow G63 0BQ.

SISTER LIVING

Lady Fiona Mary, *b* 1932: *m* 1966, Peter Alexander O'Brien Hannon, 2nd son of late Ven Archdeacon Gordon Hannon, of Ardreigh House, Cultra, co Down, and has issue living, Catherine Mary, *b* 1968: *m* 1991, Mark Tremayne Boobbyer (*see* B Rennell), — Veronica Maeve, *b* 1971: *m* 1992, Jasper E. Bark, son of Roy Bark, of Station Rd, Dalton-in-Furness, Cumbria. *Residence* – The Fort House, Dundooan, Coleraine, co Derry BT52 2PX.

HALF-SISTERS LIVING

Lady Cairistiona Anne (Kirstie), *b* 1955; *ed* Ruskin Sch of Fine Art: *m* 1982, Philip Patrick Saggers, son of Gordon F. Saggers, of PO Box 43, Lockhart 2656, NSW, Australia, and has issue living, Susanna Mary, *b* 1984, — Marina Lilias, *b* 1986, — Georgina Frances, *b* 1989. *Residence* – 42 Cook St, Randwick, NSW 2031, Australia.

Lady Lilias Catriona Maighearad, *b* 1960; *ed* St Andrews Univ (BSc): *m* 1990, Jonathan Dillon Bell, and has issue (*see* Borthwick, Bt, colls). *Residence* – 40 Colwyn St, Ngaio, Wellington, New Zealand.

AUNT LIVING (*daughter of 6th Duke*)

Lady Jean Sybil Violet, *b* 1920; DL Ayr and Arran Dist: *m* 1947 (*m diss* 1957), Col John Patrick Ilbert Fforde, CBE, who *d* 1993, and has issue living, Charles John Graham (Sannox House, Currie, Isle of Arran), *b* 1948: *m* 1998, Linda Rose Carrigan. *Residence* – Strabane, Brodick, Isle of Arran KA27 8DD.

WIDOW LIVING OF SEVENTH DUKE

SUSAN MARY JOCELYN (*Dowager Duchess of Montrose*), da of late Dr John Mervyn Semple, of Gilgil, Kenya, and widow of Michael Raleigh Gibbs, of Nakuru, Kenya: *m* 1952, as his 2nd wife, the 7th Duke of Montrose, who *d* 1992. *Residence –* Nether Tillyrie, Milnathort, Kinross-shire KY13 0RW.

COLLATERAL BRANCHES LIVING

Issue of late Brig Lord (Douglas) Malise Graham, 2nd son of 5th Duke, *b* 1883, *d* 1974: *m* 1919, Hon Rachael Mary Holland, who *d* 1977, da of 2nd Viscount Knutsford:—
Ivar Malise (Danny, Hurstpierpoint, W Sussex), *b* 1920; *ed* Eton, and Trin Coll, Camb (MA); Archives Dip (London): *m* 1958 (*m diss* 1973), Isabel Mary, da of late C. B. Ewart, of Limpsfield Surrey, and formerly wife of A. W. Carpenter, and has issue living, Alastair David (22 Leyborne Av, W13 9RB), *b* 1959: *m* 1989, Janet Deans, da of Henry Cunison Deans Rankin, of Campsie Knowe, Carnock, Fife, and has issue living, Helen Rankin *b* 1995, Fiona Ewart *b* 1998, — Lucy Helen, *b* 1963; *ed* Bryanston, and Queen's Coll, Oxford: *m* 1997, Jeremy Charles Hawes, son of John Hawes, of New Yatt, Oxon. —— Euan Douglas, CB (Hill Farm, Heddington, Calne, Wilts), *b* 1924; *ed* Eton, and Ch Ch, Oxford (MA); CB 1985: *m* 1st, 1954 (*m diss* 1970), Pauline Laetitia, da of late Hon David Francis Tennant (*see* B Glenconner, colls), and formerly wife of Capt Julian Lane Fox-Pitt-Rivers (*see* By Forster, 1980 Edn); 2ndly, 1972, Caroline Esther, da of Sheriff Kenneth W. B. Middleton of Cobblers Cottage, Ledwell, Oxon, and has issue living (from 1st *m*), Andrew Douglas (adopted son), *b* 1964, — (by 2nd *m*), Sarah Caroline, *b* 1973, — Alexandra Katherine, *b* 1976.

Issue of late Lord Alastair Mungo Graham, Capt RN, yst son of 5th Duke, *b* 1886, *d* 1976: *m* 1st 1916, Lady Meriel Olivia Bathurst, who *d* 1936, da of 7th Earl Bathurst; 2ndly, 1944, Sheelagh Violet Edgeworth, who *d* 1985, da of late Essex Edgeworth Reade (B Templemore colls):—
(By 1st *m*) Ian James (Chantry Farm, Campsey Ash, Suffolk), *b* 1923: *ed* Winchester, and Trin Coll, Dublin (BA): Dir, Maya Corpus Program, Peabody Museum, Harvard Univ, Camb, Mass, USA. —— Robin Angus, *b* 1926. —— Lilias Violet, *b* 1917. —— Margaret Christina, *b* 1919: *m* 1960, Thomas Colin Ernest Campbell-Preston, MC, TD, who *d* 1999, of 1 Bishop's Way, Stradbroke, Suffolk IP21 5JR, and has an adopted son, Patrick, *b* 1964; *ed* Eton, and Trin Coll, Camb.

PREDECESSORS – (1) PATRICK Graham, on of the Lords of the Regency during the minority of James II, was *cr Lord Graham* (peerage of Scotland) 1445; *d* about 1465; *s* by his son **(2)** WILLIAM, 2nd Lord; *d* 1472; *s* by his son **(3)** WILLIAM, 3rd Lord; fought with gallantry at the battle of Sauchyburn 1488; *cr Earl of Montrose* 1505; fell at Flodden 1513; *s* by his son **(4)** WILLIAM, 2nd Earl; *d* 1571; *s* by his grandson **(5)** JOHN, 3rd Earl; was Chancellor of Scotland 1599-1604, and Viceroy of Scotland 1604-8; *d* 1608, having *m* 1563, Hon Jean Drummond, and had three sons of whom the 2nd, William, was *cr* a *Baronet* 1625, of Braco while to the Earldom *s* the el son **(6)** JOHN, 4th Earl; was Pres of the Council in Scotland 1626; *s* by his son **(7)** JAMES, 5th Earl; having served with the Covenanters 1638-40, espoused the royal cause, and was in 1644 *cr Marquess of Montrose* (peerage of Scotland), and appointed Capt-Gen and Com-in-Ch of all the forces to be raised in Scotland for the King's service; having gained a number of brilliant victories over the Parliamentarians, he was surprised and totally defeated at Philiphaugh 13 Sept 1645; he then left Scotland, and after the execution of the King joined Charles II at the Hague, from whence in 1650 he returned, and having raised a small force was defeatd at Strachan 17 April 1650, and being afterwards taken prisoner was on 20 May following sentenced by the Scottish Parliament to be hanged, &c, which sentence was carried out on the following day and his quartered remains after being exposed were interred beneath the gallows, from whence however they were removed at the Restoration and buried in state in the aisle of the Cathedral Church of St Giles, 14 May 1661; *s* by his son **(8)** JAMES, PC, 2nd Marquess, who was immediately after the return of Charles II, restored to his honours and estates; appointed an Extraordinary Lord of Session 1668; *s* by his son **(9)** JAMES 3rd Marquess; was Pres of the Guards and Pres of the Council; *d* 1684; *s* by his son **(10)** JAMES, KG, PC, 4th Marquess; Lord Pres of the Council in Scotland 1706, a Representative Peer 1707-27, Keeper of the Privy Seal 1709-13, Principal Sec of State to George I, and Keeper of the Great Seal of Scotland 1716-33; resigned the patent Marquess of Montrose, and has a new Charter granted 1706 with various limitations, *cr Lord Aberuthven, Mugdock and Fintrie, Viscount Dundaff, Earl of Kincardine, Marquess of Graham and Buchanan* and *Duke of Montrose* (Peerage of Scotland) 1707; *d* 1742; *s* by his son **(11)** WILLIAM, 2nd Duke, who had in 1731 *s* his brother David who had in 1722 been *cr Baron Graham* and *Earl Graham* (peerage of Great Britain), with remainder to his brothers; *d* 1790; *s* by his son **(12)** JAMES, KG, KT, PC, 3rd Duke; was successively MP for Richmond and Great Bedwin, a Lord of the Treasury, Paymaster of the Forces, Master of the Horse, Lord Justice Gen of Scotland, Lord-Lieut of cos Stirling and Dunbarton, Pres of Board of Trade, and Joint Postmaster Gen; *d* 1836; *s* by his son **(13)** JAMES, KT, 4th Duke; *b* 1799; sat as MP for Cambridge 1826-30, Lord Steward of the Household 1852, Chancellor of the Duchy of Lancaster 1858-9, and Postmaster-Gen 1866: *m* 1836, Hon Caroline Agnes Beresford, who *d* 1894 (having *m* 2ndly, 1876, William Stuart Stirling-Crawford, who *d* 1883; 3rdly, 1888, Marcus Henry Milner), da of 2nd Baron Decies; *d* 1874; *s* by his son **(14)** DOUGLAS BERESFORD MALISE RONALD, KT, 5th Duke; *b* 1852; Hon Brig-Gen and Lord-Lieut of co Stirling; Lord Clerk Register of Scotland 1890-1925, and Chancellor of the Order of the Thistle 1917-25; High Commr for Gen Assembly of Church of Scotland 1916: *m* 1876 *Dame* Violet Hermione, GBE, LLD, who *d* 1940, da of Sir Frederick Ulrick Graham, 3rd Bt, of Netherby, Cumbria; *d* 1925; *s* by his el son **(15)** JAMES, KT, CB, CVO, VD, LLD, 6th Duke; *b* 1878; S Africa 1901, attached to Naval Brig, European War 1914-19 with Auxiliary Naval Patrol; Lord-Lieut of co Bute 1920-53; sometime Assist Private Sec (unpaid) to Chancellor of the Exchequer (Rt Hon J. Austen Chamberlain, MP); Lord High Commr to Gen Assembly of Church of Scotland 1942 and 1943: *m* 1906, Lady Mary Louise Douglas-Hamilton, OBE, who *d* 1957, da of 12th Duke of Hamilton; *d* 1954; *s* by his el son **(16)** JAMES ANGUS, 7th Duke, *b* 1907; Min of Agric, Lands and Natural Resources, S Rhodesia 1962-65, of Agric, Rhodesia 1964-65, and External Affairs and Defence, Rhodesia 1966-68; Lt-Cmdr RNVR 1939-45 War: *m* 1st, 1930 (*m diss* 1950), Isobel Veronica, who *d* 1990, da of late Lt-Col Thomas Byrne Sellar, CMG, DSO; 2ndly, 1952, Susan Mary Jocelyn, da of late Dr John Mervyn Semple, of Gilgil, Kenya, and widow of Michael Raleigh Gibbs; *d* 1992; *s* by his eldest son **(17)** JAMES 8th Duke and present peer; also Marquess of Montrose, Marquess of Graham and Buchanan, Earl of Montrose, Earl of Kincardine, Earl of Graham, Viscount Dundaff, Lord Graham, and Lord Aberuthven, Mugdock and Fintrie.

Moore, Viscount; son of Earl of Drogheda.

Moore, family name of Earl of Drogheda.

MOORE OF LOWER MARSH, BARON (Moore) (Life Baron 1992)

JOHN EDWARD MICHAEL MOORE, PC, son of Edward Moore, of Brighton; *b* 26 Nov 1937; *ed* Licensed Victuallers' Sch, Slough, and LSE (BSc); late Royal Sussex Regt, Korea 1955-57; Member London Borough Council of Merton 1971-74, Vice-Chm Conservative Party 1975-79, Parly Under Sec for Energy 1979-83, Min of State, Economic Sec at the Treasury June-Oct 1983, Financial Sec 1983-86, Sec of State for Transport 1986-87, Health and Social Services, Social Security, 1988-89; Chm Dean Witter Internat Ltd 1975-79 (Dir 1968-79), Energy Saving Trust 1992-96 (since when Pres), Credit Suisse Asset Management Ltd since 1992, and Monitor Europe since 1992; Dir Swiss American Corporation since 1992, Monitor Inc since 1992, G. Tech since 1992, Blue Circle Industries since 1993, and Rolls Royce since 1994 (Dep Chm since 1996); Member Court of Governors, LSE since 1977 Member Advisory Boards of Sir Alexander Gibb & Ptnrs (now ret), and Marvin & Palmer Assocs Inc, Council Member Inst of Dirs; MP Croydon Central (*C*) Feb 1974-92; *cr* PC 1986, and *Baron Moore of Lower Marsh*, of Lower Marsh in the London Borough of Lambeth (Life Baron) 1992: *m* 1962, Sheila Sarah, da of Richard Tillotson, of Illinois, USA, and has issue.

ᴀʀᴍꜱ – Azure, a dolphin naiant argent between three bunches of grapes stalked and leaved gold. Cʀᴇꜱᴛ – A griffin statant erect azure billety or and bezanty, beak, forelegs and wings also or, holding in the dexter foreclaw a double-warded key wards upward gold. Sᴜᴘᴘᴏʀᴛᴇʀꜱ – On either side a griffin statant erect azure, that to the dexter bezanty, that to the sinister billety or, the beak, forelegs and wings of each also or, the compartment comprising two grassy mounts with marshland between them all proper.
Address – c/o House of Lords, SW1.

SONS LIVING

Hon Martin, *b* 1970.
Hon Richard, *b* 1972.

DAUGHTER LIVING

Hon Stephanie Jane, *b* 1968: *m* 1994, David Mortimer Man, son of William Mortimer Man (*see* Earldom of Jowitt), and has issue living, Oliver Wynn, *b* 1995, — Lucas Richard, *b* 1997.

MOORE OF WOLVERCOTE, BARON (Moore) (Life Baron 1986)

·MORIBUS·ET·CONSILIO·

PHILIP BRIAN CECIL MOORE, GCB, GCVO, CMG, QSO, PC; *b* 6 April 1921, son of late Cecil Moore, ICS; *ed* Cheltenham Coll, and Brasenose Coll, Oxford; Prin Private Sec to First Lord of the Admiralty 1957-58, British Dep High Commr, Singapore 1961-65, Dir of Public Relations, Min of Defence, 1965-66, Assist Private Sec to HM 1966-72, Dep Private Sec 1972-77, Private Sec and Keeper of the Queen's Archives 1977-86; Permanent Lord in Waiting and Extra Equerry to HM The Queen; Chm Trustees King George VI and Queen Elizabeth Foundation of St Catharine's 1986-97; 1939-45 War as Fl-Lieut Bomber Comd RAF; *cr* CMG 1966, CB (Civil) 1973, KCVO 1976, KCB 1980, GCVO 1983, GCB 1985, and *Baron Moore of Wolvercote*, of Wolvercote, City of Oxford (Life Baron) 1986: *m* 1945, Joan Ursula, da of Capt M. E. Greenop, DCLI, and has issue.

Arms – Gules on a fess between two lions passant guardant or three moorcocks sable crested gules. **Crest** – A moorcock proper gorged with a crown or holding in its dexter claw a quill pen proper. **Supporters** – *Dexter*, a wolf proper crowned or gorged with a collar argent fimbriated or thereon roses gules barbed and seeded proper and cross crosslets sable; *sinister*, a stag proper attired and unguled or crowned also or gorged with a collar argent fimbriated or thereon cross crosslets sable and roses gules barbed and seeded proper therefrom a chain reflexed behind the back ending in a ring gold, the compartment comprising a grassy mount growing therefrom on each side between a thistle and a shamrock both proper a rose gules stalk and leaves vert barbed and seeded to the front thereof on the dexter side a rugby football and similarly on the sinister side a cricket ball proper. **Motto** – Moribus Et Consilio.
Residence – Hampton Court Palace, E Molesey, Surrey. *Clubs* – Athenaeum and MCC.

DAUGHTERS LIVING

Hon Sally Jane, *b* 1949: *m* 1980 (*m diss* 1984), Richard Gerald Grindon Leachman, and has issue living, Lucinda, *b* 1980. *Residence* – 20 Marlborough Buildings, Bath, Avon.

Hon Jill Georgina, *b* 1951: *m* 1971 (*m diss* 1990), Peter Gabriel, and has issue living, Anna Marie, *b* 1974, — Melanie, *b* 1976.

MORAN, BARON (Wilson) (Baron UK 1943)

(RICHARD) JOHN McMORAN WILSON, KCMG, 2nd Baron; *b* 22 Sept 1924; *s* 1977; *ed* Eton, and King's Coll, Camb; Sub-Lt RNVR in 1939-45 War; 3rd Sec, British Embassy, Ankara 1948-50, Tel Aviv 1950-53, 2nd Sec, Rio de Janeiro 1953-56, 1st Sec FO 1956-59, Washington 1959-61, FO 1961-65, Counsellor British Embassy, S Africa 1965-68, and Head of W Africa Deptm FCO 1968-73, and concurrently Ambassador to Chad 1970-73, Hungary 1973-76, and Portugal 1976-81; UK High Commr to Canada 1981-84; formerly Chm Wildlife and Countryside Link, Regional Fisheries Advisory Cttee, Welsh Region, NRA, and Pres Welsh Salmon and Trout Anglers' Association; Vice-Chm Atlantic Salmon Trust; Chm Salmon and Trout Assocn; Pres Radnorshire Wildlife Trust; author of *A Life of Sir Henry Campbell-Bannerman* 1973 (Whitbread Prize for biography), and *Fairfax* 1985; KCMG 1981: *m* 1949, Shirley Rowntree, da of George James Harris, MC, of Bossall Hall, York, and has issue.
Address – c/o House of Lords, SW1.

SONS LIVING

Hon JAMES McMORAN (65 Upland Rd, Brookline, Mass 02146, USA), *b* 6 Aug 1952; *ed* Eton, and Trin Coll, Camb: *m* 1980, Hon (Mary) Jane Hepburne-Scott, yst da of 10th Lord Polwarth and has issue living, David Andrew McMoran, *b* 6 Nov 1990, — Alistair Thomas Hay, *b* 1993.

Hon William Edward Alexander, *b* 1956; *ed* Eton, and Inns of Court Sch of Law; barrister: *m* 1989, Juliette E. C., da of Maj Mungo Walker, of Empshott, Hants (*see* Walker, Bt, *cr* 1868, colls), and has issue living, Samuel, *b* 19—, — Edward Mungo John, *b* 1995.

DAUGHTER LIVING

Hon Juliet, b 1950; ed St Mary's Sch, Calne (Scholar), and Newnham Coll, Camb; Solicitor: m 1972, Hon Jeffrey Richard de Corban Evans, of 5 Campden House Court, 42 Gloucester Walk, W8, and has issue (see B Mountevans).

BROTHER LIVING

Hon Geoffrey Hazlitt, CVO, b 1929; ed Eton, and King's Coll, Camb (BA); FCA; late Roy Horse Guards; Chm of Southern Electric plc 1993-96, Dep Chm of Johnson Matthey plc 1995-98, formerly Dir Blue Circle Industries and Invesco English and International Trust, Chm of Delta plc 1982-94, formerly Pres British Electrotechnical and Allied Manufacturers Association, Dep Pres Engineering Employers Federation, Chm 100 Group of Finance Directors and Chm of W Midlands and Wales Region of Nat Westminster Bank; CVO 1989: m 1955 (Barbara) Jane, only da of late W. E. H. Hebblethwaite, of Itchen Stoke, Alresford, Hants, and has issue living, Nicholas Charles Hazlitt, b 1957, — Hugo William Hazlitt, b 1963, — and two adopted das, Laura Jane, b 1966, — Jessica Harriet, b 1967: m 1st, 1992, Simon C. Newson, yr son of J. A. Newson, of Bury, W Sussex; 2ndly, 1997, Maj Nicholas George Christopher Graf Strachwitz Hamilton, elder son of Christopher Graf Strachwitz Hamilton, of Dorset, and of S Tirol, Austria.

PREDECESSOR

PREDECESSOR – (1) CHARLES McMORAN Wilson, MC, MD, FRCP, son of John Forsythe Wilson, MD; b 1882; Pres Royal Coll of Physicians, London 1941-50; Consulting Physician to St Mary's Hosp; cr Knt 1938, and Baron Moran, of Manton, co Wilts (peerage of UK) 1943: m 1919, Dorothy, MBE, who d 1983, da of Samuel Felix Dufton, DSc; d 1977; s by his el son (2) (RICHARD) JOHN McMORAN, 2nd Baron and present peer.

MORAY, EARL OF (Stuart) (Earl S 1562)
(Title pronounced "Murry")

Salvation through Christ the Redeemer

DOUGLAS JOHN MORAY STUART, 20th Earl; b 13 Feb 1928; s 1974; ed Hilton Coll Natal and Trin Coll, Camb (BA); FRICS; a JP of Perthshire (1968): m 1964, Lady Malvina Dorothea Murray, el da of 7th Earl Mansfield and Mansfield, and has issue.

Arms – Quarterly: 1st and 4th the royal arms of Scotland (a lion rampant within a double tressure flory counterflory gules) surrounded with a bordure componée argent and azure, Moray; 2nd or, a fesse checky azure and argent, Stewart of Doune; 3rd or, three cushions within a double tressure flory counterflory gules, Randolph, Earl of Moray. Crest – A pelican in her piety, proper. Supporters – Two greyhounds argent, collared gules.
Residences – Doune Park, Doune, Perthshire; Darnaway Castle, Forres, Morayshire. Club – New (Edinburgh).

SON LIVING

JOHN DOUGLAS (Lord Doune), b 29 Aug 1966.

DAUGHTER LIVING

Lady Louisa Helena, b 1968.

BROTHERS LIVING

Hon Charles Rodney Stanford (6 Lynch Rd, Farnham, Surrey; Relugas Mill, Dunphail, Moray), b 1933; ed Stowe, and McGill Univ, Montreal (B Com 1958); late 2nd Lt The Queen's Bays: m 1st, 1961 (m diss 1986), Sasha A., el da of Lt-Col R. G. Lewis of The Old Rectory, Upper Swell, Stow on the Wold; 2ndly, 1986, Frauke, only da of Hans Stender, of Marne, Schleswig-Holstein, and has issue living (by 1st m), James Benjamin, b 1962, — Justin Nicholas Moray, b 1964, — Duncan Douglas, b 1967.

Hon James Wallace Wilson (twin), b 1933; ed Stowe, and McGill Univ, Montreal (BA 1958), late 2nd Lieut 13/18th Hussars: m 1958, Jane-Scott, only da of Group Capt Henry Gordon Richards, OBE, of Louisville, Kentucky, USA, and has issue living, Elizabeth May, b 1967; ed Westminster, and Yale Univ. Residences – Dunphail, Moray; 67 Cloncurry St, SW6. Clubs – Atlantic Cavalry (Montreal), Highland (Inverness).

DAUGHTERS LIVING OF EIGHTEENTH EARL

Lady Mary Anne, b 1926: m 1st, 1945 (m diss 1960), Leonard Byng, ARBS, who d 1974; 2ndly, 1961, Col John Bovill Denham, OBE, late Scots Gds, who d 1990, only son of late Sir Edward Brandis Denham, GCMG, KBE, and has issue living, (by 1st m) Rupert Wingfield, b 1946; ed Harrow, and New Coll, Oxford: m 1987, Mrs Francesca Stewart-Liberty, — Francis John Stuart, b 1956; ed Eton: m 1086, Caroline Margaret, only da of late G. E. Stevenson, of Lymington, Hants, and has issue living, Toby James Findhorn b 1986, Maximillian Rupert Stuart b 1989, — Charlotte Victoria, b 1947: m 1991, Julian L. C. de Wette, — Elizabeth, b 1949: m 1st, 1970, George Sulimirski, yst son of late Prof Tadeusz Sulimirski, of 26 Bishops Mansions, Bishops Park Rd, SW6; 2ndly, 1983, Comte Hervé le Bault de la Morinière, of Knoyle Place, East Knoyle, Salisbury, Wilts SP3 6AF, son of Comte Jean le Bault de la Morinière, and has issue living (by 2nd m), Louis Jean Victor b 1987, John Hervé b 1990, Camilla b 1985, — Lucy Anne, b 1954: m 1st, 1975 (m diss 1984), Isidore Brandel; 2ndly, 1990, Francis Robin Christopher Stickney (see Forbes, Bt, cr 1823), and has issue living (by 1st m), Lara Rebecca b 1977, (by 2nd m) (see Forbes, Bt, cr 1823), — (by 2nd m), Charles Edward, b 1966; ed

Harrow, and Univ of Kent at Canterbury, — Harriet, *b* 1963. *Residence* – Stoke Farthing House, Broad Chalke, Salisbury, Wilts SP5 5EE.

Lady Sarah Gray (*Lady Sarah Stuart*), *b* 1928: *m* 1947 (*m diss* 1977), 4th Baron Hillingdon, who *d* 1978. *Residence* – 62 Pembridge Villas, W11 3ET.

Lady Arabella (*Lady Arabella Stuart*), *b* 1934; resumed the surname of Stuart 1983: *m* 1956 (*m diss* 1981), (Charles) Mark Edward Boxer, cartoonist and publisher, who *d* 1988, and has issue living, Charles Stephen, *b* 1961: *m* 1984, Katie, da of Peter Forshall, — Henrietta Sophia, *b* 1958. *Residence* – 44 Elm Park Rd, SW3 6AX.

COLLATERAL BRANCHES LIVING

Issue of late Hon James Gray Stuart, CH, MVO, MC, PC (3rd son of 17th Earl) who was *cr Viscount Stuart of Findhorn* 1959 (see that title).

Grandchildren of late Charles Stuart, elder son of late John Alexander Stuart, of Carnock, great-great-grandson of late Archibald Stuart, 3rd son of 4th Earl:—
Issue of late Edgar Francis Stuart, *b* 1864, *d* 1940: *m* 1885, Margaret Jones, who *d* 1935:—
Herbert (Prestwick, Manchester), *b* 1893. —— Francis Gerald, *b* 1896. —— Alan Bruce, *b* 1897. —— Three das.

Granddaughter of late Richard Edgar Stuart, 6th son of late Charles Stuart (ante):—
Issue of late Charles William Stuart, *b* 1895, *d* 1921: *m* 1920, Bessie Lee, da of Walter W. Cook, of Milford, Utah, USA:—
Maxine Charles, *b* (*posthumous*) 1922: *m* 1944, Charles Maxwell Letz, and has issue living, Vicki Diane, *b* 1947.

Grandson of late James Stuart, 4th son of Charles Stuart (ante):—
Issue of late Charles Edward Stuart, *b* 1902, *d* 1982: *m* 1931, Blanche Wilma Bouvette, who *d* 1965:—
James Henry (2600, Hewlett Rd, Kelowna, BC, Canada V1W 4B4), *b* 1934: *m* 1955, Anna Frances Ebl, and has issue living, Charles Allan (811 Fenwick Place, Port Moody, BC, Canada V3H 1C1), *b* 1964: *m* 1993, Valerie Ann Kish, — Heather Marie, *b* 1961: *m* 1985, Antony Vincent Esposito, of 2951 Keets Drive, Coquitlam, BC, Canada V3C 4S6, and has issue living, Christopher James *b* 1990, Michael Jonathan *b* 1992, — Sheila Christine, *b* 1962: *m* 1st, 1983, John Stephen Beliveau; 2ndly, 1995, Bruce Robert Lawson, of 15776 101 Av, Surrey, BC, Canada V4N 2R4, and has issue living (by 2nd *m*), Tyler James *b* 1997.

PREDECESSORS – (1) JAMES Stuart, natural son of James V by Margaret, da of 5th Lord Erskine (*de jure* 17th Earl of Mar), *cr Earl of Moray*, and *Lord Abernethy and Strathearn* (peerage of Scotland) 1562; was Regent of Scotland when Queen Mary surrendered her crown to her infant son James VI: *m* 1562, Lady Agnes Keith (who *d* 1588 having *m* 2ndly 1572, Colin Campbell, Lord Lorne, afterwards 6th Earl of Argyll), da of 3rd Earl of Marischal; was murdered by one of his foes, Hamilton of Bothwellhaugh 1570; *s* by his da (2) ELIZABETH *Countess of Moray*, who *m* 1580, Sir James Stuart, who, in 1590 *s* his father as 2nd *Lord Doune* (see * infra); Sir James on his marriage assumed the earldom, and was known as the "Bonny Earl of Moray"; he was murdered in 1592 by the followers of the 6th Earl (afterwards 1st Marquess) of Huntly; the Countess *d* 1591; *s* by their son (3) JAMES, 3rd Earl: *m* 1607, Lady Anne Gordon, da of the instigator of his father's murder, he having previously, through the King's mediation, become reconciled to the Marquess of Huntly, obtained in 1611 from James VI a new investiture of the whole earldom of Moray to himself and his heirs male, and failing which to his brother Sir Francis and the heirs male of his body; *d* 1638; *s* by his son (4) JAMES, 4th Earl, who *s* as 3rd *Lord St Colme* 1642/3 (see † infra),: *m* 1627, Lady Margaret Home, who *d* 1683, da of 1st Earl of Home, *d* 1653; *s* by his son (5) ALEXANDER, KT, 5th Earl, *b* 1634; was Justice Gen 1675, Lord of the Treasury 1678, Sec of State and an Extraor Lord of Session 1680, and Commr to the Parliament of Scotland 1686: *m* 1658, Emilia, who *d* 1683, da of William Balfour, of Pitcullo; *d* 1700; *s* by his son (6) CHARLES, KT, 6th Earl, *b circa* 1660; *cr a Baronet* (Scotland) 1681: *m* 16—, Lady Anne Campbell, who *d* 1734, da of 9th Earl of Argyll, and widow of 4th Earl of Lauderdale; *dsp* 1735, when the baronetcy became ext; *s* by his brother (7) FRANCIS, 7th Earl, *b* 1673: *m* 1st, 1698, Elizabeth, da of Sir John Murray of Drumcairn; 2ndly, 1700, Hon Jean Elphinstone, who *d* 1739, da of 4th Lord Balmerinoch; *d* 1739; *s* by his son (8) JAMES, KT, 8th Earl, *b* 1708: *m* 1st, 1734, Grace, who *d* 1738, da of George Lockhart of Carnwath, and widow of 3rd Earl of Aboyne; 2ndly, 1740, Lady Margaret Wemyss, who *d* 1779, da of 4th Earl of Wemyss; *d* 1767: *s* by his son (9) FRANCIS, 9th Earl, *b* 1737; a Representative Peer 1784-96: *cr Baron Stuart of Castle Stuart* (peerage of Great Britain) 1796: *m* 1763, Hon Jane, who *d* 1786, el da of John, 12th Lord Gray; *d* 1810; *s* by his son (10) FRANCIS, KT, 10th Earl, *b* 1771; was Lord Lieut of Elgin: *m* 1st, 1795, Lucy, who *d* 1798, da of Gen John Scott, of Balcomie, co Fife; 2ndly, 1801, Margaret Jane, da of Sir Philip Ainslie, Knt, of Pilton, co Edinburgh; *d* 1848; *s* by his el son (11) FRANCIS, 11th Earl: *d* unmarried 1859; *s* by his brother (12) JOHN, 12th Earl; a Capt in the Army; *d* unmarried 1867; *s* by his half-brother (13) ARCHIBALD GEORGE, 13th Earl; a Lt-Col in the Army; *d* 1872; *s* by his brother (14) GEORGE PHILIP, 14th Earl, *b* 1816; *s* to the *Lordship of Gray* (*cr* 1444-5) under special remainder 1878; *d* 1895, when the Lordship of Gray (see that title) was adjudged by the Committee for Privileges of the House of Lords to Eveleen, who *d* 1918, wife of late James Maclaren Smith (who received Roy Licence 1897, to assume for himself and wife the additional surname and arms of Gray), and da of late Lady Jane Pounden, da of Francis, 10th Earl of Moray (ante), and the peerages of 1561, 1581, 1611, and 1796, devolved on his cousin (15) EDMUND ARCHIBALD, 15th Earl; *b* 1840; assumed in 1878 the additional surname and arms of Gray, on succeeding to the estates of Margaret, Lady Gray, which he discontinued on his succession to the Earldom: *m* 1877, Anna Mary, who *d* 1915, da of late Rev George J. Collinson, of Clapham; *d* 1901; *s* by his brother (16) FRANCIS JAMES, 16th Earl, *b* 1842; assumed in 1895, the additional surname and arms of Gray, which he discontinued in succeeding to the Earldom: *m* 1879, Gertrude Floyer, who *d* 1928, da of late Rev Francis Smith; *d* 1909; *s* by his brother (17) MORTON GARY, 17th Earl; assumed the additional surname and arms of Gray on succeeding to the Gray and Kinfauns estates 1901 (relinquished on succession to the title): *m* 1890, Edith Douglas, who *d* 1945, da of Rear-Adm George Palmer; *d* 1930; *s* by his son (18) FRANCIS DOUGLAS, MC, 18th Earl; *b* 1892; Lord-Lieut of Morayshire 1935-43; European War 1914-18 as Capt Scottish Horse and RFC (wounded MC): *m* 1924, Barbara, who *d* 1996, aged 92, da of John Archibald Murray, of New York; *d* 1943; *s* by his brother (19) (ARCHIBALD) JOHN MORTON, 19th Earl: *m* 1922, Mabel Helen Maud, who *d* 1968, da of Ben Wilson, of Battlefields, Zimbabwe; *d* 1974; *s* by his el son (20) DOUGLAS JOHN MORAY, 20th Earl and present peer; also Lord Abernethy and Strathearn, Lord Doune, Lord St Colme, and Baron Stuart of Castle Stuart.

Sir JAMES Stuart, of Doune, co Perth was *cr Lord Doune* (peerage of Scotland) 1581, with remainder to his heirs male whatsoever (a charter in confirmation 1588 gave a novodamus of the same with remainder to his heirs male whatsoever bearing the name and arms of Stuart); Extraor Lord of Session, Scotland 1584-6: *m* 1564, Lady Margaret Campbell, who *d* 1592, da of 4th Earl of Argyll; *d* 1590; *s* by his son (2) JAMES, 2nd Lord, but styled by courtesy Earl of Moray in right of his wife (see ante).

†HENRY Stuart, yr son of 1st Lord Doune (ante) was *cr Lord St Colme* (peerage of Scotland) 1611 with remainder to his heirs male and assigns whatsoever: *m* 1603, Lady Jean Stuart, (who *d* 1623, having *m* 2ndly, 16—, Nichol Bellenden), da of co-heir of 5th Earl of Atholl; *d* 1612; *s* by his son (2) JAMES, *b* 16—; Col in Swedish Ser; *d* 1642/3; *s* by his kinsman (3) JAMES, 4th Earl of Moray (see ante).

Moreton, Lord; son of Earl of Ducie.

Moreton, family name of Earl of Ducie.

Morgan, Vaughan-, surname of Barony of Reigate.

MORLEY, EARL OF (Parker) (Earl UK 1815)

Reward is sure to the faithful

JOHN ST AUBYN PARKER, KCVO, 6th Earl; *b* 29 May 1923; *ed* Eton; *s* 1962; Lt-Col (ret) R Fus; NW Europe 1944-45, and Palestine 1945-46, with KRRC, transferred R Fus 1947, Korea 1952-53, Middle East 1953-55, and 56; Comdg 1st Bn R Fus 1965-67; Hon Col Devon ACF 1979-87, Hon Col 4th Bn Devonshire and Dorset Regt 1987-92; a JP for Plymouth, and a DL for Devon; Vice Lord Lieut of Devon 1978-82, Lord Lieut 1982-98; Pres of Plymouth Incorporated Chamber of Trade and Commerce, since 1970, of West Country Tourist Board 1971-89, and Fedn of Chamber of Commerce and Traders Assocns, Cornwall 1972-79, Chm of Farm Industries Ltd, Truro 1970-85, a Member of Devon and Cornwall Cttee of National Trust 1969-84; Member of Governing Body of Plymouth Polytechnic 1975-82 (Chm 1977-82); Chm Plymouth Sound Ltd 1974-94; Dir Lloyd's Bank 1974-78 and Lloyd's Banking Management 1979-86; Chm Devon and Cornwall Regional Board 1974-89; a Gov of Seale-Hayne Agric Coll 1973-93; KCVO 1998: *m* 1955, Johanna Katherine, da of Sir John Molesworth-St Aubyn, 14th Bt, and has issue.

Arms – Sable, a buck's head cabossed, between two flaunches, argent. **Crest** – A cubit arm couped below the elbow, the sleeve azure, cuffed and slashed argent, the hand grasping a stag's attire gules. **Supporters** – *Dexter*, a stag argent, collared or, pendent from the collar a shield vert, charged with a horse's head, couped argent, bridled or, *sinister*, a greyhound sable, collared or, pendent from the collar a shield gules, charged with a ducal coronet or.
Seat – Saltram, Plympton, Devon. *Residence* – Pound House, Yelverton, S Devon.

SON LIVING

MARK LIONEL (*Viscount Boringdon*), *b* 22 Aug 1956; *ed* Eton; Lt R Green Jackets: *m* 1983, Carolyn Jill, da of Donald McVicar of Meols, Wirral, Cheshire, and has issue:—

DAUGHTERS LIVING—*Hon* Alexandra, *b* 1985, — *Hon* Olivia, 1987, — *Hon* Helena Georgia, *b* 1991.

DAUGHTER LIVING

Lady Venetia Katherine, *b* 1960: *m* 1997, Francis Jonathan Longstreth Thompson, elder son of Prof Francis Michael Longstreth Thompson, CBE, of Wheathampstead, Herts.

BROTHER LIVING *(Raised to the rank of an Earl's son 1963)*

Hon Nigel Geoffrey, *b* 1931; *ed* Eton, and Trin Coll, Camb; late Grenadier Guards; with Shell Petroleum Co, Ltd 1955-91: *m* 1965, Georgina Jane, el da of Sir Thomas Gordon Devitt, 2nd Bt (*cr* 1916), and has issue living, Edward Geoffrey, *b* 1967; *ed* Eton, and Brasenose Coll, Oxford: *m* 1992, Alice Victoria, da of Thomas Elliott, of Ivy House, Slawston, Leics, and has issue living, Oliver James *b* 1996, Harry Richard *b* 1997, Cordelia Rose *b* 1994, — Theresa Hilaria, *b* 1966; *ed* Homerton Coll, Camb: *m* 1994, Simon Maurice William Latham, eldest son of Robert Sidney Latham, of The Old Granary, Reigate, Surrey, and has issue living, Toby Robert Simon *b* 1995, Annabel Lydia Sophie *b* 1998. *Residence* – Combe Lane Farm, Wormley, Godalming, Surrey.

PREDECESSORS – (1) JOHN Parker, MP for Devonshire 1762-84; *cr Baron Boringdon*, of Boringdon, co Devon (peerage of Great Britain) 1784; *d* 1788; *s* by his son (2) JOHN, 2nd Baron; *cr Viscount Boringdon* and *Earl of Morley* (Peerage of United Kingdom) 1815; *d* 1840; *s* by his son (3) EDMUND, 2nd Earl; *b* 1810: *m* 1842, Harriet Sophia, who *d* 1897, da of Montagu Edmund Parker, of Whiteway, Devon, and widow of William Coryton, of Pentillie Castle, Cornwall; *d* 1864; *s* by his son (4) ALBERT EDMUND, PC, 3rd Earl; *b* 1843; as Lord-in-Waiting to HM Queen Victoria 1868-74, Under-Sec for War 1880-85, First Commr of Works 1886, and Chm of Committees and Dep Speaker of House of Lords 1889-1905: *m* 1876, Margaret, who *d* 1908, da of late Robert S. Holford (Lindsay, Bt) of Westonbirt, Gloucestershire; *d* 1905; *s* by his son (5) EDMUND ROBERT, 4th Earl; *b* 1877; sometime Capt TF; *d* 1951; *s* by his brother (6) MONTAGU BROWNLOW, 5th Earl; *b* 1878; Capt Grenadier Guards; *d* 1962; *s* by his nephew (7) JOHN ST AUBYN (el son of late Hon John Holford Parker (yst son of 3rd Earl), by his wife, Hon Marjory Katherine Elizabeth Alexandra St Aubyn, who *d* 1987, da of 2nd Baron St Levan), 6th Earl and present peer; also Viscount and Baron Boringdon.

Morley, Hope-, family name of Baron Hollenden.

Mornington, Earl of; grandson of Duke of Wellington.

MORRIS, BARON (Morris) (Baron UK 1918)

Always faithful

MICHAEL DAVID MORRIS, 3rd Baron; *b* 9 Dec 1937; *s* 1975; *ed* Downside: *m* 1st, 1959 (*m diss* 1962), Denise Eleanor, only da of Morley Richards; 2ndly, 1962 (*m diss* 1969), Jennifer, only da of Sq-Ldr Tristram Gilbert; 3rdly, 1980, Juliet Susan, da of Anthony Buckingham, and has issue by 2nd and 3rd *m*.

𝕬rms – Barry wavy of eight argent and azure, two codfish naiant proper, on a chief of the second, a two-masted schooner in full sail, also proper. 𝕮rest – A caribou's head couped at the neck proper, charged on the neck with a trefoil or. 𝕾upporters – On either side a caribou charged on the shoulder with a trefoil or.

SONS LIVING (*By 3rd marriage*)

Hon THOMAS ANTHONY SALMON, *b* 2 July 1982.
Hon James, *b* 1983.

DAUGHTERS LIVING (*By 2nd marriage*)

Ann Maria (adopted da), *b* 1962.
Hon Michaela Mary, *b* 1965.

(*By 3rd marriage*)

Hon Lucy Juliet, *b* 1981.

BROTHER LIVING

Hon (Edward) Patrick (twin) (Dormer Cottage, Petham, Canterbury, Kent), *b* 1937; *ed* Downside: *m* 1963, Mary Beryl, el da of Lt-Col D. H. G. Thrush, of Freshwinds, S Canterbury Rd, Canterbury, Kent, and has issue living, Edward Patrick, *b* 1965, — Elizabeth Mary, *b* 1968.

SISTER LIVING

Hon Clodagh Mary, *b* 1936: *m* 1964, Lt-Col Thomas Hugh Francis Farrell, CBE, TD, DL, of 22 Wood Lane, Beverley, North Humberside, and has issue living, James Thomas Hugh, *b* 1966: *m* 1996, Caroline Diana Juliet, elder da of James D. N. Ford, of Jarnac, France, and has issue living, Camilla Beatrice Juliet *b* 1999, — Sophia Mary, *b* 1965: *m* 1995, Marco I. R. Betti-Berutto, only son of Carlo Betti-Berutto, of Rome, and of Mrs Marilena Scala Leon, of Newington, Oxon, and has issue living, Thomas Federico Alexis *b* 1997.

PREDECESSORS – (1) *Rt Hon Sir* EDWARD PATRICK Morris, KCMG, son of Edward Morris, of St John's Newfoundland; *b* 1858; Solicitor, Newfoundland 1884; Bar Newfoundland 1885, and a QC 1896; sat for St John's in Newfoundland Parliament 1885-1919; was a Member of Whiteway Cabinet 1889-97, Acting Attorney-Gen 1890-95, Attorney-Gen and Min of Justice of Newfoundland 1902-07, Prime Min of Newfoundland 1909-18, and a Member of British War Cabinet Feb 1916 to Jan 1918; a Member of Imperial Defence Cttee 1909-18; *cr Baron Morris*, of St John's in the Dominion of New-foundland, and of City of Waterford (peerage of United Kingdom) 1918: *m* 1901, Isabel Langrishe, who *d* 1934, da of late Rev William Legallais; *d* 1935; *s* by his son (2) MICHAEL WILLIAM, 2nd Baron; *b* 1903; Bar Inner Temple 1925 (disbarred at own request); Solicitor 1931: *m* 1st, 1933 (*m diss* 1946), Jean Beatrice, who *d* 1989, el da of Lt-Col David Edward Maitland-Makgill-Crichton (E Lauderdale, colls); 2ndly, 1960, Mary, who *d* 1991, da of late Rev Alexander Reginald Langhorne, and formerly wife of Anthony Robert Agate, MRCS, LRCP; *d* 1975; *s* by his el son (3) MICHAEL DAVID, 3rd Baron and present peer.

Morris, family name of Baron Killanin.

Morris, family name of Baron Naseby.

MORRIS OF CASTLE MORRIS, BARON (Morris) (Life Baron 1990)

BRIAN ROBERT MORRIS, son of late Capt William Robert Morris, RN, of Cardiff; *b* 4 Dec 1930; *ed* Cardiff High Sch, and Worcester Coll, Oxford (MA, DPhil); Fellow Shakespeare Inst, Birmingham Univ 1956-58; Lecturer Reading Univ 1960-65, Sr Lecturer York Univ 1967-71, Prof of English Lit Sheffield Univ (also Dep Dean and Public Orator) 1971-80, Principal St David's Univ Coll, Lampeter 1980-91; Chm Museums and Galleries Commn 1985-90 (Member since 1975), Vice-Pres Council for Nat Parks since 1985, Museums Assocn since 1985, Welsh Advisory Cttee, British Council since 1983, and Anthony Panizzi Foundation since 1987; Member of Council, Poetry Soc since 1980, Member Nat Library of Wales 1981-91, and British Library Board 1980-91; Trustee Nat Portrait Gallery since 1977, and Nat Heritage Memorial Fund 1980-91; Gen Ed New Mermaid Dramatists since 1964, and New Arden Shakespeare 1974-82; author and poet; served 1st Batn Welch Regt 1949-51, and 4th Batn Welch Regt (TA) 1951-56; *cr Baron Morris of Castle Morris*, of St Dogmaels, co Dyfed (Life Baron) 1990: *m* 1955, Sandra Mary, da of late Percival Samuel James, and has issue. *Residence* – The Old Hall, Foolow, Eyam, Derbys S30 1QR.

SON LIVING

Hon Christopher Justin Robert, *b* 1959: *m* 1995, Nirmala Devi Rajagopal, of Kuala Lumpur, Malaysia.

DAUGHTER LIVING

Hon Lindsay Alison Mary, *b* 1957: *m* 19—,—Boxall.

MORRIS OF GRASMERE, BARONY OF (Morris) (Extinct 1990)

SON LIVING OF LIFE BARON

Hon (Charles) Christopher (Ladywood, White Moss, Ambleside, Cumbria LA22 9SF), *b* 1929: *m* 1951, Cynthia Prudence, da of late Sir (Alfred) Alan Lethbridge Parsons, KCIE, and has issue.

DAUGHTER LIVING OF LIFE BARON

Hon Heather Mary, *b* 1925: *m* 1st, 1946 (*m diss* 1972), Tom Berry Caldwell; 2ndly, 1972, Alfred G. Davey, of Coach House, Kirk Hammerton, York, and has issue (by 1st *m*).

MORRIS OF KENWOOD, BARON (Morris) (Baron UK 1950)

PHILIP GEOFFREY MORRIS, 2nd Baron; *b* 18 June 1928; *s* 1954; *ed* Loughborough Coll; late Flying Officer RAF; a JP for Inner London: *m* 1958, Hon Ruth Joan Gertrude Rahle Janner (a Member Gen Advisory Council IBA since 1987), da of late Baron Janner (Life Baron), and has issue. *Residence* – 35 Fitzjohn's Av, NW3 5JY.

SON LIVING

Hon JONATHAN DAVID, *b* 5 Aug 1968: *m* 1996, Melanie, only da of Robin Klein.

DAUGHTERS LIVING

Hon Diane Susan, *b* 1960, *ed* St Paul's Sch and Central Sch of Speech and Drama (Dip Stage Management): *m* 1981, Cary Haskell Zitcer of 2 Sidmouth Rd, NW2 5JX, and has issue living, Natasha Esther, *b* 1986, — Emily Margaret, *b* 1988.

Hon Caroline Harriet, *b* 1961.

Hon Linda Jane, *b* 1965: *m* 1991, Paul M. Gelernter, of 26A Leighton Gdns, NW10 3PT, son of David Gelernter, and of Mrs Jeanne Canning.

SISTER LIVING

Hon Hilary Zara, *b* 1932: *m* 1964, Ronald Graham Lewis, of Zaraz, Littlewick Green, Maidenhead, Berks.

PREDECESSORS – **(1)** HARRY Morris, son of late Jacob Morris; *b* 1893; was MP for Sheffield Central 1945-50 and for Sheffield Neepsend Feb-March 1950; *cr Baron Morris of Kenwood*, of Kenwood, City of Sheffield (peerage of United Kingdom) 1950: *m* 1924, Florence, who *d* 1982, da of Henry Isaacs, of Leeds; *d* 1954; *s* by his only son **(2)** PHILIP GEOFFREY, 2nd Baron and present peer.

MORRIS OF MANCHESTER, BARON (Morris) (Life Baron 1997)

AFRED (ALF) MORRIS, AO, QSO, PC, son of late George Henry Morris, of Manchester; *b* 23 March 1928; *ed* Ruskin Coll, Oxford, St Catherine's Coll, Oxford (MA 19—), and Manchester Univ; Hon Fell Manchester Metropolitan Univ 1990; Hon MA Salford 1997, Hon LLD Univ of Manchester 1998; former schoolmaster; MP for Manchester Wythenshawe (Lab and Co-op) 1964-97; PPS to Min of Agric, Fisheries and Food 1964-67, and to Lord Pres of the Council and Leader of the House of Commons 1968-70; promoted Chronically Sick and Disabled Persons Act, 1970, as a private member; Memb General Advisory Council, BBC 1968-74 and 1983-96; Chm PLP Food and Agric Group 1971-74 (Vice-Chm 1970-71); first Min for Disabled People 1974-79; Chm World Planning Group appointed to draft charter for the 1980s for disabled people worldwide 1979-80; Opposition Front Bench Spokesman on Social Services and disabled people's rights 1979-93; Co-op Parliamentary Group 1982-84, and ANZAC Group of MPs and Peers since 1982; Jt Treasurer, British-American Parliamentary Group 1983-97; Pres Soc of Chiropodists and Podiatrists since 1997; first recipient of FM Lord Harding's Award for distinguished service to disabled people 1971; Louis Braille Memorial Award for outstanding services to the blind 1972; Trustee of Crisis at Christmas and Earl of Snowdon's Fund for Handicapped Students; Paul Harris Fell of Rotary International; author; *cr* PC 1979, QSO 1989, AO 1991, and *Baron Morris of Manchester*, of Manchester in co of Greater Manchester (Life Baron) 1997: *m* 1950, Irene, da of Abel Jones, of Manchester, and has issue.

Arms – Gules on a pile reversed throughout argent a pile reversed throughout gules thereon three bees volant in pale or. **Crest** – A koala sejant erect guardant gules gorged with a plain collar attached thereto a chain reflexed over the back or. **Supporters** – On either side a kiwi argent legged and gorged with a plain collar or and holding in the beak also or a rose gules barbed seeded slipped and leaved or.
Residence – 20 Hitherwood Drive, SE19 1XB.

SONS LIVING

Hon Paul Gwilym, *b* 1954; *ed* Purley Gram Sch, Croydon Technical Coll, Lanchester Univ, and Sussex Univ: *m* 19—, Frances, da of ...... Allen, and has issue living, Tom, *b* 1983, — Amy, *b* 1988, — Katie, *b* 1993. *Residence* – ....

Hon Stephen Charles, *b* 1957; *ed* Warlingham Secondary Sch, Hendon Police Coll, Ruskin Coll, Oxford, and Univ of Kent at Canterbury: *m* 1980, Karen Sylvia, da of ...... Wright, and has issue living, Laura, *b* 1984.

DAUGHTERS LIVING

Hon Catherine, *b* 1951; *ed* Warlingham Secondary Sch, Elizabeth Fry Coll, Keswick Hall, Univ of E Anglia: *m* 1984, Stefan Knapp, and has issue living, Rory, *b* 1986, — Ivan, *b* 1987.
Hon Gillian, *b* 1959: *ed* Warlingham Secondary Sch, Croydon Technical Coll, and Univ of South Bank.

Morrison, family name of Viscount Dunrossil.

Morrison, family name of Baron Margadale.

MORRISON OF LAMBETH, BARONY OF (Morrison) (Extinct 1965)

DAUGHTER LIVING OF LIFE BARON (*By 1st marriage*)

Hon Mary Joyce, *b* 1921: *m* 1st, 1941 (*m diss* 1948), Horace Williams (afterwards Hon Horace Williams), son of Baron Williams of Barnburgh (Life Baron); 2ndly, 1948, George Norman Mandelson, who *d* 1988, and has issue living (by 2nd *m*), Miles, *b* 1949, — *Rt Hon* Peter Benjamin, MP, *b* 1953; *ed* Hendon Co Gram Sch, and St Catherine's Coll, Oxford (BA); Councillor Lambeth Borough Council 1979-82; Producer *Weekend World* London Weekend TV 1982-85; Dir Campaigns and Communications Lab Party 1985-90; Lab Party Campaign Manager 1996-97; Min Without Portfolio Cabinet Office 1997-98, Sec of State for Trade and Industry and Pres Board of Trade (resigned Dec 1998); MP (*Lab*) Hartlepool since 1992; PC 1998. *Residence* – 12 Bigwood Rd, NW11.

MORTON, EARL OF (Douglas) (Earl S 1458)

Held fast

JOHN CHARLES SHOLTO DOUGLAS, 21st Earl; *b* 19 March 1927; *s* 1976; Property Consultant, Ptnr Dalmahoy Farms, Chm Edinburgh Polo Club; Lord Lieut of W Lothian: *m* 1949, Mary Sheila, da of late Rev Canon John Stanley Gibbs, MC, of Didmarton House, Badminton, Glos, and has issue.

Arms – Quarterly: 1st and 4th argent, a man's heart gules, ensigned with an imperial crown or, on a chief azure, three mullets of the field, *Douglas*; 2nd and 3rd argent, three piles issuing from the chief gules, and in chief two mullets of the field, *Douglas of Lochleven.* **Crest** – A wild boar proper sticking in the cleft of an oak tree, fructed vert, with a lock holding the clefts of the tree together azure. **Supporters** – Two savages, wreathed round the temples and waist, and holding in the exterior hand a club reversed, all proper.
Residence – The Old Mansionhouse, Dalmahoy, Kirknewton, Midlothian EH27 8EB.

SONS LIVING

JOHN STEWART SHOLTO (*Lord Aberdour*- pronounced Aberdare) (Haggs Farm, Kirknewton, Midlothian), *b* 17 Jan 1952; *ed* Dunrobin Castle Sch, and Aberdeen Univ; Ptnr Dalmahoy Farms: *m* 1985, Amanda Kirsten, yr da of David John Macfarlane Mitchell, of Castle St, Kirkcudbright, and has issue:—

SON LIVING— *Hon* John David Sholto (*Master of Aberdour*), *b* 28 May 1986.
DAUGHTERS LIVING—*Hon* Katherine Florence, *b* 1989, — *Hon* Jennifer Mary, *b* 1991.

Hon (Charles) James Sholto, *b* 1954; Ptnr Dalmahoy Farms: *m* 1981, Anne, da of late William Gordon Morgan, of Neapuke, Waikato, NZ, and has issue living, James William Sholto, *b* 1984, — Rebecca Katherine, *b* 1982, — Jillian Rosamond Florence, *b* 1986.

DAUGHTER LIVING

Lady Mary Pamela, *b* 1950: *m* 1973, Richard Callander, of Saughland House, Pathhead, Midlothian, 2nd son of late Maj John David Callander, of Prestonhall, Midlothian, and has issue living, James Edward, *b* 1979, — Sarah Mary, *b* 1977, — Emma Louise, *b* 1981.

HALF-SISTER LIVING

Helen Alice (*Baroness de Mauley*) (Langford, Little Faringdon, Lechlade, Glos), *b* 1921: *m* 1st, 1947, Lt-Col Brian Leslie Abdy Collins, OBE, MC, RE, who *d* 1952; 2ndly, 1954, 6th Baron de Mauley, and has issue living, (by 1st *m*) Thomas Abdy (Willow Cottage, Jumps Rd, Churt, Surrey), *b* 1948: *m* 1982, Anna Mary, el da of Col Ian. R. Critchley, OBE, of Greenden, Farnell, by Breckin, and has issue living, Alice Susanna Abdy *b* 1983, Eleanor Katherine Abdy *b* 1986, Phoebe Helen Abdy *b* 1988, — (Brian) James Douglas (Church Farm, Little Faringdon, Lechlade, Glos), *b* 1952: *m* 1st, 1976 (*m diss* 1988), Philippa Martha Gausel, da of Sir Rowland John Rathbone Whitehead, 5th Bt; 2ndly, 1989, Emma Charlotte, da of late Sir Neill Cooper-Key (*see* V Rothermere), and has issue living (by 1st *m*), Henry James Abdy *b* 1980, Rosie Alice Lousie *b* 1978 (by 2nd *m*), Esmond Gerald Beau *b* 1997, Elspeth Peggy *b* 1990, Cicely Violet *b* 1992, Christabel Lily *b* 1993.

COLLATERAL BRANCHES LIVING

Grandchildren of late Hon (Archibald) Roderick Sholto Douglas (infra):—
Issue of late Roderick Walter Sholto Douglas, *b* 1908, *d* 1990: *m* 1st, 1935 (*m diss* 1949), Elizabeth Margaret, who *d* 1977, el da of late Stephen Clement Paston Cooper (*see* Cooper, Bt, colls, cr 1821); 2ndly, 1950, Margaret (Buckstone, Banket, Zimbabwe), da of late J. M. Tennent, of Troon, Ayrshire:—
(By 1st *m*) Alastair Sholto (PO Box 27, Raffingora, Zimbabwe), *b* 1949: *m* 1974, Diane Adams, and has issue living, Michael Bruce Sholto, *b* 1979, — Chantal Bernardene, *b* 1974, — Fay Robyn, *b* 1977. —— Anna Winona, *b* 1936: *m* 1965, Thomas Charles Bushby, of 9 Morton Jaffray Drive, Eastlea, Harare, Zimbabwe, and has issue living, Lucinda Irene, *b* 1966. —— Juliet Elizabeth, *b* 1941: *m* 1975, Graham Peters, of 40 Parel Vallei Rd, Somerset West, S Africa. —— (By 2nd *m*) Bruce Sholto, *b* 1951.

Issue of late Brig Patrick Sholto Douglas, MC, *b* 1912, *d* 1977: *m* 1st, 1940 (*m diss* 1959), Maude Carol Hermione, da of George Orr, of Kilduff House, Drem, E Lothian; 2ndly, 1963, Alexa Granger, who *d* 1998, da of late Adm John Ewan Cameron, CB, MVO, and widow of George Howard Usher Crookshank:—
(By 1st *m*) Katharine Diana (2 Russell Place, Edinburgh), *b* 1942; *m* 1969, Peter Robin Campbell Hendriks, and has issue living, Timothy Ivan Mark, *b* 1970, — Alice Sophie, *b* 1973.

Issue of late Maj Peter Frederic Sholto Douglas, DSO, *b* 1916, *d* 1989: *m* 1942, Ursula, who *d* 1998, da of late Henry Somers Rivers, of Sawbridgeworth, Herts:—
†Roderick Gavin Sholto, *b* 1944; *ed* Univ Coll of Rhodesia and Nyasaland, and Univ Coll, Lond (Sch of Library, Archive & Information Studies); BA, Dip Lib (Lond), ALA; Chief Archivist, Nat Archives of Zimbabwe: *m* 1991, Pamela Jean (who *m* 2ndly, 1996, Neil Anthony Milne Welch, of PO Box BW192, Borrowdale, Harare, Zimbabwe), da of late Basil

Norman Maggs, and *dsp* 1995. —— Sara, *b* 1947: *m* 1974, Peter David Newbery, of Giwonde Farm, PO Box 119, Centenary, Zimbabwe, and has issue living, Nicholas David, *b* 1982, — Eloise, *b* 1978.

Issue of late Hon (Archibald) Roderick Sholto Douglas, 3rd son of 19th Earl, *b* 1883, *d* 1971: *m* 1907, Winona Constance De Maraisville, who *d* 1951, da of Col Walter Ancell Peake, DSO, of Burrough-on-the-Hill, Leics:—
Rosemary (27 Sefton St, SW15), *b* 1915: *m* 1943, Capt Winfred Marlet Curtis, RM, who *d* 1960, and has issue living, Winona Penelope, *b* 1951: *m* 1973, Richard Granville Peddar, of 12 Lower Richmond Rd, SW15, and has issue living, Adam Winfred Richard *b* 1985, Alexander David Roderick *b* 1987, Theresa Adelina Alice *b* 1980.

Grandchildren of late Hon William Sholto Douglas (infra):—
Issue of late Ian Fitzroy Sholto Douglas, *b* 1916, *d* (19 July) 1998: *m* 1st, 1946, Heather Joan, who *d* 1985, 4th da of late Lt-Col Alexander John Hew Maclean of Ardgour (*see* B Inverclyde, 1968 Edn); 2ndly, 1988, Mrs Hester Kathleen McCall-McCowan, who *d* (27 July) 1998, da of late Maurice Richard Lyndon White, and widow of David McCall-McCowan, of Moniaive, Dumfriesshire:—
(By 1st *m*) William Hew Sholto (The Gables, Station Rd, Balfron, Stirlingshire), *b* 1947; *ed* Harrow; late Major 1st Bn Argyll and Sutherland Highers: *m* 1986, Frances Mary, da of Brig Robert William Riddle, of Old Harestanes, Blyth Bridge, Peeblesshire, and has issue living, Peter Sholto, *b* 1987, — Charles Robert Douglas, *b* 1989, — Andrew William, *b* 1993, — Kerry Ann Heather, *b* 1991. —— Peter James (Wester Knocklae, Balmaclellan, by Castle Douglas, Kirkcudbrightshire), *b* 1952; *ed* Gordonstoun. —— Elizabeth Heather Winifred, *b* 1948: *m* 1st, 1971 (*m diss* 1983), Edward Inman; 2ndly, 1985, Paul William Alexander Brown, of 118 Spirea Drive, Oakwood, Dayton, Ohio, USA, and has issue living (by 1st *m*), James Michael, *b* 1974, — Heather Louise, *b* 1977. —— Jane Charlotte Georgiana, *b* 1950.

Issue of late Ronald George Sholto Douglas, *b* 1926, *d* 1996: *m* 1st, 1952 (*m diss* 1957), Margaret Jean Gai Eliott-Drake, only da of Ivor Herbert McClure, DSO, OBE, of Sutton, Prov Quebec, Canada; 2ndly, 1960 (*m diss* 1977), Valerie, yr da of William Quarterman, of 104 Cliff Rock Rd, Rubery, Birmingham; 3rdly, 1983, Heather Grey (Dalmahoy, Oneriri Rd, Kaiwaka, N Island, NZ), da of James Philip Law, of Point Chevalier, NZ:—
(By 1st *m*) Roderick Olaf William Sholto (St Catherine's Lodge, Grange Rd, Edinburgh EH9 1UQ), *b* 1953. —— Malcolm David Sholto (25 Culver Rd, Newbury, Berks), *b* 1955: *m* 1979, Barbara Elizabeth, da of Charles Hughes, of Newbury, Berks, and has issue living, James Robert Sholto, *b* 1982, — Michael Charles Sholto, *b* 1984. —— Fiona Anne Georgiana, *b* 1956; BSc: *m* 1981, Dr Robert Anderson Somerville, of 16 Grange Rd, Edinburgh EH9 1UJ, son of Charles Somerville, of Edinburgh, and has issue living, Ian Douglas, *b* 1986, — Anne Margaret, *b* 1985, — Catherine Mary, *b* 1988. —— (By 2nd *m*) Shona Fay, *b* 1962; BA: *m* 1983, Dr Roderick McDiarmid Johnstone, of 66 The Lanes, Over, Cambs CB4 5NQ, only son of Dr Robert Douglas Johnstone, of Pitlochry, Perthshire, and has issue living, Peter William Douglas, *b* 1993.

Issue of Hon William Sholto Douglas, 4th son of 19th Earl, *b* 1886, *d* 1932: *m* 1914, Hon Ethel Georgiana Frances Somerset, who *d* 1981, da of 3rd Baron Raglan:—
Jean Georgiana Ethel, OBE, *b* 1922; OBE (Civil) 1991: *m* 1949, Maj Peter Edward Findlay Heneage, son of late Lt-Col Sir Arthur Pelham Heneage, DSO, and has issue living, Thomas Peter William (2 Westmorland Terrace, SW1), *b* 1950: *m* 1st, 1980 (*m diss* 1990), Shaunagh Anne Henrietta, el da of George Silver Oliver Annesley Colthurst, of Pitchford Hall, Shrewsbury (*see* Colthurst, Bt); 2ndly, 1997, Carol M. Vogel, of New York, USA, and has issue living (by 1st *m*), Henry Robert *b* 1983, Elizabeth Anne Sophia *b* 1981, — Charles Arthur (Bailey Hill House, Birdbrook, Essex), *b* 1952: *m* 1978, Sarah Elizabeth, yst da of Col Arthur Harold Newmarch Reade, LVO Queen's Own Hus, of The Post House, Ipsden, Wallingford, Oxon, and has issue living, Frederick Rory Winwood *b* 1990, Sophia Georgiana *b* 1980, Alice Rose *b* 1983, — Robert John (Newport House, North Carlton, Lincoln), *b* 1956: *m* 1984, Maryann Louise, only da of J. N. Milne, of Preston Priory, Ledbury, and has issue living, William Peter *b* 1986, Georgiana Isabella *b* 1988, — Katherine Julia, *b* 1960: *m* 1991, Malcolm J. P. Moir, of 10 Upper Addison Gdns, W14, elder son of Nigel Moir, of Town Farm, Bacton, Suffolk, and has issue living, Jemima Mary *b* 1994, Matilda *b* 1996. *Residence* – North Carlton Old Hall, Lincoln.

Grandchildren of late Capt George Sholto Douglas, only son of Adm Hon George Henry Douglas, 2nd son of 17th Earl:—
Issue of late Brig Archibald Sholto George Douglas, CBE, *b* 1896, *d* 1981: *m* 1928, (Violet) Patricia, who *d* 1989, 4th da of late Maj Arthur Pearson Davison, TD, of 18 Alexander Sq, SW3:—
Colin Sholto Archibald (18 Upshire Gdns, The Warren, Bracknell, Berks), *b* 1932; *ed* Eton: *m* 1st, 1958 (*m diss* 1971), Jean, who *d* 1978, da of late Brig George Streynsham Rawstorne, CBE, MC; 2ndly, 1972 (*m diss* 1982), Sally Anne, only da of David Charles Humphrey Townsend, of Grindon, co Durham, and has four children (by 1st *m*), Malcolm Sholto Colin, *b* 1966, — Laura Jean, *b* 1968, — (by 2nd *m*) Archie Sholto James, *b* 1972, — Euan Sholto David, *b* 1975. —— James Sholto Arthur (Good Mondays Farm, Dauntsey, Chippenham, Wilts), *b* 1935; *ed* Eton; Capt 15th/19th Hussars: *m* 1st, 1966 (*m diss* 1979), Tedda Ann, da of Albert Charles Webber, of Litton Cheney, Dorchester, Dorset; 2ndly, 1979, Mrs Elizabeth Ann Cripps, da of late Maj Montague Howard Crocker, of Minety House, Malmesbury, Wilts, and formerly wife of Nicholas Cripps, of Cat Island, Bahamas, and has four children (by 1st *m*), Justin Sholto James, *b* 1972, — Harry Sholto Gavin, *b* 1974, — Camilla Patricia Ann *b* 1971, — (by 2nd *m*) Toby Sholto Arthur, *b* 1982. —— Gavin Sholto George (Heiton Mill, nr Kelso, Roxburghshire), *b* 1945; *ed* Gordonstoun: *m* 1982, Amanda Jane, elder da of late Christopher Evelyn Twiston Davies, of Drax House, Tilshead, nr Salisbury, and of Mrs Simon Gilbey, of Mains of Solszarie, Bridge of Cally, Perthshire (*see* Gilbey, Bt, colls), and has issue living, Alice Violet, *b* 1983, — Charlotte Rose, *b* 1985. —— Joanna Patricia Margaret, *b* 1948: *m* 1972, Roger D. Day, of Newcotts Farm, N Newton, Bridgwater, Som, and has issue living, Gregory Laramy, *b* 1972, — Lorna Elizabeth, *b* 1974.

Issue of late Capt David Sholto William Douglas, *b* 1899, *d* 1980: *m* 1940, Elizabeth Sarah Ione (Lynwick House, Rudgwick, W Sussex), only da of late Maj George Edward Capel Cure, of Blake Hall, Ongar, Essex:—
Sheena Elizabeth, *b* 1948: *m* 1973, Richard James Wright, of Lynwick House, Rudgwick, W Sussex, only son of George William James Hamilton Wright, of Bessingby Hall, Bridlington, N Yorks, and has issue living, Charles Anthony, *b* 1979. —— The late Capt D. S. W. Douglas also had a da, Ione Lavinia Margaret, *b* 1946: *m* 1983 (*m diss* 1994), Richard Zatloukal, of 3 Burbury Court, 56 Redcliffe Sq, SW10.

Issue of late Lieut-Col John Sholto Henry Douglas, OBE, *b* 1903, *d* 1960: *m* 1955, Celia (Fir Tree Cottage, Broadmeadows, Yarrowford, Selkirk), only da of late Maj J. H. McInnes Skinner, of East Carleton Manor, Norfolk, and widow of Roderick Christopher Musgrave:—
Robin Sholto John (Heron Cottage, Biddenden, Ashford, Kent TN27 8HH), *b* 1956: *m* 1983, Ann Elisabeth Forssell, and has issue living, James Sholto Edward, *b* 1989, — Anna Louisa Victoria, *b* 1991, — Olivia Laura Elizabeth, *b* 1996.
—— John Sholto James (39A Wandsworth Common Northside, SW18 2SO), *b* 1959: *m* 1997, Mieke Elisabeth van den Bergh, and has issue living, George Sholto, *b* 1998.

Grandsons of late Right Rev Hon Arthur Gascoigne Douglas, DD, DCL, Bishop of Aberdeen and Orkney, 5th son of 17th Earl:—
Issue of late Sholto James Douglas, *b* 1866, *d* 1950: *m* 1909, Grace Elizabeth, who *d* 1968, da of Sir James Henry Gibson-Craig, 3rd Bt (Gibson-Craig-Carmichael, Bt):—
Rev Canon Archibald Sholto, TD, *b* 1914; *ed* Selwyn Coll, Camb (MA); formerly V of Siddington, Hon Canon of Chester Cathedral (1978); 3rd class Chap to Forces, Cheshire Regt (TA); formerly Major King's Own Scottish Borderers (TA); appointed Chap to High Sheriff of Cheshire 1960. *Residence* – Monks Heath Hall Farm, Chelford Rd, Nether Alderley, Macclesfield, Cheshire SK10 4SY. —— Hugh Alastair, *b* 1915; formerly Conservator of Forests, Ghana: *m* 1955, Elisabeth, da of late Col John Meredith Hulton, CBE, DSO, and has issue living, Angela Elizabeth, *b* 1956; PhD: *m* 1984, Jeremy Byron Searle, — Coleena Jane, *b* 1958: *m* 1978, Nicholas Hutson Reid, of Malindi, The Highlands, E Horsley, Surrey. *Residence* – Broadlands House, Brockenhurst, Hants.

Descendants of Hon Edward Gordon Douglas-Pennant (brother of 17th Earl), who was *cr Baron Penrhyn* 1866 (see that title).

PREDECESSORS – (1) JAMES Douglas, 4th Feudal Lord of Dalkeith: *m* 1459, Joanna, 3rd da of King James I of Scotland; *cr Earl of Morton* (peerage of Scotland) 1458 *d* 1493; *s* by his son (2) JOHN, 2nd Earl, *b* 1466: *m* 14—, Janet, da of Patrick Crichton, of Cranstoun Riddell; *d* 1513, *s* by his son (3) JAMES, 3rd Earl; not having male issue made an entail of his estate and honours upon James Douglas, husband of his 3rd da Elizabeth: *m* 1507, Katherine Stewart, natural da of King James IV of Scotland; *d* 1548, *s* by his son-in-law (4) JAMES (ante), 4th Earl, *b* 1516; not having male issue he entailed the earldom upon his nephew Archibald Douglas, 8th Earl of Angus, and his heirs male, failing which to William Douglas, of Lochleven; was twice Chancellor and sometime High Adm and also Regent of Scotland: *m* 1543, Elizabeth, da of 3rd Earl (ante); tried for being accessory to the murder of Lord Darnley, and, being found guilty, was publicly executed at the Market Cross, Edinburgh, 2 June 1581, by "The Maiden", a machine he had himself introduced into Scotland; after his execution and forfeiture the Crown conferred the Earldom of Morton upon JOHN, Lord Maxwell, son of Beatrix, 2nd da of 3rd Earl (ante), by her marriage with Robert, Lord Maxwell; the grant of this honour was, however, revoked by the Act of Indemnity in 1585 to the heir of entail, and in recompense he was *cr* Earl of Nithsdale, while the Earldom of Morton passed to his nephew (5) ARCHIBALD Douglas, 5th Earl of (ante) (also 8th Earl of Angus), *b* 1555: *m* 1st, 1573, Mary, who *d* 1575, da of John, Earl of Mar; 2ndly 1575 (*m diss*), Margaret, da of 4th Earl of Rothes; 3rdly, 1587, Jean, da of 8th Lord Glamis *d* 1588; *s* by his kinsman (6) *Sir* WILLIAM, 6th Earl (a descendant of Sir Harry Douglas of Lugton and Lochleven, 4th son of Sir John Douglas of Dalkeith), *b* 1539-40: *m* 1554, Agnes, da of 4th Earl of Rothes; *d* 1606; *s* by his grandson (7) *Rt Hon Sir* WILLIAM, KG (son of Robert Douglas yr of Lochleven, el son of 6th Earl), 7th Earl, *b* 1582; was Gentleman of the Bedchamber to James VI and Charles I, High Treasurer for Scotland 1630-35, Capt of the Yeomen of the Guard, and 1641 High Chancellor; sold Dalkeith and other estates, and received in return the Islands of Orkney and Zetland, with their whole jurisdiction and royalties redeemable on payment by the Crown of £30,000; in 1638 Aberdour was erected into a burgh of Barony, and his title was altered to *Earl of Morton* and *Lord Aberdour*: *m* 1604, Lady Ann Keith, da of 5th Earl Marischal, *d* 1648; *s* by his son (8) ROBERT, 8th Earl: *m* 16—, Anne, who *d* 1654, da of Sir Edward Villiers of Brokesby; *d* 1649; *s* by his son (9) WILLIAM, 9th Earl; procured a new grant of the Islands of Orkney and Zetland, but the original being contested those islands were annexed to the Crown by Act of Parliament 1669: *m* 1662, Lady Grizel Middleton, who *d* 1666, da of 1st Earl of Middleton; *d* 1681; *s* by his uncle, (10) *Sir* JAMES, 10th Earl: *m* 16—, Ann, who *d* 1700, da and co heir of Sir James Hay, 1st Bt of Smithfield, *d* 1686: *s* by his son, (11) JAMES, 11th Earl; a strenuous supporter of the Union; *d* unmarried 1715; *s* by his brother, (12) ROBERT, 12th Earl; *d* unmarried 1730; *s* by his brother, (13) GEORGE, 13th Earl, *b* 1662; MP for Orkney and Sutherlandshire 1722-30, Vice-Adm of Scotland 1733-38: *m* 1st, 16—, a da of Alexander Muirhead of Linhouse, co Edinburgh; 2ndly, 17—, Frances, da of William Adderley, of Halstow, Kent; *d* 1738; *s* by his son, (14) JAMES, KT, 14th Earl, *b* 1702, was a Lord of the Bedchamber 1739, a Representative Peer 1739-68; Grand Master Mason of Scotland 1739-40; Lord Clerk Register of Scotland 1761-68; Pres Royal Society 1764-68; arranged finance for Capt James Cooke's 1st voyage of discovery; in 1742 the Earldom of Orkney and Lordship of Zetland were by Act of Parliament disannexed from the Crown, and vested irredeemably in him, a right which he sold to Sir Laurence Dundas, 1st Baron Dundas (M Zetland): *m* 1st, before 1731, Agatha, who *d* 1748, da of James Halyburton of Pitcur; 2ndly, 1755, Bridget, who *d* 1805, da of Sir John Heathcote, 2nd Bt, of Normanton; *d* 1768; *s* by his son (15) SHOLTO CHARLES, 15th Earl; *b* 1732; a Lord of Police: *m* 1758, Katherine, who *d* 1823, da of Hon John Hamilton, 2nd son of 6th Earl of Haddington; *d* 1774; *s* by his son, (16) GEORGE, KT, 16th Earl, *b* 1761; a Representative Peer 1784-91, Chamberlain of the Queen's Household, and Lord-Lieut of co Fife; *cr Baron Douglas of Lochleven* (peerage of Great Britain) 1791: *m* 1814, Susan Elizabeth, da of Sir Francis Buller-Yarde-Buller, 2nd Bt; *dsp* 1827, when the Barony of Douglas became ext and the Scottish peerages devolved upon his cousin, (17) GEORGE SHOLTO, 17th Earl (son of Hon John Douglas, 2nd son of 14th Earl); *b* 1789; was a Representative Peer: *m* 1817, Frances Theodora, who *d* 1879, da of Rt Hon Sir George Henry Rose, GCH; *d* 1858; *s* by his son, (18) SHOLTO JOHN, 18th Earl; *b* 1818, was a Representative Peer: *m* 1st, 1844, Helen, who *d* 1850, da of James Watson of Saughton, Midlothian, 2ndly, 1853, Lady Alice Anne Caroline Lambton, who *d* 1907, da of 1st Earl of Durham; *d* Dec 1884; *s* by his son (19) SHOLTO GEORGE WATSON, 19th Earl, *b* 1844; a Representative Peer for Scotland: *m* 1877, Hon Helen Geraldine Maria Ponsonby, who *d* 1949, da of 2nd Baron de Mauley; *d* 1935; *s* by his grandson (20) SHOLTO CHARLES JOHN HAY (son of Sholto Charles Watson, Lord Aberdour), 20th Earl; *b* 1907; *d* 1976; *s* by his cousin (son of Hon Charles William Sholto Douglas, 2nd son of 19th Earl, *b* 1881, *d* 1960: *m* 1st, 1920, Alice Agnes, who *d* 1924, only da of Lt-Col William Augustus Lane Fox-Pitt, of Presaddfed, Anglesey; 2ndly, 1926, Florence, who *d* 1985, elder da of Maj Henry Thomas Timson, of Stydd House, Lyndhurst) (21) JOHN CHARLES SHOLTO, 21st Earl and present peer; also Lord Aberdour.

MORTON OF HENRYTON, BARONY OF (Morton) (Extinct 1973)

DAUGHTER LIVING OF LIFE BARON

Hon Anne Margaret, *b* 1926, called to the Bar (Lincolns Inn 1979); former Cllr Kensington and Chelsea Borough Cncl 1960-62; Chm Consumer Protection Advy Cttee since 1973; Chm Inner London Juvenile Courts 1970-87 (appointed to panel 1961); Co-Founder and Sec of London Adventure Playground Assn 1962-69; *m* 1947, Peter Andrew Hopwood Viney, DFC (B Southborough, 1963 Edn), and has issue living, Nicholas Morton, *b* 1948: *m* 1981, Jane Fiona Maud, yr da of Benjamin Bernard Woulfe Goodden, and formerly wife of Graham Holt, — Alison Margaret, *b* 1951: *m* 1970, Christopher Patrick Maguire, — Elizabeth Frances, *b* 1956.

MORTON OF SHUNA, BARONY OF (Morton) (Extinct 1995)

SONS LIVING OF LIFE BARON

Hon Alistair Charles Ralph, *b* 1958; *ed* R High Sch, Edinburgh, and Glasgow Univ (MA): *m* 1983, Jacqueline Anne, da of William Brown, of Edinburgh.

Hon Kenneth John, *b* 1960; *ed* Broughton High Sch, Edinburgh, and Edinburgh Univ: *m* 1984, Isobel Ann, da of John McLean Cowan, of Greenock.

Hon Douglas William, *b* 1963; *ed* Broughton High Sch, Edinburgh.

WIDOW LIVING OF LIFE BARON

MURIEL (*Baroness Morton of Shuna*), da of Charles Miller, of Edinburgh: *m* 1956, Baron Morton of Shuna, PC (Life Baron), who *d* 1995. *Residence* – 25 Royal Circus, Edinburgh EH3 6TL.

Mosley, family name of Baron Ravensdale.

MOSTYN, BARON (Lloyd Mostyn) (Baron UK 1831, Bt GB 1778)

My help is from the Lord

ROGER EDWARD LLOYD LLOYD MOSTYN, MC, 5th Baron, and 6th Baronet; *b* 17 April 1920; *s* 1965; *ed* Eton, Capt 9th Queen's R Lancers; 1939-45 War in Middle East (wounded, despatches, MC): *m* 1st, 1943 (*m diss* 1957), Yvonne Margaret, da of A. Stuart Johnson, of Henshall Hall, Congleton, Cheshire; 2ndly, 1957, Sheila Edmondson (SHAW), OBE, DL, da of Maj Reginald Fairweather, of Stockwell Manor, Silverton, Devon, and has issue by 1st *m*.

Arms – Quarterly: 1st and 4th, per bend sinister ermine and ermines, a lion rampant or, *Mostyn*; 2nd and 3rd gules, a Saracen's head affrontée, erased at the neck proper, wreathed about the temples argent and sable, *Lloyd*. Crests – 1st, on a mount vert, a lion rampant or; 2nd, a Saracen's head, as in the arms; 3rd a stag trippant proper, attired or, charged on the shoulder with an escutcheon of the second, thereon a chevron of the first, between three men's heads in profile, couped at the neck, also proper. Supporters – *Dexter*, a stag proper, attired or, charged on the shoulder with an escutcheon gules, thereon a chevron argent, between three men's heads couped in profile proper; *sinister*, a lion

or, charged on the shoulder with an escutcheon argent thereon a cross engrailed and fleurettée sable, between four Cornish choughs proper.
Seat – Mostyn Hall, Mostyn, Flintshire. *Club* – Royal Automobile.

SON LIVING (By 1st marriage)

Hon LLEWELLYN ROGER LLOYD (9 Anderson St, SW3), *b* 26 Sept 1948; *ed* Eton; late Capt Army Legal Sers; Bar Middle Temple 1973; in chambers Gray's Inn: *m* 1974, Denise Suzanne, da of Roger Duvanel, and has issue living, Gregory Philip Roger, *b* 31 Dec 1984, — Alexandra Stefanie, *b* 1975.

DAUGHTER LIVING (By 1st marriage)

Hon Virginia Yvonne Lloyd, *b* 1946: *m* 1st, 1973, John Robert Hodgkinson; 2ndly, 1983, James R. K. Price, and has issue living (by 1st *m*), Dominic, *b* 1974, — Thomas, *b* 1976.

SISTER LIVING

Hon Elizabeth Mary Gwenllian Lloyd, *b* 1929: *m* 1st, 1950 (*m diss* Jan 1957), David Nicholas Goldsmith Duckham; 2ndly (May) 1957, John Henry Russell, and has issue living (by 1st *m*), Kiloran Mary, *b* 1953.

COLLATERAL BRANCHES LIVING   (Male line in special remainder to Baronetcy)

Grandchildren of late Edward Hugh Lloyd Mostyn, el son of late Rev Canon Hon Hugh Wynne Lloyd Mostyn, 5th son of 2nd Baron:—
Issue of late Hugh Wynne Lloyd Mostyn, *b* 1903, *d* 1975: *m* 1933, Eileen Grace, who *d* 1985, da of Arthur Walsh Titherley, DSc PhD, FRIC, of Itchen Abbas Manor, Winchester:—
Roger Hugh Lloyd (42 Lichfield Lane, Mansfield, Notts), *b* 1941; *ed* Lancing; MB, BS London; MRCS England, FRCP London: *m* 1967, Mary Frances, da of Capt Edward Fothergill Elderton, AFRaeS, ACGI, of Ryde, and has issue living, Christopher Edward, *b* 1968, — James William, *b* 1970, — David Thomas, *b* 1981. —— Rosemary Eleanor Lloyd, *b* 1933: *m* 1974, Rev J. D. Thorp, and has issue living, Simon Robin Hugh, *b* 1975. —— Jean Grant Lloyd, *b* 1935: *m* 1956, John Harold Matthews, Film and TV Dir and Producer, of 792 Victoria Rd, Ryde, Sydney, NSW 2112, Australia, and has issue living, Nicholas Stuart, *b* 1958: *m* 1980, Debra Young, and has issue living, Michael Lloyd *b* 1984, Daniel James *b* 1989, — Sarah Jo, *b* 1964: *m* 1988, Dennis Brian Heape.

Grandchildren of late Lt-Col James Pryce Lloyd Mostyn (infra):—
Issue of late Maj Edwyn Inigo Lloyd Mostyn, MC, Scots Gds, *b* 1921, *d* 1978: *m* 1st, 1942 (*m diss* 1964), Avice Louise Trevor, da of Cdr Sir Hugh Trevor Dawson, 2nd Bt, CBE, RN (ret); 2ndly, 1964, Mrs Janet Hope Rutherford, da of late Eric Cecil Barnes, CMG, of Polmear, Frogham, nr Fordingbridge; 3rdly, 1975, Angela Noel, who *d* 1995, da of late Maj Noel William (Bob) Leaf, 15/19th King's Royal Hus, and widow of Ralph Leyland:—
(By 1st *m*) James Michael Lloyd (Grannies Cottage, Crudgington Green, Telford, Shropshire), *b* 1952: *m* 1st, 1974, Susan Hough; 2ndly, 1997, Patricia Sutton-Jones, and has issue living (by 1st *m*), Neil James Lloyd, *b* 1982, — Sarah Louise Lloyd, *b* 1977, — Joanna Mary Lloyd, *b* 1979. —— Caroline Anne Lloyd (Oddicombe, Pitt, Winchester), *b* 1954: *m* 1979 (*m diss* 1999), John J. Baggerman, son of K. J. Baggerman, of Twyford, Hants, and has issue living, John Benjamin, *b* 1985, — Frederick Edwyn Karel, *b* 1991. —— Louise Avice Lloyd, *b* 1956: *m* 1995, Michael Christian Wigan, of Ashe House, Overton, Hants, son of late Maj Derek Wigan, of Drewitts, W Sussex, and has issue living, Lara Catherine, *b* 1997. —— Annabel Alix Lloyd (Eiche Strasse 24, 67098 Bad Durkheim, Germany), *b* 1957.

Grandson of late Rev Canon Hon Hugh Wynne Lloyd-Mostyn (ante):—
Issue of late Lt-Col James Pryce Lloyd Mostyn, *b* 1879, *d* 1968: *m* 1915, Alix Doreen, who *d* 1956, da of late Maj-Gen Inigo Richmund Jones, CVO, CB:—
David Henry Lloyd, *b* 1923, 1939-45 War as Rifleman Rifle Bde, and with Queen's R Regt (invalided): *m* 1956, Betty, da of late James Francis O'Connor, of Applecross, W Aust, and has had issue, †Christopher James, *b* and *d* 1964, — Sarah May (adopted da), *b* 1964. *Residence* – 41 Marion Way, Gooseberry Hill, W Australia 6076.

Not in remainder to Barony.

Grandchildren of late Alfred Norman Mostyn Lloyd (infra):—
Issue of late Cmdr Norman Mostyn Lloyd, RD, RNR, *b* 1911, *d* 1986: *m* 1941, Ethel Kathleen, who *d* 1986, da of late Edward Crouch:—
Edward Mostyn (15 Sussex St, SW1V 4RR), *b* 1943. —— Margaret Gwynedd, *b* 1944: *m* 1966, Douglas Havers, of Svanen, Soren Larson & Sonners, Nykobing Mors, Denmark.

Grandson of late Ven William Henry Cynric Lloyd, yr son of late Bell Lloyd, next brother of 2nd baronet and 1st Baron:—
Issue of late Alfred Norman Mostyn Lloyd, *b* 1868, *d* 1941: *m* 1st, 1895, Harriet, who *d* 1904, da of late Canon Crompton, of Breightmet, Pinetown Estate, Natal; 2ndly, 1910, Alice Rivière, who *d* 1944, da of Henry Ainsworth Condron:—
(By 2nd *m*) Alfred Anson, *b* 1914; Doc Econ (Hon Cas); *ed* Michaelhouse: *m* 1941, Elaine, da of late Horace Burdon, and has issue living, Patricia Burdon, *b* 1943, — Barbara Ann, *b* 1948: *m* 1971, Robert John Kendall Slater, of 24 Burleigh Cres, Durban North 4051, S Africa, and has issue living, Kendall Lloyd *b* 1972, Stuart James *b* 1974.

Granddaughter of late Charles Banastre Lloyd, son of Maj-Gen Benastre Pryce Lloyd, son of Llewelyn Lloyd, yst brother of 2nd Bt and 1st Baron:—
Issue of late Llewelyn Lloyd, *b* 1883, *d* 1960: *m* 1920, Jessie Elizabeth, da of James Thomas Forrester:—
Daphne Ellen Kate, *b* 1921: *m* 19— (*m diss* 1949), — Read, of Johannesburg, and has issue living, Arland Everard, *b* 1944, — Susan, *b* 1946.

PREDECESSORS – (1) EDWARD Lloyd, Secretary of War, *d* 1795, having in 1778 been *cr* a *Baronet*, with remainder to his nephew (2) *Sir* EDWARD PRYCE Lloyd, 2nd Bt; MP for Flint Borough 1806-07 and 1812-32; *b* 1768; *cr Baron Mostyn*, of Mostyn, co Flint (peerage of United Kingdom) 1831; *d* 1854; *s* by his son (3) EDWARD, 2nd Baron; sat as MP for Flintshire (LC) 1831-37, 1841-42, and 1847-54, and Lichfield 1846-47; was Lord-Lieut of Merionethshire; assumed in 1831 by Roy licence the additional surname of Mostyn; *d* 1884; *s* by his grandson (4) LLEWELYN NEVILLE VAUGHAN (son of late Hon Thomas Edward Mostyn Lloyd-Mostyn, 3rd Baron); *b* 1956; High Sheriff of Flint 1928, and Vice-Adm of N Wales and Carmarthen 1898-1929; bore Royal Standard of the Principality of Wales at Coronation of King George V 1911: *m* 1879, Lady Mary Florence Edith Clements, OBE, who *d* 1933, sister of 4th Earl of Leitrim; *d* 1929; *s* by his son (5) EDWARD LLEWELYN ROGER, 4th Baron *b* 1885; High Sheriff of Flintshire 1928: *m* 1918, Constance Mary, who *d* 1976, only child of late W. H. Reynolds, of Flintshire 1928: *m* 1918, Constance Mary, who *d* 1976, only child of late W. H. Reynolds, of Aldeburgh, *d* 1965; *s* by his el son (6) ROGER EDWARD LLOYD, MC, 5th Baron and present peer.

MOTTISTONE, BARON (Seely) (Baron UK 1933)

I hope in God

DAVID PETER SEELY, CBE, 4th Baron, *b* 16 Dec 1920; *s* 1966; Capt RN (ret); FIERE; FIPM; Hon D Litt; DL of Isle of Wight 1981-1985, Lord Lieut of Isle of Wight 1986-95, and Gov Isle of Wight 1992-95; served World War II 1939-40; Special Assist to Ch of Allied Staff, Malta, 1956-58, in Command HMS *Cossack*, Far E Fleet 1958-59; Capt 1960, Dep of Dir of Signals, Admiralty 1961-63, in Command of HMS *Ajax* and 24th Escort Sqdn Far E Fleet (despatches) 1964-65, and Naval Adviser to UK High Comnr in Canada 1965-66; Dir of Distributive Industry Training Board 1969-75; Dir Cake and Biscuit Alliance 1975-82; Chm Bureau of Applied Sciences 1987-91, and Dir Associated Information Services 1987-90; CBE (Civil) 1984: *m* 1944, Anthea Christine, da of Victor McMullan, and has issue.

Arms – Azure, three ears of wheat banded or between two martlets in pale, and as many wreaths of roses in fesse argent. **Crest** – In front of three ears of wheat banded or, the trunk of a tree fesswise eradicated and sprouting to the dexter proper. **Supporters** – On either side a sea-horse (hippocampus) azure, gorged with a mural crown and charged on the shoulder with a maple leaf or.
Residence – The Old Parsonage, Mottistone, Isle of Wight. *Clubs* – Royal Yacht Squadron, Royal Cruising, Island Sailing, Royal Commonwealth Society (Fellow), Royal Naval Sailing Association.

SONS LIVING

Hon PETER JOHN PHILIP, *b* 29 Oct 1949: *m* 1972 (*m diss* 1975), Joyce, da of Mrs Ellen Cairns, of St Ninians, Stirling; 2ndly, 1982, Linda, da of W.A. Swain, of Judds House, Bulphan Fen, Upminster, Essex, and has issue living (by 1st *m*), Christopher David Peter, *b* 1 Oct 1974. — (by 2nd *m*), Richard William Anthony, *b* 1988, — Penelope Jane, *b* 1984, — Jennifer Elizabeth, *b* 1986, — Caroline Anne, *b* 1990. *Residence* – Alendale, Uckfield Lane, Hever, Kent TN8 7LJ.

Hon Patrick Michael, *b* 1960; *ed* Harrow, and Trin Coll, Camb: *m* 1984, Susannah Shelley, da of Cdr J. C. Q. Johnson, of Brook, IoW, and has issue living, Thomas Charles Rupert, *b* 1989, — Theodore Michael John *b* 1998, — Clementine Mary, *b* 1991. *Residence* – Dunsbury Farm, Brook, Isle of Wight P030 4EL.

DAUGHTERS LIVING

Hon Diana Mary, *b* 1954: *m* 1977, Edward Anthony Spours Nicholson, and has issue living, Alexander James Edward, *b* 1988, — Zoë Mary Louisa, *b* 1990, — Henrietta Cristina, *b* 1994. *Residence* – Staple Ash House, Froxfield Green, Petersfield, Hants GU32 1DH.

Hon Victoria Anne, *b* 1957: *m* 1984, Christopher Russell, son of late John Russell, and has issue living, John Hugh *b* 1987, — Emily, *b* 1985, — Kate, *b* 1989, — Alice, *b* 1991. *Residence* – Ningwood Manor, Ningwood, Isle of Wight.

PREDECESSORS – (1) *Rt Hon* JOHN EDWARD BERNARD Seely, CB, CMG, DSO, TD, 4th son of Sir Charles Seely, 1st Bt; *b* 1868; Lord Lt for Hants and Isle of Wight, Lt-Col and Hon Col 72nd Hampshires Anti-Aircraft Bde RA (TA), and 7th Hussars (Canadian Mil), Maj-Gen in the Army; S Africa 1900-1901, with 4th Bn Imperial Yeo (DSO), 1914-18 War; commanded Canadian Cavalry Bde 1915-18; Under-Sec of State for the Colonies 1908-11, Under-Sec of State for War 1911-12, Sec of State for War and Pres of Army Council 1912-14, Warfare Member of Munitions Council 1918, Parliamentary Under-Sec to Min of Munitions, and Dep Min of Munitions 1918, and Under-Sec of State for Air 1919; MP for I of W (*C*) 1900-1906, for Liverpool, Abercromby Div 1906-10, for Ilkeston Div of Derbyshire 1910-22, for I of W (*L*) 1923-24; *cr Baron Mottistone*, of Mottistone, co Southampton (Peerage of UK) 1933: *m* 1st, 1895, Emily Florence, who *d* 1913, da of Hon Sir Henry George Louis Crichton (E Erne); 2ndly, 1917, Hon Evelyn Izme, JP, who *d* 1976, da of 1st Viscount Elibank, and widow of Capt George Crosfield Norris Nicholson, RFC (*see* Nicholson, Bt, *cr* 1912) *d* 1947, *s* by his el surviving son (2) (HENRY) JOHN ALEXANDER, OBE, FRIBA, 2nd Baron, *b* 1899; Surveyor of Fabric, St Paul's

Cathedral Architect to St George's Chapel, Windsor; Capt 72nd Hampshire Anti-Aircraft Bde (RA)(TA) 1914-18 War in Italy, 1939-45 War as Fl Lt Aux AF; *d* 1963; *s* by his brother **(3)** (ARTHUR) PATRICK WILLIAM, TD, 3rd Baron, *b* 1905; Lt-Col Anti-Aircraft Regt RA (TA): *m* 1939 (*m diss* 1949), Wilhelmina Josephine Philippa, da of Jonkheer Frans I Van Haeften (Brocklehurst, Bt); *d* 1966; *s* by his half-brother **(4)** DAVID PETER, 4th Baron and present peer.

Mountbatten, family name of Duke of Edinburgh.

Mountbatten, family name of Marquess of Milford Haven.

MOUNTBATTEN OF BURMA, COUNTESS (Knatchbull) (Earl UK 1947)

IN HONOUR BOUND

PATRICIA EDWINA VICTORIA KNATCHBULL, *Countess Mountbatten of Burma*, CBE, *b* 14 Feb 1924; *s* 1979; Col-in-Ch of Princess Patricia's Canadian LI; CD; DStJ; JP Kent 1971, DL 1973, Vice Lord Lieut 1984; Patron Legion of Frontiersmen of the Commonwealth since 1983; Vice-Pres BRCS; 1939-45 War in WRNS in UK and S-E Asia; CBE (Civil) 1991: *m* 26 Oct 1946, 7th Baron Brabourne, CBE, and has had issue.

Arms – Quarterly: 1st and 4th, azure, a lion rampant double queued barry of ten, argent and gules, armed and langued of the last, crowned or, within a bordure compony of the 2nd and 3rd; 2nd and 3rd, argent, two pallets sable charged on the honour point with an escutcheon of the arms of late Princess Alice (namely, the Royal Arms differenced with a label of three points argent, on the centre point charged with a rose gules barbed vert, and each of the other points with an ermine spot sable). **Supporters** – On either side a lion double queued and crowned all or.
Residences – Newhouse, Mersham, Ashford, Kent TN25 6NQ; 39 Montpelier Walk, SW7 1JH.

SONS LIVING AND DECEASED

NORTON LOUIS PHILIP (*Lord Romsey*) (Broadlands, Romsey, Hants SO51 9ZD), *b* 8 Oct 1947; *ed* Gordonstoun, and Kent Univ; High Steward of Romsey since 1980: *m* 20 Oct 1979, Penelope Meredith, only da of Reginald Eastwood, of Palma de Mallorca, Spain, and has issue:—

> SON LIVING— *Hon* Nicholas Louis Charles Norton, *b* 15 May 1981.
>
> DAUGHTERS LIVING AND DECEASED—*Hon* Alexandra Victoria Edwina Diana, *b* 5 Dec 1982, — *Hon* Leonora Louise Marie Elizabeth, *b* 25 June 1986, *d* 22 Oct 1991.

Hon Michael-John Ulick KNATCHBULL (1 Horbury Mews, W11 3NL), *b* 24 May 1950; *ed* Gordonstoun, and Reading Univ: *m* 1st, 1 June 1985 (*m diss* 1997), Melissa Clare, actress, only da of Hon Mr Justice (Sir John Arthur Dalziel) Owen, of Bickerstaff House, Shipston-on-Stour, Warwickshire; 2ndly, 6 March 1999, Mrs Susan Penelope Henderson, da of Cedric Coates, of The Old Rectory, Epperstone, Notts, and formerly wife of William Dalton Alexander Henderson, and has issue living (by 1st m), Kelly Louise Doreen, *b* 30 March 1988.

Hon Philip Wyndham Ashley KNATCHBULL (41 Montpelier Walk, SW7 1JH) *b* 2 Dec 1961; *ed* Gordonstoun, Kent Univ, and London Internat Film Sch: *m* 16 March 1991, Mrs Atalanta Vereker, da of late John Cowan, and formerly wife of Hugo Dominic Charles Medlicott Vereker (*see* V Gort, colls), and has issue living, Daisy Isadora, *b* 5 Oct 1992.

†*Hon* Nicholas Timothy Charles KNATCHBULL, *b* 18 Nov 1964; *k* with his grandfather, Earl Mountbatten of Burma, and grandmother, Doreen, Lady Brabourne, 1979.

Hon Timothy Nicholas Sean KNATCHBULL, *b* (twin) 18 Nov 1964; *ed* Gordonstoun, Atlantic Coll, Christ's Coll, Camb, and Kennedy Sch, Harvard Univ, USA: *m* 1998, Isabella Julia, 2nd da of David Mark Norman (*see* Sheffield, Bt).

DAUGHTERS LIVING

Lady Joanna Edwina Doreen, *b* 5 March 1955; *ed* Benenden, Atlantic Coll, Kent Univ, and Columbia Univ, USA: *m* 1st, 3 Nov 1984 (*m diss* 1995), Baron Hubert Henry Francois du Breuil, 2nd son of Baron Bertrand Pernot du Breuil, of Paris; 2ndly, 19 Nov 1995, Azriel Adrian Sorin Zuckerman, elder son of Bercu Zuckerman, of Bucharest, Rumania, and has issue living (by 1st *m*), Eleuthera Roselyne Patricia, *b* 13 May 1986.

Lady Amanda Patricia Victoria, *b* 26 June 1957; *ed* Benenden, Gordonstoun, Kent Univ, Peking Univ, and Goldsmiths Coll: *m* 31 Oct 1987, Charles V. Ellingworth, of 3 Stowe Rd, W12 2PT, eldest son of William Ellingworth, of Laughton, Leics, and has issue living, Luke John William, *b* 27 Jan 1991, — Joseph Louis Vincent, *b* 2 Dec 1992.

SISTER LIVING

Lady Pamela Carmen Louise, *b* 1929; Lady-in Waiting to HM The Queen on her tour to Australia and New Zealand 1953-54: *m* 1960, David Nightingale Hicks, who *d* 1998, and has issue living, Ashley Louis David, *b* 1963: *m* 1990, Allegra Marina, elder da of Dottor Carlo Tondato, of Turin, and has issue living, Angelica Margherita Edwina *b* 1992, Ambrosia Maria Elisabeth *b* 1997, — Edwina Victoria Louise, *b* 1961: *m* 1984, Jeremy A. R. Brudenell, 2nd son of (John) Michael Brudenell, FRCS, FRCOG, of Hever, Kent, and has issue living, Maddison May *b* 1994, Jordan Anne *b* 1995, — India Amanda Caroline (Hibiscus Hill, PO Box 255, Harbour Island, Bahamas), *b* 1967; has issue living (by David Flint Wood), Felix Austen *b* 1997. *Residences* – Albany, Piccadilly, W1V 9RP; The Grove, Brightwell Baldwin, Oxon OX9 5PF.

PREDECESSOR – **(1)** *Adm of the Fleet* Louis Francis Albert Victor Nicholas Mountbatten, KG, GCB, OM, GCSI, GCIE, GCVO, DSO, PC, FRS (discontinued by R Warrant 1917 the style of HSH and Prince and the appellation of Battenberg, and became known as Lord Louis Mountbatten in lieu of HSH Prince Louis Francis of Battenberg), 2nd son of 1st Marquess of Milford Haven (*see* Royal Family), *b* 25 June 1900; Adm of the Fleet 1956, Hon Lt-Gen in the Army and Air Marshal RAF, Col Life Guards, and Col Comdt RM 1965-79; Ch of Combined Operations and a Member of Ch of Staff's Cttee 1942-43; Supreme Allied Cdr SE Asia 1943-47, Viceroy of India March - Aug 1947; Gov-Gen of India 1947-48, Flag Officer Comdg First Cruiser Sqdn 1948-50, Fourth Sea Lord 1950-52, C-in-C Med 1952-54, and C-in-C Allied Forces, Med 1953-54, First Sea Lord 1955-59, Ch of Defence Staff and Chm of Chs of Staff Cttee 1959-65; Gov, Capt, and Steward of Isle of Wight 1965-79, and Lord Lieut 1974-79; *cr Viscount Mountbatten of Burma*, of Romsey, co Southampton (peerage of UK), with remainder to heirs male of his body, and in default of such issue to his el da, Patricia Edwina Victoria, and the heirs male of her body; and in default of such issue to every other da successively in order of seniority of age and priority of birth, and to the heirs male of their bodies 1946, and *Baron Romsey*, of Romsey, co Southampton, and *Earl Mountbatten of Burma* (peerage of UK), with similar special remainders to the above mentioned 1947: *m* 1922, Hon Dame Edwina Cynthia Annette Ashley, CI GBE, DCVO, LLD, who *d* 1960, el da of 1st Baron Mount Temple (ext); assassinated 1979; *s* by his el da **(2)** Patricia Edwina Victoria, present peeress; also Viscountess Mountbatten of Burma, and Baroness Romsey.

Mount Charles, Earl of; son of Marquess Conyngham.

MOUNT EDGCUMBE, EARL OF (Edgcumbe) (Earl GB 1789)

ROBERT CHARLES EDGCUMBE, 8th Earl; *b* 1 June 1939; *s* 1982; formerly Farm Manager for Lands and Survey, NZ: *m* 1960 (*m diss* 1988), Joan Ivy, da of Ernest Wall, of 3 RD Otorohanga, NZ, and has issue.

Arms – Gules, on a bend ermines, cottised or, three boars' heads argent. **Crest** – A boar statant argent, gorged with a wreath of oak vert, fructed or. **Supporters** – Two greyhounds argent, guttee de poix, and gorged with a collar, dovetailed gules,
Seat – Mount Edgcumbe, Plymouth. *Residence* – Empacombe House, Cremyll, Mount Edgcumbe, Cornwall PL10 1HZ.

DAUGHTERS LIVING

Lady (Valerie) Denise (Empacombe House, Cremyll, Mount Edgcumbe, Cornwall PL10 1HZ), *b* 1960.
Lady Megan Frances (14 Grey St, Kawerau, Bay of Plenty, NZ), *b* 1962; Horticulturalist.
Lady Tracy Anne, *b* 1966: *m* 1988, Colin Rush, of Opotiki, Bay of Plenty, NZ, and has issue living, Shaun, *b* 1987, — Jamie Lee (da), *b* 1989.
Lady Vanessa Erina Michelle (2 Anderton Quay Cottages, Millbrook, Torpoint, Cornwall PL10 1DU), *b* 1969; has issue living (by Ralph Winsor), Tobias Richard, *b* 1989, — Coral Erina, *b* 1991.
Lady Alison Nicole (Empacombe House, Cremyll, Mount Edgcumbe, Cornwall PL10 1HZ), *b* 1971.

HALF BROTHERS LIVING

PIERS VALLETORT, *b* 23 Oct 1946: *m* 1971 (*m diss* 19—), Hilda Warn, and has issue living, Prudence, *b* 1972, — Angela, *b* 1975. *Residence* – ....
Christopher George Mortimer, *b* 1950: *m* 1985 (*m diss* 1991), Marian Frances, da of Murray Stevenson, and has issue living, Douglas George Valletort, *b* 31 Oct 1985, — Emma Louise (adopted stepda), *b* 1983. *Residence* – Flat 2, 51 Cook St, Hamilton East, NZ.

AUNT LIVING (Sister of 7th Earl)

Erina Shelley, *b* 1898: *m* 1930, John Richard Sutton, MICE, of 16 Awatea Rd, Parnell, Auckland, NZ, and has issue living, Gillian Mary Edgcumbe, *b* 1941.

DAUGHTER LIVING OF SIXTH EARL

Lady Hilaria Agnes, *b* 1908: *m* 1933, Lt-Col Denis Lucius Alban Gibbs, DSO, Queen's R Regt, who *d* 1984, and has had issue, Jillianne Bridget, *b* 1935: *m* 1st, 1959 (*m diss* 1973), Maj Martin John Minter-Kemp, RWF (rct); 2ndly, 1974, Anthony Alan Russell Cobbold, of The Vineyard, Weston under Redcastle, Shrewsbury, and *d* 1994, leaving issue (by 1st *m*), Robin John Edgcumbe *b* 1963: *m* 19—, Penelope Garner, Emma Hilaria *b* 1960, Penelope Claire *b* (twin) 1963: *m* 19—, Tom Dickins, — Margaret Hilaria (USA), *b* 1937: *m* 1961 (*m diss* 1989), Rev Mark Lyon Thornewill, RN (ret), and has issue living, John-Mark Judah *b* 1961: *m* 1985, Araby Jane Wedekind (and has issue living, Benjamin Aaron *b* 1985, Alice Hilaria *b* 1988), Luke Thomas *b* (twin) 1961: *m* 1997, Carrie ......, Christopher Shane Kenelm *b* 1968: *m* 19—, Wendy Bissett, Jeremy Lyon *b* 1970, Joanna Lilian *b* 1965: *m* 19—, Taylor Hay, — Rosamund Lucia (*Lady Woodard*), *b* 1941: *m* 1963, Rear Adm Sir Robert Nathaniel Woodard, KCVO, DL, RN, of Restormel Manor, Lostwithiel, Cornwall PL22 0HN, and has issue living, Rupert Piers Nathaniel *b* 1964: *m* 1990, Anna Culley (and has issue living, Oliver *b* 1992, Benjamin *b* 1994, Harry *b* 1997), Jolyon Robert Alban *b* 1969, Melissa Lucia Rosamund *b* 1967, — Penelope Mary, *b* 1949: *m* 1st, 1970, Douglas Arthur Dale; 2ndly, 1985, Timothy Roger Douglas-Riley, of Smallack House, Crownhill, Devon, and has issue living (by 2nd *m*), Henrietta Lucia *b* 1987, Venetia Louise *b* 1988. *Residence* – Aldenham, Deer Park Lane, Tavistock, Devon.

MOTHER LIVING

Meta, da of late Charles Robert Lhoyer, of Nancy, France: *m* 1st, 1935 (*m diss* 1943), George Aubrey Valletort Edgcumbe, brother of 7th Earl, who *d* 1977; 2ndly, 1967, Arthur Edward Blucher, who *d* 1988. *Residence* – Summit Drive, Torbay, Auckland, NZ.

STEPMOTHER LIVING

Una Pamela EDGCUMBE BARON, da of late Edward Lewis George, of Perth, W Australia: *m* 1st, 1944, as his 2nd wife, George Aubrey Valletort Edgcumbe, brother of 7th Earl, who *d* 1977; 2ndly, 1989, Kenneth Baron. *Residence* – 77 Arapiki Rd, Stoke, Nelson, NZ.

COLLATERAL BRANCHES LIVING

Grandchildren of late Richard Gerald Valletort Edgcumbe, 3rd son of late Edward Mortimer Edgcumbe (infra):—
Issue of late Edward Mortimer Edgcumbe, *b* 1904, *d* 1983: *m* 1941, Mary MacArthur (27 Tuhaere St, Orakei, Auckland, New Zealand), da of John Stone:—
Richard John, *b* 1946. —— Margaret Ann, *b* 1942: *m* 1981, William Kendrick Smithyman, of 66 Alton Ave, Northcote, Auckland, NZ.

Granddaughter of late Edward Mortimer Edgcumbe, yr son of late Hon George Edgcumbe, yst son of 2nd Earl:—
Issue of late Ernest Athole Edgcumbe, *b* 1870, *d* 1937: *m* 1896, Louisa Charlotte, who *d* 1949, da of William Martin, of Auckland, New Zealand:—
Jessie Hilaria, *b* 1911: *m* 1934, Leslie Reeves, who *d* 1986, of 4a Chelsea Place, Hamilton, NZ and has issue living, Gaynor Hilaria Ann, *b* 1936: *m* 1957, Arthur Herbert Lidington, of 20 Chelsea Place, Hamilton, NZ, and has issue living, Brett Arthur (378 Cobham Drive, Hamilton, NZ) *b* 1961: *m* 1987, Sonia Jane Haines (and has issue living, Reid Arthur *b* 1992, Fraser Oliver *b* 1994, Braidy Millie Kristina *b* 1998), Janine Lesley *b* 1959: *m* 1979, Graeme William Pickering, of 18 Maeroa Rd, Hamilton, NZ (and has issue living, Samuel Thomas *b* 1987, Hannah Louise *b* 1991).

PREDECESSORS – (1) *Rt Hon* Richard Edgcumbe, PC, many years MP for Cornwall, St Germans, and Plympton, was successively a Lord of the Treasury, Joint Vice-Treasurer, Receiver-Gen, Treasurer of War, Paymaster-Gen, for Ireland, Chancellor of the Duchy of Lancaster, and Lord-Lieut of Cornwall &c; *cr Baron Edgcumbe*, of Mount Edgcumbe, co Devon (peerage of Great Britain) 1742; *d* 1758; *s* by his el son (2) Richard, PC, 2nd Baron; MP for Plympton 1747-54, and for Penryn 1754-8; was Lord-Lieut of Cornwall, and successively a Lord Commr of the Admiralty, and Comptroller of the Household, &c; *d* unmarried 1766; *s* by his brother (3) George, 3rd Baron; and Adm of the Blue; MP for Plympton 1754-61, and Lord-Lieut of Cornwall; *cr Viscount Mount Edgcumbe and Valletort* (peerage of Great Britain) 1781, and *Earl of Mount Edgcumbe* (peerage of Great Britain) 1789; *d* 1795; *s* by his son (4) Richard, 2nd Earl; was Lord-Lieut of Cornwall; *d* 1839; *s* by his son (5) Ernest Augustus, 3rd Earl; *b* 1797: *m* 1831, Caroline Augusta, da of Rear-Adm Charles Feilding; *d* 1861; *s* by his son (6) William Henry, GCVO, PC, 4th Earl; sat as MP for Plymouth (C) 1859-61; was Lord-Lieut of Cornwall 1877-1917, Lord Chamberlain of HM Queen Victoria's Household 1879-80, Lord High Steward of HM Queen Victoria's Household June 1885 to Jan 1886, and July 1886 to Aug 1892, and ADC to HM Queen Victoria 1887-97; a Member of Council to HRH the Prince of Wales 1901-17, and Keeper of the Seal of the Duchy of Cornwall 1907-17: *m* 1858, Lady Katherine Elizabeth Hamilton, who *d* 1874, da of 1st Duke of Abercorn, KG; 2ndly, 1906, his cousin, Caroline Cecilia, who *d* 1909, da of late Hon George Edgcumbe, and widow of 3rd Earl of Ravensworth; *d* 1917; *s* by his only son, (7) Piers Alexander Hamilton, 5th Earl; *b* 1865; Dep Warden of the Stanneries 1913-44: *m* 1911, Lady Edith Villiers, who *d* 1935, da of 5th Earl of Clarendon; *d* 1944; *s* by his kinsman (8) Kenelm William Edward, TD (only son of Richard John Frederick Edgcumbe, MVO, el son of Hon George Edgcumbe, yst son of 2nd Earl), 6th Earl, *b* 1873: *m* 1906, Lilian Agnes, who *d* 1964, da of Col Arthur Chandos Arkwright, of Hatfield Place, Witham, Essex; *d* 1965; *s* by his kinsman (9) Edward Piers (el son of George Valletort Edgcumbe, el son of Edward Mortimer Edgcumbe, 2nd son of Hon George Edgcumbe, yst son of 2nd Earl), 7th Earl; *b* 1903: *m* 1944, Victoria Effie, who *d* 1979, yr da of Robert Campbell, of N Ireland and NZ; *d* 1982; *s* by his nephew (10) Robert Charles (el son of George Aubrey Valletort Edgcumbe, brother of 7th Earl), 8th Earl and present peer; also Viscount Mount Edgcumbe and Valletort, and Baron Edgcumbe.

MOUNTEVANS, BARON (Evans) (Baron UK 1945)

Liberty

(Edward Patrick) Broke Andvord Evans, 3rd Baron; *b* 1 Feb 1943; *s* 1974; *ed* Rugby, and Trin Coll, Oxford: *m* 1974, Johanna, da of Antonius Keyzer, of The Hague.

Arms – Argent two bars wavy azure between three boar's heads sable. Crest – Between two cross crosslets fichee sable a demi lion erased reguardant or holding between the paws a boar's head erased also sable. Supporters – On either side a king penguin proper.
Address – c/o House of Lords, SW1.

BROTHER LIVING

Hon Jeffrey Richard de Corban (5 Campden House Court, 42 Gloucester Walk, W8 4HU), *b* 13 May 1948; *ed* Nautical Coll, Pangbourne, and Pembroke Coll, Camb: *m* 1972, Hon Juliet Wilson, da of the 2nd Baron Moran, and has issue living, Alexander Richard Andvord, *b* 1975, — Julian James Rowntree, *b* 1977.

SISTER LIVING

Hon Lucinda Mary Deirdre Evans, *b* 1951 (has retained her maiden name); journalist: *m* 1980, John E. Hooper.

UNCLE LIVING (*son of 1st Baron*)

Hon Edward Broke, VRD, *b* 1924; *ed* Wellington Coll; Cdr (E) RNR (ret): *m* 1947, Elaine Elizabeth, da of Capt (S) W. W. Cove, RN, and has issue living, Julian Phillip Broke, *b* 1956, — William Garth, *b* 1959, — Rosemary, *b* 1948. *Residence* – 15 York Mansions, Prince of Wales Drive, SW11.

PREDECESSORS – (1) *Adm Sir* EDWARD RATCLIFFE GARTH RUSSELL Evans, KCB, DSC, 2nd son of late Frank Evans, Bar-at-law, of 5 New Square, Lincoln's Inn, WC; *b* 1881; served as Second Officer of relief ship *Morning* during National Antarctic Expedition 1902-4, and made two voyages to Polar regions to relief of *Discovery*; was Second in Command of British Antarctic Expedition 1910, succeeding Capt Scott in command 1912-13; European War 1914-19 with Dover Patrol in command of *Broke* and as Senior Officer, Ostend; Rear-Adm Comdg Roy Australian Navy 1929-31, Com-in-Ch, Africa Station 1933-5, and at The Nore 1935-9; Rector of Aberdeen Univ 1936-42; Regional Commr for London Defence Area 1939-45; *cr Baron Mountevans*, of Chelsea, co London (peerage of United Kingdom) 1945: *m* 1st, 1904, Hilda Beatrice who *d* 1913, da of late Thomas Gregory Russell, Bar-at-law, of Christchurch, New Zealand; 2ndly, 1916, Elsa, who *d* 1963, da of late Richard Andvord, of Oslo, Norway; *d* 1957; *s* by his el son (2) RICHARD ANDVORD, 2nd Baron; *b* 1918; Chm of Norwegian Export Centre and Anglo-Swedish Parl Group; late Lt RNVR: *m* 1940, Deirdre Grace, who *d* 1997, da of John O'Connell, of Buxton House, Buxton Hill, Co Cork; *d* 1974; *s* by his el son (3) (EDWARD PATRICK) BROKE ANDVORD, 3rd Baron and present peer.

Mountgarret, Baron, title of Viscount Mountgarret on Roll of HL.

MOUNTGARRET, VISCOUNT (Butler) Sits as BARON (Baron UK 1911) (Viscount I 1550)

I was humbled, I am now exalted

RICHARD HENRY PIERS BUTLER, 17th Viscount; *b* 8 Nov 1936; *s* 1966; senior known heir to Earldoms of Ormonde and Ossory; *ed* Eton and RMA, late Capt Irish Guards: *m* 1st, 1960 (*m diss* 1969), Gillian Margaret, only da of Cyril Francis Stuart Buckley, of 41 St Leonard's Ter, SW3; 2ndly, 1970, Jennifer Susan Melville, da of Capt D. M. Wills, of Barley Wood, Wrington, Som, and formerly wife of D. W. Fattorini, of Sawley Hall, Ripon; 3rdly, 1983, Mrs Angela Ruth Waddington, eldest da of Maj Thomas Porter, of Church Fenton, Tadcaster, and formerly wife of John Waddington, of Masham, Yorks, and has issue by 1st *m*.

Arms – Quarterly, 1st and 4th, perfesse sable and azure, a quadrangular castle with four towers between three martlets all argent, *Rawson*; 2nd and 3rd, or, a chief indented azure, a crescent for difference, *Butler*. **Crests** – 1st, An eagle's head per fesse sable and azure, goutté d'or holding in the beak two annulets interlaced paleways or, *Rawson*. 2nd, out of a ducal coronet or, a plume of five ostrich feathers argent, therefrom a falcon rising of the last, *Butler*. **Supporters** – *Dexter*, a falcon wings inverted argent, armed, membered, and belled or; *sinister*, a male griffin argent, armed, collared , and chained or.
Residence – Stainley House, S Stainley, Harrogate. *Clubs* – White's, Pratt's.

SONS LIVING (*By 1st marriage*)

Hon PIERS JAMES RICHARD, *b* 15 April 1961; *ed* Eton: *m* 1995, Laura Brown GARY, da of Mrs Albert Dickens Williams, Jr, of Lake Forest, Illinois, USA, and has issue living, Alexa, *b* 1997. *Residence* – Illinois, USA. *Clubs* – White's, Union (New York).
Hon Edmund Henry Richard, *b* 1963; *ed* Stowe: *m* 1988 (*m diss* 1989), Adelle L., only da of M. Lloyd, of New York, USA.

DAUGHTER LIVING (*By 1st marriage*)

Hon Henrietta Elizabeth Alexandra BUTLER, *b* 1964; has resumed her maiden name: *m* 1991 (*m diss* 1992), Robert Cluer, only son of Henry Cluer, of S Africa.

SISTER LIVING

Hon Sarah Elizabeth Ann *b* 1932: *m* 1955 (*m diss* 1976), Geoffrey Kenneth Raynar, and has issue living, Rupert James Geoffrey, *b* 1957, — James Augustine, *b* 1962. *Residence* – 52 St Anne's Drive, Headingley, Leeds.

PREDECESSORS – **(1)** *Hon* RICHARD Butler, 2nd son of 8th Earl of Ormonde; Kt 1547, *cr Viscount Mountgarret* (peerage of Ireland) 1550*: *m* 1st, Eleanor, da of Theobald Butler, of Neigham, co Kilkenny; 2ndly, Catherine, da of Peter Barnewall, of Stackall, co Meath; 3rdly, 1541, Anne, da of 4th Lord Killeen; *d* 1571, *s* by his son (by 1st *m*) **(2)** EDMUND, 2nd Viscount; sat in Parliament 1585 and was Deputy and Sheriff of co Kilkenny 1576: *m* his 1st cousin, Grizel Fitzpatrick, da of Barnaby, 1st Lord of Upper Ossory; *d* 1602; *s* by his son **(3)** RICHARD, 3rd Viscount; sat as MP in several Parliaments; was appointed Gen of the Irish Forces 1642, and, having been outlawed, was in 1652, after his death, excepted from pardon; *m* 1st, Margaret, da of Hugh O'Neill, Earl of Tyrone; 2ndly, Thomasine Elizabeth, who *d* 1625, da of Sir William Andrews, of Newport Pagnell, Bucks; 3rdly, Margaret, who *d* 1655, da of Richard Branthwaite, and widow of Sir Thomas Spencer, Bt; *s* by his son (by 1st *m*) **(4)** EDMUND, 4th Viscount, who in 1660 received a pardon for all treasons, rebellions, etc, from Charles II, and was restored to his estates, &c 1661: *m* 1st, Lady Dorothy Touchet, who *d* 1635, 2nd da of 2nd Earl of Castlehaven; 2ndly, 1635, Anne, da of Sir Thomas Tresham, and widow of William Thatcher; 3rdly, 1637, Elizabeth, da of Sir George Simeon, and widow of William Conyers; *d* 1679; *s* by his son (by 1st *m*) **(5)** RICHARD, 5th Viscount; Capt Jacobite Army at Siege of Londonderry 4 June 1689: *m* 1st, 1661, Emilia, who *d* 1682, da of William Blundell, of Crosby, Lancs; 2ndly, his 3rd cousin, Margaret, da of Richard Shee, and widow of Gilbert Butler; *d* 1706; *s* by his son (by 1st *m*) **(6)** EDMUND, 6th Viscount; Lt-Col of Horse in the Irish Army of James II, led the forlorn hope against the City of Londonderry, 1689, and, being taken prisoner, was afterwards outlawed and his estates forfeited; in 1721 claimed his seat in Parliament and took the oath of fidelity; in 1715 the outlawry was reversed: *m* 1st, Mary Buchanan; 2ndly, 1715, Elizabeth, da of John Bryan, and widow of Oliver Grace; *d* 1735; *s* by his el son **(7)** RICHARD, 7th Viscount: *m* 1711, Catherine, who *d* 1739, da of John O'Neill, of Shanes Castle, co Antrim; *dsp* 1736 *s* by his brother **(8)** JAMES, 8th Viscount; served in Austrian Army in Campaign on the Rhine 1735: *m* 1736, Margaret, who *d* 1764, 2nd da of 11th Lord Trimlestown; *dsp* 1743; *s* by his brother **(9)** EDMUND, 9th Viscount: *m* Anne, who *d* 1773, da of Toby Purcell, of Ballymartin, co Kilkenny; *d* 1750; *s* by his son **(10)** EDMUND, 10th Viscount; *b* 1771; *d* 1779; *m* 1744, Charlotte, who *d* 1778, 2nd da of Sir Simon Bradstreet, 1st Bt; *s* by his son **(11)** EDMUND, 11th Viscount; MP co Kilkenny 1776-79: *m* 1768, Lady Henrietta Butler, who *d* 1785, 2nd da of 1st Earl of Carrick; *d* 1793; *s* by his son **(12)** EDMUND, 12th Viscount; *b* 1771; *cr Earl of Kilkenny* (peerage of Ireland) 1793: *m* Mildred, who *d* 1830, eldest da of Most Rev Robert Fowler, Archbishop of Dublin; *d* 1846, when the earldom expired, and the minor honours devolved upon his nephew **(13)** HENRY EDMUND, 13th Viscount, son of Hon Henry, 3rd son of 11th Viscount, by Anne, da of John Harrison, Esq, of Newton House, co York; *b* 1816: *m* 1844, Frances Penelope, who *d* 1886, only child of Thomas Rawson, of Nidd Hall, Knaresboro'; *d* 1900; *s* by his son **(14)** HENRY EDMUND, 14th Viscount; *b* 1844; assumed by R Licence 1891 the surname of Rawson-Butler, and the additional arms of Rawson, but in 1902 by R Licence resumed the surname of Butler only; DL and JP W Riding of Yorks, High Sheriff 1895, DL co Kilkenny and for City of York; Lieut 1st LG; *cr Baron Mountgarret*, of Nidd, W Riding of York (peerage of UK) 1911: *m* 1st, 1868, Mary Eleanor, who *d* 1900, da of late St John Chiverton Charlton, of Apley Castle, Shropshire; 2ndly, 1902, Robina Marion, who *d* 1944, el da of Col Edward Hanning Hanning-Lee, JP (formerly Comdg 2nd Life Guards), of The Old Manor House, Bighton, Alresford, Hants; *d* 1912; *s* by his son **(15)** EDMUND SOMERSET, 15th Viscount, *b* 1875: *m* 1897, Cecily, who *d* 1961, (having *m* 2ndly, 1919, as his 2nd wife, Lieut-Col Charles Hoare, DSO, who assumed by R Licence 1927 the surname of Grey in lieu of his patronymic), da of late Arthur Grey; *d* 1918; *s* by his half-brother **(16)** PIERS HENRY AUGUSTINE, 16th Viscount; *b* 1903: *m* 1st, 1931 (*m diss* 1941), Eglantine Marie Elizabeth (who *d* 1990, having *m* 2ndly, 1956, Rear Adm Patrick Vivian McLaughlin, CB, DSO, who *d* 1969), da of late William Lorenzo Christie, of Jervaulx Abbey, Yorks; 2ndly, 1941, (Elsie) Margarita, who *d* 1968, da of Sir John Nicholson Barran, 2nd Bt; *d* 1966; *s* by his only son **(17)** RICHARD HENRY PIERS, 17th Viscount and present peer; also Baron Mountgarret.

*The 1st Viscount is also said to have been *cr Baron of Kells*, but there is no mention of this title in the grant.

MOUNTMORRES, VISCOUNTCY OF (de Montmorency) (Extinct 1951)

DAUGHTER LIVING OF SEVENTH VISCOUNT

Hon Carolie Madge Warrand, *b* 1920; *ed* Chelsea Coll of Physical Education and W London Sch of Physiotherapy (MCSP); Physiotherapist, Superintendent of Poole Gen Hospital 1965-81; 1939-45 War in WAAF: *m* 1947, Douglas Morris, and has had issue, Andrew John, *b* 1957; 3rd Engr Officer RFA; *ka* S Atlantic Campaign 1982, — Diana Pauline, *b* 1954. *Residence* – Danebury Hill, 15 Greenwood Ave, Lilliput, Poole, Dorset.

Mount Stuart, Lord; son of Marquess of Bute.

MOWBRAY, SEGRAVE and STOURTON, BARON (Stourton) (Baron E 1283; *Baron E 1295; Baron E 1448)
(Title pronounced "Mo-bray, Seagrave and Sturton")

I will be loyal during my life

Badge of the Barons Stourton

CHARLES EDWARD STOURTON,* CBE, 26th Baron Mowbray, 27th Baron Segrave, and 23rd Baron Stourton; *b* 11 March 1923; *s* 1965; *ed* Ampleforth Coll, and Ch Ch, Oxford; Opposition Whip, House of Lords 1967-70 and 1974-78, Deputy Chief Whip 1978-79; a Lord-in-Waiting to HM 1970-74, and 1979-80; Knt of Sovereign Mil Order of Malta; CBE (Civil) 1982; 1939-45 War in NW Europe as Lt Grenadier Gds (wounded); Member Nidderdale RDC 1954-58, and Securicor 1961-64; Dir Securicor (Scotland) Ltd 1964-70; Chancellor Primrose League 1974-83; a Trustee College of Arms since 1975; Dir ERIC (Jersey) Ltd, ERIC (Ghana) Ltd, GDC (Ghana) Ltd, ERIC (Suisse) SA, ERIC (Canada) Inc; Kt of Sacred and Mil Constantinian Order of St George: *m* 1st, 1952, Hon Jane Faith de Yarburgh Bateson, who *d* 1998, only da of 5th Baron Deramore; 2ndly, 1999, Joan Marianne, only surv child of late Capt Herbert Edmund Street, 20th Hussars, and widow of Capt Sir Guy Hope Holland, 3rd Bt (ext 1997), and has issue by 1st *m*.

𝕬rms – Quarterly of six; 1st sable, a bend or between six fountains, *Stourton*; 2nd gules, on a bend between six crosses crosslet argent, an escutcheon or, charged with a demi-lion rampant, pierced through the mouth by an arrow, within a double tressure flory counterflory of the first, *Howard*; 3rd gules, a lion rampant argent, *Mowbray*; 4th sable, a lion rampant argent, *Segrave*; 5th gules, three lions passant guardant or, a label of three points argent, *Plantagenet*; 6th gules, a lion, rampant, within a bordure engrailed or, *Talbot*. 𝕮rest – A demi Monk proper, habited in russet, his girdle or and wielding in his dexter hand a scourge also or, thereon five knotted lashes. 𝕾upporters – *Dexter*, a lion rampant argent, ducally crowned or; *sinister*, a sea-dog sable, scaled and finned or. 𝕭adges – A drag or sledge.
Residences – 23 Warwick Sq, SW1; Marcus, by Forfar, Angus. *Clubs* – Pratt's, Turf, White's, Beefsteak.

SONS LIVING *(By 1st marriage)*

Hon EDWARD WILLIAM STEPHEN (Estate Office, Allerton Park, nr Knaresborough, N Yorks HG5 0SE), *b* 17 April 1953; *ed* Ampleforth: *m* 1980, Penelope (Nell) Lucy, el da of Dr Peter Brunet, of Jesus Coll, Oxford, and has issue living, James Charles Peter, *b* 12 Dec 1991, — (Sarah) Louise, *b* 1982, — Isabel Laura, *b* 1983, — Camilla Charlotte, *b* 1987, — Francesca Jane, *b* 1988.

Hon James Alastair (21 Moreton Place, SW1V 2NL), *b* 1956; *ed* Ampleforth, and Magdalene Coll, Camb (MA); with Sotheby's since 1979; Dep Chm Sotheby's Europe since 1997; Proprietor, The Stourton Press; Kt of Honour and Devotion Sovereign Mil Order of Malta: *m* 1993 (*m diss* 1997), Hon Sophia Ulla Stonor, yst da of 7th Baron Camoys.

SISTER LIVING *(In remainder to the Baronies of Mowbray, Segrave and Stourton)*

Hon Patricia Winifred Mary, *b* 1924; sometime in Foreign Office: *m* 1948, Frederick Petre Crowder, QC, MP, who *d* 1999 (*see* B Petre, colls, 1980 Edn), and has issue living, Richard John (Candie House, Candie Rd, St Peter Port, Guernsey GY1 1UP, CI), *b* 1950; *ed* Eton: *m* 1st, 1973 (*m diss* 1977), Belinda Jane, el da of Capt Matthew Page-Wood (*see* Page-Wood, Bt); 2ndly, 1984, Lucy E., eldest da of Michael Charlesworth, and has issue living (by 2nd *m*), George William Stourton *b* 1997, Louisa Ann *b* 1995, — John George (Polmear Lodge, St Martins, Guernsey, CI), *b* 1954; *ed* Eton: *m* 1984, Carolyn, only da of Donald Griffiths, of Elie, Fife, and has issue living, Charles Petre Gordon *b* 1990, Anna Jane *b* 1992.

AUNT LIVING *(Daughter of 24th Baron)*

Hon Charlotte Mary (2 Arthington Av, Harrogate), *b* 1904.

WIDOW LIVING OF SON OF TWENTIETH BARON STOURTON

BEATRICE CICELY (*Hon Mrs Edward P. J. Corbally Stourton*) (Arlonstown Cottage, Dunsany, Navan, co Meath), da of late H. E. Page, of Wragby, Lincs, and Titchwell, Norfolk: *m* 1934, Hon Edward Plantagenet Joseph CORBALLY STOURTON, who *d* 1966, having assumed in 1927, the additional name of Corbally, and has issue (*see* colls, infra).

COLLATERAL BRANCHES LIVING *(All of whom are in remainder to Baronies of Mowbray, Segrave and Stourton)*

Issue of late Maj Hon John Joseph Stourton, TD, yr son of 21st Baron Stourton, *b* 1899, *d* 1992: *m* 1st, 1923 (*m diss* 1933), Kathleen Alice, who *d* 1986, da of late Robert Louis George Gunther, of 8 Prince's Gdns, SW, and Park Wood, Englefield Green, Surrey; 2ndly, 1934 (*m diss* 1947), Gladys Leila, who *d*

1953, da of Col Sir William James Waldron, of Ascot Cottage, Winkfield, Berks, and 77 Cromwell Rd, SW7:—

(By 1st *m*) Michael Godwin Plantagenet, *b* 1926; *ed* Eton; Maj Grenadier Guards (ret); FRICS, QUALAS; ADC to Comdt RMA Sandhurst 1951-52, Adj 1st Bn Grenadier Guards 1953-55, and Staff Capt HQ London Dist 1955-57; Land Agent to HRH the late Duke of Gloucester, Barnwell Manor Estate 1966-71; partner Curtis & Henson 1966-68, since when Savills: *m* 1955, Lady Joanna Lambart, da of FM 10th Earl of Cavan, KP, GCB, GCMG, GCVO, GBE, and has issue living, Thomas Michael John, *b* 1965, — Henry Matthew, *b* 1971, — Julia (*Lady Rasch*), *b* 1958: *m* 1987, Sir Simon Anthony Carne Rasch, 4th Bt, and has issue (see that title), — Clare Elizabeth, *b* 1962: *m* 1993, Charles Francis Houghton Beckford, HM Foreign Office, 2nd son of Maj Adrian Beckford, of Hook Norton, Oxon, and has issue living, Jack Michael *b* 1997, Joseph Patrick *b* (twin) 1997, Rosalie Emma *b* 1999. *Residence* – The Old Rectory, Gt Rollright, Oxon. —— John Ralph, *b* 1930; *ed* Eton, and Magdalene Coll, Camb (MA); late Lieut Grenadier Guards; JP co Fermanagh 1977; Dir Liebig's Extract of Meat Co Ltd 1957-68, Brooke Bond Liebig Ltd 1968-74, Interocean Shipping Agency 1974-92: *m* 1st, 1958 (*m diss* 1965), Virginia, twin da of late Basil Colin Shrubra Hordern, of The Old Rectory, Fernhurst, Sussex; 2ndly, 1967 (*m diss* 1984), Caroline Honor, yr da of late Col J. C. O'Dwyer, of Magheracross, Ballinamallard, co Fermanagh, and has issue living (by 1st *m*), Lucilla Mary, *b* 1959: *m* 1989, John Michael Joseph Royden, elder son of Sir Christopher John Royden, Bt, — (by 2nd *m*) Georgina Caroline, *b* 1969: *m* 1998, (Thomas) Edward Hohler (*see* Stucley, Bt), — Jemima Nicola, *b* 1971: *m* 1992, Marcelo Novoa, who *d* 1997, and has issue living, Oscar *b* 1995. *Residence* – Sulgrave Farm Cottage, Sulgrave, Banbury, Oxon OX17 2HH. —— Mary (*Countess of Gainsborough*), *b* 1925: *m* 1947, 5th Earl of Gainsborough. *Residence* – Horn House, Exton, Leics LE15 7QU. —— Monica Kathleen (*Lady Greig*), *b* 1928: *m* 1955, Sir (Henry Louis) Carron Greig, KCVO, CBE, DL, lately Gentleman Usher to HM, and has issue living, Louis Stourton, *b* 1956; *ed* Eton, and St Edmund Hall, Oxford; a Page of Honour to HM 1970-73, — Jonathan, *b* 1958; *ed* Eton, and Downing Coll, Camb, — George Carron, *b* 1960; *ed* Eton, and St Peter's Coll, Oxford: *m* 1995, Kathryn Elizabeth, only da of Don Terry, of Texas, USA, and has issue living, Jasper Louis Carron *b* 1998, — Laura Monica, *b* (twin) 1960; Lady-in-Waiting to HRH The Princess of Wales 1989-96: *m* 1984, James Leopold Somerset Lonsdale (*see* B Raglan, colls, 1990 Edn), and has had issue, †Thomas Louis James *b* 1991 *d* 1992, Arthur Leopold Greig *b* 1995, Leonora Diana Fiona *b* 1986, Rosanna Monica *b* 1988, Esme Laura *b* (twin) 1995. *Residence* – Brook House, Fleet, Hants GU13 8RF.

Issue of late Hon Edward Plantagenet Joseph CORBALLY STOURTON, DSO, 4th son of 20th Baron Stourton, *b* 1880, *d* 1966, having assumed in 1927 the additional name of Corbally: *m* 1934, Beatrice Cicely (ante), da of H. E. Page:—

Nigel Edward, *b* 1937; late Capt Grenadier Guards: *m* 1st, 1960 (*m diss* 1975), Frances Deirdre Morton, da of Patrick Lancaster, of Wapsbourne Manor, Sheffield Park, Sussex; 2ndly, 1995, Lavinia Frances Elizabeth, only da of late Capt John Pitman, of Foxley House, Malmesbury, and widow of 5th Baron Fermoy, and has issue living (by 1st *m*), Edward Richard, *b* 1961, — Nicholas Simon, *b* 1963, — Patrick Henry, *b* 1965. *Residence* – Axford House, nr Marlborough, Wilts. —— Vanessa Mary, *b* 1935.

Granddaughter of late Auberon Joseph Stourton, el son of late Hon Albert Joseph Stourton (infra):—
Issue of late Eudo Philip Joseph Stourton, *b* 1900, *d* 1975: *m* 1927, Cicely Frances, who *d* 1982, da of late Henry Hyman Haldin, KC, of 17 Montagu Sq, W1 (Leon, Bt):—

Veronica Philippa, *b* 1929: *m* 1954, Philip Biden Derwent Ashbrooke, who *d* 1993, of La Grande Maison, St John, Jersey, CI, and has issue living, Auberon Francis Biden, *b* 1956; *ed* Ampleforth, and St John's Coll, Camb; Maj King's Royal Hussars, — Sophia Mary Veronica (*Viscountess Stormont*), *b* 1959: *m* 1985, Alexander David Mungo, Viscount Stormont, elder son of 8th Earl of Mansfield and Mansfield, and has issue (see that title).

Grandchildren of late Capt Herbert Marmaduke Joseph Stourton, OBE, 2nd son of late Hon Albert Joseph Stourton, 6th son of 19th Baron Stourton:—
Issue of late Sir Ivo Herbert Evelyn Joseph Stourton, CMG, OBE, KPM, *b* 1901, *d* 1985: *m* 1st, 1926, Lilian Marguerite, who *d* as a result of enemy action 1942, da of George Dickson; 2ndly, 1945, Virginia (The Old Bakery, Kimpton, Andover, Hants) (who *m* 2ndly, 1986, William Hilary Young, CMG), da of late Sir Horace James Seymour, GCMG, CVO (*see* M Hertford, colls):—

(By 1st *m*) Nigel John Ivo, OBE (Arbour Hill, Patrick Brompton, Bedale, N Yorks DL8 1JX), *b* 1929; OBE (Civil) 1981, Knt of Sovereign Mil Order of Malta: *m* 1956, Rosemary Jennifer Rushworth, da of Hon Mr Justice (Sir Myles John) Abbott, Ch Justice of Bermuda, and has issue living, Edward John Ivo (c/o BBC Television Centre, Wood Lane, W12 7RJ), *b* 1957; TV journalist, presenter BBC *One O'Clock News* 1993-99, since when presenter *Today*; Knt Sovereign Mil Order of Malta: *m* 1980, Margaret, eldest da of Sir James Napier Finnie McEwen, 2nd Bt, and has issue living, Ivo James Benedict *b* 1982, Thomas Edward Alexander *b* 1987, Eleanor Mary Elizabeth *b* 1984, — Julian Nicolas (25 Lower Addison Gdns, W14 8BG), *b* 1959: *m* 1992, Margaret A., da of late A. J. Barsham, of Broadwater, Weybridge, Surrey, and has issue living, Frederick John Nigel *b* 1994, — Christopher Nigel Paul (37 Patience Rd, SW11), *b* 1965: *m* 1992, Melissa, yr da of Hon Sir Richard Storey, 2nd Bt, and has issue living, Oria *b* 1998, — Lavinia Margaret Grace, *b* 1962: *m* 1986, Frank Nicholson, and has issue (*see* Lawson-Tancred, Bt). —— Simon Nicholas (Hume Hall, Hume, Kelso, Roxburgh TD5 7TW), *b* 1932: *m* 1st, 1975, Pamela, who *d* 1994, da of Charles James Baker, of Letcombe Manor, Wantage, Berks, and widow of Alexander J. Scratchley, MC; 2ndly, 1998, Valli J. Mitchell, formerly of Joiners Cottage, Hume. —— Felicity Magdalen (40 East Witton, Leyburn, N Yorks), *b* 1927. —— (By 2nd *m*) (Barbara) Jane, *b* 1947: *m* 1974, Maj (Archibald) Graham Buchanan-Dunlop, of Broughton Place, Broughton, Biggar, Lanarks, and has issue living, (Archibald) Roderick, *b* 1979, — David Erskine, *b* 1981.

Issue of late Magdalen Mary Charlotte Stourton, *b* 1899, *d* 1981: *m* 1st, 1925 (*m diss* 1936), Archibald Ashworth Baillie Hay, DSO, MC, who *d* 1965; 2ndly, 1936 (*m diss* USA 1943), Robert Ducas, who *d* 1978; 3rdly, 1947 (*m diss* 1956), William Brian Buchel:—

(By 2nd *m*) Robert Ivo DUCAS (Flat 10, 24 Lowndes St, SW1 9JE), *b* 1937: *m* 1963, Patricia, who *d* 19—, yr da of P. Provatoroff, of Crippenden Manor, Cowden, Kent, and has issue living, Annoushka, *b* 1966: *m* 1990, John A. C. Ayton, eldest son of Antony Ayton, of Jordans End, Jordans, Bucks, and has issue living, Oliver Henry Cleeve *b* 1995, Marina Isobel Provatoroff *b* 1993, Chloe Patricia *b* 1998. —— Magdalen June Ruth (Flat 5, 46 Oakley St, SW3 5HA), *b* 1938: *m* 1959, Hon James Donald Diarmid Ogilvy, and has issue (*see* E Airlie).

Issue of late Barbara Bertha Mary Stourton, *b* 1900, *d* 1980: *m* 1st, 1924 (*m diss* 1929), Capt Eric Charlton Tunnicliffe, R Welch Fus, who *d* 1953; 2ndly, 1929, Capt Frank Ashton Bellville, who *d* 1937; 3rdly, 1946, Capt Steuart Harrison-Wallace, DSO, RN, who *d* 1963:—

(By 1st *m*) †Nigel Arthur TUNNICLIFFE, late Gren Gds, *b* 1928: *m* 1957 (*m diss* 1980), Diana Edith, da of late Cdr Peter Du Cane, CBE, RN (*see* Pole, Bt, *cr* 1628, 1985 Edn), and formerly wife of Hon Jeremy John Cubitt (*see* B Ashcombe, colls), and *d* 1982, leaving issue, Brigid Serena, *b* 1963: *m* 1st, 1990 (*m diss* 1996), Richard L. Pavry; 2ndly, 1998, John Rynne, of 50 Musard Rd, W6 8NW. —— Elizabeth Anne, *b* 1926: *m* 1947, William Alexander Mackenzie, of Lower Hendre Farm, St Weonards, Herefords HR2 8PD, and has issue living, Michael Alexander Edward (The Square, Inver, Dunkeld, Perthshire PH8 0JR), *b* 1949; *ed* Stanbridge Earls Sch, —— Margaret Anne, *b* 1955: *m* 1975, George Champion Streatfeild, of Denmark House, Longtown, Hereford, and has issue living, Guy Alexander Champion *b* 1981, Victoria Jane *b* 1978, Alice Elizabeth *b* 1983. —— (By 2nd *m*) Patricia Barbara (Sadlers House, Hardington Mandeville, Yeovil, Som BA22 9PQ), *b* 1931: *m* 1965 (judicial separation 1992), Alfred Charles Gladitz, and has issue living, Rupert Ivo Charles (c/o John Swire & Sons (UK) Ltd, GPO Box 1, Hong Kong), *b* 1969; *ed* Ampleforth, and Gonville & Caius Coll, Camb (BA).

Issue of late Gytha Mary Stourton, *b* 1904, *d* 1992: *m* 1934, Frederick Ramon de Bertodano, 8th Marqués del Moral (Spain), who *d* 1955:—

Alfonso Michael George DE BERTODANO STOURTON (Ferraz 73, Madrid 28008), *b* 1937: *m* 1968, Carolina Garcia de la Riva, da of Abel Garcia, of Murcia, Spain, and has issue living, Miguel Ramon Marcos, *b* 1969, — Ignacio José Roberto, *b* 1970, — Gonzalo Alberto, *b* 1974, — Jaime Felipe, *b* 1982, — Carolina Isabel, *b* 1978. —— Helen Gytha Mary, *b* 1935: *m* 1957, Jean le Goaëc, of Mas de la Condamine, 83570 Cotignac, France, and has issue living, Yann Charles Ramon (49120 Neuvy en Mauges, France), *b* 1959: *m* 1996, Isabelle, da of Pierre Cardo, and has issue living, Jean-Pierre *b* 1997, Marie-Aimée *b* 1998, — Michel Patrick Roland, *b* 1962: *m* 1999, Beatrice, da of Xavier Stroebel, of Reims, — Annik Marie Nicole, *b* 1958: *m* 1982, Bruno Gaschet, of Le Petit St Georges, La Cabotiere, Vieg-Excmplet, 36400 La Châtre, France, and has issue living, Guillaume *b* 1986, Loïc *b* 1991, Astrid *b* 1984, Aurore *b* 1995, — Katarina Nancy Gytha *b* 1960: *m* 1981, Dr Mark de Caestecker, of Bethesda, Maryland, USA, and has issue living, Sebastian *b* 1986, Christian *b* 1990, Cassandra *b* 1983, Nathania *b* 1992, — Sophie Marie-Helena, *b* 1971, — Isabelle Marie-Anne, *b* 1974.

Issue of late Mary Jeanne Stourton, *b* 1913, *d* 1987: *m* 1938, 6th Baron Camoys, who *d* 1976:—
See that title.

Granddaughter of late Bertha Mary Philippa Stourton (*m* 1894, Major Frederick Bartholomew Stapleton-Bretherton (B Petre)), 4th da of late Hon Albert Joseph Stourton, 6th son of 19th Baron Stourton:—
Issue of late Mary Henrietta Stapleton-Bretherton (resumed her maiden name by deed poll 1960), *b* 1906, *d* 1995: *m* 1940 (*m diss* 1953), Col John Pell Archer-Shee, MC, late 10th Hussars, son of late Lt-Col Sir Martin Archer-Shee, CMG, DSO:—
Mary Pauline Daphne Thérèse ARCHER-SHEE, *b* 1941. *Residence* – 44 Cornwall Gdns, SW7.

BRANCHES FROM YOUNGER SONS OF 17TH BARON STOURTON

Descendants of late Hon Edward Marmaduke Joseph VAVASOUR (3rd son of 17th Baron Stourton); assumed the surname of Vavasour by sign-manual 1826 in lieu of his patronymic, and was *cr* a *Baronet* 1828:—
See Vavasour, Bt.

Grandchildren of late Lt-Col Philip Joseph LANGDALE, OBE, 3rd son of late Charles Joseph Langdale, 3rd son of late Hon Charles Joseph Langdale, MP (4th son of 17th Baron Stourton), who assumed the surname of Langdale in lieu of his patronymic 1814:—
Issue of late Joyce Elizabeth Mary, *b* 1898, *d* 1995: *m* 1st, 1922 (*m diss* 1955), 2nd Viscount FitzAlan of Derwent, who *d* 1962; 2ndly, 1956, 10th Earl Fitzwilliam, who *d* 1979:—
(By 1st *m*) *Hon* Alathea Gwendolen Alys Mary, *b* 1923; Dame of Honour and Devotion, Sovereign Mil Order of Malta: *m* 1953, as his 2nd wife, Hon Edward Frederick Ward (*see* E Dudley, 1985 Edn), who *d* 1987. *Residence* – 21b Ave du Temple, Lausanne, Switzerland. —— †*Hon* Elizabeth Anne Marie Gabrielle, *b* 1934; High Sheriff Cambs 1993, DL 1994: *m* 1st, 1952 (*m diss* 1960), Sir Vivyan Edward Naylor-Leyland, 3rd Bt, who *d* 1987; 2ndly, 1975, Sir Stephen Lewis Edmonstone Hastings, MC, and *d* 1997, leaving issue (by 1st *m*) (*see* Naylor-Leyland, Bt).

Issue of late Alathea Pauline Mary Alys Langdale, *b* 1902, *d* 1979: *m* 1923 (*m diss* 1936), 2nd Baron Manton, who *d* 1968:—
See that title.

Issue of late Ursula Dorothy Mary Langdale, *b* 1903, *d* 1969: *m* 1931, Lt-Col Norman Birch, who *d* 1960:—
Michael Edward Stafford BIRCH, *b* 1933. *Residence* – Walkington Park, Beverley, E Yorks. —— Timothy Malcolm Stafford BIRCH, *b* 1937. *Residence* – 1 Little Weighton Rd, Walkington, Beverley, E Yorks.

Grandchildren of late Dorothy Mary Paula Walpole (*m* 1st, 1919, Maj Austin Edward Scott Murray, MC; 2ndly, 1945, Col Colin Kayser Davy, MC), elder da of late Pauline Mary Langdale (Mrs Horace Walpole) (infra):—
Issue of late Anne Mary Scott Murray, *b* 1920, *d* 1991: *m* 1944, Maj Rupert Leonard Eversley Milburn, who *d* 1974:—
See Milburn, Bt.

Granddaughter of late Pauline Mary Langdale (*m* 1887, Col Horace Walpole, KRRC), yr da of late Charles Joseph Langdale (ante):—
Issue of late Maude Mary Winifred Walpole, *b* 1897, *d* 1968: *m* 1st, 1921, Cyril James Wenceslas Torr, HM Foreign Ser, who *d* 1940; 2ndly, 1946, Vicomte Theophile de Lantsheere, CVO, who *d* 1958:—
(By 1st *m*) Jean Rosita Mary (*Lady Nevile*), MBE, *b* 1923; served 1939-45 War with VAD; MBE (Civil) 1984: *m* 1944, Capt Sir Henry Nicholas Nevile, KCVO, Lord Lieut Lincs 1975-95, who *d* 1996, of Aubourn Hall, Lincoln, and has issue living, Christopher James (Manor Farm, Aubourn, Lincoln), *b* 1954: *m* 1981, Sarah Caroline, yr da of Sir Peter William

Youens, KCMG, CMG, OBE, and has issue living, Charles Cato *b* 1990, Zita Stephanie *b* 1984, Nyasa Jane *b* 1986, — Hugh Simon (21 Cromwell Grove, W6 7RQ), *b* 1960: *m* 1989, Joanna Mary, elder da of Timothy Seymour Bathurst (*see* E Bathurst, colls), and has issue living, Max Henry *b* 1994, Thomas Michael *b* 1996, Alexander James *b* 1999, — Sarah Rosita Mary, *b* 1945: *m* 1968, Roger Hudson, of 38 Kensington Place, W8, and has issue living, Toby *b* 1970, George *b* 1972, — Elizabeth Jane Mary (*Lady Arnold*), *b* 1947: *m* 1st, 1970, Robin Irwin Smithers, who *d* 1979; 2ndly, 1984 (*m diss* 1993), Sir Thomas Richard Arnold, MP, and has issue living (by 1st *m*), Christian Alexander Langley *b* 1971, Lucian James Angelo *b* 1974, (by 2nd *m*) Emily Minna Mary *b* 1986, — Jill Gabriel Anne Mary, *b* 1950: *m* 1982, David Hughes, of Hop Hill, Aubourn, Lincoln, and has issue living, Anthony James Alleyne *b* 1983, Ralph Nicholas Alleyne *b* 1985.

Grandchildren of late Alfonso Otho GANDOLFI-HORNYOLD, 2nd Duke Gandolfi, elder son of late Thomas Charles Gandolfi Hornyold, 1st Duke Gandolfi, eldest son of late John Vincent Hornyold (formerly Gandolfi), by his wife Charlotte Mary, 2nd da (by 1st *m*) of late Hon Charles Joseph Langdale, MP (ante):—
Issue of late Maria Teresa Gandolfi-Hornyold, *b* 1910, *d* 1988: *m* 1932, Luigi Acchiappati, who *d* 1972:—
Gianantonio ACCHIAPPATI (33 rue George Sand, 75016 Paris), *b* 1933: *m* 1966, Pierrille, da of Count Alfred de Bertier de Sauvigny, and has issue living, Ugo, *b* 1968, — Gaîa Francesca, *b* 1971. — Pierluigi (15 via Zenale, 20121 Milan, Italy), *b* 1934: *m* 1968, Chiara, da of Giorgio Bicchi. —— †Elena, *b* 1936: *m* 1964, Francis Buck (18 rue Pierre Brasseur, Luxembourg), and *d* 1977, having had issue, †Laurent, *b* 1965; *d* 1976, — Nicolas, *b* 1968, — Frédérique, *b* 1973. —— Nicoletta (33 via Dei Serragli, Florence, Italy), *b* 1937.

Grandsons of late Thomas Charles GANDOLFI-HORNYOLD, 1st Duke Gandolfi (ante):—
Issue of late Ralph Vincent GANDOLFI-HORNYOLD, 3rd Duke Gandolfi, *b* 1881, *d* 1938: *m* 1927, Beatrix Purdey (who *d* 1992, having *m* 2ndly, 1940, Lt-Col (Cuthbert) Euan Charles Rabagliati, MC, DFC, late King's Own Yorkshire LI, who *d* 1978, of Villa Valentine, Domaine de la Roseraie, Mougins, France AM), da of Frederick Scott Oliver, of Edgerston, nr Jedburgh, Roxburghshire:—
Antony Frederick Gandolfi HORNYOLD (*Duke Gandolfi*) (Blackmore House, Hanley Swan, Worcester WR8 0ES. *Club* – Brooks's), *b* 1931; *s* his father as 4th Duke Gandolfi (*cr* 1899), and as 17th Marquis (*cr* 1529 and 1899) 1938; *ed* Ampleforth, and Trin Coll, Camb; late 2nd Lieut KOSB; a Knight of Sovereign Mil Order of Malta: *m* 1993, Caroline Mary Katherine, MVO, da of late Maj Patrick Dudley Crichton-Stuart (*see* M Bute, colls). —— Simon Ralph William HORNYOLD (Villa Matilda, Calle 17, Vedado, Havana, Cuba), *b* 1933; *ed* Ampleforth; late 2nd Lieut 16th/5th Lancers: *m* 1st, 1965 (*m diss* 19—), Catherine Alice, da of John Charles Roberts; 2ndly, 19—, Bernadette, da of William Bernard Erskine, and has issue living (by 1st wife), Anthony Vincent, *b* 1964, — (by 2nd wife), Joshua Jacob, *b* 1986, — Jedediah, *b* 1989.

Grandchildren of late Henry HORNYOLD-STRICKLAND, FSA (assumed by Royal Licence 1932 for himself and his issue the addl surname and arms of Strickland: *m* 1920, Hon Mary Constance Elisabeth Christina, CBE, eldest da of 1st Baron Strickland), only son of late Alfred Joseph Hornyold (infra):—
Issue of late Lt-Cdr Thomas Henry HORNYOLD-STRICKLAND, DSC, RN, *b* 1921, *d* 1983; *s* his grandfather (1st Baron Strickland) as 7th Count della Catena (*cr* 1745 by Grand Master (Pinto) of Malta); assumed by Royal Licence 1938 the arms of Matthews quarterly with his own: *m* 1951, Angela Mary, OBE, DL Cumbria (Sizergh Castle, Kendal, Cumbria LA8 8AE), eldest da of late Francis Henry Arnold Engleheart, of The Priory, Stoke-by-Nayland, Suffolk:—
Henry Charles HORNYOLD-STRICKLAND, *b* 1951; *ed* Ampleforth, Exeter Coll, Oxford (BA), and INSEAD Fontainebleau (MBA); 8th Count della Catena; Knight of Honour and Devotion Sovereign Mil Order of Malta: *m* 1979, Claudine Thérèse, da of Clovis Poumirau, of Hossegor, France, and has issue living, Hugo Francis Clovis, *b* 1979, — Thomas Paul Clovis, *b* 1985. *Residences* – Sizergh Castle, Kendal, Cumbria LA8 8AE; 56 Ladbroke Rd, W11 3NW. —— Robert Francis (The Tower House, Buckland Dinham, Som BA11 2QS), *b* 1954; *ed* Ampleforth; Knight of Honour and Devotion Sovereign Mil Order of Malta: *m* 1983 (*m diss* 1996), Teresa Mary, da of Richard Fawcett, and has issue living, Francis Richard, *b* 1986, — Rollo Michael, *b* 1988, — Zoë Clementine, *b* 1991. —— John Jarrard, *b* 1956; *ed* Ampleforth; Knight of Honour and Devotion Sovereign Mil Order of Malta: *m* 1996, Jane Elizabeth Crawshay, da of John Fothergill, of Richmond, Surrey, and has issue living, Katharine Alice, *b* 1996. —— Edward Thomas, *b* 1960; *ed* Ampleforth: *m* 1999, Belinda E., 2nd da of Col David Scarborough, of Edvin Loach, Herefords. —— Clare Edeline, *b* 1953: *m* 1981, Anthony Prince, of 26 Abingdon Court, Abingdon Villas, W8 6BT. —— Alice Mary, *b* 1959: *m* 1988, Charles Loftie, of Bowerbank, Pooley Bridge, Cumbria, and has issue living, William Thomas Crozier, *b* 1991, — Alexander Edward Henry, *b* 1996, — Eleanor Sophie, *b* 1992.

Issue of late Edeline Winifred Hornyold-Strickland, *b* 1922, *d* 1981: *m* 1943, Norman Coppock, who *d* 1982:—
Michael Thomas COPPOCK, *b* 1949; *ed* More House Sch: *m* 1975, Susan Ann, da of John B. Davies, of 41 Mill Lane, Southport, Lancs, and has issue living, David Michael, *b* 1978, — Andrew Joseph, *b* 1983, — Sarah Louise, *b* 1976. *Residence* – 13 Saunders St, Southport, Lancs PR9 0HP.

Granddaughter of late Alfred Joseph HORNYOLD, 3rd son of late John Vincent HORNYOLD (ante):—
Issue of late Dorothy Hornyold, *b* 1892, *d* 1918: *m* 1917, Hon Charles Hugh Clifford (later 11th Baron Clifford of Chudleigh), who *d* 1962:—
See that title.

Grandchildren of late Maj Washington Charles Thomas HIBBERT, elder son of late Mrs Hubert Aloysius Tichborne Hibbert (infra):—
Issue of late Maj Hugh Washington HIBBERT, The Queen's Bays, *b* 1911, *d* 1985: *m* 1st, 1938 (*m diss* 1949), Lady Patricia Margery Kathleen Mackay, who *d* 1973, elder da of 2nd Earl of Inchcape; 2ndly, 1952, Angela Mary, formerly wife of Richard Miles Backhouse (*see* Backhouse, Bt), previously widow of Capt Count Richard Dudley Melchior Gurowski, Scots Gds, and eldest da of late Peter Haig Thomas (*see* E Normanton, 1971 Edn):—
(By 1st *m*) Michael Washington HIBBERT (3a Crabtree Lane, SW6 6LP), *b* 1946; *ed* Ampleforth: *m* 1st, 1972 (*m diss* 1996), Gisela, da of Paul Thomsen, of Odense, Denmark; 2ndly, 1997, Donatella, da of Ferruccio Cordenons, of Corso Italia 47, 33080 Porcia, Pordenone, Italy, and has issue living (by 1st *m*), Peter Michael Washington, *b* 1974, — Jasper Erik Washington, *b* 1978. —— †Bridget Anne, *b* 1939: *m* 1966, Edward Alan Mervyn Molyneux Herbert, who *d* 1994, and *d* 1976, leaving issue (*see* E Carnarvon, colls). —— Elizabeth Caroline (Gifford Hall, Broughton Gifford, Melksham, Wilts SN12 8LY), *b* 1943: *m* 1st, 1965, Capt Jeremy Michael Porter, RN (*see* V Charlemont, colls, 1995 Edn), who *d* 1985;

2ndly, 1991, Kenneth Royce Anderson, and has issue living (by 1st *m*), James Robert, *b* 1967: *m* 1995, Elizabeth Mary, da of Michael Lyne, and has issue living, Lucy Annabel Clare *b* 1999, — Toby Hugh Washington, *b* 1969.

Issue of late Violet Margaret Hibbert, *b* 1907, *d* 1986: *m* 1936, Lt-Cdr Llewellyn Somerset Edward Llewellyn, RN (ret), who *d* 1940:—
Virginia Mary LLEWELLYN, *b* 1937. *Residence* – 77 Cadogan Gdns, SW3.

Grandson of late Mrs Francis FFRENCH DAVIS (infra):—
Issue of late Capt Francis Holdsworth FFRENCH DAVIS, RASC, *b* 1907, *ka* in Italy 1944: *m* 1940, Ingrid Margaret Mary (who *m* 2ndly, 1948, as his 2nd wife, Maj Edmond Myles Pery-Knox-Gore (*see* E Limerick, colls), who *d* 1965), eldest da of late Maj Henry Blake MacDermot, KC, of 19 Fitzwilliam Sq, Dublin:—
Francis Conor FFRENCH DAVIS (Knockharley, Brownstown, Navan, co Meath), *b* 1941: *m* 1962, Prudence Mary Fiona, da of John Evelyn Smith Wright, of Javea, Alicante, Spain, and has issue living, Francis Dermot (Milltown, Rathkenny, Navan, co Meath), *b* 1964; *ed* Glenstal Abbey; has issue living (by Philippa Hinde), Clara Louise *b* 1995, Katherine Rowena *b* 1999, — Dominic John (Gordon Cottage, Lambourn, Berks), *b* 1965; *ed* Glenstal Abbey: *m* 1996, Avery Joan, da of late John William Whitfield, of Manor Farm, Woolstone, Berks, and has issue living, Francis Benedict *b* 1996, Daisy Joan *b* 1999, — Stephen Luke (Cadiz, Spain), *b* 1967; *ed* Ampleforth, and Trin Coll, Dublin (LLB); Bar King's Inn, Dublin; has issue living (by Angela Murphy), Samuel Luke *b* 1995, — Michael James, *b* 1969; *ed* Glenstal Abbey, — Nicola Marguerite, *b* 1977; *ed* Univ Coll, Cork (BA), — Sarah Jane Victoria, *b* 1985.

Grandchildren of late Mary Hornyold (Mrs Hubert Aloysius Tichborne Hibbert), eldest da of late John Vincent Hornyold (ante):—
Issue of late Marguerite Mary Julia Hibbert, *b* 1872, *d* 1964: *m* 1899, Capt Francis ffrench Davis:—
Peter Charles FFRENCH DAVIS (Flat 34, 77 Hallam St, W1N 5LR), *b* 1912; *ed* Ampleforth, and Trin Coll, Camb (BA); late Member London Stock Exchange; served 1939-45 War as Capt Welsh Gds.

Issue of late Angela Mary Hibbert, *b* 1877, *d* 1972: *m* 1st, 1905, as his 2nd wife, Brig-Gen Paul Aloysius Kenna, VC, DSO, who was *ka* 1915; 2ndly, 1919, Col Allen Victor Johnson, DSO, who *d* 1939 (*see* Johnson, Bt, *cr* 1818, colls, 1939 Edn):—
(By 1st *m*) Kathleen, *b* 1906: *m* 1936, Lt-Cdr Lionel Rupert Knyvet Tyrwhitt, DSO, DSC, RN, who was *ka* 1942, brother of Vera Ruby, Baroness Berners. *Residence* – 23 Fitzmaurice Place, Bradford-on-Avon, Wilts BA15 1EL. —— Celia Mary Ethel, *b* 1909. *Residence* – 23 Fitzmaurice Place, Bradford-on-Avon, Wilts BA15 1EL.

Granddaughter of late Arthur Joseph LANGDALE, 6th son of late Hon Charles LANGDALE, MP (ante):—
Issue of late Gertrude Pietrina Josephine Mary Stourton, *b* 1882, *d* 1915: *m* 1907, Adm James Ughtred Farie, CMG, who *d* 1957:—
Margaret Jean Mary FARIE, *b* 1912; a Benedictine Nun, as Dame Jean Farie, of Stanbrook Abbey, Worcs.

Grandchildren of late Henry Joseph STOURTON, son of late Hon Philip Henry Joseph STOURTON, 6th son of 17th Baron Stourton:—
Issue of late Violet Mary Annette, OBE, *b* 1873, *d* 1961: *m* 1893, Francis Joseph Siltzer, who *d* 1924:—
Derek Henry SILTZER, *b* 1897; *ed* Oratory Sch: *m* 1938, Merlyn Seaforth, da of William Densham, of Melbourne, Australia, and widow of Keith Poulton. *Residence* – 8B Longwood, Darling Point, Sydney, NSW, Australia.

Granddaughter of late Amy Mary Josephine Stourton (Mrs Frederic Dundas Harford), yr da of late Henry Joseph Stourton (ante):—
Issue of late Joan Mary Harford, *b* 1897, *d* 1983: *m* 1920, Lt-Col Sir Alexander Bannerman, 11th Bt, who *d* 1934:—
See that title.

PREDECESSORS – (1) *Sir* JOHN Stourton, Knt, was Sheriff of Wilts 1434, and of co Gloucester 1438, and Treasurer of the Household 1445; served in the Wars of France and Normandy; *cr Baron Stourton*, of Stourton, co Wilts (peerage of England) 1448; *d* 1462; *s* by his son (2) WILLIAM, 2nd Baron; *d* 1478-9; *s* by his el son (3) JOHN, 3rd Baron; *s* by his son (4) FRANCIS, 4th Baron; *d* (young) 1486-7; *s* by his uncle (5) WILLIAM, 5th Baron; *dsp* 1522; *s* by his brother (6) EDWARD, 6th Baron; appointed by Act of Parliament a Justice of the Peace for assessing and collecting £163,000 by a poll-tax; *d* 1535; *s* by his son (7) WILLIAM, 7th Baron; *d* 1548; *s* by his son (8) CHARLES, 8th Baron, was executed 16 March 1557, at Salisbury, in a halter of silk, for murdering two men named Hartgill; *s* by his el son (9) JOHN, 9th Baron; restored in blood by Act of Parliament 1575, and inherited the barony; was one of the peers on the trial of Queen Mary of Scotland; *s* by his brother (10) EDWARD, 10th Baron; *d* 1632; *s* by his son (11) WILLIAM, 11th Baron; *s* by his grandson (12) WILLIAM, 12th Baron; *s* by his el son (13) EDWARD, 13th Baron *dsp* 1720; *s* by his brother (14) THOMAS, 14th Baron; *dsp* 1743; *s* by his nephew (15) CHARLES, 15th Baron, son of Charles, 3rd son of 12th Baron; *d* 1753-4; *s* by his brother (16) WILLIAM, 16th Baron; *m* 1749, Winifred, el da and in her issue co-heir of Philip Howard, ot Buckenham, Norfolk, and in her issue co-heiress of her uncles, the 8th and 9th Duke of Norfolk, to the Baronies of Mowbray and of Segrave (see * infra) and of Howard, Greystock, Ferrers of Wemme, Furnival, Strange of Blackmere, Giffard of Brimmesfield, and Braose of Gower, &c; *d* 1781; *s* by his son (17) CHARLES PHILIP, 17th Baron; *d* 1816; *s* by his son (18) WILLIAM JOSEPH, 18th Baron; *d* 1846; *s* by his son (19) CHARLES, 19th Baron; *b* 1802: *m* 1825, Hon Mary Lucy, da of 6th Baron Clifford; *d* 1872; *s* by his el surviving son (20) ALFRED JOSEPH, 20th Baron, in whose favour the abeyances of the Baronies of Mowbray and Segrave (see ‡ infra) were terminated.

‡(1) ROGER de Mowbray was summoned to the Parliament of England as *Baron Mowbray* 1283; having previously been summoned by Simon de Montfort, when in rebellion *temp* Henry III, such summons was declared void by Act of Parliament; *d* 1298; *s* by his son (2) JOHN, 2nd Baron; summoned to Parliament in two reigns: *m* Alice, da and co-heir of William, Baron de Braose; was executed at York 1322 for his connection with the rising of the Northern Earls against the Despencers; his estates were forfeited, but an attainder did not follow; *s* by his son (3) JOHN, 3rd Baron; served in the wars of Scotland and France, and was summoned to Parliament *temp* Edward III; *d* 1361; *s* by his son (4) JOHN, 4th Baron; summoned to Parliament *temp* Edward III: *m* Elizabeth, da and heir of John, 3rd Baron Segrave (see † infra), by which marriage the Segrave estates and the dignity of Lord Segrave were vested in him; slain near Constantinople 1368; *s* by his el son (5) JOHN, 5th Baron; *cr Earl of Nottingham* (peerage of England) 1337; *d* unmarried 1382, when the ear-

ldom expired; *s* by his half brother **(6)** THOMAS, KG, 6th Baron; summoned as *Earl of Nottingham* (peerage of England) 1383-86; and *cr* Earl Marshal 1386, and *Duke of Norfolk* (peerage of England) 1397: *m* 1st, Elizabeth, da of heir of John, Lord Strange of Blackmere; and 2ndly, Elizabeth, da and co-heir of Richard FitzAlan, Earl of Arundel and Surrey; by the latter he left two sons Thomas and John, and two das Margaret, wife of Sir Robert Howard, and Isabel, wife of James, 6th Lord Berkeley; *d* 1399; *s* by his el son **(7)** THOMAS, 2nd Earl, and Dukedom of Norfolk being erroneously withheld from him, joined the rebellion of the nobles against Henry IV, 1405, and being arrested, was beheaded at York without trial; *dsp*; *s* by his brother **(8)** JOHN, 3rd Duke; in 1425 declared by Parliament to to be entitled to the dukedom; *s* by his son **(9)** JOHN, 4th Duke, obtained a confirmation of the dukedom; went as Ambassador to negotiate peace between England and France: *m* Eleanor, da of William, Baron Bourchier; *s* by his son **(10)** JOHN, 5th Duke; *cr Earl of Warren and Surrey* (peerage of England); *d* 1475, when the Dukedom of Norfolk, and Earldoms of Nottingham, Warren, and Surrey expired, while the Baronies of Mowbray and Segrave devolved upon his da **(11)** ANNE, who in infancy was affianced to Richard, Duke of York, 2nd son of Edward IV; he was murdered with his brother in the Tower 1483, and the Duchess *dsp*, when the baronies became abeyant between the sons of Sir Robert Howard and Lord Berkeley (*see* 6th Baron Mowbray), and remained so until the abeyance was terminated in favour of **(12-22)** JOHN Howard, *cr Baron Howard* (peerage of England) 1470, and *Duke of Norfolk* (peerage of England) 1483, with which peerages the Baronies of Mowbray and Segrave were merged until 1777, when they again became abeyant, and remained so until 1877, when the abeyances were terminated in favour of **(23)** ALFRED JOSEPH Stourton (ante), as senior co-heir of Margaret, wife of Sir Robert Howard (*see* 6th Baron Mowbray); *b* 1829: *m* 1865, Mary Margaret, who *d* 1925, da of late Matthew Corbally, MP; *d* 1893; *s* by his el son **(24)** CHARLES BOTOLPH JOSEPH, 24th Baron Mowbray, 25th Baron Segrave, and 21st Baron Stourton; *b* 1867; claimed as Lord Mowbray to be placed Premier Baron of England, and unsuccessfully claimed ancient Earldom of Norfolk (1312) 1906: *m* 1893, Mary, who *d* 1961, only child of late Thomas Angus Constable, of Manor House, Otley, *d* 1936; *s* by his el son **(25)** WILLIAM MARMADUKE, MC, 25th Baron Mowbray, 26th Baron Segrave, 22nd Baron Stourton, *b* 1895; Capt Grenadier Guards: *m* 1921, Sheila, who *d* 1975, da of late Hon Edward Walford Karslake Gully, CB (V Selby, colls); *d* 1965; *s* by his only son **(26)** CHARLES EDWARD, 26th Baron Mowbray, 27th Baron Segrave, 23rd Baron Stourton and present peer.

† **(1)** NICHOLAS de Segrave, one of the most active leaders of the Baron *temp* Henry III, was summoned to Parliament of England in the King's name as *Baron Segrave* 1295; *d* 1295; *s* by his son **(2)** JOHN, 2nd Baron; summoned to Parliament 1296-1325; was Constable of the English Army in Scotland; taken prisoner at the battle of Bannockburn, and imprisoned by the Scots for a year; *d* 1325; *s* by his grandson **(3)** JOHN, 3rd Baron: *m* Margaret, sole heiress of Thomas de Brotherton, Earl of Norfolk, 5th son of Edward I; *d* 1353; *s* by his da **(4)** ELIZABETH, wife of John, 4th Baron Mowbray (see * ante).

*The question of whether the barony of Segrave was created in 1283 or 1295 is discussed in the preface to *The Complete Peerage*, Vol I.

MOYLE, BARONY OF (Moyle) (Extinct 1974)

SON LIVING OF LIFE BARON (*By 1st m*)

Rt Hon Roland Dunstan (19 Montpelier Row, Blackheath, SE3 0RL), *b* 1928; PC 1978: *m* 1956, Sheleagh Patricia, da of Bernard Hogan.

MOYNE, BARON (Guinness) (Baron UK 1932)

Judge not

NOLI·JUDICARE

JONATHAN BRYAN GUINNESS, 3rd Baron; *b* 16 March 1930; *s* 1992; *ed* Eton (King's Scholar), and Trin Coll, Oxford (MA); Dir Arthur Guinness, Son & Co 1961-88, and Leopold Joseph & Sons 1963-91; Chm Monday Club 1970-72: *m* 1st, 1951 (*m diss* 1963), Ingrid Olivia Georgia, da of late Maj Guy Richard Charles Wyndham, MC (*see* B Egremont, colls); 2ndly, 1964, Suzanne, da of Harold William Denis Lisney, of Cadaqués, Gerona, Spain, and formerly wife of Timothy Phillips, and has issue by 1st and 2nd *m*.

꩜rms – Per saltire gules and azure, a lion rampant or; on a chief ermine two ducal coronets each enfiling as many arrows in saltire of the third. ꩜rest – A boar passant quarterly or and gules charged with a mullet counterchanged. ꩜upporters – On either side a Cingalese macaque sejant proper.
Residences – Bosalverne, Greenbank, Alverton, Penzance, Cornwall.
Club – Beefsteak.

SONS LIVING (*By 1st marriage*)

Hon JASPER JONATHAN RICHARD, *b* 9 March 1954; *ed* Eton: *m* 1985, Camilla Alexandra, da of Robie David Corbett Uniacke, and has issue living, Amber, *b* 1989, — Claudia, *b* 1992. *Residence* – Arniano, Murlo, Siena, Italy.
Hon Valentine Guy Bryan, *b* 1959; *ed* Eton, and Ch Ch, Oxford: *m* 1986, Lucinda Jane, only da of Cdr Miles James Rivett-Carnac, RN (*see* Rivett-Carnac, Bt), and has issue living, Tara Victoria, *b* 1991, — Madeleine Rose, *b* 1997. *Residence* – 87 Hereford Rd, W2 5BB.

(*By 2nd marriage*)

Hon Sebastian Walter Denis, *b* 1964; *ed* Eton: *m* 1987 (*m diss* 1991), Silvie Dominique, da of Eric A. Fleury, of 7 Chemin de Verdiers, Geneva, Switzerland. *Residence* –

DAUGHTERS LIVING (*By 1st marriage*)

Hon Catherine Ingrid, *b* 1952; resumed her maiden name 1988: *m* 1st, 1983 (*m diss* 1988), James Donald, Lord Neidpath, son of 12th Earl of Wemyss; 2ndly, 1990, Robert Fleetwood Hesketh (*see* E Scarbrough, 1995 Edn), and has issue living (by 1st *m*) (*see* E Wemyss), — (by 2nd *m*), a son, *b* 1992, — Anna, *b* 1991, — Violet, *b* (twin) 1991. *Residences* – Meols Hall, Southport, Lancs; 36 Porchester Terr, W2.

(*By 2nd marriage*)

Hon Daphne Suzannah Diana Joan, *b* 1967: *m* 1987, Spyros Niarchos, 2nd son of late Stavros Niarchos, of Villa Marguns, St Moritz, Switzerland, and has issue living, Nicolas Stavros, *b* 1989, — Alexis Spyros, *b* 1991. *Address* – 41 Park St, W1.

THE THIRD BARON HAS FURTHER ISSUE (*by Susan Mary, da of Ronald Taylor, of Oldham, Lancs*)

Thomas Julian William Jon TAYLOR, *b* 1986. —— Diana Gloria Isolde Rose Dimilo TAYLOR, *b* 1981. —— Aster Sophia Mary TAYLOR, *b* 1984.

BROTHER LIVING

Hon Desmond Walter, *b* 1931; *ed* Gordonstoun, and Ch Ch, Oxford (MA); Hon LLD Trin Coll, Dublin; Pres Irish Georgian Soc 1958-91; author: *m* 1st, 1954 (*m diss* 1981), HSH Princess (Hermione) Marie-Gabrielle (Mariga) Petronella Sophia Devota Florestine, who *d* 1989, elder da of HSH Prince Albrecht Eberhard Karl Gero-Maria von Urach, Count of Württemberg; 2ndly, 1985, Penelope, da of Graham Cuthbertson, and has issue living (by 1st *m*), Patrick Desmond Karl Alexander (Furness, Naas, co Kildare), *b* 1956; *ed* Winchester, and Trin Coll, Dublin (MA): *m* 1st, 1985 (*m diss* 1989), Felicity Casey; 2ndly, 1990, Louise, da of Robin Arundel, and has issue living (by 1st wife), Jasmine *b* 1976, (by 2nd *m*), Tom *b* 1991, Celeste *b* 1990, Lily *b* 1995, — Marina, *b* 1957; *ed* Cranborne Chase. *Residence* – Leixlip Castle, co Kildare.

HALF-BROTHERS LIVING

Hon Finn Benjamin, *b* 1945; *ed* Winchester, Ch Ch, Oxford (MA), and Inst of Animal Genetics, Edinburgh Univ (PhD); Biologist: *m* 1989, Mary Wilson, formerly wife of James Patrick Donleavy, author, and da of late Benjamin Wilson Price, of Baltimore, Maryland, USA. *Residence* – Chute Forest House, Chute, Andover, Hants SP11 9DS.

Hon Kieran Arthur, *b* 1949; *ed* Winchester, and Ch Ch, Oxford (MA); Botanist: *m* 1983, Mrs Vivienne Halban, da of André-Jacques van Amerongen, DFC, MB, BCh, MRCOG, FRCOG, of Grafton House, Blisworth, Northants, and has issue living, Malachy, *b* 1986, — Lorcan, *b* 1989, — Kate, *b* 1985. *Residence* – Knockmaroon House, Castleknock, co Dublin.

Hon Erskine Stuart Richard, *b* 1953; *ed* Winchester, and Edinburgh Univ; Wilts CC 1979-81, MFH Tedworth 1981-84, Farmer, Trustee Guinness Trust Housing Assocn 1979-89: *m* 1984, Louise Mary Elizabeth, only da of late Patrick Dillon-Malone, and has issue living, Hector, *b* 1986, — Arthur, *b* 1991, — Matthew Richard, *b* 1992, — Samuel, *b* 1995, — Molly, *b* 1985. *Residence* – Fosbury Manor, Marlborough, Wilts.

HALF-SISTERS LIVING

Hon Rosaleen Elisabeth, *b* 1937; *ed* St Anne's Coll, Oxford (MA): *m* 1965, Sudhir Mulji, and has issue living, Sachin Sudhir, *b* 1967, — Kabir Jayantilal Bryan, *b* 1970, — Sangita Rosaleen, *b* 1966, — Gopali Sharda Elisabeth, *b* 1975. *Residence* – 150 Malcha Marg, New Delhi 110021, India.

Hon Fiona Evelyn, *b* 1940; *ed* Cranborne Chase, and McGill Univ, Canada; Hon DUniv Edinburgh 1998; Zoologist. *Residence* – Isle of Rhum, Inner Hebrides.

Hon Thomasin Margaret, *b* 1947; *ed* Cranborne Chase, and Farnham Coll of Art; Potter and Painter; has issue living, Luke GUINNESS, *b* 1980. *Residence* – Biddesden House, Andover, Hants.

Hon Catriona Rose, *b* 1950; *ed* Cranborne Chase, Winchester Co High Sch, and LMH Oxford (MA); Botanist and Farm Manager. *Residence* – Biddesden Farm, Andover, Hants.

Hon Mirabel Jane, *b* 1956; *ed* Cranborne Chase, and E Anglia Univ (BA); MFH Tedworth 1986-93; author of *Biddesden Cookery* 1987: *m* 1984, Patrick Ian (Tom) Helme, son of A. R. Helme, of Butcher's Barn, Danehill, Sussex, and has issue living, Toby Anthony Bryan, *b* 1992, — Alice Mirabel, *b* 1987, — Tyga Elisabeth, *b* 1990, — Lily, *b* 1994. *Residence* – Mount Orleans, Collingbourne Ducis, Marlborough, Wilts.

UNCLE LIVING (*son of 1st Baron*)

Hon Murtogh David, *b* 1913: *m* 1949, Nancy Vivien Laura, who *d* 1975, only da of late Cyril Edward Tarbolton, of Hampstead, NW. *Residence* – 117 E 80th St, New York, NY 10021, USA.

AUNT LIVING (*daughter of 1st Baron*)

Hon Grania Maeve Rosaura (*Dowager Marchioness of Normanby*), *b* 1920; Hon LLD Dublin, JP N Yorks 1971-83, Pro Chancellor Dublin Univ 1985-95; formerly Section Officer WAAF: *m* 1951, 4th Marquess of Normanby, KG, CBE, who *d* 1994. *Residence* – Lythe Hall, Whitby, N Yorks.

WIDOW LIVING OF SON OF SECOND BARON

Felicity, only da of late Sir Andrew Hunter Carnwath, KCVO, of 37 Riverview Gdns, SW13: *m* 1962, Hon Diarmid Edward Guinness, who *d* 1977, and has issue (see colls, infra). *Residence* – 2 Keats Grove, NW3.

MOTHER LIVING

Hon Diana Freeman-Mitford (*Hon Lady Mosley*), 3rd da of 2nd Baron Redesdale: *m* 1st, 1929 (*m diss* 1934), Hon Bryan Walter Guinness (later 2nd Baron Moyne), who *d* 1992; 2ndly, 1936, Sir Oswald Ernald Mosley, 6th Bt, who *d* 1980. *Residence* – Temple de la Gloire, 91400 Orsay, France.

COLLATERAL BRANCH LIVING

Issue of late Hon Diarmid Edward Guinness, 3rd son of 2nd Baron, *b* 1938, *d* 1977: *m* 1962, Felicity (ante), only da of late Sir Andrew Hunter Carnwath, KCVO, of 37 Riverview Gdns, SW13:—
Ewan Diarmid, *b* 1965; *ed* Eton: *m* 1995, Claire Elizabeth, da of late Alan Perry, of E Horsley, Surrey, and has issue living, Aidan Diarmid, *b* 1997, — Kirsty Elizabeth, *b* 1999. —— Camilla, *b* 1963. —— Lorna, *b* 1967; *ed* Edinburgh Univ. —— Harriet, *b* 1970.

PREDECESSORS – (1) *Rt Hon* WALTER EDWARD GUINNESS, DSO, TD, 3rd son of 1st Earl of Iveagh; *b* 1880; Lt-Col Suffolk Yeomanry; S Africa 1900-1901 (despatches), 1914-18 War (DSO and Bar); was a County Councillor for London 1907-10, MP for Bury St Edmunds 1907-31, Under-Sec of State for War 1922-23, Financial Sec to Treasury 1923-24 and 1924-25, Min of Agriculture and Fisheries 1925-29 Joint Parliamentary Sec to Min of Agriculture and Fisheries 1940-41, Sec of State for the Colonies and Leader of the House of Lords 1941-42, Dep Min of State in Middle East 1942-44, and Min Resident for United Kingdom in Middle East Jan to Nov 1944; *cr Baron Moyne* of Bury St Edmunds, co Suffolk (peerage of United Kingdom) 1932: *m* 1903, Lady Evelyn Hilda Stuart Erskine, who *d* 1939, da of 14th Earl of Buchan; *d* (assassinated in Cairo) 1944; *s* by his son (2) BRYAN WALTER, 2nd Baron; *b* 1905; Bar Inner Temple 1930; formerly Major Royal Sussex Regt; Poet and Novelist, Hon Fellow Trin Coll, Dublin, Member of Irish Academy of Letters, Gov Nat Gallery of Ireland, FRSL: *m* 1st, 1929 (*m diss* 1934), Hon Diana Freeman-Mitford, 3rd da of 2nd Baron Redesdale; 2ndly, 1936, Elisabeth, who *d* 1999, 3rd da of late Capt Thomas Arthur Nelson, of Achnacloich, Connel, Argyll; *d* 1992; *s* by his eldest son (3) JONATHAN BRYAN, 3rd Baron and present peer.

MOYNIHAN, BARON (Moynihan) (Baron UK 1929, Bt 1922)

COLIN BERKELEY MOYNIHAN, 4th Baron, and 4th Baronet; *b* 13 Sept 1955; *s* 1991 (claim to Barony admitted by Committee for Privileges of House of Lords, and a writ issued summoning him to Parliament in the Upper House 1997); *ed* Monmouth Sch, and Univ Coll, Oxford (Pres Oxford Union Soc 1976); World Gold Medallist for Lightweight Rowing 1978 (Silver 1981), and Olympic Silver Medallist 1980; Political Assist to Foreign Sec 1983, Under Sec of State Dept of Environment (Min of Sport) 1987-90, Dept of Energy 1990-92; Sr Foreign Affairs Spokesman House of Lords since 1997; Freeman City of London 1978; Trustee Oxford Univ Boat Club 1980-83, Sports Aid Trust 1983-87; MP for Lewisham East (*C*) 1983-92; *m* 1992, Gaynor-Louise, only da of Paul Goodwin Metcalf, of Healing, S Humberside, and has issue.

Arms – Azure, a chevron between in chief three mullets argent and in base a rose also argent barbed and seeded proper. Crest – A demi-knight in armour affrontee, resting the sinister hand on the hip proper, and supporting with the dexter hand a spear also proper, flowing therefrom a forked pennon argent, charged with a Maltese Cross sable. Supporters – On either side an owl argent gorged with a Baron's coronet or.
Address – House of Lords, SW1. *Clubs* – Brooks's, Vincents.

SONS LIVING

Hon NICHOLAS EWAN BERKELEY, *b* 31 March 1994.
Hon George Edward Berkeley, *b* 1995.

DAUGHTER LIVING

Hon India Isabella Sarah, *b* 1997.

SISTER LIVING

Hon Melanie June, *b* 1957: *m* 1983, Peter-John Stuart Corbett, and has issue living, Edward John Patrick, *b* 1990, — Poppy Ann, *b* 1986, — Daisy Angelica Jak, *b* 1988. *Residence* – Pipers Cottage, Oakridge Lynch, Stroud, Glos.

HALF-SISTERS LIVING

Hon Imogen Anne Ierne, *b* 1932: *m* 1st 1953 (*m diss* 1965), Michael Edward Peter Williams; 2ndly 1965, Charles Ivan Vance, and has issue living (by 2nd *m*), Jacqueline Belinda Ierne *b* 1963.
Hon Juliet Jane Margaretta, *b* 1934: *m* 1st, 1958, Thomas Edwin Bidwell Abraham, who *d* 1976; 2ndly, 1978, Harry Hougham Sparks, and has issue living (by 1st *m*), James Bidwell, *b* 1959, — John Richard, *b* 1960.

DAUGHTERS LIVING OF THIRD BARON (*By 2nd marriage*)

Hon Miranda Dorne Ierne, *b* 1959: *m* 1977 (*m diss* 1985), Horace Harry O'Garrow Omowale X, and has issue living, Saskia Beulegh Ierne, *b* 1979, — and further issue (by Bruce Howard Gillard), Ayisha Naomi MOYNIHAN GILLARD, *b* 1990.

(*By 3rd marriage*)

Hon Antonita Maria Carmen Fernandez, *b* 1969.
Hon Aurora Luzon Maria Dolores, *b* 1971.
Hon Kathleen Maynila Helen Imogen Juliet, *b* 1974,

WIDOW LIVING OF SECOND BARON

JUNE ELIZABETH, da of Arthur Stanley Hopkins: *m* 1st, 1952, as his 2nd wife, the 2nd Baron Moynihan, who *d* 1965; 2ndly, 1967, Neville Barton Hayman, who *d* 1994.

PREDECESSORS – (1) *Sir* BERKELEY GEORGE ANDREW Moynihan, KCMG, CB, son of late Capt Andrew Moynihan, VC, 8th King's Regt; *b* 1865; and eminent Surg; Pres of Roy Coll of Surgs of England 1926-32; *cr* a Baronet 1922, and *Baron Moynihan*, of Leeds, co York (peerage of United Kingdom) 1929: *m* 1895, Isabella Wellesley, who *d* 1936, da of Thomas Richard Jessop, FRCS, JP; *d* 1936; *s* by his son (2) PATRICK BERKELEY, OBE, TD, 2nd Baron, *b* 1906; Chm Exec Cttee, Liberal Party 1947-50, and Chm of N-W Metropolitan Regional Hosp Board 1960-65: *m* 1st, 1931 (*m diss* 1952), Ierne Helen, who *d* 1991, el da of late Cairnes Derrick Carrington Candy; 2ndly, 1952, June Elizabeth (who *m* 2ndly, 1967, Neville Barton Hayman), yr da of Arthur Stanley Hopkins, *d* 1965; *s* by his el son (3) ANTONY PATRICK ANDREW CAIRNES BERKELEY, 3rd Baron, *b* 1936; Lieut Coldstream Gds: *m* 1st, 1955 (*m diss* 1958), Ann, da of Reuben Stanley Herbert, of Greenfield Cottage, Therfield, Royston; 2ndly, 1958 (*m diss* 1967), Shirin Roshan Berry, da of late Ahmed Quereshi; 3rdly, 1968 (*m diss* 1979), Luthgarda Maria Beltran Dela Rosa, da of Alfonzo Fernandez, of 160 P. Gomez, Caloocan City, Philippines; 4thly, 1981, Editha Eduarda, da of late Maj-Gen Eduardo Ruben, of Bulacan, Philippines; *d* 1991*; *s* by his half-brother (4) COLIN BERKELEY, 4th Baron and present peer.

*The Committee for Privileges found that the 3rd Baron's divorce from his fourth wife was invalid, and his subsequent marriage in 1990 to Jinna Sabiaga was bigamous, and that Daniel, the son of this union was therefore ineligible for succession to the peerage. The Committee further found that DNA testing proved that Andrew, the son born to the 3rd Baron's fourth wife after *in vitro* fertilisation was not Lord Moynihan's son.

MOYOLA, BARON (Chichester-Clark) (Life Baron 1971)

JAMES DAWSON CHICHESTER-CLARK, PC, son of late Capt James Jackson Lenox-Conyngham Chichester-Clark, DSO, RN (M Donegall, colls); *b* 12 Feb 1923; *ed* Eton; Maj (ret) Irish Gds; 1939-45 War (wounded); a DL of co Derry; a Member of House of Commons of N Ireland 1960-73, Ch Whip 1963-66, Leader 1966-67, Min of Agric 1967-69 and Prime Min 1969-71; *cr* PC 1967, and *Baron Moyola*, of Castledawson, co Londonderry (Life Baron) 1971: *m* 1959, Moyra Maud, da of Brig Arthur de Burgh Morris, CBE, DSO, and widow of Capt T. G. Haughton, and has issue.

Arms – Quarterly, 1st gules three swords erect in pale proper, hilts and pommels or, a canton argent, charged with a trefoil vert, *Clark*; 2ndly, chequy or and gules, a chief vair, *Chichester*; 3rd azure fretty argent *Etchingham*; 4th, azure on a bend or three daws gules, *Dawson*. **Crest** – Out of a mural crown a arm embowed in armour, the hand holding a dagger, all proper, charged with a trefoil vert. **Supporters** – On either side, a heron's wing addorsed and gorged with a baron's coronet proper.
Residence – Moyola Park, Castledawson, co Derry.

DAUGHTERS LIVING

Hon Fiona, *b* 1960: *m* 1994, William Rodney David Fisher, son of Leonard Fisher, of Lurgan, co Armagh.

Hon Tara Olivia, *b* 1962: *m* 1984, Edward Thomas Whitley, son of John Whitley, of Hamsey Lodge, Lewes, Sussex, and has issue living, James Edward Dawson, *b* 1997.

Muff, family name of Baron Calverley.

Mulgrave, Earl of; son of Marquess of Normanby.

Mulholland, family name of Baron Dunleath.

MULLEY, BARONY OF (Mulley) (Extinct 1995)

DAUGHTERS LIVING OF LIFE BARON

Hon Deirdre, *b* 1951.
Hon Corinne MULLEY, *b* 1953: *m* 1983, Nicholas Stevens, of Stafford.

WIDOW LIVING OF LIFE BARON

JOAN DOREEN (*Baroness Mulley*), da of Alexander Morris Phillips, of London: *m* 1948, Baron Mulley, PC, who *d* 1995. *Residence* – 3 Denny Crescent, SE11 4UY.

MUNSTER, EARL OF (FitzClarence) (Earl UK 1831)

Neither rashly nor fearfully

ANTHONY CHARLES FITZ-CLARENCE, 7th Earl; *b* 21 March 1926; *s* 1983; *ed* St Edward's Sch, Oxford, privately in Switzerland, and at Central Sch of Art and Crafts, London; served RN 1942-47; graphic designer 1950-79; Daily Mirror Newspapers 1957-66, IPC Newspaper Div (*Sun*) 1966-69, Freelance Designer 1969-71; stained glass conservator for Burrell Collection 1979-83, conservator with Chapel Studio 1983-89; MSIA 1960-69, FRSA 1987: *m* 1st, 1949 (*m diss* 1966), Louise Marguerite Diane, da of Louis Delvigne, of Liège, Belgium; 2ndly, 1966 (*m diss* 1979), Mrs Pamela Margaret Hyde, da of Arthur Spooner; 3rdly, 1979, Dorothy Alexa, MusB (Edin), LRAM, who *d* 1995, yst da of late Lt-Col Edward Boyd Maxwell, OBE, MC; 4thly, 1997, Halina Winska, MD, PhD (Sr Lecturer and Hon Consultant Rheumatologist, Univ Coll London), da of late Mieczyslaw Winski-Lubicz, and has issue by 1st and 2nd *m*.

Arms – The Arms of King William IV (without the escutcheon of the arch-treasurer of the IIR empire, and without the crown of Hanover), debruised by a baton sinister azure, charged with three anchors or. **Crest** – On a chapeau, gules, turned up ermine, a lion statant guardant crowned with a ducal coronet or, and gorged with a collar azure, charged with three anchors or. **Supporters** – *Dexter*, a lion guardant, ducally crowned or; *sinister*, a horse argent; each gorged with a collar azure, charged with three anchors or.

Address – c/o House of Lords, SW1A 0PW. *Club* – Carlton.

DAUGHTERS LIVING (By 1st marriage)

Lady Tara Francesca, *b* 1952: *m* 1979, Ross Jean Heffler, eldest son of Dr Leon Heffler, of Connecticut, USA, and has issue living, Leo Edward Michael, *b* 1985, — Alexandra Louise, *b* 1982. *Residence* – 146 Ramsden Rd, SW12 8RE.
Lady Finola Dominique, *b* 1953: *m* 1981, Jonathan Terence Poynton, yr son of D. R. Poynton, of Woodford, Cheshire, and has issue living, Oliver Maximillian Christo, *b* 1984, — Chloë Nona, *b* 1982. *Residence* – 1732 Fell St, San Francisco, CA 94117, USA.

(By 2nd marriage)

Lady Georgina Abigail, *b* 1966: *m* 1st, 1993 (*m diss* 1995), Paul Robert Phillips, yr son of Peter Phillips, of Blaby, Leics; 2ndly, 1997, John Adam, of 27 Heather Mead, Frimley, Camberley, Surrey GU16 5QA, and has issue living (by 2nd *m*), Thomas Charles, *b* 1999.

ADOPTED STEPDAUGHTER LIVING

Agnieszka FITZCLARENCE, *b* 1980.

WIDOW LIVING OF SIXTH EARL

VIVIAN (*Vivian, Countess of Munster*), da of late Benjamin Schofield, JP, of Greenroyde, Rochdale, Lancs, and stepda of late Judge A. J. Chotzner, MP: *m* 1939, as his 2nd wife, the 6th Earl of Munster, who *d* 1983. *Residence* – 1 Arundel Court, Jubilee Place, Chelsea Green, SW3.

COLLATERAL BRANCH LIVING

Granddaughter of late Capt Hon George FitzClarence, 3rd son of 1st Earl:—
Issue of late Lionel Ashley Arthur FitzClarence, *b* 1870, *d* 1936: *m* 1913, Theodora Frances Maclean, who *d* 1948, da of late Evan A. Jack, of 1 The Grove, Boltons, S Kensington, SW:—
Mary Theodora Annette, *b* 1914: *m* 1948, Adam Gluszkiewicz, and has issue living, Anna Judita, *b* 1949. *Residence* – 14 Ellesmere Orchard, Westbourne, nr Emsworth, Hants.

PREDECESSORS – **(1)** GEORGE FitzClarence, FRS, el natural son of King William IV, by the great comic actress Dorothy Bland, known as Mrs Jordan; *b* 1794: Maj-Gen in the Army, Lieut of the Tower, and Gov of Windsor Castle: *cr Baron Tewkesbury, Viscount FitzClarence* and *Earl of Munster* (peerage of United Kingdom) 1831, with remainder to his brothers, Frederick, Adolphus and Augustus primogeniturely: *m* 1819, Mary Wyndham, who *d* 1842, natural da of George, 3rd Earl of Egremont; *d* 1842; *s* by his son **(2)** WILLIAM GEORGE, 2nd Earl, *b* 1824; Capt late 1st Life Guards: *m* 1855, Wilhelmina, who *d* 1906, da of late Hon John Kennedy-Erskine; *d* 1901; *s* by his el son **(3)** GEOFFREY GEORGE GORDON, DSO, 3rd Earl, *b* 1859; Major Lothian Regt; Afghan War 1879-80, S Africa 1881, S Africa 1889-1902 (DSO); *d* 1902; *s* by his brother **(4)** AUBREY, 4th Earl, *b* 1862; a Gentleman Usher to Queen Victoria and to King Edward VII 1885-1902; *d* 1928; *s* by his nephew **(5)** GEOFFREY WILLIAM RICHARD HUGH, KBE, PC (son of late Maj Hon Harold Edward FitzClarence, MC, 7th son of 2nd Earl), 5th Earl, *b* 1906; Lord-in-Waiting to HM 1932-38, Paymaster-Gen 1938-39, Under-Sec of State for War 1939, Purl Under-Sec, of State for India and Burma 1943-44, Under-Sec of State for Home Affairs 1944-45, Parl Under-Sec of State for Colonies 1951-54, Min without Portfolio 1954-57, and Lord Lieut of Surrey 1957-73: *m* 1928, Hilary, who *d* 1979, only child of late Edward Kenneth Wilson, of Cannizaro, Wimbledon; *d* 1975; *s* by his kinsman **(6)** EDWARD CHARLES (son of late Brig-Gen Charles FitzClarence, VC, IG, el son of late Capt Hon George FitzClarence (by his wife, Violet Spencer-Churchill, grandda of 6th Duke of Marlborough), 3rd son of 1st Earl), 6th Earl, *b* 1899; Capt IG, served 1939-45 War: *m* 1st, 1925 (*m diss* 1930), Monica Sheila Harrington, who *d* 1958, da of Sir Henry Mulleneux Grayson, 1st Bt, KBE; 2ndly, 1939, Mrs Vivian Schofield, da of late Benjamin Schofield, JP, of Greenroyde, Rochdale, Lancs; *d* 1983; *s* by his only son **(7)** ANTHONY CHARLES, 7th Earl and present peer; also Viscount FitzClarence, and Baron Tewkesbury.

Murray, family name of Duke of Atholl.

Murray, family name of Earl of Dunmore.

Murray, family name of Earl of Mansfield and Mansfield.

MURRAY OF EPPING FOREST, BARON (Murray) (Life Baron 1985)

LIONEL (LEN) MURRAY, OBE, PC, *b* 2 Aug 1922; *ed* Wellington (Salop) Gram Sch, Univ of London, and New Coll, Oxford (Hon Fellow 1975); Hon DSc Aston 1977, and Salford 1978, Hon LLD St Andrews 1979, and Leeds 1985; Head of Economic Dept TUC 1954-69, Assist-Gen TUC 1969-73, and Gen-Sec 1973-84; OBE (Civil) 1966, PC 1976, and *Baron Murray of Epping Forest*, of Telford, co Shropshire (Life Baron) 1985; *m* 1945, Heather Woolf, and has issue.
Residence – 29 The Crescent, Laughton, Essex.

SONS LIVING

Hon Stephen William, *b* 1959.
Hon David Paul, MBE, *b* 1960; Sqdn/Ldr RAF; MBE (Mil) 1996; *m* 1984, Moira Denise, da of Fl/Lt Patrick Joseph Roche, of Stillorgan, Dublin, and has issue living, Joseph, *b* 1987, — Elizabeth, *b* 1985. *Address* – 5 Pinewood Av, Peterborough PE8 6BS.

DAUGHTERS LIVING

Hon Nicola Ruth, *b* 1954.
Hon Sarah Isobel, *b* 1959: *m* 1983, Ian Cook, of 88 Beamish Close, Northweald, Epping, Essex, and has issue living, Georgia, *b* 1987, — Jodie, *b* 1990.

MURRAY OF GRAVESEND, BARONY OF (Murray) (Extinct 1980)

SON LIVING OF LIFE BARON

Hon Timothy John, *b* 1966.

DAUGHTER LIVING OF LIFE BARON

Hon Catherine Anne, *b* 1964.

WIDOW LIVING OF LIFE BARON

MARGARET ANNE (*Baroness Murray of Gravesend*) (13 Parrock Rd, Gravesend, Kent), da of Frederick Charles Wakeford: *m* 1960, Baron Murray of Gravesend (Life Baron), who *d* 1980.

Murray, Erskine-, family name of Lord Elibank.

MURTON OF LINDISFARNE, BARON (Murton) (Life Baron 1979)

HENRY OSCAR MURTON, OBE, TD, PC, only son of late Henry Edgar Crossley Murton, of Hexham, Northumberland; *b* 8 May 1914; *ed* Uppingham Sch; Lt-Col (ret) R Northumberland Fus (TA); Staff Capt 149 Inf Bde (TA) 1937-39, Army Staff Coll Course 1938-39, tsc, 1939-45 War; GSO 1, HQ Salisbury Plain Dist 1942-44; GSO1 SD1, War Office 1944-46; a JP for Poole, Dorset; Man Dir Henry A. Murton Ltd, Departmental Stores, Newcastle-upon-Tyne and Sunderland 1949-57; MP for Poole (*C*) 1964-79; Sec Conservative Parly Cttee for Housing, Local Govt and Land 1964-67, Vice-Chm 1967-70; Chm Conservative Parly Cttee for Public Building and Works 1970; PPS to Min of Local Govt and Development 1970-71; an Assist Govt Whip 1971-72; a Lord Commnr HM Treasury 1972-73; Second Dep Chm of Ways and Means, House of Commons 1973-74, First Dep Chm 1974, and Dep Speaker and Chm 1976-79; a Dep Chm Cttees, House of Lords, 1981, and a Dep Speaker, House of Lords, 1983; Member Joint Select Cttee of Lords and Commons on Private Bill Procedure 1987-88, Freeman, City of London; Freeman, Wax Chandlers Co; a Past Master Clockmakers' Co; Chancellor of Primrose League 1983-88; *cr* OBE (Mil) 1946, TD 1947 (clasp 1951), PC 1976, and *Baron Murton of Lindisfarne*, of Hexham, co Northumberland (Life Baron) 1979: *m* 1st, 1939, Constance Frances, who *d* 1977, el da of late Fergus O'Loughlin Connell, of Low Fell, co Durham; 2ndly, 1979, Pauline Teresa, yst da of late Thomas Keenan, JP, of Johannesburg, and has had issue by 1st *m*.

Arms – Argent a lion tricorporate sable on a chief sable three crosses of St Cuthbert argent. **Crest** – In front of a blackcock drumming proper, three crosses of St Cuthbert argent. **Supporters** – *Dexter*, A lion guardant sable langued and armed gules gorged with a circlet of St Cuthbert crosses linked argent pendent therefrom an escallop or. *Sinister*, A like lion similarly gorged pendent therefrom a portcullis gold the compartment comprising a grassy mount proper surrounded by water barry wavy azure and argent.
Residence – 49 Carlisle Mansions, Carlisle Place, SW1P 1HY.

SON LIVING (By 1st marriage)

Hon (Henry) Peter John Connell, *b* 1941: *m* 1962 (*m diss* 1972), Louisa, da of late Maj Percy Montagu Nevile, late The Green Howards, of Skelbrooke Park, Yorks.

DAUGHTER DECEASED (By 1st marriage)

Hon Melanie Frances Isobel Connell, *b* 1946: *m* 1971, Ian Lee Vickery, of Amersham, Bucks, and *d* 1986, leaving issue.

MUSKERRY, BARON (Deane) (Baron I 1781, Bt I 1710)

Nothing is difficult to the strong and faithfull

ROBERT FITZMAURICE DEANE, 9th Baron, and 14th Baronet; *b* 26 March 1948; *s* 1988; *ed* Sandford Park Sch, Dublin, and Trin Coll, Dublin (BA, BAI); Man Dir Stride Mane Ltd, Dir Bridco Ltd, NBUSA Ltd: *m* 1975, Rita Brink, of Pietermaritzburg, S Africa, and has issue.

𝕬rms – Argent, two bars gules. 𝕮rest – Out of a ducal coronet or, a demi sea-otter proper. 𝕾upporters – Two angels habited azure, holding in their exterior hands medallions proper.
Seat – Springfield Castle, Drumcollogher, co Limerick. *Residence* – 727 Ridge Rd, Durban 4001, S Africa.

SON LIVING

Hon JONATHAN FITZMAURICE, *b* 7 June 1986.

DAUGHTERS LIVING

Hon Nicola, *b* 1976.
Hon Catherine, *b* 1978.

SISTER LIVING

Hon Betty Charlotte, *b* 1951; (BA); *m* 1974, Jonathan Dugdale Sykes, of The Kennels, Springfield, Drumcollogher, co Limerick, and has issue living, Daniel Jonathan, *b* 1980, — Karen Betty, *b* 1985.

WIDOW LIVING OF SON OF SEVENTH BARON

Dorothy, da of late Charles George Cook, of Liverpool: *m* 1st, 1936, Hon Matthew Fitzmaurice Tilson Deane, who *d* 1956; 2ndly, 1968, James Edward Anderton.

WIDOW LIVING OF SEVENTH BARON

MURIEL DOREEN SELLARS (*Muriel, Baroness Muskerry*) (44 Woodlands Rd, Liverpool 17; Cowdray, and Irish Clubs), da of late Arthur Gibson Simpson, of Carlisle: *m* 1964, and his 2nd wife, the 7th Baron Muskerry, who *d* 1966.

COLLATERAL BRANCH LIVING

Issue of late Hon Hamilton Robert Tilson Grogan Fitzmaurice DEANE-MORGAN el son of 4th Baron, *b* 1873, *d* 1907. *m* 1904, Eva, who *d* 1958 (having *m* 2ndly, 1911, Godfrey William Edward Massy), el da of William Bolton, of The Island, co Wexford:—
Eileen (*posthumous*), *b* 1907.

PREDECESSORS – (1) *Sir* MATTHEW Deane, Knt; *cr* a *Baronet* 1710; *d* 1710; *s* by his son (2) *Sir* ROBERT, 2nd Bt; *d* 1714; *s* by his son (3) *Sir* MATTHEW, 3rd Bt; MP for co Cork; *d* 1747; *s* by his el son (4) *Sir* MATTHEW, 4th Bt; MP for Cork City; *s* by his son (5) *Sir* ROBERT, PC, 5th Bt; MP for Tallagh; *d* 1770; *s* by his son (6) *Sir* ROBERT TILSON, 6th Bt; MP for co Cork; *cr Baron Muskerry* peerage of Ireland; 1781; *d* 1818; *s* by his el son (7) JOHN THOMAS FITZMAURICE, CB, 2nd Baron; *dsp* 1824; *s* by his brother (8) MATTHEW FITZMAURICE, 3rd Baron; *d* 1868; *s* by his grandson (9) HAMILTON MATTHEW TILSON FITZMAURICE, 4th Baron (son of Hon Robert Tilson Fitzmaurice Deane), 2nd son of TILSON FITZMAURICE, 4th Baron (son of Hon Robert Tilson Fitzmaurice, 2nd son of 3rd Baron, by Elizabeth Geraldine, who *d* 19—, da and co-heir of Hamilton Knox Grogan-Morgan, MP, of Johnstown Castle, co Wexford), *b* 1954; a Representative Peer for Ireland: *m* 1st, 1872, Flora Georgina, who *d* 1902, da of late Hon Chichester Thomas Foster-Skeffington; 2ndly, 1905, Lydia, who *d* 1915, only da of J. L. Booth; 3rdly, 1916, Adeline, who *d* 1950, da of late P. Ryan, of The Turrets, Charleville, Ireland; *d* 1929, *s* by his son (10) ROBERT MATTHEW FITZMAURICE, 5th Baron; *b* 1874: *m* 1906, Charlotte, who *d* 1960, da of John William Henry Irvine, of Mervyn, Rosslare, co Wexford; *d* 1952; *s* by his brother (11) MATTHEW CHICHESTER CECIL FITZMAURICE, 6th Baron; *b* 1875: *m* 1915, Helen Henrietta Blennerhassett, who *d* 1952, da of late Brig-Surg Lieut-Col Rodolph Harman, Army Med Ser; *d* 1954; *s* by his kinsman, (12) MATTHEW FITZMAURICE TILSON (son of late Hon Matthew James Hastings Fitzmaurice Deane, 3rd son of 3rd Baron), 7th Baron; *b* 1874: *m* 1st, 1897, Mabel Kathleen Vivienne, who *d* 1954, da of late Charles Henry Robinson, MD, FRCSI; 2ndly, 1964, Muriel Doreen Sellars, da of late Arthur Gibson Simpson, of Carlisle; *d* 1966; *s* by his yst son (13) HASTINGS FITZMAURICE TILSON, 8th Baron; MB, BCh, BAO, DMR (Lond), Consultant Radiologist; *m* 1944, Betty Fairbridge, who *d* (20 Aug) 1988, eldest da of George Wilfred Reckless Palmer, of Glenstone, Grahamstown, S Africa; *d* (14 Oct) 1988; *s* by his only son (14) ROBERT FITZMAURICE, 9th Baron and present peer.

MUSTILL, BARON (Mustill) (Life Baron 1992)

MICHAEL JOHN MUSTILL, son of Clement William Mustill, of Sandholme Cottage, Pateley Bridge, Yorks; *b* 10 May 1931; *ed* Oundle, and St John's Coll, Camb; Bar Gray's Inn 1955, QC 1968, Recorder 1972-78, Judge of High Court of Justice (Queen's Bench Div) 1978-92, a Lord of Appeal in Ordinary 1992-97; Chm Civil Service Appeal Tribunal 1971-78; Ktd 1978; *cr Baron Mustill*, of Pateley Bridge, co N Yorks (Life Baron) 1992: *m* 1st, 1960 (*m diss* 1983), Beryl Reid, da of John Alban Davies, of Chandlers Ford, Hants; 2ndly, 1991, Caroline, da of —, and formerly wife/widow of —Phillips, and has issue.

Naas, Lord; son of Earl of Mayo.

Nairne, Lord; title borne by Viscount Mersey.

Nairne, Master of; son of Viscount Mersey.

NAPIER and ETTRICK, LORD (Napier) (Lord S 1627, Baron UK 1872, Bt S 1666)

FRANCIS NIGEL NAPIER, KCVO, 14th Lord Napier, 5th Baron Ettrick, and 11th Baronet of Thirlestane; Chief of the name of Napier; *b* 5 Dec 1930; *s* 1954; *ed* Eton, and RMA Sandhurst; Hon DLitt Napier Univ 1993. Maj Scots Gds (Reserve), a DL for Ettrick and Lauderdale 1974-94; a Member of Queen's Body Guard for Scotland (Royal Company of Archers) since 1953; a Freeman of City of London, and Liveryman of Grocers' Co; Memb Standing Council of Scottish Chiefs, and Exec Cttee of Standing Council of the Baronetage; Pres of London (Prince of Wales') Dist of St John Ambulance Bde 1975-83; served in Malaya 1950-51 (invalided); Adjt 1st Bn Scots Gds 1955-57, Equerry to HRH Prince Henry, Duke of Gloucester 1958-60; Dep Ceremonial and Protocol Sec, Commonwealth Relations Office 1962-66; Conservative Whip, House of Lords 1970-71; on behalf of HM The Queen handed over the Instruments of Independence to Tuvalu (Ellice Islands) 1978; Private Sec, Comptroller and Equerry to HRH The Princess Margaret, Countess of Snowdon 1973-98, since when Treasurer and Equerry; MVO (4th Class) 1980; CVO 1985; CStJ 1988; KStJ 1991; KCVO 1992: *m* 1958, Delia Mary, yr da of Archibald D. B. Pearson, and has issue.

Arms – Quarterly: 1st and 4th argent, a saltire engrailed cantoned of four roses gules, barbed vert, *Napier*; 2nd and 3rd or, on a bend azure, a mullet pierced between two crescents of the field, within a double tressure flory-counterflory of the second, *Scott of Thirlestane*; below the shield on a compartment, the top of an embattled tower argent, masoned sable, issuant therefrom six lances disposed saltirewise proper, three and three, with pennons azure, *Scott.* **Crest** – A dexter arm erect couped below the elbow proper, grasping a crescent argent, *Napier.* **Supporters** – *Dexter*, an eagle, wings expanded proper; *sinister*, a chevalier in coat of mail and steel cap, all proper, holding in the exterior hand a lance with a pennon azure.
Residences – Down House, Wylye, Wiltshire BA12 0QN; Nottingham Cottage, Kensington Palace, W8 4PU. *Clubs* – White's, Pratt's, Royal Caledonian Hunt.

SONS LIVING

Hon FRANCIS DAVID CHARLES (*Master of Napier*), *b* 3 Nov 1962; *ed* Stanbridge Earls; Lloyd's 1983-97; Napier Garden Co since 1999: *m* 1993, Zara Jane, only da of Hugh Dermot McCalmont, and has issue living, William Alexander Hugh, *b* 10

June 1996, — Sophie Eleanor Rose, b 1999. *Residence* – The Thatched Cottage, Pages Lane, Higham, Bury St Edmunds, Suffolk IP28 6NJ. *Clubs* – Turf, Pratt's.
Hon Nicholas Alexander John, b 1971; *ed* Milton Abbey.

DAUGHTERS LIVING

Hon Louisa Mary Constance, b 1961: *m* 1987 (*m diss* 1997), Alexander Morrison, elder son of Peter Morrison, and has issue living, Oliver Charles Francis, b 1989, — Hugo Peter Alexander, b 1992. *Residence* – Yew Tree Cottage, Kingston Lisle, Wantage, Oxon OX12 9QL.
Hon Georgina Helena Katherine, b 1969: *m* 1995, Capt Jonathan Walker, Gren Gdns, only son of Sir David Alan Walker, and has issue living, Amelia Rose Katherine, b 1997.

BROTHER LIVING

Hon (Charles) Malcolm (Bardmony House, Alyth, Perthshire; 1 Newton Spicer Drive, Highlands, Harare, Zimbabwe; Cavalry, Turf, Pratt's, Civil Service (Capt Town) Clubs), b 1933; *ed* Canford; late Lt 1st R Dragoons, and late Lt Lothians and Border Yeo (TA); served Middle East 1952-53; a Member of Queen's Body Guard for Scotland (Royal Company of Archers); a Dir of Cos, and a Founder Member of Council of Anglo Rhodesian Soc: *m* 1969, Lady Mariota Cecilia Murray, yr da of 7th Earl of Mansfield and Mansfield, and has issue living, Eloise Dorothea, b 1970, — Maryel Cecilia, b 1973, — Cecilia Frances Stephanie, b 1976.

WIDOW LIVING OF SON OF TWELFTH LORD

Helen Catherine (Kippilaw, St Boswells, Roxburghshire), yr da of late J. M. Sanderson, of Linthill, Melrose: *m* 1967, as his 2nd wife, Cdr Hon Neville Archibald John Watson Ettrick Napier, RN, who *d* 1970.

WIDOW LIVING OF SON OF THIRTEENTH LORD

Juliet Elizabeth Hargreaves (Underhill, Treyford, Midhurst, Sussex), only da of Sir Alexander Charles Durie, CBE: *m* 1968, Hon (John) Greville Napier, who *d* 1988, and has issue (infra).

COLLATERAL BRANCHES LIVING

Issue of late Hon (John) Greville Napier, 3rd son of 13th Lord, b 1939, d 1988: *m* 1968, Juliet Elizabeth Hargreaves (ante), only da of Sir Alexander Charles Durie, CBE, of The Garden House, Windlesham, Surrey:—
Lucilla Fleur Scott, b 1969; BA: *m* 1994, Richard Anthony Agace Ferard (*see* B Biddulph, colls). —— Araminta Elizabeth Muir, b 1972: *m* 1997, Andrew James Perham, eldest son of Dr (Timothy) Geoffrey Maslen Perham, of Plymouth, Devon.

Issue of late Maj Hon Alastair John George Malcolm Napier, TD, yst son of 12th Lord, b 1909, d 1984: *m* 1933, Geraldine, who *d* 1983, da of late James Dunlop, of The Bield, Ayr:—
Diana Elizabeth, BA(Hons), SRN, SCM, b 1939: *m* 1967, Maj Robin Edward Doveton Harris, MBE, MC, late 14th/20th King's Hus, of Eden Croft, Wetheral, Carlisle, Cumbria, and has issue living, Gerald Neville Napier, b 1975, — Serita Catherine, b 1968: *m* 1993, Nicholas David Mark Sleep, — Meralynn Elizabeth, b 1970, — Chania Rozanthe, b 1973.

Branch from 3rd son of 11th Lord

Grandson of late Com Hon Archibald Lenox Colquhoun William John George Napier, RN, 3rd son of 11th Lord:—
Issue of late William Puleston Scott Napier, b 1925, d 1986: *m* 1949, Rosemary Heather (Los Arcos, Almeria, Spain), da of late Capt R. H. A. McLaren, of Uphall, Ashill, Norfolk:—
Lenox Scott, b 1953; *ed* Rugby: *m*, and has issue living, one son. Resides in Spain.

Branch from yr sons of 10th Lord

Grandchildren of late Hon Mark Francis Napier, 4th son of 10th Lord:—
Issue of late Major Claude Inverness Napier, b 1880, d 1946: *m* 1917, Lillian, who *d* 1972, el da of Lt-Com Alfred Francey, RN:—
Mark Francis (Northfield House, Northfield, Somerton, Som, TA11 6SL), b 1925: *m* 1951, Mary Frances, da of late Prof A. W. Ling, MSc, and has issue living, Charles Algernon (3 Manor Close, Kingsdon, Somerton, Som), b 1953: *m* 1977, Heather, el da of Dennio Harding, and has issue living, Sebastian Charles Bruce b 1979, Sophie Ann Frances b 1982, — Robert Bruce (37 King Ina Rd, Somerton, Som), b 1959: *m* 1980, Susan Ellen, yst da of Ceril Parsley, and has issue living, Matthew Victor Mark b 1988, Gemma Marie b 1984, — Claudia Frances, b 1962. —— Margaret Emily, b 1919: *m* 1945, Peter Hincks, of The Hatch, Upton, Langport, Som. —— Eleanor Rosemary Jean, b 1921: *m* 1942, Capt Frank Wilson.

Grandson of late Philip Henry Napier, yst son of late Hon Mark Francis Napier (ante):—

Issue of late Nigel Claud Oliver Napier, b 1913, d 1994: m 1st, 1945, Lucy Margaret, who d 1980, da of late Capt Arthur Walter Brown, MBE, JP; 2ndly, 1983, Hazel Therese, eldest da of late Joseph Dolan:—
(By 1st m) Alastair Denis, b 1946; ed Stowe.

Branch from 2nd son of 9th Lord

Grandchildren of late Maj Francis Horatio Napier, OBE, LLD, FRCS, el son of late Hon William Napier, 2nd son of 9th Lord:—
Issue of late Maj Archibald John Robert Napier, b 1894, d 1967: m 1926, Lilian Gray Delphin, who d 1979, da of Christopher Delphin Petersen, of Oslo:—
William Francis Andrew (22 Rushton Terrace, Mt Nasura, Armadale, Perth, W Australia 6112), b 1927: m 1954, Rosemary, da of late Charles William Jacobs, BEM, and has issue living, Stephen Charles Edward, b 1955, — Anne-Marie, b 1956. —— Robert Anthony Peter (162 Boldmere Rd, Sutton Coldfield, W Midlands), b 1940: m 1983, Mrs Teresa Dent. —— Charlotte Esmé Mary-Rose, b 1930: m 1956, Richard Harry Rose, of 7 Church Lane, E Huntspill, Highbridge, Somerset, and has issue living, Nicholas Henry Napier (15 Rue Baudelique, 75018 Paris), b 1957: m 1989 (m diss 1997), Laure Anne, da of late Alain Legréau, of Draguignan, France, and has issue living, Dominic Henry b 1991, Pierre Anthony b 1992, — Alistair Donald, b 1964, — Yvonne Charlotte, b 1958: m 1988, Hugh Alexander Norman, of 15 Hay St, Marshfield, Wilts, and has issue living, Alexander Henry b 1988, Thomas Martin b 1990, — Mary Eleanor, b 1961.

Issue of late Cdr Laurence Egerton Scott Napier, DSO, RN, b 1896; d 1969: m 1st, 1921 (m diss 19—), Nora Creina, da of Owen Christian, of Port Elizabeth, S Africa; 2ndly, 1930 (m diss 19—), Florence Sylvia Jack, who m 2ndly, 19—, — Tizzard, of Cape Town:—
(By 2nd m) Patricia, b 1931: m 1952, Robert Louis Moseley, of 1 De Klerks Drive, De Klerkshof, Edenvale, Transvaal.

Granddaughter of late Maj-Gen William John Napier, CB, CMG, 3rd son of late Hon William Napier (ante):—
Issue of late Brig Arthur Francis Scott Napier, b 1890, d 1971: m 1915, Phyllis Grace, who d 1978, da of late Edward Fleming:—
Margaret Esmé Scott (Runnymede, 69 Newland, Sherborne, Dorset), b 1920: m 1st, 1942 (m diss 1946), Capt Ephraim Stewart Cook Spence, A & SH; 2ndly, 1946, her cousin, Maj Alexander Napier, Indian Army (ret), who d 1954 (infra); 3rdly, 1957, John Whittingdale, FRCS, who d 1974, and has issue living (by 2nd m) (infra), — (by 3rd m) John Flasby Lawrance, OBE, MP, b 1959; ed Winchester, and Univ Coll, Lond (BSc Econ); Political Sec to Prime Minister 1988-90; MP S Colchester and Maldon (C) 1992-97, Maldon and E Chelmsford since 1997; OBE (Civil) 1990: m 1990, Ancilla Campbell Murfitt, and has issue living, Henry John Flasby b 1993, Alice Margaret Campbell b 1995.

Grandson of late Archibald Scott Napier, yst son of late Hon William Napier (ante):—
Issue of late Major Alexander Napier, Indian Army, b 1904, d 1954: m 1946, his cousin, Mrs Margaret Esmé Scott (SPENCE) (who m 3rdly, 1957, John Whittingdale, FRCS, who d 1974), da of late Brig Arthur Francis Scott Napier (ante):—
Charles Scott, b 1947; ed Wellington Coll, and Exeter Univ (BA).

Branch from 2nd son of 8th Lord

Granddaughters of late Francis Napier-Clavering, 2nd son of late Rev John Warren Napier-Clavering, 3rd son of Maj Hon Charles Napier, 2nd son of 8th Lord:—
Issue of late Maj-Gen Noel Warren Napier-Clavering, CB, CBE, DSO, b 1888, d 1964: m 1921, Margaret, who d 1983, da of T. W. Vigers, of Montville, St Peter Port, Guernsey:—
Diana Margaret (Dressors, Eversley, Hants), b 1926: m 1950, John Evelyn Gray Todd, Lt RN, who d 1978, and has issue living, Michael John Clavering (Rocky Hill House, 1 Old England Rd, Ipswich, Mass 01938, USA), b 1951: m 1983, Eileen Margaret Nemoy, of Los Angeles, California, and has issue living, Jenna Lauren b 1984, — David Matthew (Trezise, St Martin, Helston, Cornwall TR12 6EF), b 1953, — Philip Napier (Dressors, The Street, Eversley, Hants RG27 0PJ), b 1956, — Brian William, b 1958.

Issue of late Maj Francis Donald Napier-Clavering, MC, b 1892, d 1969: m 1920, Dorothy Avison, who d 1979, da of V. A. Holroyd, of Leamington:—
Jean Margaret Avison, b 1922; a JP for Leics, DL 1984: m 1943, Capt James Gordon Hartridge, RA, of The White House, Groby, Leics, and has issue living, David John, b 1944; ed Oundle: m 1968, Deborah Jane Robson, of Groby, Leics, and has issue living, Andrew Charles Napier b 1974, Anthea Frances b 1969, Jessica Mary b 1972, — Susan Margaret Anne (The Dower House, Shenley Church End, Bucks), b 1950; MCSP: m 1980, David Peter Hadfield, MICE, of Johannesburg, and has issue living, Christopher John b 1984, Alastair David b 1987. —— Anne Katherine, b 1924: m 1948, Eric G. Wood-Hill, of Icknield Close, Bidford-on-Avon, Warws B50 4BZ, and has issue living, Geoffrey Napier (New House Farm, Dorsington, Stratford upon Avon, Warwicks), b 1951; MBA, BSc: m 1980, Jennifer Margaret Hilton, and has issue living, Joanna Claire b 1981, Eve Katherine b 1984, — Heather Anne, b 1953: m 1st, 1978 (m diss 1983), Robert David William Reddall, of Barnes, SW13; 2ndly, 1987, Michael Harley, and has issue living (by 2nd m), Timothy James Alexander b 1987, Victoria Louise b 1989. —— Francis Alison Eve (Linden Cottage, Broughton, Hants), b 1929: m 1951 (m diss 1988), Maj Richard Mansel Colvile, RGJ (ret), and has issue living, Julia Francis, b 1955: m 1977, Nicholas Stephen Gallop, MSc, of Chalk House, Porton, Wilts, and has issue living, Hugh Alexander Colvile b 1986, Katherine Anna b 1981, Georgina Claire b 1983, — Philippa Katherine, b 1957: m 1982, George Edward Sampson, of The Cottage, Hall Lane, Taddington, Derbyshire, son of late D. N. Sampson, of Sandiway, Grindleford, Derbyshire, and has issue living, Elizabeth Jill b 1986, Claire Joanna b 1988, Caroline Louisa b 1990, — Joanna Caroline, b 1959; BSc: m 1980, Michael Christopher Watkiss, of The Manor, Willington, Bedfordshire, and has issue living, Benjamin Michael b 1984, Alistair James b 1987, Edward George b 1990, Robert David b 1993, — Fiona Patricia, b 1966.

Grandchildren of late Capt Arthur Lenox NAPIER, OBE, 4th son of late Rev John Warren Napier-Clavering (ante):—
Issue of late Brig John Lenox Clavering Napier, CBE, *b* 1898, *d* 1966: *m* 1925, Grace Edythe Muriel, who *d* 1999, aged 99, da of late Col Charles Augustus Young, CB, CMG (V Guillamore, colls):—
†*Rev* Charles John Lenox, *b* 1929; *ed* Radley, and at Univ Coll, Oxford (MA): *m* 1964, Jane Noel, da of Rev Gerard Noel Davidson, and *d* 1998, leaving issue, William John Noel, *b* 1965: *m* 1990, Lynne Margaret, yr da of Geoffrey Wright, of Radnor Cliff, Folkestone, Kent, — Henry Lenox Charles, *b* 1967, — Anna Clare, *b* 1970. —— Gerald William Alistair (Dunterton Glebe House, Milton Abbot, Tavistock, Devon) *b* 1932; *ed* Radley, and Gonville and Caius Coll, Camb (MA); Col late RE (ret): *m* 1962, Marjorie Currie, da of Robert Torrance, and has issue living, Alexander John Robert (11 Oak Park Drive, Convent Station, New Jersey 07960, USA), *b* 1963: *m* 1988, Nicola, da of late John Sykes, of Penrose Cottage, Stansted, Essex, and has issue living, Jack Alexander Luke *b* 1992, Sam Augustus James *b* 1994, Molly Rose *b* 1997, — Mark, *b* 1964: *m* 1994, Fiona A., da of M. S. King, OBE, of Blantyre, Malawi, — George (Apartado de Correos 311, 07620 Llucmajor, Mallorca, Spain), *b* 1967: *m* 1995, Helen M., yr da of J. W. Brown, of Eltham, London. —— Jean Elizabeth Alison (46 Causewayend, Coupar Angus, Blairgowrie PH13 9DX), *b* 1931: *ed* Roedean; MCSP: *m* 1970 (*m diss* 1988), John Alexander Seivwright.

Granddaughters of late Claude Gerald Napier-Clavering, 6th son of late Rev John Warren Napier-Clavering (ante):—
Issue of late Mark NAPIER, *b* 1898, *d* 1983; discontinued by deed poll 1924 the use of the surname of Clavering: *m* 1st, 1921 (*m diss* 1945), Elizabeth, who *d* 1974, da of late Sir (Samuel) Squire Sprigge, MD, FRCS, FRCP; 2ndly, 1946, Frances Alice (14 William Morgan Dr, Toronto, Ontario, Canada M4H 1E8), da of Dr Henry Allen Turner, of Millbrook, Ontario:—
(By 1st *m*) Julyan (a da), *b* 1922: *m* 1946, Cawthra Falconbridge Mulock, artist and writer, who *d* 1998, of Falconfield, RR2 Station Main, Newmarket, Ontario L3Y 3V9, Canada, and has issue living, Richard Cawthra (48 Parkside Drive, Barrie, Ontario, Canada L4N 1W9), *b* 1948; *ed* New Sch, Kings Langley, — Julian Napier (40 Chester Hill Rd, Toronto, Ontario, Canada M4K 1X3), *b* 1950; *ed* Michael Hall, Forest Row: *m* 1993, Andrea Risk, — Mark Ettrick (Makarios, 17902 St Croix Isle Drive, Tampa, Florida 33647, USA), *b* 1951; *ed* Michael Hall, Forest Row: *m* 1982, Miranda Ramsay, and has issue living, Jonathan *b* 1990, Geoffrey *b* 1992, — Nigel Falcon (27 Stadium St, SW10 0PU), *b* 1955; *ed* Sussex Univ (BA). — Ruth (The Old School House, Fawley, Wantage, Oxon), *b* 1923: *m* 1944, Capt Timothy Algernon Lumley-Smith, 17th/21st Lancers, who *d* 1979, son of Maj Sir Thomas Gabriel Lumley Lumley-Smith, DSO, and has issue living, Elizabeth, *b* 1947, — Sarah, *b* 1949, — Jane, *b* 1951.

Issue of late Alan NAPIER, *b* 1903, *d* 1988, film actor; discontinued the use of the christian name William and the surname of Clavering on being naturalised an American citizen 1952: *m* 1st, 1930 (*m diss* 1944), Nancy Bevill, who *d* 1970, da of Frank Pethybridge; 2ndly, 1944, Aileen Dickens Bourchier, who *d* 1961, da of late Ernest Bourchier Hawksley:—
(By 1st *m*) Jennifer Mary (PO Box 476, Occidental, California 95465, USA), *b* 1931: *m* 1950, Robert E. Nichols, and has issue living, David (5249 SW 117 Ave, Cooper City, Florida 33330, USA), *b* 1954: *m* 1986, Kalam Koehring, and has issue living, Travis Napier *b* 1990, Tyler Koehring *b* 1994, — Christie Catherine, *b* 1952: *m* 1993, James Stark, of 1465 Hayes St, San Francisco, Calif 94117, USA.

Granddaughter of late Col Edward Napier, 4th son of Maj Hon Charles Napier (ante):—
Issue of late Major Egbert Napier, *b* 1867, *ka* 1916: *m* 1901, Evangeline, who *d* 1936, da of J. G. Dreyer, of Copenhagen, Denmark, and Valschrivierdrift, Orange River Colony:—
Evangeline Mary, *b* 1904: *m* 1925, Percy Henry Vincent Fosbery, and has issue living, Napier, *b* 1926, — Anthony Vincent (T. H. Ranch (Est 1879), Chilcotin Valley, BC, Canada), *b* 1929.

Grandson of late Adm William Rawdon Napier, CB, CMG, DSO, 2nd son of late Com Lenox Napier, RN (infra):—
Issue of late Lieut-Com Mark Napier, RN, *b* 1911, *d* 1962: *m* 1945, Hon Jean Astley (12 Grassmere Close, Felpham, Bognor Regis, W Sussex PO22 7NU), da of 21st Baron Hastings:—
Brian Mark Lenox (119 Kingsmead Av, Worcester Park, Surrey KT4 8UT), *b* 1946: *m* 1970, Melinda, el da of James Prideaux, of 110 East End Rd, Finchley, and has issue living, Mark Anthony Rawdon, *b* 1975, — Jemima Sarah Lenox, *b* 1972.

Granddaughter of late Com Lenox Napier, RN, 6th son of late Maj Hon Charles Napier (ante):—
Issue of late Patrick Ronald Napier, *b* 1879, *d* 1911: *m* 1903, Kathleen Hilda Mary, who *d* 1948, 2nd da of late James O'Reilly Nugent (Nugent, Bt, *cr* 1795, colls):—
Patricia Marion Barbara, *b* 1904; a nun. *Residence* – La Rameé, 5902, Jauchelette, Belgium.

PREDECESSORS – **(1)** *Rt Hon Sir* ARCHIBALD Napier, PC, son of John Napier, one of the most eminent Philosophers of his age, and inventor of logarithms, of Merchistoun, Midlothian; *b* 1575; Gentleman of the Bedchamber to James VI of Scotland; accompanied the King to England and was one of the Bearers of the Canopy in State Procession of 1603; appointed Treasurer Depute of Scotland for life, and a Lord of Session 1623; Lord Justice-Clerk and Master of Cermonies 1623-4, and an Extraor Lord of Session 1626; *cr* a Baronet 1627, and *Lord Napier*, of Merchistoun (peerage of Scotland) 1627: *m* 1619, Lady Margaret Graham, who *d* (circa) 1628, da of 4th Earl of Montrose, and sister of the celebrated 1st Marquess; *d* 1645; *s* by his son **(2)** ARCHIBALD, 2nd Lord; a zealous Loyalist; distinguished himself in the royal cause during the Civil Wars, and was particularly excluded from Cromwell's Act of Grace and Pardon 1654: *m* 1641, Lady Elizabeth Erskine, who *d* 1683, da of 8th Earl of Mar; *d* 1660; *s* by his son **(3)** ARCHIBALD, 3rd Lord; Chief of the name of Napier; obtained an extension of the patent with limitation to his heirs female and their heirs male and female, and failing which to his sisters without children and their heirs whatsoever, the female heir being compelled to take the name and arms of Napier; *d* 1683, when the Baronetcy became dormant (*ooo* Napier, Bt, *v* 1027), *s* by his nephew **(4)** *Sir* THOMAS Nicolson (son of Jean, el da of 2nd Lord by Sir Thomas Nicolson, 3rd Bt, of Carnock), 4th Lord, *b* 1669; *d* unmarried 1686; *s* by his aunt **(5)** MARGARET Brisbane, Baroness Napier, 2nd da of 2nd Lord: *m* 1676, John Brisbane, who *d* 1684, Sec to Admiralty; *d* 1706; *s* by her grandson **(6)** FRANCIS (son of Elizabeth (Mistress of Napier), by her marriage with Sir William Scott, 2nd Bt, of Thirlestane, *cr* 1666), 6th Lord, *b* 1705; assumed the name of Napier, and *s* to his father's *Baronetcy of Nova Scotia* 1725; was Lord of Police 1761: *m* 1st, 1729, Lady Henrietta Hope, who *d* 1745, da of 1st Earl of Hopetoun; 2ndly, 1750, Henrietta Maria, who *d* 1795, da of Capt George Johnston; *d* 1773; *s* by his son **(7)** WILLIAM, 7th Lord, *b* 1730; a Lieut-Col in the Army, and DAG Forces in Scotland: *m* 1754, Hon Mary Anne, who *d* 1774, da of 8th Lord Cathcart; *d* 1775; *s* by his son **(8)** FRANCIS, DCL, 8th Lord, *b* 1758; was Lord-Lieut and Sheriff Principal of co Selkirk; a Representative Peer 1796, 1802, and 1807; Grand Master Mason of Scotland; 1st Lord High Commr to Gen Assembly of Church of Scotland 1802-16: *m* 1784, Maria Margaret, who *d* 1821, el da of Lt-Gen Sir John Clavering, KCB; *d* 1823; *s* by his son **(9)** WILLIAM JOHN, 9th Lord; *b* 1786; Capt RN; served at Battle of Trafalgar; Representative Peer 1824-32, Ambassador to China 1833, and Lord of Bedchamber to King William IV 1830-33: *m* 1816, Elizabeth, who *d* 1883, da of Hon James Cochrane Johnstone (E Dundonald); *d* 1834; *s* by his son **(10)** FRANCIS, PC, KT, LLD, 10th Lord, *b* 1819; Envoy Extraor and Min Plen to USA 1857-9 and to The Hague 1859-61, Ambassador to Russia 1861-4 and to Prussia 1864-6, Gov of Madras 1866-72, and Acting Viceroy of India 1872; *cr Baron Ettrick*, of Ettrick, co Selkirk (peerage of United Kingdom) 1872: *m* 1845, Anne Jane Charlotte, CI, da of late Robert Manners, Lockwood, of Dun-y-Greig, Glamorgan; *d* 1898; *s* by his el son **(11)** WILLIAM JOHN GEORGE, 11th Lord, *b* 1846; Sec to Legation at Stockholm 1887-8 and Tokio 1888-91: *m* 1st, 1876, Harriet Blake Armstrong, who *d* 1897, da of late Edward Lumb, of Wallington Lodge, Surrey; 2ndly, 1898, Grace, who *d* 1928, da of late James Cleland Burns; *d* 1913; *s* by his el son **(12)** FRANCIS EDWARD BASIL, 12th Lord, *b* 1876; *m* 1899, Hon Clarice Jessie Evelyn Hamilton, who *d* 1951, da of 9th Lord Belhaven and Stenton; *d* 1941; *s* by his el son **(13)** WILLIAM FRANCIS CYRIL JAMES HAMILTON, TD, 13th Lord, *b* 1900; Lieut-Col King's Own Scottish Borderers; 1939-45 Comdg 6th Batn of his Regt; an AAG War Office 1943-44; a Co Councillor for Selkirkshire 1946-48; a Member of Roy Co of Archers (Queen's Body Guard for Scotland): *m* 1928, (Violet) Muir, who *d* 1992, el da of Sir Percy Wilson Newson, 1st Bt, and last; *d* 1954; *s* by his el son **(14)** FRANCIS NIGEL, 14th Lord and present peer; also Baron Ettrick.

The Napiers of Merchistoun are co-heirs general of the Celtic Earls of Lennox. Elizabeth, wife of John Napier of Merchistoun, was grand-da of Margaret (wife of Robert Menteith of Rusky), da of Duncan, 8th Earl of Lennox (executed 1425).

NAPIER OF MAGDALA, BARON (Napier) (Baron UK 1868)
(Title pronounced "Napier of Magdahla")

Break thou the chains

ROBERT ALAN NAPIER, 6th Baron; *b* 6 Sept 1940; *s* 1987; *ed* Winchester, and St John's Coll, Camb (MA): *m* 1964, Frances Clare, eldest da of late Alan Frank Skinner, OBE, of Monks Close, Woolpit, Suffolk, and has issue.

Arms – Gules, on a saltire between two mural crowns in pale, and as many lions passant in fesse or, a rose of the field. **Crest** – Upon a mount vert, a lion passant or, gorged with a collar gules, therefrom a chain reflexed over the back and broken, gold, supporting with the sinister forepaw a flagstaff in bend sinister proper, flowing therefrom a banner argent, charged with a cross couped gules. **Supporters** – *Dexter*, a soldier of the corps of Royal Engineers holding in the exterior hand a musket all proper; *sinister*, a Sikh Sirdar habited and holding in the exterior hand a matchlock all proper.
Residence – The Coach House, Kingsbury St, Marlborough, Wilts SN8 1HU.

SON LIVING

Hon JAMES ROBERT, *b* 29 Jan 1966; *ed* Winchester, and Edinburgh Univ: *m* 1992, Jacqueline, eldest da of A. Stephen, of Inverkeithing, Fife.

DAUGHTER LIVING

Hon Frances Catherine, *b* 1964: *m* 1992, Simon Andrew Cholerton, of 5 Prince St, N Parramatta, NSW 2151, Australia, and has issue living, Nicholas Geoffrey, *b* 1991, — Frances Barbara Clare, *b* 1990.

BROTHERS LIVING

Hon Andrew Perceval, *b* 1947; *ed* Winchester, and Imperial Coll, Lond. *Residence* – Orchard Lodge, Ashtead Woods Rd, Ashtead, Surrey KT21 2ET.
Hon Michael Elibank, *b* 1953, *ed* Trinity Coll, Glenalmond, St John's Coll, Camb (MA), and Newcastle Univ (PhD).

SISTERS LIVING

Hon Jane Elizabeth, *b* 1942: *m* 1964, Christopher Thomas Butler-Cole, of The Old Manse, Carlops, Penicuik, Midlothian EH26 9NH, and has issue living, Thomas Falcon, *b* 1967, — Emma, *b* 1966: *m* 1988, Philip Stephen Aiken, of 447 Gilmerton Rd, Edinburgh EH17 7JJ, and has issue living, Amanda Joy *b* 1990, Melanie Louise *b* 1992.
Hon Ruth Kathleen (twin), *b* 1947: *m* 1972, John Arthur Self, PhD, and has issue living, Martin David, *b* 1974, — Pamela Clare, *b* 1976.

WIDOW LIVING OF FIFTH BARON

ELIZABETH MARIAN (*Dowager Baroness Napier of Magdala*), yst da of late Edmund Henderson Hunt, FRCS, of Cheniston, Farnham, Surrey; *m* 1939, Brig the 5th Baron Napier of Magdala, OBE, who *d* 1987. *Residence* – 51 Moorside Rd, Brookhouse, Lancaster LA2 9PJ.

COLLATERAL BRANCHES LIVING

Granddaughters of late Lt-Col Hon Henry Dundas Napier, CMG, 5th son of 1st Baron:—
Issue of late Col Arthur Henry Gurney Napier, OBE, RE, b 1900, d 1978: m 1937, Rosemary Evelyn, who d 1993, 2nd da of Charles George Lumley Cator (Blois, Bt):—
Mary-Rose, b 1938. —— Angela Marina, b 1940: m 1979, James Denis Merrik Naper, of Newtown House, Loughcrew, Oldcastle, co Meath, eldest son of late Capt Nigel William Ivo Naper, MC (see V Valentia, colls, 1973-74 Edn), and has issue living, Merrik Henry Nigel, b 1980, — Alexander Denis James, b 1981, — Isabel Carola Rosemary, b 1983. —— Belinda Jane, b 1946: m 1968, Michael Alan Fishwick Leather, of Heath Farm House, Heath Lane, Childer Thornton, Wirral, Ches, and has issue living, James Napier Fishwick, b 1971, — Giles Napier Fishwick, b 1973.

Grandson of late Lt-Col Hon Charles Frederick Hamilton Napier, 7th son of 1st Baron:—
Issue of late Charles Campbell Napier, b 1903, d 1989: m 1931, Violet Mushla Burnie, who d 1992:—
Peter Charles Cornelis, b 1936: m 1st, 1962 (m annulled 19—), Sylvia Walker, da of Charles Kimball-Fitts, of Lincoln, Mass, USA; 2ndly, 1996, Elena Nikolaeva, of St Petersburg, Russia, and has issue living, (by 1st m) Arianne Campbell, b 1962, — Tanya Kimball, b 1968. Residence – 42 Pinckney St, Boston, MA 02114, USA.

Issue of late Hon Sir Albert Edward Alexander Napier, KCB, KCVO, QC, yst son of 1st Baron; b 1881, d 1973: m 1917, Gladys, who d 1978, da of late FM Sir George Stuart White, VC, GCB, OM, GCSI, GCMG, GCIE, GCVO:—
Patricia Mary Stuart, b 1918: m 1948, Philip E. R. English, of 14 Milborne Grove, SW10 9SN, and has issue living, Georgina Frances (130 Branksome Rd, SW2 5JA), b 1958, — Philippa Katharine, b 1962.

PREDECESSORS – (1) Sir ROBERT CORNELIS Napier, GCB, GCSI, son of Major Charles Frederick Napier, RA, b 1810; a distinguished Field-Marshal in British Army, who commanded Abyssinian Expedition 1868, and captured the fortress of Magdála; Com-in-Ch of Indian Forces 1870-76, and Gov of Gibraltar 1876-82; cr Baron Napier of Magdála, in Abyssinia, and of Caryngton, co Chester (peerage of United Kingdom), 1868: m 1st, 1840, Anne Sarah, who d 1849, da of George Pearse, DL; 2ndly, 1861, Mary Cecilia, CI, who d 1930, da of Maj-Gen Edward William Smyth Scott, RA; d 1890; s by his el son (2) ROBERT WILLIAM, 2nd Baron, b 1845; ADC to Com-in-Ch in India 1870-76, and to Gov of Gibraltar 1876-81, and Assist Mil Sec 1881-82: m 1885, Hon Eva Maria Louisa, who d 1930, da of 4th Baron Macdonald, and widow of Capt Algernon Langham, Grenadier Guards; d 1921; s by his brother (3) JAMES PEARSE, 3rd Baron, b 1849; Col (ret); Afghanistan 1878-9 (medal): m 1876, Mabel Ellen, who d 1907, da of late Lieut-Col Windsor Parker, of Clopton Hall, Rattlesden; d 1935; s by his half-brother (4) EDWARD HERBERT SCOTT, 4th Baron, b 1861; formerly Lieut 1st Vol Batn Princess Charlotte of Wales's (Berkshire Regt); in Indian State Railways 1884-1909: m 1900, Florence Martha, who d 1946, da of late Gen John Maxwell Perceval, CB, of Dillon House, Downpatrick, co Down; d 1948; s by his son (5) (ROBERT) JOHN, OBE, 5th Baron, b 1904, Brig late RE, MICE, served Waziristan 1936-37 (despatches), European War 1939-45 in Sicily and Italy (despatches): m 1939, Elizabeth Marian, yst da of late Edmund Henderson Hunt, FRCS, of Cheniston, Farnham, Surrey; d 1987; s by his eldest son (6) ROBERT ALAN, 6th Baron and present peer.

NASEBY, BARON (Morris) (Life Baron 1997)

MICHAEL WOLFGANG LAURENCE MORRIS, PC, son of late Cyril Laurence Morris, FRIBA, of Pinner, Middx; b 25 Nov 1936; ed Bedford Sch, and St Catharine's Coll, Camb (MA 1960); Nat Service P/O, RAF and NATO Wings; Dir Benton & Bowles (advertising agency) 1971-81; Founder, AM International Public Affairs Consultants 1976-92; MP for Northampton South (C) 1974-97; PPS to Min of State, Northern Ireland Office 1979-81; Memb Public Accounts Cttee 1979-92; Memb Council of Europe and Western European Union 1983-91, and Speaker's Panel of Chairmen 1984-92; Chm Ways and Means Cttee and Dep Speaker 1992-97; Govr Bedford Sch since 1982 and Chm since 1989; cr PC 1994, and Baron Naseby, of Sandy, co Beds (Life Baron) 1997: m 1960, Ann Phyllis, da of late Percy Appleby, of Bedford, and has issue.

Arms – Azure a pall argent cotised or between three lotuses the corollas outwards argent. Crest – Upon a helm with a wreath argent and azure behind and grasping two pikes in saltire or beribboned azure an eagle displayed argent beaked and legged or. Supporters – On either side a horse statant erect reguardant argent maned tailed and unguled and supporting between the forelegs a mace or. Motto – Cogito ergo sum.
Residence – Caesar's Camp, Sandy, Beds SG19 2AD. Clubs – Carlton, George Row (Northampton), John O'Gaunt Golf, Port Stanley Golf, MCC, All England Lawn Tennis, Royal St George's Golf.

SONS LIVING

Hon Julian, b 1961; ed Bedford Sch, and Birmingham Univ Medical Sch: m 1987, Ann Elizabeth, da of Howard Rowley, FRCOG, and has issue living, Oliver Charles Laurence, b 1992. Residence – Cooper's Lodge, Sandy, Beds 3G19 2AD.
Hon Jocelyn, b 1972; ed Bedford Sch, and Keble Coll, Oxford.

DAUGHTER LIVING

Hon Susannah, b 1965; ed Bedford High Sch: m 1997, Edward Peter Willett, son of Edward Willett, of Bromley, Kent.

NATHAN, BARON (Nathan) (Baron UK 1940)

Labour ennobleth

ROGER CAROL MICHAEL NATHAN, 2nd Baron; *b* 5 Dec 1922; *s* 1963; *ed* Stowe, and at New Coll, Oxford (MA), Hon LLD Sussex, FSA, FRSA, FRGS; Solicitor 1950; retired as Senior Partner Herbert Oppenheimer Nathan & Vandyk 1986; Hon Life Associate Member Bar Assocn of City of New York; Chm House of Lords Select Cttee on Murder and Life Imprisonment 1988-89; Pres Jewish Welfare Board 1967-71, Hon Pres Central British Fund for Jewish Relief and Rehabilitation (Chm 1970-77); Chm RSA 1975-77 (Vice-Pres since 1977); Vice-Chm Cancer Research Campaign since 1987 (Chm Exec Cttee 1970-75, Treasurer 1979-87); Member Royal Commission on Environmental Pollution 1979-89, and House of Lords Select Cttee on European Communities 1983-88 and 1989-92; Chm Environment Sub-Cttee 1983-87 and 1989-92; Pres UK Environmental Law Assocn 1987-92, Nat Soc for Clean Air 1987-89, and Vice-Pres since 1992, and Soc of Sussex Downsmen 1987-92; Chm Animal Procedures Cttee 1990-93; Chm Sussex Downs Conservation Board 1992-97; Member House of Lords Select Cttee on Science and Technology since 1994; Master Gardeners' Co 1963; 1939-45 War, as Capt 17th/21st Lancers (twice wounded, despatches): *m* 1950, Philippa Gertrude, da of late Maj J. B. Solomon, MC, of Sutton, Sussex, and has issue.

Arms – Or, a fesse cottised sable over all a sword erect gules, on a canton of the second a roll of parchment proper. **Crest** – A kiln enflamed proper. **Supporters** – *Dexter*, a lion; *sinister*, a hind argent; each charged on the shoulder with a grenade sable fired proper.
Residences – Collyers Farm, Lickfold, Petworth, Sussex. *Clubs* – Athenæum, Cavalry and Guards.

SON LIVING

Hon RUPERT HARRY BERNARD, *b* 26 May 1957; *ed* Charterhouse, and Durham Univ (BA): *m* 1987, Ann, da of A. S. Hewitt, of Aldingbourne, Chichester, Sussex. *Residence* – Hareswood, Heyshott, Midhurst, Sussex GU29 0DA.

DAUGHTERS LIVING

Hon Jennifer Ruth, *b* 1952.
Hon Nicola Janet Eleanor, *b* 1954.

SISTER LIVING

Hon Joyce Constance Ina (*Hon Lady Waley-Cohen*), *b* 1920; *ed* St Felix Sch, and at Girton Coll, Camb (MA); a JP for Somerset 1959-87 and formerly of Mddx 1949-59; Member of Board of Govs, Westminster Hosp Group 1952-68, Chm of Westminster Children's Hosp 1952-68, and Chm of Gordon Hosp 1961-68; Chm of Governing Bodies of Girls Schs Assocn 1974-79 (Member since 1963), Member of Indep Schs Information Ser Council and Management Cttee 1972-86, Chm Indep Schs Joint Council 1977-80 and Pres of Indep Schs Info Ser 1981-86; Gov of Taunton Sch 1978-90, Wellington Coll 1979-90 and St Felix Sch, Camb 1945-83 (Chm 1970-83): *m* 1943, Sir Bernard Nathaniel Waley-Cohen, 1st Bt, who *d* 1991. *Residence* – Honeymead, Simonsbath, Minehead, Som TA24 7JX.

PREDECESSOR – **(1)** HARRY LOUIS Nathan, TD, PC, son of late Michael Henry Nathan, JP; *b* 1889; Under-Sec of State for War and Vice-Pres of Army Council 1945-46, and Min of Civil Aviation 1946-48; MP for NE Div of Bethnal Green (*L*) 1929-35, and for Central Div of Wandsworth 1937-40; 1914-18 War as Maj and Temporary Lt-Col London Regt (severely wounded); *cr Baron Nathan*, of Churt, co Surrey (peerage of UK) 1940, and a PC 1946: *m* 1919, Eleanor Joan Clara, JP, MA, Chm London CC 1948, who *d* 1972, da of late Carl Stettauer: *d* 1963; *s* by his only son **(2)** ROGER CAROL MICHAEL, 2nd Baron, and present peer.

Needham, family name of Earls of Kilmorey.

NEILL OF BLADEN, BARON (Neill) (Life Baron 1997)

(FRANCIS) PATRICK NEILL, QC, son of late Sir Thomas Neill; *b* 8 Aug 1926; *ed* Highgate, and Magdalen Coll, Oxford; served Rifle Bde 1944-47; Bar, Gray's Inn 1951, Bencher 1971, Treasurer 1990; QC 1966; Judge of Courts of Appeal of Jersey and Guernsey 1977-94; Chm Press Cncl 1978-83; first Chm Cncl for Securities Industry 1978-85; Chm DTI Cttee of Inquiry into Regulatory Arrangements at Lloyd's 1986-87; Warden of All Souls' Coll, Oxford 1977-95 (Fell 1950-77); Vice-Chancellor of Oxford Univ 1985-89; *cr* Kt 1983, and *Baron Neill of Bladen*, of Briantspuddle, co Dorset (Life Baron) 1997: *m* 1954, Caroline Susan, da of Sir Piers Debenham, 2nd Bt, and has had issue.

Residence – 8 Milborne Grove, SW10.

SONS LIVING AND DECEASED

Hon Timothy Piers Patrick, *b* 1955.
Hon Robin Charles Richard, *b* 1956.
Hon Jonathan Francis Kenrick, *b* 1960: *m* 1991, Lucy, yr da of Frank Mullens, of McMahon's Point, Sydney, NSW, Australia.
Matthew Piers Thomas, *b* 1965: *m* 1990, Kirstin R., da of Ian Tegner, of 44 Norland Sq, W11, and *d* 1993, leaving issue, Cecilia, *b* 19—.

DAUGHTERS LIVING

Hon Harriet Susan Anne, *b* 1962: *m* 1987, Douglas Michael Free, son of Thomas Free, of Metheringham, Lincs.
Hon Emma Charlotte Angela, *b* 1967.

NELSON, EARL (Nelson) (Earl UK 1805)

Let him wear the palm who has deserved it

PETER JOHN HORATIO NELSON, 9th Earl, *b* 9 Oct 1941; *s* 1981; Pres Royal Naval Commando Assocn, and Nelson Soc; Vice Pres Jubilee Sailing Trust; Patron Internat Fingerprint Soc, and Clapton Assocn Football Club: *m* 1st, 1969, Maureen Diana, da of Edward Patrick Quinn, of Kilkenny; 2ndly, 1992, Tracy, da of Raymond Cowie, of Morden, Surrey, and has issue by 1st and 2nd *m*.

Arms – Or, a cross patonce sable surmounted by a bend gules, thereon another bend engrailed of the field, charged with three hand-grenades of the second, fired proper; a chief of augmentation wavy argent, thereon waves the sea, from which issuant in the centre a palm tree, between a disabled ship on the dexter and a battery in ruins on the sinister, all proper. Crests – 1st, over a naval crown or, the chelenk or diamond plume of triumph, presented to the 1st Lord Nelson, by the Grand Signor, Sultan Selim III; 2nd, the stern of the San Joseph, Spanish man-of-war, floating in waves of the sea proper. Supporters – *Dexter*, a sailor habited and armed with a cutlass, with a pair of pistols in his belt proper, his right hand supporting a pike also proper, thereon hoisted a commodore's flag gules, and his left holding a palm branch; *sinister*, a lion reguardant in his mouth two broken staffs, and flowing from the one the Spanish, and from the other the French ensign, and in the dexter forepaw a palm branch all proper.
Address – c/o House of Lords, SW1. *Club* – St James's.

SONS LIVING (By 1st marriage)

SIMON JOHN HORATIO (*Viscount Merton*), *b* 21 Sept 1971: *m* 1993 (*m diss* 1997), Ikuko, da of Hideo Umekage.

(By 2nd marriage)

Hon Edward James Horatio, *b* 1994.

DAUGHTER LIVING (*By 1st marriage*)

Lady Deborah Jane Mary, *b* 1974.

BROTHER LIVING

Francis Edward Horatio, *b* 1947: *m* 1973, —, and has issue living, William, *b* 1975, — Emma, *b* 1974. Resides in New Zealand.

DAUGHTER LIVING OF EIGHTH EARL

Lady Sarah Josephine Mary, *b* 1947: *m* 1978, Dr John Clive Roberts, MB, BS, FFARCS, of Long Acre, Riverside Rd, Dittisham, Dartmouth, Devon TQ6 0HF.

MOTHER LIVING

Kathleen Mary (306 Chartleigh House, Beach Rd, Sea Point, Cape Town 8001, S Africa), da of William Burr, of Torquay: *m* 1941, Capt Hon John Marie Joseph Horatio Nelson, who *d* 1970.

WIDOW LIVING OF EIGHTH EARL

Mary Winifred (*Mary, Countess Nelson*) (9 Pwlldu Lane, Bishopston, Swansea), da of W. Bevan, of Swansea: *m* 1945, the 8th Earl Nelson, who *d* 1981.

COLLATERAL BRANCHES LIVING　*(The heirs male are in remainder to Earldom)*

Issue of late Lt-Col Hon Charles Sebastian Joseph Horatio Nelson, 3rd son of 5th Earl, *b* 1896, *d* 1964: *m* 1916, Kathleen Cook, who *d* 1980:—
Mary Teresa Muriel, *b* 1917; 1939-45 War with S African Air Force: *m* 1946, Cornelius Johannes Erasmus, and has issue living, Anthony Charles, *b* 1953, — Martina Kathleen, *b* 1947.

Grandchildren of late Charles Burrard Nelson, 3rd son of late Rear Adm Hon Maurice Horatio Nelson, 3rd son of 2nd Earl:—
Issue of late Cmdr John Charles Horatio Nelson, RN, *b* 1905, *d* 1994: *m* 1934, Alice Helen (95 Beech Grange, Landford, Salisbury SP5 2AN), 3rd da of late Col Robert Maximilian Rainey-Robinson, CB, CMG:—
Antony Burrard Horatio (Westbury Estate, Mavanhalla, Masinagudi PO, Nilgiris 643 223, S India), *b* 1935: *m* 1st, 1960 (*m diss* 1989), Judith Constance, da of late Brig Thomas Farquharson Ker Howard, DSO, of Goldenhayes, Woodlands, Southampton; 2ndly, 1990, Vasanthi Muriel, da of late Charles Jacob Vedanayakam, of Bangalore, India, and has issue living (by 1st *m*), Thomas Antony Horatio, *b* 1963, — Edward Maximilian, *b* 1971, — Teresa Helen, *b* 1962: *m* 1982, Giles Patrick Denis Ormerod, of Druids Lodge Stables, Druids Lodge, Salisbury, Wilts, elder son of Brig Denis Leonard Ormerod, CBE, and has issue living, Maurice Benedict Giles *b* 1986, Eden Francis Charles *b* 1988, Robin Paul Gervase *b* 1997, — Rebecca Anne, *b* 1975: *m* 1994, Oliver Crosthwaite Eyre, of Warrens Farm, Bramshaw, nr Lyndhurst, Hants, yst son of Antony Francis John Crosthwaite Eyre, and has issue living, George Oliver Douglas *b* 1996, James John *b* 1998, — (by 2nd *m*), Jayanna Bridget, *b* 1990, — Antonia Kavitha, *b* 1996. —— Joanna Elizabeth, *b* 1940: *m* 1962, Henry Bruce Milne, of Dowerfield, Long Bredy, Dorchester, yr son of late Henry Philip Manfield Milne, of Cadogan Square, SW1, and has one son and three das, Robert Henry, *b* 1968: *m* 1991, Gillian Helen, elder da of Derek Lazenby, of Ahare House, Castletown, Gorey, co Wexford , — Emma Alice, *b* 1970, — Sarah Elizabeth, *b* 1973, — Kate Mary, *b* 1978.

Grandchildren of late Capt George Henry Eyre Eyre-Matcham, eldest son of William Eyre Eyre-Matcham, grandson of Catherine Matcham, sister of 1st Baron:—
Issue of late Constance Valentine, *b* 1897, *d* 1984: *m* 1923, Cdr Edmund Valentine Jeffreys, RN:—
George William Eyre Jeffreys (Newhouse, Redlynch, Salisbury, Wilts), *b* 1931; *ed* Radley: *m* 1960, June, da of Alexander Bennett, of Godshill Wood, Hants, and has issue living, Sarah Kezia Eyre, *b* 1963, — Elizabeth Jemima Eyre, *b* 1964: *m* 1995, Michael David Cornish, of 12 Ashcombe St, SW6, and has issue living, George David Eyre *b* 1997, — Rachel Jane Eyre, *b* 1968: *m* 1998, Richard Evelyn Southall, of 13 St Loo Court, SW3. —— Catharine Elizabeth Eyre, *b* 1933: *m* 1953, Anthony William Lane, who *d* 1992, of Loosehanger Park, Redlynch, Salisbury, Wilts, and has issue living, Harriet Elizabeth Lane, *b* 1954; has resumed her maiden name: *m* 1974 (*m diss* 19—), David Geoffrey Crusher, of Northallerton, N Yorks, — Caroline Mary, *b* 1956: *m* 1986, Gordon Smith, of 2 Church Row, Aston Abbots, nr Aylesbury, Bucks, and has issue living, Daniel Harry *b* 1989, Sarah Valentine *b* 1987, — Georgina Margaret, *b* 1959: *m* 1981, (William) David Owen Bowe, of Manor House, Over Silton, Northallerton, N Yorks, and has issue living, William David *b* 1983, Matthew George *b* 1990, Emily Jane *b* 1985, Jessica Elizabeth *b* 1987, — Victoria Anne Michell, *b* 1962, — Florence Sophia, *b* 1967.

PREDECESSORS – (1) *Sir* Horatio Nelson, KB, 5th son of late Rev Edmund Nelson, R of Hillborough and of Burnham Thorpe, Norfolk, *b* 1758; one of the most eminent Naval Commanders of any age, having gained the celebrated victory of the Nile on 1 Aug, 1798, was in Nov of the same year *cr Baron Nelson*, of the Nile, and of Burnham Thorpe, co Norfolk (peerage of GB), and in 1799 was *cr Duke of Bronté*, in the kingdom of Sicily, which title he was afterwards permitted to use by royal sanction; on 2 April, 1802, he completely defeated the Danish fleet off Copenhagen, and on May 22 following was *cr Viscount Nelson of the Nile* and *of Burnham Thorpe*, co Norfolk (peerage of UK), and on 18 Aug of the same year was *cr Baron Nelson of the Nile* and *of Hillborough*, co Norfolk, with remainder to his father and the heirs male of the body, and failing them to the heirs male of the body severally and successively of his sisters Mrs Susannah Bolton and Mrs Catherine Matcham; on 21 Oct, 1805, having gained the ever memorable victory of Trafalgar he was mortally wounded, his remains being honoured with a public funeral in St Paul's Cathedral on 9 Jan 1806: *m* 1787, Frances Herbert, da of William Woodward, Sen Judge of Nevis, WI, and widow of Josiah Nisbet, MD; the barony of 1798 and the viscountcy became extinct, and the barony of 1801 and the Dukedom of Bronté devolved upon his brother **(2)** WILLIAM, DD, 2nd Baron; *cr Viscount Merton of Trafalgar* and *of Merton*, co Surrey, and *Earl Nelson*, of Trafalgar and of Merton, co Surrey (peerage of UK) 1805, with a similar remainder to that of the Barony (*cr* 1801); *d* 1835; *s* by his nephew **(3)** THOMAS BOLTON, 2nd Earl, el son of Susannah Bolton (ante), who in accordance with the Act of Settlement 46 Geo III, cap 3, assumed the surname of Nelson; *b* 1786: *m* 1821, Frances Elizabeth, da and heir of John Maurice Eyre, of Landford and Brickworth, co Wilts; *d* 1835, when the Duchy of Bronté reverted to Charlotte Mary, only da of the 1st Earl, and wife of Samuel, 2nd Baron Bridport, and the Earldom devolved upon his son **(4)** HORATIO, 3rd Earl, *b* 1823; *m* 1845, Lady Mary Jane Diana Agar, who *d* 1904, da of 2nd Earl of Normanton; *d* 1913; *s* by his el son **(5)** THOMAS HORATIO, 4th Earl; *b* 1857, *d* 1947; *s* by his brother **(6)** EDWARD AGAR HORATIO, 5th Earl; *b* 1860: *m* 1889, Geraldine, who *d* 1936, da of late Henry H. Cave, of Horton Crescent, Rugby; *d* 1951; *s* by his el son **(7)** ALBERT FRANCIS JOSEPH HORATIO, 6th Earl; *b* 1890; a lecturer in Astronomy and Anthropology; 1914-19 War with Aust Imperial Force, 1939-44 War as Major: *m* 1st, 1924 (*m diss* 1925), Amelia, who *d* 1937, widow of John C. Scott; 2ndly, 1927 (in Scotland) and 1942 (in England) Marguerite Helen, who *d* 1969, da of Capt J. M. O'Sullivan, of Tipperary; *d* 1957; *s* by his brother **(8)** HENRY EDWARD JOSEPH HORATIO, 7th Earl; *b* 1894; *d* 1972; *s* by his brother **(9)** GEORGE JOSEPH HORATIO, 8th Earl; *b* 1905: *m* 1945, Mary Winifred, da of W. Bevan, of Swansea; *d* 1981; *s* by his nephew **(10)** PETER JOHN HORATIO (son of late Capt Hon John Marie Joseph Horatio Nelson, yst son of 5th Earl), 9th Earl and present peer; also Viscount Merton of Trafalgar, and Baron Nelson of the Nile and of Hillborough.

NELSON OF STAFFORD, BARON (Nelson) (Baron UK 1960, Bt UK 1955)

HENRY ROY GEORGE NELSON, 3rd Baron and 3rd Baronet; *b* 26 Oct 1943; *s* 1995; *ed* Ampleforth, and King's Coll, Camb (MA); CEng, FIMechE, MIEE; Dir TIB plc: *m* 1968, Dorothy, da of Leslie Caley, of Tibthorpe Manor, Driffield, E Yorks, and has issue.

Arms – Argent, a cross flory sable, a chief gules thereon between a Stafford knot and a rose of the first, barbed and seeded proper, a pale also of the first, charged with a sword erect of the third. **Crest** – An arm embowed resting on the elbow in armour proper, the gauntlet grasping a cross flory fitchée sable between two roses gules, barbed and seeded also proper. **Supporters** – *Dexter*, a lion guardant or charged on the shoulder with a thunderbolt azure; *Sinister*, a grey horse proper gorged with a coronet composed of four fleur-de-lys with chains affixed thereto and reflexed over the back also or, and charged on the shoulder with a Stafford knot gold.
Residence – Eastlands, Tibthorpe, nr Driffield, E Yorks YO25 9LD.

SON LIVING

Hon ALISTAIR WILLIAM HENRY, *b* 3 June 1973; *ed* Ampleforth, and Loughborough Univ.

DAUGHTER LIVING

Hon Sarah Jane, *b* 1981.

BROTHER LIVING

Hon James Jonathan (82 Tachbrook St, SW1V 2NB), *b* 1947; *ed* Ampleforth, and McGill Univ, Canada; Man Dir F & C Ventures Ltd since 1985: *m* 1977, Lucy Mary, el da of Roger Gopsill Brown, of Chestnut House, Albrighton, Shropshire and has issue living, Camilla Amy, *b* 1982, — Lara Kitty, *b* 1986, — Eloise Violet, *b* 1988.

SISTERS LIVING

Hon Caroline Jane, *b* 1942: *m* 1964, Michael John Henry Ford, of Lower Moorhayne Farm, Yarcombe, nr Honiton, Devon EX14 9BE, and has issue living, James Mortimer Henry, *b* 1965, — Andrew Michael Felix, *b* 1967, — Annabel Emma Jane, *b* 1972.
Hon Sally Louise, *b* 1955: *m* 1975, Peter Robert Jolliffe Tritton, of Weasel Cottage, Brent Pelham, nr Buntingford, Herts SG9 0HH, and has issue living, Jonathan James Hedley, *b* 1981, — Emma Pamela Louise, *b* 1986.

WIDOW LIVING OF SECOND BARON

PAMELA ROY (*Dowager Baroness Nelson of Stafford*), yr da of late Ernest Roy Bird, MP, of New House Farm, Roberts-bridge, Sussex: *m* 1940, 2nd Baron Nelson of Stafford, who *d* 1995. *Residence* – Forest Lodge Cottage, Penselwood, Wincanton, Somerset BA9 8LL.

PREDECESSORS – (1) *Sir* GEORGE (HORATIO) Nelson, son of late George Nelson, of 66 Muswell Hill Rd, N; *b* 1887; Chm of The English Electric Co Ltd, and other Cos; *cr* a Bt 1955, and *Baron Nelson of Stafford*, of Hilcote Hall, co Stafford (peerage of United Kingdom) 1960: *m* 1913, Florence Mabel, who *d* 1962, only da of late Henry Howe, JP, of Leics; *d* 1962; *s* by his only son (2) HENRY GEORGE, 2nd Baron, *b* 1917; Dir Gen Electric Co plc 1968-87, Chm 1968-83, Dep Man Dir English Electric Co Ltd 1949-56, Man Dir 1956-62, Chm and Ch Exec 1962-68; Dir Bank of England 1961-87; 1st Chancellor of Aston Univ, Birmingham, etc: *m* 1940, Pamela Roy, yr da of late Ernest Roy Bird, MP, of New House Farm, Robertsbridge, Sussex; *d* 1995; *s* by his elder son (3) HENRY ROY GEORGE, 3rd Baron and present peer.

NETHERTHORPE, BARON (Turner) (Baron UK 1959)

Work itself is pleasing

JAMES FREDERICK TURNER, 3rd Baron; *b* 7 Jan 1964; *s* 1982; *ed* Harrow; Dir UBS London: *m* 1989, (Elizabeth) Curran, da of Edward William Fahan, of Redding, Conn, USA, and has issue.

𝔞rms – Argent on a Cross gules between four garbs vert five millrinds erect or a chief of stone masonry proper. 𝔠rest – A lion passant guardant gules gorged with a collar sable charged with bezants, supporting with the dexter paw a cornucopia inverted or the fruit proper. 𝔰upporters – *Dexter*, a bull; *sinister*, a ram, both argent horned and unguled or and gorged with a collar sable charged with bezants. *Residence* – Boothby Hall, Boothby Pagnell, Grantham, Lincs NG33 4DQ.

SON LIVING

Hon ANDREW JAMES EDWARD, *b* 24 March 1993.

DAUGHTERS LIVING

Hon Megan Anna Curran, *b* 1994.
Hon Nell Katherine Elizabeth, *b* 1997.

BROTHER LIVING

Hon Patrick Andrew, *b* 1971.

SISTERS LIVING

Hon Anna Elizabeth, *b* 1961: *m* 1986, Simon M. Edwards, elder son of late Roland Edwards.
Hon Kate Belinda, *b* 1967: *m* 1993, Rupert J. Ivey, 3rd son of John Ivey, of 1 Bemish Rd, SW15.

UNCLES LIVING (*sons of 1st Baron*)

Hon Edward Neil (The Limes, S Anston, Sheffield), *b* 1941; *ed* Rugby, at Roy Agricultural Coll, Cirencester, and London Univ; FRICS; QALAS; Dip FBA; FBIM; Chm of Edward Turner Cos, and Invesco Enterprise Trust plc; a Member of Yorks and Humberside Regional Economic Planning Council 1975-79; Member S Yorks Residuary Body 1985-89; Pres Assocn of Yorkshire and Humberside Chambers of Commerce since 1997; Dep Chm Regional Chamber for Yorkshire and Humberside since 1998; a Member of Co of Cutlers in Hallamshire; Memb of Council of the BIM 1976-81, 1982-88; Gen Commissioner of Tax since 1973; High Sheriff of S Yorks 1983: *m* 1963, Gillian Mary, el da of late C. J. King, and has issue living, Charles James, *b* 1966; Major, The Royal Regt of Fusiliers since 1998: *m* 1992, Sarah Eastwood, and has issue living, Edward Nicholas *b* 1995, Henry James *b* 1997, — Sara Jane, *b* 1971.

Hon (Philip Noel) Nigel (Parsonage House, Helions Bumpstead, Suffolk), *b* 1949; *ed* Rugby, and Worcester Coll, Oxford; Vice-Pres of The Northern Trust Co 1970-82; Man Dir Barclays Merchant Bank 1983-85, since when Man Dir Lazard Bros & Co Ltd: *m* 1st, 1973, Anne Rachel, da of R. Brown, of Somerton, Oxon; 2ndly, 1988, Mrs Jennifer (Annie) Goodwin, yst da of Capt David Armstrong, of Hepple, Morpeth, Northumberland, and has issue living (by 1st *m*), Lucy Victoria, *b* 1977, — Catherine Louise, *b* 1979, — Georgina Anne, *b* 1983.

WIDOW LIVING OF SECOND BARON

BELINDA (*Belinda, Baroness Netherthorpe*) (Boothby Hall, Boothby Pagnell, Grantham, Lincs NG33 4DQ), only da of late Frederick Hedley Nicholson, of Boothby Pagnell, Lincs: *m* 1960, the 2nd Baron Netherthorpe, who *d* 1982.

PREDECESSORS – **(1)** JAMES Turner, son of late Albert Edward Mann Turner, of Anston, Yorks; *b* 1908; Pres of NFU 1945-60, R Assocn of British Dairy Farmers and of R Agric Soc; *cr* Knt 1949, and *Baron Netherthorpe*, of Anston, W Riding of Yorkshire (peerage of the UK) 1959: *m* 1935, Margaret Lucy, who *d* 1995, da of James Arthur Mattock; *d* 1980; *s* by his el son **(2)** JAMES ANDREW, 2nd Baron; *b* 1936; Dep Chm and Ch Exec of Dalgety Ltd, a Dir of Lazard Bros & Co Ltd and of Babcock Internat Ltd: *m* 1960, Belinda, da of Frederick Hedley, of Boothby Pagnell, Lincs; *d* in a motor accident 1982; *s* by his el son **(3)** JAMES FREDERICK, 3rd Baron and present peer.

Nevill, family name of Marquess of Abergavenny.

Neville, family name of Baron Braybrooke.

NEWALL, BARON (Newall) (Baron UK 1946)

FRANCIS STORER EATON NEWALL, 2nd Baron; *b* 23 June 1930; *s* 1963; *ed* Eton, and RMA; Capt (ret) 11th Hussars; Adjt Roy Gloucestershire Hussars 1956-58; a DL of Greater London since 1988; Co Chm and Dir; Chm British Greyhound Racing Board 1985-97; Conservative Whip, House of Lords 1976-79; Member Council of Europe and W European Union 1983-98; Merchant Taylors' Co: *m* 1956, Pamela Elizabeth, el da of Edward Hugh Lee Rowcliffe, TD (*see* Farrington, Bt, 1990 Edn), and has issue.

Arms – Per pale azure and gules two lions passant guardant in pale or on a chief ermine a rose of the second barbed and seeded between a lotus flower and a sprig of New Zealand fern all proper. Crest – Issuant from an astral crown or an eagle wings elevated sable breathing flames proper. Supporters – On either side a pegasus gorged with an astral crown or.
Residences – Wotton Underwood, Aylesbury, Bucks. *Clubs* – Cavalry and Guards'.

SONS LIVING

Hon RICHARD HUGH EATON (17 Manchuria Rd, SW11) *b* 19 Feb 1961: *m* 1996, Keira N., 2nd da of Robert Glen, of Forest Hill.
Hon David William Norton (The Power House, Cromwell Grove, W6), *b* 1963; *ed* Eton, and RMA Sandhurst: *m* 1998, Georgina G., yr da of late Peter Lee, of How Caple Court, Herefords.

DAUGHTER LIVING

Hon Miranda Jane, *b* 1959: *m* 1986, Timothy Guy Lawson, son of Derek C. Lawson, of Bradford Abbas, Dorset, and has issue living, George Thomas Guy, *b* 1987, — Sam Frederick Guy, *b* 1989, — Eliza Daisy, *b* 1991. *Residence* – Mawley Cottage, Victoria Rd, Quenington, Cirencester, Glos.

SISTER LIVING

Hon Diana Olive (Tower House, Reybridge, Chippenham, Wilts), *b* 1927: *m* 1956 (*m diss* 1967), John Leonard Joly, and has issue living, Harriet Diana, *b* 1960.

PREDECESSOR – (1) *Marshal of the RAF Sir* CYRIL LOUIS NORTON Newall, GCB, OM, GCMG, CBE, AM, son of late Lt-Col William Potter Newall, Indian Army; *b* 1886; entered Roy Warwickshire Regt 1905, transferred to Indian Army 1909, to RFC 1914 and to RAF 1919; Dir of Operations and Intelligence, Air Min and Dep Ch of Air Staff 1926-31, Comdg Wessex Area, Air Defence 1931, and AOC Middle East 1931-35, Ch of Air Staff 1937-40, and Gov-Gen of New Zealand 1941-46; *cr* 1946, *Baron Newall*, of Clifton-upon-Dunsmoor, Co Warwick (peerage of UK) 1946: *m* 1st, 1922, Mary Dulcie Weddell, who *d* 1924; 2ndly, 1925, Olive Tennyson Foster, who *d* 1988, only da of Horace Tennyson Foster, and Mrs Francis Storer Eaton, of Boston, USA; *d* 1963; *s* by his only son (2) FRANCIS STORER EATON, 2nd Baron, and present peer.

NEWBOROUGH, BARON (Wynn) (Baron I 1776, Bt GB 1742)

Gentle in manner, vigorous in action

ROBERT VAUGHAN WYNN, 8th Baron, and 10th Baronet; *b* 11 Aug 1949; *s* 1998; *ed* Milton Abbey: *m* 1st, 1981 (*m diss* 1988), Mrs Sheila Christine Wilson, da of William A. Massey; 2ndly, 1988, Mrs Susan Elizabeth Hall, da of late Andrew Lloyd, of Aston Hall, Shropshire, and has issue by 1st *m*.

𝖆rms – Sable, three fleurs-de-lis argent. 𝕮rest – A dexter cubit arm erect, holding in the hand a fleur-de-lis or. 𝕾upporters – Two lions gules, the *dexter* gorged with a plain collar charged with three fleurs-de-lis or, the *sinister* gorged with a plain collar argent charged with three crosses patée gules.
Seat – Rûg, Corwen, Denbighshire, N Wales LL21 0EH. *Residence* – Peplow Hall, Peplow, Market Drayton, Shropshire TF9 3JP. *Club* – Royal Thames Yacht.

DAUGHTER LIVING (*By 1st marriage*)

Hon Lucinda Rosamond, *b* 1982.

SISTERS LIVING

Hon (Anne) Patricia Rosamund, *b* 1947: *m* 1970, Anthony George Budgen, of Boreatton House, Baschurch, Shrewsbury, Shropshire SY4 2EP, and has issue living, Mark George, *b* 1972; *ed* Ellesmere Coll, RAC Cirencester, and Harper Adams Agric Coll, — Nadine Patricia Mary, *b* 1975; *ed* St Mary's, Wantage, and Newcastle Univ.

Hon Diana Heather Marion, *b* 1951: *m* 1979, Capt Ralph Peter Kinloch Carmichael, Royal Scots Dragoon Gds (ret), of The Old Rectory, Woolstaston, Church Stretton, Shropshire SY6 6NN, and has issue living, William Ralph, *b* 1983; *ed* Milton Abbey, — Sophie Emma, *b* 1980; *ed* Moreton Hall, and Hurtwood House.

UNCLE LIVING (*son of 6th Baron*)

Hon CHARLES HENRY ROMER, *b* 26 May 1923; Lt-Com RN (ret), served World War II 1942-45: *m* 1947, Hon Angela Hermione Ida Willoughby, da of late 11th Baron Middleton, and has issue living, Antony Charles Vaughan (49 Crescent Lane, SW4 9PU), *b* 1949; *ed* Eton, and Balliol Coll, Oxford: *m* 1st, 1973 (*m diss* 1986), Jane Slane Sloan, el da of Rev William Thompson, of Oxnam Manse, Jedburgh, Roxburghshire; 2ndly, 1996, Mrs Victoria Jane Domenge, eldest da of Sir Derek Boorman, KCB, of Lower Rowling, Kent, — Andrew Guy, LVO (Babylon, Eton, Windsor, Berks SL4 6DU) *b* 1950: *ed* Eton, Gonville and Caius Coll, Camb; Cdr RN (ret); Equerry to HRH The Duke of Edinburgh 1982-84; Bursar Eton Coll since 1998; LVO 1984: *m* 1st, 1978 (*m diss* 1986), Susanjane, el da of late Selwyn Willis Fraser-Smith, CBE, MC; 2ndly, 1988, Shelagh Jean Macsorley, yr da of Prof Ian King Macsorley Smith, of Welwyn Garden City, Herts, and has issue living (by 1st *m*), Alexander Charles Guy *b* 1980; *ed* Pangbourne. *Residence* – Bunkersland, Withleigh, Tiverton, Devon EX16 8JN.

DAUGHTER LIVING OF FIFTH BARON (*By 2nd marriage*)

Hon Juno Odette Denisa Palma (changed to Blanche-Neige Juno Palma Odette Denisa), *b* 1940: *m* 1963 (*m diss* 1992), Philip Wolfe-Parry, LDS, RCS, and has issue living, Edward Thomas Wilton, *b* 1972. *Residence* – 206 Grand Drive, SW20 9NB.

MOTHER LIVING

Rosamund Lavington, da of late Maj Robert Barbour, of Bolesworth Castle, Tattenhall, Chester: *m* 1945 (*m diss* 1971), as his 1st wife, the 7th Baron Newborough, DSC, who *d* 1998. *Residence* – Rectory Cottage, Woolstaston, Church Stretton, Shropshire SY6 6NN.

WIDOW LIVING OF SEVENTH BARON

JENNIFER CAROLINE ACLAND (*Jenny Baroness Newborough*), yst da of late Capt Cecil Charles Acland Allen, RN: *m* 1971, as his 2nd wife, the 7th Baron Newborough, DSC, who *d* 1998. *Residence* – Rûg, Corwen, Denbighshire, N Wales LL21 0EH.

COLLATERAL BRANCH LIVING

Issue of late Hon Arthur Romer Wynn, brother of 6th Baron, *b* 1885, *d* 1964: *m* 1915, Gladys Catherine, who *d* 1988, da of late Richard Hanbury Joseph Gurney (Buxton, Bt):—
John Christopher Watkin (1 Margaret Lilly Way, Aldborough, Norwich NR11 YPA), *b* 1917: *m* 1946, Cynthia Maureen, da of late William Dodwell, and has issue living, Nicholas Romer (7 Princes Close, Brandon, Suffolk IP27 0LH), *b* 1952: *m* 1980, Julie-Ann, elder da of David Turrell, of Scottburgh, Natal, S Africa, and has issue living, Dane Ryan *b* 1980, Sherry Robyn *b* 1979, Jaime Michelle *b* 1986, — Gareth Rowland (Willow Garth, Warley Rd, West End, Halifax HX1 4HT), *b* 1958: *m* 1982, Karen, only da of Kenneth Lake, of Bulawayo, Zimbabwe, and has issue living, Richard Douglas *b* 1985, Michael Andrew *b* 1988, — Ann Richenda Dodwell (The Old Chapel, Chapel Rd, Roughton, Norwich NR11 8AF), *b* 1947: *m* 1973 (*m diss* 1982), Thomas William Everett, and has issue living, Mark William Christopher *b* 1976, Glen Stephen *b* 1978. ⸺ Rosemary Vera Georgina WYNN, *b* 1919; has resumed surname of Wynn: *m* 1st, 1941 (*m diss* 1966), John Richard Boydell; 2ndly, 1966 (*m diss* 1969), John Leicester Goldsmith.

Grandchildren of late Hon Arthur Romer Wynn (ante):—
Issue of late Dennis Gurney Wynn, *b* 1922; *d* 1983: *m* 1950, Joan Edith (The Mount, Ketton, Stamford, Lincs PE9 3TE), da of Alfred Pearman Bentley, of St Mary's Hall, Kings Lynn, Norfolk:—
Simon Charles (80 Chevening Rd, Queen's Park, NW6 6EA), *b* 1952: *ed* R Sch of Mines, Imp Coll: *m* 1984, Alison Rona, only da of Frank Cropper, of Moolham Mill, Ilminster, Som, and has issue living, Victoria Rona, *b* 1987, — Fiona Emily, *b* 1991. ⸺ Mark Gurney (28A Windsor Rd, W5 5PP), *b* 1957: *m* 1990, Donna Marie, da of Gyula Lennert, of 23 Bulwer St, Vanderbijlpark, S Africa, and has issue living, Alexander Antony *b* 1993. ⸺ Sarah Frances, *b* 1954: *m* 1994, Philip Knight, of White Post Cottage, Farnsfield, Newark, Notts NG22 8HX, and has issue living, Paul Alistair *b* 1995, Emma Joanna *b* 1997. ⸺ Rebecca Helen, *b* 1966.

PREDECESSORS – (1) THOMAS WYNN, Equerry to George II, Clerk to Board of Green Cloth, and MP for Carnarvon 1713-47; *cr* a *Baronet* 1742; *s* by his son (2) Sir JOHN, 2nd Bt, MP for co Carnarvon 1754-61; *s* by his son (3) Sir THOMAS, 3rd Bt; MP for co Carnarvon 1761-74, Lord-Lieut of Carnarvonshire, and Col of Carnarvon Militia; *cr Baron Newborough* (peerage of Ireland) 1776: *m* 2ndly, Maria Stella Patronilla Chiappini; *d* 1807; *s* by his el son (4) THOMAS JOHN, 2nd Baron; MP for Carnarvonshire 1826-31; *d* unmarried 1832; *s* by his brother (5) SPENCER BULKELEY, 3rd Baron, *b* 1803; High Sheriff of Anglesey 1847: *m* 1834, Frances Maria, who *d* 1857, *m* da of late Rev Walter de Winton, of Hay Castle, Brecon; *d* 1888; *s* by his grandson (6) WILLIAM CHARLES (son of late Hon Thomas John Wynn), 4th Baron; *b* 1873; Lieut Welsh Guards: *m* 1900, Grace Bruce, who *d* 1939, da of late Col Henry Montgomerie Carr; *d* as a result of illness contracted on active ser 1916; *s* by his brother (7) THOMAS JOHN, 5th Baron; *b* 18/8; formerly Lieut RNR: *m* 1st, 1907 (*m diss* 1938), Vera Evelyn Mary, who *d* 1940, da of late Capt Philip Montagu, 12th Lancers, of Down Hall, Dorset, and widow of Henry L. Winch; 2ndly, 1939 (*m diss* 1947), Denisa Josephine, who *d* 1987, da of late Lazar Braun, of Subotica, Yugoslavia; 3rdly, 1947, Katherine Rudkin, who *d* 1979, da of Henry Stephen Murray, of Victoria, Australia; *d* 1957; *s* by his cousin (8) ROBERT VAUGHAN, OBE (son of late Hon Charles Henry Wynn, 3rd son of 3rd Baron), 6th Baron, *b* 1877; S Africa 1899-1902 (despatches twice); 1914-18 War with 9th Lancers (despatches four times, Brevet Lt-Col): *m* 1913, Ruby Irene, who *d* 1960, da of late Edmund Wigley Severne; *d* 1965; *s* by his son (9) ROBERT CHARLES MICHAEL VAUGHAN, DSC, 7th Baron, *b* 1917; High Sheriff Merioneth 1963; 2nd Lieut 9th Lancers SR, 5th Inniskilling Dragoon Gds, and Lieut 16/5th Lancers 1935-39, invalided 1940, took part in Dunkirk evacuation as a civilian, commn'd RNVR in command of MTB 74, St Nazaire (wounded, despatches, DSC, prisoner in Colditz, escaped): *m* 1st, 1945 (*m diss* 1971), Rosamund Lavington, da of late Maj Robert Barbour, of Bolesworth Castle, Tattenhall, Chester; 2ndly, 1971, Jennifer Caroline Acland, yst da of late Capt Cecil Charles Acland Allen, RN; *d* 1998 (his ashes were fired from a cannon on the Rûg Estate, in accordance with his wishes); *s* by his only son (10) ROBERT VAUGHAN, 8th Baron and present peer.

NEWBURGH, EARL OF (Rospigliosi) (Earl S 1660)
(Title pronounced "Newbrough")

FILIPPO GIAMBATTISTA CAMILLO FRANCESCO ALDO MARIA ROSPIGLIOSI, 12th Earl; *b* 4 July 1942; *s* 1986; 11th Prince Rospigliosi (Holy Roman Empire), 14th Prince of Castiglione, 11th Duke of Zagarolo, Marquis of Giuliana, Count of Chiusa, Baron of La Miraglia and Valcorrente, Lord of Aldone, Burgio, Contessa and Trappeto, and conscribed Roman Noble, Patrician of Venice, Genoa, Pistoia, Ferrara and Ravenna: *m* 1972, Baronessa Donna Luisa, da of Count Annibale Caccia Dominioni, and has issue.

Arms – Not yet matriculated in line of the present Earl.
Residence – Piazza St Ambrogio 16, 20123, Milan, Italy.

DAUGHTER LIVING

Princess BENEDETTA FRANCESCA MARIA (*Mistress of Newburgh*), *b* 4 June 1974.

BROTHER LIVING

Prince Francesco Guido Carlo Antonio Maria, *b* 1947: *m* 1974, Clothilde, da of Henri Rival de Rouville, and has issue living, *Prince* Alessandro Giulio Enrico Francesco, *b* 1978. *Residence* – Viale Elvezia 24, Milan 20154, Italy.

COLLATERAL BRANCHES LIVING

Issue of late Princess Elena Rospigliosi (Duchessa Antonio Lante della Rovere), sister of 11th Earl, *b* 1904, *d* 1974: *m* 1926, Duke Antonio Lante Montefeltro della Rovere, who *d* 1954:—
Don Pietro (*Duke Lante della Rovere*) (Fundo Millaray, Casilla 176, Rengo, Chile), *b* 1928; a Roman Noble, and Noble of Foligno: *m* 1st, 1953, Marianne La Fourcalde Ithuralde, who *d* 19—; 2ndly, 1989, his cousin, Donna Livia, 6th da of late Don Filippo, Prince Lancellotti, of Rome, and has issue living (by 1st *m*), *Don* Marcantonio Maria Francesco, *b* 1957, — *Donna* Angela Maria, *b* 1956: *m* 19—, Ruben Perez, — *Donna* Patrizia, *b* 1959: *m* 19—, Andres Calvo Larrain, — *Donna* Livia Francesca, *b* 1963: *m* 19—, Eduardo Gildemeister, of Correa, Fundo los Coipos, Casilla 103, San Vicente de Tagua Tagua, Chile. —— †*Don* Ludovico, *b* 1931: *m* 1958, Lya Medez Marquez (Calle Los Cortijos, Edificio Country Suites, Urbanization Campoalegro, Caracas, Venezuela), and *d* 1986, leaving issue, *Don* Federico Maria, *b* 1959, — *Donna* Alessandra, *b* 1963, — *Donna* Elena, *b* 1965. ——*Don* Francesco (Via L. Bodio No 10, Rome), *b* 1933: *m* 1957, Carla dei Marchesi Spinola di Pasturana, and has issue living, *Don* Antonio *b* 1962, — *Donna* Silvia, *b* 1965. ——*Don* Alessandro (Via L. Bodio No 10, Rome), *b* 1936: *m* 1964, Marina Punturieri, and has had issue, *Don* Francesco, *b* 1966; *d* 19—, — *Donna* Lucrezia, *b* 19—. ——*Don* Federico (Calle Rengo 550, Los Angeles, Chile), *b* 1938: *m* 1965, Marcella Sandrez, and has issue living, *Don* Francesco René Maria Baltazar, *b* 1966, — *Don* Pietro Alessandro Maria Gaspar, *b* 1971. ——*Donna* Anna Vittoria (Carmelo delle Tre Madonne, Rome, Italy), *b* 1927; a Carmelite Nun (Sister Maria Carmela del Bambin Gesu). ——*Donna* Angela (Via Bitossi No 34, Rome), *b* 1930: *m* 1950, Massimo Igliori, engineer, who *d* 19—, and has issue living, Ulisse Maria, *b* 1961, — Alessandro, *b* 1963, — Paola, *b* 1952, — Benedetta, *b* 1954, — Maria Gaia, *b* 1959.

Grandchildren of late Prince Francesco Luigi Giuseppe Rospigliosi, uncle of 11th Earl:—
Issue of late Princess Francesca Rospigliosi, *b* 1921, *d* 1998: *m* 1949, Alexander Clausen Schmidt, who *d* 1972:—
William Francis (4000 Cathedral Av NW, Apt 518, Washington DC 20016, USA), *b* 1950. —— Camillo Alexander (5311 Augusta St, Bethesda, Maryland 20852, USA), *b* 1953. —— Laura Maria, *b* 1952: *m* 1988, Joseph Pizzarello, of 8507 Fountain Valley Drive, Gaithersburg, Maryland 20879, USA.

Grandchildren of late Prince Ludovico Guardino Carlo Francesco Rospigliosi, uncle of 11th Earl:—
Issue of late Prince Guglielmo Camillo Carlo Rospigliosi, *b* 1908, *d* 1990: *m* 1933 (*m diss* 1958), Hon Helen Lyon-Dalberg-Acton, da of 2nd Baron Acton:—
Prince Ludovico Giulio Francesco Maria (42 Viale Morin, Forte dei Marmi, Lucca, Italy), *b* 1934; Knt of Honour and Devotion Sovereign Mil Order of Malta, Knt of Justice of Constantinian Order of St George, and Officer of Order of Ad Merito Melitensi: *m* 1960, Giovanna Sallier de la Tour, da of 8th Marquis of Cordon, and has issue living, *Prince* Camillo Carlo Felice Francesco Maria, *b* 1969, — *Princess* Maria Lucrezia Elena Carolina Margherita Vittoria, *b* 1966, — *Princess* Olimpia Francesca Maria, *b* 1975. —— *Prince* Guardino Riccardo Carlo Francesco (119 Whitchurch Rd, Tavistock, Devon), *b* 1938; Knt of Justice of Constantinian Order of St George: *m* 1st, 1961 (*m diss* 1975), Veronica, da of Lt-Col Wilfred York Price, OBE, MC, of Devauden, Chepstow; 2ndly, 1976, Mrs Patricia Harvey, da of Robert Campbell, of Langley, Bucks, and has issue living (by 1st *m*), *Prince* Pericles Stephen Guardino Francesco Maria, *b* 1961: *m* 1987, Pauline Cheron Lyzette, da of Lloyd Power, and has had issue, *Prince* Guardino Lloyd James Francesco Maria *b* 1986, *Prince* Caspian Guglielmo Paul Francesco Maria *b* 1988, *Prince* Emerich Cornelius York Francesco Maria *b* 1990, *Princess* Alexandra Helen Veronica Francesca Maria *b* 1984, *d* 1985, — *Prince* Saladin Gabriel Charles Francesco Maria, *b* 1964, — *Prince* Joseph Darius Francesco Maria, *b* 1970, — (by 2nd *m*) *Princess* Elissa Alicia Elena Francesca Maria, *b* 1977, — *Princess* Ezinna Margherita Barbara Francesca Maria, *b* 1979. —— *Princess* Giovanna Maria Carolina Annuziata (47B Josephine Av, SW2 2JL), *b* 1935: *m* 1961 (*m diss* 1989), Giles Frere Wordsworth, who *d* 1992, and has issue living, Andrew Guardino Theodore (35 Kensington Sq, W8 5HH), *b* 1962: *m* 1997, Frances Wilson, — Catherine Columbine Maria Annuziata, *b* 1964, — (Anne) Lucy Susannah, *b* 1966: *m* 1990, Amin Khaled Fridi, of 24 Abbots Park, SW2, 3QD, son of Tahar Fridi, of Algiers, Algeria.

Issue of late Princess Ottavia Rospigliosi, aunt of 11th Earl, *b* 1878, *d* 1968: *m* 1898, Roberto Vimercati Sanseverino, Count of Castel Palazzo, who *d* 1945:—
Count Lionello, *b* 1911: *m* 1936, Oretta dei Conti Ceriana Mayneri, and has issue living, *Count* Ludovico, *b* 1940: *m* 1964, Donna Agnese Tosti dei Duchi di Valminuta, and has issue living, *Count* Ottaviano *b* 1966, *Count* Girolamo *b* 19—, *Countess* Roberta, *b* 1942. —— *Countess* Francesca, *b* 1917: *m* 1939, Enrico Budini Gattai, and has issue living, Antonello, *b* 1940, — Leopoldo, *b* 1942, — Roberto, *b* 1946, — Federico, *b* 1948, — Francesco, *b* 1949, — Ferdinando, *b* 1951, — Ruggero, *b* 1955, — Rodolfo, *b* 1957, — Giulia, *b* 1938, — Maria Vittoria, *b* 1944, — Nicoletta, *b* 1953, — Cristina, *b* 1957. —— *Countess* Laura, *b* 1923: *m* 1945, Don Livio Calenda dei Baroni di Tavani, Gen BA (R) Italian Air Force, and has had issue, *Don* Landolfo, *b* 1946, — †*Don* Michelangelo, *b* 1953; *d* 1995, leaving issue, *Don* Niccolo *b* 1985, *Don* Ludovico *b* 1987, — *Donna* Maria Nuvola, *b* 1947, — *Donna* Maria Gloria, *b* 1951, — *Donna* Maria Luce (twin), *b* 1951, — *Donna* Benedetta, *b* 1955, — *Donna* Candida, *b* 1962. *Residence* – 18 via Lorenzo de' Medici, Forte dei Marmi, Italy.

Grandchildren of late Princess (Maria) Maddalena Clementina Rospigliosi (Countess Ardicino della Porta) (infra):—
Issue of late Count Giovanni Ubaldo della Porta, *b* 1914, *d* 1967: *m* 1946, Emma Bregolisse (Frontone, nr Pesaro, Italy):—
Count Ferdinando, *b* 1951. —— *Count* Carlo, *b* 1956. —— *Countess* Giuliana, *b* 1947.

Issue of late Princess (Maria) Maddalena Clementina Rospigliosi, aunt of 11th Earl, *b* 1889, *d* 1966: *m* 1909, Ardicino della Porta, Count of Carpine, Biscina and Frontone:—
Count Carlo (Le Carpini, Montone, Perugia, Italy), *b* 1920: *m* 1949, Laura Pignatti Morano, Countess of Custoza, and has issue living, *Count* Giammaria, *b* 1950: *m* 1982, Donna Monica, Princess Borghese, and has issue living, *Count* Giacomo Maria *b* 1984, *Countess* Maria Laura *b* 1987, — *Count* Roberto, *b* 1954: *m* 1981, Carla Cassinelli, and has issue living, *Count* Carlo *b* 1982, *Count* Clemente *b* 1985, *Countess* Caterina *b* 1990, — *Count* Giulio, *b* 1956: *m* 1987, Alessandra Barattolo, and has issue living, *Countess* Beatrice *b* 1988, *Countess* Ottavia *b* 1991, — *Countess* Anna Barbara, *b* 1951: *m* 1979, Marchese Augusto Montani Fargna, and has issue living, Francesco *b* 1983, Letizia *b* 1980, Maria Angelica *b* 1987, — *Countess* Maria Camilla, *b* 1962: *m* 1985, Luigi Grandi, and has issue living, Ludovico *b* 1987, Giammaria *b* 1994, Clementina *b* 1990. — *Countess* Maria-Veronica, *b* 1964. — *Count* Enzo Maria *b* 1922. — *Countess* Laura, *b* 1911: *m* 1951, Lorenzo Scotti Douglas, Count of Vigoleno, who *d* 1965. — *Countess* Lucia, *b* 1912: *m* 1938, Professor Gaetano Gentile, and has issue living, Giovanni, *b* 1939: *m* 1964, Giovanna Ferragamo, — Fortunato, *b* 1945, — Maddelena, *b* 1940: *m* 1966, Giuseppe Passetti, — Ludovica, *b* 1943. — *Countess* Maria, *b* 1917: *m* 1940, Count Josef Forni, and has issue living, *Count* Carlo Francesco Giuseppe Gaetano Ardicino Salvatore, *b* 1941, — *Count* Giulio Maria Giuseppe Pietro Canisio Gaetano Anastasio, *b* 1946, — *Countess* Anna Maria Maddalena d'Pazzi Giulia Francesca de'Paolo Giuseppina Antonia Gaetana, *b* 1942, — *Countess* Teodolinda Maria Assunta Laura Antonia Giuseppina Giocchina, *b* 1943, — *Countess* Maria Cristina Beatrice Paola Giuseppina Antonia Gaetana, *b* 1944, — *Countess* Elena Maria Teresa, *b* 1949.

Grandchildren of late Lady Nicoletta Maria Nazarena Gioacchina Margherita Giustiniani-Bandini, 4th da of 8th Earl, *b* 1863, *d* 1938: *m* 1881, Mario, Duke Grazioli, who *d* 1936:—
Issue of late Pio, Duke Grazioli, *b* 1886, *d* 1954: *m* 1st, 1908, Donna Rufina Lancellotti, who *d* 1942, da of Don Filippo Massimo, 1st Prince Lancellotti; 2ndly, 1948, Cleo Conversi, of Casal de Pazzi, Rome:—
(By 1st *m*) *Donna* Caterina, *b* 1913: *m* 1940, Count Gabriele Emo Capodilista Maldura, who *d* 1983, and has issue living, *Count* Giorgio (45 Brunswick Gdns, W8; 32 Via In Piscinula, 00186 Rome), *b* 1941: *m* 1976, Christiane Hoberg, and has issue living, *Count* Alvise Luca *b* 1981, *Count* Pietro Antonio *b* 1990, *Countess* Rufina *b* 1978, *Countess* Beatrix *b* 1984, — *Count* Giovanni (48 Cheyne Walk, SW3), *b* 1944: *m* 1st, 1981 (*m diss* 1988), Lady Arabella Avice Diana Sackville, only da of 10th Earl De La Warr; 2ndly, 1989, Madeleine Maria, yst da of C. J. de Jong, of Glassenbury Park, Kent, and has issue living (by 2nd *m*), *Count* Gabriele Filippo *b* 1990, *Countess* Olimpia *b* 1992. *Residence* – Palazzo Grazioli, 102 Via del Plebiscito, 00186 Rome, Italy. — (By 2nd *m*) *Don* Riccardo, *b* 1943; Baron of Castelporziano, Nobile di San Marino, and Duke of Magliano: *m* 1st, 19—, Clara Randaccio; 2ndly, 19—, Donna Patrizia Musso di Peralta, and has issue living (by 2nd *m*), *Donna* Giorgiana Pia Olimpia, *b* 1986. *Residence* – Ansedonia V Ginepro 10, Orbetello Scalo, Grosseto, Tuscany, Italy.

Grandchildren of late Pio, Duke Grazioli (ante):—
Issue of late Don Massimiliano Grazioli, *b* 1911, kidnapped (presumed *d*) 1977: *m* 1942, Isabella Perrone, who *d* 1988:—
Don Giulio (*Duke Grazioli*), *b* 1943: *m* 1989, Princess Alexandra Wolodimeroff Scherbatoff, and has issue living, *Donna* Anastasia, *b* 1986. *Residence* – Palazzo Grazioli, 102 Via del Plebiscito, 00186 Rome, Italy.

Issue of late Donna Anna Grazioli, *b* 1916, *d* 1987: *m* 1942, Don Francesco, Marquis of Caravita, Prince of Sirignano:—
Don Giuseppe, *b* 1944. — *Don* Alvaro Pietro, *b* 1945. — *Donna* Nila, *b* 1951: *m* 1975, Ricardo Pintado Rivero, and has issue living, Ricardo Pintado Caravita di Sirignano, *b* 1975, — Tazio Pintado Caravita di Sirignano, *b* 1978, — Diego Pintado Caravita di Sirignano, *b* 1983. *Residences* – Palazzo Grazioli, 102 Via del Plebiscito, 00186 Rome, Italy; Villa Castello, Capri, Naples, Italy; Paseo de la Reforma 1670, 11000 Mexico DF.

Issue of Lady (Maria) Isabella Giovanna Teresa Gioacchina Giustiniani-Bandini, 6th da of 8th Earl, *b* 1867, *d* 1963: *m* 1898, the 1st Baron Howard of Penrith, who *d* 1939 (see that title).

Descendants of the late Lady Elisabetta Bandini (*m* 1841, Marchese Agostino Trionfi), 2nd da of Maria Cecilia, Countess of Newburgh (*see* 1969 and earlier edns).

Descendants of late Lady Cristina Bandini (*m* 1845, Count Marcello Marcelli Fiori), 3rd da of Maria Cecilia, Countess of Newburgh (*see* 1969 and earlier edns).

Descendants of late Lady Maria Bandini (*m* 1849, Federico Pucci Boncambi, Count Palatine, Noble of Perugia), yst da of Maria Cecilia, Countess of Newburgh (*see* 1969 and earlier edns).

PREDECESSORS – (1) *Sir* JAMES Levingston, a zealous royalist; was *cr Viscount Newburgh* (peerage of Scotland) 1647, and *Lord Levingston*, of Flacraig, *Viscount Kynnaird* and *Earl of Newburgh* (peerage of Scotland) 1660, with remainder to his heirs whatsoever; *d* 1670; *s* by his son (2) CHARLES, 2nd Earl; *d* 1694, when the viscountcy of 1647 expired, and the peerages of 1660 devolved upon his da (3) CHARLOTTE MARIA, who *m* 1st, Thomas, el son of 2nd Baron Clifford, and 2ndly, 1724, Hon Charles Radcliffe, brother of the beheaded 3rd Earl of Derwentwater, who in 1731, on the death of his nephew, assumed the title of 5th Earl of Derwentwater. (Charles Radcliffe was attainted 1716 and imprisoned in Newgate, whence he escaped, but being engaged in the rising of 1745 was taken prisoner and summarily executed on his former attainder): the Countess *d* 1755; *s* by her son (by her 2nd *m*) (4) JAMES BARTHOLOMEW, 4th Earl; unsuccessfully claimed the Derwentwater estates; *d* 1786; *s* by his son (5) ANTHONY JAMES, 5th Earl; in 1788, by Act of Parliament, the Derwentwater estates were charged with £2,500 a year to the Earl and the heirs male of his body; *dsp* 1814; *s* by his kinsman (6) VINCENT, 6th Earl, and 6th *Prince Giustiniani* (*cr* 1644) of the Papal States, son of Cecilia Mahony, only child of Anne Clifford, da of Charlotte Maria, Countess of Newburgh (ante) (by her 1st *m*), by Benedict, 5th Prince Giustiniani; he did not take proceedings to establish his claim to the earldom; *d* 1826; *s* by his only da (7) MARIA CECILIA AGATHA ANNA JOSEPHA LAURENTIA DONATA MELCHIORA BALTHASSARA GASPARA, Princess Giustiniani, who *s* her grandfather as Duchess of Mondragone; naturalized by Act of Parliament 1857, and her claims to peerages were allowed 1848: *m* 1815, Charles Bandini, 4th Marquis of Lanciano and Rustano (*cr* 1753) in the Papal States; *d* 1877; *s* by her son (8) SIGISMUND NICHOLAS VENANTIUS GAETANO FRANCIS, 8th Earl, *b* 1818; *cr Prince Giustiniani-Bandini* by Pope Pius IX (with the precedence held by his ancestors the Princes Giustiniani) 1863; *s* as *Duke of Mondragone* (Kingdom of Naples) 1878; assumed in 1850 the additional surname of Giustiniani, as adopted heir to his uncle, James, Cardinal Giustiniani, Bishop of Albano; naturalized by Act of Parliament 1857 (20th and 21st Vic chap 7): *m* 1848, Maria Sophia Angelica, who *d* 1898, da of the Cavaliere Giuseppe Maria Massani; *d* 1908; *s* by his only son (9) CHARLES, 9th Earl, *b* 1862: *m* 1885, Donna Maria Lanza di Trabia, who *d* 1949, da of the Prince of Trabia and Butera, of Palermo; *d* 1941; *s* by his da and only surviving child (10) MARIA SOFIA GIUSEPPINA, Countess of Newburgh, *b* 1889; Pres Ladies of Charity: *m* 1922, Count Manfredi Gravina di Ramacca, High Commr Danzig, ADC to HM the King of Italy, who *d* 1932; *d* 1977; *s* by her kinsman (11) GIULIO CESARE TADDEO COSIMO, Prince Rospigliosi (son of late Prince Giambattista Pio Sigismondo Francesco Rospigliosi, son of Lady Elena Maria Concetta Isabella Gioacchina Giuseppa Giustiniani-Bandini (*Princess Camillo Rospigliosi*), 3rd da of 8th Earl), 11th Earl of Newburgh, *b* 1907: *m* 1940, Donna Giulia, da of Don Guido Carlo dei Duchi Visconti di Modrone, Count of Lonate Pozzolo; *d* 1986; *s* by his elder son (12) FILIPPO GIAMBATTISTA CAMILLO FRANCESCO ALDO MARIA, Prince Rospigliosi, 12th Earl of Newburgh and present peer; also Viscount Kynnaird and Lord Levingston.

NEWBY, BARON (Newby) (Life Baron 1997)

RICHARD MARK NEWBY, OBE, son of Frank Newby, of Rothwell; *b* 14 Feb 1953; *ed* Rothwell Gram Sch, and St Catherine's Coll, Oxford (BA 1974, MA 1987); Administration Trainee, HM Customs and Excise 1974; Private Sec to Permanent Sec 1977-79; Principal Planning Unit 1979-81; joined SDP HQ Staff 1981, Nat Sec 1983-88; Rosehaugh plc Executive 1988-90, Dir of Corporate Affairs 1991; Dir Matrix Communications Consultancy Ltd (formerly Matrix Public Affairs Consultants) since 1992; Chm Reform Publications Ltd since 1993; Dir External Communications, Lib-Dem General Election Team 1996-97; Chm Centre for Reform Management Cttee since 1998; Memb Lib-Dem Economy and Industry Team, House of Lords; Memb House of Lords Select Cttee on the Monetary Policy Cttee of the Bank of England; *cr* OBE 1990, and *Baron Newby*, of Rothwell, co W Yorks (Life Baron) 1997: *m* 1978, Hon Ailsa Ballantyne Thomson, da of Baron Thomson of Monifieth, KT, PC (Life Baron), and has issue.

Residence – 4 Rockwells Gdns, Dulwich Wood Park, SE19 1HW. *Clubs* – Reform, MCC.

SONS LIVING

Hon Mark George, *b* 1985; *ed* Dulwich Coll.
Hon Roger James Swift, *b* 1987; *ed* Dulwich Coll.

NEWCASTLE, DUKEDOM OF (Pelham-Clinton) (Extinct 1988)

DAUGHTERS LIVING OF NINTH DUKE (*by his 2nd wife, Lady Diana Montagu-Stuart-Wortley-Mackenzie, who d 1997, da of 3rd Earl of Wharncliffe*)

Lady Patricia PELHAM-CLINTON-HOPE, *b* 1949; film actress; resumed maiden name 1974, and again 1983: *m* 1st, 1971 (*m diss* 1974), Alan Pariser; 2ndly, 1981 (*m diss* 1983), Nick Mancuso, actor, of Toronto; has issue living, Dorian Henry Navarr PELHAM-CLINTON-KOLE, *b* 1990. *Residence* – 6901 Washington Rd, W Palm Beach, Florida 33450, USA.
Lady Kathleen Marie Gabrielle PELHAM-CLINTON, *b* 1951; has resumed the surname of Pelham-Clinton: *m* 1st, 1970 (*m diss* 19—), Edward Vernon Reynolds; 2ndly, 19— (*m diss* 19—), a Thai gentleman; has issue living (by Alan Dawson), Roxanna DAWSON, *b* 1973. *Residence* – The Cottage, Ballinakil, Kilfinny, nr Croom, Limerick.

COLLATERAL BRANCHES LIVING

Granddaughter of late Henry William Pelham-Clinton, 2nd son of late Lord Charles Pelham-Clinton, 2nd son of 4th Duke:—
Issue of late Henry Charles Frederick Pelham-Clinton, *b* 1892, *d* 1968: *m* 1920, Dorothy Charlotte Middleton, who *d* 1969, da of late Capt J. Carlon, Royal Canadian Regt:—
Ethne Mary, *b* 1923: *m* 1951, Jasper Picton Hubbard, and has issue (*see* B Addington, colls). *Residence* – Hammonds, Lewes Heath, Horsmonden, Tonbridge, Kent TN12 8EE.

Granddaughters of late Lord Charles Pelham-Clinton (ante):—
Issue of late Hubert Edward Pelham-Clinton, *b* 1862, *d* 1913: *m* 1st, 1893, Louisa Brooks, who *d* 1911, da of late E. Macaulay Arnaud, of Bath, and widow of Henry Fitzwilliam Browne; 2ndly, 1911, Helen, who *d* 1963, da of James William Halcrow, of Burton-on-Trent:—

(By 2nd wife) Marjorie, *b* 1910: *m* 1940, Edward Date Long, who *d* 1982, and has issue living, Richard Pelham (58 Northcroft Lane, Newbury, Berks RG13 1BN), *b* 1941; *ed* Harrow, Queen's Coll, Camb (MA), and Stanford Univ, Calif (MBA): *m* 1973 (*m diss* 1985), Roslyn Vera, only da of late Capt Gordon Britton, RN, and has issue living, Camilla Elizabeth *b* 1978, Zoë Rebecca *b* 1980, — Alison Jean, *b* 1945: *m* 1969, Gerry Rowe, of 1887 Stonepath Crescent, Mississauga, Ont L4X 1Y1, Canada, and has issue living, Jonathan Oliver *b* 1974, Deborah Elizabeth *b* 1971. —— Georgiana Elizabeth May, *b* 1913; legally adopted 1916 by her aunt, Elizabeth, who *d* 1946, widow of Charles Stapleton Pelham-Clinton: *m* 1951, John Stuart Bordewich, MVO, who *d* 1986, and has issue living, John Peter Pelham, *b* 1955. *Residence* – Highgrove House, 32 Winchester Rd, Worthing, Sussex.

Descendants of Sir Henry Clinton, half-brother of Sir Edward Clinton (great great grandfather of Henry, 2nd Duke of Newcastle, who *s* 1768 by special remainder):—

See E Lincoln, colls.

Newdegate, FitzRoy-, family name of Viscount Daventry.

Newport, Viscount; son of Earl of Bradford.

Newry and Morne, Viscount, see Earl of Kilmorey.

NEWTON, BARON (Legh) (Baron UK 1892)
(Name pronounced "Lee")

RICHARD THOMAS LEGH, 5th Baron; *b* 11 Jan 1950; *s* 1992; *ed* Eton, and Ch Ch, Oxford; Solicitor: *m* 1978, Rosemary Whitfoot, yr da of Herbert Whitfoot Clarke, of Eastbourne, Sussex, and has issue.

𝕬rms – Gules, a cross engrailed argent, in the chief point, on an inescutcheon sable, semée of estoiles, an arm in armour embowed of the second, the hand proper holding a pennon silver, all within a bordure wavy or. 𝕮rest – Issuant out of a ducal coronet or, a ram's head argent, armed or, in the mouth a laurel slip vert; the whole debruised by a pallet wavy azure. 𝕾upporters – Two mastiffs proper, collared sable.
Residence – Laughton Park Farm, Laughton, Lewes, E Sussex BN8 6BU.

SON LIVING

Hon PIERS RICHARD, *b* 25 Oct 1979.

DAUGHTER LIVING

Hon Alessandra Mary, *b* 1978.

BROTHER LIVING

Hon David Piers Carlis, *b* 1951; *ed* Eton, and RAC Cirencester; FRICS: *m* 1974, Jane Mary, da of John Roy Wynter Bee, of West End, Surrey, and has issue living, Hugo Peter David, *b* 1979, — Thomas John Rowland, *b* 1984, — Charlotte Mary, *b* 1976, — Katherine Anna, *b* 1991. *Residence* – Cubley Lodge, Ashbourne, Derbys DE6 2FB.

WIDOW LIVING OF FOURTH BARON

PRISCILLA, da of late Capt John Egerton-Warburton (*see* Grey-Egerton, Bt, colls), and widow of Maj (William Matthew) Viscount Wolmer, el son of 3rd Earl of Selborne: *m* 2ndly, 1948, Maj the 4th Baron Newton, who *d* 1992; 3rdly, 1994, as his 2nd wife, Frederick Charles Horace Fryer (*see* E Peel, colls, 1985 Edn). *Residence* – Vernon Hill House, Bishop's Waltham, Hants.

COLLATERAL BRANCHES LIVING

Issue of late Maj Hon Sir Francis Michael Legh, KCVO, yst son of 3rd Baron, *b* 1919, *b* 1984; *m* 1948, Ruadh Daphne, who *d* 1973, da of late Alan Holmes-Watson:—
Nicholas Charles, *b* 1951; *ed* Eton: *m* 1980, Annabel G., da of Peter Hawkings, of Greywell, Hants, and has issue living, Lucy Henrietta, *b* 1982, — Alice Sophia, *b* 1985. *Residence* – Orchard House, Littlestone-on-Sea, New Romney, Kent.
—— Laura Helen (*Hon Mrs Simon Weinstock*) *b* 1954: *m* 1979, Hon Simon Andrew Weinstock, who *d* 1996, son of Baron Weinstock (Life Baron), and has issue living, Pamela Helen, *b* 1982, — Celia Rose, *b* 1985, — Laetitia Anne Daphne, *b* 1990.

Issue of late Lieut-Col Hon Sir Piers Walter Legh, GCVO, KCB, CMG, CIE, OBE, yr son of 2nd Baron, *b* 1890, *d* 1955: *m* 1920, Sarah Polk, who *d* 1955, da of late Judge James C. Bradford, of Nashville, Tennessee, USA, and widow of Capt Hon Alfred Thomas Shaughnessy (*see* B Shaughnessy):—
Diana Evelyn, *b* 1924; High Sheriff Cornwall 1988-89: *m* 1st, 1945 (*m diss* 1948), 4th Earl of Kimberley; 2ndly, 1951, Lt-Col Norman Robert Colville, MC, FSA, who *d* 1974, and has issue living (by 2nd *m*), James Charles David, *b* 1952; *ed* Eton; a Page of Honour to HM 1966-68: *m* 1983, Fiona, da of John Gaylor, of Bromley, Kent, and has issue living, Robert John James *b* 1984, Sarah Elizabeth Rose *b* 1986, Lucy Isabelle Amy *b* 1988. *Residences* – Penheale Barton, Launceston, Cornwall; 11 Kensington Sq, W8.

PREDECESSORS – (1) WILLIAM JOHN Legh, son of late William Legh; *b* 1828; MP for S Lancashire (*C*) 1859-65 and for Cheshire 1868-85; *cr Baron Newton*, of Newton-in-Makerfield, co Lancaster (peerage of United Kingdom) 1892: *m* 1856, Emily Jane, who *d* 1901, da of late Ven Charles Nourse Wodehouse, Archdeacon of Norwich; *d* 1898; *s* by his el son (2) THOMAS WODEHOUSE, PC, 2nd Baron; *b* 1857; Paymaster-Gen 1915-16, and Assist Under-Sec of State for Foreign Affairs 1916; sat as MP for Lancashire SW, Newton Div (*C*) 1886-1898: *m* 1880, Evelyn, who *d* 1932, da of late William Henry Bromley-Davenport, MP, of Capesthorne, Cheshire; *d* 1942; *s* by his son (3) RICHARD WILLIAM DAVENPORT, TD, 3rd Baron; *b* 1888; Capt Yeo; Hon Attaché at Vienna and Constantinople 1912-14; Hon Col 7th Batn Cheshire Regt (TA) 1939-50: *m* 1914, Hon Helen Winifred Meysey-Thompson, who *d* 1958, da of 1st Baron Knaresborough; *d* 1960; *s* by his el son (4) PETER RICHARD, 4th Baron; *b* 1915; Maj Grenadier Guards; a Lord Commr of the Treasury 1955-57, Vice-Chamberlain HM Household 1957-59, Treasurer 1959-60, Capt Yeomen of the Guard, and Assist Ch Whip House of Lords 1960-62; Joint Parl Sec Min of Health 1962-64, Min of State for Education and Science April to October 1964; MP Petersfield Div of Hants (*C*) 1951-60: *m* 1948, Priscilla (who *m* 3rdly, 1994, as his 2nd wife, Frederick Charles Horace Fryer (*see* E Peel, colls, 1985 Edn)), da of late Capt John Egerton-Warburton (*see* Grey-Egerton, Bt, colls), and widow of Maj (William Matthew) Viscount Wolmer, el son of 3rd Earl of Selborne; *d* 1992; *s* by his elder son (5) RICHARD THOMAS, 5th Baron and present peer.

Newton, family name of Barony of Eltisley

NEWTON OF BRAINTREE, BARON (Newton) (Life Baron 1997)

ANTONY (TONY) HAROLD NEWTON, OBE, PC, son of Harold Newton, of Dovercourt, Harwich; *b* 29 Aug 1937; *ed* Friends' Sch, Saffron Walden, and Trinity Coll, Oxford; Pres Oxford Union Conservative Assoc 1958, Pres Oxford Union 1959; sometime Vice-Chm Federation of Univ Conservative and Unionist Assocs; economist; former Sec and Research Sec, Bow Group; Assist Dir CRD 1970-74 (Head of Economic Section 1965-70); MP for Braintree (*C*) 1974-97; Assist Govt Whip 1979-81; a Lord Commr of the Treasury (Govt Whip) 1981-82; Parliamentary Under-Sec DHSS 1982; Min for the Disabled 1983-84, for Social Security and the Disabled 1984-86, and for Health 1986-88;

Chancellor of the Duchy of Lancaster and Min for Trade and Industry 1988-89; Sec of State for Social Security DSS 1989-92; Lord Pres of the Council and Leader of the House of Commons 1992-97; *cr* OBE 1972, PC 1988, and *Baron Newton of Braintree*, of Coggeshall, co Essex (Life Baron) 1997: *m* 1st, 1962 (*m diss* 1986), Janet Diane, elder da of Philip Huxley, of Sidcup; 2ndly, 1986, Patricia, widow of John Gilthorpe, and da of ......, of ......, and has issue by 1st *m*.
Address – c/o House of Lords, Westminster, SW1A 0PW.

DAUGHTERS LIVING (*By 1st marriage*)

Hon Polly Jane, *b* 19—: *m* 1998, Roger Alan Blitz.
Hon Jessica, *b* 19—: *m* 1998, Jonathan P. de Mounteney, son of John Mounteney-Smith, of Broadway, Hants.

NICHOLLS OF BIRKENHEAD, BARON (Nicholls) (Life Baron 1994)

DONALD JAMES NICHOLLS, PC, yr son of William Greenhow Nicholls; *b* 25 Jan 1933; *ed* Birkenhead Sch, Liverpool Univ (LLB), and Trinity Hall, Camb (BA, LLB); Hon Fellow, Trinity Hall, Camb 1986, Hon LLD Liverpool 1987; Bar, Middle Temple, 1958, Bencher 1981, Treasurer 1997; QC 1974; Judge of the High Court of Justice, Chancery Div 1983-86, Lord Justice of Appeal 1986-91, Vice-Chancellor 1991-94, since when a Lord of Appeal in Ordinary; Memb of Senate of Inns of Court and Bar 1974-76; Non-permanent Judge of the Hong Kong Court of Final Appeal since 1998: *cr* Kt 1983, PC 1986, and *Baron Nicholls of Birkenhead*, of Stoke D'Abernon, co Surrey (Life Baron) 1994: *m* 1960, Jennifer Mary, yr da of late William Ewart Chambers Thomas, MB, BCh, MRCOG, JP, of Stalybridge, Cheshire, and has issue.

Arms – Sable two bars each between two cotises set on the outer edge with birch leaves or. **Crest** – A demi-mole sable holding between the paws a daffodil slipped and leaved or. **Supporters** – On either side a cormorant wings displayed and inverted sable beaked and legged or. **Motto** – Let equity prevail.
Address – House of Lords, SW1A 0PW. *Club* – Athenaeum.

SONS LIVING

Hon John Peter, *b* 1963; *ed* Winchester, and Trinity Hall, Camb: *m* 1991, Divya Bhatia, and has issue living, Thomas Raj, *b* 1995, — Ayesha Emma, *b* 1996.
Hon Christopher William, *b* 1971; *ed* Winchester, and Trinity Hall, Camb.

DAUGHTER LIVING

Hon Gillian Mary, *b* 1965; *ed* Lady Eleanor Holles Sch, Hampton, and Exeter Univ: *m* 1990, Stephen Christie, and has issue living, Edward Stephen Donald, *b* 1997.

NICHOLSON OF WINTERBOURNE, BARONESS (Nicholson) (Life Baroness 1997)

EMMA HARRIET NICHOLSON, 3rd da of late Sir Godfrey Nicholson, 1st and last Bt, by his wife Lady Katharine Constance Lindsay, da of 27th Earl of Crawford and Balcarres; *b* 16 Oct 1941; *ed* Ports-down Lodge Sch, Sussex, St Mary's Sch, Wantage, and Royal Academy of Music (LRAM 19—, ARCM 19—); FRSA 1990; Computer Software Programmer and Engineer, ITC (now ICL) 1962-66; Computer Consultant John Tyzack & Partners 1967-69; Computer and General Management Consultant, McLintock Mann and Whinney Murray 1969-74; Dir of Fundraising, The Save the Children Fund 1977-85; Founder and Board Memb Stichting Redt de Kinderen (Netherlands) 1982-88; Founder and Memb Comité d'Honneur, Sauvez Les Enfants (France) 1983; MP for Devon West and Torridge (*C* until Dec 1995, then Lib Dem) 1987-97; Vice-Chm Conservative Party 1983-87; PPS to Michael Jack as Min of State, Home Office 1992-93, Ministry of Agric, Fisheries and Food 1993-95, and HM Treasury 1995; Memb Liberal Democrat Foreign Affairs Team, House of Lords; Front

Bench Spokesperson on Data Protection, House of Lords 1998; Founder and Chm AMAR Appeal since 1991 and Chm The AMAR Internat Charitable Foundation since 1995; Memb many charitable organisations, etc; author of many articles and pamphlets; *cr Baroness Nicholson of Winterbourne*, of Winterbourne, co Berks (Life Baroness) 1997: *m* 1987, Sir Michael Harris Caine, who *d* 1999, only son of late Sir Sydney Caine, KCMG.

𝔄rms – ......
Address – House of Lords, Westminster, SW1A 0PW. *Clubs* – Reform; National Liberal.

NICKSON, BARON (Nickson) (Life Baron 1994)

DAVID WIGLEY NICKSON, KBE, son of late Geoffrey Wigley Nickson; *b* 27 Nov 1929; *ed* Eton, and RMA Sandhurst; DL Stirling and Falkirk 1982, Vice Lord-Lt 1997; FRSE; Brig Queen's Body Guard for Scotland (Royal Company of Archers); Chancellor Glasgow Caledonian Univ since 1993; Hon DUniv Stirling, Napier, and Paisley; Coldstream Guards 1949-54; Dir William Collins plc 1959-76 (Vice-Chm and Group Man Dir 1976-83); Dir Radio Clyde Ltd 1981-85, and Scottish & Newcastle plc since 1981 (Dep-Chm 1982, Chm 1983-89); Chm Clydesdale Bank plc 1991-98 (Dir since 1981, Dep-Chm 1990-91); Dep-Chm General Accident plc 1993-98 (Dir since 1981); Dir Edinburgh Investment Trust plc 1981-94, Hambros plc 1991-98, and National Australia Bank 1991-96; Pres CBI 1986-88 (Chm for Scotland 1979-81); Chm Countryside Commn for Scotland 1983-85, Member National Economic Devpt Council 1985-88, Sr Salaries Review Body 1989-95, Scottish Devpt Agency 1989-91, and Scottish Enterprise 1990-93; Chm Atlantic Salmon Trust 1988-97, Scottish Salmon Strategy Task Force 1997; Pres Assocn of Scottish District Salmon Fishery Boards since 1997; Dep Pres Imperial Cancer Research Fund (Life Gov 1994); CBE 1981, KBE 1987; *cr Baron Nickson*, of Renagour, in the District of Stirling (Life Baron) 1994: *m* 1952, (Helen) Louise, da of late Lt-Col Louis William La Trobe Cockcraft, DSO, MVO, and has issue.
Residence – Renagour House, Aberfoyle, Stirling FK8 3TF. *Clubs* – Boodle's, MCC, Flyfishers.

DAUGHTERS LIVING

Hon Felicity, *b* 1955: *m* 1980, James Lewis, and has issue living, Emily, *b* 1984, — Sophie, *b* 1986, — Harriet, *b* 1989.
Hon Lucy, *b* 1959: *m* 1984, Melfort Campbell, and has issue living, Iona, *b* 1987, — Araminta, *b* 1988, — Alice, *b* 1990.
Hon Rosemary, *b* 1963: *m* 1st, 1986 (*m diss* 1992), George Petronanos; 2ndly, 1992, Maj Alastair Campbell, and has issue living (by 1st *m*), Andrew, *b* 1988, — (by 2nd *m*) Alexander, *b* 1995, — James, *b* 1999.

NICOL, BARONESS (Nicol) (Life Baroness 1983)

OLIVE MARY WENDY NICOL, da of late James Rowe-Hunter (*d* 1962), by his wife Harriet Hannah (*d* 1932); *b* 21 March 1923; *ed* Cahir Sch, Ireland; Civil Service 1943-48; Trustee United Charities 1967-86; JP (1972) Cambridge; Member Cambridge City Council 1972-82; Supplementary Benefits Tribunal 1976-78; Careers Service Consultative Panel 1978-81; *cr Baroness Nicol*, of Newnham, co Cambs (Life Baroness) 1983: *m* 1947, Alexander Douglas Ian Nicol, CBE, son of late Alexander Nicol and has issue.
Residence – 39 Grantchester Rd, Newnham, Cambridge CB3 9ED.

SONS LIVING

Hon Adrian Timothy, *b* 4 March 1949: *m* 1st, 1973 (*m diss* 1984), Valerie Joan, da of Alan Gilbert, of Mobberley, Cheshire; 2ndly, 1991, Christine Susan, da of Herbert John Barnes, of Paignton, Devon, and has issue living (by 1st wife), one son and one da, — (by 2nd wife), Thomas Alexander, *b* 1988, — James Edward Jack, *b* 1991.
Hon Colin Douglas, *b* 1950: *m* 1992, June, da of Donald Alexander Smith, of Hull.

Hon Jane Lesley, *b* 1954: *m* 1984, Edward John, only son of J. E. John, of Margam, Port Talbot, W Glam.

Nicolson, family name of Baron Carnock.

Nivison, family name of Baron Glendyne.

Noel, family name of Earl of Gainsborough.

NOEL-BAKER, BARONY OF (Noel-Baker) (Extinct 1982)

SON LIVING OF LIFE BARON

Hon Francis Edward (Prokopion, Euboea, Greece *Clubs* – Travellers', Special Forces and Athens) *b* 1920; *ed* Westminster and King's Coll, Camb (Exhibitioner); MP for Brentford and Chiswick (*Lab*) 1945-50, and for Swindon 1955-68; Chm UN Parly Cttee 1966-69 and Parly Lab Party Overseas Devpt Cttee 1964-68; Chm of British Greek Parly Group 1958-69 and of North Euboean Enterprises Ltd from 1963; Hon Pres of Union of Forest Owners of Greece 1968; Dir of Fini Fisheries of Cyprus 1976; Gov of Campion Sch Athens 1974-78; Memb Ecology Party 1978 and Soil Assoc 1979; Pres European Council for Villages and Small Towns (ECOVAST): *m* 1957, Barbara Christina, yr da of late Joseph Sonander, of Swenden, and has issue.

NOEL-BUXTON, BARON (Noel-Buxton) (Baron UK 1930)

DO IT WITH THY MIGHT

MARTIN CONNAL NOEL-BUXTON, 3rd Baron; *b* 8 Dec 1940; *s* 1980; *ed* Bryanston, and at Balliol Coll, Oxford; resumed by deed poll 1964, the surname of NOEL-BUXTON; Solicitor 1966: *m* 1st, 1964 (*m diss* 1968), Miranda Mary, who *d* 1979, el da of late Maj Hugo Atherton Chisenhale-Marsh, of Gaynes Park, Epping, Essex; 2ndly, 1972 (*m diss* 1982), Sarah Margaret Surridge, only da of Neil Charles Wolseley Barrett, TD, of Twickenham Rd, Teddington; 3rdly, 1986, Mrs Abigail Marie Granger, da of Eric Philip Richard Clent, and has issue living by 2nd and 3rd *m*.

Arms – Argent, a lion rampant tail elevated and turned over the head sable, between two mullets of the second. **Crest** – A buck's head couped gules, attired or, gorged with a collar of the last, therefrom pendent an escutcheon argent, charged with an African's head sable.
Address – c/o House of Lords, SW1.

SON LIVING (*By 2nd marriage*)

Hon CHARLES CONNAL, *b* 17 April 1975; *ed* Eton.

DAUGHTERS LIVING (*By 2nd marriage*)

Hon Lucy Margaret, *b* 1977.

(*By 3rd marriage*)

Hon Antonia Helen Isabella, *b* 1989.

BROTHER LIVING

Hon Simon Campden (The Orchard, High St, Bathford, Bath BA17 7TG), *b* 1943; *ed* Bryanston, and Balliol Coll, Oxford: *m* 1981, Alison D., da of S. J. Liddle, of Exmouth, Devon, and has issue living, Christopher John Noel, *b* 1988, — Katherine Helen, *b* 1983.

HALF-BROTHER LIVING

Hon Richard Christopher (Stretchney, Diptford, nr Totnes, S Devon), *b* 1950; *ed* Bryanston: *m* 1988, Annabel, da of Peter Hawker (*see* B Ravensdale, colls), and has issue living, Sarah, *b* 1990, — Rosie, *b* 1993.

HALF-SISTER LIVING

Hon Clare Elizabeth Anne, *b* 1954: *m* 1977, Owen Hampden Inskip, only son of His Honour late Judge (John Hampden) Inskip (*see* B Maclay, 1973-74 Edn), and has issue living, Thomas Hampden, *b* 1986, — Victoria Anne, *b* 1983. *Residence* – Park Farm, Shipton Moyne, nr Tetbury, Glos GL8 8PR.

AUNTS LIVING (*daughters of 1st Baron*)

Hon Jane Elizabeth Noel BUXTON, *b* 1925; relinquished surname of Noel by Public Declaration, 1957.

Hon Sarah Edith Noel NOEL-BUXTON, *b* 1928: *m* 1955, John Goldsborough Hogg, and has issue living, Sarah Jane, *b* 1956: *m* 1981, David Henry Houldsworth (*see* E Morton, colls, 1963 Edn), — Joanna Wynfreda, *b* 1960. *Residence* – Old Broad Oak, Brenchley, Kent.

PREDECESSORS – (1) NOEL EDWARD Noel-Buxton, PC, 2nd son of Sir Thomas Fowell Buxton, 3rd Bt, GCMG, by his wife, Lady Victoria Noel, da of 1st Earl of Gainsborough; *b* 1869; Min of Agriculture and Fisheries Jan to No 1924, and June 1929 to June 1930; sat as MP for Whitby Div of N Riding of Yorkshire (*L*) 1905-6, and for Norfolk, N Div 1910-18, and (*Lab*) 1922-30; assumed by deed poll (enrolled at College of Arms) 1930 the additional surname of Noel before that of Buxton; *cr Baron Noel-Buxton*, of Aylsham, Norfolk (peerage of United Kingdom) 1930: *m* 1914, Lucy Edith, who *d* 1960, da of late Major Henry Pelham Burn; *d* 1948; *s* by his son (2) RUFUS ALEXANDER Buxton, 2nd Baron, *b* 1917; Research Assist, Agricultural Economics Inst, Oxford 1940-43, Lecturer to HM Forces 1942-45, Producer N American Ser, BBC 1946-48, with *Farmers' Weekly* 1950-52: *m* 1st, 1939 (*m diss* 1947), Helen Nancy, who *d* 1949, yr da of late Col Kenneth Hugh Munro Connal, CB, OBE, TD, DL, of Monktonhead, Monkton, Ayrshire; 2ndly, 1948, Margaret Elizabeth, who *d* 1978, el da of Stephanus Abraham Cloete, of Pretoria, S Africa; *d* 1980; *s* by his el son (3) MARTIN CONNAL, 3rd Baron and present peer.

NOLAN, BARON (Nolan) (Life Baron 1994)

MICHAEL PATRICK NOLAN, PC, yr son of James Thomas Nolan, of London; *b* 10 Sept 1928; *ed* Ampleforth, and Wadham Coll, Oxford; RA 1947-49, TA 1949-55; Bar Middle Temple 1953 (Bencher 1975), QC 1968, Member Bar Council 1973-74, and Member Senate of Inns of Court and Bar 1974-81 (Treasurer 1977-79), Bar NI 1974, QC (NI) 1974, Recorder of Crown Court 1975-82, Judge of High Court of Justice (Queen's Bench Div) 1982-91 (Presiding Judge Western Circuit 1985-88), Lord Justice of Appeal 1991-93, Lord of Appeal in Ordinary 1993-98; Chm Cttee on Standards in Public Life 1994-97; Chancellor Essex Univ since 1997; *cr* Knt 1982, PC 1991, and *Baron Nolan*, of Brasted, co Kent (Life Baron) 1994: *m* 1953, Margaret, yr da of late Alfred Noyes, CBE, the poet, essayist and critic, and has issue.
Residence – Tanners, Brasted, Westerham, Kent TN16 1NH.

SON LIVING

Hon Michael Alfred Anthony, *b* 1955; *ed* Ampleforth, St Benet's Hall, Oxford (MA), and City Univ (Dip Law); Bar Middle Temple 1981: *m* 1984, Adeline Mei Choo, da of Henry S. H. Oh, of Singapore, and has issue living, Hugh, *b* 1986, — Felix, *b* 1992, — Sophia, *b* 1989. *Residence* – 17 Girdler's Rd, W14 0P5.

DAUGHTERS LIVING

Hon Patricia Margaret, *b* 1954: *m* 1979, Brig Richard John Morris, son of late Lt-Col John Morris, and has issue living, Henry John Richard, *b* 1982, — Benjamin Michael Joseph, *b* 1985, — Alice Rose, *b* 1988.
Hon Sheila Mary, *b* 1957: *m* 1981, Charles William Edward Hume, and has issue living, Thomas Charles, *b* 1982, — Joshua Michael, *b* 1986, — Samuel Donald, *b* (twin) 1986, — Lucy Margaret, *b* 1984.
Hon Anne Teresa, *b* 1959: *m* 1995, Simon John Yorke, yr son of late Maj Richard Henry Yorke, of Hill Head House, Whalton, Northumberland. *Residence* – 89 Mandrake Rd, SW17 7PX.
Hon Clare Elizabeth, *b* 1965.

NORBURY, EARL OF (Graham-Toler) (Earl I 1827)

Faithful to my king and country

NOEL TERENCE GRAHAM-TOLER, 6th Earl; *b* 1 Jan 1939; *s* 1955: *m* 1965, (Rosamund Margaret) Anne, da of late Francis Mathew, and has issue.

𝕬rms – Quarterly: 1st and 4th argent, a cross fleury gules charged with a plain cross couped of the field between four leaves vert, a crescent for difference, *Toler*; 2nd and 3rd argent, a trefoil slipped vert, on a chief sable three escallops or, *Graham*. 𝕮rest – On a ducal coronet a fleur-de-lis or. 𝕾upporters – *Dexter*, a horse or, bridled gules; *sinister*, a fawn proper. *Residence* – Woodlands, Seer Green, Bucks HP9 2UL. *Club* – RAC.

SON LIVING

RICHARD JAMES (*Viscount Glandine*), *b* 5 March 1967.

DAUGHTER LIVING

Lady Patricia Margaret, *b* 1970.

PREDECESSORS – (1) JOHN Toler, KC, 3rd son of late Daniel Toler, of Beechwood, co Tipperary; *b* 1745; Solicitor-Gen for Ireland 1789-98, Attorney-Gen 1798-99, and Ch Justice of Common Pleas 1800-27; MP for Tralee 1776-83, for Philipstown 1783-90, and for Newborough 1790-99; *cr Baron Norbury*, of Ballycrenode, co Tipperary (peerage of Ireland) 1800, and *Viscount Glandine* and *Earl of Norbury*, of Glandine, Kings Co (peerage of Ireland) 1827, with special remainder to his 2nd son, Hector John: *m* 1778, Grace, who *d* 1822 (having been *cr Baroness Norwood*, of Knockalton, co Tipperary (peerage of Ireland) 1797), da of late Hector Graham; *d* 1831; *s* by his son (2) HECTOR JOHN, 2nd Earl, *b* 1781, assumed, by Roy licence 1825, the additional surname and arms of Graham; *s* his el brother in his mother's Barony of Norwood and his father's Barony of Norbury 1832: *m* 1808, Elizabeth, who *d* 1859, only child of late William Brabazon; was murdered 1830; *s* by his son (3) HECTOR JOHN, 3rd Earl; *b* 1810: *m* 1848, Lady Steuart Lindsay, da of 1904, sister of 7th Earl of Lindsay; *d* 1873; *s* by his son (4) WILLIAM BRABAZON LINDSAY, 4th Earl; *b* 1862: *m* 1908, Lucy Henrietta Katharine, who *d* 1966, da of late Rev Hon William Charles Ellis (B Howard de Walden); *d* 1943; *s* by his kinsman (5) RONALD IAN MONTAGU (son of late Lt-Col James Otway Graham-Toler, son of late Hon Otway Fortescue Graham-Toler, 2nd son of 2nd Earl), 5th Earl, *b* 1893; formerly Capt Roy Inniskilling Fusiliers: *m* 1st, 1919 (*m diss* 1933), Simonne Evangeline Julie Caroline, da of Hans Apeness, of 22 Rue de Thermes, Calais; 2ndly, 1933, Margaret, who *d* 1984, da of John Kevan Greenhalgh, of Hoylake, Cheshire; *d* 1955; *s* by his son (6) NOEL TERENCE, 6th Earl and present peer; also Viscount Glandine, Baron Norbury, and Baron Norwood.

NORFOLK, DUKE OF (Fitzalan Howard) (Duke E 1483)

Virtue alone is unconquerable

MILES FRANCIS STAPLETON FITZALAN HOWARD, KG, GCVO, CB, CBE, MC, 17th Duke, and Premier Duke and Earl of England; *b* 21 July 1915; *s* as 12th Baron Beaumont 1971, 4th Baron Howard of Glossop 1972, and 17th Duke of Norfolk, Earl Marshal and Hereditary Marshal of England 1975 (when he assumed the additional forename of Stapleton by deed poll); *ed* Ampleforth, and Ch Ch Oxford (MA); Maj-Gen (ret) late Gren Gds; a DL for W Sussex; Knt of Sovereign Mil Order of Malta; Knt Grand Cross of Order of Pius IX 1977; Head of British Mil Mission to Russian Forces in Germany 1957-59, Comdg 70th Bde, King's African Rifles 1961-63, and GOC 1st Div 1963-65, Dir of Management and Support Intelligence, Min of Defence 1965-66, and Dir of Ser Intelligence, Min of Defence 1966-67; a Dir of Robert Fleming & Co, Ltd since 1969; Chm Arundel Castle Trustees Ltd; Pres The Building Societies Assocn 1982-86; Hon Student Ch Ch, Oxford, 1983; Hon Master of Bench Inner Temple since 1984; Hon Joint Treas (with the Duchess of Norfolk) Help the Aged since 1987; 1939-45 War in France, N Africa, Sicily, Italy, and NW Europe (despatches, MC); CBE (Mil) 1960, CB (Mil) 1966, KG 1983, GCVO 1986: *m* 1949, Anne Mary Teresa, CBE, da of late Wing-Cdr Gerald Joseph Constable-Maxwell, MC, DFC, AFC (*see* L Herries of Terregles, colls), and has issue.

Arms – Quarterly: 1st gules, a bend between six cross-crosslets fitchée argent; on the bend an escutcheon or, charged with a demi-lion rampant, pierced through the mouth by an arrow, within a double tressure flory counterflory of the first, *Howard*; 2nd gules, three lions passant guardant in pale or, in chief a label of three points argent, *Thomas of Brotherton*; 3rd checky or and azure, *Warren*; 4th gules, a lion rampant or, *Fitzalan*; behind the shield two gold batons in saltire, enamelled at the ends sable (as *Earl Marshal*). **Crest** – 1st, issuant from a ducal coronet or, a pair of wings gules each charged with a bend between six cross-crosslets fitchée argent; 2nd, on a chapeau gules, turned up ermine, a lion statant guardant with tail extended or, ducally gorged argent, *Thomas of Brotherton*: 3rd, on a mount vert a horse passant argent, holding in the mouth a slip of oak fructed proper. **Supporters** – *Dexter*, a lion argent; *sinister*, a horse argent, holding in his mouth a slip of oak vert, fructed proper.
Seat – Arundel Castle, Sussex BN18 9AB. *Residences* – Carlton Towers, Goole, Yorks DN14 9LZ; Bacres, Hambleden, Henley-on-Thames, Oxon. *Club* – Pratt's (Hon Member).

SONS LIVING

EDWARD WILLIAM (*Earl of Arundel and Surrey*), *b* 2 Dec 1956; *ed* Ampleforth, and Lincoln Coll, Oxford (MA): *m* 1987, Georgina Susan, yr da of John Temple Gore (*see* E Eglinton, 1990 Edn), and has issue:—

            SONS LIVING—Henry Miles (*Lord Maltravers*), *b* 3 Dec 1987, — *Hon* Thomas Jack, *b* 1992, — *Hon* Philip, *b* 1996.
            DAUGHTERS LIVING—*Lady* Rachel Rose, *b* 1989, — *Lady* Isabel Serena, *b* 1994.

Seat – Arundel Castle, Sussex BN18 9AB.

Lord Gerald Bernard, *b* 1962; *ed* Ampleforth: *m* 1990, Emma Georgina Egerton, da of late Dr Desmond James Cecil Roberts, of Woodhill, Mayfield, Sussex, and has issue living, Arthur, *b* 1991, — Florence, *b* 1993, — Grace, *b* 1994. *Seat* – Carlton Towers, Goole, Yorks DN14 9LZ.

DAUGHTERS LIVING

Lady Tessa Mary Isabel, *b* 1950: *m* 1971, Roderick Francis Arthur Balfour, and has issue (*see* E Balfour, colls). *Residence* – Burpham Lodge, Burpham, Arundel, Sussex.

Lady Carina Mary Gabriel, *b* 1952: *m* 1983, Sir David Paradine Frost, OBE, author and broadcaster, son of late Rev W. J. Paradine Frost, of Tenterden, Kent, and has issue living, Miles Paradine, *b* 1984, — Wilfred, *b* 1985, — George Paradine, *b* 1987.

Lady Marcia Mary Josephine, *b* 1953, actress (as Marsha Fitzalan): *m* 1977 (*m diss* 1995), Patrick Geoffrey Ryecart, actor, yr son of Rev John Reginald Ryecart, of Dovercourt, Essex, and has issue living, Frederick William Hamlet, *b* 1987, — Mariella Celia, *b* 1982, — Jemima Carrie, *b* 1984. *Residence* – Bacres Stable Cottage, Hambleden, Henley-on-Thames, Oxon RG9 6SX.

BROTHERS LIVING (*Raised to the rank of a Duke's sons*, 1975)

Lord Michael, GCVO, CB, CBE, MC, *b* 1916; *ed* Ampleforth, and Trin Coll, Camb (MA); Maj-Gen late Scots Gds, and Knight of Sovereign Order of Malta; DL Wilts 1974-93; Ch of Staff London Dist 1958-61, Comdg 4th Guards Bde Group 1961-64, Cdr Allied Command, Europe Mobile Forces (Land Component) 1964-66, Ch of Staff, S Command 1967-68, and GOC London Dist and Maj-Gen Comdg the Household Div 1968-71, Marshal of Diplo Corps 1971-81; Hon Col Camb Univ OTC 1968-71; Col Queen's Lancs Regt 1970-78, Col Life Guards and Gold Stick to HM 1979-99; Extra Equerry to HM since 1999; Chm Council of TA & VR Assocs 1973-81, Pres 1981-84, Patron 1984-93; Hon Recorder British Commonwealth Ex-Service League since 1992; 1939-45 in N-W Europe (despatches, MC), Palestine 1945-46, Malaya 1948-49; MBE (Mil) 1949, MVO (4th class) 1952, CBE (Mil) 1962, CB (Mil) 1968, KCVO 1971, GCVO 1980; Freedom City of London 1985: *m* 1st, 1946, Jean Marion, who *d* 1947, da of Sir Hew Clifford Hamilton-Dalrymple, 9th Bt; 2ndly, 1950, Jane Margaret, who *d* 1995, da of late Capt W. P. Meade Newman; 3rdly, 1997, Victoria Winifred, da of late Col Reginald Edmund Maghlin Russell, CVO, CBE, DSO, and widow of Maj Sir Mark Baring, KCVO (*see* E Cromer, colls), and has issue living, (by 1st *m*) Jean Mary, *b* 1947; Extra Lady in Waiting to HRH The Princess of Wales 1986-91, Lady in Waiting 1991-96: *m* 1976, Max Eben Lecky Pike, of 12 Alexandra Av, SW11, and has issue living, Molly Ann *b* 1979, Amy Mary *b* 1981, — (by 2nd *m*) Thomas Michael, OBE, *b* 1952; *ed* Ampleforth, and Oxford Univ (MA); Col late Scots Gds; OBE (Mil) 1996: *m* 1st, 1977 (*m diss* 1992), Penelope Jan, da of Capt David Christopher Richard Walters, RN; 2ndly, 1996, Joanna Mary, 2nd da of Robert Seymour Don, of N Elmham, Norfolk (*see* M Hertford, colls, 1960 Edn), and has issue living (by 1st *m*), Edward Michael *b* 1979, Flora Eleanor Meg *b* 1982, — Richard Andrew *b* 1953; *ed* Ampleforth, and Corpus Christi Coll, Oxford (MA): *m* 1990, Josephine Nina, da of Peter Johnsen, and has issue living, Frederick Peter *b* 1996, Lydia Nina *b* 1991, Artemis Cecilia Maria *b* 1993, — Henry Julian Nicholas (Foxcombe House, S Harting, Petersfield, Hants), *b* 1954; *ed* Ampleforth: *m* 1987, Claire Louise, eldei da of Georg Wilhelm von Mallinckrodt, KBE (*see* Darell, Bt, 1995 Edn), and has issue living, George Henry *b* 1991, Luke Valentine *b* 1996, Milo Nicholas *b* (twin) 1996, Marina Katherine *b* 1994, — Alexander Rupert (40 Kensington Place, W8), *b* 1964: *m* 1992, Hon Joanna Elizabeth Venables-Vernon, yr da of 10th Baron Vernon, and has issue living, William *b* 1995, Edmund Alexander *b* 1998, — Isabel Margaret, *b* 1951: *m* 1975, Peter Christopher Bickmore, of The Old Rectory, Cuxham, Watlington, Oxon (*see* E Perth, colls, 1985 Edn), and has issue living, Andrew Ralph *b* 1979, Rupert Nicholas *b* 1985, Fiona Clare *b* 1981. *Residence* – Fovant House, Fovant, Salisbury, Wilts. *Clubs* – Pratt's, Buck's.

Lord Martin, *b* 1922; *ed* Ampleforth, and Trin Coll, Camb; late Capt Gren Gds; JP N Yorks 1966, and DL 1982; High Sheriff 1979-80; 1939-45 War (wounded), Palestine 1945-46: *m* 1948, Bridget Anne, da of late Lt-Col Arnold Ramsay Keppel (*see* E Albemarle, colls), and has issue living, Philip Arnold Bernard Richard, *b* 1963, — Clare Launa, *b* 1949: *m* 1970, Simon Richard Browne Wood, of Brockfield Farmhouse, York YO19 5XJ, son of Lt-Col B. W. Wood, KOYLI, and has issue living, Charles Browne Martin *b* 1973; *ed* Eton, Alethea Launa Rose *b* 1975, Miranda Bridget Sarah *b* 1978, — Sarah Anne, *b* 1951: *m* 1985, Francis Jacques Roos, of 11 Ennismore Gdns, SW7, only son of Jean Jacques Roos, and has issue living, Theodore Martin *b* 1985, Maximilian Augustus *b* 1985, — Amanda Josephine Margaret, *b* 1953: *m* 1985, Robert C. Pascall, 2nd son of Clive Pascall, of 17 Priory Av, W4, and has issue living, Laurence Blaise Philip *b* 1989, Joshua Ralph Joseph *b* 1992, — Rose Bridget, *b* 1957: *m* 1979, Nicholas ffolliott Woodhead, of The Cottage, Holtby, York, eldest son of Col Michael ffolliott Woodhead, OBE, and has issue living, Christopher Archie ffolliott *b* 1985, Frederick Michael Martin *b* 1986, Hubert Nicholas Philip *b* 1989. *Residence* – Brockfield Hall, York YO19 5XJ.

Lord Mark, OBE, *b* 1934; *ed* Ampleforth; late Coldstream Gds; Chm Assocn of Investment Trust Cos 1981-83; Dir Robert Fleming Holdings Ltd 1971-94; Treas Scout Assocn 1986-96; OBE (Civil) 1994: *m* 1961, Jacynth Rosemary, da of Sir Martin Alexander Lindsay of Dowhill, 1st Bt, CBE, DSO, and has issue living, Amelia, *b* 1963, — Eliza, *b* 1964: *m* 1987, Timothy Francis Bell, of 26 Melrose Gdns, W6 7RW, yr son of John Bell, and has issue living, Tamara Alexandra *b* 1992, Leonora Ianthe *b* 1995. *Residence* – 13 Campden Hill Sq, W8 7LB.

SISTERS LIVING (*Raised to the rank of a Duke's daughters*, 1975)

Lady Mariegold Magdalene, *b* 1919: *m* 1957, Gerald James Auldjo Jamieson, who *d* 1992, son of late Sir Archibald Auldjo Jamieson, KBE, MC, and has issue living, Simon David Auldjo (Yarrow House, N Elmham, Dereham, Norfolk NR20 5LD), *b* 1959: *m* 1995, Lady Laura Margaret Fortescue, 2nd da of 7th Earl Fortescue, and has issue living, Jerry Jocelyn *b* 1996, Hugh Archibald *b* 1997, — James Gerard Auldjo: *m* 1999, Serena L., yst da of Martin Hugh Pym, of Barnfield, Charing, Kent (*see* B Bruntisfield, 1980 Edn), *b* 1963. *Residence* – 226 Cranmer Court, Whiteheads Grove, SW3 3HD.

Lady Miranda Mary, *b* 1927: *m* 1947, Hon Christopher Anthony Robert Emmet, JP, who *d* 1996, of Seabeach House, Halnaker, W Sussex, el son of late Baroness Emmet of Amberley (Life Baroness), and has issue living, Robert Anthony Bernard (Seabeach House, Halnaker, W Sussex), *b* 1958: *m* 1987, Francesca Lavinia Elizabeth, eldest da of Sebastian Snow, and of Mrs Anthony Longland, of The Old Vicarage, Stinsford, Dorset, and has issue living, Jules Anthony Christopher *b* 1990, Marcus Guy *b* 1992, Cosima Maria *b* 1996, — Teresa Miriam, *b* 1949: *m* 1969, Anthony Andrew Myers, of Hainbury Mill Farm, Ilchester, Somerset BA22 8LB, and has issue living, Adrian Anthony Geoffrey (27a Godolphin Rd, W12 8JF), *b* 1972: *m* 1996, Louise Claire, eldest da of John I. Denny, CMG, Nicholas Andrew Robert *b* 1973, — Catriona Mary (The Old Barn, Clevelode, Malvern, Worcs), *b* 1951: *m* 1st, 1978 (*m diss* 1983), Paul Striberry; 2ndly, 1984, Christopher John Russell-Pavier, who *d* 1994, and has issue living (by 2nd *m*), Charles Adey *b* 1992, Anna Louise *b* 1985, — Rowena Mary Gabriel (56 Redcliffe Square, SW10), *b* 1954: *m* 1st, 1975 (*m diss* 1981), Michael F. Hallinan; 2ndly, 1981 (*m diss* 1998), Jonathan Malcolm Green, and has issue living (by 2nd *m*), Thomas Oliver *b* 1984, James Edward *b* (twin) 1984, Iona Alice *b* 1989.

Lady Mirabel Magdalene, *b* 1931: *m* 1952, Bernard Kelly, el son of late Sir David Victor Kelly, GCMG, MC, and has issue living, Dominic Noël Miles Charles David (Romden Cottage, Smarden, Kent), *b* 1953: *m* 1981, Miranda, da of Lance Macklin, and has issue living, Sabine Mirabel Jemima Noelle *b* 1983, Alice Beatrice Noelle *b* 1985, Celina *b* 1987, — Anthony Noël Francis, *b* 1955, — Crispin Bernard Noël (Wright's Farm, Combe, Hungerford, Berks RG17 9EL), *b* 1956: *m* 1982, Frances, yr da of Sir Charles William Richards Pickthorn, 2nd Bt, and has had issue, Alexander *b* 1985, Christian *b* and *d* 1987, Rowan *b* 1998, Jessica *b* 1988, — David Mark Noël, *b* 1959: *m* 1992, Alexandra Mary Romana, 3rd da of Joseph Czernin (*see* B Howard de Walden), and has issue living, Frederick David Joseph *b* 1996, Natasha Mary Gabriella *b* 1994, — Benedict Bernard Noël d'Arenberg (Knockwood, Nether Wallop, Hants SO20 8EL), *b* 1960: *m* 1988, Elizabeth A., yr da of Alexander Eaglestone, of Oxford, and has issue living, Thomas Alexander Noël *b* 1990, Humphrey Martin Noël *b* 1992, Marcus Benedict Noël *b* 1995, Joseph Francis Noël *b* 1998, — Sebastian Charles Noël, *b* 1972; has issue living (by Annabel Bradford), Olivia Mirabel *b* 1999, — Justin Ghislain Octavius Noël, *b* 1974, — Anne-Louise Marie-Noële Miranda Josephine, *b* 1962: *m* 1987, Charles Richard Francis Arkwright, of 55 Perrymead St, SW6 3SN, elder son of late Col Peter Arkwright, OBE, of Willersey House, nr Broadway, Worcs, and has issue living, Arabella *b* 1988, Rebecca *b* 1990, Harriet *b* 1994, Charlotte *b* (twin) 1994. *Residence* – Flat 72, Piper Building, Peterborough Rd, SW6 3EF.

DAUGHTERS LIVING OF SIXTEENTH DUKE

Lady Anne Elizabeth (*Lady Herries of Terregles*), *b* 1938 (see that title).

Lady Mary Katharine, DCVO, *b* 1940; *hp* to Lordship of Herries of Terregles; Lady-in-Waiting to HRH Princess Alexandra, Hon Lady Ogilvy, since 1964; CVO 1982, DCVO 1995: *m* 1986, Gp Capt Anthony Mumford, CVO, OBE. *Residences* – North Stoke Cottage, N Stoke, Arundel, W Sussex BN18 9LS; Lantonside, Glencaple, Dumfries.

Lady Sarah Margaret, *b* 1941; DL W Sussex 1993: *m* 1988, as his 2nd wife, Nigel Hugh Clutton, yr son of late Robin John Clutton, of Woodcote, Rotherfield, Sussex. *Residence* – The Dover House, Poling, Arundel, W Sussex.

Lady (Theresa) Jane (*Countess of Ancram*), *b* 1945: *m* 1975, Michael Andrew Foster Jude, Earl of Ancram, MP, PC, elder son of 12th Marquess of Lothian, and has issue (see that title).

DAUGHTERS LIVING OF FIFTEENTH DUKE

Lady Katherine Mary, *b* 1912; has Order of Mercy: *m* 1940, Lieut-Col Joseph Anthony Moore Phillips, DSO, MBE, DL, late King's Dragoon Guards, who *d* 1990, and has had issue, Anthony Bernard Moore, *b* 1953; lost at sea during Whitbread Yacht Race 1989. *Residence* – W Sussex.

Lady Winefride Alice, *b* 1914: *m* 1943, Lt-Col John Edward Broke Freeman, late Oxfordshire and Buckinghamshire LI, who *d* 1986, son of late Sir Philip Horace Freeman, KCVO, KBE, and has issue living, Charles Philip Broke (Buxhall Vale, Stowmarket, Suffolk), *b* 1947: *m* 1982, Hilary Jane, yr da of Henry Val Faker, of Brentwood, Essex, and has had issue, Thomas *b* 1988, Isabella *b* 1986 (*dec*), Cordelia Mary Antonia *b* 1989, and an adopted son, Barnabas *b* 1980, — Mary Gwendoline, *b* 1945: *m* 1967, Martin Richard de Laszlo, of 57 Coniger Rd, SW6, and has issue living, Rupert *b* 1968, Oliver *b* 1971, Lydia *b* 1980, — Virginia Phyllis Theresa, *b* 1949: *m* 1978, Ian Ramsay Hope Henderson, of 20 Westbourne Park Rd, W2, and has issue (*see* B Faringdon, colls). *Residence* – St Catherine's Cottage, Aldingbourne, W Sussex.

COLLATERAL BRANCHES LIVING

Descendants of late Rt Hon Lord Edmund Bernard Fitzalan-Howard, KG, GCVO, DSO (3rd son of 14th Duke), who was *cr Viscount Fitz Alan of Derwent* 1921:—
See V Fitz Alan of Derwent (ext).

Granddaughter of 2nd Baron Howard of Glossop, 2nd son of Rt Hon Lord Edward George Fitzalan-Howard (who was *cr Baron Howard of Glossop* 1869), 2nd son of 13th Duke:—
Issue of late Hon Philip Granville James Fitzalan Howard, Lt WG, *b* 1895, *d* of wounds received in action 1918: *m* 1916, Gladys Cecily Clara (who *d* 1966, having *m* 2ndly, 1920 (*m diss* 1931), Capt Henry James Fosbery Mills, formerly KRRCR, son of Sir James Mills, KCMG; 3rdly, 1931, Maj P. G. Riviere), da of late Lieut-Col Charles Edward Norton, CMG:—
Philippa Gwendolen Mary (*posthumous*), *b* 1918: *m* 1940, Major Edward Guy Tyler, MC, Irish Guards, and has issue living Peter Edward, *b* 1944; *ed* Ampleforth, — Virginia Anne, *b* 1941: *m* 1965, Carlos Mejia, of 26 Mallord St, SW3 6DU, and has issue living, Carlos-Felipe *b* 1967, Mariana Luisa *b* 1971, Elena Isabel *b* 1975. *Residence* – 22 Mallord St, SW3 6DU.

Grandchildren of late Sir (Edward) Stafford Howard, KCB, 2nd son of late Henry Howard, MP, only son of late Lord Henry Thomas Howard-Molyneux-Howard, MP, brother of 12th Duke:—
Issue of late Maj Sir Algar Henry Stafford Howard, KCB, KCVO, MC, TD, *b* 1880, *d* 1970: *m* 1921, Hon Violet Ethel Meysey-Thompson, who *d* 1960, da of 1st and last Baron Knaresborough, and widow of Capt Alexander Moore Vandeleur:—
Anne Violet, *b* 1923: *m* 1952, John Cahill, of Doneen, Castleisland, co Kerry, and has issue living, John Anthony, *b* 1956, — Colin Algar, *b* 1958, — Peter Francis, *b* 1960, — Elizabeth Mary, *b* 1953, — Alice, *b* 1962, — Angela Violet, *b* 1964, — Rosemary, *b* 1967. —— Elizabeth Helen, *b* 1924: *m* 1958, Harold William Norman Suckling, and has issue living, Penelope Anne, *b* 1959: *m* 1st, 1985 (*m diss* 1989), See-Ming Ong, of Wimbledon; 2ndly, 1996, Peter Rhodes Bristow, of Brisbane, Australia, and has issue living (by 2nd husband), Katherine Helen *b* 1994. *Residence* – The Knowle, The Street, Geldeston, Beccles, Suffolk NR34 0LB.

Issue of late Capt Stafford Vaughan Stepney Howard, Coldstream Gds (Res), *b* 1915, *d* 1991: *m* 1st, 1936 (*m diss* 1940), Ursula Priscilla Marie Gabrielle, who *d* 1997, yr da of Lt-Col Sir James Nockells Horlick, 4th Bt, OBE, MC; 2ndly, 1940, (Mary) Gracia (Blind Cottage, Challock Lees, Ashford, Kent TN25 4AU), da of late George Wilder Neville, of Portsmouth, Virginia, USA:—
(By 1st *m*) Nicholas Stafford (Johnby Hall, Penrith, Cumbria CA11 0UU), *b* 1937; *ed* Eton, Magdalen Coll, Oxford, and Churchill Coll, Camb: *m* 1966, Phyllis Bethan, da of late Lewis Duckett, of Essex House, Dursley, Glos, and has issue living, Henry James Stafford, *b* 1972, — Cecilia Charlotte, *b* 1968: *m* 1992, Graham David Hewett. —— (By 2nd *m*) (Murray Bernard) Neville Cyprian, OBE (Greystoke Castle, Penrith, Cumbria CA11 0TG), *b* 1942; *ed* Eton, and RMA Sandhurst; Lt-Col Coldstream Gds; OBE (Mil) 1985: *m* 1969, Lavinia Zaria, da of late Lt-Col Philip Lewis (*see* E Dartmouth, colls, 1995 Edn), and has issue living, Alexander Philip Wilder, *b* 1971, — Catherine Anne Cardwell, *b* 1972. —— Amanda Arianwen Cecilia, *b* 1941: *m* 1967, Michael Noel Francis Cottrell, who *d* 1996, of Laurenden Forstal, Challock Lees, Ashford TN25 4AU, son of late Sir Edward Baglietto Cottrell, CBE, and has issue living, Edward Stafford Cyprian, *b* 1969; *ed* RMA Sandhurst: *m* 1995, Louise Mary, da of Paul William Burnand, and has issue living, Felix Michael Wilder *b* 1997, Rufus Guy Stafford *b* 1998, — Philip Howard Edward (92 Ragged Staff Wharf, Queensway Quay, Gibraltar), *b* 1971: *m* 1993, Eugenie Cumming, and has issue living, William Howard Edward *b* 1994, Natasha Mary *b* 1997, — Camilla Mary Josephine, *b* 1973, — Charlotte Lucinda Gracia, *b* 1981. —— Arianwen Catherine Cardwell, *b* (twin) 1942: *m* 1968, Christopher Neville Neve, and has issue living, Thomas Wilder Neville, *b* 1971, — Eleanor Marged Deborah, *b* 1972.

Grandchildren of late Robert Mowbray Howard, 3rd son of late Henry Howard, MP (ante):—

Issue of late Major Henry Ralph Mowbray HOWARD-SNEYD, OBE, *b* 1883, *d* 1950, having assumed by R licence 1950 the additional surname and arms of Sneyd: *m* 1st, 1911 (*m diss* 1931), Helen Millicent, who *d* 1967, da of late William Dodge James, CVO (Forbes, Bt, *cr* 1823); 2ndly, 1931, Janet Emma Jameson (HIBBERT), only da of late John Duthie, of Cults House, Aberdeenshire:—
(By 2nd *m*) Thomas Henry Gavin HOWARD-SNEYD (35 Fursecroft, George St, W1; Brooks's Club), *b* 1940: *m* 1963, Serena Patience, yr da of Thomas Lumley, of Ashcombe House, Lewes, and has issue living, Henry Lyulph, *b* 1965: *m* 1995, Ursula, da of Michael McCarthy, and has issue living, Chiara Zuleika *b* 1997, — Justin Andrew *b* 1966: *m* 1998, Amanda Susannah, da of late Nigel Horton Hastin, and has issue living, Sam Nigel Hurricane *b* 1998, — Antonia Caroline, *b* 1969.
——— (By 1st *m*) Diana Katherine *b* 1913: *m* 1938, Richard Marcus Beresford, who *d* 1968, and has issue living, Christopher Charles Howard (Dryden House, Burton's Way, Chalfont St Giles, Bucks HP8 4BW), *b* 1946: *m* 1973, Philippa Susan Yates, and has issue living, Nicholas Charles Marcus *b* 1979, Antonia Charlotte *b* 1975, Fiona Caroline *b* 1977, — Patricia Mary, *b* 1941: *m* 1st, 1964, (*m diss* 1977), Christopher Arthur Rollo Wells; 2ndly, 1978, Cyril Godfrey Lea, of 59 Ember Lane, Esher, Surrey, KT10 8EF, and has issue living (by 1st *m*), Gavin Marcus *b* 1965: *m* 1996, Melinda Jane Johnson (and has issue living, Tabitha Emily Charlotte *b* 1998), Amanda Clare *b* 1967: *m* 1996, Timothy Wentworth Eyre Evans (and has issue living, Gabriel Wentworth *b* 1997, Montgomery Marcus *b* 1998), — Katherine Anne, *b* 1943: *m* 1st, 1965 (*m diss* 1969), Robert Noel Hutchings; 2ndly, 1969, Jeffrey Osman Streater, of 16 Upstall St, Camberwell, SE5 9JE, and has issue living (by 2nd *m*), Olivia Katherine Nermin *b* 1974. *Residence* – Walnut House, Benefield Rd, Oundle, Peterborough PE8 4EU. ——— Joan Margery, *b* 1921: *m* 1945, Hubert Murray Sturges, and has issue living, William Henry (Lower Tytherly Farm, Hinton Charterhouse, Bath), *b* 1949: *m* 1973, Virginia Mary, da of Cdr R. FitzGerald, DSC, RN (ret), of Crondall, Surrey, and has issue living, Tom Woody *b* 1979, Robin Millie *b* 1977, — Rosemary Jane, *b* 1946: *m* 1st, 1971 (*m diss* 1975), Alastair William MacDonald; 2ndly, 1977 (*m diss* 1988), Simon John Harley Quantock Shuldham; 3rdly, 1993, Timothy Joseph Minett, of Ty-Uchaf, Hebron, Whitland, Carmarthenshire SA34 0XU, and has issue living (by 2nd *m*), Lucinda Clare *b* 1979, Catherine Emma *b* 1981. *Residence* – Springmount, Berwick St John, Shaftesbury, Dorset SP7 OIIQ.

Grandsons of late Henry Howard, MP (ante):—
Issue of late Rt Hon Sir Esme William Howard, GCB, GCMG, CVO, who was *cr Baron Howard of Penrith* 1930 (see that title).

Descendants of late Rt Hon Charles Howard (son of late Sir William Howard, son of late Sir Philip Howard, el son of late Lord William Howard, 2nd son of 4th Duke), who was *cr Earl of Carlisle* 1661 (see that title).

Descendants of late Col Sir Francis Howard, 2nd son of late Lord William Howard (ante):—

Grandchildren of late George Howard, son of late Sir Henry Howard, GCMG, KCB, son of late Sir Henry Francis Howard, GCB, son of Henry Howard, 4th in descent from Col Sir Francis Howard (ante):—
Issue of late Capt Henry Howard, Quarter-Master Corps, US Army, *b* 1907, *d* 1955: *m* 1st, 1928 (*m diss* 1930), Vara, da of William Doherty; 2ndly, 1941, Natalie Bayard, who *d* 1996 (who *m* 2ndly, 1956, Kenneth Douglas Robertson, who *d* 1982), da of late Rev Grenville Merrill, of Merillton, Newport, Rhode Island, USA:—
(By 2nd *m*) George, *b* 1944: *m* 1977, Ilse Bay Tarafa, of Hamburg, Germany. *Residence* – Dorset, Vermont 05251, USA.
——— Natalie Bayard, *b* 1942: *m* 1st, 1967, Peter Alan Gordon, of Montreal, Canada; 2ndly, 1997, William Thompson Baker, Jr, of New York, and has issue living, (by 1st *m*) Jonathan Kingman, *b* 1970. *Residences* – 49 East 86 St, New York, NY 10028, USA; Corby Close, 12 Lukeman Lane, Stockbridge, Mass 01262, USA. ——— Mary Mowbray, *b* 1948: *m* 1978, Robert Charczuk, of New York, and Russia, and has issue living, William George Howard, *b* 1984. *Residence* – West Stockbridge, Mass 01266, USA.

Grandchildren of late Sir Henry Howard, GCMG, KCB, son of Sir Henry Francis Howard, GCB (ante):—
Issue of late Com Henry Mowbray Howard, OBE, *b* 1873, *d* 1953: *m* 1917, Norah Florence Annie, who *d* 1974, da of Maj John Dunlop Watson:—
Henry Edmund, DSC, RN (16 Normandy Court, Station Close, Wickham, Hants PO17 5JZ), *b* 1923; is Capt (ret); 1939-45 War (DSC): *m* 1945, Sheila, yr da of Colin McNab Brown, of Paisley, and has issue living, Henry Colin Francis, MBE, *b* 1947; is Major RM (ret): *m* 1975, Katharine, da of Kenneth Charles Harold Rowe, MBE, JP, and has issue living, Thomas William *b* 1977, Charles Philip *b* 1979, Jane *b* 1982, — Catherine Jane, *b* 1950: *m* 1973, Edward Bruce Williams, of North Corner, Ashford Hill, Berks, and has issue living, Alasdair Edward Bruce *b* 1975, Peter Henry Bruce *b* 1978, Simon Bruce *b* 1982. ——— Joan Cecilia (4 Lansdowne House, Lansdowne Rd, W11), *b* 1917: *m* 1942, Capt Brent Elworthy Hutton-Williams, MBE, who *d* 1989, and has issue living, Christopher Brent (53 Chatsworth Av, Wimbledon, SW20), *b* 1948: *m* 1974, Caroline Oppenheimer, and has issue living, Beatrice Rose *b* 1980, — Charlotte Fiona Janet, *b* 1944: *m* 1st, 1969 (*m diss* 1975), David Fennell; 2ndly, 1975 (*m diss* 19—), Michael Harrison; 3rdly, 1990, John Mather, of 74 Oakley St, SW3, and has issue living (by 1st *m*), Benedict Nicholas *b* 1971 (by 2nd *m*), Toby Lawrence Brent *b* 1978.

(*In remainder to Barony of Beaumont only*)

Issue of late Lady Miriam Fitzalan Howard, 2nd da of Mona Josephine Tempest, Baroness Beaumont (in her own right) (11th holder of the title), *b* 1924, *k* in an accident 1996: *m* 1952, Lt-Cdr Theodore Bernard Peregrine Hubbard, RN (*see* E Lindsey, colls):—
See E Lindsey, colls.

Issue of late Hon Ivy Mary Stapleton, yr da of 10th Baron Beaumont, *b* (*posthumous*) 1895; *d* 1967: *m* 1929, Richard Gerald Micklethwait, who *d* 1976, of Ardsley, Barnsley, Yorks:—
Richard Miles MICKLETHWAIT (Preston Hall, Uppingham), *b* 1934; *ed* Ampleforth, and Ch Ch, Oxford; late Capt Grenadier Guards; DL Leics 1997: *m* 1961, Jane Evelyn, da of late William Melville Codrington, CMG, MC (*see* Codrington, Bt (*cr* 1721), colls), and has issue living, (Richard) John, *b* 1962; *ed* Ampleforth, and Magdalen Coll, Oxford; Business Ed *The Economist* since 1993: *m* 1992, Mrs Fevronia C. Barnard, only da of Michael Read, of Château Rouvres sur Aube,

France, and has issue living, Richard Thomas *b* 1997, Guy William *b* 1999, Edward Hugh *b* (twin) 1999, — William James, *b* 1964: *m* 1999, Alicia Elizabeth, 2nd da of Sir Dallas Edmund Bernard, 2nd Bt. ——— Imogen Mary, *b* 1931: *m* 1961, Maj John Lachlan Macdonald of Tote, of Tote House, Isle of Skye, and 50 Chelsea Park Gdns, SW3, and has issue living, Charles Lachlan, *b* 1964: *m* 1994, Juliet E., da of John Drysdale, of Brill House, Brill, Bucks, and has issue living, Alexander Lachlan *b* 1995, Maximilian John *b* 1996, Geordie Charles *b* 1999, — Andrew Kenneth, *b* 1965, — Lisabel Mary, *b* 1969: *m* 1999, Robert Miles, son of David Miles, of London.

Grandchildren of late John Stapleton, brother of 8th Baron Beaumont:—
Issue of late Bryan Stapleton, *b* 1871, *d* 1941: *m* 1st, 1912, Geraldine Emma, who *d* 1916, da of late Col John
Henry Crowdy, RE; 2ndly, 1918, Ruth Jane, who *d* 1954, da of late Richard James Friel, of Waterford:—
(By 2nd *m*) Thomas, *b* 1920; *ed* Univ Coll, Oxford (BM and BCh, MA, DM); FRCP London; FRACP and MD Sydney; late Capt RAMC. *Residence* - The Foundry Cottage, Lane End, High Wycombe, Bucks HP14 3JS. ——— (By 1st *m*) Anne Dunscomb, *b* 1914: *m* 1940, David Edwyn Clark, who *d* 1987, and has issue living, Anthony Miles Stapleton (317-3176 Plateau Boulevard, Coquitlam, BC, Canada V3E 3J2), *b* 1941; PhD Newfoundland: *m* 1970, Ruth Christine, da of late Rev Frederick Guy Harrison, and has issue living, David Crispin Stapleton *b* 1973 (has issue living (by Jennifer Lee, da of Lloyd King, of 1324 Hornby St, Coquitlam, BC, Canada), Aidan Natis Miles KING *b* 1993), Natasha Alexandra *b* 1971: *m* 1993, Scott Charpentier, — Bryan Stapleton (412 Muritai Rd, Eastbourne, Wellington, NZ), *b* 1944: *m* 1971, Nicolien, da of Leslie Lulofs, of 14 Beaumont Rd, Oaklands, Johannesburg, and has issue living, Graham Leslie *b* 1975, Bronwyn *b* 1972, — Geraldine Anne (Apt 1013, 155 Balliol St, Toronto, Ont, Canada, M4S IC4), *b* 1947. *Residence* - 4/378 Muritai Rd, Eastbourne, Wellington, NZ.

Issue of late Louis Henry Stapleton, *b* 1874, *d* 1949: *m* 1908, Annetta Lima Smith, who *d* 1956, da of late A. Perossi:—
Diana Enid Violet Dorothea, *b* 1911: *m* 1939, Dr Allan William Vaughan Eley, late Major RAMC, who *d* 1965, and has had issue, †Ian Miles Stanley Vaughan, *b* 1944; *ed* Oratory Sch, Woodcote; *d* 1983, — Nigel Louis Allan, *b* 1949; *ed* Oratory Sch, Woodcote, — †Bridget Diana Lilian Annetta, *b* 1940: *m* 1965, Derek Frank Gardner, and *d* 1966. *Residence* - The Cottage, Sonning Common, Oxon.

Grandchildren of late Dr Christopher Robert Stapleton, PhD, 4th son of late Bryan John Stapleton (infra):—
Issue of late Alice Veronica Enid Stapleton, *b* 1912, *d* 1994: *m* 1930, John Tyler Walls, of USA:—
John Tyler WALLS, *b* 1931. ——— Christopher Stapleton WALLS, *b* 1933, — Julian Davis WALLS, *b* 1934. ——— Alice Enid Stapleton, *b* 1941. ——— Naomi Anne, *b* 1947. ——— Collette Aurora, *b* 1948.

Grandchildren of late Cdr Gregory Stapleton, RN, 3rd son of late Bryan John Stapleton, half-brother of 8th Baron Beaumont:—
Issue of late Maj Gregory Joseph Kenneth Stapleton, IA, *b* 1908, *d* 1982: *m* 1945, Margarita (Langton Herring, Weymouth, Dorset), only da of Henry Fitzroy Chamberlayne, of Stonythorpe, Warwick:—
Miles Gregory Rowland (Manor Farm, Pengover, Liskeard, Cornwall), *b* 1948; *ed* Beaumont; formerly Capt Laker Airways; Capt Cyprus Airways: *m* 1973, Delia Felicity Mary, da of Maj Benjamin Harold Dunkey, of 190 Cooden Drive, Bexhill-on-Sea, and has issue living, Zoe Yvonne, *b* 1975, — Margarita Louisa, *b* 1979, — Sarah Jane, *b* 1988.

Issue of late Joseph Mark Hugh Stapleton, *b* 1909, *d* 1967: *m* 1948, Elizabeth (28 Cavendish Rd, Woking, Surrey), da of Sidney M. Vanheems, of Ealing (Papal Chamberlain to Pope Pius XII):—
Elizabeth Mary, *b* 1949: *m* 1973, Michel Paul René Meuret, of 35 Impasse Marcel Aymé, 39000 Lons-le-Saunier, France, and has issue living, Nicolas Mark, *b* 1976, — Caroline Anne, *b* 1982, — Anne-Lise Antoinette, *b* 1985. ——— Anne Mary, *b* 1951: *m* 1983, Hendrich Lattul, of 29 Moorholme, Woking, Surrey, and has issue living, Virginia Helena, *b* 1985, — Tanya Maria, *b* 1989. ——— Monica Mary, *b* 1953: *m* 1980, Thierry René Wertheimer, of 7 rue du May, 60129 Glaignes, Orrouy, France, and has issue living, Christian Simon, *b* 1982, — Francis Mark, *b* 1985, — Mark Alastair, *b* 1988, — Claire Monica, *b* 1987.

Issue of late Marie Josephine Stapleton, *b* 1905, *d* 1983: *m* 1928, Joseph Gregory Littledale, who *d* 1993:—
Gregory Bruno LITTLEDALE, *b* 1932; *ed* Beaumont Coll, Old Windsor; late Royal Fus; Fellow Swimming Teachers' Assocn; Member British Computer Soc: *m* 1st, 1957 (*m diss* 1966), Patricia Jane, da of Leonard Howard, of Dover, Kent; 2ndly, 1969 (*m diss* 1993), Naomi Abigail, da of G. F. A. Martin, and has issue living (by 2nd *m*), Mark Gregory, *b* 1976, — Joanna Kerra, *b* 1973; has issue living, Dale Joshua *b* 1994, Kai Jordan *b* 1998, — Tamsyn Greer *b* 1983. *Residence* - 6B Lyngford Rd, Taunton, Som.

Issue of late Elizabeth Charlotte Josephine Stapleton, *b* 1907, *d* 1995: *m* 1st, 1941, as his 2nd wife, Maj Francis John Angus Skeet, late Royal Dublin Fus, who *d* 1943; 2ndly, 1945, Maj Casimir Paul Francis Rowland William Blennerhasset, who *d* 1994:—
(By 2nd *m*) (*See* Blennerhassett, Bt).

Issue of late Antonia Marianne Angela Winefrede Stapleton, *b* 1911, *d* 1969: *m* 1939, Guy George Morris Pritchett, solicitor, of 7 Flower Walk, Guildford (who *m* 2ndly, 1972, Katherine Mary Elfrida, da of Capt John Alick Woodhouse, CBE, RN):—
Malcolm Morris PRITCHETT (19 Hare Hill Close, Pyrford, Woking, Surrey), *b* 1941; *ed* Beaumont and Imperial Coll, London; Consulting Eng; CEng, FIMM: *m* 1963, Lamorna Jill, da of David Bayly Pike, OBE, of Hailsham, Sussex, and has issue living, Clare Marion, *b* 1965: *m* 1987, Charles Croft, of Brighton, — Karen Fiona, *b* 1967, — Sally Antonia, *b* 1970. ——— Roger Morris (Canopus, 7 Bramerton Lodge, East Hill Lane, Bramerton, Norfolk NR14 7EQ), *b* 1943; *ed* Beaumont Coll; Solicitor: *m* 1st, 1969 (*m diss* 1990), Vivien, da of Francis Brothers, of Guildford; 2ndly, 1990, Magdelene Joanne Esvyra Sylvyra Margrette, da of late S/Ldr Elbert Bendt Dall, and has issue living (by 1st *m*), Rupert Francis Morris, *b* 1974; *ed* Eton, — Emma Caroline *b* 1977. ——— Helen Monica, *b* 1945: *m* 1966, Ian Strickland, FRICS, of 2 Kings Rd, Walton-on-Thames, Surrey, and has issue living, Alexander Peter, *b* 1967, — Matthew Douglas, *b* 1968, — Luke Gregory, *b* 1979, — Natasha Jane, *b* 1970. ——— Antonia Mary, *b* 1947: *m* 1971, Philip Roger Wellesley-Davies, of Manor Cottage, Whitchurch-on-Thames, Oxon RG8 7ET, and has issue living, William George, *b* 1971, — Edward James, *b* 1978, — Henry Charles, *b* 1980, — Antonia Louise, *b* 1975.

Issue of late Anne Penrodas Mary Helen Stapleton, *b* 1914, *d* 1986: *m* 1946, Xavier Philip Mary Spruyt de Bay, who *d* 1983:—
Philip Michael SPRUYT DE BAY, *b* 1950: *m* 1st, 1979 (*m diss* 1988), Lucy Therese Frances, yst da of Air Commodore Noel Holroyd Fresson, DFC, RAF, of Sydenham House, Lewdown, Devon; 2ndly, 1993, Elizabeth Jane Stephenson, da of Lt-Col Anthony Loftus St George Stephenson Clarke, of the Manor House, Seend, Wilts, and has issue living, (by 2nd *m*) Chella Antonia, *b* 1995. *Residence* – 29 Westover Rd, SW18. —— Helen Mary DE BAY (18 Holloway, Bath BA2 4PU), *b* 1947; has resumed her maiden name: *m* 1971 (*m diss* 1996), Jeremy Charles Stewart Fulford Smithies, and has issue living, Roland Jeremy Xavier Spruyt de Bay, *b* 1973, — Frances Mary Barbara, *b* 1976.

PREDECESSORS – (1) *Sir* JOHN Howard, KG, an eminent Yorkist, distinguished himself in the French Wars of Henry VI, and in 1468 was appointed Treasurer of the King's Household; summoned to Parliament of England as *Baron Howard* 1470-83, and 1483 was *cr Earl Marshal of England*, and *Duke of Norfolk* (peerage of England), his son and heir being at the same time *cr Earl of Surrey* (peerage of England); as Earl Marshal he was authorized to bear either in the king's presence or absence a golden staff tipped at each end with black, the upper part thereof to be adorned with the royal arms, and the lower with those of his own family, and to support the dignity a grant was made of £20 a year for ever; was subsequently constituted High Steward of England, and Lord Adm of England, Ireland, and Aquitaine for life; killed at Bosworth Field 1485, and was attainted the same year; *s* by his son (2) THOMAS, KG, 2nd Duke; having been taken prisoner at Bosworth his Earldom was attainted and he suffered imprisonment three years in the Tower; was restored 1489; appointed Lord Treasurer 1501, and in 1513 commanded the English Army at Flodden Field, when the Scots were routed and James IV slain; *cr Earl Marshal* of England (for life) 1510, and *Duke of Norfolk* (peerage of England) 1514; *d* 1524; *s* by his son (3) THOMAS, KG, 3rd Duke; *cr Earl of Surrey* by patent (peerage of England) 1514; was High Admiral 1513, Lord Dep of Ireland 1520, Treasurer of England 1522, Earl Marshal by patent 1533; attainted 1547, imprisoned in the Tower seven years, and restored 1553; *d* 1554; *s* by his grandson (4) THOMAS, KG, 4th Duke (son of Henry, KG, Earl of Surrey, a distinguished statesman, soldier, and poet, who was accused of treason and executed during his father's lifetime 1547; restored in blood 1554: being found guilty of high treason for communicating with Mary, Queen of Scots, he was beheaded 1572, when all his honours were forfeited; *s* by his son (5) PHILIP, who in right of his mother (Mary, da and heir of Henry Fitzalan, Earl of Arundel) as owner of Arundel Castle became (according to the admission of Parliament 1433) 13th *Earl of Arundel* (a feudal honour-peerage of England), and *Baron Maltravers* (peerage of England) 1330 (see † infra); restored in blood 1581; attainted of high treason 1589 and *d* a prisoner in the Tower 1595; *s* by his son (6) THOMAS, KG, 14th Earl, who during the reign of Elizabeth only bore the courtesy title of Lord Maltravers; restored by Act of Parliament 1604 to all the honours and precedence of his father; in 1627 the titles of *Baron FitzAlan, Baron Clun*, and *Baron Oswaldestre* (peerage of England), were annexed by Act of Parliament to the Earldom of Arundel, which peerages were entailed to descend to the heirs male of his body, with remainder to his heirs male, failing which to his heirs general; constituted Earl Marshal 1621, and *cr Earl of Norfolk* 1644; *m* 1606, Alethea, da of 7th Earl of Shrewsbury, becoming in her own right *Baroness Furnivall, Strange of Blackmere and Talbot; d* 1646; *s* by his son (7) HENRY FREDERICK, 15th Earl of Arundel, who had in 1640 been summoned to Parliament of England as Baron Mowbray; *d* 1652; *s* by his el son (8) THOMAS, 16th Earl of Arundel; restored by Act of Parliament 1660 to Dukedom of Norfolk, with precedence of 1st Duke, and in 1661 obtained an Act confirming the same, with remainder to the male issue of his grandfather, and to other collateral branches; *d* unmarried 1677; *s* by his brother (9) HENRY, KG, 6th Duke, who in 1669 had been created *Baron Howard*, of Castle Rising, and in 1672 *Earl of Norwich* (peerage of England), with remainder to various collateral branches, and hereditary *Earl Marshal* of England; was Lord-Lieut of cos Berks and Surrey; *d* 1684; *s* by his son (10) HENRY, KG, 7th Duke; Constable and Gov of Windsor Castle; *dsp* 1701; *s* by his nephew (11) THOMAS, 8th Duke; *dsp* 1732; *s* by his brother (12) EDWARD, 9th Duke; *dsp* 1777, when the Earldom of Norwich and Barony of Howard of Castle Rising expired, the Baronies of Mowbray and Segrave (*see* B Mowbray), and the Baronies of Howard, Braose of Gower, Greystock, Ferrers of Wemme, Talbot, Strange of Blackmere, Furnivall, and Giffard of Brimmesfield fell into abeyance, and the dukedom devolved upon his kinsman (13) CHARLES, 10th Duke, grandson of Charles, 4th son of 15th Earl of Arundel; *d* 1786; *s* by his son (14) CHARLES, PC, 11th Duke; *d* 1815; *s* by his cousin (15) BERNARD EDWARD, KG, 12th Duke, great grandson of Charles Bernard, 8th son of 15th Earl of Arundel; by Act of Parliament 1824 the office of Earl Marshal and Hereditary Marshal of England were empowered to be executed by Roman Catholics; *d* 1842; *s* by his son (16) HENRY CHARLES, KG, 13th Duke; Master of the Horse 1846-52; *d* 1856; *s* by his son (17) HENRY GRANVILLE, 14th Duke; *b* 1815; MP for Limerick 1851-2; assumed by R licence 1842 the additional surname of FitzAlan: *m* 1839, Augusta Mary Minna Catherine, who *d* 1886, da of 1st Baron Lyons; *d* 1860; *s* by his son (18) HENRY, KG, PC, GCVO, 15th Duke, *b* 1847; was Postmaster-Gen Aug 1895 to March 1900, and Lord-Lieut of Sussex 1905-17; received Roy Victorian Chain 1911: *m* 1st, 1877, Lady Flora Paulyna Hetty Barbara Abney-Hastings, who *d* 1887, da of Countess of Loudoun, and of the 1st Baron Donington; 2ndly, 1904, Hon Gwendolen Mary Constable-Maxwell (*Lady Herries of Terregles* in her own right), who *d* 1945, el da of 11th Lord Herries of Terregles; *d* 1917; *s* by his only surviving son (by 2nd *m*) (19) BERNARD MARMADUKE, KG, GCVO, GBE, TD, PC, 16th Duke; *b* 1908; Joint Parl Sec Min of Agric 1941-45; KG 1937, received R Victorian Chain 1953: *m* 1937, Hon Lavinia Mary Strutt, LG, CBE, who *d* 1995, da of 3rd Baron Belper; *d* 1975; *s* by his kinsman (20) MILES FRANCIS, KG, GCVO, CB, CBE, MC, 17th Duke and present peer; also Earl of Arundel (see † infra), Earl of Surrey, Earl of Norfolk, Baron Maltravers, Baron FitzAlan, Baron Clun, Baron Oswaldestre (Oswestry), Baron Beaumont (see * infra), and Baron Howard of Glossop (†† infra).

†According to the claim of John FitzAlan in 1433, which was upheld by the Crown, the Earldom of Arundel was held by tenure of Arundel Castle, Sussex. William de Albini, of Buckenham, Norfolk, acquired Arundel in 1138 on his marriage to Queen Adeliza of Louvain, widow of Henry I, and was recognized from 1139 variously as Earl of Sussex, Chichester, or (more usually) Arundel (1) RICHARD FitzAlan, Lord of Clun and Oswestry, Salop (8th Earl, according to Admission of 1433), grandson of John Fitzalan by Isabel, da of William de Albini, 5th Earl of Arundel and sister and co-heir of Hugh, 6th Earl of Arundel; was summoned to Parliament 1292 as *Earl of Arundel*; served at Carlaverock 1300: *m* before 1285, Alasia di Saluzzo, da of Thomas, Marquis of Saluzzo; *d* 1302; *s* by his son (2) EDMUND, 2nd (or 9th) Earl, *b* 1285: *m* 1305, Alice, da of William de Warenne, and sister and heir of John Earl of Surrey; executed and attainted 1326, when the Castle and Honour of Arundel was granted to Edmund, Earl of Kent, son of Edward I, but in 1331, his son (3) RICHARD, 3rd Earl, was restored in blood; assumed the Earldom of Surrey 1361: *m* 1st, 1321 (annulled 1344) Isabel, da of Sir Hugh le Despencer; 2ndly, 1345, Lady Eleanor, da of Henry, Earl of Lancaster, and widow of John de Beaumont; *d* 1376; *s* by (4) RICHARD, KG, 4th Earl, *b* 1346: *m* 1359, Elizabeth de Bohun, da of William, Earl of Northampton; 2ndly, 1390, Philippa Mortimer, da of Edmund, Earl of March and widow of John Hastings; attainted and executed 1397 when Arundel was granted to John Holand, Duke of Exeter, but in 1400, his son (5) THOMAS, KG, 5th Earl, *b* 1381, was restored to the Earldoms of Arundel and Surrey: *m* 1405, Beatrice, da of John I, King of Portugal; *d* 1415, when representation of the Warennes Earls of Surrey passed to his sister and co-heir, of whom the descendants of the eldest, Elizabeth, Duchess of Norfolk, opposed the claim of the heir male to the Earldom of Arundel; however in 1415 (6) JOHN, *de jure* 6th Earl and Lord Maltravers (§ infra) (grandson of John, 1st Lord Arundel, brother of 4th Earl) *s* to the Castle and Honour of Arundel and said to have been summoned to Parliament as *Earl of Arundel* 1416 but not afterwards: *m* before 1407, Eleanor, da of Sir John Berkeley of Beverstone, Glos; *d* 1421; *s* by his son (7) JOHN, KG, 7th Earl; *b* 1408; Capt of Rouen 1432; his petition to be considered as Earl of Arundel by tenure of Arundel was allowed 1433; *cr Duke of Touraine* (France) 1434: *m* 1st, Constance Cornwall, da of John Lord Fanhope; 2ndly, before 1429, Maud, da of Robert Lovell and widow of Sir Richard Stafford; *d* from wounds at Beauvais 1435; *s* by his son (8) HUMPHREY, 8th Earl; *b* 1429, *d* 1438; *s* by his uncle (9) WILLIAM, KG, 9th Earl, *b* 1417; Warden of Cinque Ports and Constable of Dover Castle: *m* 1438, Joan, da of Richard Nevill, Earl of Salisbury and sister of the Kingmaker; *d* 1487, *s* by his son (10) THOMAS, KG, KB, 10th Earl, *b* 1450; *m* 1464, Margaret Woodville, da of Richard, 1st Earl Rivers; *d* 1524;

s by his son **(11)** WILLIAM, KG, KB, 11th Earl, *b c* 1476; *m* 1st, Elizabeth Willoughby, da of Lord Willoughby de Broke: 2ndly, 1511, Anne Percy, da of 4th Earl of Northumberland; *d* 1534; *s* by his son **(12)** HENRY, KG, PC, 12th Earl, *b* 1512; distinguished at taking of Boulogne; Lord Chamberlain 1546-50, High Constable at Coronations of Edward VI and Mary I: *m* 1st, Catherine Grey, who *d* 1532, da of 2nd Marquess of Dorset; 2ndly, 1545, Mary, da of Sir John Arundell of Lanherne, and widow of Robert Radclyffe, Earl of Sussex; *d* 1580; *s* by his grandson **(13)** PHILIP Howard, 13th Earl (ante).

§**(1)** JOHN Maltravers, *b* about 1290; taken prisoner at Bannockburn 1314; Steward of Household to Edward III 1328; summoned to Parliament 1330, by which he is held to be 1st Lord Maltravers; Keeper of Channel Islands 1348: *m* 1st, Milicent, da of Maurice Lord Berkeley; 2ndly, Agnes, da of William de Bereford of Burton, Leics, and widow of (i) Sir John d'Argentine and (ii) Sir John de Nerford; *d* 1364, when the Barony is held to have fallen into abeyance between the two das of his son John who *d* 1349; on the death sp of the elder about 1397, the surviving **(2)** ELEANOR s: *m* 1st, John, son of Richard FitzAlan, 3rd Earl of Arundel; 2ndly, 1384, Reynold, 2nd Baron Cobham of Sterborough; *d* 1405; *s* by her son **(3)** JOHN, 3rd Baron *b* 1364; not summoned to Parliament: *m* Elizabeth, da of Edward, Baron Le Despencer; *d* 1390; *s* by his son **(4)** JOHN Lord Arundel and Maltravers, who *s* as 6th Earl of Arundel (ante).

***(1)** HENRY de Beaumont, yr son of Louis de Brienne and grandson of John de Brienne, King of Jerusalem, came to England *temp* Edward I and having secured the favour of that monarch obtained high employment from the crown, was rewarded with large territorial grants and made King of the Isle of Man for life; on Mar 4, 1309 he was sworn of the Privy Council and summoned to Parliament as a *Baron of England*: he *m* Alice, da and heiress of Alexander Comyn, Earl of Buchan, in whose right he became Constable of Scotland and was summoned to Parliament (in right of his wife) 1334; *s* by his son **(2)** JOHN, 2nd Baron; summoned to Parliament as a Baron 25 Feb 1342; *d* 1342; *s* by his son **(3)** HENRY, 3rd Baron; *d* 1368; *s* by his son **(4)** JOHN, KG, 4th Baron; summoned to Parliament 1383-93; *d* 1396; *s* by his son **(5)** HENRY, 5th Baron; *d* 1413; *s* by his son **(6)** JOHN, KG, 6th Baron; *cr Viscount Beaumont* 1440, being the first person honoured with the title of Viscount in England; was Lord High Chamberlain of England; *s* by his son **(7)** WILLIAM, 2nd Viscount; *d* 1507, when the Viscountcy expired and the Barony became abeyant between the descendants of his sister Joane and so continued until 1840, when the abeyance was terminated in favour of **(8)** MILES THOMAS Stapleton, of Carlton, co York, 8th Baron; *b* 1805: *m* 1844, Isabella Anne, who *d* 1916, da of 3rd Baron Kilmaine; *d* 16 Aug 1854; *s* by his son **(9)** HENRY, 9th Baron, *b* 1848; present at battle of Ulundi 1879: *m* 1888, Violet, OBE, who *d* 1949, only da of Frederick Wootton Isaacson, MP, of 18 Upper Grosvenor Street, W; *d* 1892; *s* by his brother **(10)** MILES, 10th Baron, *b* 1850; Lieut-Col Comdg 20th Hussars: *m* 1893, Ethel Mary, who *d* 1937, da of Sir Charles Henry Tempest, 1st Bt (*ext*), of Heaton, Lancashire; *d* 1895, when the title remained in abeyance between his two das until 1896, when it was determined in favour of the el da **(11)** MONA JOSEPHINE TEMPEST, OBE, *b* 1894: *m* 1914, 3rd Baron Howard of Glossop (†† *infra*), who *d* 1972; *d* 1971; *s* by her el son **(12)** MILES FRANCIS, KG, GCVO, CB, CBE, MC, 12th Baron, and present peer (also 17th Duke of Norfolk).

††**(1)** *Lord* EDWARD GEORGE Fitzalan-Howard, PC, 2nd son of 13th Duke of Norfolk; *b* 1818; Vice Chamberlain of HM Household 1846-52, and Dep Earl Marshal 1861-3; MP for Horsham (*L*) 1848-52, and Arundel 1852-68; *cr Baron Howard of Glossop* (peerage of UK) 1869: *m* 1st, 1851, Augusta, who *d* 1862, only da and heiress of Hon George Henry Talbot (E Shrewsbury); 2ndly, 1863, Winifred Mary, who *d* 1909, da of Ambrose de Lisle, of Garendon Park, Leics; *d* 1883: *s* by his son **(2)** FRANCIS EDWARD, 2nd Baron, *b* 1859: *m* 1st, 1883, Clara Louisa, who *d* 1887, da of late John Greenwood, MP, of Swarcliffe Hall, Ripley, Yorks; 2ndly, 1891, Hyacinthe, who *d* 1930, da of late William Scott-Kerr, of Chatto and Sunlaws, Roxburghshire; *d* 1924; *s* by his son **(3)** BERNARD EDWARD, MBE, 3rd Baron, *b* 1885: *m* 1914, Mona Josephine Tempest, *Baroness Beaumont* in her own right, who *d* 1971 (ante); *d* 1972; *s* by his el son **(4)** MILES FRANCIS, KG, GCVO, CB, CBE, MC, 4th Baron and present peer (also 17th Duke of Norfolk).

NORMANBY, MARQUESS OF (Phipps) (Marquess UK 1838)

Rest in virtue

CONSTANTINE EDMUND WALTER PHIPPS, 5th Marquess; *b* 24 Feb 1954; *s* 1994; *ed* Eton, and Worcester Coll, Oxford; Co Dir and Author: *m* 1990, Mrs Nicola St Aubyn, yr da of Milton Shulman, and formerly wife of Edward St Aubyn (*see* B St Levan, colls), and has issue.

Arms – Quarterly: 1st and 4th sable, a trefoil slipped within an orle of eight mullets argent *Phipps*; 2nd, paly of six argent and azure, a bend gules, *Annesley*; 3rd, the arms of King James II within a border compony ermine and azure (granted to Lady Catherine Darnley). Crest – A bear's paw erased and armed gules, holding a trefoil as in the arms. Supporters – *Dexter*, an unicorn ermine, armed, unguled, crined, and tufted or, and gorged with a chaplet of roses; *Sinister*, a goat ermine, armed and unguled azure, gorged at the dexter.
Seat – Mulgrave Castle, Whitby, N Yorkshire YO21 3RJ. *Town Residence* – More House, 52 Tite St, SW3 4JA.

SONS LIVING

JOHN SAMUEL CONSTANTINE (*Earl of Mulgrave*), *b* 26 Nov 1994.
Lord Thomas Henry Winston, *b* 1997.

DAUGHTER LIVING

Lady Sibylla Victoria Evelyn, *b* 1992.

BROTHER LIVING

Lord Justin Charles, *b* 1958: *m* 1985, Rachel, da of Charles Stainsby, of The Manse, Chadlington, Oxon, and has issue living, William David, *b* 1990, — Elsie Clare, *b* 1986, — Anna Matilda, *b* 1988, — Katherine Maria, *b* 1991, — Martha Elizabeth, *b* 1996, — Margaret Frances, *b* 1998. *Residence* – Cowbridges, Dean, Oxon OX7 3LB.

SISTERS LIVING

Lady Lepel Sophia, *b* 1952: *m* 1975, Richard Kornicki, and has issue living, Edmund Barnabas, *b* 1976, — Dunstan Benedick, *b* 1977, — Aniela Eurydice Pelagia, *b* 1979.

Lady Evelyn Rose, *b* 1955: *m* 1986, Hon James Ernest Buchan, 3rd son of 3rd Baron Tweedsmuir, and has issue (*see* B Tweedsmuir). *Residence* – 37 Gloucester Crescent, NW1 7DL.

Lady Peronel Katharine, *b* 1959: *m* 1990, Kleber Cruz Jaramillo, son of Jose Domingo Cruz Sarango, of Cruzpamba, Ecuador, and has issue living, Lucas Oswald, *b* 1994, — Mariel Katharine, *b* 1996, — Elena Isabel, *b* 1998. *Residence* – Claymoor Farm, Kettleness, Whitby, N Yorks YO21 2RY.

Lady Henrietta Laura, *b* 1962: *m* 1982, Adam Charles Sedgwick, who *d* 1985, eldest son of late John Humphrey Gerrie Sedgwick.

Lady Anne Elizabeth Grania, *b* 1965.

WIDOW LIVING OF FOURTH MARQUESS

Hon GRANIA MAEVE ROSAURA GUINNESS (*Dowager Marchioness of Normanby*), da of 1st Baron Moyne: *m* 1951, the 4th Marquess of Normanby, KG, CBE, who *d* 1994. *Residence* – Lythe Hall, Whitby, N Yorkshire.

COLLATERAL BRANCHES LIVING

Granddaughters of late Lord Henry George Russell Phipps, 3rd son of 2nd Marquess:—
Issue of late Vivian Louis Augustus Phipps, *b* 1884, *d* 1971: *m* 1921, Marie Elaine, who *d* 1974, da of G. E. Elliott, of the Logan, Qld:—
Maurine Elaine, *b* 1921: *m* 1943, James Fitz-Gibbon Hunter, who *d* 1988, of 43 Lutzow St, Wellers Hill, Qld 4121, and has issue living, Kenneth James (18 Soden St, Yeerongpilly, Qld 4105), *b* 1955: *m* 1985, Sally-Anne Jefferies, and has issue living, James Richard *b* 1989, Gabrielle Jane *b* 1987, — Ross Vivian (30 Hof St, Mount Gravatt East, Qld 4122), *b* 1961: *m* 1996, Nerida Small, — Helen Maurine, *b* 1945: *m* 1966, Anthony Beresford Lewis, BEc, ACA, AASA, of 24 Glen St, Hawthorn, Victoria 3122, Australia, and has issue living, Nicholas Anthony Hunter *b* 1971; BCom, Georgia Helen *b* 1969: *m* 1994, Christopher Charles Hoelter, of Apt 14B Regal Crest, 9 Robinson Rd, Mid Levels, Hong Kong, — Barbara Elaine, *b* 1948: *m* 1st, 1969 (*m diss* 1981), Richard Wilfred Armstrong, BEcon; 2ndly, 1981, Antonio Ammendola, of 814 Hamilton Rd, McDowall, Qld 4053, — Julie Margaret, *b* 1952: *m* 1977, Roger Murray Harcourt, of 1272 Chambers Flat Rd, Chambers Flat, Qld 4133, and has issue living, Andrew Behan *b* 1979, David James *b* 1982, Anthony Roger *b* 1984, Michael Douglas *b* 1986. —— Daphne Margaret, *b* 1929: *m* 1948, Barry E. Valttila, of 3 Michele Place, Turramurra, NSW 2074, and has issue living, Christopher Tony (Box 119 PO, Palm Beach, Queensland 4221), *b* 1953: *m* 1977, Mirja Karina Heimonen, of Helsinki, Finland, and has issue living, Eric Antti *b* 1983, Esa Christian *b* 1978, Elina Carita *b* 1985, Emmanita Aleksandra *b* 1987, — Jan Linda, *b* 1955, — Gaye Helen, *b* 1964.

Grandchildren of late Vivian Louis Augustus Phipps (ante):—
Issue of late Vivian Henry Blakeney Phipps, *b* 1923, *d* 1991: *m* 1944, Elizabeth Catherine (52 Beltana Cres, Buddina, Qld 4575), da of Hubert Franklin Blundell:—
Douglas Vivian (19 Burnett St, Mooloolaba, Qld 4557), *b* 1945: *m* 1st, 1968 (*m diss* 19—), Rosemary Florence McGill; 2ndly, 1980, Robyn Raynor Fraser, and has issue living (by 1st *m*), Justine Danielle, *b* 1969. —— Paul Russell (17 Tallawa Place, Wurtulla, Qld 4575), *b* 1953: *m* 1977, Robyn Faith Binns, and has issue living, Russell Adam, *b* 1980, — Lauren Elizabeth, *b* 1982. —— Catherine Margaret, *b* 1948: *m* 1st, 1969 (*m diss* 1973), — —; 2ndly, 1977, Rolf Christian Schnase, of Kapilano Cres, Mountain Creek, Mooloolaba, Qld 4557, and has issue living (by 1st *m*), Darren DUPREE, *b* 1971, — (by 2nd *m*) Kelly Anne, *b* 1978.

Issue of late Hervey Owen Phipps, *b* 1925, *d* 1982: *m* 1947, Eda Margaret (9 Seaview Terr, Moffatt Beach, Caloundra, Queensland 4551), da of Donald McNab:—
David Owen (4 Ferrar St, Mt Lawley, Perth, W Australia 6050), *b* 1948: *m* 1970, Palma Mary Mammino, and has issue living, Anthony Owen, *b* 1970, — Paul Ryman, *b* 1972. —— John Russell (13 Seaview Terr, Moffat Beach, Caloundra, Qld 4551), *b* 1949: *m* 1972, Elizabeth Gayle Strickland, and has issue living, Elaine Ann, *b* 1973, — Melissa Jane, *b* 1974, — Andra Susan, *b* 1979. —— Wendy Jane, *b* 1950: *m* 1st, 1969 (*m diss* 1981), Michael George Luland; 2ndly, 1981, Roderick Miles Nash, of 6 Greber Rd, Beerwah, Qld 4519, and has issue living (by 1st *m*), Shane Conrad (48 Heidelberg St, E Brisbane, Qld 4169), *b* 1971: *m* 1998, Anita Maree, da of Clive Martin Small, — Christopher Michael, *b* 1973, — Katherine Flavelle, *b* 1974, — (by 2nd *m*) Daniel Owen Miles, *b* 1985, — Emma Jane, *b* 1983. —— Susan Margaret, *b* 1955: *m* 1980, John Francis Miguel, of 38 Peachester Rd, Beerwah, Qld 4519, and has issue living, Benjamin John, *b* 1981, — Anna Jane, *b* 1983.

(*In remainder to the Earldom of Mulgrave only*)

Grandson of late Charles Stewart Phipps (infra):—
Issue of late Charles Francis Douglas Phipps, *b* 1905, *d* 1984: *m* 1935, Kathleen Louise Conlan, who *d* 1982:—
John Douglas Stewart, *b* 1936: *m* 1963, Colleen May, who *d* 1989, da of late James Sinclair Moore, of Cloverdale, BC, and has issue living, Karleen Louise, *b* 1964: *m* 1998, Edward John Zelinski, son of James Zelinski, of London, Ontario, Canada, — Kimberley Ann, *b* 1966, — Kelly Patricia, *b* 1968: *m* 1989, Craig Douglas Ervin, son of Douglas Allan Ervin, of Mission, BC, and has issue living, Kelsey Shaye *b* 1995, Chase Douglas *b* 1997. *Residence* – 2095 Beach Av, Apt 802, Vancouver, BC, Canada V6G 1Z3.

Grandchildren of late Maj Charles Edmund Phipps, son of late Col Hon Sir Charles Beaumont Phipps, KCB, 2nd son of 1st Earl of Mulgrave:—
Issue of late Charles Stewart Phipps, *b* 1871, *ka* 1917: *m* 1902, Edith Annie Webber, who *d* 1946, da of late Capt Francis Douglas:—
Emma Doreen Stewart, *b* 1914: *m* 1st, 1936 (*m diss* 1961), Alvah Robert Hager, who *d* 1988; 2ndly, 1964, Ian Hugh Doughty McDiarmid, of 3770 East Blvd, Vancouver, BC, Canada, and has issue living, (by 1st *m*) Robert Stewart (2706 West 50th Av, Vancouver, BC, Canada V6P 1B7), *b* 1937: *m* 1961, Judith Frances, da of Alvin R. Brown, of Vancouver, BC, and has issue living, Leslie Frances *b* 1965: *m* 1990, James Gregory Carter, of 4489 Harris Place, N Vancouver, BC, Canada (and has issue living, Taylor Howard *b* 1992, Jordan Robert *b* 1995, Alison Frances *b* 1997), Shelley Bronwyn *b* 1967: *m* 1990, Craig Andrew Boyd Ferris, of 2412 W 49th Av, Vancouver, BC, Canada (and has issue living, Jack Brown Hager *b* 1995, Alexander Robert Hager *b* 1997), — Rosemary Douglas, *b* 1941: *m* 1966, Roger Phillip Thomas, of 212-41st St, Manhattan Beach, Cal 90266, USA, and has issue living, Lisa Michelle *b* 1967, Victoria Mary *b* 1970.

Issue of late Albert Edmund Phipps, *b* 1873, *d* 1945: *m* 1899, Sydney Florence, who *d* 1951, da of Washington Boultbee, of Ancaster, Ontario:—
Stewart Beaumont, *b* 1900: *m* 1st, 1921, Frances Peacey Brown-Constable, who *d* 1951; 2ndly, 1952, Edith Patricia Allison, da of late Dr Allison Smith, and has issue living, (by 1st *m*) Barbara Phyllis, *b* 1923: *m* 1946, Thomas H. Gordon, — Diana Averill, *b* 1937: *m* 1958, Willem Otto Jan Groeneveld Meijer, — (by 2nd *m*) Geoffrey Allison, *b* 1953: *m* 1973, Leslie Elizabeth, da of Douglas D. Clarke, of Vic, BC. —— Norman Ernest, QC, *b* 1907: *m* 1944, Dorothy, da of late Albert Edward Kendal-Quarry, and has issue living, David, *b* 1945, — Penelope, *b* 1948: *m* 1972, Barry E. Tobias. —— Phyllis Lepel, *b* 1902: *m* 1925, David Eric Cumberland, who *d* 1964, and has issue living, David Keith, *b* 1930: *m* 19—, Mary Fenn. —— Ruth Audrey, *b* 1910.

Issue of late Augustus Henry Constantine Phipps, *b* 1882, *d* 1946: *m* 1909, Agnes Fraser who *d* 1971, da of late Murdoch Maclachlan, of Kilmun, Scotland:—
Charles Norman, *b* 1912: *m* 1940, Margaret Patricia, da of George F. Saunders, of W Vancouver, British Columbia. —— Harriet Patricia, *b* 1914: *m* 1942, William Henry Brown, who *d* 1971, and has issue living, John Arthur, *b* 1943, — Margaret Evelyn, *b* 1945: *m* 1965, Michael Barclay John Shannon, and has issue living, Michael William *b* 1965.

Grandchildren of late Rt Hon Sir Eric Clare Edmund Phipps, GCB, GCMG, GCVO (infra):—
Issue of late Lt-Col Mervyn Constantine Sanford Phipps, *b* 1912, *d* 1983: *m* 1941, Joyce Kathleen (1 Stalbridge Rd, Stourton Caundle, Sturminster Newton, Dorset), da of John Patrick Goode, of Foxhall, Letterkenny, co Donegal:—
Magdalene Frances, *b* 1942: *m* 1970, Fergus Rogers, of 12 Holly Mount, Hampstead, NW3. —— Caroline Mary, *b* 1943: *m* 1965, José Vives i López, of Sant Pere 15, 4°, Caldetes, Barcelona, Spain, and has issue living, Alexandre Constantine, *b* 1968, — Catalina Rosa, *b* 1965, — Lucieta, *b* 1967, — Marina, *b* 1974. —— Elizabeth Helen (74b Queenstown Rd, SW11), *b* 1945. —— Dorothy Charlotte (1 Stalbridge Rd, Stourton Caundle, Sturminster Newton, Dorset), *b* 1950: *m* 1979 (*m diss* 1982), Jay Patrick O'Boyle, of 11533 19th Av NE, Seattle, Washington 98124, USA, and has issue living, Marlon Orion Sandford, *b* 1982. —— Mary Ann, *b* 1953: *m* 1973, Nicholas Fforde, of 104 Stonefall Av, Starbeck, Harrogate, N Yorks HG2 7NT, and has issue living, Timothy Constantine, *b* 1977, — Emily Frances, *b* 1973, — Sophie Veronica, *b* 1974, — Sarah Maria, *b* 1980.

Issue of late Lieut Alan Phipps, RN, *b* 1915, *ka* in Leros 1943: *m* 1940, Hon Veronica Nell Fraser (*Hon Lady Maclean of Dunconnel*) (who *m* 2ndly, 1946, Sir Fitzroy Hew Maclean of Dunconnel, 1st Bt, KT, CBE, who *d* 1996), da of 15th Lord Lovat:—
Jeremy Julian Joseph, CB, *b* 1942; Maj-Gen The Queen's Own Hussars; CB (Mil) 1997: *m* 1974, Susan Louise, da of Lt-Cdr Wilfrid Hornby Crawford, RN, of Huntington, Haddington, E Lothian, and has issue living, Jake Shimi Alan, *b* 1975, — Jemma Louise Rose, *b* 1977. —— Susan Rose, *b* 1941: *m* 1st, 1959 (*m diss* 1968), Richard St Clair de la Mare (grandson of late Walter de la Mare, OM, CH); 2ndly, 1968 (*m diss* 1986), Derek Marlowe, who *d* 1996, in Los Angeles, Calif; 3rdly, 1986, as his 2nd wife, Nicolas Vincent Somerset Paravicini, of Glyn Celyn House, Brecon, Powys, and has issue living (by 1st *m*), Caspar James, *b* 1962, — Adam John, *b* 1964, — Laura Frances Albinia, *b* 1960: *m* 1992, Henry Alexander Boothby (*see* Boothby, Bt, colls), — Selina-Rose, *b* 1963: *m* 1991, Andrew John Harley, of 290 Portobello Rd, W10, — (by 2nd *m*) Benjamin, *b* 1969.

Grandchildren of late Sir Constantine Edmund Henry Phipps, KCMG, CB, son of late Hon Edmund Phipps, 3rd son of 1st Earl of Mulgrave:—
Issue of late Rt Hon Sir Eric Clare Edmund Phipps, GCB, GCMG, GCVO, *b* 1875, *d* 1945: *m* 1st, 1907, Yvonne, who *d* 1909, da of late Comte de Louvencourt, of 94 Rue de Courcelles, Paris; 2ndly, 1911, Frances Georgina, who *d* 1988, da of late Herbert Ward:—
(By 2nd *m*) John-Francis (43 Leckford Rd, Oxford), *b* 1933: *m* 1st, 1956 (*m diss* 1972), Charm Alys, yr da of Eric Quick; 2ndly, 1975, Rosemary Carol Anne Tecla (*née* Shirtcliffe), and has issue living (by 1st *m*), Jonathan Eric, *b* 1957, — Anna-Rose, *b* 1959, — Isabel Emma, *b* 1961, — (by 2nd *m*), William Donald *b* 1978, — Sophie Sarita Mary, *b* 1976. —— William Anthony Dominic (31 Chepstow Villas, W11), *b* 1936; late Able Seaman, RCN: *m* 1960, Henrietta Frances, da of late Henry Taylor Lamb, MC, RA (*see* E Longford, 1995 Edn), and has issue living, Frederick Fabian Aeneas, *b* 1961, — Samuel Cornelius Dominic, *b* 1964: *m* 1990, Clunie Fiona Mary, yst da of Gen Sir (James) Michael Gow, GCB (*see* Scott, Bt, *cr* 1907, colls), and has issue living, Stella Phoebe Scarlett *b* 1991, — Lucian Percy Denis, *b* 1966, — Theresa Pansy Frances, *b* 1963. —— Mary, *b* 1923: *m* 1949, Bonar Sykes, who *d* 1998, son of late Maj-Gen Rt Hon Sir Frederick Hugh Sykes, GCSI, GCIE, GBE, KCB, CMG, and has issue living, Hugh Bonar, *b* 1950; *ed* Eton, and The Queen's Coll, Oxford: *m* 1st, 1983, Marie-Odile Daulton, who *d* 1985; 2ndly, 1997, Helen Gabrielle Maughan (*née* Green), — David Eric, *b* 1953; *ed* Eton, — James Richard, *b* 1956; *ed* Eton, — Alan Geoffrey (Talkin Head Farm, Brampton, Cumbria), *b* 1960; *ed* Eton, and Univ Coll, London: *m* 1st, 1984 (*m diss* 1989), Kate Judith Hughes; 2ndly, 1989, Harriet Dean, and has issue living, (by 2nd *m*) Roland Charles *b* 1992. *Residence* – Conock Manor, nr Devizes, Wilts. —— Margaret Ann, *b* 1925: *m* 1st, 1949, George Anthony Cary, who *d* 1953; 2ndly, 1956, Donald Struan Robertson, Emeritus Professor of Greek, Camb Univ, who *d* 1961, and has had issue (by 1st *m*) Christopher Alexander George, *b* 1950: *ed* Westminster, and Trin Coll, Camb: *m* 1973, Joanna Buczkowska, and *d* 1983, leaving issue, Catherine Alexandra Joanna *b* 1979. *Residence* – 2 Richmond Rd, Cambridge CB4 3PU.

PREDECESSORS – (1) CONSTANTINE Phipps; *cr Baron Mulgrave*, of New Ross, co Wexford (peerage of Ireland) 1767; *d* 1775; *s* by his el son (2) CONSTANTINE JOHN, PC, 2nd Baron; Capt RN; went a voyage with a view to discover a NE passage; sat as MP for Newark; was Joint Paymaster of the Forces, and Lord of Trade Commn for Indian Affairs; *cr*

Baron Mulgrave, of Mulgrave, co York (peerage of Great Britain) 1790; *d* without male issue 1792, when the English barony became extinct, and the Irish peerage devolved upon his brother **(3)** HENRY, GCB, 3rd Baron; was a Gen in the Army, Col 31st Foot, and Lord-Lieut of E Riding of York, Chancellor of Duchy of Lancaster, Sec of State for Foreign Affairs, and First Lord of the Admiralty; *cr Baron Mulgrave*, of Mulgrave, co York (peerage of Great Britain) 1794, and *Viscount Normanby* and *Earl of Mulgrave* (peerage of United Kingdom) 1812; *d* 1831; *s* by his son **(4)** CONSTANTINE HENRY, KG, GCB, 2nd Earl; *b* 1797; a distinguished statesman and diplomatist; was Gov-Gen of Jamaica 1832-4, Lord Privy Seal 1834, Lord-Lieut of Ireland 1835-9, Sec of State for the Colonies 1839, and for the Home Depart 1839-41, and Ambassador to France 1846-52, and to Court of Tuscany 1854-8; *cr Marquess of Normanby* (peerage of United Kingdom) 1838: *m* 1818, Hon Maria Liddell, da of 1st Baron Ravensworth; *d* 1863; *s* by his son **(5)** GEORGE AUGUSTUS CONSTANTINE, PC, GCB, GCMG, 2nd Marquess, *b* 1819; sat as MP for Scarborough (*L*) 1847-51, and 1852-8; was successively Gov of Nova Scotia, Queensland, New Zealand, and Victoria: *m* 1844, Laura, who *d* 1885, da of late Capt Robert Russell, RN; *d* 1890; *s* by his el son **(6)** *Rev* CONSTANTINE CHARLES HENRY, 3rd Marquess; *b* 1846; V of St Mark's, Worsley, 1872-90, and Canon of St George's Chapel, Windsor 1891-1907: *m* 1903, Gertrude Stansfield, OBE, who *d* 1948, yr da and co-heiress of late Johnston J. Foster, of Moor Park, Ludlow; *d* 1932; *s* by his son **(7)** OSWALD CONSTANTINE JOHN, KG, CBE, 4th Marquess, *b* 1912; Lieut 5th Bn Green Howards, 1939-45 War in France (wounded, prisoner, MBE); PPS to Sec of State for Dominion Affairs 1944-45 and to Lord Pres of the Council 1945, a Lord in Waiting to HM King George VI 1945; Chm King's Coll Hospital 1948-78 (Fellow); Chm Nat Art-Collections Fund 1981-86; Lord Lieut and Custos Rotulorum N Riding of Yorks 1965-74 and N Yorks 1974-87, Pres TA&VR Assocn N England 1971-74 and N Yorks and Humberside 1980-83, Hon Col Cmdt Green Howards 1970-82, High Steward York Minster 1980-88: *m* 1951, Hon Grania Maeve Rosaura Guinness, da of 1st Baron Moyne; *d* 1994; *s* by his elder son **(8)** CONSTANTINE EDMUND WALTER, 5th Marquess and present peer; also Earl of Mulgrave, Viscount Normanby, and Baron Mulgrave.

The Annesley and Darnley quarterings came to this family by the marriage of William Phipps to Lady Catherine Annesley, da and heir of 3rd Earl of Anglesey, by his wife, Lady Catherine Darnley (Duchess of Buckingham), natural da of James II by Catherine Sedley, Countess of Dorchester. William and Lady Catherine Phipps were the parents of 1st Baron Mulgrave.

NORMAND, BARONY OF (Normand) (Extinct 1962)

DAUGHTER LIVING OF LIFE BARON (*By 1st marriage*)

Hon Patricia Drake, *b* 1917: *m* 1948, Douglas William Gourlay, who *d* 1988, and has issue. *Residence* – Goldielea, Dalbeattie Rd, Dumfries.

WIDOW LIVING OF SON OF LIFE BARON

Elizabeth Ann (15 Ravelston Heights, Edinburgh), da of late James Cumming, of Deneholm, Biggar, Lanarkshire: *m* 1945, Hon William Normand, who *d* 1967, and has issue.

NORMANTON, EARL OF (Agar) Sits as BARON SOMERTON (UK 1873) (Earl I 1806)

SHAUN JAMES CHRISTIAN WELBORE ELLIS AGAR, 6th Earl of Normanton, and 9th Baron Mendip; *b* 21 Aug 1945; *s* 1967; *ed* Eton, Capt Blues and Royals; patron of three livings: *m* 1970, Victoria Susan, only da of late John H. C. Beard, and has issue.

Arms – Azure, a lion rampant or. **Crest** – A demi-lion rampant or. **Supporters** – Two lions, the *dexter* per bend, and the *sinister* per bend sinister, or and azure, both plain collared and chained gules, each charged on the shoulder with a crescent.
Seat – Somerley, Ringwood, Hampshire BH24 3PL. *Residence* – Flat 6, 28 Hans Place, SW1. *Clubs* – White's, Royal Yacht Squadron.

The beaten path is the safe path

SON LIVING

JAMES SHAUN CHRISTIAN WELBORE ELLIS (*Viscount Somerton*), *b* 7 Sept 1982.

DAUGHTERS LIVING

Lady Portia Caroline, *b* 1976.
Lady Marisa Charlotte, *b* 1979.

BROTHER LIVING

Hon Mark Sidney Andrew (Bathealton Court, Bathealton, Taunton, Somerset TA4 2AJ), *b* 1948; *ed* Gordonstoun; Lt Blues & Royals: *m* 1st, 1973 (*m diss* 1979), Rosemary, da of Maj Philip Marnham; 2ndly, 1985, Arabella Clare, da of late John Gilbert Gilbey (*see* Barwick, Bt, ext, 1985 Edn), and formerly wife of Thomas Charles Blackwell, and has issue living (by 2nd *m*), Max John Andrew *b* 1986, — Charles Christopher Edward, *b* 1989.

PREDECESSORS – (1) CHARLES AGAR, DD, 3rd son of Henry Agar, MP, and yr brother of James, 1st Viscount Clifden, was successively Dean of Kilmore, Bishop of Cloyne, Archbishop of Cashel, and Archbishop of Dublin and Primate of Ireland; *cr Baron Somerton* (peerage of Ireland) 1795, *Viscount Somerton* 1800, and *Earl of Normanton* (peerage of Ireland) 1806; *d* 1809; *s* by his son (2) WELBORE ELLIS, 2nd Earl; *b* 1778: *m* 1816, Diana, da of 11th Earl of Pembroke; *d* 1868; *s* by his son (3) JAMES CHARLES HERBERT WELBORE ELLIS, 3rd Earl, *b* 1818, MP for Wilton 1841-52: *m* 1856, Hon Caroline Susan Augusta, who *d* 1915, da of 6th Viscount Barrington; *d* 1896; *s* by his el surviving son (4) SIDNEY JAMES, 4th Earl; *b* 1865: *m* 1894, Lady Amy Frederica Alice Byng, who *d* 1961, da of 4th Earl of Stafford; *d* 1933; *s* by his only son (5) EDWARD JOHN SIDNEY CHRISTIAN WELBORE ELLIS, 5th Earl; *b* 1910: *m* 1st, 1937 (*m diss* 1943), Hon Barbara Mary, only da of late Sir Frederick Frankland, 10th Bt, and of Baroness Zouche, and formerly wife of Brig Otho Leslie Prior-Palmer; 2ndly, 1944, Lady Fiona, who *d* 1985, da of 4th Marquess Camden, and formerly wife of Maj Sir (John) Gerard Henry Fleetwood Fuller, 2nd Bt; *d* 1967; *s* by his son (6) SHAUN JAMES CHRISTIAN WELBORE ELLIS, 6th Earl and present peer; also Viscount and Baron Somerton, and Baron Mendip (see * infra).

*(1) *Rt Hon* WELBORE ELLIS, FRS, MP, only surv son of Most Rev Welbore Ellis, Bishop of Meath, was Sec at War 1762-65, Treas of the Navy 1777-82, and Sec of State for America and the Colonies 1782; *cr* 1794, *Baron Mendip*, of Mendip, Somerset (peerage of Great Britain) with remainder to the three el sons of his sister Anne by her husband, Henry Agar, of Gowran: *m* 1st, 1747, Elizabeth, who *d* 1761, da and heir of Hon Sir William Stanhope, KB; 2ndly, 1765, Anne, who *d* 1803, sister and heir of the Rt Hon Hans Stanley; *d* 1802; *s* by his gt-nephew (2) HENRY WELBORE Agar-Ellis, 2nd Viscount Clifden, whose father, James Agar, MP, son of Anne (ante) was Postmaster Gen of Ireland, and was *cr Baron Clifden*, of Gowran, co Kilkenny (peerage of Ireland) 1776, and *Viscount Clifden*, of Gowran (peerage of Ireland) 1781; *b* 1761; MP for co Kilkenny 1783-89; assumed the surname of Ellis by Roy licence 1804: *m* 1792, Lady Caroline Spencer, who *d* 1813, da of 4th Duke of Marlborough; his only son, George James Welbore Agar-Ellis, FRS, MP, was *cr Baron Dover* (peerage of UK) 1831: *m* 1822, Lady Georgiana Howard, who *d* 1860, da of 6th Earl of Carlisle; predeceased him in 1833; *d* 1836; *s* by his grandson (3) HENRY, 3rd Viscount, *b* 1825, who had *s* his father in 1833 as 2nd Baron Dover; Gentleman of the Privy Chamber to the Prince Consort: *m* 1861, Eliza Horatia Frederica, VA (Lady of the Bedchamber to Queen Victoria), who *d* 1896, da of Frederick Charles William Seymour; *d* 1866; *s* by his only son (4) HENRY GEORGE, 4th Viscount; *b* 1863; *d unm* 1895; *s* by his uncle (5) LEOPOLD GEORGE FREDERICK, 5th Viscount, *b* 1829; MP for Kilkenny (L) 1857-74: *m* 1864, Hon Harriet Stonor, who *d* 1914, da of 3rd Baron Camoys; *d* 1899, when the Barony of Dover became ext, and the other honours passed to his kinsman (6) THOMAS CHARLES Agar-Robartes, 2nd Baron Robartes (son and heir of Thomas James Agar-Robartes, who was *cr Baron Robartes*, of Lanhydrock and Truro, Cornwall 1869, son of Hon Charles Bagenal-Agar (who *m* 1804, Anna Maria Hunt, heiress of Lanhydrock, great-niece of Henry Robartes, 3rd Earl of Radnor, Viscount Bodmin, and Baron Robartes of Truro, all of which titles became ext 1757) yst son of 1st Viscount Clifden), 6th Viscount, *d* 1844; Lord-Lieut of Cambs 1906-15, and MP for Cornwall, E (L) 1880-82: *m* 1878, Mary, who *d* 1921, da of late Francis Henry Dickinson, of Kingweston, Som; *d* 1930; *s* by his 2nd son (7) FRANCIS GERALD, KCVO, 7th Viscount, *b* 1883; Counsellor of Embassy, Madrid 1926-27, a Member of Council, Duchy of Cornwall 1939-52, and a Lord-in-Waiting to HM 1940-45; *d* 1966; *s* by his brother (8) ARTHUR VICTOR, MC, 8th Viscount, *b* 1887; Lt Gren Gds; acting Maj Gds Machine Gun Regt in 1914-18 War: *m* 1st, 1920 (*m diss* 1945), Patience Mary, who *d* 1956, da of Arthur Francis Basset (Salusbury-Trelawny, Bt); 2ndly, 1948, Margaret, da of Ray Carter of St Louis, USA, formerly wife of John Harvey Thursky, and widow of John Eaton Monins; *d* 1974, when the Viscountcy and Barony of Clifden, and the Barony of Robartes became ext, and the Barony of Mendip devolved upon (9) SHAUN JAMES CHRISTIAN WELBORE ELLIS Agar, 6th Earl of Normanton (ante).

Norreys of Rycote, Lord, son of Earl of Lindsey and Abingdon.

NORRIE, BARON (Norrie) (Baron UK 1957)

God provides for us

GEORGE WILLOUGHBY MOKE NORRIE, 2nd Baron; *b* 27 April 1936; *s* 1977; *ed* Eton, and RMA; commissioned 11th Hussars, 1956; ADC to C-in-C Middle East Command 1961-62; GSO 3 (Int) 4th Guards' Bde 1967-69; Acting Maj Roy Hussars 1969-70; Dir, Fairfield Nurseries (Hermitage), Ltd, Dir Internat Garden Centre (UK) 1984-86, Dir Hilliers (Fairfield) Ltd 1989, Pres British Trust for Conservation Volunteers since 1987, Dir Conservation Practice Ltd 1988-92, House of Lords European Communities sub Cttee F (Environment) 1988, Vice Pres Council for National Parks since 1990, Vice Pres Tree Council since 1990; Council for National Parks; Pres R British Legion, Newbury Branch 1971-96; Freeman of City of London 1999: *m* 1st, 1964 (*m diss* 1996), Celia Marguerite, da of Maj John Pelham Mann, MC (*see* Mann, Bt, colls); 2ndly, 1997, Mrs Pamela Ann McCaffry, only da of Maj Sir Arthur Ralph Wilmot, 7th Bt, and has issue by 1st *m*.

𝔄rms – Quarterly: 1st and 4th, ermine on a pale gules three helmets argent *Norrie*; 2nd and 3rd, or on a chevron azure between two poplar trees eradicated in chief proper and a mullet of six points in base of the second a key the ward downwards of the first *Moke*. ℭrests – An elephant's head erased sable tusked argent supporting with the trunk a garb or; 2nd, a stag's head couped holding in the mouth a branch of poplar proper between the attires a key as in the arms pendent from a chain or. 𝔖upporters – On either side a dark bay racehorse supporting between the forelegs a frond of New Zealand fern proper.
Residence – Chapel-on-the-Water, Ramsbury, Wilts SN8 2QN. *Clubs* – Cavalry and Guards, MCC, White's.

SON LIVING (By 1st marriage)

Hon MARK WILLOUGHBY JOHN, *b* 31 March 1972: *m* 1998, Carol J., eldest da of Michael Stockdale, of Wetherby, Yorks.

DAUGHTERS LIVING (By 1st marriage)

Hon Clare Marguerite, *b* 1966; *m* 1995, Dr Richard Stanton, son of John Stanton, of Finchley, London.
Hon Julia Jocelyn, *b* 1968: *m* 1998, Oliver C. Skelding, only son of Simon Skelding, of Fulham, SW10.

HALF-BROTHER LIVING

Hon Guy Bainbridge (Old Church Farm, Broughton, Stockbridge, Hants SO20 8AA; Cavalry & Guards', City of London and White's Clubs), *b* 1940; *ed* Eton; Lt-Col (ret) R Hussars; GSO 1 (DS) Staff Coll, Camberley 1977-8; Member HM Body Guard of Hon Corps of Gentlemen at Arms 1990; Dir Wellington Members Agency Ltd 1991-96; Stace Barr Ltd 1996-98; SBA Underwriting Ltd since 1998: *m* 1968, Sarah Georgina, da of Maj George Rudolph Hanbury Fielding, DSO (*see* E Denbigh, colls), and has issue living, Andrew Guy, *b* 1970, — James Adam George, *b* 1973.

SISTER LIVING

Hon Rosemary (*Viscountess Daventry*), *b* 1926: *m* 1959, 3rd Viscount Daventry, and has issue. *Residence* – Temple House, Arbury, Nuneaton, Warwickshire CV10 7PT.

HALF-SISTERS LIVING

Hon Sarah Merryweather, *b* 1943; GGSM: *m* 1974, Charles Lyon Stephenson, TD, of The Cottage, Great Longstone, Bakewell, Derbys (*see* Stephenson, Bt, colls).
Hon Annabel Mary Adelaide (19 Lillyville Rd, SW6 5DP), *b* 1945: *m* 1988, Ian Ronald Malcolm, elder son of late Colin Ronald Malcolm, of Newent, Glos.

WIDOW LIVING OF FIRST BARON

PATRICIA MERRYWEATHER (*Patricia, Baroness Norrie*) (The Old Vicarage, Leckhampstead, Newbury, Berks), da of late Emerson Bainbridge, MP, of Auchnashellach, Ross-shire; DStJ: *m* 1938, as his 2nd wife, the 1st Baron Norrie, who *d* 1977.

PREDECESSOR – (1) *Sir* (CHARLES) WILLOUGHBY (MOKE) Norrie, GCMG, GCVO, CB, DSO, MC, son of Maj George Edward Moke Norrie, Duke of Wellington's Regt; *b* 1893; Lt Gen late 11th Hussars and 10th R Hussars, and Hon Col 10th Inf Bn (The Adelaide Rifles); Comd 1st Armoured Div 1940, and 30 Corps 1941-42; Gov of S Aust 1944-52, and Gov

Gen of NZ 1952-57; Chancellor of Order of St Michael and St George 1960-68; *cr Baron Norrie*, of Wellington, NZ, and Upton, co Gloucester (peerage of UK) 1957: *m* 1st, 1921, Jocelyn Helen, who *d* 1938, da of late Richard Gosling (Dyer, Bt); 2ndly, 1938, Patricia Merryweather (DStJ), da of late Emerson Bainbridge, MP; *d* 1977; *s* by his el son (2) GEORGE WILLOUGHBY MOKE, 2nd Baron and present peer.

North, family name of Earl of Guilford.

NORTH, BARONY OF (North) (Baron E 1554) (Abeyant 1942)

JOHN DUDLEY NORTH, 13th Baron; Lieut RN; *ka* 1941, when the Barony fell into abeyance (see infra).

SISTERS LIVING OF THIRTEENTH BARON (*Co-heiresses to the Barony; raised to the rank of a Baron's daughters 1947*)

Hon DOROTHY ANNE, *b* 4 May 1915: *m* 1st, 1937 (*m diss* 1950), William Robert Alexander Clive Graham, Lieut Sherwood Foresters; 2ndly, 1950, Major John Edward Richard Bowlby, 1st Royal Dragoons (*see* V Valentia, 1985 Edn), and has issue living, (by 1st *m*) Penelope Virginia, *b* 1940, — (by 2nd *m*) Gina Anne, *b* 1954: *m* 1982, Dominic Poole, yr son of Richard Poole, of Ringwood, Hants, and has issue living, Alana *b* 1985, Auriel Martha *b* 1987. *Residence* – 51 Shawfield St, SW3.

Hon SUSAN SILENCE, *b* 19 Jan 1920; assumed by deed poll 1943 the additional surname of Beauchamp: *m* 1944, Frederick Guy Beauchamp, MD, MRCS, who *d* 1981, and has issue living, Susan Donne, *b* 1944: *m* 1965 (*m diss* 1969), Hon Nicholas Charles Cavendish (later 6th Baron Chesham), and has issue living, James North Cavendish *b* 1972, — Sally North, *b* 1945: *m* 1st, 1966 (*m diss* 1967), Michael Robert Parkin; 2ndly, 1973, Bryn Haworth, — Elizabeth Silence, *b* 1950: *m* 1976, Jean-Pierre Guillemet, and has issue living, Lucie Susan Germaine *b* 1977, Alice Elizabeth Felicie *b* 1980.

WIDOW LIVING OF THIRTEENTH BARON

MARGARET, da of R. W. H. Glennie, of Cape Province, S Africa: *m* 1st, 1940, the 13th Baron North, who was *ka* 1941; 2ndly, 1943, Lieut Weldon Bernard James, US Marine Corps. Resides in USA.

COLLATERAL BRANCHES LIVING

Grandchildren of late Hon Roger Archibald Percy North, 2nd son of 11th Baron, *b* 1863, *d* 1907: *m* 1896, Robina Ramsay Walker, who *d* 1937, da of late Edwin Barton, of Wallerawang, NSW:—
Issue of late Lt-Col Roger Edward Francis Guilford North, *b* 1897, *d* 1980: *m* 1st, 1927 (*m diss* 1937), Audrey Edith Durani, who *d* 1957, da of late Mr Justice (Alfred Edward) Martineau; 2ndly, 1939, Isabel Floyd-Jones Carpender Burn, who *d* 1983, da of late Noel Lispenard Carpender, of Long Island, USA:—
(By 1st *m*) Roger Robin NORTH (Vine Cottage, Roseacre Gdns, Chilworth, Guildford, Surrey), *b* 1929; *ed* King's Sch, Canterbury; late Lt RASC and King's African Rifles: *m* 1961, Gillian Mary, yr da of late Lt-Col William Augustus Putnam. —— Desmond Peter (twin) (The Orchard, Hale St, East Peckham, Tonbridge, Kent), *b* 1929; *ed* King's Sch, Canterbury; late Lt RASC; with Colonial Admin Ser, N Nigeria 1951-55: *m* 1960, Amanda Mary, yr da of Philip Henry Bevington Legge, and has issue living, Rupert Caspar Guilford *b* 1964; *ed* Cokethorpe: *m* 1988, Sara Catherine Lucy, da of Peter W. Jackson, of Forest Row, Sussex, and has issue living, Caspar John Guilford *b* 1991, — Jason Edward Guilford *b* 1967; *ed* Sherborne, — Emma Sophie, *b* 1962. —— Neil Dermot (17 Clanricarde Gdns, W2), *b* 1932; *ed* King's Sch, Canterbury. —— (By 2nd *m*) Edward John (Mossberga Rockneby, Sweden), *b* 1940; *ed* Fettes Coll: *m* 1967, Margreth Ekstrom, of Spanga, Sweden, and has issue living, Tom Nicholas, *b* 1971, — Peter James, *b* 1974.

Issue of late Cdr William Frederic George North, RN, *b* 1898; *d* 1977: *m* 1st, 1924 (*m diss* 1949), Hon Dorothy Hennessy, who *d* 1961, da of 1st Baron Windlesham; 2ndly, 1949, Joan Mabel, who *d* 1997, da of late Henry Reginald Fussell, of Southey Hall, Gt Bookham, Surrey, and widow of Wing Cdr Richard Griffith Shaw, of Littlecot, Bartley, Hants:—
(By 1st *m*) Moylena Robin (Sister Frances, Inst of BVM, 30 Constitution Hill, Norwich NR3 4BU), *b* 1925. —— Diana Bridget, *b* 1928: *m* 1st, 1954 (*m diss* 1958), Lt-Col Michael Edward Ovens, MC; 2ndly, 1958 (*m diss* 19—), Afzal Qureshi. —— (By 2nd *m*) (William) Simon Giles (Mossland, Shawford, Winchester), *b* 1950; *ed* Radley: *m* 1980, Angela Joan, da of late John Edward Heslop, of Downs Farm, nr Penarth, S Glamorgan, and has issue living, William James Edward, *b* 1985, — Emma Harriet, *b* 1983. —— Jeremy Frederic George (Eldon House, Eldon Lane, Braishfield, Romsey, Hants), *b* 1952; *ed* Radley: *m* 1985, Helen Suzanna Margaret, da of Sidney James Best, of 3 Norman Rd, St Cross, Winchester, and has issue living, Joseph Frederic Jeremy, *b* 1986, — Benjamin William James *b* 1989.

Grandchildren of late Hon Mina Susan Georgina North, eldest da of 11th Baron:—
Issue of late Dudley Francis North FitzGerald, b 1891, d 1960: m 1921, Hermine, who d 1955, da of late George
Kiely, of Toronto:—
Michael Francis FITZGERALD, b 1921; ed Dartmouth Coll; Lt-Cdr RN; 1939-45 War: m 1943, Anne Lise, da of late Einar
Winther, of Copenhagen, and has issue living, Robin Michael (The Old Baker, 3/5 Silver St, Buxton, Huntingdon,
Cambs), b 1944; ed Downside: m 1969, Allessandra Lyn, da of Cecil Davis, of Richmond, Surrey, and has issue living,
James Dudley b 1972, Sarah Emily b 1974, — Christopher Francis (21 Palace Gdns Terrace, W8), b 1945; ed Downside,
and Lincoln Coll, Oxford (MA): m 1st, 1968 (m diss 1984), Jennifer Georgina, da of George Willis, of Sherborne, Dorset;
2ndly, 1986, Jill, da of late Dr Douglas Freshwater, of Upton-upon-Severn, Worcs, and has issue living (by 1st m),
Matthew Francis b 1973, Francesca Marie b 1975, Julia Louise b 1978, — Mary Anne Lise (104 Merton Hall Rd, SW19),
b 1961; ed Yeovil Coll, and Surrey Univ (BSc), — Emma Theresa b 1967; ed Yeovil Coll, and Balliol Coll, Oxford (MA,
DPhil, MBA): m 1990, David Martin Wheeler, of Pinfold House, Frog Lane, Holt, Clwyd LL13 9HJ. Residence - 36 Lower
Market St, Hove, E Sussex BN3 1AT. —— †Gerald Dudley b 1922; ed Dartmouth Coll; 1939-45 War in RN and as Pilot
RAF: m 1956, Doreen, who d 1969, da of late Alexander Spence Muter, of Middlesbrough, and d 1987, leaving issue,
Susan Hermine (42 Weston Cres, Mount Pleasant, Stockton, Cleveland), b 1957.

Issue of late Col John Sidney North FitzGerald, CVO, MBE, MC, b 1893, d 1976: m 1933 (m diss 1948), Joyce
Mary, da of late Dr Edward William Hedley, MBE, and widow of Thomas Cecil Barber (see Barber, Bt, colls):—
Georgiana Mary, b 1935: m 1956, John Kenneth Humphrey Pettit, JP, of Stepstones, Scotlands Close, Haslemere, Surrey,
and has issue living, Timothy John (Woodend, Bramley, nr Guildford, Surrey), b 1959: m 1987, Susan Julia, da of John
Butterfield, and has issue living, Henry Alexander b 1994, Olivia Georgiana Butterfield b 1990, Annabel Kathleen b 1992,
— Richard Kenneth, b 1963: m 1992, Dyane Lesley, da of Victor Martin Chapman, and has issue living, Charles Edward
b 1995, Isabella Hetty Mary b 1993, — Nicola Susan Mary, b 1957.

Granddaughter (by 1st m) of late Capt Thomas Yates Benyon (infra):—
Issue of late John Wicht Yates Benyon, b 1921, d 1983: m 1966, Joan (9 Avenue Alexandra, Fresnaye, Cape
Town, S Africa), da of W. E. Robertson, of Little Brak, S Africa:—
Kendal Joanna YATES BENYON, b 1968.

Grandchildren of late Hon Christina Philippa Agnes North, OBE, yst da of 11th Baron, b 1869, d 1950,
having m 1st, 1890, Capt Thomas Yates Benyon, formerly 4th Hus, who d 1893; 2ndly, 1903, Col
Alexander Heirom Ogilvy Spence, CIE, CBE, formerly IA, who d 1936:—
Issue of late Capt Thomas Yates Benyon, b (posthumous) 1893, d 1958: m 1st, 1918 (m diss 1928), Louise, who d
1970 da of J. J. Wicht, of Cape Town; 2ndly, 1934, Joan Ida Bishop, da of John Bayley Walters:—
(By 2nd m) Thomas Yates BENYON (The Old Rectory, Adstock, Winslow, Bucks, MK18 2HY; Pratt's Club), b 1942; ed
Wellington Sch, and RMA; late Lt Scots Gds; Chm Milton Keynes Health Authority; MP for Abingdon (C) 1979-83: m
1968, Olivia Jane, yr da of late Humphrey Scott-Plummer, of Mainhouse, Kelso (see B Kinross, 1995 Edn), and has issue
living, Thomas Yates, b 1975, — Oliver William Yates, b 1980, — Clare Julia Yates, b 1969: m 1993, John Robert Hayns,
elder son of D. M. Hayns, of Malpas, Cheshire, and has issue living, Micah Luke b 1997, — Camilla Lucinda Joan Yates,
b 1972: m 1997, Clayton Sinclair, son of W. Sinclair, of Tamahere, NZ. —— Sarah Joan Yates (1 Gladstone Terrace,
Ripon, N Yorks HG4 1PR), b 1936: m 1st, 1956 (m diss 1967), Roy Ramsey; 2ndly, 1967 (m diss 1985), Andrew Harrison,
and has issue living, (by 1st m) David Andrew, b 1960, — Deborah Jacqueline, b 1958, — (by 2nd m) Rachel Sarah, b
1970: m 1995, Dean Gregory, of Scarborough, Yorks, and has issue living, Owen Josef b 1997. —— Belinda Jane Yates,
b 1939: m 1966, John Douglas Lennie, Rosemount, 3 Newbattle Terrace, Edinburgh EH10 4RU, and has issue living,
Joanna Yates, b 1966, — Rosalind Benson, b 1969: m 1992, Kenneth James Wilson, and has issue living, Jennifer Jane b
1997.

Issue of late Christa Marie Margaret Ogilvy Spence, b 1907; d 1982: m 1928, Col Noel Stanley Alington, MC,
late IA, and Foreign and Political Dept, India:—
James Giles Roger ALINGTON (46 Atholl Rd, Camps Bay, Cape Province, S Africa), b 1929: m 1960, Jean Vosloo, da of
Thomas Bell, of Harare, Zimbabwe, and has issue living, Julian Giles, b 1963.

Grandchildren of late Frederick Keppel North, son of Charles North, el son of late Frederick North,
grandson of Fountain North, grandson of Hon Roger North, yst son of 4th Baron:—
Issue of late Roger North, b 1901, d 1985: m 1934, Pamela Susan, who d 1997, da of late Rev Henry William
Leycester O'Rorke, of The Manor House, N Litchfield, Hants:—
Thomas Frederick NORTH (Rougham Hall, King's Lynn, Norfolk), b 1942; ed Eton, and Trin Coll, Camb; barrister-at-law
Inner Temple 1966: m 1974, Sally Catherine, da of late Lt-Col G. M. Strover, of Leigh Delamere House, Leigh Delamere,
Chippenham, Wilts, and has had issue, †Charles, b 1976; d 1993, — Alec Roger, b 1979, — Amy, b 1977, — Sophie, b
1983. —— Valerie Susan (Lady Guinness), b 1937: m 1967, Sir John Ralph Sidney Guinness, of 9 Hereford Sq, SW7, and
has had issue, Rupert Edward Roger, b 1971, — †Peter John Charles, b 1974; d 1978, — Lucy Arabella, b 1970: m 1996,
Olav Ostin, of Mill Farm, Gt Fransham, Norfolk NR19 2JF, only son of late Jacques Ostin, and of Mme Ene Balder, of
Megeve, France, and has issue living, Sigismond Endel b 1998. —— Christine, b 1938: m 1963, Alan Blakemore, of
Hatchford Park Nurseries, Cobham, Surrey, and has issue living, Emily Jasmine Alice, b 1964, — Flora Marianne Sophie,
b 1966, — Lily Isabella Katherine Bonnie, b 1968, — Jessica Mary Cassandra, b 1972. —— Grace Elizabeth, b 1946; BA,
MB, BChir: m 1975, Alan Barlow, of Janet Cottages, Rougham, Norfolk, and has issue living, Edward Francis, b 1978, —
Katherine Clare, b 1980.

Issue of late Charles Percy Frederick North, b 1906, d 1971: m 1937, Judith, who d 1991, da of Harry Leon
Hamlin, of Stoneyhill Farm, Amagansett, Long Island, USA:—
Mary Grace (30 Sutton Place, New York City, NY 10022, USA), b 1939: m 1969, William Ellsworth Clow, who d 1970;
has issue living, Miranda Judith, b 1980. —— Melissa Judith, b 1944: m 1976, Michael Nicholas Edmund Chassay
RIBA, of 17 Powis Terrace, W11, and has issue living, Claney Charles Arcade, b 1980, — Dixie Cleopatra, b 1976.

Granddaughter of late Charles North (ante):—
Issue of late Marjoribanks Keppel North, b 1865, d 1949: m 1905, Edith Beatrice, JP, who d 1973, only da of Sir
George John Armytage, 6th Bt:—
Arabella, b 1909; 1939-45 War as Ch Com ATS: m 1950, Louis Euan Babington Morgan, who d 1978.

Granddaughter of late Marjoribanks Keppel North (ante):—
Issue of late George Montagu North, *b* 1906, *d* 1953: *m* 1940, June Margaret (who *m* 2ndly, 1956, Robert Burton Kenward), da of late Francis Edward Harrison, OBE, of York:—
Lavinia Keppel, *b* 1940: *m* 1970, Peter Jocelyn Jeffries, of Brownings House, Ide Hill, Sevenoaks, Kent TN14 6JT, and has issue living, Charles Jocelyn, *b* 1973, — Alexandra Keppel, *b* 1971.

PREDECESSORS – (1-9) GEORGE AUGUSTUS NORTH, 9th *Baron North*, of Kirtling, co Camb (by writ of summons 1554) and 3rd Earl of Guilford (*see* E Guilford), *b* 1757; *d* 1802, when the Earldom of Guilford devolved upon his brother, and the Barony of North became abeyant, and remained so until 1841, when it was terminated in favour of his 2nd da **(10)** SUSAN; *b* 1797: *m* 1835, Col John Sidney Doyle, MP (who in 1838 assumed the surname of North); *d* 1884; *s* by her son **(11)** WILLIAM HENRY JOHN, 11th Baron, *b* 1836; Bailiff Grand Cross of Sovereign Order of Malta, Pres of that Sovereign Order in Great Britain, and Hon Pres of Committee of Privileges of Maltese Nobility; *m* 1858, Frederica, who *d* 1915, da of Com R. Howe Cockerell, RN; *d* 1932; *s* by his son **(12)** WILLIAM FREDERICK JOHN, 12th Baron, *b* 1860: *m* 1885, Arabella Valerie Keppel, who *d* 1965, da of late Charles North (E Guilford, colls); *d* 1938; *s* by his grandson **(13)** JOHN DUDLEY (son of late Hon Dudley William John North, MC, only son of 12th Baron), 13th Baron, *b* 1917; Lt RN: *m* 1940, Margaret (who *m* 2ndly, 1943, Lieut Weldon Bernard James, US Marine Corps), da of R. W. H. Glennie, of Cape Province, S Africa; *ka* 1941 in HMS *Neptune*, when the Barony again fell into abeyance.

NORTHAMPTON, MARQUESS OF (Compton) (Marquess UK 1812)
(Name pronounced "Cumpton")

SPENCER DOUGLAS DAVID COMPTON, 7th Marquess; *b* 2 April 1946; *s* 1978; *ed* Eton; patron of nine livings; a DL of Northants: *m* 1st, 1967 (*m diss* 1973), Henriette Luisa Maria Bentinck, only da of late Baron Bentinck, Netherlands Ambassador to France; 2ndly, 1974 (*m diss* 1977), Annette Marie, da of Charles Anthony Russell Smallwood; 3rdly, 1977 (*m diss* 1983), Rosemary Ashley Morritt, only da of P. G. M. Hancock, of Truro, and formerly wife of Hon Lionel John Charles Seymour Dawson-Damer (*see* E Portarlington); 4thly, 1985 (*m diss* 1988), Ellen (Fritzi), only da of late Hermann Erhardt, of Munich, and formerly wife of Hon Michael Orlando Weetman Pearson (later 4th Viscount Cowdray); 5thly, 1990, Mrs Pamela Martina Raphaela Kyprios, and has issue by 1st, 3rd and 4th *m*.

Arms – Sable, a lion passant guardant or, between three esquires' helmets argent. **Crest** – On a mount a beacon fired proper, behind it a ribbon inscribed with the words, *Nisi Dominus*. **Supporters** – *Dexter*, a dragon ermine, ducally gorged and chained or; *sinister*, an unicorn argent, horned, maned, hoofed, and tufted sable.
Seats – Castle Ashby, Northampton NN7 1LQ; Compton Wynyates, Tysoe, Warwick CV35 0UD.

SON LIVING (*By 1st marriage*)

DANIEL BINGHAM (*Earl Compton*), *b* 16 Jan 1973.

DAUGHTERS LIVING (*By 1st marriage*)

Lady Lara Katrina COMPTON, *b* 1968; has resumed her maiden name: *m* 1994 (*m diss* 1996), Peter A. Falter, yst son of late Charles Falter, of Hampstead, London.

(*By 3rd marriage*)

Lady Emily Rose, *b* 1980.

(*By 4th marriage*)

Lady Louisa Cecilia, *b* 1985.

BROTHER LIVING

Lord William James Bingham, *b* 1947; *ed* Bryanston: *m* 1st, 1973, Marlene, who *d* 1994, da of late Francis Hosie; 2ndly, 1996, Mrs Sarah Langdale, and has issue living (by 1st *m*), James William, *b* 1974, — Clare Victoria Frances, *b* 1980. *Residence* – Chadstone Old Rectory, Castle Ashby, Northampton NN7 1LH.

SISTERS LIVING

Lady Judith (59 Buckingham Gate, SW1E 6AJ) *b* 1943; *ed* Royal Coll of Music, and London Univ: *m* 1970, Sir Adrian Christopher Swire, and has issue living, Merlin Bingham, *b* 1973, — Samuel Compton, *b* 1980, — Martha Virginia, *b* 1972: *m* 1997, Alexander Peter Allfrey (*see* Fox, Bt, ext 1959).
Lady Elizabeth, *b* 1944; DL Ross and Cromarty, Skye and Lochalsh 1990: *m* 1968, Ian Hamish Leslie Melville, and has issue (*see* E Leven and Melville, colls).

COLLATERAL BRANCHES LIVING

Grandsons of late Lord Alwyne Frederick Compton, DSO, 3rd son of 4th Marquess:—
Issue of late Capt Edward Robert Francis Compton, 2nd Dragoons (R Scots Greys) *b* 1891, *d* 1977: *m* 1st, 1918, Sylvia, who *d* 1950, da of late Lt-Col Alexander Haldane Farquharson (Ross, Bt, *cr* 1672, colls); 2ndly, 1952, Mary Elizabeth, who *d* 1957, da of Sydney Dawson, of Cambridge, and formerly wife of Allen Wilson; 3rdly, 1958, Sallie Whitney, who *d* 1979, da of Dr Leonard Sanford, of New York, and widow of 2nd Baron Sysonby:—
(By 1st *m*) Alwyne Arthur Compton FARQUHARSON OF INVERCAULD, MC (Invercauld, Braemar, Aberdeenshire), *b* 1919; *ed* Eton; Capt R Scots Greys; 1939-45 War (wounded, MC); officially recognised in the surname of Farquharson of Invercauld, and as Chief of Clan Farquharson by warrant of Lord Lyon 1949, and uses his former surname as a third christian name: *m* 1st, 1949, Frances Strickland Lovell (GORDON), who *d* 1991, da of late Robert Pollard Oldham, of Seattle, Washington, USA, and widow of Capt Hon James Henry Bertie Rodney, MC (*see* B Rodney); 2ndly, 1993, Patricia Gabriella Estelle, da of Henry Simms Norman Simms-Adams, of Brancaster Hall, Norfolk, and widow of Nicholas John Dennys Parry de Winton. —— Robert Edward John COMPTON (Newby Hall, Ripon, Yorks), *b* 1922; *ed* Eton; late Maj Coldstream Guards; High Sheriff of N Yorks 1978, and a DL of N Yorks: *m* 1951, Ursula Jane (AITKEN), da of late Maj Robert Orlando Kenyon-Slaney (*see* B Kenyon, colls), and has issue living, James Alwyne (43A Upcerne Rd, SW10; Spilsbury Farm, Tisbury, Wilts SP3 6RU), *b* 1953: *m* 1st, 1980 (*m diss* 1986), Rebecca, only da of Sir Alan Lewis Wigan, 8th Bt, and formerly wife of John Dominic Spearman (*see* Spearman, Bt, colls); 2ndly, 1989, Lady Tania Frances Meade, yr da of 7th Earl of Clanwilliam, and has issue living (by 1st *m*), Philip *b* 1980, Clephane *b* 1983, Lara Ellen *b* 1985, (by 2nd *m*), Frederick Alwyne *b* 1996, Sophie *b* 1993, — Richard Clephane (50 Southerton Rd, W6; The Manor House, Marton-le-Moor, Ripon, N Yorks HG4 5AT), *b* 1957: *m* 1982, Lucinda Jane Astell, yr da of Gerald Arthur Hohler (*see* Stucley, Bt), and has issue living, Orlando Edward de Grey *b* 1986, Ludovic Hugh *b* 1989, Theodosia Alexandra *b* 1992.

Granddaughters of late Lt-Cdr Clare George Vyner, RN, who assumed by Royal Licence the surname of Vyner in lieu of his patronymic (and the arms of Vyner quarterly) 1912, yr son of late Lord Alwyne Frederick Compton, DSO (ante):—
Issue of late Henry Vyner, *b* 1932, *d* 1996: *m* 1st, 1958 (*m diss* 1982), Margaret, only da of late Capt Ralph Heathcote, DSO, RN, of Gressingham, Lancs, and formerly wife of Hon Hugo John Laurence Phillips (later 3rd Baron Milford); 2ndly, 1982, Mrs (Charlotte) Claire Pemberton (Blacklands House, Forton, Chard, Som TA20 2NG), da of late Capt Frederick Harold Deming Courtney:—
(By 1st *m*) Harriet de Grey (8 Palace Gdns Terr, W8 4RP), *b* 1959. —— Violet Elizabeth, *b* 1962: *m* 1995, Richard J. H. Edge, son of Paul Edge, of Woodbridge, Suffolk, and has issue living, George Henry, *b* 1997, — Isobel Rose, *b* 1999.

PREDECESSORS – (1) *Sir* HENRY Compton, Knt, was summoned to Parliament as *Baron Compton*, of Compton, co Warwick (peerage of England) 1566; in 1587 was at the trial of the Queen of Scots, and was one of the principal commanders of the forces that besieged the Earl of Essex; *d* 1589; *s* by his son (2) WILLIAM, KG, 2nd Baron; Lord Pres of the Marches and dominion of Wales, and Lord-Lieut of Warwickshire; *cr Earl of Northampton* (peerage of England) 1618; *d* 1630; *b* by his son (3) SPENCER, KB, 2nd Earl; was Master of the Robes to Charles, Prince of Wales, and a zealous partisan of James I; *k* at battle of Hopton Heath 1642; *s* by his son (4) JAMES, 3rd Earl; an earnest Royalist; sat as MP for Warwickshire 1640-2; was Lord-Lieut of co Warwick, Constable of the Tower of London, and Recorder of Coventry, Tamworth, and Northampton; commanded the Cavalry at first battle of Newbury 1643, and raised the siege of Banbury 1644, etc; *d* 1681; *s* by his son (5) GEORGE, PC, 4th Earl; Constable of the Tower of London, and Lord-Lieut of Warwickshire; bore the King's sceptre and cross at Coronation of William and Mary; *d* 1727; *s* by his el son (6) JAMES, 5th Earl; MP for co Warwick 1710-11, when he was summoned to House of peers in his father's barony of Compton: *m* Elizabeth, in her own right Baroness Ferrers of Chartley, sister and heir of Robert Shirley, Viscount Tamworth; *d* without male issue 1754, when the Barony of Compton devolved upon his da Charlotte (wife of 1st Marquess of Townshend, who also in 1770 inherited from her mother the Baronies of Ferrers of Chartley, Bourchier, Lovaine, and Basset of Drayton), and the Earldom devolved upon his brother (7) GEORGE, 6th Earl; was a Lord of the Treasury 1742; sat as MP for Tamworth 1726-7, and for Northampton 1727-54; *dsp* 1758; *s* by his nephew (8) CHARLES, 7th Earl, son of Hon Charles, MP, 3rd son of 4th Earl; *dsp* 1763; *s* by his brother (9) SPENCER, 8th Earl; sat as MP for Northampton 1761-3; was Lord-Lieut of Northamptonshire, Recorder of Northampton, and a Groom of the Bedchamber; *d* 1796; *s* by his son (10) CHARLES, 9th Earl, *cr Baron Wilmington*, of Wilmington, co Sussex, *Earl Compton*, and *Marquess of Northampton* (peerage of United Kingdom) 1812; *d* 1828; *s* by his son (11) SPENCER JOSHUA ALWYNE, 2nd Marquess; *b* 1790; was Pres of Royal Soc: *m* 1815, Margaret, da of Maj-Gen Douglas Maclean Clephane; *d* 1851; *s* by his son (12) CHARLES, 3rd Marquess; assumed in 1831 by Roy licence the additional and principal surname of Douglas; *dsp* 1877; *s* by his brother (13) WILLIAM, KG, 4th Marquess, *b* 1818; Adm in the Navy; assumed 1851 the additional surname of Maclean, and in 1878 that of Douglas: *m* 1844, Eliza, who *d* 1877, da of late Adm Hon Sir George Elliot, KCB; *d* 1897; *s* by his el surviving son (14) WILLIAM GEORGE SPENCER SCOTT, KG, *b* 1851; Private Sec to Lord-Lieut of Ireland 1880-82 and Lord-Lieut of Warwickshire 1912-13; Special Envoy to Foreign Courts to announce Accession of King George V; MP for Warwickshire, S-W, or Stratford-on-Avon, Div 1885-6, and for Yorkshire, W Riding, S Part, Barnsley Div (*L*) March 1889 to Sept 1897: *m* 1884, Hon Mary Florence Baring, who *d* 1902, da of 2nd Baron Ashburton; *d* 1913; *s* by hs el son (15) WILLIAM BINGHAM, 6th Marquess, DSO, *b* 1885, Maj R Horse Guards; Lt Col Comdg Warwickshire Yeo; a Com of Order of Leopold II of Belgium; CStJ; European war 1914-18 (wounded, DSO 1919): *m* 1st, 1921 (*m diss* 1942), Lady Emma Marjory Thynne, OBE, who *d* 1980, da of 5th Marquess of Bath; 2ndly, 1942 (*m diss* 1958), Virginia Lucie, who *d* 1997, da of late David Rimington Heaton, DSO, of Brockfield, Crownhill, S Devon; 3rdly, 1958, Elspeth Grace, who *d* 1976, el da of late William Ingham Whitaker, DL (V Melville); *d* 1978; *s* by his el son (16) SPENCER DOUGLAS DAVID, 7th Marquess and present peer; also Earl of Northampton, Earl Compton, and Baron Wilmington.

NORTHBOURNE, BARON (James) (Baron UK 1884, Bt GB 1791)

I love for ever

CHRISTOPHER GEORGE WALTER JAMES, 5th Baron, and 6th Baronet; *b* 18 Feb 1926; *s* 1982; *ed* Eton, and Magdalen Coll, Oxford (MA), FRICS; patron of two livings: *m* 1959, Marie Sygne, el da of Henri Louis Claudel, of Chatou-sur-Seine, and has issue.

Arms – Gules, a dolphin embowed or. **Crest** – An ostrich argent, beaked and legged or. **Supporters** – Two eagles argent, collared gules; each having pendant from the collar a shield charged with the arms. *Seat* – Coldharbour, Northbourne, Deal, Kent. *Residence* – 11 Eaton Place, SW1. *Clubs* – Brook's, Royal Yacht Sqdn.

SONS LIVING

Hon CHARLES WALTER HENRI, *b* 14 June 1960, *ed* Eton, and Magdalen Coll, Oxford: *m* 1987, Catherine Lucy, only da of W. Ralph Burrows, of Prescot, Lancs, and has issue living, Henry Christopher William, *b* 3 Dec 1988, — Alexander Oliver Charles, *b* 1996, — Anastasia Aliki, *b* 1992. *Residence* – Northbourne Court, Northbourne, Kent CT14 0LW.
Hon Anthony Christopher Walter Paul, *b* 1963, *ed* Eton, and Magdalen Coll, Oxford: *m* 19—, Johnina Macdonald. *Residence* – Evistones, Otterburn, Northumberland.
Hon Sebastian Richard Edward Cuthbert, *b* 1966, *ed* Eton, Magdalen Coll, Oxford, and INSEAD Fontainebleau: *m* 19—, Anna Gregory.

DAUGHTER LIVING

Hon Ophelia Mary Katherine Christine Aliki, *b* 1969; *ed* St Mary's Ascot, King's Sch Canterbury, and Exeter Univ.

SISTERS LIVING

Hon Gwenllian Ellen, *b* 1929: *m* 1st, 1952 (*m* annulled 1960), Michael Hugh Rose (infra); 2ndly, 1960, Thomas Jeffrey Hemsley, of 10 Denewood Rd, Highgate, N6, and has issue living, (by 2nd *m*) William Thomas James, *b* 1962, — Matthew Walter David, *b* 1963, — Michael Richard, *b* 1965.
Hon Elizabeth Sarah, *b* 1933: *m* 1960, Michael Edward Willis Fleming, and has issue living, John Michael, *b* 1961: *m* 1997, Rachel Jane, only da of Rear Adm Hubert Walter Elphinstone Hollins, CB, of Waunllan, Llandyfriog, Newcastle Emlyn, Cardiganshire, — Penelope Katherine, *b* 1965: *m* 1990, Jaume Simon Gispert, son of Luis Simon Gispert, of Barcelona, and has issue living, Luc *b* 1995, Sara *b* 1990. *Residence* – Little Betteshanger, Betteshanger, Deal, Kent.
Hon Susan Jane, *b* 1936: *m* 1961, Michael Hugh Rose (ante), of Le Sirondole, Panzano-in-Chianti (Florence), Italy, son of late Rt Rev Alfred Carey Wollaston Rose, formerly Bishop of Dover, and has issue living, Michael Justin, *b* 1966, — Nell Susanna, *b* 1961, — Emma Katherine, *b* 1963, — Sophy Elizabeth, *b* 1969.
Hon Katherine Viola, *b* 1940: *m* 1963, John Wharton Hersey, and has issue living, Robert Alexander, *b* 1964, — John Paul, *b* 1966, — Daniel Anthony James, *b* 1971. *Residence* – Thorneyburn Old Rectory, Tarset, Northumberland.

WIDOW LIVING OF SON OF SECOND BARON

Lady Serena Mary Barbara Lumley, da of 10th Earl of Scarbrough: *m* 1923, as his 2nd wife, Hon Robert James, who *d* 1960, and has issue living (see colls, infra). *Residence* – St Nicholas, Richmond, Yorkshire.

COLLATERAL BRANCHES LIVING

Grandchildren of late Lt-Col Hon Cuthbert James, CBE, MP (infra):—
Issue of late Thomas James, *b* 1906, *d* 1976: *m* 1st, 1932 (*m diss* 1940), Lady Germaine Elizabeth Olive Eliot, who *d* 1991, da of 8th Earl of St Germans; 2ndly, 1940 (*m diss* 1953), Julia Mary, who *d* 1974, da of late Charles Solomon, of 36 Queen's Grove, St John's Wood, NW; 3rdly, 1953, Rosemary Heartsease Beare, who *d* 1979, da of late Maj George Frederick Crisp Molineux-Montgomerie (see D Beaufort, colls, 1976 Edn), and widow of Capt Reginald Dilworth Howard, RN:—
(By 2nd *m*) Antony Nigel (18 Toorang Av, N Balwyn, Victoria 3104, Australia), *b* 1944; *ed* Dover Coll, and in France: *m* 1973, Therese Macormack, of Melbourne, Aust, and has issue living, Alexander Robert, *b* 1974, — Charles Henry Thomas, *b* 1976, — Francesca Danielle, *b* 1980. —— Georgina Mary, *b* 1948: *m* 1972, Christopher Watts, of 45 Woodley Lane, Cuppernham, Romsey, Hants, SO5 8JR, and has issue living, Ian Charles, *b* 1973, — Mark Andrew, *b* 1976.

Issue of late Lt-Col Hon Cuthbert James, CBE, MP, 2nd son of 2nd Baron, *b* 1872, *d* 1930: *m* 1905, Florence Marion, who *d* 1933, da of late Hussey Packe (E Kimberley):—
Joan Rosamund, *b* 1917: *m* 1949, Maj Launcelot James Francis Brydon, and has issue living, Robert Alexander (49 Melody Rd, SW18 2QW), *b* 1954; *ed* Stowe: *m* 1983 (*m diss* 1987), Francesca Camilla Roberta Ierne, da of Henry John William Phillips, of 46 Hornton St, W8 (see B Hothfield, 1985 Edn), and has issue living, Lara Daisy Edina Charlotte *b* 1984, — Nadia Mary BRYDON, *b* 1952; has resumed her maiden name: *m* 19— (*m diss* 19—), Sol Alan Saad. *Residence* – The Village House, Brasted, Kent TN16 1HU.

Granddaughter of late Hon Robert James (infra):—

Issue of late Arthur Walter James, b 1904, d 1981: m 1st, 1929 (m diss 1932), Zita Mary, da of Nico Jungman; 2ndly, 1932, Mary, who d 1976, yr da of late Albany Hawke Charlesworth, and formerly wife of late Lionel Cyril Gibbs:—
(By 2nd m) Lucinda Evelyn, b 1933: m 1st, 1953 (m diss 1967), Andrew Duff Tennant (see B Glenconner, colls); 2ndly, 1967, Rupert Oliver Steel, of Winterbourne Holt, Newbury, Berks, and has issue living (by 1st m) (see B Glenconner, colls), — (by 2nd m) James Oliver, b 1971, — Emily Jane, b 1970: m 1998, Edward Henry Duff Andrewes, son of William Andrewes, of Lindridge Priory, Tenbury Wells, Worcs.

Issue of late Hon Robert James, 3rd son of 2nd Baron, b 1873, d 1960: m 1st, 1900, Lady Evelyn Kathleen Wellesley, who d 1922, da of 4th Duke of Wellington; 2ndly, 1923, Lady Serena Mary Barbara Lumley (ante), da of 10th Earl of Scarbrough:—
(By 2nd m) Ursula Mary-Rose (Baroness Westbury), b 1924: m 1947, 5th Baron Westbury. Residence – Barton Cottage, Malton, Yorks. —— Serena Fay, b 1929: m 1955 (m diss 1963), Colin Griffith Campion, and has issue living, Marcus Robert Guy, b 1961: m 19— (m diss 1998), — Georgina Serena, b 1955: m 19— (m diss 1997), ... Ratcliff, — Christina Fay CAMPION, b 1957; has resumed her maiden name: m 1977 (m diss 19—), William J. Martin, — Meriona Patricia, b 1958: m 1983 (m diss 1995), John R. C. Armstrong. Residence – St Nicholas Cottage, Richmond, Yorks.

Issue of late Hon Wilfrid James, 4th son of 2nd Baron, b 1874, d 1908: m 1900, Margaret Anne, who d 1957, da of John Stogdon:—
Henry Norman, b 1903: m 1st, 1933 (m diss 1946), Constance Margaret, only da of Capt J. D. Macdonald, of Bucklebury Place, Woolhampton, Berks; 2ndly, 1946, Kathleen Mary, who d 1959, da of late Charles William Hewtson; 3rdly, 1967, Marjorie, da of late Charles William Hewtson, and has issue living, (by 2nd m) John Henry (Woodlands Farm, Adisham, nr Canterbury, Kent), b 1947; ed King's Sch, Canterbury: m 1970, Karen Lesley, da of Fl Lt Leslie A. Montgomery, MBE, of Ickwell Green, Biggleswade, Beds, and has issue living, Nicholas John b 1976, Lisa Maria b 1973, — Margaret Anne, b 1950: m 19—, — Speer, of New Mexico, USA. Residence – Woodlands, Adisham, nr Canterbury, Kent.

PREDECESSORS – (1) Sir WALTER JAMES Head, 2nd son of Sir Thomas Head (Knt), of Langley Hall, Berks; was sometime Warden of the Mint; assumed in 1778 by Act of Parliament the surname of James only, and in 1791 was cr a Baronet; d 1829; s by his grandson (2) Sir WALTER CHARLES, 2nd Baronet (son of late John James, Minister Plenipotentiary to the Netherlands); b 1816; MP for Hull (C) 1837-47; cr Baron Northbourne, of Betteshanger, co Kent (peerage of United Kingdom) 1884: m 1841, Sarah Caroline, who d 1890, da of Cuthbert Ellison, of Hebburn Hall, Durham; d 1893; s by his son (3) WALTER HENRY, 2nd Baron; b 1846; MP for Gateshead (L) 1874-93: m 1868, Edith Emmeline Mary, who d 1929, da of late John Newton Lane, of King's Bromley Manor, Lichfield; d 1923; s by his son (4) WALTER JOHN, 3rd Baron, b 1869: m 1894, Laura Gwenllian, who d 1952 (having m 2ndly, 1935, William Curtis Green, RA), da of late Adm Sir Ernest Rice, KCB, of Sibertswold Place, Kent; d 1932; s by his son (5) WALTER ERNEST CHRISTOPHER, 4th Baron, b 1896: m 1925, Katherine Louise, JP, who d 1980, da of George A. Nickerson, of Boston, Mass, USA; d 1982; s by his son (6) CHRISTOPHER GEORGE WALTER, 5th Baron and present peer.

NORTHBROOK, BARON (Baring) (Baron 1866, Bt GB 1793)

By uprightness and labour

FRANCIS THOMAS BARING, 6th Baron and 8th Baronet; b 21 Feb 1954; s 1990; ed Winchester, and Bristol Univ: m 1987, Amelia Sarah Elizabeth, elder da of Dr Reginald David Taylor, of Hursley, Winchester, and has issue.

Arms – 1st and 4th, azure, a fesse or, in chief a bear's head proper, muzzled and ringed of the second differenced by a portcullis azure. Baring; 2nd and 3rd, gules, a cross patée fitchée or between three fish hauriant argent within an orle of eight cross-crosslets of the second, Herring. Crest – A mullet erminois, two of the points resting on the pinions of a pair of wings conjoined and elevated argent. Supporters – On either side a bear proper, muzzled and charged on the shoulder with a portcullis or.
Address – c/o House of Lords, SW1.

DAUGHTERS LIVING

Hon Arabella Constance Elizabeth, b 1989.
Hon Venetia Harriet Anne, b 1991.
Hon Cosima Evelyn Maud, b 1994.

SISTERS LIVING

Hon Laura Anne, b 1952: m 1982, Ewen Cameron Stewart Macpherson, eldest son of late Brig George Philip Stewart Macpherson, OBE, TD, of The Old Rectory, Aston Sandford, Bucks, and has issue living, James Francis Stewart, b 1983, — George Malcolm Stewart, b 1985. Residence – The Old Rectory, Aston Sandford, nr Aylesbury, Bucks.
Hon Alexandra Grace, b 1957: m 1981, (Philip) Strone (Stewart) Macpherson, yr son of late Brig George Philip Stewart Macpherson, OBE, TD (ante), and has issue living, Philip Strone Alexander Stewart, b 1985, — Temora Anne, b 1988, — Clementina Grace, b 1989. Residence – Armsworth Park House, Old Alresford, Hants SO24 9RH.
Hon Catherine Margaret, b 1965: m 1992, (Edward) Sherard (Bourchier) Wrey, yr son of Sir (Castel Richard) Bourchier Wrey, 14th Bt, and has issue (see that title). Residence – East Stratton House, nr Winchester, Hants.

AUNT LIVING *(daughter of 5th Baron)*

Hon Anne (Westwood, W Meon, Petersfield, Hants), *b* 1917.

WIDOW LIVING OF FIFTH BARON

ROWENA MARGARET *(Rowena, Baroness Northbrook)*, da of late Brig-Gen Sir William Henry Manning, GCMG, KBE, CB: *m* 1951, the 5th Baron Northbrook, who *d* 1990.

COLLATERAL BRANCHES LIVING *(In remainder to Baronetcy only)*

Grandchildren of late Godfrey Nigel Everard Baring, 4th and yst son of late Thomas Charles Baring, MP, elder son of Rt Rev Charles Baring, DD, Bishop of Durham, 4th and yst son of 2nd baronet:—
    Issue of late Desmond Charles Nigel Baring, *b* 1914, *d* 1991: *m* 1938, Mary Eileen, JP, who *d* 1998, da of Benjamin Walter Warner:—
PETER (Dower Cottage, Ardington, Wantage, Oxon), *b* 12 Sept 1939; *ed* Eton: *m* 1973, Rose, da of George Nigel Adams, of Fernham Manor, Faringdon, Oxon, and has issue living, Samuel Nigel, *b* 1987, — Mark George, *b* 1990. —— Nigel (The Lodge, Ardington, Wantage, Oxon), *b* 1940; *ed* Eton: *m* 1968, Jane Finola, elder da of Francis Byrne, of 76 Rivermead Court, Hurlingham, SW6, and has issue living, Lorne Benjamin Nigel, *b* 1970; *ed* Eton, and RMA Sandhurst, — Edward Francis Desmond, *b* 1972, — Lucinda Anne, *b* 1980. —— (Margaret) Anne, *b* 1944: *m* 1976, Hugh Barkly Gonnerman Dalgety, of Millards Hill House, Trudoxhill, Frome, Som, and has issue living, Richard Hugh, *b* 1977, — Thomas Arthur, *b* 1984, — Katherine Anne, *b* 1979.

Descendants of late Rt Hon Alexander Baring, DCL (2nd son of Sir Francis Baring, 1st Bt), who was *cr Baron Ashburton* 1835:—
See that title.

Descendants of late Lieut-Gen Charles Baring, eldest son of late Henry Bingham Baring, MP, eldest son of late Henry Baring (*d* 1848), 3rd son of Sir Francis Baring, 1st Bt:—
See Baring, Bt.

Descendants of late Edward Charles Baring, 5th son of late Henry Baring (*d* 1848) (ante), who was *cr Baron Revelstoke* 1885:—
See that title.

Grandchildren of late Thomas Baring, 8th son of Henry Baring (*d* 1848) (ante):—
    Issue of late Richard Baring, *b* 1902, *d* 1940: *m* (1 Jan) 1922, Violetta Archer, who *d* 1931; 2ndly, 1932, Margaret, who *d* 1974, da of Henry Thomas Sutton, of Zanesville, Ohio, USA:—
(By 1st *m*) Cecilia Maureen Anne (105 Canfield Gdns, NW6 3DY), *b* (Oct) 1922.

    Issue of late Edward Thomas Baring, *b* 1903, *d* 1980: *m* 1st, 1926 (*m diss* 1949), Virginia, da of John Barry Ryan, of New York; 2ndly, 1950, Pauline Alison, da of late Frank Fawcett Copland, of Sydney, and formerly wife of Timothy Walter Boden:—
(By 1st *m*) Thomas Michael, TD (Westhay House, Axminster, Devon EX13 5XH), *b* 1927; Lt-Col Derbyshire Yeo; Comdg Leics and Derbys Yeo: *m* 1st, 1953 (*m diss* 1965), Hon Sarah Katherine Elinor Norton, da of 6th Baron Grantley, and formerly wife of 3rd Viscount Astor, 2ndly, 1966, Gillian Ann Rosemary, da of Arthur Rupert Woolley, DSO, OBE, of Tisbury, Wilts, and formerly wife of John Graham, and has an adopted son (from 1st *m*), Edward Richard Philip, *b* 1962: *m* 1996, Marianne V., yst da of Lawrence Stanton, and has issue living, James Edward *b* 1997, Emily Sarah *b* 1998, — and issue living (by 2nd *m*), Constance Nina, *b* 1970. —— (Edward) Patrick (Oriel House, Church Rd, Pimperne, Dorset DT11 8UB), *b* 1932: *m* 1960, Antonia Miriam, da of late Anthony Wentworth Guinness, of Stoke House, Stoke Albany, Market Harborough, Leics, and has issue living, Anthony Shawn, *b* 1961: *m* 1991, Kirsty A., yst da of Sidney Edmond Jocelyn Ackland (the actor Joss Ackland), — Jonathan Patrick Fortune (49D New King's Rd, SW6), *b* 1965: *m* 1994, Lady Elizabeth Clementine Ogilvy, yst da of 13th Earl of Airlie, KT, GCVO, PC, and has issue living, Samuel Fortune Patrick *b* 1995, — Sonya Hermione, *b* 1963, — Lucita Catherine Marianne, *b* 1968. —— Christopher John (6 Charter Oak Lane, Greenwich, Conn 06830, USA), *b* 1939: *m* 1971, Katherine Gayle, da of Lee Warren Jones, of Dayton, Ohio, USA.

Descendants of late Rt Hon Sir Evelyn Baring, GCB, OM, GCMG, KCSI, CIE, 9th son of late Henry Baring (*d* 1848) (ante), who was *cr Earl of Cromer* 1901:—
See that title.

Grandchildren of late Maj Francis Charles Baring, elder son of late William Henry Baring, only son of late William Baring, MP, 4th and yst son of late Sir Francis Baring, 1st Bt:—
    Issue of late Major Thomas Esmé Baring, OBE, *b* 1882, *d* 1957: *m* 1913, Deirdré Mary Hughes, who *d* 1973, da of Hughes Martin, JP, formerly of Tullaghreine, Carrigtwohill, co Cork:—
Maurice Bingham, TD, *b* 1916; *ed* Eton, and at Magdalene Coll, Camb (BA 1939, MA 1949); is Capt Rifle Bde (TA): *m* 1941, (Loveday) Anne Monica who *d* 1997, da of late Capt John Tillie Coryton (V St Vincent, colls), and has issue living, Lynda Anne (16 Cambridge St, SW1), *b* 1944: *m* 1967, Clive Edward Theo Corke, and has issue living, Philip Clive *b* 1979, Shauna Bingham *b* 1972, Anthea Lynda *b* 1973, — Shirley Bingham (Binghams, Culmer Lane, Wormley, nr Godalming, Surrey GU8 5SP), *b* 1948: *m* 1991, Andrew David Johnstone. *Residence* – Culmer House, Wormley, nr Godalming, Surrey. —— Hugo Charles, MBE, MC, *b* 1919; *ed* Eton, and at Magdalene Coll, Camb; formerly Maj Rifle Bde; 1939-45 War in Middle East and Italy (despatches, MC, MBE); MBE (Mil) 1945: *m* 1946, Elisabeth Price, who *d*

1977, only da of late Maj John Price Wylie, DSO, Sherwood Foresters, and has issue living, Anthony Hugo (7, 574 New South Head Rd, Point Piper, NSW 2027, Australia), *b* 1947; *ed* Eton: *m* 1976, Anne Crerar, da of late Stuart G. MacGillivray, of Australia, and has issue living, Nicholas Anthony *b* 1979, Jessica Emily *b* 1977, Eloise Annabelle *b* 1982, — Michael William, *b* 1950; *ed* Eton: *m* 1974, Fayne Smith, and has issue living, Christopher William *b* 1977, Tanya Elizabeth *b* 19—. *Residence* – Koromiko Station, Gladstone, nr Masterton, Wairarapa, NZ.

Issue of late Arthur Francis Charles Baring, *b* 1887, *d* 1964: *m* 1906, Margaret McIntyre, who *d* 1966, da of late George Moore, of Adelaide, S Australia:—
†Ian Douglas, *b* 1915: *m* 1937, Doris Mary Emily Luckhurst, who *d* 1984, and was *k* in a motor accident 1969, leaving issue, Douglas Sydney (10 Bennett Av, Heathmont, Victoria 3135, Australia), *b* 1938: *m* 1960, Jean Melville Leslie, and has issue living, David Ian Alan *b* 1963: *m* 1987, Lisa Joanne Chapman (and has issue living, Trent Andrew Jesse *b* 1990, Joshua David *b* 1992), Jeanette Anne *b* 1965: *m* 1987, Keven Anthony Beekman (and has issue living, Ashley Stewart *b* 1991, Laura Rhiannon *b* (twin) 1991). —— Evelyn Charles, *b* 1924: *m* 1951, Joan Margot Winter, and has issue living, Peter Charles, *b* 1952: *m* 19—, Marie Bernadette Maloney, and has issue living, Eliot FitzRoy *b* 1985, Alexander St John *b* 1989, — Graham John (107 Argyle St, St Kilda, Victoria 3182, Australia), *b* 1954: *m* 1992, Ingrid Frances Draeger, and has issue living, Isabella Tess *b* 1993, — Rodney Alan, *b* 1958: has issue living (by Fredariki Josephine Alsop), Oscar Alan *b* 1989. —— Jean Margaret, *b* 1922: *m* 1944, Arthur Gilmour Lees, of 5/4 Broad St, Labrador, Queensland 4215, Australia, and has issue living, Suzanne Leonie Margaret (23 Scala St, London W1), *b* 1949; has issue living, Alexander Lees FAWDREY *b* 1989, Sophie Serena Lees FAWDREY *b* 1992, — Judith Anne, *b* 1951: *m* 1991, Adnan Rashed, of 4/72 Burfitt St, Leichhardt, NSW 2040, Australia.

Issue of late Major Dudley William Baring, Hampshire Regt, and RASC, *b* 1892, *d* 1952: *m* 1919, Cecilia Mary, who *d* 1971, da of late Col Michael Rowan Gray Buchanan, OBE, of Ettrickdale, Isle of Bute (M Bute, colls):—
Francis William, VRD and bar, *b* 1920; *ed* Bradfield Coll; Cdr RNR; 1939-45 War: *m* 1967, Elsie Violet, RD, only da of late William Charles Redding. *Residence* – 71 Clarence Gate Gdns, NW1 6QR.

Grandchildren of late Major Dudley William Baring (ante):—
Issue of late Lieut-Com Michael John Baring, RN, *b* 1921, *d* 1955: *m* 1946, Pamela Anne (The Yews, Swarraton, Alresford, Hants) (who *m* 2ndly, 1959, Capt John Ridgeway Berridge Longden, RN (ret)), da of late Col Frederick Adolphus Fleming Barnardo, CIE, CBE, BSc, MD, MRCP, FRCS:—
†Jeremy Michael Stuart, *b* 1948; *ed* Wellington Coll; *dunm* 1982. —— (Angela) Jane, *b* 1946: *m* 1st, 1969 (*m diss* 1991), William George Stirling Home Drummond Moray (*see* D Buccleuch, colls, 1995 Edn); 2ndly, 1997, Simon G. F. Cox, of Farthinghoe, Northants, and has issue living (by 1st *m*), Anne Christian, *b* 1971, — Frances Tara, *b* 1974, — Georgina Jane, *b* 1979.

PREDECESSORS – **(1)** FRANCIS Baring, MP for Grampound 1784-90, for Calen 1796-1802, and for Chipping Wycombe 1802-6; was an eminent London merchant, and a Director of the HEIC 1779-92, and Chairman thereof 1792-3; *cr* a *Baronet* 1793: *m* 1767, Harriet, da and co-heiress of William Herring, of Croydon, cousin and co-heiress of Thomas Herring, Archbishop of Canterbury; *d* 1810; *s* by his son **(2)** *Sir* THOMAS, 2nd Bt; sat as MP for Chipping Wycombe 1806-31; *d* 1848; *s* by his son **(3)** *Sir* FRANCIS THORNHILL, 3rd Bt; *b* 1796; sat as MP for Portsmouth 1826-65; was Chancellor of the Exchequer 1839-41, and First Lord of the Admiralty 1849-52; *cr Baron Northbrook*, of Stratton, co Hants (peerage of United Kingdom) 1866: *m* 1st, 1825, Jane, who *d* 1838, da of Hon Sir George Grey, 1st Bt; 2ndly, 1841, Lady Arabella Howard, who *d* 1884, da of 1st Earl of Effingham; *d* 1866; *s* by his son **(4)** *Rt Hon* THOMAS GEORGE, GCSI, DCL, LLD; *b* 1826; *cr Viscount Baring* and *Earl of Northbrook* (peerage of United Kingdom) 1876; a Lord of the Admiralty 1857-58, Under-Sec for War 1861, for India 1861-64, and for Home Depart 1864-66, Sec to Admiralty 1866, Under-Sec for War 1868-72, Gov-Gen of India 1872-6, and First Lord of the Admiralty 1880-85; Lord-Lieut of Hampshire; MP for Penryn and Falmouth (*L*) 1857-66; *m* 1848, Elizabeth Harriet, who *d* 1867, da of late Henry Charles Stuart, of Crichel House Dorset; *d* 1904; *s* by his son **(5)** FRANCIS GEORGE, 2nd Earl, *b* 1850; MP for Winchester (*L*) 1880-85, and for N, or Biggleswade, Div of Bedfordshire (LU) 1886-92; ADC to his father when Gov-Gen of India 1873-6; High Steward of Winchester and Freeman of that City: *m* 1st, 1894, Ada Ethel Sophie, who *d* 1894, da of Col C. Davidson, CB; 2ndly, 1899, Florence Anita Eyre, CBE, who *d* 1946, da of late Eyre Coote, of West Park, Hants, and widow of Sir Robert John Abercromby, 7th Bt; *d* 1929, when the Earldom and Viscountcy became ext, and the Barony of Northbrook devolved upon his cousin **(6)** FRANCIS ARTHUR (son of late Hon Francis Henry Baring, 3rd son of 1st Baron), 4th Baron; *b* 1882: *m* 1st, 1914, Evelyn Gladys Isabelle, who *d* 1919, da of late John George Charles, of 39 St George's Rd, SW1 (*see* M Sligo, 1919 Edn); 2ndly, 1941, Constance Maud, who *d* 1976, da of late Frank Griffin, of Kew Gardens, Surrey; *d* 1947; *s* by his son **(7)** FRANCIS JOHN, 5th Baron, *b* 1915: *m* 1951, Rowena Margaret, da of late Brig-Gen Sir William Henry Manning, GCMG, KBE, CB; *d* 1990; *s* by his only son **(8)** FRANCIS THOMAS, 6th Baron and present peer.

NORTHCHURCH, BARONY OF (Davidson) (Extinct 1985)

SONS AND DAUGHTERS OF LIFE BARONESS

See V Davidson.

Northcote, family name of Earl of Iddesleigh.

NORTHESK, EARL OF (Carnegie) (Earl S 1647)
(Name pronounced "Carneggie")

Spot without stain

DAVID JOHN MACRAE CARNEGIE, 14th Earl; *b* 3 Nov 1954; *s* 1994; *ed* Eton: *m* 1979, Jacqueline May, elder (adopted) da of David Lorne Dundas Reid, of Quinta das Murtas, Rua Eduardo van Zeller, Sintra 2710, Portugal (*see* Reid, Bt, colls), and has issue.

Arms – Quarterly; 1st and 4th, or, an eagle displayed azure, armed, beaked and membered sable and (*as an Honourable Augmentation*) charged on the breast with a naval crown of the field; 2nd and 3rd, argent, a pale gules (*Earldom of Northesk*). Crests – 1st, the stem of a battleship of the line with three lanthorns all proper, inflamed gules; 2nd, issuant from a naval crown or a demi-leopard proper holding a rose argent, barbed and seeded vert. Supporters – two leopards reguardant proper gorged of three (visible) roses argent, barbed and seeded vert, and each leopard sustaining a banner of Saint George. Mottoes – (over the first crest) "Trafalgar"; (over the second crest) "Britannia Victrix"; (below the compartment) "Tache Sans Tache".

SON LIVING

ALEXANDER ROBERT MACRAE (*Lord Rosehill*), *b* 16 Nov 1980.

DAUGHTERS LIVING

Lady Sarah Louise Mary, *b* 1982.
Lady Fiona Jean Elizabeth, *b* 1987.
Lady Sophie Margaret Jean *b* 1990.

SISTERS LIVING

Lady Karen Jean, *b* 1951: *m* 1977, Hon Patrick Vavasseur Fisher, of Kilverstone Hall, Thetford, Norfolk IP24 2RL, and has issue (*see* B Fisher, *cr* 1909).
Lady Mary Barbara, *b* 1953: *m* 1977, William Patrick Stirling Damerell, of Hatchery House, Barrow, Bury St Edmunds, Suffolk, and has issue living, Charles, *b* 1980, — Thomas *b* 1982, — Robert, *b* 1985.

AUNT LIVING (*Daughter of 12th Earl*)

Lady Susan Jean, *b* 1930: *m* 1955, David Blackall Connell, MD, BS, of Lower Wreyland, Lustleigh, Newton Abbot, Devon TQ13 9TS, and has issue living, Timothy Robert, *b* 1956: *m* 1st, 1983 (*m diss* 19—), Susanne HAMMER-JENSEN, da of Fru Birthe Jensen, of Hadsund, Denmark; 2ndly, 1997, Terttu, da of Dr Rauno Heikinheimo, of Tampere, Finland, and has issue living, (by 1st *m*) Simon *b* 1984, Emilie *b* 1987, (by 2nd *m*) Oskar *b* 1998, — Alistair Douglas, *b* 1960: *m* 1995, Karen, da of C. Ashton, of Upper Hutt, New Zealand, — Caroline Lisa, *b* 1958: *m* 1980, David John Wilson, of Duchy Home Farm, Broadfield Farm, Tetbury, Glos, eldest son of Rev John Wilson, of Netherton, Peterborough, and has issue living, Seth Thomas David *b* 1982, Luke Alexander *b* 1984, Joshua Peter Arthur *b* 1987, Benjamin Montague *b* 1990.

WIDOW LIVING OF THIRTEENTH EARL

BROWNIE ELIZABETH (*Dowager Countess of Northesk*), da of John Scott Grimason, and widow of Carl L. Heimann: *m* 1989, as his 2nd wife, the 13th Earl of Northesk, who *d* 1994. *Residence* – 7 Church St, SW6 3LD.

COLLATERAL BRANCHES LIVING

Granddaughters of late Isabella Eliza Butter CARNEGY OF LOUR, da of late Patrick Carnegy, CIE, son of late Maj-Gen Alexander Carnegy, CB, 2nd son of late Patrick Carnegy of Lour (*b* 1757), great-grandson of Hon Patrick Carnegie of Lour, 3rd son of 2nd Earl:—
Issue of late Lt-Col Ughtred Elliott Carnegy CARNEGY OF LOUR, DSO, MC, *b* 1886, *d* 1973: *m* 1919, Violet, MBE, who *d* 1965, da of late Henry William Henderson, of West Woodhay House, Newbury, Berks:—
Elizabeth Patricia CARNEGY OF LOUR (*Baroness Carnegy of Lour*), *b* 1925; *cr* Baroness Carnegy of Lour 1982 (see that title). ——— Christian Margaret (*Lady Smith*), *b* 1927: *m* 1952, Sir John Lindsay Eric Smith, CH, CBE, FRIBA, of Shottesbrooke Park, White Waltham, Berks, and has had issue, Adam Carnegy Eric, *b* 1953; *ed* St Catherines Coll, Oxford, RAC, and Western Seminary, Sacramento, Calif: *m* 1983, Katherine, da of Herbert McDuffee, of Shingle Springs, California, USA, and has issue living, Spencer McDuffee *b* 1984, Arthur James Yeshua *b* 1987, Joseph Oswald Eric *b* 1990, — Bartholomew Evan Eric, *b* 1955: *m* 1987, Catherine Nicola Blanche, da of Gavin Rowan Hamilton, of Stenton, E

Lothian (see Blakiston, Bt, colls), and has issue living, Matthew John Patrick b 1988, Thomas Oswald Rowan b 1994, Oliver b 1996, Emily (Millie) Blanche Christian b 1989, — Emma Victoria Eric, b 1956; ed St Anne's Coll, Oxford; d 1983, — Serena Mary (Hon Mrs Nicholas Soames), b 1959; ed St Anne's Coll, Oxford: m 1993, as his 2nd wife, Hon (Arthur) Nicholas Winston Soames, eldest son of Baron Soames (Life Baron), and has issue (see that title), — Clare Elizabeth Dido, b 1962; ed St Anne's Coll, Oxford: m 1996, Simon Robert Alexander Sheffield (see Sheffield, Bt), and has issue (see that title).

      Grandchildren of Col Charles Gilbert Carnegy, MVO, el son of late Maj-Gen Alexander Carnegy, CB (ante):—
        Issue of late Rev Canon Patrick Charles Alexander Carnegy, b 1893, d 1969: m 1928, Joyce Eleanor who d 1995, da of late W. Percy Townsley, of Roundhay, Leeds:—
Patrick Charles (5 The Causeway, Elsworth, Cambridge), b 1940; ed Rugby and Trin Hall, Camb (MA). —— Colin David (The Parsonage, Stapleford, Salisbury, Wilts), b 1942; ed Rugby and Jesus Coll, Oxford (MA): m 1973, Rosemary Frances Deschamps, da of Saunders Edward Chamier, of Wadhurst, Sussex, and has issue living, Charles Alexander, b 1975, — Edward William, b 1977, — Francis Henry, b 1981, — Henrietta Claire, b 1983. —— Daphne Joyce (4 Ingram Rd, N2), b 1947; ed Nottingham Univ (BA).

      Granddaughter of late Rev Preb Frederick William Carnegy, 3rd son of late Gen Alexander Carnegy, CB (ante):—
        Issue of late Hector David Carnegy, LRAM, b 1913, d 1982: m 1942, Pamela Alice Burnell (9 Browning Av, Bournemouth, Dorset BH5 1NR), da of Henry Stafford Burnell Tubbs, of Winteradeen, Browning Av, Boscombe, Dorset:—
Alison Sandra Christabel, b 1944. Residence – 9 Browning Av, Bournemouth, Dorset BH5 1NR.

      Grandson of late James Souter Carnegy (infra):—
        Issue of late Colin Charles Macpherson Carnegy, b 1885, d 1931: m 1922, Mary Teresa, da of Michael Diaz Infante, of Léon, Mexico:—
†Charles William, b 1923; d 1978. Residence – Guadalajara, Mexico.

      Grandchildren of late Charles Carnegy, yst son of Patrick Carnegy of Lour (b 1757) (ante):—
        Issue of late James Souter Carnegy, b 1847, d 1915: m 1877, Jean Joyce, who d 1923, da of late Hon Charles Macpherson, of New Brunswick:—
James William Macpherson, b 1893. —— Marguerite Sophia Macpherson: m 1910, James Henry Nelson, who d 19—. Residence – Guadalajara, Mexico.

        Issue of late Robert Bower Carnegy, b 1849, d 1936: m 1896, Fanny Jane, who d 1949, da of T. A. H. Dodd, formerly of Newcastle-upon-Tyne:—
†Francis Anthony Roberts, b 1900; m 1925, Valentine, who d 1969, da of Theodore Taupmann, and d 1996, having had issue, †Derek Francis, b 1928; Lt-Cdr RN (ret); m 1961, Judith, who d 1991, only da of late David C. Herbert, and d 1993, leaving issue, Miles Bower b 1962, Angus (3 Hockley Cottages, Cheriton, Hants) b 1964; MB BS: m 1992, Mary-Ann Benson, da of late Ronald Benson Malam, — Julian Roy (66 Cromford Way, New Malden, Surrey), b 1931: m 1957, Vivien, da of late Stewart Kay-Menzies, and has issue living, Christopher Roy b 1961, Diana Elizabeth b 1959: m 1st, 1983 (m diss 1986), David John Burchell; 2ndly, 1990, Adrian John Kill (and has issue living (by 2nd husband), Jonathan Douglas b 1991, Christopher David b 1991, Nicola Grace b 1988, Rebecca Maria b 1993). Residence – Greathed Manor, Lingfield, Surrey.

PREDECESSORS – (1) Sir JOHN Carnegie, Knt, Sheriff of Forfarshire, was cr Lord Lour 1639, and Earl of Ethie 1647, which titles after the Restoration he exchanged for those of Lord Rosehill and Inglismaldie, of Rosehill, and Earl of Northesk (peerage of Scotland), with precedence in 1639 and 1647 respectively, and with remainder to heirs male and of entail in his estate; d 1667; s by his son (2) DAVID, 2nd Earl; d 1677; s by his son (3) DAVID, 3rd Earl; d 1688; s by his son (4) DAVID, PC, 4th Earl, a Representative Peer, Lord of Police, and Sheriff of co Forfar; d 1729; s by his el son (5) DAVID, 5th Earl; d unmarried 1741; s by his brother (6) GEORGE, 6th Earl; an Adm of the White; d 1792; s by his son (7) WILLIAM, GCB, 7th Earl; a distinguished Adm, who was 3rd in command at the memorable battle of Trafalgar; d 1831; s by his son (8) WILLIAM HOPETOUN, 8th Earl; b 1794; m 1843, Georgina Maria, da of late Adm Hon Sir George Elliot, KCB (E Minto); d 1878; s by his son (9) GEORGE JOHN, 9th Earl, b 1843; a Representative Peer for Scotland: m 1865, Elizabeth, who d 1933, da of late Adm Sir George Elliot, KCB; d 1891; s by his el son (10) DAVID JOHN, 10th Earl, b 1865; a Representative Peer for Scotland: m 1894, Elizabeth Boyle, who d 1950, da of late Maj-Gen George Skene Hallowes: d 1921; s by his son (11) DAVID LUDOVIC GEORGE HOPETOUN, 11th Earl, b 1901; a Representative Peer for Scotland 1959-63: m 1st, 1923 (m diss 1928), Jessica, da of late F. A. Brown, of USA; 2ndly, 1929, Elizabeth, who d 1991, da of late Anthony A. Vlasto, formerly of Binfield Park, Bracknell, Berks, d 1963; s by his kinsman (12) JOHN DOUGLAS (son of late Lt-Col Hon Douglas George Carnegie, 2nd son of 9th Earl), 12th Earl; b 1895; 1914-18 War as Maj RFA (despatches): m 1920, Dorothy Mary, who d 1967, da of Col Sir William Robet Campion, KCMG, DSO (B Byron); d 1975; s by his yr son (13) ROBERT ANDREW, 13th Earl, b 1926; Cattle Breeder, Council Member British Charolais Cattle Soc, Author of Dairy of an Island Glen: m 1st, 1949, Jean Margaret, who d 1989, yr da of Capt John Duncan George MacRae (see M Bristol, 1985 Edn); 2ndly, 1989, Mrs Brownie Elizabeth Heimann, da of John Scott Grimason, and widow of Carl L. Heimann; d 1994; s by his only surv son (14) DAVID JOHN MACRAE, 14th Earl and present peer.

NORTHFIELD, BARON (Chapman) (Life Baron 1975)

(WILLIAM) DONALD CHAPMAN, son of William Henry Chapman; *b* 25 Nov 1923; *ed* Barnsley Gram Sch, and Emmanuel Coll, Camb (MA); Snr Scholar of Emmanuel Coll Research into Agric and Econs, Camb 1943-46; Camb City Councillor 1945-47; Gen Sec Fabian Soc 1948-53; G Gibbon Fellow, Nuffield Coll, Oxford 1971-73; Visiting Fellow Centre for Contemporary European Studies, Univ of Sussex since 1973; Chm of HM Development Commnrs 1973-79, and of Telford New Town Development Corpn 1975-87; MP for Northfield Div of Birmingham (*Lab*) 1951-70; *cr* Baron Northfield, of Telford in co Shropshire (Life Baron) 1975.
Address – c/o House of Lords, SW1.

Northington, Baron; title of Baron Henley on Roll of HL.

Northland, Viscount; son of Earl of Ranfurly

NORTHUMBERLAND, DUKE OF (Percy) (Duke GB 1766, Bt E 1660)

Hope in God

RALPH GEORGE ALGERNON PERCY, 12th Duke, and 15th Baronet; *b* 16 Nov 1956; *s* 1995; *ed* Eton, and Ch Ch Oxford: *m* 1979, (Isobel) Jane Miller, da of John Walter Maxwell Miller Richard, of Edinburgh, and has issue.

ᴁrms – Quarterly: 1st and 4th grand quarters, 1st and 4th counterquartered 1st and 4th or, a lion rampant azure; 2nd and 3rd gules, three lucies hauriant argent, *Lucy*; 2nd and 3rd azure, five fusils conjoined in fesse or, *Percy*; 2nd and 3rd grand quarters quarterly 1st and 4th or, three bars wavy gules, *Drummond*; 2nd and 3rd or, a lion's head erased within a double treasure flory counterflory gules, *Drummond, coat of augmentation.* Ꞓrest – On a chapeau gules, turned up ermine a lion statant, the tail extended, azure. Ꮪupporters – *Dexter*, a lion rampant azure; *sinister*, a lion rampant guardant or, ducally crowned of the last, gorged with a collar compony argent and azure.
Seats – Alnwick Castle, Northumberland NE66 1NQ; Syon House, Brentford, Middx TW8 8JF.

SONS LIVING

GEORGE DOMINIC (*Earl Percy*), *b* 4 May 1984; Page of Honour to HM 1996-98; *ed* Eton.
Lord Max Ralph, *b* 1990.

DAUGHTERS LIVING

Lady Catherine Sarah, *b* 1982.
Lady Melissa Jane, *b* 1987.

BROTHER LIVING

Lord James William Eustace, *b* 1965; *ed* Eton, and Bristol Univ. *Residence* – Linhope Lodge, Powburn, Alnwick, Northumberland NE66 4LZ.

SISTERS LIVING

Lady Caroline Mary, *b* 1947: *m* 1974, Count Pierre de Cabarrús, and has issue living, Chiara Thérèse Cecilia, *b* 1974, — Diana Marie, *b* 1977. *Residence* – Syon House, Brentford, Middx TW8 8JF.
Lady Victoria Lucy Diana, *b* 1949: *m* 1975 (*m diss* 19—), (John) Aidan Cuthbert (*see* Milnes Coates, Bt), and has issue

living, David Hugh, b 1987, — Alice Rose, b 1978, — Lucy Caroline, b 1982, — Mary Belinda, b 1984. *Residence* – Abbey-lands, Alnwick, Northumberland NE66 2JY.

Lady Julia Helen, b 1950: m 1983, Nicholas Robert Craig Harvey (*see* B Somers, colls, 1985 Edn), and has issue living, Christopher Hugh, b 1988, — Georgina Elizabeth, b 1986, — Laura Mary, b 1992. *Residence* – The Lainston Dairy, Spar-sholt, nr Winchester, Hants SO21 2LR.

AUNT LIVING (*Daughter of 8th Duke*)

Lady Elizabeth Ivy, OBE (*Dowager Duchess of Hamilton and Brandon*), b 1916; was a Train Bearer to The Queen at Coronation of King George VI; Chm of Lamp of Lothian Collegiate Trust since 1967, Board of Govs, Yehudi Menuhin Sch 1969-89, and Exec Cttee of Friends of St Mary's; DL E Lothian 1984-89; OBE (Civil) 1988: m 1937, 14th Duke of Hamilton and Brandon, who d 1973. *Residence* – North Port, Lennoxlove, Haddington, E Lothian.

WIDOWS LIVING OF SONS OF EIGHTH DUKE

Hon Clayre Campbell, 2nd da of 4th Baron Stratheden and Campbell, CBE, and formerly wife of Hon Nicholas Ridley, MP (later Baron Ridley of Liddesdale, PC) (*see* V Ridley): m 1979, as his 2nd wife, Lord Richard Charles Percy, who d 1989. *Residence* – 212 Lambeth Rd, SE1 7JY.

Mary Elizabeth, da of Ralph Lea: m 1955, Lord Geoffrey William Percy, who d 1984, and has issue (see colls, infra). *Residence* – Barton House, Monkleigh, Bideford, N Devon EX39 5JX.

WIDOW LIVING OF TENTH DUKE

Lady Elizabeth Diana Montagu Douglas Scott (*Dowager Duchess of Northumberland*), da of 8th Duke of Buccleuch: m 1946, the 10th Duke of Northumberland, KG, GCVO, TD, PC, FRS, who d 1988. *Residences* – Friar's Well, Alnwick, Northumberland NE66 2LJ; Clive Lodge, Albury, Surrey GU5 9AB.

COLLATERAL BRANCHES LIVING

Issue of late Lord Richard Charles Percy, 3rd son of 8th Duke, b 1921, d 1989: m 1st, 1966, Sarah Jane Elizabeth, who d 1978, da of Petre Norton, of The Manor House, Whalton, Northumberland; 2ndly, 1979, Hon Clayre Campbell (ante), formerly wife of Hon Nicholas Ridley, MP (later Baron Ridley of Liddesdale, PC) (*see* V Ridley), and 2nd da of 4th Baron Stratheden and Campbell, CBE:—
(By 1st m) Algernon Alan, b 1969. —— Josceline Richard, b 1971.

Issue of late Lord Geoffrey William Percy, 4th and yst son of 8th Duke, b 1925, d 1984: m 1955, Mary Elizabeth (ante), da of Ralph Lea:—
Diana Ruth, b 1956.

Grandchildren of late Col Lord William Richard Percy, CBE, DSO (infra):—
Issue of late Henry Edward Percy, b 1925, d 1985: m 1952, Eileen Ruth Morley, da of late Lt-Col Wilmot-Smyth Caulfeild, MC (*see* V Charlemont, colls):—
George Robert, b 1953. —— James Edward Caulfeild, b 1958: m 1st, 1986 (*m diss* 1989), Gay P. Lovell-Badge, da of Mrs John Cator, and stepda of John Cator, of Woodbastwick, Norfolk; 2ndly, 1993, Hon Zara Jane Digby, only da of 12th Baron Digby. —— Lavinia Mary, b 1955. —— Susan Clare, b 1961: m 1990, George M. Woodruff, 2nd son of late James Woodruff, DFC, of Belcombe Court, Bradford-on-Avon, Wilts, and has issue living, James Frederick, b 1992, — Charlotte Lettice, b 1995.

Issue of late Col Lord William Richard Percy, CBE, DSO, 5th son of 7th Duke, b 1882, d 1963: m 1922, Mary, who d 1984, da of late Capt George Sitwell Campbell Swinton:—
Gerald (The Granary, Nunnery Place, Thetford, Norfolk IP24 2PZ), b 1928: m 1st, 1954 (*m diss* 1975), Jennifer, da of late John Brougham Home-Rigg, of Eastern Transvaal; 2ndly, 1983, Victoria, da of late Dr Roger Henderson, MD, FRCP, and has issue living (by 1st m), Richard John (2 Cottesmore Gdns, W8 5PR), b 1957: m 1987 (*m diss* 1995), Deborah Patricia, yr da of Guy Norman, of Brockham, Surrey, and has issue living, Natasha Elizabeth b 1988, Sabrina Catherine b 1990, — Andrew Alan (2 Cottesmore Gdns, W8 5PR), b 1963: m 1988, LaNora Lynn, yr da of J. R. Scott, of Scottsdale, Arizona, USA, and has issue living, Ayden Jay b 1992, Callum Zane b 1994, — Katherine Susan (2 Cottesmore Gdns, W8 5PR), b 1955: m 1982 (*m diss* 1986), John Bentley, — Diana Mary (2 Cottesmore Gdns, W8 5PR), b 1965.

Issue of late Rt Hon Lord Eustace Sutherland Campbell Percy (7th son of 7th Duke), who was *cr* *Baron Percy of Newcastle* 1952 (see that title, ext 1958).

Grandchildren of late Algernon Hugh Heber-Percy, elder son of late Algernon Heber-Percy (b 1845), eldest son of late Algernon Charles Heber-Percy, son of late Rev Hon Hugh Heber-Percy, Bishop of Carlisle, 3rd son of 1st Earl of Beverley, 2nd son of 1st Duke:—
Issue of late Brigadier Algernon George William HEBER-PERCY, DSO, b 1904, d 1961: m 1939 (*m diss* 1950), Daphne Wilma Kenyon, who d 1995, da of late Eustace Bowles (*see* E Macclesfield, colls, 1995 Edn):—
Algernon Eustace Hugh (Hodnet Hall, Hodnet, Market Drayton, Shropshire TF9 3NN), b 1944; ed Harrow; late Lieut. Grenadier Guards; DL Shropshire 1986, High Sheriff 1987, Lord Lieut 1996: m 1966, Hon Margaret Jane Lever, yst da of 3rd Viscount Leverhulme, KG, and has issue living, Algernon Thomas Lever b 1984, — Emily Jane, b 1969: m 1996, Richard Hugh Cave, yst son of Sir Charles Edward Coleridge Cave, 4th Bt, and has issue (see that title), — Lucy Ann, b 1970, — Sophie Daphne, b 1980. —— Zara Mary, b 1940: m 1st, 1961 (*m diss* 1980), Gavin Nicholas Tait; 2ndly, 1980,

Humphrey Swire, and has issue living (by 1st *m*) Lucinda Clare, *b* 1962: *m* 1st, 1983 (*m diss* 1994), James Henderson, son of Lt-Col James B. Henderson; 2ndly, 1995, John G. Mellor, and has issue living (by 1st *m*), Eliza Jennifer Jane *b* 1992, — Arabella Kate Louise, *b* 1965: *m* 1995, James Richard Lindsay, and has issue (*see* E Crawford, colls). —— Jane Maude, *b* 1942: *m* 1965, Maj Harold Antony McArthur Pyman, The Life Gds, of Windwhistle, Sampford Arundel, Som TA21 9QX, son of late Gen Sir Harold English Pyman, GBE, KCB, DSO, and has issue living, Richard Anthony, *b* 1968: *m* 1997, Corinna Harriet Loveday Richards, and has issue living, Edward Cyril Siegfried *b* 1998, — Victoria Clare, *b* 1966: *m* 1996, Kim Anthony Knott, and has issue living, Tom Sorrel Somerset *b* 1998, India Rose McArthur *b* 1997.

Issue of late Lt-Col Cyril Hugh Reginald HEBER-PERCY, DSO, MC, *b* 1905, *d* 1989: *m* 1st, 1933 (*m diss* 1944), Anne, yst da of late Charles Tuller Garland, of Moreton Morrell, Warwicks; 2ndly, 1944 (*m diss* 1959), Diana, only da of late Raymond Augustus Edward Radclyffe, of Lew, Oxon; 3rdly, 1959, Pamela, elder da of Kinmont Willie Armstrong-Lushington-Tulloch, of Shanbolard, Moyard, co Galway, widow of Capt Thomas Ansell Fair-hurst, The Life Guards, and formerly wife of Maj (George) Derek Cooper, MC, late The Life Guards:—
(By 1st *m*) †Alan Cyril *b* 1935; *ed* Eton: *m* 1st, 1962, Susan Mary, only da of late Michael Charles St John Hornby (*see* E Dudley, colls, 1985 Edn), and formerly wife of John George Vanderbilt Henry, Marquess of Blandford (later 11th Duke of Marlborough); 2ndly, 1980, Mrs Charlotte Gwynne (Eyford Knoll, Upper Slaughter, Glos), 2nd da of late Lt Cdr Sir Cyril Hugh Kleinwort, RNVR (*see* Kleinwort, Bt, colls), and *d* 1998, leaving issue (by 1st *m*), Larissa Anne, *b* 1968: *m* 1997, Justin St C. Hardy, son of Robin Hardy. —— William David, MBE (Glawcoed, Talybont-on-Usk, Brecon, Powys LD3 7JR), *b* 1939; *ed* Eton; late Assist Adviser, Aden; MBE (Civil) 1966: *m* 1969, Christine, da of Terence Horatio Gates, and has issue living, Peter Hugh, *b* 1971, — Robin Virginia, *b* 1969. —— (By 2nd *m*) Cyril Raymond (Folly Farmhouse, Farmington, Glos), *b* 1945; *ed* Eton: *m* 1st, 1971, Mrs Heather Joan Miller; 2ndly, 1988, Mrs Ann Elizabeth Francis, da of late John Douglas Rowley, of Bristol, Avon, and has issue living (by 1st *m*), Tamara Joan, *b* 1972, — Zara Ana, *b* 1976.

Issue of late Robert Vernon HEBER-PERCY, *b* 1911, *d* 1987: *m* 1st, 1942 (*m diss* 1947), Ann Jennifer Evelyn Elizabeth, only child of Sir Geoffrey Storrs Fry, 1st Bt, KCB, CVO; 2ndly, 1985, Lady Dorothy Lygon, yst da of 7th Earl Beauchamp, KG:—
(By 1st *m*) Victoria Gala, *b* 1943: *m* 1960, Peter Zinovieff, and has issue living, Leo, *b* 1963: *m* 1988, Annabelle Charlotte, only da of Hon Simon Dawson Eccles (*see* V Eccles), and has issue living, Kyril *b* 1991, Peter *b* 1995, Aloysha *b* 1988, — Kolinka, *b* 1966, — Sofka, *b* 1961; has issue living (by Vassilis Papadimitriou), Anna Alexandra *b* 1992, Lara *b* 1995. *Residences* – 50 Stevenage Rd, SW6; Faringdon House, Faringdon, Oxon.

Grandchildren of late Josceline Reginald HEBER-PERCY (infra):—
Issue of late Cdr David Josceline Algernon HEBER-PERCY, DSC, RN, *b* 1909, *d* 1971: *m* 1942, Olivia Mary, who *d* 1996, yr da of late R. W. O'Brien, of Drogheda:—
Michael David (Beechenwood Farm, Hillside, Odiham, Hants), *b* 1943; AADip Hons; ARIBA: *m* 1965, Sarah, yr da of late Alastair Gilmour, and has issue living, Colin Michael (Manor Cottage, Tidcombe, Marlborough, Wilts SN8 3SL), *b* 1968, — Paul David (8 Hopgood St, W12), *b* 1970. —— Carol Margaret Katherine, *b* 1947: *m* 1st, 1970 (*m diss* 1974), Robert Ward Woolner; 2ndly, 1974, Richard Edward Warcup Ashby, Dip Arch RIBA, of Empshott Lodge, Liss, Hants, and has issue living (by 2nd *m*), Sam David Frederick, *b* 1981, — Daisy Katharine, *b* 1974, — Poppy Elizabeth Patricia, *b* 1976, — Holly Patricia, *b* 1979. —— Angela Mary, *b* 1949: *m* 1970, Henry Robert Boileau Fawcett, of Delmonden Manor, Hawkhurst, Kent, and has issue living, Joseph Dylan, *b* 1983, — Emily, *b* 1972, — Kate, *b* 1975.

Granddaughter of late Algernon HEBER-PERCY (*b* 1845) (ante):—
Issue of late Josceline Reginald HEBER-PERCY, *b* 1880, *d* 1964: *m* 1904, Katharine Lousia Victoria, who *d* 1964, da of late Lord Algernon Malcolm Arthur Percy (son of 6th Duke):—
Dorothy Elizabeth (*Elizabeth, Lady Walker-Okeover*) *b* 1913: *m* 1938, Col Sir Ian Peter Andrew Munro Walker-Okeover, 3rd Bt, DSO, TD, JP, who *d* 1982.

Grandsons of late Alan William HEBER-PERCY (infra):—
Issue of late Capt Hugh Alan HEBER-PERCY, OBE, *b* 1897, *d* 1976: *m* 1926, Monica Violet, who *d* 1977, da of late Edmond Waterton Coningsby Erskine (E Mar and Kellie, colls), and widow of Lt-Col G. D. Maynard:—
Robin Erskine (Box 1232, Somerset West, CP 7130, S Africa), *b* 1927; *ed* Hilton Coll, Natal; 1945 War with S African Engineer Corps: *m* 1953, Ann, da of John Gaw. —— Philip Reginald (14 Edgecliffe Park, Bartle Rd, Gillitts, Natal 3610), *b* 1929; *ed* Hilton Coll, Natal; Chartered Accountant: *m* 1952, Cherie, da of Johannes van Wyk, and has issue living, Robyn, *b* 1954: *m* 1976, Anthony David Burgess (PO Box 511, Pietermaritzburg 3200, S Africa), son of Roy Burgess, and has issue living, Trevor *b* 1983, Bruce *b* 1985, — Julia, *b* 1956: *m* 1993, Andries Burger Laubscher, of 15 Gavin Av, Pine Park 2194, son of Nicholaas Laubscher, — and two adopted das, Renée, *b* 1959: *m* 1981, Dr Andrew Scogings, and *d* 1998, — Kim, *b* 1961: *m* 1985, Peter Adie (PO Box 249, Victoria Falls, Zimbabwe), son of Martin Adie. —— John Kellie (34 Kingswood Dr, Chirnside Park, Victoria 3116, Australia), *b* 1935; *ed* Hilton Coll, Natal: *m* 1961, Rosalind Marion, da of late W. H. Gathercole, and has issue living, Gillian Dorothy, *b* 1965: *m* 1987, Michael Alan Heber-Percy (who assumed the surname of Heber-Percy in lieu of his patronymic DIXON, and has issue living, Abigail Brianna *b* 1996), — Helen Marjorie, *b* 1968.

Grandsons of late Algernon Charles Heber-Percy (ante):—
Issue of late Alan William HEBER-PERCY, *b* 1865, *d* 1946: *m* 1st, 1893, Hon Susan Alice Portman, who *d* 1933, da of 2nd Viscount Portman; 2ndly, 1936, Mabel, who *d* 1953, da of late Sir William Darracott, and widow of E. Herbert Hinds:—
(By 1st *m*) Bryan, *b* 1903; formerly Capt RA: *m* 1936, Etelka, da of Istvan Kuiti, of Hungary. —— †Peter, OBE, *b* 1908; *ed* Wellington Coll; is Lt Col 55th Anti-Aircraft Regt RA (TA); 1939-45 War in Middle East and Italy (OBE); OBE, (Mil) 1945: *m* 1st, 1930 (*m diss* 1947), (Josephine) Sylvia, who *d* 1990, el da of late Brig-Gen Cyril Randall Crofton, CBE, of Trobridge, Crediton; 2ndly, 1947, Elsa Maria, da of late Giamcomo Nission, of Pisa, Italy, and *d* 1997, leaving issue (by 1st *m*), (Sylvia) Venetia, *b* 1932: *m* 1953, David Gerald Stern, of Bednall Hill, Bednall, Staffs, son of late Lt-Col Sir Albert Gerald Stern, KBE, CMG (Orr-Lewis, Bt), and has had issue, Mark David Robin *b* 1955 *d* 1981, Sylvia Louise *b* 1957, — (Susan) Deirdre, *b* 1938: *m* 1958, Anthony Benedict Xavier Fenwick (*see* B Lilford, colls), — (by 2nd *m*) Sandra Caroline, *b* 19—. *Residence* – Il Gualdo, Punta Ala, Grossetto, Italy.

Grandchildren of late Alan William HEBER-PERCY (ante):—

Issue of late Group Capt John HEBER-PERCY, RAF (ret), *b* 1910, *d* 1975: *m* 1st, 1940 (*m diss* 1949), Eve Robertson; 2ndly, 1950, Marie Elise Teixeira de Mattos, who *d* 1992:—
(By 1st *m*) *Rev* Christopher John (19 Bellfield Av, Holderness Rd, Kingston-upon-Hull HU8 9DS); *b* 1941; ordained priest 1969: *m* 1964, Lyndis Elizabeth, yst da of Rt Rev John Henry Lawrence Phillips, Lord Bishop of Portsmouth, and has issue living, William John, *b* 1965, — Thomas Henry, *b* 1967, — Anna, *b* 1970. —— Susan Elizabeth, *b* 1943: *m* 1965, Karl John Sabbagh, of 76 Sheen Park, Richmond, Surrey TW9 1UP, and has issue living, Jonathan Christopher, *b* 1978, — Isabella Mary, *b* 1972, — Susanna Jane *b* 1975. —— Josceline Mary, *b* 1946: *m* 1969, Richard Newell, FRCS, of 11 Windsor Terrace, Penarth, S Glamorgan CF64 1AA, and has issue living, Adam Richard Eric, *b* 1971, — Benjamin Rhodri, *b* 1972, — Victoria Claire, *b* 1975, — Charlotte Jessica Eve, *b* 1981.

Grandchildren of late Josceline Hugh Percy, son of late Rev Henry Percy, son of late Rt Rev Hon Hugh Percy, Bishop of Carlisle (ante):—
Issue of late Josceline Richard Percy, *b* 1894, *d* 1971: *m* 1929, Mary, who *d* 1964, da of Harold Nicholson, of Oak House, Farnworth, Bolton:—
Hugh Edward, *b* 1938; *ed* Gonville and Caius Coll, Camb (BA), and Manchester Coll of Commerce; Associate of Library Assocn: *m* 1969, Barbara, only da of —Mulholland, of Lancaster. *Residence* - —. —— Eleanor Mary, *b* 1940: *m* 1962, James Rolf Adams, of 1170 Keeler Av, Berkeley, Cal, USA, and has issue living, Katherine Charlotte, *b* 1963, — Ruth Susannah, *b* 1965.

PREDECESSORS – (1) ALGERNON Seymour, 7th Duke of Somerset (see † *infra*), was *cr Baron Warkworth*, of Warkworth Castle, co Northumberland and *Earl of Northumberland* (peerage of Great Britain) 1749, with remainder to Sir Hugh Smithson, 4th Bt (see * *infra*), who in 1740 *m* Lady Elizabeth, the Duke's only surviving child; *d* 1750; *s* by his son-in-law (2) *Sir* HUGH Smithson, KG, 2nd Earl; assumed by Act of Parliament 1750 the surname of Percy, in lieu of his patronymic; *cr Earl Percy* and *Duke of Northumberland* (peerage of Great Britain) 1766, and *Lord Lovaine, Baron of Alnwick* (peerage of Great Britain) 1784, with remainder to his 2nd son Algernon; *d* 1786; *s* by his el son (3) HUGH, KG, 2nd Duke; *d* 1817; *s* by his el son (4) HUGH, KG, 3rd Duke; was Viceroy of Ireland, Lord-Lieut and Vice Adm of Northumberland, and Chancellor of Univ of Cambridge, etc; *dsp* 1847; *s* by his brother (5) ALGERNON, KG, PC, 4th Duke; a distinguished Adm; *cr Baron Prudhoe*, of Prudhoe Castle, co Northumberland (peerage of United Kingdom) 1816; was First Lord of the Admiralty 1852; *d* 1865, when the Barony of Prudhoe became extinct, the Barony of Percy devolved upon the 7th Duke of Atholl, and the Baronetcy, the Earldom of Percy, and Dukedom reverted to his kinsman (6) GEORGE, PC, 5th Duke, el son of Algernon, 2nd Baron Lovaine (ante) who had in 1790 been *cr Earl of Beverley* (peerage of Great Britain); *b* 1778, sat as MP for Beeralston 1808-30; was a Lord of the Treasury 1804-6, and Capt of Yeomen of the Guard 1842-6: *m* 1801, Louisa Harcourt, da of Hon James Archibald Stuart-Wortley (E Wharncliffe); *d* 1867; *s* by his son (7) ALGERNON GEORGE, KG, PC, 6th Duke, *b* 1810; was a Lord of the Admiralty 1858, Vice-Pres of Board of Trade 1859, and Lord-Privy Seal 1878-80; MP for Beeralston (*C*) 1831-2 and for N Northumberland 1852-65; Lord-Lieut of Northumberland, and of co and city of Newcastle-on-Tyne: *m* 1845, Louisa, who *d* 1890, da of late Henry Drummond, of Albury Park, Surrey; *d* 1899; *s* by his el son (8) HENRY GEORGE (who in 1887 had in his father's lifetime been called to the House of Lords in the Barony of Lovaine), 7th Duke, *b* 1846: *m* 1868, Lady Edith Campbell, who *d* 1913, da of 8th Duke of Argyll, KG, KT; *d* 1918; *s* by his el surviving son (9) ALAN IAN, KG, CBE, MVO, 8th Duke, *b* 1880; Pres of Roy Institution; Lord-Lieut of Northumberland 1918-30: *m* 1911, Lady Helen Magdalen Gordon-Lennox, GCVO, CBE, JP, who *d* 1965, da of 7th Duke of Richmond; *d* 1930; *s* by his el son (10) HENRY GEORGE ALAN, 9th Duke, *b* 1912; Lieut Grenadier Guards; *ka* 1940; *s* by his brother (11) HUGH ALGERNON, 10th Duke, KG, GCVO, TD, PC, FRS, *b* 1914, a Lord-in-Waiting to HM May to June 1940, Lord Steward of HM Household 1973-88, Pres N Area Royal British Legion 1957-84, Hon Treas Royal Nat Life-Boat Inst, Co Councillor Northumberland 1944-55, Alderman 1955-57, Member Hill Farming Advisry Cttee for England and Wales 1946-60, and of other Nat Forestry and Agric Cttees, Pres Court of Durham Univ 1956-63, Master of Percy Fox Hounds 1950-88 Chancellor Univ of Newcastle upon Tyne 1964-88; 1939-45 War as Capt RA, Capt Northumberland Hus (TARO) 1949-64, Hon Col 7th Bn RNF 1948-70, Dep Hon Col Northumbrian Vols TAVR 1971-75, Hon Col 6th (V) Bn RRF 1975-88, Pres TAVR Assocn for N England 1968-71: *m* 1946, Lady Elizabeth Diana Montagu Douglas Scott, da of 8th Duke of Buccleuch; *d* 1988; *s* by his eldest son (12) HENRY ALAN WALTER RICHARD, 11th Duke; *b* 1953, *dunm* 1995; *s* by his brother (13) RALPH GEORGE ALGERNON, 12th Duke and present peer; also Earl of Northumberland, Earl Percy, Earl of Beverley, Baron Percy, Baron Warkworth, and Lord Lovaine, Baron of Alnwick.

†(1) ALGERNON Seymour, Earl of Hertford (afterwards 7th Duke of Somerset); summoned to Parliament 1722 by writ on death of his mother, Lady Elizabeth Percy, da and heir of 11th Earl of Northumberland in the erroneous belief that he had inherited the Barony of Percy (*cr* 1299), which was attainted in 1406, and by sitting in 1723 a barony of writ was thereby created, and he became *Baron Percy* (*cr* 1723); *s* by his da (2-5) *Lady* ELIZABETH, who *m* the 1st Duke of Northumberland (ante), the Barony being merged in the Dukedom until the death of 4th Duke in 1865, when it devolved upon his grand-nephew (6-10) JOHN JAMES HUGH HENRY Stewart-Murray, 7th Duke of Atholl (grandson of Lady Emily Frances Percy, sister of 5th Duke of Northumberland who *m* the 1st Baron Glenlyon); *d* 1917, when the Barony became merged in the Dukedom of Atholl until the death of the 9th Duke 1957, when it passed to (11) the 10th Duke of Northumberland (ante).

*(1) HUGH Smithson, a zealous royalist, *cr Baronet* 1660; *d* 1670; *s* by his son (2) *Sir* JEROME, 2nd Bt; *d* 1684; *s* by his son (3) *Sir* HUGH, 3rd Bt; conformed to doctrines of the Church of England; he having been born a Roman Catholic; *d* 1729; *s* by his son (4) HUGH, 4th Bt, who was *cr Duke of Northumberland* (ante).

NORTON, BARON (Adderley) (Baron UK 1878)

JAMES NIGEL ARDEN ADDERLEY, 8th Baron; *b* 2 June 1947; *s* 1993; *ed* Downside: *m* 1st, 1971 (*m diss* 1989), Jacqueline Julie, el da of Guy W. Willett, of Alderney, CI; 2ndly, 1997, Frances Elizabeth, yr da of George Frederick Rothwell (*see* B Middleton, colls), and has issue by 1st *m*.

䒜rmš – Argent, on a bend azure, three mascles of the field. Crest – On a chapeau azure, turned up ermine, a stork argent. Šupporterš – On either side a stork argent, gorged with a chain or, pendent therefrom an escutcheon azure, charged with a mascle also argent. *Residence* – 11 Picaterre, Alderney, CI.

SON LIVING (*By 1st marriage*)

Hon EDWARD JAMES ARDEN, *b* 19 Oct 1982.

DAUGHTER LIVING (*By 1st marriage*)

Hon Olivia Fleur Elizabeth, *b* 1979.

BROTHER LIVING

Hon Nigel John, *b* 1950; *ed* Downside, and RMA Sandhurst; Maj Life Guards: *m* 1991, Teresa M. A., da of Maj John Mills, and has issue living, Fleur Charlotte Alice, *b* 1992.

It is an honour to add justice to law

AUNTS LIVING (*Daughters of 6th Baron*)

Hon Rosemary Etheldreda, *b* 1913: *m* 1949, Rev John Paul Drake, and has issue living, Simon Francis, *b* 1956: *m* 1981, Vanessa, da of Robert Sewell, of Oaklands, Brundall, Norwich, — Catherine Elisabeth, *b* 1950: *m* 1974, John William Grace. *Residence* – 3 The Cloisters, Welwyn Garden City, Herts AL8 6DU.

Hon Elisabeth Joan, *b* 1919: *m* 1943, Professor (Alexander) Colin Patton Campbell, MB, ChB, MSc, FRCP (Edin), FRCPath, who *d* 1996, and has had issue, Andrew Colin, *b* 1943; MA, BM, BCh, D Phil, MRCPath; *d* 1990, — Richard Hubert Alexander (189 Hale Rd, Hale, Cheshire), *b* 1946; MB, ChB, FRCP (Edin), FRCP (Lond): *m* 1976, Candace, da of Clifford W. Richardson, of Stratford St Andrew, Suffolk, — Rosamund Elizabeth, *b* 1950; MA Oxon. *Residence* – The Priory House, Ascott-under-Wychwood, Oxon OX7 6AW.

Hon Mary, *b* 1922; European War 1939-45 as 3rd Officer WRNS: *m* 1950, Hugh Montgomery Campbell, who *d* 1980, son of late Rt Rev and Rt Hon Bishop Henry Colville Montgomery Campbell, KCVO, MC, PC, DD, formerly Lord Bishop of London, and has issue living, Philip Henry, *b* 1951; PhD, DSc, FRAS, FInstP: *m* 1980, Judith Margaret, who *d* 1992, da of Joseph William Yelton, of 7 Park Lane, Earls Colne, Colchester, — Elisabeth Mary, *b* 1954, — Veronica, *b* 1958: *m* 1987, Jeffrey Mark Berman, eldest son of Dolph L. Berman, of Cincinnati, Ohio, USA. *Residence* – 16 Ashworth Rd, W9.

WIDOW LIVING OF SEVENTH BARON

BETTY MARGARET (*Dowager Baroness Norton*), only da of late James McKee Hannah, of Domaine de Fontvieille, Aix-en-Provence, France: *m* 1946, Major the 7th Baron Norton, OBE, who *d* 1993. *Residence* – Fillongley Hall, Coventry.

COLLATERAL BRANCH LIVING

Issue of late Group Capt Hon Michael Charles Adderley, OBE, AFC, yr son of 6th Baron, *b* 1917, *d* 1992: *m* 1953, Margrethe Anne, MRCVS, who *d* 1986, only da of Karl Gerhardt Ornbo:—
Charles Henry, *b* 1954: *m* 1982, Jane Elizabeth, da of Sydney Atherton, of Ilkley, W Yorks. —— Anthony John, *b* 1955. —— David Michael, *b* 1962. —— Jane Margrethe, *b* 1957: *m* 1982, Kenneth Blackburn, of Glen Haven, Long Moss Lane, Whitestake, Preston, Lancs PR4 4XN, and has issue living, Emma Margrethe, *b* 1986, — Sara Elisabeth, *b* (twin) 1986.

PREDECESSORS – (1) *Rt Hon Sir* CHARLES BOWYER Adderley, KCMG, el son of late Charles Clement Adderley, of Hams Hall, Warwickshire, and Norton, co Stafford; *b* 1814; Pres of Board of Health, and Vice-Pres of Committee of Privy Council for Education 1858-9, Under-Sec of State for Colonies 1866-8, and Pres of Board of Trade 1874-8; MP for N Staffordshire (C) 1841-78; *cr Baron Norton*, of Norton-on-the-Moors, co Stafford (peerage of United Kingdom) 1878: *m* 1842, Hon Julia Anne Eliza, who *d* 1887, da of 1st Baron Leigh; *d* 1905; *s* by his son (2) CHARLES LEIGH, 2nd Baron; *b* 1846: *m* 1870, Caroline, who *d* 1922, da of Sir Alexander Dixie, 10th Bt; *d* 1926; *s* by his el son (3) RALPH BOWYER, 3rd Baron, *b* 1872: *m* 1899, Mary Louisa, who *d* 1939, da of Robert Watson, formerly of Ballydarton, co Carlow, and widow of Inglis Brady; *d* 1933; *s* by his brother (4) RONALD WOLSTAN FLEETWOOD, 4th Baron, *b* 1885: *m* 1931, Hylda, who *d* 1950, da of late Robert William Tovey, of Cheltenham, and widow of Hilary George Dunbar, of Glasgow; *d* 1944; *s* by his uncle (5) HENRY ARDEN (2nd son of 1st Baron), 5th Baron; *b* 1854: *m* 1881, Grace, who *d* 1944, da of late William Bruce Stopford-Sackville, of Drayton House, Thrapston; *d* 1945; *s* by his only son (6) HUBERT BOWYER ARDEN, 6th Baron; *b* 1886; a Lay Guardian of the Sanctuary of Our Lady of Walsingham, Norfolk: *m* 1912, Elizabeth, who *d* 1952, da of late William John Birkbeck, of Stratton Strawless Hall, Norfolk; *d* 1961; *s* by his el son (7) JOHN ARDEN, OBE, 7th Baron; *b* 1915; 1939-45 War in N Africa, Sicily and Italy as Major RE (despatches); Assist Master Oundle Sch; a Lay Guardian of the Sanctuary of Our Lady of Walsingham: *m* 1946, Betty Margaret, only da of late James McKee Hannah, of Domaine de Fontvieille, Aix-en-Provence, France; *d* 1993; *s* by his elder son (8) JAMES NIGEL ARDEN, 8th Baron and present peer.

Norton, family name of Baron Grantley.

Norton, family name of Baron Rathcreedan.

NORTON OF LOUTH, BARON (Norton) (Life Baron 1998)

PHILIP NORTON son of late George Ernest Norton, of Louth; *b* 5 March 1951; *ed* Sheffield Univ (BA 1972, PhD 1977), and Pennsylvania Univ (MA 1975); Lecturer in Politics, Hull Univ 1977-82, Senior Lecturer in Politics 1982-84, Reader in Politics 1984-86, since when Prof of Govt; Dir Centre for Legislative Studies since 1992; FRSA 1995; author; *cr Baron Norton of Louth*, of Louth, co Lincs (Life Baron) 1998.

Residence – 30 Mizzen Rd, Hull, E Yorkshire HU6 7AG. *Clubs* – Royal Commonwealth Soc, Royal Over-Seas League.

NORWICH, VISCOUNT (Cooper) (Viscount UK 1952)

JOHN JULIUS COOPER, CVO, 2nd Viscount; *b* 15 Sept 1929; *s* 1954; *ed* Eton, and at New Coll, Oxford (BA honours 1952); late RN; writer and broadcaster; HM Foreign Ser 1952-64; Third Sec, British Embassy, Belgrade 1956-57, and Second Sec, British Embassy, Beirut 1957-60; CVO 1993: *m* 1st, 1952 (*m diss* 1985), Anne Frances May, el da of late Hon Sir Bede Edmund Hugh Clifford, GCMG, CB, MVO (*see* B Clifford of Chudleigh, colls); 2ndly, 1989, Hon Mrs Mary Philipps, twin da of 1st Baron Sherfield, GCB, GCMG, and has issue by 1st *m*.

Arms – Or three lions rampant gules on a chief azure a portcullis chained between two fleur-de-lys of the first. **Crest** – On the battlements of a tower argent a bull passant sable armed and unguled or. **Supporters** – On either side a unicorn argent gorged with a collar with chain reflexed over the back or pendent from the collar of the dexter a portcullis chained and from that of the sinister a fleur-de-lys both gold. *Residence* – 24 Blomfield Rd, W9 1AD. *Club* – Beefsteak.

I hate and I love

SON LIVING (By 1st marriage)

Hon JASON CHARLES DUFF BEDE, *b* 27 Oct 1959; architect. *Residence* – 14 Alexander St, W2 5NT.

DAUGHTER LIVING (By 1st marriage)

Hon Alice Clare Antonia Opportune (Artemis) COOPER, *b* 1953; writer; prefers to be known as Cooper: *m* 1986, Antony James Beevor (*see* Duff-Gordon, Bt, 1964 Edn), and has issue living, Adam John Cosmo, *b* 1993, — Eleanor Allegra, *b* 1990. *Residence* – 54 St Maur Rd, SW6 4DP.

PREDECESSOR – **(1)** *Rt Hon Sir* ALFRED DUFF COOPER, GCMG, DSO, PC, son of late Sir Alfred Cooper, FRCS (D Fife); *b* 1890; appointed Private Sec to Parliamentary Under-Sec of State for Foreign Affairs, 1922; was Financial Sec, War

Office 1928-29, and again (in National Govt) 1931-33, Financial Sec to Treasury 1934-35, Sec of State for War 1935-37, First Lord of the Admiralty 1937-38, Min of Information 1940-41, Chancellor of Duchy of Lancaster 1941-43, British Envoy to French National Committee in N Africa 1943-44, and Ambassador Extraor and Plen to France 1944-47; European War 1914-19 as Lieut Grenadier Guards (despatches, DSO); sat as MP for Oldham (C) 1924-29, and for St George's Div of Westminster 1931-45; *cr Viscount Norwich*, of Aldwick, co Sussex (peerage of United Kingdom) 1952: *m* 1919, Lady Diana Olivia Winifred Maud Manners, who *d* 1986, da of 8th Duke of Rutland; *d* 1954; *s* by his only son (2) JOHN JULIUS, 2nd Viscount and present peer.

Nottingham, Earl of, see Earl of Winchilsea and Nottingham.

Nugent Baron (Austria), see Earl of Westmeath colls.

Nugent, family name of Earl of Westmeath.

NUNBURNHOLME, BARON (Wilson) (Baron UK 1906)

For laws and kings

CHARLES THOMAS WILSON, 5th Baron; *b* 27 May 1935; *s* 1998; *ed* Eton; Page of Honour to HM King George VI 1950-52; Member London Stock Exchange 1956-66: *m* 1969 (*m diss* 19—), Linda Kay, only da of Cyril James Stephens, of Woodlands, Challock Lees, Ashford, Kent, and has issue.

Arms – Or, an ancient ship sable, on a chief azure three ducal coronets of the first. Crest – Between two ducal coronets or a demi-wolf sable, holding between the paws a like coronet. Supporters – On either side a Benedictine nun, holding in the anterior hand a rosary, all proper.
Residence – The County House, Garrigill, nr Alston, Cumbria CA9 3EY.

SON LIVING

Hon STEPHEN CHARLES, *b* 29 Nov 1973; *ed* Nottingham Univ.

DAUGHTER LIVING

Hon Nathalia Ellen, *b* 1971.

HALF-BROTHER LIVING

Hon (David) Mark, *b* 1954; *ed* Eton: *m* 1983 (*m diss* 1989), Amanda Christian, da of late Roger Hayward, of Gardiners Hall, Stoke Ash, nr Eye, Suffolk. *Residence* – 2 Stoke Newington Common, N16 7ET.

SISTER LIVING

Hon Charmaine Elizabeth Violet Cecilia, *b* 1930: *m* 1957, William Rippon Bissill, who *d* 1983, and has had issue, John James Rippon, *b* 1957; *d* 1980, — William Henry, *b* 1960; *d* 1994, — Kathleen Mary Florence, *b* 1966: *m* 1991, Mark Adair Hodson, and has issue (*see* Hodson, Bt). *Residence* – Cranmer House, Aslockton, Notts.

DAUGHTERS LIVING OF FOURTH BARON

Hon Lorraine Mary Charmaine, *b* 1959.

Hon Tatiana Ines Alexandra, *b* 1960: *m* 1988, Nigel L. Dent, of Lake Cottage, Shillinglee Park, Chiddingfold, Sussex, 2nd son of Robin Dent, of Olivers, Painswick, Glos, and has issue living, Frederick, *b* 1989, — Harry Barnaby Nigel, *b* 1991, — Romilly Eve, *b* 1996.

Hon Ysabelle (6 Pottery Fields, off Mill Lane, Nettlebed, Henley-on-Thames, Oxon RG9 5AE), *b* 1963.

Hon Ines Monica (twin), *b* 1963: *m* 1988, Anthony Richard Leslie Garton, yst son of late Anthony Charles Garton, and has issue living, Tristan John Leslie, *b* 1990.

WIDOW LIVING OF THIRD BARON

ALEX, only da of Capt Douglas Hockly, of 10 Eastgate, Tenterden, Kent: *m* 1st, 1953, as his 2nd wife, the 3rd Baron Nunburnholme, who *d* 1974; 2ndly, 1975, Harry Oliver John Carter Jonas. *Residence* – Fishers Well, Brill, Constantine, nr Falmouth, Cornwall TR11 5QA.

COLLATERAL BRANCH LIVING

Issue of late Col Hon Guy Greville Wilson, CMG, DSO, TD, 2nd son of 1st Baron, *b* 1877, *d* 1943: *m* 1st, 1904, Lady Isabel Innes-Ker, who *d* 1905, da of 7th Duke of Roxburghe; 2ndly, 1911, Avery, who *d* 1982, da of late Geoffrey Fowell Buxton, CB (*see* Buxton, Bt, colls):—

(By 2nd *m*) Jeremy Charles, DFC, *b* 1923; F/Lt RAF (ret): *m* 1944, June Patricia, da of late Thomas Townsend Bucknill, and has issue living, Peter Richard (The Red House, Hougham, Grantham, Lincs NG32 2JD), *b* 1945: *m* 1972, Penelope Ann Verney, da of late Lt-Col Robert Edward Gabbett, MBE, MC, of Ballaghtobin, Kilkenny, and has issue living, Philippa Louise *b* 1974, Susanna Clark *b* (twin) 1974, — Thomas Charles (The Old Rectory, Upper Clatford, Andover, Hants SP11 7QP), *b* 1946. *Residence* – Fulmer Cottage, Fulmer, Bucks. —— Malise Joy, *b* 1913, JP. *m* 1942, Lieut-Col Archibald William Antony Smith, DSO, Coldm Gds, who *d* 1989, and has issue living, Antony Luke (28 Beveridge St, Barrow-on-Soar, Loughborough, Leics LE12 8PL), *b* 1943; Maj TAVR: *m* 1985, Penny, da of late Maj David R. W. R. Watts-Russell, of Biggin Hall, Benefield, Northants, — Rupert Malise (273 Trinity Rd, Wandsworth, SW18 3SH), *b* 1944; Coldm Gds (ret): *m* 1976, Angela, yr da of late Dr R. M. Castillo, and has issue living, Rowena Jane *b* 1978, Jessica Malise *b* 1980. *Residence* – Snipe Hall, Wymondham, Melton Mowbray, Leics. —— Alison Ann, *b* 1914: *m* 1938, Brig John Edmund Swetenham, DSO, 5th Dragoon Guards and R Scots Greys, who *d* 1982, and has issue living, (John) Foster (Pound Farmhouse, Rayne, Braintree, Essex), *b* 1939; Capt R Scots Greys (ret): *m* 1964, Marion, yr da of late G. A. Parker, of Bayways, Great Bookham, Surrey, and has issue living, Jeremy Edmund *b* 1967; Maj The Royal Scots Dragoon Gds: *m* 1993, Sandrine, da of Dr Jean-Pierre Martin, of Montgeron, France, Charlotte *b* 1966: *m* 1992, Richard Hamilton Fleetwood Fuller, only son of late Edward Hamilton Fleetwood Fuller, of Weybridge, Surrey (and has issue living, Henry Hamilton Fleetwood *b* 1997, Mary Pargiter Fleetwood (Page) *b* 1995). *Residence* – Oak House, Marton, Sinnington, York.

PREDECESSORS – (1) CHARLES HENRY Wilson, son of late Thomas Wilson (*b* 1792), of Cottingham and Hull, Yorkshire, by Susannah West (*b* 1796); *b* 1833; Chm of the Hull Seamen's Orphan Asylum; MP for Kingston-upon-Hull (*L*) 1874-85, and for W Div of Kingston-upon-Hull 1885-1905; *cr Baron Nunburnholme*, of the City of Kingston-upon-Hull (peerage of United Kingdom) 1906: *m* 1871, Florence Jane Helen, OBE, who *d* 1932, da of late Col William Henry Charles Wellesley, formerly 7th Fusiliers; *d* 1907; *s* by his el son (2) CHARLES HENRY WELLESLEY, CB, DSO, 2nd Baron; *b* 1875; S African War 1899-1902, European War 1914-19, Sheriff of Hull 1899-1901, and Lord-Lieut of E Riding of Yorkshire 1908-24; MP for Hull, W Div (*L*) Jan 1906 to Oct 1907: *m* 1901, Lady Marjorie Cecilia, who *d* 1968, da of 1st Marquess of Lincolnshire; *d* 1924; *s* by his el son (3) CHARLES JOHN, 3rd Baron; *b* 1904: *m* 1st, 1927 (*m diss* 1947) Lady Mary Beatrice Thynne, who *d* 1974, da of 5th Marquess of Bath; 2ndly, 1953, Alex (who *m* 2ndly 1975, H. O. J. C. Jonas), only da of Capt Douglas Hockly, of 10 Eastgate, Tenterden, Kent; *d* 1974; *s* by his el son (4) BEN CHARLES, 4th Baron; *b* 1928; Maj Royal Horse Guards: *m* 1958 (*m diss* 1986), Ines Dolores Jeanne, only da of Gérard Walravens, of Brussels (sometime Belgian Ambassador to Turkey); *d* 1998; *s* by his brother (5) CHARLES THOMAS, 5th Baron and present peer.

OAKSEY, BARON TREVETHIN AND (Lawrence) (Baron UK 1921 and 1947)

JOHN GEOFFREY TRISTRAM LAWRENCE (*Baron Oaksey*), OBE, 4th Baron Trevethin and 2nd Baron Oaksey; *b* 21 March 1929; *s* 1971; *ed* Eton, New Coll, Oxford, and Yale Univ; late P/O RAFVR and Lt 9th Lancers; OBE 1985: *m* 1st, 1959 (*m diss* 1987), Victoria Mary, el da of Maj John Dennistoun, MBE, of Antwick, Stud House, Letcombe Regis, Berks; 2ndly, 1988, Mrs Rachel Crocker, and has issue by 1st *m*.

𝕬rms – Per chevron argent and gules, two crosses raguly in chief of the last, and a lamb in base holding with the dexter foreleg a banner and staff, all of the first, the banner charged with a cross couped azure. Crest – A dragon's head erased sable between two bugle horns counter-embowed or. Supporters – *Dexter*, a Guernsey bull; *sinister*, a hart both proper.
Residence – Hill Farm, Oaksey, Malmesbury, Wilts SN16 9HS. *Club* – Brooks's.

SON LIVING (*By 1st marriage*)

Hon PATRICK JOHN TRISTRAM, *b* 29 June 1960: *m* 1987, Lucinda H., eldest da of Demetri Marchessini, of Wilton Cres, SW1, and of Mrs Nicholas Peto, of Dean Manor, Charlbury, Oxon, and has issue living, Oliver John Tristram, *b* 17 May 1990, — Calypso Helen, *b* 1987. *Residence* – 21 Dewhurst Rd, W14.

DAUGHTER LIVING (*By 1st marriage*)

Hon Sara Victoria, *b* 1961: *m* 1987, Mark FitzHerbert Bradstock, eldest son of David FitzHerbert Bradstock, MC, of Clanville Lodge, Andover, Hants. *Residence* – Mabberleys, E Garston, nr Newbury, Berks.

SISTERS LIVING

Hon (Mary) Elizabeth (*Hon Lady Adams*), *b* 1922: *m* 1954, Sir Philip George Doyne Adams, KCMG, HM Foreign Ser (ret), and has issue living, Geoffrey Doyne, *b* 1957: *m* 1985, Anne Louise, yr da of John Jennings, of St Brelade, Jersey, CI, — Justin Alexander, *b* 1961, — Lucy Victoria, *b* 1955, — Harriet Mary, *b* 1959. *Residences* – 54 Sussex Sq, W2; The Malt House, Ditchley, Enstone, Oxon.

Hon (Enid) Rosamond (*Hon Lady Dundas*), *b* 1924: *m* 1950, Group Capt Sir Hugh Spencer Lisle Dundas, CBE, DSO, DFC, RAF (ret), who *d* 1995, and has issue (*see* M Zetland, colls). *Residence* – 55 Iverna Court, W8.

COLLATERAL BRANCH LIVING

Issue of late Hon Alfred Clive Lawrence, CBE, el son of 1st Baron Trevethin, *b* 1876, *d* 1926: *m* 1924, Mildred Margaret, who *d* 1964, having *m* 2ndly, 1929, 1st Viscount Hailsham, who *d* 1950, da of late Rev Edward Parker Dew, of Breamore, Hants:—
Domini Margaret, *b* 1925: *m* 1979, Arnold Frank Morgan. *Residence* – Teddards, Filching, Polegate, E Sussex BN26 5QA.

PREDECESSORS – (1) *Rt Hon* ALFRED TRISTRAM Lawrence, PC, son of David Lawrence, surg of Pontypool, Monmouthshire, *b* 1843; a Judge of High Court of Justice (King's Bench Div) 1904-21, and Lord Ch Justice of England 1921-2; *cr Baron Trevethin*, of Blaengawney, co Monmouth (peerage of United Kingdom) 1921: *m* 1875, Jessie Elizabeth, who *d* 1931, da of George Lawrence, JP, *d* 1936; *s* by his second son (2) CHARLES TREVOR, 2nd Baron *b* 1879; Lt-Col late RHA and RFA; *d* 1959; *s* by his brother (3) *Rt Hon Sir* GEOFFREY, 3rd Baron, DSO, TD, *b* 1880; Judge of High Court of Jutice (King's Bench Div) 1932-44, Lord Justice of Appeal 1944-47, and Lord of Appeal in Ordinary 1947-57; *cr Baron Oaksey*, of Oaksey, co Wilts (Peerage of UK) 1947: *m* 1921, Marjorie, who *d* 1984, OBE, TD, da of late Cdr Charles Napier Robinson, RN; *d* 1971; *s* by his son (4) JOHN GEOFFREY TRISTRAM, 4th Baron Trevethin, 2nd Baron Oaksey and present peer.

OAKSHOTT, BARONY OF (Oakshott) (Extinct 1975) (see Oakshott, Bt)

O'Brien, family name of Baron Inchiquin

O'BRIEN OF LOTHBURY, BARONY OF (O'Brien) (Extinct 1995)

SON LIVING OF LIFE BARON (By 1st marriage)

Hon Michael John (The Lodge, Thursley, nr Godalming, Surrey GU8 6QF) *b* 1933: *m* 1964, Marion Sarah, da of late Walter Graham Blackie, and has issue, James Leslie Graham, *b* 1967: *m* 1994, Patricia M., elder da of Patrick Raison, of France, — Charles John, *b* 1972, — Sarah Christina, *b* 1969.

WIDOW LIVING OF LIFE BARON

Mrs MARJORIE VIOLET TAYLOR (*Baroness O'Brien of Lothbury*), da of Albert Cecil Ball: *m* 1989, as his 2nd wife, Baron O'Brien of Lothbury, GBE, PC, who *d* 1995. *Residence* – 3 Peter Av, Oxted, Surrey RH8 9LG.

O'CATHAIN, BARONESS (Bishop) (Life Baroness 1991)

DETTA O'CATHAIN, OBE, da of late Caoimhghin O'Cathain, of Dublin; *b* 3 Feb 1938; *ed* Laurel Hill, Limerick, and Univ Coll, Dublin (BA); formerly Group Economist with Tarmac plc, and Man Dir Milk Marketing Board; Dir Tesco plc since 1985, British Airways plc since 1993, BNP (UK Holdings) plc since 1995, Thistle Hotels plc since 1996, and South East Water plc since 1997; Man Dir The Barbican Centre 1990-94; Pres Chartered Inst of Marketing since 1997; OBE (Civil) 1983; *cr Baroness O'Cathain*, of The Barbican in the City of London (Life Baroness) 1991: *m* 1968, William Ernest John Bishop.
Residences – Eglantine, Tower House Gdns, Arundel, W Sussex; 121 Shakespeare Tower, Barbican, EC2Y 8DR.

Of Mar, family name of the Countess of Mar

Ogilvy Lord, son of Earl of Airlie.

Ogilvy, family name of the Earl of Airlie

OGMORE, BARON (Rees-Williams) (Baron UK 1950)

Faithful unto Death

GWILYM REES REES-WILLIAMS, 2nd Baron; *b* 5 May 1931; *s* 1976; *ed* Mill Hill: *m* 1967, Gillian Mavis, da of Maurice Keith Slack, of Hindley, Lancs, and has issue.

Arms – Azure two bars wavy argent on a chief arched of the second between as many hurts, each charged with a quatrefoil or a hurt thereon a sun in splendour of the third. **Crest** – A tiger's head couped proper charged on the neck with three chevronels couped gules. **Supporters** – *Dexter*, a tiger proper charged on the shoulder with three chevronels couped gules; *sinister*, a horse argent.
Residence – 4 Foster Rd, Chiswick, W4 4NY.

DAUGHTERS LIVING

Hon Christine Ann, *b* 1968.
Hon Jennet Elizabeth, *b* 1970.

BROTHER LIVING

Hon MORGAN (50 Novello St, SW6 4JB), *b* 19 Dec 1937; *ed* Mill Hill; Lt R Regt of Wales (TA): *m* 1st, 1964 (*m diss* 1970), Patricia, only da of C. Paris Jones, of Constantine Bay, Padstow; 2ndly, 1972 (*m diss* 1976), Roberta, da of late Capt Alec Stratford Cunningham-Reid, DFC; 3rdly, 1990, Beata, da of Zdislaw Solski, and has issue living (by 3rd *m*), Tudor David, *b* 11 Dec 1991, — Dylan, *b* 1994.

SISTER LIVING

Hon (Joan) Elizabeth HARRIS, *b* 1936; *ed* Croham Hurst Sch, and Mont Olivet, Lausanne; resumed surname of Harris by deed poll 1986: *m* 1st, 1957 (*m diss* 1969), Richard St John Harris, actor; 2ndly, 1971 (*m diss* 1975), Rex Carey Harrison (later Sir Rex Harrison), who *d* 1990, actor; 3rdly, 1981 (*m diss* 1985), Peter Michael Aitken (*see* B Beaverbrook, colls), and has issue living (by 1st *m*), Damian David, *b* 1958: *m* 1981, Annabel Joan, only da of late Robert Noel Brand Brooks (*see* B Crawshaw, colls), and has issue living, Ella *b* 1989, — Jared Francis, *b* 1961: *m* 1989, Jacqueline, yst da of Ralph I. Goldenberg, of Chicago, Illinois, USA, — Jamie St John, *b* 1963. *Residence* – 7 Grove Court, Drayton Gdns, SW10.

PREDECESSOR – (1) *Rt Hon* DAVID Rees Rees-Williams, TD, son of late William Rees Williams, FRCVS, of Garth Celyn, Bridgend, Glam; *b* 1903; Parl Under-Sec of State of Colonies 1947-50, and for Commonwealth Relations 1950-51; Min of Civil Aviation June-Oct 1951; MP for S Div of Croydon (*Lab*) 1945-50; carried the coronet at Investiture of HRH The Prince of Wales 1969, *cr Baron Ogmore*, of Bridgend, co Glam (peerage of UK) 1950: *m* 1930, Alice Alexandra Constance, JP, who *d* 1998, da of late Alderman Walter Robert Wills (Lord Mayor of Cardiff 1945-46); *d* 1976; *s* by his el son (2) GWILYM REES, 2nd Baron, and present peer.

O'HAGAN, BARON (Strachey) (Baron UK 1870)

Buas no bar
Victory or death

Tenez le vraye
Keep the truth

Mihi re non me rebus

CHARLES TOWNELEY STRACHEY, 4th Baron; *b* 6 Sep 1945; *s* 1961; a Page of Honour to HM 1959-62; *ed* Eton, and New Coll, Oxford (MA); Independent Member European Parliament 1973-75, Jnr Opposition Whip 1977-79, MEP (*C*) Devon 1979-94: *m* 1st, 1967 (*m diss* 1984), HSH Princess Tamara, el da of HSH Prince Michael Imeretinsky, of La Colla, Route de Castellar, Menton, France, and formerly wife of Lt-Cmdr Thomas Mervyn Smith-Dorrien-Smith, of Tresco Abbey, Isles of Scilly; 2ndly, 1985 (*m diss* 1995), Mrs Mary Claire Parsons, only da of Rev Leslie Roose-Francis, of Trencoth, Blisland, Bodmin, Cornwall; 3rdly, 1995, Mrs Elizabeth Lesley Eve Macnamara, only da of late Hubert Smith, of Amara, Whipton Lane, Exeter, and has issue by 1st and 2nd *m*.

Arms – Quarterly: 1st and 4th ermine, a bend and on a chief azure a fleur de lis or, *O'Hagan*; 2nd and 3rd argent, a fesse and in chief three mullets sable, *Towneley*. **Crests** – 1st, upon a fasces fessewise proper, a cubit arm vested gules, cuffed ermine, the hand holding a dagger erect, both also proper, *O'Hagan*; 2nd, upon a perch or, a hawk close proper, beaked and belled gold; round the perch a ribbon gules, *Towneley*. **Supporters** – On either side a lion or, collared gemel sable, pendant therefrom an escutcheon argent, charged with a dexter hand couped gules.
Residence – The Old Rectory, Weare Giffard, Bideford, Devon EX39 4QP. *Clubs* – Pratt's, Beefsteak.

DAUGHTERS LIVING (*By 1st marriage*)

Hon Nino Natalia O'Hagan, *b* 1968; *ed* Queen's Coll, Oxford (BA), and Courtauld Inst (MA): *m* 1998, Harry James Bradbeer, of 50 Huntingdon St, N1 1BP, yr son of Thomas Linthorn Bradbeer, FRCS, of Dunsford, Exeter.

(*By 2nd marriage*)

Hon Antonia Philippa Mary, *b* 1986.

BROTHER LIVING (*Raised to the rank of Baron's son 1963*)

Hon RICHARD TOWNELEY, *b* 29 Dec 1950; *ed* Eton, and Bath Acad of Art, Corsham: *m* 1983, Sally Anne, yr da of late Frederick Cecil Cross, of Upcompton, Compton Bishop, Som, and has issue living, Columba O'Hagan, *b* 28 Feb 1985, — Amy Lauren, *b* 1989. *Residence* – Lower House Farm, Godney, Wells, Som BA5 1RX.

SISTERS LIVING (*Raised to the rank of a Baron's daughters 1963*)

Hon Frances Towneley, *b* 1948: *m* 1967, Hon Hugh Marcus Thornley Gibson, of The Fold, Parwich, Ashbourne, Derbys (*see* B Gibson).
Hon Jane Towneley STRACHEY, *b* 1953; has resumed her maiden name: *m* 1972 (*m diss* 1977), William Stone.

AUNT LIVING (*Daughter of 3rd Baron*)

Hon Helen Frances Alice, *b* 1912; late VAD: *m* 1940, Capt Ian Desmond Curry, RA, who *d* 1969, having assumed by deed poll 1942 the surname of Curry-Towneley-O'Hagan, and has issue living, Padraic Desmond (29 Baron's Court Rd, W14 9DZ), *b* 1946: *m* 1971, Judith Patricia, only da of Hon Robin Sandbach Borwick (*see* B Borwick), and has issue living, Fiann James *b* 1974; BSc London Univ (1997), Dickon Padraic *b* 1977. *Residence* – 24 Burgh St, Islington, N1.

MOTHER LIVING

Lady Mary Sophia Palmer, da of 3rd Earl of Selborne; Lady-in-Waiting to HM when HRH Princess Elizabeth 1944-7, and Extra Lady-in-Waiting 1947-9: *m* 1st, 1944, Hon (Thomas) Anthony Edward Towneley Strachey, who *d* 1955 (having assumed by deed poll 1938, the additional Christian name of Towneley, and his mother's maiden name of Strachey in lieu of his patronymic), only son of 3rd Baron; 2ndly, 1981, as his 2nd wife, (Francis) St John Gore, CBE (*see* Gore, Bt, colls). *Residence* – Grove Farm, Stoke-by-Nayland, Colchester, Essex C06 4SL.

PREDECESSORS – (1) *Rt Hon Sir* THOMAS O'Hagan, KP, only son of late Edward O'Hagan; *b* 1812; was Solicitor-Gen for Ireland 1860-1, Attorney-Gen 1861-5, a Justice of the Common Pleas in Ireland 1865-8, and Lord Chancellor of Ireland 1868-74 and 1880-1; sat as MP for Tralee (*L*) 1863-5; *cr Baron O'Hagan*, of Tullahogue, co Tyrone (peerage of United Kingdom) 1870: *m* 1st, 1836, Mary, who *d* 1868, da of Charles Hamilton Teeling, of Belfast; 2ndly, 1871, Alice Mary, who *d* 1921, da and co-heiress of Col Charles Towneley, of Towneley, Lancashire; *d* 1885; *s* by his son **(2)** THOMAS TOWNELEY, 2nd Baron, *b* 1878; Lieut Grenadier Guards; *d* (in S Africa) 1900: *s* by his brother **(3)** MAURICE HERBERT TOWNELEY, 3rd Baron; *b* 1882; Hon Major RHA (TA) and Hon Col 4th (Cadet) Batn Essex Regt and 6th Batn Essex Regt (TA), Assist Private Sec (unpaid) to First Lord of Admiralty 1906-7, a Lord-in-Waiting to King Edward VII 1907-10, and Dep Speaker and Dep Chm House of Lords 1950-61; assumed by Roy licence 1909, the additional surname and arms of Towneley: *m* 1st, 1911, Hon Frances Constance Maddalena Strachey, who *d* 1931, only da of 1st Baron Strachie; 2ndly, 1937, Evelyn Violet, who *d* 1965, da of Harry Thornton Ross, and widow of Lt-Col Henry Osbert Samuel Cadogan, R Welch Fusiliers; *d* 1961; *s* by his grandson **(4)** CHARLES TOWNELEY Strachey (son of late Hon (Thomas) Anthony Edward Towneley Strachey, who assumed by deed poll 1938, the additional Christian name of Towneley, and his mother's maiden name of Strachey in lieu of his patronymic), 4th Baron and present peer.

OLIVER OF AYLMERTON, BARON (Oliver) (Life Baron 1986)

PETER RAYMOND OLIVER, PC, son of late David Thomas Oliver, Fellow of Trin Hall, Camb, by his wife Alice Maud, da of George Kirby; *b* 7 March 1921; *ed* The Leys, and Trin Hall, Camb (Hon Fellow 1980); served in WWII 1941-45, 12th Bn RTR (despatches); Bar Lincoln's Inn 1948, Bencher 1973, QC 1965, Judge of High Court (Chancery Div) 1974-80, a Lord Justice of Appeal 1980-86, a Lord of Appeal in Ordinary 1986-92; Member of Restrictive Practices Court 1976-80; Chm Review Body on Chancery Div of High Court 1979-81; *cr* Kt 1974, PC 1980, and *Baron Oliver of Aylmerton*, of Aylmerton, co Norfolk (Life Baron) 1986: *m* 1st, 1945, Mary Chichester, who *d* 1985, da of late Sir Eric Keightley Rideal, MBE, FRS; 2ndly, 1987, Wendy Anne, widow of late Ivon Lloyd Lewis Jones, and had issue by 1st *m*.

Arms – Per chevron gules and vert in chief two crosses moline or and in base a chaplet of olive also or a bordure ermine. **Crest** – Within a crown pallisado or a grassy mount thereon a representation of the tower of the church of St. John the Baptist at Aylmerton proper issuing therefrom a cubit arm proper holding a crescent ermine. **Supporters** – *Dexter*, a lion purpure the dexter paw in a mail gauntlet argent; *sinister*, an American bald-headed eagle holding in the dexter claw a quill pen all proper. **Motto** – Trwy weithred y dysgir.
Residence – The Canadas, Sandy Lane, Aylmerton, nr Cromer, Norfolk NR27 9ND.

SON LIVING (*By 1st marriage*)

Hon David Keightley Rideal, *b* 1949; *ed* Westminster, and Trin Hall, Camb: *m* 1st, 1972 (*m diss* 1987), Maria Luisa, da of Juan Mirasierras, of Avenida Reina Vittoria, Madrid; 2ndly, 1988, Judith Britannia Caroline, da of David Henry John Griffiths Powell, and has issue living (by 1st *m*), Daniel, *b* 1974, — Thomas, *b* 1976, — (by 2nd *m*) Rhodri, *b* 1990, — Alexander, *b* 1993. *Address* – 13 Old Square, Lincoln's Inn, WC2A 3UA.

DAUGHTER LIVING (*By 1st marriage*)

Hon Sarah Chichester OLIVER, *b* 1951; has resumed her maiden name: *m* 1974 (*m diss* 1983), James Robert Goldsack, and has issue living, Katie Louise, *b* 1980, — Rebecca, *b* 1983.

OLIVIER, BARONY OF (Olivier) (Extinct 1989)

SONS LIVING OF LIFE BARON (*By 1st marriage*)

Hon (Simon) Tarquin, *b* 1936; *ed* Eton, Christ Church, Oxford (MA), and Univ of W Indies, Trinidad (CAS); late Coldstream Guards; film producer and writer: *m* 1st, 1965 (*m diss* 1975), Riddelle, yr da of Patrick Boyce Riddell Gibson;

2ndly, 1989, (Sahnebat) Zelfa Draz, of Istanbul, and has issue living (by 1st *m*), H. Tristan R., *b* 1966: *m* 1st, 1993, Vanessa A., yst da of Prof R. A. Gabriel, of Forest Row, E Sussex; 2ndly, 1998, Emma Philippa Lucy, only da of John Jervois, of Leavenheath, Suffolk, — Isis, *b* 1967: *m* 1989, Paul D. Fairclough, and has issue living, Léo-Joseph *b* 1997, Luke Dominic *b* 1999, — Clavelle Athene P., *b* 1972.

(By 3rd marriage)

Hon Richard, *b* 1961; *ed* UCLA; film and theatre dir: *m* 1987, Shelley Marie Dupuis (*née* Herrich), of Canada, and has issue living, Troilus (Troy), *b* 1988, — (Natalie) Alessandra, *b* 1990.

DAUGHTERS LIVING OF LIFE BARON *(By 3rd marriage)*

Hon Tamsin, *b* 1963: *m* 1995, Simon Dutton, actor, and has issue living, Wilfred Laurence, 1997.
Hon Julianne Rose H. K. (Julie Kate), *b* 1966.

WIDOW LIVING OF LIFE BARON

JOAN, CBE (*Baroness Olivier*) (the actress Joan Plowright), da of William Ernest Plowright, and formerly wife of Roger Gage: *m* 1961, as his 3rd wife, Baron Olivier, OM (Life Baron), who *d* 1989. *Address* – c/o ICM Ltd, Oxford House, 76 Oxford St, W1N 0AX.

O'Neill, family name of Baron Rathcavan

O'NEILL, BARON (O'Neill) (Baron UK 1868)

Honours follow us without seeking

The Red Hand of Ireland

RAYMOND ARTHUR CLANABOY O'NEILL, TD, 4th Baron; *b* 1 Sept 1933; *s* 1944; *ed* Eton and R Agric Coll, Cirencester; Maj N Irish Horse (AVR IIA); Lt-Col (RARO), formerly Hon Col D (N Irish Horse) Sqdn RY; a DL for co Antrim; HM Lieut for co Antrim since 1994: *m* 1963, Georgina Mary, da of Lord George Francis John Montagu Douglas Scott (*see* D Buccleuch), and has issue.

ℨrms – Quarterly: 1st and 4th per fesse wavy, the chief argent, and the base representing waves of the sea, in chief a dexter hand couped at the wrist gules, in base a salmon naiant proper, *O'Neill*; 2nd and 3rd checky, or and gules, a chief vair, *Chichester*. ℭrests – 1st, an arm embowed in armour, the hand grasping a sword, all proper; 2nd, a stork rising, with a snake in its beak, all proper. ℌupporters – On either side a lion gules, gorged with an antique crown argent, pendant therefrom an escutcheon, the *dexter* charged with the arms of O'Neill, and the *sinister* with those of Chichester.
Seat – Shane's Castle, Antrim BT41 4NE. *Club* – Turf.

SONS LIVING

Hon SHANE SEBASTIAN CLANABOY, *b* 25 July 1965: *m* 1997, Celia, eldest da of Peter Hickman, of Campden Hill Sq, W8.
Hon Tyrone Alexander, *b* 1966.
Hon Rory St John, *b* 1968.

SISTER LIVING

Hon Fionn Frances Bride (10 Octavia St, SW11 3DN), *b* 1936; *ed* Heathfield, and St Anne's Coll, Oxford: *m* 1961 (*m diss* 1975), John Albert Leigh Morgan, CMG (later Sir John Morgan, KCMG), HM Amb to Mexico (ret 1989), and has issue living, John Edward Rustand, *b* 1964: *m* 1996, Natasha C., elder da of Randal MacDonnell, of London and Devon, — Mary Ann Frances, *b* 1962: *m* 1989, Charles Anthony Warneford Gibson, only son of Group Capt Phillip G. Gibson, of Manor Farm House, Sawtry, Cambs, and has issue living, Alexander Shane Warneford *b* 1991, Frederick John Philip *b* 1993, Benjamin James Campbell *b* 1995, Georgia Fionn Margaret *b* 1998, — Catherine Martha Annabel, *b* 1966.

WIDOW LIVING OF BROTHER OF THIRD BARON

Katharine Jean (*Baroness O'Neill of the Maine*), da of late William Ingham Whitaker, DL, of Pylewell Park, Lymington, Hants: *m* 1944, Baron O'Neill of the Maine, PC (Life Baron), who *d* 1990, and has issue (see colls infra). *Residence* – Lisle Court, Lymington, Hants.

COLLATERAL BRANCHES LIVING

Issue of late Rt Hon Terence Marne O'Neill (*Baron O'Neill of the Maine*), brother of 3rd Baron, *b* 1914, *d* 1990; raised to the rank of a Baron's son 1930, and *cr* Baron O'Neill of the Maine (Life Baron) 1970: *m* 1944, Katharine Jean (ante), da of late William Ingham Whitaker, DL, of Pylewell Park, Lymington, Hants (*see* V Melville, 1970 Edn):—

Hon Patrick Arthur Ingham (48 Forbes St, Newtown, NSW 2042, Australia), *b* 1945; *ed* Eton; Lieut QRI Hussars; Reporter ABC, TV Producer, Councillor Nat Trust of Australia NSW 1986-87: *m* 1st, 1975 (*m diss* 1984), Anne, da of Douglas Lillecrapp, of Adelaide, S Australia; 2ndly, 1984, Stella Mary, da of late Sir Alexander Russell Downer, KBE, of Williamstown, S Australia, and has issue living (by 1st *m*), Sophie Katherine, *b* 1976, — Elizabeth Mary, *b* 1981. —— *Hon* Penelope Anne, *b* 1947: *m* 1st, 1970 (*m diss* 1982), Christopher William Kerr Devas (*see* M Lothian, colls); 2ndly, 1984, Lt-Cdr William Victor Crutchley, RN (ret), son of Adm Sir Victor Crutchley, VC, KCB, DSC (*see* Parker, Bt, *cr* 1844, 1948 Edn), and has issue living (by 1st *m*), William Thomas, *b* 1975, — (by 2nd *m*) Arthur Percy, *b* 1987, — Daisy Alice, *b* 1986. *Residence* – Mappercombe Manor, Powerstock, Bridport, Dorset.

Issue of late Rt Hon (Robert William) Hugh O'Neill (*Baron Rathcavan*), yst son of 2nd Baron, *b* 1883, *d* 1982; *cr* a Baronet 1929, and *Baron Rathcavan* 1953:—
See that title.

PREDECESSORS – (1) *Rev* WILLIAM Chichester, el son of Rev Edward Chichester, a descendant of John Chichester, yr brother of 2nd Earl of Donegall (*see* M Donegall, colls) in 1855 succeeded to the estates of his cousin Earl O'Neill (extinct), and in that year assumed by Roy licence the surname of O'Neill; *b* 1813; *cr Baron O'Neill*, of Shanes Castle, co Antrim (peerage of United Kingdom) 1868: *m* 1st, 1839, Henrietta, who *d* 1857, da of late Hon Robert Torrens, a Judge of the Common Pleas in Ireland; 2ndly, 1858; Elizabeth Grace, who *d* 1905, da of the Ven John Torrens, DD, Archdeacon of Dublin; *d* 1883; *s* by his son (2) EDWARD, 2nd Baron, *b* 1839; MP for co Antrim (C) 1863-80: *m* 1873, Lady Louisa Katherine Emma Cochrane, who *d* 1942, da of 11th Earl of Dundonald; *d* 1928; *s* by his grandson (3) SHANE EDWARD ROBERT (el son of late Capt Hon Arthur Edward Bruce O'Neill, MP, Household Cav, *ka* 1914, el son of 2nd Baron), 3rd Baron; *b* 1907; Lieut-Col N Irish Horse: *m* 1932, Anne Geraldine Mary (who *m* 2ndly, 1945 (*m diss* 1952), 2nd Viscount Rothermere; 3rdly, 1952, Ian Lancaster Fleming, who *d* 1964 (Rose Bt, *cr* 1874, colls), and *d* 1981), da of Hon Guy Lawrence Charteris (E Wemyss); *ka* in Italy 1944; *s* by his son (4) RAYMOND ARTHUR CLANABOY, 4th Baron and present peer.

O'NEILL OF BENGARVE, BARONESS (O'Neill) (Life Baroness 1999)

ONORA SYLVIA O'NEILL, CBE, only da of late Hon Sir Con Douglas Walter O'Neill, GCMG (*see* B Rathcavan, colls), by his 1st wife, Rosemary Margaret, *née* Pritchard (who *m* 1957, Sir Terence Willcocks Garvey, KCMG; *b* 23 Aug 1941; *ed* St Paul's Girls' Sch, Somerville Coll, Oxford (MA 19—), and Harvard Univ (PhD 19—); Assist then Assoc Prof, Barnard Coll, Columbia Univ, New York 1970-77; Lecturer then Prof of Philosophy, Univ of Essex 1978-92; Principal, Newnham Coll, Camb since 1992; Visiting Prof Australian Nat Univ 1984, Univ of Santa Clara, California 1985, and Wissenschaftskolleg, Berlin 1989-90; Pres Aristotelian Soc 1988-89; Chm Nuffield Council on Bioethics 1996-98; Trustee, Nuffield Foundation since 1997 (Chm 1998); Foreign Hon Memb American Acad of Arts and Sciences 1993; FBA 1993; author; *cr* CBE 1995, and *Baroness O'Neill of Bengarve*, of The Braid, co Antrim (Life Baroness) 1999: *m* 1963 (*m diss* 1976), Edward John Nell, son of Edward John Nell, of Brooklyn, NY, USA, and has issue.

Arms – ......
Address – Newnham College, Cambridge, CB3 9DF.

SONS LIVING

Hon Adam Edward O'Neill NELL, *b* 1967.
Hon Jacob Rowan NELL, *b* 1969.

O'NEILL OF THE MAINE, BARONY OF (O'Neill) (Extinct 1990) (see B O'Neill)

ONSLOW, EARL OF (Onslow) (Earl UK 1801, Bt E 1674 (with precedency of 1660))

MICHAEL WILLIAM COPLESTONE DILLON ONSLOW, 7th Earl, and 11th Baronet (of 2nd creation); *b* 28 Feb 1938; *s* 1971; *ed* Eton, and Sorbonne; Insurance Broker: *m* 1964, Robin Lindsay, only da of Maj Robert Lee Bullard III, of Atlanta, Georgia, USA, and of Lady Aberconway, and has issue.

Arms – Argent, a fesse gules, between six Cornish choughs proper. Crest – An eagle sable, preying on a partridge or. Supporters – Two falcons close proper, belled or.
Residence – Temple Court, Clandon Park, Guildford. *Club* – Beefsteak.

Quick without impetuosity

SON LIVING

RUPERT CHARLES WILLIAM BULLARD (*Viscount Cranley*), *b* 16 June 1967; *ed* Eton.

DAUGHTERS LIVING

Lady Arabella Ann Teresa, *b* 1970.
Lady Charlotte Emma Dorothy, *b* 1977.

SISTER LIVING

Lady Teresa Lorraine, *b* 1940: *m* 1961, Auberon Alexander Waugh, the writer (*see* E Carnarvon, colls, 1973-74 Edn), and has issue living, Alexander Evelyn Michael (Stoke Bruerne Park, Towcester, Northants NN12 7RZ), *b* 1963: *m* 1990, Elizabeth Beatrice, da of Alexander Surtees Chancellor (*see* Debenham, Bt, colls), and has issue living, Auberon Augustus *b* 1998, Mary Eulalia *b* 1993, Sally Alexandra *b* 1995, — Nathaniel Thomas Biafra, *b* 1968, — (Margaret) Sophia Laura, *b* 1962: *m* 1986, Julian Watson, of Great Highleigh, Exebridge, Dulverton, Somerset, only son of Vice Adm Sir Philip Alexander Watson, KBE, LVO, of The Hermitage, Bodicote, Banbury, Oxon, and has issue living, Constance Mary Alabama *b* 1990, Beatrice Teresa Arizona *b* 1992, Esther Harriet Domenica Oklahoma *b* 1994, Cecily Laura Jacoba Louisiana *b* 1998, — Daisy Louisa Dominica, *b* 1967: *m* 19—, Peter de Sales La Terrière, 3rd son of Ian Cameron de Sales La Terrière, and has issue living, Panda Sarah *b* 1997. *Residence* – Combe Florey House, Taunton, Somerset.

WIDOW LIVING OF SIXTH EARL

NINA, MBE (*Jo, Countess of Onslow*) (Sturdee's, Freeland, Oxford), yr da of Thomas Sturdee; MBE (Civil) 1953: *m* 1962, as his 2nd wife, the 6th Earl of Onslow, who *d* 1971.

COLLATERAL BRANCHES LIVING

Branch from 2nd son of 2nd Earl

Grandchildren of late Vivian Isidore Onslow (infra):—
Issue of late Arthur Charles Vivian Onslow, *b* 1920, *d* 1997: *m* 1951, Patricia Taylor, who *d* 1996:—
Anthony Ernest Edward (33 Old Fox Close, Caterham, Surrey, CR3 5QV), *b* 1955. —— David Peter, *b* 1959. —— Anne Rose, *b* 1957: *m* 1994, Ronald Hector Mowat, Ch Petty Officer, RN, of 4 Duncan St, Thurso, Caithness KW14 7HZ.

Grandchildren of late Arthur Edward Onslow, 4th son of late Lt-Col Arthur Edward Mainwaring-Ellerker-Onslow, 3rd son of late Col Hon Thomas Cranley Onslow, MP, 2nd son of 2nd Earl:—
Issue of late Vivian Isidore Onslow, *b* 1888, *d* 1979: *m* 1st, 1912, Lily, who *d* 1918, elder da of Charles Edward Henson, of Hope House, The Vineyard, Richmond, Surrey; 2ndly, 1919, Annie Dorothea Rose, who *d* 1972, elder da of Frank Charles Davis, of Evercreech, nr Bath:—
(By 2nd *m*) Denzil Isidore Charles (5 Christopher Way, Shepton Mallet, Som), *b* 1924: *m* 1945, Iris Frances Warren, who *d* 1992, and has issue living, John M. (Little Silvers, Upton Noble, nr Frome, Som), *b* 1948: *m* 1972, Susan Jane Mary Nicholls, and has issue living, Stuart John *b* 1977, — Dennis Raymond (5 Christopher Way, Shepton Mallet, Som), *b* 1949, — Andrew Martin (33 Wyville Rd, Frome, Som), *b* 1954: *m* 1981 (*m diss* 1988), Wendy Jacqueline Baker, and has issue living, Martin Andrew *b* 1983, Matthew John *b* 1984, — Brian S. (34 Blenheim Rd, Street, Som), *b* 1957: *m* 1978, Susan Jane Parsons, and has issue living, Neil Ian *b* 1984, Michelle Claire *b* 1981, — Daphne Carol, *b* 1945; *m* 1st, 19—, — Howell; 2ndly, 1991, Derek Robert Jack, of Knowberry, Whitstone Rd, Shepton Mallet, Som, and has issue living (by 1st *m*), Wayne Lee *b* 1967, Darren Shaun *b* 1970, — Sheila Rose, *b* 1946: *m* 1970, Raymond William Withers, of Home, Weymouth Rd, Evercreech, Som and has issue living, Paul Neil *b* 1970, Mark Andrew *b* 1973, Tony Clive *b* 1980, — Pamela Susan (1 Bolters Lane, Downside, Shepton Mallet, Som), *b* 1952: *m* 1969 (*m diss* 19—), Peter John Gregory, and has issue living, Dean Marcus *b* 1972, Mandy Lea *b* 1969, Tina Clare Angelina *b* 1970, — Christine Ann, *b* 1953: *m* 1975, Glenn Robert Davies, of 34 Wickham Lane, Shepton Mallet, Som, and has issue living, Alan Robert *b* 1975, Gary Martin *b* 1977, — Linda Dawn (16 Westover, Nunney, Frome, Som), *b* (twin) 1954: *m* 1973 (*m diss* 1984), Laurence Vernon Whittaker, and has issue living, Steven Raymond *b* 1974, Timothy Laurence *b* 1977, — Sandra Jane, *b*

1959: *m* 1977, Philip Roy Farmer, of 14 Douglas Drive, Shepton Mallet, Som, and has issue living, Trevor Philip *b* 1979, Jennifer Ann *b* 1980, — Wendy Janice, *b* 1961: *m* 1987, Alan William Coubrough, of 3 Naisholt Rd, Shepton Mallet, Som, and has issue living, Craig William *b* 1990, Adam James *b* 1997. —— Constance Vivien, *b* 1934: *m* 1st, 1960, Stanley W. Crabb: 2ndly, 19—, — — Tombs.

Branch from 2nd son of 1st Earl

Granddaughter of late Frederick Horace Onslow, son of late Capt Arthur Onslow, son of 2nd son of 1st Earl:—
Issue of late Arthur Onslow, *b* 1871, *d* 1937: *m* 1893, Emily, who *d* 1952, da of W. A. Howe, and has issue living:—
Valentine Charlotte, *b* 1900. *Residence* – Addison House, Niagara-on-the-Lake, Ontario, Canada.

(Male line in remainder to the Barony and Baronetcy)

Branch from 1st son of 1st son of 2nd son of brother of 1st Baron

Grandchildren of late William Cleveland Onslow, son of late Major Pitcairn Onslow, el son of Rev George Walton Onslow, el son of George Onslow, MP (*b* 1721), el son of late Lt-Gen Richard Onslow, nephew of 1st Baron Onslow, and uncle of 1st Earl:—
Issue of late Guy Cleveland Onslow, *b* 1884, *d* 1952: *m* 1916, Angela Mary, who *d* 1974, da of Robert Pearce, of Ripley Court, Surrey:—
Guildford Arthur Richard, *b* 1921: *ed* Camb Univ (BA 19—): *m* 1945, Ilse, only da of Julius Sahm. *Residence* – 7 New Rd, Croxley Green, Rickmansworth, Herts. —— Rose Saltern, *b* 1918. *Residence* – 9 Rose Lane, Ripley, Woking, Surrey.

Branch from 2nd son of 1st son of 2nd son of brother of 1st Baron

Grandchildren of late Maj-Gen James William MACARTHUR-ONSLOW, VD, eldest son of late Capt Arthur Alexander Walton Onslow, RN (infra):—
Issue of late James Arthur MACARTHUR-ONSLOW, *b* 1898, *d* 1959: *m* 1925, Constance Faith, who *d* 1962, da of George Herbert, of Sydney:—
James William Macleay (Glen Ripple, Bonnell's Rd, M/S 2131, Toowoomba, Qld 4352, Aust), *b* 1932; *ed* Knox Gram Sch, Wahroonga, NSW: *m* 1964, Margaret Alice, da of Colin Basil Peter Bell, of Kenmore, Brisbane, Qld, and has issue living, James Stuart Macleay, *b* 1966, — Julienne Elizabeth, *b* 1969. —— Susan Helen, *b* 1935: *m* 1962, Brig Ian Henry Hayman (ret), Austn Staff Corps, of 57 Epping Rd, Double Bay, NSW 2028, Australia, and has issue living, Rosemary Susan (41 Lamrock Av, Bondi Beach, NSW 2026, Aust), *b* 1963, — Charlotte Elizabeth, *b* 1966: *m* 1995, Andrew Ferris Lennox, FRACS, and has issue living, William Thomas Onslow *b* 1997, Henry Alexander Onslow *b* 1999. —— Sandra Ruth (Old Boree, Gundaroo, NSW 2620, Aust), *b* 1936.

Grandsons of late Arthur John MACARTHUR-ONSLOW, 2nd son of late Capt Arthur Alexander Walton Onslow, RN (infra):—
Issue of late Lt-Col Richard Walton MACARTHUR-ONSLOW, Australian Light Horse, *b* 1904, *d* 1981: *m* 1928, Lois Ruth, who *d* 1976, da of H. B. Greene, of Barncleuth Sq, Sydney, NSW:—
Richard Bowring (Cannanbri, Walcha, NSW 2354), *b* 1934: *m* 1960, Christina Helen Huntly Gordon, da of Ronald Arthur McWilliam, of Vaucluse, Sydney, NSW, and has issue living, Richard Matthew, *b* 1962, — Rohan James, *b* 1964, — Lachlan Robert Hugh, *b* 1972. —— John Walton, *b* 1943. —— William Robert (45 Raglan St, Tamworth, NSW 2340), *b* 1945: *m* 1977, Sarah, da of L. B. Bettington, of Fernside, Rylstone, NSW, and has issue living, Felicity Georgina, *b* 1979, — Jane Belinda, *b* 1982.

Granddaughter of late Capt Arthur Alexander Walton Onslow, RN, el son of Arthur Pooley Onslow, el son of Rev Arthur Onslow, 2nd son of George Onslow, MP (ante):—
Issue of late Brig-Gen George Macleay MACARTHUR-ONSLOW, CMG, DSO, VD, *b* 1875, *d* 1931: *m* 1907, Violet Marguerite, who *d* 1981, da of late W. F. Gordon, of Manar, near Braidwood, NS Wales:—
Faith MacLeay (Cranmer Cottage, Dorchester-on-Thames, Wallingford, Oxon OX10 7HP), *b* 1910: *m* 1941, Ivan Lloyd Phillips, CBE, DPhil (Oxon), Malayan Civil Ser, who *d* 1984, and has issue living, Hugh Gerard Lloyd (25A Lorne Av, Killara, NSW 2071, Aust), *b* 1946: *m* 1972, Rosalind, who *d* 1995, da of late H. B. Mackenzie-Wood, of Sunninghill, Mt Ousley, NSW, and has issue living, Hugh Edward Paul *b* 1976, Julian Thomas *b* 1979, Clare Elizabeth *b* 1974.

Grandchildren of late Francis Arthur MACARTHUR-ONSLOW, 5th son of Capt Arthur Alexander Walton Onslow, RN (ante):—
Issue of late Maj-Gen Sir Denzil MACARTHUR-ONSLOW, CBE, DSO, ED, *b* 1904, *d* 1984: *m* 1st, 1927 (*m diss* 1950), Elinor Margaret, who *d* 1979, da of late Gordon Caldwell, formerly of 4 Albert Hall Mansions, SW7; 2ndly, 1950, Dorothy Wolseley, AO, MB, BS (*Lady Macarthur-Onslow*) (Mount Gilead, Campbelltown, NSW 2560, Australia), only child of late W. D. Scott, of Bellevue Hill, NSW:—
(By 1st *m*) (Denzil) Ion (2A Holt St, Double Bay, NSW 2028, Australia), *b* 1928; Lt (ret) R NSW Lancers: *m* 1957, Jenifer Marie, da of late James Crooks, CVO, FRCS, of 46 Harley St, W1, and has issue living, Rupert Gordon (228 Barker St, Randwick, NSW 2031, Australia), *b* 1962: *m* 1989, Lucienne Mary Elizabeth, yr da of Neville George Green, of Sydney, NSW, and has issue living, Benjamin George *b* 1995, Lucy Marie *b* 1997, — Sophie Rose, *b* (Nov) 1957: *m* 1st, 1987, Julian Henry Nettlefold, yr son of Edward Michael Nettlefold, of Abbey House, Milton Lilbourne, Pewsey, Wilts; 2ndly, 1993, Peter D. Stork, elder son of Kenneth Stork, of Mayfield, E Sussex, and has issue living (by 1st *m*), Harry Michael Frederick *b* 1989, (by 2nd *m*) James Kenneth Macarthur *b* 1993, Frederick George Louis *b* 1996, — Verena Marie, *b* 1960: *m* 19—, James Ashley Woodford Craven, of 2A Holt St, Double Bay, NSW 2028, son of Cmdr J. H. W. Craven, DSC, RN (ret), of Burradoo, NSW, and has issue living, Edward James Macarthur *b* 1995, Elinor Rose Macarthur *b* 1998. —— Neil Gordon, ED (27 Kemmis St, Randwick, NSW 2031, Australia), *b* 1930; Lt-Col comdg 1/15 Armd Regt R NSW Lancers: *m* 1964, Regina de Tessier, da of late Reginald de Tessier Prevost, of Bellevue Hill, NSW,

and has issue living, Duncan Reginald, *b* 1966, — Airlie, *b* 1969. —— Euan (East Tinwald, Lochmaben, Dumfriesshire), *b* 1934. —— Diana Florence, *b* 1931: *m* 1952 (*m diss* 1968), Geoffrey Brian Kewley, and has issue living, Robin Geoffrey, *b* 1953, — Martin William, *b* 1959. —— (By 2nd *m*) Lee, *b* 1952; Capt Sydney Univ Regt, Reserve of Officers. —— Katrina, *b* 1953: *m* 1993 (*m diss* 1998), Sir Charles John Spinney Hobhouse, 7th Bt.

Issue of late Lt-Col Edward Macarthur-Onslow, DSO, ED, Australian Imperial Forces, *b* 1909, *d* 1980: *m* 1932, Winifred Hall, who *d* 1987, da of late William Hall Owen, of Wollongong, NSW:—
Annette Rosemary, *b* 1933. —— Pamela Jane, *b* 1936: *m* 1st, 1958 (*m diss* 1968), Paterson James Saunders; 2ndly, 1971, Arthur Leslie Harrison, of S Shields, co Durham, now of Box 200 PO, Camden, NSW 2570, and has issue living (by 1st *m*), Kirkland Robert Macarthur, *b* 1961, — Christopher Philip, *b* 1962. —— Phoebe (Macquarie Grove, PO Box 2, Camden, NSW 2570), *b* 1939: *m* 1963 (*m diss* 1981), Hugh Geddes Atkinson, and has issue living, Jason Hugh, *b* 1959, — Rachel Ann, *b* 1963.

Grandchildren of late Arthur Loftus Onslow, el son of late Douglas Arthur Onslow, CE (infra):—
Issue of late Douglas Arthur George Onslow, *b* 1901, *d* 1966: *m* 1925, Margaret Forbes Kilgour, who *d* 1985, da of Maj John Merrick Rayner, AMIME, of Maji Chemka, Thomson's Falls, Kenya:—
Richard Douglas Loftus (4 Castlestead, Pateley Bridge, Harrogate, N Yorks HG3 5QF), *b* 1928; *ed* Michaelhouse, Balgowan, S Africa, and Natal Univ; Kenya 1952-53 with KAR: *m* 1st, 1966 (*m diss* 1968), Mrs Elizabeth Frances Bateman, da of J. Gordon Elsworthy; 2ndly, 1968, Countess Ethel Elisabeth Olga Maria von Rietberg, da of HSH late Prince Ferdinand Andreas Joseph Maria of Leichtenstein (Brunner, Bt, colls), and has an adopted da (with 2nd wife), Merith Margaret Andrea, *b* 1972. —— Patricia Margaret Daisy, *b* 1941: *m* 1st, 1960 (*m diss* 1972), Christopher David Kennedy; 2ndly, 1972, Edmond Francis Dorset Fellowes (*see* Twysden, Bt, ext, 1985 Edn), of 69 High St, Heytesbury, Warminster, Wilts BA12 OEB, and has issue living (by 1st *m*), Mark Edward Lucian, *b* 1966. —— Prudence Katherine Barbara, *b* 1946: *m* 1970, Lt-Col Robin Timothy Keigwin, Irish Gds, of Low Mains Farm, Masham, Ripon, N Yorks HG4 4PS, and has issue living, Richard Skarratt, *b* 1973, — Michael Douglas, *b* 1975.

Grandchildren of late Douglas Arthur George Onslow (ante):—
Issue of late Desmond Merrick Onslow, *b* 1929, *d* 1983: *m* 1954, Sylvia Patricia Melody Wiggins, of PO Box 45, Fourways 2055, S Africa:—
Roger, *b* 1965. —— Debra Susan, *b* 1955: *m* 1977, David Alan Brokenshire, and has issue living, Rhett David, *b* 1982. —— Vanessa Mary, *b* 1960.

Grandsons of late Douglas Arthur Onslow, CE, el son of late Lt-Col William Campbell Onslow, 2nd son of Rev Arthur Onslow (ante):—
Issue of late Francis Robert Douglas Onslow, *b* 1878, *d* 1938: *m* 1925, Mabel, who *d* 1974, da of William Strachan, of Edinburgh:—
Rt Hon Sir Cranley Gordon Douglas, KCMG, MP, *b* 1926; *cr Baron Onslow of Woking* (Life Baron) 1997 (see that title). —— Ian Denzil, *b* 1929; *ed* Harrow, and Grenoble Univ, France: *m* 1954, Marjorie, da of Albert Domville, of Stockton Heath, and has issue living, Christopher Denzil, *b* 1956; *ed* Harrow: *m* 1st, 1984 (*m diss* 1990), Veronica Jane, yst da of Capt John Stanley Mitcalfe, OBE, VRD, RNR (rct); 2ndly, 1993, Paula Louise Howell, only da of late John Jenkins, MICE, of Inkberrow, Worcs, and has issue living (by 2nd wife), Edward John Denzil *b* 1991, Alice Louise Daisy *b* 1994, — Mark Loftus Domville, *b* 1958; *ed* Pangbourne: *m* 1983, Judith Heather, da of Peter Smith, of E Grinstead, Sussex, — Michael Piers David, *b* 1963; *ed* Harrow, and Stirling Univ; Major The Royal Scots (The Royal Regt): *m* 1993, Lesley Alison, eldest da of late Kenneth Jolly, of Gt Baddow, Essex, and has issue living, James Douglas *b* 1997, Emily Deborah *b* 1995, — Robert Douglas, *b* 1965; *ed* Kings Sch, Bruton, and Glasgow Caledonian Univ: *m* 1995, Joanna C., only da of David Wallace, of Tighnabruaich, Argyll, and has issue living, Oliver Jolyon David, *b* 1997, Henry Dennis *b* 1999, — Victoria Penelope Diana *b* (twin) 1965: *m* 1993, Jolyon Robert Lydall Savill, who *d* (March) 1993, only son of John L. L. Savill. *Residence* – 3 Jubilee Cottages, 43 Middle Rd, Lymington, Hants SO41 9HE.

Granddaughters of late Maj Arthur Hughes-Onslow, el son of late Henry John Hughes-Onslow, 5th son of late Rev Arthur Onslow (ante):—
Issue of late Cdr Sir Geoffrey Henry Hughes-Onslow, KBE, DSC, RN, *b* 1893, *d* 1971: *m* 1918, Hon Eileen Mabel Lowther Crofton, who *d* 1972, da of 4th Baron Crofton:—
Auriole Kathleen, *b* 1919: *m* 1945, Rev Simon Charles David Fergusson, who *d* 1982 (*see* Fergusson, Bt). —— Judith Eileen, *b* 1923: *m* 1945, Lt John Thornton Lorimer, DSO, RNVR, of Kirkangus, Barr, Ayrshire, and has issue living, Patrick James, *b* 1946: *m* 1976, Julia Caroline, da of Alexander Patrick Pringle, DFC, of Gemilston, Kirkmichael, Ayrshire, and has issue living, James Seth Patrick *b* 1979, William Reuben John *b* 1980, Cressida Flora Kate *b* 1984, — Bridget Katharine Eileen (22 Birkbeck Rd, W3), *b* 1948. —— Mary, *b* 1929: *m* 1952, Lt Cdr George Stewart Wright, VRD, RNR, of Wainsford House, Everton, Lymington, Hants, and has issue living, Nicholas Peter, *b* 1960, — Christopher George, *b* 1964.

Grandchildren of late Capt Oliver Hughes-Onslow, eldest son of late Maj Denzil Hughes-Onslow, 2nd son of late Henry John Hughes-Onslow (ante):—
Issue of late Andrew George Hughes-Onslow, *b* 1920; *d* 1979: *m* 1944, Betty (who *m* 2ndly, 1994, as his 2nd wife, Maj David George Crichton, LVO (*see* E Erne, colls), who *d* 1997), da of late Col Maurice George Lee, MC, RFC:—
James Andrew (42 Knatchbull Rd, SE5 9QY; *Club* – Boodle's), *b* 1945; *ed* Eton; journalist: *m* 1982, Christina L., da of Peter Hay, of Melbourne, Australia, and has issue living, Andrew Peter, *b* 1985, — Flora Alice, *b* 1988, — Marina, *b* 1990, — Harriet, *b* 1993. —— Elizabeth Mary, *b* 1949: *m* 1978, John Randolph Hustler, of Ripsley House, Liphook, Hants GU30 7JH, son of late William Mostyn Collingwood Hustler, of 31 Melton Court, SW7, and has issue living, Charles James, *b* 1982, — Frederick Randolph, *b* 1986, — Willa Victoria, *b* 1983. —— Sarah Jane, *b* 1954: *m* 1975, Michael Williamo, of Werrington Park, Launceston, Cornwall PL15 8TR, and has issue living, Thomas Edward, *b* 1976, — George Michael, *b* 1979, — Camilla Ruth, *b* 1984.

Issue of late Capt Timothy Neil Hughes-Onslow, Rifle Bde, *b* 1924, *d* 1995: *m* 1950, Susan (112 Swan Court, SW3 5RU), da of Sir William Francis Stratford Dugdale, 1st Bt (*cr* 1936):—
Archibald Edward Neil (82 Mercers Rd, N19 4PR), *b* 1954; *ed* Eton, BNC Oxford, and Oxford Polytechnic; townplanner; has issue living (by Mary Ryan, solicitor), Daniel, *b* 1987, — Max, *b* 1989, — Euan Williams, *b* 1993. —— Richard Luke

(42 Agate Rd, W6 OAH. *Club* – White's), *b* 1958; *ed* Eton: *m* 1988, Christine S., da of Charles Doughty, of Mill House, Denham Bridge, Buckland Monachorum, Devon, and has issue living, George Oliver, *b* 1995, — Iona Margaret, *b* 1992. —— Henrietta, *b* 1951: *m* 1980, David W. A. Cole, of 17 Heslop Rd, SW12, son of Sir David Cole, KCMG, MC, and has issue living, Timothy David, *b* 1985, — Lucy, *b* 1983.

Issue of late Capt Fergus Erskine Hughes-Onslow, Rifle Bde, *b* 1929, *d* 1994: *m* 1955, Rose Ariel (Lower Norsebury, Stoke Charity, Winchester, Hants SO21 3PR), da of late Anthony Ewart Ledger Hill, OBE, DL, of Twyford Lodge, Twyford, Hants:—
Anthony Charles, *b* 1957: *m* 1991, Laura A., da of L. W. Newton, and of late Mrs M. A. J. Clark, of W2, and has issue living, Harry Arthur, *b* 1992, — Fergus Ambrose, *b* 1996, — Serena Alice, *b* 1995. —— Olivia, *b* 1960: *m* 1985, Michael J. W. Winterton, of The Old Rectory, Willand Old Vicarage, Cullompton, Devon, son of late Cdr David Winterton, RN, of Vale House, Halstock, Yeovil, Som, and has issue living, Alexander John, *b* 1993, — Hermione Rose, *b* 1987, — Lucy, *b* 1989. —— Belinda Marion, *b* 1962; has issue living (by Paolo Scaburri), Elsa, *b* 1996.

Grandson of late Maj Denzil Hughes-Onslow, 2nd son of Henry John Hughes-Onslow (ante):—
Issue of late Lt-Com Reginald Hughes-Onslow, RN (ret), *b* 1895, *d* 1947: *m* 1934 (*m diss* 1946), Daphne Helen Anne, who *d* 1992, da of late Col Robert Hanbury Brudenell Bruce, DSO (*see* M Ailesbury, colls, 1990 Edn):—
Denzil James (The Old Bake House, Culworth, nr Banbury, Oxon), *b* 1939; *ed* Ampleforth; late 2nd Lt R Armoured Corps: *m* 1973, Chloé Elizabeth, da of Mme de Vic, of St Cloud, Paris, and has issue living, Sophie Anne Rose, *b* 1974.

Branch from 2nd son of 2nd son of brother of 1st Baron

Descendants of late Adm Sir Richard Onslow, GCB, who was *cr* a Bt 1797, 2nd son of late Lt-Gen Richard Onslow (infra):—
See Onslow, Bt.

Branch from 1st son of 3rd son of 2nd son of brother of 1st Baron

Grandchildren of late Maj George Arthur Onslow, 5th and yst son of Capt Andrew George Onslow, of Oxenhall, Newent, eldest son of Richard Foley Onslow, of Stardens, Glos, eldest son of Ven Richard Francis Onslow, Archdeacon of Worcester, eldest son of Very Rev Arthur Onslow, Dean of Worcester, 3rd son of Lt-Gen Richard Onslow, nephew of 1st Baron and uncle of 1st Earl:—
Issue of late Adm Sir Richard George Onslow, KCB, DSO, *b* 1904, *d* 1975: *m* 1932, Kathleen Meriel (*Lady Onslow*) (Little Ryton House, Ryton, Shrewsbury, Shropshire SY5 7LW), el da of Edmund Taylor, of Longnor Bank House, Shrewsbury:—
Richard Edmund (Preston Bagot House, Preston Bagot, Henley-in-Arden, Warwicks B95 5DR), *b* 1933; Cdr RN: *m* 1961, Mary-Jean, el da of Brig Kenneth James Garner-Smith, OBE, of Aird House, by Inverness, and has issue living, Richard James (Burnhouse, Stow, Selkirkshire TD1 2RX), *b* 1962; *ed* Eton; Capt Blues & Royals: *m* 1992, Lucinda Caroline, da of Patrick Alexander Campbell Fraser (*see* Baird, Bt, 1995 Edn), of Borthwickshiels, Hawick, Roxburghshire, and has issue living, Charles Patrick *b* 1995, Alexander James *b* 1997, Rosa Kalitza *b* 1998, — Robert Denzil, *b* 1965; *ed* Eton, and Magdalen Coll, Oxford; bar-at-law: *m* 1995, Tamara Forsyth, yr da of Robert Trench Fox, CBE (*see* B Ashtown, colls), and has issue living, Sacha Llewellyn *b* 1997, Georgia Macdonald *b* 1998. —— Denzil John (The Bank House, Richards Castle, Shropshire), *b* 1939: *m* 1967, Susan, da of late B. Leach, and has issue living, Andrew John, *b* 1968, — James Denzil, *b* 1970: *m* 1998, Michaela Jayne, da of late Edward Sims, of Bridgend, Glam, — Tamsin Sarah, *b* 1976.

Issue of late Maj John Onslow, Duke of Cornwall's LI, *b* 1906, *d* 1985: *m* 1956, Susan (Oaklea, Vicarage Hill, Loxwood, W Sussex), da of late Roland Percival Neville Towle:—
Andrew George (Rylstone, Grove Park, SE5 8LT), *b* 1957: *m* 1991, (Elizabeth) Jane, yr da of Lt-Col James Barratt Owen, of Beechwood, Bengate, Appleby-in-Westmorland, and formerly wife of — Evans, and has issue living, Harry James Rufus, *b* 1992, — James Andrew Quintus, *b* 1995, — Frederica Jane, *b* 1993. —— Simon John (65 St Margarets Rd, Twickenham, TW1 2LL) *b* 1960: *m* 1993, Clare, da of Norman Lonsdale, of Bridlemere Court, Newmarket, Suffolk, and has issue living, Jack, *b* 19—, — Lucy, *b* 1997. —— Jane Elizabeth, *b* 1958; *d* 1975. —— Sarah Margaret, *b* 1962: *m* 1990, Simon F. Harrison, of Ironstone Cottage, Lower St, Fittleworth, W Sussex, son of R. F. Harrison, of Pulborough, W Sussex, and has issue living, Rupert Edward John, *b* 1996, — Emily Jane Elizabeth, *b* 1992. —— Rachel Evelyn Mary, *b* 1967.

Issue of late Maj Charles Edward Onslow, MC, *b* 1912, *d* 1969: *m* 1955, Margaret Mary Lee, who *d* 1994, da of Rev William Marsh Lee Evans, R of Saxby, Brigg, Lincs:—
John Edward, *b* 1956: *m* 1986, Dora Helen, da of late Christopher Wyborn Armstrong, OBE, of Kwetu Farm, Gilgil, Kenya, and has issue living, Jasper Denzil, *b* 1994, — Kate Helen, *b* 1997. *Address* – Gogar Farm, Rongai, Kenya.

Granddaughters of late Capt Andrew George Onslow (ante):—
Issue of late Major George Arthur Onslow, *b* 1876, *d* 1956: *m* 1st, 1902, Charlotte Riou, who *d* 1932, yst da of late Rev Riou George Benson; 2ndly, 1933, Maud Elliot, who *d* 1986, yr da of late George Steele Travers Harris:—
(By 1st *m*) Kathleen Theodosia, *b* 1914: *m* 1945, Edward Godfrey Purvis Sherwood, who *d* 1989, of Applegarth, Hayton, Carlisle, CA4 9HT, and has had issue, Edward Patrick Charles (71 High Sett, Hills Rd, Cambridge CB2 1NZ), *b* 1946: *m* 1975, Margaret Anne, da of late John Van Vechten Veeder, and *d* 1991, leaving issue, Edward Godfrey DeWitt *b* 1978, Peter David Onslow *b* 1980, Claire Margaret Letham *b* 1987, — Andrew Godfrey Purvis (2 Pelham Terr, Lewes, E Sussex BN7 1TY), *b* 1950: *m* 1974, Mary Helen, da of Hon Francis Michael Hepburne-Scott (*see* L Polwarth), and has issue living, Gideon *b* 1976, Samuel *b* 1979, Phoebe *b* 1983, Lucie *b* 1987, — Thomas James Mulso (26 Highclere Rd, New Malden, Surrey KT3 3HJ), *b* 1951: *m* 1980, Barbara, da of Kenneth Walter Emberson, of 2 Newlands Park, Copthorne, Crawley, W Sussex, and has had issue, David Mathew *b* and *d* 1986, Nathan John *b* 1988, Joanna Ruth *b* 1984, — Charlotte Claire, *b* 1947. —— Denzil Octavia (St Andrew's House, 2 Tavistock Rd, W11 1BA), *b* 1919.

Grandchildren of late Augustus Paul Lumsden Onslow, 4th son of Rev Arthur Andrew Onslow, 2nd son of Ven Richard Francis Onslow (ante):—
Issue of late Augustus Charles Albert Foley Onslow, *b* 1888, *d* 1965: *m* 1914, Winifred May, who *d* 1971, da of late W. R. Williams, of Thornton Heath, Surrey:—
Winston Hillier Gopal (108 Culvert Rd, SW11), *b* 1915: *m* 1939, Kathleen Edis, who *d* 1975, and has issue living, Veronica Vivien, *b* 1943: *m* 1969, Alan Roy Wood, Surveyor, of 33 Greenways Cres, Shoreham by Sea W Sussex BN43 6HR, and has an adopted da, Lucille Ann, *b* 1973: *m* 1992 (*m diss* 1994), — Tovey, and has issue living, Aaron Patrick *b* 19—. —— Patricia Doreen (1 Airey Houses, Scocles Rd, Minster, Isle of Sheppey, Kent), *b* 1927: *m* 1956, Ronald George Coombs, who *d* 1992, and has issue living, Anne Patricia, *b* 1957: *m* 1st, 1985, Stephen David Smart; 2ndly, 1997, Christopher Smith, of 178 Minster Rd, Sheerness, Kent, and has issue living, Sam Kenneth *b* 1988, Ben *b* 1990.

Issue of late Frederick Hewitt Lumsden Onslow, *b* 1897, *d* 1969: *m* 1939, Olive Eveline, who *d* 1998, da of Ernest Spicer:—
Frederick Winston Lumsden, *b* 1940: *m* 1964, Elizabeth Maude, da of Frank Berenger Benger, and has issue living, Robert Frederick, *b* 1970, — Gillian Elizabeth, *b* 1966, — Vivien Gail, *b* 1967. *Residence* – Red Chimneys, Chalk Lane, E Horsley, Leatherhead, Surrey.

Branch from 3rd son of 3rd son of 2nd son of brother of 1st Baron

Grandchildren of late Henry Phipps Onslow (infra):—
Issue of late Thomas Phipps Onslow, *b* 1907, *d* 1990: *m* 1945, Mrs Pauline Calvert, who *d* 1970, da of Kenneth L. Shoobridge, of Coniston, Glenora, Tasmania:—
William Phipps (Kentdale, Bushy Park, Tasmania 7140), *b* 1947: *m* 1974, Victoria, da of Paul L. Abbott, of Woodstock, Calder, Tasmania, and has issue living, Fiona Louise, *b* 1975, — Lucie Jane, *b* 1976, — Annabel Rose, *b* 1979. —— Jane Elizabeth (64 Wellington St, Mosman Park 6012, W Australia), *b* 1945: *m* 1969 (*m diss* 1993), Christopher Goodwin Morley, and has issue living, Hamish Charles Thomas, *b* 1977, — Emma Patricia, *b* 1970: *m* 1998, Cameron Alan Moir, — Georgina Joan, *b* 1972.

Granddaughter of late Rev Phipps Onslow, son of late Phipps Vansittart Onslow, yst son of Very Rev Arthur Onslow, DD (ante):—
Issue of late Henry Phipps Onslow, *b* 1869, *d* 1945: *m* 1898, Maisie, who *d* 1959, da of Hon T. Playford, of Drysdale, Norton's Summit, S Australia:—
Margaret Louise, *b* 1921: *m* 1946, Charles Edward Rollins, who *d* 1990, and has issue living, Phillip Charles (Bourbon, Tea Tree Rd, Richmond, Tasmania 7025), *b* 1947: *m* 1970, Suzanne Mary Martin, of Montrose, Tasmania, and has issue living, Richard *b* 1973, Elizabeth *b* 1976, — Susan Louise, *b* 1951. *Residence* – 12 Burnett St, Church Hill, New Norfolk, Tasmania 7140.

PREDECESSORS – **(1)** *Sir* THOMAS Foote, Knt, Lord Mayor of London 1649; was *cr* a *Baronet* 1660; *d* 1687; his son-in-law **(2)** ARTHUR Onslow (husband of his da Mary), successively MP for Bramber, Sussex, Surrey, and Guildford; was *cr* a *Baronet* 1674 (with precedency of 1660); *d* 1688; *s* by his son **(3)** *Sir* RICHARD, PC, 2nd Bt, was successively MP for Guildford, Surrey, and St Mawes; was a Lord of the Admiralty, Speaker of House of Commons, High Steward of Guildford, Gov of the Levant Co, a Lord of the Treasury, Chancellor and Under-Treasurer of the Exchequer, and a Teller of the Exchequer for life; *cr Baron Onslow*, of Onslow, co Salop, and of Clandon, co Surrey (peerage of Great Britain) 1716, with remaining to his uncle, Denzil Onslow, and aftrwards to the heirs male of his father; *d* 1717; *s* by his son **(4)** THOMAS, 2nd Baron; *d* 1740; *s* by his son **(5)** RICHARD, 3rd Baron; *dsp* Oct 1776; *s* by his heir male of his grandfather **(6)** GEORGE, PC (son of Arthur Onslow, PC, MP, who was Speaker of the House of Commons 1727-61), 4th Baron who in May of the same year had been *cr Baron Cranley*, of Imber Court (peerage of Great Britain); was successively MP for Rye and Surrey Out-Ranger of Windsor Forest, a Lord of the Treasury, Lord-Lieut of Surrey, Treasurer of the Household and a Lord of the Bedchamber; *cr Viscount Cranley* and *Earl of Onslow* (peerage of United Kingdom) 1801; *d* 1814; *s* by his son **(7)** THOMAS, 2nd Earl; sat as MP for Guildford 1784-1807; *d* 1827; *s* by his son **(8)** ARTHUR GEORGE, 3rd Earl; *d* 1870, without surviving male issue; *s* by his grandnephew **(9)** WILLIAM HILLIER, GMCG, PC, (son of George Augustus Cranley (son of Hon Thomas Cranley, 2nd son of 2nd Earl, by Mary Harriet Ann, da of Lieut-Gen William F. B. Loftus)), 4th Earl; *b* 1853; a Lord in Waiting to Queen Victoria 1880 and 1886-7, Under-Sec of State for Colonies Feb 1887 to Feb 1888, Parliamentary Sec to Board of Trade Feb to Nov 1888, Gov and Com-in-Chief of New Zealand 1888-92, Under-Sec of State for India July 1895 to Nov 1900, Under-Sec of State for the Colonies 1900-1903, Pres of Board of Agriculture 1903-5, and Dep Speaker and Chm of Committees of House of Lords 1905-11: *m* 1875, Hon Florence Coulstoun, who *d* 1934, da of 3rd Baron Gardner; *d* 1911; *s* by his el son **(10)** RICHARD WILLIAM ALAN, 5th Earl; *b* 1876; High Steward of Guildford; entered Diplo Ser 1901; was Assist Private Sec of State for Foreign Affairs 1909-11 and Private Sec to Permanent Under-Sec of State for Foreign Affairs (Rt Hon Sir Arthur Nicolson, Bt, GCB) 1911-13; European War 1915-19 (OBE, Legion of Honour); appointed a Lord-in-Waiting to HM 1919, Civil Lord of the Admiralty 1920, Parliamentary Sec to Min of Agriculture 1921, to Min of Health 1921 and 1923, and to Board of Education 1923 (resigned Jan 1924), Under-Sec of State for War 1924, and Paymaster-Gen 1928 (resigned 1929); Chm of Committees and Dep Speaker in House of Lords 1931-44; became Hon Col 30th (Surrey) Anti-Aircraft Btn, RE (TA) 1927: *m* 1906, Hon Violet Marcia Catherine Bampfylde, CBE, ARRC, who *d* 1954, da of 3rd Baron Poltimore; *d* 1945; *s* by his son **(11)** WILLIAM ARTHUR BAMPFYLDE, KBE, MC, TD, 6th Earl, *b* 1913; Col late RAC, High Steward of Guildford 1947-71, Capt of the Yeoman of the Guard 1951-60: *m* 1st, 1936 (*m diss* 1962), Hon Pamela Louisa Eleanor Dillon, who *d* 1992, only da of 19th Viscount Dillon; 2ndly, 1962, Nina, MBE, da of Thomas Sturdee; *d* 1971; *s* by his son **(12)** MICHAEL WILLIAM COPLESTONE DILLON, 7th Earl and present peer; also Viscount and Baron Cranley, and Baron Onslow.

ONSLOW OF WOKING, BARON (Onslow) (Life Baron 1997)

CRANLEY GORDON DOUGLAS ONSLOW, KCMG, PC, son of late Francis Robert Douglas Onslow (*see* E Onslow, colls); *b* 8 June 1926; *ed* Harrow, Oriel Coll, Oxford (MA 1953), and Geneva Univ; RAC 1944-48 and Co of London Yeo (TA) 1948-52; Foreign Office 1951-60; MP for Woking (*C*) 1964-67; Chm 1922 Cttee 1984-92; Chm Conservative Aviation Cttee 1970-72 and 1979-82; Parliamentary Under-Sec for Aerospace and Shipping DTI 1972-74; Opposition Spokesman on Health and Social Security 1974-75, and on Defence 1975-76; Memb UK Delegation, Council of Europe and WEU 1977-81; Chm Select Cttee on Defence 1981-82; Minister of State FCO 1982-83; Chm Redifon MEL Ltd and Nautical Museums Trust; Liveryman, Worshipful Co of Fishmongers; *cr* PC 1988, KCMG 1993, and *Baron Onslow of Woking*, of Woking, co Surrey (Life Baron) 1997: *m* 1955, Lady June Ann Hay, da of 14th Earl of Kinnoull, and has issue.
Residence – c/o House of Lords, Westminister SW1A OPW. *Club* – Travellers'.

SON LIVING

Hon Richard Alan Douglas, *b* 1956; *ed* Harrow, and Oriel Coll, Oxford (MA 19—): *m* 1985, Phyllida K......, da of Michael Moore, of Folly Farm, Lindsey, Suffolk, and has issue living, Thomas Cranley Douglas, *b* 1992, — Isabella, *b* 1990.

DAUGHTERS LIVING

Hon Sandra (Sue) Dorothy, *b* 1958; *ed* LSE (BSc 19—): *m* 1982, J...... Bartlett K...... Smith, of Dayton, Ohio, USA, and has issue living, Jonathan Christopher, *b* 1990, — Claerwen Helen, *b* 1988.
Hon Caroline Diana, *b* 1959; *ed* Manchester Univ (BA 19—): *m* 1987, Joseph V...... Martino, yr son of late J...... Martino, of New York USA.
Hon Katharine (Kash) Denise, *b* 1961: *m* 1987, Nigel P...... Steer, son of Robert Steer, of Liphook, Hants.

OPPENHEIM-BARNES, BARONESS (Oppenheim-Barnes) (Life Baroness 1989)

SALLY OPPENHEIM-BARNES, PC, da of late Mark Viner, of Sheffield; *b* 26 July 1930; *ed* Sheffield High Sch, and Low-ther Coll, N Wales; former Social Worker with ILEA; Vice-Chm Conservative Parl Prices and Consumer Protection Cttee 1971-73, and Chm 1973-74; Chm Nat Consumer Council 1987-89; Chm Nat Waterways Trust 1988-89; Front Bench Opposition Spokesman on Prices and Consumer Protection 1974-79; Member Shadow Cabinet 1975-79, Min of State for Consumer Affairs, Dept of Trade, 1979-82; Member House of Commons Cttee for Privileges 1986-89, Non-Exec Dir Main Board of Boots Co plc 1982-93, Non-Exec Dir Fleming High Income Invest-ment Trust plc 1989-97, Non-Exec Dir HFC Bank plc 1989-98, and Nat Vice-Pres Townswomen's Guild 1989-90; former Pres Glos Dist of British Red Cross; MP Gloucester (*C*) 1970-87; *cr* PC 1979, and *Baroness Oppenheim-Barnes*, of Gloucester, co Glos (Life Baroness) 1989: *m* 1st, 1949, Henry Myer Oppenheim, who *d* 1980; 2ndly, 1984, John Barnes, and has issue by 1st *m*.
Residence – Quietways, The Highlands, Painswick, Glos.

SON LIVING (*By 1st marriage*)

Hon Phillip Anthony Charles Lawrence OPPENHEIM, *b* 1956; *ed* Harrow, and Oriel Coll, Oxford (MA); MP Amber Valley (*C*) 1983-97; Under Sec of State Dept of Trade and Industry 1995-(July) 1996, Exchequer Sec to the Treasury 1996-97.

DAUGHTERS LIVING (*By 1st marriage*)

Hon Carolyn Jeanette, *b* 1951; *ed* Benenden, and London Univ (BA): *m* 1973, Martin Robert Selman, and has issue living, David Benjamin, *b* 1978; *ed* Eton, and Magdalen Coll, Oxford, — Victoria Esther Jeanette, *b* 1977; *ed* Lady Margaret Hall, Oxford (BA), — Henrietta Amy Charlotte, *b* 1982.
Hon Rosanne, *b* 1954: *m* 1st, 1984 (*m diss* 1988), David B. Williams; 2ndly, 1993, Stephen James Mattick, and has issue living (by 2nd *m*), Olivia Daisy Amelia, *b* 1993. *Residence* – Pettett's Barn, Hinxton, Cambs CB10 1RF.

ORAM, BARON (Oram) (Life Baron 1975)

ALBERT EDWARD ORAM, son of late Henry Oram; *b* 13 Aug 1913; *ed* Brighton Gram Sch, and London Univ (BA Hons); Research Officer Co-operative Party 1946-55; MP for East Ham South (*Lab* and *Co-op*) 1955-75; Co-ordinator of Development Programmes Internat Co-operative Alliance 1973-74; Development Administrator Intermediate Tech Development Group 1974-76; a Lord in Waiting to HM 1976-78; *cr Baron Oram*, of Brighton in co of E Sussex (Life Baron) 1975: *m* 1956, Frances Joan, da of Arthur Charles Barber, of Lewes, Sussex, and has issue.
Residence – 19 Ridgeside Av, Patcham, Brighton, BN1 8WD.

SONS LIVING

Hon Mark, *b* 1967.
Hon Robin, *b* 1968.

ORANMORE AND BROWNE, BARON. Sits as BARON MEREWORTH (UK 1926) (Browne) (Baron I 1836)

Boldly and faithfully

DOMINICK GEOFFREY EDWARD BROWNE, 4th Baron; *b* 21 Oct 1901; *s* 1927; *ed* Eton, and Ch Ch, Oxford: *m* 1st, 1925 (*m diss* 1936), Mildred Helen, who *d* 1980, dau of late Hon Thomas Henry Frederick Egerton (*see* D Sutherland, colls); 2ndly, 1936 (*m diss* 1950), Oonagh, who *d* 1995, da of late Hon Arthur Ernest Guinness (*see* E Iveagh colls), and formerly wife of Hon Philip Leyland Kindersley; 3rdly, 1951, Constance Vera (film actress, Sally Gray), da of late Charles Edward Stevens, and has issue by 1st and 2nd *m*.

Arms – Argent, an eagle displayed with two heads sable, langued gules. **Crest** – A gryphon's head erased argent. **Supporters** – *Dexter*, a knight in ancient armour belted azure, garnished or, holding in his right hand a battle-axe chained proper, charged on the blade with a cross pattee or, on his left an ancient pointed shield gules, charged with two lioncels or, supported by a band from the right shoulder gules, studded and garnished or; *sinister*, a knight, also in chain armour, with a circuit of blue silk, belted gules, leaning his left hand on an ancient two-handed sword, thereon a shield argent, charged with an eagle displayed with two heads sable, langued gules. **Motto** – "Fortiter et fideliter."
Residence – 52 Eaton Place, SW1.

SONS LIVING (*By 1st marriage*)

Hon DOMINICK GEOFFREY THOMAS, *b* 1 July 1929: *m* 1957 (*m diss* 1974), Sara Margaret, da of late Dr Herbert Wright, of 59 Merrion Sq, Dublin.

Hon Martin Michael Dominick, *b* 1931; *ed* Eton: *m* 1958, Alison Margaret, only da of late John Bradford, and has issue living, Shaun Dominick, *b* 1964: *m* 1990, Elizabeth Jane, yr da of Rev Rex Bird, of The Rectory, Monks Eleigh, Suffolk, and has issue living, Hugo Dominick *b* 1997, Ophelia Alexandra *b* 1994, Katharine (Katya) Elizabeth *b* 1995, — Cara Margaret, *b* 1961: *m* 1988 (*m diss* 1992), Philip William Howard (*see* Howard-Lawson, Bt).

(*By 2nd marriage*)

Hon Garech Domnagh, *b* 1939; *ed* Le Rosey: *m* 1981, Princess Harshad Purna Devi (JADEJA) of Morvi, da of late HH Sri Mahendra Maharaja of Morvi, of The New Palace, Morvi, India. *Residences* – 13 rue de la Douzaine, Fort George, St Peter Port, Guernsey, CI; Luggala, Roundwood, co Wicklow.

DAUGHTER LIVING (*By 1st marriage*)

Hon Judith, *b* 1934: *m* 1958 (Ralph) Michael Haslam, and has issue living, Christopher William Dominick, *b* 1960, — David Oliver Myles, *b* 1962: *m* 1995, Clare Elizabeth Jane, 2nd da of late Lt-Col J. J. B. Pope, MBE, of Upton Grove, Tetbury, Glos, — Carina Judith, *b* 1965: *m* 1998, John Philip Drummond Gibson, yst son of late Sir Alexander Drummond Gibson, CBE, of Glasgow. *Residence* – The Orangery, Felix Hall, Kelvedon, Essex CO5 9DG.

Noreen Anne, da of Seán MacSherry, of co Down: *m* 1963, Hon Tara Browne, who was *k* in a motor accident 1966, and has issue living (see colls infra).

COLLATERAL BRANCH LIVING

Issue of late Hon Tara Browne, yst son of 4th Baron, *b* 1945, *k* in a motor accident 1966: *m* 1963, Noreen Anne (ante), da of Seán MacSherry of co Down:—

Dorian Clifford, *b* 1963. —— Julian Dominick, *b* 1965.

PREDECESSORS – (1) DOMINICK Browne, PC, MP for and Lord-Lieut of Co Mayo, was *cr Baron Oranmore and Browne* (peerage of Ireland) 1836; *b* 1787: *m* 1811, Catherine Anne, el da and co-heir of Henry Monck; *d* 1860; *s* by his son (2) GEOFFREY DOMINICK AUGUSTUS FREDERICK, 2nd Baron, *b* 1819; was Representative Peer for Ireland; assumed *vitâ patris* the additional surname of Guthrie on his marriage: *m* 1859, Christina, who *d* 1887, only child and heiress of late Alexander Guthrie, of The Mount, Ayrshire; *d* 1900; *s* by his only son (3) GEOFFREY HENRY BROWNE, KP, PC, 3rd Baron; *b* 1861; a Representative Peer for Ireland, and a Senator for S Ireland; *cr Baron Mereworth*, of Mereworth Castle, Kent (peerage of United Kingdom) 1926: *m* 1901, Lady Olwen Verena Ponsonby, who *d* 1927, da of 8th Earl of Bessborough, KP; *d* 1927; *s* by his son (4) DOMINICK GEOFFREY EDWARD BROWNE, 4th Baron and present peer; also Baron Mereworth.

Orford, Earldom of, see Baron Walpole.

Oriel, Baron, title of Viscount Massereene and Ferrard on Roll of HL.

ORKNEY, EARL OF (Fitz-Maurice) (Earl S 1696)

OLIVER PETER ST JOHN, 9th Earl; *b* 27 Feb 1938; *s* 1998 (has not yet established his right to the peerages); *ed* Woodbridge Sch, Univ of BC (BA 1960), LSE (MSc 1963), and London Univ (PhD 1972); Lecturer Univ Coll, London 1963-64, Univ of Manitoba 1964-66, Assist Prof 1966-72, since when Associate Prof of Political Science, Univ of Manitoba; Visiting Prof Carleton Univ 1981-82; Member Royal Inst of Internat Affairs since 1962, Canadian Inst of Internat Affairs since 1964 (Pres Winnipeg Branch 1971-73), UN Assocn of Canada 1980, and Canadian Assocn for the Study of Intelligence and Security; author: *m* 1st, 1963 (*m diss* 1985), Mary Juliet, da of late Walter Graham Scott-Brown, CVO, of 61 Harley St, W1, and Little Down, Monkwood, Alresford, Hants; 2ndly, 1985, Mrs Mary Barbara Huck, da of Dr David B. Albertson, of 4206 Cedar Glen Rd, Victoria, BC, and has issue by 1st *m*.

Arms – Not matriculated at Lyon Office at time of going to press.
Residence – 595 Gertrude Av, Winnipeg, Manitoba, Canada R3L 0M9.

SON LIVING (*By 1st marriage*)

OLIVER ROBERT (*Viscount Kirkwall, Master of Orkney*), *b* 19 July 1969; *ed* McMaster Univ, Hamilton (BA): *m* 1997, Consuela Hazel, da of Joseph Ronald Davies, of Dundas, Ontario. *Residence* – 47 James St, Dundas, Ontario, Canada L9H 2J5.

DAUGHTERS LIVING *(By 1st marriage)*

Lady Juliet Elizabeth, *b* 1964.
Lady Nicola Jane, *b* 1966.
Lady Lucy Margaret, *b* 1972.

COLLATERAL BRANCHES LIVING

Granddaughter of late Isabella Annie Fitz-Maurice (*m* 1882, Sir Frederick Robert St John, KCMG (*see* V Bolingbroke and St John, colls)), 2nd da of late Capt Hon James Terence Fitz-Maurice, 5th son of 5th Earl:—
Issue of late Terence Alexander St John, *b* 1896; assumed by deed poll (enrolled at the College of Arms) 1933 the surname of de St John in lieu of his patronymic, but subsequently reverted to St John, *d* 1951: *m* 1st, 1923 (*m diss* 1932), Simone Suzanne Marie Anne, only da of Jean Baptiste Guthman, of Paris; 2ndly, 1947, Mrs Winifred Gladys West, da of Charles Giles, and formerly wife of George Lewis Barry West:—
(By 1st *m*) Rosemary Anne, *b* 1927.

Grandchildren of late Dorothy Emily Olga St John (*m* 1906, Sir Henry Crofton Lowther, GCVO, KCMG), 2nd da of late Isabella Annie, Lady St John (ante):—
Issue of late Oliver Peter Lowther, *b* 1910, *d* 1990: *m* 1937, Jean (9 Church Close, Bourton, Salisbury SP8 6DU), da of Clarence John Inder, of NZ:—
James Brabazon LOWTHER (Ramridge Dene, Ramridge Park, Weyhill, Andover, Hants SP11 0QP), *b* 1939; *ed* Harrow.

Issue of late Esmée Katalin Lowther, *b* 1913, *d* 1992: *m* 1936, Cmdr John Harry Roughton, RN, who *d* 1970:—
Jeremy John Lowther ROUGHTON (31 Whitehouse Estate, Cromer, Norfolk NR27 0EP), *b* 1944; *ed* Hawkhurst Court, Sussex. —— Priscilla Dorothy (15 Myrtle Rd, Eastbourne, E Sussex), *b* 1937: *m* 1969, John Paul, who *d* 1997. —— Jacqueline Eoméc, *b* 1951. *m* 1973, Gonzalo Amador Salazar, of 14 Kingfisher Drive, Ham, Richmond-on-Thames, Surrey, and has issue living, Rodrigo James, *b* 1977, — Marcel Oliver, *b* 1981, — Andrea Soña, *b* 1974, — Olympia Gabriella, *b* 1976.

Grandchildren of late Cecil Edward Arthur Fitz-Maurice, only son of late Cecil Henry Fitz-Maurice, 3rd and yst son of late Lt-Col William Edward Fitz-Maurice (2nd son of John, Viscount Kirkwall, eldest son of Mary, in her own right Countess of Orkney), brother of 5th Earl:—
Issue of late Mildred Lillian Fitz-Maurice, *b* 1902, *d* 1994: *m* 1938, Capt John Major Leslie Bostock, 11th Lancers (Probyn's Horse), who *d* 1959:—
Christopher John BOSTOCK, *b* 1942; *ed* Tonbridge, and Edinburgh Univ (BSc), PhD: *m* 1st, 1963 (*m diss* 1990), Yvonne Pauline, da of William James Kendrick, of Preston, Lancs; 2ndly, 19—, Patricia, da of Edward James Roberts, of Widnes, Ches, and has issue living, (by 1st *m*) Jason Guy, *b* 1969, — Joanna Clare, *b* 1963, — Camilla Jane, *b* 1967. —— Josephine Mary, *b* 1939: *m* 1964, Geoffrey Francis Stonehouse, of 7 Parkside Close, E Horsley, Surrey, and has issue living, Nicholas John, *b* 1965, — Rachel Ann, *b* 1967, — Stephanie Jane, *b* 1969, — Sarah, *b* 1972.

PREDECESSORS – **(1)** *Lord* GEORGE Hamilton, KT, PC, 5th son of Lord William Douglas (*cr* Duke of Hamilton for life), by Anne, Duchess of Hamilton, was *cr Lord Dechmont, Viscount Kirkwall,* and *Earl of Orkney* (peerage of Scotland) 1696, with remainder to the heirs whatsoever of his body; was a Field Marshal in the Army, Gov of Edinburgh Castle, Lord-Lieut of Lanarkshire, a Lord of the Bedchamber, Gov of Virginia, and a Representative Peer; *d* 1737; *s* by his da **(2)** ANNE, wife of William, 4th Earl of Inchiquin; *d* 1756; *s* by her da **(3)** MARY, wife of Murrough, 1st Marquess of Thomond; *d* 1790; *s* by her da **(4)** MARY, wife of Hon Thomas Fitzmaurice, 2nd son of John, Earl of Shelburne, and brother of 1st Marquess of Lansdowne; *d* 1831; *s* by her grandson **(5)** THOMAS JOHN HAMILTON, 5th Earl; *b* 1803; a Representative Peer: *m* 1826, Hon Charlotte Isabella, who *d* 1883, da of 3rd Baron Boston; *d* 1877; *s* by his son **(6)** GEORGE WILLIAM HAMILTON, KCMG, 6th Earl, *b* 1827; a Representative Peer. *m* 1872, Amelia, widow of the Baron de Samuel, a peer of Portugal; *d* 1889; *s* by his nephew **(7)** EDMOND WALTER (son of late Hon Henry Warrender Fitzmaurice, 2nd son of 5th Earl), 7th Earl, *b* 1867; Lieut-Col 3rd Batn Oxfordshire LI: *m* 1829, Constance Macdonald, who *d* 1946, da of late David Gilchrist; *d* 1951; *s* by his kinsman **(8)** CECIL O'BRYEN (yr son of late Douglas Frederick Harold Fitz-Maurice, son of late Major Douglas Commerell Menzies Fitz-Maurice, el son of late Com Hon Frederick O'Bryen Fitz-Maurice, RN, 3rd son of 5th Earl), 8th Earl, *b* 1919; succession approved by Lyon Court 1955; Driver RASC; European War 1939-45, Korea 1950-51: *m* 1953, Rose Katherine Durk, who *d* 1995, da of late Joseph William Durk Silley, of Brixham, Devon; *d* 1998; *s* by his kinsman **(9)** OLIVER PETER (only son of late Lt-Col Frederick Oliver St John, DSO, MC, eldest son of late Isabella Annie Fitz-Maurice (Lady St John), 2nd da of late Capt Hon James Terence Fitz-Maurice, 5th son of 5th Earl), 9th Earl and present peer, also Viscount Kirkwall, and Lord Dechmont.

ORMATHWAITE, BARONY OF (Walsh) (Extinct 1984)

SISTER LIVING OF SIXTH BARON

Hon Anne Elizabeth, *b* 1911: *m* 1948, as his 2nd wife, Peter Edward Bromley-Martin, who *d* 1968 (Rouse-Boughton, Bt, colls). *Residence* – The Pheasantry, Builth Wells, Powys, LD2 3NP.

COLLATERAL BRANCH LIVING

Issue of late Hon Nigel Christoper Walsh, 6th son of 2nd Baron, *b* 1867, *d* 1931: *m* 1904, Pauline, who *d* 1956, yst da of late Henry Francis Makins, of 180 Queen's Gate, SW:—
Geraldine Lettice (9 Abbotsbury House, W14), *b* 1909.

ORME, BARON (Orme) (Life Baron 1997)

STANLEY (STAN) ORME, PC, son of Sherwood Orme, of Sale, Cheshire; *b* 5 April 1923; *ed* elementary and technical schs, Nat Council of Labour Colls, and WEA; Hon DSc Salford 1985; Warrant Offr, Air-Bomber Navigator, RAF Comber Cmd 1942-47; MP for Salford West (Lab) 1964-83, and for Salford East 1983-97; Min of State, Northern Ireland Office 1974-76; DHSS 1976; Min of State for Social Security 1976-77; Min for Security and Memb of Cabinet 1977-79; Opposition Spokesman for Health and for Social Services 1979-80, on Industry 1980-83, and on Energy 1983-87; Chm PLP 1987-92; *cr* PC 1974, and *Baron Orme*, of Salford, co Greater Manchester (Life Baron) 1997: *m* 1951, Irene Mary, da of Vernon Fletcher Harris of Worsley, Lancs.
Residence – 8 Northwood Grove, Sale, Cheshire M33 3DZ.

ORMONDE, MARQUESSATE OF (Butler) (Extinct 1997)

DAUGHTERS LIVING OF SEVENTH AND LAST MARQUESS

Lady Constance Ann, *b* 1940: *m* 1965, Henry Lea Soukup, of 618 North Washington, Hinsdale, Illinois, USA, and has issue living, Andrew Butler, *b* 1969, — Meghan Ormonde, *b* 1971.
Lady Violet Cynthia Lilah, *b* 1946: *m* 1971, Donald Leroy Robb, of 2734 North Racine St, Chicago, Illinois 60614, USA.

DAUGHTER LIVING OF SIXTH MARQUESS

Lady Martha, *b* 1926; DL Oxon 1998: *m* 1950, Sir Ashley Charles Gibbs Ponsonby, 2nd Bt, MC, late Coldm Gds, of Woodleys, Woodstock, Oxon OX20 1HJ.

COLLATERAL BRANCH LIVING

(In remainder to the Earldoms of Ormonde and Ossory only)

Descendants of the late Hon Richard Butler (yr son of 8th Earl), who was *cr Viscount Mountgarret* 1550, of whom the 17th Viscount is the senior known heir to the Earldoms of Ormonde and Ossory see that title.

PREDECESSORS – (1) THEOBALD FitzWalter, who accompanied Henry II into Ireland, was *cr Chief Butler of Ireland* 1177; *d* about 1206; *s* by his son (2) THEOBALD, 2nd Butler, who in 1221 assumed the surname of Le Botiler or Butler; *d* 1230; *s* by his son (3) THEOBALD, 3rd Butler; *d* 1248; *s* by his son (4) THEOBALD, 4th Butler; sat as a Baron in the Parliament of Ireland; granted the Prisage of Wines; *d* 1285; *s* by his el son (5) THEOBALD, 5th Butler; sat in Parliament of Ireland as a Baron; *s* by his brother (6) *Sir* EDMOND, Knt, 6th Butler; was Lord Dep of Ireland 1312, and Ch Gov of Ireland with title of Lord Justice 1314: received the feodum of Karrik, Macgriffyn, and Roscrea 1315, and sometimes styled Earl of Karryk (Carrick); *d* 1321; *s* by his son (7) JAMES, *cr Earl of Ormonde* (peerage of Ireland) 1328; had a renewed grant of the Prisage of Wines, and grant of the Regalities, etc, of co Tipperary, with the rights of a Palatine in that co for life; *d* 1337; *s* by his son (8) JAMES, 2nd Earl; was Lord Justice of Ireland; *d* 1382; *s* by his son (9) JAMES, 3rd Earl; erected the Castle of Gowran, and was usually known as Earl of Gowran, and afterwards purchased the Castle of Kilkenny; was Lord Justice of Ireland; *d* 1405; *s* by his son (10) JAMES, 4th Earl; prevailed upon Henry V to create a King of Arms in Ireland, by the title of Ireland King of Arms (altered by Edward VI to Ulster King of Arms) and he gave lands for ever to the College of Arms, London; was Lord Dep of Ireland 1405, and Lord-Lieut of Ireland 1420, 1425, and 1442; *d* 1452; *s* by his son (11) JAMES, KG, 5th Earl, who had in 1449 been *cr Earl of Wiltshire* (peerage of England); was Lord Dep of Ireland 1451; constituted Lord High Treasurer of England 1459; fell into the hands of the Yorkists at Towton, and was beheaded at Newcastle 1461, when both Earldoms were forfeited; *s* by his son (12) JOHN, who having been at Towton was attainted; he was afterwards restored in blood, and became 6th Earl of Ormonde; was ambassador to the principal courts of Europe: *d* unmarried 1478; *s* by his brother **(13)** THOMAS, PC, who having been attainted was restored by Act of Parliament became 7th Earl; *d* 1515; *s* by his kinsman **(14)** PIERCE, great-grandson of the 3rd Earl; he assumed the Earldom, but was compelled to relinquish it to Sir Thomas Boleyn (father of Queen Anne, Consort of Henry VIII), who in 1525, was *cr* Viscount Rochford, and in 1529 Earl of Wiltshire, in peerage of England, and in 1527 Earl of Ormonde, in peerage of Ireland; as a recompense for this abandonment he was in 1527 *cr Earl of Ossory* (peerage of Ireland), and in 1538, a year before the death of Thomas Boleyn, *Earl of Ormonde* (ante) without surviving male issue, he was restored to the original Earldom, and became 8th Earl of Ormonde; *d* 1539; *s* by his son **(15)** JAMES, 9th Earl, who in 1536 has been *cr Viscount Thurles*, in 1541 was confirmed by Act of Parliament in Earldom of Ormonde; *d* 1546; *s* by his son **(16)** THOMAS, KG, 10th Earl; was Lord High Treasurer of Ireland; *d* without surviving male issue; *s* by his kinsman **(17)** WALTER, 11th Earl, son of John, 3rd son of 9th Earl; *d* 1632; *s* by his grandson **(18)** JAMES, KG, PC, 12th Earl; was six times Lord-Lieut of Ireland; *cr Marquess of Ormonde* (peerage of Ireland), 1642, *Baron Butler*, of Llanthony, and *Earl of Brecknock* (peerage of England) 1660, *Duke of Ormonde* (peerage of Ireland) 1661, and *Duke of Ormonde* (peerage of England) 1682: *m* Elizabeth Preston in her own right *Lady Dingwall*: *d* 1688; *s* by his grandson **(19)** JAMES, KG, 2nd Duke, who in 1680 had *s* his father as *Baron Butler*, of Moore Park (peerage of England, *cr* 1666), and in 1684 his grandmother as *Lord Dingwall* (peerage of Scotland, *cr* 1609); was Lord High Constable of England at Coronation of William and Mary, Capt Gen and Com in Ch of the Land Forces, Warden of the Cinque Ports, and Constable of Dover Castle; in 1715 was attainted of high treason, all his English honours were forfeited, and an Act was passed to annul the regalities and liberties of the co Palatine of Tipperary; *d* in exile 1745; *s* by his brother **(20)** CHARLES, who in 1683 had been *cr Baron Butler*, of Werston (peerage of England), and in 1693 *Baron Cloughgrenan, Viscount Tullogh*, and *Earl of Arran* (peerage of Ireland); this nobleman assumed the style of 14th Earl of Ormonde, and did not assume the Irish Dukedom or Marquessate, which had been confirmed upon his father, although the proceedings of the English legislature did not affect the Irish dignities; *d* 1758, when his own honours and the Marquessate and Dukedom of Ormonde became extinct, the Lordship of Dingwall and the Barony of Butler, of Moore Park, reverted to the heir gen (*see* Bs Lucas of Crudwell and Dingwall), and the Earldoms of Ormonde and Ossory and the Viscountcy of Thurles became vested in his kinsman **(21)** JOHN, great-grandson of Richard, yr brother of the 12th Earl; he did not however assume the titles; *d* 1766; *s* by his cousin **(22)** WALTER, who did not assume the titles; *d* 1783; *s* by his son **(23)** JOHN, 17th Earl of Ormonde by decision of House of Lords 1791; *d* 1795; *s* by his el son **(24)** WALTER, KP, 18th Earl; *cr Baron Butler*, of Llanthony, Mon (peerage of UK) 1801, and *Marquess of Ormonde* (peerage of Ireland) 1816; disposed of the grant of the Prisage of Wines (*see* Theobald, 4th Butler) to the crown for £216,000; *d* 1820, when the Marquessate of Ormonde and the Barony of Butler, of Llanthony, became extinct, and the other honours reverted to his brother **(25)** JAMES, KP, 19th Earl; *cr Baron Ormonde*, of Llanthony, co Monmouth (peerage of United Kingdom) 1821, and *Marquess of Ormonde* (peerage of Ireland) 1825; was Lord-Lieut of co Kilkenny; *d* 1838; *s* by his son **(26)** JOHN, KP, 2nd Marquess, *b* 1808: *m* 1843, Frances Jane, da of Gen Hon Sir Edward Paget, GCB (M Anglesey), *d* 1854; *s* by his son **(27)** JAMES EDWARD WILLIAM THEOBALD, PC, KP, 3rd Marquess, *b* 1844; Commodore Roy Yacht Squadron: *m* 1876, Lady Elizabeth Harriett Grosvenor, who *d* 1928, da of 1st Duke of Westminster; *d* 1919; *s* by his brother **(28)** JAMES ARTHUR WELLINGTON FOLEY, 4th Marquess; *b* 1849: *m* 1887, Ellen, who *d* 1951, da of late Gen Anson Stager, USA; *d* 1943; *s* by his son **(29)** JAMES GEORGE ANSON, 5th Marquess, *b* 1890; Major late Life Guards: *m* 1915, Hon Sybil Inna Mildred Fellowes, who *d* 1948, da of 2nd Baron de Ramsey; *d* 1949; *s* by his brother **(30)** (JAMES) ARTHUR NORMAN, CVO, MC, 6th Marquess *b* 1893: *m* 1924, Jessie Carlos, who *d* 1969, da of late Charles Carlos Clarke; *d* 1971; *s* by his cousin **(31)** JAMES HUBERT THEOBALD CHARLES, MBE, 7th and last Marquess; also Earl of Ormonde, Earl of Ossory, Viscount Thurles, and Baron Ormonde.

Orr, family name of Baron Boyd-Orr

ORR-EWING, BARON (Orr-Ewing) (Life Baron 1971, Bt UK 1963)

†(CHARLES) IAN ORR-EWING, OBE; Life Baron, and 1st Baronet, son of late Archibald Ian Orr-Ewing (*see* Orr Ewing, Bt, colls, *cr* 1886); *b* 10 Feb 1912; *ed* Harrow, and Trin Coll, Oxford (MA); late Wing-Cdr RAFVR; CEng; PPS to Min of Labour 1952-55, Parl Under-Sec Air Min 1957-59, Parl and Financial Sec to Admiralty 1959, and Civil Lord of Admiralty 1959-63; Joint Vice-Chm of 1922 Cttee 1966-70; Chm Metrication Board 1972-77; 1939-45 War in N Africa, Italy and NW Europe (despatches, OBE); MP (*C*) for Hendon (North) 1950-70; *cr* Bt (UK) 1963, and *Baron Orr-Ewing*, of Little Berkhamsted, co Hertford (Life Baron) 1971: *m* 1939, Joan Helen Veronica, only da of late Gordon McMinnies, of Talbot Hotel, Stow-on-the-Wold, Glos, and has issue. Lord Orr-Ewing *d* 19 Aug 1999.

Arms – Argent, on a chevron ensigned with a banner between in chief two mullets and in base a representation of the path of two electrons rotating round a nucleus gules a pair of wings conjoined in lure between two lymphads sails furled penons and flags flying or. **Crest** – A demi-lion rampant gules holding in the dexter paw a mullet azure and resting the sinister paw on a portcullis chained or.
Address – c/o House of Lords, SW1A 0PW.

SONS LIVING

(In remainder to Baronetcy only)

Hon (ALISTAIR) SIMON (The Old Farmhouse, Fifield, Chipping Norton, Oxon; 29 St James's Gdns, W11 4RF), *b* 10 June 1940; *ed* Harrow, Grenoble Univ, and Trin Coll, Oxford, FRICS; *ha* to Baronetcy: *m* 1968, Victoria, da of late Keith Cameron, of Fifield House, Milton-Under-Wychwood, Oxon, and has issue living, Archie Cameron, *b* 1969, — James Alexander, *b* 1971: *m* 1998, Polly M., elder da of Giles Gleadell, of Clapham, SW4, and has issue living, Alma Gillian *b* 1998, — Georgina Victoria, *b* 1974.

Hon (Ian) Colin (The Old Bakehouse, Shalbourne, Marlborough, Wilts SN8 3RR), *b* 1942; *ed* Harrow, and Trin Coll, Oxford: *m* 1st, 1973 (*m diss* 1980), Deirdre, el da of Lance Japhet, of Sandhurst, Johannesburg; 2ndly, 1986, Fleur P. M., yr da of late Dr Gavin Knight, of Blackwood, Gwent, and has issue living (by 1st *m*), Francis Ian Lance, *b* 1975: *m* 1997, Amy L., da of Dr Hartmut Kopsch, of Dover, Kent, — Bridget Joanna, *b* 1977, — (by 2nd *m*) Cordelia, *b* 1988, — Daisy Caroline, *b* 1990.

Hon Malcolm Archie (The Priory, Syresham, nr Brackley, Northants NN13 5HH), *b* 1946; *ed* Harrow, and Munich: *m* 1973, Clare Mary, da of Brig George Robert Flood, MC, of Cheverell Mill, Little Cheverell, Devizes, Wilts, and has issue living, Edward Archie, *b* 1990, — Harriet Kate, *b* 1975, — Charlotte Rose, *b* 1978.

Hon Robert James (31 Emperor's Gate, SW7), *b* 1953; *ed* Harrow; Bar Inner Temple 1976: *m* 1982, Susannah, da of Mark Bodley Scott, of Uppfield, Sonning-on-Thames, Berks, and has issue living, William Robert, *b* 1985, — Jack Alexander Bodley, *b* 1987, — Alice Josephine, *b* 1989, — Lucy Katharine McMinnies, *b* 1995.

Orrery, Earl of see Earl of Cork and Orrery.

OWEN, BARON (Owen) (Life Baron 1992)

DAVID ANTHONY LLEWELLYN OWEN, CH, PC, son of Dr John William Morris Owen; *b* 2 July 1938; *ed* Bradfield, Sidney Sussex Coll, Camb (Hon Fell 1977), and St Thomas's Hosp (BA, MB BChir, MA); Neurological and Psychiatric Registrar 1964-66, and Research Fell Med Unit 1966-68, St Thomas's Hosp; PPS to MOD (Admin) 1967, Parly Under Sec of State for Defence for RN 1968-70, Parly Under Sec of State Dept of Health and Social Security 1974, Min of State Dept of Health and Social Security 1974-76, and FCO 1976-77, Sec of State for Foreign and Commonwealth Affairs 1977-79; Founder Memb SDP 1981, Chm SDP Parly Cttee 1981-82, Dep Leader SDP Oct 1982-83, SDP Leader following resignation of Rt Hon Roy Jenkins after election June 1983-87, resigned over merger with Liberal Party 1987, re-elected SDP Leader 1988; Head of European Community's Peace Effort in Yugoslavia Aug 1992-95; Gov Charing Cross Hosp 1966-68, Patron Disablement Income Group since 1968, Chm Humanitas; MP Plymouth Sutton (*Lab*) 1966-74, and Plymouth Devonport (*Lab* 1974-81, *SDP* 1981-92); *cr* PC 1976, CH 1994, and *Baron Owen*, of the City of Plymouth (Life Baron) 1992: *m* 1968, Deborah, da of late Kyrill Schabert, of Long Island, NY, and has issue.
Residences – 78 Narrow St, Limehouse, E14 8BP; The Old Rectory, Buttermere, nr Marlborough, Wilts.

SONS LIVING

(Hon) Tristan Llewellyn (does not use courtesy title), *b* 1970.
(Hon) Gareth Schabert (does not use courtesy title), *b* 1972.

DAUGHTER LIVING

(Hon) Lucy Mary (does not use courtesy title), *b* 1979.

OXFORD AND ASQUITH, EARL OF (Asquith) (Earl UK 1925)

JULIAN EDWARD GEORGE ASQUITH, KCMG, 2nd Earl; *b* 22 April 1916; *s* 1928; *ed* Ampleforth, and Balliol Coll, Oxford (Scholar, MA); formerly Lt RE; appointed Assist Dist Commr Palestine 1942, Dep Ch Sec, Tripolitania 1949, Adviser to Prime Min of Libya 1951, Administrative Sec, Zanzibar 1955, and Administrator, St Lucia 1958; Gov and Com-in-Ch of Seychelles 1962-67, and Commr for British Indian Ocean Territory 1965-67; Constitutional Commr Cayman Islands 1971, and Turks and Caicos Islands 1973-74; CMG 1961, KCMG 1964: *m* 1947, Anne Mary Celestine, who *d* 1998, da of late Sir (Charles) Michael Palairet, KCMG, and has issue.

𝔄rms – Sable, on a fesse between three cross-crosslets argent a portcullis of the field. 𝔠rest – Issuant out of clouds proper, a mascle gules. 𝔖upporters – On either side a lion purpure, charged on the shoulder with an open book argent, edged or.
Residence – The Manor House, Mells, Frome, Somerset.

SONS LIVING

RAYMOND BENEDICT BARTHOLOMEW MICHAEL (*Viscount Asquith*), OBE, *b* 24 Aug 1952; *ed* Ampleforth, and Balliol Coll, Oxford; 1st Sec British Embassy, Moscow 1983-85, Counsellor, British Embassy, Kiev 1992-97; Dir Dessna Co Ltd since 1997; OBE (Civil) 1992: *m* 1978, Clare, el da of late Francis Anthony Baring Pollen (*see* Pollen, Bt, colls), and has issue:—

SON LIVING — *Hon* Mark Julian, *b* 13 May 1979.
DAUGHTERS LIVING — *Hon* Magdalen Katharine, *b* 1981, — *Hon* Frances Sophia, *b* 1984, — *Hon* Celia Rose, *b* 1989, — *Hon* Isabel Anne, *b* 1991.

Hon Dominic Anthony Gerard, *b* 1957: *m* 1988, Louise E., only da of John E. Cotton, of Wollaton, Nottingham, and has issue living, Gabriela Elizabeth Louise, *b* 1989.

DAUGHTERS LIVING

Lady (Mary) Annunziata (75 Ladbroke Grove, W11), *b* 1948.
Lady Katharine Rose Celestine (Upper Leigh Farm, Salisbury, Wilts SP3 6AP), *b* 1949: *m* 1st, 1970 (*m diss* 1976), Adam Nicholas Ridley (later Sir Adam Ridley) (*see* V Ridley, colls); 2ndly, 1985, (John) Nathaniel Micklem Page, 2nd son of Sir (Arthur) John Page, MP.
Lady Clare Perpetua Frances, *b* 1955.

SISTER LIVING (*Raised to the rank of an Earl's daughter* 1928)

Lady Helen Frances, OBE (Tynts Hill, Mells, Frome, Som), *b* 1908; BA Somerville Coll, Oxford, 1930; OBE (Civil) 1965.

COLLATERAL BRANCHES LIVING

Issue of late Hon Herbert Asquith, 2nd son of 1st Earl, *b* 1881, *d* 1947: *m* 1910, Lady Cynthia Charteris, who *d* 1960, da of 11th Earl of Wemyss and March:—
Michael Henry (149 Rusthall Av, W4 1BL), *b* 1914; *ed* Winchester, and Balliol Coll, Oxford (MA); served with Friends Ambulance Unit 1940-5: *m* 1st, 1938 (*m diss* 1952), Diana Eveline Montagu, da of late Lieut-Col Perceval Lawrence Montagu Battye, MC, of 21A Prince Edward Mansions, W1; 2ndly, 1953, Helga Birgitta Ebba Elisabeth, who *d* 1998, only da of late Dr Walther Sigmund Casimir Ritter, of Carlsbad, and has had issue, (by 1st *m*) Stephen Andrew Romily Michael (Hinchwick Manor, Stow-on-the-Wold, Glos), *b* 1944; *ed* Nautical Coll, Pangbourne: *m* 1st, 1963 (*m diss* 1975), Nicola, da of late Lt-Cdr Sir Peter Markham Scott, CBE, DSC (by his 1st wife, Elizabeth Jane Howard); 2ndly, 19—, Mrs Clare Frances Boyt, eldest da of late Lt-Col John Richard Guy Stanton, MBE, DL, of Snelston Hall, Ashbourne, Derbys (*see* B Castlemaine, 1960 Edn), and formerly wife of Henry Denis Ernest Boyt, and has issue living (by 1st *m*), Daniel *b* 1964, Emily Rachel *b* 1965: *m* 1988, Mark Charles Francis Derrington Bailey, of 99 Taybridge Rd, SW11 5PX (*see* St Clair-Ford, Bt, colls, 1985 Edn) (and has issue living, Frederick Peter Romilly Derrington *b* 1990, Helena Emily Derrington *b* 1992), Lucy Kate *b* 1967 (by 2nd *m*), Thomas Ivo *b* 1980, Portia *b* 1978, — Peter Edward, *b* 1947, — Annabel Laura Marguerite, *b* 1939; *ed* Somerville Coll, Oxford (BA 1960): *m* 1961, Jasper R. Ungoed-Thomas, of 13 Westbourne Park Rd, W2 5PX, son of late Hon Mr Justice (Sir Lynn) Ungoed-Thomas, and *d* 1971, leaving issue, David Stephen Jerome *b* 1962, Michael Fergus Jonathan *b* 1965, Harry Owen Nathaniel *b* 1969.

Grandchildren of late Hon Herbert Asquith (ante):—
Issue of late Simon Anthony Roland Asquith, *b* 1919, *d* 1973: *m* 1942, Vivien Lawrence (44 Gilpin Av, East Sheen SW14 8QY), da of late Maj Sir Lawrence Evelyn Jones, 5th Bt, MC, TD (*cr* 1831):—
Conrad Robin, *b* 1945; *ed* Westminster, and Ch Ch Oxford: *m* 1977, Patricia, da of L. E. Sproston, of Stoke-on-Trent, and has issue living, Daisy, *b* 1976, — Lily, *b* 1978. *Residence* – 69c Nightingale Lane, Clapham, SW12. —— Ivon Shaun (21

Minster Rd, Oxford OX4 1LY), *b* 1946; *ed* Westminster, and Ch Ch, Oxford: *m* 1982 (*m diss* 1985), Pauline R., da of Lt-Cdr Paul Murray-Jones, RN (ret), and formerly wife of Hon (Maurice) Sebastian Balliol Brett (*see* V Esher), and has issue living, Thomas, *b* 1982, — and further issue (by Katherine Tanya Jury), William, *b* 1985, — Rosamund Eloise, *b* 1991. —— Rosalind Lucy *b* 1948; has issue (by John Fordham), Frederick Simon Asquith FORDHAM, *b* 1985, — Leo Robin Asquith FORDHAM, *b* 1989. *Residence* – 51 Muswell Av, N10 2EH.

Issue of late Brig-Gen Hon Arthur Melland Asquith, DSO, 3rd son of 1st Earl, *b* 1883, *d* 1939: *m* 1918, Hon Betty Constance, who *d* 1962, da of 3rd Baron Manners:—
April Mary (*Hon Mrs W. Keith Rous*) (prefers to be known by her former style), *b* 1919: *m* 1943, as his 2nd wife, 5th Earl of Stradbroke, who *d* 1983, having survived his brother, the 4th Earl, by four days. —— Jean Constance, *b* 1920: *m* 1945, Lawrence Leif Toynbee (*see* E Carlisle, colls, 1956 Edn), and has issue living, Rosalind Catherine, *b* 1946: *m* 1st, 1972, Joe Pennybacker, who *d* 1994, of Ganthorpe Hall, Terrington, York; 2ndly, 1997, (John) Philip Watson, and has issue living (by 1st *m*), Thomas Rupert Blaise *b* 1975, Kitty Shushanik *b* 1983, — Celia Jane, *b* 1948: *m* 1966, Jeremy George Marshall Caulton, of 19 Berriman Rd, N7, and has issue living, Elisabeth Amy *b* 1967, — Clare Anne, *b* 1949: *m* 1980, Andrew David Huxley, of 48 Gillespie Rd, N5, and has issue living, Coral Susan Toynbee *b* 1984, — Rachel Mary Agnes, *b* 1950: *m* 1976, Richard Alexander Fletcher, of Low Pasture House, Nunnington, York YO62 5XQ, and has issue living, Humphrey Alexander *b* 1981, Eleanor Constance *b* 1978, Alice Catherine *b* 1983, — Sarah Alice, *b* 1953: *m* 1990, Dr Robert Towler, of 6 Evelyn Mansions, Carlisle Place, SW1, and has issue living, Frederick James Edward *b* 1991, Madeline *b* 1993, — Frances Veronica, *b* 1958: *m* 1987, John Samuel Wilson, of 87 Lambert Rd, SW2. *Residence* – Chapel Cottage, Ganthorpe, Terrington, York. —— Susan Penelope, *b* 1922: *m* 1946, (Evelyn) Basil Boothby, CMG, who *d* 1990 (*see* Boothby, Bt, colls). *Residence* – 23 Holland Park Avenue, W11. —— Christine, *b* 1926: *m* 1952, John Hatch Clark, who *d* 1997, and has issue living, John Jasper, *b* 1958, — Lucy Caroline, *b* 1953: *m* 1980, William Francis Sebastian Rickett, son of Sir Denis Hubert Fletcher Rickett, KCMG, CB, of 9 The Close, Salisbury, Wilts, and has issue living, Oliver Patrick Oscar *b* 1983, Rosanna Madeleine *b* 1986, — Emma Victoria, *b* 1955. *Residence* – Old Laundry Cottage, Clovelly, N Devon.

Grandchildren of late Rt Hon Sir Cyril Asquith, 4th son of 1st Earl, who was *cr Baron Asquith of Bishopstone* (Life Baron) 1951 (infra):—
Issue of late Hon Luke Asquith, *b* 1919, *d* 1994: *m* 1954, (Ethel) Meriel (31 Trossachs Rd, SE22 8PY), da of Maurice C. Evans, of Arrow Lawn, Eardisland, Herefordshire:—
Lucy, *b* 1962: *m* 1988, Nicholas John Troop, yr son of Robert Troop, of Barnes, SW, and has issue living, Vanessa Charlotte, *b* 1990, — Laura Alexandra, *b* 1993. *Residence* – 136 Sulgrave Rd, W6 7PU. —— Anne (*Hon Mrs Roderick A. Cavendish*), *b* 1965: *m* 1989, Hon Roderick Alexander Cavendish, only son of 7th Baron Waterpark, and has issue (see that title). *Residence* – 25 Archel Rd, W14 9QJ.

Issue of late Hon Paul Asquith, *b* 1927, *d* 1984: *m* 1st, 1953 (*m diss* 1963), Helena Mary Bridgeman (raised to the rank of a Viscount's da 1996), sister of 3rd Viscount Bridgeman; 2ndly 1963, Caroline Anne (41 Quarrendon St, SW6), yr da of Sir John Gawen Carew Pole, 12th Bt (*cr* 1628), DSO, TD:—
(By 1st *m*) Jonathan Paul (8 Colinette Rd, SW15 6QQ), *b* 1956: *m* 1984, Sarah Ann, yst da of Peter Noel Negretti (*see* B Eden of Winton), and has issue living, (Paul) William, *b* 1988, — Matthew Henry George, *b* 1994, — Harriet Mary Rose, *b* 1991. —— (Mary) Clare, *b* 1954: *m* 1986, Rory Patrick Macnamara, of 8 Castello Av, SW15 6EA, elder son of Carroll Macnamara, of Invercharron House, Ross-shire, and has issue living, (Charles) Frederick *b* 1988, — Katharine Rose, *b* 1990, — Flora Mary, *b* 1993. —— (By 2nd *m*) Rupert (36 Redburn St, SW3 4BX), *b* 1965: *m* 1996, Alexandra C. M., da of Harry Morton Neal, of Great Sarratt Hall, Sarratt, Herts. —— Emily Anne, *b* 1964: *m* 1998, Christopher Michael Bowes Daly, yr son of Lt-Col Denis James Daly, of the Royal Hospital, Chelsea (*see* E Harewood, colls, 1971 Edn).

Issue of late Rt Hon Sir Cyril Asquith (*Baron Asquith of Bishopstone*), 4th son of 1st Earl; *cr* Baron Asquith of Bishopstone (Life Baron) 1951; *b* 1890, *d* 1954: *m* 1918, Anne Stephanie, who *d* 1964, elder da of Sir Adrian Donald Wilde Pollock, KCMG (*see* Pollock, Bt, colls, 1964 Edn):—
Hon Frances Rose (*Hon Lady Stephenson*), *b* 1925: *m* 1951, Rt Hon Sir John Frederick Eustace Stephenson (*see* E Shrewsbury, colls, 1960 Edn), who *d* 1998, and has issue living, David Guy (32A Mill St, Wantage, Oxon OX12 9AQ), *b* 1954, — Daniel Paul (223A Munster Rd, SW6 6BU), *b* 1960, — Mary (55 Lightsfield, Oakley, Basingstoke, Hants RG23 7BY), *b* 1952: *m* 1972 (*m diss* 1996), Philippe G. Wines, and has issue living, Daniel Philippe Glyn *b* 1983, Katharine Valerie Rose *b* 1972: *m* 1998, Nicholas Ashcroft, Polly Victoria Jane *b* 1976, Lucy Helen Mary *b* 1979, — Laura Jane, *b* 1958: *m* 1st, 1980, D. J. Nicholas Bodington, son of late Maj W. J. Bodington, DFC, of Manor Farm, Beercrocombe, Som; 2ndly, 1987, Andrew F. Sykes, of 7 Oakhill Rd, SW15 2QJ, yr son of late Sir Richard Adam Sykes, KCMG, MC, of Wilsford-cum-Lake, Salisbury, and has issue living (by 2nd *m*), Matthew John *b* 1991, Sam Richard *b* 1995, Amelia Anne *b* 1989. *Residence* – 26 Doneraile St, SW6.

PREDECESSOR – (1) Rt Hon Sir HERBERT HENRY Asquith, KG, son of late Joseph Dixon Asquith, of Croft House, Morley, Yorkshire, *b* 1852; a KC, High Steward of Oxford, and an Elder Brother of the Trinity House; MP for Fifeshire, E Div (*L*) 1886 to Nov 1918, and for Paisley Feb 1920 to Oct 1924; Sec of State for Home Depart Aug 1892 to June 1895, Chancellor of the Exchequer Dec 1905 to April 1908, Prime Min and First Lord of the Treasury April 1908 to Dec 1916 (also Sec of State for War and Pres of Army Council March to Aug 1914, and Chm of Cabinet War Committee Nov 1915 to Dec 1916), and Leader of Liberal Party 1908-26; *cr Earl of Oxford and Asquith* (peerage of United Kingdom) and *Viscount Asquith*, of Morley, W Riding, co York, Feb 1925: *m* 1st, 1877, Helen Kelsall, who *d* 1891, el da of late Dr Frederick Melland, of Rusholme, Manchester; 2ndly, 1894, Emma Alice Margaret (Margot), who *d* 1945, da of Sir Charles Tennant, 1st Bt; *d* 1928; *s* by his grandson (2) JULIAN, only son of late Raymond Asquith (el son of 1st Earl), who was *ka* in the battle of the Somme 1916, 2nd Earl and present peer; also Viscount Asquith.

OXFUIRD, VISCOUNT OF (Makgill) (Viscount S 1651, Bt NS 1627)
(Title pronounced "Oxfurd" and Name pronounced "McGill")

GEORGE HUBBARD MAKGILL, CBE, 13th Viscount and 13th Baronet; *b* 7 Jan 1934; *s* 1986; *ed* St Peter's Sch, Cambridge, NZ, and Wanganui Collegiate Sch; commd RAF GD Branch 1955-58; CBE (Civil) 1997: *m* 1st, 1967 (*m diss* 1977), Alison Campbell, elder da of late Neils Max Jensen, of Randers, Denmark; 2ndly, 1980, Valerie Cunitia Mary, only da of Maj Charles Anthony Steward, of The Platt, Crondall, Farnham, Surrey, and has issue by 1st and 2nd *m*.

𝕬rms – Gules, three martlets argent. 𝕮rest – a phoenix in flames proper. 𝕾upporters – *Dexter*, a horse at liberty argent, gorged with a Viscount's coronet, and thereto affixed a chain, maned and hooved or; *sinister*, a bull sable, horned, unguled, collared and chained or.
Address – c/o House of Lords, SW1A 0PW.

SONS LIVING (*By 1st marriage*)

Hon IAN ARTHUR ALEXANDER (*Master of Oxfuird*), *b* 14 Oct 1969.
Hon Robert Edward George, *b* (twin) 1969.
Hon Hamish Max Alistair, *b* 1972.

(*By 2nd marriage*)

Hon Edward Anthony Donald, *b* 1983.

SISTER LIVING

Barbara Frances Katherine, *b* 1939. *Residence* – 3/46-48 Hastings Parade, North Bondi, Sydney, NSW 2026, Australia.

DAUGHTER LIVING OF TWELFTH VISCOUNT (*By 1st marriage*)

Hon Diana Mary Robina, CVO (Clouds Lodge, E Knoyle, Salisbury, Wilts, and 2 Iverna Court, W8 6TY), *b* 1930; FCO 1961-90; Protocol Consultant since 1990; Hon Steward of Westminster Abbey since 1977; Vice Pres International Cttee Operation Raleigh; Vice-Pres Women of the Year Luncheon, Action on Addiction; Consultant to Princess Helena College; Dean of Westminster's representative Queen Anne's Sch, Caversham; Gov St John and St Mary's First Sch, Hindon, Wilts; Freedom of the City of London 1989; Jubilee Medal 1977, MVO 1971, LVO 1983, CVO 1990; Order of Al Kawkab (5th class) (1966), Knight of Order of White Rose of Finland (1969), Order of the Stor (1971), Order of the Sacred Treasure (5th class) (1971), Order of Independence of United Arab Emirates (1989).

WIDOW LIVING OF TWELFTH VISCOUNT

MAUREEN (*Maureen, Viscountess of Oxfuird*), yst da of late Lt-Col Arthur Tilson Shaen Magan, CMG, of co Meath, and formerly wife of Col John Herbert Gillington, OBE, MC: *m* 1955, as his 2nd wife, the 12th Viscount of Oxfuird, who *d* 1986. *Residence* – Fornham House, Fornham St Martin, Bury St Edmunds, Suffolk IT31 1SR.

COLLATERAL BRANCHES LIVING

Grandchildren of late Capt John Edward Makgill (*infra*):—
Issue of late Rodney Devereux Makgill, *b* 1901, *d* 1955: *m* 1923, Laura, who *d* 1998, da of late Richard Reynolds, of Cambridge, Auckland, New Zealand:—
Richard John (Matahi Rd, Manawahe, RD, Matata, NZ), *b* 1926: *m* 19—, Marjorie Ann Jamieson, and has had issue, Stuart Rodney, *b* 1956, — †Roy Malcolm, *b* 1961: *m* 1987 (*m diss* 19—), Sheila Hiorns, and *d* 1997, leaving issue, Rebecca Jane *b* 1987, — Janet, *b* 1952, — Yvonne, *b* 1954. —— Patricia Ruth, *b* 1923: *m* 1946, Alfred Bridger, who *d* 1987, of 44 Kiwi Rd, Devonport, Auckland, NZ, and has issue living, Peter James, *b* 1949, — Patricia Ellen, *b* 1947: *m* 1st, 1967, Bruce Wallace Nicklin; 2ndly, 19—, Roger Wilson, of Tutaetoko Rd, PO Box 385, Opotiki, NZ, and has issue living (by 1st *m*), David John *b* 1969, Jeffrey Bruce *b* 1971 (has issue living, Tamara Lee *b* 1992, Chelsea Justine *b* 1996), Tracey Rochelle *b* 1973: *m* 1997, Johnny Green, (and has issue living Hayley Marie *b* 1993, Natasha Cherie *b* 1998), (by 2nd *m*) Tania Frances *b* 1979, Stephen James *b* 1981, — Susan, *b* 1957: *m* 1978, Grant Brendon Nauman of 62 Hamilton St, Latrobe 7307, Tasmania, and has issue living, Megan Louise *b* 1981, Laura Marie *b* 1982, Raelene Anna *b* 1984, Nicola Lee *b* 1986. —— Muriel Ann (13 Virginia Beeches, Callow Hill, Virginia Water, Surrey GU25 4LT), *b* 1927: *m* 1955, Thomas William Tyrwhitt Drake, and has issue living, Richard William (31 Elaine Grove, Oak Village, NW5 4QG), *b* 1957: *m* 19—, Sarah McGill, and has issue living, — Hugh Charles (Flat 8, 14/F, Block F, Garden Vista, Shatin, Hong Kong), *b* 1959: *m* 1992, Rebecca Pang Lai King, and has issue living Natalie *b* 1996, — Penelope Elizabeth, *b* 1964: *m* 19—, David Hynds, of 13 Addiscombe Rd, Weston-super-Mare, Avon BS23 4LT, and has issue living. —— Nancy Margaret (28 Beaumaris Way, Takanini, New Zealand), *b* 1929: *m* 1954, Edward Smith, and has issue living, Nigel, *b* 1957: *m* 1984, Stephanie Littlejohn, — Deborah Ann, *b* 1954: *m* 1986, Fred Hickling, and has issue living, Amy *b* 1988, — Sandra, *b* (twin) 1957: *m* 1981, Glen Pryor, and has issue living, Luke *b* 1983, Kate *b* 1986.

Issue of late Robert John Makgill, *b* 1910, *d* 1983: *m* 1940, Marjorie Wardell-Johnson, who *d* 1981:—
John Wardell (2 Belloc St, Cambridge, NZ), *b* 1944: *m* 1971, Valerie Joan Turner, and has issue living, Braedon, *b* 1973, — Amanda, *b* 1977. —— Hugh Haldane (83 Ngarua Rd, Waitoa, NZ), *b* 1948: *m* 1970, Pamela Ann Jones, and has issue living, Lisa, *b* 1972, — Claudia, *b* 1974, — Joanna, *b* 1977. —— Simon Redding (Lamb St, RD3 Cambridge, NZ), *b* 1949: *m* 1970, Jane Gifford, and has issue living, Matthew Simon, *b* 1977, — Louise Clare, *b* 1973, — Miriam Jane, *b* 1975, — Emily Ann, *b* 1980. —— Robert Cloan (Hemans St, Cambridge, NZ), *b* 1950: *m* 1970, Josephine Mary Uden, and has issue living, Robert, *b* 1971, — Dylan, *b* 1975.

Issue of late Geoffrey Haldane Makgill, *b* 1915, *d* 1984: *m* 1945, Elizabeth McNiven, of Auckland, NZ:—
Penelope Ann, *b* 1947: *m* 1973, John Bryce Scott, of Puketawa, Roberts Rd, RD2, Cambridge, NZ, and has issue living, William Ruediger Makgill, *b* 1975, — Geoffrey Robert, *b* 1977.

Issue of late Capt John Edward Makgill, 3rd son of 10th baronet, *b* 1874, *d* 1938: *m* 1897, Muriel Ravenscroft, who *d* 1946, da of late Hon Henry de Bohun Devereux (V Hereford, colls):—
Margaret Philippa (1/3 Matai Rd, Green Lane, Auckland 5, NZ), *b* 1919: *m* 1946 (*m diss* 1968), Alexander Hamilton Brown.

Issue of late David Makgill, 4th son of 10th baronet, *b* 1880, *d* 1934: *m* 1909, Margaret Elizabeth, who *d* 1948, da of late Ven Archdeacon Palmer:—
†John Palmer, *b* 1910: *m* 1938, Lucie Warner, and *d* 1995, leaving issue, Alan Richard John (Pukeone, Taurangaruru Rd, No 3 RD, Waiuku, NZ), *b* 1941: *m* 1985, Heather Dawn, yr da of Norman Douglas, and has issue living, Iona Amie *b* 1987, — Jennifer Ann, *b* 1939: *m* 19—, Bruce Hinton, of Te Toro No 4 RD, Waiuku, New Zealand, and has issue living, Stuart Bruce *b* 1963, Wendy Lucille *b* 1960, Barbara Anne *b* 1961. —— David Comins (Highfields, 348 Gleeson Rd, Waiuku 1852, NZ), *b* 1918: *m* 1949, Ena Mary Thompson, who *d* 1997, da of Col Keyworth, of Much Wenlock, Salop, and has issue living, Fiona Margaret, *b* 1951: *m* 1979, Donald John Macdonald, of 13 Westhead Rd, RD3, Waiuku, and has issue living, Scott Donald *b* 1983, Jenny Marie *b* 1981. —— Stephen Stewart (395 Tarpon Blvd, Fripp Is, S Carolina 29920, USA), *b* 1929: *m* 1955, Joan Woods, and has issue living, Stephen Stewart (8301 Old Deer Trail, Raleigh, N Carolina 27615, USA), *b* 1958: *m* 1986, Diane Corcoran, and has issue living, Roess *b* 1998, — Kathleen Palmer, *b* 1956: *m* 1981, Gregory Sisk, of 2405 Cliff's Edge Drive, Austin, Texas 78733, USA, and has issue living, Diana Michelle *b* 1991, — Heather Woods, *b* 1961: *m* 1989, William Lyon, of 12 Arrowhead Rd, Convent Station, NJ 07961, USA, and has issue living, Sean William *b* 1987, Victoria Leigh *b* 1985, — Allison Ashwell, *b* 1963. —— Margaret May (48L Ravelston St, St Kilda, Dunedin, NZ), *b* 1912: *m* 1933, Geoffrey Hall Dadley, who *d* 1994, and has had issue, David Francis, *b* 1934: *m* 1954 (*m diss* 1969), Joan Muriel Proctor, and *d* 1986, leaving issue, John David (25 Grampian St East, Tokoroa, Waikato, NZ) *b* 1954: *m* 1st, 1974 (*m diss* 1989), Sharon Joy Ludwig; 2ndly, 1994, Raewyn Rangi (and has issue living (by 1st *m*) Stephen Roland David *b* 1979, Keri Anne *b* 1976 (has issue living by Rodney Cheetham) Kayla Marie DADLEY *b* 1998), Jolene Marie *b* 1978, (by 2nd *m*) Chenay Jasmine *b* 1994), Geoffrey Harold (158 Gridley Rd, Te Puke, RD8, Bay of Plenty, NZ) *b* 1956: *m* 1st, 1981 (*m diss* 1987), Marie Joan Shergold; 2ndly, 1990, Jan Burt (and has issue living (by 1st *m*) Adrian Brent *b* 1983, (by 2nd *m*) Micaela Rae *b* 1990, Rhiannon Frances *b* 1992), Raewyn Anne *b* 1958: *m* 1982, Lance Noel Worthington, of 50 Trig Rd, Whitford, Auckland, NZ (and has issue living, Mark Noel *b* 1986, Amber Chanelle *b* 1984, Tegan Joan *b* 1993), Barbara Joan *b* 1959: *m* 1978, John Kleber Brooks, of 17A Montecito Place, Golf Park, Howick, Auckland, NZ (and has issue living, Benjamin John *b* 1985 Chantel Summer *b* 1982), Lorraine Sandra *b* 1961: *m* 1986, Barry Myers, of 20 Old Penang Rd, Kariong, NSW 2250 Australia (and has issue living, Samantha Louise *b* 1985, Nichol Lee, *b* 1986), — Peter Geoffrey (128 Lancaster Rd, Birkdale, Auckland 10, NZ), *b* 1936: *m* 1964, Germaine Wormald, and has issue living, Sandra Elizabeth *b* 1965: *m* 1989, Stuart Wright, of 85 Alton Av, Hillcrest, Auckland 10, NZ (and has issue living, Jason Oliver *b* 1994, Sarah Ashley *b* 1992), Helen Deborah (19/27 Fortune Rd, Coomera, Qld 4210, Australia) *b* 1967: *m* 1993 (*m diss* 1999), Mark Goddard, — Anthony Eric, *b* 1942: *d* 1969, — Marian Roes, *b* 1940: *m* 1962, Keith John Kingsford Wormald, of 10 Prichard St, Arrowton, Central Otago, NZ, and has issue living, Geoffrey John (7 Weymouth Court, Grange Rd, Sutton, Surrey SM2 6SH) *b* 1964: *m* 1994, Sarah Bennett (and has issue living, Lucy Elizabeth *b* 1997), Kirsten Anne *b* 1965, — Robin Margaret (248 Range Rd, Papamoa, Bay of Plenty, NZ), *b* 1943: *m* 1972 (*m diss* 1990), Peter Clarke, and has issue living, Michael Anthony (c/o Boyd Farm, Church Lane, E Boldre, Lymington, Hants SO42 7WS) *b* 1973, Stephen Matthew *b* 1974, — Rosemary Gwendolyn (22 Tiritiri Rd, Birkdale, Auckland 10, NZ), *b* 1944, — Katherine Ruth DADLEY (10 Porterfield Rd, Macandrew Bay, Dunedin, Otago, NZ), *b* 1949; has resumed her maiden surname: *m* 1973 (*m diss* 1978), Ian Thornton; has issue living, Matthew Antony DADLEY *b* 1983. —— Alice Mary, *b* 1913: *m* 1939, Col Guy Priestley Sanders, DSO, RNZ Engineers (ret), of Meldon, 5 Castor Bay Rd, Castor Bay, Auckland, NZ, and has issue living, Guy Makgill (30 Platina St, Remuera, Auckland, NZ), *b* 1940: *m* 1972, Jennifer Chave, and has issue living, Timothy Guy *b* 1982, Stephanie Claire *b* 1977, Katherine Alice *b* 1979, — David William Priestley (60 County Rd, Torbay, Auckland, NZ), *b* 1955: *m* 1988, Gael Frances McKitterick, and has issue living, Ben William *b* 1989, Jonathan Guy *b* 1992, — Philippa Anne SANDERS (Glenmohr Rd, Waipu, NZ), *b* 1944; has resumed her maiden name: *m* 1966 (*m diss* 1979), Thomas James Finlayson, and has issue living, Nicholas James *b* 1968, Tobias David *b* 1977, — Penelope Margaret, *b* 1950: *m* 1975, Grant Lyndon Christianson, of 86 Matipo Rd, Mairangi Bay, Auckland, NZ, and has issue living, David Grant *b* 1979, Michael Scott *b* 1981.

Grandchildren of late Arthur Makgill (infra):—
Issue of late Mungo Ian Makgill, *b* 1911, *d* 1986: *m* 1935, Eugenia Louise (31a View Rd, Waiuku, NZ), da of Samuel Massey, of Belfast:—
Ian James (49 Penny Av, Mt Roskill, NZ), *b* 1946: *m* 1975, Marie Louise Howley, of Auckland, and has issue living, Angela Louise, *b* 1979, — Philippa Suzanne, *b* 1982, — Jennifer Marie, *b* 1986. —— Margaret May, *b* 1935. —— Elizabeth Marion, *b* 1938. —— Roberta Louise, *b* 1942: *m* 1961, James Samuel Brambley, of 16 Hogan St, Pukekohe, NZ, and has issue living, Douglas James, *b* 1965: *m* 1986, Fiona Thelma McNally, and has issue living, Samuel James *b* 1988, Eli Sean *b* 1992, Renee Vivienne *b* 1989, — Marie-Anne, *b* 1962: *m* 1990 (*m diss* 1993), Michael Walker, — Louise Anne, *b* 1963: *m* 1987, Wayne Robert Callander, and has issue living, Terence Reece Wayne *b* 1996, Amy Louise *b* 1993, — Vanessa Jane, *b* 1972. —— Colleen Barbara, *b* 1944: *m* 1965, Herbert James Lovell, of 88 Ranfurly Rd, Alfriston, Manurewa, NZ, and has issue living, Scott James, *b* 1966: *m* 1989, Monique Adriana van Meygaarden, and has issue living, Brent William *b* 1991, Shaun Adrian *b* 1994, — Anna Elizabeth, *b* 1968: *m* 1988, Michael John Cutts, — Kirstene Margaret, *b* 1972.

Issue of late Arthur Makgill, 5th son of 10th baronet; *b* 1882; *d* 1954: *m* 1911, Mabel Sophia Elizabeth, who *d* 1932, da of William Marsh:—
Douglas Malcolm (25 Astley House, Everill Orr Village, 53 Allendale Rd, Mt Albert, Auckland, NZ), *b* 1922: *m* 1945, Myra Louisa, da of Osborne John Morton Pine, of Sandringham, NZ, and has issue living, Ray Malcolm (40 Lavery Place, Mairangi Bay, North Shore, Auckland, NZ), *b* 1945: *m* 1969 (*m diss* 1985), Linda Anne Elliment, and has issue

living, Daniel Ray *b* 1970, Jamie Douglas *b* 1972, Donna Marie *b* 1974, — Joy Louisa, *b* 1953: *m* 1st, 1973 (*m diss* 1979), Karl Verdun Morris; 2ndly, 1981, Jeffrey John Wills, of Seven Mile Rd, 5 HRD, Oamaru, S Island, NZ, and has issue living (by 2nd *m*), Kyle Phillip *b* 1985, Ann Marie Frances *b* 1982, Nicola Susan *b* (twin) 1985, — Lynette Jane, *b* 1955: *m* 1979, Peter Leslie Guinibert, of 20 Western Av, Auckland, NZ, and has issue living, Matthew John *b* 1985, David James *b* 1987. —— Deborah Elizabeth Mary (20/36 McLeod Rd, Henderson, Waitakere, NZ), *b* 1914: *m* 1939, Capt John Lawrence Clarkson, who *d* 1993, and has issue living, David John (11 Edkins Rd, Kere Kere, Bay of Islands, NZ), *b* 1940: *m* 1st, 1965 (*m diss* 19—), Helen Gable, of Toowoomba, Qld; 2ndly, 19—, Catherine de Boer, and has issue living (by 1st *m*), Sean *b* 1969, Fiona *b* 1968 (by 2nd *m*), Euan *b* 1979, — Peter (PO Box 308, Paihia, Bay of Islands, NZ), *b* 1945: *m* 1968, Patricia Goffin, of Howick, Auckland, and has issue living, Stephen *b* 1973, Wayne *b* 1980, Michelle *b* 1971, — Alan Richard (PO Box 30, Kohu Kohu, N Hokianga, NZ), *b* 1946: *m* 1970, Susanne Price, of Otahuhu, Auckland, and has issue living, Jonathan *b* 1977, Melissa *b* 1978, — Christine, *b* 1947: *m* 1971, John Fryer, of 83A Glengarry Rd, Glen Eden, Waitakere City, NZ, and has issue living, Nicholas *b* 1976, Kirsten *b* 1974.

PREDECESSORS – **(1)** Sir JAMES Makgill of Cranston Riddell, Midlothian, 2nd son of David Makgill of Cranston Riddell; *s* by his el brother David 1619; *cr a Baronet* (Nova Scotia) 1627 with remainder to heirs male whatsoever; Lord of Session 1629; MP for co Edinburgh 1630; *cr Viscount of Oxfuird* and *Lord Makgill of Cousland* (peerage of Scotland) 1651, with remainder to his heirs male of tailzie and provision whomsoever; member of Cttee of Estates 1651; Lord of Session 1661: *m* 1st, 1621, Katherine, el da of John Cockburn of Ormiston; 2ndly, 1646, Christian, who *d* 1664, da of Sir William Livingston of Kilsyth; *d* 1663; *s* by his 6th but 1st surv son **(2)** ROBERT, 2nd Viscount, *b* 1651; Capt of Militia Troop of Horse, Midlothian 1682: *m* 1st, 1666, Henrietta Livingston, who *d* 1683, da of 2nd Earl of Linlithgow; 2ndly, 1684, Lady Jean Ramsay, who *d* 1696, da of 2nd Earl of Dalhousie, and widow of 11th Lord Ross of Halkhead; *d* 1705, when his Peerages and Baronetcy became dormant; *s* (according to the decision of the Cttee of Privileges of House of Lords 1977) by his kinsman **(3)** DAVID Makgill of Rankeilour, Fife, *de jure* 3rd Viscount and 3rd Viscount and 3rd Baronet (despite Christian, da of 2nd Viscount having been served heir of tailzie and provision, when in 1706 she wrongly assumed the title of Viscountess Oxfuird and *d* 1707 having married Hon William Maitland, 6th son of the 3rd Earl of Lauderdale, her son and heir Robert Maitland Makgill, voted as Viscount Oxfuird at the election on Representative Peers 1733), only child of Sir James of Rankeilour (*d* 1661), grandson of Sir James of Rankeilour, Clerk Register Lord of Session, Lord Provost of Edinburgh, and an Ambassador to Queen Elizabeth I (*d* 1579), great-uncle of 1st Viscount and 1st Bt: *m* 1693, Janet, da and heir of John Craig of Ramornie, Advocate; *d* 1717; *s* by his el son **(4)** JAMES, *de jure* 4th Viscount and 4th Bt; *b* 16—: *m* 1720, Jean, da of Sir Robert Anstruther of Balkaskie; *d* 1747; *s* by his kinsman **(5)** JOHN, *de jure* 5th Viscount and 5th Bt, son of Arthur of Kemback (*d* 1725), son of the Rev John of Kemback (*d* 1673), 3rd son of James, of Rankeilour, Fifeshire (*d* 1661) (ante); *b* 1676: *m* 1706, Agnes, da of John Lindsay of Wormeston, Crail; *d* 1762; *s* by his el son **(6)** ARTHUR, *de jure* 6th Viscount and 6th Bt; *b* 1709; Capt Comdt Scottish Regt in Dutch Ser; matric arms as heir male of Rankeilour 1771; *d* unm 1733; *s* by his brother **(7)** GEORGE, *de jure* 7th Viscount and 7th Bt; *b* 1723; joined army of Prince Charles Edward Stuart; pardoned and served as Capt 12th Foot: *m* Agnes, who *d* 1799, da of Major Mungo Law, of Pittilock, Falkland; *d* 1797; *s* by his only son **(8)** JOHN, *de jure* 8th Viscount and 8th Bt; *b* 1790: *m* 1811, Eliza, who *d* 1860, el da of William Dalgleish of Scotscraig, Fifeshire, *d* 1817; *s* by his son **(9)** GEORGE, *de jure* 9th Viscount and 9th Bt; *b* 1812: *m* 1833, Harriet, who *d* 1890, da of Amos Strettell, of Binderton House, Sussex; *d* 1878; *s* by her el son **(10)** JOHN, *de jure* 10th Viscount and 10th Bt; *b* 1836; established his right to the Baronetcy 1906: *m* 1866, Margaret Isabella, who *d* 1920, da of Robert Haldane, of Cloanden, Perthshire; *d* 1906, *s* by his el son **(11)** GEORGE, *de jure* 11th Viscount and 11th Bt; *b* 1868: *m* 1891, Frances Elizabeth, who *d* 1947, da of Alexander Innes Grant, of Merchiston, Otago, NZ; *d* 1926; *s* by his el son **(12)** JOHN DONALD ALEXANDER ARTHUR, 12th Viscount, *b* 1899; claim to Viscountcy admitted by Cttee for Privileges of House of Lords, and a writ issued summoning him to Parliament in the Upper House 1977: Hon Maj Coldm Gds: *m* 1st, 1927 (*m diss* 1943), Esther Lilian, who *d* 1996, da of Sir Robert Bromley, 6th Bt; 2ndly, 1955, Maureen, yst da of Lt-Col Arthur Tilson Shaen Magan, CMG, of co Meath, and formerly wife of Col John Herbert Gillington, OBE, MC; *d* 1986; *s* by his nephew **(13)** GEORGE HUBBARD, CBE (only son of late Sqdn Ldr Richard James Robert Haldane Makgill, RNZAF Air, who was *k* in a flying accident 1948), 13th Viscount and present peer; also Lord Makgill of Cousland.

Oxmantown, Lord, son of Earl of Rosse.

Page, family name of Baron Whaddon

Paget, family name of Marquess of Anglesey.

Paget de Beaudesert, Lord; Grandson of Marquess of Anglesey

Pakenham, Baron; title of Earl of Longford, on Roll of HL.

Pakenham, family name of Earl of Longford

Pakington, family name of Baron Hampton

PALMER, BARON (Palmer) (Baron UK 1933, Bt UK 1916)

Through the cross to the palm

ADRIAN BAILIE NOTTAGE PALMER, 4th Baron and 4th Baronet; *b* 8 Oct 1951; *s* 1990; *ed* Eton, and Edinburgh Univ; Member Exec Council of Historic Houses Assocn since 1981, Scottish Rep to European Landowning Organisation 1986-92, and Member of Council of Scottish Landowners' Fedn 1986-92; Vice-Chm Historic Houses Assoc for Scotland 1993-94, Chm 1994-99; Sec Royal Caledonian Hunt since 1989; Pres Palm Tree Silk Co (St Lucia); Chm Country Sports Defence Trust since 1994; Member Queen's Body Guard for Scotland (Royal Co of Archers 1990-96): *m* 1977, Cornelia Dorothy Katharine, da of Rohan Wadham, DFC, of Dog Kennel, Exning, Newmarket, Suffolk, and has issue.

ᴁrms – Per saltire azure and gules two palmers' staves in saltire between four escallops or. Crest – Upon a mount vert in front of a palm tree proper three escallops fesseways or. Supporters – On either side a palmer, supporting with the exterior hand a palmer's staff proper. *Seat* – Manderston, Duns, Berwickshire.

SONS LIVING

Hon HUGO BAILIE ROHAN, *b* 5 Dec 1980; *ed* Eton.
Hon George Gordon Nottage, *b* 1985.

DAUGHTER LIVING

Hon Edwina Laura Marguerite, *b* 1982.

BROTHER LIVING (*Raised to the rank of a Baron's son* 1991)

Hon Mark Hugh Gordon, *b* 1954; *ed* Eton; News Editor *The Sunday Telegraph* 1994-96: *m* 1982, Irene, da of Guillermo Aranda, of Los Angeles, Calif, USA, and has issue living, Henry Gordon William, *b* 1987, — Olivia Lorna Aranda, *b* 1990. *Residence* – 38 Anhalt Rd, SW11.

DAUGHTERS LIVING AND DECEASED OF THIRD BARON

Hon Amanda Victoria, *b* 1949; *d* 1954.

Hon Carol Lylie (*Rev Lady Wodehouse*), *b* 1951; ordained priest 1994: *m* 1973, John Armine, Lord Wodehouse, son of 4th Earl of Kimberley, and has issue (see that title). *Residence* – Kingswood, Henley Rd, Medmenham, Marlow, Bucks SL7 2EU.

Hon Vanessa Marguerite, *b* 1954: *m* 1977, Robert William St John, son of Lt-Col Charles A. R. L. St John, of Glebe Manor, Pook Lane, Havant, Hants, and has issue living, Edward Robert Cecil, *b* 1982, — Camilla Victoria Celia, *b* 1980, — Laura Zoë Lylie, *b* 1985, — Melissa Lucy Amanda, *b* 1986. *Residence* – 20 Sudbrooke Rd, SW12 8TG

MOTHER LIVING

Lorna Eveline Hope (*Hon Lady Palmer*), DL Berks 1989, da of late Maj Charles William Hugh Bailie, of Manderston, Berwickshire (*see* Miller, Bt, ext, 1942 Edn): *m* 1950, Col Hon Sir Gordon William Nottage Palmer, KCVO, OBE, TD, yr son of 2nd Baron, who *d* 1989. *Residences* – Harris House, Mortimer, Berks; Edrom Newton, Duns, Berwickshire.

WIDOW LIVING OF THIRD BARON

VICTORIA ELLEN (*Victoria, Baroness Palmer*), only da of late Capt Joseph Arthur Ronald Weston-Stevens, of Woolley Cottage, The Thicket, Maidenhead: *m* 1941, the 3rd Baron Palmer, OBE, who *d* 1990. *Residence* – Fieldfares, Ferry Lane, Medmenham, Marlow, Bucks SL7 2EZ.

COLLATERAL BRANCH LIVING

Issue of late Hon Arnold Nottage Palmer, FRCM, yr son of 1st Baron, *b* 1886, *d* 1973: *m* 1911, Marjorie, who *d* 1966, da of late Alexander Freeland, of Lingfield, Surrey:—
Susan Helen (Fir Tree Farm, Hampstead Norris, Berks), *b* 1912. —— Felicity Amy (Coombe Farm, Frilsham, Hermitage, Newbury, Berks), *b* 1913.

PREDECESSORS – (1) SAMUEL ERNEST Palmer, el son of late Samuel Palmer, of Northcourt, Hampstead, NW; *b* 1858; was a Director of Huntley & Palmers, Ltd, biscuit manufacturers, of Reading, and founder of Roy Coll of Music Patrons' Fund, the Berkshire Scholarship, and Ernest Palmer Fund for Opera Study, also two Scholarships at Guildhall; *cr* a *Baronet* 1916, and *Baron Palmer* of Reading, co Berks (peerage of United Kingdom) 1933: *m* 1881, Amy Christiana, who *d* 1947, only da of late Alderman George Swan Nottage, Lord Mayor of London; *d* 1948; *s* by his son (2) (ERNEST) CECIL NOTTAGE, 2nd Baron; *b* 1882; Dep Chm of Huntley & Palmers Ltd, biscuit manufacturers of Reading: *m* 1909, Marguerite, who *d* 1959, da of late William McKinley Osborne, of USA; *d* 1950; *s* by his son (3) RAYMOND CECIL, 3rd Baron, *b* 1916; Chm Huntley and Palmers Ltd, biscuit manufacturers, of Reading, 1969-80: *m* 1941, Victoria Ellen, only da of late Capt Joseph Arthur Ronald Weston-Stevens, of Woolley Cottage, The Thicket, Maidenhead; *d* 1990; *s* by his nephew (4) ADRIAN BAILIE NOTTAGE (son of late Col Hon Sir Gordon William Nottage Palmer, KCVO, OBE, TD, yr son of 2nd Baron), 4th Baron and present peer.

Palmer, family name of Baroness Lucas of Crudwell

Palmer, family name of Earl of Selborne.

PALUMBO, BARON (Palumbo) (Life Baron 1991)

PETER GARTH PALUMBO, son of late Rudolph Palumbo; *b* 20 July 1935; *ed* Eton, and Worcester Coll, Oxford (MA); Hon FRIBA; Gov LSE 1976-4, Chancellor Portsmouth Univ since 1992; Chm Arts Council of GB 1989-94, Tate Gallery Foundation 1986-87, Painshill Park Trust 1986-96, Serpentine Gallery since 1994; Trustee and Hon Treas Writers' Scholars' Educational Trust 1984-99, Trustee Mies van der Rohe Archive since 1977, Tate Gallery 1978-85, Whitechapel Art Gallery Foundation 1981-87, and Natural History Museum since 1994; Member Salters' Company since 1965, Council Royal Albert Hall 1995-99; Hon FRIBA 1986, Hon FFB 1994, Hon FIStructE 1994, Hon DLitt Portsmouth 1993; National Order of the Southern Cross of Brazil; *cr Baron Palumbo*, of Walbrook, City of London (Life Baron) 1991: *m* 1st, 1959, Denia, who *d* 1986, da of late Maj Lionel Wigram; 2ndly, 1986, Hayat, elder da of late Kamel Morowa, and has issue by 1st and 2nd *m*.

Arms – Vert, a pale or, over all an escarbuncle counterchanged. Crest – The top of a dovecot or, perched on its conical roof vert a dove wings elevated and addorsed gold. Supporters – *Dexter*, an alsation dog; *sinister*, a fox proper, each resting the exterior foreleg on a rectangular plinth gold, the compartment comprising a circle of paving stones proper.
Residence – Bagnor Manor, Bagnor, Newbury, Berks RG20 8AG. *Clubs* – White's, Athenaeum, Pratt's, Garrick.

SONS LIVING *(By 1st marriage)*

Hon James Rudolph (Onslow Gdns, SW7), *b* 1963; *ed* Eton; Memb Citizen's Charter Advisory Panel.

(By 2nd marriage)

Hon Philip Rudolph, *b* 1992.

DAUGHTERS LIVING *(By 1st marriage)*

Hon Annabella Jane, *b* 1961: *m* 1991, Hugh H. C. Adams, of Hunts Green, Newbury, Berks, yr son of Geoffrey Adams, of Chilton Foliot, Wilts.
Hon Laura Elizabeth, *b* 1967; *ed* London Univ: *m* 1994, Neel Tikkoo, son of Ravi Tikkoo, of USA, and has issue living, Lydia Rose, *b* 1997, — Gemma Kira, *b* 1998.

(By 2nd marriage)

Hon Petra Louise, *b* 1989.
Hon Lana Rose, *b* 1991.

PANNELL, BARONY OF (Pannell) (Extinct 1980)

DAUGHTER LIVING OF LIFE BARON

Hon Hilary, *b* 1940.

PARGITER, BARONY OF (Pargiter) (Extinct 1982)

SONS LIVING OF LIFE BARON

Hon Donald (41 Douglas Rd, Maidstone), *b* 1921: *m* 1947.

Hon Russell Ashby (173 Macquarie St, Hobart, Tasmania 7000), *b* 1924; MB, BS London; a Fellow of Roy Australian and NZ Coll of Psychiatrists; DPM England; FRC Psych; Consultant Psychiatrist, R Hobart Hosp: *m* 1954, Elizabeth Edwina, da of John George Jamieson Coghill.

DAUGHTER LIVING OF LIFE BARON

Hon Isobel, *b* 1931; Pharmaceutical Chemist: *m* 1964, Ernest Cooper-Heyman, who *d* 1982. *Residence* – The Folly, 81 Woodlands Lane, Chichester, W Sussex PO19 3PF.

PARK OF MONMOUTH, BARONESS (Park) (Life Baroness 1990)

DAPHNE MARGARET SYBIL DÉSIRÉE PARK, CMG, OBE, da of late John Alexander Park; *b* 1 Sept 1921; *ed* Rosa Bassett Sch, Somerville Coll, Oxford (MA), and Newnham Coll, Camb; Cdr Women's Transport Ser FANY in NW Europe and N Africa 1943-48; FO 1948, 2nd Sec Moscow 1954, 1st Sec Leopoldville 1959, Lusaka 1964, Consul-Gen Hanoi 1969-70, Chargé d'Affaires Ulan Bator 1972, FCO 1973-79; Principal Somerville Coll, Oxford 1980-89; Member of Board of Sheffield Devpt Corpn 1989-92, Dir Devpt Trust Zoological Soc of London 1989-90; a Gov of BBC 1982-87; Member British Library Board 1981-86, Chm Legal Aid Advisory Cttee to Lord Chancellor 1986-92; pro Vice-Chancellor Oxford Univ, and Chm Royal Commn on Historical Monuments of England 1989-94; Gov Ditchley Foundation since 1989, Trustee Jardine Educational Foundation 1990-98, Great Britain Sasakawa Foundation since 1994; Pres Soc for Promotion of Training of Women since 1996; Hon LLD Bristol 1988, Mount Holyoke Coll 1992; Fell of Chatham House, FRSA: *cr* OBE (Civil) 1960, CMG 1971, and *Baroness Park of Monmouth*, of Broadway, co Hereford and Worcester (Life Baroness) 1990.

Address – c/o House of Lords, SW1A 0PW. *Clubs* – Naval and Military, Royal Commonwealth Society, Oxford and Cambridge, Special Forces.

Parker, family name of Earl of Macclesfield

Parker, family name of Earl of Morley.

PARKINSON, BARON (Parkinson) (Life Baron 1992)

CECIL EDWARD PARKINSON, PC, son of Sidney Parkinson, of Carnforth, Lancs; *b* 1 Sept 1931; *ed* Royal Lancaster Gram Sch, and Emmanuel Coll, Camb; CA 1960; Chm Hemel Hempstead Conservative Assocn 1966-69, Herts 100 Club 1968-69, Sec Conservative Parly Finance Cttee 1971-72, PPS to Michael Heseltine as Min for Aerospace and Shipping Dept of Trade and Industry 1972-74, Assist Govt Whip 1974, Min of State Dept of Trade 1979-81, Chm Conservative Party and Paymaster Gen 1981-83, Chancellor Duchy of Lancaster 1982-83, Sec of State Trade and Industry June-Oct 1983 (resigned), Sec of State for Energy 1987-89, for Transport 1989-90 Chm Conservative Party since 1997; MP (*C*) Enfield W Nov 1970-74, Herts S 1974-83, and Hertsmere 1983-92; *cr* PC 1981, and *Baron Parkinson*, of Carnforth, co Lancs (Life Baron) 1992: *m* 1957, Ann Mary, da of late Frank Anthony Jarvis, of Hatching Green, Harpenden, Herts, and has issue.

Arms – Quarterly gules and azure, a fret throughout argent, on a chief per pale azure and gules a hart's head caboshed between two lion's heads guardant or, langued argent, all within a bordure ermine. **Crest** – A crown palisado, therein a grassy mount and thereon a crane statant proper holding in its beak a rose gules barbed and seeded, slipped and leaved proper. **Supporters** – *Dexter*, a crane statant reguardant proper; *sinister*, a hart rampant reguardant also proper, attired or, the compartment comprising a grassy mount proper with on each side and growing therefrom three roses gules barbed and seeded, slipped and leaved all proper.
Clubs - Hawks, Pratt's, Beefsteak, Garrick.

DAUGHTERS LIVING

Hon Mary, *b* 1959.
Hon Emma, *b* 1961: *m* 1991, John Owrid.
Hon Joanna, *b* 1963: *m* 1988, Mark Bamber.

PARMOOR, BARON (Cripps) (Baron UK 1914)

Do not trust in appearances

(FREDERICK ALFRED) MILO CRIPPS, 4th Baron; *b* 18 June 1929; *s* (Oct) 1977; *ed* Ampleforth, and Corpus Christi Coll, Oxford.

Arms – Chequy ermines and argent, on a chevron vert five horseshoes or. **Crest** – An ostrich's head couped argent, gorged with a coronet of fleurs-de-lis, and holding in the beak a horseshoe or. **Supporters** – On either side a seahorse proper, supporting a pennon ermines charged with a swan rousant argent, beaked and legged gules, ducally gorged and lined or.
Residence – Dairy, Sutton Veny, Warminster, Wilts BA12 7A.

COLLATERAL BRANCHES LIVING

Grandsons of late Maj Hon Leonard Harrison Cripps, CBE (infra):—
Issue of late Maj (Matthew) Anthony Leonard Cripps, CBE, DSO, TD, QC, *b* 1913, *d* 1997: *m* 1941, Dorothea Margaret, who *d* 1992, da of late George Johnson-Scott, of Hill House, Ashby-de-la-Zouche:—
(MICHAEL LEONARD) SEDDON (Bessemers, Moor Wood, Lane End, High Wycombe, Bucks HP14 3HZ), *b* 18 June 1942; *ed* Eton: Bar Middle Temple 1965, Lincoln's Inn 1969, Inner Temple 1975, Circuit Judge 1998: *m* 1971, Anne, da of Maj Millward-Shennan, of Moorside, Caldy-in-Wirral, and has issue living, Henry William Anthony, *b* 2 Sept 1976; *ed* Shiplake Coll, and Univ of W of England, — Stephanie Margaret Julia, *b* 1974. ——— Jeremy George Anthony (1986 S State Route 100, Tiffin, Ohio 44883, USA), *b* 1943; *ed* Eton, Case Western Res Univ, Cleveland, Ohio (MA), and Union Inst, Cincinnati (PhD); FCA; Certified Public Accountant, Ohio; Prof of Accountancy, Heidelberg Coll, Tiffin, Ohio: *m* 1972, Mary Elizabeth, only da of Walter Howe, of Golf Manor, Cincinnati, and has issue living, Scott Anthony Charles, *b* 1978, — Clark Robert Leonard, *b* 1980, — Lynne Margaret, *b* 1983. ——— (Richard) James Nigel (46 Lilyville Rd, SW6 5DW), *b* 1956; *ed* Eton, and St Catharine's Coll, Camb (MA); Solicitor: *m* 1987, Margaret Jude, 3rd da of late Sam S. Mullin, of Osterville, Mass, USA, and has issue living, Leonard Samuel Anthony, *b* 1989, — John Richard Charles, *b* 1991, — Frederick Alfred Michael, *b* 1992, — Julia Margaret Ruth, *b* 1994.

Issue of late Major Hon Leonard Harrison Cripps, CBE, 3rd son of 1st Baron, *b* 1887, *d* 1959: *m* 1913, Miriam Barbara, who *d* 1960, da of late Rt Hon Sir Matthew Ingle Joyce:—
Charles Thomas Joyce, *b* 1916; *ed* Eton, and Ch Ch, Oxford; formerly Capt Roy Tank Regt; formerly a Member of London Stock Exchange: *m* 1941, Noreen, da of late Dr Hugh Pierce, of 24 Upper Duke St, Liverpool, and has issue living, Charles Hugh, *b* 1946; *ed* Eton, — Paul Alfred (7 Pont St, SW1X 9EJ), *b* 1950; *ed* Eton, Sorbonne, and LSE. *Residence* – 41 Somerset Rd, Wimbledon, SW19.

Grandchildren of late Rt Hon Sir (Richard) Stafford Cripps, CH, QC, FRS (infra):—
Issue of late Sir John Stafford Cripps, CBE, *b* 1912, *d* 1993: *m* 1st, 1936 (*m diss* 1971), Ursula, da of late Arthur Cedric Davy, of Whirlow Court, Sheffield; 2ndly, 1971, Ann Elizabeth (*Lady Cripps*) (Fox House, Filkins, Lechlade, Glos), da of Edwin G. K. Farwell, of Swanage, Dorset:—
(By 1st *m*) †David Stafford, *b* 1940; *ed* Bryanston, and Reading Univ: *m* 1968 (*m diss* 1981), Bridget Ayerst, and *d* 1990, leaving issue, Jennifer Bridget, *b* 1969, — Nicola Ann, *b* 1971, — Angela Claire, *b* 1973. —— Timothy Francis (10 High St, Harston, Cambridge), *b* 1943; *ed* Eton, and Trinity Coll, Camb *m* 1969, —. —— Christopher John (Pear Tree Cottage, Viney Hill, Lydney, Glos), *b* 1947; *ed* Bryanston, King's Coll, Camb, and Architectural Assocn; PhD Liverpool 1981: *m* 1976, Alyson, only da of Cyril Laverick, of 17 Bluebell Grove, Stockton-on-Tees, and has issue living, Joe John Allan, *b* 1978, — Rosie Helen Zoë, *b* 1985. —— Richard Andrew (3 Moat Cottages, Filkins, Lechlade, Glos), *b* 1953; *ed* Bryanston, and Southampton Univ. —— Judith Ursula (10 Brookside, Headington, Oxford), *b* 1938; *ed* Somerville Coll, Oxford: *m* 1964, Sarjit Heyer, who *d* 1974, and has issue living, Jasdev Philip, *b* 1968, — Daleep Andrew, *b* 1971, — Amrik Frances, *b* 1967. —— Rachel Theresa, *b* 1945; *ed* Sussex Univ: *m* 1969, (James Oriel) Bernard Rosedale, MB BS, of Thornsend, Kingsbury Hill, Marlborough, Wilts, and has issue living, Nicholas Oriel Rupert, *b* 1972, — Lawrence Andrew, *b* 1974, — Benjamin James, *b* 1976, — Katherine Jane, *b* 1978.

Issue of late Rt Hon Sir (Richard) Stafford Cripps, CH, QC, FRS, *b* 1889, *d* 1952, yst son of 1st Baron: *m* 1911, *Dame* Isobel, GBE, who *d* 1979, da of late Com Harold William Swithinbank, DL, of Denham Court, Denham, Bucks:—
Enid Margaret, MBE (PO Box 829, Kumasi, Ashanti, Ghana), *b* 1921; MBE (Civil) 1995: *m* 1953, Joseph E. Appiah, and has issue living, (Kwame) Anthony Akroma-ampim Kusi (Harvard Univ, Boston, Mass, USA), *b* 1954; *ed* Bryanston, and Clare Coll, Camb; Prof at Harvard Univ, Dept of African American Studies, — Isobel Takyiwah, *b* 1955; *ed* Badminton Sch, and Sussex Univ: *m* 1980, Klaus Endresen, of Statsrad Ihlens Vei 2, 2010 Strømmen, nr Oslo, Norway, and has issue living, Kristian Gyamfi *b* 1981, Anthony Finn *b* 1984, Per Kojo *b* 1987, — Anthony Sch, Kumasi, Roedean, Sussex Univ, and Leeds Univ: *m* 1982, Olawale Edun (PO Box 50853, Falomo, Ikoyi, Lagos, Nigeria), and has issue living, Dabalunde Adetomiwa Stafford *b* 1984, Adedeji Olamide *b* 1986, Adedamola Oluwatobi *b* 1989, — Theresa Jane (Abena), *b* 1962; *ed* Sidcot Sch, and St Godric's Coll.

PREDECESSORS – (1) *Rt Hon Sir* CHARLES ALFRED Cripps, KCVO, KC, son of late Henry William Cripps, QC, of Beechwood, Marlow; *b* 1852; appointed Attorney-Gen to successive Princes of Wales 1895, 1901, and 1910 (also a Member of Council), Chancellor and Vicar-Gen to Diocese of York 1900, Chm of Canterbury House of Laymen and a Member of its Committee 1910, a Member of Judicial Committee of Privy Council 1914, British Representative on Council of League of Nations Jan 1924, and Ch British Representative to League of Nations Assembly Sept 1924; was Vicar-Gen of Province of Canterbury 1902-24, First Chm of House of Laity in National Church Assembly 1920-24, Lord Pres of the Council Jan to Nov 1924, and June 1929 to Aug 1931, and Leader of Labour Party in House of Lords Oct 1928 to Aug 1931; sat as MP for Mid, or Stroud, Div of Gloucestershire (C) 1895-1900, for Stretford Div of Lancashire (S-E) 1901-6, and for Bucks, S or Wycombe Div Jan 1910 to Jan 1914; *cr Baron Parmoor*, of Frieth, co Bucks (peerage of United Kingdom) 1914: *m* 1st, 1881, Theresa, who *d* 1893, sixth da of Richard Potter, of Rusland Hall, Lancashire; 2ndly, 1919, Marian Emily, who *d* 1952, da of late Rt Hon John E. Ellis, of Wrea Head, Scalby, Yorkshire; *d* 1941; *s* by his son (2) ALFRED HENRY SEDDON, 2nd Baron; *b* 1882; Bar Middle Temple 1907; Bursar, Queen's Coll Oxford 1928-45 (Fellow 1929); *d* (Mar) 1977; *s* by his brother (3), FREDERICK HEYWORTH, DSO, TD; *b* 1885; author of *Life's a Gamble*, 1958; Lt-Col R Bucks Hussars Yeo, 1914-18 War in Dardanelles, Palestine and France (wounded, DSO and Bar Belgian Croix de Guerre); 1939-45 War as temp Lt-Cdr RNVR: *m* 1927 (*m diss* 1951), Violet Mary Geraldine, who *d* 1983, da of Sir William Nelson, 1st Bt, and formerly wife of (1) George Richard Francis Rowley, and (2) the 2nd Duke of Westminster; *d* (Oct) 1977; *s* by his son (4) (FREDERICK ALFRED) MILO, 4th Baron and present peer.

Parnell, family name of Baron Congleton.

PARRY, BARON (Parry) (Life Baron 1975)

GORDON SAMUEL DAVID PARRY, son of late Rev Thomas Lewis Parry; *b* 30 Nov 1925; *ed* Trin Coll, Carmarthen, and Liverpool Univ; House Master Co Secondary Sch, Haverfordwest 1952-62, Inst of Educn, Liverpool Univ 1962-63, House Master Haverford West 1963-67, and Warden of Pembrokeshire Teachers' Centre 1967-1976; Chm Wales Tourist Board 1978 (ret); Member British Tourist Authority 1978-84; Pres: Wales Spastics Soc, Pembrokeshire Spastics Soc, and Pembrokeshire Multiple Sclerosis Soc, former Member of Council of Open Univ (and Chm Educn

Cttee); Vice-Pres Mentally Handicapped Soc for Wales, Pres British Inst of Cleaning Science, Pres British Cleaning Council; Pres Milford Docks Co, Pres Tidy Britain Group, Chm Clean World International; Fellow Tourism Soc, FRSA, Fellow Hotel and Catering and Institutional Management Assocn, Hon Fellow James Cook Univ, Australia, Hon Fell Institute of Wastes Management, Hon Fell Trinity Coll, Carmarthen, Hon Fell Univ of Glamorgan, Hon Dr of Education, Swansea Institute of Higher Education; DL Dyfed 1993; *cr Baron Parry*, of Neyland in co Dyfed (Life Baron) 1975: *m* 1948, Glenys Catherine, da of Jack Leslie Incledon, and has issue.

Residence – Willowmead, 52 Port Lion, Llangwm, Haverfordwest, Dyfed SA62 4JT.

DAUGHTER LIVING

Hon Catherine Anne, *b* 1955.

Parsons, family name of Earl of Rosse.

PATEL, BARON (Patel) (Life Baron 1999)

NAREN (NARENDRAKUMAR BABUBHAI) PATEL, son of Babubhai Patel, of Sojitra, India; *b* 11 May 1938; *ed* St Andrews Univ (MB, ChB 1964, MRCOG 1969, FRCOG 1988); Consultant Obstetrician, Ninewells Hospital, Dundee; Pres Royal Coll of Obstetricians and Gynaecologists 1995; past Chm Academy of Medical Royal Colleges; *cr* Kt 1997, and *Baron Patel*, of Dunkeld in Perth and Kinross (Life Baron) 1999: *m* 1970, Helen Linda, da of Wilfed Dally, of Edzell, Scotland, and has issue.

Residence – 19 Canisp Crescent, Gowrie Park, Dundee, Angus DD2 4TP.

SONS LIVING

Hon Mark, *b* 1975; *ed* Selwyn Coll, Cambridge.
Hon Neil, *b* (twin) 1975; *ed* Univ Coll, Oxford, and Edinburgh.

DAUGHTER LIVING

Hon Susan, *b* 1971; *m* 1997, Maxime Lalondrelle.

Paton, Noel-, family name of Baron Ferrier.

PATTEN, BARON (Patten) (Life Baron 1997)

JOHN HAGGITT CHARLES PATTEN, PC, son of late Jack Patten, of Great Bookham, Surrey; *b* 17 July 1945; *ed* Wimbledon Coll, and Sidney Sussex Coll, Camb (MA 1971, PhD 1972); MP for Oxford (C)

1979-83 and for Oxford West and Abingdon 1983-97; PPS to Ministers of State at the Home Office 1980-81; Parliamentary Under-Sec of State for Northern Ireland 1981-83, and for Health 1983-85; Min of State for Housing, Urban Affairs and Construction 1985-87; Min of State, Home Office 1987-92; Sec of State for Education 1992-94; Adviser to CCF Charterhouse plc since 1995; non-exec Dir Alfred McAlpine plc since 1996, and EPR Ltd since 1997; Memb Advisory Board, Thomas Goode & Co Ltd since 1997, and non-exec Dir since 1999; non-exec Dir Baldwins Industrial Services plc since 1998; non-exec Chm Cortecs plc since 1998; UK Adviser Lockheed Martin since 1997; Fell of Hertford Coll, Oxford 1972-94; Hon Fell Harris Manchester Coll, Oxford; Liveryman of Worshipful Co of Drapers; *cr* PC 1990, and *Baron Patten*, of Wincanton, co Som (Life Baron) 1997: *m* 1978, Louise Alexandra Virginia Charlotte, 2nd da of late John Rowe of Norfolk, and has issue.
Address – c/o House of Lords, Westminster, SW1A 0PW.

DAUGHTER LIVING

Hon Mary-Claire, *b* 1986.

PAUL, BARON (Paul) (Life Baron 1996)

SWRAJ PAUL, son of late Payare Paul, of Jalandhar, India; *b* 18 Feb 1931; *ed* Univ of Punjab (BSc 1949), and Massachusetts Institute of Technology (BSc 1952, MSc 1952), Hon PhD American Coll of Switzerland (1986), Hon DSc Hull (1992), Hon DHL Chapman Univ, California (1956), Hon Dr Univ of Bradford (1997), Hon DLitt Univ of Westminster (1997), Hon DPhil Guru Nanak Dev Univ, Amritsar (1998), Hon Dr Univ of Central England (1999), Hon DSc Univ of Buckingham (1999); Dir Apeejay-Surrendra Gp, India 1952-66, came to England 1956, founded Natural Gas Tubes Ltd 1968; Chm Caparo Gp Ltd since 1978, Caparo Industries plc since 1980, and Caparo Inc, USA since 1988; awarded Order of Padma Bhushan of India 1983; *cr Baron Paul*, of Marylebone, City of Westminster (Life Baron) 1996: *m* 1956, Aruna, da of Ramnath Vij, of Calcutta, and has had issue.

Arms – Azure on each of three piles rayonny or one issuing from the dexter and one from the sinister a pile gules. **Crest** – Issuing from a lotus or a girl child proper vested azure holding aloft in the dexter hand a dove wings elevated argent. **Supporters** – On either side an Indian elephant azure tusked unguled and grasping with the trunk a torch enflamed or.
Address – Caparo Group Ltd, Caparo House, 103 Baker St, W1M 2LN. *Clubs* – MCC, RAC, Royal Calcutta Turf, Royal Calcutta Golf, Cricket of India (Bombay).

SONS LIVING

Hon Ambar, *b* 1957; *ed* Harrow, and Carnegie Mellon Univ, USA: *m* 1983, Gauri, dau of Kailash Lamba, of New Delhi, and has issue living, Akhil (son), *b* 1985, — Anika (da), *b* 1988.
Hon Akash, *b* (twin) 1957; *ed* Harrow, Carnegie Mellon Univ, and Massachusetts Institute of Technology: *m* 1983, Nisha, da of Cmdr O...... P...... Gill, of Bombay, and has issue living, Arush (son), *b* 1986, — Ashma (da), *b* 1991.
Hon Angad, *b* 1970; *ed* Harrow, and Massachusetts Institute of Technology. *Residence* – Ambika House, 9a Portland Place, W1.

DAUGHTERS LIVING AND DECEASED

Hon Anjli, *b* 1959; *ed* Roedean: *m* 1981, Gurinderjit Punn, son of Jit Singh Punn, and has issue living, Shalin (son), *b* 1985, — Shaila (da), *b* 1987. *Residence* – 84 Harborne Rd, Edgbaston, Birmingham.
Ambika, *b* 1963: *d* 1968.

Paulet, family name of Marquess of Winchester.

Peake, family name of Viscount Ingleby.

PEARCE, BARONY OF (Pearce) (Extinct 1990)

WIDOWS LIVING OF SONS OF LIFE BARON

(Jennifer) Christine, da of late Rev J. W. G. Westwood, of Eynsham, Oxfordshire: *m* 1987, as his 2nd wife, Hon (Richard) Bruce (Holroyd) Pearce, QC, who *d* 1987, and has issue living, Edward William, *b* 1981, — Erica Harriet, *b* 1982. *Residence* – Sweethawes, Kings Sutton, nr Banbury, Oxfordshire.

Julia, yr da of C. D. Hill, of Tyrrellswood, Leatherhead, Surrey: *m* 1st, 1969, Hon James Edward Holroyd Pearce, QC, who *d* 1985; 2ndly, 1987, Ian Strickland Ball, and has issue living (by 1st *m*), Edward *b* 19—, — Robert, *b* 19—, — Ianthe, *b* 19—, — Barbara, *b* 19—. *Residence* – Turf Lodge, Sheep Plain, Crowborough, Sussex TN6 3ST.

PEARSON, BARONY OF (Pearson) (Extinct 1980)

SON LIVING OF LIFE BARON

Hon Graham Thomas (Pinette, Whangarei Heads Rd, RD 4, Whangarei, New Zealand), *b* 1935: *m* 1963, Diana, da of Vice-Adm Sir Maxwell Richmond, KBE, CB, DSO, of Whangarei Heads, New Zealand, and has issue.

DAUGHTER LIVING OF LIFE BARON

Hon Lois Jean, *b* 1938: *m* 1961, Rt Rev Canon Robin Jonathan Norman Smith, of Hertford House, Abbey Mill Lane, St Albans, Herts AL3 4HE, and has issue.

Pearson, family name of Viscount Cowdray.

PEARSON OF RANNOCH, BARON (Pearson) (Life Baron 1990)

MALCOLM EVERARD MACLAREN PEARSON, son of late Col John MacLaren Pearson; *b* 20 July 1942; *ed* Eton; Hon Dr Laws (Edinburgh); Founded Pearson Webb Springbett (PWS) Group of Reinsurance Brokers 1964, Chm PWS Holdings plc 1970-86 and since 1988; Founded Rannoch Trust 1984; Member Council for National Academic Awards 1983-92 (Hon Treas 1986-92); Member House of Lords Select Cttee on European Communities 1991-96; Hon Pres Rescare (Nat Soc for Mentally Handicapped People in Residential Care) since 1994; Patron British Chinese Herbal Medicine Practitioners since 1998; *cr Baron Pearson of Rannoch*, of Bridge of Gaur, in the District of Perth and Kinross (Life Baron) 1990: *m* 1st, 1965 (*m diss* 1970), Francesca Frua, da of Giuseppe Frua de Angeli; 2ndly, 1977 (*m diss* 1995), Hon (Francesca) Mary Charteris, only da of Baron Charteris of Amisfield, GCB, GCVO, QSO, OBE, PC (Life Baron); 3rdly, 1998, Caroline, 3rd da of Major Hugh Launcelot St Vincent Rose, and has issue by 1st and 2nd *m*.

Residence – Rannoch Barracks, Rannoch Station, Perthshire PH17 2QE. *Club* – White's.

DAUGHTERS LIVING (*By 1st marriage*)

Hon Silvia Maria Francesca, *b* 1966: *m* 1995, Piers Alfred Le Marchant, and has issue (*see* Le Marchant, Bt, colls).

(*By 2nd marriage*)

Hon Marina MacLaren, *b* 1980.
Hon Zara Alexandra Mary, *b* 1984.

PEART, BARONY (Peart) (Extinct 1988)

SON LIVING OF LIFE BARON

Hon Emerson Frederick, *b* 1948: *m* .

WIDOW LIVING OF LIFE BARON

SARAH ELIZABETH (*Baroness Peart*), da of Thomas Lewis, of Aberystwyth: *m* 1945, Baron Peart (Life Baron), PC, who *d* 1988.

Pease, family name of Baron Gainford.

Pease, family name of Baron Wardington.

PEDDIE, BARONY OF (Peddie) (Extinct 1978)

SON LIVING OF LIFE BARON

Hon Ian James Crofton (36 Chiswick Staithe, Hartington Rd, W4 3TP), *b* 1945; *ed* Gordonstoun, and Univ Coll, London (LLB); Bar Inner Temple 1971; QC, Recorder SE Circuit since 1997: *m* 1976, Susan Renee, el da of Edmund John Brampton Howes, of 13 Wheelers Av, Penn, Bucks, and has issue living, Kate Chloe, *b* 1982.

PEEL, EARL (Peel) (Earl UK 1929, Bt GB 1800)

WILLIAM JAMES ROBERT PEEL, 3rd Earl and 8th Baronet; *b* 3 Oct 1947; *s* 1969; *ed* Ampleforth, Tours Univ, France, and Roy Agric Coll, Cirencester; Vice-Chm Game Conservancy Trust since 1990; a Member of the Council of the Prince of Wales, Duchy of Cornwall, since 1993, Lord Warden of the Stannaries and Keeper of the Privy Seal of the Duchy since 1994: *m* 1st, 1973, Veronica Naomi Livingston, da of Maj John Alastair Livingston Timpson, MC, Scots Gds (*see* Houstoun-Boswall, Bt); 2ndly, 1989, Hon Mrs Charlotte Clementine Hambro, yr da of late Baron Soames, GCMG, GCVO, CH, CBE, PC (Life Baron), and has issue by 1st and 2nd *m*.

ꓮrms – Argent, three sheaves of as many arrows proper two and one, banded gules, on a chief azure a bee volant or. Ꞔrest – A demi-lion rampant argent, gorged with a collar azure charged with three bezants and holding between the paws a shuttle or. Ꙍupporters – *Dexter*, a lion reguardant argent, gorged with a chain or, pendant therefrom an escutcheon azure, thereon a representation of the Speaker's mace erect of the second; *sinister*, a griffin reguardant or, gorged with a gold chain, pendant therefrom an escutcheon azure, charged with a representation of the Speaker's mace of the first.
Residence – Kilgram Grange, Jervaulx, Ripon, N Yorks HG4 4PQ. *Club* – Turf.

SON LIVING (*By 1st marriage*)

ASHTON ROBERT GERARD (*Viscount Clanfield*), *b* 16 Sept 1976.

DAUGHTERS LIVING (*By 1st marriage*)

Lady Iona Joy Julia, *b* 1978.

(*By 2nd marriage*)

Lady Antonia Mary Catherine, *b* 1991.

BROTHER LIVING

Hon Robert Michael Arthur, *b* 1950; *ed* Eton, and Hertford Coll, Oxford: *m* 1973, Fiona Natalie, da of Charles Davidson, of Dunhampstead House, Droitwich, Worcs, and has issue living, Kathryn Beatrice, *b* 1978, — Hermione Juliet, *b* 1979, — Eleanor Lindsay, *b* 1981. *Residence* – Berryhill Farm, Coedkernew, Newport, Gwent.

COLLATERAL BRANCHES LIVING (*In remainder to Viscountcy and Baronetcy only*)

Issue of late Major Hon (Arthur) George Villiers Peel, 2nd son of 1st Viscount, *b* 1868, *d* 1956: *m* 1906, Lady Agnes Lygon, who *d* 1960, da of 6th Earl Beauchamp:—
Juliet Agnes, *b* 1919: *m* 1942, Maj George Thorne, MC, ERD, DL, late Grenadier Guards (B Penryhn), of 24 Swallowfield Park, Reading, and has issue living, Robert George (Ovington House, Ovington, Alresford, Hants), *b* 1943; *ed* Eton, and RAC, Cirencester; with Barclays Bank: *m* 1990, Mrs Sarah Veronica Bond, formerly wife of late Brian David Bond, and da of James Frederick Priestley, — Ian David Peel (Beauchamp Barn, Kneesall, Newark, Notts NG22 0AS), *b* 1944; *ed* Eton, RMA, and Trin Coll, Oxford; late Capt Grenadier Guards; High Sheriff Notts 1986: *m* 1992, Paula Nkechi Enwezoh, and has issue living, Davina Nkechi Rozelle *b* 1992, — Viola Georgina Juliet, *b* 1948: *m* 1976, Nicholas Guy Halsey, TD, DL, of The Golden Parsonage, Gt Gaddesden, Hemel Hempstead, Herts, and has issue (*see* Halsey, Bt).

Grandchildren of late Rev Hon Maurice Berkeley Peel, MC, 4th son of 1st Viscount:—
Issue of late Major David Arthur Peel, MC, Irish Guards, b 1910, ka 1944: m 1936, Hon Sara Carola Vanneck (Huntingfield Hall, Halesworth, Suffolk, 1P19 0QA), da of 5th Baron Huntingfield:—
Jonathan Sidney, CBE, MC (Barton Hall, Barton Turf, Norwich, NR12 8AU), b 1937; ed Norwich Sch, Eton, and St John's Coll, Camb (MA); Capt Rifle Bde (ret); a Page of Honour to HM 1951-53; a Dir Norwich Union Insurance Gp; Chm Pleasureworld plc; Malaya 1957 (MC); Congo 1960-61; JP, DL, CC and Vice Lord-Lieut Norfolk 1980; High Sheriff 1984; Chm National Trust Properties Cttee since 1990, Dep Chm National Trust since 1992, Chm Broads Authority since 1985, Chm County Council Planning and Transport Cttee 1989-93, Chm National Trust E Anglia Region 1981-90, Vice-Pres Norfolk Naturalists Trust, Chm Norwich Sch, and How Hill Trust for Environmental Education; CBE 1994: m 1965, Jean Fulton, da of Air Ch Marshal Sir Denis Hensley Fulton Barnett, GCB, CBE, DFC, and has issue living, Robert Denis, b 1976, — Ruth Miranda, b 1966, — Emily Sara, b 1967: m 19—, Mario de Pina Antunes, and has issue living, Anibal-Jorge b 1991, — Anne Louise, b 1970, — Delia Mary, b 1974. —— Charles David (15 Ranelgh Rd, W5 5RJ), b 1940; ed Eton, and at Norwich Sch; ARIBA: m 1973, Catherine Anne, da of Duncan Mackintosh, CBE, of Woodfolds, Oaksey, Wilts, and has issue living, Thomas David, b 1975, — Elisabeth Alison, b 1977. —— Julia Victoria Mary, b 1939: m 1970, Nicholas Longe (High Sheriff of Suffolk 1984-85), of Hasketon Manor, Woodbridge, Suffolk, son of late Lt-Col R. B. Longe, of Hasketon Manor, Woodbridge, Suffolk, and has issue living, William Martin Peel, b 1972, — David John Hastings, b 1975.

(In remainder to Baronetcy only)

Grandchildren of late Lawrence Moore Peel, 3rd son of Capt Robert Moore Peel, el son of late Rt Hon William Yates Peel, MP, 2nd son of 1st baronet:—
Issue of late Lionel Victor Moore Peel, b 1901, d 1937: m 1924, Muriel Mildred (9295 McNaught Rd, Chilliwack, BC, Canada), da of M. A. Murphy, of Chilliwack, BC:—
Robert John (50769 Yale Rd East, RR1, Rosedale, BC, Canada), b 1927: m 1949, Mona Jean, yst da of A. A. E. Batchelor, and has issue living, Robert Lionel, b 1952: m 1972, Sheila, 6th da of Austin Byrnes, of Chilliwack, BC, — Rodney Robin, b 1955, — Darcy Edward, b 1965, — Susan Holly, b 1958. —— Lionel Brian, b 1931: m 1952, Beverly Ann, only da of Harvey G. Cook, of Cultus Lake, BC, Canada, and has issue living, Brian Gregory, b 1954: m 1973, Sylvia, da of Clarence Hala, of Chilliwack, BC, and has issue living, James Nathan b 1974, Jason Randall b 1976, — and two adopted das, Kathryn Patricia, b 1964, — Kimberley Ann, b 1965. —— Iris Patricia, b 1929: m 1952, Lorne Albert Gehman, and has issue living, Blair Lee, b 1957, — Lane Peel, b 1958, — Dane Robert, b 1959, — Christie Robin, b 1962, — Regen Corey Gehman, b 1965, — Shannon Dee, b 1954.

Grandchildren (by 2nd m) of late William Charles Peel (infra):—
Issue of late Frederick William Peel, b 1900, d 1978; admitted to British nationality 1936; assumed the forename of William in lieu of his second christian name of de Layney: m 1924, Martha Grace, da of William Young, of Memphis, Tennessee:—
Frederick William (PO Box 292, Paris, Tennessee, USA), b 1925; Lt-Col USAF (ret): m 1st, 1945, Clareleen Popham, of Carothersville, USA; 2ndly, 1954, Clare Elizabeth, da of F. B. Hooever, of Enid, Oklahoma, and has issue living (by 1st m), Frederick William, b 1947, — Martha Frances, b 1949, — (by 2nd m) John Hoover, b 1962: m 1985, Karen Denise, da of W. Sanders, of Paris, Tennessee, — Traci de Layney, b 1955. —— †Robert Dudley, b 1937; Maj USAF: m 1963, Mary Elizabeth (2933 Caballero Drive, Jacksonville, Florida 32217, USA), da of Lawrence J. McDonald, and d 1982, leaving issue, Elizabeth Anne, b 1987, Jeffrey Alan Styerwalt, and has issue living, Sean William b 1990, Brian Robert b 1992, — Mary Martha, b 1966: m 1991, Christian Simon Bahn, — Katherine Louise, b 1970. —— Robert de Layney (3908 Leon Drive, Plano, Texas 75074, USA), b 1939; Lt-Col USAF (rct); Capt Southwest Airlines: m 1976, Christine Ann, da of Walter Trimailo, and has issue living, Delaney Anne, b 1978, — Kathryn Eve, b 1985.

Issue of late Evelyn Ker Semer Peel, b 1909, d 1993; assumed the names of Lincoln Henry Tracy in lieu of his christian names: m 1946, Hazel Pearl Gener:—
Kevin John (66 Chislehurst Rd, Lesmurdie, W Australia 6076), b 1946: m 1967, Cheryl Anne, da of Albert George Lawrence, of 2 Nereus Place, Madora Bay, W Australia, and has issue living, Gary John, b 1970, — Christopher James, b 1973.

Issue of late Laurence Donald Tracy Peel, b 1917, d 1983: m 1950, Corinne Beatrix Crutchley:—
Suzanne Caroline, b 1951: m 1970, Paul Raymond Martin, of The Rectory, Wood Lane, Bunwell, Norfolk NR16 1TF, and has issue living, Philip Andrew b 1977, — Joanna Corinne Judith, b 1984.

Granddaughters of late Rev Frederick Peel, 3rd son of late Rt Hon William Yates Peel, MP (ante):—
Issue of late William Charles Peel, b 1863, d 1930: m 1st, 1889, Marion Georgiana Frances, who d 1897, da of Libert Chandler, of USA; 2ndly, 1900, Leonie Rose, da of Constant Hallu, of Nampcel, France:—
(By 2nd m) Estelle Frances (Cedarwood, Lows Lane, Palgrave, Diss, Norfolk IP22 1AE), b 1901: m 1st, 19—, T. S. Patterson; 2ndly, 19—, Christopher Lewis, who d 1942. —— Dorothy Léonie, b 1911: m 1938, Donnington Dade, who d 1976.

Grandson of late Col Frederick Peel, 2nd son of late Lt-Col Edmund Yates Peel, 2nd son of Lt-Gen Rt Hon Jonathan Peel, MP, 5th son of 1st baronet:—
Issue of late Archibald Peel, b 1878, d 1932: m 1908, Mary, da of late Henry Whiteley, of Wakefield, Yorkshire, and adopted da of Reuben Thomas Saunders, formerly of Raskelf, 215 Capstone Rd, Bournemouth:—
Maurice, b 1910: m (March) 1935, Louisa Myrtle, da of late John Newby Carter, and has issue living, Maurice Newby, b (Dec) 1935, — Alfred George, b 1940, — Stanley Charles, b 1946, — Cyril Ronald, b 1952, — Violet Ethel, b 1937: m 1959, Kevin George Anderson, of 59 Bladin St, Laverton, Melbourne, Australia, and has issue living, Kevin John b 1960, Brett Lewin b 1961, Steven Maurice b 1963, Vanessa Lee b 1968, — Lorraine Ruth, b 1945.

Grandchildren of late Alfred Michael John Russell Peel, 4th son of late Archibald Peel (b 1828), 3rd son of Lt-Gen Rt Hon Jonathan Peel, MP (ante):—
Issue of late Archibald John Russell Peel, b 1907, d 1978: m 1946, Patricia Virtue, who d 1980, only da of Col Baldwin Millard, of 61 Fitzjohn's Av, NW3:—

Jeremy Robert (Willow Cottages, La Pouquelaye, St Helier, Jersey, CI), *b* 1946: *m* 1st, 1970 (*m diss* 1974), Shirley Ann Brett; 2ndly, 1984, Angela Betty, only da of Edward David Neal, of La Rosa, St Peter, Jersey, and has issue living (by 1st *m*), Mark Jeremy Russell, *b* 1971. —— Michael John Russell, *b* 1952. —— Caroline Georgiana, *b* 1948: *m* 1970, Paul Fisher Bancroft, of Caroline House, South Rd, Oundle, Peterborough, and has issue living, Adam Fisher, *b* 1973, —— Oliver Robert, *b* 1976, — Jonathan Guy, *b* 1979, — Imogen Georgiana Patricia, *b* 1984. —— Elizabeth Francesca (3/14 Flemington St, Frewville, S Australia 5063), *b* 1950: *m* 1972 (*m diss* 1978), Andrew Swart.

Grandsons of late Lt-Col Charles Algernon Peel, only son of late Horace Peel, 3rd son of late Sir Charles Lennox Peel, GCB, eldest son of late Laurence Peel, 6th son of 1st baronet:—
Issue of late Jeremy Charles Peel, *b* 1934, *d* 1988: *m* 1960 (*m diss* 1971), Sheila Mary Rose, da of Capt Charles Elphinstone Fordyce (*see* B Windlesham, 1990 Edn):—
Robert Frederick Charles (6 Terrick Cottages, Terrick, Aylesbury, Bucks), *b* 1962: *m* 1991, Dr Elizabeth Mary, yr da of Geoffrey Green, of Ayr, Ontario, Canada, and has issue living, Kate, *b* 19—, — Alice Lucy Elizabeth, *b* 1998. —— James Arthur Lennox (The Garden Flat, 120 St John's Hill, SW10), *b* 1964: *m* 1987, Belinda Margaret Emma, yr da of Nicholas Smith, of Charney Bassett, Oxon.

PREDECESSORS – **(1)** *Rt Hon* ARTHUR WELLESLEY Peel, 5th son of late Rt Hon Sir Robert Peel, 2nd Bt, of Drayton Manor, Staffordshire; *b* 1829; Parliamentary Sec to Poor Law Board 1868-71, and to Board of Trade 1871-3, Patronage Sec to Treasury 1873-4, Under-Sec for Home Depart April to Dec 1880, and Speaker (four times elected to House of Commons Feb 1884 to April 1895); MP for Warwick (*L*) 1865-85, and for Warwick and Leamington 1886-95; *cr Viscount Peel*, of Sandy, co Bedford (peerage of United Kingdom) 1895: *m* 1962, Adelaide, who *d* 1890, da of William Stratford Dugdale, of Merevale, Warwickshire; *d* 1912; *s* by his el son **(2)** *Rt Hon* WILLIAM ROBERT WELLESLEY, GCSI, GBE, 2nd Viscount; *b* 1867; MP for Manchester (S Div) 1900-1906, and for Taunton 1906-12; appointed Joint Parliamentary Sec (unpaid), National Ser Depart 1917, Under-Sec of State for War 1919, and Chancellor of Duchy of Lancaster 1921 (also Min of Transport (unpaid) 1921); was Sec of State for India 1922-4, and again 1928-9, and Lord Privy Seal Sept to Nov 1931; *cr Viscount Clanfield*, of Clanfield, co Southampton, and *Earl Peel* (peerage of United Kingdom) 1929: *m* 1899, Hon Eleanor (Ella) Williamson, who *d* 1949, da of 1st Baron Ashton (ext); *d* 1937; *s* by his son **(3)** ARTHUR WILLIAM ASHTON, 2nd Earl *b* 1901; Lord Lt of Lancs 1948-50: *m* 1946, Kathleen, who *d* 1972, da of Michael McGrath of Ballycullane, co Cork; *d* 1969; *s* by his son **(4)** WILLIAM JAMES ROBERT, 3rd Earl and present peer; also Viscount Peel, and Viscount Clanfield.

*****(1)** ROBERT Peel, 3rd son of late Robert Peel, of Peele Fold, Lancashire; *b* 1750; was an eminent Cotton Spinner, MP for Tamworth 1790-1818, and contributed £10,000 towards promoting the war with France; *cr a Baronet* 1800: *m* 1st, 1783, Ellen, da of William Yates, of Spring Side, near Bury; 2ndly, 1805, Susanna, who *d* 1824, da of late Francis Clerke; *d* 1830; *s* by his el son **(2)** *Rt Hon* ROBERT, 2nd Bt; *b* 1788; sometime MP for Oxford Univ, and subsequently for Tamworth (*C*); appointed Under-Sec of State for the Colonies 1810, Ch Sec for Ireland 1812, and Sec of State for Home Depart 1828; was First Lord of the Treasury and Prime Minister 1834-5 and 1841-6: *m* 1820, Julia, who *d* 1859, yst da of Gen Sir John Floyd, 1st Bt; *d* 1850; *s* by his el son **(3)** *Rt Hon Sir* ROBERT, GCB, 3rd Bt; *b* 1822; sat as MP for Tamworth (LC) 1850-80, for Huntingdon (*C*) 1884-5, and for Blackburn 1885-6; was a Lord of the Admiralty 1852-7, and Ch Sec for Ireland 1861-5: *m* 1856, Lady Emily Hay, who *d* 1924, da of 8th Marquess of Tweeddale; *d* 1895; *s* by his only son **(4)** ROBERT, 4th Bt; *b* 1867: *m* 1897, Mercedes, da of Baron de Graffenried, formerly of Thun, Switzerland; *d* 1925; *s* by his only son **(5)** ROBERT, 5th Bt; *b* 1898: *m* 1920, Beatrice Gladys, the distinguished comedienne, who *d* 1989, aged 94, da of late John Lillie; *d* 1934; *s* by his only son **(6)** ROBERT, 6th Bt; *b* 1920; Ordinary Seaman RN; *ka* 1942; *s* by his kinsman **(7)** ARTHUR WILLIAM ASHTON (*ante*).

Pelham, family name of Earl of Chichester.

Pelham, family name of Earl of Yarborough.

Pellew, family name of Viscount Exmouth.

Pemberton, Leigh-, family name of Baron Kingsdown.

PEMBROKE and MONTGOMERY, EARL OF (Herbert) (Earl E 1551 and 1605)

One I will serve

HENRY GEORGE CHARLES ALEXANDER HERBERT, 17th Earl; *b* 19 May 1939; *s* 1969; *ed* Eton, and Oxford Univ; late RHG; Hereditary Visitor of Jesus Coll, Oxford; Film Maker: *m* 1st, 1966 (*m diss* 1981), Claire Rose, da of Douglas Gurney Pelly (*see* Pelly Bt, colls); 2ndly, 1988, Miranda Juliet, da of Cmdr John Somerville Kendal Oram, of Bulbridge House, Wilton, Salisbury, Wilts (*see* E Cairns, 1985 Edn), and has issue by 1st and 2nd *m*.

𝕬rms – Per pale azure and gules, three lions rampant argent. 𝕮rest – A wyvern wings elevated vert, holding in the mouth a sinister hand couped at the wrist gules. 𝕾upporters – *Dexter*, a panther guardant argent, incensed, spotted or, vert, sable azure, and gules, alternately, ducally collared azure; *sinister*, a lion argent, ducally collared or. *Seat* – Wilton House, Salisbury, Wilts SP2 0BZ.

SON LIVING (*By 1st marriage*)

WILLIAM ALEXANDER SIDNEY (*Lord Herbert*), *b* 18 May 1978.

DAUGHTER LIVING (*By 1st marriage*)

Lady Sophia Elizabeth, *b* 1966.
Lady Emma Louise, *b* 1969.
Lady Flora Katinka, *b* 1970.

(*By 2nd marriage*)

Lady Jemima Juliet, *b* 1989.
Lady Alice Mary, *b* 1991.
Lady Katie Ella, *b* 1997.

SISTER LIVING

Lady Diana Mary, *b* 1937.

COLLATERAL BRANCHES LIVING

Descendants of late Henry Herbert (el son of late Maj-Gen Hon William Herbert, 5th son of 8th Earl), who was *cr Earl of Carnarvon* 1793 (see that title).

PREDECESSORS – (1) *Sir* WILLIAM Herbert, KG, KB, was Ch Gentleman of the Privy Chamber, Master of the Horse 1549, twice Gov of the Forces sent into Picardy, twice Gov of Calais, and Capt Gen of the Army beyond the Seas, etc; *cr Baron Herbert*, of Cardiff, and *Earl of Pembroke* (peerage of England) 1551; *d* 1570; *s* by his el son (2) HENRY, KG, 2nd Earl; *d* 1601; *s* by his son (3) WILLIAM, KG, 3rd Earl; was Lord Chamberlain of the Household; *d* 1630; *s* by his brother (4) PHILIP, KG, 4th Earl, who in 1605 had been *cr Baron Herbert*, of Shurland, Isle of Sheppey, co Kent, and *Earl of Montgomery* (peerage of England); was Lord Chamberlain to the Household, and Chancellor of Oxford Univ; *d* 1655; *s* by his son (5) PHILIP, 5th Earl; *d* 1669; *s* by his el son (6) WILLIAM, 6th Earl; *d* unmarried 1674; *s* by his half-brother (7) PHILIP, 7th Earl; *d* without male issue 1683; *s* by his brother (8) THOMAS, KG, PC, 8th Earl; was Ambassador to States Gen 1689, Lord Privy Seal 1700, seven times one of the Lord Justices, Lord High Adm of England 1702 and 1708-9, and Lord Pres of the Council 1702; at the Coronation of George I carried the sword styled "Curtana"; *d* 1733; *s* by his son (9) HENRY, 9th Earl; a Lieut-Gen in the Army; *d* 1750; *s* by his son (10) HENRY, 10th Earl; was a Lieut-Gen in the Army, and Col 1st Dragoons; *d* 1794; *s* by his son (11) GEORGE AUGUSTUS, KG, 11th Earl; *d* 1827; *s* by his son (12) ROBERT HENRY, 12th Earl; *d* 1862; *s* by his nephew (13) GEORGE ROBERT CHARLES, 13th Earl of Pembroke, and 10th Earl of Montgomery, who had already in 1861 *s* as 2nd Baron Herbert of Lea (son of Hon Sidney Herbert, 2nd son of 11th Earl, an eminent statesman, who *m* 1846, Elizabeth, da of Lieut-Gen Charles Ashe A'Court; and *d* Aug 1861, having in Jan of that year been *cr Baron Herbert of Lea* (peerage of United Kingdom)), *b* 1850; *m* 1874, Lady Gertrude Frances Talbot, who *d* 1906, da of 18th Earl of Shrewsbury; *d* 1895; *s* by his brother (14) SIDNEY, GCVO, PC, 14th Earl; *b* 1853; a Lord of Treasury 1885-6 and July 1886 to Aug 1892, and Lord Steward of the Household to Queen Victoria July 1895 to Jan 1901, and to King Edward VII 1901-3; MP for Wilton (C) 1877-85, and for Croydon 1886-95; *m* 1877, Lady Beatrix Louisa Lambton, who *d* 1944, da of 2nd Earl of Durham; *d* 1913; *s* by his el son (15) REGINALD, MVO, 15th Earl; *b* 1880; Lieut-Col Roy Horse Guards; Mayor of Wilton 1932-34, 1942-45, and 1954-55: *m* 1904, Lady Beatrice Eleanor, CBE, who *d* 1973, da of late Lord Alexander Victor Paget (M Anglesey); *d* 1960; *s* by his el son (16) SIDNEY CHARLES, CVO, 16th Earl; *b* 1906; Equerry to HRH The Duke of Kent 1935-42; Private Sec and Comptroller to HRH the Duchess of Kent 1942-48; Lord Lieut of Wilts 1954-69: *m* 1936, Lady Mary Dorothea Hope, CVO, who *d* 1995, da of 1st Marquess of Linlithgow; *d* 1969; *s* by his son (17) HENRY GEORGE CHARLES ALEXANDER, 17th Earl and present peer; also Baron Herbert of Cardiff, Baron Herbert of Shurland, and Baron Herbert of Lea.

PENDER, BARON (Denison-Pender) (Baron UK 1937)

PERSEVERO

I persevere

JOHN WILLOUGHBY DENISON-PENDER, 3rd Baron; *b* 6 May 1933; *s* 1965; *ed* Eton; late Capt City of London Yeo (TA); late Lt 10th Hussars; Vice-Pres Royal Sch for the Deaf since 1992: *m* 1962, Julia, da of Richard Nevill Cannon, OBE, of Coombe Place, Lewes, and has issue.

Arms – Quarterly: 1st and 4th gules, on a bend nebuly argent two lions' heads erased of the first, *Pender*; 2nd and 3rd per bend sable and argent two bendlets between a unicorn's head erased in chief and three cross-crosslets in base all counterchanged, *Denison*; Crests – 1st, a demi-lion or resting the sinister paw upon a terrestrial globe, and grasping in the dexter paw a seax proper, pomel and hilt gold, *Pender*; 2nd, in front of a sun rising in splendour a dexter arm in bend proper, vested gules gutte-d'eau, cuff erminois, the fore-finger pointing to an estoile or *Denison*. Supporters – On either side a figure of Hermes standing on a cable-grapnel, the dexter holding in the exterior hand a Caduceus and the sinister a flash of lightning all proper.
Residence – North Court, Tilmanstone, Kent CT14 OJP. *Clubs* – White's, Pratt's.

SON LIVING

Hon HENRY JOHN RICHARD (*Club* – White's), *b* 19 March 1968: *m* 1994, Vanessa Jane, da of John Eley, of NSW, Australia, and has issue living, Molly Jane, *b* 1998.

DAUGHTERS LIVING

Hon Emma Charlotte, *b* 1964: *m* 1992, Matthew Christopher Anthony Brett (*see* V Esher), and has issue (see that title).
Hon Mary Anne Louise, *b* 1965.

BROTHER LIVING

Hon Robin Charles (Jessups, Mark Beech, Edenbridge, Kent; *Club* – White's), *b* 1935; *ed* Eton; late Lt 11th Hussars; High Sheriff Kent 1993; a Member of Stock Exchange: *m* 1966, Clare Nell, da of Lt-Col James Currie Thomson, MBE, TD, DL, of Stable Court, Walkern, Stevenage (*see* Borthwick, Bt, colls), and has issue living, Jocelyn Andrew (25 Hamble St, SW6 2RT), *b* 1967: *m* 1995, Georgina Rachel, 2nd da of late Charles William Fane, of Ashmansworth, Newbury, Berks (*see* E Westmorland, colls), and has issue living, Maximilian Robin *b* 1997, — Peter Robin, *b* 1972, — Sacha Louise, *b* 1969: *m* 1993, Jonathan David Forbes (*see* Ropner, Bt, *cr* 1952), and has issue (see that title).

SISTER LIVING

Hon Ann Camilla (*Hon Lady Dent*), *b* 1931: *m* 1952, Sir Robin John Dent, KCVO, of 44 Smith St, SW3, who *d* 1999, in Cairo, and has issue living, Annabel Jane, *b* 1954: *m* 1981, James John Meade, of Pitt Vale Farm House, Pitt, Winchester, Hants SO22 5QW, son of late J. A. Meade, of 6 Fulham Park House, Chesilton Rd, SW6 5AA, and has issue living, Thomas Edward *b* 1988, Katherine Anne *b* 1984, Susanna Clare *b* 1986, — Jennifer Ann, *b* 1957: *m* 1982, Andrew Everard Martin Smith, elder son of late Julian Ronald Martin Smith, MC, of Ringstead Bury, Hunstanton, Norfolk, and has issue living, David Julian *b* 1984, Henrietta Camilla *b* 1986, Rosanna Marcia *b* (twin) 1986.

COLLATERAL BRANCH LIVING

Issue of late Maj Hon Richard Ernest Denison-Pender, TD, yr son of 1st Baron, *b* 1914, *d* 1984: *m* 1939, Louise, who *d* 1973, only da of late Henry Gilbey Riviere:—
James Henry, *b* 1942: *m* 1st, 1971, Gillian, yst da of late John C. Barnett, of Threepwood Hall, Haydon Bridge, Northumberland; 2ndly, 1994, Caroline Anne, da of Maj Timothy Stuart Lewis (*see* V Daventry, 1995 Edn), and formerly wife of Sir (Frederick Douglas) David Thomson, 3rd Bt, and has issue living (by 1st *m*), Jamie Alexander, *b* 1973, — Nicholas John, *b* 1974. —— Michael Richard (The Hazard, Sandwich Bay, Kent), *b* (twin) 1942: *m* 1972, Nadine, yr da of late Henri Villiger, of Aigle, Switzerland, and has issue living, Dominic Michael, *b* 1975. —— Linda Louise, *b* 1948: *m* 1973, John Edward Bayman, of Middle Cottage, Sandwich Bay, Kent, and has issue living, Alexander Christian Gray, *b* 1976, — Caroline Louise, *b* 1975.

PREDECESSORS – (1) JOHN CUTHBERT DENISON Denison-Pender, el son of late Sir John Denison-Pender, GBE, KCMG; *b* 1882; sometime Capt in the Army; a County Councillor for London 1910-19; European War 1914-18 in France and Belgium; MP for E. of Newmarket Div, of Cambridgeshire (*C*) 1913-18, and for Balham and Tooting Div of Wandsworth 1918-22; *cr Baron Pender*, of Porthcurnow, co Cornwall (peerage of United Kingdom) 1937: *m* 1906, Irene, who *d* 1943, da of late Sir Ernest de la Rue, KCVO, of 26 Belgrave Square, SW; *d* 1949; *s* by his son (2) JOHN JOCELYN, CBE, 2nd Baron, *b* 1907: *m* 1930, Camilla Lethbridge, who *d* 1988, da of late Willoughby Arthur Pemberton (Lethbridge, Bt, colls); *d* 1965; *s* by his el son (3) JOHN WILLOUGHBY, 3rd Baron and present peer.

Pennant, Douglas-, family name of Baron Penrhyn.

PENNEY, BARONY OF (Penney) (Extinct 1991)

SONS LIVING OF LIFE BARON (*by 1st marriage*)

Hon Martin Charles (16 Gainsborough Court, College Rd, Dulwich, SE21 7LT), *b* 1938; *ed* Cranleigh, and Gonville and Caius Coll, Camb (MA): *m* 1961, Margaret Heather, da of Sqdn-Ldr H. Almond, DSO, DFC, of Basingstoke, and has issue living, Claire Virginia, *b* 1962: *m* 1997, Gareth H. Ardern, yr son of Derek Ardern, of Itteringham, Norfolk, — Kathryn Jane, *b* 1964: *m* 1989, Christopher J. Coleman, only son of John Coleman, of Monte Carlo, Monaco, and has issue living, Hugo John *b* 1994, Charles Thomas *b* 1998, Rosanna Eleanor *b* 1991.

Hon Christopher Charles (The Coach House, Langton Way, Blackheath SE3 7TJ), *b* 1941; *ed* Cranleigh, Gonville and Caius Coll, Camb (MA), and Guy's Hosp, FRCP, FRCR: *m* 1968, Margaret, da of Henry Bell Fairley, of Stockport, and has issue living, Richard William, *b* 1970.

WIDOW LIVING OF LIFE BARON

ELEANOR JOAN (*Baroness Penney*), da of George Quennell, of Brentwood, Essex: *m* 1945, as his 2nd wife, Baron Penney, OM, KBE, FRS (Life Baron), who *d* 1991. *Residence* – Orchard House, E Hendred, Wantage, Oxon OX12 8TJ.

PENNOCK, BARONY OF (Pennock) (Extinct 1993)

SON LIVING OF LIFE BARON

Hon David Roderick Michael, *b* 1944; *ed* Rugby, and Merton Coll, Oxford: *m* 1969, Jane Pinhard, and has issue, three sons and one da. *Residence* – Iridge Place, Hurst Green, Sussex TN19 7PN.

DAUGHTERS LIVING OF LIFE BARON

Hon Susan Lorna, *b* 1948: *m* 1970, David Frederick McLaren Selby, of Goodchild's Hill, Stratfield Saye, Reading, Berks, and has issue, two sons and one da.

Hon Claire Elizabeth, *b* 1958: *m* 1985, Peter Vivian Walford, son of Edward Walford, of Norton, Cleveland, and has issue living, two sons and two das. *Residence* – Beston Farm, Halden Lane, Benenden, Cranbrook, Kent TN17 4BJ.

WIDOW LIVING OF LIFE BARON

LORNA (*Baroness Pennock*), da of Percival Pearse, of Morpeth: *m* 1944, Baron Pennock (Life Baron), who *d* 1993. *Residence* – 21 Launceston Place, W8 5RL.

Penny, family name of Viscount Marchwood.

PENRHYN, BARON (Douglas-Pennant) (Baron UK 1866)
(Title pronounced "Penrin")

With an even mind

MALCOLM FRANK DOUGLAS-PENNANT, DSO, MBE, 6th Baron; *b* 11 July 1908; *s* 1967; *ed* Eton; Col (ret) late KRRC; 1939-45 in N Africa and N-W Europe; MBE (Mil) 1943, DSO 1945: *m* 1954, Elisabeth Rosemary, da of late Brig Sir Percy Robert Laurie, KCVO, CBE, DSO, and has issue.

Arms – Quarterly: 1st and 4th per bend sinister ermine and ermines, a lion rampant or, *Pennant*; 2nd and 3rd grand quarters quarterly, 1st and 4th argent, a man's heart gules, ensigned with an Imperial crown proper, on a chief azure, three mullets of the field; 2nd and 3rd argent, three piles gules, on the two outer ones a mullet of the field, *Douglas*. **Crests** – 1st, Out of a ducal coronet an antelope's head argent, maned and tufted or, charged on the neck with a cross crosslet sable, for distinction; 2nd a sanglier, statant, between two clefts of an oak tree, with a chain and lock holding them together all proper, and above it the motto *"Lock sicker,"* – (Be secure). **Supporters** – On either side an antelope proper, collared and chain reflexed over the back or, and pendant from the collar of the dexter supporter an escutcheon gules, charged with the bust of a man's head affrontée proper.
Residence – Littleton Manor, Littleton, Winchester SO22 6QU. *Clubs* – Naval and Military; Fly Fishers.

DAUGHTERS LIVING

Hon Gillian Francis, *b* 1955: *m* 1997, Robin Erskine Greenwood, son of late Peter Longworth Greenwood, of South Cadbury, Som. *Residence* – 43 Quarrendon St, SW6 3ST.

Hon Rosemary (*Hon Lady Troubridge*), *b* 1957: *m* 1984, Sir Thomas Richard Troubridge, 7th Bt.

BROTHER LIVING

Hon NIGEL (The Swallows, 43 Kingsdon, Somerton, Som TA11 7JX), *b* 22 Dec 1909; *ed* Eton, and Clare Coll, Camb (BA 1931); formerly Maj RM: *m* 1st, 1935, Margaret Dorothy, who *d* 1938, da of T. G. Kirkham, of Westholm, Jordanhill, Glasgow; 2ndly, 1940, Eleanor Stewart, who *d* 1987, da of late Very Rev H. N. Craig, Dean of Kildare; 3rdly, 1993, Stella Mary, yr da of late Stanley Bradwell, MC, DCM, of Buxton, Derbys, and widow of Rev John Robert Wingfield-Digby, and has issue living, (by 1st *m*) Simon (Mulberry House, Old Church Rd, Colwall, Worcs WR13 6HB), *b* 1938; *ed* Eton, and Clare Coll, Camb (BA): *m* 1963, Josephine Maxwell, yr da of late Robert Upcott, and has issue living, Edward Sholto *b* 1966, Hugo Charles *b* 1969, Sophie Margaret *b* 1964: *m* 1989, Michael Robert Trotter, yst son of John Trotter, of London (and has issue living, Hugo William *b* 1991, Archie Milo *b* 1994, Claudia Rosanna *b* 1997), Harriet Josephine *b* 1972, — (by 2nd *m*) Philip Morton (Tisbury House, Tisbury, Salisbury SP3 6PZ), *b* 1947; *ed* Eton: *m* 1975, Sarah Frances Jane, yr da of Maj-Gen Ronald Edward Coaker, CB, CBE, MC, of Seaton Old Rectory, Uppingham, Rutland, and has had issue, John Morton Ronald *b* 1987, Anna Susan *b* 1979; *d* 1993, Camilla Faith *b* 1981, — Brigid Elizabeth (8 Margrath Av, Cambridge CB4 3AH), *b* 1943: *m* 1972 (*m diss* 1988), Richard H. Peat, and has issue living, Harry Mark Richard *b* 1974, Laura Katharine Alice *b* 1976.

SISTER LIVING

Hon Susan Victoria, *b* 1918. *Residence* – Adam's Cottage, Horningsham, Warminster, Wilts BA12 7LG.

COLLATERAL BRANCHES LIVING

Grandchildren of late Claud Douglas-Pennant (infra):—
Issue of late Henry Douglas-Pennant, *b* 1925, *d* 1986: *m* 1957, Pamela (who *m* 2ndly, 1988, Very Rev Patrick Reynolds Mitchell, KCVO, formerly Dean of Windsor, of Wolford Lodge, Dunkeswell, Honiton, Devon EX14 0SQ), da of late Alfred Gaspard Le Marchant (*see* Le Marchant, Bt, colls):—
Rupert Henry (Flat C, 55 Sulgrave Rd, W6 7QH), *b* 1963: *m* 1994, Caroline Mary, da of Michael Fass, of Braid Rd, Edinburgh. —— †Andrew Claud, *b* 1967; *d* 1993. —— †Edward Alfred, *b* (twin) 1967; *d* 1989. —— Venetia, *b* 1960: *m* 1988, (Charles) Liell Philip Francklin, elder son of Cmdr (Mavourn Baldwin) Philip Francklin, DSO, of Gonalston Hall, Notts, and has issue living, John-Liell Philip Henry, *b* 1996, — Flora Pamela Irene, *b* 1990, — Katharine Josephine, *b* 1992. *Residence* – 62 Brodrick Rd, SW17 7DY.

Granddaughter of late Lieut-Col Hon Archibald Charles Henry Douglas-Pennant, 2nd son of 1st Baron:—
Issue of late Claud Douglas-Pennant, *b* 1867, *d* 1955: *m* 1922, Christian Eleanor Margaret, who *d* 1968, da of Sir Harry (William Henry Neville) Goschen, 1st Bt, KBE:—
Margaret, *b* 1956: *m* 1956, Patrick John Lloyd, of Valaford, W Anstey, S Molton, Devon EX36 3PW, and has issue living, John Philip (107 Cremorne Rd, Sydney 2090, NSW, Australia), *b* 1960: *m* 1992, Kathryn O'Neill, and has issue living, Harry Felix *b* 1994, Bertie Hugh *b* 1997, — Phyllida Christian, *b* 1957.

Grandchildren of late Archibald Douglas-Pennant, 5th and yst son of late Lt-Col Hon Archibald Charles Henry Douglas-Pennant (ante):—
Issue of late Ian Douglas-Pennant, *b* 1906, *d* 1941: *m* 1931, Mary, who *d* 1980, da of late Maj John Williams, of Scorrier House, Scorrier, Cornwall:—

Daphne Mary DOUGLAS-PENNANT, *b* 1932; has resumed her maiden name: *m* 1st, 1953 (*m diss* 1964), Capt Maurice Douglas Evans, RM (ret); 2ndly, 1965 (*m diss* 1992), Francis Seymour Hurndall-Waldron, and has issue living (by 1st *m*), Jeremy Douglas, *b* 1958, — Claire Douglas, *b* 1954, — Rosemary Douglas, *b* 1956. *Residence* – White Lodge, Kilmington, Warminster, Wilts BA12 6RG.

Issue of late Rodney Archibald Douglas-Pennant, *b* 1913, *d* 1993: *m* 1st, 1945, Mrs Rosemary June Delap, who *d* 1946, da of late John Wilfred Munroe, and formerly wife of Capt William Frederick Delap, of Ol Kalou, Kenya; 2ndly, 1947, Agnes Nydia (Nancye), who *d* 1984, only child of late Arthur Robertson Brailey, FRCS; 3rdly, 1985, Mrs Olivia Joan Herbert (Little White House, Church Lane, Longworth, Oxon OX13 5DX), yst da of late Alexander Henry Melvill Wedderburn, CBE (*see* Wedderburn, Bt, colls), and formerly wife of Richard Weston Herbert:—
(By 2nd *m*) Hugh Archibald, *b* 1951; *ed* Eton: *m* 1st, 1976 (*m diss* 1982), Henrietta, da of Col Oliver Berger, of Warwick Sq, SW1; 2ndly, 1983, Sarah Rosamund, yst da of late Lt-Col Jocelyn Eustace Gurney, DSO, MC, of Tacolneston Hall, Norwich, and has issue living (by 1st *m*), Oliver Andrew, *b* 1979, — (Lucy) Annabel, *b* 1977, — (by 2nd *m*) Ian Christopher, *b* 1986, — David Arthur, *b* 1989. *Residence* – Churchgate House, Stansfield, Sudbury, Suffolk CO10 8LT. —— Anthea Rose, *b* 1948: *m* 1983, Andrew Lachlan Sutherland, and has issue living, Diana Elizabeth, *b* 1983, — Sarah Felicity, *b* 1985. *Residence* – Hillingdon, RMB 8230, Hamilton, Victoria 3300, Australia.

PREDECESSORS – (1) *Hon* EDWARD GORDON Douglas-Pennant, brother of 17th Earl of Morton; *b* 1800; assumed in 1841 by Roy licence the additional surname of Pennant; sat as MP for Carnarvonshire (*C*) 1841-66; was Lord-Lieut of co Carnarvon; *cr Baron Penrhyn*, of Llandegai, co Carnarvon (peerage of United Kingdom) 1866: *m* 1st, 1833, Juliana Isabella Mary, who *d* 1842, el da and co-heiress of George Hay Dawkins Pennant, of Penrhyn Castle; 2ndly, 1846, Lady Maria Louisa FitzRoy, who *d* 1912, 2nd da of 5th Duke of Grafton; *d* 1886; *s* by his son (2) GEORGE SHOLTO GORDON, 2nd Baron; *b* 1836; MP for Carnarvonshire (*C*) 1866-8 and 1874-80: *m* 1st, 1860, Pamela Blanche Rushout, who *d* 1869, da of Sir Charles Rushout Rushout, 2nd Bt; 2ndly, 1875, Gertrude Jessy, who *d* 1940, da of late Rev Henry Glynne; *d* 1907; *s* by his el son (3) EDWARD SHOLTO, 3rd Baron; *b* 1864; MP for Northamptonshire, S Div (*C*) 1895-1900: *m* 1887, Hon Blanche Georgiana FitzRoy, who *d* 1944, da of 3rd Baron Southampton; *d* 1927; *s* by his son (4) HUGH NAPIER, 4th Baron; *b* 1894; Hon Col 6th Batn Roy Welch Fusiliers; Lord-Lieut of Caernarvonshire 1933-41: *m* 1922 (*m diss* 1941), Hon Sybil Mary Hardinge, who *d* 1985, da of 3rd Viscount Hardinge; *d* 1949; *s* by his kinsman (5) FRANK (el son of late Lieut-Col Hon Archibald Charles Henry Douglas-Pennant, 2nd son of 1st Baron), 5th Baron; *b* 1865; Lt-Col KRRC: *m* 1st, 1892 (*m diss* 1903), Maud Eleanora, who *d* 1936, da of late Col John Hardy, 9th Lancers; 2ndly, 1905, Alice Nellie, who *d* 1965, da of Sir William Charles Cooper, 3rd Bt; *d* 1967; *s* by hs son (6) MALCOLM FRANK, DSO, MBE, 6th Baron and present peer.

PENTLAND, BARONY OF (Sinclair) (Extinct 1984) (see Sinclair, Bt, cr 1704)

Pepys, family name of Earl of Cottenham.

Perceval, Viscount; son of Earl of Egmont.

Perceval, family name of Earl of Egmont.

Percy, Earl; son of Duke of Northumberland.

Percy, family name of Duke of Northumberland.

PERCY OF NEWCASTLE, BARONY OF (Percy) (Extinct 1958)

DAUGHTER LIVING OF FIRST BARON

Hon Dorothy Anne, *b* 1926; *ed* Durham Univ (MB and BS 1949): *m* 1957, Major Thomas Robert Hales Eustace, Roy Irish Fusiliers, and has issue living, James Maurice Percy, *b* 1960: *m* 1986, Gay Rosemary, da of late Alan Oughton, of The Vale, Findon, Sussex, and has issue living, Henry Alan *b* 1988, David James *b* 1991, — Alicia Mary, *b* 1958, — Katharine (Katrina) Anne, *b* 1965: *m* 1988, Andrew J. McGladdery, only son of Dr John Arthur McGladdery, of 28 Beresford Gdns, Hadleigh, Essex, and has issue living, Charles Eustace *b* 1992. *Residence* – Glebe House, Boughton Aluph, Ashford, Kent.

PERRY OF SOUTHWARK, BARONESS (Perry) (Life Baroness 1991)

PAULINE PERRY, da of late John George Embleton Welch, of Sunderland; *b* 15 Oct 1931; *ed* Girls' High Sch, Wolverhampton, and Girton Coll, Camb (MA); Secondary Sch Teacher, UK, USA and Canada 1953-56 and 1959-61; Lecturer in Philosophy Manitoba Univ 1956-59, and Mass Univ 1961-62, Lecturer in Educn Exeter Univ (part-time) 1963-66, Oxford Univ 1966-70, Access Course Tutor 1966-70; HMI 1970-74, Staff Inspector 1975-81, HM Chief Inspector of Schs 1981-86; Vice-Chancellor South Bank Univ (formerly Polytechnic) 1987-93; Freelance Journalist and Broadcaster; Pres Lucy Cavendish Coll, Camb since 1994, Governing Body of Inst of Development Studies 1987-94, British Council's Cttee on Internat Co-operation in Higher Educn 1987-95, Economic and Social Research Council 1988-91, Member of Prime Minister's Advisory Panel on the Citizens Charter 1993-97; Chm DTI Export Group for the Education and Training Sector 1993-98, Review Body on Crown Appointments since 1998; Member of the Nat Advisory Council for Education and Training Targets 1993-95, and Board of Governors of the South Bank Centre 1992-95; Council Member Foundation for Educn Business Partnerships 1990-91; Non-exec Dir Addenbrooke's Hospital Trust since 1999; Rector's Warden Southwark Cathedral 1990-94; Freeman of the City of London 1992, Liveryman of the Worshipful Co of Bakers 1992; Companion of the Institute of Management 1993; Hon FCP 1987, Hon FRSA 1988, Hon Fellow Sunderland Polytechnic 1990, Hon LLD Bath 1991; Hon D Litt Sussex 1992; Hon LLD Aberdeen 1994; author; *cr Baroness Perry of Southwark*, of Charlbury, co Oxfordshire (Life Baroness) 1991: *m* 1952, George Walter Perry, and has issue.

Arms – Sable, in dexter chief a sun in splendour issuant and in base a pear slipped and leaved gold (PERRY), on an inescutcheon of pretence argent, a cross of lozenges, in the first quarter a crescent enclosing a quaver and in the fourth quarter a cinquefoil gules (WELCH). **Supporters** – *Dexter*, a marmalade tom cat proper; *sinister*, upon a pile of three books, the spines visible bound gules, the pages edged gold, a Persian cat sable, the nose, breast and feet argent, each supporting between the forepaws a quill argent penned or.
Address – House of Lords, London SW1A 0PW.

SONS LIVING

Hon Christopher George, *b* 1953; *ed* Abingdon: *m* 1987, Elizabeth Mary Edwardes, and has issue living, one da.
Hon Timothy John Welch, *b* 1962; *ed* Beckett's Sch, Chesham, Bucks: *m* 1984, Jeannie Ross McKenzie.
Hon Simon Jeremy Welch, *b* 1966; *ed* Sevenoaks.

DAUGHTER LIVING

Hon Hilary Anne Welch, *b* 1955: *m* 1st, 1975 (*m diss* 1990), John Hayward; 2ndly, 1990, Thomas Charles Winstone, and has issue (by 1st *m*), one da, — (by 2nd *m*) two das.

PERRY OF WALTON, BARON (Perry) (Life Baron 1979)

WALTER LAING MACDONALD PERRY, OBE, FRSE, FRS, son of Fletcher S. Perry; *b* 16 June 1921; *ed* Ayr Acad, Dundee High Sch, and St Andrew's Univ (MB ChB, MD, DSc); FRCP (Edin); Dir Dept of Biological Standards, Nat Inst for Medical Research, 1952-58, Prof of Pharmacology, Edinburgh Univ 1958-68 (Vice-Principal 1967-68), Vice-Chancellor The Open Univ 1969-81; Pres Videotel International; Consultant United Nations Univ; *cr* OBE (Civil) 1957, Ktn 1974, and *Baron Perry of Walton*, of Walton, co Bucks (Life Baron) 1979: *m* 1st, 1946 (*m diss* 1971), Anne Elizabeth Grant; 2ndly, 1971, Cathcrine Ililda, da of Ambrose Crawley, and has issue by 1st and 2nd *m*.
Residence – 2 Cramond Rd South, Edinburgh EH4 6AD. *Club* – Scottish Arts.

SONS LIVING (*By 1st marriage*)

Hon Michael John (9 Queens Av, Perth), *b* 1948: *m* 1970, Kathleen Anne Sutherland Elliott, and has issue living, Lindsay, *b* 1973, — Hannah, *b* 1976.
Hon Alan Malcolm (43 Meadway, NW11 7AX) *b* 1950: *m* 1976, Naomi Melanie, da of Dr Abraham Freedman, MD, FRCP, of 21B Chesterford Gdns, NW3, and has issue, three sons.
Hon Niall Fletcher (53 Putnoe Lane, Bedford), *b* 1953: *m* 1979, Sandra Buchanan, and has issue living, Jennifer, *b* 1985, — Lesley-Anne, *b* 1987.

(*By 2nd marriage*)

Hon Robin Charles Macdonald, *b* 1973.
Hon Colin Stuart Macdonald, *b* 1979.

DAUGHTER LIVING (*By 2nd marriage*)

Hon Jennifer Joan, *b* 1981.

PERTH, EARL OF (Drummond) (Earl S 1605, Viscount S 1686)

Courage crowns honour

JOHN DAVID DRUMMOND, PC, 17th Earl of Perth and 11th (13th but for the attainder) Viscount Strathallan; *b* 13 May 1907; *s* 1951; *ed* Downside, and Camb Univ; Hon LLD St Andrews 1986 (Member of Court 1967-86), Hon FRIBA 1978, Hon FRIAS 1988, Hon FSA 1994; a Representative Peer for Scotland 1952-63, Hereditary Thane of Lennox and Hereditary Steward of Menteith and Strathearn; Lt Intelligence Corps; seconded to War Cabinet Officers 1942-43, and to Min of Production 1944-45; Min of State for Colonial Affairs 1957-62; First Crown Estate Commr 1962-77; Chm of the Reviewing Cttee on the Export of Works of Art 1972-76; Trustee of Nat Library of Scotland; Principal of Fund Raising Committee Museum of Scotland; PC 1957: *m* 1934, Nancy Seymour, who *d* 1996, da of Reginald Fincke, of New York City, USA, and has issue.

Arms – Or, three bars wavy gules. Crest – A falcon rising proper. Supporters – Two wild men wreathed about the temples and loins with oak, and each holding a club resting on his exterior shoulder, proper, standing on a compartment semée of caltraps.
Residence – Stobhall, by Perth PH2 6DR. *Clubs* – White's, Puffin's.

SONS LIVING

JOHN ERIC (*Viscount Strathallan*) (46 Tite St, SW3 4JA; *Club* – Boodle's), *b* 7 July 1935; *ed* Downside, Trin Coll, Camb (BA), and Harvard Univ, USA (MBA): *m* 1st, 1963 (*m diss* 1972), Margaret Ann, da of late Robin Gordon; 2ndly, 1988, Mrs Marion V. G. Elliot, and has issue living by 1st *m* :—

SONS LIVING (*by 1st marriage*)— *Hon* James David (Stobhall, by Perth PH2 6DR), *b* 24 Oct 1965, — *Hon* Robert Eric (41 Victoria Rd, W8 5RD), *b* 1967.

Hon James Reginald (Churchill House, Dinder, nr Wells, Somerset BA5 3RW), *b* 1938; *ed* Downside, and Trin Coll, Camb: *m* 1st, 1961 (*m diss* 1985), Marybelle, da of late Capt Charles Gordon; 2ndly, 1988, Ferelith Alison, da of late Mark Palmer (*see* Palmer, Bt, *cr* 1886, colls), and formerly wife of Ashley Gordon Down.

SISTERS LIVING

Lady Angela Alice Maryel, *b* 1912: *m* 1st, 1937 (*m diss* 1959), Count Alessandro Augusto Giovanni Giacinto Barnaba Manassei di Collestatte, who *d* 1962 (Lyle, Bt); 2ndly, 1960, Viggo de Wichfeld, who *d* 1994 (*see* B Massy, colls, 1945 Edn), and has issue living, (by 1st *m*) John Paul James Alessandro Camillo, *b* 1937: *m* 1965 (*m diss* 1975), Hon Susan Barbara, da of the 7th Viscount Sidmouth, and has issue living, Hugo Alexander *b* 1969, Marina Catherine *b* 1967, — Michael David (14 Queen Anne's Grove, W4 1HN) *b* 1947: *m* 1978, Vanessa Bettine, who *d* 1985, only da of late Cdr William Gordon Jack, RN (*see* B Tollemache, colls), and has issue living, Nicholas Jason *b* 1980, Polly Teresa *b* 1978, Clare Alexandra *b* 1981, Miranda Frances Vanessa *b* 1985, — Alessandra Mary MANASSEI (154 Via dei Serragli, 50124 Florence, Italy), *b* 1939; has resumed her maiden name: *m* 1959, Francesco Montesi Righetti. *Residence* – 41 Lennox Gdns, SW1X 0DF.

Lady Gillian Mary, *b* 1920: *m* 1946, John Murray Anderson, MC, and bar, who *d* 1991, late Capt Seaforth Highlanders, and has issue living, James Ian (Roro Lodge, Glenlyon, Aberfeldy, Perthshire PH15 2PW), *b* 1952; Member of Queen's Body Guard for Scotland (Royal Company of Archers): *m* 1st, 1981 (*m diss* 1985), Victoria Anne, twin da of late Henry Robert Hildyard, of South Hartfield House, Coleman's Hatch, Sussex (*see* B Kindersley, 1980 Edn); 2ndly, 1988, Hon Emily Mary Astor, da of 3rd Viscount Astor, and formerly wife of Alan Gregory, and has issue living (by 1st *m*), Alice Mona *b* 1983 (by 2nd *m*), Thomas Alexander *b* 1990, Rory John *b* 1991, Liza Kate *b* 1993, Isobel Nancy *b* (twin) 1993, — Sarah Mary, *b* 1947, — Elisabeth Jane, *b* 1949, — Camilla Gillian, *b* 1957: *m* 1st, 1979 (*m diss* 1992), Matthew Aidan Craig Balfour, 2nd son of John Valentine Balfour, of Walnut Tree Farm, Birling (*see* B Plunkett, 1968 Edn); 2ndly, 1993, Mark Ronald Shearring, 3rd son of Ronald George Shearring, and has issue living (by 1st *m*), Alexander John *b* 1986, Emily Kate Mary *b* 1984. *Residence* – Wilderwick House, E Grinstead, W Sussex RH19 3NS.

COLLATERAL BRANCHES LIVING

Issue of late Col Hon Sir Maurice Charles Andrew Drummond, KBE, CMG, DSO, Black Watch, 3rd son of 10th Viscount Strathallan, *b* 1877; *d* 1957: *m* 1904, Ida Mary, who *d* 1966, da of late George James Drummond (see colls, infra):—
Maurice James David, *b* 1907; *ed* Eton; Bar Lincoln's Inn 1952: Hon Lieut-Col (ret) Seaforth Highlanders, and a Member of Queen's Body Guards for Scotland (Royal Company of Archers). *Residence* – 55 Homecross House, Fishers Lane, W4 1YA.

Granddaughter of late Maj-Gen Lawrence George Drummond, CB, CBE, MVO, only son of late Adm Hon Sir James Robert Drummond, GCB, 2nd son of 6th Viscount Strathallan:—
Issue of late Lindsay Drummond, *b* 1891, *d* 1951: *m* 1924, Susan Cynthia Frances, who *d* 1981, da of late Alick William Cradock-Hartopp (*see* Cradock-Hartopp, Bt):—
Olivia Joan, *b* 1929: *m* 1957, Maj James Stuart Perry, Special Air Service Regt, and has issue living, Marcus Lindsay, *b* 1957, — Oliver James, *b* 1958. *Residence* – The Mill House, Winchelsea, E Sussex.

Grandchildren of late Edgar Atheling Drummond, 2nd son of late Andrew Robert Drummond, grandson of Hon Robert Drummond, 3rd son of 4th Viscount Strathallan:—
Issue of late Major Cyril Augustus Drummond, b 1873; d 1945: m 1st, 1897, Edith Belle, who d 1917, da of L. I. Wilkins; 2ndly, 1930, Mildred Joan (HARRINGTON) (who d 1977, having m 3rdly, 1948, Air Commodore John Charles Quinnell, CB, DFC, who d 1983), da of late Horace Humphrys:—
(By 2nd m) Maldwin Andrew Cyril, OBE, b 1932; ed Eton; commn'd Rifle Brigade 1950; JP Hants 1963, DL 1976, and High Sheriff 1980; Commodore Royal Yacht Sqdn 1991-96; Hon DSc; OBE (Civil) 1990: m 1st, 1955 (m diss 1977), Susan Dorothy Maria Gabrielle, da of Sir Kenelm Henry Ernest Cayley, 10th Bt; 2ndly, 1978, Gillian Vera, yr da of Charles Gavin Clark (see Royden, Bt, 1995 Edn), and formerly wife of Alexander Graham Athol Turner Laing, and has issue living (by 1st m), Frederica Elizabeth, b 1957: m 1984, Maj Miles Templer, 17th/21st Lancers, of Jackdaw House, Salterton, nr Salisbury, Wilts SP4 6AN, son of late Field Marshal Sir Gerald Walter Robert Templer, KG, GCB, GCMG, KBE, DSO, and has issue living, Gerald b 1986, (Robert) Benjamin b 1987, — Annabella Virginia, b 1959: m 1st, 1980 (m diss 1988), Christopher E. Robinson, 17th/21st Lancers; 2ndly, 1995, Xavier N. C. Villers, of 51 Sutherland St, SW1, and of Bogota, Colombia, and has issue living (by 1st m), Edward b 1982, Jeremy b 1984, (by 2nd m), Suzanna b 1996, — (by 2nd m), Aldred Robert Alexander, b 1978. Residences – Cadland, Fawley, Southampton; and Wester Kames Castle, Port Bannatyne, Isle of Bute. Clubs – Royal Yacht Squadron, White's, Pratt's, Leander. —— †Robert Edgar Atheling (Bend'or), b 1933; ed Eton, and Ch Ch Oxford; commn'd Life Guards 1951: m 1st, 1958 (m diss 1967), Mrs Phyllis Field Samper, who d 1985, da of late Marshall Field III, of New York City, USA; 2ndly, 1978 (m diss 1983), Athenaïs, Countess de Mortemart, formerly wife of 6th Earl of Rosslyn; 3rdly, 1985, (Maria) Alba (Stanswood Mews, Fawley, Southampton), da of late João Damasceno, of Rio de Janeiro, Brazil, and d 1994, leaving issue (by 1st m), Maldwin Marshall (Box 2449, Hobe Sound, Florida 33475, USA), b 1959, — Fiona Mary DRUMMOND (38 Brynmaer Rd, SW11 4EW), b 1960; has resumed her maiden name: m 1980 (m diss 1992), Albemarle John Cator (see Cayley, Bt, 1960 Edn), and has issue living, John b 1983, Robert Henry b 1985, — Bettina (19 Ox Hill Rd, Newtown, Connecticut 06470, USA), b 1963: m 19—, Jack O'Neil, — (by 3rd m) Marina Christina Frederica Phyllis Damasceno, b 1985. —— Annabella Frances Serena, b 1938: m 1st, 1957 (m diss 1961), David Arthur Talbot Rice (see B Dynevor, colls); 2ndly, 1961 (m diss 1972), Gerardo Hochschild; 3rdly, 1973, John Philip Pochna, of rue Aristide Briard, Putanges pont Ecrepin, 61210 Orne, France, and has issue living (by 2nd m), Maurice Leo Robert (98 Denbigh St, SW1V 2EX), b 1962: m 1989, Jessica Margaret, da of William Frederick Baldwin, of 2011 Pacific Building, Seattle, WA 98104, USA, and has issue living, Jack b 1996, Luke b 1998, Annabella b 1993, — Fabrizio Gerald Arturo, b 1963, — Agustin Emil, b 1965.

Grandchildren of late Capt Eric Roderick Brook Drummond, 4th son of late Capt Cecil George Assheton Drummond, 5th and yst son of late Andrew Robert Drummond (ante):—
Issue of late Geoffrey Brook Drummond, b 1905, d 1976: m 1939, Mary Barbara, da of late James Arthur Unitt, MRCS, LRCP, of Quorn, Leics:—
Frederick Brook (Enderby Hall, Enderby, Leics), b 1946: m 1st, 1974 (m diss 1979), Gillian Victoria, da of Donald Leslie Bridges; 2ndly, 1980, Mrs Evelyn Clare Ann Jackson, da of late James Allan, and has issue living (by 1st m), Roland Brook, b 1975, — (by 2nd m) Leigh James Brook, b 1981, — Kimberley Brook, b 1985. —— Cherry Barbara, b 1940: m 1959, Derek Cyril Gibbs, of 147 Leicester Rd, Glen Parva, Leicester, and has issue living, Nicholas Cary, b 1960, — Alistair Corin, b 1972, — Scarlett Kathryn, b 1961.

Grandchildren of late Gerald Morton Drummond, yr son of late Rev Morton Drummond, 5th son of late Charles Drummond (b 1790) eldest son of late Charles Drummond (b 1759), yr son of Hon Robert Drummond (ante):—
Issue of late Group-Capt Edward Morton Drummond, RAF, b 1898, d 1993: m 1922, Edith Daphne Eunice, who d 1989, da of late Wilfred Doneraile Stanhope Taylor (see M Headfort, colls, 1990 Edn):—
David James Morton (Blacklands, Meshaw, S Molton, Devon EX36 4NG), b 1925; European War 1943-45 as Lieut Black Watch: m 1st, 1949 (m diss 19—), Cecily Winifred Jillian, who d 1996, only da of Cmdr Alan Douglas Bruford, VRD, RN (ret), of Hailsham, Sussex; 2ndly, 19—, Diana Mary, only da of late Frederick Turner, of Barnstaple, Devon, and has had issue (by 2nd m), †James Edward Morton, b 1966; d 1992, — Lilias, b 1962: m 1984, Raymond Frederick Roulstone, of Church House, S Molton, Devon, and has issue living, Madeline Drummond b 1988, April Drummond b 1989, — Amanda, b 1963: m 1989, Roger William John Gregory, and has issue living, Callum Drummond b 1992, Harriet Drummond b 1994. —— Charmian Eunice, b 1923; 1939-45 War in WAAF: m 1951, George Geoffrey Gundry-White, of 49 Tooting Bec Gdns, SW16 1RF, and has had issue, Timothy (33 Hilldown Rd, SW16 3DZ), b 1955: m 1978, Linda Morton, and has issue living, Francis b 1981, Hannah b 1984, — Patrick (4 Rock Bank, Whaley Bridge, Stockport, Ches SK12 7LE), b 1957: m 1995, Dale Culliford, and has issue living, Toby b 19—, — Alexander, b (twin) 1957; k 1989, — Jasper (56 Copers Cope Rd, Beckenham, Kent BR3 1RJ), b 1959: m 19—, Jacqueline Pratt, and has issue living, Matthew Anthony b 1988, Rebecca Rose b 1993, — Henry Simon (50 Rectory Grove, SW4 0ED), b 1960; has issue living, Caspar b 1993, — Katherine Jane Louise (47 Park Rd, Enfield, Middx EN3 6SR), b 1952; has issue living, Joanna Helen Lawrence b 1992, Stephanie Andrea Lawrence b (twin) 1992, — Madeleine Anne (PO Box 351, Fruitvale, BC, Canada V0G 1L0), b 1954: m 1976, Juris Harlamovs, and has an adopted son, James Aleksandrs George b 1990, — Laura, b (twin) 1955: m 1977, (Peter) Nicholas Rowlatt, of 30 Chillerton Rd, SW17 9BG, and has issue living, Chloe Elizabeth b 1981, Elizabeth Mary b 1983, Mary Daphne b 1987. —— Jean, b 1927: m 1948, Gerald Charles Grenfell Robins, of Wawcott House, Elcot, Newbury, Berks RG20 8NH, and has issue living, Charles David Anthony (Wawcott House, Elcot, Newbury, Berks), b 1953; ed Cookham House, Newbury: m 19—, Lisa Flynn, and has issue living, Samuel Gerald b 19—, Effie b 19—, — Angela Daphne, b 1955: m 1979, Henry Clark Umpleby, of Orchard House, Claverton Village, Bath, Som, and has issue living, Simon Henry Charles b 1982, Nicholas Henry Gerald b 1982, Madeleine Rose b 1985, — Marion Geraldine, b 1960: m 1989, Alistair Walker, of Wardsgarth, Brightwalton, Newbury, Berks.

Grandson of late Capt Eric Arthur Drummond, RN (infra):—
Issue of late Ronald Nigel Drummond, b 1925, d 1978: m 1st, 1948 (m diss 19—), Josephine Marie, da of Jules Pourbaise, Comte de Bey; 2ndly, 1960, Dinah (41 Glanymor, Aberavon, Dyfed), da of Ralph Adams:—
(By 1st m) Iain Stewart, b 1950.

Grandchildren of late Lt-Col Arthur Berkeley Drummond, el son of late Rev Arthur Hislop Drummond (infra):—
Issue of late Capt Eric Arthur Drummond, RN, b 1900, d 1970: m 1st, 1924 (m diss 1938), Molly Beryl, da of Hugh William Crott, of Ledbury, Herefordshire; 2ndly, 1938 (m diss 1947), Elnah Raymond Russell, da of H. R. Wilding, of London; 3rdly, 1954, Mrs Barbara Clarke, who d 1972, el da of late Wilfred Barnard Faraday, Recorder of Barnstaple and Bideford:—
(By 1st m) John Berwick Lindsay (Windrush, Cradley, Malvern, Worcs WR13 5LF), b 1927: m 1953, Daphne Mary, el da of late Rev Edward Percy Woollcombe, OBE, late R of Sutton, Surrey, and has issue living, Richard John (Muhlenredder 14, 22958 Kuddewörde-Rotenbek, Germany), b 1963: m 1990, Andrea Bettina, eldest da of Peter Kutz, of Hamburg, and has issue living, Jennifer Frances b 1993, Kristin Stephanie b 1997, — Penelope Anne (17 Comeragh Rd, W14 9HP), b

1954: *m* 1980 (*m diss* 1986), Simon John Rickman, of Devonshire, — Sarah Jane, *b* 1958: *m* 1987, Robert Sidney Isaac, of Hardings Knapp, Upper Goosehill, Broughton Green, Droitwich, Worcs WR9 7ED, and has issue living, Elizabeth Jane *b* 1990, — Catriona Caroline, *b* 1961: *m* 1984, Royston Kim Lewis, of 66 Early Rd, Witney, Oxon OX8 6EU, and has issue living, Alexander Daniel *b* 1991, Laura Kirsty *b* 1988. ——— Charles Iain (Lochranza, 32 Monument Lane, Chalfont St Peter, Bucks SL9 0HX), *b* 1932; *ed* St Edmund Hall, Oxford (BA): *m* 1962, Christine Mary, only da of Eric Stevenson Browne, of Greenleas Rd, Wallasey, Ches, and has issue living, Clare Elizabeth, *b* 1967: *m* 1995, Simon Michael Selby, and has issue living, Alexander Jamie *b* 1996. ——— (By 2nd *m*) Fiona Elnah Russell, *b* 1940: *m* 1st, 1963 (*m diss* 1967), Julian Patrick Selby Ormond; 2ndly, 1967, Robert Adrian Cowell, of Hatfield Priory, Hatfield Peverel, Essex, and has issue living, (by 2nd *m*) John Maximilian Arthur, *b* 1972: *m* 1999, Claudia Annabel, da of Samuel Sieve, of London, — Sophia Russell Lilian, *b* 1969: *m* 1999, Michael Bailey Robinson, of Boston and Maine, USA. ——— Deirdre Georgina, *b* 1944: *m* 1969, Nigel Builder.

Grandchildren of late Rev Arthur Hislop Drummond, 2nd son of late Rev Arthur Drummond, 4th son of late Charles Drummond (*b* 1759) (ante):—
Issue of late Malcolm Cyril Drummond, *b* 1880; *d* 1945: *m* 1st, 1906, Zina Lilias, who *d* 1931, da of George Macartney Ogilvie, formerly ICS; 2ndly, 1934, Margaret Triquet, who *d* 1988, da of late Rev Arthur Browning, of Pangbourne Rectory, Berks:—
(By 1st *m*) (Arthur Malcolm) James (Glengairn, 7 Aberdeen Rd, Tarland, Aberdeenshire AB34 4UA) *b* 1911; late Capt R Berks Regt: *m* 1st, 1938 (*m diss* 1952), Moyra Blanche, who *d* 1982, da of late Frederick Barnard Elliot, CBE (B Emly), 2ndly, 1954, Patricia, da of late Guy Cave, and has issue living (by 1st *m*), Hamish Guy (PO Box 310, Grand Cayman, BWI), *b* 1939: *m* 1964, Valerie Louise, da of late Tyril McLaughlin, of Cayman Islands, BWI, and has issue living, Andrew Simon Hamish *b* 1970, Katherine Nicola *b* 1966, and two adopted das, Deborah Ann Eileen *b* 1961, Charmaine Alexandra *b* 1963, — (by 2nd *m*), David James, *b* 1960; RAF: *m* 1984, Beverly, da of John Steward, of Camb, and has issue living, Matthew Thomas *b* 1993, Rebecca Gemma *b* 1984, Emily Lisa *b* 1986, Francesca Claire *b* 1989, — Nicola Gesina, *b* 1956: *m* 1999, Gordon Summers, of Huntly, Aberdeenshire, — Alexina Mary, *b* 1957: *m* 1977, Arthur John Menzies, of Coirmoir, Torphins, Aberdeenshire, and has issue.

Grandchildren of late George James Drummond, son of George Drummond, el son of George Harley Drumond, el son of George Drummond (*b* 1758), grandson of Andrew Drummond, next brother of 4th Viscount Strathallan:—
Issue of late George Henry Drummond, *b* 1883, *d* 1963: *m* 1st, 1917, Helena Kathleen, who *d* 1933, da of T. Grattan Holt; 2ndly, 1940, Honora Myrtle Gladys (Grand Island Hotel, Ramsay, IoMan), da of late Lt-Col Duncan Wilfrid Lambart Spiller, DSO:—
(By 2nd *m*) George Albert Harley DE VERE DRUMMOND (The Barn, 6 Bannatyne Gdns, Bannatyne, Christchurch, Barbados, W Indies), *b* 1943: *m* 1st, 1971 (*m diss* 1974), Rachel, da of Michael Manley; 2ndly, 1982, Debra Jane, only da of R. B. Hankins, of Hertford, and has issue living (by 1st *m*), George Manley de Vere *b* 1971 — (by 2nd *m*), Sarah Georgina Joy de Vere, *b* 1982, — Jade Alexandra de Vere, *b* 1984. ——— Annabella Elizabeth, *b* 1941. ——— Omega Margaret (63 Bagley Wood Rd, Kennington, Oxford OX1 5LY), *b* 1944: *m* 1961, Robert A. Y. Pouget, and has issue living, Antoine Xavier, *b* 1962, — Robert Harley, *b* 1965, — Alexandre, *b* 1967, — William Francis, *b* 1975. ——— Isobel Camilla (Millie) (Cortijo San Clemente, 18400 Orgiva (Granada), Spain), *b* 1946.

Issue of late David Robert Drummond, Lt Scots Guards, *b* 1884, *ka* 1914: *m* 1907, Hilda Margaret (who *d* 1972, having *m* 2ndly, 1936, Maj John Elgee Gunning, JP, who *d* 1950), da of late Alfred Hellver Harris, of Donnington, Chichester:—
Joan Cécile (Amesbury Abbey, Amesbury, Wilts SP4 7EX), *b* 1909: *m* 1st, 1933 (*m diss* 1939), Maurice James Newcomb; 2ndly, 1942 (*m diss* 1949), Maj Charles St John Colthurst, RA, who *d* 1985; 3rdly, 1950 (*m diss* 1970), Arthur Raywid; 4thly, 1971, Alan James Fuller Eberle, MBE, BM, BCh, who *d* 1988, and has issue living, (by 1st *m*) Nicholas James (27 Bishops Court Drive, Bishops Court, Cape 7700, S Africa), *b* 1935: *m* 1966, Lorna Faith Maree, and has issue living, Graeme James *b* 1970, Angela Jean *b* 1973, — (by 2nd *m*) Joanna, *b* 1948: *m* 1975, Martin Butler, of 43/299 Burns Rd, Lane Cove, NSW 2066, Australia. ——— Violet Hilda, *b* 1911: *m* 1st, 1933 (*m diss* 1945), John Peter Pardoe; 2ndly, 1948, Anthony Swetenham, and has issue living, (by 1st *m*) Julian Hugh (Brinkley House, Newmarket, Suffolk), *b* 1935; *ed* Eton: *m* 1960, Camilla Guendolen, da of late Arthur Gruffydd Tudor-Evans, of The Grange, N Rode, Cheshire, and has issue living, Simon David *b* 1962: *m* 1995, Fiona Deirdre, da of Gordon John Barrett, of Cherry Hill House, Highmoor, Henley on Thames (and has issue living, Maximillian Thomas *b* 1998, Isabella Laura *b* 1996), Joanna Clare *b* 1963, Fiona Mary *b* 1965: *m* 1994, Nigel M. Powell, yr son of Stephen Powell, of Whatton, Nottingham (and has issue living, Annabel Alice *b* 1994, Poppy Clare *b* 1996, Olivia Rose *b* 1999). *Residence* – Highfield, Mandeville Rd, Saffron Walden, Essex.

Issue of late Capt Alexander Victor Drummond, *b* 1888; *d* 1937: *m* 1914, Ellen Pauline Matthew (the actress, Pauline Chase), who *d* 1962, da of Ellis Bliss, of Washington, USA:—
Jane (Parkfield, 127 Tinderbox Rd, Blackmans Bay, Tas 7052), *b* 1925: *m* 1946 (*m diss* 1965), Irving Howbert, late Lt US Naval Reserve, and has issue living, William Irving, *b* 1948, — Anne Noelle, *b* 1950, — Janet Scott, *b* 1953.

Grandchildren of late Capt Alexander Victor Drummond (ante):—
Issue of late (Alexander) Peter Drummond, *b* 1927, *d* 1987: *m* 1954 (*m diss* 1976), Anne Audrey Ruth, da of Frank Seamer, of Leigh, Kent:—
Harrie Malcolm, *b* 1962. ——— Alexandra Elspeth, *b* 1957: *m* 1993, William George Mennell. ——— (Marina) Jane, *b* 1959: *m* 1983, Patrick John Horsman, and has issue living, Thomas John, *b* 1982, — Alexander James, *b* 1985, — George Maxwell, *b* 1989.

Grandchildren of late Capt Algernon Heneage Drummond, only son of Rev Heneage Drummond, Rector of Leckhamstead, yst son of John Drummond (*b* 1766), yr brother of George Drummond (*b* 1758) (ante):—
Issue of late Algernon Cecil Heneage Drummond, *b* 1880, *d* 1975: *m* 1917, Janetta, who *d* 1958, da of late Col John Ormsby Vandeleur, CB (D St Albans, colls):—
Spencer Heneage, DSC (Keeper's Cottage, Petersfield, Hants), *b* 1922; Capt RN; 1939-45 War (DSC); MPhil: *m* 1949, Patricia Pauline, who *d* 1998, da of late Lt-Col Michael Keane, OBE, RAMC, and has issue living, Crispin Heneage (11 Clifton Rd, Winchester, Hants), *b* 1955: *m* 1st, 1981 (*m diss* 1996), Marta A. Tuey, of Boston, Mass, USA; 2ndly, 1997, Mrs Anne-Marie Palmer (*née* Foster), and has issue living, (by 1st *m*) Lewis Spencer Heneage *b* 1987, Kate Elinor *b* 1984, Juliet Vandeleur *b* 1988, (by 2nd *m*) Patricia Elizabeth *b* 1998, — Hereward John Heneage (3 Sleepers Hill Gdns, Winchester, Hants), *b* 1959: *m* 1987, Felicia J. B., elder da of George Anthony Shepherd, CMG, of Meonstoke, Hants,

and has issue living, Thomas Anthony Heneage *b* 1988, Frederick Algernon Heneage *b* 1991, Isabella Mary Heneage *b* 1989, Lucinda Jane Heneage *b* 1993, — Deirdre Mary, *b* 1953: *m* 1977, Peregrine Tatton Eyre Massey, and has issue (*see* B Massy, colls). — Ianthe Mary, *b* 1960, — Helena Mhairi, *b* 1963: *m* 1990, Andrew P. Johnstone, only son of Rev B. Johnstone, of Sydney, NSW, Australia, and has issue living, William Drummond *b* 1993, Alistair James *b* 1996, Stephanie Margaret *b* 1994. —— John Vandeleur Heneage (9 Upper Wheelan St, Newlands, Cape 7700, S Africa), *b* 1924; Pilot, E and S African Harbour Sers (ret): *m* 1951, Annette, da of Dr Alan William Stuart Sichel, MD, LLD, DO, DOMS (Pres BMA 1951-52), of Cape Town, and has issue living, Anthony Christopher Heneage (6 York Rd, Claremont, Cape), *b* 1954: *m* 1990, Fiona, da of John Nugent, of Linthorpe, Cleveland, and has issue living, Charlotte *b* 1992, — Richard Stuart Heneage, *b* 1962, — Hugo Alistair Heneage (6 Grove Rd, Mowbray, Cape), *b* 1965: *m* 1990, Karen, da of Leslie Joubert, of Mowbray, Cape, — Amanda Elizabeth, *b* 1956. —— Margaret Frederica, *b* 1926: *m* 1949, John Ironside Money, of Tanglewood, 72 Skinburness Rd, Silloth, Carlisle, Cumbria CA5 4QF, and has issue living, Paul, *b* 1950, — Brian, *b* 1953, — Colin, *b* 1956, — Olivia Margaret, *b* 1959.

Issue of late Lieut-Com Geoffrey Heneage Drummond, VC, RNVR, *b* 1886, *d* on active ser 1941: *m* 1918, Maude Aylmer Tindal, who *d* 1967, da of late Lt-Col Bernard Tindal Bosanquet, of Claysmore, Enfield:—
(Geoffrey) Mortimer Heneage, RN, *b* 1920; *ed* Eton; Lieut-Com; European War 1939-45: *m* 1956, Sarah Madeline, da of Richard Walter Spencer, of Warsash, Southampton, and has issue living, John Richard Geoffrey, *b* 1957; *ed* Eton, and Christ's Coll, Camb (MA); is Cmdr RN: *m* 1996, Constance Catherine Laura, da of Dr Nikolay Andreyev, of Cambridge, and has issue living, Laura Tatiana Rowena *b* 1996, — Charles Mortimer Geoffrey, *b* 1958, *ed* Pangbourne: *m* 1997, Caroline N. A., yst da of late Prof Meulemans, of Beaulieu sur Mer, France, — Caroline Jane, *b* 1963; *ed* St Swithuns, and Seale Hayne Agric Coll (BSc): *m* 1998, Philip Alexander Ward, son of E. R. Ward, of Tempellow, Cornwall. *Residence* – Faringdon, Hill Head, Hants. *Club* – Royal Naval. —— Aylmer Merelina, *b* 1919. *Residence* – 4 Minto St, Newington, Edinburgh EH9 1RG. —— Iris Mary Elizabeth, *b* 1926; 1939-45 War in WRNS: *m* 1947, Lt-Cdr John Munro Crosland Fenton, DSC, RN, of Bar Ewing, Balmaclellan, by Castle Douglas, Kirkcudbright, and has issue living, Jeremy John Crosland (2 Royal Crescent, Edinburgh EH3 6PZ), *b* 1949; *ed* Glenalmond, and Magdalene Coll, Camb (MA), — James Heneage Crosland (Balfour Cottage, Abernyte, by Inchture, Perthshire PH14 9ST), *b* 1952; *ed* Glenalmond, Durham Univ (BSc), and London Univ (PhD); Member British Antarctic Survey 1973-78: *m* 1986, Susan Claire, da of H. J. Wrenn, of Harmby, Yorkshire, and has issue living, Mairi Alice *b* 1989, — Geoffrey Eric Crosland (Grove Cottage, Blackford, nr Wedmore, Som BS28 4NG), *b* 1954; *ed* Glenalmond, and St John's Coll, Oxford (BA, MSc): *m* 1980, Elizabeth Tyrie, yst da of Prof J. K. T. L. Nash, of Shandon, Jordans, Bucks, and has issue living, Rosemary Tyrie *b* 1985, Isabel Shield *b* 1988, Lucy Crosland *b* 1991.

Issue of late Maurice John Heneage Drummond, *b* 1894, *d* 1975: *m* 1922, Celia, who *d* 1964, da of late Rev John Vaughan, Canon of Winchester:—
Rev Canon Christopher John Vaughan (77 Markham Rd, Capel, Surrey RH5 5JT) *b* 1926; *ed* Winchester, Magdalen Coll, Oxford (MA) and Ridley Hall, Camb; 1939-45 War in R Signals: *m* 1960, Gwyneth May, da of George Timmis, of Hanchurch, Staffs, and has issue living, Peter John Vaughan, *b* 1963: *m* 19—, Kate, da of Geoffrey Bryan, of Walton on Thames, and has issue living, Timothy John Vaughan *b* 1994, Lucy Rose *b* 1996, — Gillian Clare *b* 1961: *m* 1988, Rowland Nathaniel Howarth, son of Rev Robert Francis Harvey Howarth, and has issue living, Peter Nathaniel *b* 1990, Annabel Clare *b* 1993. —— *Rev* Joscelin Maurice Vaughan (3 Fryth Mead, St Albans, Herts), *b* 1929; *ed* London Univ (Dip Th BD) and Wycliffe Hall, Oxford; late Lt RN: *m* 1st 1962, Christine Mary, who *d* 1987, da of Alfred George Read, of 187 Lower Dale Rd, Derby; 2ndly, 1988, Susan Helena, widow of Rev Canon Andrew Michael Bowman, and da of William Bolitho Rowe, of St Just in Penrith, Cornwall, and has issue living (by 1st *m*), Andrew Paul Graham, *b* 1970, — Lydia Rosalind, *b* 1964; BA, PhD, PGCE, FRGS: *m* 1989, Stephen Keith Pierce, of Hastings, Sussex. —— Rosalind Margaret Vaughan (83 Riverside, Cambridge CB5 8HN), *b* 1924; MA, PhD; Assoc Prof of English, City Univ, New York: *m* 1st, 1947 (*m diss* 1955), Mark Arthur Monson Roberts, MA; 2ndly, 1965, Spencer Depas, who *d* 1990, and has issue living (by 1st *m*), Julian Francis; *ed* Winchester, and Caius Coll, Camb (MA): *m* 1991, Margarethe Gross, and has issue living, Alexander *b* 1992, Hilary *b* 1990, — (by 2nd *m*), Sophie Margaret, *b* 1967; has issue living, Spencer Zeke *b* 1990, Maya Lina *b* 1993.

PREDECESSORS – (1) *Hon* JAMES Drummond, 2nd son of 2nd Lord Drummond († infra); was *cr Lord Maderty* (peerage of Scotland) 1609; *d* 1632; *s* by his son (2) JOHN, 2nd Lord; joined Montrose after the battle of Kilsyth and was imprisoned; *s* by his son (3) DAVID, 3rd Lord; resigned his honours 1664, and obtained a new grant with remainder to his heirs male, and failing whom to his nominee and his heirs; *d* 1684; *s* by his brother (4) WILLIAM, 4th Lord; held a high command in the army raised in 1648 to rescue Charles I; was taken prisoner at battle of Worcester, but effecting his escape went to Russia, in which country he attained the rank of Lieut-Gen; after the Restoration became Maj-Gen of the Forces in Scotland, Gen of the Ordnance, and a Lord of the Treasury; *cr Lord Drummond of Cromlix*, and *Viscount Strathallan* (peerage of Scotland) 1686, with remainder to the heirs male of his body, which failing, to heirs male whatsoever; *d* 1688; *s* by his son (5) WILLIAM, 2nd Viscount; *d* 1702; *s* by his son (6) WILLIAM, 3rd Viscount; *dsp* 1711; *s* by his cousin (7) WILLIAM, 4th Viscount, son of Hon Sir James, 2nd son of 1st Lord Maderty; having espoused the cause of the Chevalier in 1745, he was slain at Culloden 1746, and the names of himself and eldest son were included in the bill of attainder of that year; *s* by his son (8) JAMES, 5th Viscount, who was not attainted until after he had *s* to title; *d* 1766; *s* by his el son (9) JAMES; *d* 1775; *s* by his brother (10) ANDREW JOHN, a Gen in the Army; petitioned unsuccessfully in 1787 for a restoration of the honours; *d* unmarried 1817; *s* in representation of his family by his cousin (11) JAMES ANDREW JOHN LAURENCE CHARLES, 2nd son of Hon William, 2nd son of 4th Viscount, sat as MP for Perthshire 1812-24; was restored to his ancestral honours by Act of Parliament 1824, and was afterwards a Representative Peer; *d* 1851; *s* by his son (12) WILLIAM HENRY, 7th Viscount; *b* 1810; was a Representative Peer and a Lord-in-Waiting to HM Queen Victoria: *m* 1833, Christina Maria Hersey, who *d* 1867, da of Robert Baird, of Newbyth; *d* 23 Jan 1886; *s* by his son (13) JAMES DAVID, 8th Viscount, *b* 1839; a retired Lieut-Col and a Representative Peer for Scotland: *m* 1st, 1868, Ellen, who *d* 1873, da of late Cudbert B. Thornhill, CIE; 2ndly, 1875, Margaret, who *d* 1920, da of late W. Smythe, of Methven Castle, Perthshire; *d* 1893; *s* by his el son (14) WILLIAM HUNTLY, 9th Viscount; *b* 1871; *s* as 15th Earl of Perth 1902 (see infra): *m* 1911, Anna, who *d* 1967, da of Jakob Strauss, of Prague, Czechoslovakia; *d* 1937; *s* by his half-brother (15) *Rt Hon* (JAMES) ERIC, GCMG, CB, 16th Earl, and 10th Viscount Strathallan; *b* 1876; a PC (*cr*1933); was Private Sec to Under-Sec for Foreign Affairs 1906-12, and to Prime Min 1912-15, and to Sec of State for Foreign Affairs 1915-19; first Sec-Gen of League of Nations 1919-33; Ambassador Extraor and Plen to Rome 1933-39; sometime Dep Leader of Liberal Party in House of Lords: *m* 1904, Hon Angela Mary Constable-Maxwell, who *d* 1965; yst da of 11th Lord Herries of Terregles; *d* 1951; *s* by his son (16) JOHN DAVID, 17th Earl, 11th Viscount Strathallan, and present peer; also Lord Drummond, Lord Maderty, and Lord Drummond of Cromlix.

**(1) *Hon* JOHN Drummond, KT, 2nd son of 3rd Earl of Perth, having held several high offices of State, was in 1684 *cr Lord Drummond of Gilstoun*, and *Viscount Melfort* (peerage of Scotland) 1685, and *Lord Drummond of Riccarton, Castlemaine and Gilstoun*, *Viscount Forth* and *Earl of Melfort* (peerage of Scotland) 1686, with remainder to the heirs male of his body by his second wife, and failing which to the heirs male of his body by his first wife, which Earldom he resigned into the King's hands 1688, when it is said the lands and honours were created into a new Earldom in favour of his wife for life with remainder to John, Viscount Forth, Lord of the Regality of Forth, and the heirs male of his body, whom failing to the heirs female of his body, whom failing to his heirs whatsoever; on the revolution he joined James II

in France, and was by him in 1692 *cr Marquess of Forth* and *Duke of Melfort*; and in 1701, Louis XIV accepted the Earl as Duke of Melfort, in the peerage of France; title attainted by Act of Parliament 1695, which attainder, however, did not affect the issue of his first *m*; *d* 1714; *s* by his el son, by 2nd wife (2) JOHN, 2nd Earl and Duke of Melfort; *d* 1754; *s* by his son (3) JAMES, 3rd Earl and Duke; *d* 1766; *s* by his el son (4) JAMES LEWIS, 4th Earl and Duke, who became, on the death of the 12th Earl of Perth (*cr* 1605), heir male to that peerage; *dsp* 1800; *s* by his brother (5) CHARLES EDWARD, 5th Earl and Duke of Melfort, and 13th Earl of Perth; a Roman Catholic Prelate; *d* 1840; *s* by his nephew (6) GEORGE, 6th Earl and Duke, and 14th Earl of Perth, who, in 1853, was restored in blood by Act of Parliament to the dignities of Earl of Perth (*cr* 1605), Viscount Forth, Lord Drummond, and Lord Drummond of Riccartoun, Castlemains and Gilstoun, he having in 1841 established his right to the French honours; *d* 1902, when the Earldom of Melfort became dormant, and the Lordship of Drummond (*cr* 1487) devolved upon his kinsman (7) WILLIAM HUNTLY, 9th Viscount Strathallan (ante), also 15th Earl of Perth (*cr* 1605) (see † infra).

†(1) *Sir* JOHN Drummond of Cargill and Stobhall, PC, Ambassador to England 1483, was in 1487 *cr Lord Drummond* (peerage of Scotland); defeated the Earl of Lennox at Tillymoss 1489; and suppressed the rebellion; was Constable of Stirling Castle and Justiciary of Scotland, *d* 1519; *s* by his great-grandson (2) DAVID, 2nd Lord; joined the Association on behalf of Queen Mary at Hamilton 1568; *s* by his son (3) PATRICK, 3rd Lord; embraced the reformed religion; *s* by his el son (4) JAMES, 4th Baron; was a distinguished courtier *temp* James VI; *cr Earl of Perth* (peerage of Scotland) 1605, it is said with remainder to his heirs male whatsoever, but the patent is not in existence; *s* by his brother (5) JOHN, 2nd Earl, as it is said, "heire of tailzie"; joined the Association on behalf of Charles I 1641; *s* by his son (6) JAMES, 3rd Earl; joined Montrose 1645, and was taken prisoner at Philiphaugh; *d* 1675; *s* by his son (7) JAMES, KT, 4th Earl; was Chancellor of Scotland; said to have had a regrant of his honours after resignation; *cr Earl of Perth, Lord Drummond, Baron Stobhall and Montifex* 1686; in 1693 James II, after his deposition, *cr* him Marquess of Drummond and Duke of Perth (titles acknowledged and confirmed in 1701 by Louis XIV of France), and conferred upon him numerous high offices; *d* 1716; *s* by his son (8) JAMES, who was styled "2nd Duke of Perth," and who, having been attainted in 1715, could not succeed to the Earldom of Perth; *s* by his el son (9) JAMES, "3rd Duke"; wounded at Culloden; attainted 1746; *s* by his brother (10) JOHN, "4th Duke"; attainted 1746; *dsp* 1747; *s* by his uncle (11) JOHN, "5th Duke", *d* 1757; *s* by his brother (12) EDWARD, "6th Duke"; *dsp* 1760; *s* by his second cousin (13) JAMES Lundin, grandson of John, 2nd son of 3rd Earl (see * ante), who assumed the name of Drummond, and also the style of Earl of Perth; *s* by his son (14) JAMES, who assumed the Earldom; *cr Lord Perth, Baron Drummond of Stobhall* (peerage of Great Britain) 1797; *d* 1800, when the Lordship of Perth, Baron Drummond of Stobhall became extinct, and the next heir male to the earldom was (15) JAMES LEWIS, 4th Duke of Melfort (see * ante); *d* 1800; *s* by his brother (16) CHARLES EDWARD, 5th Duke of Melfort; *d* 1840; *s* by his nephew (17) GEORGE, 6th Duke of Melfort; in 1841, established his right to the Dukedoms of Melfort and Perth, and to be Comte de Lussan and Baron de Valrose, etc, in France; obtained a reversal of all attainders by Act of Parliament 1853: *m* 1st, 1831, the Baroness Albertine von Rotberg Rheinweiler, who *d* 1842, and widow of Gen Comte Rapp; 2ndly, 1847, Susan Harriet, who *d* 1886, da of Thomas Henry Bermingham Daly Sewell, of Athenry, and widow of Col Burrowes, of Dangan Castle, Meath: *d* 1902, when the French Dukedom became ext; and the Earldom of Melfort, the Viscountcy of Forth, and the Lordship of Drummond of Riccartoun, Castlemaine and Gilstoun became extinct or dormant, while the Lordship of Drummond and the Earldom of Perth passed to his kinsman (18) WILLIAM HUNTLY, 9th Viscount Strathallan (ante).

Pery, family name of Earl of Limerick.

Pestell, see Baron Wells-Pestell.

PESTON, BARON (Peston) (Life Baron 1987)

MAURICE HARRY PESTON, son of Abraham Peston; *b* 19 March 1931; *ed* Bellevue, Bradford, Hackney Downs, London, London Sch of Economics, and Princeton Univ, USA (BSc Econ); Prof of Economics, Queen Mary Coll, London Univ 1965-88, since when Emeritus Prof (Fellow 1992); *cr Baron Peston*, of Mile End, Greater London (Life Baron) 1987: *m* 1958, Helen, da of Joseph Conroy, and has issue.

Address – Queen Mary Coll, London Univ, E1.

SONS LIVING

Hon Robert James Kenneth, *b* 1960.
Hon Edmund Charles Richard, *b* 1964.

DAUGHTER LIVING

Hon Juliet Clare Elaine, *b* 1961.

Petersham, Viscount; son of Earl of Harrington.

PETRE, BARON (Petre) (Baron E 1603)
(Name pronounced "Peter")

Nothing without God

JOHN PATRICK LIONEL PETRE, 18th Baron; *b* 4 Aug 1942; *s* 1989; *ed* Eton, and Trin Coll, Oxford; DL Essex 1991; Officer Brother of the Order of St John of Jerusalem; patron of three livings (but being a Roman Catholic cannot present): *m* 1965, Marcia Gwendolyn, only da of Alfred Plumpton, and has issue.

𝕬rms – Gules, a bend or between two escallops argent. 𝕮rest – Two lions' heads erased and addorsed; the dexter or, collared azure; the sinister azure, collared or. 𝕾upporters – Two lions reguardant; the *dexter* or, collared azure; the *sinister* azure, collared or.
Seats – Ingatestone Hall, Essex; Writtle Park, Essex.

SONS LIVING

Hon DOMINIC WILLIAM, *b* 9 Aug 1966; *ed* Worth Abbey, and Exeter Univ: *m* 1998, Marisa Verna, only da of Anthony J. Perry, of Holland Park, London, and has issue living, a da, *b* 1999.
Hon Mark Julian, *b* 1969; *ed* Worth Abbey, and Merton Coll, Oxford.

DAUGHTER LIVING

Hon Clare Helen, *b* 1973; *ed* New Hall, and Royal Holloway Coll, Univ of London.

AUNT LIVING (*daughter of 16th Baron*)

Hon Elisabeth Mary Lionel Margaret, *b* (*posthumous*) 1915: *m* 1935, Robert Peter Healing, who *d* 1991, and has had issue, Michael Lionel Kingsbury, *b* 1936; *ed* Eton; Maj Gren Gds: *m* 1966, Amanda Mary, da of Frank R. Rabone, of Gatcombe Park, Minchinhampton, Glos, and *d* 1970, — Julian Robert Peter (31 Alderney St, SW1; La Maison du Phare, Contis, France; *Clubs* – City of London, White's), *b* 1939: *m* 1970, Sabine Marie Louise Françoise, da of Christian de Sorbier de Pougnadoresse, ot Magescq, France, and has issue living, William Michael Christian *b* 1972: *m* 1997, Joanna O. S., elder da of Robert Izzard, of Crowborough, E Sussex, Lionel Michael Louis *b* 1974, Hugo Michael Peter *b* 1978, — Susan Elisabeth, *b* 1945: *m* 1966, Edward Reymond Carbutt (*see* de Montmorency, Bt, colls, 1995 Edn), of Mount Hall, Gt Horkesley, Colchester, and has issue living, James Michael Edward *b* 1972, Laura Frances Victoria *b* 1981, — Carolyn Margaret (twin), *b* 1945: *m* 1972, Christopher Sands Clayton, of 1 Fawcett St, SW10 9HN, and Sundial Cottage, The Priory, Kemerton, nr Tewkesbury, Glos, son of Archibald Sands Clayton (*see* By of Goddard, 1980 Edn), and has issue living, Alexander Michael Sands *b* 1976, Camilla Mary Louise, *b* 1973, Henrietta Catherine Rose *b* 1983. *Residence* – The Priory, Kemerton, Glos.

WIDOW LIVING OF SEVENTEENTH BARON

MARGUERITE EILEEN (*Dowager Baroness Petre*), da of late Ion Wentworth Hamilton: *m* 1941, Capt the 17th Baron Petre, who *d* 1989.

COLLATERAL BRANCHES LIVING

Grandchildren of late Francis William Petre, 2nd son of late Hon Henry William Petre, 2nd son of 11th Baron:—
Issue of late Bernard Francis Petre, *b* 1884, *d* 1942: *m* 1922, Constance, who *d* 1975, yst da of late Capt F. J. Easther, RN, of Dunedin, New Zealand:—
Francis John (18 Ketton Place, St Albans, Christchurch 5, NZ), *b* 1923; Italy 1943-5 with New Zealand Forces: *m* 1947, Patricia Josephine, who *d* 1990, da of Walter Corcoran, of Dunedin, New Zealand, and has issue living, John Bernard (540 Tay St, Invercargill, NZ), *b* 1949: *m* 1972, Kathleen Cullen, and has issue living, Brendan John *b* 1973, Damian Roy *b* 1977, Matthew Patrick *b* 1982, Rebecca Maree *b* 1980, — David Christopher (144 Albert St, Palmerston North, NZ), *b*

1954: *m* 1978, Meryl Kemp, and has issue living, Denis Christopher *b* 1985, Michael Francis *b* 1987, Amy Elizabeth *b* 1981, Josephine Mary *b* 1982, — Gerard Michael (307 Lyttelton St, Spreydon, Christchurch, NZ), *b* 1959, — Frances Mary, *b* 1948: *m* 1974, Michael Pucilowski, of 10 Briar Place, Christchurch, NZ, and has issue living, Anna Gabrielle *b* 1976, Jane Frances *b* 1978, — Philippa Josephine, *b* 1951: *m* 1983, James Frederick Goater, of Nagoya, Japan, and has issue living, Oliver James *b* 1984, Georgina Naomi *b* (twin) 1984. ⸺Robert Cargill (16 Milburn St, Corstorphine, Dunedin, NZ), *b* 1925: *m* 1954, Emily Waiwaha Kohere, and has issue living, Robert Bernard, *b* 1961, — Christopher Andrew, *b* 1962: *m* 1997, Janine Miller, and has issue living, Quentin Cargill *b* 1998, — Mary Ellen, *b* 1955: *m* 1977, Neville James Forrest, and has issue living, James Andrew *b* 1980, Garth Alan *b* 1982, — Raewyn Kura, *b* 1957: *m* 1979, Martin Allen Hay, and has issue living, Larry Dwain *b* 1981, Kura Anne *b* 1984, — Jennifer Anne, *b* 1965: *m* 1991, Wayne David Pitcaithly, and has issue living, Rebekah Emily *b* 1996, Kate Elizabeth *b* 1998. ⸺Constance Elizabeth Mary, *b* 1931: *m* 1955, Lambertus Jacobus Gerardus Snellaert, of 4 Bentley Av, Glenfield, Auckland 10, NZ, and has issue living, Peter William, *b* 1957, — Michael John (10 Sunward Rise, Glenfield, Auckland 10, NZ) *b* 1961: *m* 1982, Bernadette Patricia Cleary, and has issue living, Sarah Louise *b* 1989, Claire Michelle *b* 1991, — Philip Bernard (2/89 Moore St, Northcote, Auckland 10, NZ), *b* 1965; has issue living (by Sheryle Anne Greenfield), Darryl Elizabeth *b* 1996, — Jacqueline Mary, *b* 1956: *m* 1978, Daniel Tangata of 16 Market St, St Kilda, Dunedin, NZ, and has issue living, Nicholas Tobias *b* 1981, Benjamin Daniel *b* 1991, Helen Frances *b* 1983, Anna Elizabeth *b* 1990, — Catherine Elizabeth (32 Montgomery Av, Karori, Wellington, NZ), *b* 1959: *m* 1982 (*m diss* 19—), Peter Gembitsky.

Issue of late Joseph Austin Petre, *b* 1893, *d* 1972: *m* 1st, 1921, Eleanor Irene, who *d* 1935, da of late H. H. Norton, of Auckland, NZ; 2ndly, 1940, Leonora Agnes, who *d* 1941, da of late Robert M. Sunley, of Christchurch, NZ:—
(By 2nd *m*) Anthony John (3 Paulus Terr, Cashmere, Christchurch, NZ), *b* 1941: *m* 1967, Barbara Ann, da of late Charles Armstrong, of Geraldine, NZ, and has issue living, Robert Joseph, *b* 1973, — Ruth Leonora, *b* 1968, — Adrienne Joanne, *b* 1970.

Grandchildren of late Sebastian Henry Petre, 4th son of late Hon Henry William Petre (ante):—
Issue of late William Petre, *b* 1888, *d* 1955: *m* 1925, Marjorie Gwladys, who *d* 1982, da of Archibald Dacres Bruce (Smythe, Bt):—
Ann Mary HALES (8 Priory Rd, Cambridge), *b* 1926: *m* 1955, John Edward Turner Hales-Tooke, who *d* 1992, and has issue living, Jonathan Petre Turner Paul, *b* 1957: *m* 1994, Breda Flaherty, and has issue living, Ben William Flaherty *b* 1999, — Hugh Benedict Milton, *b* 1959, — Giles Anthony Raphael, *b* 1964. ⸺Mary Elise, *b* 1929: *m* 1951, Leonard Pardoe, and has issue living, Sebastian William Joseph, *b* 1956: *m* 1980, Amanda Walley, and has issue living, Charles Edward Adam *b* 1990, Harry *b* 1993, — Matthew James Wentworth, *b* 1960; Bar Inner Temple 1992, — Louise Mary Anne, *b* 1952; has issue living, Claudia Louise Isobel Chapman *b* 1993. *Residence* – 7 Hereford Sq, SW7.

Issue of late Capt Bernard Francis Petre, *b* 1891, *d* 1977: *m* 1926, Mary Lucy, da of late Archibald Dominic Smith-Sligo, of Inzievar, Oakley, Fife:—
Michael Henry Charles, *b* 1930: *m* 1959 (*m diss* 1980), Christian Margaret Lilias, da of John Franc McIntyre (*see* E Perth, colls, 1985 Edn), and has issue living, Benedict Francis Joseph, *b* 1967, — Gavin Ruaraidh Joseph, *b* 1969, — Tanya Mairi, *b* 1961: *m* 1981, Nicholas Lunn, — Helena Mary Alathea, *b* 1964, — Kathryne Maria, *b* 1965, — Elspeth Moira, *b* 1972.

Grandchildren of late Robert George Petre, 6th son of late Hon Henry William Petre (ante):—
Issue of late Francis William Petre, *b* 1902, *d* 1993: *m* 1st, 1932 (*m diss* 1944), Gertrude Fey, da of Philip Lowery Wright, of Bicton, Napier, NZ; 2ndly, 1947, Athalie Millicent (28 Hautana Square, Lower Hutt, NZ), da of Albert Henry Eaton, of Raumati South, NZ:—
(By 1st *m*) John Lowery (Mangaotaki, Piopio, NZ), *b* 1934: *m* 1962, Susan Helen, da of Edwin Thomas Durrant, of Auckland, NZ, and has issue living, Michael, *b* 1964, — Daniel, *b* 1966: *m* 1995, Renelle Lea Bickerton, and has issue living, Alice *b* 1997, — Sally, *b* 1963: *m* 1992, Philip Roger Shanks, of Gisborne, NZ, and has issue living, Jack Haig *b* 1992, Lily Mac *b* 1995. ⸺(By 2nd *m*) Robert Bruce, *b* 1952. ⸺Ann Mary Elizabeth, *b* 1948: *m* 1972, Robert Joseph Stella, of Lower Hutt, NZ, and has issue living, Daniel John, *b* 1976, — Nicholas James, *b* 1979, — Lucy Jane, *b* 1982. ⸺Eleanor Jane, *b* 1954: *m* 1976, John Kane, of Wellington, NZ, and has issue living, Alexander John Petre, *b* 1985, — Michael Petre, *b* 1993, — Eleanor Mary Petre *b* 1989, — Juliet Athalie Petre, *b* 1991.

Granddaughter of late Capt Hon Frederick Charles Edmund Petre, 3rd son of 11th Baron:—
Issue of late Reginald William Petre, *b* 1851, *d* 19—: *m* 1889, Caroline, da of J. Alexander Preston, of Baltimore, USA:—
Constance Achsah Ridgeley, *b* 1897: *m* 1921, William Carrington Stettinius, and has issue living.

Grandson of late Francis Loraine Petre, OBE, only son of late Hon Edmund George Petre, 5th son of 11th Baron:—
Issue of late Maj-Gen Roderic Loraine Petre, CB, DSO, MC, late Dorset Regt, *b* 1887, *d* 1971: *m* 1922, Katharine Sophia, who *d* 1973, da of Herbert W. Bryans, of The Priory, Bradford-on-Avon, Wilts:—
His Honour Judge Francis Herbert Loraine (The Ferriers, Bures, Suffolk CO8 5DL), *b* 1927; *ed* Downside, and Clare Coll, Camb (BA); Bar Lincoln's Inn 1952; a Circuit Judge 1972-97; Regular Judge, Central Criminal Court 1982-93; Chm Police Complaints Authority 1989-92: *m* 1958, Mary Jane, da of late Everard C. X. White, and has issue living, Jonathan Charles Loraine (29 Algarve Rd, SW8), *b* 1959: *m* 1987, Emma Victoria, twin da of Neil Hobson, of London, and has issue living, Robert Francis *b* 1989, Eleanor Mary Rosamond *b* 1993, — William Francis, *b* 1963, — Hugh Robert Edward, *b* 1970, — Harriet Mary, *b* 1961: *m* 1987, Mark William Hinton, of 58 Nasmyth St, W6, elder son of Dr Michael Hinton, of Sandwich, Kent.

Grandchildren of late Alfred William Ralph Petre, 4th son of late Sir George Glynn Petre, KCMG, CB (infra):—
Issue, if any, of Charles Petre (*b* 1895), Alfred Ralph Petre (*b* 1896), and George Ernest Petre (*b* 1899).

Grandchildren of late Capt Charles Bernard Petre, KRRC, 6th son of late Sir George Glynn Petre, KCMG, CB (infra):—

Issue of late Capt Robert Charles Petre, *b* 1912; rode winner of 1946 Grand National; *d* 1996: *m* 1st, 1934 (*m diss* 1975), Mary Delphine, who *d* 1995, eldest da of late Maj Claude Chichester, of Tunworth Down, Basingstoke; 2ndly, 1975, Mrs Sonia Greenish (13 Stafford Terr, W8; Little Bignor Farm, Kirdford, Billingshurst, W Sussex), da of Capt Redfern:—
(By 1st *m*) Charles Henry (Tunworth Down House, Basingstoke, Hants RG25 2NB; White's Club), *b* 1936; *ed* Downside, and Ch Ch Oxford: *m* 1963, Melanie Beatrix, eldest da of late Henry Peregrine Rennie Hoare (*see* E Cadogan), and has had issue, †Robert Henry, *b* 1968; *ed* Eton; *d* 1992. — Fenella Delphine, *b* 1967: *m* 1997, C. Andrew H. Gray, eldest son of Hugh Gray, of Hindhead, Surrey, and has issue living, Jonathan Robert Petre *b* 1998. —— Robert Bernard (Down Farm House, Tunworth, Basingstoke, Hants RG25 2LE; Boodle's Club), *b* 1938; *ed* Downside; late 2nd Lieut (Res) Scots Guards: *m* 1970, Caroline, da of Lt-Col Peter Jackson, of Wappenham, Towcester, and has issue living, Edward Robert, *b* 1976, — Georgina Sarah, *b* 1974. —— Claudia Mary Delphine, *b* 1943: *m* 1971, Ambrose Patrick Eustace Scott-Moncrieff, and has issue living, Chloë, *b* 1976.

Grandchildren of late Sir George Glynn Petre, KCMG, CB, 2nd son of late Henry William Petre, son of 2nd son of 9th Baron:—
Issue of late Rear-Adm Walter Reginald Glynn Petre, DSO, *b* 1873, *d* 1942: *m* (Jan) 1906, Agnes Marie, who *d* 1963, yst da of Capt Eugene Cadic, of Rennes, France:—
Walter George Glynn (La Mouette, Sark, Channel Isles), *b* (Oct) 1906; *ed* Oratory Sch; Sqdn-Ldr RAF: *m* 1939, Myra Millicent, who *d* 1984, only da of late Arthur Willows, of Rushton Manor, near Kettering, and has issue living, Michael Bernard (Four Winds, Cookham Dean, Berks), *b* 1946: *m* 1978, Pauline Carole McCormack, da of late Lionel Alfred Weston, and has issue living, Nicholas Lionel Charles Glynn *b* 1980, Simon Robert Glynn *b* 1983, — Geraldine Marie, *b* 1944: *m* 1st, 1967 (*m diss* 1987), David Robin Petre-Mears; 2ndly, 1992, Michael Guest, of La Mouette, Sark, Channel Isles, and has issue living (by 1st *m*), Edward Petre (Baytree Cottage, Sark, Channel Isles) *b* 1968: *m* 1995, Sarah Louise Hayden (and has issue living, Alexander David *b* 1996, Siobhan Elizabeth *b* 1998), Justin *b* 1972, — Anne Rosalie, *b* 1949: *m* 1988, Michael Francis Efrussy, of 31A Cambridge Rd, Sidcup, Kent DA14 6PT, and has issue living, Luke Michael *b* 1986, Faye Anna *b* 1987. —— †Henry Edward, *b* 1907; *ed* Oratory Sch; Lt-Cdr RNR: *m* 1939, Rosemary Sonia (10 Camden Rd, Eastbourne, E Sussex), da of late Benjamin Gottschalk of 26 Ulster Place, NW1, and *d* (18 Jan) 1994, leaving issue, Cecilia Marie, *b* 1940: *m* 1964, Douglas Milton Wiggins, MBE, of Holly House, Earls Lane, Deddington, Banbury, Oxon, and *d* (27 June) 1994, leaving issue, Nicholas James Petre *b* 1974: *m* 1998, Sarah Moisey, Emma Jane *b* 1966: *m* 1988, David Hamish Easdale, of The Laurels, Melford Rd, Sudbury, Suffolk, son of Hamish Easdale, of Polkerris, Camp Rd, Gerrards Cross, Bucks (and has issue living, Harriet Victoria *b* 1994), Katherine Blanche *b* 1968, Henrietta Clare *b* 1969: *m* 1998, Adam Bromfield, of 48 Cricklade Av, SW2, — Teresa Jane Glynn, *b* 1944: *m* 1976, George Andrew Hutchinson, of 3 Westdean Cottages, Westdean, Seaford, Sussex, and has issue living, Rupert Charles Petre *b* 1981, Amanda Jane Petre *b* 1979, — Sonia Rosemary, *b* 1946: *m* 1966, Dr Robert Hancock, of 8 Daisy Lane, Hurlingham, SW6, and has issue living, Benjamin Charles Petre *b* 1971, Toby Charles Petre *b* 1974, Bertie Petre Oliver *b* 1979, Scarlett *b* 1981. —— Mary Katherine Gabrielle, *b* 1909. —— Marie Madeleine Ethel, *b* 1913: *m* 1944, Maj-Gen Desmond Alexander Bruce Clarke, CB, CBE, late RA, who *d* 1986, of Elm Cottage, Caldbeck, Cumbria, and has issue living, Desmond Walter Robert (Old Dairy Cottage, Winchester Hants): *b* 1945; Capt RA: *m* 1970, Fiona, da of John Harrison, of The Barn Cottage, Wilmington, Sussex, and has issue living, Duncan Robert Petre *b* 1971, Sebastian Alexander *b* 1982, Philippa Kate *b* 1975, — Dominic Michael Bernard (15 Norfolk Mansions, Prince of Wales Drive, SW11), *b* 1949, — Damian Anthony John (4 School Terrace, Reading, Berks), *b* 1958: *m* 1986, Imogen, da of Rev David Cooke, of The Rectory, Stone, Bucks, and has issue living, Edward *b* 1986, Henry *b* 1988, George *b* 1989, — Antoinette Marie Edwina, *b* 1947: *m* 1978, David Ward, of The Green, Caldbeck, Cumbria, and has issue living, Andrew *b* 1981, Robin *b* 1982, Rachel *b* 1979, — Amicie Mary Bernadette, *b* 1950, *m* 1972, David Heath Thompson, of Northfields, Sudbury, Suffolk, and has issue living, Joseph Andrew *b* 1975, Toby *b* 1977, Benedict *b* 1985, Jessica *b* 1983.

Grandson of late Rear-Adm Walter Reginald Glynn Petre, DSO (ante):—
Issue of late Major Gerard Malcolm Mary Laurence Petre, Essex Regt, *b* 1916; *ka* in France 1944: *m* 1941, Pamela Marian (who *m* 2ndly, 1946, Col Desmond John H. Bannister, MBE, MC, Devonshire Regt, of Wisteria Cottage, N Cheriton, Wincanton, Som), da of Capt G. B. Pratt, RA (ret):—
Andrew Charles Malcolm Glynn, *b* 1944; *ed* Downside: *m* 1977, Alison Ord, and has issue living, Marcus, *b* 1982, — Emma, *b* 1984. *Residence* – 19 Halsey Drive, Hemel Hempstead, Herts HP1 3SE.

Grandsons of late Lt-Col Oswald Henry Philip TURVILLE-PETRE, el son of Edward Henry Petre, 3rd son of Henry William Petre (ante) *b* 1862, *d* 1941 (having assumed for himself and issue by Roy licence 1907, the additional surname and arms of Turville):—
Issue of late Prof Edward Oswald Gabriel TURVILLE-PETRE, *b* 1908, *d* 1978: *m* 1943, Joan Elizabeth (18 Hungate St, Aylsham, Norfolk), da of Sam Blomfield, of Colchester:—
Thorlac Francis Samuel (c/o Dept of English, Nottingham University, Nottingham), *b* 1944; *ed* Magdalen Coll Sch, Oxford, and Jesus Coll, Oxford (MA, BLitt): *m* 1967, Ingrid Elisabeth, da of Rudolf Zimmerlund, of Stockholm, and has issue living, Francis Gustaf, *b* 1971, — Crispin Gabriel, *b* 1974. —— Merlin Oswald, *b* 1946: *m* 1973, Christine Margaret, da of Ivor Lee-Smith, of Newbury, Berks, and has issue living, Daisy Kate, *b* 1975, — Martha Amanda, *b* 1978. —— †Brendan Arthur Auberon, *b* 1948; *d* 1981.

Grandchildren of late Maj Myles Seymour Edward Petre, Duke of Cornwall's LI (infra):—
Issue of late Martin Anthony Chaworth Petre, *b* 1940, *d* 1991: *m* 1968, Selina Frances Gladstone (who *m* 2ndly, 1993, Maj David Hastings, of Cary Hill House, Castle Cary, Som), da of Brig Philip William Gladstone Pope, DSO, MC, of Cross House, Henstridge, Som:—
Edward Myles Chaworth, *b* 1971. —— Henrietta Claire Gladstone, *b* 1969: *m* 1997, Capt Simon J. King, son of Dr George King, of Widnes, Ches. —— Isabel Mary Hartshorne, *b* 1973.

Grandson of Bertram Edward Petre, yr son of Edward Henry Petre, 3rd son of late Henry William Petre (ante):—
Issue of late Major Myles Seymour Edward Petre, Duke of Cornwall's LI, *b* 1913, *ka* 1942: *m* 1938, Audrey Catherine, who *d* 1982, da of Col John Nevile Chaworth-Musters, DSO, OBE, TD, of Annesley Park, Nottingham:—
Robin David Oswald (Flaxbourne, Blenheim, NZ), *b* 1942; *ed* Ampleforth, and RMAS; Maj (ret) 17th/21st Lancers: *m* 1968, Cecily Constance, el da of late Simon Scrope, of Flaxbourne House, Gt Ouseburn, Yorks, and has issue living, Diana Audrey Constance, *b* 1969: *m* 1998, Jamie Douglas Daer Reid, yr son of Maj-Gen Peter Daer Reid, CB, of The Border House, Cholderton, nr Salisbury (*see* Jackson, Bt (*cr* 1815), colls, 1995 Edn), — Nicola Mary Catherine, *b* 1971.

Grandchildren of late Louis William Henry Petre, son of Philip William Petre, yr son of late Hon George William Petre, 2nd son of 9th Baron:—
 Issue of late Edward Philip William Petre, *b* 1869, *d* 1923: *m* 1890, Zoila Rosa del Carmen Larenas, who *d* 1953:—

Luis Enrique, *b* 1898; is a Bank Director: *m* 19—, Else Newman Etienne, and has issue living, Agnes Petre Newman, *b* 1924: *m* 1945 (*m diss* 1952), Fernando Zilleruedo Vargas, Lieut Chilean Air Force, and has issue living, Fernando *b* 1951, Marie-Agnes *b* 1946, Marie-Luz *b* 1948. —— Anna Lucie, *b* 1894: *m* 1923, Col Aquiles Vergara Vicuña, Bolivian Army. *Residence* –

PREDECESSORS – **(1)** *Sir* JOHN Petre, Knt, only son of Sir William Petre, a Sec of State to Henry VIII and Edward VI; MP for Essex 1584-87; *cr Baron Petre*, of Writtle, co Essex (peerage of England) 1603; *d* 1613; *s* by his son **(2)** WILLIAM, 2nd Baron; MP for Essex 1597-1601; *d* 1637; *s* by his son **(3)** ROBERT, 3rd Baron; *d* 1638; *s* by his el son **(4)** WILLIAM, 4th Baron; *d* a prisoner in the Tower 1683; *s* by his brother **(5)** JOHN, 5th Baron; *d* unmarried; *s* by his brother **(6)** THOMAS, 6th Baron; Lord-Lt of Essex; *d* 1707; *s* by his son **(7)** ROBERT, 7th Baron; *d* 1713, *s* by his son **(8)** ROBERT JAMES, 8th Baron; *d* 1742; *s* by his son **(9)** ROBERT EDWARD, 9th Baron: *m* Anne Howard, niece of Edward, 9th Duke of Norfolk, and who became at his death a co-heir to the Baronies of Howard, Furnivall, Strange of Blackmere, Talbot, Braose of Gower, Dacre of Gillesland, Greystock, Ferrers of Wemme, Gifford of Brimsfield and Verdon; *d* 1801; *s* by his son **(10)** ROBERT EDWARD, 10th Baron; *d* 1809; *s* by his son **(11)** WILLIAM HENRY FRANCIS, 11th Baron; *d* 1850; *s* by his el son **(12)** WILLIAM BERNARD, 12th Baron; *b* 1817; *m* 1843, Mary Teresa, el da of Hon Charles Thomas Clifford; *d* 4 July 1884; *s* by his el son **(13)** *Right Rev* WILLIAM HENRY JOSEPH, 13th Baron, *b* 1847; Domestic Prelate at the Court of the Vatican; *d* 1893; *s* by his brother **(14)** BERNARD HENRY PHILIP, 14th Baron, *b* 1858: *m* 1899, (Etheldreda Mary) Audrey, who *d* 1959, da of Rev William Robinson Clark, MA, DD, LLD, DCL, FRS (Canada), formerly V of Taunton, Preb of Wells, and Professor of Philosophy in Trin Coll, Toronto; *d* 1908; *s* by his brother **(15)** PHILIP BENEDICT JOSEPH, 15th Baron; *b* 1864: *m* 1888, Julia Mary, who *d* 1931, el da of late George Cavendish Taylor, of 42 Elvaston Place, SW; *d* 1908; *s* by his son **(16)** LIONEL GEORGE CARROLL, 16th Baron; *b* 1890; Capt Coldstream Guards: *m* 1913, Catherine Margaret (who *m* 2ndly, 1921, Col Sir Frederic Carne Rasch, 2nd Bt, CVO, DSO (*d* 1963), and *d* 1983), da of Hon John Boscawen; *d* of wounds received in action 1915; *s* by his only son **(17)** JOSEPH WILLIAM LIONEL, 17th Baron; *b* 1914; Capt Essex Regt: *m* 1941, Marguerite Eileen, da of Ion Wentworth Hamilton; *d* 1989; *s* by his only son **(18)** JOHN PATRICK LIONEL, 18th Baron and present peer.

PEYTON OF YEOVIL, BARON (Peyton) (Life Baron 1983)

·PATIOR·POTIOR·

JOHN WYNNE WILLIAM PEYTON, PC, son of late Ivor Eliot Peyton, by his wife Dorothy Helen; *b* 13 Feb 1919; *ed* Eton and Trin Coll, Oxford; served in 1939-45 War with 15/19 Hussars (PoW 1940-45); Barrister-at-law, Inner Temple 1945; MP for Yeovil Divn of Somerset 1951-83; Min of Transport 1970; Min for Transport Industries DoE 1970-74; Chm Texas Instruments Ltd 1974-90; *cr* PC 1970, and *Baron Peyton of Yeovil*, of Yeovil, co Somerset (Life Baron) 1983: *m* 1st, 1947 (*m diss* 1966), Diana, da of late Douglas Clinch, of Durban; 2ndly, 1966, Mary Constance, da of late Col Hon (Everard) Humphrey Wyndham, MC (*see* Egremont, B), and previously wife of Ralph Hamilton Cobbold, and has issue living, by 1st *m*.

𝔄rms – Sable a cross engrailed in the first quarter a mullet Or. ℭrest – A griffin sejant or. 𝔖upporters – *Dexter*, on a mount vert with four oak sprigs growing therefrom fructed or a bull rampant reguardant in trian aspect sable armed membered the tail tuft and muzzle or unguled gules holding in the mouth an oak sprig fructed or and a shamrock slipped vert; *sinister*, on a mount vert growing therefrom four shamrocks slipped proper a griffin segreant reguardant or grasping in the beak a shamrock slipped proper and an oak sprig fructed gold.
Residences – The Old Malt House, Hinton St George, Somerset TA17 8SE; 6 Temple West Mews, West Square, SE11 4TJ.

SON LIVING (By 1st marriage)

Hon Thomas Richard Douglas, *b* 1950; *ed* Eton: *m* 1981, Vivien, da of Dr Jack Birks, CBE, and has issue living, Joseph Anthony Charles, *b* 1986, — Davey Christopher William, *b* 1990. *Residence* – 21 Ardbeg Rd, SE24 9JL.

DAUGHTER LIVING (By 1st marriage)

Hon Sarah Grenville, *b* 1948: *m* 1st, 1971, Dugald Graham-Campbell; 2ndly, 1996, Rex Chester, and has issue (by 1st *m*). *Residence* – Elms House, Twyford, Winchester, Hants SO21 1QF.

Philipps, family name of Baron Milford.

Philipps, family name of Viscount St Davids.

Philipps, family name of Baron Strange of Knokin.

PHILLIMORE, BARON (Phillimore) (Baron UK 1918, Bt UK 1881)

Pray for a brave soul

FRANCIS STEPHEN PHILLIMORE, 5th Baron and 6th Baronet; *b* 25 Nov 1944; *s* 1994; *ed* Eton, and Trin Coll, Camb: *m* 1971, Nathalie, da of late Michel Anthony Pequin, of Paris, and has issue.

Arms – Sable, three bars indented erminois, in chief an anchor between two cinquefoils or. Crest – In front of a tower argent, thereon a falcon volant proper holding in the beak a lure gold, three cinquefoils fessewise or. Supporters – On either side an owl proper, each charged with an anchor or.
Residence – Coppid Hall, Binfield Heath, nr Henley-on-Thames, Oxon RG9 4JR.

SONS LIVING

Hon TRISTAN ANTHONY STEPHEN, *b* 18 Aug 1977. —— *Hon* Julian Michel Claud, *b* 1981.

DAUGHTER LIVING

Hon Arabella Maroussia Eleanor, *b* 1975.

SISTER LIVING

Hon (Marion) Miranda PHILLIMORE, *b* 1946; has resumed her maiden surname: *m* 1973 (*m diss* 1985), Thomas Walter Montagu Douglas Scott, and has issue (*see* D Buccleuch, colls). *Residence* – 65 Cloncurry St, Bishop's Park, SW6 6DT.

AUNT LIVING (*Daughter of 2nd Baron*)

Hon Phœbe Margaret Dorothy (*Hon Lady Rose*), *b* 1912: *m* 1937, Sir Charles Henry Rose, 3rd Bt (*cr* 1909), who *d* 1966. *Residence* – Hardwick Hall, Whitchurch, Oxon.

SISTER LIVING OF THIRD BARON (*raised to the rank of a Baron's daughter* 1949)

Hon Frances Phoebe, *b* 1938: *m* 1st, 1961 (*m diss* 1978), Colin John Francis Lindsay-MacDougall of Lunga (*see* E Crawford, colls); 2ndly, 1980, Joseph Peter Gibson, son of Charles Gibson, of Kelty Hill, Kelty, Fife, and has issue (by 1st *m*) (*see* E Crawford, colls). *Residence* – Gyles House, Pittenweem, Fife, Scotland KY10 2NG.

WIDOWS LIVING OF SONS OF SECOND BARON

Sheila Bruce, da of John Farquhar MacLeod, JP, MB, ChB, of Peterculter, Aberdeenshire: *m* 1944, Col Hon Robert George Hugh Phillimore, OBE, who *d* 1984, and has issue (see colls infra). *Residence* – Brook Cottage, Mill Rd, Shiplake, Oxon RG9 3LW.

Margaret, da of late Gibson Lamb Caldwell, of Kenwood Place, Wheeling, W Virginia, USA: *m* 1946, Hon Miles Godfrey Walter Phillimore, who *d* 1972, and has issue (see colls infra). *Residence* –

WIDOW LIVING OF THIRD BARON

MARIA *(Maria, Baroness Phillimore)*, da of Ilya Slonim, by his wife Tatiana Litvinov: *m* 1983, as his 2nd wife, the 3rd Baron Phillimore, who *d* 1990. *Residence* – ....

COLLATERAL BRANCHES LIVING

Issue of late Col Hon Robert George Hugh Phillimore, OBE, 3rd son of 2nd Baron, *b* 1913, *d* 1984: *m* 1944, Sheila Bruce (ante), da of John Farquhar MacLeod, JP, MB, ChB, of Peterculter, Aberdeenshire:—
Annabel Margaret, *b* 1947: *m* 1978, Hugo Massey Gamble, of The Mill House, Shiplake, Oxfordshire RG9 3LY, son of late Brig Geoffrey Massey Gamble, CMG, OBE, of The Little White Cottage, Rotherfield Greys, Henley-on-Thames, and has issue living, James Hugo Phillimore, *b* 1979, — Lucinda Diana MacLeod, *b* 1981, — Rosemary Leigh Phillimore, *b* 1984. — Lindsay Mary MacLeod (Ellanore House, Ellanore Lane, West Wittering, Sussex PO26 8AN), *b* 1951: *m* 1977, Charles F. Dewhurst, son of late Col F. W. Dewhurst, of Pound Cottage, Buckland Monachorum, Yelverton, S Devon, and has issue living, Robert Edward Charles, *b* 1984, — Anna Elizabeth MacLeod, *b* 1987. —— (Sheila) Leigh, *b* 1952: *m* 1978, Matthew W. J. Thorne, of The Mount, Bannerdown Rd, Batheaston, Bath BA1 8EG, son of Robin Thorne, CMG, OBE, of The Old Vicarage, Old Heathfield, Sussex, and has issue living, Robin Lindsey Phillimore, *b* 1983, — Andrew Robert Wadman, *b* 1986, — Edward Matthew MacLeod, *b* 1989, — Aelene Elizabeth, *b* 1981, — Marini Annabel, *b* 1992. —— Elizabeth Anne Haig, *b* 1955: *m* 1978, Timothy H. S. Brutton, of Greenmoor Hill Farm, Woodcote, Reading, Berks RG8 0RT, son of Rev R. S. Brutton, of 7 North St, Langton Matravers, Dorset, and has issue living, Emma Penelope Phayre, *b* 1981, — Victoria Anne Haig, *b* 1983, — Clare Elizabeth Macleod, *b* 1986.

Issue of late Hon Miles Godfrey Walter Phillimore, 4th and yst son of 2nd Baron, *b* 1915, *d* 1972: *m* 1946, Margaret (ante), da of late Gibson Lamb Caldwell, of Kenwood Place, Wheeling, W Virginia:—
Dorothy Eleanor Barbara PHILLIMORE (6752 First Av NW, Seattle, Washington 98117, USA), *b* 1949; has resumed her maiden surname: *m* 1st, 1973, Robert William Drumm; 2ndly, 1982 (*m diss* 19—), Wayne Amos Rayfield, and has issue living, (by 2nd *m*) Margaret Leona Sarah, *b* 1984, — Elizabeth, *b* 19—.

PREDECESSORS – **(1)** *Rt Hon Sir* ROBERT JOSEPH Phillimore, DCL; 1810; *cr a Baronet* 1881; MP for Tavistock (LC) 1855-7, and Judge of the High Court of Admiralty 1867-83, and of Court of Arches 1867-75: *m* 1844, Charlotte Anne, who *d* 1892, da of late John Denison, MP, of Ossington, Newark, and sister of 1st Viscount Ossington; *d* 1885; *s* by his el son **(2)** *Rt Hon* WALTER GEORGE FRANK, GBE, DCL, LLD, 2nd Bt; *b* 1845; was a Judge of the High Court of Justice 1897-1913, and a Lord Justice of Appeal 1913-16; Pres English Church Union 1919-20; Chm of Naval Prize Tribunal 1918-28; *cr Baron Phillimore*, of Shiplake, Oxfordshire (peerage of United Kingdom)1918: *m* 1870, Agnes, who *d* 1929, el da of late Charles Manners Lushington, MP for Canterbury (E Iddesleigh); *d* 1929; *s* by his son **(3)** GODFREY WALTER, MC, 2nd Baron; *b* 1879; Capt late Highland LI; European War 1914-16 (MC): *m* 1st, 1905, Dorothy Barbara, who *d* 1915, el da of Lieut-Col Arthur Balfour Haig, CVO, CMG; 2ndly, 1923, Marion (BRYCE), who *d* 1950, da of late Maj-Gen Cecil Robert St John Ives; *d* 1947; *s* by his grandson **(4)** ROBERT GODFREY son of late Capt Hon Anthony Francis Phillimore (*ka* 1940) (el son of 2nd Baron), 3rd Baron, *b* 1939; late Lieut 9th/12th Royal Lancers: *m* 1st, 1974 (*m diss* 1982), Amanda, da of Carlo Hugo Gonzales-Castillo, by his wife Aida Aramburu; 2ndly, 1983, Maria, da of Ilya Slonim, by his wife Tatiana Litvinov; *d* 1990; *s* by his uncle **(5)** CLAUD STEPHEN (2nd son of 2nd Baron), 4th Baron, *b* 1911: *m* 1944, Anne Elizabeth, who *d* 1995, da of Maj Arthur Algernon Dorrien Smith, DSO, of Tresco Abbey, Isle of Scilly; *d* 1994; *s* by his son **(6)** FRANCIS STEPHEN, 5th Baron and present peer.

PHILLIPS, BARONY OF (Phillips) (Extinct 1992)

SON LIVING OF LIFE BARONESS

Hon Morgan David, *b* 1939; *ed* St Paul's Sch, and at Downing Coll, Camb (BA); PGCE, Univ of London.

DAUGHTER LIVING OF LIFE BARONESS

Hon Gwyneth Patricia, MP (c/o House of Commons, SW1A 0AA), *b* 1930; *ed* Fulham Co Secondary Sch, and Convent of Nôtre Dame, Battersea; MP for Exeter (*Lab*) 1966-70, for Crewe since 1974, and for Crewe and Nantwich since 1983: Parl Sec to Board of Trade 1967-70; a Dir of Film Production Assocn of Gt Britain: *m* 1954 (*m diss* 1975), John Elliott Orr Dunwoody, MB, BS, and has issue, two sons and one da.

PHILLIPS OF ELLESMERE, BARON (Phillips) (Life Baron 1994) (extinct 1999)

DAVID CHILTON PHILLIPS, KBE, son of late Charles Harry Phillips, of Ellesmere, Shropshire; *b* 7 March 1924; *ed* Oswestry Boys' High Sch, and Univ Coll, Cardiff (BSc 1948, PhD 1951); Hon DSc Leicester 1974, Wales 1975, Chicago 1978, Warwick 1982, Exeter 1982, Birmingham 1987, Glasgow 1990, Glamorgan 1993, Bath 1993, Hon DUniv Essex 1993, Stirling 1995, Hon PhD Weizmann Inst of Science 1990; FRS 1967 (Vice-Pres 1972-73 and 1976-83); Sub Lt RNVR 1944-47; Post-doctoral Fell, Nat Research Council of Canada 1951-53; Research Offr, Nat Research Laboratories, Ottawa, Canada 1953-55; Research Worker, Royal Inst, London 1956-66; Prof of Molecular Biophysics, Univ of Oxford 1966-90, since when Hon Prof; Fell of Corpus Christi Coll, Oxford 1966-90, since when Hon Fell; Fullerian Prof of Physiology, Royal Inst 1979-83; Dir of Celltech Ltd 1982; Biological Sec of The Royal Society 1976-83; memb Medical Research Council 1974-78; Royal Society Assessor 1976-83; Chm Advisory Board of Research Councils 1983-93; Gov De Montfort Univ since 1993; Royal Medal of Royal Society 1975, Prix Charles Léopold Mayer, French Academy of Sciences, 1979, Wolf Prize for Chemistry, Wolf Foundation, Israel 1987; *cr* Kt 1979, KBE 1989, and *Baron Phillips of Ellesmere*, of Ellesmere, co Shropshire (Life Baron) 1994: *m* 1960, Diana Kathleen, da of late Maj Edward Maitland Hutchinson, RA, of Chalfont St Giles, Bucks, and *d* 23 Feb 1999, leaving issue.
Residence – 35 Addisland Court, Holland Villas Rd, W14 8DA. *Club* – Athenaeum.

DAUGHTER LIVING

Hon Sarah, *b* 1962: *m* 1988, Paul William Matthewson, son of William Maurice Matthewson, of Preston, Lancs, and has issue living, Samuel Tosh, *b* 1991, — Isabella Rose, *b* 1993. *Residence* – 133 North End Rd, NW11 7HT.

PHILLIPS OF SUDBURY, BARON (Phillips) (Life Baron 1998)

ANDREW WYNDHAM PHILLIPS, OBE, son of Alan Clifford Phillips, of Sudbury, Suffolk; *b* 15 March 1939; *ed* Uppingham, and Trinity Hall, Cambridge; Solicitor 1964; Founder Partner of Bates, Wells and Braithwaite, London 1970; Memb Scott Trust since 1992; Founder Dir of National Lottery Charities Board 1994-96; Founder Chm of Legal Action Group 1971-76; Founder Chm of Citizenship Foundation since 1989; Company Dir; *cr* OBE 1996, and *Baron Phillips of Sudbury*, of Sudbury, co Suffolk (Life Baron) 1998: *m* 1968, Penelope Ann, da of late Edward Bennett, of Bridgwater, Som.
Residence – River House, The Croft, Sudbury, Suffolk CO10 1HW.

PHILLIPS OF WORTH MATRAVERS, BARON (Phillips) (Life Baron 1999)

NICHOLAS ADDISON PHILLIPS, PC, son of Michael Pennington Phillips, of ......; *b* 21 Jan 1938; *ed* Bryanston, and King's Coll, Camb (MA 19—); RNVR 1956-58; Bar, Middle Temple 1962; Jr Counsel to MOD and Treasury in Admiralty Matters 1973-78; QC 1978; Recorder of the Crown Court 1982; Judge of the High Court of Justice (Queen's Bench Division) 1987-95; a Lord Justice of Appeal 1995-99, since when a Lord of Appeal in Ordinary; Chm Council of legal Education 1992-97; Govr of Bryanston Sch since 1975 (Chm 1981); *cr* Kt 1987, PC 1995, and *Baron Phillips of Worth Matravers*, of Belsize Park in the London Borough of Camden (Life Baron) 1999: *m* 1972, Mrs Christylle Marie-Thérèse Rouffiac, da of Maurice Doreau, of ......, and has issue.
Address – o/o House of Lords, Westminster, SW1A 0PW. *Club* – Brooks's.

DAUGHTERS LIVING

Hon Rebecca, *b* 1973; *ed* Bryanston, and Corpus Christi Coll, Camb.
Hon Marie, *b* 1976; *ed* Bryanston, South Hampstead, and Robinson Coll, Camb.

Phipps, family name of Marquess of Normanby.

PIERCY, BARON (Piercy) (Baron UK 1945)

JAMES WILLIAM PIERCY, 3rd Baron; *b* 19 Jan 1946; *s* 1981; *ed* Shrewsbury, and Edinburgh Univ (BSc); AMIEE, FCCA.

Arms – Per fesse indented gules and argent in chief three pierced mullets of the last and in base a lion rampant guardant sable. **Crest** – Issuant from a bezant in front of two spears in saltire points upwards proper a demi lion guardant sable charged on the shoulder with a pierced mullet argent. **Supporters** – Not recorded at time of going to press.
Residence – 36 Richford St, W6 7HP.

BROTHER LIVING

Hon MARK EDWARD PELHAM, *b* 30 June 1953; *ed* Shrewsbury, and New Coll, Oxford; Barrister-at-law (Lincoln's Inn): *m* 1979, Vivien Angela, da of His Honour Judge Evelyn Faithfull Monier-Williams, and has issue living, William Nicholas Pelham, *b* 11 March 1989, — Katherine Henrietta, *b* 1982, — Olivia Charlotte, *b* 1984, — Harriet Lavinia, *b* 1987. *Residence* – 39 Carson Rd, W Dulwich, SE21 8HT.

SISTERS LIVING

Hon Charlotte Mary, *b* 1947; *ed* Badminton Sch, Florence Univ, and Heatherley Sch of Fine Art: *m* 1st, 1966 (*m diss* 1985), Paolo Emilio Taddei; 2ndly, 1985, as his 2nd wife, (William Guy) David Ropner (*see* Ropner, Bt, *cr* 1904, colls), and has issue living (by 1st *m*), Guido, *b* 1970, — Caroline Rachel, *b* 1967, — (by 2nd *m*) (*see* Ropner, Bt, *cr* 1904, colls).
Hon Lavinia Caroline, *b* (twin) 1947: *ed* Badminton Sch, and St Hugh's Coll, Oxford (MA): *m* 1971, Nicholas John Elliot Sealy, FCA, of Timber Hill, Chobham, Surrey (*see* E Chichester, colls, 1995 Edn), and has issue living, Edward John Pelham, *b* 1975, — Lucinda Clare, *b* 1977.
Hon Henrietta Jane, *b* 1951; *ed* Badminton Sch, and St Andrew's Univ (MA): *m* 1985, Tullio Luigi Giuseppe Tomba, of via Corona 40, Campoformido (UD), Italy, and has issue living, Tommaso Piercy, *b* 1987, — Francesco Piercy, *b* 1989.

AUNT LIVING (*Daughter of 1st Baron*)

Hon Joanna Elizabeth (Gable Cottage, 55 Witney St, Burford, Oxon OX18 4RZ), *b* 1923; *ed* St Paul's, and Somerville Coll, Oxford: *m* 1968, James Francis Turner.

WIDOW LIVING OF FIRST BARON

VERONICA (*Veronica, Baroness Piercy*) (Fair View House, Marton, Sinnington, York Y06 6RD), da of late John Hordley Warham: *m* 1964, as his 2nd wife, the 1st Baron Piercy, who *d* 1966.

PREDECESSORS – **(1)** WILLIAM Piercy, CBE, son of late (Augustus) Edward Piercy; *b* 1886; Economist and Financier; Chm of Industrial & Commercial Finance Corporation Ltd 1945-64, a Dir of Bank of England 1946-56, and Chm Wellcome Trust 1960-65; *cr Baron Piercy*, of Burford, co Oxford (peerage of UK) 1945: *m* 1st, 1915, Mary Louisa, OBE, who *d* 1953, da of late Hon Thomas Henry William Pelham, CB (E Chichester, colls); 2ndly, 1964, Veronica, da of John Hordley Warham; *d* 1966; *s* by his son **(2)** NICHOLAS PELHAM, 2nd Baron, *b* 1918: *m* 1944, Oonagh Lavinia, JP, who *d* 1990, da of late Maj Edward John Lake Baylay, DSO; *d* 1981; *s* by his el son **(3)** JAMES WILLIAM, 3rd Baron and present peer.

PIKE, BARONESS (Pike) (Life Baroness 1974)

IRENE MERVYN PARNICOTT PIKE, DBE, da of Ivan Samuel Pike, of Okehampton, Devon; b 16 Sept 1918; ed Hunmanby Hall, E Yorks; and Reading Univ (BA); 1939-45 War with WAAF: MP for Melton Div of Leics (C) 1956-74; Assist Postmaster-Gen 1959-63, and Joint Parl Under-Sec of State, Home Office 1963-64; Chm WRVS 1974-81; a co Councillor W Riding of Yorks 1955-57; a Dir of Watts, Blake and Bearne since 1964; Chm Broadcasting Complaints Commn 1981-85; cr Baroness Pike, of Melton, co Leicestershire (Life Baroness) 1974, and DBE (1981).

Arms – Or on a cross gules a churchwarden's staff headed of a mitre or on a chief sable a castleford fine stoneware teapot proper. Supporters – On either side a fox, that on the dexter gorged with a wreath of ivy, and that on the sinister with a wreath of rosemary proper, and each resting the interior hind foot on a portcullis or, the compartment comprising a grassy mount proper.
Residence – Hownam, Kelso, Roxburgh.

PILKINGTON, BARONY OF (Pilkington) (Extinct 1983)

SON LIVING OF LIFE BARON (By 1st marriage)

Rev Hon John Rowan, b 1932; ed Rugby, and Magdalene Coll, Camb (MA): m 1964, Celia Collison, and has issue.
Residence – 38 Main Rd, Emsworth, Hants PO10 8AU.

DAUGHTER LIVING OF LIFE BARON (By 1st marriage)

Hon Jennifer Margaret, b 1933: m 1958, Dennis Jones, of Swallow Cottage, Burbage, Leics and has issue.

PILKINGTON OF OXENFORD, BARON (Pilkington) (Life Baron 1996)

Rev PETER PILKINGTON, son of late Frank Pilkington, of Newcastle-upon-Tyne; b 5 Sept 1933; ed Dame Allan's Sch, Newcastle-upon-Tyne, Jesus Coll, Camb (BA 1955, MA 1959), and Westcott House, Cambridge; Deacon 1959, Priest 1960; Curate of Bakewell, Derbys 1959-62; Assist Master and Chaplain, Eton Coll 1962-75; Headmaster, King's Sch, Canterbury 1975-86; High Master, St Paul's Sch, London 1986-92; Hon Canon of Canterbury Cathedral 1975-90, since when Canon Emeritus; memb of Parole Board 1990-95; Chm of Broadcasting Complaints Commn 1992-95; cr Baron Pilkington of Oxenford, of West Dowlish, co Somerset (Life Baron) 1996: m 1966, Helen, who d 1997, da of Charles Wilson, of Riseholme, Lincoln, and Elleron Lodge, N Yorks, and has issue.
Residence – Oxenford House, nr Ilminster, Somerset TA19 0PP. Club – Garrick, Beefsteak.

DAUGHTERS LIVING

Hon Celia, b 1970; ed Francis Holland Sch, and Middlesex Univ.
Hon Sarah, b 1972; ed St Paul's Girls' Sch, and Manchester Univ.

PITKEATHLEY, BARONESS (Pitkeathley) (Life Baroness 1997)

JILL ELIZABETH PITKEATHLEY, OBE, da of Roland Wilfred Bisson, of St Sampson's, Guernsey; *b* 4 Jan 1940; *ed* Ladies' Coll, Guernsey, and Bristol Univ (BA 1960); Social Worker 1961-64; Voluntary Service Co-ordinator, Manchester and Essex 1970-83; Nat Consumer Cncl 1983-86; Dir Nat Cncl for Carers 1986, until merger with Assoc of Carers 1988, since when Chief Exec, Carers Nat Assoc; Memb Health Advisory Service since 1993; Vice-Pres Community Cncl for Berks since 1990; Memb RSA since 1992; Chm New Opportunities Fund since 1998; author of books on welfare, etc; cr OBE 1993, and *Baroness Pitkeathley*, of Caversham in the Royal County of Berkshire (Life Baroness) 1997: *m* 1961 (*m diss* 1978), William Pitkeathley, son of Joseph Pitkeathley, of Dudley, Worcs, and has issue.
Address – House of Lords, Westminster, SW1A 0PW

SON LIVING

Hon Simon; *b* 1964.

DAUGHTER LIVING

Hon Rachel; *b* 1966.

PITT OF HAMPSTEAD, BARONY OF (Pitt) (Extinct 1994)

SON LIVING OF LIFE BARON

Hon Bruce Michael David, *b* 1945; *ed* King Alfred Sch, Hampstead, and Univ Coll, London (LLB); Bar Gray's Inn 1970; Member Senate of Inns of Court and Bar Council 1975-76; Recorder SE Circuit since 1993. *Residence* – 6 Heath Drive, NW3. *Club* – MCC.

DAUGHTERS LIVING OF LIFE BARON

Hon Phyllis Leonora, *b* 19—.
Hon Amanda, *b* 19—.

WIDOW LIVING OF LIFE BARON

DOROTHY ELAINE (*Baroness Pitt of Hampstead*), da of Aubrey Alleyne: *m* 1943, Baron Pitt of Hampstead, who *d* 1994. *Residence* – 6 Heath Drive, NW3.

PLANT, BARONY OF (Plant) (Extinct 1986)

SONS LIVING OF LIFE BARON

Hon John Sydney Sampson (6 Swallow Croft, Leek, Staffs), *b* 1931: *m* 1953, Mary, da of John Clayton, and has issue.
Hon Christopher Victor Howe (Flat 4, 178 Dyke Rd, Brighton, E Sussex), *b* 1945: *m* 1966, Marian, da of John Parkes, and has issue.

DAUGHTER LIVING OF LIFE BARON

Hon Jennifer Edna Jane, *b* 1939: *m* 1973, Raymond John Brian Pilbeam, and has issue living, Nicholas Colin Emmerton, *b* 1962, — Sarah Jane Emmerton, *b* 1964. *Residence* –

PLANT OF HIGHFIELD, BARON (Plant) (Life Baron 1992)

RAYMOND PLANT, son of late Stanley Plant; *b* 19 March 1945; *ed* Havelock Sch, Grimsby, King's Coll, London (BA), and Hull Univ (PhD); Sr Lecturer in Philosophy Manchester Univ 1967-69, Prof of Politics Southampton Univ since 1979; Master of St Catherine's Coll, Oxford since 1994; Stevenson Lecturer Glasgow Univ 1981, Agnes Cumming Lecturer Univ Coll, Dublin 1988, Stanton Lecturer Camb Univ 1989-90 and 1990-91, Sarum Lecturer Oxford Univ 1991, Ferguson Lecturer Univ of Manchester 1994; Hon D Litt Guildhall Univ, Hon D Litt Hull Univ; Chm Labour Party Commn on Electoral Systems since 1991; author and contributor to *New Statesman and Society, The Independent, The Times,* etc; *cr Baron Plant of Highfield,* of Weelsby, co Humberside (Life Baron) 1992: *m* 1967, Katherine Sylvia, da of late Jack Dixon, and has issue.
Residence – 6 Woodview Close, Bassett, Southampton S02 8P2.

SONS LIVING

Hon Nicholas, *b* 1969
Hon Matthew, *b* 1971.
Hon Richard, *b* 1976.

PLATT, BARONY OF (Platt) (Extinct 1978) (see Platt, Bt).

PLATT OF WRITTLE, BARONESS (Platt) (Life Baroness 1981)

BERYL CATHERINE PLATT, CBE, da of Ernest Myatt; *b* 18 April 1923; *ed* Westcliffe High Sch for Girls, and Girton Coll, Camb, MA and Hon Fellow; Hon DSc City Univ, Salford, Cranfield Inst and Nottingham Trent, Hon D Univ Open Univ, Middlesex Univ and Essex Univ, Hon DEng Bradford, Hon D Tech Brunel and Loughborough, Hon LLD Cantab, Hon DSc Westminster, Hon FIMechE, FRAeS, Hon FICE, Hon FIStructE, FIGasE, Eur Ing, Hon Fellow Wales Poly, Ealing Coll of Higher Educn, UMIST, Manchester Poly, FRSA, FITD, Hon FCP, FEng, Hon Fell Women's Engineering Soc; Member of Court, Essex Univ since 1964, Cranfield Inst since 1988, and House of Lords Select Cttee on Science and Technology 1982-85, 1990-94 and since 1997; Chm Equal Opportunities Commn 1983-88, Women's Working Group of Industry Matters 1986-90 Meteorological Office Advisory Cttee since 1995; Pres Inst of Training and Development 1985-87, Camb Univ Engineers Assocn since 1987, Essex Assocn of Local Councils; Vice-Pres Parliamentary and Scientific Cttee since 1996; Patron WISE (Women into Science and Engineering), Women in Banking and Finance, Chelmsford Hospice, and Interact, Chancellor of Middlesex Univ since 1994; Liveryman of Worshipful Co of Engineers 1988 (Assistant of the Court 1996), Freeman of the City of London; DL Essex since 1983; CBE 1978; *cr Baroness Platt of Writtle,* of Writtle, co Essex (Life Baroness) 1981: *m* 1949, Stewart Sydney Platt, and has issue.

𝕬rms – Vert, four seaxes in cross their blades outwards proper hilts quillons and pommels or and as may aerofoils in saltire argent all between four plates. 𝕾upporters – *Dexter,* Perched upon the stock of an anchor a kingfisher, wings elevated and addorsed proper. *Sinister,* A lion, the wings also elevated and addorsed, supporting a patriarchal cross gules the compartment comprising a grassy mount springing therefrom founts of water proper. 𝕸otto – Love God and everyone.
Address – The House of Lords, SW1A 0PW.

SON LIVING

Hon Roland Francis (Headley House, 40 Headley Chase, Brentwood, Essex CM14 5BN), *b* 1951; FCA: *m* 1982, Louise M., yr da of Lionel Jackson, of 56 Chelmsford Rd, Shenfield, Essex, and has issue, one son and two das.

DAUGHTER LIVING

Hon Victoria Catherine, *b* 1953; MA, FCA, ATII: *m* 1984, Rhodri Davies, son of His Honour Judge John Davies, QC, and has issue, three das.

PLOWDEN, BARON (Plowden) (Life Baron 1959)

EDWIN NOEL PLOWDEN, GBE, KCB, son of late Roger H. Plowden, of Strachur Park, Argyll; *b* 6 Jan 1907; *ed* Switzerland, and Pembroke Coll, Camb (Hon Fellow); Hon DSc Pennsylvania State Univ, and Aston Univ, Hon D Litt Loughborough Univ, Visiting Fellow of Nuffield Coll, Oxford 1956-64; in Min of Economic Warfare 1939-40, in Min of Aircraft Production 1940-46 (Ch Executive and a Member of Aircraft Supply Council 1945-46); in Treasury as Ch Planning Officer and Ch of Economic Planning Board 1947-53, Vice-Chm Temporary Council Cttee of NATO 1951-52, Adviser on Atomic Energy Organisation 1953-54, and Chm UK Atomic Energy Authority 1954-59, of Cttee on Control of Public Expenditure 1959-61, of Cttee of Enquiry into Organisation of Representational Sers Overseas 1963-64, of Cttee of Enquiry into future of UK Aircraft Industry 1964-65, of Standing Advisory Cttee on Pay of Higher Civil Ser 1968-70, of Cttee of Enquiry into Structure of Electricity Supply Industry 1974-75, and of Cttee of Enquiry into CBI's aims and organisation 1974-75, Pres of Tube Investments, Ltd since 1976 (Chm 1963-76), Chm of Equity Capital for Industry Ltd 1976-83 and of Police Complaints Board 1976-81, Dep Chm Cttee of Inquiry on the Police 1977-79, Independent Chm Police Negotiating Board 1979-82, and Chm Top Salaries Review Body 1981-89 (Member 1977-81) and Pres of London Graduate Sch of Business Studies 1976-90 (Chm of Governing Body 1964-76); Dir C. Tennant, Sons & Co Ltd 1938-49, Commercial Union Assurance Co Ltd 1946-78, and Nat West Bank Ltd 1960-77; Member Ford European Advisory Council 1976-83, Internat Advisory Board SE Bank NA 1982-87, Chm CBI Cos Cttee 1976-80, Vice-Chm CBI Presidents Cttee 1977-80; *cr* KBE (Civil) 1946, KCB (Civil) 1951, GBE (Civil) 1987, and *Baron Plowden*, of Plowden, co Salop (Life Baron) 1959: *m* 1933, Dame Bridget Horatia, DBE, JP, da of late Adm Sir Herbert William Richmond, KCB (Bell, Bt, *cr* 1885), and has had issue.

Arms – Azure a fesse dancettee, the upper points terminating in fleurs-de-lys or. Crest – A buck passant sable, attired or. *Residences* – Martels Manor, Dunmow, Essex; 11 Abingdon Gdns, Abingdon Villas, W8 6BY. *Club* – Brooks's.

SONS LIVING

Hon William Julius Lowthian (49 Stockwell Park Rd, SW9), *b* 1935; *ed* Eton, King's Coll, Camb, and California Univ: *m* 1960, Veronica Mary, only da of Lieut-Col Derek Ernest Frederick Orby Gascoigne (*see* B O'Neill, 1990 Edn), and has issue living, Benedict Edmund, *b* 1963, — Luke Piers, *b* 1967, — Frances Helen, *b* 1965, — Eleanor Mary, *b* 1969.
Hon Francis John (44 Hasker St, SW3), *b* 1945; *ed* Eton, and Trin Coll, Camb: *m* 1984, Mrs Geraldine Miles, elder da of late Gerald Wickman, of Orton Longueville, Peterborough, and has issue living, George Frederick, *b* 1995.

DAUGHTERS LIVING AND DECEASED

Hon Anna Bridget, CBE, *b* 1938; *ed* Newhall, Chelmsford, and at Institute of Archæology, London Univ; CBE (Civil) 1997; *dunm* 1997.
Hon Penelope Christina (43 Lansdowne Gdns, SW8), *b* 1941; *ed* St Mary's Convent, Ascot, and New Hall, Camb: *m* 1st, 1965 (*m diss* 1975), Christopher Roper (*see* E Lovelace, colls, 1985 Edn); 2ndly, 1981, Rees T. Martin, and has issue living (by 2nd *m*), Henry, *b* 1984.

PLUMB, BARON (Plumb) (Life Baron 1987)

(CHARLES) HENRY PLUMB, son of Charles Plumb, of Ansley Warwicks, by his wife Louise, da of Henry Fisher, of Over Whitacre, Warwicks; *b* 27 March 1925; *ed* King Edward VI Sch, Nuneaton; Hon DSc Cranfield (1983); DL Warwick 1977; FRSA 1970, FRAgS 1974; Member of Council NFU since 1959, Vice Pres 1964-65, Dep Pres 1966-69, Pres 1970-79; Chm British Agricultural Council 1975-79; Member Duke of Northumberland's Cttee of Enquiry on Foot and Mouth Disease 1967-68; Pres Royal Agricultural Soc of England, etc; Pres Nat Fedn of Young Farmers' Clubs 1976-86; MEP (C) The Cotswolds 1979, Chm Agricultural Cttee 1979-82, Leader European Democratic Group 1982-87, since when Pres European Parl; Chancellor Coventry Univ since 1996; *cr* Kt 1973, and *Baron Plumb*, of Coleshill, co Warwicks (Life Baron) 1987: *m* 1947, Marjorie Dorothy, da of Thomas Victor Dunn, of Bentley, Warwicks, and has issue.
Residence – The Dairy Farm, Maxstoke, Coleshill, Warwicks B46 2QJ.

SON LIVING

Hon John Henry, *b* 1951; *ed* Solihull Sch, Wye Coll and London Univ (BSc 1973): *m* 1975, Beatrix, da of David Somoza, of Buenos Aires, Argentina, and has issue living, David Henry, *b* 1979, — Alison Ruth, *b* 1976, — Liliane, *b* 1983. *Residence* – Southfields, Coleshill, Warwicks B46 3EJ.

DAUGHTERS LIVING

Hon Elizabeth Marjorie, *b* 1948: *m* 1st, 1971 (*m diss* 1982), (John Sten) Robert Arbuthnot (*see* Arbuthnot, Bt, *cr* 1823, colls); 2ndly, 1982, Maj Anthony Holman, and has issue living (by 2nd *m*), Thomas Henry, *b* 1984, — Charles Anthony, *b* 1986. *Residence* – 9 Wilderness Mount, Seal Hollow Rd, Sevenoaks, Kent.

Hon Christine Mary, *b* 1950: *m* 1973, Benjamin John Mayo, FEng, and has issue living, Katharine Elizabeth, *b* 1977, — Sarah Louise, *b* 1979, — Stephanie Caroline, *b* 1983. *Residence* – The Garth, Kirkby Lane, Great Broughton, N Yorks.

PLUMER, VISCOUNTCY OF (Plumer) (Extinct 1944)

DAUGHTERS LIVING OF SECOND VISCOUNT

Hon (Anne) Cynthia Veronica Tempest, *b* 1921: *m* 1952, John Frederick Martyn Leapman, and has issue living, Joanna Mary Martyn, *b* 1953: *m* 1978, Colin Denis Keogh, of The Manor Farm, North Oakley, nr Basingstoke, Hants RG26 5TT, only son of J. D. Keogh, of 87 St Andrew's Rd, Hurlingham, Johannesburg, and has issue, Thomas Henri John *b* 1983, William Edward Colin *b* 1987, Katharine Emma *b* 1984, Georgina Anne *b* 1990, — Emma Hilda Martyn, *b* 1956: *m* 1982, Nicholas Richard Hunter Jones, of 69 Calbourne Rd, SW12, yst son of Col H. E. Hunter Jones, of Church Farm, Langham, Essex, and has issue living, Samuel *b* 1984, Timothy *b* 1987, Theodore *b* 1991, Rosanna *b* 1997, — Sarah Anne Martyn, *b* 1961: *m* 1987, Frederick Ellyer Cohen, only son of late Sebag Cohen, of Loge de Tisserand, Trinity, Jersey, CI, and has issue living, Harry *b* 1990, Charles *b* 1992, Emily *b* 1988, Alexandra *b* 1994. *Residence* – Highcliff, St John, Jersey.

Hon Rosemary Diana Lavinia, *b* 1929: *m* 1949, Frederick Henry Lowry-Corry (*see* F. Belmore, colls). *Residence* – Edwardstone Hall, Boxford, Suffolk.

PLUMMER OF ST MARYLEBONE, BARON (Plummer) (Life Baron 1981)

(ARTHUR) DESMOND (HERNE) PLUMMER, TD, son of late Arthur Herne Plummer; *b* 25 May 1914; *ed* Hurstpierpoint Coll, and Coll of Estate Management; JP co London, DL Greater London; Member of St Marylebone Borough Council 1952-65 (Mayor 1958-59), LCC for St Marylebone 1960-65, ILEA 1964-76, GLC for Cities of London and Westminster 1964-73 and for St Marylebone 1973-76; Opposition Leader 1966-67 and 1973-74; Leader GLC 1967-73; Member of Court, Lond Univ, 1967-77; Member of Lloyd's; Chm Horserace Betting Levy Board 1974-82, Epsom and Walton Downs Training Grounds Man Board 1974-82 and National Stud 1975-82; Pres Portman Building Soc since 1990, London Anglers' Assocn since 1976, Thames Angling Preservation Soc since 1970, and Metropolitan Assocn of Building Societies 1983-89; KStJ 1986 FAI; FRICS; FRSA; served 1939-46 with RE, Lt-Col (Temp); *cr* Knt 1971, and *Baron Plummer of St Marylebone*, in the City of Westminster (Life Baron) 1981: *m* 1941, Ella Margaret, who *d* 1998, da of Albert Holloway, and has issue.

ⁿArms – Barry wavy argent and azure on a chief vert three stirrups argent. Crest – On the battlements of a tower proper two surveyor's ranging rods in saltire compony argent and gules enfiling a stirrup argent. Supporters – Two herons proper standing on a grassy mount and extending the inner leg above a portcullis chained gold and set amid madonna lilies growing from each mount proper. Motto – Erectus non elatus
Residence – 4 The Lane, Marlborough Place, St John's Wood, NW8 OPN *Clubs* – Carlton, RAC and MCC.

DAUGHTER LIVING

Hon Sally Jane PLUMMER, *b* 19—; has retained her maiden name: *m* 1991, Richard F. Lowe, son of late W. Lowe, of Danehill, W Sussex

Plumptre, family name of Baron FitzWalter.

PLUNKET, BARON (Plunket) (Baron UK 1827)

Quick, without impetuosity

ROBIN RATHMORE PLUNKET, 8th Baron, *b* 3 Dec 1925; *s* 1975; *ed* Eton; late Capt Rifle Bde: *m* 1951, Jennifer Bailey, da of Bailey Southwell, of Crocodile Leap Farm, Olivenhoutpoort, S Africa.

Arms – Sable, a bend between in sinister chief a tower and in dexter base a portcullis, all or. **Crest** – A horse passant argent, charged on the side, with a portcullis sable. **Supporters** – *Dexter*, an antelope or; *sinister*, a horse argent; each gorged with a collar, and pendent therefrom by a chain a portcullis sable.
Residences – Rathmore, Chimanimani, Zimbabwe; 39 Lansdowne Gdns, SW8.

BROTHER LIVING

Hon SHAUN ALBERT FREDERICK SHERIDAN (11 Ennismore Gdns, SW7. *Club* – White's), *b* 5 April 1931; *ed* Eton and L'Institut de Touraine; formerly Lt Irish Gds, and Dist Comdt, Kenya Police (Reserve); a Fellow of Institute of Directors: *m* 1st, 1961 (*m diss* 1979), Judith Ann, el da of late Gerard Patrick Power of Lapworth, Warwickshire; 2ndly, 1980, Elisabeth, who *d* 1986, da of late Helge Drangel, of Stockholm, and formerly wife of late Thomas de Sancha; 3rdly, 1989, Andrea Barbara, da of late Andre Milos, of Budapest, and formerly wife of Sheldon Reynolds, and has issue living (by 1st *m*), Tyrone Shaun Terence, *b* 1966; a Page of Honour to HM The Queen (ret 1979), — Loelia Dorothée Alexandra, *b* 1963: *m* 1999, Dr George Santis, 2nd son of Kypros Santis, of Larnaca, Cyprus.

COLLATERAL BRANCHES LIVING

Issue of late Flight-Lieut Hon Brinsley Sheridan Bushe Plunket, RAF Vol Reserve, 2nd son of 5th Baron, *b* 1903, *d* on active ser 1941: *m* 1927 (*m diss* 1940), Aileen Sibell Mary PLUNKET (she *m* 2ndly, 1956 (*m diss* 1965), Valerian Stux-Rybar, who *d* 1990, resumed the surname of Plunket, and *d* 1999), da of late Hon Arthur Ernest Guinness (*see* E Iveagh, colls, 1995 Edn):—
Doon Aileen (*Dowager Countess Granville*), 1931: *m* 1958, 5th Earl Granville, MC, who *d* 1996. *Residence* – Callernish, N Uist, Western Isles.

Grandchildren of late David Pierce Conyngham Plunket, elder son of late Most Rev Hon Benjamin John Plunket, DD (infra):—
Issue of late Simon Patrick Conyngham Plunket, Lt 12th Lancers, *b* 1932, *d* 1968: *m* 1955, Susan Diana (who *m* 2ndly, 1972, Martin John Faber Morrison; and 3rdly, 1979, Maj Richard Harden, of Hunters Hill Farm, Nether Silton, nr Thirsk, N Yorks), da of late Robert Vivian Fairney, of Hartley End House, Hartley Wintney, Hants:—
Piers Robert Conyngham, *b* 1959: *m* 1989, Cordelia M., da of Colin Hart, of Charlbury, Oxon, and of Hon Mrs Patrick Penny, and has issue living, Simon Tuam Conyngham, *b* 1991, — Oliver David Conyngham, *b* 1994. —— Sara Doon, *b* 1957: *m* 1979, Luca Matteo Cumani, son of Sergio Cumani, of Milan, and has issue living, Matthew Sergio Simon, *b* 1981, — Francesca Deepsea, *b* 1983.

Issue of late David Archer Lee Plunket, *b* 1936, *d* 1997: *m* 1964, Philippa Susan (Flat 2, 57 Sinclair Rd, W14 0NR), yr da of late Capt Brian St George Daly, Lancashire Fus, of Templeogue House, co Dublin:—
Emma Elizabeth Lee, *b* 1966. —— Arabella Susan, *b* 1969: *m* 1994, Richard H. Bather, son of John Bather, of Longford Grange, Derbys, and has issue living, Thomas David, *b* 1996, — Jack Herbert, *b* 1998.

Grandson of late Most Rev Hon Benjamin John Plunket, DD, Bishop of Meath 1919-25, 2nd son of 4th Baron:—
Issue of late Benjamin William Alan Plunket, MVO, *b* 1912, *d* 1981: *m* 1943, Pamela, who *d* 1990, da of Charles Whatley, of Burderop, Swindon:—
Charles Patrick Benjamin, MBE, *b* 1947; *ed* Harrow; Maj; served NI (MBE (Mil) 1994): *m* 1990, Fiona, yr da of Gerald James, of Aston Rowant, Oxfordshire, and has issue living, Emily Lee, *b* 1991, — Olivia Kate, *b* 1993. *Residence* – Belle Isle, Lisbellaw, co Fermanagh.

Granddaughter of late Hon Charles Bushe Plunket, 2nd son of 3rd Baron:—
Issue of late David Darley Donnybrook Plunket, *b* 1869, *d* 1956: *m* 1900, Helen Rosanna, who *d* 1951, da of late Thomas Greene, of 49 St Stephen's Green, Dublin:—
Rosamond Sylvia, *b* 1908: *m* 1939, Air Commodore Henry Sam Francis Temple Jerrard, CBE, RAF, who *d* 1961, and has issue living, David Grattan (Hillside, Newcourt Av, Bray, co Wicklow), *b* 1944: *m* 1969, Noreen, da of Alphonsus Reginald Timothy Nolan, of Alvenor, Meath Rd, Bray, co Wicklow, — Helen Frances, *b* 1941: *m* 1962, John Patrick Roe. *Residence* – Hillside, Newcourt Av, Bray, co Wicklow.

Grandson of late Hon Arthur Cecil Crampton Plunket, 4th son of 3rd Baron:—
Issue of late Henry Coote Lifford Plunket, *b* 1875, *d* 1955: *m* 1912, Emily Evelyn Marjorie, who *d* 1968, da of late Severne Rowlands, of Ipswich, Queensland:—
Arthur Robert Lifford, *b* 1914: *m* 1938, Elies, da of Hugo Krieger, of Prague. *Residence* – 130 Sevenoaks Rd, Borkwood Park, Orpington, Kent.

PREDECESSORS – **(1)** WILLIAM CONYNGHAM Plunket, MP for Charlemont in Irish Parliament 1798-1800, and for Dublin Univ 1812-27, Ch Justice of the Common Pleas in Ireland 1827-30, and Lord Chancellor of Ireland 1830-34 and 1835-41; *cr Baron Plunket*, of Newtown, co Cork (peerage of United Kingdom) 1827; *d* 1854; *s* by his el son **(2)** THOMAS SPAN, DD, 2nd Baron; was Lord Bishop of Tuam, Killala and Achonry 1839-66; *s* by his brother **(3)** JOHN, QC, 3rd Baron; *b* 1793: *m* 1824, Charlotte, who *d* 1886, da of Rt Hon Charles Kendal Bushe, Lord Ch Justice of Ireland; *d* 1871; *s* by his son **(4)** *Most Rev* WILLIAM CONYNGHAM, DD, 4th Baron, *b* 1828; Bishop of Meath 1876-84 and Archbishop of Dublin 1884-97: *m* 1863, Anne Lee, who *d* 1889, da of Sir Benjamin Lee Guinness, 1st Bt, and sister of 1st Barons Ardilaun and Iveagh; *d* 1897; *s* by his el son **(5)** WILLIAM LEE, GCMG, KCVO, KBE, 5th Baron, *b* 1864; Gov of New Zealand 1904-10; Bore Standard of the Dominion of New Zealand at Coronation of King George V 1911: *m* 1894, Lady Victoria Alexandrina Hamilton-Temple-Blackwood, who *d* 1968, da of 1st Marquess of Dufferin and Ava; *d* 1920, *s* by his el son **(6)** TERENCE CONYNGHAM, 6th Baron; *b* 1899; Lt Rifle Brig (Reserve); European War 1918: *m* 1922, Dorothé Mabel, who *d* 1938, da of late Joseph Lewis, and widow of Capt Jack Barnato, RAF; *d* 1938: *s* by his el son **(7)** PATRICK TERENCE WILLIAM SPAN, KCVO; 7th Baron; *b* 1923; Lt-Col Irish Gds; Equerry to King George VI 1948-52 and to Queen Elizabeth II 1952-75; Dep Master of the Household 1954-75; *d* 1975; *s* by his brother ROBIN RATHMORE, 8th Baron and present peer.

Plunkett, family name of Baron Dunsany.

Plunkett, family name of Baron Louth.

PLURENDEN, BARONY OF (Sternberg) (Extinct 1978)

DAUGHTERS LIVING OF LIFE BARON

Hon Rosanne Monica Michelle STERNBERG, *b* 1960; has retained her maiden name: *m* 19—, Robert William Kenneth Harris, elder son of K. A. Harris, of Lanwardleigh, Devon, and has issue living, Jessica Rosanne, *b* 1990.
Hon Francesca Nicola, *b* 1962: *m* 1989, Douglas G. Allen, eldest son of B. G. Allen, of Scott City, Kansas, USA.

WIDOW LIVING OF LIFE BARON

DOROTHEE MONICA (*Baroness Plurenden*) (Lidostrasse 63, 6314 Unterägeri, Switzerland), da of Maj Robert Bateman Prust, OBE, of Vancouver, BC, Canada: *m* 1951, Baron Plurenden (Life Baron), who *d* 1978.

PLYMOUTH, EARL OF (Windsor-Clive) (Baron E 1529, Earl UK 1905)

I trust in God

OTHER ROBERT IVOR WINDSOR-CLIVE, 3rd Earl; *b* 9 Oct 1923; *s* 1943; *ed* Eton, and Trin Coll, Camb; late Capt Coldstream Guards; is a KStJ, a DL Shropshire, and an FRSA: *m* 1950, Caroline Helen, only da of Edward Rice, of Dane Court, Eastry, Kent, and has issue.

Arms – Quarterly: 1st and 4th argent, on a fesse sable, three mullets or, *Clive*; 2nd and 3rd gules, a saltire argent, between twelve cross crosslets or, *Windsor*. **Crest** – 1st, a griffin statant argent, gorged with a ducal crown gules; 2nd, a stag's head at gaze, couped at the neck argent, attired or. **Supporters** – On either side an unicorn argent, horned, maned, and hoofed or.
Residences – The Stables, Oakly Park, Ludlow, Shropshire; 48 Burton Court, SW3.

SONS LIVING

IVOR EDWARD OTHER (*Viscount Windsor*) (Oakly Park, Ludlow, Shropshire; 6 Oakley St, SW3), *b* 19 Nov 1951; *ed* Harrow: *m* 1979, Caroline Anne, da of Frederick Nettlefold (*see* Scarsdale, V), and has issue:—

     SONS LIVING — *Hon* ROBERT OTHER IVOR, *b* 25 March 1981, — *Hon* Frederick John Richard, *b* 1983, — *Hon* Edward, *b* 1994.
     DAUGHTER LIVING — *Hon* India Harriet, *b* 1988.

Hon Simon Percy, *b* 1956; *ed* Harrow.
Hon David Justin (29 Cheyne Court, Flood St, SW3), *b* 1960: *ed* Harrow, and RAC Cirencester; Commodity Broker: *m* 1986, Camilla Jane, eldest da of John Squire, of Marbella, Spain, and of Mrs John Ticehurst, of 43 Smith Terr, SW3, and has issue living, Alexander, *b* 1993.

DAUGHTER LIVING

Lady Emma WINDSOR CLIVE, *b* 1954; has resumed her maiden name: *m* 1975 (*m diss* 1992), Robert Arthur Smith-Dorrien-Smith, and has issue living, Adam Robert, *b* 1978, — Michael Horace, *b* 1987, — Frances Marcella, *b* 1980. *Residence* – The Granary, Yeabridge, S Petherton, Som TA13 5LW.

BROTHER LIVING

Hon Richard Archer Alan, *b* 1928; *ed* Eton, and Trin Coll, Camb; late Lieut RA; Chm of Bayfine Ltd 1973-85: *m* 1st, 1955 (*m diss* 1968), Joanna Mary, el da of Edward Corbet Woodall, OBE (Crawley-Boevey, Bt colls); 2ndly, 1968, Hon (Mary) Alice Chancellor, da of 4th Baron Hylton, and has issue living (by 1st *m*), Stephen Miles, *b* 1956; *ed* Eton, — Cathryn Harriet, *b* 1958: *m* 1983, Thomas P. Macfarlane, son of late Craig Macfarlane, and has issue living, Cosmo *b* 1987, Ivo *b* 1988, Pascoe Quintus *b* 1996, Rose *b* 1990, Jessie *b* 1994, — (by 2nd *m*) Nell, *b* 1974. *Residence* – Combe, Nettlecombe, Taunton, Somerset.

SISTERS LIVING

Lady Clarissa, *b* 1931: *m* 1953, Major Keith Maclean Forbes Egleston, late Rifle Bde, of 7 Ernest Gdns, W4, and has issue living, Hugo Vivyan, *b* 1955; *ed* Eton: *m* 1996, Caroline, da of Arthur Clements, of Weybridge, Surrey, and has issue living, Suzannah Olivia *b* 1998, — Sarah Caroline, *b* 1956, — Harriet Gilian, *b* 1962: *m* 1988, Simon Richard Alsop, only son of B. G. P. Alsop, of Ashtead, Surrey, and has issue living, George Richard Percy *b* 1996, Thomas Ivor Gilbert *b* 1998.
Lady Rosula Caroline, *b* 1935; OStJ: *m* 1962, Maj Sir Alan Glyn, ERD, who *d* 1998, of 17 Cadogan Place, SW1X 9SA, late Royal Horse Guards, MP for Clapham Division of Wandsworth 1959-64 and for Berkshire Division of Windsor and Windsor and Maidenhead 1970-92, son of late John Paul Glyn, RHG, and has issue living, Mary Caroline, *b* 1963: *m* 1993, Capt Adrian John Weale, son of Dr K. E. Weale, of Elmwood Rd, Chiswick, W4 and has issue living, Robert Kenneth *b* 1994, Ivo Alan *b* 1996, — Anne Serena, *b* 1964.

COLLATERAL BRANCHES LIVING (*In remainder to Barony of Windsor only*)

Issue of late Lady Gillian Mary Windsor-Clive, da of 2nd Earl, *b* 1922, *d* 1961: *m* 1st, 1941 (*m diss* 1947), Wilfred Wooller, Lieut RA, who *d* 1997; 2ndly, 1947, Lieut Albertus Jacobus de Haan, DFC (Netherlands), Croix de Guerre (Belgium), R Netherlands Navy, who *d* 1991:—
(By 2nd *m*) Julian Jan Ivor (Southfield House, Forthampton, Glos GL19 4RA), *b* 1948; *ed* Gresham's Sch, Holt; FCA, ATII: *m* 1972, Juliet Clare, da of late Maj Henry Benjamin Van der Gucht, MC (*see* Strickland-Constable, Bt, colls) and has issue living, Luke Archer, *b* 1973; *ed* Eton, Cheltenham, and Reading Univ, — Tom Julian, *b* 1976; *ed* Cheltenham, and Brighton Univ, — Sophia Gilian, *b* 1979; *ed* Malvern Girls' Coll, and Liverpool Univ. ——— Archer Anthony (Cookeridge Farm, Bromfield, Ludlow, Shropshire), *b* 1950; *ed* Gresham's Sch, Holt. *m* 1st, 1975 (*m diss* 1987), Amanda Ball; 2ndly, 1987, Vivien Whittall, and has issue living (by 1st *m*), Toby Archer, *b* 1976, — Laura Mary Emma, *b* 1979, — (by 2nd *m*) Hugo Julian Archer, *b* 1992, — Frances Catherine, *b* 1988, — Hannah Gillian, *b* (twin) 1988. ——— Andrew David (Thameside Cottage, Longworth, Oxon), *b* 1954; *ed* Northease Manor, Lewes: *m* 1981, Emma Katherine, yst da of Cdr Christopher William Stuart Dreyer, DSO, DSC, and has issue living, Nicholas Jacobus, *b* 1986, — Alice Olivia, *b* 1991. ——— Valentine Nicholas, *b* 1956; *ed* Stanbridge Earls Sch: *m* 1985, Virginia Ann, da of Bruce Balentyne Kerr, and has issue living, Alexander Bruce, *b* 1988, — Melissa Gilian, *b* 1990.

Grandsons of late Lt-Col Hon George Herbert Windsor Windsor-Clive, son of late Harriet, Baroness Windsor:—

Issue of late Lt-Col George Windsor-Clive, CMG, *b* 1878, *d* 1968: *m* 1912, Sidney Guendolen, who *d* 1935, da of Charles Carmichael Lacaita, of Selham, Sussex (Doyle, Bt):—

Robert Charles (The Pleck, Ashford Carbonel, Ludlow, Shropshire SY8 4DB), *b* 1919; *ed* Eton, and RMC; Brig (ret) late Coldm Gds; 1939-45 War (wounded despatches): *m* 1949, Olive Mary, yr da of Lt-Col Francis Longueville, DSO, MC, and has issue living, George Francis (Balak Farm, Marridge Hill, Ramsbury, Wilts), *b* 1954; *ed* Eton, and RAC Cirencester; late Lt Coldm Gds, late Maj (TA) Royal Yeo; Man Dir Windsor Clive Int Ltd: *m* 1988, Anna Georgina, da of Antony Noel Gordon Leaf (*see* Farquhar, Bt, colls), and has issue living, Thomas Robert *b* 1992, John Antony *b* 1993, — Annabel Mary, *b* 1951: *m* 1979, Mark Savage, of Castlett Farm Cottage, Guiting Power, Cheltenham, Glos, son of late G. A. R. Savage, and has issue living, Gabriel Frances *b* 1984, Victoria Mary *b* 1987. —— Francis Archer (Toneys, Bromsberrow, nr Ledbury, Herefordshire), *b* 1922; *ed* Eton; late Capt Coldm Gds; 1939-45 War (wounded, despatches): *m* 1945, Anne Gertrude, el da of late Lt-Col Francis Longueville, DSO, MC, and has had issue, Edward Archer (54 Oxberry Av, SW6), *b* 1946; *ed* Ampleforth, and RMA Sandhurst; Maj late Coldm Gds: *m* 1982, Grania M. S., da of M. E. F. S. FitzGerald, of Hill Place, Haywards Heath, Sussex, and has issue living, Robert *b* 1985, Sophie Anne *b* 1983, — Robert Ivor (Cefn Ceist, Michaelchurch, Escley, Herefordshire), *b* 1950; *ed* Ampleforth, and RAC Cirencester: *m* 1980 (*m diss* 1990), Aricelli Romero, and has issue living, Francisco Alexis *b* 1982, Ana Willow *b* 1984, — Other John (Oaklands, Whiteleaved Oak, Bromsberrow, nr Ledbury), *b* 1958; *ed* Ampleforth, and RMA Sandhurst; Maj Coldm Gds, — William Henry (Bury Court, Redmarley, Glos), *b* 1960; *ed* Belmont Abbey, and RAC Cirencester: *m* 1989, Jane, da of J. R. Lawther, of Little Arley, Birtsmorton, nr Malvern, Worcs, and has issue living, Jasper Charles *b* 1998, Harriet Ann *b* 1990, Phoebe Jane *b* 1993, — Frances Anne, *b* 1948; BEd (Cantab): *m* 1972, Maj Andrew Stow, RE, of Perrins Court, Bromsberrow, nr Ledbury, Herefordshire, and *d* 1992, leaving issue, Catherine Mary *b* 1974, Isobel Anne *b* 1976, Elizabeth Rose (twin) *b* 1976. —— Everard Ivor (The Leys, Stoke Bliss, Tenbury Wells, Worcs), *b* 1925; *ed* Eton; late Col Coldm Gds; 1939-45 War.

PREDECESSORS – **(1)** *Sir* ANDREWS Windsor, KB, distinguished himself in the French wars of Henry VIII, and was made a Knight Banneret at the battle of the Spurs 1513; summoned to Parliament of England as *Baron Windsor*, of Stanwell, co Bucks 1529; *d* 1543; *s* by his son **(2)** WILLIAM, KB, 2nd Baron; *d* 1558; *s* by his son **(3)** EDWARD, 3rd Baron; distinguished himself at St Quentin, and in 1566 entertained Queen Elizabeth at his seat at Bradenham; *d* 1574; *s* by his el son **(4)** FREDERICK, 4th Baron; *d* unmarried 1585; *s* by his brother **(5)** HENRY, 5th Baron; *d* 1605: *s* by his son **(6)** THOMAS, 6th Baron; was a Rear-Adm; *dsp* 1642; *s* by his nephew **(7)** THOMAS Windsor-Hickman, PC, 7th Baron, son of Hon Elizabeth Windsor by her marriage with Dixie Hickman, of Kew; assumed the additional surname of Windsor; commanded a Regt of Horse at Naseby 1646; was Lord-Lieut of Worcestershire, and Gov of Jamaica 1661-2; *cr Earl of Plymouth* (peerage of England) 1682; *d* 1687; *s* by his grandson **(8)** OTHER, 2nd Earl; *d* 1727; *s* by his son **(9)** OTHER, 3rd Earl; *d* 1732; *s* by his son **(10)** OTHER LEWIS, 4th Earl; was Custos Rotulorum of cos Flint, Glamorgan, and Cheshire; *d* 1777; *s* by his son **(11)** OTHER HICKMAN, 5th Earl; *d* 1799; *s* by his son **(12)** OTHER ARCHER, 6th Earl; *dsp* 1833, when the Barony of Windsor became abeyant between his sisters Maria, wife of 2nd Marquess of Downshire, and Harriet, wife of Hon Robert Henry Clive (E Powis), and the earldom reverted to his uncle **(13)** ANDREWS, 7th Earl; *d* unmarried 1837; *s* by his brother **(14)** HENRY, 8th Earl; *dsp* 1843, when the earldom became extinct. In 1855 the abeyance of the Barony of Windsor was terminated in favour of **(15)** HARRIET Clive (ante); *b* 1797; assumed in 1855 by Roy licence the additional surname of Windsor: *m* 1819, Hon Robert Henry Clive, MP, 2nd son of 1st Earl of Powis; *d* 1869; *s* by her grandson **(16)** ROBERT GEORGE Windsor-Clive, GBE, CB, PC, 1st Earl, only son of Hon Robert, MP, by Lady Mary Selina Louisa Bridgeman, da of 2nd Earl of Bradford; *b* 1857; Lord-Lieut of Glamorganshire 1890-1923; Paymaster-Gen 1891-2, and 1st Commr of Works 1902-5; *cr Viscount Windsor*, of St Fagans, co Glamorgan, and *Earl of Plymouth*, in co Devon (peerage of United Kingdom) 1905: *m* 1883, Alberta Victoria Sarah Caroline, who *d* 1944, da of late Rt Hon Sir Augustus Berkeley Paget, PC, GCB; *d* 1923; *s* by his son **(17)** IVOR MILES, PC, 2nd Earl; *b* 1889; was Parliamentary Private Sec (unpaid) to Sec of State for Home Depart (Rt Hon W. C. Bridgeman, MP), 1922, and Under-Sec of State for Dominion Affairs Jan to June 1929; became Parliamentary Sec to Min of Transport (in National Govt) Nov 1931, and Parliamentary Under-Sec, Colonial Office Sept 1932; Parliamentary Under-Sec, Foreign Office July 1936; Hon Freeman of Cardiff 1936; elected Pro-Chancellor of Univ of Wales 1941; bore Standard of Wales at Coronation of King George VI; sat as MP for Shropshire, Ludlow Div (C) Jan 1922 to Mar 1923: *m* 1921, Lady Irene Corona Charteris, who *d* 1989, da of 7th Earl of Wemyss; *d* 1943; *s* by his son **(18)** OTHER ROBERT IVOR, 3rd Earl and present peer; also Baron Windsor, and Viscount Windsor.

Pollington, Viscount; son of Earl of Mexborough.

Pollock, family name of Viscount Hanworth.

POLTIMORE, BARON (Bampfylde) (Baron UK 1831, Bt E 1641)

MARK COPLESTONE BAMPFYLDE, 7th Baron, and 12th Baronet; *b* 8 June 1957; *s* 1978; *ed* Radley: *m* 1982, Sally Anne, da of Dr Norman Miles, of Southwell, Notts, and has issue.

Arms – Or, on a bend gules, three mullets argent. Crest – A lion's head erased sable ducally crowned or. Supporters – Two lions reguardant, sable, ducally crowned gules, gorged with a collar gemelle or, and pendant therefrom an escutcheon of the arms of Bampfylde.
Residence – North Hidden Farm, Hungerford, Berks RG17 0PY.

To rejoice in the Lord

SONS LIVING

Hon HENRY ANTHONY WARWICK, *b* 3 June 1985.
Hon Oliver Hugh Coplestone, *b* 1987.

DAUGHTER LIVING

Hon Lara Fiona Brita, *b* 1990.

SISTER LIVING

Christine Margaret Hermione, *b* 1948: *m* 1st, 1970 (*m diss* 1977), Peter William Denby Roberts (*see* Roberts, Bt, colls, cr 1909); 2ndly, 1977, Patrick Joseph Scott Plummer, of Mainhouse, Kelso, Roxburghshire (*see* B Kinross, 1995 Edn), and has issue living (by 1st *m*) (*see* Roberts, Bt, cr 1909, colls), — (by 2nd *m*) Anthony Guy, *b* 1978.

UNCLE LIVING (*son of 6th Baron*)

Hon David Cecil Warwick (Coombe Lea, Malmesbury, Wilts), *b* 1924; *ed* Eton; late Capt KRRC, 1939-45 War (wounded): *m* 1950, Jean Margaret, da of late Lt-Col Patrick Kinloch Campbell, and has issue living, Michael Hugh Warwick (Tower Farm Cottage, Towerhead Rd, Banwell, N Somerset BS29 6PQ), *b* 1951; *ed* Milton Abbey; late Capt Queen's Own Hus: *m* 1981, Sarah Fenella, da of Cdr Michael Edward St Quintin Wall, RN, of Ivy House, Lambourn, Berks RG16 7PB (*see* B de Mauley, colls), and has issue living, Edward David Warwick *b* 1986, Laura Margaret *b* 1989, — Richard Ian David (31 Fernhurst Rd, SW6 7JN), *b* 1953; *ed* Milton Abbey; late Capt 15th/19th R Hus: *m* 1st, 1980 (*m diss* 1989), Sara, da of late Maj Kenneth Spicer Few, of Cambridge; 2ndly, 1990, Charlotte Mary, yr da of late Lt-Col John Monsell Christian, MC, and formerly wife of John Angus Harcourt Gold (*see* By Trent), and has issue living (by 2nd *m*) Camilla *b* 1994, — John Spencer Warwick (225 Main St, Groton, MA 01450, USA), *b* 1960; *ed* Radley, and Bristol Univ; MBA Cranfield: *m* 1990, Mrs Nicola Duffain, yr da of Sir Charles Henry McLeod, 3rd Bt.

MOTHER LIVING

Brita Yvonne (Stable Cottage, Donnington Grove, Newbury, Berks), only da of late Baron (Rudolph) Cederström (*see* B De Ramsey, 1972-73 Edn): *m* 1st, 1947, Capt Hon Anthony Gerard Hugh Bampfylde, who *d* 1969; 2ndly 1975, Guy Elmes, who *d* 1998, and has issue by 1st *m*.

COLLATERAL BRANCHES LIVING

Granddaughter of late Hon Charles Warwick Bampfylde, 2nd son of 2nd Baron:—
Issue of late Richard Warwick Bampfylde, *b* 1903, *d* 1942: *m* 1932, Ethe (who *m* 2ndly, 19—, Joseph Sweeney), da of late Mauris Edwards:—
Sonya, *b* 1937: *m* 1959, Ronald Patrick Trevor Lyttle. *Residence* – 1070A Avenue Rd, Toronto 12, Ontario, Canada.

Issue of late Hon Francis Warwick Bampfylde, 3rd son of 2nd Baron, *b* 1885, *d* 1940: *m* 1911, Margaret Harriet, who *d* 1968, da of late Robert Martin, of Belfast:—
Caroline Warwick, *b* 1920. *m* 1942 (*m diss* 1951), Wing-Cdr Dean Lenthal Swift, Roy Australian Air Force; 2ndly, 1951 (*m diss* 1984), Edward Foster James, CMG, OBE, HM Foreign Ser, and has issue living, (by 2nd *m*) David Peter (18 Girdlers Rd, W14 0PU), *b* 1954, — Susan Alexandra Caroline, *b* 1952; HM Foreign Ser; *m* 1st, 1979 (*m diss* 1982), Timothy Ison; 2ndly, 1996, Robert Marshall, of 3 Firview, Liphook, Hants GU30 7JD, — Penelope Sarah (twin), *b* 1954: *m* 1981, Christopher Wyndham Hume Stewart-Moore, of 71 Milson Rd, W14 0LH (*see* Llewellyn, Bt, cr 1922, 1995 Edn), and has issue living Henry Wyndham Hume *b* 1983, Eliza Caroline Clare *b* 1987. *Residence* – Springfield House, W Clandon, Surrey.

PREDECESSORS – (1) JOHN Bampfylde; MP for Penryn 1640; *cr a Baronet* 1641; *s* by his son (2) Sir COPLESTONE, 2nd Bt; *d* 1691; *s* by his grandson (3) Sir COPLESTONE WARWICK, 3rd Bt; MP for Exeter and Devon; *d* 1727; *s* by his son (4) Sir RICHARD WARWICK, 4th Bt; MP for Devon; *d* 1776; *s* by his son (5) Sir CHARLES WARWICK, DCL, 5th Bt; MP for Exeter; was assassinated 1823; *s* by his son (6) Sir GEORGE, 6th Bt; *b* 1786; was Vice-Lieut of Devon, and a Lord-in-Waiting to Queen Victoria; *cr Baron Poltimore* of Poltimore, co Devon (peerage of United Kingdom) 1831: *m* 2ndly, 1836, Caroline, da of Gen Frederick William Buller; *d* 1858; *s* by his son (7) AUGUSTUS FREDERICK GEORGE WARWICK, PC, 2nd Baron; *b* 1837; Treasurer of Queen Victoria's Household 1872-4: *m* 1858, Florence Sara Wilhelmine, who *d* 1909, da of late Richard Brinsley Sheridan, of Frampton Court, Dorset; *d* 1908; *s* by his son (8) COPLESTONE RICHARD GEORGE WARWICK, 3rd Baron; *b* 1859: *m* 1881, Hon Margaret Harriet Beaumont, who *d* 1931, da of 1st Baron Allendale; *d* 1918; *s* by his el son (9) GEORGE WENTWORTH WARWICK, 4th Baron, *b* 1882: *m* 1st, 1910, Cynthia Rachel, who *d* 1961, da of late Hon Gerald William Lascelles (E Harewood, colls); 2ndly, 1962, Barbara Pitcairn (WALKER), who *d* 1969, da of Peter Nicol, of Kirkintilloch; *d* 1965, *s* by his brother (10) ARTHUR BLACKETT WARWICK, 5th Baron, *b* 1883: *m* 1st, 1916,

Catharine Frances Graham, who *d* 1938, da of late Gen Hon Sir David Macdowell Fraser, GCB (L Saltoun, colls); 2ndly, 1939 (*m diss* 1948), Mrs Mabel Violet Blanche Meyrick, da of late Col Arthur Hill Sandys Montgomerie, of Grey Abbey, co Down; *d* 1967, *s* by his brother (11) HUGH DE BURGH WARWICK, 6th Baron; *b* 1888: *m* 1918, Margaret Mary, who *d* 1981, da of 4th Marquis de la Pasture (*cr* France 1768); *d* 1978, *s* by his grandson (12) MARK COPLESTONE (son of late Capt Hon Anthony Gerard Hugh Bampfylde, el son of 6th Baron), 7th Baron and present peer.

POLWARTH, LORD (Hepburne-Scott (Lord S 1690)
(Name pronounced "Hebburn-Scott")

The moon will replenish her horns

FIDES · PROBATA · CORONAT

Approved faith crowns

HENRY ALEXANDER HEPBURNE-SCOTT, TD, 10th Lord; *b* 17 Nov 1916; *s* 1944; *ed* Eton, and King's Coll, Camb (MA); Hon LLD, St Andrews, Aberdeen, Hon DLitt, Heriot Watt; D Univ Stirling; FRSE; FRSA, Hon FRIAS; a Representative Peer for Scotland 1945-63; a Member of Queen's Body Guard for Scotland (Royal Company of Archers), Vice-Lord Lt Borders Region (Roxburgh, Ettrick and Lauderdale); a partner in the firm of Chiene & Tait, chartered accountants 1950-68; Chm Scottish Council (Development & Industry) 1956-66 (Pres 1966-72), and General Accident Insurance Gp 1968-72; Min of State Scottish Office 1972-74; Chancellor Aberdeen Univ 1966-86; a Dir of Bank of Scotland 1950-71 and 1974-87 (Gov 1968-72) of ICI Ltd 1969-72 and 1974-81; a Dir of Canadian Pacific Ltd 1975-86, Sun Life Assurance Co of Canada 1975-84, Halliburton Co 1974-87, The Weir Group Ltd, and Commonwealth Development Finance Co Ltd; Member Franco-British Council, Chm Scottish Forestry Trust since 1987, Member House of Lords Select Cttee on Overseas Trade 1984-85; 1939-45 War as Capt Lothians and Border Horse: *m* 1st, 1943 (*m diss* 1969), Caroline Margaret, who *d* 1982, da of late Capt Robert Athole Hay (*see* Hay, Bt, colls, *cr* 1635, 1980 Edn); 2ndly, 1969, Jean, da of late Adm Sir Angus Edward Malise Bontine Cunninghame Graham of Gartmore and of Ardoch, KBE, CB, and formerly wife of Charles Eliot Jauncey, QC (later Lord Jauncey of Tullichettle, Life Baron), and has issue by 1st *m*.

Arms – Quarterly, 1st and 4th grand quarters quartered; 1st, vert, a lion rampant argent *Hume*; 2nd, argent, three papingoes vert *Pepdie*; 3rd, gules; three piles engrailed argent *Polwarth*; 4th, argent, a cross engrailed azure *St Clair of Herdmanston*, over all on an escutcheon azure, an orange with the stalk erect, slipped proper, and over it an Imperial Crown; 2nd grand quarter or, two mullets and a crescent in base azure *Scott of Harden*; 3rd grand quarter quartered; 1st and 4th gules, on a chevron argent a rose between two lioncels combatant of the first *Hepburne of Humbie*; 2nd and 3rd argent, three dock leaves vert *Foulis* **Crest** – 1st, a lady richly attired holding in her dexter hand the sun and in her sinister a half-moon all proper *Scott of Harden*; 2nd issuing out of a man's heart, or, an arm from the elbow proper, brandishing a scimitar of steel, with cross and pommel of gold, *Polwarth*; 3rd an oak tree proper, and a horse passant argent, saddled and bridled gules *Hepburne of Humbie* **Supporters** – *Dexter*, a lion rampant reguardant argent, lanugéd gules; *sinister*, a mermaid — holding in her sinister hand and resting on her shoulder a mirror all proper.
Residence – Wellfield Parva, Hawkchurch, Axminster, Devon EX13 5UT. *Clubs* – Brooks's, Pratt's, New (Edinburgh).

SON LIVING (*By 1st marriage*)

Hon ANDREW WALTER (*Master of Polwarth*) (72 Cloncurry St, SW6), *b* 30 Nov 1947; *ed* Eton, and Trin Hall, Camb: *m* 1971, Isabel Anna, da of late Maj John Freville Henry Surtees, OBE, MC, of Down House, Wylye, Wilts, and has issue living, William Henry, *b* 1973, — Robert Mungo, *b* 1974, — Georgina Mary, *b* 1979, — Caroline Rose, *b* 1983.

DAUGHTERS LIVING (*By 1st marriage*)

Hon Sarah Margaret, *b* 1944: *m* 1977, John Alexander Hamish Macnab of Barravorich, of 16 Cupar Rd, SW11, and has issue living, Lucy Margaret, *b* 1978, — Clare Sarah, *b* 1980.

Hon Diana Mary, *b* 1946: *m* 1977, Richard James Bradshaw, of 397 Wellesley St East, Toronto, Ontario, Canada M4X 1H5, and has issue living, James Edward Merton, *b* 1983, — Jenny Alexandra, *b* 1979.

Hon Mary Jane, *b* 1955: *m* 1980, Hon James McMoran Wilson, of 65 Upland Rd, Brookline, Mass 02146, USA, el son of 2nd Baron Moran, KCMG, and has issue (*see* B Moran).

BROTHER LIVING (*Raised to the rank of a Baron's son* 1945)

Hon Francis Michael, MC, *b* 1920; *ed* Eton, and King's Coll, Camb; a FRICS; sometime Maj Lothians and Border Horse, 1939-45 War; a Consultant Smiths Gore, Chartered Surveyors; 1939-45 War (MC): *m* 1946, Marjorie Hamilton, da of Horatio John Ross (Lighton, Bt), and has issue living, James Patrick (Larkhill, Lauder, Berwickshire), *b* 1947; *ed* Eton; late Capt The Black Watch: *m* 1972, Christian Diana, da of Maj John Freville Henry Surtees, OBE, MC, of Down House, Wylye, Wilts, and has issue living, Walter Robert *b* 1974, George James *b* 1983, Emily May *b* 1977, — Michael Francis (Wester Newhouse, Lilliesleaf, Melrose, Roxburghshire), *b* 1959: *m* 1984, Viola Susan, da of Christopher Heywood, of 3 The Drive, SW20, and has issue living, Francis Hedley *b* 1987, Malcolm Ross *b* 1988, — Mary Helen, *b* 1949: *m* 1974, Andrew Godfrey Purvis Sherwood (*see* E Onslow, colls) *Residence* – Newhouse, Lilliesleaf, Melrose, Roxburghshire.

COLLATERAL BRANCHES LIVING

Issue of late Hon Patrick John Hepburne-Scott, yst son of 9th Lord, *b* 1899; *d* 1982: *m* 1st, 1925, Cona, who *d* 1961, da of late Cyril Fielding Smith, of Dublin; 2ndly, 1963, Margaret Mary, who *d* 1982, da of late Arthur George Riddell, of Harrow, Middx:—
(By 1st *m*) Ann Harriet, *b* 1929: *m* 1963, Colin Andrew Baxter, of Red Tiles, West Linton, Peeblesshire, and has issue living, Patrick Ian (Girdwoodend Farm, Auchengray, Lanarkshire), *b* 1968.

Grandsons of late Hon Henry Robert Hepburne-Scott, 2nd son of 7th Lord:—
Issue of late James Cospatrick Hepburne-Scott, *b* 1882, *d* 1942: *m* 1907, Lady Isobel Alice Adelaide Kerr, who *d* 1975, da of 9th Marquess of Lothian:—
Michael Henry, *b* 1909; Maj late 16th/5th Lancers; late Dep Assist Dir of Army Legal Sers, War Office: *m* 1st, 1931 (*m diss* 1949), Frances Elizabeth, who *d* 1984, da of late Rev George Victor Collier, of Sotwell, Wallingford, Berks; 2ndly, 1949 (*m diss* 1986), Mrs Rohilla Ada May Pelz, da of Albert Smith, and has had issue (by 1st *m*), †David Michael Cospatrick, *b* 1935; *ed* Eton and King's Coll, Camb (MA); Assist Master, Westminster Sch; *d* 1992, — Walter Francis (Pantiles, Beeches Rd, Farnham Common, Bucks SL2 3PS), *b* 1944; *ed* Eton; MB BS, MRCGP, LLB: *m* 1st, 1968 (*m diss* 1977), Fiona Mary, da of Frey Richard Ellis, MD, of 27 Links Rd, Epsom, Surrey; 2ndly, 1983, Teresa Gail, da of Frederick John Major, and has issue living (by 1st *m*), Henry Walter *b* 1970: *m* 1996, Rebecca Ann, da of Robert Crawford (and has issue living, Charlotte Ann *b* 1998), George Walter *b* 1971, Edward Walter *b* 1974, — (by 2nd *m*), Angela Susan, *b* 1949: *m* 1st, 1973, Othmar Schimek, who *d* 1991; 2ndly, 1992, John Llewelyn Davies, of Throughham Slad Manor, Bisley, Glos GL6 7AW, and has issue living (by 1st *m*), Othmar *b* 1974, Isabelle Alice *b* 1983. —— †Walter Schomberg, *b* 1910; ARIBA, and Capt late RE: *m* 1945, Deborah, who *d* 1993, only child of late Tudor Ralph Castle, Lt Queen's Roy Regt (D Norfolk, colls), and *d* 1998, having had issue, James Ralph Schomberg (Northfield, Prestonpans, E Lothian), *b* 1947; *ed* Nautical Coll, Pangbourne, — †(Lyulph) Mark Esme, *b* 1949: *m* 1980, Jane Anne, elder da of Peter Telford, of 11 Grange Close, Southam, Leamington Spa, Warwicks, and *d* 1997.

PREDECESSORS – **(1)** *Rt Hon Sir* PATRICK Hume, PC, and Extraor Lord of Session 1693 Lord High Chancellor of Scotland 1696, and First Lord of the Treasury and of the Admiralty etc, was *cr Lord Polwarth*, of Polwarth, co Berwick (peerage of Scotland) 1690, and *Earl of Marchmont, Viscount Blasonberry*, and *Lord Polwarth*, of Polwarth, Redbraes and Greenlaw peerage of Scotland) 1697: *d* 1724; *s* by his son **(2)** ALEXANDER, KT, PC, 2nd Earl; was a Senator of the College of Justice, and Ambassador to Denmark and Prussia; *d* 1740; *s* by his son **(3)** HUGH, 3rd Earl; was First Lord of Police in Scotland; *d* 1793, when the earldom, viscountcy and lordship of 1697 became extinct, and the lordship of 1690 became vested in the grandda of the 3rd Earl of Marchmont **(4)** ANNE, *de jure* Lady Polwarth (da of Sir John Paterson), 3rd Bt, who *m* Anne, el da of the 3rd Earl of Marchmont; she *d* 1822, before any decision regarding her claim to the Lordship had been reached; her aunt **(5)** DIANA (yst da of 3rd Earl of Marchmont), became *de jure* Lady Polwarth: *m* 1754, Walter Scott, MP, of Harden, co Roxburgh, Chieftain of the Scotts of Sinton, *d* 1827; her only son and heir **(6)** HUGH Scott, was MP for Berwick 1780-4; assumed the additional surname of Hepburn; in 1835 he claimed and was allowed the peerage becoming 6th Lord; *d* 1841; *s* by his son **(7)** HENRY FRANCIS, 7th Lord; was a Representative Peer, Lord-Lieut of Selkirkshire, and a Lord-in-Waiting to Queen Victoria; *d* 1867; *s* by his son **(8)** WALTER HUGH, 8th Lord, *b* 1838; Capt Roy Co of Archers (King's Body Guard for Scotland); Lord-Lieut of co Selkirk 1878-1919: *m* 1st, 1863, Lady Mary Hamilton-Gordon, who *d* 1914, da of 5th Earl of Aberdeen; 2ndly, 1915, Katherine Grisell, who *d* 1938, da of late Rev Hon John Baillie; *d* 1920; *s* by his el son **(9)** WALTER GEORGE, 9th Lord; *b* 1864: *m* 1888, Edith Frances, who *d* 1930, da of Sir Thomas Fowell Buxton, 3rd Bt; *d* 1944; *s* by his grandson **(10)** HENRY ALEXANDER (son of late Capt Hon Walter Thomas Hepburne-Scott), 10th Lord and present peer.

Pomeroy, family name of Viscount Harberton.

Ponsonby, family name of Earl of Bessborough.

Ponsonby, family name of Baron de Mauley.

Ponsonby, family name of Baron Sysonby.

PONSONBY OF SHULBREDE, BARON (Ponsonby) (Baron UK 1930)

FREDERICK MATTHEW THOMAS PONSONBY, 4th Baron; *b* 27 Oct 1958; *s* 1990; *ed* Holland Park Sch, Univ Coll, Cardiff, and Imperial Coll, London; a Cllr London Borough of Wandsworth since 1990.

Arms – Gules, a chevron between three combs argent. **Crest** – Out of a ducal coronet azure three arrows, points downwards, one in pale and two in saltire, entwined at the intersection by a snake proper.

SISTERS LIVING AND DECEASED

Hon Julia Mary, *b* 1960.
Hon Charlotte, *b* 1961; *d* 1979.
Hon Rachel Elizabeth Emma, *b* 1964.

AUNTS LIVING (*daughters of 2nd Baron*)

Hon Laura Mary, *b* 1935. *Residence* – 17 South End, Kensington Sq, W8.
Hon Rose Magdalen, *b* 1940: *m* 1966, Brian David Owen-Smith, MB, FRCP, DPhys Med, of 48 Westgate, Chichester, Sussex PO19 3EU, and has issue living, Timothy Clive Owen, *b* 1968, — Emma Elizabeth Jane, *b* 1971.
Hon Catherine Virgina, *b* 1944: *m* 1972, Ian Macdonald Affleck Russell, of Shulbrede Priory, Lynchmere, Haslemere, Surrey, and has issue living, Harriet Mary, *b* 1977, — Joanna Elizabeth, *b* 1979.

PRO·REGE GREGE LEGE

For the king, the law, and the people

MOTHER LIVING

Ursula Mary, yr da of Cdr Thomas Stanley Lane Fox-Pitt, OBE, RN (ret) (*see* Lowther, Bt, *cr* 1824, 1964 Edn): *m* 1st, 1956 (*m diss* 1973), Hon Thomas Arthur Ponsonby (later 3rd Baron Ponsonby of Shulbrede), who *d* 1990; 2ndly, 1974, as his 2nd wife, John Ingham Brooke (*see* Hewett, Bt, 1990 Edn). *Residence* – 95 Elgin Crescent, W11.

WIDOW LIVING OF THIRD BARON

MAUREEN ESTELLE (*Baroness Ponsonby of Shulbrede*), da of Alfred William Windsor, and formerly wife of Dr Paul Campbell-Tiech: *m* 1973, as his 2nd wife, the 3rd Baron Ponsonby of Shulbrede, who *d* 1990. *Residence* – 261 Kennington Rd, SE11 6BY.

PREDECESSORS – (1) ARTHUR AUGUSTUS WILLIAM HARRY Ponsonby, son of late Gen the Rt Hon Sir Henry Frederick Ponsonby, GCB, PC (E Bessborough, colls); *b* 1871; in Diplo Ser 1894-1903, Private Sec to Prime Min (Rt Hon Sir Henry Campbell-Bannerman GCB, MP) 1905-08, Under-Sec of State for Foreign Affirs Jan to Nov 1924, and leader of the Opposition in House of Lords Sept 1931 to Sept 1935; appointed Under-Sec of State for Dominion Affairs June 1929, Parliamentary Sec to Min of Transport Nov 1929, and Chancellor of Duchy of Lancaster March 1931 (resigned Aug 1931); sat as MP for Stirling Dist (*L*) May 1908 to Nov 1918, and for Sheffield, Brightside Div (*Lab*) Nov 1922 to Jan 1930; *cr Baron Ponsonby of Shulbrede*, of Shulbrede, Sussex (peerage of United Kingdom) 1930: *m* 1898, Dorothea, who *d* 1963, da of late Sir Charles Hubert Hastings Parry, 1st Bt (ext); *d* 1946; *s* by his only son (2) MATTHEW HENRY HUBERT, 2nd Baron; *b* 1904: *m* 1929, Hon Elizabeth Mary Bigham, who *d* 1985, da of 2nd Viscount Mersey; *d* 1976; *s* by his only surviving son (3) THOMAS ARTHUR, 3rd Baron, *b* 1930; a Councillor Royal Borough of Kensington 1956-65, an Alderman Royal Borough of Kensington and Chelsea 1964-74, an Alderman GLC 1970-77 (Chm of Council 1976-77), Opposition Chief Whip, House of Lords, 1982-90, a Gov of LSE 1970-90: *m* 1st, 1956 (*m diss* 1973), Ursula Mary, yr da of Cdr Thomas Stanley Lane Fox-Pitt, OBE, RN (*see* Lowther, Bt, *cr* 1824, 1964 Edn); 2ndly, 1973, Maureen Estelle, da of Alfred William Windsor, and formerly wife of Dr Paul Campbell-Teich; *d* 1990; *s* by his only son (4) FREDERICK MATTHEW THOMAS, 4th Baron and present peer.

Ponsonby of Sysonby, Baron; title of Earl of Bessborough on Roll of HL.

POOLE, BARON (Poole) (Baron UK 1958)

DAVID CHARLES POOLE, 2nd Baron; *b* 6 Jan 1945; *s* 1993; *ed* Gordonstoun, Ch Ch Oxford, and INSEAD Fontainebleau; Member Stock Exchange: *m* 1st, 1967 (*m diss* 19—), Fiona, da of John Donald, of 69 Rivermead Court, SW6; 2ndly, 1975, Philippa, da of late Mark Reeve, of Lower Brook House, King's Somborne, Hants; 3rdly, 1995, Mrs Lucinda Edsell, and has issue by 1st *m*.

𝔄rms – Per saltire or, and barry undy argent and azure, in chief and in base a portcullis chained also azure. ℭrest – A lion's gamb erased or, enfiled by a crown composed of four trident heads set upon a rim azure. 𝔖upporters – On either side a crane proper about the neck a purse azure garnished gold. *Residence* – 7 Farmer St, W8; *Clubs* – Buck's, Royal Yacht Squadron, Groucho's.

SON LIVING (*by 1st marriage*)

Hon OLIVER JOHN, *b* 30 May 1972; *ed* Eton, and St Anne's Coll, Oxford.

DAUGHTERS LIVING OF FIRST BARON (*by 1st marriage*)

Hon Caroline (*Hon Lady Lucas-Tooth*), *b* 1934: *m* 1955, Sir Hugh John Lucas-Tooth, 2nd Bt. *Residences* – 41 Lancaster Rd, W14 1QJ; Parsonage Farm, E Hagbourne, Didcot, Oxon.

Hon Alison Victoria, *b* 1936: *m* 1961, Dr Fitz Zankel, and has issue living, Michael Rudolph, *b* 1962, — Thomas Joseph, *b* 1964, — Olivia, *b* 1977. *Residence* – Staudgasse 75, Vienna.

Hon Sheila Marian, *b* 1940: *m* 1st, 1966 (*m diss* 19—), Anthony William Paul (Cob) Stenham; 2ndly, 1980, George Ian Kenneth Ireland. *Residence* – 74 Clancarty Rd, SW6.

WIDOW LIVING OF FIRST BARON

BARBARA ANN (*Dowager Baroness Poole*), only da of E. A. Taylor, of Kinsbourne Green, Harpenden, Herts: *m* 1966, as his 3rd wife, the 1st Baron Poole, CBE, TD, PC, who *d* 1993. *Residence* – 24 Campden Hill Gate, Duchess of Bedford Walk, W8 7QH.

PREDECESSOR – (1) *Rt Hon* OLIVER BRIAN SANDERSON Poole, CBE, TD, son of late Donald Louis Poole, of Lloyd's; *b* 1911; an Underwriting Member of Lloyd's, Chm Lazard Bros & Co, Dir S. Pearson & Sons, etc; Joint Hon Treas Conservative Party 1952-55, Chm 1955-57, Dep Chm 1957-59, Joint Chm May-Oct 1963, and Vice-Chm 1963-64; commn'd Life Guards 1932, Warwickshire Yeo 1933-45, Lt-Col (Hon Col) TA, served 1939-45 War (despatches thrice, American Legion of Merit, etc); MP Oswestry Div of Shropshire (C) July 1945-Feb 1950; MBE (Mil) and OBE (Mil) 1943, CBE (Mil) 1945, *cr Baron Poole*, of Aldgate, City of London (peerage of United Kingdom) 1958, and PC 1963: *m* 1st, 1933 (*m diss* 1951), Betty Margaret, who *d* 1988, yr da of late Capt Dugald Stewart Gilkison, Cameronians (Scottish Rifles) (*see* B Vernon, colls, 1969 Edn); 2ndly, 1952 (*m diss* 1965), Mrs Daphne Wilma Kenyon Heber-Percy, who *d* 1995, da of late Eustace Bowles (*see* E Macclesfield, colls, 1995 Edn); 3rdly, 1966, Barbara Ann, only da of E. A. Taylor, of Kinsbourne Green, Harpenden, Herts; *d* 1993; *s* by his only son (2) DAVID CHARLES, 2nd Baron and present peer.

POPPLEWELL, BARONY OF (Popplewell) (Extinct 1977)

SON LIVING OF LIFE BARON

(*Hon*) John Arnold, *b* 1928: *m* 1951.

WIDOW LIVING OF LIFE BARON

LAVINIA (*Baroness Popplewell*), OBE, da of Samuel Rainbow, of Sherburn-in-Elmet: *m* 1922, Baron Popplewell (Life Baron), who *d* 1977.

Porchester, Lord; son of Earl of Carnarvon.

PORRITT, BARONY OF (Porritt) (Extinct 1994) (see Porritt, Bt)

PORTARLINGTON, EARL OF (Dawson-Damer) (Earl I 1785)

Virtue is the way of life

GEORGE LIONEL YUILL SEYMOUR DAWSON-DAMER, 7th Earl; *b* 10 Aug 1938; *s* 1959; *ed* Eton; a patron of two livings; a Page of Honour to HM 1953-55; a Dir G. S. Yuill & Co Pty Ltd, of Sydney, Austn Stock Breeders Co Ltd, Brisbane, and other Cos: *m* 1961, Davina, el da of late Sir Edward Henry Windley, KCMG, KCVO (V Brookeborough, colls), and has issue.

Arms – Azure, a chevron ermine, between three arrows points downwards, or, barbed and flighted proper; on a chief argent three martlets sable, and on a canton gules a mullet or. Crest – A cat's head erased at the neck, and affrontée, or a tabby colour, holding in the mouth a rat sable. Supporters – Two heraldic tigers proper.
Residences – Gledswood, Melrose, Roxburghshire TD6 9DN; 118 Wolseley Rd, Piper Point, NSW 2027, Australia.

SONS LIVING

CHARLES GEORGE YUILL SEYMOUR (*Viscount Carlow*), *b* 6 Oct 1965; Page of Honour to HM the Queen 1979-81; *ed* Eton.
Hon Edward Lionel Seymour, MVO, *b* 1967; Capt; Equerry to HM Queen Elizabeth the Queen Mother 1992-94; MVO 1994.
Hon Henry Lionel Seymour, *b* 1971.

DAUGHTER LIVING

Lady Marina Davina, *b* 1969. *Residence* – The Garden Flat, 14 Wetherby Gdns, SW5.

BROTHER LIVING

Hon Lionel John Charles Seymour (1 Rose Bay Av, Bellevue Hill, NSW 2023), *b* 1940; *ed* Eton: *m* 1st, 1965 (*m diss* 1975), Rosemary Ashley Morrett, da of P. G. M. Hancock, of Truro; 2ndly, 1982, Ashley Judith, da of W/Cdr W. Mann, of W Australia.

PREDECESSORS – (1) WILLIAM HENRY Dawson, MP for Portarlington and for Queen's Co; *cr Baron Dawson*, of Dawsons' Court, Queen's co (peerage of Ireland) 1770, and *Viscount Carlow* (peerage of Ireland) 1776; *d* 1779; *s* by his son (2) JOHN, 2nd Viscount; *cr Earl of Portarlington* (peerage of Ireland) 1785; sat as MP for Portarlington; *d* 1798; *s* by his son (3) JOHN, 2nd Earl; was Col 23rd Dragoons; present at numerous battles in the Peninsula, and Waterloo; in 1808 *s* to the estates of George Damer, 2nd and last Earl of Dorchester; *d* unmarried 1845; *s* by his nephew (4) HENRY JOHN REUBEN, KP, 3rd Earl, son of Capt Hon Henry Dawson (who assumed by sign manual the additional surname of Damer), by Eliza, da of Capt Edmund Joshua Moriarty, RN, and grandda of 1st Earl of Carhampton, *b* 1822; was a Representative Peer: *m* 1847, Lady Alexandrina Octavia Maria Vane, who *d* 1874, da of 3rd Marquess of Londonderry: *d* 1889; *s* by his cousin (5) LIONEL SEYMOUR WILLIAM (son of late Col Rt Hon George Lionel Dawson-Damer, 3rd son of 1st Earl), 4th Earl, *b* 1832; MP for Portarlington (C) 1857-65: *m* 1855, Hon Harriet Lydia Montagu, da of 6th Baron Rokeby (*ext*); *d* 1892; *s* by his el son (6) GEORGE LIONEL HENRY SEYMOUR, 5th Earl; *b* 1858: *m* 1881, Emma Andalusia Frere, who *d* 1929, da of late Lord Nigel Kennedy; *d* 1900; *s* by his son (6) LIONEL ARTHUR HENRY SEYMOUR, 6th Earl; *b* 1883; formerly Lt Irish Gds: *m* 1907, Winnafreda, who *d* 1975, only child of late George Skelton Yuill, of, 37 Chesham Place, SW; *d* 1959; *s* by his grandson (7) GEORGE LIONEL YUILL SEYMOUR (el son of late Air Commodore George Lionel Seymour, Viscount Carlow, only son of 6th Earl), 7th Earl and present peer; also Viscount Carlow, and Baron Dawson.

PORTER OF LUDDENHAM, BARON (Porter) (Life Baron 1990)

GEORGE PORTER, OM, FRS, son of late John Smith Porter; *b* 6 Dec 1920; *ed* Thorne Gram Sch, Leeds Univ (BSc), and Emmanuel Coll, Camb (MA, PhD, ScD); RNVR Radar Officer 1941-45; Demonstrator in Physical Chemistry, Camb Univ, 1949-52, Assist Dir of Research in Physical Chemistry, Camb Univ, and Fellow Emmanuel Coll 1952-54; Assist Dir British Rayon Research Assocn 1954-55; Prof of Physical Chemistry, Firth Prof and Head of Dept of Chemistry, Sheffield Univ, 1955-66; Dir The Royal Institution 1966-86, Pres The Royal Society 1985-90; Research Prof Imperial Coll since 1987; Chm Centre for Molecular Sciences since 1990, and Chancellor Leicester Univ since 1986; Hon Doctorates Oxford (DSc), Cambridge (LLD) and 30 other Univs in UK and abroad; Nobel Prize (joint) for Chemistry 1967, Faraday Medal (Royal Soc of Chemistry) 1981, Davy Medal 1971, Rumford Medal 1978 and Copley Medal 1990 (Royal Society); author and contributor to learned journals; *cr* Knt 1972, OM 1989, and *Baron Porter of Luddenham*, of Luddenham, co Kent (Life Baron) 1990: *m* 1949, Stella Jean, da of late Col George Arthur Brooke, of Leeds, Maidstone, Kent, and has issue.

Residence – The Old Rectory, Luddenham, Faversham, Kent ME13 0TE. *Club* – Athenaeum.

SONS LIVING

Dr the Hon John Brooke, *b* 1952; *ed* Oundle, Emmanuel Coll, Camb (BChir 1977, MB 1978), and Univ Coll Hosp, London; FRCP (UK), FRCPath: *m* 1989, Suzanne Margaret, da of late David William Church, of Beaconsfield, Bucks, and has issue living, William John, *b* 1991. *Residence* – 18 St Paul's Place, Islington, N1 2QF.

Dr the Hon Andrew Christopher George, *b* 1955; *ed* Oundle, Westminster, Bristol Univ and Linacre Coll, Oxford (DPhil): *m* 1997, Margaret Jane, da of James Philip Dallman, of Hayes, Kent, and has issue living, Alexander Jonathan DALLMAN-PORTER, *b* 1998. *Residence* – 64 Grafton Rd, W3 6PF.

PORTLAND, EARL OF (Bentinck) (Earl GB 1689)

TIMOTHY CHARLES ROBERT NOEL BENTINCK, 12th Earl; *b* 1 June 1953; *s* 1997; *ed* Harrow, and E Anglia Univ (BA); a Mediatised Count of the Holy Roman Empire; is an Actor: *m* 1979, Judith Ann, da of John Robert Emerson, of Cheadle, Staffs, and has issue.

Arms – Azure, a cross-moline argent. **Crest** – Out of a ducal coronet proper two arms counter-embowed, vested gules, on the hand gloves, or, each holding an ostrich feather argent. **Supporters** – Two lions double queued, the *dexter* or; the *sinister* sable.
Address – House of Lords, SW1A 0PW.

SONS LIVING

WILLIAM JACK HENRY (*Viscount Woodstock*), *b* 19 May 1984; *ed* Harrow.
Hon Jasper James Mellowes, *b* 1988.

SISTERS LIVING

Lady Sorrel Deirdre BENTINCK, *b* 1942; resumed her maiden name 1990: *m* 1972 (*m diss* 1988), Sir John Philip Lister Lister-Kaye, 8th Bt, and has issue. *Residence* – 18 Rankeillor St, Edinburgh EH8 9HZ.

Lady Anna Cecilia BENTINCK, *b* 1947; has resumed her maiden name: *m* 1st, 1965 (*m diss* 1974), Jasper Hamilton Holmes; 2ndly, 1975 (*m diss* 1977), Nicholas George Spafford Vester; has issue living (by Arnold George Francis Cragg, son of Rt Rev Kenneth Cragg, of Ascott-under-Wychwood, Oxon), Gulliver Jack Bentinck CRAGG, *b* 1978, — George Finn Gareth Bentinck CRAGG, *b* 1980, — Charlotte-Sophie Camden Bentinck CRAGG, *b* 1988. *Residence* – 64 Croftdown Rd, NW5 1EN.

AUNT LIVING (*sister of 11th Earl of Portland*)

Countess Brydgytte Blanche (Rykstraatweg, 242 Haren, Groningen, Netherlands), *b* 1916: *m* 1937, Jonkheer Adriaan Hendrik Sibble Van der Wyck, who *d* 1973, Capt Royal Netherlands Horse Artillery (Res), and Attorney to the Queen of the Netherlands, and has issue living, *Jonkheer* Evert Rein Robert Henry, *b* 1945, — *Jonkheer* Douglas Roderick Arthur Duncan, *b* 1955, — Caroline Norah Frédérique Adrienne, *b* 1938: *m* 1961, K. J. A. Baron Collot d'Escury, Estate Agent of Crown Property, Zeeland, and has issue living, Guyon Adolf André *b* 1962, Robert Willem Frederick *b* 1970, Juliette Brydgytte Blanche *b* 1963, Marina Caroline Norah *b* 1965, — Brydgytte Agnes Dawn (Boerenstreek 1, Gaast, Friesland, Holland), *b* 1940: *m* 1968 (*m diss* 1990), Paul Heinz Maria Dirk Vermeer, and has issue living, Robert Paul Adriaan Henry Simon *b* 1968, Fiona Victoria Regina Brydgytte *b* 1970, Nadia Norah Noel *b* 1971, — Reina Jeanne Woltera, *b*

1942; a nurse: *m* 1973, H. W. van Harrenveld, Judge of the Courts of Justice at Zutphen, of De Buitenhof, Brummen, Geldersland, and has issue living, Hugo Johannes Hendrik *b* 1974, Diederik Godard Adriaan Roelant *b* 1980, Wendela Blanche Catherine *b* 1977.

DAUGHTER LIVING OF NINTH DUKE OF PORTLAND (*By 1st marriage*)

Lady Mary Jane, *b* 1929: *m* 1st, 1963 (*m diss* 1978), Alexander Constantine Georgiades, of Pilton, Oundle, Northants; 2ndly, 1978, Prof Stephen Richards Graubard, and has issue living (by 1st *m*), William James, *b* 1967, — David Constantine, *b* 1969. *Residence* – 8 Maple Av, Cambridge, Mass 02139, USA.

DAUGHTER LIVING OF SEVENTH DUKE OF PORTLAND

Lady Alexandra Margaret Anne CAVENDISH-BENTINCK, *b* 1916; CStJ. *Seats* – Welbeck Abbey, Worksop, Notts; Welbeck Woodhouse, Worksop, Notts; Langwell, Berriedale, Caithness; Bothal Castle, Northumberland.

WIDOW LIVING OF NINTH DUKE OF PORTLAND

KATHLEEN ELSIE (*Duchess of Portland*), da of Arthur Barry, of Montreal, and formerly wife of Arthur Richie Tillotson: *m* 1948, as his 2nd wife, the 9th Duke of Portland, CMG, who *d* 1990.

WIDOW LIVING OF ELEVENTH EARL OF PORTLAND

JENIFER (*Jenifer, Countess of Portland*), only da of late Reginald Hopkins, of 91 Kingsley Way, N2: *m* 1974, as his 2nd wife, the 11th Earl of Portland, who *d* 1997. *Residence* – Little Cudworthy, Dolton, N Devon EX19 8PU.

COLLATERAL BRANCHES LIVING

Granddaughters of late William Charles Philip Otto Aldenburgh-Bentinck, 6th Count Bentinck (great great grandson of Hon William Bentinck, yr son of 1st Earl), Count of the Holy Roman Empire, who received 1886 a Royal Licence to bear in England the title of Count of the Holy Roman Empire, with permission for all other descendants, both male and female, of his father to bear the title of Count or Countess before their christian names:—
Issue of late William Frederick Charles Henry Aldenburg-Bentinck, 7th Count Bentinck; *b* 1880, *d* 1959: *m* 1923, Adrienne (LABOUCHERE), da of late Philip Ernst Vegelin van Claerbergen, of The Hague:—
Countess Sophie Mechtild Marie, *b* 1924: *m* 1950, Count Enrico Gaetani dell'Aquila d'Aragona, and has issue living, *Donna* Benedetta Rita Maria, *b* 1953, — *Donna* Jacobella Immacolata Scolastica, *b* 1956, — *Donna* Giovannella Maria, *b* 1961. *Residence* – 43 Pizzofalcone, Naples, Italy. —— *Countess* Isabelle Adrienne, *b* 1925: *m* 1951, Count Aurel Ladislaus Franz Heinrich Ernst zu Ortenburg, and has issue living, *Count* Franz Wilhelm Friedrich Ladislaus, *b* 1953, — *Count* Philipp Wilhelm, *b* 1955, — *Countess* Nadine Marie Elisabeth Johanna, *b* 1957: *m* 1981, Count Albrecht von Brandenstein-Zeppelin. *Residences* – 8601 Schloss Birkenfeld, Germany; Kasteel Middachten, De Steeg, Netherlands.

Granddaughter of late Count Godard John George Charles Aldenburg-Bentinck, yst son of Lt-Gen Charles Anthony Ferdinand Aldenburg Bentinck, 4th Count Bentinck:—
Godard Adrian Henry Jules (9th Count Bentinck, and Baron Aldenburg), *b* 1887, *d* 1968: *m* 1st, 1921, Jacoba, who *d* 1949, da of late Jacobus Johannes van den Heuvel; 2ndly, 1961, Alida (22 Saxen Weimarlaan, Amsterdam, Holland), da of late Frits Vlieger:—
(By 1st *m*) *Countess* Louise Andrienne Jacoba, *b* 1923: *m* 1954, George Léon Alex de Brauwere dit de Steelant, who *d* 1992, and has issue living, Alain George Francois (25 Kazernestraat, The Hague, Netherlands), *b* 1961; attorney (Bar of Supreme Court of Netherlands): *m* 1994, Gemma Anna Maria Wilhelmina Bakx, — Jemima Sophie Adrienne, *b* 1958; architect: *m* 1980, Ir G. R. Scherpbier, of 21 Hugo de Grootplein, Delft. *Residence* – Zuylestein, Leersum, Utrecht, Netherlands.

PREDECESSORS – (1) HANS WILLIAM Bentinck, KG, PC (whose el brother Eusebius Borchard was Baron Bentinck of Diepenheim and Schoonheten in the Netherlands), having first served William, Prince of Orange, as a Page of Honour, eventually became his confidential adviser, and after that Prince's accession to the British throne, was appointed Groom of the Stole and First Gentleman of the Bedchamber; commanded a Dutch Regt of Horse Guards, and as a Lieut-Gen took a distinguished part at the battle of the Boyne 1690; *cr Baron Cirencester, Viscount Woodstock*, and *Earl of Portland* (peerage of Great Britain) 1689; *d* 1709; *s* by his son **(2)** HENRY, 2nd Earl; was Gov and Capt Gen of Jamaica, and sometime MP for Southampton; *cr Marquess of Titchfield* and *Duke of Portland* (peerage of Great Britain) 1716: *m* 1704, Elizabeth da of the 2nd Earl of Gainsborough (*cr* 1682); *d* 1726; *s* by his son **(3)** WILLIAM KG, 2nd Duke; *d* 1762; *s* by his son **(4)** WILLIAM HENRY CAVENDISH, KG, 3rd Duke; was MP for Weobley 1761-2, Viceroy of Ireland 1782, First Lord of the Treasury 1783 and 1807, Sec of State for Home Depart 1794, Pres of the Council 1801, Chancellor of Oxford Univ, High Steward of Bristol, and Lord Lieut of Notts; assumed the additional surname of Cavendish by Roy licence 1801; *d* 1809; *s* by his son **(5)** WILLIAM HENRY, PC, DCL, FRS, 4th Duke; was Lord-Lieut of Middlesex; assumed by Roy licence in 1795 the additional surname of Scott; *d* 1854; *s* by his son **(6)** WILLIAM JOHN Cavendish-Bentinck-Scott, 5th Duke, *b* 1800; sat as MP for Lynn 1824-6; *d* 1879; *s* by his kinsman **(7)** WILLIAM JOHN ARTHUR CHARLES JAMES, KG, GCVO, TD, PC (el son of late Lieut-Gen Arthur Cavendish-Bentinck, 2nd son of Lord William Charles Augustus Cavendish-Bentinck, 3rd son of 3rd Duke), 6th Duke; *b* 1857; Hon Col 4th and 7th Batns Sherwood Foresters; sometime Lord-Lieut of Notts; Master of the Horse 1886-92 and 1895-1905, and Chancellor of Order of the Garter 1937-43; received Roy Victorian Chain 1953; *m* 1889, *Dame* Winifred, DBE, who *d* 1954, only da of late Thomas Yorke Dallas-Yorke, of Walmsgate, Louth; *d* 1943; *s* by his el son **(8)** WILLIAM ARTHUR HENRY, KG, 7th Duke; *b* 1893; Junior Lord of the Treasury 1927-29, and 1932; MP for Newark Div of Notts (*U*) 1922-43; Chancellor of Nottingham Univ 1927-29; Lt-Col Cmdg Notts Yeo (Sherwood Rangers) 1933-36; Lord Lieut of Notts 1939-62: *m* 1915, Hon Ivy Gordon-Lennox, DBE (Maid of Honour to Queen Alexandra 1912-15), who *d* 1982, da of Lord Algernon Charles Gordon-Lennox (D Richmond); *d* 1977; *s* by his kinsman

(9) FERDINAND WILLIAM, KBE, CMG, MCel son of (William George) Frederick Cavendish-Bentinck, grandson of Maj-Gen Lord Frederick Cavendish-Bentinck, CB, MP (4th son of 3rd Duke), 8th Duke, b 1888; Private Sec to Gov of Uganda 1925-27; Member for Agric and Natural Resources in Kenya; Speaker of Kenya Legislative Council: m 1st, 1912 (m diss 1950), Wentworth Frances, who d 1964, da of late William James Hope-Johnston (E Annandale and Hartfell, colls); 2ndly, 1950, Gwyneth Ethel, MBE, who d 1996, da of late John Wesley Edward, of Chettlewood Estate, and Montpellier, Jamaica, BWI and widow of Col David Alexander John Bowie, MC, RA; d 1980; s by his brother (10) VICTOR FREDERICK WILLIAM, CMG, 9th Duke, b 1897; Chm Joint Intelligence Sub Cttee on Chs of Staff 1939-45, Foreign Office Advisor to Dir of Plans 1942-45, and Ambassador to Poland 1945-47: m 1st, 1924 (m diss 1948), Clothilde Bruce, who d 1984, da of late James Bruce Quigley, of Dallas, Texas; 2ndly, 1948, Kathleen Elsie, da of Arthur Barry, of Montreal, and formerly wife of Arthur Richie Tillotson; d 1990, when the Dukedom became extinct and the Earldom passed to his kinsman (11) HENRY NOEL, 11th Earl, b 1919; Lieut Coldstream Gds; 1939-45 War (twice wounded); author of several works on environmental conservation, and sometime producer at the BBC: m 1st, 1940, Pauline, who d 1967, da of late Frederick William Mellowes, of Penn House, Reynolds Close, Hampstead, NW; 2ndly, 1974, Jenifer, only da of late Reginald Hopkins, of 91 Kingsley Way, N2; d 1997; s by his only son (12) TIMOTHY CHARLES ROBERT NOEL, 12th Earl and present peer; also Viscount Woodstock and Baron Cirencester.

♦ The 1st Earl of Portland had issue a 2nd son, Hon William Bentinck, who was cr a Count of the Holy Roman Empire by Charles VI of Austria 1732, for himself and his descendants. In 1845 by decree of the German Diet, the Counts Bentinck obtained recognition of their right to the dignities and privileges of the Mediatised Houses (Reichsunmittelbar) of Germany with the style of Erlaucht. His great great grandson, Lt-Col Count Henry Charles Adolphus Frederick William Aldenburg-Bentinck, 5th Count Bentinck, resigned his rights as head of the family 1874 to his yr brother, William Charles Philip Otho Aldenburg-Bentinck. The 5th Count d 1903, leaving issue, Count Robert Charles Bentinck, b 1875: m 1915, Lady Norah Ida Emily Noel, who d 1939, da of 3rd Earl of Gainsborough, and d 1932, leaving issue an only son, Count Henry Noel Bentinck, who s 1990 his kinsman as 11th Earl of Portland (ante).

PORTMAN, VISCOUNT (Portman) (Viscount UK 1873)

A CLEAN HEART AND A CHEERFUL SPIRIT

CHRISTOPHER EDWARD BERKELEY PORTMAN, 10th Viscount; b 30 July 1958; s 1999; m 1st, 1983 (m diss 1987), Caroline, da of Terence Ivan Steenson, of Caversham, Berks; 2ndly, 1987, Patricia Martins, elder da of Bernardino Pim, of Rio de Janeiro, Brazil, and has issue by 1st and second marriages.

Arms – Quarterly: 1st and 4th or, a fleur-de-lis azure, Portman; 2nd and 3rd gules, a chevron ermine, between ten crosses patée argent, six in chief and four in base, Berkeley. Crests – 1st, a talbot sejeant or; 2nd, a unicorn passant gules, armed and crined or. Supporters – Dexter, a savage, wreathed about the head and waist with ivy, in his dexter hand a club resting on the shoulder, proper; sinister, a talbot or.
Residence – 38 Seymour St, W1H 6BP.

SONS LIVING (By 1st marriage)

Hon LUKE OLIVER BERKELEY, b 31 Aug 1984.

(By 2nd marriage)

Hon Matthew Bernardo Berkeley, b 1990.
Hon Daniel Edward Berkeley, b 1995.

HALF-BROTHERS LIVING

Hon Alexander Michael Berkeley, b 1967: m 1992, Emma Esma, da of Christopher Morgan, of Ste Saturnin-les-Apt, Vaucluse, France, and has issue living, Maximilian, b 1996.
Hon Justin Trevor Berkeley, b 1969.
Hon Piers Richard Berkeley, b 1971: m 1995, (Alexandra) Lucy, only da of Lt-Col Sir Christopher Peile Thompson, 6th Bt, and has issue living, Willow Isabella, b 1998.
†Hon Matthew Gerald Berkeley, b 1973; d as the result of a motorcycle accident 1990.

SISTER LIVING

Hon Claire Elizabeth, b 1959: m 1983, (Anthony) Henry Robinson (see B Heytesbury, 1990 Edn), and has issue living, Anthony, b 1984, — James, b 1985, — Patrick, b 1987.

HALF-AUNT LIVING (*Half-sister of 9th Viscount*)

Suna (Synöve Isobel) (Portman Lodge, Durweston, Blandford, Dorset DT11 0QA), *b* 1939: *m* 1st, 1968 (*m diss* 1970), Martin George Anthony Wilkinson; 2ndly, 1970 (*m diss* 1981), Simon Thomas Paul Boyle; 3rdly, 1997, Patric Morrissey, and has issue living (by 1st *m*), Heron Berkeley, *b* 1968, — (by 2nd *m*) Kestrel Berkeley, *b* 1970, — Storm Simon, *b* 1979.

DAUGHTERS LIVING OF FIFTH VISCOUNT

Hon Sheila Constance (*Viscountess Knutsford*), *b* 1927: *m* 1951, 6th Viscount Knutsford. *Residence* – Broadclyst House, Exeter.

Hon Rosemary, *b* 1931: *m* 1951, Derrick Allix Pease (*see* Pease, Bt, *cr* 1920), who *d* 1998. *Residence* – Folly Farm, Ashill, Ilminster, Somerset.

MOTHER LIVING

Rosemary Joy, eldest da of Charles Farris, of Coombe Bissett, Wilts: *m* 1st, 1956 (*m diss* 1966), Edward Henry Berkeley Portman, later 9th Viscount Portman, who *d* 1999; 2ndly, 1967, John R. Maitland. *Residence* – 14 High St, Woodstock, Oxford OX20 1TF.

WIDOW LIVING OF NINTH VISCOUNT

PENELOPE ANNE HASSARD (*Dowager Viscountess Portman*), yr da of Trevor Allin, of N Moreton, Berks: *m* 1966, as his 2nd wife, 9th Viscount Portman, who *d* 1999. *Residence* – Clock Mill, Clifford, Hereford HR3 5HB.

COLLATERAL BRANCHES LIVING

Grandson of late Berkeley Portman, el son of late Hon Maurice Berkeley Portman (infra):—
Issue of late Com Maurice Percy Berkeley Portman, RN, *b* 1884, *d* 1928: *m* 1918, Joan Wycliffe, who *d* 1971, da of late Maj-Gen Charles William Thompson, CB, DSO:—
Berkeley Charles Berkeley, *b* 1919; *ed* Wellington Coll; late Lt RN: *m* 1944, Sheila Margaret Penelope, da of late Capt F. D. Mowat, RN, and has issue living, Rodney John Berkeley (3 Harley Gdns, SW10) *b* 1947; *ed* Wellington Coll, and Trin Coll, Camb: *m* 1st, 1976 (*m diss* 1992), Angela, only da of Maj John Cartwright Pringle, MC, of Pyt House, Tisbury, Wilts; 2ndly, 1997, Mrs Rosalind Jeannette Hanbury, da of late Derrick Allix Pease (*see* Pease, Bt, *cr* 1920), and has issue living (by 1st *m*), Guy Seymour Berkeley *b* 1977; *ed* Stowe, John Berkeley *b* 1982, Olivia Joan *b* 1979, — Celia Rose Berkeley, *b* 1946: *m* 1972, Anthony William Charlton Edwards, of Salterton House, nr Salisbury, Wilts, and has issue living, Berkeley Humfrey Charlton *b* 1978, Marcella Louise Charlton *b* 1973, Imogen Patricia Charlton *b* 1975, Hermione Celia Charlton *b* 1982, — Lucy Joan Berkeley, *b* 1953: *m* 1983, Ian Parsons, eldest son of Edward Victor Parsons, of Harlow, Essex, and has issue living, Hugh Stanley *b* 1988, Jessie Catherine *b* 1986, Elspeth Caroline *b* 1990, — Edwina Penelope Berkeley, *b* 1956: *m* 1986, Timothy J. Hicks, yst son of William Hicks, of Church Farm, Leckhampton, Glos, and has issue living, James *b* 1988, Frederick *b* 1991, Camilla *b* 1986, Chloë *b* 1989, — Rachel Mary Berkeley, *b* 1961; composer, received Academy Award for Best Original Musical or Comedy Score 1997: *m* 1995, Count Uberto Pasolini Dall'Onda, son of Count Pasolini Dall'Onda, and of Contessa Visconti di Modrone, of Rome, and has issue living, Anna Gwendolen *b* 1995, Giulia Ginevra *b* 1998. *Residence* – Danley Hill, Lynchmere, nr Haslemere, Surrey. *Clubs* – Army and Navy, Royal and Ancient.

Grandchildren of late Com Maurice William Portman, 2nd son of late Hon Maurice Berkeley Portman (infra):—
Issue of late Brigadier Guy Maurice Berkeley Portman, CB, TD, *b* 1890, *d* 1961; *m* 1922, Miriam Katharine, who *d* 1975, da of George William Taylor (*see* E Wilton, 1953 Edn):—
Anthony Seymour Berkeley, *b* 1928; *ed* Eton; late Lieut Dorset Regt; High Sheriff Hants 1992: *m* 1961, Penelope Helen Kathleen, da of Derrick Warner Candy, of Kingston Warren, Wantage, Oxon, and has issue living, Michael Henry Berkeley (New House, Farmington, Cheltenham, Glos GL54 3ND), *b* 1962: *m* 1992, Alison Grethe Sabin, only da of R. A. Bench, of Minchinhampton, Glos, and has issue living, Guy Ralph Berkeley *b* 1996, Henry Edmund Berkeley *b* 1997, — Jonathan Guy Berkeley, *b* 1965. *Residence* – Rushmore Farm, Upton, Andover, Hants. *Club* – Boodle's. —— Lusia Edwina, *b* 1931: *m* 1952, Christopher David Howard, who *d* 1991, of Ryton Corner, Ryton, Shrewsbury, and has issue living, Davinia Elizabeth, *b* 1953: *m* 1981, James William Vernon, elder son of Sir Nigel John Douglas Vernon, 4th Bt and has issue (*see* Vernon, Bt), — Belinda Jane, *b* 1956: *m* 1981, Timothy Michael Evans, elder son of Geoffrey Evans, of Stanyeld, Church Stretton, Shropshire, and has issue living, Alice Valerie Katherine *b* 1983, Camilla Rose Lusia *b* 1986, Florence Diana Elizabeth *b* 1991.

Granddaughter of late Hon Maurice Berkeley Portman, 3rd son of 1st Viscount:—
Issue of late Cecil Berkeley Portman, *b* 1869, *d* 1915: *m* 1902, Florence Wyndham, who *d* 1967, da of late Maj Lachlan Forbes:—
Marigold Florence Lavinia, *b* 1903: *m* 1929, Raymond Patterson, who *d* 1984, and has issue living, Alan Noel (c/o 2685 Queenswood Drive, Victoria, BC, Canada), *b* 1936: *m* 1965 (*m diss* 1975), Mary Elizabeth Ann, da of Jeffrey Boys, of Vancouver, and has issue living, Jeremy Patrick *b* 1967, Samantha Jeanne *b* 1969, Jennifer Anne *b* 1970, — Robert George (745 Greenlea Drive, Victoria, BC), *b* 1944: *m* 1974, Susan Veronica Mary, da of Henry Martyn, of Falmouth, Cornwall, and has issue living, Mark Richard Murray *b* 1978, Claire Elizabeth Olive *b* 1980, — Janet Murray, *b* 1930: *m* 1949, David Blanchet, who *d* 1981, of 1230 Gladwin Drive, North Vancouver, BC, and has issue living, Julia Claire Janet *b* 1949. *Address* – 2685 Queenswood Drive, Victoria, British Columbia, Canada.

Grandson of late Montagu Berkeley Portman, yst son of late Hon Maurice Berkeley Portman (ante):—

Issue of late Lieut-Col Gerald Berkeley Portman, RA, *b* 1903, *d* 1954: *m* 1st, 1928 (*m diss* 1945), Joan, da of late Col G. Turner; 2ndly, 1945 (*m diss* 1950), Cicely Falkener, da of Godfrey Oliver, of Port Hill, Northam, Devon; 3rdly 1950, Mai Elisabeth, who *d* 1979, da of Samuel Wohlin, of Lidingo, Brevik, Sweden:—
(By 2nd *m*) Michael Berkeley (Port Hill, Northam, Devon; *Clubs* – Cavalry and Guards', MCC), *b* 1947; *ed* Wellington Coll, and RMA; Lt-Col Light Dragoons: *m* 1979, Penelope Jane, elder da of late Brig Harry Wilkinson Bishop, FRCVS, and has issue living, Edward Berkeley, *b* 1983, — Lucy Serena, *b* 1985.

PREDECESSORS – (1) EDWARD BERKELEY Portman, son of Edward Berkeley Portman, of Bryanston; *b* 1799; sat as MP for Dorsetshire (*L*) 1823-32, and for Marylebone 1833; was *cr Baron Portman*, of Orchard Portman, co Somerset, 1837, and *Viscount Portman* (peerage of United Kingdom) 1873: *m* 1827, Lady Emma Lascelles, who *d* 1865, da of 2nd Earl of Harewood; *d* 1888; *s* by his el son (2) WILLIAM HENRY BERKELEY, GCVO, 2nd Viscount, *b* 1829; MP for Shaftesbury 1852-7, and Dorsetshire (*L*) 1857-85: *m* 1st, 1855, Hon Mary Selina Charlotte Wentworth-Fitzwilliam, who *d* 1899, da of late Viscount Milton, son of 5th Earl Fitzwilliam; 2ndly, 1908, Frances Maxwell, who *d* 1939, da of late Boyd Alexander Cuninghame, RN, of Craigends, co Renfrew, and widow of Andrew James J. Livingstone Learmonth; *d* 1919; *s* by his el son (3) HENRY BERKELEY, 3rd Viscount, *b* 1860: *m* 1901, Emma Andalusia Frere, who *d* 1929, da of late Lord Nigel Kennedy, and widow of the 4th Earl of Portarlington; *d* 1923; *s* by his brother (4) CLAUD BERKELEY, 4th Viscount, *b* 1864: *m* 1st, 1888 (*m diss* 1897), Mary Ada, who *d* 1900, da of late Major Francis Hastings Toone Gordon Cumming (Gordon Cumming, Bt, colls); 2ndly, 1898, Harriette Mary, who *d* 1939, da of late William Stevenson; *d* 1929; *s* by his son (5) EDWARD CLAUD BERKELEY, 5th Viscount, *b* 1898; Capt Life Guards: *m* 1926, Hon Sybil Mary Douglas-Pennant, who *d* 1975, da of 3rd Baron Penrhyn; *d* 1942; *s* by his uncle (6) SEYMOUR BERKELEY (5th son of 2nd Viscount), 6th Viscount; *b* 1868; *d* 1946; *s* by his brother (7) GERALD BERKELEY, 7th Viscount, *b* 1875: *m* 1902, Dorothy Marie Isolde, who *d* 1964, da of Sir Robert Sheffield, 5th Bt: *d* 1948: *s* by his el son (8) GERALD WILLIAM BERKELEY, 8th Viscount, *b* 1903: *m* 1st, 1926 (*m diss* 1946), Marjorie Josephine Wernham Bentley, who *d* 1981, da of George Bentley Gerrard, of Montreal; 2ndly, 1946, Nancy Maureen, who *d* 1998, da of Capt Percy Herbert Franklin, RN (ret); *d* 1967; *s* by his nephew (9) EDWARD HENRY BERKELEY (el son of late Hon Michael Berkeley Portman, yr son of 7th Viscount), 9th Viscount, *b* 1934: *m* 1st, 1956 (*m diss* 1966), Rosemary Joy, eldest da of Charles Farris, of Coombe Bissett, Wilts; 2ndly, 1966, Penelope Anne Hassard, yr da of Trevor Allin, of N Moreton, Berks; *d* 1999; *s* by his eldest son (10) CHRISTOPHER EDWARD BERKELEY, 10th Viscount and present peer; also Baron Portman.

PORTSMOUTH, EARL OF (Wallop) (Earl GB 1743)

QUENTIN GERARD CAREW WALLOP, 10th Earl; *b* 25 July 1954; *s* (Oct) 1984; *ed* Eton, and Millfield; Hereditary Bailiff of Burley, New Forest; Pres Basingstoke Conservative Assocn since 1992; Dir Grainger Trust plc: *m* 1st, 1981 (*m diss* 1985), Candia Frances Juliet, writer, da of late Colin Edgar McWilliam, of Edinburgh; 2ndly, 1990, Annabel, eldest da of Dr Ian Fergusson, of Tudor Place, Richmond Green, Surrey, and has issue by 1st and 2nd *m*.

Arms – Argent, a bend wavy sable. **Crest** – A mermaid proper holding in the dexter hand a comb and in the sinister a looking glass the frame lozenge-wise attached thereto a handle or. **Supporters** – Two chamois or wild goats sable. (These arms were resumed (and Royal Licence granted in 1995) by the 5th Earl, together with the family surname of Wallop).
Seat – Farleigh House, Farleigh Wallop, Basingstoke, Hants RG25 2HT. *Clubs* – Buck's, International Assocn of Cape Horners, and Royal Yacht Sqdn.

SON LIVING (*By 1st marriage*)

OLIVER HENRY RUFUS (*Viscount Lymington*), *b* 22 Dec 1981.

DAUGHTERS LIVING (*By 1st marriage*)

Lady Clementine Violet Rohais, *b* 1983.

(*By 2nd marriage*)

Lady Rose Hermione Annabel, *b* 1990.

SISTERS LIVING (*Raised to the Rank of an Earl's daughters* 1994)

Lady Lucinda Ruth, *b* 1956: *m* 1984, as his 2nd wife, Patrick Anthony Ewen Bellville, only surv son of late Anthony Seymour Bellville, of The White House, Bembridge, Isle of Wight, and has issue living, Blaise Anthony Valentine, *b* 1985, — Oscar Rupert Kintzing, *b* 1986, — Archie Seymour, *b* 1988. *Residence* – Manor Farm House, Cliddesden, Basingstoke, Hants.

Lady Emma Geraldine Anne, *b* 1958: *m* 1981, Gerald Thomas Cordingley, son of late Thomas Cordingley, and has issue living, Katie Madelaine, *b* 1983, — Venetia Ruth, *b* 1985, — Jennifer Rose, *b* 1991. *Residence* – Cheesecombe Farm, Hawkley, nr Liss, Hants.

HALF-UNCLE LIVING *(son of 9th Earl by 2nd marriage)*

Hon Nicholas Valoynes Bermingham (15 Tregunter Rd, SW10), *b* 1946; *ed* Stowe: *m* 1969, Lavinia, only da of David Karmel, CBE, QC, of 108 Eaton Place, SW1, and has issue living, Henry Robert Newton, *b* 1974, — Victoria Urania Sophia, *b* 1972.

AUNT LIVING *(Daughter of 9th Earl by 1st marriage)*

Lady (Anne) Camilla Eveline, *b* 1925: *m* 1944, Lord Rupert Charles Montacute Nevill, Life Guards, who *d* 1982, and has had issue *(see M Abergavenny)*. *Residences* – Old House Farm, Glynde, Lewes, Sussex; 35 Upper Addison Gdns, W14.

HALF-AUNT LIVING *(Daughter of 9th Earl by 2nd marriage)*

Lady Jane Alianora Borlase, *b* 1939. *Residence* – 1 Broadmere, Farleigh Wallop, Basingstoke, Hants.

WIDOW LIVING OF SON OF NINTH EARL

Julia *(Viscountess Lymington)*, only da of late W. Graeme Ogden, DSC, of The Old Manor, Rudge, Frome, Somerset, and formerly wife of Peter Robin Kirwan-Taylor, of Bridgehampton, NY, USA: *m* 1974, as his 3rd wife, Oliver Kintzing, Viscount Lymington, elder son of 9th Earl, who *dvp* (June) 1984. *Residence* – 5 Venner House, 47 Bourne St, SW1W 8UR.

COLLATERAL BRANCHES LIVING

Issue of late Hon Oliver Malcolm Wallop, yr son of 8th Earl, *b* 1905, *d* 1980: *m* 1st, 1929, Jean, who *d* 1943, da of Edward Small Moore, of New York; 2ndly, 1944 *(m diss* 1954), Mrs Alberta Jannopolis Hines; 3rdly, 1954, Carolyn, who *d* 1973, da of Harvey Parker Towle, MD, and formerly wife of Henry Sturgis Russell:—
(By 1st *m*) Edward John (68 Hanna Creek Rd, Big Horn, Wyoming 82833, USA), *b* 1930: *m* 1st, 1952 *(m diss* 1959), Carrol Robertson; 2ndly, 1962, Victoria Neison, only da of H. Lyman Stebbins, of New York; 3rdly, 1986, Tessa Janet, only da of late Douglas Neale Dalton, of Bridgnorth, Shropshire, and has issue living (by 1st *m*), John Michael, *b* 1955, — (by 2nd *m*), Andrew Gerard, *b* 1965, — Sam Huntington, *b* 1972, — Harriet Walker, *b* 1968 (adopted da), — Alexandra Marcina, *b* 1969. —— Malcolm (Upper Wallop, Big Horn, Wyoming 82833, USA), *b* 1933: *m* 1st, 1955 *(m diss* 1966), Josephine Vail Stebbins; 2ndly, 1967, Judith Warren, formerly wife of —Goodwin, and has issue living (by 1st *m*), Malcolm Moncreiffe (Henry), *b* 1957, — (Oliver) Mathew, *b* 1960, — Paul Stebbins, *b* 1963, — Amy Vail, *b* 1962. —— Jean Margaret *(Countess of Carnarvon)*, *b* 1934: *m* 1956, 7th Earl of Carnarvon, KCVO, KBE. —— Carolyn Walker, *b* 1939: *m* 1963, Irving Newman Alderson, of Bones Brothers Ranch, Birney, Montana, USA, and has issue living, Natalie Moore, *b* 1963, — Jean, *b* 1965, — Mary Roberts, *b* 1968.

Grandchildren of late Maj Barton Newton Wallop William-Powlett, late Royal Fusiliers (City of London Regt), only son of late Maj William Barton Powlett Wallop William-Powlett, son of Rev Hon Barton Wallop, brother of 2nd Earl:—
Issue of late Capt Newton James Wallop William-Powlett, DSC, RN, *b* 1896, *d* 1963: *m* 1929, Barbara Patience (who *d* 1997, having *m* 2ndly, 1966, Vice Adm Sir Peveril Barton Reibey Wallop William-Powlett, KCB, KCMG, CBE, DSO (infra)), da of Sir Bernard Eyre Greenwell, 2nd Bt, MBE:—
Oliver Newton Wallop, *b* 1933; *ed* Eton; Lieut RNR; JP, DL and High Sheriff Devon 1989. *Residence* – Cadhay, Ottery St Mary, Devon EX11 1QT. —— Ann Patience Wallop, *b* 1930: *m* 1953, Maj Thomas Noel Thistlethwayte, late 60th Rifles, of Summerhayes, Throwleigh, Okehampton, Devon EX20 2HX, and has issue living, Rupert Thomas Newton (Downs Farm, Homersfield, Harleston, Norfolk IP20 0NS), *b* 1955: *m* 1982, Elisabeth Anne, only da of Francis Cator *(see* Storey, Bt), and has issue living, Emma *b* 1983, Katharine *b* 1985, — Jane Camilla, *b* 1957: *m* 1991, Timothy L. S. Dodd, of 56 Chancellor's Rd, W6 9RS, only son of Lewis Dodd, of Newport, Dyfed, and has issue living, Peter Alexander *b* 1992, Jeremy Arran *b* 1994, Matthew Ralph *b* 1997. —— Sara Elisabeth Wallop, *b* 1936: *m* 1st, 1960 *(m diss* 1998), Hon Edward David Bruce; 2ndly, 1998, (George) Alastair Lean, OBE, of Birkhill, Muckhart, by Dollar, Clackmannanshire, and has issue (by 1st *m*) *(see* E Elgin).

Issue of late Vice Adm Sir Peveril Barton Reibey Wallop William-Powlett, KCB, KCMG, CBE, DSO, *b* 1898, *d* 1985: *m* 1st, 1923, Helen Constance, who *d* 1965, da of late J. Forbes Crombie, of Aberdeen; 2ndly, 1966, Barbara Patience, who *d* 1997, widow of his elder brother, Capt Newton James Wallop William-Powlett, DSC, RN (ante):—
(By 1st *m*) Olivia Pansy Wallop, *b* 1925: *m* 1950, Lt-Col John Clairmont Wood, of Coombe Down, Beaminster, Dorset, and has issue living, Giles Powlett Clairmont, *b* 1954: *m* 1988, Frances Mary Catherine Stewart, and has issue living, Robert *b* 1991, Rollo *b* 1992, — Charlotte Knollys Olivia, *b* 1953: *m* 1977, Philip Gilbert Herbert Bradley, and has issue living, William *b* 1980, Piers *b* 1982, Timothy *b* 1985, — Louisa Ella Delamotte, *b* 1959: *m* 1987, Richard Charles Hawker, who *d* 1992, and has issue living, John Henry Gore *b* 1988, Constance Rose Knollys *b* 1990. —— Helen Vernon Wallop, *b* 1927: *m* 1951, Lt Cdr Henry Victor Bruce of Salloch, RN, of Rodfield Cottage, Ovington, Alresford, Hants, and 39 Ashley Gdns, Ambrosden Av, SW1P 1QE, and has issue *(see* E Elgin, colls). —— Judith Jean Wallop *(Lady Colman)*, *b* 1936: *m* 1955, Sir Michael Jeremiah Colman, 3rd Bt, of Malshanger, Basingstoke, Hants, and has issue.

Issue of late Maj Peter de Barton Vernon Wallop William-Powlett, MC, *b* 1903, *d* 1988: *m* 1935, Hon Katherine Elizabeth Keyes, who *d* 1996, da of 1st Baron Keyes:—
Barton Roger Wallop (Piercewebbs, Clavering, Saffron Walden, Essex), *b* 1938: *m* 1962, Judith, elder da of Colin Silk, of 13 Highdown Rd, Lewes, and has issue living, Patrick Henry Wallop, *b* 1964: *m* 1999, Gillian Baillie, da of late Kenneth Alan Hartley, — Thomas Wallop (The Old Manse, Newport, Saffron Walden, Essex), *b* 1968: *m* 1998 Tamsin, da of David Edward Sidney Pearce, — Katherine Wallop, *b* 1965: *m* 1990, Dr D. Joshua Danziger, of 31 Goodge St, W1, son of Dr Arnold M. Danziger, of Wilmslow, Cheshire, and has issue living, Samson Peter *b* 1995. —— Mary Wallop, *b* 1936: *m* 1957, Jonathan Janson, Lieut RNVR, of Howgate Farm, Bembridge, I of W PO35 5QN, and has issue living, Nicola Claire Wallop, *b* 1959: *m* 1985, Richard Henry Alexander Southby, of The Red House, Overbury, Tewkesbury, Glos GL20 7PB, and has issue (*see* Southby, Bt), — Lucinda Katrina, *b* 1961: *m* 1991, Andrew Peter Watt, of 17 Ritherdon Rd, SW17 8QE, 2nd son of Cdr Alexander Strachan Watt, of Ditcheatt, Somerset, and has issue living, Georgiana Louisa Janson *b* 1993, Arabella Perdita *b* 1995, — Sara Arabella, *b* 1965.

PREDECESSORS – **(1)** JOHN WALLOP, MP for Hants 1714-20; was a Lord of the Treasury 1747, Lord-Lieut of Hants, Lord Warden and Keeper of the New Forest, Vice-Adm of Hants, and Vice-Adm and Gov of the Isle of Wight; *cr Baron Wallop*, of Farley Wallop, co Southampton, and *Viscount Lymington* (peerage of Great Britain) 1720, and *Earl of Portsmouth* (peerage of Great Britain) 1743; *d* 1762; *s* by his grandson **(2)** JOHN, 2nd Earl; *d* 1797; *s* by his el son **(3)** JOHN CHARLES, 3rd Earl; *dsp*, 1853; *s* by his brother **(4)** NEWTON, 4th Earl; *b* 1772; assumed by Roy licence in 1794 for himself and issue the surname and arms of Fellowes only: *m* 2ndly, 1820, Lady Catherine, da of 1st Earl Fortescue; *d* 1854; *s* by his son **(5)** ISAAC NEWTON, 5th Earl, *b* 1825; resumed (but without Roy licence) the family surname and arms of Wallop: *m* 1855, Lady Eveline Alicia Juliana Herbert, who *d* 1906, el da of the Earl of Carnarvon; *d* 1891; *s* by his el son **(6)** NEWTON, 6th Earl, *b* 1856, MP for Barnstaple. (*L*) 1880-85, and for Devon, N, or S Molton Div 1885-91: *m* 1885; Beatrice Mary, who *d* 1935, only child of late Edward Pease, of Summer House, Bewdley, and Greencroft West, Darlington; *d* 1917; *s* by his brother **(7)** JOHN FELLOWES, 7th Earl, *b* 1850; *d* 1925; *s* by his brother **(8)** OLIVER HENRY, 8th Earl; *b* 1861: *m* 1897, Marguerite, who *d* 1938, da of late S. J. Walker, of Frankfort, Kentucky, and Chicago, Illinois, USA; *d* 1943; *s* by his son **(9)** GERARD VERNON, 9th Earl, *b* 1898; 1914-18 War as Lieut 2nd Life Gds and Guards Machine Gun Regt; MP for Basingstoke Div of Hants (*C*) May 1929-Feb 1934; Chm Country Landowners' Assocn 1947-49; Vice-Pres European Electors' Union, Kenya 1952, Pres 1953; Chm Forestry Advisory Cttee, Kenya 1954-61; Vice-Chm E Africa Natural Resources Cttee 1964-84: *m* 1st, 1920 (*m diss* 1936), Mary Lawrence, who *d* 1964, da of Waldron Kintzing Post, of Bayport, LI, USA; 2ndly, 1936, Bridget Cory (OStJ), who *d* 1979, only da of late Capt Patrick Bermingham Crohan, RN, of Owlpen Old Manor, Uley, Glos; *d* (Oct) 1984; *s* by his grandson **(10)** QUENTIN GERARD CAREW (only son of Oliver Kintzing, Viscount Lymington, *b* 1923: *m* 1st, 1952 (*m diss* 1954), Maureen, only da of Lt-Col Kenneth Bridges Stanley, of 58 Kingston House, Princes Gate, SW7; 2ndly, 1954 (*m diss* 1974), Ruth Violet, who *d* 1978, yr da of Brig-Gen Gerald Carew Sladen, CB, CMG, DSO, MC (*see* Ewing, Bt, colls, 1964 Edn); 3rdly, 1974, Julia, only da of W. Graeme Ogden, DSC, of The Old Manor, Rudge, Frome, Somerset, and formerly wife of Peter Robin Kirwan-Taylor; *dvp* (June) 1984), 10th Earl and present peer; also Viscount Lymington, and Baron Wallop.

POULETT, EARLDOM OF (Poulett) (Extinct 1973) (Barony of Poulett of Hinton St George, E 1627, Extinct or Dormant 1973)

WIDOW LIVING OF EIGHTH EARL

MARGARET CHRISTINE (*Countess Poulett*), (Le Cercle, Rue du Croquet, St Aubin, Jersey), da of Wilfred John Peter Ball, of Reading: *m* 1968, as his 3rd wife, the 8th Earl Poulett, who *d* 1973, when the Earldom became extinct and the Barony became extinct or dormant.

Powell, see Baron Baden-Powell.

Powerscourt, Baron; title of Viscount Powerscourt on Roll of HL.

POWERSCOURT, VISCOUNT (Wingfield) Sits as BARON POWERSCOURT (UK 1885)
(Viscount I 1743)
(Name pronounced "Poërscourt")

Fidelity is of God

MERVYN NIALL WINGFIELD, 10th Viscount; *b* 3 Sept 1935; *s* 1973; *ed* Stowe; late Lt Irish Gds: *m* 1st, 1962 (*m diss* 1974), Wendy Ann Pauline, elder da of Ralph C. G. Slazenger; 2ndly, 1979 (*m diss* 1995), Pauline, da of W. P. Van, of San Francisco, USA, and has issue by 1st *m*.

Arms – Argent, on a bend gules, three pairs of wings conjoined in lure of the field. Crest – A demi-eagle wings displayed argent, gazing on the sun proper. Supporters – Two pegasi argent, maned, hoofed, and wings addorsed or.
Residence – Thailand.

SON LIVING (*By 1st marriage*)

Hon (MERVYN) ANTHONY, *b* 21 Aug 1963.

DAUGHTER LIVING (*By 1st marriage*)

Hon Julia Margaret, *b* 1965.

BROTHER LIVING

Hon Guy Claude Patrick (PO Box 186, Applegate, Calif 95703-0186, USA), *b* 1940; *ed* Millfield.

SISTER LIVING

Hon Grania Sybil Enid (*Hon Lady Langrishe*), *b* 1934: *m* 1955, Sir Hercules Ralph Hume Langrishe, 7th Bt, who *d* 1998. *Residence* – Arlonstown, Dunsany, co Meath.

COLLATERAL BRANCHES LIVING

Granddaughter of late Maj-Gen Hon Maurice Anthony Wingfield, CMG, CVO, DSO, yst son of 7th Viscount:—
Issue of late Brig Anthony Desmond Rex Wingfield, DSO, MC, *b* 1908, *d* 1995: *m* 1935, Juliet Constance, who *d* 1980, da of late William Burroughs Stanley, DL, of Coolamber Manor, Westmeath, and of Lillybrook, Budleigh Salterton:—
Deirdre Jocelyn, *b* 1936: *m* 1969, Basil Tiernay Pegg, of The Old Rectory, Ovington, Alresford, Hants SO24 0RF, and has issue living, Jonathan Mark, *b* 1973, — Camilla Louise, *b* 1971.

Grandchildren of late Richard William Wingfield (*infra*):—
Issue of late Noel Sparks Wingfield, *b* 1907, *d* (Feb) 1992: *m* 1933, Mary Joan, who *d* (Sept) 1992, da of R. H. Wood:—
Patrick Noel (Belvedere North, PO Goromonzi, Zimbabwe), *b* 1934: *m* 1st, 1960 (*m diss* 1971), Jean, da of David Morris Williams, of Blantyre, Nyasaland; 2ndly, 1973, Margaret, da of J. H. McKenzie Finch, of Canterbury, Kent, and has had issue, (by 1st *m*) Richard David Noel, *b* 1966, — Sandra Joan, *b* 1963; *d* 1976, — (by 2nd *m*) Jeremy James, *b* 1974, — Clare Muriel, *b* 1975. —— Jenepher Cynthia (44 Cambridge Rd, Avondale, Harare, Zimbabwe), *b* 1937: *m* 1961, Guy Colin Hensman, who *d* 1993, and has issue living, David Guy, *b* 1965, — Bridget Ann, *b* 1963.

Granddaughter of late Richard Robert Wingfield, el son of late Rev Hon Edward Wingfield, 3rd son of 4th Viscount:—
Issue of late Richard William Wingfield, *b* 1849, *d* 1918: *m* 1889, Jessie Emily (who *d* 1936, having *m* 2ndly, 1920, Thomas Edward Broster, who *d* 1941), da of Benjamin Mitchell Kennedy:—
Clare Mary Sophia (64 Jabulani, Sutton Lane, Warner Beach, Amanzimoti, S Africa), *b* 1904: *m* 1926, Sydney William Hall Kennard, who *d* 1970, and has issue living, David George (Private Bag 1549, Grahamstown 6140, S Africa), *b* 1929; *ed* Hilton Coll, Natal: *m* 1956, Isabelle, da of late Maurice Henry de Vere Pennefather, of Fort Victoria, Zimbabwe, and has issue living, Roland Derek *b* 1958, Nigel Hugh *b* 1961, Kate Ellen *b* 1971, — Desmond Richard (2 Wharncliffe Gdns, Beacon Bay, S Africa), *b* 1935; *ed* Hilton Coll, Natal: *m* 1956, Cynthia Norma, da of late Dr William Beck, of Potchefstroom, and has issue living, Mark William *b* 1959, Grant Richard *b* 1961, Brett Wingfield *b* 1964, Leigh Mary *b* 1957.

Grandchildren of late Capt Anthony Edward Foulis Wingfield, elder son of Sir Anthony Henry Wingfield, elder son of George John Wingfield, 2nd son of Rev Hon Edward Wingfield (ante):—
Issue of late Gervase Christopher Brinsmade Wingfield, *b* 1931, *d* 1964: *m* 1958, Mary Margaret (Hackney Lodge, Melton, Woodbridge, Suffolk) (who *m* 2ndly, 1973, Dennis Henry Bagshaw Neal), da of Dennis McGuinn, of Haverford, Penn, USA:—
Andrew Nicholas Brinsmade, ED, *b* 1959; *ed* Worth, and Bristol Univ; Maj Royal Hong Kong Regt (The Volunteers), and The Royal Yeo; Solicitor: *m* 1989, Caroline Jane Victoria, yst da of John Francis Felix Porter, of The Old Bakery, Martock, Som, and has issue living, Edward Nicholas Anthony, *b* 1991, — Henry John Gervase, *b* 1994. *Clubs* – Cavalry and Guards', Hong Kong Jockey. —— Nicola Caroline McGuinn, *b* 1961: *m* 1986, Mark Godfrey Jerram, of Van Cottage, Compton Chamberlayne, Salisbury, Wilts SP3 5DB, only son of Maj Geoffrey Forster Jenner Jerram, of Lower Wraxall

Farmhouse, nr Dorchester, Dorset, by his wife, Anne (*née* Brigg) (*see* Prince-Smith, Bt, 1970 Edn), and has issue living, Alexander Geoffrey Wingfield, *b* 1989, — Dominic Alistair, *b* 1990. —— Philippa Susan (*Hon Mrs Anthony Monckton*), *b* 1962: *m* 1985, Capt Hon Anthony Leopold Colyer Monckton, yst son of 2nd Viscount Monckton of Brenchley, and has issue (see that family).

Grandchildren of late Edward Rhys Wingfield, el son of late Capt Edward Ffolliott Wingfield (*infra*):—
Issue of late Lieut-Col Mervyn Edward George Rhys Wingfield, Gloucestershire Regt, *b* 1872, *d* 1952: *m* 1919, Florence Marguerite Erle, who *d* 1990, da of late Col Richard Erle Benson, E Yorkshire Regt:—
Charles Talbot Rhys, *b* 1924; *ed* Eton, and Ch Ch, Oxford; late Lieut Coldstream Guards; DL Glos 1963, and High Sheriff 1962; France 1944 (wounded): *m* 1954, Hon Cynthia Merial Hill, da of 6th Baron Sandys, and has issue living, Richard Mervyn Rhys, *b* 1967, — Venetia Blanche, *b* 1956: *m* 1978, Richard Crosbie Dawson (*see* Sutton Bt, colls, 1985 Edn), and has issue living, Anthony Charles *b* 1983, George Robert *b* 1985, Charlotte Rose *b* 1990, — Olivia Patricia, *b* 1958, — Diana Mary, *b* 1961: *m* 1986, Robert Anthony Copley, and has issue (*see* Cs Loudoun, colls). *Residence* – Barrington Park, Burford, Oxon. *Club* – Cavalry and Guards'. —— David de Cardonnel Ffolliott Rhys, *b* 1933; *ed* Bradfield Coll: *m* 1982, Mrs Mary Ann E. L. Harrison. —— Jonathan Fitzuryan Rhys (Fayre Court, Fairford, Glos), *b* 1935; *ed* Eton: *m* 1970 (*m diss* 1986), Judith, da of Albert George James Gibbins, of Mount Pleasant, Stocklane, Langford, Bristol, and widow of Hon Philip John Inman (*see* B Inman), and has issue living, Annabel Lucy, *b* 1973, — Felicity Jane, *b* 1975. —— Mary Florence Eleanor, *b* 1920: *m* 1945, Sqdn-Ldr Neville Thomas Cole, RAF, and has issue living, Michael Duncan Mervyn, *b* 1946, — Edward Charles Ffolliott George, *b* 1954, — Rachel Elizabeth Rosemary, *b* 1948. *Residence* – Windrush Lodge, Nazeing, Essex. —— Elizabeth Marguerite, *b* 1926.

Grandsons of late Maj William Jocelyn Rhys Wingfield, 2nd son of late Edward Rhys Wingfield (ante):—
Issue of late Maj William Thomas Rhys Wingfield, TD, Northamptonshire Yeo *b* 1907, *d* 1976: *m* 1936, Katherine Patricia, who *d* 1998, only child of late Maj-Gen Sir (William) James (Norman) Cooke-Collis, KBE, CB, CMG, DSO:—
Jocelyn James (Coastguard House, Morston, Holt, Norfolk NR25 7BH), *b* 1937; *ed* Eton; Maj (ret) LI; Divisional Dir Overseas (Latin America, Middle East, Pacific), Save the Children Fund: *m* 1968, Sara Elizabeth, only da of Sir (Edward John) Patrick (Boschetti) ffolkes, 6th Bt, and has issue living, Serena Geraldine Rhys, *b* 1969, — Camilla Patricia Rhys, *b* 1971. — †Robert Talbot Rhys *b* 1940; *ed* Stowe and Trin Coll, Dublin (PhD); with British Geological Survey. *m* 1969, Anne Mary (The Spring House, Grimston, nr Melton, Leics LE14 3BZ), da of Lt-Col T. W. Hamilton, of Nunholm House, Dumfries, and *d* 1999, leaving issue, James Hamilton Rhys, *b* 1971, — Charles Timothy Rhys, *b* 1974. —— George Anthony Rhys (Hearne House, North Wootton, Shepton Mallet, Som), *b* 1942; *ed* Eton and Trin Coll, Dublin; with IBM: *m* 1968, Gloria, da of Bernard Bolingbroke-Kent, of Cerne Easter, Westerham, Kent, and has issue living, Rupert Bolingbroke Rhys, *b* 1972; *ed* Eton, — Michael Somerset Rhys, *b* 1975; *ed* Blundell's.

Granddaughter of late Edward Rhys Wingfield (ante):—
Issue of late Sir Charles John Fitzroy Rhys Wingfield, KCMG, *b* 1877, *d* 1960: *m* 1905, Lucy Evelyn, who *d* 1977, da of late Sir Edmund Douglas Veitch Fane, KCMG, of Boyton Manor, Wilts:—
Diana Evelyn, *b* 1907: *m* 1935, Baron Alessandro Corsi di Turri, who *d* 1987, and has issue living, *Baron* Raimondo (Via Rovani 6, 20052 Monza, Italy), *b* 1937; Kt of Honour and Devotion Sov Mil Order of Malta, Kt of Justice Sacred Mil Constantinian Order of St George: *m* 1964, Donna Maria Francesca di Lorenzo, and has issue living, Carlo Alessadro *b* 1965, Diana Lucrezia *b* 1970, — Antonio Giuliano (Via Massimi 27, 00136 Rome, Italy), *b* 1941: *m* 1st, 1967 (*m diss* 1978), Maria Grazia Barbiani; 2ndly, 1979, Giovanna Attanasio, and has issue living (by 1st *m*), Flavio Alessandro *b* 1968, (by 2nd *m*) Benedetta Lucy, *b* 1983. *Residence* – 1 Via Masaccio, 00196 Rome, Italy.

Grandchildren of late Capt Cecil John Talbot Rhys Wingfield, 5th and yst son of late Edward Rhys Wingfield (ante):—
Issue of late Maj Edward William Rhys Wingfield, KRRC, *b* 1905, *d* 1984: *m* 1935, Lady Norah Beryl Cayzer Jellicoe (Salterbridge, Cappoquin, co Waterford), da of 1st Earl Jellicoe;—
Philip John (Salterbridge, Cappoquin, co Waterford), *b* 1938; *ed* Eton: *m* 1971, Susan Johanna, da of late Maj-Gen Ronald Edward Coaker, CB, CBE, MC, of Seaton Old Rectory, Uppingham, and has issue living, Edward Mervyn, *b* 1973; *ed* Eton, Trinity Coll, Dublin, and RMA Sandhurst; commn'd Royal Green Jackets 1997, — Venetia Sophic, *b* 1975, — Sarah Jane, *b* 1978. —— Jacqueline, *b* 1936: *m* 1967, Brig Anthony Chester Vivian, CBE, ADC, Col RWF, of 22 Henning St, Battersea, SW11 3DR. —— Elizabeth Jane, *b* 1941: *m* 1995, Peter Joseph Magnier.

Granddaughters of late Major Charles George Lewis Wingfield, 2nd son of late Capt Edward Ffolliott Wingfield, 3rd son of late Rev Hon Edward Wingfield (ante):—
Issue of late Charles Trevor Wingfield, *b* 1889, *d* 1924: *m* 1914, Liliane Laure Agnes, who *d* 1979, only child of late Vladimir Czerny, of Petrograd, Russia:—
Tatiana Elianore Lucile Beatrice *b* 1916: *m* 1947, Brig Alan Godfrey Drake-Brockman, OBE, who *d* 1976, and has issue living, Trevor Vivian, *b* 1950. —— Yvonne Angéle Primrose Czerny (61 Prevost Martin, Geneva, Switzerland), *b* 1917.

Grandchildren of late Lt-Col Rev William Edward Wingfield, DSO (*infra*):—
Issue of late John Anthony David Wingfield, *b* 1905, *d* 1983: *m* 1934, Eileen Earle, who *d* 1982, da of late Hugh Melville, of Durban, S Africa:—
Anthony Richard Melville, *b* 1941; *ed* St Andrews, Grahamstown. —— John Mervyn (4 Lewis Cres, Gt Abingdon, Cambs CB16 AG), *b* 1944; *ed* St Andrews, Grahamstown, Rand Univ (BSc), and Trin Coll, Camb (BA): *m* 1970, Diana Kay, da of F. C. Harris, of Newlands, Cape Town, and has issue living, Richard John, *b* 1972, — David Mervyn, *b* 1975, — Christopher Robert, *b* 1978. —— Robert Edward Melville (9918-227th Place SW, Edmonds, Washington 98020, USA), *b* 1950; *ed* St Andrews, Grahamstown, and Rand Univ (BSc); Civil Engr: *m* 1979, Carol, da of P. Jansen, of Seattle, USA, and has issue living, Jeremy, *b* 1981, — Joanna Ruth, *b* 1980. —— Elizabeth Melville, *b* 1936; BSc (Hons) Rand Univ, MSc London: *m* 1963, Hugh Vincent Williams, MSc, of 04 Glen St, Kenmare, Krugersdorp, Transvaal, and has issue living, Katharine Elizabeth, *b* 1965, — Julia Margaret Frances, *b* 1969, — Susan Eileen Isabella, *b* 1970.

Grandson of late Capt Richard Thomas Wingfield, el son of late Rev Hon William Wingfield, 4th son of 4th Viscount:—

Issue of late Lieut-Col Rev William Edward Wingfield, DSO, *b* 1867, *d* 1927: *m* 1896, Elizabeth Mary, who *d* 1939, a da of late George Frederic Trench (B Ashtown, colls):—

Mervyn Robert George, DSO, DSC, *b* 1911; Capt RN (ret); an ADC to HM 1962-67; formerly Naval Attaché, British Embassy, Athens, and Dir of Underwater Weapons at Admiralty; 1939-45 War (DSO, DSC and Bar, despatches); DSO 1942: *m* 1936, Sheila Mary, da of late Maj J. H. P. Leschallas, formerly of Lynchmere House, Lynchmere, Sussex, and has issue living, Richard Mervyn (Chiltern House, Hardwick Rd, Whitchurch, Pangbourne, Berks, RG8 7HW), *b* 1942; *ed* Wellington, Pembroke Coll, Camb (MA) and Southampton Univ (MSc); CEng; MICE: *m* 1969, Diana, da of P. M. Long-hurst, of Lodsworth, Sussex, and has issue living James Richard *b* 1973, Caroline Sarah *b* 1976, — William Peter (47 Combemartin Rd, SW18), *b* 1948; *ed* Wellington Coll, and Sussex Univ (BA): *m* 1975, Patricia Jane, da of G. A. Slatter, of Hastings, Sussex, — Cicely (2 Spencer Rd, S Croydon), *b* 1940: *m* 1964, David Barry Knowles, Lt-Cdr RN, who *d* 1967, and has issue living, Alastair David *b* (Nov) 1964, Melanie Kathleen *b* 1966. *Residence* – Fair Winds, Highfield Cres, Hindhead, Surrey.

Granddaughter of late Brig-Gen Cecil Vernon Wingfield-Stratford, CB, CMG, 3rd son of late John Wingfield-Stratford, only son of late Hon John Wingfield Stratford, 2nd son of 3rd Viscount:—

Issue of late Esmé Cecil Wingfield-Stratford, DSc, *b* 1882, *d* 1971: *m* 1915, Barbara Elizabeth, who *d* 1976, da of late Lt-Col Francis Henry Lancelot Errington (B Congleton):—

Roshnara Barbara Wɪɴɢꜰɪᴇʟᴅ-Sᴛʀᴀᴛꜰᴏʀᴅ-Oʀʀ, *b* 1916; assumed by deed poll 1970, for herself and her issue by 2nd *m* the surnames of Wingfield-Stratford-Johnstone, and subsequently assumed the surname of Orr in lieu of Johnstone by deed poll 1998: *m* 1st, 1941 (*m diss* 1949), Maj Richard John Wrottesley, MC (later 5th Baron Wrottesley); 2ndly, 1950, Lt-Col Norman David Melville Johnstone, MBE, Gren Gds, who *d* 1995; 3rdly, 1998, Ronald Henry Davidson Orr, of Lake View House, Station Rd, Kirby Bellars, Leics LE14 2ED, and has had issue, (by 1st *m*) (*see* B Wrottesley), — (by 2nd *m*) Esmé Edward Melville Wɪɴɢꜰɪᴇʟᴅ-Sᴛʀᴀᴛꜰᴏʀᴅ-Jᴏʜɴsᴛᴏɴᴇ (Chateau de Sours, 33750 St Quentin de Baron, France), *b* 1950: *m* 1972, Sara, da of Maj Richard Francis Birch Reynardson, and has issue living, Rupert Leo Esmé *b* 1975, Dickon *b* 1978, Harry Crocker *b* 1983, — Victoria Rose Charlotte, *b* 1954: *m* 1982, William John Corby, of 38 rue de la Liberté, Preignac, Langon, France, only son of R. A. Corby, of Kilbracken, Hudnall Common, Berkhamsted, Herts, and has issue living, Roshnara *b* 1983, Diana *b* 1986, Christina *b* 1988.

Grandchildren of late Francis Mervyn Wingfield-Stratford, 7th and yst son of late John Wingfield-Stratford, only son of late Hon John Wingfield-Stratford, 2nd son of 3rd Viscount (ante):—

Issue of late Mervyn Verner Wingfield-Stratford, *b* 1907; *d* 1982: *m* 1935, Anne Helen, who *d* 1998, da of late Douglas Charles Stewart-Sandeman, of Martins Heron, Bracknell, Berks:—

(Mervyn) Peter Douglas (28 Lansdowne Rd, Holland Park, W11), *b* 1936; LIM Citizen and Goldsmith of London: *m* 1969, Jane, da of late Dr Edward Worsley Burstal, of Lutterworth, and has issue living, James Richard Mervyn, *b* 1973, — Annabel Jane, *b* 1971. —— Georgina Isabel, *b* 1939: *m* 1962, John L. M. Modley, Lt RE, and has issue living, Drummond, *b* 1963, — Alexander, *b* 1965.

PREDECESSORS – (1) Rɪᴄʜᴀʀᴅ Wingfield, MP for Boyle; *cr Baron Wingfield*, of Wingfield, co Wexford, and *Viscount Powerscourt* (peerage of Ireland) 1743; *d* 1751; *s* by his el son **(2)** Eᴅᴡᴀʀᴅ, 2nd Viscount; MP for Stockbridge 1756-61; *d* unmarried; *s* by his brother **(3)** Rɪᴄʜᴀʀᴅ, 3rd Viscount; *d* 1788; *s* by his son **(4)** Rɪᴄʜᴀʀᴅ, 4th Viscount; *d* 1809; *s* by his son **(5)** Rɪᴄʜᴀʀᴅ, 5th Viscount; *d* 1823; *s* by his son **(6)** Rɪᴄʜᴀʀᴅ, 6th Viscount, *b* 1815; many years MP for Bath: *m* 1836, Lady Elizabeth Frances Charlotte Jocelyn, who *d* 1884, da of 3rd Earl of Roden; *d* 1844; *s* by his son **(7)** Mᴇʀᴠʏɴ, KP, PC, 7th Viscount, *b* 1836; was a Representative Peer; *cr Baron Powerscourt*, of Powerscourt, co Wicklow (peerage of United Kingdom) 1885: *m* 1864, Lady Julia Coke, who *d* 1931, el da of 2nd Earl of Leicester; *d* 1904; *s* by his son **(8)** Mᴇʀᴠʏɴ Rɪᴄʜᴀʀᴅ, KP, MVO, 8th Viscount, *b* 1880; was Comptroller of the Household to Lord-Lieut of Ireland 1906-7; appointed Lieut of co Wicklow 1901; elected a Member of Senate of S Ireland 1921: *m* 1903, Sybil, who *d* 1946, da of late Walter Pleydell-Bouverie; *d* 1947; *s* by his son **(9)** Mᴇʀᴠʏɴ Pᴀᴛʀɪᴄᴋ, 9th Viscount, *b* 1905: *m* 1932, Sheila Claude, writer, who *d* 1992, da of late Lt-Col Claude Beddington, of 33 Grosvenor St, W1; *d* 1973; *s* by his el son **(10)** Mᴇʀᴠʏɴ Nɪᴀʟʟ, 10th Viscount and present peer; also Baron Wingfield, and Baron Powerscourt.

POWIS, EARL OF (Herbert) (Earl UK 1804)
(Title pronounced "Po-is")

JOHN GEORGE HERBERT, 8th Earl; *b* 19 May 1952; *s* 1993; *ed* Wellington Coll, and McMaster Univ, Ontario, Canada (MA, PhD); formerly Lecturer McMaster Univ, and Assist Prof of English Literature Redeemer Coll, Ontario 1990-92; patron of twelve livings: *m* 1977, Marijke Sophia, eldest da of Maarten N. Guther, of Ancaster, Ontario, Canada, and has issue.

Arms – Per pale azure and gules, three lions rampant argent. **Crest** – A wyvern wings elevated addorsed vert, gorged with a ducal coronet or, holding in the mouth a sinister hand couped at the wrist gules. **Supporters** – *Dexter*, an elephant argent; *sinister*, a griffin, wings elevated, argent, ducally gorged gules, and charged with five mullets in saltire sable.
Seat – Powis Castle, Welshpool, Powys.

Ung je serviray
One will I serve

SONS LIVING

JONATHAN NICHOLAS WILLIAM (*Viscount Clive*), *b* 5 Dec 1979.
Hon Alexander Sebastian George, *b* 1994.

DAUGHTERS LIVING

Lady Stephanie Moira Christina, *b* 1982.
Lady Samantha Julie Esther, *b* 1988.

BROTHERS LIVING

Hon Michael Clive, *b* 1954, *ed* Wellington Coll, Christ's Coll, Camb, and London Business Sch: *m* 1978, Susan Mary, da of late Guy Baker, of Welshpool, Powys, and has issue living, Thomas Guy Clive, *b* 1981, — Mark Philip Clive, *b* 1983, — Joanna Frances Clare, *b* 1987. *Residence* – Wicken Hall, Wicken, Ely, Cambs CB7 5XT.

Hon Peter James, *b* 1955; *ed* Wellington Coll; MSI: *m* 1978 (*m diss* 1998), Terri, yr da of Sean McBride, of Callan, co Kilkenny, and has issue living, Oliver George Laurie, *b* 1983, — Sophie Louise Mary, *b* 1980, — Lucy Alison Julia, *b* 1988. *Residence* – 23 Fairford Close, Haywards Heath, W Sussex R16 3EF.

Hon Edward David, *b* 1958; *ed* Bryanston, Lancaster Univ (BSc), and Spurgeon's Coll (BA); ACMA: *m* 1985, Diana Christine, eldest da of Cedric Shore, and has issue living, David Andrew, *b* 1988, — Joy Sarah, *b* 1986.

ADOPTIVE SISTERS

Lorraine Elizabeth, *b* 1961: *m* 1981, Roger Samuel Jones, and has issue living, Martin William, *b* 1986, — Caroline Lorraine, *b* 1989. *Residence* – Three Brooks, Harthall, Tenbury Wells, Worcs.

Nicola Wendy, *b* 1962: *m* 1985, Robert Thomas Buxton, and has issue living, Kim Sally, *b* 1991. *Residence* – Blackfor Barn, Chirbury, Montgomery, Powys.

UNCLE LIVING (*brother of 7th Earl*) (*Raised to the rank of an Earl's son*, 1991)

Hon Andrew Clive, *b* 1933; *ed* Repton; late Capt Royal Norfolk Regt; Film Dir, Editor and Producer: *m* 1st, 1963 (*m diss* 1971), Carol Mae, yr da of late John Charlton; 2ndly, 1983, Edith Ann, yr da of late Alexander Dominguez, of Glendale, Calif, USA, and has had issue (by 1st *m*), Nicholas Mark, *b* 1963, — †Hugo Clive, *b* 1965; *d* 1985, — (by 2nd *m*), Timothy James, *b* 1987, — Amanda Colleen, *b* 1983.

WIDOW LIVING OF SON OF FOURTH EARL

VIDA, only da of late Capt James Harold Cuthbert, DSO, Scots Guards; is an OStJ; appointed a Lady-in-Waiting to HRH the Duchess of Gloucester 1944: *m* 1st, 1934, Squadron-Leader Viscount Clive, RAF (17th Baron Darcy de Knayth) who was *ka* 1943, only surviving son of 4th Earl, 2ndly, 1945, Brig Derek Schuldham Schreiber, MVO, who *d* 1972 (B Faringdon), and has issue (by 1st *m*) (*see* Bs Darcy de Knayth). *Residences* – 59 Cadogan Place, SW1; Fir Hill, Droxford, Hants.

WIDOW LIVING OF BROTHER OF SEVENTH EARL

(Monica) Brenda, only da of Laurence Edmund Swann, of The Cottage, Bilting Lane, Ashford, Kent: *m* 1955, Hon David Mark Herbert, who *d* 1996, having been raised to the rank of an Earl's son, 1991, and has two adopted children (infra). *Residence* – 46 Northchurch Rd, N1 4EJ.

WIDOW LIVING OF SEVENTH EARL

Hon KATHARINE ODEYNE DE GREY (*Dowager Countess of Powis*), da of 8th Baron Walsingham: *m* 1949, the 7th Earl of Powis, who *d* 1993. *Residence* – Marrington Hall, Chirbury, Montgomery, Powys.

COLLATERAL BRANCHES LIVING

Adopted children of late Hon David Mark Herbert (who was raised to the rank of an Earl's son 1991), brother of 7th Earl, *b* 1927, *d* 1996: *m* 1955, (Monica) Brenda (ante), only da of Laurence Edmund Swann, of The Cottage, Bilting Lane, Ashford, Kent:—
Charles Clive, *b* 1959; *ed* Bryanston, and William Ellis Sch. —— Emma Katherine Elaine, *b* 1961: *m* 1985 (*m diss* 1996), Simon Smyth Hore, son of Julian Smyth Hore, of Grenfell, Australia.

Issue of late Squadron-Leader Mervyn Horatio Herbert, RAF (*Viscount Clive*) (only surviving son of 4th Earl), who *s* his mother as 17th *Baron Darcy de Knayth* 1929 (see that title).

Descendants of late Hon Robert Henry Clive (2nd son of 1st Earl) who *m* 1819 Harriet, *Baroness Windsor* in her own right (*see* E Plymouth).

PREDECESSORS – **(1)** ROBERT Clive (el son of Richard Clive of Styche, Salop), having served three years in the Civil Service of the HEIC, he entered that Co's Military Ser and subsequently became one of its most distinguished Generals, and to him England owed, to a very substantial extent, the establishment of her dominion in India. He avenged the outrage of the "Black Hole of Calcutta" by completely routing, in the Grove of Plassey, the forces of the Surajah Dowlah amounting to 70,000, and by dethroning the Surajah, events which gave rapid ascendency to the British power. When Gov of Calcutta he defeated the Dutch by sea and land and obtained from them a beneficial treaty for the E India Co. He was subsequently Pres of Bengal, and sat as MP for Shrewsbury 1760-74; *cr Baron Clive*, of Plassey, co Clare (peerage of Ireland) 1762; KB 1764; *d* 1774; *s* by his son **(2)** EDWARD, 2nd Baron; was Lord-Lieut of cos Salop and Montgomery; *cr Baron Clive*, of Walcot, co Salop (peerage of Great Britain) 1794, and *Baron Powis*, of Powis Castle, co Montgomery, *Baron Herbert of Chirbury*, co Salop, and *Viscount Clive* and *Earl of Powis* (peerage of United Kingdom) 1804: *m* 1784, Henrietta Antonia, who *d* 1830, da of Herbert Arthur Herbert, Earl of Powis (and sister and heiress of George Edward Henry Arthur, the last Earl of Powis of the family of Herbert); *d* 1839; *s* by his son **(3)** EDWARD, KG, 2nd Earl; *b* 1785; assumed the surname and arms of Herbert by Roy licence 1807; was Lord-Lieut of co Montgomery: *m* 1818, Lady Lucy Graham, da of 3rd Duke of Montrose; *d* 1848; *s* by his son **(4)** EDWARD JAMES, 3rd Earl; *b* 1818; MP for N Shropshire (C) 1843-8; Lord-Lieut of Montgomeryshire; *d* 1901; *s* by his nephew **(5)** GEORGE CHARLES (son of late Lt-Gen the Rt Hon Sir Percy Egerton Herbert, KCB, MP, 2nd son of 2nd Earl), 4th Earl; *b* 1862; Hon Col 4th Batn, S Wales Borderers, a GCStJ; sometime Prior for Wales, Order of St John; was Lord-Lieut for Salop 1896-1951: *m* 1890, Hon Violet Ida Eveline Lane-Fox (*Baroness Darcy de Knayth* in her own right), who *d* 1929, da and co-heiress of 12th Baron Conyers; *d* 1952; *s* by his kinsman **(6)** EDWARD ROBERT HENRY, CBE, TD (son of late Col Edward William Herbert, CB, son of late Hon Robert Charles Herbert, 4th son of 2nd Earl), 5th Earl; *b* 1889: *m* 1932, Ella Mary, who *d* 1987, da of late Col William Hans Rathborne, formerly wife of Col Frank Alan George Macartney, OBE, MC, DL, IA, and previously widow of Capt Peter Douglas Colin Eliot, IA; *d* 1974; *s* by his brother **(7)** CHRISTIAN VICTOR CHARLES, 6th Earl; Maj RAOC, Bar Inner Temple 1932, Private Sec to Gov and C-in-C British Honduras 1947-55, and to Gov of British Guiana 1955-64, author of a monograph on The Dog in Sherlock Holmes; *dunm* 1988; *s* by his kinsman **(8)** GEORGE WILLIAM (son of late Rt Rev Percy Mark Herbert, KCVO, DD, son of late Maj-Gen Hon William Henry Herbert, 5th son of 2nd Earl), 7th Earl; *b* 1925; FRICS, Fellow Land Agents' Soc: *m* 1949, Hon Katharine Odeyne de Grey, da of 8th Baron Walsingham; *d* 1993; *s* by his eldest son **(9)** JOHN GEORGE, 8th Earl and present peer; also Viscount Clive, Baron Herbert of Chirbury, Baron Powis, and Baron Clive.

Powlett, Orde-, family name of Baron Bolton.

Powys, family name of Baron Lilford.

Pratt, family name of Marquess Camden.

PRENTICE, BARON (Prentice) (Life Baron 1992)

REGINALD ERNEST PRENTICE, PC, son of Ernest George Prentice, of Thornton Heath, Surrey; *b* 16 July 1923; *ed* Whitgift Sch, and LSE (BSc); RA 1942-46, served Italy and Austria 1944-46; JP Croydon 1961; Min of State Dept of Educn and Science 1964-66, Min of Public Building and Works 1966-67, Min of Overseas Devpt 1967-69, Alderman GLC 1970-71, Opposition Spokesman on Employment 1972-74, Sec of State for Educn and Science 1974-75, Min for Overseas Dept 1975-76, Min for Social Security 1979-81; Member Exec Cttee Nat Union of Conservative Assocs 1988-90, Pres Assocn of Business Execs since 1983; Co Dir and Consultant on Public Affairs; MP East Ham North (*Lab*) 1957-74, Newham North East (*Lab*) 1974-77, Newham North East (*C*) 1977-79, and Daventry (*C*) 1979-87; *cr* PC 1966, Knt 1987, and *Baron Prentice*, of Daventry, co Northants (Life Baron) 1992: *m* 1948, (Vera May) Joan, da of Mrs Rosa Godwin, of Hatfield Heath, Herts, and has issue.

Residence – Wansdyke, Church Lane, Mildenhall, Marlborough, Wilts SN8 2LU.

DAUGHTER LIVING

Hon Christine Ann, *b* 1951.

Preston, family name of Viscount Gormanston.

Primrose, family name of Earl of Rosebery.

PRIOR, BARON (Prior) (Life Baron 1987)

JAMES MICHAEL LEATHES PRIOR, PC, son of late Charles Bolingbroke Leathes Prior, of Norwich; *b* 11 Oct 1927; *ed* Charterhouse, and Pembroke Coll, Camb; Parl Private Sec to Pres of Board of Trade 1963, to Min of Power 1963-64, to Rt Hon Edward Heath (as Leader of Opposition) 1965-70; Min of Agriculture, Fisheries and Food 1970-72, Lord Pres of Council and Leader of House of Commons 1972-74, Opposition front bench spokesman on Employment 1974-79, Sec of State for Employment 1979-81, for Northern Ireland 1981-84; a Dep Chm Conservative Party 1972-74 (Vice-Chm 1965); Dir United Biscuits (Holdings) 1984-94, Barclays Bank 1984-89, Barclays International 1984-89, J. Sainsbury 1984-92, Chm The General Electric Co plc 1984-98; Chm Allders plc 1989-94, East Anglian Radio plc 1992-96, and Royal Veterinary Coll 1990-98; Member Tenneco European Advisory Council 1986-97 and American International Group Advisory Council; commn'd Royal Norfolk Regt 1946, served in India and Germany; farmer; MP Lowestoft (Suffolk) (*C*) 1959-83, and Waveney 1983-87; *cr* PC 1970, and *Baron Prior*, of Brampton, Suffolk (Life Baron) 1987: *m* 1954, Jane Primrose Gifford, 2nd da of late Air Vice-Marshal Oswyn George William Gifford Lywood, CB, CBE, and has issue.

Address – House of Lords, SW1A 0PW.

SONS LIVING

Hon David Gifford Leathes, *b* 1954: *m* 1987, Caroline, da of Peter Holmes, of The Old Rectory, Shotesham, Norwich, and has issue living, Nicholas James Peter, *b* 1988, — Helena Caitlin Elizabeth, *b* (twin) 1988. *Residence* – Swanington Manor, Norwich, Norfolk NR9 5NR.

Hon Simon Gilman Leathes, *b* 1956 *m* 1985, Vivien Ann, da of Peter George Keely, of The Cottage, Ringsfield Rd,

Beccles, Suffolk, and has issue living, Alice Rebecca, *b* 1986. *Residence* – Church Farm, Shadingfield, Beccles, Suffolk NR34 8DF.

Hon Jeremy James Leathes, *b* 1962: *m* 1988, Camilla Sarah, elder da of Julian Riou Benson, of The Old Rectory, Abbots Ann, Andover, Hants, and has issue living, Oliver James Leathes, *b* 1991, — Edward Thomas Leathes, *b* 1993, — William Michael Leathes, *b* 1995. *Residence* – Hill House, The Street, Wissett, Halesworth, Suffolk IP19 0JH.

DAUGHTER LIVING

Hon Sarah-Jane Leathes, *b* 1959: *m* 1982, David Alexander Roper, and has issue living, Lucy Victoria, *b* 1987, — Alexandra Florence, *b* (twin) 1987, — Rosanna Jane, *b* 1989. *Residence* – Widbrook House, Sutton Rd, Cookham, Berks SL6 9RD.

PRITCHARD, BARONY OF (Pritchard) (Extinct 1995)

DAUGHTERS LIVING OF LIFE BARON

Hon Rosemary Gail, *b* 1946: *m* 1st, 1967 (*m diss* 1971), Ernest Raymond Anthony Travis; 2ndly, 1980 (*m diss* 1984), Ian Barby; 3rdly, 1985, Michael Withers, of PO Box N7776, Nassau, Bahamas, and has issue (by 2nd and 3rd *m*).

Hon Diana Gillian Amanda (The Colonel's Cottage, Stoneleigh Abbey, Kenilworth, Warwicks CV8 2LF), *b* 1948: *m* 1st, 1969 (*m diss* 1977), David Huntington Williams; 2ndly, 1984 (*m diss* 1993), Harry Johnson, only son of Henry Edward Johnson, of Offchurch Bury, Warwicks, and has issue by both marriages.

WIDOW LIVING OF LIFE BARON

DENISE ARFOR (*Baroness Pritchard*), da of Frank Huntbach: *m* 1941, Baron Pritchard (Life Baron), who *d* 1995. *Residence* – West Haddon Hall, West Haddon, Northampton NN6 7AU.

Prittie, family name of Baron Dunalley.

PRYS-DAVIES, BARON (Prys-Davies) (Life Baron 1983)

GWILYM PRYS PRYS-DAVIES, son of William Davies, by his wife Mary Matilda; *b* 8 Dec 1923; assumed by Deed Poll 1982 the surname of Prys-Davies in lieu of his patronymic; *ed* Towyn Sch, and Univ Coll of Wales, Aberystwyth; served in RN 1942-46; Faculty of Law, Univ Coll of Wales, Aberystwyth 1946-52; admitted Solicitor 1956; Partner, Morgan Bruce & Nicholas, Solicitors, Cardiff, Pontypridd and Porth since 1957; Special Adviser to Sec of State for Wales 1974-78; Chm Welsh Hosps Bd 1968-74; Member Welsh Council 1967-69; Member Economic and Social Cttee, EEC 1978-82; OStJ; *cr Baron Prys-Davies*, of Llanegryn, co Gwynedd (Life Baron) 1983: *m* 1951, Llinos, da of Abram Richard Evans, and has issue, three das.

Residence – Lluest, 78 Church Rd, Tonteg, Pontypridd, Mid Glamorgan.

DAUGHTERS LIVING

Hon Catrin Prys, *b* 1957: *m* 1980, Andrew Peter Waugh, and has issue living, Matthew Prys, *b* 1989, — Owen Prys, *b* 1992, Daniel Prys, *b* 1995, — Jonathan Prys, *b* 1997.
Hon Ann Prys, *b* 1959.
Hon Elin Prys, *b* 1963.

PUTTNAM, BARON (Puttnam) (Life Baron 1997)

DAVID TERENCE PUTTNAM, CBE, son of late Capt Leonard Arthur Puttnam, RA, of Winchmore Hill; *b* 25 Feb 1941; *ed* Minchenden Gram Sch, London; Hon LLD Bristol 1983, Hon DLitt Leicester 1986, Hon LittD Leeds 1992, Hon Fell Manchester Univ 1990, Hon DLitt Bradford 1993, Humberside 1996, and Sunderland 1996; Film Producer; Chm Enigma Productions Ltd since 1978; Chm Nat Film & TV Sch Ltd; Dir Anglia TV Group plc; Chm and Chief Executive Offr, Columbia Pictures 1986-88; Pres Council for Protection of Rural England 1985-92; Tstee, Tate Gallery 1985-92, Nat Energy Foundation and Landscape Foundation; Vice-Pres BAFTA; Visiting Prof, Film Dept, Bristol Univ since 1985; FRGS, FRSA, FRPS; Officier dans l'Ordre des Arts et des Lettres (France) 1991; recipient of many Academy Awards; *cr* CBE 1983, Kt 1995, and *Baron Puttnam*, of Queensgate in the Royal Borough of Kensington and Chelsea (Life Baron) 1997: *m* 1961, Patricia Mary, da of Maj John Frederick Jones, of Folkestone, Kent, and has issue.

Arms – Or within an orle of roses a gateway composed of a central arch between two lesse arches and surmounted by a segmental pediment gules. **Crest** – A harp standing on a closed book fesswise proper bound gules. **Supporters** – *Dexter*, a curlew proper gorged with a plain collar argent charged with square billets sable; *sinister*, a stork proper gorged with a plain collar argent charged with square billets sable.
Address – Enigma Productions, 13-15 Queen's Gate Place Mews, SW7 5BG.

SON LIVING

Hon Alexander David, *b* 1966.

DAUGHTER LIVING

Hon Deborah Jane, *b* 1962: *m* 1985, Lloyd Daniel Gilman Grossman, son of late David K. Grossman, of Marblehead, Massachusetts, USA, and has issue living, Florence Grace, *b* 1989, — Constance Catherine, *b* 1992.

PYM, BARON (Pym) (Life Baron 1987)

FRANCIS LESLIE PYM, MC, PC, only son of late Leslie Ruthven Pym, MP, of Penpergwm Lodge, Abergavenny, Mon, and Hazells Hall, Sandy, Beds; *b* 13 Feb 1922; *ed* Eton, and Magdalene Coll, Camb; a DL for Cambs since 1973; Hon Fell Magdalene Coll, Camb 1979; served World War II 1941-45 as Capt 9th Queen's Royal Lancers (despatches, MC 1945); Memb Herefords CC 1958-62, MP for Cambs (*C*) 1961-83, and for Cambs South East 1983-87; Parl Sec to Treasury and Govt Chief Whip 1970-73, Sec of State Northern Ireland 1973-74, Opposition Spokesman: Agriculture 1974-76, House of Commons Affairs and Devolution 1976-78, Foreign and Commonwealth Affairs 1978-79; Sec of State for Defence 1979-81; Chancellor of Duchy of Lancaster, Paymaster Gen and Leader of House of Commons 1981, Lord Pres of the Council and Leader of House of Commons 1981-82, Foreign Sec 1982-83, Pres Atlantic Treaty Assocn 1985-88; Chm English-Speaking Union 1987-92; *cr* PC 1970, and *Baron Pym*, of Sandy, co Beds (Life Baron) 1987: *m* 1949, Valerie Fortune, elder da of Francis John Heaton Daglish, and has issue.

Arms – Quarterly, 1st and 4th sable on a fesse engrailed between three owls or a trefoil slipped vert between two cross crosslets of the first all within a bordure of the second (*Pym*); 2nd vert on a cross engrailed ermine a lion rampant reguardant sable in the dexter canton a mullet or (*Kingsley*); 3rd sable three salmon haurient per pale argent and or (*Orde*). **Crest** – Upon a mount vert a hind's head erased or gorged with a collar nebuly azure and holding in the mouth a trefoil slipped vert. **Supporters** – *Dexter*, rampant upon a sandy mount with tussocks of grass proper a warhorse in trian aspect sable mane tail and hooves or on its head a chanfron and on the neck a crinet both argent gorged with a double chain pendent therefrom a portcullis gold; *sinister*, rampant upon a like mount a bull in trian aspect sable armed and unguled or also gorged with a double chain and pendent therefrom a portcullis gold. **Motto** – Ubi Seritur Ibi Floreat. *Residence* – Everton Park, Sandy, Beds SG19 2DE. *Club* – Buck's.

SONS LIVING

Hon (Francis) Jonathan, *b* 1952; *ed* Eton, and Magdalene Coll, Camb; Partner, Travers Smith Braithwaite, Solicitors since 1984: *m* 1981, Laura Elizabeth Camille, yr da of Robin Alfred Wellesley, and has issue living, (Francis) Matthew, *b* 1984, — Oliver Quintin, *b* 1988, — Katharine Camille, *b* 1985. *Residence* – 53 Ridgway Place, SW19 4SP.
Hon Andrew Leslie, *b* 1954; *ed* Eton, and RAC Cirencester: *m* 1976, Ruth Alison, da of Benjamin Peter Skelton, and has issue living, Benjamin Ruthven, *b* 1979, — Jessica Mary, *b* 1982. *Residence* – The Elms, Everton, Sandy, Beds SG19 2JU.

DAUGHTERS LIVING

Hon Charlotte Hazell, *b* 1950: *m* 1984, Ian Nye Lightbody, and has issue living, Thomas Hugh, *b* 1986, — Helena Rosamund, *b* 1988.
Hon Sarah Lucy, *b* 1958: *m* 1985, Peter Walton, and has issue living, James Peter, *b* 1986, — Victoria Lucy, *b* 1988.

QUEENBOROUGH BARONY OF (Paget) (Extinct 1949)

DAUGHTER LIVING OF FIRST BARON (*By 2nd marriage*)

Hon Cicili Carol, *b* 1928: *m* 1949, Capt Robert Victor John Evans, and has had issue, John Almeric, *b* 1950: *m* 1980, Patricia L., da of late R. W. Westall, of Birchfield Farm, Sundridge, Kent, and has issue living, William *b* 1983, James *b* 1986, — Michael Hugh, *b* 1956: *m* 1989, Penelope M., da of David Rosling, of Little Saxbys Farm, Cowden, Kent, and has issue living, Hugo Robert *b* 1987, Rory *b* 1999, — Camilla Carol, *b* 1952; *d* 1963, — Patricia Antoinetta (Flat 5, 95 Belgrave Rd, SW1V 2BQ), *b* 1959. *Residence* – The Old Farmhouse, Headcorn, Kent.

Queensberry, Duke of; title borne by Duke of Buccleuch.

QUEENSBERRY, MARQUESS OF (Douglas) (Marquess S 1682, Bt S 1668)

DAVID HARRINGTON ANGUS DOUGLAS, 12th Marquess, and 11th Baronet; *b* 19 Dec 1929; *s* 1954; *ed* Eton; late 2nd Lieut Roy Horse Guards; Prof of Ceramics, Roy Coll of Art since 1959; Sr Fell Royal Coll of Art 1990: *m* 1st, 1956 (*m diss* 1969), Ann, da of Maurice Sinnett Jones, and formerly wife of George Arthur Radford; 2ndly, 1969 (*m diss* 1986), Alexandra Mary Clare Wyndham, da of Guy Wyndham Sich, and has issue by 1st and 2nd wives.

Arms – Quarterly: 1st and 4th argent, a King's heart crowned gules, on a chief azure, three stars of the first, *Douglas*; 2nd and 3rd azure, a bend between six cross crosslets fitchée or, *Mar.* the whole within a bordure or, charged with the double tressure flory-counter gules. Crest – A heart gules, crowned and winged. Supporters – Two flying horses argent winged or. *Residence* – 24 Brook Mews North, W2 3BW.

SONS LIVING (*By 2nd wife*)

SHOLTO FRANCIS GUY (*Viscount Drumlanrig*), *b* 1 June 1967. *Residence* – 51 Hormead Rd, W9 3NQ.
Lord Milo Luke Dickon, *b* 1975.
Lord Torquil Oberon T., *b* 1978.

DAUGHTERS LIVING (*By 1st wife*)

Lady Emma Cathleen, *b* 1956: *m* 1986, Damon Lewis Vincent Heath, and has issue living, Cato Douglas Ross, *b* 1988, — Tyro Kenyon Zane (da), *b* 1992, — Juno Vera Ann, *b* 1998.
Lady Alice, *b* 1965: *m* 1995, Simon Melia, and has issue living, Hero Himalya, *b* 1998.

(*By 2nd wife*)

Lady Kate Cordelia Sasha, *b* 1969.

ADOPTED STEPDAUGHTER LIVING

Victoria Jane Ann DOUGLAS, *b* 1953: *m* 1997, Heddon Edward Johnson, and has issue living, Hadrian Benedict DOUGLAS-JOHNSON, *b* 1976, — Tristan Tancred DOUGLAS-JOHNSON, *b* 1980, — Merlin Brodie DOUGLAS-JOHNSON, *b* 1986, — Quin Marmaduke DOUGLAS-JOHNSON, *b* 1990, — Poppy Ceceilia Ann DOUGLAS-JOHNSON, *b* 1993. *Residence* – Higher Kingston Russell Farmhouse, Winterbourne Abbas, Dorchester, Dorset DT2 9ED.

THE TWELFTH MARQUESS ALSO HAS ISSUE (*by Ann Carey*)

Ambrose Jonathan CAREY, *b* 1961: *m* 1995, Christina Rachel, yr da of Sir Michael Weir, KCMG, and has issue living, Angus Hugh Douglas, *b* 1996.

HALF-BROTHER LIVING

Lord Gawain Archibald Francis (2 Archery Sq, Walmer, Deal, Kent), *b* 1948; *ed* Downside, and Royal Acad of Music; LRAM: *m* 1971, Nicolette, yr da of Col Frank Alfred Eustace, OBE, RM, of Hong Kong, and has issue living, Jamie Sholto, *b* 1975, — Dalziel Frances, *b* 1971: *m* 1995, Michael O'Halloran, — Elizabeth Meriel, *b* 1974, — Natasha Rose, *b* 1976, — Margarita Consuela, *b* 1978, — Mary Anne, *b* 1981.

SISTER LIVING

Lady Jane Katherine, *b* 1926: *m* 1949 (*m diss* 1985), David Arthur Cory-Wright (*see* Cory-Wright, Bt). *Residence* – 14a Fore St, Buckfastleigh, Devon TQ11 0BT.

AUNT LIVING (*natural daughter of 10th Marquess*)

Violet Dorothy May (DOUGLAS), *b* 1912: *m* 1965, Joseph Vincent Conaghan, who *d* 1977.

COLLATERAL BRANCHES LIVING

Issue of late Lord Cecil Charles Douglas, 2nd son of 10th Marquess, *b* 1898, *d* 26 Feb 1981: *m* 1927, Ruby, who *d* 9 May 1981, formerly wife of — St Bede Kirkley, 2nd da of George de Vere Fenn:— Susan Jean, *b* 1939: *m* 1965, Baron (Joachim) Botho Carl Waldemar Georg Hasso von Bose, Kt of Justice, Johanniterorden (Bailiwick of Brandenburg). *Residence* – Apt 1203, 1166 Bay St, Toronto, Ont M5S 2X8, Canada. *Club* – White's.

Grandchildren of late Lord Sholto George Douglas, 4th son of 9th Marquess:—
Issue of late Sholto Augustus Douglas, *b* 1900 (became a French citizen 1938), *d* 1950: *m* 1925, Isabelle, who *d* 1993, da of late François Raymon:—
Douglas Bruce Georges, *b* 1926. —— Robert, *b* 1933: *m* 1963, Nicole Bourgeois, and has issue living, Marie Christine, *b* 1965. —— Noel (son), *b* 1939. —— Elisabeth Georgette, *b* 1927: *m* 1952, Jean Masoin, artist, and has issue living, Sybil Elisabeth, *b* 1953: *m* 1985, Daniel Rohemer, and has issue living, Alexandre *b* 1988, Louis *b* 1990, Aurelia *b* 1986. —— Sybil, *b* 1931: *m* 1966, Nigel Paul Mitchell-Carruthers, of 308, Route de Grasse, Vence, 06 France, and has issue living, Bruce Nigel Lawrence, *b* 1968: *m* 19—, Cecile, — and has issue living, Pauline *b* 19—, Laurie *b* 19—, Eve *b* 19—, — Cecilia Elisabeth, *b* 1973. —— Marguerite Jeannette, *b* 1941: *m* 1st, 1969 (*m diss* 1973), Jean Demol; 2ndly, 1974, Count Xavier de Chagny, and has issue living (by 1st *m*), Ysabelle, *b* 1965; has issue living, Quentin *b* 1992, Joel *b* 1995, — (by 2nd *m*), Godefroy, *b* 1975. —— Marie-Jeanne, *b* 1944: *m* 1st, 1970, Horace Warren Hastings-Hodgkins, who *d* 1972; 2ndly, 1978, Wesley Alan Christie (c/o Nat Westminster Bank, 5 Broad St, Wokingham, Berks) and has issue living (by 1st husband), Warren Sholto Olivier (116 Clifton Rd, Emmbrook, Wokingham, Berks), *b* 1966; MA Cantab: *m* 1992, Pamela, da of Kuldip Khosla, and has issue living, Jamie *b* 1995, Thomas Paul *b* 1998, — Julian Percy Herbert, *b* 1967, — Alistair John Hughes, *b* 1970, — (by 2nd husband), Michael Ian Jerôme, *b* 1974, — Jasmine Elisabeth Céline, *b* 1976.

Grandchildren of late Arthur Henry Johnstone-Douglas, elder son of Robert Johnstone-Douglas, 2nd son of Henry Alexander Douglas, brother of 6th and 7th Marquesses:—
Issue of late Robert Sholto Johnstone-Douglas, *b* 1871, *d* 1958: *m* 1913, Bettina, who *d* 1961, da of late Harman Grisewood:—
Robert Arthur, *b* 1914. —— Elizabeth Gwendolen Teresa, *b* 1916: *m* 1st, 1954, as his 2nd wife, 6th Earl of Craven, who *d* 1965; 2ndly, 1966, Kenneth Kruger Harmood Banner, of Peelings Manor, Pevensey, Sussex, who *d* 1995.

Grandchildren of late Archibald Charles Douglas, 2nd son of late Rt Rev Henry Alexander Douglas, Bishop of Bombay, 5th son of late Henry Alexander Douglas (ante):—
Issue of late Archibald Andrew Henry Douglas, *b* 1902, *d* 1997: *m* 1935 (*m diss* 1980), Marjorie Gordon, who *d* 1992, elder da of late Dr. H. Grey Brown:—
(Archibald) Sholto Gordon (10 Coleford Rd, Wandsworth, SW18), *b* 1937; *ed* Loretto: *m* 1984, Mrs Victoria Ann Adam, only da of late James Bonnyman, of Sarasota, Florida, USA. —— Ian Andrew McClelland (6 Ansley Rd, Houghton, Cambs PE17 2DQ), *b* 1939; *ed* Loretto; W/Cmdr RAF: *m* 1967, Jennifer, da of L. F. Merrett, of Plymouth, and has issue living, Andrew James Sholto, *b* 1973, — Kirsten Lucy, *b* 1969. —— (Katherine) Veronica, *b* 1943; *ed* Moreton Hall, and King's Coll, Durham (BA): *m* 1963, Richard Ninian Barwick Clegg, QC, of Ford Farm, Wootton Courtenay, Somerset, only son of late Sir Cuthbert Barwick Clegg, TD, and has issue living, Aidan Charles Barwick, *b* 1966: *m* 1996, Colette, da of Edward Fanning, and has issue living, James Richard Barwick *b* 1999, — Sebastian James Barwick, *b* 1969, — Flavia Mary Rosabel, *b* 1968. —— (Ursula) Rosemary, *b* (twin) 1943; *ed* Moreton Hall, and Girton Coll, Camb (BA): *m* 1968, William Harvey Righter, of 10 Quick St, N1 8HL, Reader in English and Comparative Lit, Warwick Univ, who *d* 1997.

Grandchildren of late (Hon) John Douglas, CMG (infra):—
Issue of late (Hon) Edward Archibald Douglas, *b* 1877, *d* 1947: *m* 1907, Annette Eileen, who *d* 1966, 2nd da of Hon Mr Justice Virgil Power (a Puisne Judge of Supreme Court, Queensland), of Rockhampton, Queensland:—
Sir Edward Sholto, *b* 1909; *ed* St Ignatius Coll, Sydney; 1939-45 War as Major Austn Imperial Force; Kt 1977: *m* 1939, Mary Constance, da of late C. M. Curr, of Buckie, NS Wales. *Residence* – 81 Markwell Street, Hamilton, Brisbane, Queensland. —— Gavin James, *b* 1926; *ed* Downlands Coll, Toowoomba, and Queensland Univ (MB and BS 1948); FRACS 1955; *m* 1951, Clare, da of J. H. McHugh of Townsville Queensland, and has issue living, Edward John, *b* 1952, — Andrew Benedict (4 Burdekin St, Mundingburra, Townsville, Queensland 4812), *b* 1957, — Gavin Gerard (14 Hammond, Mysterton, Townsville, Queensland 4812), *b* 1958; *ed* Downlands Coll, Toowoomba, and James Cook Univ of N Qld (BCom 1982): *m* 1985, Sally Maree, da of B. W. Desailly, of Townsville, Qld, and has issue living, Matthew Liam *b* 1987, Benjamin James *b* 1988, Nicholas Edward *b* 1990, William Gavin *b* 1994, Anna Elizabeth *b* 1992, Julia Sally *b* 1998, — Christopher James (6/18 Peerless Av, Mermaid Beach, Queensland 4218), *b* 1962, — Margot Anne (18 Cannan St, S Townsville, Queensland 4810), *b* 1953, — Helen Penny (7/469 Pine Ridge Rd, Runaway Bay, Queensland 4215), *b* 1955, — Annette Josefa, *b* 1960: *m* 1982, Roger Michael Pell, of 12 Pine Cone Court, Bunya, Queensland 4055, — Mary Patrice, *b* 1964. *Residence* – 361 Stanley St, North Ward, Townsville, Queensland 4810. —— Andrew Brice, *b* 1931; *ed* Downlands Coll, Toowoomba: *m* 1957, Lorraine, da of R. J. Lawson, of Brisbane, and has issue living, Rev Sholto Francis (207 Lesmurdie Rd, Lesmurdie, W Australia 6076), *b* 1958; *ed* Downlands Coll, Toowoomba, Queensland Univ (BA 1980), Monash Univ (Dip Ed 1987), and Melbourne Univ (B Theol 1988); ordained priest 1988, — David James (36 Collins St, Clayfield, Brisbane, Queensland 4011), *b* 1960; *ed* Downlands Coll, Toowoomba, and Queensland Univ (B Comm 1983), CPA 1994: *m* 1991, Karen Sharmaine, da of B. H. Emerson, of Dover, UK, and has issue living, James Francis Emerson *b* 1998, Alexandra Helena *b* 1993, — Maxwell Richard (17 Hayward St, Paddington, Brisbane, Queensland 4064), *b* 1966; *ed* St Joseph's Coll, Brisbane, and Queensland Univ (BSc 1986), — Andrew Brice Christopher (16 St Martin's Terrace, Buderim, Queensland 4556), *b* 1968; *ed* St Joseph's Coll, Brisbane, and Queensland Univ (BA 1988); LLB 1991: *m* 1998, Lynette, da of L. W. E. E. Evans, of Brisbane. *Residence* – 17 Sutherland Av, Ascot, Brisbane, Queensland 4007.

Issue of late Henry Alexander Cecil Douglas, *b* 1879, *d* 1952: *m* 1st, 1910, Flora Isabel, who *d* 1910, da of Charles Hugh Macdonald, formerly of Kilcoy, Queensland; 2ndly, 1914, Catherine Cecilia, who *d* 1977, da of late T. C. Beirne, MLC, of Queensland:—
(By 2nd *m*) Alexander Michael (21 Palm Av, Ascot, Brisbane, Queensland 4007), *b* 1926; *ed* Downlands Coll, Queensland: *m* 1954, Morna Therese, da of Michael Patrick O'Rourke of Brisbane, Queensland, and has issue living, Henry Alexander Michael (53 Watson St, Wilston, Brisbane, Queensland 4051), *b* 1955; *ed* St Joseph's Coll, Brisbane, and Queensland Univ (MB BS) 1978: *m* 1984, Frances Michelle, da of Eric Donnelly, of Brisbane, and has issue living, Eric Michael *b* 1987, Joseph Henry *b* 1988, Alexandra Kate *b* 1991, Annabelle Rose *b* 1994, — Richard John (36 Neulans Rd,

Indooroopilly, Brisbane, Queensland 4068), *b* 1957; *ed* St Joseph's Coll, Brisbane, and Queensland Univ (BCom, LLB), Bar Q'land 1980, Senior Counsel 1998: *m* 1981, Rosemary Nerida, da of Rodney Malcolm Wylie, of Brisbane, and has issue living, Sally Elizabeth *b* 1985, Madeline Rosemary *b* 1988, Heather Louise *b* 1990, Julia Clare *b* 1991, — Alexander Rodney (3 Montevideo Drive, Robina, Gold Coast, Queensland 4226), *b* 1958; *ed* St Joseph's Coll, Brisbane, and Queensland Univ (MB BS) 1981: *m* 1983, Susan Kim, da of C. Primmer, of Rockhampton, Queensland, — Andrew Beirne (136 Oriel Rd, Ascot, Brisbane, Queensland 4007), *b* 1960; *ed* St Joseph's Coll, Brisbane, and Queensland Univ (BCom) 1982: *m* 1988, Elizabeth Jane, da of D. Pie, of Brisbane, and has issue living, James Beirne *b* 1990, Kate Elizabeth *b* 1993, Eliza Charlotte *b* 19—, — James Patrick (7 Overstrand Mansions, Prince of Wales Drive, London SW11 4HA), *b* 1965; *ed* St Joseph's Coll, Brisbane: *m* 1995, Heather Patricia, da of J. Rigg, of Southport, Lancs. —— Sybil Catherine *b* 1918: *m* 1943, Alan B. Bryan, FCA, Lt Cdr R Aust Navy (ret), and has issue living, Alan Douglas, *b* 1944; MB BS, FRACP: *m* 1972, Margaret Suzanne van Rompaey, and has issue living, Thomas Charles *b* 1975, Sophie Elizabeth *b* 1973, Olivia Catherine *b* 1977, Chloe Margaret *b* 1979, — Henry Beirne, *b* 1947; MB BS: *m* 1982, Patricia Mary Johnson, and has issue living, Henry William *b* 1986, Michael Charles *b* 1987, Brigid Catherine Cecilia *b* 1984, — Edward Alan, *b* 1954; BComm: *m* 1st, 1982 (*m diss* 1990), Heather Joy Killen; 2ndly, 1990, Felicity York Sharples, and has issue living (by 2nd *m*), Isobel Rose *b* 1992, — Neil Beirne, *b* 1959; BBus: *m* 1983, Lisa Marie Walsh, and has issue living, Edward George Peter *b* 1986, George Bernard Joseph *b* 1990, Lucy Cecilia *b* 1985, Harriet Catherine *b* (twin) 1986, Annie Beatrice *b* 1992, Charlotte Mary *b* (twin) 1992, — Mary Christine, *b* 1949: *m* 1973, David Walter Drake, BComm, FCA, and has issue living, Alexander Bryan *b* 1974, Nicholas Thomas *b* 1977, Douglas Romeo *b* 1983, Elizabeth Sybil *b* 1980. *Residence* – 14 Inverness St, Ascot, Brisbane, Queensland 4007.

Issue of late Hugh Maxwell Douglas, Lieut Australian Forces, *b* 1881, *d* of wounds received in action 1918: *m* 1904, Hannah Elizabeth, 2nd da of E. L. Thornton, formerly of Warwick, Queensland:—
Henry Alexander (PO Box 226, Toowoomba, Queensland 4350), *b* 1908: *m* 1938, Ethel Audrey, da of late Dr A. E. Malaher, and has issue living, Henry John (Gympie Rd, Northgate, Queensland 4013), *b* 1942: *m* 1966, Susan da of E. Clark, of Balgowlah Heights, Sydney, and has issue living, Geoffrey Peter *b* 1970, Ian Andrew *b* 1971, Elizabeth Jane *b* 1967: *m* 1989, Conrad Cholakos, Kathryn Ann *b* 1973, — Kathrine (PO Box 226, Toowoomba, Queensland 4350), *b* 1938: *m* 1961 (*m diss* 1982), John Francis Douglas, and has issue living, Andrew *b* 1963, Grahame *b* 1965, James *b* 1968.

Grandchildren of late (Hon) John Douglas, CMG, 7th son of Henry Alexander Douglas (brother of 6th and 7th Marquesses), 3rd son of Sir William Douglas, 4th Bt:—
Issue of late (Hon) Robert Johnstone Douglas, *b* 1883, *d* 1972; Puisne Judge of Supreme Court of Qld: *m* 1912, Alice Mary, da of late Andrew Ball, of Townsville, Qld:—
†Robert Andrew, AM (18 Lawson St, Hermit Park, Townsville, Qld), *b* 1915; *ed* St Joseph's Coll, Nudgee, and Melbourne Univ (MB, BS); FRACP 1967; FRCP Lond 1979; formerly Maj Australian Army Med Corps Middle East, New Guinea, and Tarakan 1940-45; AM (1984): *m* 1949, Barbara, da of late Rev John Shaw, of Adelaide, S Australia, and widow of Harry Buzolich, of Melbourne, and *d* 1998, leaving issue, Robert John (13 Drewett St, Surrey Hills, Melbourne, Vic 3127), *b* 1950; *ed* James Cook Univ (BA), and Melbourne Univ (MBA): *m* 1983, Lynne, da of late Capt James Erskine Muirhead of Melbourne, and has issue living, James Robert *b* 1986, Sarah Jane *b* 1984, — Sholto James Shaw, *b* 1962, — Catriona, *b* 1952: *m* 1983, Geoffrey Charles Beames, MB BS, FRANZCP, and has issue living, Alexander Thomas *b* 1986, Michael Robert Charles *b* 1988, Catherine Alice *b* 1990, — Barbara Selina, *b* 1953: *m* 1974, Philip William Hale, and has issue living, Nathan Alexander *b* 1974, Emily Angela *b* 1975, — Sarah, *b* 1955. —— Beatrice Rose Mary, *b* 1919: *m* 1947, Cornelius James Howard, who *d* 1980, of 984 Burke Rd, Deepdene, Melbourne, Vic 3103, Aust, and has issue living, Catherine Mary, *b* 1952: *m* 1977, Peter Capell Dobson, MB, BS, MRCOG, FRCS Ed, FRACOG, of 26 Wimba Av, Kew, Vic 3101, Aust, and has issue living, Michael Howard *b* 1980, Elizabeth Mary *b* 1978, Sarah Catherine *b* 1982, Alice Jane *b* 1985, — Elizabeth Anne, *b* 1953: *m* 1978, Christopher John Dawson, of 33 Dorking Rd, Box Hill, Victoria 3128, Australia, and has issue living, Emma Catherine *b* 1984, Juliet Beatrice *b* 1986, Maria Irene *b* 1988, Tess Elizabeth *b* 1992.

Grandchildren of late (Hon) Robert Johnstone Douglas (ante):—
Issue of late (Hon) James Archibald Douglas, *b* 1917; Puisne Judge of Supreme Court of Queensland, Maj AIF; *d* 1984: *m* 1943, Marjorie Mary (Greyleaves, Morgan St, Ascot, Brisbane, Queensland), da of late James Campbell Ramsay, of Ballarat:—
Robert Ramsay, RFD (18 Towers Street, Ascot, Brisbane, Qld 4007), *b* 1944; *ed* Villanova Coll, Coorparoo, and Qld Univ (LLB); Bar Qld 1968; QC 1982; W Cmdr RAAF Res; Judge Advocate, Aust Defence Forces; Knight of Honour and Devotion Sovereign Mil Order of Malta: *m* 1970, Jennifer Farmar, da of Frank Wilmot Horton, of Blenheim, NZ, and has issue living, Robert Horton, *b* 1970, — William John Archibald, *b* 1975, — Charlotte Mary, *b* 1972. —— Francis Maxwell (4 Wiston Gardens, Double Bay, Sydney, NSW 2028), *b* 1946; *ed* Villanova Coll, Coorparoo, Qld Univ (BA, LLB), and Camb Univ (LLB); Bar Qld 1969, Bar NSW 1975, QC 1988: *m* 1st, 1970 (*m diss* 1995), Sigrun Baldvinsdottir, da of Baldvin Einarsson, of Reykjavik, Iceland; 2ndly, 1995, Lisa Ann, da of Dr Remo Cantamessa, FRCS(Ed), FRACS, of Brisbane, Qld, and has issue living, (by 1st *m*) James Baldvin, *b* 1974, — Helga Sigrun, *b* 1979, — Sara Kristin *b* 1989, — (by 2nd *m*) Sholto Francis Alexandre, *b* 1996, — Alexandre Louis James, *b* 1998. —— James Sholto (9 Lucinda Street, Taringa, Brisbane, Qld 4068), *b* 1950; *ed* Villanova Coll, Coorparoo, Qld Univ (BA, LLB), and Camb Univ (LLB); Bar Qld 1973, QC 1989: *m* 1980, Margaret Anne, da of Francis Xavier Kennedy, of Brisbane, and has issue living, Francis Sholto *b* 1983, — Hannah Mary, *b* 1986. —— Catherine Alice Mary (9 Glostermin, Whyenbah St, Hamilton, Qld 4007), *b* 1948; BA, LTCL, ASDA: *m* 1974 (*m diss* 1977), Roger John Stredwick; 2ndly, 1981, William Charles Edward McCourt, of Brisbane.

Grandson of late Walter Douglas-Irvine, 3rd son of late Lord William Robert Keith Douglas, MP (infra):—
Issue of late Rev Henry Archibald DOUGLAS (who reverted to that surname only 1919), *b* 1883, *d* 1962: *m* 1913, Beatrice Alice, who *d* 1976, da of Thomas William Gratrix, of Liverpool:—
Walter Francis Edward (32 St Leonard's St, Stamford, Lincs), *b* 1917; *ed* Exeter Coll, Oxford (BA 1938, MA 1950): *m* 1944, Eugenie Nellie, who *d* 1988, yst da of Gustave Felix Chaudoir, of Highgate, N, and has issue living, Francis Gustave (12 Woodlands, Kerry Pike, co Cork), *b* 1946; *ed* New Univ of Ulster (BSc 1971, MA 1976), and Univ of Hull (PhD 1993): *m* 1976, Hilary Agnes, who *d* 1996, only child of G. A. Deane, of Armoy, co Antrim, and has issue living, Niall Edward *b* 1978, Aoife Lucy *b* 1983, — Mark Gavin (60 Church St, Market Deeping, Lincs PE6 8AL), *b* 1958: *m* 1981 (*m diss* 1992), Sally Knew, has issue living (by Michelle Allot), Poppy Eugénie Allot DOUGLAS *b* 1997, Scarlett Georgina Allott DOUGLAS *b* 1998, — Ruth Mary, *b* 1947; *ed* St Martin's Coll of Art (Dip AD 1969), and Goldsmiths' Coll (PGCE 1988, MA 1992): *m* 1971, William Francis Wright of 10A Tower Av, Chelmsford, Essex, and has issue living, Henry Joseph *b* 1967, Francis Reuben *b* 1973, Barnabas Mark *b* 1981, Rebecca Elizabeth *b* 1976; *ed* Goldsmith's Coll (BSc 1999) (has issue living [by Caswell Andrew Coggins], Jack Andrew COGGINS *b* 1996), — Josephine Eugenie, *b* 1950: *m* 1st, 1973 (*m diss* 1981), Alan Michael Locker; 2ndly, 1984 (*m diss* 1999), Peter John Jarmakowiecz (uses surname of Jakins), and has had issue (by 1st *m*), Benjamin Harvey *b* 1974; *ed* St Andrews Univ (MA 1997), and E Anglia Univ

(PGCE 1998): *m* 1998, Anne, yst da of John Banister, of Louth, Lincs, Joseph Charles *b* 1978, Samuel William *b* and *d* 1980, — Rachel Margaret, *b* 1954: *m* 1974, Richard David Palmer, and has issue living, George Richard *b* 1982, Thomas Jonathan *b* 1983, John Henry *b* 1987, Lucy *b* 1991.

Granddaughters of late Robert Keith Douglas, 5th son of late Charles Irvine Douglas (infra):—
Issue of late Maj Archibald William Douglas, *b* 1907, *d* 1998: *m* 1934, Barbara Middlemost, who *d* 1970, yr da of late Herbert Pratt Bairstow:—
Janet Valerie, *b* 1937: *m* 1959, His Honour Judge (John Percival) Harris, DSC, of Tudor Court, Fairmile Park Rd, Cobham, Surrey KT11 2PP, and has issue living, Steven Oliver (Puzzletree Cottage, Stoke St Michael, Somerset), *b* 1965; *ed* Wellington Coll, and Bristol Univ (BSc); *m* 1993, Diana Elizabeth Jonas, and has issue living, Jack Lawrence *b* 1996, Samuel Noah *b* 1998, — Juliet Caroline, *b* 1961: *m* 19—, Alistair Charles Timms, of Heath End, Bowlhead Green, Godalming, Surrey GU6 6NW, and has issue living, Charles Benjamin Alistair *b* 1991, Amelia Charlotte *b* 1993, — Charlotte Beatrice (12 Ruvigny Gdns, SW15 1JR), *b* 1963: *m* 1992 (*m diss* 1997), Nicholas Michael Frederick Fuller. — Alison Rosemary, *b* 1939: *m* 1967, Brian Woodcock, of La Cohue, Hérupe, St John, Jersey, and has issue living, James William, *b* 1970; *ed* Uppingham, Buckingham Univ (BA), and Hughes Hall, Camb, — Sara Jane, *b* 1969: *m* 1998, Alasdair Gordon Patrick Crosby.

Grandchildren of late Charles Irvine Douglas, 4th son of late Lord William Robert Keith Douglas, MP (who was raised to the rank of a Marquess's yr son 1837), 4th son of Sir William Douglas, 4th Bt, and brother of 6th and 7th Marquesses:—
Issue of late John Campbell Douglas, *b* 1876, *d* 1960: *m* 1910, Violet Douglas, who *d* 1972, da of late C. J. Daniell, of Cuyim, Punta del Este, Uruguay:—
(Charles) Sholto, *b* 1915; European War 1939-45 as Major King's Own Scottish Borders: *m* 1941, Christian Frances, who *d* 1990, da of late Maj-Gen Francis James Marshall, CB, CMG, DSO, and has issue living, Helen Frances, *b* 1942: *m* 1971, Clive Eden Walker (37 Hans Schoeman St, Malanshof, Randburg 2194, S Africa), and has issue living, Alice Megan *b* 1973, Mary Louise *b* 1976, — Katharine Ann, *b* 1943: *m* 1st, 1969 (*m diss* 1983), Timothy MacDermot-Roe; 2ndly, 1984, Robert Athelston Price, of Urlar Farm, Aberfeldy, Perthshire, and has issue living (by 1st *m*), Charles Alexander *b* 1974, Katherine Emma *b* 1972, (by 2nd *m*) Robert John Crossley *b* 1984, Sarah Margaret *b* 1986, — Margaret Jean, *b* 1945: *m* 1976, David Eric Short, of PO Box 880, Harrismith 9880, S Africa, and has issue living, Alan Douglas *b* 1977, Brian Eric *b* 1979. *Residence* – Old School House, Little Ballinluig, Grandtully, Perthshire. ——— Violet Katherine, *b* 1910: *m* 1st, 1935, John Griffith O'Donoghue, who *d* 1976; 2ndly, 1982, Brig F. W. Sandars, DSO, of La Guarida, Jesús Pobre, Gata de Gorgos, Alicante, Spain, and has issue living (by 1st *m*), Susan, *b* 1936: *m* 1956, A. L. K. Liddle, and has issue living, Nicholas John Kestell *b* 1958, Alan Digby Simon *b* 1959, Juliet Susan *b* 1965, — Margaret Ann (Peggy), *b* 1938: *m* 1960, Christopher James Waller, Queen's Roy Irish Hussars, and has issue living, Sarah Louise *b* 1961, Celia Katherine *b* 1963. *Residence* – Drumcowie, Malin, co Donegal. ——— Margaret Elizabeth, *b* 1918: *m* 1945, John Craigmyle Cooper, and has issue living, Ian Alexander Douglas, *b* 1947, — Peter Craigmyle, *b* 1952, — Margaret Jane, *b* 1948. *Residence* – Cherryhill Farm, RRI, Freelton, Ontario, Canada.

Granddaughter of late Sir John Douglas KCMG, 7th son of late Gen Sir James Dawes Douglas, son of Maj James Sholto Douglas, grandson of Sir John Douglas, 3rd Bt:—
Issue of late Francis William Douglas; *b* 1874, *d* 1953; *m* 1908, Violet Eleanor Jane, who *d* 1956, da of late John More O'Ferrall:—
Helen Sholto, *b* 1910: *m* 1st, 1932, Edward William Eric Mann, who was *ka* 1943; 2ndly, 1950, Wilfred Harry Levita, of 6 Hans Crescent, SW1.

PREDECESSORS – (1) *Sir* WILLIAM Douglas, 9th Feudal Baron of Drumlanrig; entertained James VI at his mansion; *cr Lord Douglas of Hawick and Tibbers*, and *Viscount Drumlanrig* (peerage of Scotland) 1628, and *Earl of Queensberry* (peerage of Scotland) 1633, with remainder to his heirs male bearing the surname and arms of Douglas; *d* 1640; *s* by his son (2) JAMES, 2nd Earl; a zealous Royalist; *d* 1671; *s* by his son (3) WILLIAM, PC, 3rd Earl; Justice-Gen of Scotland 1680-2, Extraordinary Lord of Session 1681, and High Treasurer of Scotland and Constable and Gov of Edinburgh Castle 1682; *cr Lord Douglas of Kinmont, Middlebie and Dornoch, Viscount Nith, Torthorwald and Ross, Earl of Drumlanrig and Sanquhar*, and *Marquess of Queensberry* (peerage of Scotland) 1682, with remainder to his heirs male whatsoever, and *Marquess of Dumfriesshire*, and *Duke of Queensberry* (peerage of Scotland) 1683, with remainder to heirs male; *d* 1695: *s* by his el son (4) JAMES, KG, 2nd Duke; Lord High Treasurer of Scotland, Sec of State and Lord High Commr, and First Commr on the part of Scotland to discuss the measure of the Union; in 1806 surrendered the Marquessate of Dumfriesshire and the Dukedom of Queensberry, and in the same year received a new grant of those honours extending the remainder to the heirs of entail descended from William, 1st Earl of Queensberry; *cr Baron Ripon, Marquess of Beverley* and *Duke of Dover* (peerage of Great Britain) 1708 with special remainder to his 2nd son Charles and yr sons in tail male; *d* 1711; *s* (according to decision of House of Lords 1812) by his el surviving son in the Marquessate and Earldom of Queensberry, the Viscountcy of Drumlanrig, and the Lordship of Douglas of Hawick and Tibbers, these not being mentioned in the resignation and regrant of 1706, were not affected by it and descended according to the original limitation, and in the Dukedom and other titles (by his nomination) by his second surviving son, Charles (infra) (5) JAMES, 3rd Marquess; an idiot, probably from birth, who never used the titles; *d* 1715; *s* by his brother (6) CHARLES, 3rd Duke, who had in 1706 been *cr Viscount Tibbers* and *Earl of Solway* (peerage of Scotland), with remainder to the heirs of his father not in succession to the Dukedom of Queensberry; *d* without surviving issue 1778, when the English honours expired and the Scottish peerage devolved upon (7) WILLIAM, KT (only son of William, 2nd Earl of March, el son of William, 1st Earl of March, 2nd son of 1st Duke, who had been *cr Earl of March, Viscount Peebles, and Lord Douglas of Neidpath, Lyne and Munard* (peerage of Scotland) 1697, with remainder to heirs male of body, failing which to heirs to entail of the Lordships and lands of Neidpath), 4th Duke, who in 1731 had *s* his father as 3rd Earl of March (ante), and in 1748 his mother as 4th *Earl of Ruglen* (peerage of Scotland, *cr* 1665); *cr Baron Douglas of Amesbury* (peerage of Great Britain) 1768; *d* 1810, when the Barony of Douglas of Amesbury and the Earldom of Ruglen became ext, and the Earldom of March and inferior dignities (*cr* 1697) passed to the 8th Earl of Wemyss (grandson of Lady Anne Douglas, daughter of 1st Duke of Queensberry and sister of 1st Earl of March, on whom the lordships and lands of Neidpath were entailed), the Dukedom of Queenberry, Marquessate of Dumfriesshire, Earldom of Drumlanrig and Sanquhar, Viscountcy of Nith, Torthorwald, and Ross, and Lordship of Douglas of Kinmont, Middlebie and Dornoch reverted to the 3rd Duke of Buccleuch (grandson of Lady Jane Douglas, el da of 2nd Duke of Queensberry), and the Marquessate and Earldom of Queensberry, Viscountcy of Drumlanrig, and Lordship of Douglas of Hawick and Tibbers devolved upon his kinsman and heir male (8) *Sir* CHARLES Douglas, 5th Bt of Kelhead (4th in descent from Sir James Douglas of Kelhead, who was created a baronet of Nova Scotia 1668 with remainder to heirs of his body, el surviving son of Col Sir William Douglas of Kelhead, 2nd son of 1st Earl of Queensberry), who became the 6th Marquess of Queensberry; *cr Baron Solway*, of Kinmount, co Dumfries (peerage of United Kingdom) 1833; *dsp* 1837, when the Barony of Solway became ext, and he was *s* in the Scottish honours by his brother (9) JOHN, 7th Marquess; *d* 1856; *s* by his son (10) ARCHIBALD WILLIAM, PC, 8th Marquess; *b* 1818: *m* 1840, Caroline Margaret, who *d* 1904, da of Gen Sir William Robert Clayton, 5th Bt; was MP for Dumfriesshire (LC) 1847-56, and Comptroller of the Household 1853-6; *d* 1858; *s* by his son (11) JOHN

SHOLTO, 9th Marquess, b 1844: m 1st, 1866 (m diss 1887) Sibyl, who d 1935, da of late Alfred Montgomery; 2ndly, 1893 (m diss 1894), Ethel, da of Edward Charles Weeden, of Eastbourne; d 1900; s by his el surviving son (12) PERCY SHOLTO, 10th Marquess, b 1868: m 1st, 1893, Anna Maria, who d 1917, da of late Rev Thomas Walters, V of Boyton, Cornwall; 2ndly, 1918, Mary Louise, who d 1956, da of late Richard Bickel, of Cardiff, and widow of Ernest Morgan; d 1920; s by his el son (13) FRANCIS ARCHIBALD KELHEAD, 11th Marquess, b 1896; Capt Black Watch (Roy Highlanders); European War 1914-19 (twice wounded); sometime a representative Peer for Scotland: m 1st, 1917 (m diss 1925), Irene Clarice, who d 1977, da of H. W. Richards, of Regent's Park, NW; 2ndly, 1926 (m diss 1946), Kathleen Sabine, who d 1959, da of late Harrington Mann; 3rdly, 1947, Muriel Beatrice Margaret (CHUNN), who d 1992, da of late Arthur John Rowe Thornett; d 1954; s by his el son (14) DAVID HARRINGTON ANGUS, 12th Marquess and present peer; also Earl of Queens-berry, Viscount Drumlanrig, and Lord Douglas of Hawick and Tibbers.

QUIBELL, BARONY OF (Quibell) (Extinct 1962)

DAUGHTER LIVING OF FIRST BARON (By 1st marriage)

Hon Edith Ellen, b 1904: is Pres of Roy So for Prevention of Cruelty to Animals, Scunthorpe, a Dir of Quibell & Hardy Ltd, builders and contractors, and a JP for Parts of Lindsey, Lincolnshire; was Mayoress of Scunthorpe 1953-4: m 1954, Eric Bennard Cuthbert, who assumed by deed poll 1962 the surname of Bennard in lieu of his patronymic. Residence –

Quin, Wyndham, family name of Earl of Dunraven

QUINTON, BARON (Quinton) (Life Baron 1983)

ANTHONY MEREDITH QUINTON, FBA, son of late Surgeon Capt Richard Frith Quinton, RN (d 1935), by his wife, late Gwenllyan Letitia (d 1978); b 25 March 1925; ed Stowe, and Ch Ch Oxford (BA 1948); served 1939-45 War with RAF; Fell of All Souls Coll Oxford 1949-55; Fell of New Coll Oxford 1955-78; Pres of Trin Coll Oxford 1978-87; Member Arts Council of Great Britain 1979-82; FBA 1977; cr Baron Quinton, of Holywell, City of Oxford and co Oxfordshire (Life Baron) 1983; m 1952, Marcelle, da of late Maurice Wegier, of New York, and has issue.

Arms – Argent a tilting spear in bend sable grip butt and coronal or between two bends also sable and in chief three roses gules barbed and seeded proper and in base as many martlets also gules. Crest – A quintain proper Supporters – Dexter, a fox rampant proper; sinister, a griffin segreant per fess azure and or both gorged with a coronet flory gold.
Residences – The Mill House, Turville, Henley-on-Thames, Oxon RG9 6QL; A11, Albany, Piccadilly, W1V 9RD. Clubs – Garrick, Beefsteak, Brooks's.

SON LIVING

Hon Edward Frith, b 1957; ed Winchester, and Imp Coll, London: m 1987, Sarah Eve, da of A. W. Travis, of Western Samoa, and has issue living, Olivia, b 19—, — Ella Susannah, b 1994. Residence – ....

DAUGHTER LIVING

Hon Joanna, *b* 1955: *m* 1st, 1974 (*m diss* 1981), Francis Joseph Fitzherbert-Brockholes (*see* B De Freyne, 1971 Edn); 2ndly, 1981 (*m diss* 1994), Jonathan Nelson, of New York, NY, USA; 3rdly, 1995, William Bateman II, of S Carolina, and has issue living (by 2nd *m*).

QUIRK, BARON (Quirk) (Life Baron 1994)

(CHARLES) RANDOLPH QUIRK, CBE, son of late Thomas Quirk, of Lambfell, Isle of Man, *b* 12 July 1920; *ed* Cronk y Voddy Sch, Douglas High Sch, Univ Coll, London (MA 1949, PhD 1951, DLitt 1961) and Yale Univ; has many honorary doctorates; Hon Master of the Bench, Gray's Inn 1982; 1939-45 War with RAF; Lecturer in English, Univ Coll, London 1947-54; Commonwealth Fund Fell, Yale Univ and Univ of Michigan, USA 1951-52; Reader in English Language and Literature, Univ of Durham 1954-58; Prof of English Language, Univ of Durham 1958-60, Univ of London 1960-68; Quain Prof of English Language and Literature, Univ Coll, London 1968-81; Vice-Chancellor, Univ of London 1981-85; memb Board of British Council 1983-91, and Council of RADA since 1985; Gov of English Speaking Union 1980-85; FBA 1975 and Pres of British Academy 1985-89; Chm British Library Advisory Cttee 1983-98, and Hornby Educational Trust 1979-93; Trustee of Wolfson Foundation since 1987; author of many works on English language and literature; *cr* CBE 1976, Kt 1985, and *Baron Quirk*, of Bloomsbury in the London Borough of Camden (Life Baron) 1994: *m* 1st, 1946 (*m diss* 1979), Jean, who *d* 1995, da of Ellis Gauntlett Williams; 2ndly, 1984, Gabriele, da of Judge Helmut Stein, and has issue by 1st *m*.

Address – University College London, Gower St, WC1E 6BT. *Club* – Athenaeum.

SONS LIVING (*By 1st marriage*)

Hon Eric Randolph (c/o Fox Brooks Marshall, St Peter's Square, Manchester M2 3DN), *b* 1951; *ed* Highgate, and Univ Coll, London (LLB 1972); Solicitor 1975: *m* 1977 (*m diss* 1995), Patricia Anne, da of Stanley Lawrence Hemsworth, of 70 Wood Lane, Ashenhurst, Huddersfield, W Yorks, and has issue living, Richard, *b* 1983, — Catharine, *b* 1979, — Sara, *b* 1980.

Hon Robin Antony (Tornquiststrasse 3, 20259 Hamburg, Germany), *b* 1955; *ed* Highgate, and Univ Coll, London (BA 1978).

RADNOR, EARL OF (Pleydell-Bouverie) (Earl GB 1765, Bt GB 1714)
(Name pronounced "Pleddel-Booverie")

My country is dear; liberty is dearer

JACOB PLEYDELL-BOUVERIE, 8th Earl, and 11th Baronet; *b* 10 Nov 1927; *s* 1968; *ed* Harrow, and Trin Coll, Camb; patron of two livings: *m* 1st, 1953 (*m diss* 1962), Anne Garden Farquharson, da of Donald Farquharson Seth-Smith, MC; 2ndly, 1963 (*m diss* 1985), Margaret, da of late Robin Fleming, of Catter House, Drymen; 3rdly, 1986, Mrs A. C. Pettit, previously wife of late Anthony Pettit, and has issue by 1st and 2nd *m*.

Arms – Quarterly: 1st and 4th, per fesse or and argent, an eagle displayed, with two heads sable, on the breast an escutcheon gules, charged with a bend vair, *Bouverie* 2nd and 3rd, argent a bend gules, guttée d'eau between two ravens sable, a chief checky, or and sable, *Pleydell*. Crest – A demi-eagle with two heads displayed sable, ducally gorged or, and charged on the breast with a cross crosslet argent. Supporters – Two eagles reguardant, wings elevated sable, ducally gorged or, each charged on the breast with a cross crosslet argent.
Residence – Longford Castle, Salisbury, Wilts SP5 4EF.

SONS LIVING (By 1st marriage)

WILLIAM (*Viscount Folkestone*), *b* 5 Jan 1955; *ed* Harrow, and RAC Cirencester: *m* 1996, (Auriol) Melissa, only da of James Keith Edward Stanford, of Manor Farm, Droop, Haselbury Bryan, Dorset, and has issue:—

SON LIVING— *Hon* Jacob, *b* 7 April 1999.
DAUGHTER LIVING— *Hon* Hope, *b* 1997.

Hon Peter John, *b* 1958; *ed* Harrow, and Trin Coll, Camb: *m* 1986, Hon Jane Victoria Gilmour, only da of Baron Gilmour of Craigmillar, PC (Life Baron), and has issue living, Timothy, *b* 1987, — Jamie, *b* 1989, — Lara Caroline, *b* 1993, — Clare Anne, *b* (twin) 1993. *Residence* – Newcourt Farmhouse, Downton, Wilts SP5 3JF. *Club* – Pratt's.

DAUGHTERS LIVING (By 2nd marriage)

Lady Lucy, *b* 1964.
Lady Martha, *b* (twin) 1964.
Lady Belinda, *b* 1966.
Lady Frances, *b* 1973.

BROTHER LIVING

Hon Reuben (Bleak House, Slindon, W Sussex BN18 0RP), *b* 1930; *ed* Harrow; late 2nd Lt Roy Scots Greys: *m* 1956, Bridget Jane, el da of late John Fowell Buxton (*see* Buxton, Bt, colls), and has issue living, Edward (29 Malcolm St., Fremantle, Western Australia 6160), *b* 1957: *m* 1984, Nichola, da of Dr John Wood, of Blackheath, SE3, and has issue living, Nathan John *b* 1987, Joshua Edward *b* 1989, Monica Alice *b* 1990, Jessica Anne *b* 1994, — Jasper John (29 Clapham Common Southside, SW4), *b* 1964: *m* 1991, Katherine Jane, only da of Richard Christopher Wordsworth Pelly (*see* Pelly, Bt, colls), and has issue living, Josiah Edwin *b* 1997, Rufus Noah *b* (twin) 1997, — Rosalind Mary, *b* 1960: *m* 1988, Dr Jonathan Hugh Higham, of 30 Princes St, Dunstable, Beds, eldest son of J.A.E. Higham, of New York, and Chichester, Sussex.

HALF-BROTHER LIVING

Hon Richard Oakley (Lawrence End, Peters Green, Luton, Beds), *b* 1947; *ed* Harrow, and RAC Cirencester; DL Herts 1992, High Sheriff 1998: *m* 1978, Victoria M., yr da of late Frank Waldron, of Pond House, Kidmore End, nr Reading, and has issue living, David Oakley, *b* 1979, — Bartholomew Richard, *b* 1981, — Harriot Isobel, *b* 1984.

SISTERS LIVING

Lady Jane, *b* 1923; DL E Riding Yorks 1998: *m* 1945, Richard Anthony Bethell, who *d* 1996, of Manor Farm House, Long Riston, Hull (Cotterell, Bt), and has issue living, Hugh Adrian (Rise Park, Hull), *b* 1952; *ed* Eton, and Exeter Univ: *m* 1983, Sarah Elizabeth, eldest da of Maj Thomas Edward St Aubyn, CVO, of Dairy House Farm, Ashford Hill, Newbury, Berks (*see* B St Levan, colls), and has issue living, Oliver Anthony *b* 1985, Edward *b* 1987, Nicholas *b* 1990, — William Anthony (Arnold Manor, Long Riston, nr Hull), *b* 1957: *m* 1983, Elizabeth Anne, yr da of Lt-Col Charles Samuel Madden, of co Dublin, and has issue living, Christopher Frederick *b* 1988, Harriet Primrose *b* 1986, — Camilla, *b* 1946: *m* 1966, Peter Charles Freeman Gregory-Hood (*see* V Hood, colls), — Sarah, *b* 1948: *m* 1966, David Ratcliffe Brotherton, of Whitwell-on-the-Hill, York, and has issue living, Toby Ratcliffe *b* 1972, Serena *b* 1970.

Lady Harriot, *b* 1935: *m* 1965, Mark Iain Tennant, of 30 Abbey Gdns, NW8 9AT, and Dalfluig Castle, by Alford, Aberdeenshire (*see* B Glenconner, colls).

AUNTS LIVING (Daughters of 6th Earl)

Lady Margaret, *b* 1903: *m* 1923, Lt-Col Gerald Barry, MC, who *d* 1977 (*see* Barry, Bt, colls).

Lady Helen, OBE, *b* 1908: OBE (Civil) 1946, DL Berks: *m* 1931, Major Hon David John Smith, CBE, who *d* 1976 (*see* V Hambleden). *Residence* – King's Copse House, Bucklebury, Berks.

COLLATERAL BRANCHES LIVING

Issue of late Capt Hon Edward Pleydell-Bouverie, MVO, RN, 2nd son of 6th Earl, *b* 1899, *d* 1951: *m* 1936, (Alice) Pearl, who *d* 1996, aged 101, da of late Major Edward Barrington Crake, Rifle Brig, and widow of 2nd Baron Montagu of Beaulieu:—
Robin (20 Manson Mews, SW7 5AF; Curles Close, Bucklers Hard, Hants SO42 7XA), *b* 1937: *m* 1st, 1960 (*m diss* 1975), Anne-Louise, who *d* 1996, da of Bruce Durham; 2ndly, 1978, Felicity Ruth, yr da of David Towers Downer, DFC, of Holland Park, W11, and has issue living (by 2nd *m*), Nicholas Edward, *b* 1983, — Camilla, *b* 1981.

Issue of late Hon Bartholomew Pleydell-Bouverie, 3rd son of 6th Earl, *b* 1902, *d* 1965: *m* 1st, 1927, Lady Doreen Clare Hely-Hutchinson, who *d* 1942, da of 6th Earl of Donoughmore; 2ndly, 1949, Mrs Katharine Bradley Martin, who *d* 1977, da of late Robert E. Tod, of New York:—
(By 1st *m*) Simon (The Castle House, Deddington, Oxon), *b* 1928; *ed* Harrow; late 2nd Lt Life Guards: *m* 1961, Vivien Eleanor, only da of Sir Richard Michael Keane, 6th Bt, and has issue living, David Archie, *b* 1964, — Grania Clare, *b*

1962: *m* 1991, Niels David Scott, son of Wolf Scott, of Geneva, Switzerland, and of Fredensborg, Denmark, and has issue living, Finn *b* 1992, — Juliet Rose, *b* 1968, — Alice Susan, *b* 1970: *m* 1996, (Mark) Christian Meade Brotherton, yst son of Ven (John) Michael Brotherton, Archdeacon of Chichester. —— Penelope Jane, OBE, *b* 1932; OBE (Civil) 1995: *m* 1955, Michael Francis Meredith-Hardy, of Radwell Mill, Baldock, Herts SG7 5ET, and has issue living, Richard, *b* 1957; *ed* Eton, and Birmingham Poly: *m* 1987, Nicola Louise, eldest da of Hugh Morgan Lindsay Smith, of Bank Farm, Brandon Creek, Downham Market, Norfolk, and has issue living, Hugo *b* 1994, Alexandra *b* 1990, Isobel *b* 1992, — Luke, *b* 1959: *m* 1987, Clare M, yst da of late William T. Minogue, of Kew, Melbourne, Australia, and has issue living, William Michael, *b* 1992, Katherine Jane *b* 1988, Georgina Ann *b* 1990, — John Octavian, *b* 1962, — Paul Bartholomew, *b* 1966.

Issue of late Maj Hon Peter Pleydell-Bouverie, KRRC, yst son of 6th Earl, *b* 1909, *d* 1981: *m* 1st, 1938 (*m diss* 1946), Audrey Evelyn, who *d* 1968, da of late William Dodge James, CVO, JP, DL, of West Dean Park, Sussex (Forbes, Bt), formerly wife of Marshall Field, of Chicago, USA, and previously widow of Capt Muir Dudley Coats, MC; 2ndly, 1947, Audrey, who *d* 1997, da of late Capt Archibald Glen Kidston, JP, of Tyrcelyn, Builth Wells, Radnorshire, and Gwenyfed, Three Cocks, Breconshire, and formerly wife of late Anthony Seymour Bellville:—
(By 2nd *m*) James, *b* 1950; *ed* Harrow: *m* 1995, Ann Elisabeth, eldest da of late Neil Aul Mactaggart, of Nassau (*see* Mactaggart, Bt, colls), and has issue living, Jeremy *b* 1998. *Residence* – The Bell House, Man O' War Cay, Abaco, Bahamas.

Granddaughter of late Col Hon Stuart Pleydell-Bouverie, DSO, OBE, TD, 2nd son of 5th Earl:—
Issue of late Christopher Pleydell-Bouverie, *b* 1901, *d* 1949: *m* 1930 (*m diss* 1939), Kathleen Adele, who *d* 1981, da of late William Henry Carpenter Gelshenen, of New York, and 7 Cadogan Gardens, SW:—
Anne Patricia, *b* 1933: *m* 1953, Peter James Grant, Lieut Queen's Own Cameron Highlanders (TA Reserve), and has issue living, Charles Ludovic, *b* 1956; *ed* Eton, — Laura Marguerite, *b* 1959. *Residence* – Standon House, Standon, Herts.

Issue of late Hon Kenelm Pleydell-Bouverie, 6th son of 4th Earl, *b* 1852, *d* 1921: *m* 1905, Evelyn Bertie Charlotte, who *d* 1936, da of late David Maitland Makgill-Crichton (E Lauderdale, colls):—
Bertrand Eric (Middle Leaze, Coleshill, Swindon, Wilts), *b* 1914; *ed* Trin Coll, Camb (BA 1939); 1939-45 War (despatches): *m* 1950, Pamela, adopted da of late Lt-Col Roderick William Macdonald, CIE, DSO, and has issue living, Rupert William (Waverley House, Monkwood, Alresford, Hants SO24 0HB), *b* (Dec) 1950; *ed* Harrow; FCA: *m* 1978, Evelyn Marie, da of Capt John A. Conlon, of Manor Croft, W Ayton, Yorks, and has issue living, Matthew Alexander *b* 1979; *ed* Harrow, Edward Richard *b* 1984, — Nigel Justin, *b* 1955; *ed* Harrow, UBC, Canada and Univ Coll, Cardiff, — Prunella Sarah, *b* 1952: *m* 1976, Thomas Paul Miller, of 44 Bloomfield Terrace, SW1, and Lyemarsh Farmhouse, Mere, Wilts, and has issue living, Thomas Bertrand *b* 1984, Jessica Frances *b* (twin) 1984.

Grandchildren of late Wilfred Pleydell-Bouverie, 2nd son of late Adm Frederick William Pleydell-Bouverie, el son of late Rev Hon Frederick Pleydell-Bouverie, 4th son of 2nd Earl:—
Issue of late Hugh Wyndham Pleydell-Bouverie, *b* 1900, *d* 1979: *m* 1926, Viola Elizabeth, who *d* 1990, da of Walter Holloway Usher:—
Robin Wyndham (Longford Manor, PO Box 140, Harding, 4680 Natal), *b* 1935: *m* 1960, Jean Elizabeth Vermaak, and has had issue, Kim Wyndham (Sheepwalk Ridge, PO Box 301, Harding, Natal), *b* 1965: *m* 1989, Janine von Falkenhausen, and has issue living, Scott Wyndham *b* 1993, Bianca Lee *b* 1991, — Penelope Ann, *b* 1961: *m* 1985, James Craig Blaker, and has issue living, Byron Lance *b* 1993, Cayley Ann *b* 1989, — Carolyn, *b* 1963: *m* 1988, — Johnson, and *d* 1996, leaving issue, Jarryd Lee *b* 1989, Sarah Jane *b* 1991, Jenna Carrie *b* 1995, — Lynn Michelle, *b* 1968: *m* 1994, Lance Craig Rorich (Glen Read, PO Box 135, Swartberg, 4710 Natal), — Rozanne, *b* 1977. —— Peter Hugh *b* 1943. —— Joy, *b* 1927: *m* 1950, Neville Ramsay Barrett, of 15 Pepworth, Rd, Scottsville, Pietermaritzburg 3201, S Africa, and has issue living, Roger Hugh (8 Dan Pienaar Rd, Port Shepstone 4240, S Africa), *b* 1950: *m* 1974, Sally Taylor, and has issue living, Mark Hugh *b* 1975, Leigh *b* 1977, — Maureen, *b* 1953: *m* 1978, Neil Maxwell (PO Box 1, Winterton 3340, S Africa), and has issue living, Greg *b* 1985, Kirsty *b* 1983, — Judy, *b* 1959: *m* 1981, Wadham Hewstone Hull, of 1 Sakabula Lane, Yellow Wood Park, Durban 4011, S Africa, and has issue living, Lindsay *b* 1984, Tarryn *b* 1986. —— Monica Viola, *b* 1937: *m* 1960, Norman Alexander John Herring, of Chertsey, Cedarville, Natal 4720, S Africa, and has issue living, Kerry, *b* 1961: *m* 1986, Gavan Gray, of 17 Cowan Rd, Hilton, Natal 3245, S Africa, and has issue living, Darren Alexander *b* 1993, Hayley *b* 1991, — Deborah, *b* 1963: *m* 1984, Graeme Holloway, of 61 Dennis Rd, Hayfields, Pietermaritzburg, Natal 3201, S Africa, and has issue living, Christy *b* 1988, Tatum *b* 1991.

Grandchildren of late Seymour Pleydell-Bouverie, 2nd son of Philip Pleydell-Bouverie, son of Hon Philip Pleydell-Bouverie, MP, 5th son of 2nd Earl:—
Issue of late Lieut-Com Philip Hales Pleydell-Bouverie, RNVR, *b* 1900, *d* 1951: *m* 1st, 1923 (*m diss* 1927), Alice Margaret, da of William Alfred Ingram, of 5 Highbury Grove, N5; 2ndly, 1927, Beth Olivia, who *d* 1948, adopted da of late Brig-Gen Ronald Maclachlan, Rifle Brig, and formerly wife of John Fitzhardinge Berkeley Gage (*see* V Gage, colls); 3rdly, 1945, Kathleen, who *d* 1982, da of J. T. Fell, of Bristol:—
(By 1st *m*) Patricia, *b* 1924: *m* 1949, John Marshall, Solicitor, and has issue living, Roland (Wedgewood, Tothill, Burghclere, Newbury, Berks RG20 9ED), *b* 1950; *ed* Bloxham Sch: *m* 1978, Mary West, — Richard James (18 Arthur St, Double Bay, NSW 2028, Australia), *b* 1954; *ed* Radley: *m* 1978, Wendy Miranda Playfair Williams, and has issue living, Angus James *b* 1982, Hamish Playfair *b* 1984, Hugo Radnor *b* 1989, James Roland *b* 1992, — Sheila Ann, *b* 1953: *m* 1977, Philip Gray Clifton King, of 12 Leven Av, Talbot Woods, Bournemouth BH4 9LL. *Residence* – Hill House, Andover Rd, Newbury. —— (By 2nd *m*) Lois, *b* 1928: *m* 1950, Gunther Wolff, and has issue living, Adrian, *b* 1957: *m* 1982, Mary Anne Schuetter, and has issue living, Adam David *b* 1986, Kirsten Marie *b* 1988. —— Xenia, *b* 1929: *m* 1964, Alec Ronald Ayliffe, of RD3 Drury, NZ, and has issue living, Gillian Xenia, *b* 1966.

PREDECESSORS – (**1**) WILLIAM Des Bouveries, an eminent Turkey merchant; *cr a Baronet*, 1714; *d* 1717; *s* by his el son (**2**) *Sir* EDWARD, 2nd Bt; *d* 1736; *s* by his brother (**3**) *Sir* JACOB, 3rd Bt; was MP for and Recorder of New Sarum; *cr Lord Longford*, Baron of Longford, and *Viscount Folkestone* (peerage of Great Britain) 1747; *d* 1761; *s* by his son (**4**) WILLIAM, 2nd Viscount; *cr Baron Pleydell-Bouverie*, of Coleshill, co Berks, and *Earl of Radnor* (peerage of Great Britain) 1765, with remainder to the earldom in default of male issue to the male descendants of his father; *d* 1776; *s* by his son (**5**) JACOB, 2nd Earl; *d* 1828; *s* by his son (**6**) WILLIAM, 3rd Earl; *b* 1779; sat as MP for Salisbury 1802-28: *m* 2ndly, Anne Judith, da of Sir Henry Paulet St John Mildmay, 3rd Bt; *d* 1869; *s* by his son (**7**) JACOB, 4th Earl, *b* 1815; was Lord-Lieut of Wilts: *m* 1840, Lady Mary Augusta Frederica Grimston, who *d* 1879, da of 1st Earl of Verulam; *d* 1889; *s* by his el son (**8**) WILLIAM, 5th Earl, *b* 1841; was Treasurer of the Household 1885-6 and 1886; sat as MP for Wiltshire S (C) 1874-85, and for Enfield Div of Middlesex 1885-9: *m* 1866, Helen Matilda, who *d* 1929, da of late Rev Henry Chaplin, of Blankney, Lincoln; *d* 1900; *s* by his el son **(9)** JACOB, CIE, CBE, 6th Earl, *b* 1868; MP for Wilts S, or Wilton, Div (C) 1892-1900, and Lord-Lieut for Wilts 1925-30: *m* 1891, Julian Eleanor Adelaide, who *d* 1946, da of late Charles Balfour, of Newton Don; *d* 1930; *s* by his son **(10)** WILLIAM, KG, KCVO, 7th Earl, *b* 1895; Keeper of Privy Seal to Prince of Wales 1933; Lord Warden of the Stannaries 1933-65; Chm of Rothamsted Experimental Station 1938-64, and Forestry Commn 1952-63; Official Verderer of New Forest 1964-66: *m* 1st, 1922 (*m diss* 1942), Helena Olivia (*d* 1985) (who *m* 2ndly, 1943, Brig Montacute William Worrell Selby-Lowndes, DSO, who *d* 1972), da of late Charles Robert Whorwood Adeane, CB (B Leconfield, colls); 2ndly, 1943, (Anne) Isobel Graham, OBE, who *d* 1998, da of Lt-Col Richard Oakley, DSO, and widow of Richard Thomas Reynolds Sowerby; *d* 1968; *s* by his son **(11)** JACOB, 8th Earl and present peer; also Viscount Folkestone, Baron Longford (peerage of GB), and Baron Pleydell-Bouverie.

RADSTOCK, BARONY OF (Waldegrave) (Extinct 1953)

GRANDDAUGHTERS LIVING OF FIFTH BARON

Issue of late Com Hon John Montagu Granville Waldegrave, DSC, RN, only son of 5th Baron, *b* 1905, *k* on active ser 1944: *m* 1940, Lady Hersey Margaret Boyle (who *d* 1993, having *m* 2ndly, 1947, John Goring (*see* Goring, Bt, colls), who *d* 1990), da of 8th Earl of Glasgow:—
Horatia Marion, *b* 1941: *m* 1970, Oliver John Diggle, of Waterfall House, Swanton Morley, Dereham, Norfolk NR20 4QD, and has issue living, John Wyndham Hugh, *b* 1974, — Rowena Mary, *b* 1972, — Emma Georgiana, *b* 1977. —— Griselda Hyacinthe, *b* 1943: *m* 1967, Charles D. S. Drace-Francis, CMG (c/o FCO (Lisbon), King Charles St, SW1), and has issue living, James, *b* 1969, — Alexander John, *b* 1971, — Teresa, *b* 1979.

RAGLAN, BARON (Somerset) (Baron UK 1852)

MUTARE·VEL·TIMERE·SPERNO

I scorn to change or fear

FITZROY JOHN SOMERSET, 5th Baron; *b* 8 Nov 1927; *s* 1964; *ed* Westminster, and Magdalen Coll, Oxford; Capt Welsh Guards (Reserve of Officers); JP, and a DL for Mon; Chm of Cwmbran New Town Development Corpn; a Crown Estate Commr since 1970: *m* 1973 (*m diss* 1981), Alice, yr da of Peter Baily, of Great Whittington, Northumberland.

Arms – Quarterly: 1st and 4th azure, three fleurs-de-lis or, *France*; 2nd and 3rd gules, three lions passant guardant in pale or, *England*; the whole within a bordure compony argent and azure. Crest – A portcullis or, nailed azure, with chains pendant therefrom gold. Supporters – *Dexter*, a panther argent, spotted of various colours, fire issuant from the mouth and ears proper, gorged with a plain collar and chained or; *sinister*, a wyvern, wings endorsed, vert, holding in the mouth a sinister hand, couped at the wrist, gules.
Seat – Cefntilla Court, Usk, Gwent.

BROTHER LIVING

Hon GEOFFREY, *b* 29 Aug 1932; *ed* Westminster, and Royal Agricultural Coll; is Lt Grenadier Guards (Reserve); a co Councillor of Berks 1966-75, District Councillor of Newbury 1978-83, and co-Councillor of Oxon 1988-93: *m* 1956, Caroline Rachel, da of late Col (Edward) Roderick Hill, DSO, JP (*see* E St Aldwyn, colls, 1980 Edn), and has issue living, Arthur Geoffrey, *b* 27 April 1960. — Belinda Caroline, *b* 1958: *m* 1989, Nicholas Gant Boyd, eldest son of Cmdr Christopher Dennis Boyd, DSC, RN, of London, — Lucy Ann, *b* 1963: *m* 1998, Richard Scott-Watson, FRCS. *Residence* – Manor Farm, Stanford-in-the-Vale, Faringdon, Oxon.

SISTER LIVING

Hon Cecily, *b* 1938: *m* 1961 (*m diss* 1982), Jonkheer Jan T. P. Steengracht van Moyland, Capt late Irish Guards, and has issue living, *Jonkheer* Henry Jan Berrington, *b* 1963; *ed* Eton, and Bristol Univ (BA), — *Jonkvrowe* Suzanna Cecily, *b* 1968; *ed* Univ of E Anglia (MA): *m* 1998, Henry Trevenen Davidson Graham, son of late Judge William Murray Graham, CMG, CBE. *Residence* – 30 St Catherine's Hill, Bruton, Som.

COLLATERAL BRANCHES LIVING

Issue of late Brig Hon Nigel FitzRoy Somerset, CBE, DSO, MC, 3rd and yst son of 3rd Baron, *b* 1893, *d* 1990: *m* 1922, Phyllis Marion Offley, who *d* 1979, da of late Dr Henry Offley Irwin, of Boulder, W Australia:—
David Henry FitzRoy (White Wickets, Boars Head, Crowborough, Sussex TN6 3HE), *b* 1930; *ed* Wellington Coll, and Peterhouse, Camb (BA 1952, MA 1956); Chief Cashier of Bank of England 1980-88, since when Fellow of Peterhouse: *m* 1955, Ruth Ivy, da of Wilfred Robert Wildbur, of Kings Lynn, Norfolk, and has issue living, Henry Robert FitzRoy (Paul's Farm, Leigh, Tonbridge, Kent TN11 8RX), *b* 1961; *ed* Wellington Coll, and Trin Hall, Camb (BA 1983, MA 1988): *m* 1992, Jane Laird, da of Dr Peter Gordon, of Currie, Edinburgh, and has issue living, George Henry FitzRoy *b* 1999, Alice Caroline Laird *b* 1993, Claire Sophie Westwood *b* 1995, — Louise Charlotte, *b* 1956; *ed* Girton Coll, Camb (BA 1978, MA 1982): *m* 1981, John Roberts Beach, of Coppice Cottage, Ashton-under-Hill, Worcs WR11 6SS, son of Gen Sir Hugh Beach, GBE, KCB, MC, and has issue living, Charles Thomas FitzRoy *b* 1993, Georgiana Emily Estelle *b* 1989. —— Susan Mary, *b* 1923: *m* 1953 (*m diss* 1977), Patrick William Mackenzie Dean, and *d* 1996, leaving issue, James FitzRoy (East Mere House, nr Lincoln LN4 2JR), *b* 1954: *m* 1987 (*m diss* 19—), Charlotte Janet Rose, da of Timothy Heathcote Unwin, MFH, of Downhams Farm, Coberley, Glos, and has issue living, Alastair William Mackenzie *b* 1988, Laura Rosemary *b* 1990, — Julia Mary Mackenzie, *b* 1956: *m* 1986, Alexander Archibald Scott, who was shot and *k* by his groom 1994, and has issue (*see* Scott, Bt, *cr* 1962), — Veronica Jane Somerset, *b* 1958: *m* 1984, Peter Francis Howard Stephens, of Manor House, Old Somerby, Grantham, Lincs NG33 4AF, and has issue living, George Howard Somerset *b* 1988, Eleanor Veronica *b* 1990, Marina Rosamond *b* 1994, — Rosemary Elizabeth (16 Springvale Terrace, W14 0AE), *b* 1964.

PREDECESSORS – **(1)** *Field-Marshal Lord* FITZROY JAMES HENRY Somerset, GCB, son of 5th Duke of Beaufort; *b* 1788; distinguished himself in the Peninsula, and lost an arm at Waterloo; was many years Mil Sec to Duke of Wellington, and Master-Gen of the Ordnance 1854; commanded the English troops in the Crimea 1854-5, and gained the victories of the Alma, Inkerman, and Balaclava; *cr Baron Raglan*, of Raglan, co Monmouth (peerage of United Kingdom) 1852: *m* 1814, Lady Emily Harriet, da of 3rd Earl of Mornington; *d* 28 June 1855, whilst commanding the troops before Sebastopol; *s* by his son **(2)** RICHARD HENRY FITZROY, 2nd Baron, *b* 1817: *m* 1st, 1856, Lady Georgiana Lygon, who *d* 1865, da of 4th Earl Beauchamp; 2ndly, 1871, Mary Blanche, who *d* 1916, da of Sir Walter Rockliff Farquhar, 3rd Bt; *d* 3 May 1884; *s* by his son **(3)** GEORGE FITZROY HENRY, GBE, CB, 3rd Baron, *b* 1857; Under-Sec of State for War Nov 1900 to Aug 1902, and Lieut-Gov of the Isle of Man 1902-19; *m* 1883, Lady Ethel Jemima Ponsonby, who *d* 1940, da of 7th Earl of Bessborough; *d* 1921; *s* by his el son **(4)** FITZROY RICHARD, 4th Baron, *b* 1885; Maj Grenadier Guards; Lt-Col and Brevet Col Monmouthshire Militia 1930-35, Lord-Lieut of Monmouthshire 1942-64, and Pres, National Museum of Wales 1957-62: *m* 1923, Hon Julia Hamilton, who *d* 1971, da of 11th Lord Belhaven and Stenton; *d* 1964; *s* by his 2nd son **(5)** FITZROY JOHN, 5th Baron, and present peer.

Ramsay, Lord; son of Earl of Dalhousie.

RAMSAY OF CARTVALE, BARONESS (Ramsay) (Life Baroness 1996)

MARGARET MILDRED (META) RAMSAY, da of Alexander and Sheila Ramsay, of Glasgow; *b* 12 July 1936; *ed* Hutchesons' Girls' Gram Sch, Glasgow Univ (MA 1958, MEd 1961), and Graduate Inst of International Studies, Geneva; Pres Students' Rep Council, Glasgow Univ 1958-59 and Scottish Union of Students 1959-60; Associate Sec for Europe, Co-ordinating Secretariat, Nat Unions of Students, Leiden, Netherlands 1960-63; Mangr, Fund for International Student Co-operation 1963-67; joined HM Diplomatic Service 1969, served Stockholm 1970-73 and Helsinki 1981-85; Counsellor, FCO 1987-91 (ret); Foreign Policy Adviser to Leader of Opposition 1992-94; Special Adviser to Shadow Sec of State for Trade and Industry 1994-95; Chm Atlantic Council of UK since 1997; Baroness in Waiting (Govt Whip) to HM since Dec 1997; *cr Baroness Ramsay of Cartvale*, of Langside, City of Glasgow (Life Baroness) 1996.
Address – House of Lords, Westminster, SW1A 0PW. *Clubs* – Reform, University Women's, Royal Scottish Automobile (Glasgow).

Ramsay, family name of Earl of Dalhousie.

Ramsbotham, family name of Viscount Soulbury.

RANDALL OF ST BUDEAUX, BARON (Randall) (Life Baron 1997)

STUART JEFFREY RANDALL, son of late Charles Randall; *b* 22 June 1938; *ed* Univ Coll, Cardiff (BSc Elect Engrg 19—); MP for Hull West (Lab) 1983-97; PPS to Rt Hon Roy Hattersley as Dep Leader of the Labour Party and Shadow Chancellor of the Exchequer 1984-85; Front Bench Spokesman on Agriculture, Fisheries and Food 1985-87, and on Home Affairs 1987-92; *cr Baron Randall of St Budeaux*, of St Budeaux, co Devon (Life Baron) 1997: *m* 1963, Gillian Michael, and has issue.
Address – c/o House of Lords, Westminster, SW1A 0PW.

DAUGHTERS LIVING

Hon Jennifer, *b* 19—.
Hon Joanna, *b* 19—.
Hon Emma, *b* 19—.

Ranfurly, Baron; title borne by Earl of Ranfurly on Roll of HL.

RANFURLY, EARL OF (Knox) Sits as BARON RANFURLY (UK 1826) (Earl I 1831)

I move and prosper

GERALD FRANCOYS NEEDHAM KNOX, 7th Earl; *b* 4 Jan 1929; *s* 1988; *ed* Wellington Coll; Lt Cdr RN (ret); Stockbroker, Sr Ptnr Brewin Dolphin & Co 1982: *m* 1955, Rosemary, only da of late Air Vice-Marshal Felton Vesey Holt, CMG, DSO, and has issue.

𝕬rms – Gules, a falcon volant or, within an orle, wavy on the outer, and engrailed on the inner edge, argent. 𝕮rest – A falcon close, standing on a perch proper. 𝕾upporters – Two falcons, wings inverted proper, beaked, membered, belled, ducally collared and lined, or.
Residence – Maltings Chase, Nayland, Colchester, Essex.

SONS LIVING

EDWARD JOHN (*Viscount Northland*), *b* 21 May 1957; *ed* Leys Sch, and Loughborough Univ (BSc): *m* 1st, 1980 (*m diss* 1984), Rachel Sarah, da of Frank Hilton Lee; 2ndly, 1994, Johanna Humphrey, da of late Sqdn Ldr Harry Richard Walton, MBE, and has issue living (by 2nd *m*), *Hon* Adam Harry, *b* 7 Dec 1994, — *Hon* Helen Catherine, *b* 1996. *Residence* – 9 Parkgate, SE3 9XF.
Hon Rupert Stephen, *b* 1963; *ed* Ipswich Sch.

DAUGHTERS LIVING

Lady Elizabeth Marianne, *b* 1959: *m* 1986, Simon Empson, and has issue living, Lucy, *b* 1987, — Victoria, *b* 1989, — Alice, *b* 1993.
Lady Frances Christina, *b* 1961: *m* 1981, Henry Gordon-Jones, and has issue living, Alexandra, *b* 1983, — Susannah, *b* 1985, — Louise, *b* 1988.

BROTHER LIVING

Rev Thomas Anthony, *b* 1931; *ed* Wellington Coll, and St Chad's Coll, Durham (BA): *m* 1959, Susan Phoebe, da of late Arthur Pollard Matthews, of Mount Creek Manor, Chattanooga, Tennessee, USA, and has issue living, James Michael (Focus Windsurfing, Magharees, Castlegregory, co Kerry, Republic of Ireland), *b* 1962, — David Andrew (125 Oswald

Rd, Manchester), *b* 1965, — Anne Margaret, *b* 1960: *m* 1991, Herbert Musisi, of 87 Dorset Rd, E7. *Residence* – The Rectory, 41 Leighton Rd, Toddington, Beds.

DAUGHTER LIVING OF SIXTH EARL

Lady Caroline, *b* 1948: *m* 1975, John Edward Simmonds, and has issue living, Lucy, *b* 1976, — Zara, *b* 1980, — Rose, *b* 1987.

WIDOW LIVING OF SIXTH EARL

HERMIONE (*Hermione, Countess of Ranfurly*, OBE, CStJ), eldest da of Griffith Robert Poyntz Llewellyn, of Baglan Hall, Abergavenny: *m* 1939, the 6th Earl of Ranfurly, KCMG, who *d* 1988. *Residence* – Great Pednor, Chesham, Bucks.

COLLATERAL BRANCHES LIVING

            Grandchildren of late Octavius Newry Knox, 3rd son of Hon John Henry Knox, MP, 3rd son of 1st Earl:—
            Issue of late Leonard Needham Knox, *b* 1879, *d* 1956: *m* 1924, Berthe Hélène, who *d* 1982, da of late Henri Joseph Brel:—
Sir John Leonard, *b* 1925; *ed* Radley, Worcester Coll, Oxford (BA 1951, MA 1958), and Paris Univ: Bar Lincoln's Inn 1953; Bencher 1977; Attorney-Gen to Duchy of Lancaster 1984-85, Judge of High Court of Justice (Chancery Div) 1985-96, Dep Chm Parl Boundary Commn for England 1987-95, Judge of Employment Appeal Tribunal 1989-96; late Lieut RA; Knt 1985: *m* 1st, 1953, Anne Jacqueline, who *d* 1991, da of Herbert Mackintosh, of Frensham, Surrey; 2ndly, 1993, Benedicta Eugenie, da of late Léon Jean Goossens, CBE, FRCM, and widow of Robin Philip Cooksey, and has issue living (by 1st *m*), Thomas Francis Needham, *b* 1964, — Diana Jane, *b* 1957: *m* 1981, John Martyn Gurney Barclay, of 18 King Edward Rd, Jordanhill, Glasgow G13 1QW, yst son of Oliver Rainsford Barclay, of 8a Southland Rd, Leicester, and has issue living, Robert James *b* 1986, David Timothy *b* 1988, Frances Elizabeth *b* 1991, — Catherine Mary, *b* 1959: *m* 1983, David Alan Robinson, of 42 Wychwood Grove, Chandlers Ford, Hants, and has issue living, Edward John *b* 1989, Thomas George *b* 1991, Alistair David *b* 1993, — Margaret Lucy, *b* 1960: *m* 1986, Philip Stack Hanson Budden, of 43 Hook Rd, Ampfield, Romsey, Hants, and has issue living, Peter James *b* 1993, Lucy Anne *b* 1992, Jennifer Helen *b* 1996. *Address* – c/o Royal Courts of Justice, Strand, WC2A 2LL. —— Lucy Mary, *b* 1927: *m* 1960, Peter James Denholm, and has issue living, William Leonard, *b* 1962: *m* 1988, Michelle Leanne Jenson, and has issue living, Caitlin Gemma *b* 1997, Aleesha Gemma *b* (twin) 1997, — John Peter, *b* 1964: *m* 1987, Michelle Tracey O'Connor, and has issue living, Jack David *b* 1998, — Eva Mary, *b* 1969. *Residence* – Lot 5, Phillips Rd, Byford, W Australia 6122.

(In remainder to Viscountcy of Northland)

            Granddaughter of late Vesey Edmond Knox, el son of Rev Francis Edmond Knox, 2nd son of Hon Vesey Knox, 3rd son of 1st Viscount Northland:—
            Issue of late Charles Thomas Gisborne Knox, *b* 1868, *d* 1957: *m* 1893, Ethel Flora, who *d* 1935, da of Surg-Gen Archibald Henry Fraser:—
Ethel Eileen, *b* 1894: *m* 1941, Benjamin Joseph Redding.

            Grandson of late Rev Charles Beresford Knox, son of late Rev James Spencer Knox, son of late Rt Rev Hon William Knox, DD, Bishop of Derry, 4th son of 1st Viscount Northland:—
            Issue of late Rev Charles Edward Leslie Beresford Knox, *b* 1864, *d* 1956: *m* 1903, Ethel Margaret, who *d* 1952, da of late Rev Francis John Dickson, of Ribchester, Lancashire:—
Charles Francis BERESFORD-KNOX (5 Dukes Meadow, Stapleford, Cambridge CB2 5BH), *b* 1917; *ed* Tonbridge and Keble Coll, Oxford (BA 1939, MA 1985); late Capt RA: *m* 1941, Margaret Eugenie Morgan, and has issue living, Richard Charles (8 Finches Close, Stapleford, Camb CB2 5BL), *b* 1944: *m* 1967, Doris Frey, and has issue living, Christopher David *b* 1982, Nicholas James *b* 1984, — John Edward (14 Park Rd, Limpsfield, Oxted, Surrey RH8 0AW), *b* 1949: *ed* Keble Coll, Oxford (BA 1971), and Nottingham Univ (MA 1973): *m* 1979, Jacqueline Rosalind Wildash, and has issue living, Anna Louise *b* 1983, Lucy Elizabeth *b* 1985.

            Grandson of late Rev Thomas Knox, son of late Ven Hon Charles Knox, 6th son of 1st Viscount Northland:—
            Issue of late Com Vesey Knox, RN, *b* 1847, *d* 18-: *m* 1885, Helen, da of late Benjamin William Leigh, of Manchester and Valparaiso:—
Albert Vesey Bent, *b* 1887. *Residence* –

PREDECESSORS – **(1)** THOMAS KNOX, MP for Dungannon; *cr Baron Welles*, of Dungannon, co Tyrone (peerage of Ireland) 1781, and *Viscount Northland* (peerage of Ireland) 1791; *d* 1818: *s* by his son **(2)** THOMAS, 2nd Viscount; *cr Baron Ranfurly* (peerage of United Kingdom) 1826, and *Earl of Ranfurly* (peerage of Ireland) 1831; *d* 1840; *s* by his son **(3)** THOMAS, 2nd Earl; *d* 1858; *s* by his son **(4)** THOMAS, 3rd Earl; *b* 1816; *m* 1848, Harriet, who *d* 1891, da of James Rimington, Esq, of Broomhead Hall, co York; *d* 1858; *s* by his el son **(5)** THOMAS GRANVILLE HENRY STUART, 4th Earl; *d* 1875; *s* by his brother **(6)** UCHTER JOHN MARK, GCMG, PC, 5th Earl, *b* 1856; a Lord-in-Waiting to Queen Victoria 1895-7, and Gov of New Zealand 1897-1904: *m* 1880, Hon Constance Caulfeild, who *d* 1932, da of 7th Viscount Charlemont; *d* 1933; *s* by his grandson **(7)** THOMAS DANIEL, KCMG (son of late Capt Thomas Uchter Caulfeild, Viscount Northland, only son of 5th Earl), 6th Earl, *b* 1913; ADC to Gov and Com-in-Ch of Commonwealth of Australia 1936-38, Gov and Com-in-Chief of the Bahamas 1953-56; co-founder, with wife, of the Ranfurly Library Service: *m* 1939, Hermione, OBE, da of Griffith Robert Poyntz Llewellyn, of Abergavenny; *d* 1988; *s* by his kinsman **(8)** GERALD FRANCOYS NEEDHAM (son of late Capt John Needham Knox, RN (by his wife Monica, only da of late Maj-Gen Sir Gerald Kitson, KCVO, CB, CMG), elder son of late Edward Knox, OBE, grandson of late Hon John Knox, MP, 3rd son of 1st Earl), 7th Earl and present peer; also Viscount Northland, Baron Welles, and Baron Ranfurly.

RANK, BARONY OF (Rank) (Extinct 1972)

DAUGHTER LIVING OF FIRST BARON

Hon Shelagh Mary, *b* 1923: *m* 1st, 1945 (*m diss* 1955), Fred M. Packard, late Lieut Signal Corps US Army; 2ndly, 1957, Major Rosslyn Fairfax Huxley Cowen, MBE, and has issue living, (by 1st *m*) Frederick Arthur Rank, *b* 1949, — Susan Mary, *b* 1947, — (by 2nd *m*) Andrew Edward, *b* 1958: *m* 1985, Nicola, yr da of D. Baker, of Park Lane, Reigate, and has issue living, Fergus *b* 1988, Lucy *b* 1986, — Stuart Huxley, *b* 1960; Maj The Blues and Royals: *m* 1999, Elizabeth, da of William Holland, of Chaceley Lodge, Chaceley, Glos. *Residence* – Shawdon, Glanton, Northumberland.

RANKEILLOUR, BARON (Hope) (Baron UK 1932)

But hope is unbroken

PETER ST THOMAS MORE HENRY HOPE, 4th Baron; *b* 29 May 1935; *s* 1967; *ed* Ampleforth.

𝖆rms – Azure, on a chevron or between three bezants, a bay leaf slipped vert, a bordure ermine. 𝖈rest – A broken globe surmounted of a rainbow proper.
Residence – Achaderry House, Roy Bridge, West Inverness-shire.

SISTER LIVING

Hon Anne Mary, *b* 1936: *m* 1958, John Stephen Dobson, JP, and has issue living, Dominic Stephen Christopher Charles, *b* 1959, — Philippa Mary, *b* 1961, — Catherine Teresa, *b* 1962: *m* 1988, Hamish Lindsay McNair, only son of Archibald Alister Jourdan (Archie) McNair, of Hurlingham Court, SW6, and of Istan, Malaga, Spain, and has issue living, Mungo Alexander *b* 1992, Matilda Rose *b* 1994. *Residence* – Papplewick Lodge, Nottinghamshire NG15 8FE.

DAUGHTERS LIVING OF SECOND BARON

Hon Bridget (25 Kings Court North, Kings Rd, SW3 5EQ), *b* 1920: *m* 1942, Lt-Col George Henry Hugh Coles, Prince of Wales Own Regt of Yorks, who *d* 1992, and has issue living, Caroline Mary, *b* 1942: *m* 1965, Lt-Col Rodney Gilbert Stapleton Cotton, RA, of The Old Parsonage, Yarlington, Som BA9 8DJ, and has issue living, Nicholas Henry Stapleton *b* 1968; Capt The Queen's Royal Lancers, Martha Louise *b* 1966: *m* 1994, Damien John Byrne Hill, son of Graham Byrne Hill, of Lawn Crescent, Kew, Surrey (and has issue living, Cosmas George Nicholas *b* 1995, William Francis Stapleton *b* 1997), — Elisabeth Helena Anne *b* 1944: *m* 1967, Maj Hugh Rollo Gillespie, Queens R Irish Hussars, of The Old Rectory, Kirby Wiske, Thirsk, Yorks, and has issue living, Simon Rollo *b* 1970, James Hugh *b* 1973, Alice Catherine Mary *b* 1976, — Mary-Jane, *b* 1948: *m* 1987, Timothy C. Gibson, of 149 Blythe Rd, W14 0HL, son of Henry L. Gibson, of the Old Vicarage, Little Missenden, Bucks, and has issue living, Benjamin Henry *b* 1987, Kate Louise *b* 1989.

Hon Jean Margaret (*Hon Lady Wilson*), *b* 1923: *m* 1st, 1942 (*m diss* 1955), Capt Anthony Paul; 2ndly, 1958, Lt-Gen Sir Alexander James Wilson, KBE, MC, of 151 Rivermead Court, Ranelagh Gdns, SW6 3SF (*see*, Starkey, Bt, 1985 Edn), and has had issue (by 1st *m*) (Anthony) Hugh (23 Ludlow, Birch Hill, Bracknell, Berks RG12 7BZ), *b* 1951: *m* 1973, Jacqueline Anne, da of Richard Francis Winstone, and has issue living, Nicholas Anthony *b* 1975, Richard James *b* 1980, — Sarah Margaret, *b* 1943: *m* 1st, 1965 (*m diss* 1980), Nigel John Kington Blair-Oliphant; 2ndly, 1981, Peter Tait, of 15 Westfields Av, SW13, son of Lt-Col W. E. Tait, of Bromsgrove, Worcs, and has issue living (by 1st *m*), Richard Mark *b* 1967, David Iain *b* 1969, — Susan Caroline, *b* 1949; *d* 1986, — (by 2nd *m*) William Robert Bevil (6 Roundmead Av, Loughton, Essex), *b* 1959: *m* 1994, Lisa, only da of Colin Roby, of Cleveleys, Lancs, — Rupert James, *b* 1961.

Hon Barbara Mary, *b* 1930: *m* 1954, William Edward Peter Louis Drummond-Murray of Mastrick, Slains Pursuivant of Arms, Kt Grand Cross of Order of Malta (E Perth, colls), and has issue living, Andrew Philip (115 Fortess Rd, NW5 1TX), *b* 1958: *m* 1981 (*m diss* 1997), Susan Fiona Dorinthea, da of Prof Donald Michie, DPhil (*see* B Aberconway), and has issue living, John Douglas *b* 1986, Jessica Katharine *b* 1983, Laura Catriona *b* 1988, — James (Flat 2, City View Court, Overhill Rd, SE22 0PZ), *b* 1959; Kt of Order of Malta: *m* 1989, Namkhang, da of Mak Tonwong, of Thailand, Robert (23 Lincoln Rd, Bolton BL1 4HA), *b* 1965; Kt of Order of Malta, — Walter David, *b* 1973, — Isabel Mary (54 Queen Charlotte St, Edinburgh EH6 7EX), *b* 1966. *Residence* – 6/2 Huntingdon Place, Edinburgh EH7 4AT.

WIDOW LIVING OF THIRD BARON

MARY SIBYL (*Baroness Rankeillour*), da of late Lt-Col Wilfred Ricardo, DSO, of Hook Hall, Surrey: *m* 1933, the 3rd Baron Rankeillour, who *d* 1967. *Residence* – Papplewick Lodge, Papplewick, Notts.

COLLATERAL BRANCH LIVING

Issue of late Hon Richard Frederick Hope, OBE, yst son of 1st Baron, *b* 1901, *d* 1964: *m* 1938, Helen Sybil Mary, who *d* 1971, da of late Alfred Charlemagne Lambart (E Cavan, colls):—
MICHAEL RICHARD (The Old Vicarage, Thurton, Norwich, Norfolk NR14 6AG), *b* 21 Oct 1940; *ed* Downside: *m* 1964, Elizabeth Rosemary, el da of Col Francis H. Fuller, of Wakelins, Genesis Green, Wickhambrook, Newmarket, Suffolk, and has issue living, James Francis (172B Trinity Rd, SW17 7HT), *b* 1968; *ed* Downside, — Henrietta Mary (8 Percy Rd,

W10 9QA), *b* 1965, — Louisa Mary, *b* 1966: *m* 1996, Inno Van den Berg, of 75 Honeybrook Rd, SW12 0DZ, and has issue living, Frederick *b* 1998. —— Simon James (51 Fairview Rd, Norbury, SW16 5PX), *b* 1941; *ed* Downside. —— Margaret Mary (6 Belmont Villas, Gore Rd, Eastry, Sandwich, Kent CT13 0LT), *b* 1945: *m* 1966 (*m diss* 19—), Neil Arnold Slater, and has issue living, Richard Benjamin Arnold, *b* 1968, — Katherine Helen, *b* 1970.

PREDECESSORS – **(1)** *Rt Hon* JAMES FITZALAN Hope, son of late James Robert Hope-Scott QC (*see* M Linlithgow, colls); *b* 1870; was Parliamentary Private Sec (unpaid) to successive Postmaster-Gens (Duke of Norfolk and Marquess of Londonderry) 1896-1901, to Pres of Board of Trade (Rt Hon G. W. Balfour, MP) 1901, and to Colonial Sec (Rt Hon A Lyttelton, MP) 1904-5, Treasurer of HM's Household 1915-16, a Junior Lord of the Treasury 1916-18, Financial Sec to Min of Munitions 1919-21, and Chm of Committees and Dep Speaker in House of Commons 1921-4 and 1924-9; sat as MP for Sheffield, Brightside Div (*C*) 1900-1906, and for Sheffield, Central Div 1908-29; *cr Baron Rankeillour*, of Buxted, co Sussex (peerage of UK) 1932: *m* 1st, 1892, Mabel Helen, OBE, who *d* 1938, da of Francis Riddell, of Cheeseburn Grange, Northumberland; 2ndly, 1941, Lady Beatrice Minnie Ponsonby Moore, who *d* 1966, da of 9th Earl of Drogheda, and widow of Capt Struan Robertson Kerr-Clark, Seaforth Highlanders; *d* 1949; *s* by his son **(2)** ARTHUR OSWALD JAMES, GCIE, MC, 2nd Baron; *b* 1897; was Parliamentary Private Sec (unpaid) to Min of Mines 1924-9, a Junior Lord of the Treasury 1935-7, Treasurer of HM's Household 1937-9, Gov of Madras 1940-46, and MP for Warwickshire, Nuneaton Div (*C*) 1924-29, and for Birmingham, Aston Div 1931-9; European War 1914-18 as Capt Coldstream Guards (MC): *m* 1919, Grizel, who *d* 1975, da of Brig-Gen Sir Robert Gordon Gilmour, 1st Bt, CB, CVO, DSO; *d* 1958; *s* by his brother **(3)** HENRY JOHN, 3rd Baron; *b* 1899; Lt-Col Scots Guards: *m* 1933, Mary Sibyl, da of late Lt-Col Wilfred Ricardo, DSO, of Hook Hall, Surrey; *d* 1967; *s* by his only son **(4)** PETER ST THOMAS MORE HENRY, 4th Baron and present peer.

RATHCAVAN, BARON (O'Neill) (Baron UK 1953, Bt UK 1929)

HUGH DETMAR TORRENS O'NEILL, 3rd Baron and 3rd Baronet; *b* 14 June 1939; *s* 1994; *ed* Eton; Capt IG; Chm NI Tourist Board since 1988: *m* 1983, Mrs Sylvie Marie-Therese Chittenden, da of late Georges Wichard, of Provence, France, and has issue.

Arms – Quarterly: 1st and 4th per fesse wavy, the chief argent, and the base representing waves of the sea, in chief a dexter hand couped at the wrist gules, in base a salmon naiant proper. *O'Neill*; 2nd and 3rd checky, or and gules, a chief vair, *Chichester*; a mullet for difference. **Crest** – 1st, an arm embowed in armour, the hand grasping a sword, all proper; 2nd a stork rising, with a snake in its beak, all proper. **Mottoes** – Invitum sequitur honos (Honours follow us without seeking), and Lamh dearg Eirin (*The Red hand of Ireland*). **Supporters** – On either side a heron proper standing on a billet fessewise wavy argent charged with a bar wavy azure.
Residences – 14 Thurloe Place, SW7 2RZ; Cleggan Lodge, Ballymena, co Antrim BT43 7JW. *Clubs* – Beefsteak, Garrick.

SON LIVING

Hon FRANÇOIS HUGH NIAL, *b* 26 June 1984.

SISTER LIVING

Hon Mary-Rose, *b* 1935: *m* 1960, David Stewart Wellesley Blacker (*see* E Peel, 1980 Edn), of Huttons Ambo Hall, Malton, York, and has issue living, Barnaby Stewart Hugh, *b* 1961: *m* 1988, Colleen Mary, eldest da of Alexander McConnell, of Palmerston North, NZ, and has issue living, Carrick, *b* 1994, Julia Adelaide *b* 1989, — William O'Neill, *b* 1962, — Rohan David Peel, *b* 1966.

HALF-SISTERS LIVING

Hon Rosetta Anne, *b* 1954: *m* 1977, Maj John Michael Anthony Paxman, Coldm Gds, and has issue living, Truscote Phelim, *b* 1985, — Musidora Anne, *b* 1980, — Zena Binny Lavinia, *b* 1982. *Residence* – Ballylina House, Borissokane, co Tipperary.

Hon Moira Louisa, *b* 1961. *Residence* – Upper Ardbane, Downings, co Donegal.

Hon Grania Elizabeth, *b* 1963: *m* 1991, Thomas Crawford, and has issue living, Rosa Doreen, *b* 1993. *Residence* – 9 Craufurd Crescent, Barmill, Beith, Argyllshire.

WIDOWS LIVING OF SONS OF FIRST BARON

Anne-Marie (*Hon Lady O'Neill*), da of late Bertil Ljungström, of Stockholm, and formerly wife of M. Lindberg: *m* 1961, as his 3rd wife, Hon Sir Con Douglas Walter O'Neill, GCMG, who *d* 1988. *Residence* – 45 Godfrey St, SW3.

Virginia Lois, da of late John Douglas Legge, MC (*see* E Dartmouth, colls): *m* 1966, Hon Nial Arthur Ramleh O'Neill, who *d* 1980. *Residence* – Crowfield House, Crowfield, Ipswich, Suffolk IP6 9TP.

WIDOW LIVING OF SECOND BARON

BRIDGET DOREEN (*Dowager Baroness Rathcavan*), da of late Maj Hon Richard Coke (*see* E Leicester, colls), and formerly wife of Thomas Richard Edwards-Moss (*see* Edwards-Moss, Bt): *m* 2ndly, 1953, at his 2nd wife, the 2nd Baron Rathcavan, PC (NI), who *d* 1994. *Residence* – Killala Lodge, Killala, co Mayo.

COLLATERAL BRANCH LIVING

Issue of late Hon Sir Con Douglas Walter O'Neill, GCMG, 2nd son of 1st Baron, *b* 1912, *d* 1988: *m* 1st, 1940 (*m diss* 1954), Rosemary Margaret, only da of late Harold Pritchard, FRCP; 2ndly, 1954, Baroness Carola Hertha Adolfine Emma Harriet Luise (Mady), who *d* 1960, eldest da of late Baron Max von Holzing-Berstett, and widow of Baron Wilhelm Pleikart Marschall von Bieberstein; 3rdly, 1961, Mrs Anne-Marie Lindberg (ante), da of late Bertil Ljungstöm, of Stockholm, and formerly wife of M. Lindberg:—

(By 1st *m*) Rowan Peter Hugh (Jerome House, Front St, Churchill, Bristol), *b* 1944; *ed* Eton, and Worcester Coll, Oxford (BA 1966); Capt The Parachute Regt, commn'd 1967: *m* 1990, Mrs Elizabeth A. Wilson, da of late Edgar Goad, of Oxshott, Surrey. —— Onora Sylvia O'NEILL (*Baroness O'Neill of Bengarve*), *b* 1941; *cr* Baroness O'Neill of Bengarve (Life Baroness) 1999 (see that title).

PREDECESSORS – (1) *Rt Hon* (ROBERT WILLIAM) HUGH O'Neill, PC, 3rd son of 2nd Baron O'Neill; *b* 1883; Bar Inner Temple 1909; Maj Roy Irish Rifles; HM's Lieut for co Antrim 1948-59; European War 1915-17 in Roy Irish Rifles, and on Staff, Palestine 1918, as Dep Judge Advocate-Gen; Chm of Conservative Private Members 1922 Cttee in House of Commons 1935-39, and Under-Sec of State for India and Burma 1939-40; Pro Chancellor Queen's Univ, Belfast 1922; unsuccessfully contested Stockport (*C*) Jan 1906; sat as MP for Antrim County, Mid Antrim Div (*U*) Feb 1915-Oct 1922, for Antrim County Nov 1922-Feb 1950, and for N Div of Antrim Feb 1950-Oct 1952; sat for Antrim County (Parliament of N Ireland) May 1921-April 1929 (was first Speaker of that Parliament June 1921-May 1929); *cr* PC (Ireland) 1921, (N Ireland) 1922, and (GB) 1937, a *Baronet* 1929, and *Baron Rathcavan*, of The Braid, co Antrim (peerage of UK) 1953: *m* 1909, Sylvia, who *d* 1972, da of Walter A Sandeman, of Morden House, Royston; *d* 1982; *s* by his el surv son (2) PHELIM ROBERT HUGH, PC, 2nd Baron, *b* 1909; Maj RA; MP (UU) for N Antrim (UK Parl) 1952-59, and in Parl of NI 1959-73 (U and later Alliance) (Parl suspended March 1972), Min of Educn 1969 and Agric 1969-71; PC (NI) 1969: *m* 1st, 1934 (*m diss* 1944), Clare Désirée, who *d* 1956, da of Detmar Blow (*see* B Tollemache, colls); 2ndly, 1953, Mrs Bridget Doreen Edwards-Moss, da of late Maj Hon Richard Coke (*see* E Leicester, colls); *d* 1994; *s* by his only son (3) HUGH DETMAR TORRENS, 3rd Baron and present peer.

RATHCREEDAN, BARON (Norton) (Baron UK 1916)

You may break but shall not bend me

CHRISTOPHER JOHN NORTON, 3rd Baron; *b* 3 June 1949; *s* 1990; *ed* Wellington Coll, and RAC Cirencester: *m* 1978, Lavinia Anne Ross, da of Alan George Ross Ormiston, of Coln Orchard, Arlington, Bibury, Glos (*see* E Harewood, colls), and has issue.

Arms – Per fesse or and azure, in chief a lion passant sable and in base a maunch ermine. **Crest** – A tiger's head couped at the neck, holding in the mouth a broken spear in bend proper. **Supporters** – On either side a tiger reguardant proper, collared and chained argent, the collar of that on the dexter side charged with three roses gules, and that on the sinister side with three trefoils vert.
Residence – Stoke Common House, Purton Stoke, Swindon, Wilts SN5 9LL.

DAUGHTERS LIVING

Hon Jessica Charlotte, *b* 1983.
Hon Serena Clare, *b* 1987.

BROTHER LIVING

Hon ADAM GREGORY, *b* 2 April 1952: *m* 1980, Hilary Shelton, only da of Edmon Ryan, of Anchorage, Kentucky, USA, and has issue living, Emily Beatrice, *b* 1984, — Georgina Christine Ryan, *b* 1988. *Residence* – 60 Marmora Rd, E Dulwich, SE22 0RY. *Club* – Savile.

SISTER LIVING

Hon Elizabeth Ann, *b* 1954: *m* 1988, Alistair Scott, elder son of Prof James S. Scott, of Byards Lodge, Knaresborough, N Yorks.

WIDOW LIVING OF SECOND BARON

ANN PAULINE (*Dowager Baroness Rathcreedan*), JP, da of late Surg-Capt William Bastian, RN: *m* 1946, Maj the 2nd Baron Rathcreedan, TD, who *d* 1990. *Residence* – 8 Pearces Orchard, Fair Mile, Henley-on-Thames, Oxon RG9 2LF.

PREDECESSORS – (1) CECIL WILLIAM Norton, son of late William Norton, R of Baltinglass, Ireland; *b* 1850; a Junior Lord of the Treasury 1905-10, Assist Postmaster-Gen 1910-16, and Assist Parliamentary Sec (unpaid), Min of Munitions and Supply in the House of Lords 1919-21; MP for W Div of Newington July 1892 to Jan 1916; *cr Baron Rathcreedan*, of Bellehatch Park, Oxon (peerage of United Kingdom) 1916: *m* 1st, 1880, Cecilia Lafayette, who *d* 1898, da of James Kennedy, of The Limes, co Down, and widow of William Thomas Cavendish, of Thornton Hall, Bucks, and Crakemarsh Hall, Stafford; 2ndly, 1903, Marguerite Cecil, who *d* 1955, da of Sir Charles Philip Huntington, 1st Bt; *d* 1930; *s* by his son **(2)** CHARLES PATRICK, TD, 2nd Baron, *b* 1905, Bar Inner Temple 1931, Solicitor 1936, Maj 4th Batn Oxford and Bucks LI (TA), European War 1939-45 (prisoner): *m* 1946, Ann Pauline, da of late Surg-Capt William Bastian, RN; *d* 1990; *s* by his elder son **(3)** CHRISTOPHER JOHN, 3rd Baron and present peer.

RATHDONNELL, BARON (McClintock-Bunbury) (Baron I 1868)

Power is stronger by unity

THOMAS BENJAMIN MCCLINTOCK-BUNBURY, 5th Baron; *b* 17 Sept 1938; *s* 1959; *ed* Charterhouse, and RNC Dartmouth: *m* 1965, Jessica Harriet, da of George Gilbert Butler (*see* B Dunboyne, colls) and has issue.

Arms – Quarterly: 1st and 4th argent, on a bend sable, three chess-rooks of the field; 2nd and 3rd per pale gules and azure, a chevron ermine, between three escallops argent. **Crest** – 1st, two swords in saltire argent, hilted or, pierced through a leopard's face of the last; 2nd, a lion passant proper. **Supporters** – *Dexter*, a lion; *sinister*, a leopard; both proper, each gorged with a collar ermine, and charged on the shoulder with an escallop argent.
Seat – Lisnavagh, Rathvilly, co Carlow.

SONS LIVING

Hon WILLIAM LEOPOLD, *b* 6 July 1966.
Hon George Andrew Kane, *b* 1968.
Hon James Alexander Hugh, *b* 1972.

DAUGHTER LIVING

Hon Sasha Anne, *b* 1976.

SISTERS LIVING

Hon Katharine Alexandra (Coole Stables, Rathvilly, co Carlow), *b* 1940: *m* 1960, James Joseph Doyle, who *d* 1993.

Hon Hermione Jane, *b* 1943: *m* 1988, Callum Macleod, of 34 Newell St, Pt Chevalier, Auckland, NZ.

Hon Pamela Rosemary (The Middle Lodge, Kilruddery, Bray, co Wicklow), *b* 1948.

PREDECESSORS – (1) JOHN M'CLINTOCK, MP for co Louth 1857-9; *b* 1798; was Lord-Lieut of co Louth and Col Louth Militia; *cr Baron Rathdonnell*, of Rathdonnell, co Donegal (peerage of Ireland) 1868, with remainder to the issue male of his deceased brother, Capt William Bunbury McClintock-Bunbury, RN, MP; *d* 1879; *s* by his nephew **(2)** THOMAS KANE (son of late Capt M'Clintock-Bunbury, RN, MP) (ante), by Pauline Caroline Diana Mary, da of Sir James Stronge, 2nd Bt, 2nd Baron, *b* 1848; was HM's Lieut for co Carlow 1890-1929 (High Sheriff 1876), and a Representative Peer: *m* 1874, Katherine Anne, who *d* 1925, da of Right Hon Henry Bruen, PC, of Oak Park, co Carlow; *d* 1929; *s* by his son **(3)** THOMAS LEOPOLD, MBE, 3rd Baron, *b* 1881; High Sheriff of Carlow 1908-9; *m* 1912, Ethel Synge, who *d* 1922, da of late Robert Wilson Ievers, CMG; *d* 1937; *s* by his son **(4)** WILLIAM ROBERT, MC, 4th Baron; *b* 1914; Major 15th/19th Hussars: *m* 1937, Pamela (who *d* 1989, having *m* 2ndly, 1961, Major Hugh Caruthers Massy, who *d* 1987), el da of late John Malcolm Drew, of Eversley, near Milnthorpe, Westmorland; *d* 1959; *s* by his son **(5)** THOMAS BENJAMIN, 5th Baron and present peer.

RAVENSDALE, BARON (Mosley) (Baron UK 1911, Bt GB 1781)

Custom rules the law

NICHOLAS MOSLEY, MC, 3rd Baron, and 7th Baronet; *b* 25 June 1923; *s* to barony 1966, and to baronetcy 1980; *ed* Eton, and Balliol Coll, Oxford; 1939-45 War in Italy (MC) as Capt, Rifle Bde; writer, author of *Accident, Hopeful Monsters* (Whitbread Book of the Year Award 1991), etc: *m* 1st, 1947 (*m diss* 1974), Rosemary Laura, who *d* 1991, da of late Marshal of the RAF Sir John Maitland Salmond, GCB, CMG, CVO, DSO (*see* B Lucas of Crudwell, colls); 2ndly, 1974, Verity Elizabeth, 2nd da of late N. J. B. (Jack) Raymond, of Winslade Down, Basingstoke, Hants, and formerly wife of (John) Adrian Bailey, and has issue by 1st and 2nd *m*.

Arms – Quarterly, 1st and 4th, sable, a chevron between three pickaxes argent, *Mosley*; 2nd and 3rd argent, on a bend sable, three popinjays or, collared gules, *Curzon*. **Crest** – An eagle displayed ermine. **Supporters** – *Dexter*, a raven proper; *sinister*, a popinjay proper collared gules.
Residence – 2 Gloucester Crescent, NW1 7DS.

SONS LIVING (*By 1st marriage*)

Hon SHAUN NICHOLAS, *b* 5 Aug 1949; *ed* Bryanston, and Hertford Coll, Oxford: *m* 1979, Teresa Frances, da of Daniel Clifford, and has issue living, Daniel Nicholas, *b* 10 Oct 1982, — Matthew, *b* 1985, — Francis, *b* 1988, — Aidan, *b* 1991, — Thomas Kieran, *b* 1993, — Monica Collette, *b* 1996.

Hon Ivo Adam Rex, *b* 1951; *ed* Bryanston, and New Coll, Oxford: *m* 1977, Xanthe Jennifer Grenville, yst da of Sir Michael Bernard Grenville Oppenheimer, 3rd Bt, and has issue living, Nathaniel Inigo, *b* 1982, — Felix Harry, *b* 1985, — Scipio Louis, *b* 1988, — Noah Billy, *b* 1990. *Residence* – Courtyard, Neopardy, Crediton, Devon.

Hon Robert, *b* 1955; *ed* Bedales: *m* 1980, Victoria McBain, and has issue living, Gregory, *b* 1981, — Orson, *b* 1994, — Vija, *b* 1985.

(*By 2nd marriage*)

Hon Marius, *b* 1976.

DAUGHTER LIVING (*By 1st marriage*)

Hon Clare Imogen, *b* 1959.

BROTHER LIVING (*Raised to the rank of a son of a Baroness* 1967)

Hon Michael (Durham Cottage, Christchurch St, SW3), *b* 1932; *ed* Eton, and London Sch of Economics.

HALF-BROTHERS LIVING (*In remainder to the baronetcy only*)

(Oswald) Alexander (31 rue de l'Université, 75007 Paris France), *b* 1938; *ed* St Martin de France, Pontoise, and Ohio State Univ: *m* 1975, Charlotte Diana, da of George Gosselin Marten, MVO, DSC (*see* By Alington), and has issue living, Louis, *b* 1983.

Max Rufus, *b* 1940; *ed* Stein an der Traun, Germany, and Ch Ch, Oxford; Barrister-at-law, Gray's Inn 1964; Pres Internat Motor Sports Fedn since 1991; Pres Federation Internationale de l'Automobile 1993: *m* 1960, Jean Marjorie, da of James Taylor, and has issue living, Alexander James, *b* 1970, — Max Patrick, *b* 1972.

SISTER LIVING (*Raised to the rank of a daughter of a Baroness* 1967)

Hon Vivien Elisabeth (11 Mulberry Walk, SW3), *b* 1921: *m* 1949, Desmond Francis Forbes Adam, who *d* 1958 (*see* Adam, Bt, colls, *cr* 1917).

WIDOW LIVING OF SIXTH BARONET

Hon DIANA MITFORD (*Hon Lady Mosley*) (1 rue des Lacs, 91400 Orsay, France), da of 2nd Baron Redesdale, and formerly wife of Hon Bryan Walter Guinness (afterwards 2nd Baron Moyne): *m* 1936, as his 2nd wife, Sir Oswald Ernald Mosley, 6th Bt, who *d* 1980.

COLLATERAL BRANCHES LIVING *(male line in special remainder to the Barony only)*

Issue of late Lady Alexandra Naldera Curzon, CBE, yst da of 1st Marquess Curzon of Kedleston, *b* 1904, *d* 1995: *m* 1925 (*m diss* 1955), Maj Edward Dudley Metcalfe, MVO, MC, who *d* 1957:—
David Patrick METCALFE (15 Wilton St, SW1. *Clubs* – White's, Buck's), *b* 1927; *ed* Eton; late Lieut IG; Member of Lloyd's: *m* 1st, 1957 (*m diss* 1964), Alexandra Irene, who *d* 1966, da of Michael Boycun, and widow of Sir Alexander Korda, 2ndly, 1968 (*m diss* 1973), Anne Marie Jeanne, da of late Comte Jacques de Chauvigny de Blot; 3rdly, 1979, Mrs Sally Howe, da of Edward E. Cullen, of Philadelphia, USA, and formerly wife of Ralph Howe, and has issue living (by 1st *m*), Julian Edward (Alexander House, 7 North Terrace, SW3 5DB), *b* 1959: *m* 1992, Melanie Frances, da of John Michael Willson, of La Boussaque, Claviers, France, and has issue living, Michael John *b* 1993, Billy Alexander *b* 1995, — Charles Michael (70 Oxford Gdns, W10 5UN), *b* 1962: *m* 1989, Elizabeth Beach, da of Warren Zimmermann, of Southdown Farm, Great Falls, Virginia, USA, and has issue living, Louis Warren Zimmermann *b* 1993, — Zara Naldera, *b* 1957: *m* 1989, as his 2nd wife, Jonathan Halsey Luke Colchester, son of late Rev Halsey Sparrowe Colchester, CMG, OBE, — (by 2nd *m*), Edward George Anthony, *b* 1970. —— Davina Naldera, *b* 1930: *m* 1966, as his 2nd wife, (John) Hugo Eastwood, of 12 Passmore St, SW1 8HP, and has issue living, Philip Hugo (4 Lydon Rd, SW4), *b* 1966: *m* 1997, Sophie L., da of late John Harrison, of Chelsea, — Emma Alexandra, *b* 1969. — Linda Mary (14 Elvaston Place, SW7 5QF; 2195 Ibis Isle, Apt 3, Palm Beach, Florida 33480, USA), *b* (twin) 1930: *m* 1965, Henry Tilford Mortimer, who *d* 1993, and has issue living, John Metcalfe, *b* 1966, — Alexander Dudley, *b* 1969.

(In remainder to the Baronetcy only)

Issue of late Edward Heathcote Mosley, 2nd son of 5th baronet, *b* 1899, *d* 1980: *m* 1st, 1923 (*m diss* 1932), Sylvia, who *d* 1977, da of late Lt-Col Herbert Alfred Johnson, of Allestree Hall, Derby; 2ndly, 1943, Edith Victoria, who *d* 1990, da of late Thomas Leach, of Malvern.
(By 1st *m*) John Ronald (Flat 31, Chestnut House, East St, Blandford Forum, Dorset, DT11 7DU), *b* 1926; *ed* Stowe: *m* 1st, 1956 (*m diss* 1970), Primrose Antoinette, 2nd da of late F. G. Hadwen; 2ndly, 1972, Caroline Rosalind, 2nd da of late H. H. S. Hillier, and has issue living (by 1st *m*), Clare, *b* 1958: *m* 1985, Mark Bicknell, of 66 Camberwell Grove, SE5, son of F. A. Bicknell, of Putney, and has issue living, Augustus Ivo Guy *b* 1990, Cecilia *b* 1994, — Charlotte Louise, *b* 1960. —— Veronica, *b* 1924: *m* 1954, Peter Hawker, of Coln House, Coln Rogers, Cheltenham, Glos, and *d* 1996, leaving issue, Annabel (*Hon Mrs Richard Buxton*), *b* 1957: *m* 1988, Hon Richard Christopher Noel-Buxton, son of 2nd Baron Noel-Buxton.

Issue of late John Arthur Noel Mosley, yst son of 5th baronet, *b* 1901, *d* 1972: *m* 1st, 1925 (*m diss* 1936), Caroline Edith Sutton, who *d* 1986, da of late Lt-Col George D. Timmis of Matson House, Glos; 2ndly, 1936, Anne Marie Vaudescal-Vartejanu, who *d* 1983:—
(By 1st *m*) Simon James (Flat 4, 59 Onslow Gdns, SW7), *b* 1927; *ed* Eton and Ch Ch, Oxford (MA); Solicitor 1957, ret 1993; late Lt Coldm Gds: *m* 1957, Maria, da of Iraklis Zeri, of Athens, and has issue living, George Christopher (23 The Little Boltons, SW10 9SU), *b* 1959; *ed* Eton: *m* 1992, Ana-Maria, da of Miguel Rincon, of Jerez, Spain, and of Mrs V. Anderson, of London, and has issue living, Oliver Simon *b* 1994, Max Alexander *b* 1996, — Claire Amalia, *b* 1964: *m* 1997, Fabian Bachrach, of 29 Bethune St, West Village, New York, USA.

Granddaughter of late Capt John William Paget Mosley, only son of late Lt-Col John Edward Paget Mosley, 2nd son of Capt William Bayley Mosley, 3rd son of Rev John Peploe Mosley, 2nd son of 1st baronet::—
Issue of late John Herbert Mosley, *b* 1912, *d* 1986: *m* 1st, 1935 (*m diss* 1947), Ethel Marcia Hancock; 2ndly, 1949 (*m diss* 1950), Mrs Elaine Verna Savory; 3rdly, 1951 (*m diss* 1955), Elizabeth Anna Maria Stefak; 4thly, 1962 (*m diss* 1973), Lyla Fay Hemus, of Auckland, NZ:—
(By 1st *m*) Christine Ann, *b* 1941: *m* 1964, Clive Dearden, of Llwyn-Onn-Isaf, Panorama Rd, Barmouth, Gwynedd, and has issue living, Rosemary Ann, *b* 1969, — Heather Jane, *b* 1971.

Granddaughter of late Oswald Feilden Mosley (infra):—
Issue of late Capt Oswald Henry Feilden Mosley, late RAC, *b* 1913, *d* 1996: *m* 1st, 1941, Mary Angela, da of late Louis de Las Casas (*see* Heathcoat-Amory, Bt, 1942 Edn); 2ndly, 1952, Olga Marie Noelie, da of George Ackroyd:—
(By 1st *m*) Sheila Dorothy, *b* 1942: *m* 1970, Paul Piers Brissault Minet, and has issue living, (Isobel) Louise, *b* 1971: *m* 1994, Timothy Arthur, and has issue living, Caitlin *b* 1996, — Anthea, *b* 1973. *Residence* – 3 Apsley Court, Pickforde Lane, Ticehurst, E Sussex TN5 7BJ.

Grandson of late Rev Oswald Henry Mosley, 4th son of Capt William Bayley Mosley (ante):—
Issue of late Oswald Feilden Mosley, *b* 1880, *d* 1946: *m* 1912, Ida, da of late William Palmer, of St Mary Church, Torquay:—
Robert Anthony (15 Dolvin Rd, Tavistock, S Devon PL19 9EA. *Club* – RAF), *b* 1920; formerly Sqdn Ldr RAF; is a Dir of Vieux Temps of Monte Carlo: *m* 1944 (*m diss* 1954), Renee Carmen Cecily Assouad, and has had issue, Anthony Noel (16 Edgecombe Way, St Ann's Chapel, Gunnislake, Cornwall PL18 9HJ), *b* 1949, — Bertha Mary Isobel *b* 1945: *m* 1968, Alistair Maciver, and *d* 1988, leaving issue, Neil Anthony *b* 1970, Katherine Anne May *b* 1968.

PREDECESSORS – (1) GEORGE NATHANIEL Curzon, KG, GCSI, GCIE, PC, FRS, el son of 4th Baron Scarsdale; *b* 1859; Under-Sec of State for India 1891-92, Under-Sec of State for Foreign Affairs 1895-8, Viceroy and Gov-Gen of India 1898-1904 and again 1904-5, Lord Privy Seal 1915-16, Lord Pres of the Council and Leader of the House of Lords, and Sec of State for Foreign Affairs 1919-24 (also Leader of House of Lords), and again Lord Pres of the Council and Leader of the House of Lords 1924-52; *cr Baron Curzon of Kedleston*, co Derby (peerage of Ireland) 1898, and *Baron Ravensdale*, of Ravensdale, co Derby, with special remainder, in default of issue male, to his el da and the heirs male of her body, failing whom to his other das in like manner in order of primogeniture, *Viscount Scarsdale*, of Scarsdale, co Derby, with special remainder in default of issue male, to his father (the 4th Baron Scarsdale, whom he succeeded in the Barony) and the heirs male of his body, *Earl Curzon of Kedleston*, co Derby (all in peerage of UK) 1911, and *Earl of Kedleston*, co Derby, and *Marquess Curzon of Kedleston* (peerage of UK) 1921; *s* as 5th Baron Scarsdale and 9th Baronet (both of Scotland and England) 1916: *m* 1st, 1895, Mary Victoria, CI, who *d* 1906, el da of late Levi Zeigler Leiter, of Washington, USA; 2ndly, 1917, *Dame* Grace Elvina Trilla, GBE, who *d* 1958, da of late J. Monroe Hinds, of Alabama, USA, and widow of Alfred Duggan, of Buenos Aires; *d* 1925, when the Irish Barony of 1898, the Earldom of 1911, and the Marquessate of 1921, became ext, while the Barony (*cr* 1761) and the Viscountcy of Scarsdale, together with the two Baronetcies, passed to his nephew, Richard Nathaniel Curzon (see that title), and the Barony of Ravensdale devolved by special remainder upon his el da (2) MARY IRENE; *b* 1896; Treasurer of Musicians' Benevolent Fund; *cr Baroness Ravensdale of Kedleston*, of Kedleston, co Derby (Life Baroness) 1958; *d* 1966, when the Barony of Ravensdale (*cr* 1911) devolved on her nephew (3) NICHOLAS Mosley, MC (el son of Lady Cynthia Blanche Mosley (2nd da of 1st Marquess Curzon of Kedleston and 1st Baron Ravensdale), who *d* 1933, having *m* 1920, as his 1st wife, Sir Oswald Ernald Mosley, 6th Bt), 3rd Baron, and present peer.

*(1) JOHN PARKER MOSLEY, son of Nicholas Mosley; *cr* a *Baronet* 1781; *s* by his grandson (2) *Sir* OSWALD, 2nd Bt; MP for N Div of Staffs; *d* 1871; *s* by his son (3) *Sir* TONMAN, 3rd Bt; *d* 1890; *s* by his son (4) *Sir* OSWALD, 4th Bt; High Sheriff of Staffs; *d* 1915; *s* by his son (5) *Sir* OSWALD, 5th Bt; *d* 1928; *s* by his son (6) *Sir* OSWALD ERNALD, 6th Bt; leader of *New Party* Feb 1931; *d* 1980; *s* by his son (7) *Sir* NICHOLAS, 7th Bt, who succeeded as 3rd Baron Ravensdale (see ante).

RAVENSWORTH, BARON (Liddell) (Baron UK 1821, Bt E 1642)

One and the same

ARTHUR WALLER LIDDELL, 8th Baron, and 13th Baronet; *b* 25 July 1924; *s* 1950; *ed* Harrow; formerly Radio Engineer, British Broadcasting Corporation: *m* 1950, Wendy, adopted da of J. Stuart Bell, of Studio House, Cookham, Berks, and has issue.

Arms – Argent, fretty gules, on a chief of the second three leopards' faces or. **Crest** – A lion rampant sable, semée of billets or, and crowned with an Eastern coronet gold. **Supporters** – On either side a leopard or, semée of golps, gorged with a mural crown purpose.
Seat – Eslington Park, Whittingham, Alnwick, Northumberland.

SON LIVING

Hon THOMAS ARTHUR HAMISH, *b* 27 Oct 1954; *ed* Gordonstoun, and RAC Cirencester: *m* 1983, Linda, da of late Henry Thompson, of Hawthorn Farm, Brunton Lane, Gosforth, Newcastle-upon-Tyne, and has issue living, Henry Arthur Thomas, *b* 27 Nov 1987, — Alice Lorina, *b* 1986. *Residence* – Mountain, Whittingham, Northumberland.

DAUGHTER LIVING

Hon Jane Alice, *b* 1952: *m* 1984, Michael James Crowhurst Rubie, only son of late Henry Edward Rubie, of Rustington, W Sussex, and has issue living, Sophia Amy Elizabeth, *b* 1986. — Isabel Emma Mary, *b* 1988, — Francesca Louise, *b* 1991. *Residence* – Red Briars, 35 Drax Av, SW20 0EQ.

SISTER LIVING (*Raised to the rank of a Baron's daughter* 1951)

Hon Sophie Harriet, *b* 1927: *ed* Central High Sch, Newcastle-on-Tyne, and King's Coll, Durham Univ; ordained Deaconess 1980, Deacon 1987: *m* 1981, Leslie Charles William Woodhams, of 31 Hanover Close, Shaftgate Av, Shepton Mallet, Som BA4 5YQ.

SISTER LIVING OF SEVENTH BARON

Hon Beatrice Sophie, *b* 1906: *m* 1931, Edward Richard Speyer, and has issue living, Jocelyne Isolda, *b* 1933: *m* 1958, Alan Richard Tait, and has issue living, Matthew Edward *b* 1960, — Valentine Antonia, *b* 1938: *m* 1974, Nicholas John Windsor Gaffney, of Flat 1, 13 South Hill Park Gdns, Hampstead, NW3. *Residence* –

COLLATERAL BRANCHES LIVING

Grandchildren of late Capt Augustus Frederick Liddell, CVO, son of late Col Hon George Augustus Liddell, 6th son of 1st Baron:—
Issue of late Guy Maynard Liddell, CB, CBE, MC, *b* 1892, *d* 1958: *m* 1926 (*m diss* 1943), Hon Calypso Baring, who *d* 1974, da of 3rd Baron Revelstoke:—
Peter Lorillard (1 Pennington Place, Tunbridge Wells, Kent TN4 0AQ), *b* 1927, *ed* Oxford Univ (MA 1954): *m* 1st, 1951 (*m diss* 1966), Anne Jamieson, da of Capt F. M. Cannon, US Naval Res Med Corps, of San Rafael, California, USA; 2ndly, 1970, Joan Frances Hopkinson, and has issue living, (by 1st *m*) Peter Guy (290 Stainland Rd, Holywell Green, Halifax, W Yorks HX4 9EH), *b* 1952; *ed* Sevenoaks: *m* 1st, 1977 (*m diss* 1989), Elaine Patricia, eldest da of Harold Mountford Wenzel, of 41 Sedley Rise, Loughton, Essex; 2ndly, 1993, Hilary Lazenby, and has issue living, (by 1st wife) Thomas Edward *b* 1984, (by 2nd wife) Rose Alice *b* 1992, — John David (4503 Romlon St, Apt 103, Beltsville, Maryland 20705, USA), *b* 1954; *ed* Sevenoaks: *m* 1994, Jana Berg, — Thomas Andrew (4503 Romlon St, Apt 103, Beltsville, Maryland 20705, USA), *b* 1960: *m* 1999, Victoria Gilbert, — Alice, *b* 1958: *m* 1987, Paul Richard Wells, of Chellington House, Bridgend, Carlton, Beds MK43 7LP, son of Fl Cmdr Oliver Wells, of Ickwell, Beds, and has issue living, Harry Augustus

b 1992, Georgina Charlotte *b* 1988. —— Elizabeth Gay, *b* 1928: *m* 1st, 1946 (*m diss* 1970), Carl Paulson; 2ndly, 1973, Alexander van de Pol, of 615 Palos Verdes Drive West, Palos Verdes Estates, CA 90274, USA, and has issue living (by 1st *m*), Jay, *b* 1950: *m* 1982, Diane Plummer, and has issue living, Kyle *b* 1983, Scott *b* 1985, Derek *b* 1987, — Mark, *b* 1957, — Sandra, *b* 1947: *m* 1977, Harry Reese. —— Anne Jennifer (1261 NE 11th St, Bend, Oregon 97701, USA), *b* 1931: *m* 1951 (*m diss* 19—), Joseph Enzensperger, and has issue living, Joseph, *b* 1952, — Janet, *b* 1957, — Ann, *b* 1959.

(The male line is in remainder to Baronetcy)

Grandchildren of late Lt-Col Geoffrey William Liddell, DSO (infra):—
Issue of late Maj Charles Henry Liddell, MC, *b* 1917, *d* 1998: *m* 1944, Pamela Mary (Fullerton Grange, Andover, Hants SP11 7LA), da of late Maj Antony Hubert Gibbs, JP, of Pytte, Clyst St George, Devon:—
James Edward Cory (Cottonworth House, Fullerton, Andover, Hants), *b* 1947; *ed* Eton, and RAC Cirencester: *m* 1970, Rachel Anne, yr da of late Maj George De Pree, 60th Rifles, KRRC, of Little Knelle Farm, Beckley, Rye, Sussex (*see* E Galloway, colls), and has issue living, Tom Edward Charles, *b* 1977; *ed* Milton Abbey, and RAC, Cirencester, — Hugh Geoffrey, *b* 1980; *ed* Milton Abbey, — Georgie Sophia, *b* 1975. —— (Mary) Susan, *b* 1944: *m* 1964, Rev Antony Michael Ansell, of 4 Vincent Sq Mansions, SW1P 2NT (*see* Fuller, Bt, 1969 Edn), son of late Col Sir Michael Picton Ansell, CBE, DSO, and has issue living, Michael James Kirkpatrick, *b* 1970; *ed* Harrow, — Harriet Mary, *b* 1966: *m* 1994, Robert Henry Mortimer Lanyon, and has issue (*see* B Amherst of Hackney), — Alexandra Jane, *b* 1968: *m* 1991, Andrew Dunnett, son of Rev Robert Dunnett. —— Alice Margaret, *b* 1950: *m* 1973, Christopher Nicholas Allen, of Newman Street Farm, Doulting, Shepton Mallet, Som, son of Douglas Allen, and has issue living, Luke Llewellyn Liddell, *b* 1985; *ed* Kings Coll, Bruton, — Jack Basil Charles Liddell, *b* 1987, — Gus Douglas Oliver Liddell, *b* 1989.

Grandsons of late Edward Henry Liddell, eldest son of late Very Rev Henry George Liddell, DD, eldest son of late Rev Henry George Liddell, 2nd son of 5th Bt:—
Issue of late Lieut-Col Geoffrey William Liddell, DSO, *b* 1884, *d* 1955: *m* 1915, his 2nd cousin, Mary Sophia who *d* 1987, da of late Charles Lyon Liddell (see 1985 Edn):—
Thomas Lyon, *b* 1920; *ed* Radley, and Worcester Coll, Oxford; 1939-45 War as Capt Rifle Bde: *m* 1951, Susan Mary, da of late C. R. V. Coutts, of the Court Lodge, Chelsfield, Kent, and has issue living, Edward Henry (9B Engadine St, SW18 5BJ), *b* 1953; *ed* Eton, and Magdalene Coll, Camb: *m* 1988 (*m diss* 19—), Hon Anna Kinnaird, 2nd da of 13th Lord Kinnaird, and has issue living, Patrick Edward Charles *b* 1991, — Roderick William (12 Grand'rue, Kriegsheim, Brumath 67170, France), *b* 1955; *ed* Eton, and Worcester Coll, Oxford: *m* 19—, Marie Françoise, yst da of Cmdt Michel Dujol, of Calaman, Cahors, France, and has issue living, Loic *b* 1979, Theo Antonin Thomas *b* 1981, Jessica *b* 1996, — David Lyon (Orchard House, Church Rd, Barcombe, Sussex BN8 5TW), *b* 1959; *ed* Eton, and Trin Coll, Camb: *m* 1990, Chloë Camilla Margot, yst da of Dennis Percy Bertlin, of Castlefield, Bletchingley, Surrey, and has issue living, Rupert Henry *b* 1996, Freya Margot *b* 1994, Phoebe Camilla *b* 1998, — Emma Mary (4 Vicarage Rd, SW14), *b* (twin) 1955; *ed* Wycombe Abbey, and St Hilda's Coll, Oxford: *m* 1981, Charles William Taaffe Munro Mackenzie, who *d* 1998, 2nd son of John Hugh Munro Mackenzie of Mornish, and has issue living, (Charles) Alexander Munro *b* 1983, (Kenneth) Thomas Munro *b* 1986, (Charlotte) Annabella Jemima *b* 1990. *Residence* – 10 Lowdells Drive, East Grinstead, W Sussex BN8 5TW. —— William Adrian (Westover, Goodworth Clatford, Andover, Hants), *b* 1924; *ed* Radley, and Magdalene Coll, Camb (BA 19-, MA 19-); late Lt RNVR; 1939-45 War (despatches): *m* 1956, Anne Primrose, da of late Group Capt R. W. G. Lywood, of Bay Cottage, Scilly, Kinsale, co Cork, and has issue living, William George (40 Chilton Rd, Camden, Bath, BA1 6DR), *b* 1958; *ed* Eton, Keble Coll, Oxford, and St Mary's Hosp (MRCP, MRCGP): *m* 1996, Dr Morag MacDougall, da of late Colin MacDougall, of Broomswell, Suffolk, and has issue living, Geoffrey Charles *b* 1997, — Mary Clare, *b* 1960: *m* 1992, Ralph Wynne Griffith, — Caroline Sophia, *b* 1962: *m* 1988, Dominick Percival Ian Reyntiens (*see* Bruce, Bt, *cr* 1628, colls). —— Geoffrey Andrew (April Cottage, Abbots Ann, Andover, Hants SR1 7AZ), *b* 1926; *ed* Radley; late RN; 1939-45 War: *m* 1958, Jillian Mary (CLIFTON-BROWNE), da of David Walkinshaw, and has issue living, Charles David Andrew (Stables House, Winton Hill, Stockbridge, Hants SO21 6HL), *b* 1960; *ed* Marlborough: *m* 1986, Victoria Elizabeth, da of Geoffrey Herbert Jolly, of The Old Vicarage, New Chapel Lane, Horwich, Bolton, Lancs, and has issue living, Marcus Andrew *b* 1988, Caitlin Alice *b* 1991, Frances *b* 1994.

Grandchildren of late Sir Frederick Francis Liddell, KCB, KC, 2nd son of late Very Rev Henry George Liddell, DD (ante):—
Issue of late Henry George Magniac Liddell, *b* 1902, *d* 1985: *m* 1932, Amelia Lydia, who *d* 1981, da of William Albert Walker, of Gadzema, Rhodesia:—
Eric Henry George, *b* 1935: *m* 1958, Jane-Anne, da of late Walter John Hoskins, RA, of Elston, Shrewton, Wilts, and has issue living, Karen Anne, *b* 1961, — Jacqueline Toni, *b* 1962: *m* 1987, Rodney Alan Penaluna, — Bridget Alice, *b* 1964. *Address* – 6 Stirling Rd, PO Box 67555, Bryanston 2021, Transvaal, S Africa.

Issue of late Maurice Arthur Liddell, OBE, *b* 1905, *d* 1976: *m* 1937, Alix, OBE, who *d* 1981, da of late Adm Mark Edward Frederick Kerr, CB, MVO (*see* M Lothian, colls):—
Virginia Sarah Alix, *b* 1941: *m* 1962, Simon Claude Ashton, CBE, FCA, who *d* 1986, of 27 Newton Rd, W2, and has issue living, Guy Julian Claude, *b* 1964: *m* 1991, Claire Chapman, — Melanie Isabel, *b* 1967: *m* 1994, Hugh Giles Keyworth Broughton, and has issue living, Stanley Simon Keyworth *b* 1997, — Jessica Alix, *b* 1970. —— Judith Rose, *b* 1944: *m* 1968, David Mark Jackson, BM, BCh, FFARCS, of The Old Vicarage, Church Walk, Ashton Keynes, Wilts, and has issue living, Luke Hadley, *b* 1970, — Felix Mark, *b* 1973.

Granddaughter of late Lionel Charles Liddell, MVO, yst son of late Very Rev Henry George Liddell, DD (ante):—
Issue of late Philip Liddell, *b* 1904, *d* 1976: *m* 1944, Elizabeth Jane Boret (31 Centre Drive, Newmarket, Suffolk CB8 8AN), da of late Colledge Leader, of Newmarket:—
Susan Jane, *b* 1946: *m* 1970, Anthony Gatehouse Hide, of Machell Place, Newmarket, Suffolk, and has issue living, Philip Edward, *b* 1973, — Timothy David, *b* 1982, — Lucinda Jane, *b* 1971.

PREDECESSORS – (1) THOMAS Liddell, a zealous supporter of Charles I; *cr Baronet* 1642; *d* 1650; *s* by his son (2) *Sir* THOMAS, 2nd Bt; *d* 1697; *s* by his son (3) *Sir* HENRY, 3rd Bt; *d* 1723; *s* by his grandson (4) *Sir* HENRY, 4th Bt; MP; *cr Baron Ravensworth*, of Ravensworth Castle (peerage of Great Britain) 1747; *d* 1784, when the barony became extinct, and the baronetcy devolved upon his nephew (5) *Sir* HENRY GEORGE, 5th Bt; *d* 1791; *s* by his son (6) *Sir* THOMAS HENRY, 6th Bt; *cr Baron Ravensworth* (peerage of United Kingdom) 1821; *d* 1855; *s* by his son (7) HENRY THOMAS, 2nd Baron; *b* 1797; MP for Northumberland (C) 1826-39, for N Durham 1837-47, and for Liverpool 1853-5; *cr Baron Eslington*, of

Eslington Park, co Northumberland, and *Earl of Ravensworth* (peerage of United Kingdom) 1874: *m* 1820, Isabella Horatia, da of late Lord George Seymour (M Hertford); *d* 1878; *s* by his son **(8)** HENRY GEORGE, 2nd Earl, *b* 1821; MP for Northumberland S (*C*) 1852-78: *m* 1st, 1852, Diana, who *d* 1890, da of late Orlando Gunning-Sutton, RN; 2ndly, 1892, Emma Sophie Georgiana, who *d* 1939 (having *m* 3rdly, 1904, James William Wadsworth), da of late Hon Richard Denman, and widow of Capt Oswin Cumming Baker Cresswell; *d* 1903; *s* by his brother **(9)** ATHOLE CHARLES, 3rd Earl, *b* 1833: *m* 1866, Caroline Cecilia (who *d* 1909, having *m* 2ndly, 1906, as his 2nd wife, her cousin, 4th Earl of Mount Edgcumbe), da of late Hon George Edgcumbe; *d* 1904, when the Earldom became ext, but the Barony of Ravensworth passed to his cousin **(10)** ARTHUR THOMAS (son of late Rev Hon Robert Liddell, 5th son of 1st Baron), 5th Baron, *b* 1837: *m* 1866, Sophia Harriett, who *d* 1918, da of Sir Thomas Walker, 2nd Bt; *d* 1919; *s* by his el son **(11)** GERALD WELLESLEY, 6th Baron, *b* 1869: *m* 1899, Isolda Blanche, who *d* 1938, da of Charles Glyn Prideaux Brune, of Prideaux Place, Cornwall; *d* 1932; *s* by his son **(12)** ROBERT ARTHUR, ED, 7th Baron, *b* 1902; Major RA (TA); *d* 1950; *s* by his cousin **(13)** ARTHUR WALLER (son of late Hon Cyril Arthur Liddell, 2nd son of 5th Baron), 8th Baron and present peer.

RAWLINGS, BARONESS (Rawlings) (Life Baroness 1994)

PATRICIA ELIZABETH RAWLINGS, da of late Louis Rawlings; *b* 27 Jan 1939; *ed* Oak Hall, Surrey, Le Manoir, Lausanne, Switzerland, Univ of Florence, Univ Coll, London (BA 1979), and LSE (Post Graduate Dip in Internat Relations 1982-83); Hon LittD Buckingham Univ 1998; memb British Red Cross Soc since 1964, Chm Appeals, London Branch, National Badge of Honour 1981, Hon Vice-Pres since 1988; Dir English Chamber Orchestra and Music Soc since 1980; Board Memb British Association for Central and Eastern Europe since 1994; Chm Council King's Coll London since 1998; Memb Conservative Women's National Cttee 1983-88 and since 1994; MEP Essex SW (*C*) 1989-94; Bulgarian Order of the Rose, Silver Cross 1991, Brazilian Order of the Southern Cross (Grand Official) 1997; *cr Baroness Rawlings*, of Burnham Westgate, co Norfolk (Life Baroness) 1994: *m* 1962 (*m diss* 1967), David Wolfson (later Baron Wolfson of Sunningdale).

Arms – Quarterly barry wavy of six argent and azure and argent on a cross gules between in the second and third quarters an escallop azure a seax fesswise point to the sinister or surmounted by an ostrich plume palewise argent between in chief and in a base a bee volant proper on a bordure azure twelve mullets or. **Supporters** – On a grassy mount vert growing therefrom lilies argent slipped and leaved vert on the *dexter* a lion rampant or armed langued and gorged with a riband azure dependent from the knot thereof a rose argent and on the *sinister* an elephant ermine gorged with a chain or dependent therefrom a portcullis sable.
Address – c/o House of Lords, SW1A 0PW.

RAWLINSON OF EWELL, BARON (Rawlinson) (Life Baron 1978)

Mon dieu et mon Roi

PETER ANTHONY GRAYSON RAWLINSON, PC, QC, son of late Lt Col Arthur Richard Rawlinson, OBE, of Ferring, Sussex (*see* Grayson, Bt, 1990 Edn), who *d* 1984; *b* 26 June 1919; *ed* Downside and Christ's Coll, Camb (Exhibitioner, Hon Fellow); Bar Inner Temple 1946, QC 1959; Recorder of Salisbury 1961-62, Solicitor-Gen 1962-64, and Attorney Gen 1970-74; Chm of Senate of Four Inns and Bar 1975-76, Pres 1986, Recorder of Kingston upon Thames since 1975; Chm of the Bar 1975-76; Leader of Western Circuit 1975-82; Treas Inner Temple 1984; Hon Fellow Coll of America's Trial Lawyers, and Hon Member America's Bar Assocn; MP for Epsom (*C*) 1955-74, and Epsom and Ewell 1974-78; 1939-45 War as Maj Irish Gds in N Africa (despatches); author of *A Price Too High* (autobiography 1989), *The Jesuit Factor* (1990), and five works of fiction; *cr* Knt 1962, PC 1964, and *Baron Rawlinson of Ewell*, of Ewell, co Surrey (Life Baron) 1978: *m* 1st, 1940 (*m diss* 1954) (*m* annulled by Sacred Rota, Rome), Haidée da of late Gerald Kavanagh; 2ndly, 1954, Elaine Angela, da of late Vincent Luis Dominguez, of Rhode Island, USA (*see* Grayson, Bt, 1980 Edn), and has had issue by 1st and 2nd *m*.

Arms – Or between three towers sable each charged with a sword point upwards argent a pall reversed sable thereon in chief a lymphad argent and in chevron a lion head erased or between two roses argent barbed and seeded proper. **Crest** – On a mount vert within a circlet of acorns and harps or a duck proper holding in the beak an escallop argent. **Supporters** – *Dexter*, a pegasus sable, maned, hooved and crowned gold; *sinister*, a llama or gorged with a ribbon blue celeste and argent the ends flottant upwards.
Residence – East Wing, Wardour Castle, Tisbury, Wilts SP3 6RH. *Clubs* – White's, Pratt's, MCC.

SONS LIVING (*By 2nd marriage*)

Hon Michael Vincent, *b* 1957: *m* 1982, Maria Alexandra Hilda Madeline de Lourdes, only da of late Anthony Charles Garton.
Hon Anthony Richard, *b* 1963: *m* 1996, Una S., elder da of John M. Shannon, of The Peak, Hong Kong, and of Much Marcle, Herefordshire.

DAUGHTERS LIVING AND DECEASED (*By 1st marriage*)

Hon Mikaela, *b* 1941: *m* 1964, Jonathan Irwin, of Sandymount House, Digby Bridge, Sallins, co Kildare, and has issue living, Charles, *b* 1965, — Luke, *b* 1967, — Jago, *b* 1972, — Samson, *b* 1982.
Hon Dariel, *b* 1943: *m* 1965, Harry John Gerard Garnett, of 32 Northumberland Pl, W2, and has issue living, Sophia, *b* 1968: *m* 1994, Tim Beddow, son of late C. M. Beddow, — Natasha, *b* 1970.
Hon Haidée, *b* 1948: *m* 1st, 1968, (William) Richard Annesley; 2ndly, 1985, Maj Ralph Cowdy, and *d* 1997, leaving issue (by 1st *m*), Peter, *b* 1970, — Arabella, *b* 1972.

(*By 2nd marriage*)

Hon Angela Lorraine (*Baroness Swaythling*), *b* 1962; resumed maiden name until remarriage: *m* 1st, 1991, Mathew Steinmann; 2ndly, 1996, 5th Baron Swaythling, and has issue (by 2nd *m*) (see that title).

RAYLEIGH, BARON (Strutt) (Baron UK 1821)

JOHN GERALD STRUTT, 6th Baron; *b* 4 June 1960; *s* 1988; *ed* Eton, RMA Sandhurst, and RAC Cirencester; late Lieut Welsh Gds: *m* 1991, Annabel Kate, yst da of Maj (William) Garry Patterson, Life Guards (*see* B Monson), and has issue.

Arms – Azure, on a chevron argent, between three cross-crosslets fitchée or, as many leopards' faces proper. Crest – A demi-lion azure, gorged with a mural crown, holding in the dexter paw a cross-crosslet fitchée or, and resting the sinister on a shield sable, charged with a chevron argent, between three cross-crosslets fitchée also or. Supporters – *Dexter*, a reindeer or, collared and attired sable; *sinister*, a monkey proper, banded round the loins and chained, chain reflexed over the back or.
Seat – Terling Place, Chelmsford, Essex.

SONS LIVING

Hon JOHN FREDERICK, *b* 29 March 1993.
Hon William Hedley Charles, *b* 1994.
Hon Hugo Richard, *b* 1998.

SISTERS LIVING

Tenax propositi
Tenacious of purpose

Anne Caroline (*Hon Mrs Bernard Jenkin*), *b* 1955: *m* 1988, Hon Bernard Christison Jenkin, yr son of Baron Jenkin of Roding, PC (Life Baron).
Mary Jean, *b* 1957: *m* 1981, Roderick Joseph Fraser, and has issue (*see* L Lovat, colls). *Residence* – Berwicks Farm House, Hatfield Peverel, Chelmsford, Essex.

UNCLE LIVING (*Son of 4th Baron by 1st marriage*)

Hon Hedley Vicars, *b* 1915; *ed* Eton, and Trin Coll, Camb; Capt (ret) Scots Guards. *Residence* – Mulroy, Carrigart, Letterkenny, co Donegal. *Club* – Brooks's.

HALF-UNCLE LIVING (*Son of 4th Baron by 2nd marriage*)

Hon Guy Robert, *b* 1921; *ed* Eton, and Trin Coll, Camb (BA 1943). *Residence* – The Old Rectory, Terling, Chelmsford, Essex CM3 2QE.

AUNT LIVING (*Daughter of 4th Baron by 1st marriage*)

Hon Daphne (*Dowager Baroness Acton*), *b* 1911: *m* 1931, 3rd Baron Acton, who *d* 1989. *Residence* – 46 Clarence Rd, Moseley, Birmingham B13 9UH.

MOTHER LIVING

Hon Jean Elizabeth Davidson, da of 1st Viscount Davidson: *m* 1952, Hon Charles Richard Strutt, 2nd son of 4th Baron, who *d* 1981. *Residence* – Berwick Place, Hatfield Peverel, Chelmsford, Essex.

COLLATERAL BRANCHES LIVING

Grandchildren of late Capt Geoffrey St John Strutt, CBE, yr son of late Hon Richard Strutt, 3rd son of 2nd Baron:—
Issue of late W/Cmdr Antony Geoffrey Strutt, OBE, RAF, *b* 1913, *d* 1995: *m* 1st, 1939 (*m diss* 1951), Ebba, da of Lief Lunderbye, of Oslo; 2ndly, 1951, Millicent (Molly) Edith (36 Cliff Rd, Roundham, Paignton, Devon TQ4 6DH), da of Aubrey Stephen Waters, of London:—
(By 1st wife) Vivienne Ebba, *b* 1940: *m* 1968, Richard Maitland Sands, of The Mill House, Preston St Mary, Sudbury, Suffolk CO10 9ND, and has issue living, Richard Jonathan Neville, *b* 1974. —— (By 2nd wife) Peter Antony (Hartland, Mortimer Av, Paignton, Devon TQ3 1LR), *b* 1949: *m* 1997, Patricia Françoise Marie, da of Patrick Hervé Vallée, of Dowar-an-Illis, Belle-Isle en Terre, France, and has issue living, James Peter Benjamin, *b* 1989, — Alexander Antony Andrew, *b* 1993. —— Stephen Nigel (Quarter Farm, Bathgate, W Lothian EH48 4JU), *b* 1952: *m* 1978, Liselotte Groth, of Denmark, and has issue living, Michael-Joshua, *b* 1982, — Philip, *b* 1993, — Camilla Isabel, *b* 1979, — Heidi-Carolina, *b* 1980, — Daisy, *b* 1984, — Susanna, *b* 1986, — Marie-Claire, *b* 1987, — Marvbel, *b* 1990, — Annabelle, *b* 1992, — Katrina, *b* 1995. —— Michael Geoffrey (Mountain View, Doon Castle, Sheeaune, Westport, co Sligo), *b* 1958: *m* 1992, Barbara E. Young, and has issue living, Daniel, *b* 19—, — Georgina, *b* 19—. —— Ian David (36 Cliff Rd, Roundham, Paignton, Devon TQ4 6DH), *b* 1965: *m* 1998, Emma Louise Hayman. —— Denise Olivia (14 East St, Ashburton, Devon), *b* 1955: *m* 1975 (*m diss* 1990), Richard Lyndale, and has issue living, Oliver Corrin, *b* 1984. —— Pamela Jane, *b* 1957: *m* 1st, 1980 (*m diss* 1994), Ian Fielding: 2ndly, 1995, Geoffrey Thompson, of 2 Sunniside Terrace, Cladon Village, S Tyneside SR6 7XE, and has issue living (by 1st *m*), Niki, *b* 1984, — Charlotte Emily, *b* 1989.

Issue of late Lt Stephen Alistair Strutt, RNVR, *b* 1918, *d* 1949: *m* 1941, Felicity Anne (who *d* 1976, having *m* 2ndly, 1959, Brig David Campbell Mullen, CBE, who *d* 1968), da of Mervyn Sorley MacDonnell:—
Paul Alistair, *b* 1944; *ed* Ampleforth; Maj: *m* 1977, Charlotte Yvonne, da of Brig Mortimer Cecil Lanyon, MBE, MC (*see* B Amherst of Hackney, colls), and has issue living, Richard Alistair Robert, *b* 1986, — Louisa Anne, *b* 1982. *Residence* – Flaxmans, W Tytherley, nr Salisbury, Hants SP5 1NR. —— Stephen Mark Alistair, *b* 1948; *ed* Ampleforth, and RAC Cirencester; late Maj Gren Gds: *m* 1980, Christina Mary Amoroso, da of Dr Eric Amoroso Centeno, and has issue living, Edward Alistair James, *b* 1985, — Catherine Mary Felicity Erica, *b* 1983. *Residence* – St Catherine, Bath, Som BA1 8HA. —— Lucinda Alistaire, *b* 1942: *m* 1976, Lt-Col Angus Iain Ramsay, and *dsp* 1986.

Grandchildren of late Hon Edward Gerald Strutt, CH, 5th son of 2nd Baron:—
Issue of late Gerald Murray Strutt, *b* 1880, *d* 1955: *m* 1910, Rhoda, OBE, who *d* 1968, 2nd da of late Collingwood Hope, CBE, KC, formerly Recorder of Bolton, of Crix, Hatfield Peverel, Essex:—
Pamela, *b* 1911: *m* 1935, Richard Gatty, JP, who *d* 1975, yr son of late Sir Stephen Herbert Gatty, KC, and has had issue, Jonathan *b* 1937: *m* 1st, 1962 (*m diss* 1984), Valerie Cynthia, da of Alfred H Adcock; 2ndly, 1984, Cheryll, (Pepper Arden, Northallerton, N Yorks), da of George Mansfield, of Risca, Gwent, and *d* 1991, leaving issue (by 1st *m*), Fiona Katherine Adelaide *b* 1963: *m* 1992, Maj Torquil MacLeod, The Black Watch (RHR) (and has issue living, Alexander Jonathan Hardinge *b* 1994, Hector John *b* 1996, Sophie *b* 19—, Eleanor Katharine *b* 1995), Philippa Margaret *b* 1965: *m* 1988, Jean-Louis Alexandre Lanteri-Laura, of 49 Wolfington Rd, SE27 0RH (and has issue living, Titus Guido *b* 1991, Giulietta Eve *b* 1989), (by 2nd *m*) Richard George *b* 1984, — Jessica Margaret, *b* 1938, — Rhoda Pamela, *b* 1943: *m* 1964, John David Bucknill, of The Grange, Grateley, Andover, Hants SP11 8JR and has issue living, Stephen *b* 1965: *m* 1993, Amanda Jane Cotton (and has issue living, Benjamin George *b* 1997, Rosanna *b* 1995), Gemma Martha *b* 1967: *m* 1990, Michael Anthony Hughes, Charlotte *b* 1969. *Residence* – Pepper Arden, Northallerton, N Yorks. —— Ursula Joyce, *b* 1917; 1939-45 War in WRNS: *m* 1948, Maj James Richard Edwards Harden, OBE, DSO, MC, DL, and has issue living, David James (Nanhoron, Pwllheli, Gwynedd), *b* 1954: *m* 1983, Bettina Clare Lascelles, only da of Col Brian Charles Lascelles Tayleur, OBE, 14/20th King's Hussars, of Nairobi, Kenya, and has issue living, Edward Richard *b* 1986, Matilda Claire *b* 1984, — Thérèse Annabella, *b* 1949: *m* 1st, 1972 (*m diss* 1979), Charles Herbert Pelham (*see* E Chichester, colls); 2ndly, 1980, Capt Nigel John Pearson, RN, and has issue living (by 2nd *m*), James Nicholas *b* 1985, Lucinda Christine *b* 1987, — Carolyn Emily, *b* 1952: *m* 1986, Colin Ransford Galloway, and has issue living, Miles Malcolm Ransford *b* 1989, Tanya *b* 1991, Zoë *b* 1992. *Residence* – Hendy, Nanhoron, Pwllheli, Gwynedd.

Issue of late John James Strutt, *b* 1881, *d* 1968: *m* 1914, Hon Agnes Roger Dewar, who *d* 1919, da of 1st Baron Forteviot:—
Joan Eleanor (173 Cranmer Court, SW3), *b* 1916.

Issue of late Capt Edward Jolliffe Strutt, *b* 1884, *d* 1964: *m* 1912, Amélie, who *d* 1954, da of late Frederic Devas:—
Sir Nigel Edward, TD (Sparrows, Terling, Chelmsford, Essex; Brooks's and Farmers' Clubs), *b* 1916; *ed* Winchester, and Wye Coll (Fellow 1970); Maj Essex Yeo (ret); a DL for Essex; High Sheriff 1966; Hon Fellow of Roy Agric Soc of England 1971 (Pres 1982-83); Hon DSc Cranfield 1979, Hon DUniv Essex 1981, Hon D Ph Anglia Poly Univ 1993, Johann Heinrich von Thünen Gold Medal, Kiel Univ, 1974; Massey Ferguson Award for sers to Agriculture 1976; 1939-45 War as Capt 104th (Essex) Yeo RHA (TA); Middle East 1939-45 (wounded, prisoner); Knt 1972. —— Gillian Leonora, *b* 1918: *m* 1st, 1941 (*m diss* 1959), Rt Hon Harold Anthony Nutting (later 3rd Bt), who *d* 1999; 2ndly, 1961, Brig Oliver George Brooke, CBE, DSO, of The Manor House, Gt Cheverell, Devizes (*see* V Brookeborough, colls, 1985 Edn), who *d* 1987.

Granddaughter of late Capt Edward Jolliffe Strutt (ante):—
Issue of late Lt-Col Mark Frederic Strutt, MC, TD, *b* 1913, *d* 1982: *m* 1946, Estelle Elaine, da of Capt Sir Thomas Reedham Berney, 10th Bt, MC, and widow of Maj Kenneth William Bols, IA (Strickland-Constable, Bt, colls):—
Charlotte Olivia, *b* 1947: *m* 1969, Bruce Dudley Ryder, of Crix, Hatfield Peverel, Essex, and has issue living (*see* E Harrowby, colls).

PREDECESSORS – **(1)** *Lady* CHARLOTTE MARY GERTRUDE FITZGERALD, da of James, 1st Duke of Leinster, and wife of Col Joseph Holden Strutt, MP for Maldon 1790-1827, was *cr Baroness Rayleigh*, of Terling Place, co Essex (peerage of United Kingdom) 1821; *s* by her son **(2)** JOHN JAMES, 2nd Baron; *b* 1796: *m* 1842, Clara Elizabeth Latouche, who *d* 1900, da of late Capt Richard Vicars, RE; *d* 1873; *s* by his son **(3)** JOHN WILLIAM, OM, PC, DCL, LLD, DSc, FRS, 3rd Baron, *b* 1842; sometime Lord-Lieut of Essex; the eminent scientist; Nobel Prizeman, Chancellor of Camb Univ, Hon Professor of Natural Philosophy at Roy Institution, and Scientific Adviser to the Trinity House; four years Professor of Experimental Physics in Camb Univ: *m* 1871, Evelyn Georgiana Mary, who *d* 1934, da of late James Maitland Balfour, of Whittinghehame, Prestonkirk; *d* 1919; *s* by his el son **(4)** ROBERT JOHN, 4th Baron; *b* 1875; a FRS; Pres of British Asso 1938, and of Roy Institution 1945: *m* 1st, 1905, Lady Mary Hilda Clements, who *d* 1919, da of 4th Earl of Leitrim; 2ndly, 1920, Kathleen Alice, OBE, who *d* 1980, da of late John Coppin-Straker, of Stagshaw House, Northumberland, and widow of Capt James Harold Cuthbert, DSO, Scots Guards; *d* 1947; *s* by his son **(5)** JOHN ARTHUR, 5th Baron, *b* 1908: *m* 1934, Ursula Mary, who *d* 1982, da of late Lt-Col Richard Hugh Royds Brocklebank, DSO, of 18 Hyde Park Sq, W; *d* 1988; *s* by his nephew **(6)** JOHN GERALD (only son of late Hon Charles Richard Strutt, 2nd son of 4th Baron), 6th Baron and present peer.

RAYNE, BARON (Rayne) (Life Baron 1976)

MAX RAYNE, el son of Phillip Rayne; *b* 8 Feb 1918; *ed* Central Foundation Sch, and Univ Coll, London (Hon LLD 1968; Hon Fellow 1966); served with RAF 1940-45; Dir First Leisure Corporation plc 1984-99 (Dep Chm 1984-92, Chm 1992-95); Dir Housing Corporation (1974) Ltd 1974-78, and Dir of other companies; Gov of St Thomas's Hosp 1962-74, Special Trustee of St Thomas's Hosp 1974-92; Gov of Royal Ballet Sch 1966-79; Gov of Malvern Coll since 1966; Gov of Centre for Environmental Studies 1967-73; Member of Gen Council of King Edward VII's Hospital Fund for London 1966-96; Memb RADA Council since 1973, South Bank Board 1986-92, Council, St Thomas's Hosp Med Sch 1965-82; Trustee of Henry Moore Foundation since 1988; Hon Vice-Pres of Jewish Care since 1966; Vice-Pres of Yehudi Menuhin Sch since 1987 (Gov 1966-87); Chm Royal Nat Theatre 1971-88; Founder Patron of The Rayne Foundation since 1962; Hon Fell of Darwin Coll, Camb 1966, Univ Coll London 1966, LSE 1974, Royal Coll of Psychiatrists 1977, King's Coll Hosp Med Sch 1980, Univ Coll, Oxford 1982, King's Coll, London 1983, Westminster Sch 1989, Royal Coll of Physicians 1992, UMDS, Guy's and St Thomas's 1992; Officier, Légion d'Honneur 1987 (Chevalier 1973); *cr* Knt 1969, and *Baron Rayne*, of Prince's Meadow in Greater London (Life Baron) 1976: *m* 1st, 1941 (*m diss* 1960), Margaret, da of Louis Marco, of London; 2ndly, 1965, Lady Jane Antonia Frances Vane-Tempest-Stewart, el da of 8th Marquess of Londonderry, and has issue by 1st and 2nd *m*.

Arms – Per fess dancetty azure and gules a caduceus between in chief two roses or. **Crest** – Upon a wreath or and azure issuant from a circlet or a mount vert thereon a lion passant gold murally crowned azure holding in the dexter forepaw a key erect wards outwards or. **Supporters** – *Dexter*, a lion or crowned and gorged with a chain pendant therefrom two triangles interlaced azure; *sinister*, a lion azure crowned and gorged with a like chain pendant therefrom a fleur-de-lys gold.
Residence – 33 Robert Adam St, W1M 5AH.

SONS LIVING (*By 1st marriage*)

Hon Robert Anthony, *b* 1949: *m* 1973, Jane, da of late Robert Blackburn, and has issue.

(*By 2nd marriage*)

Hon Nicholas Alexander, *b* 1969.
Hon Alexander Philip, *b* 1973.

DAUGHTERS LIVING (*By 1st marriage*)

Hon Madeleine Barbara, *b* 1943: *m* 1964, Alan Rayner.
Hon Susan Ann, *b* 1945: *m* 1965 (*m diss* 1974), John Rubin.

(*By 2nd marriage*)

Hon Natasha Deborah, *b* 1966: *m* 1992, Nicholas J. Capstick-Dale, son of J. R. Capstick-Dale.
Hon Tamara Annabel, *b* 1970.

Raynham, Viscount; son of Marquess Townshend.

RAZZALL, BARON (Razzall) (Life Baron 1997)

(EDWARD) TIMOTHY RAZZALL, CBE, son of Leonard Humphrey Razzall, Master of the Supreme Court; *b* 12 June 1943; *ed* St Paul's, and Worcester Coll, Oxford (BA 1965); Admitted a Solicitor 1969; Partner, Frere Cholmeley (now Frere Cholmeley Bischoff) 1973-95; Partner, Argonaut Associates since 1995; Dir Cala plc since 1973, Chm C. & B. Publishing plc since 1997 and Dir Milner Estates plc since 1998 and Star Mining Corp NL since 1993; Councillor, London Borough of Richmond-upon-Thames 1974-98, Chm Policy and Resources Cttee and Dep Leader 1983-97; Treasurer, Liberal Party 1987-88, since when of Lib Dems: *cr* CBE 1993, and *Baron Razzall*, of Mortlake in the London Borough of Richmond (Life Baron) 1997: *m* 1st, 1965 (*m diss* 1974), Christine, da of Thomas Birkett, of Preston, Lancs; 2ndly, 1982, Deirdre Bourke, da of late Duncan Taylor-Smith, of Stavordale, Som and has issue by 1st *m*.

Address – Argonaut Associates, 14-16 Regent St, WC2E 7DU. *Clubs* – National Liberal, MCC.

SON LIVING (*By 1st marriage*)

Hon James Timothy, *b* 1972; *ed* St Paul's.

DAUGHTER LIVING (*By 1st marriage*)

Hon Katharine Mary, *b* 1970; *ed* Westminster, and Pembroke Coll, Oxford.

REA, BARON (Rea) (Baron UK 1937, Bt UK 1935)
(Name pronounced "Ree")

Ready for everything

(JOHN) NICOLAS REA, 3rd Baron and 3rd Baronet, *b* 6 June 1928; *s* 1981; *ed* Dartington Hall, Dauntsey's Sch, and Christ's Coll, Camb (MA, MD); DPH, DCH, DObst, FRCGP: *m* 1st, 1951 (*m diss* 1991), Elizabeth Anne, da of late William Hensman Robinson, of Woking; 2ndly, 1991, Judith Mary, da of late Norman Powell, of Lytham St Anne's, Lancs, and has issue by 1st *m*.

Arms – Or, on a fesse wavy azure between three stags courant gules, a lymphad sails furled of the field. **Crest** – A stag at gaze gules, resting the dexter foreleg on an anchor or. **Supporters** – On either side a stag gules, charged on the shoulder with a bezant, thereon an anchor azure. *Residence* – 11 Anson Rd, N7 0RB.

SONS LIVING (*by 1st marriage*)

Hon MATTHEW JAMES, *b* 28 March 1956; *ed* William Ellis Sch, and Sheffield Univ; has issue living, Ivan REA *b* 1992, — Ellis Kelsey Haslam REA (a da), *b* 1989.

Dr the *Hon* Daniel William, *b* 1958; *ed* William Ellis Sch, Bristol Univ, and UCH Medical Sch: *m* 1983, Hon Rebecca Llewelyn Davies, yst da of late Baron Llewelyn-Davies (Life Baron), and has issue living, William Alexander, *b* 8 Oct 1991, — Edward Inigo, *b* 1994, — Séan, *b* 1996. *Residence* – 4 Queensgate Villas, Victoria Park Rd, E9.

Hon Quentin Thomas, *b* 1961; *ed* William Ellis Sch, and Manchester Univ: has issue living (by Jane, da of Dr Allen Trevor Bevan, of Colchester, Essex), Thomas, *b* 1999, — Peggy, *b* 1995.

Hon John Silas Nathaniel, *b* 1965; *ed* William Ellis Sch: *m* 1993, Andrea, yst da of Roy Ross, of Barrington, Rhode Island, USA, and has issue living, Isabelle, *b* 1998.

BROTHER LIVING (*Raised to the rank of a Baron's son,* 1989)

Hon Charles Julian (62 Dukes Av, N10), *b* 1931; *ed* Bryanston, and Downing Coll, Camb (MA, Dip Ed): *m* 1st, 1951 (*m diss* 1964), Bridget, da of late Charles Montagu Slater; 2ndly, 1964, Anne Bernadette, da of William Robson, and has issue living (by 1st *m*), Steven (29 Farm Lane, Gt Bedwyn, Marlborough, Wilts SN8 3LU), *b* 1956: *m* 1983, Julia Louise, da of late David George Edward Wyatt, and has issue living, Benjamin David *b* 1992, Madeleine Louise *b* 1987, — Julia, *b* 1952: *m* 1973, Lalith (Kim) Kamlani, of 53 Lancaster Rd, N7, and has issue living, Joshua Rasheed *b* 1993, Neema Sunaina *b* 1977, Layla Latika *b* 1978, — (by 2nd *m*), William, *b* 1965, — James, *b* 1968, — Lucy, *b* 1966, — Kate, *b* 1972.

Helen Margaret, da of late Bernhard Hermann Richardson, of Edinburgh, and formerly wife of Donald Crawford Reid: *m* 1959, as his 3rd wife, Hon Findlay Russell Rea, who *d* 1984. *Residence* – Weald Cottage, Weald, Sevenoaks, Kent TN14 6PY.

COLLATERAL BRANCH LIVING

Issue of late Hon Findlay Russell Rea, 3rd son of 1st Baron, *b* 1907, *d* 1984: *m* 1st, 1932 (*m diss* 1946), (Margaret) Hermione, eldest da of late Col Kenneth Hope Bruce, DSO; 2ndly, 1947 (*m diss* 1959), Eileen, da of late Lt-Col Isaac Wardle, IA, and formerly wife of John Lionel Clemence; 3rdly, 1959, Helen Margaret (ante), da of late Bernhard Hermann Richardson, of Edinburgh, and formerly wife Donald Crawford Reid:—

(By 1st *m*) Benjamin Russell (15 The Knolls, Epsom, Surrey KT17 3ND), *b* 1936: *ed* Bryanston, and Trin Coll, Oxford: *m* 1st, 1964 (*m diss* 1972), Angela, only da of Arthur Jackson Bradley; 2ndly, 1973, Dorinda Anne, da of late Stanley Cutting, of Bath, Avon, and has issue living (by 1st *m*), Susannah, *b* 1968, — (by 2nd *m*) James Russell, *b* 1973, — Thomas Russell, *b* 1975. —— Joanna, *b* 1934; JP Lancaster: *m* 1st, 1957 (*m diss* 1982), Robert Cecil Seeckts, yr son of late George Seeckts; 2ndly, 1984, Peter John Bartram, of Whasdyke, Windermere, Cumbria LA23 1JN, el son of late George Hylton Bartram, of Sunderland, and has issue living (by 1st *m*), Richard Philip (South View, Main Rd, Kingsley, Hants GU35 9ND), *b* 1966: *m* 1992, Virginia Bull, — Rosemary Anne, *b* 1958: *m* 1991, Maj Ian Alexander Orr, KOSB, — Sarah Elizabeth, *b* 1960: *m* 1990, Derek Charles Culey, of 22 Orlando Av, Mosman, NSW 2088, Australia, — Katherine Mary, *b* 1963: *m* 1990, Gerald Francis Deslandes, of 6 Chandos Rd South, Chorlton, Manchester M21 0TF.

PREDECESSORS – (1) WALTER RUSSELL REA, son of late Rt Hon Russell Rea, MP of Tanhurst, Dorking, Surrey, and Dean Stanley Street, SW1; *b* 1873; a Merchant Banker, and Pres of Free Trade Union; was Comptroller of HM's Household 1931-2; sat as MP for Scarborough (L) 1906-18, for N Div of Bradford 1923-4, and for Dewsbury 1931-5; *cr* a *Baronet* 1935, and *Baron Rea*, of Eskdale, co Cumberland (peerage of United Kingdom) 1937: *m* 1st, 1896, Evelyn, who *d* 1930, da of J. J. Muirhead, JP, of Edinburgh; 2ndly, 1931, Jemima, who *d* 1964, da of Rev Alexander Ewing; *d* 1948; *s* by his el son (2) PHILIP RUSSELL, OBE, PC, 2nd Baron, *b* 1900; Foreign Office 1945-50; Liberal Leader in House of Lords 1955-67; Pres of Liberal Party 1955; a Dep Speaker House of Lords 1950-78; 1939-45 War as Lt-Col KRRC attached Special Forces (despatches): *m* 1922, Lorna, who *d* 1978, da of late Lewis O. Smith, of Glasgow; *d* 1981; *s* by his nephew, (JOHN) NICOLAS (son of late Hon James Russell Rea, 2nd son of 1st Baron), 3rd Baron and present peer.

READING, MARQUESS OF (Rufus Isaacs) (Marquess UK 1926)

SIMON CHARLES HENRY RUFUS ISAACS, 4th Marquess; *b* 18 May 1942; *s* 1980; *ed* Eton, and Tours Univ France; Lt 1st The Queen's Dragoon Gds 1961-64; Member of London Stock Exchange 1970-74; Dir Flying Hospital Inc, Nelson Recovery Trust, and Cheltenham and Gloucester College Trust; Pres Dean Close Sch since 1990: *m* 1979, Melinda Victoria, yr da of Richard J. G. Dewar, of Shoelands House, Seale, Surrey, and has issue.

Arms – Sable, a bend between two leopards' faces or, on a chief argent a fasces fesscwise proper. **Crest** – In front of a leopard's head couped sable, a faces as in the arms. **Supporters** – On either side a leopard proper, round the neck a collar or, pendent therefrom an escutcheon argent charged with a human head affrontée proper, erased at the neck, ducally crowned or.
Residence – Jaynes Court, Bisley, Glos GL6 7BE. *Clubs* – Cavalry and Guards'; MCC; All England Lawn Tennis.

SON LIVING

JULIAN MICHAEL (*Viscount Erleigh*), *b* 26 May 1986.

DAUGHTERS LIVING

Either do not attempt or complete

Lady Sybilla Alice, *b* 1980.

Lady Natasha Rose Eleanor, *b* 1983.

BROTHERS LIVING

Lord Antony Ian Michael, *b* 1943; *ed* Gordonstoun: *m* 1st, 1972 (*m diss* 1976), Ann Pugsley; 2ndly, 1983, Heide Lund, of Vancouver, BC, and has issue living (by 2nd *m*), Tallulah Elke Margot, *b* 1987, — Ruby Jacqueline Kirsten, *b* 1989.

Lord Alexander Gerald, *b* 1957; *ed* St Paul's Sch, and Oriel Coll, Oxford (MA); Bar (Middle Temple) 1982; California Bar 1988: *m* 1993 (*m diss* 1997), Marjorie Frances BACH, da of Howard Goldbach, of LA, USA.

SISTER LIVING

Lady Jacqueline Rosemary Margot (42 Glebe Place, SW3 5JE), *b* 1946: *m* 1976 (*m diss* 19—), Sir Mark Wilfrid Home Thomson, 3rd Bt (*cr* 1925).

AUNTS LIVING (*Daughters living of 2nd Marquess*)

Lady Joan Alice Violet (*Baroness Zuckerman*), *b* 1918; formerly a JP for Birmingham and Hunstanton: *m* 1939, Prof Baron Zuckerman, OM, KCB, FRS (Life Baron), who *d* 1993. *Residence* – The Shooting Box, Burnham Thorpe, King's Lynn, Norfolk.

Lady Elizabeth Anne Mary, *b* 1921: formerly Junior Com ATS: *m* 1945, Maj Derek Francis Hornsby, KRRC, who *d* 1971 (B Belper), and has issue living, Richard Gerald (38 Grosvenor Gdns Mews South, SW1W 0LB), *b* 1948: *m* 1980 (*m diss* 1997), Maria Lara, of San Francisco, California, and has issue living, Simon Daniel *b* 1983, Rachael Sarah *b* 1982, Annabel Alice *b* 1991, — David Julian (109 Winchester St, SW1), *b* 1953: *m* 1975 (*m diss* 1995), Julie Ann Witford, and has issue living, Alexander Keith *b* 1977, Samuel Florian *b* 1985, Michael David *b* 1987. *Residence* – 29 Warwick Sq, SW1V 24B.

WIDOW LIVING OF THIRD MARQUESS

Margot Irene (*Dowager Marchioness of Reading*) (Glebe Farm House, Cornwell, nr Chipping Norton, Oxon OX7 67X), yr da of late Percival Augustus Duke, OBE: *m* 1941, the 3rd Marquess of Reading, MBE, MC, who *d* 1980.

PREDECESSORS – (1) *Sir* Rufus Daniel Isaacs (later Rufus Isaacs), GCB, GCSI, GCIE, GCVO, PC, son of late Joseph Michael Isaacs, merchant and shipbroker, of London; *b* 1860; sat as MP for Reading (*L*) 1904-13; appointed Solicitor-Gen March 1910, Attorney-Gen Oct 1910 (with a seat in the Cabinet from June 1912), and Lord Chief Justice of England 1913-21; Pres Anglo-French Mission to USA 1915, Special British Representative to USA 1917, High Commr in USA, and Ambassador Extraor and Plen on Special Mission 1918-19, Viceroy of India 1921-6, and Sec of State for Foreign Affairs (in National Government) Aug to Nov 1931, became Capt of Deal Castle 1926, and Lord Warden of the Cinque Ports 1934; *cr Baron Reading*, of Erleigh, Berks (peerage of United Kingdom) 1914, *Viscount Reading*, of Erleigh, Berks (peerage of United Kingdom) 1916, *Viscount Erleigh*, of Erleigh, Berks, and *Earl of Reading* (peerage of United Kingdom) Nov 1917, and *Marquess of Reading* (peerage of United Kingdom) 1926: *m* 1st, 1887, *Dame* Alice Edith, GBE, CI, who *d* 1930, da of Albert Cohen, merchant, of London; 2ndly, 1931, *Dame* Stella, GBE (*Baroness Swanborough*), who *d* 1971, da of the late Charles Charnaud; *d* 1935; *s* by his son (2) Gerald, GCMG, CBE, MC, TD, PC, QC, 2nd Marquess; *b* 1889; a Bencher and Treasurer of Middle Temple; was Joint Parliamentary Under-Sec of State for Foreign Affairs 1951-53, and Joint Min of State for Foreign Affairs 1953-7: Hon Col Inns of Court Regt (TA) 1947-59: *m* 1914, Hon Eva Violet Mond, CBE, JP, who *d* 1973, da of 1st Baron Melchett; *d* 1960; *s* by his son (3) Michael Alfred, MBE, MC, 3rd Marquess *b* 1916; Major Queen's Bays and on Staff; served in World War II *m* 1941, Margot Irene, yr da of late Percival Augustus Duke, OBE, of Brockham Warren, Box Hill, Dorking, Surrey; *d* 1980; *s* by his son (4) Simon Charles Henry, 4th Marquess and present peer, also Earl of Reading, Viscount Reading, Viscount Erleigh, and Baron Reading.

REAY, LORD (Mackay) (Lord S 1628, Bt NS 1627)
(Name pronounced "Ray")

Hugh William Mackay, 14th Lord and 14th Baronet; *b* 19 July 1937; *s* 1963; *ed* Eton, and Ch Ch, Oxford; is Chief of the Clan Mackay, and Baron Mackay van Ophemert in the Netherlands; Member of European Parl, Strasbourg, since 1973; a Lord in Waiting since 1989, Under-Sec Dept of Trade and Industry 1989-92: *m* 1st, 1964 (*m diss* 1978), Hon Annabel Térèse Fraser, da of 15th (*de facto*) Lord Lovat; 2ndly, 1980, Hon Victoria Isabella Warrender, only da of 1st Baron Bruntisfield, and has issue by 1st and 2nd *m*.

Arms – Azure, on a chevron argent, between three bears' heads couped argent, muzzled gules, a roebuck's head erased, between two hands grasping daggers, the points turned towards the buck's head, all proper. Crest – A dexter arm erect couped at the elbow, the hand grasping a dagger also erect proper. Supporters – *Dexter*, a pikeman armed at all points; *sinister*, a musketeer, both proper.
Residences – Ophemert in Gelderland, Netherlands; 98 Oakley St, SW3. *Clubs* – Turf, Beefsteak, Puffin's, Pratt's.

SONS LIVING (*By 1st marriage*)

Hon Æneas Simon (*Master of Reay*), *b* 20 March 1965; *ed* Westminster, and Brown Univ, USA.
Hon Edward Andrew, *b* 1974.

DAUGHTERS LIVING (*By 1st marriage*)

Hon Laura Elizabeth, *b* 1966.

(*By 2nd marriage*)

Hon Antonia Alexandra, *b* 1981.
Hon Isabel Violet Grace, *b* 1985.

SISTERS LIVING

Hon Elizabeth Mary, *b* 1938: *m* 1962 (*m diss* 1979), Nicholas Hardwick Fairbairn, QC, MP (later Sir Nicholas Fairbairn), who *d* 1995, and has issue living, Charlotte Elizabeth, *b* 1963: *m* 1992, G. Ross Pople, yr son of late Lennard Pople, of Wanganui, NZ, and has issue living, Jake Alexander *b* 1994, Clara Mary *b* 1998, — Anna-Karina, *b* 1966: *m* 1996, John G. Henderson, son of Richard Henderson, of Blairston, Ayr, — Francesca Katharine Nichola, *b* 1969. *Residence* – 38 Moray Place, Edinburgh.

Hon Margaret Anne (Upper Huntlywood, Earlston, Berwickshire), *b* 1941: *m* 1976, Allen Leslie Christian, of Upper Huntlywood, Earlston, Berwicks, and 1501 Ocean Bay Drive, Key Largo, Florida, USA.

WIDOW LIVING OF THIRTEENTH LORD

CHARLOTTE MARY (*Charlotte, Lady Reay*), da of late William Younger, of Ravenswood, Melrose: *m* 1936, the 13th Lord, who *d* 1963.

COLLATERAL BRANCHES LIVING

Granddaughter of late Baron Theodoor Philip Mackay, 2nd son of Johan François Hendrik Jacob Ernestus Mackay, brother of 10th Lord:—
Issue of late Baron Constantyn Willem Ferdinand Mackay, *b* 1870, *d* 1955: *m* 1st, 1898, Jonkvrouw Petronella Adamina Hoeufft, who *d* 1933; 2ndly, 1937, Dr C. Frida Katz, who *d* 1963:—
Baroness Margaretha Clara Françoise, *b* 1909: *m* 1937, Rev Henri Jean Louis André Couvée, who *d* 1969, and has issue living, Jean Pierre Henri, *b* 1939, — Petronella Adamina, *b* 1941, — Agnès Madeleine Adélaide, *b* 1943. *Residence* – Huize Aelbrecht van Beijeren, Theo Mann-Bouwmeesterlaan 1, 2597 GT, The Hague.

Grandchildren of late Baron Æneas Mackay (infra):—
Issue of late Lt-Col Baron Daniel Mackay, *b* 1900, *d* 1969: *m* 1927, Henriette Constance Adèle, who *d* 1986, da of Dr Alfred Joan Labouchere, of Zeist, Netherlands:—
Baron Donald (279 Irislaan, 2343 CM Oegstgeest, Netherlands), *b* 1928; Lt-Col RNAF (ret): *m* 1968 (*m diss* 1987), Danielle Christine da of Dr Hendrik Gerrit Beins. —— *Baron* Alfred Alexander (248 Parkweg, Voorburg, Netherlands), *b* 1930: *m* 1965, Diana Margaret, da of Sydney Jesty Elwin, of Strathfield, NSW, and has issue living, *Baron* Andrew Robert, *b* 1967, — *Baroness* Caroline Jane, *b* 1969. —— *Baron* Eric Joan Maurits (Van Calcarlaan 21, Wassenaar, Netherlands), *b* 1938: *m* 1963, Susan Jane, da of Francis McNeill, and has issue living, *Baron* Patrick Joan, *b* 1967, — *Baroness* Alexandra, *b* 1966: *m* 1999, Jan Willem Eduard Rempt, son of Herman Eduard Rempt, — *Baroness* Helen Danielle, *b* 1969, — *Baroness* Madeline, *b* 1971.

Issue of late Baron Reinhold Alexander Mackay, *b* 1903, *d* 1990: *m* 1930, Greta Ernestina, who *d* 1995, da of Jan Adrian Smito, of The Hague:—
Baroness Sonja Gratia, *b* 1931: *m* 1953, Hendrick Willem Balthasar Croiset van Uchelen, and has issue living, Eric Alexander, *b* 1958, — Helen Astrid, *b* 1955.

Grandchildren of late Baron Theodoor Philip Mackay (ante):—
Issue of late Baron Æneas Mackay, *b* 1872, *d* 1932: Jonkvrouwe Hermina Clasina, who *d* 1945, da of Lieut-Gen Jonkheer J. C. C. den Beer Poortugael, Min of War, and Privy Councillor:—
Baron Theodoor Philip (Provinciënlaan 3-53, Heemstede, Netherlands), *b* 1911: former Burgomaster: *m* 1941, Zsófia Friderika Emma, who *d* 1999, da of late Dr Andor Henrik Ráthonyi Reusz, of Budapest, Hungary, and has issue living, *Baron* Æneas (Postbus 29, 1230 AA Loosdrecht, Netherlands), *b* 1942; is a Dir: *m* 1975 (*m diss* 19—), Yvonne Marie-Blanche, da of Frans Wyers, and has issue living, *Baron* Randolph Philip *b* 1977, *Baron* Patrick James *b* 1979, — *Baroness* Marguerite Louise, *b* 1943: *m* 1964, Dr Bernhard Rudolf Grüninger, of La Chaux de Fonds, Rue de la Prairie 76, Switzerland, and has issue living, Daniel Robert *b* 1966, Marie-Anne *b* 1968, — *Baroness* Lilian Mary, *b* 1945: *m* 1970, Jan Willem Stuart, of Heemstede, and has issue living, Wendelien *b* 1972, Marguérite *b* 1974, — *Baroness* Zsófia Alexandra, *b* 1951: *m* 1979, Dr Frederik Christiaan Musch, Secretary of Bank of International Settlements, Basle, Switzerland, and has issue living, Willem Heiko *b* 1980, Onno Frederick Roger *b* 1984, Clare Alexandra *b* 1982. —— *Baroness* Erica, *b* 1916: *m* 1974, Jonkheer Gerard Beelaerts van Blokland, former Netherlands Ambassador to Russia, who *d* 1997.

Issue of late Baron Dirk Rijnhard Johan Mackay, *b* 1876, *d* 1960: *m* 1st, 1906, Johanna Elisabeth Blaauw, who *d* 1920; 2ndly, 1927 (*m diss* 1937), Violet, da of Edward Egerts; 3rdly, 1939, Helena Esme Egerts, who *d* 1990, sister of his 2nd wife:—
(By 1st *m*) †*Baron* Johan Jacob, *b* 1909: *m* 1936, Elisabeth E., da of William Clarence Holman, and *d* 1995, leaving issue, *Baron* Derrik Philip (Casilla 16131, Santiago, Chile), *b* 1937: *m* 1964, Juanita Carmiña Hederra Sepulveda, da of Agusto Hederra Silva, and has issue living, *Baron* Cristian Andrès *b* 1965: *m* 1993, Maria Consuelo Diaz Fernandez, da of Patricio Diaz Carrasco (and has issue living, *Baroness* Maria Consuelo Magdalena *b* 1994, *Baroness* Sofia Bernardita *b* 1995), *Baron* Alejandro Andrès *b* 1967, *Baron* Matias Andrès *b* 1972, — *Baron* John Hugo (Casilla 116, Talca, Chile), *b*

1941: *m* 1971, Sylvia Bravo Perucca, da of Ladislao Bravo, and has issue living, *Baron* John Donald, *b* 1973, *Baroness* Sylvia Francisca *b* 1972, — *Baroness* Johanna Elizabeth, *b* 1939: *m* 1970, German del Rio, and has issue living, German Andrès *b* 1971, Juan Ignacio *b* 1972, — *Baroness* Marie Louise, *b* 1952. —— *Baron* Johan Hugo (29 Ary Schefferstr, 2597 VN, The Hague, Holland), *b* 1914, Commodore, RNN (ret): *m* 1945, Margaret, da of Pearse John Herbert, and has issue living, *Baron* Alexander Rijnhard (Keizersgracht 12E, 1015 CP Amsterdam, Netherlands) *b* 1950: *m* 1st, 1972 (*m diss* 1987), Maria Paula Hermanna, da of Bernardus Petrus Maria Marquering; 2ndly, 19—, Tine Elizabeth, da of Nicolaas Johannes Maria Taverne, and has issue living (by 1st *m*), *Baron* Robert Bernard *b* 1975, *Baron* Michiel Christiaan *b* 1978, — *Baron* Donald Johan, *b* 1964, — *Baroness* Carol Huguette, *b* 1954: *m* 1991, Dr Eric Paul Jozef Myjer, and has issue living, Florian Hugo Bob *b* 1992, Sandrijn Margaret Maria *b* 1988. —— *Baron* Eric Rijnhard Alexander, *b* 1917: *m* 1943, Gertrud, da of Paul Moritz Robert Ernst Brückmann, and has issue living, *Baron* Æneas, *b* 1944: *m* 1971, Joke, da of Eduard Strelitski, and has issue living, *Baron* Alexander *b* 1975, *Baroness* Fleur *b* 1977, — *Baron* Paul, *b* 1946: *m* 1st, 1971 (*m diss* 1974), Cornelie Elisabeth, da of Dr Jan Cornelis Steye Marie Nijenbandring de Boer; 2ndly, 1982, Ulrike Borgwardt, and has issue living, (by 2nd *m*) *Baron* Laurens Johannes *b* 1985, *Baron* Ernst Julian *b* 1987, *Baron* Rembert Helias *b* 1990, — *Baron* Eric, *b* 1953: *m* 1982, Geertje, da of Dr Boschma, and has issue living, *Baron* Barthold *b* 1987, *Baron* Christiaan *b* 1991, *Baroness* Charlotte *b* 1985. —— *Baroness* Helene Gérardine, *b* 1907: *m* 1926, Rodney Frederick Jarrett Sterwin, who *d* 1981, and has issue living, Peter Philip, *b* 1930, — Angela Helen, *b* 1929.

Grandchildren of late Baron Daniel Mackay (*b* 1878) (infra):—
Issue of late Baron Donald Theodoor Mackay, *b* 1910, *d* 1992: *m* 1st, 1939 (*m diss* 1945), Jonkvrouwe Alexandra Frederica, da of Jonkheer Bonifacius Christiaan de Savornin Lohman; 2ndly 1945, Kathleen, da of Percy Shaw Pearce:—
(By 2nd *m*) *Baron* Niall (2 Nobold Court, Gold St, Clipston, Leics), *b* 1956: *m* 1985, Jennifer Mary, da of Hugh Butcher, and has issue living, *Baron* Calum Hugh, *b* 1989, — *Baroness* Georgia Kathleen, *b* 1992. —— *Baroness* Moira, *b* 1952.

Granddaughter of late Baron Theodoor Philip Mackay (ante):—
Issue of late Baron Daniel Mackay, *b* 1878, *d* 1962: *m* 1st, 1906 (*m diss* 1921), Helene Hommel, who *d* 1926; 2ndly, 1921, Marie Françoise, who *d* 1959, da of Hugo François Lamaison; 3rdly, 1960, Anna Minke, who *d* 1985, da of Johannes Weyer:—
(By 2nd *m*) *Baroness* Maria Constantia (Voorsterweg 153, Tonden, 6975 AD Tonden, Gelderland, Holland), *b* 1922: *m* 1947, (*m diss* 1961) Johan Barthold Frans Bosch Ridder van Rosenthal, and has issue living, Lodewijk Hendrik Nicolaas, *b* 1948: *m* 1972, Erica van Hoorn, and has issue living, Eelco *b* 1976, Saskia *b* 1974, — Roelina Gijsbertha Gerardina, *b* 1951: *m* 1978, Christiaan van Haersma Buma, and has issue living, Michiel *b* 1981, Robert *b* 1983, — Nicolette, *b* 1953: *m* 1975, Pieter Roodenburgh, and has issue living, Frederiek *b* 1980, Roelien Anne *b* 1978. —— *Baroness* Juliana Anna (C19 De Nieuwenhof, Voorst, Netherlands) *b* 1925: *m* 1950 (*m diss* 1960), Count Rutger Jan Moritz Albert Schimmelpenninck, who *d* 1998, and has issue living, *Count* Gerrit Marius, *b* 1951, — *Countess* Marie Danielle, *b* 1952.

Granddaughter of late Baron Willem Karel Mackay, yst son of late Johan François Hendrik Jacob Ernestus Mackay (ante):—
Issue of late Baron Barthold Mackay, *b* 1871, *d* 1945: *m* 1898, Jonkvrouwe Alpheda Louise, who *d* 1935, da of Jonkheer Cornelis Charles van der Wyck:—
Baroness Johanna Elisabeth, *b* 1907: *m* 1st, 1936, Capt Patrick Alexander Agnew, Seaforth Highlanders (TA) (*ka* 1943) (*see* Agnew, Bt *cr* 1629, colls); 2ndly, 1944 (*m diss* 1965), Lt-Col William Stanley Baird. *Residence* – Laan van Rijnwijk/ Flat 35c, Zeist, Holland.

PREDECESSORS – (**1**) *Sir* DONALD Mackay, Knt, el son of Huistean Du of Farr, and Strathnaver; *b* 1590; a distinguished royalist soldier, was *cr* a *Baronet* 1627, and *Lord Reay* peerage of Scotland, 1628, with remainder to his heirs male for ever bearing the name and arms of Mackay: *m* 1st, 1610, Barbara Mackenzie, sister of 1st Earl of Seaforth; 2ndly, before 1631, (marriage annulled) Rachel Winterfield or Harrison; 3rdly, Elizabeth, da of Robert Thomson, of Greenwich; 4thly, Marjorie, da of Francis Sinclair of Stirkoke; *d* 1649; *s* by his son (**2**) JOHN, 2nd Lord, who espoused the royal cause: *m* 1st, 1636, Isabel Sinclair; 2ndly, Barbara, da of Col Hugh Mackay of Scourie; *d* about 1681; *s* by his grandson (**3**) GEORGE, FRS (son of late Donald Mackay, Master of Reay), 3rd Lord: *m* 1st, 1702, Margaret, da of Lt-Gen Hugh Mackay of Scourie; 2ndly, Janet, da of John Sinclair of Ulbster and widow of Benjamin Dunbar, yr, of Hempriggs; 3rdly, 1713, Mary, da of John Doull of Thuster, WS; *d* 1748; *s* by his son (**4**) DONALD, 4th Lord: *m* 1st, 1732, Marion, who *d* 1740, da of Sir Robert Dalrymple; 2ndly, 1741, Christian, who *d* 1763, da of James Sutherland, of Pronsie; *d* 1761; *s* by his el son (**5**) GEORGE, 5th Lord: *m* 1st, 1758, his cousin, Marion, who *d* 1759, da of late Col Hon Hugh Mackay; 2ndly, 1760, Elizabeth, who *d* 1780, da of late John Fairlie, Collector of Customs at Ayr; *d* 1768; *s* by his half-brother (**6**) HUGH, *d* unmarried 1797; *s* by his cousin (**7**) ERIC (son of late Hon George Mackay, 3rd son of 3rd Lord), 7th Lord; *b* 1773; *d* 1847; *s* by his brother (**8**) ALEXANDER, 8th Lord; *b* 1775: *m* 1809, Marion, who *d* 1865, da of Col Gall, and widow of David Ross; *d* 1863; *s* by his son (**9**) ERIC, 9th Lord; *d* unmarried 1875; *s* by his kinsman (**10**) ÆNEAS (son of Barthold John Christiaan Mackay (who was *cr* Baron Mackay van Ophemert, of the Netherlands), great-grandson of the Hon Æneas Mackay, Brig-Gen in Dutch Ser, 2nd son of 2nd Lord), 10th Lord; *b* 1806; was Min of State, and Vice-Pres of Privy Council of the Netherlands: *m* 1837, Mary Catherine Anne Jacoba, who *d* 1886, da of Baron Fagel, Privy Councillor of the Netherlands; *d* 1876; *s* by his son (**11**) DONALD JAMES, KT, GCSI, GCIE, PC, 11th Lord; *b* 1839; naturalized by Act of Parliament 1877, and *cr Baron Reay*, of Durness (peerage of United Kingdom) 1881; Lord-Lieut of co Roxburgh 1892, Gov of Bombay 1885-90, Under-Sec of State for India 1894-5, and first Pres of British Acad 1902-7: *m* 1877, Fanny Georgiana Jane, CI, who *d* 1917, da of late Richard Hasler, of Aldingbourne, Sussex, and widow of Capt Alexander Mitchell, MP, of Stow; *d* (Aug) 1921, when the United Kingdom Barony (*cr* 1881) became ext, and he was *s* in the Scottish titles by his cousin (**12**) *Baron* ERIC (only son of late Baron Æneas Mackay, son of Johan François Hendrik Jacob Ernestus Mackay, brother of 10th Lord), 12th Lord, *b* 1870: *m* 1901, Baroness Maria Johanna Bertha Christina Van Dedem, who *d* 1932; *d* (Nov) 1921; *s* by his el son (**13**) ÆNEAS ALEXANDER, 13th Lord; *b* 1905; naturalized a British subject 1938; in Foreign Office 1939-47; a Representative Peer 1955-9: *m* 1936, Charlotte Mary, da of late William Younger, of Ravenswood, Melrose; *d* 1963; *s* by his only son (**14**) HUGH WILLIAM, 14th Lord and present peer.

REDCLIFFE-MAUD, BARONY OF (Redcliffe-Maud) (Extinct 1982)

SON LIVING OF LIFE BARON

Hon Sir Humphrey John Hamilton MAUD, KCMG (31 Queen Anne's Grove, W4), *b* 1934; *ed* Eton, and King's Coll, Camb; Instructor in Classics, Minnesota Univ 1958-59; entered Foreign Service 1959, Madrid 1961-63, Havana 1963-65; FO 1966-67; Cabinet Office 1968-69; Paris 1970-74; Nuffield Coll, Oxford (Econs) 1974-75; Head of Financial Relations Dept, FCO 1975-79; Minister, Madrid 1979-82, HM Ambassador to Luxembourg 1982-85, Assist Under-Sec of State (Econ & Commercial Affairs) 1985-88, High Commr to Cyprus 1988-90, HM Ambassador to Argentina 1990-93, Commonwealth Sec-Gen (Econ & Social Affairs) 1993-99; CMG 1982, KCMG 1993: *m* 1963, Maria Eugenia Gazitua, and has issue living, three sons. *Residence* – 31 Queen Anne's Grove, Bedford Park, Chiswick W4 1HW. *Clubs* – United Oxford and Cambridge Univ, Garrick.

DAUGHTER LIVING OF LIFE BARON

Hon Caroline Mary Stewart, *b* 1939: *m* 1967, Very Rev Joel Wilson Pugh, of 9 The Close, Salisbury, Wilts SP1 2EB, and has issue living, one son and one da.

REDESDALE, BARON (Mitford) (Baron UK 1902)

God careth for us

RUPERT BERTRAM MITFORD, 6th Baron; *b* 18 July 1967; *s* 1991; *ed* Milton Abbey, Highgate, and Newcastle Univ (BA): *m* 1998, Helen J., eldest da of David Shipsey.

Arms – Quarterly; 1st and 4th argent, a fesse between three moles sable, *Mitford*; 2nd and 3rd azure, three lozenges conjoined in fesse or, a canton ermine, *Freeman*. Crest – 1st, two hands couped at the wrist proper, grasping a sword erect piercing a boar's head erased sable, *Mitford*; 2nd, a demi-wolf argent, charged on the shoulder with a fesse dancettée gules, and holding between the paws a lozenge or, *Freeman*. Supporters – On either side an eagle wings expanded sable, beaked and membered or, charged on the breast with a lozenge also or, and gorged with a wreath of shamrock vert. *Residences* – 2 St Mark's Sq, NW1 7TP; The School House, Rochester, Newcastle upon Tyne NE19 1RH; The School House, Exbury, nr Southampton, Hants SO4 1AE.

SISTERS LIVING AND DECEASED

Hon Emma, *b* 1959: *m* 1985, George Frederick Wady, of Green Batt House, The Pinfold, Alnwick, Northumberland, yr son of George Wady, of Frinton-on-Sea, Essex, and has issue living, Alexander Bertram, *b* 1989. — Philippa Bryony, *b* 1992.

Hon Tessa, *b* 1960: *m* 1990, Paul Dominic Priestman, of 19 Pembridge Mews, W11 3EQ, yr son of Martin Priestman, of Great Gransden, Cambs.

Hon Georgina Kathryn Mercia (Kate), *b* 1961; *d* 1985.

Hon Victoria-Louise (13 Lansdowne Rd, W11 3AG), *b* 1962: *m* 1988 (*m diss* 19—), Patrick James Padgett, yr son of James Padgett, of Asheville, N Carolina, USA, and has issue living, Harland James Bertram, *b* 1994.

Hon Henrietta Jane, *b* 1965.

Hon Georgina Clementine, *b* 1968.

DAUGHTERS LIVING OF SECOND BARON

Hon Diana (*Hon Lady Mosley*), *b* 1910: *m* 1st, 1929 (*m diss* 1934), Hon Bryan Walter Guinness (afterwards 2nd Baron Moyne), who *d* 1992; 2ndly, 1936, as his 2nd wife, Sir Oswald Ernald Mosley, 6th Bt, who *d* 1980. *Residence* – Temple De La Gloire, 91400 Orsay, France.

Hon Deborah Vivien (*Duchess of Devonshire*), DCVO, *b* 1920; Trustee Royal Collection; DCVO 1999: *m* 1941, 11th Duke of Devonshire, KG, MC, PC. *Residences* – Chatsworth, Bakewell, Derbyshire; 4 Chesterfield Street, W1 7HG.

WIDOW LIVING OF FIFTH BARON

SARAH GEORGINA CRANSTOUN (*Dowager Baroness Redesdale*), yr da of Brig Alston Cranstoun Todd, OBE, of Bramblehurst, Limes Lane, Buxted, Sussex: *m* 1958, the 5th Baron Redesdale, who *d* 1991. *Residences* – 2 St Mark's Sq, NW1 7TP; The School House, Rochester, Newcastle-upon-Tyne NE19 1RH; The School House, Exbury, nr Southampton, Hants SO4 1AE.

COLLATERAL BRANCH LIVING

Issue of late Major Hon Clement Bertram Ogilvy Freeman-Mitford, DSO, el son of 1st Baron, b 1876, ka 1915: m 1909, Lady Helen Alice Willington Ogilvy, (who d 1973, having m 2ndly, 1918 (m diss 1931), Capt Henry Courtney Brocklehurst, who was ka 1942 (Brocklehurst, Bt), and 3rdly, 1933, Lt-Col Harold Bligh Nutting), da of 11th Earl of Airlie:—
Rosemary Ann, b 1911: m 1932, Cdr Richard James Bailey, OBE, RN, who d 1969, and has had issue, Richard Lee Clement, b 1933; ed Charterhouse: m 1959, Barbara Joyce (49 Lawrence Gardens, Mill Hill, NW7), el da of S. G. Ede, of Fowey, Cornwall, and d 1996, leaving issue, Samantha Kate b 1967, — Michael Lee George, b 1934; ed Charterhouse: m 1st, 1964 (m diss 1976), Diana Jane, da of late Maj Laurence Deacon; 2ndly, 1979, Diana Maria Teresa, who d 1986, da of Bruno Cainero, of Udine, Italy, and d 1994, leaving issue (by 1st m), Anthony Michael George b 1966, Clementine Jane b 1969, (by 2nd m) Francesca Diana b 1980, — Ann Clementine, b 1936: m 1964, Peter Calver, of Whitcliffe Grange Farm, Ripon, N Yorks, only son of late Sir Robert Henry Sherwood Calver, QC, — Diana Penelope (8 Manor Court, Lawton Avenue, Carterton, Oxon OX18 3JY), b 1940: m 1960 (m diss 1979), William Henry Gordon Leaf, and has issue living, James-William Richard Tyrrell b 1963, Jessica Frances Rosemary b 1961, — Lavinia Jessica Iris, b 1944: m 1st, 1965 (m diss 1974), Antony Carlson; 2ndly, 1975, Hugh Brewis Bailey, MRCS, LRCP, of Hillcrest, 214 Newmarket Rd, Norwich NR4 7LA, and has issue living (by 1st m), Sarah Rosemary Iris b 1967: m 1992, Spiros Mouzakitis, of Avliotes, Corfu, Greece, Lucy b 1969, (by 2nd m), David Andrew Robert b 1977, — Annabel Lee Christine, b 1945: m 1974, Malcolm Valentine (The Lodge, Caston, Attleborough, Norfolk NR17 1DD) and has issue living, Richard William b 1976, Clare Rosemary b 1978. Residence – Mitford Cottage, Westwell, Burford, Oxon OX8 4JU. —— Clementine Mabell Kitty (Lady Beit), b (posthumous) 1915: m 1939, Sir Alfred Lane Beit, 2nd Bt, who d 1994. Residences – Russborough, Blessington, co Wicklow, Ireland; 2 Little Boltons, SW10 9LP.

PREDECESSORS – (1) This family descends from John Mitford of London, merchant (d 1720), 3rd son of Robert Mitford of Mitford Castle, Northumberland. John Mitford, Speaker of House of Commons and Lord Chancellor of Ireland; was cr Baron Redesdale 1802. His son was cr Earl of Redesdale 1877, both titles becoming ext 1886. The latter devised his estates to his cousin Algernon Bertram Mitford. (1) Sir ALGERNON BERTRAM Freeman-Mitford, GCVO, KCB, son of Henry Reveley Mitford, of Exbury House, Hants; b 1837; Sec to HM's Commrs of Public Works and Buildings 1874-6; MP for Stratford-on-Avon (C) 1892-5; assumed by Roy licence 1886 the additional surname and arms of Freeman; cr Baron Redesdale, of Redesdale, co Northumberland (peerage of UK) 1902: m 1874, Lady Clementine Gertrude Helen Ogilvy, who d 1932, da of 7th Earl of Airlie; d 1916; s by his el surviving son (2) DAVID BERTRAM OGILVY, 2nd Baron; b 1878; Capt late Northumberland Fusiliers; a Member of Select Committee of Peerages in Abeyance 1925: m 1904, Sydney, who d 1963, da of late Thomas Gibson Bowles (sometime MP for King's Lynn), of 25 Lowndes Sq, SW; d 1958; s by his brother (3) BERTRAM THOMAS CARLYLE OGILVY, DSO, 3rd Baron; b 1880; Capt RN; High Sheriff of Oxon 1935: m 1925, Mary Margaret, who d 1967, da of late Thomas Cordes, JP, DL; d 1962; s by his brother (4) JOHN POWER BERTRAM OGILVY, 4th Baron, b 1885: m 1914 (marriage annulled in Germany on her petition 1914), Marie Anne, da of Friedrich Viktor von Friedlander-Fuld, of Berlin, d 1963; s by his nephew (5) CLEMENT NAPIER BERTRAM (son of Hon (Ernest) Rupert Bertram Ogilvy Freeman-Mitford, 5th son of 1st Baron), 5th Baron, b 1932; commn'd The Black Watch 1951, served 4th Bn King's African Rifles in Kenya and Uganda, and 3rd Bn in Malaya; Pres Guild of Cleaners and Launderers 1968-70; Chm Mitford's Advertising 1970-77, Vice-Pres Corporate Communications Europe, Africa and Middle East, Chase Manhatten Bank: m 1958, Sarah Georgina Cranstoun, yr da of Brig Alston Cranstoun Todd, OBE, of Bramblehurst, Limes Lane, Buxted, Sussex; d 1991; s by his only son (6) RUPERT BERTRAM, 6th Baron and present peer.

REDMAYNE, BARONY OF (Redmayne) (Extinct 1983)

SON LIVING OF LIFE BARON

Hon Sir NICHOLAS JOHN REDMAYNE, 2nd Bt, who s to baronetcy (cr 1964), 1983 (see Redmayne, Bt).

REES, BARON (Rees) (Life Baron 1987)

PETER WYNFORD INNES REES, PC, son of late Maj-Gen Thomas Wynford Rees, CB, CIE, DSO, MC, Indian Army, of Goytre Hall, Abergavenny; b 9 Dec 1926; ed Stowe, and Ch Ch, Oxford; Scots Guards 1945-48; Bar 1953, QC 1969, Oxford Circuit; PPS to Solicitor-Gen 1972; Min of State, HM Treasury 1979-81, Min for Trade 1981-83, Chief Sec to Treasury and Member of Cabinet 1983-85; Member of Court and Council of Museum of Wales; Chm and Dir of Companies, Dep Chm Leopold Joseph plc; MP Dover (C) 1970-74, Dover and Deal 1974-83, and Dover 1983-87; cr PC 1983, and Baron Rees, of Goytre, co Gwent (Life Baron) 1987: m 1969, Mrs Anthea Peronelle Wendell, da of late Maj Hugh John Maxwell Hyslop, Argyll and Sutherland Highrs, and formerly wife of Maj Jac Wendell, Gren Guards.

Arms – Argent two chevrons ermines between three ravens proper. Crest – Upon a chapeau turned up ermines a peacock holding in its beak an oak sprig proper. Supporters – Two Bengal tigers rampant, the Dexter on a grassy mount growing therefrom two tea-plant flowers, and the Sinister on a like mount growing therefrom as many lotus flowers all proper.
Residences – Goytre Hall, Abergavenny, Gwent; 39 Headfort Place, SW1X 7DE. Clubs – Boodle's, Beefsteak, Pratt's, White's.

REES-MOGG, BARON (Rees-Mogg) (Life Baron 1988)

WILLIAM REES-MOGG, son of late Edmund Fletcher Rees-Mogg, JP, of Cholwell House, Som; b 14 July 1928: ed Charterhouse, and Balliol Coll, Oxford (MA, Pres Oxford Union 1951); Visiting Fell Nuffield Coll, Oxford, 1968-72, Hon LLD Bath 1977; High Sheriff Somerset 1978; with Financial Times 1952-60, Chief Leader Writer 1955-60, Assist Ed 1957-60, joined Sunday Times 1960, City Ed 1960-61, Political and Economic Ed 1961-63, Dep Ed 1964-67, Ed the Times 1967-81; Treas Inst of Journalists 1960-63, 1966-68 (Pres 1963-64), Vice-Chm Conservative Party's Nat Advisory Cttee on Political Educn 1961-63, Pres English Assocn 1983-84, Dir The Times Ltd 1968-81, Times Newspapers Ltd 1978-81, Vice-Chm Board of Govs BBC 1981-86; Chm Pickering & Catto (Publishers) since 1983, and Sidgwick & Jackson 1985-88; Chm Arts Council 1982-89; Chm Broadcasting Standards Council 1988-93; author of His Majesty Preserved (1954), Sir Anthony Eden (1956), How to Buy Rare Books (1985), etc; cr Kt 1981, and Baron Rees-Mogg, of Hinton Blewitt, co Avon (Life Baron) 1988: m 1962, Gillian Shakespeare, yr da of Thomas Richard Morris, JP, Mayor of St Pancras 1962, of 53 Queen Alexandra Mansions, WC1, and has issue.

Arms – Quarterly: 1st and 4th, on a fesse pean between six ermine spots, the two exterior in chief and the centre spot in base, surmounted by a crescent gules, a cock or, Mogg; 2nd and 3rd, gules, a chevron engrailed erminois between three swans argent, wings elevated or, Rees. Crests – Mogg, between two spearheads erect sable a cock proper; Rees, a swan argent, wings elevated or, holding in the beak a water-lily slipped proper. Motto – Cura pii Diis sunt.
Residences – Bilboa House, Mells, Somerset; 17 Pall Mall, SW1. Club – Garrick.

SONS LIVING

Hon Thomas Fletcher, b 1966; ed Downside: m 1996, Modwenna Vivien Hornby, da of Hon Edward Frederic Northcote (see E Iddesleigh), and has issue living, William Robert, b 1996, — Beatrice Dorothea Julia, b 1999. Residence – Cholwell Home Farm House, Cholwell, Temple Cloud, Som BS39 5OW.

Hon Jacob William, b 1969; ed Eton, and Trinity Coll, Oxford.

DAUGHTERS LIVING

Hon Emma Beatrice, *b* 1962; *ed* St Hugh's Coll, Oxford: *m* 1990, David William Hilton Brooks Craigie (who assumed the surname of Craigie in lieu of his patronymic 1990), son of late Maj Robin Brooks, and of Mrs Brian Ford, of London, and has had issue, Wilfrid Hingeston, *b* 1994, — Stanley Mogg, *b* and *d* 1994, — Maud, *b* 1991, — Myfanwy Eileen, *b* 1997.

Hon Charlotte Louise, *b* 1964; *ed* Heythrop Coll, London Univ.

Hon Annunziata Mary, *b* 1979.

Reidhaven, Viscount; son of Earl of Seafield.

REIGATE, BARONY OF (Vaughan-Morgan) (Extinct 1995)

DAUGHTERS LIVING OF LIFE BARON AND FIRST BARONET

Hon Julia Redmond, *b* 1943; *ed* Courtauld Inst of Art, London Univ (BA), and Oxford Poly (MA); author of *The Flowering of Art Nouveau Graphics*, 1990: *m* 1st, 1962 (*m diss* 1978), Henry Walter Wiggin; 2ndly, 1986, Dr Joseph Austin King, son of late William Thayer King, of Kingsport, Tennessee, USA, and has issue (by 1st *m*) (*see* Wiggin, Bt colls). *Residences* – 5 Alexa Court, 73 Lexham Gdns, W8 6JL; 132 Caroline St, Fredericksburg, VA 22401, USA.

Hon Deborah Mary, *b* 1944: *m* 1966, Michael Whitfeld, of Querns, Goring Heath, Reading, RG8 7RH (E Howe, colls), and has issue living, Nicholas John, *b* 1968, — Mark David, *b* 1971, — Melanie Katherine, *b* 1976.

WIDOW LIVING OF LIFE BARON AND FIRST BARONET

EMILY REDMOND (*Baroness Reigate*), da of late William Redmond Cross, of New York, USA; Chm of Council Royal Sch of Needlework 1966-76, Member Advisory Council Victoria and Albert Museum, author of *An Illustrated Guide to Lace*, 1986: *m* 1940, Baron Reigate, PC (Life Baron and 1st baronet), who *d* 1995. *Residence* – 36 Eaton Sq, SW1W 9DH.

REILLY, BARONY OF (Reilly) (Extinct 1990)

DAUGHTER LIVING OF LIFE BARON (*By 1st marriage*)

Hon Victoria Wentworth, *b* 1941: *m* 1973, Daniel Špička, of U Mrázovky 7, Prague 5, The Czech Republic, and has issue living, Katherine Wentworth, *b* 1974, — Lucie Wentworth, *b* 1977.

WIDOW LIVING OF LIFE BARON

ANNETTE ROSE (*Baroness Reilly*), da of late Brig-Gen Clifton Inglis Stockwell, CB, CMG, DSO: *m* 1952, as his 2nd wife, Baron Reilly (Life Baron), who *d* 1990. *Residence* – 3 Alexander Place, SW7 2SG.

REITH, BARONY OF (Reith) (Baron UK 1940, disclaimed 1972)

Whatsoever

QUÆCUNQUE

CHRISTOPHER JOHN REITH, *b* 27 May 1928; *s* as 2nd Baron 16 June 1971, disclaimed his peerage for life 21 April 1972; *ed* Eton, and Worcester Coll, Oxford (MA); late RN: *m* 1969, (Penelope Margaret) Ann, el da of late Henry Rowland Morris, of Beeston, Notts, and has issue.

𝕬rms – Or, a cross engrailed sable between four mullets gules, on a chief of the last a lion passant of the field. 𝕮rest – An eagle rising reguardant proper. 𝕾upporters – (borne by Barons Reith) Two eagles, wings addorsed proper.
Residence – Whitebank Farm, Methven, Perthshire.

SON LIVING

Hon JAMES HARRY JOHN, *b* 2 June 1971.

DAUGHTER LIVING

Hon Julie Katharine, *b* 1972.

SISTER LIVING

Hon Marista Muriel, *b* 1932; *ed* St George's, Ascot, and St Andrews Univ (MA); Ist Dir Insite Trust for Consultancy and Training in Heritage Interpretation: *m* 1960, Rev Robert Murray Leishman, MA, Psychoanalytic Psychotherapist and has issue living, Mark Murray, *b* 1962, — Iona Marista, *b* 1963, — Martha Katharine, *b* 1965, — Kirsty Jane, *b* 1969. *Residence* – 9/23 St Leonards Crag, Edinburgh EH8 9SP.

PREDECESSOR – (1) *Rt Hon Sir* JOHN CHARLES WALSHAM REITH, KT, GCVO, GBE, CB, TD, DCL, LLD, 5th son of late Very Rev George Reith, DD, of Aberdeen, and Glasgow; *b* 1889, first Gen Man and Man Dir of British Broadcasting Co Ltd 1922-26, Dir Gen of BBC 1926-38; Min of Information, Jan to May 1940; Min of Transport, May to Oct 1940; Min of Works and Bldgs, and 1st Commr of Works 1940-42; *cr Baron Reith*, of Stonehaven, co Kincardine (peerage of UK) 1940: *m* 1921, Muriel Katharine, who *d* 1977, yr da of late John Lynch Odhams, of Southwick, Sussex; *d* 1971; *s* by his only son (2) CHRISTOPHER JOHN, 2nd Baron, until he disclaimed his peerage 1972.

REMNANT, BARON (Remnant) (Baron UK 1928, Bt UK 1917)

Let him who has deserved the palm bear it

Palmam ferat qui meruit

JAMES WOGAN REMNANT, CVO, 3rd Baron, and 3rd Baronet; *b* 23 Oct 1930; *s* 1967; *ed* Eton; National Service Lt Coldstream Guards; FCA; Partner, Touche Ross & Co 1958-70; Chm of Institutional Investors Cttee 1977-78; a Church Commnr for England 1976-84; Chm of Assocn of Investment Trust Cos 1977-79; Past Pres Nat Council of YMCAs; Past Pres London Central YMCA, Trustee Royal Jubilee Trusts (previously Hon Treas and Chm); previously Chm Nat Provident Inst, Dir Bank of Scotland (and London Bd), TR Technology plc, Dir London Merchant Securities plc, previously Chm Touche, Remnant & Co, TR City of London Trust plc, TR Energy plc, TR Pacific Investment Trust plc, Dep Chm Ultramar plc, Dir Union Discount Co of London plc, Australian Mercantile Land and Finance Co Ltd, Australia and New Zealand Banking Group and other cos; Pres Nat Florence Nightingale Foundation; Chm Learning Through Landscapes Trust; Bailiff of Egle of Order of St John; Master Salters' Co 1995; CVO 1979, GCStJ 1993: *m* 1953, Serena Jane, only da of Cdr Sir Clive Loehnis, KCMG, RN (ret) (*see* E Harrowby, colls), and has issue.

𝕬rms – Sable, a bend vair between two sheldrakes proper all within two flaunches argent and charged with a cinquefoil gules. 𝕮rest – Between rushes a sheldrake proper, holding in the beak a rose gules, barbed, seeded, leaved and slipped proper. 𝕾upporters – On either side a dolphin proper charged with a cinquefoil gules.
Residence – Bear Ash, Hare Hatch, Reading, Berks RG10 9XR.

SONS LIVING

Hon PHILIP JOHN (Ham Farm House, Baughurst, nr Basingstoke, Hants RG26 5SD), *b* 20 Dec 1954; *ed* Eton and New Coll, Oxford: *m* 1977, Caroline Elizabeth Clare, da of late Capt Godfrey Herbert Richard Cavendish (*see* D Devonshire, colls), and has issue living, Edward James, *b* 2 July 1981, — Eleanor Clare, *b* 1983, — Sophie Caroline, *b* 1986.

Hon Robert James (Jardine Pacific Vietnam Ltd, 16 Han Thuyen St, Hai Ba Trung Dis, Hanoi, Socialist Republic of Vietnam) *b* 1956; *ed* Eton: *m* 1981 (*m diss* 1991), Sherrie, el da of Frederick Cronn, and has issue living, Christopher Michael, *b* 1982, — Jack Preston, *b* 1989. Mr Remnant has adopted (1987) his step-son, Shannon Lynn, *b* 1973.

Hon Hugo Charles, *b* 1959; *ed* Eton, and Newcastle Univ (BSc): *m* 1993, Annabelle Rachel, only da of T. R. Reynolds, of Tollard Royal, Dorset, and has issue living, Benjamin, *b* 1998.

DAUGHTER LIVING

Hon Melissa Clare, *b* 1963; *ed* Wycombe Abbey, and Exeter Univ: *m* 1990, David Wilson Bradley, of 1 Thessaly Lodge, Gloucester Rd, Stratton, Cirencester, Glos GL7 2LJ, yr son of J. W. A. Bradley, of Halls Court, Chesterton, Cambs, and has issue living, Arabella Jasmine, *b* 1994.

SISTER LIVING

Hon Susan Frances, *b* 1938: *m* 1967, Alan Tyser, of West Hanney House, Wantage, Oxon OX12 0LN, and has issue living, Harry, *b* 1968.

COLLATERAL BRANCH LIVING

Issue of late Hon Peter Farquharson Remnant, yr son of 1st Baron, *b* 1897, *d* 1968: *m* 1923, Betty, who *d* 1965, da of late William George Tanner, of Frenchay, Glos:—

Dawn, *b* 1927: *m* 1951, Antony Stewart Hooper, and has issue living, Susan Jane, *b* 1952: *m* 1984, Vyvyan James Kinross, and has issue living, Alastair Ben Chabaud *b* 1988, Amy Joanna *b* 1989, — Mary Sandra, *b* 1953; has issue living, Lauren Alexandra HOOPER *b* 1994, — Carol Ann, *b* 1956; PhD. —— Merrial, *b* 1934: *m* 1st, 1954 (*m diss* 1960), Arthur James Wesley-Smith; 2ndly, 1962, Henry James Stockley, who *d* 1967; 3rdly, 1968, Ivor John Crosthwaite, DSO, and has issue living, (by 1st *m*) Shane, *b* 1955: *m* 1982, Nigel de Northop Winser, and has issue living, Philip Bede *b* 1984, Kate Anne *b* 1987, — Linda, *b* 1957: *m* 1985 (*m diss* 1992), Matthew Dominic Flowers, and has issue living, Patrick *b* 1987, and further issue (by Ben Henry Weeks), Sydney Elgar WESLEY-WEEKS (a da) *b* 1993, and Tilda Elgar WESLEY-WEEKS *b* 1998, — (by 2nd *m*) Marian Julia, *b* 1963; has issue living, Lauren Merriel STOCKLEY *b* 1981.

PREDECESSORS – **(1)** JAMES FARQUHARSON Remnant, CBE, son of late Frederick William Remnant, of Southwold, Suffolk; *b* 1863; a Member of Select Committee on Taxation of Land Values (Scotland) 1904, of Roy Commn on Canals and Inland Navigation 1906-10, of Select Committee on Police Day of Rest 1908-9, of Home Office Committee on Conditions and Pay of Police 1919, and of Rating Machinery Committee 1924; MP for Holborn Div of Finsbury (C) March 1900 to Nov 1918, and for Holborn (U) Dec 1918 to June 1928; *cr* a *Baronet* 1917, and *Baron Remnant*, of Wenhaston, co Suffolk (peerage of United Kingdom) 1928: *m* 1892, Frances Emily, who *d* 1944, da of late Robert Gosling, of Hassobury, Essex; *d* 1933; *s* by his el son **(2)** ROBERT JOHN FARQUHARSON, MBE, 2nd Baron, *b* 1895: *m* 1924, Norah Susan, who *d* 1990, da of late Lt-Col Alexander John Wogan-Browne; *d* 1967; *s* by his only son **(3)** JAMES WOGAN, 3rd Baron and present peer.

RENDELL OF BABERGH, BARONESS (Rendell) (Life Baroness 1997)

RUTH BARBARA RENDELL, CBE; da of late Arthur Grasemann, of Loughton, Essex; *b* 17 Feb 1930; *ed* Loughton County High School; FRSL; crime novelist; books include *From Doon with Death* (1964), *To Fear a Painted Devil* (1965), *The Secret House of Death* (1968), *A Guilty Thing Surprised* (1970), *One Across Two Down* (1971), *No More Dying Then* (1971), *Some Lie and Some Die* (1973), *A Demon in my View* (1976; filmed 1991), *A Judgement in Stone* (1977), *Make Death Love Me* (1979), *The Lake of Darkness* (1980; televised as *Dead Lucky* 1988), *Master of the Moor* (1982; televised 1994), *The Speaker of Mandarin* (1983), *The Killing Doll* (1984), *The Tree of Hands* (1984; filmed 1989), *An Unkindness of Ravens* (1985), *The Bridesmaid* (1989), *Kissing the Gunner's Daughter* (1992), *The Crocodile Bird* (1993), *Simisola* (1994), *The Keys to the Street* (1996), *Road Rage* (1997), and (as Barbara Vine) *A Dark-Adapted Eye* (1986), *A Fatal Inversion* (1987), *House of Stairs* (1989), *Gallowglass* (1990), *King Solomon's Carpet* (1991), *Asta's Book* (1992), *No Night Is Too Long* (1994), and *The Brimstone Wedding* (1996); Arts Council National Book Award for Genre Fiction 1981, CW4 Gold Dagger Awards 1976, 1987, 1988 and 1990, Silver Dagger Award 1984, Mystery Writers of America 3 Edgar Allen Poe Awards 1974, 1984 and 1987, Sunday Times Award for Literary Excellence 1990, Cartier-CWA Diamond Dagger Award 1991; *cr* CBE 1996, and

Baroness Rendell of Babergh, of Aldeburgh, co Suffolk (Life Baroness) 1997: *m* 1950 (*m diss* 1975 and *re-m* 1977), Donald John Rendell, who *d* 1999, son of Charles Rendell, of Exeter, Devon, and has issue.

𝔄rm𝔰 – Gules three interlaced chevronels argent each ensigned by a brimstone butterfly displayed proper. 𝔖upporter𝔰 – On either side a polar bear statant erect proper gorged with a plain collar gobony gules and or fimbriated gules. *Residences* – 11 Maida Av, Little Venice, W2 1SR; Edinburgh House, Crag Path, Aldeburgh, Suffolk. *Clubs* – Groucho, Detection.

SON LIVING

Hon Simon, *b* 1953; *ed* Univ of Denver, Colorado: *m* 1991, Donna, da of Frederick Mundil, and has issue living, Phillip James, *b* 1991, — Graham Patrick, *b* 1993.

RENDLESHAM, BARON (Thellusson) (Baron I 1806)
(Name pronounced "Tellusson")

By labour and honesty

CHARLES ANTHONY HUGH THELLUSSON, 8th Baron; *b* 15 March 1915; *s* 1943; *ed* Eton; late Capt R Signals: *m* 1st, 1940 (*m diss* 1947), Margaret Elizabeth, da of Lt Col Robin Rome; 2ndly, 1947, Clare, who *d* 1987, da of late Lt-Col D. H. G. McCririck, and has issue by 1st and 2nd *m*.

𝔄rm𝔰 – Quarterly, wavy or and argent: in the 1st and 4th quarters, two wings barwise in pale and expanded towards the dexter sable, each charged with a trefoil slipped in fesse, the point towards the sinister or; in the 2nd and 3rd quarters, an oak tree eradicated vert, thereon an escutcheon placed bendwise gules, an charged with three guttés argent. ℭre𝔰t – A demi-greyhound salient argent, collared sable, between two wings elevated and expanded sable, each charged with a trefoil slipped or. 𝔖upporter𝔰 – Two greyhounds reguardant argent, plain collared sable.

SON LIVING (*By 2nd marriage*)

Hon CHARLES WILLIAM BROOKE, *b* 10 Jan 1954; *ed* Eton: *m* 1st, 1983 (*m diss* 19—), Susan, yst da of E. R. Fielding, of Monte Carlo, Monaco; 2ndly, 1988, Lucille Clare, da of Rev Henry Ian Gordon Cumming (*see* Gordon Cumming, Bt, colls), and has issue living (by 2nd *m*), Amy Elizabeth, *b* 1993.

DAUGHTERS LIVING (*By 1st marriage*)

Hon Caroline, *b* 1941: *m* 1960 (*m diss* 19—), Sir William Burton Nigel Goring, 13th Bt. *Residence* – 25 Queen's Gate Terrace, SW7.

(*By 2nd marriage*)

Hon Sarah Ann, *b* 1949: *m* 1989, Keir H. Helberg, of Washington, DC, USA.

Hon Antonia, *b* 1956: *m* 1981 (*m diss* 1996), Hugo Giles Stephen Astley Kirby, eldest son of Giles Kirby, of The Manor House, S Harting, Petersfield, Hants, and has issue living, Nicholas Charles Astley, *b* 1983, — Natasha Alexandra, *b* 1985.

Hon Jaqumine, *b* 1960: *m* 1987, Charles Nigel Bromage (*see* Cayzer, Bt, colls, 1990 Edn), and has issue living, Maximilian Charles, *b* 1993, — Iona Catherine, *b* 1997.

BROTHER LIVING (*Raised to the rank of a Baron's son* 1945)

Hon Peter Robert, *b* 1920; *ed* Eton; is Capt KRRC: *m* 1st, 1947 (*m diss* 1950), Pamela, who *d* 1968, da of late Oliver Ivan Parker (E Macclesfield, colls), and formerly wife of Maj Timothy Tufnell, MC; 2ndly, 1952, Celia, da of James Walsh, and has issue living, (by 2nd *m*) James Hugh, *b* 1961: *m* 1995, Jennifer L, elder da of Ralph Owers, of Sunningdale, Berks, and has issue living, Abigail *b* 1998, — Peter Richard, *b* 1962.

PREDECESSORS – (1) PETER ISSAC THELLUSSON, son of Peter Thellusson, MP for Malmesbury 1796-7, a wealthy London merchant, and the descendant of a French Protestant nobleman; *cr Baron Rendlesham* (peerage of Ireland) 1806; *d* 1808; *s* by his el son (2) JOHN, 2nd Baron; *d* 1832; *s* by his brother (3) WILLIAM, 3rd Baron; was in Holy Orders; *d* 1839; *s* by his brother (4) FREDERICK, 4th Baron; *b* 1798: *m* 1838, Eliza Charlotte, da of Sir George Beeston Prescott, 2nd Bt, and widow of James Duff, *d* 1852; *s* by his son (5) FREDERICK WILLIAM BROOK, 5th Baron *b* 1840; MP for Suffolk E (C) 1874-85: *m* 1861, Lady Egidia Montgomerie, who *d* 1880, da of 18th Earl of Eglinton, KT; *d* 1911; *s* by his el son (6) FREDERICK ARCHIBALD CHARLES, *b* 1868: *m* 1st, 18—, Lillian, who *d* 1931, da of late J. Manly, JP, of Kingston, Jamaica; 2ndly, 1931, Dolores Olga, who *d* 1959, da of Sir William Lewis Salusbury-Trelawny, 10th Bt, and widow of Henry

Harcourt Williams; *d* 1938; *s* by his brother **(7)** PERCY EDWARD, 7th Baron; *b* 1874; *m* 1922, Gladys Dunlop, OBE, who *d* 1933, da of Andrew Vans Dunlop Best; *d* 1943; *s* by his nephew **(8)** CHARLES ANTHONY HUGH (son of late Lieut-Col Hon Hugh Edmund Thellusson, DSO, 3rd son of 5th Baron), 8th Baron and present peer.

Renfrew, Baron of; title borne by Prince of Wales.

RENFREW OF KAIMSTHORN, BARON (Renfrew) (Life Baron 1991)

(ANDREW) COLIN RENFREW, son of late Archibald Renfrew, of Giffnock, Glasgow; *b* 25 July 1937; *ed* St Alban's Sch, and St John's Coll, Camb (BA, PhD, ScD); Hon D Litt Sheffield Univ 1987, D (honoris causa) Athens Univ 1991, FSA 1968, FSAScot 1970, FBA 1980; RAF 1956-58; Reader in Prehistory & Archaeology Sheffield Univ 1965-72, Research Fellow St John's Coll, Camb 1965-68, Bulgarian Govt Scholarship 1966, Visiting Lect California Univ at Los Angeles 1967, Prof of Archaeology and Head of Dept Southampton Univ 1972-81, since when Disney Prof of Archaeology and Head of Dept Camb Univ; Fellow St John's Coll, Camb 1981-86, since when Master Jesus Coll, Camb; Member Royal Commn for Historic Monuments of England 1977-87, Historic Buildings and Monuments Commn Advisory Board since 1983, Historic Buildings and Monuments Commn Science Panel 1983-89; Chm Nat Curriculum Art Working Group 1990-91; Freeman City of London; author; *cr Baron Renfrew of Kaimsthorn*, of Hurlet, District of Renfrew (Life Baron) 1991: *m* 1965, Jane Margaret, da of Ven Walter Frederick Ewbank, of Penrith, Cumbria, and has issue.
Residence – The Master's Lodge, Jesus College, Cambridge CB5 8BL. *Clubs* – Athenaeum, United Oxford and Cambridge.

SONS LIVING

Hon Alban, *b* 1970.
Hon Magnus, *b* 1975.

DAUGHTER LIVING

Hon Helena, *b* 1968: *m* 1996, Jonathan P. Knight, elder son of Philip Knight, of Otford, Kent.

RENNELL, BARON (Rodd) (Baron UK 1933)

(JOHN ADRIAN) TREMAYNE RODD, 3rd Baron; *b* 28 June 1935; *s* 1978; *ed* Downside, and RNC Dartmouth; Lieut RN, former Scottish Rugby International, Dir Tremayne Ltd: *m* 1977, Phyllis Caroline, da of Thomas David Neill, of Portadown co Armagh, and has issue.

Arms – Argent, two trefoils slipped sable on a chief of the second, three crescents of the first. **Crest** – A representation of the Colossus of Rhodes, over the shoulder a bow, in the dexter hand an arrow and in the sinister a cup, all proper. **Supporters** – On the either side a Cornish chough, wings elevated and addorsed proper, charged on the breast with a trefoil slipped argent. *Address* – c/o White's Club, 37 St James's St, SW1.

SON LIVING

Hon JAMES RODERICK DAVID TREMAYNE, *b* 9 March 1978.

DAUGHTERS LIVING

Hon Sophie Mary Jane *b* 1981.
Hon Rachel, *b* 1987.
Hon Lilias, *b* 1989.

DAUGHTERS LIVING OF SECOND BARON

Recte omnia duce Deo
With God for guide, all is right

Hon Joanna Phoebe D'HAUTEVILLE-RODD, *b* 1929: *m* 1966 (*m diss* 1995), Comte Gérard de Renusson d'Hauteville, yr son Marquis d'Hauteville. *Residence* – 6 du Bellay, 9 rue Puget, 06100 Nice, France

Hon Juliet Honor, *b* 1930: *m* 1957, Brian Boobbyer, and has issue living, Philip Christopher, *b* 1963, — Mark Tremayne, *b* 1967: *m* 1991, Catherine Mary, elder da of Peter Alexander O'Brien Hannon (*see* D Montrose). *Residence* – Little Rodd, Presteigne, Powys.

Hon Mary Elizabeth Jill, *b* 1932: *m* 1st, 1954, Michael William Langan Dunne; 2ndly, 1985, Christopher Bridges Daniell, and has issue living (by 1st *m*), John Francis Jeremy, *b* 1957, — Stephen Michael Damian, *b* 1961: *m* 19—, Anna Louise Garbett, and has issue living, Edward John Francis *b* 1996, Henrietta Elizabeth Grace *b* 1992, — Mary Jemima, *b* 1955: *m* 1985, Philip Lord, and has issue living, Daniel Norsen *b* 1992, Crispin Hugh *b* 1995, Harriet Frances *b* 1990, — Teresa (Tilly) Mary Claire, *b* 1962: *m* 1993, Thomas A. Calvert, yr son of David J. Calvert, of Westmore, Shropshire, and has issue living, Jack *b* 1995, Bertram David *b* 1999, Susannah Honor *b* 1997, — Miranda Mary, *b* 1966: *m* 1995, Baron William Charles Taxis Bordogna Valnigra, yst son of Baron Franz Taxis Bordogna Valnigra, and has issue living, Isabella Mary Alice *b* 1997, Annabelle Mary *b* 1999. *Residence* – Ashley Farm, Stansbatch, Leominster, Herefordshire.

Hon Rachel Georgiana, *b* 1935: *m* 1964 (*m diss* 1983), Richard Douglas Blythe, and has issue living, Joseph Matthew Gerard, *b* 1968, — Matthew Francis, *b* 1970. *Residence* – 14 Lawson Way, Darlington, Perth, W Australia 60700.

PREDECESSORS – (1) *Rt Hon Sir* (JAMES) RENNELL RODD, GCB, GCMG, GCVO, son of late Major James Rennell Rodd; *b* 1858; was Envoy Extraor and Min Plen to Stockholm 1904-8, and Ambassador Extraor and Min Plen to Italy 1908-19; sat as MP for St Marylebone 1928-32 (*C*); *cr Baron Rennell*, of Rodd, co Hereford (peerage of United Kingdom) 1933: *m* 1894, Lilias Georgina, who *d* 1951, da of late James Alexander Guthrie, of Craigie, Forfar; *d* 1941; *s* by his el son (2) FRANCIS JAMES RENNELL, 2nd Baron, KBE, CB, 2nd Baron; *b* 1895, Pres R Geographical Soc 1945-48, Visiting Fellow of Nuffield Coll, Oxford: *m* 1928, Hon Mary Constance Vivian Smith, who *d* 1981, da of 1st Baron Bicester; *d* 1978; *s* by his nephew (3) (JOHN ADRIAN) TREMAYNE, 3rd Baron and present peer (only surv son of late Cdr Hon Gustaf Guthrie Rennell Rodd, OBE, RN, yst son of 1st Baron)

RENTON, BARON (Renton) (Life Baron 1979)

Virtue is in action

DAVID LOCKHART-MURE RENTON, KBE, TD, PC, QC, son of late Maurice Waugh Renton, MD CM, DPH; *b* 12 Aug 1908; *ed* Oundle, and Univ Coll Oxford (BCL, MA, Hon Fell 1981); Bar Lincoln's Inn 1933, Member of Bar Council 1939, QC 1954, a Bencher 1962, and Treasurer 1979; a Member of Senate of Inns of Court 1967-71 and 1975-79; a DL of Cambs; Parl Sec Min of Fuel and Power 1955-57, and of Min of Power 1957-58, Joint Parl Under-Sec of State, Home Office 1958-61, Min of State, Home Office 1961-62; Recorder of Rochester 1963-68, and of Guildford 1968-71; Pres Conservation Soc 1970-71; Pres Statute Law Soc since 1980; Pres National Council for Civil Protection 1980-91; Pres Parl Arts and Heritage Group since 1992; a Member Commn on the Constitution 1971-73; Chm of Cttee on the Preparation of Legislation 1973-75; Chm Nat Soc for Mentally Handicapped Children 1977-82, Pres 1982-88; 1939-45 War as Maj RA; MP for Hunts (*C*) 1945-79; Patron National Law Library; Patron Hunts Div Conservative Assocn; Patron DEMAND (Design & Manufacture for Disability), Royal British Legion (Hunts), and Ravenswood Foundation; *cr* PC 1962, KBE (Civil) 1964, and Baron Renton, of Huntingdon in co Cambs (Life Baron) 1979: *m* 1947, Claire Cicely, who *d* 1986, yst da of late Walter Atholl Duncan, and has issue.

Arms – Azure a horse forcene on a chief or a sword point to the dexter gules between a portcullis chained and hunting horn stringed azure. Crest – In front of a horse's head erased or a hunting horn stringed azure. Supporters – *Dexter*, a lion guardant purpure gorged with a fine chain pendant therefrom a millrind gold. *Sinister*, a stag guardant proper gorged with a like chain pendant therefrom a fetterlock enclosing a heart gold.
Residences – Moat House, Abbots Ripton, Huntingdon; 16 Old Buildings, Lincoln's Inn, WC2. *Clubs* – Carlton; Pratt's.

DAUGHTERS LIVING

Hon Caroline Mary, *b* 1948: *m* 1st, 1970 (*m diss* 1974), Peter Dodds Parker; 2ndly, 1977 (*m diss* 1993), Robin Warwick Antony Parr; 3rdly, 1999, Peter Henry Arthur Stanley, of Cundall Hall, Helperby, Yorks (*see* E Derby, colls), and has issue living by 1st and 2nd *m*.
Hon Clare Olivia (11 Flodden Rd, SE5), *b* 1950; Barrister-at-law: *m* 1982, Timothy John Whittaker Scott, and has issue.
Hon Davina Kathleen, *b* 1954.

RENTON OF MOUNT HARRY, BARON (Renton) (Life Baron 1997)

RONALD TIMOTHY (TIM) RENTON, PC, yr son of late Ronald Kenneth Duncan Renton, CBE; *b* 28 May 1932; *ed* Eton, and Magdalen Coll, Oxford (MA 19—); Dir Silvermines Ltd 1967-84, ANZ Banking Group 1968-75; former Man Dir Tennant Trading; Dir Fleming Continental European Investment Trust plc 1992-99, since when Chm; MP (*C*) for Sussex Mid 1974-97; Chm Conservative Employment Cttee, PPS to John Biffen as Chief Sec to Treasury 1979-81; Pres Conservative Trade Unionists 1980-84 (Vice-Pres 1978-80); PPS to Sir Geoffrey Howe as Chancellor and Foreign Sec 1983-84; Parliamentary Under-Sec, FCO 1984, Min of State, FCO 1984-87; Min of State, Home Office 1987-89; Govt Chief Whip 1989-90; Min for the Arts 1990-92; Memb Select Cttee on National Heritage since 1995; Chm British Hong Kong Parliamentary Group 1992-97; Memb Advisory Board Know-How Fund for Central and Eastern Europ, FCO 1992-97; Vice-Chm British Council 1992-98; Chm Outsider Art since 1995; author of *The Dangerous Edge* 1994, *Hostage to Fortune* 1997; *cr* PC 1989, and *Baron Renton of Mount Harry*, of Offham, co E Sussex (Life Baron) 1992: *m* 1960, Alice Blanche Helen, da of late Sir James Fergusson of Kilkerran, 8th Bt, and has issue.
Address – House of Lords, SW1A 0PW. *Club* – Garrick.

SONS LIVING

Hon Alexander James Torre, *b* 1961.
Hon Daniel Charles Antony, *b* 1965.

DAUGHTERS LIVING

Hon Christian Louise, *b* 1963: *m* 1993, Lloyd Michael Gudgeon, elder son of Samuel Gudgeon, and has issue living, Alfred Joseph, *b* 1988.
Hon (Katherine) Chelsea, *b* (twin) 1965: *m* 1995, Mark R. Etherington, son of Richard Etherington, of Bideford, Devon, and has issue living, Anna Louise Una, *b* 1998.
Hon Penelope Sally Rosita, *b* 1970.

RENWICK, BARON (Renwick) (Baron UK 1964, Bt UK 1927)

To work is to pray

HARRY ANDREW RENWICK, 2nd Baron and 3rd Baronet; *b* 10 Oct 1935; *s* 1973; *ed* Eton: *m* 1st, 1965 (*m diss* 1989), Susan Jane, da of late Capt Kenneth Stephen B. Lucking, Cheshire Regt; 2ndly, 1989, Mrs Homayoun Mazandi, da of late Maj Mahmoud Yazdanparst Pakzad, and formerly wife of Joe Mazandi, of LA, Calif, USA, and has issue by 1st *m*.

Arms – Argent, a husbandman in the act of sowing-proper, on a chief azure a thunderbolt between two bulls, heads caboshed or. **Crest** – a thunderbolt or. **Supporters** – *Dexter*, a black poodle proper; *sinister*, a tabby cat proper.
Residence – 47 Cheyne Walk, SW3.

SONS LIVING (*By 1st marriage*)

Hon ROBERT JAMES, *b* 19 Aug 1966.
Hon Michael David, *b* 1968.

SISTERS LIVING AND DECEASED

Hon Susan Mary, *b* 1930; a JP for Hants: *m* 1st, 1955 (*m diss* 1984), Hon Sir John Francis Harcourt Baring (later 7th Baron Ashburton); 2ndly, 1997, Andre Newburg. *Residence* – 13 Alexander St, W2.
Hon Jennifer, *b* 1932: *m* 1st, 1954 (*m diss* 1967), Antony Duncan Rowe; 2ndly, 1973 (*m diss* 1978), Roy Philip Arthur, who *d* 1994; 3rdly, 1978 (*m diss* 1989), Robert Ian MacDonald, and *d* 1989, leaving issue (by 1st *m*), Giles Timothy Robert (Flat 4, 38 Redcliffe Gdns, SW10), *b* 1956: *m* 1st, 1986 (*m diss* 1991), Karma Nabulsi; 2ndly, 19—, Ann Serena Joan Musgrave Jameson, — Antonia Tanya, *b* 1959: *m* 1983, Henry James Stone, and has issue living, Benjamin James *b* 1986, Liam Henry *b* 1988, Jacob Antony *b* 1991, Harry Edward *b* 1993, Gemma Elizabeth *b* 1984.
Hon Belinda Anne, *b* 1934: *m* 1959, as his 2nd wife, John Horatio Gordon Shephard, formerly Capt Gren Gds, who *d* 1993, of The Barn, Elcot, Newbury, Berks, and has issue living, William, *b* 1962, — Sarah, *b* 1959: *m* 1st, 1988 (*m diss* 1993), Stephen P.M. Clarke; 2ndly, 1993, Alexander J. H. Scrimgeour, of 103 Strathville Rd, SW18.

MOTHER LIVING

Dorothy Mary (Miserden House, Stroud, Glos), da of late Maj Harold Parkes, of the Dial House, Alveston, Stratford-on-Avon: *m* 1st, 1929 (*m diss* 1953), Sir Robert Burnham Renwick, KBE, 2nd Bt (later 1st Baron Renwick), who *d* 1973; 2ndly, 1953, John FitzAdam Ormiston, who *d* 1994.

PREDECESSORS – **(1)** HARRY BENEDETTO Renwick, KBE, son of Andrew Renwick, of Windsor, *b* 1861; *cr* a *Baronet* 1927: *m* 1897, Frederica Louisa, da of Robert Laing, of Stirling; *d* 1932; *s* by his only son **(2)** *Sir* ROBERT BURNHAM, KBE, 2nd Bt *b* 1904; Industrialist; Chm of Airbourne Forces, 1943-45; Controller of Communications Air Min and Communications Equipment, Min of Aircraft Production 1942-45; Chm Asso TV 1961; *cr Baron Renwick*, of Coombe, co Surrey (peerage of UK) 1964: *m* 1st, 1929 (*m diss* 1953), Dorothy Mary, da of late Maj Harold Parkes, of the Dial House, Alveston, Stratford-on-Avon; 2ndly, 1953, Edith Joan, who *d* 1994, only da of late Sir Reginald Clarke, CIE; and widow of Maj John Ogilvie Spencer, WG; *d* 1973; *s* by his only son **(3)** HARRY ANDREW, 2nd Baron and present peer.

RENWICK OF CLIFTON, BARON (Renwick) (Life Baron 1997)

ROBIN WILLIAM RENWICK, KCMG, son of Richard Renwick, of Edinburgh; *b* 13 Dec 1937; *ed* St Paul's, Jesus Coll, Cambridge (Hon Fellow 1992), and Univ of Paris (Sorbonne); Hon LLD Wits

Univ, Johannesburg 1991, Hon DLitt William and Mary Coll, Williamsburg, Virginia 1993; entered Foreign Service 1963, Dakar 1963-64, FO 1964-66, New Delhi 1966-69; Priv Sec to Min of State, FCO 1970-72; First Sec, Paris 1972-76; Councillor, Cabinet Office 1976-78; Head of Rhodesia Dept, FCO 1978-80; Political Adviser to Lord Soames as Govr of Rhodesia 1980; Visiting Fell, Center for Internat Affairs, Harvard 1980-81; Head of Chancery, Washington 1981-84; Assist Under-Sec of State, FCO 1984-87; Amb to S Africa 1987-91, and to Washington 1991-95 (ret); Memb Exec Cttee The Pilgrims since 1998; co dir; author; FRSA; *cr* CMG 1980, KCMG 1989, and *Baron Renwick of Clifton*, of Chelsea in the Royal Borough of Kensington and Chelsea (Life Baron) 1997: *m* 1965, Annie Colette, da of Jean-Jacques Giudicelli, of Paris, France, and has issue.

Address – c/o Robert Fleming & Co Ltd, 25 Copthall Av, EC2R 7DR. *Clubs* – Hurlingham, Travellers', Brooks's.

SON LIVING

Hon John, *b* 1966; *ed* St Paul's, and St Andrews Univ.

DAUGHTER LIVING

Hon Marie-France, *b* 1977; *ed* Madeira Coll, Washington, DC, and Univ Coll, London.

REVELSTOKE, BARON (Baring) (Baron UK 1885)

By uprightness and labour

JOHN BARING, 5th Baron; *b* 2 Dec 1934; *s* 1994; *ed* Eton.

Arms – Azure, a fesse or, in chief a bear's head proper, ringed or, differenced by a hurt, thereon a mullet erminois. **Crest** – A mullet erminois, between two wings argent. **Supporters** – *Dexter*, a bull argent; *sinister*, a bear proper, muzzled or, each charged on the shoulder with a mullet erminois.
Residence – Lambay Island, Rush, co Dublin.

BROTHER LIVING

Hon JAMES CECIL, *b* 16 Aug 1938; *ed* Eton: *m* 1st, 1968 (*m diss* 19—), Aneta Laline Dennis, yr da of late Erskine Arthur Hamilton Fisher, of Mickleham, Surrey; 2ndly, 1983, Sarah, da of William Edward Stubbs, MBE, and has issue living (by 1st *m*), Alexander Rupert, *b* 1970, — Thomas James, *b* 1971, — (by 2nd *m*), Flora Aksinia, *b* 1983. *Residence* –

COLLATERAL BRANCHES LIVING

Issue of late Brig-Gen Hon Everard Baring, CVO, CBE, 4th son of 1st Baron, *b* 1865, *d* 1932: *m* 1904, Lady Ulrica Duncombe, who *d* 1935, da of 1st Earl of Feversham:—
Helen, *b* 1906: *m* 1939, as his 2nd wife, Maj Gordon Bentley Foster, who *d* 1963, and has issue living, Rosanna (*Hon Mrs Oliver James*), *b* 19—: *m* 1965, Hon Oliver Francis Wintour James, and has issue (*see* B James of Rusholme), — Mary Helen, *b* 1942: *m* 1981, John Duncan, of The Old Vicarage, Salton, York. *Residence* – Sleightholmedale, Kirkbymoorside, York.

Grandchildren of late Hon Hugo Baring, OBE, yst son of 1st Baron:—
Issue of late Francis Anthony Baring, *b* 1909, *ka* 1940: *m* 1933, Lady Rose Gwendolen Louisa McDonnell, DCVO, who *d* 1993, da of 7th Earl of Antrim:—
Nicholas Hugo (43 Sutherland Place, W2 5BY; The Old Rectory, Ham, Marlborough, Wilts SN8 3QR) *b* 1934; *ed* Eton, and Magdalene Coll, Camb; late Lieut Coldstream Gds; Trustee Nat Gallery since 1989 (Chm since 1991): *m* 1972, Diana, da of late Lt-Col Charles Crawfurd, and has issue living, Francis Charles, *b* 1973, — Tobias Keith Alexander, *b* 1976, — Edward Randal, *b* 1979. —— Peter, *b* 1935; *ed* Eton, and Magdalene Coll, Camb: *m* 1960, Teresa Anne, CBE (1998), da of late Hon Sir Maurice Richard Bridgeman, KBE (*see* V Bridgeman), and has issue living, Guy Francis, *b* 1965; *ed* Eton, and Bristol Univ: *m* 1995, Tessa Jean, da of His Honour Judge Andrew Brooks, of Mains of Kynachan, Strath Tummel, and has issue living, Eliza Rose *b* 1998, — Max Maurice, *b* 1967, — Hugo John, *b* 1970; has issue (by Annabel Clare, da of Roderick Mullion, of 27 FitzWilliam Sq, Dublin 2), Maud May *b* 1998. —— Susan Violet, *b* 1938: *m* 1962, Henry Joseph Rogaly, of 56 Croftdown Rd, NW5, and has issue living, Benjamin Nelson, *b* 1963, — Sarah Rose, *b* 1965, — Rachel Frances, *b* 1968, — Jessica Hilary, *b* 1971.

PREDECESSORS – (1) EDWARD CHARLES Baring, son of late Henry Baring, MP (*see* B Northbrook, colls); *b* 1828; was head of mercantile firm of Baring Brothers and Co Bishopsgate Street, EC; *cr Baron Revelstoke*, of Membland, co Devon (peerage of United Kingdom) 1885: *m* 1861, Louisa Emily Charlotte, who *d* 1892, da of John Crocker Bulteel, of Flete, Devon; *d* 1897; *s* by his son (2) JOHN, 2nd Baron, GCVO, *b* 1863; a partner in the firm of Baring Bros and Co, and a Director of Bank of England; a Member of Council of HRH the Prince of Wales 1907-29, Receiver-Gen of Duchy of Cornwall 1908-29, and Lord-Lieut for Middlesex 1926-9; *d* 1929; *s* by his brother (3) CECIL, 3rd Baron; *b* 1864: *m* 1902, Maude, who *d* 1922, da of late Pierre Lorillard, *d* 1934; *s* by his son (4) RUPERT, 4th Baron; *b* 1911; 2nd Lieut RAC (TA):

m 1934 (*m diss* 1944), Hon Florence (Flora) Fermor-Hesketh, who *d* 1971, da of 1st Baron Hesketh; *d* 1994; *s* by his elder son **(5)** JOHN, 5th Baron and present peer.

RHODES, BARONY OF (Rhodes) (Extinct 1987)

DAUGHTERS LIVING OF LIFE BARON

Hon Pamela JUDSON-RHODES (18 Aiken Ave, Princeton, NJ 08540, USA), *b* 1927: *m* 1st, 1953 (*m diss* 1969), Walter L. Hemphill; 2ndly, 1990, S. Sheldon Judson, and has issue (by 1st *m*).
Hon Helen, *b* 1929: *m* 1954, John Sutcliffe, JP, DL, of Lower Carr, Carr Lane, Oldham, Lancs OL3 5ND, and has issue.

Rhys, family name of Baron Dynevor.

Rice, Spring, family name of Baron Monteagle of Brandon.

RICHARD, BARON (Richard) (Life Baron 1990)

IVOR SEWARD RICHARD, QC, son of Seward Thomas Richard, of 30 Heol Nant Castan, Rhiwbina, Cardiff; *b* 30 May 1932; *ed* Cheltenham, and Pembroke Coll, Oxford (BA 1953, MA 1970, Hon Fellow 1981); Bar Inner Temple 1955, QC 1971, Bencher 1985; Delegate at Assembly for Council of Europe 1965-68, and Western European Union 1965-68; PPS to Sec of State for Defence 1966-69, Parly Under-Sec of State for Defence (Army) 1969-70, Opposition Spokesman Broadcasting, Posts and Telecommunications 1970-71, Dep Opposition Spokesman Foreign Affairs 1971-74, UK Permanent Rep to UN 1974-79, Chm Rhodesia Conference, Geneva, 1976, UK Commr to Commn of European Communities 1981-85; Opposition Leader of House of Lords 1992-97, Lord Privy Seal and Leader of House of Lords 1997-98; Member Fabian Soc and Lab Lawyers; MP Barons Court (*Lab*) 1964-74; *cr Baron Richard*, of Ammanford, co Dyfed (Life Baron) 1990: *m* 1st, 1956 (*m diss* 1962), Geraldine Maude, da of Alfred Moore, of Hartlepool, co Durham; 2ndly, 1962 (*m diss* 1985), Alison Mary, da of Joseph Imrie, of Alverstoke, Hants; 3rdly, 1989, Janet, da of John Jones, of Oxford, and has issue by 1st, 2nd and 3rd *m*.
Address – 2 Paper Buildings, Temple, EC4.

SONS LIVING (*By 1st marriage*)

Hon David Seward, *b* 1959.

(*by 2nd marriage*)

Hon Alun Seward, *b* 1963.

(by 3rd marriage)

Hon William John, *b* 1990.

DAUGHTER LIVING *(By 2nd marriage)*

Hon Isobel Margaret Katherine, *b* 1966.

Richards, family name of Baron Milverton.

RICHARDSON, BARON (Richardson) (Life Baron 1979, Bt UK 1963)

JOHN SAMUEL RICHARDSON, LVO, *Life Baron* and 1st *Baronet*, son of late Maj John Watson Richardson, of Sheffield (Roberts, Bt) (*cr* 1919); *b* 16 June 1910; *ed* Charterhouse, and Trin Coll, Camb (MA BChir, MD, Hon Fellow 1979) Hon DSc, NUI Hull, Hon DCL Newcastle, Hon LLD Nottingham, Liverpool; FRCP London; Hon FRCP Ed; Hon FRCP Glasgow; Hon FRCPsych; Hon FRCS; Hon FRCGP; Hon FFCM; a Consulting Physician St Thomas's Hosp since 1947, to Metropolitan Police 1957-80, to Army 1964-75, and to London Transport 1964-80; Chm Council for Postgraduate Med Educ in England and Wales 1972-80; Hon Master of The Bench of Gray's Inn 1974; Pres of Gen Med Council 1973-80, Chm of Joint Consultants Cttee 1967-72; Pres of R Soc of Medicine 1969-71, and British Med Assocn 1970-71; Master of Soc of Apothecaries of London 1971-72; Pres of International Soc of Internal Med 1966-70; 1939-45 War, as Lt-Col RAMC; LVO 1943; Knt 1960; *cr* a *Baronet* (UK, of Ecclesall, West Riding, co York) 1963, and *Baron Richardson*, of Lee, co Devon (Life Baron) 1979: *m* 1933, Sybil Angela Stephanie, who *d* 1991, da of A. Ronald Trist, of Stanmore, Middx, and has issue.

𝕬rms – Sable on a fess engrailed or between in chief an open book proper bound gules edged gold between two mullets and in base a swan argent, a lion passant guardant also gules. 𝕮rest – The head of a rhinoceros erased sable behind the horn a scroll inscribed with words "Till time ceases" (in letters gules). 𝕾upporters – Two horses reguardant the dexter a Grey, with Saddlecloth of the Metropolitan Police Force, the sinister also a Grey, with Saddlecloth of the Royal Army Medical Corps, both saddled, bridled, with headstall, horse-hair plume and breast girth all with silver buckles and bosses proper.
Residence – Windcutter, Lee, nr Ilfracombe, N Devon.

DAUGHTERS LIVING

Hon Elizabeth-Ann, *b* 1937: *m* 1st, 1960 (*m diss* 1970), Angus Gavin Lockhead Jack (*see* Inglefield-Watson, Bt, colls, 1995 Edn); 2ndly, 1971, Gregory Edmund Stafford, LLB, of 49 Deodar Rd, SW15, and has issue living (by 1st *m—see* Inglefield-Watson, Bt, colls, 1995 Edn), — (by 2nd *m*), Samuel, *b* 1975.

Hon Susan Clare, *b* 1940: *m* 1970, Robert Wales, of 2 Thorne St, SW13, and has issue living, Duncan John Richardson, *b* 1970.

RICHARDSON OF CALOW, BARONESS (Richardson) (Life Baroness 1998)

Rev KATHLEEN MARGARET RICHARDSON, OBE, da of Francis Fountain, of Chesterfield; *b* 24 Feb 1938; *ed* St Helena Sch, Chesterfield, Stockwell Coll (Cert Ed 1958), Deaconess Coll, Ilkley, and Wesley House, Camb; Hon DLitt Bradford 1994; school teacher 1958-61; Wesley Deaconess, Champness Hall, Rochdale 1961-64; Lay Worker, Team Ministry, Stevenage 1973-77; Minister, Denby Dale and Clayton West Circuit 1979-87; ordained Presbyter 1980; Chm West Yorks District 1987-95; Pres Methodist Conference 1992-93; Moderator, Free Churches' Council 1995-99; a Pres, Churches Together in England 1995-99; Co-ordinating Sec, Inter-Church and Other Relationships, Methodist Church since 1995; *cr* OBE 1996, and *Baroness Richardson of Calow*, of Calow, co Derbyshire (Life Baroness) 1998: *m* 1964, Ian David Godfrey Richardson, son of Sidney Richardson, of Rochdale, and has issue.

Address – House of Lords, Westminster, SW1A 0PW.

DAUGHTERS LIVING

Hon Kathryn Jane, *b* 1966: *m* 1993, Robert Hickmott, and has issue living, Christian Charles, *b* 1997, — Alexander Lewis, *b* 1999.

Hon Claire Margaret, *b* 1968: *m* 1999, Mark Robert Lawson.

Hon Anne Elizabeth, *b* 1970.

RICHARDSON OF DUNTISBOURNE, BARON (Richardson) (Life Baron 1983)

GORDON WILLIAM HUMPHREYS RICHARDSON, KG, MBE, PC, el son of late John Robert Richardson; *b* 25 Nov 1915; *ed* Nottingham High Sch, and Gonville and Caius Coll, Camb (BA, LLB); 1939-45 War as Maj S Notts Hus Yeo, RHA; Bar Gray's Inn 1946; Hon Bencher 1973; Chm Pilgrim Trust 1984-89; a Member of Bar Council 1951-55; Chm J. Henry Schroder Wagg & Co Ltd 1962-72, and Schroders Ltd 1966-73; Chm of Industrial Development Advisory Board 1972-73; a Dir of Bank of England 1967-75; Gov of Bank of England 1973-83; Chm R Inst of Internat Affairs 1984-87; one of HM Lieuts City of London since 1974, and a DL of Glos; *cr* MBE (Mil) 1944, PC (1976), KG (1983), and *Baron Richardson of Duntisbourne*, of Duntisbourne, co Glos (Life Peer) 1983; *m* 1941, Margaret Alison, el da of late Very Rev Hugh Richard Lawrie Sheppard, Canon and Precentor of St Paul's Cathedral, and has issue.

Arms – Argent a fess wavy bleu celeste between in chief three swords in pale points upwards fesswise gules and in base a pair of scales sable on a bordure also gules eight bezants. **Crest** – A seated female figure representing the Bank of England proper habited argent crined and murally crowned or resting the sinister hand on an oval cartouche carved or the field argent thereon a cross gules and holding in the palm of the extended dexter hand a terrestrial globe also proper. **Supporters** – On either side a griffin segreant gules the wings elevated and bezantly gorged with coronet of sword hilts gold.

Address – c/o Morgan Stanley UK Group, 25 Cabot Sq, Canary Wharf, E14 4QA. *Clubs* – Athenaeum, Brooks's.

SON LIVING

Hon Simon Bruce Sheppard, *b* 1944: *m* 1979, Miriam Ann, da of George Harrison Gibson. *Residence* – River House, Bromham Park, Bromham, Beds MK43 8HH.

DAUGHTER LIVING

Hon Sarah (*Hon Lady Riddell*), LVO, *b* 1942; LVO 1993: *m* 1969, Sir John Charles Buchanan Riddell, 13th Bt, CVO, DL, and has issue.

RICHMOND and GORDON, DUKE OF (Gordon Lennox) (Duke (Richmond) E 1675, Duke (Lennox) S 1675, Duke (Gordon) UK 1876)

CHARLES HENRY GORDON LENNOX, 10th Duke of Richmond and Lennox, and 5th Duke of Gordon; also Duke of Aubigny in France; *b* 19 Sept 1929; *s* 1989; *ed* Eton, and William Temple Coll, Rugby; Hereditary Constable of Inverness Castle; Lord Lieut W Sussex 1989-94; late 2nd Lt KRRC; Chancellor Sussex Univ 1985-98; a Chartered Accountant; formerly Member of House of Laity of General Synod for Diocese of Chichester, and of Central and Exec Cttee of World Council of Churches, and Chm of Board for Mission and Unity of General Synod; a Church Commr; Chm Goodwood Group of Companies since 1969: *m* 1951, Susan Monica, da of Col Cecil Everard Montague Grenville-Grey, CBE (*see* Morrison-Bell, Bt (*cr* 1905), colls), and has issue.

Arms – Quarterly: 1st and 4th grand quarters, the Royal arms of Charles II (viz quarterly; 1st and 4th, France and England quarterly; 2nd, Scotland; 3rd Ireland), the whole within a bordure compony argent and gules charged with eight roses of the second, barbed and seeded proper, *Lennox*; over all an escutcheon gules, three buckles or, *Aubigny*; 2nd and 3rd grand quarters quarterly, 1st azure, three boars' heads couped or, *Gordon*; 2nd or, three lions, heads erased gules, *Badenoch*; 3rd or, three crescents within a double tressure counterflory gules, *Seton*; 4th azure, three cinquefoils argent, *Fraser*. **Crests** – 1st, a bull's head erased sable horned or, *Lennox*; 2nd, on a chapeau gules, turned up ermine, a lion statant guardant or, ducally crowned gules, and gorged with a collar compony of four pieces, argent and gules charged with eight roses of the last, *Richmond*; 3rd, out of a ducal coronet, a Stag's head affrontée proper, attired with ten tynes or. **Supporters** – *Dexter*, a unicorn argent, armed, crined and unguled, or; *sinister*, an antelope argent, also crined, and unguled, or, each supporter gorged with a collar compony as the crest. *Residence* – Molecomb, Goodwood, Chichester, W Sussex PO18 0PZ.

SON LIVING

CHARLES HENRY (*Earl of March and Kinrara*), *b* 8 Jan 1955; *ed* Eton: *m* 1st, 1976 (*m diss* 1989), Sally, da of late Maurice Clayton; 2ndly, 1991, Hon Janet Elizabeth Astor, da of 3rd Viscount Astor, and has issue:—

SONS LIVING (by 2nd *m*)—Charles Henry (*Lord Settrington*), *b* 20 Dec 1994, — *Hon* William Rupert Charles, *b* 1996.
DAUGHTER LIVING (by 1st *m*)—*Lady* Alexandra, *b* 1985.

Seat – Goodwood House, Chichester, W Sussex PO18 0PX.

DAUGHTERS LIVING

Lady Ellinor Caroline, *b* 1952.
Lady Louisa Elizabeth, *b* 1967: *m* 1997, Benjamin Collings, yr son of Roger Collings, of Pitfour, Doctors Lane, Kington, Herefords. *Residence* – The Old Rectory, Presteigne, Powys.

ADOPTED DAUGHTERS LIVING

Maria, *b* 1959 *m* 1989, Christopher Handy. —— Naomi, *b* 1962; actress (as Nimmy March): *m* 1996, Gavin C. Burke, son of M. Burke, of Maldon, Essex.

BROTHER LIVING

Lord Nicholas, KCMG, KCVO, *b* 1931; *ed* Eton and Worcester Coll, Oxford; HM Diplomatic Ser (Paris) 1975-79; HM Amb to Spain 1984-89; a Gov of BBC since 1990; Chm of Trustees Historic Churches Preservation Trust since 1997; late 2nd Lt KRRC; MVO (4th class) 1957, CMG (Civil) 1978, KCMG 1986, KCVO 1988: *m* 1958, Mary, only da of late Brig Hudleston Noel Hedworth Williamson, DSO, MC (*see* Williamson, Bt, colls), and has issue living, Anthony Charles, *b* 1969, — Sarah Caroline, *b* 1960: *m* 1988, Dominic Caldecott, yst son of Andrew Caldecott, of Ramsbury, Wilts, and has issue living, Frederick Arthur Nicholas *b* 1989, Thomas Andrew *b* (twin) 1989, Rufus George *b* 1993, a da *b* 1997, — Henrietta Mary, *b* 1962: *m* 1992, Michael Lindsell, son of W. M. Lindsell, of Lymington, Hants, and has issue living, Albert James *b* 1993, Arthur Richard *b* 1996, Alice Elizabeth Anne *b* 1998, — Lucy Elizabeth, *b* 1965: *m* 1996, Mark R. D. Cornell, son of Brig John Cornell, of Marlborough, Wilts. *Residence* – South Nore, W Wittering, Chichester, Sussex PO20 8AT.

COLLATERAL BRANCHES LIVING

Grandchildren of late Brig-Gen Lord Esmé Charles Gordon Lennox, KCVO, CMG, DSO (infra):—
Issue of late Capt Reginald Arthur Charles Gordon Lennox, OBE, *b* 1910, *d* 1965: *m* 1942, Pamela Cicely, who *d* 1997, da of Capt Christopher Digby Leyland, Life Gds (Cotterell, Bt):—
James David Charles *b* 1944: *m* 1973 (*m diss* 1979), Sally Cooper, da of John Roger Cooper Brain, and has issue living, Henry, *b* 1976. —— Clare Evelyn, *b* 1946: *m* 1967, Edmund Clive Lardner-Burke.

Issue of late Brig-Gen Lord Esmé Charles Gordon Lennox, KCVO, CMG, DSO, 2nd son of 7th Duke, *b* 1875, *d* 1949: *m* 1st, 1909 (*m diss* 1923), Hon Hermione Frances Caroline Fellowes, who *d* 1971, da of 2nd Baron De Ramsey; 2ndly, 1923, Rosamond Lorys, who *d* 1961, da of late Vice-Adm Norman Craig Palmer, CVO:—
(By 2nd *m*) Sara Carolyn (*Lady Fergusson*), *b* 1933: *m* 1st, 1956, Sir William Andrew Malcolm Martin Oliphant Montgomery Cuninghame, 11th Bt, who *d* 1959; 2ndly, 1959, Sir Ewen Alastair John Fergusson, GCMG, GCVO, son of late Sir Ewen Macgregor Field Fergusson, and has issue living, (by 2nd *m*) Ewen Alexander Nicholas, *b* 1965, — Anna Rosamund Harriot, *b* 1961, — Iona Frances, *b* 1967. *Address* – c/o Coutts & Co, 440 Strand, WC2R 0QS.

Grandsons of late Maj Lord Bernard Charles Gordon Lennox, 3rd son of 7th Duke:—
Issue of late Lt-Gen Sir George Charles Gordon Lennox, KBE, CB, CVO, DSO, *b* 1908, *d* 1988: *m* 1931, Nancy Brenda, who *d* 1993, da of Maj Sir Lionel Edward Hamilton Marmaduke Darell, 6th Bt, DSO:—
Bernard Charles, CB, MBE (Hill House, Eversley, Hants), *b* 1932; *ed* Eton, a Page of Honour to HM 1946-49; Maj-Gen late Gren Gds; British Comdt and GOC British Sector W Berlin 1983-85; Senior Army Member Royal Coll of Defence Studies 1986-88, Lieut-Col Gren Gds 1989-95; Chm Guards' Polo Club since 1992; MBE (Mil) 1968, CB (Mil) 1986: *m* 1958, Sally-Rose, only da of late John Weston Warner, and has issue living, Edward Charles, *b* 1961, a Page of Honour to HM 1974-77; Capt Gren Gds: *m* 1989, Katharine Elizabeth, eldest da of (Robert) Martin Mays-Smith, and has issue living, Alexander Charles *b* 1990, Rosie Jennifer *b* 1992, Laura Clare *b* 1995, — Angus Charles (The Malt House, Newbury, Berks RG20 9HL), *b* 1964: *m* 1990, Camilla Douglas, elder da of Ian Alan Douglas Pilkington (*see* B Faringdon, colls), and has issue living, Geordie Charles *b* 1998, Iona Alice *b* 1993, Emily Charlotte *b* 1995, — Charles Bernard, *b* 1970. —— David Henry Charles (Saxham Hall, Bury St Edmunds, Suffolk IP29 5JW), *b* 1935; *ed* Eton; Col Gren Gds; High Sheriff Suffolk 1999: *m* 1982, Elizabeth C., da of late Gen Sir William Gurdon Stirling, GCB, CBE, DSO, and has issue living, Flora Louise, *b* 1983.

Issue of late Rear Adm Sir Alexander Henry Charles Gordon Lennox, KCVO, CB, DSO, *b* 1911, *d* 1987: *m* 1936, Barbara, who *d* 1987, da of late Maj-Gen Julian Steele:—
Michael Charles, *b* 1938; *ed* Eton, and RNC Dartmouth; Capt RN: *m* 1974, Jennifer Susan, da of late Capt Hon Vicary Paul Gibbs (*see* B Aldenham, colls), and has issue living, Hamish Charles, *b* 1980, — Lucinda Jean, *b* 1975, — Charlotte Louise, *b* 1978. *Residence* – Fishers Hill, Iping, Midhurst, W Sussex. —— Andrew Charles, *b* 1948; *ed* Nautical Coll, Pangbourne, and RNC Dartmouth; Cmdr RN: *m* 1973, Julia Jane Neill, da of late Dr J. Neill Morrison, and has issue living, Simon Charles, *b* 1978, — Hugo Charles, *b* 1980. *Residence* – Bridge House, Westbourne, Emsworth, Hants.

Grandson of late Rt Hon Lord Walter Charles Gordon Lennox, 4th son of 6th Duke:—
Issue of late Capt Victor Charles Hugh Gordon Lennox, *b* 1897, *d* 1968: *m* 1st, 1923 (*m diss* 1928), Mrs Anne Dorothy Bridge, who *d* 1963, da of late Edward Cazalet Browne; 2ndly, 1932 (*m diss* 1940), Diana Elizabeth Constance, who *d* 1982, da of late Adm Sir Charles Edmund Kingsmill, of Ballybeg, Ottawa; 3rdly, 1958, Norah Julia Wensley, who *d* 19—, da of Edward Guy Schofield, of Leeds:—
(By 2nd *m*) (Henry) George Charles (Veraz, Chevry, 01170 Gex, France), *b* 1934; Official UNHCR (ret): *m* 1958, Odile Steinmann, of Grenoble, France, and has issue living, Ian Charles (41 rue Plantamour, 1201 Geneva, Switzerland), *b* 1958: *m* 1989, Rev Jeltje, elder da of Owen Aukema, of Holland, Michigan, USA, and has two adopted children, Jefferson Charles *b* 1995 (adopted 1996), Sushila Louise Odile *b* 1994 (adopted 1994), — Philip George Hugh (Ch des Bergeronettes, 01280 Prevessin-Moëns, France), *b* 1962: *m* 1987, Junko, da of late Prof Tomio Higuchi, and has issue living, Thomas Charles *b* 1991, Alec George *b* 1993, — Geneviève Anne (Riedstrasse 39A, 8352 Elsau, Switzerland), *b* 1961: *m* 1993, Rainer Frick, son of Wilhelm Frick, of Basel, Switzerland, and has issue living, Adrian Bruno *b* 1996, Melchior Bernard *b* 1998.

PREDECESSORS – (1) CHARLES Lennox, KG, illegitimate son of King Charles II, by Louise Renée de Penancoet de Kerouaille (who was *cr* by HM *Baroness Petersfield, Countess of Fareham*, and *Duchess of Portsmouth* for life, and by Louis XIV of France Duchess d'Aubigny); *b* 1672; *cr Baron of Settrington*, of Settrington, co York, *Earl of March, Duke of Richmond* (peerage of England) 1675, and *Lord of Torboulton*, of Torbolton, *Earl of Darnley* and *Duke of Lennox* (peerage of Scotland) 1675; *d* 1723; *s* by his son (2) CHARLES, KG, KB, PC, 2nd Duke, *b* 1701; was High Constable of England at coronation of George II, Master of the Horse and on four occasions a Lord Justice to administer the government during the absence of the king; in 1734, on the death of his grandmother, he became *Duke d'Aubigny* (*cr* 1684) in France; *d* 1750; *s* by his son (3) CHARLES, KG, 3rd Duke, *b* 1735; carried the sceptre at the Coronation of George III; was Ambassador to France 1765, Principal Sec of State 1766, and Master-Gen of the Ordnance 1782; *dsp* 1806; *s* by his nephew (4) CHARLES, KG, 4th Duke, *b* 1764; a Gen in the Army; MP for Sussex 1790-1806; was Lord-Lieut of Ireland 1807-13, and Gov-Gen of Canada 1818-19: *m* Charlotte, da of Alexander, 4th Duke of Gordon; *d* 1819; *s* by his son (5) CHARLES, KG, PC, 5th Duke; *b* 1791; was Lord-Lieut of Sussex; assumed in 1836 by patent the additional surname of Gordon; the title of Duke D'Aubigny was confirmed to him and registered by Parliament of France 1777, and reconfirmed 1816 by Louis XVIII; *m* 1817, Lady Caroline Paget, da of 1st Marquess of Anglesey; *d* 1860; *s* by his son (6) CHARLES HENRY, KG, PC, DCL, LLD, 6th Duke of Richmond and Lennox; *b* 1818; Lord-Lieut of co Banff, and an Elder Brother of Trinity House; MP for W Sussex (*C*) 1841-60; ADC to Com-in-Ch (Duke of Wellington and Viscount Hardinge) 1845-54, Pres of Poor Law Board 1859, and of Board of Trade 1867-8 and 1885, Lord Pres of Council 1874-80, *ex officio* Keeper of the Great Seal of Scotland, Sec for Scotland and Vice-Pres of Committee of Council on Education in Scotland 1885-6; *cr Earl of Kinrara*, and *Duke of Gordon* (peerage of United Kingdom) 1876: *m* 1843, Frances Harriet, who *d* 1887, el da of late Algernon Frederic Greville; *d* 1903; *s* by his son (7) CHARLES HENRY, KG, GCVO, CB, 7th Duke; *b* 1845; sat as MP for W Sussex (*C*) 1869-85, and for SW, or Chichester, Div of Sussex 1885-8; Hereditary Constable of Inverness Castle, an ADC to Queen Victoria, King Edward VII, and King George V 1896-1920, Lord-Lieut and Custos Rotulorum of cos Elgin and Banff 1903-28, and Chancellor of Aberdeen Univ 1917-28; bore Sceptre with Dove at Coronation of King George V 1911: *m* 1st, 1868, Amy Mary, who *d* 1879, el da of late Percy Ricardo, of Bramley Park, Guildford; 2ndly, 1882, Isabel Sophie, who *d* 1887, da of William George Craven; *d* 1928; *s* by his son (8) CHARLES HENRY, DSO, MVO, 8th Duke, *b* 1870; Lieut-Col Reserve of Officers; S Africa 1900 (despatches, DSO); accompanied

Special Mission to Foreign Courts to announce Accession of King George V 1910; appointed Lord Lt of co Elgin 1928: *m* 1893, Hilda Madaleine, DBE, who *d* 1971, el da of Henry A. Brassey, of Preston Hall, Aylesford; *d* 1935; *s* by his son (9) FREDERICK CHARLES, 9th Duke, *b* 1904; 1939-45 War as Fl Lt RAF; bore Septre with the Dove at Coronations of King George VI and Queen Elizabeth II; *m* 1927, Elizabeth Grace, who *d* 1992, da of late Rev Thomas William Hudson, formerly V of Wendover, Bucks; *d* 1989; *s* by his elder son (10) CHARLES HENRY, 10th Duke and present peer; also Earl of March, Earl of Darnley, Earl of Kinrara, Baron of Settrington, and Lord of Torboulton.

RIDLEY, VISCOUNT (Ridley) (Viscount UK 1900, Bt GB 1756)

CONSTANS   FIDEI

Constant in loyalty

MATTHEW WHITE RIDLEY, KG, GCVO, TD, 4th Viscount, and 8th Baronet; *b* 29 July 1925; *s* 1964; *ed* Eton, and Balliol Coll, Oxford; ARICS; served in Coldstream Guards 1943-46; Hon Col Queen's Own Yeomanry (TA) 1982-86; HM's Lord Lieut and Custos Rotulorum of Northumberland since 1984, a DL, JP, and Alderman for Northumberland; Lord Steward of HM Household since 1989; Chm of Northumberland Co Council 1967-79; Chancellor of Univ of Newcastle-upon-Tyne 1989-99; Chm of Internat Dendrology Soc 1988-93; Pres ACC 1979-84; Member of Council of TAVRAS 1984-93; ADC to Gov of Kenya 1952-53; *cr* KG 1992, GCVO 1994, KStJ: *m* 1953, Lady Anne Katherine Lumley, da of 11th Earl of Scarbrough, and has issue.

Arms – Gules, on a chevron argent between three falcons proper, as many pellets. Crest – A bull passant the tail turned over the back gules. Supporters – Two bulls gules, each gorged with a collar gemelle or and charged on the shoulder with three mullets, pierced argent.
Seat – Boston House, Blagdon, Seaton Burn, Newcastle-upon-Tyne NE13 6DB.

SON LIVING

Hon MATTHEW WHITE, *b* 7 Feb 1958; *ed* Eton, and Magdalen Coll, Oxford (DPhil); author and journalist: *m* 1989, Anya Christine, da of Dr Robert Hurlbert, of Houston, Texas, and has issue living, Matthew White, *b* 27 Sept 1993, — Iris Livia, *b* 1997. *Residence* – Blagdon, Seaton Burn, Newcastle upon Tyne NE13 6DD.

DAUGHTERS LIVING

Hon Cecilia Anne, *b* 1953: *m* 1978, Berkeley Arthur Cole, and has issue (*see* E Enniskillen).

Hon Rose Emily, *b* 1956: *m* 1980, Owen William Paterson, MP, yr son of A. D. Paterson, of Oaklands, Tarporley, Cheshire, and has issue living, Felix Charles, *b* 1986, — Edward Owen, *b* 1988, — Evie Rose, *b* 1992. *Residence* – Shellbrook Hill, Ellesmere, Shropshire SY12 9EW.

Hon Mary Victoria, *b* 1962: *m* 1991, John James, son of P. L. James, of Meesden Hall, Herts, and has issue living, Joseph Nathaniel, *b* 1995, — Theodore Patrick, *b* 1997.

COLLATERAL BRANCHES LIVING

Issue of late Rt Hon Nicholas Ridley (*Baron Ridley of Liddesdale*), yr son of 3rd Viscount, *b* 1929, *d* 1994; *cr* a Life Baron 1992: *m* 1st, 1950 (*m diss* 1974), Hon Clayre Campbell, da of 4th Baron Stratheden and Campbell; 2ndly, 1979, Judith Mary (*Baroness Ridley of Liddesdale*), da of Dr Ernest John Coponet Kendall, of Epsom, Surrey:—
Hon Jane, *b* 1953: *m* 1986, Stephen Francis Thomas, yr son of Capt Sir William James Cooper Thomas, 2nd Bt (*cr* 1919), and has issue (see that title). *Residence* – Flat 6, 31 Dorset Square, NW1 6QJ. —— *Hon* Susanna, *b* 1955: *m* 1987, Charles Christopher Hugh Rickett, son of Christopher Owen Rickett, of Little Benhams, Rusper, Sussex, and has issue living, Benjamin Christopher, *b* 1988, — Matthew Charles, *b* 1991, — William Oliver Nicholas, *b* (twin) 1991. *Residence* – 5 Scraesburgh Cottages, Jedburgh. —— *Hon* Jessica Clayre, *b* 1957: *m* 1991, David M. G. Fletcher, son of Col Derek Fletcher, and has issue living, Oscar, *b* 1995, — Daisy Columba, *b* 1992, — Grace, *b* 1994. *Residence* – 46 Bolingbroke Rd, W14.

Grandson of late Major Hon Sir Jasper Nicholas Ridley, KCVO, OBE, 2nd son of 1st Viscount:—
Issue of late Jasper Alexander Maurice Ridley, Lieut King's Roy Rifle Corps, *b* 1913, *d* on active ser in Italy 1943: *m* 1939, (Helen Laura) Cressida Bonham Carter, who *d* 1998, da of Baroness Asquith of Yarnbury (Life Baroness):—
Sir Adam Nicholas, *b* 1942, *ed* Eton, and Balliol Coll, Oxford; Kt 1985; *m* 1st, 1970 (*m diss* 1976), Lady Katherine Rose Celestine Asquith, da of 2nd Earl of Oxford and Asquith; 2ndly, 1981, Margaret Anne (Biddy), yst da of Frederic L.

Passmore, of Cobbetts, Virginia Water, Surrey, and has issue living (by 2nd *m*), Jasper, *b* 1987, — Luke, *b* (twin) 1987, — Jo (a son), *b* 1988.

(In remainder to the Baronetcy only)

Grandson of late Henry Colborne Maunoir Ridley, only son of late Rev William Henry Ridley, el son of late Rev Henry Colborne Ridley, 3rd son of 2nd baronet:—
Issue of late Capt William Henry Wake Ridley, OBE, RN, *b* 1887, *d* 1955: *m* 1913, Vera, who *d* 1965, da of Charles Walker, formerly of Launceston, Tasmania, and widow of Gerald Stuart Eardley-Wilmot (Eardley-Wilmot, Bt, colls):—

William Terence Colborne, CB, OBE, *b* 1915; Rear-Adm; Port Adm HM Naval Base, Rosyth, 1971-72; 1939-45 War in SW Pacific (despatches twice); OBE (Mil) 1954, CB (Mil) 1968: *m* 1st, 1938, Barbara, who *d* 1989, da of R. L. Allen, of Hartford, Cheshire; 2ndly, 1993, Joan Elaine, née Dowding, widow of Rev John William Leneve Norman, and has issue living (by 1st *m*), Peter William Wake (24 Entry Hill Park, Bath, Avon BA2 5ND), *b* 1939; Capt RN: *m* 1965, Jenifer, da of Capt W. J. M. Teale, RN, and has issue living, Timothy Jaspar William *b* 1967, Nicolas Henry Sumner *b* 1971. *Residence* – 4 Hill View Rd, Bath, Avon BA1 6NX.

Grandson of late Rev Oliver Matthew Ridley, 3rd son of late Rev Henry Colborne Ridley (ante):—
Issue of late Major Edward Keane Ridley, *b* 1861, *d* 1947: *m* 1903, Ethel Janet, who *d* 1962, da of late Alexander Forbes Tweedie:—

Edward Alexander Keane, CB (c/o Coutts & Co, 440 Strand, WC2), *b* 1904; *ed* Wellington, and Keble Coll, Oxford (BA 1925, MA 1955); Solicitor 1928; Principal Assist Treasury Solicitor 1956-69; CB (Civil) 1963.

Grandchildren of late Frank Colborne Ridley, 5th son of late Rev Oliver Matthew Ridley (ante):—
Issue of late Keith Vivian Colborne Ridley, *b* 1904, *d* 1977: *m* 1933, Joan Madeline Marling (8 Mill Place, Lisvane, Cardiff CF4 5TF), da of late Rev Ernest Marling Roberts:—

Richard Nicholas (53 Pelham St, SW7 2NJ), *b* 1939; *ed* Sherborne: *m* 1st, 1963 (*m diss* 1973), Susan Gwynne, da of R. E. Haddingham; 2ndly, 1974 (*m diss* 1982), Penelope Anne, da of Roger Melville Brewer; 3rdly, 1984, Wendy Ann, da of Denis Hand-Bowman, of Pippins, Old Lane, Crowborough, E Sussex, and has issue living (by 1st *m*), Caroline Lois, *b* 1964, — Jacqueline Claire, *b* 1966, — (by 2nd *m*) Michael James, *b* 1976, *ed* Granville Coll, Bideford, and Southampton Univ (BEng), — Nicholas Mark, *b* 1979; *ed* Rendcomb Coll, Cirencester, and Bristol Univ, — (by 3rd *m*) Serena Eloise, *b* 1988. —— Henry Colborne (835, W Wolfram, Chicago, Ill, 60657, USA), *b* 1944; *ed* Denstone Coll: *m* 1969, Mary Randall, da of Alfred Acierto, of Chicago, and has issue living, Emily Marling, *b* 1971, — Elisa Acierto, *b* 1975. —— Gillian Elizabeth, *b* 1937: *m* 1st, 1960 (*m diss* 1980), John Hunt; 2ndly, 1983, Peter Dignus Garside, of 8 Mill Place, Lisvane, Cardiff, and has issue living (by 1st *m*), Graham (38 Cromwell Rd, Banbury, Oxon), *b* 1961: *m* 1986 (*m diss* 1993), Cheryl Haidon, da of Gordon Taylor, of Stratford-upon-Avon, — Adam Christopher Jonathan, *b* 1974, — Robin Nicholas Andrew, *b* 1976, — Natalie Victoria, *b* 1962: *m* 1988, Simon Halling, of 21 Whiteacre Close, Thornhill, Cardiff CF4 9DG.

Granddaughter of late Rev Oliver Matthew Ridley (ante):—
Issue of late Clarence Oliver Ridley, OBE, *b* 1869, *d* 1951: *m* 1st, 1896, Anne Arabella, who *d* 1898, da of Gregory William Eccles, formerly of 6 Melrose Rd, Southfields, SW; 2ndly, 1900, Gertrude Henrietta, who *d* 1951, second da of Henry Houseman (ante):—

(By 2nd *m*) Barbara Frances, *b* 1907: *m* 1937, Thomas C. S. Bullick, who *d* 1976, and has issue living, Timothy John, *b* 1938; *ed* Bryanston, and Worcester Coll, Oxford (MA): *m* 1965, Tessa Mary, yst da of Walter Lucian Garstang, and has issue living, David Christopher *b* 1973, Claire Elizabeth *b* 1966, Judith Catherine *b* 1969: *m* 1997, Graham Alexander Cox, — Caroline Bridget, *b* 1941: *m* 1965, Anthony Townsend Parker, of 9 Holton Rd, Buckingham, and has issue living, Rachel *b* 1966, Alison *b* 1968, Jessica *b* 1971, — Sheila Mary, *b* 1945: *m* 1969, Geoffrey Scott Clark, RN, of 1 Mount Way, Princes Risborough, Bucks HP17 9BQ, and has issue living, Jeremy Scott *b* 1971, Jonathan Thomas *b* 1974.

PREDECESSORS – (1) MATTHEW White, only surviving son of Matthew White, Sheriff of Northumberland 1756; *cr* a *Baronet* 1756, with remainder to the heirs-male of his sister, Elizabeth, wife of Matthew Ridley, of Heaton; *d* 1763; *s* by his nephew (2) *Sir* MATTHEW WHITE RIDLEY, 2nd Bt; *b* 1745: MP, for Newcastle-upon-Tyne: *m* 1777, Sarah, da of Benjamin Colborne, of Bath; *d* 1813; *s* by his el son (3) *Sir* MATTHEW WHITE, 3rd Bt; *b* 1778; MP for Newcastle-upon-Tyne: *m* 1803, Laura, da of George Hawkins; *d* 1836; *s* by his el son (4) *Sir* MATTHEW WHITE, 4th Bt; *b* 1807; MP for Northumberland N (*C*) 1859-60: *m* 1841, Cecilia Anne, da of Sir James Parke (who became subsequently Lord Wensleydale); *d* 1877; *s* by his el son (5) *Sir* MATTHEW WHITE, 5th Bt; *b* 1842; *cr Viscount Ridley* and *Baron Wensleydale*, of Blagdon and Blyth, co Northumberland (peerage of United Kingdom) 1900; MP for Northumberland N (*C*) 1868-85, and for Blackpool Div of Lancashire N Aug 1886 to Dec 1900; Under Sec of State for Home Depart 1878-80, Financial Sec to Treasury 1885-6, and Sec of State for Home Depart 1895-1900: *m* 1873, Hon Mary Georgina Marjoribanks, who *d* 1899, da of 1st Baron Tweedmouth; *d* 1904; *s* by his son (6) MATTHEW WHITE, 2nd Viscount; *b* 1874; MP for Stalybridge (*C*) 1900-1904: *m* 1899, Hon Rosamond Cornelia Gladys Guest, who *d* 1947, da of of 1st Baron Wimborne; *d* 1916; *s* by his el son (7) MATTHEW WHITE, CBE, 3rd Viscount, *b* 1902; Chm of Northumberland Co Council 1940-46 and 1949-52, and Regional Controller, N Region, Min of Production 1942-49; Hon Col Northumberland Hussars (TA) 1962-64: *m* 1924, Ursula, OBE, who *d* 1967, da of Sir Edwin Landseer Lutyens, OB, KCIE, PRA, LLB (E Lytton); *d* 1964; *s* by his el son (8) MATTHEW WHITE, 4th Viscount and present peer; also Baron Wensleydale.

RIDLEY OF LIDDESDALE, BARONY OF (Ridley) (see V Ridley)

RIPPON OF HEXHAM, BARONY OF (Rippon) (Extinct 1997)

SON LIVING OF LIFE BARON

Hon Anthony Simon Yorke, *b* 1959.

DAUGHTERS LIVING OF LIFE BARON

Hon Fiona Carolyn, *b* 1947; *ed* Sherborne Girls' Sch.

Hon Sarah Lovell, *b* 1950; *ed* Sherborne Girls' Sch, St Paul's Girls' Sch, and St Anne's Coll, Oxford (MA); Solicitor 1978, Bar New York 1980: *m* 1978 (*m diss* 1988), Michael Taylor, and has issue living, James Geoffrey Bethune, *b* 1979, — Alexander Edward Yorke, *b* 1982.

Hon Penelope Ann, *b* 1953: *m* 1984, Simon Rae, and has issue living, Albertine Helen Yorke, *b* 1985.

WIDOW LIVING OF LIFE BARON

ANN LEYLAND (*Baroness Rippon of Hexham*), OBE, da of Donald Yorke, MC, of Prenton, Ches: *m* 1946, Baron Rippon of Hexham, PC, QC (Life Baron), who *d* 1997. *Residence* – The Old Vicarage, Broomfield, nr Bridgwater, Som.

RITCHIE-CALDER, BARONY OF (Calder) (Extinct 1982).

SONS LIVING OF LIFE BARON

(*Hon*) Nigel David Ritchie (does not use courtesy title) (26 Boundary Rd, Northgate, Crawley, Sussex RH10 2BJ), *b* 1931; *ed* Merchant Taylors' Sch, and at Sidney Sussex Coll, Camb (MA); author and television script writer; Editor of *New Scientist* 1962-66: *m* 1954, Elisabeth, da of Alfred James Palmer and has issue.

Hon Angus Lindsay Ritchie, *b* 1942; *ed* Wallington Co Sch, King's Coll, Camb (MA), and Univ of Sussex (D Phil): an author, Reader in Literature and staff tutor in arts, Open Univ in Scotland 1979-93: *m* 1st, 1963 (*m diss* 1983), Jennifer, da of Prof David Daiches; 2ndly, 1986, Catherine Kyle, and has issue.

Hon Allan Graham Ritchie (233A Rotherhithe St, SE16 1XW), *b* 1944; *ed* New Sherwood Sch, Ewell Tech Coll, and London Univ (BSc, PhD); Balloon Pilot and Mathematician: *m* 1st, 1967, Anne Margaret, da of Robert A. Wood; 2ndly, 1983, Lilian Lydia, da of Edward Godfrey, and has issue.

DAUGHTERS LIVING OF LIFE BARON

Hon Fiona Catherine Ritchie, *b* 1929; *ed* Rosebery Co Sch, Epsom, London Sch of Economics (BSc Econ); writer: *m* 1949, Ernest Rudd, DSc (Econ), PhD, of 19 South Parade, York YO2 2BA, and has issue.

Hon Isla Elizabeth Ritchie CALDER (38 Well Court, Edinburgh EH4 3BE) *b* 1947; *ed* Nonsuch Co Sch, Cheam, St George's, Edinburgh, Froebel Inst of Education, Roehampton, and Open Univ (BA); business consultant; resumed surname of Calder by deed poll: *m* 1971 (*m diss* 1983), Alan Evans.

WIDOW LIVING OF LIFE BARON

MABEL JANE FORBES (*Baroness Ritchie-Calder*) (41/45 Leamington Terrace, Edinburgh EH10 4JS), da of Dr David McKail, of Glasgow: *m* 1927, Baron Ritchie-Calder, CBE, (Life Baron), who *d* 1982.

RITCHIE OF DUNDEE, BARON (Ritchie) (Baron UK 1905)

Honour is acquired by virtue

(HAROLD) MALCOLM RITCHIE, 5th Baron; *b* 29 Aug 1919; *s* 1978; *ed* Stowe and Trin Coll, Oxford (MA); 1939-45 War as Capt KRRC: *m* 1948, Anne, da of late Col Charles G. Johnstone, MC, of Durban, S Africa, and has issue.

Arms – Argent, an anchor sable, on a chief of the last three lions' heads erased of the first of the first. **Crest** – Out of an Eastern crown or a unicorn's head argent, armed of the first and charged on the neck with an anchor sable. **Supporters** – On either side a unicorn gules, gorged with an Eastern Crown or, the *dexter* charged on the shoulder with a purse or, the *sinister* with a balance, also or.
Residence – The Roundel, Springsteps, Winchelsea, Sussex.

SON LIVING

Hon (CHARLES) RUPERT RENDALL, *b* 15 March 1958: *m* 1984 (*m diss* 1990), Tara, da of Howard J. Koch, Jr, of USA.

DAUGHTER LIVING

Hon Philippa Jane, *b* 1954.

COLLATERAL BRANCH LIVING

Grandchildren of late Lt-Col Hon Harold Ritchie, DSO (infra):—
    Issue of late Maj Ian Charles Ritchie, RA, *b* 1908, *d* 1983: *m* 1st, 1931 (*m diss* 1946), Ann Dundas, da of late Gen Sir Robert Dundas Whigham, GCB, KCMG, DSO; 2ndly, 1946, Mrs Pamela Eveleen Elizabeth White (Highway House, Hog's Back, Seale, Farnham, Surrey), only da of Reginald Vickers, of Broomwood, Kettlewell Hill, Woking:—
(By 1st *m*) Harold Bruce (PO Box 431, Eltham, Victoria 3095, Australia), *b* 1933; *ed* Repton: *m* 1st, 1967 (*m diss* 1975), Shirley Anne, da of Gordon Steele, of Bury St Edmunds; 2ndly, 1977, Nancy Leith, da of Frank Richard Andrewartha, of Maryborough, Victoria, Australia, and has issue living, (by 1st *m*) Ian Angus Dundas, *b* 1972, — (by 2nd *m*) Fionnah Alice Ellen, *b* 1979. ⸻ Fiona, *b* 1934: *m* 1967 (*m diss* 1975), Kenneth Stewart Donaldson, and *d* 1992.

    Issue of late Lieut-Col Hon Harold Ritchie, DSO (with Bar), The Cameronians (Scottish Rifles), yr son of 1st Baron, *b* 1876, *ka* 1918: *m* 1907, Ella, who *d* 1956 (she *m* 2ndly, 1922, Surg-Lieut-Col Evelyn John Hansler Luxmoore, MC, Life Guards, who *d* 1955), da of late Robert Chambers Priestley, of Terriers House, High Wycombe, Bucks:—
William Nigel, *b* 1914; is a Flt-Lt RAF Vol Res: *m* 1939, Baroness Sibylla, da of late Baron von Hirschberg of Murnau, Bavaria, and has issue living, James Antony Gregor (108A Dartmouth Rd, NW2), *b* 1945; *ed* Harrow, and Ch Ch Oxford, — Andrew William (53 Egerton Gdns, SW3), *b* 1947; *ed* Harrow, and Trin Coll, Camb, — Caroline Elisabeth (*Hon Mrs Hugh Gathorne-Hardy*) *b* 1943: *m* 1971, Hon Hugh Gathorne-Hardy (*see* E Cranbrook). *Residence* – Mariners, Bradfield, Berks.

PREDECESSORS – (1) *Rt Hon* CHARLES THOMSON Ritchie, PC (whose el brother was *cr* a *Baronet* 1903), son of late William Ritchie, of Rockhill, Broughty Ferry, *b* 1838; MP for Tower Hamlets (C) Feb 1874 to Nov 1885, for Tower Hamlets, St George Div 1885 to 1892, and for Croydon May 1895 to Dec 1905; Sec to the Admiralty June 1885 to Jan 1886, Pres of Local Govt Board Aug 1886-1892 (with a seat in the Cabinet from April 1887), Pres of Board of Trade (with seat in the Cabinet) June 1895 to Oct 1900, Sec of State for Home Depart Oct 1900 to Aug 1902, and Chancellor of the Exchequer Aug 1902 to Sept 1903; *cr Baron Ritchie of Dundee*, of Welders, Chalfont St Giles, co Buckingham (peerage of United Kingdom) Dec 1905: *m* 1858, Margaret, who *d* 1905, da of late Thomas Ower, of Perth; *d* Jan 1906; *s* by his el surviving son (2) CHARLES, 2nd Baron; *b* 1866; was Chm of Port of London Authority 1925-41, and Pres of Dock and Harbour Authorities Asso 1938-41: *m* 1898, Sarah Ruth, who *d* 1950, da of late Louis Jennings MP: *d* 1948; *s* by his el surviving son (3) JOHN KENNETH, PC, 3rd Baron; *b* 1902; Chm of London Stock Exchange 1959-65: *m* 1945, Joan Beatrice, who *d* 1963, da of late Rev Henry Charles Lenox Tindall, of Peasmarsh, Sussex; *d* 1975; *s* by his brother (4) COLIN NEVILLE OWER, 4th Baron; *b* 1908; Headmaster of Brickwall Sch, E Sussex: *m* 1943, Anne Petronill, who *d* 1989, da of Henry Curteis Burra, of Rye, and formerly wife of John Francis Burra Huntley; *d* 1978; *s* by his brother (5) HAROLD MALCOLM, 5th Baron, and present peer.

RIVERDALE, BARON (Balfour) (Baron UK 1935, Bt UK 1929)

IN ·ARDUIS· FIDELIS

Faithful in difficulties

ANTHONY ROBERT BALFOUR, 3rd Baron, and 3rd Baronet; *b* 23 Nov 1960; *s* 1998.

Arms – Per chevron argent and sable, in chief two crosses pattée of the second and in base a sun in splendour per pale or and of the first. Crest – In front of a dragon's head sable a sun as in the arms. Supporters – On either side a dragon sable, each charged on the wing, the dexter with a garb, and the sinister with a cross pattée or.
Residence –

SISTERS LIVING

Nancy Ann, *b* 1963.
Kate Frances, *b* 1967.

HALF-UNCLE LIVING (*Son of 2nd Baron by 2nd marriage*)

Hon DAVID ROWLAND, *b* 15 May 1938; *ed* Harrow, and Queens' Coll, Camb (BA 1960).

HALF-AUNT LIVING (*Daughter of 2nd Baron by 2nd marriage*)

Hon Frances Christian, *b* 1946; *ed* Wycombe Abbey, and New Hall, Camb.

GREAT AUNT LIVING (*Daughter of 1st Baron*)

Hon Primrose Keighley, *b* 1913: *m* 1st, 1933, Oliver Grahame Hall, who *d* 1974, having assumed by deed poll 1945 the christian name of Claude in lieu of Oliver, and the surname of Muncaster in lieu of his patronymic; 2ndly, 1975, David John Minnitt, CMG, and has issue living, (by 1st *m*), Martin Grahame Muncaster (Clouds Hill, Lynchmere, Haslemere), *b* 1934: *m* 1959, Iona Gilbert, and has issue living, Timothy Grahame MacGeoch *b* 1960, Oliver Martin Keighley *b* 1964, Miranda Jane *b* 1962, — Clive Muncaster (c/o Whitelocks, Sutton, Pulborough, Sussex), *b* 1936: *m* 1959, Ursula Mary, el da of late Capt Edward Brotherton-Ratcliffe, and has issue living, Maximilian Nicholas Clive *b* 1960, Peregrine Luke (96 West Hill, Hitchin, Herts SG5 2HX) *b* 1962: *m* 1986, Catherine Margaret, da of Michael Andrew Holford, of Icknield House, Westmill Lane, Ickleford, Hitchin, Herts (and has issue living, Dominic Peregrine *b* 1992, Harriet Mary *b* 1988, Georgina Margaret *b* 1990), Crispin Claude *b* 1965, Caspar Amadeus *b* 1967, Quentin Augustine *b* 1971. *Residence –* Whitelocks, Sutton, Pulborough, Sussex. *Club –* Lansdowne.

WIDOW LIVING OF SON OF FIRST BARON

Daphne Cecelia, da of A. C. Moss, of Rochfort, Bathampton, Bath: *m* 1971, as his 2nd wife, Major Hon Francis Henry Balfour, TD, who *d* 1994. *Residence –* Holcombe Cottage, Holcombe Lane, Bathampton, Bath, Som BA2 6UN.

COLLATERAL BRANCH LIVING

Issue of late Major Hon Francis Henry Balfour, TD, son of 1st Baron, *b* 1905; *d* 1994: *m* 1st, 1932, Muriel Anne, who *d* 1970, da of late Eng Rear Adm Ralph Berry; 2ndly, 1971, Daphne Cecelia (ante), da of A. C. Moss, of Rochfort, Bathampton, Bath:—
(By 1st *m*) Arthur Michael (Wynthrop, Chorleywood Rd, Rickmansworth, Herts), *b* 1938; *ed* Oundle, and Bristol Univ (BSc 1960); a GIMechE: *m* 1962, Rita Ann, el da of L. C. Fance, of 21 Ashley Close, Charlton Kings, Cheltenham, Glos, and has issue living, Edward Francis, *b* 1965, — James Henry, *b* 1966, — Anna Louise, *b* 1971. —— Jeremy Ralph (151 Knowle Lane, Brentry, Bristol), *b* 1948; *ed* Oundle, and Plymouth Poly (BSc): *m* 1974, Wendy May, da of W. H. Seal, of 153 Southdown Rd, Bath, and has issue living, Robert Henry, *b* 1980, — Rebecca Ann, *b* 1983. —— Bridget Anne, *b* 1933: *m* 1957, Ewan Peter Graham, of 8 Shrimpton Close, Knotty Green, Beaconsfield, Bucks, and has issue living, Philip James, *b* 1959, — Stephen Paul, *b* 1960, — Adam Timothy, *b* 1964. —— Frances Elizabeth, *b* 1934: *m* 1958, Charles David Plows, MB, and has issue living, Ian Julian, *b* 1960, — Christopher Mark, *b* 1962.

PREDECESSORS – (1) ARTHUR Balfour, GBE, son of late Herbert Balfour; *b* 1873; a Steel Manufacturer, Chm of Arthur Balfour & Co, Ltd, and of C Meadows & Co, Ltd, of Sheffield, Chm of Advisory Council for Scientific and Industrial Research 1937-57, Vice-Consul for Denmark 1899-1947, Master Cutler of Sheffield 1911-12, Pres of Asso of British Chambers of Commerce 1923-4, and of British Council 1947-50; *cr* KBE (Civil) 1923, a *Baronet* 1929, *Baron Riverdale*, of Sheffield, co York (peerage of United Kingdom) 1935, and GBE (Civil) 1942: *m* 1899, Frances Josephine Keighley (a CStJ), who *d* 1960, da of late Charles Henry Bingham; *d* 1957; *s* by his el son (2) ROBERT ARTHUR, 2nd Baron, *b* 1901; Chm and Pres Balfour & Darwins Ltd and a Dir of Subsidiary Cos of the Group; DL S Yorks; Master Cutlers' Co Sheffield; Pres Sheffield Chamber of Commerce, Member Exec Council of Assocn of British Chambers of Commerce (Pres 1957-58), and of many other commercial enterprises; served 1939-45 War as Lt-Cmdr RNVR; Chevalier of Order of the Crown of Belgium, Officer of Order of Leopold II of Belgium, etc: *m* 1st, 1926, Nancy Marguerite, who *d* 1928, da of late Engineer Rear-Adm Mark Rundle, DSO; 2ndly, 1933, Christian Mary, who *d* 1991, da of late Maj Arthur Rowland Hill (*see* V Hill, colls, 1990 Edn); *d* 1998; *s* by his grandson (3) ANTHONY ROBERT (only son of late Hon Mark Robin Balfour, eldest son of 2nd Baron), 3rd Baron and present peer.

RIX, BARON (Rix) (Life Baron 1992)

BRIAN NORMAN ROGER RIX, CBE, son of late Herbert Dobson Rix, of E Yorks; *b* 27 Jan 1924; *ed* Bootham Sch, York; Hon MA Hull 1981, Open Univ 1983, Hon DUniv Essex 1984, Hon LLD Manchester 1986, Hon DSc Nottingham 1987, Hon LLD Dundee 1994, Hon LLD Exeter 1997; served 1939-45 War in RAF also a Bevin Boy; actor-manager 1948-77 (particularly noted for a series of successful farces at the Whitehall Theatre), actor in films and on television, BBC TV and Radio presenter; Dir and Theatre Controller Cooney-Marsh Group 1977-80; Sec-Gen Royal Soc for Mentally Handicapped Children and Adults (MENCAP) 1980-87, Chm 1988-98, since when Pres; Chm Independent Development Council for People with Mental Handicap 1981-88; Member Arts Council 1986-93 (Chm Drama Panel until 1993), Member Barbican Centre Cttee 1993-96, Chm Friends of Normansfield since 1976, Chm Libertas since 1987; Hon Vice-Pres Radio Soc of GB; Hon Fell of Royal Soc of Med; DL Greater London 1987, Vice Lord Lieut 1988-98; author; *cr* CBE (Civil) 1977, Knt 1986, and Baron Rix, of Whitehall, in the City of Westminster, and of Hornsea in Yorkshire (Life Baron) 1992: *m* 1949, Elspet Jeans (actress as Elspet Gray), da of late James MacGregor-Gray, of Surrey, and has issue.

꩜rms – Per chevron double arched points upwards gules and or, in chief a rose argent between two suns in splendour also or and in base chevronwise a Greek mask of comedy vert and a like mask of tragedy sable. ꩜rest – The upper part of a ship's wheel or, standing thereon an avocet wings elevated proper, gorged with a cronal studded gold, pendant therefrom a cross crosslet fitchy sable. ꩜upporters – On either side a labrador dog or, the compartment comprising a grassy mount proper, growing therefrom roses argent barbed and seeded proper, slipped and leaved vert.
Residence – 8 Ellerton Rd, Wimbledon Common, SW20 0EP. *Clubs* – Garrick, Lord's Taverners (Pres 1970), MCC, Yorkshire County Cricket.

SONS LIVING

Hon James MacGregor, *b* 1958; *ed* St Paul's Sch, and Univ of Kent at Canterbury (BA): *m* 1980, Helen Middleton Murry, and has issue living, Benjamin, *b* 1982, — Jack, *b* 1984. *Residence* – 47 Ritherdon Rd, SW17 8QE.

(*Hon*) Jonathan Robert MacGregor, *b* 1960; does not use courtesy title; *ed* St Paul's Sch, and Warwick Univ (BEd): *m* 1991, Caroline Cook, and has issue living, Isabel, *b* 1998.

DAUGHTERS LIVING

Hon Elspet Shelley, *b* 1951. *Residence* – 8/10 Woodlawn Crescent, Whitton, Middx.

Hon Louisa MacGregor, *b* 1955; *ed* Queen's Gate Sch, and LAMDA; actress: *m* 1st, 1981 (*m diss* 1992), Jonathan Coy, actor; 2ndly, 1994, Richard Ommaney, and has issue living (by 1st *m*), Jolyon, *b* 1985, — Charlotte Elizabeth, *b* 1983. *Residence* – 30 Richmond Rd, SW20 0PQ.

ROBBINS, BARONY OF (Robbins) (Extinct 1984)

SON LIVING OF LIFE BARON

Hon Richard, *b* 1927; *ed* Dauntsey's Sch, and New Coll, Oxford: *m* 1st, 1952 (*m diss* 1961); 2ndly, 1961, Mrs Brenda Dorothy Rooker Roberts, da of late Douglas Edward Clark, and has issue by 1st *m*. *Residence* – 20 Muswell Av, N10 2EG.

DAUGHTER LIVING OF LIFE BARON

Hon Anne, *b* 1925; *ed* N London Collegiate Sch, and Univ Coll, London: *m* 1958, Christopher Johnson, of 39 Wood Lane, N6 5UD, and has issue.

ROBENS OF WOLDINGHAM, BARONY OF (Robens) (Extinct 1999)

ALFRED ROBENS, PC, son of late George Robens, of Manchester; *b* 18 Dec 1910; Hon DCL Newcastle; Hon LLD Leicester and Manchester; Hon MIMinE; a Fellow of Manchester Coll of Science and Tech; a Member of Manchester City Council 1942-45, PPS to Min of Transport 1945-47, Parl Sec to Min of Fuel and Power 1947-51, Min of Labour and National Ser April to Oct 1951, and Dep Chm of National Coal Board Oct 1960 to Feb 1961, and Chm 1961-71; a Member of Roy Commn on Trade Unions and Employers' Assocns 1965-68, a Gov of Queen Elizabeth Training Coll for Disabled since 1951, and of London Sch of Economics since 1965, Chm of Board of Govs, Guy's Hosp since 1965, a Dir of Bank of England, and of Times Newspapers since 1966; Pres of Advertising Assocn 1963-67; Chm of Joint Steering Cttee for Malta 1967; Chancellor of Univ of Surrey 1966-77. Chm of Council of Manchester Business Sch since 1964, a Member of NEDC 1962-72, Dep Chm of Foundation on Automation and Human Development since 1962, Chm of Special Cttee of Enquiry into Health and Safety of Persons in Employment, of Vickers Ltd, and of Johnson Matthey Ltd; R Soc of Arts, Albert Medal 1977; MP for Wansbeck Div of Northumberland (*Lab*) 1945-50, and for Blyth 1950-60; *cr* PC 1951, and *Baron Robens of Woldingham*, of Woldingham, co Surrey (Life Baron) 1961: *m* 1936, Eva, da of Frederick Powell, of Manchester. Lord Robens of Woldingham *d* 27 June 1999.

Residence – Salcombe Court, Cliff Rd, Salcombe, Devon TQ8 8JQ.

ROBERTHALL, BARONY (Hall) (Extinct 1988)

DAUGHTERS LIVING OF LIFE BARON (*By 1st marriage*)

Hon Felicity Margaret, *b* 1936; *ed* Oxford High School for Girls, and Lady Margaret Hall, Oxford; editorial and writing consultant: *m* 1957, Thomas Skidmore, of 44 Halsey St, Providence, Rhode Island 02906, USA, and has issue.

Hon Anthea Mary, *b* 1939; *ed* Oxford High Sch for Girls, and Lady Margaret Hall, Oxford; Journalist: *m* 1966, (David) Max Wilkinson, 112 Hemingford Rd, N1 1DE, and has issue.

WIDOW LIVING OF LIFE BARON

PERILLA THYME (*Baroness Roberthall*), da of late Sir Richard Vynne Southwell, and formerly wife of Patrick Horace Nowell-Smith: *m* 1968, as his 2nd wife, Baron Roberthall, KCMG, CB (Life Baron), who *d* 1988. *Residence* – Quarry, Trenance, Newquay, Cornwall.

Roberts, family name of Baron Clwyd.

ROBERTS OF CONWY, BARON (Roberts) (Life Baron 1997)

(IEUAN) WYN PRITCHARD ROBERTS, PC son of late Rev Evan Pritchard Roberts, of Anglesey; *b* 10 July 1930; *ed* Harrow, and Univ Coll, Oxford; journalist with *The Liverpool Post* 1952-54; News Assist, BBC 1954-57; Welsh Controller and Exec Producer, TWW 1957-68; Programme Exec, Harlech TV 1969; MP for Conwy (*C*) 1970-97; PPS to Sec of State for Wales 1970-74; Opposition Front Bench Spokesman on Welsh Affairs 1974-79; Parliamentary Under-Sec, Welsh Office 1979-87; Min of State for Wales 1987-94; Memb Gorsedd, Royal Nat Eisteddfod 1966; *cr* Kt 1990, PC 1991, and *Baron Roberts of Conwy*, of Talyfan, co Gwynedd (Life Baron) 1997: *m* 1956, Enid Grace, da of William Williams, of Anglesey, and has issue.

Arms – Paly of six argent and vert a cross patonce gules on a chief engrailed of three arches also gules three ancient lamps argent. Crest – A demi lion with dragon's wings gules armed argent and grasping with both paws a trumpet the bell downwards or. Supporters – On either side a dragon gules armed argent dimidiating a lion gules armed argent each supporting with the exterior fore foot a plain carnyx argent garnished and the bell downwards or.
Residence – Tan y Gwalia, Conwy, Gwynedd LL32 8TY. *Clubs* – Savile, Cardiff and County (Cardiff).

SONS LIVING

Hon Rhys, *b* 1956; *ed* John Bright's Sch and Reading Univ.
Hon Geraint, *b* 1958; *ed* St David's Coll.
Hon Huw, *b* 1960; *ed* Aberconwy Sch: *m* 1990, Sian Bassett, and has issue living, Rhidian Wyn, *b* 1993, — Garmon Huw, *b* 1995.

Roberts, see Baron Goronwy-Roberts.

Robertson, family name of Baroness Wharton.

ROBERTSON OF OAKRIDGE, BARON (Robertson) (Baron UK 1961 Bt UK 1919)

WILLIAM RONALD ROBERTSON, 2nd Baron, and 3rd Baronet; *b* 8 Dec 1930; *s* 1974; *ed* Charterhouse; Maj (ret) R Scots Greys: *m* 1972, Celia Jane, yr da of William Elworthy, of the Manor House, Winterborne Monkton, Dorchester, Dorset, and has issue.

Arms – Gules, two swords in saltire argent, hilted and pommelled gold, the points downwards, between in chief a sun in splendour, in base a fleur-de-lis or, and in fesse two wolves' heads erased of the second. Crest – Issuant from a coronet of fleur-de-lis or, a demi-wolf argent, gorged with an Eastern crown gold supporting with the dexter paw a lance proper thereon a pennon per fesse gules and argent. Supporters – *Dexter*, a grey charger in review order; *sinister*, a springbok proper.

SON LIVING

Hon WILLIAM BRIAN ELWORTHY, *b* 15 Nov 1975.

SISTER LIVING

Hon (Catherine) Fiona, *b* 1939: *m* 1965, Allan Claude Chapman, DL, and has issue living, Caroline Fiona, *b* 1968, — Katharine Jean, *b* (twin) 1968: *m* 1993, David J. Cook, son of Dr John Cook, of Bagshot, Surrey, and has issue living, James Harry *b* 1998.

AUNT LIVING

Helen Millicent (*Helen, Lady Vincent*), *b* 1905: *m* 1938, Sir Lacey Eric Vincent, 2nd Bt (*cr* 1936), who *d* 1963.

PREDECESSOR – (1) *Field-Marshal Sir* WILLIAM ROBERT Robertson, GCB, GCMG, GCVO, DSO, son of late Thomas Charles Robertson; *b* 1860; enlisted in 16th Lancers 1877; commissioned as 2nd Lieut 3rd Dragoon Guards 1888; Chitral Relief Force 1895 (severely wounded DSO), S Africa 1900 as DAAG, Army Head Quarters, European War 1914-19, becoming Ch of Imperial Gen Staff (Legion of Honour, KCB, Lieut-Gen, Croix de Guerre, Orders of Crown of Italy, of White Eagle of Serbia with Swords, of Chia Ho of China, of St Alexander Nevsky of Russia and of Rising Sun of Japan, GCMG, thanked by Parliament, granted £10,000); *cr* a *Baronet* 1919: *m* 1894, Mildred Adelaide, who *d* 1942, da of late Lieut-Gen T. C. Palin, Indian Army, *d* 1933; *s* by his son (2) BRIAN HUBERT, GCB, GBE, KCMG, KCVO, DSO, MC, 2nd Bt, *b* 1896; mil Gov of British Zone, Germany 1947-49, UK High Commr for Germany 1949-50, C-in-C, MELF 1950-53, Chm of British Transport Commn 1953-61; Col Comdr RE 1950-60, and REME 1951-61; *cr Baron Robertson of Oakridge*, of Oakridge, Glos (peerage of UK) 1961: *m* 1926, Edith Christina, OStJ, who *d* 1982, da of James Black Macindoe, of Glasgow; *d* 1974; *s* by his son (3) WILLIAM RONALD, 2nd Baron and present peer.

ROBINS, BARONY OF (Robins) (Extinct 1962)

DAUGHTERS LIVING OF FIRST BARON

Hon Diana Mary Wroughton, *b* 1920: *m* 1940, Col John Offley Crewe-Read, OBE, who *d* 1996, of Croft House, Aston Tirrold, nr Didcot, Oxon, and has issue living, David Offley (Werg's Farm, Old Burghclere, Hants; The Pine Mine, Wandsworth Bridge Rd, SW6), *b* 1944: *m* 1st, 1966, Lisa, elder da of H. J. Dyer, of Odiham; 2ndly, 1999, Emma Louise, da of late Ian Garton, and of Mrs Michael James, of Playford, Suffolk, and has issue living (by 1st wife), Caspian Dante David Offley *b* 1967, Daniel Osiris John *b* 1972, Gabriella Diana *b* 1974, (by 2nd wife), Beatrice Florence Sweet-Honey-Bee *b* 1997, — Christopher Thomas Malcolm (1450 Kastner Place, Suite 100B, Sandford, Florida 32771, USA), *b* 1951: *m* 1980 (*m diss* 1989), Belinda, yst da of Sir Reginald Bennett, VRD, of 19 Elm Lodge, River Gardens, Stevenage Rd, SW6, and has issue living, Chloe Evelyn *b* 1985, Madeleine Brittain *b* 1988, — Joanna Christina (17 The Little Boltons, SW10 9LJ), *b* 1941: *m* 1st, 1962 (*m diss* 1969), Capt John Anthony Frank Morton, late RHA; 2ndly, 1974, Alasdair James Hew Saunders (*see* Culme-Seymour Bt, colls), and has issue living (by 1st *m*), Dominic Jonathan Ellis *b* 1964, Serena Mary Louise *b* 1966, (by 2nd *m*) Thomas Alasdair *b* 1978, Alice Elizabeth *b* 1975.

Hon Philippa Mary Ellis, *b* 1923: *m* 1st, 1946, Col Patrick James Danvers McCraith, MC, TD, DL, who *d* 1998; 2ndly, 1999, William Weatherley, of Mortlake, Victoria, Australia, and has issue living (by 1st *m*), Michael Ellis, *b* 1949: *m* 1981 (*m diss* 19—), Sarah Anne, el da of William Bromley, of Apperley, Gerrards Cross, Bucks, and has issue living, Flora Kate Mary *b* 1982, Alice Clementine *b* 1985, — Sally Victoria, *b* 1947: *m* 1971, Patrick George Francis Lort-Phillips, Lt-Col 9th/12th Lancers (V Cobham, colls, 1972-73 Edn), and has issue living, Harry Patrick Francis *b* 1975, Charles Arthur Ellis *b* 1980, Alexandra Mary *b* 1972. *Residence* – Cranfield House, Southwell, Notts.

Robinson, family name of Baron Martonmere.

ROBOROUGH, BARON (Lopes) (Baron UK 1938, Bt UK 1805)

Do to another as you would be done by

HENRY MASSEY LOPES, 3rd Baron, and 6th Baronet; *b* 2 Feb 1940; *s* 1992; *ed* Eton; late Lieut Coldstream Guards: *m* 1st, 1968 (*m diss* 1986), Robyn Zenda Carol, eldest da of John Bromwich, of Stamford Hill, Bacchus Marsh, Victoria, Australia; 2ndly, 1986, Sarah Anne Pipon, 2nd da of Colin Baker, of The Glebe House, Peter Tavy, Tavistock, Devon, and has issue by 1st and 2nd *m*.

𝕬rms – Quarterly: 1st and 4th, azure, a chevron or charged with three bars gemells; gules between three eagles rising of the second on a chief of the second five lozenges of the first; 2nd and 3rd, in a landscape field a fountain proper, thereout issuing a palm-tree also proper. 𝕮rests – 1st, a lion sejant erminois gorged with a collar gemelle gules, the dexter forepaw resting on a lozenge azure; 2nd, a dexter arm couped and embowed, habited purpure, purfled and diapered or, cuffed argent, holding in the hand proper a palm-branch vert. 𝔰upporters – *Dexter*, a lion proper gorged with a collar gemel and charged on the shoulder with a lozenge azure; *sinister*, a bull also proper, charged on the shoulder with a like lozenge.
Seat – Maristow, Roborough, S Devon. *Residence* – Bickham House, Roborough, S Devon.

SONS LIVING (*By 1st marriage*)

Hon MASSEY JOHN HENRY, *b* 22 Dec 1969; *ed* Eton, and — Coll, Durham: *m* 1996, Jean Campbell Sorell, da of Hon Mr Justice Underwood, of Newtown, Tasmania, and of Mrs Sally Sorell, of Sandy Bay, Tasmania, and has issue living, Henry Massey Peter, *b* 30 July 1997, — Ralph George Franco, *b* 1999.
Hon Andrew James, *b* 1971; *ed* Plymouth Coll: *m* 1993, Kristina Marie Overbeck.

DAUGHTERS LIVING (*By 1st marriage*)

Hon Katie Victoria, *b* 1976.
Hon Melinda Claire, *b* 1978.

(*By 2nd marriage*)

Hon Emily Jane, *b* 1987.
Hon Louisa Constance, *b* 1989.

BROTHER LIVING

Hon George Edward, *b* 1945; *ed* Eton, and RAC Cirencester: *m* 1975, Hon Sarah Violet Astor, da of 2nd Baron Astor of Hever, and has issue living, Harry Marcus George, *b* 1977; *ed* Eton, — Lorna Violet, *b* 1979, — Sabrina Helen, *b* 1983. *Residence* – Gnaton Hall, Yealmpton, Plymouth, Devon PL8 2HU.

PREDECESSORS – (1) MANASSEH MASSEY LOPES, son of late Mordecai- Rodrigues Lopes, of Clapham, SW; *b* 1755; was successively MP for Evesham, South Devon, Barnstaple, and Westbury; *cr* a Baronet 1805 with special remainder to his nephew, Ralph Franco, son of his yr sister, Esther, wife of Abraham Franco, of London: *m* 1795, Charlotte, who *d* 1833, da of late John Yeates, of Monmouthshire; *d* 1831; *s* by his nephew (2) RALPH (ante), 2nd Bt; *b* 1788; assumed by Roy licence 1831 the surname of Lopes in lieu of his patronymic and the arms of Lopes quarterly with those of Franco; sat as MP for Westbury (C) 1832-7 and 1841-7, and for South Devonshire (C)1849-54: *m* 1817, Susan Gibbs, who *d* 1870, el da of late A. Ludlow, of Heywood House, Wilts; *d* 1854; *s* by his el son (3) (LOPES) MASSEY, PC, 3rd Bt; *b* 1818; sat as MP for Westbury (C) 1857-68, and Devonshire, S Div 1868-85, and was a Civil Lord of the Admiralty 1874-80: *m* 1st, 1854, Hon Bertha Yarde Buller, who *d* 1872, da of 1st Baron Churston; 2ndly, 1874, Louisa, who *d* April 1908, da of Sir Robert William Newman, 1st Bt (*cr* 1836); *d* Jan 1908; *s* by his only son (4) HENRY YARDE BULLER, 4th Bt; *b* 1859; sat as MP for Grantham (C) 1892-1900; *cr* Baron Roborough, of Maristow, co Devon (peerage of United Kingdom) Jan 1938: *m* 1891, Lady Albertha Louisa Florence Edgcumbe, who *d* 1941, da of 4th Earl of Mount Edgcumbe; *d* April 1938; *s* by his only son (5) MASSEY HENRY EDGCUMBE, 2nd Baron; *b* 1903, Major Royal Scots Greys, Hon Col Devon Army Cadet Force, 1939-45 War with RAC (wounded twice), ADC to Gov-Gen of S Africa 1936, DL Exeter 1946, Vice-Lieut 1951-58, Lord Lieut and Custos Rotulorum 1958-78, High Steward Barnstaple, 1st Pres Devon Historical Buildings Trust 1965-78, and

Memb of Duchy of Cornwall Council 1958-68: *m* 1936, Helen, who *d* 1998, only da of late Lt-Col Edward Alfred Finch Dawson, Rifle Bde, of Launde Abbey, Leics; *d* 1992; *s* by his elder son **(6)** HENRY MASSEY 3rd Baron and present peer.

ROBSON OF KIDDINGTON, BARONY OF (Robson) (Extinct 1999)

SON LIVING OF LIFE BARONESS

Hon (Erik) Maurice William (Kiddington Hall, Woodstock, Oxon; Erchless Castle, Struy, by Beauly, Inverness), *b* 1943; *ed* Eton, and Ch Ch, Oxford (MA); FCA: *m* 1985, Chloe Annabel, elder da of Richard Arthur Edwards, of Ipswich, Suffolk (*see* B Hylton, colls), and has issue living, James Patrick, *b* 1990, — Natasha Lilly, *b* 1993.

DAUGHTERS LIVING OF LIFE BARONESS

Hon Kristina Elizabeth, *b* 1946: *m* 1967, Iain McLaren Mason, of 17 Crick Rd, Oxford.
Hon Vanessa Jane, *b* 1949; MB BS London 1974: *m* 1973, Dr Jonathan Martin Potter, of Tyler Hall, Tyler Hill, Canterbury, Kent, and has issue living, Lawrence Eliot, *b* 1975, — Jesica Louise, *b* 1977, — Rebecca Jane, *b* 1981.

ROCHDALE, VISCOUNT (Kemp) (Baron UK 1913, Viscount UK 1960)

I hope for light

ST JOHN DURIVAL KEMP, 2nd Viscount; *b* 15 Jan 1938; *s* 1993; *ed* Eton: *m* 1st, 1960 (*m diss* 1974), Serena Jane, da of late (James Edward) Michael Clark-Hall, of Wissenden, Bethersden, Kent; 2ndly, 1976, Elizabeth, da of Robert Norman Rossiter Boldon, and formerly wife of James Michael Anderton, and has issue by 1st *m*.

𝔄rms – Argent, a chevron engrailed gules between two estoiles in chief azure, and a rose of the second in base barbed and seeded proper. 𝔊rest – A cubit arm erect, vested argent, cuffed azure, the hand proper grasping a chaplet vert encircling a rose as in the arms. 𝔖upporters – On either side a ram or, charged on the shoulder with a rose gules, slipped and leaved proper.
Address – c/o House of Lords, SW1A 0PW.

SONS LIVING (*By 1st marriage*)

Hon JONATHAN HUGO DURIVAL, *b* 10 June 1961; *ed* Stowe: *m* 1994, Ming Xian, only da of Mr and Mrs Zhu, of Shanghai.
Hon Christopher George, *b* 1969.

DAUGHTERS LIVING (*By 1st marriage*)

Hon Joanna Victoria, *b* 1964.
Hon Susanna Jane, *b* 1965.

PREDECESSORS – **(1)** GEORGE Kemp, CB, son of late George Tawke Kemp, of Beechwood, Rochdale; *b* 1866; Chm of Kelsall & Kemp, Ltd, woollen manufacturers, and Lord-Lieut of Middx; S Africa 1900-1902 with Imperial Yeo (despatches), 1914-19 War in Gallipoli and Egypt as Brig-Gen; MP for Heywood Div of Lancs (*L*) 1895-1906, and for N-W Div of Manchester 1910-12; *cr Baron Rochdale*, of Rochdale, co Palatine of Lancaster (peerage of United Kingdom) 1913: *m* 1896, Lady Beatrice Mary Egerton, MBE, who *d* 1966, da of 3rd Earl of Ellesmere; *d* 1945; *s* by his son **(2)** JOHN DURIVAL, OBE, TD, 1st Viscount; *b* 1906; 1939-45 War in Europe, Pacific (US Forces) and India (despatches), Col late RA (TA), Hon Brig; DL Cumbria 1948-83; Chm Kelsall & Kemp, Rochdale, 1950-71, Dep-Chm W Riding Worsted & Woollen Co Ltd, 1969-72, Williams & Glyn's Bank Ltd, 1973-77, and other Cos; *cr Viscount Rochdale*, of Rochdale, co Palatine of Lancaster (peerage of UK) 1960: *m* 1931, Elinor Dorothea, CBE, who *d* 1997, da of late Ernest Hubert Pease, of Mowden, Darlington; *d* 1993; *s* by his only son **(3)** ST JOHN DURIVAL, 2nd Viscount and present peer; also Baron Rochdale.

Roche, family name of Baron Fermoy.

ROCHESTER, BARON (Lamb) (Baron UK 1931)

FOSTER CHARLES LOWRY LAMB, 2nd Baron; *b* 7 June 1916; *s* 1955; *ed* Mill Hill, and Jesus Coll, Camb (MA); formerly Capt 23rd Hussars; joined ICI Ltd 1946, Labour Manager, Alkali Div 1955-63 Personnel Manager, Mond Div 1964-72; Pro-Chancellor of Univ of Keele 1976-86; DL Cheshire 1979; DUniv Keele 1986: *m* 1942, Mary Carlisle, BA, da of Thomas Benjamin Wheeler, CBE, and has issue.
Residence – 337 Chester Rd, Hartford, Northwich, Cheshire CW8 1QR.

SONS LIVING

Hon DAVID CHARLES, *b* 8 Sept 1944; *ed* Shrewsbury and Sussex Univ: *m* 1969, Jacqueline Agnes, da of John Alfred Stamp, of Torquay, and has issue living, Daniel, *b* 1971, — Joe, *b* 1972. *Residence –* The Anchorage, 1 Beresford Av, Twickenham, Middx TW1 2PY.
Hon Timothy Michael, *b* 1953; *ed* Shrewsbury, and The Queen's Coll, Oxford; formerly a professional cricketer; Sec/Gen Man Middx County Cricket Club 1984-87; Cricket Sec, Test and County Cricket Board, 1988-96; Chief Exec England and Wales Cricket Board (ECB) since 1997: *m* 1978, Denise Ann, da of John Buckley, of Frinton-on-Sea, Essex, has issue living, Nicholas, *b* 1985, — Sophie, *b* 1983.

DAUGHTER LIVING

Hon Elizabeth Mary, *b* 1951: *m* 1974, Thomas Meredith McIlroy, and has issue living, Samuel, *b* 1975, — Duncan, *b* 1977, — John Benjamin, *b* 1979, — Catherine, *b* 1989.

BROTHER LIVING

Rev Hon Roland Hurst Lowry, *b* 1917; *ed* Mill Hill, and Jesus Coll, Camb, (BA 1938, MA 1942); sometime Chap RAF; Gen Sec of British Evangelical Council 1967-82: *m* 1943, Vera Alicia, da of late A. H. Morse, and has issue living, Andrew Michael (5 Flint Lane, South Darley, Matlock, Derbys), *b* 1951: *m* 1974, Helen, da of late Eric Mitchell, of 30 Fisher Av, Rugby, and has issue living, Benjamin James *b* 1980, Rebecca Mary Alicia *b* 1982, — Rosemary Elizabeth, *b* 1947: *m* 1969, David Michael John Pike, of 3 Laburnum Rd, Weston-super-Mare, and has issue living, Martin John *b* 1973, Sarah Louise *b* 1971, — Hilary Jennifer, *b* 1949: *m* 1972, Prof Howard Jackson, of 11 Fox Hill, Selly Oak, Birmingham, and has issue living, Nathan Dieter *b* 1976, Kirsten Renate *b* 1978, Lydia Ruth *b* 1985, — Valerie Judith, *b* 1955: *m* 1978, Joseph George Unsworth, of 73 Elwyn Drive, Halewood Village, Merseyside L26 0DX and has issue living, Joseph Jonathan *b* 1993, Jodi Ann *b* 1980, Amy Ruth *b* 1983, Mia Dawn *b* 1986. *Residence –* 74 Rutland Av, Halewood Village, Merseyside L26 0TP.

SISTER LIVING

Hon Muriel Joan Lowry, *b* 1921; *ed* Oxford Univ (BA 1943, MA 1957); Senior Lecturer in Education, Loughborough Coll of Education; PT tutor counsellor, Open Univ, 1977-84; formerly 3rd Sec, British Embassy, Oslo: *m* 1947 (*m diss* 1957), William Oswald Collier (*see* B Monkswell, colls). *Residence –* Cloudberry Cottage, 8 Unicorn St, Bloxham, Oxon OX15 4QA.

WIDOW LIVING OF SON OF FIRST BARON

Elizabeth Anne, da of late D. A. Saul, and step-da of J. B. Allan, of 187 Queen's Gate, SW7: *m* 1952, Hon Kenneth Henry Lowry Lamb, CBE, who *d* 1995, and has issue (see colls infra). *Residence –* 25 South Terr, SW7 2TB.

COLLATERAL BRANCH LIVING

Issue of late Hon Kenneth Henry Lowry Lamb, CBE, yst son of 1st Baron, *b* 1923, *d* 1995: *m* 1952, Elizabeth Anne (ante), da of late D. A. Saul, and step-da of J. B. Allan, of 187 Queen's Gate, SW7:—
Stephen Ernest Henry (28 Southernhay Av, Clifton, Bristol BS8 5TJ), *b* 1957: *m* 1990, Sue M., elder da of W. J. Turner, of Clevedon, Avon. —— Sarah Elizabeth Hurst, *b* 1955. —— Caroline Mary Anne, *b* 1966: *m* 1992, Paul J. O. Knight, Lieut RN, son of Dr Peter Knight, of Austin, Texas.

PREDECESSOR – (1) ERNEST HENRY LAMB, CMG, el son of late Benjamin Lamb, of Thorndown, Windlesham, Surrey, and Shorne, Rochester, Kent, *b* 1876; a retired Transport Contractor; was Paymaster-Gen (in National Govt) 1931-35; represented Min of Labour in House of Lords 1931-5; Vice-Pres of Methodist Church 1941-2, and of British Council of

Churches 1942-4; sat as MP for Rochester (*L*) 1906-10, and 1910-18; *cr Baron Rochester*, of Rochester, co Kent (peerage of United Kingdom) 1931: *m* 1913, Rosa Dorothea, who *d* 1979, yr da of late William John Hurst, JP, of Drumaness, Ballynahinch, co Down; *d* 1955; *s* by his el son (2) FOSTER CHARLES LOWRY, 2nd Baron and present peer.

ROCKLEY, BARON (Cecil) (Baron UK 1934)

JAMES HUGH CECIL, 3rd Baron; *b* 5 April 1934; *s* 1976; *ed* Eton, and New Coll, Oxford; Master Salters' Co 1998: *m* 1958, Lady Sarah Primrose Beatrix Cadogan, el da of 7th Earl Cadogan, and has issue.

Arms – Barry of ten argent and azure, over all six escutcheons, three, two, and one, sable, each charged with a lion rampant of the first, and for difference a crescent gules charged with another crescent or, a crescent gules for difference. **Crest** – Six arrows in saltire or, barbed and flighted argent, girt together with a belt gules, buckled and garnished gold, over the arrows a morion cap proper. **Supporters** – On either side a lion ermine, gorged with a collar or pendent therefrom an escutcheon, the dexter sable a lion argent, and the sinister gules, three tilting spears erect or, headed argent.
Residence – Lytchett Heath, Poole, Dorset BH16 6AE.

Late, but in earnest

SON LIVING

Hon ANTHONY ROBERT, *b* 29 July 1961; *ed* Eton, and Camb Univ: *m* 1988, Katherine Jane, da of G. A. Whalley, of Chipperfield, Herts, and has issue living, William Evelyn, *b* 7 July 1996, — Emily Sarah, *b* 1991, — Lydia Elizabeth, *b* 1994.

DAUGHTERS LIVING

Hon Caroline Anne, *b* 1960: *m* 1985, Mark G. Preston, yr son of Simon Preston, of Lowfield Farm, Tetbury, Glos, and has issue living, Hugh Simon, *b* 1987, — Edward James, *b* 1989, — Lucy Camilla, *b* 1991.

Hon Camilla Sarah, *b* 1965; Social Ed *Harpers & Queen* since 1998: *m* 1998, Henry Nicholas Mountain (*see* Mountain, Bt).

BROTHER LIVING

Hon Charles Evelyn (Wilcote House, Charlbury, Oxon), *b* 1936; *ed* Eton: *m* 1965, Jennifer Anne, da of Duncan Mackinnon, of Swinbrook House, Burford, Oxon, and has issue living, David *b* 1971, — Arabella Elizabeth, *b* 1967, — Lucinda, *b* 1970.

SISTER LIVING

Hon Elizabeth Anne, *b* 1939: *m* 1961, Capt Andrew Lyon Wills, late Life Guards, who *d* 1998 (*see* Wills, Bt (*cr* 1904), colls). *Residence* – Gavelacre House, Longparish, Andover, Hants.

PREDECESSORS – (1) *Rt Hon Sir* EVELYN Cecil, GBE, el son of late Lieut-Col Lord Eustace Brownlow Henry Gascoyne Cecil (M Salisbury, colls); *b* 1865; MP for Herts E, or Hertford Div (*C*) 1898-1900, for Aston Manor 1900-1918, and for Aston Div of Birmingham 1918-29; *cr Baron Rockley*, of Lytchett Heath, co Dorset (peerage of United Kingdom) 1934: *m* 1898, Hon Alicia Margaret Amherst, CBE, who *d* 1941, da of 1st Baron Amherst of Hackney; *d* 1941; *s* by his son (2) ROBERT WILLIAM EVELYN, 2nd Baron; *b* 1901: *m* 1933, Anne Margaret, who *d* 1980, da of late Adm Hon Sir Herbert Meade-Featherstonhaugh, GCVO, CB, DSO (E Clanwilliam, colls); *d* 1976; *s* by his el son (3) JAMES HUGH, 3rd Baron and present peer.

Rodd, family name of Baron Rennell.

RODEN, EARL OF (Jocelyn) (Earl I 1771, Bt E 1665)

To do my duty

ROBERT JOHN JOCELYN, 10th Earl, and 14th Baronet; *b* 25 Aug 1938; *s* 1993: *m* 1st, 1970 (*m diss* 1982), Sara Cecilia, da of late Brig Andrew Dunlop, of Que Que, Zimbabwe; 2ndly, 1986, Ann Margareta Maria, da of late Dr Gunnar Albert Philip Henning, of Göteborg, Sweden, and has issue by 1st and 2nd *m*.

Arms – Azure, a circular wreath or torse argent and sable, with four hawks' bells conjoined thereto in quadrangle or. Crest – A falcon's leg erased at the thigh proper, belled or. Supporters – Two falcons proper, wings inverted belled or.
Residence – Doon House, Cashel, co Galway, Ireland.

SON LIVING (*By 2nd marriage*)

SHANE ROBERT HENNING (*Viscount Jocelyn*), *b* 9 Dec 1989.

DAUGHTER LIVING (*By 1st marriage*)

Lady Cecilia Rose, *b* 1976.

BROTHER LIVING

Hon James Michael, *b* 1943; *ed* Stowe, and Trin Coll, Dublin. *Residence* – Glynsk, Cashel, Connemara, co Galway.

COLLATERAL BRANCH LIVING

Issue of Lt-Cdr Hon Thomas Alan Jocelyn, RN, 2nd son of 9th Earl, *b* 1941, missing, feared lost at sea, 1991: *m* 1966 (*m diss* 1982), Fiona Alice, da of Capt Rudland Dallas Cairns, DSC, RN (*see* Simpson, Bt, ext):—
Charles Patrick, *b* 1978. —— Moira Anne, *b* 1969. —— Caragh Clodagh, *b* 1975.

PREDECESSORS – (1) ROBERT Jocelyn, successively Solicitor-Gen, Attorney-Gen, and Lord High Chancellor of Ireland, and twelve times a Lord Justice in the absence of the Viceroy, was *cr Baron Newport*, of Newport (peerage of Ireland) 1743, and *Viscount Jocelyn* (peerage of Ireland) 1755; *d* 1756; *s* by his son (2) ROBERT, 2nd Viscount; was MP for Old Leighlin 1743, and Auditor-Gen of Ireland 1750; *s* by his kinsman as 5th Bt 1770 (see * infra); *cr Earl of Roden*, of High Roding, co Tipperary (peerage of Ireland) 1771; *d* 1797; *s* by his son (3) ROBERT, KP, 2nd Earl; was MP for Dundalk, and joint Auditor-Gen for Ireland; *d* 1820; *s* by his son (4) ROBERT, KP, PC, 3rd Earl, *b* 1788; was MP for Dundalk, Auditor-Gen of the Exchequer in Ireland, and Custos Rotulorum of co Louth; *cr Baron Clanbrassil*, of Hyde Hall, co Herts (peerage of United Kingdom) 1821; *s* by his grandson (5) ROBERT, 4th Earl; was a Lord-in-Waiting to HM 1874-80; *d* unmarried 1880; *s* by his uncle (6) JOHN STRANGE, 5th Earl (2nd son of 3rd Earl), *b* 1823; *m* 1851, Hon Sophia Hobhouse, who *d* 1916, 2nd da of 1st Baron Broughton; *d* 1897, when the Barony of Clanbrassil became ext and he was *s* in other honours by his kinsman (7) WILLIAM HENRY (son of late Hon John Jocelyn, 4th son of 2nd Earl), 6th Earl, *b* 1842; *d* 1910; *s* by his brother (8) ROBERT JULIAN, 7th Earl, *b* 1845; Lieut-Col in the Army: *m* 1882, Ada Maria, who *d* 1931, da of late Col Soame Gambier Jenyns, CB; *d* 1915; *s* by his son (9) ROBERT SOAME, 8th Earl; *b* 1883; Capt (ret) N Irish Horse, and a Representative Peer: *m* 1905, Elinor Jessie, who *d* 1962, da of late Joseph Charlton Parr; *d* 1956; *s* by his son (10) ROBERT WILLIAM, 9th Earl; *b* 1909; Capt RN, served European War 1939-45 (despatches thrice): *m* 1937, Clodagh Rose, who *d* 1989, da of late Edward Robert Kennedy (*see* Kennedy, Bt, colls, 1990 Edn); *d* 1993; *s* by his eldest son (11) ROBERT JOHN, 10th Earl and present peer; also Viscount Jocelyn and Baron Newport.
*(1) ROBERT Jocelyn, of Hyde Hall; *cr* a *Baronet* 1665; *d* 1712; *s* by his son (2) *Sir* STRANGE 2nd Bt; *d* 1734; *s* by his el son (3) *Sir* JOHN, 3rd Bt; *d* unmarried 1741; *s* by his brother (4) *Sir* CONVERS, MD, 4th Bt; Sheriff of Hertford 1745; *d* unmarried 1770; *s* by his kinsman (5) ROBERT, 2nd Viscount Jocelyn (see ante) grandson of Thomas, 3rd son of 1st Bt.

RODGER OF EARLSFERRY, BARON (Rodger) (Life Baron 1992)

ALAN FERGUSON RODGER, son of late Prof Thomas Ferguson Rodger, CBE, of Glasgow; *b* 18 Sept 1944; *ed* Kelvinside Academy, Glasgow, Glasgow Univ (MA, LLB), and New Coll, Oxford (DCL, MA, DPhil); Hon Bencher Lincoln's Inn 1992; Research Fellow Balliol Coll, Oxford 1969-70, Fellow and Tutor in Law New Coll, Oxford 1970-72, Member Faculty of Advocates 1974, Clerk of Faculty 1976-79, Standing Jr Counsel (Scotland) to Dept of Trade 1979, QC 1985, Advocate Depute 1985-88, Home Advocate Depute 1986-88, Solicitor Gen for Scotland 1989-92, Lord Advocate of Scotland 1992-96, since when Lord Justice-Gen and Lord Pres of the Court of Session; Member Mental Welfare Commn for Scotland 1982-85, Maccabaeah Lect British Academy 1991; FBA 1991, FRSE 1992; *cr Baron Rodger of Earlsferry*, of Earlsferry in the District of NE Fife (Life Baron) 1992.
Address – Lord Advocate's Chambers, Regent Rd, Edinburgh EH7 5BL. *Club* – Athenaeum.

RODGERS OF QUARRY BANK, BARON (Rodgers) (Life Baron 1992)

WILLIAM THOMAS RODGERS, PC, son of William Arthur Rodgers, of Liverpool; *b* 28 Oct 1928; *ed* Quarry Bank High Sch, Liverpool, and Magdalen Coll, Oxford; Parl Under Sec Dept of Economic Affairs 1964-67, Foreign Office (Leader of UK Delegation to Council of Europe & Assembly of Western European Union) 1967-68, Min of State Board of Trade 1968-69, Treasury 1969-70, Min of Defence 1974-76, Sec of State for Transport 1976-79; Gen-Sec Fabian Soc 1953-60 (member until 1981); Chm Expenditure Cttee Trade & Industry 1971-74; Dir-Gen RIBA 1987-94; MP for Stockton-on-Tees (*Lab* 1962-81, *SDP* 1981-83) 1962-74, and Teesside, Stockton 1974-83; author of *Hugh Gaitskell* (1963), *The People into Parliament* (1966), *The Politics of Change* (1982), *Government and Industry* (1986), etc; *cr* PC 1975, and *Baron Rodgers of Quarry Bank*, of Kentish Town in the London Borough of Camden (Life Baron) 1992: *m* 1955, Silvia, da of Hirsch Szulman, of London, and has issue, three das.
Residence – 43 North Hill, N6 4BE. *Club* – Garrick.

RODNEY, BARON (Rodney) (Baron GB 1782, Bt GB 1764)

Eagles do not bring forth doves

GEORGE BRYDGES RODNEY, 10th Baron, and 10th Baronet; *b* 3 Jan 1953; *s* 1992; *ed* Eton: *m* 1996, Jane, da of H...... Rowan Blakeney, of The Old Rectory, Hatherop, Glos, and has issue.

Arms – Or: three eagles displayed with wings inverted purpure. **Crest** – On a ducal coronet or, an eagle, wings displayed and inverted purpure. **Supporters** – Two eagles, wings inverted purpure, beaked and membered or, each sustaining with the interior claw a banner of St George, the staves proper, each enfiled with a naval coronet gold.
Residence – 38 Pembroke Rd, W8 6NU.

SON LIVING

Hon JOHN GEORGE BRYDGES, *b* 5 July 1999.

SISTER LIVING

Hon Anne, *b* 1955; resumed her maiden name 1982: *m* 1st, 1982 (*m diss* 19—), Hugh Lusted, PhD, of San Francisco, Calif, USA; 2ndly, 1991, Alexander Constantine Basil D'Janoeff, son of late Constantine V. D'Janoeff, of Windsor, Berks, and has issue living (by 2nd *m*), Katya Alexandra Elisabeth, *b* 1994.
Residence – 3 Avenue Court, Draycott Av, SW3.

AUNT LIVING (*daughter of 8th Baron*)

Hon Diana Rosemary (5222 Sark Rd, Victoria, BC, Canada V8Y 2M3), *b* 1924; *ed* Havergal Coll, and McGill Univ, Canada (BA 1949); served World War II with WRCNS 1943-45.

WIDOW LIVING OF SON OF EIGHTH BARON

Penelope Jane, da of late Capt Eric S. Garner, of Easton, Northants: *m* 1974, as his 2nd wife, Hon Michael Christopher Rodney, who *d* 1993. *Address* – PO Box 11, Pender Is, BC, Canada V0N 2M0.

WIDOW LIVING OF NINTH BARON

REGINE ELISABETH LUCIENNE THERESE MARIE GHISLAINE (*Dowager Baroness Rodney*), yr da of late Chevalier Robert Egide Marie Ghislain Pangaert d'Opdorp, of Château Rullingen, Looz, Belgium: *m* 1951, the 9th Baron Rodney, who *d* 1992.
Residence – 38 Pembroke Rd, W8 6NU.

COLLATERAL BRANCHES LIVING

Issue of late Hon Michael Christopher Rodney, yst son of 8th Baron, *b* 1926, *d* 1993: *m* 1st, 1953 (*m diss* 1973), Anne, da of David Yuile, of Montreal, Canada; 2ndly, 1974, Penelope Jane (ante), da of late Capt Eric S. Garner, of Easton, Northants:—
(By 1st *m*) Patricia Anne, *b* 1955; *ed* Univ of BC (MSN 1988, PhD 1997): *m* 1995, John Joseph Thomasson, of Hamilton, Ontario, Canada. ——Jocelyn Marjorie, *b* 1959; *ed* Univ of Alberta (BEd 1982): *m* 1981, Norman Marc Langlois, of Edmonton, Alberta, Canada, and has issue living, Christopher Paul Rodney, *b* 1985, — Shaun Jocelyn, *b* 1990, — Jordan Anne, *b* 1996. ——Jennifer Susan, *b* 1964; *ed* Univ of Calgary (BEd 1989): *m* 1991, Jay David Todesco, of Calgary, Alberta, Canada, and has issue living, Matthew Michael, *b* 1993.

Grandchildren of late Lt-Cdr Mervyn Harley Rodney, eldest surv son of late Hon Robert William Henry Rodney (infra):—
Issue of late Cdr Nigel Robert Harley Rodney, RN, *b* 1917, *d* 1992: *m* 1946, Patricia Ann Merlyn (Ashen House, Northleigh, Colyton, Devon), da of late Lt-Col Harley Wentworth Ashburner, DSO:—
Nicholas Simon Harley (17 rue da Labruyere, 78000 Versailles, France), *b* 1947: *m* 1973, Maité Bernadette Edith, da of Henri Pinet des Ecots, of Château de Curty, Imphy, 58 Nièvre, France, and has issue living, Victoria Segolène Jehanne, *b* 1997. —— Christopher Lossie Charles, *b* 1957. —— Julia Diana, *b* 1951. —— Emma Gabrielle, *b* 1952: *m* 1975, Charles Ainslie Guest, of Glebe House, Southleigh, Colyton, Devon, son of Dennis William Guest, of 20A Watchbell St, Rye, Sussex, and has issue living, Henry Harley, *b* 1983, — Charles Humphrey, *b* 1985, — Oliver Hugo, *b* 1987.

Issue of late Maj John Armand Rodney, MC, *b* 1921, *d* 1992: *m* 1951, Gertrude Evelyn (147 Gloucester Rd, SW7 4TH), yr da of late Capt Simon John James:—
Peter Miles (171 Elms Crescent, SW4 8QQ), *b* 1953; *ed* Radley, and Magdalene Coll, Camb: *m* 1980, Marianne Hilary, da of George Robert Downes, and has issue living, Lydia Jane Louise, *b* 1983, — Katharine Amelia Laura, *b* 1985. —— David James (Craig-y-Dorth Cottage, Mitchell Troy Common, nr Monmouth, NP5 4JQ), *b* 1965; *ed* Haileybury, and RMA Sandhurst; commn'd Coldm Gds 1985: *m* 1989, Sally L— M—, elder da of Dr David Norman Howell Owen, of Bryn-y-Mor, Fishguard, Pembrokeshire, and has issue living, Harry John Melville, *b* 1992, — Oliver Hugh James, *b* 1994.

Granddaughters of late Hon Robert William Henry Rodney, 2nd son of 6th Baron:—
Issue of late Group Capt Ivor Morgan Rodney, OBE, RAF (ret), *b* 1896, *d* 1954: *m* 1931, Althea Caroline Winifred, who *d* 1978, el da of late Sir Gerald Woods Wollaston, KCB, KCVO, FSA, late Garter Principal King of Arms:—
Prudence Jane, *b* 1936: *m* 1960, Keith Hyde Wollaston, TD, of 29 Archery Sq, Walmer, Kent CT14 7HP, and has issue living, Andrew James Rodney, *b* 1961: *m* 1991, Alison Wishart, and has issue living, George William Woods *b* 1996, Amelia Grace *b* 1995, Olivia Lucy Hyde *b* 1997, — Rachel Althea Rodney, *b* 1963: *m* 1st, 1989 (*m diss* 1994); 2ndly, 1995, Samuel Andrew Roland Hatfield, and has issue living (by 2nd *m*), India Rose Rodney *b* 1995, Althea Georgina Catcheside *b* 1997, — Frances Jane Rodney, *b* 1964: *m* 1993, Said El Moumni and has issue living, Sarah *b* 1994, Rebecca *b* 1998, — Catherine Mary Rodney, *b* (twin) 1964: *m* 1991, Robert Dickson, and has issue living, Wendy Elizabeth *b* 1992. —— Alicia Henrietta Althea, *b* 1937: *m* 1960, David John Pentin, of 16 St Dunstan's Terrace, Canterbury, Kent, and has issue living, John Mark, *b* 1964: *m* 1995, Sheena Nicholette Forster, and has issue living, Natasha Alexandra *b* 1997, — Richard Harley, *b* 1969, — Caroline Louise, *b* 1962: *m* 1987, Mark Kendall Blamey, and has issue living, Jacob John *b* 1992, Joseph Peter *b* 1994, — Edward Michael, *b* 1971.

Grandson of late Frederick James Rodney, son of late Hon Mortimer Rodney, 7th son of 2nd Baron:—
Issue of late Reginald George Rodney, *b* 1873, *d* 1933: *m* 1916, Patricia Lissette du Châstel, who *d* 1964, da of late William James MacGrath, of co Tipperary:—
Philip Harley Brydges (61 Knighton Rd, Wembury, Plymouth), *b* 1917: *m* 1951, Janet Barker, and has issue living, Julie Rose Patricia, *b* 1954: *m* 1976, Andrew George Lewis Leftley, and has issue living, Ian Andrew Philip *b* 1985, Nicola Caroline *b* 1979, — Faye Jessica Frances Corisande, *b* 1958: *m* 1991, Graham George Tongue, and has issue living Martin Terence Philip *b* 1994.

PREDECESSORS – **(1)** *Adm Sir* GEORGE BRYDGES Rodney, (son of Henry Rodney, greatgrandson of Sir John Rodney, by Jane (cousin german to Edward VI), da of Sir Henry Seymour, brother of 1st Duke of Somerset and Queen Jane Seymour), an eminent Naval Commander, who, having gained numerous victories, eventually in 1782 defeated the French fleet under the Comte de Grasse, whom he took prisoner, the result of this success was the peace of Versailles 20 Jan 1783; *cr Baronet* 1764, and *Baron Rodney*, of Rodney Stoke, co Somerset (peerage of Great Britain) 1782; granted by Parliament a pension of £2,000 a-year to himself and his successors (commuted 1924); successively MP for Saltash, Okehampton, Penrhyn, and Northampton; *d* 1792; *s* by his son **(2)** GEORGE, 2nd Baron; sat as MP for Northampton; *d* 1802; *s* by his el son **(3)** GEORGE, 3rd Baron; was Lord-Lieut of Radnor; *d* 1842; *s* by his brother **(4)** THOMAS JAMES, 4th Baron; assumed the additional surname and arms of Harley by Roy licence 1805; *d* unmarried 1843; *s* by his brother **(5)** SPENCER, 5th Baron; was Rector of Elmley, Kent; *d* unmarried 1846; *s* by his nephew **(6)** ROBERT DENNETT, 6th Baron, son of Capt Hon Robert, RN, 4th son of 2nd Baron; *b* 1820: *m* 1850, Sarah, who *d* 1882, da of late John Singleton; *d* 1864; *s* by his son **(7)** GEORGE BRYDGES HARLEY DENNETT, 7th Baron; *b* 1857: *m* 1st, 1891 (*m diss* 1902), Hon Corisande Evelyn Vere Guest, who *d* 1943, da of 1st Baron Wimborne; 2ndly, 1903, Charlotte Eugenia, who *d* 1939, da of late Edmund Probyn, of Longhope and Huntley, Gloucestershire; *d* 1909; *s* by his el son **(8)** GEORGE BRIDGES HARLEY GUEST, 8th Baron; *b* 1891: *m* 1917, Lady Marjorie Lowther, who *d* 1968, da of 6th Earl of Lonsdale; *d* 1973; *s* by his 2nd son **(9)** JOHN FRANCIS, 9th Baron; *b* 1920; 1939-45 War as Lieut Commandos (despatches); Delegate to Council of Europe and Western European Union: *m* 1951, Régine Elisabeth Lucienne Thérèse Marie Ghislaine, yr da of late Chevalier Robert Egide Marie Ghislain Pangaert d'Opdorp, of Château Rullingen, Looz, Belgium; *d* 1992; *s* by his only son **(10)** GEORGE BRYDGES, 10th Baron and present peer.

ROGERS OF RIVERSIDE, BARON (Rogers) (Life Baron 1996)

RICHARD GEORGE ROGERS, son of Dada Gairinger Rogers, of Trieste, Italy; *b* 23 July 1933; *ed* Architectural Assoc, London (AA Dip 1959), and Yale Univ, USA (March 1962, Fulbright, Edward D. Stone, and Yale Scholar), Dir Richard Rogers Partnership Ltd; winner of International Competition for Pompidou Centre, Paris 1977; winner of Lloyd's International Competition for Headquarters, London 1978; has been responsible for many major architectural projects, including World Headquarters for Wellcome Foundation, UK 1986, London Docklands Development 1984, and Billingsgate Market Conversion 1985; Visiting Lecturer, UCLA, Princeton, Columbia, Harvard and Cornell Universities, USA; Chm Trustees of the Tate Gallery 1984; Exhibitor RA 1986; awarded

Gold Medal of RIBA 1985; Chevalier of the Legion of Honour of France 1986; *cr* Kt 1991, and *Baron Rogers of Riverside*, of Chelsea, Royal Borough of Kensington and Chelsea (Life Baron) 1996: *m* 1st, 1960 (*m diss* 19—), Susan J. da of Marcus Brumwel, of Cornwall; 2ndly, 1973, Ruth, da of Frederick Elias, of Long Island, USA, and has issue by 1st and 2nd *m*.
Address – Thames Wharf, Rainville Rd, W6 9HA.

SONS LIVING (*By 1st marriage*)

Hon Ben M., *b* 1963; *ed* Oxford Univ.
Hon Zadoc D., *b* 1964; *ed* Manchester Univ; has issue living, Eve, *b* 19—.
Hon Ab, *b* 1968; *ed* Liverpool Univ.

(*By 2nd marriage*)

Hon Roo, *b* 1975; *ed* Colombia, NY, USA.

ADOPTED SON LIVING

Bo, *b* 1983.

ROLL OF IPSDEN, BARON (Roll) (Life Baron 1977)

ERIC ROLL, KCMG, CB, son of Mathias Roll; *b* 1 Dec 1907; *ed* Birmingham Univ (BCom, PhD), Hon DSc, Hull, Hon DSoc Sci Birmingham, Hon LlD Southampton; Prof of Economics and Commerce, Univ Coll of Hull (1935-46); Special Rockefeller Foundation Fellow, USA 1939-41; Member, later Dep Head Brit Food Mission to N America, and UK Dep Member and UK Exec Officer, Combined Food Board, Washington 1941-46; Assist Sec, Min of Food, 1946-47; Under-Sec HM Treasury 1948, Min UK Delegation to OEEC, 1949, Dep Head, UK Delegation to NATO, Paris 1952-53, Under Sec Min of Agric, 1953-57, Exec Dir Internat Sugar Council 1957-59; Chm UN Sugar Conference 1958; Dep Sec Min of Agric 1959-61; Dep Leader, UK Delegation for negotiations with the EEC, 1961-63; Econ Min and Head of UK Treasury Delegation, Washington, Exec Dir for the UK Internat Monetary Fund and Internat Bank for Reconstruction and Development 1963-64 and Permanent Under-Sec of State, Dept of Economic Affairs, 1964-66; Dir of Bank of England 1968-77, Chm and later Hon Chm Book Development Council since 1967; Dir Times Newspapers Ltd 1967-83, and Indep Member NEDC 1971-80; Chancellor, Southampton Univ 1974-84; Chm S. G. Warburg & Co Ltd and Mercury Securities Ltd 1974-84, and a Dir of other Cos; Pres S. G. Warburg Group plc 1987-95; Senior Adviser, Warburg Dillon Read; *cr* CMG 1949, CB (Civil) 1956, KCMG 1962, and *Baron Roll of Ipsden*, of Ipsden, co Oxford (Life Baron) 1977: *m* 1934, Winifred, who *d* 1998, only da of Elliott Taylor, and has issue.
Club – Brooks's.

DAUGHTERS LIVING

Hon Joanna, *b* 1944.
Hon Elizabeth, *b* 1946: *m* 1st, 1970 (*m diss* 1975), Hon Robin James Greenhill, who *d* 1986, yr son of Baron Greenhill of Harrow, GCMG, OBE; 2ndly, 19—, Peter Foldes, and has issue.

ROLLO, LORD (Rollo) (Lord S 1651, and Baron UK 1869)

Fortune makes way through everything

LA FORTUNE PASSE PARTOUT

DAVID ERIC HOWARD ROLLO, 14th Lord; *b* 31 March 1943; *s* 1997; *ed* Eton; Capt Gren Gds: *m* 1971, Felicity Anne Christian, only da of Lt-Cmdr John Bruce Lamb, DSC, RN, of Burrow House, Tywardreath, Cornwall, and has issue.

𝕬rms – Or, a chevron between three boars heads erased azure, armed proper langued gules. 𝕮rest – A stag's head couped at the neck proper. 𝕾upporters – Two stags proper.
Residence – Pitcairns, Dunning, Perthshire PH2 9BX.

SONS LIVING

Hon JAMES DAVID WILLIAM (*Master of Rollo*), *b* 8 Jan 1972; *ed* Eton, and Edinburgh Univ. *Residence* – 55 Iverna Gdns, W8 7TP.
Hon Thomas Stapylton, *b* 1975; *ed* Milton Abbey.
Hon William Eric John, *b* 1978; *ed* Bradfield.

BROTHER LIVING

Hon James Malcolm, *b* 1946; *ed* Eton, and Ch Ch, Oxford (MA): *m* 1968, Henrietta Elizabeth Flora, who *d* 1998, da of Maj Alasdair David Forbes Boyle (*see* E Glasgow, colls), and has issue living, Malcolm Howard, *b* 1981; *ed* Fettes, — Helen Beatrice, *b* 1985. *Residence* – Milkhouse, Barr, Girvan, Ayrshire.

SISTER LIVING

Hon (Erica) Helen Susan, *b* 1939: *m* 1970, Valentine Edward Dillon. *Residence* – 45 Sandford Rd, Dublin.

HALF-UNCLES LIVING (*Son of 12th Lord by 2nd marriage*)

Hon John Dunning, *b* 1931.

(*Son of 12th Lord by 3rd marriage*)

Hon Simon David Paul (60 Green Leas, Sunbury on Thames, Middx TW17 7PG), *b* 1939; *ed* Eton: *m* 1964, Valerie Ernestine, yr da of Robert William Gaspard Willis, of Newton Green, Sudbury, Suffolk, and has issue living, Michelle Leila, *b* 1971, — Dominique Ruth, *b* 1977.

AUNT LIVING (*Daughter of 12th Lord by 1st marriage*)

Hon Jean Helen, *b* 1926: *m* 1952, Lt-Col Robert Henry Heywood-Lonsdale, MBE, MC, DL, Grenadier Gds, of Mount Farm, Churchill, Oxon (*see* V Valentia, 1965 Edn), and has issue living, Thomas Norman (Mount Farm, Churchill, Oxon), *b* 1953; *ed* Eton: *m* 1987 (*m diss* 1995), Sara Lonsdale, da of Strachan Bongard, of Toronto, and has issue living, James Alexander *b* 1989, Oliver Robert *b* (twin) 1989, Edward David *b* 1990, — (Helen) Jane, *b* 1957: *m* 1994, David Richard Langley Cleave, of Greenslade Farmhouse, Lower Brailes, nr Banbury, Oxon, son of late Alan Cleave, of Sundridge, Kent, and has issue living, Robert Oliver Rollo *b* 1996, Iona Jessamy Africa *b* 1998, — Clare Jean, *b* 1961: *m* 1987, James Hugh Leslie Melville, and has issue (*see* E Leven and Melville, colls), — Emma Lucinda, *b* 1962: *m* 1989, Matthew Donald Knight, of Sockneys Wood, Willards Hill, Robertsbridge, E Sussex, eldest son of Nicholas P. Knight, of Eltham, SE9 and has issue living, Laura Emma *b* 1991, Sophie Lucinda *b* 1993, Martha Emily *b* 1994.

WIDOW LIVING OF BROTHER OF TWELFTH LORD

Diana Joan (Barley Thorpe, Oakham, Rutland), da of late Edward Castell Wrey (*see* Wrey Bt): *m* 1st 1932 (*m diss* 1946), Jocelyn Abel Smith, who *d* 1966; 2ndly, 1946, as his 2nd wife, Hon William Hereward Charles Rollo, MC (who was raised to the rank of a Baron's son 1946), who *d* 1962.

WIDOW LIVING OF SON OF TWELFTH LORD

Bridget Mary (30 King St, Nairn), da of Brig James Erskine Stirling, DSO (*see* D Devonshire colls, 1980 Edn): *m* 1948, Capt Hon David Ian Rollo, MBE, MC, who *d* 1981, and has issue living (see colls infra).

WIDOW LIVING OF THIRTEENTH LORD

SUZANNE (*Suzanne, Lady Rollo*), 2nd da of William Howard Brinton Hatton, of Broome House, Clent, Worcs: *m* 1938, Capt the 13th Lord Rollo, who *d* 1997. *Residence* – Flat 1, Pitcairns, Dunning, Perthshire.

COLLATERAL BRANCHES LIVING

Issue of late Capt Hon David Ian Rollo, MBE, MC, yst son of 12th Lord, *b* 1921; *d* 1981: *m* 1948, Bridget Mary (ante), da of late Brig James Erskine Stirling, DSO (*see* D Devonshire, colls, 1980 Edn):—
(Norman) Hamish (Burnbrae, Burghclere, Newbury, Berks), *b* 1955; *ed* Radley; Col: *m* 1979, Nicole, yst da of Vincent J. Sullivan, of Larchdale, Ashford, Kent, and has issue living, Andrew David, *b* 1981, — Euan Christopher, *b* 1983. —— Joanna Mary (3 Jenner Rd, N16), *b* 1949. —— Carolyn Louise, *b* 1952: *m* 1st, 1973, Gordon Wilson; 2ndly, 1981, Ronald Mitchell, of Bogside of Brodie, Auldearn, Nairn, and has issue living, (by 1st *m*) Kirsty Jane MITCHELL, *b* 1974: *m* 1996, Paul Bigsby, and has issue living, Megan Carolyn *b* 1997, — (by 2nd *m*), Jake David, *b* 1984, — Abigail Betty, *b* 1982. —— Harriet Clarissa Jane, *b* 1960: *m* 1983, Julian P. Spencer, of 12 Streathbourne Rd, SW17 8QX, elder son of late Michael Spencer, and has issue living, George Hector, *b* 1990, — Alexander James, *b* 1993, — Edward Aeneas, *b* 1997.

Issue of late Hon William Hereward Charles Rollo, MC (who was raised to the rank of a Baron's son 1946), yr brother of 12th Lord, *b* 1890, *d* 1962: *m* 1st, 1917 (*m diss* 1946), Lady Kathleen Nina Hill, who *d* 1960, da of 6th Marquess of Downshire; 2ndly, 1946, Mrs Diana Joan Abel Smith (ante), da of late Edward Castell Wrey (*see* Wrey, Bt):—
(By 1st *m*) (Peter) Andrew, MBE (Cold Blow, Oare, Marlborough, Wilts), *b* 1919; Lieut RN (ret); Far East 1945; MBE (Mil) 1946 *m* 1953, Patricia Mary, who *d* 1985, da of late Capt Charles Cairn Best, and has issue living, William Raoul, *b* 1955; *ed* Eton; Maj Blues and Royals: *m* 1987, Annabel Evadne, only da of Lt-Cdr Sir Howard Christian Sheldon Guinness, VRD, RNR, of The Manor House, Glanvilles Wootton, Sherborne, Dorset (*see* Smith-Marriott, Bt, colls, 1973-74 Edn), and has issue living, Andrew *b* 1996, Katie *b* 1989, Laura Evadne *b* 1991, — Susan Rose, *b* 1957: *m* 1998, Gregory Kenneth Palm.

Grandchildren of late Hon Gilbert de Ste Croix Rollo, yst son of 10th Lord:—
Issue of late Alexander David Rollo, *b* 1909, *d* 1974: *m* 1st, 1934 (*m diss* 19—), Maud Mary Venn; 2ndly, 1952, Margaret Valmai, who *d* 1961, only da of William Slaney Wilmot:—
(By 2nd *m*) Calum John Slaney, *b* 1953: *m* 1980, Lindsay Froggatt.

Issue of late Maj Robert Duncan Rollo, *b* 1911, *d* 1986: *m* 1936, Violet Augustine, da of late Russell Charles Stanhope (*see* E Harrington, colls):—
Gilbert Mark (Monadhliath House, Aviemore, Inverness-shire PH22 1QT), *b* 1937: *m* 1968, his first cousin once removed, Paulette Beatrice, da of late Lt-Col Aubrey Charles Stanhope, DFC, USAF (*see* E Harrington, colls), and has issue living, Duncan Andrew, *b* 1971, — Catherine Ann, *b* 1969, — Clare Elizabeth, *b* 1976, — Caroline Jane, *b* 1979. —— Charles (21 Countess Rd, Amesbury, Wilts), *b* 1950. —— Mary Rose, *b* 1938: *m* 1st, 1960, Noel Keaveney, of Cork; 2ndly, 1988, John Curry, of 2 Rosery Court, Dinton, Wilts, and has issue living (by 1st *m*), Catherine Ruth, *b* 1961, — Deborah Maeve, *b* 1963.

PREDECESSORS – (1) *Sir* ANDREW Rollo; *cr Lord Rollo*, of Duncrub (peerage of Scotland) 1651, with remainder to his heirs male whatsoever; *s* by his son (2) JAMES, 2nd Lord; *d* 1669; *s* by his son (3) ANDREW, 3rd Lord; *d* 1700; *s* by his son (4) ROBERT, 4th Lord; was implicated in the rising of 1715, but having surrendered he obtained the benefit of the Act of Grace 1716; *d* 1758; *s* by his el son (5) ANDREW, 5th Lord; served as Brig-Gen in the first American War; *d* without surviving issue 1765; *s* by his brother (6) JOHN, 6th Lord; *d* 1783; *s* by his son (7) JAMES, 7th Lord; *d* 1784; *s* by his son (8) JOHN, 8th Lord; served with the Guards in Flanders 1793-5; *d* 1846; *s* by his son (9) WILLIAM 9th Lord; *b* 1809: *m* 1834, Elizabeth, da of John Rogerson; *d* 1852; *s* by his son (10) JOHN ROGERSON, 10th Lord; *b* 1835; was a Representative Peer for Scotland 1860-68; *cr Baron Dunning* (peerage of UK) 1869: *m* 1857, Agnes Bruce, who *d* 1906, el da of Lt-Col Trotter, of Ballindean House, co Perth; *d* 1916; *s* by his el son (11) WILLIAM CHARLES WORDSWORTH, CB, 11th Lord; *b* 1860; formerly Lt-Col and Hon Col 3rd Batn Black Watch (Roy Highlanders): *m* 1882, Mary Eleanor, who *d* 1929, da of late Beaumont Williams Hotham; *d* 1946; *s* by his nephew (12) JOHN ERIC HENRY (son of late Hon Eric Norman Rollo, 2nd son of 10th Lord), 12th Lord; *b* 1889: *m* 1st, 1915, Helen Maud, who *d* 1928, da of Frederick Chetwynd-Stapylton; 2ndly, 1930 (*m diss* 1936), Phyllis Carina, only da of late Bernard Sanderson; 3rdly, 1937, Mrs Lily Marie Cockshut (who *d* 1989, having *m* 3rdly, 1949, Richard Andrew Perceval Leach, who *d* 1981), da of Max Seiflow, of Hatch End, Middlesex; *d* 1947; *s* by his el son (13) ERIC JOHN STAPYLTON, 13th Lord, *b* 1915; Capt Grenadier Gds; JP Perthshire: *m* 1938, Suzanne, 2nd da of William Howard Brinton Hatton, of Broome House, Clent, Worcs; *d* 1997; *s* by his elder son (14) DAVID ERIC HOWARD, 14th Lord and present peer; also Baron Dunning.

ROMNEY, EARL OF (Marsham) (Earl UK 1801, Bt E 1663)

Not for himself, but for his country

MICHAEL HENRY MARSHAM, 7th Earl, and 13th Baronet; *b* 22 Nov 1910; *s* 1975; *ed* Sherborne; formerly Maj RA; 1939-45 War: *m* 1939, Frances Aileen, who *d* 1995, da of late Maj James Russell Landale, Indian Army.

Arms – Argent, a lion passant in bend gules, between two bendlets azure. **Crest** – A lion's head erased gules. **Supporters** – Two lions azure, semée of cross crosslets and each gorged with a naval coronet or.
Residence – Wensum Farm, West Rudham, King's Lynn, Norfolk PE31 8SZ.

COLLATERAL BRANCHES LIVING

Grandchildren of late Hon Sydney Edward Marsham, yst son of 4th Earl:—
Issue of late Col Peter William Marsham, MBE, *b* 1913, *d* 1970: *m* 1946, Hersey (Waterloo Cottage, Gayton, King's Lynn, Norfolk), da of late Maj Hon Richard Coke (*see* E Leicester, colls):—
JULIAN CHARLES (Gayton Hall, King's Lynn, Norfolk), *b* 28 March 1948; *ed* Eton: *m* 1975, Catriona Ann, da of Robert Christie Stewart, of Arndean, Dollar, Perthshire (*see* B Cochrane of Cults, colls), and has issue living, David Charles, *b* 1977, — Michael Julian, *b* 1979, — Laura Clare, *b* 1984. —— Lavinia, *b* 1950: *m* 1973, Simon James Macdonald Lockhart of The Lee, of Thornton Hill, Fossoway, Kinross, and has issue (*see* E Ducie, colls). —— Sarah, *b* 1954: *m* 1982, Maxwell Colin Bernard Ward, of Stobshiel House, Humbie, East Lothian, and has issue (*see* E Bangor, colls).

Grandchildren of late Walter John Marsham, 2nd son of late Rev Hon John Marsham (infra):—
Issue of late John Edward Marsham, *b* 1910, *d* 1990: *m* 1st, 1937 (*m diss* 1970), Jean Frances, who *d* 1986, da of late Reginald Cambden Clare Hayward; 2ndly, 1970, Mrs Evelyn Moore, who *d* 19—, da of Lesley George Rush:—
(By 1st *m*) Richard John, *b* 1946: *m* 1964, Janet Anne Wilson, and has issue living, Gary Frederick, *b* 1964: *m* 1988 (*m diss* 19—), his cousin, Celaine Margaret, da of late Donald James Griffin (infra), and has issue living, Cassandra Dawn *b* 1989, — Stephen John, *b* 1967. —— Gillian Dawn (Flat 1, 5 Laburnham Rd, Maidenhead, Berks), *b* 1938: *m* 1st, 1956, Donald James Griffin, who *d* 1959; 2ndly, 1961 (*m diss* 1964), Alan Henry Craig; 3rdly, 1968, Abdul Hanif Rashid, who *d* 1971; 4thly, 19— (*m diss* 1979), Thomas William McConnell; 5thly 1980 (*m diss* 1985, re-*m* 1990), David Alfred Forisky, and has issue living (by 1st *m*), Pauline Elizabeth, *b* 1956: *m* 19—, Keith Gough, of 33 Heywood Court Crescent, Woodlands Park, Maidenhead, Berks SL6 3NB; has issue living, Darrell Colin GRIFFIN *b* 1981, John BUSHNELL *b* 1986, Gillian Dawn GRIFFIN *b* 1976, — Celaine Margaret (18 South Rd, Maidenhead, Berks), *b* 1959: *m* 1988 (*m diss* 19—), her cousin, Gary Frederick Marsham, and has issue (ante), — (by 3rd *m*) Kris Hanif (New York City, USA), *b* 1970; assumed forename of Kris by deed poll 19— in lieu of Aftab.

Grandsons of late Rev Hon John Marsham, 2nd son of 3rd Earl:—
Issue of late Capt Cyril Montagu Charles Marsham, DCM, *b* 1871; *d* 1943: *m* 1911, Gladys Helen, who *d* 1965, da of late Douglas Kingsford, Bar-at-law:—
Peter (Kings Acre, Coddington, Ledbury, Herefordshire), *b* 1912; *ed* Clifton: *m* 1938, Margaret, da of Benjamin Harral, of Cawthorne, Barnsley, Yorkshire, and has issue living, John Kingsford (Follybrook House, Newcastle-on-Clun, Shropshire), OBE, *b* 1942; *ed* Bryanston, and RMC Sandhurst; Lt-Col 3rd LI; OBE (Mil) 1993: *m* 1978, Olwen, da of late Joshua Adamson, of Brisbane, Australia, and has issue living, Robert Edward Harral *b* 1981, Anne Kingsford *b* 1979, — Robert Harral, *b* 1946; *ed* Abbotsholme Sch, — Marion Caroline, *b* 1939: *m* 1st, 1961 (*m diss* 1978), Richard Naylor; 2ndly, 1981 (*m diss* 1989), Dr George Richard Castellain Walton, and has issue living (by 1st *m*), Charles Gray Marsham *b* 1962: *m* 1991, Denise Jones (and has issue living, Toby Peter Hollinshead *b* 1993), Michael Harry Richard *b* 1970, Margaret Kingsford *b* 1964: *m* 1991, Giles Emerson (and has issue living, Poppy Charlotte Kingsford *b* 1992). —— Richard Douglas Hollinshead (Llwynglas, Penrhiwllan, Llandyssul, Dyfed), *b* 1913; Maj (ret) Worcester Regt: *m* 1947 (*m diss* 1981), Shirley, da of late John Hannah, of The Mill House, Mathon, Malvern, Worcestershire, and has issue living, Richard Charles Hannay, *b* 1948, — David John Hollinshead, *b* 1954, — Catherine Elizabeth (Flat 5, 32 Arcadia St, Coogee, NSW 2034, Australia), *b* 1952.

Granddaughters of late Hugh Sydney Marsham Townshend, el son of late Hon Robert Marsham-Townshend, 2nd son of 2nd Earl:—
Issue of late Capt Thomas Marsham-Townshend, Scots Guards, *b* 1915, *ka* 1944: *m* 1940, Averil Innes (who *d* 1993, having *m* 2ndly, 1945, Col John Robert Stephenson Clarke, OBE, MC, Scots Guards, who *d* 1993), da of late Major Lewis Frederic Innes Loyd:—
June (26 Kildare Terrace, W2 5LX), *b* 1942: *m* 1st, 1962, Bryan Montagu Norman; 2ndly, 1980 (*m diss* 1997), Sir Ian Niall Rankin, 4th Bt and has issue (by 2nd *m*) (*see* Rankin, Bt), and an adopted da (from 1st *m*), Emily Kate, *b* 1975. —— Susan (*posthumous*), *b* 1944: *m* 1972, Dr Piero Studiati Berni, of Molina di Quosa, Pisa, Italy, and has issue living, Cesare Studiati, *b* 1972, — Viola, *b* 1975.

(In remainder to Barony of Romney and Baronetcy)

Grandson of late Major Charles George Field-Marsham, elder son of late Robert Henry Bullock-Marsham, 2nd son of late Robert Bullock-Marsham, el son of late Rev Hon Jacob Marsham, DD, 3rd son of 2nd Baron:—
Issue of late Charles Austen FIELD-MARSHAM, Lieut Life Guards, *b* 1910, *ka* 1941: *m* 1935, Joan Helen (who *d* 1988, having *m* 2ndly, 1950, as his 2nd wife, Major Robert Edward Field-Marsham, who *d* 1996, elder brother of her first husband), da of late Percy Llewellyn Nevill (*see* Abergavenny, colls, 1985 Edn):—

Rupert Charles Edward (29 Roxborough St West, Toronto, Canada), *b* 1938; *ed* Eton, and McGill Univ; 2nd Lt R Armoured Corps: *m* 1st, 1963 (*m diss* 1973), Marilyn, da of Dr G. B. Maugham, of Westmount, Montreal; 2ndly, 1973, Lindsay Ruth, da of late Robert Dale-Harris (by his wife, Leslie, da of late Leslie Howard, the actor), and has issue living (by 1st *m*), Robert Scott, *b* 1964, — Rupert Charles, *b* 1968, — (by 2nd *m*), George Robert, *b* 1975, — Mark Austen, *b* 1977, — Jacob Edward, *b* 1979.

Grandsons of late Robert Anstruther MORRIS-MARSHAM, yr son of Robert Henry Bullock-Marsham (ante):—
Issue of late Richard Henry Anstruther Morris-Marsham, *b* 1905, *d* 1975: *m* 1st, 1929 (*m diss* 1951), Iris Rose Sophia, da of Capt Dennis Larking, CMG, RN; 2ndly, 1951, Eileen Reba (Jacaranda, 4 Chiltley Lane, Liphook, Hants), only da of late Victor di Halfalla Nahum, of Italy, and formerly wife of Neville Blond, CMG, OBE:—
(By 1st *m*) David Charles Robert (32 Alderbrook Rd, Clapham, SW12 8AE), *b* 1930; *ed* Eton, and Merton Coll, Oxford: *m* 1976, Margaret Lindelia, da of late Robert Crawford, and has issue living, Victoria Harriet, *b* 1978, — Charlotte Rose, *b* 1979. ──Jack Richard (Brookside, Ewen, Cirencester, Glos GL7 6BU), *b* 1936; *ed* Eton: *m* 1st, 1963 (*m diss* 1978), Agnes Margaret (Molly), da of late Maj-Gen Walter Rutherfoord Goodman, CB, DSO, MC; 2ndly, 1978, Ann Christine Humphreys, who *d* 1980, da of late Howard Sargent Backhouse; 3rdly, 1983, Serena Sybil Newmark, da of late Gp Capt Geoffrey Kinglake Fairtlough, and has issue living (by 1st *m*), James Jonathan (Garden House, High Rd, Ashton Keynes, Wilts SN6 6NX), *b* 1964: *m* 1991, Susan Marie, elder da of Henry Menzel, of Falmouth, Cornwall, and has issue living, Jessica Rose *b* 1993, — Dominic Rutherfoord (35 Furness Rd, SW6 2LJ), *b* 1967: *m* 1996, Veronica M., yr da of late Maj C. R. C. Inglis, of Brecon, — Tiffany Jane, *b* 1969: *m* 1997, (Julius) Andrew G. Beilby, of 4 Petley Rd, W6 9ST, son of Guy Beilby, of Evenlode, Glos, and of Mrs John Hills, of E Witton, N Yorks.

Grandchildren of late Rev Cloudesley Dewar Bullock-Marsham, 3rd son of Robert Bullock-Marsham (ante):—
Issue of late Cloudesley Henry Bullock-Marsham, *b* 1879, *d* 1928: *m* 1911, Algitha, who *d* 1972, da of late Rev Hon Algernon Robert Parker (E Macclesfield, colls):—
Cloudesley George (Horton Cottage, Rolvenden Layne, Cranbrook, Kent TN17 4NP), *b* 1917; *ed* Eton; Maj 297th (Kent Yeo) Field Regt RA (TA); 1939-45 War (prisoner): *m* 1941, Suzanne, da of Dudley Holloway. ──Algernon James (Brambly Hedge, Grove Lane, Iden, Rye, E Sussex TN31 7PX), *b* 1919; *ed* Eton, and Ch Ch, Oxford; Capt KRRC; 1939-45 War (prisoner): *m* 1948, Elizabeth, da of Air Vice-Marshal Malcolm Henderson, CB, CIE, DSO, and has issue living, Charles James Lessels, *b* 1950; *ed* Eton: *m* 1973, Jane-Anne Holland, and has issue living, Andrew Cloudesley *b* 1977, Joanna *b* 1976. ──Vere Frances, *b* 1913: *m* 1932, (George) Ronald Pigé Leschallas, who *d* 1991, and has issue living, Anthony George, *b* 1933: *m* 1954, Marie-Louise Yvonne Renner, and has issue living, (Anthony) Simon *b* 1955: *m* 1st, 1987 (*m diss* 1992), Amanda Nanci, da of Maj James Le Coq, of Seething, Norfolk; 2ndly, 1995, Joanna E. G., 3rd da of Jeremy Lywood, of Ashford Court, Ludlow, Shropshire (and has issue living (by 1st *m*), Marie-Clair *b* 1988, (by 2nd *m*), Hubert Edmund Pige *b* 1998, Katya Camilla *b* 1997), William Henry *b* 1963: *m* 1992, Emma C., elder da of David Huxtable, of Bosham, W Sussex (and has issue living, Henry Oliver Pigé *b* 1994, Archie William Pigé *b* 1996), Marie-Louise Sophie *b* 1957, Joanna Clare *b* 1960: *m* 1989, Edward Anthony Morys Berry (*see* V Kemsley, colls), — James Ronald Percy, *b* 1943: *m* 1967, Rosemary Elizabeth, only da of late Rev Hon Andrew Charles Victor Elphinstone, and has issue (*see* L Elphinstone), — Lavinia Frances, *b* 1934: *m* 1965, Christopher William Trelawny Hare, and has issue living, Henry William Trelawny *b* 1966: *m* 1999, Isabel, da of Giles le Maitre, Jonathan Christopher Trelawny *b* 1968, James Frederick Trelawny *b* 1971: *m* 1997, Anna Mary Louise, da of Kenneth Thomas Moore, FRCS, — Suzanne Vere (*Lady Jones*), *b* 1939: *m* 1965, Gen Sir (Charles) Edward Webb Jones, KCB, CBE, late Royal Green Jackets, and has issue living, Hume Richard Webb *b* 1967; Maj The Royal Green Jackets: *m* 1998, Davina Henrietta, da of Maj Sir Shane Gabriel Basil Blewitt, KCVO (*see* Buxton, Bt, colls), Benjamin Edward Webb *b* 1978, Jemma Suzanne *b* 1971.

PREDECESSORS – (1) *Sir* JOHN Marsham, MP, one of the six Clerks of the Court of Chancery 1638-44 and 1660-80; *cr* a Baronet 1663; *s* by his son (2) *Sir* JOHN, 2nd Bt; *d* 1692; *s* by his son (3) *Sir* JOHN, 3rd Bt; *d* unmarried 1696; *s* by his uncle (4) *Sir* ROBERT, Knt, 4th Bt; was one of the six clerks in Chancery 1680-95; sat as MP for Maidstone 1698-1703; *d* 1703; *s* by his son (5) *Sir* ROBERT, 5th Bt; was Gov of Dover Castle; sat as MP for Maidstone 1708-16; *cr Baron of Romney*, of Romney, co Kent (peerage of Great Britain) 1716; *d* 1724; *s* by his son (6) ROBERT, DCL, FRS, 2nd Baron; *d* 1793; *s* by his son (7) CHARLES, 3rd Baron, successively MP for Maidstone and Kent; in 1799 entertained George III at the Mote, when HM reviewed about 6,000 of the Kentish Volunteers; was Lord-Lieut of Kent; *cr Viscount Marsham* and *Earl of Romney* (peerage of UK) 1801; *d* 1811; *s* by his son (8) CHARLES, 2nd Earl; was successively MP for Hythe and Downton; *d* 1845; *s* by his son (9) CHARLES, 3rd Earl; *b* 1808; sat as MP for W Kent (*C*) 1841-5: *m* 1832, Lady Margaret Harriet Montagu-Douglas-Scott, who *d* 1846, da of 4th Duke of Buccleuch; *d* 1874; *s* by his son (10) CHARLES, 4th Earl; *b* 1841; was a Lord-in-Waiting to HM Queen Victoria 1889-92: *m* 1863, Lady Frances Augusta Constance Muir-Campbell-Rawdon-Hastings, who *d* 1910, da of 2nd Marquess of Hastings; *d* 1905; *s* by his el son (11) CHARLES, 5th Earl; *b* 1864; Hon Lieut-Col (ret) 4th Batn Bedfordshire Regt, and Pres of Marine So: *m* 1890, Anne Louisa, who *d* 1936, da of Sir Edward Henry Scott, 5th Bt (*cr* 1821); *d* 1933; *s* by his son (12) CHARLES, 6th Earl; *b* 1892: *m* 1918, Marie Henrietta, who *d* 1976, da of Sir Colin Richard Keppel, GCVO, KCIE, CB, DSO (E Albemarle, colls); *d* 1975; *s* by his cousin (13) MICHAEL HENRY (son of Lt-Col Hon Reginald Hastings Marsham, OBE, 2nd son of 4th Earl), 7th Earl and present peer; also Viscount Marsham, and Baron Romney.

Romsey, Lord; son of Countess Mountbatten of Burma.

Ronaldshay, Earl of; son of Marquess of Zetland.

ROOTES, BARON (Rootes) (Baron UK 1959)

Forwards into the Future

NICHOLAS GEOFFREY ROOTES, 3rd Baron; *b* 12 July 1951; *s* 1992; *ed* Harrow; Journalist, Author and Copywriter: *m* 1976, Dorothy Anne, formerly wife of Jonathan Burn-Forti, of Barnes, SW, and da of Cyril Wood, of Swansea.

Arms – Ermine within an orle azure a bugle horn sable garnished or stringed gules. **Crest** – On a wreath argent and vert a cubit arm bendwise in armour or the hand proper grasping a spear in bend also proper flying therefrom a forked pennon barry argent and azure semée of plates and bezants. **Supporters** – On either side a horse argent gorged with a chain pendent therefrom a wheel or.
Residence – 2 Cedars Rd, Barnes, SW13 0HP.

SISTER LIVING

Hon Sally Hayter, *b* 1947: *m* 1968, Andrew Beauchamp St John, of Cul-na-Cloich, Glenalmond, Perthshire (*see* B St John of Bletso, colls).

WIDOW LIVING OF SON OF FIRST BARON

Elizabeth Margaret, da of late Rev Humphrey Gordon Barclay, CVO, MC, and widow of Lt Norman Lewis Philips (E Ducie, colls): *m* 1944, Hon Brian Gordon Rootes, who *d* 1971, and has issue (*see* colls infra). *Residence* – No 11, Isles Court, Ramsbury, Wilts SN8 2QW.

WIDOW LIVING OF SECOND BARON

MARIAN (*Marian, Baroness Rootes*), da of late Lt-Col Herbert Roche Hayter, DSO, and widow of Wing-Cdr James Hogarth Slater, AFC, RAF: *m* 1946, the 2nd Baron Rootes, who *d* 1992. *Residence* – Oakhill Cottage, Froxfield, Marlborough, Wilts SN8 3JU.

COLLATERAL BRANCH LIVING

Issue of late Hon Brian Gordon Rootes, yr son of 1st Baron, *b* 1919, *d* 1971: *m* 1944, Elizabeth Margaret (ante), da of late Rev Humphrey Gordon Barclay, CVO, MC, and widow of Lt Norman Lewis Philips (E Ducie, colls):—
WILLIAM BRIAN (Drummond Park, Loglealmond, Perthshire PH1 3TJ), *b* 8 Nov 1944: *m* 1969, Alicia Graham, yst da of late Frederick Graham Roberts, OBE, of East Farm House, Piddlehinton, Dorset, and has issue living, Talitha Alice Louise, *b* 1973, — Annabel Catherine Natasha, *b* 1976.

PREDECESSORS – (1) *Sir* William Edward Rootes, GBE, son of late William Rootes, of Hawkhurst, Kent; *b* 1894; Chm of Rootes, Ltd; Chm of Dollar Exports Council 1951-60, and of successor body, W Hemisphere Exports Council 1961-64: *m* 1st, 1916 (*m diss* 1951) Nora, who *d* 1964, da of Horace Press; 2ndly, 1951, Ruby Joy (Ann), who *d* 1968, da of Capt Gordon Duff, widow of Sir Charles Thomas Hewitt Mappin, 4th Bt, and formerly wife of Sir Francis Henry Grenville Peek, 4th Bt; *d* 1964; *s* by his el son (2) (WILLIAM) GEOFFREY, 2nd Baron, *b* 1917; Chm Chrysler UK Ltd (formerly Rootes Motors Ltd) 1967-73, Pres Inst of Motor Industry 1973-75, Chm Soc of Motor Manufacturers and Traders 1972-73 (Pres 1960-61), etc; Member Council of Warwick Univ 1956-74, Vice-Pres Game Conservancy 1975-79: *m* 1946, Marian, da of late Lt-Col Herbert Roche Hayter, DSO, and widow of Wing-Cdr James Hogarth Slater, AFC, RAF; *d* 1992; *s* by his only son (3) NICHOLAS GEOFFREY, 3rd Baron and present peer.

Roper, Trevor-, family name of Baron Dacre of Glanton.

ROSEBERY, EARL OF (Primrose) (Earl S 1703 Bt S 1651)

FIDE ET FIDUCIA

By faith and trust

NEIL ARCHIBALD PRIMROSE, 7th Earl, and 9th Baronet; *b* 11 Feb 1929; *s* 1974; *ed* Stowe, and New Coll, Oxford; patron of three livings; a DL for Midlothian: *m* 1955, (Alison Mary) Deirdre, da of late Ronald William Reid, MS, FRCS (*see* Chaytor, Bt, colls, 1980 Edn), and has issue.

ᴀrms – Quarterly: 1st and 4th vert three primroses within a double tressure flory counterflory or *Primrose*; 2nd and 3rd argent, a lion rampant, double queued sable *Cressy*. ᴄrest – A demilion gules holding in the dexter paw a primrose or. ᵴupporters – Two lions or.
Seat – Dalmeny House, South Queensferry, W Lothian E1130 9TQ.

SON LIVING

HARRY RONALD NEIL (*Lord Dalmeny*), *b* 20 Nov 1967: *m* 1994, Caroline J., eldest da of Ronald Daglish and of Mrs William Wyatt-Lowe, of Hemel Hempstead.

DAUGHTERS LIVING

Lady Lucy Catherine Mary, *b* 1955: *m* 1976, (Anthony Gavin) Charles Luis Garton, 2nd son of late Anthony Charles Garton, of West Hyde House, W Hyde, Herts, and has issue living, James Anthony Leo, *b* 1986, — Camilla Mary Eva, *b* 1982.

Lady Jane Margaret Helen, *b* 1960: *m* 1989, Michael S. E. Kaplan, son of R. Kaplan, of Cambridge, Mass, USA, and has issue living, Felix Balthazar Inigo, *b* 1991.

Lady Emma Elizabeth Anne, *b* 1962: *m* 1984, William G. Lamarque, yr son of late W. G. Lamarque, and has issue living, Victor George, *b* 1986, — Francesca, *b* 1988.

Lady Caroline Sara Frances, *b* 1964.

COLLATERAL BRANCHES LIVING

(Not in remainder to United Kingdom Earldom)

Grandchildren of late Ralph Gore Primrose, son of late Edward Montagu Primrose, son of late Hon Francis Ward Primrose, MP, 2nd son of 3rd Earl:—
Issue of late Gerald Edward David Primrose, *b* 1914, *d* 1988: *m* 1950, Anne Loletta (350 La Prenda, Millbrae, Calif 94030, USA), da of late James Ranney Broughton, of Atwood, Ontario, Canada:—
James Ralph, *b* 1952: *m* 1983, Jane Porter, da of Lewis Weyburn Saxby, Jr, of Toledo, Ohio, and has issue living, Andrew Gerald, *b* 1988, — Nicholas James, *b* 1991. *Residence* – 242 Sydney Drive, Alamo, CA 94507, USA.

Issue of late Neil Primrose, *b* 1918, *d* 1979: *m* 1944, Margaret Verna (14560 Sunset Drive, White Rock, BC, Canada V4B 2V9), da of late Henry James Francis, of Portsmouth:—
David Neil (2278 Midas St, Abbotsford, BC, Canada V2S 4R2), *b* 1945; CGA: *m* 1966, Anna Joyce, da of late F. C. Walters, of White Rock, BC, and has issue living, David Francis Neil, *b* 1966; CGA: *m* 1989, Cynthia Lee, da of Dennis C Rumpel, of Abbotsford, BC, and has issue living, Natalie Nicole *b* 1998, — Douglas James Baird, *b* 1970; BA, BEd: *m* 1994, Tracey Michelle, da of Ian N. Gillies, of Abottsford, BC, — Amy Irene, *b* 1979, — Tanya Margaret, *b* 1983. —— Margaret Jane Elizabeth, *b* 1948: *m* 1971, Robert Noboru Maikawa, of 5382 Frances St, Burnaby, BC, Canada V5B 1T5, and has issue living, Paul Robert, *b* 1974, — Steven Anthony, *b* 1976, — Andrea Margaret, *b* 1990. —— Deirdre Katherine, *b* 1951: *m* 1971, Thomas Kevin Ruffen, of 812 East 51st Av, Vancouver, BC, Canada V5X 1E5, and has issue living, Jessica Kirsten, *b* 1973. —— Ann Jennifer, *b* 1954: *m* 1973, Christopher John Barber, of Box 34 Morello Rd, RR1, Nanoose Bay, BC, Canada V0R 2R0, and has issue living, Matthew John, *b* 1975, — Daniel Morgan, *b* 1977, — Jennifer Erin, *b* 1978.

PREDECESSORS – (1) ARCHIBALD Primrose, Clerk of the Privy Council, *cr* a *Baronet* (NS) by Charles II, 1651, and after the Restoration (1661) was appointed a Lord of Session and Lord Clerk Register with the title of Lord Carrington; *d* 1679; *s* by his son (2) Sir WILLIAM, 2nd Bt; was Clerk of the Notaries; *d* 1687; *s* by his son (3) Sir JAMES, 3rd Bt; MP for Edinburghshire 1702-3; *cr Lord Primrose and Castlefield*, and *Viscount Primrose* (peerage of Scotland) 1703, with remainder to the heirs male of his father; *d* 1706; *s* by his el son (4) ARCHIBALD, 2nd Viscount; *d* unmarried 1716; *s* by his brother (5) HUGH, 3rd Viscount; a Lieut-Col in the Army; *dsp* 1741, when the peerages expired, and the baronetcy devolved upon his kinsman (6) JAMES, 6th Bt, who had in 1723 *s* his father as 2nd *Earl of Rosebery* (see*infra); *d* 1755; *s* by his son (7) NEIL, KT, 3rd Earl; a Representative Peer 1768-84; *d* 1814; *s* by his son (8) ARCHIBALD JOHN, KT, PC, 4th Earl, *b* 1783; was unsuccessively MP for Helston and Cashel, and Lord-Lieut of Linlithgowshire; *cr Baron Rosebery*, of Rosebery, co Edinburgh (peerage of United Kingdom) 1828: *m* 1st, 1808, Harriet, da of Hon Bartholomew Bouverie (E Radnor); *d* 1868; *s* by his grandson (9) ARCHIBALD PHILIP, KG, KT, PC (el son of Archibald, Lord Dalmeny, MP, by Lady Catherine Lucy Wilhelmine Stanhope, da of 4th Earl Stanhope), 5th Earl; *b* 1847; Lord-Lieut of cos Linlithgow 1873-1929, and Edinburgh 1884-1929, an Elder Brother of Trinity House, Lord Rector of Aberdeen Univ 1878-81, Under-Sec of State for Home Depart 1881-3, Lord Rector of Edinburgh 1882-5, Lord Privy Seal and First Commr of Works and Public Buildings Feb to June 1885, temporary Keeper of the Great Seal of Scotland 1885, Sec of State for Foreign Affairs 1886 and Aug 1892 to March 1894, and Premier, First Lord of the Treasury, and Lord Pres of the Council March 1894 to June 1895, and Lord Rector of Glasgow 1899-1902; Special Envoy to Court of Vienna to announce Accession of King George V 1910; held Canopy at Coronations of Kings Edward VII and George V: *cr* KG 1892, KT 1895, *Baron Epsom*, of Epsom, co Surrey, and *Viscount Mentmore*, of Mentmore, and *Earl of Midlothian* (peerage of United Kingdom) 1911; received Victorian Chain 1917: *m* 1878, Hannah, who *d* 1890, da and heiress of the late Baron Meyer de Rothschild; *d* 1929; *s* by his son (10) ALBERT EDWARD HARRY MAYER ARCHIBALD, KT, DSO, MC, PC, 6th Earl; *b* 1882; doyen of British Turf as racehorse owner, and breeder; Steward of Jockey Club 1929-32, and 1945-48; MP for Midlothian (*L*) 1906-10; Regional Commr for Scotland 1941-45; Sec of State for Scotland 1945; Chm of Nat Liberal Party 1945-47: *m* 1st, 1909 (*m* *diss* 1919), Lady Dorothy Alice Margaret Augusta Grosvenor, who *d* 1966, sister of 3rd Duke of Westminster; 2ndly, 1924, Hon Dame Eva Isabel Marian Strutt, DBE, JP, LLD, who *d* 1987, da of 2nd Baron Aberdare, and formerly wife of 3rd Baron Belper; *d* 1974, *s* by his yr son **(11)** NEIL ARCHIBALD, 7th Earl and present peer; also Earl of Midlothian, Viscount Rosebery, Viscount Inverkeithing, Viscount Mentmore, Lord Primrose and Dalmeny, Lord Dalmeny and Primrose, Baron Rosebery, and Baron Epsom.

(1) ARCHIBALD Primrose, 4th son of Sir Archibald Primrose, 1st Bt (ante), MP for Edinburgh 1695, Gentleman of the Bedchamber to Prince George of Denmark, and a Commr for the Treaty of the Union, was *cr Lord Primrose and Dalmeny* and *Viscount of Rosebery* (peerage of Scotland) 1700, with remainder to his issue male and female successively, and in default thereof to the heirs of entail in the lands of Rosebery; and *Lord Dalmeny and Primrose, Viscount Inverkeithing*, and *Earl of Rosebery* (peerage of Scotland) 1703, with remainder to his issue male and female successively; was a Representative Peer 1708- 14; *d* 1723; *s* by his son **(2)** JAMES, 2nd Earl, *b* 1741; *s* as 6th Bt (see ante).

Rosehill, Lord; son of Earl of Northesk.

ROSKILL, BARONY OF (Roskill) (Extinct 1996)

SON LIVING OF LIFE BARON

Hon Julian Wentworth (8 Leigh Rd, N5 1SS), *b* 1950; *ed* Winchester; Solicitor 1974: *m* 1975, Catherine Elizabeth, 2nd da of Maj William Francis Garnett, of Quernmore Park, Lancaster LA2 9HJ, and has issue, Matthew Wentworth, *b* 1979, — Oliver Wentworth, *b* 1981.

DAUGHTERS LIVING OF LIFE BARON

Hon Jane Elisabeth Sybil, *b* 1948: *m* 1973, David Christopher Roberts, of 133 Albert Street, NW1 7NB.
Hon Katharine Lucy, *b* 1953: *m* 1977, Nicholas Richard Melville Williams, of 37 Perrymead St, SW6 3SN, and has issue, George Nicholas Melville, *b* 1981, — Olivia Katharine Elisabeth, *b* 1978.

WIDOW LIVING OF LIFE BARON

ELISABETH WALLACE (*Baroness Roskill*), 3rd da of late Thomas Frame Jackson: *m* 1947, Baron Roskill, PC (Life Baron), who *d* 1996. *Residence* – Heatherfield, Newtown, Newbury, Berks RG20 9DB.

Rospigliosi, family name of Earl of Newburgh.

ROSS OF MARNOCK, BARONY OF (Ross) (Extinct 1988)

WIDOW LIVING OF LIFE BARON

ELIZABETH JANE ELMA (*Baroness Ross of Marnock*), BEM, da of J. Aitkenhead, of Ayr: *m* 1948, Baron Ross of Marnock, MBE, PC, who *d* 1988, and has issue two das.

ROSS OF NEWPORT, BARONY OF (Ross) (Extinct 1993)

SONS LIVING OF LIFE BARON

Hon James Gibb, *b* 1956. *Residence* – 65 Brocklehurst St, SE19.
Hon Huw Weston, *b* 1960. *Residence* – 61B Pyle St, Newport, IoW.

DAUGHTERS LIVING OF LIFE BARON

Hon Lesley Priscilla, *b* 1950: *m* 19—, Finian O'Sullivan, of 44 Station Rd, Netley, Southampton, Hants.
Hon Judith Caroline, *b* 1952: *m* 1983, Theodore Kiendl, of 65 Tyrwhitt Rd, Brockley, SE14.

WIDOW LIVING OF LIFE BARON

BRENDA MARIE (*Baroness Ross of Newport*), da of Arthur Ivor Hughes, of Stanmore, Middx: *m* 1949, Baron Ross of Newport (Life Baron), who *d* 1993. *Residence* – Herb Cottage, Skyborry Green, Knighton, Powys LD7 1TW.

ROSSE, EARL OF (Parsons) (Earl I 1806, Bt I 1677)

For God and the King

WILLIAM BRENDAN PARSONS, 7th Earl and 10th Baronet; *b* 21 Oct 1936; *s* 1979; *ed* Grenoble Univ, and Ch Ch, Oxford (MA); late 2nd Lt Irish Guards; UN Official 1963-80, appointed to Ghana, Dahomey, Mid-West Africa, Algeria, Iran, as First UN Volunteer Field Dir, and Bangladesh as UN Disaster Relief Co-ordinator; Memb Irish Govt's Advisory Council on Development Co-operation 1983-88; Dir Historic Irish Houses and Gardens Assoc 1980-91, Agency for Personal Services Overseas 1981-89, Birr Scientific and Heritage Foundation since 1985, and Lorne House Trust since 1993; Trustee of the Tree Register of the British Isles since 1989, and of Quest Campus, Charleville Castle, Ireland since 1997; Hon Fell of Institution of Engineers of Ireland 1994: *m* 1966, Alison Margaret, el da of late Maj John Davey Cooke-Hurle, of Startforth Hall, Barnard Castle, co Durham, and has issue.

Arms – Gules, three leopards' faces argent. Crest – A cubit arm proper, grasping a poleaxe gules. Supporters – Two ounces argent, spotted sable, and gorged with a plain collar gules, charged with four bezants.
Seat – Birr Castle, Birr, co Offaly.

SONS LIVING

(LAURENCE) PATRICK (*Lord Oxmantown*), *b* 31 March 1969; *ed* Aiglon Coll, Switzerland.
Hon Michael John Finn, *b* 1981; *ed* Gordonstoun.

DAUGHTER LIVING

Lady Alicia Siobhan Margaret Nasreen, *b* 1971; *ed* Kingston Univ (B Eng 1993).

BROTHER LIVING

Hon Desmond Oliver Martin (Womersley Park, Doncaster), *b* 1938; *ed* Eton: *m* 1965, Aline Edwina, da of George Alexander Macdonald, MB, of Gable End, Priors Marston, Rugby, and has issue living, Rupert Alexander Michael, *b* 1966, — Desmond Edward Richard, *b* 1968.

COLLATERAL BRANCHES LIVING

Grandchildren of late Hon Richard Clere Parsons, 5th son of 3rd Earl:—
Issue of late Lieut-Col William Frederic Parsons, DSO, *b* 1879, *d* 1956: *m* 1915, Clara Helena who *d* 1972, da of late Hon Edward Gerald Strutt (B Rayleigh, colls):—

(Desmond) Richard (Flat 5, 113 Ifield Rd, SW10 9AS), *b* 1916; *ed* Lancing, and Trin Coll, Camb (BA 1938); late 2nd Lieut Essex Regt. —— Nancy Olivia, *b* 1919.

Issue of late Arthur David Clere Parsons, *b* 1881, *d* 1955: *m* 1914, Doris, who *d* 1970, da of late Norman Charles Cookson, of Oakwood, Wylam, Northumberland:—
(Arthur) Christopher (Hatchwood House, Odiham, Hants; Army and Navy, and City of London Clubs), *b* 1919; 1939-45 War as Maj RA: *m* 1945, Veronica Rosetta de Courcy, el da of Maj-Gen Sir Guy de Courcy Glover, KBE, CB, DSO, MC (B Kingsale, colls), and has issue living, John Christopher, CVO (The Old Stables, Kensington Palace, W8 4PU; Brooks's Club), *b* 1946; Dep Treas to HM since 1987; LVO 1992, CVO 1998: *m* 1982, Hon Anne Constance Manningham-Buller, yst da of 1st Viscount Dilhorne, and has issue living, Michael Reginald *b* 1983, David Guy *b* 1985, Lilah Veronica *b* 1988, — Rosemary Anne, *b* 1948: *m* 1975, John Bernard Burke, of Western House, Lowick, Berwick-upon-Tweed, Northumberland TD15 2UD, and has issue living, Edward Christopher *b* 1981, Henrietta Celia *b* 1979, Juliet Rosemary *b* 1985, — Daphne Phoebe, *b* 1951: *m* 1971, Hugh Richard Oliver-Bellasis, of Wootton House, Wootton St Lawrence, Basingstoke, Hants RG23 8PE, and has issue living (*see* Bates, Bt, *cr* 1880, colls). —— Norman Charles (Pigdon House, nr Morpeth, Northumberland NE61 3SE), *b* 1925: *m* 1953, Katharine Alison, who *d* 1992, 2nd da of Col H. H. Gardiner, MC, late RA, and has had issue, †Giles Randal, *b* 1957; *d* 1983, — Deborah Anne, *b* 1954: *m* 1988, Timothy Harvey Noel Martin, of 154 Loughborough Rd, Nottingham NG2 7JE, and has issue living, Toby Charles Parsons *b* 1991, Harry William Parsons *b* 1994, — Clare Elizabeth, *b* 1959: *m* 1991, Emanuele Trucco, and has issue living, Alistair Alessandro *b* 1999, Emily Valeria *b* 1994, Francesca Alison *b* 1996, — Katharine Mary, *b* 1963: *m* 1987, Alexander Bruce Gentles, of Montgomery House, Stukeley Park, Great Stukeley, Huntingdon, Cambs PE17 5AQ, and has issue living, Angus Alexander *b* 1999. —— Theodora Phoebe, MBE, *b* 1915; MBE (Civil) 1989: *m* 1939, Lt-Cdr James Bertram Everard Wainwright, DSO, OBE, RN, who *d* on active ser 1943, and has had issue, Andrew Christopher James, *b* 1943: *m* 1972, Liza Philpott, and has issue living, Benjamin Andrew *b* 1973, Katherine Louise Parsons *b* 1975, Jennifer Susan *b* 1978, — Susan Rosalind, *b* 1941, *d* 1989: *m* 1967, Richard Edward Dawson. *Residence* – 4 Fairlop Walk, Elmbridge Village, Cranleigh, Surrey GU6 8TW. —— Phyllis Rosemary, *b* 1918: *m* 1st, 1945, as his 2nd wife, Capt Ian Stanley Akers-Douglas, Berks Yeo, who *d* 1952 (*see* V Chilston, colls); 2ndly, 1965, John Anthony Cobham Shaw, of 1 Garden Cottages, Amesbury Abbey, Amesbury, Wilts SP4 7EX (*see* By Cobham).

Issue of late Rev Canon Richard Edward Parsons, *b* 1888, *d* 1971: *m* 1917, Hester Katherine, who *d* 1954, da of late Maj John William Ainslie Drummond (E Perth, colls):—
Rev Desmond John (Priors House, Croft Lane, Crondall, Hants GU10 5QF), *b* 1925; *ed* Eton; late Lt Irish Gds; Organising Sec and Dep Warden, Moor Park Coll for Adult Education 1950-61, and a Gov 1961: *m* 1968, Althea Hermione, da of Charles Anthony Stanley Prowse (*see* Millais, Bt, 1985 Edn), and has issue living, Benedict Desmond Drummond, *b* 1969, — Francesca Katherine, *b* 1972. —— Agnes Mary, *b* 1918: *m* 1941, Maj Cosmo Rex Ivor Russell (*see* B Ampthill, colls). —— Hester Clere, *b* 1920: *m* 1940, David Hastings Gerald Russell, late Lt RNVR (*see* B Ampthill, colls). —— Elizabeth Frances, *b* 1923. —— Rachel Anne (38 Ridgeway Rd, Farnham, Surrey), *b* 1927.

Grandchildren of late Rev Randolph Cecil Parsons (infra):—
Issue of late John Cecil Lawrence Parsons, *b* 1905, *d* 1978: *m* 1940 (*m diss* 1958), Mary Lovell:—
Michael Charles (12 Addicott Rd, Weston-super-Mare), *b* 1950. —— Cynthia, *b* 1948: *m* 1967, John Ryman, and has issue living, Julie Angela, *b* 1968.

Granddaughter of late Hon Lawrence Parsons, son of 2nd Earl:—
Issue of late Rev Randolph Cecil Parsons, *b* 1852, *d* 1941: *m* 1901, Florence Emily, who *d* 1946, da of William Ashton:—
Joan Mary (12 Addicott Rd, Weston-super-Mare), *b* 1906; LRAM.

PREDECESSORS – **(1)** LAWRENCE Parsons; *cr* a Baronet 1677; was attainted by King James's Parliament 1689, and sentenced to death; *d* 1698; *s* by his son **(2)** Sir WILLIAM, 2nd Bt; *d* 1740; *s* by his grandson **(3)** Sir LAWRENCE, 3rd Bt; was MP for King's Co 1741; *d* 1749; *s* by his son **(4)** Sir WILLIAM, 4th Bt; was MP for King's Co; *d* 1791; *s* by his son **(5)** Sir LAWRENCE, 5th Bt; successively MP for Dublin University and King's Co; in 1807 *s* his father's half-brother as 2nd *Earl of Rosse* (see *infra*); was a Representative Peer, and last Joint Postmaster-Gen for Ireland; *d* 1841; *s* by his son **(6)** WILLIAM, KP, 3rd Earl; *b* 1800; sat as MP for King's Co (*L*) 1821-34; was a Representative Peer, Pres of Royal Soc, Chancellor of Dublin Univ; erected upon his estate at Parsonstown between the years 1828 and 1845 an enormous telescope at the cost of more than £20,000: *m* 1836, Mary, who *d* 1885, da and el co-heir of John Wilmer Field, of Heaton Hall, co York; *d* 1867; *s* by his son **(7)** LAWRENCE, KP, DCL, FRS, 4th Earl; *b* 1840; a Representative Peer and Chancellor of Dublin Univ; Lieut and Custos Rotulorum of King's Co (High Sheriff 1867): *m* 1870, (Frances) Cassandra, who *d* 1921, da of 4th Baron Hawke; *d* 1908; *s* by his son **(8)** WILLIAM EDWARD, 5th Earl, *b* 1873; a Representative Peer, and Lieut and Custos Rotulorum of King's co; Major Irish Guards: *m* 1905, Frances Lois, who *d* 1984, having *m* 2ndly, 1920, 5th Viscount de Vesci (*d* 1958), da of Sir Cecil Edmund Lister-Kaye, 4th Bt; *d* of wounds received in action 1918; *s* by his son **(9)** LAURENCE MICHAEL HARVEY, KBE, 6th Earl; *b* 1906; FSA, FRSA, FRAS, Hon FRIBA, MRIA, VMH, Vice-Chancellor Dublin Univ 1949-64, Chm Georgian Group 1947-68, and Standing Commn on Museums and Galleries; Dep Chm National Trust: *m* 1935, Anne, who *d* 1992, only da of late Lt-Col Leonard Charles Rudolph Messel, OBE, TD (and granddaughter of Linley Sambourne, in whose house at 18 Stafford Terr, W8, she assembled the Victorian Soc 1957), and formerly wife of late Ronald Owen Lloyd Armstrong-Jones, MBE, QC (*see* E Snowdon); *d* 1979; *s* by his son **(10)** WILLIAM BRENDAN, 7th Earl and present peer; also Baron Oxmantown.

*(1) LAWRENCE Parsons, 2nd son of Sir Lawrence, 3rd Bt (ante), was *cr Baron Oxmantown* (peerage of Ireland) 1792, with remainder to his nephew Sir Lawrence Parsons, 5th Bt (ante), *Viscount Oxmantown* (peerage of Ireland) 1795, without the special remainder, and *Earl of Rosse* (peerage of Ireland) 1806, with remainder to his nephew aforesaid; *d* 1807, when the Viscountcy became ext, and he was *s* in the other honours by his nephew **(2)** Sir LAWRENCE, 2nd Earl and 5th Bt (ante).

ROSSLYN, EARL OF (St Clair Erskine) (Earl UK 1801, Bt S 1666)

PETER ST CLAIR ERSKINE, 7th Earl, and 10th Baronet; *b* 31 March 1958; *s* 1977; *ed* Eton, and Bristol Univ (BA); Metropolitan Police 1980-94, since when Thames Valley Police: *m* 1982, Helen M., eldest da of C. R. Watters, of Christ's Hospital, Sussex, and has issue.

Arms – Quarterly: 1st, argent, a cross engrailed sable, *St Clair*; 2nd, argent, a pale sable, *Erskine*; 3rd azure, a bend between six cross crosslets fitchée or, *Mar*; 4th argent, on a chevron between three roses gules, a fleur-de-lis of the field, *Wedderburn*. **Crest** – A demi-phoenix in flames, wings expanded and elevated proper. **Supporters** – Dexter, an eagle, wings inverted proper, gorged with a plain collar argent, thereon a rose gules; *sinister*, a griffin, wings elevated proper, beaked and membered or.
Address – c/o House of Lords, SW1A 0PW.

SONS LIVING

JAMIE WILLIAM (*Lord Loughborough*), *b* 28 May 1986.
Hon Harry, *b* 1995.

DAUGHTERS LIVING

Lady Alice, *b* 1988.
Lady Lucia, *b* 1993.

SISTER LIVING

Lady Caroline, *b* 1956: *m* 1991, Michael Francis Marten, son of Lt-Col Francis William Marten, CMG, MC (*see* B Vernon, 1964 Edn).

MOTHER LIVING

Athenaïs, da of late Louis Victor de Mortemart, Duc de Vivonne: *m* 1st, 1955 (*m diss* 1962), 6th Earl of Rosslyn, who *d* 1977; 2ndly 1978 (*m diss* 1983), as his 2nd wife, Robert Edgar Atheling (Bend'or) Drummond (*see* E Perth, colls), who *d* 1994.

PREDECESSORS – (1) *Rt Hon* ALEXANDER Wedderburn, PC, MP for the Ayr Burghs 1761-8, for Castle Rising 1774, for Okehampton 1774-8, and for Bishops Castle 1778-80, having been Solicitor-Gen, and Attorney-Gen was in 1780 *cr Baron Loughborough*, of Loughborough, co Leicester (peerage of Great Britain); was Lord High Chancellor of Great Britain 1793-1801; *cr Baron Loughborough*, of Loughborough, co Surrey (peerage of Great Britain) 1795, with remainder to his nephew Sir James Erskine, 6th Bt (see *infra) and Earl of Rosslyn* (peerage of United Kingdom) 1801, with similar remainders; *dsp* 1805; *s* by his nephew (2) JAMES, GCB, PC, 2nd Earl; assumed the additional surname of St Clair by Roy licence 1805; sat as MP for Castle Rising 1782-84, for Morpeth 1784-90 and for Kirkcaldy 1796-1805; was Director-Gen of Chancery in Scotland 1785-1837, a Lieut-Gen in the Army, Lord-Lieut of Fifeshire, and Lord Pres of the Council 1834-5; *d* 1837; *s* by his son (3) JAMES ALEXANDER, PC, 3rd Earl; *b* 1802; was a Gen in the Army, Col 7th Hussars, Master of the Buckhounds 1841-6, and Under-Sec of State for War 1859: *m* 1826, Frances, da of Lieut-Gen William Wemyss; *d* 1866; *s* by his son (4) FRANCIS ROBERT, PC, 4th Earl; *b* 1833; High Commr to Gen Assembly of Church of Scotland 1874, 1878, 1879, and 1880, and Capt of Corps of Gentlemen-at-Arms 1886-90; *d* 1890: *m* 1866, Blanche Adeliza, who *d* 1933, da of Henry FitzRoy, and widow of Col Hon Charles Henry Maynard; *s* by his el son (5) JAMES FRANCIS HARRY, 5th Earl, *b* 1869: *m* 1st, 1890 (*m diss* in Scotland 1902), Violet Aline, who *d* 1945, da of late Robert Charles de Grey Vyner (B Lucas, colls); 2ndly, 1905 (*m diss* 1907), Georgeiana, then a member of the dramatic profession, who *d* 1917, yr da of George Robinson, of Minneapolis, USA; 3rdly 1908, Vera Mary, who *d* 1975, da of late Eric Edward Bayley, formerly Lt 17th Lancers; *d* 1939; *s* by his grandson (6) ANTHONY HUGH FRANCIS HARRY (son of late Francis Edward Scudamore, Lord Loughborough, el son of 5th Earl), 6th Earl, *b* 1917: *m* 1955 (*m diss* 1962), Athenaïs (who *m* 2ndly, 1978 (*m diss* 1983), as his 2nd wife, Robert Edgar Atheling (Bend'or) Drummond (*see* E Perth, colls), who *d* 1994), only da of late Louis Victor, Duc de Vivonne, and *d* 1977; *s* by his only son (7) PETER, 7th Earl and present peer; also Baron Loughborough.

*(1) CHARLES Erskine, successively MP for cos Clackmannan and Stirling; *cr* a *Baronet* 1666: *s* by his el son (2) *Sir* JAMES, 2nd Bt; *k* at battle of Landen 1693, unmarried; *s* by his brother (3) *Sir* JOHN, 3rd Bt; MP for Clackmannan; *d* 1739; *s* by his el son (4) *Sir* CHARLES, 4th Bt; *k* at battle of Laffeldt 1747, unmarried; *s* by his brother (5) *Sir* HENRY, 5th Bt; a Lieut-Gen in the Army; sat as MP for Ayr and for Anstruther: *m* Janet, da of Peter Wedderburn (Lord Chesterhall), a Lord of Session; *s* by his son (6) *Sir* JAMES, 6th Bt, who *s* his uncle as 2nd Earl of Rosslyn (ante).

ROSSMORE, BARON (Westenra) (Baron I 1796 and UK 1838)

After battles, rewards

WILLIAM WARNER WESTENRA, 7th Baron; *b* 14 Feb 1931; *s* 1958; *ed* Eton, and Trin Coll, Camb (BA 1957); is 2nd Lieut Somerset LI: *m* 1982, Valerie Marion, da of Brian Tobin, of Ballough, Riverstown, Birr, co Offaly, and has issue.

Arms – Quarterly: 1st and 4th per bend or and argent, in chief a tree eradicated vert, and in base waves of the sea, therein a seahorse naiant, reguardant, all proper, *Westenra*; 2nd and 3rd quarterly, 1st and 4th azure, three mullets argent, *Murray*; 2nd and 3rd gules, three martlets within a bordure or, *Cairnes*. Crest – A lion rampant proper. Supporters – *Dexter*, a trooper of the 5th Dragoons in uniform, and holding in his right hand a sword, point downwards; *sinister*, a black charger of the same regiment, caparisoned proper.
Address – c/o Lloyds Bank plc, 6 Pall Mall, SW1.

SON LIVING

Hon BENEDICT WILLIAM, *b* 6 March 1983.

SISTER LIVING

Hon Brigid Mary WESTENRA, *b* 1928; has resumed her maiden name: *m* 1956 (*m diss* 1969), Hon Jonathan Alan Howard (*see* B Strathcona and Mount Royal).

COLLATERAL BRANCH LIVING

Issue of late Hon Richard Westenra, 2nd son of 5th Baron, *b* 1893, *d* 1944: *m* 1st, 1919 (*m diss* 1936), Alice Florence, who *d* 1975, da of Maxwell Vandeleur Blacker-Douglas, of Seafield, Millbrook, Jersey, Channel Islands; 2ndly, 1936, Mrs Margaret Cecilia Sullivan Hope, who *d* 1979, da of Rev George Sullivan Edgcombe:—
(By 1st *m*) Cynthia Zia Hester, *b* 1920: *m* 1947 (*m diss* 1957), Eric Miles, son of Alfred Shakespear Miles, of Buenos Aires, Argentina, and has issue living, Richard Christopher (37 St Peter's Sq, W6 9NW), *b* 1955: *m* 1982, Sarah Dawson, and has issue living, Robert Henry Shakespear *b* 1988, Henry Blacker Shakespear *b* 1990, Katharine Westenra *b* 1985, — Caroline Rose, *b* 1948: *m* 1970, James Peter Stansfeld-Huelin, of La Vallonerie, La Blinerie, St Clements, Jersey, CI, and has issue living, Alicia Antoinette *b* 1975, Rosanna Arlette *b* 1978, — Sylvia Claire, *b* 1950: *m* 1979, Guy Robert William Woods, of Homestead, Rue De La Fontaine, St Lawrence, Jersey, CI (*see* Pelly, Bt, 1990 Edn), and has issue living, Serena Sylvia *b* 1982.

PREDECESSORS – (1) ROBERT Cuninghame, son of late Col David Cuninghame; *b* 17-; a Gen in the Army, and Col 5th Dragoons; MP for Tulske 1751-60, for Armagh 1761-8, for Monaghan 1769-96, and for E Grinstead 1788-9; *cr Baron Rossmore*, of Monaghan, co Monaghan (peerage of Ireland) 1796, with remainder to his wife's nephews, Henry Alexander Jones (who *dsp*) and Warner William and Henry Westenra: *m* 1754, Elizabeth, who *d* 1824, 2nd da and co-heiress of the late Col John Murray; *d* 1801; *s* by his nephew (2) WARNER WILLIAM Westenra, 2nd Baron; *b* 1765; MP for co Monaghan 1800-1801; *cr Baron Rossmore*, of co Monaghan (peerage of United Kingdom) 1838: *m* 1st, 1791, Marianne, who *d* 1807, da of late Charles Walsh, of Walsh Park, co Tipperary; 2ndly, 1819, Lady Augusta Charteris, who *d* 1840, da of Francis, Lord Elcho; *d* 1842; *s* by his el son (3) HENRY ROBERT, 3rd Baron; *b* 1792; was MP for co Monaghan 1818-32 and 1834-42, and afterwards Lord-Lieut thereof: *m* 1st, 1820, Anne Douglas Hamilton, who *d* 1844; 2ndly, 1846, his cousin, Julia Ellen Josephine, who *d* 1912, da of Henry Lloyd, of Farinrory, co Tipperary; *d* 1860; *s* by his el son (4) HENRY CAIRNES, 4th Baron; Cornet 1st Life Guards; *d* 1874; *s* by his brother (5) DERRICK WARNER WILLIAM, 5th Baron, *b* 1853; Lieut of co Monaghan: *m* 1882, Mittie, OBE, who *d* 1953, da of Richard Christopher Naylor, of Hooton Hall, Cheshire; *d* 1921; *s* by his el son (6) WILLIAM, 6th Baron; *b* 1892; European War 1914-18, European War 1939-45 as Lieut RNVR: *m* 1927, Dolores Cecil, who *d* 1981, formerly wife of late Col Maurice George Lee, MC, RFC, of Christchurch, NZ, and da of late Lieut-Col James Alban Wilson, DSO, Indian Army, of West Barton, Yorkshire; *d* 1958; *s* by his only son (7) WILLIAM WARNER, 7th Baron, and present peer.

ROTHERMERE, VISCOUNT (Harmsworth) (Viscount UK 1919, Bt UK 1910)

He who acts diligently acts well

(HAROLD) JONATHAN ESMOND VERE HARMSWORTH, 4th Viscount, and 4th Baronet; *b* 3 Dec 1967; *s* 1998; *ed* Gordonstoun, and Duke Univ, N Carolina, USA; Chm Daily Mail and General Trust plc since 1998; patron of three livings: *m* 1993, Claudia C., da of Terence J. Clemence, of Wilton Crescent, SW1, and has issue.

𝕬rms – Azure, two scrolls of paper in saltire or, banded in the centre gules, between four bees volant of the second. 𝕮rest – Between two ostrich feathers or a cubit arm erect proper, the hand grasping a roll of paper or. 𝕾upporters – On either side a gladiator fully habited and accoutred, the dexter holding in the exterior hand a sword, and the sinister holding on the exterior arm a shield all proper, each charged on the breast with a fountain.
Address – Northcliffe House, 2 Derry St, Kensington, W8 5TT.

SON LIVING

Hon VERE RICHARD JONATHAN HAROLD, *b* 20 Oct 1994.

DAUGHTER LIVING

Hon Eleanor Patricia Margaret, *b* 1996.

SISTERS LIVING

Hon Geraldine Theodora Mary Gabriel, *b* 1957: *m* 1st, 1981 (*m diss* 1990), David John, Lord Ogilvy, el son of 13th Earl of Airlie, KT, GCVO, PC; 2ndly, 1997, Glyn Meurig Maxwell, and has issue living (by 1st *m*) (*see* E Airlie), — (by 2nd *m*), Alfreda, *b* 1997.
Hon Camilla Patricia Caroline, *b* 1964: *m* 1989, Andrew R. Yeates, and has issue living, Sebastian Andrew Alexander Vere, *b* 1990, — Alexander Samuel Jonathan Vere, *b* 1993, — Imogen Camilla Patricia Geraldine, *b* 1995, — India Charlotte Caroline Sarah, *b* 1996.

HALF UNCLE LIVING (*Son of 2nd Viscount by 3rd marriage*)

Hon Esmond Vyvyan, *b* (June) 1967; *ed* Eton, Brown Univ, RI, and Harvard Law Sch, Mass. *Residence* – 359 Beacon St, Boston, Mass, USA.

AUNTS LIVING (*Daughters of 2nd Viscount by 1st marriage*)

Hon Lorna Peggy Vyvyan (*Hon Lady Cooper-Key*), *b* (Oct) 1920: *m* 1941, Sir (Edmund Mc) Neill Cooper-Key, who *d* 1981 (*see* Wigram, Bt, colls, 1973-74 Edn), and has had issue, Adrian Astley Vere, *b* 1942; *ed* Eton; *d* as the result of a motor accident in Spain 1963, — (Kevin) Esmond Peter, *b* 1943; *ed* Le Rosey, Millfield, and Carleton Univ, Canada: *m* 1st, 1971 (*m diss* 1976), Lady Mary Gaye Georgiana Lorna Curzon, da of 6th Earl Howe; 2ndly, 1980, Anna (who *m* 2ndly, 1987, Thomas C. U. M. Lundstrom, of Hurdcott House, Hurdcott, Winterbourne Earls, Salisbury, Wilts), da of Count Wilhelm Wachtmeister, Swedish Ambassador to USA, and *d* 1985, leaving issue (by 1st *m*), Pandora Lorna Mary *b* 1973, (by 2nd *m*) Cosmo *b* 1980, Cara *b* 1981, — Emma Charlotte, *b* 1958: resumed her maiden name until re-marriage: *m* 1st, 1985 (*m diss* 19—), Hilary Ord Chittenden, son of late N. G. Chittenden; 2ndly, 1989, (Brian) James Douglas Collins, and has issue (by 2nd *m*) (*see* E Morton). *Residence* – Floralies, Ave de Grande Bretagne, Monte Carlo, Monaco.
Hon Esme Mary Gabriel, CVO, *b* 1922: a Lady of the Bedchamber to HM 1967-71, and an Extra Lady of the Bedchamber to HM, 1974-93, since when an Extra Woman of the Bedchamber to HM; CVO 1980: *m* 1st, 1942, 3rd Earl of Cromer, KG, GCMG, MBE, PC, who *d* 1991; 2ndly, 1993, as his 2nd wife, (Reinier) Gerrit Anton van der Woude, late Capt Gren Guards, who *d* 1999.

WIDOW LIVING OF THIRD VISCOUNT

MAIKO JOEONG-SHUN LEE, of Kyoto, Japan (*Dowager Viscountess Rothermere*): *m* 1993, as his 2nd wife, 3rd Viscount Rothermere, who *d* 1998. *Residence* – 36 Rue du Sentier, Paris 75002, France.

PREDECESSORS – (1) *Rt Hon* HAROLD SIDNEY Harmsworth, 2nd son of late Alfred Harmsworth, Bar-at-Law; *b* 1868; sometime Ch Proprietor of the *Daily Mail, Evening News*, etc, Chm of Associated Newspapers, Ltd, and a Director of the Amalgamated Press, Ltd; was Director-Gen of Roy Army Clothing Depart 1916, and Pres of Air Council 1917-18; *cr* a *Baronet*, 1910, *Baron Rothermere*, of Hemstead, co Kent (peerage of UK) 1914, and *Viscount Rothermere*, of Hemsted, co Kent (peerage of UK) 1919: *m* 1893, Mary Lilian, who *d* 1937, da of George Wade Share, of Forest Hill, SE; *d* 1940; *s* by his 3rd but only surviving son (2) ESMOND CECIL, 2nd Viscount; *b* 1898, was MP Isle of Thanet Div, Kent 1919-29; Chm of Assoc Newspapers, and *Daily Mail* and General Trust, Pres Newspaper Press Fund 1935-37, Chm Newspaper Proprietors' Assoc 1934-61, Chm Newsprint Supply Co 1940-59, Trustee Reuters New Agency: *m* 1st, 1920 (*m diss* 1938), Margaret Hunam, who *d* 1991 (having *m* 2ndly, 1938 (*m diss* 1946), as his 2nd wife, Capt Thomas Andrew Hussey, CBE, RN, who *d* 1980, and 3rdly, 1947, as his 2nd wife, Sir John Lionel Reginald Blunt, 10th Bt, who *d* 1969), da of late William Lancelot Redhead, of Carville Hall, Brentford; 2nd, 1945 (*m diss* 1952), Ann Geraldine Mary, who *d* 1981, el da of Hon Guy Lawrence Charteris (*see* E Wemyss), and widow of 3rd Baron O'Neill; 3rdly 1966, Mary, who *d* 1993, el da of Kenneth Murchison, of Dallas, Texas, and formerly wife of Richard Ohrstrom, of The Plains, Virginia; *d* 1978; *s* by his el son (3) VERE HAROLD ESMOND, 3rd Viscount, *b* 1925; Chm Associated Newspapers Ltd 1970-92, and Daily Mail and

General Trust plc 1978-98; FRSA; Cmdr of several foreign orders: *m* 1st, 1957, Mrs Patricia Evelyn Beverley Brooks, who *d* 1992, da of John William Matthews, FIAS, and formerly wife of Capt Christopher John Brooks (*see* B Crawshaw, colls); 2ndly, 1993, Maiko Joeong-shun Lee, of Kyoto, Japan; *d* 1998; *s* by his only son (4) (HAROLD) JONATHAN ESMOND VERE, 4th Viscount and present peer; also Baron Rothermere.

ROTHERWICK, BARON (Cayzer) (Baron UK 1939, Bt UK 1924)

(HERBERT) ROBIN CAYZER, 3rd Baron, and 3rd Baronet; *b* 12 March 1954; *s* 1996; *ed* Harrow and RAC Cirencester; *hp* to his kinsman's Baronetcy (cr 1904); late Life Guards: *m* 1982 (*m diss* 1994), Sara Jane, only da of Robert James McAlpine (*see* McAlpine, Bt, colls), and has issue.

Arms – Per chevron azure and argent, two estoiles or and an ancient ship with three masts, sails furled sable, pinions flying gules; a chief invected of the third charged with a rose gules barbed and seeded proper between two fleurs-de-lis of the first. **Crest** – A sea-lion erect proper, gorged with a naval crown and holding in his dexter paw an estoile gold. **Supporters** – *Dexter*, a lion; and *sinister*, a Bengal tiger proper; each gorged with a naval crown or, and grasping a flagpole also proper, flying therefrom a banner gules, thereon a lozenge argent charged with a lion rampant, also gules.
Seat – Cornbury Park, Charlbury, Oxon OX7 3HA.

SONS LIVING

Hon HERBERT ROBIN, *b* 10 July 1989.
Hon Henry Alexander, *b* 1991.

DAUGHTER LIVING

Hon Harriette Jane, *b* 1986.

BROTHERS LIVING

Hon Charles William, *b* 1957; *ed* Harrow; late Life Guards: *m* 1985, Amanda Cosbie Sara, 2nd da of John Squire, of Marbella, Spain, and has issue living, (Charles) William, *b* 1991, — Victoria Amanda, *b* 1989. *Residence* – Finstock Manor, Finstock, Oxon OX7 3DG.
Hon Avon Arthur, *b* 1968.

SISTER LIVING

Hon Robina Jane, *b* 1953: *m* 1981, Olivier Debarge, and has issue living, Alexandra Jane *b* 1982, — Iona Amelia, *b* 1986. *Residence* – 3 Redesdale St, SW3.

AUNT LIVING (*Daughter of 1st Baron*)

Hon Molly Angela (*Hon Lady Wyldbore-Smith*), *b* 1917: *m* 1944, Maj-Gen Sir Francis Brian Wyldbore Wyldbore-Smith, CB, DSO, OBE (*see* Smith-Marriott, Bt, colls). *Residence* – Grantham House, Grantham, Lincs NG31 6SS.

WIDOW LIVING OF SON OF FIRST BARON

Baroness Sybille de Selys Longchamps: *m* 1982, as his 2nd wife, Hon (Michael) Anthony (Rathborne) Cayzer, who *d* 1990.

COLLATERAL BRANCH LIVING

Issue of late Hon (Michael) Anthony (Rathborne) Cayzer, yr son of 1st Baron, *b* 1920 *d* 1990: *m* 1st, 1952, Hon Patricia Helen Browne, who *d* 1981, da of 4th Baron Oranmore and Browne; 2ndly, 1982, Baroness Sybille de Selys Longchamps (ante):—
(By 1st *m*) (Linda) Kinvara, *b* 1953: *m* 1st, 1979 (*m diss* 1989), Timothy James Douro Hoare, eldest son of Michael Douro Hoare, of Downland Court, Ditchling, Sussex; 2ndly, 1994, Alan James Holder, and has issue living (by 1st *m*), Sam Patrick Douro, *b* 1981, — (by 2nd *m*), Turoe James, *b* 1994, — Sasha Kinvara, *b* 1995. *Residence* – Model Farm, Kings Langley, Herts. ——Rosanne (*Hon Mrs Hugh Tollemache*), *b* 1956: *m* 1986, Hon Hugh John Hamilton Tollemache, yst son of 6th Baron Tollemache, and has issue. *Residence* – Sandbourne House, Earl's Croome, Worcs WR8 9DG. —— Verena Brigid, *b* 1961: *m* 1985, R. Ian Molson, 3rd son of William M. Molson, of Montreal, Canada, and has

had issue, Edward Charles, *b* 1987, — Camilla Rose, *b* 1989; *d* 1995, — Sophie Natasha, *b* 1995, — Louisa Rose, *b* 1996. *Residence* – 14 Mallord St, SW3 6DU.

PREDECESSORS – **(1)** HERBERT ROBIN Cayzer, 5th son of Sir Charles (William) Cayzer, 1st Bt (*cr* 1904), of Gartmore, Perthshire; *b* 1881; Chm British & Commonwealth Steamship Co Ltd, Clan Line Steamers Ltd, Union Castle Mail Steamship Co Ltd, and other Cos; MP for S Div of Portsmouth (*C*) 1918-22, and 1923-39; *cr* a *Baronet* 1924, and *Baron Rotherwick*, of Tylney, co Southampton (peerage of United Kingdom) 1939: *m* 1911, Freda Penelope, who *d* 1961, da of late Col William Hans Rathbone, formerly of Scripplestown and of Kilcogy, co Cavan; *d* 1958; *s* by his el son **(2)** (HERBERT) ROBIN, 2nd Baron, *b* 1912; Major The Greys (Supplementary Res), Middle East 1939-45; Dep Chm Caledonia Investments plc; *m* 1952, Sarah Jane, who *d* 1978, only da of Sir Michael Nial Slade, 6th Bt; *d* 1996; *s* by his eldest son **(3)** (HERBERT) ROBIN, 3rd Baron and present peer.

ROTHES, EARL OF (Leslie) (Earl S before 1457)
(Title pronounced "Roth-ez")

IAN LIONEL MALCOLM LESLIE, 21st Earl; *b* 10 May 1932, *s* 1975; *ed* Eton; late Sub-Lieut RNVR: *m* 1955, Marigold, only da of late Sir David Martyn Evans Bevan, 1st Bt, and has issue.

𝔄rms – Quarterly: 1st and 4th, Argent on a bend azure three buckles or, *Leslie*; 2nd and 3rd or, a lion rampant, gules, debruised by a ribbon sable, *Abernethy*. ℭrest – A demi-griffin proper. 𝔖upporters – Two griffins proper.
Residence – Tanglewood, W Tytherley, Salisbury, Wilts.

SONS LIVING

JAMES MALCOLM DAVID (*Lord Leslie*), *b* 4 June 1958.
Hon Alexander John, *b* 1962; *ed* Eton: *m* 1990, Tina L., da of Dr T. E. Gordon, of Westmoreland Drive, Orlando, Florida, USA. *Residence* – Whitefield House, Monimail, Cupar, Fife KY15 7SB.

SISTERS LIVING

Lady Jean, CBE *b* 1927; CBE 1991: *m* 1949, Roderick Robin Mackenzie (Troubridge, Bt). *Residence* – Kingfisher House, Ampfield, Hants.
Lady Evelyn, *b* 1929: *m* 1949, Gerard William Mackworth Mackworth-Young (*see* Young, Bt *cr* 1813, colls), who *d* 1984. *Residence* – Fisherton Mill, Fisherton de la Mere, Warminster, Wilts BA12 OPZ.

WIDOW LIVING OF SON OF NINETEENTH EARL

Coral Angela, da of late George Henry Pinckard, JP, of Combe Court, Chiddingfold, Surrey, and 9 Chesterfield St, W1: *m* 1932, Hon John Wayland Leslie, late Flight-Lieut RAF Vol Reserve, who *d* 1991. *Residence* – The Dower House, Headbourne Worthy, Winchester, Hants SO23 7JG.

COLLATERAL BRANCHES LIVING

Issue of late Hon John Wayland Leslie, late Flight-Lieut RAF Vol Reserve, yr son of 19th Earl, *b* 1909, *d* 1991: *m* 1932, Coral Angela (ante), da of late George Henry Pinckard, JP, of Combe Court, Chiddingfold, Surrey, and 9 Chesterfield St, W1:—
Alastair Pinckard, TD, *b* 1934; *ed* Eton; formerly Capt RSF (TA); Member Queen's Body Guard for Scotland (Royal Company of Archers): *m* 1963, Rosemary, da of late Cdr Hubert Wyndham Barry, RN, of Hill House, Broughton, Hants (*see* Barry, Bt, colls), and has had issue, †David John, *b* 1967; *d* 1989, — Fiona Jane, *b* 1965: *m* 1990, Richard Alan Patrick de Klee, yst son of Col Murray de Klee, OBE, of Auchnacraig, Isle of Mull, and has issue living, Frederick Leslie Blair *b* 1993, Lachlan Richard John *b* 1996, — Ann Mary, *b* 1973: *m* 1997, Kelvin Mullins. *Residence* – Seasyde House, by Errol, Perthshire PH2 7TA. —— Amber Elizabeth, *b* 1939: *m* 1964, Beresford Robert Winder White, and has issue living, Rupert Beresford, *b* 1966, — Alexander Richard Beresford, *b* 1968. *Residence* – Dumpford Manor House, Trotton, nr Rogate, Petersfield, Hants.

Issue of late Hon Edward Courtenay Haworth-Leslie, 2nd son of Mary Elizabeth, Countess of Rothes, *b* 1840, *d* 1911: *m* 1890, Caroline Edith, who *d* 1948, da of Thomas Tregenna Biddulph, of The Earee, Shoalhaven, NS Wales:—
Edward Biddulph, *b* 1895; 1914-18 War as Cpl AIF in France. —— Martin Tregenna, *b* 1896; Lt Australian Reserve of Officers; 1914-18 War in Egypt, Gallipoli, and France (wounded): *m* 1st, 1928, Nettie Margaret, who *d* 1943, da of William Harper, of Napier, NZ; 2ndly, 1945, Joyce Enid, da of Rev Alfred James Gardner, of Chatswood, NSW, and widow of Rev L. M. Dunstan, and has issue living, (by 1st *m*), Mary Haworth, *b* 1936. —— Norman Evelyn, *b* 1898: *m* 1944, Helen Thomson, da of James Thomson Robertson.

PREDECESSORS – **(1)** GEORGE Leslie, *cr* Lord *Leslie* (peerage of Scotland 1445), and *Earl of Rothes* (peerage of Scotland) before 1457; *d* 1488; *s* by his grandson **(2)** GEORGE, 2nd Earl; *d* 1513; *s* by his brother **(3)** WILLIAM, 3rd Earl; killed at Flodden 1513; *s* by his son (4) GEORGE, 4th Earl, Extraordinary Lord of Session; *d* 1558; *s* by his son (5) ANDREW, 5th Earl; *d* 1611; *s* by his grandson (6) JOHN, 6th Earl, one of the first signatories of National Covenant 1638; *d* 1641; *s* by his son (7) JOHN, 7th Earl; carried the Sword of State at the Coronation of Charles II at Scone 1651; was taken a prisoner at battle of Worcester, his estates were forfeited, and he was kept in confinement 1651-8; on the Restoration he was constituted Pres of the Council, and an Extraordinary Lord of Session, was High Commr to the Parliament at Edinburgh 1663, and Keeper of the Privy Seal 1664, Gen of the Forces in Scotland 1666, and Lord High Chancellor for life 1667; obtained in 1663 a charter conferring the *Earldom of Rothes*, and the Lordship of Leslie, regranted as *Leslie and Ballenbreich* in default of male issue upon his el da and her descendants male and female, with the stipulation that the Earldoms of Rothes and Haddington should not be united, and in 1680 was *cr Lord Auchmuty and Caskieberry, Viscount Lugtown, Earl of Leslie, Marquess of Ballenbreich*, and *Duke of Rothes* (peerage of Scotland); *d* without male issue 1681, when the peerages of 1680 expired, and the Earldom of Rothes and inferior honours devolved upon his el da (8) MARGARET, wife of Charles, 5th Earl of Haddington; *d* 1700; *s* by her el son (9) JOHN Hamilton, 9th Earl; assumed the surname of Leslie; appointed a Scottish Representative Peer 1708; *d* 1722; *s* by his son (10) JOHN, KT, 10th Earl; a Lieut-Gen in the Army, and Com-in-Ch of the Forces in Ireland and a Representative Peer; *d* 1767; *s* by his son (11) JOHN, 11th Earl; *dsp* 1773; *s* by his el sister (12) JANE ELIZABETH, wife of George Raymond Evelyn; *d* 1810; *s* by her son (13) GEORGE WILLIAM, 13th Earl; *d* 1817; *s* by his da (14) HENRIETTA ANNE, wife of George Gwyther; assumed the name of Leslie; *d* 1819; *s* by her son (15) GEORGE WILLIAM EVELYN, 15th Earl; *b* 1809: *m* 1831, Louisa, who *d* 1886, da of Col Anderson Morshead, RE; *d* 1841; *s* by his son (16) GEORGE WILLIAM EVELYN, 16th Earl; *d* unmarried 1859; *s* by his sister (17) HENRIETTA ANDERSON MORSHEAD: *m* 1861, Hon George Waldegrave, who assumed the additional surname of Leslie, yst son of 8th Earl Waldegrave; *dsp* 10 Feb 1886; *s* by her aunt (18) MARY ELIZABETH (2nd da of Henrietta Anne (ante No 14)), *b* 1811: *m* 1835, Martin E. Haworth, who *d* Nov 1886, having in March of that year assumed the additional surname of Leslie; *d* 1893; *s* by her grandson (19) NORMAN EVELYN (son of late Martin Leslie Haworth, who *d* before his mother *s* to the Earldom), 19th Earl; *b* 1877; a Representative Peer for Scotland: *m* 1900, Lucy Noël Martha (who *d* 1956, having *m* 2ndly, 1927, Col Claud Macfie, DSO, who *d* 1963), only child of late Thomas Dyer-Edwardes, of Prinknash Park, Gloucester, and Charmandean, Broadwater, Sussex; *d* 1927; *s* by his son (20) MALCOLM GEORGE DYER EDWARDES, 20th Earl *b* 1902; Representative Peer for Scotland 1931-59; Member Queen's Body Guard for Scotland (Royal Company of Archers), Maj Gen List 1940; Dir of Tyres 1941-45, Chm Trinidad Petroleum Co Ltd, Butterworth & Co (Publishers) Ltd, Nat Mutual Life Assurance Soc, Dep Chm British Electric Traction Ltd, Dir Inst of Opthalmology, Rothes Chair in Public Health Opthalmology established at London Univ 1977: *m* 1926, Beryl Violet, who *d* 1994, only da of James Lionel Dugdale, of Crathorne Hall, Yorks; *d* 1975; *s* by his son (21) IAN LIONEL MALCOLM, 21st Earl and present peer; also Lord Leslie and Ballenbreich.

Rothesay, Duke of; title borne by Prince of Wales.

ROTHSCHILD, BARON (Rothschild) (Baron UK 1885, Bt UK 1847)

Concord, integrity, industry

(NATHANIEL CHARLES) JACOB ROTHSCHILD, GBE, 4th Baron, and 5th Baronet; *b* 29 April 1936; *s* 1990; *ed* Eton, and Ch Ch, Oxford; Chm J. Rothschild Holdings plc since 1971, Chm Board of Trustees National Gallery since 1985, Member of Council RCA since 1986, Chm Nat Heritage Memorial Fund since 1991, and Chm Trustees Heather Trust since 1998; Hon FBA 1998; Cdr of Order of Henry the Navigator (Portugal) 1985; GBE (Civil 1998): *m* 1961, Serena Mary, da of Sir Philip Gordon Dunn, 2nd Bt (ext), and has issue.

Arms – Quarterly: 1st or, an eagle displayed sable langued gules; 2nd and 3rd azure, issuing from the dexter and sinister sides of the shield, an arm embowed proper, grasping five arrows points to the base argent; 4th or, a lion rampant proper, langued gules, over all an escutcheon gules, thereon a target, the point to the dexter proper. Crest – 1st (*centre*), issuant from a ducal coronet or, an eagle displayed sable; 2nd (*dexter*), out of a ducal coronet or, between open buffalo horns per fesse or and sable, a mullet of six points or; 3rd (*sinister*), out of a ducal coronet or, three ostrich feathers, the centre one argent, the exterior ones azure. Supporters – (of the Austrian Barony), — *Dexter*, a lion rampant or; *sinister*, an unicorn argent.
Residences – 28 Warwick Av, W9; Stowell Park, Marlborough, Wilts; *Club* – White's

SON LIVING

Hon NATHANIEL PHILIP VICTOR JAMES, *b* 1971; *ed* Wadham Coll, Oxford: *m* 1995 (*m diss* 1998), Iona Annabelle, da of Max Neilson.

DAUGHTERS LIVING

Hon Hannah Mary, *b* 1962: *m* 1994, William Lord Brookfield, eldest son of William Brookfield, of Ocala, USA, and has issue living, Nell Tomoka, *b* 1994, — Clemency Ruth, *b* 1997, — Rose, *b* 1998.

Hon Beth Matilda, *b* 1964: *m* 1991, Antonio Goffredo Tomassini, son of Georgio Tomassini, and has issue living, Ferdinand, *b* 1992, — Edoardo, *b* 1994, — Tess, *b* 1996.

Hon Emily Magda, *b* 1967: *m* 1998, Julian David Warren Freeman-Attwood, son of Maj Harold Warren Freeman-Attwood, and has issue living, Ivy Antarctica, *b* 1999.

SISTERS LIVING

Hon Sarah (known as Hon Sarah DANIEL), *b* 1934; *ed* St Hilda's Coll, Oxford; has issue living (by James Douglas-Henry), Thomas James DANIEL, *b* 19—: *m* 1993, Emily Louise Gilmour, yr da of John Robert Purvis, CBE, of Gilmerton, St Andrews, Fife, — Sharon, *b* 19—; has issue living, Jack *b* 19—, Patrick *b* 19—.

Hon Miranda, *b* 1940: *m* 1st, 1962, Boudjemåa Boumaza, who *d* 1964; 2ndly, 1967, Iain Thomas Watson, and has issue living, (by 1st *m*), Da'ad, *b* 19—: *m* 19—, ... de Gunzbourg, and has issue living, Patrice *b* 19—.

HALF-SISTERS LIVING

Hon Emma Georgina, *b* 1948; *ed* Somerville Coll, Oxford: *m* 1991, Prof Amartya Kumar Sen, FBA.

Hon Victoria Katherine, *b* 1953; *ed* Bedford Coll, London: *m* 1997, Simon James Holliday Gray.

AUNT LIVING *(Sister of 3rd Baron)* *(Raised to the rank of a Baron's daughter 1938)*

Hon Miriam Louisa, CBE, FRS (1985), *b* 1908; Hon Fell of St Hugh's Coll Oxford; Hon DSc Oxford, Leicester, Hull, Göteborg, North Western Univ, Open Univ, Essex, and Cambridge; Prof Roy Free Hosp, and a Trustee of British Museum; CBE (Civil) 1982: *m* 1943 (*m diss* 1957), George Lane, MC, and has had issue, Charles Daniel, *b* 1948; has issue living (by Carmen Wheatley), Alexander *b* 19—, Olivia *b* 19—, — (Mary) Rozsika, *b* 1945: *m* 19— (*m diss* 19—), Kim Parker; has issue living (by Andrew Samuel), Joel *b* 19—, Lydia *b* 19—, — Charlotte Theresa, *b* 1951; has issue living (by Jim Grant), Miriam *b* 19—, Naomi *b* 19—, — Johanna Miriam, *b* 1951 (adopted da): *m*, and has issue. *Residence* – Ashton Wold, Peterborough PE8 5LZ.

WIDOW LIVING OF SON OF THIRD BARON

Anita Patience, 3rd da of James Edward Alexander Rundel Guinness, of Coldpiece Farm, Hook, Hants RG27 8LQ: *m* 1981, Hon Amschel Mayor James Rothschild, who *d* 1996, and has issue (see colls, infra). *Address* – Home Farm, Rushbrooke, Bury St Edmunds, Suffolk IP30 0ER.

COLLATERAL BRANCHES LIVING

Issue of late Hon Amschel Mayor James Rothschild, yr son of 3rd Baron Rothschild, *b* 1955, *d* 1996: *m* 1981, Anita Patience (ante), 3rd da of James Edward Alexander Rundel Guinness, of Coldpiece Farm, Hook, Hants RG27 8LQ:—
James Amschel Victor, *b* 1985. —— Kate Emma, *b* 1982. —— Alice Miranda, *b* 1983.

(In remainder to Baronetcy only)

Grandchildren of late Leopold DE ROTHSCHILD, CVO, son of late Baron Lionel Nathan de Rothschild, el brother of 1st baronet:—
Issue of late Major Lionel Nathan DE ROTHSCHILD, OBE, *b* 1882, *d* 1942: *m* 1912, Marie-Louise Eugenie, who *d* 1975, da of late Edmond Beer, of Paris:—
Edmund Leopold, CBE, TD, *b* 1916; *ed* Harrow, and Trin Coll, Camb (MA); Hon LLD Memorial Univ of Newfoundland 1961, Hon DSc Salford Univ; Order (1st Class) of the Sacred Treasure of Japan; Major RA (TA); Dir of N. M. Rothschild & Sons Ltd; 1939-45 War (wounded); CBE (Civil) 1997: *m* 1st, 1948, Elizabeth Edith, who *d* 1980, da of late Marcel Lentner, of Vienna, Austria; 2ndly, 1982, Anne Evelyn, JP, widow of Lt-Col J. Malcolm Harrison, OBE, TD, and has issue living (by 1st *m*), Nicholas David, *b* 1951: *m* 1985, Caroline J. L., da of late Lawrance Darvall, of Reading, Berks, and has a da, Chloë Alix Irina *b* 1990, — (David) Lionel, *b* 1955: *m* 1991, Louise de C., yst da of late Dr P. M. de C. Williams, of Boar's Hill, Oxford, and has issue living, Leopold James *b* 1994, Amschel Nathaniel *b* 1995, Elizabeth Naomi *b* 1992, — Katherine Juliette, *b* 1949: *m* 1971, Marcus Ambrose Paul Agius, and has issue living, Marie-Louise Eleanor *b* 1977, Lara Sophie Elizabeth *b* 1980, — Charlotte Henrietta, *b* (twin) 1955: *m* 1990, Nigel S. Brown, yr son of late Michael G. H. Brown. *Residence* – Exbury House, Exbury, Southampton. —— Leopold David, CBE, *b* 1927; *cr* CBE (Civil) 1985; Member of Council of Winston Churchill Memorial Trust since 1990. —— Rosemary Leonora, *b* 1913: *m* 1st, 1934 (*m diss* 1942), Maj Hon Denis Gomer Berry, TD, Gren Gds, who *d* 1983 (*see* V Kemsley, colls); 2ndly, 1942, John Antony Seys, who *d* 1989, of No 31 The Mansion, Albury Park, Guildford, Surrey GU5 9BB, and has had issue (by 1st *m*) (*see* V Kemsley, colls), — (by 2nd *m*) David Godfrey Antony (Aston House, Blackheath, Guildford, Surrey, GU4 8RD), *b* 1947: *m* 1978, Nicola Barrington Baird, and has issue living, Alexander Antony David *b* 1980, Philip Christopher Hugh *b* 1984. —— Naomi Louisa Nina, *b* 1920: *m* 1st, 1941, Jean Pierre Reinach, who was *ka* 1942; 2ndly, 1947, Bertrand Goldschmidt, and has issue living, (by 1st *m*) Jocelyne Marguerite Marie-Louise, *b* 1942: *m* 1965, Claude Brice, of Paris, and has issue living, Thomas *b* 1967, Anne *b* 1965: *m* 1998, Felix Doissart (and has issue living, Arthur *b* 1997, Théodore *b* (twin) 1997, Ulysse *b* 1998), — (by 2nd *m*) Paul Lionel, *b* 1952: *m* 1st, 1982 (*m diss* 1997), Cynthia Hampton; 2ndly, 1998, Aline Guichard, and has issue living (by 1st *m*), Olivia *b* 1983, Mathilde *b* 1985, — Emma Louise, *b* 1955: *m* 1987, David

Machover (and has issue living, Edouard *b* 1986, Philippe *b* 1987, Louise *b* 1990). *Residence* – 11 Boulevard Flandrin, Paris, XVI.

Issue of late Anthony Gustav DE ROTHSCHILD, *b* 1887, *d* 1961: *m* 1926, Yvonne, who *d* 1977, da of late Robert Cahen d'Anvers, of Paris:—

Sir Evelyn Robert Adrian (Ascott, Wing, Leighton Buzzard, Beds), *b* 1931; *ed* Harrow and Trin Coll, Camb; Kt 1989: *m* 1st, 1966 (*m diss* 1971), Jeanette, who *d* 1981, da of late Ernest Bishop; 2ndly 1973, Victoria, da of Lewis Schott, and has issue living (by 2nd *m*), Anthony James, *b* 1977, — David Mayer, *b* 1978, — Jessica, *b* 1974. ——— Renée Louise Marie, *b* 1927: *m* 1955, Peter David Robeson. *Residence* – Fences Farm, Tyringham, Newport Pagnell, Bucks.

PREDECESSORS – (1) ANTHONY de Rothschild, second son of Nathan Mayer Rothschild, of Frankfurt-am-Main, who was *cr* a Baron of the Austrian Empire 1822; *b* 1810; a merchant and banker in London; *cr* a *Baronet* 1847 with remainder to the issue of the sons of his elder brother Lionel: *m* 1840, Louise, who *d* 1910, da of late Abraham Montefiore, of Stamford Hill, Middlesex; *d* 1876; *s* by his nephew (2) NATHANIEL MAYER, GCVO, PC (el son of late Baron Lionel Nathan de Rothschild, MP, the first Member of the Jewish persuasion to enter Parliament), 2nd baronet; *s* by special remainder, his uncle, *Sir* ANTHONY, as 2nd Baronet 1876, and *cr Baron Rothschild*, of Tring, co Hertford (peerage of United Kingdom) 1885; Lord-Lieut of Bucks 1887-1915; MP for Aylesbury (*L*) 1865-85: *m* 1867, Emma Louisa, who *d* 1935, da of Baron Mayer Carl de Rothschild, of Frankfurt-am-Main; *d* 1915; *s* by his el son (3) LIONEL WALTER, 2nd Baron, *b* 1868; a Trustee of British Museum, Lieut for City of London; FRS; MP for Bucks, Mid, or Aylesbury Div (LU) 1899-1910; *dunm* 1937; *s* by his nephew (4) NATHANIEL MAYER VICTOR, GBE, GM, FRS (only son of Hon (Nathaniel) Charles Rothschild, 2nd son of 1st Baron), 3rd Baron, *b* 1910; Col Intelligence Corps 1939-45 War, Assist Dir of Research, Zoology Dept, Camb Univ 1950-70, Chm Agricultural Research Council 1948-58, Chm N. M. Rothschild and Sons 1975-76, and Rothschilds Continuation Ltd 1976-88, Chm Shell Research Ltd 1963-70, etc, Dir Gen Central Policy Review Staff, Cabinet Office, 1971-74, author: *m* 1st, 1933 (*m diss* 1945), Barbara, who *d* 1989 (having *m* 2ndly, 1949 (*m diss* 19—), Rex Warner, who *d* 1986, and 3rdly, 1961, Nico Hadjikyriakou-Ghika, who *d* 1994), da of late St John Hutchinson, KC, Bar-at-law, Recorder of Hastings; 2ndly, 1946, Teresa Georgina, MBE, who *d* 1996, da of late Robert John Grote Mayor, CB, of 26 Addison Av, W11; *d* 1990; *s* by his elder son (5) (NATHANIEL CHARLES) JACOB, 4th Baron and present peer.

Rous, family name of Earl of Stradbroke.

ROWALLAN, BARON (Corbett) (Baron UK 1911)

God feeds the ravens

JOHN POLSON CAMERON CORBETT, 4th Baron; *b* 8 March 1947; *s* 1993; *ed* Eton, and RAC Cirencester; ARICS: *m* 1st, 1971 (*m diss* 1983), Susan Jane Dianne, da of James A. Green, of New Farm House, South Linden, Longhorsley, Northumberland; 2ndly, 1984 (*m diss* 1994), Sandrew Filomena, da of William Bryson, of Holland Green, Kilmaurs, Ayrshire; 3rdly 1995, Claire, da of Robert Laidler, of Gateshead, Tyne and Wear, and has issue by 1st and 2nd *m*.

Arms – Quarterly, 1st and 4th argent, a key fesse-wise, wards downwards between two ravens sable, *Corbett*; 2nd and 3rd, azure, a chevron or between two bears' heads couped argent muzzled gules in chief, and in base a cross moline of the third, *Polson*. **Crest** – A branch of an oak proper, thereon a raven sable. **Supporters** – *Dexter*, a salmon proper, holding in its mouth a jewelled ring or; *sinister*, a seal also proper.
Residence – Meiklemosside, Fenwick, Ayrshire KA3 6AY.

SONS LIVING (*By 1st marriage*)

Hon JASON WILLIAM POLSON CAMERON, *b* 21 April 1972; *ed* Glenalmond, and RAC Cirencester.

(*By 2nd marriage*)

Hon (Jonathan Arthur) Cameron, *b* 1985.

DAUGHTERS LIVING (*By 1st marriage*)

Hon Joanna Gwyn Alice Cameron, *b* 1974.

(By 2nd marriage)

Hon Soay Mairi Cameron, *b* 1988.

SISTERS LIVING

Hon Sarah Elizabeth Cameron, *b* 1949: *m* 1968, (Lachlan) Roderick Maclean, and has issue living, Iona Charlotte, *b* 1969, — Sophy Emma, *b* 1972. *Residence* – 8 Elthiron Rd, SW6.

Hon Anne Mary Cameron, *b* 1953: *m* 1972, Rodney John Turner, and has issue living, James Anthony, *b* 1975; *ed* Milton Abbey, — Charles Rory, *b* 1981; *ed* Eton, — Nicola Anne Maria, *b* 1974, — Arabella Mary Claire, *b* 1984. *Residence* – Prescott House, Tiverton, Devon EX16 5NB.

Hon Rosalind Eleanor Cameron, *b* 1958: *m* 1977, Jeremy Michael Sacher, and has issue living, Harry, *b* 1987, — Chloe Emma, *b* 1979, — Charlotte Daisy, *b* 1982. *Residence* – 11 Lansdowne Crescent, W11 2NJ.

UNCLE LIVING (Son of 2nd Baron)

Hon Joseph Mervyn, *b* 1929; *ed* Eton, and Corpus Christie Coll, Camb (BA 1953); late 2nd Lieut Royal Scots Fusiliers: *m* 1960, Hon Catherine Lyon-Dalberg-Acton, da of 3rd Baron Acton, CMG, MBE, TD, and has issue living, Sebastian Antony (Chittlegrove, Rendcomb, nr Cirencester, Glos GL7 7DG), *b* 1963; *ed* Eton, and RAC Cirencester: *m* 1991, Mrs Doran Elizabeth Ann McPherson, only da of late Alan Leary, and has issue living, George Alan Cameron *b* 1993, — Victoria, *b* 1961: *m* 1988, Hugh Merrill, MVO, son of Eric Merrill, of Monkseaton, Tyne & Wear, and has issue living, James Joseph *b* 1989, Guy Charles *b* 1992, Thomas Hugh *b* 1994. *Residence* – The Old Rectory, Coates, nr Cirencester, Glos.

AUNT LIVING (Daughter of 2nd Baron)

Hon Fiona Elizabeth Cameron, *b* 1942: *m* 1st, 1966 (*m diss* 1972), David Henry Amherst Cecil (*see* B Amherst of Hackney, colls); 2ndly, 1974, William Garry Patterson, late Maj Life Guards, and has issue living (by 1st *m*) (*see* B Amherst of Hackney, colls), — (by 2nd *m*), Joseph Robert William, *b* 1981. *Residence* – Kisby's Farm, Ecchinswell, Newbury, Berks RG15 8TS.

MOTHER LIVING

Eleanor Mary, da of late George Frederic Boyle (*see* E Glasgow, colls): *m* 1st, 1945 (*m diss* 1962), Capt Hon Arthur Cameron Corbett, Ayrshire Yeo (later 3rd Baron Rowallan), who *d* 1993; 2ndly, 1963, Col (Richard) Derek Cardiff, late Scots Guards. *Residence* – 8 Melton Court, Old Brompton Rd, SW3.

PREDECESSORS – **(1)** ARCHIBALD CAMERON Corbett, son of late Thomas Corbett, JP, of South Park, Cove, Dunbartonshire; *b* 1856; sat as MP for Tradeston Div of Glasgow (*L*) 1885-1911; *cr Baron Rowallan*, of Rowallan, co Ayr (peerage of United Kingdom) 1911: *m* 1887, Alice Mary, who *d* 1902, only da of John Polson, of Castle Levan, by Gourock; *d* 1933; *s* by his son **(2)** THOMAS GODFREY POLSON, KT, KBE, MC, TD, 2nd Baron, *b* 1895; Lt-Col RSF; Ch Scout of British Commonwealth and Empire 1945-59, Gov of Tasmania 1959-63; Hon Freeman of Edinburgh 1957: *m* 1918, Gwyn Mervyn (CStJ), who *d* 1971, da of Joseph B. Grimond, of St Andrews, Fife, *d* 1977; *s* by his son **(3)** ARTHUR CAMERON, 3rd Baron, *b* 1919; Capt Ayrshire Yeo; 1939-45 War (despatches, Croix de Guerre): *m* 1st, 1945 (*m diss* 1962), Eleanor Mary, da of late George Frederic Boyle (*see* E Glasgow, colls); 2ndly, 1963 (*m annulled* 1970), April Ashley; *d* 1993; *s* by his eldest son **(4)** JOHN POLSON CAMERON, 4th Baron and present peer.

ROWLEY, BARONY OF (Henderson) (Extinct 1968)

WIDOW LIVING OF LIFE BARON

MARY ELIZABETH (*Baroness Rowley*), da of Ernest Verrall Barnes, of Finchley, N, and widow of Harold Gliksten, of London: *m* 1958, Baron Rowley (Life Baron), who *d* 1968.

ROXBURGHE, DUKE OF (Innes Ker) (Duke S 1707, Bt S 1625)
(Title pronounced "Roxbrough", Name pronounced "Innez Carr", Seat pronounced "Fleurs")

For Christ and country danger is sweet

GUY DAVID INNES-KER, 10th Duke, 11th Baronet, and Premier Baronet of Scotland or Nova Scotia; *b* 18 Nov 1954; *s* 1974; *ed* Eton, Magdalene Coll, Camb, and RMA; Lt Blues and Royals (RHG and 1st Dragoons): *m* 1st, 1977 (*m diss* 1990), Lady Jane Meriel Grosvenor, da of 5th Duke of Westminster; 2ndly, 1992, Virginia Mary, elder da of David Wynn-Williams, and of Mrs Christopher Edwards, and has issue by 1st and 2nd *m*.

Arms – Quarterly: 1st and 4th grand quarters counter quartered, 1st and 4th, vert on a chevron between three unicorn's heads erased argent, as many mullets sable; 2nd and 3rd, gules, three mascles or, 2nd and 3rd grand quarters, argent three stars of five points azure. **Crests** – 1st, a unicorn's head erased argent, armed and maned or: 2nd, a boar's head erased proper, langued gules. **Supporters** – Two savages wreathed about the head and middle with laurel, and holding in their exterior hands a club resting on the shoulder all proper.
Seat – Floors Castle, Kelso, Roxburghshire.

SONS LIVING (*By 1st marriage*)

CHARLES ROBERT GEORGE (*Marquess of Bowmont and Cessford*), *b* 18 Feb 1981.
Lord Edward Arthur Gerald, *b* 1984; *ed* Eton.

(*By 2nd marriage*)

Lord George Alastair, *b* 1996.

DAUGHTERS LIVING (*By 1st marriage*)

Lady Rosanagh Viola Alexandra, *b* 1979.

(*By 2nd marriage*)

Lady Isabella May, *b* 1994.

BROTHER LIVING

Lord Robert Anthony, *b* 1959; *ed* Gordonstoun; Lieut Blues and Royals; served in S Atlantic Campaign (despatches), 1982: *m* 19—, Dr Katherine Christina Mary PELLY, elder da of Capt A. M. Jones, RN, of Warsash, Hants, and has issue living, Eliza Henrietta, *b* 1997. *Residence* – Battlesden House, nr Woburn Abbey, Beds.

COLLATERAL BRANCHES LIVING

Descendants of Thomas Ker, of Ferniehirst, brother of Walter Ker, great-great-grandfather of 1st Earl of Roxburghe:—
See M Lothian.

(*In remainder to Baronetcy only*)

Descendants of Alexander Innes, yr brother of James Innes, of Cromey, great-grandfather of 1st baronet:—

Grandchildren of late Arthur Charles Innes-Cross (who assumed the additional surname of Cross by Roy Licence 1888), son of Arthur Innes, of Dromantine, co Down, 8th in descent from Alexander Innes:—
Issue of late Arthur Charles Wolseley Innes, MC, Irish Guards, who relinquished the additional surname of Cross 19—; *b* 1888, *d* 1940: *m* 1915, Etta Maud, who *d* 1971, da of William Bradshaw, of Ordley Hill:—
William Anthony Wolseley, *b* 1935; *ed* Eton. *Residence* – 35 Whittingstall Rd, SW6. —— Anne, *b* 1929: *m* 1959, Roger I. C. Ryland, and has issue living, Charles John (Towngate House, Tidebrook, Wadhurst, E Sussex TN5 6PE), *b* 1962: *m* 1990, Jane M., elder da of Prof Charles Fowler Cullis, of Cuckfield, Sussex, and has issue living, Anna Elizabeth *b* 1991, Arabella Kate *b* 1994, Imogen *b* 1996, — Anna, *b* 1960. *Residence* – 19B British Grove, W4 2NL.

PREDECESSORS – (1) *Sir* ROBERT Ker, Knt; *cr Lord Roxburghe* peerage of Scotland, before 31 March 1600, *Lord Ker of Cessford and Cavertoun*, and *Earl of Roxburgh* (peerage of Scotland) 1616, which honours in 1648 were by charter confirmed in remainder to his grandson Hon William Drummond, who was 4th son of his da Jean by her marriage with the 2nd Earl of Perth, and after him upon the three sons successively of his grand-da Jean, by her marriage with the 3rd Earl of Wigton, with the express stipulation that whoever should succeed should marry Jean, the da of his deceased son Harry, and failing her the next eldest da Anne, and failing her the next da Margaret, and a final remainder to heirs male whatsoever; was Keeper of the Privy Seal 1637; *d* 1650; *s* by his grandson (ante) **(2)** WILLIAM Drummond, 2nd Earl; assumed the surname of Ker, and *m* his cousin Jean, according to the stipulation of the remainder; *d* 1675; *s* by his son **(3)** *Rt Hon* ROBERT, 3rd Earl; *d* 1682; *s* by his el son **(4)** ROBERT, 4th Earl; *d* unmarried 1693; *s* by his brother **(5)** JOHN, KG; was Sec of State 1704; *cr Viscount Broxmouth, Earl of Kelso, Marquess of Bowmont and Cessford*, and *Duke of Roxburghe* (peerage of Scotland) 1707, with remainder to the heirs who should inherit the Earldom of Roxburghe; *d* 1741; *s* by his son **(6)** ROBERT, 2nd Duke, who in 1722 had been *cr Baron Ker*, of Wakefield, co York, and *Earl Ker* (peerage of Great Britain); *d* 1755; *s* by his son **(7)** JOHN, KG, KT, 3rd Duke; *d* unmarried 1804 when the peerages of Great Britain (*cr* 1722) expired, and the Scottish honours devolved upon his kinsman **(8)** WILLIAM, 4th Duke, who in 1797 had *s* as 7th *Lord Bellenden of Broughton*, peerage of Scotland, *cr* 1661; *dsp* 1805, when the Lordship of Bellenden of Broughton became extinct and the Scottish peerages remained dormant until 1812, when they were successfully claimed by **(9)** JAMES Innes, great-grandson of Lady Margaret (ante), 3rd grand-da of the 1st Earl, by her marriage with Sir James Innes, 3rd Bt (see†infra), assumed in 1767 by Roy licence the additional surname of Norcliffe, and relinquished it in 1807 on the death of his first wife; *d* 1823; *s* by his only son by his 2nd *m* **(10)** JAMES HENRY ROBERT, KT, 6th Duke; *b* 1816; *cr Earl Innes* (peerage of United Kingdom) 1837; was Lord-Lieut of Berwickshire, and a Lieut-Gen of Royal Co of Archers: *m* 1836, Susanna Stephania, da of Lieut-Gen Sir James Charles Dalbiac, KCH, *d* 1879; *s* by his son **(11)** JAMES HENRY ROBERT, 7th Duke, *b* 1839; MP for Roxburghshire (*L*) 1870-74; Lord-Lieut of co Roxburgh, and one of HM Queen Victoria's Body Guard of Scotland: *m* 1874, Lady Emily Anne Spencer-Churchill, OBE, VA, who *d* 1923, da of 6th Duke of Marlborough; *d* 1892; *s* by his el son **(12)** HENRY JOHN, KT, MVO, 8th Duke, *b* 1876; bore Queen Consort's Crown at Coronation of King Edward VII 1902, and St Edward's Staff at Coronation of King George V 1911; was Chancellor of the Order of the Thistle: *m* 1903, Mary, who *d* 1937, da of late Ogden Goelet, of Newport, USA; *d* 1932; *s* by his only son **(13)** GEORGE VICTOR ROBERT JOHN, 9th Duke, *b* 1913: *m* 1st, 1935 (*m diss* 1953), Lady Mary Evelyn Hungerford Crewe-Milnes, da of 1st Marquess of Crewe (ext); 2ndly, 1954, (Margaret) Elisabeth (who *d* 1983, having *m* 3rdly, 1976, as his 2nd wife, Jocelyn Olaf Hambro, MC, who *d* 1994), da of late Capt Frederick Bradshaw McConnel, Gordon Highlanders, of Knockdalian, Colmonell, Ayrshire, and formerly wife of Lt-Col James Cunningham Church, MC; *d* 1974; *s* by his el son **(14)** GUY DAVID, 10th Duke, and present peer; also Marquess of Bowmont and Cessford, Earl of Roxburghe, Earl of Kelso, Earl Innes, Viscount Broxmouth, Lord Roxburghe, and Lord Ker of Cessford and Cavertoun.

†**(1)** *Rt Hon Sir* ROBERT Innes (19th Baron of Innes, co Moray, from 1160); MP for Elgin and Forres-shire 1639-41; *cr* a *Baronet* with remainder to heirs male whatsoever 1625; *d* 1658; *s* by his son **(2)** *Sir* ROBERT, 2nd Bt; MP for Moray 1661-78; *s* by his son **(3)** *Sir* JAMES, 3rd Bt: *m* Lady Margaret Ker (ante), da of Harry, son of 1st Earl of Roxburghe; *s* by his son **(4)** *Sir* HARRY, 4th Bt; MP for Moray in Union Parliament 1707; *d* 1721; *s* by his son **(5)** *Sir* HARRY, 5th Bt; *d* 1762; *s* by his son **(6)** *Sir* JAMES, 6th Bt, who *s* as 5th Duke of Roxburghe (ante).

ROYLE, BARONY OF (Royle) (Extinct 1975)

DAUGHTER LIVING OF LIFE BARON

Hon Joan Mary (Abbotswell, Frogham, Fordingbridge, Hants), *b* 1920: *m* 1st, 1942 (*m diss* 1963), Gordon Dixon; 2ndly, 1975, Albert Ralph Roberts, who *d* 1980; 3rdly, 1987, Rev John Atcherley Davies, of 6 Durlston Crescent, Christchurch, Dorset BH23 2ST, and has issue (by 1st *m*), one son.

Royle, family name of Baron Fanshawe of Richmond.

RUFFSIDE, VISCOUNTCY OF (Brown) (Extinct 1958)

DAUGHTER LIVING OF FIRST VISCOUNT

Hon Audrey Pellew, *b* 1908; *cr Baroness Hylton-Foster* (Life Baroness) 1965 (see that title).

RUGBY, BARON (Maffey) (Baron UK 1947)

PASS FRIEND

ROBERT CHARLES MAFFEY, 3rd Baron; *b* 4 May 1951; *s* 1990; a Farmer: *m* 1974, Anne Penelope, yr da of David Hale, of Somerden, Chiddingstone, Kent, and has issue.

Arms – Ermine, a fort with two towers proper, issuant from the base a pile reversed sable, a chief dancette or, surmounted by a pile azure, charged with an increscent argent. **Crest** – A gauntlet fessewise grasping a lantern proper. **Supporters** – On either side an Afghan hound proper gorged with a collar with chain reflexed over the back or.
Residence – Grove Farm Cottage, Frankton, Rugby.

SONS LIVING

Hon TIMOTHY JAMES HOWARD, *b* 23 July 1975.
Hon Philip Edward, *b* 1976.

BROTHERS LIVING

Hon Christopher Alan, *b* 1955; *ed* Malvern: *m* 1st, 1977 (*m diss* 1981), Barbara Anne, yr da of Guthrie Stewart, of Auckland, NZ; 2ndly, 1982, Katherine, elder da of Viv Rutherfurd, of Waiuku, Auckland, NZ, and has issue living (by 2nd *m*), Aaron John, *b* 1983, — Leigh Alan, *b* 1984. *Residence* – Hamiltons Rd, RD4, Waiuku, NZ.

Hon Mark Andrew, *b* 1956; *ed* Harrow, and Ecole de Commerce, Neuchâtel, Switzerland: *m* 1983, Angela Mary, da of Derek J. Polton, of The Pennies, Draycote, Rugby, and has issue living, Thomas Henry, *b* 1988, — Georgina Louise, *b* 1986. *Residence* – The Flat, Grove Farm, Frankton, Rugby.

SISTERS LIVING

Hon (Selina) Penelope, *b* 1952; has issue living, Tamas Henry, *b* 1990, — Angelica Helena, *b* 1986. *Residence* – McDougal Rd, Julatten, Queensland 4880, Australia.

Hon Alicia Dorothy, *b* 1960: *m* 1981 Richard M. Morton, 2nd son of John Morton, of Draycote, Rugby, and has issue living, Samuel Richard, *b* 1986, — John Alan Kynaston, *b* 1990, — Eleanor Margaret, *b* 1984. *Residence* – Manor Farm, Draycote, Rugby.

UNCLE LIVING (*Son of 1st Baron*)

Hon Simon Chelmsford Loader (Charterhouse, EC1), *b* 1919; *ed* Rugby; formerly Lt Coldstream Guards; 1939-45 War in France (wounded): *m* 1949 (*m diss* 1962), Andrée Norma, da of George Middleton, of London, and has issue living, Penelope Anne, *b* 1950: *m* 1973, Richard Patrick James Lacy, of The Moat Farmhouse, Mill Green, Edwardstone, Sudbury, Suffolk, and has issue living (*see* Lacy, Bt).

AUNT LIVING (*Daughter of 1st Baron*)

Hon Penelope Loader (*Hon Lady Aitken*), MBE (2 North Court, Great Peter St, SW1), *b* 1910; MBE (Civil) 1955; JP: *m* 1938, Sir William Traven Aitken, KBE, MP, who *d* 1964, and has issue living, Jonathan William Patrick, *b* 1942; *ed* Eton, and Ch Ch, Oxford (MA); Dir TV-am 1981-88; Min of State for Defence 1992-94, Chief Sec to HM Treasury; MP for Thanet South (*C*) 1974-97; PC 1994 (resigned 1997): *m* 1979, Lolicia Olivera, da of O. A. Azucki, of Zürich, Switzerland, and has issue living, William *b* 1982, Victoria *b* 1980, Alexandra *b* (twin) 1980, — Maria Penelope Katharine, *b* 1945; actress: *m* 1st, 1968, Mark Richard Durden-Smith; 2ndly, 1972 (*m diss* 1980), Nigel Davenport; 3rdly, 1991, Patrick J. McGrath, and has issue living (by 2nd *m*), Jack *b* 1973; actor.

WIDOW LIVING OF SECOND BARON

MARGARET (*Margaret, Baroness Rugby*), da of Harold Bindley, of Burton-on-Trent: *m* 1947, the 2nd Baron Rugby, who *d* 1990. *Residence* – Grove Farm, Frankton, Rugby.

PREDECESSORS – (1) *Sir* JOHN LOADER Maffey, GCMG, KCB, KCVO, CSI, CIE, son of late Thomas Maffey, of Rugby; *b* 1877; entered ICS 1899, Priv Sec to HE The Viceroy 1916-20, Ch Cmmr NWFP India 1921-24, Gov-Gen of the Sudan 1926-33; Permanent Under-Sec of State for Colonies 1933-37; UK Rep res in Eire 1939-49; *cr Baron Rugby*, of Rugby, co Warwick (peerage of UK) 1947: *m* 1907, Dorothy Gladys, OBE, who *d* 1973, da of late Charles Lang Huggins, JP, of Hadlow Grange, Buxted; *d* 1969; *s* by his el son (2) ALAN LOADER, 2nd Baron, 1939-45 War as Fl Lt RAF, Farmer: *m* 1947, Margaret, da of Harold Bindley, of Burton-on-Trent; *d* 1990; *s* by his 2nd son (his eldest son, Hon John Richard, *b* 1949, *dvp* in Egypt 1981), ROBERT CHARLES, 3rd Baron and present peer.

RUNCIE, BARON (Runcie) (Life Baron 1991)

Rt Rev and *Rt Hon* ROBERT ALEXANDER KENNEDY RUNCIE, MC, PC, son of late Robert Dalziel Runcie, of Crosby, Merseyside; *b* 2 Oct 1921; *ed* Merchant Taylors', Crosby, Brasenose Coll, Oxford (MA), and Westcott House, Camb (Dip Theol); served European War 1939-45 Scots Guards (MC 1945); Hon Bencher Gray's Inn 1981; Hon DD Oxford 1980, Camb 1981, St Andrews 1989, Yale 1989, London 1990, and other Univs, Hon DLitt Keele 1981, Hon DCL Kent 1982, and Hon LittD Liverpool 1983; ordained priest 1949, Curate All Saints Gosforth 1950-52, Chaplain and Vice-Pres Westcott House, Camb, 1953-56, Dean Trin Coll, Camb, 1956-60, Principal Cuddesdon Theol Coll 1960-70, Bishop St Albans 1970-80, Archbishop of Canterbury 1980-91, since when High Steward Camb Univ; Anglican Chm Anglican-Orthodox Joint Doctrinal Commn 1973-80; Teape Lecturer Delhi Univ 1962, and Nobell Lecturer Harvard Univ 1987; Freeman Cities of London, Canterbury and St Albans; Freeman Merchant Taylors' Co, Grocers' Co and Butchers' Co; author; PC 1980, Royal Victorian Chain 1991; *cr Baron Runcie*, of Cuddesdon, co Oxfordshire (Life Baron) 1991: *m* 1957, (Angela) Rosalind, da of late J. W. Cecil Turner, MC, of Cambridge, and has issue.

Arms – Argent, on a fess sable between three roses gules barbed and seeded proper as many crosses patonce also argent. Crest – A horse statant argent, crined, maned, unguled and the tail sable, gorged with a chaplet of roses gules barbed and seeded proper, resting the dexter foreleg upon a millrind gold.
Residence – 26a Jennings Rd, St Albans, Herts AL1 4PD. *Clubs* – Athenaeum, Cavalry and Guards', and MCC.

SON LIVING

Hon James (36 Liverpool Rd, St Albans, Herts AL1 3UJ), *b* 1959; *ed* Marlborough, and Trin Hall, Camb (MA): *m* 1985, Mrs Marilyn Elsie Kellagher, da of late John Campbell Imrie, of Redroofs, Markinch, Fife, and has issue living, Charlotte Susan Elizabeth, *b* 1989.

DAUGHTER LIVING

Hon Rebecca, *b* 1962; *ed* St Albans High Sch for Girls, Haileybury, and St Mary's Coll, Durham: *m* 1994, (Thomas Michael) Christopher Tabor, only son of G. M. Tabor, of South Cerney, Glos and has issue living, Matthew Alexander Runcie, *b* 1996, — Edward Michael Runcie, *b* 1998. *Residence* – 10c Clarendon Gdns, Little Venice, W9 1AY.

RUNCIMAN OF DOXFORD, VISCOUNT (Runciman) (Viscount UK 1937 Bt UK 1906)

WALTER GARRISON RUNCIMAN, CBE, 3rd Viscount; *b* 10 Nov 1934; *s* 1989; *ed* Eton, and Trin Coll, Camb (Fellow 1959-63, and since 1971); Hon DSc (Soc Sci) Edinburgh, Hon D. Univ York; Chm Andrew Weir & Co Ltd and Runciman Investments Ltd; Jt Dep Chm Securities & Investments Board; Pres of Gen Council of British Shipping 1986-87; CBE 1987, FBA: *m* 1963, Ruth, DBE, Chm Mental Health Act Commn since 1994, da of Joseph Hellman, of Johannesburg, and formerly wife of Denis Mack Smith, of Oxford, and has issue.

Arms – Per fesse or and azure a lymphad oars in action, the sail charged with a thistle leaved and slipped proper, flags flying to the dexter gules. Crest – A seahorse erect gules, holding in the fore fins a thistle as in the arms. Supporters – On either side a seahorse or gorged with a chain pendent therefrom a grappling iron azure.
Seat – Doxford, Chathill, Northumberland. *Residence* – 44 Clifton Hill, NW8 0QE. *Club* – Brooks's.

SON LIVING

Dr the Hon DAVID WALTER, *b* 1 March 1967; *ed* Eton, and Trin Coll, Camb: *m* 1997, Beatrice (Bee) D., yr da of A. N. Wilson.

DAUGHTERS LIVING

Hon Lisa, *b* 1965.
Hon Catherine, *b* 1969.

UNCLE LIVING *(Son of 1st Viscount)*

Hon Sir James Cochran Stevenson (*Hon Sir Steven Runciman*), CH, *b* 1903; *ed* Eton, and Trin Coll, Camb (MA, Fellow); Hon LittD, Oxford, and Camb, Hon LLD Glasgow; Hon DLitt Durham, London, St Andrews, and Birmingham; Hon DPh Salonika 1951; Hon DD, Wabash, Indiana, and Ball State, Indiana, Hon DHL Chicago and New York, and Author, a FBA, and a Knight Cdr of Order of Phoenix of Greece; Prof of Byzantine Art and History at Istanbul Univ 1942-45; Representative of British Council in Greece 1945-47; Onassis Foundation International Award for Culture 1998; Knt 1958, CH 1983. *Residence* – Elshieshields, Lockerbie, Dumfriesshire.

PREDECESSORS – (1) WALTER Runciman, son of late Walter Runciman, of Dunbar; *b* 1847; head of firm of Walter Runciman & Co, Ltd, shipowners of Newcastle, London, etc, Chm of Anchor Line, Ltd, Glasgow, and a Member and Chm of various other shipping organisations; MP for Hartlepool (*L*) 1914-18; *cr* a *Baronet* 1906, and *Baron Runciman*, of Shoreston, co Northumberland (peerage of United Kingdom) 1933: *m* 1868, Ann Margaret, who *d* 1933, el da of late John Lawson, of Blakemoor Northumberland; *d* Aug 1937; *s* by his only son (2) WALTER, 2nd Baron; *b* 1870; Chm of United Kingdom Provident Institution 1920-31; Pres of Chamber of Shipping of United Kingdom 1926; was Parliamentary Sec to Local Govt Board 1905-07, Financial Sec to the Treasury 1907-08, Pres of Board of Education 1908-11, Pres of Board of Agriculture and Fisheries, and Commr of HM Woods, Forests, and Land Revenues 1911-14, Pres of Board of Trade 1914-16, again Pres of Board of Trade (in National Govt) 1931-7, and Lord Pres of the Council 1938-9; Head of Mission to Czechoslovakia 1938; sat as MP (*L*) for Oldham 1899-1900, for Dewsbury 1902-18, for Swansea, W Div 1924-9, and for St Ives Div of Cornwall 1929-37; *cr Viscount Runciman of Doxford*, of Doxford, co Northumberland (peerage of United Kingdom) June 1937: *m* 1898, Hilda (MP for Cornwall, St Ives Div (*L*) 1928-9), who *d* 1956, da of late James Cochran Stevenson (sometime MP for South Shields), of Westoe, South Shields: *d* 1949; *s* by his el son (3) WALTER LESLIE, OBE, AFC, AE, 2nd Viscount; *b* 1900, Elder Brother of Trinity House, Hon Air Commodore, Chm of Council of Armstrong Coll, Durham 1935-37, Dir-Gen British Overseas Airways Corporation 1940-43, Air Attaché British Embassy, Teheran 1943-46, Pres Royal Inst of Naval Architects 1951-61, Pres Chamber of Shipping of UK 1952, Chm of Trustees Nat Maritime Museum 1961-72, Chm British Hall-Marking Council 1974-83, and Pres Marine Soc 1974-89: *m* 1st, 1923 (*m diss* 1928), Rosamond Nina, who *d* 1990, da of late Rudolph Chambers Lehmann, of Fieldhead, Bourne End, Bucks; 2ndly, 1932, Katharine Schuyler, who *d* 1993, aged 90, yst da of late William R. Garrison, of New York; *d* 1989; *s* by his only son (4) WALTER GARRISON, 3rd Viscount and present peer; also Baron Runciman.

RUNCORN, BARONY OF (Vosper) (Extinct 1968)

WIDOW LIVING OF LIFE BARON

HELEN NORAH, da of late Sir (Joseph) Crosland Graham, of Clwyd Hall, Ruthin, Denbighshire; a JP for SW London, a Member of Merton Sutton and Wandsworth Area Health Authority (Teaching), and of Westminster Hosp (Special Trustee 1974-88; a Gov of Westminster Hosp Teaching Group 1972-74; Member of R Dental Hosp Sch Council 1978-82), and Roehampton Trustee 1976-1989; Chm Richmond, Twickenham and Roehampton Health Authority, and Member Charing Cross and Westminster Medical Sch Council 1982-88; Member Hammersmith and Queen Charlotte's Special Health Authority 1988-94; Member Council for Action Research since 1988; Member of Industrial Tribunal, London South since 1989: *m* 1st, 1966, as his 2nd wife, Baron Runcorn (Life Baron), who *d* 1968; 2ndly, 1976, Dr James Earle, FRC Path, MD, of 18 Hillside, Wimbledon SW19.

RUSHCLIFFE, BARONY OF (Betterton) (Extinct 1949)

DAUGHTERS LIVING OF FIRST BARON

Hon Averil Diana, *b* 1914: *m* 1st, 1939, Major Richard Wyndham-Quin Going, KOSB, who was *ka* in Normandy 1944; 2ndly, 1946, Col Charles Walter Philipps Richardson, DSO, KOSB (Foley-Philipps, Bt), who *d* 1993, and has issue living, (by 1st *m*) Christopher Wyndham (15 Wycombe Place, SW18), *b* 1944, Capt 9th/12th Royal Lancers (POW's): *m* 1975 (*m diss* 1989) Elisabeth Susan, da of James Christie Brownlow, of The Old Rectory, Kelling, Holt, Norfolk, and has issue living, Richard Wyndham *b* 1980, Emily Sarah *b* 1978, — Penelope Clare, *b* 1942: *m* 1965, Col Arthur David Bentley Brooks, The Queen's R Irish Hussars, of Higher Barns, Malpas, Cheshire, and has issue living, Jonathan Wyndham *b* 1970, Emma Frances *b* 1968: *m* 1995, Guy Charles Myddelton, of Chirk Castle, nr Wrexham, N Wales (*see* M Lansdowne), — (by 2nd *m*) Mark Rushcliffe (Priors Court, W Hanney, Wantage, Oxon), *b* 1947: *m* 1973, Cherry

Victoria, yst da of Sidney Smart, of Coopers, Woolstone, Faringdon, Oxon, and has had issue, Hugo Charles Rushcliffe *b* 1981, Melanie Clare *b* 1974, *d* 1994, Davina Kate *b* 1976. *Residence* – Sutton Manor, Sutton Scotney, Winchester, Hants.

Hon Claudia Violet, *b* 1917: *m* 1937, Maj Derek Swithin Allhusen, CVO, 9th Lancers, and has issue living, Timothy Frederick (Capstitch House, Compton Abbas, Shaftesbury, Dorset), *b* 1942: *m* 1965, Annabel Victoria, only da of late John Creighton Morris, and has issue living, Nicolas Christian *b* 1970, Alexia Suzanne *b* 1966, Lara Victoria *b* 1968, — Rosemary Claudia, *b* 1944: *m* 1973, Maj Jeremy Grimble Groves, 17th/21st Lancers, Member HM's Body Guard of the Hon Corps of Gentlemen at Arms, of Cole Henley Manor, Whitchurch, Hants RG28 7QD and has issue living, Anthony Grimble *b* 1975, Clare Nicola Claudia *b* 1977. *Residence* – The Manor House, Claxton, Norwich.

RUSSELL, EARL (Russell) (Earl UK 1861)

What will be, will be

CONRAD SEBASTIAN ROBERT RUSSELL, 5th Earl; *b* 15 April 1937; *s* 1987; *ed* Eton, and Merton Coll, Oxford; Reader in History, Bedford Coll, London Univ until 1979; Prof of History, Yale Univ 1979-84, Astor Prof of British History, Univ Coll, London 1984-90, since when Prof of British History, King's Coll, London; Sir Henry Savile Visiting Prof, Merton Coll Oxford 1994-95; Ford's Lecturer Oxford Univ 1987-88: *m* 1962, Elizabeth, da of Horace Sanders, of 43 Stockwood Rd, Chippenham, Wilts, and has issue.

Arms – Argent, a lion rampant gules, on a chief sable, three escallops of the field, over the centre escallop a mullet. **Crest** – A goat stantant argent, armed and unguled or. **Supporters** – *Dexter*, a lion gules; *siniser*, an heraldic antelope gules, armed, unguled, tufted, ducally gorged and chained, the chain reflexed over the back or; each supporter charged on the shoulder with a mullet argent.
Address – c/o House of Lords, SW1A 0PW.

SONS LIVING

NICHOLAS LYULPH (*Viscount Amberley*), *b* 12 Sept 1968; *ed* William Ellis Sch, Camden.
Hon John Francis, *b* 1971; *ed* William Ellis Sch, Camden.

DAUGHTER LIVING OF FOURTH EARL

Lady Sarah Elizabeth, *b* 1946. Resides in Oxford.

HALF-SISTER LIVING (*Daughter of 3rd Earl by 2nd marriage*)

Lady Katharine Jane, *b* 1923: *m* 1948, Rev Charles William Stuart Tait, and has issue living, David Alexander, *b* 1951, — Jonathan Francis, *b* 1955, — Andrew Michael Philip, *b* 1961, — Benjamin Peter, *b* 1965, — Anne Elizabeth, *b* 1953.

MOTHER LIVING

Patricia Helen, da of Harry Evelyn Spence: *m* 1936 (*m diss* 1952), as his 3rd wife, the 3rd Earl Russell, who *d* 1970. Resides in Devon.

PREDECESSORS – **(1)** *Lord* JOHN RUSSELL, KG, 3rd son of 6th Duke of Bedford; *b* 1792; sat as MP for Tavistock (*L*) 1813-17, 1818-19, and 1830-2, for Huntingdonshire 1820-6, for Bandon 1826-30, for S. Devonshire 1832-5, for Stroud 1835-41, and for London 1841-61; was Sec for Home Depart 1835-9, for the Colonies 1839-41 and 1855, Sec for Foreign Affairs 1852-3 and 1859-65, Premier and First Lord of the Treasury 1846-52 and 1865-6, and Lord Pres of the Council 1854-5; *cr Viscount Amberley* and *Earl Russell* (peerage of United Kingdom) 1861: *m* 1st, 1835, Adelaide, who *d* 1838, da of Thomas Lister, of Armitage Park, and widow of 2nd Baron Ribblesdale; 2ndly, 1841, Lady Frances Anna Maria Elliot, who *d* 1898, da of 2nd Earl of Minto, GCB; *d* 1878; *s* by his grandson **(2)** JOHN FRANCIS STANLEY (son of John, Viscount Amberley, MP, by Hon Katherine Louisa, da of 2nd Baron Stanley of Aderley), 2nd Earl, *b* 1865; tried by his Peers at Westminster 1901 (free pardon granted by His Majesty and recorded in proceedings of House of Lords July 1911): Parliamentary Sec to Min of Transport June 1929, and Under Sec of State for India Dec 1929-31: *m* 1st 1890 (*m diss* 1901), Mabel Edith, who *d* 1908, da of Sir Claude Edward Scott, 4th Bt (*cr* 1821); 2ndly, 1901 (*m diss* 1915), Mollie, da of George Cooke; 3rdly, 1916, Mary Annette (an authoress), who *d* 1941, da of H. Herron Beauchamp, and widow of Count (Henning August) Von Arnim; *d* 1931; *s* by his brother **(3)** BERTRAND ARTHUR WILLIAM OM, 3rd Earl, *b* 1872; Philosopher and Mathematician: *m* 1st, 1894 (*m diss* 1935), Alys Whitall who *d* 1951, da of late Robert Pearsall Smith; 2ndly, 1921 (*m diss* 1935), Dora Winifred, MBE, who *d* 1986, da of late Sir Frederick William Black, KCB; 3rdly, 1936 (*m diss* 1952), Patricia Helen, da of Henry Evelyn Spence; 4thly, 1952, Edith, who *d* 1978, da of late Edward Bronson Finch, of New York; *d* 1970; *s* by his son **(4)** JOHN CONRAD, 4th Earl, *b* 1921; served RNVR, Admin Assist HM Treasury: *m* 1946 (*m diss* 1955), Susan Doniphan, who *d* 1990, da of late Nicholas Vachel Lindsay, American poet; *d* 1987; *s* by his half-brother **(5)** CONRAD SEBASTIAN ROBERT, 5th Earl and present peer; also Viscount Amberley.

Russell, family name of Baron Ampthill.

Russell, family name of Duke of Bedford.

Russell, family name of Baron de Clifford.

Russell, Hamilton-, family name of Viscount Boyne.

RUSSELL OF KILLOWEN, BARONY OF (Russell) (Extinct 1986) (see Russell, Bt, cr 1916)

RUSSELL OF LIVERPOOL, BARON (Russell) (Baron UK 1919)

SIMON GORDON JARED RUSSELL, 3rd Baron; *b* 30 Aug 1952; *s* 1981; *ed* Charterhouse, Trin Coll, Camb, and INSEAD, France: *m* 1984, Gilda F., yst da of F. Albano, of Salerno, Italy, and has issue.

Arms – Per saltire sable and or, in chief an estoile argent, two roses in fesse gules, barbed and seeded proper, and in base a thistle leaved and slipped of the second. **Crest** – An owl wings expanded argent, beaked and legged or, resting the dexter claw on an estoile azure. **Supporters** – On either side an owl argent beaked and legged or, gorged with a chaplet of roses gules, leaved vert.
Address – c/o House of Lords, SW1A 0PW.

SONS LIVING

Hon EDWARD CHARLES STANLEY, *b* 2 Sept 1985.
Hon William Francis Langley, *b* 1988.

DAUGHTER LIVING

Hon Leonora Maria Kiloran, *b* 1987.

BROTHERS LIVING (*Raised to the rank of a Baron's sons*, 1983)

Hon Adam Mark Haslingden, *b* 1957.
Hon Daniel Charles Edward, *b* 1962.

SISTERS LIVING *(Raised to the rank of a Baron's daughters, 1983)*

Hon Emma Kiloran, *b* 1955.
Hon Annabel Tacy, *b* 1959: *m* 1987, Lt-Col Mark Ralph Michael Eliot, 1st Queen's Dragoon Gds, son of Maj Morrell Geffery Eliot, MBE, and has issue living, Caspar Laurence Robin, *b* 1989, — Ralph Morrell Arthur, *b* 1992, — Barnaby Alexander Wynne, *b* 1995.
Hon Lucy Leonora Catherine, *b* 1968.

AUNT LIVING *(Daughter of 2nd Baron by 1st marriage)*

Hon Anne Philippa *b* 1924: *m* 1947, Gershom Radcliffe Layton Warren, late Maj Canadian Army, who *d* 1991, of 15 Williams St, Taupo, NZ.

HALF-AUNT LIVING *(Daughter of 2nd Baron by 2nd marriage)*

Hon Crystal (Ann Boleyn's Cottage, Grandmother's Rock Lane, Beach, Bittern, nr Bristol, Avon), *b* 1936: *m* 1955 (*m diss* 1969), John Mark Essington-Boulton, and has issue living, James Clive (83 Belmont Hill, Blackheath, SE13 5AX), *b* 1958; has issue (by Susan J., da of Robert Bray), Oliver Langley ESSINGTON-BOULTON *b* 1998, — Nicolette (L'Esperou, 31265 Vaudreville, France), *b* 1956: *m* 1978 (*m diss* 1994), Jean-Sebastien Joly.

MOTHER LIVING

Kiloran Margaret (*Hon Mrs Langley G. H. Russell*) (Ash Farm, Stourpaine, Blandford, Dorset), da of late Hon Sir Arthur Jared Palmer Howard, KBE, CVO (*see* B Strathcona and Mount Royal, colls): *m* 1951, Capt Hon Langley Gordon Haslingden Russell, MC, who *d* 1975.

PREDECESSORS – (**1**) *Sir* EDWARD RICHARD Russell, son of late Edward Haslingden Russell, of London; *b* 1834; editor of *Liverpool Daily Post and Mercury*, MP for Glasgow, Bridgeton Div (*L*) 1885-7; *cr Baron Russell of Liverpool*, of Liverpool, co Palatine of Lancaster (peerage of United Kingdom) 1919: *m* 1st, 1858, Eliza Sophia, who *d* 1901, da of Stephen Bradley, of Bridge, Canterbury; 2ndly, 1902, Jean Stewart, who *d* 1927, da of late Alexander Macdonald, of Campbeltown, Argyllshire, and Joseph, and widow of Joseph McFarlane; *d* 1920; *s* by his grandson (**2**) EDWARD FREDERICK LANGLEY, CBE, MC (son of late Richard Henry Langley Russell, 2nd son of 1st Baron), 2nd Baron, *b* 1895; Bar Gray's Inn 1931; Brig The King's Regt (Liverpool) and 20th Lancers (IA); Assist Judge Advocate Gen British Expeditionary Force 1930-40, Dep Judge Advocate Gen at 1st Army Headquarters 1942-43, and Allied Force Head-quarters 1943-45, to Middle East Forces 1945-46, and to British Army of the Rhine 1946-51, and Assist Judge Advocate Gen 1951-54; an author: *m* 1st, 1920 (*m diss* 1933), Constance Claudine, who *d* 1974, yr da of late Col Philip Cecil Harcourt Gordon, CMG, RAMC; 2ndly, 1933 (*m diss* 1946), (Joan) Betty, who *d* 1997, da of late David Ewart, OBE, MD, FRCS, of Chichester; 3rdly, 1946, Alix, who *d* 1971, only da of late Marquis de Bréviaire d'Alaincourt, and widow of Comte de Richard d'Ivry; 4thly, 1972, Selma, who *d* 1977, da of —, and widow of A. W. Brayley; *d* 1981; *s* by his grand-son (**3**) SIMON GORDON JARED (son of late Capt Hon Langley Gordon Haslingden Russell, MC, only son of 2nd Baron), 3rd Baron and present peer.

RUSSELL-JOHNSTON, BARON (Russell-Johnston) (Life Baron 1997)

(DAVID) RUSSELL RUSSELL-JOHNSTON, son of late David Knox Johnston, of Edinburgh; *b* 28 July 1932; assumed the surname of Russell-Johnston in lieu of his patronymic by deed poll 1997; *ed* Portree High Sch, Isle of Skye, and Edinburgh Univ (MA 1957); Nat Service Commn with Intelligence Corps 1958; History Teacher, Liberton Secondary Sch, Edinburgh 1961-63; Memb Executive, Scottish Liberal Party since 1961, Vice-Chm 1963, Chm 1970-74, Leader 1974-88, Pres 1988-94; Research Assist, Scottish Liberal Party 1963-64; MP for Inverness (*L*) 1964-83, and for Inverness, Nairn and Lochaber (*L* until 1988, then *Lib Dem*) 1983-97; Liberal Spokesman on Foreign and Commonwealth Affairs 1970-75 and 1979-85, Scotland 1970-73, 1975-83 and 1985-87; Alliance Spokesman on Scotland and Euro Community Affairs 1987; Lib Dem Spokesman on Foreign and Commonwealth Affairs 1988-89, and Europe and East/West Relations 1989-97; MEP (*L*) 1973-75 and 1976-79 (Vice Pres Political Cttee 1976-79); Pres Scottish Lib Dems 1988-94; Memb Royal Commn on Scottish Local Government 1966-69; Vice-Pres Euro Lib Dem and Reform Parties 1990-92; Vice-Chm Board of Governors, Westminster Foundation for Democracy 1992-97; Pres Parliamentary Assembly of the Council of Europe since 1999; author; *cr* Kt 1985, and *Baron Russell-Johnston*, of Minginish in Highlands (Life Baron) 1997: *m* 1967, Joan Graham, da of Donald Menzies, of Inverness, and has issue.
Address – c/o House of Lords, Westminster, SW1A 0PW. *Club* – Scottish Liberal (Edinburgh).

Hon Graham, *b* 1972.
Hon David, *b* 1974.
Hon Andrew, *b* 1978.

Ruthven of Canberra, Viscount; son of Earl of Gowrie.

Ruthven, Hore-, family name of Earl of Gowrie.

Ruthven of Freeland, Lord (Ruthven) (Lordship S 1651) (see E Carlisle).

RUTLAND, DUKE OF (Manners) (Duke E 1703)

POUR Y PARVENIR

To obtain your object

DAVID CHARLES ROBERT MANNERS, 11th Duke; *b* 8 May 1959; *s* 1999; patron of eleven livings, but being a Roman Catholic cannot present; Dir Belvoir Management Ltd; Chm Historic Houses Assocn, E Midlands until 1999; Pres Grantham Branch Air Crew Assocn; Memb Civilian Cttee 47F ATC Sqdn, Game Conservancy, Salmon and Trout Assoc, and CLA Cttee for Leics; Pres Belvoir Cricket Club; Freeman City of London, and Liveryman Gunmakers' Co: *m* 1992, Emma Louise, da of John Watkins, of Heartease, Knighton, Powys, and has issue.

꩜rms – Or, two bars azure, a chief quarterly, azure and gules; in 1st and 4th quarters two fleurs-de-lis, and in the 2nd and 3rd a lion passant guardant, all or. ꩜rest – On a chapeau gules, turned up ermine, a peacock in pride proper. ꩜upporters – Two unicorns, armed, ungules, maned and tufted, or.
Seats – Belvoir Castle, Grantham, Lincs; Haddon Hall, Bakewell, Derbys.
Club – Turf.

SON LIVING

CHARLES JOHN MONTAGUE (*Marquess of Granby*), *b* 3 July 1999.

DAUGHTERS LIVING

Lady Violet Diana Louise, *b* 1993.
Lady Alice Louisa Lilly, *b* 1995.
Lady Eliza Charlotte, *b* 1997.

BROTHER LIVING

Lord EDWARD JOHN FRANCIS, b 29 May 1965. Residence – Haddon Hall, Bakewell, Derbyshire.

SISTER LIVING

Lady Helen Teresa Margaret (preferred style Lady Theresa Chipman), b 1962: m 1997, Dr John M. W. Chipman, son of Lawrence Carroll Chipman, and of Maria Isabel Prados, of Montreal, Canada.

HALF-SISTER LIVING

Lady Charlotte Louisa, b 1947.

UNCLES LIVING (Sons of 9th Duke)

Lord John, b 1922; ed Eton, and New Coll, Oxford; formerly Capt Life Guards, and 2nd Special Air Ser Regt: m 1957, Mary Diana, who d 1997, yst da of late Lieut-Col Lancelot Geoffrey Moore, DSO, and has issue living, (Richard John) Peveril, b 1963: m 1996, Hilary C., da of late Neil Hewitson, of Rushlake Green, Sussex, — Elizabeth (Libby) Diana, b 1959: m 1986, Alexander Charles Thomas Wriothesley Russell, and has issue (see D Bedford, colls), — Lucy Rachel, b 1961; an Extra Lady in Waiting to HRH The Duchess of York 1989-96. Residences – Reservoir Cottage, Knipton, Grantham, Lincolnshire; Haddon Hall, Bakewell, Derbyshire.
Lord Roger David, b 1925; ed Eton; formerly 2nd Lt Grenadier Guards: m 1965, Finola St Lawrence, only da of Thomas Edward Daubeney, of Ampney St Peter, Glos, and has issue living, Moira Violet Joanna, b 1966, — Phœbe Constance Adeliza, b 1968. Residence – Marsh End Farm, Broads Green, Heddington, Wilts.

AUNTS LIVING (Daughters of 9th Duke)

Lady Ursula Isabel, b 1916; was a Train Bearer to the Queen at Coronation of King George VI: m 1st, 1943 (m diss 1948), Anthony Freire Marreco, late Lieut RNVR; 2ndly, 1951, Robert Erland Nicolai d'Abo, who d 1970, and has issue living, (by 2nd m) (John) Henry Erland (West Wratting Park, Cambs), b 1953; ed Eton: m 1989, Tatjana Maria Margareta Nina Schoeller, and has issue living, Anoushka Maria Violet b 1991, Celina Maria Isobel b 1996, — Richard Winston Mark, b 1956; ed Eton, — Louisa Jane (Hon Mrs John P. Ramsay), b 1955: m 1981, Hon John Patrick Ramsay, yst son of 16th Earl of Dalhousie. Residences – West Wratting Park, Cambs; 29 Kensington Sq, W8.
Lady Isabel Violet Kathleen, b 1917: m 1st, 1936 (m diss 1951), as his 2nd wife, Group Capt (Thomas) Loel Evelyn Bulkeley Guinness, OBE, Auxiliary Air Force (Reserve), who d 1988; 2ndly, 1953, Sir Robert George Maxwell Throckmorton, 11th Bt, who d 1989, and has issue living, (by 1st m) William Loel Seymour (10 Bourne St, SW1), b 1939: m 1971, Agnes Elizabeth Lynn, only da of Ian T. M. Day, and has issue living, Sheridan William b 1972, Thomas Seymour b 1973, — Serena Belinda Rosemary (Marchioness of Dufferin and Ava), b 1941: m 1964, 5th Marquess of Dufferin and Ava, who d 1988. Residences – Coughton Court, Alcester, Warwickshire; Molland, South Molton, N Devon.

WIDOW LIVING OF TENTH DUKE

FRANCES HELEN (Frances, Duchess of Rutland), da of late Charles Sweeny, and of late Margaret, Duchess of Argyll: m 1958, as his 2nd wife, the 10th Duke of Rutland, CBE, who d 1999. Residences – Belvoir Castle, Grantham, Lincs; Haddon Hall, Bakewell, Derbys.

COLLATERAL BRANCHES LIVING

Grandchildren of late Rev William Manners-Sutton, 2nd son of late Frederick Manners-Sutton, 3rd son of late Capt John Manners-Sutton, MP, 2nd son of late Lord George Manners-Sutton, 3rd son of 3rd Duke:—
Issue of late Frederick William Manners-Sutton, b 1865, d 1946: m 1902, Winifred Grace Richardson, who d 1970:—
John Lumley, b 1914: m 1949, Elizabeth Mary Gylda Eliot, da of A. N. G. Irving, of Lesmurdie, W Aust, and has issue living, John Frederick, b 1955, — Elizabeth Marjorie Inez (61 Riley Rd, Dalkeith, Western Australia 6009, Australia), b 1950: m 1987, Barry Spencer Clements, MB ChB, MRCP, only son of Sydney Ernest Clements, of Johannesburg, and has issue living, Christopher James b 1989, Michael Alexander b 1992, — Melanie Grace, b 1952: m 1978, Robert James Champion de Crespigny, of 1 Edwin Terr, Gilberton 5081, Adelaide, son of James Vivian Champion de Crespigny, of Melbourne, Victoria, Australia, and has issue living, Stuart James b 1980, Angus Robert b 1982, Lachlan Thomas b 1984, James John b 1987, Georgina Melanie b 1993. Residence – 3 Buckingham St, Gilberton 5081, Adelaide, S Australia. —— Evelyn Mabel (Tarcoola, Shepparton, Victoria 3630, Australia), b 1909: m 1928, John Kenneth Finlay, MBE, who d 1970, and has issue living, Chester Manners, b 1932, — Warwick Henry (Campbells Bend, Murchison, Victoria 3610, Australia), b 1934: m 1973, Anne Elizabeth Jones, and has issue living, Gareth John b 1974, Jocelyn Edwina b 1976, — John Lexton (Thalia, RMB 4067, Violet Town, Victoria 3669, Australia), b 1936: m 1961, Sandra Marion, elder da of Donald Hugh Bayne, of Barambah, Nagambie, Victoria, Australia, and has issue living, Mark John b 1966, Sarah Elizabeth b 1961, Catherine Deborah b 1963.

Descendants of late Rt Hon Thomas Manners-Sutton, 5th son of late Lord George Manners-Sutton (ante), who was cr Baron Manners 1807 (see that title).

PREDECESSORS – (1) *Sir* THOMAS Manners, KG, 13th Baron de Ros (*see* B de Ros), was *cr Earl of Rutland* (peerage of England) 1525; *d* 1543; *s* by his son (2) HENRY, KG, 2nd Earl; was Constable of Nottingham Castle, and Pres of the North; he completed the re-building of Belvoir Castle; *d* 1563; *s* by his son (3) EDWARD, KG, 3rd Earl; *d* 1587 without male issue, when the Barony of de Ros reverted to his da Elizabeth, wife of Lord Burleigh (*see* M Exeter), and the earldom devolved upon his brother (4) JOHN, 4th Earl; *d* 1588; *s* by his el son (5) ROGER, 5th Earl; *dsp* 1612; *s* by his brother (6) FRANCIS, KG, 6th Earl; who in 1616 had been *cr Baron Roos*, of Hamlake (peerage of England); in 1618 *s* his cousin, son of Elizabeth, Baroness de Ros (ante), as 17th Baron de Ros; *d* 1632, when the Barony of Roos of Hamlake expired, and the other honours devolved upon his brother (7) GEORGE, 7th Earl; *dsp* 1641, when the Barony of de Ros reverted to Katherine, wife of George Villiers, 1st Duke of Buckingham (*cr* 1623), and the earldom devolved upon his cousin (8) JOHN, 8th Earl; *d* Sept, 1679; *s* by his son (9) JOHN, 9th Earl, who in April, 1679, had been summoned to Parliament as *Baron Manners of Haddon*, co Derby (peerage of England); was Lord-Lieut of Leicestershire; *cr Marquess of Granby* and *Duke of Rutland* (peerage of England) 1703; *d* 1711; *s* by his son (10) JOHN, KG, 2nd Duke; *b* 1676; successively MP for Derbyshire, Leicestershire, and Grantham, and Lord-Lieut of Leicestershire: *m* 1st, 1693, Catharine Russell, who *d* 1711, da of William, Lord Russell, 2nd son of 1st Duke of Bedford; 2ndly, 1713, Hon Lucy Sherard, who *d* 1751, da of 2nd Baron Sherard; *d* 1721; *s* by his son (11) JOHN, KG, PC, 3rd Duke; *b* 1696; was Lord-Lieut of co Leicester 1721-79, Chancellor of Duchy of Lancaster 1727-36, Lord Steward of the Household 1755-61, and Master of the Horse 1761-66: *m* 1717, Hon Bridget Sutton, who *d* 1734, da of 2nd Baron Lexinton; *d* 1779; *s* by his grandson (12) CHARLES, KG, PC (son of late John, Marquess of Granby, el son of 3rd Duke), 4th Duke; was MP for Camb Univ 1774-9, and Viceroy of Ireland 1784-7: *m* 1775, Lady Mary Isabella Somerset, who *d* 1831, da of 4th Duke of Beaufort; *d* 1787; *s* by his son (13) JOHN HENRY, KG, 5th Duke; *b* 1778; was Lord-Lieut of co Leicester, Recorder of Grantham, Cambridge, and Scarborough, and Col Leicestershire Militia: *m* 1799, Lady Elizabeth Howard, who *d* 1825, da of 5th Earl of Carlisle, KG; *d* 1857; *s* by his son (14) CHARLES JOHN CECIL, KG, 6th Duke; *b* 1815; sat as MP for Stamford (C) 1837-52, and for N Leicestershire 1852-7; *d* 1888; *s* by his brother (15) JOHN JAMES ROBERT, KG, GCB, PC, DCL, LLD, 7th Duke, First Commr of Works (with a seat in the Cabinet) 1852, 1858-9 and 1866-7, Postmaster-Gen 1874-80 and 1885-6, and Chancellor of Duchy of Lancaster July 1886 to Aug 1892; sat as MP for Newark (C) 1841-7, for Colchester 1850-57, for Leicestershire N 1857-85, and for E, or Melton, Div of Leicestershire 1885-8; *cr Baron Roos of Belvoir*, co Leicester (peerage of United Kingdom) 1896: *m* 1st, 1851, Catherine Louisa, who *d* 1854, da of late Col George Marlay, CB; 2ndly, 1862, Janetta, who *d* 1899, da of Thomas Hughan, of Airds; *d* 1906; *s* by his son (16) HENRY JOHN BRINSLEY, KG (who had been called to the House of Lords in his father's Barony of Manners of Haddon 1896, and *s* as 8th Duke of Rutland and 2nd Baron Roos of Belvoir 1906), 8th Duke; *b* 1852; Principal Private Sec to Marquess of Salisbury June 1885 to Jan 1886, and Aug 1886 to March 1888; Lord-Lieut of Leicestershire 1900-25; MP for E, or Melton, Div of Leicestershire (C) 1888-95: *m* 1882, Marion Margaret Violet, who *d* 1937, da of late Col Hon Charles Hugh Lindsay, CB; *d* 1925; *s* by his yr son, (17) JOHN HENRY MONTAGU, 9th Duke; *b* 1886: *m* 1916, Kathleen, who *d* 1989, da of Francis John Tennant (B Glenconner, colls); *d* 1940; *s* by his el son (18) CHARLES JOHN ROBERT, CBE, 10th Duke, *b* 1919; Chm E Midlands Economic Planning Council 1971-74, CC Leics, DL and JP, Area Pres E Midlands Conservatives; Master Belvoir Foxhounds 1940-47, subsequently Joint Master: *m* 1st, 1946 (*m diss* 1956), Anne Bairstow, da of late Maj William Cumming Bell, of Binham House, Edgerton, Huddersfield; 2ndly, 1958, Frances Helen, da of late Charles Sweeny, of 70 South Audley St, W1, and of late Margaret, Duchess of Argyll; *d* 1999; *s* by his elder son (19) DAVID CHARLES ROBERT, 11th Duke and present peer; also Marquess of Granby, Earl of Rutland, Baron Manners of Haddon, and Baron Roos of Belvoir.

Ryder, family name of Earl of Harrowby.

RYDER OF EATON HASTINGS, BARON (Ryder) (Life Baron 1975)

SYDNEY THOMAS (DON) RYDER, son of John Ryder; *b* 16 Sept 1916; *ed* Ealing County Gram Sch; Editor of *Stock Exchange Gazette* 1950-60; Joint Man Dir Kelly Iliffe Holdings, and Associated Iliffe Press Ltd 1961-63, Man Dir 1961-63, Dir IPC 1963-70, Man Dir Reed Paper Gp 1963-68 and Chm and Ch Exec Reed Internat, Ltd (formerly Reed Gp, Ltd) 1968-75; Pres of Nat Materials Handling Centre 1970-75; Vice-Pres of Roy Soc of Prevention of Accidents 1973-88, Dir of Metropolitan Estate and Property Corpn, Ltd 1972-75; Member of Council BIM 1970-75, of British Gas Board 1972-78, and Reserve Pension Board 1973-75, of UK S Africa Trade Assocn 1974-75, and Govt Ch Industrial Adviser 1975-77; *cr* Knt 1972, and *Baron Ryder of Eaton Hastings*, of Eaton Hastings, Oxon (Life Baron) 1975: *m* 1950, Eileen, da of William Dodds, and has issue.

Arms Not exemplified at time of going to press.

SON LIVING

Hon Michael John, *b* 1953.

DAUGHTER LIVING

Hon Jill Patricia, *b* 1950.

RYDER OF WARSAW, BARONESS (Cheshire) (Life Baroness 1978)

(MARGARET) SUSAN CHESHIRE, CMG, OBE, da of late Charles Ryder; *b* 3 July 1923; *ed* Benenden; Hon LLD Liverpool 1973, Exeter 1980, London 1981, Hon DLitt Reading 1982, Hon LLD Leeds 1984, Hon DCL Kent 1986, Hon LLD Cambridge 1989, DUniv Essex 1993: Founder and Social Worker, Sue Ryder Foundation for the Sick and Disabled of all age groups; co-Founder of The Ryder-Cheshire Foundation, and Trustee of The Leonard Cheshire Foundation; 1939-45 War with FANY and Special Operations Executive: Polonia Restituta (1965), Golden Order of Merit of Poland (1976); Medal of Yugoslav Flag with Gold Wreath and Diploma (1971), Polish Order of Smile (1981), Cdr's Cross of the Order of Polonia Restituta 1992, and Author of *And The Morrow is Theirs*, 1975; *cr* OBE (Civil) 1957, CMG 1976, and *Baroness Ryder of Warsaw*, of Warsaw in Poland and of Cavendish, co Suffolk (Life Baroness) 1978: *m* 1959, as his 2nd wife, Group Capt (Geoffrey) Leonard Cheshire (*Baron Cheshire*) (Life Baron), VC, OM, DSO, DFC, who *d* 1992, and has issue.
Address – Sue Ryder Home, Cavendish, Sudbury, Suffolk CO10 8AY.

SON LIVING

Hon Jeromy Charles, *b* 1960.

DAUGHTER LIVING

Hon Elizabeth Diana, *b* 1962.

RYDER OF WENSUM, BARON (Ryder) (Life Baron 1997)

RICHARD ANDREW RYDER, OBE, PC, son of (Richard) Stephen Ryder, of Green Bradley Hall, Newmarket, Suffolk; *b* 4 Feb 1949; *ed* Radley, and Magdalene Coll, Camb (BA 1971); Journalist; Partner M. Ryder and Sons; Chm Eastern Counties Radio; Political Sec to PM 1975-81; MP for Norfolk Mid (*C*) 1983-97; PPS to Fin Sec to the Treasury 1984, and to Sec of State for Foreign Affairs 1984-86; Chm Conservative Foreign and Commonwealth Council 1984-89; Govt Whip 1986-88; Parliamentary Sec MAFF 1988-89; Economic Sec to the Treasury 1989-90; Paymaster-Gen July-Nov 1990; Parliamentary Sec to the Treasury (Govt Chief Whip) 1990-95; *cr* OBE 1981, PC 1990, and *Baron Ryder of Wensum*, of Wensum, co Norfolk (Life Baron) 1997: *m* 1981, Caroline, MBE, da of late Sir David Stephens, KCB, CVO, and has had issue.
Address – c/o House of Lords, Westminster, SW1A 0PW.

SON DECEASED

Jack, *b* and *d* 1989.

DAUGHTER LIVING

Hon Meg Clemency, *b* 1983; *ed* Godolphin and Latymer Sch.

SAATCHI, BARON (Saatchi) (Life Baron 1996)

MAURICE SAATCHI, son of Nathan David Saatchi, of London; *b* 21 June 1946; *ed* LSE (BSc); Chm Saatchi & Saatchi Co plc 1984-94; Founder M & C Saatchi Agency Ltd 1995; Memb Bd The London First since 1992: Chm Megalomedia plc since 1995; Governor, LSE; Memb Council, RCA; *cr Baron Saatchi*, of Staplefield, co West Sussex (Life Baron) 1996: *m* 1984, Josephine Hart, and has issue.
Address – M & C Saatchi, 36 Golden Square, W1R 4EE.

SON LIVING

Hon Edward, *b* 1985.

SACKVILLE, BARON (Sackville-West) (Baron UK 1876)

The day of my life

LIONEL BERTRAND SACKVILLE-WEST, 6th Baron; *b* 30 May 1913; *s* 1965; *ed* Winchester, and Magdalen Coll, Oxford (BA); late Capt Coldm Guards, and a Member of Lloyd's; patron of eleven livings; 1939-45 War (prisoner): *m* 1st, 1953, Jacobine Napier, who *d* 1971, da of J. R. Menzies-Wilson, of Fotheringhay Lodge, Nassington, Peterborough, and widow of Capt John Hichens, RA; 2ndly, 1974 (*m diss* 1983), Arlie Roebuck, who *d* 1991, da of Charles Woodhead, of Romany Rye, Brisbane, Aust, widow of Maj Hugh Dalzell Stewart, W Yorks Regt, and formerly wife of Maj-Gen Sir Francis Wilfred de Guingand, KBE, CB, DSO; 3rdly, 1983, Jean, da of late Arthur Stanley Garton, of Danesfield, Marlow, Bucks, and widow of Maj Sir Edward Henry Bouhier Imbert-Terry, 3rd Bt, and has issue by 1st *m*.

Arms – Quarterly: 1st and 4th argent, a fesse dancette sable, *West*; 2nd and 3rd or and gules, a bend vair, *Sackville*. Crests – 1st, out of a ducal coronet or, a griffin's head azure, beaked and eared gold; 2nd out of a coronet composed of a fleur-de-lis or, an estoile argent. Supporters – On either side a griffin azure, beaked and eared or, ducally gorged gold, therefrom pendent an escutcheon, that on the dexter charged with the arms of West, and that on the sinister with the arms of Sackville.
Seat – Knole, Sevenoaks, Kent.

DAUGHTERS LIVING (*By 1st marriage*)

Hon Teresa, *b* 1954: *m* 1979, (Alastair) Rupert Marlow, of 11 Gladstone St, SE1, son of Capt C. N. Marlow, RN, of Greenhill House, Upper Westwood, Wilts, and has issue living, Sebastian Edward, *b* 1985, — Julia Catherine, *b* 1982, — Rebecca Clare, *b* 1983.
Hon Catherine Jacobine SACKVILLE-WEST (36 Iffley Rd, W6), *b* 1956; resumed her maiden name 1984: *m* 1980 (*m diss* 1983), Stuart Cooper Bennett, elder son of H. M. Bennett, of Pasadena, Calif, USA.
Hon Sophia Anne, *b* 1957: *m* 1988, Guy R. Elliott, of 11 Sinclair Gdns, W14, only son of Robert Elliott, of Little Ashley Farm, Bradford-on-Avon, Wilts.
Hon Victoria Mary, *b* 1959: *m* 1989, Jonathan G. F. Lang, of 61 Richbourne Terr, SW8, yr son of John Lang, of Nairobi, Kenya, and has issue living, Leo John Bertrand, *b* 1993, — Clementine Jacobine Eva, *b* 1991.
Hon Sarah Elizabeth, *b* 1960: *m* 1992, (Edward) Simon Rendall, yr son of Peter Godfrey Rendall, of Burford, Oxon, and has issue living, Frederick Thomas Inigo, *b* 1994, — Edward Bertrand Montague, *b* 1996.

BROTHER LIVING

HUGH ROSSLYN INIGO, MC (Knole, Sevenoaks, Kent; Brooks's Club), *b* 1 Feb 1919; *ed* Winchester, and Magdalen Coll, Oxford (MA); late Capt R Tank Regt; ARICS; Admin Officer, N Nigeria 1946-59; 1939-45 War (wounded, MC, French Croix de Guerre): *m* 1957, Bridget Eleanor da of Capt Robert Lionel Brooke Cunliffe, CBE, RN (*see* Cunliffe, Bt, colls), and has issue living, Robert Bertrand (Gardener's Cottage, Knole, Sevenoaks, Kent TN15 0RP), *b* 1958: *m* 1st, 1985 (*m diss* 1992), Catherine Dorothea, elder da of Geoffrey Bennett, of Smelthouses, N Yorks: 2ndly, 1994, (Margot) Jane, da of Mark MacAndrew, of Holmwood House, Holmwood, Dorking, Surrey, and has issue living (by 2nd *m*), Freya *b* 1998, — William Lionel Cunliffe (Flat 9, Cleveland Court, 90 Cleveland St, W1P 5DR), *b* 1967: *m* 1993 (*m diss* 1998), Annika, da of Kurt Lennartsson, of Västeras, Sweden, and of Birgitta Dellastrand, of Köping, Sweden, — Mary Cecilie, *b* 1960, — Elizabeth Anne, *b* 1962, — Jane Eleanor, *b* 1964.

PREDECESSORS – (1) *Hon* MORTIMER Sackville-West (4th son of 5th Earl De La Warr); *b* 1820; held several high appointments in Royal Household, and was *cr Baron Sackville*, of Knole, co Kent (peerage of United Kingdom), 1876, with special remainder, failing heirs male of his body, to his brothers Lionel and William Edward respectively in like manner (*see* E De La Warr, colls): *m* 1st, 1847, Fanny Charlotte, da of late Maj-Gen William Dickson, CB; 2ndly, 1873, Elizabeth, da of late Charles William Faber, Esq, of Northaw House, Barnet; *d* 1888; *s* by his brother (2) LIONEL SACKVILLE, GCMG, 2nd Baron; *b* 1827; was Min to Argentine Republic 1872-8, to Madrid 1878-81, and to Washington 1881-8; *dspl* 1908, when a suit was brought by Henri Ernest Jean Baptist Sackville-West under the Declaration of Legitimacy Act, claiming to be el legitimate son of the 2nd Baron by Josephine Duran de Ortega (Pepita), but in 1910 the petition was dismissed, and then *s* to the Barony under the special remainder the 2nd Baron's nephew (3) LIONEL EDWARD (el son of late Lieut-Col Hon William Edward Sackville-West), 3rd Baron, *b* 1867; a Director of Bank of Liverpool and Martins: *m* 1890, his cousin, Victoria Sackville-West, who *d* 1936, natural da of 2nd Baron Sackville; *d* 1928; *s* by his brother (4) CHARLES JOHN, KBE, CB, CMG, 4th Baron, *b* 1870; Maj-Gen, late King's Roy Rifle Corps; British Representative at Supreme War Council, Versailles 1918 and 1919, Mil Attaché at Paris 1920-4, and Lieut-Gov of Guernsey 1925-9: *m* 1st, 1897, Maud Cecilia, who *d* 1920, da of late Matthew John Bell, of Bourne Park, Kent (B St Leonards); 2ndly, 1924, Anne (BIGELOW), who *d* 1961, da of late William Meredith, of New York; *d* 1962; *s* by his son (5) EDWARD CHARLES, 5th Baron, *b* 1901, *d* 1965; *s* by his cousin (6) LIONEL BERTRAND (el son of Hon Bertrand George Sackville-West, yst brother of 4th Baron), 6th Baron and present peer.

Sackville, family name of Earl De La Warr.

SAINSBURY, BARONY OF (Sainsbury) (Extinct 1998)

SONS LIVING OF LIFE BARON (*By 1st marriage*)

Hon Sir John Davan, *b* 1927; *cr* Baron Sainsbury of Preston Candover (Life Baron) 1989 (see that title).

Hon Simon David Davan, *b* 1930; *ed* Eton, and Trin Coll, Camb; formerly Vice-Chm and a Director of J. Sainsbury Ltd; a Trustee Nat Gallery since 1991.

Rt Hon Sir Timothy Alan Davan (c/o FLAG, Suite 23, Buckingham Court, 78 Buckingham Gate, SW1E 6PE; Boodle's Club), *b* 1932; *ed* Eton, and Worcester Coll, Oxford; MP for Hove (C) 1973-97; Govt Whip 1983-87, Parl Under-Sec Min of Defence 1987-89, Parl Under-Sec of State Foreign & Commonwealth Office 1989-90, Min of State, Dept of Trade & Industry 1990-94; Chm Trustees of Somerset House Trust; PC 1992, and Ktd 1995: *m* 1961, Susan Mary, da of Brig James Alastair Harry Mitchell, CBE, DSO, and has issue living, (Timothy) James, *b* (Feb) 1962: *m* 1995, Margaret, eldest da of Edward Alexander Martin (*see* Barry, Bt, colls), and has issue living, Hector *b* 1997, — Alexander, *b* 1968, — Camilla Davan, *b* (Dec) 1962: *m* 1987, Shaun Anthony Woodward, MP, and has issue living, Tom *b* 1989, Ella *b* 1991, Olivia *b* 1993, Kate *b* 1996, — Jessica Mary, *b* 1970: *m* 1997, Peter Doimi de Frankopan.

DAUGHTER LIVING OF LIFE BARON (*By 2nd marriage*)

Hon Paulette Ann, *b* 1946: *m* 1970, James Anderson, and has issue living, Lindsey (a da), *b* 19—.

SAINSBURY OF PRESTON CANDOVER, BARON (Sainsbury) (Life Baron 1989)

JOHN DAVAN SAINSBURY, KG, eldest son of Baron Sainsbury (Life Baron); *b* 2 Nov 1927; *ed* Stowe, and Worcester Coll, Oxford (Hon Fell 1982); Hon Bencher Inner Temple 1985, Hon FIGD 1973, Hon DSC Econ London 1985, Hon DLitt South Bank Univ 1992, Hon LLD Bristol 1993, Hon FRIBA 1993, Albert Medal RSA 1989; Dir J Sainsbury plc 1958-92, Vice-Chm 1967-69, Chm 1969-92, since when Pres; Dir The Royal Opera House, Covent Garden, 1969-85, Chm 1987-91, Chm Friends of Covent Garden 1969-81, Dir The Royal Opera House Trust 1974-84, and 1987-97; Chm Benesh Inst of Choreology 1986-87, and Dulwich Picture Gallery since 1994; Gov Royal Ballet Sch 1965-76, and 1987-91, Gov Royal Ballet since 1987 (Chm since 1995); Dir The Economist 1972-80; Joint Hon Treas European Movement 1972-75, Memb Council Retail Consortium 1975-79 (Pres 1993-97), Nat Cttee for Electoral Reform 1976-85, and President's Cttee CBI 1982-84; Vice-Pres Contemporary Arts Soc since 1984 (Hon Sec 1965-71, Vice-Chm 1971-74), Trustee National Gallery 1976-83, Westminster Abbey Trust 1977-83, Tate Gallery 1982-83, Rhodes Trust 1984-98; Dir Friends of the Nelson Mandela Children's Fund since 1996; Pres Sparsholt Coll, Hants 1993-2000; *cr* Kt 1980, *Baron Sainsbury of Preston Candover*, of Preston Candover, co Hants (Life Baron) 1989, and KG 1992: *m* 1963, Anya (Anya Linden, Royal Ballet ballerina), formerly wife of Igor Tamarin, and da of George Charles Eltenton, and has issue.

Arms – Azure, on a fess dancetty between three cornucopiae bendwise or, as many lyres gules. **Crest** – A mural crown azure, thereon a leopard sejant proper supporting a corinthian column gold. **Supporters** – On either side rampant upon a cornucopia or a leopard proper, the compartment comprising a grassy mount all proper.
Address – House of Lords, SW1A 0PW. *Club* – Garrick.

SONS LIVING

Hon (John) Julian, *b* 1966.
Hon Mark Leonard, *b* 1969.

DAUGHTER LIVING

Hon Sarah Jane, *b* 1964: *m* 1990, Robert Joseph Neville Galmoye Butler-Sloss, elder son of Hon Mr Justice (Joseph William Alexander) Butler-Sloss, and has issue living, Samuel Robert John, *b* 1997, — Lucy Ann Josephine, *b* 1995.

SAINSBURY OF TURVILLE, BARON (Sainsbury) (Life Baron 1997)

DAVID JOHN SAINSBURY, son of Sir Robert Sainsbury, and nephew of late Baron Sainsbury (Life Baron); *b* 24 Oct 1949; *ed* King's Coll, Camb (BA 1963), and Columbia Graduate Sch of Business, New York (MBA 1971); Hon DSc Salford 1989; Hon LLD Cantab 1997; joined J. Sainsbury plc 1963, Dir since 1966, Financial Controller 1971-73, Financial Dir 1973-90, Dep Chm 1988-92, Chm 1992-98; Under Sec of State Trade and Industry since 1998; Chm Savacentre Ltd 1984-93; Dir Shaw's Supermarkets Inc; Visiting Fell, Nuffield Coll, Oxford; Chm Governing Body, London Business Sch since 1991; Tstee, SDP 1982-90 (Memb Steering Cttee 1981-82); Columbia Business Sch Award for Distinguished Leadership in Business 1990; Hon FEng 1994; author; *cr Baron Sainsbury of Turville*, of Turville, co Bucks (Life Baron) 1997: *m* 1973, Susan Carole, da of K. M. Reid, and has issue.
Address – c/o J. Sainsbury plc, Stamford House, Stamford St, SE1 9LL.

DAUGHTERS LIVING

Hon Clare Natasha, *b* 1974.
Hon (Anya) Lucy, *b* 1976.
Hon Francesca Elizabeth, *b* 1978.

ST ALBANS, DUKE OF (Beauclerk) (Duke E 1684)
(Name pronounced "Bo-clare")

AUSPICIUM MELIORIS ÆVI

A pledge of better times

MURRAY DE VERE BEAUCLERK, 14th Duke; *b* 19 Jan 1939; *s* 1988; *ed* Tonbridge; a Chartered Accountant, a Liveryman of Drapers' Co; patron of two livings, Hereditary Grand Falconer, and Hereditary Registrar of Court of Chancery; Gov-Gen Royal Stuart Soc: *m* 1st, 1963 (*m diss* 1974), Rosemary Frances, only da of Dr Francis Harold Scoones, JP, MRCS, LRCP, of 83 Abbotsbury Rd, W14; 2ndly, 1974, Cynthia Theresa Mary, da of late Lt-Col William James Holdsworth Howard, DSO, and formerly wife of Sir Anthony Robin Maurice Hooper, 2nd Bt, and has issue by 1st *m*.

𝔄rms – Quarterly: 1st and 4th grand quarters the royal arms of King Charles II, 1st and 4th France and England, quarterly; 2nd Scotland; 3rd Ireland; the whole debruised by a baton sinister gules, charged with three roses argent, *Beauclerk*; 2nd and 3rd grand quarters quarterly gules and or, in the 1st quarter a mullet argent *de Vere*. 𝔄rest – On a chapeau gules, turned up ermine, a lion statant guardant or, ducally crowned per pale argent and gules, and gorged with a plain collar gules, charged with three roses argent. 𝔖upporters – *Dexter*, an antelope argent, armed and unguled or; *sinister*, a greyhound argent, each collared as the crest.
Residence – 16 Ovington St, SW3 2JB. *Club* – Hurlingham.

SON LIVING (*By 1st marriage*)

CHARLES FRANCIS TOPHAM DE VERE (*Earl of Burford*), *b* 22 Feb 1965; *ed* Sherborne, Hertford Coll, Oxford (MA), and Edinburgh Univ; founder and Pres De Vere Soc; Vice-Pres Royal Stuart Soc since 1989; Pres Shakespeare Oxford Soc 1995-97; Liveryman Drapers' Co 1990: *m* 1994, Louise Ann Beatrice Fiona, eldest da of Col Malcolm Vernon Robey, of Canada, and has issue.

SON LIVING— James Malcolm Aubrey Edward de Vere (*Lord Vere of Hanworth*), *b* 2 Aug 1995.

Residence – Benton Lodge, 125 Benton St, Hadleigh, Suffolk IP7 5AY. *Club* – Brooks's.

DAUGHTER LIVING (*By 1st marriage*)

Lady Emma Caroline de Vere, *b* 1963; *ed* Roedean, St John's Coll, Camb (BA), and Univ of E Anglia: *m* 1991, David Craig Shaw Smellie, son of late Prof (Robert) Martin Stuart Smellie, of Hyndland, Glasgow, and has issue. *Residence* – 1A Templar St, Myatt's Fields, Camberwell, SE5 9JB.

HALF-BROTHERS LIVING

Lord Peter Charles de Vere, *b* 1948; *ed* Eton: *m* 1972 (*m diss* 19—), Beverley June, da of late Alva Edwin Bailey, of Cal, USA, and has had issue, Robin, *b* 1971; *d* 1973, — Angela Grace de Vere, *b* 1974. *Residence* – 2726 Shelter Island Drive 332, San Diego, California 92106, USA.

Lord James Charles Fesq de Vere (Barn House, Midgham, Reading, Berks RG7 5UG), *b* 1949; *ed* Eton.

Lord John William Aubrey de Vere, *b* 1950; *ed* Eton: *m* 1986, Carolyn Ann Heath, da of Mrs B. Wilkinson, of Isle of Wight, and has issue living, Kiatsi Sofia, *b* 1984. Lord John has further issue (by Joanna, da of Stanislav Kolaczinski, of Warsaw, Poland), Annamary, *b* 1998. *Address* – c/o Save The Children Fund (Hungary), 17 Grove Lane, SE5 8SP.

HALF-SISTER LIVING

Lady Caroline Anne de Vere, *b* 1951; *ed* Fritham House, Queen's Gate Sch, Open Univ (BA), and Southampton Univ (MSc, Dip SW): *m* 1970 (*m diss* 1986), Neil St John ffrench Blake, and has issue living, Clare Eleanor de Vere, *b* 1972, — Kate Juliana de Vere, *b* 1977. *Residence* – Barn House, Midgham, Reading, Berks RG7 5UG.

WIDOW LIVING OF THIRTEENTH DUKE

SUZANNE MARIE ADELE (*Dowager Duchess of St Albans*), da of late Emile William Fesq, of Mas Mistral, Vence, France AM: *m* 1947, as his 2nd wife, Col the 13th Duke, OBE, who *d* 1988. *Residence* – 64 West St, Newbury, Berks RG13 1BD.

COLLATERAL BRANCHES LIVING

Granddaughter of late William Nelthorpe Beauclerk, JP, DL, LLD, el son of Capt Lord Frederick Charles Peter Beauclerk, JP, RN, 2nd surv son of 8th Duke:—
Issue of late Major Aubrey Nelthorpe Beauclerk, *b* 1879, *d* 1916: *m* 1911, Vera Eileen May, who *d* 1975, having *m* 2ndly, 1919, Capt Gerald Andrew Greig, late R Scots Fusiliers, who *d* 1950, da of late Capt W. H. Francis, formerly 28th Regt:—
Daphne Diana de Vere, *b* 1911: *m* 1933, Count Claude Antoine Chauvin de Précourt, who *d* 1971, and has issue living, François Charles Christian (36 rue de la Résistance, 78150 Le Chesnay, France), *b* 1936: *m* 1962, Sabine, da of the late Comte de Vautibault, of Laval, Mayenne, France and has issue living, Claude Henri Aubrey *b* 1963, Rémy François Xavier *b* 1972, Ghislaine *b* 1967: *m* 1991, Jean du Puytison, of Versailles (and has issue), — Philippe Etienne (27 Rue Borgnis-Desbordes, Versailles, 78000, France), *b* 1938: *m* 1st, 1961, Marie-Noelle, who *d* 1989, da of René Gasquet, of Neuilly-sur-Seine, France; 2ndly, 1992, Catherine, da of Robert Treppier, of Paris, and has issue living (by 1st *m*), Aude Emilie *b* 1962: *m* 1989, Geoffrey de Monteynard, son of Comte Jean de Monteynard, of Versailles (and has issue), Laure Sabine Pierrette *b* 1963: *m* 1997, Thierry Hano, of Paris (and has issue), Clarisse Agnes *b* 1966: *m* 1991, Nicolas Demont, of Versailles (and has issue), Marguerite *b* 1972: *m* 1996, Baron Frederic de Ravinel, of Paris, — Jean Yves (Le Bouscatel, Bouchet de la Lauze, Ponteils par Génolac, 30, France), *b* 1943: *m* 1970, Nathalie, da of Dr Dubel, of France, and has issue living, Jeremy Adrian *b* 1978, Penelope *b* 1971, — Anne Victoria, *b* 1944: *m* 1996, Nigel E. L. Foxell, son of Rev Canon W. J. Foxell. *Residence* – Kennards, Amberley, W Sussex BN18 9NQ.

Grandchildren of late Maj Aubrey Nelthorpe Beauclerk (ante):—
Issue of late Hermione de Vere Beauclerk, *b* 1915, *d* 1969: *m* 1939, James Dewar, MBE, GM, AE, FCA, who *d* 1983:—
Peter de Vere BEAUCLERK-DEWAR, RD and bar (22 Faroe Rd, Brook Green, W14 0EP; Holm of Huip, by Stronsay, Orkney Is; New (Edinburgh), and Puffins Clubs), *b* 1943; recognised in the surname and arms of Beauclerk-Dewar by Lyon Court 1965; *ed* Ampleforth; Lt-Cdr RNR; RD 1980 and bar 1990; Member Queen's Body Guard for Scotland (Royal Co of Archers); Falkland Pursuivant Extraor 1975, 1982, 1984, 1986, 1987, 1991, 1994, 1996, 1997 and 1999; Silver Stick Usher at HM Silver Jubilee Thanksgiving Ser 1977; Usher at HM Queen Elizabeth the Queen Mother's 80th Birthday Thanksgiving Ser 1980; JP (Inner London), FSA Scot, FIMgt, FFA, FHG (Hon); co-author of *The House of Nell Gwyn* 1974, and author *The House of Dewar* 1991; Vice-Pres Royal Stuart Soc since 1995; NADFAS Lecturer since 1998; a Liveryman of Haberdashers' Co; OStJ, Kt of Sovereign Mil Order of Malta, Kt of Sacred Mil Order of Constantine St George, Cdr of Merit with Swords 'Pro Merito Melitensi' 1989: *m* 1967, Sarah Ann Sweet Verge, el da of Maj Lionel John Verge Rudder, late DCLI, of Fairford, Glos, and has issue living, James William Aubrey de Vere (1 Sterndale Rd, W14 0HT), *b* 1970; *ed* Ampleforth, — Alexandra Hermione Sarah, *b* 1972, — Emma Diana Peta, *b* 1973, — Philippa Caroline Frances, *b* 1982. ——Gillian de Vere BEAUCLERK (Lamberts, Stourton Caundle, Dorset DT10 2JJ), *b* 1944; assumed surname of Beauclerk by deed poll 1990: *m* 1st, 1964 (*m diss* 1978), Peter John Lawrence Silley, of Park House, Eynsford, Kent; 2ndly, 1978 (*m diss* 1990), Robert Erskine Beveridge, and has had issue (by 1st *m*), Natasha Margaret, *b* 1965, — Tanya Anne, *b* 1967; *d* 1984.

Grandchildren of late Charles Robert Beauclerk, son of late Charles George Beauclerk, grandson of late Lord Sydney Beauclerk, 5th son of 1st Duke:—
Issue of late William Topham Sidney Beauclerk, *b* 1864, *d* 1950: *m* 1910, Lola de Penalver, who *d* 1972, da of Enrique, Conde de Penalver y Marqués de Arcos in Spain:—
Rafael Charles, MBE, *b* 1917; *ed* Downside; 1939-45 War as Capt Intelligence Corps (MBE (Mil) 1945, French Croix de Guerre); Marques Valero de Urria in Spain; MBE (Mil) 1945: *m* 1957, Noirine Mary, who *d* 1997, el da of James Bowen, of Bowen's Cross, co Cork, and has issue living, William Rafael (6 Queen Anne Gdns, Leatherhead, Surrey KT22 7JE; 15 rue de Béarnid, 78670 Medan, France), *b* 1961; *ed* Worth; Lieut RN (ret) served in HMY *Britannia*; ARICS: *m* 1986, Margaret Eleanor, da of Lesley James Mountjoy, of Totteridge, London, and has issue living, Alexander Charles *b* 1990, Cameron *b* 1993, Charlotte *b* 1987, — Dolores Mary, *b* 1958; SRN: *m* 1981, Dr Richard M. Makower, son of C.S. Makower, MC, of 37 Piercing Hill, Theydon Bois, Essex, and has issue living, Timothy *b* 1984, Oliver William *b* 1992, Emily Elizabeth *b* 1987. ——Diana Mary, *b* 1924. *Residences* – Villa Etchè Biskiak, Av des Chênes, Biarritz, France; 31 Marryat Rd, Wimbledon, SW19.

PREDECESSORS – (1) *Sir* CHARLES Beauclerk, KG, FRS, natural son of Charles II, by Eleanor Gwyn; *b* 1670; *cr Baron Heddington*, co Oxford, and *Earl of Burford* (peerage of England) 1676, and *Duke of St Albans* (peerage of England) 1684; Hereditary Registrar of the Court of Chancery 1698; Hereditary Master Falconer of England 1685; Capt of Band of Gentlemen Pensioners; a Lord of the Bedchamber, Lord Lieut of Berks, High Steward of Windsor and of Wokingham and Col of Princess Anne of Denmark's Regt of Horse: *m* 1694, Lady Diana de Vere (1st Lady of the Bedchamber and Lady of the Stole to Caroline, Princess of Wales, later Queen Caroline), who *d* 1742, el da and heir of 20th and last Earl of Oxford, KG; *d* 1726; *s* by his son (2) CHARLES, KG, KB, 2nd Duke; *b* 1696; successively MP for Bodmin and Windsor, Constable and Gov of Windsor Castle and Lord Warden of the Forests; a Lord of the Bedchamber; Lord Lieut of Berks and High Steward of Windsor and of Wokingham: *m* 1722, Lucy, who *d* 1752, da of Sir John Werden, 2nd Bt; *d* 1751; *s* by his son (3) GEORGE, 3rd Duke; *b* 1730; a Lord of the Bedchamber, Lord Lieut of Berks and High Steward of Windsor: *m* 1752, Jane who *d* 1778, da and heir of Sir Walter Roberts, 6th Bt; *dsp* 1786; *s* by his 1st cousin once removed (4) GEORGE (grandson of Lord William, 2nd son of 1st Duke), 4th Duke; *b* 1758; Lt-Col 3rd Foot Gds; *d unm* 1787; *s* by his 1st cousin once removed (5) AUBREY, (son of Adm Lord Vere of Hanworth, 3rd son of 1st Duke, who *d* 1781, having in 1750 been *cr Baron Vere of Hanworth* (peerage of GB)), 5th Duke; *b* 1740; successively MP for Thetford and Aldborough: *m* 1763, Lady Catherine Ponsonby, who *d* 1789, da of 2nd Earl of Bessborough; *d* 1802, *s* by his son (6) AUBREY, 6th Duke; *b* 1765; Lt-Col 34th Foot: *m* 1st, 1788, Jane, who *d* 1800, da of John Moses, of Hull; 2ndly, 1802, Louisa Grace, who *d* 1816, da of John Manners, MP, of Grantham Grange, Lincs, by Lady Louisa Manners (later Tollemache), Countess of Dysart; *d* 1815; *s* by his son (7) AUBREY, 7th Duke; *b* 1815; *d* 1816; *s* by his uncle (8) WILLIAM, 8th Duke; *b* 1766; Cdr RN; High Sheriff of Denbigh and Lincs: *m* 1st, 1791, Charlotte, da of Rev Robert Carter Thelwall, of Redbourne Hall, Lincs; 2ndly, 1799, Maria Janetta, who *d* 1822, da of John Nelthorpe, of Little Grimsby Hall, Lincs; *d* 1825; *s* by his son (9) WILLIAM AUBREY DE VERE, 9th Duke; *b* 1801; LLD Cantab: *m* 1st, 1827, Harriet (actress), da of Matthew Mellon, and widow of Thomas Coutts, banker of London; 2ndly, 1839, Elizabeth Catherine, who *d* 1893, da of Gen Joseph Gubbins, of Kilfrush, co Limerick; *d* 1849; *s* by his son (10) WILLIAM AMELIUS AUBREY DE VERE, PC, 10th Duke; *b* 1840; Lord Lieut Notts; Capt of HM's Yeomen of the Guard 1873-74 Col 1st Notts (Robin Hood) Rifle Vols; offered but declined KG 1875: *m* 1st, 1867, Sybil Mary, who *d* 1871, da of Gen Hon Charles Grey; 2nd, 1874, Grace, who *d* 1926, da of Ralph Bernal Osborne, MP, of Newtown Anner, co Tipperary; *d* 1898; *s* by his el son (11) CHARLES VICTOR ALBERT AUBREY DE VERE, 11th Duke; *b* 1870; Capt S Notts Yeo, formerly Lieut R Scots; *dunm* 1934; *s* by his half-brother (12) OSBORNE DE VERE, TD, 12th Duke; *b* 1874; Capt 17th Lancers and Maj S Notts Hussars; High Sheriff and DL co Waterford: *m* 1918, Lady Beatrix Frances, GBE, who *d* 1953, da of the 5th Marquess of Lansdowne, KG, and widow of 6th Marquess of Waterford, KP; *dsp* 1964; *s* by his 2nd cousin (13) CHARLES FREDERIC AUBREY DE VERE, OBE (only son of Aubrey Topham Beauclerk, 3rd son of Lord Charles Beauclerk, 5th surv son of 8th

Duke), 13th Duke, *b* 1915; Col Intelligence Corps, 1939-45 War in Mediterranean, Dir Films Div, Central Office of Information, Gov-Gen Royal Stuart Soc: *m* 1st, 1938 (*m diss* 1947), Nathalie Chatham, who *d* 1985, da of late Percival Field Walker, of Rythe Court, Thames Ditton, Surrey; 2ndly, 1947, Suzanne Marie Adèle, da of Emile William Fesq, of Mas Mistral, Vence, France AM; *d* 1988; *s* by his eldest son **(14)** MURRAY DE VERE, 14th Duke and present peer; also Earl of Burford, Baron Hedington, and Baron Vere of Hanworth.

ST ALDWYN, EARL (Hicks Beach) (Earl UK 1915, and Bt E 1619)

All in good time

MICHAEL HENRY HICKS BEACH, 3rd Earl, and 11th Baronet; *b* 7 Feb 1950; *s* 1992; *ed* Eton, and Ch Ch Oxford (MA): *m* 1982, Gilda Maria, only da of late Barão Saavedra, of Rua Paula Freitas 104, Copacabana, Rio de Janeiro, and has issue.

Arms – Quarterly: 1st and 4th, vaire, argent and gules, a canton azure charged with a pile or, *Beach*; 2nd and 3rd, gules, a fesse wavy between three fleurs-de-lis or, a crescent for difference, *Hicks*. **Crest** – A demi-lion rampant argent, ducally gorged or, and holding in the paws an escutcheon azure, charged with a pile or. **Supporters** – *Dexter*, a knight armed cap-à-pie in the middle of the fourteenth century, his jupon charged with the arms of *Beach*, namely, vaire argent and gules, on a canton azure a pile or; *sinister*, a knight similarly vested, his jupon charged with the arms of *Hicks*, namely, gules a fesse wavy between three fleur-de-lis, or, a crescent argent for difference.
Residences – Williamstrip Park, Cirencester, Gloucestershire GL7 5AT; 17 Hale House, 34 De Vere Gdns, W8 5AQ. *Clubs* – Leander, White's, Pratt's.

DAUGHTERS LIVING

Lady Atalanta Maria, *b* 1983.
Lady Aurora Ursula, *b* 1988.

BROTHERS LIVING AND DECEASED

†*Hon* Peter Hugh, *b* 1952; *ed* Eton; painter; *dunm* 1990.

Hon DAVID SEYMOUR, *b* 25 May 1955; *ed* Eton; a Page of Honour to HM 1969-71: *m* 1993, Katrina (Kate) Louise Susannah, da of Michael Henriques, of Winson Manor, Cirencester, Glos, and has issue living, Peter Etienne, *b* 1998, — Lucy Susan, *b* 1996. *Residence* – The Upper Mill, Coln St Aldwyns, Glos GL7 5AJ. *Club* – Pratt's.

AUNT LIVING (sister of 2nd Earl) (raised to the rank of an Earl's daughter 1920)

Lady Delia Mary, *b* 1910: *m* 1934, Brigadier Sir Charles Michael Dillwyn-Venables-Llewelyn, 3rd Bt, MVO, who *d* 1976. *Residence* – Llysdinam, Newbridge-on-Wye, Powys LD1 6NB.

COLLATERAL BRANCHES LIVING (In remainder to the Baronetcy only)

Grandson of late William Frederick Hicks Beach, 2nd son of 8th Bt:—
Issue of late Michael Hicks Beach, *b* 1872, *d* 1953: *m* 1907, Helène, who *d* 1941, da of Arthur Des Fosses, formerly of Montreal:—
Michael, *b* 1909: *m* 1st, 1932, Dorothy, da of late Robert Stratton, formerly of Nottingham; 2ndly, 1944, Eunice, who *d* 1973, da of late Rudolph J. Thanisch, of Boston, Mass, USA; 3rdly, 1974, Grace Vera, da of late Henry Moos, Sr, of Union City, NJ, USA, and widow of Charles Arthur Rankin, and has issue living (by 1st *m*), Heather Diane HICKS BEACH (417 Hampton Court, Falls Church, Va 22046, USA), *b* 1935; has reverted to maiden name: *m* 1957 (*m diss* 1970), Edward Lionel Peck, and has issue living, Brian Michael *b* 1960, Heather Anne *b* 1959: *m* 1989, Michael Lindner (and has issue living, Noah William *b* 1994).

Grandchildren of late Michael Hicks Beach (ante):—
Issue of late Frederick Edward Hicks Beach, *b* 1911, *d* 1972: *m* 1st, 1933 (*m diss* 1947), Harriet Green (who *m* 2ndly, 1947, Oren Clark Burt); 2ndly, 1947, Lois (5230 101st St, Jacksonville Florida, 32210, USA), da of John W. Lainhart, of Washington, DC, USA:—
(By 1st *m*) Frances Helene BURT (934 East 40th St, Brooklyn, NY 11210), *b* 1942; has issue living, Liam Christopher, *b* 1981.

Issue of late John Hugh Hicks Beach, *b* 1915, *d* 1982: *m* 1945, Jeanne Potter (55 Clinton Rd, Bedford Hills, NY 10507, USA), da of Herbert McGuhy, of Bedford Hills:—
John Hugh, *b* 1960. —— Lucinda (21 Sunset Place, N Salem, NY 10560, USA), *b* 1948: *m* 1971 (*m diss* 1996), Timothy F. Quinn, and has issue living, Tressan Lucinda, *b* 1977, — Holly Bebhinn, *b* 1979. —— Priscilla, *b* 1950: *m* 1982, Ferdinand Travis Hopkins IV, of Hickory Ridge Rd, Brewster, NY 10509, USA.

Grandchildren of late Ellis Hicks Beach, 3rd son of late William Frederick Hicks Beach (ante):—
Issue of late Maj William Whitehead Hicks Beach, TD, *b* 1907, *d* 1975: *m* 1939, Diana (Witcombe Park, Gloucester), da of Christopher Gurney Hoare:—

†Mark William, *b* 1943: *m* 1966, Cecilia Ruth (Witcombe Farm, Great Witcombe, nr Glos), el da of Douglas Allan Wright, and *d* 1998, leaving issue, Andrew William, *b* 1970, — Frederick David, *b* 1980, — Lucinda Jane, *b* 1975. —— Elizabeth Anne, *b* 1940: *m* 1st, 1962 (*m diss* 1975), Simon Erne St Houlston Clarke; 2ndly, 1987, Peter Malcolm Hinson, and has issue living (by 1st *m*), Martin, *b* 1963, — Timothy, *b* 1965. —— Rosemary Gillian, *b* 1944: *m* 1965, Maj Gen David Murray Naylor, CB, late Scots Gds (*see* Holt, Bt, *cr* 1935, 1985 Edn), and has issue living, Nicholas John, *b* 1967: *m* 1995, Clare E. M., eldest da of G. Jacobs, of Balmullo, Fife, — Duncan Hugh, *b* 1968, — Christopher William, *b* 1972. *Residence* – Minster Hill, Huttons Ambo, N Yorks.

Grandchildren of late William Frederick Hicks Beach (ante):—
Issue of late Edward Howe Hicks Beach, *b* 1875, *d* 1967: *m* 1903, Alberta Louise, who *d* 1946, da of William Penn Jaynes, of Vancouver:—

Edward Adryan (PO Box 1373, La Pine, Oregon 97739-0138, USA), *b* 1915: *m* 1st, 1936 (*m diss* 1940), Evelyn, da of Clarence Dale, of Los Angeles, Cal, USA; 2ndly, 1940, Linnéa Maria, da of late Andrew Holst, of Los Angeles, Cal, USA, and has issue living (by 2nd *m*), Edward Erick (RR1 Box 60Y, Custer, S Dakota 57730, USA), *b* 1941: *m* 1991, Betty-May, da of late Henry Carl Snider, and has issue living, Christine Elizabeth *b* 1970, — Frederick Howe (5181 Heil Avenue, Huntington Beach, Calif 92649, USA), *b* 1944: *m* 1970, Kathleen Mary, da of Roy Edward Tincher, of 421 Rainier Way, Hemet, Calif 92543, USA, and has issue living, Chad Edward *b* 1977, Cara Leigh *b* 1983. —— Clara Violet Louise, *b* 1905: *m* 1954, Ralph Elmer Wilson, of 4181 Lincoln Av, Culver City, Cal 90230, USA

Grandsons of late Maj Archibald William Hicks Beach, son of late Rt Hon William Wither Bramston Beach, MP, son of late William Beach, MP, son of 2nd son of 6th Bt:—
Issue of late William Guy Hicks Beach, *b* 1891, *d* 1953: *m* 1st, 1914 (*m diss* 1932), Fanny Muriel, da of Ninian B. Stewart, of Dunloe, Wemyss Bay, and 14 Park Circus, Glasgow; 2ndly, 1932, Mrs Beatrice Mary Uniacke, who *d* 1975, da of Arthur Johnstone, formerly Indian Police:—

(By 1st *m*) Peter Stewart, OBE (Boscobel, Hammer Lane, Grayshott, Hindhead, Surrey), *b* 1924; Capt RN; 1939-45 War (despatches); OBE (Mil) 1968: *m* 1950, Victoria Margaret, who *d* 1986, da of Ralph Victor Nelson, and has had issue, †Richard Stewart Nelson, *b* 1951; *d* 1966, — Sally Elizabeth, *b* 1953: *m* 1980, Anthony Michael Farnfield, and has issue living, Johanna *b* 1983. —— Geoffrey Robert Wither (Cucumber Hall, Fressingfield, Suffolk), *b* 1925: *m* 1952, Rosemary Wendy Wolseley-Charles, and has issue living, Nicholas Charles, *b* 1960; *ed* Charterhouse, and Bristol Univ; scriptwriter, — Fiona Susan, *b* 1955: *m* 1981, Anthony Arthur Edwards, of 107 Mycenae Rd, SE3, son of A. A. Edwards, of Swansea, and has issue living, Benjamin Nicholas Owen *b* 1984, Samuel Dafydd William *b* 1989, Rosamund Margretta Victoria *b* 1986.

PREDECESSORS – (1) WILLIAM Hicks of Beverston Castle, co Gloucester, only son of Sir Michael Hicks, descended from Robert Hicks of Bristol, a merchant in London, and father of the famous Sir Baptist Hicks, created (1628) Viscount Campden, from whom spring the Noels, Earls of Gainsborough; *b* 1596; *cr* a *Baronet* 1619; *d* 1680; *s* by his son (2) WILLIAM, 2nd Bt; *d* 1703; *s* by his son (3) HENRY, 3rd Bt; twice *m*; *d* 1755; *s* by his only son (4) ROBERT, 4th Bt; *d* 1768; *s* by his cousin (5) JOHN BAPTIST (son of Charles Hicks), 5th Bt; *d* 1792: *s* by his cousin (6) HOWE (son of Howe Hicks, of Witcombe, Gloucestershire), 6th Bt; *b* 1722: *m* 1739; *d* 1801; *s* by his son (7) WILLIAM, 7th Bt; *d* 1754: *m* 1st, 1785, Judith, who *d* 1787, da of Edward Witcombe; 2ndly, 1793, Anne Rachael, da of T. L. Chutc, who *d* 1839; *d* 1834; *s* by his great nephew (8) MICHAEL (son of Michael Hicks-Beach, of Netheravon, Wilts, whose father assumed the additional surname of Beach), 8th Bt; MP for E Gloucestershire 1854: *m* 1832, Harriet Victoria, who *d* 1900, da of John Stratton, of Farthinghoe Lodge; *d* 1854; *s* by his son (9) MICHAEL EDWARD, PC, DCL, 3rd Bt; *b* 1837; MP for E Gloucestershire (*C*) 1864-85, and for W Div of Bristol 1885-1906; Parl Sec to Poor Law Board March to Aug 1868, Under-Sec for Home Office Aug to Dec 1868, Ch Sec for Ireland 1874-8, Sec of State for the Colonies 1878-80, a Member of Committee of Council on Education in Scotland and Chancellor of the Exchequer 1885-6, again Ch Sec for Ireland July 1886 to March 1887, Pres of Board of Trade Feb 1888 to Aug 1892, a Church Estates Commr 1892-5, and again Chancellor of the Exchequer 1895-1902; *s* to the Baronetcy 1854, and was *cr Viscount St Aldwyn*, of Coln St Aldwyn, co Gloucester (peerage of the United Kingdom) 1906, and *Viscount Quenington*, of Quenington, co Gloucester, and *Earl St Aldwyn*, of Coln St Aldwyn, co Gloucester (peerage of United Kingdom) 1915: *m* 1st, 1864, Caroline Susan, who *d* 1865, da of late John Henry Elwes, of Colesborne Park, Cheltenham (Bromley-Wilson, Bt); 2ndly, 1874, Lady Lucy Catherine Fortescue, who *d* 1940, da of 3rd Earl Fortescue; *d* 1916; *s* by his grandson (10) MICHAEL JOHN, GBE, TD, PC (son of late Capt Michael Hugh, Viscount Quenington, MP, Gloucestershire Hussars Yeo, son of 1st Earl, *ka* 1916, by his wife, Marjorie, who *d* 1916, da of late Henry Dent Brocklehurst, of Sudeley Castle, Winchcombe), 2nd Earl, *b* 1912; Major 1st Royal Gloucestershire Hussars; JP and DL Glos, and Vice-Lieut 1981-87; Min of Agriculture, Fisheries and Food 1955-58, Chief Whip House of Lords, and Capt Hon Corps of Gentlemen-at-Arms 1958-64 and 1970-74: *m* 1948, Diana Mary Christian (SMYLY), who *d* (10 July) 1992, da of late Henry Christian George Mills (*see* B Hillingdon, colls, 1990 Edn); *d* (29 Jan) 1992; *s* by his eldest son (11) MICHAEL HENRY, 3rd Earl and present peer; also Viscount St Aldwyn, and Viscount Quenington.

St Andrews, Earl of; son of Duke of Kent.

St Aubyn, family name of Baron St Levan.

ST AUDRIES, BARONY OF (Fuller-Acland-Hood) (Extinct 1971)

(See also Fuller-Acland-Hood, Bt, ext)

WIDOW LIVING OF SON OF FIRST BARON

Phyllis Lily Frances (Wootton House, nr Glastonbury, Somerset), da of late Dr Denys B. I. Hallett, of 2 Old Palace Terr, The Green, Richmond, Surrey: *m* 1939, Hon (Arthur) John Palmer Fuller-Acland-Hood, who *d* 1964, and has issue living (see colls, infra).

COLLATERAL BRANCH LIVING

Issue of late Hon (Arthur) John Palmer Fuller-Acland-Hood, yr son of 1st Baron, *b* 1906, *d* 1964: *m* 1939, Phyllis Lily Frances (ante), da of late Dr Denys Bouhier Imbert Hallett, of 2 Old Palace Terr, The Green, Richmond, Surrey:—
Elizabeth Periam (*Lady Gass*) (Fairfield, Stogursey, Bridgwater, Som) *b* 1940; High Sheriff Som 1994, DL 1995, Lord Lieut since 1998: *m* 1975, Sir Michael David Irving Gass, KCMG, who *d* 1983. —— Mary Mildred ACLAND-HOOD (9 Fentiman Rd, SW8), *b* 1941; has retained the surname of Acland-Hood: *m* 1st, 1961, Timothy Stephen (Toby) Hodder-Williams, who *d* 1969; 2ndly, 1975, Frank Thomas Blackaby, and has issue living (by 2nd *m*), John Christopher ACLAND-HOOD, *b* 1979, —— Susan Elizabeth ACLAND-HOOD, *b* 1977. —— Sylvia (The Rectory, Exford, Minehead, Som TA24 7LX), *b* 1944: *m* 1991, Rev Robin J. Ray.

SAINT BRIDES, BARONY OF (James) (Extinct 1989)

SON LIVING OF LIFE BARON (*By 1st marriage*)

Hon Roderick Morrice, *b* 1956; *ed* Emmanuel Coll, Camb: *m* 1981, Harriet Sophie, yst da of Cdr John Benians, RN, of Waterfield, Headley, Hants, and has issue living, Caspian, *b* 1985, — Pasco, *b* 1987. *Residence* – Hopkiln Cottage, Gracious St, Selborne, Hants.

DAUGHTERS LIVING OF LIFE BARON (*By 1st marriage*)

Hon Laura Catherine, *b* 1948; *ed* Sussex Univ (BA): *m* 1981, Robert Lacy Tatton Sykes, elder son of Geoffrey Sykes, of Kirribilli, NSW, Australia. *Residence* – The Old House, Ibthorpe, Andover, Hants SP11 0BJ.

Hon Clare Veronica JAMES, *b* 1950; *ed* London Univ (BSc); translator; has retained her maiden name: *m* 1st, 1970 (*m diss* 1978), Dr Patrick Duncan; 2ndly, 1995, Marek Osolinski, and has issue living (by 1st *m*), Patrick, *b* 1973, — (by 2nd *m*), Robin James, *b* 1994. *Residence* – Fräkenvägen 6, SE-192 48 Sollentuna, Sweden.

WIDOW LIVING OF LIFE BARON

GENEVIEVE CHRISTIANE (*Baroness Saint Brides*), da of late Robert Henri Houdin, and widow of Prof Reymond Sarasin: *m* 1968, as his 2nd wife, Baron Saint Brides, GCMG, CVO, MBE, PC (Life Baron), who *d* 1989. *Residence* – Cap Saint-Pierre, 83990 Saint-Tropez, France.

St Clair, family name of Lord Sinclair.

St Cyres, Viscount; son of Earl of Iddesleigh.

ST DAVIDS, VISCOUNT (Philipps) (Viscount UK 1918, Bt E 1621)

COLWYN JESTYN JOHN PHILIPPS, 3rd Viscount, and 15th Baronet; *b* 30 Jan 1939; *s* 1991; *ed* Sevenoaks Sch, and King's Coll, London (Cert Advanced Mus Studies 1989); late 2nd Lieut Welsh Guards; a Lord in Waiting to HM 1992-94: *m* 1965, Augusta Victoria Correa Larrain, da of late Don Estanislao Correa Ugarte, of Santiago, Chile, and has issue.

Arms – Argent, a lion rampant sable, ducally gorged and chained or, langued and taloned gules. Crest – A lion as in the arms. Supporters – *Dexter*, a knight vested in chain armour, the jupon charged with the arms of *Philipps* and resting his exterior hand upon the hilt of his sword; *sinister*, a knight vested in plate armour, his jupon charged with arms of *Wogan* (or, on a chief sable, three martlets of the field) and resting the exterior hand upon the hilt of the sword; both standing upon a battlemented wall, all proper.
Address – c/o House of Lords, SW1 0PW.

SONS LIVING

Hon RHODRI COLWYN, *b* 16 Sept 1966; *ed* Worth.
Hon Roland Augusto Jestyn Estanislao, *b* 1970; *ed* Downside.

SISTERS LIVING

Hon Rowena Frances (418 Wellington St, Clifton Hill, Vic 3068, Australia), *b* 1940: *m* 1959 (*m diss* 1977), David Elford, and has had issue, Richard, *b* 1962; *d* 1990. — Wendy, *b* 1960. — Suzanne, *b* 1964. — Leone, *b* 1965.
Hon Myfanwy Ann (23 Pyrland Rd, Islington, N5), *b* 1944: *m* 1968, Anthony John Frederick Smith, and has issue living, Tobias Peter John, *b* 1971. — Benjamin Cosby, *b* 1973.
Hon Rhiannon Elizabeth (39 Spice Court, Asher Way, E1 9JD), *b* 1946: *m* 1974 (*m diss* 1991), Donald Hudson Chapman.
Hon Eiddwen Sara, *b* 1948: *m* 1986, Clive Geoffrey Owen, of 4 Quarry Rd, Kenilworth, Warwicks CV8 1AE, and has issue living, David James, *b* 1987. — Philip Michael, *b* 1990.

Patriotism my motive

WIDOW LIVING OF SECOND VISCOUNT

EVELYN MARJORIE (*Marjorie, Viscountess St Davids*), only da of late Dr John Edmund Guy Harris, of The Heritage, Bray-on-Thames, Berks: *m* 1959, as his 3rd wife, the 2nd Viscount St Davids, who *d* 1991. *Residence* – 15 St Mark's Crescent, Regent's Park, NW1 7TS.

COLLATERAL BRANCHES LIVING

(Male line in remainder to Baronetcy only)

Descendants of late Laurence Richard Philipps (*cr Baron Milford* 1939), 6th son of 12th Baronet, *b* 1874, *d* 1962 (see that title)

(In remainder to Baronies of Strange of Knokin, Hungerford and de Moleyns)

Issue of late Hon Lelgarde de Clare Elizabeth Rawdon Philipps, only da of 1st Viscount St Davids, by his 2nd wife, Elizabeth Frances, Baroness Strange of Knokin, Hungerford and de Moleyns (in her own right), *b* 1918, *d* 1984: *m* 1950 (*m diss* 1967), Colin Charles Evans:—
Roland Anthony Christopher EVANS (78 Dundela Park, Sandycove, co Dublin), *b* 1951; *ed* Portora Royal Sch: *m* 1978, Annette Matilda, da of Alfred Hunter, of Carrick Henry, co Sligo, and has issue living, Rebecca Lara, *b* 1982. —— William Harold Sandford EVANS (Aglish, The Curragh, Castlebar, co Mayo), *b* 1953; *ed* St George's Sch, Nenagh: *m* 1979, Elizabeth Ann, da of Sean James Smith, of Castlebar, co Mayo, and has issue living, Billy Sean, *b* 1980, — Kayleigh Elizabeth, *b* 1988, — Bronwyn Mary, *b* 1990. —— (Lorna) Susan (11 Fairoak Chase, Brockla, Whitchurch, Bridgend, Glamorgan), *b* (twin) 1953.

PREDECESSORS – This family is of great antiquity in South Wales, being descended from Cadifor ap Collwyn, Lord of Dyfed (*d* 1089). His great-grandson, Sir Aaron ap Rhys, attended Richard I into the Holy Land 1190, where he behaved so gallantly against the Saracens, that he is said to have received from Richard the Knighthood of the Sepulchre of Our Saviour, his arms of a lion rampant sable, and the addition of a "Crown and Chain". Sir Thomas Philipps, Knt, of Picton Castle, accompanied Henry VIII twice to France. His descendant **(1)** Sir JOHN Philipps, Knt, of Picton, co Pembroke; MP for Pembroke 1597-98 and Oct-Dec 1601; *cr* a *Baronet* 1621: *m* Anne, da of Sir John Perrott, of Haroldston; *d* 1629; *s* by his el son **(2)** RICHARD, 2nd Bt: *m* Elizabeth, da of Sir Erasmus Dryden, Bt; *d* 16—; *s* by his son **(3)** ERASMUS Philipps, 3rd Bt; MP for Pembroke 1654-55 and Jan-April, 1659: *m* 1st, Cicely, da of Thomas, Earl of Winchilsea; 2ndly, Katharine, el da and co-heir of Edward D'Arcy, of Newhall, co Derby; *d* 1697; *s* by his 2nd son **(4)** JOHN, 4th Bt; MP for Pembroke 1695-1702, and for Haverfordwest 1718-1722: *m* 1697, Mary, da of Anthony Smith; *d* 1736; *s* by his el son **(5)** ERASMUS, 5th Bt; MP for Haverfordwest 1726-43; *d* 1743; *s* by his brother **(6)** JOHN, 6th Bt; MP for Carmarthen 1741-47, for Petersfield 1754-61, and for co Pembroke 1761-64: *m* Elizabeth, da of Henry Shepperd; *d* 1764; *s* by his only son **(7)** RICHARD, 7th Bt; MP for co Pembroke 1765-70 and 1786-1812, Lord-Lieut of co Pembroke 1786; *cr Baron Milford* 1776: *m* 1764, Mary, da of James Philipps, of Penty Park; *d* 1823, when the Barony of Milford became ext and the Baronetcy passed to his kinsman **(8)** ROWLAND HENRY Philipps-Laugharne-Philipps (descendant of Hugh Philipps, 3rd son of 1st Bt), 8th Bt: *m* 1812, Elizabeth, who *d* 1834, da of James Frampton; *d* 1823; *s* by his brother **(9)** WILLIAM, 9th Bt; *b* 1794: *m* 1829, Elizabeth, who *d* 1865, da of George White; *d* 1850; *s* by his only son **(10)** GODWYN, 10th Bt; *b* 1840; *d* 1857; *s* by his kinsman **(11)** *Rev Sir* JAMES EVANS Philipps, 11th Bt; *b* 1793: *m* 1822, Mary Anne, who *d* 1833, da of Benjamin Bickley; *d* 1873; *s* by his son **(12)** *Rev Sir* JAMES ERASMUS, 12th Bt; *b* 1824; V of Warminster 1859-1897, and Canon of Salisbury: *m* 1859, Hon Mary Margaret, who *d* 1913, da of late Rev Hon Samuel Best; *d* 1912; *s* by his el son **(13)** JOHN WYNFORD, 13th Bt; *b* 1860; *cr Baron St Davids*, of Roch Castle, co Pembroke (peerage of UK) 1908, and *Viscount St Davids*, of Lydstep Haven, co Pembroke (peerage of UK) 1918: *m* 1st, 1888, Nora, who *d* 1915, da of late I. Gestenberg, of Stockleigh House, Regent's Park, NW; 2ndly, 1916, Lady Elizabeth Frances (*Baroness Strange of Knokin, Hungerford, and de Moleyns* in her own right), who *d* 1974 (see † infra), da of late Maj Hon Paulyn Francis Cuthbert Rawdon-Hastings; *d* 1938; *s* by his 3rd but only surviving son **(14)** JESTYN REGINALD AUSTEN PLANTAGENET, 2nd Viscount; *b* 1917; Lieut RNVR; founder Regent's Boat Club 1966, co-founder Inland Waterways Assocn, Cttee Memb House of Lords Yacht Club, and founder and patron Pirate Club; Queen Elizabeth II's Silver Jubilee Medal: *m* 1st, 1938 (*m diss* 1954), Doreen Guinness, who *d* 1956, only da of Capt Arthur Craven Jowett, of Coverdale, Toorak, Melbourne, Australia; 2ndly, 1954 (*m diss* 1959), Elisabeth Joyce, elder da of Dr E. Alec Woolf, of Hove, Sussex; 3rdly, 1959, (Evelyn) Marjorie, only da of Dr John Edmund Guy Harris, of The Heritage, Bray-on-Thames, Berks; *d* 1991; *s* by his only son **(15)** COLWYN JESTYN JOHN, 3rd Viscount and present peer; also 16th Baron Strange of Knokin, 25th Baron Hungerford, 23rd Baron de Moleyns, and 3rd Baron St Davids.

†**(1)** Sir WALTER Hungerford, KG; served with distinction in France; was Steward of the Household to Henry VI; summoned to Parliament of England as *Baron Hungerford* 1426-49; *d* 1449; *s* by his son **(2)** ROBERT, 2nd Baron; summoned to Parliament 1450-5: *m* Margaret, only da of William, *Baron Botreaux* (peerage of England, *cr* 1386); *d* 1458; *s* by his son **(3)** ROBERT, 3rd Baron, who had previously 1445-52 been summoned to Parliament of England as *Baron de Moleyns* (or *Molines*); was never summoned as Baron Hungerford; joined the Lancastrian interests, and being made prisoner at the battle of Hexham his honours and estates were attainted, and he was beheaded at Newcastle 1463; *s* by his son **(4)** THOMAS, who espoused the cause of Edward IV, but subsequently exerted his influence for the restoration of Henry VI, he was seized and beheaded as a traitor 1479: he left issue by his first *m* **(5)** MARY, who obtained the reversal of her father's and grandfather's attainders, and was styled Baroness Hungerford, Botreaux, and Molines (or de Moleyns); she *m* Edward Hastings, son and heir of William, 1st *Baron Hastings* (peerage of England, *cr* 1461); *s* by her son **(6-15)** GEORGE, 6th Baron; *cr Earl of Huntingdon* 1529; in which peerage the Baronies of Hungerford, Botreaux, de Moleyns (or Molines) and Hastings were merged until 1789, when the 10th Earl *dsp*, and was *s* by his sister **(16)** ELIZABETH, wife of John Rawdon, 1st *Earl of Moira* (peerage of Ireland, *cr* 1762): *d* 1808; *s* by her son **(17)** FRANCIS, KG, GCB, who in 1793 had *s* his father as 2nd Earl of Moira; a Gen in the Army, Lord-Lieut of the Tower Hamlets, Constable of the Tower of London, and successively Gov-Gen of India and Gov and Com-in-Ch of Malta; assumed the name of Hastings in addition to that of Rawdon; *cr Baron Rawdon*, of Rawdon, co York (peerage of Great Britain) 1783, and *Viscount Loudoun, Earl of Rawdon*, and *Marquess of Hastings* (peerage of United Kingdom) 1816: *m* Flora Mure-Campbell, *Countess of Loudoun*, in her own right; *d* 1826; *s* by his son **(18)** GEORGE AUGUSTUS FRANCIS, 2nd Marquess, who in 1840 *s* his mother as 7th Earl of Loudoun: *m* 1831, Barbara, *Baroness Grey de Ruthyn* (peerage of England, *cr* 1324); he *d* 1844; *s* by his el son **(19)** PAULYN REGINALD SERLO, 3rd Marquess; *d unm* 1851; *s* by his brother **(20)** HENRY WEYSFORD CHARLES PLANTAGENET, 4th Marquess, who in 1858 *s* to his mother's Barony of Grey de Ruthyn; *d* 1868, when the Barony of Rawdon, the Viscountcy of Loudoun, the Earldoms of Moira and Rawdon, and the Marquessate of Hastings became extinct and the Baronies of Grey de Ruthyn, Hastings, Hungerford, Botreaux, and de Moleyns (or Molines) became abeyant between his sisters, and the Earldom of Loudoun and minor Scottish honours devolved upon his el sister **(21)** EDITH MAUD Abney-Hastings, in whose favour in 1871, the abeyance of the Baronies of Hastings, Hungerford, Botreaux and de Moleyns (or Molines) was terminated; *b* 1833: *m* Charles Frederick Clifton, who in 1859 assumed the names of Abney-Hastings, and in 1880 was *cr Baron Donington*, of Donington Park, co Leicester (peerage of United Kingdom); she *d* 1874; *s* by his son **(22)** CHARLES EDWARD HASTINGS, 11th Earl of Loudoun, *b* 1855; an Hereditary Bearer of one of the Golden Spurs: *m* 1880, Hon Alice Mary Elizabeth Fitzalan-Howard, who *d* 1915, da of 1st Baron Howard of Glossop; *d* 1920, when the Barony of Donington devolved upon his brother Gilbert Theophilus Clifton Clifton-Hastings-Campbell, and the Earldom of Loudoun upon his niece, Edith Maud, el da of late Major Hon Paulyn Francis Cuthbert Rawdon-Hastings, while the Baronies of Botreaux, de Moleyns (or Molines), Hungerford, and Hastings fell into abeyance between the das of late Major Hon Paulyn Francis Cuthbert Rawdon-Hastings, brother of 11th Earl of Loudoun, the abeyance in the Baronies of Hungerford and de Moleyns, as well as in the Barony of Strange of Knokin (*cr* by writ 1299) (see * infra) being shortly afterwards in Feb 1921 terminated in favour of the el **(23)** ELIZABETH FRANCES, Viscountess St Davids (ante).

*(1) JOHN le Strange, son of John le Strange, of Knokin, co Salop, was summoned by writ to Parliament 1299 and 1308-9 as *Lord Strange de Knokin*; *d* 1309; *s* by his son **(2)** JOHN; summoned to Parliament 1311; *d* 1311; *s* by his son **(3)** JOHN; summoned to Parliament 1312-13; *d* 1323; *s* by his brother **(4)** ROGER; summoned to Parliament 1341-47; *d* 1349; *s* by his son **(5)** ROGER; summoned to Parliament 1355-82; *d* 1382; *s* by his son **(6)** JOHN; summoned to Parliament 1383-97: *m* Maud, da and co-heir of John, Lord Mohun de Dunster (*cr* 1299); *d* 1387; *s* by his son **(7)** RICHARD, *b* 1381; in 1431 became (through his mother) *Lord Mohun de Dunster*; *d* 1449; *s* by his son **(8)** JOHN; summoned to Parliament 1446-72; *d* 1477; *s* by his only da **(9)** JOAN: *m* 1482, George, Lord Stanley, KG, son of the 1st Earl of Derby, who in right of his wife was summoned to Parliament as Lord Strange de Knokin 1482-96; *d* 1513; *s* by her el son **(10)** THOMAS, *b* 1485, who in 1504 had *s* as 2nd Earl of Derby, as well as to the Barony of Stanley (*cr* 1456); *d* 1521; *s* by his son **(11)** EDWARD, 3rd Earl, *b* 1509; *d* 1572; *s* by his son **(12)** HENRY, 4th Earl, *b* 1521; summoned to Parliament in his father's Barony of Strange de Knokin 1558-75; *d* 1593; *s* by his son **(13)** FERDINANDO, 5th Earl, *b* 1559; summoned to Parliament in his father's Barony of Strange of Knokin 1588-92; *d* 1594; when the Earldom of Derby devolved upon his brother, and the Baronies of Strange de Knokin, Mohun de Dunster, and Stanley fell into abeyance between his daughters and co-heirs, until in 1921 the abeyance in the Barony of Strange of Knokin was determined in favour of **(14)** ELIZABETH FRANCES, Viscountess St Davids (ante).

ST GERMANS, EARL OF (Eliot) (Earl UK 1815)

PEREGRINE NICHOLAS ELIOT, 10th Earl; *b* 2 Jan 1941; *s* 1988; *ed* Eton; patron of three livings: *m* 1st, 1964 (*m diss* 1990), Hon Jacquetta Jean Frederica Lampson, da of 1st Baron Killearn; 2ndly, 1991 (*m diss* 1995), Elizabeth Mary, eldest da of Basil James Williams, of France, and has issue by 1st *m*.

Arms – Argent, a fesse gules, between double cottises wavy azure. Crest – An elephant's head argent, plain collared gules. Supporters – Two eagles reguardant, wings displayed and inverted proper, each charged on the breast with an ermine spot sable.
Seat – Port Eliot, St Germans, Cornwall.

SONS LIVING (*By 1st marriage*)

JAGO NICHOLAS ALDO (*Lord Eliot*), *b* 24 March 1966; *ed* Millfield.
Hon Louis Robert, *b* 1968; *ed* Eton.
Hon Francis Michael, *b* 1971; *ed* Eton.

SISTER LIVING

Lady Frances Helen Mary, *b* 1943: *m* 1965 (*m diss* 1987), Charles Maurice, Earl of Shelburne, el son of 8th Marquess of Lansdowne.

Press close upon those who take the lead

WIDOW LIVING OF SON OF EIGHTH EARL

Marie Frances Richmond, da of late Geoffrey Mervyn Cooper, of Preston Candover, Hants (*see* Cooper, Bt, *cr* 1863, colls), and widow of A. R. Lusk, of Comrie, Perthshire: *m* 2ndly, 1983, Capt Hon (Montagu) Robert (Vere) Eliot, Gren Gds (ret), who *d* 1994.

COLLATERAL BRANCH LIVING

Issue of late Hon Edward Granville Eliot, brother of 7th and 8th Earls, *b* 1878, *d* 1950: *m* 1907, Clare Louisa, who *d* 1927, da of late William Robert Phelips (E Bessborough, colls):—
Margaret Augusta, *b* 1914: *m* 1943, Richard Alan John Asher, MD, FRCP, who *d* 1969, and has issue living, Peter (90 Malibu Colony, Malibu, Calif 90265, USA), *b* 1944; *ed* Westminster; Sr Vice-Pres Sony Music: *m* 1st, 1970 (*m diss* 1983) Betsy Doster; 2ndly, 1983, Wendy Worth, and has issue living (by 2nd *m*), Victoria Jane *b* 1984, — Jane, *b* 1946; actress and author: *m* 19—, Gerald Scarfe, artist, and has issue living, Alexander David *b* 1981, Rory Christopher *b* 1983, Katie Geraldine *b* 1974, — Clare, *b* 1948: *m* 1975, John Gillies, of 6 Hillbury Rd, SW17 8JT, and has issue living, Sarah *b* 1978, Helen *b* 1980. *Residence* – 6A Hillbury Rd, SW17.

PREDECESSORS – (1) EDWARD Eliot, MP for Cornwall, and Receiver Gen of Duchy of Cornwall; *cr Baron Eliot*, of St Germans, Cornwall (peerage of Great Britain) 1784; assumed the additional surname of Craggs by Roy licence 1789; *d* 1804; *s* by his son (2) JOHN, 2nd Baron; *cr Earl of St Germans* (peerage of United Kingdom) 1815, with remainder to his brother; *dsp* 1823; *s* by his brother (3) WILLIAM, 2nd Earl; was successively Ambassador to the States Gen and to Munich, MP for Liskeard, and a Lord of the Treasury; *d* 1845; *s* by his son (4) EDWARD GRANVILLE, GCB, PC, 3rd Earl; *b* 1798; sat as MP for Liskeard 1824-32, and for Cornwall, E (C) 1837-45; was a Lord of the Treasury 1827-32, Envoy to Spain 1835, Ch Sec for Ireland 1841-5, Postmaster-Gen 1845, Lord-Lieut of Ireland 1852-5, Lord Steward of the Household 1857-8 and 1859-66, and Special Dep Warden of Stannaries 1852-77: *m* 1824, Lady Jemima Cornwallis, da and co-heiress of 2nd and last Marquess Cornwallis; *d* 1877; *s* by his son (5) WILLIAM GORDON CORNWALLIS, 4th Earl; sat as MP for Devonport (*L*) 1866-8; called to the Upper House in his father's Barony of Eliot 1870, *d* unm 1881; *s* by his brother (6) HENRY CORNWALLIS, 5th Earl, *b* 1835; in RN 1848-53 and Foreign Office 1855-81: *m* 1881, Hon Emily Harriet Labouchere, who *d* 1933, da of 1st Baron Taunton (ext); *d* 1911; *s* by his yr son (7) JOHN GRANVILLE CORNWALLIS, 6th Earl, *b* 1890; Capt R Scots Greys: *m* 1918, Lady Blanche Linnie Somerset, who *d* 1968, da of 9th Duke of Beaufort, *d* 1922; *s* by his cousin (8) GRANVILLE JOHN (el son of Col Hon Charles George Cornwallis Eliot, CVO, 6th son of 3rd Earl), 7th Earl; *b* 1867, *d* 1942; *s* by his brother (9) MONTAGUE CHARLES, KCVO, OBE, 8th Earl; *b* 1870; a Gentleman Usher to King Edward VII 1901-8, and a Groom in Waiting 1908-10, a Gentleman Usher to King George V 1911-36, Groom of the Robes 1920-36, and an Extra Groom in Waiting 1924-36, and 1937-60; European War 1914-19 as Lieut-Com RNVR: *m* 1910, Helen Agnes, who *d* 1962, da of late Arthur Post, of New York; *d* 1960; *s* by his el son (10) NICHOLAS RICHARD MICHAEL, 9th Earl *b* 1914; Capt Duke of Cornwall's LI, served European War 1939-45: *m* 1st, 1939 (*m diss* 1947), Helen Mary, who *d* 1951, yr da of late Lt-Col Charles Walter Villiers, CBE, DSO (E Clarendon, colls); 2ndly, 1948 (*m diss* 1959), Margaret Eleanor, who *d* 1967, only da of late Lt-Col William Francis George Wyndham, MVO, of Heathfield Lodge, Midhurst, Sussex, and formerly wife of (i) Hugh Wharton Earle, and (ii) Basil Francis Eyston; 3rdly, 1965, (Mary) Bridget, who *d* 1998, da of late Sir Thomas Shenton Whitelegge Thomas, GCMG, OBE, and formerly wife of Lt-Col Jack Leslie Larry Lotinga; *d* 1988; *s* by his only son (11) PEREGRINE NICHOLAS, 10th Earl and present peer; also Baron Eliot.

ST HELENS, BARON (Hughes-Young) (Baron UK 1964)

RICHARD (RORY) FRANCIS HUGHES-YOUNG, 2nd Baron; *b* 4 Nov 1945; *s* 1980; *ed* Nautical Coll, Pangbourne: *m* 1983, Mrs Emma R. Talbot-Smith, and has issue.

Arms – Or three piles sable each charged with a fountain. Crest – A dexter cubit arm proper charged with a fountain a hand grasping an arrow fesswise proper. Supporters – *Dexter*, a wolf gules; *sinister*, a griffin sable; each charged on the shoulder with a portcullis or.

SON LIVING

Hon HENRY THOMAS, *b* 7 March 1986.

DAUGHTER LIVING

Hon Lara Elizabeth, *b* 1987.

SISTERS LIVING

Hon Henrietta Maria, *b* 1940: *m* 1970, Brian Turnbull Julius Stevens, of Sutton Warbington, Long Sutton, Hants, and has issue living, (Flora) Matilda Julius, *b* 1973, — Harriet Maria Julius, *b* 1975, — Louisa Elizabeth Julius, *b* 1976.

Hon Selina Lilian, *b* 1944: *m* 1969, Jonathan Basil Morton Peto (*see* Peto, Bt, colls, *cr* 1927), of Bealings House, Woodbridge, Suffolk.

Hon Louisa Nina, *b* 1949: *m* 1974, Maj James Francis Arbuthnott, Black Watch (*see* V Arbuthnott, colls), of Stone House Cottage, Stone, Kidderminster, Worcs.

PREDECESSOR – (1) MICHAEL HENRY COLIN Hughes-Young, MC, son of Brig-Gen Henry George Young, CIE, DSO, of Skeffington Lodge, Antrim; *b* 1912; Lt-Col The Black Watch; a Lord Commnr of Treasury 1958-62, Dep Govt Ch Whip 1959-64, Treasurer to HM Household 1962-64; MP for Central Div of Wandsworth (C) 1955-64; *cr Baron St Helens*, of St Helens co Palatine of Lancaster (Peerage of UK) 1964: *m* 1939, Elizabeth Agnes, who *d* 1956, yst da of Capt Richard Blakiston-Houston (Blakiston, Bt); *d* 1980; *s* by his only son (2) RICHARD FRANCIS, 2nd Baron and present peer.

St John, Viscount; title borne by Viscount Bolingbroke.

St John, family name of Viscount Bolingbroke.

St John, family name of Earl of Orkney.

ST JOHN OF BLETSO, BARON (St John) (Baron E 1559, Bt E 1660)
(Title pronounced "Sinjun of Bletso")

Following his allotted fate

ANTHONY TUDOR ST JOHN, 21st Baron, and 18th Baronet; *b* 16 May 1957; *s* 1978; *ed* Diocesan Coll, Cape Town, Cape Town Univ (BA, BSc, and London Univ (LLM)); Solicitor; Consultant to Smith New Court plc, and Chm Eurotrust Internat; Cross Bencher, House of Lords; Extra Lord in Waiting to HM since 1998: *m* 1994, Dr Helen Jane, eldest da of Michael Westlake, of Bath, Avon, and has issue.

Arms – Argent, on chief gules, two mullet, or. Crest – On a mount vert, a falcon rising or, belled of the last, ducally gorged gules. Supporters – Two monkeys proper.
Residences – 10 Pencombe Mews, Denbigh Rd, W11 2SJ; Woodlando, Llanishen, nr Chepstow, Gwent NP6. *Club* – Hurlingham.

SONS LIVING

Hon OLIVER BEAUCHAMP, *b* 11 July 1995.
Hon Alexander Andrew, *b* 1996.

DAUGHTERS LIVING

Hon Athene Emma, *b* 1998.
Hon Chloe, *b* 1999.

AUNT LIVING *(Sister of 20th Baron)*

(Raised to the rank of a Baron's daughter, 1977)

Hon Elaine Julia Barbara, *b* 1921: *m* 1939, Lt-Col John Francis Whidborne (ret), RA, and has had issue, Stephen Barham, *b* 1940; *ed* Blundell's; *dunm* 1965, — Richard St John, MBE (14 Berrylands, Liss Forest, Liss, Hants GU33 7DB), *b* 1942; *ed* Blundell's; Maj (ret) AAC; Air Accidents Investigation Branch, Dept of Transport; MBE (Mil) 1973, FRAeS 1993: *m* 1st, 1965, Linda Beverley, who *d* 1975, da of Cyril Trevor Sherwood, of Child Okeford, Dorset; 2ndly, 1978, Jennifer, da of F. E. Gould, of Sempringham House, Sleaford, Lincs, and has issue living (by 1st *m*), Nicholas St John *b* 1969, James Oliver St John *b* 1973; BSc, ARICS, — Julia Lauretta, *b* 1943. *Residence* – Holly Mount, Pethybridge, Lustleigh, Devon TQ13 9TG.

DAUGHTER LIVING OF EIGHTEENTH BARON

Hon Katherine Barbara, *b* 1907: *m* 1945, George William Uttley, MA, BSc, late Fl-Lt RAF, and has issue living, Alathea St John, *b* 1947.

WIDOW LIVING OF TWENTIETH BARON

KATHERINE (*Katherine, Baroness St John of Bletso*) (By The Sea, Kalk Bay, Cape, S Africa), yst da of late Alfred von Berg, of Gonville House, Manor Fields, SW15: *m* 1955, the 20th Baron St John of Bletso, who *d* 1978.

COLLATERAL BRANCHES LIVING

Granddaughters of late Lt-Col Hon Rowland Tudor St John, Durham LI, 3rd son of 16th Baron:—
Issue of late Rev Oliver John Frank Lockwood St John, DSC, *b* 1914, *d* 1972: *m* 1938, Elva Rosemary (29 Bay Rd, Alverstoke, Hants), da of Alfred John Skinn, MB, ChB, of Hong Kong:—
Vyvian Elaine, *b* 1940: *m* 1972, Patrick Nelson Maudsley, of 18 Tudor Way, Wellingborough, Northants, and has issue living, Ruth Claire, *b* 1973. —— Juliet Rosemary, *b* 1943; SRN: *m* 1967, Brian William Ellis Johnson, ARIBA, of 131 Grosvenor Av, N5, and has issue living, George St John, *b* 1969, — Hugh William Nicholas, *b* 1979, — Katherine Alice (twin), *b* 1969. —— Diana Hazel Susan, *b* 1946; BA: *m* 1970, Ewart John Holmes, ARIBA, MRTPI, of Harpers Cottage, Main St, Avebury, Marlborough, Wilts SN8 1RF, and has issue living, Rowland St John, *b* 1973, — Oliver John, *b* 1975, — Genevieve Anne, *b* 1979. —— Margaret Vanessa Lucy, *b* 1948: *m* 1969, George Marlay Spencer, and has issue living, Rachel Marlay, *b* 1972, — Abigail, *b* 1974.

Grandchildren of late Rev Hon Edmund Tudor St John, 3rd son of 14th Baron:—
Issue of late Col Edmund Farquhar St John, CMG, DSO, *b* 1879, *d* 1945: *m* 1921, Henrietta Frances, who *d* 1989, da of late Col James Alexander Dalmahoy, MVO, WS:—
(Edmund) Oliver, WS, *b* 1927; *ed* Trin Coll, Glenalmond: WS 1953: *m* 1959, Elizabeth Frances, only da of late Lieut-Col Henry Rice Nicholl, of High Lipwood, Haydon Bridge, Northumberland, and has issue living, Charles Henry Oliver, *b* 1963: *m* 1991, Emma Catherine Sewell, elder da of Henry Moore, of Shucknall Court, Hereford, and has issue living, Edward Milo Oliver *b* 1999, Poppy Rebecca Harriet *b* 1995, — Nicola Rosemary, *b* 1960: *m* 1995, John William McKenzie Barber, son of Prof William J. Barber, OBE, of 306 Pine St, Middletown, Connecticut, USA, and has issue living, Henry William St John *b* 1996, Benjamin Charles St John *b* 1997, — Emma Harriet, *b* 1968. *Residence* – Spittal, Biggar, Lanarkshire. —— Frances Dalmahoy, *b* 1931. *Residence* – Bletsoe, 26 St Andrew's St, Brechin, Angus.

Issue of late Maj Beauchamp Tudor St John, *b* 1880, *d* 1965: *m* 1910, Madeleine Ethel, who *d* 1982, da of late J. Ellis Goodbody, of Thornville, Limerick:—

†Roger Ellis Tudor, CB, MC, *b* 1911; *ed* Wellington Coll; Maj-Gen (ret); Dep Col (Northumberland) R Regt of Fusiliers 1968-69; Comd, British Army Staff and Mil Attaché Washington 1963-65, and Pres of Regular Commns Board 1965-67; 1939-45 War (despatches, MC), Kenya 1955 (despatches); CB (Mil) 1965: *m* 1943, Rosemary Jean Douglas (Harelaw, Virginia Water, Surrey GU25 4AS), da of late Ronald Vickers, and *d* 1998, leaving issue, Henry Edward Tudor (29 Windmill Heights, N Leigh, Witney, Oxon OX8 6ZD), *b* 1949; *ed* Eton, and Coll of Estate Management (BSc, FRICS), FAAV; Partner Cluttons Daniel Smith, Chartered Surveyors: *m* 1983 (*m diss* 1997), Kerra, eldest da of late John Lockhart, of Calgary, Alberta, Canada, and has issue living, Oliver Tudor Lockhart *b* 1984, Atlanta Victoria *b* 1987, — Angela Lucy, *b* 1944: *m* 1970, Maj Christopher Rohan Delacombe, late R Scots, only son of late Maj-Gen Sir Rohan Delacombe, KCMG, KCVO, KBE, CB, DSO, and has issue living, Caroline May *b* 1971, Sophie Clare *b* 1973, Katharine Joyce *b* 1975, — Jane Margaret, *b* 1946, — Alice Rosemary, *b* 1950: *m* 1974, Hugh Martyn Williams, of Lower Willsworthy, Peter Tavy, Tavistock, Devon PL19 9NB, and has issue living, Patrick *b* 1986, Emily *b* 1979, Florence *b* 1980, Martha *b* 1985, Veronica *b* 1991. ──── Michael Beauchamp, DSC (The Old Thatch, Leggs Lane, Heyshott, nr Midhurst, Sussex), *b* 1915; Cdr (ret) RN; 1939-45 War with Submarines (DSC): *m* 1944, Pamela Patience, da of late Sir Arthur Rundell Guinness, KCMG, and has issue living, Andrew Beauchamp (Cul-na-Cloich, Glenalmond, Perthshire), *b* 1945: *m* 1968, Hon Sally Hayter Rootes, da of 2nd Baron Rootes, — Clare Pamela, *b* 1947: *m* 1968, David Waldorf Astor, of Bruern Grange, Milton-under-Wychwood, Oxon, and has issue (*see* V Astor), — Hermione Patience, *b* 1951: *m* 1973, William Stanhope Owen, of Merriscourt Farm House, Churchill, Oxon OX76 6QX, and has issue living, Sam Arthur Stanhope *b* 1975, Georgina Hermione *b* 1974.

Grandchildren of late Cdr Richard St John, RN, 4th and yst son of late Rev Hon Edmund Tudor St John (ante):—
Issue of late Capt John Richard St John, *b* 1917, *d* 1988: *m* 1st, 1943 (*m diss* 1951), Helen Mary, da of late H. O. Coleman; 2ndly, 1952, Diana Elwell (40 Arkwright Rd, NW3 6BH), yst da of late Col Edward Stockley Sinnott, CMG, TD:—
(By 1st *m*) Tudor Richard, *b* 1946: *m* 1977, Marlyn, only da of G. Foster. ──── Lucinda Jill, *b* 1944; ARCM: *m* 1968, Andrew Jon Cameron-Beaumont, FRICS, and has issue living, Richard Peregrine, *b* 1973, — Charlotte Lucinda, *b* 1971; BSc. *Residence* – Tideford Farmhouse, Tideford, Cornwall. ──── (By 2nd *m*) Clare Sylvia, *b* 1955. ──── Katharine Elinor Margaret, *b* 1957: *m* 1st, 1976 (*m diss* 1986), Erik Austin Flakoll; 2ndly, 1993, Albert Sidney Griffin, of Kentucky, USA.

Grandchildren of Richard Fleming St Andrew St John, son of Henry St Andrew St John, son of Rev John Francis Seymour St John, 2nd son of the Very Rev Hon St Andrew St John, DD, 2nd son of 10th Baron:—
Issue of late Winstan St Andrew St John, MRCS, LRCP, *b* 1872, *d* 1962: *m* 1909, Violet Julia Louisa, da of late Henderson James Twigg, of Petane Grange, Petane, Hawks Bay, New Zealand:—
Orford Henderson St Andrew, *b* 1910; *ed* Wellington Coll, and at Hertford Coll, Oxford (BA 1932); 1939-45 War as Capt Gen List (Movement Control, attached Intelligence). Resides in Spain.

Issue of late Major Edward Churchill St John, *b* 1878, *d* 1956: *m* 1906, Irene, who *d* 1956, da of Col Charles Edward Shepherd, formerly Indian Army:—
Catherine Margaret, *b* 1907.

Issue of late Lieut-Com Arthur Beauchamp St John, RN (ret), *b* 1884, *d* 1948: *m* 1914, Lucinda Mary Stanley, da of late Hon John French, of Miramar, Queenstown, co Cork, and Rotra House, Frenchpark, co Roscommon:—
Œnône Mary, *b* 1917: *m* 1st, 1943, John Francis Elton Watkins; 2ndly, 1953, Leslie James Ashton, of 1 Victoria Flats, Livingstone Av, Gwelo, Zimbabwe, and has issue living (by 1st *m*), Mary Veronica, *b* 1946: *m* 1969, Donald Hodder (c/o Standard Bank, Cecil Sq, Harare, Zimbabwe). ──── Deirdre Mary, *b* 1919: *m* 1944, Harold Drummond-Hay Oxenham Leach, of PO Box 1409, Port Shepstone 4240, Natal, S Africa, and has issue living, Susan Mary, *b* 1945: *m* 1965, Christopher Forbes Johnson, and has issue living, Russell Forbes *b* 1968, Catherine Amber *b* 1966, — Peta Mary, *b* 1947: *m* 1967, Clive Charles Lilford, and has issue living, Grant Charles *b* 1968, Karen *b* 1970, — Lucinda Margaret, *b* 1950, — Mary Louisa, *b* 1951.

Granddaughters of late Maj Edward Churchill St John (ante):—
Issue of late Lt-Col Edward Richard Gordon St John, RA, *b* 1911, *d* 1986: *m* 1943, Mary Aderyn, who *d* 1993, da of Rev H. Jones-Davies:—
Catherine Aderyn, *b* 1944: *m* 1968, Friedrich Kuebart, of 44795 Bochum, Plasshofstr 21, W Germany, and has issue living, Patrick Alexander, *b* 1975, — Oliver Edward, *b* 1978. ──── Margaret Joan, *b* 1949. *Residence* – 19 Selwyn Rd, Birmingham 16.

Granddaughters of late George Beauchamp Fleming St John, son of Rev George St John, son of Rev John Francis Seymour St John (ante):—
Issue of late Harry Beauchamp St John, *b* 1886, *d* 1957: *m* 1919, Mary Katherine, who *d* 1947, da of late Moreton Hyde Fitzhardinge, of Sydney, NSW:—
Barbara Margaret (Unit 20, Chatswood Garden Village, 5 Hart St, Lane Cove 2066, NSW, Australia), *b* 1920. ──── Gladys, *b* 1922; 1939-45 War in AWAS: *m* 1945, Norman Wycliffe Fairfax, who *d* 1986, and has issue living, John Beauchamp, *b* 1949, — Helen Margaret, *b* 1947. *Residence* – 133 Woodburn St, Evans Head, NSW 2473, Australia.

Grandchildren of late Rev Harris Fleming St John, son of late Fleming St John, son of late Rev John Francis Seymour St John (ante):—
Issue of late Oliver Stukeley Fleming St John, *b* 1881, *d* 1955: *m* 1st, 1913, Agnes Jane, who *d* 1916, da of Arthur Jenkins, of Pencombe, Herefordshire; 2ndly, 1924, Elizabeth Sarah Ross, who *d* 1933:—
(By 2nd *m*) Paul Fleming, *b* 1928: *m* 1953, Lesley Patricia, yst da of Albert Edwin Marsh, of Perth, W Australia, and has issue living, Brian Fleming, *b* 1954, — Peter Michael, *b* 1957: *m* 1981, Loretta Anne-Marie, elder da of John Toniolo, of Perth, W Australia, — Nola Margaret, *b* 1955: *m* 1980, Stewart Parkinson, yr son of John Parkinson, of Perth, and has issue living, Hannah Jane *b* 1983, — Pauline Maree Teresa, *b* 1960: *m* 1979, Graham Leslie Waddell, of Perth, — Julie Frances, *b* 1964. ──── Rev Oliver Peter Fleming (St Joseph's Presbytery, PO Box 45, Kulin, W Australia 6535), *b* 1929. ──── Michael Fleming, *b* 1932: *m* 1958, Teresa Josephine, da of Thomas W. Murphy, of Finchley, N3, and has issue

living, Nicholas Fleming (23 Scampton Close, Boston Rd, Bicester, Oxon OX6 8LG), *b* 1961: *m* 1989, Catherine Clare, da of James Smith, of Winton House, Westcliff-on-Sea, Essex, and has issue living, Thomas James *b* 1992, Charlotte Louise *b* 1995, — Andrew Thomas (32 Kenbrook House, Leighton Rd, Kentish Town NW5 2QN) *b* 1963: has issue living (by Jessica Earle), Jona Benito Sᴛ Joʜɴ-Eᴀʀʟᴇ *b* 1991, Ruby Maria Sᴛ Joʜɴ-Eᴀʀʟᴇ *b* 1995. — Philip Ambrose (56 Ida St, Bassendean, Perth, Western Australia 6054), *b* 1965: *m* 1986 (*m diss* 19—), Catherine Anne, da of Stanley John Simpson, of Perth, W Australia; has issue (by Dana Anning), Alexander Sᴛ Joʜɴ Aɴɴɪɴɢ *b* 1998, Georgiana Sᴛ Joʜɴ-Aɴɴɪɴɢ *b* 1993, — Robert Oliver (9 Victoria Av, Church End, Finchley, N3 1BD), *b* 1968. *Residence* – 9 Victoria Av, Finchley, N3. ⸺ Joan Fleming, *b* 1925: *m* 1947, Stanley John Simpson, of 13 Byron St, Leederville, Perth, W Australia 6007 and has issue living, Christopher John, *b* 1950, — Peter James, *b* 1952, — John Andrew, *b* 1957, — Richard Stephen Francis, *b* 1960, — Pauline Mary, *b* 1948: *m* 1968, Kenneth Gerald Glasgow (c/o BP Australia, Port-Hedland, W Aust), — Catherine Anne, *b* 1966.

Grandchildren of late Lt-Col Sir Henry Beauchamp St John, KCIE, CBE, Indian Army, only son of late Col Sir Oliver Beauchamp Coventry St John, KCSI, el son of Oliver St John, 2nd son of late Thomas St John (*b* 1765), 3rd son of Very Rev Hon St Andrew St John, DD (ante):—
Issue of late Lt-Col Oliver Charles Beauchamp St John, CMG, *b* 1907; *d* 1976: *m* 1st, 1935, Elizabeth Mary, who *d* 1957, da of Philip Lambton; 2ndly, 1966, Mary (Masseys, East Boldre, Brockenhurst, Hants, SO42 DWE), da of John Greenway, and widow of John Gillum Maxwell-Gumbleton:—
(By 1st *m*) Simon Lambton Beauchamp, *b* 1940: *m* 1971, Margaret Lee, step-da of Perry Leslie Owen, of Tampa, Florida, USA, and has issue living, Ryan Christopher Beauchamp, *b* 1972, — Erin Elizabeth, *b* 1975. ⸺ Sarah Mary (23 Fir Tree Close, SW16 1TF), *b* 1937: *m* 1957 (*m diss* 1980), Michael Geoffrey Morvaren Mayhew, and has issue living, Nicholas Morvaren (c/o The Naval Secretary, Min of Defence, Whitehall, SW1), *b* 1959; Lt Cmdr RN: *m* 1st, 1987 (*m diss* 1995), Katherine Cherry; 2ndly, 19—, Kathleen Susan, da of Robert Wood, of York, PA, USA, and has issue living (by 2nd *m*), Peri Margaret *b* 1998, — Charles Geoffrey (19 Priestley Drive, Larksfield, Kent ME20 6TX), *b* 1966: *m* 1989, Michele D. Crosby, and has issue living, Joshua Charles *b* 1991, Emily Victoria *b* 1992, Natasha Crosby *b* 1997, — Hamish St John, *b* 1968: *m* 1993, Julia Ann Jarvis, and has issue living, Jack St John *b* 1998, — Amanda Elizabeth, *b* 1962. ⸺ Victoria Anne, *b* 1942: *m* 1983, Brian Richard Easton, of 17 Abbots Way, Beckenham, Kent. ⸺ Vanessa Margaret, *b* 1944: *m* 1964, Nicholas John Connolly, of Monks Gate Cottage, Monks Gate, Horsham, and has issue living, Rupert St John, *b* 1965; *ed* — Coll, Oxford (MA), and Warwick Univ (MSc), — Philippa Joan, *b* 1964; *ed* Leeds Univ, and Penn State Univ, USA; MEng, CEng MICE, MIStructE, — Victoria Maria, *b* 1967; MA (Oxon).

Grandchildren of late Philip George St John, 5th and yst son of late Lt-Col Oliver Henry Beauchamp St John, el son of Lt-Gen Robert St John, 3rd son of Thomas St John (*b* 1765), 3rd son of Very Rev Hon St Andrew St John, DD (ante):—
Issue of late Capt Anthony Philip St John, RA, *b* 1925, *d* 1990: *m* 1st, 1947 (*m diss* 1951), Joyce Elizabeth, who *d* 1988, da of late George Edward Alleyne Dawes; 2ndly, 1959, Shelagh Marie James (Christophers, Budleigh Salterton, Devon):—
(By 1st *m*) David Warren (4 Nottingham Rd, Somercotes, Derbys DE55 4JJ), *b* 1950: *m* 1977 (*m diss* 1999), Dawn Yvonne, da of John Barry Price. ⸺ (By 2nd *m*) Oliver Philip, *b* 1959. ⸺ Trudie Sophia, *b* 1961. ⸺ Katherine Emma, *b* 1963: *m* 19—, Gordon Pulham.

Grandchildren of late Com Thomas Charles St Andrew St John, 3rd son of late Lt Gen Robert St John (ante):—
Issue of late Robert Henry Beauchamp St John, *b* 1878, *d* 1956: *m* 1st, 1901, Agnes Mary Sybil, who *d* 1915, da of late Capt Frederick Shelton, Argyll and Sutherland Highlanders; 2ndly, 1916, Edith Mary, da of late Capt Cape Hutton, of Ives, Bucks:—
(By 1st *m*) Dorothy Mary Beaufort, *b* 1902: *m* 1962, Magnus Karl Olof Friman.

Issue of late St John St Andrew Newell St John, *b* 1884, *d* 1962: *m* 1910, Mary Audrey, who *d* 1957, da of C. E. Hicks, of North Battlefold, Saskatchewan, Canada:—
Andrew Charles (1416 Collett St, Merritt, BC, Canada V1K 1K7), *b* 1927: *m* 1952, Cecile Marie, da of W. J. Calnan, of Vancouver, British Columbia and has issue living, Marie Patricia, *b* 1953: *m* 1974, Robert Anthony Parent, of 15520 Royal Av, White Rock, BC, Canada V4B 1N3, and has issue living, Robert Michael *b* 1975, Jennifer Marie *b* 1979, Michelle Elizabeth *b* 1981, — Janet Mary, *b* 1956: *m* 1978, Ian Lorne Creighton, of 28-5955 Oakdale Rd, Burnaby, BC, Canada V5H 4S5, and has issue living, Ian Michael *b* 1983, Alexander William *b* 1987, — Jillian Eleanor, *b* 1966: *m* 1989, Bradley Allen Lyle, of 203-1150 W 12th Av, Vancouver BC, Canada V6H-L6. ⸺ Mary Cecilia, *b* 1912: *m* 1932, Walter Davidson, who *d* 19—. ⸺ Ella Monica, *b* 1917: *m* 1942, W. H. Davis, Pilot Officer Roy Canadian Air Force, who *d* 19—, and has issue living, Ralph Austin, *b* 1947, — Marion Elizabeth, *b* 1950, — Anne Roberta, *b* 1954. ⸺ Hilda Margaret, *b* 1925: *m* 1949, Victor Leon Charbonneau, who *d* 19—, and has issue living, Kenneth Lawrence, *b* 1960, — Susan Hilda, *b* 1952, — Catherine Ann, *b* 1962.

Grandchildren of late Rev Canon Frederick de Porte St John (infra):—
Issue of late Roland Tyrwhitt St John, MBE, *b* 1914, *d* 1991: *m* 1st, 1949, Margaret, who *d* 1972, da of late Ven Archdeacon Reginald Beatty Massey; 2ndly, 1976, Marjorie Jean (6 Campbell St, Toowoomba, Queensland 4350, Australia), widow of Rev David J. T. Richardson:—
(By 1st *m*) David Henry (26 Gladstone St, Indooroopilly, Queensland 4068, Australia), *b* 1951; *ed* Qld Univ (BSc, PhD); Prof, Dept of Mining, Minerals & Materials Engrg, Queensland Univ: *m* 1976, Helen Jennifer, da of late Donald McLeod, of Brisbane, and has issue living, Andrew Timothy, *b* 1980, — Robin Thomas, *b* 1983. ⸺ Paul Michael (52 Yuletide St, Holland Park, Brisbane, Queensland 4121), *b* 1953; *ed* Qld Univ (BSc): *m* 1987, Frances Julia, da of John Thompson McDonald, of Toowoomba. ⸺ Nigel Alexander (6 Garfield Av, Carnegie, Vic 3163), *b* 1958; *ed* Qld Inst of Technology (BAppSc), and Qld Univ (PhD): *m* 1991, Heather Anne, da of Roy Ernest Willis, and has issue living, Luke William, *b* 1998. ⸺ Julian Andrew, *b* 1963; has issue living, Isabella Rainbow, *b* 1994. ⸺ Philippa Robin, *b* 1955; *ed* Qld Univ (BA): *m* 1988, Kim Graham Grady, of PO Box 110, Mount Nebo, Queensland 4520, and has issue living, Alicia St John, *b* 1988, — Jessica St John, *b* 1990.

Issue of late Edward Henry St John, *b* 1916, *d* 1994: *m* 1st, 1940, Sylvette, who *d* 1954, elder da of Jean Meer Cargher, of Strasbourg, Alsace; 2ndly, 1955, Valerie Erskine (40 Alexandra Crescent, Bayview, NSW 2104, Australia; Mt Elliot, Holgate, NSW), da of late Henry John Winslow, of 2a Stanley Crescent, W11:—
(By 1st *m*) Madeleine Sᴛ Joʜɴ, *b* 1941; *ed* Sydney Univ (BA); has resumed her maiden name: *m* 1965 (*m diss* 1972), Christopher Roger Tillam. ⸺ Colette, *b* 1944: *m* 1980, Stephen Louis Lippincott, and has issue living, Aaron, *b* 1985.

—— (By 2nd *m*) Oliver Winslow, *b* 1956. —— Edward Erskine (25 Ryries Parade, Cremorne, NSW 2090, Australia), *b* 1960: *m* 1988, Susan Elizabeth, da of Sydney Young, of Albury, and has issue living, Henry William, *b* 1993, — Thomas Sydney, *b* 1997. —— Patrick Graeme (28 Marcel Av, Clovelly, NSW 2031, Australia), *b* 1963; *ed* NSW Univ (BComm, LLB): *m* 1992, Karen Leanne, da of late Peter John Reginald O'Loughlin, of Sydney, and has issue living, Katherine Jane, *b* 1994, — Emma Louise, *b* 1996.

Grandchildren of late Henry St John (*b* 1852), yst son of late Frederick St John (*b* 1809), 5th and yst son of Very Rev Hon St Andrew St John, DD (ante):—
Issue of late Rev Canon Frederick de Porte St John, *b* 1879, *d* 1963: *m* 1908, Hannah Phœbe Mabel, who *d* 1950, da of late Samuel Lucas Charles Pyrke, JP, of Tamworth, NS Wales:—
Florence Anne, *b* 1924; *ed* Sydney Univ: *m* 1955, Frank Heller, BSc, PhD, of 84 Wood Vale, N10, and has issue living, Michael Guy St John, *b* 1957, — Juliet Margarethe, *b* 1961, — Clare Andrea, *b* 1964. —— Pamela Mary ST JOHN (River Glen, 1/590 Riversdale Rd, Camberwell, Vic 3124, Aust), *b* 1925; BA (Melb), BEd (Melb); Dip Adv Studies in Ed; Cert KTC (Adelaide); resumed the surname of St John 1972; Lecturer at Inst of Early Childhood Development, Melbourne, 1967-84: *m* 1st, 1946 (*m diss* 1959), Ronald Fry, late RN, who *d* 1971; 2ndly, 1976 (*m diss* 1977), Edward John Minchin, solicitor, and has issue living (by 1st *m*), Jeremy William ST JOHN (205 William St, Melbourne, Vic, Australia), *b* 1952; *ed* Melbourne Univ (LLB); Bar and Solicitor 1975; Bar-at-law 1983: *m* 1st, 1978 (*m diss* 1985), Christine Fay Barrow; 2ndly, 1990, Jillian Margaret Rivers, and has issue living (by 1st *m*), Emily Catherine *b* 1980, Polly Louise *b* 1982, (by 2nd *m*) Thomas Rivers *b* 1994, Phoebe Rivers *b* 1991, — Jennifer Jane, *b* 1949; BEd (Special Educn) Melbourne, TITC (Melbourne), TTCTD (Melbourne): *m* 1977, Jonathan Hugh Beverley Crosskill, and has issue living, Nicholas William *b* 1980, Richard Campbell *b* 1982, Edward Daniel *b* (twin) 1982, — Catherine Mary, *b* 1957; BEd, Melbourne: *m* 1st, 1978 (*m diss* 1981), David Kenneth Hitchcock; 2ndly, 1981 (*m diss* 1992), Kim Leigh Mark Savery, and has issue living (by 2nd *m*), Elliot Henry *b* 1986, Amelia Kate *b* 1983.

Issue of late Ambrose St John, *b* 1896, *d* 1968: *m* 1925, Mary Kathleen (34 Kemp St, Port Macquarie, NSW 2444), da of Peter Gaffney, of Sydney, NSW:—
Kevin Joseph (34 Kemp St, Port Macquarie, NSW 2444), *b* 1926. —— Desmond Henry (115 Wallace St, Macksville, NSW 2447), *b* 1932: *m* 19—, Mavis Duncan, of Rockhampton, Qld, and has issue living, Lorelle *b* 19—, — Deborah, *b* 19—, — Sandra, *b* 1963. —— Marlene Illina, *b* 1936: *m* 1962, David Steuart, of 6/25 Banksia Rd, Caringbah, NSW 2229, and has issue living, Jason, *b* 1967, — Nicole, *b* 1963.

Granddaughters of late Oliver St John, 5th and yst son of late Frederick St John (*b* 1809) (ante):—
Issue of late Oliver Beauchamp St John, *b* 1895, *d* 1970: *m* 1st, 1921 (*m diss* 19—) Winifred Lyndall Fox, of Hastings, Sussex; 2ndly, 1944, Josephine Lorna, who *d* 1969, da of W. Kurtze, of Saskatoon, Canada:—
(By 1st *m*) Patricia Jocelyn (3171 Henderson Rd, Victoria, BC, Canada V8P 5A3), *b* 1922: *m* 1941, Prof John Alexander McCarter, PhD, FRSC, and has issue living, David Graham (511 Hibiscus Av, London, Ont, Canada N6H 3P2), *b* 1946: *m* 1968, Janice Evelyn, da of R. E. Yates, of Walkerton, Ont, Canada, and has issue living, Robert Alexander *b* 1974, James Graham *b* 1976, Peter Jonathan *b* 1979, Jennifer Irene *b* 1982, — Robert Malcolm, *b* 1948: *m* 1971 (*m diss* 19—), Bonnie Gail, da of Lorne E. Davis, of London, Ont, and has issue living, Alexis Lauren *b* 1979, Jacqueline Brie *b* 1982, — William Alexander (Box 250, Lillooet, BC, Canada V0K 1V0), *b* 1955, — Patricia Lyndall McCARTER (10114 Resthaven Rd, Sydney, BC, Canada V8L 3G5), *b* 1953; has resumed her maiden name; *ed* Victoria Univ (BEd): *m* 1976 (*m diss* 1997), René Groulx, and has issue living, Donald William *b* 1979, Samuel Alexander *b* 1986, Sarah Denise *b* 1976; *ed* Victoria Univ (BSc). —— Josephine Lyndall (No. 115, 22515-116th Av, Maple Ridge, BC, Canada V2X 0L1), *b* 1925: *m* 1947 (*m diss* 1974), Walter H. Cudmore, and has issue living, Rodney William (2487 Valleyview Drive, Kamloops, BC, Canada V2C 4E2), *b* 1949: *m* 19—, Leonora Marie Dixon, — Donald MacKenzie, *b* 1953, — Richard Michael (8878-214B St, Langley, BC, Canada V1M 1Y3), *b* 1957, — Diane Louise, *b* 1962: *m* 19—, James B. Kempton, of 1472 Helen Drive, Port Coquitlam, BC, Canada V3C 2X8.

Descendants, if any, of Capt Hon Henry St John, RN (*b* 17—), and Rev Hon Ambrose St John (*b* 1743), 3rd and 4th sons of 10th Baron.

PREDECESSORS – (1) OLIVER St John (descended from John St John, el son of Sir Oliver St John of Bletso, who *m* Margaret, great-granddaughter of Roger de Beauchamp, who was summoned to Parliament of England as *Baron Beauchamp of Bletshoe* 1363-79, since when that title has not been assumed), *cr Baron St John of Bletso*, co Beds (peerage of England) 1559; *d* 1592; *s* by his el son (2) JOHN, 2nd Baron; was one of the peers who sat on the trial of Mary, Queen of Scots; *d* without male issue 1596, when the Barony of Beauchamp devolved upon his da Anne, wife of William, Lord Howard, el son of the 1st Earl of Nottingham, and the Barony of St John devolved upon his brother (3) OLIVER, 3rd Baron; *d* 1618; *s* by his el son (4) OLIVER, 4th Baron; *cr Earl of Bolingbroke* (peerage of England) 1624; *d* 1646; *s* by his grandson (5) OLIVER, 2nd Earl; *d* 1688; *s* by his brother (6) PAULET, 3rd Earl; *d* unm 1711, when the earldom became extinct and the barony devolved upon his kinsman (7) PAULET ST ANDREW, 7th Baron, who had previously *s* his father as 4th Bt (see * infra); *d* 1714; *s* by his uncle (8) WILLIAM, 8th Baron; *d* unm 1720; *s* by his brother (9) ROWLAND, 9th Baron; *d* unm 1722; *s* by his brother (10) JOHN, 10th Baron; *d* 1757; *s* by his son (11) JOHN, 11th Baron; *d* 1767; *s* by his el son (12) HENRY BEAUCHAMP, 12th Baron; *d* 1805; *s* by his brother (13) ST ANDREW, 13th Baron; *d* 1817; *s* by his son (14) ST ANDREW BEAUCHAMP, 14th Baron; *b* 1811: *m* 1838, Eleanor, who *d* 1899, da of late Vice-Adm Sir Richard Hussey-Hussey, GCMG, KCB; *d* 1874; *s* by his son (15) ST ANDREW, 15th Baron, *b* 1840: *m* 1868, Ellen Georgiana, who *d* 1890, da of late Edward Senior, Poor Law Commr, Ireland; *d* 1887; *s* by his brother (16) BEAUCHAMP MOUBRAY, 16th Baron; *b* 1844; Lord-Lieut of Bedfordshire: *m* 1st, 1869, Helen Charlotte, who *d* 1909, 2nd da of late Harry Thornton, of Kempston Grange, Beds; 2ndly, 1911, Ethel Susan, who *d* 1945, da of late John Habington Barneby Lutley, of Brockhampton, Herefordshire; *d* 1912; *s* by his son (17) HENRY BEAUCHAMP OLIVER, 17th Baron; *b* 1876; *d* 1920; *s* by his brother (18) MOUBRAY ST ANDREW THORNTON, 18th Baron; *b* 1877: *m* 1st, 1905, Evelyn Geraldine, who *d* 1918, yst da of late Capt Andrew Hamilton Russell (formerly 58th Regt), of The Heath House, Petersfield, Hants; 2ndly, 1923, Elizabeth May, who *d* 1978, da of Lloyd Griffith, of Hurst Court, Ore, Hastings, and widow of Col Edward Charles Ayshford Sanford, CMG, of Nynehead Court, Som; *d* 1934; *s* by his only son (19) JOHN MOUBRAY RUSSELL, 19th Baron; *b* 1917; *d* 1976; *s* by his cousin (20) ANDREW BEAUCHAMP, TD (3rd son of Lt-Col Hon Rowland Tudor St John, DLI, 3rd son of 16th Baron), 20th Baron; *b* 1918: *m* 1955, Katharine, yst da of late Alfred von Berg, of 5 Gonville House, Manor Fields, SW15; *d* 1978; *s* by his only son (21) ANTHONY TUDOR, 21st Baron and present peer.

*The Hon Sir Rowland St John, 4th son of the 3rd Baron St John of Bletso (see ante), had, with other issue (1) OLIVER, *cr* a *Baronet* 1660; *d* 1661; *s* by his son (2) Sir ANDREW, 2nd Bt; *d* 1708; *s* by his son (3) Sir ST ANDREW, 3rd Bt; *s* by his son (4) Sir PAULET ST ANDREW, 4th Bt, who succeeded as 7th Baron St John of Bletso (see ante).

ST JOHN OF FAWSLEY, BARON (St John-Stevas) (Life Baron 1987)

NORMAN ANTONY FRANCIS ST JOHN-STEVAS, PC, son of late Stephen S. Stevas, by his wife, late Kitty St John O'Connor; *b* 18 May 1929; *ed* Ratcliffe, Fitzwilliam Coll, Camb (BA 1950, MA 1954), Ch Ch, Oxford (BCL 1954), and Yale Univ; Life Fellow Emmanuel Coll, Camb 1996; Bar Middle Temple 1952; jurisprudence tutor Ch Ch 1953-55, and Merton Coll 1955-57; legal, ecclesiastical and political correspondent on *The Economist* 1959-64; Min of State for Educn and Science with special responsibility for the Arts 1973-74, Opposition Spokesman for the Arts 1974, Member Shadow Cabinet, Min for the Arts 1979-81, Leader of House of Commons and Chancellor of Duchy of Lancaster 1979-81, Member Parly Select Cttee on Foreign Affairs since 1983; Chm Booker McConnell Prize 1985, Vice-Pres Theatres Advisory Council since 1983, Member of Council of RADA since 1983, Nat Soc for Dance since 1983, Nat Youth Theatre since 1983, RCA since 1985, etc; Trustee: Royal Soc of Painters in Watercolours since 1984, Decorative Arts Soc since 1984, and Royal Philharmonic Orchestra since 1985, Chm Royal Fine Art Commn since 1985; Master Emmanuel Coll, Camb 1991-96; author and editor, *Walter Bagehot* (1959), and subsequently edited his literary, historical and political works; MP Chelmsford (*C*) 1964-87; OStJ 1980, Order of Merit (Italy) 1965, FRSL 1966; *cr* PC 1979, and *Baron St John of Fawsley*, of Preston Capes, co Northants (Life Baron) 1987.

𝕬rms – Tierced in fesse azure, gules and azure per pale counterchanged, in the azure an open crown or, in the gules a lion passant guardant gold, armed and langued azure. 𝕮rest – A fallow deer's head erased proper, in the mouth a chaplet of laurel vert, the attires per fesse, the dexter azure and gules, the sinister gules and azure. 𝕾upporters – *Dexter*, a monkey proper; *sinister*, a lion argent winged or, both crowned with a crown rayonny also or and each rampant on a grassy mount, the dexter having a primrose growing therefrom, the sinister a lily all proper.
Residence – The Old Rectory, Preston Capes, Daventry, Northants. *Clubs* – White's, Garrick, Pratt's.

ST JUST, BARONY OF (Grenfell) (Extinct 1984)

DAUGHTERS LIVING OF SECOND BARON (*By 1st marriage*)

Hon Laura Clare (*Hon Lady Phillips*), *b* 1950: *m* 1980, Sir (Gerald) Hayden Phillips, KCB, Permanent Sec, Lord Chancellor's Dept, and Clerk to the Crown in Chancery, and has issue living, Thomas Peter, *b* 1987, — Florence Leslie, *b* 1981, — Louisa Henrietta, *b* 1984.

(*By 2nd marriage*)

Hon Kathrine (Katya), *b* 1957; resumed her maiden name 1985: *m* 1st, 1981 (*m diss* 1985), Oliver John Gilmour (later Hon Oliver John Gilmour); 2ndly, 1990, Roger N. Middleton, and has issue (by 1st *m*) (*see* B Gilmour of Craigmillar), — (by 2nd *m*), Tamara Sophia, *b* 1992, — Tatiana Maria, *b* 1994. *Residence* – Le Bailly, Loiret, France.
Hon Natasha Jeannine Mary, *b* 1959.

St Leger, family name of Viscount Doneraile.

ST LEONARDS, BARONY OF (Sugden) (Extinct 1985)

NATURAL BROTHERS LIVING OF FOURTH AND LAST BARON

Arthur Herbert (1 Abbey Park, Killester, Dublin 5), *b* 1942: *m* 1967, Phyllis, da of late Patrick Muldoon, of Whitehall, and has issue living, Arthur John, *b* 1968.

Philip Hugh (17 Craigford Drive, Artane, Dublin 5), *b* 1944: *m* 1965, Roseanna Mary da of Michael Hill, of Clonshaugh, and has issue living, Philip Hugh, *b* 1966, — Mark Anthony, *b* 1974, — Edward Charles, *b* 1977, — Derek Peter, *b* 1978, — Rebecca Julie, *b* 1969.

Hugh David (1 Merchants Rd, East Wall, Dublin 3), *b* 1947: *m* 1983, Caroline, da of Denis Galavan, of Artane, Dublin.

MOTHER LIVING OF FOURTH AND LAST BARON

Julia Sheila (17 Craigford Drive, Artane, Dublin 5), da of late Philip Wyatt, of Curragh, co Kildare: *m* 1949, Arthur Herbert Sugden, who *d* 1958.

ST LEVAN, BARON (St Aubyn) (Baron UK 1887, Bt UK 1866)

Complete in himself

JOHN FRANCIS ARTHUR ST AUBYN, DSC, 4th Baron, and 5th Baronet; *b* 23 Feb 1919; *s* 1978; *ed* Eton, and Trin Coll, Camb (BA); Fellow of Roy Soc for Encouragement of Art, FRSA 1974; admitted a solicitor 1948; sometime Lt RNVR; High Sheriff of Cornwall 1974, DL 1977, Vice Lord Lieut since 1992; Pres London Cornish Assocn 1987-97; Pres Cornwall Branch, Council for Protection of Rural England 1975-90, Pres Friends of Plymouth City Museums and Art Gallery since 1985, Vice Pres Penzance YMCA, Royal Bath and SW Cos Soc (Vice Pres 1989), Truro Branch Royal Naval Assocn; Vice Pres Royal Cornwall Agric Assocn (formerly Pres); Patron Normandy Veterans Assocn, Cornwall Branch; Bard of Cornwall 1995; Pres Cornwall Maritime Trust since 1994, St Ives Soc of Artists since 1978, and Penwith & Isles of Scilly District Scouts since 1985; KStJ; author *Illustrated History of St Michael's Mount*: *m* 1970, Susan, yr da of late Maj-Gen Sir John Noble Kennedy, GCMG, KCVO, KBE, CB, MC.

Arms – Ermine, on a cross gules, five bezants, all within a bordure wavy of the second. **Crest** – A rock proper, therefrom a Cornish chough rising sable, the whole debruised with a bendlet sinister wavy ermine. **Supporters** – Two lions or, each gorged with a chain proper and pendant therefrom an escutcheon, that of the dexter, per fesse azure and argent, in chief a naval crown between two laurel branches saltirewise or, in base the frame of a vessel proper; that of the sinister, sable, charged with five bezants.

Residence – St Michael's Mount, Marazion, Cornwall, TR17 0HT. *Clubs* – Brooks's, Royal Yacht Squadron.

BROTHERS LIVING

Hon (OLIVER) PIERS, MC, *b* 12 July 1920; *ed* Wellington Coll, and St James's Sch, Maryland, USA; High Sheriff of E Sussex 1982-83; Pres Cornwall Branch, Council for Protection of Rural England since 1990; Vice-Pres Penzance YMCA; 1939-45 War as Capt 60th Rifles and Parachute Regt (despatches, MC): *m* 1948, Mary Bailey, who *d* 1987, da of Bailey Southwell, of Crocodile Leap Farm, Olievenhoutpoort, S Africa, and has issue living, James Piers Southwell (Tredrea Manor, St Erth, Hayle, Cornwall TR27 6JS), *b* 1950; *ed* Eton, and Magdalen Coll, Oxford: *m* 1981, Mary Caroline, yst da of Peter Ward Bennett, OBE, of Dene House, Glynde, Sussex, and has issue living, Hugh James *b* 14 June 1983, Felix John *b* 1992, Clemency Lara *b* 1985, Louisa Mary *b* 1987, — Nicholas Francis, MP (c/o House of Commons, SW1), *b* 1955; *ed* Eton; MP Guildford (C) since 1997: *m* 1980, Jane Mary, only da of William F. Brooks, of Bishopswood House, Bishopswood, Herefordshire, and has issue living, Henry Francis *b* 1981, Edward Nicholas *b* 1995, Katharine Mary *b* 1983, Alice Jane *b* 1986, Camilla Bailey *b* 1990, — Fiona Mary (*Hon Mrs Robert Boyle*), *b* 1952; author of *The Butler's Guide* (co-author) (1982), *A Portrait of Georgian London* (1985), etc: *m* 1987, Hon Robert William Boyle, of 30 Durand Gdns, SW9 0PP, son of 14th Earl of Cork and Orrery, and has issue (*see* E Cork). *Residence* – Hogus House, Ludgvan, Penzance, Cornwall TR20 8EZ. *Clubs* – Brooks's, House of Lords Yacht.

Hon Giles Rowan, LVO, *b* 1925; *ed* Wellington Coll, at Glasgow Univ, and at Trin Coll, Oxford; FRSL; 1939-45 War as Ordinary Seaman RN (invalided); author (works include *A Victorian Eminence* (1957), *The Royal George* (1963), *Edward VII* (1979), *The Year of Three Kings* 1483 (1983), and *Queen Victoria, A Portrait* (1991)); LVO 1977. *Residence* – Apartment 2, Saumarez Park Manor, Route de Saumarez, Câtel, Guernsey GY5 7TH. *Clubs* – Beefsteak, House of Lords Yacht.

SISTERS LIVING

Hon Jessica Gwendolen, *b* 1918: *m* 1939, John Patrick Koppel, late Maj Welsh Gds, and has issue living, Patrick Anthony (PO Box 415, Brookshire, Texas, USA), *b* 1944: *m* 1st, 1967 (*m diss* 1971), Jacqueline Ann, da of J. N. Fairrie; 2ndly, 1974, Jerry, who *d* 19—, da of Cecil White; 3rdly, 1996, Debra Kay Bristow, — Lamorna Jessica, *b* 1940: *m* 1st, 1964 (*m diss* 1974), Ian Clinton Elliot; 2ndly, 1974, Alastair Michael Hyde Villiers (*see* D Roxburghe, 1968 Edn), of 17 Lansdowne Crescent, W11, and has issue living (by 1st *m*), Patrick Ian *b* 1965, Shane Robert *b* 1970, (by 2nd *m*) Katherine Alexandra Hyde *b* 1979, — Susan Katherine Dorothy, *b* 1942: *m* 1963, Richard Noël Dobbs, of Flat B3 Montevetro, Battersea Church Rd, SW11 3NA, and has issue living, Richard Francis Conway (188 Broomwood Rd, SW11 6JY) *b* 1966: *m* 1996, Catherine Hardman (and has issue living, Annie Louise *b* 1997), Alexander Noel *b* 1967, Jessica Katherine Ann *b* 1971. *Residence* – Goodworth House, Goodworth Clatford, Andover, Hants.

Hon Philippa Catherine, *b* 1922: *m* 1948, Evelyn Charles Lacy Hulbert-Powell, late Lieut Queen's Roy Regt, who *d* 1985, and has issue living, Charles George Lacy (Old Place Farm, Mayfield, E Sussex), *b* 1952: *m* 1978, Sara Mary Philomena, el da of late Jurat Michael Walter Bonn, of Oaklands, St Peter, Jersey (*see* Buxton, Bt, colls), and has issue living, John Charles Lacy *b* 1984, Catherine Mary Lacy *b* 1980, Emma Sara Lacy *b* 1982, Victoria Elizabeth Lacy *b* 1987, — Francis Peter Lacy, *b* 1961, — Elizabeth Catherine Lacy, *b* 1950: *m* 1976, Lt-Cdr Richard Charles Harden, RN, and has issue (*see* Ingram, Bt), — Veronica Mary Lacy, *b* 1954: *m* 1979, John Robert Maclean, DL, of Westfield House, Spynie, Elgin, Morayshire, and has issue living, Hugh Charles *b* 1984, Charlotte Louise *b* 1982, Anastasia Mary *b* 1986, — Teresa Philippa Lacy, *b* 1956: *m* 1993, Paul H. C. T. Isolani-Smyth, of Flat 181, Elm Park Mansions, Park Walk, SW10 0AX, only son of C. T. Isolani, CBE, LVO, of Pont St, SW1. *Residence* – Old Place Farm Bungalow, Mayfield, Sussex TN20 6PN.

COLLATERAL BRANCHES LIVING

Grandchildren of Hon Lionel Michael St Aubyn, MVO (infra):—
   Issue of late Lt-Cdr Geoffrey Piers St Aubyn *b* 1922, *d* 1964: *m* 1958, Valerie Elizabeth, who *d* 1964, only da of late Wing-Cdr B. W. T. Hare, of Curtisknowle, Totnes:—
Michael Piers, *b* 1959: *m* 1987, Astrid E., da of Richard Edward Walter Lumley, of Roundwood, Windlesham, Surrey, and has issue living, Thomas Piers, *b* 1991, — Matilda Elizabeth, *b* 1994, — Isabella Astrid, *b* 1996. *Residence* – The Old Rectory, Kingscote, Tetbury, Glos. ——— Rupert Trelawny, *b* 1963. ——— Camilla Elizabeth, *b* 1961: *m* 1988 (*m diss* 1997), Jonathan Chiam Elichaoff, elder son of Michael Elichaoff, of Finchley, N3, and has issue living, Zak Nicholas Piers, *b* 1993.

   Issue of late Capt Hon Lionel Michael St Aubyn, MVO, yst son of 1st Baron, *b* 1878, *d* 1965: *m* 1915, Lady Mary Theresa Parker, who *d* 1932, da of 3rd Earl of Morley:—
Thomas Edward, CVO (Dairy House Farm, Ashford Hill, Newbury, Berks), *b* 1923; late Maj 60th Rifles; Lieut HM Body Guard of Hon Corps of Gentlemen at Arms 1990-93; High Sheriff Hants 1979, DL 1984; CVO 1993: *m* 1953, Henrietta Mary, only da of Sir Henry Grey Studholme, 1st Bt, CVO, MP, and has issue living, Sarah Elizabeth, *b* 1955: *m* 1983, Hugh Adrian Bethell (*see* E Radnor), — Caroline Mary, *b* 1957: *m* 1980, Andrew H. Llewellyn, of Church Acre, Rhode Lane, Uplyme, Lyme Regis, Dorset, — Judith Clare, *b* 1962.

(In remainder to the Baronetcy only)

Granddaughter of late Col Edward St Aubyn (infra):—
   Issue of late Lieut-Col Guy Stewart St Aubyn, OBE, *b* 1870, *d* 1924: *m* 1899, Florita, who *d* 1925, da of late Pascoe du Pre Grenfell, of Wilton Park, Bucks:—
Violet Susan May, *b* 1909: *m* 1929, Raymond Lort-Phillips, Capt Scots Guards, who *d* 1980, and has had issue, Guy Stewart (6 Les Champs Farm, Grouville, Jersey, Channel Isles), *b* 1930; *ed* Eton, and RMA Sandhurst; late Capt Welsh Guards: *m* 1st, 1956, Norah Eugenie, who *d* 1986, da of late Baron Hans Rodolphe de Jenner, of Schloss Landshütte, nr Berne, Switzerland, and formerly wife of late John Patrick O'Leary; 2ndly, 1996, Jennifer Mary, da of late George Henry Darlow, of Kempston, Beds, and formerly wife of Robin Ernest Richard Rumboll, and has issue living (by 1st *m*), Piers Wickham (51 Harcourt St, Hawthorn, Melbourne, Vic 3122, Australia) *b* 1957: *m* 1986, Virginia, da of late Ronald Hodgson, of Vaucluse, Sydney, Australia (and has issue living, Harry Burgess *b* 1991), Giles Raymond (13 McHugh Crescent, Whitfield, Cairns, Qld 4870, Australia) *b* 1958: *m* 1985, Kathleen, da of Sydney Miles, of Randfontein, S Africa (and has issue living, Guy Dylan *b* 1986, Ben Raymond *b* 1988), Edward St Aubyn (20 Alfred St, Richmond, Melbourne, Vic 3121, Australia) *b* 1966, — †Peregrine Edward Grenfell, *b* 1937; *ed* Charterhouse, and at Trin Coll, Camb (BA Hons); Solicitor 1962: *m* 1st, 1963 (*m diss* 1981), Carolyn Diana Brougham, only da of late George A. B. Docker, of 13 Prospect Place, Watlington, Oxon; 2ndly, 1984, Lamorna (who *m* 3rdly, 1990, Michael F. Good), da of Roger St Aubyn (infra), and formerly wife of Capt David Julian Cotton, and *d* 1988, leaving issue (by 1st *m*), Penelope Samantha *b* 1964: *m* 1994, Campbell Gordon, son of late Donald Gordon, of Montreal, Canada (and has issue living, Edward Peregrine Lysander *b* 1997), Venetia Nike *b* 1968: *m* 1996, Andrew R. Eliot, yr son of Robin Eliot, of Lelant, Cornwall, — Anthony Frederick Fitzroy (PO Box 478, St Helier, Jersey JE4 5SL, CI), *b* 1944; *ed* Eton, and RMA Sandhurst; late Capt Gren Gds: *m* 1st, 1971, Saranne Frances, who *d* 1984, da of James Harold Alexander, of co Dublin, and formerly wife of 10th Baron Calthorpe; 2ndly, 1995, Melanie Susan Clara, da of Clifford Dargie, of Johannesburg, S Africa, and has issue living (by 2nd wife), Michaela Susan Alexandra *b* 1991. *Residence* – Camellia Cottage, Gorey, Jersey.

Grandchildren of late Col Edward Geoffrey St Aubyn, DSO, 2nd son (by 2nd *m*) of Col Edward St Aubyn (infra):—
   Issue of late Roger St Aubyn, *b* 1906, *d* 1985: *m* 1st, 1939 (*m diss* 1957), Baroness Sophie Helene, da of Baron Heinrich von Puthon; 2ndly, 1957 (*m diss* 1968), Lorna, elder da of Capt Alastair Mackintosh:—
(By 1st *m*) Lamorna, *b* 1944: *m* 1st, 1965 (*m diss* 1983), David Julian Cotton, Capt RGJ, TAVR; 2ndly, 1984, Peregrine Edward Grenfell Lort-Phillips, who *d* 1988 (ante); 3rdly, 1990, Michael Frankland Good, of Thellusson Lodge, Church Walk, Aldeburgh, Suffolk IP15 5DT, and has issue living (by 1st *m*), Caroline Mary Sophie, *b* 1966: *m* 1990, Julian Chamberlen, of 11 Glenrosa St, SW6 2QY, eldest son of Nicholas Chamberlen, of Church Farmhouse, Berwick, E Sussex, and has issue living, Ralph Hugo *b* 1997. ——— Diana, *b* 1945: *m* 1970, Daniel Romer-Lee, of 35 Napier Av, SW6 3PS, and has issue living, Christopher Daniel, *b* 1972, — Serena Isabel Hilaria, *b* 1974. ——— (By 2nd *m*) Edward (Le Petit Canadeau, 900 94 Route du Cas, Le Castellet 83330, Var, France), *b* 1960; *ed* Westminster, and ...... Coll, Oxford; writer: *m* 1987 (*m diss* 1990), Nicola, yr da of Milton Shulman, writer. ——— Alexandra (112 Highlever Rd, W10 6PL), *b* 1958.

Issue of late Col Edward St Aubyn, 4th son of 1st baronet, *b* 1837, *d* 1914: *m* 1st, 1866, Edith, who *d* 1875, da of late Adm Hon Keith Stewart, CB, son of 8th Earl of Galloway; 2ndly, 1879, Eugenia Susannah, who *d* 1886, da of David Barclay Chapman, of Downshire House, Roehampton, and widow of George Henry FitzRoy; 3rdly, 1891, Ada Mary, who *d* 1948, da of late Col Sir Robert Thomas White-Thomson, KCB (Ferguson-Davie, Bt):—

(By 3rd *m*) Hildegarde Ada, *b* 1894.

PREDECESSORS – **(1)** EDWARD ST AUBYN, *b* 1799 (son of Sir John St Aubyn, FRS, FSA, FLS, 5th and last Bt (*cr* 1671), by Miss Juliana Vinicombe, whom he *m* 1822); *cr* a *Baronet* 1866: *m* 1828, Emma, who *d* 1887, da of Gen Knollys; *d* 1872; *s* by his son **(2)** JOHN 2nd Bt; *b* 1829; MP for Cornwall W (*L*) 1858-85, and for W, or St Ives, Div of Cornwall (LU) 1885-7; Mayor of Devonport 1890 and 1891; *cr Baron St Levan*, of St Michael's Mount, Cornwall (peerage of United Kingdom) 1887: *m* 1856, Lady Elizabeth Clementina Townshend, who *d* 1910, da of 4th Marquess Townshend: *d* 1908; *s* by his son **(3)** JOHN TOWNSHEND, CB, CVO, 2nd Baron, *b* 1857; Col and Hon Brig-Gen late Grenadier Guards, and Dep Warden of the Stannaries of Cornwall and Devon: *m* 1st, 1892, Lady Edith Hilaria Edgcumbe, who *d* 1931, da of 4th Earl of Mount Edgcumbe; 2ndly, 1933, Julia Georgiana Sarah, who *d* 1938, da of Sir George Orby Wombwell, 4th Bt, and widow of 2nd Earl of Dartrey; *d* 1940; *s* by his nephew **(4)** FRANCIS CECIL (son of late Hon Arthur James Dudley Stuart St Aubyn, 4th son of 1st Baron), 3rd Baron, *b* 1895: *m* 1916, Hon Clementina Gwendolen Catharine Nicolson, JP, who *d* 1995, da of 1st Baron Carnock; *d* 1978; *s* by his el son JOHN FRANCIS ARTHUR, 4th Baron, and present peer.

ST OSWALD, BARON (Winn) (Baron UK 1885)

All for God and my country

CHARLES ROWLAND ANDREW WINN, 6th Baron; *b* 22 July 1959; *s* 1999; *ed* New School, King's Langley: *m* 1985, Louise Alexandra, da of Stewart MacKenzie Scott, and has issue.

Arms – Ermine, on a fesse vert, three eagles displayed or. **Crest** – A demi-eagle or, collared ermine. **Supporters** – Two dragons reguardant vert, each gorged with a cord or, and pendant therefrom an escutcheon gules, each charged with a rose argent.
Seat – Nostell Priory, Wakefield, W Yorks.

SON LIVING

Hon ROWLAND CHARLES SEBASTIAN HENRY, *b* 15 April 1986.

DAUGHTER LIVING

Hon Henrietta Sophia Alexandra, *b* 1993.

SISTER LIVING

Hon Geva Charlotte Caroline, *b* 1955: *m* 1987, (John) Simon Blackett, and has issue (*see* Blackett, Bt, colls). *Residence* – Clunie Cottage, Braemar, Aberdeenshire AB35 5XQ.

WIDOW LIVING OF SON OF SECOND BARON

Alice, da of late Moncure Perkins, of Virginia, USA: *m* 1924, Maj Hon Reginald Henry Winn, Gren Gds, who *d* 1985, and has issue (see colls infra). *Residence* – 59 Whitelands House, Cheltenham Terr, SW3.

WIDOW LIVING OF FIFTH BARON

CHARLOTTE DENISE EILEEN (*Dowager Baroness St Oswald*), only da of late Wilfrid Haig Lloyd (*see* Oakeley, Bt, 1985 Edn): *m* 1954, the 5th Baron St Oswald, who *d* 1999.

COLLATERAL BRANCHES LIVING

Issue of late Hon Charles John Frederic Winn, 2nd son of 2nd Baron, *b* 1896, *d* 1968: *m* 1st, 1919 (*m diss* 1925), Hon Olive Cecilia Paget, who *d* 1974, da of 1st Baron Queenborough; 2ndly, 1929 (*m diss* 1938), Katherine, da of Henry Van Hevkelom; 3rdly, 1938, Mrs Theodora Thorpe Dixon, who *d* 1978:—
(By 1st *m*) Susan Mary Sheila, *b* 1923: *m* 1st, 1946 (*m diss* 1971), Capt Hon Geoffrey Denis Erskine Russell, late Irish Guards, now 4th Baron Ampthill; 2ndly, 1972, Col Edward Remington-Hobbs, DSO, OBE, who *d* 1997, of 31 Melton Court, SW7 3JQ, and has issue (by 1st *m*) (*see* B Ampthill). —— (By 2nd *m*) Michael Peter Anthony (4 Battery Place, Charleston, South Carolina 29401, USA), *b* 1933: *m* 1963, Caroline Knowlton Lipscomb, of New York, and Southport, Conn, USA, and has issue living, Charles Michael Anthony, *b* 1967.

Issue of late Maj Hon Reginald Henry Winn, Gren Gds, 3rd son of 2nd Baron, *b* 1899, *d* 1985: *m* 1924, Alice (ante), da of late Moncure Perkins, of Virginia, USA:—
Elizabeth Susan (Neville House, 15 Onslow Gdns, SW7), *b* 1925. —— Anne, *b* 1926: *m* 1947 (*m diss* 19—), Hon Mark Hugh Wyndham, MC, 12th R Lancers, and has issue (*see* B Egremont). *Residence* – Thatched Cottage, Chilson, Charlbury, Oxon.

Grandchildren of late Hon Cecil Henry Winn (infra): —
Issue of late Maj Henry John Winn, DSO, MC, *b* 1914, *d* 1991: *m* 1960, Pamela Sylva (Exelby House, Exelby, Bedale, N Yorks), only da of late Ernest Charles de Rougemont, CBE:—
Martin John (93 Palace Rd, SW2), *b* 1961: *m* 1986, Caroline Anne, da of Douglas da Costa, of 6 Clifton Gdns, W9, and has issue living, Hugo John, *b* 1991, — Hannah Louise, *b* 1993, — Eleanor Mary Heather, *b* 1997. —— Fiona Jane, *b* 1962: *m* 1988, Bruce J. Moriarty, of 7 Habgood St, E Fremantle, W Australia 6158, son of Donald Moriarty, of Halifax, Nova Scotia, Canada, and has issue living, Ryan James, *b* 1996, — Kate Sylva, *b* 1998.

Issue of late Hon Cecil Henry Winn, 5th son of 1st Baron, *b* 1866, *d* 1934: *m* 1913, Alice Marjorie Iris, who *d* 1964, da of late Henry Darley, of Aldby Park, York:—
(Geoffrey) Mark Victor, *b* 1918; late Capt RE; 1940-45 War in NW Europe and SE Asia: *m* 1st, 1958, Alice Alexandra, who *d* 1991, da of late Peter Haig-Thomas (*see* E Normanton, 1971 Edn); 2ndly, 1994, Mrs H. (Patsy) Macmillan, and has issue living (by 1st *m*), Geoffrey George WINN-DARLEY, *b* 1966, assumed the additional surname and arms of Darley by Royal licence 1985: *m* 1997, Sara L., da of Giles Shepherd-Cross, of Skewsby, York, and has issue living, Serena Alice *b* 1999, — Alice Rosemary *b* 1960: *m* 1993, Christopher Milan Nenadich, of Lakes Farm, Sutton, Hereford, and has issue living, Megan Rose *b* 1993, Eliza Emily May *b* 1996, — Iris Alexandra, *b* 1964. *Residence* – Aldby Park, Buttercrambe, York.

PREDECESSORS – **(1)** ROWLAND Winn (el son of late Charles Winn, of Nostell Priory, Yorkshire, and Appleby Hall, Lincolnshire); *b* 1820; MP for N Lincolnshire (*C*) 1868-85; a Lord of the Treasury 1874-85; was *cr Baron St Oswald*, of Nostell, co York (peerage of United Kingdom) 1885; *m* 1854, Harriet Maria Amelia, who *d* 1926, da of late Col Henry Dumaresq; *d* 1893; *s* by his el son **(2)** ROWLAND, 2nd Baron; *b* 1857; sat as MP for Pontefract (*C*) 1885-93: *m* 1892, Mabel Susan, who *d* 1919, da of Sir Charles Forbes, 4th Bt, of Newe, Aberdeenshire; *d* 1919; *s* by his son **(3)** ROWLAND GEORGE, 3rd Baron; *b* 1893; Capt Coldm Gds: *m* 1915, Eve Carew, who *d* 1976, da of Charles Greene; *d* 1957; *s* by his el son **(4)** ROWLAND DENYS GUY, 4th Baron, *b* 1916; Maj King's R Irish Hus, DL of W Riding of Yorks and of York, a Lord in Waiting 1959-62; Joint Parliamentary Sec, Min of Agric, Fisheries and Food 1962-64; Member European Parliament, Strasbourg 1973-84; served Middle East 1940-44, SE Asia 1945 (wounded, despatches), Korea 1950-52 (MC): *m* 1st, 1952 (*m diss* 1955), Laurian, da of Sir (George) Roderick Jones, KBE; 2ndly, 1955, Marie Wanda, who *d* 1981, yr da of late Sigismund Jaxa-Chamiec, of Filtrowa, Warsaw, Poland; *d* 1984; *s* by his brother **(5)** DEREK EDWARD ANTHONY, 5th Baron; *b* 1919; Capt Parachute Regt (Regular Army Reserve); European War 1939-45 in Middle East and N Africa (wounded); ADC to Gov-Gen of NZ 1943-45; Malayan Police Service 1948-51: *m* 1954, Charlotte Denise Eileen, only da of late Wilfrid Haig Lloyd (*see* Oakeley, Bt, 1985 Edn); *d* 1999; *s* by his only son **(6)** CHARLES ROWLAND ANDREW, 6th Baron and present peer.

ST VINCENT, VISCOUNT (Jervis) (Viscount UK 1801)

RONALD GEORGE JAMES JERVIS, 7th Viscount; *b* 3 May 1905; *s* 1940; *ed* Sherborne; 1939-45 War as acting Lt-Cdr RNVR, JP Som 1950-55: *m* 1945, (Constance) Phillida Anne, only da of late Lieut-Col Robert Hector Logan, OBE, late Loyal Regt, and has issue.

Arms – Sable, a chevron ermine, between three martlets argent. **Crest** – Out of a naval coronet or, encircled round the rim by a wreath of laurel vert, a demi-pegasus argent, wings elevated azure, thereon a fleur-de-lis gold. **Supporters** – *Dexter*, an eagle, wings elevated, grasping in the left claw a thunderbolt, all proper; *sinister*, a pegasus argent, wings elevated azure, thereon a fleur-de-lis or.
Residence – Les Charrières, St Ouen, Jersey.

SONS LIVING

Hon EDWARD ROBERT JAMES, *b* 12 May 1951; *ed* Radley: *m* 1977, Victoria Margaret, only da of late Wilton J. Oldham, of Jersey, and has issue living, James Richard Anthony, *b* 1982, — Emma Margaret Anne, *b* 1980. *Residence* Colinas Verdes 26, Bensafrim, Lagos 8600, Algarve, Portugal.
Hon Ronald Nigel John, *b* 1954; *ed* Eton, and Durham Univ: *m* 1983, Gillian Lois, da of Geoffrey Sharp, and has issue living, David Stephen, *b* 1988, — Sarah Frances, *b* 1986, — Ruth Margaret, *b* 1991. *Residence* – The Brooms, Congleton, Cheshire.

DAUGHTER LIVING

Hon Cassandra Phillida Anne RINGSELL, *b* 1949: reverted to her former married surname by deed poll 1980: *m* 1st, 1970 (*m diss* 1976), Martyn Leslie Ringsell; 2ndly, 1979 (*m diss* 1981), James E. M. Colbeck-Welch, and has issue living (by 1st *m*), Brett George Jervis, *b* 1972, — Christopher Charles Robert, *b* 1974.

COLLATERAL BRANCHES LIVING

Issue of late Col Hon St Leger Henry Jervis, DSO, 5th son of 3rd Viscount, *b* 1863, *d* 1952: *m* 1905, Hilda Maud, who *d* 1942, only da of late Thomas Collier:—
Hilda Violet Ursula, *b* 1909: *m* 1934 (*m diss* 1949), Lieut-Col John Alexander Goschen, OBE, Gren Gds (afterwards 3rd Viscount Goschen), who *d* 1977. *Residence* – Pitminster Lodge, Taunton, Som.

Grandsons of Edward St Vincent Parker-Jervis, son of late Edward John Parker-Jervis, el son of late Hon Edward Swynfen Parker-Jervis, yst son of 2nd Viscount:—
Issue of late Lieut St Vincent John Parker-Jervis, RNVR, *b* 1891, *d* 1931: *m* 1917, Marianita (who *m* 2ndly, 19—, John Frederick Harker), yr da of late C. T. Roller, of Burnham, Bucks:—
Antony St Vincent, *b* 1919; *ed* Ampleforth Coll; Capt Roy Canadian Horse Artillery; head of Mathematics Dept, St George's Sch, BC, 1961-86: *m* 1942, Doris Beauchamp, who *d* 1996, da of late George Beauchamp Taverner, of Winryl, East Close, Middleton-on-Sea, Sussex, and Midhurst, Longwood Drive, Roehampton, SW, and has issue living, Nicholas St Vincent (6474 109th St, Delta, BC, Canada V4E IH3), *b* 1943; *ed* Univ of BC (BA) and Oxford Univ (Dip Ed): *m* 1st, 1967 (*m diss* 1976), Patsy K., da of Masao Hayashi, of Steveston, BC; 2ndly, 1976, Hazel Anne, da of Edward Lester Pierrot, and widow of Robert Frank Wright, and has issue living (by 2nd *m*), John St Vincent *b* 1980, Laura Anne *b* 1978, — Antony Leigh, *b* 1947: *m* 1981, Lisa Robbyn Marie, da of George Edmond Joseph Ayotte, and has issue living, Sarah Marie Grace *b* 1983, — Hilary Anne, *b* 1950. *Residence* – 6258 Vine St, Vancouver, BC, Canada V6M 4A8. — Noel John, *b* 1920: *ed* Ampleforth, and Univ of British Columbia (BA); formerly Prof of English, Univ of Alberta; late Lance-Bombardier, Roy Canadian Artillery: *m* 1st, 1950 (*m diss* 1954), Jean Mary Columbus; 2ndly, 1956, Betty, 3rd da of late Jasper Rutherford, and has issue living, (by 2nd *m*) Jonathan Rutherford, *b* 1962. *Residence* – 3549 Cardiff Place, Victoria, BC, Canada.

Granddaughters of late Maj Edward Mainwaring Parker-Jervis, MC (infra):—
Issue of late Robert St Vincent Parker-Jervis, *b* 1908, *d* 1973: *m* 1st, 1936 (*m diss* 1946), Lucy, who *d* 1966, only da of Maj William Edward Burrill, of The Greens, Masham, Ripon; 2ndly, 1946, Pamela Violet, who *d* 1981, da of late Capt Alexander Moore Vandeleur, Life Gds (By Knaresborough), and formerly wife of Lt-Col Lennox John Livingstone-Learmonth, DSO, MC:—
(By 1st *m*) Diana Elizabeth, *b* 1937: *m* 1958, Roger Parker-Jervis (infra). —— (By 2nd *m*) Linda, *b* 1946: *m* 1970, Brig Michael Lord, of Orchard Farm, Tutts Clump, nr Reading, Berks, and has issue living, Simon James Austin, *b* 1972, — Guy Robert Thomas, *b* 1974, — Patrick Michael Jervis, *b* 1977. —— Sally-Anne *b* 1947: *m* 1981, John William Parsons, CBE, *d* 1997, of Townsend House, Corfe Castle, Dorset, son of late Frederick John Parsons, of Wareham, Dorset, and has issue living, Timothy John Jervis, *b* 1987, and two adopted children, Dominic William Robert, *b* 1989, — Victoria Hannah Vandeleur, *b* 1990. —— Angela, *b* 1949: *m* 1984, (Peter) Jeremy Woodland Payne, of 50 Narbonne Av, SW4 9JT, son of Dr R. F. Payne, of Huxtable Farm, Devon, and has issue living, Christopher William, *b* 1992, — Emily Louise, *b* 1989.

Granddaughter of late William Robert Parker Jervis, 3rd son of late Hon Edward Swynfen Parker-Jervis, yst son of 2nd Viscount:—
Issue of late Major Edward Mainwaring Parker-Jervis, MC, *b* 1880, *d* 1935: *m* 1906, Eleanor Dora, who *d* 1955, da of Alfred Charles Lyon, formerly of Albrighton Hall, Albrighton, Shropshire:—
Rosemary Eleanor, *b* 1914: *m* 1940, Brig Francis Peter Barclay, DSO, MC, late Royal Norfolk Regt, who *d* 1992, and has had issue, Robin Peter, *b* 1943; *ed* Harrow, and RMA Sandhurst, 2nd Lieut 1st East Anglian Regt; *d* 1964 as a result of a mountain accident while serving in Aden, — Christopher Thomas, *b* 1946; *ed* Harrow. *Residence* – Little Dunham Lodge, King's Lynn, Norfolk.

Grandchildren of late Humphrey Parker-Jervis (infra):—
Issue of late Capt John Humphrey Parker-Jervis, RE, *b* 1923, *d* 1989: *m* 1956, Elizabeth Margaret (Martens Hall Farm, Longworth, Abingdon, Oxon), da of Richard Durrant Trotter, of Brin House, Flichity, Inverness:—
Simon Humphrey, *b* 1961: *m* 1997, Béatrice, elder da of Bernard Mathivon, of Meudon, France, and has issue living, Emma, *b* 1999. —— Fiona Mary, *b* 1965. —— Mary Clare, *b* 1966: *m* 1993, Andrew Hank Shaw, son of Stephen Shaw, of Crockham Hill, Kent, and has issue living, George Angus John, *b* 1995, — Fergus Humphrey, *b* 1997.

Grandsons of late Thomas Swynfen Parker-Jervis, 8th son of late Hon Edward Swynfen Parker-Jervis (ante):—
Issue of late Humphrey Parker-Jervis, *b* 1889, *d* 1948: *m* 1922, Helen Frances, who *d* 1998, aged 100, da of Sir John Ralph Starkey, 1st Bt:—
Christopher Thomas (Lane Cottage, Watledge, Nailsworth, Glos), *b* 1929; *ed* Radley; Lt-Cdr RN (ret): *m* 1959, Gillian Bowden, and has issue living, Edward Christopher, *b* 1960; *ed* Abingdon, and St Catherine's Coll, Oxford: *m* 1990, Sarah Jane, only da of Rev John Musgrave Shorrock, of Bredgar Vicarage, Sittingbourne, Kent, and has issue living, James Oliver *b* 1997, Helen Alexandra *b* 1993, — William Thomas, *b* 1965; *ed* Abingdon, and Aberdeen Univ, — Sarah Belinda, *b* 1967.

Issue of late George Parker-Jervis, *b* 1895, *d* 1973: *m* 1924, Ruth Alice, who *d* 1990, da of late Charles Edward Farmer:—
James (Templewood, Brechin, Angus DD9 7PT), *b* 1926; *ed* Eton; Lt-Cdr RN (ret): *m* 1956, Sybil Anne, da of late Thomas Prain Douglas Murray, MBE, TD, of Templewood, Brechin, Angus, and widow of Hon John Michael Inigo Cross (*see* V Cross), and has issue living, Andrew Swynfen (Home Farm House, Little Walden, Saffron Walden, Essex CB10 1XE), *b* 1959; *ed* Eton, and Edinburgh Univ: *m* 1990, Victoria L., yst da of late Rowan B. Hutchison, and of Mrs D. Allen, of Rendham Court, Saxmundham, Suffolk, and has issue living, Rowan Swynfen *b* 1995, Clovis George Balfour *b* 1997, Holly Audrey *b* 1993, — Harriet Anne, *b* 1957: *m* 1985, Frederick Gibson, son of late F. W. Gibson, and has issue living, James Frederick *b* 1989, Rosie Alice *b* 1993. —— Nicholas (The Manor House, South Littleton, Evesham, Worcs), *b* 1927; *ed* Eton, and at Magdalene Coll, Camb: *m* 1960, Elisabeth Henley, da of J. T. Morgan, of Llaneinydd, St

Nicholas, Glam, and has issue living, George Rhidian, *b* 1961, — Thomas Fabyan, *b* 1974, — Catherine Elisabeth, *b* 1964: *m* 1995, Harry M. Crossley, elder son of Martin Crossley, of Auchtermuchty, Fife, and has issue living, Barnaby Horace *b* 1996, Suzannah Janet *b* 1999. ——— Roger, *b* 1931; *ed* Eton, and Magdalene Coll, Camb: *m* 1958, Diana Elizabeth, da of late Robert St Vincent Parker-Jervis (ante), and has issue living, Edward Swynfen, *b* 1959: *m* 1997, Alison Kingsbury, and has issue living, Edward John *b* 1995, Juliette Elizabeth *b* 1997, — Guy, *b* 1960: *m* 1985 (*m diss* 1993), Linda Johnston, — Lucy Alice, *b* 1966: *m* 1989, Julian Guy Rutherford, yr son of Ian Rutherford, of Childwickbury, Herts, and has issue living, Patrick Ian *b* 1999, Laura Diana *b* 1992, Chloë Jane Lucy *b* 1994. *Residence* – The Old Schoolhouse, Brill, Bucks.

PREDECESSORS – (1) *Adm Rt Hon Sir* JOHN Jervis, GCB, 2nd son of late Swynfen Jervis, of Meaford, Staffordshire; *b* 1734; a celebrated Naval Commander, who in 1797 obtained a splendid victory over the Spanish Fleet at Cape St Vincent; First Lord of the Admiralty 1801-4; MP for Launceston 1783-4, for Great Yarmouth 1784-90, and for Chipping Wycombe 1790-94: *m* 1783, his cousin, Martha, who *d* 1816, da of late Rt Hon Sir Thomas Parker, Lord Ch Baron of the Exchequer; *cr Baron Jervis*, of Meaford, co Stafford, and *Earl of St Vincent* (peerage of Great Britain) 1797, and *Viscount St Vincent*, of Meaford, co Stafford (peerage of United Kingdom) 1801, with remainder to his nephews, William Henry Ricketts and Edward Jervis Ricketts successively, and after them to his niece Mary, wife of 7th Earl of Northesk, and her heirs male; *d* 1823, when the barony and earldom became extinct and the viscountcy devolved upon his surviving nephew (2) EDWARD JERVIS Ricketts, 2nd Viscount; *b* 1767; assumed by Roy licence 1823 the surname of Jervis only; *d* 1859; *s* by his grandson (3) CARNEGIE ROBERT JOHN, 3rd Viscount; *b* 1825: *m* 1848, Lucy Charlotte, who *d* 1900, da of John Baskervyle Glegg, of Withington Hall, Cheshire; *d* 1879; *s* by his son (4) JOHN EDWARD LEVESON, 4th Viscount; *b* 1850; *d* of wounds received at battle of Abu Klea Jan 1885; *s* by his brother (5) CARNEGIE PARKER, 5th Viscount; *b* 1855: *m* 1885 (*m diss* 1896), Rebecca May, da of late James Baston, of Barrow-in-Furness; *d* 1908; *s* by his brother (6) RONALD CLARGES, 6th Viscount; *b* 1859: *m* 1894, Marion Annie, who *d* 1911, da of late James Brown, of Orchard, Carluke, and Petit Menage, Jersey; *d* 1940; *s* by his son (7) RONALD GEORGE JAMES, 7th Viscount and present peer.

SALISBURY, MARQUESS OF (Gascoyne-Cecil) (Marquess GB 1789)

Late, but seriously

ROBERT EDWARD PETER GASCOYNE-CECIL, 6th Marquess; *b* 24 Oct 1916; *s* 1972; *ed* Eton; DL Dorset 1974; patron of seven livings, Capt Gren Gds; MP for W Bournemouth (*C*) 1950-54: *m* 1945, Marjorie Olein, da of late Capt Hon Valentine Maurice Wyndham-Quin, RN (*see* E Dunraven), and has had issue.

Arms – Quarterly: 1st and 4th barry of ten argent and azure, over all six escutcheons, three, two, and one, sable, each charged with a lion rampant of the first, a crescent gules for difference, *Cecil*; 2nd and 3rd argent, on a pale sable, a conger's head erased and erect or, charged with an ermine spot, *Gascoyne*. **Crests** – 1st, six arrows in saltire or, barbed and feathered argent, banded gules, buckled and garnished gold, surmounted by a morion or steel cap proper; 2nd, a conger's head erased and erect or, charged with an ermine spot. **Supporters** – On either side a lion ermine.
Seat – Hatfield House, Hatfield.

SONS LIVING AND DECEASED

ROBERT MICHAEL JAMES (*Rt Hon Viscount Cranborne*) (The Manor House, Cranborne, Wimborne, Dorset), *b* 30 Sept 1946; *ed* Eton, and Ch Ch Oxford; MP for Dorset South (*C*) 1979-87; DL Dorset 1988; Pres Hertfordshire Agricultural Soc since 1998; called to House of Lords in his father's Barony of Cecil 1992; Lord Privy Seal and Leader of House of Lords 1994-97, Shadow Leader House of Lords 1997-Dec 1998; PC 1994: *m* 1970, Hannah Ann, da of Lt-Col William Joseph Stirling of Keir (*see* Stirling-Maxwell, Bt, dormant), and has issue:—

SONS LIVING— *Hon* Robert Edward William, *b* 18 Dec 1970; a Page of Honour to HM 1983-86; *ed* King's Sch, Canterbury, — *Hon* James Richard, *b* 1973.

DAUGHTERS LIVING— *Hon* Elizabeth Ann, *b* 1972: *m* 1998, Stephen M. Buscher, eldest son of H. Buscher, of Snowmass, Colorado, USA, — *Hon* Georgiana, *b* 1977, — *Hon* Katherine, *b* 1977 (twin).

†*Lord* Richard Valentine, *b* 1948; *ed* Eton; Capt Gren Gds (despatches 1973); *d* 1978.
Lord Charles Edward Vere (21 Hollywood Rd, SW10), *b* 1949; *ed* Eton, and Ch Ch Oxford: *m* 1993, Virginia Edith, yr da of late Paul Zervudachi, of Morges, Switzerland, and Levanto, Italy.
Lord Valentine William (11 Shalcomb St, SW10), *b* 1952; *ed* Eton; a Page of Honour to HM Queen Elizabeth The Queen Mother 1966-67; Maj Gren Gds.
Lord Michael Hugh (PO Box 49428, Nairobi, Kenya), *b* 1960; *ed* Eton; Gren Gds: *m* 1986, Camilla Julia, yr da of late Maj Richard Jervoise Scott, TD (*see* Scott, Bt, *cr* 1962, colls), and has issue living, Hubert George, *b* 1992, — Edward William James, *b* 1996, — Daisy Alice Julia, *b* 1989.

DAUGHTER LIVING

Lady Rose Alice Elizabeth, *b* 1956: *m* 1st, 1985 (*m diss* 19—), Mark G. Flawn Thomas, yst son of Peter Flawn Thomas, of Shortbridge Mill, Piltdown, Sussex; 2ndly, 1996, Malachy Dunne.

COLLATERAL BRANCHES LIVING

Issue of late Lord (Edward Christian) David Cecil, CH, CLit, author, yr son of 4th Marquess, *b* 1902, *d* 1986: *m* 1932, Rachel, who *d* 1982, da of late Sir Desmond McCarthy:—
Jonathan Hugh, *b* 1939; *ed* Eton, and New Coll, Oxford; actor: *m* 1st, 1963 (*m diss* 1976), Vivien Sarah Frances, el da of late David Granville Heilbron, of 2 Clevedon Drive, Glasgow, W2; 2ndly, 1976, Anna Sharkey. ——— Hugh Peniston (The University, Leeds, Yorks), *b* 1941; *ed* Eton, and New Coll Oxford (BA): *m* 1972, Mirabel, da of Richard Walker, OBE, of The Close, Withington, Glos, and has issue living, Conrad Richard James, *b* 1973, — David Edward Hugh, *b* 1978, — Clementine Rachel Amelia, *b* 1975, — Stella, *b* 1984. ——— Alice Laura, *b* 1947: *m* 1975, Angelo Hornak, yr son of late Herman Hornak, and has issue living, Leo David, *b* 1979, — Francesca Rachel, *b* 1981.

Grandchildren of late Rt Rev Lord William Rupert Ernest Gascoyne-Cecil, DD, Bishop of Exeter, 2nd son of 3rd Marquess:—
Issue of late Randle William Gascoyne-Cecil, *b* 1889, *ka* 1917: *m* 1st, 1914 (*m diss* 1916), Dorothy Janaway, who *d* 19—; 2ndly, 1916, Elizabeth Claire, who *d* 1972, da of George Turner:—
(By 2nd *m*) Anne Mary (*posthumous*), *b* 1918; 1939-45 War as 2nd Officer WRNS: *m* 1945, David Bryce Wilson, Lt-Cdr RCNVR, and Canadian Foreign Ser (ret), and has issue living, Andrew David Randle (Canadian Foreign Ser, 13 Lynhaven Crescent, Nepean, Ontario K2E 5K3), *b* 1956: *m* 1988, Susan Blyth-Schofield, — Elizabeth Anne, *b* 1946: *m* 1982, Bruno Fascinato, of 52 Manitoba St, Guelph, Ontario, Canada N1E 3B9, and has issue living, Francesco Bruno Bruce *b* 1980, David Tullio Charles *b* 1986, — Carolyn Susan Mary, *b* 1948: *m* 1972, Simon Roger Williams (c/o Canadian High Commn, Canberra, Australia), — Jennifer Laura Eve *b* 1951: *m* 1982 (*m diss* 1994), Nyle Belkov, — Deborah Rosalind Louise (702 Parkdale Av, Ottawa, Ontario K1Y 1J4), *b* 1952. *Residence* – 371 Daly Av, Ottawa, Ontario, Canada K1N 6G8.

Issue of late Lt-Col Victor Alexander Gascoyne-Cecil, *b* 1891, *d* 1977: *m* 1915, Fairlie Estelle Caroline, who *d* 1980, da of late Lt-Col Arthur Watson, of Dublin:—
Rupert Arthur Victor CECIL, DFC, *b* 1917; MA Oxon; PhD; Wing-Cdr (ret) RAFVR; relinquished by deed poll 1955, the surname of Gascoyne; Vice-Prin of Linacre Coll, Oxford; 1939-45 War (DFC and Bar): *m* 1st, 1940 (*m diss* 1974), Helen Moira Rosemary Phillips, only child of late Col Roland Luker, CMG, MC; 2ndly, 19—, Anna Teresa, da of Donald Hodson, of 10 Wood Lane, Highgate, N6 (*see* V Arbuthnott, 1970 Edn), and has issue living (by 1st wife), Desmond Hugh, CMG (38 Palace Rd, E Molesey, Surrey KT8 9DL), *b* 1941; *ed* Magdalen Coll Sch, Queen's Coll, Oxford (MA), and Berne Univ; Under-Sec, HM Dip Serv; Sr Advisor to BNFL; CMG 1996: *m* 1964, Ruth Elizabeth, da of Dr Werner Sachs, of 19 Tideswell Rd, SW15, and has issue living, Thomas Desmond *b* 1966: *m* 1997, Dr Alison J. N., da of G. R. Wyborn, of Walton-on-Thames, Surrey (and has issue living, Tobias Thomas George *b* 1998), Nicholas David *b* 1968: *m* 1997, Joanna L., da of A. J. Barron, of Godalming, Surrey (and has issue living, Christopher James *b* 1999), Andrew Peter *b* 1971, Sarah Ruth *b* 1972, — Timothy Rupert (27 King's Rd, Flitwick, Bedford), *b* 1944; *ed* Magdalen Coll Sch, Exeter Coll, Oxford (MA), and Munich Univ: *m* 1977, Ursula Margaret, da of John Christopher Rotton, of Compton, Sussex, and has issue living, Robert *b* 1977, Thomas *b* 1979, — June Elizabeth (4 Pleasant Place, Bathford, Bath BA1 7TL), *b* 1946: *m* 1968 (*m diss* 1994), Michael Durnford Robb, and has issue living, Geoffrey Edward *b* 1972, Joanna Frances *b* 1970, — (by 2nd wife) Flora, *b* 1971, — Maud, *b* 1972. ——— †Anthony Robert, *b* 1921: *m* 1st, 1944 (*m diss* 1951), Mary Hood, only da of late Rev Ernest James Simpson, of Great Burstead Vicarage, Billericay, Essex; 2ndly, 1952, Alison Julia (Woodlands, Butts Green, Sandon, Chelmsford, Essex), only da of late H. C. Foster, of Little Baddow, Essex, and *d* 1998, leaving issue (by 1st *m*), Michael Anthony (Acorns, School Rd, Wickham Bishops, Essex), *b* 1946: *m* 1st, 1969 (*m diss* 1990), Carol Ann, only da of Samuel Oxford; 2ndly, 1996, Christine Mary Olive, only da of Gordon Llewellyn Elliott, of 14 Lime Tree Close, Gt Kingshill, Bucks, and has issue living (by 1st *m*), Jonathan Michael *b* 1971, Christopher Anthony *b* 1973, Victoria Ruth *b* 1976: *m* 1996, Douglas Edmund Buist, Elizabeth Carol *b* 1980, — Jennifer Jean Mary, *b* 1947: *m* 1981, John Warwick Mills, of Thorington Hall, Wherstead, Ipswich, Suffolk, and has issue living, George Frederick Cecil *b* 1986, Eleanor Mary Cecil *b* 1984, — (by 2nd *m*) Richard David (Chestnut Cottage, Butts Green, Sandon, Chelmsford, Essex CM2 7RN), *b* 1953: *m* 1978, Judith Westhorp, only da of late Geoffrey Roberts, OBE, of 5 Arley Close, Chester, and has issue living, James Anthony *b* 1981, Andrew Peter *b* 1985, Helen Elizabeth *b* 1982, — Caroline Alison (30 Poplar Grove, W6 7RE), *b* 1955, — Rosalind Julia, *b* 1962: *m* 1993, David Platt, of 2 Ilgars Cottage, Mosses Lane, S Woodham Ferrers, Chelmsford, Essex, son of Malcolm Platt, of The Wirral, Merseyside.

Grandchildren of late Lieut-Col Lord Eustace Brownlow Henry Gascoyne-Cecil, 3rd son of 2nd Marquess:—
Issue of late Rt Hon Evelyn Cecil, GBE, who was *cr Baron Rockley* 1934:—
(See that title)

PREDECESSORS – (1) *Rt Hon Sir* ROBERT Cecil, KG, PC, yr son of William Cecil, 1st Baron Burghley (*see* M Exeter); was Sec of State 1596-1612, Chancellor of Duchy of Lancaster 1597-9, Lord Privy Seal 1597-1612, and Lord High Treasurer 1608-12; *cr Baron Cecil*, of Essendon, co Rutland (peerage of England) 1603, *Viscount Cranborne* (peerage of England) 1604, and *Earl of Salisbury* (peerage of England) 1605; *d* 1612; *s* by his son (2) WILLIAM, KG, 2nd Earl; *d* 1668; *s* by his grandson (3) JAMES, KG, 3rd Earl; *d* 1683; *s* by his son (4) JAMES, 4th Earl; having become a convert to the Roman Catholic faith the House of Commons in 1689 resolved that he be impeached for high treason, but the prosecution was not proceeded with; *d* 1694; *s* by his son (5) JAMES, 5th Earl; carried King Edward's staff at the coronation of George I; *d* 1728; *s* by his son (6) JAMES, 6th Earl; *d* 1780; *s* by his son (7) JAMES, KG, 7th Earl; *cr Marquess of Salisbury* (peerage of Great Britain) 1789; sat as MP for Bedwin; was Lord Chamberlain of the Household 1783-1804, and Lord-Lieut of Herts; *d* 1823; *s* by his son (8) JAMES BROWNLOW, KG, PC, DCL, 2nd Marquess; *b* 1791; was Lord Pres of the Council 1858-9, and Lord-Lieut of Middlesex; in 1821 assumed by Roy licence the additional surname of Gascoyne: *m* 1821, Frances Mary, da and heir of late Bamber Gascoyne; 2ndly, 1847, Lady Mary Catherine Sackville-West, da of 5th Earl De la Warr; *d* 1868; *s* by his 2nd son (9) ROBERT ARTHUR TALBOT, KG, GCVO, PC, 3rd Marquess; *b* 1830; MP for Stamford (C) 1853-68; Sec of State for India 1866-7 and 1874-8, and for Foreign Affairs 1878-80, Special Ambassador at Conference on Eastern Affairs held at Constantinople 1876-7, 2nd Plen for Great Britain at Congress of Berlin 1878, Prime Minister and Sec of State for Foreign Affairs June 1885 to Feb 1886, Prime Minister and First Lord of the Treasury June 1886 to Jan 1887, Prime Minister and Sec of State for Foreign Affairs Jan 1887 to Aug 1892, and again Prime Minister and Sec of State for Foreign Affairs June 1895 to Nov 1900, and Prime Minister and Lord Privy Seal 1900-1902: *m* 1857, Georgina, CI, VA, who *d* 1899, da of late Hon Sir Edward Hall Alderson, a Baron of the Court of Exchequer; *d* 1903; *s* by his son (10) JAMES EDWARD HUBERT, KG, GCVO, CB, PC, 4th Marquess; *b* 1861; sometime High Steward of Westminster and Hertford; served in Herts Yeo, Bedfordshire Regt (TA), and RA (TA), becoming Maj-Gen; S Africa 1900 (despatches, CB); was Under-Sec of State for Foreign Affairs 1900-1903, Lord Privy Seal 1903-5, Lord Privy Seal and Pres of Board of Trade 1905, and Lord Pres of the Council and Dep Leader of the House of Lords (also temporary Chancellor of the Duchy of Lancaster) 1922-4, and again Lord Privy Seal 1924-9 (also Leader of the House of Lords 1925-9, and of Opposition 1929-31); appointed Lord High Steward 1937; bore St Edward's Crown at Coronation of King George VI; sat as MP for Darwen Div of N-E Lancashire (*C*) 1885-92 and for Rochester 1893-1903: *m* 1887, Lady Cicely Alice Gore, who *d* 1955, second da of 5th Earl of Arran; *d* 1947; *s* by his son (11) ROBERT ARTHUR JAMES, KG, PC, 5th Marquess *b* 1893; MP for S Dorset (*C*) 1929-41; called to House of Lords in his father's Barony of Cecil 1941; Sec of State for Dominions Affairs 1940-42 and 1943-45, for Colonies 1942 and for Commonwealth Relations 1952, Lord Privy Seal 1942-43 and 1951-52, and Lord Pres of the Council 1952-57; Leader of House of Lords 1942-43 and 1951-57; Chancellor Liverpool Univ 1951-71; Chancellor of Order of the Garter 1960-72: *m* 1915, Elizabeth Vere, who *d* 1982, da of late Col Rt Hon Lord Richard Frederick Cavendish, CB, CMG (D Devonshire); *d* 1972; *s* by his son (12) ROBERT EDWARD PETER, 6th Marquess and present peer; also Earl of Salisbury, Viscount Cranborne, and Baron Cecil.

SALMON, BARONY OF (Salmon) (Extinct 1991)

SON LIVING OF LIFE BARON

Hon David Neville Cyril (Holne Cott, Holne, nr Ashburton, Devon), *b* 1935: *m* 1st, 1958 (*m diss* 1972), Heather Turner-Laing; 2ndly, 1973, Mrs Sarah Harrison, da of Herman L. Eberts, of Montreal, Canada, and formerly wife of Noel Harrison, and has issue living, Alexander, *b* 19—, — Marc, *b* 19—.

DAUGHTER LIVING OF LIFE BARON

Hon Gai Rencie, *b* 1933: *m* 1st, 1955, Martin Treves, who *d* 1970; 2ndly, 1973, Geoffrey Robinson, CBE, and has issue (by 1st *m*), William Martin, *b* 1960, — George Thomas, *b* 1963, — Toby Charles, *b* 1966, — Emma Elizabeth Rencie, *b* 1959.

Saltersford, Baron; title of Earl of Courtown on Roll of HL.

SALTOUN, LADY (Fraser) (Lordship S 1445)
(Title pronounced "Salton")

FLORA MARJORY FRASER, *Lady Saltoun; b* 18 Oct 1930; *s* 1979; Chief of the name of Fraser: *m* 6 Oct 1956, Capt Alexander Arthur Alphonso David Maule Ramsay of Mar, Grenadier Guards (ret) (*see* E Dalhousie, colls), and has issue.

Arms – Azure, three fraises argent. Crests – *Dexter*, on a mount a flourish of strawberries leaved and fructed proper. *Sinister*, an ostrich holding in its beak a horseshoe proper. Supporters – Two angels proper with wings expanded and vested in long garments or.
Residence – Inverey House, Braemar, Aberdeenshire AB35 5YB.

DAUGHTERS LIVING

Hon KATHARINE INGRID MARY ISABEL FRASER, *b* 11 Oct 1957; assumed the surname and arms of Fraser by Warrant of Lord Lyon King of Arms 1973: *m* 3 May 1980, Capt Mark Malise Nicolson, Irish Guards, only son of late Maj Malise Allen Nicolson, MC, of Frog Hall, Tilston, Malpas, Cheshire, and has issue living, Alexander William Malise FRASER *b* 5 July 1990, — Louise Alexandra Patricia, *b* 1984, — Juliet Victoria Katharine, *b* 1988. *Residence* – Cairnbulg Castle, Fraserburgh, Aberdeenshire AB43 5TN.

Hon Alice Elizabeth Margaret, *b* 8 July 1961: *m* 1990, David Ramsay, yr son of Ronald Ramsey, of St James, Barbados, and has issue living, Alexander David, *b* 1991, — George, *b* 1995, — Oliver, *b* (twin) 1995, — Victoria Alice, *b* 1994.

Hon Elizabeth Alexandra Mary RAMSAY OF MAR, *b* 15 April 1963.

COLLATERAL BRANCHES LIVING

Issue of late Rear Adm Hon George Fraser, DSO, RN, 2nd son of 18th Lord, b 1887, d 1970: m 1st, 1920, Elizabeth FRASER SPENCER STANHOPE, who d 1964, having assumed by Roy licence 1945, the additional surnames of Spencer Stanhope, da of late John Montague Spencer-Stanhope (Milborne-Swinnerton-Pilkington, Bt, colls); 2ndly, 1934, Margaret Elizabeth, who d 1999, da of Reginald Barnes, of St Ermin's, Westminster:—

(By 1st m) Simon Walter (Mains of Tilliefoure, Monymusk, Inverurie, Aberdeenshire AB51 7JB; New Club), b 1924; ed Eton: m 1st, 1950 (m diss 1962), Jean Madeline Frances, da of late Prof John Masson Gulland, FRS, of 8 Great Stuart St, Edinburgh; 2ndly, 1962 (m diss 1971), Yvonne, da of Edwin Valère Newby; 3rdly, 1971 (m diss 1976), Cheryl Mary Eleanor, da of David Lloyd McNeil Williams of Summerfield House, Cheshire, and formerly wife of Richard Charles Sheffield (see Sheffield, Bt, colls); 4thly, 1976 (m diss 1983), Meryl, da of John Ingham, of Halifax, W Yorks; 5thly, 1987, Marjorie, who d 1995, widow of late Neil W. Cameron, MD, ChB, and da of late Sydney Donaldson; 6thly, 1995, Avice Moira, da of late James Finlayson Cunningham, MB, ChB, of Eyemouth and Monymusk, and has had issue (by 1st m) Isabel Madeline, b 1951, — Elspeth Caroline, b 1954; MB, ChB 1978 Aberdeen, MRCGP 1982, — (by 2nd m) Alistair John (Jowett House, Bark House Lane, Cawthorne, Barnsley, S Yorks S75 4AS), b 1963: m 1989, Marie-Catherine Elizabeth, da of James Sigston, of Prenton, Wirral, and has issue living, Alexander James Walter b 1995, Robert Conrad b 1997, — Deborah Gail, b 1965, — (by 3rd m) James David, b 1971, — †William Alexander, b 1972; d 1998. —— (By 2nd m) Robert Andrew Gerard (Suikerbos, Gordons Bay, Cape Province, S Africa), b 1935: m 1964, Sarah Elizabeth, da of Brig Gerald Edward Peck, CBE, DSO, and has issue living, David Alexander George, b 1966, — Fiona Elizabeth, b 1965. —— Patrick George (Silverhill, Kenilworth, Cape Province, S Africa), b 1938: m 1975, Patricia Aletta, da of late Dr Peter John Frost, and has issue living, Alexandra Nelle, b 1979, — Sophie Elizabeth, b 1981, — Camilla Mary, b 1981.

Issue of late Brig Hon William Fraser, DSO, MC, yst son of 18th Lord, b 1890, d 1964: m 1919, Pamela Cynthia, who d 1975, da of late Cyril Francis Maude (V Hawarden, colls), and widow of Maj William La Touche Congreve, VC, DSO, MC:—
Sir David William, GCB, OBE (Vallenders, Isington, Alton, Hants GU34 4PP; Turf and Pratt's Clubs), b 1920; Gen late Gren Gds; ed Eton, and Ch Ch, Oxford; Hon DLitt Reading 1992; 1939-45 War; Malaya 1948: Cyprus 1958, Cameroun 1961, and Borneo 1964; GOC 4th Div 1969-71, Asst Ch of Defence Staff 1971-73, and Vice-Ch of Gen Staff 1973-75, UK Mil Rep to NATO 1975-77, Comdt R Coll of Defence Studies 1977-80; ADC (Gen) 1977; Col Royal Hampshire Regt 1981-87; Chm of Treloar Tst and Gov body of Treloar Coll 1982-93; OBE (Mil) 1952, KCB (Mil) 1973, GCB (Mil) 1980; a DL of Hants since 1982: m 1st, 1947 (m diss 1952), Anne, da of late Brig Edward William Sturgis Balfour, CVO, DSO, OBE, MC (E Balfour); 2ndly, 1957, Julia Frances Oldridge, da of late Maj C. James Oldridge de la Hey, and has issue living, (by 1st m) Antonia Isabella, b 1949: m 1st, 1972 (m diss 1975), Thomas Harney; 2ndly 1975 (m diss 1979), Thomas Bantock; 3rdly, 1981, Timothy Hanbury, of Willow Cottage, E Walton, Kings Lynn, Norfolk, and has issue living (by 2nd m), Amaryllis Eva b 1975, (by 3rd m) Edan William Samson b 1985, — (by 2nd m) (Alexander) James (23a Lansdowne Rd, W11 3AG), b 1960: m 1997, Stephanie Mary, eldest da of Alastair Struthers, of Craigmaddie, Milngavie, and has issue living, Iona Elizabeth b 1999, — Simon William David (Mountfield Court, Robertsbridge, E Sussex), b 1963: m 1991, Lucinda Anne, elder da of Thomas Edward Sydney Egerton, of Chaddleworth, Newbury, Berks, and has issue living, a son b 1994, a son b 1996, a da b 1998, — Arabella Katharine, b 1958: m 1984, Lt-Col Gordon Thomas Riddell Birdwood, Blues and Royals, of 31 Alexander St, W2, son of Lt-Col Richard Birdwood, MC, DL, of Horwood House, Horwood, Bideford, Devon and has issue living, a da b 1993, — Lucy Caroline (Hon Mrs Alexander Baring), b 1965: m 1992, Hon Alexander Nicholas John Baring, of 109 Portobello Rd, W11, yr son of 7th Baron Ashburton, KCVO, and has issue (see that title).

Issue of late Hon Mary Alexandra Fraser, da of 18th Lord, b 1892, d 1969: m 1st, 1918, Lt-Cdr John Robert Auber Codrington, RN, who d 1918 (V Hambleden); 2ndly, 1928, Maj Arthur Balcarres Wardlaw Ramsay, DL, JP (B Magheramorne, colls), who d 1956:—
(By 2nd m) Euphan Mary (Lady Hanbury-Tenison), b 1931: m 1955, Sir Richard Hanbury-Tenison, KCVO, JP, Lord Lieut of Monmouthshire, of Clytha Park, Mon, and has issue living, John Wardlaw (Bettws, Clytha Hill, Raglan, Mon), b 1957: m 1993, Laura Katharine, only da of Sir Robert Lucian Wade-Gery, KCMG, KCVO, of 7 Rothwell St, NW1, — William Ayscough, b 1962: m 1997, Mina Choi, — Capel Thomas, b 1965: m 1992, Beatrice Hannah, eldest da of Alan Hutchison, of Wern-y-Cwm, Abergavenny, and has issue living, William Augustus b 1992, — Sarah, b 1956: m 1984, Dr Martin S. Tolley, yr son of Canon George Tolley, of Dore, Sheffield, and has issue living, Thomas b 1986, Sophie Margaret b 1989, Felicity Ruth b 1993, — Laura Mary, b 1966: m 1991, A. John Femi-Ola. —— Elizabeth Mary, b 1934: m 1955, Simon Anthony Helyar Walker-Heneage, of The Old Rectory, Wanstrow, Shepton Mallet, Somerset BA4 4TQ, and has issue living, James Arthur, b 1957: m 1987, Charlotte Elizabeth, da of late Roland Shott, of North Farm House, Ashmore, Wilts, and has issue living, Eliza Mary b 1993, — Celia Mary, b 1956: m 1990, Paul Maxwell Gurowich, of 6 Loder Rd, Brighton, son of Peter Gurowich, of 10 Godwin Close, Winchester, and has issue living, Timothy Peter b 1991, and an adopted son, Aaron Finbarr Simon b 1994 (adopted 1997), — Arabella Jane, b 1959: m 1985, Nicholas David Douro Hoare, of 66 Winchedon Rd, SW6, son of Michael Douro Hoare, of Downsland Court, Ditchling, Hassocks, Sussex, and has issue living, Thomas b 1988, Charlie b 1997, — Sophie Dionysia b 1962: m 1988, Nicholas John Gibson Wright, son of David John Vernon Wright, of 11 Davenant Rd, Oxford, and has issue living, Flora Clemence Elizabeth b 1990, Lily Dionysia b 1992, — Sarah Phoebe, b 1974.

PREDECESSORS – (1-6) Sir LAURENCE Abernethy; cr Lord Saltoun, of Abernethy (peerage of Scotland) 1445, and the title passed in regular succession for five generations; in 1587 the 6th Lord was s by his son (7) GEORGE, 7th Lord; s by his son (8) JOHN, 8th Lord; s by his son (9) ALEXANDER, 9th Lord; dsp 1668; s by his cousin (10) ALEXANDER, 10th Lord, son of Margaret, da of 7th Lord, by her m with Alexander Fraser, of Philorth; title confirmed by patent 1670 and ratified by Parliament; wounded at battle of Worcester; d 1693; s by his grandson (11) WILLIAM, 11th Lord; d 1716; s by his son (12) ALEXANDER, 12th Lord; d 1748; s by his el son (13) ALEXANDER, 13th Lord; d unm 1751; s by his brother (14) GEORGE, 14th Lord; d 1782; s by his son (15) ALEXANDER, 15th Lord; d 1793; s by his son (16) ALEXANDER GEORGE, 16th Lord; a Lieut-Gen in the Army, and Representative Peer; dsp 1853; s by his nephew (17) ALEXANDER, 17th Lord, son of Hon William, 3rd son of 15th Lord; was a Representative Peer: m 1849, Charlotte, 2nd da of Thomas Browne Evans, Esq, of Dean House, Oxfordshire; d 31 Jan 1886; s by his son (18) ALEXANDER WILLIAM FREDERICK, CMG, 18th Lord; b 1851; a Representative Peer for Scotland, and Capt King's Body Guard for Scotland (Roy Co of Archers): m 1885, Mary Helena, who d 1940, sister of Sir Henry Christopher Grattan-Bellew, 3rd Bt; d 1933; s by his el son (19) ALEXANDER ARTHUR, MC, 19th Lord; b 1886; a Representative Peer for Scotland 1935-63; Capt Gordon Highlanders; a Member of Roy Co of Archers (Queen's Body Guard for Scotland); 1914-18 War (prisoner, MC): m 1920, Dorothy Geraldine, who d 1985, da of Sir Charles Glynne Earle Welby, 5th Bt, CB; d 1979; s by his only da (20) FLORA MARJORY, present peeress.

SAMUEL, VISCOUNT (Samuel) (Viscount UK 1937)

TURN NOT ASIDE

DAVID HERBERT SAMUEL, 3rd Viscount; *b* 8 July 1922; *s* 1978; *ed* Balliol Coll, Oxford (MA); PhD Hebrew Univ, Jerusalem 1953; Sherman Prof Emeritus of Physical Chemistry Weizmann Inst of Science, Rehovot, Israel, and Pres Shenkar Coll of Textile Technology and Fashion, Ramat Gan, Israel; Research Fellow, Chemistry Dept, Harvard Univ, Camb, Mass, USA 1957-58; Research Fell, Chemical Biodynamics Lab (LRL), Univ of California, Berkeley 1965-66; Visiting Royal Soc Prof, Zoology Dept (MRC Neuroimmunology Unit), Univ Coll, London 1974-75; Visiting Prof, Pharmacology Dept, Yale Univ Sch of Medicine 1983-84; McLaughlin Prof, Medical Sch McMaster Univ, Hamilton, Ont 1984; Dep Chm of Scientific Council Weizmann Inst 1963-65, Dean, Faculty of Chemistry, Weizmann Inst 1971-73, Dir Centre for Neurosciences and Behavioural Research, Weizmann Inst, 1977-87; Member US-Israel Educational (Fulbright) Foundation Bd 1969-74 (Chm 1974-75); Member Advisory Bd, Bat-Sheva de Rothschild Foundation for the Advancement of Science in Israel 1970-83; Academic Advisory Cttee, Everyman's (Open) Univ 1976-83; Bd of Governors, Bezallel Acad of Arts and Design since 1976; Council, Israel Chemical Soc 1977-83; Member Israel Exec Cttee, America-Israel Cultural Foundation 1978-88 (Chm 1985-88); a Gov Tel-Aviv Museum since 1980; Member Council Anglo Israel Assoc, London since 1982; titular Member Cttee for Chemical Education of Internat Union of Pure and Applied Chemistry 1982-91; Member Advisory Cttee and Bd of Trustees, Israel Centre for Psychobiology since 1973, and Bd of Trustees, Menninger Foundation, Topeka, KS, USA; co-editor of *Aging of the Brain* (1983), Member Editorial Bd of *Journal of Labelled Compounds and Radiopharmaceuticals*; *Brain Behaviour and Immunity*; *Alzheimer Disease and Related Disorders*, and author or co-author of over 300 scientific publications; 1939-45 War as Capt RA in India, Burma and Sumatra (despatches): *m* 1st, 1950 (*m diss* 1957), Esther, da of late J. Berelowitz, of Cape Town, S Africa; 2ndly, 1960 (*m diss* 1979), Mrs Rinna Dafni, da of late Meir Grossman, of Herzliyah, Israel; 3rdly, 1980 (*m diss* 1993), Mrs Veronika Engelhardt Grimm, da of late Ernest Engelhardt, of Toronto, Canada; 4thly, 1997, Eve Black, and has issue by 1st and 2nd *m*.

𝔄rms – Or, a bend between two caps of liberty gules, on a chief sable a balance of the first. ℭrest – In front of a sun rising or a dove wings elevated and addorsed, holding in the beak an olive branch proper. 𝔖upporters – On either side a lion or, the *dexter* gorged with a collar gules and resting the interior hind leg on a stump of oak eradicated and sprouting proper; the *sinister* gorged with an Eastern Crown also gules and resting the interior hind leg on a stump of olive eradicated and sprouting also proper.
Address – 54 Rehov Hanasi, Harishon, Rehovot, Israel.

DAUGHTERS LIVING *(By 1st marriage)*

Hon Judith (prefers to be known as *Hon Mrs Samuel Daliot*), *b* 1951, *ed* Technion-Israel Inst of Technology, and Architectural Assocn London (BArch 1972): *m* 1987, Dr Daniel Daliot, MD, and has issue living, Jonathan, *b* 1988, — Talya, *b* 1990. *Residence* – 5 Lipsky St, Tel Aviv, Israel.

(By 2nd marriage)

Hon Naomi Rachel (prefers to be known as *Hon Mrs Samuel-Wilf*), *b* 1962; *ed* Hebrew Univ, Jerusalem Law Sch (LLB 1987); with Legal Dept, Israel Police Force since 1990: *m* 1992, Nir Wilf, and has issue living, Ittamar, *b* 1994. *Residence* – 43 Hatishbi St, Haifa, Israel.

BROTHER LIVING

Hon DAN JUDAH (154 Hillspoint Rd, Westport, CT 06880, USA; The Barns, Old Mill Farm, Mill Lane, Sidlesham, Chichester, Sussex), *b* 25 March 1925; *ed* Rugby, and at Balliol Coll, Oxford (MA); formerly Maj Yorkshire Hussars; with Sch of Advanced Intern Studies, Wash 1950-51; Gen Manager of Shell Co of Thailand 1962-66, with Shell Oil Co, New York 1966-67, Pres of Belgian Shell Co 1967-70, Gen Man, Regional Marketing, Shell Internat Chemical Co, London 1971-72, Marketing Co-ordinator (Oil) 1973-75, Group Personnel Co-ordinator 1976-77, Regional Co-ordinator W Hemisphere 1977-81, and a Dir of Shell Internat Petroleum Co, London 1973-81; Pres and Chief Exec Offr Scallop Corpn, New York 1981-86; Business Consultant, Member Bd of Directors Witco Corpn, New York, Canadian Overseas Packaging Industries, and of Measurement Specialties Inc; Chm Board of Management SEATO Graduate Sch of Eng, Bangkok 1963-66, and UK Trustee of Asian Inst of Technology 1966-68, and 1973-91; Member Bd of Directors Council of the Americas, New York 1981-86, British-American Educational Foundation, New York, and Asian Inst of Technology Foundation; Dir Foundation for Management Educn, London 1975-77; Cdr of Order of Roy Crown of Thailand; Officer Order of Crown of Belgium: *m* 1st, 1957 (*m diss* 1977), Nonni (Esther), da of late Max Gordon, of Johannesburg, S Africa; 2ndly, 1981 (*m diss* 1992), Heather, da of late Angus Cumming, of Haywards Heath, and has issue living (by 1st *m*), Jonathan Herbert, *b* 1965, — Lia Miriam, *b* 1961: *m* 1987, Glenn H. Album, — Maia Tessa, *b* 1963, — (by 2nd *m*), Benjamin Angus, *b* 1983, — Sasha Tamar, *b* 1982.

AUNT LIVING

Hon Nancy Adelaide, *b* 1906; *ed* Oxford Univ (BA 1928, MA 1955): *m* 1935, Arthur Gabriel Salaman, MB, BCh, MRCS, LRCP, and has issue living, John Redcliffe (5 Brooklyn Close, Rhiwbina, Cardiff), *b* 1937; *ed* Bedales, and at Clare Coll, Camb (MA) MB, MChir, FRCS: *m* 1961, Patricia Faith, da of Edward G. Burkett, and has issue living, Robert Arthur *b* 1965, Paul William *b* 1971, Janet Susan *b* 1967, Mary Elizabeth *b* 1967. — William Herbert, *b* 1940; *ed* Bedales, and at Clare Coll, Camb (BA): *m* 1963, Alison Spears, da of Dr Philippe Sidney de Quetteville Cabot, and has issue living, Clare Rachel *b* 1966, Rachel Isabel *b* 1968, Anna Beatrice *b* 1970, — Susan Caroline (23a High St, Littleport, Ely, Cambs CB6 1HE), *b* 1936: *m* 1960, Reginald Valentine Clery, and has issue living, Daniel Philip *b* 1964, Emma Juliet *b* 1962, Louisa Caroline *b* 1967, — Juliet Miriam, *b* 1942: *m* 1961, Reuben Selek, who *d* 1994, and has issue living, Gull *b* 1963, Oren *b* 1965, Netta *b* 1971, Tal *b* 1979. *Residence* – Moshav Givat Joav, Golan Heights, Israel 12946.

PREDECESSORS – (**1**) *Sir* HERBERT LOUIS SAMUEL, GCB, OM, GBE, PC, son of late Edwin Louis Samuel, of Claremont, Prince's Park, Liverpool, and 9 Kensington Gore, SW, banker; *b* 1870; Under-Sec of State of Home Dept 1905-9, Chancellor of Duchy of Lancaster, 1909-10, Postmaster Gen 1910-14, Pres of Local Govt Board 1914-16, again Postmaster Gen 1915, again Chancellor of Duchy of Lancaster 1915-16, Sec of State for Home Dept 1916, British Special Commr to Belgium 1919, High Commr for Palestine 1920-25, again Sec of State for Home Dept 1931-2; MP for Cleveland Div, N Riding of Yorks (*L*) 1902-18, and for Darwen Div of Lancs 1929-35; Chm Liberal Party Organization 1917-29, Leader of Liberal Parliamentary Party 1931-35, and Dep Leader of Liberal Party in the House of Lords 1941-4, and Leader 1944-55; *cr Viscount Samuel*, of Mount Carmel and of Toxteth, City of Liverpool (peerage of UK) 1937: *m* 1897, Beatrice, who *d* 1959, yst da of late Ellis Abraham Franklin; *d* 1963; *s* by his el son (**2**) EDWIN HERBERT, CMG, 2nd Viscount; *b* 1898; Palestine Civil Ser 1920-48; Dir of Broadcasting, Palestine 1945-48, Prin of Inst of Public Admin in Israel 1945-78; Senior Lecturer in British Instns, Hebrew Univ, Jerusalem 1954-69; author of *A Lifetime in Jerusalem, A Cottage in Galilee*, and other short stories: *m* 1920, Hadassah, who *d* 1986, da of Judah Goor, of Tel Aviv; *d* 1978; *s* by his el son (**3**) DAVID HERBERT, 3rd Viscount and present peer.

Samuel, family name of Viscount Bearsted.

SAMUEL OF WYCH CROSS, BARONY (Samuel) (Extinct 1987)

DAUGHTER LIVING OF LIFE BARON

Hon Carole, *b* 1942: *m* 1963, Geoffrey Clive Henry Lawson, and has issue.
Hon Marion, *b* 1944: *m* 1964, Guy Antony Naggar, and has issue.

WIDOW LIVING OF LIFE BARON

EDNA (*Baroness Samuel of Wych Cross*), da of Harry Nedas, of London: *m* 1936, Baron Samuel of Wych Cross (Life Baron), who *d* 1987.

SANDBERG, BARON (Sandberg) (Life Baron 1997)

MICHAEL GRAHAM RUDDOCK SANDBERG, CBE, son of Gerald Arthur Clifford Sandberg, of Thames Ditton, Surrey; *b* 31 May 1927; *ed* St Edward's Sch, Oxford; served in 6th Lancers (IA) and King's Dragoon Gds 1945; joined Hong Kong and Shanghai Banking Corporation 1949, Chm 1977-86; Treasurer, Univ of Hong Kong 1977-86; Chm British Bank of the Middle East 1980-86; Dir Internat Totalisator Systems Inc, New World Development Co Ltd, Windsor Ind Corporation, Pricoa Group, Broadstreet Inc, and A. S. Watson & Co Ltd; Memb Exec Council of Hong Kong 1978-86; Chm Board of Stewards, Royal Hong Kong Jockey Club 1981-86 (Hon Steward 1986); Pres Surrey CCC 1987-88; JP Hong Kong 1972-86; author of *The Sandberg Watch Collection* (1998); Freeman of the City of London and Liveryman of the Worshipful Co of Clockmakers; FCIB 1977 (Vice-Pres 1984-87); FRSA 1983; *cr* OBE 1977, CBE 1982, Kt 1986, and *Baron Sandberg*, of Passfield, co Hants (Life Baron) 1997: *m* 1954, Carmel Mary Roseleen, da of Joseph Donnelly, of Dublin, and has issue.

Arms – Argent on a chevron or fimbriated vert a robin redbreast (Erithacus rubecula) proper all between three trefoils slipped vert. **Crest** – A pearl proper between two wings displayed argent. **Supporters** – *Dexter*, a Chinese dragon or, *Sinister*, a dragon sans wings or.
Residences – Waterside, Passfield, Liphook, Hants GU30 7RT; Domaine de la Haute Germaine, 06510 Le Broc, Alpes Maritimes, France. *Clubs* – Cavalry and Guards', White's, MCC, Surrey CCC, Hampshire CCC, Portland.

SONS LIVING

Hon Michael, *b* 1954; *ed* Downside, and Christ Coll, Camb: *m* 1978, Ann Marilyn Hutson, and has issue living, James Michael Hutson, *b* 1985, — Mark Alexander, *b* 1990, — Robert David, *b* 1993, — Natasha Katharine, *b* 1987.
Hon Paul, *b* 1956; *ed* Downside, and Munich Univ.

DAUGHTERS LIVING

Hon Marion, *b* 1959; *ed* Convent of The Sacred Heart, Woldingham: *m* 1994, Capt Robert Alasdair Davidson Lawrence, MC, and has issue living, Maximilian Myles, *b* 1994, — Matilda Rosaleen Sandberg, *b* 1997.
Hon Deirdre Elizabeth, *b* 1964; *ed* Convent of The Sacred Heart, Woldingham: *m* 1997, Steven William Sorton.

SANDERSON OF AYOT, BARONY OF (Sanderson) (Baron UK 1960, disclaimed 1971)

ALAN LINDSAY SANDERSON, *b* 12 Jan 1931; *s* as 2nd Baron 15 Aug 1971, disclaimed his peerage for life 28 Sept 1971; *ed* Uppingham; MB, BS London; MRCP London; MRC Psych: *m* 1959, Gertrud, da of Herman Bocshsler, and has issue.

Arms – Paly of six argent and azure on a bend sable a mullet of the first between two annulets or. **Crest** – A talbot passant argent pied and eared sable resting the dexter forepaw on an annulet or. **Supporters** – (borne by Barons Sanderson of Ayot). On either side a talbot oojant erect argent pied and eared sable.
Residence – 2 Caroline Close, W2.

SON LIVING

Hon MICHAEL, *b* 6 Dec 1959; *ed* St Paul's Sch, York Univ (BA), and The Wharton Sch, Pennsylvania (MBA).

DAUGHTERS LIVING

Hon Evelyn, *b* 1961.
Hon Frances, *b* 1963.
Hon Andrea, *b* 1964.
Hon Stephanie, *b* 1970.

BROTHER LIVING

Hon Murray Lee (twin) (PO Box 20516, Kitwe, Zambia), *b* 1931; *ed* Rugby, at Trin Coll, Oxford, and at King's Coll, Camb; a Co Dir; Admin Officer, Kenya, 1956-63: *m* 1st, 1966 (*m diss* 1972), Muriel, da of late George Williams; 2ndly, 1973, Eva, da of Rev David Simfukwe, and has issue living, (by 2nd *m*) Basil, *b* 1974, — Constance, *b* 1976.

SISTER LIVING

Hon Pauline Maud, *b* 1929; MA Oxford; Dr de l'Université de Paris: *m* 1952, Robert Henry Matarasso, who *d* 1982, and has issue living, Pascale, *b* 1955, — Antoine, *b* 1957, — François, *b* 1958, — Veronique, *b* 1964.

PREDECESSORS – **(1)** BASIL Sanderson, MC, son of Harold Arthur Sanderson, of Jenkyn Place, Bentley, Hants; *b* 1894; Dir of Shipping in Port, Min of Shipping 1939-41, Head of Port Transit Control, Min of War Transport 1941-45, and Man Dir of Shaw Sevill & Albion Co, Ltd 1945-59, and Chm 1947-63; *cr Baron Sanderson of Ayot*, of Welwyn, co Hertford (peerage of UK) 1960: *m* 1927, Evelyn Constance, who *d* 1940, da of Joseph Bruce Ismay, of Costelloe, co Galway, and London; *d* 1971; *s* by his el son **(2)** ALAN LINDSAY, 2nd Baron, until he disclaimed his peerage, 1971.

SANDERSON OF BOWDEN, BARON (Sanderson) (Life Baron 1985)

(CHARLES) RUSSELL SANDERSON, son of Charles Plummer Sanderson, by his wife, Martha Evelyn, da of Joseph Gardiner, of Glasgow; *b* 30 April 1933; *ed* Trin Coll, Glenalmond, Scottish Coll of Textiles, Galashiels, and Bradford Coll; commn'd R Signals 1952, served 51 (Highland) Inf Div Signal Regt (TA) 1953-56, KOSB (TA) 1956-58; DL Ettrick and Lauderdale 1989; Chm Central & Southern Area, Scottish Conservative Unionist Assocn, 1974-75, Vice-Pres 1975-77, Pres 1977-79; Vice-Chm Nat Union of Conservative Assocns 1979-81 (Member Exec Cttee since 1977), Chm Exec Cttee 1981-86; Gov St Mary's Sch, Melrose, 1977-87, Chm since 1998, and Gov Scottish Coll of Textiles 1980-87, Member of Council Trin Coll, Glenalmond, since 1982, Chm since 1994; Ptnr Chas P. Sanderson, Wool and Yarn Merchants, Melrose, 1978-87; Chm Edinburgh Financial Trust (Yorkshire and Lancashire Trust, renamed 1984) 1983-87, Chm Shires Investment Trust 1984-87, Member Scottish Council Independent Schools 1984-87, Member Cttee Gvng Bodies Assocn 1984-87, Dir Clydesdale Bank 1985-87, Chm since 1999; Commr Gen Assembly Church of Scotland 1972; a Min of State, Scottish Office, 1987-90; Chm Scottish Conservative Party 1990-93; Chm Scottish Mortgage Trust since 1993; Dir United Auctions Ltd 1993-99, Watson & Philip plc (now Alldays plc) 1993-99, Edinburgh Woollen Mills Ltd 1993-97, and Woolcombers Ltd 1991-94; Chm Hawick Cashmere Co since 1991, and Yorkshire Bank since 1999; Memb Napier Univ Court (Chancellor's Assessor) since 1996; *cr* Kt 1981, and *Baron Sanderson of Bowden*, of Melrose in the District of Ettrick and Lauderdale (Life Baron) 1985: *m* 1958, Frances Elizabeth, da of Donald Alfred Ramsden Macaulay, of Rylstone, Skipton, Yorks, and has had issue.

Arms – Per pale, dexter bendy sable and or, sinister azure, a chevron per pale azure and or, in dexter chief a ram's head affrontee argent horned gules, in sinister chief a fleur de lys issuant from a crescent argent. **Crest** – A cock or armed, crested and wattled sable supporting in the dexter claw a buckle of the first. **Supporters** – *Dexter* a Connemara pony proper; *Sinister* — a Cashmere goat proper. **Motto** – Persevere.
Residence – Becketts Field, Bowden, Melrose, Roxburgh TD6 0ST

Hon (Charles) David Russell, *b* 1960; *ed* Glenalmond, and Leeds Univ (BA): *m* 1990, Laura, yr da of H. G. Purdie, of Coatbridge, Lanarks, and has issue. *Residence* – Deansyde, Denholm, Hawick, Roxburghshire.
Hon Andrew Bruce Plummer, *b* 1968; *ed* Glenalmond; *d* 1991.

DAUGHTERS LIVING

Hon (Evelyn) Claire, *b* 1961; *ed* St Leonard's Sch, Newnham Coll, Camb (BA), and Edinburgh Univ; MBChB: *m* 1986, Thomas M. Walker, only son of K. P. Walker, of Glenairlie, Kilmalcolm.
Hon (Frances) Georgina, *b* 1963; *ed* St Leonard's Sch, and Queen Margaret's Coll, Edinburgh: *m* 1990, Peter James Holland Riley, son of Maj J. C. Riley, of Chislehurst, Kent.

SANDFORD, BARON (Edmondson) (Baron UK 1945)

CUICUNQUE FERIENTI APERIETUR

Rev JOHN CYRIL EDMONDSON, DSC, 2nd Baron; *b* 22 Dec 1920; *s* 1959; *ed* Eton; Cdr RN (ret); 1939-45 War with Eastern Med Fleet, Allied Landings in N Africa, Sicily and Normandy (DSC); on Staff of C-in-C Far East 1951-53, and Cdr Home Fleet Flagship 1955-56; Curate of St Nicholas, Harpenden, 1958-63; Exec Chap to Bishop of St Albans 1965-68; Conservative Whip, House of Lords 1966-70; a Parl Sec, Min of Housing and Local Govt June to Oct 1970, and a Parl Under Sec of State Dept of Environment 1970-73, and of Dept of Education and Science 1973-74, Chm of Herts Council of Social Ser 1966-69, and Chm of Church Army Board 1969-70; Pres of Council for Environmental Education 1975-84; Chm of Community Task Force 1977-82; Pres Assoc of District Councils 1980-86, since when a Vice-Pres; Church Commissioner 1981-88; Dir Ecclesiastical Insurance Office 1978-89; Chm Redundant Churches 1982-89; Founder Sandford Award for Heritage Educn, and Heritage Educn Trust; Chm Conference on SE Regional Planning 1981-88; Pres Anglo-Swiss Soc 1976-83; Vice-Pres of Youth Hostels Assocn 1977-89: *m* 1947, Catharine Mary, da of Rev Oswald Andrew Hunt, and has issue.

Arms – Azure, a cross couped and pointed between, in chief two lions combatant, and in base as many swans, wings elevated and addorsed respectant, all or. **Crest** – In front of a portcullis or a dexter arm embowed in armour fessewise, the hand clenched proper. **Supporters** – On either side a pikeman of Honourable Artillery Company armed and accoutred supporting with the exterior hand a pike erect proper, the dexter charged with a portcullis chained or, and the sinister with an oak tree eradicated and fructed also proper, the trunk pierced by three arrows or flighted azure (the badge of the Edmondson family).
Residence – 27 Ashley Gdns, Ambrosden Av, SW1P 1QD.

SONS LIVING

Hon JAMES JOHN MOWBRAY (1023 East 21st Av, Vancouver, BC, V5V 1S6, Canada), *b* 1 July 1949; *ed* Eton, York Univ, and Univ of British Columbia; school counsellor: *m* 1st, 1973 (*m diss* 1985), Ellen Sarah, da of Jack Shapiro, of Toronto; 2ndly, 1985, Linda, da of Blair Wheeler, of Nova Scotia, and has issue living (by 1st *m*), Sarah Juliette, *b* 1977, — (by 2nd *m*) Devon John, *b* 1986.
Hon Nicholas Mark (237 Abbotsfield Rd, Pitsmoor, Sheffield), *b* 1956; *ed* Eton: *m* 1983 (*m diss* 1998), Joanna, da of Gordon Snee, of Willingham, Lincs, and has issue living, Rachel Alice, *b* 1986, — Amber May, *b* 1989.

DAUGHTERS LIVING

Hon Margaret Catharine, *b* 1947; *ed* Downe House Sch, Trin Coll, Dublin, and Bristol Univ; social worker: *m* 1977, (Charles Alan) Simon Holland, of Barncroft, Brightwell-cum-Sotwell, Wallingford, Oxon, and has issue living, Hereward Julian, *b* 1984, — Hannah Catharine, *b* 1979, — Venetia Frances, *b* 1981.
Hon Frances Mary, *b* 1953; *ed* Downe House Sch, and Bristol Univ; research scientist: *m* 1979, Geoffry Wharton, of Vorgebirgstrasse 5, 50677 Köln, Germany, elder son of Robert Wharton, of Grand Forks, N Dakota, USA, and has issue living, Lionel Thomas, *b* 1982, — John Lorenz, *b* 1984.

BROTHER LIVING

Hon Anthony James Kinghorn, *b* 1924; *ed* Eton, and Harvard Univ; Capt (ret) Gren Gds: *m* 1st, 1947 (*m diss* 1969), Olivia Charlotte, yst da of late Rev Oswald Andrew Hunt; 2ndly, 1969, Hilary Pauline, da of late Lt-Col Edward Shirley Trusler, OBE, and has had issue (by 1st *m*), Charles Anthony (Burhill, Buckland, nr Broadway, Worcs WR12 7LY), *b* 1949; *ed* Shrewsbury: *m* 1st 1978 (*m diss* 1989), Isabella, da of Thomas Wright, of Glasgow; 2ndly, 1996, Rhian, da of

Ralph Cowles, of Warwick, and has issue living (by 1st *m*), Andrew James *b* 1982, Sarah Isabella *b* 1979, Gemma Lavinia *b* 1981, (by 2nd wife), Toby Benjamin *b* 1994, Amelia Clementine *b* 1997, — Simon Andrew (Conde de Aranda, No 3 4th Floor, 28001 Madrid, Spain), *b* 1955; MA; MFA: *m* 1st, 1981 (*m diss* 1988), Louise Caroline Marion, da of Donald Alistair Blair, of 9 Roedean Terrace, Brighton; 2ndly, 1992, Maria Martin Hernandez-Cañizares, da of Cristobal Martin Garcia, of Madrid, — Anthony James (Somerford Lakes Reserve, Somerford Keynes, Cirencester, Glos), *b* 1957: *m* 1987 (*m diss* 1997), Olivia, 5th da of Dr Charles Dansie, of Welwyn, Herts, and has issue living, James *b* 1989, Charlotte *b* 1987, — Elizabeth Anne (14 Davies Drive, Devizes, Wilts SN10 2RL), *b* 1951: *m* 1979 (*m diss* 1996), Nigel A. Urquhart, el son of Sir Andrew Urquhart, KCMG, MBE, and has issue living, Tamsin Elizabeth *b* 1984, Madeleine Emma *b* 1987, — (by 2nd *m*) †Rupert James Kinghorn, *b* 1972, *d* 1979.

PREDECESSOR – **(1)** *Sir* ALBERT JAMES Edmondson, son of late James Edmondson, of Weston, Herts; *b* 1886; Major Hon Artillery Co; Parliamentary Private Sec to Min of Pensions 1924-29 and 1931-34, an Assist Govt Whip 1937, a Junior Lord of the Treasury 1939, Vice-Chamberlain of HM's Household 1939, Treasurer of HM's Household 1942-5, Dep Ch Whip 1942-5, and High Steward of Banbury 1947; sat as MP for Banbury Div of Oxfordshire (C) 1922-45; *cr Baron Sandford*, of Banbury, co Oxford (peerage of United Kingdom) 1945: *m* 1911, Edith Elizabeth, who *d* 1946, da of George James Freeman; *d* 1959; *s* by his el son **(2)** *Rev* JOHN CYRIL, 2nd Baron and present peer.

SANDHURST, BARON (Mansfield) (Baron UK 1871)

(JOHN EDWARD) TERENCE MANSFIELD, DFC, 5th Baron; *b* 4 Sept 1920; *s* 1964; *ed* Harrow; 1939-45 War as Flight-Lt, RAFVR Bomber Command (DFC): *m* 1st, 1942 (*m diss* 1946), Priscilla Ann, who *d* 1970, da of late J. Fielder Johnson; 2ndly, 1947, Janet Mary, el da of late John Edward Lloyd, of Long Island, New York, USA, and has issue by 2nd *m*.

Arms – Argent, on a chevron embattled azure, between three maunches sable an Eastern crown or; on a chief enrailed of the third a lion of the fourth combatant with a tiger cowed proper. Crest – Out of an Eastern crown argent, a griffin's head sable beaked or, between two branches of laurel proper. Supporters – *Dexter*, A horse argent mane and tail sable, charged on the shoulder with a rose gules barbed and seeded proper, holding in the mouth a branch of laurel vert; *sinister*, a tiger cowed proper, gorged with a collar therefrom a chain reflexed over the back sable.
Residence – La Volière, Les Ruisseaux, St Brelade, Jersey, CI. *Clubs* – RAF, United (Jersey), MCC.

SON LIVING (By 2nd marriage)

Hon GUY RHYS JOHN (1 Crown Office Row, Temple, EC4Y 7HH; Leander Club, MCC; United (Jersey)), *b* 3 March 1949; *ed* Harrow, and Oriel Coll, Oxford (MA); Bar Middle Temple 1972, QC 1994, Recorder of the Crown Court since 1993, Memb Gen Cncl of the Bar since 1997 (Chm Legal Aid Remuneration Cttee since 1998): *m* 1976, Philippa St Clair, el da of late Digby Everard Verdon-Roe, of 5 Hameau de Bosquet, 41 Avenue Victoria, 06110 Le Cannet, France, and has issue living, Edward James, *b* 12 April 1982; *ed* Eton, — Alice Georgina, *b* 1980; *ed* Wycombe Abbey, and Bristol Univ.

DAUGHTER LIVING (By 2nd marriage)

Hon Victoria Elizabeth, *b* 1957; *ed* Benenden, and Univ of Bordeaux: *m* 1978, (Charles) James Sharp Bentley, 2nd son of late Kenneth Bentley, of Balmuir House, by Dundee, and has issue living, James William Nicholas, *b* 1982, — Sophie Katharine, *b* 1985. *Residence* – South Fen House, Fen End, Kenilworth, Warwicks CV8 1NQ.

WIDOW LIVING OF SON OF FOURTH BARON

Evelyn Cecil, yr da of late Sir Ronald Barry Keefe: *m* 1961, as his 2nd wife, Hon Ralph Geoffrey Knyvet Mansfield, 2nd son of 4th Baron, who *d* 1983, and has issue (see colls infra). *Residence* – Wendover, 40 Old Rd, Frinton-on-Sea, Essex CO13 9BZ.

COLLATERAL BRANCH LIVING

Issue of late Hon Ralph Geoffrey Knyvet Mansfield, 2nd son of 4th Baron, *b* 1926, *d* 1983: *m* 1st, 1952 (*m diss* 1960), Hélène Gertrude, who *d* 1975, only da of late James Montague Coutts Duffus of Dalclaverhouse, of The Mansion House, Claverhouse, by Dundee; 2ndly, 1961, Evelyn Cecil (ante), yr da of late Sir Ronald Barry Keefe:—
(By 1st *m*) (Penelope) Sara Hélène, *b* 1953: *m* 1983, Dr C. Neale Muir, of Sheldon Park, Allan Rd, Forrestdale, Western Australia. ——— Trudé Charlotte Victoria, *b* 1955; MPS; *m* 1983, M. Timothy Borrett, of Beckwith Farm, Great Holland, Essex, and has issue living, Alexandra Victoria, *b* 1984, — Katherine Frances, *b* 1986. ——— Tessa Emily Henrietta, *b* 1959: *m* 1981, Steven Williams, of Middleton Cheney, Banbury, Oxon, and has issue living, James Matthew Thomas, *b*

1995. —— (By 2nd *m*) Morley Rafael Kate, *b* 1965: *m* 1988, Bernard Reignier, ingénieur, of Château Malard, Bordeaux, France, and has issue living, Sheldon, *b* 1992, — Tom Samuel, *b* 1994.

PREDECESSORS – (1) *Gen Rt Hon Sir* WILLIAM ROSE Mansfield, GCB, GCSI, PC, DCL, *b* 1819; Col 38th Foot; served in Sutlej Campaign 1845-6, commanded 53rd Regt in the Punjab 1848-9; employed in Peshawar operations 1851-2; appointed responsible military adviser to ambassador at Constantinople 1855, and accompanied Lord Stratford de Redcliffe to the Crimea; was Ch of Staff during Indian Mutiny Campaign 1857-9, Com-in-Ch in India 1865-70, and Com of Forces in Ireland 1870-5; *cr Baron Sandhurst*, of Sandhurst, co Berks (peerage of United Kingdom) 1871: *m* 1854, Margaret, da of Robert Fellowes, of Shotesham Park, Norfolk; *d* 1876; *s* by his son (2) WILLIAM, GCSI, GCIE, GCVO, PC, 2nd Baron, *b* 1855; a Lord-in-Waiting to HM Queen Victoria 1880-85, Under-Sec of State for War 1886 and 1892-5, and Gov of Bombay 1895-1900; appointed Lord Chamberlain of the Household 1912, a Member of Govt Committee for Employment of Disabled Soldiers and Sailors 1915, and again Lord Chamberlain of the Household 1916 and Jan 1919; Treasurer of St Bartholomew's Hospital 1908-21; *cr Viscount Sandhurst*, of Sandhurst, Berks (peerage of United Kingdom) 1917: *m* 1st, 1881, Lady Victoria Alexandrina Spencer, CI, who *d* 1906, da of 4th Earl Spencer; 2ndly, 1909, Eleanor Mary Caroline, OBE, who *d* 1934, da of late Matthew Arnold, and widow of Hon Armine Wodehouse, CB, MP; *d* 1921, when the Viscountcy became ext, and he was *s* in the Barony by his brother (3) JOHN WILLIAM, 3rd Baron, *b* 1857: *m* 1888, Edith Mary, who *d* 1939, da of late John Higson, JP, of Oakmere Hall, Hartford, Cheshire; *d* 1933; *s* by his son (4) RALPH SHELDON, OBE, 4th Baron, *b* 1892: *m* 1917, Victoria Morley, who *d* 1961, da of Edward Berners Upcher, formerly of Kirby Cane, Sheringham; *d* 1964; *s* by his el son (5) JOHN EDWARD TERENCE, 5th Baron and present peer.

Sandilands, family name of Lord Torphichen.

Sandon, Viscount; son of Earl of Harrowby.

SANDWICH, EARL OF (Montagu) (Earl E 1660)

After so many shipwrecks (I find) a port

JOHN EDWARD HOLLISTER MONTAGU, 11th Earl; *b* 11 April 1943; *s* 1995; *ed* Eton, and Trin Coll, Camb (MA): *m* 1968, (Susan) Caroline, only da of late Rev Canon Perceval Ecroyd Cobham Hayman, of Rogate Vicarage, W Sussex, and has issue.

Arms – Quarterly: 1st and 4th argent three fusils, conjoined in fesse gules within a bordure sable, *Montagu*; 2nd and 3rd or, an eagle displayed vert, beaked and membered gules, *Monthermer*. Crest – A griffin's head couped at the neck or, wings elevated sable. Supporters – *Dexter*, a triton proper, crowned with an Eastern crown or, and holding in his right hand a trident sable; *sinister*, an eagle with wings expanded vert, beaked and membered gules.
Address – c/o House of Lords, SW1A 0PW.

SONS LIVING

LUKE TIMOTHY CHARLES (*Viscount Hinchingbrooke*), *b* 5 Dec 1969; *ed* Westminster Sch, and Columbia Univ, NY, USA.
Hon Orlando William, *b* 1971; *ed* Marlborough: *m* 1996, Laura Ann, da of Richard Charles Roundell (*see* E Dartmouth, colls).

DAUGHTER LIVING

(*Lady*) Jemima Mary (does not use courtesy title), *b* 1973,

BROTHER LIVING

Hon (George Charles) Robert, *b* 1949; *ed* Eton: *m* 1970, Donna Marzia, da of Conte Brigante Colonna, and has issue living, Oliver Drogo, *b* 1974; *ed* Bryanston, and Edinburgh Univ, — Cosimo Ralph, *b* 1988, — Fiamma Fleur, *b* 1971, — Bona Frances, *b* 1972. *Residence* – The Old Manor, Evershot, Dorset DT2 0JR.

SISTERS LIVING AND DECEASED

(*Lady*) Sarah Jane Helen MONTAGU (does not use courtesy title), *b* 1935; resumed her maiden name: *m* 1959 (*m diss* 1971), Alessandro Ballarin, and has issue living, Caterina Teresa, *b* 1960, — Antonia Barbara, *b* 1964.

(*Lady*) (Elizabeth) Anne (does not use courtesy title), *b* 1937: *m* 1961, Torquil Patrick Alexander Norman, and has issue (*see* Norman, Bt, *cr* 1915). *Residence* – 62 Gloucester Crescent, NW1 7EG.

Lady Katharine Victoria, *b* 1945: *m* 1965, Nicholas Victor Hunloke (*see* D Devonshire, 1980 Edn), and has issue living, Edward Perceval, *b* 1969; *ed* Bryanston, and Wolverhampton Univ., — Henrietta Yvery, *b* 1968: *m* 1998, Lucien Henry Valentine Thynne (*see* M Bath, colls), — Matilda Anne, *b* 1972. *Residence* – The Old Rectory, Poulshot, Devizes, Wilts SN10 1RT.

Lady Julia Frances MONTAGU, *b* 1947; resumed her maiden name: *m* 1st, 1972 (*m diss* 1976), Martin Lee Oakley; 2ndly, 1976 (*m diss* 1987), Peter Gerald Edward Body, and *d* 1995, leaving issue (by 2nd *m*), Timothy, *b* 1982.

AUNT LIVING (*daughter of 9th Earl*)

Lady Elizabeth, *b* 1917. *Residence* – 11 York Mansions, Prince of Wales Drive, SW11.

COLLATERAL BRANCH LIVING

Issue of late Hon (William) Drogo Sturges Montagu, Flying Officer Auxiliary Air Force, 2nd son of 9th Earl, *b* 1908, *k* in an aeroplane accident on active ser 1940: *m* 1st, 1931 (*m diss* 1935), Tanis Eva Bulkeley, who *d* 1993, da of late Benjamin Seymour Guinness; 2ndly, 1935, Hon Janet Gladys (CAMPBELL) (who *d* 1988, having *m* 3rdly, 1942, Major Thomas Edward Dealtry Kidd, MBE, Roy Canadian Artillery), da of 1st Baron Beaverbrook:—
(By 1st *m*) John Dru (Hall Place, W Meon, Hants GU32 1LX), *b* 1932; is Lt RNR: *m* 1st, 1958, Sarah Maria (Sari), da of Manolo de Palacio, of Serrano 39, Madrid; 2ndly, 1977, Maria Elena (Minna), eldest da of late Richard Guy Buckmaster, and has issue living (by 1st *m*), Sophie, *b* 1959, — Bridget Doon, *b* 1961, — Claire Mary, *b* 1962, — Sarah Tanis (Sarita), *b* 1965: *m* 1993, Christopher M. Hawkins, and has issue living, Chester *b* 1998, Ava *b* 1994, — (by 2nd *m*), Paul Patrick Drogo, *b* 1979, — Kyra, *b* 1978. —— (By 2nd *m*) William Drogo (Garland's Cottage, Beard's Yard, High St, Langport, Som), *b* 1936: *m* 1st, 1965 (in Barbados, WI), Bonnie Mackenzie; 2ndly, 1969, Edna Maud Ahlers, and has issue living (by 1st *m*), Michael Drogo, *b* 1966, — (by 2nd *m*), Nicola Lilian, *b* 1971, — Monette Edna, *b* 1973.

PREDECESSORS – (1) *Rt Hon Sir* EDWARD Montagu, KG, PC, son of late Sir Sidney Montagu, yst brother of 1st Earl of Manchester; *b* 1625; a distinguished Parliamentary Gen, and afterwards Lord High Adm of England, in which capacity he induced the whole fleet to support the Restoration of 1660; MP for Huntingdonshire 1644-7; *cr Baron Montagu*, of St Neots, Hunts, *Viscount Hinchingbrooke* and *Earl of Sandwich* (peerage of England) 1660: *m* 1642, Hon Jemima Crewe, who *d* 1674, da of 1st Baron Crewe; *ka* 1672 in the great sea-fight with the Dutch off Sole Bay; *s* by his son (2) EDWARD, 2nd Earl; *b* 1648; was Ambassador at Lisbon 1678: *m* 1668, Hon Mary Boyle, who *d* 1671, da of 2nd Earl of Cork; *d* 1689; *s* by his son (3) EDWARD, 3rd Earl; *b* 1670; was Lord-Lieut of co Huntingdon: *m* 1689, Hon Elizabeth Wilmot, who *d* 1757, da of 2nd Earl of Rochester; *d* 1729; *s* by his grandson (4) JOHN, 4th Earl; *b* 1718; was successively a Sec of State and First Lord of the Admiralty; sponsored the voyages of discovery made by Capt James Cooke, who named the Sandwich Islands in his honour; *d* 1792; *s* by his son (5) JOHN, 5th Earl; *b* 1744; *d* 1814; *s* by his son (6) GEORGE JOHN, 6th Earl; *b* 1773; *d* 1818; *s* by his son (7) JOHN WILLIAM, PC, 7th Earl; *b* 1811; was Master of the Buckhounds, 1858-9, and Lord-Lieut of Huntingdonshire: *m* 1st, 1838, Lady Mary Paget, who *d* 1859, da of 1st Marquess of Anglesey, KG; 2ndly, 1865, Lady Blanche Egerton, da of 1st Earl of Ellesmere; *d* 1884; *s* by his son (8) EDWARD GEORGE HENRY, KCVO, 8th Earl, *b* 1839; Lord-Lieut of Hunts 1891-1916; MP for Huntingdon (C) 1876-84; *d* 1916; *s* by his nephew (9) GEORGE CHARLES (son of late Rear-Adm Hon Victor Alexander Montagu, CB, 2nd son of 7th Earl), 9th Earl; *b* 1874; Assist Private Sec to Board of Agriculture 1898-1900; MP for S Div of Hunts (C) 1900-6: *m* 1st, 1905, Alberta, who *d* 1951, da of late William Sturges, of New York; 2ndly, 1952, Ella Lillian (Amiya), who *d* 1986, da of late George Sully, of N Petherton, Somerset; *d* 1962; *s* by his elder son (10) ALEXANDER VICTOR EDWARD PAULET, 10th Earl (until he disclaimed his peerages for life 1964); *b* 1906; MP for S Div of Dorset (C) 1941-62; Chm Tory Reform Cttee, House of Commons 1943, Pres Anti-Common Market League 1962-84: *m* 1st, 1934 (*m diss* 1958), (Maud) Rosemary, who *d* 1998, having resumed her maiden name by deed poll 1961, da of late Maj Ralph Harding Peto (*see* Peto, Bt, *cr* 1855, colls); 2ndly, 1962 (*m annulled* 1965), Lady Anne Holland-Martin, MBE, who *d* 1981, yst da of 9th Duke of Devonshire, widow of Christopher John Holland-Martin, MP, and formerly wife of Lt-Col Henry Philip Hunloke; *d* 1995; *s* by his elder son (11) JOHN EDWARD HOLLISTER, 11th Earl and present peer; also Viscount Hinchingbrooke, and Baron Montagu, until he disclaimed his peerages 1964.

SANDYS, BARON (Hill) (Baron UK 1802)
(Title pronounced "Sands")

RICHARD MICHAEL OLIVER HILL, 7th Baron; *b* 21 July, 1931; *s* 1961; late Lieut R Scots Greys; a DL of Worcs; FRGS; patron of one living; a Lord-in-Waiting to HM Jan to March, 1974; Opposition Whip, House of Lords 1974-79; Dep Ch Whip and Capt Yeomen of the Guard 1979-83: *m* 1961, Patricia Simpson, da of late Capt Lionel Hall, MC, of Parkgate, Lower Beeding, Sussex.

Arms – Quarterly: 1st and 4th or, a fesse dancettée, between three cross crosslets fitchée gules, *Sandys*; 2nd and 3rd sable, on a fesse argent, between three leopards passant guardant or, spotted of the field, as many escallops gules, *Hill*. **Crests** – 1st, a griffin segreant per fesse or and gules, *Sandys*; 2nd, a reindeer's head couped at the neck gules, attired and plain collared or, *Hill*. **Supporters** – Two griffins, with wings elevated per fesse, or and gules, each gorged with a collar dancettée, of the last. *Seat* – Ombersley Court, Droitwich, Worcestershire. *Club* – Cavalry and Guards'.

Probum non pænitet
The honest man has not to repent

SISTER LIVING

Hon Cynthia Meriel, *b* 1929: *m* 1954, Charles Talbot Rhys Wingfield (*see* V Powerscourt, colls). *Residence* – Barrington Park, Burford, Oxon.

COLLATERAL BRANCHES LIVING

Descendants of Arthur Blundell Hill, 3rd Marquess of Downshire, eldest son of Mary, Baroness Sandys:—
Of whom ARTHUR ROBIN IAN, 8th Marquess of Downshire, is *hp* to the Barony.

PREDECESSORS – **(1)** MARY, wife of 2nd Marquess of Downshire, inherited the estates of her uncle, Edwin, 2nd and last Baron Sandys, *cr* 1743, and was *cr Baroness Sandys*, of Ombersley, co Worcester (peerage of United Kingdom) 1802, with remainder to her sons Arthur Moyses William, Arthur Marcus Cecil, Arthur Augustus Edwin, and George Augustus successively, and failing them to her el son Arthur Blundell; *d* 1836; *s* by her 2nd son **(2)** ARTHUR MOYSES WILLIAM, 2nd Baron; a Lieut-Gen in the Army; *d unm* 1860; *s* by his brother **(3)** ARTHUR MARCUS CECIL, PC, 3rd Baron; assumed in 1861 by Roy licence the surname of Sandys, in lieu of Hill: *m* 1837, Louisa, who *d* 1886, da of Joseph Blake; *d* 1863; *s* by his son **(4)** AUGUSTUS FREDERICK ARTHUR, 4th Baron, *b* 1840: *m* 1872, Augusta, who *d* 1903, da of Sir Charles Des Vœux, 2nd Bt; *d* 1904; *s* by his brother **(5)** MICHAEL EDWIN MARCUS, 5th Baron, *b* 1855: *m* 1886, Marjorie Clara Pentreath, who *d* 1929, da of late John Morgan, of Brighton; *d* 1948; *s* by his kinsman **(6)** ARTHUR FITZGERALD SANDYS HILL (son of late Arthur Blundell George Sandys Hill, el son of late Lord George Augustus Hill, MP, 5th son of Mary, Baroness Sandys), 6th Baron; *b* 1876; Lieut-Col RE: *m* 1924, Cynthia Mary, who *d* 1990, da of late Col Frederic Richard Thomas Trench-Gascoigne, DSO; *d* 1961; *s* by his son **(7)** RICHARD MICHAEL OLIVER, 7th Baron and present peer.

Saumarez, family name of Baron de Saumarez.

Savernake, Viscount; grandson of Marquess of Ailesbury.

SAVILE, BARON (Lumley-Savile) (Baron UK 1888)

GEORGE HALIFAX LUMLEY-SAVILE, 3rd Baron; *b* 24 Jan 1919; *s* 1931; *ed* Eton; a DL for W Yorks, a JP for Dewsbury and patron of two livings; CStJ; formerly Capt Duke of Wellington's Regt; Burma 1943-44 attached Lincolnshire Regt.

Arms – Argent, on a bend sable, three owls affrontée of the first, within a bordure wavy of the second. Crest – An owl affrontée argent, debruised by a bendlet sinister wavy sable. Supporters – Two talbots ermine, each gorged with a collar wavy sable, pendent therefrom an escutcheon or charged with a popinjay vert, collared gules.
Seat – Walshaw, Hebden Bridge, W Yorks. *Residence* – Gryce Hall, Shelley, via Huddersfield, W Yorks. *Club* – Brooks's.

BROTHER LIVING

Hon HENRY LEOLINE THORNHILL (*Clubs* - White's, Buck's, Guards'); *b* 2 Oct 1923; *ed* Eton; late Lieut Grenadier Guards; European War 1939-45 (wounded); *m* 1st, 1946 (*m diss* 1951), Presiley June, only da of Maj G. H. E. Inchbald, of 28/2 Porchester Gdns, W2; 2ndly, 1961, Caroline Jeffie, who *d* 1970, da of Peter Julian Clive, of Biarritz, France (*see* By Muir-Mackenzie, 1970 Edn); 3rdly, 1972, Margaret Ann, ARCM, da of Edward Matthew Phillips, of Vancouver, BC, and widow of Peter Alexander Bruce (*see* E Elgin, colls, 1970 Edn), and has issue living, (by 1st *m*) John Anthony Thornhill, *b* 1947, — (by 3rd *m*), James George Augustus, *b* 1975, — Peter Edward Henry (triplet), *b* 1975, — Robin William Matthew (triplet), *b* 1975. *Residence* – Walshaw, Hebden Bridge, W Yorks HX7 7AX.

SISTER LIVING

Hon Deirdre Barbara Elland, *b* 1928: *m* 1948, Col Kent Kane Parrot, US Air Force (ret), who *d* 1995, and has issue living, Jonathan Kent (483 Peregrine Drive, Indialantic, Florida 32903, USA), *b* 1950: *m* 1976, Theresa Marie Mell, — Richard Halifax (443 North Palm Drive, Apt E, Beverly Hills, CA 90210, USA), *b* 1952, — Barbara Elland, *b* 1959: *m* 1982, Howard R. Katz, of 5507 Grove St, Chevy Chase, Maryland 20815, USA. *Residence* – 5506 Grove St, Chevy Chase, Maryland 20815, USA.

PREDECESSORS – (1) JOHN Savile, GCB, PC, natural son of 8th Earl of Scarbrough, *b* 1818; Envoy Extraor and Min Plen to Saxony 1866-67, to Swiss Confederation 1867-68, and to Brussels 1868-83, and Ambassador Extraor and Min Plen to Italy 1883-88; assumed by Roy licence 1887 the surname of Savile in lieu of Lumley; *cr Baron Savile*, of Rufford, Notts (peerage of United Kingdom) 1888, with remainder, in default of male issue, to his nephew, John Savile Lumley, only son of late Rev Frederick Savile-Lumley; *d* 1896; *s* under the special remainder by his nephew (2) JOHN, KCVO, 2nd Baron, *b* 1853; served in Foreign Office and Diplo Ser; assumed by Roy licence 1898 the surname of Savile after that of Lumley, and the arms of Savile only: *m* 1st, 1894, Gertrude Violet, who *d* 1912, da of late Charles Francis Webster-Wedderburn, and widow of Horace Augustus Helyar, of Coker Court, Somerset; 2ndly, 1916, Esmé Grace Virginia, who *d* 1958, only da of late John Hyem Wolton, and formerly wife of Capt Claude Levita; *d* 1931; *s* by his el son (3) GEORGE HALIFAX, 3rd Baron and present peer.

Savile, family name of Earl of Mexborough.

SAVILLE OF NEWDIGATE, BARON (Saville) (Life Baron 1997)

MARK OLIVER SAVILLE, PC, son of Kenneth Vivian Saville, of Hastings, Sussex; *b* 20 March 1936; *ed* Rye Gram Sch, and Brasenose Coll, Oxford (BA 1959, BCL 1960); Nat Service as 2nd Lieut Royal Sussex Regt 1954-56; Bar, Middle Temple 1962, Bencher 1983; QC 1975; Judge of the High Court of Justice (Queen's Bench Division) 1985-94; a Lord Justice of Appeal 1994-97, since when a Lord of Appeal in Ordinary; *cr* Kt 1985, PC 1994, and *Baron Saville of Newdigate*, of Newdigate, co Surrey (Life Baron) 1997: *m* 1961, Jill, da of Frederick Gray, of Altrincham, Cheshire, and has issue.
Address – c/o House of Lords, Westminster, SW1A 0PW.

SONS LIVING

Hon William Christian, *b* 1962; *ed* Marlborough.
Hon Henry Oliver, *b* 1964; *ed* Marlborough: *m* 1995, Jane Michaela Grace, and has issue living, Thomas Henry, *b* 1998.

SAWYER, BARON (Sawyer) (Life Baron 1998)

LAWRENCE (TOM) SAWYER, Dep Gen Sec Nupe, later UNISON 1981-94; Gen Sec, Labour Party 1994-98; Memb NEC, Labour Party 1981-94; Chm Labour Party 1990-91; *cr Baron Sawyer*, of Darlington, co Durham (Life Baron) 1998.
Address – c/o House of Lords, SW1A 0PW.

SAYE and SELE, BARON (Fiennes) (Baron E 1447 and 1603)
(Name pronounced "Fines")

Ask for a brave spirit

Seat – Broughton Castle, Banbury, Oxon.

NATHANIEL THOMAS ALLEN FIENNES, 21st Baron; *b* 22 Sept 1920; *s* 1968; *ed* Eton, and New Coll, Oxford; relinquished by deed poll 1965 the additional surnames of Twisleton and Wykeham; 1939-45 War in Rifle Bde (despatches twice); DL Oxon 1979: *m* 1958, Mariette Helena, only da of late Maj-Gen Sir (Arthur) Guy Salisbury-Jones, GCVO, CMG, CBE, MC (*see* de Bunsen, Bt, ext, 1995 Edn), and has issue.

Arms – Quarterly: 1st and 4th azure, three lions rampant or, *Fiennes*; 2nd and 3rd argent, a chevron between three moles sable, *Twisleton*. Crests – 1st, a wolf sejant proper, gorged with a spiked collar, the line therefrom reflexed over the back or, *Fiennes*; 2nd, an arm embowed, vested sable, cuffed argent, holding in the hand proper a mole spade or, headed and armed of the second, *Twisleton*. Supporters – Two wolves argent, gorged and lined as the crest.

SONS LIVING

Hon RICHARD INGEL, *b* 19 Aug 1959.
Hon Martin Guy, *b* 1961: *m* 1996, Pauline Kang Chai Lian, only da of Kang Tiong Lam, and has issue living, Guy, *b* 1997, — Ned Richard Ling, *b* 1999.
Hon William John, *b* 1970.

DAUGHTER LIVING

Hon Susannah Hersey (twin), *b* 1961; painter.

BROTHER LIVING

Very Rev Hon Oliver William TWISLETON-WYKEHAM-FIENNES (Home Farm House, Colsterworth, Lincs), *b* 1926; *ed* Eton, and New Coll, Oxford (MA); late Lt Rifle Bde; KStJ; Dean of Lincoln 1968-89, Dean Emeritus 1989: *m* 1956, Juliet, yr da of late Dr Trevor Heaton, of 3 St Martins Sq, Chichester, and has issue living, Adam Hugh, *b* 1961, — James William, *b* 1964: *m* 1996, Caroline H., elder da of John Newton-Davies, of Sandridge, Herts, and of Mrs Diana Whiteside, of Chailey, Sussex, and has issue living, Georgina Lucy *b* 1998. — Celia Ruth, *b* 1957: *m* 1979, James Long-Howell, only son of Lt-Col J. D. Howell, of Maenillar, Pembrey, Dyffd, and has issue living, George David Henry *b* 1992, Emily Myfanwy *b* 1987, Charlotte Angharad *b* 1990, — Laura Charlotte, *b* 1959: *m* 1988, Roger Hughes, son of late Gordon Hughes, of Turton, Lancs, and has issue living, Charles Oliver Edmund *b* 1989, Lucy Venetia *b* 1994.

COLLATERAL BRANCHES LIVING

Grandchildren of late Hon Eustace Edward Twisleton-Wykeham-Fiennes (2nd son of 17th Baron), who was *cr* a *Baronet* 1916:—
See Twisleton-Wykeham-Fiennes, Bt.

Grandchildren of late Gerard Yorke Twisleton-Wykeham-Fiennes, CBE, eldest son of late Rev Hon Wingfield Stratford Twisleton-Wykeham-Fiennes, 4th son of 16th Baron:—
Issue of late Gerard Francis Gisborne Twisleton-Wykeham-Fiennes, OBE, *b* 1906, *d* 1985: *m* 1st, 1934, Norah, who *d* 1960, el da of Thomas Davies, of Llangollen; 2ndly, 1962, Jean (29 Wentworth Rd, Aldeburgh, Suffolk), formerly wife of — Kerridge, and da of late James Valentine, of Dovercourt:—
(By 1st *m*) Jeremy, *b* 1937; *ed* Winchester, and Clare Coll, Camb: *m* 1st, 1962 (*m diss* 19—), Else Brekke, da of Niels Larsen, of Knuthenborg Park, Bandholm, Denmark; 2ndly, 19—, —, and has issue living (by 1st *m*), Sine, *b* 1962, — Nicole Juana, *b* 1968. —— Michael Wynn (Burcott Manor, nr Wells, Som), *b* 1941; *ed* Winchester, New Coll, Oxford, and Harvard: *m* 1966, Rosalie Ruth, da of Stanley Sheppard, of Street, Som, and has issue living, Rupert Yorke, *b* 1969, — Hugo Barnabas, *b* 1971, — Joshua Gisborne, *b* 1974, — Ivo Martindale, *b* 1978. —— Gerard Ivor, *b* 1946; *ed* Winchester, and Hertford Coll, Oxford: *m* 1973, Jane, da of Neil Digney, of Wimbledon, and has issue living, David Gerard, *b* 1982, — Clare Elizabeth, *b* 1976. —— Joslin Mary, *b* 1939; *ed* Newnham Coll, Camb: *m* 1963, Pierre Michael Landell-Mills, of 2954 Macomb St, NW Washington, DC 20008, USA, and has issue living, Julius Paul, *b* 1965, — Nicholas Vladimir, *b* 1967, — Natalia Norah, *b* 1972. —— Bronwen Margaret, *b* 1944: *m* 1967, Oliver Addis, of 389 Bobbin Head Rd, N Turramurra, NSW 2074, Australia, and has issue living, Thomas Oliver, *b* 1970, — Helen Mary, *b* 1968, — Harriet Jane, *b* 1972, — Sarah Elizabeth Ruth *b* 1975.

Issue of late Richard Nathaniel Twisleton-Wykeham-Fiennes, MRCVS, *b* 1909, *d* 1988: *m* 1st, 1941 (*m diss* 1948), Mary Morwenna Daphne, da of late Rev James Rashleigh Hale, sometime V of Yalding, Maidstone; 2ndly, 1948, Alice Isobel, who *d* 1986, da of late William Cowie, of Singapore, and formerly wife of Robert Tremlett, of Mbale, Uganda:—
(By 2nd *m*) (Richard) George, *b* 1950; *ed* Winchester, and Coll of Estate Mgmnt (BSc), ARICS: *m* 1974, Julia Florence, da of Raymond Humphrey, of Winchester, and has issue living, Felix George, *b* 1978, — Eleanor Florence, *b* 1983, — Isobel Joanna, *b* 1986, — Arabella Julia, *b* 1988. —— Frances Elizabeth, *b* 1947; *ed* St Paul's Girls' Sch, and York Univ (BA); JP: *m* 1969, Col Michael Philip Kenneth Beatty, CBE, TD, DL (Staffs 1980), High Sheriff 1994-95, late Royal Mercian and Lancastrian Yeo, of Tixall Farmhouse, Tixall, Stafford ST18 0XT, and has issue living, Geraldine Alice Martindale, *b* 1971, — Rosanna Mary Gisborne, *b* 1973, — Katherine Margaret Barrett, *b* 1980, — Caroline Diana Charlotte, *b* 1986.

Issue of late Sir John Saye Wingfield Twisleton-Wykeham-Fiennes, KCB, QC, *b* 1911, *d* 1996: *m* 1937, Sylvia Beatrice, who *d* 1979, da of late Rev Charles Robert Loraine McDowall (Burdett, Bt, *cr* 1665):—
Nicholas John (21 Chalfont Rd, Oxford OX2 6TL), *b* 1940; *ed* Winchester, and Merton Coll, Oxford: *m* 1st, 1969 (*m diss* 1990), Vicki Karen, da of W. Alan Thomas, of Stourbridge, Worcs; 2ndly, 1993, Angela Helen, only da of late Rev Geoffrey Walker Ellison, of Withington, Glos, and has issue living (by 1st *m*), Alexander William, *b* 1971, — John Edward, *b* 1973, — Katherine Margaret, *b* 1974. —— William Gerard (April Cottage, Main St, Clanfield, Oxon OX18 2QH), *b* 1946; *ed* Winchester, New Coll, Oxford, and Imperial Coll, London: *m* 1976, Rosalind Dalzel, da of William Dalzel Pritchard, of Alderton, Glos, and has issue living, Timothy Gerard, *b* 1985, — Lucy Anne, *b* 1981. —— Judith Mary (5 Parliament Court, Parliament Hill, NW3 2TS), *b* 1938.

Issue of late Michael Yorke Twisleton-Wykeham-Fiennes, *b* 1912, *d* 1989: *m* 1957, Jacqueline (Woodcote, Oaks Rd, Tenterden, Kent), da of Rev Edward Montmorency Guilford:—
Toby Jonathan (18 Shrublands Rd, Berkhamstead, Herts HP4 3HY), *b* 1961: *m* 1989, Hilary Linda, elder da of D. T. McGladdery, of Newton Abbot, Devon, and has issue living, Thomas Michael, *b* 1995, — Emily Leonora, *b* (triplet) 1995, — Caroline Leandra, *b* (triplet) 1995. —— Peter Guilford (9 Hillier Rd, SW11 6AX), *b* 1963: *m* 1993, Anna, only da of Judge Martin Graham, of Highgate, N6, and has issue living, Alexander Dylan, *b* 1995, — Natalie Geraldine, *b* 1991, — Esme Imogen, *b* 1999.

Grandchildren of late Alberic Arthur Twisleton-Wykeham-Fiennes, 2nd son of late Rev Hon Wingfield Stratford Twisleton-Wykeham-Fiennes (ante):—
Issue of late Sir Maurice Alberic Twisleton-Wykeham-Fiennes, *b* 1907, *d* 1994: *m* 1st, 1932 (*m diss* 1964), Sylvia Joan, who *d* 1996, da of Maj David Finlay, late 7th Dragoon Gds; 2ndly, 1967, Erika Hueller (*Lady Twisleton-Wykeham-Fiennes*) (11 Heath Rise, Kersfield Rd, SW15 3HF), da of Dr Herbert Hueller von Huellenried, of Vienna:—
(By 1st *m*) Mark (29 Therapia Rd, SE22 0SF), *b* 1933; *ed* Eton: *m* 1st, 1962, Jennifer Anne Mary Alleyne, who *d* 1993, da of late Brig Henry Alleyne Lash, Indian Army, of Bridge End, Churt, Surrey; 2ndly, 1996, Caroline Jane, da of late ...... Corris Evans, and has issue living (by 1st *m*), Ralph Nathaniel, *b* 1962: *m* 1993 (*m diss* 1997), Alexandra Elizabeth, da of Anthony Charles Edward Kingston, of Betchworth, Surrey, — Magnus Hubert, *b* 1965: *m* 1995, Maya Dokic, — Jacob Mark, *b* 1970, — Joseph Alberic, *b* (twin) 1970, — Martha Maria, *b* 1964, — Sophia Victoria, *b* 1967. —— Alberic George (19 Pendarves Rd, SW20), *b* 1947; *ed* Lyceum Alpinum, Zuoz; MS, FRCS: *m* 1985, Louise Emily Jane, eldest da of Gordon Bidlake, of Bere Alston, Devon, and has issue living, Emily Elizabeth, *b* 1989, — Alice Henrietta, *b* 1991. —— Elizabeth (c/o National Westminster Bank, 27 Horseferry Rd, SW1P 2AZ), *b* 1935: *m* 1965, Lt-Col Richard James Heslop Randall, who *d* 1984, and has issue living, William Basil, *b* 1966, — Michael Matthew Shaun, *b* 1968, — Roland Patrick James, *b* 1970. —— Antonia Susan Maria (c/o Royal Bank of Scotland, Huntly, AB54 8AD), *b* 1939: *m* 1970 (*m diss* 1989), John Houlton Ewing Mocatta, and has issue living, Antonia Irena Maria, *b* 1971, — Marie-Gabrielle, *b* 1974. —— Henrietta Celia, *b* 1943: *m* 1987, Stephen René Molivadas, DFC, of 4701 Willard Av, Suite 703, Chevy Chase, Maryland 20815, USA.

Grandsons (by 2nd *m*) of late Maj Cecil Wingfield Twisleton-Wykeham-Fiennes (infra):—
Issue of late Anthony Patrick Twisleton-Wykeham-Fiennes, *b* 1927, *d* 1989: *m* 1966, Prudence Jane (30 View St, Woollahra, NSW 2025, Australia), da of late George Woodward Pearce:—
Nicholas Mark, *b* 1969. —— Nathaniel Woodward, *b* 1973.

Granddaughter of late Caryl Wentworth Twisleton-Wykeham-Fiennes, 3rd son of Rev Hon Wingfield Stratford Twisleton-Wykeham-Fiennes (ante):-

Issue of late Maj Cecil Wingfield Twisleton-Wykeham-Fiennes, RMLI, *b* 1897, *d* 1972: *m* 1st, 1920, Margaret Annie, who *d* 1921, da of Philip Robinson, of Egginton, Derby; 2ndly, 1923 (*m diss* 1936), Jessie Mary Goddard, who *d* 1993, da of Nicholas Goddard Jackson, of Duddington, Northants; 3rdly, 1940, Elizabeth Stockton, who *d* 1961, da of George Perry Fiske, of New York:—

(By 2nd *m*) (Kathleen) Patricia, *b* 1925: *m* 1958, Richard Graham Shedden, MC, who *d* 1997, of Bowers Barn, Blandford Forum, Dorset, and has issue living, Simon Rory Lindesay, *b* 1963: *m* 1993 (*m diss* 1995), Juliet Lawley, — Emma Lavinia, *b* 1959: *m* 1994, Patrick R. Mant, and has issue living, Alexandra Remington *b* 1996.

Granddaughter of late Rev Hon Wingfield Stratford Twisleton-Wykeham-Fiennes (ante):—

Issue of late Lt-Col John Temple Twisleton-Wykeham-Fiennes, *b* 1877, *d* 1970: *m* 1929, Constance Astbury, who *d* 1939, da of late David Ross, of Holywood, co Down:—

Bridget Susan Winifred, *b* 1935: *m* 1956, Melvin Marriott, and has issue living, Crispin John Fiennes (37 Greenwood Av, Singapore), *b* 1966: *m* 1996, Jane Alison, da of Leonard Charles Skilton, — Josephine Susan, *b* 1957, — Esmeralda Jane, *b* 1959, — Prudence Ann, *b* 1964, — Samantha Sara, *b* 1968.

PREDECESSORS – (1) *Sir* JAMES Fiennes, Constable of Dover, Warden of the Cinque Ports and Lord Treasurer of England; summoned to Parliament 1446-7-9, and said to have been *cr Lord Saye and Sele* by patent 1447; was imprisoned in the Tower as a partisan of the Duke of Suffolk, and in 1450 was beheaded by Jack Cade's mob at the Standard in Cheapside; *s* by his son (2) WILLIAM, 2nd Lord; was Constable of Porchester and Pevensey Castles, and Vice-Adm of England; summoned to Parliament 1451-69; killed at the Battle of Barnet 1471; *s* by his son (3) HENRY, 3rd Lord; bore the title of Lord Saye but was not summoned to Parliament; *d* 1476; *s* by his son (4) RICHARD, *de jure* 4th Lord; was not summoned to Parliament; *s* by his son (5) EDWARD, *de jure* 5th Lord; did not assume the title; *s* by his son (6) RICHARD, *de jure* 6th Lord, who did not assume the title; *d* 1573; *s* by his son (7) RICHARD, KB; obtained confirmatory recognition of his claim to the Barony, and in 1603 was *cr* by letters patent *Baron Saye and Sele* (peerage of England), with remainder to his heirs-gen with precedence of that date; *d* 1613; *s* by his son (8) WILLIAM, 8th Baron; was a Commr of the Public Safety, and a distinguished leader in the contest between the Parliament and Charles I, and at his residence at Broughton the secret discussions of resistance to the Court took place; *cr Viscount Saye and Sele* (peerage of England) 1624; *d* 1662; *s* by his el son (9) JAMES, 2nd Viscount; *d* 1674 without surviving male issue, when the barony became abeyant between his das, Elizabeth, wife of John Twisleton, and Frances, wife of Andrew Ellis, and the viscountcy devolved upon his nephew (10) WILLIAM, 3rd Viscount, son of Col Hon Nathaniel Fiennes, Speaker of Cromwell's Upper House, who was 2nd son of the 8th Baron; *d* 1696; *s* by his son (11) NATHANIEL, 4th Viscount; *d* unm 1710; *s* by his cousin (12) LAWRENCE, 5th Viscount (son of Col Hon John, one of Cromwell's Lords, who was 3rd son of 8th Baron); *dsp* 1742; *s* by his cousin (13) RICHARD, 6th Viscount (son of Rev Richard Fiennes); *d* 1781, when the viscountcy expired, and the abeyance of the barony of Saye and Sele, which owing to the death of one of the two co-heirs had belonged de jure since 1715 to (14) CECIL, *de jure* Baroness Saye and Sele (da of John Twisleton, of Barley Hall, ante), then to her son (15) FIENNES, *de jure* 11th Baron Saye and Sele, and subsequently to his son (16) JOHN, *de jure* 12th Baron Saye and Sele was terminated in favour of the latter's son (17) THOMAS Twisleton, 13th Baron, great-great-grandson of Elizabeth, da of 2nd Viscount (ante); Gen in the Army and Col 9th Foot; *d* 1788; *s* by his son (18) GREGORY WILLIAM, 14th Baron; assumed in 1825 the additional surnames of Fiennes and Eardley; *d* 1844; *s* by his son (19) WILLIAM THOMAS, 15th Baron; *d* unm 1847; *s* by his cousin (20) FREDERICK, DCL, 16th Baron, 3rd son of the Ven Hon Thomas James Twisleton, DD, by Anne, da and co-heir of Benjamin Ashe; *b* 1799; assumed by Roy licence 1849 the additional surnames of Wykeham-Fiennes: *m* 1st, 1827, Hon Emily Wingfield, who *d* 1837, da of the 4th Viscount Powerscourt; 2ndly, 1857, Hon Caroline Leigh, da of the 1st Baron Leigh; *d* 1887; *s* by his el son (21) JOHN FIENNES, 17th Baron, *b* 1830: *m* 1856, Lady Augusta Sophia Hay, who *d* 1915, da of 10th Earl of Kinnoull; *d* 1907; *s* by his son (22) GEOFFREY CECIL, 18th Baron; *b* 1858; was Comptroller of HM's Household 1912-15: *m* 1884, Marion Ruperta Murray, who *d* 1946, da of late Major Robert Bartholomew Lawes, of Old Park, Dover; *d* 1937; *s* by his el son (23) GEOFFREY RUPERT CECIL, 19th Baron; *b* 1884; Bar Inner Temple 1911; *d* 1949; *s* by his brother (24) IVO MURRAY, OBE, MC, 20th Baron; *b* 1885; Lt-Col RA; High Steward of Banbury 1959-68: *m* 1919, Hersey Cecilia Hester, who *d* 1968, da of late Capt Sir Thomas Dacres Butler, KCVO (E Minto, colls); *d* 1968; *s* by his el son (25) NATHANIEL THOMAS ALLEN, 21st Baron and present peer.

SCANLON, BARON (Scanlon) (Life Baron 1979)

HUGH PARR SCANLON, son of Hugh Scanlon; *b* 26 Oct 1913; *ed* Stretford Elem Sch and Nat Council of Labour Colls; Hon DCL Univ of Kent at Canterbury 1988; Pres Amalgamated Engineering Union 1967-78; Chm Engineering Industry Training Board since 1975; Member British Gas Corpn since 1977; *cr Baron Scalon*, of Davyhulme, co Greater Manchester (Life Baron) 1979: *m* 1943, Nora, da of James Markey, and has issue living, two das.

Residence – 23 Seven Stones Dr, Broadstairs, Kent.

SCARBROUGH, EARL OF (Lumley) (Earl E 1690)

A sound conscience is a wall of brass

RICHARD ALDRED LUMLEY, 12th Earl; *b* 5 Dec 1932; *s* 1969; *ed* Eton, and Magdalen Coll, Oxford; late Lt Queen's Own Yorks Dragoons, and 2nd Lt 11th Hussars; ADC to Gov and C-in-C Cyprus 1956; Hon Col 1st Bn Yorkshire Vols 1975-88; Pres Northern Area, R British Legion 1984-93; Trustee Leeds Castle Foundation since 1981; DL S Yorks 1974, Lord Lieut since 1996; Memb Royal Commn on Historical MSS since 1994: *m* 1970, Lady Elizabeth Ramsay, Lady of the Bedchamber to HM Queen Elizabeth The Queen Mother since 1994, da of 16th Earl of Dalhousie, and has issue.

꽃rms – Argent, a fesse gules, between three popinjays vert, collared of the second. Crest – A pelican in her piety, proper. Supporters – Two parrots, wings expanded, vert beaked and membered gules.
Residence – Sandbeck Park, Maltby, Rotherham, S Yorks. *Clubs* – White's, Pratt's, Jockey.

SONS LIVING

RICHARD OSBERT (*Viscount Lumley*), *b* 18 May 1973; Page of Honour to HM Queen Elizabeth The Queen Mother 1988-89.
Hon Thomas Henry, *b* 1980; Page of Honour to HM Queen Elizabeth The Queen Mother 1995-97.

DAUGHTER LIVING

Lady Rose Frederica Lily, *b* 1981.

SISTERS LIVING

Lady Elizabeth (*Baroness Grimthorpe*), DCVO, *b* 1925; appointed a Lady of the Bedchamber of HM Queen Elizabeth, The Queen Mother 1973; CVO 1983, DCVO 1995: *m* 1954, 4th Baron Grimthorpe. *Residence* – Westow Hall, York.
Lady Anne Katharine (*Viscountess Ridley*), *b* 1928: *m* 1953, 4th Viscount Ridley, KG. *Residence* – Boston House, Blagdon, Seaton Burn, Northumberland.
Lady (Jane Lily) Serena, *b* 1935: *m* 1963, Hugh Wiley of Oak Hill, Palmyra, Virginia 22963, USA, and has issue living, Justin Hugh, *b* 1964, — Marcus Thomas, *b* 1966, — Peter Alexander, *b* 1971.

DAUGHTER LIVING OF TENTH EARL

Lady Serena Mary Barbara, *b* 1901; is a DStJ, and a JP for Richmond: *m* 1923, Hon Robert James, who *d* 1960 (*see* B Northbourne, colls). *Residence* – St Nicholas, Richmond, Yorkshire.

PREDECESSORS – (1) *Sir* RICHARD Lumley, Knt, garrisoned Lumley Castle on behalf of the Royal cause, and was a principal commander under Prince Rupert; *cr Viscount Lumley* (peerage of Ireland) 1628; *s* by his grandson (2) RICHARD, PC, 2nd Viscount; commanded a regt of Horse at Battle of Sedgemoor 1685; was a Gentleman of the Bedchamber to Prince of Orange, Lieut-Gen of Forces in Flanders, Lord-Lieut of Durham and Northumberland, and Chancellor of the Duchy of Lancaster, etc; *cr Baron Lumley*, of Lumley Castle, co Durham (peerage of England) 1681, and *Viscount Lumley* and *Earl of Scarbrough* (peerage of England) 1690; *d* 1721; *s* by his el son (3) RICHARD, KG, 2nd Earl; *d* unm 1740; *s* by his brother (4) THOMAS, KB, 3rd Earl; assumed the surname of Saunderson by Roy licence 1723; *d* 1752; *s* by his son (5) RICHARD, PC, 4th Earl; was Cofferer of the Household, Dep Earl Marshal of England, and Joint Vice-Treasurer of Ireland; *d* 1782; *s* by his el son (6) GEORGE AUGUSTA (*sic*), 5th Earl; *d* unm 1807; *s* by his brother (7) RICHARD, 6th Earl; sat as MP for Lincoln city; *d* 1832; *s* by his brother (8) JOHN, 7th Earl; assumed the surname of Savile by Act of Parliament; was Preb of York and Rector of Winteringham; *d* 1835; *s* by his son (9) JOHN, 8th Earl; assumed by Roy licence 1836 the additional and principal surname of Savile; was Lord-Lieut of Nottinghamshire; *d* unm 1856; *s* by his cousin (10) RICHARD 9th Earl, son of Frederick Lumley-Savile, son of Hon Frederick Lumley (5th son of 4th Earl); *b* 1813: *m* 1846, Frederica Mary Adeliza, who *d* 1907, da of late Andrew Robert Drummond; *d* 1884; *s* by his son (11) ALDRED FREDERICK GEORGE BERESFORD, KG, GBE, KCB, TD, 10th Earl, *b* 1857; late Hon Col (sometime Comdg) Yorkshire Dragoons (Yeo), and Bailiff Grand Cross of Order of St John of Jerusalem (Sub-Prior thereof 1923-43); Lord-Lieut of W Riding of Yorkshire 1892-1904; S Africa 1900 with Imperial Yeo; Director-Gen of Territorial and Vol Forces 1917-21 with rank of Maj-Gen: *m* 1899, Lucy Cecilia, who *d* 1931, el da of Cecil Dunn Gardner, and widow of Robert Ashton; *d* 1945; *s* by his nephew (12) (LAWRENCE) ROGER, KG, GCSI, GCIE, GCVO, Royal Victorian Chain, TD, PC (son of late Brig-Gen Hon Osbert Victor George Atheling Lumley, CMG, 3rd son of 9th Earl), 11th Earl, *b* 1896; World War I 1915-18 with 11th Hus; MP for E Hull 1922-29 and for York 1931-37; Gov of Bombay 1937-43; Lord Lieut W Riding 1948-69; Lord Chamberlain 1952-63; Grand Master of United Grand Lodge of English Freemasons 1951-67, and Pro Grand Master 1967-69; a Permanent Lord-in-Waiting to HM 1963-69; Chancellor of Durham Univ; High Steward of York Minster: *m* 1922, Katharine Isabel, DCVO, who *d* 1979, da of late Robert Finnie McEwen, of Bardrochat, Ayrshire, and Marchmont, Berwickshire (B Napier of Magdala); *d* 1969; *s* by his only son (13) RICHARD ALDRED, 12th Earl and present peer; also Viscount and Baron Lumley.

SCARMAN, BARON (Scarman) (Life Baron 1977)

LESLIE GEORGE SCARMAN, OBE, PC, son of late George Charles Scarman; *b* 29 July, 1911; *ed* Radley, and Brasenose Coll, Oxford (MA, Hon Fellow 1966); Hon LLD Exeter, Glasgow, London, Keele, Freiburg, Warwick and Bristol; Bar Middle Temple 1936; QC 1957; Bencher 1961; a Judge of High Court of Justice (Probate, Divorce and Admiralty Div, now Family Div) 1961-72; Chm Law Commn 1965-72; Lord Justice of Appeal 1972-77, since when a Lord of Appeal in Ordinary; Chancellor, Warwick Univ since 1978; author of *Pattern of Law Reform*, 1967, and *English Law — The New Dimension*, 1975; 1939-45 War as Wing Cdr RAFVR (OBE); *cr* OBE (Mil) 1945, Knt 1961, PC 1972, and *Baron Scarman*, of Quatt, co Shropshire (Life Baron) 1977: *m* 1947, Ruth Clement, da of late Clement Wright, ICS.

Address – c/o House of Lords, SW1.

ADOPTED SON LIVING

John Clement, *b* 1946.

SCARSDALE, VISCOUNT (Curzon) (Baron GB 1761, Viscount UK 1911, Bt (S) 1636 and (E) 1641)

FRANCIS JOHN NATHANIEL CURZON, 3rd Viscount, 7th Baron, and 11th Baronet; *b* 28 July 1924; *s* 1977; *ed* Eton; late Capt Scots Gds; 30th Lord of Kedleston, and patron of three livings (but being a Roman Catholic cannot present): *m* 1st, 1948 (*m diss* 1967), Solange Yvonne Palmyre Ghislaine, who *d* 1974, da of late Oscar Hanse, of Mont-sur-Marchienne, Belgium; 2ndly, 1968, Mrs Helene Gladys Frances Lubbock, only da of late Maj William Ferguson Thomson, of Kinellar, Aberdeenshire, and has issue by 1st and 2nd *m*.

Arms – Argent, on a bend sable, three popinjays or, collared gules. **Crest** – A popinjay rising, wings displayed and inverted or, collared gules. **Supporters** – Two female figures, the *dexter*, representing Prudence, habited argent, mantled azure, holding in her sinister hand a javelin, entwined by a remora proper; the *sinister* representing Liberality, habited argent mantled purpure, and holding in both hands a cornucopia proper. **Mottoes** – Let Curzon holde what Curzon helde; Recte et suaviter.

Seat – Kedleston, Derby. *Residence* – Tullich, Strathcarron, Ross-shire. *Club* – County (Derby).

Justly and mildly

SONS LIVING (By 1st marriage)

Hon PETER GHISLAIN NATHANIEL, *b* 6 March 1949; *ed* Ampleforth: *m* 1983 (*m diss* 1996), Mrs Karen Osborne (*née* Jackson), and has issue living, Danielle Solange, *b* 1983.

Hon David James Nathaniel (33 Lingfield Rd, SW19), *b* 1958; *ed* Stowe: *m* 1981, Ruth, da of late John Ernest Linton, of Wavertree, Liverpool, and has issue living, Andrew Linton Nathaniel, *b* 1986, — Emma Rachel, *b* 1983.

(By 2nd marriage)

Hon Richard Francis Nathaniel (Cumberhill Lodge, Kedleston, Derby), *b* 1969; *ed* Shiplake, and RAC Cirencester: *m* 1999, Emma Rachel Hilary, da of late Vincent Maguire, of Little Waltham, Essex.

Hon James Fergus Nathaniel (53 Rutland Gate, SW7), *b* 1970; *ed* Eton, and Edinburgh Univ (MA).

DAUGHTER LIVING (By 1st marriage)

Hon Annette Yvonne (12 Kaab Ibn Malek St, Hegaz Sq, Heliopolis, Cairo, Egypt), *b* 1953: *m* 1979, Capt Hani Talaat Latief, of 16 Salah el Din St, Heliopolis, Cairo, and has issue living, Sagi, *b* 1982, — Shadi, *b* 1989.

SISTER LIVING (Raised to the rank of a Viscount's daughter, 1980)

Hon Christian Avril (The House of the Pines, Virginia Ave, Virginia Water, Surrey), *b* 1923.

DAUGHTERS LIVING OF SECOND VISCOUNT

Hon Anne Mildred, *b* 1923; 1942-44 War in ATS: *m* 1942 (*m diss* 1960), Maj Walter James Latimer Willson, DSO, Gren Gds, who *d* 1994, son of Sir Walter Stuart James Willson, and has had issue, Simon James Curzon (46 Warwick Rd, W5 5PX), *b* 1942: *m* 1st, 1968, Sarah, el da of Douglas Ferris Hewat Jaboor, MB, of La Maison De la Fontaine, Mont Perrine, St Lawrence, Jersey (*see* Aykroyd, Bt, *cr* 1920, 1985 Edn); 2ndly, 1979, Sandra, da of Harold Singer, of Tillsonburg, Canada, and has issue living (by 1st *m*), Alexander James Alfred Curzon *b* 1969, Benjamin William Curzon *b* 1971, (by 2nd *m*) Simone Junia Singer Curzon *b* 1981, — Nicholas William Curzon, *b* 1951; *d* 197—, — Jacqueline Anne Curzon, *b* 1945: *m* 1967, Anthony Julian Bavin, and *d* 1992.

Hon Juliana Eveline (Castledown, Portroe, Nenagh, co Tipperary), *b* 1928: *m* 1st, 1948 (*m diss* 1952), George Derek Stanley Smith, who *d* 1963; 2ndly, 1953 (*m diss* 1956), Frederick Nettlefold; 3rdly, 1956 (*m diss* 1962), as his 2nd wife, Sir Dudley Herbert Cunliffe-Owen, 2nd Bt; 4thly, 1962 (*m diss* 1972), as his 3rd wife, John Roberts (*see* Roberts, Bt, colls, *cr* 1909), and has issue living, (by 1st *m*) Charles Peregrine, *b* 1952; *ed* Eton, — Venetia Mary, *b* 1950, — (by 2nd *m*) Caroline Anne (*Viscountess Windsor*), *b* 1954: *m* 1979, Ivor Edward Other, Viscount Windsor, el son of 3rd Earl of Plymouth, — (by 3rd *m*) (*see* Cunliffe-Owen, Bt), — (by 4th *m*) (*see* Roberts, Bt, colls, *cr* 1909).

Hon Diana Geraline, *b* 1934.

COLLATERAL BRANCH LIVING

(In remainder to Baronetcies only)

Descendants of Assheton Curzon (2nd son of 4th baronet), who was *cr* Viscount Curzon 1802 (*see* E Howe).

PREDECESSORS – From the muniments at Kedleston this family can trace descent from Robert de Courson, Seigneur of Courson, nr Lisieux, Normandy, who was granted Fishead, Oxon, W Lockinge, Berks, etc by William I. His grandson, Richard de Courson, was granted Knights' fees of Croxall, Kedleston, Edinghall and Twyford, cos Derby and Stafford. Richard's 2nd son Stephen (who *m* Elfrica, da of Olav King of Man) held Fauld, Staffs. The senior line terminated in Mary, da and heir of Sir George Curzon of Croxall, who *m* c 1612, Edward Sackville, 4th Earl of Dorset, KC, the second line being Curzon of Kedleston, and the third, Curzon of Waterperry (Bts ext 1750); **(1)** JOHN Curzon (*cr* a *Baronet* of Scotland 1636 and of England 1641), el son of John Curzon of Kedleston, MP for Derbys; *d* 1686; *s* by his son **(2)** *Sir* NATHANIEL, 2nd Bt; *d* 1718; *s* by his el son **(3)** *Sir* JOHN, 3rd Bt; sat as MP for Derbyshire 1702-27; *d* unmarried 1727; *s* by his brother **(4)** *Sir* NATHANIEL, 4th Bt; sat as MP for Derbyshire 1727-58; his 2nd son was *cr* Viscount Curzon (*see* E Howe); *d* 1758; *s* by his el son **(5)** *Sir* NATHANIEL, 5th Bt; *cr* Baron Scarsdale, of Scarsdale, co Derby (peerage of Great Britain) 1761; was Chm of Cttees in House of Lords 1775-90; *d* 1804; *s* by his son **(6)** NATHANIEL, 2nd Baron; *d* 1837; *s* by his el son **(7)** NATHANIEL, 3rd Baron; *d* unmarried 1856; *s* by his nephew **(8)** *Rev* ALFRED NATHANIEL, 4th Baron (2nd son of the Rev Hon Alfred Curzon, 2nd son of 2nd Baron), *b* 1831; R of Kedleston: *m* 1856, Blanche, who *d* 1875, da of Joseph Pocklington Senhouse, of Netherhall, Cumberland; *d* 1916; *s* by his el son **(9)** GEORGE NATHANIEL, KG, GCSI, GCIE, PC, FRS, 5th Baron, 1st Earl and 1st Marquess Curzon of Kedleston: *b* 1859; Under-Sec of State for India Nov 1891 to Aug 1892, Under-Sec of State for Foreign Affairs 1895-98, Viceroy and Gov-Gen of India 1898-1904, and again 1904-5, Lord Warden of the Cinque Ports and Constable of Dover Castle 1904-5, Lord Privy Seal 1915-16, Pres of first Air Board May to Dec 1916 (also became a Member of Cabinet War Council July 1916), Lord Pres of the Council and Leader of the House of Lords (with a seat in the War Cabinet) Dec 1916 to Nov 1919, and Sec of State for Foreign Affairs Nov 1919 to Jan 1924 (also Leader of the House of Lords), and again Lord Pres of the Council and Leader of the House of Lords Nov 1924 to March 1925; sat as MP for SW Lancashire, Southport Div (*C*) 1886-98; bore Standard of Empire of India at Coronation of King George V 1911; *cr* Baron Curzon of Kedleston, co Derby (peerage of Ireland) 1898, *Baron Ravensdale*, of Ravensdale, co Derby, with special remainder in default of issue male to his el da and the heirs of her body, failing whom to his other das in like manner in order of primogeniture, *Viscount Scarsdale*, of Scarsdale, co Derby, with special remainder in default of issue male, to his father (the 4th Baron Scarsdale, whom he succeeded in the Barony) and the heirs male of his body, and *Earl Curzon of Kedleston*, co Derby (all in peerage of UK) 1911; KG 1916; *cr* Earl of Kedleston, co Derby and Marquess Curzon of Kedleston (peerage of UK) 1921; *s* as 5th Baron Scarsdale and as 9th Baronet (both of Scotland and England) 1916; received Roy Victorian Chain 1903: *m* 1st, 1895, Mary Victoria, CI, who *d* 1906 (had Kaisar-i-Hind gold medal), el da of Levi Zeigler Leiter, of Dupont Circle, Washington, USA; 2ndly, 1917, *Dame* Grace Elvina Trilla, GBE, who *d* 1958, da of J. Monroe Hinds, of Alabama, USA, widow of Alfred Duggan, (M Curzon of Kedleston (ext)); *d* 1925, when the Irish Barony of 1898, the Earldom of 1911, and the Marquessate and Earldom of 1921 became ext, and the Barony of Ravensdale devolved by special remainder upon his el da Mary Irene, and the Barony (*cr* 1761) and Viscountcy of Scarsdale, together with the two Baronetcies, passed to his nephew **(10)** RICHARD NATHANIEL (son of late Col Hon Alfred Nathaniel Curzon, 2nd son of 4th Baron Scarsdale and in special remainder to the Viscountcy), 2nd Viscount; *b* 1898, 1914-18 War with R Scots Greys; 1939-45 War as Maj RA in Middle East; sometime Hon Attaché Diplo Ser, and Vice-Pres British Boxing Board of Control: *m* 1st, 1923 (*m diss* 1946), Mildred Carson, who *d* 1969, da of William Roland Dunbar, of Huyton, Lancs; 2ndly, 1946, Ottilie Margarete Julie, who *d* 1998, da of Charles Pretzlik, of 155 Sloane St, SW1, and formerly wife of James Harris; *d* 1977; *s* by his first cousin **(11)** FRANCIS JOHN NATHANIEL (son of late Hon Francis Nathaniel Curzon, 3rd son of 4th Baron), 3rd Viscount and present peer; also Baron Scarsdale.

SCHON, BARONY OF (Schon) (Extinct 1995)

DAUGHTERS LIVING OF LIFE BARON

Hon Susan Henriette, *b* 1941: *m* 1964, Richard Henry Keller, of Hillmorton, Wills Grove, Mill Hill Village, NW7.
Hon Yvonne Catherine, *b* 1944: *m* 1979, Norman Saville, of 21 Hillview Rd, Mill Hill Village, NW7.

Schreiber, family name of Baron Marlesford.

SCOTLAND OF ASTHAL, BARONESS (Scotland) (Life Baroness 1997)

PATRICIA JANET SCOTLAND, da of Arthur Leonard Scotland, of Ilford, Essex; *b* 19 Aug 1955; *ed* London Univ (LLB 1977); Bar Middle Temple 1977, Master 1997; QC 1991; Memb Antigua Bar; former Memb Commn for Racial Equality; Memb Millenium Commn since 1994; Chm HMG Caribbean Advisory Group; Head of Chambers, 1 Gray's Inn Sq; *cr Baroness Scotland of Asthal*, of Asthal, co Oxfordshire (Life Baroness) 1997: *m* 1985, Richard Martin Mawhinney, son of Raymond Johnston Mawhinney and has issue.
Address – 1 Gray's Inn Sq, WC1R 5AG.

SONS LIVING

Hon Matthew Jackson MAWHINNEY, *b* 1992.
Hon Benjamin James MAWHINNEY, *b* 1994.

Scott, family name of Earl of Eldon.

Scott, Hepburne-, family name of Lord Polwarth.

Scott, Montagu Douglas, family name of Duke of Buccleuch.

Scrymgeour, Lord; son of Earl of Dundee.

Scrymgeour, family name of Earl of Dundee.

SEAFIELD, EARL OF (Ogilvie-Grant) (Earl S 1701)

IAN DEREK FRANCIS OGILVIE-GRANT, 13th Earl; *b* 20 Mar 1939; *s* 1969; *ed* Eton; recognised in the surname of Ogilvie-Grant by warrant of Lord Lyon 1971: *m* 1st, 1960 (*m diss* 1971), Mary Dawn Mackenzie, el da of Henry Illingworth, of 35 Gloucester Sq, W2; 2ndly, 1971, Leila, da of Mahmoud Refaat, of Cairo, and has issue by 1st *m*.

Arms – Quarterly; 1st and 4th grand quarters, quarterly, 1st and 4th, argent, a lion passant guardant gules, crowned with an imperial crown or, and 2nd and 3rd, argent, a cross engrailed sable, *Ogilvie*; 2nd and 3rd grand quarters, gules, three antique crowns or, *Grant*. **Crests** – *Dexter*, a lady richly attired from the waist upwards proper wearing a pointed fifteenth century head-dress argent, *Ogilvie; sinister*, a burning hill between two Scots Pine saplings proper, *Grant*. **Supporters** – *Dexter*, a lion rampant guardant or, armed gules: *sinister*, a savage or naked man bearing upon his shoulder a club proper and wreathed about the head and middle with a laurel vert.
Seat – Old Cullen, Cullen, Banffshire.

SONS LIVING (By 1st marriage)

Hon JAMES ANDREW (*Viscount Reidhaven* and *Master of Seafield*), *b* 30 Nov 1963; *ed* Harrow.

Hon Alexander Derek Henry, *b* 1966; *ed* Eton: *m* 1995, Mrs Lucy Clare Naylor-Leyland, da of Henry Potts, of Eglingham Hall, Alnwick, Northumberland, and formerly wife of Michael Alexander Robert Naylor-Leyland (*see* Naylor-Leyland, Bt, colls).

SISTER LIVING

Lady Pauline Anne, *b* 1944: *m* 1st, 1964 (*m diss* 1970), James Henry Harcourt Illingworth; 2ndly, 1972 (*m diss* 1976), Sir William Gordon Gordon-Cumming, 6th Bt; 3rdly, 1976, Hugh Richard Sykes; 4thly, 1989, David John Nicholson, of Revack Lodge, Grantown-on-Spey, Morayshire, and has issue living (by 3rd *m*), Harry Peter Derek, *b* 1977.

COLLATERAL BRANCHES LIVING   *In remainder to the Earldom, the Barony of Strathspey, and the Baronetcy (cr 1625)*

Descendants of late Trevor Ogilvie Grant (2nd son of 10th Earl), who *s* as 4th Baron Strathspey 1915 (see that title).

Grandchildren of late William Robert Ogilvie-Grant, son of late Capt Hon George Henry Essex Ogilvie-Grant, 6th son of 6th Earl:—

Issue of late Eleanora Ogilvie-Grant, *b* 1892, *d* 1956: *m* 1st, 1913 (*m diss* 1926), Lt-Com Reginald William Blake, RN (ret), who *d* 1927; 2ndly, 1926, Lt-Com Sir Roger Thomas Twysden, 10th Bt, who *d* 1934:—
(By 1st *m*) Pamela Rosemary, *b* 1916: *m* 1937, Col Leslie Brindley Bream Beuttler, OBE, Duke of Wellington's Regt, who *d* 1978, and has had issue, †Michael Simon Brindley Bream, *b* 1940; *d* 1988, — Nicholas Randolph Kerr (Château de la Môle, La Môle 83129, France), *b* 1943: *m* 1979, Martine Andriveau, — Caroline Jane (*Hon Mrs Alan Clark*), *b* 1942: *m* 1958, Rt Hon Alan Kenneth McKenzie Clark, of Saltwood Castle, Hythe, Kent (*see* B Clark, ext), and has issue living, James Alasdair Kenneth *b* 1960: *m* 1st, 1985 (*m diss* 1988), Sarah Marian, yst da of A. Dawes, of Wexham Place, Fulmer, Bucks; 2ndly, 1988 (*m diss* 1992), Sally Ruth, da of late Peter Smith, of Codsall, Staffs; 3rdly, 1995, Julie Jane, yst da of Col Nigel Flower, of Camberley, Surrey (and has issue living (by 3rd *m*), Angus George McKenzie *b* 1997), Andrew McKenzie *b* 1962: *m* 1993, Sarah G., da of Nigel Harris, of Muscat, Sultanate of Oman (and has issue living, Albert McKenzie *b* 1996, Archibald Randolph *b* 1998). *Residence* – Finca Villordo, Benalmàdena-Pueblo, Malaga, Spain. —— Lavinia Elizabeth, *b* 1921: *m* 1954, Lt-Col Charles Edward Morton, TD, City of London Yeo (TA) (Durrant, Bt), who *d* 1988, and has issue living, Roger Thomas (Green Lanes, Gt Coxswell, nr Faringdon, Oxon), *b* 1957, — Louise Jean (Cuckoo Cage Farm, Rangemore, nr Burton on Trent, Staffs DE14 9SF), *b* 1955. *Residence* – The Old Stables, Hollybush Park, Newborough, nr Burton on Trent, Staffs DE13 8SF.

Issue of late Marjorie Elspeth Ogilvie-Grant, *b* 1894, *d* 1967: *m* 1921, Capt Ronald Fitzhardinge Speir, formerly RE (B Gifford):—
(John Hugh) Anthony SPEIR (PO Box 5389, Cresta 2118, S Africa), *b* 1925; Capt S African Inf Corps: *m* 1st 1946 (*m diss* 1952), Isobel, da of James Snart, of Leicester; 2ndly, 1974, Joan Margaret, da of A. Valentine, of Krugersdorp, S Africa, and has issue living (by 1st *m*), Helen Joanna (9 Orchard St, Madison, NJ 07940, USA), *b* 1948: *m* 1969 (*m diss* 1997), David George Thomson, and has issue living, Iain James Speir *b* 1973, Caroline Louise Speir *b* 1976, — Fiona Margaret, *b* 1951: *m* 1973, Michael John Haughey, of 11 Blenheim Rd, Bedford Park, W4 1UB, and has issue living, Barnaby Michael Fitzhardinge Speir *b* 1975, Tobias John Thomas Speir *b* 1983, Michael Gabriel Bartholomew Speir *b* 1986, Rachel Mary Speir *b* 1974, Bethany Joy Speir *b* 1978, Tamara Jane Speir *b* 1979: *m* 1999, Thomas Parker. —— Elizabeth Jean (Flat 5, 13 Upper Phillimore Gdns, W8 7HF), *b* 1922. —— Diana Marigold (1 North St, St Andrews, Fife), *b* 1932.

Issue of late Alison Jean Ogilvie-Grant, *b* 1896, *d* 1970: *m* 1923, Capt Reginald Cornwallis Hargreaves, MVO, MC, formerly Rifle Bde, who *d* 1974:—
Basil John Alexander HARGREAVES (Barn House, Sawbridge Rd, Litchfield, Conn 06759, USA), *b* 1925: *m* 1st, 1960 (*m diss* 1972), Anne Mary Beatrice Stacey; 2ndly, 1980, Mrs Barbara Ann Baker (*née* Court), and has issue living (by 1st *m*), Charles John Cornwallis, *b* 1966. —— Alison June (Swallowfield, Enton Green, Godalming, Surrey), *b* 1928: *m* 1978, Ronald Burns, who *d* 1995.

PREDECESSORS – (1) *Sir* WALTER Ogilvie, Knt, was *cr Lord Ogilvie of Deskford* (peerage of Scotland) 1616; *s* by his son **(2)** JAMES, 2nd Lord, *cr Earl of Findlater* (peerage of Scotland) 1638, and obtained in 1641 a new patent with remainder to his daughter Elizabeth and her husband Sir Patrick Ogilvy, who at his death became **(3)** PATRICK and ELIZABETH, Earl and Countess of Findlater; the Earl *d* 1658; *s* by his son **(4)** JAMES, 3rd Earl, *d* 1711; *s* by his son **(5)** JAMES, 4th Earl, who had in 1698 been *cr Lord Ogilvy of Cullen* and *Viscount Seafield* (peerage of Scotland), with remainder, failing heirs male of the body, to heirs of entail, and in 1701 *Lord Ogilvy of Deskford*, and *Cullen, Viscount Reidhaven*, and *Earl of Seafield* (peerage of Scotland), with the same special remainder; was an eminent lawyer, and held successively the offices of Solicitor Gen and Sec of State for Scotland, Lord Chief Baron of the Exchequer, High Commr to the Gen Assembly of the Church, Keeper of the Great Seal in Scotland, and Pres of the Court of Session; *d* 1730; *s* by his son **(6)** JAMES, 5th Earl of Findlater and 2nd Earl of Seafield; *d* 1764; *s* by his son **(7)** JAMES, 6th Earl of Findlater and 3rd Earl of Seafield; *d* 1770; *s* by his son **(8)** JAMES, 7th Earl of Findlater and 4th Earl of Seafield; *d* 1811, when the Earldom of Findlater expired, and the peerages of 1698 and 1701 reverted to his heir-general **(9)** *Sir* LEWIS ALEXANDER Grant of Grant, 9th Bt, who became 5th Earl of Seafield; assumed 1811 the additional surname of Ogilvie; MP for Elginshire 1790-96; *d* unmarried 1840; *s* by his brother **(10)** FRANCIS WILLIAM, 6th Earl of Seafield; MP for various Scottish constituencies 1802-40; was Lord-Lt of co Inverness, and a Representative Peer; *d* 1853; *s* by his son **(11)** JOHN CHARLES, KT, 7th Earl, *b* 1815; having been a Representative Peer, was *cr Baron Strathspey*, of Strathspey, cos Inverness and Moray (peerage of UK) 1858: *m* 1850, Hon Caroline Henrietta Stuart, who *d* 1911 (having succeeded in 1884 to the Grant and Seafield estates, and having devised them in trust for the 11th Earl and his successors in the title), da of 11th Lord Blantyre; *d* 1881; *s* by his son **(12)** IAN CHARLES, 8th Earl, *b* 1851; *dsp* 1884, when the Barony of Strathspey became ext *s* in Scottish peerages of 1698 and 1701 to his uncle **(13)** JAMES, 9th Earl, 4th son of 6th Earl, by Mary Anne, da of John Charles Dunn, of St Helena and Higham House; *b* 1817; sat as MP for Elgin and Nairnshire (*C*) 1868-74; *cr Baron Strathspey* (peerage of UK) 1884: *m* 1st, 1841, Caroline Louisa, who *d* 1850, da of late Eyre Evans, of Ash Hill Towers, Limerick; 2ndly, 1853, Constance Helena, who *d* 1872, da of Sir Robert Abercromby, 5th Bt; 3rdly, 1875, Georgiana Adelaide, da of late Gen Frederick Nathaniel Walker, KCH, of Manor House, Bushey, and widow of William Stuart, of Aldenham Abbey, Herts; *d* 1888; *s* by his el son **(14)** FRANCIS WILLIAM, 10th Earl, *b* 1847: *m* 1874, Ann (Nina) Trevor Corry, who *d* 1935, da of late Maj George Thomas Evans, of Ash Hill Towers, co Limerick, and Clooneavin, Otago, NZ; *d* 1888; *s* by his el son **(15)** JAMES, 11th Earl, *b* 1876; 30th Chief of the Clan Grant; Capt Queen's Own Cameron Highlanders: *m* 1898, Mary Elizabeth Nina, who *d* 1962, da of late Joseph Henry Townend, MD, JP, of Christchurch, NZ; *ka* 1915, when the Barony of Strathspey and the Baronetcy devolved upon his brother, but in the Scottish Peerages he was *s* by his only child **(16)** NINA CAROLINE, Countess of Seafield, *b* 1906: *m* 1930 (*m diss* 1957), Derek Studley-Herbert (who *d* 1960, having assumed by deed poll 1939, the additional surnames of Ogilvie-Grant), F/O RAFVR, and late Gren Gds; *d* 1969; *s* by her only son **(17)** IAN DEREK FRANCIS, 13th Earl, and present peer; also Viscount Seafield, Viscount Reidhaven, Lord Ogilvie of Cullen, and Lord Ogilvie of Deskford and Cullen.

Seaford, Baron; see Baron Howard de Walden and Seaford.

Seager, family name of Baron Leighton of St Mellons.

SECCOMBE, BARONESS (Seccombe) (Life Baroness 1991)

JOAN ANNA DALZIEL SECCOMBE, DBE, da of late Robert John Owen, of Solihull, W Midlands; *b* 3 May 1930; *ed* St Martin's Sch, Solihull; JP Solihull 1968, Chm of Bench 1981-84, Chm Lord Chancellor's Advisory Cttee Solihull 1978-93, CC W Midlands 1977-81; Chm Trading Standards Cttee 1979-81, Midlands Electrical Consultative Council 1981-90, Conservative Women's Nat Cttee 1981-84, and Nat Union of Conservative and Unionists Assocn 1987-88 (Vice-Chm 1984-87), Vice-Chm Conservative Party 1987-97; Member W Midlands Police Cttee 1977-81, and 1985-91; Gov Nuffield Hosps since 1988 (Dep Chm since 1992), Chm of Trustees Nuffield Hosps Pension Fund; *cr* DBE 1984, and *Baroness Seccombe*, of Kineton, co Warwicks (Life Baroness) 1991: *m* 1950, Henry Lawrence Seccombe, and has issue.

𝕬rms – Per pale gules and vert, a chevron ermine between three bugle horns argent, stringed or, on a chief per pale vert and gules three roses argent barbed or, on each another rose gules barbed and seeded proper.
Residence – Linden Cottage, The Green, Little Kineton, Warwicks CV35 0DJ.

SONS LIVING

Hon Philip Stanley, *b* 1951; *ed* Rugby, and RAC Cirencester: *m* 1978, Isabel Elizabeth Urquhart, and has issue living, Charles Stanley, *b* 1982, — Olivia Elizabeth, *b* 1984.
Hon Robert Murray, *b* 1954; *ed* Stowe, Brasenose Coll, Oxford, and Lancaster Univ: *m* 1995, Tatyana Sergeyevna Karpenko, and has issue living, Anna Tatyana, *b* 1995.

SEEBOHM, BARONY OF (Seebohm) (Extinct 1990)

SONS LIVING OF LIFE BARON

Dr the Hon Richard Hugh, *b* 1933; *ed* Winchester, Magdalene Coll, Camb (MA 1964), and Magdalen Coll, Oxford (DPhil 1964); late 2nd Lieut RA; Tube Investments Ltd 1960, HM Treasury 1968, Department of Trade and Industry 1982; a Reference Sec Monopolies and Mergers Commn 1990-93: *m* 1966, Margaret Evelyne, da of late Cdr Edward Rolf Frederick Hok, OBE, RN, of Long Crendon, Aylesbury, Bucks, and has issue living, Henrietta Lucy, *b* 1967, — Sophia Kate, *b* 1968, — Charlotte Emily, *b* 1970, — Laura Frances Harriet, *b* 1973. *Residence* – Stable Cottage, Flatford Lane, E. Bergholt, Colchester, Essex C07 6UN.

DAUGHTERS LIVING OF LIFE BARON

Hon Victoria, CBE, *b* 1937; author and journalist (as Victoria Glendinning); Hon DLitt Southampton 1994, Ulster 1995, and Dublin 1995; FRSL; CBE (Civil) 1998: *m* 1st, 1958 (*m diss* 1981), Prof Oliver Nigel Valentine Glendinning; 2ndly, 1982, Terence de Vere White, who *d* 1994; 3rdly, 1996, Kevin O'Sullivan, and has issue living (by 1st *m*), Paul Alexander, *b* 1959, — Hugo Frederic, *b* 1961, — Matthew Nigel, *b* 1962, — Simon Benjamin, *b* 1964. *Address* – c/o David Higham Assocs, 5-8 Lower John St, W1R 4HA.

Hon Caroline, *b* 1940; writer: *m* 1st, 1962 (*m diss* 1967), Roger John Smith; 2ndly, 1974 (*m diss* 1993), Walter H. Lippincott, and has issue living (by 2nd *m*), Hugh, *b* 1983, — Sophie, *b* 1979. *Residence* – 19 River Drive, Titusville, NJ 08560, USA.

Seely, family name of Baron Mottistone.

SEFTON OF GARSTON, BARON (Sefton) (Life Baron 1978)

WILLIAM HENRY SEFTON, son of George Sefton; b 5 Aug 1915; ed Duncombe Rd Sch, Liverpool; Liverpool Co Council 1953 (Leader 1964-78); Chm and Leader, Merseyside Co Council 1974-77, since when a Member, Dep Chm Runcorn Development Corpn 1967-74, since when Chm; a Member of NW Economic Planning Corpn since 1975; cr Baron Sefton of Garston, of Garston, co Merseyside (Life Baron) 1978: m 1940, Phyllis, da of — Kerr.
Residence – 88 Tramway Rd, Liverpool L17 7AZ.

SEGAL, BARONY OF (Segal) (Extinct 1985)

DAUGHTERS LIVING OF LIFE BARON

Hon Maureen (2 Park Town, Oxford OX2 6SH), b 1935: m 1956, Jeremy Hadfield, who d 1988, and has issue.
Hon Valery, b 1943: m 1967, Paul Nicholas David Pelham, of Manor Farm House, Manningford Bohun, Pewsey, Wilts SN9 6JR, and has issue.

SELBORNE, EARL OF (Palmer) (Earl UK 1882)

The palm is for virtue

JOHN ROUNDELL PALMER, KBE, 4th Earl; b 24 March 1940; s 1971; ed Eton, and Ch Ch, Oxford (MA); DL Hants 1982; FIBiol, FRAgS, Hon LLD Bristol 1989; FRS; Vice Chm of The Apple and Pear Development Council 1971-73; Treas of Bridewell Royal Hosp (King Edward's Sch, Witley) 1972-83, and Chm Hops Marketing Board 1978-82; Chm Agricultural and Food Research Council 1983-89; Pres South of England Agric Soc 1984, and Royal Agric Soc of England 1988; Chm Joint Nature Conservation Cttee 1991-97; Memb Royal Commn on Environmental Pollution 1993-98; Chm House of Lords Select Cttee on Science and Technology 1993-97; Pres Royal Geographical Soc (with IBG) since 1997; Chancellor, Southampton Univ since 1996; cr KBE (Civil) 1987: m 1969, Joanna Van Antwerp, yr da of Evan James, of Upwood Park, Abingdon, Oxon, and has issue.

𝕬rms – Argent, two bars sable, charged with three trefoils slipped of the field; in chief a greyhound courant of the second, collared or. 𝕮rest – A mount vert, thereon a greyhound sejant sable, collared or, charged on the shoulder with a trevoil slipped argent. 𝕾upporters – On either side a greyhound sable, collared or, and charged on the shoulder with a trefoil slipped argent.
Residence – Temple Manor, Selborne, Alton, Hants. *Clubs* – Brooks's, Farmers'.

SONS LIVING

WILLIAM LEWIS (*Viscount Wolmer*), b 1 Sept 1971; ed Eton, and Ch Ch Oxford.
Hon George Horsley, b 1974; ed Eton, and Leeds Univ.
Hon Luke James (twin), b 1974; ed Eton, and Goldsmith's Coll, London.

DAUGHTER LIVING

Lady Emily Sophia, b 1978; ed Bryanston.

BROTHER LIVING

Hon Henry William (Burhunt Farm, Selborne, Alton, Hants), *b* 1941; *ed* Eton, and Ch Ch, Oxford (MA); Dir The Centre for Interfirm Comparison since 1985; Dep Chm St Paul's Girls' Sch since 1995; FIMgt: *m* 1968, Minette, el da of late Sir Patrick William Donner, of Hurstbourne Park, Whitchurch, Hants, and has issue living, Benjamin Matthew, *b* 1970, — Robert Henry, *b* 1972, — Charles William, *b* 1978, — Laura Cecilia, *b* 1976.

SISTER LIVING *(raised to the rank of an Earl's daughter* 1985*)*

Lady Katherine Elizabeth, *b* 1938: *m* 1958, Hon David Laurence Robert Nall-Cain, of Cairnfold, Wooler, Northumberland NE71 6QT *(see* B Brocket).

AUNTS LIVING *(Daughters of 3rd Earl)*

Lady Anne Beatrice Mary, *b* 1911; *ed* Somerville Coll, Oxford (BA 1934): *m* 1935, Rev John Salusbury Brewis, who *d* 1972 (Duckworth-King, Bt, colls), and has issue living, Thomas William (West Garth, Bailes Lane, Normandy, Guildford, Surrey GU3 2AX) *b* 1937; *ed* Eton, and New Coll, Oxford: *m* 1983, Susan Alison Virginia, da of late Lt-Col J. A. Mackay, — Robert Salusbury (Benham's Farm, Benham's Lane, Blackmoor, Liss, Hants), *b* 1939; *ed* Eton, and Magdalen Coll, Oxford: *m* 1965, Irena, el da of late Wiktor Grubert, and has issue living, Paul William Salusbury *b* 1966, Edward George *b* 1969, Eleanor Anne *b* 1975, — Mary Elizabeth Maud, *b* 1947: *m* 1970, David Allison Osborne Tweedie, of 31 Oxberry Av, SW6, eldest son of late Dr Reid Tweedie, of Sungei Siput, Perak, Malaysia, and has issue living, Jeannie Anne Cecilia *b* 1973; *ed* Exeter Univ, Katherine Grace *b* 1975; *ed* St Andrews Univ, — Susan Amy, *b* 1949; *ed* King's Coll, London: *m* 1975, Edward Crispin Akers Martineau, of Moorland, Box End Rd, Bromham, Bedford. *Residence* – Benham's House, Benham's Lane, Blackmoor, Liss, Hants.

Lady Mary Sophia, *b* 1920: Lady-in-Waiting to HRH Princess Elizabeth 1944-7, and Extra Lady-in-Waiting 1947-9: *m* 1st, 1944, Maj Hon (Thomas) Anthony Edward Towneley Strachey, who *d* 1955, only son of 3rd Baron O'Hagan; 2ndly, 1981, as his 2nd wife, (Francis) St John Gore, CBE *(see* Gore, Bt, colls), and has issue (by 1st *m*) *(see* B O'Hagan). *Residence* – Grove Farm, Stoke-by-Nayland, Colchester, Essex C06 4SL.

MOTHER LIVING

Priscilla, da of late John Egerton-Warburton *(see* Grey-Egerton, Bt, colls): *m* 1st, 1936, William Matthew, Maj Viscount Wolmer, who *d* on active ser 1942; 2ndly, 1948, 4th Baron Newton, who *d* 1992; 3rdly, 1994, as his 2nd wife, Frederick Charles Horace Fryer *(see* E Peel, colls, 1985 Edn). *Residence* – Vernon Hill House, Bishop's Waltham, Hants.

COLLATERAL BRANCHES LIVING

Issue of late Maj Hon Robert Jocelyn Palmer, MC, late Coldstream Guards, 3rd son of 3rd Earl, *b* 1919, *d* (30 Nov) 1991: *m* 1950, Anne Rosemary, Baroness Lucas of Crudwell, and Lady Dingwall (in her own right), who *d* (31 Dec) 1991:—
Ralph Matthew, *b* 1951, who *s* his mother as *Baron Lucas of Crudwell and Lord Dingwall* 1991 (see those titles). —— *Hon* Timothy John (West Woodyates Manor, Salisbury, Wilts), *b* 1953; *ed* Eton, and Balliol Coll, Oxford: *m* 1984, Adèle Cristina Sophia, 4th da of late Lt-Col Hon Henry Anthony Camillo Howard *(see* B Howard of Penrith, colls), and has issue living, Henry Jocelyn, *b* 1987, — Robert Dominic, *b* 1993, — Nan Cristina, *b* 1985, — Isabella Spring, *b* 1989. —— *Hon* Anthea Amabel, *b* 1956; assumed by deed poll 1963 the additional christian name of Amabel.

Issue of late Hon Edward Roundell Palmer, yst son of 3rd Earl, *b* 1926, *d* 1974: *m* 1957, Joanna Constance (who *d* 1994, having *m* 2ndly, 1982, John Bernard Bruce), el da of Sir Edmund Castell Bacon, 14th Bt, KG, KBE, TD:—
Francis Mark Bacon, *b* 1958. —— Matthew Roundell, *b* 1965. —— Henrietta Cecilia, *b* 1960. —— Lucinda Beatrice, *b* 1962.

Grandsons of late Hon (William Jocelyn) Lewis Palmer (infra):—
Issue of Rev Stephen Roundell Palmer, *b* 1923, *d* 1990: *m* 1952, Joyce (21 Windy Ridge, Beaminster, Dorset DT8 3SP), da of Rev Walter Darling Topping:—
William Jocelyn (Smoky Hole, Woodhouse Fields, Uplyme, Dorset DT7 3SJ), *b* 1953: *m* 1992, Catharine Hossenlopp, and has issue living, Sophie Juliette Hossenlopp, *b* 1992, — Chloé Celine Hossenlopp, *b* 1994. —— Andrew Nicholas (15 Northlands Gdns, Southampton SO15 2NL), *b* 1955: *m* 1981 (*m diss* 1996), Anne-Marie Foster, and has issue living, Thomas John, *b* 1986, — Rebecca Louise, *b* 1982, — Frances Mary Laura, *b* 1984, — Alice Rose, *b* 1987, — Isobel Margaret Jane, *b* 1989, — Catherine Anna Sophia, *b* 1992.

Issue of late Hon (William Jocelyn) Lewis Palmer, yst son of 2nd Earl, *b* 1894, *d* 1971: *m* 1922, Hon Dorothy Cecily Sybil Loder, who *d* 1986, da of 1st Baron Wakehurst:—
Penelope Jane, *b* 1925: *m* 1965, David George Jamison, BM, of Les Fontenelles, Forest, Guernsey, CI.

PREDECESSORS – (1) *Rt Hon Sir* ROUNDELL Palmer, PC, *b* 1812; MP for Plymouth (*L*) 1847-52 and 1853-7, and for Richmond 1861-72; was Solicitor-Gen 1861-3, Attorney-Gen 1863-6, and Lord High Chancellor 1872-4, and 1880-85; *cr Baron Selborne*, of Selborne, co Southampton (peerage of United Kingdom) 1872, and *Viscount Wolmer* and *Earl of Selborne* (peerage of United Kingdom) 1882: *m* 1848, Lady Laura Waldegrave, who *d* 1885, 3rd da of 8th Earl Waldegrave; *d* 1895; *s* by his only son (2) WILLIAM WALDEGRAVE, KG, PC, GCMG, 2nd Earl, *b* 1859; was Under-Sec of State for Colonies 1895-1900, First Lord of the Admiralty 1900-05, High Commr for S Africa and Gov of Transvaal 1905-10, and Pres of Board of Agriculture and Fisheries 1915-16; sat as MP for E or Petersfield Div of Hampshire (LU) 1885-92, and for W Div of Edinburgh 1892-5: *m* 1883, Lady Beatrix Maud Cecil, who *d* 1950, da of 3rd Marquess of Salisbury; *d* 1942; *s* by his son (3) ROUNDELL CECIL, CH, PC, 3rd Earl, *b* 1887; Asst Postmaster-Gen 1924-29; Min of Economic Warfare 1942-45; MP for Newton Div, SW Lancs (LU) 1910-18, and Aldershot (C) 1918-40; called to House of Lords in his father's Barony of Selborne 1941: *m* 1st, 1910, Hon Grace Ridley, who *d* 1959, da of 1st Viscount Ridley; 2ndly, 1966, Mrs Valerie Irene Josephine Margaret de Thomka Bevan, who *d* 1968, da of late J. A. N. de Thomka de Thomkahaza, Sec of State for Hungary; *d* 1971; *s* by his grandson (4) JOHN ROUNDELL (el son of late William Matthew, Maj Viscount Wolmer, el son of 3rd Earl), 4th Earl and present peer, also Viscount Wolmer, and Baron Selborne.

SELBY VISCOUNT (Gully) (Viscount UK 1905)

Nec temere nec tarde

Neither rashly nor slowly

EDWARD THOMAS WILLIAM GULLY, 5th Viscount; *b* 21 Sept 1967; *s* 1997; *ed* Harrow: *m* 1992 (*m diss* 1995), Charlotte Cathrine, yr da of Rolph Brege, of Lomma, Sweden, and has issue.

𝕬rms – Argent, a lion rampant sable between four escallops gules, on a chief of the last as many escallops or. 𝕮rest – Between two wings erect or, an arm vested sable, cuffed argent, the hand grasping a sword erect proper. 𝕾upporters – *Dexter*, an owl sable, charged with a balance or; *sinister*, an eagle sable, charged with a portcullis or.
Seat – Island of Shuna, Argyll. *Residence* – Ardfern House, by Lochgilphead, Argyll.

SON LIVING

Hon CHRISTOPHER ROLF THOMAS, *b* 18 Oct 1993.

SISTER LIVING

Hon Catherine Mary Albinia, *b* 1971.

UNCLE LIVING (*son of 3rd Viscount*)

Hon (James) Edward Hugh Grey (Island of Shuna, Arduaine, by Oban, Argyll; Dunmor, Easdale, Isle of Seil, by Oban, Argyll), *b* 1945; *ed* King's Sch, Canterbury: *m* 1971, Fiona Margaret, only da of late Ian Strathaird Mackenzie, of Iona, and has issue living, James Ian Mackenzie, *b* 1975; *ed* Glenalmond, and Durham Univ, — Andrew Donald Mackenzie, *b* 1977; *ed* Glenalmond, and Durham Univ.

AUNT LIVING (*daughter of 3rd Viscount*)

Hon (Helen) Alexandra Briscoe (*Hon Lady Roche*), JP, *b* 1934: *m* 1st, 1952 (*m diss* 1965), Roger Moreton d'Hauteville Frewen, later Frewen di Tuttavilla (name assumed by deed poll 1971) who *d* 1972; 2ndly, 1971, Sir David O'Grady Roche, 5th Bt, and has had issue (by 1st *m*), Jonathan Briscoe Moreton (The Sheephouse, Brede, Rye, Sussex TN31 6BS), *b* 1953: *m* 1979, Anita Louise, yr da of late Nils J. L. Grebstad, of Sykkylven 6230, Norway 66, and has issue living, Antonia *b* 1987, — Robert Edward Jerome (Park Hall, Healaugh, Richmond, N Yorks), *b* 1957: *m* 1989, Rolline Charlotte, yr da of late Alexander Fergus Forbes Williamson (*see* B Forres, colls), and has issue living, Jerome Fergus d'Estoutville *b* 1995, Jennie Selina McMorrough *b* 1992, — Charles Grey Justin, *b* 1959, — Selina Veronica Clara, *b* 1955; *k* in a motor accident 1972, — (by John Foster) Emma Catherine Gully FOSTER, *b* 1964: *m* 1st, 1985 (*m diss* 1986), Jonathan Colin Fraser Bower, only son of Colin Bower, of 6 Hestercombe Av, SW6; 2ndly, 1989 (*m diss* 1991), Richard Goddard, of Hong Kong; 3rdly, 1998, Charles Sykes, — (by 2nd *m*) (*see* Roche, Bt). *Residences* – Bridge House, Starbotton, Skipton, N Yorks BD23 5HY; 20 Lancaster Mews, W2 3QE.

WIDOW LIVING OF FOURTH VISCOUNT

MARY THERESA (*Viscountess Selby*), da of late Capt Thomas Folliott Powell, of 10 Pelham Crescent, SW7: *m* 1965, the 4th Viscount Selby, who *d* 1997. *Residence* – Ardfern House, Lochgilphead, Argyll.

PREDECESSORS – (1) *Rt Hon* WILLIAM COURT Gully, son of late James Manby Gully, MD of The Priory, Great Malvern, *b* 1835; Recorder of Wigan 1886-95, and Speaker of the House of Commons 1895-1905; MP for Carlisle (*L*) 1886-1905; *cr Viscount Selby*, of the City of Carlisle (peerage of United Kingdom) 1905: *m* 1865, Elizabeth Anne Walford, who *d* 1906, el da of late Thomas Selby, of Whitley and Wimbish, Essex; *d* 1909; *s* by his el son (2) JAMES WILLIAM HERSCHELL, 2nd Viscount; *b* 1867: *m* 1st, 1893 (*m diss* 1909), Ada Isabel, who *d* 1931, da of late Alexander George Pirie, of Stoneywood House, Aberdeen; 2ndly, 1909, Dorothy Evelyn, who *d* 1951, da of late Sir William Grey, KCSI; *d* 1923; *s* by his son (3) THOMAS SUTTON EVELYN, 3rd Viscount; *b* 1911; Paymaster Lieut-Com RNR (ret): *m* 1933, Veronica Catherine Briscoe-George, who *d* 1996, da of late Albert Joseph George, and of Mrs Briscoe-George, of Aldford House, Park Lane, W1, and of Starbotton, Yorks; *d* 1959; *s* by his son (4) MICHAEL GUY JOHN, 4th Viscount; *b* 1942; FCA: *m* 1965, Mary Theresa, da of late Capt Thomas Folliott Powell, of 10 Pelham Crescent, SW7; *d* 1997; *s* by his only son (5) EDWARD THOMAS WILLIAM, 5th Viscount and present peer.

SELKIRK, EARLDOM OF; see Baron Selkirk of Douglas.

Selkirk, Master of; see Baron Selkirk of Douglas.

SELKIRK OF DOUGLAS, BARON (Douglas-Hamilton) (Earl S 1646, disclaimed 1994) (Life Baron 1997)

JAMES ALEXANDER DOUGLAS-HAMILTON, PC, QC, 2nd son of 14th Duke of Hamilton; *b* 31 July 1942; *s* as 11th Earl of Selkirk 23 Nov 1994 (claim to Earldom admitted by Lyon Court 14 March 1996, but disclaimed his peerages for life 28 Nov 1994); *ed* Eton, Balliol Coll, Oxford (MA, Pres Union 1964), and Edinburgh Univ (LLB); QC 1996; Officer TAS 6/7th Bn Cameronians Scottish Rifles 1961-66, TAVR 1971-73, Capt 2nd Bn Lowland Vols; Advocate 1968-74; Scottish Conservative Whip 1977, a Lord Commr of the Treasury 1979-81, PPS to Malcolm Rifkind, MP, 1983-87 (as Min Foreign Office 1983-86, and as Sec of State for Scotland 1986-87), Parly Under Sec of State for Home Affairs and Environment inc local govt Scottish Office 1987-89, Parly Under-Sec of State for Home Affairs and Environment 1989-92 with addl responsibility for local govt finance 1989-Sept 1990, and with addl responsibility for the arts in Scotland Sept 1990-92, Parly Under-Sec of State for Educn and Housing Scottish Office 1992-95, Min of State for Home Affairs and Health with responsibility for roads, transport and construction Scottish Office 1995-97; Hon Sec Conservative Parly Constitutional Cttee and Conservative Parly Aviation Cttee; Chm Scottish Parly All-Party Penal Affairs Cttee 1983; Hon Pres Scottish Amateur Boxing Assoc 1975-99; Pres Royal Commonwealth Soc (Scotland) 1979-87, and Scottish National Council UN Assoc 1981-87; Member of Council National Trust for Scotland 1977-82; Member Queen's Body Guard for Scotland (Royal Company of Archers); Hon Air Commodore No 2 (City of Edinburgh) Maritime HQ Unit 1995, and Pres International Rescue Corps 1995; MP Edinburgh W (*C*) 1974-97; PC 1996; author; *cr Baron Selkirk of Douglas*, of Cramond, City of Edinburgh (Life Baron) 1997: *m* 1974, Hon (Priscilla) Susan Buchan, da of 2nd Baron Tweedsmuir, and has issue.
Address – House of Lords, SW1A 0PW.

SONS LIVING

Hon (JOHN) ANDREW (*Master of Selkirk*), *b* 8 Feb 1978.
Hon Charles Douglas, *b* 1979.
Hon James Robert, *b* 1981.
Hon Harry Alexander, *b* (twin) 1981.

PREDECESSORS – **(1)** *Lord* WILLIAM Douglas, KG, PC, 4th son of 1st Marquess of Douglas; *b* 1634; a Commr of Treasury 1686-89 and an Extraor Lord of Session 1686-89 and 1689-94; *cr Lord Daer and Shortcleuch and Earl of Selkirk* (peerage of Scotland) 1646, and *Duke of Hamilton; Marquess of Clydesdale, Earl of Arran, Lanark and Selkirk, Lord Aven, Machansire, Polmont and Daer* (peerage of Scotland) 1660 for life only; having resigned his Lordships and Earldom into the King's hands, who in 1688 re-conferred them, with the precedence of 1646, upon his 3rd son, Charles, and his yr sons primogeniturely (provided that, if the said son Charles, or any of his brothers or the heirs male of their bodies succeeded to the Dukedom of Hamilton, *cr* 1643, the Earldom should pass to the then Duke's next brother), and with further remainder to his Grace's other heirs male; in conformity with the new patent the 3rd son **(2)** CHARLES, PC, *b* 1662, became 2nd Earl; was Lord Clerk Register 1696 and 1733, a Lord of the Bedchamber and a Representative Peer; *d* 1739; *s* by his brother **(3)** JOHN, 3rd Earl, *b* 1664, who in 1697 had been *cr Lord Hilhouse, Viscount Riccartoun*, and *Earl of Ruglen* (peerage of Scotland), with remainder to heirs of his body whatsoever; *d* 1744; *s* in Earldom of Ruglen, and in peerages of 1697 by his da Anne, while the honours of 1646 reverted to his grand-nephew **(4)** DUNBAR Hamilton (grand-son of Lord Basil, 6th son of 1st Earl), 4th Earl, *b* 1722; resumed the paternal surname of Douglas, was a Representative Peer: *m* 1758, Helen, who *d* 1802, da of late Hon John Hamilton; *d* 1799; *s* by his 7th son **(5)** THOMAS, 5th Earl, *b* 1771; a Representative Peer; founder of Red River Settlement in Manitoba: *m* 1807, Isabella, who *d* 1871, da of Andrew Black-burn; *d* 1820; *s* by his son **(6-9)** DUNBAR JAMES, 6th Earl; *d* 1886; *s* by his kinsman the 12th Duke of Hamilton, the Earl-dom being held in fiduciary fee until 1940, when it devolved under the terms of special destination upon **(10)** (GEORGE) NIGEL, KT, GCMG, GBE, AFC, PC, AE, QC (2nd son of 13th Duke of Hamilton), 10th Earl, *b* 1906; Group-Capt Auxiliary Air Force, Commanded 603 City of Edinburgh Sqdn of AAF 1934-38, Dep Keeper Palace of Holyrood House 1937-72, Member Edinburgh Town Council 1935-40, Lord in Waiting to HM 1951-53, Paymaster-Gen 1953-55, Chancellor Duchy of Lancaster 1955-57, First Lord of the Admiralty 1957-59, UK Commr for Singapore and Commr-Gen SE Asia, etc: *m* 1949, Audrey Durrell, who *d* (21 Dec) 1994, da of late Maurice Drummond-Sale-Barker, and *d* (23 Nov) 1994, when it devolved under the terms of special destination (confirmed by a ruling by the Lyon Court 14 March 1996) upon **(11)** JAMES ALEXANDER (2nd son of 14th Duke of Hamilton), 11th Earl, also Lord Daer and Shortcleuch, until he disclaimed his peerage 28 Nov 1994; *cr Baron Selkirk of Douglas*, of Cramond, City of Edinburgh (Life Baron) 1997.

SELSDON, BARON (Mitchell-Thomson) (Baron UK 1932, Bt UK 1900)

God will provide

MALCOLM McEACHARN MITCHELL-THOMSON, 3rd Baron, and 4th Baronet; *b* 27 Oct 1937; *s* 1963; *ed* Winchester: *m* 1st, 1965, Patricia Anne, da of Donald Smith; 2ndly, 1995, Gabrielle, da of Richard Godfrey Melville-Williams, and has issue by 1st *m*.

Arms – Per pale argent and gules between three mascles a stag's head cabossed all counter-changed. **Crest** – A dexter hand couped at the wrist proper grasping a cross-crosslet fitchée in bend sinister gules. **Supporters** – Two sea-horses proper, crined sable, finned or.
Address – c/o House of Lords, SW1.

SON LIVING (By 1st marriage)

Hon CALLUM MALCOLM McEACHARN, 7 Nov 1969.

SISTER LIVING

Hon Mary Gail, *b* 1939: *m* 1963, Patrick John O'Kelly, MB, BCh, and has issue living, Sebastian Patrick Sean, *b* 1964, — Shane, *b* 1968, — Niall, *b* 1970.

HALF-SISTER LIVING

Hon Petrina Frances Anne, *b* 1945: *m* 1967, James Geoffrey Lennox Pugh, late Gren Gds, of Whitelands, Rudford, Glos, and has issue living, Henry William Geoffrey, *b* 1974, — Emma Louise, *b* 1969.

PREDECESSORS – **(1)** *Sir* MITCHELL Thomson, 4th son of late Andrew Thomson, of Seafield, Alloa, by Janet, da of William Mitchell, *b* 1846; was Lord Provost of Edinburgh 1897-1900; assumed by Roy licence 1900 the additional surname of Mitchell; *cr a Baronet* 1900: *m* 1st, 1876, Eliza Flowerdew, who *d* 1877, da of late William Lowson, of Balthaycock, Perthshire; 2ndly, 1880, Eliza Lamb, who *d* 1926, da of late Robert Cook, shipowner, of Leith; *d* 1918; *s* by his son **(2)** *Rt Hon Sir* WILLIAM LOWSON, KBE, 2nd Bt, *b* 1877; was Parliamentary Sec to Min of Food 1920-21, and to Board of Trade 1921-2, and Postmaster-Gen 1924-9; MP for N-W Div of Lanarkshire (*U*) 1906-10, for N Down Div of co Down 1910-18, for Maryhill Div of Glasgow 1918-22, and for S Div of Croydon 1923-32; *cr Baron Selsdon*, of Croydon, co Surrey (peerage of United Kingdom) 1932: *m* 1st, 1909 (*m diss* 1932), Anne Madeleine, who *d* 1946, da of late Sir Malcolm Donald McEacharn, of Galloway House, Garlieston, and Goathland, Melbourne; 2ndly, 1933, Effie Lilian Loder, who *d* 1956, da of late Lieut-Col Charles Brennan, of Mullingar; *d* 1938; *s* by his son **(3)** PATRICK, 2nd Baron *b* 1913: *m* 1st, 1936 (*m diss* 1944), Phoebette, who *d* 1991, da of Crossley Swithinbank, of Donnington Grove, Newbury; 2ndly, 1944, Dorothy (who *m* 2ndly, 1972, Charles Larking, and *d* 1988), da of late Frederick John Greenish, of Honnington Hall, Lincoln; *d* 1963; *s* by his only son **(4)** MALCOLM McEACHARN, 3rd Baron and present peer.

SELWYN-LLOYD, BARONY OF (Lloyd) (Extinct 1978)

DAUGHTER LIVING OF LIFE BARON

Hon Joanna Elizabeth, *b* 1952.

SEMPILL, LORD (Sempill) (Lord S 1489)

JAMES WILLIAM STUART WHITEMORE SEMPILL, 21st Lord; *b* 25 Feb 1949; *s* 1995; *ed* Oratory Sch, St Clare's Hall, Oxford (BA), and Hertford Coll, Oxford: *m* 1977, Josephine Ann Edith, da of Joseph Norman Rees, of Kelso, and has issue.

ᴬrms – Argent, a chevron checky gules and of the field, between three hunting horns sable, garnished and stringed of the second. ᴄrest – A stag's head argent, attired with ten tines azure, collared with a Prince's crown or. ᔆupporters – Two greyhounds argent collared gules.
Residences – 3 Vanburgh Place, Leith, Edinburgh EH6 8AE.

SON LIVING

Hon FRANCIS (*Master of Sempill*), *b* 4 Jan 1979.

DAUGHTER LIVING

Hon Cosima, *b* 1983.

BROTHER LIVING

Hon Ian David Whitemore CHANT-SEMPILL, *b* 1951; *ed* Oratory Sch; Lt-Col Gordon Highlanders: *m* 1980, Amanda, yr da of Anthony Dallas, of Blackmoor, Burghfield, Berks, and has issue living, Hamish Anthony Stuart, *b* 1987, — Clementine Ann Constance, *b* 1985. *Residence* – The Bell House, Sutton Veny, nr Warminster, Wilts BA12 7AW.

HALF-SISTER LIVING

Hon Frances Marion, *b* 1942: *m* 1976, David Ian Russell, and has issue (*see* Russell, Bt, *cr* 1916, colls). *Residence* – 4 Westover Rd, SW18 2RG.

HALF-AUNTS LIVING (*daughters of 19th Lord by 2nd marriage*)

Hon Janet Cecilia FORBES-SEMPILL, *b* 1942. *Residence* – Keil Cottage, Muir of Fowlis, nr Alford, Aberdeenshire.
Hon Kirstine Elizabeth DARANYI-FORBES-SEMPILL, *b* 1944: *m* 1st, 1968 (*m diss* 1989), John Michael Cable (who assumed by deed poll 1968 the additional surname of Forbes before his patronymic); 2ndly, 1990, Béla Peter de Darányi, and has issue living (by 1st *m*), William Richard Craigievar FORBES-CABLE, *b* 1970; *ed* Glenalmond, and Leeds Univ: *m* 1999, Shona M., da of Capt D. M. Waters, AM, of Hobart, Australia, and Inverness, — Malcolm Dunbar Craigievar, *b* 1972, *ed* Glenalmond, and UEA. *Residence* – Davidston House, Drummuir by Keith, Banffshire AB55 3PX.
Hon Brigid Gabriel, *b* 1945: *m* 1983 (*m diss* 1991), Jeremy Menuhin, yst son of late Sir Yehudi Menuhin, OM, KBE (later Baron Menuhin), and has issue living, Petroc Forbes, *b* 1988, — Nadja Cecilia, *b* 1985. *Residence* – 41 Rochester Rd, NW1 9JJ.

COLLATERAL BRANCHES LIVING

Issue of late Rear Adm Hon Arthur Lionel Ochoncar Forbes-Sempill, yst son of 17th Lord:—
See Forbes, Bt (*cr* 1630), of Craigievar, Aberdeenshire.

Grandchildren of late Alexander William Pirie, 2nd son of late Hon Evelyn Courtenay Forbes-Sempill (Hon Mrs Pirie) (infra):—
Issue of late Ridley Gordon Pirie, *b* 1936, *d* 1984: *m* 1962, Eva Maria Lenel (28 Hubert Rd, Winchester, Hants):—
Edward Duncan PIRIE, *b* 1968. —— Fernanda, *b* 1964.

Issue of late Hon Evelyn Courtenay Forbes-Sempill, da of 17th Lord, *b* 1868, *d* 1934: *m* 1894, Lieut-Col Duncan Vernon Pirie, OBE, JP, DL, a Member of King's Body Guard for Scotland (Royal Company of Archers), who *d* 1931:—
Douglas Gordon PIRIE, *b* 1910; *ed* Winchester, and Edinburgh Univ; is a Member of Queen's Body Guard for Scotland (Royal Company of Archers); 2nd Lieut Coldm Gds (SR) 1935, Private Sec and ADC to Gov of Mauritius 1937-40, Private Sec to Gov of Kenya 1946-47, in Colonial Office 1947-50, and in HM Foreign Ser 1950-53; 1939-45 War as Lt-Col Coldm Gds (despatches, Legion of Honour): *m* 1954, Jean Frances Caroline Alicia Dorothea Grant, yst da of late Evelyn George Massey Carmichael of Carmichael, OBE, JP, FSA (Colquhoun, Bt), and has had issue, †Douglas Alastair Carmichael *b* 1957; *d* 1989. *Residences* – The Old House, Milland, Liphook, Hants; 70 Pelham Court, Fulham Rd, SW3. *Club* – Boodle's.
—— Valérie Marguerite (Old Rectory House, Coombe Bissett, Salisbury, Wilts), *b* 1906: *m* 1962, Henry Ernest Spry, CBE, who *d* 1967.

Grandchildren of late Hon Evelyn Courtenay Forbes-Sempill (ante):—
Issue of late Evelyn Jean-Gordon Pirie, *b* 1895, *d* 1981: *m* 1926, Col Owen Evelyn Wynne, OBE, RE, who *d* 1974, son of Gen Sir Arthur Singleton Wynne, GCB:—
Robert Owen WYNNE (18 Britten St, SW3), *b* 1930; *ed* Wellington, and RMA Sandhurst; late Lieut KOYLI, served in Malaya 1950-51. —— Evelyn Valerie, *b* 1928; *ed* St Andrews Univ (MA 1950): *m* 1957, Thomas Syme Drew, of Fossens House, Methill Rd, Alyth, Perthshire, son of late Maj-Gen Sir James Syme Drew, KBE, CB, DSO, MC, and has issue living, Rachel Jean, *b* 1961: *m* 1986, John David Barstow, of Thorpe Hall, Ampleforth, N Yorks, and has issue living, Marcus Thomas James *b* 1990, Julia Victoria *b* 1992.

Grandchildren of late Lt-Col James Ochoncar Forbes, yr son of late Hon James Ochoncar Forbes, brother of 17th Lord:—
Issue of late Lt-Col Patrick Walter Forbes, OBE, *b* 1914, *d* 1979: *m* 1939, Margaret Hawthorne (Gardeners Cottage, Breda, Alford AB3 8NN, Aberdeenshire), da of C. H. Lydall, of Brightling, Sussex:—
Andrew Iain Ochoncar, *b* 1945; MA (Oxon); Maj (ret) Gordon Highlanders; *hp* to baronetcy of Forbes of Craigievar (*cr* 1630). —— Mhairi Margaret, *b* 1942. —— Shelagh Anne, *b* 1948.

Granddaughter of late Charlotte Elizabeth Henrietta Grant of Druminnor (who *m* 1886, Philip Alexander Holland, both of whom and their issue assumed in 1896 the surname of Grant), only surviving da and heir of Hon Elizabeth Forbes, el sister of 17th Lord, who *m* 1864, Robert Grant of Druminnor:—
Issue of late Alexander Philip Foulerton Grant of Druminnor, MBE, *b* 1887, *d* 1961: *m* 1916, Maud Annie, who *d* 1963, da of late John Dyer, of Cheltenham:—
Rachel Ann, *b* 1922: *m* 1941, Maurice Richard Pope, and has two children, Richard John, *b* 1953, — Diana Mary Ann, *b* 1955: *m* 1978, Laramy Walter Badcock Day.

Grandchildren of late Alexander Mansfield Forbes, son of Hon Sarah Forbes 2nd sister of 17th Lord, who *m* 1852, Duncan Forbes (*see* Forbes, Bt (*cr* 1630), of Craigievar, colls):—
Issue of late Duncan Alexander Forbes, *b* 1888, *d* 1964: *m* 1918, Sybil Dorothy, who *d* 1948, da of late John Mitchell, of Ceylon:—
Duncan, MC (18 Thornton Close, Girton, Cambridge), *b* 1922; Emeritus Reader in History of Modern Political Thought, Camb Univ, and a Fellow of Clare Coll, Camb: *m* 1947, Sheila, da of Rev Clement John Morton, and has issue living, Duncan Alastair (80 Southfield Rd, Oxford), *b* 1949; Fellow and Bursar, Mansfield Coll, Oxford: *m* 1971, Angela, da of Francis Ralph Sargent, and has issue living, Joy Mary *b* 1972, Katherine Dorothy *b* 1976, — Ian (Peat Hill, Westgate, Bishop Auckland, co Durham), *b* (twin) 1949: *m* 1973, Pamela, da of Dr Douglas Bailey, and has issue living, Nicholas Iain *b* 1973, Helen Catherine *b* 1977, Susan Claire *b* 1980 (has issue living, Bethany Riley *b* 1998), — Helen Morag, *b* 1954: *m* 1986, Mark Fitton, and has issue living, Jessica Elisabeth *b* 1990, Ruth *b* 1992. —— Katharine Ann (Inveroy, Roy Bridge, Inverness-shire), *b* 1926: *m* 1947 (*m diss* 1956), Albert Cook, and has issue living, Rosemary Ann, *b* 1948: *m* 1979, Timothy Cresswell Skipper, of Gyfeile, Maesymeillion, Llandysul, Dyfed, and has issue living, Andrew James *b* 1979, Peter Timothy *b* 1983, — Valerie, *b* 1952: *m* 1986, Timothy Dix, of 2 Drimsdale, S Uist, Western Isles, and has issue living, Alasdair John *b* 1987, Iain Timothy *b* 1989.

Issue of late Mhari Margaret Forbes, *b* 1891, *d* 1975: *m* 1st, 1918 (*m diss* 1935), Arthur Haydn Parry, who *d* 1944; 2ndly, 1935, Maj Stuart Frederick Maxwell Ferguson, MC, RA, who *d* 1975:—
(By 1st *m*) Mhari Elisabeth Forbes (Broadmead Copse, Wanborough, Guildford, Surrey), *b* 1921.

Grandchildren of late Most Rev Walter John Forbes Robberds, DD, son of Rev Frederick Walter Robberds and Hon Caroline Anne Forbes, yst sister of 17th Lord:—
Issue of late Ethel Margaret Robberds, *b* 1901, *d* 1984: *m* 1938, John Whitehead, who *d* 1985:—
Janet Margaret, *b* 1939; *ed* St Andrews Univ (MA): *m* 1968, Peter John Low, of 21 Corbar Rd, Buxton, Derbys, and has issue living, Caroline Margaret, *b* 1969, — Elizabeth Hilary, *b* 1971, — Polly Alexandra, *b* 1973.

Issue of late Katharine Frances Robberds, *b* 1904, *d* 1980: *m* 1924, Francis David Jefferson Buist, who *d* 1980:—
Mary (Beech Cottage, 1 Glen Court, Dunblane, Perthshire FK15 0DY), *b* 1926: *m* 1st, 1945 (*m diss* 1966), Roland Sydney Hill, who *d* 1972; 2ndly, 1967, William James Drysdale, who *d* 1979, and has issue living (by 1st *m*), Andrew Forbes (Leask Cottage, Collieston, Aberdeenshire), *b* 1955; MA (Hons) Edinburgh; FSA Scot: *m* 1983, Linda Joan Knox, — David Jefferson, *b* 1957, — Susan Frances, *b* 1946: *m* 1969, Donald Drysdale, CA, of Ardlochan, 49 Roselea Drive, Milngavie, Glasgow, and has issue living, Michael Christopher *b* 1972, Alastair Nicholas *b* 1974, Lisa Jane *b* 1977, — Alison Margaret, *b* 1949; MA Edinburgh: *m* 1st, 1971, Iain Taylor Carruthers, who *d* 1986; 2ndly, 1988, Eugene Charles Henry O'Neale, of 23 Warriston Cres, Edinburgh EH3 5LB, and has issue living (by 1st *m*), Angus St John Hornsby *b* 1983, Catherine Lucy Forbes *b* 1974, Jessica Rose *b* 1977. —— Margaret Brora, *b* 1930: *m* 1954, Charles Richard Butterworth, of Maus House, Hilton, Dornoch, Sutherland IV25 3PW, and has issue living, Emma Mary, *b* 1955: *m* 1980, Francis Anderson Murray, of Ardmore House, Edderton, Tain, Ross-shire IV19 1LB, and has issue living, Angus Francis Hugh *b* 1984, Frederick Richard Finnbarr *b* 1986, Lucy Anne *b* 1983, — Charlotte Clunes, *b* 1958: *m* 1981, Gordon Bruce Dickie, of Poundland, Moniaive, Dumfriesshire, and has issue living, Alice Katharine Brora *b* 1983, Arabella Rose *b* 1984, Flora Sophia Elizabeth *b* 1988.

PREDECESSORS – (1) *Sir* JOHN Sempill, Knt, *cr* Lord Sempill (peerage of Scotland) about 1489; *k* at Flodden 1513; *s* by his son (2) WILLIAM, 2nd Lord; *d* about 1550; *s* by his son (3) ROBERT, 3rd Lord, known as "The Great Lord Sempill"; *s* by his grandson (4) ROBERT, 4th Lord; was Ambassador from James VI to Spain 1596; *s* by his son (5) HUGH, 5th Lord; *d* 1639; *s* by his el son (6) FRANCIS, 6th Lord; *dsp* 1644; *s* by his brother (7) ROBERT, 7th Lord; *d* 1675; *s* by his son (8) FRANCIS, 8th Lord; *dsp* 1684; *s* by his sister (9) ANNE, wife of Robert Abercromby, who in 1685 was *cr* Lord Glassford for life; obtained in 1688 a new charter settling the Lordship of Sempill, in default of male issue, upon her daughters without division by her then or any future husband; *d* 1695: *s* by her el son (10) FRANCIS, 10th Lord; *d* unmarried; *s* by his brother (11) JOHN, 11th Lord; *d* unmarried 1716; *s* by his brother (12) HUGH, 12th Lord; commanded left wing of Govt Army at Culloden 1746; *d* 1746; *s* by his son (13) JOHN, 13th Lord; *d* 1782; *s* by his son (14) HUGH, 14th Lord; *b* 1758: *m* 1787, Maria, da of Charles Mellish, of Ragnal, Notts: *d* 1830; *s* by his son (15) SELKIRK, 15th Lord; *d* unmarried 1835; *s* by his sister (16) MARIA JANET: *m* 1836, Edward Candler, who were both allowed by Roy Licence 1853 to assume the name and arms Sempill only; *dsp* 1884; *s* by her kinsman (17) *Sir* WILLIAM Forbes, 8th Bt of Craigievar, grandson of Hon Sarah, el da of 13th Lord, *b* 1836; assumed in 1885, the additional and principal surname of Sempill: *m* 1st, 1858 (*m diss* 1861), Caroline Louisa, who *d* 1872, da of Sir Charles Forbes, 3rd Bt, of Newe; 2ndly, 1862, Frances Emily, who *d* 1887, da of Sir Robert Abercromby, 5th Bt; 3rdly, 1890, Mary Beresford, who *d* 1930, da of late Henry Sherbrooke, of Oxton, Notts; *d* 1905; *s* by his son **(18)** JOHN, 18th Lord, *b* 1863; Hon Col 5th Bn Gordon Highlanders (TA), a Representative Peer for Scotland: *m* 1892, Gwendolen, who *d* 1944, da of late Herbert Prodgers, of Hington St Michael, Chippenham, Wilts; *d* 1934; *s* by his son **(19)** WILLIAM FRANCIS, AFC, 19th Lord, *b* 1893; a Representative Peer for Scotland, Wing-Cdr RNAS and Col RAF, a pioneer in aviation: *m* 1st, 1919, Eileen Marion, who *d* 1935, da of Sir John Lavery, RA; 2ndly, 1941, Cecilia Alice, who *d* 1984, da of B. E. Dunbar-Kilburn, of Ledwell, Sandford St Martin, Oxon; *d* 1965; *s* in the baronetcy of Forbes of Craigievar by his brother Sir Ewan Forbes of Brux, 11th Bt (*see* Forbes, Bt, *cr* 1630), and in the Lordship by his el da **(20)** ANN MOIRA, Lady Sempill, *b* 1920; late Petty Officer WRNS: *m* 1st, 1941 (*m diss* 1945), Capt Eric Holt, Manchester Regt, who *d* (31 Jan) 1995; 2ndly, 1948, Lt-Col Stuart Whitemore Chant, OBE, MC, late Gordon Highlanders (who *d* 1991, having assumed by decree of Lyon Court 1966 the additional surname of Sempill); *d* (6 July) 1995; *s* by her elder son **(21)** JAMES WILLIAM STUART WHITE-MORE, 21st Lord and present peer.

SEROTA, BARONESS (Serota) (Life Baroness 1967)

BEATRICE SEROTA, DBE, da of Alexander Katz; *b* 15 Oct 1919; *ed* London Sch of Economics (BSc Econ); a JP of Inner London; a Member of LCC 1954-65 (Chm of Children's Cttee 1958-65) and of GLC (Lambeth) 1964-67; a Member of Advisory Council in Child Care and Central Training Council in Child Care 1958-68, of Advisory Council on Penal System 1966-68; Chm of Health Education Council 1967-69, a Baroness in Waiting to HM 1968-69, and Min of State, Dept of Health and Social Security 1969-70; Pres of National Council for Unmarried Mother and Her Child since 1971; a Member of Community Relations Comm 1971; *cr Baroness Serota*, of Hampstead in Greater London (Life Baroness) 1967, and DBE 1992: *m* 1942, Stanley Serota, FICE, and has issue.

Residence – The Coach House, 15 Lyndhurst Terr, NW3.

SON LIVING

(*Hon*) *Sir* Nicholas Andrew (does not use courtesy title), *b* 1946; *ed* Haberdashers' Askes Sch, Christ's Coll, Camb (BA), and Courtauld Inst of Art (MA); Hon DArts City of London Polytechnic 1990, Hon DLitt City Univ 1990, Hon DArts Univ of Plymouth 1993, Hon DLitt Univ of Keele 1994; Sr Fellow RCA 1996, Hon Fellow Queen Mary and Westfield Coll London Univ 1988, Goldsmiths' Coll London Univ 1994; Dir Whitechapel Art Gallery 1976-88, Trustee Public Art Development Trust 1983-88, Dir Tate Gallery since 1988; Hon FRIBA 1992; *cr* Kt 1999: *m* 1973, Angela Mary Beveridge, and has issue, two das.

DAUGHTER LIVING

Hon Judith Alexandra Anne, *b* 1948; *ed* Royal Manchester Coll of Music: *m* 1973, Francis John Pugh, and has issue living, Rebecca Sarah, *b* 1975, — Ellen Martha, *b* 1978.

Settrington, Lord; grandson of Duke of Richmond.

SEWEL, BARON (Sewel) (Life Baron 1995)

JOHN BUTTIFANT SEWEL, CBE, son of ...... Sewel, of ......; *b* ...... 19—; Dean of the Faculty of Economic and Social Sciences, Univ of Aberdeen since 19—; Under Sec of State Scottish Office (Agriculture) 1997; *cr* CBE 19—; and *Baron Sewel*, of Gilcomstoun, in the District of the City of Aberdeen 1995: *m* 19—, da of ......, of ......, and has issue.

Address – University of Aberdeen, Aberdeen AB9 1FX.

Seymour, Lord; son of Duke of Somerset.

Seymour, family name of Duke of Somerset.

Seymour, family name of Marquess of Hertford.

SHACKLETON, BARONY OF (Shackleton) (Extinct 1994)

DAUGHTER LIVING OF LIFE BARON

Hon Alexandra Mary Swinford SHACKLETON, *b* 1940; *ed* Trin Coll, Dublin; has resumed her maiden name: *m* 1969 (*m diss* 1998), Richard Charles Bergel, MB, BS, and has issue. *Address* – c/o Lloyds Bank, 26 Hammersmith Broadway, W6 7AH.

WIDOW LIVING OF SON OF LIFE BARON

Lady Caroline Harriet Hastings, da of 15th Earl of Huntingdon: *m* 1970, Hon Charles Edward Ernest Shackleton, who *d* 1979. *Address* – c/o Coutts & Co, 16 Cavendish Sq, W1.

WIDOW LIVING OF LIFE BARON

BETTY MURIEL MARGUERITE (*Baroness Shackleton*), da of late Capt Charles E. Homan, Elder Brother of Trinity House: *m* 1938, Baron Shackleton, KG, OBE, FRS, PC, who *d* 1994. *Address* – c/o Lloyds Bank, 39 High St, Lymington, Hants SO41 9ZF.

SHAFTESBURY, EARL OF (Ashley-Cooper) (Earl E 1672, Bt E 1622)

ANTHONY ASHLEY-COOPER, 10th Earl, and 11th Baronet; *b* 22 May 1938; *s* 1961; *ed* Eton, and Ch Ch, Oxford; late Lt 10th Hussars; Hon Citizen S Carolina, USA; Chm London Philharmonic Orchestra Council 1966-80; patron of five livings: *m* 1st, 1966 (*m diss* 1976), Mrs Bianca Maria Le Vien, da of late Gino de Paolis; 2ndly, 1976, Mrs Christina Eva Casella, da of Nils Montan, and has issue by 2nd *m*.

𝕬rms – Quarterly: 1st and 4th argent, three bulls passant sable, armed and unguled or. *Ashley;* 2nd and 3rd gules, a bend engrailed between six lions rampant or, *Cooper.* 𝕮rest – On a chapeau gules, turned up ermine, a bull statant sable, armed, unguled and ducally gorged or. 𝕾upporters – *Dexter,* a bull sable, armed, unguled, ducally gorged and chain reflexed over the back or; *sinister,* a talbot azure, ducally gorged or.

Residence – St Giles's House, Wimborne, Dorset, BH21 5NH. *Clubs* – Turf, Pratt's.

SONS LIVING (*By 2nd marriage*)

ANTHONY NILS CHRISTIAN (*Lord Ashley*), *b* 24 June 1977.
Hon Nicholas Edmund Anthony, *b* 1979.

SISTER LIVING (*Raised to the rank of an Earl's daughter* 1962)

Lady Frances Mary Elizabeth (La Combe, 30126 Tavel, Gard, France), *b* 1940.

WIDOW LIVING OF SON OF NINTH EARL

Julian, da of late Capt George Gerald Petherick (*see* E Radnor, 1976 Edn): *m* 1946, Maj Hon (Anthony) John Percy Hugh Michael Ashley Cooper, yr son of 9th Earl, who *d* 1986, and has issue (see colls, infra). *Residence* – 46 High St, Sixpenny Handley, Salisbury SP5 5ND.

MOTHER LIVING

Françoise, da of George Souilier: *m* 1st, 1937, as his 2nd wife, Lord Ashley, who *d* 1947, el son of 9th Earl; 2ndly, 1947, Col François Goussault, French Air Force, who *d* 1984. *Residence* – 6 Square d'Astorg, Residence St Honoré, 78150 Le Chesnay, France.

COLLATERAL BRANCH LIVING

Issue of late Maj Hon (Anthony) John Percy Hugh Michael Ashley Cooper, yr son of 9th Earl, *b* 1915, *d* 1986: *m* 1946, Julian (ante), da of late Capt George Gerald Petherick (*see* E Radnor, 1976 Edn):—
Susan Mary Jeane, *b* 1946. —— Caroline Sibell PETHERICK-BRIAN, *b* 1948; has issue living (by Robert Keith Petherick-Brian, of Windsworth, St Martin-by-Looe, Cornwall PL13 1NZ), Henry Charles Sebastian, *b* 1984, — Alexander Edward Arlington, *b* 1986, — Victoria Sibell Camda, *b* 1983, — Henrietta Caroline Aurelia, *b* 1988. — Elizabeth Julian, *b* 1950.
—— Mary Patricia, *b* 1953: *m* 1984, Robert John Elkington, son of late J. D. R. Elkington, of Haworth House, Kintbury, Berks, and has issue living, Louisa Alice Rosemary, *b* 1986, — Edwina Amy Charlotte Julian, *b* 1989.

PREDECESSORS – (1) *Sir* JOHN Cooper, sometime MP for Poole; *cr Baronet* 1622, *d* 1631; *s* by his son (2) *Sir* ANTHONY ASHLEY, PC, an able and prominent statesman, who having originally espoused the royal cause, afterwards joined the Parliamentarians, and eventually assisted to restore the monarchy; *cr Baron Ashley,* of Wimborne St Giles, co Dorset (peerage of England) 1661, and *Baron Cooper,* of Paulett, co Somerset, and *Earl of Shaftesbury* (peerage of England) 1672; was Lord-Lieut of Dorset, Chancellor of the Exchequer 1667-72, Lord High Chancellor of England 1672-3, and Lord Pres of the Council 1679; *d* 1683; *s* by his son (3) ANTHONY ASHLEY, 2nd Earl; *d* 1699; *s* by his son (4) ANTHONY, 3rd Earl; designated by Voltaire as the boldest English philosopher; *d* 1713; *s* by his son (5) ANTHONY, 4th Earl; *d* 1771; *s* by his el son (6) ANTHONY ASHLEY, 5th Earl; *d* 1811; *s* by his brother (7) CROPLEY ASHLEY, 6th Earl; *b* 1768; was Chm of Committees in House of Lords; *d* 1851; *s* by his son (8) ANTHONY Ashley-Cooper, KG, PC, 7th Earl; was Lord-Lieut of Dorsetshire; sat as MP for Woodstock (*C*) 1826-30, for Dorchester 1830, for Dorsetshire 1831-46 and for Bath 1847-51; *d* 1 Oct 1885; *s* by his son (9) ANTHONY, 8th Earl; *b* 1831; sat as MP for Hull (LC) 1857-9, and for Cricklade 1859-65: *m* 1857, Lady Harriet Augusta Anne Seymourina Chichester, who *d* 1898, only da of 3rd Marquess of Donegall; *d* 1886; *s* by his son (10) ANTHONY, KP, GCVO, CBE, PC, 9th Earl; *b* 1869; Capt 10th Hussars; Lieut-Col and Hon Col Comdg N Irish Horse 1902-12, and HM's Lieut for co Antrim 1911-16; Hon Brig-Gen Hon Col Special Cav, and RGA; was Mil Sec to Gov of Victoria (Baron Brassey) 1896-8, Lord Mayor of Belfast 1907-8, HM's Lieut 1903-11, Commr of Congested Dists Board for Ireland 1902-14, Chamberlain to Queen Mary (when Princess of Wales) 1901-10, Lord Chamberlain to Queen Mary 1910-22, Chm of National Advisory Council for Juvenile Employment (England and Wales) 1928-31, and Lord Steward of HM's Household 1922-36; Chancellor of Belfast Univ 1910-23; Lord-Lieut for Dorset 1916-52; European War 1914-18; Chm of Dorset Co Council 1924-46: *m* 1899, Lady Constance Sibell Grosvenor (a DJStJ), who *d* 1957, da of late Earl Grosvenor; *d* 1961; *s* by his grandson (11) ANTHONY (son of late Anthony, Lord Ashley, el son of 9th Earl), 10th Earl and present peer; also Baron Ashley, and Baron Cooper.

SHANNON, EARL OF (Boyle) Sits as BARON CARLETON (GB 1786) (Earl I 1756)

Let us be judged by our actions

RICHARD BENTINCK BOYLE, 9th Earl; *b* 23 Oct 1924; *s* 1963; late Capt Irish Guards: *m* 1st, 1947 (*m diss* 1955), Donna Catherine Irene Helen (Katie Boyle, the broadcaster), da of the Marchese Demetrio Imperiali di Francavilla; 2ndly, 1957 (*m diss* 1979), Susan Margaret, da of late John Russell Hogg (M Lothian); 3rdly, 1994, Mrs Almine Barton, da of late Rocco Catorsia de Villiers, of Cape Town, S Africa, and has issue by 2nd *m*.

Arms – Per bend embattled argent and gules, a crescent for difference. Crest – Out of a ducal coronet or a lion's head per pale embattled argent and gules, and charged with a crescent for difference. Supporters – Two lions, the *dexter* per pale embattled gules and argent, the *sinister* per pale embattled argent and gules, each charged with a crescent for difference.
Residence – Pimm's Cottage, Man's Hill, Burghfield Common, Berks RG7 3BD. *Club* – White's.

SON LIVING (By 2nd marriage)

RICHARD HENRY JOHN (*Viscount Boyle*), *b* 19 Jan 1960; *ed* Northease Manor Sch, Lewes, Sussex.

DAUGHTERS LIVING (By 2nd marriage)

Lady Georgina Susan, *b* 1961.
Lady Caroline Mary Victoria, *b* 1965: *m* 1990, Mark Nowell Waters, only son of P.N. Waters, of Guildford, Surrey, and has issue living, Oliver Robert Nowell, *b* 1991, — Max Alexander, *b* 1993. *Residence* – Snowberry Cottage, Somersway, Shalford, Surrey GU4 8EQ.

COLLATERAL BRANCHES LIVING

Grandchildren of late Vice-Adm Hon Robert Francis Boyle, MVO, 3rd son of 5th Earl:—
Issue of late Cdr Vivian Francis Boyle, RN, *b* 1902, *d* 1962: *m* 1929, Margaret Ruth Howard, who *d* 1992, da of Charles Howard Tripp, of Timaru, New Zealand:—
Robert Francis (180 Moana Av, Tahunanui, Nelson, NZ), *b* 1930; logging consultant: *m* 1956, Janet Eleanor Ashley, da of Selwyn Ashley Cooper, of Rotorua, NZ, and has issue living, David de Crespigny (8 Ferriman St, Brunswick West, Victoria 3055, Australia) *b* 1959: *m* 1996, Lesley Anne Paton, and has issue living, Mara Eleanor Paton *b* 1997, — Robert Andrew, *b* 1961, — Judith Eleanor, *b* 1957: *m* 1st, 1987 (*m diss* 1992), Abid Ilahi; 2ndly, 1994, Nikiforos Papadakis, and has issue living (by 2nd *m*), Andreas Boyle *b* 1997, Krysianna Boyle *b* 1995. —— Moyra Anne Howard (17B Sylvia Rd, St Heliers, Auckland, NZ), *b* 1936: *m* 1960, William Francis Leonard, who *d* 1997, and has issue living, Mark Francis (French Farm, Akaroa, NZ), *b* 1961; has issue living (by Julie Innes Sigley), Ruby Innes *b* 1994, Frances Rose *b* 1995, — Zucchi Philippa Jane, *b* 1962: *m* 1988, Alastair Salmond, of Wellington, NZ, and has issue living, Oscar William *b* 1991, Hannah June *b* 1992, — Virginia Anne, *b* 1965: *m* 1992, George Kenneth Cooke, of Auckland, NZ.

Grandsons of Capt Hon Edward Spencer Harry Boyle, RN, 5th son of 5th Earl:—
Issue of late Lt-Cdr Patrick Spencer Boyle, RNVR, *b* 1905, *d* 1978: *m* 1st, 1932, Vera Maude Radcliffe Agnew, who *d* (Feb) 1940, da of Daniel Radcliffe, JP, LLD, of Pen-y-Lan, Cardiff; 2ndly, (Aug) 1940, Rita (13 Springfield, E Oakley, Basingstoke, Hants), da of late Cecil Berens, JP:—
(By 1st *m*) Michael Patrick Radcliffe (Saint Cross House, Whitchurch, Hants RG28 7AS), *b* 1934; *ed* Eton; Capt (ret) IG; CC Hants 1970, High Sheriff 1976, and DL 1982; Member Hants Police Authority since 1970 (Vice Chm 1974-76, Chm 1976-88); CStJ: *m* 1st, 1962 (*m diss* 1995), Lady Nell Carleton Harris, da of 6th Earl of Malmesbury; 2ndly, 1995, Mrs Alexandra Mary Hilda Seymour, da of Maj Sir Victor Basil John Seely, 4th Bt, and has issue living (by 1st *m*), Robert Algernon Radcliffe (Boodle's Club), *b* 1963; *ed* King's Sch, Bruton; Major Irish Gds (ret): *m* 1987, Fiona Elisabeth Maule, yst da of Col George Patrick Maule Ramsay (*see* E Dalhousie, colls), and has issue living, George Patrick Radcliffe *b* 1998, — Rupert Alexander (14 Redcliffe Gdns, SW10 9EX), *b* 1968, — Maria, *b* 1964. —— (By 2nd *m*) David Spencer (2 St John's Gdns, W11 2NO), *b* 1942; *ed* Winchester, and Trin Coll, Camb: *m* 1980, Melanie Georgiana, only da of late William Robert Brudenell Foster (*see* M Ailesbury, colls, 1976 Edn), and has issue living, James Patrick W., *b* 1983, — Fennella, *b* 1982.

PREDECESSORS – (1) HENRY Boyle, PC, MP for co Cork 1715-56, Speaker of the Irish House of Commons, fifteen times Lord Justice of Ireland, and Chancellor of the Exchequer and Commr of the Treasury; *cr Baron Castle Martyr, Viscount Boyle*, and *Earl of Shannon* (peerage of Ireland) 1756; *d* 1764; *s* by his son (2) RICHARD, KP, PC, 2nd Earl; was successively MP for Dungarvan and for co Cork, Master-Gen of the Ordnance 1766-70, and Vice-Treasurer of Ireland 1781, etc; *cr Baron Carleton*, of Carleton, co York (peerage of Great Britain) 1786; *d* 1807; *s* by his son (3) HENRY, KP, 3rd Earl; was Custos Rotulorum of co Cork, and Clerk of the Pells in Ireland; *d* 1842; *s* by his son (4) RICHARD, 4th Earl; *b* 1809: *m* 1832, Emily Henrietta, da of Lord George Seymour (M Hertford); *d* 1868; *s* by his son (5) HENRY BENTINCK, 5th Earl. *b* 1833: *m* 1st, 1859, Lady Blanche Emma Lascelles, who *d* 1863, da of 3rd Earl of Harewood; 2ndly, 1868, Julia Charlotte, who *d* 1921, da of Sir William Edmund Cradock-Hartopp, 3rd Bt; *d* 1890; *s* by his el son (6) RICHARD HENRY, 6th Earl, *b* 1860: *m* 1895, Nellie, who *d* 1910, da of late Charles Thompson, of 14 Park Sq, NW; *d* 1906; *s* by his el son (7) RICHARD BERNARD, 7th Earl, *b* 1897; Lt Roy Fusiliers; (*ka* 1917); *s* by his brother (8) ROBERT HENRY, 8th Earl; *b* 1900; Capt Indian Army; ADC to Gov of Madras 1923; *m* 1923, Marjorie, who *d* 1981, da of S. A. Walker, of Ootacamund, India; *d* 1963; *s* by his only son (9) RICHARD BENTINCK, 9th Earl and present peer; also Viscount Boyle, Baron Castle Martyr, and Baron Carleton. (*Note*, this title derived from Shannon Park, co Cork and *not* the River Shannon.)

SHARP OF GRIMSDYKE, BARONY OF (Sharp) (Extinct 1994)

SON LIVING OF LIFE BARON

Hon Richard Simon, *b* 1956.

DAUGHTER LIVING OF LIFE BARON

Hon Victoria Madeleine, *b* 1956 (twin): *m* 19—, — Chappatte.

WIDOW LIVING OF LIFE BARON

MARION (*Baroness Sharp of Grimsdyke*), da of ...... Freeman: *m* 1950, Baron Sharp of Grimsdyke, CBE (Life Baron), who *d* 1994.

SHARP OF GUILDFORD, BARONESS (Sharp) (Life Baroness 1998)

MARGARET LUCY SHARP, da of late Osmund Hailstone, AFC, of Hadlow and Southborough, Kent; *b* 21 Nov 1938; *ed* Tonbridge Girls' Gram Sch, and Newnham Coll, Camb; Civil Servant 1960-63; Univ Lecturer, LSE 1963-72; Economic Adviser NEDO 1977-81; Snr Research Fell, Univ of Sussex since 1981; Founder Memb SDP 1981; Memb Exec Cttee Save British Science 1986-96; *cr Baroness Sharp of Guildford*, of Guildford, co Surrey (Life Baroness) 1998: *m* 1962, Thomas (Tom) Sharp, CBE, and has issue.
Residence – 96 London Rd, Guildford, Surrey GU1 1TH.

DAUGHTERS LIVING

Hon Helen, *b* 1965; *ed* Sydenham Sch, and Loughborough Univ (M Eng).
Hon Elizabeth, *b* 1967; *ed* Sydenham Sch, Emmanuel Coll, Camb (BA), and Sheffield Univ (MSc, PhD).

SHARPLES, BARONESS (Swan) (Life Baroness 1973)

PAMELA SWAN, da of Keith William Newall; *b* 11 Feb 1923; *ed* Southover Manor, Lewes; 1939-45 War as LACW with WRAF; *cr Baroness Sharples*, of Chawton, in Hampshire (Life Baroness) 1973: *m* 1st, 1946, Sir Richard Christopher Sharples, KCMG, OBE, MC, Gov of Bermuda, who *d* (assassinated in Bermuda) 1973; 2ndly, 1977, Patrick David de Laszlo, who *d* 1980; 3rdly, 1983, Robert Douglas Swan, who *d* 1995, and has issue by 1st *m*.

Arms – Argent, a chevron vert between in chief two copper beech trees eradicated, and in base a white tailed tropicbird (Phaethon Lepturus), a volant proper, for *Sharples*, on an escutcheon of pretence the Arms of *Newall*, Per saltire argent and gules, a crozier in fesse or between three bustards, wings elevated and addorsed, counterchanged.
Supporters – On either side a Great Dane dog, resting the interior hind foot proper on a portcullis or.
Residence – Nunswell, Higher Coombe, Shaftesbury, Dorset.

SONS LIVING (*By 1st marriage*)

Hon Christopher John SHARPLES (72 Elm Park Rd, SW3), *b* 1947; *m* 1975, Sharon, el da of late Robert Sweeny, of Montague Sq, W1; and has issue.

Hon David Richard SHARPLES, *b* 1955: *m* 1981 (*m diss* 1988), Annabel (Anna), 2nd da of Col Thomas Armitage Hall, OBE, of Chiselhampton House, Oxford.

DAUGHTERS LIVING (*By 1st marriage*)

Hon Fiona, *b* 1949: *m* 1981 (*m diss* 1982), Alexander Paterson; has issue living, Natalie Louise SHARPLES, *b* 1975.
Hon Miranda, *b* 1951: *m* 1981, Nicholas Larkins, elder son of Dr N. Larkins, of Sydney, Australia, and has issue living, Harry Claud, *b* 1985, — Amelia Kate (Kitty), *b* 1989. *Residence* – The Old Rectory, Stoke Wake, Blandford, Dorset.

SHAUGHNESSY, BARON (Shaughnessy) (Baron UK 1916)

With a strong hand

WILLIAM GRAHAM SHAUGHNESSY, CD, 3rd Baron; *b* 28 Mar 1922; *s* 1938; *ed* Bishop's Coll Sch, Bishop's Univ, Lennoxville, Canada, and Columbia Univ, New York; Major (ret) Canadian Gren Gds; Dir Arbor Memorial Services Inc, Toronto, since 1972, Memb Joint Select Cttee on Statutory Instruments since 1985, and Delegated Powers Scrutiny Cttee (Hoel) since 1993; Executive Assist to Canadian Min of Finance 1949-51; Pres of Royal Commonwealth Soc, Montreal, Canada 1959-61; Trustee, The Last Post Fund; 1939-45 War in NW Europe (despatches); CD 1955: *m* 1944, Mary, only da of late John Whitley, of Letchworth, and has issue.

Arms – Per fesse gules and azure, in chief two mill-rinds, and in base an ancient harp or, within a bordure engrailed ermine. **Crest** – Issuing from an antique crown or, a dexter cubit arm in armour and gauntleted, grasping a two-headed battle-axe, all proper. **Supporters** – *Dexter*, an Irish wolfhound proper, gorged with a collar argent charged with three trefoils vert; *sinister*, a beaver proper, gorged with a collar argent, charged with three maple leaves gules.
Address – c/o House of Lords, SW1A 0PW.

SONS LIVING AND DECEASED

†*Hon* Patrick John, *b* 1944; *d* 1982.
Hon MICHAEL JAMES, *b* 12 Nov 1946.

DAUGHTERS LIVING

Hon Brigid Mary, *b* 1948.
Hon Marion Kathleen, *b* 1951.

COLLATERAL BRANCHES LIVING

Granddaughters of late Capt Hon Alfred Thomas Shaughnessy (*infra*):—
Issue of late Capt Thomas Bradford Shaughnessy, *b* 1915, *d* 1994: *m* 1949, Margot, who *d* 1991, da of late William D. Chambers, of Montreal:—
Amanda Marguerite Polk (21 Laing Rd, Old Chelsea, Quebec, Canada J0X 1N0), *b* 1951. ——— Roxane Elizabeth, *b* 1952: *m* 1984, Thomas Herbert McGreevy, of 7 Barrie Av, Toronto, Ont, Canada M6C 1E1, son of John McGreevy, of Quebec City, Canada, and has issue living, Julian Thomas Gray, *b* 1989, — Sarah Paige, *b* 1986, — Madeleine Claire Elizabeth, *b* 1989. ——— Tara Evelyn, *b* 1954: *m* 1983, Alain Du Bois, of 50 Tunstall Av, Senneville, Quebec H9X 1T2, Canada, son of Leopold Du Bois, of Magog, Quebec, Canada, and has issue living, Louis Shaughnessy, *b* 1985, — Chella Evelyn, *b* 1988.

Issue of late Capt Hon Alfred Thomas Shaughnessy, Canadian Expeditionary Force, yr son of 1st Baron, *b* 1887, *ka* 1916: *m* 1912, Sarah Polk, who *d* 1955 (having *m* 2ndly, 1920, Lieut-Col Hon Sir Piers Walter Legh, GCVO, CMG, CIE, OBE, who *d* 1955 (*see* B Newton, colls)), da of late Judge James C. Bradford, formerly of Nashville, Tennessee, USA:—
Alfred James (*posthumous*) (The Grange, Yattendon, nr Newbury, Berks), *b* 1916; late Capt Gren Gds (Reserve): *m* 1948, Jean Margaret, da of late George Lodge, of Kirkella, Yorks, and has issue living, Charles George Patrick (534 15th St, Santa Monica, Calif 90402, USA), *b* 1955: *m* 1983, Susan, da of Sydney Fallender, of Los Angeles, Cal, USA, and has issue living, Jenny Johanna *h* 1990, Madelyn Sarah *b* 1995. — David James Bradford (3815 Marfield Av, Tarzana, Calif 91356, USA), *b* 1957: *m* 1985, Anne-Marie, da of Thomas Schoettle, of Indianapolis, USA, and has issue living, Amy Jean *b* 1990, Kathryn Anne *b* 1992, Josephine Sarah *b* 1997. ——— Elizabeth Sarah Polk (78 Melton Court, Old Brompton Rd, SW7 3JQ), *b* 1913; resumed the surname of Stafford 1976 until re-marriage: *m* 1st, 1932 (*m diss* 1946), 2nd Baron Grenfell, who *d* 1976; 2ndly, 1946, Maj Berkeley Buckingham Howard Stafford, KRRC, who *d* 1966; 3rdly, 1969 (*m diss* 1975), Trevor Walton King; 4thly, 1983, Cdr (Arnold) Derek Arthur Lawson, RN, who *d* 1984, and has issue living (by 1st *m*) (*see* B Grenfell).

PREDECESSORS – **(1)** THOMAS GEORGE Shaughnessy, KCVO, son of Thomas Shaughnessy, of Limerick; *b* 1853 (Milwaukee, USA); was Pres Canadian Pacific Railway 1899-1918 (Chm of Board of Directors); also a Director of all this Co's allied lines; *cr Baron Shaughnessy,* of City of Montreal, Dominion of Canada, and of Ashford, co Limerick (peerage of United Kingdom) 1916: *m* 1880, Elizabeth Bridget, who *d* 1937, da of N. Nagle, of Milwaukee, USA; *d* 1923; *s* by his son **(2)** WILLIAM JAMES, KC, 2nd Baron; *b* 1883; KC Canada; a Director of Canadian Pacific Railway Co, of Canadian Bank of Commerce, and other Cos: *m* 1911, Marion Laura, who *d* 1936, da of late Robert Kilgour Graham, of Montreal, Canada; *d* 1938; *s* by his only son **(3)** WILLIAM GRAHAM, 3rd Baron and present peer.

Shaw, family name of Baron Craigmyle.

Shaw, family name of Baron Kilbrandon.

SHAW OF NORTHSTEAD, BARON (Shaw) (Life Baron 1994)

MICHAEL NORMAN SHAW, eldest son of late Norman Shaw, FCA; *b* 9 Oct 1920; *ed* Sedbergh; FCA; MP Brighouse and Spenborough (*L* and *C*) 1960-64, Scarborough and Whitby (*C*) 1966-74, Scarborough 1974-92; Parly Private Sec to Ministry of Labour and Nat Service 1962-63, to Sec of State for Trade and Industry 1970-72, and to Chancellor of the Duchy of Lancaster 1973-74; memb UK Delegation to European Parliament 1974-79; JP Dewsbury 1953, DL W Yorks 1977; *cr* Kt 1982, and *Baron Shaw of Northstead,* of Liversedge, co West Yorks (Life Baron) 1994: *m* 1951, Joan Mary Louise, da of late Sir Alfred Law Mowat, DSO, OBE, MC, JP, DL, 2nd and last Bt, and has issue.

Arms – Or issuant from a triple mount in base three trees an arrow in flight fesswise to the dexter between their trunks all proper on a chief wavy azure an estoile argent between two roses also argent barbed and seeded proper each environed by a crescent gold. **Crest** – Out of a circle of roses argent barbed and seeded proper the hulk of a lymphad azure rising therefrom a square stone tower also proper all in front of a sun in splendour gold. **Supporters** – On either side a ram argent gorged bezanty armed or and unguled sable each resting the interior hind foot upon a fishing net covering a glass float all upon a compartment representative of a quayside proper.
Residence – Duxbury Hall, Liversedge, W Yorks WF15 7NR.

SONS LIVING

Hon Charles Michael Mowat, *b* 1952; *ed* Sedbergh: *m* 1979, Sarah, da of late Dr ...... Bremner, of ......, and has issue living, Roland Charles, *b* 1984, — Jeremy Bremner, *b* (twin) 1984, — Lucy Kathleen, *b* 1986. *Residence* – ....
Hon James William, *b* 1955; *ed* Sedbergh. *Residence* – 39 Carrara Wharf, Ranelagh Gdns, SW6 3UJ.
Hon Jonathan David, *b* 1957; *ed* Sedbergh: *m* 1985, Gillian Susan, yr da of Rollo Belsham, of Fifehead Cottage, Fifehead Magdalen, Marnhull, Gillingham, Dorset. *Residence* – 215 Hammersmith Grove, W6 0NP.

SHAWCROSS, BARON (Shawcross) (Life Baron 1959)

HARTLEY WILLIAM SHAWCROSS, GBE, PC, QC, son of late John Shawcross, MA; b 4 Feb 1902; ed Dulwich Coll, and Geneva; Hon LLM Liverpool; Hon LLD Columbia (USA), Bristol, Michigan, Lehigh (USA), Sussex, London and Liverpool; Hon DCL New Brunswick, and Hull; Hon Member Royal Coll of Surgeons, and Royal Coll of Obstetricians & Gynaecologists; Bar Gray's Inn 1925, Bencher 1939, KC 1939, and Treasurer 1955; a Member of Bar Council (Chm 1952-57), Hon Fellow of American Bar Foundation, and Hon Member of American and New York Bars; Recorder of Salford 1941-45, and Kingston upon Thames 1946-61; Attorney-Gen 1945-51 and Pres of Board of Trade April to Oct 1951; a Prin Delegate for UK to Assemblies of UN 1945-49, Ch Prosecutor for UK before Internat Mil Tribunal Nuremberg 1945-46, and UK Member of Permanent Court of Arbitration, The Hague 1950-67, Chm Royal Commn on the Press 1961-62, Med Research Council 1961-65, Sussex Discharged Prisoners' Aid Soc 1962-66, and City Panel on Take-Overs and Mergers 1968-80; a JP for Sussex; Dir: Caffyns Ltd (Dep Chm); sometime Dir Observer Newspapers Ltd, Shell Transport & Trading Co Ltd, Morgan et Cie SA, Hawker Siddeley Group Ltd, Times Newspapers Ltd, Thames Television Ltd (Chm 1969-74), Upjohn (UK) Ltd (Chm), Rank Hovis Macdougall Ltd; sometime Consultant to Hawker Siddeley, Rank Hovis, and J.P. Morgan; Chm Morgan Guaranty Trust Co's Internat Advisory Council 1967-74; Past Pres of Rainer Foundation (formerly London Police Court Mission), and of British Hotels and Restaurants Assocn; a sometime Member of Exec of Internat Commn of Jurists, and of Council of Internat Chamber of Commerce; Chm of Friends of Atlantic Union, Internat Law Section, British Inst of Internat & Comparative Law, and Justice (British Branch Internat Commn of Jurists); Member of Court, London Univ; Chancellor of Sussex Univ 1965-85; Indep Chm of Press Council 1974-78; MP for St Helens (L) 1945-58; cr Knt 1945, PC 1946, Baron Shawcross, of Friston, co Sussex (Life Baron) 1959, and GBE (Civil) 1974: m 1st, 1924, Rosita Alberta, who d 1943, da of William Shyvers, of Upminster Lodge, Essex; 2ndly, 1944, Joan Winifred, who d 1974, da of Hume Mather, of Carlton Lodge, Tunbridge Wells, and has issue by 2nd m.

Arms – Per pale azure and gules on a saltire between four annulets argent an ermine spot sable. Crest – Upon the battlements of a tower proper a martlet gules holding in the beak a cross paty fitchy or. Supporters – Dexter, a lion argent gorged with a chain sable pendant therefrom an escutcheon also sable charged with a balance or; sinister, a griffin sable armed and langued azure gorged with a chain, pendent therefrom a portcullis or.
Residences – Friston Place, Sussex; Anchorage, St Mawes, Cornwall; I-One Albany, Piccadilly, W1V 9RP. Address – 60 Victoria Embankment, EC4Y 0JP. Clubs – Buck's, White's, Garrick, Pratt's, Royal Automobile, Royal Cornwall Yacht, Royal Yacht Squadron, New York Yacht, and Travellers' (Paris).

SONS LIVING (By 2nd marriage)

Hon William Hartley Hume (46 Blomfield Rd, W9), b 1946; ed Eton, and Univ Coll, Oxford: m 1st, 1972 (m diss 1980), Marina Sarah, da of late Col Esmond Pelham Warner, TD, of Cambridge; 2ndly, 1981 (m diss 1987), Michal E., da of A. J. Levin, of London; 3rdly, 1993, Hon Mrs Olga Polizzi, eldest da of Baron Forte (Life Baron), and has issue living (by 1st m), Conrad Hartley Pelham, b 1977, — (by 2nd m) Eleanor Joan Georgina, b 1983.
Hon Hume, b 1953; ed Eton.

DAUGHTER LIVING (By 2nd marriage)

Hon Joanna, b 1948; ed Benenden, and St Bartholomew's Hosp Med Sch: m 1986, Charles Russell Peck, eldest son of Russell Peck, of Cambridge, Mass, USA, and has issue living, Henry Russell Hartley, b 1988, — Alice Joan, b 1989.
Residence – Flint Cottage, Friston Place, nr Eastbourne, Sussex BN20 0AN.

Sheffield and Stanley of Alderley, Baron (see Stanley of Alderley).

Shelburne, Earl of; son of Marquess of Lansdowne.

SHEPHERD, BARON (Shepherd) (Baron UK 1946)

MALCOLM NEWTON SHEPHERD, PC, 2nd Baron; *b* 27 Sept 1918; *s* 1954: Capt of HM Body Guard of Hon Crops of Gentlemen-at-Arms 1964-67; Dir Mitchell Cotts & Co (FE) Ltd 1946-50, Chm and Man Dir Fielding, Brown and Finch (FE) Ltd 1950-64; Dep Speaker and Ch Whip, House of Lords 1964-67; a Min of State Commonwealth Office 1967-70, and Dep Leader House of Lords 1968-70; Lord Privy Seal and Leader of the House of Lords 1974-76; Dep Chm of Sterling Group of Cos since 1976; Chm of Practice and Procedure Select Cttee House of Lords 1976-78, of Medical Research Council 1973-79, of Civil Ser Pay Research Unit Board since 1978, of Packaging Council since 1978, Chm National Bus Co 1978; Pres Centre Européen de L'Enterprise Publique 1984-85, and Inst of Road Transport Engrs since 1987; Chm House of Lords Cttee European Community Affairs, Telecom-Transport-Energy, 1987-89; Internat Consultant, Sun Hung Kai Securities, Sun Hung Kai Bank, Hong Kong; 1939-45 War as Lt RASC in N Africa, Sicily, and Italy; PC 1965: *m* 1941, Allison, who *d* 1998, da of Patrick Redmond, of 56 Carrick Knowe, Parkway, Edinburgh, and has issue.

Residence – 29 Kennington Palace Court, Sancroft St, SE11.

SONS LIVING

Hon GRAEME GEORGE, *b* 6 Jan 1949: *m* 1971, Eleanor, da of —, and has issue living, Patrick Malcolm, *b* 19—. *Residence* – Apt 19B Tower One, University Heights, 23 Pokfield Rd, Mid Levels, Hong Kong.
Hon Douglas Newton, *b* 1952.

SISTER LIVING

Hon Margaret Eleanor, *b* 1922: *m* 1949, Theodore Leonard Bates, and has issue living, Andrew Michael, *b* 1952, — Suzanne Katherine Michele, *b* 1960. *Residence* – Justacott, 3 Victoria Cottages, Lydiate Lane, Lynton, N Devon.

PREDECESSOR – **(1)** *Rt Hon* GEORGE ROBERT Shepherd, PC, son of late George Robert Shepherd of Spalding, Lincolnshire, *b* 1881; Ch Opposition Whip, and a Dep-Speaker, House of Lords and a Member of Parliamentary Committee of Labour Party; National Agent of Labour Party 1928-46; was a Lord-in-Waiting to HM Oct 1948 to July 1949; Capt of Yeomen of the Guard July to Oct 1949, and Capt of Gentlemen-at-Arms and Ch Govt Whip in House of Lords Oct 1949 to Oct 1951; *cr* PC 1951, *Baron Shepherd*, of Spalding, co Lincoln (peerage of UK) 1946: *m* 1915, Ada, who *d* 1975, da of late Alfred Newton, of Halstead, Essex; *d* 1954; *s* by his son **(2)** MALCOLM NEWTON, 2nd Baron and present peer.

SHEPPARD OF DIDGEMERE, BARON (Sheppard) (Life Baron 1994)

ALLEN JOHN GEORGE SHEPPARD, KCVO, son of late John Baggott Sheppard; *b* 25 Dec 1932; *ed* Ilford County Sch, and LSE (BSc Econ); Hon Dr International Management Centre 1989, Brunel Univ 1994, South Bank Univ 1994, Univ of East London 1997, Westminster Univ 1998; Ford UK and Ford Europe 1958-68, Rootes/Chrysler 1968-71, British Leyland 1971-75, Grand Metropolitan 1975-96 (Chm 1987-96); Chm London First since 1992, and Dir London Development Partnership; Co-Chm London Pride Partnership 1994-98; Chm Advsy Board, Prince of Wales's Trusts 1995-98, Vice-Pres Business in the Community (Chm 1994-97); Dep Chm International Business Leaders Forum since 1990; Chm Prince's Youth Business Trust 1990-94; Chm Group Trust plc since 1994; Chm McBride plc since 1993; Chm CB Railways since 1996, and Unipart Group of Companies since 1996; Dir High-Point Rendel Group plc since 1997; Memb Board of Management, Conservative Party 1992-98; Memb Exec Cttee of Animal Health Trust; Board Memb, Blue Cross; Vice-Pres United Response, and Brewers Licensed Retailers Assoc; Memb House of Lords Finance & Staff; Gov of LSE; FCMA, FCIS, CIMgt; *cr* Kt 1990, *Baron Sheppard of Didgemere*, of Roydon, co Essex (Life Baron) 1994, and KCVO 1997: *m* 1st, 1958 (*m diss* 1980), Damaris, da of late David Jones; 2ndly, 1980, Mary da of Harry Stewart, of London.

Arms – ......
Address – c/o House of Lords, SW1A 0PW.

SHEPPARD OF LIVERPOOL, BARON (Sheppard) (Life Baron 1998)

Rt Rev DAVID STUART SHEPPARD, son of late Stuart Morton Winter Sheppard, Solicitor; *b* 6 March 1929; *ed* Sherborne, Trinity Hall, Camb (MA 1956, Hon Fell 1983), and Ridley Hall Theological Coll; Hon LLD Liverpool 1981, Hon DTech Liverpool John Moores Univ 1987, Hon DD Cantab 1991; Hon DD Exeter 1998; ordained Deacon 1955, Priest 1956; Curate of St Mary's, Islington 1955-57; Warden and Chaplain, Mayflower Family Centre, Canning Town 1957-69; Bishop Suffragan of Woolwich 1969-75; Bishop of Liverpool 1975-97; Nat Service 2nd Lieut Royal Sussex Regt 1947-49; played cricket for Cambridge Univ 1950-52, Sussex 1947-62 and England 1950-63; Freeman of the City of Liverpool 1995; author; *cr Baron Sheppard of Liverpool*, of West Kirby, co Merseyside (Life Baron) 1998: *m* 1957, Grace, da of late Rev Bryan Raymund Isaac, of Bridport, Dorset, and has issue.
Residence – 11 Melloncroft Drive, West Kirby, Wirral, Merseyside CH48 2JA.

DAUGHTER LIVING

Hon Jenny, *b* 1962: *m* 1989, Donald Sinclair.

SHERBORNE, BARONY OF (Dutton) (Extinct 1985)

COLLATERAL BRANCH LIVING

Issue of late Vice-Adm Hon Arthur Brandreth Scott Dutton, CB, CMG (raised to rank of a Baron's son 1920), brother of 6th Baron, *b* 1876, *d* 1932: *m* 1914, Doriel, who *d* 1941, da of Sir John Adam Hay, 9th Bt (*cr* 1635):—

Julia Meliora, *b* 1914: *m* 1939, Bertram Salisbury Butler, formerly Sqdn-Ldr RAFVR, of Burton Manor, Pulborough, Sussex, and has issue living, Doriel Julia Primrose, *b* 1941: *m* 1964, Gavin Fleming Crawford, of 7 Woodsford Sq, Addison Rd, W14, and has issue living, Charles William Norrie *b* 1970, Caroline Doriel *b* 1966, Sarah Elizabeth *b* 1968: *m* 1994, James Edward More Newman. —— (Doriel) Rowena, *b* 1916: *m* 1940, Ian Norman Bayles, DFC, Wing-Cdr RAFVR, of Chatsworth Park, Tabilk, Vic, Aust, and has had issue, Alastair Ian (Balthayock, Avenel, Victoria 3664, Australia) *b* 1941: *m* 1967, Judith Alison, el da of Geoffrey Ryan, of Willowmavin, Vic, Aust, and has issue living, Emma Rowena *b* 1970, Fiona Alison *b* 1973, — Archibald James Norman (1 River Av, Echuca Village, Victoria 3564, Australia), *b* 1948: *m* 1975, Sally Ishbel, el da of Sir Alec (Alexander Reid) Creswick, of Allanvale, Avenel, Vic, Aust, and has issue living, Timothy James Creswick *b* 1981, Edward Ian Alexander *b* 1984,   Aprilla Rowena, *b* 1946: *m* 1st, 1968: *m* 1st, 1968 (*m diss* 1979), John Beaufort Somerset; 2ndly, 1979, Anthony George Hodgson, of S Yarra, Melbourne, Aust, and *d* 1995, leaving issue (by 1st *m*), Sarah Penelope *b* 1970, Catherine Rowena *b* 1971, — Amanda Mary, *b* 1951: *m* 1st, 1976 (*m diss* 1987), Capt David Maurice Stirling Home Drummond Moray, Scots Gds (ret) (*see* D Buccleuch, colls, 1995 Edn); 2ndly, 1987, John Dorman Elliott, of Toorak, Melbourne, Aust, and has issue living (by 1st *m*), Edwina Alice *b* 1980, (by 2nd *m*) Alexandra Louisa Amanda *b* 1989, — Ayliffe Julia (twin), *b* 1951: *m* 1977, John Wallis Caldwell, of Milong, Yourg, NSW, and has issue living, William John Bayles *b* 1982, Hugh Ian Wallis *b* 1984, Camilla Ayliffe *b* 1980. *Residence* – Chatsworth Park, Tabilk, Vic, Aust.

SHERFIELD, BARON (Makins) (Baron UK 1964)

CHRISTOPHER JAMES MAKINS, 2nd Baron; *b* 23 July 1942; *s* 1996; *ed* Winchester, and New Coll, Oxford; HM Diplo Ser 1964-75; Fellow of All Soul's Coll 1963-77: *m* 1975, Mrs Wendy Catherine Cortesi, elder da of late John Whitney, of Evergreen, Colorado, USA, and has issue.

Arms – Argent or a fesse embattled counter embattled gules between in chief two falcons proper belled or, and in base a lion's face of the second, an annulet or between two besants. **Crest** – A dexter arm embowed in armour proper encircled by an annulet or and holding a flagstaff, therefrom flowing a banner argent charged with a lion's face gules. **Supporters** – *Dexter*, a lion sable pendent from a chain about the neck or a bezant charged with a model representing an atom of lithium 6 sable, *Sinister*, a bald headed eagle rising proper adorned likewise about the neck the bezant charged with a lawn tennis racquet erect gules.
Residence – 3034 P St NW, Washington, DC 20007, USA.
Clubs – Pratt's, Metropolitan (Washington).

DAUGHTER LIVING

Hon Marian Whitney, *b* 1980.

BROTHER LIVING

Hon DWIGHT WILLIAM, *b* 2 March 1951; *ed* Winchester, and Ch Ch, Oxford: *m* 1983, Penelope Jane, da of Donald R. L. Massy Collier. *Residence* – Beaurepaire House, Basingstoke, Hants RG26 5EH.

SISTERS LIVING

Hon Mary (*Viscountess Norwich*), *b* 1935: *m* 1st, 1959 (*m diss* 1984), as his 2nd wife, Hon Hugo John Laurence Philipps (later 3rd Baron Milford); 2ndly, 1989, as his 2nd wife, 2nd Viscount Norwich, CVO, and has issue (by 1st *m*) (*see* B Milford). *Residence* – 24 Blomfield Rd, W9.
Hon Cynthia, *b* (twin) 1935: *m* 1967, Oliver James Colman, and has issue (*see* Colman, Bt). *Residence* – 7 Tor Gdns, W8.
Hon Virginia, *b* 1939; *ed* Lady Margaret Hall, Oxford: *m* 1972, David Michael Shapiro, and has issue living, Adam, *b* 19—, — Jacob, *b* 19—, — Jeremy, *b* 19—. *Residence* – 14 Woodstock Rd, W4.
Hon Patricia, *b* 1946: *m* 1st, 1966, Michael Ordway Miller, of Muir Beach, Calif, USA; 2ndly, 1980, Loring Sagan, and has issue. *Residence* – 488 Old County Rd, Tahoe City, CA ......, USA.

PREDECESSOR – (1) ROGER MELLOR Makins, GCB, GCMG, FRS, son of late Brig-Gen Sir Ernest Makins, KBE, CB, DSO; *b* 1904; Fellow of All Souls' Coll, Oxford, and Winchester Coll 1963-79 (Warden 1974-79); Bar Inner Temple 1927; Ambassador to USA 1952-56, Joint Permanent Sec to The Treasury 1956-60; Chm UK Atomic Energy Authority 1960-64; Chancellor Reading Univ 1970-92; *cr Baron Sherfield*, of Sherfield-on-Loddon, co Southampton (Peerage of UK) 1964: *m* 1934, Alice Brooks, who *d* 1985, eldest da of late Hon Dwight F. Davis, of Washington, DC, USA, sometime Gov of the Philippines; *d* 1996; *s* by his elder son (2) CHRISTOPHER JAMES, 2nd Baron and present peer.

Shirley, family name of Earl Ferrers.

SHINWELL, BARONY OF (Shinwell) (Extinct 1986)

SON LIVING OF LIFE BARON

Hon Samuel, *b* 19—.

Hon Mrs P. Sellers.

Shore, family name of Baron Teignmouth.

SHORE OF STEPNEY, BARON (Shore) (Life Baron 1997)

PETER DAVID SHORE, PC, son of late Robert Norman Shore; *b* 20 May 1924; *ed* Quarry Bank Gram Sch, Liverpool, and King's Coll, Camb; MP (Lab) for Stepney 1964-74, for Tower Hamlets, Stepney and Poplar 1974-83, and for Bethnal Green and Stepney 1983-97; Head of Lab Research Dept 1959-64, PPS to Harold Wilson as Prime Minister 1965-66; Joint Parliamentary Sec, Ministry of Technology 1966-67, and Dept of Economic Affairs 1967; Sec of State for Economic Affairs 1967-69; Min Without Portfolio and Dep Leader of House of Commons 1969-70; Opposition Spokesman on Europe 1971-74; Trade Sec 1974-76; Environment Sec 1976-79; Memb Shadow Cabinet and Chief Opposition Spokesman on Foreign Affairs 1979-80, Treasury and Economic Affairs 1981-83, Trade and Industry and Shadow Leader of the House 1983-87; Memb Select Cttee on Foreign Affairs 1987-97; Memb Nolan Cttee 1995; *cr* PC 1967, and *Baron Shore of Stepney*, of Stepney in London Borough of Tower Hamlets (Life Baron) 1997: *m* 1948, Elizabeth Catherine, CB, da of late Edward Murray Wrong, and has had issue, two sons (one dec'd), and two das.
Residence – 23 Dryburgh Rd, SW15 1BN.

Short, family name of Baron Glenamara.

SHREWSBURY AND WATERFORD, EARL OF (Chetwynd-Talbot) (Earl E 1442, I 1446, and GB 1784)

Ready to accomplish

CHARLES HENRY JOHN BENEDICT CROFTON CHETWYND CHETWYND-TALBOT, 22nd Earl, and Premier Earl (on the Roll) in peerages both of England and Ireland; *b* 18 Dec 1952; *s* 1980; *ed* Harrow; is Hereditary Lord High Steward of Ireland, and patron of eleven livings; DL Stafford 1994: *m* 1974, Deborah Jane, only da of Noel Staughton Hutchinson, of Ellerton House, Sambrook, Shropshire, and has issue.

𝕬rms – Quarterly, 1st and 4th, gules, a lion rampant, within a bordure engrailed or, *Talbot*; 2nd and 3rd azure, a chevron between three mullets or, *Chetwynd*. 𝕮rest – 1st, on a chapeau gules, turned up ermine, a lion statant, with the tail extended or, *Talbot*; 2nd, a goat's head erased argent, attired or, *Chetwynd*. 𝕾upporters – Two talbots argent. 𝕭adge – A talbot passant argent. *Seat* – Wanfield Hall, Kingstone, Uttoxeter, Staffs.

SONS LIVING

JAMES RICHARD CHARLES JOHN (*Viscount Ingestre*), *b* 11 Jan 1978.
Hon Edward William Henry Alexander, *b* 1981.

DAUGHTER LIVING

Lady Victoria Jane, *b* 1975.

BROTHER LIVING

Hon Paul Alexander Anthony Bueno, *b* 1957; *ed* Eton, and Ch Ch, Oxford (BA): *m* 1982, Sarah Elizabeth, da of late Simon Hildebrand Melville Bradley, of Thundridge, Ware, Herts (*see* V Hampden), and has issue living, Harry, *b* 1985, — Jack, *b* 1987, — Rory Arthur Alton, *b* 1995. *Residence* – Gunville House, Grateley, nr Andover, Hants SP11 8JQ.

SISTERS LIVING

Lady Charlotte Sarah Alexandra, *b* 1938: *m* 1965, Camillo Cavazza dei Conti Cavazza, of Isola del Garda, 25010 S Felice del Benaco, Brescia, Italy, who *d* 1981, and has issue living, Sigmar, *b* 1966, — Eric, *b* 1969, — Christian, *b* 1979, — Lars-Patrick, *b* (twin) 1979, — Livia, *b* 1967: *m* 19—, Alessandro Bonù, — Ilona, *b* 1972, — Alberta, *b* 1977.

Lady (Josephine) Sylvia-Rose, *b* 1940: *m* 1965, Stafford Antony Saint, and has issue living, Stafford Alexander Antony Talbot, *b* 1970, — Helen Elizabeth Charlotte, *b* 1966, — Victoria Nadine Mary, *b* 1968. *Residence* – Ledburn Farm, Ledburn, Leighton Buzzard, Beds.

Lady Catharine Laura, *b* 1945; LRAM: *m* 1966, Richard Sebastian Endicott Chamberlain, and has issue living, Thomas Endicott, *b* 1973; *ed* Radley, — Sophie Anne Zacyntha *b* 1968, — Caroline Amy, *b* 1971. *Residence* – Stocks Farm, Burley St, nr Ringwood, Hants.

Lady Marguerite Mary, *b* 1950: *m* 1st, 1970 (*m diss* 1984), Guy William Brisbane; 2ndly, 1984, Andrew Wynne, and has issue living (by 1st *m*), Duncan Guy Talbot, *b* 1975; *ed* Berkhamsted. *Residence* – 18 Campbell Drive, Beaconsfield, Bucks HP9 1TF.

MOTHER LIVING

Nadine Muriel, yr da of late Brig-Gen Cyril Randell Crofton, CB, of Trobridge, Crediton, Devon: *m* 1936 (*m diss* 1963), as his 1st wife, the 21st Earl, who *d* 1980. *Residence* – The House, Lower Ascott, Leighton Buzzard, Beds.

COLLATERAL BRANCHES LIVING

Branch from 3rd son of 2nd Earl Talbot

Grandson of late Brig-Gen Arthur Hervey Talbot, son of late Charles Arthur Talbot, elder son (by 1st *m*) of late Rev Hon Arthur Chetwynd-Talbot, 3rd son of 2nd Earl Talbot:—

Issue of late Lieut-Col Douglas Hervey Talbot, DSO, MC, *b* 1882, *d* 1927: *m* 1914, Dorothy Helen Roylance, who *d* 1978, da of late William Roylance Court, JP (Walker, Bt, *cr* 1886):—

Bryan Hervey (Aston Lodge, Aston, Runcorn, Cheshire), *b* 1916; *ed* Marlborough Coll; 1940-46 War as Fl Lt RAFVR: *m* 1940, Katherine, who *d* 1977, da of R. J. Hughes, of Llandudno, and has issue living, Andrew Hervey (La Montjoie, Sargé-lès-Le Mans, 72190 France), *b* 1946: *m* 1st, 1972 (*m diss* 1976), Hilda Margaret Priscilla Williams, SRN; 2ndly, 1979 (*m diss* 1996), Danielle Claude, yst da of Roger Basil Boulay, of 9 rue de Verneil, Lavernat, 72500 France; 3rdly, 19—, Axelle Sabrina, yst da of Jean-Claude Martineau, of 13 rue des Platanes, Château-du-Loir, 72500 France, and has issue living, (by 2nd *m*), Jessie Sarah *b* 1983, Kate *b* 1986, Miriam *b* 1990, (by 3rd *m*), Stuart Hervey *b* 1999, — Howard Douglas (Burnt Thatch, Aston, Runcorn, Cheshire), *b* 1948: *m* 1972, Christine Anne, da of W. A. A. Dutton, of Hoole Bank, Chester, and has issue living, Charles Aston Hervey *b* 1981, Bridget Louisa *b* 1975, Sophie Katharine *b* 1977, — Marie-Luize (3 Maidenhead Rd, Stratford-upon-Avon, Warwicks), *b* 1942: *m* 1st, 1966 (*m diss* 1981), John Bernard Haycraft; 2ndly, 1984 (*m diss* 1986), Graham John Ollis, and has issue living (by 1st *m*), Alexander Richard *b* 1969: *m* 1998, Rataya Torrey Mathias, of USA (and has issue living, Satchel Jaron *b* 1997), Oliver Talbot *b* 1972 (has issue living (by Helen Victoria Wimperis), Samuel Eban Talbot *b* 1997), Simon Hervey *b* 1973, — Wendy Robina Roylance, *b* 1949: *m*

1973, Rodger Price, of Hilltop, Sutton Weaver, Runcorn, Cheshire, and has issue living, Hannah Roylance *b* 1975, Madeleine Kate *b* 1977.

Grandson of late Col Hervey Talbot, yr son (by 1st *m*) of late Rev Hon Arthur Chetwynd-Talbot (ante):—
Issue of late Arthur Aston Talbot, *b* 1881, *d* 1918: *m* 1912, Mary Winifred, who *d* 1964, da of late A. Battiscombe, of Hinton Court, Hereford:—
Patrick Edward Aston (Beau Coin Lodge, Le Mont au Roux, St Brelade, Jersey JE3 8BY, CI), *b* 1913; CEng, MRAeS; RAF 1934-38, RAE 1939-46: *m* 1936, Gwyneth, yr da of late Lt-Col Herbert Gaussen Sargeaunt, RA, and has issue living, David Nugent Aston (Ontario, Canada), *b* 1939: *m* 1st, 1962 (*m diss* 1971), Carole, da of Oakley Pawson, of Ontario; 2ndly, 1979, Rachel, who *d* 1988, yr da of Dr Frank Edmund Hampton, of Lincs, and has issue living (by 1st *m*), John Oakley Aston *b* 1964, Jeanne Davida *b* 1962, Rachel Millicent *b* 1966, (by 2nd *m*) Georgina Amy *b* 1980, — Maryan Gwyneth, *b* 1938; BA (1959); Chevalier l'Ordre des Arts et des Lettres: *m* 1974, John Roberts (*see* Roberts, Bt, *cr* 1909, colls), of 2 Douro Terrace, St Helier, Jersey, CI.

Grandchildren of late Rev Arthur Henry Chetwynd-Talbot, yst son (only son by 2nd *m*) of late Rev Hon Arthur Chetwynd-Talbot (ante):—
Issue of late Sqdn-Ldr John Arthur Chetwynd-Talbot, AFC, *b* 1905, *d* 1993: *m* 1st, 1929 (*m diss* 1963), Helen Mary, who *d* 1969, eldest da of late Adm Cyril Samuel Townsend, CB; 2ndly, 1963, Betty Verral, who *d* 1999, yr da of late Rev Augustus George Allton:—
(By 1st *m*) John Edward (Old Swan Cottage, Wilton, nr Salisbury, Wilts SN8 3SS), *b* 1934; *ed* Harrow; Sub-Lieut (A) RNVR 1955-57: *m* 1st, 1959 (*m diss* 1964), Sonja Ann, da of late Roger Walker, of South Corner, Duncton, Sussex; 2ndly, 1967, Belinda Bess, yr da of Maj Euan James Leslie Warren Gilchrist, MC, DFC, RA, of Monk Sherborne House, Monk Sherborne, Hants, and has issue living (by 1st *m*), Jane Sonja, *b* 1960: *m* 1984, Simon Barkes, of Fawler End, Kingston Lisle, Wantage, Oxon, son of B. R. Barkes, of Wimbledon, and has issue living, Benjamin *b* 1989, Harriet Maria Eleanora *b* 1987, Serena Jane *b* 1991, — Sarah Ann, *b* 1962: *m* 1983, Michael W. Morris, son of M. E. Morris, of Myrtle Cottage, Llandogo, Gwent, and has issue living, Rebecca Sarah *b* 1984, Chloe *b* 1985, — (by 2nd *m*) Edward John, *b* 1969, — Mary Rowena, *b* 1968: *m* 1995, Andreas J. Söllner, yr son of Wolfgang Söllner, of Erlangen, Germany, — Prudence Ankaret, *b* (twin) 1969. —— Susan Mary, *b* 1930: *m* 1954, William Byars Thomson, of Holt Valley Farm, Clayton, Hassocks, Sussex BN6 9PL, and has issue living, Geoffrey Charles Byars (Thorngreen, Kinrossie, by Perth), *b* 1958: *m* 1990, Judy, da of Cdr D. M. G. Brittan, of Yelverton, S Devon, and has issue living, James David Byars *b* 1994, Rose Elizabeth *b* 1991, Daisy Isobel *b* (twin) 1994, — *Rev* Richard William Byars (All Saints' Vicarage, Piddletrenthide, Dorset), *b* 1960: *m* 1991, Alexandra Jane Foster, and has issue living, Jack William Byars *b* 1993, Frederick Michael Byars *b* 1994, — Mary Rose Byars, *b* 1962; MB BS: *m* 1987, Peter George Shears, of Wovies, Southdown Av, Lewes, Sussex, and has issue living, William Peter George *b* 1996, Annalie Florence *b* 1993, Helena Rose *b* 1994. —— Ankaret Helen, *b* 1932: *m* 1955, John Orcheston Dean, of High Valley Farm, RR1, Macdonald's Corner, Ontario, Canada K0G 1M0, and has issue living, John Anthony, *b* 1962, — Joanna Elizabeth, *b* 1956: *m* 1979, David Knight Wilson, of 60 Evelyn Av, Ottawa, Ontario, Canada, and has issue living, Lucas Knight *b* 1983, Amanda Helen *b* 1981, — Philippa Ankaret, *b* 1958: *m* 1979, Russel Ray Pedley, of RR1, S Slocan, BC, Canada, and has issue living, Sidney Matthew *b* 1982, Jasmine Ankaret *b* 1981, — Louise Helen, *b* 1960: *m* 1979, Douglas William Moody, and has issue living, Jonathan William *b* 1979, Adam Douglas *b* 1982, Simon Jeffrey *b* 1984.

Issue of late Rev Arthur Charles Ashton Chetwynd-Talbot, *b* 1907, *d* 1987: *m* 1945, Pamela Mountjoy, who *d* 1998, da of late Hugh John Say, of Dartford, Kent:—
Clare Eveline (29 Holloway, Bath, Avon), *b* 1946: *m* 1968 (*m diss* 1976), Malcolm Garfield Green, and has issue living, Timothy Ashton Garfield, *b* 1969, — Caroline Anne, *b* 1971.

Branch from 4th son of 2nd Earl Talbot

Grandchildren of late Rt Hon Sir George John Talbot, eldest son of late Rt Hon John Gilbert Talbot, elder son of late Hon John Chetwynd-Talbot, QC, 4th son of 2nd Earl Talbot:—
Issue of late Capt Thomas George Talbot, CB, QC, *b* 1904, *d* 1992: *m* 1933, Hon Cynthia Edith Guest, who *d* 1994, yr da of 1st Viscount Wimbourne:—
Charles John, *b* 1947: *m* 1st, 1978 (*m diss* 1992), Phyllida R., eldest da of late Rev Michael McCormick; 2ndly, 1993, Nicola Mary, da of late George Boulton, of Upland, Hillydeal Rd, Otford, Sevenoaks, Kent, and has issue living (by 1st *m*), Richard Charles, *b* 1980: — Francis Michael, *b* 1982, — Hugo Peter, *b* 1983, — (by 2nd *m*) George Thomas *b* 1992, — Henrietta, *b* 1995. *Residence* – Falconhurst, Markbeech, Edenbridge, Kent TN8 5NR. —— Meriel Cornelia, *b* 1935: *m* 1966, Prof Robert David Hugh Boyd, MB, FRCP, of The Stone House, Skellorn Green, Adlington, Macclesfield, Cheshire, and has issue living, Thomas Dixon, *b* 1967, — Diana Charlotte, *b* 1969, — Lucy Madeleine, *b* 1974. —— Joanna, *b* 1938: *m* 1964, Alan Malcolm Smith, of Edells, Markbeech, Edenbridge, Kent, and has issue living, Bertram Thomas, *b* 1967, — Emily Mary, *b* 1965, — Flora, *b* 1971. —— Mary Gertrude, *b* 1942.

Grandchildren of late John Edward Talbot, 3rd son of late Rt Hon John Gilbert Talbot (ante):—
Issue of late Lt-Col Evan Arthur Christopher Talbot, MBE, Gren Gds, *b* 1903, *d* 1975: *m* 1926, Felicite Annette Cynthia, who *d* 1985, da of Lt-Col William Edward Long:—
Christopher Michael Edward, *b* 1928; late Lt RN: *m* 1962, Suzanne Barbara, el da of late Arthur Dulley, and has issue living, Sarah Josephine, *b* 1964: *m* 1990, Hugh S. Muirhead, son of Richard Muirhead, of Greenfields, Plumpton, Sussex, and has issue living, Archie Patrick Talbot *b* 1995, Jack Richard Caradoc *b* 1998, Madeleine Rose England *b* 1994, — Miranda Meriel, *b* 1966: *m* 1998, James Frederick Brian Napier (*see* Gooch, Bt, *cr* 1746), — Alice Elizabeth, *b* 1969: *m* 1997, Adam Charles Dickens, son of Rev Harry Dickens, of Grayshott, Hants, and has issue living, Thomas Arthur Charles *b* 1998. —— Catherine TALBOT (11 rue Maitre Cornille, 13990 Fontvieille, France), *b* 1930; has resumed her maiden name: *m* 1958 (*m diss* 1978), Clement Francis Kelly, and has issue living, Anthea Jane, *b* 1959: *m* 1981 (*m diss* 1991), C. Coulson — Felicity Ankarot, *b* 1962: *m* 1992, Gordon Jones.

Granddaughter of late Rt Rev Edward Stuart Talbot, DD, Lord Bishop of Winchester, son of late Hon John Chetwynd-Talbot, QC (ante):—
Issue of late Rt Rev Neville Stuart Talbot, MC, DD, Bishop of Pretoria 1920-32, *b* 1879, *d* 1943: *m* 1918, Cecil Mary, who *d* 1921, da of William Seymour Eastwood, of West Stoke House, Chichester:—

Elizabeth, *b* 1919; late Flight Officer WAAF; a JP: *m* 1946, Fl Lt Ronald Arthur Chalk, who *d* 1993, and has issue living, Gilbert John (103 Elgin Crescent, W11 2JF; Foxcote Grange, Andoversford, Cheltenham, Glos), *b* 1947: *m* 1975, Gillian Frances Audrey, only da of Sir Gervase Ralph Edmund Blois, 10th Bt, MC, and formerly wife of Hugh Christopher Riddle, and has issue (*see* Blois, Bt), — Sarah Elizabeth, *b* 1950: *m* 1982, Nicholas John Squire, of Park Farm, Euston, Thetford, Norfolk IP124 2QT, and has issue living, Guy Charles *b* 1985, Hugo Edward John *b* 1987, Amanda Elizabeth *b* 1984, Octavia Clare *b* 1991. *Residence* – 3 Wildwood Court, Cedars Village, Chorleywood, Herts WD3 5GG.

Branch from 5th son of 2nd Earl Talbot

Granddaughter of late George Canning Talbot, son of late Rev Hon George Gustavus Chetwynd-Talbot, 5th son of 2nd Earl Talbot:—
Issue of late Major John Arthur William Talbot, *b* 1876, *d* 1918: *m* 1906, Barbara Grace, who *d* 1938, el da of late Rowland Ticehurst, of Crickley, Witcombe, Gloucestershire:—
Lettice Mary, *b* (Dec) 1907: *m* 1934, George Butt Miller, who *d* 1958, and has issue living, Thomas Butt (La Planque, Torteval, Guernsey), *b* 1935; *ed* Eton, and New Coll, Oxford (MA); Solicitor 1966: *m* 1965, Jane Mary, only da of late C. C. Roberts, of Bepton Old Rectory, Midhurst, — Robert Cottrell Butt (80 Alderney St, SW1), *b* 1947; *ed* Worksop Coll, Trin Coll, Dublin (BA), and Edinburgh Univ (M Litt): *m* 1971, Patricia Georgina, da of late Dr G. McBrien, of Bath, and has issue living, George Talbot *b* 1974; *ed* Sherborne, and Reading Univ, Caroline Mary *b* 1978; *ed* Royal Sch, Bath, and Swansea Univ, — John Richard Butt (The Glebe House, Kilninor, Gorey, co Wexford), *b* 1950; *ed* Stanbridge Sch, and Duke Univ, N Carolina, — Barbara Blanche, *b* 1938, — Mary Ruth (Calebrook House, Charlton Musgrove, Wincanton, Som), *b* 1939: *m* 1989, George Blaug. *Residence* – Berrywood House, Donhead, Shaftesbury, Dorset.

Branch from 6th son of 2nd Earl Talbot

Granddaughter of late Lieut-Col Gerald Francis Chetwynd-Talbot, 3rd son of late Rev Hon William Whitworth Chetwynd-Talbot, 6th son of 2nd Earl Talbot:—
Issue of late Sir Gerald Francis Chetwynd-Talbot, KCVO, CMG, OBE, *b* 1881, *d* 1945: *m* 1920, Hélène, who *d* 1975, da of S. Jarislowsky, of Paris, and widow of Capt Charles Labouchere, French Army:—
Isobel Helen Henrietta, *b* 1923: *m* 1942, Antony Mackenzie Smith, OBE, MC, and has issue living, Peter (30 Prothero Rd, SW6 7LZ) *b* 1946: *m* 1973, Sandra Gay-French, and has issue living, Helen Sarah *b* 1974, Alexandra Anne *b* 1976, Harriet Isobel *b* 1981, — Duncan John Gerald (10c Windsor Rd, W5 5PD), *b* 1951, — Jane Elizabeth, *b* 1947: *m* 1972, Robin Martin, and has issue living, James Benedict *b* 1973, Edward Barnaby *b* 1975, Peter Nicholas *b* 1983, — Catherine Isobel, *b* 1957; MD Sydney 1982: *m* 1979, Dr Simon Hawke, of Claphatch Farm, Claphatch Lane, Wallcrouch, nr Wadhurst, E Sussex, and has issue living, Edward Antony John *b* 1995, Henrietta *b* 1984, Charlotte *b* 1986. *Residence* – Backfields End, Winchelsea, Sussex TN36 4AB.

Branch from 8th son of 2nd Earl Talbot

Grandchildren living of late Gilbert Edward Chetwynd-Talbot, 5th son of late Col Hon Sir Wellington Patrick Manvers Chetwynd-Talbot, KCB, 8th son of 2nd Earl Talbot:—
Issue of late Maj Patrick Gilbert Murray Chetwynd-Talbot, *b* 1905, *d* 1979: *m* 1928, Audrey, who *d* 1995, yst da of late Julius Ernst Guthe, JP, of Kepwick Hall, Northallerton, Yorks:—
Humphrey John Patrick (The Three Horseshoes, 31 Staploe, St Neots, Cambs PE19 4JA), *b* 1930; *ed* Winchester, and Univ Coll, Oxford (MA): *m* 1953, Anne, twin da of late Capt Edward Glyn de Styrap Jukes-Hughes, CBE, RN, of Stourbridge House, Milton-on-Stour, Gillingham, Dorset, and has issue living, Kathryn Helen Anne, *b* 1957: *m* 1979, Sidney Anthony George Abrahams, of Woodfield, Honeydon Rd, Colmworth, Beds MK44 2LZ, and has issue living, Thomas Anthony Talbot *b* 1985, Annika Kathryn Anne *b* 1983, Harriett Laila *b* 1988, — Jennifer Mary, *b* 1958; *ed* St Hugh's Coll, Oxford (MA); MBA: *m* 1983, Martin Paul Rigby, late Capt RGJ, of Buckden Wood, Perry Rd, Buckden, Cambs PE18 9QX, son of John Rigby, of Camberley, Surrey, and has issue living, Dominic John Vaughan *b* 1992, Eloise Jennifer *b* 1989, Alice Helen Elizabeth *b* 1992, — Annabel Jean, *b* 1961; *ed* Exeter Univ (B Ed Hons). —— Michael Gilbert (Sunny Lawn, Tweentown, Cheddar, Som BA27 3JE), *b* 1931; *ed* Eton, and RMA Sandhurst; late Capt RA: *m* 1st, 1956 (*m diss* 19—), Bridget Adele, yr da of late Sidney Terence Evelyn Pook Ennion, of Colbourne, IoW; 2ndly, 1980, Kathleen (Kay) R. M. Gibson, who *d* 19—; 3rdly, 1995, Muriel M. V. Radaman, and has issue living (by 1st *m*), Rupert Edward Terence Gilbert, *b* 1962, — Tobias John Michael, *b* 1963, — Juliet Emma Serena, *b* 1958. —— Janet Ivory Audrey, *b* 1932: *m* 1954, Donald Craufurd Robertson, of 35 Gloucester Rd, Richmond, Surrey TW9 3BS, and has issue living, James Craufurd, *b* 1958; *ed* Washington Univ, Missouri, USA (PhD); lecturer at Univ of W Indies: *m* 1998, Muriel Sturtz, PhD, — William Alexander (6 Ivy Gdns, Crouch End, N8 9JE), *b* 1959: *m* 1998, Janice Wardrope, — David Kenneth Craufurd (2 Avenue Gdns, SW14 8BP), *b* 1964.

Issue of late Capt (Edward) Hugh Frederick Chetwynd-Talbot, MBE, RA, *b* 1909, *d* 1998: *m* 1935, Cynthia Phœbe Duncan (Mead Acre, Milton Lilbourne, Pewsey, Wilts), da of late Noel McGrigor Phillips, of Stoke d'Abernon Manor, Cobham:—
Mark Patrick (Scencliffe Grange, Coxwold, York), *b* 1941; *ed* Wellington Coll, and RMA Sandhurst; Maj late Coldm Gds: *m* 1970, Elizabeth Ann, da of Sacheverel O. F. Bateman, of Mortham Tower, Barnard Castle, co Durham, and has issue living, Nicholas John, *b* 1971: *m* 1997, Penelope J., da of ...... Toulmin, of Thorp Arch, Yorks, — Lara Katherine, *b* 1973. —— Anthea, *b* 1939: *m* 1st, 1963, Philip Simon Antill, who *d* 1996; 2ndly, 1999, Roger H. Moat, of Scofton Farm House, Worksop, Notts, and has issue living (by 1st *m*), Vanessa Cicely, *b* 1964: *m* 1989, Andrew Robinson, and has issue living, Thomas *b* 1992, Abigail *b* 1994, — Juliet Willa, *b* 1966: *m* 1995, Neil Goodwin, and has issue living, Sophie *b* 1997, Leah *b* 1998, — Helen Meriel, *b* 1969, — Jemima Louise, *b* 1971. —— Meriel, *b* 1944: *m* 1964, Mark Alexander Wyndham Baker, of The Old School, Fyfield, Abingdon, Oxon, and has issue (*see* Macnaghten, Bt, colls).

Branch from 9th son of 2nd Earl Talbot

Grandchildren of late Charles Fleming Chetwynd Chetwynd-Talbot (infra):—

Issue of late Charles John Huyshe Chetwynd Chetwynd-Talbot, *b* 1910, *d* 1991: *m* 1936, Jane (VAUGHAN), who *d* 1989, eldest da of late David Wheldon Jones, of Blaenyddol, Ffestiniog, N Wales:—
John Vaughan Chetwynd (8 Kinecroft, Wallingford, Oxon), *b* 1941; *ed* Eton; Page to Earl of Shrewsbury at Coronation of HM Queen Elizabeth II. —— Frances Elizabeth, *b* 1947: *m* 1974, Peter Henry Mayes, of Blakenhall Lodge, The Green, Barton-under-Needwood, Staffs, and has issue living, Tomasine Lucy, *b* 1977, — Rebecca Jane, *b* 1979.

Grandchildren of late Charles Alexander Price Chetwynd-Talbot, son of Hon Gerald Chetwynd-Talbot, 9th son of 2nd Earl Talbot:—
Issue of late Charles Fleming Chetwynd Chetwynd-Talbot, *b* 1879, *d* 1933: *m* 1906, Margaret Dorothy, who *d* 1969, da of Lt-Col Dunbar Fraser Huyshe, formerly RHA:—
Gilbert Alexander Lucius Chetwynd, *b* 1918; *ed* Eton: Lt-Col (ret) late Comdg 14th/20th King's Hussars; formerly Assist Mil Sec to C-in-C, Middle East; Sec, Albany, Piccadilly, 1967-83; 1939-45 War in Iraq, Syria, Persia (despatches), and Italy. *Residences* – Mansion Basement, Albany, Piccadilly, W1; Pleasant Cottage, Brightwell-cum-Sotwell, Wallingford, Oxon. *Club* – Cavalry. —— Geraldine Cecil Barbara, *b* 1907; formerly Subaltern First Aid Nursing Yeo. *Residences* – Mansion Basement, Albany, Piccadilly, W1; Pleasant Cottage, Brightwell-cum-Sotwell, Wallingford, Oxon.

Issue of late Gilbert Patrick Chetwynd-Talbot, *b* 1887, *d* 1958: *m* 1921 (*m diss* 1929), Alice Alethea, da of C. H. Christopher Moller, of Lindsey House, Cheyne Walk, Chelsea, SW:—
Christopher Patrick Chetwynd, RD, *b* 1922; *ed* Harrow, and Corpus Christi Coll, Camb; 1939-45 War as Lieut RNVR; Lt-Cdr RNR (ret) 1957-81: *m* 1955, Rosalind Mary, da of Air Vice-Marshal Christopher Neil Hope Bilney, CB, CBE, and has two adopted children, Patrick Nicholas Chetwynd, *b* 1958, — Harriet Susan, *b* 1959: *m* 1998, Duncan A. Cavenagh, son of Dr A. J. M. Cavenagh, of Brecon, Powys, and has issue living, Alexander Patrick *b* 1999. —— Barbara Maud Mary, *b* 1924: *m* 1949, Douglas Scott.

Branch from 3rd son of 1st Baron Talbot

Granddaughters of late Capt Henry FitzRoy George Talbot, DSO, RN (infra):—
Issue of late Vice Adm Sir (Arthur Allison) Fitzroy Talbot, KBE, CB, DSO, *b* 1909, *d* 1998: *m* 1st, 1940, Joyce Gertrude, who *d* 1981, elder da of late Frank Edwin Linley, of 28 Lower Sloane St, SW1, and of Tower Park, Fowey, Cornwall, 2ndly, 1983, Elizabeth Mary, who *d* 1995, da of Rupert Handley Ensor, formerly wife of Capt Richard Steel, RN, and widow of Sir Esmond Otho Durlacher:—
(By 1st *m*) Anthea Jane, *b* 1944: *m* 1969, James Arthur Hubert Charrington, of Cherry Orchard, Shaftesbury, Dorset, and has issue living, Melissa Clare, *b* 1970, — Lucinda Rose, *b* 1973. —— Elizabeth, *b* 1945: *m* 1969, Michael Shuttleworth, of Hathersage, Derbys, and has issue living, Ashton FitzRoy, *b* 1972, — Henry Ashton, *b* 1974.

Granddaughter of late Maj Henry Charles Talbot, son of Rev Henry George Talbot, el son of Very Rev Charles Talbot, yr son of late Rev George Talbot, 3rd son of 1st Baron:—
Issue of late Capt Henry Fitzroy George Talbot, DSO, RN, *b* 1874, *d* 1920: *m* 1904, Susan Blair Athol, who *d* 1951, only da of late William Allison:—
Nesta Cecil, *b* 1905: *m* 1929, Capt John Hext Lewes, OBE, RN, who *d* 1992, and *d* 1994, leaving issue, John William Talbot, RN (Y Fron, Maesycrugiau, Pencader, Carmarthenshire. *Club* – United Service), *b* 1931; is Lt-Cdr; Korea 1950-51; *m* 1st, 1954 (*m diss* 1963), Mary Georgiana, who *d* 1992, da of late Pascoe Anthony George Glyn (*see* B Wolverton, colls, 1990 Edn); 2ndly, 1967, Margaret Jane, da of Owen Fenner Clayton, of Sydney, NSW, Australia and has issue living, (by 1st *m*) John Pascoe *b* 1955, James Glyn *b* 1959: *m* 1984, Helen Lohmann, of Reading, Penn, USA (and has issue living, Maxwell John Pascoe *b* 1985), Alice Mary Rhiannon *b* 1957, (by 2nd *m*) Owain Vaughan *b* 1967, Angharad Hope *b* 1972, — Loveday Elisabeth Talbot, *b* 1932: *m* 1956, Robert George Gee, of Llanllyr, Talsarn, Lampeter, Dyfed, and has issue living, Matthew George Cooper *b* 1960, Patrick Robert Cooper *b* 1963: *m* 1991, Miranda Whitelaw Dunn (and has issue living, William Benedict Robert Cooper *b* 1992), Emma Louise Moya *b* 1962: *m* 1990, Nicholas Eric Hugh Barran (and has issue: *see* Barran, Bt, colls), — Gwenllian Anne Talbot, *b* 1934: *m* 1955, Capt John Franklin Kidd, RN, of Llanfair, Llandyssul, Dyfed, and has issue living, John Christopher William *b* 1957: *m* 1995, Carine Celia Ann, elder da of J. St G. Coldwell, of Somerton, Oxford, and widow of Sir Richard John Maitland, 9th Bt (and has issue living, Eleanor Rhianwen *b* 1996, Katharine Eilir *b* (twin) 1996), Elisabeth Ceridwen *b* 1958.

Grandsons of late Maj Edward Frederick Talbot-Ponsonby, 3rd but eldest surv son of late Charles William Talbot-Ponsonby (infra):—
Issue of late Lt-Col John Arthur Talbot-Ponsonby, *b* 1907, *d* 1969: *m* 1st, 1931 (*m diss* 1956), Frances Elizabeth, who *d* 1980, only da of late Douglas H. Fraser; 2ndly, 1957, Daphne TALBOT-PONSONBY (who *d* 1976, having *m* 2ndly, 1972, Capt Thomas Hanbury), el da of late Percival Augustus Duke, OBE, and formerly wife of Capt Jack Brittain-Jones, CBE:—
(By 1st *m*) Michael Clement (Hinton Manor, Hinton Parva, nr Swindon, Wilts), *b* 1932: *m* 1956, Judith Katharine Gibson, who *d* 1985, and has issue living, Caroline Frances, *b* 1958: *m* 1990, Patrick E. F. Pilkington, of Tullynally Castle, Castle Pollard, co Westmeath, eldest son of late Maj Nigel Pilkington, of Purley, Surrey, and has issue living, Hubert Edward *b* 1991, John Nigel *b* 1993, Patrick Cecil *b* 1994, Oliver George *b* 1997, — Charlotte Jane, *b* 1963: *m* 1992, William M. E. O'Leary, eldest son of David O'Leary, of Upper House, Knucklas, Knighton, Powys, and has issue living, Arthur *b* 1997, Lettice *b* 1994, Olive *b* 1998, — Lucy Elizabeth, *b* 1965: *m* 1999, Hervé Barois, and has issue living, Loic *b* 1994, Florence *b* 1995, — Katherine Louisa, *b* 1967. —— Peter William (Tocknells House, Painswick, Glos GL6 6TR), *b* 1938: *m* 1st, 1962 (*m diss* 1988), Sarah Vansittart, da of late Sir Eric Vansittart Bowater; 2ndly, 1988, Jane Faye, da of Jean Lancelot d'Espeissis, of Perth, W Australia, and has issue living (by 1st *m*), Nina Karen, *b* 1964: *m* 1997, Rupert Duncan Brown (*see* Falkiner, Bt), — Jessica, *b* 1965: *m* 1987, Andrew J. Saunders, of 19 Ensor Mews, SW7, — Frederica Ella, *b* 1972: *m* 1994, Hamish Erskine Allen, late Capt Devonshire and Dorset Regt, son of Maj John Allen, of Launceston, Cornwall, — (by 2nd *m*) Frederick James, *b* 1990.

Grandchildren of late Charles George Talbot-Ponsonby, 4th son of late Charles William Talbot-Ponsonby (infra):—
Issue of late Edward FitzRoy Talbot-Ponsonby, *b* 1916, *d* 1996: *m* 1st, 1938 (*m diss* 1960), Bertha Marie Louise Muriel, who *d* 1999, elder da of late Horatio Claude Barber, of Trinity Hill, Jersey; 2ndly, 1960 (*m diss* 1967), Mrs Shirley Rhona Mearns; 3rdly 1967, Anja Edith Boudewijn:—

(By 1st *m*) Nigel Edward Charles (Langrish House, Langrish, Petersfield, Hants), *b* 1946; *ed* Harrow: *m* 1977, Robina Helen, eldest da of Lt-Cmdr Henry Victor Bruce, DL, RN (ret) (*see* E Elgin, colls), and has issue living, Charles Henry FitzRoy, *b* 1981. — James Nigel Edward, *b* 1986. — Alexander John Bruce, *b* 1987. —— Suzanne Molly, *b* 1939: *m* 1957 (*m diss* 1973), Lt James Granville Lucas, RN, and has issue (*see* Lucas, Bt, colls).

Grandchildren of late Cmdr Frederick William Talbot-Ponsonby, RN, 5th son of late Charles William Talbot-Ponsonby (infra):—
    Issue of late Evelyn John Talbot-Ponsonby, *b* 1915, *d* 1997: *m* 1943, Hilary (38 Kitsbury Rd, Berkhamsted, Herts HP4 3EA), only da of Thomas Kingsley Curtis, of 82 Highgate West Hill, N6:—
Rev Preb Andrew (Llan Farm House, Clunbury, Craven Arms, Shropshire), *b* 1944; *ed* Harrow, and Leeds Univ (Dip Theol 1966); ordained priest 1970: *m* 1st, 1968, Alice Margaret, who *d* 1989, elder da of Raymond Whittier Baldwin, of Alderley Edge, Ches (*see* Barlow, Bt, *cr* 1902, colls, 1990 Edn); 2ndly, 1991, Rev Jill, da of Cecil Frank Robert Sims, of Shirley, Southampton, and has issue living (by 1st *m*), Daniel Frederick, *b* 1971; *ed* Shrewsbury, and Oriel Coll, Oxford (MA, DPhil): *m* 1999, Rachel Cairns, — Thomas Martin, *b* 1973; *ed* Shrewsbury, and Clare Coll, Camb (MA), — William Peter, *b* 1975; *ed* Shrewsbury, and Oriel Coll, Oxford (MPhys), — Henry James, *b* 1981. —— Christopher (38 Kitsbury Rd, Berkhamsted, Herts HP4 3EA), *b* 1950; *ed* Harrow. —— Simon (West Barns, Home Farm, Abbots Leigh, Bristol), *b* 1952; *ed* Harrow, and Nottingham Univ (BSc); CEng: *m* 1st, 1976 (*m diss* 1990), Hilary, da of Eric Cropper; 2ndly, 1998, Anne Christine Bruce, who *d* 1998, elder da of William Harold Wakely. —— Elizabeth Hannah, *b* 1945: *m* 1969, Dr John Michael Beck, of 4 St Mary's Av, Harrogate, and has issue living, Mark Thomas Coulton, *b* 1972, — George Samuel Curtis, *b* 1975, — Charles Edward Frank, *b* 1979, — Tess Adwoa Margaret Nora, *b* 1970, — Ruth Mary Ann, *b* 1977. —— Celia, *b* 1947: *m* 1971, David McTeer, G/Capt RAF, and has issue living, Stuart Paul, *b* 1973, — Ian James, *b* 1975, — Philip John, *b* 1977.

Granddaughter of late Charles William TALBOT-PONSONBY (who assumed by Roy Licence 1866, the additional surname of Ponsonby), el son of late Adm Sir Charles Talbot, KCB, 2nd son of late Very Rev Charles Talbot (ante):—
    Issue of late Cmdr Frederick William Talbot-Ponsonby, RN, *b* 1879, *d* 1930: *m* 1913, Hannah, who *d* 1952, da of late John Ritchie Findlay, of Aberlour, Banffshire:—
Felicity Philippa (*Lady Scott*), *b* 1918: *m* 1951, Lt-Cmdr Sir Peter Markham Scott, CH, CBE, DSC, FRS, late RNVR, who *d* 1989 (Bruce, Bt, *cr* 1804, colls), and has issue living, Richard Falcon (The Depot, Weeton Lane, Dunkeswick, Harewood, Leeds LS17 9LP), *b* 1954: *m* 1st, 1981 (*m diss* 1992), Jillian Elizabeth Gomersall; 2ndly, 1995, Jane F., only da of Noel Schofield, of Rossett Green, Harrogate, N Yorks, and has issue living (by 1st *m*), Lucy Jane Elizabeth *b* 1983, (by 2nd *m*) Christopher Robert *b* 1996, — Dafila Kathleen, *b* 1952: *m* 1980, Dr Timothy Clutton-Brock, of White Roses, Reach, Cambs, and has issue living, Peter *b* 1983, Amber *b* 1981. *Residence* – The New Grounds, Slimbridge, Gloucestershire GL2 7BS.

Grandchildren of late Maj Francis Arthur Bouverie Talbot, 2nd son of late Adm Sir Charles Talbot, KCB (ante):—
    Issue of late Vice-Adm Sir Cecil Ponsonby Talbot, KCB, KBE, DSO, *b* 1884, *d* 1970: *m* 1912, Bridget, who *d* 1960, da of late R. B. D. Bradshaw, of Fairfield, Barrow-in-Furness:—
John (Lodge House, Smeeth, Ashford, Kent TN25 6QZ), *b* 1925; *ed* Radley; Lt-Col RA (ret), formerly Defence Attaché Sofia, then Vienna: *m* 1954, Janet Wyndham, da of late Lt-Gen Sir William Wyndham Green, KBE, CB, DSO, MC, and has issue living, David John (Heatherland House, 12 The Flats, Blackwater, Camberley, Surrey), *b* 1960: *m* 1983, Margret Manson, da of late Douglas Gordon McKenzie Cameron, of Dunfermline, Fife, and has issue living, Charles Edward Cameron *b* 1987, James Alexander St John *b* 1989, Sholto Richard John *b* 1993, — Anthony Francis Wyndham (23 Wandle Rd, Wandsworth, SW17), *b* 1961: *m* 1989, Melody Jane, da of Peter Sidney Hallett, of Sydney, NSW, Australia, and has issue living, Imogen Primrose Claire *b* 1993, Samantha Jasmine *b* 1995, Bridget Eleanor Wyndham *b* 1997, — Peter Charles (85 Hewlett St, Bronte, Sydney, NSW, Australia), *b* 1964: *m* 1990, Jacqueline Margaret, da of David Parkes, of The Old Rectory, Wrington, Bristol, and has issue living, Ella Parkes *b* 1995, Mia Parkes *b* 1997. —— Barbara Bridget, *b* 1919: *m* 1940, Cdr Richard Molyneux Favell, DSC, JP, DL, RN, who *d* 1995, of Shell Cottage, Penberth, St Buryan, Cornwall (High Sheriff Cornwall 1963), and *d* 1996, leaving issue, Frances Barbara Molyneux (*Lady Banham*), *b* 1943; High Sheriff of Cornwall 2000: *m* 1965, Sir John Michael Middlecott Banham, of Penberth, St Buryan, N Penzance, Cornwall TR19 6HJ, and has issue living, Mark Richard Middlecott *b* 1968, Serena Frances Tamsin *b* 1970, Morwenna Bridget Favell *b* 1972, — Bridget Alathea, *b* 1946: *m* 1970, David Llewelyn Hugh-Jones, of The Thatched Cottage, Penberth, St Buryan, N Penzance, and has issue living, Tristan Llewelyn *b* 1973, Rupert Favell *b* 1977, Demelza Alice *b* 1971: *m* 1996, Renny Haswell Henderson, son of late W. H. Henderson, of Carmarthen, Carenza Bridie *b* 1978, — Julia Alice, *b* 1949: *m* 1976, Derek Robin Bryant, of Chynance, St Buryan, N Penzance, and has issue living, Frank Favell Ingram *b* 1981, Rebecca Sophie *b* 1978, Rachel Jessica *b* 1980.

Grandson of late Col George Reginald FitzRoy Talbot, only son of late Maj-Gen FitzRoy Somerset Talbot, only son of late Col George Talbot, 3rd son of late Very Rev Charles Talbot (ante):—
    Issue of late Col Granville FitzRoy Talbot, *b* 1908, *d* 1978: *m* 1938, Kathleen Betty (Lapworth Cottage, Elstead, Surrey), only da of Gerald Townend, of Woking:—
John FitzRoy (Daggers House, Hope, Derbyshire), *b* 1945; *ed* Uppingham, and St Thomas's Hosp, London; MB, BS, FRCS, FRC Oph, LRCP; Consultant Ophthalmic Surg and Hon Lecturer, Sheffield Med Sch: *m* 1972, Esmé, yst da of late Dr Robert de Brath Ashworth, of Holdfast Hall, Warfield, Berks (*see* B Ravensdale, colls, 1990 Edn), and has issue living, Fleur Katharine FitzRoy, *b* 1978, — Emily Sarah FitzRoy, *b* 1980, — Ann Adele FitzRoy, *b* 1987.

PREDECESSORS – **(1)** *Sir* GILBERT Talbot, Lord Chamberlain to Edward III, was summoned to Parliament of England 1331; *d* 1346; *s* by his son **(2)** RICHARD, 2nd Baron, and a Knight Banneret; was summoned to Parliament 1331-55; *d* 1356, possessed of immense estates; *s* by his son **(3)** GILBERT, 3rd Baron; summoned to Parliament 1362-86; *d* 1387; *s* by his son **(4)** RICHARD, 4th Baron; summoned to Parliament as Ricardo *Talbot de Blackmere* in his father's lifetime 1387: *m* Ankaret, da and heiress of John, 5th Baron *Strange of Blackmere*; *d* 1396; *s* by his son **(5)** GILBERT, 5th Baron; *d* 1419; *s* by his da **(6)** ANKARET; *d* unmarried 1431; *s* by her uncle **(7)** JOHN, KG, 7th Baron, who having *m* 1408, Maud (*suo jure* Baroness Furnivall), da of Thomas (Nevill) Lord Furnivall, in 1409 had been summoned to Parliament as *Johann Talbot de Furnyvall*; became Lord Justice of Ireland 1412, and was Lord-Lieut thereof 1414-21; was a celebrated warrior and gloriously sustained the cause of Henry VI throughout his French realm; his successes were, however, in 1429, checked by the Maid of Orleans at Patay, when his army was routed and himself taken prisoner; he was soon exchanged and again pursued a career of victory; *cr Earl of Shrewsbury* (peerage of England) 1442, and *Earl of Waterford* (peerage of Ireland) 1446; was Ambassador to France 1443: appointed Lieut of the Duchy of Aquitaine 1453, and on 20 July of that year was killed at the battle of Castillon; *s* by his son **(8)** JOHN, KG, KB, 2nd Earl; was Lord Chancellor of Ireland 1446, and Lord High Treasurer of England 1457; *k* at the battle of Northampton 1460, while fighting for the Red Rose; *s* by his son (9) JOHN, 3rd Earl; d 1473; s by his son (10) GEORGE, KG, 4th Earl; served with distinction at the battle of Stoke; d 1528; s by his son (11) FRANCIS, KG, PC, 5th Earl; summoned to Parliament in lifetime of his father; was one of the few public men who, having served Queen Mary, was admitted to the Privy Council of Elizabeth; d 1560; s by his son (12) GEORGE, KG, 6th Earl; had the charge of Mary, Queen of Scots, for many years, and assisted at her execution; appointed Lord High Steward of England at the arraignment of the Duke of Norfolk, and Earl Marshal after the Duke's execution; d 1590; s by his son (13) GILBERT, KG, 7th Earl; d without male issue, when the Baronies of Talbot, Furnivall, and Strange of Blackmere became abeyant between his three daughters, eventually devolving upon the last surviving Alathea, wife of Thomas, 14th Earl of Arundel; s in the earldom by his brother (14) EDWARD, 8th Earl; d 1617; s by his kinsman (15) GEORGE, 9th Earl, descendant in the 4th generation of Sir Gilbert, 3rd son of 2nd Earl; d 1630; s by his nephew (16) JOHN, 10th Earl; d 1653; s by his son (17) FRANCIS, 11th Earl; killed in a duel with George Villiers, 2nd Duke of Buckingham, 1667; s by his son (18) CHARLES, KG, 12th Earl; held some of the most important offices in the state, and was a prominent statesman *temp* William and Mary, Anne, and George I; conformed to the Protestant cause 1679; cr *Marquess of Alton* and *Duke of Shrewsbury* 1694; dsp 1717, when the marquessate and dukedom expired and the earldom reverted to his cousin (19) GILBERT, 13th Earl, son of Hon Gilbert, 2nd son of 10th Earl; was in Holy Orders of Church of Rome; d 1743; s by his nephew (20) GEORGE, 14th Earl; dsp 1787; s by his nephew (21) CHARLES, 15th Earl; dsp 1827; s by his nephew (22) JOHN, 16th Earl; d 1852; s by his cousin (23) BERTRAM ARTHUR, 17th Earl; d 1856; s by his kinsman (24) HENRY JOHN Chetwynd-Talbot (infra), CB, PC, 18th Earl; who, in 1849, had s as 3rd *Earl Talbot* and 5th *Baron Talbot* (see * infra); was an Adm and Capt of Corps of Gentlemen-at-Arms, etc; d 1868; s by his son (25) CHARLES JOHN, 19th Earl; b 1830; sat as MP for N Staffordshire 1859-65, and for Stamford 1868; was Capt of Hon Corps of Gentlemen-at-Arms 1874-7: m 1855, Anne Theresa, who d 1912, da of Com Richard Howe Cockerell, RN; d 1877; s by his son (26) CHARLES HENRY JOHN, KCVO, 20th Earl; b 1860; was Lord High Steward of Ireland: m 18 June 1882, Ellen Mary, who d 1940, da of late Charles Rowland Palmer-Morewood (B Byron), and former wife of Alfred Edward Miller Mundy, of Shipley Hall, Derby; d 1921; s by his grandson (27) JOHN GEORGE CHARLES HENRY ALTON ALEXANDER CHETWYND (son of late Charles John Alton Chetwynd, Viscount Ingestre, MVO, who d 1915), 21st Earl, b 1914; Staff-Lieut to HRH The Duke of Gloucester 1940-42; served in World War II as Capt RA in Middle East and Italy 1942-44; Pres Staffordshire Agric Soc, and Assoc of Agric: m 1st, 1936 (m diss 1963), Nadine Muriel, yr da of late Brig-Gen Cyril Randell Crofton, CB; 2ndly, 1963, Doris Aileen Mortlock, who d 1993; d 1980; s by his el son (28) CHARLES HENRY JOHN BENEDICT CROFTON CHETWYND, 22nd Earl and present peer; also Earl of Waterford, Earl Talbot, Viscount Ingestre, and Baron Talbot.

*(1) CHARLES Talbot, PC, eighth in descent from Hon Sir Gilbert Talbot, 3rd son of 2nd Earl of Shrewsbury; sat successively as MP for Tregony and Durham; was an eminent lawyer, and in 1723 attained the summit of his profession on being constituted Lord High Chancellor of England; cr *Baron Talbot*, of Hensol, co Glamorgan (peerage of Great Britain) 1723; d 1737; s by his son (2) WILLIAM, PC, 2nd Baron; was Lord Steward of the Household; cr *Earl Talbot* (peerage of Great Britain), 1761, and *Baron Dinevor*, of Dynevor, co Carmarthen (peerage of Great Britain), 1780, with remainder to his da Cecil, wife of George Rice, MP, and her issue male; d 1782, when the earldom expired, the barony of Dinevor passed to his da (ante), and the Barony of Talbot reverted to his nephew (3) JOHN CHETWYND, 3rd Baron; sat as MP for Castle Rising, cr *Viscount Ingestre* and *Earl Talbot* (peerage of Great Britain) 1784, and assumed by Roy licence the additional surname and arms of Chetwynd; d 1793; s by his son (4) CHARLES, KG, 2nd Earl; was Viceroy of Ireland, and Lord-Lieut of Staffordshire; d 1849; s by his son (5) HENRY JOHN (ante) 3rd Earl, who in 1856 s as 18th Earl of Shrewsbury.

SHUTTLEWORTH, BARON (Kay-Shuttleworth) (Baron UK 1902, Bt UK 1850)

Kind kin when known keep

CHARLES GEOFFREY NICHOLAS KAY-SHUTTLEWORTH, 5th Baron, and 6th Baronet; b 2 Aug 1948; s 1975; ed Eton; DL Lancs 1986, Lord Lieut since 1996; Dir Abbey National plc since 1996 (Dep Chm 1996-99); Memb Council of Duchy of Lancaster since 1998; FRICS: m 1975, Ann Mary, High Sheriff Lancs 1999, da of James Whatman, of Northcote Hill, Shamley Green, Surrey, and formerly wife of late Daniel Henry Barclay, and has issue.

Arms – Quarterly; 1st and 4th, argent, three shuttles sable, tipped and threaded or; 2nd and 3rd, argent, two bendlets sable between as many crescents azure, between the bendlets three ermine spots. Crests – 1st, a cubit arm in armour proper, grasping in the gauntlet a shuttle as in the arms, *Shuttleworth*; 2nd, on a crescent azure a goldfinch proper, *Kay*. Supporters – *Dexter*, a weaver habited in cap and apron proper, holding in the exterior hand a shuttle as in the arms; *sinister*, a seaman holding in his exterior hand a ship's lamp, all proper.
Residences – Leck Hall, Carnforth, Lancs LA6 2JF; 14 Sloane Av, SW3 3JE.

SONS LIVING

Hon THOMAS EDWARD, b 29 Sept 1976.
Hon David Charles, b 1978.
Hon William James, b 1979.

BROTHERS LIVING

Hon Robert James, b 1954; ed Eton; late Lieut Coldstream Guards Res: m 1995, J. Claire D., eldest da of Michael Pridham, of Pudleston, Herefords.

Hon Edward Roger Noël, *b* 1962; *ed* Eton: *m* 1996, Noemi, yr da of Delfin Cortez, of the Philippines, and has issue living, Ellen Anne, *b* 1998.

SISTER LIVING

Hon Sarah Rachel Jane, *b* 1950: *m* 1st, 1970 (*m diss* 1984), Richard Francis Foster (*see* M Ailesbury, colls, 1976 Edn), 2ndly, 1988, Peter Figgins, and has issue living (by 1st *m*), Edward William Thomas *b* 1978. — Henrietta Victoria, *b* 1973, — Georgiana Pamela, *b* 1975, — (by 2nd *m*) Tom, *b* 1990. *Residence* – 102 Kenyon St, SW6 6LB.

PREDECESSORS – **(1)** *Sir* JAMES PHILLIPS Kay-Shuttleworth, el son of late Robert Kay, of Brookshaw, Bury, Lancashire; *b* 1804; was Sec to the Committee of the Privy Council on Education 1839-49; *cr* a Baronet 1850: *m* 1842, Janet, who *d* 1872, only child and heiress of Robert Shuttleworth, of Gawthorpe Hall, whose surname he assumed by Roy licence in addition to his patronymic; *d* 1877: *s* by his el son **(2)** *Sir* UGHTRED JAMES, PC, 2nd Bt, *b* 1844; Under-Sec of State for India Feb to April 1886, Chancellor of Duchy of Lancaster April to Aug 1886, Parliamentary Sec to Admiralty 1892-5, and Lord-Lieut and Custos Rotulorum of Lancashire 1908-28; MP for Hastings (*L*) 1869-80, and for Clitheroe Div of N-E Lancashire 1885-1902; *cr Baron Shuttleworth*, of Gawthorpe, co Palatine of Lancaster (peerage of United Kingdom) 1902: *m* 1871, Blanche Marion, who *d* 1924, da of late Sir Woodbine Parish, KCH; *d* 1939; *s* by his grandson **(3)** RICHARD UGHTRED PAUL (son of late Capt Hon Lawrence Ughtred Kay-Shuttleworth, RFA (el son of 1st Baron), who was *ka* 1917), 2nd Baron, *b* 1913; Flying Officer RAF Vol Reserve, and a JP and Co Councillor for Lancashire; *ka* during Battle of Britain 1940; *s* by his brother **(4)** RONALD ORLANDO LAWRENCE, 3rd Baron, *b* (*posthumous*), 1917; Capt RA (TA); *ka* in N Africa 1942; *s* by his cousin **(5)** CHARLES UGHTRED JOHN, MC (son of late Capt Hon Edward James Kay-Shuttleworth) (2nd son of 1st Baron), who *d* (accidentally *k* during 1914-18 War) 1917, 4th Baron; *b* 1917: *m* 1947, Anne Elizabeth, who *d* 1991, da of late Col Geoffrey Francis Phillips, CBE, DSO (*see* V Ridley, colls, 1971 Edn); *d* 1975; *s* by his el son **(6)** CHARLES GEOFFREY NICHOLAS, 5th Baron and present peer.

Siddeley, family name of Baron Kenilworth.

SIDMOUTH, VISCOUNT (Addington) (Viscount UK 1805)

JOHN TONGE ANTHONY PELLEW ADDINGTON, 7th Viscount; *b* 3 Oct 1914; *s* 1976; *ed* Downside, and Brasenose Coll, Oxford; Colonial Ser E Africa 1938-54; Cttee Chm and Council Member, Nat Farmers Union 1962-69; Member Agric Research Council 1964-74; Member Central Council for Agric Co-operation 1970-73; Kt of Malta: *m* 1st, 1940, Barbara Mary Angela, who *d* 1989, el da of Bernard Rochford, OBE, of 7 Prince's Gate, SW7; 2ndly, 1993, Marie Thérèse, da of His Honour late Sir Joseph (Alfred) Sheridan, and widow of Francis Anthony Baring Pollen (*see* Pollen, Bt, colls), and has had issue.

Liberty under a pious king

Arms – Per pale ermine and ermines, a chevron charged with five lozenges counter-changed, between three fleurs-de-lis or. **Crest** – A cat-a-mountain sejant guardant proper, bezantée, the dexter forepaw resting on an escutcheon azure, charged with a mace erect, surmounted with a regal crown or, within a bordure engrailed argent. **Supporters** – Two stags, the *dexter* ermines, the *sinister* ermine, both attired and gorged with a chain, pendent therefrom a key, all or.
Residence – 12 Brock St, Bath, Avon BA1 2LW.

SONS LIVING AND DECEASED (*By 1st marriage*)

†*Hon* Christopher John, *b* 1941; *ed* Downside, and Brasenose Coll, Oxford: *m* 1963, Clio Mona, who *d* (8 April) 1986, only da of John Peristiany, of 15 Karneadou St, Athens, and *d* (2 June) 1986.

Hon JEREMY FRANCIS, *b* 29 July 1947; *ed* Ampleforth: *m* 1st, 1970, Grete, da of — Henningsen, of Randers, Denmark; 2ndly, 1986, Una, eldest da of James Coogan, of 54 Compton Bassett, Calne, Wilts, and of Mrs Susana Newman, and has issue living (by 1st wife), Steffan, *b* 1966, — Laura Grete, *b* 1975, — (by 2nd wife) John, *b* 29 Nov 1990, — Anna Frances, *b* 1988, — Olivia Barbara, *b* 1994. *Residence* – Highway Manor, nr Calne, Wilts SN11 8SR.

DAUGHTERS LIVING (By 1st marriage)

Hon Veronica Mary, *b* 1944: *m* 1st, 1982 (*m* annulled 1987), Allan Gilfillan (Sam) Mainds, eldest son of late George Mainds; 2ndly, 1989, Michael Jeremy Hodges, only son of late Capt Michael Hodges, RN; has issue living, Philippa Clare, *b* 1969. *Residences* – 54a Cornwall Gdns, SW7 4BG; 1 The Cottage, Berwick St James, Salisbury, Wilts SP3 4TN.

Hon Susan Barbara (27 Ellerby St, SW6), *b* 1945: *m* 1st, 1965 (*m diss* 1975), Count John Paul James Alessandro Camillo Manassei di Collestatte (*see* E Perth); 2ndly, 1990, as his 2nd wife, Anthony Andrew Ward Kimpton (*see* B Hazlerigg, 1990 Edn), and has issue (by 1st *m*) (*see* E Perth).

Hon Janet Teresa, *b* 1949: *m* 1972, Anthony Goodman, and has issue living, Joanna Louise, *b* 1973, — Frances Julia, *b* 1975, — Isabel Alice *b* 1979.

Hon Pauline Rosemary, *b* 1951: *m* 1973, Paul Cristopher Clare, of Glenarth, Aberarth, Aberaeron, Dyfed, and has issue living, Tomas Aeron, *b* 1980, — John Joseph, *b* 1988, — Jennifer Rose, *b* 1982.

Hon Mary Margaret (Kidge), *b* 1956: *m* 1978, James Alexander Burns, and has issue living, Julia Isabel, *b* (Feb) 1985, — Miriam Janet, *b* (Dec) 1985.

BROTHERS LIVING

Hon Hiley William Dever, *b* 1917; Lt-Cdr RN (ret); 1939-45 War: *m* 1st, 1942, Brenda Swanney, who *d* 1990, da of late Robert Charles Wallace, CMG, PhD, DSc, Principal of Queen's Univ, Kingston, Canada; 2ndly, 1993, Rita, widow of Alec T. Cousins, and has issue living (by 1st *m*), Robert Hiley, *b* 1944, — Charles Haviland, *b* 1949, — Frances Clare, *b* 1947. *Residence* – 1420 Sylvan Court, Sarnia, Ontario, Canada N7S 4A3.

Hon Raymond Thomas Casamajor, MC, *b* 1919; *ed* Downside; Major (ret) RHA, 1939-45 War in Commandos (MC): *m* 1947, Veronique, who *d* 1970, da of Emile Wirtz, of Antwerp, Belgium, and has issue living, Peter John Gerald (Highway Farm, Calne, Wilts SN11 8SR), *b* 1948: *m* 1977, Rosemary Anita, da of Richard Anthony Lamb, of Knighton Manor, Broadchalke, Wilts, and has issue living, Paul Anthony *b* 1979, Michael Peter *b* 1980, Edmund John *b* 1983, Raleigh Thomas *b* 1987, — Donald Emile (216 Varsity Estates Link, Calgary, Alberta, Canada T3B 4C9), *b* 1949; Prof: *m* 1973, Jean Margaret, da of David Alexander Baikie, and has issue living, Jack Alexander *b* 1974, Leo Nicholas *b* 1976, Oliver Thomas *b* 1979, Zoe Veronica *b* 1977, — Francis Henry, *b* 1955, — Lucy Anne (8 Radcliffe Av, NW10 5XS), *b* 1952, — Carol Jacqueline, *b* 1953, — Antonia Veronica, *b* 1956: *m* 1996, Col David J. Clements, MBE, — Edwina Gillian, *b* 1959: *m* 1983, Yukinobu Mori, of Tokyo, Japan, and Riyadh, Saudi Arabia, and has issue living, Henry Addington *b* 1984, George Addington *b* 1987, Richard Addington *b* 1990. *Residence* – Strattons, Highway, nr Calne, Wilts SN11 8SR.

Hon Gurth Louis Francis, *b* 1920; *ed* Downside, and Brasenose Coll, Oxford (MA); 1939-45 War with RAF (Air Crew): *m* 1950, Patience Gillian, da of late Col L. E. Travers, RE, and has issue living, Martin Gerald Francis (6 Palm Av, Palmerston North, NZ), *b* 1952: *m* 1978, Lynne Elizabeth Mautner, and has issue living, Benjamin Richard Francis *b* 1980, Lauren Elizabeth *b* 1982, — David Anthony Brian (32 Aitken Av, Queenscliff, Sydney, NSW 2096, Australia), *b* 1955: *m* 1979, Mary-Anne Delmont, and has issue living, Daniel Anthony Travers *b* 1985, Emma Teresa *b* 1982, — Mark Nicholas Guy, *b* 1957, — Mary Clare, *b* 1951: *m* 1975, Trevor Roberts, of 11 Edwin St, Fairlight, NSW 2094, Australia, and has issue living, Dafydd Wynn *b* 1982, Owen Wynn *b* 1986, Gareth Wynn *b* 1988, Halina Clare *b* 1980, — Catherine Dorothy, *b* 1953: *m* 1975, Richard James Lumley, of 3 Edwards Bay Rd, Mosman, Sydney, NSW 2088, Australia, and has issue living, Roger Gurth *b* 1988, Justine Molly *b* 1982, Rebecca Patience *b* 1984, Philippa Catherine *b* 1986, — Deirdre Anne, *b* (twin) 1955: *m* 1981, Derek Trow, of 7 Waterhouse St, Curtin, ACT 2605, Australia, and has issue living, Gareth Michael Addington *b* 1986, Jeremy Frederick Addington *b* 1989, Miriam Johanna Addington *b* 1987, Veronica Catherine Addington *b* 1993, — Monica Jane *b*, (twin) 1957: *m* 1983, Glenn Richard Batchelor, of Amaroo, 91 Sweeneys Lane, Eltham, Victoria 3095, Australia, and has issue living, Richard Mark *b* 1986, Kate Betty *b* 1986, Jessica Patience *b* 1988, — Barbara Mary, *b* 1961: *m* 1987, John William Waugh, of 7 Wisdom Place, Hughes, ACT 2605, Australia, and has issue living, Henry William Addington *b* 1990, Olivia Charlotte *b* 1988, Cecilia Jane *b* 1992, — Jane Margaret, *b* 1964: *m* 1984, Stephen Hall, of 19 Gladstone Rd, Northcote, Auckland, NZ, and has issue living, Edward James *b* 1989, Jonathon Gurth *b* 1991, Harriet Patience *b* 1993, Grace Elizabeth *b* 1996. *Residence* – 11 Edwin St, Fairlight, NSW 2094, Australia.

Hon Leslie Richard Bagnall, DFC; *b* 1923; *ed* Downside; Lt-Col (ret) late RA; Comdg Essex Yeo 1965-66; Malaya 1948, Korea 1951-52 (DFC): *m* 1955, Anne, el da of Capt Trevor Hume (Lacy, Bt), and has issue living, William Leslie Hume, *b* 1956: *m* 1981, Sally Jane, da of Brig D. G. Russell, of Fletching, Sussex, and has issue living, Alexander William Russell *b* 1987, Jason Robin Mark *b* 1989, — Richard Charles Raymond, *b* 1958: *m* 1989, Deryn Victoria, da of Col R. H. Johnson, of San Antonio, Texas, USA, and of Mrs Joan Pepita Nell Brown, of Bourton on the Hill, Glos, and has issue living, Raleigh Richard *b* 1996, Constance Victoria Nell *b* 1993, Honor Pepita *b* (twin) 1996, — Sarah Anne Clare, *b* 1961, — Alice Mary Cynthia, *b* 1964: *m* 1992, Julian Guy Rogers-Coltman, elder son of Lt-Cmdr Wyndham Julian Rogers-Coltman, RN, of Berryburn, Ancroft, Northumberland, and has issue living, Charles Wyndham *b* 1994, Hugh Leslie *b* 1997, Thomas Uvedale *b* 1998. *Residence* – Polebridge, Sutton Veny, Warminster, Wilts. *Club* – Army and Navy.

SISTERS LIVING

Hon Prudence Mary, *b* 1916: *m* 1939, Lieut-Com Hugo Edward Forbes Tweedie, DSC, RN, who *d* 1986, son of late Adm Sir Hugh Justin Tweedie, KCB, and has issue living, Alexander Hugh Carmichael (Harewood Cottage, Ugley Green, Bishops Stortford, Herts CM22 6HW), *b* 1942: *m* 1966, Wendy, da of Basil Henry Francis Templer, and has issue living, Michael Hugh Quarter *b* 1970, Richard *b* 1976, Lisa Ann *b* 1967: *m* 1997, Guy Franklin, Jessica Margret *b* 1968: *m* 1994, Adrian Stone (and has issue living, Oscar *b* 1998), — Dominic James Drumelzier, *b* 1945: *m* 1st, 1972, Maia Knoetzer; 2ndly, Dr Judith Atkinson; 3rdly, 19—, Shanthie Naidoo, and has issue living (by 2nd *m*), James *b* 1975, Hugh *b* 1976, — Julian Michael Forbes (Mombiti, Manston Rd, Sturminster Newton, Dorset DT10 1BQ), *b* 1947: *m* 1970, Shirley, da of late Leslie Mousley, of Machakos, Kenya, and has issue living, Nicola *b* 1976, Zoe *b* 1987, — Stephen John Oliver, *b* 1952: *m* 1987, Ruth ......, and has issue living, Owen *b* 1987, Ben *b* 1989, Martin *b* 1992, Julia *b* 1994, — Teresa Frances, *b* 1940: *m* 1964, Nicolas Alexander Victor Garratt Carp, of The Old Vicarage, Morebath, Tiverton, Devon EX16 9AL, and has issue living, Sarah Frances *b* 1965, Juliet Anne *b* 1967, Victoria Teresa *b* 1970: *m* 1995, Waleed Al-Hussaini, Lucy Beatrice *b* 1973, — Monica Mary, *b* 1954: *m* 1978, Ian Richard Newbery, of 17 Braidley Rd, Bournemouth, Dorset BH2 6JX, and has issue living, Guy Francis *b* 1983, John Forbes *b* 1985, — Prudence Margaret, *b* 1956: *m* 1992, Dr Malcolm Courts. *Residence* – 14 Fernbank, St Stephen's Rd, Bournemouth, Hants BH2 6JP.

Hon Mary Octavia, *b* 1927: *m* 1st, 1953, David Christopher Leeming; 2ndly, 1959, David Tilling Wroth, who *d* 1986; 3rdly, 1989, Maj R. William Ingall, DSO, and has issue living, (by 1st *m*) David Tobias, *b* 1955. *Residence* – Santiani, Moscari, Mallorca, Spain.

Hon Elizabeth Clare, *b* 1928. *Residence* – Coachmans Cottage, Pewsey, Wilts.

PREDECESSORS – (1) *Rt Hon* HENRY Addington; MP for Devizes 1784-1805, Speaker of the House of Commons 1789-1801, First Lord of the Treasury (Prime Minister) and Chancellor of the Exchequer 1801-4, Pres of the Council 1805-6, Lord Privy Seal 1806, Home Sec 1812-22, High Steward of Westminster and Reading, Gov of the Charterhouse, and Dep Ranger of Richmond Park, etc; *cr Viscount Sidmouth* (peerage of United Kingdom) 1805; *d* 1844; *s* by his son **(2)** WILLIAM LEONARD, 2nd Viscount; *b* 1794; was in Holy Orders: *m* 1820, Mary, who *d* 1894, el da of Rev John Young, Rector of Thorpe Malsor, co Northampton; *d* 1864; *s* by his son **(3)** WILLIAM WELLS, 3rd Viscount, *b* 1824; MP for Devizes 1863-4: *m* 1848, Georgiana Susan, who *d* 1896, da of late Very Rev Hon George Pellew, DD; *d* 1913; *s* by his el son **(4)** GERALD ANTHONY PELLEW BAGNALL, 4th Viscount, *b* 1854: *m* 1881, Ethel Mary, who *d* 1954, only da of late Capt Louis Charles Henry Tonge, RN; *d* 1915; *s* by his el son **(5)** GERALD WILLIAM, 5th Viscount, *b* 1882; Capt Devonshire Regt and Chm of Honiton Rural Dist Council; European War 1914-18 in India, Mesopotamia, Aden and Salonika: *m* 1915, Mary Murdoch, who *d* 1983, da of late Sir Donald Campbell Johnstone, formerly Ch Judge of Ch Court, Punjab; *d* 1953; *s* by his brother, **(6)** RAYMOND ANTHONY, 6th Viscount; *b* 1887: *m* 1913, Gladys Mary Dever, who *d* 1983, da of late Thomas Francis Hughes, Commr of Imperial Chinese Customs; *d* 1976; *s* by his el son **(7)** JOHN TONGE ANTHONY PELLEW, 7th Viscount and present peer.

Sidney, family name of Viscount De L'Isle.

SIEFF, BARONY OF (Sieff) (Extinct 1972)

SON LIVING OF LIFE BARON

Hon Sir Marcus Joseph, OBE, *b* 1913: *cr Baron Sieff of Brimpton*, 1979 (see that title).

WIDOW LIVING OF SON OF LIFE BARON

Elizabeth (*Baroness Haslam*), da of late William Norman Pitt, of Hampton, Middx: *m* 1st, 1975, as his 2nd wife, Hon Michael David Sieff, CBE, who *d* 1987; 2ndly, 1996, as his 2nd wife, Baron Haslam (Life Baron).

GRANDCHILDREN OF LIFE BARON

Issue of late Hon Michael David Sieff, CBE, el son of late Baron Sieff, *b* 1911, *d* 1987: *m* 1st, 1932 (*m diss* 1975), Daphne Madge Kerin, who *d* 1988 (having *m* 2ndly, 1976, Sir Michael Hadow, KCMG, who *d* 1993), da of Cyril Aaron Michael, of London; 2ndly, 1975, Elizabeth (ante) (who *m* 2ndly, 1996, as his 2nd wife, Baron Haslam), da of late William Norman Pitt, of Hampton, Middx:—
(By 1st *m*) Jonathan, *b* 1933; *ed* Marlborough: *m* 1st, 1959 (*m diss* 1966), Nicole, only da of Francis Moschietto, of 8 Avenue St Michael, Monte Carlo; 2ndly, 1966 (*m diss* 19—), Angela, da of Brig Douglas Pringle, of 14c The Precincts, Canterbury; 3rdly, 1986, Candy Seymour-Smith, and has issue living (by 1st *m*), Mark, *b* 1959, — Patrick, *b* 1963, — (by 2nd *m*) Rebecca, *b* 1967. —— (By 2nd *m*) Daniel Marcus, *b* 1977. —— Elizabeth Anne, *b* 1980.

SIEFF OF BRIMPTON, BARON (Sieff) (Life Baron 1980)

MARCUS JOSEPH SIEFF, OBE, yr son of late ISRAEL MOSES, Baron Sieff (Life Baron *cr* 1966), *b* 2 July 1913; *ed* Manchester Gram Sch, St Paul's, and Corpus Christi Coll, Camb (BA); Hon LLD St Andrews 1983, Hon Dr Babson Coll, Mass, 1984, Hon DLitt Reading 1986, D Univ Stirling 1986, Hon Dr of Laws Leicester 1988; Marks and Spencer Ltd, Vice-Chm and Assist Managing Dir 1965-67, Vice-Chm 1965, Joint Managing Dir 1967-83, Dep Chm 1971, Chm 1972-84, Pres 1984-85, since when Hon Pres; Chm First Internat Bank of Israel Trust Ltd since 1983, Non-Exec Chm *The Independent* since 1986, Non-Exec Dir Wicks plc, and Sock Shop Internat plc; a Member of BNEC 1965-71; Chm of Export Cttee for Israel 1965-68; Hon Pres of Joint Israel Appeal since 1984, Vice Pres Policy Studies Inst (formerly PEP) since 1975, Pres Anglo-Israel Chamber of Commerce 1975; a Trustee Nat Portrait Gallery 1986-92; Hon Master of the Bench Inner Temple 1987, Hon FRCS 1984; Col RA, 1939-45 War in Middle East and Italy (despatches); OBE (Mil) 1944; *cr* Knt 1971, and *Baron Sieff of Brimpton*, of Brimpton, co Berks (Life Baron) 1980: *m* 1st, 1937 (*m diss* 1947), Rosalie Fromson; 2ndly, 1951 (*m diss* 1953), Elsie Florence Gosen; 3rdly, 1956 (*m diss* 1962), Brenda Mary Beith; 4thly, 1963, Mrs Pauline Lily Moretzki, who *d* 1997, da of Friedrich Spatz, and has issue by 1st, 3rd and 4th *m*.

Arms – Sable a lion rampant argent crowned with an Eastern Crown and holding between forepaws 2 triangles interlaced and eradiated or, on a chief argent a lyre azure between 2 pairs paintbrushes in a saltire proper. **Supporters** – *Dexter*, a lion holding aloft two interlaced triangles or, depressing a cornucopia replenished proper and gorged with a plain collar sable tied about with a fishing line knotted in front and pendent there from a "Grey Wulf" trout fly proper. *Sinister*, an Owl proper gorged with a like collar tied about with a fishing line knotted in front and pendent there from a "Red Wulf" trout fly proper. **Crest** – A demi-lion as in the arm supporting a caduceus or. **Motto** – "Without knowledge there is no understanding".
Address – Michael House, Baker St, W1A 1DN.

SON LIVING (*By 1st marriage*)

Hon David Daniel, *b* 1939; *ed* Repton: *m* 1962, Jennifer, da of H. Walton, of Salford Priors, Worcs, and has issue living, Simon Marcus, *b* 1965: *m* 1995, Diana J. A., da of late John Ward, of Guildford, Surrey, — Jonathan David, *b* 1966: *m* 1995, Hayley Anne, yr da of Elliott Bernerd, of Chelsea, SW, and has issue living, Jack Elliott *b* 1996, — Jemima Jasmine, *b* 1997.

DAUGHTERS LIVING (*By 3rd marriage*)

Hon Amanda Jane, *b* 1958.

(*By 4th marriage*)

Hon Daniela Frederica, *b* 1965.

Silchester, Baron; title of Earl of Longford on Roll of HL.

SILKIN, BARONY OF (Silkin) (Baron UK 1950, disclaimed 1972)

ARTHUR SILKIN, *b* 20 Oct 1916; *s* as 2nd Baron 11 May 1972, disclaimed his peerage for life 18 May 1972; *ed* Dulwich Coll, and Peterhouse, Camb (BA honours); formerly with Civil Ser Coll (ret 1976); 1939-45 War as F/O RAF: *m* 1969, Audrey, da of late Thomas Bennett.
Residence – 33 Woodnook Rd, SW16 6TZ.

WIDOW LIVING OF SON OF FIRST BARON

Sheila Marian (*Baroness Silkin of Dulwich*) (see that title).

COLLATERAL BRANCHES LIVING

Issue of late Rt Hon Samuel Charles (*Baron Silkin of Dulwich*), QC, PC, 2nd son of 1st Baron, *b* 1918; *cr* Baron Silkin of Dulwich (Life Baron) 1985; *d* 1988: *m* 1st, 1941, Elaine Violet, who *d* 1984, da of late Arthur Stamp, of London; 2ndly, 1985, Sheila Marian (ante), da of A. E. Jeal, and widow of Walter Swanston:—
(By 1st *m*) (*see* By Silkin of Dulwich).

Issue of late Rt Hon John Ernest Silkin, MP, yst son of 1st Baron, *b* 1923, *d* 1987: *m* 1950, Rosamund John, actress, who *d* 1998, formerly wife of Lt-Cdr Russell Lloyd, RNVR, and da of Frederick Jones:—
Rory Lewis, *b* 1954.

PREDECESSOR – **(1)** *Rt Hon* LEWIS Silkin, CH; *b* 1889: Min of Town and Country Planning 1945-50, Dep Leader of Labour Party, House of Lords 1955, and MP for Peckham Div of Camberwell (*Lab*) 1946-50; *cr Baron Silkin*, of Dulwich, co London (peerage of UK) 1950: *m* 1st, 1915, Rosa Neft, who *d* 1947; 2ndly, 1948, Frieda M., who *d* 1963, da of late Rev Canon Pilling, of Norwich, and widow of J. F. F. Johnson; 3rdly, 1964, Marguerite Schlageter, who *d* 1975; *d* 1972; *s* by his el son **(2)** ARTHUR, 2nd Baron, until he disclaimed his peerage 1972.

SILKIN OF DULWICH, BARONY OF (Silkin) (Extinct 1988)

SONS LIVING OF LIFE BARON

Hon CHRISTOPHER LEWIS, *b* 12 Sept 1947; *hp* to his uncle Baron Silkin (disclaimed 1972); *ed* Dulwich, and Middlesex Tech Coll (LLB); admitted a solicitor 1977.
Hon Peter David Arthur, *b* 1952; *ed* Dulwich, and Sussex Univ (MA); Member of Inst of Public Finance and Accountancy 1985: *m* 1974 (div 1982), Frances, da of Dr Patrick Kemp, of Woking. *Residence* – 28 Phoebeth Rd, SE4 1JP.

DAUGHTERS LIVING OF LIFE BARON

Hon Charlotte Ann, *b* 1944; *ed* James Allen's Girls Sch, and Lady Spencer Churchill Coll, Oxford (BEd): *m* 1965, Francis Josephs, MA, and has issue living, Thomas Daniel, *b* 1972, — Anna Frances, *b* 1975.
Hon Patricia Jane SILKIN, *b* (twin) 1947; *ed* James Allen's Girls Sch, and Sussex Univ (BA); has reverted to her maiden name: *m* 1970, Michael Johnson, BA, PhD.

WIDOW LIVING OF LIFE BARON

SHEILA MARIAN (*Baroness Silkin of Dulwich*), da of A. E. Jeal, and widow of Walter Swanston: *m* 1985, as his 2nd wife, Baron Silkin of Dulwich, QC, PC, who *d* 1988.

SILSOE, BARON (Eve) (Baron UK 1963, Bt UK 1943)

DAVID MALCOLM TRUSTRAM EVE, QC, 2nd Baron, and 2nd Baronet, *b* 2 May 1930; *s* 1976; *ed* Winchester, Ch Ch, Oxford (MA), and Columbia Univ, New York; Bar Inner Temple 1955; Bar Auditor Inner Temple 1965-70; Bencher 1970; QC 1972; late 2nd Lt RWF, and Lt, Queen Victoria's Rifles (TA): *m* 1963, Bridget Min, da of Sir Rupert Charles Hart-Davis, of The Old Rectory, Marske-in-Swaledale, Richmond, N Yorks, and has issue.

Arms – Sable, two swords, points upwards, in saltire argent pommels and hilts or, on a chief of the second a closed book gules, garnished of the third, between two torteaux. Crest – Issuant from a mural crown or, an apple tree fructed, the trunk entwined by a serpent proper. Supporters – On either side a Kashmir goat argent, horned winged and gorged with a mural crown or.
Residence – Neals Farm, Wyfold, Reading, Berks, RG4 9JB.

SON LIVING

Hon SIMON RUPERT TRUSTRAM, *b* 17 April 1966.

DAUGHTER LIVING

Hon Amy Comfort Trustram, *b* 1964.

BROTHER LIVING

Hon Peter Nanton Trustram, OBE, (twin) (Barton End Hall, nr Nailsworth, Glos GL6 0QQ; Flat D, 163 Pavilion Rd, SW1; Ski Club of Great Britain and Royal Anglo-Belgian), *b* 1930; *ed* Winchester, and Ch Ch, Oxford (MA; Col R Green Jackets (ret); late 2nd Lt RWF, and Lt Queen Victoria's Rifles (TA); US Armed Forces Staff Coll 1972, British Army Staff, Washington 1972-73, Cmdg Officer Oxford Univ Officers Training Corps 1973-75; Defence and Mil Attaché, Brussels 1980-83; Gen Man Churchill Hosp 1985-88; OBE (Mil) 1978: *m* 1961, Petronilla Letiere Sheldon, da of late Jannion Steele Elliott, of Dowles Manor, Bewdley, Worcs, and has issue living, Richard Malcolm Jannion Trustram, *b* 1963: *m* 1988, Albinia Julia, elder da of late Maj Christopher Wyndham Diggle (*see* Thompson, Bt, colls, *cr* 1890), and has issue living, Alexander Christopher Peter Trustram *b* 1993, James Arthur Richard Trustram *b* 1996, — Nicholas Dominic Peter Trustram, *b* 1965.

PREDECESSORS – (1) *Sir* (ARTHUR) MALCOLM TRUSTRAM Eve, GBE, MC, TD, QC, son of late Sir Herbert Trustram Eve, KBE; *b* 1894; Chm of War Damage Commn 1941-49, of War Works Commn 1945-49, and of Burnham Cttees on Teachers' Salaries 1950-53; First Crown Estate Commr 1954-62, and First Church Estates Commr 1954-69; *cr a Baronet* 1943, and *Baron Silsoe*, of Silsoe, co Bedford (peerage of UK) 1963: *m* 1st, 1927, Marguerite, who *d* 1945, da of late Sir Augustus Meredith Nanton; 2ndly, 1946, Margaret Elizabeth, who *d* 1993, da of late Henry Wallace Robertson, of Ayton, Berwicks; *d* 1976; *s* by his el son (2) DAVID MALCOLM TRUSTRAM, 2nd Baron, and present peer.

SIMEY, BARONY OF (Simey) (Extinct 1969)

SON LIVING OF LIFE BARON

Hon Thomas Iliff (Coed Nant Gain, Cilcain Rd, Pontnewydd, Mold, Clwyd CH7 5NJ), *b* 1938; *ed* St Christopher's Sch, Letchworth; Chartered Architect 1965; Consultant in Community Building Initiatives, Lesotho, 1977-86: *m* 1963, Fiona, da of A. G. Porteous, of Menstrie, Clackmannanshire, and has issue.

WIDOW LIVING OF LIFE BARON

MARGARET BAYNE (*Baroness Simey*), (3 Blackburne Terr, Blackburne Pl, Liverpool L8 7PJ), da of John Aiton Todd: *m* 1935, Baron Simey (Life Baron), who *d* 1969.

SIMON, VISCOUNT (Simon) (Viscount UK 1940)

Jan David Simon, 3rd Viscount, *b* 20 July 1940; *s* 1993; *ed* Westminster, Dept of Navigation, Southampton Univ, and Sydney Technical Coll; Dep Chm of Cttees, House of Lords, since 1998; Dep Speaker House of Lords since 1999: *m* 1969, Mary Elizabeth, da of John Joseph Burns, of Sydney, NSW, Australia, and has issue.

Arms – Gules three lotus flowers in pale proper between two flaunches or each charged with a lion rampant of the field. Crest – Upon a well proper an eagle rising or. Supporters – *Dexter*, a guillemot; *sinister*, a monal proper.

DAUGHTER LIVING

Hon Fiona Elizabeth Christie, *b* 1971.

SISTER DECEASED

Hon Gemma Louise, *b* 1934: *m* 1956, Brian Hunter, and *d* 1994, leaving issue, Ian *b* 1957, — Alan, *b* 1958.

WIDOW LIVING OF SECOND VISCOUNT

Such is my name

(James) Christie (*Dowager Viscountess Simon*), da of William Stanley Hunt: *m* 1930, 2nd Viscount Simon, CMG, who *d* 1993. *Residence* – 2 Church Cottages, Abbotskerwell, Newton Abbot, Devon TQ12 5NY.

PREDECESSORS – (1) *Rt Hon Sir* John Allsebrook Simon, GCSI, GCVO, OBE, PC, QC, only son of late Rev Edwin Simon, a Congregational Min; *b* 1873; was Solicitor-Gen 1910-13, Attorney-Gen (with a seat in the Cabinet) 1913-15, Sec of State for Home Depart 1915-16, Sessional Chm and Dep Leader of Ind Liberal Party in House of Commons 1922-4, and Chm of Indian Statutory Commn 1927-30, R101 Airship Inquiry 1930, and Roy Commn on Population 1943-6; appointed Sec of State for Foreign Affairs (in National Govt) 1931, Sec of State for Home Affairs and Dep Leader of House of Commons 1935, and Chancellor of the Exchequer 1937 (also Member of War Cabinet 1939); Lord High Chancellor 1940-45; sometime Leader of Liberal National Party; High Steward of Oxford Univ; European War 1917-18 as Maj RAF (despatches); sat as MP for SW or Walthamstow, Div of Essex (*L*) 1906-18; and for Yorkshire W Riding, Spen Valley Div 1922-40; *cr Viscount Simon*, of Stackpole Elidor, co Pembroke (peerage of United Kingdom) 1940: *m* 1st, 1899, Ethel Mary, who *d* 1902, da of Gilbert Venables; 2ndly, 1917, Kathleen, DBE, who *d* 1955, da of Francis Eugene Harvey, of Wexford, and widow of T. Manning, MD; *d* 1954; *s* by his only son (2) John Gilbert, CMG, 2nd Viscount, *b* 1902; Manager P & O London 1936-40, with Min of War Transport 1940-46, Man Dir (later Joint Dep Chm) P & O 1947-58, Chm Port of London Authority 1958-71, sometime Pres Chamber of Shipping, Royal Inst of Naval Architects, Inst of Naval Engrs, Internat Assocn of Ports and Harbours, and Royal National Inst for the Deaf, etc; Memb N Atlantic Assembly, Dep Speaker House of Lords: *m* 1930, (James) Christie, da of William Stanley Hunt; *d* 1993; *s* by his only son (3) Jan David, 3rd Viscount and present peer.

SIMON OF GLAISDALE, BARON (Simon) (Life Baron 1971)

Jocelyn Edward Salis Simon, PC, son of late Frank Cecil Simon, of 51 Belsize Park, NW3; *b* 15 Jan 1911; *ed* Gresham's Sch, Holt, and Trin Hall, Camb; Bar Middle Temple 1934, KC 1951, and Bencher 1958; Joint Parl Under-Sec of State, Home Office 1957-58, Financial Sec to the Treasury 1958-59, Solicitor-Gen 1959-62, Pres of Probate, Divorce and Admiralty Div of High Court 1962-71, and a Lord of Appeal in Ordinary 1971-77; 1939-45 War as Maj RTR, and Lt-Col Staff; MP for W Middlesbrough (*C*) 1951-62; *cr* Knt 1959, PC 1961, and *Baron Simon of Glaisdale*, of Glaisdale, in N Riding, co York (Life Baron) 1971: *m* 1st, 1934, Gwendolen Helen, who *d* 1937, da of E. J. Evans; 2ndly, 1948, Fay Elizabeth Leicester, JP, da of Brig H. Guy A. Pearson, of Jersey, and has issue by 2nd *m*.

Arms – Per saltire sable and ermine, a pair of scales or between in fess two roses argent barbed and seeded proper, and in pale two crescents ermine. Crest – A cock's head erased azure combed and wattled gules between two palm branches vert, holding in the beak two roses argent clipped leaved barbed and seeded proper. Supporters – *Dexter*, a man habited in the robes of a Doctor of Civil Law in the University of Cambridge proper, and holding in his dexter hand a book or; *sinister*, a man habited in the robes of the President of the Probate Divorce and Admiralty Division of the High Court proper. *Address* – c/o House of Lords, SW1.

SONS LIVING (By 2nd marriage)

Hon Peregrine Charles Hugo, *b* 1950; *ed* Westminster, and Trin Hall, Camb (MA); Bar Middle Temple 1973, QC 1991, Bencher 1999; Recorder of the Crown Court: *m* 1980, Francesca, da of Maj T. W. E. Fortescue Hitchins, of Border Lodge, Brewham, Som, and has issue, Alexander Edward Orlando, *b* 1986, — Ferdinand William Hugo, *b* 1989, — Polly Harriet Artemis, *b* 1982, — Lucy Persephone Frances, *b* 1984. *Residence* – Midge Hall, Glaisdale, Whitby, N Yorks.

Hon (Benedict) Mark Leicester, *b* 1953; *ed* Marlborough, Trin Hall, Camb (MA), and Wolfson Coll, Oxford (BLitt): *m* 1980, Patricia, da of Ricardo Hernandez Amozurrutia, of Mexico City, and has issue, Isaak David, *b* 1989, — Jael Daniela, *b* 1984. *Residence* – 33 South Parade, Oxford.

Hon (Dominic) Crispin Adam, *b* 1958; *ed* Westminster, and Lincoln Coll, Oxford (MA): *m* 1983, Georgina Frances, da of R. G. Brown, of Chestnut House, Albrighton, Shropshire, and has issue, Freddie, *b* 1991, — Clementine, *b* 1993. *Residence* – Cotte Farm, Combe Hay, Bath, Avon.

SIMON OF HIGHBURY, BARON (Simon) (Life Baron 1997)

DAVID ALEC GWYN SIMON, CBE, son of late Roger Albert Damas Jules Simon, of Shoreham, Sussex; *b* 24 July 1939; *ed* Christ's Hosp, Gonville and Caius Coll, Camb (MA 1961), and INSEAD (MBA 1966); Hon DSc (Econ) Hull 1990, Univ of North London 1995, Hon LLD Bath 1998; Marketing Dir, British Petroleum Oil UK 1980-82, Man Dir BP Oil UK 1980-82, Man Dir BP Oil International 1982-85, a Group Man Dir 1986-95, Chief Operating Offr 1990-92, Group Dep Chm 1990-95, Group Chief Exec 1992 95, since when Chm; Memb Court of Bank of England 1995-97; Non-exec Dir Grand Metropolitan plc 1989-96, and The RTZ Corporation plc 1995-97; Memb Supervisory Board Allianz AG 1996-97, International Council and UK Advisory Board INSEAD 1985-97, and Advisory Council Deutsche Banl 1991-97; Minister for Trade and Competitiveness in Europe, Department of Trade and Industry and HM Treasury since 1997; Liveryman of Worshipful Co of Tallow Chandlers and Worshipful Co of Carmen; *cr* CBE 1991, Kt 1995, and *Baron Simon of Highbury*, of Canonbury in the London Borough of Islington (Life Baron) 1997: *m* 1st, 1964 (*m diss* 1987), Hanne, da of Ehrling Mohn, of Oslo, Norway; 2ndly, 1992, Sarah, da of Frederick Roderick Smith, of Much Wenlock, Shropshire, and has issue by 1st *m*.

Address – Department of Trade and Industry, Room 8.E.10, 1 Victoria St, SW1H 0ET. *Clubs* – Brooks's, Groucho.

SON LIVING (By 1st marriage)

Hon Nicholas, *b* 1964; *ed* Highgate.
Hon Alexander, *b* 1967; *ed* Highgate.

SIMON OF WYTHENSHAWE, BARON (Simon) (Baron UK 1947)

ROGER SIMON, 2nd Baron, *b* 16 Oct 1913; *s* 1960 (but does not use the title); *ed* Gresham's Sch, Holt, and at Gonville and Caius Coll, Camb; European War 1940-45: *m* 1951 (Anthea) Daphne, da of Sidney George William May, and has issue.
Residence – Oakhill, Chester Avenue, Richmond, Surrey.

SON LIVING

(*Hon*) MATTHEW (does not use courtesy title), *b* 10 April 1955; *ed* St Paul's Sch, and Balliol Coll, Oxford (BA, PhD); Lecturer; CEng, MIMechE

DAUGHTER LIVING

Hon Margaret, *b* 1953.

BROTHER LIVING

Hon Brian, *b* 1915; *ed* Gresham's Sch, Holt, and Trin Coll, Camb; European War 1940-45: *m* 1941, Joan Home, da of late Capt Home Peel, DSO, MC (By Emmott), and has had issue, †Alan, *b* 1943; *d* 1991, — Martin, *b* 1944. *Residence* – 11 Pendene Rd, Leicester.

PREDECESSOR – (1) ERNEST DARWIN Simon, son of late Henry Simon, of Lawnhurst, Didsbury; *b* 1879; an Engineer and Contractor, and Pres of Simon Carves Ltd, and of Henry Simon Ltd; Lord Mayor of Manchester 1921-2; Parliamentary Sec to Min of Health (in National Govt) Sept to Oct 1931; was Chm of British Broadcasting Corporation 1947-52; sat as MP for Withington Div of Manchester (*L*) 1923-4 and 1929-31; *cr Baron Simon of Wythenshawe*, of Didsbury, City of Manchester (peerage of United Kingdom) 1947: *m* 1912, Shena Dorothy, who *d* 1972, da of John Wilson Potter, of Westminster, SW1; *d* 1960; *s* by his el son (2) ROGER, 2nd Baron and present peer.

SIMPSON OF DUNKELD, BARON (Simpson) (Life Baron 1997)

GEORGE SIMPSON, son of late William Simpson, of Dundee; *b* 2 July 1942; *ed* Morgan Acad, Dundee, and Dundee Inst of Technology (Dip in Business Admin 19—); Snr Accountant, Scottish Gas 1964-68; Snr Financial Position, Brit Leyland 1969-77; Fin Dir Leyland Truck & Bus Ltd 1978-79; Man Dir Coventry Climax 1980-82, Freight Rover 1983-85, and Rover Group Commercial Vehicles 1986-87; Chief Exec Leyland DAF 1987-88; Chm and Chief Exec Rover Group plc 1989-92; Memb Supervisory Board, DAF NV 1989-94; Chm Rover Group and Dep Chief Exec British Aerospace plc (Parent co) 1992-94; Chief Exec Lucas Industries plc 1994-96; Man Dir GEC plc since 1996; Non-Exec Dir ICI plc since 1995, Pilkington plc since 1992, and NW Venture Capital Fund Ltd; Pres SMMT since 1995 (formerly Vice Pres); Vice-Pres Inst of the Motor Industry; Industrial Prof, Univ of Warwick since 1991; Memb Govt Advisory Cttee on Business and Environment 1991-93; Memb Senate, Engineering Council; FCCA, ACIS, FIMI, FCIT, FRSA; *cr Baron Simpson of Dunkeld*, of Dunkeld in Perth and Kinross (Life Baron) 1997: *m* 1963, Eva, da of William Chalmers, of Dundee, and has issue.

Address – c/o General Electric Co plc, 1 Bruton St, W1 8AQ. *Clubs* – Royal Birkdale Golf, New Zealand Golf, Pine Valley Golf, Gleneagles Golf.

SON LIVING

Hon George Anthony, *b* 1965; *ed* Ulster Univ (BSc), and Queen's Coll, Oxford (MBA).

DAUGHTER LIVING

Hon Gillian, *b* 1966; *ed* Oxford Polytechnic (BEd).

SINCLAIR, LORD (St Clair) (Lord S about 1449, confirmed 1488-9)

(Title pronounced "Sinclair" and name pronounced "St Clair")

CHARLES MURRAY KENNEDY ST CLAIR, CVO, 17th Lord; *b* 21 June 1914; *s* 1957; *ed* Eton, and Magdalene Coll, Camb; a Representative Peer for Scotland 1959-63; Major late Coldstream Guards; is a Member of Queen's Body Guard for Scotland (Roy Co of Archers); HM's Lord Lieut for Dumfries and Galloway (District of Stewartry) 1982-89; Portcullis Pursuivant of Arms 1949-57, and York Herald 1957-68; Hon Genealogist to Roy Victorian Order 1960-68; an Extra Equerry to HM Queen Elizabeth the Queen Mother since 1953; Palestine 1939 (despatches), 1939-45 War (wounded); LVO 1953, CVO 1990: *m* 1968, Anne Lettice, yr da of Sir Richard Charles Geers Cotterell 5th Bt, CBE, TD, and has issue.

𝕬rms – Argent, a cross engrailed azure. 𝕮rest – A swan, wings expanded and elevated proper gorged with a ducal coronet and chained or. 𝕾upporters – Two gryphons sable, armed and beaked and winged or, beaked and membered or.
Residence – Knocknalling, St John's Town of Dalry, Castle Douglas DG7 3ST.

SON LIVING

Hon MATTHEW MURRAY KENNEDY (*Master of Sinclair*), *b* 9 Dec 1968; *ed* Glenalmond, and RAC Cirencester; ARICS. *Residence* – Knocknalling, St John's Town Dalry, Castle Douglas DG7 3ST. *Club* – New (Edinburgh).

DAUGHTERS LIVING

Hon Laura Anne, *b* 1972.
Hon Annabel Lettice, *b* 1973.

COLLATERAL BRANCHES LIVING

Grandchildren of late Hon Lockhart Matthew St Clair, CIE, CBE, 4th son of 14th Lord:—
Issue of late Maj-Gen George James Paul St Clair, CB, CBE, DSO, *b* 1885, *d* 1955: *m* 1911, Charlotte Theresa Orme, who *d* 1961, da of late Major Archibald Cosmo Little (E Shrewsbury):—
Malcolm Archibald James, TD, *b* 1927; *ed* Eton; is a Farmer; MP for S-E Div of Bristol (C) 1961-63; Lt-Col Comdg R Glos Hussars (TA) 1967-69: *m* 1955, Mary-Jean, only da of Wing-Cdr Caryl Liddell Hargreaves, of Broadwood House, Sunningdale, Berks (B Ravensworth, colls), and has issue living, Hugh Alan Charles (The Priory, Long Newnton, Tetbury, Glos), *b* 1957; *ed* Eton, and USA; writer: *m* 1988, Raffaella F., elder da of late George Barker, of Bintry House, Itteringham, Norfolk, and has issue living, Roman George *b* 1988, Lorne Patrick *b* 1991, — Andrew David Paul, *b* 1960; *ed* Eton, and Guildhall Sch of Music and Drama, — Vanessa Alice Rosabelle, *b* 1971; *ed* St Mary's Calne, and Manchester Univ (BA). *Residence* – The Priory, Long Newnton, Tetbury, Glos. *Club* – White's. —— Rosabelle Evelyn Teresa, *b* 1919. —— Guendolen Helen Charlotte (Berkley House, The Chipping, Tetbury, Glos), *b* 1920: *m* 1966, Maurice Owen Griffith Cleaver, who *d* 1975.

Grandson of late Adm William Home Chisholme St Clair, el son of late Com Hon Charles St Clair (infra):—
Issue of late Capt Frederic Cathcart Guy St Clair, RN, *b* 1878, *d* 1931: *m* 1913, Maude Sophie Childers, who *d* 1962, yr da of Capt S. H. Childers Thompson, RN (ret), formerly of Taplow, Bucks:—
Derek Charles ST CLAIR-STANNARD, MBE, *b* 1919; formerly in HM Foreign Ser; Public Relations Officer to Roy Agricultural Soc of England 1960-70; 1939-45 War as Lt RNVR (MBE); assumed by deed poll 1939, the additional surname of Stannard; MBE (Mil) 1945: *m* 1953, Elizabeth Ann, da of Douglas Charles Baskett, and has issue living, Matthew Peter, *b* 1954: *m* 1981, Sally Elizabeth, eldest da of Capt R. Heptinstall, RN, and has issue living, Guy Roger *b* 1982, Oliver Simon Charles *b* 1984, Chloe Elizabeth *b* 1989, — Lucie, *b* 1955: *m* 1981, Richard John Shelbourne, yr son of G. R. Shelbourne, of Langore, Cornwall, and has issue living Frederick John Philip *b* 1988, India Lucie *b* 1982, Arabella Frances *b* 1984, Tatiana Francesca Sophia *b* 1993, — Sophie Alexandra, *b* 1958: *m* 1985, Richard Sean de Courcy O'Grady, eldest son of late Patrick de Courcy O'Grady, and has issue living, Ludovic Patrick *b* 1989, Harriet Rose *b* 1987, — Josephine Camilla, *b* 1965: *m* 1996, John Maurice Owen only son of David Owen, of Milnrow, Greater Manchester. *Residence* – The Priory, 33 Church St, Godalming, Surrey GU7 1EL.

Grandchildren of late Percival James St Clair, el son of James Andrew St Clair (infra):—
Issue of late Rodney Samuel St Clair, *b* 1919, *d* 1964: *m* 1942, Beatrice Wyatt Walker (Trefusis, Boomi, NS Wales 2405):—
Malcolm Clive, *b* 1943: *m* 1971, Julie Murphy, and has issue living, Rodney James, *b* 1973, — Timothy, *b* 1975. —— Rosslyn Violet, *b* 1947: *m* 1971, Iain Couper, and has issue living, Samuel Boyd, *b* 1971, — Rachel Kate, *b* 1974. —— Linda Helen, *b* 1953: *m* 1974, Ronald Coulton, and has issue living, Christopher Ronald, *b* 1980, — Sarah Jane, *b* 1977.

Granddaughters of late James Andrew St Clair, 5th son of Hon Charles St Clair, 3rd son of 13th Lord:—
Issue of late Charles Archibald St Clair, *b* 1878, *d* 1917: *m* 1913, Madeline Smith:—
Joan Madeline, *b* 1914.

Issue of late Christopher Fenwick St Clair, *b* 1882, *ka* 1918: *m* 1914, Ethel Maud Cheesbrough:— Erica Webster, *b* 1916: *m* 1940, Duncan Cannon McConnel, and has issue living, Christopher David, *b* 1951: *m* 1984, Susan Jane Underdown, and has issue living, Caitlin Jane St Clair *b* 1990, — Rosemary Robina St Clair, *b* 1941: *m* 1987, Graham Kensley Neumann, — Diana Rose, *b* 1946: *m* 1968, Arthur Edmund de Norbury Rogers, and has issue living, Andrew de Norbury *b* 1970, Scott McConnel *b* 1972, James McConnel *b* 1974. *Residence* – Cressbrook, Toogoolawah, Queensland 4313, Australia.

PREDECESSORS – **(1)** WILLIAM Sinclair, 3rd Earl of Orkney (*cr* 1379); a Lord of Parliament as *Lord Sinclair* about 1449; *cr Earl of Caithness* 1455; resigned the Earldom of Orkney to the Crown 1470 and the Earldom of Caithness later; *s* by his son **(2)** WILLIAM; *s* by his son **(3)** HENRY, who in 1488 was confirmed as a Peer of Parliament as *Lord Sinclair* (peerage of Scotland); *k* at Flodden Field 1513; *s* by his son **(4)** WILLIAM, 4th Lord; *d* 1570; *s* by his son **(5)** HENRY, 5th Lord; *d* 1601; *s* by his grandson **(6)** HENRY, 6th Lord; *d* 1602; *s* by his brother **(7)** JAMES, 7th Lord; *d* 1607; *s* by his brother **(8)** PATRICK, 8th Lord; *d* 1617; *s* by his son **(9)** JOHN, 9th Lord; *d* 1676; *s* by his grandson **(10)** HENRY (son of John St Clair by Catherine, Mistress of Sinclair, da of 9th Lord Sinclair), 10th Lord; obtained a charter under the Great Seal 1677 confirming all the honours, precedence, and dignities, etc, enjoyed by his predecessors, with remainders respectively to his brother Henry and his father's brothers Robert, George, and Matthew, and failing them to his own heirs male whatsoever; *d* 1723, his el son **(11)** JOHN, having been engaged in the Rebellion of 1715 was attainted, and never assumed the title; *dsp* 1750; his brother **(12)** JAMES also did not assume the title; a Gen in the Army and a distinguished diplomatist; *d* 1762, when the Lordship became dormant and remained so until 1782, when through **(13)** CHARLES (son of Matthew (ante)), *de jure* 11th Lord; *s* by his son **(14)** ANDREW, *de jure* 12th Lord, the House of Lords confirmed the claim of his son **(15)** CHARLES, who thus became 13th Lord, and the first of his line who held the title without descent from the original Lords; was a Representative Peer, *d* 1863; *s* by his son **(16)** JAMES, 14th Lord; *b* 1803; a Representative Peer: *m* 1830, Jane, da of Archibald Little, Esq, of Shabden Park, Surrey, *d* 1880; *s* by his son **(17)** CHARLES WILLIAM, 15th Lord, *b* 1831; a Representative Peer; Col in Army; Crimean Campaign 1854-55: *m* 1870, Margaret Jane, who *d* 1935, da of James Murray, of 16 Bryanston Square, W; *d* 1922; *s* by his son **(18)** ARCHIBALD JAMES MURRAY, MVO, 16th Lord; *b* 1875; Extra Equerry to HRH Prince Arthur of Connaught 1914-38; a Representative Peer for Scotland: *m* 1906, Violet Frances, who *d* 1953, da of late Col John Murray Kennedy, MVO, of Knocknalling, Dalry, Galloway; *d* 1957; *s* by his only son **(19)** CHARLES MURRAY KENNEDY, 17th Lord and present peer.

Sinclair, family name of Earl of Caithness.

Sinclair, family name of Baron Pentland.

Sinclair, family name of Viscount Thurso.

SINCLAIR OF CLEEVE, BARON (Sinclair) (Baron UK 1957)

JOHN LAWRENCE ROBERT SINCLAIR, 3rd Baron; *b* 6 Jan 1953; *s* 1985; *ed* Winchester, Bath Univ and Manchester Univ; teacher.

Arms – Or a cross engrailed sable in the first quarter a sword erect proper on a chief also sable three martlets gold. **Crest** – In front of a saltire argent a dove proper beaked and legged gules in the beak an olive branch also proper. **Supporters** – *Dexter*, a griffin sable; *sinister*, a unicorn argent. Each gorged with a chaplet or white may leaved and flowered proper.

SISTERS LIVING

Hon Juliet, *b* 1951: *m* 1983, A. Philip Wallis, only son of A. P. Wallis, of Beaumont, Essex.
Hon Jane, *b* 1955: *m* 1982, Robert Anthony John Holliday, son of R. F. Holliday, of Ashwellthorpe, Norfolk, and has issue living, James Robert Sinclair, *b* 1984, — Fiona Jane, *b* 1987. *Residence* – Larkfield, Hawstead, Bury St Edmunds, Suffolk.

WIDOW LIVING OF SECOND BARON

PATRICIA (*Baroness Sinclair of Cleeve*), da of Lawrence Hellyer, of The Hawke, Lockerbie, Dumfriesshire: *m* 1950, Lt-Col, the 2nd Baron Sinclair of Cleeve, OBE, who *d* 1985.

PREDECESSORS – (1) ROBERT JOHN SINCLAIR, KCB, KBE, son of Robert Henry Sinclair, *b* 1893, Pres of Imperial Tobacco Co Ltd; Chm Finance Corp for Industry and of Bristol Waterworks Co; Dir-Gen of Army Requirements, War Office 1939-42; Ch Executive, Min of Production 1943-45; Pres of Fedn of British Industries 1949-51; a Member of Security Commn 1966-77; Pro-Chancellor of Bristol Univ 1946-70, and High Sheriff Som; *cr Baron Sinclair of Cleeve*, of Cleeve, co Somerset (peerage of UK) 1957: *m* 1917, Mary Shearer, who *d* 1984, da of late Robert Shearer Barclay; *d* 1979; *s* by his son (2) JOHN ROBERT KILGOUR, OBE, 2nd Baron, *b* 1919; Lt-Col Queen's Own Highlanders, Mil Attaché, Leopoldville 1960-63, with SHAPE 1964-66, and Min of Defence 1967-69; served 1939-45 War (despatches): *m* 1950, Patricia, da of Lawrence Hellyer, of The Hewke, Lockerbie, Dumfriesshire; *d* 1985; *s* by his only son (3) JOHN LAWRENCE ROBERT, 3rd Baron and present peer.

SINHA, BARON (Sinha) (Baron UK 1919)

ARUP KUMAR SINHA, 6th Baron; *b* 23 April 1966; *s* 1999: *m* 1993 (*m diss* 1995), Deborah Jane, da of Tony Tidswell.

Arms – Argent, on a chevron ermine between in chief two lotus flowers and in base an Adjutant bird, three fountains all proper. **Crest** – A demi-tiger supporting a fasces erect proper. **Supporters** – On either side an Adjutant bird proper, collared or.
Address – c/o House of Lords, SW1.

BROTHER LIVING

Hon DILIP KUMAR, *b* 28 May 1967.

SISTERS LIVING

Hon Sheila Joelle, *b* 1978.
Hon Leila, *b* 1983.

AUNT LIVING (*Daughter of 2nd Baron by 2nd marriage*)

Hon Sheila, *b* 1923: *m* 1st, 1944, Dev Kumar Das, who *d* 1951; 2ndly, 1964, Prof C. L. Mukherjee, who *d* 1972; 3rdly, 1989, Sanat Lahiri, who *d* 1996, and has issue living (by 1st *m*), Deep (Sydney, NSW, Australia), *b* 1947: *m* 19—, Svetlana Malinovsky, and has issue living, Shanti *b* 1983, Sona *b* 19—, Krystal *b* 19—, — Lolita (*Baroness Sinha*), *b* 1944: *m* 1965 (New Delhi, India), 5th Baron Sinha, who *d* 1999, — (by 2nd *m*), Dev Kumar, *b* 1964: *m* 1986, Hena Verma, and has issue living, Rahoul (a son) *b* 1993, Devika *b* 1987. *Residence* – Flat A1, 67B Ballygunge Circular Rd, Calcutta 7, 00019 India.

HALF-AUNT LIVING (*Daughter of 2nd Baron by 1st marriage*)

Hon Bina, *b* 1917: *m* 19—, Narendra Deva, who *d* 1996, and has issue living, one son and one da.

DAUGHTER LIVING OF FOURTH BARON

Hon Caroline, *b* 1973: *m* 19—, ..., and has issue living, Amanda PARKER, *b* 1991, — Iris PARKER, *b* 1999. *Residence –* Promila Mansion (4th Floor), Suite 9A, 214-16 A. J. C. Bose Rd, Calcutta 17, India.

DAUGHTER LIVING OF THIRD BARON

Hon Anjana, *b* 1950: *m* 19— (*m diss* 19—), S. Lahiri, son of late Sanat Lahiri (ante). *Residence –* D216 Saket, New Delhi 17, India.

WIDOW LIVING OF FIFTH BARON

LOLITA (*Baroness Sinha*), da of late Dev Kumar Das, by his wife, Hon Sheila Sinha, da of 2nd Baron Sinha: *m* 1965 (in India), the 5th Baron Sinha, who *d* 1999. *Residence –* 2 Highfield Rd, Billericay, Essex CM11 2PF.

COLLATERAL BRANCHES LIVING

Issue of late Hon Sisir Sinha, 2nd son of 1st Baron, *b* 1890, *d* 1950: *m* 1917, (*please give full names and maiden name of wife, and her year of death*):—
Indrajit (7 Lord Sinha Rd, Calcutta, India), *b* 1918: *m* 1951, Sunanda, da of late S. Seu, of Calcutta, and has issue living, Premola, *b* 1954 (*please give full details of marriage/issue, as applicable, and full present address*). — Anita, *b* 1921.

Issue of late Hon Sushil Kumar Sinha, 3rd son of 1st Baron, *b* 1895, *d* 1968: *m* 1st, (Oct) 1919, a da (*full names, please*), who *d* (Dec) 1919, of late Sir Atul Chandra Chatterjee, GCIE, KCSI, ICS; 2ndly, 1921, Romola, da of Dr S. K. Mullick:—
(By 2nd *m*) Arun, *b* 1939; nuclear physicist in USA (*please give full present address, etc*). — Leila, *b* 1937.

PREDECESSORS – (1) *Rt Hon Sir* SATVENDRA PRASANNA Sinha, KCSI, PC, KC (the first Indian to be created a peer), son of Siti Kanatha Sinha, of Raipur, Birbhum, Bengal, *b* 1864; was a Member of Viceroy's Council 1909-10, Advocate-Gen and a MLC, Bengal 1916-19; Under-Sec of State for India Jan 1919 to Nov 1920, and Gov of Bihar and Orissa Nov 1920 to Nov 1921; represented India at Special War Conference 1917 and 1918; appointed a Member of Judicial Committee of Privy Council 1926; *cr Baron Sinha*, of Raipur, Presidency of Bengal (peerage of United Kingdom) 1919: *m* 1880, Gobindo Mohini, who *d* 1938, da of Krislo Chunder Mitter, Zemindar of Maheta, District Burdwan, India; *d* 1928; *s* by his son (2) AROON KUMAR, 2nd Baron; *b* 1887; writ of summons to House of Lords granted 1939: *m* 1st, 1916, Pryatama (Rani), who *d* 1919, el da of Rai Bahadur Lalit Mohan Chatterjee; 2ndly, 1919, Nirupama, who *d* 1975, yr da of Rai Bahadur Lalit Mohan Chatterjee (ante); *d* 1967; *s* by his son (3) SUDHINDRO PROSANNO, 3rd Baron; *b* 1920: *m* 1945, Madhabi, who *d* 1996, da of late Monoranjan Chatterjee, of Calcutta; *d* 1989; *s* by his son (4) SUSANTA PRASSANNA, 4th Baron, *b* 1953; tea broker: *m* 1972 (*m diss* 1991), Patricia, da of Dennis Edward Orchard; *d* 1992; *s* by his uncle (5) ANINDO KUMAR (2nd son of 2nd Baron), 5th Baron, *b* 1930; Sales Manager at Unilever and at Pilkington Bros: *m* 1965 (New Delhi, India), Lolita, da of late Dev Kumar Das (by his wife, Hon Sheila Sinha, da of 2nd Baron Sinha); *d* 1999; *s* by his son (6) ARUP KUMAR, 6th Baron and present peer.

Skeffington, family name of Viscount Massereene and Ferrard.

SKELMERSDALE, BARON (Bootle-Wilbraham) (Baron UK 1828)

In the haven there is rest

ROGER BOOTLE-WILBRAHAM, 7th Baron; *b* 2 April 1945; *s* 1973; *ed* Eton, Lord Wandsworth Coll, Basingstoke; Proprietor of Broadleigh Gdns 1972, Man Dir Broadleigh Nurseries, Ltd 1973; a Lord in Waiting to HM 1980-86, Parliamentary Under-Sec Dept of Environment 1986-87, Dept of Health and Social Security 1987-88, Dept of Social Security 1988-89, N Ireland Office 1989-90, since when Consultant in Parl Affairs; Dir Broadleigh Nurseries Ltd: *m* 1972, Christine Joan, only da of Phillip Roy Morgan, of Evercreech, Somerset, and has issue.

𝕬rms – Quarterly: 1st and 4th argent, three bendlets wavy azure, *Wilbraham*; 2nd and 3rd gules, on a chevron engrailed, between three combs argent, as many crosses partée fitchée, of the field. *Bootle*. 𝕮rest – 1st, a wolf's head erased argent; 2nd, a demi-lion reguardant proper, holding in the paws an escutcheon gules, charged with a cross flory argent. 𝕾upporters – *Dexter*, a wolf argent; gorged with a plain collar azure, and pendent thereform an escutcheon charged with the ancient arms of Wilbraham, viz azure, two bars argent, and a canton sable, thereon a wolf's head erased argent; *sinister*, a wolf proper, collared or, and from the collar pendent an escutcheon as the dexter.
Address – c/o House of Lords, SW1A 0PW.

SON LIVING

Hon ANDREW, *b* 9 Aug 1977.

DAUGHTER LIVING

Hon Carolyn Ann, *b* 1974.

SISTERS LIVING

Hon Lavinia, *b* 1937: *m* 1969, Robert Brian Noel Massey, of Waterstone House, Itchenor, nr Chichester, Sussex, and has issue living, Harry, *b* 1975, — Archibald Edmonds, *b* 1977.
Hon Olivia, *b* 1938: *m* 1961 (*m diss* 1975), Anthony John Hoole Lowsley-Williams (*see* Makins, Bt, 1967 Edn), and has issue living, Richard Edward, *b* 1962, — (Hugh) Sebastian, *b* 1964, — Benjamin Christopher, *b* 1968. *Residence* – Villa Santa Rosa, 36 Paseo de Coca, Los Barrios 11370, Cadiz, Spain.
Hon Daphne, *b* 1946: *m* 1980 (*m diss* 1992), Jocelyn Peter Gore Graham, son of Brig Peter Alastair John Gore Graham, of Chalkpit Cottage, Blewbury, Oxon, and has issue living, Tamsin Christobel, *b* 1985. *Residence* – 1 Canynge Square, Clifton, Bristol BS8 3LA.

PREDECESSORS – **(1)** EDWARD Bootle-Wilbraham; *b* 1771; MP for Westbury 1795-6, for Newcastle-under-Lyme 1796-1812, and for Dover 1818-28; *cr Baron Skelmersdale* (peerage of United Kingdom) 1828; *d* 1853; *s* by his grandson **(2)** EDWARD, GCB, PC (son of Hon Richard Bootle-Wilbraham, MP), 2nd Baron; *b* 1837; Lord-in-Waiting to HM Queen Victoria 1866-8, Capt of Yeomen of the Guard 1874-80, and Lord Chamberlain of HM's Household 1885-6, 1886-92, and 1895-8; *cr Earl of Lathom* (peerage of United Kingdom) 1880: *m* 1860, Lady Alice Villiers, who *d* 1897, 2nd da of 4th Earl of Clarendon; *d* 1898; *s* by his el son **(3)** EDWARD GEORGE, 2nd Earl, *b* 1864: *m* 1889, Lady Wilma Pleydell-Bouverie, who *d* 1931, only surviving da of 5th Earl of Radnor; *d* 1910; *s* by his only son **(4)** EDWARD WILLIAM, 3rd Earl; *b* 1895: *m* 1927, Marie Xenia, who *d* 1974, da of E. W. de Tunzelman, of Singapore, and formerly wife of Ronald William Morrison; *d* 1930, when the Earldom of Lathom became ext, and the Barony of Skelmersdale devolved upon his kinsman **(5)** ARTHUR GEORGE, MC (el son of late Col Arthur Bootle-Wilbraham, a grandson of 1st Baron), 5th Baron; *b* 1876; *d* 1969; *s* by his cousin **(6)** LIONEL, DSO, MC (only son of Lionel Bootle-Wilbraham, grandson of 1st Baron), 6th Baron, *b* 1896; Lt-Col Coldm Gds: *m* 1936, Ann, who *d* 1974, da of late Percy Cuthbert Quilter (Quilter, Bt, colls); *d* 1973; *s* by his son **(7)** ROGER, 7th Baron and present peer.

SKIDELSKY, BARON (Skidelsky) (Life Baron 1991)

ROBERT JACOB ALEXANDER SKIDELSKY, son of late Boris Jacob Skidelsky, of Vladivostock, Russia; *b* 25 April 1939; *ed* Brighton Coll, and Jesus Coll, Oxford (MA, DPhil); Hon DLitt Buckingham 1997, Hon Fell Jesus Coll, Oxford 1997, Research Fellow Nuffield Coll, Oxford 1965-68, British Acad 1968-70, Assoc Prof of History John Hopkins Univ, USA 1970-76, Head of Dept of History,

Philosophy and European Studies N London Poly 1976-78, Prof of Internat Studies Warwick Univ 1978-90, since when Prof of Pol Ec Warwick Univ; Chm Charleston Trust 1987-92; Member Policy Cttee SDP 1988-90, and Lord Chancellor's Advisory Council on Public Records 1988-93; Principal Opposition Spokesman, Culture, Media and Sport, House of Lords 1997-98, since when on Treasury Affairs; Chm Social Market Foundation since 1989; Pres Hands Off Reading Campaign 1994-97; FRHistS 1973, FRSL 1978, FBA 1994; author; *cr Baron Skidelsky*, of Tilton, co E Sussex (Life Baron) 1991: *m* 1970, Augusta Mary Clarissa, da of late John Humphrey Hope, of E Harptree, Som, and has issue.

Residence – Tilton House, Firle, E Sussex. *Club* – United Oxford and Cambridge.

SONS LIVING

Hon Edward, *b* 1973; *ed* Eton.
Hon William, *b* 1976; *ed* Eton.

DAUGHTER LIVING

Hon Juliet, *b* 1981.

Slane, Viscount; grandson of Marquess Conyngham.

SLATER, BARONY OF (Slater) (Extinct 1977)

SON LIVING OF LIFE BARON

Hon Brian, *b* 1948. *Residence* – 30 Corscombe Close, Rudds Hill, Ferryhill, co Durham.

DAUGHTER LIVING OF LIFE BARON

Hon Elizabeth, *b* 1934: *m* 1955, Frank Davison, of 1 Seymour Grove, Eaglescliffe, Cleveland.
Mrs Kingsmill Pennefather,

SLIGO, MARQUESS OF (Browne) (Marquess I 1800) Sits as BARON MONTEAGLE (UK 1806)

Follow the right

JEREMY ULICK BROWNE, 11th Marquess; *b* 4 June 1939; *s* 1991; *ed* St Columba's Coll, and RAC Cirencester: *m* 1961, Jennifer June Lushington, only da of Maj (George) Derek Cooper, MC, late The Life Guards, of Dunlewey, Gweedore, co Donegal, and of Mrs Cyril Heber-Percy, and has issue.

𝕬rms – Sable, three lions passant in bend between four bendlets argent. 𝕮rest – An eagle displayed vert. 𝕾upporters – *Dexter*, a talbot proper, gorged with a baron's coronet; *sinister*, a horse argent. *Seat* – Westport House, Westport, co Mayo.

DAUGHTERS LIVING

Lady Sheelyn Felicity, *b* 1963.
Lady Karen Lavinia, *b* 1964.
Lady Lucinda Jane, *b* 1969.
Lady Clare Romane, *b* 1974.
Lady Alannah Grace, *b* 1980.

AUNTS LIVING *(sisters of 10th Marquess) (raised to the rank of a Marquess's daughters 1953)*

Lady Sheelah Annette, *b* 1908: *m* 1930, John Dalrymple Winn Treherne, who *d* 1972, and has had issue, Roland Dalrymple, *b* 1935; *ed* Eton; *d* 1992. — Oona Cicely (Long Meadow, Hasketon, Woodbridge, Suffolk), *b* 1930: *m* 1950 (*m diss* 1973), Christopher Paul Mansel Campbell Methuen Campbell, who *d* 1998, and has issue (*see* B Methuen, colls). *Residence* – Long Meadow, Hasketon, Woodbridge, Suffolk.
Lady Noreen, *b* 1910: *m* 1931, Clive Ali Chimmo Branson, who was *ka* in Far East 1944, and has issue living, Rosa (46 Southwood Av, Highgate, N6 5RZ), *b* 1933: *m* 1st, 1954 (*m diss* 1966), Alan Hopkins; 2ndly, 1971, Henry Joseph Hooper, who *d* 1990, and has issue living (by 1st *m*), Michael Stephen *b* 1958: *m* 1986, Eileen Jane Eccles, Peggy Anne *b* 1955: *m* 1st, 1975 (*m diss* 1983), Thomas Aquineas Prendeville; 2ndly, 1987, Anthony George Francis Godfrey, of 10 Colmans Court, 46 Morris Rd, E14 (and has issue living (by 2nd *m*) Joel Nathaniel John *b* 1994, Isolde Iona Hephzibah *b* 1989). *Residence* – 46 Southwood Av, Highgate, N6 5RZ.

WIDOW LIVING OF BROTHER OF TENTH MARQUESS

Fiona, da of late John Glenn, of E Grinstead, Sussex: *m* 1962, as his 2nd wife, Capt Lord Ulick Browne, RA (who was raised to the rank of a Marquess's son 1953), who *d* 1979, and has issue (see colls infra). *Residence* – 32 The Little Boltons, SW10.

WIDOW LIVING OF TENTH MARQUESS

JOSÉ (*Dowager Marchioness of Sligo*), da of late William Gauche, of —: *m* 1930, the 10th Marquess of Sligo, who *d* 1991. *Residence* –

COLLATERAL BRANCHES LIVING

Issue of late Capt Lord Ulick Browne, RA (raised to the rank of Marquess's son 1953), brother of 10th Marquess, *b* 1915, *d* 1979: *m* 1st, 1942, Mrs Elma Valerie Warren, who *d* 1959, da of Capt Andrew Burmanoff, Russian Hussars; 2ndly, 1962, Fiona (ante), da of late John Glenn, of E Grinstead, Sussex:—
(By 2nd *m*) SEBASTIAN ULICK, *b* 27 May 1964; *ed* Rugby: *m* 1984 (*m diss* 1992), Christina Maria, yst da of late Luis Suaznabar, of Bolivia, and has issue living, Christopher Ulick, *b* 14 Nov 1988, — Camilla, *b* 1986. —— Ulicia Catherine, *b* 1962: *m* 1993, Giles P. T. Edwards, only son of Peter Guy Edwards, of Low Walworth Hall, Darlington, co Durham, and has issue living, Charlotte Fiona Mary, *b* 1994, — Emily Jill, *b* 1996.

Grandsons of late Major Percy Howe Browne, 2nd son of Lord Richard Howe Browne (infra):—
Issue of late Lieut-Com Anthony Howe Browne, RN, *b* 1905, *ka* 1940: *m* 1931, Joyce Mary Le Roy (who *d* 1981, having *m* 2ndly, 1946, Squadron Leader Graham Doody, ACA, who *d* 1981), da of John Collin, of Trumpington, Cambridge:—
Patrick Ulick Anthony Howe (27 Lanhill Rd, W9; Brook Farm, Fowlmere, nr Royston, Herts), *b* 1935; *ed* Eton; and Magdalene Coll, Camb: *m* 1962, Gerd, da of Anders Hamer, of Norway, and has issue living, Patrick Alexander Howe, *b* 1965, — Anthony Howe, *b* 1967, — Cecilie Howe, *b* 1963. —— Michael John Le Roy (27 Lanhill Rd, W9), *b* 1936: *m* 1959 (*m diss* 1969), Sarah Ruth, da of James Edward Kenneth Sprot, of Natal, and has issue living, Richard Howe, *b* 1962, — Jeremy Ulick, *b* 1963.

Granddaughters of late Lord Richard Howe Browne, 6th son of 2nd Marquess:—
 Issue of late Cyril Edward Browne, OBE, *b* 1873, *d* 1960: *m* 1902, Alice Christina, who *d* 1962, da of Frederick
 Thomas Lewin, DL, of Castlegrove, near Tuam, co Galway, and Cloghans, co Mayo:—
Phyllis Marion Alice, *b* 1913; *ed* Trin Coll, Dublin (Mod BA): *m* 1st, 1941, Harold Hugh Brodie Ind, who *d* 1977; 2ndly,
1982, Kingsmill Pennefather, of Elsinore, Delgany, co Wicklow, and has issue living (by 1st *m*), Peter Lewin Brodie
(Beechcroft, 90 Forest Rd, Horsham, W Sussex RH12 4HL), *b* 1944; *ed* Eton, and Trin Coll, Dublin (BA): *m* 1st, 1982,
Peta Mary Wyldbore (*née* Butler); 2ndly, 1996, Karen Margaret Skinner (*née* Swift), and has issue living (by 1st *m*), Lisa
Peta Alice *b* 1983, — Christina Isabel Mary, *b* 1942; *ed* Trin Coll, Dublin (BA): *m* 1970, W/Cdr Robin Worthington Scott,
of Throstlenest, Summer Bridge, Harrogate, York, and has issue living, Gervase Roderick John *b* 1971; *ed* Repton, and
Edinburgh Univ, Nicholas Hugo Howe *b* 1972; *ed* Repton, and Edinburgh Univ, — Miranda Eleanor Phyllis (78 Redford
Park, Greystones, co Wicklow), *b* 1946: *m* 1971, John Morris O'Connor, Assist Prof of Philosophy, Case Western Reserve
Univ, Cleveland, and has issue living, Amanda Evelyn Alice *b* 1974. —— Marjory Maud, *b* 1916: *m* 1954, Charles
Hastings Doyne, and has issue living, Charles Philip (Greenside House, Hampsthwaite, Harrogate, N Yorks HG3 2EU), *b*
1955; *ed* Sherborne, and Aston Univ (BSc): *m* 1987, Sarah Mary, da of Michael S. Benson, of High Pines, Dane Hill,
Sussex, and has issue living, Samuel Charles Michael *b* 1992, Alice Sarah Mary *b* 1990. *Residence* – Fountains Bent,
Darley Rd, Birstwith, Harrogate, N Yorks HG3 2PN.

(In remainder to Earldom of Altamont, Viscountcy of Westport, and Barony of Mount Eagle only)

Granddaughters of late Capt Perceval Altamont Browne, only surv son of John Denis Browne, 4th son
 of Rt Hon Denis Browne, MP, 2nd son of 2nd Earl of Altamont:—
 Issue of late Percy Frederick Browne, *b* 1872, *d* 1959: *m* 1904, Ruth Reynolds, who *d* 1957, da of John Reynolds
 Warren, of Berea, Durban, S Africa:—
Nancye Maud (The Cottage, 12 Mayfair Av, Newlands, Cape Town 7700, S Africa), *b* 1905: *m* 1945, Maj Aubrey James
Rous, and has issue living, Patrick James (Happy Hollow Lane, Austin, Texas 78703, USA), *b* 1947. —— Moya Lennox
(1005-2012 Fullerton Av, N Vancouver, BC, Canada V7P 3P3), *b* 1917: *m* 1944, Richard Read Birtwistle, who *d* 1983, and
has issue living. Susan Lennox, *b* 1947: *m* 1972, Capt Dan Collinson Koch, of 1945 Russel Way, W Vancouver, BC V7V
3B3, Canada, and has issue living, Michael Richard Collinson *b* 1975, Christopher John Collinson *b* 1978, James Daniel
Collinson *b* 1990.

Grandchildren of late Percy Frederick Browne (ante):—
 Issue of late Patrick Warren Browne, *b* 1908, *d* 1944: *m* 1936, Ada Elizabeth Minnie Barnes, who *m* 2ndly, 1946
 (*m diss* 1954), Charles Edward Hatton Duprez, and has resumed the surname of Browne:—
Michael Lewis, *b* 1940. —— (Phillip) Anthony (1735 Fraser Court, Washington DC 20009, USA), *b* 1941; *ed* Boxgrove
Sch, Guildford. —— Patricia Ruth, *b* 1937: *m* 19—, David Heather, and has issue living, Lucy, *b* 19—.

Grandchildren of late George Robert Browne, eldest son of Rev George Browne, 5th son of late Rt Hon
 Denis Browne, MP (ante):—
 Issue of late George Denis Gun Browne, *b* 1874, *d* 1946: *m* 1901, Gertrude Bessie, who *d* 1953, yst da of John
 Robert Sutton Hudson:—
Denis George Robert Anthony Gun (Fairmead Court, 6 College Rd, Rondebosch, S Africa 7700), *b* 1907: *m* 1960, Violet
Ailsa, da of Charles Henry Stewart-Hess, of Wallasey, Cheshire. —— Gertrude Frances Hester (PO Village of
Happiness, Natal, S Africa 4280), *b* 1905: *m* 1st, 1931, George Ryder Runton, who *d* 1935; 2ndly, 1945, Roger Sydney
McCulloch, and has issue living (by 1st *m*), Aileen Frances (PO Box 405, Grabouw, S Africa 7160), *b* 1932: *m* 1950, John
Geoffrey Harrison, who *d* 1975, and has issue living, Michael John (PO Box 114, Goroka, Eastern Highland Prov, Papua
New Guinea) *b* 1952: *m* 1983, Diana, da of late Maj P. M. Gratwicke, of Bognor Regis (and has issue living, John Philip
b 1983, Rachael Elizabeth *b* 1986), Rosemary Ann *b* 1954: *m* 1991, David Ames, of 53 Kempe Rd, NW6 6SN, — (by 2nd
m) Jane Ann Louise, *b* 1946: *m* 1968, Marie Denise Guiot-Pascau, of 138 Mermoz Av, Candiac, Prov Quebec J5R 4R8,
Canada, and has issue living, Daniel François *b* 1973, Grant Ivan *b* 1975, Neal Gregory *b* 1977.

Grandchildren of late Robert Denis Browne, eldest son of late Rev Robert Browne, 2nd son of late Rev
 George Browne (ante):—
 Issue of late Robert John Denis Browne, FRCGP, *b* 1907, *d* 1985: *m* 1949, Norah Mary (1536 Pershore Rd, Stir-
 chley, Birmingham, W Midlands), da of David Haywood, of Burton-on-Trent:—
Stephen Denis (178 Pineapple Rd, Stirchley, Birmingham B30 2TY), *b* 1950; MRCGP: *m* 1978, Patricia Marian, da of
William George Delahaye, of Birmingham, and has issue living, Elizabeth Anne, *b* 1979, — Sarah Jayne, *b* 1981.
—— Anthony David (120 Howard Rd, Westbury Park, Bristol BS6 7XA), *b* 1958; MSc: *m* 1983, Susan Elizabeth, da of
John Frederick Hole, of Stourbridge, and has issue living, David Alexander, *b* 1989, Daniel Benjamin *b* 1991, Sophie
Elizabeth *b* 1994. —— Margaret, *b* 1952: *m* 1973, John Charles Williams, of 197 Longbridge Lane, Longbridge,
Birmingham B31 4JX, and has issue living, Rachel, *b* 1977: *m* 1998, Robert William Jones, of 382 Frankley Beeches Rd,
Birmingham B31 5NH, — Ruth Emma, *b* 1979.

Issue of late Terence Francis Denis Browne, *b* 1910, *d* 1987: *m* 1947, Avril Honor, who *d* 1973, da of William T.
 Thompson, of Rustington, Sussex:—
Peter Malyon Denis (16 Gaywood Rd, Ashtead, Surrey KT21 1BL), *b* 1953; *ed* Monkton Combe Sch. —— Ian Anthony
Denis (16 Gaywood Rd, Ashtead, Surrey KT21 1BL), *b* 1956; *ed* Monkton Combe Sch.

Grandchildren of late Rev Robert Browne (ante):—
 Issue of late Ambrose George Denis Browne, *b* 1875, *d* 1954: *m* 1st, 1915, Alice Winifred who *d* 1938, da of late
 Sir William Henry White, KCB, 2ndly, 1941, Gertrude Mariana, who *d* 1973, yr da of late Rev John Kipling
 Quarterman, MA, of Blackheath, SE3:—
(By 1st *m*) William Robert Anthony Denis (1334 St Patrick St, Oak Bay, Vic, Vancouver, BC, Canada), *b* 1924; FRICS, RI
(BC); European War with RM: *m* 1st, 1949 (*m diss* 1967), Eileen Beatrice Louise, da of Horace Hugh Perceval Hunt, of
High Ham, Somerset; 2ndly, 1967, Hildegard, da of Johann Cremer, of Dorsetn, W Germany, and has issue living (by 1st
m), James Anthony Ulick Denis, *b* 1956, — Caroline Elizabeth Anne Denis, *b* 1952, — (by 2nd *m*) Andrew Christopher
Denis *b* 1972. —— Winifred Anne Denis, *b* 1921: *m* 1950, John Henry Bateman, MA, of The Orchard, 18A Chapel Lane,
Wilmslow, Ches.

Grandchildren of late Henry Browne, 2nd son of late George Browne, 3rd son of late Maj John Browne, el son of Col Rt Hon Arthur Browne, MP, 2nd son of 1st Earl of Altamont:—
Issue of late Ernest Henry Browne, *b* 1863, *d* 1928: *m* 19—, Beatrice Brownrigg, who *d* 1964:—
Ernest Henry (126 Ohiro Bay Parade, Wellington, S2, NZ), *b* 1913. —— Beatrice Mary (92 Cabra Park, Phibsborough, Dublin), *b* 1911.

Granddaughter of late Rev John Denis Browne, son of late George Townshend Browne, son of late Col Rt Hon Arthur Browne, MP (ante):—
Issue of late Rev Valentine John Augustus (altered by deed poll 1897 to Valentine Denis) Browne, *b* 1843, *d* 1933: *m* 1884, Frances Elizabeth, da of late William Rose, Bar-at-law:—
Rosalind Frances, *b* 1885.

PREDECESSORS – (1) JOHN Browne, son of Peter Browne of Westport, grandson of Sir John Browne, 1st Bt (*cr* 1636) (*see* B Kilmaine), was MP for Castlebar 1749-60; *cr Baron Mount Eagle* of Westport, co Mayo (peerage of Ireland) 1760, *Viscount Westport* (peerage of Ireland) 1768, and *Earl of Altamont* (peerage of Ireland) 1771; *d* 1776; *s* by his son (2) PETER, 2nd Earl, sat as MP for co Mayo; *d* 1780, *s* by his son (3) JOHN DENIS, KP, PC, 3rd Earl; sat as MP for co Mayo; *cr Marquess of Sligo* (peerage of Ireland) 1800, and *Baron Monteagle*, of Westport, co Mayo (peerage of United Kingdom) 1806; *d* 1809; *s* by his son (4) HOWE PETER, KP, PC, 2nd Marquess, *b* 1788: *m* 1816, Hester Catherine, el da of 13th Earl of Clanricarde; *d* 1845; *s* by his son (5) GEORGE JOHN, 3rd Marquess, *b* 1820: *m* 1st, 1847, Louisa Ellen Frances Augusta Smythe, who *d* 1852, da of 6th Viscount Strangford; 2ndly, 1858, Julia Catherine Anne Nugent, who *d* 1859, el da of 9th Earl of Westmeath; 3rdly, 1878, Isabelle, who *d* 1927, da of late Vicomte de Peyronnet; *d* 1896; *s* by his brother (6) JOHN THOMAS, 4th Marquess; *b* 1824; sat as MP for co Mayo 1857-68; *d* 1903; *s* by his brother (7) HENRY ULICK, 5th Marquess; *b* 1831: *m* 1855, Catharine Henrietta, who *d* 1914, da of late William Stephens Dicken, Dep Inspector-Gen Indian Med Ser; *d* 1913; *s* by his el son (8) GEORGE ULICK, 6th Marquess; *b* 1856; in 1916 *s* to *Earldom of Clanricarde* (*cr* 1800) appointed Lieut and Custos Rotulorum for co Mayo 1914: *m* 1887, Agatha Stewart, who *d* 1965, da of late J. Stewart Hodgson, of Haslemere; *d* 1935; *s* by his only son (9) ULICK DE BURGH, MC, 7th Marquess; *b* 1898; Capt (ret) The Greys; European War 1914-19 (MC); *d* 1941; *s* by his uncle (8) ARTHUR HOWE, KBE, CB (3rd son of 5th Marquess), 8th Marquess; *b* 1867; Col late S Staffordshire Regt and Roy Munster Fusiliers; on Gen Staff, Special Intelligence Directorate, War Office 1914-19 (KBE); Principal Assist Sec, Imperial War Graves Commn 1919-30: *m* 1919, Lilian Whiteside, who *d* 1953, da of Charles Chapman, and widow of Major A. F. Mann; *d* 1951; *s* by his brother (9) TERENCE MORRIS, 9th Marquess; *b* 1873; was Sup Bengal Police 1894-1907, *d* 1952; *s* by his nephew (10) DENIS EDWARD (el son of late Lieut-Col Lord Alfred Eden Browne, DSO, 5th son of 5th Marquess), 10th Marquess; *b* 1908: *m* 1930, José, da of William Gauche; *d* 1991; *s* by his only son (11) JEREMY ULICK, 11th Marquess, and present peer; also Earl of Altamont, Earl of Clanricarde, Viscount Westport, Baron Mount Eagle, and Baron Monteagle.

*(1) ULICK BURKE or de Burgh, great grandson of Ulick de Bourke, MacWilliam Eighter, feudal Lord of Clanricarde, collateral heir male of Earls of Ulster; Gov of Connaught; *cr Baron of Dunkellin*, and *Earl of Clanricarde* (peerage of Ireland) 1543; *d* 1544; *s* by his son (2) RICHARD, 2nd Earl; was Lord-Lieut of Ireland; *d* 1582; *s* by his son (3) ULICK, 3rd Earl; his 4th son, John, was *cr Viscount Burke*, of Clanmories, co Mayo (peerage of Ireland) 1629, with remainder to the issue male of his father, which title, on the death of the 2nd Viscount, merged into the Earldom; *d* 1601; *s* by his son (4) RICHARD, 4th Earl; *cr Baron Somerhill* and *Viscount Tunbridge* (peerage of England) 1624, and *Earl of St Albans* (peerage of England) 1628; *d* 1635; *s* by his son (5) ULICK, 5th Earl; *cr Marquess of Clanricarde* (peerage of Ireland) 1646; *d* without male issue 1658, when the English peerages and the Marquessate became extinct, and the Irish Earldom devolved upon his cousin (6) RICHARD, 6th Earl, el son of Sir William Burke, 3rd son of 3rd Earl; *d* 1666; *s* by his brother (7) William, 7th Earl; *d* 1687; *s* by his son (8) RICHARD, 8th Earl: *s* by his brother (9) JOHN, 9th Earl, Col of a regiment of foot in the army of James II; being taken prisoner at the battle of Aghrim 1691, was outlawed and attainted, and his estates were forfeited; his children however claimed their several remainders prior to the sale of the forfeitures and recovered the same; in 1701 the Earl was, by Act of Parliament, acquitted of his treasons and attainder; and restored to his estates; *d* 1722; *s* by his son (10) MICHAEL, 10th Earl; *d* 1726; *s* by his son (11) JOHN SMITH, 11th Earl; resumed by sign manual the ancient surname of De Burgh, *d* 1782; *s* by his son (12) HENRY, KP, PC, 12th Earl; Gov of co Galway; *cr Marquess of Clanricarde* (peerage of Ireland) 1789; *dsp* 1795, when the Marquessate became extinct; *s* in Earldom by his brother (13) JOHN THOMAS, 13th Earl; a Gen in the Army and Gov of co Galway; *cr Earl of Clanricarde* (peerage of Ireland) 1800, with remainder to his two daughters and their issue male according to priority of birth; *d* 1808; *s* by his son (14) ULICK JOHN, KP, PC, 14th Earl; *b* 1802; was Under-Sec for Foreign Affairs 1826-7, Ambassador at St Petersburg 1838-40, Postmaster-Gen 1846-52, Lord Privy Seal 1858, and Lord-Lieut of co Galway, etc; *cr Marquess of Clanricarde* (peerage of Ireland) 1825, and *Baron Somerhill*, of Somerhill, co Kent (peerage of United Kingdom) 1826: *m* 1825, Hon Harriet, who *d* 1876, da of Rt Hon George Canning and of his wife Viscountess Canning in her own right; *d* 1874; *s* by his son (15) HUBERT, 2nd Marquess; *b* 1832; assumed in 1862 the additional surname of Canning, by Roy licence, as heir of his maternal uncle, the 1st Earl Canning; MP for co Galway (*L*) 1867-71; *d* 1916, when the Marquessate of Clanricarde and the Barony of Somerhill became ext, and the Barony of Dunkellin, and Earldom of Clanricarde (*cr* 1543), and the Viscountcy of Bourke became ext, while the Earldom of Clanricarde (*cr* 1800) devolved under special remainder upon his cousin (16) GEORGE ULICK, 6th Marquess of Sligo (ante).

SLIM, VISCOUNT (Slim) (Viscount UK 1960)

A recompense is fairer from a depth

JOHN DOUGLAS SLIM, OBE, 2nd Viscount; *b* 20 July 1927; *s* 1970; Lt-Col (ret) A&SH and Special Air Ser Regt; DL Greater London 1988; FRGS 1983; *cr* OBE (Mil) 1973: *m* 1958, Elisabeth, da of Arthur Rawdon Spinney, CBE, and has issue.

𝔄rms – Gules semée of swords erect argent a lion rampant or, on a canton quarterly azure and also argent a mullet of seven points gold. 𝔠rest – Out of a Crown Vallary or a peacock in its pride proper gorged with a collar and with line reflexed over the back gold. 𝔖upporters – *Dexter*, a British soldier in jungle-green battle dress with web equipment the exterior hand supporting a rifle with bayonet affixed; *Sinister*, a Gurkha rifleman in North-West Frontier dress with web equipment the exterior hand supporting a rifle all proper. *Address* – c/o Lloyds Bank, 6 Pall Mall, SW1. *Clubs* – White's, Special Forces.

SONS LIVING

Hon MARK WILLIAM RAWDON, *b* 13 Feb 1960: *m* 1992, Harriet Laura, yr da of Jonathan Harrison, of Beds, and has issue living, Rufus William Rawdon, *b* 15 April 1995.

Hon Hugo John Robertson, *b* 1961; *ed* Eton, and St John's Coll, Oxford (MA); Senior Lecturer, Oxford Brookes Univ; Trustee of Oxfam GB; FRGS: *m* 1991, M. B. Rebecca, da of late Prof Philip Abrams, and of Prof Sonia Jackson, of Bristol, and has issue living, Solomon Joseph Abrams, *b* 1997, — Jessica Charlotte Abrams, *b* 1994.

DAUGHTER LIVING

Hon Mary Ann, *b* 1964; BA.

SISTER LIVING

Hon Una Mary, *b* 1930: *m* 1st, 1953 (*m diss* 1979), Maj Peter Nigel Stewart Frazer, Grenadier Guards; 2ndly, 1980, Ronald Rowcliffe, of Bamson, Puddington, Tiverton, Devon, and has issue living (by 1st *m*), Sarah Juliet, *b* 1953: *m* 1978, Robert M. Whyte, and has issue living, Jemima Jane *b* 1979, Arabella Rose *b* 1980, Clementine Elisabeth *b* 1983, — (Jennifer) Jane, *b* 1956: *m* 1989, Colin P. G. Farrant, son of Michael Farrant, of Crawley, Hants, and has issue living, Luke *b* 1991, Annabel Mary *b* 1993, — Emma Mary, *b* 1965: *m* 1995, Julian M. A. Samengo-Turner, yst son of William Samengo-Turner, of Montegabbione, Italy, and has issue living, Felix Frazer Fabio *b* 1997.

PREDECESSOR – (1) *Sir* WILLIAM JOSEPH SLIM, KG, GCB, GCMG, GCVO, GBE, DSO, MC, son of late John Slim of Bristol; *b* 1891; Field Marshal; GOC-in-C 14th Army 1943-45, Allied Land Forces, SE Asia 1945-46, Dep Chm Rly Exec 1948, CIGS 1948-53, Gov-Gen of Aust 1953-60, and Gov and Constable Windsor Castle 1964-70; *cr Viscount Slim*, of Yarralumla, ACT, and of Bishopston, City and Co of Bristol (peerage of UK) 1960: *m* 1926, Aileen, who *d* 1994, da of Rev J. A. Robertson, of Edinburgh; *d* 1970; *s* by his son (2) JOHN DOUGLAS, 2nd Viscount and present peer.

SLYNN OF HADLEY, BARON (Slynn) (Life Baron 1992)

GORDON SLYNN, son of late John Slynn; *b* 17 Feb 1930; *ed* Sandbach Sch, Goldsmiths' Coll, and Trin Coll, Camb; Hon Fellow Buckingham 1982, St Andrew's Coll Sydney Univ 1991, Liverpool Poly 1992, and Goldsmiths' Coll 1993, Hon LLD Birmingham 1983, Buckingham 1983, Exeter 1985, Univ of Technology Sydney 1991, Bristol Poly 1992, Sussex 1992, Stetson, USA 1993, Staffs 1994, Pace, New York 1995, Pondicherry 1997, Strathclyde 1999, and London 1999, Hon DCL Durham 1989, and City Univ 1994, Hon Decanus Legis Mercer Univ USA 1986, Hon Fellow American Coll of Trial Lawyers 1992, Memb American Law Inst 1993; Pres Bar Assocn for Commerce, Finance and Industry since 1999; Bar Gray's Inn 1956 (Treasurer 1988), Recorder 1971, Hon Recorder Hereford 1972-76, Junior Counsel to Treasury 1968-74, QC 1974, Leading Counsel to Treasury 1974-76, a Judge of the High Court of Justice (Queen's Bench Div) 1976-81, Pres Employment Appeal Tribunal 1978-81, Advocate-Gen Court of Justice European Communities 1981-88, Judge 1988-92, since when a Lord of Appeal in Ordinary; Visiting Prof of Law Durham Univ 1981-88, Univ of Technology Sydney since 1990, and National Univ of India since 19—; Chief Steward Hereford since 1978; Gov Internat Students' Trust 1979-85, and since 1992, Chm Exec Council Internat Law Assocn since 1988; Master of Broderers' Co 1994-95; Commandeur d'honneur de Bontemps de Medoc et des Graves, Commandeur Confrerie de St Cumbert, Chevalier de Tastevin; contributor to learned journals, and author of *Introducing a European Legal Order;* Grand Croix Ordre de Merite of Luxembourg 1998; KStJ; *cr* Knt 1976, and *Baron Slynn of Hadley,* of Eggington, co Beds (Life Baron) 1992; *m* 1962, Odile Marie Henriette, da of late Pierre Boutin.

Arms – Argent, on a chevron gules between three leopards' heads proper as many garbs or, on a chief azure three saltires couped argent. **Crest** – Within a crest coronet or a tawny owl holding in the dexter claw a quill erect proper, the leg ringed or.
Address – Royal Courts of Justice, Strand, WC2. *Clubs* – Athenaeum, Beefsteak, Garrick.

SMITH, BARONY OF (Smith) (Extinct 1998)

SONS LIVING OF LIFE BARON *(By 1st marriage)*

Hon Martin Rodney, *b* 1942.
Hon Andrew Edward Rodney, *b* 1948.
Hon Robert Aidan Rodney, *b* 1956.

DAUGHTER LIVING OF LIFE BARON *(By 1st marriage)*

Hon Elinor, *b* 1950; *m* 1981 (*m diss* 19—), Stephen Foster Kelly.

WIDOW LIVING OF LIFE BARON

SUSAN (*Baroness Smith*), da of Dr Rowdon Marrian Fry; *m* 1971, as his 2nd wife, Baron Smith, KBE, who *d* 1998. *Residence* – Dower Cottage, Marlow Common, Bucks. *Club* – MCC.

Smith, family name of Baron Bicester.

Smith, family name of Baron Colwyn.

Smith, family name of Viscount Hambleden.

Smith, family name of Baron Kirkhill.

SMITH OF CLIFTON, BARON (Smith) (Life Baron 1997)

TREVOR ARTHUR SMITH, son of late Arthur James Smith, of Newnham-on-Severn, Glos; *b* 14 June 1937; *ed* LSE (BSc 1958); Hon LLD Dublin 1992, Hull 1993, Belfast 1995, Nat Univ of Ireland 1996, DHL Alabama 1998; School Teacher, LCC 1958-59; Temp Assist Lecturer, Exeter Univ 1959-60; Res Offr, Acton Soc Trust 1960-62; Lecturer in Politics, Hull Univ 1962-67; Visiting Assoc Prof. California State Univ, Los Angeles 1969; Lecturer (later Snr Lecturer) in Political Studies, Queen Mary Coll (later Queen Mary and Westfield Coll), London 1967-83, Head of Dept 1972-85, Dean of Social Studies 1979-82, Prof 1983-91, Pro-Principal 1985-87, Snr Pro-Principal 1987-89, Snr Vice-Principal 1989-90; Vice Chancellor and Hon Prof, Univ of Ulster 1991-99; Dir Jab Ownership Ltd 1978-85, New Society Ltd 1986-88, Statesman and Nation Publishing Co Ltd 1988-90, and Gerald Duckworth & Co Ltd 1990-95; Chm Political Studies Assoc of UK 1988-89, Vice-Pres 1989-91, Pres 1991-93; Govr Sir John Cass and Redcoats Sch 1979-84, Univ of Haifa 1985-92, and Bell Education Trust 1988-93; Memb Tower Hamlets DHA 1987-91 (Vice-Chm 1989-91); Vice-Pres Patients Assoc of UK 1988-97; Dep Pres Inst of Citizenship Studies since 1991; Pres Belfast Civic Trust 1995-99; Memb UK Socrates Council 1993-99 (Chm 1996-99), Administrative Board, Internat Assoc of Univs 1995-96, Chm Conference of Rectors in Ireland 1987, Editorial Board, *Government and Opposition* since 1995, Board of *A Taste of Ulster* 1996-99, and Board of Opera Northern Ireland 1997-99; Trustee, Joseph Rowntree Reform Trust Ltd 1975-87, since when Chm; FRHistS 1996, CIMgt 1992, FRSA 1994, FICPD 1998; Hon Memb of Senate of Fachhochschule, Augsburg 1994; *cr* Kt 1996, and *Baron Smith of Clifton*, of Mountsandel, co Londonderry (Life Baron) 1997: *m* 1st, 1960 (*m diss* 1973), Brenda Susan, da of late G.W.F. Eustace, of Ashford, Middx; 2ndly, 1979, Julia Donnithorne, da of E.J.D. Bullock, of Ewell, Surrey, and has issue by 1st and 2nd *m*.

Arms – Sable between two haunches argent fretty sable four fusils conjoined in pale throughout each per pale argent and or per chevron counterchanged. **Crest** – A sacred ibis's head proper gorged with a plain collar or. **Supporters** – On either side a sacred ibis proper gorged with a plain collar or.
Address – House of Lords, SW1A 0PW. *Club* – Reform.

SONS LIVING (By 1st marriage)

Hon Adam James William, *b* 1964; *ed* Newcastle Univ: *m* 1992, Brenda Anne Lynn, and has issue living, Heather Dawn Veronica, *b* 1994, — Abigail Rebecca Lynn, *b* 1996.
Hon Gideon Matthew Kingsley, *b* 1966; *ed* William Ellis Sch, London: *m* 1991, Catherine Dorothy Mary Mothersole, and has issue living, Matthew James Kingsley, *b* 1994.

DAUGHTER LIVING (By 2nd marriage)

Hon Naomi Thérèse Donnithorne, *b* 1981; *ed* Methodist Coll, Belfast.

SMITH OF GILMOREHILL, BARONESS (Smith) (Life Baroness 1995)

ELIZABETH MARGARET SMITH, da of late Frederick William Moncrieff Bennett; *b* 4 June 1940; *ed* Hutchesons' Girls' Gram Sch, Univ of Glasgow (MA), and Jordanhill Coll of Education (postgraduate); Hon LLD Glasgow 1998; teacher 1964-68; Scottish Sec, Great Britain-USSR Assoc 1982-88, since when Consultant on Russian Training Programmes; Member of Press Complaints Commn since 1995; Pres Scottish Opera 1998, Pres Birkbeck Coll 1998; Memb Advisory Board, Know How Fund 1998; Non-Exec Dir Deutsche Scotland 1996; Memb BP Advisory Board for Scotland 1996; Chm Edinburgh Festival Fringe Soc since 1995; DL City of Edinburgh 1996; Member Governing Body British Assocn for Central and Eastern Europe since 1996; *cr Baroness Smith of Gilmorehill*, of Gilmorehill in the District of the City of Glasgow (Life Baroness) 1995: *m* 1967, Rt Hon John Smith, QC, MP, who *d* 1994, son of late Archibald Leitch Smith, of Dunoon, Argyll, and has issue.
Address – c/o House of Lords, SW1A 0PW.

DAUGHTERS LIVING

Hon Sarah Elizabeth, *b* 1968; *ed* Univ of Glasgow.
Hon Jane Bennett, *b* 1971; *ed* Heriot-Watt Univ.
Hon Catherine Anne, *b* 1973; *ed* Univ of Glasgow.

Smith, Buchanan-, surname of Barony of Balerno.

Smith, Walker-, family name of Barony of Broxbourne.

SNOW, BARONY OF (Snow) (Extinct 1980)

SON LIVING OF LIFE BARON

Hon Philip Charles Hansford, *b* 1952; *ed* Eton, and Balliol Coll, Oxford; writer; Member Royal Inst of Internat Affairs, and Council Member China Soc: *m* 1987, Amanda C., elder da of Sir Clive Anthony Whitmore, of E Sussex, and has issue living, Alexander Daniel Hansford, *b* 1994, — Renata Maria Hansford, *b* 1992. *Residence* – 39 Alderney St, SW1V 4HH.

Snow, surname of Barony of Burntwood.

SNOWDON, EARL OF (Armstrong-Jones) (Earl UK 1961)

ANTONY CHARLES ROBERT ARMSTRONG-JONES, GCVO, 1st Earl, son of late Ronald Owen Lloyd Armstrong-Jones, MBE, QC, of Plas Dinas, Caernarvonshire; *b* 7 Mar 1930; *ed* Eton, and Jesus Coll, Camb; Sr Fellow Royal Coll of Art 1986, Hon DUniv Bradford 1989, Hon LLD Bath 1989, Hon LLD Southampton 1993, Hon DLitt Portsmouth 1993; Constable of Caernarvon Castle since 1963; *cr* Viscount Linley, of Nymans, co Sussex, and *Earl of Snowdon* (peerage of UK) 1961; GCVO 1969: *m* 1st, 6 May 1960 (*m diss* 1978), HRH The Princess Margaret Rose, yr da of HM late King George VI; 2ndly, 1978, Lucy Mary, only da of Donald Brook Davies, of Enniskerry, co Wicklow, and formerly wife of Michael Lindsay-Hogg (*see* Lindsay-Hogg, Bt), and has issue by 1st and 2nd *m*.

What God wills will be

Arms – Sable on a chevron argent, between in chief two fleurs-de-lis, and in base an eagle displayed or, four pallets gules. **Crest** – A stag statant gules attired collared and unguled or between two arms embowed in armour the hands proper each grasping a fleur-de-lis gold. **Supporters** – *Dexter*, a griffin, and *sinister*, an eagle, each with wings elevated and addorsed or.
Residence – 22 Launceston Place, W8 5RL. *Clubs* – Buck's, Leander, Hawkes, Oxford and Cambridge.

SON LIVING (*By 1st marriage*)

DAVID ALBERT CHARLES (*Viscount Linley*), *b* 3 Nov 1961; *ed* Bedales; Commr for Exhibition of 1851 and Member Board of Management since 1998: *m* 8 Oct 1993, Hon Serena Alleyne Stanhope, only da of Charles Henry Leicester, Viscount Petersham (*see* E Harrington), and has issue living, *Hon* Charles Patrick Inigo, *b* 2 July 1999.

DAUGHTERS LIVING (*By 1st marriage*)

Lady Sarah Frances Elizabeth, *b* 1964; *ed* Bedales, and Royal Academy Sch: *m* 1994, Daniel Chatto, yr son of late Thomas Chatto, and has issue living, Samuel David Benedict, *b* 1996, — Arthur Richard Nathaniel, *b* 1999.

(*By 2nd marriage*)

Lady Frances, *b* 1979.

SOAMES, BARONY OF (Soames) (Extinct 1987)

SONS LIVING OF LIFE BARON

Hon (Arthur) Nicholas Winston, *b* 1948; *ed* Eton; 2nd Lieut 11th Hussars (PAO) 1967-70; Extra Equerry to HRH the Prince of Wales 1970-72; Memb Select Cttee on European Legislation 1983-84; MP for Crawley (*C*) since 1983; Parl Private Sec to Min of State for Employment and Chm Conservative Party (Mr John Gummer) 1984-92, Parly Sec, Dept of Agriculture, Fisheries and Food 1992-94, Min of State Armed Forces 1994-97: *m* 1st, 1981 (*m diss* 1988), Catherine N., eldest da of Capt Anthony E. Weatherall, of Cowhill Tower, Dumfries; 2ndly, 1993, Serena Mary, da of Sir John Lindsay Eric Smith, CH, CBE (*see* E Northesk, colls), and has issue living (by 1st *m*), Arthur Harry David, *b* 1985, — (by 2nd *m*), Isabella Mary Christian, *b* 1996.

Hon Jeremy Bernard, *b* 1952; *ed* Eton: *m* 1978, Susanna, elder da of late (James) David (Agar) Keith, of W Barsham Hall, Fakenham, Norfolk, and has issue living, Archie Christopher Winston, *b* 1988, — Gemma Mary, *b* 1979, — Flora Caroline, *b* 1982.

Hon Rupert Christopher, *b* 1959; *ed* Eton: *m* 1988, Camilla Rose, eldest da of Sir Thomas Raymond Dunne, KCVO, of Gatley Park, Leominster, Herefords (HM's Lord Lieut of Herefordshire and Worcestershire), and has issue living, Arthur Christopher, *b* 1990, — Jack, *b* 1994, — Daisy, *b* 1992.

DAUGHTERS LIVING OF LIFE BARON

Hon Emma Mary SOAMES, *b* 1949; has resumed her maiden name; journalist; editor of *Tatler* 1988-90, and *ES* Magazine since 1992: *m* 1981 (*m diss* 1989), James N. M. MacManus, eldest son of Dr Niall MacManus, of 8 Warwick Sq, SW1, and has issue living, Emily Fiona, *b* 1983. *Residence* – 26 Eland Rd, SW11.

Hon Charlotte Clementine (*Countess Peel*), *b* 1954: *m* 1st, 1973 (*m diss* 1982), (Alexander) Richard Hambro, 2nd son of Jocelyn Olaf Hambro, MC; 2ndly, 1989, as his 2nd wife, 3rd Earl Peel, and has issue (by 1st *m*), Clementine Silvia, *b* 1976, — (by 2nd *m*) (*see* E Peel). *Residence* – Kilgram Grange, Jervaulx, Ripon, N Yorks HG4 4PQ.

WIDOW LIVING OF LIFE BARON

Hon MARY SPENCER-CHURCHILL, DBE (*Baroness Soames*), yst da of late Rt Hon Sir Winston Leonard Spencer-Churchill, KG, OM, CH, TD, FRS (*see* D Marlborough, colls), and of late Baroness Spencer-Churchill, GBE: *m* 1947, Baron Soames, GCMG, GCVO, CH, CBE, PC (Life Baron), who *d* 1987.

SOMERLEYTON, BARON (Crossley) (Baron UK 1916, Bt UK 1863)

All good is from above

SAVILE WILLIAM FRANCIS CROSSLEY, GCVO, 3rd Baron and 4th Baronet; *b* 17 Sept 1928; *s* 1959; *ed* Eton; Capt (ret) Coldstream Guards; co Councillor E Suffolk 1967-73; DL Suffolk 1964; JP Lowestoft 1969; a Lord in Waiting to HM The Queen 1978-92, and Master of the Horse to HM 1991-98; a Dir of E Anglian Water Co; Chm E Anglia Regional Branch, Historic Houses Assocn, and of Assocn of Masters of Harriers and Beagles, Pres of E Region, YMCA, and Gov Lowestoft Coll of Further Education; patron of one living; KCVO 1994, GCVO 1999: *m* 1963, Belinda Maris, OBE, eldest da of late Capt Vivian Loyd, RFA, of Kingsmoor, Ascot, and has issue.

Arms – Gules, a chevron indented ermine between two cross-crosslets in chief, and a saltire coupled in base or. **Crest** – A demi-hind erased proper, charged with two bars holding between the feet a cross-crosslet or. **Supporters** – On either side a hind proper, semée of cross-crosslets or. *Seat* – Somerleyton Hall, Lowestoft, Suffolk. *Clubs* – White's, Pratt's.

SON LIVING

Hon HUGH FRANCIS SAVILE, *b* 27 Sept 1971; a Page of Honour to HM The Queen 1983-84.

DAUGHTERS LIVING

Hon Isabel Alicia Claire, *b* 1964: *m* 1991, Mark Cator, and has issue (*see* Storey, Bt).

Hon Camilla Mary Lara, *b* 1967: *m* 1993, William Aldwin (Sandy) Soames, eldest son of Robert Harold Soames, of Toppesfield, Essex, and has issue living, Milo, *b* 1995, — Tommy, *b* 1997, — Mary Alicia Claire, *b* 1999.

Hon Alicia Phyllis Belinda, *b* 1969: *m* 1998, Robert E. C. Pawson, only son of Michael Pawson, of Windsor Forest, Berks.

Hon Louisa Bridget Vivien, *b* 1974.

BROTHER LIVING

Hon (Richard) Nicholas, TD (Westfield Farm, Settrington, Malton, York. *Clubs* – Cavalry and Guards', Pratt's, Royal Yacht Sqdn); *b* 1932; *ed* Eton and RMA; DL N Yorks 1988, High Sheriff 1989; Capt 9th Queen's R Lancers (ret); Maj Queens Own Yeo (TA); Comdg Officer Queens Own Yeomanry (TA) 1973-76, Col Gen Staff (TA) 1978; appointed Aide-de-Camp TAVR to HM The Queen 1980; a Member of Hon Corps of Gentlemen-at-Arms: *m* 1st, 1958, Alexandra Anne Maitland, who *d* 1990, only da of W/Cdr Charles Donald Graham Welch, RAF of Perrot Farm, Graffham, Sussex; 2ndly, 1995, Mrs Priscilla Ann Kennedy, twin da of late Maj Alastair Graham, MC (*see* Graham, Bt, *or* 1002, colls), and has issue living (by 1st *m*), John Dickon Francis, *b* 1966; *ed* Eton, and RMA Sandhurst; Capt 9/12th Royal Lancers: *m* 1997, Sarah F. B., yst da of Maj John Bayfield Freeland, of Kintbury, Berks, — Amanda Carolyn, *b* 1960: *m* 1st, 1984 (*m diss* 1992), Patrick James Auchinleck Darling, only son of Lt Cdr Gerald Ralph Auchinleck Darling, RD, QC, of Crevenagh, Omagh, co Tyrone; 2ndly, 1992, Edward P. U. Mead, son of Humphrey Mead, of Normandy, and of Mrs Peter Cadbury, of Alresford, Hants, and has issue living (by 1st *m*), Shaunagh Edwina Auchinleck *b* 1986, (by 2nd *m*) Arthur Silas *b* 1993, Leila Alexandra *b* (twin) 1993, — Lucinda Mary, *b* 1962: *m* 1980, Masood Oloumi, of Yazdi, and has issue living, Lilly *b* 1985, Rose *b* 1989.

SISTER LIVING

Hon Mary, *b* 1926; JP Huntingdon and Peterborough 1966: *m* 1950, Maj William Birkbeck, DL, Coldm Gds (ret), of Bainton House, Stamford, Lincs, and has issue living, Anthony William Savile (Meddoms Farm Barn, Hornton, Banbury, Oxon OX15 6EA), *b* 1956; *ed* Eton: *m* 1991, Hon Davina Mary Bewicke-Copley, yr da of 6th Baron Cromwell, and has issue living, Elizabeth (Beth) *b* 1993, Kate *b* 1994, — Victoria Mary, *b* 1951: *m* 1981 (*m diss* 1995), Adauto Santos, of Rio de Janeiro, — Priscilla Bridget, *b* 1952: *m* 1987, John Kenneth Scott Moncrieff, WS, of 23 Cluny Drive, Edinburgh, elder son of David Charles Scott Moncrieff, CVO, TD, WS, and has issue living, Robert David *b* 1991, Iona Mary *b* 1988, Isabel Ann *b* 1989, — Rosetta Sybil, *b* 1958: *m* 1987, Iain James Russell, of The Weavers House, Knockfarrel, by Dingwall, Ross-shire IV15 9TQ, only son of James Seckham Russell, of Croyard House, Beauly, Inverness-shire, and of Seafield, co Waterford, and has issue living, Oliver George Seckham *b* 1988, Alastair William James *b* 1991, Patrick Alexander Bazaine *b* 1993, Douglas Anthony Iain *b* 1997.

COLLATERAL BRANCH LIVING

Grandchildren (by 1st *m*) of late Capt Hon John de Bathe Crossley (*infra*):—
Issue of late Anthony Everard Savile Crossley, *b* 1920, *d* 1993: *m* 1956, Jean Margaret Gillian (Milima, Warhurst Rd, MSF 115 Gympie, Qld 4570, Australia), eldest da of David Oliphant Russell, of Kipkarren River, Kenya:—
John de Bathe (Milima, Warhurst Rd, MSF 115 Gympie, Qld 4570, Australia), *b* 1958: *m* 1982, Yvonne Theresa van Tongeren, da of late Michael Lodewyk (formerly van Tongeren), of Cairns, Qld, and has issue living, Peter Hugh de Bathe, *b* 1988, — Rowena Lauren, *b* 1985, — Angela Louise, *b* 19—. —— Timothy Elgon Savile (6 Arkana Terrace, Moranbah, Qld 4744, Australia), *b* 1963: *m* 1993, Rachael Anne, da of Michael Green, of Jesslands, Warra, Qld and has issue living, Nicholas Anthony Savile, *b* 1995, — Annabelle Lucinda, *b* 1998. —— Marguerite, *b* 1957: *m* 1982, William Anthony Peat Darbishire, of 324 Pinjarra Rd, Pinjarra Hills, Qld 4069, Australia, and has issue living, George William Urie, *b* 1995, — Amanda Flora, *b* 1983. —— Julia, *b* 1960: *m* 1996, James Iain Harry Macdonald-Buchanan, and has issue (*see* B Bicester, colls).

Issue of late Capt Hon John de Bathe Crossley, 2nd son of 1st Baron, *b* 1893, *d* 1935: *m* 1st, 1918 (*m diss* 1930), Dorothy Frances who *d* 1955, da da of Capt Sir George Everard Cayley, 9th Bt; 2ndly, 1930, Sybelle Winifred, who *d* 1963, da of Cyril Augustus Drummond (E Perth, colls):—
(By 2nd *m*) (Elizabeth) Belinda (New Farm House, Longdown, Marchwood, Hants), *b* 1932: *m* 1959 (*m diss* 1974), 3rd Baron Montagu of Beaulieu.

PREDECESSORS – **(1)** Francis Crossley, son of John Crossley, of Halifax, *b* 1817; MP for Halifax (*L*) 1852-9, and for the North-West Riding of Yorkshire 1859-72; *cr* a *Baronet* 1863: *m* 1845, Martha Eliza, who *d* 1891, da of Henry Brinton; *d* 1872; *s* by his only son **(2)** *Sir* Savile Brinton, GCVO, PC, 2nd Bt; *b* 1857; MP for N, or Lowestoft, Div of Suffolk (LU) 1885-92, and for Halifax 1900-1906; Paymaster-Gen 1902-5, and a Lord-in-Waiting to HM 1918-24; *cr Baron Somerleyton*, of Somerleyton, co Suffolk (peerage of United Kingdom) 1916: *m* 1887, Phyllis, CBE, yst da of Gen Sir Henry Percival de Bathe, KCB, 4th Bt; *d* 1935; *s* by his el son **(3)** Francis Savile, MC, 2nd Baron; *b* 1889; Major late 9th Lancers and a Director of John Crossley & Sons Ltd, of Halifax: *m* 1924, Bridget, MBE, who *d* 1983, da of William Douro Hoare, CBE, of Guessons, Welwyn, Herts; *d* 1959; *s* by his el son **(4)** Savile William Francis, 3rd Baron and present peer.

SOMERS, BARON (Cocks) (Baron GB 1784, Bt GB 1772)
(Title pronounced "Summers")

To be useful, rather than conspicuous

PHILIP SEBASTIAN SOMERS COCKS, 9th Baron, and 9th Baronet; *b* 4 Jan 1948; *s* 1995; *ed* Elston Hall, Newark, and Craig-y-Parc, Cardiff.

Arms – Quarterly; 1st and 4th sable, a chevron between three stags' attires argent, *Cocks*; 2nd and 3rd vert, a fesse dancettée ermine, *Somers*. **Crest** – On a mount vert, a stag lodged and reguardant argent, attired and hoofed sable. **Supporters** – Two lions, each gorged with a collar dancettée vert. *Address* – 19 Kempson Rd, SW6 4PX.

SISTERS LIVING (*Raised to the rank of a Baron's daughters* 1997)

Hon Anne (Anna) Gwenllian SOMERS COCKS, *b* 1950; *ed* St Anne's Coll, Oxford (MA), and Courtauld Inst, London Univ (MA); writer: *m* 1st, 1971 (*m diss* 1977), Martin Alan Walker; 2ndly, 1978 (*m diss* 1990), John Julian Savile Lee Hardy; 3rdly, 1991, Umberto Allemandi, and has issue living (by 2nd *m*), Maximilian John Lee, *b* 1980, — Katherine Isabella Eugenia, *b* 1982. *Residence* – San Defendente 52, Canale d'Alba, Piedmont, Italy.

Hon Frances Mary SOMERS COCKS, *b* 1953; *ed* Somerville Coll, Oxford (MA); teacher and writer; has issue living (by Stephen Bell), Abraham Alexander SOMERS COCKS, *b* 1995. *Residence* – 39 Rylett Rd, W12 9ST.

MOTHER LIVING

Marjorie Olive, da of late Arthur Julius Weller: *m* 1946, John Sebastian Somers Cocks, CVO, CBE, who *d* 1964. *Residence* – 19 Kempson Rd, SW6 4PX.

COLLATERAL BRANCHES LIVING

Grandchildren of late Rev Canon Philip John Cocks, 3rd son of late Rev Henry Bromley Cocks (infra):—

Issue of late Henry Bromley Cocks, *b* 1896, *d* 1967: *m* 1922, Edith Hazel, who *d* 1976, da of late F. H. Melville Walker, of Christchurch, NZ:—

ALAN BROMLEY (55 La Trobe St, Pakuranga, Auckland, NZ), *b* 28 May 1930: *m* 1955, Pamela Fay, da of A. H. Gourlay, of Christchurch, NZ, and has issue living, Martin Bromley (10 Clipper Place, Cockle Bay, Auckland, NZ), *b* 14 Sept 1957; *m* 1982, Carol Anne, da of A. L. White, of Auckland, NZ, and has issue living, Jonathan Bromley *b* 18 Aug 1985, Stephen Michael *b* 1987, — Lynette Marguerite, *b* 1960: *m* 1981, Kevin Mark Steadman, of PO Box 23, Renwick, Marlborough, NZ, and has issue living, Ryan David *b* 1990, Rachel Marguerite *b* 1993, — Gillian Fay, *b* 1962: *m* 1989, Christean Lenard Mitchell, of 3602 Flagstone Drive, Carrollton, Texas 75007, USA, and has issue living, Tyler Christean *b* 1994, Breanna Nicole *b* 1998, — Judith Grace Somers (4a Wood St, Papakura, Auckland, NZ) *b* 1973; *ed* Auckland Univ, NZ (BSc). —— Pamela Somers, *b* 1927; *ed* Canterbury Coll, NZ (MA): *m* 1968, Allan John Hall, LLB, of 6 Ann St, Gisborne, NZ, and has issue living, Veronica Ann, *b* 1970; *ed* Victoria Univ (BA, LLB), — Rosemary Megan, *b* 1972; *ed* Otago Univ (MB, ChB).

Issue of late John Reginald Cocks, *b* 1898, *d* 1973: *m* 1920, Mary Dillworth, who *d* 1973, da of late Charles Dilworth Fox, of Christchurch, NZ:—

John Alexander (RD, Turua, NZ), *b* 1921. —— Timothy Charles (3 Leal Place, Manly, Whangaparaoa 1463, NZ), *b* 1923: *m* 1949, June Alice, da of J. C. Fantham, and has issue living, Ross Basil SOMERS (RD1, Bruntwood, Cambridge, NZ), *b* 1951; assumed the surname of Somers in lieu of his patronymic 1993, and abandoned the forename of Basil: *m* 1972, Janice Evelyn, yst da of late Pat Russell, of Silverdale, and has issue living, Wayne Gregory *b* 1976, Michael Bryce *b* 1977, Joananna Karen *b* 1982, — Barry John SOMERS, (58 Citrus Av, Waihi Beach, Auckland, NZ), *b* 1954; assumed the surname of Somers in lieu of his patronymic 1993: *m* 1980, Raewyn Louisa, da of R. P. Gavin, of Tuakau, and has issue living, Philip Gavin *b* 1984, Ryan John *b* 1987, — Helen Julie, *b* 1958: *m* 1984, William Roy McCready, of Yarborough Station, RD1, Kohu Kohu, NZ, and has issue living, Richard James *b* 1987, Daniel Thomas *b* 1992, Carol Anne *b* 1985. —— Kathleen Mary, *b* 1922: *m* 1946, Archibald Stewart Gray, of 22 Hillcrest St, Tirau, Waikato, NZ, and has issue living, Peter Stewart (Parapara Rd, Tirau, Waikato, NZ), *b* 1946: *m* 1984, Mary Elizabeth, da of Robert Hyndman, of Hamilton, NZ, and has issue living, Simon Peter *b* 1988, Timothy Stephen *b* 1996, — Sidney Charles (103 Matai St, Te Anau, South Island, NZ), *b* 1948: *m* 1976, Susan Mary, 2nd da of Robin Sim, of Queenstown, NZ, and has issue living, Rebekah Susan *b* 1978, Catherine Amy *b* 1980, — Mary Kathleen, *b* 1949: *m* 1971, John Edward Bray, of PO Ahaura, West Coast, South Island, NZ, and has issue living, Rachael Janine *b* 1975, Helen Mary *b* 1977, Carissa Anne *b* 1979, — Barbara Elizabeth, *b* 1951: *m* 1974, Ian Goodall, of 48 Orakei Rd, Remuera, Auckland 5, NZ, and has issue living, Elizabeth Anne *b* 1976, Hilary Jean *b* 1978. —— Phoebe Somers (7B Waerenga Rd, Otaki, NZ), *b* 1925: *m* 1949, Roland Hunter, who *d* 1994, and has issue living, James Reginald (PO Box 53, Putaruru, NZ), *b* 1953: *m* 1975, Anna Margaret, only da of Michael Malanchak, of Lower Hutt and has had issue, James Michael Roland *b* and *d* 1977, David James Robert *b* 1979, Brian Benjamin *b* 1980, Roseanna Marie *b* 1985, — Roger Paul (RD Turua, NZ), *b* 1956: *m* 1984, Stephanie Gaye, yst da of Colin William Wallace, and has issue living, Donne Kirstin *b* 1997, — Ann Helen, *b* 1950: *m* 1st, 1970 (*m diss* 1987), Brian Edward Turner; 2ndly, 1987, Peter Terrance Spicer, of 208 Chapel St, Masterton, NZ, and has issue living (by 1st *m*), Pamela Ann *b* 1972, Melanie Rose *b* 1973, — Janet Clair, *b* 1951: *m* 1971, Randall John Papworth, of 115 Te Pene Av, Titahi Bay, NZ, and has issue living, Michael Randall *b* 1974 (has issue living, Mikayla Joy ROLTON *b* 1993), Suzanne Mary *b* 1971 (has issue living, Kisha Marijke LAVEN *b* 1992), Elizabeth Carol *b* 1972 (has issue living, Jaime Carol CALLENDAR *b* 1997), — Peggy Jane, *b* 1958: *m* 1977, Steven Daryl Mathie, of 2 Bermer Rd, Belmont, Lower Hutt, and has issue living, Bruce Thomas *b* 1981, Jennifer Louise *b* 1983.

Issue of late Ven Hubert Maurice Cocks, BD, *b* 1901, *d* 19—: *m* 1928, Mary, who *d* 1990, da of C. D. Matson of Fendalton, Christchurch, NZ:—

Rev Michael Dearden Somers (Robbs Rd, Whitecliffe, RD Coalgate, NZ), *b* 1928; *ed* Canterbury Coll, NZ (MA 1951), and Oxford (MA 1957); V of Hororata, Canterbury, NZ 1953-93, Chap W Sweden 1993-98: *m* 1st, 1958, Barbara Phyllis, el da of Hector Frank Allan, of Nelson, NZ; 2ndly, 1983, Gertrud Birgitta, yst da of Johan Axel Evald Svaren, of Sjösa, Sweden, and has issue living (by 1st *m*), Richard Martin, *b* 1966, — Charlotte Elizabeth, *b* 1959, — Andrea Jane, *b* 1961, — Stephanie Anne, *b* 1963. —— Jonathan Somers (113 Worcestor St, Ashhurst, Manawatu, NZ), *b* 1933: *m* 1st, 1962, Audrey Geraldine, who *d* 1987, da of Aubrey William Scott, of Burnham, NZ; 2ndly, 1991, Jennifer Marianne, da of William Rudd Pratt, of Apiti, NZ, and has issue living (by 1st *m*), Jeremy Andrew Somers (125 Oxford St, Ashhurst 5451, NZ), *b* 1964: *m* 1996, Angel Merle, da of Owen George Fox, of Palmerston North, NZ, — Jennifer Mary, *b* 1963.

Grandchildren of late Frederic Armine Cocks, 4th son of late Rev Henry Bromley Cocks, eldest son of Rev Henry Somers Cocks, only child of Hon Reginald Somers Cocks, 4th son of 1st Baron:—
Issue of late Douglas Edgar West Cocks, *b* 1901, *d* 1981: *m* 1925, Olive May, da of late Joseph Messines:—
Peter Douglas, *b* 1937: *m* 19—, Joan, da of John Brentnall Lees, of Christchurch, NZ, and has issue living, Paul Brentnall, *b* 1964: *m* 1989, Leanne Sutherland, and has issue living, Jake Peter *b* 1991, Sophie Rosalie Joan *b* 1994, — Sheryll Anne, *b* 1962. *Residence* – Adams Rd, RD6, W Melton, Christchurch, NZ. —— Patricia Somers, *b* 1928: *m* 1953, Walter Percival Ussher, and has issue living, Simon Walter, *b* 1956, — Julie Helen, *b* 1960: *m* 1983, Paul Raymond Quinn, of Boxhill North, Melbourne 3129, Australia, and has issue living, Jarrod Jeffrey *b* 1984, Alistair Paul *b* 1986, Bradley David *b* 1988. *Residence* – 6 Burrows Av, Karori, Wellington, NZ. —— Helen Marion (4 Roberta Drive, Spreydon, Christchurch 2, NZ), *b* 1930: *m* 1952 (*m diss* 1976), Kenneth William Barr, and has issue living, Deborah Jane, *b* 1956: *m* 19—, Stuart Stephenson, and has issue living, Dominic Robert *b* 1988, Simon Salvatore *b* 1990, Tobias Douglas Stuart *b* 1993, — Janine Patricia, *b* 1959: *m* 1988, Alistair James, and has issue living, Fergus Douglas *b* 1995, Emily Jessica *b* 1998, — Elizabeth Kate MESSINA, *b* 1962; assumed surname of MESSINA: *m* 1st, 1989 (*m diss* 1995), Beat Gasser; 2ndly, 1998, James Palmer.

Issue of late Armine Christopher Somers Cocks, *b* 1903, *d* 1989: *m* 1936, Ella (Flat 4, 83 Cranford St, Christchurch 1, NZ), da of J. Buzan:—
Robin Fraser (17 Ashbrook Lane, Lower Cashmere, Christchurch 2, NZ), *b* 1944: *m* 1969, Anita Josephine, da of K. A. J. Smith, of Christchurch, NZ, and has issue living, Rodney Somers, *b* 1969, — Calvin James, *b* 1972, — Penelope Jane, *b* 1974. —— Denis Somers (97 Mount Pleasant Rd, Mount Pleasant, Christchurch 8, NZ), *b* 1947; BA: *m* 1971, Allison Elspeth, da of late D. W. Cook, of Dacre, Southland, NZ, and has issue living, Bede Somers, *b* 1979, — Gretchen Emma, *b* 1976. —— Diane Beverley, *b* 1939: *m* 1962, Douglas Bernard Charles Williams, of 85 Breezes Rd, Christchurch 7, NZ, and has issue living, Shane Douglas, *b* 1962, — Brent Charles, *b* 1965. —— Juliet Elizabeth (7 Searells Rd, Wainoni, Christchurch 5, NZ), *b* 1940; NZRN: *m* 1964 (*m diss* 19—), Donald Martin Stirton, and has issue living, Rachel, *b* 1972, — Sally Somers *b* 1976.

Issue of late Charles John Somers Cocks, *b* 1904, *d* 1975: *m* 1932, Hazel, da of William Steel, of Christchurch, NZ:—
Geoffrey Somers (9 Rossall St, Christchurch, NZ), *b* 1934: *m* 1st, 1959, Madeline Mary, who *d* 1980, da of R. J. Coulter, of Ashburton, NZ; 2ndly, 1985, Sharon May Fountain, and has issue living (by 1st *m*), Richard Somers, *b* 1962, — Mark Somers, *b* 1967, — Elizabeth Mary, *b* 1968, — Charlotte Ann, *b* 1972. —— Ian Somers, *b* 1940; APANZ: *m* 1961, Beverley Claire, da of G. W. Kearney, of Christchurch, NZ, and has issue living, Tracey Jane, *b* 1962, — Sarah Hilary, *b* 1964. —— Sandra Christine, *b* 1944; *ed* Canterbury Univ, NZ (BA): *m* 1968, Thomas Desmond Keenan, MD, ChB, of 7 St Andrews Sq, Christchurch, NZ, and has issue living, Timothy James, *b* 1969, — Caroline Mary, *b* 1971, — Emily Jane, *b* 1974, — Anna Elizabeth, *b* 1976.

Issue of late Patrick Somers Cocks, *b* 1905, *d* 1994: *m* 1943, Evelyn May (20B Glenharrow Av, Avonhead, Christchurch 4, NZ), da of Lealand Bertram Iles:—
Barbara Mary, *b* 1944: *m* 1975, Graeme Clifford Wynn, of 3550 W 19th Av, Vancouver, BC, Canada, and has issue living, Jonathan Blakeley Somers, *b* 1984, — Louise Jane, *b* 1978. —— Yvonne Dawn (21050 Sitting Bull, Apple Valley, CA 92307, USA), *b* 1946: *m* 1967 (*m diss* 1983), — ...... Newton, and has issue living, John Patrick, *b* 1975, — Roxanne Leah, *b* 1972. —— Cynthia Joan, *b* 1950. —— Marion Elizabeth, *b* 1952: *m* 1st, 1970 (*m diss* 1978), Kenneth Michael Tate; 2ndly, 1979, Dennis Erwyn Young, of 23 Meadowville Av, Spreydon, Christchurch, NZ, and has issue living, (by 1st *m*) Rachael Marion, *b* 1971, — (by 2nd *m*) Heather Jane, *b* 1980.

Grandson of late Rev Henry Bromley Cocks (ante):—
Issue of late Charles Richard Cocks, *b* 1877, *d* 1944: *m* 1926, Fanny, da of S. E. Hubbard, of Dunedin, New Zealand:—
Charles Bromley, *b* 1928; *ed* Canterbury Coll, New Zealand (LLB 1956).

PREDECESSORS – (1) CHARLES Cocks, MP for Reigate; *cr* a *Baronet* 1772, and *Baron Somers*, of Evesham, co Worcester (peerage of Great Britain) 1784; *d* 1806; *s* by his son (2) JOHN SOMERS, 2nd Baron; MP for Grampound, Lord-Lieut of Herefordshire, and Recorder of Gloucester; *cr Viscount Eastnor* and *Earl Somers* (peerage of United Kingdom) 1821; *d* 1841; *s* by his son (3) JOHN SOMERS, 2nd Earl; *b* 1788; was Lord-Lieut of Herefordshire, and Col Hereford Militia: assumed the additional surname of Somers by Roy licence 1841; *d* 1852; *s* by his son (4) CHARLES SOMERS, 3rd Earl; *b* 1819; sat as MP for Reigate (C) 1852-7: *m* 1850, Virginia, who *d* 1910, da of late James Pattle, BCS; *d* 1883, when the viscountcy and earldom became extinct and the barony devolved upon his kinsman (5) PHILIP REGINALD Cocks, 5th Baron (son of late Lieut-Col Hon Philip James Cocks, MP, 3rd son of 1st Baron), *b* 1815: *m* 1859, Camilla, who *d* 1904, da of late Rev William Newton, V of Old Cleeve, Somerset; *d* 1899; *s* by his grand-nephew (6) ARTHUR HERBERT TENNYSON, KCMG, DSO, MC (son of late Herbert Haldane Somers Cocks, a descendant of 3rd son of 1st Baron), 6th Baron; *b* 1887; Lieut-Col late 1st Life Guards; was a Lord-in-Waiting to HM King George V 1924-6, and Gov of Victoria, Australia 1926-31; Ch Scout of United Kingdom and the British Commonwealth 1941-4; European War 1914-19 (MC, DSO): *m* 1921, (Daisy) Finola, CBE, who *d* 1981, da of late Capt Bertram Meeking; *d* 1944; *s* by his uncle (7) ARTHUR PERCY SOMERS (4th son of late Arthur Herbert Cocks, CB, brother of 5th Baron), 7th Baron; *b* 1864; European War 1915-17 with Canadian Forces: *m* 1896, Benita, who *d* 1950, da of late Major Luther Sabin, of USA; *d* 1953; *s* by his son (8) JOHN PATRICK SOMERS, 8th Baron, *b* 1907; Prof Royal Coll of Music, Dir of Music, Epsom Coll: *m* 1st, 1935, Barbara Marianne, who *d* 1959, da of Charles Henry Southall, of Norwich; 2ndly, 1961, Dora Helen, who *d* 1993, da of late John Mountfort; *d* 1995; *s* by his kinsman (9) PHILIP SEBASTIAN SOMERS (son of late John Sebastian Somers Cocks, CVO, CBE, son of late Philip Alphonso Somers Cocks, CMG, son of late Hon John James Thomas Somers Cocks, brother of 5th Baron), 9th Baron and present peer.

*John Somers, Lord Chancellor 1697-1700, *cr Baron Somers*, of Evesham 1697, and *d* 1716 when his title became ext. His sister and co-heir, Mary, *m* Charles Cocks, of Worcester, by whom she was mother of John Cocks, father of 1st Baron, of second creation (ante).

SOMERSET, DUKE OF (Seymour) (Duke E 1547, Bt E 1611)

FOY · POVR · DEVOIR

Faith for duty

JOHN MICHAEL EDWARD SEYMOUR, 19th Duke and 17th Baronet; *b* 30 Dec 1952; *s* 1984; *ed* Eton; DL Wilts 1993 FRICS; patron of two livings: *m* 1978, Judith-Rose, elder da of John Hull, of 33 Edwardes Sq, W8, and has issue.

Arms – Quarterly: 1st and 4th or, on a pile gules, between six fleurs-de-lis azure, three lions of England; 2nd and 3rd gules, two wings conjoined in lure or, *Seymour*. **Crest** – Out of a ducal coronet or, a demi-phoenix in flames proper. **Supporters** – *Dexter* a unicorn argent, armed, unguled, and crined, or, gorged with a ducal coronet, per pale azure and gold, and chained of the last; *sinister*, a bull azure, armed, unguled, ducally gorged and chained, or.
Seats – Maiden Bradley, Warminster, Wilts; Berry Pomeroy, Totnes, S Devon.

SONS LIVING

SEBASTIAN EDWARD (*Lord Seymour*), *b* 3 Feb 1982.
Lord Charles Thomas George, *b* 1992.

DAUGHTERS LIVING

Lady Sophia Rose, *b* 1987.
Lady Henrietta Charlotte, *b* 1989.

BROTHER LIVING

Lord Francis Charles Edward, *b* 1956; *ed* Eton; solicitor: *m* 1982, Patricia (Paddy), da of Col Anthony John Irvine Poynder, MC, RE, of Gassons, Slindon, Sussex, and has issue living, Webb Edward Percy, *b* 1990, — Poppy Hermione Alexandra, *b* 1988, — Leonora Hermione Jane, *b* 1995, — Hermione Anne Tara, *b* 1997. *Residences* – Tollard House, Tollard Royal, Salisbury, Wilts SP5 5PP; 27 Palliser Rd, W14.

SISTER LIVING

Lady Anne Frances Mary, *b* 1954.

AUNT LIVING (*Daughter of 17th Duke*)

Lady Susan Mary, *b* 1913; late Divisional Pres British Red Cross So, Warminster. *Residence* – Sunnyside, Maiden Bradley, Wilts.

WIDOW LIVING OF EIGHTEENTH DUKE

GWENDOLINE COLLETTE (JANE) (*Jane, Duchess of Somerset*), da of late Maj John Cyril Collette Thomas, N Staffordshire Regt, of Burn Cottage, Bude, Cornwall: *m* 1951, Maj the 18th Duke of Somerset, who *d* 1984. *Residence* – Maiden Bradley, Warminster, Wilts.

COLLATERAL BRANCHES LIVING

Descendants of late Rt Hon Francis Seymour-Conway (4th son of Hon Sir Edward Seymour, 4th Bt, grandfather of 8th Duke), who was *cr Baron Conway of Ragley* 1703 (*see* M Hertford).

PREDECESSORS – **(1)** Sir EDWARD Seymour, KG, KB, PC, el surv son of Sir John Seymour of Wolf Hall, Wilts (by Marjorie, da of Sir Henry Wentworth, KB, of Nettlestead, Suffolk, a descendant of Edward III) and brother of Queen Jane Seymour; *b* c 1500: *m* 1st, c 1527, Katherine (whom he repudiated and who probably *d* before 1535), da and co-heir of Sir William Fillol, of Woodlands, Dorset; 2ndly, c 1535, Anne (who *d* 1582, having *m* 2ndly, Francis Newdegate), da of Sir Edward Stanhope, of Rampton Notts; *cr Viscount Beauchamp* (peerage of England), with remainder to heirs male of his body *hereafter to be begotten*, 1536, and *Earl of Hertford* (peerage of England) with remainder to his issue male by his present or any future wife 1537, *Baron Seymour* and *Duke of Somerset* (peerage of England) with a special remainder to his issue male by his 2nd wife, failing which to his male descendants by his 1st and any other wife 1547; Protector of the Realm to his nephew Edward VI 1547-1549; found guilty of felony 1 Dec 1551, and executed on Tower Hill, 22 Jan 1552; attainted 12 April 1552, by Act of Parliament, and all his honours forfeited. His el surv son by his 2nd wife **(2)** Sir EDWARD, KB; *b* 1539; *cr Baron Beauchamp* and *Earl of Hertford* (peerage of England) 1559; Ambassador to Brussels 1605: *m* 1st (secretly) 1560, Lady Katherine (sister of Lady Jane Grey), da of Henry Grey, Duke of Suffolk; on discovery of this marriage he was fined £15,000 (later remitted to £3,000) "for seducing a virgin of the blood royal" and he and his wife imprisoned in the Tower; the *m* was pronounced invalid 1561, but validity was established in 1606; she *d* 1568 in captivity at Cockfield Hall, Suffolk; he *m* 2ndly c 1595, Frances Howard, who *d* 1598, da of 1st Lord Howard of Effingham; 3rdly, 1601, Frances Howard (who *d* 1639, having *m* 3rdly Ludovic Stuart, 1st Duke of Richmond), da of 1st Viscount Howard of Bindon, and widow of Henry Pranell; *d* 1621; *s* by his grandson (3) WILLIAM, KG, KB, PC (2nd but eventually el son and heir of Edward Lord Beauchamp, who *d* 1612, el son of 1st Earl by 1st wife) 2nd Earl; *b* 1587; bore King Edward's staff at Coronation of Charles I 1626; Gov of Prince of Wales (Charles II) 1641-43; Royalist Lt-Gen of South-West and S Wales 1642-43; restored to Barony of Seymour and Dukedom of Somerset 1660: *m* 1st (secretly) 1610, Lady Arabella Stuart, da and heir of 5th Earl of Lennox and 1st cousin of James I, for which they were both imprisoned in the Tower, where she *dsp* 1615; 2ndly, 1617, Lady Frances Devereux, who *d* 1674, sister and co-heir of 3rd Earl of Essex: *d* 1660; *s* by his grandson (4) WILLIAM, 3rd Duke (son and heir of Henry, Lord Beauchamp); *b* 1652; *d* unm 1671; *s* by his uncle (5) JOHN, 4th Duke, *b* 1629; *m* 1661, Sarah (who *d* 1692, having *m* 3rdly, 1682, 2nd Baron Coleraine) da and co-heir of Sir Edward Alston, MD, and widow of George Grimston; *d* 1675, when the Marquessate of Hertford became ext and his estates passed to his niece Elizabeth (sister of 3rd Duke) who *m* 1676 the 2nd Earl of Ailesbury; *s* by his kinsman (6) FRANCIS (3rd Baron Seymour of Trowbridge) 5th Duke (son of Charles 2nd Baron, son of Francis 1st Baron (*cr* 1641), yr brother of 2nd Duke) *b* 1658; *d* 1678, having been shot at the door of his inn at Lerice, Italy, by Horatio Botti, a Genoese nobleman, who alleged his wife had been insulted by the Duke's companions; *s* by his brother (7) CHARLES, KG, 6th Duke ("The Proud Duke") *b* 1662; Master of the Horse 1702-12 and 1714-15; *m* 1st, 1682, Lady Elizabeth Percy (Mistress of the Robes to Queen Anne), who *d* 1722, da and heir of 11th Earl of Northumberland and widow of Henry Cavendish, Earl of Ogle, and Thomas Thynne of Longleat; 2ndly, 1726, Lady Charlotte Finch, who *d* 1773, da of 7th Earl of Winchilsea and 2nd Earl of Nottingham; *d* 1748; *s* by his son (8) ALGERNON, 7th Duke; *b* 1684; summoned to Parliament as *Lord Percy* 1722 under the erroneous belief that this Barony had been vested in his mother, and took his seat, by which the Barony of Percy was *cr* by writ; *cr Baron Warkworth*, of Warkworth Castle, co Northumberland, and *Earl of Northumberland* (peerage of Great Britain) 1749, with remainder to his son-in-law, Sir Hugh Smithson, and *Baron Cockermouth*, of Cockermouth Castle, and *Earl of Egremont*, with remainder to his nephews, Sir Charles Wyndham, Bt, and Percy O'Brien (who was afterwards *cr* Earl of Thomond); *m* 1715, Frances, who *d* 1754, da of Hon Henry Thynne, son of 1st Viscount Weymouth; *d* 1750, when the Earldom of Hertford, and the Baronies of Beauchamp and Seymour of Trowbridge expired, the Barony of Warkworth and Earldom of Northumberland devolved upon his son-in-law Sir Hugh Smithson, the Barony of Cockermouth and Earldom of Egremont reverted to his nephew Sir Charles Wyndham, the Barony of Percy (*cr* 1722), passed to his da Lady Elizabeth, wife of Sir Hugh Smithson (ante), and the Barony of Seymour and Dukedom of Somerset descended to the heir male of the 1st Duke by his 1st *m* (9) EDWARD, 8th Duke, who had previously *s* as 6th Bt (see * infra); *b* 1695; MP for Salisbury 1741; *m* 1717, Mary, who *d* 1768, da and heir of Daniel Webb of Malksham, Wilts; *d* 1757; *s* by his el son (10) EDWARD, 9th Duke; *b* 1718, *d* unm 1792; *s* by his brother (11) WEBB, 10th Duke; *b* 1718: *m* 1769, Anna Marie, who *d* 1802, da and heir of John Bonnell; *d* 1793; *s* by his son (12) EDWARD ADOLPHUS, 11th Duke; *b* 1775: *m* 1800, Lady Charlotte Douglas-Hamilton, da of 9th Duke of Hamilton and Brandon; *d* 1855; *s* by his son (13) EDWARD ADOLPHUS, KG, 12th Duke, *b* 1804; MP for Totnes (L) 1834-55; First Lord of the Admiralty 1859-66; *cr Earl of St Maur* (peerge of UK) 1863; *d* 1885, when the Earldom of St Maur became extinct, and the Dukedom of Somerset and Barony of Seymour passed to his brother (14) ARCHIBALD HENRY ALGERNON, 13th Duke, *b* 1810; *d* 1891; *s* by his brother (15) ALGERNON PERCY BANKS, 14th Duke, *b* 1813: *m* 1845, Horatia Isabella Harriet, who *d* 1915, da of John Philip Morier, HM Min at Dresden; *d* 1894; *s* by his el son (16) ALGERNON, 15th Duke *b* 1846; bore the Orb at Coronations of King Edward VII and King George V: *m* 1877, Susan Margaret, who *d* 1936, yr da of Charles Mackinnon; *d* 1923; *s* by his cousin (17) EDWARD HAMILTON, KBE, CB, CMG (son of late Rev Francis Payne Seymour), 16th Duke, *b* 1860; Brig-Gen; in March 1925 he established before the Cttee for Privileges of the House of Lords his right to the Dukedom as grandson of Capt Francis Edward Seymour, RN, el son of Col Francis Compton Seymour (grandson of 8th Duke), who *m* 1787, Leonora, widow of John Hudson (who *d* 1786 in Calcutta): *m* 1881, Rowena, who *d* 1950, da of George Wall, of Colombo; *d* 1931; *s* by his son (18) EVELYN FRANCIS EDWARD, DSO, OBE, 17th Duke, *b* 1882; Lt-Col (ret) R Dublin Fusiliers and Devonshire Regt, Col Gen Staff, and Lord-Lieut for Wilts; S Africa 1901-02 (Queen's medal with five clasps), 1914-18 War (despatches, DSO, OBE); bore the Sceptre at Coronation of King George VI: *m* 1906, Edith Mary, who *d* 1962, only child of W. Parker, JP, of Whittington Hall, Derbyshire; *d* 1954; *s* by his only son (19) PERCY HAMILTON, 18th Duke, *b* 1910; Maj Wilts Regt, DL and Pres British Legion for Wilts: *m* 1951, Gwendoline Collette (Jane), da of late Maj John Cyril Collette Thomas, N Staffordshire Regt, of Burn Cottage, Bude, Cornwall; *d* 1984; *s* by his elder son (20) JOHN MICHAEL EDWARD, 19th Duke and present peer; also Baron Seymour.

*(1) EDWARD Seymour, MP for Devon (el son of Sir Edward Seymour, who was el son of 1st Duke of Somerset by his 1st *m*); *cr a Baronet* 1611; *d* 1613; *s* by his son (2) *Sir* EDWARD, KB, 2nd Bt; was MP for Devon; *d* 1659; *s* by his son (3) EDWARD 3rd Bt; sat as MP for Devon; *d* 1688; *s* by his son (4) *Sir* EDWARD, PC; promoted the impeachment of Lord Clarendon, and was Speaker of the Long Parliament, *d* 1708; *s* by his son (5) *Sir* EDWARD, 5th Bt; *d* 1741; *s* by his son (6) *Sir* EDWARD, 6th Bt, who *s* as 8th Duke of Somerset (ante).

Somerset, family name of Duke of Beaufort.

Somerset, family name of Baron Raglan.

Somerton, Viscount; son of Earl of Normanton.

Somerton, Baron; title of Earl of Normanton on Roll HL.

SONDES, EARLDOM (Milles-Lade) (Extinct 1996)

WIDOW LIVING OF FIFTH EARL

PHYLLIS (*Countess Sondes*), da of Martin Kane, of USA, and widow of Robert J. Schmertz; Patron Friends of Lees Court, Hyperbaric Oxygen Trust, and Specialised Oncology Nurse Grants; Pres Sheldwich Cricket Club; Dir Qualified Cancer Care Ltd; Ptnr Gosmere Farms Ptnrship; and Council Memb The Game Conservancy Trust: *m* 1986, as his 4th wife, the 5th Earl Sondes, who *d* 1996, when the title became extinct. *Residence* – Stringman's Farm, Badlesmere, Faversham, Kent ME13 0LA.

NOTE

The Barony as well as the Earldom became extinct on the death of the 5th Earl. The younger sons of the 1st Baron, viz Henry WATSON (*b* 1755, *d* 1833), Charles WATSON (*b* 1761, *d* 1769), and George WATSON (*b* 1768, *d* 1824), all died without leaving issue.

SOPER, BARONY OF (Soper) (Extinct 1998)

DAUGHTERS LIVING OF LIFE BARON

Hon Ann Loveday Dean, *b* 1931; BSc: *m* 1952 (*m diss* 1979), Prof Gabriel Horn, MD, and has issue living, 2 sons and 2 da. *Residence* – 54 St Barnabas Rd, Cambridge.

Hon Bridget Mary Dean, *b* 1933: *m* 1956, Owen H. Kemmis, MA (*dec*), and has issue living, one son. *Residence* – Garden Flat, 30 Parliament Hill, NW3 2TN.

Hon Judith Catharine Dean, *b* 1942; BSc: *m* 1970, Alan Jenkins, BEd, and has issue living, one son and one da. *Residence* – 12 Brookland Hill, NW11.

Hon Caroline Susan Dean, *b* 1946; BA: *m* 1975, Terence Blacker, MA, el son of Gen Sir Cecil Hugh Blacker, KCB, OBE, MC, and has issue living (*see* Buxton, Bt, colls). *Residence* – 91 Wendell Rd, W12.

SORENSEN, BARONY OF (Sorensen) (Extinct 1971)

DAUGHTER LIVING OF LIFE BARON

Hon Moira Muriel, *b* 1917: *m* 1951, Derek Gerald Clark, JP, of 15 Crossing Rd, Epping, Essex, CM16 7BQ, and has issue.

Jennifer (37 Nassington Rd, NW3), da of Alan Adams, of Stocksfield, Newcastle-upon-Tyne: *m* 1960, Hon Michael Malcolm Reginald Sorensen, who *d* 1978.

Soskice, surname of Barony of Stow Hill.

SOULBURY, VISCOUNT (Ramsbotham) (Viscount UK 1954)

JAMES HERWALD RAMSBOTHAM, 2nd Viscount; 21 March 1915; *s* 1971; *ed* Eton, and Magdalen Coll, Oxford: *m* 1949, Anthea Margaret, who *d* 1950, da of late David Wilton.

Not by force but by virtue

Arms – Sable on a chevron or between three plates each charged with a cross pattée gules a ram's head erased of the field. **Crest** – A plate charged with a ram's head erased per pale gules and sable. **Supporters** – On either side a raven proper charged with a plate thereon a cross pattée gules.
Address – c/o House of Lords, SW1.

BROTHER LIVING

Hon Sir PETER EDWARD, GCMG, GCVO, DL, *b* 8 Oct 1919; *ed* Eton, and Magdalen Coll, Oxford; NW Europe 1944-45 as Lt-Col Intelligence Corps (despatches, Croix de Guerre with palm); a Member of HM Diplo Ser; British High Commr in Cyprus 1969-71, Ambassador to Iran 1971-73, and Ambassador to USA 1974-77; Gov and C-in-C Bermuda 1977-80; CMG 1964, KCMG 1972, GCVO 1976, GCMG 1977: *m* 1st, 1941, Frances Marie, who *d* 1982, da of Hugh Massie Blomfield; 2ndly 1985, Dr Zaida Mary Hall, previously wife of late Ruthven Hall, and has issue living (by 1st *m*), Oliver Peter (11 Silverless St, Marlborough), *b* 1943: *m* 1965, Meredith Anne, only da of Brian Jones, of The White House, Easton Royal, Pewsey, Wilts, and has issue living, Edward Herwald *b* 1966, Benedict *b* 1967, Alexander *b* 1969, — Simon Edward (36 Bensham Lane, Croydon), *b* 1949: *m* 1976, Sandra Cayley, and has issue living, David Peter *b* 1981, Elizabeth Sarah *b* 1978, Allison Frances *b* 1983, — Mary Frances, *b* 1945: *m* 1st, 1981, Charles Gray, who *d* 1982; 2ndly, 1993, Christopher John Courtenay Coulston, of 84 St Edward's Rd, Gosport, Hants, and *dsp* 1994. *Residence* – East Lane, Ovington, Alresford, Hants SO24 0RA.

SISTER LIVING

Hon Joan Eleanor, *b* 1917: *m* 1950, Major Robert Hardress Standish O'Grady, MC, Irish Guards, and has issue living, Jeremy Robert (32 Addison Av, W11 4QR), *b* 1953, — Jane Elizabeth (The Cottage, 141 St Mark's Rd, W10), *b* 1952, — Selina Joan (The Cottage, 141 St Mark's Rd, W10), *b* 1956. *Residences* – 32 Addison Av, Holland Park, W11; Midford Place, Midford, Bath, Avon.

PREDECESSORS – **(1)** *Rt Hon Sir* HERWALD Ramsbotham, GCMG, GCVO, OBE, MC, son of Herwald Ramsbotham, JP, of London; *b* 1887; Min of Pensions 1936-39, 1st Commr of Works 1939-40, Pres of Board of Education 1940-41, Chm of Assistance Board 1941-48, and Gov-Gen of Ceylon 1949-54; MP for Lancaster (*C*) 1929-41; *cr Baron Soulbury*, of Soulbury, co Buckingham (peerage of UK) 1941, and *Viscount Soulbury*, of Soulbury, co Buckingham (peerage of UK) 1954; *m* 1st, 1911, Doris Violet, CStJ, who *d* 1954, da of Sinauer de Stein; 2ndly, 1962, Ursula, who *d* 1964, da of late Amand Jerome, and widow of Frederick Wakeham; *d* 1971; *s* by his el son **(2)** JAMES HERWALD, 2nd Viscount and present peer; also Baron Soulbury.

SOULSBY OF SWAFFHAM PRIOR, BARON (Soulsby) (Life Baron 1990)

ERNEST JACKSON LAWSON SOULSBY, son of William George Lawson Soulsby; *b* 23 June 1926; *ed* Queen Elizabeth Gram Sch, Penrith, and Edinburgh Univ; MRCVS, DVSM, PhD, MA (Cantab), Fellow Wolfson Coll, Camb; Veterinary Officer City of Edinburgh 1949-52, Lecturer in Clinical Parasitology Bristol Univ 1952-54, and Animal Pathology Camb Univ 1954-63, Prof of Parasitology Pennsylvania Univ 1964-78, since when Prof of Animal Pathology Camb Univ; Pres Royal Coll of Veterinary Surgeons 1984, Sr Vice-Pres 1985; Ford Foundn Visiting Prof at Ibadan Univ 1964, Richard Merton Guest Prof at Justus Liebig Univ 1974-75; Expert Advisor and Consultant for many Scientific Groups and Organisations; lecturer and contributor to learned journals; Hon AM 1972, Hon DSc (Pennsylvania Univ 1984), Hon DVSM (Edinburgh 1991); R. N. Chaudhury Gold Medal, Calcutta Sch of Tropical Medicine, 1976, Behring-Bilharz Prize, Cairo 1977, Ludwig-Schunk Prize, Justus Liebig Univ 1979, etc; *cr Baron Soulsby of Swaffham Prior*, of Swaffham Prior, co Cambs (Life Baron) 1990: *m* 1962, Georgina Elizabeth Annette, da of John Whitmore Williams, of Cambridge, and has issue.

Residence – Old Barn House, Swaffham Prior, Cambs CB5 0LD. *Clubs* – Farmers', and United Oxford & Cambridge University.

SON LIVING

Hon John Angus Lawson, *b* 1954.

DAUGHTER LIVING

Hon Katrina Yvonne, *b* 1950: *m* 19—, — Bulloch.

Souter, family name of Baron Audley.

SOUTHAMPTON, BARON (FitzRoy) (Baron GB 1780)

The ornament and recompense of virtue

(CHARLES) JAMES FITZROY, 6th Baron; *b* 12 Aug 1928; *s* 1989; *ed* Stowe; Master of Easton Harriers 1968-69 and 1970-71, and of Blankney Foxhounds 1971-72: *m* 1st, 1951, Pamela Anne, who *d* 1997, da of late Edward Percy Henniker, of Clematis, Yelverton, S Devon; 2ndly, 1997, Mrs Alma Slater (*née* Pasqual), of Tarlac, nr Manila, formerly wife of Bryan Slater, and has had issue by 1st and 2nd *m*.

𝔄rms – Quarterly: 1st and 4th, France and England quarterly; 2nd, Scotland; 3rd, Ireland; the whole debruised by a baton sinister compony argent and azure, and with a crescent for difference. ℭrest – On a chapeau gules, turned up ermine, a lion statant guardant or, ducally crowned azure, and gorged with a collar counter compony argent and azure. 𝔖upporters – *Dexter*, a lion guardant or, ducally crowned azure, gorged with a collar compony argent and blue; *sinister*, a greyhound argent gorged as the dexter.
Residence – Stone Cross, Chagford, Newton Abbot, Devon.

SONS LIVING AND DECEASED (By 1st marriage)

†Charles, *b* 1954; *ed* Gresham's Sch, Holt: *m* 1975, Joanna Dana (who *m* 2ndly, 1977, Paul Farrant), da of late Chandos Robert Henry Brudenell-Bruce (*see* M Ailesbury, colls), and was *k* in a motor accident (Oct) 1975, *sp*.

Hon EDWARD CHARLES, *b* 8 July 1955; *ed* Gresham's Sch, Holt, and RAC Cirencester: *m* 1978, Rachel Caroline Vincent, 2nd da of Peter John Curnow Millett, of West Underdown, Drewsteignton, Devon, and has issue living, Charles Edward Millett, *b* 18 Jan 1983, — Fiona Joan Margaret, *b* 1979, — Sarah Barbara Sibell, *b* 1981, — Julia Rachel Caroline, *b* 1984.
Residence – Venn Farm, Morchard Bishop, Crediton, Devon EX17 6SQ.

(By 2nd marriage)

Hon Charles James, *b* 1998.

DAUGHTER LIVING *(By 1st marriage)*

Hon Geraldine Anne, *b* 1951: *m* 1st, 1969 (*m diss* 19—), Gavin Prescott; 2ndly, 1977, Richard G. Fuller, and has issue living (by 2nd *m*), Joshua FitzRoy, *b* 1978, — Oliver, *b* 1981, — Victoria, *b* 1983. *Residence* – Strete House, Strete, Whimple, nr Exeter, Devon.

COLLATERAL BRANCHES LIVING

Descendants of late Capt Rt Hon Edward Algernon FitzRoy, MP (Speaker of House of Commons 1928-43), 2nd son of 3rd Baron, *b* 1869, *d* 1943: *m* 1891, Muriel, CBE, da of late Lieut-Col Hon Archibald Charles Henry Douglas-Pennant (*see* B Penrhyn, colls), who was *cr* Viscountess Daventry 1943 (see that title).

Grandchildren of late Capt Frederick Henry FitzRoy, RD, RNR, 3rd son of late Maj-Gen William FitzRoy, eldest son of late William Simon Haughton FitzRoy (infra):—
Issue of late Capt William Wentworth STEWART-FITZROY, RN, *b* 1907, *d* 1998; assumed by deed poll 1958 the additional surname of Stewart before his patronymic for himself and for his issue: *m* 1st, 1934, Margaret Patricia, who *d* 1984, da of late Douglas Stewart Grant, of New York, USA; 2ndly, 1988, Evelyn (407 Russell Av, Apt 413, Gaithersburg, Maryland 20877, USA), da of late James Wallace Nichol, of Washington, DC, and widow of Col John Fogg Twombly III, US Army:—
(By 1st *m*) Allan Wentworth (12 St George's Av, Warblington, Havant, Hants), *b* 1935; *ed* Nautical Coll, Pangbourne, and RNC Dartmouth; Cmdr RN: *m* 1960, Susan Elizabeth, da of late Capt Horace Gerald Southwood, CBE, DSC, RN, and has issue living, Louise, *b* 1962: *m* 1988, Col Michael John Stone, late Duke of Wellington's Regt, and has issue living, Maxallan Arthur John, *b* 1994, Alexandra Susan Joy *b* 1990, — Jane, *b* 1964: *m* 1987, Rupert John Eastell, and has issue living, Tom Jonathan *b* 1992, Georgina Jane *b* 1994, — Helen, *b* 1967: *m* 1997, Jonathan Poley. —— Douglas James Fitzflaad (51 Brondesbury Villas, Kilburn, NW6 6AJ), *b* 1943; *ed* Epsom Coll. —— Roderick Charles FITZROY (14 Maritime St, Leith, Edinburgh EH6 6SB), *b* 1947; *ed* Sherborne; late Intelligence Corps; relinquished the surname of Stewart by deed poll 1976: *m* 1st, 1972 (*m diss* 19—), Susan Mary, da of H. C. Ruse, of Arbroath; 2ndly, 1995, Linda Jane Breckenridge, of Oban, Argyll, and has issue living (by 1st *m*), James, *b* 1973, — Amanda Jane, *b* 1976. —— Anne Patricia (135 E 50th St, New York, NY 10022, USA), *b* 1936; MBA, CPA.

Grandson of late Capt George Dartmouth FitzRoy, 2nd son of late William Simon Haughton FitzRoy (infra):—
Issue of late Gordon Duncan Seymour FitzRoy, *b* 1868, *d* 1936: *m* 1st, 1891, Marie E., who *d* 1894, widow of Howell Turner, MD, of Norwich; 2ndly, 189—, N. Adalia Leasure, of Arkansas City, Kansas, USA:—
(By 2nd *m*) Francis George, *b* 1903.

Grandchildren of late Ferdinand Trevor FitzRoy (infra):—
Issue of late Eric Hamilton FitzRoy, *b* 1906, *d* 1987: *m* 1938, Grace Perrier, who *d* 1989:—
Helen Eugene, *b* 1942: *m* 1965, John Henry Hemphill, of 16 Cameron Av, Artarmon, NSW 2064, Australia, and has issue living, Michael John, *b* 1968: *m* 1996, Amy Caroline Tucker, — Robert Eric, *b* 1969: *m* 1999, Christine Elizabeth McKenna, — Peter Douglas, *b* 1976.

Issue of late Herbert Crommelin FitzRoy, OAM, *b* 1907, *d* 1987: *m* 1932, Dorothy Muriel Broad, who *d* 1988:—
John Trevor Hill (5/29 Pine St, East Brighton, Vic 3187, Australia), *b* 1932: *m* 1959, Aileen Gertrude Cushing, and has issue living, Paul John (82 Queen St, Bayswater, W Australia 6053), *b* 1961: *m* 1996, Christine Catherine O'Hara, and has issue living, Ella Rose *b* 1998, — Andrew John, *b* 1965, — Nicholas John, *b* 1968, — Kathryn Mary, *b* 1960: *m* 1988, Dale Malcolm Smart, and has issue living, Rachelle Alexandra *b* 1990, Rebecca Courtney *b* 1992, — Elizabeth Mary, *b* 1962: *m* 1996, Martin Daniel Kjendle, and has issue living, Maia Eliza FitzRoy *b* 1998, — Virginia Mary, *b* 1966: *m* 1994, Peter Anthony Wilkins, and has issue living, Oliver Harrison *b* 1995, Alexandra Georgia *b* 1993, Chloe Eliza *b* 1997. —— Peter Trevor (54 Barkley Av, Armadale, Vic 3143, Australia), *b* 1936: *m* 1966 (*m diss* 19—), Barbara Ann Gnall, and has issue living, Jill Elizabeth, *b* 1967, — Christine Brooke, *b* 1975. —— David Hamilton (530 Johnson's Creek Rd, Alexandra, Vic 3714, Australia), *b* 1938: *m* 1959, Margaret Joyce Morris, and has issue living, Mark David, *b* 1959, — Timothy Morris, *b* 1970: *m* 1994, Danielle Kerry Maddaford, and has issue living, Darcy Foden *b* 1998, — Robyn Anne, *b* 1961; has issue living (by Shane Patrick McCarthy), Samantha Joy *b* 1990, — Lee Susan, *b* 1963, — Donna Vivian, *b* 1967: *m* 1993, Neil William Hibberd, and has issue living, Jackson William *b* 1998.

Grandchildren of late Lt-Col Ferdinand FitzRoy, RA, of The Lea, Hobart, Tasmania, 3rd son of late William Simon Haughton FitzRoy, eldest son of late Lt-Gen Hon William FitzRoy, 7th son of 1st Baron:—
Issue of late Ferdinand Trevor FitzRoy, *b* 1857, *d* 1928: *m* 1902, Maud Harvey Hamilton, who *d* 1947:—
Kathleen Mary, *b* 1904: *m* 1930, Geoffrey Cheverton Wyatt, who *d* 1964, and *d* 1989, having had issue, Anthony Trevor, *b* and *d* 1935, — Judith Ann, *b* 1933: *m* 1956, Ian Edmond Nicholson, of Binowee, Goobragandra Rd, via Tumut, NSW 2720, Australia, and has issue living, Mark Roger *b* 1960: *m* 1988, Alice Eddy Hill (and has issue living Alasdair Wyatt Hill *b* 1993, Hamish McNiece Hill *b* 1997), Jillian Ann *b* 1958: *m* 1984, Beverley de Bussy McGeoch (and has issue living, Angus Nicholson *b* 1993, Samantha de Bussy *b* 1988), Penelope Jane *b* 1964: *m* 1996, Stephen Geoffrey Edwin McLeish, Bridget Wyatt *b* 1966. —— Lorraine Elizabeth, *b* 1911: *m* 1937, Denis Steele Wyatt, who *d* 1975, and has issue living, Andrew Trevor (No 6 Johnson St, Horsham, Vic 3400, Australia), *b* 1940: *m* 1967 (*m diss* 19—), Diane Joy Frances, and has issue living, Richard Cheverton *b* 1969, Elizabeth Kathleen *b* 1971, Julia Clare *b* 1973, — Heather Elaine (now known as Hannah MORROW), *b* 1944; changed her name by deed poll 1994: *m* 1974, David Sherlock, and has issue living, Emma *b* 1975, Jessica *b* 1980.

PREDECESSORS – **(1)** *Lieut-Gen* CHARLES FitzRoy, 2nd son of Lord Augustus FitzRoy (D Grafton); *cr Baron South-ampton*, of Southampton, co Hants (peerage of Great Britain) 1780; *d* 1797; *s* by his son **(2)** GOERGE FERDINAND, 2nd Baron, was a Lieut-Gen in the Army and Col 34th Regt; *d* 1810; *s* by his son **(3)** CHARLES, 3rd Baron; *b* 1804; was Lord-Lieut of Northampton: *m* 1st, 1826, Harriet, who *d* 1860, da of late Hon Henry FitzRoy Stanhope; 2ndly, 1862, Ismania Catherine, VA, who *d* 1918, da of late Walter Nugent, a Baron of the Austrian Empire; *d* 1872: *s* by his son **(4)** CHARLES HENRY, OBE, 4th Baron, *b* 1867; Capt 10th Hussars, and Lieut-Col Yorkshire Regt: *m* 1892, Lady Hilda Mary Dundas, who *d* 1957, da of 1st Marquess of Zetland; *d* 1958; *s* by his son **(5)** CHARLES, 5th Baron, *b* 1904; late Royal Horse Guards, and Pioneer Corps; Jt Master Grove Foxhounds 1930-32; disclaimed his peerage for life 1964: *m* 1st, 1927, Margaret, who *d* 1931, da of Rev Preb Herbert Mackworth Drake, V of Berry Pomeroy, Devon; 2ndly, 1940 (*m diss* 1944), Mrs Phyllis Joan Leslie, da of Francis Archibald Lloyd; 3rdly, 1951, Rachel Christine, who *d* 1985, da of Charles Zaman, of Lille, France; *d* 1989; *s* by his only son **(6)** CHARLES JAMES, 6th Baron and present peer.

SOUTHBOROUGH, BARONY OF (Hopwood) (Extinct 1992)

ADOPTED DAUGHTER LIVING OF FOURTH BARON

Anne Mary, *b* 1960: *m* 1992, John Charles Cunningham-Jardine, of Fourmerkland, Lockerbie, Dumfriesshire (*see* Nairn, Bt, 1985 Edn), and has issue living, Hamish Michael Charles, *b* 1997, — Ewan Ronald, *b* 1999, — Serena Moyna, *b* 1993. *Residence* – Tinwald House, Tinwald, Dumfriesshire DG1 3PW.

SISTER LIVING OF FOURTH BARON

Hon Moira, *b* 1919: *m* 1st, 1940, Peter Anthony Stanley Woodwark, Fl/Lieut RAF Vol Res, who was *ka* 1943, son of late Col Sir (Arthur) Stanley Woodwark, CMG, CBE, MD, FRCP; 2ndly, 1946, Joseph McArthur Rank, Hon FRCP, who *d* 1999, and has issue living (by 1st *m*), Caroline Nicola, *b* 1943: *m* 1966, Richard Hugh Payne, of West End, Shipton Moyne, Tetbury, Glos, and has issue living, Alexander Richard *b* 1971, Hugo Frederick *b* 1981, Samantha *b* 1969, Selina Francesca *b* 1978, — (by 2nd *m*) Colin Rowland Hopwood (The Old Forge, Kemble, Glos), *b* 1948: *m* 1972, Lavinia Ruth Phillips, and has issue living, James Benjamin *b* 1974, Nicola Emily *b* 1976, Rachel Margaret *b* 1978, — Camilla Moira, *b* 1953: *m* 1971, Jeremy Allan Jennings, and has issue living, Joseph Piers *b* 1975, Timothy David *b* 1977: *m* 1998, Sarah Maxine Dunton, Katharine Moira *b* 1979, Serena Margaret *b* 1993.

Southesk, Earl of; son of Duke of Fife

SOUTHWELL, VISCOUNT (Southwell) (Viscount I 1776, Bt I 1662)
(Title pronounced "Suthell")

NEC MALE NOTUS EQUES

Not an unknown knight

PYERS ANTHONY JOSEPH SOUTHWELL, 7th Viscount, and 10th Baronet; *b* 14 Sept 1930; *s* 1960; Capt (ret) 8th Hussars: *m* 1955, Barbara Jacqueline, da of A. Raynes, and has issue.

Arms – Argent, three cinquefoils pierced gules, charged on each leaf with an annulet or the field. Crest – A demi-Indian goat argent, armed and eared gules, ducally gorged or, and charged on the body with three annulets in bend also gules. Supporters – Two Indian goats argent, ducally collared, chained, and charged on the body with three annulets gules.
Address – PO Box 2211, Paphos 8062, Cyprus.

SONS LIVING

Hon RICHARD ANDREW PYERS, *b* 15 June 1956: *m* 1985, Alison Margaret, da of Kenneth Huntington, and has had issue, †Patrick Andrew, *b* 1987; *k* in a road accident 1998.
Hon Charles Anthony John, *b* 1962: *m* 1991, Mrs Jennifer Knight, da of Francis Joseph Wynne, and has issue living, two das.

SISTERS LIVING

Evelyn Mary Elizabeth, *b* 1926: *m* 1952, Harold Hope, and has issue living, Carol, *b* 1953, — Valerie, *b* 1956. *Residence* – 19 Mortlake Street, Islington, Christchurch, New Zealand. —— Barbara Frances Magdalene, *b* 1928: *m* 1949, Peter Fowler, and has issue living, Simon Peter (29 Simla Av, Havelock North, NZ), *b* 1965: *m* 1993, Kirsty Ellen, da of Alexander Neil Macgregor, of 432 Albert St, Palmerston North, NZ, and has issue living, Jamie Frances Joan *b* 1998, — Vivienne Anne, *b* 1951: *m* 1971, Paul James Homersley, of 25 Forest Close, Shawbirch, Wellington, Shrops, and has issue living, Christian Paul *b* 1974, Katie Louise *b* 1978, — Gillian Clare, *b* 1953: *m* 1974, Adrian Harold Edward Smith, of Murivance Cottage, Town Walls, Shrewsbury SY1 1JW, and has issue living, Adam Lloyd *b* 1979, Natalie Clare *b* 1981, — Sarah Elizabeth (1 Clare Rd, Hounslow, Middx TW4 78T), *b* 1959. *Residence* – Beech Tree House, Market Drayton, Shropshire.

DAUGHTER LIVING OF SIXTH VISCOUNT

Hon Susan Mary, *b* 1926: *m* 1951, Keith Francis MacRae, of 27 Dennis Rd, Slacks Creek, via Brisbane, Queensland, and has issue living, John Francis, *b* 1952, — Paul Finlay, *b* 1955.

COLLATERAL BRANCHES LIVING

Grandchildren of late Walter Stedman Southwell, son of late Charles Josiah Southwell, el son of late Josiah Southwell (infra):—
Issue of late Capt Bertie Charles Sydney Stedman Southwell, late 59th Bn AIF, *b* 1882, *d* 1984: *m* 1921, Elsie Annie, da of late J. S. Wenden:—
Evelyn John Stedman (2 Terry St, Balwyn, Victoria 3103, Australia), *b* 1923; late 2nd Commando Squad 2/AIF: *m* 1951, Shirley Jean, da of Robert Ingram Kennison, of 94 Prospect Rd, Geelong, and has issue living, Robert John, *b* 1953, — Anne Heather, *b* 1957. —— Alec James, QC (7 Euston St, Malvern, Victoria 3144, Australia), *b* 1926; late RANR; Judge Supreme Court, Victoria: *m* 1957, Margot Rose, da of late Frank Tracy, of Mount Eliza, Victoria, and has issue living, Peter James, *b* 1961, — Kay Tracy, *b* 1962. —— Mary Joy, *b* 1924: *m* 1949, Edward Russell Wilmoth, MC, late Lt-Col AIF, of 16 Haverbrack Av, Malvern, Victoria 3144, Australia, and has issue living, Stephen Guy Russell, *b* 1952, — Peter Charles Russell, *b* 1960, — Wendy Anne, *b* 1950, — Rosemary Susan, *b* 1954, — Jennifer Mary, *b* 1959, — Sarah Jane, *b* 1962.

Granddaughter of late Thomas Martin Southwell, JP, 2nd son of late Josiah Southwell, 2nd son of late Thomas Southwell, son of Hon John Southwell, 4th son of 1st Baron:—
Issue of late Frank Marven Southwell, *b* 1859, *d* 1935: *m* 1887, Florence Isabel, who *d* 1930, da of late Rev Henry James Cotton (V Combermere, colls):—
Gladys Florence, *b* 1888. *Residence* – Alexandra House, Poyner Rd, Ludlow, Shropshire.

PREDECESSORS – (1) *Sir* THOMAS Southwell, Knt; *cr* Baronet 1662: *s* by his grandson (2) *Sir* THOMAS, PC, 2nd Bt; sat as MP for co Limerick 1702-17; *cr Baron Southwell*, of Castle Mattress (peerage of Ireland) 1717; *d* 1720; *s* by his son (3) *Sir* THOMAS, 2nd Baron; *d* 1766; *s* by his son (4) THOMAS GEORGE, 3rd Baron; sat as MP for Enniscorthy; *cr Viscount Southwell* (peerage of Ireland) 1776; *d* 1780; *s* by his son (5) THOMAS ARTHUR, 2nd Viscount; *d* 1796; *s* by his son (6) THOMAS ANTHONY, KP, 3rd Viscount; *d* 1860; *s* by his nephew (7) THOMAS ARTHUR JOSEPH, KP, 4th Viscount; *b* 1836; was Lord-Lieut of co Leitrim: *m* 1871, Charlotte Mary Barbara, who *d* 1929, da of Sir Pyers Mostyn, 8th Bt; *d* 1878; *s* by his son (8) ARTHUR ROBERT PYERS JOSEPH MARY, 5th Viscount; *b* 1872: *m* 1897, Hon Dorothy Katharine Walrond who *d* 1952, da of 1st Baron Waleran; *d* 1944; *s* by his son (9) ROBERT ARTHUR WILLIAM JOSEPH, 6th Viscount; *b* 1898; Com RN: *m* 1st, 1926 (*m diss* 1931), Violet Mary Weldon, da of Paymaster-Com Francis Weldon Walshe, MVO, OBE, RN (ret); 2ndly, 1943, Josephine, who *d* 1973, da of Denis Joseph de la Mole, and formerly wife of Capt Henry Noel Marryat Hardy, DSO, RN; *d* 1960; *s* by his nephew (10) (PYERS) ANTHONY Joseph (son of Hon Francis Joseph Southwell, 2nd son of 5th Viscount), 7th Viscount and present peer; also Baron Southwell.

SPENCER, EARL (Spencer) (Earl GB 1765, Viscount UK 1905)

God defend the right

CHARLES EDWARD MAURICE SPENCER, 9th Earl; *b* 20 May 1964; *s* 1992; *ed* Eton, and Magdalen Coll, Oxford; Patron of twelve livings; Page of Honour to HM 1977-79: *m* 1989 (*m diss* 1997), (Catherine) Victoria, only da of John Lockwood, of Barnes, SW14, and has issue.

𝕬rms – Quarterly argent and gules, in the 2nd and 3rd quarters a fret or, over all on a bend sable three escallops of the first. 𝕮rest – Out of a ducal coronet or, a griffin's head argent, gorged with a collar gemelle gules, between two wings expanded and elevated, also argent. 𝕾upporters – *Dexter*, a griffin wings elevated per fesse ermine and erminois; *sinister*, a wyvern wings elevated ermine; each chained and gorged with a collar sable, flory and counterflory, charged with three escallops, argent.
Seat – Althorp, Northampton. *Residence* – Cape Town, S Africa.

SON LIVING

LOUIS FREDERICK JOHN (*Viscount Althorp* - pronounced Altrup), *b* 14 March 1994.

DAUGHTERS LIVING

Lady Kitty Eleanor, *b* 1990, — *Lady* Eliza Victoria, *b* 1992, — *Lady* (Katya) Amelia, *b* (twin) 1992.

SISTERS LIVING AND DECEASED

Lady (Elizabeth) Sarah Lavinia, *b* 1955: *m* 1980, Neil Edmund McCorquodale, High Sheriff Lincs 1987 (*see* E Westmorland, colls, 1969 Edn), and has issue living, George, *b* 1984, — Emily, *b* 1983, — Celia, *b* 1989. *Residence* – Stoke Rochford, Grantham, Lincs.
Lady (Cynthia) Jane, *b* 1957: *m* 1978, Rt Hon Sir Robert Fellowes, GCB, GCVO, QSO (*see* V Hampden, colls), and has issue living Alexander Robert, *b* 1983, — Laura Jane, *b* 1980, — Eleanor Ruth, *b* 1985.
Lady Diana Frances (*Diana, Princess of Wales*), *b* 1 July 1961: *m* 29 July 1981 (*m diss* 28 Aug 1996), HRH The Prince Charles Philip Arthur George, KG, KT, GCB, PC, Prince of Wales, and *d* 31 Aug 1997, leaving issue (*see* ROYAL FAMILY).

AUNT LIVING (*daughter of 7th Earl*)

Lady Anne, *b* 1920; sometime 3rd Officer WRNS, served 1939-45 War: *m* 1944, Capt Christopher Baldwin Hughes Wake-Walker, RN, who *d* 1998, and has issue (*see* Walker, Bt, *cr* 1856, colls). *Residence* – East Bergholt Lodge, Suffolk CO7 6QU.

MOTHER LIVING

Hon Frances Ruth Burke, yr da of 4th Baron Fermoy: *m* 1st, 1954 (*m diss* 1969), Edward John, Viscount Althorp, LVO (later 8th Earl Spencer), who *d* 1992; 2ndly, 1969 (*m diss* 1990), Peter Shand Kydd. *Residence* – Isle of Seil, by Oban, Argyll.

WIDOW LIVING OF EIGHTH EARL

RAINE (*Raine, Countess Spencer*), da of late Alexander George McCorquodale, of The White Lodge, Speen, Berks, and of Dame Barbara Cartland, DBE, of Camfield Place, Hatfield, Herts, and formerly wife of 9th Earl of Dartmouth; resumed her former style 1997: *m* 2ndly, 1976, as his 2nd wife, the 8th Earl Spencer, LVO, who *d* 1992; 3rdly, 1993 (*m diss* 1996), Count Jean-François de Chambrun. *Residence* – 24 Farm St, W1X 7RE.

COLLATERAL BRANCH LIVING

Issue of late Capt Hon George Charles Spencer, 3rd son of 6th Earl, *b* 1903, *d* 1982: *m* 1st, 1931 (*m diss* 1962), Barbara, who *d* 1978, only da of Benjamin Blumenthal, of Paris; 2ndly, 1966, (Kathleen Elisabeth) Sheila, who *d* 1968, yr da of late J. J. Henderson, and formerly wife of (i) William Geoffrey Lowndes, and (ii) Lt-Col Robert Fitzroy Hamilton Pascoe Stuart-French:—
(By 1st *m*) George Cecil Robert Maurice, *b* 1932: *ed* Eton; late Lieut 11th Hus. *Residence* – 314 Crane's Nest Way, West Palm Beach, Florida 33401, USA. *Club* – Cavalry and Guards'.

PREDECESSORS – Hon John Spencer, MP, 3rd son of 3rd Earl of Sunderland (D Marlborough), had issue **(1)** JOHN, sometime MP for Warwick; *cr Baron Spencer*, of Althorp, co Northampton, and *Viscount Spencer* (peerage of Great Britain) 1761, and *Viscount Althorp* and *Earl Spencer* (peerage of Great Britain) 1765; *d* 1783; *s* by his son **(2)** GEORGE JOHN, KG, 2nd Earl; was First Lord of the Admiralty 1794-1801, and Sec of State for Home Depart 1806-7; *d* 1834; *s* by his el son (3) JOHN CHARLES, 3rd Earl; MP for Northamptonshire S, and Chancellor of the Exchequer 1830-4; d 1845; s by his brother (4) FREDERICK, KG, CB, 4th Earl; b 1798; Rear-Adm; Lord Chamberlain 1846-8, and Lord Steward of the Household 1854-7: m 1st, 1830, Elizabeth Georgina, da of William Stephen Poyntz, MP, of Cowdray, Sussex; 2ndly, 1854, Adelaide Horatia Elizabeth, da of Sir Horace Beauchamp Seymour (M Hertford); d 1857; s by his son (5) JOHN POYNTZ, KG, PC, DCL, LLD, 5th Earl, b 1835; Groom of the Stole to the Prince Consort 1859-61, and to King Edward VII when Prince of Wales 1862-6, Lord-Lieut of Ireland 1868-74 and 1882-5, and of Northamptonshire 1872-1908, Lord Pres of Council 1880-83 and 1886, and First Lord of Admiralty 1892-95; MP for S Northamptonshire (L) 1857; Member of Council of Prince of Wales 1898-1910, and Member of Council of Duchy of Cornwall and Keeper of its Privy Seal 1901-7: m 1858, Charlotte Frances Frederica, VA, who d 1903, 4th da of Frederick Charles William Seymour (M Hertford, colls); d 1910; s by his half-brother (6) CHARLES ROBERT, KG, GCVO, PC, b 1857 (who had been cr Viscount Althorp, of Great Brington, co Northampton, peerage of United Kingdom 1905), 6th Earl; was Parliamentary Groom-in-Waiting to Queen Victoria Jan to July 1886, Vice-Chamberlain to the Household Aug 1892 to June 1895, Lord Chamberlain of the Household 1905-12, and Lord-Lieut of Northants 1908-22; MP for N Northamptonshire (L) April 1880 to Nov 1885, and for Mid Div of Northamptonshire 1885-95 and Oct 1900 to Dec 1905: m 1887, Hon Margaret Baring, who d 1906, da of 1st Baron Revelstoke; d 1922; s by his el son (7) ALBERT EDWARD JOHN, TD, DLitt, 7th Earl; b 1892; Capt 1st Life Gds; Lord Lieut of Northants 1952-67; Chm Advisory Council, Victoria & Albert Museum 1961-69: m 1919, Lady Cynthia Ellinor Beatrix Hamilton, DCVO, OBE (Lady of the Bedchamber to HM Queen Elizabeth the Queen Mother), who d 1972, da of 3rd Duke of Abercorn; d 1975; s by his only son (8) EDWARD JOHN, LVO, 8th Earl, b 1924; temp Equerry to HM King George VI 1950-52, and HM Queen Elizabeth II 1952-54, ADC to Gov of S Aust 1947-50, Dep Hon Col The Royal Anglian Regt (Northants) TAVR, late Capt Royal Scots Greys, served 1939-45 War (despatches), DL, Co Councillor and High Sheriff Northants: m 1st, 1954 (m diss 1969), Hon Frances Ruth Burke Roche, da of 4th Baron Fermoy; 2ndly, 1976, Raine, da of late Alexander George McCorquodale, of The White Lodge, Speen, Berks, and formerly wife of 9th Earl of Dartmouth; d 1992; s by his only surv son (9) CHARLES EDWARD MAURICE, 9th Earl and present peer; also Viscount Althorp, and Viscount and Baron Spencer.

Spencer, family name of Viscount Churchill.

Spencer-Churchill, Barony of (Ext 1977); see Marlborough, Duke of.

SPENS, BARON (Spens) (Baron UK 1959)

PATRICK MICHAEL REX SPENS, 3rd Baron; b 22 July 1942; s 1984; ed Rugby, and Corpus Christi Coll, Camb (MA, FCA); formerly Man Dir Henry Ansbacher & Co Ltd, a Dir of Morgan Grenfell & Co Ltd: m 1966, Barbara Janet Lindsay, da of Rear Adm Ralph Lindsay Fisher, CB, DSO, OBE, DSC, and has issue.

𝕬rms – Quarterly, 1st and 4th, or, a lion rampant gules within a bordure of the last charged with eight roses argent, Spens of Lathallan, in the dexter chief point a heart ensigned with an Imperial crown, both proper; 2nd and 3rd, gyronny of eight, or and sable, charged of a quarter in dexter chief per bend argent and azure, Campbell of Glendouglas; over all on an inescutcheon or, a lion rampant gules surmounted by a bend sable charged with three mascles argent, which inescutcheon is ensigned with the circlet of a Lord-Baron's coronet, Spens. 𝕮rest – A hart's head erased proper. 𝕾upporters – Dexter, an elephant; Sinister, a mallard wings close, both proper. Residence – Gould, Frittenden, Kent TN17 2DT.

SON LIVING

Hon PATRICK NATHANIEL GEORGE, b 14 Oct 1968; ed Rugby: m 1998, Hon Philippa Patricia Lennox-Boyd, yr da of 2nd Viscount Boyd of Merton. Residence – Beech House, 33a Pembroke Rd, W8.

DAUGHTER LIVING

Hon Sarah Helen, *b* 1970; *ed* Benenden, and Bristol Univ (MA).

THE THIRD BARON HAS FURTHER ISSUE
(by Elizabeth Mary, twin da of late Cmdr Ronald Hunter Blair, DSC, RN (see Hunter Blair, Bt, colls))

William Ronald Patrick SPENS, *b* 1983.

BROTHER LIVING

Hon William David Ralph (6 Roundwood View, Station Rd, Christian Malford, nr Chippenham, Wilts SN15 4BG), *b* 1943; *ed* Rugby, and Corpus Christi Coll, Camb (MA); Bar Inner Temple 1972: *m* 1967, Gillian Mary, only da of Albert Edwin Jowett, OBE, MD, FRCS, of the Old Rectory, Over Stowey, and has issue living, James Michael William, *b* 1969, — Tamsin Caroline, *b* 1971.

SISTER LIVING

Hon Mallowry Ann, *b* 1949.

AUNTS LIVING *(Daughters of 1st Baron)*

Hon Patricia Mary, *b* 1919: *m* 1946, Anthony MacGregor Grier, CMG, who *d* 1989, late Overseas Civil Ser, and has issue living, Anthony Richard MacGregor, *b* 1948: *m* 1976, Sally, el da of K. H. Ong, of Singapore, and has issue living, Alexander Anthony MacGregor *b* 1978, Cristelle Patricia *b* 1983, — Francis John Roy, *b* 1955: *m* 1st, 1976, Shelagh Elizabeth, da of Alec John Frederick Banks; 2ndly, 1990, Anjali, da of Joseph D'Souza, and has issue living (by 2nd *m*), Savitri Patricia *b* 1992, Indira Cicely *b* 1995, — Lynda Mary, *b* 1947: *m* 1981, John D. Payne, of The Gable House, Abbots Morton, Worcs WR7 4NA, son of late Percy Jennings Payne, and has issue, Robert John *b* 1983, David Roy Christopher *b* 1984. *Residence* – Oak Cottage, 5 Lewins Rd, Epsom Common, Surrey KT18 7TL.

Hon (Emily) Susan, MBE, *b* 1924; WRNS 1941-46; Foreign & Commonwealth Office 1956-72; Internat Atomic Energy Agency 1972-82; MBE (Civil) 1970. *Residence* – 47 The Drive, Hove, Sussex BN3 3JE.

WIDOW LIVING OF FIRST BARON

KATHLEEN ANNIE FEDDEN (*Dowager Baroness Spens*), (Gould, Frittenden, Kent), da of late Roger Dodds, of Bath, and Northumberland: *m* 1963, as his 2nd wife, the 1st Baron Spens, who *d* 1973.

COLLATERAL BRANCH LIVING

Issue of late Capt Robert Richard Patrick Spens, MC, Roy Norfolk Yeo, yr son of 1st Baron, *b* 1917, *ka* 1942: *m* 1939, Elisabeth Clare (who *d* 1990, having *m* 2ndly, 1955, Francis David Corbin, TD), da of George Catterall Leach:—
Charmian Helen, *b* 1940: *m* 1960, William Thomas Scott, of Meiklewood, Stirling FK8 3AF, and has issue living, Thomas Robert George, *b* 1973, — Elisabeth Charlotte, *b* 1962, — Alexandra Mary, *b* 1965: *m* 1987, Hugh Colin Graham-Watson, yr son of Charles FitzJames Graham-Watson, of La Massana, Andorra, and has issue living, Archibald Edward *b* 1990, Amber Isobel *b* 1989.

PREDECESSORS *Rt Hon Sir* (WILLIAM) PATRICK Spens, KBE, son of late Nathaniel Spens, of 1 St Mary Abbot's Court, Kensington, W; *b* 1885, Bar Inner Temple; Commr of Imperial War Graves Comm 1931-43 and 1949-65; Ch Justice of India 1943-47; Chm of Arbitral Tribunal for India and Pakistan 1947-48; MP for Ashford, Kent (C) 1933-43, and S Kensington 1950-59; *cr Baron Spens*, of Blairsanquhar, co Fife (peerage of UK) 1959: *m* 1st, Hilda Mary, who *d* 1962, da of Lt-Col Wentworth, Grenville Bowyer (B Denham, colls); 2ndly, 1963, Kathleen Annie Fedden, da of Roger Dodds, of Bath and Northumberland; *d* 1973; *s* by his el son (2) WILLIAM GEORGE MICHAEL, 2nd Baron *b* 1914; Bar Inner Temple 1945; Maj RA: *m* 1941, Joan Elizabeth, who *d* 1994, da of late Reginald Goodall, *d* 1984 *s* by his elder son (3) PATRICK MICHAEL REX, 3rd Baron and present peer.

STAFFORD, BARON (Fitzherbert) (Baron E 1640)

One I will serve

FRANCIS MELFORT WILLIAM FITZHERBERT, 15th Baron; *b* 13 March 1954; *s* 1986; *ed* Ampleforth; patron of one living (but being a Roman Catholic cannot present); DL Stafford 1994: *m* 1980, Katharine Mary, 3rd da of John Codrington, of Barnes, SW13, and has issue.

Arms – Argent, a chief vairée or and gules, over all a bend sable, *Fitzherbert*. **Crest** – A dexter cubit arm in armour erect, the hand appearing clenched within the gauntlet. **Supporters** – *Dexter*, a lion argent; *sinister* a swan, wings inverted argent, gorged with a ducal coronet per pale gules and sable.
Seat – Swynnerton Park, Stone, Staffordshire.

SONS LIVING

Hon BENJAMIN JOHN BASIL, *b* 8 Nov 1983.
Hon Toby Francis, *b* 1985.

DAUGHTERS LIVING

Hon Teresa Emily, *b* 1987.
Hon Camilla Rose Jane, *b* 1989.

BROTHERS LIVING

Hon Thomas Alastair, *b* 1955; *ed* Ampleforth; late Capt Scots Gds: *m* 1982, Deborah Susan, yr da of late Peter Alan Beak, of Brazil, and has issue living, Rory Basil Thomas, *b* 1989, — Tamara Frances, *b* 1986, — Purdita Aileen, *b* 1987.
Hon Philip Basil, *b* 1962; *ed* Ampleforth, and Durham Univ (BA): *m* 1991, Caroline T., yr da of Michael Hadcock, of Bodedern, Isle of Anglesey, and has issue living, Basil Edward, *b* 1998, — Emily Theresa, *b* 1995, — Philippa Rose, *b* (twin) 1995.

SISTERS LIVING

Hon Aileen Mary, *b* 1953: *m* 1980, Antony Robin Walhouse Littleton, and has issue (*see* B Hatherton). *Residence* – Old Walls, Hannington, Hants.
Hon Caroline Fiona, *b* 1956: *m* 1981, William Kirkland Tellwright, eldest son of late William Tellwright, of Park Springs, Shropshire, and has issue living, Turia Mary, *b* 1984, — Laura Caroline, *b* 1987. *Residence* – The Sydnall Farm, Woodseaves, Market Drayton, Shropshire.
Hon Wendy Helen, *b* 1961: *m* 1983, Jeremy John Maurice Hill, eldest son of late Lt-Col Colin Hill, of Coley Court, E Harptree, Avon, and has issue living, Thomas Colin Evelyn, *b* 1985, — Nicholas Jeremy John, *b* 1987. *Residence* – Wentworth House, Wentworth Close, Glen Lorne, Harare. *Postal Address* — PO Box BW 730, Borrowdale, Harare, Zimbabwe.

WIDOW LIVING OF FOURTEENTH BARON

MORAG NADA (*Dowager Baroness Stafford*), DStJ, yr da of late Lt-Col Alastair Campbell, of Altries, Milltimber, Aberdeenshire: *m* 1952, the 14th Baron Stafford, who *d* 1986. *Residence* – Beech Farm House, Beech, Stoke-on-Trent, Staffs.

COLLATERAL BRANCHES LIVING

Grandchildren of late Hon Mary Beatrice Theresa Fitzherbert, eldest sister of 12th and 13th Barons, *b* 1862, *d* 1949: *m* 1895, as his 2nd wife, Sir Trevor John Chichele Chichele Plowden, KCSI, who *d* 1905:—
    Issue of late Hester Mary Beatrice Chichele-Plowden, *b* 1902, *d* 1993: *m* 1922, Cdr Kenneth Gordon Poland, RNVR, who *d* 1970:—
Trevor Peter Gordon, *b* 1923; Lt-Cdr RN (ret): *m* 1st, 1944, June Mary, who *d* 1969, eldest da of Henry Bowlby, of 100 Elm Park Gdns, SW10 (*see* V Combermere, colls, 1960 Edn); 2ndly, 1969, Lorette Elizabeth Johanna, da of late Dr J. M. Durr, of Cape Town, S Africa, and has issue living (by 1st *m*), Peter Kenneth, *b* 1945, — Jill, *b* 1948, — (by 2nd *m*) Sophie Victoria, *b* 1982. —— John Michael (Fermain, W Wittering, Chichester, Sussex), *b* 1925; *ed* Downside, and Trin Coll, Camb: *m* 1952 (*m diss* 1983), Diana Mary Angela Forbes, da of late Leo Forbes O'Connor (*see* B Byron, 1985 Edn), and has issue living, Simon John Joseph, *b* 1957, — Jonathan David, *b* 1958: *m* 1997, Gordana, da of late Miroslav Toplak, of Zagreb, Croatia, — Matthew John, *b* 1963, — Sara Daphne Mary, *b* 1954, — Lucy Mary, *b* 1959: *m* 1987, (Geoffrey Roger George) Chandos Elletson, yr son of late Daniel Hope Elletson, of Parrox Hall, Lancs, and has issue living, Frederick Chandos John *b* 1990, Harry Leo Hope *b* 1996. —— †David Kenneth, *b* 1929; *ed* Downside: *m* 1st, 1958 (*m diss* 1967), Joanna Mary, eldest da of late Capt John Buller Edward Hall, RN (*see* B Ritchie of Dundee, colls, 1985 Edn); 2ndly, 1967, Isie Suzetli, only da of late Maj Louis Esselen, of S Africa, and *d* 1982, leaving issue (by 1st *m*), Kevin John (Penfold, Coach Rd, Ivy Hatch, Kent TN15 0PE), *b* 1959: *m* 1993, Jane Alison, da of Peter Hall, of 11a Downs Rd, Ramsgate, Kent, and has issue living, George Henry Peter *b* 1996, Eleanor Phoebe Jane *b* 1999, — Jeremy David (6 College Fields, Clifton, Bristol BS8 3HP), *b* 1961: *m* 1996, Sarah Winnifred, da of late Michael Wyvil Lesley, and has issue living, Rupert Oliver *b* 1997, Angus Benjamin *b* 1999, — (by 2nd *m*) Caroline Mary, *b* 1969: *m* 1996, Stefan Hans Xaver Seitz, and has issue living, Nicholas James *b* 1998. —— Michael Desmond (Lower Preshaw House, Upham, Southampton SO3 1HP), *b* 1937; *ed* Downside; *m* 1st, 1969 (*m diss* 1980), Elizabeth, da of late Philip Asprey, of Perry, Worplesdon, Surrey; 2ndly, 1981, Mrs Carolyn Mary Denison, 2nd da of late W/Cdr William James Maitland

Longmore, CBE (*see* B Forres), and has issue living (by 1st *m*), Lara Hester Mary, *b* 1969: *m* 1997, William G. A. Sussmann, of Flat 5, 9 Gloucester Av, NW1 7AU, son of Peter Sussmann, of NW11, — Emma Elizabeth, *b* 1970, — Liza Evelyne Theresa, *b* 1973, — Anna Louise, *b* 1974. —— Daphne Elizabeth Beatrice, *b* 1933: *m* 1960, Edward Kendall Thorneycroft, MBE, TD, DL, of Tigbourne Farm, Wormley, Surrey, and has issue living, Tom Edward, *b* 1962, — Mary Louise, *b* 1961: *m* 1985, Jeremy Campbell-Lamerton, of The Old Rectory, Rendlesham, Woodbridge, Suffolk, eldest son of Col Michael John Campbell-Lamerton, of Shipston-on-Stour, Warwicks, and has issue living, Harry Alexander *b* 1987, Alice Louisa *b* 1988, Olivia Rose *b* 1990, Poppy Camilla *b* 1993.

Grandchildren of late Hon Alice Mary Wilhelmina Trappes-Lomax, 3rd sister of 12th and 13th Barons: *m* 1894, Maj Richard Trappes-Lomax, JP:—
Issue of late Brig Basil Charles Trappes-Lomax, MC, *b* 1896, *d* 1963: *m* 1929, Diana Mary, who *d* 1995, da of late Cdr Arthur Edward Silvertop, RN:—
†David Edward, *b* 1930; *ed* Downside; Maj Scots Guards: *m* 1980, Gillean Hill (Great Hockham Hall, Thetford, Norfolk), and *dsp* 1993. —— John Michael (131 Southgate St, Bury St Edmunds, Suffolk), *b* 1947; *ed* Downside, and Gonville and Caius Coll, Camb. —— Alice Mary, *b* 1938: *m* 1959, John Edward Benedict Wells, of Scatho, Throwleigh, Devon, and has issue living, Benedict Swithin (Hamilton House, Vicarage Lane, Branscombe, Devon), *b* 1960; Major The King's Royal Hussars (ret): *m* 1989, Vicki Caroline, da of Stanley Alexander Maitland, of Firs Hill, High Rd, Chipstead, Surrey, and has issue living, James Edward Benedict *b* 1994, Charles Swithin *b* 1995, Thomas Alexander *b* 1997, Sophie Louise Cameron *b* 1990, Georgia Rose *b* 1991, Juliet Katherine *b* 1993, — Thomas Edward (8 Burntwood Close, SW18 3JU), *b* 1962: *m* 1990, Katherine J. Rich, and has issue living, William St George *b* 1994, Henry Benedict *b* 1996, — Katherine Mary Horatia, *b* 1959: *m* 1988, John Collingwood Almond, of Creaber, Gidleigh, nr Newton Abbot, Devon, and has issue living, Edward Collingwood *b* 1993, Lucy Horatia *b* 1991.

Issue of late Col Nicholas Hugh Trappes-Lomax, *b* 1911, *d* 1969: *m* 1938, Gertrude Maisie, who *d* 1994, da of late Lt-Col Hugh Charles Stockwell, OBE:—
Hugh Richard Nicholas (28 Blackford Av, Edinburgh EH9 2PH), *b* 1943: *m* 1968, Jocelyn Ncekei, da of Johnson Karandi, of Meru, Kenya, and has issue living, Simon Mwenda, *b* 1968: *m* 1993, Marie-Christine Michaela, da of late Michael Edward Skrutkowski, of Bromma, Sweden, — Robert Kimathi, *b* 1980, — Catherine Nkirote, *b* 1970, — Helen Kagendo, *b* 1977. —— Mark Clement, *b* 1946. —— Tessa Margaret (Laundry Cottage, Flete, Devon), *b* 1941. —— Nicola Frances, *b* 1944: *m* 1964, Anthony Miles Trevor Eastwood, of Foulscales House, Newton-in-Bowland, Clitheroe, Lancs, and has issue living, Anthony Charles, *b* 1965, — Benjamin Miles, *b* 1966, — Carl Hugh, *b* 1968.

Issue of late Maj Stephen Richard Trappes-Lomax, MC, TD, *b* 1913; *d* 1982: *m* 1952, Alison Marjorie Gundrede (The Farm House, Little London, N Walsham, Norfolk), only da of late George Algernon Perkins, of Bure House, Lamas, Norwich:—
Francis George, *b* 1955: *m* 1986, Annette Chalkley, and has issue living, Christopher Michael, *b* 1990, — Catherine Ruth, *b* 1988. *Residence* – Croft Cottage, Cann's Lane, Hethersett, Norwich NR9 3JE. —— Richard Nicholas Henry, *b* 1960. —— Mary Alison Catherine, *b* 1953: *m* 1984, Alexander Cockburn, of Rosedene, Aylsham Rd, Swanton Abbott, Norwich, elder son of Denison Cockburn, of Chipping Campden, Glos, and has issue living, George Stephen Denison, *b* 1986, — Alastair William Richard, *b* 1989. —— Clare Gundrede, *b* 1957: *m* 1983, Brian Ronald Weir Gibson, of Longworth House, Gt Wolford, Shipston-on-Stour, Warwicks, son of late Ronald Gibson, of Lowood, S Queensferry, W Lothian, and has issue living, Emma Clare, *b* 1987.

Descendants, in the female line, of brothers of 8th Baron:—
See 1969 and earlier edns.

PREDECESSORS – (1) *Sir* WILLIAM Howard, KB (3rd son of Thomas Howard, *cr* Earl of Norfolk 1644); *m* Mary, only sister of Henry, 5th (or but for attainder 14th) Baron de Stafford; in 1640 he and his wife were *cr Baron and Baroness Stafford* (peerage of England), with remainder, in default of heirs male of the body, to the heirs of their bodies, and *Viscount Stafford* (peerage of England) with remainder to his issue male; subsequently tried for complicity in Titus Oates plot, attainted 1678 and executed 1680; his wife was *cr Countess of Stafford* 1688 for life; she *d* 1693; *s* by her son (2) HENRY STAFFORD, *de jure* 2nd Baron; *cr Earl of Stafford* (peerage of England) 1688, with remainder to his brothers John and Francis; *dsp* 1719; *s* by his nephew (3) WILLIAM, 2nd Earl, and *de jure* 3rd Baron Stafford, el son of the Hon John (ante); *s* by his son (4) WILLIAM MATTHIAS, 3rd Earl, and *de jure* 4th Baron Stafford; *dsp* 1750; *s* by his uncle (5) JOHN PAUL STAFFORD, 4th Earl, and *de jure* 5th Baron Stafford; *dsp* 1762, when the earldom expired, and the barony vested in (6-7) Mary, wife of Sir George Jerningham, 5th Bt, only child of Mary Plowden, sister of 4th Earl; attainder of the 1st Viscount was reversed 1824, and on 6 July 1825, the House of Lords resolved that (8) *Sir* GEORGE WILLIAM Jerningham, 7th Bt (*cr* 1621), had made out his claim to be 8th Baron Stafford; unsuccessfully claimed the Barony of Stafford, *cr* 1299; assumed 1826 by Roy licence additional surname and arms of Stafford; *d* 1851; *s* by his son (9) HENRY VALENTINE, 9th Baron; *b* 1802; *d* 30 Nov 1884; *s* by his nephew (10) AUGUSTUS FREDERICK FITZHERBERT, son of Hon Edward (2nd son of 8th Baron), 10th Baron, *b* 1830: *d* 1892; *s* by his brother (11) FITZHERBERT EDWARD, 11th Baron, *b* 1832; *d* 1913; *s* by his nephew (12) FRANCIS EDWARD Fitzherbert-Stafford, DSO (son of late Basil Thomas Fitzherbert, of Swynnerton Park, Stone (who *m* 2ndly, 1887, Emma Eliza, Baroness Stafford, who *d* 1912), by Emily Charlotte, who *d* 1881, sister of 10th and 11th Barons), 12th Baron, *b* 1859: was Lord High Steward of Stafford; assumed by Roy licence 1913 for himself and issue the additional surname of Stafford: *m* 1903, Dorothy Hilda, who *d* 1958, 3rd da of late Albert Octavius Worthington, JP, DL, of Maple Hayes, Lichfield; *d* 1932; *s* by his brother (13) EDWARD STAFFORD JOSEPH Fitzherbert, KCB, 13th Baron; *b* 1864; Adm; Com-in-Chief African Station 1918-20; *d* 1941; *s* by his nephew (14) BASIL FRANCIS NICHOLAS (son of late Capt Hon Thomas Charles Fitzherbert, AM, brother of 12th and 13th Barons), 14th Baron, *b* 1926; Lt Scots Gds: *m* 1952, Morag Nada, yr da of late Lt-Col Alastair Campbell, of Altries, Milltimber, Aberdeenshire; *d* 1986; *s* by his eldest son (15) FRANCIS MELFORT WILLIAM, 15th Baron and present peer.

STAIR, EARL OF (Dalrymple) (Earl S 1703, Bt S 1664 and 1698)

JOHN DAVID JAMES DALRYMPLE, 14th Earl, and 15th Baronet of Stair and 11th of Killock; *b* 4 Sept 1961; *s* 1996; *ed* Harrow; commn'd Scots Gds 1982.

Arms – Quarterly: 1st, or, on a saltire azure nine lozenges of the field, *Dalrymple*; 2nd or, a chevron chequy sable and argent between three water bougets of the second, *Ross*; 3rd grand quarter, quarterly, 1st and 4th counterquartered, 1st and 4th gules, three cinquefoils ermine, 2nd and 3rd, argent, a galley sails furled sable, the whole within a border compony argent and azure, the first charged with hearts gules, and the second with mullets argent, *Hamilton of Bargany*; 2nd and 3rd gules, on a fesse between three crescents or, as many mullets azure, de *Franguetot*; 4th grand quarter, quarterly, 1st and 4th gules, on a chevron between three cinquefoils argent, as many round buckles azure, *Hamilton of Fala*; 2nd and 3rd gules, three martlets argent, *Makgill.* Crest – A rock proper. Supporters – Two storks holding in their beaks, a fish, all proper.
Seat – Lochinch Castle, Stranraer, Wigtownshire.

BROTHERS LIVING

Hon DAVID HEW, *b* 30 March 1963; *ed* Harrow.
Hon Michael Colin, *b* 1965; *ed* Stanbridge Earls: *m* 1991, Harriet Lucy, elder da of Sir Jocelyn Charles Roden Buxton, 7th Bt, VRD, RNVR, and has issue living, William Hew, *b* 1992, — Angus, *b* 1993, — Peter, *b* 1996. *Residence* – Cranstoun Riddel, Oxenfoord, Midlothian.

UNCLES LIVING (sons of 12th Earl)

Hon Hew North, TD, *b* 1910; *ed* Eton; formerly Capt 2nd Batn Black Watch (TA); Member Queen's Body Guard for Scotland (Royal Company of Archers); DL Ayrshire 1955; served 1939-45 War in Crete, N Africa and Burma 1943-45 (twice wounded): *m* 1st, 1938, Mildred Helen, who *d* 1980, da of late Hon Thomas Henry Frederick Egerton (*see* D Sutherland, colls, 1980 Edn), and formerly wife of 4th Baron Oranmore and Browne; 2ndly, 1983, Helen Margaret Wilson, da of late James Phillips, of Albany, Ballantrae, and has issue living (by 1st *m*), Robert Hew (Crailoch, Ballantrae, Ayrshire KA26 0LW), *b* 1946; *ed* Fettes: *m* 1976, Caroline Anne, da of late (Charles) Patrick Maule Hunting, CBE, TD, of The Old House, Birch Grove, Horsted Keynes, Sussex, and has issue living, Hamish Hew *b* 1979, Alastair North *b* 1982. *Residence* – Castlehill, Ballantrae, Ayrshire.
Hon Colin James, *b* 1920; *ed* Eton, and Trin Coll, Camb (BA 1941); late Maj Scots Gds; Member Queen's Body Guard for Scotland (Royal Company of Archers); DL Midlothian 1961, JP 19—; served 1939-45 War in Italy 1944-45: *m* 1st, 1945 (*m diss* 1954), Pamela Mary, only da of late Maj Lamplugh Wickham, CVO, of Star Hill, Hartley Wintney, Basingstoke (*see* M Huntly, 1936 Edn); 2ndly, 1956, Fiona Jane, only da of late Adm Sir Ralph Alan Bevan Edwards, KCB, CBE, and has issue living (by 1st *m*), Caroline Mary, *b* 1946: *m* 1973, Michael Scott, ARICS, of Troloss, Elvanfoot, Lanarkshire, son of M. M. Scott, of Cakemuir Castle, Tynehead, Midlothian, and has issue living, Alexander James *b* 1975, Camilla Rose *b* 1978, — (by 2nd *m*), Andrew David (Quarryford House, Gifford, E Lothian EH41 4PL), *b* 1959; *ed* Eton, and Downing Coll, Camb; Lt Scots Guards; Memb Queen's Body Guard for Scotland (Royal Company of Archers): *m* 1987, Bryony Winterton, da of William Anthony Major, of Shilston Barton, Modbury, S Devon, and has issue living, Hew William James *b* 1993, Thomas Alick James *b* 1995, Louisa Alice Clare *b* 1990, — Serena Jane, *b* 1957: *m* 1979, Maj James Peter Greenwell, The Blues and Royals (ret), and has issue (*see* Greenwell, Bt), — Rose Joanna, *b* 1962: *m* 1987, Charles Leighton Dudgeon, of Fala Mains, Blackshiels, Midlothian, son of John Dudgeon, of Humbie, Kirkliston, W Lothian, and has issue living, Edward John *b* 1993, Sara Rose *b* 1991. *Residence* – Oxenfoord Mains, Dalkeith, Midlothian. *Club* – New (Edinburgh).

AUNT LIVING (daughter of 12th Earl)

Lady Jean Margaret, DCVO, *b* 1905; appointed a Woman of the Bedchamber to HM Queen Elizabeth The Queen Mother 1947; CVO 1957, DCVO 1969: *m* 1931, Lt-Col (Arthur) Niall Talbot Rankin, Scots Guards, who *d* 1965 (*see* Rankin, Bt).

WIDOW LIVING OF THIRTEENTH EARL

DAVINA KATHARINE (*Countess of Stair*), da of late Hon Sir David Bowes Lyon, KCVO (*see* E Strathmore, colls): *m* 1960, Col the 13th Earl of Stair, KCVO, MBE, who *d* 1996. *Residence* – Lochinch Castle, Stranraer, Wigtownshire.

COLLATERAL BRANCHES LIVING (In special remainder to Earldom)

Grandchildren of late Col Hon North de Coigny DALRYMPLE-HAMILTON, MVO, 2nd son of 10th Earl:—
Issue of late Adm Sir Frederick Hew George Dalrymple-Hamilton of Bargany, KCB; *b* 1890, *d* 1974: *m* 1918, Gwendolen, who *d* 1974, da of Sir Cuthbert Edgar Peek, 2nd Bt:—
North Edward Frederick DALRYMPLE-HAMILTON OF BARGANY, CVO, MBE, DSC (3 New Court, Sutton Manor, Sutton Scotney, Winchester, Hants SO21 3JX. *Clubs* – Pratt's, MCC, New (Edinburgh)), *b* 1922; *ed* Eton; Capt RN (ret) and Lieut Queen's Body Guard for Scotland (Royal Company of Archers); DL Ayrshire 1973, JP 1980; 1940-45 War (DSC), Korea 1952-53 (MBE); MBE (Mil) 1953, MVO (4th class) 1954, CVO 1961: *m* 1st, 1949, Hon Mary Helen Colville, who *d* 1981, el da of 1st Baron Clydesmuir; 2ndly, 1983, Geraldine Inez Antoinette, widow of Maj Rowland Beech, MC, of Park Leaze, Ewen, Cirencester, and da of late Maj Frank Harding, and has issue living (by 1st *m*), North John Frederick,

OBE, TD, DL (Lovestone House, Bargany, Girvan, Ayrshire KA26 9RF), *b* 1950; *ed* Eton, and Aberdeen Univ (MA Hons); a Page of Honour to HM Queen Elizabeth The Queen Mother 1964-66; Member Queen's Body Guard for Scotland (Royal Company of Archers), Col late Queen's Own Yeo (TA); DL Ayrshire 1995; TD 1986, OBE (Mil) 1992: *m* 1980, Sally-Anne, da of Robert Boothby How, of Ladies Lake, St Andrews, Fife, and has issue living, Hew North Robert *b* 1981, Edward James Robin *b* 1986, Catherine Mary Anne *b* 1982, — James Hew Ronald (Well Cottage, Barton End, Horsley, Glos GL6 0SF), *b* 1955; ARICS: *m* 1986, Pippa M. D., only da of Maj David Metcalfe, of Minchinhampton, Glos, and has issue living, Frederick David George *b* 1990, Jack Louis Robert *b* 1994, Clementine Mary *b* 1989. —— Christian Margaret, MBE, *b* 1919; a DL of Wigtown; MBE 1989. *Residence* – Cladyhouse, Cairnryan, Stranraer, Wigtown. —— Graeme Elizabeth, *b* 1926: *m* 1948, Alexander Grant Laing, MC, who *d* 1988, of Relugas, Forres, Moray IV36 0QL (Grant, Bt, *cr* 1924), and has issue living, Alasdair North Grant (Logie House, Forres, Moray IV36 0QN), *b* 1949; *ed* Eton; Lt Scots Guards: *m* 1979, Hon Lucy Ann Anthea Low, yr da of 1st Baron Aldington, and has issue living, Alexander William Grant *b* 1982, Frederick Charles Grant *b* 1985, Emma Mary Grant *b* 1980, — Fergus Hew Grant (Craggan, Grantown on Spey, Morayshire), *b* 1951; *ed* Gordonstoun: *m* 1979, Priscilla Mary, yr da of late Michael Telfair Keith, TD, of Hoe Hall, Dereham, Norfolk (*see* Mann, Bt), and has issue living, Michael Hew Grant *b* 1984, Iona Rose Grant *b* 1982, Henrietta Mary Grant *b* 1986, Elizabeth Ruby Grant *b* 1988, — Carolyn Margaret Grant, *b* 1952: *m* 1981, Capt James Melville John Balfour, RGJ (*see* E Harewood, colls, 1972-73 Edn), and has issue living, Edward James Melville *b* 1982, Laura Elizabeth *b* 1984, Margaret Carolyn *b* 1985, — Fiona Mary Grant (*Hon Mrs Jonathan Warrender*), *b* 1954: *m* 1979, Hon Jonathan James Warrender, of Minuntion, Pinmore, Girvan, Ayrshire KA26 0TE, yr son of 2nd Baron Bruntisfield, and has issue (see that title).

Granddaughter of late George North Dalrymple, el son of Hon George Grey Dalrymple, 2nd son of 9th Earl:—
Issue of late Maj Walter Grey North Hamilton Dalrymple, *b* 1896, *d* 1969: *m* 1929 (*m diss* 1946), Melisande Germaine Violet Craigie, who *d* 1969, da of Robert G. Hunter, of London:—
Dawn Mary Kathleen, *b* 1930: *m* 1956, Peter Humphrey Methuen, of Elliston, St Boswells, Roxburghshire TD6 0HJ, and has issue living, Piers Harry North Dalrymple (6 Warwick Sq, SW1V 2AA), *b* 1966: *m* 1997, Rebecca Harriet, eldest da of Colin Thomson, of Lymington, Hants.

Granddaughter of late Walter Francis Dalrymple, yr son of Hon George Grey Dalrymple (ante):—
Issue of late Basil Walter Dalrymple, *b* 1891, *d* 1977: *m* 1st, 1920, (*m diss* 1925), Aileen Eugenie, only da of late Maj Charles May Hayes Newington, late King's and Cheshire Regts; 2ndly, 1930, Erica Isolde, who *d* 1977, da of late Lt-Col P. N. G. Reade, RA:—
(By 1st *m*) Elizabeth Mary Wetherell, *b* 1920; late Com ATS: *m* 1945 (*m diss* 1954), Anthony Edward Home Phillips, Sub-Lt RNVR, who *d* 1989, only son of late Sir Herbert Phillips, KCMG, OBE, and has issue living, Anthony Jeremy Herbert Home (USA), *b* 1947.

Descendants of late Hon Sir Hew Dalrymple, MP (3rd son of 1st Viscount Stair), who was *cr* a *Baronet* 1698:—
See Hamilton-Dalrymple, Bt.

Descendants of late Robert Dalrymple-Horn-Elphinstone (2nd son of late Robert Dalrymple-Horn-Elphinstone, el son of late Hew Dalrymple, 2nd son of late Hon Sir Hew Dalrymple (ante)), who was *cr* a *Baronet* 1828:—
See Elphinstone-Dalrymple, Bt.

PREDECESSORS – (1) JAMES Dalrymple, a Lord of Session as Lord Stair, was *cr* a *Baronet* (of Stair) 1664; appointed Pres of Court of Session 1671; removed from that office 1681, and reappointed in 1688, after the revolution; *cr Lord Glenluce and Stranraer* and *Viscount Stair* (peerage of Scotland) 1690; *d* 1695; *s* by his son (2) JOHN, PC, 2nd Viscount; was Lord Justice Clerk, Lord Advocate for Scotland, and a Principal Sec of State, which latter office he resigned in consequence of the part he took in the massacre of Glencoe; *cr Lord Newliston, Glenluce and Stranraer, Viscount Dalrymple* and *Earl of Stair* (peerage of Scotland) 1703, with remainder to the heirs male of his father; *d* 1707; *s* by his son (3) JOHN, KT, 2nd Earl; an eminent military commander; attained the rank of Field Marshal, and was sometime ambassador to France; his brother Hon William (heir presumptive), having *m* the Countess of Dumfries, a peeress in her own right, he in 1707 surrendered all his honours to the Crown, and obtained a new charter empowering him to name as his successor any male descendant of the 1st Viscount, and in virtue of this authority he in 1747, shortly before his death, nominated by deed his nephew John, 2nd son of his 2nd brother George; this nomination was contested, and the House of Lords decided in favour of the 2nd son of Hon William and the Countess of Dumfries (ante) viz (4) JAMES, 3rd Earl: *dsp* 1760: *s* by his el brother (5) WILLIAM, 4th Earl, who had previously *s* as 4th *Earl of Dumfries*; *dsp* 1768, when the Earldom of Dumfries devolved upon his nephew Patrick Macdowal, Esq, and the Earldom of Stair passed to his cousin (6) JOHN, 5th Earl, who had been nominated for the title by the 2nd Earl; *d* 1789; *s* by his son (7) JOHN, 6th Earl; a Representative Peer, and sometime Ambassador to Prussia, *dsp* 1821; *s* by his cousin (8) JOHN WILLIAM HENRY, 7th Earl, son of Gen William Dalrymple, Lieut-Gov of Chelsea Hospital; *dsp* 1840; *s* by his kinsman (9) JOHN HAMILTON, KT, 8th Earl, who had previously *s* as 5th Bt (see * infra); was a Gen in the Army; *cr Baron Oxenfoord*, of Cousland, co Edinburgh (peerage of United Kingdom) 1841, with remainder to his brother; *d* 1853; *s* by his brother (10) NORTH HAMILTON, 9th Earl; *b* 1776: *m* 1st, 1817, Margaret, da of J. Penny, of Arrad; *d* 1864; *s* by his son (11) JOHN HAMILTON, KT, 10th Earl, *b* 1819; sat as MP for Wigtownshire 1841-56; was Lord High Commr to Gen Assembly of Church of Scotland 1869-71; many years Lord-Lieut of Ayrshire and Lord-Lieut of co Wigtown: *m* 1846, Louisa Jane Henrietta Emily, who *d* 1896, da of the Duc de Coigny; *d* 1903; *s* by his son (12) JOHN HEW NORTH GUSTAVE HENRY, 11th Earl, *b* 1848; Provost of Stranraer 1900-1909, and Lord High Commr to Gen Assembly of Church of Scotland 1910: *m* 1878 (*m diss* 1905), Susan Harriet, who *d* 1946, da of Sir James Grant-Suttie, 6th Bt; *d* 1914; *s* by his son (13) JOHN JAMES, KT, DSO, 12th Earl; *b* 1879; formerly Lieut-Col Scots Guards; MP for Wigtownshire (C) 1906-14; Lord High Commr to Church of Scotland 1927 and 1928, and Lord-Lieut of Wigtownshire 1935-61; European War 1914-19 (DSO): *m* 1904, Violet Evelyn, JP, who *d* 1968, da of Col Frederick Henry Harford; *d* 1961; *s* by his son (14) JOHN AYMER, KCVO, MBE, 13th Earl, *b* 1906; Col late Scots Gds, Capt Gen Queen's Body Guard for Scotland (Royal Company of Archers), Gold Stick for Scotland; Lord Lieut of Wigtownshire; European War 1939-45 in Middle East and Central Mediterranean (despatches): *m* 1960, Davina Katharine, da of late Hon Sir David Bowes-Lyon, KCVO (*see* E Strathmore, colls); *d* 1996; *s* by his eldest son (15) JOHN DAVID JAMES, 14th Earl and present peer; also Viscount Stair, Viscount Dalrymple, Lord Glenluce and Stranraer, Lord Newliston, and Baron Oxenfoord.

*(1) Hon JAMES Dalrymple, 2nd son of 1st Viscount: *cr* a *Baronet* (of Killock) 1698; *s* by his son (2) *Sir* JOHN, 2nd Bt; *d* 1740; *s* by his son (3) *Sir* WILLIAM, 3rd Bt; *d* 1771; *s* by his son (4) *Sir* JOHN, 4th Bt; was a Baron of the Court of Exchequer in Scotland: *m* his cousin Elizabeth Macgill, the heir and representative of the Viscount Oxenfoord, and

assumed the surnames of Hamilton and Macgill; *d* 1810; *s* by his son **(5)** *Sir* JOHN HAMILTON Dalrymple, 5th Bt, who *s* as 8th Earl of Stair (ante).

STALLARD, BARON (Stallard) (Life Baron 1983)

ALBERT WILLIAM STALLARD, son of Frederick Stallard, of Tottenham; *b* 5 Nov 1921; *ed* Low Waters Public Sch, and Hamilton Academy, Scotland; engineer 1937-65; Technical Training Officer 1965-70; mem St Pancras Borough Council 1953-59; Alderman 1962-65; mem Camden Borough Council 1965-70; Alderman since 1971; MP for St Pancras North 1970-74 and for Camden Divn of St Pancras North 1974-83; PPS Min of Agric 1973-74; PPS Min of Housing and Construction 1974-76; Assistant Govt Whip 1976-78; a Lord Commr of HM Treasury 1978-79; *cr Baron Stallard* of St Pancras, London Borough of Camden (Life Baron) 1983: *m* 1944, Julie, da of William Cornelius Murphy, of co Kerry, and has issue.
Residence – 2 Belmont Street, Chalk Farm, NW1.

SON LIVING

Hon Richard, *b* 1945; *ed* Richard Acland Sch, London; *m* 1969, Carol, da of William Packman, of Swanley, Kent, and has issue.

DAUGHTER LIVING

Hon Brenda, *b* 1949, *m* 1971 (*m diss* 1987), Colin Hills, and has issue.

STAMP, BARON (Stamp) (Baron UK 1938)

I hold in trust that which is trusted to me

TREVOR CHARLES BOSWORTH STAMP, 4th Baron; *b* 18 Sept 1935; *s* 1987; *ed* Leys Sch, Gonville and Caius Coll, Camb (BA 1956), and Yale Univ, USA (MSc 1957); St Mary's Hosp Med Sch, London; MB BChir 1961, MD 1972, FRCP 1978 (Lond): *m* 1st, 1963 (*m diss* 1971), Anne Carolynn, da of John Kenneth Churchill, of Tunbridge Wells, Kent; 2ndly, 1975 (*m diss* 1997), Carol Anne, da of Robert Keith Russell, of Farnham, Surrey, and has issue by 1st and 2nd *m*.

Arms – Gules between two garbs or three bezants in bend each charged with a horse passant sable. **Crest** – Issuant from a mount vert bezantee a demi-horse argent. **Supporters** – On either side a horse argent resting the interior hind leg on a bezant.
Residence – 15 Ceylon Rd, W14 0PY.

SON LIVING (*By 2nd marriage*)

Hon NICHOLAS CHARLES TREVOR, *b* 1978.

DAUGHTERS LIVING (*By 1st marriage*)

Hon Catherine Anne Louise, *b* 1963.
Hon Emma Caroline, *b* 1968.

(*by 2nd marriage*)

Hon Lucinda Jane, *b* 1976.

BROTHER LIVING

Hon (Josiah) Richard, *b* 1943; *ed* Winchester, and Queens' Coll, Camb (BA). *Residence* – Flat B, 11 Lymington Rd, NW6 1HX.

UNCLE LIVING (son of 1st Baron)

Hon (Jos) Colin, *b* 1917; *ed* Leys Sch, and Queens' Coll, Camb (MA); late Lt RNVR: late Dir of Marketing Sers for Europe of American Express Internat: *m* 1st, 1940 (*m diss* 1956), Althea, da of late Mrs William Dawes, of Evanston, Illinois, USA; 2ndly, 1958, Gillian Penelope, da of late Guy St J. Tatham, of Johannesburg, SA, and has issue living, (by 1st *m*) Olive Judith *b* 1941; *ed* Wellesley Coll, Mass, USA (BA): *m* 1963 (*m diss* 1975), Eugene Humphrey, and has issue living, Eugene Jos *b* 1971, Alison Dudley *b* 1968, — Althea Patricia Dawes, *b* 1943; *ed* Wellesley Coll, Mass, USA (BA), and York Univ, Toronto (PhD 1981): *m* 1981, Stephen Katz, of Toronto, — Ann Jocelyn, *b* 1945, — Rowena Jane, *b* 1953: *m* 1977, Patrick Olwell, of Nellysford, Va, and has issue living, Matthew *b* 1978, Aaron *b* 1981, — (by 2nd *m*) Robert Colin, *b* 1960; *ed* St Paul's, and Corpus Christi Coll, Camb (BA): *m* 1988, Susan Caroline, da of late John F. Lester, and has issue living, Samuel Robert Josiah *b* 1990, Olivia Joscelyne Isabel *b* 1993, — Jonathan Guy, *b* 1963; *ed* St Paul's, and Balliol Coll, Oxford (BA). *Residence* – 12 Ullswater Rd, SW13 9PJ. *Club* – Naval.

DAUGHTERS LIVING OF SECOND BARON

Hon (Nancy) Elizabeth (11 Harpes Rd, Summertown, Oxford OX2 7QJ), *b* 1931; *ed* St Andrews Univ (MA 1953).

Hon Veronica, *b* 1934; MRCS, and LRCP 1960: *m* 1961, Richard Alfred Hugh McWatters, of The Grove, Dundry, Bristol, son of late Sir Arthur Cecil McWatters, CIE, and has issue living, Rupert Charles, *b* 1967, — Philippa Mary, *b* 1964: *m* 1993, Paul Anthony Ford, son of Ronald Ford, of Cardiff, — Bridget Penelope, *b* 1965.

Hon Jessica Catherine, *b* 1936; *ed* London Univ (BA 1958): *m* 1961, John Edward Chalmers Dow, and has issue living, Charlotte Mary, *b* 1963: *m* 1990, Kevin John Davis, of Penrose, 126 King Charles's Rd, Surbiton, Surrey KT5 8QL, eldest son of F. J. Davis, of Worcester Park, Surrey, and has issue living, Emily Jessica Lycett *b* 1992, Jemima Lucy Katherine *b* 1996, — Juliette Elizabeth Chalmers, *b* 1966: *m* 1995, Daniel Hugh Chisholm (*see* B Windlesham). *Residence* – 30 Norfolk Farm Rd, Pyrford, Woking, Surrey GU22 8LH.

WIDOW LIVING OF SON OF FIRST BARON

(Alice) Mary (1 Holly Oaks, Wormingford, Colchester, Essex), elder da of late Walter Richards, and formerly wife of John Hagon: *m* 1944, as his 2nd wife, Lt-Col Hon (Arthur) Maxwell Stamp, who *d* 1984.

COLLATERAL BRANCH LIVING

Issue of late Lt-Col Hon (Arthur) Maxwell Stamp, 3rd son of 1st Baron, *b* 1915, *d* 1984: *m* 1st, 1938 (*m diss* 1943), Janet Tyler, da of B. Tyler Bryan, of Beaumont, Texas, USA; 2ndly, 1944, (Alice) Mary (ante), elder da of late Walter Richards, and formerly wife of John Hagon:—

(By 2nd *m*) Anthony Philip Josiah (Bonds Cottage, Wormingford, Colchester, Essex), *b* 1947; *ed* Winchester, and Jesus Coll, Camb (BA): *m* 1970, Rosemary Ann, only da of Hume Boggis-Rolfe, CB, CBE, of 22 Victoria Sq, SW1, and has three adopted children, Joseph Anthony, *b* 1977, — Laura Dorothea, *b* 1982. —— Marian Ellina, *b* 1945; *ed* Somerville Coll, Oxford (MA, DPhil); Prof: *m* 1967 (*m diss* 1984), Clinton Richard Dawkins, only son of Clinton John Dawkins, of Over Norton Park, Chipping Norton, Oxon. —— Alison Mary, *b* 1950; *ed* Somerville Coll, Oxford (BA): *m* 1980, Richard Cooke, of Sudbury House, Wrotham, Kent, elder son of late Canon Alfred Gordon Cooke, of The Rectory, St Columb Major, Cornwall, and has issue living, Maxwell Richard Gordon *b* 1985, Florence Mary *b* 1982, Hannah Marian *b* 1984.

PREDECESSORS – (1) Sir JOSIAH CHARLES Stamp, GCB, GBE, DSc, son of late Charles Stamp, of Yomah, Bexley; *b* 1880; was Assist Sec to Board of Inland Revenue 1916-19, Sec and Director Nobel Industries, Ltd 1919-26, and a Director of Imperial Chemical Industries, Ltd 1927-8; appointed a Member of Roy Commn on Income Tax 1919, British Member of Reparations Expert ("Dawes") Committee 1924, a Member of Coal Mins Enquiry Court 1925, a Reparation Expert for Great Britain 1929, and Chm Canadian Grain Futures Enquiry 1931; Chm and Pres of Executive of London, Midland and Scottish Railway, a Director of Bank of England, Adviser of Economic Co-ordination, Past Pres Roy Statistical Soc, and Pres National Institute of Economic Research and of Soc of Genealogists, Col Comdg Engineer and Railway Staff Corps (TA) and Hon Col Transportation, RE (Supplementary Reserve); Charter Mayor of Beckenham 1935, and Pres British Asso for Advancement of Science 1936: *m* 1903, Olive Jessie, who *d* as a result of enemy action during World War II, 16 April 1941, da of Alfred Marsh; *cr Baron Stamp*, of Shortlands, co Kent (peerage of United Kingdom) 1938; *d* as a result of enemy action during World War II, 16 April 1941; *s* by his el son (by decision of House of Lords 10 Sept 1941, and approved by HM King George VI, the decision being analogous to the Law of Property Act 1925, which provides that where two persons have died in circumstances rendering it uncertain which of them survived the other, such deaths should be presumed to have occurred in order of seniority) (2) WILFRID CARLYLE, 2nd Baron, *b* 1904: *m* 1929, Katharine Mary, who *d* 1985, da of Tom Wickett, of Redruth; *d* as a result of enemy action during World War II, 16 April 1941; *s* by his brother (3) TREVOR CHARLES, 3rd Baron, *b* 1907, MD, MRCS England and LRCP London, FRCPath, Prof Emeritus of Bacteriology, Lond Univ: *m* 1932, Frances Dawes, who *d* 1998, da late Charles Henry Bosworth, of Evanston Illinois, USA; *d* 1987; *s* by his elder son (4) TREVOR CHARLES BOSWORTH, 4th Baron and present peer.

Stanhope, family name of Earl of Harrington.

Stanley, Barony of (cr 1456); see Loudoun, Countess of.

Stanley, family name of Earl of Derby.

STANLEY OF ALDERLEY, BARON SHEFFIELD AND (Stanley) (Baron I 1783, UK 1839 and 1848 and Bt E 1660)

Without changing

THOMAS HENRY OLIVER STANLEY (*Baron Stanley of Alderley*), 8th Baron Sheffield, 8th Baron Stanley of Alderley, and 14th Baronet; *b* 28 Sept 1927; *s* 1971; *ed* Wellington Coll; Capt (ret), Coldm Gds; DL Gwynedd 1985; Member Cttee of Management RNLI since 1981, Chm Fund Raising 1985-93; Gov St Edward's Sch, Oxford: *m* 1955, Jane Barrett, da of late Ernest George Hartley, of Lower Farm, Milton-under-Wychwood, Oxon, and has issue.

Arms – Argent, on a bend azure, three bucks' heads cabossed or: a crescent for difference. Crest – On a chapeau gules, turned up ermine, an eagle with wings expanded or preying upon an infant proper, swaddled gules, handed argent. Supporters – (appertaining to the Barony of Stanley of Alderley) — *Dexter*, a stag or, gorged with a ducal crown, line reflexed over the back, and charged on the shoulder with a mullet azure; *sinister*, a lion reguardant proper, gorged with a plain collar argent charged with three escallops gules.
Residence – Trysglwyn Fawr, Rhos y Bol, Amlwch, Anglesey.

SONS LIVING

Hon RICHARD OLIVER, *b* 24 April 1956; *ed* St Edward's Sch, Oxford, and Univ Coll, London (BSc): *m* 1983, Carla Mary Angela, el da of Dr Kenneth Thomas Clyde McKenzie, of 14 The Crescent, Solihull, and has had issue, †Oliver Richard Hugh, *b* 1986, *d* 1989, — Maria Elizabeth Jane, *b* 1988, — Imogen Alexandra Ruth, *b* 1990, — Hermione Helena Rose, *b* 1992.

Hon Charles Ernest, *b* 1960; *ed* St Edward's Sch, Oxford, and Nottingham Univ (BA): *m* 1989, Beverley Ann, elder da of Michael Emmitt, of Swineshead, Lincs, and has issue living, Venetia Jane, *b* 1992, — Olivia Marie, *b* 1995, — Sophia Kate, *b* 1998. *Residence* – Hill Crest, 42 Franconia Rd, SW4 9ND.

Hon Harry John, *b* 1963; *ed* St Edward's Sch, Oxford, Univ Coll, London (LLB), and Camb Univ (LLM): *m* 1998, Shirin, elder da of Zulfikar Kassim-Lakha, of Brussels.

DAUGHTER LIVING

Hon Lucinda Maria, *b* 1958: *m* 1983, Peter Brazel, son of late Benedict Brazel, of Lyndhurst, S Australia, and has issue living, Thomas Owen, *b* 1984, — Harry Jack, *b* 1987, — Jack Alexander, *b* 1988. *Residence* – Lillypilly, 10 River Rd W, Kialla, Victoria 3631, Australia.

BROTHER LIVING (*Raised to the rank of a Baron's son* 1973)

Hon Richard Morgan Oliver, *b* 1931; *ed* Winchester, and New Coll, Oxford: *m* 1956, Phyllida Mary Katharine, da of Lt-Col Clive Grantham Austin, RHA, JP, DL (E Scarbrough), and has issue living, Martin Thomas Oliver (1 Lavender Gdns, SW11 1DH), *b* 1957; *ed* Harrow; 17th/21st Lancers (ret): *m* 1982, Georgina Mary Victoria, only da of George Grimm, of 10 Radnor Walk, SW3 and has issue living, Oliver George *b* 1984, Hugh Richard Timothy *b* 1992, Clementine Masha *b* 1986, Isabella Kate *b* 1988, — Oliver Hugh (Parsonage Farm, Bentworth, nr Alton, Hants), *b* 1959; *ed* Harrow; Coldstream Gds (ret): *m* 1985, Sophie Elizabeth, da of Nicholas Holmes, of Hook Norton Manor, Banbury, Oxon, and has issue living, Arabella Anne *b* 1989, Sabrina Laura *b* 1992, Susannah Rose *b* 1994, — Serena Emma Rose, *b* 1961: *m* 1987, Matthew Hilary Jebb (*see* Pollen, Bt, colls), of Ardsilla, Delgany, co Wicklow, and has issue living, Edwin Francis *b* 1988, Harry *b* 1990, Theodore Philip *b* 1992, Philip Lawrence *b* 1998, Rose Magdalen *b* 1994, — Laura Sylvia Kathleen, *b* 1968: *m* 1996, David J. Barbour, eldest son of Clive Barbour, of Croston, Lancs. *Residence* – Sandfield, Breach Lane, Shaftesbury, Dorset SP7 8LD.

DAUGHTER LIVING OF SIXTH BARON

Hon Edwina Maureen, *b* 1933: *m* 1st, 1953 (*m diss* 1966), John Dawnay Innes, who *d* 1966 (V Downe, colls); 2ndly, 1968, J Philip Epstein, and has issue living, (by 1st *m*), Thomas John Stanley (64 Monnow St, Monmouth), *b* 1954; *ed* Eton: *m* 1989, Irma Fingal-Rock, and has issue living, Oliver Edward Zachariah FINGAL-ROCK INNES *b* 1984, Aphrodite Irma Emilie Clementine FINGAL-ROCK INNES *b* 1987, — Richard James, *b* 1955: *m* 1987, Auriol I., yr da of R. H. F. Stanton, of Bungay, Suffolk, and has issue living, Archibald John Stanton *b* 1992, Dominic Robert *b* 1994, — Mary Clementine Adelaide, *b* 1960: *m* 1986, Alexander Nikolaevich Drewchin, of Box 920, RD1 Honesdale, Pennsylvania 18431, USA. *Residence* – 146 Benhill Rd, SE5 7LZ.

DAUGHTER LIVING OF FIFTH BARON

Hon Victoria Venetia, *b* 1917: *m* 1942, Lt-Cdr James Douglas Woods, Roy Canadian Naval VR, and has issue living, Virginia Louise, *b* 1943, — Teresa Clare, *b* 1946. *Residence* – 31 Boswell Av, Toronto 180, Ont, Canada.

PREDECESSORS – (1) *Rt Hon* JOHN Holroyd, MP for Coventry: *cr Baron Sheffield*, of Dunnamore, co Meath (peerage of Ireland) 1781, *Baron Sheffield*, of Roscommon (peerage of Ireland) 1783 with remainder to the das of his 1st *m* and their heirs male, *Baron Sheffield*, of Sheffield, co York (peerage of United Kingdom) 1802, and *Viscount Pevensey* and *Earl of Sheffield* (peerage of Ireland) 1816; Pres of Board of Agriculture 1803, and Lord of Board of Trade, etc; *d* 1821; *s* by his son (2) GEORGE AUGUSTUS FREDERICK CHARLES, 2nd Earl; *b* 1802; a Lord-in-Waiting to HM Queen Victoria 1858-9: *m* 1825, Harriet, da of 2nd Earl of Harewood; *d* 1870; *s* by his son (3) HENRY NORTH, 3rd Earl; *b* 1832; MP for Sussex E (C) 1857-65; *d* 1909, when the Irish Barony (*cr* 1781), the United Kingdom Barony (*cr* 1802), and the Earldom (*cr* 1816) became *ext*; *s* in the Irish Barony (*cr* 1783) under the special remainder by his kinsman (4) EDWARD LYULPH, PC, 4th Baron Stanley of Alderley (grandson of Lady Maria Josepha Holroyd, da of 1st Earl of Sheffield) (see * infra); *b* 1839; in 1909 *s* to *Barony of Sheffield* (*cr* 1783): MP for Oldham (L) 1880-85: *m* 1873, Mary Katharine, CBE, who *d* 1929, da of late Sir (Isaac) Lowthian Bell, 1st Bt; *d* 1925; *s* by his son (5) ARTHUR LYULPH, KCMG, 5th Baron; *b* 1875; was Director of National Bank of Australasia and of Australian Mercantile, Land, and Finance Co (Limited); formerly a Member of Woods and Forests Committee; sometime Parliamentary Private Sec (unpaid) to Postmaster-Gen (Rt Hon S. C. Buxton, MP), Private Sec (unpaid) Office of Woods and Forests, and a Member of Select Committee on Peerages in abeyance: Gov of Victoria 1914-20: MP for Cheshire, Eddisbury Div (L) Jan 1906 to Jan 1910; *m* 1905, Margaret Evelyn, who *d* 1964, da of Henry Evans Gordon, of 59 Cadogan Gdns, SW; *d* 1931; *s* by his son (6) EDWARD JOHN, 6th Baron; *b* 1907: *m* 1st, 1932 (*m diss* 1936), Lady Victoria Audrey Beatrice Chetwynd-Talbot, who *d* 1994, da of late Charles John Alton Chetwynd, Viscount Ingestre, MVO (E Shrewsbury); 2ndly, 1944 (*m diss* 1948), Louise Sylvia, who *d* 1977, da of Arthur Hawkes, and widow of Douglas Fairbanks, Sr; 3rdly, 1951 (*m diss* 1957), Thérèse, da of Gen Husson, of Toulon, France; 4thly, 1961, Kathleen Margaret, who *d* 1996, da of late Cecil Murray Wright, and widow of Sir Edmund Frank Crane; *d* 3 March 1971, *s* by his brother (7) LYULPH HENRY VICTOR OWEN, 7th Baron *b* 1915, *d* 23 June 1971; *s* by his cousin (8) THOMAS HENRY (3rd son of Lt-Col Hon Oliver Hugh Stanley, DSO, yst son of 4th Baron), 8th Baron and present peer; also Baron Stanley of Alderley, and Baron Eddisbury.
*(1) THOMAS Stanley, Bar-at-law, descended from Hon Sir John Stanley, 3rd son of 1st Baron Stanley (*see* E Derby); *cr* a *Baronet* 1660; *s* by his son (2) *Sir* PETER, 2nd Bt; was High Sheriff of Cheshire 1678; *d* 1701; *s* by his son (3) *Sir* THOMAS, 3rd Bt; *d* 1721; *s* by his el son (4) *Sir* JAMES, 4th Bt; *d* 1746; *s* by his brother (5) *Sir* EDWARD, 5th Bt; *d* 1755; *s* by his son (6) *Sir* JOHN THOMAS, 6th Bt; was a Gentleman of the Privy Chamber and Clerk of the Cheque of the Yeomen of the Guard; *d* 1807; *s* by his son (7) *Sir* JOHN THOMAS, 7th Bt; *cr Baron Stanley of Alderley* (peerage of United Kingdom) 1839: *m* Lady Maria Josepha Holroyd, da of 1st Earl of Sheffield; *d* 1850; *s* by his son (8) EDWARD JOHN, PC, 2nd Baron, who in 1848 had been *cr Baron Eddisbury*, of Winnington (peerage of United Kingdom); *b* 1802; sat as MP for Hendon 1831, and for N Cheshire 1832-41, and 1847-8; was Under-Sec of Home Dept 1834, Sec to Treasury 1835-41, Under-Sec for Foreign Affairs 1846-52, Vice-Pres of Board of Trade 1852, Pres of Board of Trade 1855-8, and Postmaster-Gen 1859-66: *m* 1826, Hon Henrietta Maria, who *d* 1895, da of 13th Viscount Dillon; *d* 1869; *s* by his son (9) HENRY EDWARD JOHN, 3rd Baron; *b* 1827; Sec of Legation at Athens 1854-9; *dsp*; *s* by his brother (10) EDWARD LYULPH, PC, 4th Baron, who *s* as 4th Baron Sheffield 1909 (ante).

Stanley of Bickerstaffe, Lord; son of Earl of Derby.

STANSGATE, VISCOUNTCY OF (Benn) (Viscount UK 1942, disclaimed 1963)

Rt Hon ANTHONY (NEIL) WEDGWOOD BENN, MP, *b* 3 April 1925; *s* as 2nd Viscount 17 Nov 1960, but made it known that he did not wish to claim the Viscountcy; disclaimed his peerage for life 31 July 1963, having unsuccessfully attempted to renounce his right of succession 1955 and 1960; *ed* Westminster, and New Coll, Oxford (MA); CIEE; FRSA; Hon LLD Strathclyde; Hon DTech Bradford; Hon DSc Aston; late PO RAFVR, and Sub-Lt Fleet Air Arm; 1939-45 War; Postmaster-Gen 1964-66, and Min of Tech 1966-70; Chm of Labour Party 1971-2; Sec of State for Industry, and Min of Posts and Telecommunications 1974-75, Sec of State for Energy 1975-79; MP for SE Div of Bristol (*Lab*) 1950-60; re-elected May 1961, but debarred from sitting by judgement of Election Court 1961; MP for SE Div of Bristol 1963-83, and for Chesterfield since 1984; PC 1964. *m* 1949, Caroline Middleton, MA, da of late James Milton De Camp, of Handasyde Court, Cincinnati, USA, and has issue.

Arms – See Benn, Bt (*cr* 1914), not used.
Residence – 12 Holland Park Av, W11.

SONS LIVING

STEPHEN MICHAEL WEDGWOOD, *b* 21 Aug 1951; *ed* Holland Park Sch, and Keele Univ: *m* 1988, Ishika Nita, da of Stuart Ashley Bowes, of Tel Aviv Univ, Ramat Hasharon, Israel, and has issue living, Daniel, *b* 10 Dec 1991, — Emily, *b* 1989.

Hilary James Wedgwood, *b* 1953: *m* 1st, 1973, Rosalind Retey, who *d* 1979; 2ndly, 1982, Sally Clark, and has issue, three sons and one da.

Joshua William Wedgwood, *b* 1958: *m* 1984, Elizabeth Feeney, and has issue, one son.

DAUGHTER LIVING

Melissa Anne Wedgwood, *b* 1957; has issue, two das.

BROTHER LIVING

Hon David Julian Wedgwood, *b* 1928; *ed* Balliol Coll, Oxford (BA 1951): *m* 1959, June Mary, el da of late Ernest Charles Barraclough, and has issue living, Piers Michael Wedgwood, *b* 1962, — Cordelia Frances Margaret Wedgwood, *b* 1964: *m* 1998, Michael G. Nestor, son of Michael Nestor, of Croydon, Surrey, and has issue living, Michael Charles Archie *b* 1999. *Residences* – 4 Liskeard Gdns, Blackheath, SE3; Stansgate Cottage, nr Steeple, Southminster, Essex.

PREDECESSOR – **(1)** (WILLIAM) WEDGWOOD Benn, DSO, DFC, PC, 2nd son of Sir John William Benn, 1st Bt (*cr* 1914); *b* 1877; Sec of State for India 1929-31, and Sec of State for Air 1945-46; sat as MP for St Geroge's Div of Tower Hamlets (L) 1906-18, for Leith 1918-27, for Aberdeen, N Div (Lab) 1928-31, and Gorton Div of Manchester 1937-41; *cr Viscount Stansgate*, of Stansgate, co Essex (peerage of United Kingdom) 1942: *m* 1920, Margaret Eadie, who *d* 1991, da of late Daniel Turner Holmers, formerly MP for Govan Div of Lanarkshire; *d* 1960; *s* by his 2nd son **(2)** ANTHONY (NEIL) WEDGWOOD, 2nd Viscount, until he disclaimed his Peerage 1963.

STEEL OF AIKWOOD, BARON (Steel) (Life Baron 1997)

DAVID MARTIN SCOTT STEEL, KBE, PC, son of Very Rev Dr David Steel, sometime Moderator of the General Assembly of the Church of Scotland; *b* 31 March 1938; *ed* Prince of Wales Sch, Nairobi, George Watson's Coll, Edinburgh, and Edinburgh Univ (MA 1960, LLB 1962, Hon LLD 1988), Hon DUniv Stirling 1991, Hon D Litt Buckingham 1993, Hon DUniv Heriot Watt Univ 1996; MP (Lib until 1988, then Lib Dem) for Roxburgh, Selkirk and Peebles 1965-83, and for Tweeddale, Ettrick and Lauderdale 1983-97; Memb Parliamentary Delegation to UN 1967; Liberal Chief Whip 1970-75; Spokesman on Foreign Affairs 1975-76; Leader of Liberal Party 1976-88; Memb Select Cttee on Privileges 1979-86; Pres Liberal International 1994-96; Rector of Edinburgh Univ 1982-85; Freeman of Tweeddale 1988, and of Ettrick and Lauderdale 1990; awarded Commander's Cross of Order of Merit (Germany) 1992; DL Ettrick and Lauderdale and Roxburghshire 1990; *cr* 1977, KBE 1990, and *Baron Steel of Aikwood*, of Ettrick Forest in the Scottish Borders (Life Baron) 1997: *m* 1962, Judith Mary, da of late William Douglas MacGregor, CBE, of Kiltane, Dunblane, Perthshire, and has issue, 2 sons and 1 da.

Address – House of Lords, SW1A 0PW.

STERLING OF PLAISTOW, BARON (Sterling) (Life Baron 1991)

JEFFREY MAURICE STERLING, CBE, son of Harry Sterling; *b* 27 Dec 1934; *ed* Reigate Gram Sch, Preston Manor County Sch, and Guildhall Sch of Music; Hon Dr Business Admin Nottingham Trent Univ 1995, Hon DCL Durham 1996; Advisor, Paul Schweder & Co, Stock Exchange, 1955-57, and G. Eberstadt & Co 1957-62, Finance Dir Gen Guarantee Corpn 1962-64, Man Dir Gula Investments Ltd 1964-69, Chm Sterling Guarantee Trust plc 1969-85, when it merged with P&O Steam Navigation Co, Chm P&O Steam Navigation Co since 1983; Member British Airways Bd 1979-82; Special Advisor to Sec of State for Industry 1982-83, and to Sec of State for Trade & Industry 1983-90; Chm Organisation Cttee World ORT (Organisation for Rehabilitation by Training) Union 1969-73 (Member Exec since 1966), Chm ORT Technical Services since 1974, Vice-Pres British ORT since 1978; Pres Gen Council of British Shipping 1990-91; Pres European Community Shipowners' Assoc 1992-94; Dep-Chm and Hon Treas London Celebrations Cttee, HM's Silver Jubilee, 1975-83; Chm Young Vic Co 1975-83, Chm of Govs Royal Ballet Sch since 1983, Gov Royal Ballet since 1986; Chm Motability since 1994; Vice-Chm and Chm of Exec Motability since 1977; Hon Fell Inst of Marine Engrs 1991; Freeman of City of London; Hon Capt RNR 1991; Elder Brother Trinity House 1991; Hon Fell Inst of Chartered Shipbrokers 1992; Hon Memb RICS 1993; Fell ISVA 1995; Hon Fell Royal Inst of Naval Architects 1997; CBE 1977, Knt 1985, and *Baron Sterling of Plaistow*, of Pall Mall, City of Westminster (Life Baron) 1991: *m* 1985, Dorothy Ann Smith, and has issue, one da.

𝕬rms – Chequy argent and sable, three lyres bendwise in bend gules. 𝕮rest – A salamander statant upon its hind legs sable, enflamed proper, and holding between the forefeet the Hebrew letter chaim argent. 𝕾upporters – *Dexter*, a retriever gules supporting with the exterior forefoot an anchor argent; *sinister*, a fallow deer gules supporting with the exterior forefoot an anchor argent.
Office- The Peninsular and Oriental Steam Navigation Company, Peninsular House, 79 Pall Mall, SW1Y 5EJ. *Clubs* – Garrick, Carlton, Hurlingham.

Stern, surname of Barony of Michelham.

Stevas, St John-, family name of Baron St John of Fawsley.

STEVENS OF LUDGATE, BARON (Stevens) (Life Baron 1987)

·PERSEVERANCE·

DAVID ROBERT STEVENS, son of late (Arthur) Edwin Stevens, CBE, of Esher, Surrey, by his wife Kathleen Alberta, da of Charles James; *b* 26 May 1936; *ed* Stowe, and Sidney Sussex Coll, Camb (MA); Dir Philip Hill Higginson Erlangers 1959-68, Hill Samuel Securities since 1968, Drayton Group 1968-74, Samuel Montagu (Man Dir) 1974-85, Chm City & Foreign since 1976, Drayton Far East since 1976, English & Internat since 1976, Consolidated Venture (formerly Montagu Boston) since 1979, Drayton Consolidated since 1980, Drayton Japan since 1980, Chm EDC for Civil Engrs 1984-86, United Newspapers since 1981 (Dir since 1974), Express Newspapers since 1985, and Chm and Chief Exec MIM Britannia Ltd (formerly Montagu Investment Management Ltd) since 1980; *cr Baron Stevens of Ludgate*, of Ludgate, in the City of London (Life Baron) 1987: *m* 1st, 1961 (*m diss* 1970), Patricia Ann, da of George Warren Rose, of St George's Hill, Weybridge, Surrey; 2ndly, 1977, Mrs Melissa Sadoff, who *d* 1989, da of Milos Milicevic and of Countess Andrassy; 3rdly, 1990, Mrs Meriza Giori, and has issue by 1st *m*.

Arms – Argent a bear rampant proper and a chief embattled azure. **Crest** – A triple mount vert thereon a crest coronet or the lesser finials (two manifest) pearled proper statant within the same a swan wings displayed proper about the neck two ribands nowed and the ends flotant to the rear gules and argent. **Supporters** – *Dexter*, a lion sejant erect and guardant or; *sinister*, a cairn terrier also sejant erect and guardant proper, the compartment comprising a grassy mount also proper. **Motto** – Perseverance.
Address – 11 Devonshire Sq, EC2M 4YR. *Club* – White's.

SON LIVING (*By 1st marriage*)

Hon Andrew David, *b* 1966.

DAUGHTER LIVING (*By 1st marriage*)

Hon Judith Ann, *b* 1964.

Stewart, family name of Earl of Galloway.

Stewart, family name of Baron Stewartby.

Stewart, Vane-Tempest-, family name of Marquess of Londonderry.

STEWARTBY, BARON (Stewart) (Life Baron 1992)

(BERNARD HAROLD) IAN (HALLEY) STEWART, RD, PC, only son of Prof Harold Charles Stewart, CBE (grandson of late Sir Halley Stewart, *see* Stewart, Bt, *cr* 1937); *b* 10 Aug 1935; *ed* Haileybury, and Jesus Coll, Camb (MA, DLitt 1978); RNVR 1954-56, Lieut-Cdr RNR (RD 1972); Dir Brown Shipley & Co (Merchant Bankers) 1971-83; PPS to Rt Hon Sir Geoffrey Howe (as Chancellor of the Exchequer) 1979-83, Under-Sec MOD (Defence Procurement) Jan-Oct 1983, Economic Sec Treasury 1983-87, Min of State for the Armed Forces 1987-88, and for NI 1988-89; Chm Throgmorton Trust plc since 1990, Dep Chm Standard Chartered plc since 1993, Member Public Expenditure Cttee 1977-79, Public Accounts Cttee 1991-92, Financial Services Authority 1993-97, and British Academy Cttee for Sylloge of Coins of British Isles since 1967; Life Gov Haileybury 1977, Trustee Sir Halley Stewart Trust since 1978, Vice-Pres St John's Ambulance for Herts since 1977, CStJ 1986, KStJ 1992; FBA 1981, FRSE 1986, FSA, FSA(Scot); author; MP Hitchin (*C*) 1974-83, and N Herts 1983-92; *cr* PC 1989, Kt Bach 1991, and *Baron Stewartby*, of Portmoak, in the District of Perth and Kinross (Life Baron) 1992: *m* 1966, Hon Deborah Charlotte Buchan, JP, da of 3rd Baron Tweedsmuir, and has issue.

Arms – Or, a fess chequy azure and argent between a portcullis with chains in chief, and a lymphad, sails furled, oars in action sable, flagged gules in base all within a bordure azure, a label of three points gules. Crest – A lymphad as in the shield between two fleurs-de-lys or. Supporters – *Dexter*, a stag proper attired or gorged with a collar engrailed gules; *sinister*, a lion proper gorged with a collar engrailed chequy argent and gules.
Address – Broughton Green, Peeblesshire ML12 6HQ. *Clubs* – New (Edinburgh), MCC, Hawks, RAC.

SON LIVING

Hon Henry Ernest Alexander Halley, *b* 1972; *ed* Haileybury, and Jesus Coll, Camb; 2nd Lieut Royal Scots.

DAUGHTERS LIVING

Hon Lydia Barbara Rose Anna Phoebe, *b* 1969.
Hon (Dorothy) Louisa Charlotte Amabel, *b* 1970: *m* 1999, Dr Andrew Murdoch Elder, yr son of Prof Murdoch Elder, of Broughton, Peeblesshire.

STEYN, BARON (Steyn) (Life Baron 1995)

JOHAN VAN ZYL STEYN, PC, son of Izak van Zyl Steyn, of S Africa; *b* 15 Aug 1932; *ed* Jan van Riebeeck Sch, Cape Town, S Africa, Univ of Stellenbosch (BA, LLB 1957), and Univ Coll, Oxford (Cape Province Rhodes Scholar 1955, MA 1957); Bar S Africa 1958-73 (Senior Counsel); Bar England 1973, QC 1979, Bencher, Lincoln's Inn 1985; High Court Judge, Commercial Court 1985, Supreme Court Rule Commn 1985-89, Chm Race Relations Cttee of Bar 1987, Presiding Judge, Northern Circuit 1989-91, Lord Justice of Appeal 1992-95, since when a Lord of Appeal in Ordinary; Memb American Law Inst (AIL) 1999; *cr* Kt 1985, PC 1995, and *Baron Steyn*, of Swafield, co Norfolk (Life Baron), 1995: *m* 1st, 1958 (*m diss* 1977), Jean Margaret, da of late Martin John Pollard; 2ndly, 1977, Mrs Susan Leonore Heard, da of E. A. L. Lewis, and has issue living by 1st *m*.
Residence – c/o House of Lords, SW1A 0PW.

SONS LIVING (*By 1st marriage*)

Hon Martin van Zyl (21 Quarry Hill Rd, Borough Green, Kent TN15 8RQ), *b* 1964; *ed* Judd Sch, Tonbridge, and Keele Univ: *m* 1994, Alison Jane, da of Graham Lawrence (Sam) Footitt, of Si Rusa, Hopgarden Lane, Sevenoaks, Kent.
Hon Deon Johan, *b* 1966; *ed* Bethany Sch, Goudhurst, Kent.

DAUGHTERS LIVING (*By 1st marriage*)

Hon Linda Jean, *b* 1968; *ed* Combe Bank Girls' Sch, Sundridge, and New Coll, Durham: *m* 1995, Robert A. Lewis, of 21 Hydethorpe Rd, SW12 0JE.
Hon Karen Margaret, *b* 1970; *ed* Tonbridge Gram Sch, Liverpool Univ, and City Univ, London; Bar Middle Temple 1995: *m* 1997, Alexander J. Glassbrook.

STOCKS, BARONY OF (Stocks) (Extinct 1975)

DAUGHTERS LIVING OF LIFE BARONESS

Hon Mary Ann, *b* 1915: *m* 1942, Arthur Patterson, CMG, who *d* 1996, and has issue.
Hon Helen Jane, JP, *b* 1920. *Residence* – 44 Regent's Park Rd, NW1.

STOCKTON, EARL OF (Macmillan) (Earl UK 1984)

ALEXANDER DANIEL ALAN MACMILLAN, 2nd Earl; *b* 10 Oct 1943; *s* 1986; *ed* Eton, Univ of Paris, and Strathclyde Univ; Chm Macmillan Publishing Ltd since 1980: *m* 1st, 1970 (*m diss* 1991), Hélène Birgitte (Bitta), da of late Alan Douglas Christie Hamilton, of Stable Green, Mitford, Northumberland; 2ndly, 1995, Miranda Elizabeth Louise, da of Richard St John Quarry, and formerly wife of (i) Peter Richard Henry Sellers, CBE, the actor, and (ii) Sir Nicholas Keith Lillington Nuttall, 3rd Bt, and has issue by 1st *m*.

꿈rms – Argent a chief or overall between three open books proper edged or and bound azure those in chief inscribed respectively in letters sable 'Miseres' and 'Discere' and that in base also in letters sable inscribed 'Succo' and as many mullets azure a lion rampant sable. Crests – Upon a helm with a wreath or azure and sable within sprigs of oak fructed or a dexter cubit arm and a sinister arm embowed both proper the dexter hand gauntletted or and with the other brandishing a two handed sword proper hilt pommel and quillons sable. Supporters – *Dexter* a lion rampant gules; *sinister* an American bald headed eagle proper the compartment comprising a crenelated wall proper in the portal thereof an anchor azure and joined on either side by two bars wavy azure to a grassy mount growing from that on the dexter a long branch and from that on the sinister a thistle both proper.
Residence – Hayne Manor, Stowford, Okehampton, Devon EX20 4DB. *Office* — 25 Eccleston Place, SW1W 9NF.

SON LIVING (*By 1st marriage*)

DANIEL MAURICE ALAN (*Viscount Macmillan of Ovenden*), *b* 9 Oct 1974.

DAUGHTERS LIVING (*By 1st marriage*)

Lady Rebecca Elizabeth, *b* 1980.
Lady Louisa Alexandra, *b* 1982.

BROTHERS LIVING AND DECEASED

Joshua Edward Andrew, *b* 1945; *ed* Balliol Coll, Oxford; *dunm* 1965.
Hon Adam Julian Robert, *b* 1948; *ed* Eton, and Univ of Strasbourg: *m* 1982, Sarah Anne Mhuire, yr da of late Dr Brian

MacGreevy, of 85 Onslow Sq, SW7, and has issue living, Frederick Maurice Brian, *b* 1990, — Joshua, *b* 1995, — Sophia Elizabeth Katherine, *b* 1985, — Alice Charlotte Rose, *b* 1987.

Hon David Maurice Benjamin, *b* 1957; *ed* Harrow: *m* 1995, Arabella Rosalind Hungerford, yr da of Peregrine Michael Hungerford Pollen (*see* Pollen, Bt, colls), and formerly wife of Giacomo Dante Algranti, and has issue living, Finn Joshua Marcus, *b* 1995, — Mabel Rachel, *b* 1998.

SISTER DECEASED

Hon Rachael Mary Georgina, *b* 1955: *m* 1982 (*m diss* 1986), Leith Corbett, only son of H. M. Corbett, of Sydney, NSW, Australia; *dsp* 1987.

AUNT LIVING (*Daughter of 1st Earl*)

Lady (Ann) Caroline, *b* 1923: *m* 1944, Julian Tufnell Faber (Fisher's Gate, Withyham, Hartfield, E Sussex TN7 4BB; Flat 4, 17-21 Sloane Court West, SW3), son of late Alfred Faber, and has had issue, Michael David Tufnell, *b* 1945; *ed* Eton, and Trin Coll, Camb: *m* 1968, Catherine Suzanne, da of Comte Robert de Braine, of Cannes, France, and has issue living, Richard Julian Robert *b* 1974, Elizabeth Anne Catherine *b* 1971, — Mark James Julian, *b* 1950; *ed* Eton, and Balliol Coll, Oxford: *m* 1983, Ann (35 Albert Bridge Rd, SW11 4PX), da of Christopher Griffith, of Natal, South Africa, and *d* 1991, leaving issue, Alexander John Julian *b* 1986, Luke Christopher Michael *b* 1990, Thomas Mark Nicholas, *b* (*posthumous*) 1992, — David James Christian, MP (House of Commons, SW1), *b* 1961; *ed* Eton, and Balliol Coll, Oxford; MP Westbury (*C*) since 1992: *m* 1st, 1988 (*m diss* 1996), Sally Elizabeth, elder da of Mrs Kenneth J. Gilbert, of Yelverton, Devon; 2ndly, 1998, Sophie Amanda, da of Martyn Hedley (*see* B Ampthill, colls), and has issue living (by 1st *m*), Henry Mark Tufnell *b* 1992, — James Edwin Charles (Neaves Park Farm, Hartfield, E Sussex TN7 4HA), *b* 1964; *ed* Eton, and Edinburgh Univ: *m* 1994, Phillida Ann, da of late Adrian Henry, FRCS, of Oxhill, Warwicks, and has issue living, Archibald Adrian *b* 1994, Francis Edwin *b* 1996, — Anne Christine Adriane (*Hon Mrs David Bernstein*) (27 Tregunter Rd, SW10 9LS), *b* 1944; JP Inner London 1994; Family Panel 1998: *m* 1st, 1970 (*m diss* 1981), Michael Roger Lewis Cockerell, eldest son of Prof Hugh A. L. Cockerell; 2ndly, 1995, Hon David Sidney Bernstein, son of late Baron Bernstein (Life Baron), and has issue living (by 1st *m*), William Michael Victor Lewis *b* 1973, Sophia Charlotte Evelyn *b* 1970: *m* 1996, Capt Philip G. R. Earl, The Life Guards, of The Garden Flat, 50 Cathcart Rd, SW10 9JQ, elder son of Col Timothy Earl, of Haddon Lodge, Stourton Caundle, Dorset.

MOTHER LIVING

Hon Katharine Margaret Alice Ormsby-Gore (*Viscountess Macmillan of Ovenden*), DBE, 2nd da of 4th Baron Harlech, KG, GCMG, PC: *m* 1942, Maurice Victor, Viscount Macmillan of Ovenden, PC, MP, who *dvp* 1984, only son of 1st Earl of Stockton, OM, PC, FRS. *Residence* – 9 Warwick Square, SW1.

PREDECESSORS – (1) Rt Hon (MAURICE) HAROLD Macmillan, OM, PC, FRS, 3rd and yst son of late Maurice Crawford Macmillan, *b* 1894, served 1914-18 War as Capt Gren Gds (thrice wounded), MP for Stockton-on-Tees 1924-29 and 1931-45, and for Bromley 1945-64, Parliamentary Sec Min of Supply 1940-42, Under-Sec of State for the Colonies Feb-Dec 1942, Min Resident in N Africa Dec 1942 — May 1945, Sec of State for Air May-July 1945, Min of Housing and Local Govt 1951-54, of Defence 1954-55, Sec of State for Foreign Affairs April-Dec 1955, Chancellor of the Exchequer 1955-57, Prime Minister and First Lord of the Treasury 1957-63, Chancellor of Oxford Univ 1960-86, Pres Macmillan Ltd 1974-86, Hon Freeman City of London 1961; *cr Viscount Macmillan of Ovenden*, of Chelwood Gate, in the County of E Sussex, and of Stockton-on-Tees, in the County of Cleveland, and *Earl of Stockton* (peerage of United Kingdom) 1984: *m* 1920, Lady Dorothy Evelyn Cavendish, GBE, who *d* 1966, 3rd da of 9th Duke of Devonshire, KG, GCMG, GCVO, PC; *d* 1986; *s* by his grandson (2) ALEXANDER DANIEL ALAN (eldest son of Maurice Victor, Viscount Macmillan of Ovenden, only son of 1st Earl), 2nd Earl and present peer; also Viscount Macmillan of Ovenden.

STODART OF LEASTON, BARON (Stodart) (Life Baron 1981)

JAMES ANTHONY STODART, PC, son of late Col Thomas Stodart, CIE, IMS; *b* 6 June 1916; *ed* Wellington; Under-Sec of State for Scotland 1963-64, Parl Sec Min of Agric, Fisheries and Food 1070-72, Min of State Min of Agric, Fisheries and Food 1972-74; MP for Edinburgh West (*C*) 1959-74; Chm Agric Credit Corpn 1975-87; Chm Cttee of Enquiry into Local Govt in Scotland 1980; *cr* PC 1974, and *Baron Stodart of Leaston*, of Humbie, in the District of E Lothian (Life Baron) 1981: *m* 1940, Hazel Jean, who *d* 1995, da of Lieut Ronald James Usher, DSC, RN (*see* Usher, Bt, colls, 1995 Edn). *Residence* – Lorimers, N Berwick, E Lothian. *Clubs* – New (Edinburgh), Cavalry and Guards', Hon Co of Edinburgh Golfers.

STODDART OF SWINDON, BARON (Stoddart) (Life Baron 1983)

DAVID LEONARD STODDART, son of late Arthur Leonard Stoddart, by his wife Queenie Victoria Price; *b* 4 May 1926; *ed* St Clement Danes and Henley Gram Schs; mem Reading County Borough Council 1954-72; MP for Swindon 1970-83; an Assistant Govt Whip 1975; a Lord Commr for HM Treasury 1976-77; *cr Baron Stoddart of Swindon*, of Reading in the Royal County of Berkshire (Life Baron) 1983: *m* 1st, 1946 (*m diss* 1960), Doreen M. Maynard; 2ndly, 1961, Jennifer, adopted da of late Mrs Lois Percival-Alwyn, of Battle, Sussex, and has issue by 1st and 2nd *m*.
Residence – Sintra, 37A Bath Rd, Reading, Berks.

SONS LIVING (*By 2nd marriage*)

Hon Howard David, *b* 1966.
Hon Mathwyn Hugh, *b* 1969.

DAUGHTER LIVING (*By 1st marriage*)

Hon Janet Victoria, *b* 1947, *m* 1967, Jack Pudney, and has issue.

STOKES, BARON (Stokes) (Life Baron 1969)

DONALD GRESHAM STOKES, TD, son of Harry Potts Stokes, of Rock Towers Hotel, Looe; *b* 22 March 1914; *ed* Blundell's Sch, and Harris Inst of Technology, Preston; F Eng; FIMechE; MSAE; FIMI; FCIT; FIRTE; Hon LLD Lancaster; Hon DTech Loughborough; Hon DSc Southampton, and Salford; late Lt-Col REME; DL for Lancs; Gen Sales Manager Leyland Motors Ltd, 1950, Dir 1954, Chm and Managing Dir Leyland Motor Corpn, 1967, and of British Leyland Motor Corpn Ltd 1968, Ch Exec 1973 (Pres 1977-79); Chm Dutton-Forshaw Motor Group Ltd and Jack Barclay Ltd 1980-90; a Member of NW Economic Planning Council 1965-70; Chm NEDC for Electronics Industry 1966-68; a Dir of National Westminster Bank 1969-81; Chm of British Arabian Advisory Co 1977-85, Vice-Pres of Employers' Eng Fedn, a Member of Council CBI, a Member of Soc of Motor Manufacturers & Traders; Dir KBH Communications Ltd 1985-96; Dir Scottish & Universal Investments Ltd 1980-92, and GWR Group 1990-94; Chm Two Counties Radio Ltd 1979-94; Dir Beherman Auto-Transports NV (Belgium) 1982-89; Fell of Keble Coll, Oxford since 1968; Pres Manchester Univ Inst of Science and Technology 1968-76; Chm The Dovercourt Motor Co Ltd 1982-90; Liveryman of Carmen Co; Officer of Order of Crown of Belgium; Cdr of the Order of Leopold II of Belgium; *cr* Knt 1965, and *Baron Stokes*, of Leyland, co Palatine of Lancaster (Life Baron) 1969: *m* 1939, Laura Elizabeth Courteney, who *d* 1995, da of Frederick C. Lamb, and has issue.

Arms – Gyronny of eight or and sable, a lion rampant double queued ermine, on a chief or an estoc erect between two speedwell flowers stalked and leaved proper. Crest – A demi lion double queued ermine, holding between the paws a piston with connecting rod argent, the crown inflamed proper. Supporters – *Dexter*, a lion reguardant double queued ermine; *sinister*, a horse argent, crined and unguled sable.
Residence – Branksome Cliff, Westminster Road, Poole, Dorset, BH13 6JW. *Club* – Royal Motor Yacht.

SON LIVING

Hon Michael Donald Gresham, *b* 1947; *ed* Southampton Univ (BSc): *m* 1st, 1970 (*m diss* 1980), Inger Anita, yr da of Douglas Percy, of Hotspur House, Hythe, Hants; 2ndly, 1986, Theresa, da of late John Edgar Papworth, and has issue.
Residence – Longfield House, Mill Bank, Fladbury, Worcs WR10 2QA.

STONE, BARONY OF (Stone) (Extinct 1986)

SON LIVING OF LIFE BARON

Hon Richard Malcolm Ellis, (15 Blenheim Rd, NW8 0LU), *b* 1937; MA (Jurisprudence) Oxford; BM BCh, MRCGP: *m* 1970, Ruth Perry, and has isuse living, one son and two das.

DAUGHTER LIVING OF LIFE BARON

Hon Adrianne Barbara Ellis, *b* 1934; LCST: *m* 1957, Clive M. Marks, of 39 Farm Av, NW2.

STONE OF BLACKHEATH, BARON (Stone) (Life Baron 1997)

ANDREW ZELIG STONE, son of late Sydney Stone, of Porthcawl; *b* 7 Sept 1942; *ed* Cardiff High Sch; Management Trainee, Marks & Spencer 1966, Israel 1967, Merchandise Manager 1973, PA to Chm 1978-80, Divisional Dir 1986, Menswear 1986, Children's Wear 1988, Ladies' Wear 1990, Dir since 1990, Jt Man Dir since 1994; Govr Welzmann Inst Foundation 1997 (Dir 1993); Pres BOTGI Group for Israel since 1997 and Adventures in Motion Pictures (Ballet Co); Trustee ABSA, Jewish Assoc of Business Ethics; Patron Interalia Inst of Arts and Science; FRSA; *cr Baron Stone of Blackheath*, of Blackheath in the London Borough of Greenwich (Life Baron) 1997: *m* 1973, Vivienne Wendy, da of Bernard Lee, and has issue.
Address – Marks & Spencer, Michael House, Baker St, W1A 1DN.

SON LIVING

Hon Daniel Marcus, *b* 1976.

DAUGHTERS LIVING

Hon Jessica Alexandra, *b* 1980.
Hon Susannah Naomi, *b* 1984.

STONHAM, BARONY OF (Collins) (Extinct 1971)

SON LIVING OF LIFE BARON

Hon Ian Grenville, *b* 1941; *ed* Queen's Coll Taunton, and Kingston Gram Sch: *m* 1968, Sandra Felicity Bell, and has issue.

Stonor, family name of Baron Camoys.

Stopford, Viscount; son of Earl of Courtown

Stopford, family name of Earl of Courtown.

STOPFORD OF FALLOWFIELD, BARONY OF (Stopford) (Extinct 1961)

SON LIVING OF LIFE BARON

Hon Thomas, *b* 1921; *ed* Manchester Gram Sch, and at Manchester Univ; European War 1939-45 as Capt RA: *m* 1943, Mary Howard, da of late Alfred James Small, of Manchester, and has issue. *Residence* – 16 Rhos Manor, Colwyn Avenue, Rhos-on-Sea, Clwyd LL28 4NP.

Stormont, Viscount; son of Earl of Mansfield and Mansfield.

Stourton, Baron; see Baron Mowbray, Segrave and Stourton.

Stourton, family name of Baron Mowbray, Segrave and Stourton.

STOW HILL, BARONY OF (Soskice) (Extinct 1979)

SONS LIVING OF LIFE BARON

Hon David William, *b* 1941; *ed* Winchester, and Trin Coll, Oxford: *m* 1966, Alison, da of Walter Black, and has issue.
Hon Oliver Cloudesley Hunter, *b* 1947; *ed* Winchester, and Trin Hall, Camb: *m* 1982, Janet L., el da of A. M. Martin, of St Louis, Missouri, USA, and has issue.

STRABOLGI, BARON (Kenworthy) (E 1318)
(Title pronounced "Strabogie")

DAVID MONTAGUE DE BURGH KENWORTHY, 11th Baron; *b* 1st Nov 1914; *s* 1953; *ed* Gresham's Sch, Holt, Chelsea Sch of Art, and Paris; a co-heir to the Baronies of Cobham and Burgh; 1939-45 War in France and Middle East as Maj and acting Lt-Col RAOC; Capt of Queen's Bodyguard of Yeomen of the Guard and Dep Chief Whip, House of Lords 1974-79; Parl Priv Sec to Lord Privy Seal 1969-70; Assist Opposition Whip, House of Lords 1970-74, a Dep Speaker and Dep Chm of Cttees, House of Lords since 1986; Extra Lord in Waiting to HM since 1998; Memb Select Cttee for Privileges 1987; Member British Section, Franco-British Council 1981; Dep Chm Bolton Building Soc 1983 (Chm 1986-87); Freeman City of London; Officier de la Légion d'Honneur: *m* 1st 1939 (*m diss* 1946), Denise, yr da of Jocelyn William Godefroi, MVO; 2ndly, 1947 (*m diss* 1951), Angela, only child of George Street, of Barton Lawn, nr Elstree, Herts; 3rdly, 1955 (*m diss* 1961), Myra Sheila Litewka; 4thly, 1961, Doreen Margaret, el da of late Alexander Morgan, of Ashton-under-Lyne, Lancs.

Arms – Argent, an eagle displayed gules surmounted by a bend vert, thereon three fleur-de-lis or. **Crest** – An eagle displayed argent, collared gules, holding in either claw a fleur-de-lis gold.
Address – House of Lords, SW1A 0PW. *Club* – Reform.

Without noise

SISTER LIVING

Hon Ferelith Rosemary Florence (*Hon Lady Hood*), *b* 1918: *m* 1946, Sir Harold Josph Hood, TD, 2nd Bt. *Residence* – 31 Avenue Rd, St John's Wood, NW8 6BS.

WIDOW LIVING OF SON OF TENTH BARON

Victoria HEWITT: *m* 1963, as his 2nd wife, Rev the Hon Jonathan Malcolm Atholl Kenworthy, who *d* 1991, and has issue (see colls infra).

COLLATERAL BRANCHES LIVING

Issue of late Rev the Hon Jonathan Malcolm Atholl Kenworthy, 2nd son of 10th Baron, *b* 1916, *d* 1991: *m* 1st, 1943, Joan Marion, who *d* 1963, da of late Claude Gilbert Gaster, of Tunbridge Wells; 2ndly, 1963, Victoria Hewitt (ante):—
(By 1st *m*) Elizabeth Joan, *b* 1944: *m* 1st, 1964 (*m diss* 1977), Geoffrey Greetham; 2ndly, 1978 (*m diss* 1986), David Woodman, and has issue living (by 1st *m*), Jonathan, *b* 1967, — Matthew, *b* 1968, — Alexander, *b* 1971, — (by 2nd *m*) Edward, *b* 1980, — Kathrine, *b* (twin) 1980. —— Brenda Marion, *b* 1946: *m* 1974, Geoffrey Collins, and has issue living, Ian Gareth, *b* 1981. —— (By 2nd *m*) ANDREW DAVID WHITLEY, *b* 25 Jan 1967. —— †James Atholl, *b* 1971; *d* 1993. —— Penelope Ruth, *b* 1964: *m* 1986, Dr Samuel B. P. Bass, son of late P. A. Bass, and has issue living, Oliver William, *b* 1993, — Laura Charlotte, *b* 1992.

Issue of late Hon Basil Frederick de la Pole Kenworthy, TD, 3rd and yst son of 10th Baron, *b* 1920, *d* 1998: *m* 1948 (*m diss* 1965), Chloë, da of late Henry Gerard Walter Sandeman (*see* B Newton, 1985 Edn):—
Forflissa Viola, *b* 1949: *m* 1970, William John Healey, and has issue living, Patrick Joseph, *b* 1975, — Charlotte Eleanor, *b* 1977, — Megan Jane Florence, *b* 1981, — Rachel Lilian, *b* 1983. —— Nicolette Elizabeth, *b* 1950: *m* 1972, Prof John Russell Vincent, of 8 Charlotte St South, Bristol 1, and has issue living, Leo Jonathan, *b* 1984. —— Emma Yseult, *b* 1958: *m* 1988, P. Sebastian Kent, of The Old Rectory, Fonthill Gifford, Tisbury, Wilts SP3 6QH, and has issue living, Miranda Jacket, *b* 1992, — Elfreda Helen, *b* 1994, — Olivia Mercedes, *b* 1996.

Grandchildren of late Rev Hon Cuthbert Reginald Leatham Kenworthy, 2nd son of 9th Baron:—
Issue of late Maj Cuthbert Reginald D'Isney Kenworthy, Gordon Highlanders, *b* 1914, *d* 1987: *m* 1st, 1941 (*m diss* 1947), Patricia Kathleen, only da of late Brig Sir Francis William Crewe Fetherston-Godley, OBE, of St Lawrence, Jersey, CI; 2ndly, 1947 (*m diss* 1958), Joan Mary, da of Lt-Col R. A. G. Stewart, RM (ret), of Winthorpe House, Newark; 3rdly, 1960, Mrs Peggy Owtram (Rose Cottage, Jubilee Lane, Boundstone, Farnham, Surrey GU10 4TA):—
(By 1st *m*) David Patrick Francis, *b* 1942. —— (By 2nd *m*) Duncan Alexander D'Isney, *b* 1950: *m* 1975, Alwyn Jean Flack, and has issue living, Stewart Alexander D'Isney, *b* 1982, — Kirsten Jane, *b* 1979. *Residence* – 3 Grasslees, Rickleton, Washington, Tyne & Wear NE38 9JA. —— Sheena Mary, *b* 1948: *m* 1969, Allan de Jager, of 8 Allambic St, The Gap, Brisbane, Queensland 1061, Australia.

PREDECESSORS – (1) MADACH, 1st Earl of Atholl (*cr* S, *circa* 1122), was nephew of Malcolm III and Duncan I, Kings of Scotland; *s* by his son (2) MALCOLM, 2nd Earl; *s* by his son (3) HENRY, 3rd Earl; *s* by his da (4) ISABELLA, Countess of Atholl: *m* Thomas of Galloway (*jure uxoris* Earl of Atholl); *s* by her son (5) PATRICK, 5th Earl; murdered 1242; *s* by his aunt (6) FERELITH, Countess of Atholl, yr da of 3rd Earl: *m* David Hastings (*jure uxoris* Earl of Atholl); one of the

Guarantors of the Treaty of Peace with Henry III 1244; *s* by her da **(7)** ADA, Countess of Atholl: *m* John of Strabolgi (or Strathbogie), son of David of Strabolgi, and grandson of Duncan, Earl of Fife, who granted the lands of Strathbogie to the above-mentioned David; *s* by her son **(8)** DAVID, 8th Earl; joined the 7th Crusade under Louis IX of France; *d* of the plague at Carthage 1270; *s* by his son **(9)** JOHN, 9th Earl; taken prisoner by the English at Battle of Methven 1306, and subsequently executed in London: *m* Margery, da of Donald, Earl of Mar, and sister of Isabel, wife of Robert Bruce, King of Scotland; *s* by his son **(10)** DAVID (de Strabolgi), 10th Earl; summoned to Parliament as Lord Strabolgi 1318; *d* 1326; *s* by his el son **(11)** DAVID, 11th Earl of Atholl, and 2nd Lord Strabolgi; summoned to Parliament as Lord Strabolgi 1329-34; a famous soldier; accompanied his kinsman, Lord Balliol, in invasion of Scotland, when a much larger force of their opponents was defeated at battle of Dupplin Moor (tactics employed became model for English armies, and also affected military procedure on the Continent); *k* at battle of Kilblane 1335; *s* by his only son **(12)** DAVID, 12th Earl of Atholl and 3rd Lord Strabolgi; summoned to Parliament as Lord Strabolgi 1335-1369; went to the wars in France with the Black Prince in 1355: *m* Catherine, da of 2nd Lord Ferrers of Groby; *dsp* 1369, when the Scottish Earldom of Atholl (*cr circa* 1122) ceased to be borne in England, and the English Barony of Strabolgi fell into abeyance between his das and co-heirs, and so remained until 1496, when it is held to have passed to the sole surviving representative of the co-heirs **(13)** Sir EDWARD Burgh, *de jure* 4th Baron (son of Thomas Burgh temp 1431-95); MP for co Lincoln: *m* 1477, Anne, da of Sir Thomas Cobham of Sterborough Castle, and widow of 2nd Baron Mountjoy; *d* 1528; *s* by his son **(14)** THOMAS, *de jure* 5th Baron; summoned to Parliament as Lord Burgh 1529: *m* 1st, 1497, Agnes, da of Sir William Tyrwhitt; 2ndly, 15—, Alice, da of William London, and widow (i) of Sir Thomas Bedingfeld and (ii) of Sir Edmund Rokewood; *d* 1550; *s* by his el surviving son **(15)** WILLIAM, 2nd Baron Burgh, and *de jure* 6th Baron Strabolgi; summoned to Parliament as Lord Burgh 1551-80: *m* 15—, Catherine, da of Edward, Earl of Lincoln; *d* 1584; *s* by his el surviving son **(16)** THOMAS, KG, 3rd Baron Burgh, and *de jure* 7th Baron Strabolgi; summoned to Parliament as Lord Burgh 1584-97; Ambassador to Scotland 1593, and Lord Dep of Ireland 1597: *m* 15—, Frances, da of John Vaughan, of Sutton-on-Derwent; *d* 1597; *s* by his el surviving son **(17)** ROBERT, 4th Baron Burgh, and *de jure* 8th Baron Strabolgi; *dsp* (about) 1600, when the Baronies fell into abeyance between his four sisters, among whose descendants they so remained until the abeyances were determined in 1916, the Barony of Strabolgi being called out of abeyance in favour of **(18)** CUTHBERT MATTHIAS Kenworthy (only surviving son of late Rev Joseph Kenworthy, R of Acworth, co York, by Harriet Elizabeth, da of Capt William Henry Cockerell Leatham, of Kirkham Abbey, Carleton, Yorkshire, and a co-heiress to the Barony), 9th Baron Strabolgi, *b* 1853; established his claim as a co-heir to the Baronies of Burgh and Cobham 1912; *m* 1884, Elizabeth Florence, who *d* 1951, da of George Buchanan Cooper, of Sacramento, California, USA; *d* 1934; *s* by his el son **(19)** JOSEPH MONTAGUE, RN, 10th Baron Strabolgi: *b* 1886; Lieut-Com (ret); with Grand Fleet, on Admiralty War Staff, and Assist Chief of Staff, Gibraltar during European War 1914-18; was Ch Opposition Whip in House of Lords 1937-45; sat as MP for Kingston-upon-Hull, Central Div (*L* afterwards *Lab*) 1919-29: *m* 1st, 1913 (*m diss* 1941), Doris Whitley, who *d* 1988, only child of late Sir Frederick Whitley-Thomson, JP, MP; 2ndly, 1941, Mrs Geraldine Mary (HAMILTON), who *d* 1970, da of late Maurice Francis; *d* 1953; *s* by his el son **(20)** DAVID MONTAGUE DE BURGH, 11th Baron Strabolgi and present peer.

(The title of Strabolgi is derived from the Aberdeenshire district of Strathbogie, being the valley of the river Bogie, which flows into the Deveron; and Strathbogie Castle was the seat of the Earls of Atholl.)

Strachey, family name of Baron O'Hagan.

STRADBROKE, EARL OF (Rous) (Earl UK 1821, Bt E 1660)

(ROBERT) KEITH ROUS, 6th Earl and 11th Baronet; *b* 25 March 1937; *s* 1983; *ed* Harrow: *m* 1st, 1960 (*m diss* 1977), Dawn Antoinette, da of Thomas Edward Beverley, of Brisbane; 2ndly, 1977, Roseanna Mary, da of late Francis Reitman, MD (*see* B Lyveden, colls), and has issue living by 1st and 2nd *m*.

Arms – Sable, a fesse dancettée or, between three crescents argent. **Crest** – A pyramid of bay leaves, in the form of a cone vert. **Supporters** – *Dexter*, a lion, gorged with a wreath of olive proper; *Sinister*, a seahorse, gorged with a wreath of olive proper, the tail resting on an anchor azure.
Seat – Henham, Wangford, Beccles, Suffolk. *Address* – Mount Fyans, RSD Darlington, Victoria 3271, Australia.

SONS LIVING (*By 1st marriage*)

ROBERT KEITH (*Viscount Dunwich*), *b* 15 Nov 1961.
Hon Wesley Alexander, *b* 1972.

(*By 2nd marriage*)

Hon Hektor Fraser, *b* 1978.
Hon Maximilian Otho, *b* 1981.
Hon Henham Mowbray, *b* 1983.

Hon Winston Walberswick, *b* 1986.
Hon Yoxford Ulysses Uluru, *b* 1989.
Hon Ramsar Fyans, *b* 1992.

DAUGHTERS LIVING *(By 1st marriage)*

Lady Ingrid Arnel, *b* 1963; has issue living, Sam, *b* 1994.
Lady (Sophia) Rayner, *b* 1964; has issue living, Jake, *b* 1993, — Olivia, *b* 1990, — Kaylon, *b* 1991, — Cerana, *b* 1992.
Lady Heidi Simone, *b* 1966: *m* 1991, Timothy Crick, and has issue living, Joshua William, *b* 1992, — Thomas Oscar, *b* 1993.
Lady Pamela Keri, *b* 1968.
Lady Brigitte Aylena, *b* 1970.

(By 2nd marriage)

Lady Zea Katherina, *b* 1979.
Lady Minsmere Matilda, *b* 1988.

BROTHER DECEASED

†*Lt-Gen the Hon Sir* William Edward, KCB, OBE, *b* 1939; *ed* Harrow, Angers Univ and RMA Sandhurst; Brig; commn'd Coldm Gds 1959, commanded 2nd Bn Coldm Gds 1979-81, and 1st Inf Bde 1983-84, Dir of Public Relations (Army) 1985-87, GOC 4 Armoured Div 1987-89, Comdt Staff Coll 1990-91, Mil Sec 1991-94, since when QMG; 27th Col Coldm Gds 1994; MBE (Mil) 1974, OBE (Mil) 1980, KCB (Mil) 1992: *m* 1970, Judith Rosemary, da of late Maj Jocelyn Arthur Persse, Rifle Bde, and *d* 1999, leaving issue, James Anthony Edward, *b* 1972; *ed* Harrow, and RMA Sandhurst; commn'd Coldm Guards 1996, — Richard William Jocelyn, *b* 1975.

HALF-BROTHER LIVING

Hon John, *b* 1950; *ed* Gordonstoun, and Kent Univ (BA): *m* 1984, Zeenat, da of late Dr K. Hameed, of Lucknow, and has issue living, Maha Magdalene, *b* 1987, — Zoya Constance, *b* 1990. *Residences* – Clovelly Court, Bideford, Devon; 94 Oakley St, SW3.

HALF-SISTERS LIVING

Lady (Christine) Caroline Catherine, *b* 1946; *ed* Cranborne Chase, Zambia Univ, and London Univ (BSc, PGCE, Dip Ed): *m* 1st, 1978, John Francis Burnett Armstrong, who *d* 1992; 2ndly, 1999, Richard M. Cox-Johnson, of 63 Frognal, NW3, and has issue living (by 1st *m*), Henry Francis Arthur Rous, *b* 1978, — John George William Rous, *b* 1982, — Catherine Julia Cecily, *b* 1986. *Residence* – Dalby, Terrington, N Yorks YO6 4PF.
Lady Henrietta Elizabeth, *b* 1947. *Residence* – Clovelly Court, Bideford, Devon.
Lady Virginia, *b* 1954: *m* 1974, Antony William Hew Gibbs, and has issue *(see* Hamilton Dalrymple, Bt). *Residence* – Home Farm, Barrow Gurney, Bristol.

DAUGHTERS LIVING OF FOURTH EARL

Lady Marye Violet Isolde, *b* 1930. *Residence* – Sacaba Beach, Malaga 29004, Spain.
Lady Penelope Anne, *b* 1932; patron of five livings; Lay Canon of St Edmundsbury Cathedral: *m* 1st, 1950 *(m diss* 1960), Com Ian Dudley Stewart Forbes, DSC, RN, who *d* 1992, and has issue *(see* Forbes, Bt, colls, *cr* 1823); 2ndly, 1961 *(m diss* 1969), John Cator *(see* Cayley, Bt, 1960 Edn); 3rdly, 1984, as his 3rd wife, Anthony James Gilbey *(see* M Linlithgow, colls, 1990 Edn). *Residence* – White Lion House, Wangford, Beccles, Suffolk NR34 8RL.

WIDOW LIVING OF FIFTH EARL

(APRIL) MARY *(Hon Mrs W. Keith Rous)* (prefers to be known by her former style), da of late Hon Arthur Melland Asquith *(see* E Oxford and Asquith, colls): *m* 1943, as his 2nd wife, the 5th Earl of Stradbroke, who *d* 1983 (having survived his elder brother, the 4th Earl, by four days). *Residence* – Clovelly Court, Bideford, N Devon.

COLLATERAL BRANCH LIVING

Issue of late Maj Hon George Nathaniel Rous, 3rd son of 3rd Earl, *b* 1911, *d* 1982: *m* 1949, Joyce, who *d* 1985, yst da of late Col Charles Harpur, OBE:
Robert Charles, *b* 1953; *ed* Harrow, and Trin Coll, Camb (MA); DL Suffolk 1995; Lay Canon of St Edmundsbury Cathedral; ARICS: *m* 1976, Teresa Mary Mercedes, da of David Keith Ford Heathcote, of Badlingham Manor, Chippenham, Cambs *(see* Sykes, Bt, *cr* 1783, 1990 Edn), and has issue living, Peter George *b* 1984; *ed* Harrow, — Laura Frances, *b* 1982; *ed* St Felix. *Residence* – Dennington Hall, Woodbridge, Suffolk IP13 8AU. —— Georgina Alice, *b* 1951; *ed* Heathfield: *m* 1975, Charles H. W. Holloway, of The Old Rectory, Whissonsett, Dereham, Norfolk NR20 5TF, and has issue living, George Henry Rous, *b* 1983, — Edward Charles, *b* 1986, — Alice Victoria Pendrill, *b* 1978, — Lucinda Rose, *b* 1980. —— Veronica Rose, *b* 1958; *ed* Heathfield: *m* 1989, James H. A. Maberly, of Red House Farm, Dennington,

Woodbridge, Suffolk IP13 8AQ, eldest son of late Lt-Col J. E. A. Maberly, and has issue living, Edward George Astley, *b* 1991, — Harry Robert Astley, *b* 1993, — Jasper James Astley, *b* 1995, — Joanna Eve Astley, *b* 1999. —— Frances Diana (*Hon Mrs Charles R. Boscawen*), *b* 1961; *ed* Heathfield: *m* 1985, Hon Charles Richard Boscawen, 3rd son of 9th Viscount Falmouth, and has issue (see that title).

Issue of late Maj Hon Peter James Mowbray Rous, 4th son of 3rd Earl, *b* 1914, *d* 1997: *m* 1942, Elizabeth Alice Mary, who *d* 1968, da of late Maj Hon Alastair Thomas Joseph Fraser, DSO (*see* L Lovat, colls, 1968 Edn):—

Michael James Mowbray (57 Parma Crescent, SW11 1LU), *b* 1945; *ed* Elston Hall, and St George's Coll, Salisbury: *m* 1989, Isabelle M. B., eldest da of François Le Chevallier, of Paris 75015. —— †Peter George Anthony Mowbray, *b* 1948; *d* as the result of an accident 1952. —— Simon Roderick (Burston, Dulverton, Som), *b* 1950; *ed* St George's Coll, and Trin Coll, Camb (MA): *m* 1978, Carol A., da of Robert Dawson, of Bolton, Lancs, and has issue living, Oliver Mowbray Abdel Rahman, *b* 1981, — Clare Elizabeth Khalida, *b* 1979, — Rebecca Mary Alice, *b* 1987, — Henrietta Florence, *b* 1988. —— (John) Sebastian (Kamusha, Box 25, Mvurwi, Zimbabwe), *b* 1953: *m* 1980, Valda Louise, da of Alastair Guy Waterhouse, of Middleton Hall, Youlgrave, Derbys, and has issue living, Justin Henry, *b* 1980, — William James, *b* 1984, — Julia Louise, *b* 1982. —— Edmund Felix, *b* 1954: *m* 1982, Jane N., elder da of Derek Willshaw, of Sussex, and has issue living, Sebastian James, *b* 1985, — Emma Jade, *b* 1982, — Elizabeth Frances, *b* 1988. —— Peter Joseph, *b* 1956. —— Christopher Hugh (3447 Zulla Rd, The Plains, VA 20198, USA) *b* 1958: *m* 1987, Elisabeth Christman, only da of Dr Stokes Jerome Smith, of Spartanburg, S Carolina, USA, and has issue living, Simon Joseph, *b* 1990, — Katherine Elisabeth, *b* 1988. —— Petronilla, *b* 1943: *m* 1966, (Thomas) Peter John Cockin, of 13 The Ferns, Carlton Rd, Tunbridge Wells, Kent TN1 2JT, and has had issue, James Francis John, *b* 1968, — John Joseph, *b* 1970, — Charles Hereward John, *b* and *d* 1974, — Michael Hereward John, *b* 1975; has issue living (by Sam Smith), Lilli Elizabeth Mary SMITH *b* 1995, — Antonia Patricia Mary, *b* 1967: *m* 1993, Nicholas Edward Osborne, of 9 Court Way, Twickenham, Middx TW2 7SA. —— Helena (Nina) Sibyl, *b* 1947: *m* 1977, Michael Clive Rashleigh Beasley, of 72 Stamford Brook Rd, W6 0XN, and has issue living, Thomas Humphrey Clovis, *b* 1979, — George Hugh Dominic, *b* 1983, — Charlotte (Lotte) Hermione Alice, *b* 1981. —— Elizabeth Anne, *b* 1951: *m* 1977, Bruce Lewis Hamilton Powell, of Broadhatch House, Bentley, Alton, Hants, and has issue living, Louis Edmund, *b* 1983, — Jemima Anne, *b* 1978, — Camilla (Millicent) Mary Augusta, *b* 1979, — Harriet Elizabeth Maud, *b* 1980. —— Philippa Mary Katherine, *b* 1960: *m* 1986, Anthony John Stratford Eyre, of Poppy Cottage, Driffield, Cirencester GL7 5PY, and has issue living, Edmund Anthony Bobo, *b* 1988, — Giles Peter Dusmet, *b* 1989, — Hew Raymond Bundu, *b* 1991, — Elena Alice, *b* 1993.

PREDECESSORS – This family descends from Sir Peter Rous, of Dennington, near Stradbroke, Suffolk, *temp* early 14th century. Henham became the principal seat in 1544. **(1)** JOHN ROUS, MP for Dunwich; *cr* a *Baronet* 1660; *s* by his son **(2)** *Sir* JOHN, 2nd Bt; High Sheriff of Suffolk *d* 1730; *s* by his son **(3)** *Sir* JOHN, 3rd Bt; *d* unmarried; *s* by his half-brother **(4)** *Sir* ROBERT, 4th Bt; *s* by his son **(5)** *Sir* JOHN, 5th Bt; was MP for Suffolk; *d* 1771; *s* by his son **(6)** *Sir* JOHN, 6th Bt; sat as MP for Suffolk 1780-96; *cr Baron Rous*, of Dennington, co Suffolk (peerage of Great Britain) 1796, and *Viscount Dunwich* and *Earl of Stradbroke* (peerage of United Kingdom) 1821: *m* 2ndly, 1792, Charlotte Maria, da of Abraham Whittaker; *d* 1827; *s* by his son **(7)** JOHN EDWARD CORNWALLIS, 2nd Earl; *b* 1794; was Lord-Lieut of Suffolk; served in Coldm Gds in Peninsular War (medal with five clasps) and in Belgian Campaign 1815: *m* 1857, Augusta, da of the Rev Sir Christopher John Musgrave, 9th Bt, and widow of Col Bonham; *d* 27 Jan 1886; *s* by his son **(8)** GEORGE EDWARD JOHN MOWBRAY, KCMG, CB, CVO, CBE, 3rd Earl; *b* 1862; Lord-Lieut and Vice-Adm of Suffolk; Gov of Victoria, Australia 1920-26, and Parliamentary Sec to Min of Agriculture and Fisheries 1928-9; European War 1914-19 (CBE): *m* 1898, *Dame* Helena Violet Alice, DBE, who *d* 1949, da of late Lieut-Gen James Keith Fraser, CMG; *d* 1947; *s* by his son **(9)** JOHN ANTHONY ALEXANDER, 4th Earl, *b* 1903; Lay Canon of St Edmundsbury Cathedral; FRSA; Cdr RN, Hon Col 660th Heavy Anti-Aircraft Regt RA (TA); Lord-Lt of Suffolk 1948-78; Agriculturalist and Forester; Vice-Pres of R British Legion (Pres Eastern Area); Vice-Pres of Assocn of Land Drainage Authorities; a CC for E Suffolk 1931-45, and an Alderman 1953-64: *m* 1929, Barbara, who *d* 1977, yr da of late Lord Arthur Hugh Grosvenor (D Westminster, colls); *d* (14 July) 1983; *s* by his brother **(5)** (WILLIAM) KEITH, 5th Earl, *b* 1907; Lt (E) RN; Lt RNVR; 1939-45 War, commanded HMS *Amethyst*, HMS *Lady Lilian* and HMS *Coltfoot* 1940-43: *m* 1st, 1935 (*m diss* 1941), Pamela Catherine Mabell, who *d* 1972, da of late Capt Hon Edward James Kay-Shuttleworth (B Shuttleworth, colls); 2ndly, 1943, April Mary, da of late Brig-Gen Hon Arthur Melland Asquith, DSO (*see* E Oxford and Asquith, colls); *d* (18 July) 1983; *s* by his el son **(6)** (ROBERT) KEITH, 6th Earl, and present peer; also Viscount Dunwich, and Baron Rous.

STRAFFORD, EARL OF (Byng) (Earl UK 1847)

MOUGUERRE

I will defend

·TUEBOR·

THOMAS EDMUND BYNG, 8th Earl, *b* 26 Sept 1936; *s* 1984; *ed* Eton, and Clare Coll, Camb: *m* 1st, 1963 (*m diss* 1981), Jennifer Mary Denise, elder da of Rt Hon William Morrison May, MP, of Mertoun Hall, Holywood, co Down; 2ndly, 1981, Julia Mary, formerly wife of Derek Nicholas Howard, and yr da of late Sir Dennis Pilcher, CBE, of Brambles, Batts Lane, Mare Hill, Pulborough, W Sussex, and has issue by 1st *m*.

ᴀrms – Quarterly: sable and argent, in the first quarter a lion rampant of the second; over all in bend sinister, a representation of the Regimental Colour of the 31st Regt of Foot. ᴄrest – 1st, out of a mural crown or, an arm, embowed gules, curfed azure, grasping the Regimental Colour of the said Regt, and pendent from the wrist by a crimson riband, the gold cross awarded to the 1st Lord Strafford, and on an escroll, the word "Mouguerre", 2nd, an heraldic antelope statant ermine, attired and crined or. ꜱupporters – *Dexter*, an heraldic antelope ermine, attired and crined or; *sinister*, a lion or.
Residence – Apple Tree Cottage, Easton, Winchester.

SONS LIVING (*By 1st marriage*)

WILLIAM ROBERT (*Viscount Enfield*), *b* 10 May 1964; *ed* Winchester, and Durham Univ: *m* 1994, Karen Elizabeth, eldest da of Graham Lord, and has issue living, *Hon* Samuel Peter, *b* 17 July 1998, — *Hon* Isaac John, *b* (twin) 1998, — *Hon* Saskia Ruth Jessica, *b* 1996. *Residence* – 5 Brierville, Durham DH1 4QE.
Hon James Edmund, *b* 1969; *ed* Winchester: *m* 1994, Whitney, eldest da of Charles McVeigh III, and has issue living, Marley McVeigh (a da), *b* 1996. *Residence* – Flat 3, 28 Gayfield Sq, Edinburgh EH1 3PA.

DAUGHTERS LIVING (*By 1st marriage*)

Lady Georgia Mary Caroline, *b* 1965: *m* 1990, Daniel S. Chadwick, yr son of Lynn Chadwick, of Lypiatt, Glos.
Lady (Harriet Clare) Tara, *b* 1967: *m* 1994, T. Christopher Wilbur, son of late Richard Wilbur, of Hawaii, and of Mrs Richard Anger, of Calif, USA.

BROTHER LIVING

Hon Julian Francis, *b* 1938; *ed* Eton; Capt Queen's R Rifles (TA): *m* 1st, 1966 (*m diss* 1983), Ingela Brita, da of Axel Berglund, of Stockholm; 2ndly, 1984, Mrs Prudence Mary Kent, da of late Albert Edward Delany, of Queensland, Australia, and formerly wife of David Kent, and has issue living (by 1st *m*), Francis Gustaf, *b* 1968; *ed* Eton, — (George Michael) Alexander, *b* 1973; *ed* Eton.

MOTHER LIVING

Maria Magdalena Elizabeth, da of late Henry Cloete, CMG, of Alphen, S Africa: *m* 1st, 1934 (*m diss* 1947), Robert Cecil Byng (later 7th Earl of Strafford), who *d* 1984; 2ndly, 1954, as his 2nd wife, James Henry Royds (*see* E Perth, 1959 Edn). *Residence* – Cedar Falls, Bishop Lydeard, nr Taunton, Som.

PREDECESSORS – **(1)** *Sir* JOHN BYNG, GCB, GCH, PC (great-grandson of the 1st Viscount Torrington, and of Thomas Wentworth, 1st Earl of Strafford of 2nd creation 1711) was one of the most distinguished military commanders during the Peninsular War; *b* 1772; *cr* Baron Strafford (peerage of United Kingdom) 1835, and *Viscount Enfield* and *Earl of Strafford* (peerage of United Kingdom) 1847: *m* 1st, 1804, Mary Stevens, who *d* 1806, da of Peter Mackenzie, of Grove House, Middlesex; 2ndly, 1808, Marianne, who *d* 1845, da of Sir Walter James James (formerly Head) 1st Bt; *d* 1860; *s* by his son **(2)** GEORGE STEVENS, PC, FRS, 2nd Earl; *b* 1806; sat as MP for Milborne Port (*L*) 1831, the Poole 1835-7, and for Chatham 1837-52; was a Lord of the Treasury 1834, Comptroller and Treasurer of HM Queen Victoria's Household 1841, and Sec of Board of Control 1846-7: *m* 1st, 1829, Lady Agnes Paget, who *d* 1845, da of 1st Marquess of Anglesey, KG; 2ndly, 1848, Hon Harriet Elizabeth Cavendish, da of 1st Baron Chesham; *d* Oct 1886; *s* by his son **(3)** GEORGE HENRY CHARLES, 3rd Earl, *b* 1830; called to the House of Lords in his father's Barony of Strafford 1874; Parliamentary Sec to Poor Law Board 1865-6, Under-Sec of State for Foreign Affairs 1870-74, a Lord-in-Waiting to HM Queen Victoria 1880, Under-Sec of State for India 1880-83, and First Civil Ser Commr (unpaid) 1880-88; Lord-Lieut of Middlesex: *m* 1854, Lady Alice Harriet Frederica Egerton, who *d* 1928, da of 1st Earl of Ellesmere, KG; *d* 1898; *s* by his brother **(4)** HENRY WILLIAM JOHN, KCVO, CB, 4th Earl, *b* 1831; Page of Honour to HM Queen Victoria 1840-47, Groom-in-Waiting 1872-4, and Equerry 1874-99: *m* 1st, 1863, the Countess Henrietta Daneskiold Samsøe, who *d* 1880; 2ndly, 1898, Cora, who *d* 1932, widow of S. Colgate, of USA; *d* 1899; *s* by his brother **(5)** FRANCIS EDMUND CECIL, 5th Earl, *b* 1835; V of St Peter's, S Kensington 1867-89, and Chap to Speaker of House of Commons 1874-89: *m* 1st, 1859, Florence Louisa, who *d* 1862, da of Sir William Miles, 1st Bt; 2ndly, 1866, Emily Georgina, who *d* 1929, el da of late Adm Lord Frederick Herbert Kerr; *d* 1918; *s* by his son **(6)** EDMUND HENRY, 6th Earl; *b* 1862; a Co Alderman for Middlesex and Herts: *m* 1894, Mary Elizabeth, who *d* 1951, da of Sir Thomas Edward Colebrooke, 4th Bt; *d* 1951; *s* by his nephew **(7)** ROBERT CECIL (son of late Hon Ivo Francis Byng, 4th son of 5th Earl), 7th Earl; *b* 1904: *m* 1st, 1934 (*m diss* 1947), Maria Magdalena Elizabeth, da of Henry Cloete, CMG, of Alphen, S Africa; 2ndly, 1948, Clara Evelyn, who *d* 1985, da of Sir Nusserwanjee Nowrosjee

Wadia, KBE, CIE; *d* 1984; *s* by his son **(8)** THOMAS EDMUND, 8th Earl and present peer; also Viscount Enfield, and Baron Strafford.

STRANG, BARON (Strang) (Baron UK 1954)

COLIN STRANG, 2nd Baron: *b* 12 June 1922; *s* 1978; *ed* Merchant Taylors' Sch, and St John's Coll, Oxford (MA, BPhil); *m* 1st, 1948, Patricia Marie, da of Meiert C. Avis, of Johannesburg, S Africa; 2ndly, 1955, Barbara Mary Hope, who *d* 1982, da of Frederick Albert Carr, of Wimbledon, SW; 3rdly, 1984, Mary Shewell, da of Richard Miles, of Sheffield, and has issue living by 2nd *m*.
Residence – Stansfield Cottage West, Hole Bottom, Todmorden, W Yorks OL14 8DD.

DAUGHTER LIVING *(By 2nd marriage)*

Hon Caroline Jane, *b* 1957.

PREDECESSORS – **(1)** WILLIAM STRANG, GCB, GCMG, MBE, was British Rep on European Advisory Commn with rank of Ambassador 1943-45, Political Advisor to Com-in-Ch, British Forces in Germany 1945-47, Permanent Under-Sec of State, Foreign Office (German Sect) 1947-49, Permanent Under-Sec of State, Foreign Office 1949-53, Chm of National Parks Commn 1954-66; a Dep Speaker of House of Lords 1962-78; *b* 1893; *cr Baron Strang* of Stonesfield, co Oxford (peerage of UK) 1954: *m* 1920, Elsie Wynne, who *d* 1974, da of late J. E. Jones, of Addiscombe; *d* 1978; *s* by his son **(2)** COLIN, 2nd Baron and present peer.

STRANGE, BARONESS (Drummond of Megginch) (Baron E 1628)

(JEAN) CHERRY DRUMMOND OF MEGGINCH (*Lady Strange*) *b* 17 Dec 1928; *s* (on termination of abeyance) 1986; *ed* St Andrews (MA) and Camb Univs; FSA (Scot); Hon FIMarE; author; Pres War Widows' Assocn since 1990; senior heir-general of Aubrey de Vere, Master Chamberlain to King Henry I: *m* 1952, Capt Humphrey ap Evans, MC, who assumed the name of Drummond of Megginch by decree of Lord Lyon 1966, son of Maj James John Pugh Evans, MBE, MC, JP, DL, of Lovesgrove, Aberystwyth, Cardiganshire, and has issue.

Arms – Parted per fess waved or and gu. Crest – Two arms ppr drawing an arrow to the head of a bow or. Supporters – *Dexter*, a naked savage wreathed about the head and middle with oak leaves, holding over his dexter shoulder a club all ppr; *sinister*, a knight armed at all points, the visor of his helmet up, a spear resting on his sinister arm and a shield hanging thereon all ppr. Motto – Marte et arte. Badge – holly.
Seat – Megginch Castle, Errol, Perthshire. *Town Residence* – 160 Kennington Rd, SE11.

SONS LIVING

Hon ADAM HUMPHREY, *b* 20 April 1953; *ed* Eton, RMA Sandhurst, and Heriot-Watt Univ: *m* 1988, Hon Mary Emma Jeronima Dewar, eldest da of 4th Baron Forteviot, and has issue living, John Adam Humphrey, *b* 3 Nov 1992, — Sophie Frances, *b* 1991.

Dr the Hon Humphrey John Jardine, *b* 1961; *ed* Eton, and Imperial Coll, London (BSc 1981); PhD 1988, DIC, MRSC, CChem, ARCS: *m* 1997, Zara Sophia, da of Sir Ian Niall Rankin, 4th Bt. *Residence* – 64 Comeragh Rd, W14.

Hon John Humphrey Hugo, *b* 1966; *ed* Eton, and St John's Coll, Camb (MA); ACA 1993. *Residence* – 160 Kennington Rd, SE11.

DAUGHTERS LIVING

Hon Charlotte Cherry, *b* 1955; *ed* Heathfield, and Dundee Coll of Commerce. *Residence* – 222, 2500 Q St NW, Washington, DC 20007, USA.

Hon Amélie Margaret Mary, *b* 1963; *ed* Heathfield, Dundee Coll of Commerce, London Poly, CFPPA Beaune Viticulture, and Ecole Agricole et Forestière, Etang sur Arroux: *m* 1990, as his 2nd wife, Philippe, 8th Marquis de MacMahon, 4th Duc de Magenta, and has issue living, Maurice Marie Patrick Bacchus Humphrey (Comte de MacMahon de Magenta), *b* 1992, — Pélagie Jeanne Marie Marguerite Charlotte Natalie, *b* 1990. *Residence* – Château de Sully, 71360 Epinac, Saone-et-Loire, France.

Hon Catherine Star Violetta, *b* 1967; *ed* Heathfield, Dundee Coll of Commerce, and Hertfords Univ: *m* 1996, Giles R. D. Herdman, yr son of Col Robert Herdman, of Dryden House, Ambrosden, Oxon. *Residence* – 33 West Sq, SE11

SISTERS LIVING

Hon Heather Mary, *b* 1931: *m* 1954, Lt-Cdr Andrew Christian Currey, RN, of The Mill House, Santon, Isle of Man, only son of late Rear Adm Harry Philip Currey, CB, OBE, and has issue living, Robert James Drummond (99 Ritherdon Rd, SW17), *b* 1955; *ed* Eton, and at London Polytechnic (BSc): *m* 1983, Diana Jane, da of Kenneth Garrod, of Aldeburgh, Suffolk, and has issue living, Cosmo Charles Drummond *b* 1985, Francesca Rose *b* 1989, — John Andrew Fairbridge, *b* 1959; *ed* Stowe, — Arabella Mary Christian, *b* 1958: *ed* Hampden House: *m* 1987, Reiner Friedhelm Gustav Gerland, son of Karl Heinz Gerland, of Kassel, W Germany, and has issue living, Oskar Gustav Christian *b* 1987.

Hon Margaret April Irene (*Hon Lady Agnew-Somerville*), *b* 1939: *m* 1963, Sir Quentin Charles Somerville Agnew-Somerville, 2nd Bt, of Mount Auldyn, Jurby Rd, Ramsey, Isle of Man, and has issue.

PREDECESSORS – **(1)** JAMES Stanley, later 7th Earl of Derby, was summoned to Parliament by writ 1628 as *Baron Strange*. The Barony followed succession of the Earldom **(2-3)** until the death of 9th Earl of Derby 1702, when it fell into abeyance between his two daughters, Lady Henrietta and Lady Elizabeth Stanley. On the death of Lady Elizabeth in 1714, the barony devolved on her sister **(4)** *Lady* HENRIETTA: *m* 1st, 1706, 4th Earl of Anglesey, who *d* 1710; 2ndly, 1714, 1st Earl of Ashburnham, who *d* 1737, and *d* 1718; *s* by her da (by 2nd *m*) **(5)** *Lady* HENRIETTA BRIDGET Ashburnham, *dunm* 1732; *s* by her great uncle **(6)** JAMES Stanley, 10th Earl of Derby, and 6th Baron Strange, who *dsp* 1736; *s* as Baron Strange and in the sovereignty of the Isle of Man by his kinsman **(7)** JAMES Murray, 2nd Duke of Atholl, KT, and 7th Baron Strange (grandson of Lady Amelia Sophia Stanley, da of 7th Earl of Derby and 1st Baron Strange, who *m* 1659, John Murray, 1st Marquess of Atholl); *d* 1764; *s* in the Barony of Strange and in the sovereignty of the Isle of Man by his da **(8)** *Lady* CHARLOTTE, *b* 1731: *m* 1753, her cousin, John Murray, 3rd Duke of Atholl; *d* 1805; disposed of sovereignty of the Isle of Man to British Govt in 1765 for £70,000; *s* by her eldest son **(9)** JOHN, 4th Duke of Atholl, and 9th Baron Strange, from whom it followed succession of the Dukedom **(10-14)** to JAMES THOMAS, 9th Duke and 14th Baron Strange; *dunm* 1957, when the Barony of Strange fell into abeyance between the representatives of the three daughters of the 4th Duke (i) Lady Charlotte Murray, who *m* 1st, 1797, Sir John Menzies, 4th Bt, who *d* 1800; 2ndly, 1801, Adm Sir Adam Drummond of Megginch, KCH, (ii) Lady Amelia Sophia Murray, who *m* 1809, 6th Viscount Strathallan (E Perth), and (iii), Lady Elizabeth Murray, who *m* 1808, Maj-Gen Sir Evan John Murray MacGregor, 2nd Bt, and so continued until 1964, when the abeyance was terminated (after petition to HM the Queen) in favour of **(15)** JOHN Drummond of Megginch (only son of Capt Malcolm Drummond, JP, DL, 9th of Megginch, and great grandson of Lady Charlotte Drummond), 15th Baron, *b* 1900; author (as John Drummond) of ten books of fact and fiction: *m* 1928, Violet Margaret Florence, who *d* 1975, formerly wife of Capt Edmund Owen Ethelwood Peel, MC, and only da of Sir Robert William Buchanan-Jardine, 2nd Bt; *d* 1982, when the barony again fell into abeyance between his three daughters, and so continued until 1986, when the abeyance was terminated (after petition to HM The Queen) in favour of the eldest da **(16)** (JEAN) CHERRY Drummond of Megginch, Baroness Strange, the present peeress.

Strange of Knokin, Hungerford, and de Moleyns, Baron; see Viscount St Davids.

Strangways, Fox-, family name of Earl of Ilchester.

Strathallan, Viscount; son of Earl of Perth.

STRATHALMOND, BARON (Fraser) (Baron UK 1955)

WILLIAM ROBERTON FRASER, 3rd Baron; *b* 22 July 1947; *s* 1976; *ed* Loretto; CA; Man Dir London Wall Members Agency 1986-91, and Dir London Wall Holdings 1986-91, Chm R. W. Sturge Ltd 1991-94; Finance Dir Owen & Wilby Underwriting Agency since 1995: *m* 1973, Amanda Rose, yr da of Rev Gordon Clifford Taylor, of St Giles-in-the-Fields Rectory, Gower St, WC1, and has issue.

Arms – Tierce in pairle azure gules and sable cinquefoils or. **Crest** – In front of a bezant gutté d'huile a stag's head erased proper. **Supporters** – *Dexter*, a pheasant; *sinister*, a grouse proper.
Address – House of Lords, SW1A 0PW

SONS LIVING

Hon WILLIAM GORDON, *b* 24 Sept 1976.
Hon George Edward, *b* 1979.

DAUGHTER LIVING

Hon Virginia Audrey Hart, *b* 1982.

SISTERS LIVING AND DECEASED

Hon Cordelia, *b* 1949: *m* 1981 (*m diss* 1986), Ralph Lyman Brown. *Residence* – 75 Carthew Rd, W6 0DU.
Hon Christina, *b* 1954: *m* 1974, Timothy Andrew Lebus, and *d* 1999, leaving issue, David Oliver, *b* 1983.

AUNT LIVING (*Daughter of 1st Baron*)

Hon Mary Joan (*Hon Lady Westbrook*), *b* 1922: *m* 1945, Sir Neil Gowanloch Westbrook, and has issue living, Fraser Gownaloch, *b* 1946: *m* 1st, 1971 (*m diss* 1993), Jane Bray; 2ndly, 1999, Mrs Ruth V. Allan, da of late Reginald Hartery, of Haslemere, Surrey, — Mary Joan, *b* 1950: *m* 1974, Robert Michael John Keene. *Residence* – White Gables, Prestbury, Ches.

WIDOW LIVING OF SECOND BARON

LETITIA (*Letitia, Baroness Strathalmond*), da of late Walter Martin Krementz, of Morristown, New Jersey, USA: *m* 1945, the 2nd Baron Strathalmond, who *d* 1976. *Residence* – 155 Fawn Lane, Portola Valley, Calif 94025, USA.

PREDECESSORS – (1) Sir WILLIAM Fraser, CBE, son of late William Fraser, of Glasgow; *b* 1888; Chm of British Petroleum Co, Ltd, 1941-56; *cr* Knt 1939, and Baron Strathalmond, of Pumpherston, co Middlothian (peerage of UK) 1955: *m* 1913, Mary Roberton, who *d* 1963, da of late Thomson McLintock, of Glasgow; *d* 1970; *s* by his son (2) WILLIAM, CMG, OBE, TD, 2nd Baron; *b* 1916; Man Dir of Kuwait Oil Co 1959-62 and Dir of British Petroleum Co Ltd 1962-74: *m* 1945, Letitia, da of late Walter Martin Krementz, of Morristown, New Jersey, USA; *d* 1976; *s* by his only son (3) WILLIAM ROBERTON, 3rd Baron and present peer.

STRATHCARRON, BARON (Macpherson) (Baron UK 1936, Bt UK 1933)

With heart and head

DAVID WILLIAM ANTHONY BLYTH MACPHERSON, 2nd Baron, and 2nd Baronet; *b* 23 Jan 1924; *s* 1937; *ed* Eton, and Jesus Coll, Camb; formerly Fl-Lt RAFVR; motoring correspondent of *The Field*; a Partner in the firm of Strathcarron & Co, a Dir of Kirchoffs (London) Ltd, of Seabourne World Express Group plc, and of Kent Internat Airport Ltd; Fellow Inst of Motor Industry, and of Chartered Inst of Transport; Chm All-Party Parl Motorcycle Group; Pres Vehicle Builders & Repairers Assocn, Driving Instructors Assocn, and Nat Breakdown Recovery Club; Pres of Guild of Motoring Writers; Chm The Order of the Road; author of *Motoring for Pleasure*: *m* 1st (Feb) 1947 (*m diss* 1947), Valerie Cole; 2ndly, 1948, Diana Hawtry, who *d* 1973, da of late Cdr R. H. Deane, of Cooden, Sussex, and formerly wife of J. N. O. Curle; 3rdly, 1974, Mary Eve, who *d* 1999, da of late John Comyn Higgins, CIE, and formerly wife of Hon Anthony Gerald Samuel (*see* V Bearsted), and has issue by 2nd *m*.

𝕬rms – Per fesse or and azure a galley of the first, masts, oars, and tackling proper, flagged gules, in the dexter chief point a hand couped fesseways holding a dagger paleways, and in the sinister a cross-crosslet fitchée of the last; over all a fese chequy of the second and argent. 𝕮rest – A cat-a-mountain sejant guardant, and having its dexter paw raised proper. 𝕾upporters – *Dexter*, a private soldier of the Cameron Highlanders in field service dress of the period 1916-18; *sinister*, a Macpherson clansman of the period 1745.

Residences – 22 Rutland Gate, SW7 1BB; Otterwood, Beaulieu, Hants

SONS LIVING (*By 2nd marriage*)

Hon IAN DAVID PATRICK, *b* 31 March 1949. *Residence* – 1 Leinster Mews, W2 3EY.
Hon Andrew Charles James, *b* 1959.

SISTER LIVING

Hon Ann Patricia (*Hon Lady Lowson*) (Oratory Cottage, 33 Ennismore Gdns Mews, SW7 1HZ) *b* 1919; is an OStJ. *m* 1936, Sir Denys Colquhoun Flowerdew Lowson, 1st Bt, who *d* 1975.

PREDECESSOR – (1) *Rt Hon* (JAMES) IAN Macpherson, PC, KC, son of James Macpherson, JP, of Inverness; *b* 1880; MP for Ross and Cromarty (*L*) 1911-18, and for Inverness-shire, Ross-shire and Cromarty, Ross and Cromatry Div 1918-35; successively Parliamentary Under-Sec of State for War, Dep Sec of State and Vice-Pres of Army Council, Ch Sec for Ireland, and Min of Pensions; *cr* a Baronet 1933, and *Baron Strathcarron*, of Banchor, co Inverness (peerage of United Kingdom) 1936: *m* 1915, Jill, who *d* 1956, da of Sir George Wood Rhodes, JP, 1st Bt; *d* 1937; *s* by his son (2) DAVID WILLIAM ANTHONY BLYTH 2nd Baron and present peer.

STRATHCLYDE, BARON (Galbraith) (Baron UK 1955)

A leader of men

THOMAS GALLOWAY DUNLOP DU ROY DE BLICQUY GALBRAITH, PC, 2nd Baron; *b* 22 Feb 1960; *s* 1985; *ed* Wellington Coll, Univ of E Anglia, and Univ of Aix-en-Provence; a Lord in Waiting 1988-89; Parl Under-Sec of State Dept of Employment, and Min for Tourism 1989-90, Under Sec of State Dept of Environment July-Sept 1990, Under Sec of State Scottish Office, Min of Agric and Fisheries 1990-92, Parl Under Sec of State Dept of Environment 1992-93, Under Sec of State Dept of Trade and Industry 1993-94, Min of State, Min for Consumer Affairs and Small Firms — to — 1994, Capt HM Body Guard of Hon Corps of Gentlemen at Arms (Ch Govt Whip, House of Lords) 1994-97, Shadow Leader House of Lords since Dec 1998; PC 1995: *m* 1992, Jane, elder da of John Skinner, of Chenies, Herts, and has issue.

Arms – Gules, three bears' heads erased argent, muzzled azure, within a bordure indented or charged with three mullets of the third, a crescent of the second for difference. **Crest** – A bear's head erased gules, muzzled argent. **Supporters** – Two bears gules, muzzled argent. *Address* – c/o House of Lords, SW1.

DAUGHTERS LIVING

Hon Elizabeth Ida Skinner, *b* 1993.
Hon Annabel Jane Simone Skinner, *b* 1996.
Hon ......, *b* 1999.

BROTHER LIVING (*raised to the rank of Baron's son* 1987)

Hon CHARLES WILLIAM DU ROY DE BLICQUY, *b* 20 May 1962; *ed* Wellington Coll, and St Andrews Univ: *m* 1992, Bridget Anne, da of Brian Reeve, of Marford, Clwyd, and has issue living, Humphrey Eldred Galloway, *b* 1994, — Alexander Charles Geoffrey, *b* 1997, — Georgina Bridget Ghislaine, *b* 1999. *Residence* – 43 Lavender Gdns, SW11 1DJ.

SISTER LIVING (*raised to the rank of a Baron's daughter* 1987)

Hon (Anne Marie) Ghislaine (du Roy), *b* 1957: *m* 1989, Peter Dilworth Kennerley, TD, of Highfield, Mauchline, Ayrshire, son of John Dilworth Kennerley, of Whitchurch, Canonicorum, Dorset, and has issue living, Samuel John Maximilian, *b* 1992, — Sarah Marie Louise, *b* 1991.

UNCLES LIVING (*sons of 1st Baron*)

Hon James Muir Galloway, CBE, *b* 1920; *ed* RN Coll, Dartmouth, Ch Ch, Oxford (MA) and R Agric Coll, Cirencester; FRICS; late Lt RN; 1939-45 War in destroyers (wounded); Co Councillor Dumfries-shire 1951-52; JP Inverness-shire 1953-54; a Dir of Buccleuch Estates Ltd since 1964; Member Home Grown Timber Advisory Cttee 1978-90; Chm Timber Growers UK 1980-83, and Chm Forestry Industry Cttee of GB 1987-90; Chm Scottish Forestry Trust since 1990; CBE 1984: *m* 1945, Anne, el da of late Maj Kenneth Paget, of Old Rectory House, Itchen Abbas, Hants, and has issue living, Brodie Thomas Paget (13 Trowlock Av, Teddington, Middx), *b* 1948: *ed* Wellington Coll and Besançon Univ; late Capt The Queen's Own Hussars: *m* 1983, Fawziah Mohammad, and has issue living, Alexander *b* 1988, Diana *b* 1984, Selina *b* 1986, — James Muir Paget (7 Saxe-Coburg Place, Edinburgh EH3), *b* 1955: *ed* Eton and RAC, Cirencester; ARICS; Member Queen's Body Guard for Scotland (Royal Company of Archers): *m* 1990, Mrs Antoinette C. Hudson, da of late Brig Peter Robert Ashburner, CBE, MC, of Wamil Hall, Mildenhall, Bury St Edmunds, Suffolk, — John Kenneth Paget (Belses Muir, Ancrum, Roxburghshire), *b* 1956: *ed* Eton: *m* 1983, Dorothy, da of John P. S. Hunter, JP, of Torbeag, Banavie, Inverness-shire, and has issue living, Donald *b* 1983, Jock *b* 1993, Anna *b* 1985, Emily *b* 1987, Flora *b* 1991, — Sara Caroline Paget, *b* 1950: *m* 1977, John Barry Ernest McCorkell, of Clanmurry House, Dromore, co Down, eldest son of Col Sir Michael McCorkell, KCVO, OBE, TD, of Ballyarnett, Londonderry, and has issue living, Harry *b* 1988, Rosanna *b* 1985. *Residence* – Rawflat, Ancrum, Roxburghshire TD8 6UW. *Clubs* – Naval and Military, Army and Navy, New (Edinburgh).

Hon Norman Dunlop Galloway, *b* 1925; *ed* Wellington Coll; a Dir of Ben Line Steamers Ltd 1968-86; 1939-45 War as Sub-Lieut RNVR: *m* 1950, Susan Patricia, el da of late Com J. H. F. Kent, of La Coupe, St Martin, Jersey, Channel Islands, and has issue living, Norman Thomas Galloway (Over Newton, Gifford, by Haddington, E Lothian EH41 4JN), *b* 1955; *ed* Wellington Coll, and Newcastle Univ; FRICS; Memb Queen's Body Guard for Scotland (Royal Company of Archers): *m* 1987, Quona Rose, da of late Maj Cecil Geoffrey Braithwaite, of Lochmalony, Cupar, and has issue living, Jake Geoffrey Kent *b* 1989, James Jan Kent *b* 1991, Thomas Norman Kent *b* 1996, Ann Rose Braithwaite *b* 1990, — Patricia Jane, *b* 1951: *m* 1981, Christopher J. Rowe, of Withy Shaw House, Goring Heath, nr Reading, Oxon RG8 7RJ, and has issue living, John Edward *b* 1983, Hamish Patrick *b* 1990, — Diana Susan, *b* 1954: *m* 1976, Andrew Guy Windham, and has issue (*see* Bowyer-Smyth, Bt). *Residence* – Over Newton, Gifford, by Haddington, E Lothian EH41 4JN.

Hon David Muir Galloway, *b* 1928; *ed* Wellington Coll, and Roy Agricultural Coll, Cirencester: *m* 1967, Marion Bingham, da of Maj Bruce Bingham Kennedy, TD, of Doonholm, Ayr, and has issue living, William James Kennedy *b* 1970; *ed* Glenalmond, Newcastle Univ (BSc), and RMA Sandhurst; Capt Royal Scots Dragoon Gds: *m* 1996, Sara Jane, yr da of Anthony Pickard, of Eshott, Northumberland, — Fiona Jane Kennedy, *b* 1968: *m* 1991, Andrew P. Robinson, son of R. L. Robinson, of Top Cottage, Thornyflat Farm, Ayr, — Mary Ida Galloway, *b* 1973, — Alice Sylvia Kennedy, *b* 1976. *Residence* – Burnbrae Lodge, Mauchline, Ayrshire.

AUNTS LIVING (*Daughters of 1st Baron*)

Hon Ida Jean Galloway, *b* 1922; 1939-45 War as 3rd Officer WRNS.
Hon Heather Margaret Anne Galloway, *b* 1930.

PREDECESSORS – (1) Thomas Dunlop Galbraith, PC, 1st Baron, son of late William Brodie Galbraith, JP, of Overton, Kilmacolm, Renfrewshire; *b* 1891; Hon FRCP Edinburgh 1960, and Hon Fellow, Roy Coll of Physicians and Surgeons, Glasgow 1961; Com RN, a Chartered Accountant, and an Hon Gov of Glasgow Acad; was a Member of Glasgow Corporation 1933-40, and Magistrate 1938-40, Joint Parliamentary Under-Sec of State for Scotland May to Aug 1945, and again Nov 1951 to April 1955, and Min of State, Scottish Office April 1955 to Oct 1958; a Gov of Wellington Coll 1947-61; Chm of North of Scotland Hydro-Electric Board 1959-67; European War 1914-18, in HMS *Audacious* and HMS *Queen Elizabeth* at Gallipoli Landings and surrender of German High Seas Fleet; European War 1939-45 on Staff of Com-in-Ch, Coast of Scotland, and as Dep British Admiralty Supply Representative in USA; MP for Pollock Div of Glasgow (*U*) 1940-55; a Freeman of Dingwall and Aberdeen; *cr* PC 1953 and *Baron Strathclyde*, of Barskimming, co Ayr (peerage of United Kingdom) 1955: *m* 1915, Ida Jean, who *d* 1985, da of late Thomas Galloway, JP, of Auchendrane, Ayrshire; *d* 1985; *s* by his grandson (2) Thomas Galloway Dunlop du Roy de Blicquy (son of late Hon Sir Thomas Galloway Dunlop Galbraith, KBE), 2nd Baron and present peer.

STRATHCONA AND MOUNT ROYAL, BARON (Howard) (Baron UK 1900)

Donald Euan Palmer Howard, 4th Baron; *b* 26 Nov 1923; *s* 1959; *ed* Eton, at Trin Coll, Camb, and McGill Univ., Montreal; late Lt RNVR; a DL for Angus; Vice-Chm Maritime Trust, and Pres of UK Pilots Assocn and Steamboat Assocn of Great Britain; a Lord in Waiting to HM and a Govt Whip 1973-74, and Parl Under-Sec of State for RAF Jan to March 1974; Joint Dep Leader of the Opposition House of Lords 1976-79; Min of State, MOD, 1979-81: *m* 1st, 1954 (*m diss* 1977), Lady Jane Mary Waldegrave, da of 12th Earl Waldegrave; 2ndly, 1978, Patricia, da of late Harvey Evelyn Thomas, and widow of John Middleton, and has issue by 1st *m*.

Arms – Quarterly, 1st and 4th argent, on a bend indented between four cross-crosslets gules, three maple leaves or; 2nd and 3rd gules, on a fess argent, between a demi-lion rampant or in chief, and a canoe of the last with four men rowing proper, in the stern a flag of the second flowing towards the dexter inscribed flag of the second flowing towards the dexter inscribed with the letters NW sable, in base a hammer surmounted of a nail in saltire of the last. Crest – On a mount vert, a beaver eating into a maple tree proper. Supporters – *Dexter*, a trooper of the Regiment of Strathcona's Horse peroper; *sinister*, a navvy standing on a railway sleeper, chaired and railed all proper.
Seat – Isle of Colonsay, Argyll. *Residence* – Townsend Barn, Poulshot, nr Devizes, Wilts SN10 1SD. *Clubs* – Brooks's, Pratt's, Royal Yacht Squadron.

SONS LIVING (By 1st marriage)

Hon (Donald) Alexander Smith, *b* 24 June 1961; *ed* Gordonstoun, and London Business Sch (MBA): *m* 1992, Jane Maree, da of R. Shaun Gibb, of Sydney, Australia, and has issue living, Angus, *b* ......, — Amelia Alexandra, *b* 1996. *Residence* – ....
Hon Andrew Barnaby, *b* 1963: *m* 1994, Katharine E., eldest da of C. Oldfield, of Uplyme, Devon. *Residence* – 16 Henning St, SW11.

DAUGHTERS LIVING (By 1st marriage)

Hon Jane Elizabeth Stirling, *b* 1955; *ed* Sherborne Sch for Girls, and Somerville Coll, Oxford: *m* 1987, Nigel Morris Jones, only son of M. H. Morris Jones, of Tarvin, Cheshire, and has issue living, Sophia Venetia, *b* 1989, — Lydia Iona, *b* 1991, — Kiloran Imogen, *b* 1993, — Eloïse Georgia, *b* (twin)1993. *Residence* – 143 Portland Rd, W11 4LR.
Hon Katharine Mary, *b* 1956: *m* 1st, 1975, Gavin Michael Jasper Strachan; 2ndly, 1982, William Evelyn Hinton Joll (*see* Agnew, Bt (*cr* 1895), 1985 Edn), and has issue living (by 2nd *m*), Harry Augustus, *b* 1983, — Flora Katharine Kiloran, *b* 1985, — Hannah Olympia, *b* 1988. *Residence* – Bushy Farm, Ripe Lane, Firle, E Sussex BN8 6LS.
Hon Caroline Anne, *b* 1959.
Hon Emma Laura Louise (twin), *b* 1963: *m* 1996, David Zuill, son of William Zuill, of Adelaide, S Australia. *Residence* –

BROTHERS LIVING

Hon Barnaby John, *b* 1925; *ed* Eton, and Trin Coll, Camb (BA Law 1948, MA 1954); appointed Commr, S Rhodesian Forestry Commn 1957; European War 1943-45 as Sub-Lt RNVR (Air Branch): *m* 1st, 1952 (*m diss* 1967), Elizabeth, da of late Frank M. Mayfield, of St Louis, Missouri, USA; 2ndly, 1970, Mary-Jane Bishop, who *d* 1994, da of late Ambrose Chambers; 3rdly, 1996, Linda F. Kitson, and has had issue (by 1st *m*) †Alan Stirling, *b* 1956; *d* 1992, — Elizabeth Kiloran, *b* 1957: *m* 1982, Vicomte Philippe de Lapérouse, of 2 White Gate Lane, St Louis, Missouri 63124, USA, eldest son of Count Bertrand de Lapérouse, of Fairhaven, NJ, USA, and has issue living, Patrick Henri Louis Léon Marie *b* 1985, Kiloran Elizabeth Diana Marie *b* 1986, Isabelle Marthe Jeanne Marie *b* 1990, — Sarah Ann Catriona, *b* 1962: *m* 1983, Dr Jeffrey Lee Thomasson, MD, of 6197 Waterman Av, St Louis, MO 63130, USA, and has issue living, Robert Howard *b* 1987, Alan Mayfield *b* 1988, Patricia Delzell *b* 1991. *Address* – 1224 River Rd, Orange Park, Florida 32073, USA; St Ann's Bay, RR4 Baddeck, Nova Scotia, Canada, BOC 1HO. *Clubs* – Brooks's, Queen's.

Hon Jonathan Alan, *b* 1933; *ed* Eton, Trin Coll, Camb, R Inst of Tech, Stockholm, and Stockholm Univ; late 2nd Lt Coldstream Guards, and Argyll & Sutherland Highlanders (TA): *m* 1st, 1956 (*m diss* 1969), Hon Brigid Mary Westenra, da of 6th Baron Rossmore; 2ndly, 1970 (*m diss* 1981), Cecilia Philipson, and has issue living (by 1st *m*), Nicola Charlotte, *b* 1958, — Kiloran Emma, *b* 1959, — (by 2nd *m*) Olof Philipson, *b* 1970. *Address* – Box 3360, Luanda, Angola.

SISTER LIVING

Hon Diana Catriona, *b* 1935: *m* 1956, Michael Leslie Ogilvie Faber, of Rodmell Hill Cottage, Mill Lane, Rodmell, E Sussex BN7 3HS, and has issue living, Rory Valdemar (1801 Hyde St, Apt 3, San Francisco, CA 94109-2143, USA), *b* 1956: *m* 1997, Julie Ann Johnson, — Guy Donald George, *b* 1959, — Laura Diana, *b* 1958: *m* 1993, John R. Percival, son of late Michael Percival, of SW1, and has issue living, Mary Diana *b* 1996, Heather Tessa *b* (twin) 1996, — Charlotte Victoria (twin), *b* 1958: *m* 1990, John E. Marais, of Calle Rossic, Bis 4, Barcelona 08003, Spain, and has issue living, Edward John *b* 1991, Maria-del-Mar *b* 1989.

COLLATERAL BRANCH LIVING

Issue of late Capt Hon Sir Arthur Jared Palmer Howard, KBE, CVO, yst son of Margaret Charlotte, Baroness Strathcona and Mount Royal, *b* 1896, *d* 1971: *m* 1922, Lady Leonora Stanley Baldwin, who *d* 1989, da of 1st Earl Baldwin of Bewdley:—

Alexander (Poronui Station, RD3 Taupo, NZ), *b* 1930; *ed* Eton, and Trin Coll, Camb (MA); Scots Gds: *m* 1959, Penelope Joanna, da of Gershom Radcliffe Layton Warren, of Saanichton BC, Canada, and has issue living, Shamus Alexander, *b* 1962, — Harry Alexander, *b* 1967, — Rory Jared, *b* 1973. —— Kiloran Margaret (*Hon Mrs Langley G. H. Russell*), *b* 1926: *m* 1951, Hon Langley Gordon Haslingden Russell, MC, who *d* 1975 (*see* B Russell of Liverpool). —— Jill, *b* 1934: *m* 1958, Peter James Scott Lumsden, and has issue living, James Herbert, *b* 1962, — Alice Margaret, *b* 1961, — Susanna Helen, *b* 1965.

PREDECESSORS – (1) *Sir* DONALD ALEXANDER Smith, GCMG, GCVO, DCL, LLD, FRS, son of late Alexander Smith, of Archieston, Scotland, *b* 1820; entered Hudson Bay Co's Ser at an early age, and was last Resident Gov of that Corporation as a governing body; was Special Commr during 1st Riel Rebellion in Red River Settlements 1869-70 (thanked by Gov-Gen in Council); appointed a MEC (first) of NW Territory 1870; represented Winnipeg and St John's in Manitoba Legislature 1871-84; elected MP for Selkirk in Canadian House of Commons 1871, 1872, 1874, and 1878, and for Montreal West 1887 and 1891, which constituency he represented until 1896; sworn PC Canada 1896, and was appointed High Commr in Great Britain for the Dominion 1896; raised a body of mounted troops — Strathcona's Horse — for service in S Africa 1900; *cr* GCMG 1896, GCVO 1908, *Baron Strathcona and Mount Royal*, of Glencoe, co Argyll, and Mount Royal, Quebec, Canada (peerage of United Kingdom) 1897, and *Baron Strathcona and Mount Royal*, of Mount Royal, Quebec, Canada, and Glencoe, co Argyll (peerage of UK) 1900, with special remainder in default of male issue to his only da Margaret Charlotte, and her heirs male: *m* 1853, Isabella Sophia, who *d* 1913, da of late Richard Hardisty, of Canada; *d* 1914, when the Barony (*cr* 1897) became ext, while in that of 1900 he was *s* under the special remainder by his only da (2) MARGARET CHARLOTTE Howard, *b* 1854: *m* 1888, Robert Jared Bliss Howard, OBE, FRCS, who *d* 1921; *d* 1926; *s* by her son (3) DONALD STIRLING PALMER Howard, 3rd Baron; *b* 1891; Major London Scottish (TA); was MP for Cumberland, N Div (*U*) 1922-26, Parliamentary Private Sec (unpaid) for Parliamentary Sec to Min of Labour 1923-4, Parliamentary Private Sec to First Lord of the Admiralty 1925-7, and Under-Sec of State for War and Vice-Pres of Army Council 1934-39; appointed Capt of Yeomen of the Guard 1931; *m* 1922, Hon Diana Evelyn Loder, who *d* 1985, da of 1st Baron Wakehurst; *d* 1959; *s* by his son (4) DONALD EUAN PALMER, 4th Baron and present peer.

STRATHEDEN AND CAMPBELL, BARON (Campbell) (Baron UK 1836)

DONALD CAMPBELL, 6th Baron; *b* 4 April 1934; *s* 1987; *ed* Eton: *m* 1957, Hilary Ann Holland, who *d* 1991, da of late Lt-Col William Derington Turner, of Simonstown, S Africa, and has issue.

Boldly and openly

Arms – Gyronny of eight or and sable, within a bordure engrailed quarterly, or and azure charged with eight buckles counterchanged. Crest – A boar's head erased, gyronny or eight, or and sable. Supporters – (*Barony of Stratheden*) On either side a buck argent, attired and hoofed or, that on the dexter gorged with a collar counter-compony gules and of the second, therefrom pendent an escutcheon gyronny of eight or and sable and that on the sinister gorged with a collar or, therefrom pendent an escutcheon gold, charged with three chaplets of laurel two and one proper. —— (*Barony of Campbell*) On either side a lion guardant gules, that on the *dexter* gorged with a collar or, pendant therefrom an escutcheon azure, charged with a saltire argent, and that on the *sinister* gorged with a wreath of shamrocks proper, therefrom an escutcheon checky or and gules. *Residence* – Ridgewood, MS 401, Cooroy, Queensland 4563, Australia.

SON LIVING

Hon DAVID ANTHONY, *b* 13 Feb 1963; *ed* Queensland, Australia: *m* 1993, Jennifer Margaret Owens, and has issue living, Rebecca Hilary, *b* 1995. *Residence* – 71 Magpie Lane, Cooroy, Queensland 4563, Australia.

DAUGHTERS LIVING

Hon Tania Ann CAMPBELL, *b* 1960; has resumed her maiden name: *m* 1984, Paul Hamment, of Melbourne. *Residence* – 36 Charles Kurg Drive, Worongary, Queensland 4213, Australia.
Hon Wendy Meriel, *b* 1969.
Hon Joyce Margaret, *b* 1971.

DAUGHTERS LIVING OF FOURTH BARON

Hon Moyra Jean, *b* 1924. *Residence* – Scraesburgh, Jedburgh, Roxburghshire TD8 6QR.
Hon Clayre (*Lady Richard Percy*), *b* 1927: *m* 1st, 1950 (*m diss* 1974), Hon Nicholas Ridley, MP (later Baron Ridley of Liddesdale, PC, Life Baron), who *d* 1993; 2ndly, 1979, as his 2nd wife, Lord Richard Charles Percy (*see* D Northumberland), who *d* 1989. *Residence* – 212 Lambeth Rd, SE1 7JY.
Hon Fiona, *b* 1932. *Residence* – 158 Lambeth Rd, SE1 7DF.

WIDOW LIVING OF FOURTH BARON

NOEL CHRISTABEL (*Noël, Baroness Stratheden and Campbell*), da of late Capt Conrad Viner, and formerly wife of George Vincent: *m* 1964, as his 2nd wife, the 4th Baron Stratheden and Campbell, CBE, who *d* 1981.

PREDECESSORS – (1) JOHN Campbell, PC; *b* 1779; a distinguished lawyer, judge, and biographical writer; sat successively as MP for Stafford, Dudley, and Edinburgh (*L*), and having held for many years the offices of Solicitor-Gen and Attorney-Gen was in 1841 appointed Lord Chancellor of Ireland, and *cr Baron Campbell*, of St Andrews, co Fife (peerage of United Kingdom); was Chancellor of the Duchy of Lancaster 1846, Lord Ch Justice of England 1850-9, and Lord High Chancellor of Great Britain 1859-61: *m* 1821, Hon Mary Elizabeth Scarlett (da of 1st Baron Abinger), who in 1836, was *cr* in her own right *Baroness Stratheden*, of Cupar, co Fife (peerage of United Kingdom); *d* 1861; *s* by his son (2) WILLIAM FREDERICK, 2nd Baron, who in 1860 had *s* his mother as 2nd Baron Stratheden, *b* 1824; MP for Cambridge (*L*) 1847-52, and for Harwich 1856-60; *d* 1893; *s* by his brother (3) HALLYBURTON GEORGE, 3rd Baron, *b* 1829: *m* 1865, Louisa Mary, who *d* 1923, el da of late Rt Hon Alexander James Beresford-Hope, MP; *d* 1918; *s* by his grandson (4) ALASTAIR, CBE (son of late Capt Hon John Beresford Campbell, DSO, son of 3rd Baron), 4th Baron, Brig Coldstream Gds, Capt Queen's Body Guard for Scotland (Roy Co of Archers); Chm Edinburgh and E Scotland Coll of Agric 1956-70, and Hill Farming Research Organisation 1958-69; Convenor Roxburgh Co Council 1960-68, Pres Assocn of Co Councils in Scotland 1966-68; Chm Historic Buildings Council for Scotland 1969-76: *m* 1st, 1923, Jean Helen St Clair, CBE, who *d* 1956, da of Col William Anstruther-Gray (Anstruther, Bt, colls); 2ndly, 1964, Mrs Noël Christabel Vincent, da of late Capt Conrad Viner; *d* 1981; *s* by his brother (5) GAVIN, 5th Baron, *b* 1901; Maj KRRC and Lieut-Col 19th (Kenya) Battn King's African Rifles: *m* 1933, Evelyn Mary Austen, who *d* 1989, da of late Col Herbert Austen Smith, CIE; *d* 1987; *s* by his only son (6) DONALD, 6th Baron and present peer; also Baron Campbell.

STRATHMORE AND KINGHORNE, EARL OF (Bowes Lyon) (Earl S 1606 and 1677, Earl UK 1937)

In Thee, O Lord, have I put my trust

MICHAEL FERGUS BOWES LYON, 18th Earl; *b* 7 June 1957; *s* 1987; a Page of Honour to HM Queen Elizabeth the Queen Mother 1971-73; a Lord in Waiting 1989-91; Capt Yeomen of the Guard (Dep Chief Whip) 1991-94; DL Angus 1994; Pres The Boys Brigade 1994-98: *m* 1984, Isobel Charlotte, yr da of Capt Anthony E. Weatherall, of Cowhill, Dumfries, and has issue.

Arms – Quarterly: 1st and 4th argent, a lion rampant azure, armed and langued gules, within a double tressure flory counterflory of the second, *Lyon;* 2nd and 3rd ermine, three bows, strings palewise proper, *Bowes.* **Royal Augmentation** (granted to the holder of the Earldom only) — An inescutcheon en surtout azure, thereon a rose argent, barbed vert, seeded or, ensigned with an Imperial Crown proper, within a double tressure flory-counterflory of the second, the said inescutcheon ensigned with an Earl's coronet proper. **Crest** – Between two slips of laurel, a lady to the girdle, habited, and holding in her right hand a thistle all proper. **Supporters** – *Dexter,* a unicorn argent, armed, unguled, maned, and tufted or; *sinister,* a lion per fesse or and gules. **Seat** – Glamis Castle, Forfar, co Angus. *Clubs* – Turf, Pratt's, Perth, White's.

SONS LIVING

SIMON PATRICK (*Lord Glamis*), *b* 18 June 1986.
Hon John Fergus, *b* 1988.
Hon George Norman, *b* 1991.

SISTERS LIVING

Lady Elizabeth Mary Cecilia, *b* 1959; *ed* St Hilda's Coll, Oxford: *m* 1990, Antony Richard Leeming, eldest son of late Richard Whiteside Leeming, of Skirsgill Park, Penrith, Cumbria, and has issue living, Richard Fergus, *b* 1992, — Andrew Michael, *b* 1996, — Teresa Mary, *b* 1994. *Residence* – Skirsgill Park, Penrith, Cumbria.

Lady Diana Evelyn, *b* 1966: *m* 1995, Christopher Bryan Godfrey-Faussett, elder son of Richard Hugh Godfrey-Faussett, of Badlesmere, Kent, and has issue living, Fergus, *b* 1998, — Laura, *b* 1997.

UNCLE LIVING *(Brother of 17th Earl; raised to the rank of an Earl's son 1974)*

Hon (Michael) Albemarle, *b* 1940; *ed* Eton, and Magdalen Coll, Oxford; Dir Coutts & Co 1969-93; Gov Peabody Trust since 1982, Hon Treasurer Family Service Units 1976-96; Trustee Distressed Gentlefolks' Aid Assoc since 1998.

AUNT LIVING *(Sister of 17th Earl; raised to the rank of an Earl's daughter 1974)*

Lady Mary Cecilia, *b* 1932; an Extra Lady-in-Waiting to HRH Princess Alexandra, Hon Lady Ogilvy, since 1970: *m* 1951, Sir Timothy James Alan Colman, KG, Lord Lieut Norfolk since 1978, of Bixley Manor, Norwich NR14 8SJ, and has issue living, James Russell, *b* 1962: *m* 1994, Sacha L., da of Robert Cotterell, of Upper Norton, Herefords, and of Mrs Elizabeth Rawlings, of Baydon, Marlborough, Wilts, and has issue living, Jake Jeremiah *b* 1994, Leilah Ophelia *b* 1996, — Matthew Geoffrey, *b* 1966: *m* 1997, Jane E., yr da of James Johnston, of Sydney, NSW, — Sarah Rose, *b* 1953; Lady-in-Waiting to HRH The Duchess of Kent since 1990: *m* 1977, Peter John Charles Troughton, of The Lynch House, Upper Wanborough, Swindon, Wilts SN4 0BZ, eldest son of late Sir Charles Hugh Willis Troughton, CBE, MC, TD, of Little Leckmelm, Ullapool, Ross-shire (*see* Fowler, Bt (ext 1933), 1966 Edn), and has issue living, Michael *b* 1981, Rose *b* 1979, Lucy *b* 1984, — Sabrina Mary, *b* 1955: *m* 1976, Christopher Arthur Penn, of 50 Sussex St, SW1V 4RG, yr son of late Lt-Col Sir Eric Charles William MacKenzie Penn, GCVO, OBE, MC, and has issue living, Rory *b* 1980, Louisa *b* 1983, — Emma Elizabeth, *b* 1958: *m* 1986 (*m diss* 1994), Richard Henry Ramsbotham, yst son of Lt-Gen Sir David Ramsbotham, GCB, CBE, and has issue living, Sophie *b* 1987.

GREAT AUNT LIVING *(Daughter of 14th Earl)*

Lady Elizabeth Angela Marguerite (*HM Queen Elizabeth The Queen Mother*), *b* 4 Aug 1900 (*see* ROYAL FAMILY): *m* 26 April 1923, HM King George VI, who *d* 6 Feb 1952. *Residences* – Clarence House, SW1; Royal Lodge, Windsor Great Park, Berkshire; Castle of Mey, Caithness.

WIDOW LIVING OF SEVENTEENTH EARL

MARY PAMELA (*Mary, Countess of Strathmore and Kinghorne*), DL Angus 1989, yr da of Brig Norman Duncan McCorquodale, MC, of Maxton House, St Boswell's, Roxburghshire: *m* 1956, the 17th Earl of Strathmore and Kinghorne, who *d* 1987. *Residence* – Glamis House, Forfar, co Angus.

COLLATERAL BRANCHES LIVING

      Issue of late Hon John Herbert Bowes Lyon, 2nd son of 14th Earl, *b* 1886, *d* 1930: *m* 1914, Hon Fenella Hepburn-Stuart-Forbes-Trefusis, who *d* 1966, da of 21st Baron Clinton:—
Katherine, *b* 1926.

      Issue of late Hon Sir David Bowes Lyon, KCVO, yst son of 14th Earl, *b* 1902, *d* 1961: *m* 1929, Rachel Pauline, who *d* 1996, da of late Col Rt Hon Herbert Spender-Clay, CMG, MC, MP (V Astor):—
Simon Alexander (St Pauls Walden Bury, Hitchin, Herts), *b* 1932; *ed* Eton; Lord Lieut of Hertfordshire 1986: *m* 1966, Caroline Mary Victoria, da of late Rt Rev Victor Joseph Pike, CB, CBE, former Bishop Suffragan of Sherborne, and has issue living, Fergus Alexander, *b* 1970, — David Victor, *b* 1973, — Andrew Simon *b* 1979, — Rosemary Pema, *b* 1968: *m* 1996, (Nicholas) David Kirkland Glazebrook, elder son of Benjamin Kirkland Glazebrook. —— Davina Katharine (*Countess of Stair*), *b* 1930: *m* 1960, 13th Earl of Stair, KCVO, MBE, who *d* 1996. *Residence* – Lochinch Castle, Stranraer, Wigtownshire.

(Not in remainder to UK Earldom)

      Grandchildren of late Capt Geoffrey Francis Bowes-Lyon (infra):—
      Issue of late Maj-Gen Sir Francis James Cecil Bowes-Lyon, KCVO, CB, OBE, MC, *b* 1917, *d* 1977: *m* 1941, Mary (Beltingham House, Bardon Mill, Hexham, Northumberland), da of late Sir Humphrey Edmund de Trafford, MC, 4th Bt:—
John Francis, *b* 1942; *ed* Ampleforth. *Residence* – D5 Albany, Piccadilly, W1. *Clubs* – Buck's, Pratt's. —— David James, *b* 1947; *ed* Ampleforth; DL Midlothian 1992: *m* 1976, (Elizabeth) Harriet, da of late Sir John Rupert Colville, CB, CVO (*see* V Colville of Culross, colls), and has issue living, James Francis John, *b* 1979; Page of Honour to HM since 1991, — Charles David, *b* 1989, — Georgina Alice, *b* 1977, — Alexandra Violet, *b* 1986. *Residence* – Heriot Water, Heriot, Midlothian. *Club* – White's. —— Fiona Ann, *b* 1944: *m* 1966, Joseph Henry Goodhart, of Great Givendale, Pocklington, York, and has issue living, James Henry, *b* 1970, — David Andrew, *b* 1971, — Camilla Bridget, *b* 1968: *m* 1994, (David) Benjamin Ridgwell, yr son of Dr Stanley Arthur Ridgwell, CBE, of London.

      Granddaughters of late Hon Francis Bowes-Lyon, 2nd son of 13th Earl:—
      Issue of late Capt Geoffrey Francis Bowes-Lyon, Black Watch (Roy Highlanders), *b* 1886, *d* 1951: *m* 1914, Edith Katharine, who *d* 1971, da of Sir Lewis Amherst Selby-Bigge, 1st Bt, KCB:—
Caroline Anne Lindsay, *b* 1916: *m* 1939, Llewellyn Ross Llewellyn, who *d* 1988, and has issue living, Llewellyn Charles (44 Drayton Gdns, SW10 9SA), *b* 1943: *m* 1966, Kathleen Mary, da of late John Charles Roche, of Nairobi, Kenya, and has issue living, Sophie Anita *b* 1971, Eleanor Loveday Caroline (Daisy) *b* 1976, — Simon Lindsay, *b* 1945: *m* 1970 (*m diss* 1992), Stella Willis, and has issue living, Fergus John *b* 1975, Emma *b* 1977. *Residence* – Casa Al Ghaba, Alfeição, 8100 Loulé, Algarve, Portugal. —— Susannah Sarah, *b* 1920: *m* 1940, Peter Hugh Dudley Ryder, MBE, Hon Lt-Col late R Armoured Corps TA Reserve, who *d* 1993 (*see* E Harrowby, colls). *Residence* – Ardmore, Riverbank Rd, Ramsey, Isle of Man.

      Granddaughter of late Hubert Ernest Bowes-Lyon (infra):—
      Issue of late Hubert Malcolm Bowes-Lyon, *b* 1907, *d* 1995: *m* 1943 (*m diss* 1964), Fanny Rose, who *d* 1969, da of late Simon Jacobs, of S Africa:—
Jennifer Merrill, *b* 1944; *ed* Tel Aviv Univ (BA): *m* 19—, Stephen Byk, and has issue living, a da, *b* 1977. *Residence* – 2 Ha Tamar St, Tiriat Ha Savionim, Yehud, Israel 5647.

      Grandchildren of late Hon Ernest Bowes-Lyon, 3rd son of 13th Earl:—
      Issue of late Hubert Ernest Bowes-Lyon, *b* 1883, *d* 1959: *m* 1st (Jan) 1905, Mary Agnes, who *d* 1914, da of James Hay Smeaton; 2ndly, 1919, Margaret, who *d* 1966, da of Frank Nuttall, of Belfast, and widow of James Graham:—
(By 1st *m*) Douglas Ian Gordon, *b* 1912; Lieut CAC (ret); served World War II: *m* 1942, Charlotte, da of late Norman Herbert Gardner, and has issue living, Douglas Malcolm (1474 Lloyd George, Verdun, Quebec, Canada H4H 2P5), *b* 1946: *m* 1975, Diana Frechette, — David Gordon (780 Edgewood Rd, Pickering, Ontario, Canada L1V 2Z9), *b* 1949; *ed* Concordia Univ (B Comm): *m* 1974, Elizabeth, da of Donald Allan Rodier, and has issue living, Marianne Elizabeth *b* 1978, Andrea Lynn *b* 1980, — Charlotte Mary Diane, *b* 1943: *m* 1965, Jean D. Wagner, of 127 Chartwell Crescent, Beaconsfield, Quebec, Canada H9W 1C2, and has issue living, Richard Steven *b* 1968, Ian Gordon *b* 1982, Andrew James *b* 1983, Heidi *b* 1970, — Deborah Jane (PO Box 1300, St John's, Newfoundland, Canada A1C 8H8), *b* 1958. —— (By 2nd *m*) Sonia Gabrielle, *b* 1922: *m* 1948, Lt-Col Stephen Otteran Murphy, MBE, of Higher Polgrain, St Wenn, Bodmin, Cornwall.

      Issue of late Hon Patrick Bowes-Lyon, 5th son of 13th Earl, *b* 1863, *d* 1946: *m* 1893, Alice Wiltshire, who *d* 1953, ward of late Capt Arthur Lister-Kaye, of Manor House, Stretton-on-Dunsmore:—
Margaret Ann (36 Cumberland Terrace, Regent's Park, NW1 4HP), *b* 1907: *m* 1945, Lt-Col Francis Arthur D'Abreu, ERD, ChM, FRCS, RAMC, who *d* (16 Nov) 1995, and has had issue, Anthony Patrick John (Mill End Reach, Hambleden, Henley-on-Thames, Oxon), *b* 1946; *ed* Stonyhurst, and London Univ (BA 1970): *m* 1967 (*m diss* 1976), Rachel Jane, da of late Maj W. Green, and has issue living, James Simon Francis *b* 1969, Catherine Jane Ann *b* 1967: *m* 1996, Ricardo Bagen Escudero, of Barcelona, — Francesca Ann, *b* 1948: *m* 1970, Kieran Patrick Fogarty, of 131 Northchurch Rd, Islington, N1, — Anna Teresa, *b* 1950: *m* 1977 (*m diss* 1990), Nicholas Robin Le Fowne Hurt, and *d* (17 April) 1995, leaving issue, Cassandra Isobel Ann *b* 1980.

      Issue of late Lieut-Col Hon Malcolm Bowes-Lyon, CBE, yst son of 13th Earl; *b* 1874, *d* 1957: *m* 1907, Winifred, who *d* 1957, da of Hector John Gurdon-Rebow, JP, formerly of Wyvenhoe Park, Essex:—
Clodagh Pamela (*Pamela, Lady Lever*) (Lessudden Cottage, St Boswells, Melrose, Roxburghshire TD6 0BH), *b* 1908: *m* 1st, 1931 (*m diss* 1952), Lord Malcolm Avondale Douglas-Hamilton, OBE, DFC, RAF, who *d* 1964 (*see* D Hamilton and Brandon); 2ndly, 1962, Sir Tresham Joseph Philip Lever, 2nd Bt, who *d* 1975.

PREDECESSORS – (1) PATRICK LYON, PC, grandson of Sir John Lyon, of Forteviot, and afterwards of Glamis, co Forfar (who *m* Jean, da of King Robert II of Scotland); was one of the hostages to the English 1424-7 for the ransom of King James I; *cr Lord Glamis* 1445, and appointed Master of the Household 1452; *d* 1459; *s* by his son (2) ALEXANDER, 2nd Lord; *dsp* 1485; *s* by his brother (3) JOHN, PC, 3rd Lord; was Justice Gen of Scotland; *d* 1497, *s* by his son (4) JOHN, 4th Lord; *d* 1500; *s* by his el son (5) GEORGE, 5th Lord; *d* 1505; *s* by his brother (6) JOHN, 6th Lord; *d* 1528; his son Lord Glamis, his widow, a kinsman, and an old priest were indicted for designs against the life of James V by poison or witchcraft; Lady Glamis was condemned to the flames and suffered on the Castle Hill at Edinburgh, July 17th, 1537, Lord Glamis was sentenced to be executed and his estates forfeited, but was respited until he attained his majority; the accuser, however, having confessed that the whole story was a fabrication his lordship was released, and in 1543 was restored by Act of Parliament to his honours and estates, and *s* as (7) JOHN, 7th Lord; *d* 1558; *s* by his son (8) JOHN, 8th Lord; was Lord Chancellor of Scotland 1575; *d* 1578; *s* by his son (9) PATRICK, PC, 9th Lord; was Capt of the Guard; *cr Earl of Kinghorne* (peerage of Scotland) 1606; *d* 1615; *s* by his son (10) JOHN, 2nd Earl; *d* 1647; *s* by his son (11) PATRICK, PC, 3rd Earl; was a Lord of the Treasury, an Extraordinary Lord of Session; obtained in 1672 a new charter extending the remainder to his heirs and assigns whatsoever, and in 1677 another charter providing that he and each successive inheritor of the title should be styled *Lord Glamis, Tannadyce, Sidlaw and Strathdichtie, Viscount Lyon,* and *Earl of Strathmore and Kinghorne; d* 1695; *s* by his son (12) JOHN, 4th Earl; *d* 1712; *s* by his el son (13) JOHN, 5th Earl, was slain in the rebellion of 1715 at battle of Sheriffmuir; *s* by his brother (14) CHARLES, 6th Earl; *b* 17—: *m* 1725; *d* 1728; *s* by his brother (15) JAMES, 7th Earl; *b* 1702: *m* (May) 1731, Mary, who *d* (Sept) 1731, da of Dr Charles Oliphant; *d* 1735; *s* by his brother (16) THOMAS, 8th Earl; *b* 1704: *m* 1736, Jean, who *d* 1778, da of James Nicholson, of West Rainton, co Durham; *d* 1753: *s* by his son (17) JOHN, 9th Earl; assumed by Act of Parliament 1767 the surname of Bowes: *m* 1767, Mary Eleanor, who *d* 1800, da and heir of George Bowes of Streatlam Castle, co Durham; *d* 1776; *s* by his el son (18) JOHN, 10th Earl; *cr Baron Bowes,* of Streatlam Castle (peerage of United Kingdom) 1815; *d* 1820; *s* by his brother (19) THOMAS, 11th Earl; resumed the surname of Lyon before that of Bowes: *m* 1800, Mary Elizabeth Louisa Rodney, who *d* 1811, da and heir of George Carpenter, of Redbourn, Herts; *d* 1846; *s* by his grandson (20) THOMAS GEORGE, 12th Earl, son of George, Lord Glamis, by Charlotte, da of Joseph Valentine Grimstead; was a Representative Peer; *d* 1865; *s* by his brother (21) CLAUDE, 13th Earl; *b* 1824; Lord-Lieut of co Forfar; a Representative Peer 1870-87; assumed the surname of Bowes Lyon in lieu of Lyon Bowes; *cr Baron Bowes,* of Streatlam Castle (peerage of United Kingdom) 1887: *m* 1852, Frances Dora, who *d* 1922, da of Oswald Smith, of Blendon Hall, Kent; *d* 1904; *s* by his son (22) CLAUDE GEORGE, KG, KT, GCVO, 14th Earl; *b* 1855; 32 years Lord Lieut, of co Angus; *cr Earl of Strathmore and Kinghorne* (peerage of United Kingdom) 1937: *m* 1881, Nina Cecilia, GCVO, who *d* 1938, da of late Rev Charles William Cavendish-Bentinck (D Portland, colls); *d* 1944; *s* by his son (23) PATRICK, 15th Earl, *b* 1884: *m* 1908, Lady Dorothy Beatrix Osborne, who *d* 1946, da of 10th Duke of Leeds; *d* 1949; *s* by his son (24) TIMOTHY PATRICK, 16th Earl, *b* 1918: *m* 1958, Mary Bridget, who *d* 1967, da of Peter Brennan, of Clonasee, co Leix; *d* 1972; *s* by his cousin (25) FERGUS MICHAEL CLAUDE (el son of Hon Michael Claude Hamilton Bowes Lyon, 5th son of 14th Earl), 17th Earl, *b* 1928; late Capt Scots Gds, and Member of Queen's Body Guard for Scotland (Royal Company of Archers); Vice Lieut co Angus 1979-87; Dir T. Cowie plc, Sunderland, co Durham: *m* 1956, Mary Pamela, yr da of Brig Norman Duncan McCorquodale, MC; *d* 1987; *s* by his only son (26) MICHAEL FERGUS, 18th Earl and present peer; also Earl of Strathmore and Kinghorne (*cr* UK 1937), Viscount Lyon, Lord Glamis, Tannadyce, Sidlaw and Strathdichtie, and Baron Bowes.

Strathnaver, Lord; son of Countess of Sutherland.

STRATHSPEY, BARON (Grant of Grant) (Baron UK 1884, Bt NS 1625)
(Title pronounced "Strathspay")

JAMES PATRICK TREVOR GRANT OF GRANT, 6th Baron, and 18th Baronet; *b* 9 Sept 1943; *s* 1992; *ed* abroad; is 33rd Chief of Clan Grant: *m* 1966 (*m diss* 1984), Linda, da of David Piggott, of Forfar; 2ndly, 1985 (*m diss* 1993), Margaret, da of Robert Drummond, of Fife, and has issue by 1st *m*.

Arms – Gules, three antique crowns or. Crest – A burning hill proper. Supporters – Two savages or naked men wreathed about the head and middle with laurel, each bearing on his exterior shoulder a club, proper.
Address – The School House, Lochbuie, Isle of Mull, Argyllshire.

DAUGHTERS LIVING (*By 1st marriage*)

Hon Carolyn Anne Maclean, *b* 1967.
Hon Philippa Jane, *b* 1971.
Hon Victoria Louise, *b* 1976.

HALF-BROTHER LIVING

Hon MICHAEL PATRICK FRANCIS, *b* 22 April 1953; *ed* Harrow, and Oriel Coll, Oxford; ARICS. *Residence* – 3 Ifield Rd, SW10 9AZ.

SISTERS LIVING

Hon (Geraldine) Janet GRANT OF GRANT, *b* 1940; resumed surname of Grant of Grant 1972: *m* 1963 (*m diss* 1972), Neil Hamish Cantlie, yr son of late Adm Sir Colin Cantlie, KCB, CB, DSC. *Residence* – 24 Denbigh Rd, W11 2SN.

Hon Jacqueline Patricia, *b* 1942: *m* 1966, Malcolm Usheen Lingen Hutton. *Residence* – Borrowstone House, Kincardine O'Neil, Aberdeenshire AB34 5AP.

HALF-SISTER LIVING

Hon Amanda Caroline, *b* 1955; *ed* St Margaret's Sch, Bushey, and Central Sch of Art and Design, London. *Residence* – 10 Nevern Place, SW5 9PR.

MOTHER LIVING

Alice, only child of late Francis Bowe, of Timaru, NZ: *m* 1st 1938 (*m diss* 1951), as his 1st wife, the 5th Baron Strathspey, who *d* 1992; 2ndly, 1953, Brig Alasdair Gillean Lorne Maclean of Pennycross, who *d* 1973. *Residence* – The School House, Lockbuie, Isle of Mull, Argyll PA62 6AA.

WIDOW LIVING OF FIFTH BARON

OLIVE (*Dowager Baroness Strathspey*), only da of late Wallace Henry Grant, of Norwich: *m* 1951, as his 2nd wife, the 5th Baron Strathspey, who *d* 1992. *Residence* – Elms Ride, W Wittering, Sussex.

COLLATERAL BRANCHES LIVING (*In remainder to Baronetcy only*) (*See* E Seafield, colls.)

PREDECESSORS – (1-5) *Sir* HUMPHREY Colquhoun, 5th Bt, of Luss (*cr* 1625), obtained 1704 a new patent with original precedence giving remainder to his son-in-law, James Grant; *d* 1718; *s* by his son-in-law (6) *Sir* JAMES, 6th Bt; *d* 1747; *s* by his son (7) *Sir* LUDOVICK, 7th Bt; sat as MP for co Moray 1741-61: *m* 2ndly, Lady Margaret Ogilvie, da of Earl of Findlater; *d* 1773; *s* by his son (8) *Sir* JAMES, 8th Bt; sat as MP for Elgin and Forres 1761-8, and was Lord-Lieut of Inverness-shire; *d* Feb 1811; *s* by his son (9) *Sir* LEWIS ALEXANDER Grant of Grant, 9th Bt, who in Oct 1811 *s* as 5th Earl of Seafield; assumed in 1811 the additional surname of Ogilvie; MP for Elginshire 1790-96; *d* unmarried 1840; *s* by his brother (10) FRANCIS WILLIAM, 6th Earl; MP for various Scottish constituencies 1802-40; Lord-Lieut of co Inverness, and a Representative Peer; *d* 1853; *s* by his son (11) JOHN CHARLES, KT, 7th Earl, *b* 1815; a Representative Peer; *cr* Baron Strathspey, of Strathspey, cos Inverness and Moray (peerage of United Kingdom) 1858: *m* 1850, Hon Caroline Henrietta Stuart, who *d* 1911, da of 11th Baron Blantyre; *d* 1881; *s* by his son (12) IAN CHARLES, 8th Earl, *b* 1851; *dsp* 1884, when the Barony of Strathspey became ext; *s* in Scotch peerages of 1698 and 1701 by his uncle (13) JAMES, 9th Earl (3rd son of 6th Earl, by Mary Anne, da of John Charles Dunn, of St Helena and Higham House), *b* 1817; MP for Elgin and Nairnshire (C) 1868-74; *cr* Baron Strathspey (peerage of United Kingdom) 1884: *m* 1st, 1841, Caroline Louisa, who *d* 1850, da of late Eyre Evans, of Ash Hill Towers, Limerick; 2ndly, 1853, Constance Helena, who *d* 1872, da of Sir Robert Abercromby, 5th Bt; 3rdly, 1875, Georgiana Adelaide, da of late Gen Frederick Nathaniel Walker, KCH, of Manor House, Bushey, and widow of William Stuart, of Aldenham Abbey, Herts; *d* 1888; *s* by his el son (14) FRANCIS WILLIAM, 10th Earl, *b* 1847: *m* 1874, Ann (Nina) Trevor Corry, da of Major George Thomas Evans, of Clooneavin, Otago, New Zealand; *d* 1888; *s* by his el son (15) JAMES, 11th Earl, *b* 1876; Capt Queen's Own Cameron Highlanders: *m* 1898, Mary Elizabeth Nina, da of late Joseph Henry Townend, MD, JP, of Christchurch, New Zealand; *ka* 1915, when the Earldom of Seafield devolved upon his only da, and he was *s* in the Barony of Strathspey and the Baronetcy by his brother (16) TREVOR, 4th Baron, *b* 1879: *m* 1st, 1905, Alice Louisa, who *d* 1945, da of late Thomas Masterman Hardy Johnston, MICE, of London, and subsequently Christchurch, New Zealand; 2ndly, 1947 Elfrida Minnie Fass, who *d* 1949, da of late Gordon William Alexander Cloete, JP, of Cape Prov, S Africa, and widow of Lt-Col George Capron, York and Lancaster Regt; *d* 1948; *s* by his son (17) DONALD PATRICK TREVOR, 5th Baron, *b* 1912; Lieut Col Gen List; recognised in the surname of Grant of Grant by decree of Lord Lyon 1950; Assist Chief Land Agent Defence Lands Sers: *m* 1st, 1938 (*m diss* 1951), Alice, only child of late Francis Bowe, of Timaru, NZ; 2ndly, 1951, Olive, only da of late Wallace Henry Grant, of Norwich; *d* 1992; *s* by his eldest son (18) JAMES PATRICK TREVOR, 6th Baron and present peer.

Strathtay and Strathardle, Earl of; grandson of Duke of Atholl.

STRAUSS, BARONY OF (Strauss) (Extinct 1993)

SONS LIVING OF LIFE BARON (By 1st marriage)

Hon Roger Anthony, b 1934.
Hon Brian Timothy, b 1935.

DAUGHTER LIVING OF LIFE BARON (By 1st marriage)

Hon Hilary Jane, b 1937.

WIDOW LIVING OF LIFE BARON

Mrs BENITA ELEONORA ARMSTRONG (Baroness Strauss): m 1987, as his 2nd wife, Baron Strauss, PC (Life Baron), who d
1993.

Strutt, family name of Baron Belper.

Strutt, family name of Baron Rayleigh.

Stuart, Viscount; son of Earl Castle Stewart.

Stuart, family name of Earl Castle Stewart.

Stuart, family name of Earl of Moray.

Stuart, Crichton-, family name of Marquess of Bute.

STUART OF FINDHORN, VISCOUNT (Stuart) (Viscount UK 1959)

DAVID RANDOLPH MORAY STUART, 2nd Viscount; *b* 20 June 1924; *s* 1971; *ed* Eton; late Lt KRRC; Maj 6/7th R Welch Fus (TA); FRICS; Page of Honour to HM 1938-40; DL of Caerns 1963-68: *m* 1st, 1945, Grizel Mary Wilfreda, who *d* 1948, da of late Theodore Fyfe, and widow of Michael Gillilan; 2ndly, 1951 (*m diss* 1979), Marian, da of late Gerald Wilson, of Kintbury, Berks; 3rdly, 1979, Margaret Anne, yr da of Cdr Peter Du Cane (*see* Pole, Bt, *cr* 1628, 1985 Edn), and has issue by 1st and 2nd *m*.

᠎Arms – Quarterly: 1st, or, a lion rampant within a double tressure flory counterflory gules, all within a bordure compony azure and argent, *Stuart*; 2nd, or, a fess chequy azure and argent, *Stewart of Downe*; 3rd, or, three cushions within a double tressure flory counterflory gules, *Randolph*; 4th gules, a lion rampant within a bordure engrailed argent, *Gray*, all within a bordure or for difference. Crest – In a nest vert a pelican feeding her young or, about her neck a collar engrailed gules. Supporters – Two capercailzie proper, their wings closed.
Residence – 38 Findhorn, Findhorn, Moray.

SONS LIVING (*By 1st marriage*)

Hon (JAMES) DOMINIC, *b* 25 March 1948; *ed* Eton: *m* 1979, Yvonne Lucienne, da of Edgar Després, of Ottawa. *Residence* – 15 Stowe Rd, W12.

(By 2nd marriage)

Hon Andrew Moray, *b* 1957.

DAUGHTERS LIVING (*By 2nd marriage*)

Hon Chloe Anne-Marie, *b* 1952.
Hon Rosalie Jane, *b* 1954.
Hon Vanessa Mary, *b* 1960.

SISTER LIVING

Hon Jean Davina (Tannachie, Findhorn, Forres, Moray IV36 0JY), *b* 1932: *m* 1st, 1951, John Reedham Erskine Berney, Lt Roy Norfolk Regt, who was *ka* in Korea 1952, son of Major Sir Thomas Reedham Berney, MC, 10th Bt; 2ndly, 1954, Percy William Jesson; 3rdly, 1985, Michael Denison Ritchie, and has had issue, (by 1st *m*) (*see* Berney, Bt), — (by 2nd *m*) Rayner Charles Percy (13 Basing St, W11), *b* 1954: *m* 1987, Gordana, da of Veljko Simakovic, of Sarajevo, Yugoslavia, — James Gray (6 Bishop's Av, E13), *b* 1959, — Belinda Clare, *b* 1957; *d* 1959, — Arabella Clare Lucy (8 Evening Court, Newmarket Rd, Cambridge CB5 8EA), *b* 1962: *m* 1983 (separated 1996), Barry Ball.

PREDECESSOR – (1) *Rt Hon* JAMES GRAY STUART, CH, MVO, MC, 3rd son of 17th Earl of Moray; *b* 1897; Ch Conservative Whip 1941-48, Sec of State for Scotland 1951-57, Chm of Unionist Party in Scotland 1950-62, and MP for Moray and Nairn 1923-59; *cr Viscount Stuart of Findhorn*, of Findhorn, co Moray (peerage of UK) 1959: *m* 1923, Lady Rachel Cavendish, who *d* 1977, da of 9th Duke of Devonshire; *d* 1971; *s* by his el son (2) DAVID RANDOLPH MORAY, 2nd Viscount and present peer.

SUDELEY, BARON (Hanbury-Tracy) (Baron UK 1838)

MEMORIA · PII · ÆTERNA

The pious are held in everlasting remembrance

Badge of the
Barons Sudeley

MERLIN CHARLES SAINTHILL HANBURY-TRACY, 7th Baron; *b* 17 June 1939; *s* 1941; *ed* Eton, and Worcester Coll, Oxford (BA); Lay Patron Prayer Book Soc; Chm Monday Club, and Vice-Chancellor Monarchist League; Chm Constitutional Monarchy Assoc; FSA; co-author of *The Sudeleys, Lords of Toddington* (1987): *m* 1st, 1980 (*m diss* 1988), Hon Mrs Elizabeth Mairi Villiers, el da of late Derek William Charles Keppel, Viscount Bury (*see* E Albemarle), and formerly wife of Alastair Michael Hyde Villiers (*see* D Roxburghe, 1968 Edn); 2ndly, 1999, Mrs Margarita Kellett, of Kingsclere, Hants.

Arms – Quarterly: 1st and 4th or, an escallop in the chief point sable, between two bendlets gules, *Tracy*; 2nd and 3rd or, a bend engrailed vert plain cotised sable, *Hanbury*. **Crest** – 1st, on a chapeau gules, turned up ermine, an escallop sable, between two wings or; 2nd, out of a mural coronet sable, a demi-lion rampant or, holding in the paws a battle-axe sable, helved gold. **Supporters** – On either side a falcon, wings elevated proper, beaked and belled or. **Badge** – A fire beacon, and in front thereof and chained thereto a panther ducally gorged, the tail nowed.
Residence – 25 Melcombe Court, Dorset Square, NW1 6EP.

WIDOW LIVING OF SIXTH BARON

ELIZABETH MARY (*Lady Collins*), da of Rear-Adm Sir Arthur Bromley, KCMG, KCVO, 8th Bt: *m* 1st, 1940, the 6th Baron, who *d* on active service 1941; 2ndly, 1965, Maj Sir Arthur James Robert Collins, KCVO, of Kirkman Bank, Knaresborough, N Yorks.

COLLATERAL BRANCHES LIVING

Granddaughter of late Hon Felix Charles Hubert Hanbury Tracy, 3rd son of 4th Baron:—
Issue of late Ninian John Frederick Hanbury Tracy, *b* 1910, *d* 1971: *m* 1st, 1935 (*m diss* 1954), Hon Blanche Mary Arundell, who *d* 1993, da of 15th Baron Arundell of Wardour; 2ndly, 1954, Daphne Mary Christian, who *d* 1983, da of late Lt-Col Vivian Henry, CB (Milbank, Bt), and widow of Maj Charles Scott:—
(By 1st *m*) Jennifer Avril, *b* 1941: *m* 1964, Martin Robert Morland, CMG, HM Ambassador to Burma 1986-90, of 50 Britannia Rd, SW6, el son of Sir Oscar Charles Morland, GBE, KCMG, and has issue living, William, *b* 1965, — Anthony, *b* 1967, — Catherine Mary, *b* 1966.

Grandchildren of late Maj Eric Thomas Henry Hanbury-Tracy, OBE, only surv son of late Lt-Col Hon Frederick Stephen Archibald Hanbury Tracy, MP, 5th son of 2nd Baron:—
Issue of late Maj Claud Edward Frederick HANBURY-TRACY-DOMVILE, TD, *b* 1904, *d* 1987; assumed by deed poll 1961 the additional surname of Domvile: *m* 1st, 1927 (*m diss* 1948), Veronica May, who *d* 1985, da of late Cyril Grant Cunard (Cunard, Bt, colls); 2ndly, 1954, Marcella Elizabeth, who *d* 1983, da of late Canon John Willis Price, Rector of Croughton, Brackley, Northants:—
(By 1st *m*) (DESMOND) ANDREW JOHN HANBURY-TRACY, *b* 30 Nov 1928; *ed* Sherborne, and RAC Cirencester: *m* 1st, 1957 (*m diss* 1966), Jennifer Lynn, only da of Dr Richard Christie Hodges, of Elizabethan House, Warwick; 2ndly, 1967, Lillian, da of late Nathaniel Laurie; 3rdly, 1988, Mrs Margaret Cecilia White, da of late Alfred Henry Marmaduke Purse, MBE, and has issue living (by 1st *m*), Nicholas Edward John, *b* 1959, — (by 2nd *m*) Timothy Christopher Claud, *b* 1968: *m* 1996, Anneliese Mary, only da of Lt-Col John Reginald Arthur, OBE, of Sunningdale, Berks. —— Charles William Justin HANBURY-TRACY (13 Ann St, Ipswich, Suffolk), *b* 1938; *ed* Sherborne, and London Univ (BA, PhD): *m* 1st, 1969 (*m diss* 1983), Sarah Jane, da of late Lt-Col George Ashley, The Cameronians (Scottish Rifles), of Rosamundford Lodge, Aylesbeare, Devon; 2ndly, 1984, Megan Joy, 2nd da of Rev Geoffrey Windsor Harrison, of Newcastle, S Africa, and has issue living (by 1st *m*), Justin, *b* 1971, — Edward Claud, *b* 1976, — Emily, *b* 1970. —— Mary Claudia Elizabeth, *b* 1931: *m* 1953, Robert Singlehurst Cross, of West End House, 1 Step Terrace, Winchester SO22 5BW, only son of late Lt-Col Charles Norman Cross, MC and bar, of Park House, Market Drayton, Shropshire, and has issue living, Edward Robert (PO Box 86762, Mombasa, Kenya), *b* 1956: *m* 1989, Suhaila ......, and has issue living, Jasmine Mary *b* 1991, — Lucy Cunard, *b* 1954: *m* 1st, 1980 (*m diss* 1985), Richard Walter Emanuel, son of late Walter Braithwaite Emanuel, of 300 Fulham Palace Rd, SW6; 2ndly, 1989, Michael Worthington, of 72 Stockton Lane, York YO31 1BN, son of late Kenneth Spencer Worthington, of 91 West Way, Stafford, and has issue living (by 2nd *m*), Simon Robert Kenneth *b* 1990, — Sylvia Mary, *b* 1961; *m* 1991, Crispin Weston, of Granary Cottage, W Milton, nr Bridport, Dorset DT6 3TN, — Anna Elizabeth, *b* 1964.

PREDECESSORS – (1) CHARLES Hanbury, 3rd son of late John Hanbury, of Pontypool Park, Mon (deriving from the same source as the Barons Bateman); *b* 1777; MP for Tewkesbury; Chm of Commn to Judge Designs for new Houses of Parliament 1835; *cr Baron Sudeley* of Toddington, co Gloucester (peerage of UK) 1838: *m* 1798, Hon Henrietta Susanna, who *d* 1839, only child and heir of Henry, 8th and last Viscount Tracy, who in the same year took by sign manual the surname and arms of Tracy in lieu of his patronymic, and assumed the surname of Hanbury-Tracy; *d* 1858; *s* by his son (2) THOMAS CHARLES, 2nd Baron; *b* 1801; assumed by Roy licence the surname of Leigh in 1806, which name in 1839 he discontinued by Roy licence, and again assumed the surname of Hanbury: *m* 1831, Emma Eliza Alicia, who *d* 1888, da of late George Hay Dawkins-Pennant, of Penrhyn Castle, co Caernarvon; *d* 1863; *s* by his el son (3) SUDELEY CHARLES GEORGE, 3rd Baron; *d* 1877; *s* by his brother (4) CHARLES DOUGLAS RICHARD, PC, FRS, 4th Baron; *b* 1840; MP for Montgomery Dist (*L*) 1863-77; a Lord-in-Waiting to Queen Victoria 1880-85, and Capt Hon Corps of Gentlemen-at-Arms 1886: *m* 1868, Ada Maria Katherine, who *d* 1928, da of late Hon Frederick James Tollemache (Cs Dysart); *d* 1922; *s* by his el son (5) WILLIAM CHARLES FREDERICK, 5th Baron, *b* 1870: *m* 1905 (*m diss* 1922), Edith Celandine who *d* 1975, da of late Lieut Lord Francis Horace Pierrepont Cecil, RN (M Exeter); *d* 1932; *s* by his nephew **(6)** RICHARD ALGERNON FREDERICK (son of late Major Hon Algernon Henry Charles Hanbury-Tracy, CMG, 2nd son of 4th Baron), 6th Baron; *b* 1911; Major Roy Horse Guards: *m* 1940, Elizabeth Mary, da of Rear-Adm Sir Arthur Bromley, KCMG, CVO: *d* on active service 1941; *s* by his kinsman **(7)** MERLYN CHARLES SAINTHILL (son of late Capt (Michael) David Charles Hanbury Tracy, who *d* on active service 1940, grandson of 4th Baron), 7th Baron and present peer.

Sudley, Baron; title of Earl of Arran on Roll of HL.

Sudley, Viscount; son of Earl of Arran.

SUFFIELD, BARON (Harbord-Hamond) (Baron GB 1786, Bt GB 1745)

Even mindedly

ANTHONY PHILIP HARBORD-HAMOND, MC, 11th Baron, and 12th Baronet; *b* 19 June 1922; *s* 1951; *ed* Eton; Maj Coldm Gds (ret); Member HM Body Guard of Hon Corps of Gentlemen-at-Arms 1973-92; 1942-45 War in N Africa and Italy; Malaya 1948-50 (MC): *m* 1952, (Elizabeth) Eve, who *d* 1995, el da of late Judge (Samuel Richard) Edgedale, QC, of Field Lodge, Crowthorne, Berks, and has issue.

Arms – Quarterly: 1st and 4th quarterly, azure and gules, four lions rampant argent, and in the entre an imperial crown or, *Harbord*; 2nd and 3rd argent, a fleur-de-lis gules, *Morden.* **Crest** – On a chapeau gules turned up ermine, a lion couchant argent. **Supporters** – *Dexter*, a lion or, charged on the shoulder with a fleur-de-lis gules, and gorged with a crown flory, chain reflexed over the back, azure; *sinister*, a leopard guardant proper, gorged with a similar coronet and chain or.
Residence – Gardener's Cottage, Gunton Park, Hanworth, Norfolk NR11 7HL. **Clubs** – Army and Navy, Pratt's.

SONS LIVING

Hon CHARLES ANTHONY ASSHETON, *b* 3 Dec 1953; *ed* Eton; formerly Capt Coldm Gds; temp Equerry to HM 1977: *m* 1st, 1983 (*m diss* 1990), Lucy Lennox Scrope, yr da of Com A. S. Hutchinson, of Langford Grange, Lechlade, Glos; 2ndly, 1999, Mrs Emma Louise Royds, elder da of Sir Lawrence Hugh Williams, 9th Bt (*cr* 1798). *Residence* – Park House, Gunton Park, Hanworth, Norfolk NR11 7HL. *Clubs* – Pratt's, City of London.

Hon John Edward Richard, *b* 1956: *m* 1983, Katharine Margaret Lucy, only child of Maj George Raymond Seymour, CVO, of The Old Vicarage, Bucklebury, Reading, Berks (*see* M Hertford, colls), and has issue living, Sam Charles Antony, *b* 1989, — George Edward Seymour, *b* 1991, — William, *b* 1996, — Alice Mary, *b* 1986. *Residence* – 28 Swanage Rd, SW18 2DY.

Hon Robert Philip Morden, *b* 1964; *ed* Harrow: *m* 1st, 1994 (*m diss* 1996), Sarah, only da of Derek Stevens; 2ndly, 1998, Anita, da of Roberto Ferruzzi, and of Mrs Anne Dunhill. *Residence* – Harbord House, Cromer, Norfolk.

DAUGHTER LIVING

Hon Caroline Mary Elaine, *b* 1960: *m* 1985, Audley William Twiston Davies, and has issue (*see* Archdale, Bt, colls). *Residences* – Mynde Park, Much Dewchurch, Ross-on-Wye, Hereford.

SISTER LIVING

Hon Charity Patricia, *b* 1917.

COLLATERAL BRANCHES LIVING

Issue of late Maurice Assheton Harbord, yst brother of 10th Baron, b 1874, d 1954: m 1st, 1905 (m diss 1918), Isabel Jessie Lowth, 4th da of Baron Frederick von Wurzburg Schade, and widow of Richard Hedley Robinson, of Kirkby Mallory Hall, Leicestershire; 2ndly, 1929, Ethel Florence, who d 1992, da of George William Goldsmith, of Hastings, and widow of Francis Tungwell Cowley:—
(By 2nd m) Patrick Rupert Shirley, b 1930: m 1955, Jean Shirley, da of Reginald George Webb, of Pebsham Farm Cottage, Bexhill-on-Sea, and has issue living, Alan Anthony (Brookwood, 44 Wadhurst Close, St Leonards-on-Sea, E Sussex), b 1956: m 1977, Nicola, only da of R. Greenhalf, of 75 Mount Rd, Hastings, and has issue living, Matthew Aaron b 1984, Stacey Jane b 1977, — Shirley Ann, b 1958: m 1984, Roy Anthony Jennings, of Owls Roost, 9 Aviemore Dr, Oakley, Basingstoke, Hants, only son of Lawrence Hamilton Jennings, of Gt Yarmouth, Norfolk. Residence – 16 Clarence Rd, Bohemia, St Leonards-on-Sea, E Sussex. — Ralph Assheton Edward, b 1932: m 1959, Angela, only da of S. D'Eath, of 5 Conqueror Rd, St Leonards, Sussex, and has issue living, Richard, b 1964. Residence – Scotsford Cottage, 12 New Town, Uckfield, E Sussex.

Grandchildren of late Capt Edward Ralph Harbord, DSO, MC (infra):—
Issue of late William Edward Harbord, b 1908, d 1992: m 1st, 1938 (m diss 1949), Vivien Sylvia, da of late Lt-Col Foster Newton Thorne, Royal Sussex Regt; 2ndly, 1950 (m diss 1959), Christine Winifred, da of late Alan Higham, of Richmond Surrey:—
(By 1st m) Charles Francis (Torres do Colegio, Monte Judeu, 8600 Lagos, Portugal), b 1943; ed Harrow: m 1st, 1973, Honor Lois, da of Tom Saul, of Seacroft, Lincs; 2ndly, 1980, Sarah Juliet, da of late Peter Blandy, of Jubilee Place, SW3, and has issue living (by 2nd m), Astrid Anne Sylvia, b 1981, — Davina Auriol Bridget, b 1986. — †David Ralph Foster, b 1947; ed Worksop Coll; Capt 15/19th Royal Hussars: m 1971, Lauretta Chinty (who m 2ndly, 1978, Nicholas Charles Wetherill Ridley), only da of Sir Hervey John William Bruce, 6th Bt (cr 1804), and d 1974. — (By 2nd m) Christopher Evelyn, b 1953; ed Albury, NSW. — Gay Diana, b 1951.

Issue of late Ralph Evelyn Harbord, b 1915, d (9 May) 1993: m 1950, Madeleine Betty Kezia, who d (23 Oct) 1993, da of late Robert Finlay-Greig:—
Robert Ralph, b 1950; ed Eton; late Lieut Royal Green Jackets: m 1984, Clare Mary Petre, da of late Capt Thomas Hornsby (see By Furnivall), and has issue living, Harry Robert Thomas, b 1991, — Charles Edward Ralph, b 1994, — Georgiana Rosamund Elizabeth b 1998. — Jeremy Julian (Clubs - St Mortiz Tobogganing); b 1953; ed Eton; late Capt The Life Guards: m 1984, Monique Katherine Marie, elder da of Maj Theobald Henry Robert Fetherstonhaugh, and has issue living, James Henry Sebastian Charles b 1988, — Sophie India Charlotte, b 1986.

Granddaughters of late Hon Ralph Harbord, 6th son of 3rd Baron:—
Issue of late Capt Edward Ralph Harbord, DSO, MC, b 1870, d 1950: m 1906, Annie Evelyn, who d 1980, da of Henry Herbert Riley-Smith, of Toulston, Tadcaster Yorks:—
Bridget, b 1907: m 1931, Noel Fraser Nickols, who d 1966. Residence – 2 Beech Court, Harrogate, N Yorks HG2 0EU. — Elizabeth Mary, b 1912; 1939-45 War as Ch Officer WRNS; a CStJ: m 1946, Capt John Michael Hodges, DSO, RN (ret), who d 1987, son of late Adm Sir Michael Henry Hodges, KCB, CMG, MVO, of The White House, Thatcham, Berks, and has issue living, Patrick Michael (Bentworth Place, Bentworth, Alton, Hants GU34 5JP), b 1948; ed Eton: m 1974, Alison Mary, da of Wing-Cdr Roy Dossetter, RAF, of Andover, Hants, and has issue living, Rupert Henry b 1982; ed Eton, Katherine Mary b 1978; ed St Swithun's, and Imperial Coll London, — Judith Evelyn, b 1952; ed Roedean: m 1982, Maj William F. A. Heal, late Royal Anglian Regt, of Burgh Parva Hall, Melton Constable, Norfolk NR24 2PU, son of Lt-Col W. A. Heal, OBE, of Denston, Suffolk, and has issue living, Jeremy William Austin b 1984, Olivia Claire Evelyn b 1983. Residence – 31 Marlborough Court, Pembroke Rd, W8 6DE. — (Dorothy) Primrose, b 1919: m 1939, Maj Edward d'Abo, KOYLI (Reserve), yr son of Gerard Louis d'Abo, of Coval Court, Sunningdale, by his wife Muriel Molesworth, da of Sir Robert Molesworth Kindersley, GBE, and sister of 1st Baron Kindersley, and has issue living, Philip Edward (The Old Squash Court, Leigh Court Close, Cobham, Surrey KT11 2HT), b 1941; ed Harrow: m 1972, Fay Mary St Claire, da of late William Barbour, and has issue living, Camilla Sophie Louise b 1973, Lucy Dorothy b 1977, — Michael David (Hillcrest House, St George's Av, Kings Stanley, Glos GL10 3HJ), b 1944; ed Harrow: m 1st, 1966 (m diss 1982), Margaret Evelyn, da of George Lyndon, of Chelmsford; 2ndly, 1982 (m diss 1993), Karen Sue, da of William Gilbert, of Michigan, USA; 3rdly, 1996, Lisa Nikola Jane, da of Arthur Weaver, of Twyning, Glos, and has issue living, (by 1st m) Benjamin Byron b 1967, Olivia Jane b 1969, (by 2nd m) Bruno George b 1984, — (Andrew Gerard) Noel (187 Amesbury Av, SW2 3BJ), b 1948; ed Harrow: m 1980, Caroline Lydia Susan, yr da of Edward Burnham, of Chelwood Beacon Cottage, Haywards Heath, W Sussex, and has issue living, Polly Primrose b 1983, Phoebe Rose b 1989, — (Penelope) Carol (Lady Baker), b (twin) 1948: m 1970, Sir Nicholas Brian Baker, who d 1997 and has issue living, Matthew Ronald Nicholas b 1976, Annabel Dorothy Clementine b 1980. Residence – 18 White Rock House, White Rock Rd, Hastings, E Sussex TN34 1LE. — Molly, b 1921: m 1st, 1941 (m diss 1946), Roy Laird-Macgregor, Lt RA; 2ndly, 1953, John Cecil Atkinson Clark, who d 1969 (Meyrick, Bt), and has issue living (by 2nd m), George Evelyn (Manor House Farm, Beckerings Park, Lidlington, Beds MK43 0RA), b 1960; ed Eton; late Maj Scottish Yeo (TA); Member Queen's Body Guard for Scotland (Royal Company of Archers): m 1986, Hon Sarah Anne Elliott, twin da of Baron Elliott of Morpeth (Life Baron), and has issue living, Edward George b 1988, Henry William b 1993, Sophie Catherine b 1990. Residence – 1c Edificio El Chambel, Calle Miguel Caño 15, Marbella 29600, Spain.

PREDECESSORS – (1) Sir WILLIAM Morden, KB, was cr a Baronet 1745; assumed by Roy licence the surname of Harbord in lieu of his patronymic; d 1770; s by his son (2) Sir HARBORD Harbord, 2nd Bt; was MP for Norwich; cr Baron Suffield, co Norfolk (peerage of Great Britain) 1786; d 1810; s by his el son (3) WILLIAM ASSHETON, 2nd Baron; d 1821; s by his brother (4) EDWARD, 3rd Baron; b 1781: m 1st, 1809, Hon Georgiana, da and heiress of George, 2nd Baron Vernon; 2ndly, 1826, Emily Harriet, da of Evelyn Shirley, of Ettington Park, Warwickshire; d 1835; s by his son (5) EDWARD VERNON, 4th Baron; dsp 1853; s by his half-brother (6) CHARLES, GCVO, KCB, PC, 5th Baron; b 1830; Lord-in-Waiting to Queen Victoria 1868-72, Lord of Bedchamber to Prince of Wales 1872-1901, and Permanent Lord-in-Waiting to King Edward VII 1901-10: m 1st, 1854, Cecilia Annetta, who d 1911, da of late Henry Baring; 2ndly, 1911, Frances Amelia Jessie, who d 1934, only da of late Major Robert Poole Gabbatt, RA, and widow of Col Charles C. Rich, RHA; d 1914; s by his el son (7) CHARLES, CB, MVO, 6th Baron; b 1855; a Groom-in-Waiting to HM Queen Victoria 1895-1901: m 1896, Evelyn Louisa, JP, who d 1951, da of late Capt Eustace John Wilson-Patten (see B Winnarleigh); d 1924; s by his el son (8) VICTOR ALEXANDER CHARLES, 7th Baron; b 1897: m 1925 (m diss 1937), Hon Olwen Gwynne Philipps, who d 1998, da of 1st Baron Kylsant (ext); d 1943; s by his brother (9) JOHN, 8th Baron; b 1907; d 1945; s by his kinsman (10) GEOFFREY WALTER (3rd son of late Hon William Harbord, 4th son of 3rd Baron), 9th Baron; b 1861: m 1902, Eliza Jane, who d 1933, da of John Mills, and widow of A. R. Beaumont, 16th Lancers; d 1946, s by his cousin (11) RICHARD MORDEN (son of late Rev Hon John Harbord, 5th son of 3rd Baron), 10th Baron; b 1865; Adm; Egyptian War 1882, European War 1914-19; assumed by Roy Licence 1917 the additional surname of Hamond: m 1913, Nina Annette Mary

Crawfuird, who *d* 1955, el da of John William Hutchison of Laurieston Hall, and Edingham, Kirkcudbright; *d* 1951; *s* by his only son **(12)** ANTHONY PHILIP, 11th Baron and present peer.

SUFFOLK AND BERKSHIRE, EARL OF (Howard) (Earl Suffolk E 1603 and Berkshire E 1626)

NOUS MAINTIENDRONS

We will maintain

MICHAEL JOHN JAMES GEORGE ROBERT HOWARD, 21st Earl of Suffolk and 14th Earl of Berkshire; *b* 27 March 1935; *s* 1941; *ed* Winchester; Nat Service Lieut RNVR: *m* 1st, 1960 (*m diss* 1967), Mme Simone Paulmier, da of Georges Litman, of Paris; 2ndly, 1973 (*m diss* 1980), Anita Robsahm, yr da of late Robin Robsahm Fuglesang, of Cuckfield, Sussex; 3rdly, 1983, Linda Jacqueline, da of Lt-Col Vincent Rudolph Paravicini, of Nutley Manor, Basingstoke, and formerly wife of 4th Viscount Bridport, and has issue living by 2nd and 3rd *m*.

Arms – Quarterly: 1st gules, a bend between six cross-crosslets fitchée argent, on the bend an escutcheon or, charged with a demi-lion rampant, pierced through the mouth with an arrow, and within a doubletressure flory-counter-flory gules, *Howard*; 2nd gules, three lions passant guardant in pale or, and a label of three points argent, *Thomas of Brotherton*; 3rd, checky or and azure, *Warren*; 4th gules, a lion rampant argent, *Mowbray*; in the centre of the four quarterings a crescent for difference. **Crest** – On a chapeau gules, turned up ermine, a lion statant guardant tail extended or, gorged with a ducal coronet argent, and charged on the body with a crescent for difference. **Supporters** – Two lions argent, each charged on the shoulder with a crescent sable.
Seat – Charlton Park, Malmesbury, Wilts, SN16 9DG.

SON LIVING (*By 2nd marriage*)

ALEXANDER CHARLES MICHAEL WINSTON ROBSAHM (*Viscount Andover*), *b* 17 Sept 1974.

DAUGHTERS LIVING (*By 2nd marriage*)

Lady Katharine Emma Frances Anita Robsahm, *b* 1976.

(*By 3rd marriage*)

Lady Philippa Mimi Jacqueline Henrietta, *b* 1985.
Lady Natasha Rose Catherine Linda, *b* 1987.

BROTHERS LIVING

Hon Maurice David Henry, *b* 1936; *ed* Eton; served with RN (Suez) 1955-57: *m* 1978, C. M. Vicky, el da of G. B. Summers, of Newcastle upon Tyne, and has issue living, Annabel Frances Victoria, *b* 1979.
Hon Patrick Greville (Far Upton Wold, Moreton-in-Marsh, Glos GL56 9TG), *b* 1940; *ed* Eton, Grenoble (France) and Heidelberg Univs, and Peterhouse, Camb (BA); Lt R Wiltshire Yeo: *m* 1966, Mary Elizabeth, da of Dr Clarence Laverne Johnson, of 140 Park Lane, W1 (*see* Royden Bt, 1980 Edn), and has issue living, Jason Patrick, *b* 1968: *m* 1991, Amanda Jane, da of Sir (James) Gerard Waterlow, 4th Bt (*cr* 1930), and has issue living, Ava Suzanne *b* 1997, — Rory Alexander, *b* 1970, — Timothy Charles, *b* 1973, — Charles Edward, *b* 1974.

WIDOW LIVING OF SON OF NINETEENTH EARL

Frances Drake, da of late Edwin Morgan Dean, of Newcastle, Northumberland, and Toronto, Canada: *m* 1939, Hon Cecil John Arthur Howard, who *d* 1985. *Residence* – 1511 Summit Ridge Drive, Beverly Hills, Calif, USA.

COLLATERAL BRANCHES LIVING

Issue of late Lt-Cdr Hon Greville Reginald Howard, yst son of 19th Earl, *b* 1909, *d* 1987: *m* 1945, Mary, who *d* 1994, da of late William Smith Ridehalgh, of Broughton Lodge, Cartmel, N Lancs:—
Caroline Margaret, *b* 1947: *m* 1st, 1965, Nigel William Stacey; 2ndly, 1970, Robert Mark Goodden, and has a da, Sarah Philippa, *b* 1968, and a son, Luke Greville Thorburn, *b* 1982.

Issue of late Hon James Knyvett Estcourt Howard, 2nd son of 18th Earl, *b* 1886, *d* 1964: *m* 1925, Nancy Induna Frances Caroline, who *d* 1972, el da of late Edgar Lubbock, LLB (B Avebury, colls):— Virginia Mary Eloise (Fayleys Lodge, Aldworth, Reading, Berks RG8 9RL), *b* 1926: *m* 1948, Capt David John Richard Ker, MC, DL, late Coldm Gds, who *d* 1997, and has issue living, David Peter James (58 Jermyn St, SW1Y 6LX; *Clubs* – White's, Turf, Beefsteak, Pratt's, The Brook (NY)); *b* 1951; Founder and Proprietor David Ker Fine Art 1980: *m* 1974, Alexandra Mary, da of Vice-Adm Sir Dymock Watson, KCB, CBE, DL, of Trebinshwyn, Brecon, and has had issue, David Edward Richard *b* 1979; *d* 1980, David Humphry Rivers *b* 1982, Clare Rose *b* 1977, — Caroline Moira, *b* 1949: *m* 1st, 1968 (*m diss* 1972), Thomas William Fellowes (*see* V Hampden, colls); 2ndly, 1988, Yonatan (Yoni) H. Cohen, — Camilla Rosanna Gian, *b* 1959.

Grandchildren of late Brig Sir Charles Alfred Howard, GCVO, DSO, yr son of Hon Greville Theophilus Howard, 2nd son of 17th Earl:—
Issue of late Lt-Col Henry Redvers Greville Howard, KRRC, *b* 1911, *d* 1978: *m* 1st 1940 (*m diss* 1946), Patience, da of Lt-Col Charles Rice Iltyd Nicholl, TD, of 52 Queen's Gate, SW7; 2ndly 1948, Odette (The Pink Cottage, Low Rd, Castle Rising, King's Lynn, Norfolk), da of Henry Clark, of Ventnor, Isle of Wight, and widow of Fl-Lt Gordon Crosby, RAF:—
(By 1st *m*) Greville Patrick Charles (Castle Rising, King's Lynn, Norfolk), *b* 1941: *m* 1st, 1968 (*m diss* 1972), Zoë, yr da of Douglas Walker, of 65 Pont St, SW1, and Paris; 2ndly, 1978, Mary Rose, who *d* 1980, yst da of Sir (Edward) John Chichester, 11th Bt; 3rdly, 1981, Mary Cortland, da of Robert Culverwell, of Bridges Court, Luckington, Wilts, and has issue living (by 3rd *m*), Thomas Henry Greville, *b* 1983; a Page of Honour to HM 1995-98, — Charles Edward John, *b* 1986, — Annabel Rosemary Diana, *b* 1984. ——— Amanda Susan Diana (Hyde Park, Stanhoe, King's Lynn, Norfolk PE31 8PX), *b* 1943: *m* 1968, Alexander Simon James Montague Burton, who *d* 1972, and has issue living, Michael Alexander Greville James, *b* 1971, — Sophie Amelia Sarah, *b* 1970. ——— (By 2nd *m*) Katharine Venetia HOWARD (Calle Sol 21, Jimena de la Frontera, C.P. 11330, Prov de Cadiz, Spain), *b* 1948: has issue living (by Miguel Mateo Salcedo), Henry Greville Michael FITZ-HOWARD, *b* 1978, — (by Alvaro Alvarez Diaz), Samara ALVAREZ HOWARD, *b* 1982, — Marta ALVAREZ HOWARD, *b* 1984, — Lucia ALVAREZ HOWARD, *b* 1985.

PREDECESSORS – (1) *Lord* THOMAS Howard, KG, PC, 2nd son of Thomas, 4th Duke of Norfolk, was summoned to Parliament in right of his mother as *Baron Howard de Walden* (peerage of England) 1597, and in 1603 was *cr Earl of Suffolk* (peerage of England); was a Commr for executing the office of Earl Marshal of England, in which capacity he was mainly instrumental in discovering the Gunpowder Plot; elected Chancellor of Cambridge University 1613; was Lord High Treasurer of England 1613-18; *d* 1626; *s* by his son (2) THEOPHILUS, KG, PC, 2nd Earl; summoned to Parliament in his father's Barony of Howard de Walden; was Lord Warden of the Cinque Ports, Constable of Dover Castle, and Capt of the Band of Gentlemen Pensioners; *d* 1640; *s* by his el son (3) JAMES, KB, 3rd Earl; *d* 1689 without male issue, when the Barony of Howard de Walden went into abeyance between his daughters, and the Earldom devolved upon his brother (4) GEORGE, 4th Earl, who *dsp* 1691; *s* by his next brother (5) HENRY, 5th Earl; *d* 1709; *s* by his son (6) HENRY, 6th Earl, who in 1706 had been *cr Baron Chesterford*, Co Essex and *Earl of Bindon*, Co Dorset (peerage of GB); was sometime Dep Earl Marshal, in which capacity in 1707 he held a Court of Chivalry; *d* 1718; *s* by his son (7) CHARLES WILLIAM, 7th Earl; *dsp* 1722, when the Barony of Chesterford and the Earldom of Bindon expired, and the Earldom of Suffolk devolved upon his uncle (8) EDWARD, 8th Earl; *d* unmarried 1731; *s* by his brother (9) CHARLES, 9th Earl; *d* 1733; *s* by his son (10) HENRY, 10th Earl; *dsp* 1745; *s* by his kinsman (11) HENRY BOWES, PC, 11th Earl, who had previously *s* as 4th *Earl of Berkshire* (see * infra); appointed Dep Earl Marshal of England 1708; *d* 1757; *s* by his grandson (12) HENRY, 12th Earl; *d* 1779; *s* by his son (13) HENRY, 13th Earl; *d* 1779; *s* by his great-uncle (14) THOMAS, 14th Earl, 3rd son of 11th Earl; *dsp* 1783; *s* by his kinsman (15) JOHN, 15th Earl, great-grandson of Hon Philip, 7th son of 1st Earl of Berkshire; was a Gen in the Army; *d* 1820; *s* by his son (16) THOMAS, 16th Earl; *d* 1851; *s* by his son (17) CHARLES JOHN, 17th Earl; *b* 1804; sat as MP for Malmesbury (*L*) 1832-41: *m* 1829, Isabella, who *d* 1891, da of Lord Henry Howard and niece of 12th Duke of Norfolk; *d* 1876; *s* by his son (18) HENRY CHARLES, 18th Earl of Suffolk and 11th Earl of Berkshire, *b* 1833; MP for Malmesbury (*L*) 1859-68: *m* 1868, Mary Eleanor Lauderdale, who *d* 1928, da of late Hon Henry Amelius Coventry; *d* 1898; *s* by his el son (19) HENRY MOLYNEUX PAGET, 19th Earl of Suffolk and 12th Earl of Berkshire, *b* 1877; Maj RFA: *m* 1904, Marguerite Hyde, who *d* 1968, da of late Levi Zeigler Leiter, of Dupont Circle, Washington, USA: *ka* 1917; *s* by his el son (20) CHARLES HENRY GEORGE, GC, 20th Earl of Suffolk, and 13th Earl of Berkshire; *b* 1906: *m* 1934, Mimi, who *d* 1966, da of late Alfred George Forde-Pigott; *d* on active service 1941; *s* by his el son (21) MICHAEL JOHN JAMES GEORGE ROBERT, 21st Earl of Suffolk, and 14th Earl of Berkshire and present peer; also Viscount Andover, and Baron Howard of Charlton.

*(1) *Hon* THOMAS Howard, KG, 2nd son of the 1st Earl of Suffolk was *cr Baron Howard of Charlton*, co Wilts, and *Viscount Andover* (peerage of England) 1622, and *Earl of Berkshire* (peerage of England) 1626; *d* 1660; *s* by his son (2) CHARLES, 2nd Earl; was summoned to Parliament in his father's Barony of Howard; *d* 1679; *s* by his brother (3) THOMAS, 3rd Earl; *d* 1706; *s* by his great-nephew (4) HENRY BOWES, 4th Earl (grandson of Hon William, 4th son of 1st Earl), who *s* as 11th Earl of Suffolk (ante).

Suirdale, Viscount; son of Earl of Donoughmore.

SUMMERSKILL, BARONY OF (Summerskill) (Extinct 1980)

DAUGHTER LIVING OF LIFE BARONESS

Hon Shirley Catherine Wynne SUMMERSKILL, *b* 1931; *ed* St Paul's Girls' Sch, and Somerville Coll, Oxford (BM, BCh and MA); MP for Halifax (*Lab*) 1964-83; an Under-Sec of State Home Office 1974-79: *m* 1957 (*m diss* 1971), John Ryman, Bar-at-law.

WIDOW LIVING OF SON OF LIFE BARONESS

Maryly Blew La Follette, da of Earle Blew: *m* 1983, as his 3rd wife, Hon Michael Brynmôr Summerskill, who *d* 1994.

Sunderland, Earl of; grandson of Duke of Marlborough

SUTHERLAND, COUNTESS OF (Sutherland) (Earl S about 1235)

ELIZABETH MILLICENT SUTHERLAND (*Countess of Sutherland*), 24th holder of the peerage, Chief of Clan Sutherland, *b* 30 Mar 1921; *s* 1963; adopted the surname of Sutherland under Scots Law 1963: *m* 1946, Charles Noel Janson, late Welsh Guards, and has issue.

Arms – Gules, three mullets or (as the ancient arms of Sutherland of that Ilk), on a bordure of the second a double tressure flory-counterflory of the first (as an Honourable Augmentation). **Crest** – A Cat-a-mountain sejant rampant proper. **Supporters** – *Dexter*, a savage man wreathed about the head and loins with laurel proper, holding in his exterior hand a club Gules resting upon his shoulder, *sinister*, another like savage sustaining in his sinister hand and against his shoulder, upon a staff ensigned by the coronet of an Earl, a bannerette gules, charged of three mullets or.
Seat – Dunrobin Castle, Golspie, Sutherland. *Residences* – 39 Edwardes Sq, W8; House of Tongue, by Lairg, Sutherland.

SONS LIVING

ALISTAIR CHARLES ST CLAIR SUTHERLAND (*Lord Strathnaver*) (Sutherland Estates Office, Golspie, Sutherland), *b* 7 Jan 1947; *ed* Eton, and Ch Ch, Oxford; Master of Sutherland; Vice Lord Lieut of Sutherland since 1993; Metropolitan Police 1969-74; IBM UK Ltd 1975-78: *m* 1st, 1968 (*m diss* 19—), Eileen Elizabeth, only da of Richard Wheeler Baker, of Princeton, USA; 2ndly, 1980, Gillian Margaret St Clair, el da of late Robert Murray, of 23 Cloch Rd, Gourock, Renfrewshire, and has issue by 1st and 2nd *m*:—

SON LIVING (*By 2nd m*) *Hon* Alexander Charles Robert, *b* 1 Oct 1981.

DAUGHTERS LIVING (*By 1st m*) *Hon* Rachel Elizabeth, *b* 1970, — *Hon* Rosemary Millicent, *b* 1972, — (*by 2nd m*) *Hon* Elizabeth Murray St Clair, *b* 1984.

Hon Martin Dearman SUTHERLAND JANSON (twin), *b* 1947; *ed* Eton: *m* 1974, Hon Mary Ann Balfour, da of 1st Baron Balfour of Inchrye, and has issue living, James Charles Harold, *b* 1975, — Nicholas George, *b* 1977, — Benjamin Edward, *b* 1979, — Alexander Martin, *b* 1981, — Christopher David, *b* 1984. *Residence* – Uppat House, Brora, Sutherland KW9 6NL.

DAUGHTER LIVING

Lady Annabel Elizabeth Hélène SUTHERLAND, *b* 1952: *m* 1982, John Vernon Bainton, of Charlton, Bungunya, Queensland, Australia, only son of late John Richard Bainton, of Point Piper, Sydney, and has issue, Edward John, *b* 1983, — Nicholas John, *b* 1988, — Laurens John, *b* 1996, — Alice Elizabeth, *b* 1985. *Residence* – 9 North Moor Rd, Oxford.

COLLATERAL BRANCHES LIVING

See E Dudley.

Descendants of late Lady Rosemary Millicent Sutherland-Leveson-Gower, RRC, yr da of 4th Duke, *b* 1893, *d* 1930: *m* 1919, Viscount Ednam, afterwards 3rd Earl of Dudley, who *d* 1969:—

See E Cromartie.

Descendants of late Lord Francis Leveson-Gower, 2nd son of 3rd Duke, who *s* his mother as 2nd Earl of Cromartie:—

See V Chaplin (ext).

Descendants of late Lady Florence Leveson-Gower, elder da of 3rd Duke, *b* 1855, *d* 1881: *m* 1876, Rt Hon Henry Chaplin, afterwards 1st Viscount Chaplin, who *d* 1923:—

See M Londonderry.

Grandchildren of late Hon Edith Helen Chaplin, DBE, elder da of late Lady Florence Chaplin (ante), *b* 1879, *d* 1959: *m* 1899, 7th Marquess of Londonderry, who *d* 1949:—

Grandchildren of late Hon Florence Chaplin (*m* 1920, Charles Richard Hoare), yr da of late Lady Florence Chaplin (ante):—
Issue of late Charles Hugh Hoare, *b* 1923, *d* 1981: *m* 1949, Gillian Leith (15 Main St, Preston, Oakham, Rutland), da of Samuel Ernest Chesterman:—
Richard Mark HOARE, *b* 1955: *m* 1986, Alison Wendy Allen (*née* McDonald), and has issue living, Edward Hugh Richard, *b* 1986. *Residence* – Wardley, Stonehouse, Oakham, Leics. —— Stephen Robin HOARE, *b* 1959. —— Caroline (Amanda) HOARE, *b* 1952.

See that title.

Descendants of late Lady Elizabeth Georgiana Leveson-Gower, VA, CI, el da of 2nd Duke, *b* 1824, *d* 1878: *m* 1844, 8th Duke of Argyll, who *d* 1900:—

See Baird, Bt, *cr* 1809, colls.

Descendants of the late Lady Evelyn Leveson-Gower, 2nd da of 2nd Duke, *b* 1825, *d* 1869: *m* 1843, 12th Lord Blantyre, who *d* 1900:—

See that title.

Descendants of late Lady Caroline Leveson-Gower, 3rd da of 2nd Duke, *b* 1827, *d* 1887: *m* 1847, 4th Duke of Leinster, who *d* 1887:—

See that title.

Descendants of late Lady Constance Gertrude Leveson-Gower, yst da of 2nd Duke, *b* 1834, *d* 1880: *m* 1852, 1st Duke of Westminster:—

See D Sutherland.

Descendants of late Lord Francis Leveson-Gower (*cr Earl of Ellesmere*), 3rd son of Elizabeth, Countess of Sutherland and 1st Duke:—

See that title.

Descendants of late Lady Charlotte Sophia Leveson-Gower, el da of Elizabeth, Countess of Sutherland and 1st Duke, *b* 1788, *d* 1870: *m* 1814, 13th Duke of Norfolk:—

See D Westminster.

Descendants of late Lady Elizabeth Mary Leveson-Gower, yr da of Elizabeth, Countess of Sutherland and 1st Duke, *b* 1797, *d* 1891: *m* 1819, 2nd Marquess of Westminster, who *d* 1869:—

PREDECESSORS – **(1)** WILLIAM of Murray (Moray, the vast northern province of which his family were the leading barons at end of 12th century) afterwards called William of Sutherland, el son of Hugh Freskin or de Moray, Lord of Duffus in Moray; *s* his father as Lord Sutherland before 1222; *cr* Earl of Sutherland after 1232; *d* 1248; *s* by his son **(2)** WILLIAM Sutherland, 2nd Earl; defeated Norse invaders of Sutherland 1263; *d* 1306/7; *s* by his el son **(3)** WILLIAM, 3rd Earl, attended Parliament at St Andrews 1308/9 as an adherent of King Robert Bruce; *d* 1330; *s* by his brother **(4)** KENNETH, 4th Earl: *m* (according to Sir Robert Gordon) Mary, da of Donald, Earl of Mar; *k* at Halidon Hill 1333; *s* by his el son **(5)** WILLIAM, 5th Earl; taken prisoner at Nevill's Cross 1346; had a blood feud with the Mackays of Strathnaver that lasted three centuries: *m* 1st, 1342, Margaret, who *d* 1346, da of King Robert I; 2ndly, 1347, Joan, da of Sir John Menteith of Rusky, and widow of Malise, 7th Earl of Strathearn, of John Campbell, Earl of Atholl, and of Maurice Moray, Earl of Strathearn; *d* about 1371; *s* by his el surv son (by 2nd wife) **(6)** ROBERT, 6th Earl, after whom his castle of Dunrobin ("Robert's Castle") was named; mentioned by Froissart as a leader of invasion of England 1388: *m* 1389, Margaret Stewart, nat da of Alexander, Earl of Buchan, "the Wolf of Badenoch", 4th son of King Robert II; *d* about 1427; *s* by his el son **(7)** JOHN, 7th Earl; knighted on battlefield near Liège 1408; resigned Earldom to his son John, Master of Sutherland 1456: *m* Margaret, who *d* 1509/10, da of Sir William Baillie of Lamington; *d* about 1460; his el surv son **(8)** JOHN, 8th Earl; *s* 1456; became an idiot 1494: *m* 1st, (according to Sir Robert Gordon) da of Alexander Macdonald, Lord of the Isles and Earl of Ross; 2ndly, Fingole, said to have been da of William, Thane of Cawdor, and widow of Sir John Munro, 11th of Foulis; 3rdly, Catherine; *d* about 1508; *s* by his son, by his first wife **(9)** JOHN, *de jure* 9th Earl; also became mentally incapable, so was ward of the Crown, his estates being administered by High Treasurer; his service as heir was opposed by his half-brother Alexander (son of 2nd marriage), who in 1509 resigned his claim; *d* 1514; *s* by his sister **(10)** ELIZABETH, Countess of Sutherland: *m* about 1500 Adam Gordon of Aboyne (who *d* 1538), *jure uxoris* 10th Earl of Sutherland, 2nd son of 2nd Earl of Huntly; constantly at war with her half-brother, who seized Dunrobin Castle; she resigned Earldom, with consent of her husband in favour of her son Alexander 1527, who was infeft in reversion; *d* 1535; *s* by their grandson **(11)** JOHN Gordon (el son of Alexander Gordon, Master of Sutherland, who *m* Lady Janet Stewart, da of 2nd Earl of Atholl, and *d* 1529/30) 11th Earl; *b* 1525; accompanied Queen Dowager to France 1550, and *cr* Knt of St Michael there; involved in Earl of Huntly's revolt, and dignities and titles forfeited 1563, when he fled to Flanders; restored by Parliament in 1567; assisted at Queen Mary's marriage to Bothwell: *m* 1st, 1545/46, Lady Elizabeth Campbell, who *dsp* about 1548, da of 3rd Earl of Argyll, and widow of James, Earl of Moray, nat son of James IV; 2ndly, 1548, Lady Helen Stuart, who *d* 1564, da of 12th Earl of Lennox and widow of 6th Earl of Erroll; 3rdly, Marion Seton, who *d* (poisoned) 1567, da of 4th Lord Seton, and widow of 4th Earl of Menteith; *d* (poisoned) at Dunrobin 1567; *s* by his only surviving son **(12)** ALEXANDER, 12th Earl, *b* 1552; Hereditary Sheriff of Inverness; acquired Lordship of Strathnaver from Earl of Huntly in exchange for Aboyne; made peace treaties with his ancestral enemies the Mackay chief and Earl of Caithness: *m* 1st, 1567 (*m diss* 1572) Lady Barbara Sinclair, el da of 4th Earl of Caithness; 2ndly, 1573, Lady Jean Gordon (who *m* 3rdly, 1599 Alexander Ogilvie of Boyne, and *d* 1629), da of 4th Earl of Huntly, and formerly wife of 4th Earl of Bothwell (afterwards husband of Mary, Queen of Scots); *d* 1594; *s* by his el son **(13)** JOHN, 13th Earl, *b* 1576, bore the Sword of State before the King at Rising of Parliament 1597, which he claimed as his hereditary right; encouraged industry in Sutherland, opening coalpits at Brora; obtained 1601 a novodamus of Earldom, which was erected into a Regality, with grant of Hereditary Shrievalty of Sutherland (his territories being specially erected into a sheriffdom), in favour, failing heirs male of his body, of his brothers and their issue male, whom all failing, to Adam Gordon; 3rd son of 1st Marquess of Huntly and his heirs male whatsoever: *m* 1600, the Hon Agnes Elphinstone, who *d* 1617, el da of 4th Lord Elphinstone; *d* 1615; *s* by his 4th but el surv son **(14)** JOHN, 14th Earl, *b* 1609; was the first man to sign the National Covenant 1638; active Covenanter during Civil War (Commr for Sutherland); Col of Horse and Foot, Sutherland; Lord Privy Seal (for Cromwell) 1656-58; bore the Sceptre at opening of 1st Parliament of Charles II 1661; obtained 1662 a novodamus of Earldom in favour of his son George, Lord Strathnaver; *m* 1st, 1632, Lady Jean Drummond, who *d* 1637, da of 1st Earl of Perth; 2ndly, 1639, Hon Anne Fraser, who *dsp* 1658, da of 7th Lord Lovat; *d* 1679; *s* by his only surv son **(15)** GEORGE, 15th Earl, *b* 1633; Commr of Great Seal (for William III) 1689; obtained 1681 a novodamus of Earldom in favour of his el son and their heirs male of the body, whom failing, to Lord Strathnaver's el da and other heirs named: *m* 1659, Lady Jean Wemyss, who *d* 1715; da and heir of line of 2nd Earl of Wemyss, and widow of Archibald, Earl of Angus, son of 1st Marquess of Douglas; *d* 1703; *s* by his son **(16)** JOHN Gordon, (later Sutherland) KT, PC, 16th Earl, *b* 1661; secured Inverness for William III; raised his own Regt of Foot, which he commanded in Flanders campaign 1694; later Lt-Gen; Commr for the Union 1706; was elected one of the first 16 Representative Peers; as Lord-Lt of all the six northern counties, he held them for George I against Jacobite Rising 1715; resumed ancient surname of Sutherland about 1670; obtained 1706 a novadamus of Earldom in favour of his son Lord Strathnaver and himself, and their heirs male of the body, whom failing the heirs female of the body of Lord Strathnaver without division, and their issue male, whom failing the Earl's heirs female: *m* 1st, 1680, Helen Cochrane, who *d* 1690, da of William Lord Cochrane (E Dundonald); 2ndly, Lady Katherine Tollemache, who *d* about 1705, da of Countess of Dysart (Duchess of Lauderdale) and widow of James, Lord Doune (E Moray); 3rdly, 1727, Frances, who *d* 1732, da of Sir James Hodgson of Bramwith Hall, Yorks, and widow of Sir Thomas Travell; *d* 1733; *s* by his grandson **(17)** WILLIAM, 17th Earl (son of William, Lord Strathnaver, by Katherine, da of William Morison of Prestongrange, E Lothian); *b* 1708; a Representative Peer; supported Govt 1745-46, present at Culloden; received £1,000 in compensation for abolition of Hereditary Shrievalty of Sutherland 1747: *m* 1734, Lady Elizabeth Wemyss who *d* 1747, da of 3rd Earl of Wemyss; *d* 1750; *s* by his only son **(18)** WILLIAM, 18th Earl *b* 1735; Lt-Col Comdt of a Bde of Highlanders; a Representative Peer: *m* 1761, Mary, who *d* 1766, da and co-heir of William Maxwell, of Preston, Kirkcudbright; *d* 1766; *s* by his only surv da **(19)** ELIZABETH, Countess of Sutherland, *b* 1765; her right to the Peerage, which was opposed by Sir Robert Gordon, descendant of 2nd son of 12th Earl, as heir male of body of Adam Gordon, Earl of Sutherland, husband of Elizabeth Countess of Sutherland **(20 ante)**, and by George Gordon of Forse, as heir male of 1st Earl, was confirmed by House of Lords 1771; raised Sutherland Fencibles 1779 and 1793: *m* 1785, the 1st Duke of Sutherland; *d* 1839 **(20-23)**; succession followed the Dukedom of Sutherland until the death of 5th Duke 1963; he was *s* in the Earldom by his niece **(24)** ELIZABETH MILLICENT (only da of late Lord Alistair St Clair Sutherland-Leveson-Gower, MC, 2nd son of 4th Duke), Countess of Sutherland and present peeress; also Lady Strathnaver.

SUTHERLAND, DUKE OF (Egerton) (Duke UK 1833, Bt E 1620)

Thus until

JOHN SUTHERLAND EGERTON, 6th Duke; *b* 10 May 1915; *s* as 5th Earl of Ellesmere 1944, and as 6th Duke of Sutherland 1963; *ed* Eton, and Trin Coll, Camb; late Capt Roy Armoured Corps (TA), and a DL for Berwickshire; 1939-45 War (prisoner): *m* 1st, 1939, Lady Diana Evelyn Percy, who *d* 1978, da of 8th Duke of Northumberland; 2ndly, 1979, Evelyn Mary, da of Maj Robert Moubray (*see* Morrison-Bell, Bt, colls).

Arms – Argent, a lion rampant gules between three pheons sable. **Crest** – On a chapeau gules, turned up ermine, a lion rampant of the first, supporting an arrow or, feathered and headed argent. **Supporters** – *Dexter*, a horse argent, ducally gorged or; *sinister*, a griffin or, ducally gorged azure.
Seats – Mertoun, St Boswell's, Roxburghshire; Lingay Cottage, Newmarket, Suffolk. *Clubs* – Jockey, White's, Turf.

SISTERS LIVING

Lady Susan Alice, *b* 1913: *m* 1933 (*m diss* 1966), Maj John Marjoribanks Askew, Gren Gds, who *d* 1996, and has issue living, Henry John (Ladykirk House, Berwick-upon-Tweed TD15 1SU; 77 Chester Row, SW1W 8JL), *b* 1940; *ed* Eton: *m* 1978, Rosemary Eileen da of Dr (Charles) Edmunds Darby Taylor, of Alnwick House, Little Shelford, Cambridge, and has issue living, Jack *b* 1984, George *b* 1986, William *b* 1992, — Sarah Caroline (*Baroness Faringdon*), *b* 1936: *m* 1959, 3rd Baron Faringdon, of Buscot Park, Faringdon, Oxon SN7 8BU. *Residence* – Stone House, Sprouston, Kelso, Roxburghshire.

Lady Margaret, CVO, *b* 1918; sometime Junior Comm ATS; was a Lady-in-Waiting to HRH Princess Elizabeth 1946-49, Extra Lady-in-Waiting to HM Queen Elizabeth the Queen Mother; CVO 1994: *m* 1948, Sir John Rupert Colville, CB, CVO, who *d* 1987, and has issue (*see* V Colville of Culross, colls). *Residence* – The Close, Broughton, nr Stockbridge, Hants.

COLLATERAL BRANCHES LIVING

Issue of late Capt Lord Alistair St Clair Sutherland-Leveson-Gower, MC, 2nd son of 4th Duke, *b* 1890, *d* 1921: *m* 1918, Elizabeth Helène, who *d* 1931 (having *m* 2ndly, 1931, Col Baron George Osten Driesen), da of Warren Gardener Demarest of New York City:—
Elizabeth Millicent (*Countess of Sutherland*); *s* as Countess of Sutherland 1963 (see that title).

Grandchildren of late Hon Francis William George Egerton, 2nd son of 3rd Earl of Ellesmere:—
Issue of late Cyril Reginald Egerton, *b* 1905, *d* 1992: *m* 1st, 1934, Mary, who *d* 1949, da of Rt Hon Sir Ronald Hugh Campbell, GCMG; 2ndly, 1954, Mary Truda, who *d* 1982, only da of late Sir (Thomas) Sydney Lea, 2nd Bt:—
(By 1st *m*) FRANCIS RONALD, *b* 18 Feb 1940; *ed* Eton, and RAC Cirencester: *m* 1974, Victoria Mary, da of Maj-Gen Edward Alexander Wilmot Williams, CB, CBE, MC, of Herringston, Dorset (*see* B Addington, 1968 Edn), and has issue living, James Granville, *b* 1975, — Henry Alexander, *b* 1977. *Residence* – Ley Farm, Stetchworth, Newmarket, Suffolk CB8 9GX. —— Lucy Helen, *b* 1937: *m* 1958, Michael Alan Pelham, JP, of Old Way House, Beaulieu, Hants SO42 7YL, and has issue living, Charles Peregrine (12A Charleville Mansions, Charleville Rd, W14 9JB), *b* 1959: *m* 1990, Clare Johanna Marina, da of Wallace Earl Britton, of 1842 Calypso Drive, Aptos, CA 95003, USA, and has issue living, Henry Cyril *b* 1992, George Marcus *b* 1994, Avanete Johanna *b* 1998, — Laura Mary (10 Hollywood Court, Hollywood Rd, SW10 9HR), *b* 1962: *m* 1996, Ronald J. Slade, eldest son of Ronald Slade, of Dulwich. —— Katharine Mary, *b* 1942: *m* 1979, Franklin Watts, of 42 Chiddingstone St, SW6, and has issue living, Angus William, *b* 1982, — Camilla Mary, *b* 1984. —— Alice Marian, *b* 1946: *m* 1971, Thomas David Fremantle, and has issue (*see* B Cottesloe, colls).

Issue of late Hon Thomas Henry Frederick Egerton, 3rd son of 3rd Earl of Ellesmere, *b* 1876, *d* 1953: *m* 1902, Lady Bertha Anson, who *d* 1959, da of 3rd Earl of Lichfield:—
Pamela Katharine, *b* 1918: *m* 1940, Lieut-Col Ralph Capel Stockley, Roy Northumberland Fusiliers, who was *ka* 1944, and has issue living, Jane Margaret, *b* 1942: *m* 1974, Gerard Balfour Chichester, of Llangoed, Erwood, Builth Wells, Powys LD2 3TJ, and has issue living, Henry Ralph *b* 1977, Charles Edmond *b* 1978, — Sally Elizabeth, *b* 1944: *m* 1978, Dr Christopher John Tudor Lewis, of Malt Office Farm, Metfield, Harleston, Norfolk IP20 0LP, and has issue living, Beatrice Emily Frances *b* 1979, and an adopted son, John Claude *b* 1976 (adopted 1983). *Residence* – Owls, Middle Hill, Englefield Green, Surrey.

Grandsons of late Capt Francis Egerton (infra):—
Issue of late Anthony Francis Egerton, *b* 1921, *d* 1985; late Lieut 60th Rifles and Fl Lieut RAF: *m* 1946, Pauline Clodagh, who *d* 1997, da of late Trevor Toulmin Seaton Leadam, of Colebrooke, Watersfield, Sussex:—
Simon Francis Cavendish, *b* 1949; *ed* Milton Abbey: *m* 1990, Juliet Susannah, only da of Robert Assheton Barrett, of Widford, Herts (*see* B Clitheroe, 1972-73 Edn), and has issue living, Isabella Louise Greville *b* 1994. *Residence* – Old Hoyle, Heyshott, Midhurst, Sussex GU29 0DX. —— Fulke Charles Granville, *b* 1952; *ed* Stanbridge Earls. *Address* – c/o Wells Fargo Bank, Sunnyvale, Calif, USA.

Issue of late Michael Godolphin Egerton, *b* 1924, *d* 1979: *m* 1st, 1951, (Pamela) Nicolette, yr da of Giulio Giorgio de Gardiol, of La Fontana, and Luserna San Giovanni, Turin, Italy, and formerly wife of Patrick William

Meade-Newman; 2ndly, 1957, Elizabeth Anne Bowring, who *d* 1994, only da of Leslie Bowring Wimble, of Romany Ridge, N Chailey, Lewes, Sussex:—
(By 2nd *m*) Mark William Godolphin (Mijas, Malaga, Spain), *b* 1958: *m* 1st, 1979 (*m diss* 1983), Nicola J. Hawkes; 2ndly, 1991, Mercedes Abadia Gomez, of Fuengirola, Spain, and has issue living (by 1st *m*), Sophia Annabel Godolphin, *b* 1983, — (by 2nd *m*) Sacha Louise, *b* 1993. ——— †Robin Michael Bowring, *b* 1962: *m* 1985, Suzanne, da of John Edward Liversidge, of Field Cottage, Westlands, Birdham, nr Chichester, Sussex, and *d* 1988, as the result of a motor accident, leaving issue, Kathryn Rebecca, *b* 1986, — Charlotte Louise, *b* 1987. ——— Nicholas, *b* 1967.

Grandson of late William Francis Egerton, son of late Adm Hon Francis Egerton, 2nd son of 1st Earl of Ellesmere:—
Issue of late Capt Francis Egerton, *b* 1896, *d* 1935: *m* 1921, Hon Doris Mary Pottinger Meysey-Thompson (who *d* 1953, having *m* 2ndly, 1938, Major John Humphrey Allison Seed, TD, DL, JP, Yorkshire Hussars (Yeo)), da of 1st Baron Knaresborough:—
David William, *b* 1930; *ed* Stowe; Capt (ret) 17th/21st Lancers: *m* 1956, Patricia Mary Treharne, da of late Archibald Allen Treharne Thomas, formerly wife of late William Rippon Bissill, and has issue living, Francis David (76 Bridge St, Osney Island, Oxford OX2 0BD), *b* 1959; *ed* Stowe, RAC Cirencester, and Keble Coll, Oxford: *m* 1995, Jess M., da of late J. Godfrey Owen, of Acton Pigot, Shropshire. *Club* – Cavalry and Guards'.

Granddaughters of late Claude Francis Arthur Egerton, 3rd son of late Lt-Col Hon Arthur Frederick Egerton, 4th son of 1st Earl of Ellesmere:—
Issue of late Lt-Col Scrope Arthur Francis Sutherland Egerton, *b* 1902, *d* 1986: *m* 1933, Marjorie, who *d* 1992, da of late Hugh Morrison, MP (*see* E Granville, 1934 Edn):—
Sarah Jane Mary, *b* 1934. ——— Susan Alexandra, *b* 1936: *m* 1957, David John Yorke, and has issue (*see* B Clitheroe). ——— Katharine Rose, *b* 1946: *m* 1973, Peter John Sanguinetti, of Sand Hall, Wedmore, Som, and has issue living, Edward Francis, *b* 1979, — Charlotte Emma Georgiana, *b* 1983.

(In remainder to Marquessate of Stafford)

Descendants of late Rt Hon Lord Granville Leveson-Gower, GCB (yst son of 1st Marquess of Stafford), who was *cr Earl Granville* 1833 (see that title).

(In remainder to Earldom of Gower)

Grandchildren of late Lt-Col Harold Boscawen Leveson-Gower (infra):—
Issue of late Charles Murrough Leveson-Gower, *b* 1933, *d* 1983: *m* 1960, Rosemary Anne (who *m* 2ndly, 1987, Ronald Patrick Thorburn, FRICS, of Straloch, by Blairgowrie, Perthshire), da of late Maj Charles John Frederick Platt, 3rd Hussars, of Muirhouselaw, St Boswells, Roxburghshire:—
Mark Broke, *b* 1961: *m* 1987, Emma Joy, elder da of Desmond O'Conor Cameron, of Horsegrove House, Rotherfield, Sussex, and has issue living, Hugh Charles, *b* 1993, — Jemima Anastasia, *b* 1996. *Residence* – 57 Swaffield Rd, SW18 34Q. ——— Henry Boscawen Boddington, *b* 1962; has assumed his wife's maiden name as an additional forename: *m* 1992, Paula Ruth, DPhil, yr da of David Boddington, of Poole, Dorset, and has issue living, Reuben Boddington, *b* 1993, Indigo Boddington *b* 1998. *Residence* – 25 Batman St, Braddon, ACT 2612, Australia. ——— Alice Victoria, *b* 1966: *m* 1993, Mark W. V. Mathewson, yr son of Niel Mathewson, of Cullaloe, Fife, and has issue living, William Niel Charles, *b* 1995, — Kate Violet, *b* 1997.

Granddaughter of late Col Charles Cameron Leveson-Gower, CMG, OBE, el son of late Capt Hugh Broke Boscawen Leveson-Gower, 2nd son of John Leveson-Gower, el son of Gen John Leveson-Gower, el son of Adm Hon John Leveson-Gower, yst son of 1st Earl Gower:—
Issue of late Lt-Col Harold Boscawen Leveson-Gower, *b* 1905, *d* 1973: *m* 1930, Kathleen May, OBE, who *d* 1984, da of late Sir Murrough John Wilson, KBE (B Inchiquin, colls):—
Anastasia (*Anastasia, Lady Studd*), *b* 1931: *m* 1958, Sir Robert Kynaston Studd, 3rd Bt, who *d* 1977, and has issue (see that title).

Issue of late Brig-Gen Philip Leveson-Gower, CMG, DSO, DL, yr son of Capt Hugh Broke Boscawen Leveson-Gower (ante), *b* 1871, *d* 1939: *m* 1899, Eleanor Marcia, who *d* 1975, da of Christopher R Nugent, JP, formerly of The Hall, Pinner, Middx:—
Elizabeth Ellen *b* 1915: *m* 1945, Mark William Harford, who *d* 1969, and has issue living, Philip Hugh (Horton Hall Farm, Horton, Chipping Sodbury, Avon BS17 6QN), *b* 1946: *m* 1982, Willa, yr da of late William Joseph Franklin, of St Mary's Mead, Witney, Oxon, and has issue living, William Scandrett *b* 1984, Harriet Kate Isabel *b* 1987, — Gerald Mark (Trewyn, Abergavenny NP7 7PG), *b* 1948: *m* 1985, Camilla Margaret, eldest da of Alistair Allan Horne, of The Old Rectory, Turville, Oxon (*see* D Buccleuch, 1976 Edn), and has issue living, Auriol Louise *b* 1987, Elizabeth Mida *b* 1989. *Residence* – 8 Court St, Sherston, Malmesbury, Wilts SN16 0LL.

Granddaughter of late Brig-Gen Philip Leveson-Gower, CMG, DSO, DL (ante):—
Issue of late Brig Hugh Nugent Leveson-Gower, *b* 1900, *d* 1979: *m* 1st, 1934 (*m diss* 1948), Avril Joy, who was *k* in a motor accident in Mexico 1978, da of late Sir John Ashley Mullens, and formerly wife of Prince George Imeritinsky; 2ndly, 1949, Rachel, who *d* 1981, yst da of Maj Harold Hunter Grotrian, of North Stainley Hall, Ripon, and formerly wife of Michael Humphrey Wilkins:—
(By 1st *m*) Lucinda Gaye (*Lady Le Marchant*), *b* 1935: *m* 1955, Sir Spencer Le Marchant (*see* Le Marchant, Bt), who *d* 1986. *Residences* – 29 Rivermill, Grosvenor Rd, SW1; The Saltings, Yarmouth, I of Wight.

Grandchildren of late Evelyn Marmaduke Gresham Leveson-Gower, 6th son of late Granville William Gresham Leveson-Gower, el son of late William Leveson-Gower (*b* 1806), el son of late William Leveson-Gower (*b* 1779), 3rd son of Adm Hon John Leveson-Gower (ante):—

Issue of late Alastair Marmaduke Gresham Leveson-Gower, *b* 1907, *d* 1990: *m* 1st, 1934, Marjorie Blackburn, who *d* 1936, da of late Herbert Cawtheray; 2ndly, 1939, Barbara, who *d* 1997, da of William George Higgins:—
(By 1st *m*) Anthony Gresham (24A Oak Tree Rd, Whitehill, Bordon, Hants GU35 9DF), *b* 1934. —— (By 2nd *m*) Robert Alastair (3 Briarwood Rd, St Johns, Woking, Surrey GU21 1XD), *b* 1946.

Issue of late Rupert Evelyn Gresham Leveson-Gower, Capt King's Own Royal Regt, *b* 1911, *d* 1985: *m* 1956, May (Manor Farm, Standlake, Witney, Oxon), da of William Humphrey Clinkard, of Great Leys Farm, Garsington, Oxon:—
Charles William Gresham (Meadow Cottage, Kencot, nr Lechlade, Glos), *b* 1959. —— Catherine Anne Gresham (97 Meadowbank Rd, Kirknewton, Midlothian EH27 8BH), *b* 1957: *m* 1986 (*m diss* 19—), David Walter Brown, and has issue living, William Charles, *b* 1992, — Alexandra Sophie Louise *b* 1990.

PREDECESSORS – **(1)** Sir THOMAS Gower, Knt; *cr* a *Baronet* 1620; *s* by his son **(2)** Sir THOMAS, 2nd Bt; a zealous partisan of Charles I; *s* by his grandson **(3)** Sir THOMAS, 3rd Bt; a Col of Foot; *d* unmarried 1689; *s* by his uncle **(4)** Sir WILLIAM Leveson-Gower, 4th Bt; sat for many years as MP for Newcastle-under-Lyme; *d* 1691; *s* by his son **(5)** Sir JOHN, 5th Bt; was Chancellor of the Duchy of Lancaster *cr Baron Gower*, of Sittenham, co York (peerage of Great Britain) 1703; *d* 1709; *s* by his son **(6)** JOHN, PC, 2nd Baron; was Lord Privy Seal, twice one of the Lords Justice during the King's absence, and Custos Rotulorum of Staffordshire; *cr Viscount Trentham* and *Earl Gower* (peerage of Great Britain) 1746; *d* 1754; *s* by his son **(7)** GRANVILLE, KG, 2nd Earl; sat successively as MP for Bishop's Castle, Westminster, and Lichfield; was a Lord of the Admiralty 1749, Lord-Lieut of Staffordshire, Lord Privy Seal 1755-7, Master of the Horse 1757, Keeper of the Great Wardrobe 1760, Lord Chamberlain 1763-5, and Pres of the Council 1768-79 and 1783-94; *cr Marquess of Stafford* (peerage of Great Britain) 1786; *d* 1803; *s* by his son **(8)** GEORGE GRANVILLE, KG, PC, 2nd Marquess; was summoned to Parliament in his father's Barony of Gower 1799; was Ambassador to Paris 1790-2: *m* 1785, Elizabeth, in her own right *Lady Strathnaver* and *Countess of Sutherland* (peerage of Scotland, see Css Sutherland, ante); *cr Duke of Sutherland* (peerage of United Kingdom) 1833; *d* 1833; *s* by his son **(9)** GEORGE GRANVILLE, KG, 2nd Duke; summoned to Parliament in his father's Barony of Gower 1826, and in 1839 *s* his mother as Baron Strathnaver and Earl of Sutherland; *b* 1786; sat as MP for St Mawes 1808; was Lord-Lieut of co Sutherland, and Custos Rotulorum of Staffordshire: *m* 1823, Harriet Elizabeth Georgiana, VA, da of 6th Earl of Carlisle; *d* 1861; *s* by his son **(10)** GEORGE GRANVILLE, KG, 3rd Duke, *b* 1828; MP for Sutherland (*L*) 1852-61; Lord-Lieut of Cromartie and Sutherland; *m* 1st, 1849, Anne, VA (*cr Countess of Cromartie, Viscountess Tarbat of Tarbat, Baroness Castlehaven of Castlehaven and Baroness Macleod of Leod* (peerage of United Kingdom) 1861, with remainder to her second surviving son Francis, and the heirs male of his body, to each other her yr sons in like manner in priority of birth, to said Francis and the heirs of his body, to each other her yr sons in like manner in priority of birth, to her daughter Florence and the heirs of her body, and to each other of her daughters in like manner in priority of birth), who *d* 1888 (when the Earldom of Cromartie devolved, in accordance with the special remainder upon her second surviving son, Francis), only child of John Hay Mackenzie; 2ndly, 1889, Mary Caroline, who *d* 1912, da of Rev Richard Mitchell, DD, and widow of Arthur Kindersley Blair, 71st Highland LI; *d* 1892; *s* by his el son **(11)** CROMARTIE, KG, 4th Duke; *b* 1851; Mayor of Longton 1895; MP for Sutherland (*L*) 1874-86; KG 1902: *m* 1884, Lady Millicent Fanny St Claire-Erskine, who *d* 1955 (having *m* 2ndly, 1914 (*m diss* 1919), Brig-Gen Percy Desmond Fitzgerald, DSO, 11th Hussars, and 3rdly, 1919, Lieut-Col Geoffrey Ernest Hawes, DSO, MC, Roy Fusiliers (ret), who *d* 1945), da of 4th Earl of Rosslyn; *d* 1913; *s* by his el son **(12)** GEORGE GRANVILLE SUTHERLAND, KT, PC, 5th Duke, *b* 1888; Lord High Commr to Gen Assembly of Ch of Scotland 1921 and 1922, Under Sec of State for Air 1922-24, Paymaster-Gen 1925-28, Under Sec of State for War 1928-29, Lord Steward of HM Household to King Edward VIII 1936, and High Steward of Kingston upon Thames 1953-63: *m* 1st, 1912, Lady Eileen Gwladys Butler, who *d* 1943, da of 7th Earl of Lanesborough; 2ndly, 1944, Mrs Clare Josephine Dunkerly, who *d* 1998, 2nd da of late Herbert O'Brien, of Calcutta, and formerly wife of (i) Alexander Blake Shakespear, CIE, of Cawnpore, and (ii) Lt-Col Vincent Ashforth Blundell Dunkerley, DSO, JP; *d* 1963; *s* in the Earldom of Sutherland and Lordship of Strathnaver by his niece, Elizabeth Millicent, da of late Capt Lord Alistair St Clair Sutherland-Leveson-Gower, MC, 2nd son of 4th Duke, and wife of Charles Noel Janson (see Cs Sutherland), and in his other honours by his kinsman **(13)** JOHN SUTHERLAND Egerton, 5th Earl of Ellesmere (see infra *), 6th Duke, and present peer; also Marquess of Stafford, Earl Gower, Earl of Ellesmere, Viscount Trentham, Viscount Brackley, and Baron Gower.

*(1) Lord FRANCIS Leveson-Gower, KG, PC, yr surv son of 1st Duke; MP for Sutherland, 1826-31 and for S Lancashire 1835-36; a Lord of the Treasury 1827, Ch Sec for Ireland 1828, and Lord-Lieut of Lancashire; assumed the name of Egerton by Roy licence on succeeding to the estates of the 3rd and last Duke of Bridgwater; *cr Viscount Brackley* and *Earl of Ellesmere* (peerage of UK) 1846; *d* 1857; *s* by his son **(2)** GEORGE GRANVILLE FRANCIS, 2nd Earl, *b* 1823: *m* 1846, Lady Mary Louisa Campbell, who *d* 1916, da of 1st Earl Cawdor; *d* 1862; *s* by his son **(3)** FRANCIS CHARLES GRANVILLE, 3rd Earl, *b* 1847: *m* 1868, Lady Katharine Louisa Phipps, who *d* 1926, da of 2nd Marquess of Normanby; *d* 1914; *s* by his el son **(4)** JOHN FRANCIS GRANVILLE SCROPE, MVO, 4th Earl, *b* 1872: *m* 1905, Lady Violet Lambton, who *d* 1972, da of 4th Earl of Durham; *d* 1944; *s* by his only son **(5)** JOHN SUTHERLAND, 5th Earl, and afterwards 6th Duke of Sutherland (ante).

Swan, family name of Baroness Sharples.

SWANN, BARONY OF (Swann) (Extinct 1990)

SONS LIVING OF LIFE BARON

Hon Richard Meredith (1 Carmel Court, Holland St, W8), *b* 1944, *ed* The Edinburgh Academy, Trin Coll, Camb, and Univ Coll, London; architect: *m* 1969, Julia, da of Ronald Coke-Steel, and has issue, Robert Edward Meredith, *b* 1973.

Dr the Hon (Gavin Michael) Peter (28 Winscombe Cres, W5), *b* 1955; *ed* The Edinburgh Academy, St Andrews Univ, Bristol Univ, and LSE; Associate Prof, London Business Sch: *m* 1989, Jenny R., yr da of Prof Walter Elkan, and has issue living, Caroline Susan Teresa, *b* 1991, — Emma Frances Ruth, *b* 1992.

DAUGHTERS LIVING OF LIFE BARON

Hon Sylvia Jane, *b* 1947: *m* 1970, Christopher William Maxwell Garnett, of Henden Hall, Biddenden, Kent TN27 8BB, and has issue living, Simon Michael John, *b* 1978, — Lucy Teresa Emma, *b* 1973, — Emma Caroline Barbara, *b* 1975.

Hon Catriona Mary Antonia, *b* 1953: *m* 1976, Robert Noble Watson, of Ballingall, nr Leslie, Fife, and has issue, James Richard, *b* 1982, — Teresa Janet, *b* 1978.

WIDOW LIVING OF LIFE BARON

TERESA ANN (*Baroness Swann*), da of late Prof Reginald Morier Yorke Gleadowe, CVO: *m* 1942, Baron Swann, FRS (Life Baron), who *d* 1990. *Residences* – Tallat Steps, Coln-St-Denys, Cheltenham, Glos; 23 Sheffield Terr, W8.

SWANSEA, BARON (Vivian) (Baron UK 1893, Bt UK 1882)

Live by the spirit of God

JOHN HUSSEY HAMILTON VIVIAN, 4th Baron, and 4th Baronet; *b* 1 Jan 1925; *s* 1934; *ed* Eton, and Trin Coll, Camb; a DL for Powys; CStJ: *m* 1st, 1956 (*m diss* 1973), Miriam Antoinette, who *d* 1975, da of A. W. F. Caccia-Birch, MC, of Guernsey Lodge, Marton, New Zealand; 2ndly, 1982, Mrs Lucy Temple-Richards, da of late Rt Rev Hugh Rowlands Gough, CMG, OBE, TD, DD of Forge House, Over Wallop, Stockbridge, Hants (*see* B Kinnaird), and has issue by 1st *m*.

Arms — Or, on a chevron azure, between three lions' heads erased proper, as many annulets gold; on a chief embattled gules, a wreath of oak or, between two martlets argent. Crests – 1st, a lion's head erased proper charged with two bezants palewise and gorged with a collar gules, thereon three annulets or, with a chain of the last; 2nd, issuant from a bridge of one arch embattled and having at each end a tower proper, a demi-hussar, in the uniform of the 18th Reg, holding in his right hand a sabre and in his left a red pennon flying to the sinister. Supporters – *Dexter*, a dragon wings elevated gules, gorged with a collar or charged with three torteaux; *sinister*, a horse argent, saddle and bridle proper, trappings gules, gorged with a collar sable charged with three bezants.
Residence – 16 Cheyne Gdns, SW3 5QT.

SON LIVING (By 1st marriage)

Hon RICHARD ANTHONY HUSSEY, *b* 24 Jan 1957; *ed* Eton, Durham Univ, and City Univ Business Sch (MBA): *m* 1996, Mrs Anna Clementine Brooking, da of Michael John Somerset Austin, of Sunbury, Melbourne, Australia, and has issue living, James Henry Hussey, *b* 25 June 1999. *Residence* – 36 Lavenham Rd, SW18 5HA.

DAUGHTERS LIVING (By 1st marriage)

Hon Amanda Ursula Georgina, *b* 1958: *m* 1985, Hugh William Lowther, and has issue (*see* Lowther, Bt, colls, *cr* 1824). *Residence* – Guilsborough Court, Guilsborough, Northants NN6 8QW.

Hon Louisa Caroline Sarah, *b* 1963: *m* 1990, Paul David Vincent, only son of Peter Vincent, of 16 Gaddum Rd, Bowdon, Cheshire, and has issue living, Beatrice Miriam Georgina, *b* 1996. *Residence* – 6 Upper Spit Rd, Mosman, NSW 2088, Australia.

SISTER LIVING

Hon Averil, *b* 1930; a JP for Herts: *m* 1953, Alexander William Houston, and has issue living, Peter Richard Vivian (Fair Dawn, Pack Horse Lane, Southstoke, Bath, Som), *b* 1954: *m* 1979, Susan Caroline, yr da of Maj Robert Evelyn Russell Smallwood (*see* Birkmyre, Bt), — Charles Robson Hamilton (Neen Sollars House, Neen Sollars, Cleobury Mortimer, Shropshire SY14 0AH), *b* 1959: *m* 1987, Emma Woodbine, yst da of late Maj Michael Woodbine Parish, MC, Notts Yeo (*see* By Trent), and has issue living, Michael Charles Woodbine *b* 1991, Florence Rose Woodbine *b* 1989, Roselle Azalea Woodbine *b* 1992, Elsie Lily Woodbine *b* 1994, — Claire Mary, *b* 1956: *m* 1985, Patrick Charles Archibald Mansel Lewis, of Capel Isaf, Manordeilo, Llandeilo, Carmarthenshire, and has issue (*see* E Wharncliffe). *Residence* – Paynters House, Datchworth, Knebworth, Herts SG3 6ST.

PREDECESSORS – **(1)** HENRY HUSSEY VIVIAN, el son of John Henry Vivian, MP, brother of 1st Baron Vivian; *b* 1821; MP for Truro (*L*) 1852-7, for Glamorganshire 1857-85, and for Swansea Dist 1885-93; *cr* a *Baronet* 1882,and *Baron Swansea*, of Singleton, co Glamorgan (peerage of United Kingdom) 1893: *m* 1st, 1847, Jessie Dalrymple, who *d* 1848, da of Ambrose Goddard, MP, of The Lawn, Swindon; 2ndly, 1853, Caroline Elizabeth, who *d* 1868, da of Sir Montague John Cholmeley, MP, 2nd Bt; 3rdly, 1870, Averil, who *d* 1934, da of Capt Richard Beaumont, RN; *d* 1894; *s* by his el son **(2)** ERNEST AMBROSE, 2nd Baron; *b* 1848; *d* 1922; *s* by his half-brother **(3)** ODO RICHARD, DSO, MVO, TD, 3rd Baron; *b* 1875; European War 1914-18 as Lieut-Col Cmdg 14th Batn Roy Irish Rifles (DSO); *m* 1906, Hon Winifred Hamilton, who *d* 1944, da of 1st Baron Holm Patrick; *d* 1934; *s* by his only son **(4)** JOHN HUSSEY HAMILTON, 4th Baron and present peer.

SWAYTHLING, BARON (Montagu) (Baron UK 1907, Bt UK 1894)

SWIFT · YET · SURE

CHARLES EDGAR SAMUEL MONTAGU, 5th Baron and 5th Baronet; *b* 20 Feb 1954; *s* 1998: *m* 1996, Hon Angela Lorraine Rawlinson, yst da of Baron Rawlinson of Ewell, PC (Life Baron), and has issue.

Arms – Or, on a mount proper, a tent argent between on the dexter a staff proper, flowing therefrom a pennon azure, charged with a lion rampant of the field, and on the sinister a palm tree also proper. **Crest** – A stag statant holding in the mouth a sprig of palm proper, in front of a flagstaff also erect proper, therefrom flowing to the dexter a banner azure, charged with a lion rampant or. **Supporters** – On either side a figure representing a soldier of ancient Judea.
Address – c/o House of Lords, SW1.

DAUGHTER LIVING

Hon Delilah Elaine, *b* 1998.

SISTERS LIVING AND DECEASED

Fiona Yvonne, *b* 1952; *d* 1982.
Hon Nicole Mary, *b* 1956: *m* 1987, Nicholas Charles Wilson Campbell, yst son of late Prof Wilson Campbell, of Warkworth, Northumberland.

UNCLE LIVING (*son of 3rd Baron*)

Hon Anthony Trevor Samuel, *b* 1931; *ed* Eton; formerly Chm Abingworth plc: *m* 1962, Deirdre Bridget, yr da of late Brig Ronald Henry Senior, DSO, TD (*see* B Joicey, 1985 Edn), and has issue living, Rupert Anthony Samuel, *b* 1965; *ed* Eton, — Damian William Samuel, *b* 1970; *ed* Eton, — Georgina Mary, *b* 1963: *m* 1995, William D. Petty, of 90 W Center St, Moab, Utah 84532, USA, eldest son of William Petty, of Denver, Colorado, USA, and has issue living, Willa Mary *b* 1997. *Residence* – 26 Broadwalk House, 51 Hyde Park Gate, SW7 5DZ.

AUNT LIVING (*daughter of 3rd Baron*)

Hon Jean Mary, *b* 1927: *m* 1951, Lintorn Trevor Highett, MC, and has issue living, Paul Lintorn, *b* 1958; *ed* Eton, — Clare Joanna, *b* 1956: *m* 1977, Nigel Godfrey Powell Day, of The Old Mill House, Mill Rd, Gt Gransden, Sandy, Beds SG19 3AG, and has issue living, Peter *b* 1986, Emma Louise *b* 1984, — Stephanie Jane, *b* 1963. *Residence* – 2A Gore St, SW7.

WIDOW LIVING OF SON OF SECOND BARON

Iris Rachel (24 Montrose Court, Exhibition Rd, SW7 2QQ), da of Solomon Joseph Solomon, RA, formerly of Hyde Park Gate, W: *m* 1923, Hon Ewen Edward Samuel Montagu, CBE, QC, who *d* 1985.

CHRISTINE FRANCOISE (NINETTE) (*Dowager Baroness Swaythling*), da of late Edgar Dreyfus, of 5 rue de Chaillot, Paris: *m* 1951, the 4th Baron Swaythling, who *d* 1998. *Residence* – 14 Craven Hill Mews, Devonshire Terrace, W2 3DY.

COLLATERAL BRANCHES LIVING

Issue of late Hon Ewen Edward Samuel Montagu, CBE, QC, 2nd son of 2nd Baron, *b* 1901, *d* 1985: *m* 1923, Iris Rachel (ante), da of Solomon Joseph Solomon, RA, formerly of 18 Hyde Park Gate, W:—
Jeremy Peter Samuel (171 Iffley Rd, Oxford OX4 1EL), *b* 1927; *ed* Hotchkiss Sch, USA, Gordonstoun, Trin Coll, Camb, and Guildhall Sch of Music; museum curator: *m* 1955, Gwen Ellen, da of Jack Ingledew, of Westhouses, Derby, and has issue living, Simon Joseph Samuel, *b* 1959: *m* 1st, 1983 (*m diss* 1989), Judith, da of late Charles Lowy, of 14 Edgware Court, High St, Edgware; 2ndly, 1990, Hepzibah, da of late Mordechai Cohen, of Jerusalem, and has issue living (by 1st *m*), Avital Rose *b* 1986, (by 2nd *m*) Aviad Mordechai *b* 1992, Ahinoam Rachel *b* 1993, Ellat Lily Amalia *b* 1998, — Rachel Mary, *b* 1956; Rabbi: *m* 1990, Francis Samuel, son of late Werner Treuherz, of Rochdale, and has issue living, Eliezer Michael Montagu *b* 1993, Isaac Raphael Menachem Montagu *b* 1998, — Sarah Ruth, *b* 1958: *m* 1980, Mark Roseman, and has issue living, Jacob Edward James *b* 1981, Abigail Shoshana *b* 1984, Kate Nechama *b* 1987. —— Jennifer Iris Rachel *b* 1931; *ed* Lady Margaret Hall, Oxford (BA), and London Univ (PhD 1960); art historian.

Grandchildren of late Hon Gerald Samuel Montagu, 3rd son of 1st Baron:—
Adopted children of late Bryan de Castro Samuel Montagu, *b* 1916, *d* 1997: *m* 1950, Elcie (9 Hesper Mews, SW5 0HH), da of late John Weiser, of 5 Rowan Walk, N2:—
Robert de Castro Samuel (6 Groveside, Gt Bookham, Surrey KT23 4LD), *b* 1956: *m* 1983, Claire Strettell, and has issue living, James de Castro Samuel, *b* 1990, — Charlotte Claire, *b* 1992, — Lydia, *b* 1959: *m* 1989, Ian Leonard Coltman, of 44 Normanton Av, Wimbledon Park, SW19 8BB, elder son of William A. Coltman, of Catterick, N Yorks.

PREDECESSORS – (1) MONTAGU Samuel-Montagu, son of late Louis Samuel, watchmaker of Liverpool; *b* 1832; founder of the banking firm of Samuel Montagu and Co, of Old Broad Street, EC; granted Roy licence 1894 to assume surnames of Samuel-Montagu (surname of Samuel not now used by descendants); MP for Tower Hamlets, Whitechapel Div (*L*) 1885-1900; *cr* a *Baronet* 1894, and *Baron Swaythling*, of Swaythling, co Southampton (peerage of United Kingdom) 1907: *m* 1862, Ellen, who *d* 1919, da of late Louis Cohen, of the Stock Exchange; *d* 1911; *s* by his el son (2) LOUIS SAMUEL, 2nd Baron, *b* 1869; head of the banking firm of Samuel Montagu and Co, of Old Broad Street, EC: *m* 1898, Gladys Helen Rachel, OBE, who *d* 1965, da of Col Albert Edward Williamson Goldsmid, MVO; *d* 1927; *s* by his son (3) STUART ALBERT SAMUEL, OBE, 3rd Baron, *b* 1898; Dir Samuel Montagu & Co Ltd, Bankers; Pres English Guernsey Cattle Soc 1950-51, and 1971-72, and of Royal Assocn of British Dairy Farmers 1972-73 (Dep Pres 1970-72 and 1973-74): *m* 1st, 1925 (*m diss* 1942), Mary Violet, who *d* 1996, eldest da of late Maj Walter Henry Levy, DSO (*see* V Bearsted, 1962 Edn); 2ndly, 1945, Jean Marcia, CBE, who *d* 1993, da of late G. C. Leith Marshall, and formerly wife of late S/Ldr G. R. M. Knox, RAF; *d* 1990; *s* by his elder son (4) DAVID CHARLES SAMUEL, 4th Baron, *b* 1928; Chm Samuel Montagu & Co Ltd, and Rothmans International plc; Pres Asso for Jewish Youth: *m* 1951, Christine Françoise (Ninette), da of late Edgar Dreyfus, of 5 rue deChaillot, Paris; *d* 1998; *s* by his only son (5) CHARLES EDGAR SAMUEL, 5th Baron and present peer.

SWINFEN, BARON (Eady) (Baron UK 1919)

ROGER MYNORS SWINFEN EADY, 3rd Baron; *b* 14 Dec 1938; *s* 1977; *ed* Westminster; late Lt R Scots; ARICS: *m* 1962, Patricia Anne, only da of late J. D. Blackmore, of Doone, Highfield Park, Dundrum, co Dublin, and has issue.

Arms – Per pale argent and vert, on a chevron between three battle-axes, as many ermine spots, all counter-charged. **Crest** – A demi-lion rampant vert, charged on the body with a battle-axe erect, and holding a like axe in bend argent. **Supporters** – *Dexter*, a lion guardant vert charged with a battle-axe argent; *sinister*, a lion guardant argent charged with a battle-axe vert.
Address – c/o House of Lords, SW1.

Through difficulties to the heights

SON LIVING

Hon CHARLES ROGER PEREGRINE SWINFEN, *b* 8 March 1971.

DAUGHTERS LIVING

Hon Georgina Mary Rose Swinfen, *b* 1964: *m* 1990, Capt Robin Edgar Douglas Liley, 2nd son of Capt Robert Liley, of Deal, Kent, and has issue living, Sophie Anne Clare, *b* 1994, — Emily Alice Mary, *b* 1996.
Hon Katherine Anne Dorothy Swinfen, *b* 1966: *m* 1993, Major Gareth Huw Davies, RTR, son of Dr Cyril Davies, of Bath.
Hon Arabella Victoria Eleanor Swinfen, *b* 1969: *m* 1994, Capt Charles E. A. Mayo, The Light Dragoons, son of Col (Edward) John Mayo, CBE, of Camberley, Surrey, and has issue living, Elizabeth Rose Anne, *b* 1996.

BROTHER LIVING

Hon (Hugh) Toby, *b* 1941; *ed* Bryanston, and Wadham Coll, Oxford.

MOTHER LIVING

Mary Aline, CBE, da of late Col Harold Mynors Farmar, CMG, DSO; author under the name of Mary Wesley: *m* 1st, 1937 (*m diss* 1945), the 2nd Baron Swinfen, who *d* 1977; 2ndly, 1952, Eric Otto Siepmann, journalist, who *d* 1970.

WIDOW LIVING OF SECOND BARON

AVERIL KATHLEEN SUZANNE (*Averil, Baroness Swinfen*), da of late Maj William Marshall Hickman Humphreys, of Broomfield House, Midleton, co Cork, and formerly wife of Lt Col Andrew Knowles, TD: *m* 1950, as his 2nd wife, the 2nd Baron Swinfen, who *d* 1977.

PREDECESSORS – **(1)** *Rt Hon Sir* CHARLES SWINFEN Eady, son of George John Eady, of Chertsey, *b* 1851; a Judge of High Court of Justice 1901-13, a Lord Justice of Appeal 1913-18, and Master of the Rolls 1918-19; *cr Baron Swinfen*, of Chertsey, co Surrey (peerage of United Kingdom), 1 Nov 1919: *m* 1894, Blanche Maude, who *d* 1946, da of late S. W. Lee of Dereham, Putney Hill, SW; *d* 15 Nov 1919; *s* by his only son **(2)** CHARLES SWINFEN, 2nd Baron; *b* 1904; Bar-at-law, Inner Temple: *m* 1st, 1937 (*m diss* 1945), Mary Aline (Mary Wesley, CBE, the author), da of Col Harold Mynors Farmar, CMG, DSO; 2ndly, 1950, Averil Kathleen Suzanne, da of late Maj William Marshall Hickman Humphreys, of Broomfield House, Midleton, co Cork, and formerly wife of Lt-Col Andrew Knowles, TD; *d* 1977; *s* by his el son **(3)** ROGER MYNORS SWINFEN, 3rd Baron and present peer.

SWINTON, EARL OF (Cunliffe-Lister) (Earl UK 1955)

DAVID YARBURGH CUNLIFFE-LISTER, 2nd Earl; *b* 21 March 1937; *s* 1972; *ed* Winchester, and Roy Agric Coll, Cirencester; JP and DL N Yorks; CC N Riding of Yorks 1961-74, and N Yorks 1973-77; a Countryside Commr 1987-93; Dep Ch Whip 1982-86, and Capt of the Queen's Body Guard of Yeomen of the Guard 1982-86; Chm RAF Menwith Hill Cttee of British/American Community Relations Cttee; FRSA 1993: *m* 1959, Susan Lilian Primrose (*Baroness Masham of Ilton*) (Life Baroness), yr da of late Sir Ronald Norman John Charles Udny Sinclair, 8th Bt (*cr* 1704), and has two adopted children.

Arms – Quarterly; 1st and 4th ermine, on a fesse sable three mullets or and (for distinction) a cross crosslet of the second, *Lister*; 2nd, sable, three conies courant argent, and (for distinction) a cross crosslet of the last, *Cunliffe*; 3rd, or, two chevronels sable, on a chief of the second three escallops of the first, *Greame*. Crests – 1st, a stag's head proper, erased or, attired sable, charged on the neck (for distinction) with a cross crosslet sable, *Lister*; 2nd a greyhound sejant argent, collared with a ring attached sable, charged on the shoulder (for distinction) with a cross crosslet sable, *Cunliffe*; 3rd, two wings endorsed semee of escallops sable, *Graeme*. Supporters – On either side a stag proper, the dexter gorged with a chain or, suspended from the dexter a rose argent, barbed and seeded proper and from the sinsiter an escallop also argent.

Residence – Dykes Hill House, Masham, Ripon, Yorks HG4 4NS.

ADOPTED SON LIVING

John Charles Yarburgh, *b* 1967.

ADOPTED DAUGHTER LIVING

Clare Caroline, *b* 1965.

BROTHER LIVING (*Raised to the rank of an Earl's son* 1974)

Hon NICHOLAS JOHN (Glebe House, Masham, Ripon, Yorks), *b* 4 Sept 1939; *ed* Winchester, and Worcester Coll, Oxford; late 2nd Lt WG; Solicitor 1966: *m* 1st, 1966 (*m diss* 1996), Hon (Elizabeth) Susan Whitelaw, eldest da of 1st Viscount Whitelaw; 2ndly 1996, Pamela Sykes, and has issue living (by 1st *m*), Mark William Philip, *b* 1970, — Simon Charles, *b* 1977; *s* his kinsman Marcus William Wickham-Boynton in Burton Agnes, E Yorks, 1989, — Lorna Mary, *b* 1968.

COLLATERAL BRANCH LIVING

Issue living of late Hon Philip Ingram Cunliffe-Lister, DFC, DSO, yr son of 1st Earl, *b* 1918, *d* 1956: *m* 1st, 1940 (*m diss* 1947), Rosina Gladys, da of A. G. Emburey, of Cambridge; 2ndly, 1947, Mary Stewart (who *d* 1978, having *m* 3rdly, 1958 (*m diss* 1969), Robert Alexander Pleasant Craigie, and resumed the surname of Cunliffe-Lister by deed poll 1973; *m* 4thly, 1977, Maj Patrick Robert Reid, MBE, MC, who *d* 1990), da of late Robert G. Leggatt, of Hamilton, Lanarks, and formerly wife of Robert Noel Stewart-Humphries:—
(By 2nd *m*) (Julian) Michael (17 Annington Rd, Eastbourne, E Sussex BN22 8NG), *b* 1949; *ed* Uppingham: *m* 1976 (*m diss* 1989), Penelope Susan, only da of Lt-Col David A. Pinner, of White Cottage, Sandhurst Lane, Little Common, Bexhill, E Sussex, and has issue living, Constance Alexandra Elise, *b* 1979. —— (By 1st *m*) Simone Philippa Judith Clare, *b* 1943; resumed her maiden name 1976: *m* 1st, 1965 (*m diss* 1980), Jack Frederick Deakin; 2ndly, 1986, Keith Howell, and has issue living (by 1st *m*), Lorna-Jane CUNLIFFE-LISTER, *b* 1970, — Deborah Simone Jackeline CUNLIFFE-LISTER, *b* 1971. *Residence* – 28 Ashenden Rd, Guildford, Surrey GU2 5XE. —— (By 2nd *m*) Madeline Frances Anne, *b* 1950. *Residence* – 76 South St, Lewes, E Sussex.

PREDECESSORS – (1) *Rt Hon Sir* PHILIP Cunliffe-Lister, GBE, CH, MC, son of late Lt-Col Yarburgh George Lloyd-Greame, of Sewerby House, Bridlington; *b* 1884; assumed by Roy licence 1924 the surname of Cunliffe-Lister; Pres of Board of Trade 1922-24, 1924-29, and 1931; Sec of State for Colonies 1931-35, and for Air 1935-38; Min Resident in W Africa 1942-44; Min of Civil Aviation 1944-45; Chancellor of The Duchy of Lancaster and Min of Materials 1951-52, and Sec of State for Commonwealth Relations 1952-55; MP for Hendon (*C*) 1918-35; *Viscount Swinton*, of Masham, co York (peerage of UK) 1935, and *Baron Masham*, of Ellington, co York and *Earl of Swinton* (peerage of UK) 1955: *m* 1912, Mary Constance, who *d* 1974, da of late Rev Charles Ingram William Boynton (Boynton, Bt colls); *d* 1972; *s* by his grandson (2) DAVID YARBURGH (son of late Maj Hon John Yarburgh Cunliffe-Lister, el son of 1st Earl), 2nd Earl, and present peer; also Viscount Swinton and Baron Masham.

SYMONS OF VERNHAM DEAN, BARONESS (Symons) (Life Baroness 1996)

ELIZABETH CONWAY SYMONS, da of late Ernest Vize Symons, CB, of Richmond, Surrey; *b* 14 April 1951; *ed* Putney High Sch for Girls, and Girton Coll, Camb (MA 19—); Admin Trainee, Dept of Environment 1974-77; Dep Gen Sec, Inland Revenue Staff Federation 1988-89 (Assist Sec 1977-88); Gen Sec Assoc of First Division Civil Servants 1989-96; Memb Gen Council, TUC 1989-96, Civil Service Coll Advisory Council, Council of Hansard Soc 1993-97, Exec Council Campaign for Freedom of Information, Council The Industrial Soc, and Council Open Univ; Commr Equal Opportunities Commn; Govr London Business Sch 1995-97; Trustee Inst of Public Policy Research 1994-97; Hon Assoc Nat Council of Women 1990-97; Parliamentary Under-Sec of State, Foreign and Commonwealth Office since 1997; Min for Overseas Territories since 1988; FRSA; *cr Baroness Symons of Vernham Dean*, of Vernham Dean, co Hants (Life Baroness) 1996: has issue (by Philip Alan Bassett).
Address – House of Lords, Westminster, SW1A 0PW.

SON LIVING

James Alexander BASSETT SYMONS, *b* 1985.

SYSONBY, BARON (Ponsonby) (Baron UK 1935)

For the king, the law, and the people

JOHN FREDERICK PONSONBY, 3rd Baron; *b* 5 Aug 1945; *s* 1956.

𝕬rms – Gules, a chevron between three combs argent. Crest – Out of a ducal coronet azure three arrows, points downards, one in pale and two in saltire, entwined at the intersection by a snake proper. Supporters – On either side a lion guardant crowned with a Saxon crown or, and charged on the shoulder with a key, wards downwards and inwards azure.
Address – c/o Birch Cullimore, Solicitors, Friars, White Friars, Chester CH1 1XS.

SISTER LIVING

Hon Carolyn Mary, *b* 1938.

PREDECESSORS – (1) *Rt Hon Sir* FREDERICK EDWARD GREY Ponsonby, GCB, GCVO, son of late Gen the Rt Hon Sir Henry Frederick Ponsonby, GCB, GCVO (E Bessborough, colls); *b* 1867; formerly Major and Brevet Lieut-Col Grenadier Guards; was an Equerry-in-Ordinary to Queen Victoria 1894-1901, Assist Keeper of the Privy Purse and Assist Private Sec to Queen Victoria 1897-1901, and Equerry-in-Ordinary, an Assist Keeper of the Privy Purse, and an Assist Private Sec to King Edward VII 1901-10; appointed an Equerry-in-Ordinary to HM King George V 1910, Keeper of HM's Privy Purse and an Extra Equerry 1914, Treasurer to the King and Keeper of the Privy Purse 1920, and Lieut-Gov of Windsor Castle and Constable of the Round Tower 1928; Receiver-Gen of Duchy of Lancaster; S Africa 1901-2, European War 1914; *cr Baron Sysonby*, of Wonersh, co Surrey (peerage of United Kingdom) June 1935: *m* 1889, Victoria Lily Hegan, who *d* 1955, da of late Col Edmund Hegan Kennard of 25 Bruton Street, W; *d* Oct 1935; *s* by his son (2) EDWARD GASPARD, DSO, 2nd Baron, *b* 1903; Lieut-Col 5th Batn Queen's Roy Regt (TA); European War 1939-40 (DSO): *m* 1936, Sallie Whitney, who *d* 1979, having *m* 3rdly, 1958, Maj Edward Robert Francis Compton (M Northampton, colls), da of Dr Leonard Cutler Sanford, of New York, USA, and formerly wife of George Edward Monkland; *d* 1956; *s* by his only son (3) JOHN FREDERICK, 3rd Baron and present peer.

Talbot, Earl; title borne by Earl of Shrewsbury.

TALBOT OF MALAHIDE, BARON (Arundell) (Baron I 1831)

Strong and faithful

(REGINALD) JOHN RICHARD ARUNDELL, 10th Baron; *b* 9 Jan 1931; *s* 1987; *ed* Stonyhurst; DL Wilts 1983, Vice Lord-Lieut since 1996; KStJ; Hereditary Lord Admiral of Malahide and Adjacent Seas: *m* 1st, 1955, Laura Duff, who *d* 1989, da of late Group-Capt John Edward Tennant, DSO, MC (*see* B Glenconner, colls); 2ndly, 1992, Mrs Patricia Mary Blundell-Brown, eldest da of late John Cuthbert Widdrington Riddell, OBE, of Felton Park, and Swinburne Castle, Northumberland, and formerly wife of late Maj Geoffrey Thomas Blundell-Brown, MBE, and has issue by 1st *m*.

𝕬rms – Quarterly: 1st and 4th, sable six martlets three two and one argent, *Arundell*; 2nd and 3rd, gules a lion rampant or within a bordure engrailed erminois, *Talbot*. Crests – 1st, a wolf passant argent, *Arundell* 2nd, on a chapeau gules doubled ermine a lion passant erminois, *Talbot* Supporters – *Dexter*, a talbot or; *sinister*, a lion gules. Motto – Deo data.
Seat – Malahide Castle, co Dublin. *Residence* – Park Gate, Donhead St Andrew, nr Shaftesbury, Dorset SP7 9EU.

SON LIVING (*By 1st marriage*)

Hon RICHARD JOHN TENNANT, *b* 28 March 1957; *ed* Stonyhurst, and RAC Cirencester; commn'd Royal Wessex Yeo (TA) 1979; JP Salisbury 1991: *m* 1984, Jane Catherine, da of Timothy Heathcote Unwin, MFH, of Dowmans Farm, Coberley, Glos, and has issue living, John Richard, *b* 25 June 1998, —

Isabel Mary, *b* 1986, — Emily Rose, *b* 1988, — Frances Laura, *b* 1990, — Lucinda Jane, *b* 1991. *Residence* – Hook Manor, Donhead St Andrew, Shaftesbury, Dorset SP7 9EU.

DAUGHTERS LIVING *(By 1st marriage)*

Hon Juliet Anne Tennant, *b* 1959: *m* 1987, Simon James Teakle, son of John Anthony Teakle, MRCVS, of Southover Old House, Lewes, Sussex, and has issue living, Humphrey, *b* 1990, — George, *b* 1991, — Sophie, *b* 1988, — Laura, *b* 1993.

Hon Catherine Mary Tennant, *b* 1960: *m* 1993, Andrew G. Allwood, only son of C. M. Allwood, of Ferndown, Dorset, and had issue living, Arthur Otto, *b* 1996, — Edward Ignatius, *b* 1997, — Mary Jane, *b* 1994.

Hon (Caroline) Rose Tennant, *b* 1962: *m* 1998, Jonathan Charles Oliver Peel, 2nd son of late Rev Edward Beechey Peel, of Stratton Audley, Oxon.

Hon Lucy Veronica Tennant, *b* 1965: *m* 1991, Christopher S. Daniel, only son of Lt Cdr J. J. S. Daniel, of W Meon, Hants, and has issue living, Jack Benedict, *b* 1995, — Poppy Laura, *b* 1997.

BROTHER LIVING *(Raised to the rank of a Baron's son 1991)*

Hon Edward Renfric, *b* 1933; *ed* Oratory Sch, and RMA Sandhurst; commn'd Duke of Cornwall's LI; Maj: *m* 1961, Margaret Ann Honoria, da of Brig John Francis Macnab, CBE, DSO, and has issue living, Lucinda Margaret Beatrice, *b* 1962: *m* 1987, Dr Steven Roy Nash, MB BS, MRCGP, son of Roy Nash, of Liskeard, Cornwall, and has issue living, Edward Mungo Steven *b* 1990, Emma Margaret Alice *b* 1988, Tertia Mary *b* 1993, Flora May *b* 1995, — Camilla Edwina Clare (82 Edith Grove, SW10 0NH), *b* 1965, — Nicola Marina Merry, *b* 1967: *m* 1992, Dominic Peter Craven Chambers, of Trafalgar Houseboat, 106 Cheyne Walk, SW10 0DG (*see* L Herries, colls). *Residence* – 12 Tower Park, Fowey, Cornwall PL23 1JB.

DAUGHTER LIVING OF EIGHTH BARON

Hon Ann Cecily Mary, *b* 1931: *m* 1955, Col Edward Reginald Edwards, and has issue living, Edward David (The Cottage, Back St, Modbury, Devon PL21 0RF), *b* 1956: *m* 1996, Sarah Elizabeth Hudson, and has issue living, Cecily Evelyn *b* 1998, — John Llewellyn, *b* 1958: *m* 1990, Susan Elizabeth Breen, and has issue living, Joshua Talbot *b* 1993, Edwin Jack *b* 1997, — Richard Reginald, *b* 1973. *Residence* – Malahide, Whiteway, Litton Cheney, Dorchester, Dorset DT2 9AG.

SISTER LIVING OF SEVENTH BARON *(Raised to the rank of a Baron's daughter 1949)*

Hon Rose Maud (Malahide, Fingal, Tasmania, Australia 7214), *b* 1915.

COLLATERAL BRANCHES LIVING

Grandchildren of late Joseph Hubert Edward Pius Talbot, 2nd son of late Reginald Aloysius Talbot, 3rd son of late John Reginald Francis George Talbot, elder son of Adm Hon Sir John Talbot, GCB, 3rd son of 1st Baroness:—
Issue of late Clive Richard Talbot, *b* 1943, *d* 1994: *m* 1965, Pamela Maureen (41 Headland Av, Seaford, E Sussex BN25 4PZ), da of Basil Coxwell, of Bahia, Brazil:—
Richard Paul (c/o MOD (Navy)), *b* 1966; *ed* RNC Dartmouth; Lt Cmdr RN, cmd'd HMSs *Kingfisher* and *Arun*: *m* 1996, Emma Katherine, da of Derek Harrison, of Guernsey, CI, and has issue living, Edward Benedict Richard, *b* 1999, — Camilla Isabel Katherine, *b* 1997. —— *Rev* Anthony John, *b* 1967; *ed* Reading Univ (BSc), and Oscott Seminary (Louvain Univ (STB)); ordained priest 1995. —— Michael Hugh Arnold, *b* 1977; *ed* Newlands Sch and Southampton Univ. —— Stephen Edward, *b* 1981; *ed* Oratory. —— Nicola Louise Cecilia, *b* 1970; *ed* Essex Univ (BSc, PhD): *m* 1997, Dr Gavin Cawley, of 8 Lindley St, Lakenham, Norwich. —— Frances Mary, *b* 1984.

Grandchildren of late Reginald Aloysius Talbot (infra):—
Issue of late Robert Peter Frederick Gerard Talbot, *b* 1916, *d* 1995: *m* 1944 (*m diss* 1983), Blanche Edna, da of late Herbert Albert Caseley:—
Anthony Robert John (59 Vandyke, Great Hollands, Bracknell, Berks), *b* 1946: *m* 1970, Patricia Ayliffe Doris, da of Arthur Edward Davis, and has issue living, Christopher Anthony Matthew, *b* 1979, — Claire Elizabeth Patricia, *b* 1976. —— Catherine Blanche Mary, *b* 1944.

Granddaughter of late John Reginald Francis George Talbot (ante):—
Issue of late Reginald Aloysius Talbot, *b* 1870, *d* 1922: *m* 1898, Mabile Mary, who *d* 1942, da of late Hon Robert Arthur Arundell (B Arundell of Wardour, colls):—
Lucy Geraldine Mary (Maryfield Residential Home, London Rd, Hook, Hants RG27 9LA), *b* 1907.

PREDECESSORS – Richard Talbot, of Malahide Castle, heir male of the ancient Lords of Malahide (barons by tenure): *m* (1) MARGARET, el da of James O'Reilly, Esq, of Ballinlough, co Westmeath (of the Milesian princely house of Breffney); she was *cr* 1831 *Baroness Talbot of Malahide* and *Lady Malahide of Malahide*, co Dublin (peerage of Ireland), with remainder to her issue male by her late husband Richard Talbot; *d* 1834: s by her el son (2) RICHARD WOGAN, 2nd Baron; *cr Baron Furnival* (peerage of United Kingdom) 1839; *d* 1849; without surviving male issue, when the Barony of Furnival became extinct, and the Barony of Talbot of Malahide devolved upon his brother (3) JAMES, 3rd Baron; *b* 1767; *d* 1850; *s* by his son (4) JAMES, LLD, FRS, 4th Baron; *b* 1805; sat as MP for Athlone (L) 1832-5; *cr Baron Talbot de Malahide* (peerage of United Kingdom) 1856: *m* 1842, Maria Margaretta, who *d* 1873, da of Patrick Murray, of Simprim, Forfarshire; *d* 1883; *s* by his son (5) RICHARD WOGAN, 5th Baron; *b* 1846: *m* 1st, 1873, Emily Harriet, who *d* 1898, da of Sir James Boswell, 2nd Bt (*ext*); 2ndly, 1901, Dame Isabel Charlotte, DBE, who *d* 1932, da of late Robert Blake Humfrey, of Wroxham House, Norwich, and widow of John Gurney, of Sprowston Hall, Norfolk; *d* 1921; *s* by his son (6) JAMES

BOSWELL, 6th Baron; *b* 1874: *m* 1924, Joyce Gunning, who *d* 1980, da of late Frederick Kerr, formerly of 84 Coleherne Court, SW5 *d* 1948; *s* by his cousin **(7)** MILO JOHN REGINALD, CMG (son of late Col Hon Milo George Talbot, CB, 4th son of 4th Baron), 7th Baron; *b* 1912; Ambassador to Laos 1955-56; *d* 1973, when the UK *Barony of Talbot de Malahide* became ext; *s* in the Irish peerage of *Baron Talbot of Malahide*, by his Kinsman **(8)** REGINALD STANISLAUS VICTOR, MC (2nd son of John Reginald Charles Talbot, grandson of Adm Hon Sir John Talbot, GCB, 3rd son of 1st Baroness), 8th Baron; *b* 1897: *m* 1924, Cecily Elizabeth, who *d* 1976, da of Maj Garstang Hodgson, of Clevedon, Som; *d* 1975; *s* by his brother **(9)** JOSEPH HUBERT GEORGE, 9th Baron, *b* 1899; Lieut Coldm Gds: *m* 1st, 1924, Hélène, who *d* 1961, da of M. Gouley, of Bessancourt, Seine-et-Oise, France; 2ndly, 1962 (*m diss* 1970), Beatrice Bros, of 20 rue Frederic, Passy, Nice; *d* 1987; *s* by his 1st cousin once removed **(10)** REGINALD JOHN RICHARD ARUNDELL (son of late Reginald John Arthur ARUNDELL, who assumed the surname and arms of Arundell in lieu of his patronymic, by Royal Licence 1945, eldest son of late Reginald Aloysius Talbot (grandson of Adm Hon Sir John Talbot, 3rd son of 1st Baroness), by his wife Mabile Mary, da of Hon Robert Arthur Arundell, 4th son of 9th Baron Arundell of Wardour), 10th Baron and present peer.

Talbot, Chetwynd-, family name of Earl of Shrewsbury.

Tamworth, Viscount; son of Earl Ferrers.

TANGLEY, BARONY OF (Herbert) (Extinct 1973)

SON LIVING OF LIFE BARON

Hon Peter Meldrum, *b* 1936: *m* 1961, Annabel Evelyn, da of Stephen Binnie, and has issue living, Julian Tangley, *b* 1964, — James Meldrum, *b* 1965; Lieut 6th QEO Rifles: *m* 1990, Helen S., only da of Peter Palmer, of White Beeches, Moss Green Lane, Brayton, N Yorks.

DAUGHTERS LIVING OF LIFE BARON

Hon Elizabeth Ann, *b* 1933; *ed* Oxford Univ (MA, BM, BCh): *m* 1960, Hon Michael Cottrell Brain, DM, of 131, Northshore Blvd E, Burlington, Ontario, Canada (*see* B Brain).

Hon Jane Katherine, *b* 1938; GRSM, LRAM: *m* 1964, George Kenneth Beattie, CBE, RD, DL, of Big Oak, Churt, Farnham, Surrey, who *d* 1994, and has issue.

Hon Alison Margaret, *b* 1943; LRAM, ARCM: *m* 1965, John Michael Bradshaw, of Cherrydale, W Clandon, Surrey, and has issue.

TANKERVILLE, EARL OF (Bennet) (Earl GB 1714)

To serve the king with good will

PETER GREY BENNET, 10th Earl; *b* 18 Oct 1956; *s* 1980; *ed* Grace Cathedral Sch (chorister), San Francisco, and Oberlin Conservatory, Ohio (B Mus), MA (Mus) San Francisco State Univ.

Arms – Gules, three demi-lions rampant argent, in the centre point a bezant. **Crest** – 1st, out of a mural coronet or, a lion's head gules, charged on the neck with a bezant; 2nd, a scaling ladder or. **Supporters** – Two lions argent, ducally crowned or, and charged on the shoulder with a torteau.
Seat – Chillingham Castle, Alnwick, Northumberland.
Residence – 139 Olympia Way, San Francisco, Cal 94131, USA.

SISTER LIVING

Lady Anne Thérèse *b* (twin) 1956: *m* 1981, Timothy Michael Poirier.

UNCLE LIVING *(son of 8th Earl by 1st m)*

Rev the Hon GEORGE ARTHUR GREY (112 Norwich Rd, Wymondham, Norfolk NR18 0SZ), *b* 12 March 1925; *ed* Radley, and Corpus Christi Coll, Camb (MA); V in Shaston Team Min 1973-80; Rector of Redenhall, Harleston, Wortwell and Needham 1980-90; author of *Electricity and Modern Physics* (1965), *Progress through Lent* (1993), *One Fold, One Shepherd* (1996): *m* 1957, Hazel (Jane) G., da of late Ernest W. G. Judson, of Bishopswood, Chard, Somerset, and has issue living, Adrian George (The Loaning, Reston, Eyemouth, Berwicks TD14 5LD), *b* 1958: *m* 1st, 1984 (*m diss* 1991), Lucinda Mary, eldest da of Ashley Bell, of Weetwood Hall, Wooler, Northumberland; 2ndly, 1991, Karel Ingrid Juliet Wensby-Scott, — Neil Robert (112 Norwich Rd, Wymondham, Norfolk NR18 0SZ), *b* 1961, — Helen Jane (26 The Quadrangle, Herne Hill, SE24 9QR), *b* 1964.

HALF-UNCLE DECEASED *(son of 8th Earl by 2nd marriage)*

Hon Ian, *b* 1935; *ed* Radley, and Corpus Christi Coll, Camb (MA); Lt RNR; *dunm* 1998.

HALF-AUNT LIVING *(daughter of 8th Earl by 2nd marriage)*

Lady Corisande, *b* 1938: *m* 1963, Lt-Cdr Timothy Bain Smith, RN, of Wickens Manor, Charing, Kent, and has issue living, James, *b* 1964; *ed* Winchester, — Charles, *b* 1966; *ed* Winchester: *m* 1993, Rebecca J. Murphy.

WIDOW LIVING OF EIGHTH EARL

VIOLET (*Dowager Countess of Tankerville*), (Estate House, Chillingham, Alnwick, Northumberland), da of Erik Pallin, of Stockholm; JP of Northumberland; has Order of Vasa of Sweden: *m* 1930, as his 2nd wife, the 8th Earl of Tankerville, who *d* 1971.

PREDECESSORS – **(1)** *Sir* JOHN Bennet, KB, el son of late Sir John Bennet, of Dawley; *cr Baron Ossulston*, of Ossulston, co Middlesex (peerage of England) 1682; he and the heirs male of his body are in special remainder to the titles of his younger brother Henry, who was *cr Baron Arlington*, of Arlington, co Middlesex, *Viscount Thetford* and *Earl of Arlington* (peerage of England) 1672: *m* 1st, 1661, Lady Elizabeth, who *d* 1672, da of 1st Earl of Middlesex, and widow of 2nd Earl of Mulgrave; 2ndly, 1673, Bridget, who *d* 1703, da of John Grubham Howe, of Langar, Nottingham: *d* 1682; *s* by his son **(2)** CHARLES, KT, 2nd Baron: *m* 1695, Lady Mary Grey, da and heiress of 1st and last Earl of Tankerville (*cr* 1695), and after the demise of his father-in-law he was *cr Earl of Tankerville* (peerage of Great Britain); *d* 1722; *s* by his son **(3)** CHARLES, KT, 2nd Earl; filled several high positions about the Court 1728-40: *m* 17-, Camilla, who *d* 1775, da of late Edward Colville, of Whitehouse, Durham; *d* 1753; *s* by his son **(4)** CHARLES, 3rd Earl; MP for Northumberland 1748-53: *m* 1742, Alicia, who *d* 1775, da of Sir John Astley, 2nd Bt (*cr* 1662, ext); *d* 1767; *s* by his son **(5)** CHARLES, 4th Earl: *m* 1771, Emma, who *d* 1836, da of Sir James Colebrook, Bt; *d* 1822; *s* by his son **(6)** CHARLES AUGUSTUS, PC, 5th Earl; *b* 1776; Joint Postmaster-Gen 1782-3 and 1784-6: *m* 1806, Corisande Armandine Sophie Leónice Helene, who *d* 1865, da of Antoine, Duke de Gramont; *d* 1859; *s* by his son **(7)** CHARLES, 6th Earl; *b* 1810; MP for N Northumberland (C) 1832-59, Capt Hon Corps of Gentlemen-at-Arms 1866-7, and Lord Steward of the Household 1867-8; summoned to House of Lords in his father's Barony of Ossulston 1859: *m* 1850, Lady Olivia Montagu, who *d* 1922, el da of 6th Duke of Manchester; *d* 1899; *s* by his second son **(8)** GEORGE MONTAGU, 7th Earl, *b* 1852: *m* 1895, Leonora Sophia, who *d* 1949, da of late J. G. van Marter, sometime of New York; *d* 1931; *s* by his el son **(9)** CHARLES AUGUSTUS KER, 8th Earl, *b* 1897: *m* 1st, 1920 (*m diss* 1930), Roberta, who *d* 1992, da of Julian Nolan, of Chicago, USA, and step-da of Dr Percy Mitchell; 2ndly, 1930, Violet, JP, da of Erik Pallin, of Stockholm; *d* 1971; *s* by his son **(10)** CHARLES AUGUSTUS GREY, 9th Earl, *b* 1921: *m* 1st, 1943 (*m diss* 1950), Virginia, who *d* ca 1967, da of late Louis M. Diether, of Vancouver, and formerly wife of — Morris; 2ndly, 1954, Georgiana Lilian Maude, who *d* 1998, da of late Gilbert Wilson, DD, MA, PhD, of Vancouver, BC; *d* 1980; *s* by his only son **(11)** PETER GREY, 10th Earl and present peer; also Baron Ossulston.

TANLAW, BARON (Mackay) (Life Baron 1971)

SIMON BROOKE MACKAY, yst son of 2nd Earl of Inchcape; *b* 30 March 1934; *ed* Eton, and Trin Coll, Camb (MA); Dir of Inchcape & Co, Ltd 1966-92; Chmn and Man Dir of Private Group of Cos since 1973; Hon Treasurer, Scottish Peers Assoc 1979-85; Pres Sarawak Assocn 1972-75; Member Council of Management, Univ of Buckingham since 1973 (Hon Fellow 1981); Member Court of Governors of London Sch of Economics and Political Science 1980-94; Fellow British Horological Inst 1996; *cr Baron Tanlaw, of Tanlawhill, co Dumfries (Life Baron)* 1971: *m* 1st, 1959, Joanna Susan, only da of late Maj John Henry Hirsch, of Sungrove Lodge, Newbury; 2ndly, 1976, Rina Siew Yong, yst da of late Tiong Cha Tan, of Kuala Lumpur, Malaysia, and has had issue by 1st and 2nd *m*.

Arms – Parted per chevron azure and argent, in chief two lymphads of the 2nd and in base a tiger's face affrontée proper, on a chief or a cross engrailed per cross indented azure and sable. **Crest** – A falcon proper, hooded gules, issuant out of a five-pointed Eastern crown or. **Supporters** – *Dexter*, a Prejevalski's mare proper; *sinister*, a roe deer also proper.
Residences – Tanlawhill, Eskdalemuir, Dumfries-shire DG13 0PQ; 31 Brompton Sq, SW3 2AE.

SONS LIVING AND DECEASED *(By 1st marriage)*

Hon James Brooke, *b* 1961: *m* 1993, Anne-Marie, yr da of Michael Barrett, of Midsomer Norton, Som.
†Joshua Alexander Brooke, *b* 1964; *d* 1967.

(By 2nd marriage)

Hon Brooke Brooke, *b* 1982.

DAUGHTERS LIVING *(By 1st marriage)*

Hon Iona Hélöise MACKAY, *b* 1960; has resumed her maiden name: *m* 1978 (*m diss* 1988), Stephen P. Hudson.
Hon Rebecca Alexandra, *b* 1967: *m* 1995, R. Mark Ayre-Smith, only son of Dr Robert Ayre-Smith, of Sydney.

(By 2nd marriage)

Hon Asia Brooke, *b* 1980.

Tarbat, Viscount; son of Earl of Cromartie.

TAVERNE, BARON (Taverne) (Life Baron 1996)

DICK TAVERNE, QC, son of late Dr Nicolaas Jacobus Marie Taverne; *b* 18 Oct 1928; *ed* Charterhouse, and Balliol Coll, Oxford; Bar-at-Law Middle Temple 1954; QC 1965; MP for Lincoln (*Lab*) 1962-72, Parliamentary Sec Home Office 1966-68, Min of State, Treasury 1968-69, Fin Sec 1969-70; resigned from Labour Party 1972; MP for Lincoln (Independent Social Democrat) 1973-74; first Dir Inst for Fiscal Studies 1971 (Chm 1979-83); Chm Public Policy Centre 1984-87; British Memb Spierenburg Cttee to examine working of Euro Commn 1979; Pres PRIMA Europe 1994-98 (Dir since 1987, Chm 1991-94); Chm OLIM Convertible Trust since 1989; Dep Chm Central European Growth Fund since 1995; Chm Axa Equity and Law since 1998 (Dir since 1972), Oxford Centre for the Environment, Ethics and Society since 1997, Alcohol and Drug Abuse Prevention and Treatment since 1996; *cr Baron Taverne*, of Pimlico in the City of Westminster (Life Baron) 1996: *m* 1955, Janice, da of late Dr Robert Samuel Fleming Hennessey, of Beckenham, Kent, and has issue.

Residence – 60 Cambridge St, SW1V 4QQ.

DAUGHTERS LIVING

Hon Suzanna, *b* 1960: *m* 19—, Marc Vlessing.
Hon Caroline, *b* 1963.

Tavistock, Marquess of; son of Duke of Bedford.

TAYLOR, BARONY OF (Taylor) (Extinct 1988)

SONS LIVING OF LIFE BARON

Hon Jeremy Stephen (12 Wymond St, Putney, SW15 1DY), *b* 1940; *ed* Highgate; a Television Executive: *m* 1964, Christina, yr da of late John Bruce Holmes, of 37 Redington Rd, NW3 (*see* L Forbes, colls, 1968 edn), and has issue.

Hon Charles Richard Herbert (3911 Argyle Terr NW, Washington DC 20011, USA), *b* 1950; *ed* Highgate, King's Coll, Camb, Queen's and St Antony's Colls, Oxon, and Wharton Business Sch, Univ of Pennsylvania; Economist, Arthur Andersen: *m* 1977, Mary-Ellen, da of late John Feeney, of 1543 North Hills Av, Willow Gr, Pa 19090, USA, and has issue.

DAUGHTER LIVING OF LIFE BARON

Hon Elizabeth Trilby Charity, *b* 1943; *ed* Univ of Sussex; Librarian, BTG International Ltd: *m* 1st, 1971 (*m diss* 1986), Paul Stephen Masterman; 2ndly, 1986, Alan George Woodruff, of 26 Lucastes Lane, Haywards Heath, W Sussex RH16 1LD.

Taylor, family name of Baron Ingrow.

TAYLOR OF BLACKBURN, BARON (Taylor) (Life Baron 1978)

THOMAS TAYLOR, CBE, son of James Taylor, *b* 10 June 1929; *ed* Blakey Moor Higher Grade Sch; Member of Blackburn Town Council 1954-76 (Leader 1972-76, and Chm Policy and Resources Cttee 1972-76); a Member of N-W Economic Planning Council, N-W and Area Health Authority; Dept Pro-Chancellor of Lancaster Univ since 1974; (Member of Council and Founder Member); a Member of Council for Education and Technology in UK, of Nat Foundation for Educational Research in England and Wales, and of Schs Council; author of Taylor Report on problems at Lancaster Univ 1973; Chm, Govt Cttee of Enquiry into Management and Govt of Schs, and of Nat Foundation for Visual Aids; JP of Blackburn, Lancs; Past Chm of Juvenile Bench; Sunday Sch Supt 1947-59, and Pres Free Church Council 1962-68; Elder of United Reform Church; Treas, Blackburn Labour Party 1964-76; Member of Norweb Board and consultant, Shorrock Security Systems Ltd, Chm Thames Internat plc and other cos: *cr* OBE (Civil) 1969, CBE (Civil) 1974, and *Baron Taylor of Blackburn*, of Blackburn, co Lancaster (Life Baron) 1978: *m* 1950, Kathleen, da of John Edward Nurton, and has issue.

Arms – Argent a bar wavy cottised wavy sable between three roses gules barbed and seeded proper all within a bordure vert thereon eight bees volant proper. **Crest** – Statant on a grassy mount proper a lion or supporting with the dexter forepaw at its base growing from the front of the mount a rose branch proper reflexed over the lion's back and ending in three roses gules barbed and seeded proper on the mid-most a bee also proper. **Supporters** – *Dexter*, a dragon statant erect gules eyed langued clawed and the barb of its tail or gorged with a bar wavy sable fimbriated argent and in its jaws an olive branch proper; *Sinister*, a bull statant erect in trian aspect gules armed and unguled and the tuft of its tail or also gorged with a bar wavy sable fimbriated argent and also holding in its mouth an olive branch proper.
Residence – 34 Tower Rd, Feniscliffe, Blackburn, Lancs.

SON LIVING

Hon Paul Nurton (1 Risdale Grove, Blackburn), *b* 1953: *m* 1978, Diane Brindle.

TAYLOR OF GOSFORTH, BARONY OF (Taylor) (Extinct 1997)

SON LIVING OF LIFE BARON

Hon (David) Louis, *b* —: *m* 19—, Kate A. M. G., yr da of Prof Robert Riddell, of Auckland, NZ.

DAUGHTERS LIVING OF LIFE BARON

Hon Ruth Diana, *b* 1958: *m* 19—, Robert J. Torday.
Hon Deborah Frances, *b* 1959: *m* 1987, Michael Stevenson, and has issue living, one son.
Hon Judith Claire, *b* 1961: *m* 1986, Paul Bridge, and has issue living, one da.

TAYLOR OF GRYFE, BARON (Taylor) (Life Baron 1968)

THOMAS JOHNSTON TAYLOR, son of John Sharp Taylor, of Glasgow; *b* 27 April 1912; *ed* Ballahouston Acad, Glasgow; Chm of Forestry Commn 1970-76, and of Morgan Grenfell (Scotland), Ltd; Chm of Economic Forestry Group 1976-82; Fellow R Soc of Edinburgh since 1977; DL, LLD (Strathclyde) since 1974; a Member of Exec Cttee, Scottish Council (Development and Industry) since 1964, of British Railways Board, and a Board Member of Scottish Television Ltd 1968-82, and of Friends Provident and Century Group 1972-82; a Dir Whiteways Laidlaw & Co 1971-88, Chm Isaac and Edith Wolfson Trust 1971-88, Trustee Dulverton Trust, Chm Scottish Peers Assocn since 1987, All Party Parliamentary Forestry Group, and Scottish Metropolitan Property Co Ltd since 1972; Vice-Chm All Party Minerals Group; *cr Baron Taylor of Gryfe*, of Bridge of Weir, Renfrewshire (Life Baron) 1968: *m* 1943, Isobel, da of Williams Wands, and has issue.

Residence – Glentyan, 33 Seagate, Kingsbarns, Fife K16 8SR. *Clubs* – Caledonian (London); Royal & Ancient.

DAUGHTERS LIVING

Hon Jill, *b* 1945: *m* 1st, 1969, Dr Thomas Egli; 2ndly, 1976, Hans Wäber.
Hon Joyce (1 Woodland Rise, Muswell Hill, N10 3UP), *b* 1948: *m* 1st, 1969 (*m diss* 1980), Alan Begbie; 2ndly, 1982, John Huw Lloyd Richards, and has issue living (by 1st *m*).

TAYLOR OF HADFIELD, BARONY OF (Taylor) (Extinct 1995)

DAUGHTERS LIVING OF LIFE BARON (*By 1st marriage*)

Hon Audrey Evelyn, *b* 1932: *m* 1952, Brian Sadler Leigh Trafford, and has had issue, John Tarleton Leigh, *b* 1960; *d* 1985, — David Jeremy Mallory, *b* 1962: *m* 1985, Stephanie Vivien, da of Roger Cambridge Ffooks, of Redhill, Surrey, and has issue living, George William Leigh *b* 1991, Henry John Jeremy *b* 1993, — Judy Evelyn (*Lady Scott*), *b* 1952: *m* 1st, 1972, Andrew Lyndon-Skeggs; 2ndly, 1982, Sir James Jervoise Scott, 3rd Bt (*cr* 1962) and has issue living, (by 1st *m*) Vanessa Evelyn *b* 1975, Tessa Angela *b* 1979, (by 2nd *m*) (*see* Scott, Bt, *cr* 1962), — Diana Barbara (*Viscountess Melgund*), *b* 1954: *m* 1983, Gilbert Timothy George Lariston, Viscount Melgund son of 6th Earl of Minto. *Residence* – Tismans, Rudgwick, Sussex.

Hon Gillian Doreen, *b* 1934: *m* 1st, 1955, Simon Edward Anthony Kimmins, VRD, of Geneva; 2ndly, 1980, Robin Geoffrey Marlar, and has issue living (by 1st *m*), Andrew Simon Taylor, *b* 1958, — Martin Charles Anthony, *b* 1965: *m* 19—, Charlotte Louise, eldest da of Raymond Haslam, of Turton, Lancs, and has issue living, Thomas Charles Anthony *b* 1991, — Robyn Elizabeth Frances, *b* 1957, — Joanna Mary Verena, *b* 1960. *Residence* – Brantyngeshay, Sample Oak Lane, Chilworth, Surrey GU4 8RE.

(*By 2nd marriage*)

Hon C. Sarah A., *b* 1961: *m* 1987, David M. Melville, son of Murray Melville, of Lymington, Hants, and has issue living, John Edward Charles, *b* 1992, — Francis David Peter, *b* 1995, — Mary Diana Christine, *b* 1993.

WIDOW LIVING OF LIFE BARON

CHRISTINE ENID (*Baroness Taylor of Hadfield*), da of Charles Hughes: *m* 1956, as his 2nd wife, Baron Taylor of Hadfield (Life Baron), who *d* 1995.

TAYLOR OF MANSFIELD, BARONY OF (Taylor) (Extinct 1991)

SON LIVING OF LIFE BARON

Hon Bernard Alfred (3 Sycamore Close, Rainworth, nr Mansfield, Notts NG2 0FX), *b* 1922: *m* 1952, Mary K. Green.

TAYLOR OF WARWICK, BARON (Taylor) (Life Baron 1996)

JOHN DAVID BECKETT TAYLOR, son of late Derief David Samuel Taylor, of Warwickshire; b 21 Sept 1952; ed Keele Univ (BA 1976); Bar-at-law, Gray's Inn, 1978; practised Midland and Oxford Circuit 1978-90; Special Advsr to Home Sec and Home Office Ministers 1990-91; Consultant, Lowe Bell Communications Ltd 1991-92; Producer/Presenter, BBC Radio and Television since 1994; Memb Solihull FPC 1986-90; Memb Greater London FEFC Cttee 1994-96; Non exec Dir NW Thames RHA 1992-93; Dir City Technology Colls Tst 1994-95; Memb Solihull District Council 1986-90; Dir Warwick Leadership Foundation, Warwick Consulting Internatnl Ltd; Vice-Pres National Small Business Bureau since 1997, British Board of Film Classification since 1998; Member Inst of Directors since 1998; Barker, Variety Club Children's Charity; Patron, Parents for Children (adoption charity); Memb Exec Cttee Sickle Cell Anaemia Relief; Memb Parliament and Industry Trust; Company Dir; Memb Aston Villa FC; LLD Warwick Univ 1999; Freedom of City of London 1999: cr Baron Taylor of Warwick, of Warwick, co Warwickshire 1996: m 1981, Jean Katherine, da of Dr Harry Binysh, of Hertfordshire, and his issue.
Address – House of Lords, Westminster, SW1A 0PW.

SON LIVING

Hon Mark Thomas Warwick, b 1997.

DAUGHTERS LIVING

Hon Laura Anne Elizabeth, b 1987.
Hon Alexandra Helen Louise, b 1995.

Taylor, Suenson-, family name of Baron Grantchester.

Taylour, family name of Marquess of Headfort.

TAYSIDE, BARONY OF (Urquhart) (Extinct 1975)

SONS LIVING OF LIFE BARON

Hon William James Lauchlan (West Kilmany House, Kilmany, Cupar, Fife), b 1944; ed Fettes Coll, and Glasgow Univ (BSc Hons); CA; Member of Inst of Taxation; m 1967, Wendy Helen, da of late William Campbell Cook, JP, and has issue living Carolyn J. L., b 1971: m 1996, Piers A.C. Coombs, elder son of Col Marcus Coombs, of Westcot, Oxon, — Suzanne E. L., b 1972: m 1998, Christopher R. F. Mallon, elder son of late Christopher Mallon, of co Armagh, — Jacqueline W. L., b 1974.
Hon Ronald Douglas Lauchlan (The Willows, Wonersh Park, Guildford, Surrey GU5 0QP; Caledonian Club, London, and Hong Kong Club), b 1948; ed Fettes Coll, and Edinburgh Univ (LLB); CA: m 1975, Dorothy May Jackson.

DAUGHTER LIVING OF LIFE BARON

Hon Hilda Louise Lauchlan, b 1950; ed St Leonards Sch, St Andrews, and Bedford Coll of Physical Education: m 1978, John Alexander Dalgety.

HILDA GWENDOLINE, BSc (*Baroness Tayside*) (Kallisté, 30 Turfbeg Place, Forfar, Angus), da of John Thomson Harris, of Dundee: *m* 1939, Baron Tayside (Life Baron), who *d* 1975.

TEBBIT, BARON (Tebbit) (Life Baron 1992)

NORMAN BERESFORD TEBBIT, CH, PC, 2nd son of Leonard Albert Tebbit, of Enfield, Middx; *b* 29 March 1931; *ed* Edmonton Co Gram Sch; RAF 1949-51, RAuxAF 1952-55; Airline Pilot 1953-70; Member Select Cttee Science and Technology, Chm Conservative Aviation Cttee, Vice Chm and Sec Conservative Housing and Construction Cttee, Sec New Town MPs, PPS to Min of State for Employment 1972-73, Parly Under Sec of State for Trade 1979-81, Min of State for Industry 1981, Sec of State for Employment 1981-Oct 1983, Sec of State for Trade and Industry Oct 1983-85, Chancellor of Duchy of Lancaster 1985-87, and Chm of Conservative Party 1985-87; MP Epping (*C*) 1970-74, and Waltham Forest, Chingford 1974-92; journalist; *cr* PC 1981, CH 1987 and *Baron Tebbit*, of Chingford, in the London Borough of Waltham Forest (Life Baron) 1992: *m* 1956, Margaret Elizabeth, da of Stanley Daines, of Chatteris, Isle of Ely, and has issue.
Address – c/o House of Lords, SW1 0PW.

SONS LIVING

Hon John Beresford, *b* 1958: *m* 1984, Penelope Robinson, and has issue living, one son and two das.
Hon William Mark, *b* 1965: *m* 1992, Vanessa Hurrell.

DAUGHTER LIVING

Hon Alison Mary, *b* 1960: *m* 1981, Raymond Shakespeare Smith, and has issue living, one son and one da.

TEDDER, BARON (Tedder) (Baron UK 1946)

ROBIN JOHN TEDDER, 3rd Baron; *b* 6 April 1955; *s* 1994; Company Director; Proprietor Glenguin Wine Co; Master of Wine; ASIA: *m* 1st, 1977, Jennifer Peggy, who *d* 1978, da of John Mangan, of New Zealand; 2ndly, 1980, (Rita) Aristea, yr da of John Frangidis, of Sydney, NSW, Australia, and has issue by 2nd *m*.

Arms – Sable, a sword enflamed palewise all proper in chief an eagle affronty volant head to sinister or. Crest – Issuant from an astral crown or a lion sejant guardant sable, armed and langued or, holding in the sinister fore-paw a sword enflamed as in the Arms. Supporters – Two representations of the God Horus all proper.
Residence – 11 Kardinia Rd, Clifton Gds, Sydney, NSW 2088, Australia.

SONS LIVING (*By 2nd marriage*)

Hon Benjamin John, *b* 1985.
Hon Christopher Arthur, *b* 1986.

DAUGHTER LIVING (*By 2nd marriage*)

Hon Jacqueline Christina, *b* 1988.

BROTHER LIVING

Hon Andrew Jonathan (Sydney, NSW, Australia), *b* 1958.

SISTER LIVING

Hon Anne Rosalinde, *b* 1963: *m* 1989, Euan Angus Johnston, son of David Johnston, of Leuchars, Fife, and has issue living, Rory, *b* 1996, — Jade, *b* 1991.

HALF-UNCLE LIVING (*son of 1st Baron by 2nd marriage*)

Hon Richard Seton (W Buckland, Luddesdown, nr Meopham, Kent), *b* 1946: *m* 1st, 1975 (*m diss* 1987), Ann-Marie Adams; 2ndly, 1989, Lesley Anne, yr da of John Coster, of Luddesdown, Kent.

AUNT LIVING (*daughter of 1st Baron by 1st marriage*)

Hon Mina Una Margaret (Openfields, Barnyards, Kilconquhar, Fife), *b* 1920; formerly Assist Librarian, British Embassy, Wash, USA; BBC, TV 1954-7, and Scottish TV Glasgow 1957-65; Dist Commr, Nat Savings, Alnwick, Northumberland.

WIDOW LIVING OF SECOND BARON

PEGGY EILEEN (*Dowager Baroness Tedder*), yr da of Samuel George Growcott, of Birmingham: *m* 1952, 2nd Baron Tedder, who *d* 1994. *Residence* – Little Rathmore, Kennedy Gdns, St Andrews, Fife.

PREDECESSORS – (1) *Marshal of the RAF Sir* ARTHUR WILLIAM Tedder, GCB, yr son of Sir Arthur John Tedder, CB; *b* 1890; 1914-18 War with Dorset Regt, and RFC; ACC Far East, Singapore 1936-38, Dir-Gen of Research and Development, Air Min 1938-40, Dep Air Member for Development and Production 1940, Dep AOC in C Middle East 1940-41, AOC in C Middle East 1941-42, AOC in C Mediterranean 1943, Dep Supreme Cdr SHAEF 1943-45, Ch of Air Staff 1946-49, and Chm of British Joint Sers Mission, Washington USA 1950; Chancellor of Camb Univ 1950-67; *cr Baron Tedder*, of Glenguin, co Stirling (peerage of UK) 1946: *m* 1st, 1915, Rosalinde, who *d* 1943, da of William McIntyre Maclardy, of Sydney, NSW; 2ndly, 1943, Mrs Marie de Seton Black, who *d* 1965, da of Col Sir Bruce Gordon Seton, CB, 9th Bt (*cr* 1663); *d* 1967: *s* by his 2nd son (2) JOHN MICHAEL, 2nd Baron: *b* 1926; FRSE; FRIC; Purdie Prof of Chemistry, Univ of St Andrews: *m* 1952, Peggy Eileen, yr da of Samuel George Growcott, of Birmingham; *d* 1994: *s* by his elder son (3) ROBIN JOHN, 3rd Baron and present peer.

TEIGNMOUTH, BARONY OF (Shore) (Extinct 1981)

WIDOW LIVING OF SEVENTH BARON

PAMELA (*Baroness Teignmouth*) (108 Kensington Church St, W8 4BH), da of late Henry Edmonds-Heath, of Hungerford, Berks, and formerly wife of George Anthony Meyer: *m* 1979, as his 2nd wife, the 7th Baron, DSC and Bar, who *d* 1981, when the title became extinct.

TEMPLE OF STOWE, EARL (Temple-Gore-Langton) (Earl UK 1822)

(WALTER) GRENVILLE ALGERNON TEMPLE-GORE-LANGTON, 8th Earl; *b* 2 Oct 1924; *s* 1988; *ed* Nautical Coll, Pangbourne: *m* 1st, 1954, Zillah Ray, who *d* 1966, da of James Boxall, of Tillington, Petworth, Sussex; 2ndly, 1968, (Margaret) Elizabeth Graham, only da of late Col Henry William Scarth of Breckness, of Skaill House, Orkney, and has issue by 1st *m.*

ᴀrms – Quarterly: 1st and 4th grand quarters, quarterly sable and or, a bend argent, *Langton*: 2nd grand quarter, gules, a fesse between three cross-crosslets fitchée or, *Gore*: 3rd grand quarter, quarterly, 1st and 4th or, an eagle displayed sable; 2nd and 3rd argent, two bars sable, each charged with three martlets or, *Temple*. ᴄrest – 1st, An eagle or and a wyvern vert, their necks entwined reguardant, *Langton*; 2nd, on a mount vert, an heraldic tiger salient argent, ducally gorged or, *Gore*; 3rd on a ducal coronet or, a martlet gold, *Temple*. ᴤupporters – *Dexter*, a lion per fesse nebuly or and gules, gorged with a ribbon of the last, pendant therefrom an escutcheon of the arms of *Langton; sinister*, a horse argent, semée of eaglets displayed sable, gorged with a ribbon gules, pendent therefrom an escutcheon of the arms of *Gore.*
Residences – The Cottage, Easton, Winchester, Hants SO23 1EH; Garth, Outertown, Stromness, Orkney.

SONS LIVING (By 1st marriage)

JAMES GRENVILLE (*Lord Langton*), *b* 11 Sept 1955; *ed* Winchester, and Bristol Univ.

Hon Robert Chandos, *b* 1957; *ed* Eton; journalist: *m* 1985, Susan Penelope, elder da of David Cavender, of The Manor House, Dowlish Wake, Ilminster, Somerset, and of Mrs Jennifer Neubauer, of Smallcombe House, Bath, and has issue living, Louis Grenville, *b* 1990, — Christopher Chandos, *b* 1993, — Georgia Ray, *b* 1989. *Residence* – 46 Brixton Water Lane, SW2 1QE.

DAUGHTER LIVING (By 1st marriage)

Lady Anna Clare, *b* 1960.

SISTER LIVING

Elspeth Dorina, *b* 1926: *m* 1950, Thomas Alfred Spry Carlyon, who *d* 1999, and has issue living, William Thomas Alfred, *b* 1951; *ed* Stowe: *m* 1988, Mrs Alison Jean Humphreys, da of C H J Bellingham, of Cornworthy, Devon, and has issue living, Sam *b* 1991, Thomas *b* (triplet) 1991, Sophie *b* (triplet), 1991, — Nicola Elspeth, *b* 1954. *Residence* – The Glebe, Colan, Newquay, Cornwall TR8 4NB.

SISTER LIVING OF SEVENTH EARL (Raised to the rank of an Earl's daughter 1941)

Lady Elizabeth Ann, *b* 1908: *m* 1927, Group-Capt Peter Bathurst, RAF, who *d* 1970 (*see* E Bathurst, colls). *Residence* – 12A Northanger Court, Grove St, Bath, Avon BA2 6PE.

COLLATERAL BRANCHES LIVING

Grandchildren of late Cdr Hubert Edwin Gore Langton, DSO, RN, 3rd son of late Col Hon Henry Powell Gore Langton, brother of 4th Earl:—
Issue of late Lt-Cdr Alaric Hubert St George Gore Langton, RN, *b* 1918, *d* 1987: *m* 1946, Margaret Edwina (Hatch Park, Hatch Beauchamp, Somerset), elder da of Lt-Col Donald McLeod Douglas, MC, of Sanderstead, Surrey:—
Chandos Alaric Graham, *b* 1949; *ed* Taunton Sch, and St Catherine's Coll, Oxford: *m* 1978, S. Fiona, da of Bernard Collins, of Pitsham Place, Midhurst, Sussex, and has issue living, Chandos James Brydges, *b* 1987, — Emma Lucilla Clare, *b* 1983, — Lucy Fiona Alice, *b* 1985. —— Grenville Julian Brydges, *b* 1954; *ed* Millfield. —— Clare Margaret, *b* (twin) 1954: *m* 1984, Peter E. Jordan, yr son of late Maj H. J. Godfrey Jordan, of Thornhill, Kiltimagh, co Mayo, and has issue living, Henry James Bourke, *b* 1987, — Oliver Charles d'Exeter, *b* (twin) 1987.

Grandchildren of late Robert Lancelot Gore-Langton (infra):—
Issue of late Montagu Grenville Gore-Langton, *b* 1919, *d* 1968: *m* 1944, Wilda Handlen, who *m* 2ndly, 1971, Geoffrey D. Smiley, of 3396, Hilton Rd, Duncan, BC, Canada:—
Robert Edward (650 Grandview, London, Ont, Canada N6K 3G6), *b* 1950; *ed* Victoria Univ, BC (BSc), and Trin Hall, Camb (PhD): *m* 1989, Dr Susan Anne Jennifer Daniel, and has issue living, Jonathan Kent, *b* 1990, — Jena Anne Catherine, *b* 1992. —— Gillian Dixie GORE-LANGTON (588A, 4678 Elk Drive, Victoria, BC V8Z 5MI, Canada), *b* 1945; has resumed her maiden name: *m* 1st, 1963 (*m diss* 1968), George Clifford Madill; 2ndly, 1971 (*m diss* 1978), John Molloy; 3rdly, 1986 (*m dioo* 10), Stanley Morib, and has issue living, (by 1st *m*) Michael George, *b* 1964, — Lance Maurice, *b* 1967, — Susan Lorraine, *b* 1965, — (by 2nd *m*) Shannon Marie, *b* 1973.

Grandchildren of late Col Hon Henry Powell Gore-Langton (ante):—
Issue of late Robert Lancelot Gore-Langton, *b* 1885, *d* 1948: *m* 1914, Winifreda Lilian Margaret, who *d* 1987, da of late Capt Arthur G. Nixon, Rifle Bde (Prince Consort's Own):—

Margaret Coëline, b 1920: m 1944, Andrew William Stewart, RCAF, of 2326 Lincoln Rd, Victoria, BC V8R 6A4, Canada, and has issue living, Ronald David (802-1498 Harwood Av, Vancouver, BC V8G 1X6, Canada), b 1961, — Heather Margaret (144 James St, Ottawa, Ont K1R 5M5, Canada), b 1948: m 1969 (m diss 1988), Peter John Lund, RCMP, of Ottawa, Ont, and has had issue, David Alexander b 1974, d 1998, Wendy Anne b 1969, — Victoria Ann, b 1953: m 1976, Michael Reginald Ziegler, of 350 Beach Drive, Victoria, BC V85 2M2, and has issue living, Tristan Brooks b 1983. —— Gillian Mary, b 1925: m 1st, 1950, Hugo Wuerzer, who d 1984; 2ndly, 1986, George Arthur Barr, and has issue living (by 1st m), Nigel John (Jordans, First Raleigh, Bideford, Devon EX39 3NJ), b 1955; ed St Edward's Sch, Oxford, Bath Univ and Birmingham Univ: m 1984, Sheila Marion, da of E. F. Thorpe, of Taunton, Som, and has issue living, James Lewis b 1985, Laura Jane b 1988, — Robert Guy (7 Killams Crescent, Taunton, Som), b 1959; ed Wellington Sch, Som, — Wendy Margaret, b 1951: m 1976, Col David H. Keenan, OBE, and has issue living, Nicholas Edward b 1983, Rosalind Jane b (twin) 1983, — Jane Felicity (The Old Police House, Northleigh, Colyton, Devon EX13 6BS), b 1956. Residence – 7442 E Saanich Rd, Saanichton, Vancouver Is, BC, Canada V8M 1W2.

Issue of late Richard Gerald Gore-Langton, b 1892, d 1978: m 1st, 1925 (m diss 1936), Laura Edith Pryor, da of late Herbert W. Bevan; 2ndly, 1936, Doreen Audrey, da of Aubrey H. Davies, MB, MRCS, LRCP:—
(By 1st m) Richard Eric Bevan (5465 Alderley Rd, Victoria, BC, Canada), b 1933: m 1957, Marjorie Joyce, da of late Thomas A. Boag, and has issue living, Richard Thomas, b 1959, — Laura Gay, b 1961: m 1993, Mark Joseph Ahern, of 813 Sayward Rd, Victoria, BC, Canada V8Y 1R5, and has issue living, Robert Bevan Joseph b 1995, Lillie Anna b 1999. —— (By 2nd m) Gerald Hugh, b 1947. —— Norman Guy, b 1950. —— Dorothy Veronica, b 1952.

PREDECESSORS – (1) RICHARD Temple-Nugent-Grenville, KG, 2nd Marquess of Buckingham (see V Cobham); assumed 1799, by Roy licence, the additional surnames of Brydges-Chandos; was cr Earl Temple of Stowe (with remainder to his grandda Anna Eliza Mary, afterwards wife of William Henry Powell Gore-Langton, MP), Marquess of Chandos, and Duke of Buckingham and Chandos (peerage of United Kingdom) 1822, (2-3) in which title the Earldom of Temple was merged until the death of the 3rd Duke of Buckingham and Chandos (ext) in 1889, when it devolved upon his nephew (4) WILLIAM STEPHEN Gore-Langton (son of late William Henry Powell Gore-Langton, MP (ante), 4th Earl, b 1847; MP for Mid Somerset (C) 1878-85; assumed by Roy licence 1892 the additional surname and arms of Temple: m 1870, Helen Mabel, who d 1919, 2nd da of Sir Graham Graham-Montgomery, 3rd Bt; d 1902; s by his son (5) ALGERNON WILLIAM STEPHEN, 5th Earl; b 1871; m 1913, Agnes Florence Regina, who d 1941, da of Charles K. de Laporte, and widow of Alfred Burrows, of Melbourne; d 1940; s by his nephew (6) CHANDOS GRENVILLE (son of late Capt Hon Chandos Graham Temple-Gore-Langton, 2nd son of 4th Earl); 6th Earl; b 1909: m 1st, 1934 (m diss 1940), Frances Vauriel Fenton, da of Maj Francis Vivian Lister, OBE, of Ashwick Grove, Oakhill, Bath; 2ndly, 1943, Joan Helen, who d 1977, da of Charles Abbott, of Penn, Bucks; d 1966; s by his brother (7) RONALD STEPHEN BRYDGES, 7th Earl; b 1910; travelling salesman in Australia; did not use the title; dunm 1988; s by his cousin (8) WALTER GRENVILLE ALGERNON (only son of late Cdr Hon Evelyn Arthur Grenville Temple-Gore-Langton, DSO, RN, yst son of 4th Earl) 8th Earl and present peer.

TEMPLEMAN, BARON (Templeman) (Life Baron 1982)

SYDNEY WILLIAM TEMPLEMAN, MBE, PC, son of late Herbert William Templeman; b 3 March 1920; ed Southall Gram Sch, and St John's Coll, Camb; Bar Middle Temple and Lincoln's Inn 1947, QC 1964, Bencher Middle Temple 1969 (Treas 1987); a Member Bar Council 1961-65 and 1970-72; Attorney Gen Duchy of Lancaster 1970-72, a Judge of High Court of Justice (Chancery Div) 1972-78; a Member Tribunal to inquire into matters relating to Vehicle & Gen Insurance Co 1971-72; a Member R Commn on Legal Services 1976-79; a Lord Justice of Appeal 1978-82, since when a Lord of Appeal in Ordinary; 1939-45 War as Maj 4/1st Gurkha Rifles in India and Burma (despatches); cr MBE (Mil) 1946, Knt 1972, PC 1978, and Baron Templeman, of White Lackington, co Somerset (Life Baron) 1982: m 1st, 1946, Margaret Joan, who d 1988, da of Morton Rowles; 2ndly, 1996, Mrs Sheila Barton Edworthy, da of late Frank Templeman, and widow of Dr John Edworthy, of 1 Rosebank Crescent, Exeter, and has issue by 1st m.

Arms – Per pale azure and gules a fess raguly between a lion passant in chief and in base a fleur-de-lys bourgeonny gold. **Crest** – An eagle or, beaked and legged and wings displayed gules, gorged with a coronet its finials of roses also gules, and supporting by the dexter claw a kukri erect with the point of the blade outwards proper. **Supporters** – Dexter a cock pheasant. Sinister a hen pheasant both guardant and in the beak of each a grain of wheat proper.
Residence – Mellowstone, Rosebank Crescent, Exeter EX4 6EJ.

SONS LIVING (By 1st marriage)

Rev the Hon Peter Morton, b 1949: m 1973, Ann Joyce, da of Peter Williams, and has issue.
Hon Michael Richard, b 1951: m 1974, Lesley Frances, da of Henry Davis, and has issue.

TEMPLETOWN, VISCOUNTCY OF (Upton) (Extinct 1981)

DAUGHTER LIVING OF FIFTH VISCOUNT

Hon (Alleyne Evelyn) Maureen Louisa, *b* 1921; late ATS: *m* 1st, 1947, Maj John Hackett, late RAOC, who *d* 19—; 2ndly, 1961 (*m diss* 1983), Michael Starkey, and has had issue (by 1st *m*), Charles John, *b* 1948; *d* 1994, in Brazil. *Residence* – 13 Malbrook Rd, SW15 6UH.

TENBY, VISCOUNT (Lloyd George) (Viscount UK 1957)

WILLIAM LLOYD GEORGE, 3rd Viscount; *b* 7 Nov 1927; *s* 1983; *ed* Eastbourne Coll, and St Catharine's Coll, Camb (Exhibitioner, BA Hons); RWF (TA); a JP for Hants: *m* 1955, Ursula, yst da of late Lt-Col Henry Edward Medlicott, DSO, and has issue.

𝔄rms – Azure over water barry wavy in base a bridge of one arch proper, on a chief argent a portcullis sable between two daffodils stalked and leaved also proper. Crest – A demi-dragon gules holding between the claws a portcullis sable. Supporters – *Dexter*, a dragon gules; *sinister* a lion or each gorged with a collar compony argent and vert; pendent from that of the dexter an escutcheon argent charged with a martlet sable, and from that of the sinister an escutcheon gules charged with a port between two towers also argent.
Residence – The White House, Dippenhall St, Crondall, nr Farnham, Surrey GU10 5PE.

SON LIVING

Hon TIMOTHY HENRY GWILYM, *b* 19 Oct 1962; *ed* Downside, and Univ Coll of Wales, Aberystwyth. *Residence* – 11 Fleet St, Summer Hill, Sydney, NSW 2130, Australia.

DAUGHTERS LIVING

Hon Sara Gwenfron, *b* 1957.
Hon Clare Mair, *b* 1961. *Residence* – 54 Russell House, Cambridge St, SW1V 4EQ.

PREDECESSORS – (1) GWILYM Lloyd George, TD, PC, 2nd son of 1st Earl Lloyd George of Dwyfor; *b* 1894; MP for Pembrokeshire (*L*) 1922-24 and 1929-50, and N Newcastle-upon-Tyne (*L and C*) 1951-57; Min of Fuel and Power 1942-45, Min of Food 1951-54, and Home Sec and Min for Welsh Affairs 1954-57; *cr Viscount Tenby*, of Bulford, co Pembroke (Peerage of UK) 1957: *m* 1921, Edna Gwenfron, who *d* 1971, da of David Jones, of Gwnfa, Denbigh; *d* 1967; *s* by his el son (2) DAVID, 2nd Viscount, *b* 1922; *d* 1983; *s* by his brother (3) WILLIAM, 3rd Viscount and present peer.

Tenison, King-, family name of Earl of Kingston.

Tennant, family name of Baron Glenconner.

TENNYSON, BARON (Tennyson) (Baron UK 1884)

MARK AUBREY TENNYSON, DSC, 5th Baron; *b* 28 March 1920; *s* 1991; *ed* RNC Dartmouth; Cdr RN 1939-45 War (despatches, DSC): *m* 1964, Deline Celeste, who *d* 1995, da of Arthur Harold Budler, of Cradock, S Africa.

ᴬrms – Gules, a bend nebuly or, thereon a chaplet vert, between three leopards' heads jessant de lys of the second. ℭrest – A dexter arm in armour, the hand in a gauntlet or, grasping a broken tilting spear enfiled with a garland of laurel. ᴪupporters – Two leopards rampant guardant gules, semée de lys and ducally crowned or.
Residence – 304 Grosvenor Sq, Duke Rd, Rondebosch, Cape Town 7700, S Africa. *Clubs* – White's, RAC.

Look backward and forward

COLLATERAL BRANCHES LIVING

Grandchildren of late Hon Lionel Tennyson, 2nd son of 1st Baron:—
Issue of late Alfred Browning Stanley Tennyson, *b* 1878, *d* 1952: *m* 1912, Hon Margaret Cicely Drummond, who *d* 1963, da of 10th Viscount Strathallan (E Perth):—
JAMES ALFRED, DSC (222A Karori Rd, Wellington 5, NZ), *b* 26 Nov 1913; Lieut-Cdr RN (ret); formerly in New Zealand Govt Ser; European War 1939 (despatches, DSC): *m* 1954, Beatrice Aventon, eldest da of Alexander Tolhurst Young, of Wellington, NZ, and has issue living, David Harold Alexander, *b* 4 June 1960; *ed* Scot's Coll, and Canterbury Univ, NZ (ME), — Alan James Drummond, *b* 1965; *ed* Scot's Coll, and Otago and Auckland Univs, NZ (MSc): *m* 1998, Susanna Ruth Brow, and has issue living, Andrew Barnard Brow, *b* 1992. —— Aubrey Drummond (Urb el Salze No 3, Escas, La Massana, Andorra), *b* 1920; Capt late Essex Regt and Sudan Defence Force; attached Sudan Govt: *m* 1966, Mai Chin Yau, and has issue living, Davina May, *b* 1969; *ed* Edgehill Coll, Devon, and Liverpool Univ (BSc): *m* 1999, Christian Erich Kreis, — Georgina Cicely, *b* 1979; *ed* Culford Sch, Bury St Edmunds, and Manchester Univ. —— Eleanor Rachel (41 Alver Quay, Gosport, Hants PO12 1SR), *b* 1915; an artist and former art teacher at Atherley Sch, Southampton; formerly Prof of Art, Baylor Univ, Waco, Texas, USA: *m* 1st, 1945 (*m diss* 1954), Maj David Rainsford Moore, Essex Regt; 2ndly, 1967 (*m diss* 19—), William Charles Bigg, RAF (ret).

Grandchildren of late Sir Charles Bruce Locker Tennyson, CMG (infra):—
Issue of late Capt Charles Julian Tennyson, *b* 1915, *ka* in Burma 1945: *m* 1937, Yvonne (who *m* 2ndly, 1947, Michael Jeans), da of Col R. B. le Cornu:—
Simon, *b* 1939. —— Penelope, *b* (twin) 1939.

Grandson of late Hon Lionel Tennyson (ante):—
Issue of late Sir Charles Bruce Locker Tennyson, CMG, *b* 1879, *d* 1977: *m* 1909, Ivy Gladys, OBE, who *d* 1958, da of late Walter J. Pretious:—
Hallam Augustine (1 Berkeley Rd, N8), *b* 1920; *ed* Eton, and Balliol Coll, Oxford; author and broadcaster: *m* 1945 (*m diss* 1971), Margot, da of late Gustav Wallach, and has issue living, Charles Jonathan Penrose, *b* 1955; *ed* Bootham Sch, York; Lecturer in Physics at London Univ: *m* 1985, Janice Hopson, and has issue living, Alexander Hallam Hopson *b* 1986, Matthew James *b* 1988, Frederick Penrose *b* 1991, — (Sita) Rosalind Joanne, *b* 1950; Dir Marylebone Centre Trust 1989-91: *m* 1980, Richard Grover.

PREDECESSORS
– (1) ALFRED Tennyson, DCL, FRS, son of late Rev George Clayton Tennyson, LLD, R of Somersby, *b* 1809; Poet Laureate 1850-92; *cr Baron Tennyson*, of Aldworth, Sussex, and Freshwater, Isle of Wight (peerage of United Kingdom) 1884: *m* 1850, Emily, who *d* 1896, da of Henry Sellwood, of Berkshire; *d* 1892; *s* by his el son (2) HALLAM, GCMG, PC, 2nd Baron, *b* 1852; Gov and Com-in-Ch of S Australia 1899-1902, and Gov-Gen of Commonwealth of Australia 1902-4; appointed Dep Gov and Steward of the Isle of Wight 1913: *m* 1st, 1884, Audrey Georgiana Florence, who *d* 1916, da of late Charles John Boyle; 2ndly, 1918, Mary Emily, who *d* 1931, da of Charles Robert Prinsep, Advocate-Gen of Calcutta, and widow of Andrew Hichens; *d* 1928; *s* by his el son (3) LIONEL HALLAM, 3rd Baron, *b* 1889; Major Rifle Brig, and Hon Col 51st (London) Anti-Aircraft Brig RA (TA): *m* 1st, 1918 (*m diss* 1928), Hon Clarissa Madeline Georgiana Felicité, who *d* 1960, da of 1st Baron Glenconner, and formerly wife of Capt William Adrian Vincent Bethell, 2nd Life Guards; 2ndly, 1934 (*m diss* 1943), Carroll, da of Howard Elting, of Chicago, USA, and widow of Joseph William Donner, of Buffalo, USA; *d* 1951; *s* by his el son (4) HAROLD CHRISTOPHER, 4th Baron, *b* 1919; Co-Founder with Sir Charles Tennyson of Tennyson Research Centre, Lincoln; *d* 1991; *s* by his brother (5) MARK AUBREY 5th Baron and present peer.

TERRINGTON, BARON (Woodhouse) (Baron UK 1918)

Labour conquers all things

Residence – 59 Pegasus Grange, Oxford OX1 4QQ.

(CHRISTOPHER) MONTAGUE WOODHOUSE, DSO, OBE, 5th Baron; *b* 11 May 1917; *s* 1998; *ed* Winchester, and New Coll, Oxford (MA); FRSL 1951; Fellow Trin Hall, Camb 1950, and Visiting Fellow Nuffield Coll, Oxford 1956-64, Visiting Prof King's Coll, London 1978, Special Member of Academy of Athens 1980; Dir-Gen Royal Inst of International Affairs 1955-59, and Dir of Studies 1955-59; Parl Sec to Min of Aviation 1961-62, and Joint Parl Under-Sec of State for Home Dept 1962-64; Dir of Education and Training CBI 1966-70; 1939-45 War in Middle East as Temporary Col Intelligence Corps (despatches twice, DSO 1943, OBE (Mil) 1944), organised resistance in occupied Greece; has American Legion of Merit, and Order of Phoenix of Greece with Swords: MP Oxford (*C*) 1959-66, and 1970-74: *m* 1945, Lady Davidema Katharine Cynthia Mary Millicent Bulwer-Lytton, who *d* 1995, 2nd da of 2nd Earl of Lytton, KG, PC, and widow of 5th Earl of Erne, and has issue.

Arms – Per fesse or and azure, issuant in chief a hurst of oak trees proper, in base two bars wavy argent. *Crest* – A demi-woodman proper issuant out of a wreath of roses argent, barbed and seeded also proper, supporting in the dexter hand an axe or. *Supporters* – On either side an Airedale terrier proper, gorged with a ducal coronet or.

SONS LIVING

Hon CHRISTOPHER RICHARD JAMES, *b* 20 Sept 1946; *ed* Winchester, and Guy's Hosp Med Sch (MB BS), FRCS 1975, FEBU 1993; FRSM 1981: *m* 1975, Hon Anna Margaret Philipps, elder da of 3rd Baron Milford, and has issue living, Jack Henry Lehmann, *b* 7 Dec 1978; *ed* Eton, and Univ Coll London, — Constance Margaret Davina, *b* 1982; *ed* Cheltenham Ladies' Coll. *Residence* – 14 Crescent Grove, SW4 7AH.

Dr the Hon Nicholas Michael John, *b* 1949; *ed* Winchester, and Ch Ch Oxford: *m* 1973, Her Honour Judge (Mary Jane) Mowat, da of late D. M. Stormont Mowat, of Long Crendon, Bucks, and has issue living, Thomas Duncan, *b* 1987.

DAUGHTER LIVING

Hon Emma Davina Mary, *b* 1954: *m* 1981, Christopher Ian Johnson-Gilbert, son of late Thomas Ian Johnson-Gilbert, of 5 Blenheim Rd, NW8, and has issue living, Hugh Christopher Ian, *b* 1991, — Cordelia Mary, *b* 1983, — Jemima Catherine, *b* 1985, — Imogen Alice, *b* 1990. *Residence* – 79 Thurleigh Rd, SW12 8TY.

DAUGHTERS LIVING OF FOURTH BARON

Hon Lavinia Valerie (24 Harcourt Terrace, SW10 9JR), *b* 1943: *m* 1974 (*m diss* 1988), Nicholas George Bolton, son of late Sir George Lewis French Bolton, KCMG, and has issue living, Carina Suzanne, *b* 1976, — Sophie Davina, *b* 1979.

Hon (Georgina) Caroline (The Little House, Quenington, Cirencester, Glos GL7 5BW), *b* 1946; Interior Designer: *m* 1996, Philip William Leatham (see By Buckland, 1973-74 Edn).

Hon Davina Mary (*Countess Alexander of Tunis*), LVO, *b* 1955; Pres SOS 1992-95; Soc of Stars 1996-99; Member of General Council, Friends of the Elderly and Gentlefolks' Help; Lady in Waiting to HRH The Princess Margaret, Countess of Snowdon, 1975-79, since when Extra Lady in Waiting; LVO 1991: *m* 1981, as his 2nd wife, 2nd Earl Alexander of Tunis, and has issue (see that title).

WIDOW LIVING OF FOURTH BARON

SUZANNE (*Baroness Terrington*), da of late Col Thomas Strutt Irwin, JP, DL, late Royal Dragoons, of Justicetown, Carlisle, and Mill House, Holton, Suffolk: *m* 1942, Maj the 4th Baron Terrington, who *d* 1998. *Residence* – 16 The Orchard, Fairford, Glos GL7 4BH.

PREDECESSORS – (1) JAMES THOMAS Woodhouse, son of James Woodhouse, of Flamborough, ER Yorks; *b* 1852; MP for Huddersfield (*L*) 1895-1906; a Railway and Canal Traffic Commr 1906-21, and Chm Losses under Defence of the Realm Commn 1915-21; *cr* Knt 1895, and *Baron Terrington*, of Huddersfield, co York (peerage of United Kingdom) 1918: *m* 1876, Jessie, who *d* 1942, da of W J Reed, formerly of Okidby, Yorkshire; *d* 1921; *s* by his el son (2) HAROLD JAMES SELBORNE, OBE, 2nd Baron, *b* 1877: *m* 1st, 1918 (*m diss* 1926), Vera Florence Annie (MP for Bucks, Wycombe Div (*L*) 1923-4), da of H. G. Bousher, and widow of Guy Ivo Sebright, son of Sir Guy Thomas Saunders Sebright, 12th Bt; 2ndly, 1927, Rena de Vere, who *d* 1973, da of late Capt William Molyneux Shapland-Swiny, 42nd Roy Highlanders (The Black Watch), and sometime ADC to HRH the late Duke of Edinburgh, of Ballymurrogh and Cloghamon, co Wexford; *d* 1940; *s* by his brother (3) HORACE MARTON, KBE, 3rd Baron, *b* 1887; Bar Inner Temple 1911, Principal Assist Sec, Min of Labour and National Ser 1941-4, Dep Speaker and Dep Chm of Committee, House of Lords 1949: *m* 1st, 1914, Valerie, who *d* 1958, da of late George Allen Phillips of Leyden House, Edenbridge, Kent; 2ndly, 1959, Mrs Phyllis Mary Haggard, who *d* 1971, da of late W. W. Drew, ICS; *d* 1961; *s* by his son **(4)** JAMES ALLEN DAVID, 4th Baron; *b* 1915; ADC to GOC Madras 1940; Member London Stock Exchange, ptnr Sheppards and Chase, Clements House, Gresham St, EC2; Dep Chm and Council Member Wider Share Ownership Council; Dep Chm of Cttees, House of Lords 1961-63; Member International Advisory Board of the American Univ, Washington, DC: *m* 1942, Suzanne, da of late Col Thomas Strutt Irwin, JP, DL, Royal Dragoons; *d* 1998; *s* by his brother **(5)** CHRISTOPHER MONTAGUE, 5th Baron and present peer.

TEVIOT, BARON (Kerr) (Baron UK 1940)

Late, but in earnest

CHARLES JOHN KERR, 2nd Baron; *b* 16 Dec 1934; *s* 1968; *ed* Eton: *m* 1965, Patricia Mary, da of late Alexander Harris, and has issue.

Arms – Quarterly: 1st and 4th gules, on a chevron argent three mullets of the field, *Kerr of Ferniehurst*; 2nd and 3rd per fess gules and vert, on a chevron argent between three mascles in chief or and a unicorn's head in base of the third, horned of the fourth, three mullets of the first, *Kerr of Cessford*; in the centre of the quarters a rose or. **Crest** – A stag's head erased proper. **Supporters** – Two border terriers proper.
Residence – The Knoll, Stockcroft Rd, Balcombe, W Sussex RH17 6LG.

SON LIVING

Hon CHARLES ROBERT, *b* 19 Sept 1971.

DAUGHTER LIVING

Hon Catherine Harriet, *b* 1976.

PREDECESSOR – **(1)** CHARLES IAIN KERR, DSO, MC, son of Charles Wyndham Rudolph Kerr (M Lothian, colls); *b* 1874; Lt-Col R Horse Guards; Junior Lord of the Treasury 1937-39, Comptroller of HM's Household 1939-40, Chm of Liberal National Party 1940-56, Ch Whip of Liberal National Party in House of Lords 1945; MP for Montrose (*L*) 1932-40; *cr Baron Teviot*, of Burghclere, co Southampton (peerage of UK) 1940: *m* 1st, 1911 (*m diss* 1930), Muriel Constance, da of late William Gordon-Canning, of Hartpury, Glos; 2ndly, 1930, Florence Angela, who *d* 1979, da of late Lt-Col Charles Walter Villiers, CBE, DSO (E Clarendon, colls); *d* 1968; *s* by his only son **(2)** CHARLES JOHN, 2nd Baron, and present peer.

TEYNHAM, BARON (Roper-Curzon) (Baron E 1616)
(Title pronounced "Tenham")

My hope is in God

JOHN CHRISTOPHER INGHAM ROPER-CURZON, 20th Baron; *b* 25 Dec 1928; *s* 1972; *ed* Eton; late Capt The Buffs (TA), and 2nd Lt Coldm Gds; Land Agent; OStJ; ADC to Gov of Bermuda 1953 and 1955 to Gov of Leeward Is 1955-56 (Private Sec 1956) and to Gov of Jamaica 1962; Palestine 1948; Pres of Inst of Commerce: *m* 1964, Elizabeth, yr da of late Lt-Col Hon David Scrymgeour-Wedderburn, DSO, Scots Gds (*see* E Dundee, colls), and has issue.

Arms – Quarterly: 1st and 4th argent, on a bend sable, three popinjays or, collared gule *Curzon*; 2nd and 3rd per fesse azure and or, a pale counterchanged, and three stags' heads eased of the second, *Roper*. **Crest** – 1st a popinjay rising, wings displayed and inverted or collared gules, *Curzon*; 2nd, a lion rampant sable, supporting on the dexter forepaw a ducal coronet or, *Roper*. **Supporters** – *Dexter*, a buck or; *sinister*, an heraldic tiger regardant argent.
Residence – Pylewell Park, Lymington, Hants. *Clubs* – Turf, House of Lords Yacht, Puffin's (Edinburgh), Ocean Cruising.

SONS LIVING

Hon DAVID JOHN HENRY INGHAM, *b* 5 Oct 1965: *m* 1985, Lucinda L., eldest da of Maj-Gen Sir Christopher John Airy, KCVO, CBE, and has had issue, Henry Christopher John Ingham (Alexis), *b* 5 Feb 1986, — †Jack, *b* and *d* 1990, — (Elizabeth) Poppy, *b* 1989.
Residence – Pylewell Park, Lymington, Hants.
Hon Jonathan Christopher James, *b* 1973.
Hon Peter Michael Alexander, *b* 1977.
Hon William Thomas, *b* 1980.
Hon Benjamin Alexander, *b* 1982.

DAUGHTERS LIVING

Hon Emma Elizabeth, *b* 1966: *m* 1988, Robert A. Murphy, yr son of Christopher Murphy, and has issue living, Doone, *b* 1989, — Willow, *b* 1990, — Jemima Kaitlin, *b* 1992. *Residence* – 38 Lancaster Rd, W11 1QR.

Hon Sophie Patricia, *b* 1967: *m* 1995, Rupert O. B. Van den Bogaerde, son of Gareth Van den Bogaerde, of SW11, and has issue living, Declan John, *b* 1997, — Jasmine Lucilla Elizabeth Jennifer, *b* 1996. *Residence* – The Mill, Pylewell, Lymington, Hants.

Hon Lucy Elspeth, *b* 1969: *m* 1991, Benjamin Hugh Fraser, and has issue (*see* L Lovat, colls). *Residences* – 45 Westwick Gdns W14; North Lodge, Pylewell Park, Lymington, Hants.

Hon Hermione Marie Hilda Edith, *b* (twin) 1973.

Hon Alice Penelope Rachael, *b* 1983.

BROTHER LIVING

Hon Michael Henry, *b* 1931; Lt (ret) RN; an OStJ: *m* 1964 (*m diss* 1967), Maria, only da of late Maj R. V. Taylor, 16th/5th Queen's R Lancers. *Residence* – Barton House, Ashurstwood, E Grinstead, W Sussex RH19 3FL.

HALF SISTERS LIVING

Hon Henrietta Margaret Fleur, *b* 1955. *Residence* – 165 Walmer Rd, W11 4EW.
Hon Holly Anne-Marie, *b* 1963. *Residence* – 19 Breer St, SW6 3HE.

WIDOW LIVING OF NINETEENTH BARON

ANNE RITA (Inwood House, Sarisbury Green, Hants), da of late Capt Leicester Charles Assheton St John Curzon-Howe, MVO, RN (*see* F. Howe, colls): *m* 1st, 1955, as his 2nd wife, the 19th Baron Teynham, who *d* 1972, 2ndly, 1975, Dr Ian Edwards, who *d* 1988.

COLLATERAL BRANCHES LIVING

      Grandchildren of late Blayney Tenison Roper (*b* 1853), elder son of Blayney Tenison Roper (*b* 1811), yst son of Very Rev Henry Roper, DD, eldest son of Rev Hon Richard Henry Roper, yst son of 8th Baron:—
      Issue of late Lt-Col Richard Blayney Roper, *b* 1897, *d* 1964: *m* 1930, Elmslie, who *d* 1962, da of late William Forbes-Garden:—
Christopher Blayney (40 Northumberland Av, Craighall Park, Johannesburg 2196, S Africa), *b* 1932; late 2nd Lt RE; CEng; an Asso of Camborne Sch of Mines: *m* 1963, Elizabeth Garthorne, 2nd da of late Andrew Ian Dalglish Brown, of Johannesburg, and has issue living, Katherine Elizabeth, *b* 1966; *ed* Univ of Witwatersrand (BSc): *m* 1989, Ian Frederick Burman, of 22D Guildford Rd, Tunbridge Wells, Kent TN1 1LS, — Margaret Jennifer, *b* 1967; *ed* Univ of Witwatersrand (BPrim Ed, BEd), — Philippa Garthorne, *b* 1969. —— Margaret Elizabeth, *b* 1935: *m* 1959, Maj John David Cousins (65 Harvey St, Taupo, NZ), late 10th Princess Mary's Own Gurkha Rifles, and has issue living, Terence David, *b* 1969; MB, ChB, — Elizabeth Mary, *b* 1972; *ed* Univ of Otago (BA, LLB).

      Grandson of late Capt Charles Cadwaladr Trevor-Roper, el son of late George Edward Trevor-Roper, 3rd son of Charles Blayney Trevor-Roper, el son of Cadwallader Blayney TREVOR-ROPER, 2nd son of Rev Hon Richard Henry Roper, yst son of 8th Baron:—
      Issue of late Flight-Lieut Richard Dacre Trevor Roper, DFC, DFM, RAF, *b* 1915, *ka* over Germany 1944: *m* 1942, Patricia Audrey (who *m* 2ndly, 1949, Frank Marvin, and 3rdly, 1955, John Derick Straight, of 292 Reading Rd, Winnersh, Berks), da of late Richard Barrie Edwards, of Nottingham:—
Charles Anthony, *b* 1943; *ed* Wellington, and Reading Univ (BSc, PhD): *m* 1967, Carol Elizabeth, da of Charles James Pape, of 4 Vauxhall Drive, Woodley, Reading, and has issue living, Dacre Gabriel, *b* 1969, — Mathew Blayney, *b* 1977.

      Granddaughter of late George Edward Trevor-Roper (ante):—
      Issue of late Capt Charles Cadwaladr Trevor-Roper, Hampshire Regt, *b* 1884, *d* of wounds received in action 1917: *m* 1913, Gertrude Alice, who *d* 1962 (having *m* 2ndly, 1925, Major Robert Hugh Poyntz, MC, late The King's Shropshire LI, who *d* 1931), da of W. G. Clabby, Indian Police:—
Anne, *b* 1916: *m* 1941, Josiah Maddocks, of 8 Northgate, Goosnargh, Preston, Lancs, and has issue living, Richard James (8 Lindle Close, Hutton, Preston, Lancs), *b* 1943: *m* 1965, Dorothy Suzanne Pallett, and has issue living, John Charles James *b* 1967, Valerie Suzanne *b* 1966, — David Hugh *b* 1950.

      Grandchildren of late Arthur Messeena Trevor-Roper (infra):—
      Issue of late Richard Teynham Trevor-Roper, *b* 1903, *d* 1968: *m* 1928, Lilian M. Prestwood, who *d* 1978:—
Richard Eric (14 Groby Rd, Glenfield, Leics), *b* 1928: *m* 1st, 1954 (*m diss* 1959), Patricia Anne McClintock; 2ndly, 1964, Marilyn Elizabeth Fox, and has issue living (by 1st *m*), Richard Patrick (64 Hinau St, Wanganui, N7), *b* 1955: *m* 1977, Michelle Anne Lhonneux, and has issue living, Michael Patrick *b* 1980, Jason Charles *b* 1982, Ryan Paul *b* 1986. —— Kathleen Edith, *b* 1931: *m* 1951, Kenneth Leslie Jones, of 139 Leicester Rd, Thurcaston, Leics, and has issue living, Nigel Kenneth, *b* 1952: *m* 1972, Gillian Ann Hardy, and has issue living, Nicola Marie *b* 1976, Abbie Eileen *b* 1978.

      Issue of late Cyril Peter Trevor-Roper, *b* 1916, *d* 1995: *m* 1940, Lorna Eileen, da of late Harry J. Smith, of Hillside Terrace, Dorchester, Dorset:—

Virginia Yvonne, b 1943: m 1981, Winston Keith Harris, of 12 Garrett Drive, Bradley Stoke, Bristol. —— Sandra Victoria, b 1946: m 19—, Colin Williams, of 10 Lytton Drive, Pound Hill, Crawley, W Sussex. —— Susan Brenda, b 1952; d 1989.

Grandchildren of Richard Henry Trevor-Roper, 4th son of Charles Blayney Trevor-Roper (ante):—
Issue of late Arthur Messeena Trevor-Roper, b 1876, d 1966: m 1902, Mary Wynifred, who d 1958, da of James Keel, of Froglands, Cheddar, Somerset:—
Margaret Elizabeth, b 1923: m 1946, Niels Peter Nielsen, who d 1971, of 23 Hampshire Rd, Aylestone, Leicester LE2 8HF, and has issue living, Niels Roger, b 1955, —— Gerald Paul, b 1958.

Issue of late Bertie William Edward Trevor-Roper, MB, MRCS, b 1885, d 1978: m 1910, Kathleen Elizabeth, who d 1964, da of William Davison:—
Hugh Redwald (Baron Dacre of Glanton), b 1914; cr Baron Dacre of Glanton 1979 (see that title). —— Patrick Dacre, MB, BCh (3 Park Sq West, NW1. Clubs – Athenaeum, Beefsteak), b 1916; ed Charterhouse, and Clare Coll, Camb (CMB, ChB, MA): FRCS England; Ophthalmic Surg, Westminster and Moorfields Eye Hosps, and late Capt New Zealand Med Corps.

Grandchildren of late Dacre Trevor-Roper, 5th son of Charles Blayney Trevor-Roper (ante):—
Issue of late Lennard Carew Trevor-Roper, b 1876, d 1948: m 1st, 1898, Margaret Helen, who d 1901, da of late James Laffan, of Killarney; 2ndly, 1909, Lisbeth Rankin, who d 1970 da of Alexander Knight Stein:—
(By 2nd m) Lennard Dacre, b 1910: m 1935, Constance May, da of John H. Barr, of Abergele, Denbighshire. —— Janet Rankin, b 1911; formerly 3rd Officer, WRNS: m 1942, Major Vivian M. E. Bateson, King's (Liverpool) Regt, who d 1959, and has issue living, Simon Vivian Ranulf, b 1946, — Julia Janet, b 1948: m 1965, John Read, and has issue living, Sean b 1965, Amber Ruth b 1966. Residence – 8 South Close, Green Lane, Morden, Surrey.

Issue of late Rev Ranulph Dacre Trevor-Roper, b 1893, d 1975: m 1916, Joan Fraser, who d 1976 da of late Robert Fraser Woodcock, MRCS, of Wigan:—
Helen Bennetta, b 1919: m 1st, 1940, Richard Stoate; 2ndly, 1957, Terence H. Summers, of 15 Pigeon House Lane, Freeland, Oxford. —— Joan Everilda (Burtle Farm, Burtle, Bridgwater, Somerset TA7 8NT), b 1923: m 1940 (m diss 1968), Owen John Howell, ARIBA, and has issue living, Robin John (91 Kingsdown Parade, Bristol 6), b 1941: m 1st, 1963 (m diss 1983), Pamela Ann, da of Alfred Raymond Reader, of Northampton; 2ndly, 1984, Claire Hunter, and has issue living, (by 1st m) Jonathan Raef b 1964, Nicholas Dacre b 1966, Christopher Noel b 1969, Benjamin James b 1970, — Jennifer Eve, b 1949: m 1970, Anthony Stephen Duval, and has issue living, Simon Joseph b 1975, Timothy James b 1978.

Grandchildren of late Rev Ranulph Dacre Trevor-Roper (ante):—
Issue of late Capt Anthony Dacre Trevor-Roper, MC, b 1921, d 1986: m 1954, Amy Frances (28 Park Rd, Stony Stratford, Bucks MK11 1LF), yst da of late Capt John Douglas Collins, of Burton Bradstock, Dorset:—
Julian Dacre (The Gate Lodge, Waresley Park Stud, Waresley, Sandy, Beds SG19 3DD), b 1956. —— Christopher Charles ffarington, b 1964. —— Mary Anne TREVOR-ROPER (164 Westbury Lane, Newport Pagnell, Bucks MK16 8PT), b 1954; has resumed her maiden name: m 1982 (m diss 19—), Michael John Frederick Charles Buswell, and has issue living, Jonathan Charles, b 1982. —— Susan Elizabeth TREVOR-ROPER (Sultanate of Oman), b 1958; ed Imperial Coll of Science (BSc), ARCS 1980; has resumed her maiden name: m 1982 (m diss 19—), Nicholas Mark Palmer, 2nd son of B. E. Palmer, of Hadley Green, Herts.

Grandson of late William Roper (b 1837), eldest son of late Charles Roper, elder son of William Roper (b 1768) (infra):—
Issue of late William Trevor Roper, b 1880, d 1956: m 1st, Elsie Beatrice, who d 1934, da of Thomas Holt, of Oxton, Cheshire; 2ndly, 1938, Janet Pegman, of Clontarf, Dublin:—
(By 1st m) Dacre Alexander (Kings Shade, 70 The Street, Capel, Dorking, Surrey RH5 5LA), b 1921; 1939-45 War as Lt RNVR: m 1st, 1945, Sylvia Mary, da of Thomas H. Jameson, of Dublin; 2ndly, 1987, Joan Hodges, of Beare Green, Surrey, and has issue living (by 1st m), Lynda Susan, b 1948.

Granddaughter of late William Trevor Roper (ante):—
Issue of late Trevor Holt Roper, b 1914, d 1988: m 1938, Hylda Florence (203 Rosses Court, Dun Laoghaire, co Dublin), da of Charles T. Marks:—
Penelope Margaret, b 1944: m 1968, David Allengame Proger, of Crowe Abbey House, Killincarrig, Delgany, co Wicklow, and has issue living, Lizanne Margaret, b 1969: m 1995, David Charles Molind, and has issue living, Owen Proger b 1997, — Philippa Jane, b 1972: m 1998, Anthony McGuinness, and has issue living, Nicholas Marc b 1999, — Nicola Kate, b 1980.

Grandchildren of late Henry Charles Roper, elder son of late Hon Sir Henry Roper, yr son of late William Roper (b 1768), 3rd son of late Rev Hon Richard Henry Roper (ante):—
Issue of late Capt Alexander John Henry Roper, TD, RA, b 1913, d 1995: m 1st, 1947, Marjorie Edith, who d 1981, da of Henry Broom Vines, of Lower Field, Bourton, Berks; 2ndly, 1983, Evelyn Joan, who d 1994, da of Herbert Vines, of Petwick Farm, Challow, Berks:—
(By 1st m) Richard Henry (Little Thatch, Wigborough, S Petherton, Som TA13 5LP), b 1948; ed Abingdon, and Bath Univ (BSc 1971): m 1st, 1978 (m diss 1992); 2ndly, 1992, Christine Frances Brammer, of Norton-sub-Hamdon, Som, and has issue living (by 2nd m), Henry Alexander Richard, b 1994, — Phoebe Miranda Jane, b 1992. —— Margaret Hilda Jane, b 1950.

PREDECESSORS – (1) Sir JOHN Roper, Knt, was cr Baron Teynham, of Teynham, co Kent (peerage of England) 1616; d 1618; s by his son (2) CHRISTOPHER, 2nd Baron; d 1622; s by his son (3) JOHN, KB, 3rd Baron; d 1627; s by his son (4) CHRISTOPHER, 4th Baron; d 1673; s by his son (5) CHRISTOPHER, 5th Baron; was Lord-Lieut of co Kent; d 1692; s by his el son (6) JOHN, 6th Baron; d unmarried; s by his brother (7) CHRISTOPHER, 7th Baron; d unmarried; s by his brother (8) HENRY, 8th Baron; conformed to the Established Church, and took his seat in the House of Lords 1715; was a Lord of the Bedchamber to George I; d 1722; s by his el son (9) PHILIP, 9th Baron; d unmarried 1727; s by his brother (10) HENRY, 10th Baron; d 1781; s by his son (11) HENRY, 11th Baron; d 1786; s by his el son (12) HENRY, 12th Baron; d unmarried 1806; *s* by his brother **(13)** JOHN, 13th Baron; *d* unmarried 1824; *s* by his cousin **(14)** HENRY FRANCIS, 14th Baron, son of Hon Francis Roper, 4th son of 10th Baron; *b* 1768; assumed in 1788 by Roy licence the surname of Curzon in lieu of his patronymic, and in 1813 by Roy licence he assumed the surnames of Roper-Curzon, in lieu of his then name: *m* 1788, Bridget, da and heiress of Thomas Hawkins, of Nash Court; *d* 1842; *s* by his el son **(15)** HENRY, 15th Baron; *dsp* 1842; *s* by his brother **(16)** GEORGE HENRY, 16th Baron, *b* 1798: *m* 1st, 1822, Eliza, who *d* 1871, da of William Joynes, of Sevenoaks; 2ndly, 1873, Elizabeth, da of late William Jay, Lieut RA; *d* 1889; *s* by his son **(17)** HENRY GEORGE, 17th Baron, *b* 1822: *m* 1860, Harriet Anne Lovell, who *d* 1916, da of the Rev Thomas Heathcote; *d* 1892; *s* by his el son **(18)** HENRY JOHN PHILIP SYDNEY, 18th Baron, *b* 1867: *m* 1895, Mabel, who *d* 1937, da of late Lt-Col Henry Green Wilkinson, Scots Guards; *d* 1936; *s* by his el son **(19)** CHRISTOPHER JOHN HENRY, DSO, DSC; 19th Baron; *b* 1896; Capt RN; Dep Chm of Cttees, House of Lords 1946-59, and Chancellor of Primrose League 1948: *m* 1st, 1927 (*m diss* 1954), Elspeth Grace, who *d* 1976, el da of William Ingham Whitaker (V Melville); 2ndly, 1955, Anne Rita (who *m* 2ndly, 1975, Dr Ian Edwards), da of Capt Leicester Charles Assheton St John Curzon-Howe, MVO, RN (E Howe); *d* 1972; *s* by his el son **(20)** JOHN CHRISTOPHER INGHAM, 20th Baron and present peer.

THATCHER, BARONESS (Thatcher) (Life Baroness 1992)

MARGARET HILDA THATCHER, LG, OM, PC, yr da of late Alfred Roberts, of Grantham, Lincs; *b* 13 Oct 1925; *ed* Grantham Girls' Sch, and Somerville Coll, Oxford (MA, BSc, Hon Fell 1970); Bar Lincoln's Inn 1954 (Hon Bencher 1975); FRS 1983, Freedom of Borough of Barnet 1980, Hon Freeman Grocers' Co 1980, Freedom Falkland Is 1983, Donovan Award USA 1981, US Medal of Freedom 1991; Chancellor Buckingham Univ 1992-98; Joint Parly Sec Min of Pensions and National Insurance 1961-64, Memb Shadow Cabinet 1967-70, Chief Opposition Spokesman on Educn 1969-70, Sec of State Educn and Science (and co-Chm Women's National Commn) 1970-74, Chief Opposition Spokesman on the Environment 1974-75, Leader of the Opposition Feb 1975-79, Prime Min and First Lord of the Treasury (first woman to hold this office) 4 May 1979-28 Nov 1990, Min for the Civil Ser 1981-90; Chancellor, William and Mary Coll, Williamsburg, Virginia, since 1994; MP Finchley (*C*) 1959-74, Barnet, Finchley 1974-83, 1983-87 and 1987-90; *cr* PC 1970, OM 1990, LG 1995 and *Baroness Thatcher*, of Kesteven, co Lincs (Life Baroness) 1992: *m* 1951, Sir Denis Thatcher, 1st Bt, MBE, TD, and has issue.

Arms – Per chevron azure and gules, in chief two lions rampant guardant, the dexter contourny, supporting between them a double-warded key wards upward or and in base a tower also or, its portal sable, therein a portcullis gold. **Supporters** – *Dexter*, on a mount of tussocks of grass proper a male figure representing an Admiral of the Fleet on active service holding in his exterior hand a pair of binoculars all proper; *sinister*, on a grassy mount vert a male figure representing Sir Isaac Newton holding in his exterior hand a pair of scales all proper.
Address – c/o House of Lords, SW1A 0PW.

SON LIVING

Hon Mark, *b* 1953; *ed* Harrow: *m* 1987, Diane, only da of T. C. Burgdorf, of Dallas, Texas, USA, and has issue living, Michael *b* 1988, — Amanda Margaret, *b* 1993. Resides in S Africa

DAUGHTER LIVING

Hon Carol, *b* (twin) 1953; journalist and broadcaster.

Thellusson, family name of Baron Rendlesham.

Thesiger, family name of Viscount Chelmsford.

THOMAS, BARONY OF (Thomas) (Extinct 1980)

SON LIVING OF LIFE BARON

Hon (William) Michael Webster *b* 1926: *m* 1952, Ann, da of late Col Philip Kirby-Green, and has issue. *Residence* – 9 Shorelands Court, Old Greenwich, CT 0686790, USA.

DAUGHTER LIVING OF LIFE BARON

Hon Sheila, *b* 1925: *m* 1948, Julian von Bergen, of Hatch Green Lodge, Hatch Green, Hatch Beauchamp, Taunton, Som, and has issue.

THOMAS OF GRESFORD, BARON (Thomas) (Life Baron 1996)

(DONALD) MARTIN THOMAS, OBE, QC, son of late Hywel Thomas, of Wrexham; *b* 13 March 1937; *ed* Grove Park Gram Sch, Wrexham, and Peterhouse, Camb (MA 1963, LLB 1961); admitted a Solicitor 1961, practised in Wrexham 1961-66; Lecturer in Law 1966-68; Bar-at-law, Gray's Inn, 1967, Bencher 1989; Junior Counsel, Wales and Chester Circuit 1968-79; QC 1979; Recorder of the Crown Court 1976; Deputy High Court Judge since 1985; Memb Criminal Injuries Compensation Board 1985-93; Chm Marcher Sound Ltd since 1992; Pres Welsh Liberal Party 1978; Pres Welsh Liberal Democrats since 1993; *cr* OBE 1982, and *Baron Thomas of Gresford*, of Gresford, co Borough of Wrexham (Life Baron) 1996: *m* 1961, Nan, da of John Kerr, of Fauldhouse, West Lothian, and has issue.
Residence – Glasfryn, Gresford, Clwyd LL12 8RG. *Clubs* – Reform, Western, Wrexham RFC.

SONS LIVING

Hon Andrew, *b* 1965; *ed* Yale Coll, and Peterhouse, Camb.
Hon Gavin, *b* 1969; *ed* Yale Coll, and Univ Coll, Swansea.
Hon Jamie, *b* 1975; *ed* Yale Coll.

DAUGHTER LIVING

Hon Claire, *b* 1964; *ed* Yale Coll.

THOMAS OF GWYDIR, BARON (Thomas) (Life Baron 1987)

PETER JOHN MITCHELL THOMAS, PC, QC, only son of late David Thomas, solicitor, of Llanrwst, Denbighshire; *b* 31 July 1920; *ed* Epworth Coll, Rhyl, and Jesus Coll, Oxford (MA); served 1939-45 War in RAF, Pilot, Bomber Command (prisoner 1941-45); Bar Middle Temple 1947, QC 1965, Bencher 1971 (Emeritus 1991), Member Wales and Chester Circuit, Dep-Chm Cheshire Quarter Sessions 1966-70, and Denbighshire Quarter Sessions 1968-70, Recorder of Crown Court 1974-88; PPS to Solicitor-Gen 1955-59, Parl Sec Min of Labour 1959-61, Parl Under-Sec of State for Foreign Affairs 1961-63, and Min of State for Foreign Affairs 1963-64, Chm Conservative Party Orgn 1970-72, and Sec of State for Wales 1970-74, Pres of Nat Union of Conservative Assocns 1973-75; a JP of Cheshire and Denbighshire; MP for Conway (*C*) 1951-66, and for Hendon South 1970-87; *cr* PC 1964, and *Baron Thomas of Gwydir*, of Llanrwst, co Gwynedd (Life Baron) 1987: *m* 1947, Frances Elizabeth Tessa, who *d* 1985, only da of late Basil Dean, CBE, theatrical producer (*see* E Warwick, 1968 Edn), and has issue.

Arms – Per pale vert and gules in pale a sword point upwards argent hilt pommel and quillons or between in chief two portcullisses also or all within a bordure engrailed of the last thereon eight pellets. **Crest** – A grassy mount proper statant thereon a stag armed and unguled or resting the dexter foreleg upon a staff raguly also or and between the attires a cross engrailed gold. **Supporters** – *Dexter*, a dragon statant erect tail nowed gules gorged with a crown rayonny gold; *Sinister*, a lamb statant erect or gorged with a crown rayonny gules.
Residences 37 Chester Way, SE11; Millicent Cottage, Elstead, Surrey. *Club* – Carlton.

SONS LIVING

Hon David Nigel Mitchell, *b* 1950. *Residence* – 72 Jerningham Rd, SE14.
Hon Huw Basil Maynard Mitchell, *b* 1953. *Residence* – 1 Regent St, Oxford.

DAUGHTERS LIVING

Hon Frances Jane Mitchell, *b* 1954: *m* 1982, Jeffrey Alex Clargo, and has issue living, two sons and one da. *Residence* – 33 Oxford Rd, Putney, SW15.
Hon Catherine Clare Mitchell, *b* 1958: *m* 1989, Martin Howe, and has issue living, two das. *Residence* – 39 Culver Rd, St Albans, Herts.

THOMAS OF MACCLESFIELD, BARON (Thomas) (Life Baron 1997)

TERENCE JAMES THOMAS, CBE, son of late William Emrys Thomas, of Carmarthen, Dyfed; *b* 13 Oct 1937; *ed* Queen Elizabeth I Gram Sch, Carmarthen, Univ of Bath Sch of Management (Postgrad Dip) and INSEAD (Advanced Management Programme); Hon DLitt Salford 1996; Hon Dr of Business Admin Manchester Metropolitan Univ 1998; Banker; held various positions in National Provincial Bank, then National Westminster Bank; seconded as Research Mangr then Nat Sales Mangr, Joint Credit Card Co (Access) 1971-72; joined Co-operative Bank plc as Market Mangr 1973, subsequently Asslst Gen Mangr, Jt Gen Mangr and Dir of Group Development; Man Dir 1988-97; FCIB, CIMgt, MCIM, FRSA; *cr* CBE 1997, and *Baron Thomas of Macclesfield*, of Prestbury, co Cheshire (Life Baron) 1997: *m* 1963, Lynda, da of William John Stevens, of Kidderminster, Worcs, and has issue.

Arms – Azure three bars potenty on the upper edge argent fracted and parted by three garbs in pale or. **Crest** – A demi lion with dragon's wings gules holding in the sinister paw three daffodils or slipped argent. **Supporters** – On either side a dragon gules dimidiating fesswise a lion also gules each gorged with a plain collar attached thereto a chain reflexed over the back and holding in the exterior forepaw three daffodils also or slipped argent.
Residence – 51 Willowmead Drive, Prestbury, Cheshire SK10 4DD.

SONS LIVING

Hon Justin, *b* 1965: *m* (*m diss*), and has issue living, Nathan, *b* 1988; has further issue, (by Catherine Booth) Owen THOMAS, *b* 1998.
Hon Neil, *b* 1967.
Hon Brendan, *b* 1969.

THOMAS OF SWYNNERTON, BARON (Thomas) (Life Baron 1981)

HUGH SWYNNERTON THOMAS, son of Hugh Whitelegge Thomas, CMG (*d* 1960), by his wife Margery Angelo Augusta, da of Frederick R. Swynnerton; *b* 21 Oct 1931; *ed* Sherborne, and Queens' Coll, Camb; Historian; *cr Baron Thomas of Swynnerton*, of Notting Hill in Greater London (Life Baron) 1981: *m* 1962, Hon Vanessa Mary Jebb, el da of 1st Baron Gladwyn, and has issue.

Arms – Quarterly argent and or cross formy flory sable surmounted of a dragon's head erased gules. **Crest** – Upon a helm with chapeau gules turned up ermine, issuant from the top of a representation of the Torre d'Arnolfo on the Palazzo Vicariale at Scarperia in Italy, argent a bull's head sable armed or. **Supporters** – Upon a compartment composed of a grassy mound proper thereon a bar embowed proper or charged with a like barrulet wavy azure, a pair of falcons wings expanded and addorsed argent, beaked, armed and belled or, legged gules, gorged with a torse or and gules and holding in the beak a quill argent penned or.
Residence – 29 Ladbroke Grove, W11. *Clubs* – Athenaeum, Beefsteak.

SONS LIVING

Hon (Charles) Inigo Gladwyn, *b* 1962; *ed* Latymer Upper Sch, and Univ of East Anglia: *m* 1997, Hon Horatia Holly Lawson, da of Baron Lawson of Blaby, PC (Life Baron).
Hon (Henry) Isambard (Tobias), *b* 1964 *ed* Latymer Upper Sch, London Coll of Printing, and St Martin's Sch of Art.

DAUGHTER LIVING

Hon Isabella Pandora, *b* 1966; *ed* St Paul's Girls' Sch, and Newnham Coll, Camb.

THOMAS OF WALLISWOOD, BARONESS (Thomas) (Life Baroness 1994)

SUSAN PETRONELLA THOMAS, OBE, da of John Arrow; *b* 20 Dec 1935; *ed* Cranborne Chase Sch, and Lady Margaret Hall, Oxford; Memb Surrey CC since 1985, DL Surrey 1996; served on various cttees; past Pres Women Liberal Democrats; *cr* OBE 1989, and *Baroness Thomas of Walliswood*, of Dorking, co Surrey (Life Baroness) 1994: *m* 1958, David Churchill Thomas, CMG, only son of David Bernard Thomas, and has issue.

SON LIVING

Hon David William Penrose, *b* 1959; *ed* Eton, and King's Coll, Camb (BA 19—); author, journalist and TV critic: *m* 1986, Clare Elizabeth, da of John Jeremy, MBE, of ...... and has issue living, Holly, *b* 1988, —— Lucy, *b* 1989. *Address* – c/o Patrick Walsh, Christopher Little, 49 Queen Victoria St, EC4.

DAUGHTERS LIVING

Hon ......, b 19—.
Hon ......, b 19—.

Thomson, surname of Barony of Tweedsmuir of Belhelvie.

THOMSON OF FLEET, BARON (Thomson) (Baron UK 1964)

KENNETH ROY THOMSON, 2nd Baron; b 1 Sept 1923; s 1976; ed Upper Canada Coll, and Camb Univ (MA); Chm Pres and Dir, Thomson Newspapers Ltd, (Owners of 40 daily newspapers in Canada), and Thomson Newspapers (Owners of 82 newspapers in USA); Chm and Dir, Internat Thomson Organisation plc Ltd, of London, Internat Thomson Organisation Ltd, and Thomson British Holdings Ltd; formerly Co-Pres, Times Newspapers Ltd; Pres and Dir of Dominion-Consolidated Holdings Ltd, The Evening Telegram Ltd, Fleet Street Publishers Ltd, Kenthom Holdings Ltd, 96015 Ontario Ltd, 373075 Ontario Ltd, Ontario Newspapers Ltd, The Standard St Lawrence Co Ltd, Thomson Internat Corp Ltd, and other Cos; 1939-45 War with RCAF: m 1956, Nora Marilyn, da of Albert Vernard Lavis, of Toronto, and has issue.

Arms – Argent, a stag's head cabossed proper on a chief azure between two mullets a hunting-horn of the first, stringed gules. Crest – A beaver sejant erect proper, blowing upon a hunting-horn argent, slung over his dexter shoulder by a ribband of the Dress Tartan proper to Thomson of that Ilk and his dependers. Supporters – Dexter, a Mississauga Indian, habited in the proper costume of his tribe, holding in his dexter hand a bow all proper; sinister, a shepherd, bearing in his sinister hand a shepherd's crook, on his head a bonnet all proper, and wearing a kilt of the usual tartan proper to Thomson of that Ilk and his dependers.
Residences – 8 Kensington Palace Gdns, W8; 8 Castle Frank Rd, Toronto 5, Ont, Canada M4W 2Z4.

SONS LIVING

Hon DAVID KENNETH ROY, b 12 June 1957: m 19— (m diss 19—).
Hon Peter John, b 1965.

DAUGHTER LIVING

Hon Lesley Lynne, b 1959.

SISTER LIVING

Hon Phyllis Audrey (c/o Thomson Organisation Ltd, PO Box 4YG, 4 Stratford Place, W1A 4YG), b 1917: m 1947, Clarence Elwood Campbell, and has issue living, Linda Christine b 1949, — Patricia Gay, b 1951, — Susan Elaine, b 1954.

PREDECESSOR – (1) Sir ROY HERBERT THOMSON, GBE, son of Herbert Thomson; b 1894; Joint Chm of Thomson Organisation (and subsidiaries including The Times and The Sunday Times) and of The Thomson Newspapers Ltd, Toronto, Canada, and founder of The Thomson Foundation; cr Baron Thomson of Fleet, of Northbridge, City of Edinburgh (peerage of UK) 1964: m 1916, Edna Alice, who d 1951, da of late John Irvine, of Drayton, Ont; d 1976; s by his only son (2) Kenneth Roy, 2nd Baron, and present peer.

THOMSON OF MONIFIETH, BARON (Thomson) (Life Baron 1977)

GEORGE MORGAN THOMSON, KT, PC, son of late James Thomson, of Monifieth, Angus; *b* 16 Jan 1921; *ed* Grove Acad, Dundee; DL Kent 1992; Hon LLD Dundee; Hon DLitt Heriot Watt; Hon DSc Aston, Hon DCL Kent; 1939-45 War with RAF; MP for E Dundee (*Lab*) 1952-72; Min of State FO 1964-66, Chancellor of Duchy of Lancaster 1966-67, and again 1969-70, Sec of State for Commonwealth Affairs 1967-68, and Min without Portfolio 1968-69; a Member of Commn of European Communities, with special responsibility for Regional Policy, and of enlarged EEC (Regional Policy) 1973-77; First Crown Estate Commissioner 1977-80; Chm Independent Broadcasting Authority 1981-88, Chm Leeds Castle Foundation; *cr* PC 1966, and *Baron Thomson of Monifieth,* of Monifieth in the district of the city of Dundee (Life Baron) 1977; KT (1981): *m* 1948, Grace, da of Cunningham Jenkins, of Glasgow, and has issue.
Address – House of Lords, SW1A 0PW.

DAUGHTERS LIVING

Hon Caroline Agnes Morgan, *b* 1954: *m* 1st, 1977 (*m diss* 1981), Ian C. Bradley; 2ndly, 1983, Roger Liddle, and has issue living (by 2nd *m*), Andrew *b* 1988.
Rev the Hon Ailsa Ballantyne (*Baroness Newby*), *b* 1956: *m* 1978, Baron Newby, OBE (Life Baron), and has issue (see that title).

Thomson, Mitchell-, family name of Baron Selsdon.

THORNEYCROFT, BARONY OF (Thorneycroft) (Extinct 1994)

SON LIVING OF LIFE BARON (*By 1st marriage*)

Hon John Hamo, LVO, *b* 1940; LVO 1992: *m* 1971, Delia, yst da of William Lloyd, of Penallt, Mon, and has issue living, Richard William Henshaw, *b* 1977, — Eleanor Blanche, *b* 1974. *Residence* – 21 St Peter's St, Islington, N1 8JD.

DAUGHTER LIVING OF LIFE BARON (*By 2nd marriage*)

Hon Victoria Elizabeth Anne, *b* 1951: *m* 1975, Richard H. Nathanson, and has issue living, Daniel, *b* 1978, — Alexander, *b* 1980, — Susannah, *b* 1985. *Residence* – 46 Oakhill Rd, SW15 2QR.

WIDOW LIVING OF LIFE BARON

Countess CARLA ROBERTI, DBE (*Baroness Thorneycroft*), da of late Count Malagola Cappi, of Ravenna, Italy, and of late Mrs George William Holt Innes (*see* Innes, Bt, *cr* 1686, colls): *m* 1949, as his 2nd wife, Baron Thorneycroft, CH, PC (Life Baron), who *d* 1994. *Residence* – 42c Eaton Sq, SW1W 9BD.

THURLOW, BARON (Hovell-Thurlow-Cumming-Bruce) (Baron GB 1792)

We have been *Faith is the sister of Justice* *Wherever fate may call*

FRANCIS EDWARD HOVELL-THURLOW-CUMMING-BRUCE, KCMG, 8th Baron; *b* 9 March 1912; *s* 1971; *ed* Shrewsbury Sch and Trin Coll, Camb (MA); Dept of Agric for Scotland 1935-37; Sec to British High Commn in NZ 1939-44, and Canada 1944-45, Private Sec to Sec of State for Commonwealth Relations 1947-49, Counsellor; British High Commn in New Delhi 1949-52; Adviser to Gov of Gold Coast 1955, Dep High Commr in Ghana 1957, and in Canada 1958; High Commr for UK in NZ 1959-63, and in Nigeria 1963-66, Dep Sec in Diplo Ser 1966-68, and Gov of Bahamas 1968-72; KStJ; CMG 1957, KCMG 1961: *m* 1949, Yvonne Diana, who *d* 1990, da of late Aubyn Wilson, of Westerlees, St Andrews, Fife, and has had issue.

Arms – Quarterly: 1st or, a saltire gules, on a chief of the last in the sinister canton a mullet of the first, charged with a crescent of the second, and for distinction a cross crosslet gold, *Bruce*; 2nd azure, three garbs or, and for distinction in the centre chief point a cross crosslet of the last, *Cumming*; 3rd argent, upon a chevron between two chevronels sable, three portcullises, with chains and rings of the field, *Thurlow*; 4th or, a cross sable, *Hovell*. **Crest** – 1st, upon a cap of maintenance proper, a dexter arm in armour from the shoulder, resting on the elbow also proper, the hand holding a sceptre erect or, the arm charged for distinction with a cross crosslet gules; 2nd a lion rampant or, holding in the dexter paw a dagger proper, charged on the shoulder for distinction with a cross crosslet azure; 3rd a raven proper, with a portcullis hung round her neck argent; 4th a greyhound couchant or, collared and line reflexed over the back sable. **Supporters** – Two greyhounds or, collared and lined sable.

Residences – 102 Leith Mansions, Grantully Rd, W9 1LJ; Philham Water, Hartland, Bideford, N Devon EX69 6EZ. *Club* – Travellers'.

SONS LIVING AND DECEASED

Hon ROUALEYN ROBERT, *b* 13 April 1952; *ed* Milton Abbey: *m* 1980, Bridget Anne Julia, only da of (Hugh) Bruce Ismay Cheape, TD, of South Lodge, Isle of Mull, and had issue living, Nicholas Edward, *b* 16 Feb 1986, — George Patrick Ranelagh, *b* 1990, — Tessa Iona Bridget, *b* 1987, — Lorna Belinda, *b* 1991. *Residence* – Old Vicarage, Mapledurham, Oxon.

†*Hon* Peter Torquil Francis, *b* 1962, *ed* Shrewsbury; *d* 1985.

DAUGHTERS LIVING

Hon (Diana) Miranda, *b* 1954: *m* 1981, Michael J. Gurney, son of late J. C. Gurney, of 19a Marloes Rd, W8, and has issue living, Mungo *b* 1982, — Rowan (a da), *b* 1984. *Residence* – Broad Lane House, Brancaster, Norfolk.

Hon Aubyn Cecilia, *b* 1958: *m* 1986, Frederick March Phillipps de Lisle, elder son of Gerard March Phillipps de Lisle, of Quenby Hall, Leics, and has issue living, James Gerard, *b* 1987, — Ralph Francis, *b* 1989, — Rosalie, *b* 1991.

BROTHERS LIVING

Rt Hon Sir (James) Roualeyn, *b* (twin) 1912; *ed* Shrewsbury, and Magdalene Coll, Camb; Bar Middle Temple 1937, a Bencher 1959, and Treas 1975; Chancellor of Diocese of Ripon 1954-57, Recorder of Doncaster 1957-59 and of York 1959-61 and Junior Counsel, Treasury (Common Law) 1959-64, a Judge of High Court of Justice (Divorce, Probate and Admiralty Div) 1964-76 and a Lord Justice of Appeal 1977-85; 1939-45 War as Lt-Col RA in Iraq, Syria, Egypt, N Africa, and E Mediterranean; Knt 1964, PC 1977: *m* 1955, Lady (Anne) Sarah Alethea Marjorie Savile, who *d* 1991, da of 6th Earl of Mexborough, and has issue living, Edward Simon (33 Malward Rd, SW12 8EN), *b* 1958: *m* 1984, Antonia Mary, elder da of Christopher Stephen Gaisford-St Lawrence, of Howth Castle, co Dublin (*see* Mostyn, Bt, colls, 1985 Edn), and has issue living, Michael Alastair *b* 1985, William James Christopher *b* 1987, Isabelle *b* 1990, — Richard Henry, *b* 1963, — Jane Mary (*Lady Gore-Booth*), *b* 1956: *m* 1980, Sir Josslyn Henry Robert Gore-Booth, 9th Bt, and has issue. *Clubs* – Pratt's, United Universities.

Hon Alexander Pascoe (Flat 211 Beddell House, Sherburn House, Sherburn, Durham DH1 2SE), OBE, *b* 1917; *ed* Shrewsbury, and at Trin Coll, Camb (MA); Colonial Admin Ser 1941-60, and Home Civil Ser 1961-78; OBE (Civil) 1960: *m* 1942, Catherine Agnes, who *d* 1995, da of Rev Hamilton Blackwood, of Scalby, Yorks, and has issue living, Charles Hamilton (13 Goldsmith Av, W3 6HR), *b* 1947; *ed* Gordonstoun, and Exeter Univ (BA Hons): *m* 1982, Dr Vimala Valencia Herman, da of late Nicholas Herman, — Nicholas Christian (Flat 26, Tippy Court, 19 Soi 35, Sukhumvit Rd, Bangkok, Thailand), *b* 1949, — Catherine Veronica, *b* 1943: *m* 1970, George Nikolaou Yannoulopoulos, of 2 Auckland Cottages, Auckland Rd, Cambridge CB5 8DP, and has issue living, Nicholas Alexis *b* 1970.

COLLATERAL BRANCHES LIVING

(Male line was in special remainder to Barony)

Granddaughters of late Lt-Col Hugh Hovell Thurlow, son of late Rev Charles Augustus Thurlow, son of late Rev Edward South Thurlow, son of late John Thurlow, yst brother of 1st Baron:—
Issue of late Brig (Edward) Guy (Lethbridge) Thurlow, CBE, DSO, *b* 1881, *d* 1966: *m* 1912, Margaret Merry, who *d* 1952, da of Lt-Col E. H. Vaughan:—
Nancy Katharine, *b* 1914: *m* 1940, Henry George Willis, who *d* 1990, of Ellesboro, Brushford, Dulverton, Som, and has issue living, Nicholas Michael Thurlow (via Cantonale 31, CH-6537 Grono, Switzerland), *b* 1942; *ed* Harrow, and London Univ (BA): *m* 1972, Ann Catherine, da of Harvey Roy (Jack) Callaway, of 5 Chestnut Circle, Mount Hope, W Virginia, USA, and has issue living, Caroline Fiona *b* 1973, Rebecca Margaret *b* 1977, — Ian Henry (Chapel Barn, Goodworth Clatford, Andover, Hants SP11 7QY), *b* 1946; *ed* Harrow, RMA Sandhurst, and Ch Ch, Oxford (BA, BPhil); Capt 4/7th Dragoon Guards (ret): *m* 1978, Mary Catherine Ileana Camilla, elder da of Radu Tilea, of 7 Kenil Court, Clinton Lane, Kenilworth, Warwicks (*see* E Carnarvon, colls, 1995 Edn), and has issue living, Nicholas Henry David *b* 1984, Edward Tilea *b* 1986, Sophie Catherine Glory *b* 1989. —— Rosemary Margaret, *b* 1919; formerly Junior Cdr ATS; has Territorial Efficiency Medal: *m* 1st, 1947, Maj Jasper John Ogilvie, MBE, Somerset LI, who *d* 1974; 2ndly, 1976, Lt-Cdr James Henry de Courcy Hughes, RN (ret), who *d* 1998, of The Old Rectory, Hinton St George, Som, and has issue living (by 1st *m*), Philip John (The Old Rectory, Hinton St George, Som; Paseo del Parque 100, 11310 Sotogrande, Cadiz, Spain), *b* 1948; FCA; *ed* Ampleforth: *m* 1981, Loreto, da of Col Eduardo Vega de Seoane y Barroso, of Madrid, and has issue living, Ian Alexander *b* 1985, William Jasper Charles *b* 1988, James Edward George *b* 1990, — David Jasper (Keepers Piece, Chedington, Beaminster, Dorset), *b* 1952; *ed* Millfield.

PREDECESSORS – (1) *Rt Hon* EDWARD Thurlow, having been Solicitor-Gen and Attorney-Gen, was in 1778 appointed Lord High Chancellor of England, and *cr Baron Thurlow*, of Ashfield, co Suffolk (peerage of Great Britain); held the Great Seal from June 1778 till April 1783 and from Dec 1783 to 1792, when he was *cr Baron Thurlow*, of Thurlow, co Suffolk (peerage of Great Britain), with remainder to his brothers; *d* unmarried 1806, when the Barony of Thurlow, of Ashfield expired, and the Barony of Thurlow, of Thurlow, devolved upon his nephew (2) EDWARD, 2nd Baron, el son of Rt Rev Thomas Thurlow, Lord Bishop of Durham; assumed in 1814 by Roy licence the additional surname of Hovell; *d* 1829; *s* by his son (3) EDWARD, 3rd Baron; *b* 1814: *m* 1836, Sarah, who *d* 1840, only da of Peter Hodgson; *d* 1857; *s* by his el son (4) EDWARD THOMAS, 4th Baron; *d* 1874; *s* by his brother (5) THOMAS JOHN, PC, 5th Baron; *b* 1838; a Lord-in-Waiting to Queen Victoria 1880-85, High Commr to Gen Assembly of Church of Scotland 1886, and Paymaster-Gen 1886; assumed in 1873 by Roy licence the additional surname of Bruce, and in 1874 the additional surname of Cumming: *m* 1864, Lady Elma Bruce, who *d* 1923, da of 8th Earl of Elgin, KT; *d* 1916; *s* by his son (6) *Rev* CHARLES EDWARD, 6th Baron; *b* 1869; V of St Andrew, and Rural Dean, Bishop Auckland 1913-22, Rural Dean of Liverpool N 1926-30, and R of Sedgefield, co Durham 1930-39: *m* 1909, Grace Catherine, who *d* 1959, da of late Rev Henry Trotter, formerly V of Ch Ch, Barnet, *d* 1952, *s* by his el son (7) HENRY CHARLES, CB, CBE, DSO, 7th Baron, *b* 1910: Maj-Gen late Seaforth Highlanders; GOC Troops, Malta 1962-63, *d* 1971; *s* by his brother (8) FRANCIS EDWARD, 8th Baron and present peer.

THURSO, VISCOUNT (Sinclair) (Viscount UK 1952, Bt GB 1786)

JOHN ARCHIBALD SINCLAIR, 3rd Viscount and 6th Baronet; *b* 10 Sept 1953; *s* 1995; *ed* Eton; Dir Lancaster Hôtel 1981-85, Cliveden House Ltd 1987-93, CEO Fitness and Leisure Holdings Ltd (formerly CEO Cranfel Holdings) since 1992; Non-Exec Dir Savoy plc 1993-98, Walker Greenbank plc since 1997 (Chm since 1999), Royal Olympic Cruise Lines since 1998; FHCIMA 1991, Master Innholder 1991; Liveryman Worshipful Co of Innholders since 1997; sits as Lib Dem in House of Lords, Frontbench spokesman on Tourism since 1997, Food since 1998: *m* 1976, Marion Ticknor, da of Louis D. Sage, of Connecticut, USA, and of Mrs Reggie Ward, and has issue.

Arms – Quarterly: 1st, azure, a ship at anchor, her oars erected in saltire, within the royal tressure or; 2nd and 3rd or, a lion rampant gules; 4th azure, a ship under sail or; over all dividing the quarters, a cross engrailed quarterly argent and sable, all within a bordure quartered or and gules, the last charged with three stars of the first. **Crest** – A star of six points waved argent, rising from a cloud proper. **Supporters** – Two red deer proper.
Seat – Dalnawillan, Altnabreac, Caithness. *Residences* – Thurso East Mains, Thurso, Caithness KW14 8HW; New Court, Wigginton, Tring, Herts HP23 6HY. *Clubs* – Brooks's, New (Edinburgh).

SONS LIVING

Hon JAMES ALEXANDER ROBIN, yr of Ulbster, *b* 14 Jan 1984.
Hon George Henry MacDonald, *b* 1989.

DAUGHTER LIVING

Hon Louisa Ticknor Beaumont, *b* 1980.

BROTHER LIVING

Hon Patrick James, *b* 1954; *ed* Fettes: *m* 1st, 1974 (*m diss* 1984), Carol North; 2ndly, 1995, Nicola, da of Bruce Wilson, of Boat of Garton, Inverness, and has issue living, (by 1st *m*) Jody Fergus Peter North, *b* 1976, — Luke Robin, *b* 1979. Mr Sinclair also has issue (by Jenny Ogg), Celeste Jennifer, *b* 1981. *Residence* – Strathmore Lodge, Westerdale, by Halkirk, Caithness.

SISTER LIVING

Hon Camilla Janet, *b* 1957: *m* 1983, Robert Bruce Sanson, of Puketotara Rd, RD3, Whangarei, NZ, and has issue living, Mevagh Janet, *b* 1989, — Nina Elizabeth, *b* 1992.

UNCLE LIVING (*son of 1st Viscount*)

Hon Angus John, *b* 1925; *ed* Eton, and New Coll, Oxford; formerly Lt Scots Gds; NW Europe 1945; BBC 1950-54, Nigerian Broadcasting Corporation 1954-58, Central Office of Information 1959-85, British Council 1985-90, Man Dir Universal Aunts Ltd since 1991: *m* 1st, 1955 (*m diss* 1967), Pamela Karen, da of Dallas Bower; 2ndly, 1968 (*m diss* 1992), Judith Anne Percy; 3rdly, 1992, Kate, da of late William Fry, and widow of Leonard Hunting, and has issue living, (by 2nd *m*) (Isaiah) William Columba Stroma, *b* 1971; *ed* Eton, and Bristol Univ. *Residence* – 19 The Chase, SW4. *Club* – Pratt's.

AUNT LIVING (*daughter of 1st Viscount*)

Hon Catherine, *b* 1919: *m* 1957, Kazimierz Zielenkiewicz, who *d* 1988, and has issue living, Clementina Stewart, *b* 1958: *m* 1st, 1981 (*m diss* 1984), Roberto Lucarini, only son of Alvaro Lucarini, of Prato-in-Toscana, Italy; 2ndly, 1990, Alain Stiegler, son of Mme Colette Stiegler, of Le Grand Pressigny, Touraine, and has issue living (by 2nd *m*), Max Casimir *b* 1990. *Residence* – The Mill House, Isle Brewers, Taunton.

WIDOW LIVING OF SECOND VISCOUNT

Margaret Beaumont (*Margaret, Viscountess Thurso*), da of late Col Josiah James Robertson, DSO, of Norwood, Wick, Caithness, and widow of Lieut Guy Warwick Brokensha, DSC, RN: *m* 1952, the 2nd Viscount Thurso, who *d* 1995. *Residence* – Thurso East Mains, Thurso, Caithness KW14 8HW.

COLLATERAL BRANCHES LIVING (*In remainder to Baronetcy only*)

Grandchildren of late Ven John Stewart Sinclair, 4th son of Rev William Sinclair, 5th son of 1st baronet (infra):—
Issue of late Very Rev Ronald Sutherland Brook Sinclair, MC, *b* 1894, *d* 1953: *m* 1924, Patience Penelope, who *d* 1988, da of Herbert Chitty, FSA:—
Christopher Ronald (5 Fentiman Rd, SW8), *b* 1936; *ed* King's Sch, Canterbury, and at Exeter Coll, Oxford; Dir Adcomm Ltd: *m* 1969, Penelope Ann, da of Edwin Alfred Springett, and has issue living, Sophie Letitia, *b* 1971.

Issue of late Maj-Gen Sir John Alexander Sinclair, KCMG, CB, OBE, *b* 1897, *d* 1977: *m* 1927, Esmé Beatrice, who *d* 1983, da of late Ven Thomas Karl Sopwith, Archdeacon of Canterbury:—
Ian Alexander Charles (The Garth, 60 Marygate, York YO30 7BH), *b* 1938; *ed* Eton, and Worcester Coll, Oxford (BA, PhD): *m* 1969, Elma Elizabeth, da of late Charles Henry Williams, of Braunton, Devon, and has issue living, Andrew George, *b* 1970, — John Charles, *b* 1972, — Elizabeth Beatrice, *b* 1974. —— Roderick John (Downgate Farm, Petersfield, Hants), *b* 1944: *m* 1st, 1970 (*m diss* 1976), Lucinda Mary, da of late Eric Martin Smith, MP; 2ndly, 1977, Sarah Margaret, da of late Brig Cyril Edwin Harold Dolphin, CBE, of 78 Heath Rd, Petersfield, Hants and has issue living (by 2nd *m*), James Alexander, *b* 1984, — Natasha Esmé, *b* 1981. —— Jean Esmé, *b* 1929: *m* 1961, Christopher Bruce Seagrim, of Hill Farm, Pulborough, Sussex, and has issue living, John Christopher (9 Shalcomb St, SW10 0HZ), *b* 1965: *m* 1994, Georgina Gay, da of Maj David Hood, MC, and has issue living, Edward Nott *b* 1999, Ochre Georgina *b* 1997, — Victoria Esmé, *b* 1962: *m* 1995, Timothy Peter Townsend, son of Ian Townsend, and has issue living, Christopher Ian *b* 1997. —— Iona (*Lady Carnegie*), *b* 1931: *m* 1955, Lt-Gen Sir Robin Macdonald Carnegie, KCB, OBE, DL, yr son of late Sir Francis Carnegie, CBE, and has issue living, Rupert Alexander (151 Ashley Gdns, SW1P 1HW), *b* 1959, — Catriona Jean, *b* 1957: *m* 1982, Simon J. N. Heale, of 11 Lansdown Crescent, Bath BA1 5EX, son of James Heale, and has issue living, James Newton *b* 1985, Charlotte Esmè Serena *b* 1987, Anna Frances *b* 1989, — Rachel Clare *b* 1962: *m* 1989, Mark Goldring, and has issue living, Rory Alexander Carnegie *b* 1995, Natasha Kate *b* 1992.

PREDECESSORS (1) *Rt Hon* John Sinclair, only son of George Sinclair; *b* 1754; a PC and Founder of the Board of Agriculture; *cr* a *Baronet*, 1786, with remainder, in default of his own male issue, to male issue of his daughters respectively: *m* 1st, 1776, Sarah, who *d* 1785, da of late Alexander Maitland, of Stoke Newington; 2ndly, 1788, Hon Diana Macdonald of Macdonald, who *d* 1845, da of 1st Baron Macdonald; *d* 1835; *s* by his son (2) *Sir* George, 2nd Bt; *b* 1790; MP for Caithness-shire (*L*) 1811-18 and 1831-41: *m* 1816, Lady Catherine Camilla Tollemache, who *d* 1863, sister of 8th Earl of Dysart; *d* 1868; *s* by his only surviving son (3) *Sir* John George Tollemache, 3rd Bt; *b* 1824; sometime Page of Honour to Queen Adelaide; MP for Caithness-shire (*L*) 1869-85: *m* 1853 (*m diss* 1878), Emma Isabella Harriet, who *d*

1889, da of late William Standish Standish, of Duxbury Park, Lancashire; *d* 1912; *s* by his grandson **(4)** ARCHIBALD HENRY MACDONALD, KT, CMG, PC (son of late Clarence Granville Sinclair, el son of 3rd baronet), 4th Bt; *b* 1890; Sec of State for Scotland (Nat Govt) 1931-32, Leader of Liberal Party in House of Commons 1935-45, Lord Rector of Glasgow Univ 1938-45, Sec of State for Air 1940-45, MP for Caithness and Sutherland (*L*) 1922-45; *cr Viscount Thurso*, of Ulbster, co Caithness (peerage of UK) 1952: *m* 1918, Marigold, who *d* 1975, da of late Lt-Col James Stewart Forbes (Forbes, Bt, colls, *cr* 1823); *d* 1970, *s* by his el son **(5)** ROBIN MACDONALD, 2nd Viscount, *b* 1922; DL and Lord Lieut Caithness, Pres Highland Soc and Brigade Pres The Boys' Brigade; Fl-Lt RAF 1939-45 War: *m* 1952, Margaret Beaumont, da of late Col Josiah James Robertson, DSO, of Norwood, Wick, Caithness, and widow of Guy Warwick Brokensha, DSC, RN; *d* 1995; *s* by his elder son **(6)** JOHN ARCHIBALD, 3rd Viscount and present peer.

Thynn, family name of Marquess of Bath.

Tiverton, Viscount; son of Earl of Halsbury.

TODD, BARONY OF (Todd) (Extinct 1997)

SON LIVING OF LIFE BARON

Dr the Hon Alexander Henry (The Chestnuts, Lower Peover, Knutsford, Cheshire), *b* 1939; *ed* The Leys Sch, Camb, and at Oriel Coll, Oxford (D Phil); Upper Warden Salters' Co 1998: *m* 1st, 1967 (*m diss* 19—), Joan Margaret, da of Frederick Wilbur Koester, of Campbell, Cal, USA; 2ndly, 1981, Patricia Mary, da of late Brig A. Harvey Jones, of Somerford Booths, Cheshire.

DAUGHTERS LIVING OF LIFE BARON

Hon Helen Jean, *b* 1941; *ed* Somerville Coll, Oxford: *m* 1963, Philip Edgar Brown, of Lesser Moorguards, West Hall, Brampton, Cumbria CA8 2BP and has issue.
Hon Hilary Alison, *b* 1946.

Toler, Graham-, family name of Earl of Norbury.

TOLLEMACHE, BARON (Tollemache) (Baron UK 1876)
(Name and Title pronounced "Tolmash")

TIMOTHY JOHN EDWARD TOLLEMACHE, 5th Baron, *b* 13 Dec 1939; *s* 1975; *ed* Eton; late Lt Coldstream Gds; DL Suffolk 1984, and Vice Lord Lieut 1994; Chm CLA Suffolk 1990-93, Dir Fortis (UK) Ltd, and other cos; Pres Suffolk Assocn of Local Councils 1978-96; Chm Council of St John in Suffolk 1982-89; Pres Friends of Ipswich Museums 1980-96, The Milk Group since 1994, SSAFA Suffolk since 1996, CAB Ipswich since 1998; Chm Historic Houses Assoc (E Anglia Region) 1979-83; Chm St Edmundsbury Cathedral Appeal 1986-90, Suffolk Historic Churches Trust (Trustees) since 1996; Pres Suffolk Family History Soc since 1988; Vice-Pres Cheshire Red Cross since 1980; Vice-Pres Suffolk Preservation Soc since 1992; Patron Suffolk Accident Rescue Service since 1983; Patron Suffolk Association for the Blind since 1992; Pres Cheshire Cereal Society since 1983, and Suffolk Agricultural Assocn 1988; a patron of four livings: *m* 1970, Alexandra Dorothy Jean, da of late Col Hugo Meynell, MC (*see* E Halifax, colls) and has issue.

I trust and am content

Arms – Argent, a fret sable. Crest – A horse's head erased argent, between two wings or, pellety. Supporters – On either side a stag guardant proper, gorged with a collar flory counterflory or.
Seat – Helmingham Hall, Stowmarket, Suffolk IP14 6EF. *Clubs* – White's, Pratt's, Special Forces.

SONS LIVING

Hon EDWARD JOHN HUGO, *b* 12 May 1976; a Page of Honour to HM The Queen 1988-90.
Hon James Henry Timothy, *b* 1980.

DAUGHTER LIVING

Hon Selina Karen, *b* 1973.

BROTHERS LIVING

Hon (John) Nicholas Lyonel (1114 San Ysidro Drive, Beverly Hills, Calif 90210, USA), *b* 1941; *ed* Eton and Trin Coll, Camb (MA) and Harvard Univ, USA (MBA): *m* 1st, 1971 (*m diss* 1974), Heide Eva Marie, da of Gunther Wiedeck, of Bonn; 2ndly, 1982, Dietlinde Hannelore, da of Hannelore Riegel, of Munich, W Germany.
Hon Michael David Douglas (Framsden Hall, Stowmarket, Suffolk IP14 6HL; White's Club), *b* 1944; *ed* Eton, and Trin Coll, Camb (MA); Dir Michael Tollemache Ltd, since 1967, David Carritt Ltd 1983-93, Artemis Fine Art (UK) Ltd 1983-93, and Partridge Fine Arts plc since 1997: *m* 1969, Theresa, da of Peter Bowring, of London, and has issue living, Lyonel John Peter, *b* 1973, — Archibald Robert Bowring (twin), *b* 1973, — Melissa Natasha, *b* 1971: *m* 1997, Sam C. Kiley, son of Dennis Kiley, of London, and has issue living, Ella *b* 1997.
Hon Hugh John Hamilton (Sandbourne House, Earl's Croome, Worcs WR8 9DG), *b* 1946; *ed* Eton; Man Dir Beshara Press Ltd: *m* 1986, Rosanne, 2nd da of late Hon (Michael) Anthony (Rathborne) Cayzer, of Great Westwood, King's Langley, Herts (*see* B Rotherwick), and has issue living, Thomas Anthony Hamilton, *b* 1987, — David Charles John, *b* 1989, — John Edward Hugh, *b* 1992.

DAUGHTER LIVING OF THIRD BARON (*by 2nd marriage*)

Hon Sybil Diana, *b* 1930: *m* 1966, Harold Diehl.

COLLATERAL BRANCHES LIVING (*All of whom are in remainder to the Earldom of Dysart*)

Grandchildren of late Henry Robert Tollemache, yr son of late Hon Hamilton John Tollemache, 4th son of 1st Baron:—
Issue of late Sqdn Ldr Anthony Henry Hamilton Tollemache, GC, RAuxAF, *b* 1913, *d* 1977: *m* 1st, 1947 (*m diss* 1960), Françoise, da of Comte Jean de Hauteclocque, French Ambassador to Canada; 2ndly, 19—, Cecilia Vernon Mary, who *d* 1993, da of late Bryce Cochrane, of McLaren Rd, Edinburgh:—
(By 1st wife) Richard Lionel (41 Lochaline St, W6), *b* 1950: *m* 1978, Caroline, da of Capt Edward Maxwell Cunningham Walker, OBE, RN, and has issue living, Max Philip Anthony, *b* 1987, — Stephanie Elizabeth Louise, *b* 1985. —— Gregory Marmaduke Anthony (6 Elms Walk, Totnes, Devon TQ9 5YQ), *b* 1954: *m* 1976, Karin —, and has issue living, Eugene Anthony, *b* 1976. —— Catherine, *b* 1948: *m* 1970, Malcolm Woolff, of The Old Granary, Malton Rd, Orwell, Herts SG8 5QN, and has issue living, Nicholas Elliot, *b* 1974, — Georgina Juliet, *b* 1975. —— Juliette, *b* 1956: *m* 1979, Jonathan Brian Cottam, of St Aubins, 35 Kingsley Av, W13 0EQ, and has issue living, Alexie Juliette Daisie, *b*

1982, — Harriet Rosie Madeleine, *b* 1986. ——— (By 2nd wife) Alexander Anthony, *b* 1958; *ed* Stowe, and Exeter Univ: *m* 1987, Nobuko Kida.

Issue of late Karin Irene Elizabeth Tollemache, *b* 1916, *d* 1981: *m* 1945, Cdr William Gordon Jack, RN, who *d* 1992:—
Michael Anthony Gordon JACK (5 Bay Noakes Rd, Chisipite, Harare, Zimbabwe), *b* 1946; *ed* Charterhouse, and Lincoln Coll, Oxford: *m* 1980, Anne, da of Hugh Fletcher, of Cape Province, S Africa, and has issue living, Julia, *b* 1981, — Diana, *b* 1984. ——— †David Lionel JACK, *b* 1954; *ed* Eton, and Bristol Univ; *d* as the result of an accident in Bermuda 1985. ——— †Vanessa Bettine, *b* 1948; *ed* East Haddon Hall, and Univ of E Anglia: *m* 1978, Michael Manassei di Collestatte, and *d* 1985, leaving issue (*see* E Perth).

Grandchildren of late Hon Hamilton James Tollemache (ante):—
Issue of late Marguerite Emily Tollemache, *b* 1880, *d* 1968: *m* 1906, Lt-Col George Cecil Minett Sorel-Cameron, CBE, late Queen's Own Cameron Highlanders, who *d* 1947:—
Robert SOREL-CAMERON, CBE, AFC, *b* 1911; *ed* Wellington Coll, and Edinburgh Univ; Air Commodore (ret) RAF; Air Attache Athens 1960-62, SE Asia 1945-47 (AFC, CBE): *m* 1939, Henrietta Grace (Jane), who *d* 1997, da of late Capt John Radford-Norcop, of The Brand Hall, Market Drayton, Shropshire, and has issue living, Alistair (49 Montgomery Rd, W4 5LZ), *b* 1940: *m* 1981, Ann Kristine, da of Kenneth Cole Harkess, MBE, of 4 Copperfields Close, Kemsing, Kent, and has issue living, George Jack *b* 1988, Henrietta Eve *b* 1986, — James (49 Evesham Rd, Stratford on Avon), *b* 1948: *m* 1972, Bridget Susan, eldest da of Alan Henry Dring, of Tinkley Lodge, Nympsfield, Stonehouse, Glos, and has issue living, Robert James *b* 1975, Peter Alan *b* 1982, Matthew George *b* 1984, Catriona Jane *b* 1973, Joanna Helen *b* 1979, — Victoria, *b* 1943: *m* 1968, Sayyid Rifaat, of 27A Crawford Place, Newbury, Berks, and has issue living, Tariq Sayyid *b* 1971, Rashid Ali *b* 1973, Samir *b* 1975, Sasha Amy *b* 1979. *Residence* – The White House, Whitwell, Norfolk NR10 4RF. ——— Hester Marguerite (*Lady Dick-Lauder*), *b* 1920: *m* 1945, Maj Sir George Andrew Dick-Lauder, 12th Bt, who *d* 1981.

Grandchildren of late Marguerite Emily Tollemache (Mrs George C. M. Sorel-Cameron) (ante):—
Issue of late Brig John Sorel-Cameron, CBE, DSO, *b* 1907, *d* 1986: *m* 1937, Catherine Nancy (Sally), who *d* 1984, yr da of late Frank Lee, of Well Head, Halifax:—
†Catriona, *b* 1940: *m* 1st, 1963 (*m diss* 1967), Allan Carruthers; 2ndly, 1968, Maurice Cleary, and *d* 1997, leaving issue (by 1st *m*), Rupert Harry Edgell, *b* 1963, — (by 2nd *m*) Angus Peter, *b* 1968.

Issue of late Agnes Sorel-Cameron, *b* 1909, *d* 1986: *m* 1933, Lt-Col Cyril Hugh Kerr-Smiley, TD, who *d* 1980:—
See Smiley, Bt, colls.

Grandchildren of late Winifred Gertrude Tollemache (Mrs Detmar Blow) (infra):—
Issue of late Richard Purcell Blow, *b* 1915, *d* 1963: *m* 1st, 1939 (*m diss* 1956), Diana Hermione, who *d* 1967 (having *m* 2ndly, 1961, Marco Blow), da of late Capt William Adrian Vincent Bethell (*see* B Glenconner, 1960 Edn); 2ndly, 1957, Catherine, who *d* 1992, da of late Donald MacAskill, of 23 Borve, Berneray, Invernessshire:—
(By 1st *m*) (Richard) David Detmar BLOW (7 Heathview Gdns, SW15), *b* 1942: *m* 1988, Laurence Marie, da of George Lécallier, of 11 rue Parmentier, Neuilly, Paris, and has issue living, John, *b* 1989. ——— (Adrian) Simon (35 Great Queen St, WC2), *b* 1943; writer. ——— (By 2nd *m*) Catherine Anne, *b* 1960.

Issue of late Jonathan Oliver Tollemache Blow, *b* 1919, *d* 1977: *m* 1962, (Elaine) Helga (The Chalet Hotel, Kandy, Sri Lanka; Hilles Edge, Stroud, Glos GL6 6NW), da of Edmund Frederick Lorenz de Silva, MBE, of Kandy, Sri Lanka, sometime MP for Kandy, Ceylonese Ambassador to France and Memb of Executive Board of UNESCO:—
Detmar Hamilton Lorenz Arthur BLOW (5 Theed St, Waterloo, SE1 8ST; Hilles, Edge, Stroud, Glos GL6 6NW. *Club* – Brooks's), *b* 1963; *ed* Harrow, and LSE (BA); Bar Middle Temple 1989; Consultant Withers, Solicitors, since 1998; Dir Modern Art Inc since 1999: *m* 1989, Isabella Delves, eldest da of Sir Evelyn Delves Broughton, 12th Bt. ——— Amaury Hugh John Jellings (Edge Farm, Edge, Stroud, Glos; *Club* – Groucho), *b* 1965; *ed* Millfield. ——— Selina Jane (42 Elizabeth St, SW1; Cherry Hill Cottage, Spoonbed Vale, Edge, Stroud, Glos), *b* 1966; *ed* Hatherop Castle, and Queen's Coll; fashion designer: *m* 1998, Dr Charles M. Levinson, son of Dr Gordon Levinson, of Richmond, Surrey, and has issue living, Augustus Hugh Hamilton Jonathan, *b* 1998.

Issue of late Clare Desirée Blow, *b* 1914, *d* 1956: *m* 1st, 1934 (*m diss* 1944), Hon Phelim Robert Hugh O'Neill (later 2nd Baron Rathcavan), who *d* 1994; 2ndly, 1944, Lt-Col Lewis Stanton Starkey, of Huttons Ambo Hall, York:—
(By 1st *m*) (*See* B Rathcavan). ——— (By 2nd *m*) †Kathleen Mary, *b* 1946: *m* 1972, John Fitzgerald Willcox Jenyns, yr son of Roger Soame Jenyns, of Bottisham Hall, Cambridge, and *d* 1994, leaving issue, Clare Eulalia Starkey, *b* 1974. *Residence* – The Grange, Huttons Ambo, York.

Granddaughter of late Hon Hamilton James Tollemache (ante):—
Issue of late Winifred Gertrude Tollemache, *b* 1882, *d* 1954: *m* 1910, Detmar Blow, JP, FRIBA, who *d* 1939:—
Lucilla, *b* 1923: *m* 1948, Philip Amyas Warre-Cornish, who *d* 1998, of The Tower, Woolstone, Faringdon, Oxfordshire SN7 7QL, and has issue living, Alexander Philip Hubert Detmar (le Sage ten Broeklaan 81, Eindhoven, The Netherlands), *b* 1949; *ed* Eton: *m* 1983, Penelope Ann, da of Dr Philip Canning Farrant, of 8 High View Rd, Sidcup, Kent, and has issue living, Katherine Mary *b* 1985, Harriet Jane *b* 1988, Anna Belinda *b* 1991, Elizabeth Alexandra *b* 1996, — James Damian, *b* 1952.

Issue of late Hon Stanhope Alfred Tollemache, 6th son of 1st Baron, *b* 1855, *d* 1934: *m* 1905, Elizabeth, who *d* 1958, da of W. Monks:—
Ina Elaine (Hanby, 94A High Rd West, Felixstowe, Suffolk), *b* 1916.

Grandchildren of late Maj Hon Douglas Alfred Tollemache, 8th son of 1st Baron:—
Issue of late Capt Humphrey Douglas Tollemache, RN, *b* 1893, *d* 1970: *m* 1924, Elsie Violet, who *d* 1981, da of late William George Raphael (Goldsmid, Bt):—
Michael Humphrey (Tollemache Hall, Offton, Ipswich IP8 4RT), *b* 1930; *ed* Eton: *m* 1968, Gay Rosemary D. O'Grady, da of H. E. O'Grady Thompson, of Castle Garde, co Limerick, and has issue living, Rosamond Sybil, *b* 1969: *m* 1993 (*m diss* 1999), Ashley P. de Laroque, only son of Charles de Laroque, of Lyndale Cottage, Chalfont St Peter, Bucks, and has issue living, Rebecca *b* 1997, — Juliet Elsie, *b* 1974. —— Jean Margherita (*Jean, Baroness Tweedsmuir*) *b* 1927: *m* 1st, 1953, Sir Francis Cullen Grant, 12th Bt, who *d* 1966; 2ndly, 1980, as his 2nd wife, 2nd Baron Tweedsmuir, CBE, CD, who *d* 1996, and has issue (by 1st *m*) (see Grant of Monymusk, Bt). *Residence* – Flat 2, The White House, 24 Dirleton Av, N Berwick, E Lothian EH39 4BQ.

Issue of late Angela Mariota Tollemache, *b* 1900, *b* 1995: *m* 1st, 1923, as his 2nd wife, 3rd Baron Belper, who *d* 1956; 2ndly, 1958, Rev (Harry) Norman Tollemache (formerly Wrigley), who *d* 1981:—
(By 1st *m*) (*See* B Belper).

Grandchildren of late Hon Ranulph Carteret Tollemache, 10th son of 1st Baron:—
Issue of late Com Lawrence Lionel Tollemache, RN, *b* 1894, *d* 1954: *m* 1926, Violet Mary (who *m* 2ndly, 1956, Laurence Reid), da of John Bayly A'Deane:—
Margaret Ngaire Yoskyl A'Deane, *b* 1928: *m* 1955, Antony Percy Jackson, of White Pines, Takapau, Hawkes Bay, New Zealand, and has issue living, Peter Lawrence, *b* 1956, — Timothy, *b* 1959, — Ashley, *b* 1961, — Alison, *b* 1958, — Ngaianne, *b* 1962. —— Annette A'Deane, *b* 1950: *m* 1st, 1974 (*m diss* 1981), Andrew Berne Vallance; 2ndly, 1984, Bryan Chesney Philpott, of Ashcott Station, RD Takapau, Hawkes Bay, NZ, and has issue living (by 1st *m*), Natasha A'Deane, *b* 1978, — (by 2nd *m*) Tamarin Mary A'Deane, *b* 1983.

Issue of late Harold Vincent Tollemache, *b* 1895, *d* 1989: *m* 1937, Marjorie Violet, who *d* 1990, da of late W. H. Lonsdale, of Rangoon:—
Laurence Ranulph (46 Preston Grove, Faversham, Kent), *b* 1938: *m* 1960, Maureen Elizabeth, da of Harold Hex, of Taunton, Som, and has issue living, Paul Laurence, *b* 1965, — Clare Elizabeth, *b* 1968.

Grandchildren of late Leila Mary Cartwright (infra):—
Issue of late Sir Charles Mortimer Tollemache Smith-Ryland, KCVO, *b* 1927, *d* 1989: *m* 1952, Hon Jeryl Marcia Sarah (*Hon Lady Smith-Ryland*) (Medbourne Old Hall, Market Harborough, Leics LE16 8DZ), da of late Hon Robert Brampton Gurdon (*see* B Cranworth):—
Robin Charles SMITH-RYLAND, *b* 1953: *m* 1st, 1982 (*m diss* 1985), Eliza S., da of late Cdr James George Greville Dugdale, RN; 2ndly, 1985, Baroness Helène von Ludinghausen. —— David James, *b* 1961. —— Sarah Yoskyl, *b* 1955: *m* 1983 (Luke Edward) Timothy Hue Williams, and has issue living, Charles Luke, *b* 1991, — Sophie, *b* 1984, — Laura, *b* 1987. —— Joanna, *b* 1959. —— Petra Louisa, *b* 1970.

Granddaughter of late Hon Mortimer Granville Tollemache, yst son of 1st Baron:—
Issue of late Leila Mary Tollemache, *b* 1896, *d* 1971: *m* 1st, 1919, Charles Ivor Phipson Smith-Ryland, Capt Warwickshire Yeo, and Lieut Coldstream Gds Res of Officers, who *d* 1929; 2ndly, 1933, Victor Hamilton Aubrey Cartwright, who *d* 19—:—
(By 1st *m*) June, *b* 1924: *m* 1st, 1945, Robert W. Bensley; 2ndly, 1970, Patrick Joseph O'Donnell, and has issue living (by 1st *m*), Robert Ward (76 Kahdena Rd, Morristown, NJ 07960-3500, USA), *b* 1954, — Charles Ivor (18 Valley View Rd, Morristown, NJ 07960-4816, USA), *b* 1958: *m* 1985, Leslie Forrest, da of John K. Thorsen, of 116 West Gaston St, Savannah, Georgia, and has issue living, Samuel Ivor *b* 1991, Eliza Knox *b* 1988, — Leila Hannah (13a Midhurst Rd, W13 9XS), *b* 1947. *Residence* – Grenan House, Kilmacthomas, co Waterford.

PREDECESSORS – (1) JOHN JERVIS Tollemache of Helmingham Hall, Suffolk, son of late Adm John Richard Delap Tollemache (formerly Halliday), maternal grandson of 4th Earl of Dysart, sat as MP for Cheshire S (C) 1841-68, and for Cheshire W 1868-72, and was *cr Baron Tollemache*, of Helmingham, co Suffolk (peerage of United Kingdom) 1876; *b* 1805: *m* 1st, 1825, Georgina Louisa, who *d* 1846, da of Thomas Best; 2ndly, 1850, Eliza-Georgiana, who *d* 1918, da of James Duff; *d* 1890; *s* by his el son (2) WILBRAHAM FREDERICK, 2nd Baron; *b* 1832: MP for Cheshire W (C) 1872-85: *m* 1st, 1858, Lady Emma Georgina Stewart, who *d* 1869, 2nd da of 9th Earl of Galloway; 2ndly, 1878, Mary, who *d* 1939, da of late Rt Hon Lord Claude Hamilton (*see* D Abercorn, colls); *d* 1904; *s* by his grandson (3) BENTLEY LYONEL JOHN (son of late Hon Lyonel Plantagenet Tollemache, el son of 2nd Baron), 3rd Baron; *b* 1883; Capt 3rd Batn Cheshire Regt, Lieut-Com RNVR, and Capt RGA: *m* 1st, 1902, Wynford Rose, who *d* 1926, only da of late Gen Sir Arnold Burrowes Kemball, KCB, KCSI; 2ndly 1928, Lynette, MBE, who *d* 1982, da of Alfred Vincent Pawson, of Nynehead Court, Somerset; *d* 1955; *s* by his kinsman (4) JOHN EDWARD HAMILTON, MC (only son of late Maj-Gen Edward Devereux Hamilton Tollemache, DSO, MC, el son of late Hon Hamilton James Tollemache, 4th son of 1st Baron), 4th Baron; *b* 1910; Maj Coldm Gds: *m* 1939, Dinah Susan, who *d* 1998, da of late Sir Archibald Auldjo Jamieson, KBE, MC; *d* 1975; *s* by his el son (5) TIMOTHY JOHN EDWARD, 5th Baron and present peer.

TOMBS, BARON (Tombs) (Life Baron 1990)

FRANCIS LEONARD TOMBS, son of Joseph Tombs; *b* 17 May 1924; *ed* Elmore Green Sch, Walsall, Birmingham Coll of Technology, and London Univ (BSc); Hon LLD Strathclyde Univ (Chancellor 1991-98), Hon DSc Aston Univ, Lodz Univ (Poland), Cranfield Inst of Technology (Pro-Chancellor and Chm of Council 1985-91), City of London Univ, Bradford Univ, Queen's Univ (Belfast), Surrey Univ and Nottingham Univ, Hon DTech Loughborough Univ of Technology, Hon DEd CNAA, Hon DSc Camb 1989, FEng, Hon FIEE, Hon FIMechE, Hon FICE, Hon FIChemE, Hon FIProdE, Hon Member British Nuclear Energy Soc; Chm Electricity Council for England and Wales 1977-80, Weir Group plc 1981-83, Turner & Newall plc 1982-89, Rolls-Royce plc 1985-92 (Dir since 1982), The Eng Council 1985-88, The Advisory Council on Science and Technology 1987-90, and Molecule Theatre Co 1985-92; Dir N M Rothschild & Sons Ltd 1981-92, Turner & Newall Int Ltd 1982-89, Turner & Newall Welfare Trust Ltd 1982-89, and Shell UK Ltd 1983-92; Liveryman and Assist Warden (Prime Warden 1993-94) Goldsmiths' Co, Freeman City of London; *cr* Knt 1978, and *Baron Tombs*, of Brailes, co Warwicks (Life Baron) 1990: *m* 1949, Marjorie, da of Albert Evans, of Walsall.

Arms – Azure, on a saltire azure fimbriated argent a sun, its four rays in saltire extended and tipped with flame all gold. Crest – Out of a crown rayonny or, each straight ray ending in a mullet or, a dexter arm embowed vested azure the hand proper holding two keys in saltire bows upwards gold. Supporters – *Dexter*, a unicorn argent, armed, unguled, bearded, maned and tufted or, sejant erect upon a grassy mount proper between two double roses growing therefrom argent on gules and both barbed and seeded, stalked and leaved proper; *sinister*, a bear proper, clawed and muzzled or, sejant erect upon a like mount between two thistles growing therefrom also proper.
Residence – Honington Lodge, Honington, Shipston-upon-Stour, Warwicks CV36 5AA.

DAUGHTERS LIVING

Hon Catherine Barbara, *b* 1950.
Hon Elisabeth Jane, *b* 1952.
Hon Margaret Clare, *b* 1958.

TOMLIN, BARONY OF (Tomlin) (Extinct 1935)

DAUGHTER LIVING OF LIFE BARON

Hon Helen Rosa, *b* 1906: *m* 1932, Prof Frank Goldby, MD, FRCP, of 1 St Mark's Court, Barton Rd, Cambridge.

TOMLINSON, BARON (Tomlinson) (Life Baron 1998)

JOHN EDWARD TOMLINSON, son of Frederick Edwin Tomlinson, of ......; *b* 1 Aug 1939; *ed* West-minster City Sch, Co-operative Coll, Loughborough, and Nottingham Univ (Dip Political Economic Social Studies); MA (Industrial Relations) Warwick 1982; Sec Sheffield Co-operative Party 1961-68; Head of Research Dept, AUEW 1968-70; Lecturer in Industrial Relations 1970-74; MP for Meriden (Lab) 1974-79; PPS to Prime Minister 1975-76; Parly Under-Sec of State, FCO 1976-79, and ODM 1977-79; Senior Lecturer in Industrial Relations and Management, later Head of Social Studies, Solihull Coll of Technology 1979-84; MEP for Birmingham West (Lab) since 1984; European Parliamentary Labour Party Spokesman on Budgeting Control since 1989; Vice-Chm, Hansard Soc

since 1993; Tstee, Industry and Parliament Trust since 1988; *cr Baron Tomlinson*, of Walsall, co West Midlands (Life Baron) 1998: *m* 1963, Marianne Solveig, da of ...... Sommar, of Stockholm, Sweden, and has issue.
Residence – 34 Bridge St, Walsall WS1 1JQ.

SONS LIVING

Hon ......, *b* 19—; *ed* ....
Hon ......, *b* 19—; *ed* ....
Hon ......, *b* 19—; *ed* ....

TOPE, BARON (Tope) (Life Baron 1994)

GRAHAM TOPE, CBE, son of late Leslie Tope, of Plymouth; *b* 30 Nov 1943; *ed* Whitgift Sch, S Croydon; MP Sutton and Cheam (*L*) 1972-74; Leader of Council, London Borough of Sutton since 1986; Pres London Liberal Democrats since 1991; UK Rep, EU Cttee of the Regions since 1994, Leader European Lib Dem and Reform Group since 1998; Lib Dem Education Spokesman in House of Lords since 1994, Assistant Whip since 1998; *cr* CBE 1991, and *Baron Tope*, of Sutton, in the London Borough of Sutton (Life Baron) 1994: *m* 1972, Margaret, da of Frank East, of Buckhurst Hill, Essex, and has issue.
Residence – 88 The Gallop, Sutton, Surrey SM2 5SA.

SONS LIVING

Hon Andrew, *b* 1974; *ed* Greenshaw High Sch, Sutton, and Sussex Univ.
Hon David, *b* 1976; *ed* Greenshaw High Sch, Sutton, and Nottingham Trent Univ.

TORDOFF, BARON (Tordoff) (Life Baron 1981)

GEOFFREY JOHNSON TORDOFF, son of Stanley Acomb Tordoff, of Marple, Cheshire, *b* 11 Oct 1928; *ed* Manchester Gram Sch, and Manchester Univ; Chm Liberal Party 1976-79, Pres 1983-84; *cr Baron Tordoff*, of Knutsford, co Cheshire (Life Baron) 1981: *m* 1953, Mary, da of Thomas Swarbrick, of Leeds, and has issue.
Residence – c/o House of Lords, SW1.

SONS LIVING

Hon Nicholas Gregory, *b* 1958.
Hon Mark Edmund, *b* 1962.

DAUGHTERS LIVING

Hon Mary Catherine, *b* 1954.
Hon Frances Jane, *b* 1956.
Hon Paula Mary, *b* 1960.

TORPHICHEN, LORD (Sandilands) (Lord S 1564)
(Title pronounced "Tor-fikken")

I hope for better things

SPERO·MELIORA

JAMES ANDREW DOUGLAS SANDILANDS, 15th Lord, *b* 27 Aug 1946; *s* 1975; *ed* King's Sch, Canterbury, Birmingham Univ and Napier Coll, Edinburgh: *m* 1976, Margaret Elizabeth, only da of late William Alfred Beale, of Boston, Mass, USA, and has issue.

Arms – Quarterly: 1st and 4th argent, on a chief an Imperial crown or, in base a thistle vert, flowered gules; 2nd and 3rd grand quarters, 1st and 4th argent, a bend azure, *Sandilands*; 2nd and 3rd argent, a man's heart proper, ensigned by an Imperial crown gules, on a chief azure, three mullets of the field, *Douglas*. **Crest** – An eagle displayed proper. **Supporters** – Two wild men, wreathed about the temples and loins with oak leaves, each holding on the exterior shoulder a club proper.
Seat – Calder House, Mid-Calder, West Lothian EH53 0HN.

DAUGHTERS LIVING

Hon Margaret Elizabeth Grizel, *b* 1979.
Hon Mary Christian Sarah, *b* 1981.
Hon Anne, *b* 1985.
Hon Alison, *b* 1990.

SISTER LIVING

Hon Alison Mary, *b* 1944: *m* 1966, David Maurice Baldwin, and has issue living, Emma Alison, *b* 1968, — Petra Josephine, *b* 1972. *Residence* – 30 Rochford Av, Shenfield, Essex.

MOTHER LIVING

Mary Thurstan, only da of Randle Henry Neville Vaudrey, of Edgbaston, Birmingham: *m* 1943 (*m diss* 1952), Hon James Bruce Sandilands, Master of Torphichen (later 14th Lord Torphichen), who *d* 1975.

WIDOW LIVING OF FOURTEENTH LORD

PAMELA MARY (*Pamela, Lady Torphichen*) (16 Moore St, Cadogan Sq, SW3), da of late John Howard Snow, and widow of Thomas Hodson-Pressinger: *m* 1973, as his 3rd wife, the 14th Lord Torphichen, who *d* 1975.

COLLATERAL BRANCHES LIVING

Issue of late Hon Walter Alexander Sandilands, yst son of 12th Lord, *b* 1888, *d* 1966: *m* 1918 (*m diss* 1930), Nancy Margaret, who *d* 1979, da of Hubert Powell, of Lewes:—
DOUGLAS ROBERT ALEXANDER (*Master of Torphichen*) (109 Royal George Rd, Burgess Hill, W Sussex); *b* 31 Aug 1926; a Driving Instructor; Memb Inst of Advanced Motorists; Memb Driving Instructors' Asscn: *m* 1st, 1949, Ethel Louise Burkitt; 2ndly 19—, Suzette Veva (*née* Pernet), and has issue living (by 1st *m*), Robert Powell (72 Lacot Rd, Greendale, nr Melbourne, Vic 3341, Australia), *b* 1950: *m* 1974, Cheryl Lin Watson, of Eastbourne, and has issue living, Ashton Powell *b* 14 April 1979, Bethany Ellen *b* 1977, — (by 2nd *m*), Bruno Charles, *b* 1977, — Edward Louis, *b* 1979. —— Jean Eleanor, *b* 1920: *m* 1st, 1947 (*m diss* 1950), Edward Cecil Doudney, who *d* 1955; 2ndly, 1955, as his 2nd wife, Col Richard Greville Acton Steel, TD, who *d* 1981, of 11 Eastleach Turville, Southrop, Cirencester, Glos GL7 3NQ, and has issue living (by 2nd *m*) James Alexander Drummond (2 The Butts, Poulton, Cirencester, Glos), *b* 1958. —— Jonet Christian WIGG, *b* 1924; has resumed surname of Wigg: *m* 1st, 1944, Capt John Osborne Wigg, RN; 2ndly, 19—, John Hine, of Houston, Texas, who *d* 1987, and has issue living (by 1st *m*), Anthony John Osborne, *b* 1955, — Coralie Ann Osborne, *b* 1945: *m* 1965, Keith Clement, — Nina Jonet Osborne, *b* 1947: *m* 1966 (*m diss* 1983), Roderic Erskine Swift, and has issue living, Damien John Erskine *b* 1968, Julian James Sheridan *b* 1971, — Amanda Jane Osborne *b* 1966: *m* 1986, Peter Dyke. *Residence* – 7 Cluny St, Southover, Lewes, E Sussex.

Granddaughters of late Hon John Hope Sandilands (*raised to the rank of a Baron's son* 1870), brother of 12th Lord:—
Issue of late James Bruce Sandilands, *b* 1883, *d* 1951: *m* 1909, Aline, who *d* 1972, da of F. G. Taylor, of Uralla, NSW:—
Helen Lucy, *b* 1909: *m* 1936, Richard Riley Trevitt, of Braeside, Uralla, NSW, and has issue living, Richard John (Sandon, Uralla, NSW), *b* 1938: *m* 1961, Mollie Juanita Blomfield, of Quirindi, NSW, and has issue living, Marcus John *b* 1964, Justin James *b* 1966, Annette *b* 1963, — Simon Bruce *b* 1942: *m* 1965, Robyn Anne Brown, of Uralla, NSW, and has issue living, Shaun Richard *b* 1967, Fiona Jane *b* 1969, — Robin Ann Lucy, *b* 1939: *m* 1965, David Edward Moore, of Perth, and has issue living, Richard Edward *b* 1966, Andrew Geoffrey *b* 1968, Amanda Gillian *b* 1969. —— Aline Dorothy, *b* 1920: *m* 1st, 1941, Godfrey Rees-Jones, RAAF, who was *ka* over Germany 1942; 2ndly, 1955, (Arthur) Harold Roberts, who *d* 1996, and has issue living, (by 2nd *m*) Marc Bruce (Down House, 90 Down Rd, Merrow, Guildford, Surrey GU1 2PZ), *b* 1959: *m* 1991, Deborah Lee Scott, and has issue living, Brendan Marc *b* 1997, — Ian Geoffrey, *b* 1964, — Julie Aline, *b* 1957: *m* 1979, Glenn Raymond Johns, of 5 Robyn Avenue, French's Forest, Sydney, NSW 2086, and has issue, Lee Michael *b* 1981, Matthew Marc *b* 1982, Adam Glenn *b* 1984. *Residence* – 8 Ocean View Drive, Alstonville, NSW 2477.

Granddaughter of late James Bruce Sandilands (ante):—
Issue of late Geoffrey Bruce Hope Sandilands, Roy Australian Air Force, *b* 1922, *k* on active ser 1944: *m* 1944, Dorothy Mary (who *m* 2ndly, 1952, Henry Myron Carlson, of 3,000 Quadra Street, Victoria, British Colombia), da of George Nelson Joyce, of Victoria, BC:—
Joyce Hope SANDILANDS (4444 Tremblay Drive Victoria, BC, Canada V8N 4W5), *b* (*posthumous*) 1945; has retained her maiden name: *m* 1st, 1964 (*m diss* 1979), D. L. Atchison, CA; 2ndly, 1996, J. Robert Whittle, and has issue living (by 1st *m*), James Geoffrey, *b* 1965, — Christine Anne, *b* 1967: *m* 1990, Steven Falconer, of Victoria, BC, Canada, and has issue living, Shayla Christine *b* 1994.

PREDECESSORS – **(1)** *Sir* JAMES Sandilands, 2nd son of the 6th feudal Baron of Calder, a Knight of Malta and Chief of that Order in Scotland, having resigned the property of the Knights of St John to Queen Mary, was *cr Lord Torphichen* (peerage of Scotland) 1564, with remainder to his heirs and assigns whatsoever; *dsp* 1579; *s* by his great-nephew, the 8th feudal Baron of Calder **(2)** JAMES, 2nd Lord; *d* 1617; *s* by his el son **(3)** JAMES, 3rd Lord; *d* unmarried 1622; *s* by his brother **(4)** JOHN, 4th Lord; *d* 1637; *s* by his el son **(5)** JOHN, 5th Lord; *d* unmarried 1649; *s* by his brother **(6)** WALTER, 6th Lord; *d* 1690; *s* by his son **(7)** JAMES, 7th Lord; a zealous supporter of the Scottish Union; was Commr of Police; *d* 1753; *s* by his son **(8)** WALTER, 8th Lord; *d* 1765; *s* by his son **(9)** JAMES, 9th Lord; was a Representative Peer; *dsp* 1815; *s* by his cousin **(10)** JAMES, 10th Lord; el son of Hon Robert, 8th son of 7th Lord; *d* 1862 *s* by his son **(11)** ROBERT, 11th Lord; *d* 1869; *s* by his nephew **(12)** JAMES WALTER, 12th Lord (el son of Rev the Hon John, 2nd son of 10th Lord, by Helen, da of James Hope, Clerk to the Signet), *b* 1846; a Representative Peer: *m* 1881, (*m diss* 1890) Francis Ellen, el da of late Lieut-Gen Charles Parke Gordon CB; *d* 1915; *s* by his second son **(13)** JOHN GORDON, 13th Lord; *b* 1886: *m* 1st, 1916, Grace Douglass, who *d* 1948, da of Winslow Pierce, of Bayville, Long Island, New York; 2ndly, 1950, Isabel Fernandez, who *d* 1976, da of Richard Bowden Daniel, of Jacksonville, Fla, USA, and widow of Richard Youel Phillips, of Greystones, Nanyuki, Kenya; *d* 1973; *s* by his son **(14)** JAMES BRUCE, 14th Lord; *b* 1917: *m* 1st, 1943 (*m diss* 1952) Mary Thurstan, only da of Randle Henry Neville Vaudrey, of Edgbaston, Birmingham; 2ndly, 1955 (*m diss* 1967), Margaret Dawson, of New York City, USA; 3rdly, 1973, Pamela Mary, da of late John Howard Snow, and widow of Thomas Hodson-Pressinger; *d* 1975; *s* by his only son **(15)**, JAMES ANDREW DOUGLAS, 15th Lord and present peer.

TORRINGTON, VISCOUNT (Byng) (Viscount GB 1721, Bt GB 1715)

I will defend

TIMOTHY HOWARD ST GEORGE BYNG, 11th Viscount, and 11th Baronet; *b* 13 July 1943; *s* 1961; *ed* Harrow and St Edmund Hall, Oxford: *m* 1973, Susan Honour, da of Michael George Thomas Webster, of Little Manor Farm, Dummer, Hants (M Conyngham), and has issue.

Arms – Quarterly, sable and argent, in the 1st quarter a lion rampant of the second. **Crest** – An heraldic antelope ermine. **Supporters** – *Dexter*, an heraldic antelope ermine, armed, unguled, maned and tufted or, standing on a ship's gun proper; *sinister*, a sea-horse also proper also on a ship's gun.
Residence – Great Hunts Place, Owslebury, Winchester, Hants. *Clubs* – White's, Pratt's, Muthaiga, Kenya.

DAUGHTERS LIVING

Hon Henrietta Rose, *b* 1977.
Hon Georgina Isabel, *b* 1980.
Hon Malaika Anne, *b* 1982.

MOTHER LIVING

Anne Yvonne, da of late Capt R. G. P. Wood, Dragoon Guards, of Durban, Natal: *m* 1st, 1942, Paymaster-Lieut Hon George Byng, RN, who *d* on active service 1944, only son of 10th Viscount; 2ndly, 1951, Howard Henry Masterton Carpenter, who *d* 1976; 3rdly, 1991, Michael Ingram Bostock. *Residence* – 12 Southgate Villas, St James Lane, Winchester, Hants SO23 9SG.

COLLATERAL BRANCHES LIVING

Grandson of late Lt-Col Alfred Molyneux Cranmer-Byng, el son of Capt Henry Byng, RN (infra):—
Issue of late Capt Launcelot Alfred Cranmer Byng, *b* 1872, *d* 1945: *m* 1st, 1894, Harriet, who *d* 1913, da of Issac Hammersley; 2ndly, 1916, Daisy Elaine, who *d* 1981, da of N. B. Beach, of Chelmsford:—
(By 2nd *m*) †John Launcelot, MC, *b* 1919; *ed* Haileybury, and King's Coll, Camb (MA 1944); Prof of History, Toronto Univ; formerly Lecturer in History at Univ of Hong Kong; 1939-45 War as Maj Airborne Forces (MC): *m* 1955, Margaret Ellen (2177 Burnhamthorpe Rd West, Apt 508, Mississauga, Ont, Canada L5L 5P9), da of R. H. Hardy, of Sevenoaks, Kent, and has issue living, COLIN HUGH, *b* 10 Sept 1960: *m* 1984, Lisa Anne, da of L. A. Dallimore, of Toronto, and has issue living, John Nicholas *b* 10 Nov 1990, Peter Joseph *b* 1994, Leslea Anne *b* 1986, Mary Margaret *b* 1988, Sarah Jaine *b* 1992, Alexandra Ruth *b* 1998, — Alison Caroline, *b* 1956: *m* 1985, Howard Lam, son of Tse Wing Lam, of Toronto, Ont, — Sheila Margaret, *b* 1962. *Residence* – 40 Baif Blvd, Richmond Hill, Ontario, Canada.

Granddaughters of late John Anstruther Byng (infra):—
Issue of late Arthur Maitland Byng, *b* 1917, *d* 1983: *m* 1965, Joan Stuart Marr (Glenbucket, Box 1146, Rustenburg 0300, Transvaal, S Africa):—
Joanne Rachel, *b* 1969. —— Ann Maitland, *b* 1970.

Granddaughters of late Major Arthur Hervey Byng, son of Capt Henry Byng, RN, eldest son of Vice-Adm Hon Henry Dilkes Byng, 4th son of 5th Viscount:—
Issue of late John Anstruther Byng, *b* 1877, *d* 1960: *m* 1915, Rachel Wyllie, da of William Hampden Brodie, of Glenbucket, Scotland:—
Julienne Wyllie, *b* 1919: *m* 1st, 1941, John Duncan, who *d* 19—; 2ndly, 1965, Courtice Jocelyn Leigh-Hunt, who *d* 1976, of No 6 Golden Pond, Private Bag 6007, 3245 Hilton, K.Z. Natal, and has issue living (by 1st *m*), Annette Jennifer (Calle Princesa 50, 08003 Barcelona, Spain), *b* 1943: *m* 19— (*m diss* 19—), Richard Valentine Copley, and has issue living, Sally Victoria *b* 1971, Julienne Borain *b* 1973, — Patricia Jane, *b* 1945: *m* 19—, Robert François Nelson, of 25A Thurlow Rd, London NW3 5PP, and has issue living, Robert Arthur Byng *b* 19—, — Julienne Rae Cranmer, *b* 1947: *m* 19—, David Martin Wilmot (PO Box 223, Hillcrest, K.Z. Natal 3650), and has issue living, Thomas James *b* 1971, Hildegard Susan Judith *b* 1972, Cecilia Mary *b* 1976. —— Mary Maitland, *b* 1923: *m* 1946, Arthur Harold Hampshire Davison, and has issue living, Ian Hampshire (16 Kemp Av, Waterval, Johannesburg 2195, S Africa), *b* 1948, — Neil Torrington (68 Heath Rd, Market Bosworth, Leics CV13 0NX), *b* 1953, — Bruce Dale, *b* 1958.

Descendants of late Rt Hon Sir John Byng, GCB, GCH (3rd son of late George Byng, MP, el son of late Hon Robert Byng, 3rd son of 1st Viscount), who was *cr Earl of Strafford* 1847 (see that title).

PREDECESSORS – **(1)** *Adm Sir* GEORGE Byng, Knt, an eminent naval commander, knighted 1704; *cr* a *Baronet* 1715, and *Baron Byng*, of Southill, co Bedford, and *Viscount Torrington* (peerage of Great Britain) 1721; sat as MP for Plymouth 1705-21, and was Treasurer of the Navy 1725, and First Lord of the Admiralty 1727; *d* 1733; *s* by his el son **(2)** PATTEE PC, 2nd Viscount; sat successively as MP for Plymouth and Bedfordshire; was Treasurer of the Navy 1724-7, and sometime Vice Treasurer and Paymaster-Gen for Ireland, and Capt of the Yeomen of the Guard; *d* 1747; *s* by his brother **(3)** GEORGE, 3rd Viscount; a Maj-Gen in the Army; *d* 1750; *s* by his el son **(4)** GEORGE, 4th Viscount; *d* 1812; *s* by his brother **(5)** JOHN, 5th Viscount; *d* 1813; *s* by his son **(6)** GEORGE, 6th Viscount; *b* 1768; was a Vice-Adm; *d* 1831; *s* by his son **(7)** GEORGE, DCL, 7th Viscount; *b* 1812; was Gov of Ceylon 1847-50, a Lord-in-Waiting to HRH the Prince Consort 1853-9, and to HM Queen Victoria 1859-84; *d* 26 April 1884; *s* by his nephew **(8)** GEORGE STANLEY, 8th Viscount (son of late Major Hon Robert Barlow Palmer Byng, 3rd son of 6th Viscount, and Elizabeth Maria Lowther (who *m* 2ndly, 1861, Rev William Winchester), da of Col Gwatkin) *b* 1841; a Lord-in-Waiting to HM Queen Victoria: *m* 1st, 1882, Alice Arabella, who *d* 1883, da of James Jameson, of Airfield, Dublin; 2ndly, 1885, Emmeline St Maur, who *d* 1912, da of Rev Henry Seymour; *d* 1889; *s* by his son **(9)** GEORGE MASTER, 9th Viscount, *b* 1886; was a Page of Honour to Queen Victoria and to King Edward VII 1899-1903; sometime a Railway and Canal Commr: *m* 1st, 1910 (*m diss* 1921), Eleanor, who *d* 1931, el da of late Edwin Souray, of Long Ditton, Surrey; 2ndly, 1923, Norah Elizabeth Ursula (FERENS), who *d* 1968, da of late Capt Robert Wood-Pottle, 5th R Irish Lancers; *d* 1944; *s* by his cousin **(10)** ARTHUR STANLEY (son of late Hon Sydney Byng, brother of 8th Viscount), 10th Viscount; *b* 1876; Lt-Col RASC; S Africa 1899-1902 (DCM), 1914-18 Was (Officer of Legion of Honour): *m* 1st, 1909 (*m diss* 1936), Louise Annette, da of Joseph Rawlins; 2ndly, 1936 (*m diss* 1952), Rosamund Ella, da of late Vice-Adm Alexander Percy Davidson, DSO; *d* 1961; *s* by his grandson **(11)** TIMOTHY HOWARD ST GEORGE (only son of late Paymaster-Lt Hon George Byng, RN, only son of 10th Viscount), 11th Viscount and present peer; also Baron Byng.

Tottenham, family name of Marquess of Ely.

TOWNSHEND, MARQUESS (Townshend) (Marquess GB 1787, Bt E 1617)

HÆC·GENERI·INCREMENTA·FIDES

Faith obtained these honours for our race

GEORGE JOHN PATRICK DOMINIC TOWNSHEND, 7th Marquess, and 12th Baronet; *b* 13 May 1916; *s* 1921; *ed* Harrow; is Patron of thirteen livings; DCL, FRSA; Chm of Anglia Television Group plc 1976-86, Anglia Television Ltd 1958-86, Anchor Enterprises Ltd 1967-88, AP Bank Ltd 1975-87, Raynham Farm Co since 1957, Norfolk Agricultural Station 1974-87, and Survival Anglia Ltd 1971-86; Vice Chm Norwich Union Life Insurance Society 1973-86, and Fire Insurance Soc 1975-86; Dir Scottish Union and National Insurance Co 1968-86, Maritime Insurance Co Ltd 1968-86, London Merchant Securities plc 1964-95, D E Longe & Co 1962-90, E Coast Grain Ltd 1962-90, and Norwich Union Holdings 1981-86; a Gov of Roy Agric Soc of England; 55 (Suffolk and Norfolk Yeo) Anti Tank Regt 1936, ADC to GOC-in-C, E Command 1936-39, Personal Assist to CIGS 1939-40, Scots Gds 1940-45: *m* 1st, 1939 (*m diss* 1960), Elizabeth Pamela Audrey, who *d* 1989, only da of Maj Thomas Luby, late Judicial Commr, ICS; 2ndly, 1960, Ann Frances, who *d* 1988, only da of late Arthur Pellew Darlow, and has issue by 1st and 2nd *m*.

Arms – Azure, a chevron ermine between three escallops argent. **Crest** – A stag statant proper, attired and unguled or. **Supporters** – *Dexter*, a stag sable attired and unguled or: *sinister*, a greyhound argent.
Seat – Raynham Hall, Norfolk. *Clubs* – White's, Norfolk, MCC.

SONS LIVING *(By 1st marriage)*

CHARLES GEORGE (*Viscount Raynham*) (Pattesley House, Fakenham, Norfolk; 22 Ebury St, SW1), *b* 26 Sept 1945; *ed* Eton: *m* 1st, 1975, Hermione, who *d* 1985, in a motor accident, da of late Lt-Cdr Robert Martin Dominic Ponsonby (*see* E Bessborough, colls, 1995 Edn); 2ndly, 1990, Mrs Alison Marshall, yr da of late Sir Willis Ide Combs, KCVO, CMG, of Wadhurst Park, E Sussex, and has issue:—

SON LIVING (*by 1st m*)—Hon THOMAS CHARLES, *b* 2 Nov 1977.
DAUGHTER LIVING (*by 1st m*)—Hon Louise Elizabeth, *b* 1979.

(By 2nd marriage)

Lord John Patrick, *b* 1962; *ed* Eton, and London Univ: *m* 1987 (*m diss* 1991), Rachel Lucy, da of FM Sir John Chapple, GCB, KBE, ADC Gen. *Residence* – 31 Coleherne Rd, SW10 9BS.

DAUGHTERS LIVING *(By 1st marriage)*

Lady Carolyn Elizabeth Ann TOWNSHEND, *b* 1940; has resumed her maiden name: *m* 1st, 1962 (*m diss* 1971), Antonio Capellini; 2ndly, 1973 (*m annulled* 1974), and has issue living (by 1st *m*), Vincenzo Charles CAPELLINI TOWNSHEND, *b* 1963: *m* 1994, Rachael, da of Mark Daniels, and has issue living, Luca *b* 1995, Sofia *b* 1996, Luisa Carolyn *b* 1998. *Residence* – 89 Elizabeth St, SW1W 9PG.

Lady Joanna Agnes TOWNSHEND, *b* 1943: *m* 1st, 1962 (*m diss* 1968), Jeremy George Courtenay Bradford; 2ndly, 1978 (*m diss* 1984), James Barry Morrissey; 3rdly, 1991, Christian Marc Boegnor, son of late Etienne Boegnor, and has issue living (by 1st *m*), Francis James Patrick, *b* 1963.

(By 2nd marriage)

Lady Katherine Ann *b* 1963: *m* 1991, Piers W. Dent, yst son of Robin Dent, of Olivers, Painswick, Glos, and has issue living, Lucia, *b* 1992.

COLLATERAL BRANCHES LIVING

Grandsons of late Ferrars Ernest Osborne Townshend, only son (by 1st *m*) of late George Ferrars Townshend (*b* 1854), 2nd son of late Rev Lord George Osborne Townshend, yr brother of 4th Marquess:—
Issue of late Henry George Townshend, *b* 1911, *d* 1979: *m* 1943, Elaine Florence (45 Pitua Rd, Te Puna, Tauranga, NZ), da of T. E. Frith, of Melbourne, Australia:—
Ferrars Edwin, *b* 1944: *m* 1980, Gillian Adams, and has issue living, Hamish Richard, *b* 1982, — Nicholas John, *b* 1984, — Rachel Louise, *b* 1987. *Residence* – 45 Pitua Rd, Tauranga, NZ. —— Anthony Stuart, *b* 1956; has issue living (by Nicola LeAnn Duxfield), Rian Alexander DUXFIELD, *b* 1997. *Residence* – 34B Holt Av, Browns Bay, Auckland, NZ.

Granddaughter of late George Ferrars Townshend, elder son (by 2nd *m*) of late George Ferrars Townshend (*b* 1854) (ante):—

Issue of late George Ferrars Vere Townshend, *b* 1897, *d* 1957: *m* 1921, Fanny Elizabeth, da of James Matthew Brassington, of Staffordshire:—
Diana Vere, *b* 1927: *m* 1949, Noel Trevor Gedye, MI StructE, AMNZIE, and has issue living, Christopher John (2/14 Minto St, Remuera, Auckland, NZ), *b* 1950; LLB: *m* 1st, 1973, Ranee Joy Murphy; 2ndly, 19—, Leigh Wilson, and has issue living (by 1st *m*), Sharl Justin *b* 1980, Nicole Jade *b* 1984, — Stephen Warren (24 Duart Av, Mt Albert, Auckland, NZ), *b* 1953: *m* 1977, Roseann Hare, — Michael Jonathan (87A Selwyn Av, Mission Bay, Auckland, NZ), *b* 1957; LLB, BCom, LLM: *m* 1984, Victoria Ruth Ohms, and has issue living, Peter Michael *b* 1991. *Residence* – 1/19 Selwyn Av, Mission Bay, Auckland 5, New Zealand.

Grandsons of late Ernest Edwin Townshend, 3rd son of late Rev Lord George Osborne Townshend (ante):—
Issue of late Clifford Edwin Townshend, *b* 1884, *d* 1958: *m* 1915, Rose Evelyn, MBE, da of John Abraham Greensill, of Picton, Marlborough, New Zealand:—
John Edwin, *b* 1918; 1939-45 with RNZAF: *m* 1943, Mary, da of William Joseph Curran Sharp, and has issue living, Keith Edwin (38A Symonds St, Onehunga, Auckland 6, NZ), *b* 1948: *m* 1981, Margaret Johanna, da of Joseph Boldero, of Kawhia, NZ, and has issue living, David John Edwin *b* 1982, James Raynham *b* 1983, — Margaret Ann Townshend (1019 Hood St, Hastings, NZ), *b* 1944; has resumed her maiden name: *m* 1st, 1963 (*m diss* 1972), Earl Dudley Gee; 2ndly, 1974 (*m diss* 1982), John Leslie Taylor, and has issue living, (by 1st *m*) Richard John Earl Townshend *b* 1969; assumed surname of Townshend by deed poll in lieu of his patronymic, Michelle Margaret *b* 1963: *m* 1984, Neville McAlister, of 11A Woodfield Av, Palmerston North, NZ, Lisa Ann *b* 1966. —— George Maling, MBE (2/26 Rothesay Bay Rd, Auckland, NZ), *b* 1921; *ed* Marlborough Coll, NZ; a JP, and a City Councillor of Napier; 1939-45 War with RNZAF: *m* 1st, 1944, Alice Joyce, who *d* 1986, el da of Alfred Wilfred Nye, of Long Bay Rd, Coromandel, NZ; 2ndly, 1987, Heather Joan Pallesen, 3rd da of Douglas Brown, of Hastings, NZ, and has issue living (by 1st *m*), Colin David, *b* 1948: *m* 1969, Jennifer Pearl, da of Ian Alfred Madsen, of Napier, NZ, and has issue living, Glen David *b* 1971, Zane Colin *b* 1972, Tara Jean *b* 1974, — Yvonne Joy, *b* 1946: *m* 1971, Brett Denize, of 27 Haseler Cres, Howick, Auckland, NZ, and has issue living, Donna Joy *b* 1972, Rowena Helen *b* 1975.

Grandchildren of late Clifford Edwin Townshend (ante):—
Issue of late Charles Roberts Townshend, *b* 1926, *d* 1987: *m* 1952, Dorothy Winifred (11 Whakarire Av, Westshore, Napier, NZ), da of Frederick Leo Luks, of Auckland, NZ:—
Robert Paul (15a Mission Rd, Napier, NZ), *b* 1965: *m* 1994, Lisa Pierrine, da of Raymond Martin Cooper, of Napier, NZ. —— Denise Kaye, *b* 1955: *m* 1980, Stephen Alexander Greer, solicitor, of 124 Puketitiri Rd, Poriati, Hawkes Bay, NZ, and has issue living, Alexander Townshend, *b* 1982, — Charles Townshend, *b* 1989, — Rebecca Ellen, *b* 1984. —— (Adopted son) Mark, *b* 1962.

PREDECESSORS – (1) Roger Townshend, MP for Norfolk 1627; *cr* a Baronet 1617; *d* 1637; *s* by his el son **(2)** *Sir* Roger; 2nd Bt; *s* by his brother **(3)** *Sir* Horatio, 3rd Bt a zealous royalist, who rendered valuable assistance in restoring the monarchy; was sometime MP for Norfolk; *cr Baron Townshend*, of Lynn Regis (peerage of England) 1661, and *Viscount Townshend*, of Raynham (peerage of England) 1682; *d* 1687; *s* by his son **(4)** Charles, KG, PC, 2nd Viscount; was Lord-Lt of Norfolk, Capt of Yeomen of the Guard 1707-11, Ambassador to the Hague 1709-10, a Lord Justice, Principal Sec of State 1714-16 and 1721-30, and Pres of the Council 1720; *d* 1738; *s* by his son **(5)** Charles, 3rd Viscount, who in 1723 had been summoned to Parliament in his father's Barony of Lynn; was Lord of the Bedchamber, Custos Rotulorum of Norfolk, and Master of the Jewels; *d* 1767; *s* by his son **6** George, PC, 4th Viscount; a Field-Marshal in the Army and a successful military commander, was *cr Marquess Townshend* (Peerage of Great Britain) 1787; sat as MP for Norfolk, Lt-Gen of the Ordnance 1763-67, and Master-Gen 1772-82, Viceroy of Ireland 1767, Gov of Jersey, &c, Lord-Lieut of Norfolk, &c: *m* 1st 1751, Charlotte, who *d* 1770, in her own right (through her mother) Baroness Ferrers of Chartley, and (through her father) Baroness Compton; 2ndly, 1773, Anne, who *d* 1819, da of Sir William Montgomery, 1st Bt; *d* 1807; *s* by his son **(7)** George, 2nd Marquess, who following the death of his mother 1770, was summoned to Parliament as *Baron Ferrers de Chartley*, and in 1784 had been *cr Earl of Leicester* (peerage of Great Britain); was Postmaster-Gen 1794-8, and Lord Steward of the Household 1799-1802; *d* 1811; *s* by his son **(8)** George Ferrers, 3rd Marquess; *dsp* 1855, when the Earldom of Leicester became extinct, the Baronies of Ferrers of Chartley, Compton, &c became abeyant, and the Barony, Viscountcy, and Marquessate of Townshend devolved upon his cousin **(9)** John, 4th Marquess; *b* 1798; was a Rear-Adm: *m* 1825, Elizabeth Jane, who *d* 1877, da of Rear-Adm Lord George Stuart, CB (M Bute); *d* 1863; *s* by his son **(10)** John Villiers Stuart, 5th Marquess, *b* 1831; MP for Tamworth (*L*) 1856-63: *m* 1865, Lady Anne Elizabeth Clementina Duff, who *d* 1925, da of 5th Earl of Fife; *d* 1899; *s* by his only son **(11)** John James Dudley Stuart, 6th Marquess, *b* 1866: *m* 1905, Gladys Ethel Gwendolen Eugénie (who *d* 1959, having *m* 2ndly, 1946, Bernard le Strange), eldest da of late Thomas Sutherst, Bar-at-law; *d* 1921; *s* by his son **(12)** George John Patrick Dominic, 7th Marquess and present peer; also Viscount Townshend, of Raynham, and Baron Townshend, of Lynn Regis.

Tracey, Hanbury-, family name of Baron Sudeley.

TRAFFORD, BARONY OF (Trafford) (Extinct 1989)

SON LIVING OF LIFE BARON

Hon Mark Russell, b 1966; ed Lancing, and Brunel Univ; Bar Lincoln's Inn 1991: m 1995, Brigitte A., elder da of John Howe, of Loughton, Essex, and has issue living, Luc Anthony, b 1999, — Jessica Laura, b 1990, — Katherine Elizabeth, b (twin) 1999. Chambers — 2 King's Bench Walk, Temple, EC4Y 7DE.

DAUGHTER LIVING OF LIFE BARON

Hon Tanya Helen, b 1968; ed Deepdene Sch, and RMA Sandhurst.

WIDOW LIVING OF LIFE BARON

HELEN (Baroness Trafford), da of Ralph Chalk, of Cambs; Hon DSc Univ of Sussex 1991; Founder Trafford Centre for Medical Research; Trustee Nurses Welfare Service, Trafford Renal Research Trust; Vice-Pres Royal Coll of Nursing since 1997; Hon Memb Royal Pharmaceutical Soc of GB since 1999: m 1960, Baron Trafford (Life Baron), who d 1989. Residence – 17 Courtfield Rd, SW7 4DA

TRANMIRE, BARONY OF (Turton) (Extinct 1994)

SONS LIVING AND DECEASED OF LIFE BARON

Hon Michael Andrew, b 1929.

†Hon Timothy Robert Scott, b 1934; ed RNC Dartmouth, and Balliol Coll, Oxford; Bar Inner Temple 1956; d 1989.

Hon Gerald Christopher (Park House, Upsall, N Yorks), b 1937; ed Eton, and RAC Cirencester; a farmer: m 1967, Alexandra Susan, da of Lt-Col S. Oliver, of 12 Maison Dieu, Richmond, Yorks, and has issue living, Robert Edmund, b 1971, — Natalia Maud Elizabeth, b 1969, — Alexandra Christian, b 1974.

DAUGHTER LIVING OF LIFE BARON

Hon Gillian Hermione Christian, b 1930: m 1960, David Poulett Wells, BM, BCh, FRCGP, of Hilperton House, Hilperton, Trowbridge, Wilts, and has had issue, Quinton Robert, b 1962, — Nicholas Michael, b and d 1966, — Fiona Mary, b 1963, — Olivia Rosalind, b 1969.

TREDEGAR, BARONY OF (Morgan) (Extinct 1962)

WIDOW LIVING OF SIXTH BARON

JOANNA, only da of Walter Henry Law-Smith, of Adelaide, S Australia: m 1st, 1938 (m diss 1954), Cdr A. B. Russell, DSO, RN; 2ndly, 1954, the 6th Baron, who d 1962, when the title became ext; 3rdly, 1967, the 9th Baron Wharton, who d 1969; 4thly, 1971, Bruce Yorke, of Casa Le Concha, Rocio de Naguëles, Marbella (Malaga), Spain.

TREFGARNE, BARON (Trefgarne) (Baron UK 1947)

DAVID GARRO TREFGARNE, PC, 2nd Baron; *b* 31 March 1941; *s* 1960; *ed* Haileybury, and Princeton Univ, USA; awarded Roy Aero Club Bronze Medal (jointly) for flight UK to Aust and back in light aircraft 1963; Opposition Whip, House of Lords 1977-79; Lord in Waiting to HM 1979-81; Under Sec, Dept of Trade 1981; Under Sec, Foreign & Commonwealth Office 1981-82; Under Sec Dept of Health & Social Security 1982-83; Under Sec for Armed Forces 1983-85, Min of State for Defence (Support) 1985-86, and (Procurement) 1986-89, Min for Trade Dept of Trade & Industry 1989-90; Chm Engineering Training Authority since 1994; Company Dir and Pres of Metcom; PC 1989: *m* 1968, Hon Rosalie Lane, da of Baron Lane of Horsell (Life Baron), and has issue.

Arms – Or, a dragon rampant gules, over all a bend azure charged with a leek of the first between two thistles stalked and leaved proper. **Crest** – A palm tree, suspended therefrom by a strap proper an escutcheon or, charged with a portcullan chained gules. **Supporters** – On either side is a Herefordshire bull proper, charged on the shoulder with an escutcheon or, thereon a portcullis chained sable.
Address – c/o Barclays Bank, Woking, Surrey GU21 1AE.

SONS LIVING

Hon GEORGE GARRO, *b* 4 Jan 1970.

Hon Justin Peter Garro (30 Kimbell Gdns, SW6 6QQ), *b* 1973: *m* 1997, Molly Elizabeth Helen, 2nd da of Robert Gaisford, of Stonegate, E Sussex.

DAUGHTER LIVING

Hon Rebecca Rosalie, *b* 1976.

BROTHERS LIVING

Hon Trevor Garro (30 Kimbell Gdns, SW6 6QQ), *b* 1944; *ed* Cheltenham; Cranfield Sch of Management 1968-69; Chm, Nesco Investments plc 1979-87, Enterprise Insurance Co Ltd since 1998; Dir Templeton Emerging Markets Investment Trust plc since 1989, Gartmore High Income Trust plc since 1999, and of other cos: *m* 1st, 1967 (*m diss* 1979), Diana Elizabeth, 2nd da of Michael Edward Gibb; 2ndly, 1979, Caroline France, da of Michael Gosschalk, of Monte Carlo, and has issue living (by 1st *m*), Rupert Michael Garro, *b* 1972, — Oliver Edward Garro, *b* 1974, — Susannah Julia, *b* 1976, — (by 2nd *m*) Mark Michael Garro, *b* 1982, — Camilla Amélie, *b* 1988.

Hon Gwion George Garro (Cherry Croft, Hewelsfield, Lydney, Glos), *b* 1953; *ed* Milton Abbey, and Merrist Wood & Usk Agric Colls; Tree Surgeon: *m* 1986, Jacqueline Louise, da of Alan Rees, of Woodspring, Brockweir, Chepstow, Gwent, and has issue living, Samuel Ivor Garro, *b* 1987, — Hannah Elizabeth, *b* 1989.

SISTER LIVING

Hon Mary Elizabeth, *b* 1946; Bar (Gray's Inn) 1971.

PREDECESSOR – (1) GEORGE MORGAN Trefgarne, son of late Rev David Garro-Jones of Milford Haven; *b* 1894; assumed by deed poll (enrolled at College of Arms) 1954 the surname of Trefgarne in lieu of his patronymic; was Parliamentary Sec, Min of Production 1942-5, Chm of Television Advisory Committee 1945-9, and Founder Chm of Colonial Development Corporation 1947-50; sat at MP for S Div of Hackney (*L*) 1924-9, and for N Div of Aberdeen (*Lab*) 1935-45; *cr Baron Trefgarne*, of Cleddau, co Pembroke (peerage of UK) 1947: *m* 1940, Elizabeth (who *m* 2ndly, 1962 (*m diss* 1966), Com Anthony Tosswill Courtney, OBE, who *d* 1988, and 3rdly, 1971, Hugh Cecil Howat Ker, and *d* 1987), yst da of late Charles Edward Churchill, of Ashton Keynes, Wilts; *d* 1960; *s* by his el son (2) DAVID GARRO, 2nd Baron and present peer.

Trefusis, Fane-, family name of Baron Clinton.

Trench, family name of Baron Ashtown.

Trench, Le Poer, family name of Earl of Clancarty.

TRENCHARD, VISCOUNT (Trenchard) (Viscount UK 1936, Bt UK 1919)

HUGH TRENCHARD, 3rd Viscount, and 3rd Baronet; *b* 12 March 1951; *s* 1987: *ed* Eton, and Trin Coll, Camb (BA 1973); Capt 4th Royal Green Jackets, TA (1973-80); Dir Kleinwort Benson Ltd 1986-96, Dover Japan Inc 1985-87, Japan Securities Dealers Assocn 1994-95, Robert Fleming and Co Ltd 1996-98, and Robert Fleming Internatnl Ltd since 1998; Member Executive Cttee British Chamber of Commerce in Japan 1993-95; Chm Securities Cttee, European Business Community in Japan 1993-95 (Vice Chm Council 1995): *m* 1975, Hon Fiona Elizabeth Morrison, da of 2nd Baron Margadale, and has issue.

Arms – Per Pale argent and azure, on the first three pallets sable, all within a bordure of the last. **Crest** – A cubit arm erect, vested azure, cuffed argent, holding in the hand a Cinqueda sword, both proper. **Supporters** – On either side an eagle close gules, each charged on the neck, the dexter with a thistle slipped and leaved and the sinister with truncheon erector.
Residence – Standon Lordship, Standon, Ware, Herts SG11 1PR.

SONS LIVING

Hon ALEXANDER THOMAS, *b* 26 July 1978; *ed* Eton, and St Hugh's Coll, Oxford; a Page of Honour to HM The Queen 1990-93.
Hon William James, *b* 1986.

DAUGHTERS LIVING

Hon Katherine Clare, *b* 1980; *ed* St Mary's Sch, Calne.
Hon Laura Mary, *b* 1987.

NOSCE TEIPSVM
Know thyself

BROTHERS LIVING

Hon John (Lower Abbott's Wootton, Whitchurch Canonicorum, Bridport, Dorset DT6 6NL), *b* 1953; *ed* Eton: *m* 1983, Clare, yst da of Edward Chandos de Burgh Marsh, of The Old Rectory, Salcott, Essex, and has issue living, Thomas Edward, *b* 1988, — Emma Clare, *b* 1991.
Hon Thomas Henry, *b* 1966; *ed* Haileybury: *m* 1997, Sarah Saunders, and has issue living, Katherine Elizabeth, *b* 1997.

WIDOW LIVING OF SECOND VISCOUNT

PATRICIA SCOTT (*Dowager Viscountess Trenchard*), da of late Adm Sir Sidney Robert Bailey, KBE, CB, DSO: *m* 1948, the 2nd Viscount Trenchard, MC, who *d* 1987. *Residence* – Abdale House, North Mymms, Hatfield, Herts.

PREDECESSOR – (1) *Marshal of the RAF Sir* HUGH MONTAGUE Trenchard, GCB, OM, GCVO, DSO, son of late Capt Henry Montague Trenchard; *b* 1873; S Africa 1900-02 with Imperial Yeo, Bushman Corps, and Canadian Scouts (dangerously wounded), S Nigeria 1904 in command (despatches), 1904-05 Comdg patrol through Ibibio and Kwa country, 1905-6 in command of Bendo-Onitsha Hinterland Expedition (despatches, DSO), 1914-18 War as Gen Officer Comdg Mil Wing of RFC as Ch of Air Staff (RAF) and as GOC-in-C, Inter-Allied Indep Air Force, thanked by Parliament, *cr* a Baronet, granted £10,000; Ch of Air Staff and Member of Air Council 1918 and 1918-30. Prin Air ADC to HM 1921-

25, and Commr of Metropolitan Police 1931-35; bore Third Sword at Coronation of King George VI; *cr* a Baronet 1919, *Baron Trenchard*, of Wolfeton, co Dorset (peerage of UK) 1930, and *Viscount Trenchard*, of Wolfeton, co Dorset (peerage of UK) 1935: *m* 1920, Katherine Isabel Salvin, who *d* 1960, da of late Edward Salvin Bowlby, of Gilston Park, Herts, and Knoydart, Inverness-shire, and widow of Capt Hon James Boyle; *d* 1956; *s* by his yr son (2) THOMAS, MC, 2nd Viscount, *b* 1923; served 1939-45 War as Capt KRRC; Dir T. Wall & Sons Ltd 1953-66, Chm Walls Meat Co Ltd 1960-66, Dir Unilever Ltd, and Unilever NV 1967-77, and other Cos; Pres Royal Inst of Public Health and Hygiene 1970-79; Member Agric Research Council 1970-79; Pres of Grocery Distribution 1974-77; Min of State Dept of Industry 1979-81, for Defence Procurement 1981-83; Chm Schlumberger Measurement & Control (UK) Ltd 1985-87: *m* 1948, Patricia Scott, da of late Adm Sir Sidney Robert Bailey, KBE, CB, DSO; *d* 1987; *s* by his eldest son (3) HUGH, 3rd Viscount and present peer; also Baron Trenchard.

TREND, BARONY OF (Trend) (Extinct 1987)

SONS LIVING OF LIFE BARON

Hon Michael St John, CBE, MP, *b* 1952; *ed* Westminster, Oriel Coll, Oxford and in Athens (Greek Govt scholarship); MP (*C*) Windsor since 1992, Deputy Chm Conservative Party 1995-98; Opposition Front Bench Spokesman on European Affairs since 1998; CBE (Civil) 1997: *m* 1987, Jill Elizabeth, elder da of L. A. Kershaw, of Oldham, Lancs, and has issue living, Edward St John, *b* 1990, — Faith Charlotte, *b* 1988, — Mary Cecilia, *b* 1994.

Dr the Hon Patrick St John, *b* 1955; FRCP 1997: *m* 1989, Susan F., da of late R. W. Saunders, of Meanwood, Leeds, and has issue living, Alexander *b* 1992, — Hector, *b* 1993, — Cassandra, *b* 1996.

DAUGHTER LIVING OF LIFE BARON

Hon Catharine Julia, *b* 1950: *m* 1966, Colin James Rawlinson.

WIDOW LIVING OF LIFE BARON

PATRICIA CHARLOTTE (*Baroness Trend*), da of late Rev Gilbert Shaw: *m* 1949, Baron Trend, GCB, CVO, PC, who *d* 1987.

TRENT, BARONY OF (Boot) (Extinct 1956)

DAUGHTERS LIVING OF SECOND BARON

Hon Barbara Jacqueline (Wilton Lodge, Lovel Rd, Winkfield, Berks), *b* 1915: *m* 1934 (*m diss* 1973), Maj Willoughby Rollo Norman, who *d* 1997, and has issue living (*see* Norman, Bt).

Hon Jocelyne Mary, *b* 1917: *m* 1947, Maj Harcourt Michael Scudamore Gold, MC, of Wheathill, Sparsholt, nr Winchester, Hants, who *d* 1982, and has issue living, John Angus Harcourt (St Mark, Snailwell Rd, Newmarket, Suffolk CB8 7DP), *b* 1958: *m* 1982 (*m diss* 1988), Charlotte Mary, yr da of late Lt-Col John Monsell Christian, MC, — Charmian Joy, *b* 1950: *m* 1st, 1969 (*m diss* 1973), Frederick James Meynell (*see* E Halifax, colls); 2ndly, 1974 (*m diss* 19—), James Richard Nicholson (*see* Nicholson Bt, *cr* 1912); 3rdly, 1982, Timothy Gilbert Culcheth Holcroft (*see* Holcroft, Bt, colls).

Hon (Margaret) Anne, *b* 1920: *m* 1st, 1940 (*m diss* 1948), Major John Edward Jocelyn Davie, Derbyshire Yeo; 2ndly, 1949, Air Vice-Marshal Somerled Douglas MacDonald, CB, CBE, DFC, who *d* 1979, and has issue living, (by 1st *m*) Simon John (55 Sutherland St, SW1), *b* 1941, — (Anne) Clare (18 Quarrendon St, SW6), *b* 1943: *m* 1964 (*m diss* 1975), Robin Gerard d'Abo, and has issue living, John Gerard Nicholas *b* 1968, Zara *b* 1966. *Residence* – Thane, Kintbury, Newbury, Berks.

Hon Elizabeth Campbell, *b* 1927: *m* 1947, Major Michael Woodbine Parish, MC, Notts Yeo, who *d* 1994, and has issue living, (Clement) Robin Woodbine (Walcot Hall, Lybury North, Shropshire), *b* 1950: *m* 1997, Lucinda Jane, da of Lt-Cmdr Wyndham Julian Rogers-Coltman, late RN, of Berryburn, Ancroft, Berwick-upon-Tweed, and has issue living, Arthur Jesse Woodbine *b* 1998, — Suzanne Woodbine, *b* 1948: *m* 1983, S. B. Kumaramangalam, of Dharmapuri, Tamil Nadu, India, and has had issue, Kim *b* 1983, *d* 1995, Melissa Zoë *b* 1984, — Caroline Woodbine, *b* 1953: *m* 1979, George Constantine Zegos, of Villa Primrose, Grammou St, Kaki-Vigla, Salamina, Greece, and has issue living, Constantine George *b* 1979, Elizabeth Miriam *b* 1984, Dimitra Winifred *b* 1986, Rose Athina *b* 1988, — Emma Woodbine, *b* 1957: *m* 1987, Charles Robson Hamilton Houston, and has issue (*see* B Swansea). *Residence* – Walcot Hall, Lydbury North, Shropshire.

TREVELYAN, BARONY OF (Trevelyan) (Extinct 1985)

DAUGHTERS LIVING OF LIFE BARON

Hon Susan Anne, *b* 1941: *m* 1961, Harald Busse, and has issue living, Allan George, *b* 1962, — Jan Michael, *b* 1963, — Nicola Andrea, *b* 1967.
Hon Catherine Mary, OBE, *b* 1943; OBE (Civil) 1977: *m* 1990, as his 3rd wife, Robert Kee.

WIDOW LIVING OF LIFE BARON

VIOLET MARGARET (*Baroness Trevelyan*) (24 Duchess of Bedford House, W8 7QN), da of late Gen Sir William Henry Bartholomew, GCB, CMG, DSO: *m* 1937, Baron Trevelyan, KG, GCMG, CIE, OBE (Life Baron), who *d* 1985.

Trevethin and Oaksey, Baron, see Oaksey.

TREVOR, BARON (Hill-Trevor) (Baron UK 1880)

(MARKE) CHARLES HILL-TREVOR, 5th Baron; *b* 8 Jan 1970; *s* 1997; *ed* Rannoch Sch; patron of two livings.

𝕬rms – Quarterly: 1st and 4th per bend sinister ermine and ermines, a lion rampant or, *Trevor.* 2nd and 3rd sable, on a fesse argent, between three leopards passant guardant or, spotted of the field, as many escallops gules, *Hill.* 𝕮rest – 1st, a wyvern, wings addorsed sable, *Trevor.* 2nd, a reindeer's head couped at the neck gules, attired and plain collared or, *Hill.* 𝕾upporters – *Dexter*, a lion ermines, gorged with a ducal coronet and chained or, the chain reflexed over the back; pendant from the collar a shield argent, charged with the crest of Trevor; *sinister* a leopard or, spotted sable, gorged with a ducal coronet and chained or, the chain reflexed over the back; pendent from the collar a shield ermines charged with the crest of Hill.
Seat – Brynkinalt, Chirk, Wrexham, N Wales LL14 5NS. *Clubs* – E India, Devonshire, Sports and Public School.

BROTHER LIVING

Hon IAIN ROBERT, *b* 12 June 1971; *ed* Trin Coll, Glenalmond, Wye Coll, and London Univ; MSc, ARICS: *m* 1998, Kate L., yr da of David Lord, of Deighton Hills, Norfolk. *Addresses* – Auch, Bridge of Orchy, Argyll; The Holt, Chirk, Wrexham, N Wales.

UNCLE LIVING (*son of 3rd Baron*)

Hon Nevill Edward (Plâs Lledrod, Llansilin, Clwyd), *b* 1931; *ed* Shrewsbury; High Sheriff Denbighshire (now Clwyd) 1965, DL 1965, JP Bcrwyn Div 1971; Jt Master Border Counties (NW) Otter Hounds 1950-59, Jt Master Sir Watkin Williams Wynn's Foxhounds 1970-79; Flying Officer RAF (ret), ADC to Com-in-Ch Fighter Command 1958-59, ADC to Ch of Air Staff 1959-61: *m* 1963, Deborah Helen Benson, only da of late William Thomas Benson Jowitt, of Crag Hill, Killinghall, Yorks, and has issue living, Caroline Anne, *b* 1965, — Diana Rosemary, *b* 1967.

WIDOW LIVING OF FOURTH BARON

SUSAN JANET ELIZABETH (*Baroness Trevor*), da of late Ronald Ivor Bence, DSC, VRD, BM, BCh, of Selly Oak, Birmingham: *m* 1967, the 4th Baron Trevor, who *d* 1997. *Residence* – Pen-y-Bryn, Whittington, Oswestry, Shropshire SY11 4DG.

PREDECESSORS – (1) *Lord* ARTHUR EDWIN HILL, 3rd son of 3rd Marquess of Downshire, KP; *b* 1819; MP for co Down (*C*) 1845-80; assumed the additional surname of Trevor 1862, on succeeding to the estates of Viscount Dungannon; *cr*

Baron Trevor, of Brynkinalt, co Denbigh (peerage of United Kingdom) 1880: *m* 1st, 1848, Mary Emily, who *d* 1855, el da of Sir Richard Sutton, 1st Bt; 2ndly, 1858, Hon Mary Catherine Curzon, who *d* 1911, sister of 4th Baron Scarsdale; *d* 1894; *s* by his el son (2) ARTHUR WILLIAM, 2nd Baron, *b* 1852; Lieut-Col 1st Life Guards, and Vice-Lieut for Denbighshire; Comdt Denbighshire Vol Regt 1917-20 (Hon Col): *m* 1st, 1894, Hon Annie Mary Eleanor Fraser, who *d* 1895, da of 17th Baron Saltoun, and formerly wife of 15th Baron Zouche; 2ndly, 1897, Rosamond, MBE, who *d* 1942, da of late Hon Edmund George Petre (*see* B Petre, colls), and widow of 4th Earl of Bantry (*ext*); *d* 1923; *s* by his half-brother (3) CHARLES EDWARD, 3rd Baron, *b* 1863: *m* 1927, Phyllis, who *d* 1990, da of J. A. Sims, of Ings House, Kirton-in-Lindsey, Lincolnshire; *d* 1950; *s* by his el son (4) CHARLES EDWIN, 4th Baron, *b* 1928; Trustee Royal Forestry Soc of England: *m* 1967, Susan Janet Elizabeth, da of late Ronald Ivor Bence, DSC, VRD, BM, BCh, of 13 Bournbrook Rd, Selly Oak, Birmingham; *d* 1997; *s* by his elder son (5) (MARKE) CHARLES, 5th Baron and present peer.

TRIMLESTOWN, BARON (Barnewall) (Baron I 1461)

I had rather die than be disgraced

RAYMOND CHARLES BARNEWALL, 21st Baron; *b* 29 Dec 1930; *s* 1997; *ed* Ampleforth.

Arms – Ermine, a bordure engrailed gules. Crest – A plume of five ostrich feathers or, gules, azure, vert, and argent, and issuant therefrom a demifalcon rising of the last. Supporters – *Dexter*, a griffin argent; *sinister*, a lion gules.
Residence – Autumn Cottage, Chiddingfold, Surrey.

SISTER LIVING

Hon Diana, *b* 1929: *m* 1954, Anthony Gerard Astley Birtwistle, and has issue living, Caroline Muriel Mary, *b* 1955: *m* 1982, Stewart Oliver, of Creek Farm, Brancaster, King's Lynn, Norfolk, son of S/Ldr H. W. Oliver, OBE, RAF, of Staithe House, Brancaster Staithe, King's Lynn, Norfolk, and has issue living, Alexander Charles James *b* 1985, George Anthony Andrew *b* 1989, Charlotte Mary Rose *b* 1983, — Emma Frances Mary, *b* 1957: *m* 1982, Oliver John Woodforde Pawle, of 33 Blenkarne Rd, SW11 6HZ, son of late Roger Pawle, OBE, of Parkstone, Dorset, and has issue living, James Roger Woodforde *b* 1985, Lucy Diana Mary *b* 1988, Victoria Louise Maria *b* 1992, — Lucinda Jane Mary, *b* 1960: *m* 1986, P. Malcolm G. Reid, of The Granary, Little Iridge Farm, Hurst Green, E Sussex TN19 7RX, yst son of Dr Kenneth Reid, of Rest Harrow, Cooden, Sussex, and has issue living, Charles Anthony Gilmore *b* 1991, Emily Louise Mary *b* 1988, Olivia Charlotte Mary *b* 1997, — Sophia Louise Mary, *b* 1964: *m* 1996, Julian Stirling Emmet Lynn, of New Cottage, Woodhurst, E Sussex TN5 6LP, son of Mrs Graeme Hamilton, of Eastling, Kent, and has issue living, Frederick Graeme Stirling *b* 1997. *Residence* – Terwick Hill House, Rogate, Petersfield, Hants GU31 5EJ.

WIDOW LIVING OF TWENTIETH BARON

MARY WONDERLY (*Baroness Trimlestown*), elder da of late Judge Thomas F. McAllister, of Grand Rapids, Michigan, USA: *m* 1977, as his 2nd wife, the 20th Baron Trimlestown, who *d* 1997.

PREDECESSORS – (1) *Sir* ROBERT Barnewall, was *cr Baron Trimlestown*, of Trimlestown, co Meath (peerage of Ireland) 1461; *s* by his son (2) CHRISTOPHER, 2nd Baron; *s* by his el son (3) JOHN; appointed Vice-Treasurer of Ireland 1522 High Treasurer 1524, and Lord High Chancellor 1534; *d* 1538; *s* by his son (4) PATRICK, 4th Baron; *s* by his el son (5) ROBERT, 5th Baron; *dsp* 1573; *s* by his brother (6) PETER 6th Baron; *d* 1598; *s* by his son (7) ROBERT, 7th Baron; *d* 1639; *s* by his grandson (8) MATTHIAS (el son of Hon Christopher Barnewall, el son of 7th Baron), 8th Baron; *d* 1667; *s* by his el son (9) ROBERT, 9th Baron; *d* 1687; *s* by his son (10) MATTHIAS, 10th Baron; *dsp* 1692; *s* by his brother (11) JOHN, 11th Baron: *m* 1703, Margaret, da and heiress of Sir John Barnewall; *s* by his el son (12) ROBERT, 12th Baron; *d* 1779; *s* by his only son (13) THOMAS, 13th Baron; a Knight of Malta; *dsp* 1796; *s* by his cousin (14) NICHOLAS (son of Hon Richard Barnewall, 3rd son of 11th Baron), 14th Baron; *b* 1726; was twice *m*; *d* 1813; *s* by his only son (15) JOHN THOMAS, 15th Baron, *b* 1773: *m* 1793, Maria Theresa, da of R. Kirwan; *d* 1839; *s* by his son (16) THOMAS, 16th Baron, *b* 1796; *m* 1836, Margaret Randalina, who *d* 1872, da of Philip Roche; *d* 1879, when the title became dormant until claimed in 1891 by his kinsman (17) CHRISTOPHER PATRICK MARY, *de jure*, 17th Baron, son of Charles Barnewall, of Meadstown, co Meath, and great-grandson of Richard Barnewall, of Fyanstown (a descendant of Hon Patrick Barnewall, 2nd son of the 7th Baron), on whom the 14th Baron, failing his own issue male, entailed his estates: he *d* 1891, before he had established his right to vote at the Election of Representative Peers; *s* by his brother (18) CHARLES ALOYSIUS, 18th Baron; *b* 1861; adjudged 18th Baron Trimlestown by Committee for Privileges of House of Lords in 1893: *m* 1st, 1889, Margaret Theresa, who *d* 1901, da of Richard John Stephens, of Brisbane; 2ndly, 1907, Mabel Florence, who *d* 1914, da of William Robert Shuff, of Torquay, Devon; 3rdly, 1930, Josephine Francesca, who *d* 1945, da of Rt Hon Sir Christopher John Nixon, PC, MD, 1st Bt; *d* 1937; *s* by his only surviving son (19) CHARLES ALOYSIUS, 19th Baron; *b* 1899, Lieut Irish Guards: *m* 1st, 1926, Muriel, who *d* 1937, da of Edward Oskar Schneider, of Mansfield Lodge, Whalley Range, Manchester; 2ndly, 1952, Freda Kathleen, who *d* 1987, da of late Alfred Watkins, of Ross-on-Wye; *d* 1990; *s* by his elder son (20) ANTHONY EDWARD, 20th Baron, *b* 1928; Irish Guards 1946-48; Naval architect with Jack Jones 1949-53; European sales exec P & O Shipping 1965-74: *m* 1st, 1963 (*m diss* 1973), Lorna Margaret Marion, who *d* 1988, da of late Charles Douglas Ramsay; 2ndly, 1977, Mary Wonderly, elder da of late Judge Thomas F. McAllister, of Grand Rapids, Michigan, USA; *d* 1997; *s* by his brother (21) RAYMOND CHARLES, 21st Baron and present peer.

TROTMAN, BARON (Trotman) (Life Baron 1999)

ALEXANDER JAMES TROTMAN, son of ...... Trotman, of ......; *b* 22 July 1933; *ed* Boroughmuir Sch, Edinburgh, and Michigan State Univ, USA (MBA 19—); served RAF 1951-55; Ford Motor Co, Europe 1955-69, Dearborn, Michigan, USA 1969-71; Dir Sales and Marketing Planning 1971-72; Exec Dir Production Planning and Research 1972-75; Chief Car Planning Manager, Car Production Development Group 1975-77; Exec Dir Ops Planning 1977-78; Assist Gen Manager, Track and Recreational Productions Ops 1978-79; Corporation Vice-Pres 1979; Vice-Pres Truck Ops Ford of Europe Inc then Pres Ford Asia-Pacific Inc 1983-84; Pres and Chm Ford of Europe Inc 1984; Exec Vice-Pres North American Auto Ops 1989; Chm, Pres and Chief Exec Offr Ford Motor Co 1993-98; Dir IBM Corporation, New York Stock Exchange, and ICI plc; *cr* Kt 1996, and *Baron Trotman*, of Osmotherley, co N Yorks (Life Baron) 1999: *m* 19—, ..., da of ......, of ......, and has issue.

Arms – ......
Address – c/o House of Lords, Westminster, SW1A 0PW.

TRUMPINGTON, BARONESS (Barker) (Life Baroness 1980)

JEAN ALYS BARKER, PC, da of late Arthur Edward Campbell-Harris; *b* Oct 23 1922; *ed* Privately; Camb City Councillor 1963-73, Cambs Co Councillor 1973-75, Mayor of Camb 1971-72, JP South Westminster 1976-82; Member Airline Users Cttee 1973-80 (Chm 1979-80); UK Representative to UN Status of Women 1979-82; Baroness in Waiting to HM 1983-85, 1991-92, 1992-97, and an Extra Baroness in Waiting since 1998; Parl Under Sec of State DHSS 1985-87, Parl Sec Agriculture 1987-92; *cr Baroness Trumpington*, of Sandwich, co Kent (Life Baroness) 1980, and PC 1992: *m* 1954, William Alan Barker, who *d* 1988, and has issue.

Arms – Gyronny of eight ermine and azure, three hedgehogs two and one, gold. Supporters – *Dexter*, a boxer bitch; *Sinister*, a bay colt, both proper.
Address – c/o House of Lords, SW1.

SON LIVING

Hon Adam Campbell, *b* 1955: *m* 1985, Elizabeth M., elder da of Eric Marsden, of Stourpaine Manor, Blandford, Dorset, and has issue living, Virginia Giverny, *b* 1987.

TRYON, BARON (Tryon) (Baron UK 1940)

DO RIGHT AND FEAR NOT

ANTHONY GEORGE MERRIK TRYON, 3rd Baron; *b* 26 May 1940; *s* 1976; *ed* Eton; a Page of Honour to HM 1954-56; Capt R Wilts Yeo; DL Wilts 1993: *m* 1973, Dale Elizabeth, who *d* 1997, el da of Barry Harper, of Melbourne, Vic, Aust, and has issue.

𝕬rms – Azure a fesse embattled between in chief three estoiles and in base a portcullis chained or. 𝕮rest – Issuant from a coronet composed of four roses set upon a rim or a bear's head sable charged with seven stars in the form of the constellation ursa major gold. 𝕾upporters – *Dexter*, an army pensioner in hospital uniform; *sinister*, a postman holding with the exterior hand a letter sack over his shoulder proper.
Residence – The Manor House, Great Durnford, Salisbury.

SONS LIVING

Hon CHARLES GEORGE BARRINGTON, *b* 15 May 1976; a Page of Honour to HM 1988-91.
Hon Edward Henry, *b* 1979.

DAUGHTERS LIVING

Hon Zoë Elizabeth, *b* 1974.
Hon Victoria Clementine, *b* 1979 (twin).

SISTER LIVING

Hon Patricia Joan Kathleen, *b* 1942: *m* 1973, C. Ranald Macdonald, of 103 Caroline St, S Yarra, Vic 3141, Aust, and has issue living, Hamish Aylmer Syme, *b* 1977, — Laura Christina, *b* 1974.

WIDOW LIVING OF SECOND BARON

ETHELREDA JOSEPHINE (*Baroness Tryon*), da of Sir Merrik Raymond Burrell, 7th Bt, CBE: *m* 1939, the 2nd Baron, who *d* 1976.

PREDECESSORS – (1) *Rt Hon* GEORGE CLEMENT Tryon, son of late Vice-Adm Sir George Tryon, KCB, *b* 1871; was Min of Pensions Oct 1922 to Jan 1924, Nov 1924 to June 1929, and Sept 1931 to June 1935, Postmaster-Gen June 1935 to April 1940, Chancellor of Duchy of Lancaster April to May 1940, First Commr of Works May to Oct 1940, and Parliamentary Sec to Min of Pensions Oct to Nov 1940; sat as MP for Brighton (*C*) 1910-40; *cr Baron Tryon*, of Durnford, co Wilts (peerage of UK) 1940: *m* 1905, Hon Averil Vivian, who *d* 1959, da of 1st Baron Swansea; *d* 1940; *s* by his son (2) CHARLES GEORGE VIVIAN, GCVO, KCB, DSO, PC, 2nd Baron, *b* 1906; Assist Keeper of HM's Privy Purse 1949-52, Keeper of The Privy Purse and Treas to HM the Queen 1952-71, and a Lord-in-Waiting to HM 1971-76: *m* 1939, Ethelreda Josephine, da of Sir Merrik Raymond Burrell, 7th Bt, CBE; *d* 1976; *s* by his son (3) ANTHONY GEORGE MERRIK, 3rd Baron and present peer.

Tufton, family name of Baron Hothfield.

TUGENDHAT, BARON (Tugendhat) (Life Baron 1993)

CHRISTOPHER SAMUEL TUGENDHAT, elder son of late Dr Georg Tugendhat, of London; *b* 23 Feb 1937; *ed* Ampleforth, and Gonville and Caius Coll, Camb; Leader and Feature Writer *Financial Times* 1960-70; Dir Sunningdale Oils 1971-76, Consultant Phillips Petroleum Internat Ltd 1972-76, British EEC Commr 1977-81, and Vice-Pres Commn of European Communities 1981-85; Dep-Chm National Westminster Bank 1990-91 (Dir 1985-91), Chm Abbey National plc since 1991; Non-Exec Dir The BOC Group, Commercial Union Assurance plc 1988-91, LWT (Holdings) plc, Eurotunnel plc, etc; Chancellor Bath Univ since 1998; MP Cities of London and Westminster (*C*) 1970-74, and

City of London and Westminster South 1974-76; *cr* Knt 1990, and *Baron Tugendhat*, of Widdington, co Essex (Life Baron) 1993: *m* 1967, Julia Lissant, da of Kenneth D. Dobson, of Keston, Kent, and has issue.

Residences – 35 Westbourne Park Rd, W2 5QD. *Club* – Buck's.

SONS LIVING

Hon James Walter, *b* 1971.
Hon Angus George Harry, *b* 1974.

Tullibardine, Marquess of; son of Duke of Atholl.

Turner, family name of Baron Netherthorpe.

TURNER OF CAMDEN, BARONESS (Turner) (Life Baroness 1985)

MURIEL WINIFRED TURNER, da of Edward Price; *b* 18 Sept 1927; Assist Gen Sec Assocn of Scientific, Technical and Managerial Staffs (ASTMS) 1970-87; Chm Ombudsman Council, Personal Investment Authority 1994-97; Deputy Speaker, House of Lords since 1997; Member: TUC Gen Council, Equal Opportunities Commn, Occupational Pensions Bd, Central Arbitration Cttee and Brokers' Registration Council; Hon LLD (Leicester Univ) 1992, *cr Baroness Turner of Camden*, of Camden in Greater London (Life Baroness) 1985: *m* 1955, Reginald Thomas Frederick Turner, MC, DFC, DFC (USA), late W/Cdr RAF.

Residence – 87 Canfield Gdns, Hampstead, NW6.

Turnour, family name of Earl Winterton.

Turton, family name of Baron Tranmire.

TWEEDDALE, MARQUESS OF (Hay) (Marquess S 1694)

EDWARD DOUGLAS JOHN HAY, 13th Marquess; *b* 6 Aug 1947; *s* 1979; presumed heir to Baronetcy of Hay of Smithfield and Haystoun (*cr* 1635); *ed* Milton Abbey Sch, and Trin Coll, Oxford (BA Hons); Hereditary Chamberlain of Dunfermline.

Arms – Quarterly: 1st and 4th, argent, three inescutcheons gules, *Hay*; 2nd, gules, three bars ermine, *Gifford of Yester*; 3rd, azure, three cinquefoils argent, *Fraser*. **Crest** – A goat's head erased argent, horned or. **Supporters** – Two bucks proper, attired or, collared azure, the collars charged with three cinquefoils argent. *Address* – c/o House of Lords, SW1.

BROTHERS LIVING

Lord CHARLES DAVID MONTAGU *b* (twin) 6 Aug 1947; *ed* Milton Abbey Sch, and Trin Coll, Oxford. *Residence* – 336a Gilmerton Rd, Edinburgh GH17 7P4.

(*Lord*) Alistair James Montagu (does not use courtesy title), *b* 1955; *ed* Eton, and Univ Coll, Oxford (MA, DPhil); Botanist; has taken Australian citizenship. *Residence* – 26 Swanson St, Erskineville, NSW 2043, Australia.

HALF-BROTHERS LIVING

Lord Andrew Arthur George (Eastridge House, Binley, Hants SP11 6HA), *b* 1959; *ed* Fettes Coll, and RAC Cirencester; partner Knight Frank; ARICS: *m* 1986, Rosanna Meryl, 2nd da of John Brabazon Booth, of Tarmens, Waterville, co Kerry, and has issue living, Angus David George, *b* 1991, — Rory Edward Hamish, *b* 1993.

Lord Hamish David Montagu *b* (twin) 1959; *ed* Fettes Coll, Wadham Coll, Oxford (BA), and King's Coll Hosp (MB BS, DA), FRCA.

AUNT LIVING (*Sister of 12th Marquess*) (*Raised to the rank of a Marquess's daughter* 1970)

Lady Marioth Christina HAY (Forbes Lodge, Gifford, E Lothian) *b* 1918, resumed by deed poll the surname of Hay 1971: *m* 1st, 1940 (*m diss* 1954), Lt-Col George Richard Trotter, R Scots Greys, who *d* 1970 (E Eglinton); 2ndly, 1954, as his 2nd wife, Sir Gifford Wheaton Grey Fox, 2nd Bt, who *d* 1959, when the title became extinct; 3rdly, 1963 (*m diss* 1971), Sir John Hastings James, KCVO, CB, who *d* 1980, and has issue living, (by 1st *m*) Richard Reginald (52 Leander Av, Hillside, Bulawayo, Zimbabwe), *b* 1941; *ed* Eton: *m* 1974, Marion M., el da of Lt-Col Ralph Maxwell Campbell, of Chasehayes, Stockland, Devon, and has issue living, Georgina Maryoth Maxwell *b* 1978, — Edward George (The Cottage, Bohunt Manor, Liphook, Hants GU30 7DL), *b* 1943; *m* 1973, Jemima Rachel McLay, el da of Niel Mills, of Upton Grey House, Hants (*see* B Hazlerigg, 1990 Edn), and has issue living, George *b* 1977, Joanna *b* 1975, — Bridget Mary, *b* 1944: *m* 1981, John Ellwood, of 2 McLaren Rd, Edinburgh EH9 2BH, son of late Capt Victor Ellwood, RFC, of 88 Harley St, W1, and has issue living, Sophy Catherine *b* 1982.

HALF-AUNT LIVING (*Half-sister of 12th Marquess*) (*Raised to the rank of a Marquess's daughter* 1970)

Lady Caroline Susan Elizabeth, *b* 1930: *m* 1st, 1953 (*m diss* 1970), Richard Noel Marshall Armitage, who *d* 1986, 2ndly, 1970, Reginald Charles Tyrrell, and has issue living, (by 1st *m*) Charles Edward Marshall, *b* 1954: *m* 1987, Judith A., only da of F. Reed, of Hampton, Middx, — Alexander James (81 Lonsdale Rd, SW13), *b* 1958; *ed* Eton: *m* 1987, Carolyn Margery, da of Peter Allen, of Portsmouth, and has issue living, Sophie Claire *b* 1987, Daisy Elizabeth Collette *b* 1990.

DAUGHTERS LIVING OF ELEVENTH MARQUESS

Lady Hélène Candida (*Dowager Viscountess Kemsley*) (Field House, Lubenham, Market Harborough, Leics LE16 9TR); a DStJ, *b* 1913: *m* 1933, 2nd Viscount Kemsley, who *d* 1999.

Lady (Marguerite) Georgina Christine, *b* 1916: *m* 1941, Capt Arthur Nicholas Coleridge, late Irish Guards (*see* B Coleridge, colls), who *d* 1988. *Residence* – 33 Peel Street, W8.

Lady (Christine) Daphne, *b* 1919: *m* 1st, 1939 (*m diss* 1947), Lieut-Col David Morley-Fletcher, TD, Rifle Brig; 2ndly, 1957, Lieut-Col Francis Robert Cameron Stewart, late Indian Army, who *d* 1995, el son of late Sir Francis Hugh Stewart, CIE, and has issue living, (by 1st *m*) Hugo David Montagu (The Old Vicarage, Padbury, Buckingham), *b* 1940; *ed* Stowe, and Trin Coll, Camb (MA); FSA: *m* 1st, Josceline Mary, yr da of late Rt Hon Lord Justice (Sir Henry Josceline) Phillimore, OBE; 2ndly, 1980, Belinda Mary, da of William Miles David, of Little Smeaton, Pontefract, Yorks, and has issue living (by 1st *m*), Gifford Henry Montagu *b* 1969: *m* 1997, Isabelle, elder da of Patrick Lemoine, of St Cyprien, France, Hester Mary Victoria *b* 1972, (by 2nd *m*) Isabella Frances *b* 1981, — Victoria Catherine Margaret, *b* 1942. *Residence* – 5 Brewery Court, Haddington, E Lothian.

Lady Frances Elizabeth Ann, *b* 1926: *m* 1956, Nigel Arthur Pearson, who *d* 1975, son of Sir Neville Arthur Pearson, 2nd Bt. *Residence* – Coedsaithpren, Nantgaredig, Carmarthen, Dyfed.

MOTHER LIVING

Hon Sonia Mary, da of 1st Viscount Ingleby: *m* 1st, 1946 (*m diss* 1958), 12th Marquess of Tweeddale, GC, who *d* 1979; 2ndly, 1966, Maj Michael William Vernon Hammond-Maude, JP, 5th R Inniskilling Dragoon Guards (ret), who *d* 1998.

WIDOW LIVING OF TWELFTH MARQUESS

NELLA DOREEN (*Marchioness of Tweeddale*) (Isle of Mull), da of M. Dutton: *m* 1959, as his 2nd wife, 12th Marquess of Tweeddale, GC, who *d* 1979.

COLLATERAL BRANCHES LIVING

Grandchildren of late Maj Malcolm Vivian Hay, of Seaton House, Aberdeen (infra):—
Issue of late Maj James Malcolm Hay of Seaton, *b* 1907, *d* 1987: *m* 1941, Mary Eleanora Basset (Markie Cottage, Glass, Huntly, Aberdeenshire), da of late Charles Ernest Basset Lothian Curzon (*see* E Howe, colls):—
Malcolm Charles HAY OF SEATON (Edinglassie, Huntly, Aberdeenshire), *b* 1956; *ed* Ampleforth, and Magdalene Coll, Camb: *m* 1983, Deborah Louise, da of Lt-Cdr Derek Malcolm Rouse, MBE, RN (ret), of The Dell, Bonchurch, IoW, and has issue living, James Malcolm Douglas, *b* 1985, — Oliver Charles Quintin, *b* 1987, — Georgina Eileen, *b* 1990, — Isabella Jane, *b* 1993, — Katharine Louise, *b* (twin) 1993. ——— Elizabeth Mary, *b* 1942: *m* 1977, David Buchanan Gillespie, of The Lodge, St Mary's Abbey, Haslemere, Surrey GU27 1GA, and has issue living, Hamish Peregrine Curzon, *b* 1979. ——— Joanna Margaret, *b* 1945: *m* 1973, Brig Ewen Duncan Cameron, OBE, The Black Watch (*see* Rugge-Price, Bt) and has issue living, Louisa Mary, *b* 1976, — Clare Elizabeth, *b* 1977. ——— Nicola Anne, *b* 1958: *m* 1983, Andrew Lachlan Rattray, of Craighall-Rattray, Blairgowrie, Perthshire, yst son of Capt James Silvester Rattray of Rattray (28th Chief), and has issue living, Thomas Alexander, *b* 1987, — Hew Lachlan, *b* 1989, — Flora Mary, *b* 1992.

Grandchildren of late James Gordon Hay, el son of Lt-Gen Lord James Hay, 2nd son of 7th Marquess:—
Issue of Maj Malcolm Vivian Hay, of Seaton House, Aberdeen, *b* 1881, *d* 1962: *m* 1st, 1902, Florence, who *d* 1943, da of Gaëtan, Comte de Thienne, of Paris; 2ndly, 1956, Alice Ivy, DStJ, who *d* 1974, da of Herbert John Wigmore, of Perth, W Australia, and widow of Walter Moncrieff Paterson, of Tilliefoure, Aberdeenshire:—
(By 1st *m*) Peter Brian (Titford Hold, Awliscombe, Honiton, Devon), *b* 1918; Maj Gordon Highlanders (ret); 1939-45 War (despatches, prisoner): *m* 1946, Marigold Armatrude, da of Col A. G. Eden, of Culver, nr Exeter, and has issue living, Angus Malcolm (Cavalry and Guards'), *b* 1947; late Capt Scots Greys, and late Capt Abu Dhabi Defence Force (Arabian Gulf): *m* 1978 (*m diss* 1984), Miranda Mary, da of late Anthony Seymour Bellville, of The White House, Bembridge, I of Wight, — James Andrew, *b* 1949: *m* 1975 (*m diss* 1979), Emma, da of (Rondle) Owen (Charles) Stable, QC, of Buckler's Hall, Much Hadham, Herts, — Charlotte Jerardine, *b* 1959: *m* 1988, John Paul Deacon, of The Dial House, Chilmark, Wilts, and has issue living, Maximilian James *b* 1989, Georgia Florence *b* 1991, Jessica Charlotte *b* (twin) 1991.

Issue of late Capt Cuthbert Joseph Hay, *b* 1882, *d* 1970: *m* 1908, Letitia Griffith, who *d* 1982, da of Frederick Heylighter Fausset, of Willsborough, co Sligo:—
Ronald Cuthbert, DSO, DSC (South Mill, Amesbury, Wilts) *b* 1916; *ed* Ampleforth; Cdr RN; 1939-45 War (DSO, DSC and Bar); DSO 1944: *m* 1944, Barbara, da of Lt-Col George Rochfort Grange, of Strathblane, Stirlingshire, and has issue living, Charles Edward Ronald (A10 Habitat, Lot 1106, DD 217 Pak Sha Wan, Sai Kung, N.T., Hong Kong), *b* 1948; *ed* Ampleforth: *m* 1975, Susan Rodica, da of Terence Prendergast, of Steeple Claydon, Bucks, and has issue living, Jeremy Charles *b* 1976, Hannah Rodica Barbara *b* 1980, — James Philip Burness, *b* 1957, — Penelope Rochfort, *b* 1946: *m* 1977, Maj John Julius Rogers, R Hussars (PWO), and has issue living, Katherine Philippa *b* 1978, Vanessa Victoria *b* 1981, Olivia Hilary *b* 1983, — Sara Elizabeth, *b* 1951: *m* 1980, Alastair Macrae, and has issue living, Calum Andrew *b* 1980, Athene Hope *b* 1983. ——— John Malcolm (Mirrabooka, 56 Mugga Way, Red Hill, Canberra, ACT), *b* 1918; *ed* Ampleforth; Lt-Cdr RN; 1939-45 War: *m* 1952, Alicia Gertrude Maria, da of Herbert Moore, of Sydncy, NSW, and has issue living, Richard Malcolm (Characene Park, RMB 605, Summer Hill Rd, Bungendore 2621, NSW, Australia), *b* 1953: *m* 1972, Maureen Loretta, da of Walter Larkin, of San Francisco, Calif, USA, and has issue living, David Richard Hay *b* 1983, Katie Elizabeth Hay *b* 1985. ——— Vivien Mary (Fiveways, Cookham, Berks) *b* 1909: *m* 1st, 1937, M. John Ripley, who *d* 1947; 2ndly, 1960, Samuel K. Jerome, who *d* 1966, and has issue living, (by 1st *m*) Michael, *b* 1939. ——— Mary Charlotte, *b* 1915: *m* 1947, Lt-Col Neil Sylvester Smith, RAF Signals, who *d* 1981, and has issue living, Stephen Neil, *b* 1948: *m* 1984, his cousin, Jaqueline Mary, yr da of Sqdn-Ldr W.D.K. Franklin, by his late wife Margaret Patricia, 2nd da of late Capt Cuthbert Joseph Hay (ante), and has issue living, Ashley Christopher *b* 1984, Simon Matthew *b* 1987, Sophia Gilliam *b* 1990, — Graham John, *b* 1957, — Diana Mary, *b* 1949: *m* 1st, 1969 (*m diss* 1976), Peter John Thompson; 2ndly, 1978, Brian Barbrec Campbell, and has issue living (by 1st *m*), Bentley Warrick James *b* 1972, Grant Peter *b* 1974, (by 2nd *m*) Reuben Gregory Barbrec *b* 1980, Zoe Louise *b* 1983.

Granddaughter of late Capt William Drummond Ogilvy-Hay-Newton, el son of John Stuart Hay-Newton, grandson of Richard Hay Newton, uncle of 7th Marquess:—
Issue of late Lieut-Col Stuart Hay, DSO, *b* 1876, *d* 1960: *m* 1908, Inna Vera Evelyn, who *d* 1971, da of late Hon Louis Guy Scott (E Clonmell, colls):—
Vera Jean, *b* 1910. *Residence* – 150 Jasmine Crescent, Princes Risborough, Aylesbury, Bucks.

Grandchildren of late William Hope Hay, el son of Maj-Gen Alexander Charles Hay (infra):—
Issue of late Lt-Col George Harold Hay, DSO, *b* 1893, *d* 1967: *m* 1935, Patricia Mary, who *d* 1998, da of Maj Etienne Hugonin, of Edinburgh:—
Alexander Douglas (Duns Castle, Berwickshire, TD11 3NW), *b* 1948: *m* 1973, Aline Mary, da of Robert Macdougall, of Edinburgh, and has issue living, Robert Alexander, *b* 1976, — Caroline Laura, *b* 1978. ——— Philip Antony, *b* 1950: *m* 1975, Helena Anne, da of Frank Sim, of Alloa, and has issue living, George Francis, *b* 1979, — Felicity Patricia, *b* 1977. ——— Caroline Mary, *b* 1944: *m* 1967, George Michael Mackinnon Thomson, and has issue living, George Jolyon Hay, *b* 1970, — Mary Emma Julia (twin), *b* 1970. ——— Barbara Elizabeth, *b* 1947: *m* 1979, Dr Michael John Chevalier Asher.

Granddaughter of late Maj-Gen Alexander Charles Hay, son of late William Hay, son of late Robert Hay (*b* 1731), grandson of late Hon William Hay, 2nd son of 1st Earl:—
Issue of late Edward George Hay, *b* 1879, *d* 1945: *m* 1917, Ascelin Frances Collett, da of late James Collett-Mason, JP, of Ashurst Place, Langton Green, Kent:—
Nora Margaret, *b* 1922: *m* 1942, John Robertson Campbell, and has issue living, David Michael Hay, *b* 1944, — Christopher William John, *b* 1949, — Stuart Calvin, *b* 1953, — Tessa Margaret, *b* 1946, — Lynn Nora Mary, *b* 1952, — Sally Anne Frances, *b* 1956.

Grandchildren of late Robert William Seton Hay (infra):—
Issue of late Robert Dino James Hay, *b* 1901, *d* 1977: *m* 1942, Laura, who *d* 1984, da of Gen N. Fochetti:—
William Robert Alexander, *b* 1947. *Residence* – Via di Trasone 5, 00199 Rome, Italy. —— Patricia Caterina Maria *b* 1944. *Residence* – Via di Trasone 5, 00199 Rome, Italy.

Grandson of late Robert James Alexander Hay, son of Robert Hay (*b* 1799), son of Robert Hay (*b* 1731) (ante):—
Issue of late Robert William Seton Hay, *b* 1878, *d* 1965: *m* 1900, Maria, who *d* 1961, da of Antonio Baratti:—
Alexander Giuseppe (4 S Lorenzo di Rabatta, 06070 Perugia, Cenerente, Italy), *b* 1906: *m* 1937, Giovanna Bice, da of Cdr Mario Dasso, and has issue living, Andrew Alexander Mario (6 Favorita Rubbiano, 06070 Perugia Cenerente, Italy), *b* 1941: *m* 1966, Maria Pia Antonietta Mancini, and has issue living, Alexander *b* 1966, Massimo *b* 1971, Maurizio *b* 1973, — Mary Grace Alexandra, *b* 1939, — Roberta Alexandra, *b* 1942, — Jane Alexandra, *b* 1948, — Daniela Alexandra, *b* 1953.

Descendants of late James Hay (4th in descent from Hon John Hay, 2nd son of 3rd Lord Hay of Yester), who was *cr* a *Baronet* 1635:—
See Hay, Bt, *cr* 1635.

PREDECESSORS – **(1)** JOHN HAY; *cr Lord Hay of Yester* (peerage of Scotland) 1488; *s* by his son **(2)** JOHN, 2nd Lord; fell at Flodden 1513; *s* by his son **(3)** JOHN, 3rd Lord; *s* by his son **(4)** JOHN, 4th Lord; was imprisoned for some years in the Tower of London, having been taken prisoner at the battle of Pinkie 1547; *d* 1557; *s* by his son **(5)** WILLIAM, 5th Lord; *s* by his el son **(6)** WILLIAM, 6th Lord; *s* by his brother **(7)** JAMES, 7th Lord; *s* by his son **(8)** JOHN, 8th Lord; commanded a Regt in the Royal Army 1639; *cr Earl of Tweeddale* (peerage of Scotland) 1646; *d* 1654; *s* by his **(9)** JOHN, PC, 2nd Earl; sat as MP for Haddingtonshire in Cromwell's Parliament; assisted at Coronation of Charles II at Scone; having been a Commr of the Treasury and an Extra Lord of Session was in 1692 appointed Lord Chancellor of Scotland; *cr Viscount Walden*, *Earl of Gifford*, and *Marquess of Tweeddale* (peerage of Scotland) 1694, with remainder to his heirs male whatsoever; *d* 1697; *s* by his son **(10)** JOHN, PC, 2nd Marquess; was High Treasurer of Scotland 1695, High Commr to the Scottish Parliament 1704, Lord Chancellor of Scotland 1704-5, and sometime a Representative Peer; *d* 1713; *s* by his son **(11)** CHARLES, 3rd Marquess; was Pres of Court of Police, Lord-Lieut of Haddingtonshire, and a Representative Peer; *d* 1715; *s* by his son **(12)** JOHN, PC, 4th Marquess; was a Representative Peer, the last person who held the office of Extraordinary Lord of Session, Sec of State for Scotland 1742-6, Principal Keeper of the Signet, and in 1761 Justice-Gen of Scotland; *d* 1762; *s* by his son **(13)** GEORGE, 5th Marquess; *d* 1770; *s* by his uncle **(14)** GEORGE, 6th Marquess; *d* unmarried 1787; *s* by his kinsman **(15)** GEORGE, 7th Marquess, grandson of Lord William, 3rd son of 2nd Marquess; was Lord-Lieut of Haddington, and a Representative Peer; *d* 1804; *s* by his son **(16)** GEORGE, KT, GCB, 8th Marquess; *b* 1787: a Field-Marshal; served with distinction in the Peninsular War; a Representative Peer, Gov and Com in Ch at Madras 1842-48, Col 2nd Life Guards, and Lord-Lieut of Haddingtonshire; *m* 1816, Lady Susan Montagu, da of 5th Duke of Manchester; *d* 1876; *s* by his son **(17)** ARTHUR, 9th Marquess; *b* 1824; Lieut-Col Grenadier Guards: *m* 1st, 1857, Helena Eleanora Charlotte Augusta, who *d* 1871, da of Count Adolf August Friedrich von Kielmansegge; 2ndly, 1873, Julia Charlotte Sophia, who *d* 1937 (having *m* 2ndly, 1887, Rt Hon Sir John Rose, GCMG, PC, 1st Bt, who *d* 1888; 3rdly, 1892, Major Sir William Eden Evans-Gordon, who *d* 1913), da of Keith Stewart Mackenzie; *d* 1878; *s* by his brother **(18)** WILLIAM MONTAGU, KT, 10th Marquess; *b* 1826: in BCS, 1845-62; MP for Taunton (*L*) 1865-8, and for Haddington Dist 1878; Lord High Commr for the Gen Assembly of Church of Scotland 1889-92, 1896, *cr Baron Tweeddale*, of Yester, co Haddington (peerage of United Kingdom) 1881: *m* 1878, Candida Louise, CBE, who *d* 1925, da of Vincenzo Bartolucci, of Cantiano, Italy; *d* 1911; *s* by his el son **(19)** WILLIAM GEORGE MONTAGU, 11th Marquess; *b* 1884; Lord-Lt of E Lothian 1944-67: *m* 1st, 1912, Marguerite Christine Ralli, who *d* 1944, step-da of Lewis Einstein; 2ndly, 1945, Marjorie Helen, who *d* 1977, da of late Henry John Wagg, OBE, and formerly wife of Lt-Col Joseph Henry Nettleford; *d* 1967; *s* by his nephew **(20)** DAVID GEORGE MONTAGU, GC son of Lt-Col Lord Edward Douglas John Hay (3rd son of 10th Marquess), and Violet Florence Catherine Bridget, da of Maj Cameron Barclay (B Decies), 12th Marquess; *b* 1921; AM 1941, Lloyd War Medal for bravery at sea and Royal Life Saving Medals: *m* 1st, 1946 (*m diss* 1958), Hon Sonia Mary Peake, da of 1st Viscount Ingleby; 2ndly, 1959, Nella Doreen, da of M. Dutton; *d* 1979; *s* by his son **(21)** EDWARD DOUGLAS JOHN, 13th Marquess and present peer; also Earl of Gifford, Earl of Tweeddale, Viscount Walden, Lord Hay of Yester, and Baron Tweeddale.

TWEEDSMUIR, BARON (Buchan) (Baron UK 1935)

Not following meaner things

WILLIAM DE L'AIGLE BUCHAN, 3rd Baron; *b* 10 Jan 1916; *s* 1996; *ed* Eton, and New Coll, Oxford; served 1939-45 War as Sqdn-Ldr RAF Vol Reserve; Author of *John Buchan, A Memoir* (1982), *The Rags of Time* (autobiography) (1990), and other works: *m* 1st, 1939 (*m diss* 1946), Nesta Irene, only da of late Lt-Col Cecil Darley Crozier, RA; 2ndly, 1946 (*m diss* 1960), Barbara Howard, who *d* 1969, da of Ernest Nash Ensor, of 24 Chivelston Court, Wimbledon Parkside, SW; 3rdly, 1960, Sauré Cynthia Mary, da of late Maj Gerald Edward Tatchell, Royal Lincs Regt, and has issue by 1st, 2nd and 3rd *m*.

𝔄rms – Azure, a fesse between three lions' heads erased argent. 𝔆rest – A sunflower proper. 𝔖upporters – *Dexter*, a stag proper, attired or, collared gules; *sinister*, a falcon proper, jessed, belled, and beaked or, armed and collared gules.
Residence – West End House, Hornton, Banbury, Oxfordshire. *Club* – Travellers'.

SONS LIVING (*By 2nd marriage*)

Hon JOHN WILLIAM HOWARD DE L'AIGLE (TOBY), *b* 25 May 1950; *ed* Magdalen Coll Sch, Oxford: *m* 1977, Amanda Jocelyn, 2nd da of late Sir Gawain Westray Bell, KCMG, CBE, of Hidcote Bartrim Manor, Chipping Campden, Glos, and has issue living, (John) Alasdair Gawain, *b* 20 Nov 1986, — Christopher Charles Westray, *b* 1988. *Address* – c/o Lloyds Bank, Wallingford, Oxfordshire.

Hon (Charles Walter) Edward Ralph, *b* 1951; *ed* Magdalen Coll Sch, and Southampton Univ (BSc); Man Dir Hill Samuel Bank 1993-96, since when Man Dir Close Brothers Corporate Finance Ltd, FCA. *m* 1982, Fiona Jane, yr da of Capt Edmund Paul Carlisle, of Penyrwrlodd, Llanigon, Hay-on-Wye, and has issue living, William Edward Francis Ewelme, *b* 1984, — Annabel Clare, *b* 1986, — Laura Yseulte, *b* 1988, — Amilia Katherine, *b* 1992. *Residence* – South Sea Farm, Kington Langley, Chippenham, Wilts. *Club* – Travellers'.

Hon James Ernest, *b* 1954; *ed* Eton, and Magdalen Coll, Oxford: *m* 1986, Lady Evelyn Rose Phipps, 2nd da of 4th Marquess of Normanby, KG, and has issue living, Nicholas Adam, *b* 1992, — Elizabeth Blanche, *b* 1989, — Rose Barbara Averil, *b* 1995. *Residence* – 37 Gloucester Crescent, NW1 7DL.

(*By 3rd marriage*)

Hon Alexander Edward, *b* 1961; *ed* Westminster, Aberdeen Univ (BSc), and Kent Univ (PhD): *m* 1993, Sarah Janet, da of George Pickles, of 22 Osbert Place, Newton Aycliffe, Darlington, and has issue living, Patrick Charles Julian, *b* 1994, — Roland Thomas Lucien, *b* 1997. *Residence* – 198 Stockbridge Rd, Winchester, Hants SO22 6RP.

DAUGHTERS LIVING (*By 1st marriage*)

Hon Perdita Caroline, *b* 1940; *ed* Springside Sch, Radcliffe Coll, Harvard Univ: *m* 1968 (*m diss* 1977), Edward Connolly, of Amherst, Mass, USA, and has issue living, Cressida, *b* 1969. *Residence* – 166 Main St, Concord, MA 01742, USA.

(*By 2nd marriage*)

Hon Deborah Charlotte (*Baroness Stewartby*), *b* 1947; JP London 1984: *m* 1966, Baron Stewartby, RD, PC (Life Baron), and has issue (see that title). *Residence* – Broughton Green, Broughton, Peebles-shire ML12 6HQ.

Hon Laura Mary Clare, *b* 1953: *m* 1980, Robin Chanter, and has issue living, Bacchante Pallas-Athene, *b* 1981, — Artemis Helen Bacchante, *b* 1982, — Aphrodite Barbara Bacchante, *b* 1984, — Demeter Violetta Bacchante, *b* 1988. *Residence* – Maison Bacchus, Gajan, 37030 St Mamert du Gard, France.

Hon Ursula Margaret Bridget, *b* (twin) 1953; *ed* Oxford High Sch, New Hall, Camb (MA), and Royal Botanic Gdns, Kew (Dip Hort): *m* 1979, Charles Thomas Wide, QC, yr son of Nicholas Wide, and has issue living, Thomas Nicholas Buchan, *b* 1984, — Emily Susan, *b* 1982. *Residence* – Church Cottage, Main St, Glapthorn, Northants PE8 5BE.

DAUGHTER LIVING OF SECOND BARON

Hon Priscilla Susan (*Baroness Selkirk of Douglas*), *b* 1949: *m* 1974, Baron Selkirk of Douglas, PC, QC (Life Baron), and has issue.

WIDOW LIVING OF SECOND BARON

JEAN MARGHERITA (*Jean, Baroness Tweedsmuir*), da of late Capt Humphrey Douglas Tollemache, RN (*see* B Tollemache, colls), and widow of Capt Sir Francis Cullen Grant, 12th Bt (*see* Grant of Monymusk, Bt): *m* 1980, as his 2nd wife, 2nd Baron Tweedsmuir, CBE, CD, who *d* 1996. *Residence* – Flat 2, The White House, 24 Dirleton Av, N Berwick, E Lothian EH39 4BQ.

COLLATERAL BRANCH LIVING

Issue of late Prof Hon Alastair Francis Buchan, CBE, yst son of 1st Baron, *b* 1918, *d* 1976: *m* 1942, Hope, who *d* 1997, da of late David Gordon Gilmour, of Ottawa, Canada:—
David John Brian Washington, OBE (20 Anhalt Rd, SW11 4NX) *b* 1947; OBE 1993: *m* 1st, 1974 (*m diss* 1980), Sarah, da of George L. Cawkwell, of 8 Moreton Rd, Oxford; 2ndly, 1981, Eugenie Elisabeth, da of Prof Charles Maechling, Jr, of Washington, DC, USA, and has issue living (by 2nd *m*), Charles, *b* 1986, — Julian Daniel, *b* 1990, — Susannah Janet, *b* 1983. —— Benjamin William Alastair (6 Franconia Rd, SW4), *b* 1948: *m* 1974, Elizabeth, da of Maj Peter Oakleigh-Walker, of The Meade, Crondall, Surrey, and has issue living, Adam Peter Alastair, *b* 1980, — Eleanor Rose, *b* 1983. —— (Anna) Virginia Pauline, *b* 1953: *m* 1983, Kenneth David Peake, of 103 The Bowery, New York City, NY 10002, USA, son of Kenneth Peake, of Penyffordd, N Wales, and has issue living, Ella Hope Dong Qiong BUCHAN PEAKE, *b* 1995.

PREDECESSORS – (1) *Rt Hon* JOHN BUCHAN, GCMG, GCVO, CH, son of late Rev John Buchan, of Glasgow; *b* 1875; a well-known writer, author of *Prester John, The Thirty-Nine Steps, Greenmantle, Mr Standfast, Huntingtower, The Island of Sheep,* and other works; sat as MP for Edinburgh, St Andrews, Glasgow and Aberdeen Univs (*C*) 1927-35; was Lord High Commr to Gen Assembly of Church of Scotland 1933 and 1934, and Gov-Gen and Com-in-Ch Dominion of Canada 1935-40; *cr Baron Tweedsmuir,* of Elsfield, co Oxford (peerage of United Kingdom) 1935: *m* 1907, Susan Charlotte, who *d* 1977, da of Capt Hon Norman de l'Aigle Grosvenor (B Ebury); *d* 1940; *s* by his son (2) JOHN NORMAN STUART, CBE, CD, 2nd Baron; *b* 1911; Rector Aberdeen Univ 1948-51, Pres Fedn of Commonwealth and British Empire Chambers of Commerce 1955-57, and Inst of Export 1963-67, Gov Commonwealth Inst 1958-77; Pres British Schs Exploring Soc 1964-85; part-author *The St Kilda Papers* (1931), and other works; 1939-45 War as Lt-Col Hastings and Prince Edward Regt (Canadian Mil), and on Staff (wounded, despatches twice); Order of Orange Nassau of the Netherlands with Swords: *m* 1st, 1948, Rt Hon Priscilla Jean Fortescue (*Baroness Tweedsmuir of Belhelvie*), PC, who *d* 1978, da of Brig Alan Fortescue Thomson, DSO, and widow of Maj Sir Arthur Lindsay Grant, 11th Bt (*cr* 1705); 2ndly, 1980, Jean Margherita, da of late Capt Humphrey Douglas Tollemache, RN (*see* B Tollemache, colls), and widow of Capt Sir Francis Cullen Grant, 12th Bt (*cr* 1705); *d* 1996; *s* by his brother (3) WILLIAM DE L'AIGLE, 3rd Baron and present peer.

TWEEDSMUIR OF BELHELVIE BARONY OF (Thomson) (Extinct 1978)

DAUGHTERS LIVING OF LIFE BARONESS

(*By 1st m*) (*see* Grant, Bt, *cr* 1705).
(*By 2nd m*) (*see* Tweedsmuir, B).

TWINING, BARONY OF (Twining) (Extinct 1967)

SONS LIVING OF LIFE BARON

Hon John Peter (3 The Ridgeway, Guildford), *b* 1929; *ed* Charterhouse, and Brasenose Coll, Oxford; Colonial Ser 1953-63; an Admin Officer, City and Guilds of London Inst; 1963-78; Chm Guildford Educational Services Ltd: *m* 1954, Mary Avice, da of late Brig Joseph Hector Dealy Bennett, CBE, and has issue.
Hon William Lawrence (10 Mill Lane, Iffley, Oxford), *b* 1934; *ed* Charterhouse, Brasenose Coll, Oxford, and Chicago Univ; Prof of Law, Queen's Univ, Belfast 1965-72 Prof of Law Univ of Warwick 1972-82; Quain Prof of Jurisprudence, Univ Coll London 1983-96, Research Prof of Law since 1996: *m* 1957, Penelope Elizabeth, da of Richard Wall Morris, of Dublin, and has issue.

Tyrone, Baron, title of Marquess of Waterford on Roll of HL.

Tyrone Earl of; son of Marquess of Waterford.

UDDIN, BARONESS (Uddin) (Life Baroness 1998)

MANZILA POLA UDDIN, da of Mr & Mrs Khan; *b* 17 July 1959; *ed* Plashet Gram Sch, and Univ of North London; Youth and Community Worker, YWCA 1980-82; Liaison Officer for Tower Hamlets Social Services 1982-84; Manger Women's Health Project 1984-88; Manager Asian Family Counselling Service 1989-90; Social worker, Manager and later Management Consultant, London Borough of Newham Social Services 1993-98; Councillor for Shadwell Ward, London Borough of Tower Hamlets Council 1990-98; Dep Leader of Labour Group 1993-94; Dep Leader of the Council 1994-95; Memb Lords European Community Cttee, All-Party Children, Women and Disablement Group, Inter-Parly Union and Commonwealth Parly Assocn, etc *cr Baroness Uddin*, of Bethnal Green in the London Borough of Tower Hamlets (Life Baroness) 1998: *m* 1976, Komar Uddin, son of Shiraj Uddin, of Chattak, Bangladesh, and has issue.
Residence – 51 Garnet St, Wapping, E1 9QT.

SONS LIVING

Hon Shamim, *b* 1978.
Hon Sabid, *b* 1980.
Hon Shareef, *b* 1986.
Hon Shakeeb, *b* 1997.

DAUGHTER LIVING

Hon Tasneem Sadia Monisha, *b* 1992.

ULLSWATER, VISCOUNT (Lowther) (Viscount UK 1921)

The office shows the man

NICHOLAS JAMES CHRISTOPHER LOWTHER, PC, 2nd Viscount; *b* 9 Jan 1942; *s* 1949; *ed* Eton, and Trin Coll, Camb; Capt Wessex Yeo (ret); Parl Under-Sec Dept of Employment 1990-93; Capt HM Body Guard of Hon Corps of Gentlemen at Arms and Ch Govt Whip, House of Lords, 1993-94, Min of State Environment 1994-95; Private Sec to HRH Princess Margaret, Countess of Snowdon since 1998; *cr* PC 1994: *m* 1967, Susan, da of James Howard Weatherby, of Cleeve House, E Knoyle, Salisbury, Wilts (*see* Wake, Bt), and has issue.

Arms – Or, six annulets, three, two, and one, sable, a crescent for difference. **Crest** – A dragon passant argent. **Supporters** – On either side a horse argent, gorged with a wreath of laurel vert and charged on the shoulder with a portcullis chained or.
Residence – The Old Rectory, Docking, King's Lynn, Norfolk PE31 8LJ.

SONS LIVING

Hon BENJAMIN JAMES, *b* 26 Nov 1975.
Hon Edward John, *b* 1981; Page of Honour to HM 1993-96.

DAUGHTERS LIVING

Hon Emma Mary, *b* 1968.
Hon Clare Priscilla, *b* 1970: *m* 1996, Mark G. Flawn-Thomas, son of Peter Flawn-Thomas, of Piltdown, Uckfield, Sussex.

SISTER LIVING (*Raised to the rank of a Viscount's daughter* 1951)

Hon Kirstin Elizabeth, *b* 1939: *m* 1st, 1966, Capt Caledon Alexander, late 7th Queen's Own Hussars; 2ndly, 1976, Antony Edward Ord Welton, and has issue living (by 1st *m*), James Caledon, *b* 1969, — Charlotte Jane, *b* 1968.

HALF-AUNTS LIVING (*Raised to the rank of a Viscount's daughters* 1950)

Hon Rosemary, *b* 1922: *m* 1945, Lt Douglas Cyril Aubrey Goolden, RNVR, and has issue living, Michael Cyril Christopher (Foxes Bank Farm, Wadhurst, E Sussex TN5 6LN), *b* 1947: *m* 1977, Siegrith, yr twin da of late Basil Vickers, of Skelmorlie, Ayrshire, and has issue living, Freya Polly Tamsin *b* 1980, Camilla Sophia Marique *b* 1984, Chloë Florence Basilia *b* 1988, — Alastair Richard Lowther, *b* 1954, — Jill Priscilla, *b* 1949: *m* 1984, Paul Douglas Marshall, son of Frank Marshall, of Hampton. *Residence* – Tile Lodge, Colemans Hatch, Hartfield, E Sussex.
Hon Jennifer LOWTHER, *b* 1932; resumed her maiden name 1989: *m* 1st, 1954 (*m diss* 1962), as his 2nd wife, 7th Earl of Lonsdale; 2ndly, 1962 (*m diss* 1972), Flt-Lt William Edward Clayfield, DFC, RAF; 3rdly, 1976 (*m diss* 1979), Rev Oswald Dickin Carter, who *d* 1986; 4thly, 1981, James Cornelius Sullivan. *Residence* – 19 Minster Yard, Lincoln LN2 1PY.

PREDECESSOR – (1) *Rt Hon Sir* JAMES WILLIAM Lowther, GCB, son of late Hon William Lowther, brother of 3rd Earl of Lonsdale; *b* 1855; Bar Inner Temple 1879, and a Bencher 1906; was 4th (unpaid) Charity Commr 1887-91, Under-Sec of State for Foreign Affairs 1891-2, Chm of Committee of Ways and Means and Dep Speaker of House of Commons 1895-1905, and Speaker 1905-21; Chm of Political Honours Commn 1923-4; sat as MP for Rutland (*C*) 1883-5, for Mid, or Penrith, Div of Cumberland 1886-1918, and for Cumberland, Penrith and Cockermouth Div 1918-21; *cr Viscount Ullswater*, of Campsea Ashe, co Suffolk (peerage of UK) 1921: *m* 1886, Mary Frances, who *d* 1944, da of late Right Hon Alexander James Beresford-Hope, MP, of Bedgebury Park, Cranbrook; *d* 1949; *s* by his great-grandson (2) NICHOLAS JAMES CHRISTOPHER (son of late Lt John Arthur Lowther, MVO, RNVR, son of late Maj Hon Christopher William Lowther, el son of 1st Viscount), 2nd Viscount and present peer.

Ulster, Earl of; son of Duke of Gloucester.

UNDERHILL, BARONY OF (Underhill) (Extinct 1993)

SONS LIVING OF LIFE BARON

Hon Terry Leonard (Fairlight, Mill Cross, Rattery, South Brent, Devon), *b* 1938: *m* 1960, Dorothy, da of late Edwin Askew, and has issue, three sons.
Hon Robert (4 Hall Rd, Wilmslow, Cheshire SK9 5BW), *b* 1948: *m* 1970 (*m diss* 1997), Christine Ann, da of late Ernest Edward Lawrence Vinsen, of 19 Cherrydown Close, E4, and has issue, one son and one da.

DAUGHTER LIVING OF LIFE BARON

Hon Joan Evelyn (88 Mansfield Rd, Selston, Notts NG16 6ER), *b* 1944; Selston Parish Cllr and CC Notts; Chm Equalities Panel of Local Govt Assocn and Chief Whip Labour Group of LGA; Chm European Wide Womens Cttee; Trustee Child Migrants Trust: *m* 1st, 1965 (*m diss* 1973), Edwin Fennell; 2ndly, 1973 (*m diss* 1989), Ian Robert Taylor; 3rdly, 1993, John Robert Stocks, and has issue (by 1st *m*), one son, — (by 2nd *m*), two sons.

WIDOW LIVING OF LIFE BARON

FLORA JANET (*Baroness Underhill*), da of Leonard George Philbrick: *m* 1937, Baron Underhill, CBE (Life Baron), who *d* 1993. *Residence* – 94 Loughton Way, Buckhurst Hill, Essex IG9 6AH.

Upton, family name of Viscountcy of Templetown.

Urquhart, surname of Barony of Tayside.

Uxbridge, Earl of; son of Marquess of Anglesey.

VAIZEY, BARONY OF (Vaizey) (Extinct 1984)

SONS LIVING OF LIFE BARON

Hon Thomas Peter John, *b* 1964; *ed* St Paul's, Worcester Coll, Oxford (BA), and City Univ (Dip Law); Bar Inner Temple 1988.
Hon Edward, *b* 1968; *ed* St Paul's (Scholar), Merton Coll, Oxford (BA), and City Univ (Dip Law); Bar Inner Temple 1995.

DAUGHTER LIVING OF LIFE BARON

Hon Polly Mary Ruth, *b* 1962; *ed* St Paul's Girls' Sch, and Lady Margaret Hall, Oxford: *m* 1991, Charles Gavin McAndrew, elder son of Nicolas McAndrew, of Kilcoy Castle, Killearnan, Muir of Ord, Ross-shire, and has issue living, Lucy Mary, *b* 1998, — Emily Rose, *b* (twin) 1998.

WIDOW LIVING OF LIFE BARON

MARINA ALANDRA (*Baroness Vaizey*); author, Gov South Bank Board since 1993; Trustee Imperial War Museum since 1991; Trustee National Museums and Galleries on Merseyside since 1986; da of Lyman Stansky, of New York, USA: *m* 1961, Baron Vaizey (Life Baron), who *d* 1984. *Residence* – 24 Heathfield Terr, W4 4JE.

VALENTIA, VISCOUNT (Annesley) (Viscount I 1642, with precedence of 1622, Bt I 1620)
(Name pronounced "Ansley")

VIRTUTIS · AMORE ·

By the love of virtue

RICHARD JOHN DIGHTON ANNESLEY, 15th Viscount and Premier Baronet of Ireland; *b* 15 Aug 1929; *s* 1983; *ed* Marlborough; BA (S Africa); Capt RA (ret): *m* 1957, Anita Phyllis, only da of William Arthur Joy, of Bristol, and has had issue.

𝕬rms – Paly of six argent and azure, over all a bend gules. 𝕮rest – A Moor's head in profile couped proper, wreathed about the temples argent and azure. 𝕾upporters – *Dexter*, a Roman soldier in armour or, short sleeves and apron gules, face, arms, and legs bare, the latter sandalled, argent: on his head a helmet gold, on the top three feathers of the second, holding in his exterior hand a shield, thereon a female's head; *sinister*, a Moorish prince proper, in armour or, wreathed round the temples argent and azure, short sleeves and apron gules, boots gold, behind him a sheaf of arrows proper, fastened by a pink ribbon, in his exterior hand a bow proper.
Residences – 1 Fairbairn Drive, Mount Pleasant, Harare, Zimbabwe; Brook House, Hope Bowdler, Church Stretton, Shropshire SY6 7DD.

SONS LIVING AND DECEASED

Hon FRANCIS WILLIAM DIGHTON, *b* 29 Dec 1959; *ed* Falcon Coll, Bulawayo: *m* 1982, Shaneen Hobbs, and has issue living, Kirsten Belinda, *b* 1986, — Sarah Ashleigh, *b* 1989. *Address* – Mazoe Citrus Estate, PO Mazowe, Zimbabwe.

†*Hon* Richard Dighton, *b* 1962; *ed* Falcon Coll, Bulawayo; *d* in a motor accident 1989.

Hon Peter John, *b* 1967; *ed* Falcon Coll, Bulawayo: *m* 1997, Deborah Ann, da of Lester Coelen, of Constantia, Cape Town, S Africa, and has issue living, William Lester Dighton, *b* 1999. *Residence* – 1 Fairbairn Drive, Mount Pleasant, Harare, Zimbabwe.

DAUGHTER LIVING

Hon Sarah Joy, *b* 1958: *m* 1980, Mark K. Frewen, of Hillside Farm, N Bergersdorp, NE Cape, S Africa, and has issue living, Matthew, *b* 1991, — Samantha, *b* 1987.

SISTERS LIVING

Hon Elizabeth Mary Jean, *b* 1926: *m* 1948, Maj James Terence Ralph Sylvester Bradley, MA, CEng, MIERE, who *d* 1987, of Knighton Manor, Durweston, Blandford, Dorset, and has issue living, Charles Robin (9 Pembroke Rd, Westbourne, Bournemouth), *b* 1959: *m* 1985, Jennifer Roberts, and has issue living, Jolyon *b* 1986, Christabel Morwenna *b* 1990, — Fiona Elizabeth (195A Quemerford, Calne, Wilts SN11 8JX), *b* 1949, — Heather Mary, *b* 1951: *m* 1978, Michael Dias do Nascimento, BVMS, MRCVS, of Quinta dos Sobreiros, Faxelhas, Apartado 75, 8300 Silves, Algarve, Portugal, and has issue living, Charles James *b* 1979, Edward Michael *b* 1980, Jorge Norman *b* 1988, — Catherine Alison, *b* 1957: *m* 1984, Toby C. Goddard, of 2 Ham Lane, Marnhull, Dorset, son of Keith Goddard, FRICS, FSVA, of Lane End, Broad Oak, Sturminster Newton, Dorset, and has issue living, Hamish Toby *b* 1989, Alexandra Catherine *b* 1987.

Hon Susan Margaret, *b* 1931: *m* 1954, Peter Lindsay Milln, and has issue living, Jeremy James (3 South St, Stafford ST16 2DX), *b* 1956, — Teresa Clare, *b* 1958: *m* 1983, John Joseph Doran, of Milloran, Ardillon, Russellstown, Mullingar, co Westmeath, and has issue living, Fabian James *b* 1985, Jonathan Lindsay *b* 1988, — Eleanor Eve MILLN (5/204 St Asaph Street, Christchurch, New Zealand), *b* 1961; has resumed her maiden name: *m* 1987 (*m diss* 1994), John Courtnay Channon, eldest son of George H. Channon, of Herons Lake, Polbrook, Bodmin, Cornwall, — Jesica Rose, *b* 1964: *m* 1995, Mark Thomas Fisher, of Trecrida Court Gardens, St Austell, Cornwall PL25 5BL, and has issue living, Mungo James *b* 1996, Piran Alexander *b* 1997. *Residence* – Nanterrow, Tregongeeves Lane, Polgooth, St Austell, Cornwall PL26 7AX.

Hon Helen Jennifer Frances, *b* 1935: *m* 1957, Simon FitzRoy Casswell, and has issue living, Edward FitzRoy (2 Harrow Cottages, Ulcombe, Maidstone, Kent ME17 1DP), *b* 1958: *m* 19—, Rosemary Tassel, and has issue living, James FitzRoy *b* 1987, Mark *b* 1989, — Jane Elizabeth (28 Down's Close, Headcorn, Ashford, Kent TN27 9UG), *b* 1962, — Karen Mary (18 Parkgate Park Rd, Westcliff-on-Sea, Essex SSO 7NY), *b* 1969; BSc, BVSc, MRCVS. *Residence* – The Limes Barn Farm, Smarden, nr Ashford, Kent.

WIDOW LIVING OF THIRTEENTH VISCOUNT

GLADYS MAY KATHLEEN (*Gladys, Viscountess Valentia*), da of late Uriah Fowler; *ed* Ridley Hall, Camb: *m* 1938, the 13th Viscount Valentia, who *d* 1951. *Residences* – Wassall House, Wincanton, Somerset; Monckton, 34 Uphills, Bruton, Somerset.

COLLATERAL BRANCHES LIVING

Issue of late Philip de Vere Annesley, brother of 13th Viscount, *b* 1879, *d* 1949: *m* 1907, Christabel Charlotte, BEM, who *d* 1955, da of late John Christopher Tomson:—
Anne Christabel de Vere (*Lady Thompson*), *b* 1909; assumed by deed poll 1941 the additional christian name of Anne: *m* 1939, Sir Richard Hilton Marler Thompson, 1st baronet (*cr* 1963), of Rhodes House, Sellindge, Ashford, Kent.

Granddaughter of late Lt-Col Clifford Reginald Templeman Annesley, DSO (infra):—
Issue of late Reginald Clifford Martin Annesley, *b* 1909, *d* 1994: *m* 1940, Ann Isabella, who *d* 1986, el da of John Robert Strachan, of Firthview, Tain, Ross-shire:—
Kathleen Elaine Vere, *b* 1941: *m* 1966, Beverley Aldington Bird, and has issue living, Clive Robert, *b* 1982, — Glynnis Ann, *b* 1970: *m* 1989, Henry Kevin Botes, and has issue living, Dean Stephen *b* 1989, Matthew Ryan *b* 1992, — Jane Claire, *b* 1972. —— Sheila Rosalind, *b* 1945: *m* 1964, Michael Stuart Allen, late BSA Police, and has issue living, Stuart David, *b* 1969, — Christopher Michael, *b* 1985, — Deborah Michelle, *b* 1966: *m* 1989, Paul Whitechurch, and has issue living, Gary Paul *b* 1990, Ashleigh Lara *b* 1994, Kirsten Michelle *b* (twin) 1994, — Nicole Paula, *b* 1983.

Grandchildren of late Lt-Col Reginald Carey Annesley, son of George, yst son of late Rev Arthur Annesley, son of late Rev Arthur Henry Annesley, DD, great-grandson of late Hon Francis Annesley, 4th son of 1st Viscount:—
Issue of late Lt-Col Clifford Reginald Templeman Annesley, DSO, *b* 1877, *d* 1971: *m* 1907, Clara Mabel, who *d* 1954, el da of Lt-Col Samuel Martin Gully, Norfolk Regt:—
Vere Bessie Mabel (18 Wykeham Place, Lymington, Hants), *b* 1910.

Issue of late Maj Martin Tyndale Annesley, *b* 1896, *d* 1965: *m* 1935, Marjorie Jex Blake, who *d* 1980, el da of Lt-Col B. E. Winter, of Lowestoft:—
Richard Bruce (St Paul's Cottage, Ellesborough Rd, Butlers Cross, Aylesbury), *b* 1937: *m* 1972, Elizabeth Mary Emily, da of late Thomas Doyle, of Armanagh, Glenbrook, co Cork, and has issue living, Charlotte Mary, *b* 1973, — Philippa Vere, *b* 1975, — Sophie Elizabeth, *b* 1977.

Descendants of late William Annesley, MP (3rd son of Hon Francis Annesley, 4th son of 1st Viscount), who was *cr Viscount Glerawly* 1766 (*see* E Annesley).

PREDECESSORS – (1) *Rt Hon Sir* FRANCIS Annesley, filled during forty years numerous high official positions in Ireland, and sat for sometime as MP for Armagh; *cr a Baronet* 1620; in 1621 obtained by patent a reversionary grant to the peerage of *Viscount Valentia* (peerage of Ireland) at the decease of the then viscount; *cr Baron Mountnorris*, of Mountnorris, co Armagh (peerage of Ireland) 1628; in 1635 he publicly offended Lord Strafford, the Lord Deputy of Ireland, and for this offence he was tried, and found guilty, and sentenced to deprivation of military rank and to be shot or beheaded at the pleasure of the General; the capital punishment was not carried out, but he suffered a long imprisonment in Dublin Castle; *d* 1660; *s* by his son (2) ARTHUR, 2nd Viscount; was Treasurer of the Navy 1667, and Lord Privy Seal 1673; *cr Baron Annesley*, of Newport Pagnel, co Bucks, and *Earl of Anglesey* (peerage of England) 1661; *d* 1686; *s* by his son (3) JAMES, 2nd Earl; *d* 1690; *s* by his el son (4) JAMES, 3rd Earl; *d* 1702; *s* by his brother (5) JOHN, 4th Earl; *d* 1710; *s* by his brother (6) ARTHUR, 5th Earl; *d* 1737; *s* by his kinsman (7) RICHARD, 6th Earl, who had previously *s* as 5th *Baron Altham* (peerage of Ireland, *cr* 1680), he being 2nd son of the 3rd Baron Altham, who was 3rd son of the 1st Earl; after the assumption of the earldom by this peer a Mr James Annesley claimed the earldom as son of Arthur, 4th Baron Altham, and alleged that in his infancy he had been kidnapped by his uncle Richard (6th Earl), and in 1743 he commenced a suit of law to recover the property from his uncle and obtained a verdict, though he did not further pursue his claim to the earldom, and his uncle continued to be recognised as earl; *d* 1761; *s* by his son (8) ARTHUR, 8th Viscount, whose claims to the Baronies of Mountnorris, Altham, and the Viscountcy of Valentia were twice confirmed by the Irish Parliament, whilst his claim to the Barony of Annesley and Earldom of Anglesey was refused by the English Parliament; *cr Earl of Mountnorris* (peerage of Ireland) 1793; *d* 1816; *s* by his son (9) GEORGE, second Earl; *d* 1844 when the Barony of Altham and Earldom of Mountnorris expired; *s* in the Baronetcy, Barony of Mountnorris, and Viscountcy of Valentia by his kinsman (10) ARTHUR, 10th Viscount, 5th in descent from Francis, 4th son of 1st Viscount; *d* 1863; *s* by his grandson (11) ARTHUR, KCVO, CB, 11th Viscount, son of Hon Arthur Annesley (el son of 10th Viscount) by Flora Mary, who *d* 1884, da of Lt-Col James Macdonald of Clanranald); Comptroller of the Household to Queen Victoria 1898-1901, and to King Edward VII 1901-05, and a Lord-in-Waiting to King George V 1915-24; *cr Baron Annesley of Bletchington*, co Oxford (peerage of UK) 1917: *m* 1878, Laura Sarah, who *d* 1933, da of Daniel Hale Webb, of Wykeham Park, and widow of Sir Algernon William Payton, 4th Bt; *d* 1927; *s* by his son (12) CARYL ARTHUR JAMES, CVO, 12th Viscount; *b* 1883; Maj 1st R Dragoons; High Steward of Banbury 1932-47; Private Sec to HRH Prince Arthur of Connaught 1922-38; *d unm* 1949, when the Barony of Annesley of Bletchington (peerage of UK) became ext; *s* in his other titles by his kinsman (13) *Rev* WILLIAM MONCKTON, 13th Viscount (el son of Rev Henry Arthur Annesley, el son of Arthur Annesley, great-grandson of Rev Martin Annesley, DD, grandson of Hon Francis Annesley, 4th son of 1st Viscount); *b* 1875; V of Brewham-cum-Redlynch, Somerset, and Cottonian Family Trustee of British Museum: *m* 1938, Gladys May Kathleen, da of late Uriah Fowler; *d* 1951; *s* by his cousin (14) FRANCIS DIGHTON, MC, MRCS, LRCP (son of late George Dighton Annesley, uncle of 13th Viscount); 14th Viscount, *b* 1888; established his succession 1959; MRCS, LRCP 1914; Brig RAMC; Cottonian Family Trustee of British Museum; European War 1914-18 (MC, Belgian Croix de Guerre), Afghanistan 1919, Waziristan 1922-23, European War 1939-45: *m* 1925, Joan Elizabeth, who *d* 1986, da of late John J. Curtis, of Sunnybrook, Sandhurst; *d* 1983; *s* by his only son (15) RICHARD JOHN DIGHTON, 15th Viscount and present peer; also Baron Mountnorris.

Vane, Earl, title of Marquess of Londonderry on Roll of HL.

Vane, family name of Baron Barnard.

Vane, Fletcher-, family name of Baron Inglewood.

Vanneck, family name of Baron Huntingfield.

VANSITTART, BARONY OF (Vansittart) (Extinct 1957)

DAUGHTER LIVING OF FIRST BARON (By 1st m)

Hon Cynthia, *b* 1922: *m* 1st, 1942 (*m diss* in California, USA 1954), Frederick C. Whitman; 2ndly, 1955, Edward Hart Mackay, and has issue living, (by 1st *m*) Michael Robert Vansittart (2518 Buchanan St, San Francisco, Calif 94115, USA), *b* 1944, — Jonathan Crocker (256-30th Av, San Francisco, Calif 94121, USA), *b* 1948, — Kevin Crocker (180 E 79th St, Apt G, New York, NY 10021, USA), *b* 1950, — Tania Vansittart (2109 Baker St, San Francisco, Calif 94115, USA), *b* 1942, — (by 2nd *m*) Robert Vansittart, *b* 1958, — Donald James Edward, *b* 1961. *Residence* – 2655 Clay St, San Francisco, Calif 94115, USA.

VARLEY, BARON (Varley) (Life Baron 1990)

ERIC GRAHAM VARLEY, PC, son of Frank Varley, of Poolsbrook, Derbys; *b* 11 Aug 1932; *ed* Ruskin Coll, Oxford; DL Derbys 1989; Engineer's Turner 1952-55, Mining Industry (Coal) Craftsman 1955-64; Assist Govt Whip 1967-68, PPS to PM (Rt Hon Harold Wilson) 1968-69, Min of State Min of Technology 1969-70, Sec of State for Energy 1974-75, for Industry 1975-79; Chief Opposition Spokesman on Employment 1978-83; Treasurer Lab Party 1981-83; Visiting Fellow Nuffield Coll 1977-81; Chm and Chief Exec Coalite Group since 1984; Steward and Bailiff of the Manor of Northstead since 1984; MP for Chesterfield (*Lab*) 1964-84; *cr* PC 1974, and *Baron Varley*, of Chesterfield, co Derbys (Life Baron) 1990: *m* 1955, Marjorie, da of Alfred Turner, of Duckmanton, Derbys, and has issue.
Residence – 189 Middlecroft Rd, Staveley, Chesterfield, Derbys.

SON LIVING

Hon —, *b* 19—.

Vaughan, Viscount; son of Earl of Lisburne.

VAUX OF HARROWDEN, BARON (Gilbey) (Baron E 1523)
(Title pronounced "Vawks of Harrowden")

Today, not tomorrow

JOHN HUGH PHILIP GILBEY, 10th Baron; *b* 4 Aug 1915; *s* 1977; *ed* Ampleforth Coll, and at Ch Ch Oxford (BA 1937); Maj Duke of Wellington's Regt (ret): *m* 1939, Maureen, da of late Hugh Gilbey, of Shellwood Bend, Leigh, Reigate, Surrey, and has issue.

𝕬rms – Quarterly, 1st and 4th gules, a fesse nebulée or, in chief a horse rampant between two estoiles and the like in base, all of the last, *Gilbey*; 2nd and 3rd: Per bend sinister ermine and erminois a lion rampant or, *Mostyn*. 𝕮rest – In front of a tower proper issuant from the battlements thereof a dragon's head gules, a fleur-de-lis or, all between two ostrich feathers argent. 𝕾upporters – *Dexter*, a griffin sable beaked or the forelegs gold; *sinister*, a buck or each gorged with a torse argent and gules pendant therefrom by a ring gold an escutcheon of the Arms of Vaux (checky, or and gules, on a chevron azure, three roses gold).
Residence – Cholmondeley Cottage, 2 Cholmondeley Walk, Richmond, Surrey.

SONS LIVING

Hon ANTHONY WILLIAM (Rusko, Gatehouse of Fleet, Kirkcudbrightshire), *b* 25 May 1940; FCA; *ed* Ampleforth: *m* 1964, Beverley Anne, only da of late Charles Alexander Walton, of Cooden, Sussex, and has issue living, Richard Hubert Gordon, *b* 16 March 1965: *m* 1996, Elizabeth F., da of M. R. Worsley, of Bolney, W Sussex, — Philip Alexander Charles, *b* 1967: *m* 1994, E. Charlotte, da of late Timothy Britton, of Hatfield Broad Oak, Essex, and has issue living, Timothy John Anthony *b* 1998, — Victoria Caroline, *b* 1969, — Elizabeth Muriel Emma, *b* 1989.

Hon William John (The Grange, Waltham St Lawrence, Twyford, Berks), *b* 1944, *ed* Ampleforth: *m* 1971, Caroline, da of Alan Ball, of The Old Mill, Ramsbury, Wilts, and has issue living, Thomas Edward, *b* 1972: *m* 1996, Beth C., yst da of Peter Martin, of Kingston, Surrey, — James William, *b* 1978, — Charlotte Katharine, *b* 1974.

Hon Michael Christopher (Pheasants Ridge, Hambleden, Henley, Oxon RG9 6SD), *b* 1949, *ed* Ampleforth, and St Andrew's Univ (MA); ARICS: *m* 1971, Linda, yst da of late Arthur Sebastian Gilbey (*see* Gilbey, Bt, colls), and has issue living, Henry John, *b* 1973: *m* 1999, Islay Mary, da of William Field Clegg (*see* B Colnbrook), — Julian Sebastian, *b* 1975, — William Michael, *b* 1979.

DAUGHTER LIVING

Hon Penelope Margaret, *b* 1942: *m* 1965, John Charles Haynes, of Lellizzick West, Padstow, Cornwall PL28 8HR, and has issue living, Charles Thomas Francis (51 Faroe Rd, W14 0EL), *b* 1967: *m* 1998, Natalie Astrid Gunn, — Edward Hugh Gordon, *b* 1976, — Alexandra Louise, *b* 1966: *m* 1991, Christopher John Courage, of Edgcote, Banbury, Oxon (*see* Reynolds, Bt), — Bridget Clare, *b* 1969.

SISTER LIVING

Hon Mary Agnes Margaret, *b* 1928. *Residence* – Dolphins, Gt Harrowden, Wellingborough.

COLLATERAL BRANCHES LIVING

Grandchildren of late Hon Harold Plantagenet Mostyn, yr brother of 7th Baron:—
Issue of late George Anthony Mostyn, *b* 1898, *d* 1972: *m* 1924, Catharine Sibylla, who *d* 1983, da of late Bernard Henry Holland, CB (*see* V Knutsford, colls):—
Richard Anthony MOSTYN (3 Flamingo Drive, Greenside, Mutare, Zimbabwe), *b* 1927; *ed* RNC Dartmouth; Lt RN (ret); FIAC (SA); LIMTA (SA): *m* 1961, Mary, da of J. J. Michie, of Marian Hill, Natal, and has issue living, Anthony Damian (25 Mynn Crescent, Bearsted, Maidstone, Kent ME14 4AR), *b* 1964; CA (Zim),: *m* 1997, Deborah Lawrenson, of Maidstone, and has issue living, Harriet Christine *b* 1997, — Christopher Francis Joseph (3 Flamingo Drive, Greenside, Mutare, Zimbabwe), *b* 1966: *m* 1996, Jody Kim, da of Henry Kasprow, of Prince George, BC, Canada, — Nicola Mary, *b* 1961: *m* 1981, Grant Taylor, of 167/2 Murray Av, Mosman Park, W Australia 6012, and has issue living, Grant Alexander *b* 1994, Alana Clare *b* 1986, — Clare Sibylla, *b* 1963: *m* 1983, Morgan Hore, of 77 Oxlow Lane, Dagenham, Essex RM9 5XD, and has issue living, Mark Patrick *b* 1983, Kevin Anthony *b* 1987. —— Valentine Francis (50 Cranley Mews, SW7), *b* 1943; *ed* Oxford Sch of Architecture, and Canterbury Sch of Architecture (Dip Arch); ARIBA: *m* 1974, Gay, da of H. Field (PO Box 1167, Malibu, Calif 90265), and has issue living, Amy Clare *b* 1974, — Sarah Jane, *b* 1977. —— Juliet Veronica, *b* 1925: *m* 1952, Anthony Lightfoot, of Valley Cottage, Brundish, nr Woodbridge, Suffolk, and has issue living, Edward Jude (644 Wickham Rd, Shirley, Croydon, Surrey CR0 8EA), *b* 1953: *ed* Framlingham Coll, and Univ Coll London; ACIB: *m* 1st 1977 (*m diss* 1982), Hilary Diane Carver; 2ndly, 1983, Gaynor Alison Clark, and has issue living (by 2nd *m*), Alexander Richard *b* 1985, Jessica Louise *b* 1984, — Dominic Anthony (Wells Yard, 5 Barnes Rd, Pulham Market, Diss, Norfolk IP21 4SP), *b* 1955, — Paul Jerome (36A Lonsdale Rd, W11 2DE), *b* 1956: *m* 1st, 1982 (*m*

diss 19—), Claudia Cecilia, only da of Claude Vaux Miéville (*see* B Hatherton, 1985 Edn); 2ndly, 1999, Virginie Helène Amandine Roudière, — Mary Victoria, *b* 1959: *m* 1998, Robert John Pendered, of Hill View, Halesworth Rd, Walpole, Halesworth, Suffolk IP19 9AZ, and has issue living, Matilda Mary *b* 1996, Emily Rachel *b* 1998, — Catherine Lucy LIGHT-FOOT (Honeysuckle Cottage, 3 Orchard Rd, Knowle, nr Braunton, Devon EX33 2DZ), *b* 1966; has resumed her maiden name: *m* 1992 (*m diss* 1993), James Hartley Berwick. ——Joan Elizabeth Verena MOSTYN, *b* 1948; *ed* Royal Coll of Art (MA): *m* 1971 (*m diss* 1977), Anthony John Dyson; has issue living (by Douglas Jones, of San Francisco, Calif), Santiago Alexis Kanjuchi Sadiq MOSTYN, *b* 1981.

Issue of late Hon Gladys Flora Mostyn, 2nd da of 7th Baron, *b* 1889, *d* 1975: *m* 1911, George Victor Bellasis Charlton, who *d* 1943:—

Eleanor Margaret Mary, *b* 1912. ——†Anne Mary Georgina, *b* 1913: *m* 1948, Hugh Dougal Fyfe Baird, who *d* 1979, and *d* 1994, leaving issue, (Rosemary) Gillian, *b* 1950: *m* 1st, 1974 (*m diss* 1980), Barry Lambert; 2ndly, 1981, Charles Davies King, and has issue living (by 2nd *m*), Patrick Charles *b* 1987. ——Joan Mary Winifrede, *b* 1916: *m* 1st, 1940, Ian Alexander Bruce Johnstone, P/O RAF, who was *ka* 1942; 2ndly, 1945, Harry James Hubert Ripper, F/O RAF, of 1A Recreation Ground, Sible Hedingham, Essex CO9 3JD, and has issue living (by 2nd *m*), Christopher James (Hillcroft House, Upper Stowe, Daventry, Northants), *b* 1946; *ed* Blackfriars Sch, Laxton, Northants: *m* 1974 (*m diss* 1998), Julie Margaret Long, of Sydney, Australia, and has issue living, Georgina Louise *b* 1977, Annabel Merry *b* 1979, Holly Charlton *b* 1981, — Judith Caroline (51 Begbroke Crescent, Begbroke, Oxon OX5 1RW), *b* 1949: *m* 1971 (*m diss* 1993), Philip William Ford, and has issue living, Adam George *b* 1975, Samantha Anne *b* 1973. ——Dorothy Mary Amy, *b* 1919: *m* 1958, Digby Michael Auden, of Dolphin House, Hardingstone, Northampton NN4 6BX, and has had issue, †Julian Michael, *b* 1961; *k* in an accident 1973, — Penelope Clare, *b* 1960: *m* 1986, Paul John Radford, formerly of Montreal, of 8 Darwin Close, Porterswood, St Albans, Herts AL3 6LH, and has issue living, Michael Julian Auden *b* 1988, Dominic Peter Auden *b* 1990, Sebastian Thomas Auden *b* 1992, Oliver Lawrence Auden *b* 1996, Catriona Helen Margaret Auden *b* 1987. ——Frances Mary Elizabeth, *b* 1924: *m* 1947, Stephen Louis Dudley Ripper, of Orchard House, High St Green, Sible Hedingham, Essex CO9 3LG, and has had issue, Anne Mary Frances, *b* 1948: *m* 1983, Anton Brooke Shellim, of 12 Moreton Av, Harpenden, Herts AL5 2ET, and has issue living, Alexander Brooke *b* 1985, Rebecca Frances *b* 1987, — †Susan Mary Margaret, *b* 1951; *dunm* 1990, — Catherine Mary Alison, *b* 1955: *m* 1st, 1974 (*m diss* 1980), George Hales; 2ndly, 1980, John Alexander Malone, of 8 Greenbank Crescent, Edinburgh EH10 5SG, and has issue living (by 2nd *m*), Martin John *b* 1988, Amy Frances *b* 1984.

Descendants of late Barbara Maria Mostyn, sister of 6th Baron, who *m* 1833, Sir Frederick William Slade, QC, 2nd Bt:—

See Slade, Bt.

PREDECESSORS – **(1)** *Sir* NICHOLAS Vaux, a distinguished soldier and statesman, was summoned to Parliament of England as *Baron Vaux of Harrowden*, 1523; *d* 1523; *s* by his son **(2)** THOMAS, 2nd Baron; *d* 1562; *s* by his son **(3)** WILLIAM, 3rd Baron; was summoned to Parliament 1563-89; *d* 1595; *s* by his grandson **(4)** EDWARD, 4th Baron; summoned to Parliament 1620; *dsp* 1661; *s* by his brother **(5)** HENRY, 5th Baron; *d* unmarried 1662, when the barony became abeyant between his surviving sister Joyce, and the heirs of his sisters Mary (Lady Symeon) and Catherine (Baroness Abergavenny), and remained so until 1838, when the abeyance was terminated in favour of the heir of Mary, the el sister **(6)** GEORGE CHARLES Mostyn, 6th Baron, son of Mary Lucinda, née Butler, by her *m* to Charles Browne-Mostyn, 2nd son of Sir Edward Mostyn, 5th Bt; *d* 1883; *s* by his grandson **(7)** HUBERT GEORGE CHARLES (el son of late Major Hon George Charles Mostyn), 7th Baron; *b* 1860; appointed Attache in Diplo Ser 1884, became a 3rd Sec 1886, and a 2nd Sec 1891; retired 1899: *m* 1st, 1886, Eleanor Margaret, who *d* 1896, da of Sir Alexander Matheson, MP, 1st Bt; 2ndly, 1902, Margaret Annette Jane Chichele, who *d* 1922, da of late Sir William Chichele Plowden, KCSI (Bass, Bt); 3rdly, 1924, Mary Winefride Teresa (Freyda), who *d* 1944, da of Sir Joseph Edward Radcliffe, 4th Bt, and widow of Capt Thomas Cecil de Trafford, Roy Fusiliers (de Trafford, Bt, colls); *d* 1935, when the Barony again fell into abeyance between his three das, and so remained until July 1938, when it was terminated by Letters Patent in favour of the el **(8)** GRACE MARY ELEANOR Mostyn, *b* 1887: *m* 1911, William Gordon Gilbey who *d* 1965; *d* 1958; *s* by her el son **(9)** *Rev* PETER HUBERT GORDON, 9th Baron, in Holy Orders of Church of Rome, a Monk of Ampleforth Abbey, *d* 1977; *s* by his brother **(10)** JOHN HUGH PHILIP, 10th Baron and present peer.

VENTRY, BARON (Daubeny de Moleyns) (Baron I 1800, Bt I 1797)
(Name pronounced "demmoleens")

To conquer is to live enough

ANDREW WESLEY DAUBENEY DE MOLEYNS, 8th Baron and 8th Baronet; *b* 28 May 1943; *s* 1987; assumed by deed poll 1966 the surname of Daubeny de Moleyns; *ed* Aldenham: *m* 1st, 1963 (*m diss* 1979), Nelly Edouard Renée, da of Abel Chaumillon, of Loma de los Riseos, Villa Angel, Torremolinos, Malaga, Spain; 2ndly, 1983, Jill Rosemary, da of Cecil Walter Oram, and has issue by 1st and 2nd *m*.

Arms – Quarterly, 1st and 4th sable, on a chief ermine three fusils gules; 2nd and 3rd per pale or and sable, two chevronels between three griffins passant counterchanged. **Crests** – 1st, a savage's head couped at the shoulders and affrontée, proper; 2nd, a goat's head erased, per chevron or and sable, attired of the 2nd, in the mouth a branch of laurel proper. **Supporters** – Two lions or, ducally collared and chained azure.
Residence – Hill of Errol House, Errol, Perthshire PH2 7TQ.

SON LIVING (*By 1st marriage*)

Hon FRANCIS WESLEY, *b* 1 May 1965; *ed* Gordonstoun.

DAUGHTERS LIVING (*By 1st marriage*)

Hon Elizabeth-Anne Stuart, *b* 1964: *m* 1990, Justin D. Byford, only son of T. J. Byford, of Belgrade, Yugoslavia, and of Mrs J. D. Campane, of Barnes, SW14.
Hon Brigitte Catherine, *b* 1967.

(*By 2nd marriage*)

Hon Lisa, *b* 1985.

SISTER LIVING

Sally Joan, *b* 1940: *m* 1964, Robin Hart, son of George Hart, of Beaulieu, Mitton Grove, Shrewsbury, and has issue living, Christopher, *b* 1965; *ed* Shrewsbury, — Penelope, *b* 1966, — Caroline, *b* 1968, — Rachel, *b* 1970.

HALF-SISTER LIVING

Valentia, *b* 1928: *m* 1950, Capt Nathaniel Duncan Spry Grant-Dalton, RHA, High Sheriff of Cornwall 1986, and has issue living, Kevin Duncan Spry (Place, St Anthony-in-Roseland, Portscatho, Truro, Cornwall TR2 5EZ), *b* 1952; *ed* Radley: *m* 1980, Amanda Charlton, da of F. E. de Smitt, of 45 Drax Av, SW20, and has issue living, Samuel Duncan Spry *b* 1985, Jolyon *b* 1991 Pippa Charlton *b* 1988, — Miranda Jane, *b* 1955: *m* 1983, Simon James Forrester, of Greenacres Farmhouse, Lower Tysoe, Warws CV39 0BY, elder son of Maj-Gen Michael Forrester, CB, CBE, DSO, MC, of West Worldham, Hants, and has issue living, Nicholas Francis *b* 1985, Frederick Richard George *b* 1990, — Nicola Frances, *b* 1957: *m* 1979, Ian Adair Campbell, of Barton House, St Anthony-in-Roseland, Portscatho, Truro, Cornwall TR2 5EZ, 2nd son of Lt-Col Robert Adair Campbell, of Altries, Maryculter, Aberdeenshire, and has issue living, Hamish Adair *b* 1982, Oliver Alistair *b* 1985, Robert Francis *b* 1988. *Residence* – Place House, St Anthony-in-Roseland, Portscatho, Cornwall TR2 5EZ.

STEP-MOTHER LIVING

Olivia Phœbe (has reverted to her former style of *Lady John Conyngham*), da of Capt Percy Neave Leathers, of Fayre Cottage, Robertsbridge, Sussex, and widow of Lord John Victor Albert Blosse Conyngham, son of 6th Marquess Conyngham: *m* 1963, as his 4th wife, Hon Francis Alexander Innys Eveleigh-Ross-de-Moleyns, who *d* 1964. *Residence* – Windmill Cottage, Yapton Rd, Barnham, Bognor Regis, W Sussex.

COLLATERAL BRANCHES LIVING

Grandchildren of late Hon John Gilbert Eveleigh-de-Moleyns (*infra*):—
  Issue of late John Andrew WAUCHOPE, *b* 1900, *d* 1956, having assumed the surname of Wauchope in lieu of his patronymic 1945: *m* 1923, Rosemary Eve, who *d* 1975, da of late Rear-Adm John Arthur Tuke:—
Andrew Dermod (The Cottage, Lochtower, Kelso TD5 8PD), *b* 1932: *m* 1957, Jennifer Siggers, and has issue living, James Andrew, *b* 1963: *m* 1992, Victoria Neil, and has issue living, Angus *b* 1995, Emma *b* 1993, Robyn (a da) *b* 1998, — Ian Simon (twin) *b* 1963: *m* 1990, Sarah Barlow, and has issue living, Lara *b* 1991, Katie *b* 1993, — Fiona Jane, *b* 1958: *m* 1981, William Elliot, and has issue living, Christopher *b* 1982, Nicola *b* 1984, — Nicola Anne, *b* 1959: *m* 1990, Douglas Dale, and has issue living, Alexander *b* 1994, Constance *b* 1995. —— Œnone Eileen Frances, *b* 1931: *m* 1952, Timothy Robert Crum Willis, of Meadowcroft, Station Rd, Great Ayton, Middlesbrough, Cleveland TS9 6HB, and has issue living, Robert Nigel Crum (68 Shandon Park, Belfast BT5 6NY), *b* 1954: *m* 1984, Paula Carol Hamilton, and has issue living,

Simon Robert Crum *b* 1987, Deborah Carol Jane *b* 1988, — Andrew James Scott (Hawkhill, 21 Broad St, Weston, CT 06883, USA), *b* 1956: *m* 1992, Linda Anne Marinaro, and has issue living, Robin Christopher Scott *b* 1994, James Michael Billopp *b* 1998, — John Douglas Charles (52 Sugden Rd, SW11 5EF), *b* 1960, — Michael Philip Bruce (56 Forth St, N Berwick, E Lothian EH39 4JJ), *b* 1966: *m* 1993, Karen Edwick, and has issue living, Georgina Chloe Edwick *b* 1995, Stephanie Megan *b* (twin) 1995.

        Issue of late Hon John Gilbert Eveleigh-de-Moleyns, brother of 6th Baron *b* 1878, *d* 1928: *m* 1899, Marguerite, who *d* 1982, aged 103, da of George Edward Noon:—
Eileen Mildred Alice, *b* 1912: *m* 1939, Harold Alan Coldham, LLB, who *d* 1996, of La Bastia, Propriano, France, and has issue living, Simon Frederick Russell, *b* 1940; MA, PhD, — Christopher Alan (Basement Flat, 11 Kildare Gdns, W2), *b* 1943, — Marie Audrey (twin), *b* 1943: *m* 1988, Julian Stephen Frere Bidwell, of 60 Lydden Grove, SW18 4LN.

        Granddaughter of late Rev William Bishop de Moleyns, 2nd son of late Major Hon Edward de Moleyns, 5th son of 1st Baron:—
        Issue of late Rev Alured Bayfield de Moleyns, *b* 1851, *d* 1925: *m* 1888, Mary Louisa, who *d* 1908, el da of John Lyon (retired Fleet Paymaster, RN):—
Alice Louisa Eveleigh, *b* 1889.

PREDECESSORS – **(1)** Thomas Mullins; *cr* a *Baronet* 1797, and *Baron Ventry*, of Ventry, co Kerry (peerage of Ireland) 1800; *d* 1824; *s* by his son **(2)** William Townsend, 2nd Baron; *d* 1827; *s* by his nephew **(3)** Thomas Townsend Aremberg, 3rd Baron; *b* 1786; resumed the ancient family name of De Moleyns by Roy licence 1841: *m* 1821, Eliza Theodora, da of Sir John Blake, 10th Bt; *d* 1868; *s* by his son **(4)** Dayrolles Blakeney, 4th Baron, *b* 1828; a Representative Peer; assumed 1874 the additional surname and arms of Eveleigh: *m* 1860, Harriet Elizabeth Frances, who *d* 1906, da of Andrew Wauchope, of Niddrie Marischal, Midlothian; *d* 1914; *s* by his el son **(5)** Frederick Rossmore Wauchope, DSO, 5th Baron, *b* 1861; *d* 1923; *s* by his brother **(6)** Arthur William, 6th Baron, *b* 1864: *m* 1897, Evelyn Muriel Stuart, who *d* 1966, da of Lansdowne Daubeney, of Norton Malreward, Somerset, *d* 1936; *s* by his el son **(7)** Arthur Frederick Daubeney, 7th Baron, *b* 1898, assumed addl christian name of Olav, received King Haakon's Freedom Medal, served in World War I in Irish Guards and RAF (Airship Branch), and World War II in Balloon Cmd and Intelligence, late Hon A/Cdre No 902 (Co of London) Balloon Sqdn AAF and Fl Lieut RAFVR; *d* 1987; *s* by his nephew **(8)** Andrew Wesley (son of late Hon Francis Alexander Innys Eveleigh-Ross-de Moleyns, yr son of 6th Baron), 8th Baron and present peer.

This family descends from Col Frederick Mullins of Burnham, Norfolk, who settled in Ireland about 1666, and *m* Jane, da and co-heir of Very Rev John Eveleigh, Dean of Ross. The Mullins family claim descent from the de Moleyns, though the descent remains to be proved. They may have taken their name from Moulins la Marche, Orne, Normandy; *see* The Complete Peerage, Vol IX, p 43, for a note on the origin of this family.

Vere of Hanworth, Lord; grandson of Duke of St Albans.

Vereker, family name of Viscount Gort.

Verney, family name of Baron Willoughby de Broke.

VERNON, BARON (Venables-Vernon) (Baron GB 1762)

or
ver non semper viret
Vernon always flourishes; or
The spring does not always flourish

JOHN LAWRANCE VENABLES-VERNON, 10th Baron; *b* 1 Feb 1923; *s* 1963; *ed* Eton, and Magdalen Coll, Oxford; Bar Lincoln's Inn 1949; a JP for Derbys; served in Cabinet Office 1953-57, Colonial Office, Kenya 1957-58, and Foreign Office 1958-60; 1939-45 War as Capt Scots Gds: *m* 1st, 1955 (*m diss* 1982), Sheila Jean, yr da of W. Marshall Clark, OBE, of Johannesburg, S Africa; 2ndly, 1982, Sally June, el da of Robin Stratford, QC, and formerly wife of (i) Colin Fyfe-Jamieson and (ii) Sir (John) Jeremy Eustace Tennyson d'Eyncourt, 3rd Bt, and has had issue by 1st *m*.

Arms – Quarterly: 1st and 4th grand quarters quarterly 1st and 4th argent, a fret sable; 2nd and 3rd or, on a fesse azure, three garbs of the field, *Vernon*; 2nd and 3rd azure, two bars argent, *Venables*. **Crests** – 1st, a boar's head erased sable, ducally gorged or, *Vernon*; 2nd, a wyvern, with wings endorsed, standing on a fish weir or trap, devouring a child, and pierced through with an arrow in fesse, all proper, *Venables*. **Supporters** – *Dexter*, a lion gules, collared, and chain reflexed over the back or; *sinister*, a boar sable, ducally gorged, and chain reflexed over the back or.
Seat – Sudbury House, Sudbury, Derby. *Residence* – 10 Ringmer Av, SW6. *Club* – Boodle's.

DAUGHTERS LIVING AND DECEASED (*By 1st marriage*)

Hon Georgina Frances, *b* 1963; *ed* Cranborne Chase, and — Coll, Camb; author (as Frances Vernon) of *Privileged Children* 1982, *Gentlemen and Players* 1984, *A Desirable Husband* 1987, *The Bohemian Girl* 1988, and *The Marquis of Westmarch* 1989; *d* 1991.
Hon Joanna Elizabeth, *b* 1965: *m* 1992, Alexander Rupert Fitzalan Howard (*see* D Norfolk).

COLLATERAL BRANCHES LIVING

Granddaughter of late Rt Hon Sir William George Granville Venables-Vernon-Harcourt, KC, MP, 2nd son of late Rev William Harcourt, 4th son of the Most Rev Hon Edward Harcourt, Archbishop of York, 3rd son of 1st Baron:—
Issue of late Robert Venables-Vernon-Harcourt, who discontinued the use of the surnames of Venables-Vernon, *b* 1878, *d* 1962: *m* 1911, Margorie Laura, who *d* 1977, da of late William Samuel Cunard (Cunard, Bt, colls):—
Mary Elizabeth, *b* 1922: *m* 1950, Com Ian Rochfort Johnston, RN, of 8 Pembroke Gardens Close, W8, and has issue living, Sarah Elizabeth, *b* 1956: *m* 1979, William James Archer Ziegler (*see* B Brownlow, colls), — Laura Catherine, *b* 1960.

Granddaughter of late Augustus George Vernon-Harcourt, FRS, el son of Adm Frederick Edward Vernon-Harcourt (*infra*):—
Issue of late Simon Evelyn Vernon-Harcourt, *b* 1882, *d* 1966: *m* 1916, Dorothy Margaret, MBE, who *d* 1987, da of late Sir Robert Hudson, GBE:—
Anne, *b* 1925.

Grandchildren of late Leveson William Vernon-Harcourt, elder son of late Leveson Francis Vernon-Harcourt, MICE, 2nd son of Adm Frederick Edward Vernon-Harcourt, 5th son of late Most Rev Hon Edward Harcourt (*ante*):—
Issue of late William Ronald Denis Vernon-Harcourt, OBE, *b (posthumous)* 1909, *d* 1999: *m* 1937, Nancy Everil (Quoin Cottage, Southwick Rd, Denmead, Portsmouth, Hants PO7 6LA), only child of late Lt-Col Bertram Henry Leatham, DSO:—
ANTHONY WILLIAM (Monks Farm, Debden Green, Saffron Walden, Essex CB11 3LX), *b* 29 October 1939; *ed* Eton, and Magdalene Coll, Camb: *m* 1966, Cherry Stanhope, da of late Thomas Corbin, of Lime Tree House, Spaldwick, Hunts, and has issue living, Simon Anthony, *b* 1969, — Edward William, *b* 1973, — Oliver Thomas, *b* 1977, — Charlotte Lucy, *b* 1968; has issue living (by Paul Kaye), Hector Thomas Vernon KAYE *b* 1998. —— Anne Dorothy, *b* 1945: *m* 1st, 1967 (*m diss* 1974), Nicholas Bloxam; 2ndly, 1983, Peter George Cobb, of The Old School House, Clanfield, Hants and has issue living (by 1st *m*) Richard William, *b* 1971, — David Vernon, *b* 1974.

Granddaughters of late Edward Evelyn Harcourt-Vernon, eldest son of late Rev Evelyn Hardolph Harcourt-Vernon, 2nd son of late Granville Harcourt-Vernon, 7th son of Most Rev Hon Edward Harcourt (*ante*):—
Issue of late Capt Egerton Gervase Edward Harcourt-Vernon, MC, Gren Gds, *b* 1899, *d* 1976: *m* 1932, Norma, da of G. W. Hatherly:—
Anne Letitia, *b* 1933. —— Pamela Teresa Marygold, *b* 1938; *ed* Bedgebury Park, Medway Coll of Technology (BSc London), and Newnham Coll, Camb (MA): *m* 1961, Prof Antony Dawson Cox, FRCP, FRCPsych, FRCPCH, of Wensley Hall, nr Matlock, Derbys DE4 2LL, and has issue living, Simon (20 Oxford Sq, W2 2PB), *b* 1962: *m* 1989, Antonia Mary, da of Edgar J. Feuchtwanger, and has issue living, George Leo Vernon *b* 1994, Thomas Gerrard Kennedy *b* 1995, — Nicholas, *b* 1964: *m* 1996, Kitty, da of late Adrian John Martin Seeker, — Hugo Francis *b* 1997. —— Rosalind Elizabeth Ida, *b* 1942: *m* 1966, Christopher Howell, of 36 Guards Club Rd, Maidenhead, and has issue living, Candida Justine, *b* 1969, — Madeleine Theresa, *b* 1977.

Grandchildren of late Herbert Evelyn Harcourt-Vernon, yst son of late Rev Evelyn Hardolph Harcourt-Vernon (*ante*):—

Issue of late Arthur Arundel Harcourt-Vernon, *b* 1895, *d* 1971: *m* 1925, Alice Margaret, who *d* 1977, da of late Rev Edward Cartwright Cayley (*see* Cayley, Bt, colls, 1976 Edn):—
Granville Patrick (57 Glengowan Rd, Toronto, Ont, Canada M4N IG3), *b* 1926; BA (Toronto), LLB, QC: *m* 1954, Deborah Perry Smith, and has issue living, Geoffrey William (20 Elmer Av, Toronto, Ont, Canada M4L 3R7), *b* 1958; BA (Toronto), BLA (Guelph): *m* 1980 (*m diss* 1994), Cynthia Jane Gunn, and has issue living, Caitlin Elizabeth Gunn *b* 1988, Julia Robin Gunn *b* 1991, — Catherine Harcourt, *b* 1956; BA (Queens), MBA (Western Ont): *m* 1987, Robert Bruce McFarran Martin, of 71 Rosedale Heights Drive, Toronto, Ont, Canada M4T 1C4, and has issue living, Richard Harcourt *b* 1988, Stephen Taylor *b* 1990, Scott Edward *b* 1993, — Susan Elizabeth *b* 1961; BSc (Queens), MBA (INSEAD): *m* 1992, Denis Pellerin, of 22 bis Rue de Sevres, 92150 Suresnes, France. ——— Hugh (176 Melrose Ave, Toronto, Ont, Canada M5M 1Z1) *b* 1930: *m* 1st, 1953, Elizabeth Virginia Richardson; 2ndly, 1978, Mrs Shirley Rose Archer, da of Cecil Ernest Woodford, of Prestatyn, Clwyd, and has issue living (by 1st *m*), Christopher Hugh (29 Kelway Blvd, Toronto, Ont, Canada M5N 1H2), *b* 1956, — Nancy Margaret (PO 685, Station Main, Digby, Nova Scotia, Canada B0V 1A0), *b* 1960, — Tannis Elizabeth, *b* 1964: *m* 19—, Richard Edward Longmore, Jr, of 20 Upper Rd, Stafford Springs, CT 06076, USA. ——— John Anthony (1565 Big Bay Point Rd, RR#4, Barrie, Ont, Canada L4M 4S6), *b* 1938: *m* 1975, Susan Elaine, da of Thomas Tinniswood Vaulkhard, of Victoria, BC, and has issue living, Mark Nicholas, *b* 1984, — Stephen Andrew, *b* 1984, — Marin Georgina, *b* 1982. ——— Joy, *b* 1934. ——— Rosemary, *b* 1935: *m* 1960, Rev John Francis Moorhead, of 79 Queen St, Sussex, New Brunswick, Canada E4E 2B2, and has issue living, Margaret Patricia, *b* 1961, — Nancy Catherine, *b* 1967, — Cynthia Mabel, *b* 1970.

PREDECESSORS – (1) GEORGE Vernon, son of Henry Vernon of Sudbury, Derby, and Anne, da and heir of Thomas Pigott by Mary, sister and heir of Sir Peter Venables, Baron of Kinderton, Cheshire; MP for Lichfield; assumed in 1728 by Roy licence the additional surname of Venables and in 1762 was *cr Baron Vernon, Baron of Kinderton*, co Chester (peerage of Great Britain), *d* 1780; *s* by his el son (2) GEORGE, 2nd Baron; sat as MP for Glamorganshire 1774; *d* 1818; *s* by his half-brother (3) HENRY, 3rd Baron; *d* 1829; *s* by his son (4) GEORGE CHARLES, 4th Baron; *d* 1838; *s* by his son (5) GEORGE JOHN, 5th Baron; *b* 1803; assumed in 1837 by sign manual the surname of Warren only for himself and subsequent issue; *d* 1866; *s* by his son (6) AUGUSTUS HENRY, 6th Baron; *b* 1829: *m* 1851, Lady Harriet Frances Maria Anson, who *d* 1898, da of 1st Earl of Lichfield: *d* 1883; *s* by his son (7) GEORGE WILLIAM HENRY, PC, 7th Baron, *b* 1854; Capt Hon Corps of Gentlemen-at-Arms 1892-4: *m* 1885, Frances Margaret, who *d* 1940, da of Francis Lawrance, of New York; *d* 1898; *s* by his el son (8) GEORGE FRANCIS AUGUSTUS, 8th Baron, *b* 1888; (*ka* as Capt Derbyshire Yeo 1915); *s* by his brother (9) FRANCIS WILLIAM LAWRANCE, 9th Baron; *b* 1889; Lt-Cdr RN: *m* 1915, Violet Miriam Nightingale, who *d* 1978, da of late Lt-Col Charles Herbert Clay; *d* 1963; *s* by his only son (10) JOHN LAWRANCE, 10th Baron and present peer.

Vernon, family name of Baron Lyveden.

VERULAM, EARL OF (Grimston) (Earl UK 1815, Bt E 1629)

JOHN DUNCAN GRIMSTON, 7th Earl and 14th Baronet; *b* 21 April 1951; *s* 1973; *ed* Eton, and Ch Ch, Oxford: *m* 1976, Dione Angela, el da of Jeremy Fox Eric Smith, of The Old Rectory, Slaugham, Handcross, W Sussex (*see* Burrell, Bt), and has issue.

Arms – Quarterly: 1st and 4th argent, on a fesse sable, three rowels of six points or pierced gules; in the dexter chief an ermine spot sable, *Grimston*; 2nd sable, a fesse dancettée between two leopards' faces or, *Luckyn*; 3rd argent, three bugle horns sable, stringed gules, *Forrester*. **Crest** – A stag's head erased proper, attired or. **Supporters** – *Dexter*, a stag reguardant proper, attired or; *sinister*, a griffin reguardant or.
Seat – Gorhambury, St Albans, Herts.

SONS LIVING

JAMES WALTER (*Viscount Grimston*), *b* 6 Jan 1978.
Hon Hugo Guy Sylvester, *b* 1979.
Hon Sam George, *b* 1983.

DAUGHTER LIVING

Lady Flora Hermione, *b* 1981.

SISTERS LIVING

Moderate things are stable

Lady Hermione Frances GRIMSTON (Old Pondyards, Redbourn Rd, St Albans, Herts), *b* 1941; resumed the surname of Grimston: *m* 1st, 1965 (*m diss* 1971), Richard John Perronet Thompson; 2ndly, 1971 (*m diss* 1982), James Darell Dickson Thompson-Schwab.

Lady Romayne Bryony, *b* 1946: *m* 1973, John Roberts Bockstoce, of 1 Hill St, S Dartmouth, Mass 02748, USA, and has issue living, John Grimston, *b* 1976.

Lady Iona Charlotte (*Countess of Mount Charles*), *b* 1953: *m* 1985, as his 2nd wife, Henry Vivian Pierpoint, Earl of Mount Charles, eldest son of 7th Marquess Conyngham. *Residence* – Slane Castle, co Meath.

COLLATERAL BRANCHES LIVING

(In remainder to Lordship of Forrester of Corstorphine only)

Issue of late Lady Elisabeth Hariot Grimston, eldest da of 6th Earl, *b* 1939, *d* 1987: *m* 1958 (*m diss* 1972), John Christopher George, Viscount Pollington (later 8th Earl of Mexborough):—
See E Mexborough.

Issue of late Lady Helen Grimston, eldest da of 3rd Earl, *b* 1879, *d* 1947: *m* 1908, Rt Hon Sir Felix Cassel, 1st Bt, who *d* 1953:—
See Cassel, Bt.

Issue of late Lady Hermione Grimston, 2nd da of 3rd Earl, *b* 1881, *d* 1924: *m* 1904, Cdr Bernard Buxton, DSO, RN, who *d* 1923:—
See Buxton, Bt, colls.

Grandchildren of late Lady Aline Grimston, 3rd da of 3rd Earl:—
Issue of late (Peter) Cedric Barnett, *b* 1910, *d* 1980: *m* 1941, Sylvia Irina, OBE (7 Upper Belgrave St, SW1), da of Lt-Col William David Kenny, OBE, of Dun Laoghaire, co Dublin:—
Ulric David BARNETT, *b* 1942; *ed* Eton, and Magdalen Coll, Oxford: *m* 1969, Marie-Jane, da of Capt de Frégate Jean Levasseur, and has issue living, Rory Nicholas, *b* 1971, — Oliver Louis, *b* 1979, — Natalie Aline, *b* 1974. *Residence* – Towersey Manor, Thame, Oxon OX9 3QR. —— Patricia (26 Stanhope Gdns, SW7), *b* 1945: *m* 1st, 1968 (*m diss* 1975), Oscar Jorge Potier; 2ndly, 1975 (*m diss* 1979), Dennis Nagle; 3rdly, 1979, Samuel Kenneth Henry Goodenough, who *d* 1983, yst son of Sir William Macnamara Goodenough, 1st Bt, and has issue living (by 1st *m*), Rupert Alexander, *b* 1969, — (by 2nd *m*), Patricia, *b* 1975. —— Susan, *b* 1947: *m* 1967 (*m diss* 1997), Capt Charles Temple Blackwood, late Gren Gds, and has issue living, James Temple, *b* 1969, — Jonathan Charles, *b* 1971.

Grandchildren (by 1st *m*) of late Lady Elizabeth Motion (infra):—
Issue of late Maj Michael Hesketh-Prichard, RA, *b* 1909, *d* 1988: *m* 1938, Venetia Alice, who *d* 1992, da of late Sir Frederick Daniel Green:—
Richard Michael HESKETH-PRICHARD (1703 Calveryman Lane, Katy, Texas 77449, USA), *b* 1939; *ed* Fettes: *m* 1965 (*m diss* 1981), Elizabeth Susan, da of late John Cuthbert Ottaway, MBE, TD, of Beech Bottom, St Albans, and has issue living, James Michael, *b* 1966; *ed* Pembroke Coll, Camb, — Thomas Richard Edward, *b* 1969, — Rebecca Sophie Venetia, *b* 1971; *ed* Exeter Univ. —— Cicely Elizabeth Theodosia (Hill Cottage, Thurloxton, Taunton, Som), *b* 1942: *m* 1966 (*m diss* 19—), Martin Charles Jacoby, FLS, and has issue living, Charles John, *b* 1967, — Katherine Venetia, *b* 1970. —— Venetia, *b* 1948; *ed* Trin Coll, Dublin (BA): *m* 1972, David Richard Lascelles, of 60 Talbot Rd, Highgate, N6, and has issue living, Harry Francis, *b* 1978, — Alice Virginia, *b* 1976.

Issue of late Lady Elizabeth Grimston, 4th da of 3rd Earl, *b* 1885, *d* 1975: *m* 1st, 1908, Maj Hesketh Vernon Hesketh-Prichard, DSO, MC, who *d* 1922; 2ndly, 1927, Maj Thomas Augustus Motion, JP, who *d* 1942:—
(By 2nd *m*) Joan Elizabeth Mary (*Lady Stuart-Smith*), *b* 1929; *ed* St Anne's Coll, Oxford; JP, DL, High Sheriff Herts 1983: *m* 1953, Rt Hon Sir Murray Stuart-Smith, Lord Justice of Appeal, of Serge Hill, Abbots Langley, Herts, and has issue living, Jeremy Hugh (Pie Corner, Abbots Langley, Herts), *b* 1955; *ed* Radley, and Camb Univ (Choral Scholar); QC 1997: *m* 1982, Hon Arabella Clare Montgomery, da of 2nd Viscount Montgomery of Alamein, and has had issue, Edward Murray *b* 1988, Sam Nicholas *b* 1990, Luke David *b* 1993, Emma Lucia *b* 1984, †Laura *b* 1986 *d* 1987, — Mark, *b* 1958; *ed* Radley, and Christ's Coll, Camb, — Thomas Richard Steven Peregrine (The Barn, Serge Hill, Abbots Langley, Herts), *b* 1960; *ed* Radley, and Camb Univ (Corpus Scholar): *m* 1986, Dr Susan Jane Evans, da of late Bryan Evans, of Ardnadam House, Ardnadam, by Dunoon, Strathclyde, and has issue living, Benjamin *b* 1989, Harry Horatio *b* 1992, Rose *b* 1987, — Kathcrine, *b* 1957: *m* 1992, Dr David Docherty, of Serge Hill, Abbots Langley, Herts, and has issue living, Flora Olivia Annie *b* 1993, Polly *b* 1997, — Jane, *b* 1961: *m* 1992, Hugh Jonathan Earle Raven, of 14 Avondale Park Gdns, W11, and has issue living, Kitty *b* 1995, Madeleine *b* 1997, — Elizabeth (twin), *b* 1961: *m* 1990, Adam Beck, elder son of Sir Philip Beck, and has issue living, Sam Benedict *b* 1994, Isabella Elizabeth *b* 1997.

Issue of late Lady Sibyl Grimston, 5th da of 3rd Earl, *b* 1887, *d* 1968: *m* 1915, Maj Hon Alastair Thomas Joseph Fraser, DSO, who *d* 1949:—
See L Lovat, colls.

Issue of late Lady Vera Grimston, SRN, yst da of 3rd Earl, *b* 1890, *d* 1970: *m* 1922, Maurice Francis Headlam, CB, CMG, who *d* 1956:—
Anthony Francis HEADLAM (c/o Child & Co, 1 Fleet St, EC4), *b* 1923; *ed* Eton (KS), and King's Coll, Camb (Scholar); 1939-45 War with KRRC: *m* 1956 (*m diss* 1977), Jill Caroline, da of late Bruce R. Campbell, of Sydney, Aust, and has issue living, Hugo Francis, *b* 1960; *ed* Eton: *m* 1994, Romany M., yr da of Vice Adm Sir Philip Alexander Watson, KBE, LVO, of Bodicote, Oxon, and has issue living, Jemima Florence Mary *b* 1996, Phoebe Frances Alexandra *b* 1998, — Caroline Ann, *b* 1963: *m* 1996, Maj Crispin Nicholas Black, MBE, Welsh Gds, yr son of John Black, of Montagu Sq, W1. —— †Christopher Grimston HEADLAM, *b* 1925; *ed* Eton (KS), and King's Coll, Camb (Scholar); 1939-45 War with RNVR: *m* 1959, Sarah, da of late Sir John Richard Hobhouse, MC, and *d* 1989, leaving issue, Thomas Walter, *b* 1962, — Catherine Sophia, *b* 1960: *m* 1994, (Richard) Charles Hindson, son of Christopher Eldred Hindson, of Scaynes Hill, W Sussex, and has issue living, John Francis *b* 1996, Camilla Sarah *b* 1998. —— James Nicholas HEADLAM, *b* 1926; *ed* Eton, and New Coll, Oxford (Scholar). *m* 1966, Elizabeth Jane, da of Sir Peter William Shelley Yorke Scarlett, KCMG, KCVO, and has issue living, Anthony John Nicholas, *b* 1969: *m* 1993, Katherine Lucinda Mary, eldest da of Ian M. Maitland Hume, of Edinburgh, — Fenella Jane, *b* 1967: *m* 1997, Francis Alan Kenyon-Slaney (*see* B Kenyon, colls), — Mary Amelia, *b* 1972.

(Male line in remainder to all peerages)

Grandchildren of late Rev Canon Hon Robert Grimson, 3rd son of 2nd Earl:—
Issue of late Sir Robert Villiers Grimston, *b* 1897, *d* 1979; *cr* a *Baronet* 1952, and *Baron Grimston of Westbury* 1964:—
See B Grimston of Westbury.

Grandson of late George Sylvester Grimston, son of late Rev Hon Francis Sylvester Grimston, 5th son of 1st Earl:—
Issue of late Francis Sylvester Grimston, CIE, *b* 1876, *d* 1969: *m* 1907, Eleanor Vincent, who *d* 1960, da of late Arthur W. L. Reddie:—
Francis Brian Sylvester (Lyn Cottage, Hound St, Sherborne, Dorset DTG 3AA; Royal Thames & Ocean Racing Clubs), *b* 1908; *ed* Cheltenham; late S/Ldr RAFVR: *m* 1940 (*m diss* 1954), Monica Katherine, who *d* 1978, da of late Col Hon Sir Maurice Charles Andrew Drummond, KBE, CMG, DSO (*see* E Perth, colls, 1980 Edn).

PREDECESSORS – **(1)** WILLIAM Luckyn (MP for St Albans), great-nephew of Sir Samuel Grimston, 3rd Bt (ext), whose surname he assumed on succeeding to the estates, was *cr Baron Dunboyne* and *Viscount Grimston* (peerage of Ireland) 1719, and in 1736 *s* his brother as 5th Bt (*cr* 1629); *d* 1756; *s* by his son **(2)** JAMES, 2nd Viscount; *d* 1773; *s* by his son **(3)** JAMES BUCKNALL, 3rd Viscount; *cr Baron Verulam*, of Gorhambury, co Herts (peerage of Great Britain) 1790; *d* 1809; *s* by his son **(4)** JAMES WALTER, 4th Viscount, who in 1808 had *s* his maternal cousin Anna Maria as 10th *Lord Forrester of Corstorphine* (see*infra); *b* 1775; MP for St Albans 1802-8; Lord-Lieut of co Herts; *cr Earl of Verulam* (peerage of United Kingdom) 1815: *m* 1807, Lady Charlotte Jenkinson, da of 1st Earl of Liverpool; *d* 1845; *s* by his son **(5)** JAMES WALTER, 2nd Earl, *b* 1809; MP for St Albans (*C*) 1830, for Newport 1831; and for Hertfordshire 1832-45; a Lord-in-Waiting to HM Queen Victoria 1852 and 1858-9, sometime Lord-Lieut of Herts: *m* 1844, Elizabeth Joanna, who *d* 1886, da of Richard Weyland, of Woodeaton, Oxford; *d* 1895; *s* by his el son **(6)** JAMES WALTER, 3rd Earl, *b* 1852; MP for Mid, or St Albans, Div of Herts (*C*) 1885-92: *m* 1878, Margaret Frances, who *d* 1927, da of Sir Frederic Ulric Graham, 3rd Bt, of Netherby; *d* 1924; *s* by his son **(7)** JAMES WALTER, 4th Earl, *b* 1880: *m* 1909, Lady Violet Constance Maitland Brabazon, who *d* 1936, da of 12th Earl of Meath; *d* 1949; *s* by his son **(8)** JAMES BRABAZON, 5th Earl; *b* 1910; Mayor of St Albans 1956-7; *d* 1960; *s* by his brother **(9)** JOHN, 6th Earl, *b* 1912; MP for St Albans (*C*) 1943-45 and 1950-59: *m* 1938, Margaret Ray, who *d* 1994, da of Walter Duncan; *d* 1973; *s* by his son **(10)** JOHN DUNCAN, 7th Earl and present peer; also Viscount Grimston, Baron Verulam, Baron Dunboyne, and Lord Forrester of Corstorphine.

*****(1)** GEORGE Forrester of Corstorphine, Midlothian, el son of Henry Forrester of Corstorphine; *cr Lord Forrester of Corstorphine* (peerage of Scotland) 1633, with remainder to his heirs male whatsoever; on the death of his only son without issue, he resigned his peerage and obtained a re-grant thereof 1651 with remainder to James Baillie, husband of his fifth da Joanna and their issue in tail male, remainder to William Baillie, husband of Lilias his sixth and yst da and their issue in tail male, remainder to the issue of James and William by their said wives, in tail general, the el da of such issue to be heir of line, with a final remainder to James Baillie and his heirs male or of entail made by him, all parties to bear the name and arms of Forrester jointly with his own: *m* 1606, Christian, da of Sir William Livingston of Kilsyth; *d* 1652; *s* by his son-in-law **(2)** JAMES Baillie (afterwards Forrester), 2nd Lord; *b* 1629; was fined £2,500 under Cromwell's Act of Grace 1654: *m* 1st, 1649, Joanna, da of 1st Lord Forrester of Corstorphine (ante); 2ndly, 1661, Janet, 3rd da and co-heir of Patrick Ruthven, 1st Earl of Forth and Brentford; *d* 1679; *s* by his brother **(3)** WILLIAM, *de jure* 3rd Lord; *b* 1632; did not assume the title: *m circa* 1650 Lilias, yst da of 1st Lord Forrester of Corstorphine (ante); *d* 1681; *s* by his son **(4)** WILLIAM, 4th Lord; *b* 16—: *m circa* 1684, Margaret, da of Sir Andrew Birnie, of Saline, Judge of Court of Session; *d* 1705; *s* by his son **(5)** GEORGE, 5th Lord; *b* 1688; Lt-Col 26th Foot (Cameronians), and Col 30th Foot, and of Horse Grenadier Guards: *m circa* 1724, Charlotte, who *d* 1743, da of Anthony Rowe; *d* 1727; *s* by his son **(6)** GEORGE, 6th Lord; *b* 1724; Capt RN; *d* unm 1748; *s* by his cousin **(7)** WILLIAM (son of Capt Hon John Forrester, RN, yst son of 4th Lord), 7th Lord: *m* 17—, Hannah—, who *d* 1825; *d* 1763; *s* by his cousin **(8)** CAROLINE, el sister of 6th Lord (who *s* under terms of special remainder); *b* 17—: *m* 17—, Capt George Cockburn of Ormiston, RN, who *d* 1770; *d* 1784; *s* by her da **(9)** ANNA MARIA: *b* 17—; *d* unm 1808; *s* by her cousin **(10)** JAMES WALTER Grimston, son of James Bucknall Grimston, 3rd Viscount Grimston, by Harriet, da and heir of Edward Walter, and Hon Harriet Forrester, yst da of 5th Lord, who in 1809 *s* as 4th Viscount Grimston (ante).

Vesey, family name of Viscount de Vesci.

VESTEY, BARON (Vestey) (Baron UK 1922, Bt UK 1913)

SAMUEL GEORGE ARMSTRONG VESTEY, 3rd Baron, and 3rd Baronet; *b* 19 March 1941; *s* 1954; *ed* Eton; Lt Scots Gds; patron of one living; DL Glos 1982; GCStJ, Chancellor Order of St John 1988-91, since when Lord Prior; Master of the Horse to HM since 1999: *m* 1st, 1970 (*m diss* 1981), Kathryn Mary, el da of John Eccles, of Moor Park, Herts; 2ndly, 1981, Celia Elizabeth, da of late Maj (Hubert) Guy Broughton Knight, MC, of Lockinge Manor, Wantage, Oxon, and has issue by 1st and 2nd *m*.

Arms – Azure, in base barry wavy of four argent and of the first an iceberg issuant proper, on a chief of the second three eggs also proper. **Crest** – In front of a springbok's head couped at the neck proper three mullets fessewise azure. **Supporters** – *Dexter*, a sheep proper; *sinister*, a bull argent.
Residence – Stowell Park, Northleach, nr Cheltenham, Glos GL54 3LE.

SONS LIVING (*By 2nd marriage*)

Hon WILLIAM GUY, *b* 27 Aug 1983; Page of Honour to HM 1995-98.
Hon Arthur George, *b* 1985.

DAUGHTERS LIVING (*By 1st marriage*)

Hon Saffron Alexandra, *b* 1971: *m* 1996, Matthew Charles Idiens, of The Home Farm, Stowell Park, Northleach, Glos GL54 3LE, only son of late Cmdr Simon Idiens, RN, and has issue living, Alfred John Simon, *b* 1997, — Megan Rose, *b* 1998.
Hon Flora Grace, *b* 1978.

From labour stability

(*By 2nd marriage*)

Hon Mary Henrietta, *b* 1992.

BROTHER LIVING

(*Raised to the rank of a Baron's son* 1955)

Hon Mark William (Foxcote Manor, Andoversford, Glos GL54 4LP), *b* 1943; *ed* Eton; 2nd Lt Scots Guards: *m* 1975, Rose Amelia, yr da of late Lt-Col Peter Thomas Clifton, CVO, DSO (*see* Bruce, Bt, *cr* 1804, colls), and has issue living, Benjamin John, *b* 1979, — Tamara Pamela, *b* 1976, — Carina Patricia, *b* 1982.

MOTHER LIVING (*Raised to the rank of a Baron's Widow* 1955)

(HELEN) PAMELA FULLERTON (MELBA) (*Pamela, Baroness Vestey*), da of late George Nesbitt Armstrong (*see* Armstrong, Bt, *cr* 1841, colls): *m* 1939, Capt Hon William Howarth Vestey, Scots Guards, who was *ka* in Italy 1944. *Residence* – Coombe Cottage, Coldstream, Victoria 3770, Australia.

COLLATERAL BRANCHES LIVING

Issue of late Hon George Ellis Vestey, 2nd son of 1st Baron, *b* 1884, *d* 1968: *m* 1909, Florence May, who *d* 1964, da of Thomas Webster, of Melling, Lancs:—
Norah (Sundial House, Manor Av, Greystones, co Wicklow), *b* 1916: *m* 1st, 1944, Maj William Bellingham Denis Dobbs, R Ulster Rifles (ret), who *d* 1982; 2ndly, 1985, William Ronald Dobbs, who *d* 1985, and has issue living, (by 1st *m*) George Denis Kildare (Sheephill, Dunganstown, co Wicklow), *b* 1947: *m* 1975, Prunella Osborne, da of Osborne David Philips, of Ballyfree House, Glenealy, co Wicklow, and has issue living, Kildare Denis David *b* 1979, Edward George *b* 1981, Daniel Osborne William *b* 1985, Emily Norah *b* 1977, — Rosemary Florence, *b* 1944: *m* 1971, David Michael Cochrane Elsworth Steen (*see* Cochrane, Bt), — Susan Norah, *b* 1951: *m* 1978, Nigel Atkinson, of 43 Bramerton St, SW3, and Cowden House, Cholderton, Salisbury, Wilts SP4 0DJ, and has issue living, Anna Venetia *b* 1980, Camilla Mary *b* 1983, Victoria Eleanor *b* 1991. —— Alice (Appleton House, Appleton-le-Street, Malton, N Yorks, YO17 0PG), *b* 1918: *m* 1st, 1939, William Ernest Legard, F/O, RAF, who was *ka* 1940 (*see* Legard, Bt, colls); 2ndly, 1943, Col Basil Perry Beale, OBE, MC, DL, RASC, who *d* 1967, and has issue living, (by 1st *m*) (*see* Legard, Bt, colls), — (by 2nd *m*) Richard Basil William, *b* 1944. *m* 1901, Giao-Li Liao, and has issue living, Jennifer Mary Alice *b* 1982, Alice Elizabeth May *b* 1986, Stephen Dudley Norman, *b* 1950: *m* 1st, 1972 (*m diss* 1978), Elizabeth Helen, da of Peter Green, of The Rookery, Kirkby Malham, Skipton, Yorks; 2ndly, 1978, Jo-Anna Mary Munt, da of Arthur Harry Cook, of Church Farm, Wavendon, Bucks, and has issue living (by 1st *m*), Zoë Helen *b* 1973, (by 2nd *m*) Rollo Basil Arthur *b* 1982, — Elizabeth Alice, *b* 1947: *m* 1975, Anthony David Stanbury, and has issue living, Alexander George Basil *b* 1978, Edward Samuel Joseph *b* 1982, Caroline Alice *b* 1976, Victoria Elizabeth Sophie *b* 1984.

Issue of late Hon Leonard Vestey, 3rd son of 1st Baron, *b* 1888, *d* 1954: *m* 1st, 1919 (*m diss* 1931), Hilda Dorothy, da of Thomas Thompson; 2ndly, 1931, Eleanor Margery (who *d* 1972, having *m* 3rdly, 1955, Dr Richard Taylor, and 4thly, 19—, Frank Fisher), widow of Capt F. W. H. Simpson, RA:— (By 1st *m*) Joyce (19 Elamang Av, Kirribilli, Sydney, NSW 2061), *b* 1920: *m* 1st, 1949 (*m diss* 1953), Henry Willis Maxwell Telling, who *d* 1993; 2ndly, 1966, Dr Thomas Hugh Strong, who *d* 1988, and has issue living, (by 1st *m*) Michael Henry Maxwell *b* 1950: *m* 1st, 1978 (*m diss* 1981), Alison Ruth Webber; 2ndly, 1981, Monika Elizabeth, who *d* 1983, da of Louis Zumsteg, of Santa Rosa, Calif, USA, and has issue living (by 1st *m*), Matthew James Maxwell *b* 1979. —— Elizabeth Anne (26 Eldon Rd, W8), *b* 1923: *m* 1946 (*m diss* 1962), Lt-Cdr Patrick Brougham, RN, and has issue living, Christopher John (34 Launceston Place, W8), *b* 1947; *ed* Radley, and Worcester Coll, Oxford (BA); Bar Inner Temple 1969, QC 1988: *m* 1974, Mary Olwen, da of Timothy Traherne Corker, of 19 Park Sq East, NW1, and has issue living, William Charles Rupert *b* 1977, Emily Clarissa *b* 1979, Miranda Jane Thérèse *b* 1982, Deborah Anne Rosemary *b* 1988, — Nicholas Dominic Leonard (Burwood Farm, One Tree Hill Rd, Guildford, Surrey GU4 8PJ), *b* 1954; *ed* Radley: *m* 1982, Susan, da of Thomas Frederick Vernon Mason, of Carbery Lodge, Farley Green, Albury, Surrey, and has issue living, Thomas Edward Alexander *b* 1988, Caroline Fiona Jane *b* 1984, Claire Emma Louise *b* 1986, — Margaret Elizabeth Jane, *b* 1948: *m* 1st, 1970 (*m diss* 1982), Hugh Robert John Simpson; 2ndly, 1982, John Arthur William Webber, of 8 Elm Rd, Beckenham, Kent BR3 4JB, and has had issue (by 1st *m*), Antony John *b* 1972 *d* 1986, Tracey Jane *b* 1975.

PREDECESSORS – (1) WILLIAM Vestey, el son of Samuel Vestey, of Liverpool; *b* 1859; was Joint Head of Blue Star Line; *cr* a *Baronet* 1913, and *Baron Vestey*, of Kingswood, co Surrey (peerage of United Kingdom) 1922: *m* 1st, 1882, Sarah, who *d* 1923, da of George Ellis; 2ndly, 1924, Evelyn, who *d* 1941, da of H. Brodstone, of Superior, Nebraska, USA; *d* 1940; *s* by his el son (2) SAMUEL, 2nd Baron; *b* 1882; High Sheriff of Gloucestershire 1953: *m* 1908, Frances Sarah, who *d* 1969, da of John Richard Howarth, of Freshfield, Lancs; *d* 1954; *s* by his grandson (3) SAMUEL GEORGE ARMSTRONG (son of late Capt Hon William Howarth Vestey, only son of 2nd Baron), 3rd Baron and present peer.

Villiers, family name of Earl of Clarendon.

Villiers, Child-, family name of Earl of Jersey.

VINCENT OF COLESHILL, BARON (Vincent) (Life Baron 1996)

RICHARD FREDERICK VINCENT, GBE, KCB, DSO, son of late Frederick Vincent, by his wife Frances Elizabeth, *née* Coleshill; *b* 23 Aug 1931; *ed* Aldenham, and RMC of Science, Shrivenham; Hon DSc Cranfield 1985; Fellow Imperial Coll 1996; Comdt RMC of Science 1980-83, Master Gen of the Ordnance, Ministry of Defence 1983-87, Vice-Chief of the Defence Staff 1987-91, and Chief 1991-92, Col Comdt REME 1983-87 and RA since 1983, Hon Col 100 (Yeo) Field Regt, RA (Volunteers) TA 1982-91, 12 Air Defence Regt 1985-91, Master Gunner, St James's Park since 1996, Field Marshal 1991; Chm North Atlantic Military Cttee 1992-96; Kermit Roosevelt Lecturer, USA 1988; Visiting Fell of Australian Coll of Defence Studies; Pres Combined Services Winter Sports Assoc 1983-90, Pres Army Skiing Assoc 1983-87; Memb Court Cranfield Institute of Technology 1981-83; Governor of Aldenham Sch since 1987; Chm Hunting Defence Ltd since 1996, Hunting Engineering Ltd since 1998 (Dir since 1996), and Hunting-Brae; Non-Exec Dir Vickers Defence Systems since 1996, and Royal Artillery Museums Ltd since 1996; Chm Imperial Coll of Science, Technology and Medicine since 1996; Master Gunner St James's Park 1996; Chancellor, Cranfield Univ since 1998; Freeman of the City of London and Memb Guild of Freemen; Freeman Wheelwrights' Co; FIMechE 1990, FRAeS 1990; awarded Jordanian Order of Merit (1st cl) and USA Legion of Merit (Degree of Commd); *cr* DSO 1972, KCB 1984, GBE 1990, and *Baron Vincent of Coleshill*, of Shrivenham, co Oxfordshire (Life Baron) 1996: *m* 1955, Jean Paterson, da of late Kenneth Stewart, and has had issue, one son (dec'd), and one da.
Residence – c/o House of Lords, SW1A 0PW.

VINSON, BARON (Vinson) (Life Baron 1985)

NIGEL VINSON, LVO, son of late Ronald Vinson, of Nettlestead Place, Wateringbury, Kent, by his 2nd wife, Bettina Myra Olivia, da of Dr Gerald Southwell-Sanders; *b* 27 Jan 1931; *ed* RNC Pangbourne; Lieut Queen's Royal Regt 1949-51; DL Northumberland 1990; foundation donor Martin Mere Wildfowl Trust; founder (Chm 1952-72) Plastic Coatings Ltd; Dir Centre for Policy Studies 1974-80; Hon Dir Queen's Silver Jubilee Appeal 1976-78; Chm Rural Development Commn 1980-90, and Industrial Participation Assocn 1971-79; Dep Chm Electra Investment Trust plc 1989-98, Chm of Trustees of the Inst of Economic Affairs 1989-96, and Trustee St George's House Windsor Castle 1989-97; FRSA; *cr* LVO 1979, and *Baron Vinson*, of Roddam Dene, co Northumberland (Life Baron) 1985: *m* 1972, Yvonne Ann, da of Dr Olaf Collin, of Forest Row, Sussex, and has issue.

Arms – Per pale gules and azure, a cross formy argent, on a chief per pale azure and gules two bull's heads caboshed argent armed or and crowned with a crown rayonny each straight ray ensigned by a mullet gold. Crest – Upon a helm with a wreath argent, azure and gules within a garland of vine leaves or a demi-ounce azure. Supporters – *dexter*— An ounce rampant sable semy of mullets or gorged with a garland of vine leaves gold; *sinister*— A horse rampant argent also gorged with a garland of vine leaves gold, the compartment comprising two grassy hillocks and in the valley between them water barry wavy of six azure and argent.
Residence – Roddam Hall, by Alnwick, Northumberland. *Address* – 34 Kynance Mews, SW7. *Club* – Boodle's.

DAUGHTERS LIVING

Hon Bettina Claire, *b* 1974.
Hon Rowena Ann, *b* 1977.
Hon Antonia Charlotte, *b* 1979.

VIVIAN, BARON (Vivian) (Baron UK 1841, Bt UK 1828)

Live, as one about to live hereafter

NICHOLAS CRESPIGNY LAURENCE VIVIAN, 6th Baron, and 6th Baronet; *b* 11 Dec 1935; *s* 1991; *ed* Eton, and Madrid Univ; commn'd 3rd Carabiniers 1955, Royal Scots Dragoon Gds 1971, Comdg Officer 16/5th The Queen's Royal Lancers 1976-79, Col MOD 1979-84, Dep Cmdr Land Forces Cyprus, and Ch of Staff 1984-87, Cmdr British Communication Zone NW Europe 1987-90, ret 1990 as Brig; sits as Conservative in House of Lords; Sec Parliamentary All Party Defence Group since 1995; Member Parliamentary Statutory Instruments Cttee since 1997; Dep Chm Assocn of Conservative Peers since 1999; Trustee Regt Assocn 16/5L and QRL since 1991; Commissioner Royal Hospital Chelsea since 1994; Special Trustee Chelsea and Westminster Hospital since 1996: *m* 1st, 1960 (*m diss* 1972), Catherine Joyce, yst da of James Kenneth Hope, CBE, DL, of West Park, Lanchester, co Durham; 2ndly, 1972, Carol, elder da of late (Frederick) Alan Martineau, MBE, JP, of Valley End House, Chobham, Surrey, and has issue by 1st and 2nd *m*.

Arms – Or, a chevron azure, between three lions' heads erased proper, as many annulets gold; on a chief embattled gules, a wreath of oak or, between two medals, that on the dexter representing the gold medal and clasp given to the first baron for his services in the actions of Sahagun, Benevente and Orthes; and that on the sinister the silver Waterloo medal. Crest – Issuant from a bridge of one arch embattled, and having at each end a tower, a demi-hussar, in the uniform of the 18th Regt holding in his right hand a sabre, and in his left a pennon flying to the sinister gules, and inscribed with gold letters, "Croix d'Orade". Supporters – *Dexter*, a grey horse caparisoned, thereon mounted a hussar of the 7th Regt of Light Dragoons (Hussars) habited, armed and accoutred, his sword drawn proper; *sinister*, a bay horse guardant, caparisoned, thereon mounted a lancer of the 12th Regt of Lancers, habited, armed and accoutred, supporting his lance, also proper.
Clubs - White's, Cavalry and Guards'.

SONS LIVING (*By 1st marriage*)

Hon CHARLES CRESPIGNY HUSSEY, *b* 20 Dec 1966; *ed* Milton Abbey.

DAUGHTERS LIVING (*By 1st marriage*)

Hon Henrietta Mary, *b* 1963: *m* 1984, Philip John Hoyland, son of Dr Hugh James Hoyland, of Clarelands, Painswick, Glos, and has issue living, Jack Nicholas Hope, *b* 1985, — George Hugh James, *b* 1991, — Francesca Mary Jane, *b* 1986. *Residences* – 14 Starmead Drive, Wokingham, Berks; Box Green, Box, Nailsworth, Glos.

(*By 2nd marriage*)

Hon Natasha Sarah, *b* 1973: *m* 1995, Capt F. A. J. (Jamie) Piggott, eldest son of F. J. R. Piggott, of Guernsey, CI, and of Mrs Susan C. M. Scott, of Antibes, France.
Hon Camilla Harriet, *b* 1976.

BROTHER LIVING

Hon Victor Anthony Ralph Brabazon (Le Gamaos, Cammao et Roucan, 30140 Generargues, France), *b* 1940; *ed* Nautical Coll, Pangbourne, and Southampton Univ; late Merchant Navy: *m* 1966, Inger Johanne, yr da of Advokat Per Gulliksen, of Sandfjord, Norway, and has issue living, Thomas Crespigny Brabazon, *b* 1971; *ed* Marlborough, and Grenoble Univ; has issue living (by Victoria Ruth Abrahams), Daisy Victoria VIVIAN *b* 1998, — Arabella Victoria, *b* 1973: *m* 1998, Benedict Nicholas Wray, of 1 Elswick St, SW6 2QR, yr son of Christopher Wray, of Putney, SW.

SISTER LIVING

Hon Sally Ann Marie Gabrielle, *b* 1930: *m* 1st, 1954 (*m diss* 1962), (William) Robin Charles Edward Cecil Lowe, son of late John Muir Lowe (actor, as John Loder); 2ndly, 1963, Charles William Munro Wilson, son of late Charles Skinner Wilson, and has issue living (by 2nd *m*), Alexander Vivian, *b* 1965; *ed* Shiplake Coll. *Residence* – 150 Cranmer Court, Whiteheads Grove, SW3 3HF.

WIDOW LIVING OF SON OF FOURTH BARON

Mary Alice (Edington Cottage, Inmead, Edington, Westbury, Wilts BA13 4QR), da of late Francis John Gordon Borthwick, WS (*see* L Borthwick, colls): *m* 1943, Lt-Cdr Hon Douglas David Edward Vivian, DSC, RN, who *d* 1973, and has issue (see colls infra).

COLLATERAL BRANCHES LIVING

Issue of late Lt-Cdr Hon Douglas David Edward Vivian, DSC, RN, yr son of 4th Baron, *b* 1915, *d* 1973: *m* 1943, Mary Alice (ante), da of late Francis John Gordon Borthwick, WS (*see* L Borthwick, colls):— Deborah Mary, OBE, *b* 1944; OBE (Civil) 1994; JP: *m* 1971, Nicholas John Hinton, CBE, who *d* 1997, of 22 Westmoreland Place, SW1V 4AE, and has issue living, Josephine Mary Vivian, *b* 1984. —— Rose Emma Margaret, *b* 1945: *m* 1st, 1965 (*m diss* 1973), James Collet Norman; 2ndly, 1973, Benjamin B. W. Goodden, of Ferryside, Riverside, Twickenham, Middx, and has issue living (by 1st *m*), Rupert Montagu, *b* 1966: *m* 1995, Tasmin La Cloche, da of Dean Edward Fischer, and has issue (*see* Wheler, Bt), — Jason Douglas, *b* 1968, — Melissa Rose, *b* 1970, — (by 2nd *m*) Timothy Simon, *b* 1980. —— Eugenie Nancy (Pear Tree Cottage, Bratton, nr Westbury, Wilts), *b* 1947: *m* 1966 (*m diss* 1988), Capt Simon N. J. Burne, 9th/12th R Lancers, and has issue living, Thomas Edward Francis, *b* 1980, — Lucy Caroline, *b* 1970. —— Victoria Alice (The Lodge, Highfield, Whittonstall, co Durham DH8 9LQ), *b* (twin) 1947: *m* 1972 (*m diss* 1999), Nicholas Charlton Dudley Craig, and has issue living, Richard Nicholas Dudley, *b* 1976, — Edward Douglas Charlton, *b* 1977, — George David Vivian, *b* 1982. —— Charlotte Claire, *b* 1950: *m* 1971, Charles Robert Dimpfl, of High Hampton, 34 Holland Rd, NW10 5AU, and has issue living, Francesca Mary, *b* 1979, — Daisy Charlotte, *b* 1985, — Nancy Alice Rose, *b* 1990.

Granddaughter of late Lieut-Col Claud Esmé Vivian, MC (infra):—
Issue of late Capt Claud Panton Vivian, RHA, *b* 1920, *d* of wounds received in action in Normandy 1944: *m* 1943, Margaret Eleanor (who *m* 2ndly, 1947, Charles Dundas Lawrie, of Plâs Gwyn, Pentraeth, Anglesey), only da of Alec E. Baird, OBE, of Hailes Brae, Colinton, Edinburgh:—
Amanda Mary Panton, *b* 1944.

Grandchildren of late Hon Claud Hamilton Vivian, 4th son of 2nd Baron:—
Issue of late Lieut-Col Claud Esmé Vivian, MC, *b* 1882, *d* 1928: *m* 1914, Emily, who *d* 1994, aged 101, da of late Col Michael Rowan Gray Buchanan, OBE (M Bute, colls):—
Ann (Cae Du, Dwyran, Anglesey), *b* 1923: *m* 1953, Desmond Brennan, MB, who *d* 1970, and has had issue, Vincent Patrick Esme, *b* 1958: *m* 1986, Jennifer Owen, and *d* 1996, leaving issue, Desmond Andrew *b* 1987, Christopher William *b* 1990, Katherine Emily *b* 1994, — Claire Patricia Ann, *b* 1956: *m* 1990, Andrew Hicks, and has issue living, Joseph Andrew *b* 1992, Elizabeth Ann *b* 1990, — Hazel Mary, *b* 1961: *m* 1992, Mark Francis Robinson, and has issue living, Cai Francis *b* 1995, Lois Siw *b* 1992.

Issue of late Capt Eric Paul Vivian, RN, *b* 1891, *d* 1961: *m* 1922, Evelyn Audrey, who *d* 1997, el da of Capt Thomas Pryse Arthur Holford, late 10th Hussars, of Duntish Court, Buckland Newton, Dorset:—
†Desmond Walter Paul, *b* 1925; *ed* Harrow; Capt 12th Lancers; served 1939-45 War (despatches twice): *m* 1949, Rose (Langford Gate, Sydling St Nicholas, Dorset), da of Capt Charles Houssemayne du Boulay, RN, of Exton House, Exton, Hants, and *d* 1974, leaving issue, Christopher John Desmond, *b* 1956; *ed* Harrow: *m* 1984, Alice Camilla, yst da of John Brian Hollingsworth, of Cruea, Llanfrothen, Penrhyndeudraeth, Gwynedd, and has issue living, Alastair Desmond *b* 1991, Hugh Maxwell *b* 1994, — Vanda Rose, *b* 1950, — Clare Veronica, *b* 1952. —— Patrick Cyril, *b* 1929; *ed* Camb Univ (BA 1950, MA 1958, MB and BCh 1953, DRCOG 1958); late Capt RAMC: *m* 1961, Pamela Mary, da of Lieut-Col Richard Rees Davies, JP, DL, of Ceris, Bangor, Caernarvonshire, and has issue living, Simon Paul Richard, *b* 1962: *m* 1st, 1988, Rose Rookmin, da of Dr Balideo Bisseru, of Lusaka, Kenya, and of Bromley, Kent; 2ndly, 1997, Isobel Suzy, only da of Michael Thornton, of Ferndown, Dorset, — Susan Caroline, *b* 1964: *m* 1999, Adam Hayward. *Residence* – Pumney, Sutton Courtenay, nr Abingdon, Berks. —— Charles Evelyn, *b* 1937. *Residence* – Hook Cottage, Hambledon, Hants.

Issue of late Capt Robert Crespigny Gwynedd Vivian, LG, *b* 1898, *d* 1984: *m* 1925, Violet Clinton, who *d* 1993, da of Clinton Holme, of Ruthin, N Wales:—
Robin Audley Clinton (B92 Res Amiral, Marina Baie des Anges, 06270 Villeneuve-Loubet, France), *b* 1936; *ed* Eton: *m* 1961, Alice Penelope, only da of late Lt Caesar Charles Hawkins, DSC, RN (*see* Hawkins, Bt, colls), and has issue living, Rupert James, *b* 1970, — Claire Jennifer, *b* 1971. —— Edith Evelyn CLINTON (Hawthorne Cottage, Pitmore Lane, Sway, Lymington, Hants), *b* 1926: *m* 1954 (*m diss* 1975), Arnold Euston More Bloomer, and has issue living, Anthony Leonard Clinton, *b* 1964: *m* 1993, Harriet Ann, only da of Timothy George Kirkbride (*see* Baker Wilbraham, Bt), and has issue living, Alice Letitia Clinton *b* 1996, — Angela Gwyneth More, *b* 1960: *m* 1988, John Jardine Hearne Slater, of 21 Saxon Rd, Hyde, Winchester, Hants SO23 7DJ, and has issue living, Sophie Eve Hearne *b* 1992, Jessica Violet Hearne *b* 1994, Charlotte Lucy Hearne *b* 1999.

PREDECESSORS – (1) *Sir* RICHARD HUSSEY Vivian, GCB, GCMG, GCH, PC, etc; *b* 1775; a Lt-Gen in the Army, and a distinguished soldier, cmdg 7th Lt Dragoons throughout the Peninsula Campaign and the Light Cavalry Bde at Waterloo; was Col 1st R Dragoons, Com of the Forces in Ireland, MP for Windsor, Equerry to George IV, and Master Gen of Ordnance 1835-41; *cr* a *Baronet* 1828, and *Baron Vivian*, of Glynn, and of Truro, co Cornwall (peerage of United Kingdom) 1841: *m* 1st, 1804, Eliza, da of Philip Champion de Crespigny, of Aldborough, Suffolk; *d* 1842; *s* by his son **(2)** CHARLES CRESPIGNY, 2nd Baron; sat as MP for Bodmin (*L*) 1837-42: was Lord-Lieut of Cornwall 1856-77: *m* 1st, 1833, Arabella, who *d* 1837, da of Rev John Middleton Scott, of Ballygannon, co Wicklow; 2ndly, 1841, Mary Elizabeth, who *d* 1907, el da of Jones Panton, of Plasgwyn, Anglesey; *d* 24 April 1886; *s* by his son **(3)** HUSSEY CRESPIGNY, GCMG, CB, PC, 3rd Baron, *b* 1834; Agent and Consul-Gen in Moldavia and Wallachia 1874-6, and in Egypt 1876-9, Min at Berne 1879-81, Envoy Extraor and Min Plen to Swiss Confederation 1881, to Denmark 1881-4, and at Brussels 1884-9, and Ambassador Extraor and Plen to Rome 1891-3: *m* 1876, Louisa Alice, who *d* 1926, da of Robert George Duff, of Wellington Lodge Ryde; *d* 1893: *s* by his only son **(4)** GEORGE CRESPIGNY BRABAZON, DSO, 4th Baron, *b* 1878; Col (ret) TA; sometime Major 17th Lancers; S Africa 1900-01, European War 1914-18 (DSO): *m* 1st, 1903 (*m diss* 1907), Barbara, da of late William Atmar Fanning; 2ndly, 1911, Nancy Lycett, MBE, who *d* 1970, da of Sir Edward Lycett Green, 2nd Bt (*cr* 1886), and widow of Capt Adrian Rose, Roy Horse Guards; *d* 1940; *s* by his son **(5)** ANTHONY CRESPIGNY CLAUD, 5th Baron; *b* 1906; European War 1939-40 in RA, Special Constabulary and War Correspondent; Theatrical Impressario: *m* 1930, Victoria Ruth Mary Rosamond, who *d* 1985, da of Capt Henry Gerard Laurence Oliphant, DSO, MVO, RN; *d* 1991; *s* by his elder son **(6)** NICHOLAS CRESPIGNY LAURENCE, 6th Baron and present peer.

Vivian, family name of Baron Swansea.

WADDINGTON, BARON (Waddington) (Life Baron 1990)

DAVID CHARLES WADDINGTON, GCVO, PC, QC, son of late Charles Waddington, JP, of The Old Vicarage, Read, Lancs; *b* 2 Aug 1929; *ed* Sedbergh, and Hertford Coll, Oxford; DL Lancs 1991; 2nd Lieut 12th Royal Lancers 1951-53; Bar Gray's Inn 1951, QC 1971, Recorder 1972, Bencher 1985; sometime Dir J. J. Broadley Ltd, J. and J. Roberts Ltd, and Wolstenholme Rink Ltd; MP Nelson and Colne (C) 1968-74, Clitheroe 1979-83, Ribble Valley 1983-90; Lord Commr HM Treasury 1979-81, Parly Under Sec Employment 1981-83, Min of State Home Office 1983-87, Govt Chief Whip 1987-89, Home Sec 1989-90, Lord Privy Seal and Leader House of Lords 1990-92, Gov of Bermuda 1992-97; *cr* PC 1987, GCVO 1994, and *Baron Waddington*, of Read, co Lancs (Life Baron) 1990: *m* 1958, Gillian Rosemary, da of Alan Green, CBE, of The Stables, Sabden, Lancs, and has issue.

DEUS NOSTER REFUGIUM ET VIRTUS

Arms – Ermine on a cross azure a lions' head gardant or langued gules between four roses gules barbed and seeded proper. Crest – An arm embowed vested azure issuing from the sleeve of a silk's gown sable the hand proper holding a wreath of four roses gules barbed and seeded proper enfiled by a sword point upwards argent, hilt, pommel and quillons gold. Supporters – *dexter*— A lion in trian aspect; *sinister*— A griffin, both or, armed and langued gules, gorged with a bar dancetty ermine edged azure, each statant erect amid reeds growing from a grassy mount proper.
Residences – Stable House, Sabden, nr Clitheroe, Lancs; Flat 4, 39 Chester Way, SE11 4UR. *Club* – Cavalry and Guards'.

SONS LIVING

Hon James Charles, *b* 1960.
Hon Matthew David, *b* 1962.
Hon Alistair Paul, *b* 1965.

DAUGHTERS LIVING

Hon Jennifer Rosemary, *b* 1965.
Hon Victoria Jane, *b* 1971.

WADE, BARONY OF (Wade) (Extinct 1988)

SONS LIVING OF LIFE BARON

Hon Donald William Mercer, *b* 1941, *ed* Silcoates Sch, and at Trin Hall, Camb (MA).

Hon Robert Alexander Mercer (The Old Rectory, Barwick-in-Elmet, Leeds, W Yorks), *b* 1943; *ed* Mill Hill, and Trin Coll, Camb (MA, LLM); Solicitor 1968: *m* 1st 1967, Jennifer Jane, da of Leslie Elliott, of Grantley Grange, High Grantley, Ripon; 2ndly, 1978, Elizabeth, da of James Lobban, of 24 Lintrathen Gdns, Dundee, and has issue living, (by 1st *m*) Michael Richard, *b* 1968, — Juliet Helen, *b* 1970, — (by 2nd *m*) Alistair James Mercer, *b* 1982, — Katherine Elizabeth, *b* 1985.

DAUGHTERS LIVING OF LIFE BARON

Hon Helen Mary, *b* 1933: *m* 1963, Rev Dr Lionel Wickham, of The Vicarage, West Wratting, Cambridge, and has issue living, three sons, and one da, of whom, the 2nd son Henry J., *b* 1966: *m* 1991, Madeleine S., eldest da of David Townley, of Wimbledon, and has issue living, Frederick Ralph Richard *b* 1996, Hugo David Edward *b* 1998, — Dorothy M. H., *b* 1972: *m* 1997, Barry W. Greenstreet, son of W. Greenstreet, of Coventry.

Hon Rosalind Beatrice, *b* 1937: *m* 1961, Richard David Morrish, solicitor, of 34 St Margaret's Rd, Horsforth, Leeds, and has issue living, Jonathan R., *b* 1964: *m* 1992, Katharine L. Brown, and has issue living, Matthew James *b* 1995, Victoria Helen *b* 1994, — Thomas Wade, *b* 1966: *m* 1993, Sarah J. Challinor, and has issue living, Rebecca Jane *b* 1997, — Judith Helen, *b* 1969.

WADE OF CHORLTON, BARON (Wade) (Life Baron 1990)

WILLIAM OULTON WADE, son of Samuel Norman Wade, of Chester; *b* 24 Dec 1932; *ed* Birkenhead Sch, and Queen's Univ, Belfast; CC Cheshire 1973-77; Dir Murray Vernon (Holdings) Ltd, John Wilman Ltd, Millers Damsell Ltd, Inward, and Fletchers Stores Ltd, Chm Marlow Wade and Partners Ltd, Consultants, Nimtech Ltd, and P.I. Political Consultants Ltd; Chm English Cheese Export Council 1982-84; Chm Parly Rural Economy Group; JP Cheshire 1967, Freeman City of London 1980, Liveryman Farmers' Co since 1980; Joint Treasurer Conservative Party 1982-90; *cr* Knt 1982, and *Baron Wade of Chorlton*, of Chester, co Cheshire (Life Baron) 1990: *m* 1959, Gillian Margaret, da of Desmond Leete, of Buxton, Derbys, and has issue.
Residence – Chorlton Lodge Farm, Chorlton-by-Backford, Chester CH2 4DB. *Clubs* – Carlton, Farmers', St James's (Manchester), City (Chester).

SON LIVING

Hon Christopher James, *b* 1961.

DAUGHTER LIVING

Hon Alexandra Jane, *b* 1964.

WAKEFIELD OF KENDAL, BARONY OF (Wakefield) (Extinct 1983)

DAUGHTERS LIVING OF FIRST BARON

Hon Joan Rosemary, OBE, *b* 1920; OBE (Civil) 1981: *m* 1944, Capt Antony Edward Montague Raynsford, RN (ret), DL, who *d* 1993, and has issue living, Richard Wakefield, *b* 1945: *m* 1979, Rosemary, da of late Brig Thomas Hayward Evill, CBE, DSO, and has issue living, Thomas Lindsay Wakefield *b* 1980, Clementina Daisy *b* 1982, — Julia Daphne (*Lady Boyd*), *b* 1948: *m* 1977, Sir John Dixon Iklé Boyd, KCMG, and has issue living, Jessica *b* 1978, Alice Clara *b* 1979, Olivia Wakefield *b* 1982. *Residences* – Milton Malsor Manor, Northampton NN7 3AR; The Old House, Kendal, Cumbria.

Hon Mary Sheila, OBE, *b* 1922; OBE 1992: *m* 1945, Brig Richard Frank Bradshaw Hensman, CBE, who *d* 1988, and has issue living, Peter Richard Wavell, *b* 1948: *m* 1973, Claire Theresa, da of Peter Wallace Henderson, MC, BM, BCh, and has issue living, Roger Edward Wavell *b* 1981, Lucinda Carolyn Barrett *b* 1978, Joanna Mary Bradshaw *b* 1980, — Suzannah Mary, *b* 1953: *m* 1977, William Ian Simpson, and has issue living, Thomas James *b* 1981, Victoria Jane *b* 1979. *Residence* – Lindum Holme, Stricklandgate, Kendal, Cumbria LA9 4QG.

Hon Ruth Isabel, *b* 1932: *m* 1st, 1955, Maj Nigel James Clarkson Webb, who *d* 1987; 2ndly, 1992, Paul Anthony Adorian, and has issue living (by 1st *m*), Edward James, *b* 1966, — Georgina Anne, *b* 1957: *m* 1981, Christopher Campbell Townsend, eldest son of Eric L. Townsend, of Sandford Orcas, Sherborne, Dorset, and has issue living, Alexander Peard *b* 1984, Rosanna Campbell *b* 1987, — Carolyn Mary, *b* 1958: *m* 1983, Jeremy Simon Seel, yst son of Kenneth Seel, of Great Rollright Manor, Chipping Norton, Oxon, and has issue living, Annabel Lucy *b* 1987, Natasha Mary *b* 1989. *Residence* – Buckstone House, Carnforth, Lancs.

WAKEHAM, BARON (Wakeham) (Life Baron 1992)

JOHN WAKEHAM, PC, son of late Maj Walter John Wakeham, of Godalming, Surrey; *b* 22 June 1932; *ed* Charterhouse; JP Inner London 1972; DL Hants 1997; CA, Member of Lloyd's, sometime Sec Small Businesses Cttee, Govt Whip 1979, Lord Commr to the Treasury 1981, Under Sec of State for Industry 1981-82, Min of State Treasury 1982-83, Parly Sec to the Treasury and Chief Whip 1983-87, Lord Privy Seal 1987-88, Lord Pres of the Council 1988-89, Leader of the House of Commons 1987-89, Sec of State for Energy July 1989-92, Lord Privy Seal, and Leader of the House of Lords 1992-94; Chm Press Complaints Commn since 1995; Chm Alexandra Rose Day since 1998; Chancellor Brunel Univ since 1998; MP Maldon (*C*) 1974-83, and Colchester S and Maldon 1983-92; *cr* PC 1983, and *Baron Wakeham*, of Maldon, co Essex (Life Baron) 1992: *m* 1st, 1965, Anne Roberta, who was *k* in the bomb explosion at the Grand Hotel, Brighton, 1984, da of late Harold Edwin Bailey; 2ndly, 1985, Alison Bridget, MBE, yr da of Ven Edwin James Greenfield Ward, LVO (*see* Buxton, Bt, colls, 1985 Edn), and has three sons.

Arms – Per fesse embattled azure and argent, a pale counter-changed, in the azure a lion's head guardant or, langued gules, and in the argent a bugle horn azure, garnished and stringed gold. **Crest** – A greyhound statant or, crowned with a mural crown checky azure and argent and supporting by the dexter fore-leg a cross raguly argent, nailed of three gold. **Supporters** – *Dexter*, a sea-lion azure, mane and head in trian aspect argent, langued gules, crowned with a crown tridenty gold; *sinister*, a sea-horse azure, head and neck argent and crowned also with a crown tridenty gold, the

compartment comprising three bars wavy azure, argent and azure, in front thereof a grassy mount, growing therefrom three double roses argent upon gules, barbed and seeded, stalked and leaved proper.
Address – c/o House of Lords, SW1. *Clubs* – Buck's, Carlton, Garrick, Royal Yacht Squadron, St Stephen's Constitutional.

ADOPTED SONS LIVING

Jonathan Martin, *b* 1972; *ed* Charterhouse.
Benedict Ian, *b* 1975; *ed* Charterhouse.

SON LIVING (*By 2nd marriage*)

Hon David Robert, *b* 1987.

WAKEHURST, BARON (Loder) (Baron UK 1934)

A sound conscience is a wall of brass

(JOHN) CHRISTOPHER LODER, 3rd Baron; *b* 23 Sept 1925; *s* 1970; *ed* Eton, King's Sch, nr Sydney, NSW, and Trin Coll, Camb (MA, LLB); Bar Inner Temple 1950; Chm Anglo & Overseas Trust plc 1968-96, The Overseas Investment Trust plc 1980-95, and Morgan Grenfell Equity Income Trust plc 1991-95, Dir Morgan Grenfell Latin American Companies Trust plc 1994-96, Dep Chm London and Manchester Group plc 1970-95; late Sub-Lt RANVR and RNVR; 1939-45 in W Pacific: *m* 1st, 1956, Ingeborg, who *d* 1977, da of Walter Krumbholz; 2ndly, 1983, Brigid, yr da of William Noble, of Cirencester, Glos, and has issue by 1st *m*.

᎐rms – Quarterly; 1st and 4th grand quarters; Azure, on a fesse between in chief a portcullis chained and in base a martlet or, three stags' heads caboshed proper, *Loder*; 2nd grand quarter, quarterly, the Royal Arms of Charles II, 1st and 4th, France and England quarterly, 2nd, Scotland, 3rd, Ireland, and overall a baton sinister gules charged with three roses argent, barbed and seeded proper, *Beauclerk*; 3rd grand quarter, quarterly gules and or, in the first a mullet argent, *de Vere*. Ꭰrest – A stag's head caboshed transfixed by an arrow bendwise point downwards all proper, between two escallops or. ᎒upporters – *Dexter*, A Russian brown bear proper; *sinister*, a greyhound argent gorged with a collar checky of the last and azure.
Residence – Trillinghurst Oast, Ranters Lane, Goudhurst, Kent TN17 1HL.

SON LIVING (*By 1st marriage*)

Hon TIMOTHY WALTER (Trillinghurst Oast, Ranters Lane, Goudhurst, Kent TN17 1HL), *b* 28 March 1958; *ed* Millfield: *m* 1987 (*m diss* 1997), Susan Elaine Hurst.

DAUGHTER LIVING (*By 1st marriage*)

Hon Christina Anne (Wiveton Hall, Wiveton, Holt, Norfolk NR25 7TE), *b* 1959: *m* 1993, Desmond James MacCarthy, and has issue (*see* Buxton, Bt, colls).

BROTHERS LIVING

Hon (James) David Gerald (Flat C, 45 Chesterton Rd, W10 6ES), *b* 1928; *ed* Geelong Gram Sch, Victoria, and Trin Coll, Camb (BA); Bar Inner Temple 1952; OStJ; late Lt Coldstream Guards.

Hon Robert Beauclerk, CBE (14 Ladbroke Grove, W11 3BQ), *b* 1934; *ed* Eton, and Trin Coll, Camb (BA); Chm Mental Health Foundation 1982-94; CBE (Civil) 1990: *m* 1973, Josette, da of Josef Bromovsky (*see* Dunn, Bt, ext, 1995 Edn), of Ottmanach, Pisheldorf, Kärnten, Austria, and has issue living, John James (Jan), *b* 1977, — Nicolai, *b* 1986, — Nell Marguerite, *b* 1983.

PREDECESSORS – **(1)** GERALD WALTER ERSKINE Loder, 5th son of Sir Robert Loder, 1st Bt; *b* 1861; was an Assist Private Sec to Pres of Local Govt Board 1888-92, and to Sec of State for India 1896-1901; sat as MP for Brighton (*C*) 1889-1905; *cr Baron Wakehurst*, of Ardingly, co Sussex (peerage of United Kingdom) 1934: *m* 1890, Lady Louise de Vere Beauclerk, who *d* 1958, el da of 10th Duke of St Albans: *d* 1936; *s* by his only son **(2)** JOHN ᴅᴇ VERE, KG, KCMG, 2nd Baron, *b* 1895; MP for E Leicester (*C*) 1924-29, and Lewes 1931-36; Gov of NSW 1937-46, and N Ireland 1952-64: *m* 1920,

Dame Margaret, DBE, who *d* 1994, da of Sir Charles Tennant, 1st Bt (B Glenconner); *d* 1970; *s* by his el son (3) (JOHN) CHRISTOPHER, 3rd Baron and present peer.

WALDEGRAVE, EARL (Waldegrave) (Earl GB 1729, Bt E 1643)
(Name and Title pronounced "Wallgrave")

Press forward

JAMES SHERBROOKE WALDEGRAVE, 13th Earl, and 17th Baronet; *b* 8 Dec 1940; *s* 1995; *ed* Eton, and Trin Coll, Camb: *m* 1986 (*m diss* 1996), Mary Alison Anthea, da of late Sir Robert Furness, of Little Shelford, Cambs, and has issue.

Arms – Per pale argent and gules. **Crest** – Out of a ducal coronet or, a plume of five ostrich feathers, the first two argent, the third per pale argent and gules, and the last two gules. **Supporters** – Two talbots sable, ears or, each gorged with a mural coronet argent.
Residence – Chewton House, Chewton Mendip, Bath BA3 4LQ.

SONS LIVING

EDWARD ROBERT (*Viscount Chewton*), *b* 10 Oct 1986; Page of Honour to HM since 1998.
Hon (Robert Arthur) Riversdale, *b* 1989.

BROTHER LIVING

Rt Hon William Arthur (*Baron Waldegrave of North Hill*), *b* 1946; *ed* Eton, Corpus Christi Coll, Oxford, and Harvard Univ; Quondam Fellow of All Souls Coll, Oxford; CPRS 1971-73; Head of Rt Hon Edward Heath's Political Office 1974-75; GEC Ltd 1975-81; Member IBA Advsy Council 1980-81 Under Sec of State DES (for higher education) 1981-83, Under Sec of State Dept of Environment 1983-85, Min of State: Dept of Environment 1985-88, Foreign & Commonwealth Office 1988-90, Dept of Health and Social Security 1990-92, Chancellor of the Duchy of Lancaster 1992-94, Min of State Agriculture, Fisheries and Food 1994-July 1995, Ch Sec to the Treasury 1995-97; JP; MP for Bristol West (*C*) 1979-97; PC 1990; *cr* a Life Baron 1999: *m* 1977, (Linda Margaret) Caroline, yr da of Maj Richard Burrows, of ?a Royal Chase, Tunbridge Wells, Kent, and has issue living, James Victor, *b* 1984, — Katharine Mary, *b* 1980, — Elizabeth Laura, *b* 1983, — Harriet Horatia, *b* 1988.

SISTERS LIVING

Lady Sarah Caroline, *b* 1931; JP and DL Som 1998: *m* 1955, Ernest George Wright, GM, CPM, late Sr-Supt Colonial Police Service (Kenya) of Honibere Farmhouse, Burton, Stogursey, Somerset, and has issue living, Thomas Geoffrey, *b* 1956; late RGJ: *m* 1986, Sophia Louise, yst da of late J. F. P. Tate, of The Old Rectory, Boscombe, Salisbury, Wilts, and has issue living, Matthew Adam Christopher *b* 1988, Katherine Elizabeth *b* 1992, — David James, *b* 1957.
Lady Jane Mary HOWARD, *b* 1934: *m* 1st, 1954 (*m diss* 1977), 4th Baron Strathcona and Mount Royal; 2ndly 1977 (*m diss* 1979), Duncan McIntosh, OBE, AFC, and has issue (by 1st *m*) (see that title).
Lady Elisabeth Jeronima (*Baroness Forteviot*), *b* 1936: *m* 1963, 4th Baron Forteviot, of Aberdalgie House, by Perth, and has issue (see that title).
Lady Anne Hermione, *b* 1937: *m* 1971, Sir John Dennis (Jack) Boles, MBE (High Sheriff Devon 1993), of Rydon House, Talaton, nr Honiton, Devon EX5 2RP.
Lady Susan Katharine (*Lady Susan Hussey*), DCVO, *b* 1939; appointed a Woman of the Bedchamber to HM The Queen 1960; CVO 1971, DCVO 1984: *m* 1959, Baron Hussey of North Bradley (Life Baron), and has issue (see that title).

COLLATERAL BRANCH LIVING

Descendants of Adm Hon Sir William Waldegrave, GCB (2nd son of 3rd Earl), who was *cr Baron Radstock* 1800 (see that title).

PREDECESSORS – (1) *Sir* EDWARD Waldegrave, Knt, sometime MP for Sudbury; when 70 years of age took up arms in the royal cause; *cr* a *Baronet* 1643; afterwards eminently distinguished as a military leader; *s* by his son (2) *Sir* HENRY, 2nd Bt; *d* 1658; *s* by his son (3) *Sir* CHARLES, 3rd Bt; *s* by his son (4) *Sir* HENRY, 4th Bt; *cr Baron Waldegrave*, of Chewton, co Somerset (peerage of England) 1686; was Comptroller of the King's Household; *d* 1689; *s* by his son (5) JAMES, KG, PC, 2nd Baron; conformed to the Church of England and took his seat in the House of Lords 1722; was Ambassador to Emperor of Germany 1727-37: *cr Viscount Chewton and Earl Waldegrave* (peerage of Great Britain) 1729; *d* 1741; *s* by his el son (6) JAMES, KG, PC, 2nd Earl; was successively a Lord of the Bedchamber, Steward of the Duchy of Cornwall, Gov to George Prince of Wales and to Prince Edward, Duke of York, and Teller of the Exchequer, &c; *d* 1763; *s* by his brother (7) JOHN, KG, 3rd Earl; sat as MP for Oxford and Newcastle-under-Lyme; was Master of the Horse, Gov of Plymouth, a Groom of the Bedchamber, and Lord-Lieut of Essex: *d* 1784; *s* by his son (8) GEORGE, 4th Earl; was Col 14th Regt: *m* his cousin, Lady Elizabeth Laura Waldegrave, da of the 2nd Earl; *d* 1789; *s* by his el son (9) GEORGE, 5th Earl; *d* 1794; *s* by his brother (10) JOHN JAMES, 6th Earl; a Lt-Col in the Army *d* 1835; *s* by son (11)

GEORGE EDWARD, 7th Earl; *dsp* 1846; *s* by his uncle (12) WILLIAM, CB (4th son of 4th Earl), 8th Earl; was a Vice-Adm; *d* 1859; *s* by his grandson (13) WILLIAM FREDERICK, PC (el son of William Frederick, Viscount Chewton, by Frances, VA, da of late Capt John Bastard, RN), 9th Earl, *b* 1851; a Lord-in-Waiting to Queen Victoria Aug 1886 to Aug 1892 and July 1895 to Aug 1896, Capt of the Yeomen of the Guard 1896-1906, and Ch Conservative Whip in the House of Lords 1896-1911: *m* 1874, Lady Mary Dorothea Palmer, DBE, who *d* 1933, da of 1st Earl of Selborne; *d* 1930; *s* by his only son (14) WILLIAM EDWARD SEYMOUR, 10th Earl, *b* 1882; *d* 1933; *s* by his uncle (15) *Rev* HENRY NOEL (2nd son of William Frederick, Viscount Chewton), 11th Earl, *b* 1854; Rector of Stoke d'Abernon, Surrey, of Marston Bigot, nr Frome, Somerset, and of Orchardleigh with Lullington: *m* 1892, Anne Katharine, who *d* 1962, da of late Rev William Pollexfen Bastard, of Buckland Court, Ashburton and Kitley, Devon; *d* 1936; *s* by his only son (16) GEOFFREY NOEL, KG, GCVO, TD, 12th Earl, *b* 1905; Vice-Lt Som 1955-60, Joint Parly Sec to Min of Agriculture, Fisheries and Food 1957-62, Chm Forestry Commn 1963-65, a Member of Prince of Wales's Council, Duchy of Cornwall 1951-58, Lord Warden of the Stanneries 1965-76; Officer of the American Legion of Merit: *m* 1930, Mary Hermione, who *d* (Nov) 1995, da of late Lt-Col Arthur Morton Grenfell, DSO (V Cobham, colls); *d* (23 May) 1995; *s* by his elder son (17) JAMES SHERBROOKE, 13th Earl and present peer; also Viscount Chewton, and Baron Waldegrave.

WALES, PRINCE OF, see Royal Family.

Walker, see Baron Gordon-Walker.

WALKER OF DONCASTER, BARON (Walker) (Life Baron 1997)

HAROLD WALKER, PC, son of late Harold Walker; *b* 12 July 1927; *ed* Manchester Coll of Technology; Fleet Air Arm 1946-48; DL S Yorks; Freeman of Doncaster; MP for Doncaster (*Lab*) 1964-83, and for Doncaster Central 1983-97; Assist Govt Whip 1967, Parliamentary Under-Sec of State for Employment and Productivity 1968-70, Opposition Front Bench Spokesman on Industrial Relations 1970-74, Parliamentary Under-Sec of State for Employment 1974-76, Min of State 1976-79, Opposition Spokesman 1979-83, Chm Ways and Means Cttee and Dep Speaker 1983-92; Memb Joint Select Cttee on Statutory Instruments; *cr* PC 1979, Kt 1992, and *Baron Walker of Doncaster*, of Audenshaw, co Greater Manchester (Life Baron) 1997: *m* 1st, 1956, Barbara, who *d* 1981, da of Cecil Hague, of Ashton-under-Lyne; 2ndly, 1984, Mary, da of Christopher Griffin, of co Tipperary, and has issue by 1st *m*.

Address – c/o House of Lords, Westminster, SW1A 0PW. *Clubs* – Westminster, Clay Lane, Doncaster Trades, RN, Catholic (all Doncaster).

DAUGHTER LIVING (By 1st marriage)

Hon Lyn, *b* 1963; *ed* Sheffield Univ.

WALKER OF WORCESTER, BARON (Walker) (Life Baron 1992)

PETER EDWARD WALKER, MBE, PC, son of Sydney Walker; *b* 25 March 1932; *ed* Latymer Upper Sch; Member Nat Exec of Conservative Party since 1956, PPS to Leader of House of Commons 1963-64, Min of Housing and Local Govt June-Oct 1970, Sec of State for Environment 1970-72, for Trade and Industry 1972-74, Min of Agriculture, Fisheries and Food 1979-83, Sec of State for Energy 1983-87, and for Wales 1987-90; non-exec Dir Tate & Lyle plc, Chm Cornhill Insurance Co, Vice Chm Dresdner Kleinwort Benson; Chm Carlton Club; author of *The Ascent of Britain* 1977, *Trust the People* 1987, and *Staying Power* 1991; MP Worcester (*C*) 1961-92; *cr* MBE (Civil) 1950, PC 1970, and *Baron Walker of Worcester*, of Abbots Morton, co Hereford and Worcester (Life Baron) 1992: *m* 1969, Tessa, da of Geoffrey Ivan Pout, and has issue.

Arms – Per pale sable and or semy of portcullises and three-turreted towers all counterchanged. Crest – Growing from a grassy mound proper, over which curls a footpath, a cedar tree all proper irradiated or. Supporters – *Dexter*, a dragon gules; *sinister*, a sea lion proper, the head and mane or, supporting a trident also proper; a compartment per bend dexter a grassy mound, growing therefrom red and yellow cowslips all proper, sinister water barry-wavy azure and argent, over all in bend a footpath proper.
Residence – Abbots Morton Manor, Gooms Hill, Abbots Morton, Worcs WR7 4LT. *Clubs* – Buck's, Pratt's, Carlton.

SONS LIVING

Hon Jonathan Peter, *b* 1970; *ed* St Paul's and Balliol Coll, Oxford.
Hon Timothy Rupert, *b* 1975; *ed* St Paul's, and Exeter Univ.
Hon Robin Caspar, *b* 1978; *ed* St Paul's, and Balliol Coll, Oxford.

DAUGHTERS LIVING

Hon Shara Jane, *b* 1971; *ed* Francis Holland Sch, and Brasenose Coll, Oxford: *m* 1998, Jonathan F. W. Smithson, only son of John Smithson, of Cambridge.
Hon Marianna Clare, *b* 1985; *ed* Godolphin and Latymer.

WALL, BARONY OF (Wall) (Extinct 1980)

SONS LIVING OF LIFE BARON

Hon Martin John, *b* 1948: *m* 1976, Margaret, da of L. J. Scott, of Alton, Hants.
Hon Robin John, *b* (twin) 1948: *m* 1977, Catharine Joan, da of H. Sara, of Salisbury.

DAUGHTER LIVING OF LIFE BARON

Hon Yvonne Marie, *b* 1942: *m* 1970, Hugh Walker.

WIDOW LIVING OF LIFE BARON

GLADYS EVELYN (*Baroness Wall*) (Wychwood, Coombe End, Coombe Hill, Kingston upon Thames, Surrey KT2 7DQ), da of William Edward Wright: *m* 1939, Baron Wall, OBE (Life Baron), who *d* 1980.

WALLACE OF COSLANY, BARON (Wallace) (Life Baron 1974)

· USQUE·AD·FINEM ·

GEORGE DOUGLAS WALLACE, son of late George Wallace, of Cheltenham; *b* 18 April 1906; *ed* Cheltenham Central Sch; 1939-45 War as Sgt RAF; Govt Whip 1947-50 and Oppn Whip 1979-86; PPS to Lord Pres of Council 1964-66, to Sec of State for Commonwealth Affairs 1966-67, and to Min of State for Housing and Local Govt 1967-68; Speaker's Panel of Chairman 1970-74; a Lord in Waiting to HM 1977-79; Pres Radio Soc of GB 1977, Pres Friends of Queen Mary's Hosp Sidcup; MP for Chislehurst (*Lab*) 1945-50, and for Norwich North 1964-74; *cr Baron Wallace of Coslany*, of Coslany, City of Norwich (Life Baron) 1974: *m* 1932, Vera, da of William Joseph Randall, of Guildford, Surrey, and has issue.

Arms – Or a turkey oak tree eradicated vert in base a portcullis chained orle-wise azure on a chief of the last a representation of Norwich Castle argent masoned proper its portal or closed by a portcullis azure all between in the flanks two roses gules barbed and seeded stalked and leaved proper. Crest – Statant within a chaplet of turkey oak vert a lion in trian aspect gules head mane and tail tufts or supporting the shaft of a spear gules headed or pendent therefrom on a crossbar by a cord azure and or a gonfalon of the arms. Supporters – *Dexter*, a horse argent; *sinister*, a lion or head and mane gules, each rampant on a hillock of two grassy mounts the innermost higher than the other both within a circular wall proper masoned or growing from the dexter hillock between two double roses argent upon gules an oak sprig proper fructed or and from the sinister hillock between two like oak sprigs another double rose argent upon gules all three roses barbed seeded stalked and leaved proper. Motto – Usque ad finem.
Residence – 44 Shuttle Close, Sidcup, Kent, DA15 8EP.

SON LIVING

Hon Michael George (17 Leamington Av, Orpington, Kent), *b* 1944: *m* 1974, Susan, da of Henry William Price, of Orpington, Kent, and has issue.

DAUGHTER LIVING

Hon Elizabeth Anne (44 Shuttle Close, Sidcup, Kent), *b* 1933; Dep Headmistress of St Mary's C of E Sch, Swanley, ret 1993.

WALLACE OF SALTAIRE, BARON (Wallace) (Life Baron 1995)

WILLIAM JOHN LAWRENCE WALLACE, son of William Edward Wallace, of Leicester; *b* 12 March 1941; *ed* Westminster Abbey Choir Sch, St Edward's Sch, Oxford, King's Coll, Cambridge (BA 1962), Nuffield Coll, Oxford, and Cornell Univ, USA (PhD Govt 1968); Lecturer in Govt, Univ of Manchester 1966-67; Dir of Studies, Royal Inst of Internat Affairs 1978-90; Hallstein Fell, St Antony's Coll, Oxford 1990-95, Reader in Internat Relations, LSE 1995-99, since when Prof; *cr Baron Wallace of Saltaire*, of Shipley, co W Yorks (Life Baron) 1995: *m* 1968, Helen Sarah, da of late Edward Rushworth, of Bradford, W Yorkshire, and has issue.
Address – Department of International Relations, London School of Economics, Houghton St, WC2A 2AD.

SON LIVING

Hon Edward, *b* 1981; *ed* Graveney Sch, Tooting.

DAUGHTER LIVING

Hon Harriet, *b* 1977; *ed* Graveney Sch, Tooting, Trinity Coll, Camb, and Harvard Univ.

Wallop, family name of Earl of Portsmouth.

WALPOLE, BARON (Walpole) (Baron GB 1723 and 1756)

ROBERT HORATIO WALPOLE, 10th Baron Walpole, and 8th Baron Walpole of Wolterton; *b* 8 Dec 1938; *s* 1989; *ed* Eton, and King's Coll, Camb; JP; patron of six livings: *m* 1st, 1962 (*m diss* 1979), Sybil Judith, who *d* 1993, da of Theodore Thomas Schofield, FDS, MRCS, LRCP, of Harpenden, Herts; 2ndly, 1980, Laurel Celia, only da of S. T. Ball, of Swindon, Wilts, and has issue by 1st and 2nd *m*.

Arms – Or, on a fesse, between two chevrons sable three crosscrosslets of the field. Crest – A Saracen's head in profile, couped at the shoulders proper, ducally crowned or, and from the coronet flowing a red cap turned down in front, tasselled, and charged with a catherine-wheel gold. Supporters – *Dexter*, an antelope argent; *sinister*, a stag argent, each gorged with a collar checky or and azure, and therefrom a chain reflexed over the back gold. *Residence* – Mannington Hall, Norwich, Norfolk NR11 7BB.

SONS LIVING (*By 1st marriage*)

Hon JONATHAN ROBERT HUGH, *b* 16 Nov 1967; *ed* Eton, and Manchester Univ.
Hon Benedict Thomas Orford, *b* 1969; *ed* Eton.

(*By 2nd marriage*)

Hon Roger Horatio Calibut, *b* 1980; *ed* Eton.
Hon Henry William, *b* 1982; *ed* The King's Sch, Canterbury.

Let him be true to himself

DAUGHTERS LIVING (*By 1st marriage*)

Hon Alice Louise, *b* 1963, *ed* Norwich High Sch, and New Hall, Camb: *m* 1990, Dr Angel Cesar Carro Sanz, yr son of Herminio Carro Sanz, of Geneva, and has issue living, Inigo Robert, *b* 1996, — Hester Nancy, *b* 1990, — Beatrice Maud, *b* (twin) 1990, — Isobel Clemency, *b* 1993.
Hon Emma Judith, *b* 1964; *ed* Norwich High Sch, and Durham Univ: *m* 1998, Timothy Roger Titus Walpole-Walsh (formerly Walsh), yr son of Brian Walsh, of Malvern, Adelaide, S Australia.

(*By 2nd marriage*)

Hon Grace Mary, *b* 1986.

SISTER LIVING

Hon Phillida Ann, *b* 1950: *m* 1st, 1973 (*m diss* 1981), Clive Grainger Morgan-Evans; 2ndly, 1983, Anthony Hurn, of Beck Farm, Calthorpe, Norwich NR11 7NG, and has issue living (by 1st *m*), Edward Grainger, *b* 1973; *ed* Framlingham Coll, — Daniel Rupert, *b* 1977; *ed* Framlingham Coll, and RAC Cirencester.

DAUGHTER LIVING OF FIFTH EARL OF ORFORD

Lady Anne Sophia, *b* 1919; VMH 1986, Hon FRHS 1988; Hon Dr Sc Exeter 1990; Chm Internat Dendrology Soc 1982-87; JP 1964-80: *m* 1st, 1939, Col Joseph Eric Palmer, CBE, TD, DL, who *d* 1980; 2ndly, 1990, Robert James Berry, of Tiniroto, Gisborne, NZ, and has issue living (by 1st *m*), John Robert Walpole (Kirkmichael House, Blairgowrie, Perthshire), *b* 1943: *m* 1st, 1971, Carolyn, da of W. H. Atkinson-Clark, of Ashintully Castle, Kirkmichael, Blairgowrie; 2ndly, 1979, Mrs Alison Ann Allinson, da of Dr Noel Ian Bartholomew, of The Old Vicarage, Norton Bavant, Warminster, Wilts, — Anthony Eric Fletcher, *b* 1945: *m* 1969 (*m diss* 1998), Nicola Mary, da of H. Maude, of Gisborne, NZ. *Address* – Hackfalls, PO Box 3, Tiniroto, via Gisborne, NZ.

WIDOW LIVING OF SEVENTH BARON

NANCY LOUISA, OBE (*Nancy, Baroness Walpole*), da of late Frank Harding Jones, of 21 Abingdon Court, W8; OBE (Civil) 1977; JP: *m* 1937, Capt the 7th Baron Walpole, TD, who *d* 1989.

COLLATERAL BRANCH LIVING

Grandchildren of late Sir Horatio George Walpole, KCB, el son of late Rt Hon Spencer Horatio Walpole, QC, 2nd son of late Thomas Walpole (*b* 1755), son of Hon Thomas Walpole, 2nd son of 1st Baron Walpole of Wolterton:—

Issue of late Maj Robert Spencer Hobhouse Walpole, *b* 1881; *d* 1975: *m* 1923, Edith Winifred, who *d* 1978, da of late S. H. Keeling, of Parkfield, Kenilworth:—

Horace Jeremy Spencer (Old Forge, Ashton Keynes, Swindon, Wilts), *b* 1924; Lt-Cmdr RN: *m* 1950, Mary Elizabeth Bruce Kidman, and has issue living, Robert Charles Spencer (Stocks Farmhouse, Meysey Hampton, nr Cirencester, Glos), *b* 1955: *m* 1st, 1975 (*m diss* 1986), Diana Rosemary Bishop; 2ndly, 1987, Judith, da of Carrick McLelland, of Wester Housebyes, Melrose, Roxburghshire, and has issue living, (by 1st *m*) Daniel Nicholas Spencer *b* 1977, Thomas James *b* 1980, Theresa *b* 1975, (by 2nd *m*) Catherine Mary *b* 1992, Helen Elspeth *b* 1995, — Caroline Mary Bruce (27 Avondale Rd, SW14 8PU), *b* 1951, — Elizabeth Jane Bruce (Barn End, 6 Downs Mill, Frampton Mansell, Stroud, Glos GL6 8JX), *b* 1953; has issue (by Dr Peter Lawrence), Emma Victoria *b* 1990, Charlotte Alice *b* 1991, — Lucy Margaret Bruce *b* (twin) 1955: *m* 1974, Stephen Ashcroft, of 1 Down Ampney, Glos, and has issue living, Simon James *b* 1975, Christopher Andrew Jeremy *b* 1981, Caroline Jennifer *b* 1978, — Charlotte Victoria Bruce, *b* 1960: *m* 1987, James Ronald Trumper, of The Bothy, The Whiteway, Cirencester, Glos, son of William Trumper, of Bloxham, Oxon, and has issue living, Fiona Jane *b* 1991.

PREDECESSORS – **(1)** *Sir* ROBERT Walpole, KG, KB, a distinguished statesman; sat as MP for Lynn Regis 1702-42; was successively a Lord of the Treasury, Chancellor of the Exchequer, a Lord Justice, sole Sec of State, and Prime Minister; made a KG 1726, while a Commoner; *cr Baron Walpole*, of Houghton, *Viscount Walpole* and *Earl of Orford* (peerage of Great Britain) 1742; *d* 1745; *s* by his son **(2)** ROBERT, KB, 2nd Earl, who had in 1723 been *cr Baron Walpole*, of Walpole, co Norfolk (with remainder to his brothers Edward and Horace, and in default thereof to the heirs male of his father, and in default thereof to the heirs male of his grandfather): *m* 1724, Margaret, afterwards in her own right Baroness Clinton; the Earl *d* 1751; *s* by his son **(3)** GEORGE, 3rd Earl, who in 1781 *s* his mother as 16th *Baron Clinton* (peerage of England, *cr* 1332); was a Lord of the Bedchamber and Ranger of St James's and Hyde Parks; *d* 1791, when the Barony of Clinton reverted to his kinsman, Robert George William Trefusis (see B Clinton), and the Earldom devolved upon his uncle **(4)** HORACE, 4th Earl; sat successively as MP for Collington, Castle Rising, and King's Lynn, but was more distinguished for literary than political attainments; was Usher of the Receipt of the Exchequer, Comptroller of the Great Roll, and Keeper of the Foreign Receipts, having retired from public life he purchased a villa at Twickenham and transformed it into the celebrated Gothic mansion known as Strawberry Hill, where he printed his own works and many curious pieces; *d* unmarried 1797, when all the honours expired except the Barony of Walpole of Walpole (*cr* 1723), which devolved upon his first cousin **(5)** HORATIO, 4th Baron, who in 1757 had *s* his father, who was brother of 1st Earl, as 2nd *Baron Walpole of Wolterton* (peerage of Great Britain, *cr* 1756), sat as MP for Lynn Regis 1747-57; *cr Earl of Orford* (peerage of United Kingdom) 1806; *d* 1809; *s* by his son **(6)** HORATIO, 2nd Earl; MP for Wigan 1780-4, and for King's Lynn 1784-1809; *d* 1822; *s* by his son **(7)** HORATIO, 3rd Earl; *b* 1783; was High Steward of Lynn, and Col W Norfolk Militia: *m* Mary, da of late William Augustus Fawkener, of Brocton Hall, Salop; *d* 1858; *s* by his son **(8)** HORATIO WILLIAM, 4th Earl, *b* 1813; MP for Norfolk 1835-7: *m* 1841, Harriet Bettina Frances, who *d* 1886, da of late Hon Sir Fleetwood Broughton Reynolds Pellew; *d* 1894; *s* by his nephew **(9)** ROBERT HORACE (son of late Hon Frederick Walpole, MP, 3rd son of 3rd Earl), 5th Earl, *b* 1854: *m* 1st, 1888, Louise Melissa, who *d* 1909, da of D. C. Corbin, of New York; 2ndly, 1917, Emily Gladys, who *d* 1988, da of Rev Thomas Henry Royal Oakes, R of Thurgarton, Norwich; *d* 1931, when the Earldom of Orford became ext, and the Baronies of Walpole and Walpole of Wolterton devolved upon his cousin **(10)** ROBERT HENRY MONTGOMERIE (son of late Horatio Spencer Walpole, descended from late Hon Thomas Walpole, brother of 1st Earl of Orford, *cr* 1806), 9th Baron, *b* 1913, Capt RA, TD: *m* 1937, Nancy Louisa, OBE, da of late Frank Harding Jones, of 21 Abingdon Court, W8; *d* 1989; *s* by his elder (but only surv) son **(11)** ROBERT HORATIO, 10th Baron, and present peer; also Baron Walpole of Wolterton.

Walsh, family name of Baron Ormathwaite.

WALSINGHAM, BARON (de Grey) (Baron GB 1780)

To be spirited, not inactive

JOHN DE GREY, MC, 9th Baron; *b* 21 Feb 1925; *s* 1965; *ed* Wellington Coll, Aberdeen Univ, and at Magdalen Coll, Oxford (MA); Lt-Col (ret) RA; patron of two livings; 1939-45 War, Palestine 1947, Korea 1951-52 (MC), Malaya 1954-56, Cyprus and Suez 1956, Aden 1957-58 and 1961-63, Far East (Borneo) 1963-65: *m* 1963, Wendy Elizabeth, elder da of Edward S. Hoare, of Southwick, Sussex, and has issue.

𝕬𝖗𝖒𝖘 – Barry of six argent and azure, in chief three annulets gules. 𝕮𝖗𝖊𝖘𝖙 – A wyvern's head, or. 𝖀𝖚𝖕𝖕𝖔𝖗𝖙𝖊𝖗𝖘 – Two wyverns regardant argent, collared azure, chained or, and charged on the breast with three annulets gules.
Residence – The Hassocks, Merton, Thetford, Norfolk 1P25 6QP. *Clubs* – Army and Navy, Farmers', Norfolk County (Norwich) Special Forces.

SON LIVING

Hon ROBERT, *b* 21 June 1969; *ed* Exeter Univ (BSc 1992): *m* 1995, Josephine Elizabeth, da of Richard Haryott, of Brickendon, Hertford, and has issue living, Thomas, *b* 23 Jan 1997. *Residence* – Merton Hall, Thetford, Norfolk IP25 6QJ.

DAUGHTERS LIVING

Hon Sarah Jane, *b* 1964; *ed* London Univ (BA 1986): *m* 1990, Bryan Muggeridge, yr son of Percy Muggeridge, of Paarl, Cape Province, S Africa. *Residence* – 14 Plein St, Paarl, 7646 Western Cape, S Africa.

Hon Elizabeth Anne, *b* 1966; *ed* Durham Univ (BA 1989): *m* 1993, Stefan Jones, only son of Roger Jones, of Yarnton House, Peopleton, Worcs, and has issue living, Archibald Willoughby, *b* 1996, — Ivan, *b* 1998. *Residence* – 17 St James's Drive, Wandsworth, SW17 7RN.

SISTERS LIVING

Hon Lavender Hyacinth, *b* 1923; European War 1942-45 with First Aid Nursing Yeo in N Africa, Italy, India and Ceylon: *m* 1946, Col William d'Arcy Garnier, late RA, who *d* 1989, and has issue living, James Hugh, *b* 1948; *ed* Wellington Coll, RMA Sandhurst, and RMCS Shrivenham: *m* 1984, Katherine Hale, yr da of late John Hale Puckle, of Foxton House, Foxton, Cambs, and has issue living, Louisa Hale *b* 1986, Sophia Elizabeth *b* 1988, Georgina Sarah *b* 1989, Olivia Caroline *b* 1991, Camilla Henrietta *b* 1994, — Richard Charles, *b* 1950; *ed* Wellington Coll, and Hull Univ: *m* 1989, Melissa (Minnie) Mary, eldest da of Anthony Meyrick Denny, of Rose Cottage, Hattingley, Alton, Hants, and has issue living, William Richard *b* 1989, Robert Anthony *b* 1993, Elizabeth Henrietta *b* 1995, — Edward Henry, QC, MP (1 Brick Court, Temple, EC4), *b* 1952; *ed* Wellington Coll, and Jesus Coll, Oxford (MA); Bar Middle Temple 1976; QC 1995; MP for Harborough (C) since 1992: *m* 1982, Anna Caroline, el da of late Michael James Mellows (*see* Heathcote, Bt, of London), and has issue living, George Edward *b* 1986, James William *b* 1991, Eleanor Katharine Rose *b* 1983, — Katharine Juliet, *b* 1958: *m* 1985, Anthony Richard Ashmore Wolstenholme, elder son of Michael Ashmore Wolstenholme, of Fitzgeorge Av, W14, and has issue living, William Michael *b* 1996, Florence Maud *b* 1990, Edwina Lavender *b* 1991. *Address* – College Farm, Thompson, Thetford, Norfolk.

Hon Margaret Isolda, *b* 1926; European War 1943-45 in WRNS: *m* 1950, Major Geoffrey Edward Ford North, MC, High Sheriff Devon 1990, and has issue living, David John Ford (Strattenborough Castle Farm, Coleshill, Oxon SN6 8TH), *b* 1959: *m* 1986, Sarah Jane, da of Gerald Barrow, of Gustard Wood, Wheathampstead, Herts, and has issue living, George Peter Ford *b* 1988, Rosanna Katharine *b* 1990, Perdita Alexandra *b* 1991, — Amanda (*Lady Weldon*), *b* 1951: *m* 1st, 1970 (*m diss* 1980), Anthony John Wigan (*see* By Tweedmouth); 2ndly, 1980, Sir Anthony William Weldon, 9th Bt, of Easton Manor, Easton Royal, Pewsey, Wilts, — Joanna Katharine (*Hon Mrs Kim Fraser*), *b* 1953: *m* 1975, Hon Kim Maurice Fraser (*see* L Lovat), — Belinda Jane, *b* 1955: *m* 1994, Simon Michael Weinstock, and has issue living, Abigail Louisa *b* 1995. *Residence* – Holmingham Farm, Bampton, Tiverton, Devon EX16 9EF.

Hon Katharine Odeyne (*Dowager Countess of Powis*), *b* 1928: *m* 1949, 7th Earl of Powis, who *d* 1993. *Residence* – Marrington Hall, Chirbury, Montgomery, Powys.

COLLATERAL BRANCHES LIVING

Grandchildren of late Nigel de Grey, CMG, OBE, yr son of late Rev Hon Arnald de Grey, 3rd son of 5th Baron:—
Issue of late John de Grey, *b* 1911, *d* 1973: *m* 1939, Averil Mary (Oliver House, Buckden, Cambs), da of late Herman Walter de Zoete, of Sproughton, Suffolk:—
Michael John (Crooked Cottage, Dunkerton, Bath), *b* 1942; *ed* Eton: *m* 1st, 1966 (*m diss* 1988), Carolyn Althea Jane, da of late John Ernest Haldane Blackie, CB, of The Bell House, Alconbury, Cambs; 2ndly, 1989, Charlotte Janet Rosamund, da of late Lt-Col Robert Arthur d'Escourt Ashe, of Newtownmountkennedy, co Wicklow, and has issue living, (by 1st *m*) Rachel Emma, *b* 1969, — Helen Sarah, *b* 1970, — (by 2nd *m*) Annabel Louise, *b* 1994. —— Anthony (54 Abbotswood Rd, SW16 1AW), *b* 1948; *ed* Eton: *m* 1975 (*m diss* 1985), Miranda Jane, da of Robert Clive Murdoch, of Westerhill, Linton, Maidstone, Kent, and has issue living, Nigel John, *b* 1981, — Alexandra Mary Carena, *b* 1984.

Issue of late Sir Roger de Grey, KCVO, Pres Royal Academy 1984-93, *b* 1918, *d* 1995: *m* 1942, Flavia Hatt (*Lady de Grey*) (5-6 Camer St, Meopham, Kent), da of late Lt-Col Clinton Irwin, MC, of Silver Bridge, Chideock, Dorset:—
Spencer Thomas, CBE, *b* 1944; *ed* Eton, and Churchill Coll, Camb (MA); CBE (Civil) 1997: *m* 1977, Hon Amanda Lucy Annan, elder da of Baron Annan (Life Baron), and has issue living, Felix Nicholas, *b* 1992, — Georgia Catherine, *b* 1988. *Residence* – 38 Stockwell Park Crescent, SW9 0DG. —— Robert Fulke, *b* 1948; *ed* Eton, and Selwyn Coll, Camb (MA):

m 1974, Muriel Janik, da of Jean-Paul Schoendoerffer, of Paris, and has issue living, Thomas George, *b* 1981, — Elisa Catherine, *b* 1976, — Alice Rose, *b* 1979. —— Emilia Jane Mary, *b* 1952; *ed* Cobham Hall, and Royal Coll of Music: *m* 1975, Timothy Crawford, son of James Crawford, of Post House, Stroud, Hants, and has issue living, George, *b* 1979, — Joseph, *b* 1988, — Harriet, *b* 1982.

PREDECESSORS – (1) *Sir* WILLIAM de Grey, Knt, having filled the offices of Solicitor-Gen, Attorney-Gen and Ch Justice of the Common Pleas, was *cr Baron Walsingham*, of Walsingham, co Norfolk (peerage of Great Britain) 1780; sat as MP for Newport, Cornwall, 1762-8, and for Cambridge University 1770; *d* 1781; *s* by his son (2) THOMAS, 2nd Baron; was for 20 years Chairman of Committees of House of Lords; *d* 1818; *s* by his el son (3) GEORGE, 3rd Baron; Lieut-Gen Peninsular Campaign; he was burned to death 26 April, 1831, his wife dying the following day; *s* by his brother (4) THOMAS, 4th Baron; was Archdeacon of Surrey, and Prebendary of Winchester, &c; *d* 1839; *s* by his son (5) THOMAS, 5th Baron; *b* 1804: *m* 1st, Augusta Louisa, da of Sir Robert Frankland Russell, 7th Bt; 2ndly, Hon Emily Elizabeth Julia Thellusson, da of 2nd Baron Rendlesham; *d* 1870; *s* by his son (6) THOMAS, 6th Baron, *b* 1843; MP for Norfolk (*C*) 1865-70, and a Lord-in-Waiting to Queen Victoria 1874-5: *m* 1st, 1877, Augusta Selina Elizabeth (Leila), who *d* 1906, da of late William Locke (*see* Cs Dysart, colls), widow of Ernest, Lord Burghersh (E Westmorland), and formerly wife of Don Luigi Caracciolo, Duke of San Teodoro; 2ndly, 1908, Marion Gwytherne-Williams, of Belvedere, St Lawrence, Isle of Wight, who *d* 1913, da of late Thomas Rhys Withers; 3rdly, 1914, Agnes Baird, who *d* 1926, da of late Frederick Shand Hemming, and widow of Richard Dawson, of Lealands, Hellingly; *d* 1919; *s* by his half-brother (7) JOHN AUGUSTUS, 7th Baron, *b* 1849; a Metropolitan Police Magistrate 1905-19; *m* 1st, 1883, Elizabeth Henrietta, who *d* 1927, da of Patrick Grant, HEICS; 2ndly, 1928, Marguerite, who *d* 1931, da of late Walter Vernon, of Trematon Lodge, Anerley, SE, and widow of Thomas Godley, of Scarborough; *d* 1929; *s* by his son (8) GEORGE, DSO, OBE, 8th Baron, *b* 1884; Lt-Col R Norfolk Regt 1914-18 War (thrice wounded): *m* 1919, Hyacinth Lambart, who *d* 1968, da of late Lt-Col Lambart Henry Bouwens, RHA; *d* 1965; *s* by his son (9) JOHN, MC, 9th Baron and present peer.

WALSTON, BARONY OF (Walston) (Extinct 1991)

SONS LIVING OF LIFE BARON (*By 1st marriage*)

Hon Oliver (Thriplow Farm, Thriplow, Royston, Herts) *b* 1941; *ed* Eton, and King's Coll, Camb; agricultural broadcaster: *m* 1st, 1966, Leslie, da of Milton A. Gordon, of New York; 2ndly, 1969, Anne Lowell, da of William H. Dunbar, of Washington, DC, and has issue.

Hon William, *b* 1942; *ed* Eton, Downside, and King's Coll Camb: *m* 1st, 1963 (*m diss* 1988), Hilary Blanche, da of William Osselton Galbraith; 2ndly, 1989, Barbara Catherine, da of Michael James Jardine, and has issue by both marriages.

Hon James Patrick Francis (Via del Biscione 78, 00186, Rome, Italy) *b* 1949; *ed* Eton, Ampleforth and Jesus Coll, Camb: *m* 1987, Nora Emilia Antonia Maria, da of Vincenzo Galli de'Paratesi.

DAUGHTERS LIVING OF LIFE BARON (*By 1st marriage*)

Hon Anne Sheridan BREWIN (who resumed surname of Brewin 1982) (Clare Cottage, Northfield End, Henley-on-Thames, Oxon RG9 2JL), *b* 1937: *m* 1st, 1960 (*m diss* 1972), Charles Edward Brewin; 2ndly, 1978 (*m diss* 1982) Edward McCririe-Hallman, and has issue by 1st *m*.

Hon Susan (RMB31, Marlee, NSW, Australia) *b* (twin) 1942.

WIDOW LIVING OF LIFE BARON

ELIZABETH ROSEMARY (*Baroness Walston*), da of late Robert Bissett-Robinson, and formerly wife of Nicholas Paul Scott, MBE, MP (later Rt Hon Sir Nicholas Scott, KBE): *m* 1979, as his 2nd wife, Baron Walston, CVO (Life Baron), who *d* 1991. *Residence* – Marquis, St Lucia, W Indies.

WALTON OF DETCHANT, BARON (Walton) (Life Baron 1989)

JOHN NICHOLAS WALTON, TD, son of Herbert Walton; *b* 16 Sept 1922; *ed* Alderman Wraith Gram Sch, and King's Coll Med Sch, Durham Univ (MD); late Col RAMC, Comdg Offr 1 (N) Gen Hosp (TA) 1963-66, Hon Col 201 (N) Gen Hosp (TAVR) 1968-73; Consultant Neurologist Newcastle Univ Hosps 1958-83, Prof of Neurology Newcastle Univ 1968-83, Chm Muscular Dystrophy Group of GB 1970-95, Member Gen Med Council 1971-89 (Chm Educn Cttee 1975-82, Pres 1982-89), Pres BMA 1980-82, Assocn for Study of Med Educn 1982-94, and Assocn of British Neurologists 1987-88, first Vice-Pres World Fedn of Neurologists 1981-89, Pres 1989-97, and Pres Royal Soc of Medicine 1984-86; Warden Green Coll, Oxford 1983-89; FRCP, DSc Newcastle; TD 1962; *cr* Knt 1979, and *Baron Walton of Detchant,* of Detchant, co Northumberland (Life Baron) 1989: *m* 1946, Mary Elizabeth, da of Joseph Harrison, of Spennymoor, co Durham, and has issue, one son and two das.

Arms – Paly wavy argent and gules, a castle triple-towered purpure, on a chief of the last three crosses formy quadrate gold. **Crest** – Issuant from clouds proper a seahorse argent the piscine part proper, crined and finned or, holding between the forelegs a cross formy quadrate fitchy at the foot purpure. **Supporters** – *Dexter—* A boar gold suspended from the neck by a riband purpure a clarion, pipes downward, gules; *sinister—* A greylag goose proper.
Residence – 13 Norham Gdns, Oxford OX2 6PS. *Clubs* – Athenaeum, United Oxford and Cambridge.

Ward, family name of Viscount Bangor.

Ward, family name of Earl of Dudley.

WARD OF WITLEY, VISCOUNTCY OF (Ward) (Extinct 1988)

DAUGHTER LIVING OF FIRST VISCOUNT

See E Dudley, colls.

WARDINGTON, BARON (Pease) (Baron UK 1936)

Peace and hope

CHRISTOPHER HENRY BEAUMONT PEASE, 2nd Baron; *b* 22 Jan 1924; *s* 1950; *ed* Eton; late Capt Scots Guards; a partner in the firm of Hoare, Govett, Ltd 1950-86; an Alderman of City of London 1960-63; Member of Council of the Stock Exchange 1963-81; Member of Corporation of Foreign Bond Holders since 1967, and of Public Works Loan Board 1964-69; Chm Athlone Trust; Chm Friends of the British Library; Trustee of Royal Jubilee Trusts; 1939-45 War (wounded): *m* 1964, Audrey (DUNFEE), da of late John White, and has one adopted son and two adopted das.

Arms – Per fesse azure and gules, a fesse nebuly ermine between two lambs passant in chief argent, and in base upon a mount proper a dove rising argent, holding in the beak a pea stalk, the blossom and pods proper. Crest – Upon the capital of an Ionic column a dove rising, holding in the beak a pea stalk as in the arms. Supporters – On either side a fox or, charged on the shoulder with a bugle horn stringed sable.
Seat – Wardington Manor, Banbury, Oxon OX17 1SW. *Residence* – 29 Moore Street, SW3 2QW.

SON LIVING

Christopher William Beaumont, *b* 1970.

DAUGHTERS LIVING

Lucy Anne, *b* 1966: *m* 1991, John Vallance Petrie, eldest son of Neil Petrie, of Sulphur Wells, NZ, and has issue living, Christopher Beaumont, *b* 1993, — Angus, *b* 1994, — Abigail, *b* 1998.
Helen Elizabeth, *b* 1967.

BROTHER LIVING

Hon WILLIAM SIMON, *b* 15 Oct 1925; *ed* Eton, New Coll, Oxford (MA), and St Thomas's Hosp Med Sch; MB and BS London; FRCS England; late Capt Gren Gds; late Consultant ENT Surgeon, Central Middx and Northwick Park Hosps: *m* 1962, Hon Elizabeth Jane Ormsby-Gore, da of 4th Baron Harlech. *Residences* – 29 Upper Addison Gdns, W14; Lepe House, Exbury, Southampton. *Club* – Royal Yacht Squadron.

PREDECESSOR – (1) JOHN WILLIAM BEAUMONT Pease, 1st Baron, son of late John William Pease, DCL, of Pendower, Newcastle-upon-Tyne, and Nether Grange, Alnmouth, Northumberland; *b* 1869; Chm of Lloyds Bank 1922-45, and of Bank of London and S America 1922-47; *cr Baron Wardington* of Alnmouth, co Northumberland (peerage of United Kingdom) 1936: *m* 1923, Hon Dorothy Charlotte, who *d* 1983, da of 1st Baron Forster, and widow of Capt Hon Harold Fox Pitt Lubbock, Grenadier Guards (*see* B Avebury); *d* 1950; *s* by his el son (2) CHRISTOPHER HENRY BEAUMONT, 2nd Baron and present peer.

WARNER, BARON (Warner) (Life Baron 1998)

NORMAN REGINALD WARNER, son of Albert Henry Edwin Warner; *b* 8 Sept 1940; *ed* Dulwich, Univ of California Berkeley (MPh 1973, Harkness Fell), and Nuffield Coll, Oxford (Gwilym Gibbon Fell); entered DHSS 1960; Principal Priv Sec of State for Social Services 1974-76; Assist Sec, Supplementary Benefit 1976-79 and Operational Planning 1979-81; Regional Controller Wales and SW Region 1981-83; Under Sec, Supplementary Benefit and Housing Benefit 1984-85; Dir Social Services Kent CC 1985-91; Chm City and E London Family Services Authority 1991-94; Man Dir Warner Consulting and Training Services 1991-97; Chm Nat Enquiry into Children's Homes 1992; Memb Local Govt Commn 1995-96; Senior Policy Adviser to Home Sec 1997-98; Chm Youth Justice Board for England and Wales since 1998; Senior Residential Fell in Euro Social Welfare and Chm Euro Inst of Social Services, Univ of Kent; Chm The Residential Forum 1993-97, and Royal Philanthropic Soc 1993-98; Tstee Leonard Cheshire Foundation and MacIntyre Care 1994-97; *cr Baron Warner*, of Brockley in the London Borough of Lewisham (Life Baron) 1998: *m* 1st, 1961 (*m diss* 1981), Anne Lesley Lawrence; 2ndly, 1990, Suzanne Elizabeth, da of Charles Clifford Reeder, and formerly wife of Jonathan Reeve, and has issue by 1st and 2nd *m*.

Residence – 8 College Gdns, Dulwich, SE21 7BE.

SONS LIVING (*By 1st marriage*)

Hon Andrew Simon, *b* 1967: *m* 1996, Karen McGroutner.

(*By 2nd marriage*)

Hon Joel James Stephen, *b* 1981.

DAUGHTER LIVING (*By 1st marriage*)

Hon Justine Emma, *b* 1969.

WARNOCK, BARONESS (Warnock) (Life Baroness 1985)

(HELEN) MARY WARNOCK, DBE, da of late Archibald Edward Wilson, of Winchester, by his wife, Ethel Mary, eldest da of Sir Felix Otto Schuster, 1st Bt; *b* 14 April 1924; *ed* St Swithun's, Winchester, and Lady Margaret Hall, Oxford (Hon Fellow 1984); has Hon Degrees from Univs of Essex, Exeter, Melbourne, St Andrews, Manchester, York, etc Fellow and Tutor in Philosophy, St Hugh's Coll, Oxford 1949-66 (Senior Research Fellow 1976-84, Hon Fellow 1985); Headmistress, Oxford High Sch 1966-72; Member, IBA 1973-81, Cttee of Inquiry into Special Educn 1974-78, R Commn on Environmental Pollution 1979-84 (Chm), Advisory Cttee on Animal Experiments (Chm 1979-86), and Cttee of Inquiry into Human Fertilization 1982-84 (Chm); Mistress of Girton Coll, Camb 1985-92; author of philosophical and educational works; *cr* DBE (Civil) 1984, and *Baroness Warnock*, of Weeke, in the City of Winchester (Life Baroness) 1985: *m* 1949, Sir Geoffrey James Warnock, Prin Hertford Coll, Oxford, 1971-88, and Vice-Cllr, Oxford Univ 1981-85, who *d* 1995, and has issue.

Residence – 3 Church St, Gt Bedwyn, nr Marlborough, Wilts SN8 3PE.

SONS LIVING

Hon Felix Geoffrey, *b* 1952; *ed* Winchester, and R Coll of Music: *m* 1975, Juliet, da of Arthur Robert Lehwalder, of 5047-18-NE, Seattle, Washington, USA, and has issue living, Daniel Arthur Richard, *b* 1985, — Eleanor Denise, *b* 1982, — Polly Patricia, *b* 1986. *Residence* – 5 Kingsbridge Rd, W10 6PU.

Hon James Marcus Alexander, *b* 1953; *ed* Winchester, and E Anglia Univ: *m* 1986, Fiona Margaret, da of Matthew Stewart Hair, and has issue, one son and one da. *Residence* – 5 Cheltenham Av, Liverpool 17 2AR.

DAUGHTERS LIVING

Hon Kathleen, *b* 1950; *ed* Oxford High Sch, and St Hugh's Coll, Oxford.

Hon Stephana (Fanny), *b* 1956; *ed* Downe House, Oxford High Sch, and Guildhall Sch of Music: *m* 1987, David E. (Bruno) Branson, son of W. E. Branson, of South Hill, Beds, and has issue living, Abigail Brigitte Edith, *b* 1989. *Residence* – 7 St Ruald's Close, Wallingford, Oxon.

Hon (Grizel) Maria, *b* 1961; *ed* Oxford High Sch, and W Surrey Sch of Art and Design: *m* 1994, Paul Jenkins, son of Keith Jenkins, of Kidlington, Oxford. *Residence* – 22 Hayes Court, Camberwell New Rd, SE5 0TQ.

Warrender, family name of Baron Bruntisfield.

WARWICK, EARL BROOKE AND OF (Greville) (Earl GB 1746)

I scarcely call these things our own

GUY DAVID GREVILLE, 9th Earl; *b* 30 Jan 1957; *s* 1996; *ed* Eton: *m* 1st, 1981 (*m diss* 1992), Mrs Susan McKinley Cobbold, da of George William McKinley Wilson, of Melbourne, Australia, and formerly wife Nicholas Sydney Cobbold; 2ndly, 1996, Louisa, yr da of Dr Peter Heenan, of Perth, W Australia, and has issue by 1st *m*.

𝔄rms – Sable, on a cross, engrailed or five pellets, all within a bordure engrailed of the second or. 𝔠rests – 1st, out of a ducal coronet gules, a demi-swan, with wings expanded and elevated argent beaked of the first; 2nd, a bear sejant argent, muzzled gules, supporting a ragged staff of the first. 𝔖upporters – Two swans, wings inverted, argent legged, beaked, and ducally gorged gules.
Residence – 4 Walter St, Claremont, Perth, W Australia 6010.

SON LIVING (*By 1st marriage*)

CHARLES FULKE CHESTER (*Lord Brooke*), *b* 27 July 1982; *ed* Eton.

SISTER LIVING

Lady Charlotte Anne, *b* 1958: *m* 1979, Hon Andrew Roy Matthew Fraser, who was *k* in a hunting accident in E Africa 1994, and has issue (*see* L Lovat, colls). *Residence* – 1 Petyt Place, Old Church St, SW3 5DJ.

MOTHER LIVING

Sarah Anne Chester, da of Alfred Chester Beatty, of Owley, Wittersham, Kent: *m* 1st, 1956 (*m diss* 1967), David Robin Francis Guy, Lord Brooke (later 8th Earl of Warwick), who *d* 1996; 2ndly, 19—, Harry Thomson Jones.

WIDOW LIVING OF SEVENTH EARL

JANINE (*Dowager Countess of Warwick*), da of Georges Detry de Mares: *m* 1963, as his 3rd wife, the 7th Earl of Warwick, who *d* 1984.

COLLATERAL BRANCHES LIVING

Issue of late Hon Maynard Greville, yst son of 5th Earl, *b* 1898, *d* 1960: *m* 1918, Dora, who *d* 1957, da of late Edward Pape, of Moor Hall, Battle, and 26 Portland Place, W.:—
Felice, *b* 1919: *m* 1940, Eric J. Spurrier, who *d* 1984, and *d* 1994, leaving issue, Neil, *b* 1952; *ed* Stowe, — Caroline Ann, *b* 1957. *Residence* – Brook End Farm, Easton Lodge, Dunmow, Essex.

(*In remainder to Barony of Brooke only*)

Grandchildren of late Lt-Col Guy George Frederick Fulke Greville, DSO, HLI, yr son of late Brooke Southwell Greville, elder son of Maj Southwell Geville, brother of 1st Baron Greville, 2nd son of late Algernon Greville, great-grandson of Hon Algernon Greville, MP, 2nd son of 5th Baron Brooke:—
Issue of late Capt Guy Eric Fulke Greville, MC, ERD, RTR, *b* 1911, *d* 1986: *m* 1st, 1934 (*m diss* 1968), Mary Henrietta d'Arcy, who *d* 1982, da of Col Sir Harry Waechter, 1st Bt, CMG; 2ndly, 19—, Rosalind Jessie Gwavas (Treetops, Llandividdy Lane, Polperro, nr Looe, Cornwall PL13 2RT), widow of John Mostyn-Walker, and da of late George Larritt Polsue:—
(By 1st wife) Guy Jonathan Fulke, *b* 1940; *ed* privately. —— René Brooke Fulke (Church Cottage, St Nicholas, Harleston, Norfolk IP20 0PS), *b* 1947; *ed* privately: *m* 1976, Marion Pearl Emma, only child of H. E. Ings, of Harrow Weald, Middx, and has issue living, Beaufort Henry d'Arcy, *b* 1977, — Brooke Southwell Guy, *b* 1981. —— Priscilla Mary Caroline, *b* 1935: *m* 1957, Dr Richard Michael Holmes, PhD, who *d* 1994, only son of Prof Eric Gordon Holmes, of Mivanza, Tanganyika, and has issue living, Guy Aladar, *b* 1960. — Michael Aristide, *b* 1966, — Jacquetta Noël Barbara, *b* 1959. —— Charlotte Anne Esther, *b* 1937: *m* 1954, Bernard Morton-Stevens, son of Bernard Morton-Stevens, of High-gate, N6, and has issue living, Robert Guy *b* 1956, — Dominic Peter, *b* 1962, — Veronica Mary, *b* 1955, — Lesley Anne, *b* 1959. —— (By 2nd wife) Brooke Peregrine Fulke (7 Sistova Rd, SW12 9QT), *b* 1966; actor: *m* 1996, Lydia Ramoutar, of Trinidad and Tobago. —— Hugh Tristan Maynard, *b* 1968.

Grandson of late Stapleton Fulke Greville, el son of late Rear-Adm Stapleton John Greville, grandson of Lt-Col Henry Francis Greville, yr brother of Capt William Fulke Greville, RN, MP, grandson of Hon Algernon Greville, MP (ante):—
Issue of late John Algernon Fulke Greville, *b* 1896, *d* 1968: *m* 1929, Frances Alice, who *d* 1989, da of Harry Bird Harper:—
John Brooke Fulke (314 Robin Hood Lane, Hall Green, Birmingham, 28), *b* 1930: *m* 1958, Maureen Constance, da of L. A. Parkhouse, and has issue living, Robert John Fulke, *b* 1960.

Granddaughter of late Rear-Adm Stapleton John Greville (ante):—
Issue of late Henry Brooke Macartney Crewe Greville, b 1870, d 1944: m 1906, Cecilia Ada, who d 1959, da of Lieut-Col Sir Frederick Thomas Arthur Hervey-Bathurst, 4th Bt:—
Margaret Ishla, b 1914. *Residence* – Ridge Hill Cottage, Kingscote, E Grinstead, Sussex.

PREDECESSORS – (1) Rt Hon Sir FULKE Greville, *de jure* 5th Lord Willoughby de Broke, a favourite courtier of Queen Elizabeth I, was successively keeper of the signet to the Council in the Marches of Wales, Treasurer of the Navy, and Chancellor of the Exchequer; obtained, *temp* James I, a grant of Warwick Castle and its dependencies; *cr Baron Brooke*, of Beauchamp's Court, co Warwick (peerage of England) 1621, with remainder to his cousin, Robert, son of Fulke Greville, of Thorpe Latimer, co Lincoln; d (stabbed by a servant) unmarried 1628; s by his kinsman (2) ROBERT, 2nd Baron, son of Fulke (ante); sat as MP for Warwick; was a distinguished Gen in the Parliamentary Army during the Civil Wars; k at the assault of Lichfield 1642; s by his el son (3) FRANCIS, 3rd Baron; s by his brother (4) ROBERT, 4th Baron; was one of the Commrs deputed to invite the return of Charles II; d 1676; s by his brother (5) FULKE, 5th Baron; was Recorder of Warwick; d 1710; s by his grandson (6) FULKE, 6th Baron; d unmarried; s by his brother (7) WILLIAM, 7th Baron; was Recorder of Warwick; d 1727; s by his son (8) Sir FRANCIS, KT, 8th Baron; was Recorder of Warwick, and Lord-Lieut of Warwickshire; *cr Earl Brooke* (peerage of Great Britain) 1746, and *Earl of Warwick* (peerage of Great Britain) 1759; d 1773; s by his son (9) GEORGE, 2nd Earl; sat as MP for Warwickshire; was a Lord of Trade and Recorder of Warwick; d 1816; s by his son (10) HENRY RICHARD, KT, 3rd Earl; b 1779; was Lord-Lieut of Warwickshire: m 1816, Sarah, widow of 3rd Baron Monson, and da of 2nd Earl of Mexborough; d 1853; s by his son (11) GEORGE GUY, 4th Earl, b 1818; MP for S Warwickshire (C) 1846-53: m 1852, Lady Anne Charteris, da of 8th Earl of Wemyss and March; d 1893; s by his el son (12) FRANCIS RICHARD CHARLES GUY, 5th Earl, b 1853; MP for Somerset E (C) 1879-85, and for Colchester 1888-92; Lord-Lieut of Essex 1901-19: m 1881, Frances Evelyn, who d 1938, da of late Col Hon Charles Henry Maynard (V Maynard (*ext*), colls); d 1924; s by his el son (13) LEOPOLD GUY FRANCIS MAYNARD, CMG, MVO, 6th Earl; b 1882; Capt 1st Life Guards; Hon Brig-Gen Overseas Mil Forces of Canada, Hon Lieut-Col TF Reserve; S African War 1900, European War 1914-19 as ADC to Com-in-Ch, and Comdg 4th and 12th Canadian Inf Brigs; Reuter's Special Correspondent during Russo-Japanese War 1904-5: m 1909, Elfrida Marjorie, who d 1943, da of Sir William Eden, 7th Bt; d 1928; s by his el son (14) CHARLES GUY FULKE, 7th Earl, b 1911, a Gov Birmingham Univ, Warwicks Kings Sch, R Shakespeare Theatre and Univ Coll Hosp; Mayor of Warwick 1951-52: m 1st, 1933 (m diss 1938), Rose, who d 1972, da of late David Cecil Bingham (*see* E Lucan, colls); 2ndly, 1942 (m diss 1949), Mary Kathleen, el da of late Percy Clifford Hopkinson, of Seabarn, Kingston Gorse, Sussex, and formerly wife of Harold Edward Bell; 3rdly, 1963, Mme Janine Detry de Marès; d 1984; s by his only son (15) DAVID ROBIN FRANCIS GUY, 8th Earl, b 1934; Warwickshire Yeo (TA), late 2nd Lieut LG: m 1956 (m diss 1967), Sarah Anne Chester, da of Alfred Chester Beatty, of Owley, Wittersham, Kent; d 1996; s by his only son (16) GUY DAVID, 9th Earl and present peer; also Baron Brooke.

Waterford, Earl of; title borne by Earl of Shrewsbury.

WATERFORD, MARQUESS OF (Beresford) Sits as BARON TYRONE (GB 1786) (Marquess I 1789, Bt I 1665)

No dependence but in the Cross

JOHN HUBERT DE LA POER BERESFORD, 8th Marquess, and 12th Baronet; b 14 July 1933; s 1934; ed Eton; Lieut Roy Horse Guards Supplementary Reserve: m 1957, Lady Caroline Olein Geraldine Wyndham-Quin, da of 6th Earl of Dunraven and Mount-Earl, and has issue.

Arms – Quarterly: 1st and 4th argent, semée of cross crosslets fitchée and three fleurs-de-lis within a bordure engrailed sable, *Beresford*; 2nd and 3rd argent, a chief indented sable, *De la Poer*. **Crest** – A dragon's head erased azure, the neck pierced with a broken tilting spear, and holding the point broken off in the mouth. **Supporters** – Two angels, habited in white robes reaching to the ankles, hair and wings inverted or, the exterior arm extended and holding a sword erect proper, pommel and hilt gold.
Seats – Curraghmore, Portlaw, co Waterford; Glenbride Lodge, Valleymount, co Wicklow. *Club* – White's.

SONS LIVING

HENRY NICHOLAS DE LA POER (*Earl of Tyrone*), b 23 March 1958: m 1986, Amanda, da of Norman Thompson, of The Castle, Borris-in-Ossary, co Leix, and has issue:—

SONS LIVING— Richard John de la Poer (*Baron Le Poer*), b 19 Aug 1987. — Hon Marcus Patrick de la Poer, b 1990.
DAUGHTER LIVING— *Lady* Camilla Juliet de la Poer, b 1996.

Residence – Luggershall Farm, Owlpen, Dursley, Glos GL11 5BX.

Lord Charles Richard de la Poer (Estancia el Pucara, 6409 Tres Lomas, Prov de Buenos Aries), *b* 1960: *m* 1984, Maria Teresa, da of Sr Gabriel Donoso Phillips, and Sra Maria Isabelle Donosa Rosselot, of Geronimo de Molina 4900, Santiago, Chile, and has issue living, William, *b* 1990, — a son, *b* 1996, — Carolina, *b* 1989.

Lord James Patrick de la Poer, *b* 1965: *m* 1989, Avril, da of Louis Murphy, of Baylough, Portlaw, co Waterford.

DAUGHTER LIVING

Lady Alice Rose de la Poer, *b* 1970.

BROTHER LIVING

Lord Patrick Tristram de la Poer, *b* 1934; *ed* Eton; Capt (ret) RHG: *m* 1964 (*m diss* 1971), Julia, formerly wife of Capt Darel Saumarez Carey, RHG, and da of late Col Thomas Cromwell Williamson, DSO, and has issue living, Valentine Tristram, *b* 1965: *m* 1993, Evelyne D., 2nd da of John Hoskin, of Harlow, Essex, and has issue living, Ferdinand John Patrick *b* 1994, Ludovic William *b* 1998, — Samantha Julia, *b* 1969. *Residence* – Fairview Cottage, Wicks Green, Binfield, Bracknell, Berks RG42 5PF.

WIDOW LIVING OF SON OF SIXTH MARQUESS

Rachel (Thatched Cottage, Church Lane, Stradbally, co Waterford), da of George Kennett Page, of Upton Lodge, Bursledon, Hants: *m* 1945, Maj Lord William Mostyn de la Poer Beresford, who *d* 1973, and has issue (see colls, infra).

COLLATERAL BRANCHES LIVING

(Branch from 2nd son of 6th Marquess of Waterford)

Issue of late Maj Lord William de la Poer Beresford, 2nd son of 6th Marquess, *b* 1905, *d* 1973: *m* 1945, Rachel (ante), da of George Kennett Page, of Upton Lodge, Bursledon, Hants:—
Meriel, *b* 1948: *m* 1970, Joseph Power, of Old Town House Stud, Shanballymore, co Cork, and has issue living, James Anthony, *b* 1972, — Richard Joseph, *b* 1982, — Rosemarie Ann, *b* 1970: *m* 1999, Marc Salingardes, of Memer, 12200 Vaihourles, France, — Jennifer Alice, *b* 1986. ——— Nicola (Englishtown, Stradbally, co Waterford), *b* 1951: *m* 1976 (legally separated 1993), Andreas Minihan, eldest son of Andrew Minihan, of Kylebeg, New Ross, co Wexford, and has issue living, Andrew Peter Mark de la Poer, *b* 1977, — Ian Michael de la Poer, *b* 1980, — William David de la Poer, *b* 1983, — Anna Rachel de la Poer, *b* 1984.

(Branch from 2nd son of 1st Earl of Tyrone) (*Male line in remainder to Earldom of Tyrone*)

Grandchildren of late George Stuart de la Poer Beresford, 2nd son of Arthur George de la Poer Beresford, 2nd son of George William de la Poer Beresford, el son of John Beresford (*b* 1796), el son of Rt Rev George de la Poer Beresford, 2nd son of Rt Hon John de la Poer Beresford (*b* 1738), 2nd son of 1st Earl of Tyrone:—
Issue of late Arthur de la Poer Beresford, *b* 1903, *d* 1931: *m* 1926, Helen, who *d* 1973, da of late Thomas Cull, of Perth, W Australia:—
John de la Poer (3 Park Way, Murray Lakes, S Yunderup, Western Australia 6208), *b* 1927; Snr Technical Officer, Commonwealth Scientific and Industrial Research Organisation (ret 1986): *m* 1951, Pamela, da of late Glen J. Sloman, of Applecross, W Aust, and has issue living, Marcus de la Poer, *b* 1952: *m* 1991, Rilla Commins, and has issue living, Celeste Pamela de la Poer *b* 1995, Natasha Ray *b* (twin) 1995, — Graham de la Poer (7 Characin Court, Sorrento, WA 6020), *b* 1954: *m* 1981, Josephine Vasallo, and has issue living, Lauren Louise *b* 1987, — Simon Stuart de la Poer (28 Gill St, N Perth, WA 6006), *b* 1961: *m* 1991, Elizabeth Parker, and has issue living, Georgia Kate de la Poer *b* 1997, — Shelley Louise, *b* 1957: *m* 1980, Graham Ekert, of 10 Boya Crescent, Boya, WA 6056, and has issue living, Cassandra Claire *b* 1985, Melissa Louise *b* 1987, Alexandra Michelle *b* 1990. ——— Margaret Pamela de la Poer, *b* 1930: *m* 1953, Lt-Col Eric McPherson McCormick, R Australian Regt (ret), of Unit 4 Nicolle Court, 42 Kenyon Circuit, Monash, ACT 2904, Australia, and has issue living, Gordon Rory (16 Bedford St, Deakin, ACT 2600, Australia), *b* 1954: *m* 1982, Alice Jeanette Robinson, and has issue living, Fergus George *b* 1984, Harriet Faith *b* 1986, — Peter James (11 McManus Place, Calwell, ACT 2905, Australia), *b* 1956: *m* 1983, Jennifer Louise Spence, and has issue living, Rory Michael *b* 1984, Mitchell James *b* 1986, Georgia Mae *b* 1991, Isabella Grace *b* 1995, — Angus Roy (231 Namatjira Drive, Fisher, ACT 2611, Australia), *b* 1957: *m* 1985, Dianna Marie McKeough, and has issue living, Thomas John *b* 1990, Ashleigh Louise *b* 1987, — Hamish John, *b* 1961.

Issue of late Major Brian de la Poer Beresford, MC, Australian Forces, *b* 1910, *ka* in New Guinea 1942: *m* (April) 1942, Valmai, only da of Merlyn B. Jones, of Perth, W Australia:—
Brian George de la Poer (*posthumous*) (3 Circe Circle, Dalkeith, W Australia), *b* 1943; Bar-at-law and Solicitor, Australia: *m* 1964, Deborah Frances, only da of Albert Francis Gamble, of Evalley, Koorda, W Australia, and has issue living, Brian James de la Poer, *b* 1967, — Victoria Jane, *b* 1965.

Grandchildren of late Arthur George de la Poer Beresford (ante):—
Issue of late George Stuart de la Poer Beresford (twin), *b* 1877, *d* 1965: *m* 1st, 1900, Margaret, who *d* 1920, da of late Edward Hooper, of Melbourne, Victoria; 2ndly, 1923, Kathleen, who *d* 1950, da of late Thomas Cull, of Perth, W Australia; 3rdly, 1950, Faith, who *d* 1984, da of Rev F. G. O'Halloran, of Perth, W Australia, and widow of Sqdn Ldr Preston Williams, MC:—

(By 1st *m*) Rosemary de la Poer, *b* 1917: *m* (Feb) 1948, Flight Lt Reginald Harold Sutton, DFC, RAAF, who *d* 1991, and *d* 1998, leaving issue, David Beresford (79 Florence Rd, Nedlands, W Australia 6009), *b* 1953: *m* 1980, Catherine Anne Brewster, and has issue living, Hannah Catherine *b* 1986, Brigitte Rose *b* 1989, — Georgia Jane, *b* (Dec) 1948: *m* 1st, 1979 (*m diss* 1988), Peter Jonathan Schofield; 2ndly, 1991, James Richard Hutchison, of 3 Airedale Av, E Hawthorn, Vic 3123, and has issue living (by 1st *m*), Jonathan Henry Beresford *b* 1986, — Rosemary Ann, *b* 1950: *m* 1974, William Richard Kilpatrick, of Allanvale, Great Western, Victoria 3377, and has issue living, Jane Regina *b* 1977, Catherine Ann *b* 1979, Annabel Clare *b* 1984.

Issue of late Marcus John de la Poer Beresford, *b* 1882, *d* 1952: *m* 1st, 1910, Alice Janet Schmidt, who *d* 1935, of Victoria, Australia; 2ndly, 1936, Edith, da of late Capt George Wilkins, of Young, NS Wales:—
(By 1st *m*) Marcus de la Poer, *b* 1912: *m* 1936, Marie Helmers, and has issue living, Marcus Edward de la Poer, *b* 1937, — Brian de la Poer, *b* 1942. —— John de la Poer, *b* 1913; S-W Pacific 1944-45 with Australian Imperial Force: *m* 1936, Helen Wilson, and has issue living, John de la Poer, *b* 1942, — Helen de la Poer, *b* 1937, — Barbara de la Poer, *b* 1940. *Residence* – Turramurra, NS Wales.

Issue of late Henry Mayo de la Poer Beresford, *b* 1889, *d* 1948: *m* 1921, Nathalie, who *d* 1963, da of late Robert Muir, of Middle Brighton, Victoria, Australia:—
Joan de la Poer (Corner Cottage, Sandy Lane, Kingswood, Surrey KT20 6LZ), *b* 1922: *m* 1965, Ralph Louis Bewick, MBE, TD, R Fusiliers (TA) (ret), who *d* 1985. —— Judith de la Poer, *b* 1930: *m* 1954 (*m diss* 1983), Lt-Col Robin William Hone, R Australian Regt (ret), who *d* 1992, and has issue living, David Christopher (57 Gainsford St, London SE1 2NB), *b* 1958: *m* 1993, Wendy Jane, da of Barry Moss, and has issue living, Luke William *b* 1995, — Carolyn Louise, *b* 1963: *m* 1984, Andrew John McLean (3 Allenby St, Clontarf, NSW 2093, Australia), and has issue living, Christopher Andrew *b* 1987, Alexandra Louise *b* 1993, Anastasia Leah *b* 1994. *Address* – Unit 1, 16 Alpha St, Kensington Park, S Aust 5068.

Issue of late Capt William Russell de la Poer Beresford, MC, *b* 1893; *d* 1938: *m* 1923, Marie Isobel, who *d* 1944, da of Samuel Cowper Ward of Adelaide, S Australia:—
Diana Mary de la Poer (139 Stanley St, N Adelaide, S Australia 5006), *b* 1924: *m* 1946, Arthur John Watson, AM, who *d* 1991, and has had issue, Christopher John Beresford (69 Highlever Rd, W10), *b* 1948: *m* 1st 1970 (*m diss* 1976), Georgiana Henry; 2ndly, 1977, Lalita Georgiana Williams, da of W. Peter Halliday, MBE, and has issue living (by 1st *m*), Michaela *b* 1970 (by 2nd *m*) Adelaide Elizabeth Beresford *b* 1982, Francesca Mary Beresford *b* 1984, — Johanna Mary Beresford *b* 1950: *m* 1st, 1972 (*m diss* 1979), Rolf Alexander Detmering; 2ndly, 1992, Geoffrey Robert Scott, of 11 Ferdinand St, Hunters Hill, NSW, Australia, and has issue living, (by Ian Darnton Hill) Phoebe Jane Beresford *b* 1981, (by 2nd *m*) Georgia Anne Beresford *b* 1992, — Robina Anne Beresford, *b* 1960: *m* 1986, Richard Goldsmith Daw, of 40 Melville St, Hawthorn, Victoria, Australia, and *d* 1994. —— Marie Suzanne de la Poer, *b* 1925: *m* 1st, 1946, Murray Frew Bonnin, solicitor, late Austn Imperial Forces, who *d* 1978; 2ndly, 1979, David Hans Heysen, of Heysen Rd, Hahndorf, S Australia 5245, son of late Sir Hans Heysen, and has issue living (by 1st *m*), John Frew, *b* 1951, — David Frew, *b* 1952: *m* 1st, 1976, Jennifer Crowe; 2ndly, 1989, Angela Jane Dunstan, and has issue living (by 2nd *m*), William Frew *b* 1990, Annabel Beresford *b* 1992.

Grandchildren of late Richard de la Poer Beresford, 3rd son of George William de la Poer Beresford (ante):—
Issue of late Claude Richard de la Poer Beresford, *b* 1888, *d* 1945: *m* 1915, Edith Marion, who *d* 1977, da of Christopher Beaven, of Adelaide, S Aust:—
Ben Richard de la Poer, *b* 1927; late RAN; ASA; Member of Australian Stock Exchange: *m* 1955, Janet Marcia, da of John Essington Grime, of The Pines, Green Point, NSW, and has issue living, William Richard de la Poer (472 Argyle St, Moss Vale, NSW 2577, Australia), *b* 1959; BVSc: *m* 1987, Sally Isobel, da of John Walsh, of Sutton Forest, NSW, and has issue living, Samantha Jane *b* 1988, Georgia Kate *b* 1993, — John Ben de la Poer, *b* 1965; BAgrSc, — Charles Patrick de la Poer (67 First Av, St Peters, S Australia 5069), *b* 1966; LLB: *m* 1992, Sarah Jane, da of Colin Hagger, of North Adelaide, S Australia, and has issue living, Kate Victoria *b* 1995, Mary Alexandra *b* 1997, — Mary Lynne de la Poer, *b* 1956; BappSc (Physio): *m* 1977, Stewart Graham Teague, of 354A Kensington Rd, Erindale, S Australia, and has issue living, Nicholas James *b* 1982, Andrew Graham *b* 1984, James Robert *b* 1986, Benjamin Stewart *b* 1988, Sarah Jane *b* 1980. *Residence* – 36 Brunswick St, North Walkerville, S Aust 5081. —— Donald Charles de la Poer (97 Arthur St, Surry Hills, NSW 2010, Australia), *b* 1933: *m* 1962 (*m diss* 1979), Ruth Tisdall, and has issue living, Peter Mark de la Poer, *b* 1965, — Susan Jane de la Poer, *b* 1964. —— Molly Clodagh de la Poer (50 Second Av, St Peters, S Australia 5069), *b* 1920: *m* 1940, Harold de Vall Amphlett, who *d* 1988, and has issue living, John de Vall, *b* 1949: *m* 1976, Margaret, da of Robert Stokes, SM and has issue living, Scott Francis *b* 1980, Mark John de Vall *b* 1982, Alice Louise *b* 1988, — Margaret de Vall, *b* 1947: *m* 1968, Daniel Knight, and has issue living, Andrew de Vall *b* 1971, (Rebecca) Anne *b* 1974.

Issue of late Guy Erroll de la Poer Beresford, *b* 1889, *d* 1944: *m* 1921, Dorothy Margaret, who *d* 1956, da of W. T. McCoy, of Adelaide:—
Richard de la Poer (5 George St, Norwood 5067, S Australia), *b* 1922; 1939-45 War in RAAF: *m* 1945, Elizabeth Leitch, and has issue living, Marcus Richard de la Poer (Brownhill Creek Rd, Mitcham, S Australia; PO Box 113, Mitcham, S Australia 5062), *b* 1950, — Melanie de la Poer (4/30 Lavender St, N Sydney, NSW 2060, Australia), *b* 1948; is a Dr. —— Bunty Margaret de la Poer, *b* 1925: *m* 1st, 1947 (*m diss* 1970), Jan Edgar Marr, late AIF; 2ndly, 1980, John Adams, of PO Box 507, Bowral, NSW 2576, Australia, and has issue living (by 1st *m*), Carolyn Ann, *b* 1950: *m* 1979, Sam Phillips, of PO Box 251, Mudgeeraba, Qld 4213, Australia, and has issue living, Jason *b* 1981, Fiona *b* 1983, — Stephanie Jane (4/111 Salerno St, Isle of Capri, Qld 4217, Australia), *b* 1951; has issue living, Rafe Marr SHOLER *b* 1984, — Katrina Louise, *b* 1957: *m* 1982, Michael Stuart Orme, of 425 Friday Hut Rd, Possum Creek, Bangalow, NSW 2479, Australia, and has issue living, Zachary Oscar *b* 1985, Alexander Mikhail *b* 1986, April Amber *b* 1993.

Grandson of late Edward Beresford, yr son of George de la Poer Beresford, el son of Rt Hon and Most Rev Marcus Gervais Beresford, DD, Archbishop of Armagh, 2nd son of Rt Rev George de la Poer Beresford (ante):—
Issue of late George Henry William de la Poer Beresford, *b* 1904, *d* 1961: *m* 1926 (*m diss* 1949), Mary Isobel, who *d* 1989, da of George Richardson, of Molesley:—
John George de la Poer (Aubawn, Lamorna Cove, Penzance, Cornwall TR19 6XW), *b* 1927: *m* 1960, Jeanne Frances, da of William Steward, of London, and has issue living, Stephen de la Poer (27 Bearton Av, Hitchin, Herts SG5 1NZ), *b* 1961: *m* 1991, Aline Rogers, and has issue living, Jack George de la Poer *b* 1994, Philip Alexander de la Poer *b* 1996, —

Mark de la Poer (25 High St, Lindfield, W Sussex RH16 2HJ), *b* 1962: *m* 1989, Sophie Grissa, and has issue living, Justin de la Poer *b* 1989, Héloïse *b* 1992, — Clare Jeanne (25 High St, Lindfield, W Sussex RH16 2HJ), *b* 1964.

Grandchildren of late George Henry William de la Poer Beresford (ante):—
Issue of late Timothy Edward de la Poer Beresford, *b* 1931, *d* 1964: *m* 1955, Mary Thom Leburn (Maureen) (who *m* 2ndly 1965, Maj Matthew Alexander Forrester, of Little Etchden, Bethersden, Kent TN26 3DS), only child of late John Waugh, of Edinburgh:—
Michael John de la Poer, *b* 1957. —— Karen Mary de la Poer, *b* 1959: *m* 1984, Gordon James Findlay.

Grandson of late Lt-Col Kennedy Beresford, el son of Maj Henry Marcus Beresford, yr son of Rt Hon and Most Rev Marcus Gervais Beresford, Archbishop of Armagh (ante):—
Issue of late Col Gervais de la Poer Beresford, MBE, MC, DSM, *b* 1895, *d* 1979: *m* 1st, 1927, Nada Celina, who *d* 1956, da of Harry L. Wormald, of Bramhall, Cheshire; 2ndly, 1957, Rosemary Helen Arnaud Gange, da of late Lt-Col G. E. Painter, RE, of Epsom, Surrey:—
(By 1st *m*) Michael Marcus Gervais de la Poer (26 Ladbroke Sq, W11), *b* 1928; *ed* Marlborough, and at Birmingham Univ; Lt 8th Hussars (Reserve): *m* 1975, Ann Veronica Nieburg, of S Africa.

Grandson of late Col William Randal Hamilton Beresford-Ash, 3rd son of late John Barré Beresford (infra):—
Issue of late Maj Douglas Beresford-Ash, *b* 1887, *d* 1976: *m* 1930, Lady Betty Helena Joanna Rous, who *d* 1969, da of 3rd Earl of Stradbroke:—
John Randal (Ashbrook, co Londonderry; Carlton Club), *b* 1938; *ed* Eton: *m* 1968, Agnès Marie Colette, da of Count Guy de Lamberterie, of Ensouleiada, Avenue de Benefiat, Cannes, and has issue living, Melanie Anne Helena Charlotte, *b* 1968, — Louisa-Jane Marie Caroline, *b* 1971, — Angélique Mary Elisa, *b* 1978.

Granddaughter of late John Barré Beresford, el son of Henry Barré Beresford, yst son of Rt Hon John de la Poer Beresford (*b* 1738) (ante):—
Issue of late Lieut-Col Marcus John Barré de la Poer Beresford, DSO, *b* 1868, *d* as a result of enemy action 1944: *m* 1914, Alma, who *d* 1968, da of David Methven, of Hillside, 31 Elsworthy Rd, Regent's Park, NW3:—
Patricia Douglas Methven, *b* 1924: *m* 1974, Maurice William Alfred Carter, of Worthing, Sussex.

(Branch from 3rd son of 1st Earl of Tyrone)

Descendants of late Most Rev Hon William Beresford, DD (3rd son of 1st Earl of Tyrone), who was *cr* Baron Decies 1812 (see that title).

PREDECESSORS – **(1)** *Sir* TRISTRAM Beresford, MP for Londonderry, was *cr* a Baronet 1665; *d* 1673; *s* by his son **(2)** *Sir* RANDAL, 2nd Bt; *s* by the son **(3)** *Sir* TRISTRAM, 3rd Bt; commanded a Regt of Foot against James II, and was attainted by Parliament; *d* 1701; *s* by his son **(4)** *Sir* MARCUS, 4th Bt: *m* 1717, Lady Catharine Poer (*Baroness La Poer* in her own right, *cr* by writ of summons 1375 *et seq*), da and heiress of James, 3rd Earl of Tyrone and Baron La Poer; *cr* Baron Beresford, of Beresford, co Cavan, and *Viscount Tyrone* (peerage of Ireland) 1720, and *Earl of Tyrone* (peerage of Ireland) 1746; *d* 1763; *s* by his son **(5)** GEORGE DE LA POER, 2nd Earl, who in 1769 *s* by his mother in the Barony of De La Poer; *cr* Baron Tyrone, of Haverfordwest, co Pembroke (peerage of Great Britain) 1786, and *Marquess of Waterford* (peerage of Ireland) 1789; *d* 1800; *s* by his son **(6)** HENRY DE LA POER, KP, PC, 2nd Marquess was Gov of co Waterford and Col of Waterford Militia; *d* 1826; *s* by his el son **(7)** HENRY DE LA POER, KP, 3rd Marquess; *d* 1859; *s* by his brother **(8)** JOHN DE LA POER, 4th Marquess; *b* 1814; was in Holy Orders, a Rural Dean, and incumbent of Mullaghbrack: *m* 1843, Christiana, da of Charles Powell Leslie, MP, of Glaslough, co Monaghan; *d* 1866; *s* by his son **(9)** JOHN HENRY DE LA POER, PC, KP, 5th Marquess, *b* 1844; Lord-Lieut of co Waterford; MP for Waterford Co (*C*) 1865-6, and Master of the Buckhounds 1885-6: *m* 1st, 1872, Florence Grosvenor, who *d* 1873, da of Major George Rowley, Bombay Army, and divorced wife of Hon John C. W. Vivian; 2ndly, 1874, Lady Blanche Elizabeth Adelaide, da of 8th Duke of Beaufort; *d* 1895; *s* by his only son **(10)** HENRY DE LA POER, KP, 6th Marquess, *b* 1875: *m* 1897, Lady Beatrix Frances Fitzmaurice, GBE, who *d* 1953 (having *m* 2ndly, 1918, 12th Duke of St Albans), da of 5th Marquess of Lansdowne; *d* 1911; *s* by his el son **(11)** JOHN CHARLES DE LA POER, 7th Marquess, *b* 1901: *m* 1930, Juliet Mary (who *d* 1987, having *m* 2ndly, 1946, Lient-Col John Eric Durnford Silcock), da of Major David Balcarres Lindsay; *d* 1934; *s* by his el son **(12)** JOHN HUBERT DE LA POER, 8th Marquess and present peer; also Earl of Tyrone, Viscount Tyrone, Baron Le Poer, Baron Beresford, and Baron Tyrone.

WATERPARK, BARON (Cavendish) (Baron I 1792, Bt GB 1755)

Secure by caution

FREDERICK CARYLL PHILIP CAVENDISH, 7th Baron, and 8th Baronet; *b* 6 Oct 1926; *s* 1948; *ed* Eton; late Lieut Grenadier Gds; Assist Dist Comdt Kenya Police Reserve 1952-54; Dir CSE Aviation 1962, Dep Chm 1983-89, Ch Exec 1989-90; Trustee RAF Museum since 1994: *m* 1951, Danièle Alice, da of Roger Guirche, of Paris, and has issue.

𝔄rms – Sable, three stags' heads cabossed argent, attired or, within a bordure of the second. 𝔠rest – On a ducal coronet or, a serpent nowed fessewise proper. 𝔖upporters – *Dexter*, a stag, per fesse indented gules and sable, attired and unguled or; *sinister*, a stag proper, attired and unguled or, and gorged with a chaplet of four roses argent and azure, alternatively.
Residences – 74 Elm Park Rd, SW3 6AU; Broadlands Stud, Somerset West, Cape Prov, S Africa. *Clubs* – Cavalry and Guards, and The Air Squadron.

SON LIVING

Hon RODERICK (RORY) ALEXANDER, *b* 10 Oct 1959: *m* 1989, Anne, da of late Hon Luke Asquith (*see* By Asquith of Bishopstone), and has issue living, Luke Frederick, *b* 17 Sept 1990, — Thomas Matthew Arthur, *b* 1997. *Residence* – 25 Archel Rd, W14 9QJ.

DAUGHTERS LIVING

Hon Caroline Laurence Patricia, *b* 1952: *m* 1979, Richard Michael George Goulding, and has issue (*see* Goulding, Bt).
Hon Juliet Enid Marie Gabrielle, *b* 1953: *m* 19—, Charles Dumaresq Nicholson, yr son of late Arthur Wilfrid Nicholson, of Hartham Park, Corsham, Wilts, and has issue living, Isabel, *b* 1986, — Claire, *b* 1988.

SISTER LIVING

Patricia Enid (Broadlands Stud, Somerset West, CP, S Africa), *b* 1925: *m* 1st, 1950 (*m diss* 1954), Frank Thomas O'Neill; 2ndly, 1958, Count Aymon de Roussy de Sales; 3rdly, 1969, her former husband, Frank Thomas O'Neill.

DAUGHTERS LIVING OF SIXTH BARON

(By 2nd marriage)

Hon Margaret, *b* 1907: *m* 1934, Wallace Edward Thomas Leaver, BSc who *d* 1972, and has issue living, Diana Cavendish, *b* 1938: *m* 1961, Charles Peter Parnell Wiggins, of East Cross, Tenterden, Kent, and has issue living, Rupert Alexander Cavendish *b* 1963, Philippa Cavendish *b* 1962, — Elizabeth Cavendish, *b* 1942. *Residence* – St Benets, Becch Hill, Bridge, Canterbury.

Hon Winifred *b* 1909: *m* 1929, Albert Frank Tribe, Trinity House Pilot, who *d* 1962, having assumed by deed poll 1944 the additional surname of Cavendish, and by letters patent, 1944 the Arms of Cavendish quarterly with Tribe, and has issue living, Barrie Cavendish (27 Strickmere, Stratford St Mary, Colchester, Essex), *b* 1930: *m* 1957, Jane McGeorge, only da of late Surg Rear-Adm David Duncan, CB, OBE, and has issue living, *Eur Ing* Alan Cavendish (128 Hill Village Rd, Four Oaks, Sutton Coldfield, W Midlands B75 5HN) *b* 1960; BSc Eng, C Eng, FI Mech E, F Weld I: *m* 1996, Susan Mary, only da of Roy Willson, Sonia Cavendish *b* 1963; BSc Chem: *m* 1990, David Richard Ellis, and has issue living, Emily Jane *b* 1996, Karen Louise *b* (twin) 1996. *Residence* – 27 Strickmere, Stratford St Mary, Colchester, Essex.

COLLATERAL BRANCH LIVING

Grandsons of late Charles Tyrell Cavendish, second son of late Hon Richard Cavendish, 2nd son of 2nd Baron:—
Issue of late Tyrell William Cavendish, *b* 1875, *d* 1912: *m* 1906, Julia Florence, who *d* 1963, only child of Henry Siegel, of New York:—
†Henry Siegel, *b* 1908; *ed* Eton, and Trin Coll Camb; European War 1939-45 as Squadron-Leader Auxiliary Air Force: *m* 1940, Diana Linda, da of Edward Hewish Ryle, and *d* 1996, leaving issue, William Henry Tyrell, *b* 1940; *ed* Eton. *Residence* – 15 Cadogan Lane, SW1. —— Geoffrey Manners (7 Gema Close, Allestree, Derby, DE22 2UL), *b* 1910; *ed* Stowe; CEng; MIEE; Member of Institution of British Radio Engineers; Diploma of Faraday House Engineering Coll; late Air Min Examiner in Scientific and Electrical Section of Aeronautical Inspection Directorates: *m* 1st, 1937, Caecilia Frances Patricia, who *d* 1968, da of Godfrey Pharazyn, of Waewaepa, Dannevirke, Hawkes Bay, NZ; 2ndly, 1967, Mrs Pamela Newman, and has issue living (by 1st *m*) Caroline Anne, *b* 1938: *m* 1964, Charles Grellan Aliaga-Kelly, BArch, ARIBA, FRTPI, FRIAI, Dublin Planning Officer (ret), of Clare Villa, Coliemore Rd, Dalkey, co Dublin, and has issue living, William John *b* 1967; *ed* Univ Coll, Dublin, — Caecilia Bridget, *b* 1941: *m* 1979, Ralph Rokeby Johnson, of Kelsey Farm, PO Box 2001, Stellenbosch, Cape 7601, S Africa; and Arthingworth, PO Box 1513, Rancho Santa Fé, Calif 92067, USA, and has issue living, Henry Ralph Cavendish *b* 1979.

PREDECESSORS – **(1)** *Rt Hon* HENRY Cavendish, PC; MP for Lismore, Teller of the Exchequer in Ireland, Collector for Cork, and a Commr for Revenue (Ireland); *cr* a *Baronet* 1755; *d* 1776; *s* by his son **(2)** *Sir* HENRY, PC, 2nd Bt; sat as MP for Lostwithiel; was Receiver-Gen in Ireland: *m* 1757, Sarah, da and heir of Richard Bradshaw, which lady was in 1792 *cr Baroness Waterpark*, of Waterpark, co Cork (peerage of Ireland), with remainder to her issue male by Sir Henry Cavendish; she *d* 1807; *s* by her son **(3)** RICHARD, 2nd Baron, who in 1804 had *s* his father as 3rd Bt; *d* 1830; *s* by his son **(4)** HENRY MANNERS, 3rd Baron; *b* 1793; was Col Derbyshire Militia, and a Lord-in-Waiting: *m* 1837, Hon Eliza Jane, VA, who *d* 1894, da of 1st Viscount Anson; *d* 1863; *s* by his son **(5)** HENRY ANSON, 4th Baron; *b* 1839: *m* 1873, Emily, who *d* 1925, da of late John Stenning; *d* 1912; *s* by his son **(6)** CHARLES FREDERICK, *b* 1883; *d* 1932; *s* by his cousin **(7)** HENRY SHEPPARD HART (el son of late William Thomas Cavendish, grandson of 2nd Baron), 6th Baron; *b* 1876; was a hunter and explorer in Africa, Patagonia, Australia, Solomon Islands, and Canada: *m* 1st, 1902 (*m diss* 1906), Isabel Emilie (an actress), who *d* 1927, da of John Wimburn Jay; 2ndly, 1906 (*m diss* 1913), May, who *d* 1969, da of William Ernest Burbridge, of Bromley, Kent; 3rdly, 1913 (*m diss* 1919), Elise, da of Emmanuel Adolphe Herran, formerly Sec to French Embassy in London: 4thly, 1920 (*m diss* 1929), Georgette, da of Ivan Zlateffmoloff Chandronnier of Bulgaria; 5thly, 1929, Jeanne, who *d* 1968, da of Pierre Lassallette; *d* 1948; *s* by his nephew **(8)** FREDERICK CARYLL PHILIP (only son of late Brig-Gen Frederick William Laurence Sheppard Hart Cavendish, brother of 6th Baron), 7th Baron and present peer.

WATKINS, BARONY OF (Watkins) (Extinct 1983)

WIDOW LIVING OF LIFE BARON

BRONWEN RICHARDS (*Baroness Watkins*), da of late Thomas Stather, of Talgarth: *m* 1936, Baron Watkins (Life Baron), who *d* 1983.
Residence – Bronafon Penyfan Rd, Brecon, Powys.

WATKINSON, VISCOUNTCY OF (Watkinson) (Extinct 1995)

DAUGHTERS LIVING OF FIRST VISCOUNT

Hon Sarah Margaret, *b* 1944: *m* 1965, David Bethune Spicer, of Vingers, West Harting, Petersfield, Hants GU31 5NX, and has issue living, Mary Bethune, *b* 1966: *m* 1998, Jason W. K. Lambert, son of late Dr K. C. Lambert, of Cambridge, — Joanna Margaret, *b* 1968, — Eliza Jane, *b* 1970: *m* 1994, Rupert Charles Melbourn Jarvis, only son of Peter Jarvis, of Lauder, Berwickshire, and has issue living, Euan David Xavier *b* 1998, — Alice Bethune, *b* 1985.

Hon Rosemary Jane, *b* 1947: *m* 1976 (*m diss* 1998), Barrie Robert Musgrave, and has issue living, Oliver Robert, *b* 1977, — Rowan Gill, *b* 1979.

WIDOW LIVING OF FIRST AND LAST VISCOUNT

VERA (*Viscountess Watkinson*), da of John Langmead, of Northwood, Ford, Sussex: *m* 1939, the 1st Viscount Watkinson, CH, PC, who *d* 1995, when the title became extinct.

Watson, family name of Baron Manton.

WATSON OF INVERGOWRIE, BARON (Watson) (Life Baron 1997)

MICHAEL GOODALL (MIKE) WATSON, son of late Clarke Carter Watson, of Dundee; b 1 May 1949; ed Invergowrie Primary Sch, Dundee High Sch, and Heriot-Watt Univ (BA 1974); Development Offr and tutor, Mid-Derbyshire WEA 1974-77; Trade Union Official ASTMS (now MSF) 1977-89 (Divisional Offr 1977-87, Regional Offr 1987-89); MP for Glasgow Central (Lab) 1989-97; Memb Select Cttee on Parliamentary Commr for Administration 1990-95, and Public Accounts Cttee 1995-97; Chm PLP Cttee on Overseas Development Aid 1991-97; Sec PLP Trade Union Group 1990-97; Memb Exec Cttee Labour Party Scot Council 1987-90; Dir P.S. Communication Consultants Ltd since 1997; author; cr Baron Watson of Invergowrie, of Invergowrie in Perth and Kinross (Life Baron) 1997: m 1986, Lorraine Thérèse, da of late William McManus, of Glasgow.

Address – House of Lords, Westminster, SW1A 0PW.

WAVELL, EARLDOM OF (Wavell) (Extinct 1953)

DAUGHTERS LIVING OF FIRST EARL

Lady (Eugénie) Pamela, b 1918: m 1942, Arthur Francis Walter Humphrys, OBE, only son of Lieut-Col Sir Francis Humphrys, GCMG, GCVO, KBE, CIE, and has issue living, Francis Wavell Harold James, b 1944, — (Henry) Owen Rookhurst, b 1946, — (Eugénie) Cecilia, b 1950.

Lady Joan Patricia Quirk, b 1923: m 1st, 1943, Capt Hon Simon Nevill Astley, 7th Hussars, who d 1946 (see B Hastings); 2ndly, 1948, Maj Harry Alastair Gordon, MC, Gordon Highlanders, who d 1965; 3rdly, 1973, Maj Donald Struan Robertson, Scots Gds, who d 1991, of Winkfield Plain Farm, Winkfield, Windsor, Berks SL4 4QU, and has issue living (by 1st m) (see B Hastings), — (by 2nd m) Anthea Leila, b 1949: m 1st, 1970 (m diss 1980), Timothy Hanbury; 2ndly, 1982, William D. Dalton, of The Old Schoolhouse, 47A Grove Lane, SE5 8SP, and has issue living (by 1st m), Jesse b 1974, Griffin b 1975, Luella b 1977, — Patricia (19 Chelsea Sq, SW3), b 1951: m 1977 (m diss 1990), Sir John Auld Mactaggart, 4th Bt.

WAVERLEY, VISCOUNT (Anderson) (Viscount UK 1952)

JOHN DESMOND FORBES ANDERSON, 3rd Viscount; b 31 Oct 1949; s 1990; ed Malvern: m 1994, Her Excellency Dr Ursula Helen Barrow, LLM, PhD, High Commr for Belize, da of Raymond Hugh Barrow, SC, Bar-at-law, of Belize City, and has issue.

Arms – Argent, a saltire engrailed between a mullet in chief and a lotus flower in base, and in each flank a crescent gules; on a chief sable three martlets of the field. Crest – A demi-lion rampant or, armed and langued azure, holding in his dexter forepaw a branch of olive proper. Supporters – Two horses argent, crined and unguled or.

Address – c/o House of Lords, SW1A 0PW

SON LIVING

Hon FORBES ALASTAIR RUPERT, b 15 Feb 1996.

SISTERS LIVING AND DECEASED

Hon Ida Christina Romaine, b 1952; k in a motor accident in Africa 1972.

Hon Patricia Mairead Janet, b 1955; resumed her maiden name 1983: m 1st, 1979 (m diss 1983), Charles R. Roberts; 2ndly, 1989, Leon Clifton, of Colorado, USA, and has issue living (by 2nd m), William Scott, b 1990, — India Rose Veronica Romaine, b 1994. Residence – Chanders, Aldworth, Berks RG8 9RU.

AUNT LIVING (*daughter of 1st Viscount*)

Hon Dame Mary Mackenzie, DBE, *b* 1916; Brig WRAC; Dir WRAC; and Hon ADC to HM, 1967-70; MBE (Mil) 1958, DBE (Mil) 1970: *m* 1973, Frithjof Pihl, of Engö, Tjøme, Norway, who *d* 1988. *Residence* – 7 Kiln Gardens, Hartley Wintney, Hants RG27 8RG.

WIDOW LIVING OF SECOND VISCOUNT

LORNA MYRTLE ANN (*Dowager Viscountess Waverley*), da of late Lt-Col Frederick Hill Ledgerwood, late IA: *m* 1948, the 2nd Viscount Waverley, who *d* 1990. *Residence* – Chanders, Aldworth, Berks RG8 9RU.

PREDECESSORS – **(1)** *Rt Hon Sir* JOHN ANDERSON, GCB, OM, GCSI, GCIE, FRS, son of late David A. P. Anderson, of Westland House, Eskbank, Midlothian; *b* 1882; entered Colonial Office 1905, became Principal Clerk National Health Insurance Commn 1912, Sec thereto 1913, Sec Min of Shipping 1917-19, Second Sec Min of Health 1919, Chm and a Commr of Board of Inland Revenue 1919, Joint Under-Sec for Ireland 1920, and Permanent Under-Sec of State for Home Depart 1922; Gov of Bengal 1932-37, Lord Privy Seal 1938-9, Sec of State for Home Depart and Min of Home Security 1939-40, Lord Pres of the Council (Member of War Cabinet) 1940-43, and Chancellor of the Exchequer 1943-45; Chm of Port of London Authority 1946-58; sat as MP for Edinburgh, St Andrews, Glasgow, and Aberdeen Univs (*National*) 1938-50; *cr Viscount Waverley*, of Westdean, co Sussex (peerage of United Kingdom) 1952: *m* 1st, 1907, Christina, who *d* 1920, da of late Andrew Mackenzie, of Edinburgh; 2ndly, 1941, Ava, who *d* 1974, da of late J. E. C. Bodley, and widow of Ralph Wigram, CMG; *d* 1958; *s* by his only son **(2)** DAVID ALASTAIR PEARSON, 2nd Viscount; *b* 1911, MRCS England and LRCP London 1936, MRCP 1946, FRCP 1957, Consultant Physician, Royal Berkshire Hospital, Reading: *m* 1948, Lorna Myrtle Ann, da of late Lt-Col Frederick Hill Ledgerwood, late IA; *d* 1990; *s* by his only son **(3)** JOHN DESMOND FORBES, 3rd Viscount and present peer.

WEATHERILL, BARON (Weatherill) (Life Baron 1992)

(BRUCE) BERNARD WEATHERILL, PC, son of late Bernard Weatherill, of Spring Hill, Guildford; *b* 25 Nov 1920; *ed* Malvern; Hon DCL Univ of William and Mary, Williamsburg, Virginia, USA 1988, Hon DCL Univ of Kent at Canterbury 1990, and Hon DL Open Univ 1993; Hon Bencher, Lincoln's Inn 1990; DL Kent 1992; commn'd 4/7th Royal Dragoon Guards 1940, transferred to IA (19th King George V's Own Lancers) and served 1939-45 War in Burma and NW Europe; Bernard Weatherill Ltd, Tailors, of Savile Row 1946-70 (Man Dir 1957-70), Pres since 1992; Lord Commr HM Treasury 1970-71, Vice-Chamberlain Royal Household 1971-72, Comptroller 1972-73, Treasurer and Dep Chief Whip 1973-74, Chm Ways and Means and Dep Speaker 1979-83, Speaker of the House of Commons 1983-92; Chm Commonwealth Speakers and Presiding Officers 1986-88; Chm Guildford Conservative Assocn 1959-63, and Member Nat Union of Conservative Party 1963-64; Trustee Prince's Youth Business Trust since 1992; Chm The Industry and Parliament Trust 1994; Convenor of Cross Bench Peers in House of Lords 1995; High Bailiff Westminster Abbey since 1989; Vice Chancellor Order of St John of Jerusalem since 1992; Freeman City of London; MP Croydon NE (*C*) 1964-92; *cr* PC 1980, and *Baron Weatherill*, of NE Croydon, London Borough of Croydon (Life Baron) 1992: *m* 1949, Lyn, da of late Henry Thomas Eatwell, of Whitehall, Sandwich Bay, Kent, and has issue.

Arms – Azure, a cross floretty or surmounting two lances in saltire proper, flying from each a forked pennon per fess gules and argent. **Crest** – A horse rampant argent supporting a mace erect or. **Supporters** – *Dexter*, a Captain in the 19th King George V's Own Lancers (Indian Army); *sinister*, a Knight of Justice of the Most Venerable Order of the Hospital of St John of Jerusalem both proper.

SONS LIVING

Hon Bernard Richard, *b* 1951; *ed* Malvern; QC 1996: *m* 1977, Sally Maxwell Fisher, and has issue living, Thomas Bernard, *b* 1984, — Julia Rosemary, *b* 1982.

Hon Henry Bruce, *b* 1953; *ed* Malvern: *m* 1978, Susan Mary Dutton, and has issue living, James Edward Bruce, *b* 1983, — Benjamin Harry Charles, *b* 1986, — Sophie, *b* 1989.

DAUGHTER LIVING

Hon Virginia, *b* 1955: *m* 1982, Alan Charles Lovell, and and has issue living, Emma Charlotte, *b* 1985, — Lucinda Mary, *b* 1986.

WEDDERBURN OF CHARLTON, BARON (Wedderburn) Life Baron (1977)

KENNETH WILLIAM WEDDERBURN, son of Herbert John Wedderburn; *b* 13 April 1927; *ed* Aske's (Hatcham) Gram Sch, Whitgift Sch, and Queen's Coll, Camb (MA, LLB), Hon DGiur, Pavia 1990, Hon DEcon, Siena 1991, Hon DJur Stockholm 1996; Bar Middle Temple 1953, QC 1990; Fellow Clare Coll, Camb 1952-64 (Hon Fellow 1997), Hon Fellow LSE 1998; Cassel Professor of Commercial Law, London Univ (LSE) 1964-92, since when Emeritus, Professor of Law; Visiting Professor Harvard Law School 1969-70; Gen Editor, *Modern Law Review* 1970-88; Chm TUC Indep Review Cttee since 1976; Hon Pres Industrial Law Soc since 1997; FBA (1981); Fl Lt RAF 1951; *cr* Baron Wedderburn of Charlton*, of Highgate, Greater London (Life Baron) 1977: *m* 1st, 1951 (*m diss* 1962), Nina, da of Dr Myer Salaman; 2ndly, 1962 (*m diss* 1969), Dorothy Enid, da of late Frederick C. Barnard, and formerly wife of William A. Cole; 3rdly, 1969, Frances Ann, da of Basil F. Knight, and has issue by 1st and 3rd *m*.
Residence – 29 Woodside Av, Highgate, N6 4SP.

SONS LIVING (*By 1st marriage*)

Hon David Roland *b* 1956; BSc, ACA.

(*By 3rd marriage*)

Hon Jonathan Michael, *b* 1972; MA.

DAUGHTERS LIVING (*By 1st marriage*)

Hon Sarah Louise, *b* 1954: *m* 1st, 1975 (*m diss* 1985), Michael Walsh; 2ndly, 1992, Hugh Edmund Brooke Faulkner, of 3 Birley Rd, N20 0HB (*see* de Trafford, Bt, colls, 1995 Edn), and has issue living (by 1st *m*), Claire, *b* 1978, — (by 2nd *m*), Lucy Grace, *b* 1993, — Amy, *b* 1995.
Dr the Hon Lucy Rachel, *b* 1960; MA.

WEDGWOOD, BARON (Wedgwood) (Baron UK 1942)

PIERS ANTHONY WEYMOUTH WEDGWOOD, 4th Baron, b 20 Sept 1954; s 1970; ed Marlborough; late Capt Royal Scots: m 1985, Mary Regina Margaret Kavanagh, da of late Edward Quinn, of Philadelphia, Pa, USA, and has issue.

Arms – Gules four mullets in cross and a canton argent. Crest – On a ducal coronet, a lion passant argent. Supporters – On either side a lion rampant queue fourchée argent supporting a staff raguly gules.
Residence – 152 Ashley Gdns, SW1.

DAUGHTER LIVING

Hon Alexandra Mary Kavanagh, b 1987.

SISTERS LIVING

Hon Susan Margaret, b 1950: m 1994, Hubert Ribeiro de Santana.
Hon Sarah Jane Edith, b 1958: m 1982, Paul J. Bitove, of Toronto, Canada, son of James Bitove, of Toronto, Canada, and has issue living, Olivia Charlotte, b 1988.

I split asunder obstacles

WIDOW LIVING OF THIRD BARON

JANE WEYMOUTH, (Harewood Cottage, Chicksgrove, Tisbury, Wilts), da of William James Poulton, of Kenjockety, Molo, Kenya: m 1st, 1949, as his 2nd wife the 3rd Baron Wedgwood, who d 1970; 2ndly, 1999, John Philip Waterer.

COLLATERAL BRANCH LIVING

Issue of late Hon Josiah Wedgwood, yr son of 1st Baron; b 1899; d 1968: m 1919, Dorothy Mary, OBE, who d 1974, da of Percy James Winser, of Knutsford:—
JOHN, CBE (156 Ashley Gdns, Thirleby Rd, SW1P 1HW; Athenæum Club), b 1919; ed Abbotsholme, and Camb Univ (MA, BCh, MD); FRCP; 1939-45 War, as Surg-Lt RNVR in Europe and Far East; Emeritus Consultant Physician at Middx Hospital (ret 1980) since when, Dir Roy Hospital & Home for Incurables; Hon Sr Lectr Middx Hospital Med Sch 1980-86, and Dir Wedgwood Ltd 1967-87; CBE (Civil) 1987: m 1st, 1943 (m diss 1971), Margaret, da of Alfred S. Mason of Bury St Edmunds, Suffolk; 2ndly, 1972, Jo Alice Tamlyn, da of late Harold Swann Ripsher, and has issue living (by 1st m), Antony John (10 Milner Place, N1; Athenæum Club), b 1944; ed Marlborough, and Trin Coll, Camb (MA); FCA; partner in KPMG: m 1970, Angela Margaret Mary Page, and has issue living, Thomas b 1978, Elizabeth b 1975, Caroline b 1981, — Simon James Josiah (18 Fournier St, E1 6QE), b 1949, — Nicholas Ralph (43 Netherford Rd, SW4), b 1951, — Judith Margaret Susannah, b 1946: m 1st, 1966 (m diss 1986), Christopher Anthony Wingfield Tracy; 2ndly, 1986, (Kevin) Dominic Hall Brennan, and has issue living (by 1st m), Emma b 1970, Victoria b 1974, Charlotte b 1976, (by 2nd m) Alexander b 1987, Roland b (twin) 1987, — Katherine Sarah, b 1955: m 1988, Ian R. Stanbury, and has issue living, Jack b 1988, Matthew b 1990. —— Josiah Ralph (3717 41st Av NE, Seattle, Washington 98105-5436, USA), b 1924; ed Bedales, Putney Sch, Putney, Vermont, Harvard Univ, and Harvard Med Sch (MD); naturalized US citizen 1951; Prof Univ of Washington, Seattle since 1963: m 1943, Virginia Lloyd, da of late Edward Eyre Hunt, of Washington, DC, and has had issue, Josiah Francis (240 Saint Ronan, New Haven, CT 06510, USA), b 1950: m 1982, Ruth Anne, da of Morris Glushien, of Gt Neck, LI, USA, and has issue living, Josiah Ruskin b 1998, — †James Cecil, b 1951; d 1973, — Jeffrey Galton (1837 127th St SE, Bellevue, WA 98005, USA), b 1953: m 1st, 1974 (m diss 1984), Cynthia Baird; 2ndly, 1985, Susan S., da of Pierce D. Smith, of Darien, Conn, USA, and has issue living (by 2nd m), Josiah Smith b 1986, Grace Madeleine b 1989, — John Ralph Christopher (7922 208th Ave NE, Redmond, WA 98053, USA), b 1964: m 1987, Kathleen, da of William Turner of Kirkland, WA, USA, and has issue living, James Turner Berkeley b 1998.

PREDECESSORS – (1) Col Rt Hon JOSIAH CLEMENT WEDGWOOD, DSO, 2nd son of late Clement Francis Wedgwood, master potter, of Barlaston, Staffordshire, b 1872; S Africa 1899-1902, European War 1914-19 as Col (DSO); Chancellor of Duchy of Lancaster (also Ch Civil Commr) Jan to Nov 1924; sat as MP for Newcastle-under-Lyme (L, Lab, and Ind) Jan 1906 to Jan 1942; cr Baron Wedgwood, of Barlaston, co Stafford (peerage of United Kingdom) 1942: m 1st, 1894 (m diss 1919), Hon Ethel Kate, who d 1952, da of 1st Baron Bowen; 2ndly, 1919, Florence Ethel, who d 1969, da of late Edward Guy Willett; d 1943; s by his son (2) FRANCIS CHARLES BOWEN, 2nd Baron; b 1898; an Artist: m 1920, Edith May, who d 1977, da of William Telfer, of Glasgow; d 1959; s by his only son (3) HUGH EVERARD, 3rd Baron, b 1921: m 1st, 1945 (m diss 1947), Jeno Annette Heather, only child of Ralph S Leake, of Bournemouth; 2ndly, 1949, Jane Weymouth, da of William James Poulton, of Kenjockety, Molo, Kenya; d 1970; s by his only son (4) PIERS ANTHONY WEYMOUTH, 4th Baron and present peer.

WEEKS, BARONY OF (Weeks) (Extinct 1960)

DAUGHTERS LIVING OF FIRST BARON

Hon Pamela Rose, *b* (Nov) 1931: *m* 1957, Lieut-Com Henry Walter Plunkett-Ernle-Erle-Drax, RN (ret) (*see* B Dunsany, colls). *Residence* – Charborough Park, Wareham, Dorset.

Hon Venetia Daphne, *b* 1933: *m* 1st, 1954, Lt-Cdr Sir Peter Troubridge, RN (ret), 6th Baronet, who *d* 1988; 2ndly, 1995, as his 2nd wife, William Frederick Eustace (Derick) Forbes (*see* V De Vesci, colls, 1990 Edn). *Residence* – Earlstoun Lodge, Dalry, Castle Douglas, Kirkcudbrightshire DG7 3TT.

WEIDENFELD, BARON (Weidenfeld) (Life Baron 1976)

Arms must yield to the gown

(ARTHUR) GEORGE WEIDENFELD, son of late Max Weidenfeld; *b* 13 Sept 1919; *ed* Piaristen Gymnasium, Vienna, Vienna Univ, and Konsular Akademie (Diplomatic Coll); Chm of Weidenfeld & Nicolson Ltd, since 1948; Gov The South Bank Board Ltd, and Trustee Nat Portrait Gallery since 1988; Member English Nat Opera Board; Vice-Chm Campaign for Oxford; *cr* Knt 1969, and *Baron Weidenfeld*, of Chelsea in Greater London (Life Baron) 1976: *m* 1st, 1952, Jane, da of J. Edward Sieff; 2ndly, 1956 (*m diss* 1961), Mrs Barbara Connolly, who *d* 1996, da of Maj George Skelton; 3rdly, 1966 (*m diss* 1973), Sandra, da of Charles Shipman Payson; 4thly, 1992, Annabelle, da of late Cdr Nicholas Whitestone, and has issue by 1st *m*.

Arms – Per fess or and vert, a fess embattled argent masoned proper, overall a weeping willow eradicated. Crest – a demi-wolf regardant sable holding in its mouth a scroll argent. Supporters – *Dexter*, an old man proper bearded argent habited in a gown and cap sable supporting in his exterior hand a tablet proper; *Sinister*, a youth proper habited in a blouse argent and breeches or, boots and peaked cap sable, a rapier the scabbard sable.
Residence – 9 Chelsea Embankment, SW3.

DAUGHTER LIVING (*By 1st marriage*)

Hon Laura Miriam Elizabeth, *b* 1953: *m* 1976, Christopher Andrew Barnett, and has issue living, Benjamin, *b* 1979, — Rowan, *b* 1981, — Nathaniel Peter Edward, *b* 1984, — Clara Aurjana, *b* 1986.

WEINSTOCK, BARON (Weinstock) (Life Baron 1980)

ARNOLD WEINSTOCK, son of Simon Weinstock; *b* 29 July 1924; *ed* London Univ (BSc Econ); FSS; Hon FRCR, Hon DSc Salford, Aston, Bath, Reading and Ulster Univs, Hon LLD Leeds Univ, and Wales Univ; Hon DTech Loughborough Univ; Hon DLaw Keele Univ, Hon DUniv Anglia Polytechnic Univ, Hon DEconSc Lond Univ, Hon Fell of Peterhouse, Camb, and LSE; Hon Master of the Bench, Gray's Inn; Man Dir General Electric Co Ltd 1963-96, since when Chm Emeritus, and a Dir Rolls-Royce (1971) Ltd 1971-73; Trustee British Museum 1985-96; Dir Friends of Ravenna Festival since 1993; Commendatore Neu'Ordine Al Merito (Italy) 1991, Officier Légion d'Honneur (France) 1992; *cr* Knt 1970 and *Baron Weinstock*, of Bowden, co Wilts (Life Baron) 1980: *m* 1949, Netta, da of late Sir Michael Sobell, and has had issue.

Arms – Dancetty argent and gules on each of three piles, two issuant in chief and one in base azure, a sun in splendour its straight rays each tipped with flame gold. **Crest** – Upon a wreath argent, or and azure on a mount vert two musical pipes saltirewise or between two stakes entwined by vines fructed proper and ensigned by a crown rayonny gules. **Supporters** – *Dexter*, a male griffin azure beaked, rayed and gorged with a crown tridenty and forelegs or; *sinister*, a horse or gorged with a wreath of trefoils the stalks entwined vert.
Club – Jockey.

SON DECEASED

Hon Simon Andrew, *b* 1952; *ed* Winchester, and Magdalen Coll, Oxford (MA): *m* 1979, Laura Helen, only da of Maj Hon Sir Francis Michael Legh, KCVO, and *d* 1996, leaving issue (*see* B Newton).

DAUGHTER LIVING

Hon Susan Gina, *b* 1955; *ed* Cranborne Chase, St Hilda's Coll, Oxford, and LSE (PhD): *m* 1980, Laurent Lacroix, and has issue, one son and two das.

WEIR, VISCOUNT (Weir) (Viscount UK 1938)

WILLIAM KENNETH JAMES WEIR, 3rd Viscount, *b* 9 Nov 1933; *s* 1975; *ed* Eton and Trin Coll, Camb (BA), Hon D Eng Glasgow, Hon FEng; Chm BICC plc since 1996; Chm The Weir Group plc 1983-99 (Vice Chm 1981-83; Chm and Chief Exec 1972-81); Dir St James's Place Capital plc, Chm The Great Northern Investment Trust Ltd 1975-82; a Dir Hambro Life 1984-86, The British Bank of the Middle East 1977-79, British Steel Corpn 1972-76, and Canadian Pacific Ltd since 1989; Member of the London Advisory Cttee of the Hong Kong and Shanghai Banking Corpn 1980-92, of the Engineering Industries Council 1975-81, and a Member of Court, Bank of England 1972-84, a Member of Queen's Body Guard for Scotland (Royal Company of Archers): *m* 1st, 1964 (*m diss* 1974), Diana Lucy, da of late Peter Lewis MacDougall, of Rockcliffe, Ont, Canada; 2ndly, 1976 (*m diss* 1989), Jacqueline Mary, el da of late Baron Louis de Chollet, of Fribourg, Switzerland, and formerly wife of Donald Alexander Cameron Marr; 3rdly, 1989, Marina, da of late Marc Sevastopoulo, of 1150 Fifth Av, New York City, and has issue by 1st and 3rd *m*.

Arms – Azure, a cogwheel or, winged argent, in chief the sun in his splendour of the second. **Crest** – A wing argent, charged with a thistle slipped proper. **Supporters** – Two winged horses argent, armed and crined or.

Residence – Rodinghead, Mauchline, Ayrshire KA5 5HU. *Club* – White's.

SON LIVING (*By 1st marriage*)

Hon JAMES WILLIAM HARTLAND, *b* 6 June 1965.

(*By 3rd marriage*)

Hon Andrew Alexander Marc, *b* 1989.

DAUGHTER LIVING (*By 1st marriage*)

Hon Lorna Elizabeth, *b* 1967.

BROTHERS LIVING

Hon Douglas Nigel, *b* 1935; *ed* Eton, and Trin Coll, Camb: *m* 1964, Penelope Anne, da of Group Capt John Whitehead, of Bent Mead, Waltham St Lawrence, Berks, and has issue living, Juliet Anne, *b* 1964, — Lucy, *b* 1966, — Nicola Jean, *b* 1969, — Joanna, *b* 1978.
Hon George Anthony (Kilmany House, Kilmany, Cupar, Fife KY15 4QW) *b* 1940; *ed* Winchester, at Trin Coll, Camb (BA), and at Mass Inst of Technology, USA (SM, PhD): *m* 1962 (*m diss* 1992), Hon Jane Caroline Anstruther-Gray, da of late Baron Kilmany (Life Baron) (*see* Anstruther of that Ilk, Bt, colls), and has issue living, William John, *b* 1971, — Edward Kenneth, *b* 1972, — Belinda Jane, *b* 1974.
Hon James Richard Canning (25 Chester St, SW1), *b* 1949; *ed* Winchester, and Strathclyde Univ (BA): *m* 1977, Haude Chantal Gabrielle, da of Marc Charpentier, of Paris, and has issue living, Victoria Dorothy Sabine, *b* 1978, — Kate, *b* 1980.

SISTER LIVING

Hon Janet Sibella, *b* 1947: *m* 1978, Francis Anthony Brinsley (James) Valentine (*see* E Lanesborough, 1985 Edn), and has issue living, Robert Harris, *b* 1983, — Sibella Margaret, *b* 1981. *Residence* – The Gate House, Astrop, nr Banbury, Oxon.

WIDOW LIVING OF SECOND VISCOUNT

DOROTHY (*Dorothy, Viscountess Weir*), da of late William Yerrington Dear, and widow of Edward F. Hutton: *m* 1973, as his 2nd wife, the 2nd Viscount Weir, who *d* 1975. *Residence* – Little Pennbrook, Lake Rd, Far Hills, NJ, USA 07931.

PREDECESSORS – (1) *Rt Hon Sir* WILLIAM DOUGLAS Weir, GCB, son of late James Weir, of Over Courance, Dumfriesshire; *b* 1877; Hon Pres of G & J Weir Holdings, Ltd, and a Director of International Nickel Co of Canada; was Scottish Director of Munitions 1915-16, Controller of Aeronautical Supplies; and a Member of Air Board 1917-18, Director-Gen of Aircraft Production, Min of Munitions 1918, Sec of State and Pres of Air Council April to Dec 1918, Director-Gen of Explosives and Chemical Supplies, Min of Supply 1939-41, and Chm of Tank Board 1943; *cr Baron Weir*, of Eastwood, co Renfrew (peerage of UK) 1918, and *Viscount Weir*, of Eastwood, co Renfrew (peerage of UK) 1938: *m* 1904, Alice Blanche, who *d* 1959, da of late John MacConnachie of Glasgow; *d* 1959; *s* by his only son (2) (JAMES) KENNETH, 2nd Viscount, *b* 1905; Engineer; (Chm of Weir Group, Ltd of Glasgow), 1955-72: *m* 1st, 1929 (Dorothy Isabel), Lucy, who *d* 1972, only da of James Fuidge Crowdy, MVO, Asst Sec to Gov Gen of Canada; 2ndly, 1973, Dorothy, da of William Yerrington Dear, and widow of Edward F. Hutton; *d* 1975: *s* by his el son (3) WILLIAM KENNETH JAMES, 3rd Viscount and present peer; also Baron Weir.

Weir, family name of Baron Inverforth.

Wellesley, family name of Earl Cowley.

Wellesley, family name of Duke of Wellington.

WELLINGTON, DUKE OF (Wellesley) (Duke UK 1814)

Fortune is the companion of valour

ARTHUR VALERIAN WELLESLEY, KG, LVO, OBE, MC, 8th Duke, Prince of Waterloo in the Netherlands (*cr* 1815), Duque da Vittoria and Marques de Torres Vedras (*cr* 1812) and Conde do Vimeiro (*cr* 1811) in Portugal, and Duque de Ciudad Rodrigo (*cr* 1812), and a Grandee (1st class) in Spain, which he became on the renunciation by his father (published in Official Gazette Madrid, 20 Feb 1968); *b* 2 July 1915; *s* 1972; *ed* Eton, and New Coll, Oxford; patron of four livings; Brig (ret) late RHG; OC RHG 1954-58, Silver Stick-in-Waiting, and Lt-Col Comdg Household Cav 1959-60, and Comdg 22nd Armd Bde 1960-61, CRAC, 1st British Corps 1962-64, and Defence Attaché Madrid 1964-67; Col C-in-C The Duke of Wellington's Regt since 1974; Dep-Col to The Princess Royal of the Blues & Royals since 1998; late Hon Col 2nd Br Wessex Regt TAVRA; Co Councillor for Hants 1967-73; DL for Hants (1975); Dir Massey Ferguson Holdings & Massy Ferguson Ltd 1973-89; Pres SE Branch of R British Legion, Member of Council, RASE, and Dep Pres 1993, Pres Atlantic Salmon Trust, Trustee Thames Salmon Trust and Lawes Agricultural Trust; a Gov of Wellington Coll since 1965; Pres and Dep Pres Game Conservancy 1976-87, Pres Rare Breeds Survival Trust 1982-86, Council for Environmental Conservation 1983-86, Chm Hants Assocn Parish Council since 1994, Pres National Canine Defence League since 1996, Pres Labrador Retriever Club since 1997; HM The Queen's Representative on Bd of Trustees of the Royal Armouries 1983-96; Vice-Pres Kennel Club since 1987; Member of Advisory Cttee, Centre for Agricultural Strategy at Reading Univ; Pres Pitt Club since 1998; 1939-45 War in Middle East, Italy, and NW Europe (MC 1941); Grand Cross Order of Isabel the Catholic (Spain) 1986, Legion d'Honneur (France); LVO 1952, OBE (Mil) 1957, KG 1990: *m* 1944, Diana Ruth, only da of late Maj-Gen Douglas Fitzgerald McConnel, of Knockdolian, CB, CBE, DSO, of Ayrshire, and has issue.

🛡rms – Quarterly: 1st and 4th gules, a cross argent, in each quarter five plates in saltire, *Wellesley:* 2nd and 3rd or, a lion rampant gules, ducally collared gold, *Cowley:* over all, in the centre chief point, an escutcheon of augmentation charged with the Union badge. 🛡rest – Out of a ducal coronet or, a demi-lion rampant gules, holding in the paws a forked pennon argent, flowing to the sinister, charged with the cross of St George, the ends gules. 🛡upporters – Two lions gules, gorged with Eastern coronets, and chained or.
Seat – Stratfield Saye House, Basingstoke, Hants, RG7 2B2. *Town Residence* – Apsley House, Piccadilly, W1V 9FA. *Club* – Cavalry and Guards.

SONS LIVING

ARTHUR CHARLES VALERIAN (*Marquess of Douro*) (Apsley House, 149 Piccadilly, W1V 9FA; The Old Rectory, Stratfield Saye, Reading, RG7 2DA), *b* 19 Aug 1945; *ed* Eton, and Ch Ch, Oxford; Dep-Chm Vendôme Luxury Group plc since 1993, Dir Sun Life Assurance Soc since 1988, Transatlantic Holdings plc since 1983, Chm Dunhill Holdings plc 1990-93, Dir Rothmans International plc 1990-93, Dep Chm Guinness Mahon Holdings plc 1988-91, Dir Continental & Industrial Trust plc 1987-90, Deltec Panamerica SA 1968-89 (late Dep-Chm), Eucalyptus Pulp Mills plc 1979-88, and GB Papers 1981-84; Member of Council Royal Coll of Art since 1992; Basingstoke Borough Councillor 1978-79; MEP (C) 1979-89; *m* 1977, Antonia Brigid Elizabeth Luise, yr da of HRH the late Prince Friedrich Georg Wilhelm Christoph of Prussia (*see* Royal Family), and has issue living:—

> SONS LIVING—Arthur Gerald (*Earl of Mornington*), *b* 31 Jan 1978; Page of Honour to HM Queen Elizabeth The Queen Mother 19—95; *ed* ......, and Ch Ch, Oxford, — *Lord* Frederick Charles, *b* 1992.
> DAUGHTERS LIVING—*Lady* Honor Victoria, *b* 1979, — *Lady* Mary Luise, *b* 1986, — *Lady* Charlotte, *b* 1990.

Lord Richard Gerald (Knockdolian, Colmonell, Girvan, Ayrshire), *b* 1949; *ed* Eton and RAC Cirencester: *m* 1973, Joanna, el da of John Sumner, of Marston St Lawrence, Oxon, and has issue living, Natasha Doone, *b* 1975, — Davina Chloe, *b* 1977.
Lord John Henry (69 Hopton St, SE1 9LF), *b* 1954; *ed* Eton: *m* 1977, Corinne, da of HE Baron Vaes, KCMG, formerly Belgian Ambassador, and has issue living, Gerald Valerian, *b* 1981, — Alexandrina Sofia, *b* 1983.
Lord (James) Christopher Douglas, *b* 1964: *m* 1994 Laura Elizabeth, only da of T. E. Wedge, and has issue living, Eleanor Rose, *b* 1995.

DAUGHTER LIVING

Lady (Caroline) Jane (42 Clarendon Rd, W11), *b* 1951.

SISTER LIVING

Lady Elizabeth (42 Wilson Av, Henley-on-Thames, Oxon), *b* 1918: *m* 1939 (*m diss* 1960), Capt Thomas Clyde, Royal Horse Guards, and has had issue, (Michael) Jeremy (Thomas), *b* 1941; *ed* Eton, and Central Sch of Speech and Drama; Actor: *m* 1970, Vanessa, da of Harold Field, and has issue living, Matthew Thomas *b* 1974, Lucy Sophia *b* 1971: *m* 1996, Shaun Roberts, — Robin *b* 1943; *d* 1950, — William Jonathan, *b* 1949; *ed* Eton.

DAUGHTER LIVING OF FIFTH DUKE

Lady Anne Maud, *b* 1910; *s* her brother (6th Duke of Wellington) as Duquesa de Ciudad Rodrigo and a Grandee (1st class) in Spain (*cr* 1812) 1943, but relinquished this title in favour of her uncle the 7th Duke of Wellington 1949: *m* 1933 (*m diss* 1963), Capt Hon David Reginald Rhys, Welsh Gds, who *d* 1991 (*see* B Dynevor). *Residence –*

COLLATERAL BRANCHES LIVING

Issue of late Capt Lord Richard Wellesley, 2nd son of 4th Duke, *b* 1879, *ka* 1914: *m* 1908, Louise Nesta Pamela, who *d* 1946, having *m* 2ndly (in New York), 1917, his younger brother, Major Lord George Wellesley, MC (ante), da of Sir Maurice FitzGerald (20th *Knight of Kerry*), CVO, 2nd Bt:—
Mary, *b* (*posthumous*) 1915. *Residence* – 12 Clarence Terr, NW1 4RD.

Grandchildren (by 1st *m*) of late Lt-Col Lord George Wellesley, MC, 4th son of 4th Duke:—
Issue of late Maj Richard Wellesley, MC, DL, *b* 1920, *d* 1984: *m* 1st, 1948 (*m diss* 1970), Ruth, da of late Peter Haig-Thomas (*see* E Normanton, 1971 Edn); 2ndly, 1970, Jill (Buckland Mead, Buckland, Faringdon, Oxon, SN7 8QR), da of late G/Capt E. Burton, RAF:—
(By 1st *m*) Charles (The Dower House, Buckland, nr Faringdon, Oxon SN7 8QR), *b* 1955: *m* 1981, Louise Charlotte, da of late Cdr Allan Miles Brittain Buxton, and has issue living, Rosanna *b* 1989, — Charlotte, *b* 1992. —— John, *b* 1962: *m* 1994, Catriona, da of Dr David Duncan, and of Mrs Anthony Fryer. —— Nesta, *b* 1951: *m* 1985, Richard Sidney Hawes, of St Mary's, Latton, Swindon, Wilts SN6 6DS, only son of Sidney Hawes, of Cirencester, Glos, and has issue living, David Richard, *b* 1992, — John Sydney, *b* (twin) 1992. —— Lucy, *b* 1953: *m* 1991, Charles Robert Collin, only son of R. F. D. Collin, of Wheatsheaf House, Brick Hill, Hook Norton, nr Chipping Norton, Oxon.

(*In remainder to Earldom of Mornington Viscounty of Wellesley and Barony of Mornington only*)

Granddaughters of late Lt-Col Frederic Henry Burton Wellesley, yr son of Lt-Col Gerald Valerian Wellesley, 2nd son of Col William Henry Charles Wellesley, 2nd son of Hon Gerald Valerian Wellesley, DD, 4th son of 1st Earl of Mornington:—
Issue of late Maj Frederic Henry Valerian Wellesley, *b* 1908, *d* 1978: *m* 1938, Nancy Evelyn (Church Hill, Crayke, Yorks), yr da of late Percy Saunders:—
Evelyn Angela Juliana, *b* 1938: *m* 1961, John Albert Searle. *Residence* – Southlands, Market Bosworth, Leics CV13 0LS. —— Helen Christabel Kate, *b* 1947: *m* 1975, Daniel Levasseur. *Residence* – La Croix de Pinet, Uriage, France. —— Rosalind Jane *b* 1954: *m* 1978, Alfred Peter Walshaw. *Residence* – The Cottage, 1 High Mickley, Stocksfield, Northumberland.

Granddaughter of late Gerald Valentine Wellesley, elder son of late Edmond Ernest Charles Wellesley, 3rd son of late Col William Henry Charles Wellesley (ante):—
Issue of late Philip Vernon Charles Wellesley, *b* 1921, *d* 1992: *m* 1952, Marguerite Victoria (50A Ellerslie Rd, N Barnstaple, Devon), da of Alfred Cameron Clark, of Barnstaple:—
Barbara Victoria, *b* 1958: *m* 1985, Roger John Sandwell, of 25 Lydhurst Av, Barnstaple, Devon.

Granddaughter of late Col William Henry Charles Wellesley (ante):—
Issue of late Major Cecil George Wellesley, OBE, *b* 1869, *d* 1932: *m* 1906, Winifred Mary (who *d* 1959, having *m* 2ndly, 1933, Lieut-Col Clifford Charles Horace Twiss, DSO, who *d* 1947), da of late Hon Reginald Parker (E Macclesfield, colls):—
Pamela (White Gate, Acrise, nr Folkestone, Kent), *b* 1909: *m* 1938, Maj-Gen Edward Noel Keith Estcourt, DSO, OBE, late RA, who *d* 1982, and has issue living, Edward James, *b* 1939; Lt-Col RA: *m* 1963, Jennifer Clare, da of Lt-Col C. A. McLaren, of High Torr, Cornwood, Ivybridge, S Devon, and has issue living, Edward Rory Charles *b* 1965, Angus James *b* 1968, — Adrian Charles (Sunnycroft, Petworth Rd, Chiddingfold, Surrey), *b* 1942: late Lt Parachute Regt: *m* 1967 (*m diss* 1991), Judith Mary, da of Col G. W. Preston, of Beck Cottage, Menethorpe, Malton, Yorks, and has issue living, Suzannah Jane *b* 1970, Charlotte Pamela *b* 1972, — Hermione Jessica Jane, *b* 1947: *m* 1970, Christopher Hugh James Cousins, of White Gate, Acrise, nr Folkestone, Kent, and has issue living, Elizabeth Pamela Juliet *b* 1977, Victoria Edwina Jane *b* 1982.

Descendants of late Hon Sir Henry Wellesley (5th son of 1st Earl of Mornington), who was *cr Baron Cowley* 1828 (see E Cowley).

PREDECESSORS – **(1)** *Rt Hon Sir* ARTHUR Wellesley, KG, GCB, etc, 3rd son of 1st Earl of Mornington, *b* 1769; entered 73rd Regt 1787; became a Gen 1808, and a Field-Marshal 1815; sat as MP for Trim in the Irish Parliament; *cr Baron Douro*, of Wellesley, co Somerset, and *Viscount Wellington of Talavera and of Wellington*, co Somerset (peerage of United Kingdom) 1809, *Earl of Wellington*, co Somerset (peerage of United Kingdom) 1812, *Marquess of Wellington* (peerage of United Kingdom) 1812, *Marquess Douro* and *Duke of Wellington* (peerage of United Kingdom) 1814, *Count of Vimeiro* in Portugal 1811, *Duke of Ciudad Rodrigo* (and a Grandee of the 1st class) in Spain 1812, *Duke of Vittoria* and *Marques of Torres Vedras* in Portugal 1812, and *Prince of Waterloo*, in the Netherlands 1815; the brilliant services of the "Great Duke" are unrivalled in military history, but they are too varied to be particularized in this volume; in recognition of these services he was awarded the highest honours that could be conferred, besides large pecuniary awards, while the Sovereigns of various European countries conferred upon him their highest titles of nobility; was Premier 1828-30 and 1834-5, Chancellor of University of Oxford, Lord High Constable of England, Lord Warden of the Cinque Ports, Constable of the Tower and of Dover Castle, Lord-Lieut of Hants, Chief Ranger of Hyde, St James's and other Parks, Com in Chief, Col of Grenadier Guards, Col-in-Chief of Rifle Brigade, etc: *m* 1806, Hon Catherine Sarah Dorothea Pakenham, who *d* 1831, 2nd da of 2nd Baron Longford; *d* 14 Sept 1852; *s* by his son **(2)** ARTHUR RICHARD, 2nd Duke, *b* 1807; sat as MP for Aldborough (*C*) 1829-30 and 1831, and for Norwich 1837-52; was Master of the Horse 1853-8, a Lieut-Gen in the Army and Lord, Lieut of Middlesex; *s* in 1863 as 6th Earl of Mornington (see infra *); *dsp* 13 Aug 1884: *s* by his nephew **(3)** HENRY, 3rd Duke, el surviving son of Maj-Gen Lord Charles Wellesley, MP (2nd son of 1st Duke), by Augusta Sophia Anne, only child of the Right Hon Henry Manvers Pierrepont (E Manvers), *b* 1846, MP for Andover (*C*) 1874-80: *m* 1882, Evelyn Katrine Gwenfra, who *d* 1939, da of late Col Thomas Peers Williams MP, of Temple House, Great Marlow; *d* 1900; *s* by his brother **(4)** ARTHUR CHARLES, KG, GCVO, 4th Duke, *b* 1849; Col (ret) late Grenadier Guards; bore Union Standard at Coronations of Edward VII 1902, and George V 1911: *m* 1872, Kathleen Emily Bulkeley Williams, who *d* 1927, da of late Robert Griffith Williams (Williams-Bulkeley, Bt, colls); *d* 1934; *s* by his el son **(5)** ARTHUR CHARLES, 5th Duke, *b* 1876: *m* 1909, Hon Lilian Maud Glen Coats, who *d* 1946, da of 1st Baron Glentanar; *d* 1941; *s* by his only son **(6)** HENRY VALERIAN GEORGE, 6th Duke, *b* 1912; Capt Duke of Wellington's Regt and Commando; *ka* 1943, when he was *s* in the Dukedom of Ciudad Rodrigo and as a Grandee (1st class) in Spain (*cr* 1812) by his sister, Lady Anne Maud, wife of Hon David Reginald Rhys, and in the British and Portuguese titles by his uncle **(7)** GERALD, KG, 3rd son of 4th Duke, 7th Duke, *b* 1885; Lt-Col Gren Gds; Surveyor of HM's Works of Art 1936-44; Chancellor of Southampton Univ 1951-62; Gov, Capt and Steward of Isle of Wight 1957-65: *m* 1914, Dorothy, who *d* 1956, da of late Robert Ashton, of Croughton, Cheshire; *d* 1972, *s* by his son **(8)** ARTHUR VALERIAN, 8th Duke and present peer; also Marquess of Wellington, Marquess Douro, Earl of Mornington (I), Earl of Wellington, Viscount Wellesley (I), Viscount Wellington of Talavera and Wellington, Baron of Mornington (I), and Baron Douro; Prince of Waterloo in Netherlands (*cr* 1815) Duque da Vittoria and Marques de Torres Vedras (*cr* 1812) and Conde do Vimeiro (*cr* 1811) in Portugal, and Duque de Ciudad Rodrigo and a Grandee (1st class) in Spain (*cr* 1812).

***(1)** RICHARD, MP, son of Henry Colley, MP, assumed in 1728 by Roy licence the surname of Wesley; sat as MP for Trim 1729-46; *cr Baron of Mornington* (peerage of Ireland) 1746; *d* 1758; *s* by his son **(2)** GARRET, 2nd Baron; sat as MP for Meath 1757-8; *cr Viscount Wesley* (changed to Wellesley by his son *ca* 1798) and *Earl of Mornington* (peerage of Ireland) 1760; *d* 1781; *s* by his son **(3)** RICHARD, KG, KP, 2nd Earl: sat as MP for Trim, 1780-1, Beeralston 1784-6, Saltash 1786-7, Windsor 1787-96 and Sarum 1796-7; was Gov-Gen of India 1798-1805, Ambassador to Spain 1809, Ch Sec of State for Foreign Affairs 1809-12, Lord-Lieut of Ireland 1821, 1833-4; *cr Marquess Wellesley* (peerage of Ireland) 1799; *dsp* 1842, when the Marquessate became extinct; *s* by his brother **(4)** WILLIAM, GCH, PC, 3rd Earl; assumed in 1778 the surname of Wellesley-Pole: sat as MP for Trim 1783-90, East Looe 1790-94, and Queen's Co 1801-21; was Postmaster-Gen in 1835; *cr Baron Maryborough* (peerage of UK) 1821; *d* 1845; *s* by his son **(5)** WILLIAM POLE, 4th Earl; assumed in 1812 the additional surnames of Tylney-Long; *d* 1857; *s* by his son **(6)** WILLIAM ARTHUR, 5th Earl; *d* unmarried 1863, when the Barony of Maryborough became ext and the honours of the first Earl devolved upon his cousin **(7)** ARTHUR RICHARD, 6th Earl, who had previously succeeded as 2nd Duke of Wellington (see ante).

WELLS-PESTELL, BARONY OF (Wells-Pestell) (Extinct 1991)

SONS LIVING OF LIFE BARON

Hon Philip, *b* 1941: *m* 1965, Holly Erin, who *d* 1998, da of Lorne Hopkins, of Conn, USA, and has issue.

Hon Richard (2 Queen's Mansions, Queen's Av, Muswell Hill N10), *b* 1945: *m* 1973, (*m diss* 1977), Claudia Marseille, step-da of Prof John Gerhart, of Berkeley, Calif, USA.

WEMYSS AND MARCH, EARL OF (Charteris) (Earl S 1633 and 1697)

This is our Charter

(FRANCIS) DAVID CHARTERIS, KT, 12th Earl of Wemyss and 8th Earl of March; *b* 19 Jan 1912; *s* 1937; *ed* Eton, and Balliol Coll, Oxford (BA); Hon LLD, St Andrews 1953 and Hon D Univ Edinburgh, 1983; a JP for E Lothian; Lord Lieut 1967-87; Lord High Commr to Gen Assembly of Church of Scotland 1959, 1960 and 1977; Lieut in the Queen's Body Guard for Scotland (R Co of Archers); Lord Clerk Register of Scotland and Keeper of HM Signet for Scotland since 1974; Chm of Roy Commn on Ancient and Historical Monuments of Scotland 1949-84, and of Scottish Cttee of Marie Curie Memorial Foundation; Vice-Chm of Marie Curie Memorial Foundation, Chm of the National Trust for Scotland 1946-69, Pres 1967-91, and Pres Emeritus since 1991; Hon Pres of the Thistle Foundation for Severely Disabled Scottish Ex-Servicemen; Pres of National Bible Soc of Scotland 1960-83; a Consultant of Wemyss and March Estate Management Co Ltd; late Capt Lovat Scouts (TA Reserve); Colonial Admin Ser, Basutoland 1937-44; Middle East 1941-44 with Basuto Troops as Maj: KT 1966: *m* 1st, 1940, Mavis Lynette Gordon, who *d* 1988, el da of late Edwin Edward Murray, of Hermanus, Cape Province, S Africa; 2ndly, 1995, Mrs Shelagh Kathleen Kennedy, da of George Ernest Thrift, of Vancouver, BC, Canada, and has issue by 1st *m*.

Arms – Quarterly: 1st and 4th argent, a fesse azure, within a double tressure flory counterflory gules, *Charteris*; 2nd and 3rd or, a lion rampant gules, armed and langued azure, *Wemyss*. Crest – A dexter hand holding up a dagger paleways proper. Supporters – Two swans, wings elevated proper, gorged with earl's coronets about their necks. *Residence* – Gosford House, Longniddry, East Lothian EH32 0PX. *Club* – New (Edinburgh).

SON LIVING *(By 1st marriage)*

JAMES DONALD *(Lord Neidpath)*, *b* 22 June 1948; *ed* Eton, Univ Coll, Oxford (BA 1969), St Antony's Coll, Oxford (D Phil 1975), and RAC Cirencester (Diploma 1978); ARICS 1984; Page of Honour to HM Queen Elizabeth the Queen Mother 1962-64; author of *The Singapore Naval Base and the Defence of Britain's Eastern Empire 1919-41*: *m* 1st, 1983 (*m diss* 1988), Catherine Ingrid, el da of Hon Jonathan Bryan Guinness (later 3rd Baron Moyne); 2ndly, 1995, Amanda Claire Marion, yst da of late Basil Percy Terence Feilding (*see* E Denbigh, colls), and has issue by 1st *m*:

SON LIVING *(by 1st marriage)*—Hon (Francis) Richard, *b* 15 Sept 1984.
DAUGHTER LIVING *(by 1st marriage)*—Hon Mary Olivia, *b* 1987.

Residence – Stanway, Cheltenham, Glos. *Clubs* – Brooks's, Pratt's, Puffin's (Edinburgh), Ogniesko Polski.

DAUGHTER LIVING *(By 1st marriage)*

Lady Elizabeth Mary, *b* 1941: *m* 1964, David Holford Benson, son of late Lt-Col Sir Reginald (Rex) Lindsay Benson, DSO, MVO, MC, and has issue living, Matthew James, *b* 1966: *m* 1997, Cecilia, elder da of Timothy Usher, and has issue living, Sophie Veronica Ivy *b* 1998, — Henrietta Katharine, *b* 1969, — Katharine Emma, *b* 1972.

BROTHER LIVING

Rt Hon Sir Martin Charles, GCB, GCVO, OBE, QSO, PC *(Baron Charteris of Amisfield)*, *b* 1913: *cr* Baron Charteris of Amisfield 1978 (see that title).

COLLATERAL BRANCHES LIVING

Grandchildren of late Capt Hon Guy Laurence Charteris, 2nd son of 11th Earl:—
Issue of late Capt Hugo Francis Guy Charteris, MC, *b* 1922, *d* 1970: *m* 1948, Virginia Mary Forbes (The Elms, Church St, Bubwith, Selby, Yorks YO8 8LW), da of late Colin Gurdon Forbes Adam, CSI (*see* Adam, Bt, *cr* 1917):—
Jamie Hugo Desmond (Corner House, Westow, York YO6 7NE), *b* 1958: *m* 1990, Kathryn Helen, only da of G. B. Shaw, of Fourstones, Hexham, Northumberland, and has issue living, Felix Guy, *b* 1992, — Esme Iris, *b* 1995, — Ruby Rose, *b* 1997. —— Frances Irene Anne (2825 Kenyon Circle, Boulder, Colorado 80303, USA), *b* 1950: *m* 1983 (*m diss* 1995),

Albert Chong, and has issue living, Ayinde (a son), *b* 1981, — Chinwe Amelia, *b* 1987. ——— (Virginia) Jane, *b* 1953: *m* 1984, Peter Charles Clark, of 41 Bloemfontein Av, W12, elder son of F. C. Clark, of Streatham, SW16. ——— Perdita Rosemary, *b* 1955: *m* 1978, Jeremy Rupert Beckett, and has had issue (*see* Beckett, Bt).

         Grandchildren of late Capt Hon Frederick William Charteris, RN, 5th son of 9th Earl:—
         Issue of late Col Nigel Keppel Charteris, CMG, DSO, OBE, *b* 1878, *d* 1967: *m* 1904, Katharine Margaret, who *d* 1961, el da of Sir John Walter Buchanan Riddell, 11th Bt:—
John Douglas (Glen Lorne House, Muirfield Drive, PO Chisipite, Harare City, Zimbabwe), *b* 1914; *ed* Radley; Maj R Scots (ret); Palestine 1936-38; 1939-45 War (despatches): *m* 1st, 1943, Mrs Catherine Pitcairn Colley, who *d* 1957, da of late Capt W. P. Nunneley, Black Watch; 2ndly, 1958 (*m diss* 1971), Jean Haigh, of Umtali, Rhodesia; 3rdly, 1982, Mrs Rosemary Gillian Druscilla Perry (*neé* Edmonds), of Zimbabwe, and has issue living, (by 1st *m*) Sarah Keppel, *b* 1945: *m* 1970, Peter Guthrie Brown, and has issue living, Robert Guthrie *b* 1973, Christopher John *b* (twin) 1973, — (by 2nd *m*) Martin Ian (Wingtip Farm, Marondera, Zimbabwe), *b* 1960: *m* 1989, Dr Helen Heath, and has issue living, Michael Samuel *b* 1991, Andrew Phillip *b* 1992, — Bridget Alison, *b* 1958: *m* 1983, Ian Donovan, of 5 Bolitree Close, Umwinsidale, Harare, Zimbabwe, and has issue living, Matthew John *b* 1989, Emma Clare *b* 1985. ——— David Nigel (Longstones Cottage, South St, Little Avebury, nr Marlborough, Wilts SN8 1QX), *b* 1920; *ed* Lancing; late Lt RNVR: *m* 1st, 1952, Euphemia Mary, who *d* 1969, da of Maj-Gen Sir (John) Drummond Inglis, KBE, CB, MC; 2ndly, 1982, Astrid Henrietta Vivian Alys (*neé* Cooper), widow of Dr A. Henderson-Begg, and has had issue (by 1st *m*), Nigel Drummond Keppel (P.O. Box CH172, Chisipite, Harare, Zimbabwe), *b* 1958: *m* 1988, Philippa Margaret, da of Maj Robert Edward Paton, of Harare, Zimbabwe, and has issue living, James David *b* 1992, Thomas Hugo *b* 1998, Alice Fiona *b* 1990, — Angela Katharine Keppel, *b* 1953: *m* 1980, Nigel A. C. Butler, and *d* 1999 (together with her husband), in Harare, Zimbabwe, leaving issue, Katharine Emma *b* 1981, Sabrina Charlotte *b* 1983, Belinda *b* 1986, Joanna Mary *b* 1988, — Helen Mary Keppel, *b* 1956: *m* 1984, Richard William Lewis Groves (c/o The Hong Kong & Shanghai Banking Corpn, 1 Queens Rd, Central, Hong Kong), son of Capt P. W. Groves, of Whitchurch, Cardiff, and has issue living, Charlotte Elizabeth *b* 1985, Francesca Katharine *b* 1987, Georgina *b* 1993. ——— Margaret Olive (Clare Park, Crondall, Farnham, Surrey), *b* 1905: *m* 1st, 1930, Lt-Cdr Michael Richard Hallam Murray, RN (ret), who *d* 1938; 2ndly, 1954, Maj Eric Cecil Lewis Copner, Devon Regt, who *d* 1968, and has issue living, (by 1st *m*) Christopher Philip Hallam (Manor Farm, Little Barugh, Malton, N Yorks YO17 6UY), *b* 1937: *m* 1967, Judith Mary, da of late Lt-Col I. D. MacInnes, and has issue living, James Michael Hallam *b* 1968, Justin Richard Hallam *b* 1973, Harriet Alexandra Hallam *b* 1970: *m* 1998, Simon Andrew Southgate, elder son of Sir Colin Southgate, — Susan Barbara (7 Dacre House, St Thomas More Estate, Beaufort St, SW3 5BH), *b* 1930: *m* 1974, Leslie Max Pritchard, who *d* 1990, — Katharine Bridget, *b* 1934: *m* 1st, 1956, Lt John Charles Brian Taite, RN, who *d* 1975; 2ndly, 1997, Dr Nigel Davison, of 3 South Dene, Stoke Bishop, Bristol BS9 2BW, and has issue living (by 1st *m*), Roderick Michael James *b* 1966, Clare Bridget *b* 1959, Caroline Rachel *b* 1960. ——— Anne Louisa (Flowerdown Residential Home, Harestock Rd, Winchester SO22 6NT), *b* 1909: *m* 1939, John Arkwright Bonham-Carter, CVO, DSO, OBE, ERD, Col Engineer & Transport Staff Corps RE (TA) (Maybank, Monkwood, Ropley, Alresford, Hants SO24 0HB), who *d* 1998, and has issue living, Richard Francis (Maybank, Monkwood, Ropley, Alresford, Hants SO24 0HB), *b* 1940; *ed* Winchester; MICE 1970: *m* 1968, Josephine Ann, who *d* 1998, elder da of late Alfred Smithson Gallimore, and of Mrs J. B. C. Rankine, of Burton Hall, Carlow, and has issue living, Nicola Jane *b* 1969, Claire Helen *b* 1972, — Nigel John (Dowlands, Thorndon, Eye, Sussex) *b* 1945; *ed* Winchester, and King's Coll, Camb (MA 1970).

         Grandsons of late Randolph Gordon Erskine Wemyss, el son of James Hay Erskine Wemyss, MP, el son of Lt-Gen William Wemyss, MP, el son of Hon James Wemyss, MP, 3rd son of 5th Earl:—
         Issue of late Capt Michael John Wemyss of that Ilk, *b* 1888; *d* 1982; recognised as Chief of the name of Wemyss by Lord Lyon 1910: *m* 1918, Lady Victoria Alexandrina Violet Cavendish Bentinck, CVO, who *d* 1994, aged 104, da of 6th Duke of Portland:—
David WEMYSS OF THAT ILK, *b* 1920; *ed* Eton, and Magdalene Coll, Camb; formerly Capt Roy Corps of Signals: *m* 1945, Lady Jean Christian Bruce, da of 10th Earl of Elgin and Kincardine, and has issue living, Michael James (Wemyss Castle, East Wemyss, Fife), *b* 1947; *ed* Gordonstoun, and RAC Cirencester; DL; FRICS 1985: *m* 1975, Charlotte Mary, da of late Lt-Col Royle Bristowe, of Brookhampton Hall, Ickleton, Cambs, and has issue living, Hermione Mary *b* 1982, Leonora Anne *b* 1986, — Charles John (Hill of Invermay, Forgandenny, Perthshire), *b* 1952; *ed* Eton, and Magdalen Coll, Camb: *m* 1978, Fiona Elizabeth, only da of late Lt-Col Sir Eric Charles William Mackenzie Penn, GCVO, OBE, MC, of Sternfield House, Saxmundham, Suffolk, and has issue living, James Michael *b* 1987, Mary Victoria *b* 1981, Elizabeth Katherine *b* 1985. *Residence* – Invermay, Forteviot, Perthshire. ——— Andrew Michael (Torrie House, Newmills, Dunfermline, Fife), *b* 1925; *ed* Eton: *m* 1967, Janet Alethea, only da of John Swire Scott, of Eredine Dalmally, Argyll, and has issue living, William John, *b* 1970, — Isabella Alethea, *b* 1968.

PREDECESSORS – **(1)** *Rt Hon* JOHN Wemyss, was *cr* by Charles I a *Baronet of Nova Scotia* 1625, *Lord Wemyss of Elcho* (peerage of Scotland) 1628, and *Lord Elcho and Methel* and *Earl of Wemyss* (peerage of Scotland) 1633; he eventually espoused the cause of the Covenant; *d* 1649; *s* by his son **(2)** DAVID, 2nd Earl; constructed at his own cost the harbour of Methil, in 1672 resigned his honours to the crown in return for a new patent with original precedency and extending the limitation to his da; *d* 1679, when the baronetcy expired and the peerages devolved upon his 2nd surv da **(3)** MARGARET; *d* 1705; *s* by her son **(4)** DAVID, PC, 4th Earl; was Lord High Adm of Scotland, a Commr for concluding the Treaty of Union, and a Representative Peer; *d* 1720; *s* by his son **(5)** JAMES, 5th Earl; *d* 1756; *s* by his el son **(6)** DAVID, *de jure* 6th Earl, who having been attainted in 1746 did not succeed to the titles and they remained dormant; *dspms* 1787, when the peerages but for the attainder would have devolved upon his younger brother **(7)** FRANCIS, *de jure* 7th Earl; *b* 1725; assumed the surname of Charteris in lieu of that of Wemyss on being made his heir by his maternal grandfather, Col Francis Charteris, of Amisfield, who *d* 1732; enabled by Act of Parliament in 1771 to retain the surname, arms and estates of Charteris of Amisfield, notwithstanding the devolution upon him of the Earldom of Wemyss, or any other title, which under the will of Col Charteris had been prohibited; assumed the Earldom of Wemyss on the death of his el brother in 1787; *d* 1808; *s* by his grandson **(8)** FRANCIS 8th Earl; *b* 1772; in 1810 on the death of the 4th Duke of Queensberry, who was also 3rd Earl of March he *s* (under special remainder, being the lineal heir male of Lady Anne Douglas, sister of 1st Earl of March) (see *infra), as 4th *Earl of March*, and in 1821 was *cr Baron Wemyss*, of Wemyss, co Fife (peerage of United Kingdom); obtained a reversal of the attainder in 1826; was Lord-Lieut of co Peebles, *d* 1853; *s* by his son **(9)** FRANCIS, 9th Earl; *b* 1796; was Lord-Lieut of Haddingtonshire: *m* 1817, Lady Louisa Bingham, who *d* 1882, da of 2nd Earl of Lucan; *d* 1 Jan 1883; *s* by his son **(10)** FRANCIS, GCVO, LLD, 10th Earl; *b* 1818; was Scotch Lord of the Treasury 1853-5, and an ADC to Queen Victoria 1881-1901, to King Edward VII 1901-10, and to King George V 1910-14; MP for E Gloucestershire (LC) 1841-6, and for Haddingtonshire 1847-83: *m* 1st, 1843, Lady Anne Frederica Anson, who *d* 1896, da of 1st Earl of Lichfield; 2ndly, 1900, Grace, who *d* 1946, da of late Major Blackburn; *d* 1914; *s* by his el surviving son **(11)** HUGO RICHARD, 11th Earl; *b* 1857; MP for Haddingtonshire (C) 1883-5, and for Ipswich 1886-95: *m* 1883, Mary Constance, who *d* 1937, da of late Hon Percy Scawen Wyndham; *d* 1937; *s* by his grandson **(12)** FRANCIS DAVID (son of late Capt Hugo Francis Lord Elcho), who was *ka* 1916, 12th Earl and present peer; also Earl of March, Viscount of Peebles, Lord Elcho and Methel, Lord Douglas of Neidpath, Lyne, and Munard, Lord Wemyss of Elcho, and Lord Wemyss of Wemyss.

*(1) Lord WILLIAM DOUGLAS, 2nd son of 1st Duke of Queensberry, *b* circa 1665; Gov of Edinburgh Castle 1702-4; received from his father on his marriage the lands of Neidpath and others in Peeblesshire; *cr Lord Douglas of Neidpath,

Lyne, and Munard, Viscount of Peebles, and *Earl of March* (peerage of Scotland) 1697, with remainder to heirs male of his body, failing which to his other heirs male and of tailzie; *m* 1693, Lady Jane Hay, who *d* 1729, da of 1st Marquess of Tweeddale; *d* 1705; *s* by his son **(2)** WILLIAM, 2nd Earl; *b* circa 1696: *m* 17-, Lady Anne Hamilton (who *s* her father as Countess of Ruglen 1744 and who *m* 2ndly, 1747, Anthony Sawyer, and *d* 1748), da of 3rd Earl of Selkirk and 1st Earl of Ruglen; *d* 1731; *s* by his son **(3)** WILLIAM, KT, 3rd Earl, *b* 1725, *s* his kinsman as 4th Duke of Queensberry 1778, and his mother as 4th Earl of Ruglen 1748; *cr Baron Douglas of Amesbury*, co Wilts (peerage of Great Britain) 1768; *d* unm 1810, when the Barony of Douglas of Amesbury and the Earldom of Ruglen became ext, the Dukedom of Queensberry reverted to the 3rd Duke of Buccleuch, the Marquessate and Earldom of Queensberry passed to his kinsman Sir Charles Douglas, 5th Bt, of Kelhead, and the Earldom of March devolved on his kinsman **(4)** FRANCIS, 4th Earl (great-great-grandson of Lady Anne Douglas, wife of 4th Earl of Wemyss, and sister of 1st Earl of March), who had *s* as 8th Earl of Wemyss 1808, but on account of his predecessor's forfeiture none of the titles was recognised by the Crown until his attainder was reversed in 1826 (ante).

WESSEX, EARL OF, SEE ROYAL FAMILY.

West, see Baron Granville-West.

West, Sackville-, family name of Baron Sackville.

WESTBURY, BARON (Bethell) (Baron UK 1861)

Ap Ithel (the old Welsh family name)

DAVID ALAN BETHELL, CBE, MC, 5th Baron; *b* 16 July 1922; *s* 1961; *ed* Harrow, and RMC Sandhurst; Capt Scots Guards; DL N Yorks 1973; Equerry to HRH the Duke of Gloucester 1947-49; KStJ 1977, Bailiff of Egle, Order of St John 1988-92, Bailiff Grand Cross 1988; 1939-45 War in N Africa and Italy (thrice wounded, despatches, MC); CBE 1994: *m* 1947, Ursula Mary-Rose, da of late Hon Robert James (*see* B Northbourne, colls), and has issue.

Arms – Argent, on a chevron engrailed azure between three boars' heads couped sable, an estoile or, all within a bordure of the third. **Crest** – Out of a crown vallery or, an eagle's head sable, between two wings azure, charged on the breast with an estoile as in the arms. **Supporters** – On either side an eagle, wings addorsed azure, ducally crowned, collared, and charged on the breast with an estoile or.
Residences – Grange Cottage, Thirlby, N Yorks YO7 2DT, 8 Ropers Orchard, Danvers St, SW3 5AX. *Club* – Jockey.

SONS LIVING

Hon RICHARD NICHOLAS, MBE, *b* 29 May 1950; *ed* Harrow, and RMA Sandhurst; Maj Scots Guards; MBE (Mil) 1979; served in NI and S Atlantic Campaign 1982 (despatches twice, wounded); Officer Brother, Order of St John; *m* 1st, 1975 (*m diss* 1991), Caroline Mary, da of Richard John Palmer, of Queen Anne's Mead, Swallowfield, Berks (*see* V Churchill); 2ndly, 1993, Charlotte Sara Jane, elder da of John Temple Gore (*see* E Eglinton, 1990 Edn), and formerly wife of Maj Sir Hervey James Hugh Bruce, 7th Bt (*cr* 1804), and has issue living (by 1st *m*), Alexander, *b* 21 Dec 1986, — Alice Mary, *b* 1979, — Rose *b* 1984. *Residence* – 60 Bromfelde Rd, SW4.

Hon James David William, *b* 1952: *m* 1st, 1974, Emma Hermione, yr da of late Maj Malise Allen Nicolson, MC, of Frog Hall, Tilston, Malpas, Cheshire; 2ndly, 1987, Mrs Sally Le Gallais, da of John Roberts (*see* Roberts, Bt, *cr* 1909, colls) and has issue living (by 1st *m*), Clare Angelina Serena, *b* 1977, — Lucinda Emma, *b* 1979, — (by 2nd *m*) Edward David John, *b* 1994, — Jessica Mary, *b* 1988. *Residence* – Clarendon House, Middleham, Leyburn, N Yorks DL8 4NP.

DAUGHTER LIVING

Hon (Celia) Mary, *b* 1955: *m* 1980, as his 2nd wife, (Lionel) Brook Holliday, yr son of late Maj Lionel Brook Holliday, OBE, TD, of Copgrove Hall, Yorks, and has issue living, Lucy, *b* 1983, — Serena, *b* 1990. *Residence* – Thirlby Grange, Thirlby, Thirsk, N Yorks YO7 2DL.

SISTER LIVING (*Raised to the rank of a Baron's daughter* 1930)

Hon Veronica Wenefryde Nefertari, *b* 1917: *m* 1941, Lieut-Col James Innes, Coldstream Guards (ret) (E Lonsdale), and has issue living, James Richard (Romanys, Lawbrook Lane, Peaslake, Guildford, Surrey) *b* 1943; Lt-Col Coldm Gds, — Peter David (Boon House, Lauder, Berwicks), *b* 1952; Capt Coldm Gds: *m* 1980, Carolyn Ann Darley, da of Julian Blackwell, of Osse Field, Appleton, Oxon, and has issue living, James David *b* 1982, Sarah Clementine *b* 1984, Laura Mary *b* 1987, — Elizabeth Mary, *b* 1947: *m* 1st, 1967 (*m diss* 1972), James Keith Alan Rugge-Price (*see* Rugge-Price, Bt); 2ndly, 1973, Edward Rice Nicholl, of Trewhitt Hall, Thropton, Northumberland NE65 7ET, and has issue (by 1st *m*) (*see* Rugge-Price, Bt), (by 2nd *m*), Katherine Sarah *b* 1974, Emily Mary *b* 1977.

COLLATERAL BRANCHES LIVING

Grandchildren of late Lionel Beresford Bethell, 3rd son of late Hon Slingsby Bethell, CB, 2nd son of 1st Baron:—
Issue of late Maj Vivian Lionel Slingsby Bethell, *b* 1897, *d* 1967: *m* 1928, Joan Ker, who *d* 1984, da of late John Manwell:—
Richard Ker Slingsby, OBE (Court Farm House, Nunney, Frome, Somerset; *Club* – Army and Navy) *b* 1928; Capt RN, OBE (Mil) 1973; DL Somerset 1991: *m* 1953, Anne, da of H. Frost, and has issue living, Helena Susan Mary, *b* 1955: *m* 1978, Cdr Nicholas J. G. Harland, RN, of Quinces, Piddlehinton, Dorset, and has issue living, Rupert Slingsby *b* 1981, Francesca *b* 1984, — Theresa Jane, *b* 1956: *m* 1979, Michael J. Stephenson, of Napier Lodge, Napier Av, SW6, and has issue living, Edward *b* 1982, Emily *b* 1984, — Jane Ker, *b* 1959: *m* 1979, David F. Fletcher, of 18 Rusholme Rd, Putney, SW15, and has issue living, Charles *b* 1992, Rosanna *b* 1987. —— Deirdre Ann, *b* 1929: *m* 1st, 1952 (*m diss* 1964), Sir Hugo Giles Edmund Sebright, 14th Bt, who *d* 1985; 2ndly, 1965, Anthony Melbourne-Hart, who *d* 1988. *Residence* – Swingletree, Stone Allerton, Wedmore, Som BS26 2NW.

Grandchildren of late Hon Slingsby Bethell, CB (ante):—
Issue of late Llwelyn Slingsby Bethell, *b* 1889, *d* 1971: *m* 1914, Margery Gladys, who *d* 1985, aged 99, da of late George Stanley Farnell, Prin of Victoria Coll, Jersey:—
Margaret Eve Slingsby, *b* 1915: *m* 1939 (*m diss* 1969), Cdr Warwick Bracegirdle, DSC, RAN, who *d* 1993, and has issue living, Simon Warwick Slingsby (30 Lower Coast Rd, Stanwell Park, NSW 2508, Australia), *b* 1941: *m* 1962 (*m diss* 1972), Carolyn, da of late Charles Hale, and has issue living, Saul *b* 1963, Joshua *b* 1982, Ruth *b* 1964, — Nicolas (12 Belgrave Terrace, Camden, Bath BA1 5JC), *b* 1944; Lt Cdr RN (ret): *m* 1975, Carol Patricia Gay, da of late Godfrey Vernon Bird, GM, of Briar Cottage, Roman Landing, W Wittering, Sussex, and has issue living, Belinda Alice *b* 1979, Isobel Louise *b* 1983, — Phillada Ann BRACEGIRDLE (11 Maplehurst Rd, Portslade, E Sussex BN41 2LR), *b* 1946: *m* 1965 (*m diss* 1986), — Lecomte; has issue living (by Gerard Vilage), Gaea VILAGE *b* 1973; *ed* Bristol Univ (BA). *Residence* – 11 Maplehurst Rd, Portslade, E Sussex BN41 2LR.

Issue of late Lt-Cdr Richard Alfred Slingsby Bethell, RN (ret), *b* 1892, *d* 1975: *m* 1930, Frances Elizabeth (Hill Close, School Lane, Litton Cheney, Dorchester, Dorset DT2 9AU), da of late Lt-Col Charles Maxwell Shurlock Henning, of Frome House, Dorchester, Dorset:—
Maxwell Slingsby, *b* 1931; *ed* Wellington Coll, and Camb Univ (MB and BCh, MA, FRCPsych): *m* 1953, Pamela Mary, da of late Hubert Fletcher, and has issue living, Charles Maxwell Slingsby, *b* 1957: *m* 1987 (*m diss* 19—), Cathryn E. Baker, — Nicola Slingsby, *b* 1953: *m* 1981, Nicholas Winer, of Maadi, Cairo, Egypt, and has issue living, Daniel *b* 1982, Rose Elvira *b* 1976, — Juliet Slingsby, *b* 1955: *m* 19— (*m diss* 19—), ... Hallam, — Zoe Melisende Slingsby, *b* 1958: *m* 1st, 1980, David W. Naylor; 2ndly, 1997, Paul Herrington, and has issue living (by 1st *m*), Nicola Joanna *b* 1980, India Rachael *b* 1986, (by 2nd *m*), Jack Slingsby *b* 1998. —— David Slingsby (14 Lombard St, Lichfield, Staffs WS13 6DR), *b* 1934; *ed* Wellington Coll, and Peterhouse, Camb (BA 1958, MA 1962); late Lieut The Cameronians: *m* 1964, Sadie Patricia Melfort, eldest da of Lt-Col P. G. M. Baldwin, of Culver House, Payhembury, Devon, and has issue living, Richard Slingsby, *b* 1965; *ed* Leicester Univ (BSc); late Lieut RN; MIEE: *m* 1994, My Dung, da of Nguyen Trong Ngoc, of Saigon, Vietnam, and has issue living, Hugh (Minh Tri) Slingsby *b* 1997, — Christopher Maunsell Slingsby (Montague House, 2 Dartmouth Hill, SE10), *b* 1966; MPhil (Cantab): *m* 1994, Nichola J., da of Morris Gray, of Alicante, Spain, — Zillah Slingsby, *b* 1968; MA (Oxon).

PREDECESSORS – (1) *Rt Hon Sir* RICHARD Bethell, DCL; sat as MP for Aylesbury 1851-9, and for Wolverhampton 1859-61; was Solicitor-Gen 1852-6, Attorney-Gen 1856-8 and 1859-61, and Lord Chancellor of England 1861-5; *cr Baron Westbury*, of Westbury (peerage of United Kingdom) 1861; *d* 1873; *s* by his son (2) RICHARD AUGUSTUS, 2nd Baron; *b* 1830; was a Registrar in Bankruptcy: *m* 1851, Mary Florence, who *d* 1901, da of Rev Alexander Fownes-Luttrell; *d* 1875; *s* by his son (3) RICHARD LUTTRELL PILKINGTON, 3rd Baron; *b* 1852: *m* 1882, Lady Agatha Manners Tollemache, who *d* 1941, sister of 9th Earl of Dysart; *d* 1930; *s* by his grandson (4) RICHARD MORLAND TOLLEMACHE (son of late Capt Hon Richard Bethell, only son of 3rd Baron), 4th Baron; *b* 1914; European War 1939-45 as Major RE; *d* 1961; *s* by his brother (5) DAVID ALAN, 5th Baron and present peer.

Westenra, family name of Baron Rossmore.

WESTMEATH, EARL OF (Nugent) (Earl I 1621)

I have resolved

WILLIAM ANTHONY NUGENT, 13th Earl; *b* 21 Nov 1928; *s* 1971; *ed* Marlborough and RMA Sandhurst; late Capt RA; sometime Senior Master, St Andrews Sch, Pangbourne (ret 1988): *m* 1963, Susanna Margaret, only da of His Hon Judge (James Charles Beresford Whyte) Leonard, of Cross Trees, Sutton Courtenay, Oxon, and has issue.

Arms – Ermine, two bars gules. **Crest** – A cockatrice, wings elevated and displayed, vert. **Supporters** – Two cockatrices, wings elevated, vert.
Residence – Farthings, Rotten Row Hill, Tutts Clump, Bradfield, Berks RG7 6LL.

SONS LIVING

SEAN CHARLES WESTON (does not use courtesy title of Lord Delvin), *b* 16 Feb 1965; *ed* Ampleforth.
Hon Patrick Mark Leonard (17 Alandale Close, Whitley Wood, Reading RG2 8JP), *b* 1966; *ed* Douai, and Lancaster Univ.

SISTER LIVING

Lady Pamela Joan, *b* 1921; sometime Section Officer WAAF: *m* 1950, Lieut-Col Peter John Barbary, OBE, GM, TD, DL, FRIBA, who *d* 1969, and has issue living, Michael John Nugent (14 Creswells Terrace, St Just, Penzance, Cornwall TR19 7QF), *b* 1951, — Joanna Clare Nugent (44 West Hill, Hitchin, Herts SG5 2HY), *b* 1955. *Residence* – Briar Rose Cottage, 17 Landeryon Gdns, Penzance, Cornwall TR18 4JN.

COLLATERAL BRANCHES LIVING

Granddaughter of late Maj-Gen St George Mervyn Nugent, son of late Christopher Edmund John Nugent, a descendant of late Oliver Nugent, brother of 13th Baron Delvin:—
Issue of late Maj-Gen Sir Oliver Stewart Wood Nugent, KCB, DSO, *b* 1860, *d* 1926: *m* 1899, Catherine Percy, who *d* 1970, da of late Thomas Evans Lees, of Betley Hall, Ches:—
Alison Joan Elliott, *b* 1909: *m* 1947, Harry Gerhard Hirschberg, LLD, of Cullentragh, Mount Nugent, co Cavan.

(In remainder to Barony of Delvin)

Grandchildren of late Brig-Gen Frank Henry BURNELL-NUGENT, CB, DSO, OBE, yst son of Albert Llewellyn Nugent, 4th son of Walter Nugent (*cr* Baron of Austria 1859, with remainder to issue male and female), 10th in descent from Andrew Nugent of Clonlost, yr son of Andrew Nugent of Donore, brother of 11th Baron Devlin:—
Issue of late Cdr Anthony Frank Burnell-Nugent, DSC, RN (ret), *b* 1906, *d* 1976: *m* 1941, Gian Mary, da of late Rear-Adm Charles Otway Alexander, of Wilford Rise, Woodbridge, Suffolk:—
Charles Anthony (*Baron Nugent*) (10 Radley Lodge, 25 Inner Park Rd, Wimbledon SW19 6DG), *b* 1942; *s* his cousin as 8th Baron Nugent 1988; *ed* Brickwall. ——— James Michael, *b* 1949; *ed* Stowe, and Corpus Christi Coll, Camb; Commodore RN: *m* 1973, Henrietta Mary, yst da of late Rt Rev Robert Wilmer Woods, KCMG, KCVO, formerly Dean of Windsor and Bishop of Worcester, and has issue living, Anthony James, *b* 1980, — Rupert Michael, *b* 1982, — Thomas Alexander, *b* 1986, — Henrietta Marie, *b* 1978. ——— Mary, *b* 1947: *m* 1967, John Richard Conway Lloyd, of Argent Manor, Stutton, Ipswich, and has issue living, John Conway, *b* 1970, — Lucy Ellen, *b* 1972: *m* 1997, Major Crispin Alexander Lockhart, The Blues and Royals (*see* L Gray, colls), and has issue (*see* that title). ——— Sheila Jane, *b* 1951: *m* 1980, Marino Gianella, of Florence, Italy, and has issue living, Francesco, *b* 1981.

PREDECESSORS – (1) RICHARD Nugent, 12th Baron of Delvin, and Lord Dep of Ireland 1528, was summoned to Parliament of Ireland 1486, 1490, and 1493; *d* 1538; *s* by his grandson (2) RICHARD, 13th Baron; *d* 1559; *s* by his son (3) CHRISTOPHER, 14th Baron; *d* 1602; *s* by his son (4) RICHARD, 15th Baron; *cr Earl of Westmeath* (peerage of Ireland) 1621; *d* 1641; *s* by his grandson (5) RICHARD, 2nd Earl; *d* 1684; *s* by his grandson (6) RICHARD, 3rd Earl; was a Capuchin Friar; *d* 1714; *s* by his brother (7) THOMAS, 4th Earl; having been outlawed for his adhesion to the cause of James II, the outlawry was afterwards reversed and his honours and estates restored; *d* 1752; *s* by his brother (8) JOHN, 5th earl; a Major-Gen in the Army; *d* 1754; *s* by his son (9) THOMAS, KP, 6th Earl; conformed to the Established Church, *d* 1792; *s* by his son (10) GEORGE FREDERICK, 7th Earl; *d* 1814; *s* by his son (11) GEORGE THOMAS JOHN, 8th Earl; was Lord-Lieut of co Westmeath, and a Representative Peer; *cr Marquess of Westmeath* (peerage of Ireland) 1822; *d* 1871, when the marquessate became extinct, and the earldom devolved upon his kinsman (12) ANTHONY FRANCIS, 9th Earl, descendant of Thomas, 2nd son of 2nd Earl, whose father was called 4th Lord Riverston (a title that had been conferred by James II after his deposition); *b* 1805; established his claim to the Earldom 1871; *d* 1879; *s* by his son (13) WILLIAM ST GEORGE, 10th Earl, *b* 1832: *m* 1866, Emily Margaret, who *d* 1906, da of late Andrew William Blake, JP, DL, of Furbough, co Galway; *d* 1883; *s* by his son (14) ANTHONY FRANCIS, 11th Earl, *b* 1870; a Representative Peer for Ireland; *d* 1933; *s* by his brother (15) GILBERT CHARLES, 12th Earl, *b* 1880: *m* 1915, Doris, who *d* 1968, da of late Charles Imlach, of Liverpool; *d* 1971; *s* by his son (16) WILLIAM ANTHONY, 13th Earl and present peer, also Baron Delvin.

WESTMINSTER, DUKE OF (Grosvenor) (Duke UK 1874, Bt E 1622)

GERALD CAVENDISH GROSVENOR, OBE, 6th Duke, and 15th Baronet; *b* 22 Dec 1951; *s* 1979; *ed* Harrow, and Sunningdale Sch; DL Cheshire 1982; Lt-Col and OC Queen's Own Yeo (TAVR) 1992; Dir Grosvenor Estate Holdings, Marcher Sound Ltd, Sutton Ridge Pty Ltd, North West Business Leadership Team, and Business in the Community; Pres Royal Nat Inst for the Blind since 1986, Scope, Arthritis Care, Game Conservancy, Abbeyfield Soc, BLESMA, Youth Clubs UK, BASC, and Drug and Alcohol Foundn; Pres of Royal Agric Soc of England; Chancellor Manchester Metropolitan Univ; Trustee Lloyds TSB, Foundn for England and Wales 1986-97, and The Civic Trust; Member of Council of National Army Museum 1988-97; Freeman of City of Chester in 1971 and of London 1981; KStJ 1991, OBE (Mil) 1995: *m* 1978, Natalia Ayesha, yst da of late Lt-Col Harold Pedro Joseph Phillips, FRGS (*see* Wernher, Bt), and has issue.

Virtue, not ancestry

Arms – Quarterly: 1st and 4th azure, a portcullis with chains pendant or, on a chief of the last, between two united roses of York and Lancaster a pale, charged with the arms of King Edward the Confessor *City of Westminster* (Augmentation); 2nd and 3rd azure, a garb or, *Grosvenor.* **Crest** – A talbot statant or. **Supporters** – Two talbots reguardant or, collared azure.
Seat – Eaton Hall, Eaton, Chester. *Clubs* – Cavalry and Guards'; MCC; Brooks's; Roy Yacht Sqdn.

SON LIVING

HUGH RICHARD LOUIS (*Earl Grosvenor*), *b* 29 Jan 1991.

DAUGHTERS LIVING

Lady Tamara Katherine, *b* 1979.
Lady Edwina Louise, *b* 1981.
Lady Viola Georgina, *b* 1992.

SISTERS LIVING

Lady Leonora Mary (*Countess of Lichfield*), LVO, *b* 1949; Lady in Waiting to HRH The Princess Royal since 1977; LVO 1997: *m* 1975 (*m diss* 1986), 5th Earl of Lichfield. *Residence* – 80 Eaton Sq, SW1.

Lady Jane Meriel, *b* 1953; resumed her maiden name 1990 until remarriage: *m* 1st, 1977 (*m diss* 1990), 10th Duke of Roxburghe; 2ndly, 1996, her 2nd cousin, Edward William Dawnay (*see* V Downe, colls). *Residence* – Hillington Hall, King's Lynn, Norfolk PE31 6BW.

DAUGHTER LIVING OF SECOND DUKE (by 1st marriage)

Lady Mary Constance, *b* 1910. *Residence* – Saighton Lodge, Saighton, Chester.

WIDOW LIVING OF SECOND DUKE

ANNE WINIFRED (*Anne, Duchess of Westminster*), only da of late Brig-Gen Edward Langford Sullivan, CB, CMG, of Glanmire House, co Cork: *m* 1947, as his fourth wife, the 2nd Duke of Westminster, who *d* 1953. *Residence* – Eaton Lodge, Eccleston, Chester.

COLLATERAL BRANCHES LIVING

Granddaughter of late Lord Arthur Hugh Grosvenor, 9th son of 1st Duke:—
Issue of late Robert Arthur Grosvenor, MC, *b* 1895, *d* 1953: *m* 1925, Doris May, who *d* 1975, da of late
    Frederick William Wignall (Tate, Bt, colls):—
Robina Jill, *b* 1930: *m* 1st, 1951 (*m diss* 1961), Michael Phillip Forsyth-Forrest; 2ndly, 1961, Ronald Mills of Court Farm,
Kenchester, Hereford, and has issue living, (by 1st *m*) Anita, *b* 1952: *m* 1st, 19— (*m diss* 19—) George Mavros; 2ndly,
1995, Nicholas J. Stabb, and has issue living (by 1st *m*), a son *b* 1988, — Tessa (*Hon Mrs Harry Fane*), *b* 1955: *m* 1st,
19—, Christopher Baldwin; 2ndly, 1984, Hon Harry St Clair Fane, yr son of 15th Earl of Westmorland, and has issue
living (by 2nd *m*) (*see* E Westmorland), — (by 2nd *m*), Robin, *b* 1962, — Serena Laura Rosanna, *b* 1965.

(In remainder to the Marquessate)

Descendants of late Rt Hon Lord Thomas Grosvenor, GCH, DCL (2nd son of 1st Marquess), who *s* his
maternal grandfather (under special remainder) as 2nd *Earl of Wilton* 1814 (see that title).

Descendants of late Rt Hon Lord Robert Grosvenor (3rd son of 1st Marquess of Westminster), who
was *cr Baron Ebury* 1857 (see that title).

PREDECESSORS – **(1)** *Sir* RICHARD Grosvenor, Knt, of Eaton, Cheshire, MP for Cheshire, was *cr a Baronet* 1622; *d*
1645; *s* by his son **(2)** *Sir* RICHARD, 2nd Bt; *d* 1664; *s* by his grandson **(3)** *Sir* THOMAS, 3rd Bt; sat as MP for Chester; *d*
1700; *s* by his el son **(4)** *Sir* RICHARD, 4th Bt; was Grand Cupbearer at the coronation of George II, *dsp* 1732; *s* by his
brother **(5)** *Sir* THOMAS, 5th Bt; was MP for Chester; *d* 1733; *s* by his brother **(6)** *Sir* ROBERT, 6th Bt; sat as MP for
Chester; *d* 1755; *s* by his son **(7)** *Sir* RICHARD, 7th Bt; *cr Baron Grosvenor*, of Eaton, co Chester (peerage of Great
Britain) 1761, and *Viscount Belgrave* and *Earl Grosvenor* (peerage of Great Britain) 1784: *m* 1776, Henrietta (who *m*
2ndly, 1802, 6th Baron de Hochepied, and *d* 1828), da of Henry Vernon, of Hilton Park, Staffs; *d* 1802; *s* by his son **(8)**
ROBERT, 2nd Earl; *cr Marquess of Westminster* (peerage of United Kingdom) 1831; was Lord-Lieut of Flintshire: *m* 1794,
Lady Eleanor Egerton, who *d* 1846, da of 1st Earl of Wilton; *d* 1845; *s* by his son **(9)** RICHARD, KG, PC, 2nd Marquess; *b*
1795; was Lord-Lieut of Cheshire: *m* 1819, Elizabeth Mary, who *d* 1891, da of 1st Duke of Sutherland; *d* 1869, *s* by his
son **(10)** HUGH LUPUS, 3rd Marquess; *b* 1825; Lord-Lieut of Cheshire, and of co London; Master of the Horse 1880-85;
MP for Chester (*L*) 1847-69; *cr Duke of Westminster* (peerage of United Kingdom) 1874: *m* 1st, 1852, Lady Constance
Gertrude Leveson-Gower, who *d* 1880, da of 2nd Duke of Sutherland, KG; 2ndly, 1882, Hon Katharine Caroline
Cavendish, CBE, who *d* 1941, da of 2nd Baron Chesham; *d* 1899; *s* by his grandson **(11)** HUGH RICHARD ARTHUR, GCVO,
DSO (only son of Victor Alexander, Earl Grosvenor), 2nd Duke; *b* 1879; Lord-Lieut of Cheshire 1906-20; S Africa 1900-02,
and 1914-18 War: *m* 1st, 1901 (*m diss* 1919), Constance Edwina, CBE, who *d* 1970, da of late Col William Cornwallis-
West (E De La Warr); 2ndly, 1920 (*m diss* 1926), Violet Mary Geraldine, who *d* 1983, da of Sir William Nelson, 1st Bt;
3rdly, 1930 (*m diss* 1947), Hon Lœlia Mary Ponsonby, who *d* 1993, da of 1st Baron Sysonby; 4thly, 1947, Anne Winifred,
only da of late Brig-Gen Edward Langford Sullivan, CB, CMG, of Glanmire House, co Cork; *d* 1953; *s* by his cousin **(12)**
WILLIAM (son of late Lord Henry George Grosvenor, 3rd son of the 1st Duke), 3rd Duke; *d* 1963; *s* by his cousin **(13)**
GERALD HUGH, DSO, PC (el son of late Capt Lord Hugh William Grosvenor, 6th son of 1st Duke) 4th Duke; *b* 1907; Lt
Col 9th Lancers; Col 9th/12th Lancers 1961-67; High Sheriff of Cheshire 1959; Lord Steward of HM Household 1964-67:
m 1945, Sally Perry, who *d* 1990, natural twin da of late Roger Ackerley (by Muriel Perry); *d* 1967; *s* by his brother
(14) ROBERT GEORGE, TD, 5th Duke, *b* 1910; Col N Irish Horse; Lord Lieut co Fermanagh 1977-79, High Sheriff 1952,
PPS to Sec of State for Foreign Affairs 1957-59, MP for Fermanagh and S Tyrone (*U*) 1955-64 and Senator, N Ireland
1964-67: *m* 1946, Hon Viola Maud Lyttelton, who was *k* in a motor accident 1987, da of 9th Viscount Cobham; *d* 1979; *s*
by his only son **(15)** GERALD CAVENDISH, 6th Duke and present peer; also Marquess of Westminster, Earl Grosvenor,
Viscount Belgrave, and Baron Grosvenor.

WESTMORLAND, EARL OF (Fane) (Earl E 1624)

Disgrace not the altar

ANTHONY DAVID FRANCIS HENRY FANE, 16th Earl; *b* 1 Aug 1951; *s* 1993; *ed* Eton; Chm (Europe) Phillips Internatnl Auctioneers; Member Orbitex North Pole Expedition 1990; Life Pres St Moritz Sporting Club; FRGS: *m* 1985, Mrs Caroline Eldred Fairey, da of Keon Hughes, and formerly wife of Charles Fairey, and has issue.

Arms – Azure, three dexter gauntlets back affrontée or. Crest – Out of a ducal coronet or, bull's head of a brindled colour, armed gold, and charged with a rose gules. Supporters – *Dexter*, a griffin, per fesse argent and or, collared, and line reflexed over the back sable; *sinister*, a pied or brindled bull, collared and lined or, at the end of the line a ring and three staples of the last.
Residence – 31 Langton St, SW10 0JL. *Club* – Turf.

DAUGHTER LIVING

Lady Daisy Caroline, *b* 1989.

BROTHER LIVING

Hon HARRY ST CLAIR, *b* 19 March 1953; *ed* Harrow; Page of Honour to HM 1966-68: *m* 1984, Tessa, da of Capt Michael Philip Forsyth-Forrest (*see* D Westminster, colls), and formerly wife of Christopher Baldwin, and has issue living, Sam Michael David, *b* 1989, — Sophie Jane, *b* 1987. *Residences* – 14 Trevor St, SW7; The Barn House, Eastcourt, Malmesbury, Wilts.

SISTER LIVING

Lady Camilla Diana, *b* 1957: *m* 1985, Howard J. Hipwood, and has issue living, Sebastian John, *b* 1988, — Rosanna Charlotte, *b* 1986. *Residence* – Fosse Tillery Farm, Brokenborough, Malmesbury, Wilts SN16 0HY.

UNCLE LIVING (*son of 14th Earl*)

Hon Julian Charles, *b* 1927; *ed* Harrow; Author; FRSL 1974: *m* 1976, Gillian, yr da of late John Kidston Swire, DL, of Hubbards Hall, Harlow, Essex. *Residence* – Rotten Row House, Lewes, E Sussex BN7 1TN.

WIDOW LIVING OF FIFTEENTH EARL

BARBARA JANE (*Dowager Countess of Westmorland*), da of Lt-Col Sir Roland Lewis Findlay, 3rd Bt: *m* 1950, the 15th Earl of Westmorland, GCVO, who *d* 1993. *Residences* – The Old Rectory, Badminton, Avon; 26 Laxford House, Cundy St, SW1.

COLLATERAL BRANCHES LIVING

Issue of late Lt-Col Hon Mountjoy John Charles Wedderburn Fane, TD, 2nd son of 13th Earl, *b* 1900, *d* 1963: *m* 1926, Agatha Isabel, who *d* 1993, da of late Lt-Col Arthur Acland-Hood-Reynardson, OBE (*see* Fuller-Acland-Hood, Bt, colls, 1990 Edn):—
Antony Charles Reynardson (Ridgemead House, Shrubbs Hill Lane, Sunningdale, Berks SL5 OLD), *b* 1927; Lt-Cdr RN (ret): *m* 1956, Caroline Mary Rokeby, da of late Hugh D. Holland, of The Crossways, Englefield Green, Surrey, and has issue living, Edward Hugh Reynardson (The Old Farmhouse, West St, Burghclere, Hants RG20 9LB), *b* 1957; *ed* Harrow: *m* 1982, Suki Serena, only da of Sir David Mitchell, of Berry Horn Cottage, Odiham, Hants, and has issue living, Arthur Charles Reynardson *b* 1992, Elizabeth Helen Clementine *b* 1986, Helena Evelyn Cecily *b* 1988, — Olivia Mary Rokeby, *b* 1960: *m* 1st, 1982 (*m diss* 1992), Adam Nicolson (*see* B Carnock, colls); 2ndly, 1993, (Richard) Mark Pemberton, of The Old Dairy, Stoughton, W Sussex PO18 9JQ (*see* Riddell, Bt), — Charlotte Evelyn Langham, *b* 1967. —— Daphne Sybil, *b* 1929.

Grandchildren of late Col William (Vere Reeve) KING-FANE, only son of late William Dashwood Fane, 5th son of late Hon Henry Fane, MP, yr son of 8th Earl:—
Issue of late Capt Henry William Newman Fane, OBE, *b* 1897, *d* 1976: *m* 1946, Dorothy Mary, who *d* 1986, only da of late Alexander Findlay, of Llantarnam, Gwent:—
Mary Helen, *b* 1947: *m* 1982, Michael Robin Fry, and has issue living, Marcus Fane, *b* 1985, — Samuel Henry Fane, *b* 1987. *Residence* – Fulbeck Hall, Grantham, Lincs.

Issue of late Lt Francis Christopher Fane, RN, *b* 1900, *d* 1947: *m* 1931, Joyce Patricia (Scots Hill, Fulbeck, Grantham, Lincs) (who *m* 2ndly, 1957, Maj Vincent Tofts, TD, late Indian Army, who *d* 1983), da of late Rev W. Hugh Hancock:—
Julian Francis, *b* 1938; *ed* Marlborough and Emmanuel Coll, Camb (MA), High Sheriff of Lincolnshire 1981, DL 1997: *m* 1965, Mary Julia, da of Michael W. Allday, of The Shrubbery, Hartlebury, Worcs, and has issue living, Andrew Julian, *b* 1967; *ed* Marlborough, — Alexandra Julia, *b* 1969. *Residence* – Fulbeck Manor, Grantham, Lincs. —— Susan Cicely, *b* 1932: *m* 1953, Lt-Col John Lindley Marmion Dymoke, MBE, DL, late R Anglian Regt, 34th Queen's Champion of

England (By Lindley, ext), High Sheriff Lincs 1979, Vice-Lord Lieut 1991 and 1995, and has issue living, Francis John Fane Marmion (Scrivelsby Grange, Horncastle, Lincs), *b* 1955; High Sheriff Lincs 1999: *m* 1982, Rosalie Mary, only da of Maj Antony Goldingham, of Marsh Farm, Uley, Glos, and has issue living, Henry Francis Marmion *b* 1984, Thomas Antony Marmion *b* 1989, Emily Rachel Marmion *b* (twin) 1984, — Philip Henry Marmion (28 Ellerby St, SW6 6EY), *b* 1957; late Maj WG: *m* 1982, Arabella, yr da of Sir Ralph Jordan Dodds, 2nd Bt, and has issue living, Edward Philip Marmion *b* 1985, William Thomas Marmion *b* 1988, — Charles Edward Marmion, *b* 1961: *m* 1990, Kathryn Jane, yst da of Rex Topham, of Otford, Kent, and has issue living, Jasper Rex Fane *b* 1993, Angus John Topham *b* 1994, Archie Charles Lindley *b* 1997. *Seat* – Scrivelsby Court, Horncastle, Lincs. *Club* – United Service. —— Rosemary Lillias, *b* 1934; BA (Soc Sci 1987) JP: *m* 1954, Derek Cecil Stevenson, MB BS, MRCS, LRCP, FRCS, who *d* 1998, and has issue living, Christopher Peter (60 Thomas St, Nedlands, W Australia 6009), *b* 1956; B Juris, LLB (UWA), LLM (Lond); Sqn Ldr RAAF: *m* 1985, Evelyn Bowen, MB BS, DObst (RCOG), and has issue living, Richard Vere *b* 1990, Harry Bowen *b* 1994, Georgina Bowen *b* 1988, — Melody Jane, *b* 1958: *m* 1980, Christopher John Chipper (PO Box 131, York, W Australia 6302), and has issue living, Simon Derek *b* 1984, Jasmin Melody *b* 1982, — Catherine Fane, *b* 1960: *m* 1985, Peter Charles Kiel, MB BS, of 63 Alderbury St, Floreat, W Australia 6014, and has issue living, Michael William Fane *b* 1989, David Peter Stevenson *b* 1991, Sarah Jane Mary *b* 1987, — Mary-Louise, *b* 1969; BSc: *m* 1993, Russell Paul Hardwick, of Lot 35 Liddelow Rd, Banjup, W Australia 6164, and has issue living, Hayley Louise *b* 1997. *Residence* – 7 Muller St, N Beach, W Australia 6020. —— Belinda Joyce (26a Cumberland Way, Bassendean, W Australia 6024), *b* (twin) 1938; ThA 1976, ThDip 1988: *m* 1971 (*m diss* 1981), Gary Douglas Phillips.

Issue of late Charles William Fane, *b* 1904, *d* 1976: *m* 1st, 1931 (*m diss* 1966), Pauline Margaret, who *d* 1994, da of Rt Rev Ernest Morell Blackie, Dean of Rochester; 2ndly, 1966, Pamela Mary, who *d* 1987, da of late Capt Robert Millington Synge (*see* Synge, Bt, colls):—
(By 1st wife) Peter William (?? Cheyne Row, SW3 5HL; Garrick Club and MCC), *b* 1939; *ed* Eton; High Sheriff of Lincs 1983-84: *m* 1969, Ruth, da of late John Paske Yeomans, and has an adopted son, Maximilian William, *b* 1978. —— Angela Pauline, *b* 1936: *m* 1964, Lt-Cdr Kenneth Patrick Bruce-Gardyne, RN, of The Old Rectory, Meonstoke, Hants, and has issue living, James Patrick, *b* 1965, — Vere Alexander, *b* 1973, — Victoria Sophie, *b* 1969. —— (By 2nd wife) Eleanor Mary (Tree Tops, Ashmansworth, Newbury, Berks), *b* 1965: *m* 1999, Jon Magnusson. —— Georgina Rachel, *b* 1966: *m* 1995, Jocelyn Andrew Denison-Pender, and has issue (*see* B Pender). —— Rose Christabel (24 Wandsworth Bridge Rd, SW6), *b* 1968.

Grandchildren of late John Lionel Richards Fane (infra):—
Issue of late Vere John Alexander Fane, *b* 1935, *d* 1997: *m* 1964, Tessa Helen Murray (18 Empire House, Thurloe Place, SW7 2RU), only da of late John Murray Prain, DSO, OBE, DL, of Longrigg, St Andrews, Fife:—
Rupert John Alexander, *b* 1967: *m* 1998, Nicola, da of Jens Dowling, of Sydney, Australia. —— Miranda Helen, *b* 1968: *m* 1997, Jamie Landale, yst son of Sir David William Neil Landale, KCVO, DL, of Dalswinton, Dumfries. *Residence* – 20 Luxemburg Gdns, W6 7EA.

Granddaughter of late Cecil Francis William Fane, 2nd son of late Robert George Cecil Fane, 7th son of late Hon Henry Fane, MP (ante):—
Issue of late John Lionel Richards Fane, *b* 1884, *d* 1945: *m* 1928 Barbara Kathleen (who *d* 1980, having *m* 3rdly, 1947, Bryan Northam Gibbs, MBE, who *d* 1965, and 4thly, 1969, John Sidney Mason, who *d* 1974), da of late Falconer Lewis Wallace, OBE, of Candacraig, Aberdeenshire (M Anglesey, colls), and formerly wife of late Capt Oliver Henry Douglas Vickers:—
Venetia Sophia Diana, MBE (Drumwhill, Mossdale, by Castle Douglas, Kirkcudbrightshire DG7 2NL), *b* 1930; MBE (Civil) 1994.

Grandchildren of late Major John Augustus Fane, el son of late Col John William Fane, MP, son of John Fane, MP (*b* 1775), el son of John Fane, MP, son of Henry Fane, yr brother of 8th Earl:—
Issue of late Francis Luther Fane, *b* 1865, *d* 1954: *m* 1st, 1906, Mary, who *d* 1927, da of late John Henry Horris of Ballarat, Victoria, Australia; 2ndly, 1929, Beatrice Jane, who *d* 1961, el da of late Harry Coppleston, of Lostwithiel, Cornwall:—
(By 2nd *m*) John Coppleston Luther (MCC, Cavalry and Guards' Club), *b* 1933; *ed* Harrow, and Emmanuel Coll, Camb; late Lt Welsh Guards; High Sheriff of Oxfordshire 1977. —— Anne Isabel (Castle Minor, Tintagel, Cornwall), *b* 1931. *m* 1954 (*m diss* 1976), Colin Irvin Richmond-Watson, and has had issue, Harry Fane (67 Woodmeadow Rd, Kings Norton, Birmingham B30 3PH), *b* 1956, — Angus Colin John, *b* 1958; *d* 1984, — Elizabeth Frances Aves RICHMOND-WATSON (Half Acre, Bix, Henley-on-Thames, Oxon RG9 6AE), *b* 1960; has resumed her maiden name: *m* 1978 (*m diss* 1982), Stuart Hogan, and has issue living, Gareth Michael Colin *b* 1978, — Sarah Eleanor (1 Kettle Rd, Norwalk, Connecticut 06850, USA), *b* 1962: *m* 1987 (*m diss* 1992), Kerry C. Baxley, of New York.

Grandchildren of late Sydney Algernon Fane, 2nd son of late Maj John Augustus Fane (ante):—
Issue of late Capt Gerard William Reginald Fane, DSC, *b* 1898, *d* 1979: *m* 1st, 1919, Constance Rhoda Elizabeth, who *d* 1969, da of Sir Nicholas Henry Bacon, 13th Bt; 2ndly, 1970, Phyllis Jane (Feering Place, Kelvedon, Colchester), da of late Hugh Jackson, of Chevington:—
(By 1st *m*) Julian Raymond, *b* 1925.

Issue of late Cdr Nigel Loftus Henry Fane, RNR, *b* 1904, *d* 1973: *m* 1st, 1935 (*m diss* 1959), Catharine Henrietta, who *d* 1968, da of Henry P. Hussey, of Bricklehurst Manor, Stonegate, Sussex; 2ndly, 1960 (*m diss* 1971), Dorothy Mai, da of John Farrington, and widow of Borras Noel Hamilton Whiteside (*see* L Belhaven and Stenton, colls, 1980 Edn):—
(By 1st *m*) Patricia Margaret, *b* 1936: *m* 1958, as his 1st wife, (Charles Henry) David Denning, of Northgate House, Church St, Ticehurst, E Sussex TN5 7AE, yr son of Lt-Gen Sir Reginald Francis Stewart Denning, KCVO, KBE, CB, and *d* 1996, leaving issue, James Henry (Enderloy House, Dell Lane, Selsley East, Stroud, Glos GL5 5JY), *b* 1959: *m* 1983, Lois Margaret, da of Arthur Green, and has issue living, Thomas Christopher David *b* 1988, Catharine Rebecca *b* 1987, Daisy Patricia *b* 1996, — Guy William (1 Woodside Cottages, Bewl Lane, Lamberhurst, Kent), *b* 1962: *m* 1998, Lindsay Caroline, da of Michael Treanor, and has issue living, Jessie Amelia *b* 1997, — Sophia Jane, *b* 1964: *m* 1987, Duncan Richard Maynard, and has issue living, Charles Hugo Patrick *b* 1996, Emily Victoria *b* 1994, — Venetia Mary, *b* 1966: *m* 1996, Nicholas Peter Evan Davidson, and has issue living, Ella Kate *b* 1997.

Grandchildren of late Hubert William Fane (infra):—
    Issue of late Maj Robert William Augustus Fane, MBE, *b* 1913, *d* 1989: *m* 1940, Elinor Valerie (Hoo Lodge, Hoo, Woodbridge, Suffolk IP13 7QJ), da of late Hon William Borthwick (*see* Borthwick, Bt, colls):—
Andrew William Mildmay, *b* 1949; *ed* Radley, and Emmanuel Coll, Camb (MA); FCA: *m* 1989, Clare Lucy, MB BS, FRCS, yr da of Francis Marx, of Coventry, Warwicks. *Residence* – Hoo House, Hoo, Woodbridge, Suffolk IP13 7QJ. —— Peter Robert Spencer, *b* 1956; *ed* Radley, and RAC Cirencester; MSc, ARICS: *m* 1997, Dorothy E., only da of Thomas Harris, of Brighton, and has issue living, Thomas Robert *b* 1997. *Residence* – Ivy Cottage, Cavenham, nr Bury St Edmunds, Suffolk IP28 6DA. —— Priscilla Margaret, *b* 1943: *m* 1975, Christopher Brewer, of Ballards Cottage, Ballards Lane, Limpsfield, Surrey, and has issue living, Simon Robert, *b* 1976; *ed* Eastbourne Coll, and Emmanuel Coll, Camb, — Charles Thomas, *b* 1979; *ed* Charterhouse. —— Lavinia Anne, *b* 1947: *m* 1974, Stephen Wright, PhD, of Downs Reach, 3 Pewley Bank, Guildford, Surrey, and has issue living, Matthew David Robert, *b* 1975; *ed* Royal Gram Sch, Guildford, Univ Coll, Lond, and Merton Coll, Oxford, — Catherine Frances, *b* 1977. —— Angela Elizabeth (36 Felden St, SW6 5AF), *b* 1954; Bar-at-Law.

    Grandchildren of late Capt Henry George Fane, 2nd son of Col John William Fane, MP (ante):—
    Issue of late Hubert William Fane, *b* 1878, *d* 1949: *m* 1911, Tilda, who *d* 1953, da of late A. von Adametz:—
Dorothy Louisa (25 Amesbury Crescent, Hove, E Sussex BN3 5RD), *b* 1917: *m* 1st, 1938, Capt Frederick James Colville, Gordon Highlanders, who was *ka* 1940 (V Colville of Culross, colls); 2ndly 1941 (*m diss* 1962), Lt-Cdr Clifford John Maddocks, RNVR, MIME, who *d* 1975; 3rdly, 1962 (*m diss* 1974), Lt-Col John Anthony Russell Freeland, late Queen's R Regt, who *d* 1989, and has issue living (by 2nd *m*), Cynthia Diana, *b* 1944: *m* 1967, John Charles Johnson Orchard, of Honington Glebe, Honington, nr Shipston-on-Stour, Warwicks, and has issue living, Alaister Mildmay Heywood *b* 1971, Alexandra Rosemary Fane *b* 1969, — Anne Susan, *b* 1948: *m* 1st, 1968 (*m diss* 1988), Richard Fullerton Evetts; 2ndly, 1989, Christopher Corder Litten, of The Lodge, Bovingdon Green, Bovingdon, Herts HP3 0LD, and has had issue (by 1st *m*), Toby James Fullerton *b* 1970, David Jason Clifford *b* and *d* 1974.

    Issue of late Francis John Fane, *b* 1885, *d* 1963: *m* 1915, Violet, who *d* 1970, da of late G. Clifford Bower, of Newquay, Bromley, Kent:—
Peter Francis George (12 Erskine Close, Pamber Heath, Hants. *Club* – Carlton), *b* 1917; *ed* Marlborough, and Emmanuel Coll, Camb (MA 1939); Capt (ret) RA; 1939-45 War (prisoner): *m* 1939, Diana, only da of late Col George Holden Hodgkinson, and has issue living, Francis Michael George (Murreyfield, Reading Rd, Burghfield Common, Reading, Berks), *b* 1941; *ed* Peterhouse, Rhodesia, and Emmanuel Coll, Camb (MA): *m* 1st, 1967 (*m diss* 1989), Anne Bridget, da of late Maj John Alfred Gordon Gribble; 2ndly, 1989, Irene, da of late Maurice Frederick Osborne Johnston, of 27 Sefton Drive, Maghull, Merseyside, and has issue living (by 1st *m*), Thomas Francis *b* 1968, Suzanne *b* 1972, — Victoria, *b* 1947; BSc 1993: *m* 1966, Martin Richard Cardale, of Castle View Hotel, Chepstow, Gwent, and has issue living, George Martin (36 Ashton Gate Rd, Bristol), *b* 1970: *m* 1998, Annica, da of Bo Henning, of Stockholm, Sweden, Miranda Lucy *b* 1968; *ed* Exeter Univ (BA 1989): *m* 1994, Stuart James Nicholson, of 6 Malcolm Rd, Borrowdale, Harare, Zimbabwe (and has issue living, Olivia Kim *b* 1998), Zara Diana *b* 1962; *ed* Exeter Univ (BA 1984): *m* 1998, Frederic Fournier, of 10 Granville Rd, Palmers Green, N13. —— Elizabeth Daphne (1 Mytchett Heath, Mytchett, Camberley, Surrey GU16 6DP) *b* 1916: *m* 1940, Lt-Col John David Logan Dickson, MC, RHA, who *d* 1958, and has issue living, Jeremy David Fane (8 Alan Rd, Wimbledon, SW19), *b* 1941; *ed* Marlborough, and Emmanuel Coll, Camb (MA): *m* 1965, Patricia, da of Laurence Cleveland Martin, MD, FRCP, and has issue living, James David Laurence *b* 1970, Lucy Camilla *b* 1971, — Sally Ann, *b* 1942: *m* 1975, Lt-Col John Alan Cubitt Blakiston, 13th/18th Royal Hus, and has issue (*see* Blakiston, Bt, colls).

    Grandsons of late Francis John Fane (ante):—
    Issue of late Maj Henry John Fane, MC, RA, *b* 1919, *d* 1993: *m* 1st, 1945 (*m diss* 1970), Agatina, da of Onorevole, Count Severio d'Ayala, of Rome; 2ndly, 1980, Mrs Anne Barclay Fane (Ovingdean, Church Place, Pulborough, W Sussex RH20 1AF), da of late Lt-Col Henry Gamble, OBE, of Instow, N Devon, formerly wife of Lt-Cdr Antony Stuart Melville-Ross, DSC, RN, and widow of his kinsman, Peter Gerald Scrope Fane, RNVR (*see* 1976 Edn):—
(By 1st *m*) Richard John George (45 Oakley St, SW3 5HA), *b* 1946; *ed* The Oratory: *m* 1989, Anne L., yst da of Peter Knox, of 27 The Rise, Sevenoaks, Kent. —— Patrick Henry (The Old Post Office, Church Hill, Coldwaltham, Pulborough, W Sussex RH20 1LG), *b* 1949; *ed* The Oratory: *m* 1976, Stephanie Anne, eldest da of A.R. Matanle, of East Wing, Beedings Castle, Nutbourne, Sussex, and has issue living, Edward Henry, *b* 1978, — George Arthur, *b* 1981, — Heloise Anne, *b* 1982.

    Granddaughter of late Col John William Fane, MP (ante):—
    Issue of late Cecil Fane, *b* 1859, *d* 1948: *m* 1st, 1892, Alice Mary, who *d* 1899, da of Rev Thomas Ward Goddard, formerly V of Nazeing, Essex; 2ndly 1913, Florence Marjorie, who *d* 1967, d of William Ferrand (B Bolton, colls):—
(By 2nd *m*) Winifred Anne, *b* 1917; late Flight Officer WAAF: *m* 1949, Philip William Dacre Stuart, and has issue living, Peter Robin (17 Wellington St, Goderich, Ont, Canada N7A 2W6), *b* 1953: *m* 1979, Susan Blaker Clinkard, and has issue living, Tyler John *b* 1985, Amanda Michelle *b* 1981, — Penelope Anne, *b* 1951: *m* 1970, Eric Douglas Honsberger, of 90 Quantrell Trail, Scarborough, Ont, Canada M1B 1L8, and has issue living, Philip John Walter *b* 1974, Stuart Douglas *b* 1979, Margaret Anne *b* 1972, Alison Michelle *b* 1976. *Residence* – 35 Front St South, Apt 1806, (Port Credit) Mississauga, Ontario, Canada L5H 2C6.

    Grandchildren of late Cecil Fane, 4th and yst son of late Col John William Fane, MP (ante):—
    Issue of late Adrian Cecil Fane, *b* 1916, *d* 1987: *m* 1952, Eliabeth Muriel (Carrickmanor Haven, Carrickbrennan Rd, Monkstown, co Dublin), da of Henry Wheeler, of Garbally, Bruff, co Limerick:—
Henry Cecil, *b* 1954; *ed* Kilkenny Coll: *m* 1st, 1979 (*m diss* 1991), Roisin Elizabeth, da of Donald Mooney, of Delgany, co Wicklow; 2ndly, 1991, Mrs Celia Margaret Wreford, da of Brian Councell, of Clevedon, Avon, and formerly wife of Anthony Wreford, and has issue living (by 1st *m*), Edwyn Charles *b* 1979, — Gareth John, *b* 1981. —— Gwendoline Ann, *b* 1953: *m* 1988, Michael John Harrison, of 36 Pearson St, Narara, NSW 2250, Australia.

    Issue of late John William Fane, *b* 1919; *d* 1982: *m* 1st, 1944 (*m diss* 19-), Doreen, da of Albert Lawrence, of Waltham Abbey, Essex; 2ndly, 1964, Gwendoline-Ann, widow of Gerald Francis Kelly (84 Addison Rd, Enfield, Middlesex):—
(By 1st *m*) Anthony John, *b* 1948. —— Sheila Rosamond, *b* 1951: *m* 19—, John Johnson, of 3 Manton Rd, Lincoln LN2 2JL.

Granddaughters of late Col Frederick John Fane, son of late Rev Frederick Adrian Scrope Fane, 2nd
son of late John Fane, MP (*b* 1775) (ante):—
Issue of late Frederick Luther Fane, MC, *b* 1875, *d* 1960: *m* 1938, Edna Mary, who *d* 1982, da of late Henry
James Meads, of Eastbourne:—
Elizabeth Anne, *b* 1946: *m* 1997, John E. Barker, twin son of late Philip Barker, of Epping, Essex. *Residence* – 22
Maunsel St, SW1P 2QN. —— Rosemary Enid, *b* 1952. *Residence* – Hoo House, Hoo, Woodbridge, Suffolk.

Grandchildren of late Charles Eugene Fane (infra):—
Issue of late Charles Irwin Fane, *b* 1912, *d* 19—: *m* 1942, Gwendoline Jolyn, da of Ernest Stainton, of Broome,
WA:—
Michael, *b* 1949. —— Fifi Antoinette, *b* 1943. —— Tania, *b* 1952.

Grandchildren of late Charles Augustus Fane, of Carnarvon, W Australia, elder son of late George
Augustus Scrope Fane, 3rd son of late John Fane, MP (ante):—
Issue of late Charles Eugene Fane, *b* 1872, *d* 1955: *m* 1909, Florence Beatrice Yeates:—
Alexander Eugene, *b* 1913: *m* 1942, Nancy Lorna, da of Ray Carron, of Brighton, Vic, and has issue living, Russell (21
Knox Dr, Barwon Heads, Victoria 3227), *b* 1952, — Sylvia, *b* 1943: *m* 1966, Donald B. Shaw, of 37 Kent St, Gladstone,
Qld 4680, — Gwendoline (13 Haines St, Hawthorn, Victoria 3122), *b* 1948: *m* 1966 (*m diss* 1981), Ray Leggett. *Residence*
– Australia. —— George Augustus, *b* 1916; *m* 1st, 19— (*m diss* 19—), Eileen Byers: 2ndly, 19—, Lena Campbell, and
has issue living (by 1st *m*), Brenda, *b* 19—, — Joy, *b* 19—, — (by 2nd *m*) Peter Eugene (230 Barker Rd, Subiaco, W
Australia 6008), *b* 1959; *ed* Univ of Western Australia, and Australia Nat Univ: *m* 1983, Debra Barnes, and has issue
living, Kristy Caroline *b* 1983, — Donald Lorne (4 Lazarus St, Geraldton 6530, W Australia), *b* 1960: *m* 1982, Gae
Pepperell, — Shirlee Margaret, *b* 1956: *m* 1983, Allan Rose, of 8 Duclas Place, Geraldton 6530, W Australia. *Residence* –
159 George Rd, Geraldton 6530, W Australia. —— Iolanthe Florence, *b* 1918: *m* 1945, Ronald LeGrange Dunlop, and has
issue living, Diana Iolanthe, *b* 1946: *m* 1970, John Joseph Pauley, of 10 Rainbow View, Ocean Reef 6027, W Australia,
and has issue living David John *b* 1974, Helen Diana *b* 1973, — Margaret Chase, *b* 1950: *m* 1979, John Robin Lanyon, of
Yarrabee, One Tree Hill Rd, Ferny Creek, Victoria 3786, Australia, and has issue living, James John *b* 1982, Thomas
Charles *b* 1985. *Residence* – 130 Abbett St, Scarborough, W Australia. —— Beatrice Mary, *b* 1922: *m* 1944, Laban
Johnson-Head, and has issue living, Stephen Johnson (207 Windward Passage, Slidell, Louisiana 70458, USA), *b* 1945: *m*
1970 (*m diss* 1985), Betsy Holter, and has issue living, Charles Johnson *b* 1974, — Susan Gail (5134 Timber Trail,
Atlanta, Georgia 30342, USA), *b* 1947: *m* 1st, 1976 (*m diss* 1983), Elgin M. Wells, jr; 2ndly, 1988, Brian Wealand Kreider,
and has issue living (by 1st *m*), Laurel Brooke *b* 1978, — Julia Kathleen, *b* 1952: *m* 1980, Charles David Adams, Capt
USAF, of 2839 Tahoe Drive, Merced, California 95340, USA, and has issue living, Royce Henry *b* 1988. Capt and Mrs
Charles D. Adams also have adopted children, Quinton Lee *b* 1984, Royal Dawn *b* 1980, Jennifer Réne *b* 1982 *Residence* –
1046 McConnell Drive, Decatur, Georgia 30033, USA. —— Gloria Sybil, *b* 1924: *m* 1958, Noel Gleed. *Residence* – 12
Grosvenor Rd, Meltham 6053, W Australia. —— Deborah Kathleen *b* 1927: *m* 1951, Murray Henderson, and has issue
living, Murray, *b* 1953, — John, *b* 1955, — Fiona, *b* 1957, — (Mrs Henderson also has issue, Margaret Enid FANE (15B,
55 Herdsman Parade, Wembley, WA 6014, Australia), *b* 1950; SFO (Third Order of St Francis); legally resumed the
surname of Fane 1982: *m* 1973 (*m diss* 1981), Steven James Kirkman, and has issue living, James Murray *b* 1977,
Genevieve Margaret *b* 1974, Priscilla Norma (39 Mistral St, Falcon, WA 6210, Australia) *b* 1976, Kathleen Deborah *b*
1979). *Residence* – MS 115, Harchs Rd, Gympe 4570, Queensland, Australia. —— Mary Patricia, *b* 1929: *m* 1955, Donald
Whiteford McLaren, who *d* 1976. *Residence* – 104 Nollamara Av, Nollamara, W Australia 6061.

PREDECESSORS – (**1**) Sir FRANCIS Fane, was *cr Baron Burghersh* and *Earl of Westmorland* (peerage of England) 1624,
and in 1626 *s* his mother as *Baron Le Despencer* (see V Falmouth); *d* 1628; *s* by his son (**2**) MILDMAY, KB, 2nd Earl; *d*
1665; *s* by his el son (**3**) CHARLES, 3rd Earl; *dsp* 1691; *s* by his half-brother (**4**) VERE, KB, 4th Earl; *d* 1693; *s* by his el
son (**5**) VERE, 5th Earl; *d* unmarried 1699; *s* by his brother (**6**) THOMAS, 6th Earl; *dsp* 1736; *s* by his brother (**7**) JOHN,
7th Earl, a Lieut-Gen in the Army and a distinguished military officer under the Duke of Marlborough; *cr Baron
Catherlough* (peerage of Ireland) 1733: *d* 1762 when the Barony of Catherlough became extinct, the Barony of Le
Despencer passed to Sir Francis Dashwood, Bt (see V Falmouth) and the Barony of Burghersh and Earldom of Westmorland devolved upon his kinsman (**8**) THOMAS, MP, the descendant of Sir Francis Fane, 3rd son of 1st Earl; *d* 1771: *s*
by his son (**9**) JOHN, 9th Earl; *d* 1774; *s* by his son (**10**) JOHN, KG, 10th Earl; *d* 1841; *s* by his son (**11**) JOHN, GCB,
GCH, 11th Earl; *b* 1784; a Gen in the Army and a distinguished military officer, was afterwards Ambassador at Berlin
1841, and at Vienna 1851, and Special Commr at Conference at Vienna 1855: *m* 1811, Lady Priscilla Anne Wellesley, da
of 3rd Earl of Mornington; *d* 1859; *s* by his son (**12**) FRANCIS WILLIAM HENRY, CB, 12th Earl, *b* 1825; Col Coldstream
Guards: *m* 1857, Lady Adelaide Ida Curzon, 2nd da of 1st Earl Howe, GCB; *d* 1891; *s* by his only surviving son (**13**)
ANTHONY MILDMAY JULIAN, CBE, 13th Earl, *b* 1859; Col, and an ADC to HM; S Africa 1902: *m* 1st, 1892, Lady Sybil Mary
St Clair-Erskine, who *d* 1910, da of 4th Earl of Rosslyn; 2ndly, 1916, Catherine Louise, who *d* 1973, da of late Rev John
S. Geale; *d* 1922; *s* by his el son (**14**) VERE ANTHONY FRANCIS ST CLAIR, 14th Earl, *b* 1893; Lt (ret) RN: *m* 1923, Hon
Diana Lister, who *d* 1983, da of 4th Baron Ribblesdale (ext), and widow of (i) Percy Lyulph Wyndham, Lt Coldstream
Gds (E Leconfield), and (ii) Capt Arthur Edward Capel, CBE; *d* 1948; *s* by his el son (**15**) DAVID ANTHONY THOMAS,
GCVO, 15th Earl, *b* 1924; Capt Royal Horse Gds, 1939-45 War (wounded); Chm Sothebys 1980-82 (Dir since 1965); Lord
in Waiting to HM 1955, Master of the Horse 1978-91; *m* 1950, Barbara Jane, da of Lt-Col Sir Roland Lewis Findlay, 3rd
Bt; *d* 1993; *s* by his elder son (**16**) ANTHONY DAVID FRANCIS HENRY, 16th Earl and present peer; also Baron Burghersh.

WESTWOOD, BARON (Westwood) (Baron UK 1944)

WILLIAM GAVIN WESTWOOD, 3rd Baron; *b* 30 Jan 1944; *s* 1991; *ed* Fettes: *m* 1969, Penelope, FCA, eldest da of late Charles Edgar Shafto, VRD, MB, of 67 Jesmond Park West, Newcastle upon Tyne NE7 7BX, and has issue.

Arms – Argent, a lion rampant gules, between three lymphads sable, flags flying to the dexter of the second. Crest – A mullet argent, charged with a thistle slipped and leaved proper. Supporters – On either side a sea-lion argent, charged on the shoulder with two anchors in saltire sable.
Residence – Ferndale, Clayton Rd, Newcastle upon Tyne NE2 1TL.

SONS LIVING

Hon WILLIAM FERGUS, *b* 24 Nov 1972; *ed* Royal Gram Sch, Newcastle, and Birmingham and Northumbria Univs.
Hon Alistair Cameron, *b* 1974; *ed* Royal Gram Sch, Newcastle, and Sheffield Univ.

BROTHER LIVING

Hon Nigel Alistair, *b* 1950; *ed* Fettes; FRICS, FRSA; Knt 1st Class Royal Norwegian Order of Merit; Hon Royal Norwegian Consul: *m* 1977, Joan Elizabeth, yr da of Reginald Ibison, CBE, of Gosforth, Newcastle-upon-Tyne, and has issue living, David Alistair, *b* 1983, — Peter Robert, *b* 1986. *Residence* – 7 Fernville Rd, Gosforth, Newcastle upon Tyne NE3 4HT.

AUNT LIVING (*daughter of 1st Baron*)

Hon Margaret Taylor Young, MBE, *b* 1913; formerly 3rd Officer, WRNS: *m* 1st, 1934, William B. Lynn; 2ndly, 1945 (*m diss* 1974), John Bruce Campbell, formerly Roy Canadian Artillery, and has issue living, (by 2nd *m*), Robert Bruce, *b* 1948, — Helen Jean Laura, *b* 1946. *Residence* – 2 Ethorpe Cresc, Gerrards Cross, Bucks SL9 8PW.

WIDOW LIVING OF SECOND BARON

MARJORIE (*Dowager Baroness Westwood*), only child of Arthur Bonwick, of Heaton, Newcastle upon Tyne: *m* 1937, the 2nd Baron Westwood, who *d* 1991.

COLLATERAL BRANCHES LIVING

　　　　Adopted da of late Hon Douglas Wilkie Westwood, 2nd son of 1st Baron, *b* 1910, *d* 1968: *m* 1939, Mary Katherine, who *d* 1987, da of John Carter:—
Carol Margaret, *b* 1945: *m* 1st, 1966 (*m diss* 1978), Maj Stephen Ralli, Rifle Bde (ret); 2ndly, 1978, Robert Alexander Karl Constantin, Baron Staël von Holstein, and has issue living (by 1st *m*) Charles Douglas Stephen, *b* 1968; *ed* Sherborne.

　　　　Issue of late Hon James Young Shaw Westwood, yst son of 1st Baron, *b* 1915, *d* 1989: *m* 1941 (*m diss* 1969), Joan, only child of Raymond Potts:—
Roger Douglas, *b* 1943; *ed* Westminster, and New Coll, Oxford (MA, Dip Ed); P/O RAFVR. *Residence* – Swallowtail Cottage, Beckley, E Sussex TN31 6TT.

PREDECESSORS – **(1)** WILLIAM Westwood, OBE, son of late William Westwood, of Dundee; *b* 1880; was National Supervisor of Ship Constructors' and Shipwrights' Asso 1913-29, and Gen Sec thereof 1929-45, Ch Industrial Adviser 1942-45, a Lord-in-Waiting to HM 1945-47, and Chm of Mineral Development Committee under Min of Fuel and Power 1946-49; *cr Baron Westwood*, of Gosforth, co Northumberland (peerage of United Kingdom) 1944: *m* 1st, 1905, Margaret Taylor, who *d* 1916, da of late William Young, of Dundee; 2ndly, 1918, Agnes Helen Flockhart, who *d* 1952 da of late James Downie, of Dundee; *d* 1953; *s* by his el son **(2)** WILLIAM, 2nd Baron, *b* 1907, FRSA, FCIS, Life Member and Former Pres Football League: *m* 1937, Marjorie, only child of Arthur Bonwick, of Heaton, Newcastle upon Tyne; *d* 1991; *s* by his elder son **(3)** WILLIAM GAVIN, 3rd Baron and present peer.

Weymouth, Viscount; son of Marquess of Bath.

WHADDON, BARON (Page) (Life Baron 1978)

(JOHN) DEREK PAGE, son of John Page; *b* 14 Aug 1927; *ed* St Bedes Coll, Manchester; BSc (Sociology) London; Dir, Cambridge Chemical Co Ltd since 1962, and Rindalbourne Ltd 1983-90; Chm Daltrade Ltd since 1983, Skorimpex-Rind Ltd since 1986, and Crag Grp since 1997; MP for Kings Lynn (*Lab*) 1964-70; Golden Insignia, Order of Merit (Poland) 1992; *cr Baron Whaddon* of Whaddon Co Cambridge (Life Baron) 1978: *m* 1st, 1948, Catherine Audrey, who *d* 1979, da of John William Halls; 2ndly, 1981, Angela Rixson, da of Luigi della Bella, of Treviso, Italy, and has issue by 1st *m*.

𝕬rms – Quarterly vert and or on a fess engrailed ermine between in dexter chief a mullet and in sinister base a harp or and in sinister chief and dexter base a rose gules barbed and seeded proper three garbs gold. 𝕮rest – Upon a wreath or, vert and gules a crown vallary or issuing therefrom, within a chaplet vert set with roses gules barbed and seeded proper, a triple trefoil slipped vert. 𝕾upporters – *Dexter*, a lion guardant proper winged or; *sinister*, a mermaid proper crined and with a tail fin or, a round shield with its boss gold on her forearm and holding in the hand proper a sword point upward argent hilt, pommel and quillons gold.

Residence – The Old Vicarage, Whaddon, Royston, Herts. *Club* – Reform.

SON LIVING (*By 1st marriage*)

Hon John Keir *b* 1955: *m* 1976, Gale Masterman.

DAUGHTER LIVING (*By 1st marriage*)

Hon Eve-Ann, *b* 1952: *m* 1972, Patrick Prentice.

WHARNCLIFFE, EARL OF (Montagu Stuart Wortley) (Earl UK 1876)

He flourishes with the honour of his ancestors

RICHARD ALAN MONTAGU STUART WORTLEY, 5th Earl; *b* 26 May 1953; *s* 1987; *ed* Wesleyan Univ, Conn; builder: *m* 1979, Mary Elizabeth, da of Rev William Wellington Reed, of Keene, NH, and has issue.

𝕬rms – Quarterly: 1st and 4th argent, on a bend between six martlets gules three bezants, a canton or charged with a fesse checky azure and argent within a double tressure flory counterflory gules, *Wortley*; 2nd or, a fesse checky azure and argent within a double tressure flory counterflory gules, *Stuart*; 3rd argent, three lozenges conjoined in fesse gules within a bordure sable, *Montagu*. 𝕮rests – 1st, a demi-lion gules, and in an escrol over the motto '*Nobilis Ira*', *Stuart*; 2nd, an eagle's leg erased or, issuant therefrom three ostrich feathers proper, charged on the thigh with a fesse checky azure and argent, *Wortley*; 3rd, a griffin's head couped or, wings endorsed and beak sable, *Montagu*. 𝕾upporters – *Dexter*, a horse argent, bridled and gorged with a collar, flory counterflory gules; *sinister*, a stag proper gorged as the dexter.

Residence – 74 Sweetser Rd, N Yarmouth, Maine 04097, USA.

SONS LIVING

REED (*Viscount Carlton*), *b* 5 Feb 1980.
Hon Christopher James, *b* 1983.
Hon Otis Alexander, *b* 1991.

BROTHER LIVING

William Ralph, *b* 1959: *m* 1985, Dorothea Jane, da of Ronald Riley, of Rochester, NH, USA, and has issue living, Brian Alan, *b* 1988, — Dorothea Jayme, *b* 1987. *Residence* – 18 Nola Av, Rochester, NH, USA.

SISTER LIVING

Anne Steele, *b* 1955: *m* 1987, Robert Losty, son of Bruce Losty, of Cheshire, Conn, USA, and has issue living, Michelle Anne, *b* 1988. *Residence* – 29 Whiffle Tree Rd, Walingford, Conn 06492, USA.

AUNT LIVING

Joan Isabella, *b* 1928: *m* 1951, Harry Atwood Bishop, Jr, who *d* 1993, and has issue living, Harry Atwood (III) (9 Colony Drive, Turner, Maine 04282, USA), *b* 1957; *ed* Univ of NH, Plymouth: *m* 1982, Julie Sayre, da of Leonard Mulligan, and has issue living, Alex MacKenzie *b* 1986, Erin Sayre *b* 1984, — Alan Stuart Wortley (25 Kerry Hill, Fairport, NY 14450, USA), *b* 1959; *ed* Syracuse Univ (BA): *m* 1989, Lisa Mary, da of Anthony Orazio Marconi, of 2805 Bayer Rd, Waterloo, NY, and has issue living, Andrew Anthony Wortley *b* 1991, Colleen Joan *b* 1994, — Wendy Anne Isabella, *b* 1952; *ed* Univ of NH, Durham (BA): *m* 1975, Dennis Charles Gillespie, of 19 Woodhaven Drive, Andover, Mass 01810, USA, and has issue living, Kelly Anne Isabella *b* 1977, Meghan Therese *b* 1980, — Linda Walters (15B Orchard Lane, Haverhill, Mass 01830, USA), *b* 1953; *ed* Springfield Coll, Mass (BS, MSM): *m* 1981, Nicolo Bimbo, and has issue living, Katherine Anne, *b* 1985. *Residence* – 18 Webber Av, Bath, Maine 04530, USA.

DAUGHTERS LIVING AND DECEASED OF FOURTH EARL

Lady Joanna Margaret, *b* 1959; *k* in a motor accident 1981.

Lady Rowena STUART WORTLEY HUNT, *b* 1961: *m* 1986, John Hunt, son of Dr H. G. Hunt, of Greenwich, and has issue living, Somerset Carlton Gerald, *b* 1987, — Fleur Aline Isabel, *b* 1989.

DAUGHTERS LIVING OF THIRD EARL

Lady Ann Lavinia Maud, *b* 1919; 1939-45 War in Mechanised Transport Corps: *m* 1939, as his 2nd wife, Cdr Vivian Russell Salvin Bowlby, RN (ret), who *d* 1972, and has issue living, Michael Robin Salvin, *b* 1947; *ed* Malvern. *Residence* – Sutton Stables, Felixkirk Rd, Sutton-under-Whitestonecliffe, Thirsk, N Yorks YO7 2PU.

Lady Barbara Maureen, *b* 1921; formerly in Women's Land Army, and Remount Depot, Melton Mowbray: *m* 1943, David Cecil Ricardo, Lieut (ret) 8th King's Roy Irish Hussars, and has issue living, Dorrien Harry Ralph *b* 1952; *ed* Scarborough Coll, — Richard Michael David, *b* 1955; *ed* Ackworth: *m* 1986, (Charlotte) Miranda, da of Michael Evelyn Brown, of East Bergholt, Suffolk, and has issue living, Frederick Michael David *b* 1989, Corisande Barbara Emily *b* 1991. *Residence* – Rose Cottage, Wortley, Sheffield S35 7DB.

Lady Mary Rosemary Marie-Gabrielle, OBE, *b* 1930; JP 1974; OBE (Civil) 1983: *m* 1953, Sir David Courtenay Mansel Lewis, KCVO, JP, KStJ, Lord Lieut of Dyfed (*see* Warner, Bt, 1985 Edn), and has issue living, Patrick Charles Archibald Mansel (Capel Isaf, Manordeilo, Llandeilo, Carmarthenshire), *b* 1953; *ed* Eton: *m* 1985, Claire Mary, only da of (Alexander) William Houston, of The Little House, Datchworth, Herts (*see* B Swansea), and has issue living, Edward Vivian *b* 1987, Robert William *b* 1989, John David *b* 1992, — Catherine Maud Leucha MANSEL LEWIS (Laurel Cottage, Welsh Newton Common, Monmouth), *b* 1955; has resumed her maiden name: *m* 1985 (*m diss* 19—), Christopher N. Hamilton, son of P. N. Hamilton, of Florence, Italy, and has issue living, Archie Balthazar *b* 1985, — Annabel Lilian El-frida, *b* 1962: *m* 1990, Guy W. C. Herbert, of 19 Highlever Rd, W10 6PP, elder son of H. R. Herbert, of Alderbury, Wilts, and has issue living, Benson *b* 1991. *Residence* – Stradey Castle, Llanelli, Dyfed SA15 4PL.

WIDOW LIVING OF SON OF SECOND EARL

Lucy, da of — Perrin: *m* 1st, 1921, Hon Edward Thomas Montagu Stuart Wortley, who *d* 1923; 2ndly, 1925, Frank Leslie Russell. *Residence* –

WIDOW LIVING OF FOURTH EARL

ALINE MARGARET (*Aline, Countess of Wharncliffe*), da of late Robert Fernie Dunlop Bruce, of Dyson Holmes House, Wharncliffe Side, nr Sheffield: *m* 1957, the 4th Earl of Wharncliffe, who *d* 1987. *Residence* – Wharncliffe House, Wortley, Sheffield.

PREDECESSORS – (1) *Rt Hon* JAMES ARCHIBALD Stuart Wortley Mackenzie (grandson of 3rd Earl of Bute, KG), successively MP for Bossiney and Yorkshire, and Lord-Lieut of co York; was *cr Baron Wharncliffe*, of Wortley, co York (peerage of United Kingdom) 1826, was Lord Privy Seal 1834 and Lord Pres of the Council 1841; *d* 1845; *s* by his son (2) JOHN, 2nd Baron; *b* 1801: *m* 1825, Lady Georgiana Elizabeth, who *d* 1884, da of 1st Earl of Harrowby; *d* 1855; *s* by his son (3) EDWARD MONTAGU STUART GRANVILLE, 3rd Baron, *b* 1827; *cr Viscount Carlton* and *Earl of Wharncliffe* (peerage of United Kingdom) 1876, with remainder to his brother, Francis Dudley; assumed in 1880 by Roy licence the additional surname of Montagu: *m* 1855, Lady Susan Charlotte Lascelles, who *d* 1927, da of 3rd Earl of Harewood; *d* 1899; *s* by his nephew (4) FRANCIS JOHN (el son of late Hon Francis Dudley Montagu Stuart Wortley), 2nd Earl, *b* 1856: *m* 1886, Ellen, who *d* 1922, da of late Lieut-Gen Sir Thomas Lionel John Gallwey, KCMG; *d* 1926; *s* by his son (5) ARCHIBALD RALPH, 3rd Earl; *b* 1892; sometime Capt Life Guards: *m* 1918, Lady Maud Lilian Elfrida Mary Wentworth-Fitzwilliam, who *d* 1979, da of 7th Earl Fitzwilliam; *d* 1953; *s* by his only son (6) ALAN JAMES, 4th Earl, *b* 1935; Master of Ecclesfield Beagles: *m* 1957, Aline Margaret, da of late Robert Fernie Dunlop Bruce, of Dyson Holmes House, Wharncliffe Side, Sheffield; *d* 1987; *s* by his kinsman (7) RICHARD ALAN MONTAGU (elder son of late Alan Ralph Montagu Stuart Wortley, only son of late Ralph Montagu Stuart Wortley, only son of late Hon Ralph Granville Montagu Stuart Wortley, brother of 2nd Earl), 5th Earl and present peer; also Viscount Carlton, and Baron Wharncliffe.

WHARTON, BARONESS (Robertson) (Baron E 1544-5)

MYRTLE OLIVE FELIX (ZIKI) ROBERTSON (*Baroness Wharton*); *b* 20 Feb 1934; *s* (on termination of abeyance) 1990: *m* 1958, Henry MacLeod Robertson, who *d* 1996, Composer and Film Producer, and has issue.
Residence – 9 Gipsy Lane, SW15.

SONS LIVING

Hon MYLES CHRISTOPHER DAVID, *b* 1 Oct 1964; *ed* King's Coll, Wimbledon: *m* 1998, Caroline Laura, da of John David Jeffrey, of Ipsden, Oxon.
Hon Christopher James, *b* 1969; *ed* Clayesmore.
Hon Nicholas Charles, *b* (twin) 1969; *ed* Clayesmore.

DAUGHTER LIVING

Hon Patricia Lesley, *b* 1966: *m* 1999, Kenneth John William Reid, son of William John Hunter Reid of Edinburgh.

SISTER LIVING

Hon Caroline Elizabeth, *b* 1935: *m* 1970, Capt Jonathan Cecil Appleyard-List, CBE, RN, and has issue living, Zoë, *b* 1973.
Residence – Birches, Stanford Common, Pirbright, Surrey.

WIDOW LIVING OF NINTH BARON

JOANNA, only da of Walter Henry Law-Smith, of Adelaide, S Australia, widow of 6th Baron Tredegar, and formerly wife of late Cmdr Archibald Boyd Russell, DSO, RN: *m* 3rdly, 1967, the 9th Baron, who *d* 1969; 4thly, 1971, Bruce Yorke.
Residence – Casa la Concha, Rocio de Naguèles, Marbella (Malaga), Spain.

PREDECESSORS – (1) Sir THOMAS Wharton, *b* 1495; MP for Appleby 1529-36, and Cumberland 1542-4; Warden of West Marches 1537, and Gov of Carlisle Castle 1541, and of Berwick Castle 1557; summoned to Parliament 1544-5 to 1566: *m* 1st, Helen, da of Sir Bryan Stapleton, of Whighill; 2ndly, 1561, Anne, widow of 2nd Baron Braye, and da of 5th Earl of Shrewsbury; *d* 1568; *s* by his son (2) THOMAS, 2nd Baron; MP for Cumberland 1544-5 and 1547-52, for Headon 1554, and for Northumberland 1555-9; summoned to Parliament 1571-2: *m* 1547, Anne, who *d* 1561, da of 1st Earl of Sussex; *d* 1572; *s* by his only son (3) PHILIP, 3rd Baron: summoned to Parliament 1580-1625: *m* 1st, 1577, Frances, who *d* 1592, da of 2nd Earl of Cumberland, 2ndly, 1597, Dorothy, da of Thomas Colley, of Sherfield, and widow of (i) John Tamworth, of Leek, and (ii) Sir Francis Willoughby, of Wollaton; *d* 1625; *s* by his grandson (4) PHILIP (son of Sir Thomas Wharton, of Aske), 4th Baron; summoned to Parliament 1639-85; Lord-Lieut. of cos Lancaster, Buckingham, and Westmorland; Speaker of the House of Lords 1642-5: *m* 1st, (about) 1632, Elizabeth, da of Sir Rowland Wandesford, of Pickhill; 2ndly, 1637, Jane, da of Arthur Goodwin; 3rdly, 1661, Anne, da of William Carr, of Ferneyhurst, Roxburghshire, and widow of Col Edward Popham; *d* 1695; *s* by his son (5) THOMAS, 5th Baron; *b* 1648; MP for Wendover 1673-9 and Bucks 1679-96; Comptroller of the Household to William of Orange 1689-1702; one of the Commrs for Union with Scotland; *cr Viscount Winchendon*, of co Bucks, and *Earl of Wharton*, co Westmorland 1706; served as Lord-Lieut of Ireland 1708-10; *cr Baron of Trim*, co Meath, *Earl of Rathfarnham*, co Dublin, and *Marquess of Catherlough* Jan 1714-15, and *Marquess of Wharton*, co Westmorland, and *Marquess of Malmesbury*, co. Wilts, Feb 1714-15: *m* 1st, 1673, Anne, who *d* 1685, da of Sir Henry Lee, 5th Bt, of Ditchley, Oxon; 2ndly, 1692, Lucy, who *d* 1717, da of 1st Viscount Lisburne (*cr* 1685); *d* 1715; *s* by his only son (6) PHILIP, 6th Baron; *cr Duke of Wharton*, co Westmorland 1718; outlawed for high treason 1728 (but declared void on a writ of error in Court of Queen's Bench 1845, and so declared by the Committee for Privileges 1915): *m* 1st, 1714, Martha, who *d* 1726, da of Maj-Gen Richard Holmes; 2ndly, 1726, Maria Theresa O'Beirne, who *d* 1777, da of Col Henry O'Beirne; *d* 1731, when all dignities became ext, except (according to the decision of the Committee for Privileges) the Barony of Wharton, which they decided fell into abeyance between his two sisters, the elder of whom survived, when the Barony devolved upon her (7) JANE, *de jure* Baroness Wharton: *m* 1st, 1723, John Holt, who *d* 1728; 2ndly, 1733, Robert Coke, of Hillingdon, Middlesex; *dsp* when, according to the decision in 1915, the Barony again fell into abeyance among the representatives of the 4th Baron; from Mary, the second of whom, by her second marriage in 1678 with Sir Charles Kemeys, 3rd Bt., of Cefn Mably, is descended (through her da Jane, who *m* Sir John Tynte, 2nd Bt) (8) CHARLES THEODORE HALSWELL Kemeys-Tynte, 8th Baron, *b* 1876; the abeyance was determined in his favour Feb 1916: *m* 1899, Dorothy, who *d* 1944, da of the late Maj-Gen Sir Arthur Edward Augustus Ellis, GCVO, CSI; *d* 1934; *s* by his son (9) CHARLES JOHN HALSWELL, 9th Baron; *b* 1908: *m* 1967, Joanna (who *m* 4thly, 1971, Bruce Yorke), da of Walter Henry Law-Smith, of Adelaide, S Australia, widow of 6th Baron Tredegar, and formerly wife of late Cmdr Archibald Boyd Russell, DSO, RN; *d* 1969; *s* by his sister (10) ELIZABETH DOROTHY, Baroness Wharton; *b* 1906: *m* 1st, 1933 (*m diss* 1946), David George Arbuthnot, who *d* 1985 (*see* Arbuthnot, Bt, colls); 2ndly, 1946 (*m diss* 1958), St John Vintcent; *d* 1974, when the barony again fell into abeyance between her two das, Hon Myrtle Olive Felix Robertson, and Hon Caroline Elizabeth Appleyard-List, and so continued until 1990, when the abeyance was terminated in favour of the elder da (11) MYRTLE OLIVE FELIX, present peeress.

WHEATLEY, BARONY OF (Wheatley) (Extinct 1988)

SONS LIVING OF LIFE BARON

Hon John Francis (Braefoot Farmhouse, Fossoway, Kinross-shire), *b* 1941; *ed* Mount St Mary's Coll, and Edinburgh Univ (BL); called to Scots Bar 1966; Advocate-Depute 1974-78; Sheriff of Perthshire and Kinross-shire since 1980; Sheriff Principal of Tayside Central and Fife since 1998; Temporary High Court Judge since 1992: *m* 1970, Bronwen Catherine, da of Alastair Fraser of 25 Strachan Cres, Dollar, and has issue living.

Hon Patrick, *b* 1943: *m* 1968, Sheena, da of late Douglas James Lawrie.

Hon Anthony, *b* 1945; *ed* Mount St Mary's Coll, Sheffield, Fordham Univ, New York, and Holy Cross Academy, Edinburgh.

Hon Michael (Millburn, Old Philipstoun, W Lothian, EH49 7RY; MCC), *b* 1949; *ed* Mount St Mary's Coll: *m* 1971, Anne, da of Thomas Barry.

DAUGHTER LIVING OF LIFE BARON

Hon Kathleen Mary Agnes, *b* 1937; *ed* Convent of the Sacred Heart, Aberdeen, and Edinburgh Univ (MA 1960); Member of Royal Fine Art Commission for Scotland and Ancient Monuments Board: *m* 1963, (Sir) Thomas (Tam) Dalyell of The Binns, MP, 11th Bt (but does not use the title), of The Binns, Linlithgow.

WHITE, BARONESS (White) (Life Baroness 1970)

EIRENE LLOYD WHITE, da of late Thomas Jones, CH, LLD, of Brynhir, Aberystwyth; *b* 7 Nov 1909; *ed* St Paul's Girls' Sch, and Somerville Coll, Oxford (Hon Fellow 1966); Min of Labour Officer 1933-37, and 1941-45; Political Correspondent *Manchester Evening News* 1945-49; a Member of Nat Exec Cttee Labour Party 1947-53, and 1958-72 (Chm 1968-69); Parl Sec, Colonial Office 1964-66, Min of State for Foreign Affairs 1966-67, and Min of State, Welsh Office 1967-70; Dep Chm, Metrication Board 1972; a Dep Speaker House of Lords 1979-89; Member of Royal Commission on Environmental Pollution; Pres of Nat Council of Women (Wales); MP for E Flint (*Lab*) 1950-70; *cr* *Baroness White*, of Rhymney, co Monmouth (Life Baroness) 1970: *m* 1948, John Cameron White, who *d* 1968.

Residences – 64 Vandon Court, Petty France, SW1H 9HF; Treberfydd, Bwlch, Brecon, Powys LD3 7PX.

White, family name of Baron Annaly.

White, family name of Baron Hanningfield.

White, family name of Baroness James of Holland Park.

WHITE OF HULL, BARONY OF (White) (Extinct 1995)

SON LIVING OF LIFE BARON (by 2nd marriage)

Hon Lucas Charles, b 1974. Residence – ....

DAUGHTERS LIVING OF LIFE BARON (by 1st marriage)

Hon Carolina, b 1959: m 19—, Daniel Blasco, and has issue living, Gordon, b 1994. Residence – ....
Hon Ana Luisa (Sita), b 1961: m 1st, 1986 (m diss 1987), Francesco Venturi; 2ndly, 1996, Alan Joseph Marshall; has issue living, Tyrian-Jade (a da), b 1992. Residence – ....

WIDOW LIVING OF LIFE BARON

VICTORIA ANN TUCKER: m 1st, 1992, as his 3rd wife, Baron White of Hull, KBE (Life Baron), who d 1995; 2ndly, 1996, Tom O'Gara. Residence – 410 Park Avenue, New York, NY 10022, USA.

Whiteley, family name of Baron Marchamley.

WHITELAW, VISCOUNT (Whitelaw) (Viscount UK 1983)

SOLERTIA ❋ DITAT ❋

†WILLIAM STEPHEN IAN WHITELAW, KT, CH, MC, PC, 1st Viscount, son of late William Alexander Whitelaw, of Monkland, Nairn (ka 1919); b 28 June 1918; ed Winchester, and Trin Coll Camb (MA); Major (ret) Scots Guards; served in 1939-45 War with Scots Guards Tank Bn in Normandy, Germany and Palestine (despatches); MP for Penrith and the Border 1955-83; Lord Commr of the Treasury 1961-62; Parl Sec to Min of Labour 1962-64; Opposition Chief Whip 1964-70; Lord Pres of the Council and Leader of the House of Commons 1970-72; Sec of State for Northern Ireland 1972-73; Sec of State for Employment 1973-74; Dep Leader of the Opposition 1975-79; Home Sec 1979-83; Lord Pres of the Council and Leader of the House of Lords 1983-88; DL (1967) Cumbria; MC 1944; cr PC 1967, CH 1974, KT 1990, and Viscount Whitelaw, of Penrith, co Cumbria (peerage of UK) 1983: m 1943, Cecilia Doriel, yr da of late Major Mark Sprot, R Scots Greys, of Riddell, by Melrose, Roxburghshire, by his wife Meliora, da of Sir John Adam Hay, 9th Bt (cr 1635), and has issue. Viscount Whitelaw d 1 July 1999.

Arms – Sable a chevron engrailed or between three boars' heads couped argent armed and langued or. Crest – A bee erect proper. Supporters – On either side a Charolais bull in trian aspect proper each with a garland about the shoulder of roses gules barbed and seeded slipped and leaved and thistles stalked and leaved proper and interlaced in front with two pairs of golf clubs fretted saltirewise gold, the compartment comprising three mounts of moorland proper growing from each of those to the fore two roses and as many thistles the roses gules barbed and seeded stalked and leaved proper and the thistles stalked and leaved also proper.
Residence – Ennim, Penrith, Cumbria. Clubs – White's, Carlton, County (Carlisle), and Royal and Ancient Golf Club of St Andrews (Captain 1969-70).

DAUGHTERS LIVING

Hon (Elizabeth) Susan (Burton Agnes, Hull, E Yorks), *b* 1944; DL E Riding Yorks 1998: *m* 1966 (*m diss* 1996), Hon Nicholas John Cunliffe-Lister and has issue (*see* E Swinton).

Hon Carolyn Meliora, *b* 1946: *m* 1st, 1973 (*m diss* 1979), Robert Donald Macleod Thomas; 2ndly, 1983, Michael Francis Graves-Johnston, of 54 Stockwell Park Rd, SW9, and has issue living (by 1st *m*), Miranda Cecilia, *b* 1974, — Rhoda Mary Macleod, *b* 1977, — (by 2nd *m*) Cleopatra Frances, *b* 1985, — Helen Mercedes, *b* 1987.

Hon Mary Cecilia, *b* 1947: *m* 1972, David Alexander Coltman, of Haystoun House, Peebles, yr son of Col Thomas Alexander Hamilton Coltman, OBE, DL, RA (*see* B Hothfield), and has issue living, Susannah Mary Lavinia, *b* 1987.

Hon Pamela Winifred, *b* 1951: *m* 1974, Malise Charles Richard Graham, of The Cottage, Sproxton, Melton Mowbray, Leics, and has issue (*see* Graham, Bt, *cr* 1783).

Whitfield, family name of Baron Kenswood.

WHITTY, BARON (Whitty) (Life Baron 1996)

(JOHN) LAWRENCE WHITTY, son of late Frederick James Whitty, of co Down; *b* 15 June 1943; *ed* Latymer Upper Sch, and St John's Coll Camb; with Hawker Siddeley 1962; Civil Service 1965-70, Ministry of Aviation, UKAEA, Ministry of Technology; Economics Dept, TUC 1970-73; Nat Res and Political Offr GMBATU (formerly General and Municipal Workers Union) 1973-85; Euro Sec, Labour Party 1994-97 (Gen Sec 1985-94); a Lord in Waiting to HM (Govt Whip) 1997-98; Memb Fabian Soc and Friends of the Earth; Under Sec of State Environment and Transport since 1998; *cr Baron Whitty*, of Camberwell, London Borough of Southwark (Life Baron) 1996: *m* 1st, 1969 (*m diss* 1986), Tanya Margaret, da of Tom Gibson, of South Shields; 2ndly, 1993, Angela, da of James Forrester, of Glasgow, and has issue by 1st *m*.

Address – House of Lords, Westminster, SW1A 0PW.

SONS LIVING (*By 1st marriage*)

Hon Michael Sean, *b* 1970.
Hon Daniel James, *b* 1972.

WICKLOW, EARLDOM OF (Forward-Howard) (Extinct 1978)

COLLATERAL BRANCH LIVING

Issue of late Hon Hugh Melville Forward-Howard, 3rd son of 6th Earl, *b* 1883; *d* 1919: *m* 1908, Mary Emily, who *d* 1941, da of Benjamin Aymar Sands, of New York, and Southampton, Long Island, USA:— Katharine Frances Theodosia, *b* 1910.

WIDGERY, BARONY OF (Widgery) (Extinct 1981)

WIDOW LIVING OF LIFE BARON

ANN (*Baroness Widgery*) (56 Jubilee Place, SW3 3QT), da of late William Edwin Kermode, of Peel, Isle of Man: *m* 1948, Baron Widgery, OBE, TD, PC (Life Baron), who *d* 1981.

WIGG, BARONY OF (Wigg) (Extinct 1983)

DAUGHTERS LIVING OF LIFE BARON

Hon Mary Cecilia, *b* 1930: *m* 1958, Robert Cartlidge, of Rois Bheinn, Abilene, Princes St, Huntly, Aberdeenshire AB5 8HB, and has issue, three das.
Hon Jean Audrey, *b* 1932: *m* 1955, Andrew Huggins, of Ty Eiddew, Garndolbenmaen, Gwynedd, N Wales, and has issue, three das.
Hon Maureen Ann, *b* 1934: *m* 1963, Alfred John Mudge, who *d* 1987, of 940 Melton Drive, Mississauga, Ont, Canada L4Y 1L1, and has issue living, two sons.

WIGODER, BARON (Wigoder) (Life Baron 1974)

BASIL THOMAS WIGODER, QC, son of Philip I. Wigoder, LRCPI, LRCSI, of 2 St John St, Deansgate, Manchester 3; *b* 12 Feb 1921; *ed* Manchester Gram Sch, and Oriel Coll, Oxford (MA); Bar Gray's Inn 1946, Bencher 1972 (Master of the Bench 1972), Treasurer 1989; a Member of Gen Council of the Bar 1970-74, a memb Crown Court Rules Cttee 1971-77, and a Recorder of the Crown Court 1972-84; Chm Liberal Party Exec 1963-65, and Liberal Party Organising Cttee 1965-66, Vice-Pres of Liberal Party 1966; Chm of Health Sers Board 1977-80, Chm of BUPA and Dir of BUPA Hospitals 1981-92, since when Vice-Pres BUPA; Ch Liberal Whip in House of Lords 1977-84; Pres of Oxford Union 1946, 1939-45 War, as Lt RA, in Middle East, Italy, and Greece; *cr Baron Wigoder*, of Cheetham, in City of Manchester (Life Baron) 1974: *m* 1948, Yoland, da of Ben Levinson, and has issue.

Arms – Gules a chevron engrailed ermine between three wigs or a chief or. Crest – On a wreath or and gules, upon a mount vert a gosling or, supporting by the dexter foot a daffodil proper, mantled gules doubled argent. Supporters – *Dexter*, a seahorse; *sinister*, a sea-griffin; both or, their piscine parts azure scaled, finned and tailed or, each gorged with a collar sable, pendent therefrom a chain ending in a broken ring sable.
Address – c/o House of Lords, SW1. *Clubs* – National Liberal, MCC.

SONS LIVING

Hon Justin, *b* 1951: *m* 1981, Heather J., da of late J. H. Bugler, and has issue living, Annabel Miriam Jane, *b* 1986, — Charlotte Abigail Lucy, *b* 1991.
Hon Charles Francis, *b* 1960: *m* 1988, Elizabeth Sophia, only da of Elmar Duke-Cohan, of Totteridge, and has issue living, Benjamin Marcus James, *b* 1990, — Natasha Sarah, *b* 1992, — Clarissa Emma, *b* 1995.
Hon Giles, *b* 1963: *m* 1993 (*m diss* 1995), Louisa eldest da of Prof Gerald Westbury.

DAUGHTER LIVING

Hon Carolyn (twin), *b* 1963.

WIGRAM, BARON (Wigram) (Baron UK 1935)

(GEORGE) NEVILLE (CLIVE) WIGRAM, MC, 2nd Baron; *b* 2 Aug 1915; *s* 1960; *ed* Winchester, and Magdalen Coll, Oxford; late Lt-Col Gren Gds; a JP and a DL for Glos; a Page of Honour to HM 1925-32, and Mil Sec and Comptroller to Gov-Gen of NZ 1946-49; a Gov of Westminster Hosp 1967; 1939-45 War: *m* 1941, Margaret Helen, who *d* 1986, da of late Gen Sir Augustus Francis Andrew Nicol Thorne, KCB, CMG, DSO (B Penrhyn), and has issue.

Arms – Argent, on a pale gules three escallops or; over all a chevron engrailed counterchanged, and on the chief waves of the sea, thereon a ship representing an English vessel of war of the 16th century, with four masts, sails furled proper, colours flying gules. Crest – On a mount vert, a hand in armour in fesse couped at the wrist proper, charged with an escallop holding a fleur-de-lis erect or. Supporters – On either side a Bengal Lancer holding in the exterior hand a lance proper.
Residence – Poulton Fields, Cirencester, Gloucestershire. *Clubs* – Cavalry and Guards', MCC.

Sweet is the love of one's country

SON LIVING

Hon ANDREW FRANCIS CLIVE, MVO (Poulton Fields Farms, Poulton, Cirencester, Glos. *Clubs* – Leander, HAC and Farmers), *b* 18 March 1949; *ed* Winchester, RMA, and RAC Cirencester; Maj Gren Gds; Extra Equerry to HRH The Duke of Edinburgh 1982-86; Steward Henley RR: *m* 1974, Gabrielle Diana, yst da of late R. D. Moore, of Wellington, NZ, and has issue living, Harry Richard Clive, *b* 20 May 1977, — Robert Christopher Clive, *b* 1980, — William Michael Clive, *b* 1984, — Alice Poppy Louise, *b* 1989.

DAUGHTERS LIVING

Hon Margaret Cherry, *b* 1942: *m* 1972 (*m diss* 1993), Lt-Col Greville John Wyndham Malet, OBE, Royal Hussars, of The Walled House, Hatherop, Cirencester, Glos, and has issue (*see* Malet, Bt, colls).
Hon Anne Celia, *b* 1945: *m* 1973, Maj Gen Evelyn John Webb-Carter, OBE, late Gren Gds, of 8 Cadogan Gardens, SW3 2RS (V Hood, colls), and has issue living, Alexander Clive, *b* 1975, — Helen Celia, *b* 1978, — Rose Evelyn *b* 1983.

PREDECESSOR – (1) CLIVE WIGRAM, GCB, GCVO, CSI, PC, son of late Herbert Wigram (see Wigram, Bt, colls), *b* 1873; Lieut-Col and Brevet Col (ret) Indian Army; was an Extra Equerry-in-Waiting to Prince of Wales 1906-10, an Equerry-in-Waiting and Assist Private Sec to King George V 1910-31, Private Sec and an Extra Equerry 1931-36 (also Keeper of HM's Privy Purse 1935-36) and Keeper of HM's Archives 1936-45; acted as Assist to Ch of Staff of the Prince of Wales during tour in India 1905-6; S Africa 1900, with Kitchener's Horse; Dep Constable and Lieut-Gov of Windsor Castle 1936-45; Permanent Lord-in-Waiting to HM King George VI 1936-52, and to HM Queen Elizabeth II 1952-60; *cr Baron Wigram*, of Clewer, co Berks (peerage of United Kingdom) 1935: *m* 1912, Nora Mary, who *d* 1956, da of late Col Sir Neville Francis Fitzgerald Chamberlain, KCB, KCVO, *d* 1960; *s* by his son (2) (GEORGE) NEVILLE (CLIVE), 2nd Baron and present peer.

WILBERFORCE, BARON (Wilberforce) (Life Baron 1964)

RICHARD ORME WILBERFORCE, CMG, OBE, PC, son of Samuel Wilberforce, of Lavington House, Petworth, Sussex; *b* 11 March 1907; *ed* Winchester, and New Coll, Oxford; Hon DCL Oxford 1967; Hon LLD London 1972 and Bristol Univ 1983; Bar Middle Temple 1932, and QC 1954; a Judge of High Court of Justice (Chancery Div) 1961-64, a Lord of Appeal in Ordinary 1964-82; High Steward of Oxford Univ 1967-90 and Chllr of Hull Univ 1978-94; appointed Chm of Court of Inquiry into power workers' dispute 1970; Fell of All Souls Coll, Oxford since 1932; Hon Fellow, New Coll, Oxford since 1965; Hon Fellow Wolfson Coll Oxford 1990; 1939-45 War as Brig late RA in Norway and Germany (OBE); *cr* OBE (Mil) 1944, CMG 1956, Knt 1961, PC 1964, and *Baron Wilberforce*, of city and co of Kingston-upon-Hull (Life Baron) 1964: *m* 1947, Yvette Marie, da of Roger Lenoan, of Paris, and has issue.

Residence – 8 Cambridge Place, W8. *Club* – Athenæum.

SON LIVING

Hon Samuel Herbert (71 Birdhurst Rise, Croydon CR2 7ES), *b* 1951; *ed* Eton: *m* 1978, Mrs Sarah L. Scorer, da of late Arthur Allen, of Northampton.

DAUGHTER LIVING

Hon Anne Catherine, *b* 1948: *m* 1975, Lindsay Stuart Burn.

Wilbraham, Bootle-, family name of Baron Skelmersdale.

WILCOX, BARONESS (Wilcox) (Life Baroness 1996)

JUDITH ANN WILCOX, da of John Freeman, of Plymouth, Devon; *b* 31 Oct 1940; *ed* St Mary's Convent, Wantage, and Univ of Plymouth; founder Channel Foods Ltd, Cornwall 1983; partner, Morinie et Cie, France since 1990; Chm of Nat Consumer Council 1990-96, National Marine Aquarium since 1999; Memb Citizens' Charter Advisory Panel, Local Govt Commn, Inland Revenue Board, Port of London Authority, and Cttee of Automobile Assoc; FRSA; *cr Baroness Wilcox*, of Plymouth, co Devon (Life Baroness) 1996: *m* 1st, 1961 (*m diss* 1986), Keith Davenport, son of Harold Cornelius Davenport, of Plymouth, Devon; 2ndly, 1986, Sir Malcolm George Wilcox, CBE, who *d* 1986, son of late George Harrison Wilcox, and has issue by 1st *m*.

Arms – Azure a cross argent between four tressures or each enclosing a fleur-de-lis surmounting and conjoined to a pentagon voided the two upper sides enarched argent. **Supporters** – On either side a lobster azure crowned or.

Residence – 17 Great College St, SW1P 3RX. *Club* – Reform.

SON LIVING (*By 1st marriage*)

Hon Simon DAVENPORT, *b* 1963; *ed* Blundell's, and Leeds Univ; Bar Inner Temple 1987.

WILLIAMS, BARONY OF (Williams) (Extinct 1966)

DAUGHTER LIVING OF FIRST BARON

Hon Gweneth Mary, *b* 1927: *m* 1st, 1947 (*m diss* 1958), Hugh Sharp Eadie, AMIEE; 2ndly, 1961, Donald Walter Alexander Brown, MB, ChB, and has issue living (by 1st *m*), Graham Edward, *b* 1949, — Dianne Claire, *b* 1951.

WIDOW LIVING OF FIRST BARON

LAVINIA (*Baroness Williams*), da of Charles Northam, of Plumstead, SE18: *m* 1921, the 1st Baron, who *d* 1966, when the title became ext.

WILLIAMS OF BARNBURGH, BARON (Williams) (Extinct 1967)

WIDOW LIVING OF SON OF LIFE BARON

Margaret Dick Chisholm (*Hon Mrs Horace Williams*), da of William Green: *m* 1952, as his 2nd wife, Hon Horace Williams, who *d* 1993. *Residence* – Flat 3, 2 Chichester Terrace, Kemptown, Brighton, Sussex.

DAUGHTER LIVING OF LIFE BARON

Hon Doris (346 Thorne Rd, Doncaster), *b* 1916: *m* 1939, Robert Kesteven Lee, who *d* 1967.

WILLIAMS OF CROSBY, BARONESS (Neustadt) (Life Baroness 1993)

SHIRLEY VIVIEN TERESA BRITTAIN NEUSTADT, PC, da of late Prof Sir George Edward Gordon Catlin, by his late wife, Vera Brittain; *b* 27 July 1930; *ed* Summit Sch, Minnesota, USA, St Paul's Girls' Sch, Somerville Coll, Oxford (Hon Fellow), and Columbia Univ, New York; PPS to Min of Health 1964-66, Parl Sec Min of Labour 1966-67, Min of State for Educn and Science 1967-69, Min of State Home Office 1969-70, Sec of State for Prices and Consumer Protection 1974-76 (also Paymaster-Gen), Sec of State for Educn and Science 1976-79; Chm Fabian Soc 1980 (Gen Sec 1960-64); Member Lab National Executive Cttee 1970-81; Co-Founder SDP 1981, Pres 1982-88; MP for Hitchin (*Lab*) 1964-74, Hertford and Stevenage (*Lab*) 1974-79, and Crosby (SDP) 1981-83; Fellow Inst of Politics Harvard 1979-80, OECD Examiner since 1979, Prof and Fellow Policy Studies Inst 1979-85, Public Service Prof of Elective Politics, Kennedy Sch of Government, Harvard since 1988, and Member Senior Advisory Cttee Inst of Politics Harvard; FBA; *cr* PC 1974, and *Baroness Williams of Crosby*, of Stevenage, co Herts (Life Baroness) 1993: *m* 1st, 1955 (*m diss* 1974), Prof Bernard Arthur Owen Williams; 2ndly, 1987, Prof Richard E. Neustadt, and has issue by 1st *m*.

Arms – Per chevron azure and or, three lions passant guardant in pale counterchanged, a bordure engrailed ermine.
Residence – The Well House, Causeway, Furneaux Pelham, Buntingford, Herts SG9 0LN.

DAUGHTER LIVING (*By 1st marriage*)

Hon Rebecca Clare, *b* 1961.

WILLIAMS OF ELVEL, BARON (Williams) (Life Baron 1985)

CHARLES CUTHBERT POWELL WILLIAMS, CBE, *b* 9 Feb 1933, son of late Dr Norman Powell Williams, DD, by his wife, Muriel de Lérisson, only surv da of late Arthur Philip Cazenove, of 51 Cadogan Pl, SW1; *ed* Westminster, and Ch Ch, Oxford, and LSE; British Petroleum Co Ltd 1958-64, Bank of London and Montreal 1964-66, Eurofinance SA, Paris 1966-70, Baring Brothers & Co Ltd 1970-77 (Man Dir 1971-77), Chm Price Commn 1977-79, Man Dir Henry Ansbacher & Co Ltd 1980-82, Ch Exec Henry Ansbacher Holdings plc, Chm Henry Ansbacher & Co Ltd 1982-85, Pres Campaign for the Protection of Rural Wales 1989-95; *cr* CBE (Civil) 1980, and *Baron Williams of Elvel*, of Llansantffraed in Elvel, co Powys (Life Baron) 1985: *m* 1975, Jane Gillian, da of Lt-Col Gervase Edward Portal, and formerly wife of Gavin Bramhall Bernard Welby.
Residence – 48 Thurloe Sq, SW7 2SX. *Clubs* – Reform, and MCC.

WILLIAMS OF MOSTYN, BARON (Williams) (Life Baron 1992)

GARETH WYN WILLIAMS, son of late Albert Thomas Williams; *b* 5 Feb 1941; *ed* Rhyl Gram Sch, and Queens' Coll, Camb (MA, LLM); Bar Gray's Inn 1965, Recorder Crown Court 1978, QC 1978, Leader Wales and Chester Circuit 1987-90, Bencher Gray's Inn 1991, Member Bar Council since 1986 (Chm 1992); Pro-Chancellor Univ of Wales since 1994; Min of State Home Office since 1998; *cr Baron Williams of Mostyn*, of Great Tew, co Oxon (Life Baron) 1992: *m* 1st, 1962 (*m diss* 19—), Pauline, da of late Ernest Clarke; 2ndly, 1994, V. M. Russell, and has issue by 1st and 2nd *m*.

Arms – Ermine, on a pile flory at the point sable a lion rampant or, armed and langued gules. Crest – A portcullis or in front of an arm embowed vested and the cuff braided sable, frilled at the wrist, the hand proper holding by its blade upwards argent a sword palewise to the front of the portcullis, its hilt, pommel and quillons gold. Supporters – *Dexter*, upon a grassy mount, growing therefrom two sweet pea flowers proper, a griffin statant erect gold; *sinister*, upon a like mount a dragon statant erect also gold, both armed and langued gules.
Residence – Poplars Farmhouse, Evenlode, Glos GL5 0NN.

SON LIVING (*By 1st marriage*)

Hon Daniel, *b* 1969.

DAUGHTERS LIVING (*By 1st marriage*)

Hon Martha, *b* 1963.
Hon Emma, *b* 1966.

(*By 2nd marriage*)

Hon Imogen, *b* 1994.

Williams, Rees-, family name of Baron Ogmore.

WILLIAMSON, BARONY OF (Williamson) (Extinct 1983)

DAUGHTER LIVING OF LIFE BARON

Hon Milba Hartley, *b* 1926: *m* 1952, Jack Fleming Eccles, CBE, of Terange, 11 Sutton Rd, Alderley Edge, Cheshire SK9, and has issue.

Williamson, family name of Baron Forres.

WILLIAMSON OF HORTON, BARON (Williamson) (Life Baron 1999)

DAVID FRANCIS WILLIAMSON, GCMG, CB, son of late Samuel Charles Wathen Williamson, of Bath; *b* 8 May 1934; *ed* Tonbridge, and Exeter Coll, Oxford (MA 1959), Hon DCL Kent (1998), Hon DEconS Limerick (1996); served in Min of Agriculture, Fisheries and Food 1958-65 and 1967-77; seconded to HM Diplomatic Service for Kennedy Round Trade Negotiations 1965-67; Dep Dir Gen Agriculture, European Commn, Brussels 1977-83; Dep Sec, Cabinet Office 1983-87; Sec-Gen European Commn, Brussels 1987-97; Non-Exec Dir Whitbread plc since 1998; Visiting Prof Univ of Bath since 1997; Kt Cmdr's Cross of Order of Merit of Federal Republic of Germany 1991, Cmdr Grand Cross Royal Order of the Polar Star of Sweden 1998, Commandeur Légion d'Honneur 1999; *cr* CB 1984, GCMG 1998, and *Baron Williamson of Horton*, of Horton, co Som (Life Baron) 1999: *m* 1961, Patricia Margaret, da of late Eric Cade Smith, of Broadclyst, Exeter, Devon, and has issue.
Residence – Thatchcroft, Broadway, Ilminster, TA19 3QZ.

SONS LIVING

Hon Timothy, *b* 1963; *ed* St Dunstan's Coll, Catford, and British Sch, Brussels.
Hon Jonathan, *b* 1965; *ed* St Dunstan's Coll, Catford, and British Sch, Brussels.

WILLIS, BARONY OF (Willis) (Extinct 1992)

SON LIVING OF LIFE BARON

(*Hon*) John Edward, *b* 1946; does not use courtesy title; *ed* Eltham Coll, Fitzwilliam Coll, Camb (MA), and Bristol Univ (Postgrad Cert in Radio, Film and TV); writer and director, dir *Johnny Go Home*, etc; Dir of Programmes for Channel Four Television since 1993: *m* 1972, Janet, da of Kenneth Sperrin, and has issue living, Thomas, *b* 1975, — Beth, *b* 1978.

DAUGHTER LIVING OF LIFE BARON

Hon Sally Ann Hale, *b* 1951: *m* 1974, Robin James Murray, and has issue living, James Edward, *b* 1980, — Alice Louise, *b* 1982, — Helen Jane, *b* (twin) 1982.

WIDOW LIVING OF LIFE BARON

AUDREY MARY (*Baroness Willis*), da of Alfred Hale: *m* 1944, Baron Willis (Life Baron), who *d* 1992.

Willoughby, family name of Baron Middleton.

WILLOUGHBY DE BROKE, BARON (Verney) (Baron E 1491)
(Title pronounced "Willoughby de Brook")

Virtue prevails

(LEOPOLD) DAVID VERNEY, 21st Baron; *b* 14 Sept 1938; *s* 1986; *ed* Le Rosey, and New Coll, Oxford; patron of two livings: *m* 1965 (*m diss* 1989), Petra Daphne, 2nd da of late Col Sir John Renton Aird, 3rd Bt, MVO, MC, Gren Gds, and has issue.

Arms – Quarterly: 1st and 4th, gules, three crosses recercellé or, a chief vair ermine and ermines; 2nd and 3rd, quarterly argent and gules, a bear sejant sable. **Crests** – 1st, a Saracen's head, affrontée, couped at the shoulders proper, ducally crowned or; 2nd, a demi-bear sable, holding in his paws a lozenge, pierced or. **Supporters** – Two antelopes argent, semée of torteaux, armed and unguled or.
Residences – Ditchford Farm, Moreton in Marsh, Glos GL56 9RD. *Club* – White's.

SONS LIVING

Hon RUPERT GREVILLE, *b* 4 March 1966.
Hon John Mark, *b* 1967.
Hon Edmund Peyto, *b* 1973.

SISTER LIVING

Hon Susan Geraldine, *b* 1942: *m* 1st, 1964 (*m diss* 1969), Jeremy James Wagg (*see* Horlick, Bt, 1969 Edn); resumed her maiden name by deed poll 1969; 2ndly, 1972, as his 2nd wife, Capt Robie David Corbett Uniacke; 3rdly, 1990, as his 2nd wife, Rupert John Orlando Lascelles (*see* E Harewood, colls), and has had issue (by 2nd *m*), Caspar John, *b* 1973, — †Kate Rachel, *b* 1975; *d* 1979. *Residence* – Tarrant Abbey, Blandford, Dorset DT11 9HU.

PREDECESSORS – (1) *Sir* ROBERT Willoughby, Knt, who took part in the victory of Bosworth, was summoned to the Parliament of England as *Lord Willoughby de Broke* 1491; was Capt Gen of the Forces sent to aid the Duke of Brittany against the French, *temp* Henry VII and subsequently Marshal of the English Army sent into France: *m circa* 1475, Blanche, da and co-heir of Sir John Champernowne, of Beer Ferrers, Devon; *d* 1502; *s* by his son (2) ROBERT, 2nd Baron; summoned to Parliament 1511: *m* 1st, Elizabeth, who *d* 1503, da and co-heir of 2nd Baron Beauchamp of Powyk; 2ndly, Lady Dorothy Grey (who *m* 2ndly, 15—, William Blount, 4th Baron Mountjoy, and *d* 1553), da of 1st Marquess of

Dorset; *d* 1522; when the barony fell into abeyance between the three das of his el son Edward Willoughby, and so remained until 1558, when the sole surviving grand-da (her sisters dying without issue) **(3)** ELIZABETH, became *de jure* Baroness: *m circa* 1534, as his second wife, Sir Fulke Greville; *d* 1560; *s* by her el son **(4)** *Sir* Fulke, *de jure* 4th Baron, *b* 1535; MP for Warwick 1586: *m circa* 1553, Lady Anne Nevill, da of 4th Earl of Westmorland; *d* 1606; *s* by his only son **(5)** *Sir* FULKE, *de jure* 5th Baron; *b circa* 1554; *cr Baron Brooke*, of Beauchamp's Court, co Warwick 1621, with remainder to his cousins Robert and William Greville; *d* 1628, when the Barony of Brooke passed to Robert Greville (see E Warwick) and the right to the Barony of Willoughby de Broke devolved on his sister **(6)** MARGARET, *de jure* Baroness; *b circa* 1561: *m* before 1584, Sir Richard Verney, of Compton Verney, co Warwick; *d* 1631; *s* by her el son **(7)** *Sir* GREVILLE, *de jure* 7th Baron; *b* circa 1587: *m* 1618, Catherine, da of Sir Robert Southwell, of Woodrising, Norfolk; *d* 1642; *s* by his el son **(8)** GREVILLE, *de jure* 8th Baron; *b circa* 1620: *m* 16—, Hon Elizabeth Wenman, who *d* 1649, da of 2nd Viscount Wenman of Tuam, *d* 1648; *s* by his only child **(9)** *Sir* GREVILLE, KB, de jure 9th Baron, *b* (posthumously) 1649: *m* 1667, Lady Diana Russell (who *m* 2ndly, 1675 the 3rd Baron Alington of Killard, and *d* 1701), da of 1st Duke of Bedford; *d* 1668; *s* by his only child **(10)** WILLIAM, *de jure* 10th Baron, *b* 1668; *d* 1683; *s* by his great-uncle **(11)** *Sir* RICHARD (3rd son of *de jure* 7th Baron), 11th *de jure* Baron, *b* 1621; established his claim to the Barony before the House of Lords 1696: *m* 1st, before 1658, Elizabeth, da and heir of George Turpin; 2ndly, circa 1677, Frances, da of Thomas Dove; *d* 1711; *s* by his son **(12)** GEORGE, 12th Baron; *b* 1659; was Dean of Windsor: *m* 1688, Margaret, who *d* 1729, da and heir of Sir John Heath; *d* 1728; *s* by his son **(13)** RICHARD, 13th Baron; *b* 1693: *m* 1st, 17—, Penelope, who *d* 1718, da of Clifton Packe; 2ndly, before 1735, Elizabeth, who *d* 1767, da of Nathaniel Williams; *dsp* 1752; *s* by his nephew **(14)** JOHN, 14th Baron, son of Hon John Verney, 3rd son of 12th Baron; *b* 1762; assumed in 1772 the additional surname of Peyto: *m* 1761, Lady Louisa North, who *d* 1798, da of 1st Earl of Guilford; *d* 1816; *s* by his son **(15)** JOHN, 15th Baron; *b* 1762; *d unm* 1820; *s* by his brother **(16)** HENRY, 16th Baron; *dsp* 1852; *s* by his nephew **(17)** ROBERT JOHN, 17th Baron, son of Hon Louisa, da of 14th Baron, by her marriage to the Rev Robert Barnard; *b* 1809; assumed in 1852 the surname of Verney in lieu of his patronymic: *m* 1842, Georgiana Jane, who *d* 1889, da of Maj-Gen Thomas William Taylor, CB, of Ogwell, Devon; *d* 1862; *s* by his son **(18)** HENRY, 18th Baron; *b* 1844: *m* 1867, Geraldine, who *d* 1894, el da of late James H. Smith-Barry, Esq, of Marbury Hall, Cheshire, and Fota Island, Cork; *d* 1902; *s* by his son **(19)** RICHARD GREVILLE, 19th Baron, *b* 1869; MP for Warwickshire, SE, or Rugby Div (C) 1895-1900: *m* 1895, Marie Frances Lisette, OBE, who *d* 1941, da of late Charles Addington Hanbury; *d* 1923; *s* by his son **(20)** JOHN HENRY PEYTO, MC, AFC, AE, 20th Baron, *b* 1896, JP, DL and Lord Lieut Warwicks 1939-67, Member Jockey Club (Steward 1944-47, and 1954-56), and National Hunt Cttee (Steward 1942-44, 1950-53 and 1964-67), Chm Tattersall's Cttee 1948-53, Pres Hunters' Improvement Soc 1957-58, Member Council of Order of St John 1946-67; Capt 17th/21st Lancers, Air Commodore RAuxAF, Cdr 605 (Co Warwick) Sqdn AAF 1936-39 (Air Efficiency Award, AFC), Hon Col Queen's Own Warwicks and Worcs Yeo (TA) 1942-63, served 1914-18 War (wounded MC), and 1939-45 War (despatches); Dep Dir Public Relations Air Min 1941-44 (Dir 1945-46): *m* 1933, Rachel, who *d* 1991, only child of Sir (Robert) Bourchier Sherard Wrey, 11th Bt; *d* 1986; *s* by his only son **(21)** LEOPOLD DAVID, 21st Baron and present peer.

WILLOUGHBY DE ERESBY, BARONESS (Heathcote-Drummond-Willoughby) (Baron E 1313)

(NANCY) JANE MARIE HEATHCOTE-DRUMMOND-WILLOUGHBY, *Baroness Willoughby de Eresby*; *b* 1 Dec 1934; *s* 1983; Joint Hereditary Lord Great Chamberlain of England; a Train Bearer to HM The Queen at the Coronation 1953; DL Lincs 1993.

Arms – Quarterly, — 1st and 4th, or fretty azure, *Willoughby*; 2nd, or three bars wavy gules, *Drummond*; 3rd, ermine three pomais each charged with a cross or, *Heathcote*.
Seats – Grimsthorpe Castle, Bourne, Lincs; Drummond Castle, Crieff, Perthshire.

AUNT LIVING (*Daughter of 2nd Earl of Ancaster*)

(Co-heiress presumptive) *(half share)*

Lady PRISCILLA, *b* 29 Oct 1909: *m* 1939, Col Sir John Renton Aird, 3rd Bt, MVO, MC, Gren Gds, who *d* 1973, and has issue (*see* Aird, Bt). *Residence* – Wingrove House, Chipping Campden, Glos.

COLLATERAL BRANCHES LIVING (*All in remainder*)

Issue of late Lady Catherine Mary Clementina Heathcote-Drummond-Willoughby, elder da of 2nd Earl of Ancaster, *b* 1906, *d* 1996: *m* 1st, 1935 (*m diss* 1948), John St Maur Ramsden, who was assassinated in Malaya 1948 (*see* Ramsden, Bt, colls); 2ndly, 1948, Charles Wedderburn Hume, who *d* 1974:—
(By 1st *m*) (ELOISE) CAROLA, *b* 26 Oct 1938; co-heiress presumptive to Barony (half share), *b* 1938: *m* 1st, 1961, George Fillmore Miller III; 2ndly, 1974, Robert E. J. Philippi, and has issue living (by 1st *m*), Sebastian St Maur, *b* 1965; Capt The Blues and Royals: *m* 1991, Emma Caroline, da of John Harries, of Esher, Surrey, and has issue living, Hermione Clementina *b* 1997, — (by 2nd *m*) James Jeremy George, *b* 1975. *Residence* – Mains of Drummond, Crieff, Perthshire.

Granddaughter of late Brig-Gen Hon Charles Strathavon Heathcote-Drummond-Willoughby, CB, CMG, son of 1st Earl of Ancaster:—
Issue of late Charles Peregrine Heathcote-Drummond-Willoughby, *b* 1905, *d* 1965: *m* 1939, Anne Eveline, who *d* 1983, da of late James Fitzsimmons:—

(Anne) Leueen WILLOUGHBY, *b* 1949; continues to be styled by her maiden name: *m* 1985, David Reid Brown, and has issue living, Peregrine WILLOUGHBY-BROWN, *b* 1985, — Breanne WILLOUGHBY-BROWN, *b* 1988. *Residence* – 509 Broadview Av, Toronto, Canada M4K 2N5.

Grandchildren of late Lady Margaret Mary Heathcote-Drummond-Willoughby (*m* 1902, Gideon Macpherson Rutherford), 2nd da of 1st Earl of Ancaster:—
Issue of late Margaret Evelyn Rutherford, *b* 1903, *d* 1984: *m* 1930 (*m diss* 1944), Lt-Cdr Reginald Arthur Forbes, RN (ret), who *d* 1975:—
See Stuart-Forbes, Bt.

Issue of late Christine Jane Rutherford, *b* 1906, *d* 1997: *m* 1934, Group Capt W. H. Poole, AFC, MM, RAF, who *d* 1971:—
David Rutherford POOLE (Wanebridge House, Malt Hill, Warfield, Bracknell, Berks RG21 6PL), *b* 1939; *ed* Charterhouse; MA: *m* 1962, Julie Anne Hoskins, and has issue living, Jennifer Alice, *b* 1968.

Issue of late Lady Mary Adelaide Heathcote-Drummond-Willoughby, yst da of 1st Earl of Ancaster, *b* 1878, *d* 1960: *m* 1903, 14th Earl of Dalhousie, who *d* 1928:—
See E Dalhousie.

PREDECESSORS – **(1)** ROBERT Willoughby, having been actively engaged in the French and Scottish wars of Edward I, was summoned to Parliament of England as Baron 1313; *s* by his son **(2)** JOHN, 2nd Baron; was one of the principal commanders at the battle of Crécy; summoned to Parliament 1332-49; *s* by his son **(3)** JOHN, 3rd Baron; served at Poitiers; *d* 1373; *s* by his son **(4)** ROBERT, 4th Baron; *d* 1390; *s* by his son **(5)** WILLIAM, 5th Baron; was a Peer of Parliament when Richard II made a formal resignation in 1399; *s* by his son **(6)** ROBERT, KG, 6th Baron; an eminent military commander, *temp* Henry VI; *cr Baron Willoughby of Monblay and Beaumesguil* and *Earl of Vendome and Beaumont*, in France, which titles expired at his death in 1452; *s* in Barony of Willoughby de Eresby by his da **(7)** JOAN, wife of Sir Richard Welles, Knt, who in right of his wife was summoned to Parliament as 7th Baron Willoughby de Eresby 1455-66; his lordship was only son of Leo, 6th Baron Welles (*cr* 1299), who was killed at the battle of Towton Field 1461, and at his decease his estates and honours were attainted; in 1468 the attainders were reversed and he became 7th Baron Welles; having become through his son involved in the vibrating fortunes of the red and white roses he was treacherously beheaded by the order of King Edward IV 1469, *s* by his son **(8)** ROBERT, 8th Baron, who having heard of the king's treachery attacked the royal army, but being defeated he was taken prisoner and immediately beheaded; *s* in both baronies by his sister **(9)** JOANE, wife of Richard Hastings, who was summoned to Parliament as Baron Welles 1482-3; he *d* 1503 when his Barony of Welles became extinct; the Baroness *d* 1506 when the old Barony of Welles became abeyant and still remains so, while the Barony of Willoughby de Eresby passed to **(10)** WILLIAM Willoughby, 10th Baron, lineal descendant of Sir Thomas Willoughby, 2nd son of 5th Baron; *d* 1525; *s* by his da **(11)** KATHERINE: *m* 1st, Charles Brandon, KG, 1st Duke of Suffolk, and 2ndly, Richard Bertie; *d* 1580; *s* by her son by her 2nd marriage **(12)** PEREGRINE Bertie, 12th Baron; summoned to Parliament 1581; *d* 1601; *s* by his son **(13)** ROBERT, KG, 13th Baron; established (through his mother, sister and heiress of 17th Earl of Oxford) his right to be hereditary Lord Great Chamberlain of England; *cr Earl of Lindsey* (peerage of England) 1626; *s* by his son **(14)** MONTAGU, KG, 2nd Earl; *d* 1666; *s* by his son **(15)** ROBERT, 3rd Earl; *d* 1701; *s* by his son **(16)** ROBERT, 4th Earl; summoned to Parliament as Baron Willoughby de Eresby in his father's lifetime; *cr Marquess of Lindsey* (peerage of Great Britain) 1706, and *Duke of Ancaster and Kesteven* (peerage of Great Britain) 1715; *d* 1723; *s* by his son **(17)** PEREGRINE, 2nd Duke; *d* 1742; *s* by his son **(18)** PEREGRINE, 3rd Duke; *d* 1778; *s* by his son **(19)** ROBERT, 4th Duke; *d* unmarried 1779, when the dukedom and all honours except the Barony of Willoughby de Eresby passed to his uncle Brownlow (see E Lindsey), and the Barony of Willoughby fell into abeyance between his grace's sisters, Priscilla, wife of 1st Baron Gwydyr, and Georgiana, wife of 1st Marquess of Cholmondeley, each of whom became Joint Hereditary Great Chamberlain; in 1780 the abeyance was terminated in favour of the former **(20)** PRISCILLA BARBARA ELIZABETH: *m* 1779, Sir Peter Burrell, Bt, who in 1796 was *cr* Baron Gwydyr; she *d* 1828; *s* by her son **(21)** PETER ROBERT, 21st Baron, who in 1820 had *s* his father as 2nd Baron Gwydyr; assumed in 1807 by sign manual the additional surname of Drummond: *d* 1865; *s* by his son **(22)** ALBERIC, 22nd Baron; was Joint Hereditary Great Chamberlain of England; *d* unmarried 1870, when the Barony of Gwydyr devolved upon his cousin Peter Robert Burrell, and the Barony of Willoughby de Eresby fell into abeyance between his sisters, Clementina, wife of 1st Baron Aveland, and Charlotte, wife of 2nd Baron Carrington each of whom became entitled to a moiety of the office of Joint Hereditary Great Chamberlain; in 1871 the abeyance was terminated in favour of **(23)** CLEMENTINA ELIZABETH, *b* 1809; assumed in 1870 by Roy licence the additional surname and arms of Drummond, and in 1872, the additional surname of Willoughby: *m* 1827, the 1st Baron Aveland; *d* 1888; *s* by her el son **(24)** GILBERT HENRY, 2nd Baron Aveland (infra), 24th Baron Willoughby de Eresby; *b* 1830; in 1872, assumed by Roy licence the additional surnames of Willoughby and Drummond; MP for Boston (*L*) 1852-56, and for Rutland 1856-67; *cr Earl of Ancaster*, in co Lincoln (peerage of United Kingdom) 1892: *m* 1863, Lady Evelyn Elizabeth Gordon, who *d* 1921, 2nd da of 10th Marquess of Huntly; *d* 1910; *s* by his son **(25)** GILBERT, GCVO, TD, 2nd Earl, *b* 1867; Parliamentary Sec to Min of Agriculture and Fisheries 1921-4 (also Dep Min therefor from Oct 1921); Joint Hereditary Lord Great Chamberlain (acting for reign of King George VI) 1936-50; sat as MP (*C*) for Lincolnshire, S Lindsey or Horncastle Div 1894-1910: *m* 1905, Eloise, OBE, JP, who *d* 1953, el da of late W. L. Breese, of New York, USA; *d* 1951; *s* by his el son **(26)** (GILBERT) JAMES, KCVO, TD, 3rd Earl, *b* 1907; Maj RA (TA); Joint Hereditary Lord Chamberlain (acting for reign of King George VI); European War 1939-45 (despatches); Lord Licut of Lincs 1950-75, and an Alderman for Kesteven Co Council 1954-75; bore St Edward's Staff at Coronation of Queen Elizabeth II; MP for Rutland and Stamford Div of Parts of Kesteven and Rutland (*C*) Nov 1933 — Feb 1950; called to House of Lords in his father's Barony of Willoughby de Eresby Jan 1951: *m* 1933, Hon (Nancy) Phyllis Louise Astor, who *d* 1975, da of 2nd Viscount Astor; *d* 1983, when the Earldom of Ancaster and Barony of Aveland became ext, and the baronetcy of Heathcote passed to his kinsman (*see* Heathcote, Bt, of London), and he was *s* in the Barony of Willoughby de Eresby by his only surv child (his only son, Timothy Gilbert, Lord Willoughby de Eresby, *b* 1936, disappeared at sea between Cap Ferrat and Corsica 1963) **(27)** (NANCY) JANE MARIE, Baroness Willoughby de Eresby, present peeress.

Wills, family name of Baron Dulverton.

WILSON, BARON (Wilson) (Baron UK 1946)

PATRICK MAITLAND WILSON, 2nd Baron; *b* 14 Sept 1915; *s* 1964; *ed* Eton, and King's Coll, Camb; 1939-45 War in Greece and Middle East (despatches): *m* 1945, Storeen Violet, who *d* 1990, da of late Maj James Hamilton Douglas Campbell of Blythswood, OBE (B Clarina, ext).

ᴀrms – Sable, a wolf salient or, on a chief of the last a pale of the first charged with a fleur-de-lys argent between two pellets. ᴄrest – A demi wolf or, the sinister paw resting on a pellet charged with a fleur-de-lys gold. ᴤupporters – *Dexter*, a rifleman; *sinister*, a bugler, both of the Rifle Brigade, in full dress proper.
Address –

PREDECESSOR – **(1)** *Sir* HENRY MAITLAND Wilson, GCB, GBE, DSO, son of Arthur Maitland Wilson, OBE, of Stowlangtoft Hall, Suffolk; *b* 1881; Field Marshal late Rifle Bde (OC 1st Bn 1927-30), and Col Comdt 1939-51; GOC-in-C British Troops in Egypt 1939-41, Mil Gov and GOC-in-C Cyrenaica, GOC-in-C British Troops in Greece, GOC, British Troops in Palestine and Transjordan, GOC, Allied Forces in Syria, and GOC 9th Army 1941, GOC-in-C, Persia and Iraq 1942-43, and Middle East 1943-44, Supreme Allied Comd in Mediterranean Theatre 1944-45 and Head of British Joint Staff Mission, Washington 1945-47, Constable of HM Tower of London 1955-60; *cr Baron Wilson*, of Libya and of Stowlangtoft, co Suffolk (Peerage of UK) 1946: *m* 1914, Hester Mary, who *d* 1979, da of Philip James Digby Wykeham, late of Tythrop House, Oxon; *d* 1964; *s* by his only son **(2)** PATRICK MAITLAND, 2nd Baron and present peer.

Wilson, family name of Baron Moran.

Wilson, family name of Baron Nunburnholme.

WILSON OF RADCLIFFE, BARONY OF (Wilson) (Extinct 1983)

DAUGHTER LIVING OF LIFE BARON

Hon Moyra Christine, *b* 1943: *m* 1st, 1964, Dr Arthur Crowther, who *d* 1979; 2ndly, 1983, Joseph Levey, who *d* 1985. *Residence* – 24 Acre Lane, Cheadle Hulme, Cheshire.

WIDOW LIVING OF LIFE BARON

FREDA (*Baroness Wilson of Radcliffe*), da of Jessie Mather, of Bolton: *m* 1976, as his second wife, Baron Wilson of Radcliffe (Life Baron), who *d* 1983. *Residence* – 10 Gisburn Drive, Walshaw, nr Bury, Lancs BL8 3DH.

WILSON OF RIEVAULX, BARONY OF (Wilson) (Extinct 1995)

SONS LIVING OF LIFE BARON

Hon Robin James, *b* 1943, *ed* Univ Coll Sch, Balliol Coll, Oxford (MA), Univ of Pennsylvania (MA, PhD), and Massachusetts Inst of Technology: *m* 1968, (Margaret Elizabeth) Joy, da of Brian Crispin, of Dawlish, and has issue, Jennifer, *b* 1975, — Catherine, *b* (twin) 1975. *Residence* – 15 Chalfont Rd, Oxford OX2 6TL.

Hon Giles Daniel John, *b* 1948; *ed* Univ Coll Sch, Brighton Coll of Education, and Open Univ (BA). *Residence* – 5 Ashley Gdns, Ambrosden Av, SW1.

WIDOW LIVING OF LIFE BARON

(GLADYS) MARY (*Baroness Wilson of Rievaulx*), da of late Rev Daniel Baldwin, of The Manse, Duxford, Cambridge: *m* 1940, Baron Wilson of Rievaulx, KG, OBE, PC, FRS (Life Baron), who *d* 1995. *Residence* – 5 Ashley Gdns, Ambrosden Av, SW1.

WILSON OF TILLYORN, BARON (Wilson) (Life Baron 1992)

DAVID CLIVE WILSON, GCMG, son of late Rev William Skinner Wilson; *b* 14 Feb 1935; *ed* Trin Coll, Glenalmond, Keble Coll, Oxford (Scholar, MA), Hon Fellow 1987, Hong Kong Univ, Columbia Univ (visiting scholar), and London Univ (PhD); Hon LLD Aberdeen Univ 1990, Chinese Univ of Hong Kong 1996, Hon DLitt Sydney Univ 1991, Abertay Univ Dundee 1994; HM Diplomatic Ser 1958-68, ed The China Quarterly Contemporary Inst SOAS London Univ 1968-74; Rejoined Diplomatic Ser 1974; Cabinet Office 1974-77, Political Adviser to Gov of Hong Kong 1977-81, Head S European Dept FCO 1981-84, Assist Under Sec of State responsible for Asia and the Pacific, FCO 1984-87, Govr and C-in-C Hong Kong 1987-92; Chm Scottish Hydro-Electric plc (Scottish and Southern Energy plc since 1998) since 1993, Chancellor, Univ of Aberdeen since 1997 (Chancellor's Assessor 1993-97), Chm Scottish Cttee of British Council since 1993, Pres Bhutan Soc of UK since 1993, Memb of Council, Glenalmond Coll since 1993, Pres Hong Kong Soc and Hong Kong Assoc since 1994; KStJ 1987; *cr* CMG 1985, KCMG 1987, GCMG 1991, and *Baron Wilson of Tillyorn*, of Finzean, in the District of Kincardine and Deeside and of Fanling in Hong Kong (Life Baron) 1992: *m* 1967, Natasha Helen Mary, da of late Bernard Gustav Alexander, and has issue.

Arms – Sable, on a chevron argent between a dragon passant guardant or in chief, and a demi-wolf argent holding in its forepaws a pearl proper in base, a Celtic cross azure. **Crest** – A talbot's head erased sable langued gules gorged of a collar argent charged with two mullets gules. **Supporters** – *Dexter*, a Chinese dragon or langued and with each leg having four claws gules; *sinister*, a lion gules langued and armed azure a compartment comprising a rock proper rising from water barry wavy of four argent and azure.
Residence – Tillyorn, Finzean, Aberdeenshire AB31 6PN. *Clubs* – Alpine, New (Edinburgh), Royal Northern and University (Aberdeen).

SONS LIVING

Hon Peter Michael Alexander, *b* 1968.
Hon Andrew Marcus William, *b* 1969.

WILTON, EARL OF (Egerton) (Earl UK 1801)

I trust to virtue, not to arms

SEYMOUR WILLIAM ARTHUR JOHN EGERTON, 7th Earl; *b* 29 May 1921; *s* 1927; *ed* Eton: *m* 1962, Diana Elizabeth Lea (NAYLOR-LEYLAND), da of Roy Galway, of St Ronans, Winkfield Row, Ascot, Berks.

Arms – Argent, a lion rampant gules, between three pheons, points downwards sable. **Crest** – Three arrows, points downwards, one in pale and two in saltire or, barbed and fledged sable, band gules, and tasseled or. **Supporters** – *Dexter*, a wyvern, wings inverted or; *sinister*, a lion argent, ducally crowned or. *Address* – c/o Messrs Warrens Boyes and Archer, 20 Hartford Rd, Huntingdon, Cambs PE18 6QE. *Club* – White's.

COLLATERAL BRANCH LIVING　(*In special remainder*)

Descendants of late Lord Robert Grosvenor (3rd son of 1st Marquess of Westminster), who was *cr Baron Ebury* 1857 (see that title):—
Of whom FRANCIS EGERTON (*Baron Ebury*), *b* 8 Feb 1934; is *hp* to the Earldom.

PREDECESSORS – (1) *Sir* THOMAS Egerton, 7th Bt, of Oulton, was *cr Baron Grey de Wilton*, of Wilton Castle, co Hereford (peerage of Great Britain) 1784, and *Viscount Grey de Wilton* and *Earl of Wilton* (peerage of United Kingdom) 1801, with remainder to the 2nd and all the younger sons successively of his da Eleanor, wife of Lord Belgrave, afterwards 1st Marquess of Westminster; *d* 1814, when the Barony of Grey de Wilton expired, the baronetcy reverted upon the lineal descendant of the 1st Bt (see Grey-Egerton, Bt), and the viscountcy and earldom devolved upon his grandson (2) Rt Hon THOMAS Grosvenor, GCH, DCL, 2nd Earl; *b* 1799; was Lord Steward of the Household; assumed in 1821 by sign manual the surname of Egerton in lieu of Grosvenor; *m* 1st, 1821, Lady Mary Margaret Stanley, da of 12th Earl of Derby; 2ndly, 1863, Isabella, who *d* 1916, da of late Major Elton Smith, of Ilminster: *d* 1882; *s* by his el son (3) ARTHUR EDWARD HOLLAND GREY, 3rd Earl; *b* 1833; sat as MP for Weymouth (*C*) 1859-65, and for Bath 1873-4: *m* 1858, Lady Elizabeth Charlotte Louisa Craven, who *d* 1919, da of 2nd Earl of Craven; *cr Baron Grey de Radcliffe* (peerage of United Kingdom) 1875; *dsp* 19 Jan 1885, when the Barony of Grey de Radcliffe became extinct, and the peerage of 1801 devolved upon his brother (4) SEYMOUR JOHN GREY, 4th Earl; *b* 1839: *m* 1862, Laura Caroline, who *d* 1916, da of late William Russell; *d* 1898; *s* by his son (5) ARTHUR GEORGE, 5th Earl, *b* 1863: *m* 1895, Hon Mariota Thelluson, who *d* 1924, da of 5th Baron Rendlesham; *d* 1915; *s* by his el son (6) SEYMOUR EDWARD FREDERICK, 6th Earl; *b* 1896: *m* 1917, Brenda, who *d* 1930, da of late Sir William Petersen, KBE, of Eigg, Inverness; *d* 1927; *s* by his son (7) SEYMOUR WILLIAM ARTHUR JOHN, 7th Earl and present peer; also Viscount Grey de Wilton.

Wiltshire, Earl of; son of Marquess of Winchester.

WIMBORNE, VISCOUNT (Guest) (Viscount UK 1918, Baron UK 1880 and 1910, Bt UK 1838)

By iron, not by the sword

IVOR MERVYN VIGORS GUEST, 4th Viscount, and 6th Baronet; *b* 19 Sept 1968; *s* 1993; *ed* Eton.

Arms – Azure, on a chevron or, between three swan's heads erased proper, as many crosses moline sable. Crest – A swan's head, erased proper, gorged with a collar or, and charged underneath with a cross moline as in the arms, between two ostrich feathers or. Supporters – On either side a figure habited as Vulcan, resting his exterior hand on an anvil and holding in front thereof a sledge hammer, all proper. *Address* – c/o House of Lords, SW1A 0PW.

HALF-SISTER LIVING

Hon Ilona Charlotte, *b* 1985.

UNCLES LIVING *(sons of 2nd Viscount)*

Hon JULIAN JOHN, *b* 12 Oct 1945; *ed* Stowe: *m* 1st, 1970 (*m diss* 1978), Emma Jane Arlette, elder da of Cdr Archibald Gray, DSO, RN, of Tilbridge, Gt Staughton, St Neots, Hunts; 2ndly, 1983, Jillian, da of late Ninian Stuart Gray Bannatine. *Address* – c/o White's Club, St James's, W1.

Hon Charles James, *b* 1950; *ed* Harrow, and RMA Sandhurst; commn'd 9th/12th Royal Lancers (Prince of Wales's) 1973, late Capt Royal Wessex Yeo; Member of Securities Institute: *m* 1976, Simone Katherine, yst da of Patrick Whinney, of Grand Havre, Guernsey, CI, and has issue living, Henry Charles, *b* 1978, — William Patrick, *b* 1981, — Catherine Elizabeth, *b* 1987. *Residence* – Truckwell Manor Farm, Lydeard St Lawrence, Taunton, Som TA4 3PT; *Club* – White's.

AUNT LIVING *(daughter of 2nd Viscount)*

Hon Frances Ann, *b* 1942: *m* 1st, 1971 (*m diss* 1987), Ernest Martin Johnson; 2ndly, 1991, Rao Gaddipati. *Residence* – PO Box 600, Germantown, NY 12526-0600, USA.

MOTHER LIVING

Victoria Ann, only da of late Col Mervyn Doyne Vigors, DSO, MC, 9th Bengal Lancers (Hodson's Horse): *m* 1st, 1966 (*m diss* 1981), the 3rd Viscount Wimborne, who *d* 1993; 2ndly, 1982, Vincent Poklewski-Koziell.

WIDOW LIVING OF THIRD VISCOUNT

VENETIA MARGARET *(Viscountess Wimborne)*, da of Richard Bridges St John Quarry, of Orchard House, Odiham, Hants, and formerly wife of Capt Frederick Grant Barker, late 11th Hus: *m* 1983, as his 2nd wife, the 3rd Viscount Wimborne, who *d* 1993. *Residence* – Fontaine l'Abbé, 27470 Serquigny, France.

COLLATERAL BRANCHES LIVING *(In remainder to the Barony of Wimborne and the Baronetcy only)*

Grandchildren of late Lt-Col Hon (Christian) Henry Charles Guest, 2nd son of 1st Baron:—
Issue of late John Spencer Churchill Guest, *b* 1913, *d* (14 May) 1997: *m* 1948, Margaret Hetherington, who *d* (21 May) 1997, da of late Henry Craft Houck, of Schenectady, NY, USA:—
Richard Lyttelton (7 James St, Norwalk, Connecticut, USA), *b* 1954: *m* 1983, Cynthia Rogers, da of late William Shelton Vaiden, of Los Osos, Calif, USA, and has issue living, Sarah Frances Vaiden, *b* 1984. —— Cornelia Schermerhorn, *b* 1952: *m* 1986, Robert Allan Mitchell, of 148 June Rd, N Salem, NY, USA, and has issue living, Andrew Moses Leonard, *b* 1993, — John Henry Guest, *b* (triplet) 1993, — Anne Elizabeth Houck, *b* (triplet) 1993.

Grandchildren of late Capt Rt Hon Frederick Edward Guest, CBE, DSO, MP, 3rd son of 1st Baron:—
Issue of late Capt Winston Frederick Churchill Guest, US Marines, *b* 1906, *d* 1982: *m* 1st, 1934 (*m diss* 1944), Helena Woolworth, da of Charles Edward Francis McCann, of New York; 2ndly, 1947, Lucy Douglas (651 North Country Rd, Palm Beach, Fla 33480, USA), da of late Alexander Lynde Cochrane, of Boston, Mass:—
(By 1st *m*) Winston (152 Wells Rd, Palm Beach, Fla 33480, USA), *b* 1936: *m* 1967, Helen, da of Joseph V. Shields, of New York, and has issue living, Winston Frederick Churchill, *b* 1968, — Spencer Randolph Harrison, *b* 1984, — Helena Woolworth, *b* 1970. —— Frederick Edward (II) (10 West 66 St, New York City 10023, USA), *b* 1938: *m* 1st, 1963, Stephanie, da of late Walter F. Wanger, by his late wife, Joan Bennett, the film actress; 2ndly, 1988, Carole, da of Frank Baldoff, of Pittsburgh, Penn, and has issue living (by 1st *m*), Frederick Edward (III), *b* 1975, — Andrew Churchill, *b* 1976, — Victoria Woolworth, *b* 1966, — Vanessa Wanger, *b* 1973. —— (By 2nd *m*) Alexander Michael Dudley Churchill (11 Knollwood Drive, Mendham, NJ 07845, USA), *b* 1954: *m* 1986, Elizabeth, da of Cyril Geacintov, and has issue living, Gregory Winston Churchill, *b* 1990.

Issue of late Raymond Richard Guest, sometime Senator of Virginia, and US Amb to Ireland 1965-69, *b* 1907, *d* 1991: *m* 1st, 1935, Elizabeth Sturgis, who *d* 1990, da of Frank Lyon Polk; 2ndly, 1953, Mrs Ellen Tuck Astor, da

of Francis Ormond French, and formerly wife of John Jacob Astor; 3rdly, 1960, HH Princess Caroline Cécile Alexandrine Jeanne (Powhatan Plantation, King George, Virginia, USA), yr da of HH late Prince Alexandre Michel Eugène Joachim Napoléon Murat:—
(By 1st *m*) Raymond Richard (Jr) (Rock Hill Farm, Front Royal, Virginia, USA), *b* 1939: *m* 1st, 1962, Patricia, da of David R. Donovan; 2ndly, 1979, Mary Scott, da of Butler Carson Derrick, and has issue living (by 1st *m*), Raymond Richard (III), *b* 1965, — Mary Elizabeth, *b* 1964. —— Elizabeth Polk, *b* 1937: *m* 1st, 1958, Edward B. Condon; 2ndly, 1965, George C. Stevens, Jr, of 3050 Avon Lane NW, Washington DC 20007, USA, and has issue living (by 1st *m*), Caroline, *b* 1959, — (by 2nd *m*) Michael Murrow, *b* 1966, — David Averill, *b* 1968. —— Virginia, *b* 1946: *m* 1st, 1975 (*m diss* 1978), William L. Van Alen, Jr, of Newtown Sq, Penn; 2ndly, 1991, E. Massie Valentine, of 102 Tonbridge Rd, Richmond, Virginia 23221, USA. —— (By 3rd *m*) Achille Murat, *b* 1961. —— Laetitia Amelia, *b* 1965: *m* 1994, Laurie C. R. Oppenheim, of 4 Tregunter Rd, SW10, and has issue living, Caroline, *b* 1995.

Issue of late Major Hon (Oscar) Montague Guest, yst son of 1st Baron, *b* 1888, *d* 1958: *m* 1924, Kathleen Susan, who *d* 1982, da of late Graham Paterson (E Huntingdon):—
Bertie Warner (Cabalva House, Whitney-on-Wye, Hereford), *b* 1925: *m* 1949, (*m diss* 1970), Margaret Rose, da of Charles Lamond Henderson, QC, and has issue living, Jonathan Bertie (Drumphin, Fowlis Wester, Crieff, Perthshire PH7 3NJ), *b* 1952: *m* 1983, Anna Faith, da of Barrington Charles Ward, of Overkerne, Ross on Wye, Hereford, and has issue living, Oliver Charles Bertie *b* 1984, Hector Jonathan *b* 1988, Rose Marie *b* 1990, — Veronica Susan GUEST, *b* 1953; resumed her maiden name 19—: *m* 1978 (*m diss* 1989), J. Crowder; has issue living (by Gary Jones), Daniel Meredith *b* 1987, Benjamin Patrick *b* 1989, — Harriet Clare, *b* 1955: *m* 19—, Prof John Barrell, of 14 Bootham Terrace, York YO3 7DH, and has issue living, Helena *b* 1992 , — Diana Charlotte, *b* 1959: *m* 1988, Charles Hicks, of 167 Barry Rd, E Dulwich, SE22 0JP, and has issue living, Sam Thomas KERRIDGE *b* 1982, Christopher James *b* 1990. —— Patrick Henry, *b* 1927: *m* 1951, Juliet Marian, da of late H. M. James, and has issue living, Peter Hugh, *b* 1952: *m* 1988, Donna Jean, da of late Donald Lee Macfarlane, of Piedmont, Calif, USA, — Matthew James, *b* 1954, — David Christian, *b* 1960: *m* 1986, Henrietta Mary, da of John Giles Selby Coode-Adams, of Feeringbury Manor, Feering, Essex (*see* Buxton, Bt, colls, 1980 Edn), and has issue living, Imogen Victoria *b* 1993, Jemima Charlotte *b* 1995, Genevieve Isla *b* 1997. *Residence* – Lower Bettws Farm, Whitney-on-Wye, Herefords. —— Cornelia Rowena, *b* 1928: *m* 1st, 1949 (*m diss* 1955), Hugh Dearman Janson; 2ndly, 1957, Peter Frederick Arthur Denman (*see* B Denman, colls), and has issue living, (by 1st *m*) Charles James, *b* 1952, — Sarah, *b* 1950, — (by 2nd *m*) (*see* B Denman, colls). *Residence* – Duke's House, 23 Lawrence St, SW3. —— Revel Sarah, *b* 1931; co-author of *Lady Charlotte; a Biography of the Nineteenth Century* (1989): *m* 1963, Robert Alan Albert, and has issue living, Justin Thomas (Cabalva Farmhouse, Whitney-on-Wye, Hereford), *b* 1965: *m* 1991, Hester Amanda Jessica, eldest da of Michael Selby Gray, of Argyll, and has issue living, Oscar Timothy *b* 1996, Charlotte Revel *b* 1991, — Corisande Charlotte, *b* 1967. *Residence* – Cabalva House, Whitney-on-Wye, Hereford HR3 6EX.

Granddaughter of late Arthur Edward Guest, brother of 1st Baron:—
Issue of late (Arthur) Rhuvon Guest, *b* 1869, *d* 1946: *m* 1901, Hilda Eugenia, who *d* 1959, da of late Adm Hon Keith Stewart, CB (E Galloway, colls):—
Pamela Margaret (51 Abingdon Villas, W8 6XA), *b* 1905.

PREDECESSORS – (1) JOSIAH JOHN Guest, son of late Thomas Guest, of Dowlais, Glamorgan; *b* 1785; MP for Honiton 1825-31, and for Merthyr Tydvil 1832-52; *cr* a *Baronet* 1838: *m* 1st, 1817, Maria Elizabeth, who *d* 1818, da of William Ranken; 2ndly, 1833, Lady Charlotte Elizabeth Bertie, who *d* 1895 (having *m* 2ndly, 1855, Charles Schreiber, MP, who *d* 1884), da of 9th Earl of Lindsey: *d* 1852; *s* by his son (2) Sir IVOR BERTIE, 2nd Bt, *b* 1835; *cr Baron Wimborne*, of Canford Magna, Dorset (peerage of United Kingdom) 1880: *m* 1868, Lady Cornelia Henrietta Maria Spencer-Churchill, who *d* 1927, el da of 7th Duke of Marlborough; *d* 1914; *s* by his el son (3) IVOR CHURCHILL, PC, 2nd Baron, *b* 1873; MP for Plymouth (*L*) 1900-1906, and for Cardiff 1906-10; Paymaster-Gen 1910-12, a Lord-in-Waiting to HM 1913-15, and Lord-Lieut of Ireland 1915-18; *cr Baron Ashby St Ledgers*, of Ashby St Ledgers, co Northampton (peerage of United Kingdom) 1910, and *Viscount Wimborne*, of Canford Magna, Dorset (peerage of United Kingdom) 1918: *m* 1902, Hon Alice Katherine Sibell Grosvenor, who *d* 1948, da of 2nd Baron Ebury; *d* 1939; *s* by his only son (4) IVOR GROSVENOR, OBE, 2nd Viscount, *b* 1903; PPS to Under-Sec of State for Air 1943-45; MP for Breconshire 1935-39: *m* 1938, Lady Mabel Edith Fox-Strangways, who *d* 1995, da of 6th Earl of Ilchester; *d* 1967; *s* by his son (5) IVOR FOX-STRANGWAYS, 3rd Viscount, *b* 1939; Chm Harris & Dixon Ltd 1972-76, Chm Harris & Dixon Holdings Ltd 1977-93; Joint Master Pytchley Hounds 1968-76: *m* 1st, 1966 (*m diss* 1981), Victoria, only da of late Col Mervyn Doyne Vigors, DSO, MC, 9th Bengal Lancers (Hodson's Horse); 2ndly, 1983, Mrs Venetia Margaret Barker, da of Richard Bridges St John Quarry, of Gaddeshill House, Everley, Hants, and formerly wife of Capt Frederick Grant Barker, late 11th Hus; *d* 1993; *s* by his only son (6) IVOR MERVYN VIGORS, 4th Viscount and present peer; also Baron Ashby St Ledgers, and Baron Wimborne.

WINCHESTER, MARQUESS OF (Paulet) (Marquess E 1551)

NIGEL GEORGE PAULET, 18th Marquess, and Premier Marquess of England; *b* 22 Dec 1941; *s* 1968; Dir Rhodesia Mineral Ventures (Pvt) Ltd, Sani-Dan Services (Pvt) Ltd, and Rhodesia Prospectors (1969) (Pvt) Ltd: *m* 1967, Rosemary Anne, da of Maj Aubrey John Hilton, of Harare, Zimbabwe, and has issue.

Arms – Sable, three swords in pile, points downwards, proper, pommels and hilts, or. **Crest** – A falcon, wings displayed or, belled of the same, and ducally collared gules. **Supporters** – Two hinds purpure, semée of estoiles, and ducally gorged or. *Residence* – 6A Main Rd, Irene 1675, Transvaal, S Africa.

Love loyalty

SONS LIVING

CHRISTOPHER JOHN HILTON (*Earl of Wiltshire*), *b* 30 July 1969: *m* 1992, Christine, da of Peter Town, of Cheam, Surrey, and has issue living, *Lady* Emma Louise, *b* 1993.
Lord Richard George, *b* 1971.

DAUGHTER LIVING

Lady Susan, *b* 1976.

BROTHER LIVING (*Raised to the rank of a Marquess's son* 1970)

Lord Timothy Guy, *b* 1944: *m* 1973, Gilian Margaret, da of late Capt Thomas Preacher, 8th Bn DLI, and has issue living, Timothy Guy, *b* 1975, — Michael Raoul, *b* 1976. *Residence* – 47 Stratford Drive, Greystone Park, Harare, Zimbabwe. *Postal Address* - PO Box BW 694, Borrowdale, Harare, Zimbabwe.

SISTER LIVING (*Raised to the rank of a Marquess's daughter* 1970)

Lady Jane Angela, *b* 1939: *m* 1972 (*m diss* 1989), Christopher John Fisher, and has issue living, Henry Nicholas, *b* 1972, — Benjamin David, *b* 1974. *Residence* – 66 Slyne Rd, Lancaster.

SISTER LIVING OF SEVENTEENTH MARQUESS (*Raised to the rank of Marquess's daughter* 1970)

Lady Eileen Cecil Theo, *b* 1917: *m* 1st, 1941, Harry Evan Martin, who *d* 1947; 2ndly, 1949, Joseph Fitton, of 470 Sonora Crescent, Campbell River, BC, Canada V9W 6V3, and has had issue (by 1st *m*), Gillian Jane (1193 S Alder St, Campbell River, BC, Canada V9W 1Z8), *b* 1942: *m* 1964, Lipot Gyula Winter, and has issue living, Edward Steven *b* 1966, Robert Ferenc *b* 1974, Peter James *b* 1978, Elizabeth Jane *b* 1964, — Elizabeth Susan, *b* 1945: *m* 1971, Luis Correia, of 21 Kenton Gdns, Kenton, Harrow, Middx HA3 8BE, — (by 2nd *m*) Francis Peter (Box 454, Quathiaski Cove, Quadra Is, BC, Canada V0P 1NO), *b* 1949: *m* 1985, Victoria Lynn, da of Donald Ralph Gregory, and has issue living, Kala Louise *b* 1985, Deanna Eileen *b* 1987, — Jonathan Paul (359 Simms Rd, Campbell River, BC, Canada V9W 1P2), *b* 1952: *m* 1991, Lona Dianne, da of Reuben Emil Croissant; has issue living, Jeffrey Duggan *b* 1983, William Elliot *b* 1984, — Theresa Mary, *b* 1951: *m* 1992, Neil Andrew Marson, of 500 Quadra St, Campbell River, BC, Canada V9W 6V1, — Margaret Anne, *b* 1956: *m* 1982, Kenneth Dodd Clippingdale, of Box 203, Heriot Bay, BC, Canada V0P 1H0, and has issue living, Robert Nathan *b* 1974, Andrew Dodd *b* 1983, — Catherine Louise, *b* 1958, — Judith Ellen, *b* 1961; *d* 1985.

COLLATERAL BRANCH LIVING

Issue of late John Valentine Paulet, uncle of 18th Marquess, *b* 1909, *d* 1970: *m* 1945, Mira Elizabeth, da of Edmund Francis Smith, of Mossel Bay, Cape Province:—
†Michael John, *b* 1945; served British S Africa Police, Salisbury, Rhodesia: *m* 1967, Gail Lisbeth, da of John Blackwood Ward, of Bulawayo, Rhodesia, and was *k* in a flying accident 1978. —— Pamela Elizabeth, *b* 1947.

PREDECESSORS – (1) *Sir* WILLIAM Paulet, KG, and *cr Baron St John of Basing* (peerage of England) 1539, *Earl of Wiltshire* (peerage of England) 1550, and *Marquess of Winchester* (peerage of England) 1551, and *Marquess of Winchester* (peerage of England) 1551; was an executor to the will of Henry VIII, and Lord Treasurer of England *temp* Edward VI and Queens Mary I and Elizabeth I; *d* 1572; *s* by his son (2) JOHN, 2nd Marquess; summoned to Parliament in his father's barony of St John; *d* 1576; *s* by his son (3) WILLIAM 3rd Marquess; summoned to Parliament in his father's barony of St John; *d* 1598; *s* by his son (4) WILLIAM, 4th Marquess; entertained Queen Elizabeth with magnificence at his seat at Basing, by which and other expenses he became involved in pecuniary difficulties; *d* 1628; *s* by his son (5) JOHN, 5th Marquess, a zealous partisan of Charles I; his seat at Basing was after a protracted siege by the Parliamentarians burned to the ground, when property of the value of £200,000 was destroyed; *d* 1675; *s* by his son (6) CHARLES, 6th Marquess; *cr Duke of Bolton* (peerage of England) 1689; *d* 1699; *s* by his son (7) CHARLES, 2nd Duke; was Lord-Lieut of Ireland 1717; *d* 1722; *s* by his el son (8) CHARLES, KG, 3rd Duke; was Lord Lieut of the Tower Hamlets and Constable of the Tower of London; *d* 1754; *s* by his brother (9) HARRY, 4th Duke; *d* 1759; *s* by his son (10) CHARLES, KB, 5th Duke; was Lieut of Tower of London, and Lord-Lieut of Hants; *d* unmarried 1765; *s* by his brother (11) HARRY, 6th Duke; was and Adm of the White; *d* 1794, when the dukedom expired, and the barony, earldom, and marquessate devolved upon his kinsman (12) GEORGE, 12th Marquess, descendant of Lord Henry, 3rd son of 4th Marquess; *d* 1800; *s* by his son (13) CHARLES INGOLDSBY, 13th Marquess; *b* 1765; assumed in 1839 the additional surname of Burroughs: *m* 1800, Anne da of John Andrews, Esq, of Shotney Hall, co Northumberland; *d* 1843; *s* by his son *b* (14) JOHN, 14th Marquess, *b* 1801: *m* 1855, the Hon Mary Montagu, who *d* 1868, el da of 6th Baron Rokeby (*ext*); *d* 1887; *s* by his son (15) AUGUSTUS JOHN HENRY BEAUMONT, 15th Marquess; *b* 1858; Major Coldstream Guards; killed at battle of Magersfontein in S Africa 1899; *s* by his brother (16) HENRY WILLIAM MONTAGU, 16th Marquess, *b* 1862; Lord-Lieut of Hants 1904-17; Chm of Hants Co Council 1905-9; Major Rifle Bde in France 1914-17: *m* 1st, 1892, Dame Charlotte Josephine, GBE, who *d* 1924, da of late Col John Stanley Howard, of Ballina Park, co Wicklow, and widow of Samuel Garnett; 2ndly, 1925, Caroline, who *d* 1949, da of Abraham Hoffnung, and widow of Major Claude Marks, DSO; 3rdly, 1952, Bapsy, who *d* 1995, da of Most Rev Khurshedi Pavry; *d* 1962, *s* by his kinsman (17) RICHARD CHARLES (only son of late Major Charles Standish Paulet, MVO, grandson of late Rev Lord Charles Paulet, 2nd son of 13th Marquess), 17th Marquess, *b* 1905, *d* 1968; *s* by his kinsman (18) NIGEL GEORGE (el son of George Cecil Paulet, el son of Cecil Henry Paulet, uncle of 17th Marquess), 18th Marquess and present peer; also Earl of Wiltshire, and Baron St John of Basing.

WINCHILSEA AND NOTTINGHAM, EARL OF (Finch Hatton) (Earl E 1628 and 1681, Bt E 1611 and 1660)

NIL SIBI CONSCIRE

Conscious of no guilt

†CHRISTOPHER DENYS STORMONT FINCH HATTON, 16th Earl of Winchilsea, 11th Earl of Nottingham, 17th Baronet of Eastwell, and 11th Baronet of Raunston; *b* 17 Nov 1936; *s* 1950; *ed* Eton, and Gordonstoun; Hereditary Lord of Roy Manor of Wye: *m* 1962, Shirley, el da of late Bernard Hatfield, of Wylde Green, Sutton Coldfield, and *d* 26 June 1999, leaving issue.

𝕬rms – Argent, a chevron between three griffins passant sable. 𝕮rest – A pegasus courant argent, wings expanded or. 𝕾upporters – *Dexter*, a pegasus wings elevated argent, ducally gorged or; *sinister*, a griffin wings elevated sable, gorged as the dexter.
Residence – South Cadbury House, nr Yeovil, Somerset.

SON LIVING

DANIEL JAMES HATFIELD (*Viscount Maidstone*), *b* 7 Oct 1967: *m* 1994, Shelley Amanda, da of Gordon Gillard, and has issue living, Hon Tobias Joshua Stormont, *b* 21 June 1998.

DAUGHTER LIVING

Lady Alice Nan Christiane, *b* 1970.

BROTHER LIVING

Hon Robin Heneage (Town House Farm House, Clemsfold, Horsham, W Sussex RH12 3PP), *b* 1939; *ed* Gordonstoun: *m* 1962, Molly Iona, yr da of Col Palgrave Dawson Turner Powell, of Damson Hill Cottage, Swanmore, Hants, and has had issue, Christopher Benjamyn *b* 1966, — Rupert Stormont, *b* 1968, — Nicola Jane, *b* 1964, *d* 1967, — Louisa Henrietta Mari (Mariska), *b* 1971.

AUNT LIVING (*Daughter of 14th Earl*)

Lady Daphne Margarita, *b* 1913: *m* 1935, Air-Commodore Whitney Willard Straight, CBE, MC, DFC, Auxiliary Air Force, who *d* 1979, and has issue living, Camilla Caroline *b* 1937: *m* 1960, Maj Michael Ian Vansittart Bowater, Scots Guards, son of late Lt-Col Sir Ian Frank Bowater, DSO, TD (*see* Bowater, Bt, *cr* 1939), — Amanda Betsy, *b* 1952.

COLLATERAL BRANCHES LIVING

Granddaughters of late Rev William Robert Finch Hatton, son of late Rev Hon Daniel Heneage Finch Hatton, brother of 10th Earl of Winchilsea and Nottingham:—
Issue of late Brig-Gen Edward Heneage Finch Hatton, CMG, DSO, late the Buffs, *b* 1868, *d* 1940: *m* 1912, Dagmar Gladys, who *d* 1975, da of late Col Francis George Archibald Wiehe, formerly 68th Durham LI:—
Ann Zephine, *b* 1912: *m* 1943, Group-Capt Maurice Ashdown Newnham, OBE, DFC, RAF, VR, and has issue living, Nicola Ann, *b* 1946. *Residence* – Briar Cottage, Duckmead Lane, Liss, Petersfield, Hants. —— Essex Dagmar FINCH HATTON, *b* 1916.

Descendants of late Hon Heneage Finch (2nd son of 1st Earl of Nottingham), who was *cr Earl of Aylesford* 1714 (see that title).

PREDECESSORS – (**1**) *Sir* MOYLE Finch, Knt, was *cr a Baronet* 1611 (of Eastwell): *m* Elizabeth, only da of Sir Thomas Heneage, Knt, of Copt Hall, Essex, which Lady was *cr Viscountess Maidstone* (peerage of England) 1623 and Countess of Winchilsea (peerage of England) 1628; Sir Moyle *d* 1614; *s* by his son (**2**) *Sir* THEOPHILUS, 2nd Bt; *dsp*; *s* by his brother (**3**) *Sir* THOMAS, 3rd Bt, who in 1633 *s* his mother as 2nd Earl; *d* 1634; *s* by his son (**4**) Heneage, 3rd Earl; an earnest royalist; having rendered efficient aid in restoring the monarchy was in 1660 *cr* by Charles II *Baron FitzHerbert of Eastwell,* co Kent (peerage of England); was Lord-Lieut of co Kent; *d* 1689; *s* by his grandson (**5**) CHARLES, 4th Earl; *d* 1712; *s* by his uncle (**6**) HENEAGE, 5th Earl; *dsp* 1726; *s* by his half-brother (**7**) JOHN, 6th Earl; *dsp* 1729, when the Barony of FitzHerbert of Eastwell became extinct, and the baronetcy, viscountcy and earldom reverted to his kinsman (**8**) DANIEL, PC, 7th Earl, who in 1682 has *s* his father as 2nd Earl of Nottingham (see * infra); was Sec of State 1689-94 and 1702-4, Lord Pres of the Council 1714-16, and Lord-Lieut of Kent; *d* 1730; *s* by his son (**9**) DANIEL, 8th Earl; *dsp* 1760; *s* by his nephew (**10**) GEORGE, KG, 9th Earl, son of Rt Hon William Finch, MP, 2nd son of 7th Earl; was Lord Lieut of co Rutland; *d* unmarried 1826; *s* by his cousin (**11**) GEORGE WILLIAM Finch Hatton 10th Earl, grandson of Hon Edward, MP (5th son of 7th Earl), who assumed without Roy Licence the additional surname of Hatton; *b* 1791, *m* 1st, 1814, Lady Georgiana Charlotte, da of 3rd Duke of Montrose; 2ndly, 1837, Emily Georgina, da of Rt Hon Sir Charles Bagot, GCB; 3rdly, 1849, Fanny Margaret, who *d* 1909, da of Edward Royd Rice, of Dane Court, Kent; *d* 1858; *s* by his son (**12**) GEORGE JAMES, 11th Earl, *b* 1815; sat as MP for Northamptonshire (*C*) 1837-41: *m* 1st, 1846, Lady Constance Henrietta Paget, who *d* 1878, da of 2nd Marquess of Anglesey; 2ndly, 1882, Lady Elizabeth Georgiana, who *d* 1904, widow of George Leopold Bryan, MP, and da of 2nd Marquess of Conyngham; *d* 1887; *s* by his half-brother (**13**) MURRAY EDWARD GORDON, 12th Earl, *b* 1851; MP for Lincolnshire S (*C*) 1884, and for Lincolnshire, Holland, or Spalding, Div 1885-7; largely interested in agricultural questions: *m* 1875, Edith, who *d* 1944, da of late Edward William Harcourt; *d* 1898; *s* by his brother (**14**) HENRY STORMONT, 13th Earl, *b* 1852: *m* 1882, Anne, who *d* 1924, da of late Adm of the Fleet Sir Henry

John Codrington, KCB; *d* 1927; *s* by his son (15) GUY MONGAGU GEORGE, OBE, DSC, 14th Earl, *b* 1885; European War 1915-18 (DSC, OBE): *m* 1910, Margaretta Armstrong, who *d* 1952, da of Anthony Joseph Drexel, of Philadelphia, USA; *d* 1939; *s* by his son (16) CHRISTOPHER GUY HENEAGE, 15th Earl, *b* 1911; Lieut RNVR: *m* 1st, 1935 (*m diss* 1946), Countess Gladys, who *d* 1978, third da of Count László Széchényi, Hungarian Min in London; 2ndly, 1946, Agnes Mary, who *d* 1964, da of late Patrick Joseph Conroy, JP, of Malvern House, Wigan; *d* 1950; *s* by his son (17) CHRISTOPHER DENYS STORMONT, 16th Earl and present peer; also Viscount Maidstone, and Baron Finch.

*(1) Sir HENEAGE Finch, Knt, PC, son of Hon Sir Heneage Finch, Speaker of the House of Commons (3rd son of Sir Moyle Finch and Elizabeth, Countess of Winchilsea), sat successively as MP for Canterbury, St Michael's, and Oxford; in 1660 was appointed Solicitor-Gen, knighted, and *cr a Baronet* (of Raunston) 1660; in 1670 became Attorney-Gen; in 1673 was made Keeper of the Great Seal, and *cr Baron Finch*, of Daventry, co Northampton (peerage of England); in 1675 was promoted to be Lord High Chancellor of England and *cr Earl of Nottingham* (peerage of England); was nominated 1677 Lord High Steward of England; *d* 1682; *s* by his son (2) DANIEL, 2nd Earl, who in 1729 *s* as 7th Earl of Winchilsea (ante).

WINDLESHAM, BARON (Hennessy) (Baron UK 1937 Bt UK 1927)

I live by force and arms

DAVID JAMES GEORGE HENNESSY, CVO, PC, 3rd Baron, and 3rd Baronet; *b* 28 Jan 1932; *s* 1962; *ed* Ampleforth, and Trin Coll Oxford (MA, Hon Fellow); DLitt (Oxon); Managing Dir of Grampian Television 1967-70; Chm of Bow Group 1959-60 and 1962-63, and a Member of Westminster City Council 1958-62; Min of State, Home Office 1970-72, Min of State, N Ireland 1972-73; Lord Privy Seal, and Leader of House of Lords 1973-74, and Leader of the Opposition, House of Lords March to Oct 1974; Man Dir of ATV Network 1975-81 (Joint Man Dir from 1974), Chm 1981; Dir of "The Observer" 1981-89, Dir of W. H. Smith 1986-95, and Vice-Pres of Roy TV Soc 1977-82; Chm of Oxford Preservn Tst 1979-89, Oxford Soc 1985-88, and Parole Bd 1982-88; Joint Dep Chm The Queen's Silver Jubilee Appeal 1977; Dep Chm Roy Jubilee Trusts 1977-80; a Trustee, The Royal Collection since 1993, Charities Aid Foundation 1977-81, the British Museum 1981-96 and Community Service Volunteers since 1981; a Member Museums and Galleries Commn 1984-86; Chm of Trustees of British Museum 1986-96, Visiting Fellow All Souls Coll, Oxford 1986; Visiting Prof Princeton Univ 1997; Prin Brasenose Coll, Oxford since 1989; *cr* PC 1973: *m* 1965, Prudence, who *d* 1986, yr da of Lt-Col Rupert T. W. Glynn, MC, of Harlesford House, Tetsworth, Oxon, and has issue.

Arms – Gules, a boar passant proper, on a chief or a trefoil slipped vert between two roses of the field, barbed and seeded also proper. **Crest** – In front of a dexter arm embowed in armour, the hand grasping a battle-axe, a trefoil slipped and a red rose stalked and leaved saltire-wise, all proper. **Supporters** – On either side an Officer of the Irish Brigade in the service of the King of France in the eighteenth century proper, the dexter supporting with the exterior hand a gold mounted and tasselled staff proper.
Address – c/o House of Lords, SW1A 0PW. *Club* – Brooks's.

SON LIVING

Hon JAMES RUPERT, *b* 9 Nov 1968; *ed* Eton, and Bristol Univ.

DAUGHTER LIVING

Hon Victoria Jane, *b* 1966; *ed* London Univ.

SISTERS LIVING

Hon Marie-Louise (*Hon Lady de Zulueta*), *b* 1930: *m* 1955, Sir Philip Francis de Zulueta, who *d* 1989, and has issue living, Francis Philip Harold, *b* 1959: *m* 1st, 1981, Miranda Jane, da of late Philip Alexander Howden, of Worminghall, Bucks; 2ndly, 1987, Pandora, formerly wife of Hon Edward Abdy Wodehouse (*see* E Kimberley), and eldest da of Mrs W. J. Germing, of Mortlake, and has issue living (by 2nd *m*), Sebastian Philip Wilham *b* 1990, Gala Marie-Louise Philomena *b* 1988, — Louise Angela Mary, *b* 1956: *m* 1982, Mark Donald Seligman, son of Spencer Walter Oscar Seligman, of 64 Bedford Gdns, W8, and has issue living, Jocelyn David *b* 1983, Lucinda Marie Joanne *b* 1985, Iona Louise *b* 1990.

Hon Rosalie Ann, *b* 1934: *m* 1960, Peter John Gervase Elwes (B Rennell), and has issue living, Luke Andrew Cary, *b* 1961: *m* 1987, Anneke Lucille, only da of Hans du Moulin, of Farnham, Surrey, and has issue living, Jake Peter *b* 1993, Tobias Robert *b* 1996, — Benedict James, *b* 1963: *m* 1991, Georgina Claire, only da of Michael Rapinet, of Northend,

Henley-on-Thames, Oxon, and has issue living, Jasper Simon *b* 1996, Samuel Joseph *b* 1997, — Marcus David, *b* 1964; has issue living, Thomas William *b* 1998, — Harriet Clare, *b* 1968.

Hon Annabel Jane, *b* 1937: *m* 1963, Ian Duncan Chisholm, MRCP, of The Manor House, Stratton on the Fosse, Bath, Avon BA3 4QU, and has issue living, Roderick Bryan Duncan, *b* 1964, — Daniel Hugh, *b* 1966: *m* 1995, Juliette Elizabeth Chalmers, yr da of John Edward Chalmers Dow (*see* B Stamp) , — Alexander James, *b* 1968: *m* 1993, Eliza, yr da of Thomas Frank Dermot Pakenham (*see* E Longford), and has issue living, Aidan Carus *b* 1996, Ciaran Thomas *b* 1998, — John Malcolm, *b* 1970.

AUNTS LIVING (*Daughters of 1st Baron*)

Hon Noreen Madeleine, *b* 1910: *m* 1931 (*m diss* 1948), Michael Bull, and has issue living, (Michael) Matthew, MBE (Castle Dewey, Warleggan, Bodmin, Cornwall PL30 4HE), *b* 1932; *ed* Ampleforth; late Maj Coldstream Guards; MBE 1969: *m* 1st, 1962, Jane, only da of Harry Inglis, of Lane Lodge, Stoke Green, Slough, Bucks; 2ndly, 1998, Helen Mary Howitt, yr da of Rev Alwyne Woodard, and has issue living, (by 1st *m*) Richard Matthew Charles *b* 1963; *ed* Manchester Univ (BA Hons), Philip Henry *b* 1969; *ed* Ampleforth: *m* 1998, Sophie Jane, yr da of Kenneth Watkins, Emma Jane, *b* 1964, — *Sir* George Jeffrey (The Old Vicarage, Arkesden, Saffron Walden), *b* 1936; *ed* Ampleforth; Kt Bach 1998: *m* 1960, Fleur-Thérèse, only da of Patrick Freeland, of Zimbabwe, and has issue living, George Sebastian Matthew *b* 1960, Rupert Frederick Alain *b* 1963, Justin Bartholomew Peter *b* 1964, Cassian Michael Thomas *b* 1968, Tamsin Emily Mary *b* 1972. *Residence* – 42 Roland Gdns, SW7.

Hon Kathleen Irene Mary, *b* 1914: *m* 1947, Wilfred Ernest Barnett, who *d* 1992, and has issue living, Robin George (Ponds House, Hurst Green, E Sussex), *b* 1951; *ed* Worth Abbey Sch: *m* 1973, Carolyn Seward, el da of Ronald E. Plummer, of Rowley, Wadhurst, Sussex, and has issue living, Max Robin Nicholas *b* 1983, Annabel Penelope *b* 1978, Julia Seward *b* 1980, Stephanie Lucinda *b* 1987, — Nicholas James (27 Mysore Rd, SW11), *b* 1955; *ed* Worth Abbey Sch: *m* 1998, Margaret, da of Colin Morrison, of Benenden, Kent. *Residence* – The Stables, The Green, Benenden, Kent TN17 4DN.

COLLATERAL BRANCH LIVING

Issue of late Maj Hon Frederick Francis George Hennessy, MBE, yr son of 1st Baron; *b* 1906, *d* 1969: *m* 1932, Merritt Jean, who *d* 1976, da of late Alfred A. Longsdon:—

Peter Grant Auguste (Cradle House Farm, Wigginton, Banbury, Oxon) *b* 1944: *m* 1968, Sally Ann, yst da of Dr Clarence Laverne Johnson (*see* Royden, Bt, 1980 Edn), and has issue living, James George, *b* 1970, — Benedict John, *b* 1978, — Katherine Ann, *b* 1973, — Sophie Elizabeth, *b* 1981. —— Maunagh Jean (Blacksmiths Cottage, Idbury, Oxon), *b* 1933: *m* 1953, Timothy William Jacques Leopold Koch de Gooreynd (*see* M Queensberry, colls, 1985 Edn), who *d* 1987, and has issue living, Peter Frederick Leopold, *b* 1958: *m* 1990, Carolyn Antonia N., yr da of Ambrose Parker, of Hereford Sq, SW7, and has issue living, Timothy Ladislas (Luke) *b* 1995, Anthony *b* 1998, Tamara Manuela *b* 1992, — Alexander Francis William, *b* 1969, — Stella Antoinette Jeanne, *b* 1954: *m* 1976, Kenneth Mannering, and has issue living, William *b* 1977, Olivia *b* 1981, Alexia *b* 1983, Miranda *b* 1986, — Manuela Enriqueta Maria, *b* 1957, — Annabel Maria Therese, *b* 1963: *m* 1990, Christopher Alexander, and has issue living, Joseph Timothy Lloyd *b* 1994. —— Susan Jane (16 Paradise Walk, SW3 4JL), *b* 1938: *m* 1st, 1963, Charles Edward Morley-Fletcher, who *d* 19—; 2ndly, 1999, David L. Pickett, and has issue living, (by 1st *m*), Michael Francis, *b* 1964: *m* 1991, (Elisabeth) Anne, elder da of David Quintin Gurney, of Bawdeswell Hall, Norfolk (*see* Boughey, Bt, colls, 1985 Edn), and has issue living, Oliver Charles *b* 1994, — Patrick Edward, *b* 1966, — Frederick Maurice, *b* 1969, — Caroline Angela Elisabeth (Minnie), *b* 1971: *m* 1997, Dorian Stephen MacDonald.

PREDECESSORS – **(1)** George Richard James Hennessy, OBE, son of late Richard Hennessy, of Bagnolet, Cognac, France; *b* 1877; High Sheriff of Hants 1910-11; European War 1915-18 as major King's Roy Rifle Corps and on Staff of 8th Div; was Parliamentary Private Sec (unpaid) to Min of Labour 1921-22, a Junior of the Treasury 1922-24, and 1924-25, Vice-Chamberlain of HM's Household 1925-28, Treasurer of HM's Household 1928-29 and (in National Govt) Sept to Nov 1931, and Vice-Chm Conservative and Unionist Party 1931-41; sat as MP for Winchester Div of Hampshire (*U*) 1918-31; *cr* a *Baronet* 1927, and *Baron Windlesham*, of Windlesham, co Surrey (peerage of United Kingdom) 1937: *m* 1898, Ethel Mary, who *d* 1951, da of late Charles Reginald Wynter; *d* 1953; *s* by his el son **(2)** James Bryan George, 2nd Baron; *b* 1903; Brig late Grenadier Guards: *m* 1st, 1929, Angela Mary, who *d* 1956, da of late Julian Duggan; 2ndly, 1957, Pamela, formerly wife Dermot A. Dinan, who *m* 3rdly 1966, William Marsden Elverston-Trickett, da of Francis Kennedy; *d* 1962; *s* by his son **(3)** David James George, 3rd Baron and present peer.

WINDSOR, FAMILY AND HOUSE NAME OF THE ROYAL FAMILY.

Windsor, Viscount; son of Earl of Plymouth.

Wingfield, family name of Viscount Powerscourt.

Winn, family name of Baron St Oswald.

WINSTANLEY, BARONY OF (Winstanley) (Extinct 1993)

SONS LIVING OF LIFE BARON (By 1st marriage)

Hon Nicholas Clayton Platt, *b* 1945.

(By 2nd marriage)

Hon Stephen Woodhouse, *b* 1957.

DAUGHTER LIVING OF LIFE BARON (By 1st marriage)

Hon Diana Christine, *b* 1960.

WIDOW LIVING OF LIFE BARON

JOYCE MARY (*Baroness Winstanley*), da of late Arthur Woodhouse: *m* 1955, as his 2nd wife, Baron Winstanley, MRCS, LRCP (Life Baron), who *d* 1993. *Residence* – Hare Hall, Dunnerdale, Broughton-in-Furness, Cumbria.

WINSTON, BARON (Winston) (Life Baron 1995)

ROBERT MAURICE LIPSON WINSTON, son of late Lawrence Winston, of London; *b* 15 July 1940; *ed* St Paul's, Univ of London (MB, BS 1964), MRCS, LRCP 1964, FRCOG 1983 (MRCOG 1971); FRSA; Senior Resident Accoucheur, The London Hosp 1965; Senior Lecturer, Inst of Obstetrics and Gynaecology 1975-81; Visiting Resident Prof, Catholic Univ of Leuven, Belgium 1976-77; Consultant Obstetrician and Gynaecologist, Hammersmith Hosp since 1978; presenter of Your Life in Their Hands, BBC TV 1979-87; Prof of Gynaecology, Univ of Texas, San Antonio 1980-81; Reader in Fertility Studies, Royal Postgraduate Medical Sch 1981-86; Prof of Fertility Studies, Univ of London since 1986; Chm British Fertility Soc 1990-93; Pres Internat Fallopius Soc 1987-88 and Progress All Party Parly Group for Research in Reproduction 1991, author of books and articles on infertility; awarded Cedric Carter Medal of Clinical Genetics Soc 1992, Victor Bonney Prize of Royal Coll of Surgeons of England 1993, and Chief Rabbinate Open Award for Contributions to Society 1993; *cr Baron Winston*, of Hammersmith, in the London Borough of Hammersmith and Fulham (Life Baron), 1995: *m* 1973, Lira Helen, da of late Simon Joseph Feigenbaum, of London, and has issue. *Residence* – 11 Denman Drive, NW11 6RE.

SONS LIVING

Hon Joel, *b* 19—; *ed* ....
Hon Benjamin, *b* 19—; *ed* ....

DAUGHTER LIVING

Hon Tanya, *b* 19—; *ed* ....

WINTERBOTTOM, BARONY OF (Winterbottom) (Extinct 1992)

SONS LIVING OF LIFE BARON *(By 1st marriage)*

Hon John (20 Pantile Rd, Oatlands Village, Weybridge, Surrey KT13 9PY), *b* 1940; *ed* Charterhouse, and Clare Coll, Camb: *m* 1980, Sheila Marie, da of Arthur Evershed, of 3 St Malo Close, Ferring, nr Worthing, W Sussex, and has issue living, Robert Ian, *b* 1981.

(By 2nd marriage)

Hon Dudley Walter Gordon (8 Shottendane Rd, SW6 5TJ), *b* 1946; *ed* Charterhouse, Kent Univ, and Wolfson Coll, Oxford; Sec Chelsea Arts Club: *m* 1st, 1978 (*m diss* 1991), Mirjana Bukvić; 2ndly, 19—, Lauren, da of Dr Brian Creighton Sproule, of Kincoppa, Elizabeth Bay Rd, Elizabeth Bay, Sydney, Australia, and has issue living (by 1st *m*), Thomas, *b* 1989, — Olga, *b* 1987.

Hon Graham Anthony, *b* 1948; *ed* Charterhouse, and RNC Dartmouth: *m* 1984 (*m diss* 19—), Caroline Joy, only da of Guy Bodgard Webster, of Cranbrook, Toddington, Beds.

DAUGHTER LIVING OF LIFE BARON *(By 2nd marriage)*

Hon Caroline Margaret Alyson, *b* 1950; *ed* Oxford Polytechnic.

WIDOW LIVING OF LIFE BARON

IRENE EVA (IRA) (*Baroness Winterbottom*), da of late Dr Walter Munk, of Berlin, and of Mount Carmel, Haifa: *m* 1944, as his 2nd wife, Baron Winterbotton (Life Baron), who *d* 1992. *Residence* – 9 Bisham Gdns, Highgate, N6 6DJ.

WINTERTON, EARL (Turnour) (Earl I 1766)
(Name pronounced "Turner")

To be, rather than seem to be

(DONALD) DAVID TURNOUR, 8th Earl (has not yet established his right to the Peerages); *b* 13 Oct 1943; *s* 1991; *ed* Waterloo Lutheran Univ, Ont (BA): *m* 1968, Jill Pauline, da of late John Geddes Esplen, of Bala, Ont, and has issue.

𝕬rms – Ermines, on a cross quarterly, pierced argent, four fers de moline sable. 𝕮rest – A lion passant guardant argent, holding in the dexter forepaw a fer de moline, sable. 𝕾upporters – Two lions argent, semée of fers de moline, sable.
Residence – 6672 Mockingbird Lanes, Mississauga, Ont L5N 5K1.

DAUGHTERS LIVING

(*Lady*) Michele Susan, *b* 1973.
(*Lady*) Amy Elizabeth, *b* 1976.

BROTHERS LIVING

ROBERT CHARLES, *b* 30 Jan 1950: *m* 1st, 1974 (*m diss* 1976), Sheila, da of Garth H. Stocking, of Brampton, Ont; 2ndly, 1983, Patricia Ann, da of William Avery, of Cambridge, Ont, and has issue living (by 2nd *m*), Sarah Elizabeth, *b* 1983, — Meagan Ann, *b* 1985. *Residence* – 553 Duke St, Cambridge, Ont N3H 3T2, Canada.
Murray John, *b* 6 Feb 1951: *ed* Univ of Waterloo, Ont (OD 1975, MSc 1979): *m* 1980, Brenda Jill, da of late Dr James Alexander Tremayne Behan, of Orillia, Ont, and has issue living, Jonathan Winterton Behan, *b* 18 April 1985. *Residence* – 4 Lansdowne Rd South, Cambridge, Ont N1S 2T3, Canada.

SISTER LIVING OF SEVENTH EARL

Margaret Ethel, *b* 1917: *m* 1939, Donald Selby McGeary, who *d* 1997, of 514-2511 Lakeshore Rd W, Oakville, Ont, Canada L6L 6L9, and has had issue, Donald Garth (33 Head St, Oakville, Ont L6K 1L4), *b* 1941: *m* 1975, Irene Claire, da of George Woodruff, of Niagara Falls, Ont, Canada, — Robert Wayne, *b* 1944; *d* 1996, — Hugh Gordon (49 Hawktree Green, Calgary, Alberta T3G 3P9), *b* 1951: *m* 1974, Karen Louise, da of Walter Warms, of 56 Thatcher Drive, Winnipeg, Canada, and has issue living, Carson Hugh *b* 1995, Whitney Anne *b* 1987, Kaitlin Diane *b* 1990, — James Douglas (3622 Balfour Court, Saskatoon, Sask S7H 4B2), *b* 1954: *m* 1976, Elaine Leslie, da of Gilbert Aulis, of 853 Cathedral Av, Winnipeg, Manitoba, Canada, and has issue living, Matthew James *b* 1980, Jordon Garth *b* 1983, Devon Elaine *b* 1985, — Wendy Louise, *b* 1948; has issue living, Timon Andrew *b* 1981, Nadia Katherine *b* 1978, Lara Jacqueline *b* 1986.

MOTHER LIVING

Evelyn Isabel, da of late Dr Charles Albert Oulton, of Saskatoon, Sask: *m* 1941, (Cecil) Noel Turnour, DFM, CD, RO, FAAO (yr brother of 7th Earl), who *d* 1987. *Residence* – 47 Kenmore Av, Cambridge, Ont N1S 3H4, Canada.

WIDOW LIVING OF SEVENTH EARL

MARION ELEANOR (*Marion, Countess Winterton*), da of late Arthur Phillips, of Stirling, Ont: *m* 1971, as his 2nd wife, the 7th Earl Winterton, who *d* 1991.

COLLATERAL BRANCHES LIVING

Grandchildren of late Donald Winterton Turnour (infra):—
Issue of late John Turnour, *b* 1938, *d* 1986: *m* 1st, 19— (*m diss* 19—), Leonie Wharton; 2ndly, 19 , Theresa Coultard.—
(By 1st *m*) Richard, *b* 1961. —— Damien, *b* 1963. —— (By 2nd *m*) Cheyne, *b* 1975. —— Sally Adele, *b* 1980.

Grandchildren of late Keppel Arthur Turnour, eldest son of late John Horatio Turnour, 5th son of late Rev Hon Adolphus Augustus Turnour, 3rd son of 2nd Earl:—
Issue of late Donald Winterton Turnour, *b* 1882, *d* 1975: *m* 1932, Muriel Mary Helen (Doll) King, who *d* 1985:—
Glenis, *b* 1933: *m* 1957, Geoffrey Ponsford (61 The Boulevarde, Mullaway, NSW 2456, Australia), and has issue living, Michael Winterton (18 The Crofts, Richmond, Vic 3121, Australia), *b* 1960: *m* 1st, 1986 (*m diss* 1995), Frances Wise; 2ndly, 1997, Jennifer Roberts, — Rowena Jane, *b* 1963: *m* 1988, Richard John Crysell, of 97 Manning Rd, Woollahra, NSW 2025, and has issue living, Thomas William *b* 1995, Anna Patricia *b* 1992, — Megan Jennifer, *b* 1967: *m* 1998, Frank Brunetti, of 742 Malvern Rd, Armadale, Vic 3143, and has issue living, Edward Michael *b* 1998. —— Roslyn, *b* 1935: *m* 1964, Ian Fox (20 Alicia St, Hampton, Vic 3188, Australia), and has issue living, David James Shoolbred, *b* 1967, — Andrew Charles Shoolbred, *b* 1969, — Robyn Margaret, *b* 1971.

Issue of late James Derwas (known as James Owen) Turnour, *b* 1883, *d* (9 Aug) 1967: *m* 1922, Moira Gwendolyne Cara Lloyd, who *d* (10 Aug) 1967:—

William Donald (PO Box 501, Armidale, NSW 2350, Australia), *b* 1923: *m* 1946, Doris Hills, and has issue living, Winifred Ann, *b* 1947: *m* 19—, Bruce Grove, — Mary Elizabeth, *b* 1949, — Barbara June, *b* 1952: *m* 1980, William Tahana (PO Box 2318, Broome, W Australia 6725), and has had issue, Sacha Joe *b* 1973, *d* 1975, Tui William *b* 1975, Zac Randall *b* 1979, Beau Edward *b* 1981, — Sally Dawn, *b* 1967. —— James Arthur (11 Stonehaven Rd, Tatura, Vic 3616, Australia), *b* 1924: *m* 1954, Nancy Sharp, and has issue living, Phillip James, *b* 1955: *m* 1995, Carol Carowther, — Robert Owen (PO Box 752, Bacchus Marsh, Vic 3340), *b* 1956, — Craig Lloyd, *b* 1961, — Heather Margaret, *b* 1958: *m* 1980, David Victor Silvagni, and has issue living, Ryan Dion *b* 1984, Lara Erin *b* 1986, Stephanie Julia *b* 1987, — Michal Ann, *b* 1959, — Kathryn Wendy, *b* 1963: *m* 1995, Charles David Kerr (PO Box 497, Castlemaine, Vic 3450), and has issue living, Alexandra Kathryn *b* 1997, — Shirley Patricia, *b* 1965: *m* 1990, Gerard Francis McCarty, and has issue living, Asha Leah *b* 1988, Mahlee Elizabeth *b* 1992, Chelsea Kathryn *b* 1994, Regan Clara *b* 1997, — Moira Eileen, *b* 1970. —— Edward Lloyd (7 Westbrook St, Cohuna, Vic 3568, Australia), *b* 1929: *m* 1953, Eileen Blanche, da of late Windsor Winston Tickell, of Kyabram, Vic, and has issue living, David James Edward, *b* 1954: *m* 1975, Angela Mae, da of Donald Peace, of Clifton Springs, Vic, and has issue living, Amber *b* 1977, — Andrew Sherring (Doc) (28 Union Rd, Windsor, Vic 3181), *b* 1956, — Edward Charles (14 Parooba Av, Camp Hill, Qld 4152), *b* 1957: *m* 1987, Rita Louise, da of Justin O'Sullivan, of Dalby, Qld, and has issue living, Matthew Edward *b* 1992, Emma Louise *b* 1997, — Ian Windsor, *b* 1959, — Jane Gwendolyn, *b* 1955: *m* 1975, Desmond Leahy (21 Valentine St, Bendigo, Vic 3550), and has issue living, Hamish Edward *b* 1984, Bridget Louise *b* 1982, Anna Eileen *b* 1986, — Louise May, *b* 1964: *m* 1993, John Timothy Murrihy, of 16 Upton Rd, Windsor, Vic 3181, and has issue living, Thomas Edward *b* 1996, Harrison John *b* 1999, Samantha Alice *b* 1994.

Issue of late Ernest Keppel (Kep) Turnour, *b* 1884, *d* 1946: *m* 1923, Grace (Gay), who *d* 1950, da of Dr James Florance, of Mooroopna, Vic—
James Florance (PO Box 448, Dromana, Vic 3936, Australia), *b* 1924: *m* 1st, 1957, Sheila Jean, who *d* 1980, da of late Athol Rupert Innes (*see* Innes, Bt, *cr* 1686, colls, 1995 Edn); 2ndly, 1987, Mrs Joan Albiston, da of late Charles Edward Cope, and has issue living (by 1st *m*), Keppel John, *b* 1959, — Quentin David (15 McCabe Place, N Melbourne, Vic 3051), *b* 1962, — Louise Marguerite, *b* 1958: *m* 1980, Gary John Ryan (6 Toora St, Ivanhoe, Vic 3079), and has issue living, Owen James *b* 1990, Edwin John *b* 1993. —— Keppel Arthur, OAM (PO Box 6383, Shepparton, Vic 3632, Australia), *b* 1926; OAM 1998: *m* 1963, Helen, da of late William George Pogue, and has issue living, Phillip Douglas, *b* 1964: *m* 1998, Alexandra, da of John Buchanan, of Clar Innis, Woodstock, Vic, — Stephen Richard (2541 Carnegie Drive, State College, PA, USA), *b* 1965: *m* 1998, Florence Amy, da of Stuart Newberger, of Corvallis, Oregon, USA, — Catherine Joy, *b* 1967. —— John Winterton (115 Mt Coot-tha Rd, Toowong, Qld 4066, Australia), *b* 1931: *m* 1956, Joan Edith Pearce, and has issue living, Matthew Dwight, *b* 1960: *m* 1983, Wendy Anne Day, and has issue living, Benjamin John *b* 1987, Elizabeth Anne *b* 1986, Victoria Grace *b* 1991, Christina Louise *b* 1993, — James Pearce (6 Isobel St, Mareeba, Qld 4880), *b* 1966, — Jennifer Joyce, *b* 1963: *m* 1988, Aime Marohasy (61 Harte St, Chelmer, Qld 4068), and has issue living, Caroline *b* 1989, — Caroline Elizabeth, *b* 1968. —— Enid Gay, *b* 1928: *m* 1954, Peter Julian Barlow, who *d* 1992 (9 Patricia Av, Blairgowrie, Vic 3942, Australia), and has issue living, Julian Peter (Longflat, Bega, NSW 2550), *b* 1955: *m* 1984, Robyn Henfrey, and has issue living, Jack Peter *b* 1985, Edward Julian *b* 1987, — Neil Richard (725 Brunswick St, N Fitzroy, Vic 3068), *b* 1961; has issue living, Ruth Dominique BAMFORD BARLOW (adopted da) *b* 1990, Isabella *b* 1998, — Gaye Madelaine, *b* 1957: *m* 1981, Simon Thomson (12 Boa Vista Rd, New Town, Tas 7008), and has issue living, Christopher Malcolm James *b* 1986, Alistair Peter *b* 1993, Katrina Gaye *b* 1983. —— Diana Grace (27 Denbigh St, Parramatta Park, Qld 4870, Australia), *b* 1934.

PREDECESSORS – (1) EDWARD TURNOUR Garth, assumed in 1744 by Roy licence the surname of Turnour; *cr Baron Winterton*, of Gort, co Galway (peerage of Ireland) 1761, and *Viscount Turnour* and *Earl Winterton* (peerage of Ireland) 1766; *d* 1788; *s* by his son (2) EDWARD TURNOUR, 2nd Earl; *d* 1831; *s* by his son (3) EDWARD, 3rd Earl; *d* 1833; *s* by his son (4) EDWARD, 4th Earl; *b* 1810: *m* 1832, Maria, who *d* 1904, da of Sir Peter Pole, 2nd Bt; *d* 1879; *s* by his son (5) EDWARD, 5th Earl, *b* 1837: *m* 1882, Lady Georgiana Susan Hamilton, who *d* 1913, da of 1st Duke of Abercorn, KG; *d* 1907; *s* by his only son (6) EDWARD, TD, PC, 6th Earl, *b* 1883; Major TA Reserve, Sussex Yeo; Under-Sec of State for India 1922-4, and 1924-29, Chancellor of Duchy of Lancaster 1937-9, Dep Sec of State for Air and Vice-Pres of Air Council 1938, Assist to Home Sec 1938-9, and Paymaster Gen 1939; MP for Horsham Div of Sussex (*C*) 1904-18, for Horsham and Worthing Div 1918-45, and for W Sussex 1945-51; *cr Baron Turnour* (peerage of UK) 1952: *m* 1924, Hon Cecilia Monica Wilson, who *d* 1974, da of 2nd Baron Nunburnholme; *d* 1962, when the UK Barony (*cr* 1952) became ext; *s* by his kinsman (7) ROBERT CHAD (el son of Cecil Turnour, grandson of Charles Chad Turnour, el son of Rev Hon Adolphus Augustus Turnour, 3rd son of 2nd Earl), 7th Earl, *b* 1915; Flight-Sergeant RCAF, with Canadian NATO Force Sqdn, Sardinia 1957-58, served 1939-45 War: *m* 1st, 1941, Kathleen Ella, who *d* 1969, da of D. B. Whyte, of Saskatoon, Sask; 2ndly, 1971, Marion Eleanor, da of late Arthur Phillips, of Stirling, Ont; *d* 1991; *s* by his nephew (8) DONALD DAVID (eldest son of late (Cecil) Noel Turnour, DFM, CD, RO, FAAO, yr brother of 7th Earl), 8th Earl and present peer; also Viscount Turnour and Baron Winterton.

Winton, Earl of; title borne by Earl of Eglinton.

WISE, BARON (Wise) (Baron UK 1951)

JOHN CLAYTON WISE, 2nd Baron; *b* 11 June 1923; *s* 1968; a Farmer: *m* 1st, 1946 (*m diss* 1986), Margaret Annie, da of Frederick Victor Snead, of Banbury; 2ndly, 1993 (*m diss* 1998), Mrs Janice Harman Thompson, da of late Albert John Harman, of NSW, Australia, and has issue by 1st *m*.

Residence – Lynn Cottage, Castle Hill, Hemyock, Devon EX15 3RU. *Club* – Farmers'.

SONS LIVING (*By 1st marriage*)

Hon CHRISTOPHER JOHN CLAYTON, *b* 19 March 1949; *ed* Norwich Sch and Southampton Univ (BSc); PhD. *Residence* – Demeter, Woodmancote, Cirencester, Glos.

Hon Martin Highfield, *b* 1950; *ed* Norwich Sch and Bristol Univ (MB, ChB, MD); FRCS. *Residence* – Chellow Bank, 4 Rawvilles Lane, Catisfield, Fareham, Hants.

SISTER LIVING

Hon Eileen Ellen, *b* 1916: *m* 1940, Sq Ldr Gerald Edmund Hastings, RAF, and has issue living, Eileen Mary, *b* 1948, — Bridget Talmine, *b* 1950. *Residence* – 19 Thomas Basset Close, Colyford, Devon.

PREDECESSOR – **(1)** FREDERICK JOHN Wise, son of Edward Wise, of Bury St Edmunds; *b* 1887; MP for King's Lynn (*Lab*) 1945-51; *cr Baron Wise*, of King's Lynn, co Norfolk (peerage of UK); 1951: *m* 1911, Kate Elizabeth, da of John Michael Sturgeon, of Horringer, Bury St Edmunds; *d* 1968; *s* by his son **(2)** JOHN CLAYTON, 2nd Baron, and present peer.

Wodehouse, Baron; son of Earl of Kimberley.

Wodehouse, family name of Earl of Kimberley.

WOLFENDEN, BARONY OF (Wolfenden) (Extinct 1985)

SON LIVING OF LIFE BARON

Hon Daniel Mark, *b* 1942: *m* 1972, Sally Frankel, and has issue, two sons.

DAUGHTERS LIVING OF LIFE BARON

Hon Priscilla, *b* 1937: *m* 1959, Lt-Col F. L. Dainty, of Thump Head Cottage, 22 Boobery, Sampford Peverell, Devon.
Hon Deborah, *b* 1943: *m* 1966, Francis Eveleigh, of Boehill, Uplowman, nr Tiverton, Devon EX16 7DZ, and has issue, one son and one da.

WIDOW LIVING OF LIFE BARON

EILEEN LE MESSURIER (*Baroness Wolfenden*), 2nd da of A. J. Spilsbury: *m* 1932, Baron Wolfenden, CBE (Life Peer), who *d* 1985. *Residence* – The White House, Westcott, nr Dorking, Surrey.

WOLFSON, BARON (Wolfson) (Life Baron 1985, Bt (UK) 1962, of St Marylebone, co London)

LEONARD GORDON WOLFSON, *Life Baron* and 2nd *Baronet*, son of Sir Isaac Wolfson, 1st Bt; *b* 11 Nov 1927; *s* his father in his baronetcy, 1991; *ed* King's Sch, Worcester; Hon Fellow St Catherine's Coll, Oxford, Wolfson Coll, Camb, Wolfson Coll, Oxford, Worcester Coll, Oxford, Univ Coll, London, and London Sch of Hygiene and Tropical Medicine; Member of Court of Benefactors R Soc of Medicine; Trustee Imperial War Museum since 1988; Hon FRCP 1977, Hon PhD Tel Aviv 1971, Hebrew Univ 1978, DCL Oxon 1972, Hon LLD Strathclyde 1972, Dundee 1979, Cantab 1982, London 1982, Hon DSc Hull 1977, Wales 1984, Hon DHL Bar Ilan Univ 1983; Patron R Coll of Surgeons; Chm and a Founder Trustee Wolfson Foundation; Chm Great Universal Stores 1981-96, and Burberrys Ltd 1978-96; *cr* Kt 1977, and *Baron Wolfson*, of Marylebone in the City of Westminster (Life Baron) 1985: *m* 1st, 1949 (*m diss* 1991), Ruth, da of Ernest A. Sterling, of London; 2ndly, 1991, Mrs Estelle Jackson widow of Michael Jackson, and has issue by 1st *m*.

Arms – Per pale dovetailed vert and or, on a chevron counterchanged between in chief two roses, also or and gules respectively, and in base an ancient hand bell proper, two pears sable and gold. **Crest** – In front of two rods of Æsculapius in saltire proper, a touch inflamed also proper.
Address – 18-22 Haymarket, SW1Y 4DQ.

DAUGHTERS LIVING (*By 1st marriage*)

Hon Janet Frances, *b* 1952: *m* 1st, 1972 (*m diss* 1989), Michael Philip Green; 2ndly, 1990, Gilbert de Botton, and has issue living (by 1st *m*), Rebecca Sarah Wolfson, *b* 1974, — Catherine Victoria Wolfson, *b* 1976. *Address* – c/o GAM, 12 St James's Place, SW1A 1NX.

Hon Laura, *b* 1954: *m* 1975, Barry Stephen Townsley, and has issue living, Charles Ralph Wolfson, *b* 1984, — Alexandra Jane Wolfson, *b* 1977, — Georgina Kate Wolfson, *b* 1979, — Isabella Edith Wolfson, *b* 1994. *Address* – c/o Townsley & Co, 44 Worship St, EC2A 2JT.

Hon Deborah, *b* 1959: *m* 19—, G— Davis. *Residence* –

Hon Elizabeth, *b* 1966: *m* 1991, Daniel Peltz, son of Dr Sam Peltz, of W1, and has issue living, Max, *b* 19—, — Isaac Henry, *b* 1995, — Francesca Edith, *b* 1992. *Residence* –

WOLFSON OF SUNNINGDALE, BARON (Wolfson) (Life Baron 1991)

DAVID WOLFSON, son of Charles Wolfson; *b* 9 Nov 1935; *ed* Clifton, Trin Coll, Camb (MA), and Stanford Univ, California (MBA); Hon Fell Hughe's Hall, Camb 1989, Hon FRCR 1978, Hon FRCOG 1989; Great Universal Stores 1960-78 and since 1993 (Dir 1973-78 and since 1993); Sec to Shadow Cabinet 1978-79, Chief of Staff, Political Office, 10 Downing St 1979-85; Chm Alexon Group plc (formerly Steinberg Group plc) 1982-86, and Next plc 1990-98 (Non-Exec Dir 1989-98); Non-Exec Dir Stewart Wrightson Holdings plc 1985-87; *cr* Knt 1984, and *Baron Wolfson of Sunningdale*, of Trevose, co Cornwall (Life Baron) 1991: *m* 1st, 1962 (*m diss* 1967), Patricia Elizabeth (later Baroness Rawlings), da of late Louis Rawlings; 2ndly, 1967, Susan E., da of Hugh Davis, and has issue by 2nd *m*.
Address – c/o House of Lords, SW1A 0PW.

SONS LIVING (*By 2nd marriage*)

Hon Simon Adam, *b* 1967.
Hon Andrew Daniel, *b* 1969.

DAUGHTER LIVING (*By 2nd marriage*)

Hon Deborah Sarah, *b* 1973.

Wolmer, Viscount; grandson of Earl of Selborne.

WOLVERTON, BARON (Glyn) (Baron UK 1869)

CHRISTOPHER RICHARD GLYN, 7th Baron; *b* 5 Oct 1938; *s* 1988; *ed* Eton; FRICS: *m* 1st, 1961 (*m diss* 1967), Carolyn Jane, yr da of late Antony Noel Hunter, of 33 Brompton Sq, SW3; 2ndly, 1975 (*m diss* 1989), Mrs Frances Sarah Elisabeth Stuart Black, eldest da of Robert Worboys Skene, of 12 Kensington Gate, W8; 3rdly, 1990 (*m diss* 1994), Gillian Konig, and has issue by 1st *m*.

Arms – Argent, an eagle displayed with two heads sable, guttée d'or. Crest – An eagle's head, erased sable, guttée d'or; in the beak an escallop argent. Supporters – On either side an eagle with wings elevated sable, guttée d'or, gorged with a collar gemel or, and holding in the beak an escallop argent. *Residence* – 97 Hurlingham Rd, SW6.

Firm to my trust

DAUGHTERS LIVING (*By 1st marriage*)

Hon Sara-Jane, *b* 1963: *m* 1993, John Francis O'Callaghan, yr son of James O'Callaghan, of co Clare, and has issue living, Edward Kit, *b* 1997.
Hon Amanda Camilla, *b* 1966.

BROTHER LIVING

Hon ANDREW JOHN, *b* 30 June 1943; *ed* Eton, and New Coll, Oxford (MA), Fellow of Corpus Christi Coll, Oxford: *m* 1st, 1965 (*m diss* 1986), Celia Laws; 2ndly, 1986, Wendy Carlin, and has issue living (by 1st *m*), Miles John, *b* 1966, — Lucy Abigail, *b* 1968, — (by 2nd *m*) Jonathan, *b* 1990, — Tessa, *b* 1987. *Residence* – 167 Divinity Rd, Oxford.

SISTERS LIVING

Hon Susan, *b* 1940: *m* 1962, Nicholas Greenaway Mills, yr son of Lt-Col Robert Breynton Yarnton Mills, OBE, MC, of Barrington Grove, Burford, Oxon, and has issue living, Charlotte Sophia, *b* 1964: *m* 1991, Capt James David Tarn Bainbridge, late 16th/5th Royal Lancers, yr son of late David Tarn Bainbridge, of Hurworth Hall, Darlington, and has issue living, Edward Breynton Tarn, *b* 1995, — Jake Riversdale Tarn, *b* 1999, — Charlotte Isabelle Greenaway *b* 1993, — Maria Louise Greenaway, *b* 1967. *Residence* – Lower Upton Farm, Burford, Oxon.
Hon Joanna Caroline, *b* 1955.

WIDOW LIVING OF SIXTH BARON

AUDREY MARGARET (*prefers to be known as Mrs Audrey Glyn*), da of late Richard Stubbs, of Haseley Manor, Oxford: *m* 1937, Maj the 6th Baron Wolverton, CBE, who *d* 1988. *Residence* – 2 Lower Upton Cottages, Burford, Oxon OX18 4LX.

COLLATERAL BRANCHES LIVING

Granddaughter of late Sir Francis Maurice Grosvenor Glyn, KCMG, 2nd son of Maurice George Carr Glyn, yr son of Hon Pascoe Charles Glyn, 6th son of 1st Baron:—
Issue of late Jeremy Christopher Glyn, *b* 1930, *d* 1984: *m* 1956, Robina Elspeth (Upton Farm, Upton, Andover, Hants), da of Sir George Arthur Harford, 2nd Bt:—
Lucinda Mary, *b* 1958.

Issue of late Hilary Beaujolais Glyn, yst brother of 6th Baron *b* 1916, *d* 1995: *m* 1938, Caroline, yst da of late William Perkins Bull, QC, of Lorne Hall, Rosedale, Toronto, Canada:—
James Hilary, *b* 1939; *ed* Eton; Man Dir N Borneo Timbers: *m* 1964 (*m diss* 1983), Lucinda March, only da of W/Cdr Gordon Stanley Keith Haywood, RAF (ret) (*see* E Darnley), and has issue living, Caspar Hilary Gordon, *b* 1969, — Marina Jane, *b* 1966: *m* 1991, Robert P. Furniss-Roe, of 14 rue des Renaudes, Paris 75017, France, son of late Henry Furniss-Roe, of Bishopsteignton, Devon, and has issue living, Olivia Sophie, *b* 1993. —— (Caroline) Ann, *b* 1941: *m* 1st, 1968 (*m diss* 1979), Padmanabh Vijai Pillai, yr son of Dr P. P. Pillai, of New Delhi; 2ndly, 1980, Gowri Shankar, of Castle Hill Cottage, Boothby Graffoe, Lincoln. —— Sarah, *b* 1948: *m* 1st, 1967 (*m diss* 1971), Richard Patrick King, only son of late Richard Francis King, of Assam, India; 2ndly, 1979 (*m diss* 1982), Nicholas John Turner, son of John Turner; 3rdly, 1984, Robert Gino Henson of Ermine House, Boothby Graffoe, Lincoln LN5 0LD, son of late John Gordon (Gino) Henson, and has issue living (by 2nd *m*), James William Hilary, *b* 1980, — (by 3rd *m*), Jessica Ann Frances, *b* 1985, — Cecilia Sarah, *b* 1990.

PREDECESSORS – (1) GEORGE CARR GLYN, 4th son of Sir Richard Carr Glyn, 1st Bt; *b* 1797; was a partner in the banking house of Glyn, Mills, Currie and Co, and Chairman of the London and North Western Railway; *cr Baron Wolverton*, of Wolverton, co Bucks (peerage of United Kingdom) 1869: *m* 1823, Marianne, da of late Pascoe Grenfell, of Taplow Court, Bucks; *d* 1873; *s* by his son **(2)** GEORGE GRENFELL, PC, 2nd Baron, *b* 1824; sat as MP for Shaftesbury (*L*) 1857-73, and was successively Joint Sec to Treasury, Paymaster-Gen, and Postmaster-Gen: *m* 1848, Georgiana Maria, who *d* 1894, da of Rev George Tufnell, of Uffington, Berks; *d* 1887; *s* by his nephew **(3)** HENRY RICHARD, 3rd Baron, *b* 1861; *dsp* 1888; *s* by his brother **(4)** FREDERICK, 4th Baron, *b* 1864; a Partner in the Metropolitan banking firm of Glyn, Mills and Co; a Lord-in-Waiting to Queen Victoria 1891-3, and Vice-Chamberlain of the Household to King Edward VII 1902-5: *m* 1895, Lady Edith Amelia Ward, CBE, who *d* 1956, da of 1st Earl of Dudley; *d* 1932; *s* by his son **(5)** NIGEL REGINALD VICTOR, 5th Baron, *b* 1904; Capt RA (TA); *d* 1986; *s* by his kinsman **(6)** JOHN PATRICK RIVERSDALE, CBE, 6th Baron, *b* 1913; Maj Gren Gds, served 1939-45 War (wounded); Dir Glyn, Mills & Co; Chm Yorkshire Bank Ltd: *m* 1937, Audrey Margaret, da of late Richard Stubbs, of Haseley Manor, Oxford; *d* 1988; *s* by his elder son **(7)** CHRISTOPHER RICHARD, 7th Baron and present peer.

Wood, family name of Earl of Halifax.

Wood, family name of Baron Holderness.

Woodhouse, family name of Baron Terrington.

Woodstock, Viscount; son of Earl of Portland

WOOLF, BARON (Woolf) (Life Baron 1992)

HARRY KENNETH WOOLF, PC, son of late Alexander Woolf; *b* 2 May 1933; *ed* Fettes, and Univ Coll, London (LLB, Fellow 1981); Hon LLD Buckingham, Bristol and London Univs, Hon Fellow Leeds Polytechnic (now Univ); Hon Fellow American Coll of Trial Lawyers since 1999; commn'd 15/19th Royal Hussars 1954, Capt Army Legal Ser 1955; Bar Inner Temple 1954, Recorder Crown Court 1972-79, Junior Counsel Inland Revenue 1973-74, First Treasury Junior Counsel in Common Law 1974-79, Judge of High Court of Justice (Queen's Bench Div) 1979-86, Presiding Judge SE Circuit 1981-84, Lord Justice of Appeal 1986-92, Lord of Appeal in Ordinary 1992, Master of the Rolls since 1996; Chm Civil Procedures Rules Cttee; Chm Civil Justice Council; Member Senate of Bar and Bench 1981-85; Chm Lord Chancellor's Advisory Cttee on Legal Educn 1987-90, Middx Justice's Advsy Cttee 1987-90, and Board of Management Inst of Advanced Legal Studies 1986-94; Chm Butler Trust 1992-98, since when Pres; Pres Law Teachers' Assocn 1985-90, Central Council for Jewish Social Services since 1988, and W London Magistrates' Assocn 1987-92 Chm St Mary's Hosp Special Trustees since 1993; Gov Oxford Centre for Hebrew Studies since 1988; Freeman Drapers' Co; *cr* Knt 1979, PC 1986, and *Baron Woolf*, of Barnes, London Borough of Richmond (Life Baron) 1992: *m* 1961, Marguerite, da of George Sassoon, and has issue.
Address – House of Lords, SW1A 0PW. *Club* – Garrick.

SONS LIVING

Hon Jeremy Richard George, *b* 1962; *ed* Clifton, Sussex Univ, and Trinity Hall, Camb: *m* 1995, Wendy F., elder da of late Bernard Pollecoff, of Barnes, SW.

Hon Andrew James David, *b* 1965; *ed* Clifton, St Paul's, Southampton Univ, and Woolfson Coll, Camb; *m* 1997, Julie, da of Dr Adrian Preston.

Hon Eliot Charles Anthony, *b* 1967; *ed* Eton, and Robinson Coll, Camb.

WOOLLEY, BARONY OF (Woolley) (Extinct 1986)

SONS LIVING OF LIFE BARON (*By 1st marriage*)

Hon (William) Graham (Hatton Hall, Hatton Heath, Cheshire), *b* 1927: *m* 1955, Joan, who *d* 1974, da of Ralph Thomas Rowlands, of Connah's Quay, Flintshire; 2ndly, 1984 (*m diss* 1994), Shirley Ann, da of Thomas Lega, of Bulolo, Papua, New Guinea, and has issue.

Hon Harold Ewart (1350, Laurier Av, Vancouver, BC, Canada), *b* 1929; MD, FRCS(C): *m* 1954, Margaret, yr da of Alderman T. S. Bennett, JP, of Worcester, and has issue.

Hon David Jeffs (Fernhill Farm, 4222 216th St, RR14 Langley, BC, Canada V3A 7R2), *b* 1934; Capt, Air Canada: *m* 1958, Freda Constance, da of Alfred W. S. Walker, of Barrow-in-Furness, and has issue.

Hon Peter Jeffs (2660 Queens Av, W Vancouver, BC, Canada), *b* (twin) 1934: MA, CA: *m* 1960, Lois, da of Edward Chanter, of Tiverton, Devon, and has issue.

DAUGHTERS LIVING OF LIFE BARON (*By 2nd marriage*)

Hon Hazel Eleanor, *b* 1938; JP: *m* 1961, William David Harper, MA, MB, BChir, of Clogwyn y Gwin, Rhyd Ddu, Beddgelert, Gwynedd, and has issue.

Hon Christine Maralyn, *b* 1946: *m* 1st, 1970 (*m diss* 1980), Barrie Scott Morgan, BSc, PhD; 2ndly, 1984, Lt-Cdr David Rodwell, MIEE, CEng, RN, of 35 Northumberland Av, Wanstead, E12.

WOOLTON, EARL OF (Marquis) (Earl UK 1956)

By fortitude and courage it shall be given

SIMON FREDERICK MARQUIS, 3rd Earl, *b* 24 May 1958; *s* 1969: *m* 1987 (*m diss* 1997), Hon Sophie Frederika, only child of 3rd Baron Birdwood, and has issue.

Arms – Sable, on a bend engrailed between two garbs or a rose gules barbed and seeded proper between two lions rampant of the field. **Crest** – Suspended from and between the antlers of a stag proper, a stirrup and leather. **Supporters** – On either side a lion rampant or, gorged with a riband azure, pendent therefrom by a chain also or, an escutcheon azure charged with a liver bird argent.
Residence – Auchnacree House, Glenogil, by Forfar, Angus DD8 3SX.

DAUGHTERS LIVING

Lady Olivia Alice, *b* 1990.
Lady Constance Elizabeth, *b* 1991.
Lady Claudia Louise, *b* 1995.

SISTER LIVING

Lady Alexandra Susan, *b* 1961: *m* 1984, Philip Roger Chandos Elletson, of The Old Rectory, Huish, nr Marlborough, Wilts, son of Roger Elletson, of The Grey House, Forton, Lancs, and has issue living, Edward Roger Chandos, *b* 1990, — Laura Katherine Elizabeth, *b* 1985, — Sophia Josephine Rose, *b* 1986.

WIDOW LIVING OF SECOND EARL

CECILY JOSEPHINE (*Countess Lloyd-George of Dwyfor*) (Ffynone, Boncath, Pembrokeshire; 47 Burton Court, SW3), elder da of Maj Sir Alexander Penrose Gordon-Cumming, MC, 5th Bt: *m* 1st, 1957, as his 2nd wife, 2nd Earl of Woolton, who *d* 1969; 2ndly, 1969 (*m diss* 1974), 3rd Baron Forres, who *d* 1978; 3rdly, 1982, as his 2nd wife, 3rd Earl Lloyd-George of Dwyfor.

PREDECESSORS – **(1)** *Sir* FREDERICK JAMES Marquis, CH, PC, DL, son of Thomas Robert Marquis, of Kirkham, Lancs; *b* 1883; *ed* Manchester Gram Sch, and Manchester Univ; Managing Dir and Chm of Lewis's and Asso Cos 1926-39 and 1945-51 and Hon Pres 1951-64; Min of Food 1940-43; Min of Reconstruction, and Member of War Cabinet 1943-45, Lord Pres of Council May to July 1945, and 1951-52, and Chancellor of Duchy of Lancaster 1952-55 (and Min of Materials 1953-54); Chm of Conservative Party 1946-55; Chancellor of Manchester Univ 1944-64; *cr Baron Woolton*, of Liverpool, co Lancaster (peerage of UK) 1939, *Viscount Woolton*, of Liverpool, co Lancaster (peerage of UK) 1953, and *Earl of Woolton*, and *Viscount Walberton*, of Walberton, co Sussex (peerage of UK) 1956: *m* 1st, 1912, Maud, who *d* 1961, da of Thomas Smith, of Manchester; 2ndly, 1962, Margaret Eluned, MB, ChB, who *d* 1983, only da of Richard Thomas; *d* 1964; *s* by his only son **(2)** ROGER DAVID, 2nd Earl, *b* 1922: *m* 1st, 1946 (*m diss* 1953), Hon Lucia Edith Lawson, only da of 4th Baron Burnham; 2ndly, 1957, (Cecily) Josephine (who *m* 2ndly, 1969 (*m diss* 1974), 3rd Baron Forres, and 3rdly, 1982, as his 2nd wife, 3rd Earl Lloyd-George of Dwyfor), elder da of Maj Sir Alexander Penrose Gordon-Cumming, MC, 5th Bt; *d* 1969; *s* by his only son **(3)** SIMON FREDERICK, 3rd Earl and present Peer; also Viscount Woolton, Viscount Walberton, and Baron Woolton.

Worlingham, Baron, title of Earl of Gosford of Roll of HL.

Worsley, Baron; son of Earl of Yarborough.

Wortley, Montagu Stuart, family name of Earl of Wharncliffe.

WRAXALL, BARON (Gibbs) (Baron UK 1928)

GEORGE RICHARD LAWLEY GIBBS, 2nd Baron; *b* 16 May 1928: *s* 1931; *ed* Eton, and RMA; late Maj N Somerset and Bristol Yeo, and late Lt Coldstream Guards.

Arms – Argent, three battle-axes erect sable within a bordure nebuly of the last. **Crest** – A dexter arm embowed in armour, the hand in a gauntlet proper bearing a battle-axe bendwise sinister sable. **Supporters** – On either side a St Kilda sheep proper, each charged on the shoulder with a portcullis chained or.
Seat – Tyntesfield, Wraxall, Bristol BS48 1NU. *Clubs* – Royal Automobile, Cavalry and Guards'.

BROTHER LIVING

Hon Sir EUSTACE HUBERT BEILBY, KCVO, CMG (Coddenham House, Coddenham, nr Ipswich; Pratt's Club), *b* 3 July 1929; *ed* Eton, and Ch Ch, Oxford; HM Diplomatic Serv 1954-86; CMG 1982, KCVO 1986: *m* 1957, Evelyn Veronica, only da of late Sydney K. Scott, of Reydon Grove Farm, Southwold, Suffolk, and has issue living, Antony Hubert, *b* 1958: *m* 1st, 1988, Caroline Jane, da of late Arthur Gould; 2ndly, 1995, Virginia Gilchrist, and has issue living, (by 1st *m*), India Florence Aurelia *b* 1989, Cosima Eleanore Hero *b* 1992, (by 2nd *m*), Orlando Hubert, *b* 19 May 1995, Felix Leo *b* 1999, — Andrew Christopher, *b* 1965: *m* 1995, Diahann Alison, da of Andrew Brown, of Brighton, and has issue living, Eleanore Frances *b* 1998, — Jonathan Charles William, *b* 1969, — Miranda Caroline, *b* 1961: *m* 1993, Andrew David Fox Jolliffe, only son of B. R. Jolliffe, of Bedford, — Alexandra Mary Henrietta, *b* 1971.

Tenacious of purpose

HALF-SISTER LIVING

Hon Doreen Albinia de Burgh, *b* 1913: *m* 1937, Charles Bathurst Norman, Bar-at-Law, and has issue living, George Alfred Bathurst (14 Orchard Rise, Richmond, Surrey), *b* 1939; Bar Inner Temple 1961; Metropolitan Stipendiary Magistrate 1981, Circuit Judge 1986: *m* 1st, 1967 (*m diss* 1967), Prudence Veronica, da of F. H. Keenlyside, of Salisbury, Rhodesia; 2ndly, 1973, Susan Elizabeth, da of James Ball, of 46 Park Av, Bromley, Kent, and has issue living (by 2nd *m*), Charles Canning Bathurst *b* 1979, Harriet Anstice Bathurst *b* 1977, — Victoria Mary Bathurst, *b* 1940: *m* 1st, 1961 (*m diss* 1967), Raymond Edward Barthorp, late Capt Northamptonshire Regt: 2ndly, 1977, Patrick Giles Andrew Eyre (*see* B Acton, 1995 Edn), and has issue living (by 1st *m*), Nicola Vivien *b* 1964, (by 2nd *m*) Toby Charles Peter *b* 1983. *Residence* – Villa Villetri, Vallée de Vaux, Jersey.

PREDECESSOR – (1) *Rt Hon* GEORGE ABRAHAM Gibbs, el son of late Antony Gibbs, of Tyntesfield, Bristol, and 16 Hyde Park Gardens, W; *b* 1873; was Parliamentary Private Sec to Sec of State for the Colonies (Rt Hon W. H. Long, MP) and Govt Whip in House of Commons 1917-21, and Treasurer of HM's Household April 1921 to Jan 1924 and Nov 1924 to Jan 1928; MP for W Div of Bristol (*U*) Jan 1906 to Jan 1928; *cr* PC 1923 and *Baron Wraxall*, of Clyst St George, co Devon (peerage of United Kingdom) 1928: *m* 1st, 1901, Victoria Florence de Burgh Long, CBE, who *d* 1920, el da of Rt Hon Walter Hume Long, MP (afterwards 1st Viscount Long of Wraxall); 2ndly, 1927, Hon Ursula Mary Lawley, OBE, RRC, who *d* 1979, da of 6th Baron Wenlock; *d* 1931; *s* by his son (2) GEORGE RICHARD LAWLEY, 2nd Baron and present peer.

WRENBURY, BARON (Buckley) (Baron UK 1915)

Rev JOHN BURTON BUCKLEY, 3rd Baron; *b* 18 June 1927; *s* 1940; *ed* Eton, and Kings Coll, Camb (MA); Solicitor 1952; a partner in the legal firm of Freshfields, of Grindall House, 25 Newgate St, EC1 1956-74, and Thomson Snell & Passmore, of 3 Lonsdale Gdns, Tunbridge Wells 1974-90; Dep Legal Adviser to National Trust 1955-56; Ordained Priest 1991: *m* 1st, 1956 (*m diss* 1961), Carolyn Joan Maule, da of Col Ian Burn-Murdoch, OBE, of Gartincaber, Doune, Perthshire; 2ndly, 1961, Penelope Sara Frances, da of Edward Fort, of The White House, Sixpenny Handley, Dorset, and has issue by 2nd *m*.

Arms – Azure, a chevron cottised between two stags' heads cabossed in chief and a garb in base all or, on a chief engrailed ermine a buckle between two crosses patée fitchée gules. Crest – On a mount vert a demi-stag at gaze gules, attired and gorged with a collar, a chain attached reflexed over the back or, supporting a garb of the last. Supporters – On either side a buck at gaze gules, collared, attired, and chained or.
Residence – Oldcastle, Dallington, near Heathfield, Sussex. *Club* – Oriental.

SON LIVING (*By 2nd marriage*)

Hon WILLIAM EDWARD, *b* 19 June 1966: *m* 1996, Emma L., only da of Peter Clementson, of Rose Cottage, Acre St, W Wittering, W Sussex.

DAUGHTERS LIVING (*By 2nd marriage*)

Hon Elizabeth Margaret, *b* 1964; resumed her maiden name 1991 until remarriage: *m* 1st, 1988 (*m diss* 1991), Capt Andrew Murray Macnaughton, Argyll and Sutherland Highers, elder son of R. M. Macnaughton, of Edinburgh; 2ndly, 1993, Dr Timothy Grey Morgan, son of Prof Colyn Grey Morgan, of Mayals, Swansea, and has issue living (by 2nd *m*), Thomas Alexander, *b* 1997, — Ellen Margaret Louise, *b* 1996.
Hon Katherine Lucy, *b* 1968: *m* 1994, Andrew Gerhard Schaale, of 38 Cambray Rd, SW12 0DY.

SISTER LIVING

Hon Mary Graham, *b* 1929: *m* 1961, (John) Richard Seymour Homan, CBE, of 30 High St, Ticehurst, Sussex TN5 7AS, and has issue living, Robert Seymour, *b* 1964, — Frances Mary, *b* 1967: *m* 1999, Gerry Jue, of 1706 Broderick St, San Francisco, CA 94115, USA, — Rosalind Clare *b* 1969.

COLLATERAL BRANCHES LIVING

Issue of late Hon Colin Burton Buckley, MB, BCh, 3rd son of 1st Baron, *b* 1899, *d* 1981: *m* 1925, Evelyn Joyce, who *d* 1987, da of Hugh C. Webster, of Lea House, Harpenden, Herts:—
Martin Christopher Burton (Crouchers, Rudgwick, Sussex RH12 3DD), *b* 1936; Bar Lincoln's Inn 1961, Registrar in Bankruptcy, Companies Court, 1988-97, since when Ch Registrar in Bankruptcy: *m* 1964, Victoria Gay, da of Dr Stanhope Furber, of Oak Cottage, Bracknell, Berks, and 14 Wimpole St, W1, and has issue living, Arthur Burton (6 Sandfield Av, Ravenshead, Notts NG15 9AR), *b* 1967: *m* 1992, Amanda Jane Ridley, and has issue living, Adam Burton *b* 1997, Catherine Alice *b* 1995, — Samuel Burton, *b* 1973, — Hannah Kate, *b* 1965; MB BS Lond 1989: *m* 1994, Lt-Cmdr Mark Emerton, RN, of 92 Farlington Av, Drayton, Portsmouth PO6 1ES, and has issue living, Rebecca Mary *b* 1997, — Amanda Victoria, *b* 1968: *m* 1991, Anthony Clarke, of 51 Maidcroft Rd, Cowley, Oxford OX4 3EW, and has issue living, Benjamin Edward *b* 1998, — Jessica Beth, *b* 1971. ——Jessica Margaret, *b* 1932: *m* 1957, Michael John Knott, of 13 Gardiner St, Headington, Oxford OX3 7AW, and has issue living, Thomas, *b* 1960, — George, *b* 1963, — Albert, *b* 1965, — Mary Louise, *b* 1968, — Martha Elizabeth, *b* 1971. ——Alison Rachel, *b* 1933: *m* 1959, Benjamin Fisher, of 133 Victoria Rd, Fulwood, Preston, Lancs PR2 4NP, and has issue living, Benjamin Edward, *b* 1960, — William David, *b* 1964, — Harry James, *b* 1968, — Charlotte Anne, *b* 1962. ——Hazel Charlotte, *b* 1934.

Issue of late Rt Hon Sir Denys Burton Buckley, MBE, 4th and yst son of 1st Baron, *b* 1906, *d* 1998: *m* 1932, Gwendolen Jane, who *d* 1985, da of late Sir Robert Armstrong-Jones, CBE, MD, FRCP, FRCS, DSc, of Plas Dinas, Caerns:—
Jane Gwenllian Armstrong (*Lady Slade*), *b* 1936: *m* 1958, Rt Hon Sir Christopher John Slade, of 16 Elthiron Rd, SW6, and has issue living, Richard Penkivil (26 Whittingstall Rd, SW6 4ED), *b* 1963: *m* 1994, Lucy Jane, da of George Cacanas, of Upper Swainswick, Bath, and has issue living, Jack Alexander *b* 1997, Thomas Patrick *b* (twin) 1997, — Lucinda Jane, *b* 1959: *m* 1985, Christopher Charles Tite, of 27 Hotham Rd, SW15 1QL, son of late Leslie J. Tite, of Nantwich, Ches, and has issue living, William Christopher James *b* 1990, Oliver Henry Charles *b* 1992, Serena Catherine Lucinda *b* 1994, — Victoria Albinia, *b* 1962: *m* 1988, Hugh J. Henderson-Cleland, of 6 Steep Hill, SW16 1UL, son of J. G. W. Henderson-Cleland, of Clapham, SW4, and has issue living, Archibald Hugh *b* 1994, Georgia *b* 1989, Charlotte May *b* 1991, Octavia Jane *b* 1997, — Amelia Caroline, *b* 1966: *m* 1992, Maj Matthew C. F. Jackson, RE, son of Cmdr M. F. Jackson, RN, of Old Portsmouth, Hants, and has issue living, Luke George Buckley *b* 1997, Brontë Eliza Jane *b* 1995. ——Catherine Elizabeth Armstrong, *b* 1938: *m* 1961, Charles Kenneth Roylance Nunneley, of 4 Grenville Place, SW7 4RU, and of Fyfield House, Pewsey, Wilts, and has issue living, Luke James Charles (30B Burghley Rd, SW19 5HN), *b* 1963: *m* 1990, Katerine Ruth, 2nd da of B. F. Panter, of Walton-on-Thames, Surrey, and has issue living, Thomas *b* 1995, Rebecca *b* 1992, Sarah *b* (twin) 1995, — Alice Georgina, *b* 1964: *m* 1989, Nicholas Bruce Chapple, of Bakers Well,

Hethfelton, Wareham, Dorset BH20 6HJ, and has issue living, Ben *b* 1994, Sally *b* 1995, — Clare Sabina, *b* 1967: *m* 1997, Christopher J. Clark, and has issue living, Charles *b* 1998, — Frances Mary, *b* 1969: *m* 1999, Giles Wilson Mervyn Crewdson (*see* B Grimthorpe). —— (Marion) Miranda Armstrong (47 Bury Walk, SW3 6QE), *b* 1945.

PREDECESSORS – **(1)** *Rt Hon* HENRY BURTON Buckley, son of late Rev John Wall Buckley, V of St Mary's, Paddington, W; *b* 1845; was a Member of the Bar Committee and of Bar Council 1882-98, a Judge of High Court of Justice 1900-1906, and a Lord Justice of Appeal 1906-15; *cr Baron Wrenbury*, of Old Castle, Sussex (peerage of United Kingdom) 1915; *m* 1887, Bertha Margaretta, who *d* 1960, da of Charles Edward Jones, of 20 Cornwall Gardens, SW; *d* 1935; *s* by his son **(2)** BRYAN BURTON, 2nd Baron, *b* 1890: *m* 1925, Helen Malise, who *d* 1981, da of His Honour John Cameron Graham, of Ballewan, Blanfield, Stirlingshire; *d* 1940; *s* by his son **(3)** JOHN BURTON, 3rd Baron and present peer.

WRIGHT OF ASHTON UNDER LYNE, BARONY OF (Wright) (Extinct 1974)

SONS LIVING OF LIFE BARON

Hon Owen Mortimor (Wingthorne, Slade Rd, Newton, Swansea), *b* 1934: *m* 1960, Barbara, da of Arthur Hudson, and has issue.
Hon Glyn David (12 Brookfield Grove, Ashton under Lyne, Lancs), *b* 1940: *m* 1965, May Elizabeth, da of George Frederick Alldridge, and has issue.

WRIGHT OF RICHMOND, BARON (Wright) (Life Baron 1994)

PATRICK RICHARD HENRY WRIGHT, GCMG, son of late Herbert Wright, of The Hermitage, Chetwode, Buckingham; *b* 28 June 1931; *ed* Marlborough, and Merton Coll, Oxford; National Service Lieut RA; entered Foreign Service 1955 and served in Beirut, Washington, Cairo, and Bahrain; Priv Sec (overseas affairs) to the Prime Minister 1974-744; Ambassador to Luxembourg 1977-79, and Syria 1979-81; Dep Under-Sec FCO 1982-84; Ambassador to Saudi Arabia 1984-86; Permanent Under-Sec FCO and Head of Diplomatic Service 1986-91; Dir of Barclays Bank 1991-96, Unilever 1991-99, BAA 1992-98, British Petroleum (now BP Amoco) since 1991, and De La Rue since 1991; Member of Security Commn since 1993; Member of Council of Royal Institute of Internat Affairs (Chm 1995-99), Royal College of Music, Order of St John, and United World Coll of the Atlantic; Vice-Pres of Home-Start; Governor of Wellington Coll, Ditchley; *Hon* Fell of Merton Coll, Oxford 1987; KStJ 1990; CMG 1978, KCMG 1974, GCMG 1989; *cr Baron Wright of Richmond*, of Richmond-upon-Thames, in the London Borough of Richmond-upon-Thames (Life Baron) 1994: *m* 1958, Virginia Anne, step da of late Col Samuel John Hannaford, of Hove, and has issue.

𝕬rms – Per fess gules and or, on a pale counterchanged between in chief two oak leaves or each charged with a quaver azure and in base as many oak leaves gules each charged with a quaver gold a doric column proper and overall a chevron per pale azure and gules. 𝕮rest – Beneath a palm tree a pelican in its piety with its young all proper. 𝕾upporters – *Dexter*, a bichon frisé rampant and in trim aspect proper; *sinister*, a stag guardant gold.
Address – c/o House of Lords, SW1A 0PW.

SONS LIVING

Hon Marcus, *b* 1959: *m* 1989, Rebecca Mary Bates, and has issue living, Jasper Louis, *b* 1991, — Tristram Theodore Stafford, *b* 1995, — Sholto Benedict, *b* 1998.
Hon Angus, *b* 1964.

DAUGHTER LIVING

Hon Olivia, *b* 1963: *m* 1989, Simon Gerard McDonald, and has issue living, Felix Dominic, *b* 1990, — Joachim James, *b* 1994, — Matilda Dorothy, *b* 1992, — Adelaide Mary, *b* 1996. *Address* – c/o Foreign & Commonwealth Office, King Charles Street, SW1A 2AH.

WROTTESLEY, BARON (Wrottesley) (Baron UK 1838, Bt E 1642)

Strength is increased by union

CLIFTON HUGH LANCELOT DE VERDON WROTTESLEY, 6th Baron and 14th Baronet, *b* 10 Aug 1968; *s* 1977; *ed* Eton, Edinburgh Univ, and RMA Sandhurst; 2nd Lieut Gren Gds.

Arms – Or, three piles sable and a canton ermine. **Crest** – Out of a ducal coronet or a boar's head ermine, crined and tusked gold. **Supporters** – On either side a unicorn argent, armed, maned, tufted, unguled, gorged with a ducal coronet, and chain reflexed over the back or pendent from the coronet an escutcheon, charged with the arms of Wrottesley.
Residence – c/o C. Hoare & Co, 32 Lowndes St, SW1X 9HZ. *Clubs* – Carlton, Lansdowne, Cavalry and Guards'.

HALF-UNCLES LIVING (*sons of 5th Baron by 3rd marriage*)

Hon STEPHEN JOHN, *b* 21 Dec 1955; *ed* Harrow; journalist: *m* 1982, Mrs Rosamund Clare Fletcher (*neé* Taylor), and has issue living, Alexandra Wynne Marie, *b* 1985, — Stephanie Victoria, *b* 1988. *Residence* – 1 Lodge Rd, Orangezicht, Cape Town 8001, S Africa.
Hon Nicholas Charles, *b* 1963; *ed* Harrow, and Cape Town Univ (BA 1985, LLB 1987, LLM 1992): *m* 1991, Denny Marian Welman, and has issue living, Mary, *b* 1994. *Residence* – 88 Stredwick Drive, Torbay, Auckland, NZ.

GRANDMOTHER LIVING

Roshanara Barbara WINGFIELD-STRATFORD-ORR, da of Esmé Cecil Wingfield-Stratford, DSc (*see* V Powerscourt, colls) assumed by deed poll 1970 the surnames of Wingfield-Stratford-Johnstone, and subsequently assumed the surname of Orr in lieu of Johnstone by deed poll 1998: *m* 1st, 1941 (*m diss* 1949), Maj Richard John Wrottesley, MC (later 5th Baron Wrottesley), who *d* 1977; 2ndly, 1950, Lt-Col Norman David Melville Johnstone, MBE, Gren Gds, who *d* 1995; 3rdly, 1998, Ronald Henry Davidson Orr, of Lake View House, Station Rd, Kirby Bellars, Leics LE14 2ED.

MOTHER LIVING

Georgina Anne, el da of late Lt-Col Peter Thomas Clifton, CVO, DSO (*see* Bruce, Bt, *cr* 1804, colls): *m* 1st, 1967 (Nevada), Hon Richard Francis Gerard Wrottesley, who *dvp* 1970; 2ndly, 1982, Lt-Col Jonathan Lovett Seddon-Brown, Scots Gds, and has issue by 1st *m* (ante). *Residence* – The Coach House, Dauntsey, Chippenham, Wilts SN15 4HP.

WIDOW LIVING OF SON OF FIFTH BARON (*by 2nd marriage*)

Judy, da of — Matthews: *m* 1981, as his 2nd wife, Hon Mark Wrottesley, son of 5th Baron, who *d* 1986.

WIDOW LIVING OF FIFTH BARON

MARY ADA VAN ECHTEN (*Baroness Wrottesley*) (18 Sonnehoogte, Thomas Rd, Kenilworth, Cape Province 7708, S Africa), only da of late Edgar Dryden Tudhope, of Kenilworth, CP, S Africa: *m* 1955, as his 3rd wife, the 5th Baron Wrottesley, who *d* 1977.

COLLATERAL BRANCHES LIVING

Issue of late Hon Mark Wrottesley, only son by 2nd *m* of 5th Baron, *b* 1951, *d* 1986: *m* 1st, 1974 (*m diss* 1978), Marie Louise du Plooy; 2ndly, 1981, Judy (*née* Matthews), formerly wife of —:—
(By 1st *m*) Caroline May, *b* 19—. ⸻ Veronica, *b* 19—.

(In remainder to Baronetcy)

Grandchildren of late Edward Algernon Wrottesley, 2nd son of late Rev Francis John Wrottesley, only son of late Rev Edward John Wrottesley, only son of late Capt Edward Wrottesley, RN, 5th son of 8th baronet:—

Issue of late Capt Arthur John Francis Wrottesley, *b* 1908, *d* (14 July) 1996: *m* 1936, Marjorie Mary, MBE, who *d* (13 March) 1996, only da of late Frank Wilde, of Moorland Rd, Edgbaston:—
David John (29 Twentywell Rd, Bradway, Sheffield S17 9PU), *b* 1940; *ed* Mill Hill Sch: *m* 1969, Christine Ann, only da of Henry Smith, of Sheffield, and has issue living, Angela Jane, *b* 1977. —— Michael Francis (17 Ordnance Hill, NW8 6PR), *b* 1945; *ed* Mill Hill Sch: *m* 1973, Francesca Jacqueline, only da of late Jack Miller, and has issue living, Alexander Francis, *b* 1976; *ed* Westminster, and King's Coll, Lond (BA 1998), — Maxim George, *b* 1980; actor. —— Elizabeth Mavis, *b* 1938; *ed* St Mary's Coll, Durham (BA 1960): *m* 1st, 1962, Capt John Michael Parr, RAEC; 2ndly, 1982, I. Breac C. MacLeod, of Anvil House, Hook Norton, Oxon OX15 5NH, and has issue living (by 1st *m*), Richard John (Laburnham Villa, Mill Rd, Wollerton, Shropshire TF9 3NE), *b* 1964: *m* 1988, Alison Jane, da of Graham Massey, of Moore, Cheshire, and has issue living, James Richard *b* 1991, Sophie Rebecca *b* 1993, Grace Florence *b* 1997. — Sarah Anne Elizabeth, *b* 1965: *m* 1992, Stephen John Ross, of 10 Canynge Rd, Clifton, Bristol BS8 3JX, yr son of Peter Ross, of Prestbury, Ches, and has issue living, Magnus Alexander *b* 1998, Amy Freya *b* 1994, — Rosalind Mary, *b* 1975. —— Letitia Marjorie, *b* (twin) 1945: *m* 1968, Graeme Allan Lythe, of 38 Vicarage Rd, East Sheen, SW14 8RU, and has issue living, Edward Graeme, *b* 1970; Lieut Queen's Own Hussars, — James Edgar, *b* 1972, — Henry Frederick, *b* 1975.

PREDECESSORS – (1) *Sir* WALTER Wrottesley, Knt, son of Sir Hugh Wrottesley (High Sheriff of co Stafford), descended in the male line from Sir Hugh de Wrottesley, KG (temp 1348), a zealous royalist, was *cr* a *Baronet* 1642; *d* 1659; *s* by his son (2) *Sir* WALTER, 2nd Bt; *d* 1686; *s* by his son (3) *Sir* WALTER, 3rd Bt; *d* 1712; *s* by his son (4) *Sir* JOHN, MP, 4th Bt; *d* 1726; *s* by his el son (5) *Sir* HUGH, 5th Bt; *d* 1729; *s* by his brother (6) *Sir* WALTER, 6th Bt; *d* 1731; *s* by his brother (7) *Sir* RICHARD, 7th Bt; was sometime MP for Tavistock, and a Principal Clerk of the Board of Green Cloth; subsequently took Holy Orders, and having been a Royal Chaplain was appointed Dean of Worcester; *d* 1769; *s* by his son (8) *Sir* JOHN, 8th Bt; was Maj-Gen in the Army, sometime MP for Staffordshire and Equerry to HRH the Duke of York; *d* 1787; *s* by his son (9) *Sir* JOHN, 9th Bt; having been successively MP for Staffordshire and Lichfield, was *cr* *Baron Wrottesley*, of Wrottesley, co Stafford (peerage of United Kingdom) 1838; *d* 1841; *s* by his son (10) JOHN, DCL, FRS, 2nd Baron; *b* 1798; was Pres of the Royal So, and one of the founders of the Astronomical So: *m* 1821, Sophia Elizabeth, da of late Thomas Giffard of Chillington, Staffordshre, *d* 1867; *s* by his son (11) ARTHUR, 3rd Baron; *b* 1824; a Lord-in-Waiting to Queen Victoria 1869-74 and 1880-85, and Lord-Lieut of Staffordshire 1871-87: *m* 1861, Hon Augusta Elizabeth Denison, who *d* 1887, da of 1st Baron Londesborough; *d* 1910; *s* by his el son (12) VICTOR ALEXANDER, 4th Baron; *b* 1873; *d* 1962; *s* by his nephew (13) RICHARD JOHN, MC (only son of late Hon Walter Bennet Wrottesley, yst son of 3rd Baron), 5th Baron, *b* 1918, Maj (Reserve); OStJ; 1935-49 War: *m* 1st, 1941 (*m diss* 1949), Roshanara Barbara, da of Esmé Cecil Wingfield-Stratford, DSC (V Powerscourt, colls); 2ndly, 1949 (*m diss* 1953), (Joyce) Marion, da of late Frederick Alexander Wallace, and formerly wife of Maj Sean Rainey; 3rdly, 1955, Mary Ada Van Echten, only da of Edgar Dryden Tudhope, of Rondebosch, CP, S Africa; *d* 1977; *s* by his grandson (14) CLIFTON HUGH LANCELOT DE VERDON (only son of late Hon Richard Francis Gerard Wrottesley, 2nd son of 5th Baron), 6th Baron and present peer.

WYATT OF WEEFORD, BARONY OF (Wyatt) (Extinct 1997)

SON LIVING OF LIFE BARON (*By 3rd marriage*)

Hon Pericles Plantagenet James Casati, *b* 1963.

DAUGHTER LIVING OF LIFE BARON (*By 4th marriage*)

Hon Petronella Aspasia, *b* 1969; journalist.

WIDOW LIVING OF LIFE BARON

VERONICA (VERUSHKA) (*Baroness Wyatt of Weeford*), widow of Baron Dr Laszlo Banzsky von Ambroz, and da of Jeno Racz: *m* 1966, as his 4th wife, Baron Wyatt of Weeford, (Life Baron), who *d* 1997. *Residence* – 19 Cavendish Av, NW8 9JD.

WYFOLD, BARON (Hermon-Hodge) (Baron UK 1919, Bt UK 1902)

HERMON ROBERT FLEMING HERMON-HODGE, 3rd Baron, and 3rd Baronet; *b* 26 June 1915; *s* 1942; *ed* Eton, and Le Rosey, Switzerland; is Capt Gren Gds (Res), formerly a Dir of Robert Fleming Holdings, Ltd.

Arms – Sable, a lion couchant erminois holding between the paws a bale of cotton proper. **Crest** – An eagle, wings addorsed and inverted or, supporting with the dexter claw an increscent argent, and looking at the rays of the sun issuant from clouds proper. **Supporters** – On either side a trooper of the Oxfordshire Yeomanry (Queen's Own Oxfordshire Hussars).
Residence – Les Trois Couronnes, Vevey, Switzerland. *Address* – 25 Copthall Av, EC2R 7DR. *Clubs* – Carlton, Pratts, Metropolitan (New York).

Glory is the reward of valour

SISTERS LIVING

Hon Lorna Frances, *b* 1911: *m* 1941, John Barkley Schuster, TD, who *d* 1984 (Parker of Waddington, By), and has issue living, Peter Jonathan, *b* 1952: *m* 1984, Emma M., elder da of Christopher Codrington, of Manor Farm House, Petersham, Surrey, and has issue living, George Barkley *b* 1989, Hannah Frances *b* 1986, — Richard Douglas (The Grange, Over Worton, Oxon), *b* 1953: *m* 1986, Jennifer C., da of David G. W. Barham, of Hole Park, Rolvenden, and formerly wife of Simon Francis Mann (*see* Mann, Bt, colls), — Joanna Valentine (Nether Worton House, Middle Barton, Chipping Norton, Oxford OX7 7AT; 63 Bourne St, SW1), *b* 1950: *m* 1971 (*m diss* 1989), Orme Roosevelt Clarke, who *d* 1992, and has issue (*see* Clarke, Bt, *cr* 1831). *Residence* – The Manor Farm, Nether Worton, Middle Barton, Oxon OX5 4AS.

Hon Dorothy Charmian, *b* 1913: *m* 1938, Maj Richard Evelyn Fleming, MC, TD, late Lovat Scouts, who *d* 1977 (Rose, Bt, *cr* 1874, colls), and has issue living, James Roland (Blanche House, Northleach, Glos), *b* 1944: *m* 1975, Kathryn Alice, da of late D. A. Rooksby, and has issue living, Christian Peter *b* 1977, Thomas Roland, *b* 1980, — Adam Richard (Curdle Hill Farm, Chadlington, Chipping Norton, Oxon OX7 3NS), *b* 1948: *m* 1979, Caroline Jane, 2nd da of Sir Hereward Wake, 14th Bt, MC, and has issue living, Hector Adam *b* 1982, Angus Richard *b* 1988, Dickon Toby Robert *b* 1995, Eleanor Kate *b* 1985, — George Andrew (York Cottage, Churchill, Oxon), *b* 1950: *ed* Gordonstoun: *m* 1979 (*m diss* 1987), Elaine, da of Peter Owen, of The Old Rectory, Mixbury, Oxon, and has issue living, Frederick Richard *b* 1981, — Roderick John (The Dower House, Sarsgrove, Churchill, Oxon), *b* 1953: *m* 1979, Diana Julia, eldest da of Sir Hereward Wake, 14th Bt, MC, and has issue living, Chloe Dorothy *b* 1989, Hermione Kisty *b* (twin) 1989, — Fergus Hermon Robert, *b* 1959, — Kathleen Alexandra (Sydenham Farm, Broadwell, Moreton-in-Marsh, Glos GL56 0YE), *b* 1941: *m* 1962 (*m diss* 1979), Capt Simon John Loder, late Gren Gds, and has issue (*see* Loder, Bt, colls), — Mary Fern, *b* 1942: *m* 1971, Jeremy Donnithorne Taylor, of Cold Harbour Farm, North Aston, Oxford, and has issue living, James Fionn *b* 1971, Katherine Clare Romayne *b* 1973, — Dorothy Frances, *b* 1955. *Residence* – Inverliver Farm, Taynuilt, Argyll.

COLLATERAL BRANCH LIVING

Issue of late Rear-Adm Hon Claude Preston Hermon-Hodge, DSC, 5th son of 1st Baron, *b* 1888, *d* 1952: *m* 1918, Gwendoline Rose, who *d* 1949, da of J. Goulding Davis, Public Works Depart, India:—
Stella Riette, *b* 1925: *m* 1949, David Ashley Courtenay, who *d* 1983, of Woodcutters, Ambersham Common, Midhurst, W Sussex GU29 0BZ, and has issue living, David Anthony Orin (9 Hedge Court, 103 Hainault Rd, Leytonstone, E11 1DU), *b* 1958: *m* 1995, Laura Maria Salvador, and has issue living Roseve *b* 1995, — Geraldine, *b* 1953: *m* 1977, Rev Douglas John Dales, of Hillside, Bath Rd, Marlborough, Wilts SN8 1NN, and has issue living, Christopher St John Douglas *b* 1981, Basil Michael Dunstan *b* 1987, Gwendoline Clare Courtenay *b* 1984.

PREDECESSORS

PREDECESSORS – (1) ROBERT TROTTER Hermon-Hodge, TD, el son of late George William Hodge, of Newcastle-upon-Tyne; *b* 1851; sat as MP for Accrington Div of N-E Lancashire (*C*) 1886-92, for S, or Henley, Div of Oxfordshire 1895-1906 and 1917-18, and for Croydon 1909-10; sometime Lieut-Col and Hon Col Comdg Queen's Own Oxfordshire Hussars Yeo; assumed by Roy licence the additional surname of Hermon 1903; *cr* a *Baronet* 1902, and *Baron Wyfold*, of Accrington, co Lancaster (peerage of United Kingdom) 1919: *m* 1877, Frances Caroline, who *d* 1929, only da of Edward Hermon, of Wyfold Court, Oxon; *d* 1937, *s* by his son (2) ROLAND HERMON, DSO, MVO, 2nd Baron; *b* 1880; Major and Brevet Lieut-Col late Reserve of Officers; S Africa 1899-1902, European War 1914-18 (DSO): *m* 1906, Dorothy, who *d* 1976, el da of Robert Fleming, of Joyce Grove, Oxfordshire, and 27, Grosvenor Square, W1; *d* 1942: *s* by his son (3) HERMON ROBERT FLEMING, 3rd Baron and present Peer.

Wyndham, family name of Baron Egremont.

WYNFORD, BARON (Best) (Baron UK 1829)

Liberty in the laws

ROBERT SAMUEL BEST, MBE, 8th Baron; *b* 5 Jan 1917; *s* 1943; *ed* Eton; Lieut-Col (ret) RWF, Croix de Guerre 1943; a DL of Dorset; MBE (Mil) 1952: *m* 1941, Anne Daphne Mametz, da of late Maj-Gen John Randle Minshull-Ford, CB, DSO, MC (Harmood-Banner, Bt), and has issue.

Arms – Sable, a cinquefoil within an orle of cross crosslets or; on a canton of the last, a portcullis of the first. **Crest** – Out of a ducal coronet or, a demi-ostrich rising argent, in its beak a cross crosslet fitchée gold, gorged with a plain collar, and pendent therefrom a portcullis sable. **Supporters** – Two eagles reguardant, wings elevated, each standing on a Roman fasces, all proper.
Seat – Wynford House, Wynford Eagle, Dorchester, Dorset.

SON LIVING

Hon JOHN PHILIP ROBERT (The Manor, Wynford Eagle, Dorchester, Dorset DT2 0ER), *b* 23 Nov 1950; *ed* Radley, Keele Univ and RAC Cirencester: *m* 1981, Fenella Christian Mary, only da of late Arthur Reginald Danks, MBE, TD (*see* B Gifford, 1995 Edn), and has issue living, Harry Robert Francis, *b* 9 May 1987, — Sophie Hannah Elizabeth, *b* 1985.

DAUGHTERS LIVING

Hon Caroline Anne Sabina, *b* 1942: *m* 1964, Edward Patrick Gundry, of 15 Genoa Av, SW15 (*see* Williams, Bt, *cr* 1915, 1980 Edn) and has issue living, David Patrick Edward, *b* 1976, — Rachel Anne, *b* 1965, — Alexandra Clare, *b* 1967: *m* 1995, Mark Simon Fraser, son of Frederick Fraser, of Durban, S Africa.

Hon Jacqueline Dorothy Mametz, *b* 1946: *m* 1969, Jeremy James Richard Pope, OBE, FRSA, of Field Cottage, Compton Abbas West, Maiden Newton, Dorset, — Rory Christian Robert, *b* 1970: *m* 1996, Natasha Jane, da of Michael Berrigan, of Lymington, Hants, and of Mrs Elfriede King, of Haslemere, Surrey, — Rupert Philip, *b* 1973, — Toby Francis, *b* 1977.

BROTHER LIVING

Hon Patrick George Mathew (Ridgeway, London Rd, Rake, Liss, Hants, Boodle's Club), *b* 1923; *ed* Wellington Coll; Lt RNVR 1941-46; Chm/Man Dir Wiggins Teape Group; Dir BAT Industries, Ranks Hovis McDougal; Past Master of Ironmongers' Co; FRSA; Offr Order of Crown of Belgium 1980; *m* 1947, Heather Elizabeth, who *d* 1999, da of Hamilton Gardner, and has issue living, Christopher John Patrick (27 Warwick Rd, N11 2SB), *b* 1948: *m* 1st, 1973 (*m diss* 1977), Anna Marion Richmond Rowe, only da of David Rowe Mitchell; 2ndly, 1977, Margherita Antonietta, da of Alberto Pietro Toninato, and has issue living (by 2nd *m*), Francesca Victoria *b* 1984, — David Robert (La Saboterie, 21420 Bouilland, France), *b* 1953: *m* 1998, Rachel Mary, da of Frank Foulkes, of Toronto, Canada, — Philip Edward Fraser, *b* 1960: *m* 1995, Catherine, yst da of Claude Legoux, of Lyon, France, and has issue living, Edward George *b* 1996, Alexander Claude *b* 1998, — Clare Phyllis, *b* 1955: *m* 1992, Philip A. Willatt, yst son of Ian Duncan Willatt, MD, of Lavant, Chichester, Sussex, and has issue living, Frederick Charles Michael *b* 1995.

DAUGHTERS LIVING OF SIXTH BARON

Hon Grace Janet Mary, *b* 1907: *m* 1930, Edward Kenneth Macleod Hilleary, MVO, of Lordington Park, Chichester, W Sussex PO18 9DX, and has issue living, Shena Sarah, *b* 1931: *m* 1954, Lt-Cdr Harry R. Cornell, RN (ret), of Walled House, Droxford, Hants, — Wendy Jemima, *b* 1933: *m* 1954, Ian Hedderwick, of 19 Boyle St, Busselton, Western Australia 6280, Australia, — Gillian Mariannc, *b* 1936: *m* 1975, Maj J. D. Bengough, The Black Watch (Royal Highland Regt) (ret), of White Lodge, Sidbury, Sidmouth, Devon.

Hon Eva Constance Edith, *b* 1909: *m* 1932, Philip Valentine Mackinnon, son of late Rt Hon Sir Frank Douglas Mackinnon, Lord Justice of Appeal, and has had issue, Michael Alexander, *b* 1936: *m* 1964, Cleodie Jean Sheila, da of Maj-Gen Harry Macdonald, CB, CIE, DSO, of Portree, Isle of Skye, and *d* 1981, leaving issue, Alan Alexander John *b* 1970, Mairi Jessie Julia *b* 1968. *Residence* – The Hyde, Walditch, Bridport, Dorset.

Hon Mary Jemima, *b* 1912: *m* 1944, Jack Hendy, and has issue living, John Giles, *b* 1948, — Peter Gerard, *b* 1953. *Residence* – 1 Portherras Cross, Pendeen, Penzance, Cornwall TR19 7DY.

COLLATERAL BRANCHES LIVING

Grandchildren of late Adm Hon Sir Matthew Robert Best, KCB, DSO, MVO, 3rd son of 5th Baron:—
Issue of late Capt George Frederic Matthew Best, OBE, RN, *b* (Dec) 1908, *d* 1994: *m* 1940, Rosemary Elizabeth (Wallhayes, Nettlecombe, Bridport, Dorset DT6 3SX), da of Maj J. Chadwick-Brooks, OBE, of Bedford Park, W4:—
John Vincent Matthew (29 Folkestone Rd, Walthamstow, E17), *b* 1948; *ed* Sussex Univ (BSc): *m* 1970, Penelope Ann, da of John H. Williams, of Washington, DC, USA, and Isle of Arran, and has issue living, Tobias Graham, *b* 1974, — Crispin Alex Sebastian, *b* 1983, — Philippa Hannah, *b* 1972. —— Annis Rosemary Georgina, *b* 1944: *m* 1971, Col Richard M. Connaughton, late RCT, of Wallhayes, Nettlecombe, Bridport, Dorset DT6 3SX, and has issue living, Michael Thomas George, *b* 1972, — Emma Caroline Jane, *b* 1974.

Grandchildren of late Capt Hon James William Best, OBE, VD (infra):—
Issue of late Rear Adm Thomas William Best, CB, *b* 1915, *d* 1984: *m* 1942, Brenda Joan (Hincknowle, Melplash, Bridport, Dorset DT6 3UG), da of late F. A. Hellaby MC, LLD, of Auckland, NZ:—
Rupert Thomas (39 Beach Rd, Emsworth, Hants PO10 7HR), *b* 1943; Cmdr RN: *m* 1971, Margaret Ludgate, da of late Maj Alan Murray, 3rd Carabiniers (Prince of Wales's Dragoon Gds), and has issue living, Thomas Matthew, *b* 1973, — William Rupert, *b* 1982, — Sarah Margaret, *b* 1976. ——James Frederick (Walnut Farm, Melplash, Bridport, Dorset DT6 3UG), *b* 1948; BA Oxon: *m* 1980, Sara Victoria, da of Brian Cole, of 49 Milverton Rd, NW6, and has issue living, Harry James, *b* 1983, — Tom, *b* 1987, — Mary-Rose Victoria, *b* 1981. ——Joanna Mavis, *b* 1945; *ed* Durham Univ (BA): *m* 1970, Maj Thomas James Knott, RE, of Hillside Riverview Rd, Pangbourne, Berks RG8 7AU, son of Lt-Gen Sir Harold Edwin Knott, KCB, OBE, MD, and has issue living, Felicity Anne, *b* 1971, — Alison Joanna, *b* 1973, — Amelia Mary, *b* 1982.

Issue of late Samuel James Best, *b* 1927, *d* 1974: *m* 1954, Jennifer Elspeth Mary (Kings House, Powerstock, Dorset), el da of Max H. Heilbut:—
Crispin John, *b* 1955. ——Jane Mary, *b* 1957. ——Susannah Catherine, *b* 1962. ——Deborah Gabriel, *b* 1966.

Issue of late Capt Hon James William Best, OBE, VD, yst son of 5th Baron, *b* 1882, *d* 1960: *m* 1914, Florence Mary Bernarda, who *d* 1961, da of Sir Elliott Lees, 1st Bt, DSO:—
Henry Nicholas, *b* 1930; *ed* Wellington Coll; former Man Dir Anglo Blackwells Ltd, and SKW Metals UK Ltd: *m* 1963, Elisabeth Rose Ursula, el da of Hans Joachim Druckenbrodt, of Marburg, W Germany, and Rittergut Minsleben, Wernigerode, E Germany, and has issue living, Frederick Henry Achim, *b* 1964, — Thomas Bernard Nicholas, *b* 1968, — Isabel Florence Christina, *b* 1972. *Residence* – Whitelackington House, Ilminster, Somerset TA19 9EF. ——Alice Mary, *b* 1919: *m* 1939, Christopher Wentworth Dilke, Lt-Col RA (*see* Dilke, Bt), who *d* 1987. *Residence* – Valehouse Farm, Whitchurch Canonicorum, Bridport, Dorset. ——Helen Margaret, *b* 1923.

Grandson of late Capt Hon John Charles Best, 2nd son of late Rev Hon Samuel Best, 3rd son of 1st Baron:—
Issue of late Capt William Best, Roy Welch Fusiliers, *b* 1874, *d* 1950: *m* 1903, Constance Adela, who *d* 1963, da of late Col Charles Wingfield, of Onslow, Shrewsbury:—
John William, MBE (Lawton Hall, Leominster, Herefordshire), *b* 1912; formerly Fl-Lt RAF; 1939-45 War (prisoner); MBE (Mil) 1964: *m* 1st, 1938 (*m diss* 1959), Mary Constance, da of Robert Charles Otter, of Royston Manor, Clayworth; 2ndly, 1959, Mary Elisabeth (CORBIN), da of late Dr Edward Lancelot Bunting, of Hardwicke Manor, Worcs, and has issue living, (by 1st *m*) Robert John (Vivod, Llangollen, Denbighshire), *b* 1946: *m* 1976, Juliet, da of Peter John Owen, of The Old Rectory, Mixbury, Brackley, Northants, and has issue living, William *b* 1981, Lucinda Emma *b* 1977, Candida Mary *b* 1979, — Antonia Mary, *b* 1948: *m* 1970, Christopher Duncan Steuart Wilson-Clarke, of Greenbanks, Coptiviney, Ellesmere, Shropshire, and has issue living, Alpha Georgia *b* 1978, Laura Alice *b* 1979.

Grandchildren of late Hon Thomas William Best, 3rd son of late Rev the Hon Samuel Best, 3rd son of 1st Baron:—
Issue of late Capt Humphrey Willie Best, CBE, DSO, RN, *b* 1884, *d* 1959: *m* 1914, Helen Grace, who *d* 1975, da of late Mrs James Meakin, of Weeford, Ashby de-la-Zouch:—
Walter John, *b* 1917: *m* 1941, Elizabeth, yst da of Kenneth M. Simpson, of Trinidad, and Forres, and has issue living, Anne Mackintosh, *b* 1944: *m* 1966, Robert Brian Massey of 8 Gilwell Rd, Valsayn Park, Trinidad, and has issue living, Stewart John *b* 1967: *m* 1998, Sarah Loraine Boyles, Ian James *b* 1972, Catherine Anne *b* 1975, — Fiona Elizabeth Wynford, *b* 1949: *m* 1972, Anthony John Cotter, of Trewalla Farm, Minions, Liskeard, Cornwall PL14 6ED, and has issue living, Andrew John *b* 1976, Heather Jane, *b* 1979. *Residence* – 10 Cronk Drean, 2nd Avenue, Douglas, Isle of Man. ——Peter Anthony (White House, Trevilson, St Newlyn East, Newquay, Cornwall TR8 5JF), *b* 1922; Flight-Lieut RAF (ret); 1939-45 War (prisoner): *m* 1st, 1948, Sheelah Gillian Vernon St John, who *d* 1979, only da of late Lt-Col D. St J. Baxter, of Chichester, Sussex; 2ndly, 1979, B. Smyth, and has issue living (by 1st *m*), Peter Kimble, *b* 1952; S/Ldr RAF: *m* 1974, Georgina Alison Gibson, and has issue living, Oliver Giles *b* 1977, Timothy Tristan *b* 1978, Gemma Lucy Gillian *b* 1982, — Jeremy Dean (Brambles, Mitchell Fruit Garden, Mitchell, Newquay, Cornwall), *b* 1954; horticulturalist: *m* 1978, Claudia Anhalies Roost, and has issue living, Timothy Peter *b* 1985, Christine Sara *b* 1984, Miriam Anna *b* 1987, — Hilary Jane *b* 1949: *m* 1971, Robert Dale Johnson, of 17 Glenwood Drive, Washington, Penn 15301, USA, and has issue living, Dale Anthony *b* 1974; 1st Lieut USAF, Jeremy Ross *b* 1976. ——Pamela Grey, *b* 1920: *m* 1947, Philip H. Hawkins, of Veryan, 6 Shuteleigh, Wellington, Som TA21 8PG, and has issue living, Jonathan Edward Spencer (Whitmore Cottage, Shawford, nr Winchester, Hants SO21 2BL), *b* 1953: *m* 1978, Sarah Sants Smith, and has issue living, Catherine Sarah *b* 1980, Emily Elizabeth *b* 1982, — Caroline Tessa, *b* 1948: *m* 1971, James Harvey Bradnock, of Russets, 8 Shuteleigh, Wellington, Som TA21 8PG, and has issue living, Thomas Philip *b* 1975; *ed* Exeter Coll, Oxford, Edward James Peter *b* 1978.

PREDECESSORS – (1) Rt Hon Sir WILLIAM DRAPER Best, DCL, 3rd son of late Thomas Best, of Haselbury Plucknett, Somerset; *b* 1767; appointed Solicitor to the Prince of Wales 1813, and Attorney-Gen 1816; sat successively as MP for Petersfield and Bridport; was a Judge of the Common Pleas 1819-24, and Chief Justice of that Court 1824-9; sometime Dep Speaker of House of Lords; *cr Baron Wynford*, of Wynford Eagle, co Dorset (peerage of United Kingdom) 1829: *m* 1794, Mary Anne, who *d* 1840, da of late Jerome Knapp; *d* 1845; *s* by his son (2) WILLIAM SAMUEL, 2nd Baron; *b* 1798: *m* 1821, Jane, who *d* 1895, da of William Thoyts, of Sulhampstead, Berks; *d* 1869; *s* by his son (3) WILLIAM DRAPER MORTIMER, 3rd Baron, *b* 1826: *m* 1857, Caroline Eliza Montague, who *d* 1913, el da of Evan Baillie, of Dochfour; *d* 1899; *s* by his brother (4) HENRY MOLYNEUX, 4th Baron, *b* 1829; *d* 1903; *s* by his cousin (5) GEORGE (son of late Rev Hon Samuel Best, 3rd son of 1st Baron), 5th Baron, *b* 1838: *m* 1870, Edith Anne, who *d* 1924, da of Matthew Henry Marsh, of Ramridge House, Andover; *d* 1904; *s* by his son (6) PHILIP GEORGE, DSO, 6th Baron; *b* 1871; Major (ret) RHA; European War 1914-19 (DSO): *m* 1906, Hon Eva Lilian Napier, who *d* 1974, da of 2nd Baron Napier of Magdala; *d* 1940; *s* by his brother (7) SAMUEL JOHN, 7th Baron, *b* 1874: *m* 1st, 1914, Evelyn Mary Aylmer, who *d* 1929, da of Maj-Gen Sir Edward Sinclair May, KCB, CMG; 2ndly, 1933, Marguerite, who *d* 1966, da of Charles Pratt, and widow of William Kenneth Allies; *d* 1943; *s* by his el son (8) ROBERT SAMUEL, 8th Baron and present peer.

Wynn, family name of Baron Newborough.

WYNNE-JONES, BARONY OF (Wynne-Jones) (Extinct 1982)

DAUGHTERS LIVING OF LIFE BARON (By 1st m)

Hon Kristin, *b* 1931: *m* 1956, Dr Charles Joseph Gallagher, who *d* 1964, and has issue.
Hon Sigrid, *b* 1935: *m* 1962, Dr Marvin Goldiner, of Oakland, Cal, USA, and has issue.

WIDOW LIVING OF LIFE BARON

RUSHEEN (*Baroness Wynne-Jones*) (16 Chelsea Embankment, SW3), da of Neville Preston: *m* 1972, as his second wife, Baron Wynne-Jones (Life Baron), who *d* 1982.

YARBOROUGH, EARL OF (Pelham) (Earl UK 1837)

CHARLES JOHN PELHAM, 8th Earl; *b* 5 Nov 1963; *s* 1991; *ed* Eton, and Bristol Univ: *m* 1990, Anna-Karin, da of George Zecevic, of Montreux, Switzerland, and has issue.

𝕬rms – The two coats of *Pelham* quarterly, viz, 1st and 4th azure, three pelicans argent vulning themselves proper; 2nd and 3rd gules, two pieces of belt erect argent decorated with buckles and studs or. 𝕮rest – A peacock in his pride argent. 𝕾upporters – *Dexter*, a bay horse reguardant, charged on the body with three ancient buckles gold; *sinister*, a water spaniel dog reguardant or, charged on the body with three crosses flory sable.
Seat – Brocklesby Park, Habrough, Lincolnshire DN41 8FB.

SONS LIVING

GEORGE JOHN SACKVILLE (*Lord Worsley*), *b* 9 Aug 1990.
Hon William Charles John Walter, *b* 1991.
Hon James Marcus, *b* 1994.

DAUGHTER LIVING

Lady Margaret Emily, *b* 1997.

SISTERS LIVING

Lady Sophia, *b* 1958: *m* 1983, (Patrick William) John Kinmont, son of Dr Patrick David Clifford Kinmont, of Carlton Ashes House, Hough-on-the-Hill, Grantham, Lincs. *Residence* – Manor Farm House, Rodmarton, Cirencester,

The love of country prevails

Glos GL7 6PE.
Lady Arabella, *b* 1960: *m* 1984, Christopher Casey, only son of late Ronald Casey, of Pecklands Farm, Stansted, Kent, and has had issue, Thomas Edward Ronald, *b* 1993, *d* 1995, — Laura Alexandra, *b* 1986, — Emma Olivia, *b* 1988. *Residence* – Park Wood Farm, nr Leighterton, Tetbury, Glos GL8 8UQ.
Lady Vanessa Petronel, *b* 1961: *m* 1st, 1987 (*m diss* 1995), Timothy Colin Brown, only son of Peter Brindley Brown; 2ndly, 1999, Rupert Michael Colvin Watson, son of Col Michael Colvin Watson, OBE, MC, TD (*see* By Buckland, 1990 Edn). *Residence* – Flat 7, 56 Redcliffe Sq, SW10.

DAUGHTERS LIVING OF FIFTH EARL

(co-heiresses to the Baronies of Fauconberg and Conyers)

Lady Diana Mary, *b* 1920; SRN 1945: *m* 1952, Robert Miller, who *d* 1990, as the result of a motor accident in Harare, and has issue living, Marcia Anne LYCETT, *b* 1954; adopted by Maj Michael H. L. Lycett, whose surname she assumed, and renamed Anthea Theresa (retains right of succession to the baronies), — Beatrix Diana, *b* 1955: *m* 1991, Simon

William Jones Armstrong (Box 49, Gilgil, Kenya), only son of late Christopher Wyborne Armstrong, OBE, of Kwetu Farm, Gilgil, Kenya. *Address* – c/o Zimbank, Box 2270, Harare, Zimbabwe.

Lady (June) Wendy, *b* 1924; late 3rd Officer WRNS; Joint Master Tynedale Hunt 1974-77: *m* 1959, as his 2nd wife, Maj Michael Hildesley Lycett Lycett, CBE, late Royal Scots Greys, Joint Master Tynedale Hunt 1975-77. *Residence* – West Grange, Scots Gap, Morpeth, Northumberland NE61 4EQ.

WIDOW LIVING OF SEVENTH EARL

FLORENCE ANN PETRONEL (*Ann, Countess of Yarborough*), da of late John Herbert Upton, of Ingmire Hall, Yorks, and formerly wife of Lieut Charles John Riddell Duffin, Scots Guards: *m* 1957, the 7th Earl of Yarborough, who *d* 1991. *Residence* – Flat 6, St Albans Mansions, Kensington Court Place, W8 5QH.

PREDECESSORS – (1) CHARLES Anderson-Pelham, MP for Beverley 1768-74, and for Lincolnshire 1774-94, was *cr Baron Yarborough*, of Yarborough, co Lincoln (peerage of Great Britain) 1794; *d* 1823; *s* by his son (2) CHARLES, DCL, FRS, 2nd Baron; sat as MP for Great Grimsby 1803-7, and for Lincolnshire 1807-23; *cr Baron Worsley*, of Appuldurcombe, Isle of Wight, and *Earl of Yarborough* (peerage of United Kingdom) 1837; *d* 1846; *s* by his son (3) CHARLES ANDERSON WORSLEY, 2nd Earl; sat as MP for Newport, Isle of Wight 1830-1, and for N Lincolnshire 1832-47; was Lord-Lieut of co Lincoln; *d* 1862; *s* by his son (4) CHARLES ANDERSON PELHAM, 3rd Earl; *b* 1835; sat as MP for Grimsby 1857-62: *m* 1858, Lady Victoria Alexandrina, who *d* 1927, da of 4th Earl of Listowel; *d* 1875; *s* by his son (5) *Rt Hon* CHARLES ALFRED WORSLEY, KG, 4th Earl; *b* 1859; Vice-Adm and Lord-Lieut for Lincolnshire; Capt of HM's Hon Corps of Gentlemen-at-Arms 1890-92, and Lieut-Col Comdg Lincolnshire Imperial Yeo 1901-7; assumed for himself and issue by Roy licence 1905 the surname and arms of Pelham only: *m* 1886, Hon Marcia Amelia Mary Lane-Fox (*Baroness Fauconberg and Conyers* in her own right), OBE, who *d* 1926, el da of 12th Baron Conyers; *d* 1936; *s* by his son (6) SACKVILLE GEORGE, MC, 5th Earl; *b* 1888; Lieut-Col Comdg Notts Yeo (Sherwood Rangers); European War 1914-19 (MC) European War 1939-45: *m* 1919, Nancye, who *d* 1977, da of late Alfred Brocklehurst; *d* 1948, when the Baronies of Fauconberg and Conyers fell into abeyance between his two daughters, and he was *s* in the Earldom and the Baronies of Yarborough and Worsley by his brother (7) MARCUS HERBERT, 6th Earl, *b* 1893; a DL for Lincs, 1950-66: *m* 1919, Hon Pamela Douglas-Pennant, who *d* 1968, da of 3rd Baron Penrhyn; *d* 1966; *s* by his son (8) JOHN EDWARD, 7th Earl, *b* 1920; Maj Grenadier Guards, Lord Lieut Lincs, High Sheriff 1964: *m* 1957, (Florence) Ann Petronel, da of late John Herbert Upton, of Ingmire Hall, Yorks, and formerly wife of Lieut Charles John Riddell Duffin, Scots Guards; *d* 1991; *s* by his only son (9) CHARLES JOHN, 8th Earl and present peer; also Baron Yarborough, and Baron Worsley.

Yarmouth, Earl of; son of Marquess of Hertford.

Yerburgh, family name of Baron Alvingham.

YORK, DUKE OF, SEE ROYAL FAMILY

Yorke, family name of Earl of Hardwicke.

YOUNG, BARONESS (Young) (Life Baroness 1971)

JANET MARY YOUNG, PC, da of John Norman Leonard Baker; b 23 Oct 1926; ed Headington Sch, Oxford, Prospect Hill Sch, New Haven, Conn, USA, Mt Holyoke Coll, USA, and St Annes Coll, Oxford (MA); Hon Fell of St Anne's Coll, Oxford: DL Oxon 1990; a Member of Oxford City Council 1957-72 (Alderman 1967-72, Leader Conservative Group Oxford City Council 1967-72); a Baroness-in-Waiting to HM 1972-73; Parl Under-Sec of State Dept of Environment 1973-74; Vice Chm Conservative Party Organization 1975-83; (Dep Chm 1977-79, Co-Chm Women's Nat Cttee 1979-83); Min of State, Dept of Educ and Science 1979-81; Chancellor of Duchy of Lancaster 1981-82 and Leader of House of Lords 1981-82; Lord Privy Seal 1982-83; Min of State, Foreign and Commonwealth Office 1983-87; Dir Nat Westminster Bank plc 1987-96, and Marks & Spencer plc 1987-97; Trustee Lucy Cavendish Coll, Camb; a Vice-Pres The West India Cttee since 1988; Chancellor of Greenwich Univ 1993-98, Member of Court of Cranfield Univ since 1992; cr Baroness Young, of Farnworth, co Palatine of Lancaster (Life Baroness) 1971, and PC 1981: m 1950, Dr Geoffrey Tyndale Young, and has issue.
Residence – 23 Northmoor Rd, Oxford.

DAUGHTERS LIVING

Hon Alexandra Janet, b 1951: m 1974, John Douglas Slater, of 12 Edgar Rd, Winchester, Hants, and has issue living, one son and one da.

Hon Rosalind Ann, b 1954: m 1977, Stephen McIntyre, of 48 Taleworth Rd, Ashtead, Surrey, and has issue living, Peter James, b 1981, — David Edward, b 1984.

Hon Juliet Marguerite, b 1962: m 1986, Stephen Paul Brown, elder son of Dr Stanley Brown, of Harborne, Birmingham, and has issue living, Simon Richard, b 1989.

Young, family name of Baron Kennet.

YOUNG OF DARTINGTON, BARON (Young) (Life Baron 1978)

MICHAEL YOUNG, son of Gibson Young, a musician; b 9 Aug 1915; ed Dartington Hall Sch, and London Univ (MA, PhD), Hon LittD Sheffield 1965, Hon Dr Open Univ 1973, Hon DLitt Adelaide 1974; Bar Gray's Inn 1939; Dir of Political and Economic Planning 1941-45, and Sec Research Dept, Labour Party 1945-51; Dir, Inst of Community Studies since 1953, and Trustee, Dartington Hall since 1942 (Dep Chm since 1980); memb NEDC 1975; Pres of Consumers Assocn 1965, Nat Extension Coll 1971, ACE 1976; Chm Mutual Aid Centre, the Tawney Soc 1982; Author; cr Baron Young of Dartington, of Dartington, co Devon (Life Baron) 1978: m 1st, 1945, Joan Lawson; 2ndly, 1960, Sasha, broadcaster and novelist, who d 1993, da of Raisley Stewart Moorsom; 3rdly, 1995, Dorit Uhlemann, and has issue by 1st, 2nd and 3rd m.
Residence – 18 Victoria Park Sq, E2 9PF.

SONS LIVING (By 1st marriage)

Hon Christopher Ivan b 1946.
Hon David Justin (18 Camden Rd, NW1), b 1949.

(By 2nd marriage)

Hon Toby Daniel Moorsom (67 Gibson Sq, N1), b 1963; ed Brasenose Coll, Oxford, Harvard and Trin Coll, Camb; co-founder and ed The Modern Review 1991. Club – Green Street.

DAUGHTER LIVING (*By 1st marriage*)

Hon Emma Dorothy *b* 1956.

(*By 2nd marriage*)

Hon Sophie Ann *b* 1961.

(*By 3rd marriage*)

Hon Gaia Inigo, *b* 199—.

YOUNG OF GRAFFHAM, BARON (Young) (Life Baron 1984)

DAVID IVOR YOUNG, PC, son of Joseph Young, by his wife, Rebecca; *b* 27 Feb 1932; *ed* Christ's Coll, Finchley, and Univ Coll, London (LLB); solicitor 1956; Chm Eldonwall Ltd 1961-75, and Manufacturers Hanover Property Services 1974-84; Dir Town & City Properties Ltd 1972-75; Chm British Organisation for Rehabilitation by Training 1975-80 (Pres 1980-82); Member Admin Cttee World Organisation for Rehabilitation by Training Union 1980-84; Chm Internat Council of Jewish Social and Welfare since 1981; Dir Centre for Policy Studies 1979-82 (Member Management Bd 1977); Member English Industrial Estates Corpn 1980-82; Chm Manpower Services Commn 1982-84; Dept of Industry Industrial Adviser 1979-80, and Special Adviser 1980-82; Member Nat Economic Development Council since 1982; Min without Portfolio 1984-85, Sec of State for Employment 1985-87, for Trade and Industry 1987-89; Pres Inst of Directors since 1993, of Jewish Care since 1990, and of Central Council for Jewish Community Services since 1993; Exec Chm Cable & Wireless plc since 1990; Dir Salomon Inc 1990-94; Trustee Royal Opera House Trust; Hon FRPS; *cr* PC 1984, and *Baron Young of Graffham*, of Graffham, co W Sussex 1984 (Life Baron): *m* 1956, Lita Marianne, da of Jonas Shaw, and has issue.

Arms – Argent eight barrulets azure overall a sword in bend proper hilt pommel and quillons or between two roundels gyronny enarched also gold and azure each within an annulet gold. **Crest** – Within a criclet of roses argent barbed and seeded proper placed alternatively with bluebell flowers also proper a lion's head azure amid a show of three oak trees proper fruited gold. **Supporters** – On either side in front of the exterior rear claws of a lion rampant reguardant or a long-haired dachshund each respectant proper.
Address – 124 Theobalds Rd, WC1X 8RX. **Club** – Savile.

DAUGHTERS LIVING

Hon Karen Debra (*Hon Lady Rix*), *b* 1957; *m* 1983, Sir Bernard Anthony Rix (Hon Mr Justice Rix), son of late Otto Rix, of London, and has issue living, Jacob, *b* 19—, — Gideon, *b* 19—, — Jonathan, *b* 19—, — Hannah, *b* 19—, — Rachel Elsie, *b* 1994.
Hon Judith A., *b* 1960, *m* 1989, Jeremy A. Amias, yr son of Alan Amias, of London.

YOUNG OF OLD SCONE, BARONESS (Young) (Life Baroness 1997)

BARBARA SCOTT YOUNG, da of late George Young, of Perth; *b* 8 April 1948; *ed* Perth Academy, Edinburgh Univ (MA 1970), and Strathclyde Univ; Hon DUniv Stirling 1995; Hon DSc Herts 1997, and Canfield 1998; Senior Administrator, Greater Glasgow Health Board 1973-78; Dir of Planning and Development, St Thomas's Health District; District Gen Administrator, NW District, Kensington, Chelsea and Westminster AHA 1979-82; District Administrator, Haringey Health Authority 1982-85; District Gen Mangr, Paddington and N Kensington Health Authority 1985-88, Parkside Health Authority 1988-91; Chief Executive, Royal Soc for the Protection of Birds (RSPB) 1991-98; Chm English Nature since 1998; Vice-Chm BBC since 1998; Pres Inst of Health Services Management 1987-88; Patron, Inst of Environmental and Ecological Management since 1993; Tstee, Nat Council for Voluntary Organisations 1993-97; Memb World Council, Birdlife International 1994-98; Vice-Pres Flora & Fauna Internat since 1998; Council Memb Forum for the Future since 1999; Memb Sec of State for the Environment's UK Round Table on Sustainability since 1995; Memb Commn on Future of the Voluntary Sector 1995-96, Cttee on the Public Understanding of Science (COPUS) 1996-97, and Min for Agriculture's Advisory Group 1997-98; AHSM 1971; author; *cr Baroness Young of Old Scone*, of Old Scone in Perth and Kinross (Life Baroness) 1997.
Address – House of Lords, Westminster, SW1A 0PW.

Young, Hughes-, family name of Baron St Helens.

YOUNGER OF LECKIE, VISCOUNT (Younger) (Viscount UK 1923, Bt 1911)

Swift and bold

Younger as the years go by

GEORGE KENNETH HOTSON YOUNGER, KT, KCVO, TD, PC, 4th Viscount, and 4th Baronet; *b* 22 Sept 1931; *s* 1997; *ed* Winchester (Fellow 1992), and New Coll, Oxford (MA); Hon LLD Glasgow 1992, Hon DLitt Napier Univ 1992, Hon DUniv Edinburgh 1992, Hon DUniv Paisley 1994; late Major Argyll and Sutherland Highlanders (TA), served BAOR and Korea 1951, Hon Col 154 Regt RCT (V) 1977-85, Brig HM Body Guard for Scotland (Royal Company of Archers); DL Stirlingshire 1968; Gov Royal Scottish Academy of Music 1962-70, Dir Royal Bank of Scotland since 1989 (Chm since 1991), Murray Johnstone Investment Trusts since 1989; Scottish Conservative Whip 1965-67, Dep-Chm Scottish Conservative & Unionist Assocn 1967-70, Joint Parl Under Sec of State for Scotland for Development 1970-74, Min of State for Defence Jan-March 1974, Chm Conservative Party in Scotland 1974-76, Sec of State for Scotland 1979-Jan 1986, Sec of State for Defence 1986-89; MP Ayr Div of Ayrshire and Bute (C) 1964-92; Chancellor of Napier Univ since 1993; Warden of Winchester Coll since 1997; *cr* PC 1979, *Baron Younger of Prestwick*, of Ayr in the District of Kyle and Carrick (Life Baron) 1992, KCVO 1993, and KT 1995: *m* 1954, Diana Rhona, eldest da of late Capt Gerald Seymour Tuck, DSO, RN (ret), of Little London, Chichester, Sussex, and has issue.

𝕬rms – Parted per saltire or and gules, a rose counterchanged, in base a martlet sable, on a chief azure three covered cups or. 𝕮rest – An armed leg couped at the thigh proper, garnished and spurred or. 𝕾upporters – *Dexter*, a lion rampant sable; *sinster*, a wolf argent; both armed and langued gules.
Seat – Leckie, Gargunnock, Stirlingshire FK8 3BN. *Clubs* – Caledonian (London), Highland Brigade.

SONS LIVING

Hon JAMES EDWARD GEORGE, *b* 11 Nov 1955; *ed* Winchester, and St Andrews Univ (MA); MBA, MCIM; Personnel Mangr Coats Patons plc 1979-84; Consultant Angela Mortimer Ltd 1984-86; Asst Dir Stephens Consultancies 1986-92; Dir MacInnes Younger 1991-96: *m* 1988, Jennie Veronica, da of William Wootton, of Chanters House, Pilton, Som, and has issue living, Alexander William George, *b* 13 Nov 1993, — Emily Evelyn, *b* 1990, — Alice Elizabeth, *b* 1992. *Residence* – The Old Vicarage, Dorton, Aylesbury, Bucks. *Club* – New (Edinburgh).

Hon Charles Gerald Alexander, *b* 1959; *ed* Winchester: *m* 1986, Sally Elizabeth, elder da of late Kenneth Mackenzie Neil Fergusson, of Blinkbonny House, Haddingfton, E Lothian, and has had issue, †Freddie *b* and *d* 1995, — Geordie Charles Kenneth, *b* 1997, — Arabella Emily, *b* 1987, — Katrina Louise, *b* 1990, — Georgina Harriet, *b* and *d* 1993, — Francesca Claire, *b* 1996.

Hon Andrew Seymour Robert, *b* 1962; *ed* Winchester: *m* 1989, Hilary Margaret, yst da of Philip Alexander Forbes Chalk, of The Barn House, Hurstbourne Priors, Whitchurch, Hants, and has issue living, Rosanna Lucy, *b* 1994, — Isobel Alexandra, *b* 1996. *Residence* – Fernhill, Cradley, Malvern, Worcs.

DAUGHTER LIVING

Hon Joanna Rosalind, *b* 1958; resumed her maiden name until remarriage: *m* 1st, 1986 (*m diss* 1989), Gregory William Rossiter Cooper, son of late Brian Cooper, of Ealing, W5; 2ndly, 1995, Cmdr John S. M. Davidson, son of late Malcolm Davidson, and of Dr Audrey Dunlop, of Greystones, Lovington, Castle Cary, Som, and has issue living (by 2nd *m*), Molly Diana Audrey, *b* 1996, — Lucy Harriet Alice, *b* 1997. *Residence* – Easter Leckie, Gargunnock, Stirling.

BROTHERS LIVING

Hon Alexander James, *b* 1933; *ed* Winchester, and Worcester Coll, Oxford (BA 1956); late Capt Argyll and Sutherland Highlanders (TA); Dir of Sir Joseph Causton & Sons, Ltd 1963-68; Managing Dir of Robt Maclehose & Co Ltd 1968-77; Dir of Simpson Label Co Ltd, Dalkeith 1980-96; Pres FINAT (European Assocn of Label Printers) 1994-96; Chm Bannockburn Group Riding for the Disabled 1996-98; served Korea 1952: *m* 1959, Annabelle Christine, da of late Gerald Furnivall, of Middle Brook, Bishop's Waltham, Hants, and has issue living, Nicholas Gerald Gilmour, *b* 1963, — Rupert Edward Alexander, *b* 1966; *ed* Winchester, and King's Coll, Aberdeen; Dir Finsbury Ltd since 1994: *m* 1995, Catherine E. P., da of David de Borman, of London, and has issue living, Alec Gilmour *b* 1998, — Amanda Charlotte Frances, *b* 1961: *m* 1st, 1981 (*m diss* 1986), Simon John Miller Richard; 2ndly, 1989 (*m diss* 1998), William Alexander Clark, and has issue living (by 2nd *m*), Ruari Alexander *b* 1990, Harry Edward *b* 1992, — Araminta Lucy, *b* 1967. *Residence* – Wester Leckie, Kippen, Stirlingshire. *Club* – Highland Brigade.

Hon Robert Edward Gilmour, *b* 1940; *ed* Winchester, and New Coll, Oxford (BA), Edinburgh Univ and Glasgow Univ; Sheriff of Glasgow and Strathkelvin 1979-82 Sheriff of Tayside Central and Fife at Stirling and Falkirk 1982-87 and at Stirling and Alloa 1987-92, since when Sheriff at Stirling: *m* 1972, Helen Jane, da of late Eric Gerald Hayes, of Tremelethen, St Mary's, Scilly Isles (*see* Muir, Bt), and has issue living, Fergus Robert, *b* 1975, — Meriel Charlotte, *b* 1973. *Residence* – Old Leckie, Gargunnock, Stirling.

SISTER LIVING

Hon Rosalind Evelyn, *b* 1937 *m* 1960, Thomas Ross Charles Cropper, JP, and has issue living, Charles Thomas Howe (Guntawang, Gulgong, NSW 2852), *b* 1962: *m* 1994, Sophia, da of Antony de Mestre, — Robert Douglas (Greenhills, Willow Tree, NSW 2339), *b* 1969, — Jill Marion, *b* 1961: *m* 1984, Michael John Hawker, of 9 Kylie Av, Killara, NSW 2071, and has issue living, William Thomas George *b* 1990, Annabel Kate *b* 1988, Emma Louise *b* 1993, — Annabel Rosalind, *b* 1966: *m* 1998, Craig Kennedy Williamson, of 29 Cascade St, Paddington, NSW 2021. *Residence* – Greenhills, Willow Tree, NSW 2339, Australia.

WIDOW LIVING OF SON OF SECOND VISCOUNT

Elizabeth Kirsteen (*Hon Lady Younger*) (3 New Buildings, Shore Rd, Old Bosham, W Sussex PO18 8JD), only da of late William Duncan Stewart, JP, of Achara, Duror, Argyll: *m* 1934, Rt Hon Sir Kenneth Gilmour Younger, KBE, who *d* 1976, and has issue (see colls infra).

COLLATERAL BRANCH LIVING

Issue of late Rt Hon Sir Kenneth Gilmour Younger, KBE, yr son of 2nd Viscount, *b* 1908, *d* 1976: *m* 1934, Elizabeth Kirsteen (ante), only da of late William Duncan Stewart, JP, of Achara, Duror, Argyll:—
James Samuel, *b* 1951; *ed* Westminster, and New Coll, Oxford: *m* 1984, Katharine Anne, da of C. K. Spencer, of Abergavenny, Gwent, and has issue living, Edward Kenneth Spencer, *b* 1986. *Residence* – 28 Rylett Cres, W12 9RL.
—— Susannah Mary (23 Av Antoine Béguère, 65100 Lourdes, France), *b* 1936; *ed* Somerville Coll, Oxford (MA).
—— Christina Lucy (41 Charlton, Singleton, W Sussex), *b* 1950; *ed* St Hilda's Coll, Oxford.

PREDECESSORS – **(1)** GEORGE Younger, el son of late James Younger, brewer, of Alloa, by Janet, who *d* 1912, da of late John McEwan, of Alloa; *b* 1851; was Chm of George Younger & Son, Ltd, of Alloa, and a Director of National Bank of Scotland, and of Lloyds Bank, Ltd; Lord-Lieut for Stirlingshire 1926-9; MP for Ayr (*C*) Jan 1906 to Oct 1922; *cr* a *Baronet* 1911, and *Viscount Younger of Leckie*, of Alloa, Clackmannanshire (peerage of United Kingdom) 1923: *m* 1879, Lucy, who *d* 1921, da of Edward Smith, MD, FRS, of Heanor Fall, Derbyshire, and Harley Street, W; *d* 1929; *s* by his son **(2)** JAMES, 2nd Viscount, *b* 1880; Lieut-Col (ret) Fife and Forfar Yeo, Vice-Lieut for Clackmannanshire, a Director of George Younger & Son, Ltd, of Alloa, and Ensign of Roy Co of Archers (King's Body Guard for Scotland); European War 1914-19 (DSO): *m* 1906, Maud, who *d* 1957, da of Sir John Gilmour, 1st Bt; *d* 1946; *s* by his son **(3)** EDWARD GEORGE, OBE, TD, 3rd Viscount, *b* 1906; Lt-Col Argyll and Sutherland Highlanders (TA); Lord Lieut Stirlingshire and Falkirk 1964-79; 1939-45 War as Col Gen Staff (OBE): *m* 1930, Evelyn Margaret, MBE, who *d* 1983, da of late Alexander

Logan McClure, KC, Sheriff of Aberdeen, Kincardine and Banff; *d* 1997; *s* by his elder son **(4)** GEORGE KENNETH HOTSON, 4th Viscount and present peer; also Baron Younger of Prestwick (Life Baron).

YPRES, EARLDOM OF (French) (Extinct 1988)

DAUGHTERS LIVING OF THIRD EARL

(By 1st marriage)

Lady Charlene Mary Olivia, *b* 1946: *m* 1965, Charles Mordaunt Milner (*see* Milner, Bt). *Address* – PO Box 41, Klatmuts, Cape, S Africa.

Lady Sarah Mary Essex, *b* 1953.

Lady Emma Mary Helena, *b* 1958: *m* 1st, 1980 (*m diss* 1989), Charles Geoffrey Humfrey, only son of Charles Michael Humfrey, of Alderney, CI; 2ndly, 1991, Christopher Francis Wolferstan Chanter, son of David Wolferstan Chanter, of The Vine House, Abbots Leigh, Bristol, and has issue living (by 1st *m*), Charles Hamish Lowndes French, *b* 1986, — (by 2nd *m*) Thomas Fulco French Wolferstan, *b* 1992.

(By 2nd marriage)

Lady Lucy Kathleen, *b* 1975.

SISTER LIVING OF THIRD EARL

Lady Patricia Mary Charlemont, *b* 1919: *m* 1942, Henry Edmund Roland Kingsbury (E Bradford, colls), who *d* 1980, and has issue living, Philip Charles Orlando (The Old Farm House, Stoke Row, Henley-on-Thames, Oxon), *b* 1944; *ed* Winchester; late 2nd Lt 15th/19th King's R Hussars: *m* 1971, Huberta Maria Daly, da of late Maj Jobst Heinrich von Reinhard, and has issue living, Julian Henry Orlando *b* 1972, Francis Alexander Lowndes *b* 1973, Oliver Philip Lambart *b* 1976, Mariella Charlotte Pauline *b* 1982, — Gerald Richard Charlemont, *b* 1945; *ed* Winchester: *m* 1975, Clico, only da of Capt Bernard MacIntyre, DSC, RN (ret), of Birdham, Sussex, and has issue living, Thomas Jake Essex Charlemont *b* 1977, Toby Bernard Richard Henry *b* 1979, Gemma Alice Olivia Charlotte *b* 1984.

WIDOW LIVING OF THIRD EARL

DEBORAH (*Countess of Ypres*), da of R. Roberts, of Liverpool: *m* 1972, as his 2nd wife, the 3rd Earl of Ypres, who *d* 1988. *Residence* – 2 Southwood Court, Northway, Hampstead Garden Suburb, NW11.

ZETLAND, MARQUESS OF (Dundas) (Marquess UK 1892, Bt GB 1762)

Try

LAWRENCE MARK DUNDAS, 4th Marquess, 6th Earl of Zetland, 7th Baron Dundas and 8th Baronet; *b* 28 Dec 1937; *s* 1989; *ed* Harrow, and Christ's Coll, Camb; late 2nd Lieut Grenadier Guards; patron of one living; DL N Yorks 1994; Steward Jockey Club since 1992, Dir British Horseracing Board since 1993: *m* 1964, Susan Rose, 2nd da of late Guy Richard Chamberlin, of Shefford House, Great Shefford, Newbury, Berks, and has issue.

ᴀrms – Argent, a lion rampant gules, within a double tressure flory counterflory, all within a bordure azure. Crest – A lion's head affrontée gules, encircled by an oak bush proper. Supporters – Two lions proper, each crowned with an antique crown or, and gorged with a chaplet of oak leaves vert; pendant from each chaplet an escutcheon, that on the *dexter* charged with the arms of *Bruce*, viz argent, a saltire and chief gules, and on a canton argent, a lion rampant azure; that on the *sinister* with the arms of *Fitzwilliam*, viz lozengy or and gules.
Seat – Aske, Richmond, N Yorks DL10 5HJ. *Town Residence* – 9 Crescent Place, SW3 2EA. *Clubs* – All England Lawn Tennis; Jockey.

SONS LIVING

ROBIN LAWRENCE (*Earl of Ronaldshay*) (Olliver, Richmond, N Yorks), *b* 5 March 1965; *ed* Harrow, and RAC Cirencester: *m* 1997, Heather (Hetti) A., elder da of Robert Hoffman, of Maryland, USA, and of Mrs Richard Cazenove, of Cottesbrooke, Northants, and has issue:—

DAUGHTER LIVING—*Lady* Eliza Constance, *b* 1998.

Lord James Edward, *b* 1967; *ed* Harrow, and RAC Cirencester: *m* 1991, Melanie C., eldest da of Robert Henry Whitefield, of The Old Rectory, Stocking Pelham, Herts, and has issue living, Milo James, *b* 1998, — Poppy Alice, *b* 1993, — Emily Rose, *b* 1994. *Residence* – The Fishing Cottage, Stitchcombe, Marlborough, Wilts SN8 2EU.

DAUGHTERS LIVING

Lady Henrietta Kate, *b* 1970: *m* 1994, (James) Mark Ptarmigan Douglas Stroyan (*see* Ropner, Bt (1904), colls, 1985 Edn), and has issue living, Archie Angus, *b* 1999, — Clementine Isabel, *b* 1997. *Residence* – 77 Bramfield Rd, SW11 6PZ.
Lady Victoria Clare, *b* 1973. *Residence* – 41 Norland Sq, Holland Park, W11 4PZ.

BROTHERS LIVING

Lord David Paul Nicholas, *b* 1945; *ed* Harrow, and Central Sch of Speech and Drama; song writer: *m* 1st, 1971 (*m diss* 1995), Corinna, da of Denys Scott, of 11 Glebe Place, SW3; 2ndly, 1997, Taina Betina, only da of Kurt Eberhard Philipp Breuckmann, and has issue living (by 1st *m*), Harry Thomas Jeingo, *b* 1981, — Daisy Star, *b* 1975. *Residence* – 17 Mandeville Courtyard, 142 Battersea Park Rd, SW11 4NB.
Lord (Richard) Bruce, *b* 1951; *ed* Harrow: *m* 1st, 1974 (*m diss* 1981), Jane Melanie, yst da of Ernest Frederick Wright, of 47 Montrose Place, SW1; 2ndly, 1983 (*m diss* 1992), Sophie Caroline, only da of late Henry Giles Francis Lascelles (*see* E Harewood, colls); 3rdly, 1995, Ruth Anne, yr da of Sir Francis Kennedy, KCMG, CBE, of Chorley, Lancs, and has issue living (by 1st *m*), Max, *b* 1978, — Emily Louisa, *b* 1980, — (by 2nd *m*) Flora, *b* 1986, — Tallulah, *b* 1988. *Residence* – 28 Overstrand Gdns, Prince of Wales Drive, SW11 4EZ.

SISTER LIVING

Lady Serena Jane, *b* 1940: *m* 1964, Capt Nigel Ion Charles Kettlewell, JP, RN, and has issue living, Robert James, *b* 1965; *ed* Sherborne, — Melissa Jane, *b* 1968: *m* 1992, John S. Nicholson, yr son of C. J. Nicholson, of E Lambrook, Som, and has issue living, Natasha Coco *b* 1998, — Charlotte Rose, *b* 1970. *Residence* – The Old Rectory, Newton Toney, Salisbury, Wilts SP4 0HA.

WIDOW LIVING OF THIRD MARQUESS

PENELOPE (*Penelope, Marchioness of Zetland*), da of late Col Ebenezer John Lecky Pike, CBE, MC, of Little Glebe, Fontwell, Sussex: *m* 1936, the 3rd Marquess of Zetland, who *d* 1989.

COLLATERAL BRANCHES LIVING (*In remainder to the Earldoms, Barony and Baronetcy*)

Grandchildren of late Frederick James Dundas (infra):—
Issue of late Group Capt Sir Hugh Spencer Lisle Dundas, CBE, DSO, DFC, *b* 1920, *d* 1995: *m* 1950, Hon (Enid) Rosamond Lawrence (*Hon Lady Dundas*) (55 Iverna Court, W8), da of 3rd Baron Trevethin and 1st Baron Oaksey:—

James Frederick Trevor (16 Norland Sq, W11 4PX), *b* (Nov) 1950: *m* 1979, Jennifer A., da of Lt-Col John Daukes, of Chaucers, Seale, nr Farnham, Surrey, and has issue living, David Lawrence Charles, *b* 1989, — Clare Jessica, *b* 1984, — Lucy Rose, *b* 1986. —— Sarah Jane DUNDAS, *b* 1953; has resumed her maiden name: *m* 1977, Terence McGlade, of Toronto, Ontario, Canada and has issue living, Victoria Rose Clare, *b* 1983, — Charlotte Amanda, *b* 1984. —— Amanda Rose, *b* 1956: *m* 1986, Thomas Nicholas McKinlay Service, of 30 Baskerville Rd, SW18 3RS, yr son of late Ian McKinlay Service, and has issue living, George McKinlay, *b* 1992, — Katherine Mary Rose, *b* 1987, — Louisa Amy, *b* 1989.

Grandchildren of late Hon John Charles Dundas, brother of 1st Marquess:—
Issue of late Frederick James Dundas, *b* 1877, *d* 1950: *m* 1913, Sylvia Mary, who *d* 1976, el da of Hugh March Phillips, of Chapel Court, Kenn, near Exeter:—
Elizabeth Mary (*Dowager Lady Muir*), *b* 1914: *m* 1936, Sir John Harling Muir, 3rd Bt, who *d* 1994. *Residence* – Bankhead, Blair Drummond, Perthshire. —— Charmian, *b* 1931: *m* 1955, Maurice R. Snowden, of Manor Cottage, Milton, Banbury, Oxon, and has issue living, John Frederick Hugh, *b* 1955, — Mark Lawrence, *b* 1957.

Grandchildren of late Hon William Fitzwilliam James Dundas (infra):—
Issue of late Robert Bruce Dundas, *b* 1900, *d* 1980: *m* 1934, Enid Mary, da of late Cdr Francis William Roberts, RN:—
David Lawrence (405 Sage St, Gridley, CA 95948-2203, USA), *b* 1936; *ed* Shrewsbury, and Balliol Coll, Oxford (Domus Exhibitioner): *m* 1968 (*m diss* 1995), Faith Dorine, da of Harold Scott, of Friendship, Jamaica, WI. —— Jennifer Elizabeth Mary *b* 1942: *m* 1963, John Warren Williams, of Combe Moor Cottage, Spreyton, nr Crediton, Devon EX17 5AW, and has issue living, Patricia Helen, *b* 1965.

Issue of late Hon William Fitzwilliam James Dundas, brother of 1st Marquess, *b* 1860, *d* 1945: *m* 1892, Mary Maud, who *d* 1945, da of late Lieut-Col H. A. Prinsep:—
Janet Elizabeth, *b* 1911.

Grandchildren of late Hon Cospatrick Thomas Dundas, brother of 1st Marquess:—
Issue of late Vice-Adm John George Lawrence Dundas, CB, CBE, *b* 1893, *d* 1952: *m* 1928, Ruth (255 Buckingham Way, San Francisco, CA 94132, USA), da of Archibald Coleman:—
John Archibald Lawrence (151 Concord St, Apt 34, Newton Lower Falls, Mass 02462, USA), *b* 1942: MD; *ed* Groton, and Harvard Univ: *m* 1967 (*m diss* 1985), Dorothy Polk, da of H. Bradford Washburn, of Boston, Mass, and has issue living, Michael Henry Lawrence, *b* 1969, — Patrick George Bradford, *b* 1973, — Matthew Colgate, *b* 1976, — Jennifer Deirdre, *b* 1971. —— Elgiva Ruth, *b* 1929; PhD: *m* 1951, Penn Thomas Watson, of 4408 Pamlico Drive, Raleigh, N Carolina, USA, and has issue living, Rom Purefoy (378 Central St, Newton, Mass 02166, USA), *b* 1955: *m* 1981, Susan Bazett, — Ruth Coleman, *b* 1952: *m* 1st, 1974 (*m diss* 1978), Jack Barry Tanenbaum; 2ndly, 1982, Jeffrey Scheuer, of 56 West 10th St, New York, NY 10011, USA, — Clare Thomas, *b* 1958: *m* 1st, 1982 (*m diss* 1992), James Acker, MD; 2ndly, 1993, Louis Gallo, of 544 Riverside Drive, Ormond Beach, Florida 32176, USA. —— Rosemary Maud, *b* 1933; MA: *m* 1954, Dr Robert Gray Patton, of 85 Parker Av, San Francisco, Calif 94118, USA, and has issue living, Mary Gray, *b* 1956: *m* 1986, Roger T. Phelps, of 325 El Cerrito Av, Piedmont, Calif 94611, — Sarah Dundas, *b* 1959: *m* 1991, Peter Feichtmeir, of 1611 7th Av West, Seattle, Washington 98119, — Susannah MacRae, *b* 1964: *m* 1995, Christopher Noble, of 120 Blvd Raspail, 75006 Paris, France. —— Deirdre Clare, *b* 1935; MA: *m* 1st, 1958 (*m diss* 1960), Clifford Enright; 2ndly, 1961, Dr Walter Munro Newton, of 325 Crest Rd, Southern Pines, N Carolina 28387, USA, and has issue living, (by 1st *m*) Iva Margaret, *b* 1959: *m* 19—, Jeremy D. C. Peele, — (by 2nd *m*) Walter Monroe, *b* 1962, — Elisabeth Dundas, *b* 1970. —— Alexandra Mary, *b* 1946; PhD: *m* 1st, 1965 (*m diss* 1973), John Andrew Todd; 2ndly, 1988, Stephen Russell Fox, PhD and has issue living (by 1st *m*), John Andrew, *b* 1970.

(*In special remainder to Baronetcy only*)

Grandson of late Thomas George Dundas (infra):—
Issue of late Thomas Archibald Dundas, *b* 1880, *d* 19—: *m* 1903, Sybil Katherine, da of late F. R. Hampshire:—
Thomas Archibald David, *b* 1904.

Grandson of late Joseph Dundas, son of late Lt-Col Thomas Dundas, son of late Thomas Dundas, MP, brother of 1st Bt:—
Issue of late Thomas George Dundas, *b* 1853, *d* 1929: *m* 1879, Mary, who *d* 1923, da of late Lieut-Col Duncan Henry Caithness Reay Davidson, of Tulloch (Mackenzie, Bt, *cr* 1703 (of Gairloch), colls):—
Ronald George, *b* 1885: *m* 1912, Olive Mary, da of Robert Scott-Day, and has issue living, Eleanor Mary, *b* 1914. *Residence* – Los Angeles, California, USA.

PREDECESSORS – (1) LAWRENCE Dundas, Comy-Gen and Contractor to the Army 1747-59; *cr* a *Baronet* 1762 with remainder to his brother Thomas; MP for Edinburgh 1768-81; *d* 1781; *s* by his son (2) *Sir* THOMAS, 2nd Bt; MP for co Stirling 1768-9; Lord-Lieut and Vice-Adm of Orkney and Shetland; *cr Baron Dundas*, of Aske, co York (peerage of Great Britain) 1794; *d* 1820; *s* by his son (3) LAWRENCE, 2nd Baron; successively MP for Richmond and York. Lord-Lieut and Vice-Adm of Orkney and Shetland; *cr Earl of Zetland* (peerage of United Kingdom) 1838; *d* 1839; *s* by his son (4) THOMAS, KG, 2nd Earl; MP for Richmond 1818-30 and 1835-9, and York 1830-32 and 1833-5; Lord-Lieut of N Riding of York, and Grand Master of Freemasons 1844; *s* by his nephew (5) *Rt Hon* LAWRENCE, KT (el son of Hon John Charles Dundas, MP, 4th son of 1st Earl, by Margaret Matilda, who *d* 1907, da of James Talbot, of Mary Ville, co Wexford), 3rd Earl, *b* 1844; MP for Richmond (*L*) 1872-3; Lord-in-Waiting to Queen Victoria 1880, and Lord-Lieut of Ireland 1889-92; *cr* KT 1900, and *Marquess of Zetland* and *Earl of Ronaldshay*, in co of Orkney and Shetland (peerage of United Kingdom) 1892: *m* 1871, Lady Lilian Selina Elizabeth Lumley, who *d* 1943, da of 9th Earl of Scarbrough; *d* 1929; *s* by his el son (6) LAWRENCE JOHN LUMLEY, KG, GCSI, GCIE, PC, 2nd Marquess, *b* 1876; formerly Capt 1st N Riding of Yorkshire Artillery, W Div RA, Major 4th Batn Green Howards, and Hon Col 62nd (Northumbrian) Anti-Aircraft Brig RA (TA), sat as MP for Hornsey Div of Middlesex 1907-16; appointed a Member of Roy Commn on Indian Public Ser 1912, Gov of Bengal 1916, and Pres of Roy Geographical So 1922 (a Trustee thereof 1925-47), and of Roy India So 1923-50; Sec of State for India 1935-40 (also for Burma 1937-40); Chm of Executive Committee of National Trust 1931-45, and Lord Lieut of N Riding of Yorkshire 1945-51; bore Sword of State at Coronation of King George VI: *m* 1907, Cicely, who *d* 1973, da of Col Mervyn Archdale, formerly 12th Lancers; *d* 1961; *s* by his el son (7) LAWRENCE ALDRED MERVYN, 3rd Marquess, *b* 1908; DL N Yorks, Treasurer Royal Masonic Institution for Girls, temp Maj Yorkshire

Yeo, served 1939-45 War in Middle East (despatches): *m* 1936, Penelope, da of late Col Ebenezer John Lecky Pike, CBE, MC, of Little Glebe, Fontwell, Sussex; *d* 1989; *s* by his eldest son **(8)** LAWRENCE MARK, 4th Marquess and present peer; also Earl of Zetland, Earl of Ronaldshay, and Baron Dundas.

ZOUCHE, BARON (Frankland) (Baron E 1308, Bt (E) 1660)
(Title pronounced "Zooch")

JAMES ASSHETON FRANKLAND, 18th Baron and 12th Baronet; *b* 23 Feb 1943; *s* to Baronetcy 1944, and to Barony 1965; Capt 15th/19th King's R Hussars: *m* 1978, Sally Olivia, yr da of Roderic M. Barton, of Brook House, Pulham, St Mary, Norfolk, and has issue.

Arms – Azure, a dolphin naiant embowed or, on a chief of the second two saltires gules. **Crest** – A dolphin hauriant argent and entwined round an anchor erect proper.
Residence – The Abbey, Charlton Adam, Somerton, Somerset TA11 7BE.

SON LIVING

Hon WILLIAM THOMAS ASSHETON, *b* 23 July 1984.

DAUGHTER LIVING

Hon Lucy Victoria, *b* 1982.

AUNT LIVING (*Daughter of Mary Cecil, Baroness Zouche*)

Hon Barbara Mary FRANKLAND, *b* 1906; resumed by deed poll 1958 her maiden surname of Frankland in lieu of that of Lucas: *m* 1st, 1926 (*m diss* 1937), Brig Otho Leslie Prior-Palmer, 9th Lancers (DSO 1945, Knt 1959), who *d* 1986; 2ndly, 1937 (*m diss* 1943), 5th Earl of Normanton, who *d* 1967; 3rdly, 1943 (*m diss* 1962), Peter Lucas, and has issue living, (by 1st *m*) Diana Mary Leslie, *b* 1929: *m* 1974, Bruno de Marco. *Residence* – Ridge House, Stockland, Honiton, Devon.

COLLATERAL BRANCHES LIVING

Issue of late W/Cmdr Hon Roger Nathaniel Frankland, RAuxAF (Res), yr son of Mary Cecil, Baroness Zouche, *b* 1909, *d* 1989: *m* 1st, 1931 (*m diss* 1947), Elizabeth Cecil, who *d* 1968, da of Arthur Cecil Sanday, of 41 Evelyn Gdns, SW7; 2ndly, 1947, Olivia, who *d* 1987, da of late Rev Hon Nigel Campbell (*see* E Cawdor), and widow of Maj Samuel John Rennie Bucknill, Irish Gds:—
(By 1st *m*) Timothy Cecil, *b* 1931; *ed* Charterhouse: *m* 1st, 1957 (*m diss* 1968), Lynette, yr da of Lt-Cmdr Ian Hope Dundas, RNVR; 2ndly, 1986, Elizabeth Greenway, and has issue living (by 1st *m*), Nicholas Charles (East Park House, Handcross, W Sussex RH17 6BD), *b* 1958: *m* 1991, Suzanne H., only da of Michael Race, of Tole House, Keymer, Sussex, and has issue living, Tallulah Cecily *b* 1992, Tatjana Camellia *b* 1994, — Mathew Curzon, *b* 1962: *m* 1999, Sarah Garnham, — Adam Christian *b* 1965. —— Frederick Mark, *b* 1934; *ed* Charterhouse, and Pembroke Coll, Camb (BA).

(In remainder to the Barony only)

Grandchildren of late Emily Anne Curzon (da of late Hon Edward Cecil Curzon, 2nd son of Harriet Anne, Baroness de la Zouche), who *m* 1861, Augustus Frederick Wentworth Gore, formerly 7th Hussars:—
Issue of late Francis Southwell Cecil Charles Gore, Lieut Middlesex Regt, *b* 1879, *ka* 1917: *m* 1904, Frances Rose Mary, who *d* 1974, only da of C. Maybrook:—
Francis Norton Wentworth, CBE, *b* 1906; Brigadier (ret) late RA; OBE (Mil) 1947, CBE (Mil) 1960: *m* 1939, Else Gurli Astrid, da of late Evald Christensen, of Copenhagen, Denmark and has issue living, Peter Wentworth (Saddlers, Mark Cross, Crowborough, Kent), *b* 1946; Capt Queen's Own Hussars: *m* 1975, Joanna Penelope, da of late John Guy Bedford, and has issue living, Emily-Jane Wentworth *b* 1977, Robert Edward Wentworth *b* 1979, — Frances Jane Wentworth, *b* 1947: *m* 1970, Maj Colijn Thomson-Moore, Irish Gds (ret), of 14 Clareville Court, Clareville Grove, SW7, and Barne, Clonmel, co Tipperary, and has issue living, Richard Charles Randal *b* 1978; *ed* Stowe, and RAC Cirencester, Alexandra Louise *b* 1977; *ed* Downe House, and Worcester Coll, Oxford. *Residence* – Vine Cottage, Point Hill, Rye, Sussex TN31 7NP.

PREDECESSORS – **(1)** WILLIAM la Zouche, Lord of Haryngworth, was summoned to Parliament of England as a Baron 1308-14; *d* 1352; *s* by his grandson **(2)** WILLIAM, 2nd Baron; summoned to Parliament during his grandfather's lifetime 1348-51, and after his grandfather's decease 1352-82; *d* 1382; *s* by his son **(3)** WILLIAM, 3rd Baron; summoned to Parliament 1383-94; *d* 1396; *s* by his son **(4)** WILLIAM, KG, 4th Baron; summoned to Parliament 1396-1414; *d* 1415; *s* by his son **(5)** WILLIAM, 5th Baron; summoned to Parliament 1426-63; *d* 1463; *s* by his son **(6)** WILLIAM, 6th Baron, who in 1466 was summoned to Parliament in right of his mother as *Baron St Maur, d* 1468; *s* by his son **(7)** JOHN, 7th Baron; was summoned to Parliament 1482-3; attainted 1485, and attainder reversed 1495; again summoned to Parliament 1509-15; *d* 1526; *s* by his son **(8)** JOHN, 8th Baron; summoned to Parliament 1529-48; *d* 1550; *s* by his son **(9)** RICHARD, 9th

Baron; was summoned to Parliament 1552; *d* 1552; *s* by his son **(10)** GEORGE, 10th Baron; summoned to Parliament 1553-66; *d* 1569; *s* by his son **(11)** EDWARD, 11th Baron; was summoned to Parliament 1571-1625; was Lieut of N and S Wales, and Constable of Dover and Warden of the Cinque Ports; *d* 1625, when the Baronies of Zouche and St Maur became abeyant between his two daus, Elizabeth and Mary, and remained so until 1815, when the abeyance of the Barony of Zouche was terminated in favour of **(12)** *Sir* CECIL Bisshopp, 8th Bt, who became 12th Baron in right of his mother, she being the descendant in the 6th generation of Elizabeth, el da of 11th Baron (ante); *d* 1828, when the baronetcy devolved upon his cousin, and the barony became abeyant between his two daus, Harriet Anne Curzon (infra), and Katherine Annabella, wife of Sir George Richard Brooke-Pechell, 4th Bt; in 1829 the abeyance was terminated in favour of his el da **(13)** HARRIET ANNE, known as Baroness de la Zouche: *m* 1808, Hon Robert Curzon, MP, son of 1st Viscount Curzon (*see* E Howe); *d* 1870; *s* by her son **(14)** ROBERT Curzon, 14th Baron; *b* 1810; was MP for Clitheroe: *m* 1850, Emily Julia, da of the Rt Hon Sir Robert Wilmot-Horton, 3rd Bt; *d* 1873; *s* by his son **(15)** ROBERT NATHANIEL CECIL GEORGE, 15th Baron; *b* 1851: *m* 1875 (*m diss* 1876), Hon Annie Mary Eleanor Fraser, who *d* 1895, 2nd da of 17th Baron Saltoun; *d* 1914; *s* by his sister **(16)** DAREA, *b* 1860; *d* 1917; *s* by her cousin **(17)** MARY CECIL (da of late Col George Augustus Curzon, grandson of late Harriet Anne, Baroness de la Zouche), *b* 1875: *m* 1901, Sir Frederick William Francis George Frankland, 10th Bt, who *d* 1937 (see * infra); *d* 1965 *s* by her grandson **(18)** *Sir* JAMES ASSHETON Frankland (only son of Hon Sir Thomas William Assheton Frankland, 11th Bt), who *s* as 12th Bt 1944 (infra); 18th Baron and present peer.

*(1) WILLIAM, son of *Sir* Henry Frankland of Thirkelby, Yorks, *b c* 1640; MP for Thirsk, *cr* a Baronet of England 1660: *m* 1662, Arabella, who *d* 1687, da of Hon Henry Belasyse, *d* 1697, *s* by his el son **(2)** *Sir* THOMAS, 2nd Bt, *b c* 1665; PMG 1690-1715 and MP for Thirsk, *m* 1683, Elizabeth, who *d* 1733, da of Sir John Russell, 4th Bt (*cr* 1629) by Frances, da of Oliver Cromwell, Lord Protector; *d* 1726; *s* by his el son **(3)** *Sir* THOMAS, 3rd Bt; a Lord of Admiralty 1730-41 and MP for Harwich and Thirsk: *m* 1st, Dinah, who *d* 1741, da of Francis Topham; 2ndly, 1743, Sarah Moseley, who *d* 1783; *d* 1747; *s* by his nephew **(4)** *Sir* CHARLES HENRY, 4th Bt (el son of Henry Frankland, 4th son of 2nd Bt) *b* 1716; Collector at Boston, Mass, 1741-57 and Consul-Gen at Lisbon 1757-67: *m* 1756, Agnes (who *m* 2ndly, 1781, John Drew, banker, and *d* 1783) da of Edward Surriage, of Marblehead, New England; *d* 1768; *s* by his brother **(5)** *Sir* THOMAS, 5th Bt, *b* 1718; Admiral of the White and MP for Thirsk. *m* 1743, Sarah Rhett, of S Carolina, who *d* 1808; *d* 1784; *s* by his el surv son **(6)** *Sir* THOMAS, FRS, 6th Bt, *b* 1750; MP for Thirsk: *m* 1773, Dorothy, who *d* 1820, da of William Smelt; *d* 1831; *s* by his only surv son **(7)** *Sir* ROBERT, 7th Bt; *b* 1784; MP for Thirsk; assumed by Roy Lic 1837 the surname of Russell after Frankland on inheriting Chequers Court, Bucks, from Sir Robert Greenhill Russell, Bt: *m* 1815, Louisa Anne, who *d* 1871, da of Lord George Murray (D Atholl); *d* 1849; *s* by his cousin in the Baronetcy but not the estates **(8)** *Sir* FREDERICK WILLIAM, 8th Bt (el son of Rev Canon Roger Frankland, yst son of 5th Bt), *b* 1793; served at Waterloo and Peninsula: *m* 1821, Katherine Margaret, who *d* 1871, da of Capt Isaac Scarth; *d* 1878; *s* by his el surv son **(9)** *Sir* WILLIAM ADOLPHUS, 9th Bt *b* 1837; Lt-Col RE: *m* 1864, Lucy Ducarel, who *d* 1928, da of Francis Adams, of Clifton, Glos; *d* 1883; *s* by his el son **(10)** *Sir* FREDERICK WILLIAM FRANCIS GEORGE, 10th Bt, *b* 1868; Maj Beds Regt Matabele and S African Wars: *m* 1st, 1890, Charlotte, who *d* 1892, da of John Augustus di Zerega, of New York; 2ndly, 1901, Mary Cecil Curzon, *Baroness Zouche*, who *d* 1965 (ante); *d* 1937; *s* by his el son **(11)** *Hon Sir* THOMAS WILLIAM ASSHETON, 11th Bt, *b* 1902; Maj 15th/19th Hussars: *m* 1st, 1931 (*m diss* 1941), Edna Maud, da of Frederick Hynde Fox; 2ndly, 1942, Pamela Catherine Mabell (ROUS), da of Capt Hon Edward James Kay-Shuttleworth (B Shuttleworth), and who *d* 1972, having *m* 3rdly, 1946 (*m diss* 1968), as his 2nd wife, Henry Michael Barclay; 4thly, 1970, Robert Hugh Pardoe; *d* 1944; *s* by his only son **(12)** *Sir* JAMES ASSHETON, 12th and present Bt, who *s* as 18th Baron Zouche (ante) 1965.

ZUCKERMAN, BARONY OF (Zuckerman) (Extinct 1993)

SON LIVING OF LIFE BARON

Hon Paul Sebastian, *b* 1945; *ed* Rugby, Trin Coll, Camb (MA), and Reading Univ (PhD): *m* 1972 (*m diss* 1987), Mrs Janette Hampel, da of R. R. Mather, of Stoke-by-Clare, Suffolk. *Residence* – The Old Rectory, Grosvenor Rd, SW1. *Club* – Brooks's.

DAUGHTER DECEASED OF LIFE BARON

Hon Stella Maria, *b* 1947: *ed* Cranborne Chase Sch, E Anglia Univ (BA) and London Univ (PhD): *m* 1977, Dr Andrew R. Norman, and *d* 1992, leaving issue, Sebastian Henry Andrew, *b* 1982, — Hester Joanna Rachel, *b* 1978.

WIDOW LIVING OF LIFE BARON

Lady JOAN ALICE RUFUS ISAACS (*Baroness Zuckerman*); JP Birmingham 1961, Norfolk 1967, da of 2nd Marquess of Reading: *m* 1939, Prof Rt Hon Baron Zuckerman, OM, KCB, FRS (Life Baron), who *d* 1993. *Residence* – The Shooting Box, Burnham Thorpe, King's Lynn, Norfolk.

LORDS SPIRITUAL

(Archbishops and Bishops of the Church of England)

ARCHBISHOPS

Canterbury (103rd), George Leonard Carey, *b* 1935 apptd 1991.
York (96th), David Michael Hope, *b* 1940 apptd 1995.

BISHOPS

London (132nd), Richard John Carew Chartres, *b* 1947, apptd 1995.
Durham (93rd), (Anthony) Michael Arnold Turnbull, *b* 1935, apptd 1994.
Winchester (96th), Michael Charles Scott-Joynt, *b* 1943, apptd 1995.
Bath and Wells (76th), James Lawton Thompson, *b* 1936, apptd 1991.
Birmingham (7th), Mark Santer, *b* 1936, apptd 1987.
Blackburn (7th), Alan David Chesters, *b* 1937, apptd 1989.
Bradford (8th), David James Smith, *b* 1935, apptd 1992.
Bristol (54th), Barry Rogerson, *b* 1936, apptd 1985.
Carlisle (65th), Ian Harland, *b* 1932, apptd 1989.
Chelmsford (8th), John Freeman Perry, *b* 1935, apptd 1996.
Chester (40th), Peter Robert Forster, *b* 1950, apptd 1996.
Chichester (99th), Eric Waldron Kemp, *b* 1915, apptd 1974.
Coventry (8th), Colin James Bennetts, *b* 1940, apptd 1998.
Derby (6th), Jonathan Sansbury Bailey, *b* 1940, apptd 1995.
Ely (67th), Stephen Whitefield Sykes, *b* 1939, apptd 1990.
Exeter (69th), (Geoffrey) Hewlett Thompson, *b* 1929, apptd 1985.
Gloucester (39th), David Edward Bentley, *b* 1935, apptd 1993.
Guildford (8th), John Warren Gladwin, *b* 1942, apptd 1994.
Hereford (103rd), John Keith Oliver, *b* 1935, apptd 1990.
Leicester (6th), Timothy John Stevens, *b* 1946, apptd 1999.
Lichfield (97th), Keith Norman Sutton, *b* 1934, apptd 1983.

Lincoln (70th), Robert Maynard Hardy, *b* 1936, apptd 1986.
Liverpool (7th), James Stuart Jones, *b* 1948, apptd 1998.
Manchester (10th), Christopher John Mayfield, *b* 1935, apptd 1993.
Newcastle (11th), (John) Martin Wharton, *b* 1944, apptd 1997.
Norwich (70th), Peter John Nott, *b* 1933, apptd 1985.
Oxford (41st), Richard Douglas Harries, *b* 1936, apptd 1987.
Peterborough (37th), Ian Patrick Martyn Cundy, *b* 1945, apptd 1996.
Portsmouth (8th), Kenneth William Stevenson, *b* 1949, apptd 1995.
Ripon (11th), David Nigel de Lorentz Young, *b* 1931, apptd 1977.
Rochester (106th), Michael James Nazir-Ali, *b* 1949, apptd 1994.
St. Albans (9th), Christopher William Herbert, *b* 1944, apptd 1995.
St. Edmundsbury & Ipswich (9th), (John Hubert) Richard Lewis, *b* 1943, apptd 1997.
Salisbury (77th), David Staffurth Stancliffe, *b* 1942, apptd 1993.
Sheffield (6th), John Nicholls, *b* 1943, apptd 1997.
Sodor & Man (79th), Noel Debroy Jones, *b* 1932, apptd 1989.
Southwark (9th), Thomas Frederick Butler, *b* 1940, apptd 1998.
Southwell (10th), George Henry Cassidy, *b* 1942, apptd 1999.
Truro (13th), William Ind, *b* 1942, apptd 1997.
Wakefield (11th), Nigel Simeon McCulloch, *b* 1942, apptd 1992.
Worcester (112th), Peter Stephen Maurice Selby, *b* 1941, apptd 1997.

PEERS' SONS, DAUGHTERS, BROTHERS AND SISTERS; WIDOWS OF SONS OF PEERS; ALSO GRANDCHILDREN OF DUKES, MARQUESSES AND EARLS
(Bearing Courtesy Titles)

Borkowy, Hon Laura *Mackenzie Stuart, B.*
Borthwick, Hon Alexandra *Borthwick, L.*
Borthwick, Hon Georgina *Borthwick, L.*
Borthwick, Hon J. Henry A. *Borthwick, L.*
Borwick, Hon Angela J. *Borwick, B.*
Borwick, Hon George S. *Borwick, B.*
Borwick, Hon Mary-Anne *Borwick, B.*
Borwick, Hon Patricia G. *McAlpine of Moffat, By.*
Borwick, Hon Robin S. *Borwick, B.*
Boscawen, Hon Charles R. *Falmouth, V.*
Boscawen, Hon Evelyn A. H. *Falmouth, V.*
Boscawen, Hon H. Edward *Falmouth, V.*
Boscawen, Hon Nicholas J. *Falmouth, V.*
Boscawen, Hon Robert T. *Falmouth, V.*
Boscawen, Hon Vere G. *Falmouth, V.*
Bossom, Hon Sir Clive *Bossom, Bt.*
Bossom, Lady Barbara J. *Guilford, E.*
Boteler, Hon Theresa C. R. *Amery of Lustleigh, B.*
Boulton, Hon Crystal Essington- *Russell of Liverpool, B.*
Boulton, (Hon) Kerena A. *Melchett, B.*
Bourke, Hon Mrs Bryan L. *Mayo, E.*
Bourke, Hon Corinne M. J. *Mayo, E.*
Bourke, Hon Eoin P. *Mayo, E.*
Bourke, Hon Harry R. *Mayo, E.*
Bourke, Hon James E. M. *Mayo, E.*
Bourke, Hon Patrick A. *Mayo, E.*
Bourke, Hon Richard T. *Mayo, E.*
Bourke, Hon E. Shân J. Legge- *Glanusk, B.*
Bourne, Hon Michael K. *Bourne, B.*
Bouverie, Lady Belinda Pleydell- *Radnor, E.*
Bouverie, Lady Frances Pleydell- *Radnor, E.*
Bouverie, Hon Hope Pleydell- *Radnor, E.*
Bouverie, Hon Jacob Pleydell- *Radnor, E.*
Bouverie, Hon Jane V. Pleydell- *Gilmour of Craigmillar, B.*
Bouverie, Lady Lucy Pleydell- *Radnor, E.*
Bouverie, Lady Martha Pleydell- *Radnor, E.*
Bouverie, Hon Peter J. Pleydell- *Radnor, E.*
Bouverie, Hon Reuben Pleydell- *Radnor, E.*
Bouverie, Hon Richard O. Pleydell- *Radnor, E.*
Bowater, Hon (Ursula M.) Lady *Dawson of Penn, Vy.*
Bowden, Hon Mary *Bowden, B.*
Bowden, Hon Robin *Bowden, B.*
Bowlby, Lady Ann L. M. *Wharncliffe, E.*
Bowlby, Hon Dorothy A. *North, By.*
Bowness, Hon Caroline *Bowness, B.*
Bowyer, Hon George P. P. *Denham, B.*
Bowyer, Hon Henry M. M. *Denham, B.*
Bowyer, Hon Jocelyn J. *Denham, B.*
Bowyer, Hon Richard G. G. *Denham, B.*
Boxall, Hon Lindsay A. M. *Morris of Castle Morris, B.*
Boyd, Hon Catherine *Jay, B.*
Boyd, Hon James C. E. *Kilmarnock, B.*
Boyd, Hon Jonathan A. L. *Kilmarnock, B.*
Boyd, Hon Robin J. *Kilmarnock, B.*
Boyd, Hon Timothy I. *Kilmarnock, B.*
Boyd, Hon Benjamin A. Lennox- *Boyd of Merton, V.*
Boyd, Hon Christopher A. Lennox- *Boyd of Merton, V.*
Boyd, Hon Edward G. Lennox- *Boyd of Merton, V.*
Boyd, Hon Sir Mark A. Lennox- *Boyd of Merton, V.*
Boyle, Lady Alice D. *Glasgow, E.*
Boyle, Hon Cara M. C. *Cork, E.*
Boyle, Hon C. Reginald *Cork, E.*
Boyle, Hon David M. G. *Glasgow, E.*
Boyle, Hon Davina C. T. *Cork, E.*
Boyle, Lady Georgina S. *Shannon, E.*
Boyle, Hon John W. *Cork, E.*
Boyle, Lady Nell C. *Malmesbury, E.*
Boyle, Hon Robert W. *Cork, E.*
Boyle, Hon Rory J. C. *Cork, E.*
Brabazon, Lady Corinna L. *Meath, E.*
Brabazon, Hon David G. N. *Meath, E.*
Brabazon, Lady Serena A. *Meath, E.*
Brabazon, Hon Anabel M. Moore- *Brabazon of Tara, B.*
Brabazon, Hon Benjamin R. Moore- *Brabazon of Tara, B.*
Bradbeer, Hon Nino N. O. *O'Hagan, B.*
Bradbury, Hon Ben *Bradbury, B.*
Bradbury, Hon John *Bradbury, B.*
Bradbury, Hon Mrs Paul *Bradbury, B.*
Bradby, Hon Josephine J. A. *Barber, B.*
Bradford, Hon Alice T. *Marchamley, B.*
Bradford, Hon Tatiana *Lucas of Chilworth, B.*
Bradley, Hon Elizabeth M. J. Sylvester *Valentia, V.*

Bradley, Hon Melissa C. *Remnant, B.*
Bradshaw, Hon Alison M. *Tangley, By.*
Bradshaw, Hon Diana M. *Polwarth, L.*
Bradstock, Hon Sara V. *Trevethin and Oaksey, B.*
Brady, Hon Charlotte M. T. *ylanmorris, B.*
Bragg, Hon Alice *Bragg, B.*
Bragg, Hon Marie-Elsa *Bragg, B.*
Bragg, Hon Tom *Bragg, B.*
Brain, Hon Elizabeth A. *Tangley, By.*
Brain, Hon Michael C. *Brain, B.*
Braine, Hon Brendan T. *Braine of Wheatley, B.*
Braine, Hon Michael R. *Braine of Wheatley, B.*
Braine, Hon Richard L. *Braine of Wheatley, B.*
Bramall, Hon Nicolas *Bramall, B.*
Brand, Hon Francis A. *Hampden, V.*
Brand, Hon Jonathan C. D. H. *Hampden, V.*
Brand, Hon Laura C. B. *Hambleden, V.*
Brand, Hon Saracha M. *Hampden, V.*
Brand, Hon Virginia L. *Bonham-Carter, B.*
Brander, Lady Evelyn J. B. *Balfour, E.*
Brandon, Hon James R. V. *Brandon of Oakbrook, B.*
Brandon, Hon Richard H. *Brandon of Oakbrook, B.*
Brandon, Hon William R. *Brandon of Oakbrook, B.*
Brandram, Lady Katherine *Royal Family.*
Brandt, Hon Henrietta J. H. *Inchyra, B.*
Branson, Lady Noreen *Sligo, M.*
Branson, Hon Stephana *Warnock, Bs.*
Brassey, Hon Chloe *Brassey of Apethorpe, B.*
Brassey, Hon Edward *Brassey of Apethorpe, B.*
Brassey, Lady Romayne E. A. *Exeter, M.*
Brassey, Hon Thomas I. *Brassey of Apethorpe, B.*
Brassey, Hon Zara *Brassey of Apethorpe, B.*
Bream, Hon Catherine F. L. *Kemsley, V.*
Brett, Hon Christopher L. B. *Esher, V.*
Brett, Hon Emma C. *Pender, B.*
Brett, Hon Guy A. B. *Esher, V.*
Brett, Hon Maurice S. B. *Esher, V.*
Brett, Hon Michael J. B. *Esher, V.*
Brett, Hon Stephen P. B. *Esher, V.*
Brewis, Lady Anne B. M. *Selborne, E.*
Breyer, Hon Joanna F. *Blakenham, V.*
Bridge, Hon Charles C. *Bridge of Harwich, B.*
Bridge, Hon Judith C. *Taylor of Gosforth, B.*
Bridgeman, Lady Alicia N. *Bradford, E.*
Bridgeman, Hon Benjamin T. O. *Bradford, E.*
Bridgeman, Hon Charles G. O. *Bradford, E.*
Bridgeman, Hon Esmond F. R. O. *Bridgeman, V.*
Bridgeman, Hon Henry G. O. *Bradford, E.*
Bridgeman, Hon Luke R. O. *Bridgeman, V.*
Bridgeman, Hon Orlando H. G. *Bridgeman, V.*
Bridgeman, Lady Serena M. *Bradford, E.*
Bridgeman, Hon William O. C. *Bridgeman, V.*
Bridges, Hon Harriet E. *Bridges, B.*
Bridges, Hon Mark T. *Bridges, B.*
Bridges, Hon Nicholas E. *Bridges, B.*
Bridges, Hon Robert O. *Bridges, B.*
Bridges, Hon Susan C. *Auckland, B.*
Brierley, Hon Caroline *Gordon-Walker, B.*
Briggs, Hon Daniel N. *Briggs, B.*
Briggs, Hon Judith S. *Briggs, B.*
Briggs, Hon Matthew W. B. *Briggs, B.*
Brightman, Hon Christopher A. J. *Brightman, B.*
Brimelow, Hon Alison J. *Brimelow, B.*
Brimelow, Hon Elizabeth A. *Brimelow, B.*
Brinckman, Hon (G. Sheira B.) Lady *Harvington, B.*
Brindle, Hon Joan K. *Darwen, B.*
Bristol, Hon Lavinia M. Maclean- *Hawke, B.*
Bristow, Hon Caroline J. *Luke, B.*
Broadbridge, Hon Mrs Howard E. *Broadbridge, B.*
Broadbridge, Hon Mrs Hugh T. *Broadbridge, B.*
Broadbridge, Hon Jemima L. *Broadbridge, B.*
Broadbridge, Hon Mrs Rupert G. *Broadbridge, B.*
Broadbridge, Hon Sophie M. *Broadbridge, B.*
Brockway, Hon Christopher F. *Brockway, B.*
Brodie, Hon Vanessa N. M. *Hawke, B.*
Brodrick, Hon Ashley R. *Midleton, V.*
Brodrick, Hon Charlotte H. *Midleton, V.*
Brodrick, Hon Hester W. *Hastings, B.*
Brodrick, Hon William M. *Midleton, V.*
Bromage, Hon Jaqumine *Rendlesham, B.*
Bromet, Hon Victoria *Braybrooke, B.*
Bronfman, Lady Caroline E. A. *Townshend, M.*
Brook, Hon Catherine M. *Hawke, B.*
Brooke, Hon Christopher A. *Brookeborough, V.*
Brooke, Hon Sir Henry *Brooke of Cumnor, By.*
Brooke, Hon (Katharine E.) Lady *Hussey of North Bradley, B.*
Brooke, Lady Melissa E. C. *Dunraven, E.*
Brooke, Hon Nancy M. *Hindlip, B.*

Coggan, Hon Dorothy A. *Coggan, B.*
Coggan, Hon Ruth E. *Coggan, B.*
Cohen, Hon Mrs Hugh L. *Cohen, By.*
Cohen, Hon John C. C. *Cohen of Brighton, B.*
Cohen, Hon Leonard H. L. *Cohen, By.*
Cohen, Hon Felicity A. Waley- *Bearsted, V.*
Cohen (Joyce C. I.) Lady Waley-, *Nathan, B.*
Cokayne, Hon Dorothy G. *Cullen of Ashbourne, B.*
Cokayne, Hon Edmund W. M. *Cullen of Ashbourne, B.*
Coke, Hon Hermione B. *Leicester, E.*
Coke, Hon Rupert H. J. *Leicester, E.*
Coke, Hon Wenman J. *Leicester, E.*
Cole, Hon Cecilia A. *Ridley, V.*
Cole, Lady Emma F. *Enniskillen, E.*
Cole, Hon Jonathan D. *Cole, B.*
Cole, Hon Juliet A. *Cole, B.*
Cole, Lady Lucy C. *Enniskillen, E.*
Cole, Hon Jane E. Butler- *Napier of Magdala, B.*
Coleridge, Hon James D. *Coleridge, B.*
Coleridge, Lady M. Georgina C. *Tweeddale, M.*
Coleridge, Hon Katharine S. *Coleridge, B.*
Coleridge, Hon Samuel J. T. *Coleridge, B.*
Coleridge, Hon Sophia T. *Coleridge, B.*
Coleridge, Hon Vanessa L. *Coleridge, B.*
Coles, Hon Bridget *Rankeillour, B.*
Collier, Hon James A. *Monkswell, B.*
Collier, Hon Laura J. *Monkswell, B.*
Collier, Hon Lorna E. *Monkswell, B.*
Collier, Hon Robert W. G. *Monkswell, B.*
Collier, Hon Muriel J. L. *Rochester, B.*
Collin, Lady Clarissa *Feversham, B.*
Collings, Lady Louisa E. *Richmond, D.*
Collins, Hon Ian G. V. *Stonham, B.*
Collins, Hon Katharine A. *Hailsham of St Marylebone, B.*
Collins, Lady Sara E. *Donoughmore, E.*
Collins, Hon Sir Stephen O. H. *Collins, By.*
Colman, Hon Cynthia *Sherfield, B.*
Colman, Lady Mary C. *Strathmore, E.*
Coltman, Hon Mary C. *Whitelaw, V.*
Colville, Hon Alexander F. G. *Colville of Culross, V.*
Colville, Hon Andrew J. *Clydesmuir, B.*
Colville, Hon C. Anthony *Colville of Culross, V.*
Colville, Hon Charles M. T. *Colville of Culross, V.*
Colville, Hon Edmund C. *Colville of Culross, V.*
Colville, Hon Hamish *Clydesmuir, B.*
Colville, Hon Harriet *Clydesmuir, B.*
Colville, Lady Joan *Jersey, E.*
Colville, Lady Margaret *Sutherland, D.*
Colville, Hon R. James I. *Colville of Culross, V.*
Colville, Hon Rachel *Clydesmuir, B.*
Colville, Hon Richard *Clydesmuir, B.*
Colville, Hon Rupert G. S. *Colville of Culross, V.*
Colvin, Hon Nichola *Cayzer, B.*
Combe, Lady Mary E. C. *Kilmorey, E.*
Combe, Lady Silvia B. *Leicester, E.*
Compton, Lady Emily R. *Northampton, M.*
Compton, Lady Lara K. *Northampton, M.*
Compton, Lady Louisa *Northampton, M.*
Compton, Lady Tania F. *Clanwilliam, E.*
Compton, Lord William J. B. *Northampton, M.*
Connell, Lady Alexandra V. C. A. *Erroll, E.*
Connell, Lady Susan J. *Northesk, E.*
Connolly, Hon Perdita C. *Tweedsmuir, B.*
Constantine, Hon Roy *Constantine of Stanmore, B.*
Conwy, Hon Charlotte S. G. Rowley- *Langford, B.*
Conwy, Hon Christopher G. H. Rowley- *Langford, B.*
Conwy, Hon John S. Rowley- *Langford, B.*
Conwy, Hon Owen G. Rowley- *Langford, B.*
Conwy, Hon Peter A. Rowley- *Langford, B.*
Conyngham, Lord F. W. Patrick *Conyngham, M.*
Conyngham, Lady Henrietta T. J. *Conyngham, M.*
Conyngham, Lady John *Conyngham, M.*
Conyngham, Lord Simon C. E. W. *Conyngham, M.*
Conyngham, Lady Tamara J. *Conyngham, M.*
Cook, Hon Sarah I. *Murray of Epping Forest, B.*
Cooke, Hon Christopher M. D. *Cooke of Thorndon, B.*
Cooke, Hon Francis M. R. *Cooke of Thorndon, B.*
Cooke, Hon James V. F. *Cooke of Islandreagh, B.*
Cooke, Hon Michael J. A. *Cook of Islandreagh, B.*
Cooke, Hon Philip M. B. *Cooke of Thorndon, B.*
Cooke, Hon Sarah M. M. *Kenyon, B.*
Cooke, Hon Victoria S. *Cooke of Islandreagh, B.*
Cookson, Hon Angela M. M. *Hemphill, B.*
Cooper, Hon Jason C. D. B. *Norwich, V.*
Cooper, Lady Maureen I. *Clancarty, E.*
Cooper, Hon Mrs A. John P. H. Ashley *Shaftesbury, E.*

Cooper, Lady Frances M. E. Ashley- *Shaftesbury, E.*
Cooper, Hon Nicholas E. A. Ashley- *Shaftesbury, E.*
Cooze, Hon Tania R. Harcourt *Coleridge, B.*
Cope, Hon Nicola L. *Cope of Berkeley, B.*
Copley, Hon David G. Bewicke *Cromwell, B.*
Copley, Hon Helen T. Bewicke- *Cromwell, B.*
Copley, Hon Thomas D. Bewicke- *Cromwell, B.*
Copsey, Hon Jenifer C. *Healey, B.*
Corbett, Hon Catherine *Acton, B.*
Corbett, Hon John P. C. *Rowallan, B.*
Corbett, Hon Joseph M. *Rowallan, B.*
Corbett, Hon Melanie J. *Moynihan, B.*
Corcuera, Lady Mary V. S. *Gosford, E.*
Cordingley, Lady Emma G. A. *Portsmouth, E.*
Corke, Hon Shirley F. *Bridges, B.*
Cormack, Hon G. R. Jean *Davies, B.*
Cormack, Lady Miranda M. *Kilmuir, E.*
Cornwallis, Hon F. W. Jeremy *Cornwallis, B.*
Cornwallis, Hon P. W. David *Cornwallis, B.*
Cornwallis, Hon Vanessa R. *Cornwallis, B.*
Corrall, Hon Sheila M. *Lowry, B.*
Corran, Hon Miranda A. *Chaplin, Vy.*
Corry, Lady Martha C. Lowry- *Belmore, E.*
Corry, Hon Montagu G. G. Lowry- *Belmore, E.*
Corry, Hon Rosemary D. L. Lowry- *Plumer, V.*
Corry, Hon Juliet E. Steuart- *Milverton, B.*
Corsar, Hon Dame Mary D. *Balerno, B.*
Cosgrave, Lady Louisa *Cathcart, E.*
Cotterell, Hon Caroline V. *Boyne, V.*
Cotterell, Hon Harriet P. S. *Camoys, B.*
Cotton, Hon David P. D. Stapleton- *Combermere, V.*
Cotton, Hon Thomas R. W. Stapleton- *Combermere, V.*
Cottrell, Hon Fiona C. M. *Manton, B.*
Coulson, Hon Elizabeth A. *Crowther-Hunt, B.*
Courtenay, Lady Camilla G. *Devon, E.*
Courtenay, Hon Camilla M. *Devon, E.*
Courtenay, Hon Charles P. *Devon, E.*
Courtenay, Hon Eleonora V. *Devon, E.*
Courtenay, Lady Mary E. *Devon, E.*
Coutanche, Hon John A. G. *Coutanche, By.*
Coutts, Hon Crispin J. A. N. Money- *Latymer, B.*
Coutts, Hon Fanny C. M. Money- *Latymer, B.*
Coutts, Hon Giles T. N. Money- *Latymer, B.*
Coutts, Hon Henry E. Money- *Latymer, B.*
Coutts, Hon Hugo N. Money- *Latymer, B.*
Coutts, Hon Penelope A. C. Money- *Emmet of Amberley, By.*
Coutts, Hon Vera C. M. Money- *Latymer, B.*
Coventry, Lady Anne D. *Coventry, E.*
Coventry, Lady Maria A. *Coventry, E.*
Cowan, Hon Mary L. *Dilhorne, V.*
Cowell, Hon Cressida *Blakenham, V.*
Cowen, Hon Shelagh M. *Rank, B.*
Cowdray, Lady Anne P. B. *Bradford, E.*
Cowdray, Hon Christopher S. *Cowdrey of Tonbridge, B.*
Cowdrey, Hon Graham R. *Cowdrey of Tonbridge, B.*
Cowdray, Hon Jeremy C. *Cowdrey of Tonbridge, B.*
Cowieson, Hon Frances F. D. *Chetwynd, V.*
Cox, Hon Christopher W. Roxbee *Kings Norton, B.*
Cox, Hon Jeremy W. Roxbee *Kings Norton, B.*
Craig, Hon Christopher C. B. *Craig of Radley, B.*
Craig, Hon Roxane Laird *Balfour of Inchrye, B.*
Craigie, Hon Emma B. *Rees-Mogg, B.*
Cram, Lady Jeanne L. *Argyll, D.*
Craufurd, Hon Caroline H. Houison *Kemsley, V.*
Craven, Hon Frances L. *Addington, B.*
Crawford, Hon Grania E. *Rathcavan, B.*
Crawford, Lady Susanna *Eglinton, E.*
Cresswell, Hon Alexandra *Lane of Horsell, B.*
Cretton, Hon Catherine A. *de Vesci, B.*
Crewdson, Hon L. Clare *Grimthorpe, B.*
Crews, Hon Anne P. *Boston, B.*
Croft, Hon Bernard W. H. P. *Croft, B.*
Crofton, Hon Mrs A. Marcus L. *Crofton, B.*
Crofton, Hon C. Marus G. *Crofton, B.*
Crofton, Hon E. Harry P. *Crofton, B.*
Crofton, Hon Freya C. *Crofton, B.*
Crofton, Hon Georgiana A. *Crofton, B.*
Crolla, Hon S. P. Rose *Cornwallis, B.*
Cronin, Hon Jane *Elton, B.*
Cronshaw, Lady Miranda *Lonsdale, E.*
Crook, Hon Catherine H. *Crook, B.*
Crook, Hon Robert D. *Crook, B.*
Crookenden, Hon (Patricia N.) Lady *Kindersley, E.*
Cropper, Hon Rosalind E. *Younger of Leckie, V.*
Cross, Hon L. G. Kilorn *Ebury, B.*

Fremantle, Hon Edward W. *Cottesloe, B.*
Fremantle, Hon Elizabeth C. J. *Cottesloe, B.*
Fremantle, Hon Katharine D. H. *Cottesloe, B.*
Fremantle, Hon Thomas F. H. *Cottesloe, B.*
French, Lady Lucy K. *Ypres, E.*
French, Hon Fulke Charles A. J. *De Freyne, B.*
French, Hon Mrs Hubert J. *De Freyne, B.*
French, Hon Patrick F. *De Freyne, B.*
French, Lady Rosemary *Inchcape, E.*
French, Lady Sarah M. E. *Ypres, E.*
Frewen, Hon Sarah J. *Valentia, V.*
Freyberg, Hon Annabel P. *Freyberg, B.*
Freyberg, Hon Christina M. G. *Freyberg, B.*
Frost, Lady Carina M. G. *Norfolk, D.*
Frost, Hon Marygold *Hillingdon, By.*
Frost, Hon Raymond *Gaitskell, Bs.*
Fuchs, Hon Rose S. I. M. ffrench- *ffrench, B.*
Fullard, Hon Glenys *Macdonald of Gwaenysgor, B.*
Fuller, Hon Geraldine, A. *Southampton, B.*
Fulton, Hon Alan *Fulton, B.*
Fulton, Hon Charity *Fulton, B.*
Fulton, Hon Duncan *Fulton, B.*
Fulton, Hon Oliver *Fulton, B.*
Gabriel, Hon Jill G. *Moore of Wolvercote, B.*
Gaddipati, Hon Frances A. *Wimborne, V.*
Gaff, Hon Elizabeth F. *Byers, By.*
Gage, Hon David B. *Gage, V.*
Gage, Hon Henry W. *Gage, V.*
Galbraith, Hon Annabel J. S. S. *Strathclyde, B.*
Galbraith, Hon Charles W. du R. de B. *Strathclyde, B.*
Galbraith, Hon David M. G. *Strathclyde, B.*
Galbraith, Hon Elisabeth I. S. *Strathclyde, B.*
Galbraith, Hon Heather M. A. G. *Strathclyde, B.*
Galbraith, Hon Ida, J. G. *Strathclyde, B.*
Galbraith, Hon James M. G. *Strathclyde, B.*
Galbraith, Hon Norman D. G. *Strathclyde, B.*
Galbraith, Hon Rose M-L. S. *Strathclyde, B.*
Gallacher, Hon Robert J. *Gallacher, B.*
Gallagher, Hon Kristin *Wynne-Jones, B.*
Galpern, Hon Maurice L. *Galpern, B.*
Gamester, Lady Jane M. *Annesley, E.*
Gannon, Hon Catherine S. *Eccles V.*
Ganzoni, Hon Mary J. *Belstead, B.*
Garber, Hon Fiona *Monteagle of Brandon, B.*
Gardiner, Hon Carol *Gardiner, B.*
Gardner, Hon Joanna M. *Gardner of Parkes, Bs.*
Gardyne, Hon Adam G. J. Bruce- *Bruce-Gardyne, B.*
Gardyne, Hon Thomas A. Bruce- *Bruce-Gardyne, B.*
Garnell, Lady Caroline L. *Bradford, E.*
Garner, Hon Christopher J. S. *Garner, B.*
Garner, Hon Joseph J. *Garner, B.*
Garnett, Hon Anne J. E. *Delamere, B.*
Garnett, Hon Dariel *Rawlinson, B.*
Garnett, Hon Sylvia J. *Swann, B.*
Garnier, Hon Lavender H. *Walsingham, B.*
Garnsworthy, Hon Charles, E. *Garnsworthy, B.*
Garton, Hon Annabel J. *Hudson, Vy.*
Garton, Hon Ines M. *Nunburnholme, B.*
Garton, Lady Lucy C. M. *Rosebery, E.*
Gaskell, Hon Jessica A. *Hillingdon, By.*
Gascoigne, Hon E. Ann *Harcourt, V.*
Gascoigne, Hon Olivia C. T. *Esher, V.*
Gaussen, Hon Diana B. *Hereford, V.*
Gaussen, Lady Mary E. *Amherst, E.*
Geddes, Hon Mrs David C. *Geddes, B.*
Geddes, Hon James G. N. *Geddes, B.*
Geddes, Hon Mrs John R. C. *Geddes, B.*
Gee, Hon Joan M. *Hives, B.*
Gee, Hon Lucy Kemp- *Cobham, V.*
Gelernter, Hon Linda J. *Morris of Kenwood, B.*
Gellhorn, Hon Olive S. *Layton, B.*
George, Hon Clare M. Lloyd *Tenby, V.*
George, Hon Robert J. D. Lloyd *Lloyd George of Dwyfor, E.*
George, Hon Sara G. Lloyd *Tenby, V.*
George, Hon Timothy H. G. Lloyd *Tenby, V.*
Gibb, Hon Annabel M. *Howie of Troon, B.*
Gibbings, Hon (Louise B.) Lady *Lambert, V.*
Gibbs, Hon Alexandra R. C. M. *Killearn, B.*
Gibbs, Hon Elizabeth B. *Howick of Glendale, B.*
Gibbs, Hon Sir Eustace H. B. *Wraxall, B.*
Gibbs, Hon George H. P. *Aldenham, B.*
Gibbs, Lady Hilaria A. *Mount Edgcumbe, E.*
Gibbs, Hon Humphrey W. F. *Aldenham, B.*
Gibbs, Hon Jessica J. M. *Aldenham, B.*
Gibbs, Hon Rosalind M. *Aldenham, B.*
Gibbs, Hon S. Marcia *Kimball, B.*
Gibbs, Lady Sarah *Lucan, E.*

Gibbs, Hon Thomas A. J. *Aldenham, B.*
Gibbs, Lady Virginia *Stradbroke, E.*
Gibson, Hon Camilla *Davidson, V.*
Gibson, Hon Clive P. *Gibson, B.*
Gibson, Hon E. Charles D. *Ashbourne, B.*
Gibson, Hon Frances P. *Phillimore, B.*
Gibson, Hon Frances T. *O'Hagan, B.*
Gibson, Hon Hugh M. T. *Gibson, B.*
Gibson, Hon Patrick M. *Ashbourne, B.*
Gibson, Hon Piers N. *Gibson, B.*
Gibson, Hon Mrs W. David *Ashbourne, B.*
Gibson, Hon W. Rodney C. *Ashbourne, B.*
Gibson, Hon William K. *Gibson, B.*
Gifford, Hon Polly A. *Gifford, B.*
Gifford, Hon Thomas A. *Gifford, B.*
Gilbert, Hon Amanda *Gilbert, B.*
Gilbert, Hon Caroline *Gilbert, B.*
Gilbert, Hon Emma D. M. Johnson- *Terrington, B.*
Gilbey, Hon Anthony W. *Vaux of Harrowden, B.*
Gilbey, Hon Mary A. M. *Vaux of Harrowden, B.*
Gilbey, Hon Michael C. *Vaux of Harrowden, B.*
Gilbey, Lady Penelope A. *Stradbroke, E.*
Gilbey, Hon William J. *Vaux of Harrowden, B.*
Giles, Lady Katharine P. *De La Warr, E.*
Gillies, Hon Jane C. *Kilmany, By.*
Gillmore, Hon Julian *Gillmore of Thamesfield, B.*
Gillmore, Hon Paul *Gillmore of Thamesfield, B.*
Gilmour, Hon Andrew J. *Gilmour of Craigmillar, B.*
Gilmour, Hon Christopher S. *Gilmour of Craigmillar, B.*
Gilmour, Hon David R. *Gilmour of Craigmillar, B.*
Gilmour, Hon Elizabeth *Cayzer, B.*
Gilmour, Hon Oliver, J. *Gilmour of Craigmillar, B.*
Gimena, Lady Anne-Marie I. Perez-Andujar *Dudley, E.*
Girling, Hon Eleanor, B. *Addison, V.*
Gladstone, Hon Josephine *Elwyn-Jones, B.*
Gladwin, Hon James *Gladwin of Clee, B.*
Glanvill, Hon Amanda *Howe of Aberavon, B.*
Glassbrook, Hon Karen M. *Steyn, B.*
Glasse, Lady Margaret N. *Caithness, E.*
Glennie, Hon Jane M. T. *Dormer, B.*
Glodek, Lady Jennifer *Atholl, D.*
Glover, Lady Sarah J. Thomson *Craven, E.*
Glyn, Hon Andrew J. *Wolverton, B.*
Glyn, Hon Joanna C. *Wolverton, B.*
Glyn, Lady Rosula C. *Plymouth, E.*
Godber, Hon A. Robin *Godber of Willington, By.*
Godber, Hon Richard T. *Godber of Willington, By.*
Godfrey, Hon S. Lois *Mitchison, By.*
Godley, Hon Christopher J. *Kilbracken, B.*
Godley, Hon Seán G. *Kilbracken, B.*
Godley, Hon Wynne A. H. *Kilbracken, B.*
Godsal, Lady Elizabeth C. *Courtown, E.*
Goff, Hon Angela E. *Airedale, By.*
Goff, Hon Juliet M. C. *Goff of Chieveley, B.*
Goff, Hon Katharine I. *Goff of Chieveley, B.*
Goff, Hon R. Thomas A. *Goff of Chieveley, B.*
Gold, Hon Jocelyne M. *Trent, By.*
Goldby, Hon Helen R. *Tomlin, By.*
Goldiner, Hon Sigrid *Wynne-Jones, B.*
Goldsmith, Lady Annabel *Londonderry, M.*
Goodale, Hon Pamela M. D. *Hirst, By.*
Goodhart, Hon Annabel F. *Goodhart, B.*
Goodhart, Hon Benjamin H. *Goodhart, B.*
Goodhart, Hon Laura *Goodhart, B.*
Goodman, Hon Janet T. *Sidmouth, V.*
Goodrich, Hon Audrey *Elton, B.*
Goodwin, Hon Gillian T. M. *Chorley, B.*
Goold, Hon James D. *Goold, B.*
Goold, Hon Michael K. *Goold, B.*
Goolden, Hon Rosemary *Ullswater, V.*
Gordon, Lady Adam G. *Huntly, M.*
Gordon, Lord Alastair N. J. *Aberdeen, M.*
Gordon, Lady Amy J. *Huntly, M.*
Gordon, Lady Anna K. *Aberdeen, M.*
Gordon, Hon Caroline R. T. *Berners, Bs.*
Gordon, Hon Christopher J. *Gordon of Strathblane, B.*
Gordon, Lord Douglas C. A. *Huntly, M.*
Gordon, Hon Michael S. *Gordon of Strathblane, B.*
Gordon, Lady Roderic A. *Huntly, M.*
Gordon, Lady Rose M.-L. *Huntly, M.*
Gordon, Hon Sam D. *Aberdeen, M.*
Gordon, Hon Sarah J. *Gordon of Strathblane, B.*
Gore, Lady Barbara S. *Eglinton, E.*
Gore, Lady Laura M. *Arran, E.*
Gore, Lady Lucy K. *Arran, E.*
Gore, Lady Mary S. *Selborne, E.*

McDonnell, Lady Rachel *Antrim, E.*
McDougall, Hon Carolyn J. *Griffiths, B.*
MacDowel, Hon Angela C. *Hazlerigg, B.*
McFadyen, Hon Anna J. *Goold, B.*
McFadzean, Hon Gordon B. *McFadzean, B.*
Macfarlane, Hon Hamish *Macfarlane of Bearsden, B.*
Macfarlane, Hon Marguerite *Macfarlane of Bearsden, B.*
McGowan, Hon A. Charlotte *Eden of Winton, B.*
McGowan, Hon Catriona C. H. *McGowan, B.*
McGowan, Hon Dominic J. W. *McGowan, B.*
McGowan, Hon Harry J. C. *McGowan, B.*
Macgowan, Hon Jane A. *Casey, By.*
McGowan, Hon Mungo A. C. *McGowan, B.*
McGrath, Hon Virginia M. *Carew, B.*
MacGreevy, Hon Catriona M. *Craigmyle, B.*
McGregor, Hon Alistair J. *McGregor of Durris, B.*
McGregor, Hon Gregor W. *McGregor of Durris, B.*
McGregor, Hon W. Ross *McGregor of Durris, B.*
McIlroy, Hon Elizabeth N. *Rochester, B.*
McIndoe, Lady Felicity A. A. *Courtown, E.*
MacInnes, Hon Janitha S. *Craigavon, V.*
McIntosh, Hon Francis R. *McIntosh of Haringey, B.*
McIntosh, Hon Philip H. S. *McIntosh of Haringey, B.*
Mackay, Hon Æneas S. *Reay, L.*
Mackay, Hon Asia B. *Tanlaw, B.*
Mackay, Lady Ailsa F. *Inchcape, E.*
Mackay, Hon Mrs Alan J. F. *Inchcape, E.*
Mackay, Baron (and Hon) Alexander W. R. *Reay, L.*
Mackay, Hon Antonia *Reay, L.*
Mackay, Hon Brooke *Tanlaw, B.*
Mackay, Hon Caroline *Mackay of Drumadoon, B.*
Mackay, Hon Colin J. *Mackay of Ardbrecknish, B.*
Mackay, Hon Cynthia *Vansittart, B.*
Mackay, Hon David F. *Mackay of Ardbrecknish, B.*
Mackay, Hon Diana *Mackay of Drumadoon, B.*
Mackay, Hon Edward A. *Reay, L.*
Mackay, Lady Elspeth *Inchcape, E.*
Mackay, Hon Fiona J. *Mackay of Ardbrecknish, B.*
Mackay, Hon Isabel V. *Reay, L.*
Mackay, Hon Iona H. *Tanlaw, B.*
Mackay, Hon Ivan C. *Inchcape, E.*
Mackay, Hon James *Mackay of Clashfern, B.*
Mackay, Hon James B. *Tanlaw, B.*
Mackay, Hon James J. T. *Inchcape, E.*
Mackay, Hon Laura E. *Reay, L.*
Mackay, Lady Lucinda L. *Inchcape, E.*
Mackay, Hon Shane L. *Inchcape, E.*
Mackay, Hon Shona R. *Mackay of Clashfern, B.*
Mackay, Hon Simon *Mackay of Drumadoon, B.*
McKenna, Lady Cecilia E. *Albemarle, E.*
Mackenzie, Hon Alasdair *Cromartie, E.*
Mackenzie, Hon Andrew C. *Mackenzie of Framwellgate, B.*
Mackenzie, Hon Brian T. *Mackenzie of Framwellgate, B.*
Mackenzie, Lady Anne M. I. *Grafton, D.*
Mackenzie, Lady Gilean F. *Cromartie, E.*
Mackenzie, Lady Jean *Rothes, E.*
Mackenzie, Hon S. A. Julia *Cromartie, E.*
Mackeson, Hon (Camilla) Lady *Keith of Castleacre, B.*
Mackie, Hon George Y. *John-Mackie, B.*
Mackie, Hon James A. *John-Mackie, B.*
Mackie, Hon John M. *John-Mackie, B.*
Mackie, Hon Mary Y. *John-Mackie, B.*
Mackinnon, Hon Eva C. E. *Wynford, B.*
Mackinnon, Hon Patricia A. *Audley, B.*
Mackinnon, Hon Patricia C. *Glentoran, B.*
Mackintosh, Hon Diana M. *Mackintosh of Halifax, V.*
Mackintosh, Hon Fiona E. A. *Listowel, E.*
Mackintosh, Hon George J. F. *Mackintosh of Halifax, V.*
Mackintosh, Hon Graham C. *Mackintosh of Halifax, V.*
Mackintosh, Hon Thomas H. G. *Mackintosh of Halifax, V.*
McLaren, (Hon Dame) Anne L. D. *Aberconway, B.*
McLaren, Hon Christopher *Aberconway, B.*
Maclaren, Lady Edith H. *Loudoun, Cs.*
McLaren, H. Charles *Aberconway, B.*
McLaren, Hon Michael D. *Aberconway, B.*
McLaren, Lady Rose M. P. *Anglesey, M.*
MacLaurin, Hon Gillian *MacLaurin of Knebworth, B.*
MacLaurin, Hon Neil R. C. *MacLaurin of Knebworth, B.*

Maclay, Hon Angus G. *Maclay, B.*
Maclay, Hon David M. *Maclay, B.*
Maclay, Hon Joseph P. *Maclay, B.*
Maclay, Hon Rebecca D. *Maclay, B.*
Maclay, Hon Thomas M. *Maclay, B.*
Maclay, Hon Mrs Walter S. *Maclay, B.*
Maclean, Hon Sir Lachlan H. C. *Maclean, Bt (cr 1631).*
Maclean, Hon Sarah E. C. *Rowallan, B.*
Maclean, Lady Sarah E. J. *Aylesford, E.*
Maclean, Hon (Veronica N.) Lady *Lovat, L.*
McLeavy, Hon Mrs Douglas J. *McLeavy, By.*
McLeavy, Hon Frank W. *McLeavy, By.*
McLeod, Hon Eva M. E. *MacLeod, Bt (cr 1924).*
Macleod, Hon Hermione J. *Rathdonnell, B.*
MacLeod, Hon Sir John M. N. *MacLeod, Bt (cr 1924).*
MacLeod, Hon Neil D. *MacLeod, Bt (cr 1924).*
MacLeod, Hon Torquil A. R. *MacLeod of Borve, Bs.*
McLintock, Hon Carla A. *Hill-Norton, B.*
McManus, Hon Alice C. E. *Hemingford, B.*
McMeekan, Hon Sarah A. V. de la P. *Decies, B.*
McMichael, Hon Paquita M. J. *Florey, B.*
Macmillan, Hon Adam J. R. *Stockton, E.*
Macmillan, Hon Daniel M. A. *Stockton, E.*
Macmillan, Hon David M. B. *Stockton, E.*
Macmillan, Lady Louisa A. *Stockton, E.*
Macmillan, Lady Rebecca E. *Stockton, E.*
Macnab, Hon Diana M. *Kilmany, B.*
Macnab, Hon Elisabeth J. *Arwyn, B.*
Macnab, Hon Sarah M. *Polwarth, L.*
Macnaghten, Hon (Beatrice) Lady *Macnaghten, B.*
McNair, Hon Duncan J. *McNair, B.*
McNair, Hon Josephine M. *McNair, B.*
McNair, Hon W. Samuel A. *McNair, B.*
McNally, Hon Imogen *McNally, B.*
McNally, Hon James G. *McNally, B.*
McNally, Hon John *McNally, B.*
McNaught, Hon Fiona *Macfarlane of Bearsden, B.*
MacNaughton, Hon L. Jane *Cowdray, V.*
McNeal, Hon Julia *Gaitskell, Bs.*
McNeile, Hon Henrietta C. L. *Ingleby, V.*
McNulty, Lady Sarah L. *Belmore, E.*
Macpherson, Hon Alexandra G. *Northbrook, B.*
Macpherson, Hon Andrew C. J. *Strathcarron, B.*
Macpherson, Hon Anne A. *Macpherson of Drumochter, B.*
Macpherson, Hon Ian D. P. *Strathcarron, B.*
Macpherson, Hon James A. *Macpherson of Drumochter, B.*
Macpherson, Hon Jennifer M. *Macpherson of Drumochter, B.*
Macpherson, Hon Laura A. *Northbrook, B.*
Macpherson, Hon Mary S. *Drumalbyn, B.*
Macpherson, Hon Sarah C. *Carew, B.*
McQuiston, Lady Silvy C. *Bath, M.*
MacRae, Hon Susan M. *Southwell, V.*
McWatters, Hon Veronica *Stamp, B.*
Maddock, Hon Anna *Maddock, Bs.*
Maddock, Hon Becki *Maddock, Bs.*
Maffey, Hon Christopher A. *Rugby, B.*
Maffey, Hon Mark A. *Rugby, B.*
Maffey, Hon Robert C. *Rugby, B.*
Maffey, Hon Selina P. *Rugby, B.*
Maffey, Hon Simon C. L. *Rugby, B.*
Maher, Hon Sarah J. *Burnham, B.*
Mainwaring, Hon Amanda *Harris, B.*
Mais, Hon Jonathan R. N. *Mais, B.*
Mais, Hon Richard J. I. *Mais, B.*
Maitland, Lady Caroline C. M. *Lauderdale, E.*
Maitland, Lady Elizabeth S. *Lauderdale, E.*
Maitland, Hon John D. *Lauderdale, E.*
Maitland, Hon Rosemary C. *Abertay, By.*
Maitland, Hon Sydney M. P. *Lauderdale, E.*
Major, Hon Charles J. G. Henniker- *Henniker, B.*
Major, Hon Mark I. P. C. Henniker- *Henniker, B.*
Major, Hon Richard A. O. Henniker- *Henniker, B.*
Makgill, Hon Diana M. R. *Oxfuird, V.*
Makgill, Hon Edward A. D. *Oxfuird, V.*
Makgill, Hon Hamish M. A. *Oxfuird, V.*
Makgill, Hon Ian A. A. *Oxfuird, V.*
Makgill, Hon Robert E. G. *Oxfuird, V.*
Makins, Hon Dwight W. *Sherfield, B.*
Makins, Hon Marian W. *Sherfield, B.*
Malcolm, Hon Annabel M. A. *Norrie, B.*
Maldura, Lady Arabella A. D. Emo Capodilista *De La Warr, E.*
Malet, Hon M. Cherry *Wigram, B.*

Malpas, Hon Venetia J. Colborne- *Manners, B.*
Maltby, Lady Sylvia V. A. *Malmesbury, E.*
Mancroft, Hon Arthur L. S. *Mancroft, B.*
Mancroft, Hon Georgia E. *Mancroft, B.*
Mancroft, Hon Maximillian M. *Mancroft, B.*
Mandelson, Hon Mary J. *Morrison of Lambeth, B.*
Manners, Lady Alice L. L. *Rutland, D.*
Manners, Lady Charlotte L. *Rutland, D.*
Manners, Lord Edward J. F. *Rutland, D.*
Manners, Lady Eliza C. *Rutland, D.*
Manners, Lord John *Rutland, D.*
Manners, Hon John H. R. *Manners, B.*
Manners, Hon Richard N. *Manners, B.*
Manners, Lord Roger D. *Rutland, D.*
Manners, Hon Thomas J. *Manners, B.*
Manners, Lady Violet D. L. *Rutland, D.*
Mansfield, Hon Guy R. J. *Sandhurst, B.*
Mansfield, Hon Mrs Ralph G. K. *Sandhurst, B.*
Mar, Lady Janet H. of *Mar, Cs.*
Mar, Lady Susan H. of *Mar, Cs.*
Marckus, Hon Rachel M. F. *King of Wartnaby, D.*
Marcow, Hon Hannah O. *Marks of Broughton, B.*
Marffy, Hon Pelline M. *Acton, B.*
Margesson, Hon Jane H. *Margesson, V.*
Margesson, Hon Rhoda F. *Margesson, V.*
Margesson, Hon Richard F. D. *Margesson, V.*
Margesson, Hon Sarah H. *Margesson, V.*
Marks, Hon Adrianne B. E. *Stone, B.*
Marks, Hon Simon R. *Marks of Broughton, B.*
Marlar, Hon Gillian D. *Taylor of Hadfield, B.*
Marlow, Hon Teresa *Sackville, B.*
Marquis, Lady Claudia L. *Woolton, E.*
Marquis, Lady Constance E. *Woolton, E.*
Marquis, Lady Olivia A. *Woolton, E.*
Marr, Hon Jacqueline *Ashley of Stoke, B.*
Marrian, Lady Emma C. *Cawdor, E.*
Marriott, Hon Dinah L. *Dacre, Bs.*
Marsh, Hon Andrew *Marsh, B.*
Marsh, Hon Christopher *Marsh, B.*
Marsh, Hon (Felicity C. F.) Lady *McFadzean of Kelvinside, B.*
Marshall, Hon Ana L. (Sita) *White of Hull, B.*
Marshall, Hon Jonathan C. W. *Marshall of Goring, B.*
Marshall, Hon Elizabeth J. Vereker- *Gort, V.*
Marshall, Hon Katherine *Kilpatrick of Kincraig, B.*
Marsham, Hon Jonathan C. W. *Marshall of Goring, B.*
Marston, Hon Vanessa M. *Cawley, B.*
Marten, Hon Mary A. S. E. *Alington, By.*
Marten, Lady Caroline *Rosslyn, E.*
Martin, Hon Jill D. *Mason of Barnsley, B.*
Martin, Hon Penelope C. *Plowden, B.*
Martin, Hon Anne E. Bromley- *Ormathwaite, B.*
Martino, Hon Caroline D. *Onslow of Woking, B.*
Mason, Hon Elizabeth *Auckland, B.*
Mason, Hon Elizabeth-Anne *Blackford, B.*
Mason, Hon Kristina E. *Robson of Kiddington, Bs.*
Massey, Hon Lavinia *Skelmersdale, B.*
Massy, Hon David H. S. *Massy, B.*
Massy, Hon Graham I. S. *Massy, B.*
Massy, Hon John H. S. *Massy, B.*
Massy, Hon Muriel O. *Massy, B.*
Massy, Hon Paul R. *Massy, B.*
Massy, Hon Sheelagh M. L. *Massy, B.*
Matarasso, Hon Pauline M. *Sanderson of Ayot, B.*
Mather, Hon (Philippa S.) Lady *Cromwell, B.*
Matheson, Hon (Jean E. M.) Lady *Middleton, B.*
Mathews, Hon M. Clair *Geddes, B.*
Matthews, Hon Emma E. *Griffiths, B.*
Matthews, Hon Ian V. *Matthews, B.*
Matthews, Hon Joanna L. C. *Derwent, B.*
Matthewson, Hon Sarah *Phillips of Ellesmere, By.*
Mattick, Hon Rosanne *Oppenheim-Barnes, Bs.*
Maud, Hon Humphrey J. H. *Redcliffe-Maud, B.*
Maude, Hon Francis A. A. *Maude of Stratford-upon-Avon, B.*
Maude, Hon Henry C. *Hawarden, V.*
Maude, Hon R. Connan W. L. *Hawarden, V.*
Maude, Hon Thomas P. C. *Hawarden, V.*
Maude, Hon Sonia M. Hammond *Ingleby, V.*
Maudslay, Hon Arabella B. R. *Jauncey of Tullichettle B.*
Mawhinney, Hon Benjamin J. *Scotland of Asthal, Bs.*
Mawhinney, Hon Matthew J. *Scotland of Asthal, Bs.*
Maxwell, Lady Avena M. C. *Harrington, E.*
Maxwell, Hon (Theodora M.) Lady *Farnham, B.*
Maxwell, Hon Diana E. *de Ros, B.*

Maxwell, Hon Finbar J. *de Ros, B.*
Maxwell, Hon Geraldine T. M. G. *Rothermere, V.*
Maxwell, Hon Jessye M. *de Ros, B.*
Maxwell, Hon Katharine G. *de Ros, B.*
Maxwell, Hon Peter T. *de Ros, B.*
Maxwell, Hon Simon R. *Farnham, B.*
May, Hon Jasper B. S. *May, B.*
May, Hon M. Jane *May, B.*
Mayall, Hon (Mary H.) Lady *Harlech, B.*
Mayhew, Hon Christopher J. *Mayhew, B.*
Mayhew, Hon David F. *Mayhew, B.*
Mayhew, Hon Henry E. B. *Mayhew of Twysden, B.*
Mayhew, Hon James, B. B. *Mayhew of Twysden, B.*
Mayhew, Hon Jerome P. B. *Mayhew of Twysden, B.*
Mayhew, Hon Judith E. A. *Mayhew, B.*
Mayhew, Hon Margaret L. *Brock, By.*
Mayhew, Hon Tristram T. B. *Mayhew of Twysden, B.*
Mayo, Hon Arabella V. E. S. *Swinfen, B.*
Mayo, Hon Christine M. *Plumb, B.*
Meade, Hon John M *Clanwilliam, E.*
Meade, Lady Sophia C. *Cranbrook, E.*
Meade, Hon Tamara L. *Clanwilliam, E.*
Means, Hon Juliet E. M. *Deedes, B.*
Meddings, Hon Susan *Delfont, B.*
Megarry, Lady Henrietta C. E. *Anglesey, M.*
Melia, Lady Alice *Queensberry, M.*
Mellish, Hon David *Mellish, B.*
Mellish, Hon Paul *Mellish, B.*
Mellish, Hon Robert *Mellish, B.*
Mellish, Hon Stephen *Mellish, B.*
Melville, Hon Sarah *Taylor of Hadfield, B.*
Melville, Hon Alan D. Leslie *Leven, E.*
Melville, Hon Archibald R. Leslie *Leven, E.*
Melville, Lady Elizabeth Leslie *Northampton, M.*
Melville, Hon Mrs George D. Leslie *Leven, E.*
Melville, Lady Jean E. Leslie *Leven, E.*
Melville, Hon Mrs Ronald J. Leslie *Leven, E.*
Menpes, Hon Marjorie *Cooper of Stockton Heath, B.*
Menuhin, Hon Brigid G. *Sempill, Ly.*
Menuhin, Hon Gerard *Menuhin, By.*
Menuhin, Hon Jeremy *Menuhin, By.*
Menuhin, Hon Krov *Menuhin, By.*
Merriman, Hon Violet G. *Merriman, B.*
Meston, Hon Elspeth M. *Meston, B.*
Meston, Hon Laura A. R. *Meston, B.*
Meston, Hon Thomas J. D. *Meston, B.*
Meston, Hon William D. *Meston, B.*
Metherell, Hon Rosamond A. *Harding-Davies, Bs.*
Methuen, Hon Robert A. H. *Methuen, B.*
Meynell, Hon Elizabeth M. *Gretton, B.*
Michie, Hon Janet R. *Bannerman of Kildonan, B.*
Middleditch, Hon Grace *Bethell, B.*
Middleton, Hon Katya *St Just, By.*
Mieczkowska, Hon Caroline S. A. *Grenfell, B.*
Milbanke, Lady Caroline M. N. Lytton- *Lytton, E.*
Miles, Hon Christine H. *Forester, B.*
Millar, Hon Alastair J. H. H. *Inchyra, D.*
Millar, Hon C. James C. H. *Inchyra, B.*
Miller, Hon Ann K. *Aylmer, B.*
Miller, Hon David P. *Miller of Hendon, Bs.*
Miller, Lady Diana M. *Yarborough, E and Fauconberg, and Conyers, By.*
Miller, Hon Honor L. *Brooke of Cumnor, B.*
Miller, Hon Michael S. *Miller of Hendon, Bs.*
Miller, Hon Paul H. *Miller of Hendon, Bs.*
Millett, Hon Andrew *Millett, B.*
Millett, Hon Richard *Millett, B.*
Milln, Hon Susan M. *Valentia, V.*
Mills, Hon Catherine G. *Hillingdon, By.*
Mills, Hon Christopher P. R. *Mills, B.*
Mills, Hon Susan *Wolverton, B.*
Mills, Hon Ursula S. *Hillingdon, By.*
Milne, Hon George A. *Milne, B.*
Milne, Hon Iain C. L. *Milne, B.*
Milner, Lady Charlene M. O. *Ypres, E.*
Milner, Hon Richard J. *Milner of Leeds, B.*
Milsom, Hon Penelope J. *Kaldor, B.*
Minnitt, Hon Primrose K. *Riverdale, D.*
Mishcon, Hon Peter A. *Mishcon, B.*
Mishcon, Hon Russell O. *Mishcon, B.*
Mitchell, Hon Charlotte M. *Boyd of Merton, V.*
Mitchison, Hon Denis A. *Mitchison, By.*
Mitchison, Hon John M. *Mitchison, By.*
Mitchison, Hon Nicholas A. *Mitchison, By.*
Mitford, Hon Georgina C. *Redesdale, B.*
Mitford, Hon Henrietta J. *Redesdale, B.*
Mitford, Hon Rupert B. *Redesdale, B.*

Miyonga, Hon Flora C. *Cottesloe, B.*
Mobbs, Hon (Pamela J. M.) Lady *Kemsley, V.*
Moffatt, Hon Ruth *Jackson of Burnley, By.*
Mogg, Hon Annunziata M. Rees- *Rees-Mogg, B.*
Mogg, Hon Charlotte L. Rees- *Rees-Mogg, B.*
Mogg, Hon Jacob W. Rees- *Rees-Mogg, B.*
Mogg, Hon Thomas F. Rees- *Rees-Mogg, B.*
Moggridge, Hon Catherine G. *Hemingford, B.*
Mole, Hon Susan M. *Hinton of Bankside, B.*
Molesworth, Hon William J. C. *Molesworth, V.*
Molloy, Hon Kathryn *Howell, B.*
Monck, Hon Charles S. *Monck, V.*
Monck, Hon George S. *Monck, V.*
Monck, Hon I. Shiela T. *Dunboyne, B.*
Monck, Hon James S. *Monck, V.*
Monckton, Hon Anthony L. C. *Monckton of Brenchley, V.*
Monckton, Hon Christopher W. *Monckton of Brenchley, V.*
Monckton, Hon J. Philip *Galway, V.*
Monckton, Hon Jonathan R. St. Q. *Monckton of Brenchley, V.*
Monckton, Hon Rachel J. *Galway, V.*
Monckton, Hon R. Wynsome *Galway, V.*
Monckton, Hon Timothy D. R. *Monckton of Brenchley, V.*
Moncreiff, Hon Mrs Donald G. F. *Moncreiff, B.*
Moncreiff, Hon Rhoderick H. W. *Moncreiff, B.*
Moncreiff Hon Robert F. A. *Moncreiff, B.*
Moncreiffe, Hon Peregrine D. E. M. *Erroll, E.*
Monro, Hon Hugh B. H. E. *Monro of Langholm, B.*
Monro, Hon Seymour H. R. H. *Monro of Langholm, B.*
Monson, Hon Andrew A. J. *Monson, B.*
Monson, Hon Anthony J. *Monson, B.*
Monson, Hon Jeremy D. A. J. *Monson, B.*
Monson, Hon Nicholas J. *Monson, B.*
Monson, Lady O. Rose M. *Grafton, D.*
Monson, Hon Stephen A. J. *Monson, B.*
Montagu, Hon Angela L. *Rawlinson, B.*
Montagu, Hon Anthony T. S. *Swaythling, B.*
Montagu, Hon Ashley F. M. N. *Manchester D.*
Montagu, Hon Delilah E. *Swaythling, B.*
Montagu, Lady Elizabeth *Sandwich, E.*
Montagu, Lady Emma *Manchester, D.*
Montagu, Hon Mrs Ewen E. S. *Swaythling, B.*
Montagu, Hon G. C. Robert *Sandwich, E.*
Montagu, (Lady) Jemima M. *Sandwich, E.*
Montagu, Hon Orlando W. *Sandwich, E.*
Montagu, Hon Jonathan Douglas-Scott- *Montagu of Beaulieu, B.*
Montagu, Lord Kimble *Manchester, D.*
Montagu, Hon Ralph Douglas-Scott- *Montague of Beaulieu, B.*
Montague, Hon Christopher *Amwell, B.*
Montague, Hon Ian *Amwell B.*
Montague, Hon Sheila E. *Amwell, B.*
Montgomerie, Hon James D. *Eglinton, E.*
Montgomerie, Hon Robert S. *Eglinton, E.*
Montgomerie, Hon Roger H. *Eglinton, E.*
Montgomerie, Hon William J. *Eglinton, E.*
Montgomery, Hon Bridget A. *Fisher, B.*
Montgomery, Hon Daphne *Bridgeman, V.*
Montgomery, Hon Henry D. *Montgomery of Alamein, V.*
Montgomery, Hon Sophie F. *Birdwood, B.*
Moore, Hon Astraea J. D. *Barnetson, B.*
Moore, Hon C. Sheila *Digby, B.*
Moore, Hon Garrett A. *Drogheda, E.*
Moore, Hon Janie St. G. *Charlemont, V.*
Moore, Lady Marina A. *Drogheda, E.*
Moore, Hon Martin *Moore of Lower Marsh, B.*
Moore, Hon Richard *Moore of Lower Marsh, B.*
Moore, Hon Stephanie *Moore of Lower Marsh, B.*
Morehead, Lady Patricia C. *Annesley, E.*
Moreton, Hon Claire A. *Ducie, E.*
Moreton, Hon Douglas H. *Ducie, E.*
Moreton, Hon James B. *Ducie, E.*
Moreton, Hon Robert M. *Ducie, E.*
Morgan, Hon Fionn F. B. *O'Neill, B.*
Morgan, Hon Owain *Elystan-Morgan, B.*
Morgan, Hon Elizabeth M. Grey *Wrenbury, B.*
Morley, Hon Andrew J. S. Hope- *Hollenden, B.*
Morley, Hon Alastair K. Hope- *Hollenden, B.*
Morley, Hon Edward Hope- *Hollenden, B.*
Morley, Hon Henry G. Hope- *Hollenden, B.*
Morley, Hon Juliette Hope- *Hollenden, B.*
Morley, Hon Robin G. Hope- *Hollenden, B.*
Moro, Hon Anne M. T. *Huntingfield, B.*

Morris, Hon Carolie M. W. *Mountmorres, V.*
Morris, Hon Caroline H. *Morris of Kenwood, B.*
Morris, Hon C. Christopher *Morris of Grasmere, B.*
Morris, Hon Christopher J. R. *Morris of Castle Morris, B.*
Morris, Hon E. Patrick *Morris, B.*
Morris, Hon Elizabeth *Hill of Luton, B.*
Morris, Hon George R. F. *Killanin, B.*
Morris, Hon Gillian *Morris of Manchester, B.*
Morris, Hon Paul G. *Morris of Manchester, B.*
Morris, Hon Stephen C. *Morris of Manchester, B.*
Morris, Hon James *Morris, B.*
Morris, Hon Jocelyn *Naseby, B.*
Morris, Hon John M. *Killanin, B.*
Morris, Hon Jonathan D. *Morris of Kenwood, B.*
Morris, Hon Julian *Naseby, B.*
Morris, Hon Lucy *Morris, B.*
Morris, Hon Michael F. L. *Killanin, B.*
Morris, Hon Michaela M. *Morris, B.*
Morris, Hon Patricia M. *Nolan, B.*
Morris, Hon Thomas A. S. *Morris, B.*
Morris, Lady V. Audrey B. *Shrewsbury, E.*
Morrish, Hon Rosalind B. *Wade, B.*
Morrison, Hon A. Sara F. S. *Long, V.*
Morrison, Hon Alasdair V. O. *Dunrossil, V.*
Morrison, Hon Alasdair G. *Dunrossil, V.*
Morrison, Hon Alastair J. *Margadale, B.*
Morrison, Hon Andrew W. R. *Dunrossil, V.*
Morrison, Hon Catriona M. *Dunrossil, V.*
Morrison, Hon Sir Charles A. *Margadale, B.*
Morrison, Hon Helena G. *Garner, B.*
Morrison, Hon Hugh *Margadale, B.*
Morrison, Hon Joanna C. *Dunrossil, V.*
Morrison, Hon Louisa M. C. *Napier and Ettrick, L.*
Morrison, Hon Mary A. *Dunrossil, V.*
Morrison, Hon Dame Mary A. *Margadale, B.*
Morrison, Hon Mrs Nial R. *Dunrossil, V.*
Morrison, Hon Philippa A. *Hives, B.*
Morrison, Hon Ranald J. *Dunrossil, V.*
Morrison, Lady Sophia L. S. *Devonshire, D.*
Morrissey, Lady Joanna A. *Townshend, M.*
Morse, Hon Jennifer *Delfont, B.*
Morton, Hon Alicia D. *Rugby, B.*
Morton, Hon Alistair C. R. *Morton of Shuna, B.*
Morton, Hon Douglas W. *Morton of Shuna, B.*
Morton, Hon Kenneth J. *Morton of Shuna, B.*
Mosley, Hon Clare I. *Ravensdale, B.*
Mosley, Hon (Diana) Lady *Redesdale, B.*
Mosley, Hon Ivo A. R. *Ravensdale, B.*
Mosley, Hon Marius *Ravensdale, B.*
Mosley, Hon Michael *Ravensdale, B.*
Mosley, Hon Robert *Ravensdale, B.*
Mosley, Hon Shaun N. *Ravensdale, B.*
Moss, Hon Susannah E. *Alvingham, B.*
Mosselmans, Hon Prudence *McCorquodale of Newton, B.*
Mostyn, Hon Llewellyn R. L. Lloyd- *Mostyn, B.*
Motion, Hon Penelope M. *Harcourt, V.*
Motl, Hon Marion A. *Molloy, B.*
Mountain, Hon Camilla S. *Rockley, B.*
Mountbatten, Lord Ivar A. M. *Milford Haven, M.*
Mountbatten, Lady Tatiana H. G. *Milford Haven, M.*
Moyle, Hon Roland D. *Moyle, By.*
Moynihan, Hon Antonita M. C. F. *Moynihan, B.*
Moynihan, Hon Aurora L. M. *Moynihan, B.*
Moynihan, Hon George E. B. *Moynihan, B.*
Moynihan, Hon India I. S. *Moynihan, B.*
Moynihan, Hon Kathleen M. H. I. J. *Moynihan, B.*
Moynihan, Hon Miranda, D. I. *Moynihan, B.*
Moynihan, Hon Nicholas E. B. *Moynihan, B.*
Mudge, Hon Maureen A. *Wigg, B.*
Muff, Hon Andrew R. *Calverley, B.*
Muff, Hon Jonathan E. *Calverley, B.*
Muff, Hon Peter R. *Calverley, B.*
Muggeridge, Hon Sarah *Walsingham, B.*
Muir, Lady Linda M. *Enniskillen, E.*
Muir, Lady Rosemary, M. *Marlborough, D.*
Mulholland, Hon Andrew H. *Dunleath, B.*
Mulholland, Hon Tara M. *Dunleath, B.*
Mulholland, Hon William A. *Dunleath, B.*
Mulji, Hon Rosaleen, E. *Moyne, B.*
Mullins, Hon Sarah, V. *Bearsted, V.*
Mumford, Lady Mary, K. *Norfolk, D.*
Mummery, Hon E. Rosamund Lockhart- *Elles, Bs.*
Mundy, Lady Bridget Miller *Minto, E.*
Munro, Hon Diana M. *Clydesmuir, B.*
Munro, Hon Marjorie A. Walker- *Biddulph, B.*
Murphy, Hon Emma E. *Teynham, B.*

Riddell, Hon (Sarah) Lady *Richardson of Duntisbourne, B.*
Ridgely, Hon Janetta *Raglan, B.*
Ridley, Hon Annabel *Hawke, B.*
Ridley, (Hon) Helen L. C. *Asquith of Yarnbury, By.*
Ridley, Hon Julia H. *Aberconway, B.*
Ridley, Hon Matthew W. *Ridley, V.*
Ridley, Hon Nicholas *Ridley, V.*
Riley, Hon F. Georgina *Sanderson of Bowden, B.*
Riley, Hon Ruth M. *Hives, B.*
Ringsell, Hon Cassandra P. A. *St Vincent, V.*
Rippon, Hon A. Simon Y. *Rippon of Hexham, B.*
Rippon, Hon Fiona C. *Rippon of Hexham, B.*
Ritchie, Hon C. Rupert R. *Ritchie of Dundee, B.*
Ritchie, Hon Jean D. *Stuart of Findhorn, V.*
Ritchie, Hon Philippa J. *Ritchie of Dundee, B.*
Rix, Hon (Karen D.) Lady *Young of Graffham, B.*
Robb, Lady Violet C. L. *Ormonde, M.*
Robbins, Hon Richard *Robbins, B.*
Roberts, Hon Ann E. *Goronwy-Roberts, B.*
Roberts, Hon Mrs David S. *Clwyd, B.*
Roberts, Hon Geraint *Roberts of Clwyd, B.*
Roberts, Hon Hugh G. A. *Clwyd, B.*
Roberts, Hon Huw *Roberts of Clwyd, B.*
Roberts, Hon Jane E. S. *Roskill, B.*
Roberts, Hon Jeremy T. *Clwyd, B.*
Roberts, Hon Joan M. *Royle, By.*
Roberts, Hon John M. *Clwyd, B.*
Roberts, Hon Juliana E. *Scarsdale, V.*
Roberts, Hon Marjorie *Macfarlane of Bearsden, B.*
Roberts, Hon Owen D. *Goronwy-Roberts, B.*
Roberts, Hon P. Jane S. *Aldington, B.*
Roberts, Hon Rhys *Roberts of Clwyd, B.*
Roberts, Hon Mrs W. H. Mervyn *Clwyd, B.*
Robertson, Hon Christopher J. *Wharton, Bs.*
Robertson, Hon Elizabeth A. *Bourne, B.*
Robertson, Lady Joan P. Q. *Wavell, E.*
Robertson, Hon Myles C. D. *Wharton, Bs.*
Robertson, Hon Nicholas C. *Wharton, Bs.*
Robertson, Hon Patricia L. *Wharton, Bs.*
Robertson, Hon William B. E. *Robertson of Oakridge, B.*
Robins, Hon Elizabeth M. G. *Lloyd of Kilgerran, B.*
Robinson, Hon Claire E. *Portman, V.*
Robinson, Hon Gai Kencie *Salmon, B.*
Robinson, Hon Mrs Richard A. G. *Martonmere, B.*
Robinson, Hon Stella H. *Hollenden, B.*
Robinson, Hon Susannah J. Maitland- *Faringdon, B.*
Robson, Hon Elizabeth *Atkin, B.*
Robson, Hon Erik M. W. *Robson of Kiddington, Bs.*
Robson, Lady J. Penelope J. *Ferrers, E.*
Roche, Hon Arabella E. B. *Fermoy, B.*
Roche, Hon E. Hugh B. *Fermoy, B.*
Roche, Hon (H. Alexandra B.) Lady *Selby, V.*
Roche, Hon Mrs John F. A. *Roche, By.*
Roche, Hon Mary C. B. *Fermoy, B.*
Roche, Hon P. Maurice B. *Fermoy, B.*
Rudd, Hon James R. D. T. *Rennell, B.*
Rodd, Hon Lilias *Rennell, B.*
Rodd, Hon Rachel *Rennell, B.*
Rodd, Hon Sophie M. J. *Rennell, B.*
Rodney, Hon Diana R. *Rodney, B.*
Rodney, Hon John G. B. *Rodney, B.*
Rodney, Hon Mrs Michael G. *Rodney, B.*
Rodwell, Hon Christine M. *Woolley, B.*
Roe, Hon Susan *Lewin, B.*
Rogers, Hon Ab *Rogers of Riverside, B.*
Rogers, Hon Ben *Rogers of Riverside, B.*
Rogers, Hon Loretta A. *Martonmere, B.*
Rogers, Hon Roo *Rogers of Riverside, B.*
Rogers, Hon Zadoc *Rogers of Riverside, B.*
Rogerson, Hon Caroline *Gilbert, B.*
Rogerson, Hon Rose T. *Ashburton, B.*
Rolfe, Hon Louise J. D. *Barnetson, B.*
Roll, Hon Elizabeth *Roll of Ipsden, B.*
Roll, Hon Joanna *Roll of Ipsden, B.*
Rollo, Hon Mrs David I. *Rollo, L.*
Rollo, Hon James D. W. *Rollo, L.*
Rollo, Hon James M. *Rollo, L.*
Rollo, Hon John D. *Rollo, L.*
Rollo, Hon Simon D. P. *Rollo, L.*
Rollo, Hon Thomas S. *Rollo, L.*
Rollo, Hon William E. J. *Rollo, L.*
Rollo, Hon Mrs William H. C. *Rollo, L.*
Rolnick, Hon Julia R. *Joseph, B.*
Rootes, Hon Mrs Brian G. *Rootes, B.*
Rootes, Hon Nicholas G. L. *Rootes, B.*
Roper, Hon Sarah-Jane L. *Prior, B.*
Ropner, Hon Charlotte M. *Piercy, B.*

Rose, Hon (Phœbe M. D.) Lady *Phillimore, B.*
Rose, Hon Susan J. *Northbourne, B.*
Rose, Lady Katherine P. Townsend- *Erne, E.*
Rosen, Hon June A. *Lever, B.*
Rosenbaum, Hon Jane E. *Ashley of Stoke, B.*
Roskill, Hon Julian W. *Roskill, B.*
Rospigliosi, Hon Helen M. G. *Acton, B.*
Ross, Hon Huw W. *Ross of Newport, B.*
Ross, Hon James G. *Ross of Newport, B.*
Ross, Hon Roxana R. C. N. *Killearn, B.*
Rothenberg, Hon Mary *Pentland, By.*
Rothschild, Hon Mrs Amschel M. J. *Rothschild, B.*
Rothschild, Hon Emma G. *Rothschild, B.*
Rothschild, Hon Hannah M. *Rothschild, B.*
Rothschild, Hon Nathaniel P. V. J. *Rothschild, B.*
Rous, Lady Brigitte A. *Stradbroke, E.*
Rous, Lady Heidi S. *Stradbroke, E.*
Rous, Hon Henham M. *Stradbroke, E.*
Rous, Lady Henrietta E. *Stradbroke, E.*
Rous, Hon Hektor F. *Stradbroke, E.*
Rous, Lady Ingrid A. *Stradbroke, E.*
Rous, Hon John *Stradbroke, E.*
Rous, Lady Marye V. I. *Stradbroke, E.*
Rous, Lady Minsmere M. *Stradbroke, E.*
Rous, Hon Maximilian O. *Stradbroke, E.*
Rous, Lady Pamela K. *Stradbroke, E.*
Rous, Hon Ramsar F. *Stradbroke, E.*
Rous, Lady S. Rayner *Stradbroke, E.*
Rous, Hon Lady *Stradbroke, E.*
Rous, Hon Mrs W. Keith *Stradbroke, E.*
Rous, Hon Wesley A. *Stradbroke, E.*
Rous, Hon Winston W. *Stradbroke, E.*
Rous, Hon Yoxford U. U. *Stradbroke, E.*
Rous, Lady Zea K. *Stradbroke, E.*
Rowcliffe, Hon Una M. *Slim, V.*
Rowlandson, Hon Antonia J. H. *Caldecote, V.*
Rowley, Lady Sibell *Beauchamp, E.*
Rowse, Hon Mrs Rosemary S. V. *Grimston of Westbury, B.*
Royle, Hon Lucinda K. F. *Fanshawe of Richmond, B.*
Rubie, Hon Jane A. *Ravensworth, B.*
Rubin, Hon Susan A. *Rayne, B.*
Ruck, Hon Catherine D. *Braybrooke, B.*
Rudd, Hon Fiona C. R. *Ritchie-Calder, B.*
Rudd, Hon Hilary A. *Peddie, B.*
Rule, Hon Miranda J. C. *Dynevor, B.*
Runcie, Hon James *Runcie, B.*
Runciman, Hon Anne E. *Cromwell, B.*
Runciman, Hon Catherine *Runciman of Doxford, V.*
Runciman, Hon David W. *Runciman of Doxford, V.*
Runciman, Hon Lisa *Runciman of Doxford, V.*
Runciman, Hon Sir Steven (J. C. S.) *Runciman of Doxford, V.*
Rundall, Lady Rosalthé F. *Harrowby, E.*
Rusbridger, Hon Lindsay M. *Mackie of Benshie, B.*
Rush, Lady Tracy A. *Mount Edgcumbe, E.*
Rushbrooke, Hon Nell *Butler of Brockwell, B.*
Russell, Hon Adam M. H. *Russell of Liverpool, B.*
Russell, Hon Ann B. *Congleton, B.*
Russell, Hon Anthony J. M. *Ampthill, B.*
Russell, Hon Catherine V. *Ponsonby of Shulbrede, B.*
Russell, Hon Daniel C. E. *Russell of Liverpool, B.*
Russell, Hon David W. E. *Ampthill, B.*
Russell, Hon Easter D. *Kennet, B.*
Russell, Hon Edward C. S. *Russell of Liverpool, B.*
Russell, Hon Mrs Edward W. C. *Ampthill, B.*
Russell, Hon Elizabeth M. G. L. *Mostyn, B.*
Russell, Hon Emma K. *Russell of Liverpool, B.*
Russell, Hon F. Damian *Russell of Killowen, B.*
Russell, Hon Frances M. *Sempill, L.*
Russell, Lord Francis H. *Bedford, D.*
Russell, Lord Hugh H. *Bedford, D.*
Russell, Lord James E. H. *Bedford, D.*
Russell, Hon John F. *Russell, E.*
Russell, Hon John H. T. *Ampthill, B.*
Russell, Hon Kathleen M. *Ashbourne, B.*
Russell, Hon Mrs Langley G. H. *Russell of Liverpool, D.*
Russell, Hon Leonora M. K. *Russell of Liverpool, B.*
Russell, Hon Lucy L. C. *Russell of Liverpool, B.*
Russell, Lady Mary *Haddington, E.*
Russell, Hon Nicole *Churston, B.*
Russell, Lord Robin L. H. *Bedford, D.*
Russell, Lord Rudolf *Bedford, D.*
Russell, Lady Sarah E. *Russell, E.*
Russell, Hon Valentine F. X. M. *Russell of Killowen, B.*

Russell, Hon William F. L. *Russell of Liverpool, B.*
Russell, Hon William S. *de Clifford, B.*
Russell, Hon Emelia R. Hamilton- *Boyne, V.*
Russell, Hon Richard G. Hamilton- *Boyne, V.*
Ryder, Hon D. A. Hugo C. *Harrowby, E.*
Ryder, Hon Emily G. H. *Harrowby, E.*
Ryder, Hon Frederick W. D. *Harrowby, E.*
Ryder, Hon Henry M. D. *Harrowby, E.*
Ryder, Hon Jill P. *Ryder of Eaton Hastings, B.*
Ryder, Hon John S. T. D. *Harrowby, E.*
Ryder, Hon Meg C. *Ryder of Wensum, B.*
Ryder, Hon Michael J. *Ryder of Eaton Hastings, B.*
Ryecart, Lady Marcia M. J. *Norfolk, D.*
Ryland, Hon (Jeryl M. S.) Lady Smith- *Cranworth, B.*
Ryman, Hon Shirley *Summerskill, Bs.*
Saatchi, Hon Edward *Saatchi, B.*
Sacher, Hon Rosalind E. C. *Rowallan, B.*
Sachs, Hon (Janet M.) Lady *Goddard, By.*
Sackville, Lady Arabella A. D. *De La Warr, E.*
Sackville, Hon Edward G. R. *De La Warr, E.*
Sackville, Hon Thomas G. *De La Warr, E.*
Sackville, Hon M. Teresa Stopford *Cowdray, V.*
Sadler, Hon Susan L. *Harris of Peckham, B.*
Sagan, Hon Patricia *Sherfield, B.*
Saggers, Lady Kirstie A. *Montrose, D.*
Saglio, Hon Tara C. *Combermere, V.*
Sain, Hon Harriet M. *Burnham, B.*
Sainsbury, Hon A. Lucy *Sainsbury of Turville, B.*
Sainsbury, Hon Clare N. *Sainsbury of Turville, B.*
Sainsbury, Hon Francesca E. *Sainsbury of Turville, B.*
Sainsbury, Hon J. Julian *Sainsbury of Preston Candover, B.*
Sainsbury, Hon Mark L. *Sainsbury of Preston Candover, B.*
Sainsbury, Hon Paulette A. *Sainsbury, B.*
Sainsbury, Hon Sarah J. *Sainsbury of Preston Candover, B.*
Sainsbury, Hon Simon D. D. *Sainsbury, B.*
Sainsbury, Hon Sir Timothy A. D. *Sainsbury, B.*
Saint, Lady J. S. Rose *Shrewsbury, E.*
St. Aubyn, Hon C. Gwendolen C. *Carnock, B.*
St. Aubyn, Hon Giles R. *St. Levan, B.*
St. Aubyn, Hon O. Piers *St. Levan, B.*
St. Clair, Hon Annabel R. *Sinclair, L.*
St. Clair, Hon Laura A. *Sinclair, L.*
St. Clair, Hon Matthew M. K. *Sinclair, L.*
St. George, Lady Henrietta F. D. *Grafton, D.*
St John, Hon Alexander A. *St. John of Bletso, B.*
St John, Hon Athene E. *St John of Bletso, B.*
St John, Hon Chloe *St John of Bletso, B.*
St. John, Hon Henry F. *Bolingbroke and St. John, V.*
St. John, Lady Juliet E. *Bolingbroke and St. John, V.*
St. John, Lady Lucy M. *Bolingbroke and St. John, V.*
St. John, Hon Nicholas A. *Bolingbroke and St. John, V.*
St. John, Lady Nicola J. *Bolingbroke and St. John, V.*
St. John, Hon Oliver B. *St. John of Bletso, B.*
St. John, Hon Oliver J. *Bolingbroke and St. John, V.*
St. John, Hon Sally H. *Rootes, B.*
St. John, Hon Vanessa M. *Palmer, B.*
St. Leger, Hon David H. *Doneraile, V.*
St. Leger, Hon Edward H. *Doneraile, V.*
St. Leger, Hon Elizabeth A. *Doneraile, V.*
St. Leger, Hon Karen J. *Doneraile, V.*
St. Leger, Hon Maeve I. M. *Doneraile, V.*
St. Leger, Hon Nathaniel W. R. St. J. *Doneraile, V.*
Salaman, Hon Nancy A. *Samuel, V.*
Sales, Hon Isobel C. *Boston, B.*
Salmon, Hon David N. C. *Salmon, B.*
Samuel, Hon Anthony G. *Bearsted, V.*
Samuel, Hon Dan J. *Samuel, V.*
Samuel, Hon Eugenie S. *Bearsted, V.*
Samuel, Hon Harry R. *Bearsted, V.*
Samuel, Hon Juliet S. *Bearsted, V.*
Samuel, Hon Michael J. *Bearsted, V.*
Samuel, Hon Natalie N. *Bearsted, V.*
Samuel, Hon Zoe E. *Bearsted, V.*
Samuels, Hon Ann *Bruce of Donington, B.*
Sandberg, Hon Michael *Sandberg, B.*
Sandberg, Hon Paul *Sandberg, B.*
Sandelson, Hon Mary F. A. *Alexander of Weedon, B.*
Sandeman, Hon Phyllis E. *Newton, B.*

Sandeman, Hon Sylvia M. *Maclehose of Beoch, B.*
Sanders, Hon Rowena M. *Hawke, B.*
Sanderson, Hon Andrea *Sanderson of Ayot, By.*
Sanderson, Hon C. David R. *Sanderson of Bowden, B.*
Sanderson, Hon Evelyn *Sanderson of Ayot, By.*
Sanderson, Hon Frances *Sanderson of Ayot, By.*
Sanderson, Hon Michael *Sanderson of Ayot, By.*
Sanderson, Hon Murray L. *Sanderson of Ayot, By.*
Sanderson, Hon Stephanie *Sanderson of Ayot, By.*
Sandilands, Hon Alison *Torphichen, L.*
Sandilands, Hon Anne *Torphichen, L.*
Sandilands, Hon Margaret E. G. *Torphichen, L.*
Sandilands, Hon Mary C. S. *Torphichen, L.*
Sandys, Hon Celia M. *Duncan-Sandys, By.*
Sandys, Hon Laura J. *Duncan-Sandys, By.*
Sanson, Hon Camilla J. *Thurso,V.*
Sarson, Hon Gillian I. J. *Hanworth, V.*
Saumarez, Hon Claire *de Saumarez, B.*
Saumarez, Hon Emily *de Saumarez, B.*
Saumarez, Hon Victor T. *De Saumarez, B.*
Savile, Lady Alethea F. C. *Mexborough, E.*
Savile, Hon C. Anthony *Mexborough, E.*
Savile, Hon James H. H. J. *Mexborough, E.*
Savile, Lady Lucinda S. C. *Mexborough, E.*
Savile, Hon Henry L. T. Lumley- *Savile, B.*
Saville, Hon Henry O. *Saville of Newdigate, B.*
Saville, Hon William C. *Saville of Newdigate, B.*
Saville, Hon Yvonne C. *Schon, E.*
Scarlett, Hon James H. *Abinger, B.*
Scarlett, Hon Mrs John L. C. *Abinger, B.*
Scarlett, Hon Peter R. *Abinger, B.*
Scarr, Lady Davina J. *Erne, E.*
Schaale, Hon Katherine L. *Wrenbury, B.*
Schreiber, Hon Nicola C. *Marlesford, B.*
Schreiber, Hon Sophie L. *Marlesford, B.*
Schüffel, Hon Shân *Edmund-Davies, B.*
Schuster, Hon Lorna F. *Wyfold, B.*
Scott, Hon (A. Drusilla) Lady *Lindsay of Birker, B.*
Scott, Hon Cecilia A. *Hawke, B.*
Scott, Hon Clare O. *Renton, B.*
Scott, Hon Elizabeth A. *Rathcreedan, B.*
Scott, Hon Elizabeth M. *Bannerman of Kildonan, By.*
Scott, Hon Helena R. C. *Eldon, E.*
Scott, Hon John J. R. C. *Eldon, E.*
Scott, Hon Mary R. *Montagu of Beaulieu, B.*
Scott, Hon Rita *Blyton, B.*
Scott, Hon Simon P. *Eldon, E.*
Scott, Hon Andrew W. Hepburne- *Polwarth, L.*
Scott, Hon Francis M. Hepburne- *Polwarth, L.*
Scott, Hon Mary J. Hepburne- *Polwarth, L.*
Scott, Hon Patrick J. Hepburne- *Polwarth, L.*
Scott, Lady Amabel C.A. Montagu Douglas *Buccleuch, D.*
Scott, Hon Charles D. P. Montagu Douglas *Buccleuch, D.*
Scott, Lord Damian T. F. C. Montagu Douglas *Buccleuch, D.*
Scott, Lady Louisa Jane T. Montagu Douglas *Buccleuch, D.*
Scruton, Hon Sophie L. *Jeffreys, B.*
Scrymgeour, Lady Flora H. V. *Dundee, E.*
Scrymgeour, Lady Lavinia R. E. *Dundee, E.*
Scrymgeour, Lady Marina P. *Dundee, E.*
Seager, Hon Douglas L. *Leighton of St. Mellons, B.*
Seager, Hon Emma E. L. *Leighton of St Mellons, B.*
Seager, Hon Simon J. L. *Leighton of St. Mellons, B.*
Sealy, Hon Lavinia C. *Piercy, B.*
Seccombe, Hon M. Robert *Seccombe, Bs.*
Seccombe, Hon Philip S. *Seccombe, Bs.*
Sedgwick, Lady Henrietta L. *Normanby, M.*
Seebohm, Hon Richard H. *Seebohm, B.*
Seely, Hon Patrick M. *Mottistone, B.*
Seely, Hon Peter J. P. *Mottistone, B.*
Seely, Hon Victoria A. *Mottistone, B.*
Selby, Hon Susan L. *Pennock, B.*
Self, Hon Ruth K. *Napier of Magdala, B.*
Selkirk, Hon Nadia *Lucas of Chilworth, B.*
Selman, Hon Carolyn *Oppenheim-Barnes, Bs.*
Sempill, Hon Cosima *Sempill, L.*
Sempill, Hon Francis *Sempill, L.*
Sempill, Hon Ian D. W. Chant- *Sempill, L.*
Sempill, Hon Janet C. Forbes- *Sempill, L.*
Sempill, Hon Kirstine E. Daranyi- Forbes- *Sempill, L.*
Senior, Hon Rosemary *Hunt of Fawley, B.*
Serota, (Hon) Nicholas A. *Serota, Bs.*
Servatius, Hon Prunella J. *Hawke, B.*

Smith, Hon Vera L. M. *Granville-West, By.*
Smith, Hon W. Henry *Hambleden, V.*
Smith, Hon Elizabeth S. Abel *De L'Isle, V.*
Smith, Hon Rebecca A. Ayre- *Tanlaw, B.*
Smith, Lady Jean M. Babington *Clanwilliam, E.*
Smith, Lady Corisande E. Bain *Tankerville, E.*
Smith, Hon Alick, L. Buchanan- *Balerno, B.*
Smith, Hon Mrs George A. Buchanan- *Balerno, B.*
Smith, Hon Jock G. Buchanan- *Balerno, B.*
Smith, Hon Robert D. Buchanan- *Balerno, B.*
Smith, Hon Lesley Delacourt- *Delacourt-Smith, By.*
Smith, Hon Stephen Delacourt- *Delacourt-Smith, By.*
Smith, Hon Adam W. G. Dixon *Dixon-Smith, B.*
Smith, Hon Elizabeth (Betsy) W. Duncan *Cottesloe, B.*
Smith, Hon Margaret B. M. Eric *Bangor, V.*
Smith, Lady Eliza M. Mays- *Iveagh, E.*
Smith, Hon Theresa C. Orme- *Kilbrandon, B.*
Smith, Hon Rose M. Owen- *Ponsonby of Shulbrede, B.*
Smith, Hon Gabrielle M. Seth- *Basing, B.*
Smith, Hon Moana E. J. Seth- *McGowan, B.*
Smith, Hon Arabella C. Stuart- *Montgomery of Alamein, V.*
Smith, Hon Sir J. Jonath Walker- *Broxbourne, By.*
Smith, Hon (Molly A.) Lady Wyldbore- *Rotherwick, B.*
Smyly, Hon Harriet L. *Grimthorpe, B.*
Smyth, Hon Patricia M. *Black, B.*
Snow, Hon Harriet F. H. *Burntwood, By.*
Snow, Hon Philip C. H. *Snow, By.*
Snowball, Hon Clarinda S. *Knollys, V.*
Soames, Hon Camilla M. L. *Somerleyton, B.*
Soames, Hon Emma M. *Soames, B.*
Soames, Hon A. Nicholas W. *Soames, B.*
Soames, Hon Jeremy B. *Soames, B.*
Soames, Hon Rupert C. *Soames, B.*
Sofer, Hon Anne H. *Crowther, By.*
Somers, Hon Sara M. *Byers, B.*
Somerset, Lord Alexander *Beaufort, D.*
Somerset, Lord Edward A. *Beaufort, D.*
Somerset, Hon Geoffrey *Raglan, B.*
Somerset, Lady Isabella E. *Beaufort, D.*
Somerset, Lord John R. *Beaufort, D.*
Somerville, Hon (M. I. April) Lady Agnew- *Strange, Bs.*
Sorensen, Hon Michael M. R. *Sorensen, By.*
Sorton, Hon Deirdre E. *Sandberg, B.*
Soskice, Hon David W. *Stowhill, B.*
Soskice, Hon Oliver C. H. *Stowhill, B.*
Soukup, Lady Constance A. *Ormonde, M.*
Soulsby, Hon John A. L. *Soulsby, B.*
Souter, Hon Amanda E. *Audley, B.*
Southby, Lady Anne A. *Linlithgow, M.*
Southey, Hon Victoria F. J. *Deedes, B.*
Southwell, Hon Charles A. J. *Southwell, V.*
Southwell, Hon Mrs Francis J. *Southwell, V.*
Southwell, Hon Richard A. P. *Southwell, V.*
Sparks, Hon Juliet J. M. *Moynihan, B.*
Sparks, Hon Rosemary *Monslow, By.*
Spencer, Hon Catherine A. *Ebbisham, B.*
Spencer, Lady Eliza V. *Spencer, E.*
Spencer, Lady K. Amelia *Spencer, E.*
Spencer, Lady Kitty E. *Spencer, E.*
Spens, Hon Emily S. *Spens, B.*
Spens, Hon Mallowry A. *Spens, B.*
Spens, Hon Patrick N. G. *Spens, B.*
Spens, Hon Philippa P. *Boyd of Merton, V.*
Spens, Hon Sarah H. *Spens, B.*
Spens, Hon William D. R. *Spens, B.*
Speyer, Hon Beatrice S. *Ravensworth, B.*
Spicer, Lady Avice E. M. *De La Warr, E.*
Spicer, Hon Sarah M. *Watkinson, V.*
Spickernell, Lady Rachel B. V. *Lansdowne, M.*
Spickova, Hon Victoria W. Reilly- *Reilly, B.*
Spurrier, Hon Elizabeth J. *Maude of Stratford upon Avon, B.*
Spziro, Hon Jane E. *Henniker, B.*
Stacey, Hon Anne C. M. *Bridgeman, V.*
Stafford, Hon Elizabeth-Anne *Richardson, B.*
Staib, Hon Mary C. *Kinnaird, L.*
Stainton, Hon (Janet B.) Lady *Forteviot, B.*
Stallard, Hon Richard *Stallard, B.*
Stamp, Hon Mrs A. Maxwell *Stamp, B.*
Stamp, Hon Jos C. *Stamp, B.*
Stamp, Hon Josiah R. *Stamp, B.*
Stamp, Hon Nancy E. *Stamp, B.*
Stamp, Hon Trevor C. B. *Stamp, B.*
Stanhope, Lady Isabella R. *Harrington, E.*

Stanhope, Hon John F. *Harrington, E.*
Stanhope, Hon Steven F. L. *Harrington, E.*
Stanhope, Lady Trina M. *Harrington, E.*
Stanhope, Hon William H. L. *Harrington, E.*
Stanley, Hon Caroline M. *Renton, B.*
Stanley, Hon Charles E. *Stanley of Alderley, B.*
Stanley, Hon Frances (Fanny) A. *Cottesloe, B.*
Stanley, Hon Frances C. B. *Fermoy, B.*
Stanley, Hon Harry J. *Stanley of Alderley, B.*
Stanley, Lady Henrietta M. R. *Derby, E.*
Stanley, Hon Lucinda M. *Stanley of Alderley, B.*
Stanley, Hon Peter H. C. *Derby, E.*
Stanley, Hon Richard M. O. *Stanley of Alderley, B.*
Stanley, Hon Mrs Richard O. *Derby, E.*
Stanley, Hon Richard O. *Stanley of Alderley, B.*
Stanton, Hon Clare M. *Norrie, B.*
Starkey, Hon A. E. Maureen L. *Templetown, V.*
Steel, Lady Rosemary V. E. *Clarendon, E.*
Steel, Hon Sophia R. E. *Hawarden, V.*
Steer, Hon Katharine (Kash) D. *Onslow of Woking, B.*
Stenham, Hon S. Marian *Poole, B.*
Stephenson, Hon (F. Rose) Lady *Asquith of Bishopstone, By.*
Stephenson, Hon Sarah M. *Norrie, B.*
Sternberg, Hon Rosanne M. M. *Plurenden, B.*
Stevens, Hon Andrew D. *Stevens of Ludgate, B.*
Stevens, Hon Henrietta M. *St. Helens, B.*
Stevens, Hon Judith A. *Stevens of Ludgate, B.*
Stevenson, Hon Deborah F. *Taylor of Gosforth, B.*
Stevenson, Hon Susan M. *Ebbisham, B.*
Stevenson, Hon Deborah S. Sinclair- *Broxbourne, By.*
Stewart, Lady Alison J. *Ducie, E.*
Stewart, Lady C. Daphne *Tweeddale, M.*
Stewart, Hon Frances J. *Kaldor, B.*
Stewart, Hon Henry E. A. H. *Stewartby, B.*
Stewart, Hon Lydia B. R. A. P. *Stewartby, B.*
Stewart, Lady Miranda K. *Beatty, E.*
Stewart, Hon Virginia *Galpern, B.*
Stewart, Hon Zoë L. *Leighton of St. Mellons, B.*
Stewart, Lord Reginald A.
  Vane-Tempest- *Londonderry, M.*
Steyn, Hon Deon J. *Steyn, B.*
Steyn, Hon Michael van Z. *Steyn, B.*
Stirling, Lady Marjorie H. *Dunmore, E.*
Stockdale, Hon (Louise) Lady *Hesketh, B.*
Stockdale, Hon Margaret V. *Faringdon, B.*
Stocks, Hon Helen J. *Stocks, By.*
Stocks, Hon Joan E. *Underhill, B.*
Stocks, Hon John R. *Stocks, By.*
Stoddart, Hon Howard D. *Stoddart of Swindon, B.*
Stoddart, Hon Mathwyn H. *Stoddart of Swindon, B.*
Stokes, Hon Michael D. G. *Stokes, B.*
Stone, Hon Caroline E. *Fraser of Allander, By.*
Stone, Hon Catherine M. *Dormer, B.*
Stone, Hon Daniel M. *Stone of Blackheath, B.*
Stone, Hon Jane T. *O'Hagan, B.*
Stone, Hon Jessica A. *Stone of Blackheath, B.*
Stone, Hon Richard M. E. *Stone, B.*
Stone, Hon Susannah N. *Stone of Blackheath, B.*
Stonor, Hon Emily M. J. *Camoys, B.*
Stonor, Hon Georgina M. H. *Camoys, B.*
Stonor, Hon Julia M. C. M. *Camoys, B.*
Stonor, Hon Ralph W. R. T. *Camoys, B.*
Stonor, Hon Sophia U. *Camoys, B.*
Stopford, Hon Mrs Edward R. B. *Courtown, E.*
Stopford, Hon Jeremy N. *Courtown, E.*
Stopford, Lady Rosanna E. A. *Courtown, E.*
Stopford, Hon Thomas *Stopford of Fallowfield, By.*
Storey, Hon Sir Richard *Buckton, By.*
Stotten, Lady Irmengarde *Ducie, E.*
Stourton, Hon Charlotte M. *Mowbray, B.*
Stourton, Hon Edward W. S. *Mowbray, B.*
Stourton, Hon James A. *Mowbray, B.*
Stourton, Lady Joanna *Cavan, E.*
Stourton, Hon Mrs Edward P. J. Corbally *Mowbray, B.*
Stowasser, Hon Helen M. *Platt, B.*
Strachey, Hon Antonia P. M. *O'Hagan, B.*
Strachey, Hon Richard T. *O'Hagan, B.*
Straight, Lady Daphne M. *Winchilsea, E.*
Straker, Hon Ann G. *Milne, B.*
Strangways, Hon Raymond G. Fox- *Ilchester, E.*
Stratford, Hon Oriel A. D. *Massereene, V.*
Strauss, Hon Brian T. *Strauss, B.*
Strauss, Hon Hilary J. *Strauss, B.*
Strauss, Hon Roger A. *Strauss, B.*
Streatfield, Lady Moyra C. *Courtown, E.*

Wellesley, Lord John H. *Wellington, D.*
Wellesley, Lady Mary L. *Wellington, D.*
Wellesley, Hon Natasha R. *Cowley, E.*
Wellesley, Lord Richard G. *Wellington, D.*
Wellesley, Lady Tara L. *Cowley, E.*
Wells, Hon Gillian H. C. *Tranmire, B.*
Wells, Hon Jane *Bernstein, B.*
Welton, Hon Kirstin E. *Ullswater, V.*
Wemyss, Lady Jean C. *Elgin, E.*
Wesley, Hon Melissa M. *Leathers, V.*
Wesolowska, Hon Pandora *Melchett, B.*
West, Hon Gerald H. G. *Granville-West, By.*
West, Hon Catherine J. Sackville- *Sackville, B.*
Westbrook, Hon Mary J. *Strathalmond, B.*
Westenra, Hon Benedict W. *Rossmore, B.*
Westenra, Hon Brigid M. *Rossmore, B.*
Weston, Hon Berenice M. *Broxbourne, By.*
Weston, Hon Caroline C. *Montagu of Beaulieu, B.*
Westropp, Victoria M. *Manton, B.*
Westwood, Hon Mrs Douglas W. *Westwood, B.*
Westwood, Hon Nigel A. *Westwood, B.*
Westwood, Hon William G. *Westwood, B.*
Whaley, Hon Lucy R. *Deedes, B.*
Wharton, Hon Frances M. *Sandford, B.*
Wharton, Hon Rebecca E. *Devon, E.*
Wheatley, Hon Anthony *Wheatley, B.*
Wheatley, Hon John *Wheatley, B.*
Wheatley, Hon Michael *Wheatley, B.*
Wheatley, Hon Patrick *Wheatley, B.*
Wheeler, Hon Katharine J. *Briggs, B.*
Wheeler, Hon Sibyl G. *Berners, Bs.*
Whetherly, Hon Rosemary G. A. *Leverhulme, V.*
Whidborne, Hon Elaine J. B. *St John of Bletso, B.*
Whitcombe, Hon Rosemary A. H. *Clydesmuir, B.*
White, Hon Caroline D. *Annaly, B.*
White, Hon Frances A. *Fisher, B.*
White, Hon Iona E. *Annaly, B.*
White, Hon Jessica J. V. *Howard de Walden, B.*
White, Hon Lavinia M. *Annaly, B.*
White, Hon Lucas C. *White of Hull, B.*
White, Hon Luke H. *Annaly, B.*
White, Hon Mary A. Mayon- *Daventry, V.*
Whitehead, Hon Annabel A. H. *Inchyra, B.*
Whitehead, Hon Lucia E. *Burnham, B.*
Whiteley, Lady Angela M. *Guilford, E.*
Whiteley, Lady Anne P. *Abergavenny, M.*
Whiteley, Hon William F. *Marchamley, B.*
Whitfeld, Hon Deborah M. *Reigate, B.*
Whitfield, Hon Anna L. *Kenswood, B.*
Whitfield, Hon Anthony J. *Kenswood, B.*
Whitfield, Hon Benjamin M. *Kenswood, B.*
Whitfield, Lady Fiona C. *Caithness, E.*
Whitfield, Hon Michael C. *Kenswood, B.*
Whitfield, Hon Steven J. *Kenswood, B.*
Whitley, Lady Mary I. M. *Cambridge, M.*
Whitley, Hon Tara O. *Moyola, B.*
Whitty, Hon David J. *Whitty, B.*
Whitty, Hon Michael S. *Whitty, B.*
Wickham, Hon Helen M. *Wade, B.*
Widdows, Hon Angela H. *Marshall of Leeds, B.*
Wide, Hon Ursula M. B. *Tweedsmuir, B.*
Wightman, Lady Rebecca M. *Dunmore, E.*
Wigoder, Hon Carolyn *Wigoder, B.*
Wigoder, Hon Charles *Wigoder, B.*
Wigoder, Hon Giles *Wigoder, B.*
Wigoder, Hon Justin *Wigoder, B.*
Wigram, Hon Andrew F. C. *Wigram, B.*
Wilberforce, Hon Samuel H. *Wilberforce, B.*
Wilbraham, Hon Andrew Bootle- *Skelmersdale, B.*
Wilbraham, Hon Carolyn A. Bootle- *Skelmersdale, B.*
Wilbur, Lady H. C. Tara *Strafford, E.*
Wilder, Hon Rachel A. *Lucas of Chilworth, B.*
Wildman, Hon Corinna *Cunliffe, B.*
Wiley, Lady J. L. Serena *Scarbrough, E.*
Wilf, Hon Naomi R. Samuel- *Samuel, V.*
Wilkinson, Hon Anthea M. *Roberthall, B.*
Wilkinson, Hon Elizabeth J. M. *Fletcher, B.*
Wilkinson, Lady Louise *Ailesbury, M.*
Wilkinson, Hon Adam Browne- *Browne-Wilkinson, B.*
Wilkinson, Hon Henrietta Browne- *Browne-Wilkinson, B.*
Wilkinson, Hon Martha Browne- *Browne-Wilkinson, B.*
Wilkinson, Hon Oliver Browne- *Browne-Wilkinson, B.*
Willett, Hon Susannah *Naseby, B.*
Willetts, Hon Sarah H. A. *Butterfield, B.*

Williams, Hon Daniel *Williams of Mostyn, B.*
Williams, Hon Emma *Williams of Mostyn, B.*
Williams, Hon Mrs Horace *Williams of Barnburgh, B.*
Williams, Hon John M. *Francis-Williams, By.*
Williams, Hon Katharine L. *Roskill, B.*
Williams, Hon Margaret de H. *Belhaven, L.*
Williams, Hon Martha *Williams of Mostyn, B.*
Williams, Lady Mary R. *Grafton, D.*
Williams, Hon Rebecca C. *Williams of Crosby, Bs.*
Williams, Hon Sarah S. R. *Dynevor, B.*
Williams, Hon Olivia, Hoole-Lowsley- *Skelmersdale, B.*
Williams, Lady C. M. Fiona Lowsley- *Bute, M.*
Williams, Hon Christine A. Rees- *Ogmore, B.*
Williams, Hon Jennet E. Rees- *Ogmore, B.*
Williams, Hon Morgan Rees- *Ogmore, B.*
Williams, Lady Penelope Wynn- *Jowitt, E.*
Williamson, Hon George A. *Forres, B.*
Williamson, Hon Guthrie J. *Forres, B.*
Williamson, Hon Jonathan *Williamson of Horton, B.*
Williamson, Hon Timothy *Williamson of Horton, B.*
Willis, Hon John E. *Willis, B.*
Willoughby, Hon Mrs Charles C. W. *Middleton, B.*
Willoughby, Hon H. E. Christopher *Middleton, B.*
Willoughby, Hon John H. F. *Middleton, B.*
Willoughby, Hon Lucy C. A. *De L'Isle, V.*
Willoughby, Hon Michael C. J. *Middleton, B.*
Willoughby, Hon T. H. Richard *Middleton, B.*
Wills, Hon Charlotte A.H. *Dulverton, B.*
Wills, Hon E. Robert H. *Dulverton, B.*
Wills, Hon Elizabeth A. *Rockley, B.*
Wills, Hon Jean C. *Elphinstone, L.*
Wills, Lady Katharine A. *Clanwilliam, E.*
Wills, Hon R. Ian H. *Dulverton, B.*
Wills, Hon Robert A. H. *Dulverton, B.*
Wills, Hon Sarah M. H. *Dulverton, B.*
Wills, Hon V. Patrick H. *Dulverton, B.*
Willson, Hon Anne M. *Scarsdale, V.*
Wilson, Lady Alexandra P. G. *Jellicoe, E.*
Wilson, Hon Andrew M. W. *Wilson of Tillyorn, B.*
Wilson, Hon D. Mark *Nunburnholme, B.*
Wilson, Hon Geoffrey H. *Moran, B.*
Wilson, Hon Giles D. J. *Wilson of Rievaulx, B.*
Wilson, Hon James M. *Moran, B.*
Wilson, Hon (Jean M.) Lady *Rankeillour, B.*
Wilson, Hon Lorraine M. C. *Nunburnholme, B.*
Wilson, Hon Margaret E. *Maybray-King, B.*
Wilson, Hon Nathalia E. *Nunburnholme, B.*
Wilson, Hon Peter M. W. *Wilson of Tillyorn, B.*
Wilson, Hon Robin J. *Wilson of Rievaulx, B.*
Wilson, Hon Sally Ann M. G. *Vivian, B.*
Wilson, Hon Shirley C. *Cunliffe, B.*
Wilson, Hon Stephen C. *Nunburnholme, B.*
Wilson, Lady Tatiana M. L. R. C. F. *Eldon, E.*
Wilson, Hon William E. A. *Moran, B.*
Wilson, Hon Ysabelle *Nunburnholme, B.*
Wilson, Hon Yvette L. *Baillieu, V.*
Wilson, Hon Christian V. G. Menzies- *Catto, B.*
Winch, Hon Jean R. V. B. *Falkland, V.*
Windsor, Lady Amelia S. T. M. M. *Kent, D.*
Windsor, Lady Davina E. A. B. *Gloucester, D.*
Windsor, Lord Frederick M. G. D. L. *Kent, D.*
Windsor, Lady Gabriella M. A. O. *Kent, D.*
Windsor, Lady Marina-Charlotte *Kent, D.*
Windsor, Lord Nicholas C. E. J. *Kent, D.*
Windsor, Lady Rose V. B. L. *Gloucester, D.*
Wingfield, Hon Cynthia M. *Sandys, B.*
Wingfield, Hon Guy C. P. *Powerscourt, V.*
Wingfield, Hon Julia *Powerscourt, V.*
Wingfield, Hon Mervyn A. *Powerscourt, V.*
Wingfield, Lady Norah B. C. *Jellicoe, E.*
Winn, Hon Henrietta S. A. *St Oswald, B.*
Winn, Hon Mrs Reginald H. *St. Oswald, B.*
Winn, Hon Rowland C. S. *St Oswald, B.*
Winn, Hon Mrs Owain G. Allanson- *Headley, By.*
Winn, Hon Susan E. Allanson- *Headley, By.*
Winnington, Lady Betty M. *Lichfield, E.*
Winstanley, Hon Diana C. *Winstanley, B.*
Winstanley, Hon Nicholas C. P. *Winstanley, B.*
Winstanley, Hon Stephen W. *Winstanley, B.*
Winston, Hon Benjamin *Winston, B.*
Winston, Hon Joel *Winston, B.*
Winston, Hon Tanya *Winston, B.*
Winstone, Hon Hilary A. W. *Perry of Southwark, Bs.*
Winterbothom, Hon Emmeline V. L. *Derwent, B.*
Winterbottom, Hon Caroline M. A. *Winterbottom, B.*
Winterbottom, Hon Dudley W. G. *Winterbottom, B.*

THE BARONETAGE

THE BARONETAGE

The ALPHABETICAL ARRANGEMENT includes (*i*) the names of Baronets, and (*ii*) the names of extinct baronetcies that are represented in the female line.

Compound surnames are arranged under the last and principal surname,
  e.g. Havelock-Allan will be found under the letter A.

The scope of EACH ARTICLE IN THE BARONETAGE is designed to include information concerning every *living* male descended in the male line from the first Baronet, and of all *living* females being issue of males so descended. For remainders to Baronetcies see article on Baronets in Preliminary Section.

DECEASED FEMALE COLLATERALS and their issue are not as a rule referred to in this work.

ISSUE of the members of two families mentioned in the work, who happen to have intermarried, are usually referred to under the father's name.

CHRISTIAN NAMES OF THE HEIR apparent or presumptive are given in capital letters.

CREATIONS:— E= England (22 May 1611 to 30 April 1707).
             NS= Nova Scotia or Scotland (28 May 1625 to 30 April 1707).
             I= Ireland (30 Sept 1619 to 31 Dec 1800).
             GB= Great Britain (1 May 1707 to 31 Dec 1800).
             UK= United Kingdom (1 Jan 1801 to present time).

Since 1929, Baronets of England, Ireland, Great Britain, and the United Kingdom have been permitted to depict their respective Badges suspended by the ribbon below the shield of arms, as was already the case in respect of Baronets of Nova Scotia.

ABDY (UK) 1850, of Albyns, Essex

Sir VALENTINE ROBERT DUFF ABDY, 6th *Baronet*; *b* 11 Sept 1937; *s* his father, *Sir* ROBERT HENRY EDWARD, 1976; *ed* Eton; Chevalier des Arts et Lettres, France, 1995: *m* 1971 (*m diss* 1982), Mathilde, da of Etienne Coche de la Ferté, and has issue.

Arms – Or, two chevronels between three trefoils slipped sable. Crest – An eagle's head couped proper, beaked azure.
Residences – 11 Avenue de Brétigny, 92380 Garches, France; 19 Belgrave Place, SW1; Hadsley House, Lefebore St, St Peter Port, Guernsey, CI.

SON LIVING

ROBERT ETIENNE ERIC, *b* 22 Feb 1978.

Firm and faithful

Sir Thomas Neville Abdy, 1st Bt, of Albyns, Essex, was MP for Lyme Regis 1847-52, and High Sheriff of Essex 1875.

ABERCROMBY (NS) 1636, of Birkenbog, Banffshire

He aims at high things

Sir IAN GEORGE ABERCROMBY, 10th *Baronet*, only son of Robert Ogilvie Abercromby, el son of David James Abercromby, 4th son of 5th baronet; *b* 30 June 1925; *s* his kinsman, *Maj Sir* ROBERT ALEXANDER, MC, DL, 1972; *ed* Lancing, and Bloxham Sch, Banbury: *m* 1st, 1950 (*m diss* 1957), Joyce Beryl, da of Leonard Griffiths, of Spencer's Wood, Berks; 2ndly, 1959, Fanny Mary Udale (Mollie), only da of Dr Graham Udale-Smith, of Sitio Litre, Puerto de la Cruz, Tenerife; 3rdly, 1976, Diana Marjorie, da of Horace Geoffrey Cockell, of Ditton House, Oxhey Woods, Herts, and widow of Capt Ian Charles Palliser Galloway, Seaforth Highlanders, of Blervie, Forres, Morayshire, and has issue by 2nd *m*.

Arms – Quarterly: 1st and 4th argent, a chevron gules between three boars' heads, erased azure, langued of the second; 2nd and 3rd grand quarters: 1st and 4th argent, a lion passant guardant gules, crowned with an imperial crown: 2nd and 3rd argent, three popinjays vert, beaked and membered gules. **Crest** – A falcon rising belled proper. **Supporters** – Two greyhounds argent, collared gules. **Motto** – Vive ut vivas (*Live, that thou mayest live*).
Clubs – Ski Club of Great Britain, Kandahar, Real Nautico (Tenerife).

DAUGHTER LIVING (*By 2nd marriage*)

Maria Amelia, *b* 1960: *m* 1988, Wellesley Theodore Octavius Wallace, son of late Dr Caleb Paul Wallace, of W Clandon, Surrey, and has issue living, James Abercromby Octavius *b* 1989, — Lucy Maria Diana, *b* 1991. *Residence* – Whitecroft, W Clandon, Surrey.

COLLATERAL BRANCH LIVING

Granddaughter of Douglas Charles Abercromby, 4th son of 6th baronet:—
Issue of late Keith Douglas Abercromby, *b* 1887 *d* 1968: *m* 1st, 1913, Eva Winifred, who *d* 1930, only da of late Harry Millward Wright; 2ndly, 1939, Mrs Hilda Brocket Lemon, who *d* 1985, da of Alan Sandys, Bar-at-Law:—
(By 1st *m*) Joan Eileen (36 Marlborough Pl, NW8 0PD), *b* 1919: *m* 1st, 1939 (*m diss* 1948), Alan James Butler Aldridge; 2ndly, 1948, Richard Lloyd Joseph Wills, CBE, MC, who *d* 1969; 3rdly, 1972, Maj-Gen James Alexander Rowland Robertson, CB, CBE, DSO, DL, and has issue living, (by 1st *m*) Gail Susan Eva, *b* 1946: *m* 1974, Raymond Henry Cornish, and has issue living, Belinda Mary Eva *b* 1975, Peta Eleanor *b* 1986.

Sir Alexander Abercromby, of Birkenbog, MP for Banffshire, 7th in descent from George Abercrombie, whose lands were erected into the Barony of Pitmedden 1513, was created a Bt of Nova Scotia 1636 with remainder to his heirs male. The 2nd baronet sat as MP for co Banff in Scottish Parliament 1694, and the 5th baronet sat at MP for the same co 1812-18. Sir George William Abercromby, DSO, 8th Bt, was convener of Banff Co Council 1929-61, and Lord-Lieut of Banffsire 1946-64. Sir Robert Alexander Abercromby, MC, 9th Bt, was Vice-Lieut of Banffshire 1965-71.

ACKROYD (UK) 1956, of Dewsbury, West Riding of Yorkshire

Sir TIMOTHY ROBERT WHYTE ACKROYD, 3rd *Baronet*; *b* 7 Oct 1958; *s* his father, *Sir* JOHN ROBERT WHYTE, 1995; *ed* Bradfield, and LAMDA; Actor; Founder and Trustee Tusk 1989, Trustee Marjorie & Dorothy Whyte Memorial Fund 1992, The Ackroyd Trust 1994, and Have a Go Holiday Project 1995.

𝕬rms – Azure on a pale between two oak leaves or a sword erect gules. 𝕮rest – A goat's head erased azure armed or charged on the neck with a rose argent barbed and seeded proper.
Residence – Flat 4, 33 Chepstow Rd, W2 5BP. *Clubs* – MCC, and Garrick.

BROTHER LIVING

ANDREW JOHN ARMITAGE, *b* 17 Sept 1961; *ed* Bradfield, and St Martin's Sch of Art; painter.

SISTERS LIVING

Jane Victoria MacLeod, *b* 1957, sculptress: *m* 1992, as his 2nd wife, David Robert Ewart Annesley, and has issue (*see* E Annesley, colls). *Residence* – 77 Park Avenue North, N8. —— Kate Georgina McBride, *b* 1963: *m* 1986, Fabrice Gilles Marion, eldest son of Roger Marion, and has issue living, Oscar Winston, *b* 1991, — Oriane Eileen, *b* 1987, — Tiphaine Jennifer, *b* 1989, — Heloise Victoria, *b* 1994. *Residence* – 39 Boulevard du Château, 92200 Neuilly-sur-Seine, France.

UNCLE LIVING (*son of 1st baronet*)

Christopher Lowell, *b* 1934; *ed* Bradfield, and Magdalene Coll, Camb (BA 1957, MA 1961): *m* 1961, Caroline Rachael, only da of late Eric Lewis, and has issue living, Marcus Lowell, *b* 1964; *ed* Manchester Univ, and Balliol Coll, Oxford, — Vivyan Katy, *b* 1962: *m* 1987, David Clive Whittaker, 2nd son of Kenneth Whittaker, and has issue living, Giles Matthew *b* 1988, Harry Lowell *b* 1992, Angus David *b* 1995.

Sir Cuthbert Lowell Ackroyd, 1st Bt, son of Benjamin Batley Ackroyd, of Dewsbury, Yorks, was Lord Mayor of London 1955-56; his son, Sir John Robert Whyte Ackroyd, 2nd Bt, commn'd RA, awarded Sword of Honour at Mons Officer Cadet Sch 1951, was an Underwriting Member of Lloyd's, a Member of Council of Zoological Soc of London, Hon Sec Royal Coll of Music, and Vice-Pres Dystonia Soc.

ACLAND (E) 1678, with precedence from 1644, of Columb-John, Devon

Unshaken

Sir JOHN DYKE ACLAND, 16th *Baronet*; *b* 13 May 1939; *s* his father, *Sir* RICHARD THOMAS DYKE, 1990; *ed* Clifton, Magdalene Coll, Camb (MA), and Univ of W Indies (MSc): *m* 1961, Viriginia, yr da of Roland Forge, of The Grange, Barnoldby-le-Beck, Lincs, and has issue.

𝕬rms – Checky argent and sable, a fesse gules. 𝕮rest – A man's hand apaumée couped at the wrist in a glove lying fessewise to the sinister, thereon a falcon perched all proper, jessed and belled or.
Seat – Killerton, Broadclyst, Devon. *Residence* – Sprydon, Broadclyst, Exeter, Devon EX5 3JN.

SONS LIVING

DOMINIC DYKE, *b* 19 Nov 1962; *ed* Edinburgh Univ (MA): *m* 1990, Sarah Anne, 3rd da of Ven Kenneth Unwin, formerly Archdeacon of Pontefract, and has issue living, Patrick, *b* 18 Nov 1993, — Finlay, *b* 1995, — Florence, *b* (twin) 1993, — Esther, *b* 1998. —— Piers Dyke, *b* 1965; *ed* Univ Coll, London (BSc, PhD); Bar Lincoln's Inn 1992: *m* 1994, Lucinda M., da of Dr John Draper Raiman, of Highams Park, E4, and has issue living, Harriet, *b* 1995, — Alice Beatrice, *b* 1996.

DAUGHTER LIVING

Holly, *b* 1972; *ed* Leeds Univ (BA).

BROTHERS LIVING

Robert Dyke, *b* 1941; *ed* Bryanston, and London Univ (MB BS); FRCS England, LRCP London: *m* 1st, 1963 (*m diss* 1983), (Susan Maureen) Sarah, da of Cmdr James Wood, RN, of Liss, Hants; 2ndly, 1983 (*m diss* 1990), Susan Ann, da of Thomas L. Bishop of Crestwood, Kentucky, USA; 3rdly, 1993, Bette, da of Leon M. Levy, of Yardley, PA, USA, and has issue living (by 1st *m*), Daniel James, *b* 1969; has discontinued use of forename Dyke; *ed* Berkely Univ, Calif, — Beatrice Maud, *b* 1966; has discontinued use of forename Dyke; *ed* Duke Univ, Calif, — (by 2nd *m*) Benjamin Thomas, *b* 1984, — Emily Grace, *b*

1986. —— Henry Dyke, b 1943; ed Clifton, and Magdalene Coll, Camb (BA); DPhil Oxon: m 1967 (m diss 1977), (Irene) Norma, da of Percy Norman Gatley, of 28 Cherry Tree Av, Runcorn, Ches. Residence – 1339 Talmadge St, Los Angeles, Calif, USA.

COLLATERAL BRANCHES LIVING

Issue of late Arthur Geoffrey Dyke Acland, 2nd son of 14th Bt, b 1908, d 1964: m 1932 (Winifred) Julian Dorothy, da of Lt-Col Sydney Roden Fothergill, JP, DL, of Lowbridge House, Kendal:—
Oliver Geoffrey Dyke, b 1934; 2nd Lt Border Regt: m 1959, Judith Veronica, 2nd da of late Peter Willans, of 18 Canonbury Park North, N1, and has issue living, Peter Geoffrey Dyke, b 1961, — Francis Oliver Dyke, b 1963, — Christopher John Dyke, b 1966. Residence – Barnsdale, Burneside, nr Kendal, Cumbria. —— Robin Julian Dyke, b 1937. —— Edward Francis Dyke, b 1942.

Grandsons of late Capt Henry Vivian Acland (infra):—
Issue of late Capt John Ernest Vivian Acland, R Westminster Regt, Canadian Army, b 1911, d 1982: m 1st, 1935, Edith Eleanor, who d 1953, da of late John Waterman of Vancouver, BC; 2ndly, 1954, Joan Wilmot:—
(By 2nd m) Peter Vivian, b 1955. —— Anthony Robert, b 1957.

Granddaughter of late Capt John Edward ACLAND (infra):—
Issue of late Capt Henry Vivian Acland, b 1883, d 1968: m 1st, 1910, Jeanne, who d 1950, only da of M. Vander Nest, formerly Min for Belgium in USA; 2ndly, 1951, Mrs Inez Sweetwood, da of Robert Everett Mutch, of Charlottetown, Prince Edward Island:—
(By 1st m) Patricia Evelyn, b 1920: m 1945, Robert Browne-Clayton, late Lt, Princess Patricia's Canadian LI, of 4534 Gordon Drive, Kelowna, BC, Canada, and has issue living, Patrick Robert (385 5th St, Campbell River, BC, Canada V9W 3X4), b 1947; ed Nôtre Dame Univ, Nelson, BC (BSc), — Peter Shane (1444 Lawrence Av, Kelowna, BC, Canada V1Y 6M8), b 1949; ed BC Univ (BSc): m 1972, Mary Elizabeth, da of W. C. Law, of Vancouver, BC, and has issue living, Nicole Ann b 1975, Celia Jeanne b 1977, — Jeanne Madeline (104 1585 West 11th Av, Vancouver, BC, Canada V6J 2B5), b 1953; ed BC Univ (BSc).

Grandchildren of late Lt-Gen Arthur Nugent FLOYER-ACLAND, CB, DSO, MC, 2nd son of late Capt John Edward ACLAND, 2nd son of late Col Charles Arthur Williams TROYTE, eldest son of late Arthur Henry Dyke TROYTE, 2nd son of 10th baronet:—
Issue of late Brig Stafford Nugent Floyer-Acland, CBE, b 1916, d 1994: m 1950, Patricia Egidia Hastings, da of late Lt-Col Richard St Barbe Emmott, IA (ret) (see Cts Loudoun, colls):—
Richard Stafford (Blakeway Farm, Harley, nr Shrewsbury, Shropshire SY5 6LT), b 1952; ed Marlborough: m 1983, Sarah Margaret, da of Henry Millington Synge, of Nesscliffe, Shropshire, and has issue living, Charles Stafford, b 1987, — Olivia Joy, b 1985, — Beatrice Rose, b 1990. —— Andrew Arthur (5 Foxcote, Andoversford, nr Cheltenham, Glos), b 1955; ed Marlborough, and Durham Univ (BA): m 1987, (Penelope) Lucy Priscilla, elder da of Julian Gerard Wathen (see Starkey, Bt, 1985 Edn), and has issue living, Toby Julian, b 1989. —— Victoria Egidia, b 1962; ed Bristol Univ (BA): m 1992, Nagi El-Bay, of Sisams Cottage, Nightingale Lane, Cleeve Prior, Worcs, eldest son of Saad El-Bay, of Heliopolis, Egypt, and has issue living, Noorah Egidia, b 1993.

Granddaughter of late Capt John Edward ACLAND (ante):—
Issue of late Capt John Bevill Acland, b 1890, d 1966: m 1914, Marjorie, who d 1977, da of H. Guernsey:—
Ione Vivienne (161 Acland Rd, Ganges, Salt Spring Is, BC), b 1915; Headmistress of Strathcona Lodge Sch, Shawnigan Lake, BC 1959-69: m 1936, Charles Clement Guthrie, who d 1966, and has issue living, Barnaby Fairbairn, b 1937; ed Univ of Victoria (BA), — Nicholas Bruce, b 1938; ed Univ of BC (BSc, BEd): m 1966, Anna Scott, and has issue living, Russell Sean b 1967, Ross Cameron b 1968, Ian Benjamin b 1970, Ryan David b 1981, Jennifer Sarah b 1974.

Descendants of late Sir Henry Wentworth Dyke Acland, KCB (4th son of 10th baronet), who was cr a Baronet 1890:—
See Acland, Bt, cr 1890.

Grandchildren of late Lt-Col Baldwyn John Dyke Acland, eldest son of late Cdr Benjamin Dyke Acland (infra):—
Issue of late John Ben Dyke Acland, b 1916, d 1991: m 1st, 1941 (m diss 1950), Beatrice Margaret, who d 1957, da of William Willes, of Newbold Comyd, Leamington Spa; 2ndly, 1950, Lorna May Woodthorpe (1 East St, Uffculme, Devon EX15 3AL), da of late Capt Harry Woodthorpe Graham, MC, of Uitenhague, S Africa:—
(By 1st m) John William Brian Dyke (6 St John's Terr, Devoran, Cornwall), b 1942; ed Bradfield, and Cambourne Sch of Mines: m 1968, Georgina Scarborough, and has issue living, Peter, b 1978, — Samantha Louise, b 1969: m 1994, her 1st cousin once removed, Wensley Grosvenor Haydon-Baillie, of Wentworth Woodhouse, Yorks, son of late Malcolm Haydon-Baillie, and of late Mrs Peter Murray-Lee, — Carina, b 1972. —— (By 2nd m) Thomas Jeremy Dyke (86 Hurstbourne Rd, Forest Hill, SE23), b 1952; ed Plymouth Coll; has issue living (by Pat England), Joseph Peter Reynolds, b 1988, — Polly Jane Reynolds, b 1993. —— Diana Jane Dyke, b 1954: m 1975, Leonardo Martinez, of Plaza San Francisco 3, Mahon, Menorca, and has issue living, Maria-Carmen, b 1977.

Grandchildren of late Cdr Benjamin Dyke Acland, 2nd son of Rev Peter Leopold Dyke Acland, 5th son of 10th baronet:—
Issue of late Capt Hubert Edward Peter Dyke Acland, b 1884, d 1953: m 1912, Dorothy Marion, who d 1958, da of Sir John Henry Thorold, 12th Bt:—
Anne Dyke, b 1915; formerly Subaltern ATS: m 1948, Ian Graham Gordon, who d 1993. Residence – The Old Laundry, Syston, nr Grantham, Lincolnshire.

Issue of late Capt Lauchlan Henry Dyke Acland, MC, *b* 1889, *d* 1969: *m* 1923, Doris Dar, who *d* 1980, da of Hugh Davidson, of 12 Queensbury Place, SW:—
Julian Dyke (11 Dunton Close, Four Oaks, Sutton Coldfield, Warwicks), *b* 1924; *ed* St Paul's Sch, Magdalen Coll, Oxford (MA, BSc), and Sheffield Univ (PhD), BM, BCh: *m* 1964, Alison, da of Arthur William Chapman, CBE, of 53 Ranmor Cres, Sheffield, and has issue living, Ann Sarah, *b* 1965.

Grandson of late Capt Hubert Edward Peter Dyke Acland (ante):—
Issue of late Roger Dyke Acland, *b* 1920, *d* 1984: *m* 1st, 1945 (*m diss* 1951), Sylvia, only child of late Nicholas Galperin, of St John's Wood, NW; 2ndly, 1951, Molly, da of David McLurg, of Washington, USA:—
(By 2nd *m*) Simon Nicholas Dyke, *b* 1953: *m* 1981, Kathleen Spellman, and has issue living, Rosemary Anjelica, *b* 1983.
Residence – Avalon, Camphill Devon Community, Hampstead Village, Buckfastleigh, Devon.

Granddaughter of late Rev Henry Dyke Acland, 3rd son of Rev Peter Leopold Dyke Acland (ante):—
Issue of late Eng-Rear-Adm Edward Leopold Dyke Acland, CB, MVO, DL, *b* 1878, *d* 1968: *m* 1910, Phyllis, who *d* 1973, da of late Connell Whipple:—
Adria Margaret (37 Church St, Henley-on-Thames, Oxon RG9 1SE), *b* 1914: *m* 1st, 1935, Arthur Francis Procter, who *d* 1970, son of late Sir Henry Edward Edleston Procter, CBE; 2ndly, 1971, Lt-Col James Hawke Dennis, TD, Chevalier of Legion of Honour, who *d* 1985, and has issue living (by 1st *m*) Susan Caroline, *b* 1939: *m* 1969, Timothy Gordon Keown, of Cockslease Farm House, Fawley, Henley-on-Thames, and has issue living, David Nigel *b* 1971, Alice Belinda *b* 1972.

Grandchildren of late Col Sir Hugh Thomas Dyke Acland, CMG, CBE, FRCS (infra):—
Issue of late Sir (Hugh) John Dyke Acland, KBE, *b* 1904, *d* 1981: *m* 1935, Katherine Wilder (Mount Peel, Canterbury, NZ), da of John Davies Ormond, of Hawkes Bay, NZ:—
John Barton Ormond (Mount Peel, Canterbury, NZ), *b* 1936: *m* 1961, Dorothy Rosemary, da of Allan Albert Hobson, of Fielding, NZ, and has issue living, John Barton, *b* 1964, — Paul Hobson, *b* 1965, — Henry Dyke, *b* 1975. — Jessica Emily, *b* 1963: *m* 1989, Richard Jeffrey Staniland, of 27 Winchendon Rd, SW6 5DR, and has issue living, George Richard Acland *b* 1993, Lucinda Katherine Acland *b* 1991, — Georgina Katharine, *b* 1969, — Alexandra Evelyn, *b* 1970. — Mark Arundel (Mount Somers Stn, Canterbury, NZ), *b* 1939: *m* 19—, Joanna, da of John Quaife, of Mount Albert Stn, Wanaka, and has issue living, David Quaife, *b* 19—, — Benjamin Napier, *b* 19—, — Hamish Ormond *b* 19—. — *Rev* Simon Henry Harper (25 Campden Hill Sq, W8 7JY), *b* 1941: *m* 1970 (*m diss* 1983), his cousin, Nicola Hornby, da of John Pavey (infra), and has issue living, Michael Bernard Pavey, *b* 1971, — Luke Simon Burgoyne, *b* 1980, — Kim Lin Ovans, *b* 1973, — Anna Katherine Hornby, *b* 1975. — Audrey Ann, *b* 1937: *m* 1960, Hamish McHardy, of Tauroa, Havelock N, NZ, and has issue living, Jonathan Forbes, *b* 1962, — Kate Acland, *b* 1961, — Rebecca Thornley, *b* 1965, — Sarah Ormond, *b* 1966, — Emma Elizabeth, *b* 1968. — Evelyn Wilder, *b* 1947: *m* 1973, James Leybourne Wallace, LLB (*see* Jackson, Bt, *cr* 1915, colls), of Sundrum, Woodbury, NZ, and has issue. — Sarah Burgoyne, *b* 1951.

Grandchildren of late Hon John Barton Arundel Acland, 6th son of 10th baronet:—
Issue of late John Dyke Acland, *b* 1863, *d* 1944: *m* 1902, Mary Eveline, who *d* 1961, el da of late Rev Canon Harry Woodford St Hill:—
Thomas St Hill (c/o ANZ Bank, Geraldine, S Canterbury, NZ), *b* 1910; 1939-45 War with NZEF: *m* 1963, Margaret Ellen, da of late John Musgrove, and widow of Cdr John Swift Sharp, OBE, RD, RNR. — Emily Mary Dyke, *b* 1905; is a JP for Somerset; 1939-45 War in ATS. *Residence* – Middle Croft, Bossington Lane, Porlock, Som.

Issue of late Henry Dyke Acland, *b* 1867, *d* 1942: *m* 1906, Elizabeth Grace, who *d* 1942, da of the Hon James Watson, MLC, of Sydney, NS Wales:—
Philippa Mabel, *b* 1914. *Residence* – 8 Dublin Street, Christchurch, New Zealand.

Issue of late Col Sir Hugh Thomas Dyke Acland, CMG, CBE, FRCS, *b* 1874, *d* 1956: *m* 1903, Evelyn Mary, who *d* 1964, da of late J. L. Ovans:—
Colin Dyke (Woodbourne, Main Road North, Paraparaumu, NZ), *b* 1906; 1939-45 War with S Africa Forces: *m* 1936, Sybil Marjorie, da of T.A. Warner, of Durban, Natal, and has issue living, Hugh Thomas Dyke (Woodbourne, Main Rd North, Paraparaumu, NZ), *b* 1940: *m* 1965, Fredericka Scott, da of G. A. Hutton, of Bangor, Darfield, N Canterbury, NZ, and has issue living, Thomas Dyke *b* 1972, Susannah Scott *b* 1967: *m* 1993, George Arthur Churchill Gould (and has issue living, Arthur *b* 1996, George *b* 1998, Augusta *b* 1994), Annabel Emily *b* 1970, — Mary Ann Warner, *b* 1936: *m* 1st, 1964 (*m diss* 1968), Josef Maria Baukes; 2ndly, 1970, Christopher John Hindmarsh, and has issue living (by 2nd *m*), John Marcos Acland *b* 1973, Brigid Acland *b* 1971, Nicola Acland *b* 1974. — Michael Dyke, *b* 1911; 1939-45 War as Lt NZ Artillery: *m* 1946, Elizabeth Vibaert, da of H. de C.McArthur, of Dunedin, NZ, and has issue living, Peter McArthur, *b* 1947, — Alastair Michael, *b* 1950, — Richard, *b* 19—. *Residence* – Christchurch, NZ. — Elizabeth Evelyn Dyke, *b* 1913; sometime Lt S African Women's Auxiliary Army Ser: *m* 1944, John Pavey, who *d* 1952, and has issue living, Timothy John *b* 1945, — Phillida Ann, *b* 1946, — Nicola Hornby, *b* 1948: *m* 1970 (*m diss* 1983), her cousin, Rev Simon Henry Harper Acland, and has issue (ante), — Miranda Jane, *b* 1950. *Residence* –

The 1st baronet, Sir John Acland, in the service of Charles I, impaired his fortune by raising and supporting a troop to garrison his house at Columb-John. He was created a baronet, but in the confusion of the civil war the letters patent were destroyed, and on the fall of the royal party he was fined £1,800. After the Restoration, new letters patent were granted, but not till the year 1677, on account of a long minority in the family, in consideration of which the patent specially granted precedency from 1644. The 10th baronet sat as MP for Devon 1812-18, and 1820-32, and for N Devon (C) 1837-57. The 11th baronet sat as MP for W Somerset, Wellington Div 1837-46 and 1865-86. John, grandson of 6th baronet, was also *cr* a baronet, 1818 (ext 1871) and assumed the additional surname of Palmer. The 12th baronet, Sir (Charles) Thomas Dyke, was Dep Warden of the Stannaries, and sat as MP for E Cornwall (L) 1882-5, and for E, or Launceston, Div of Cornwall 1885-92. The 13th baronet, Rt Hon Sir Arthur Herbert Dyke, was Vice-Pres of Committee of Council on Education (with a seat in the Cabinet) Aug 1892 to June 1895, a Member of Privy Council Committee on Industrial Research, and MP for Rotherham Div of S Part of W Riding of York (L) 1885-98. The 14th baronet, Rt Hon Sir Francis Dyke, sat as MP for Yorkshire, N Riding, Richmond Div (L) 1906-10, for Cornwall, Camborne Div 1910-22, for Devonshire, Tiverton Div 1923-4, and for Cornwall, N Div 1932-9, and was Financial Sec to War Depart 1908-10 and 1911, Under-Sec of State for Foreign Affairs 1911-15, Financial Sec to Treasury 1915, and Parliamentary Sec to Board of Agriculture and Fisheries 1915-16. The 15th baronet, Sir Richard Thomas Dyke, was MP for Barnstaple Div of Devon (L and subsequently *Common Wealth*) 1935-45, and for Gravesend Div of Kent (Lab) 1947-55.

ACLAND (UK) 1890, of St Mary Magdalen, Oxford

Sir (CHRISTOPHER) GUY (DYKE) ACLAND, MVO, 6th *Baronet, b* 24 March 1946; *s* his father, *Maj Sir* ANTONY GUY, RA, 1983; *ed* Allhallows Sch, and RMA Sandhurst; Lt-Col RA (ret); Equerry to HRH The Duke of Edinburgh 1988-90; Equerry to HM and Deputy Master of HM's Household 1994-99; MVO 1990: *m* 1971, Christine Mary Carden, yst da of late John William Brodie Waring, MB BS, of Waterdip, Totland Bay, Isle of Wight, and has issue.

𝕬rms – Checky argent and sable, a fesse gules. 𝕮rest – A man's hand apaumée couped at the wrist in glove lying fessewise to the sinister, thereon a falcon perched all proper, jessed and belled or.
Club – Royal Yacht Sqdn.

SONS LIVING

Unshaken

ALEXANDER JOHN DYKE, *b* 29 May 1973: *m* 1999, Ruperta Helen, da of Mrs Alexandra Melville, of Anchor, Shropshire. —— Hugh Antony Waring Dyke, *b* 1976.

HALF-SISTER LIVING

Gail Alison Jane, *b* 1942: *m* 1968, Anthony James Rayment, of 30 Lyall Av, Toronto, Ont M4E IV9, Canada.

SISTER LIVING

Caroline Barbara Margaret, *b* 1947; SRN, SCM: *m* 1972, Peter Desmond George Sleigh, of RD8, Waimate, S Canterbury, NZ, and has issue living, David Ralph, *b* 1972, — John Antony, *b* 1973, — Catherine Joan, *b* 1976, — Margaret Gail *b* 1980, — Susan Mary, *b* 1980 (twin).

DAUGHTER LIVING OF THIRD BARONET

(Emily) Patricia, *b* 1931: *m* 1953, Kenneth John Coles, and has issue living, Elizabeth Anne, *b* 1954. *Residence* – The Old Rectory, Newtimber, Hassocks, W Sussex.

WIDOW LIVING OF FIFTH BARONET

MARGARET JOAN (*Margaret, Lady Acland*), el da of late Maj Nelson Rooke, HLI, of Markham House, Badminton: *m* 1944, as his second wife, Maj Sir Antony Guy Acland, RA, 5th Bt, who *d* 1983. *Residence* – Merrie Cottage, Queens Rd, Freshwater, I of Wight PO40 9ES.

COLLATERAL BRANCHES LIVING

Issue of late Lt-Col James Alison Acland, DSO, younger son of 4th baronet, *b* 1919, *d* 1993: *m* 1942, Diana Marcia, only da of late James Edward Briggs, of The Elms, Troy, Monmouth:—
David James Dyke, *b* 1947; *ed* Nautical Coll, Pangbourne, RNC Dartmouth; Cdr RN (Fleet Air Arm): *m* 1975, Amanda Joy, SRN, el da of John Alan Norman, of Floods, Curland, Taunton, Som, and has issue living, Thomas Alison Dyke, *b* 1977, — Timothy John Dyke, *b* 1978. —— Ion Andrew Dyke, *b* 1949; *ed* Nautical Coll, Pangbourne; Lt-Cdr RNR (ret 1989), Master Mariner; Capt in Cmnd BT (Marine) Ltd Cableship: *m* 1976, Susan Jean, SRN, SCM, da of John Jervis Chapman, of Lake Rd, Poole, Dorset. —— Angela Marcia Dyke, *b* 1946: *m* 1981, Maurice FitzGibbon, el son of Maurice FitzGibbon, FRIC, FCS, MInstPI, of Haverbreaks, Lancaster.

Granddaughters of late Sir Reginald Brodie Dyke Acland, KC, 5th son of 1st baronet, *b* 1856, *d* 1924: *m* 1885, Helen Emma, who *d* 1943, da of late Rev Thomas Fox, R of Temple Combe, Wincanton, Som:—
Issue of late Edward Fox Dyke Acland, *b* 1891, *d* 1978: *m* 1924, Beatrice, who *d* 1972, da of late Dr J. W. Laver, of Grimston, Norfolk:—
Barbara Elizabeth, *b* 1929; FRSA, FSA: *m* 1949, Richard George Adams, Hon FRSL, author, of Benwells, 26 Church St, Whitchurch, Hants, and has issue living, Juliet Vera Lucy, *b* 1958: MA (Oxon), AM (Stanford USA): *m* 1981, Peter Johnson, FRSA, Fell of Balliol Coll, Oxford, and has issue living, Robert Alasdair Edward *b* 1994, Lucy Charlotte Acland *b* 1986, Miranda Sylvia Louise *b* 1991, *b* 1998, — Rosamond Beatrice Elizabeth, *b* 1960: *m* 1983, Michael Mahony, and has issue living, Sarah Elizabeth Louise *b* 1989, Grace Anna Kathryn *b* 1991, Maeve Evelyn Jessica *b* 1998. —— Phillis Penelope Jane, *b* 1932; SRN: *m* 1958, Glynn Meirion Owen, MBE, of 19 Fairfield, Upavon, Pewsey, Wilts, and has issue living, William Edward, *b* 1959: *m* 1992 (*m diss* 1994), Rebecca Barnacle, — Eleri Jane, *b* 1961; SRN, Registered Sick Children's Nurse: *m* 1983, Patrick Dodge, and has issue living, Thomas Patrick *b* 1986, Alan James *b* 1989, Emma Jane *b* 1992, Sian Kathleen *b* 1994, — Alys Mair, *b* 1964: *m* 1st, 1990 (*m diss* 1992), David Marles; 2ndly, 1995, Peter Goodchild, and has issue living (by 2nd *m*), Elke Marianne *b* 1997. —— Judith Sarah, *b* 1942.

Issue of late Wing-Cdr Wilfrid Reginald Dyke Acland, DFC, AFC, *b* 1894, *d* 1937: *m* 1921, Mary Strange who *d* 1991, having *m* 2ndly, 1939 Air Commodore Thomas Edward Barham Howe, CBE, AFC, who *d* 1970, da of late Thomas Marshall, of Lee-on-Solent:—

Joan Mary Louise, *b* 1923; European War 1941-5 as 3rd Officer WRNS: *m* 1946, Lt-Cdr Peter Allen Ridd Gould, RN, of Hambledon, 35 Stoke Rd, Cobham, Surrey KT11 3BG, and has issue living, Timothy Acland Ridd, *b* 1948: *m* 1976 (*m diss* 1994), Veronica Ruth Franklin, and has issue living, James Acland Ridd *b* 1979, Lucinda Jane Louise *b* 1977, — Angela Mary, *b* 1950: *m* 1970, Nicholas David Gooda, and has issue living, Edward Anthony *b* 1970; ACII: *m* 1997, Karen, da of David Duff, of Pound Hill, W Sussex, Anita Helen *b* 1973. ⸺ Cynthia Helen, *b* 1928: *m* 1953, Robert Coston Taylor, who *d* 1999, and has issue living, Frederick Robert Acland, *b* 1961; BSc, LRPS, — Pamela Harriet, *b* 1957: *m* 1983, George Goldsbrough, of 3 Yew Tree Court, Fordingbridge, Hants, only son of E. Goldsbrough, of Johannesburg, S Africa.

Granddaughter of late Capt Francis Edward Dyke Acland, 6th son of 1st baronet:—
Issue of late Herbert Arthur Dyke Acland, *b* 1886, *d* 1968: *m* 1914, Maud Kathleen, who *d* 1986, da of late Col G. E. Branson, of Broomgrove, Sheffield:—
Stephanie Jane, *b* 1924: *m* 1947, Reginald Chase, LDSRCS Eng, who *d* 1981, and has issue living, Phillip Reginald (Warwick Court, Winchester, Hants), *b* 1949: *m* 1st, 1984 (*m diss* 1985), Josephine Marian, da of W. J. Whiting, of Cheadle Hume, Cheshire; 2ndly, 1988, Josephine Eleanor Weeks, — Douglas Martyn (17 Darlaston Rd, Wimbledon, SW19), *b* 1955: *m* 1983, Noëlle Mary Rose, da of Mrs Barbara Thompson of West Broyle, Chichester, and has issue living, Guy William Thompson *b* 1989, Verity Jane *b* 1986.

Grandsons of late Col Alfred Dyke Acland, CBE, 7th son of 1st baronet:—
Issue of late Lt-Col Arthur William Acland, OBE, MC, TD, *b* 1897, *d* 1992: *m* 1926, Violet Gwendolen, who *d* 1984, yr da of late Rev Canon Hon Robert Grimston (*see* E Verulam, colls, 1985 Edn):—
David Alfred (The Manor, Notgrove, Cheltenham, Glos; *Club* – Royal Yacht Sqdn), *b* 1929; *ed* Eton, and ChCh Oxford (MA): *m* 1960, Serena Elizabeth, da of late Sir Cyril Hugh Kleinwort (*see* Kleinwort, Bt, colls), and has issue living, Harry Alexander (Durhams Farm, Chastleton, Moreton-in-Marsh, Glos GL56 0SZ), *b* 1963: *m* 1st, 1991, Catherine Juliet, MB BS, who *d* 1992, as the result of a yachting accident, da of Cmdr Richard Masterman, RNR, of Thuborough House, Sutcombe, Holsworthy, Devon; 2ndly, 1995, Diana F., yst da of Tom Chissell, of Cowgrove, nr Wimborne, Dorset, and has issue living (by 2nd *m*), Rory *b* 19—, Arabella Catherine *b* 1998, — Lucy Henrietta, *b* 1962: *m* 1988, Nicholas C. Morris, yst son of C.P. Morris, of Radnor Walk, SW3, and has issue living, Leo *b* 1991, Pandora *b* 1989. ⸺ Martin Edward (Standon Green End, Ware, Herts; *Club* – Royal Yacht Sqdn), *b* 1932; *ed* Eton; JP Herts, High Sheriff 1978, DL 1996: *m* 1956, Anne Maureen, OBE, DStJ, da of late Stanley Ryder Kunton, of Ilkley, Yorks, and has issue living, Michael Christopher Dyke (*Club* - Royal Yacht Sqdn), *b* 1958; *ed* Eton, and RNC Dartmouth; Capt RM; ADC to Lt-Gen Wilkins, Commandant-Gen RM: *m* 1988, Miranda Jane Elisabeth, eldest da of John Bradshaw, of 11 Cheyne Place, SW3, and has issue living, Tara Katherine Elisabeth *b* 1990, Susanna Rose Juliet *b* 1993, — Richard Arthur Dyke (*Club* Royal Yacht Sqdn), *b* 1962; *ed* Eton, Wye Agric Coll, and London Univ: *m* 1990, Alison Jane, da of Dr Bruce Osborne, of Westacott House, Goodleigh, Barnstaple, N Devon, and has issue living, Thomas Alexander *b* 1994, Charlotte Emma Victoria *b* 1992, Emily Rosanna *b* 1996, — Peter Edward Dyke, *b* 1964; *ed* Shiplake Coll; *m* 1995, Rachel, da of John Hodge. ⸺ Charles Robert, *b* 1937; *ed* Eton, and RMA Sandhurst; Capt Grenadier Guards.

Issue of late Brig Peter Bevil Edward Acland, OBE, MC, TD, JP, *b* 1902, *d* 1993: *m* 1927, Bridget Susan, who *d* 1996, da of late Rev Herbert Barnett (Hon Canon Ch Ch Oxford), of Farley Moor, Binfield, Bracknell, Bucks (Lethbridge, Bt, Colls):—
Maj-Gen Sir John Hugh Bevil, KCB, CBE (Feniton Court, Honiton, Devon), *b* 1928; *ed* Eton; enlisted Scots Guards 1946, commn'd 1948, Maj-Gen 1977, Equerry to HRH late Duke of Gloucester 1957-59; Malaya 1950-51; Cyprus 1951-52; Egypt 1952-53; Kenya 1960-62; Zanzibar 1962-63; Libya 1968-69; N Ireland 1970 and 1973; CO, 2nd Scots Gds 1968-71; Comd Land Forces Cyprus 1976-78; GOC SW Dist 1978-81; Comd Commonwealth Force, Rhodesia 1979-80; Hon Col Exeter Univ OTC 1981, R Devon Yeo 1983; R Wessex Yeo 1989; DL Devon 1984; Vice Lord Lieut of Devon 1994; CBE (Mil) 1978; *cr* KCB (Mil) 1980: *m* 1953, Myrtle Christian Euing, da of Brig Alastair Wardrop Euing Crawford, of Auchentroig, Stirlingshire, and has issue living, Peter John, *b* 1954: *m* 1979, Amanda, da of Brian Ryrie, of Nairobi, Kenya, and has issue living, Katharine Elisabeth *b* 1981, Elizabeth Caroline *b* 1983, — Victoria Susan, *b* 1958: *m* 1986, Thomas J. Goddard, yst son of Maj David Goddard, of The Mill, Lympstone, Devon, and has issue living, Luke *b* 1992, Rosanna *b* 1990, Helena *b* 1995. ⸺ *Sir* Antony Arthur, GCMG, GCVO (The Provost's Lodge, Eton College, Windsor, Berks SL4 6DH), *b* 1930; *ed* Eton, and Ch Ch Oxford; Hon LLD Exeter 1988, William & Mary Coll, Virginia 1990, and Reading 1992; entered Foreign Ser 1953; Prin Private Sec to Sec of State for Foreign Affairs 1972, Ambassador to Luxembourg 1975-77, and to Spain 1977-79; Permanent Under-Sec of State FCO, and Head of HM Diplomatic Service 1982-86; Ambassador to Washington 1986-91, since when Provost of Eton Coll; Chancellor of the Order of St Michael and St George since 1994; *cr* CMG, 1976, KCVO 1976, KCMG 1982, GCMG 1986, and GCVO 1991: *m* 1st, 1956, (Clare) Anne, who *d* 1984, el da of late Francis Reynolds Verdon, of Littlefields, Sidbury, Devon; 2ndly, 1987, Mrs Jennifer Joyce McGougan, da of late Col R. Dyke, OBE, and formerly wife of John McGougan, of Bicton, Devon, and has issue living (by 1st *m*), Simon Hugh Verdon, *b* 1958: *m* 1988, Josephine, elder da of Michael Valentine, and has issue living, two das, — Nicholas Antony Bevil, *b* 1960: *m* 1984, Sophia Caroline Annabel, only da of David John Yorke, of Hall Foot, Worston, Clitheroe, Lancs (*see* B Clitheroe), and has issue living, Thomas *b* 1989, Hugh *b* 1994, Olivia *b* 1990, — Katharine Mary, *b* 1965: *m* 1996, George G. Weston, 2nd son of Garfield Howard (Garry) Weston, of Ennismore Gdns, SW7.

The 1st Baronet, Sir Henry Wentworth Acland, KCB, MD, LLD, DCL, FRS (4th son of 10th baronet of creation 1678, *see* ante), a well-known scientist, was Regius Professor of Medicine at Oxford, Hon Physician to HM King Edward VII when Prince of Wales, and Member and Pres of Medical Council of United Kingdom. Adm Sir William Alison Dyke Acland, CVO, 2nd Bt, was Naval ADC to Queen Victoria 1896-9, second in command of Channel Squadron 1901-2, and Adm Sup of Gibraltar Dockyard 1902-04. Lt-Col Sir William Henry Dyke Acland, MC, AFC, TD, 3rd Bt, was Maj RFC and RAF in European War 1914-18 (wounded, despatches, MC, 4th class Order of St George (Russia), AFC) and cmd'd Royal Devon Yeo RA (TA). His brother, Capt Sir Hubert Guy Dyke Acland, DSO, RN, 4th Bt, served in European War 1914-18 (despatches, DSO), cmd'd HMAS Australia 1937-38 and HMAS and HMS Albatross 1938, and served 1939-45 War. He *m* Lalage Mary Kathleen, eldest da of Capt John Edward Acland (Acland, Bt, *cr* 1678, colls). Maj Sir Antony Guy Acland, 5th Bt, served RA 1937-58, specialising in Anti-Aircraft, Instructor Fire Control, Instructor in Gunnery, Development and Trials 1958, ret 1958 and joined Saunders-Roe on rocket development and trials projects.

Acland (Fuller-Acland-Hood), see Hood.

ADAIR (UK) 1838, of Flixton Hall, Suffolk (Extinct 1988)

Maj-Gen Sir ALLAN HENRY SHAFTO ADAIR, GCVO, CB, DSO, MC, 6th and last *Baronet*.

DAUGHTERS LIVING OF SIXTH BARONET

Bridget Mary (*Lady Darell*), *b* 1928: *m* 1953, Brig Sir Jeffrey Lionel Darell, MC, 8th Bt, Coldm Gds. *Residence* – Denton Lodge, Harleston, Norfolk. —— Annabel Violet, *b* 1937.

ADAM (UK) 1917, of Hankelow Court, co Chester

The cross gives me welcome rest

Sir CHRISTOPHER ERIC FORBES ADAM, 3rd *Baronet*, only son of late Eric Graham Forbes Adam, CMG, 2nd son of 1st baronet; *b* 12 Feb 1920; *s* his uncle, *Gen Sir* RONALD FORBES, GCB, DSO, OBE, 1982; *ed* Abinger Hill Sch, Surrey, and privately: *m* 1957, Patricia Anne Wreford, yr da of late John Neville Wreford Brown, of Maltings, Abberton, Colchester, Essex.

Arms – Argent, a mullet pierced between three cross-crosslets fitchée gules, a chief of the last thereon a pale or, charged with a rose of the second, barbed and seeded proper. Crest – A cubit arm argent holding in the hand a cross-crosslet fitchée in bend sinister, and charged on the wrist with a rose, both as in the arms.
Residence – 46 Rawlings St, SW3.

ADOPTED DAUGHTER LIVING

Sarah Anne, *b* 1960: *m* 1986, Andrew J. Allen (assumed the surname of Allen by deed poll 1964), son of Prof Alec Eden, of Torquay, Devon, and has issue living, Edward Christopher, *b* 1989, — Alicia Elizabeth, *b* 1991, — Holly Ann Georgia, *b* 1998. *Residence* – Laundry Cottage, Syon House, Brentford, Middx TW8 8JF.

DAUGHTERS LIVING OF SECOND BARONET

Barbara Forbes (*Lady Proctor*), *b* 1917: *m* 1953, as his 2nd wife, Sir (Philip) Dennis Proctor, KCB, who *d* 1983. —— Bridget Islay Forbes, MBE, *b* 1927; Col WRAC (ret); MBE (Mil) 1960. *Residence* – Ardmore, Netherhampton, Salisbury, Wilts SP2 8PU. —— Isobel Forbes, *b* (twin) 1927. *Residence* – 4 Alderville Rd, SW6 3RJ.

COLLATERAL BRANCHES LIVING

Issue of late Colin Gurdon Forbes Adam, CSI, 3rd son of 1st baronet, *b* 1889; *d* 1982: *m* 1920, Hon Irene Constance Lawley, who *d* 1976, da of 3rd Baron Wenlock:—

Rev (STEPHEN) TIMOTHY BEILBY FORBES (Woodhouse Farm, Escrick, York YO4 6HT), *b* 19 Nov 1923; *ed* Eton, and Balliol Coll, Oxford; Rifle Bde 1942-47 in France and Far East; ordained 1962; Rector of Barton-in-Fabis with Thrumpton, South-well, Notts 1964-70; priest-in-charge of Southstoke, Bath and Wells 1974-84: *m* 1954, Penelope, da of George Campbell Munday, MC, of Leverington Hall, Wisbech, Cambs, and has issue living, Anna Victoria, *b* 1955, — Catherine Mary, *b* 1956: *m* 1991, Kristan David Stone, adopted son of Stanley Stone, and has issue living, Joseph Atkinson *b* 1982, Odysseus *b* 1993, Cassandra *b* 1995, — Lucy, *b* 1960, — Sonia Clare, *b* 1966. —— Nigel Colin (Skipwith Hall, Selby, Yorks YO8 5SH), *b* 1930; JP, High Sheriff N Yorks 1976, DL 1991; *ed* Eton, and King's Coll, Camb: *m* 1st, 1954, Teresa Hermione Idena, only da of Cdr David Robertson, RN; 2ndly, 1987, (Mildred) Malise Hare, formerly wife of William Guy David Ropner (*see* Ropner, Bt, *cr* 1904, colls), and da of late Col George Armitage, MC, TD, of Newburgh House, Coxwold, Yorks, and has issue living (by 1st *m*), Charles David (Charity Farm, Skipwith, Selby, N Yorks), *b* 1957: *m* 1982, Rosalind Cecilia, da of Geoffrey Colvile, of Ivy House Farm, East Malling, Kent, and has issue living, (Crispin) Bielby *b* 1987, Hal *b* 1989, Charlotte Irene *b* 1992, — Titus Desmond, *b* 1960, — Julian Nigel Peregrine, *b* 1961: *m* 1986, Christina Maria, who *d* 1998, da of Colin Woodiwiss, of 55 Connaught St, W2, and has issue living, Luke George Nigel *b* 1987, — Harry Crispin, *b* 1962. —— Virginia Mary (The Elms, Bubwith, Selby, Yorks), *b* 1922: *m* 1948, Capt Hugo Francis Guy Charteris, MC, Scots Gds, who *d* 1970 (*see* E Wemyss, colls).

Grandchildren of late Colin Gurdon Forbes Adam, CSI (ante):—
Issue of late Desmond Francis Forbes Adam, b 1926, d 1958: m 1949, Hon Vivien Elisabeth (11 Mulberry Walk, SW3), da of Sir Oswald Ernald Mosley, 6th Bt (see B Ravensdale):—
Rupert Colin (Richardsons, Skipwith, nr Selby, N Yorks), b 1957: m 1981, Mrs Anya B. Hillman, da of Richard Cadbury Butler. —— Cynthia Rebecca, b 1950: m 1978, H. Clive Chaddock, of The Manse, Harray, Orkney, only son of H. Chaddock, of 2 Mornington Av, Crosby, Liverpool, and has issue living, Jack Colin, b 1981, — Harry Desmond, b 1984, — Benjamin Gabriel, b 1987. —— Arabella Irene (Woodland Farm, Yeoford, nr Crediton, Devon), b 1952; has issue living, Archie Desmond Hugo, b 1980, — Wilfrid Peter Jamie, b 1983, — Alfy Sholto, b 1988, — Dora Maisie Irene, b 1992.

The 1st baronet, Sir Frank Forbes Adam, CB, CIE, was Pres of Bombay Chamber of Commerce 1884-9, and Manchester Chamber of Commerce 1893, 1894, and 1903-5. The 2nd baronet, Gen Sir Ronald Forbes Adam, GCB, DSO, OBE, late RA, served in European Wars 1914-18 in France and Italy (despatches thrice), and 1939-45 in France and Belgium (despatches), was Gen Officer Comdg-in-Ch N Command June 1940 and A-G to the Forces June 1941-May 1946; Chm to British Council 1946-54, Pres Library Ass 1949, and Chm of Exec Board of UN Educn, Scientific and Cultural Organisation 1952-54.

AGNEW (NS) 1629, of Lochnaw, Wigtownshire

By counsel not by rashness

Sir CRISPIN HAMLYN AGNEW OF LOCHNAW, 11th *Baronet*; b 13 May 1944; s his father, *Sir* FULQUE MELVILLE GERALD NOEL, 1975; ed Uppingham, and RMA; Maj RHF (ret 1981); Advocate 1982; QC 1995; Rothesay Herald since 1986; a Member of Queen's Body Guard for Scotland (Royal Co of Archers); Chief of the Name of Agnew; Representor of the baronial house of Agnew of Lochnaw; Hereditary Sheriff of Wigton; a Member of Expeditions to Greenland 1966, Antarctica 1970, Nuptse Himal 1975, and Everest 1976; Leader of Expeditions to Greenland 1968, Patagonia 1972, and Api Himal 1980, author of Legal Works: m 1980, Susan Rachel Strang, journalist and broadcàster, yr da of late Jock Wykeham Strang Steel (see Steel of Philiphaugh, Bt), and has issue.

𝕬rms – Argent, a chevron between two cinquefoils in chief gules, and a saltire couped in base azure. 𝕮rest – An eagle issuant and reguardant proper. 𝕸otto – Consilio Non Impetu. 𝕾upporters – Two heraldic tigers proper collared and chained or.
Residence – 6 Palmerston Rd, Edinburgh, EH9 1TN. *Clubs* – Army and Navy.

SON LIVING

MARK DOUGLAS NOEL, yr of Lochnaw, b 24 April 1991.

DAUGHTERS LIVING

Isabel Sevilla Wilhelmina, b 1984. —— Emma Rachel Elizabeth, b 1986. —— Roseanna Celia Nancy, b 1989.

WIDOW LIVING OF TENTH BARONET

SWANZIE (*Swanzie, Lady Agnew of Lochnaw*) (2/23 Croft An Righ, Abbey Hill, Edinburgh, EH8 8DG), da of late Maj Esmc Nourse Erskine, CMG, MC (see E Buchan, colls): m 1937, Sir Fulque Melville Gerald Noel Agnew of Lochnaw, 10th Bt, who d 1975.

COLLATERAL BRANCHES LIVING

Grandchildren of late Col Quentin Graham Kinnaird Agnew, DSO, MVO, 4th son of 8th baronet:—
Issue of late Col David Quentin Hope Agnew, b 1900, d 1975: m 1928, Janet May Dilkes, who d 1980, da of late Rev Charles Herbert Malden, R of Little Gransden, Beds:—
Andrew David Quentin (Garth House, Furnace, Machynlleth, Powys), b 1929; ed Trin Coll, Glenalmond and Edinburgh Univ (BSc); PhD Bangor: m 1957, Shirley, da of late James Arnold Smithson, of Woodstock, Simonstone, Lancs, and has issue living, David James, b 1960, — Peter Jonathan, b 1963, — Robin Andrew b 1966. —— Jonathan Herbert (11 Ulting Lane, Langford, Maldon, Essex CM9 6QB), b 1933: m 1958, Mary Kathleen, who d 1982, da of late Brig Stannus Grant Gordon Fraser, MC, Indian Army (ret), and has issue living, George Archibald Quentin, b 1962, — Michael Stannus, b 1965, — Susan Louise, b 1963.

Issue of late Cdr John Andrew Agnew, RN, b 1903, d 1977: m 1934, Ysabel Augusta Aurelia, who d 1979, da of Don Ernesto Larios, of Algeciras, Spain:—

Fulke Quentin Ernesto (Monte de la Torre, Los Barrios, Provincia de Cadiz, Spain), *b* 1938; Maj RHF (ret): *m* 1970, Susan Georgina, el da of late Group Capt Frank Hastings Tyson RAF (ret), of Diss, Norfolk, and has issue living, Tomas Quentin, *b* 1972, — John Benedict, *b* 1976, — Luisa Beatriz, *b* 1973.

Issue of late Capt Patrick Alexander Agnew, Seaforth Highlanders, *b* 1908, *ka* 1943: *m* 1936, Baroness Johanna Elizabeth (who *m* 2ndly, 1944, Lt-Col William Stanley Baird), da of Baron Barthold MacKay (*see* L Reay, colls):—
Robin Andrew Patrick Mackay (MS 897, Ravensbourne, Queensland 4352, Australia), *b* 1940: *m* 1965, Diana Clyde, da of Humphrey Dinsdale Phillips and formerly wife of David Allan Bennett, and has issue living, Gordon Alexander Mackay *b* 1967. ─── Rosemary Joanna Evelyn, *b* 1938: *m* 1960, Arthur Struan Hannay Robertson, and has issue living, Duncan Struan Alexander, *b* 1961, — Jonathan Dougal, *b* 1962, — Alastair James, *b* 1967, — Patrick Hamish, *b* 1970. *Address* – Box 70245, Bryanston 2021, RSA.

Granddaughter of late Rev David Carnegie Andrew Agnew, 3rd son of 7th baronet:—
Issue of late Andrew David Carnegie Agnew, *b* 1856, *d* 1927: *m* 1882, Minnie Dale, who *d* 1928, da of David Dale Buchanan:—
Ivy Diamond Dale, *b* 1895.

Grandchildren of late Sir Stair Andrew Agnew, KCB, 5th son of 7th baronet:—
Issue of late Stair Carnegie Agnew, *b* 1872, *d* 1940: *m* 1918, Sylvia Bellville, who *d* 1974, da of late Alexander Martin Bremner, Bar-at-Law, of 1 St Petersburgh Place, W, and 3 Paper Buildings, Temple, EC:—
Lesley Stair, *b* 1919; Sister Mary Magdalene; has been Canoness Regular of Order of St Augustine since 1945.

Issue of late Col Herbert Charles Agnew, OBE, late RE, *b* 1880, *d* 1949: *m* 1919, Enys, who *d* 1985, da of late James Wason, of Merton Hall, Wigtownshire:—
John Nevin, *b* 1922; *ed* Rugby, and Ch Ch Oxford (MA); Lt-Col (ret) Coldstream Guards: *m* 1951, Margaret Scott, da of late Moffat Thomson, of Lambden, Berwickshire, and has issue living, Andrew Robert (Springfield, Lasswade, Midlothian), *b* 1956: *m* 1981, Patricia, da of late Sir Russell Fairgrieve, CBE, TD, of Pankalan, Boleside, Galashiels, Selkirk, and has issue living, Roy Duncan *b* 1984, Jonathan Michael *b* 1986, Christina Margaret *b* 1982, — James Douglas (Hendersyde, Kelso, Roxburghshire), *b* 1959: *m* 1984, Elizabeth Mary, da of late Dr John Atherton Cameron, and has issue living, Charlotte Elizabeth *b* 1987, Georgina Catherine *b* 1990, Alexandra Isobel *b* 1992, — Jean Catherine, *b* 1953: *m* 1979, Richard Swan, son of late Lt-Col Sir William B. Swan, KCVO, CBE, TD, JP, of Blackhouse, Eyemouth, Berwickshire, and has issue living, Peter Allan *b* 1982, Nicola Anne *b* 1981, Alice Margaret *b* 1984. *Residence* – Bonjedward House, Jedburgh, Scotland. ─── Patrick William, *b* 1927; *ed* Rugby, and Trin Coll, Camb (BA 1947, MA 1963): *m* 1958, Anne Meryl Turner, and has had issue, David Martin, *b* 1959; Capt RHF; *k* in a helicopter crash 1984, while serving with Frontier Force, Oman, — Stephen William, *b* 1963, — Hazel Patricia, *b* 1961.

Grandson of late Capt Douglas Agnew, RN, only son of late Thomas Frederick Agnew, 6th son of 7th Bt:—
Issue of late Maj (Frederick) Douglas Agnew, TD, *b* 1909, *d* 198-: *m* 1st, 1938 (*m diss* 1950), Barbara, da of R. T. B. Glasspool, of Calday Grange School, W Kirby; 2ndly, 1951, Vivien Elizabeth Willoughby, da of Harold Willoughby Bartlett, of Vine House, Well End, Bourne End, Bucks:—
(By 1st *m*) Jocelyn, *b* 1940: *m* 1965, Raymond Graham Jenner, of Tigh Aran-Cri, Strathview Terrace, Pitlochry PH16 5QR, and has issue living, Angus Donald Agnew, *b* 1966, — Bruce Roderick, *b* 1969.

Granddaughters of late Thomas Frederick Andrew Agnew, 6th son of 7th baronet:—
Issue of late Percy Reginald Agnew, *b* 1878, *d* 1952: *m* 1909, Ethel Adelaide Susan Wakefield, who *d* 1962:—
Maud Susan Rosemary: *m* 1941, Jarvis H. Campbell, and has issue living, John Agnew, *b* 1949: *m* 1974, Kathleen Mary, yr da of Alexander Shaw Ferguson Wilson, of The Orchard, Kilbride, Doagh, co Antrim, — Adelaide Elizabeth, *b* 1943, — Eily Jane, *b* 1945, — Dinah Mary, *b* 1953. *Residence* – The Moat Inn, Donegore, Dunadry, co Antrim. ─── Poppy Eily, *b* 1915. ─── Denise Frances, *b* 1917. ─── Nancy Marion, *b* 1919: *m* 1939, Philip Humphrey Vellacott, and has issue living, Giles Wakefield, *b* 1949, — Julia Clare, *b* 1943, — Teresa, *b* 1944. *Residence* – Tan y Bryn, Franksbridge, Llandrindod Wells.

This family descends from Andrew Agnew, who was granted the lands of Lochnaw, made Hereditary Constable of Lochnaw 1426 and subsequently granted the Hereditary Sheriffdom of Wigton 1451. Sir Andrew, 7th of Lochnaw (ktd 1595), *d* after 1616; his eldest son, Sir Patrick, 8th of Lochnaw, MP for Wigtonshire 1628-33, was granted 16,000 acres of land in Nova Scotia, erected into the Barony of New Agnew and *cr* a Baronet of Nova Scotia with remainder to his heirs male whatsoever: *m* Margaret, da of Sir Thomas Kennedy of Culzean; *d* 1661; *s* by his eldest son, Sir Andrew, 9th of Lochnaw, 2nd Bt, ktd in his father's lifetime, MP for Wigtonshire 1644-49 and 1665-71: *m* Lady Anne Stewart, da of 1st Earl of Galloway; *d* 1671; *s* by his eldest son, Sir Andrew, 10th of Lochnaw, 3rd Bt, MP for Wigtonshire 1685 and 1689-1702: *m* Jean, da of Sir Thomas Hay of Park; *d* 1702; *s* by his eldest son, Sir James, 11th of Lochnaw, 4th Bt: *m* Lady Mary Montgomerie, da of 8th Earl of Eglinton; *d* 1735; *s* by his eldest son, Sir Andrew, 12th of Lochnaw 5th Bt, Commanded 21st Royal North British Fusiliers (late RSF), Lt Gen in the Army and Gov of Carlisle Castle; received £4,000 for the abolition of the jurisdiction of the Sheriff of Wigtonshire: *m* Eleanor, da of Thomas Agnew, by whom he had 21 children; *d* 1771; *s* by his 5th son, Sir Stair, 13th of Lochnaw, 6th Bt; cotton and tobacco merchant in Glasgow: *m* 1st, Mary, da of Thomas Baillie of Polkemmet; 2ndly, Margaret, da of Thomas Naesmyth of Dunblair; *d* 1809; *s* by his grandson (eldest son of Andrew, yr of Lochnaw: *m* Hon Martha da of 26th Lord Kinsale), Sir Andrew, 14th of Lochnaw, 7th Bt, MP for Wigtonshire 1830-37, added to Lochnaw Castle in 1822, involved with the Sabbath Day Observance movement: *m* Madeline, da of Sir David Carnegie of Southesk, Bt (but for the attainder 7th Earl of Southesk); *d* 1849; *s* by his eldest son, Sir Andrew, 15th of Lochnaw, 8th Bt, Capt 93rd Highlanders and later 4th Light Dragoons, MP for Wigtonshire 1856-68: *m* Louisa, da of 1st Earl of Gainsborough; *d* 1892; *s* by his eldest son, Sir (Andrew) Noel, 16th of Lochnaw, 9th Bt, Barrister, MP for Edinburgh South 1900-06: *m* Gertrude, da of Hon Gowran Vernon; *d* 1928; *s* by his nephew (son of Charles Hamlyn Agnew, 3rd son of 8th Bt), (Sir) Fulque Melville Gerald Noel, 17th of Lochnaw, 10th Bt (did not use the title), Registrar at Fort Hare Univ, S Africa 1952-60 (dismissed for anti-apartheid activities): *m* Swanzie, da of Major Esme Erskine, CMG, MC (*see* E Buchan, colls); *d* 1975; *s* by his son, the 11th and present Bt.

AGNEW (UK) 1895, of Great Stanhope Street, St George, Hanover Square, co London.

Sir JOHN KEITH AGNEW, 6th *Baronet*; *b* 19 Dec 1950; *s* his father *Major Sir* (GEORGE) KEITH, 1994; *ed* Gresham's Sch, Holt, and RAC, Cirencester.

ᴀrms – Per saltire argent and gules, in pale two cinquefoils and in fesse as many saltires couped, all counterchanged. Crest – An eagle reguardant, wings expanded proper, each wing charged with a pale or, holding in its mouth a sword pointed upwards also proper, and resting the dexter claw on a saltire couped gules.
Seat – Rougham Hall, Bury St Edmunds. *Residence* – Lawney's Farm, Rougham, Bury St Edmunds, Suffolk IP30 9JG.

BROTHER LIVING

GEORGE ANTHONY, *b* 18 Aug 1953; *ed* Gresham's Sch, Holt, and Univ of East Anglia. *Residence* – Freewood Cottage, Bradfield St George, Bury St Edmunds, Suffolk.

Consilo et impetu

By wisdom and vigour

UNCLE LIVING (son of 3rd baronet)

Stephen William (4a Prince Alfred Parade, Newport, NSW 2106, Australia), *b* 1921; *ed* Rugby, and Trin Coll, Camb; late Lt 7th Hussars; 1939-45 War (wounded): *m* 1st, 1947 (*m diss* 1966), Elizabeth, da of late James Brooks Close, of Aldeburgh, Suffolk; 2ndly, 1967, Mrs Adene Leona Cookson, yr da of Vincent John Brady, of Sydney, and has issue living, (by 1st *m*) John Stuart (Fincham Farm, Rougham, Kings Lynn), *b* 1949; *ed* Gordonstoun, and RAC, Cirencester: *m* 1982, Diana Margaret Zoë, el da of Cmdr Christopher Ellis Baker, RN, of Cley, Norfolk, and has issue living, Jethro Luke *b* 1988, Edgar Christopher *b* 1990, Garth Stephen *b* 1992, — Bolton (Oulton Hall, Norwich, Norfolk), *b* 1950; *ed* Gordonstoun: *m* 1989, Clare Elizabeth, da of late Henry Everet Tinsley, of Langrick Grange, Boston, Lincs, and has issue living, William Henry Bolton *b* 1991, Rosemary Brooks *b* 1989, — James Brooks Close (Church Farm, Oulton, Norwich), *b* 1953; *ed* Gordonstoun, and RAC, Cirencester: *m* 1984, Judith Dianne, da of Edward Gilbert, of 5 Todman Av, Pymble, Sydney, Australia, and has issue living, Catherine Penelope *b* 1986, Louise Frances Elizabeth *b* 1988, — Stephen Hardcastle (Fred) (The Old Rectory, West Acre, Kings Lynn, Norfolk PE32 1UD), *b* 1954; *ed* Gordonstoun: *m* 1993, Mrs Amanda Gabrielle Mary Garthwaite, only da of Edward Willoughby Trafford, of Wroxham, Norfolk (*see* E Lindsay and Abingdon, colls), and has issue living, Imogen Helen *b* 1994, Emily Rose *b* 1996, — Theodore Thomas More (The Little Manor, Thorndon, Suffolk), *b* 1961; *ed* Rugby: *m* 1993, Clare Margaret, yr da of John Joseph Buxton, of Horsey Hall, Gt Yarmouth (*see* Buxton, Bt, colls), and has issue living, Madeleine Elizabeth Demetria *b* 1995, — St John Colin Kenneth (Sankence Lodge, Aylsham, Norfolk), *b* 1964; *ed* Rugby, and Sheffield Univ: *m* 1992, Jenny R., elder da of Gerald W. Youngs, of Sankence House, Aylsham, Norfolk, and has issue living, Harry Jack *b* 1995, Alfred Gerald *b* 1997, — Margaret Elizabeth Diana, *b* 1952: *m* 1977, Richard Eustace Thomas Gurney, of Heggatt Hall, Horstead, Norfolk, and has issue (*see* M Hertford, colls).

WIDOW LIVING OF FIFTH BARONET

Baroness ANNE MERETE LOUISE (*Lady Agnew*), yr da of Baron Johan Schaffalitzky de Muckadell, of Rødkilde, Fyn, Denmark: *m* 1948, Maj Sir (George) Keith Agnew, TD, 5th Bt, who *d* 1994.

COLLATERAL BRANCHES LIVING

Branch from 2nd son of 1st baronet

Grandchildren of late Charles Gerald Agnew (infra):—
Issue of late Sir Geoffrey William Gerald Agnew, *b* 1908, *d* 1986: *m* 1934, Hon Doreen Maud Jessel, who *d* 1990, da of 1st Baron Jessel:—
Jonathan Geoffrey William, *b* 1941; *ed* Eton, and Trin Coll, Camb (MA); Chm Limit plc and Gerrard Group plc, Dep Chm Nationwide Building Soc: *m* 1st, 1966 (*m diss* 1985), Hon (Agneta) Joanna (Middleton) Campbell, yr da of Baron Campbell of Eskan (Life Baron, extinct); 2ndly, 1990, Marie-Claire, elder da of Bernard Dreesmann, and has issue living (by 1st *m*), Caspar Jonathan William (83 Elms Rd, SW4 9EP), *b* 1967: *m* 1991, Annabel J., elder da of Tim Summers, of Godalming, Surrey, and has issue living, Hector Jonathan Timothy *b* 1993, Edward Thomas William *b* 1999, Daisy Matilda *b* 1995, — Lara Joanna, *b* 1969, — Katherine Agneta, *b* 1971, — (by 2nd *m*) George Jonathan Henry, *b* 1999, — Clarissa Virginia, *b* 1992. — (Morland Herbert) Julian, *b* 1943; *ed* Eton, and Trin Coll, Camb (MA): *m* 1st, 1973, Elizabeth Margaret, yst da of William B. Mitchell, of Gateside, Blanefield, Stirlingshire; 2ndly, 1993, Victoria, 2nd da of late Maj Henry Ronald Burn Callander, MC (*see* Crossley, Bt, colls), and has issue living (by 1st *m*), Thomas Julian Noel, *b* 1975, — Amelia Elizabeth, *b* 1979, — Georgina Helen, *b* 1982, — (by 2nd *m*), Benjamin Geoffrey David Callander, *b* 1996. —— Jennifer Maud, *b* 1937: *m* 1962, Paul Lazell, of 26 Fairfax Rd, Bedford Park, W4 1EW, and The Manor House, Wighton, Norfolk, only son of Henry George Leslie Lazell, of Reigate, Surrey, and has issue living, Sebastian Henry, *b* 1963: *m* 1989, Belinda Mary, elder da of Peter Beck, of Wimbledon, and has issue living, Frederick Henry *b* 1990, Hamish William *b* 1992, Alexandra Mary *b* 1995, Camilla Katherine *b* 1997, — Dominic Geoffrey Paul, *b* 1972, — Natasha Jennifer, *b* 1967: *m* 1991, Duncan James Bell, of 3 Homefield Rd, W4 2LN, yst son of late Harold Bell, of Devon, and has issue living, Joshua James *b* 1994, Tabitha Amelia *b* 1997.

Grandsons of late Charles Morland Agnew, OBE, 2nd son of 1st baronet:—
Issue of late Charles Gerald Agnew, *b* 1882, *d* 1954: *m* 1900, Olive Mary, who *d* 1946, da of late Ven William Danks, Canon of Canterbury:—
(Denys) Martin (Flat 107 Keverstone Court, 95 Manor Rd, Bournemouth BH1 3DB), *b* 1919; *ed* Eton, and Trin Coll, Camb (BA); Maj RA (Emergency Reserve); 1939-45 War (Special Forces); former Vice-Pres American Express Internat UK and Ireland: *m* 1st, 1943, Monica (BA) (1981) MA Psych (1983), DPsych (1989), PhD (1992) Univ of Colorado), da of Rev S. Foskett, MD, of Killinghall, Harrogate; 2ndly, 1949, Josephine Ann, da of Alan Ross, of Natal, S Africa; 3rdly, 1974, Rosetta Mary, da of Mrs Ethel Benjamin, of Johannesburg, S Africa; 4thly, 1988, Mrs Doreen Rosemary Wylde, who *d* 1999, of Amsterdam, Florence and London, and has issue living, (by 1st *m*) Jeremy Andrew Derrick (2110 Wood Avenue, Colorado Springs, Colorado, USA), *b* 1943; *ed* Eton, and Colorado Coll, USA (BA), Univ of Colorado (BS), Calif

Coast Univ (MS, PhD Engrg): *m* 1968, Mary Sylvia Perkins, and has issue living, Tracy Marie *b* 1974, Christine Noel *b* 1977, — (by 2nd *m*) William George Morland, *b* 1955: *m* 1984, Antonia Jane, yr da of Capt Richard Lawrence Garnons-Williams, of the Manor House, Gate Helmsley, York, — (Emma Christianne) Annabel (*Marchioness Conyngham*), *b* 1951: *m* 1987, as his 4th wife, 7th Marquess Conyngham.

Issue of late Major Alan Graeme Agnew, *b* 1887, *d* 1962: *m* 1913, Dorothy Cecil, who *d* 1959, da of late William Winstanley Strode, of Pole House, King's Langley:—
Peter Graeme, MBE; *b* 1914; Wing Com RAF Vol Reserve; MBE (Mil) 1946: *m* 1937, Mary Diana, only da of late James Philip Hervey, of Knutsford, Cheshire, and has issue living, Ian Hervey (Oak Lodge, Ifield Wood, Crawley, Sussex), *b* 1941: *m* 1964, Amanda Barbara, da of late Maj A. Wyndham-Read, and has issue living, Mark Wyndham *b* 1966, Jonathan Graeme *b* 1968, — James Philip (Trenarth Cottage, Constantine, Falmouth, Cornwall TR11 5JN), *b* 1947: *m* 1972, Carol Ann, only da of late Edward Garfield Williams, of Constantine, Cornwall, and has issue living, William Edward Philip *b* 1976, Emma Victoria *b* 1972, — Penelope Mary, *b* 1939: *m* 1961, Col Norman Thomas Davies, OBE, JP, of Lowfields Cottage, London Rd, Hartley Wintney, Hants RG27 8HY, and has issue living, Edward Peter, MBE *b* 1962; Maj Ll: *m* 1992, Susan Mary, yr da of Joseph Goble, of Harare, Zimbabwe (and has issue living, Charles Jasper Peter *b* 1995, Jemma Eliza Mary *b* 1996), Clare Mary *b* 1964: *m* 1997, Nicholas Thomas Duffield, — Diana Nicola (*Lady Ropner*), *b* 1945: *m* 1st, 1966 (*m diss* 1978), Anthony David Mayhew; 2ndly, 1983, Maj Antony Michael Tippett; 3rdly, 1996, as his 3rd wife, Sir John Bruce Woollacott Ropner, 2nd Bt, of Thorp Perrow, Bedale, N Yorks, and has issue living (by 1st *m*), Anthony James *b* 1969, Gavin Mark *b* 1971, Louisa Clare *b* 1973. *Residence* – The Linhay, Trenarth Lane, Constantine, Falmouth, Cornwall TR11 5JN.

Branch from 3rd son of 1st baronet

Grandchildren of late Victor Charles Walter Agnew (infra):—
Issue of late Lt-Col (Charles) David Agnew, 15th/19th Hussars, *b* 1916, *d* 1987: *m* 1949, Mary Lorna (Lime Walk Cottage, Long Marston, York YO26 8LR), da of late Rt Rev Henry St John Stirling Woollcombe, Bishop of Selby:—
(David) Richard Charles (Thatchover, Knole, Long Sutton, Som TA10 9HZ), *b* 1953; *ed* Harrow: *m* 1978, Charlotte Anne, yr da of John Calkim Whately-Smith (*see* B Hotham, colls), and has issue living, Dickon James, *b* 1983, — Joanna Woollcombe, *b* 1981. —— Susan Lorna, *b* 1950: *m* 1976, Alastair Philip Hunter Smart, who *d* 1992, of Yeoman's Cottage, Great Ouseburn, York YO26 9RQ, and has issue living, Angus David Alastair, *b* 1978, — Harriet Bridget *b* 1981. —— Vanda Jane, *b* 1959: *m* 1986, Julian Edward Lambton, of Pennybridge House, Pennybridge, Ulverston, Cumbria LA12 7RJ, and has issue (*see* E Durham, colls).

Granddaughter of late Walter Agnew, 3rd son of 1st baronet:—
Issue of late Victor Charles Walter Agnew, *b* 1887, *d* 1929: *m* 1913, Phyllis May Claude (who *d* 1981, having *m* 2ndly, 1932, Air Commodore Andrew George Board, CMG, DSO, DL, RAF, who *d* 1973), da of late Claude Baggallay, KC, of 32 Draycott Place, SW:—
Elizabeth Moran, *b* 1914: *m* 1938, Brig Brian Kingzett, CBE, MC, of Long Hill House, Castle Hill Lane, Mere, Warminster, Wilts, and has issue living, Charles David Brian, *b* 1942, — Sarah Elizabeth, *b* 1945.

Granddaughter of late Lt-Col Richard Leslie Agnew (infra):—
Issue of late (Richard) Mark Walter Agnew, *b* 1930, *d* 1998: *m* 1st, 1955 (*m diss* 1963), Edwina Ottilie Jane, eldest da of late Maj-Gen Sir Robert Edward Laycock, KCMG, CB, DSO (*see* E Dudley, colls); 2ndly, 1972, Lady Teresa Jane Fox-Strangways, who *d* 1989, da of 7th Earl of Ilchester, and widow of 9th Viscount Galway; 3rdly, 1992, Elspeth (The Curate's House, Melbury Osmond, Dorchester, Dorset), da of late Lt-Col A. I. Macpherson, of Lochgilphead, Argyll, and widow of Capt William Richard Dalrymple Gerard-Pearse, CBE, LVO, RN, of Dinder, Som:—
(By 1st *m*) Leonie, *b* 1956: *m* 1979, Daniel Davis, of New York, and has issue living, Benjamin Daniel, *b* 1985, — Sarah Jane, *b* 1983. *Residence* – 43 Glenridge Av, Stonybrook, NY 11790-2201, USA.

Granddaughters of late Walter Agnew (ante):—
Issue of late Lt-Col Richard Leslie Agnew, 15th/19th King's Roy Hussars, *b* 1900, *d* 1987: *m* 1st, 1927 (*m diss* 1946), Leila May, da of Brig-Gen Anthony Courage, DSO, MC; 2ndly, 1953, Hilda Dorothy, who *d* 1993, da of late Thomas Henry Spinks:—
(By 1st *m*) (Leila) Rosemary, *b* 1928: *m* 1st, 1948 (*m diss* 1959), Kenneth Malcolm Ritchie, only son of late Kenneth Leslie Ritchie; 2ndly, 1962, Robert John Lyle, of Pantyrhedyn, Gellywen, Carmarthen SA33 6EA, eldest son of late Capt Robert Charles Lyle, MC, of Weston Grange, Thames Ditton, Surrey, and has issue living (by 1st *m*), Linda Rosemary Anne, *b* 1951: *m* 1st, 1973, Fl Lt Nigel Corbishley, who *d* 1984; 2ndly, 1988, Fl Lt Michael Pichel-Juan, of The Woodhouse Arms, Corby Glen, Grantham, Lincs NG33 ANJ, and has issue living (by 1st *m*), Benjamin James *b* 1977, Jonathan Piers *b* 1979, Rupert Charles *b* 1982, — Venetia Claire, *b* 1953: *m* 1972, Robert Christopher Springett Sanders, and has issue living, Philip Malcolm *b* 1982, Katherine Joan *b* 1974, Josephine Rosemary *b* 1980, Sally-Anne Madeleine *b* 1984, — (by 2nd *m*), Richard Charles Cecil (11 Galesbury Rd, SW18 2RL), *b* 1965: *m* 1993, Joanna Mary Smith, and has issue living, Charles Oliver Thomas *b* 1997, — Lucinda, *b* 1963: *m* 1989, John Julian Peter Johnson, of Rockstone, La Rue des Vaux de l'Eglise, St Martin, Jersey JE3 6BF, CI, and has issue living, William Charles Eric *b* 1994, Elizabeth Daisy *b* 1992. —— Lavinia Mary, *b* 1933: *m* 1st, 1952 (*m diss* 1956), Geoffrey Arnold Ellert, son of John Arnold Ellert, of Oreham House, Henfield, Sussex (*see* Havelock-Allan, Bt, 1937 Edn); 2ndly, 1956, Jonathan Rashleigh, who *d* 1995, of Dumbledore, Warren Row, nr Wargrave, Berks, only son of late Vernon Leslie William Rashleigh, and has had issue (by 1st *m*), Sallyann Barbara, *b* 1954; assumed surname of Rashleigh by deed poll 1977: *m* 1st, 1973, Anthony Phillips; 2ndly, 1992, Philip M. Boreham, and has issue living (by 1st *m*), Melissa Mary *b* 1976, Victoria Claire *b* 1978, Antonia Melanie *b* 1981, — Serena, *b* 1956; assumed surname of Rashleigh by deed poll 1970: *m* 1977, Roderick Baird, and has issue living, Thomas Roderick *b* 1982, Rosemary Alice *b* 1984, Holly Madeleine *b* 1986, — (by 2nd *m*) Julian Philip, *b* 1957; *d* 1993, — Elizabeth Jane, *b* 1961: *m* 1995, Guy C. B. Hindley, son of Brian Hindley, of Rolvenden, Kent, and has issue living, Laura Alexis *b* 1997, Madeleine Florence *b* 1999.

The 1st baronet Sir William (many years senior partner in the firm of Thos Agnew and Sons, of Manchester, Liverpool, and London, and Chm of Bradbury, Agnew, and Co (Limited), proprietors and publishers of *Punch*), sat as MP for SE Lancashire (*L*) 1880-85, and for Lancashire (SE), Stretford Div 1885-6, and the 2nd baronet sat as MP for Salford, W Div (*L*) 1906-18.

AINSWORTH (UK) 1916, of Ardanaiseig, co Argyll

Sir (THOMAS) DAVID AINSWORTH, 4th *Baronet*; *b* 22 Aug 1926; *s* his half-brother, *Sir* JOHN FRANCIS, 1981; *ed* Eton; late Lieut 11th Hussars; racehorse trainer: *m* 1957, Sarah Mary, da of late Lt-Col Hugh Carr Walford, 17th/21st Lancers, and has issue.

Arms – Gules three Battleaxes two and one and as many Buckles tongues to the dexter one and two Argent; **Crest** – Between two Battleaxes blades outwards Argent a Falcon wings displayed and inverted Or beaked and legged Gules belled and jessed Gold.
Residence – Ashley House, Wootton, Woodstock, Oxon OX20 1DX.

SONS LIVING

ANTHONY THOMAS HUGH, *b* 30 March 1962; *ed* Harrow; late Lieut 11th Hussars. —— Charles David, *b* 1966; *ed* Harrow. *Residence* – 80 Elm Park Gdns, SW10.

DAUGHTERS LIVING

Serena Mary, *b* 1958: *m* 1987, Stelios Peratinos, of Brokini No 4, Corfu 49100, Greece, and has issue living, Nicholas David, *b* 1987, — George Stamatis, *b* 1988. —— Tessa Jane, *b* 1959: *m* 1986, Nicholas Cecil John Fortescue, and has issue (*see* E Fortescue, colls).

The 1st baronet, Sir John Stirling Ainsworth, was a mine-owner, and sat as MP for Argyllshire (*L*) Aug 1903 to Nov 1918.

AIRD (UK) 1901, of Hyde Park Terrace, Paddington, co London

Sir (GEORGE) JOHN AIRD, 4th *Baronet*; *b* 30 Jan 1940; *s* his father, *Col Sir* JOHN RENTON, MVO, MC, 1973; *ed* Eton, Ch Ch, Oxford (MA), and Harvard Univ (MBA); a Page of Honour to HM 1955-57: *m* 1968, Margaret Elizabeth, yr da of Sir John Harling Muir, 3rd Bt, TD, and has issue.

Arms – Gules, on a chevron between in chief two wolves' heads erased, and in base a mullet of six points within an increscent all argent, two falcons' heads erased sable. **Crest** – On a bull-headed rail fessewise, a lion rampant holding erect between the paws a spike point downwards all proper.
Residence – Grange Farm, Evenlode, Moreton-in-Marsh, Glos.

SON LIVING

JAMES JOHN, *b* 12 June 1978.

Vigilantia
By vigilance

DAUGHTERS LIVING

Rebecca, *b* 1970. — Bolinda Elizabeth, *b* 1972.

SISTERS LIVING

Susan Priscilla (The Candy-Colored Tangerine, 106 Cheyne Walk, SW10), *b* 1942. —— Petra Daphne (19 Cranbury Rd, SW6), *b* 1944: *m* 1965 (*m diss* 1989), 21st Baron Willoughby de Broke. —— Amanda Alecia (73 Epirus Rd, SW6), *b* 1946.

WIDOW LIVING OF THIRD BARONET

Lady PRISCILLA HEATHCOTE-DRUMMOND-WILLOUGHBY (*Lady Priscilla Aird*) (Wingrove House, Chipping Campden, Glos), da of 2nd Earl of Ancaster: *m* 1939, Col Sir John Renton Aird, 3rd Bt, MVO, MC, who *d* 1973.

COLLATERAL BRANCHES LIVING

Grandchildren of late Malcolm Rucker Aird (infra):—
Issue of late Malcolm Henry Aird, OBE, *b* 1899, *d* 1965: *m* 1922, Joan Meredith, who *d* 1986, da of Henry Sturgis:—
†Malcolm Robin Meredith, *b* 1923; *ed* Canford; 1939-45 War as Capt Irish Guards (wounded): *m* 1955, Barbara (Flat 4, 17 Basil St, SW3), da of J. Addison Wilson, and *d* 1999, leaving issue, Julian Malcolm, *b* 1955, — Zandra Theresa Jane, *b* 1960: *m* 1989, Michael Alistair Patrick Mercer, son of Maj P. Mercer, of Cotes, Leics, and of Mrs J. Davis, of Bradford-on-Avon, Avon. —— *Sir* Alastair Sturgis, GCVO (31 St James's Palace, SW1), *b* 1931; *ed* Eton, and RMC; late Capt 9th Lancers; Equerry to HM Queen Elizabeth The Queen Mother 1960-64, Asst Private Sec and Extra Equerry 1964-73, Comptroller of the Household to HM Queen Elizabeth the Queen Mother 1964-93, since when Private Sec, Comptroller and Equerry; LVO 1969, CVO 1976, KCVO 1984, GCVO 1997: *m* 1963, Fiona Violet, LVO, da of late Lt Col Ririd Myddleton, LVO, Coldstream Gds (*see* M Lansdowne), and has issue living, Caroline Margaret Violet, *b* 1964: *m* 1989, Major Charles John Allfrey, late The Royal Hussars (PWO), and has issue (*see* V Daventry), — Henrietta Idina, *b* 1966: *m* 1996, Johnnie N. P. Seidler, yr son of late Francis Seidler, of San Francisco, Calif, USA. —— Jeremy John (Quarry Wood Cottage, Burghclere, Newbury, Berks), *b* 1936; *ed* Eton: *m* 1967, Mary Elizabeth, da of late Lt-Col Sir William Richard De Bacquencourt Des Voeux, 9th Bt, and has issue living, David William, *b* 1968, — Catherine Rosemary Jean, *b* 1972.

Issue of late Maj Ronald Aird, MC, TD, *b* 1902, *d* 1986: *m* 1925, Viola Mary, who *d* 1965, da of Sir Godfrey Baring, 1st Bt, KBE:—
Gillian Viola, *b* 1930: *m* 1st, 1951 (*m diss* 1961), Robert Ian MacDonald; 2ndly, 1962, Christopher Michael Maude, of Feildings, Hoe Lane, Flansham, Bognor Regis, Sussex, and has issue living (by 1st *m*), Ian, *b* 1955, — Zara, *b* 1953: *m* 1980, Daniel E. Harris, — (by 2nd *m*) Victoria Viola, *b* 1968.

Issue of late Malcolm Rucker Aird, 2nd son of 1st baronet, *b* 1872, *d* 1934: *m* 1898, Nellie Margaret, who *d* 1954, da of Jeremiah Dummett, formerly of 54 Porchester Terrace, W:—
Ruth Sarah, *b* 1909: *m* 1940, Robert Ross Buchanan Brown, CBE, and has issue living, Ian Robert Aird, *b* 1946: *m* 1969 (*m diss* 1982), Tessa Elizabeth, da of Desmond Pertwee, and has issue living, Katherine *b* 1972, Emily *b* 1974, Rebecca Rose *b* 1984, — Sarah Elizabeth, *b* 1944, — Margaret Jane, *b* 1947.

The 1st baronet, Sir John, was a partner in the firm of John Aird and Co, contractors (who carried out the Assuan Dam and Assiut Barrage in Egypt), and sat as MP for Paddington, N Div (*C*) 1887-1906.

AITCHISON (UK) 1938, Lemmington, co Northumberland

Sir CHARLES WALTER DE LANCEY AITCHISON, 4th *Baronet*; *b* 27 May 1951; *s* his father, *Major Sir* STEPHEN CHARLES DE LANCEY, 1958; *ed* Gordonstoun; ARICS; late Lt 15th/19th KRH: *m* 1984, Susan, yr da of late Edward Ellis, of Hest Bank, Lancs, and has issue.

SON LIVING

RORY EDWARD DE LANCEY, *b* 7 March 1986.

DAUGHTER LIVING

Tessa Charlotte, *b* 1982.

BROTHER LIVING

(Stephen) Edward (Howden Dene Farm House, Corbridge, Northumberland), *b* 1954; *ed* Fettes: *m* 1978 (*m diss* 1998), Mrs Harriet N. Thomson, yr da of late Dr Henry Miller, and has issue living, Stephen Henry, *b* 1981, — Amanda Jo, *b* 1983, — Katherine Louise, *b* 1996.

UNCLE LIVING (*Son of 2nd baronet*)

David Lachlan, *b* 1928: *m* 1955, Dorothy Hazel, da of late S. K. Walton, of Wanwood Hill, Alston, Cumberland, and has issue living, Jeremy David, *b* 1959, — Dawn Elizabeth, *b* 1956. *Residence* – The Red House, 2 Apperley Rd, Stocksfield, Northumberland NE43 7PE.

AUNT LIVING (*Daughter of 2nd baronet*)

Shena Diana, *b* 1927. *Residence* – West Lea, Fenwick, Berwick on Tweed TD15 2PJ.

WIDOW LIVING OF THIRD BARONET

ELIZABETH ANNE MILBURN, MB, BS, el da of late Lt-Col Edward Reed, of Ghyllheugh, Longhorsley, Northumberland: *m* 1st, 1950, Maj Sir Stephen Charles de Lancey Aitchison, 3rd baronet, who *d* 1958; 2ndly, 1974, Roland Antony Cookson, CBE, DCL, who *d* 1991, of The Brow, Wylam, Northumberland.

The 1st baronet, Sir Stephen Harry Aitchison (son of John Gordon Aitchison), was a JP for City and Co of Newcastle-upon-Tyne and for Northumberland. The 2nd baronet, Sir Walter de Lancey Aitchison, FSA (Scot), was Chm and Managing Director of Walter Willson, Ltd, and of de Lancey Lands Ltd. The 3rd baronet, Major Sir Stephen Charles de Lancey Aitchison, late 13th/18th Roy Hussars, was Managing Director of Walter Willson Ltd, and of de Lancey Lands Ltd.

ALBU (UK) 1912, of Grosvenor Place, City of Westminster, and Johannesburg, Province of Transvaal, Union of South Africa.

All turns out well

Sir GEORGE ALBU, 3rd *Baronet*; *b* 5 June 1944; *s* his father, *Sir* GEORGE WERNER, 1963; *ed* Michael House, and Cedara Agric Coll, S Africa: *m* 1969, Joan Valerie, da of late Malcolm Millar, and has issue.

Arms – Per chevron raguly or and vert, in the dexter chief an acorn, in the sinister a flower of a sugar bush, both slipped and leaved, and in base a bear sejant proper. **Crest** – The battlements of a tower or, issuant therefrom a demi-bear proper, holding in the dexter paw a flower of the sugar plant as in the arms.
Residence – Glen Hamish Farm, Richmond, Natal, S Africa.

DAUGHTERS LIVING

Camilla Jane, *b* 1972: *m* 1996, Gary Neilsen, of 24 Margaret St, Silkstone, Ipswich, Qld 4304, Australia, son of Denis Neilsen, of Ipswich, Qld. — Victoria Mary, *b* 1976.

SISTERS LIVING

Susan Nomakepu (*Hon Mrs David Stapleton-Cotton*), *b* 1932: *m* 1955, Hon David Peter Dudley Stapleton-Cotton, and has issue (*see* V Combermere). *Residence* – The Old Buffers, Station Rd, Darling, Cape, S Africa. — Julia Mary ALBU, *b* 1937; has resumed her maiden name: *m* 1957 (*m diss* 1978), Hon Michael John Harbottle Grimston, and has issue (*see* B Grimston of Westbury). *Address* – PO Box 67250, Bryanston, S Africa. — Caroline, *b* 1943: *m* 1969, Philip G. Lorentz, and has issue living, William George, *b* 1971, — Charles Gordon, *b* 1975, — Marie Louise Caroline Rosie, *b* 1978. *Residence* – 21 Ridge Rd, La Lucia, Durban 4051, S Africa.

The 1st baronet, Sir George Albu (son of Simon Albu, of Berlin), was naturalized as a British subject in Transvaal 1887 and in England 1911, and was Chm and Managing Director of General Mining and Finance Corporation, Ltd. The 2nd baronet, Sir George Werner Albu, was Chm of General Mining and Finance Corporation, Ltd.

ALEXANDER (UK) 1921, of Edgehill, Stamford, Connecticut, USA

Sir DOUGLAS ALEXANDER II, 3rd *Baronet*, elder son of late Lt-Cdr Archibald Gillespie Alexander, US Coast Guard, yr son of 1st baronet; *b* 9 Sept 1936; *s* his uncle, *Sir* DOUGLAS HAMILTON, 1983: *ed* Rice Univ, Houston, Texas (MA 1961); PhD (1967) Univ of N Carolina; Pres Edgehill Investment Co: *m* 1958, Marylon, da of Leonidas Collins Scatterday, of Worthington, Ohio, USA, and has issue.

Arms – Azure, on a chevron between three lymphads, sails furled, oars in action or, as many grenades fired proper. Crest – In front of a talbot's head erased sable, gorged with a collar gemelle gules, two crescents or.
Residence – 2499 Windsor Way Court, Wellington, Florida 33414, USA.

SONS LIVING

DOUGLAS GILLESPIE, *b* 24 July 1962; *ed* Reed Coll, Portland, Oregon (BA 1984).
—— Andrew Llewellyn, *b* 1967, *ed* Bowdoin Coll, Brunswick, Maine (BA 1989).

BROTHER LIVING

Vita perit labor non moritur

Life perishes, labour never dies

Archibald Bonsall (6540 Cholla Drive, Scottsdale, Arizona 85253, USA), *b* 1940: *m* 1967, Catherine Clair, da of John Cyril Biggins, of Montclair, New Jersey, USA, and has issue living, Sean Hamilton, *b* 1970, — Cristina Cripps, *b* 1969.

SISTER LIVING

Margery Griffith, *b* 1945: *m* 1st, 1969 (*m diss* 1971), Richard Danch Cleland; 2ndly, 1972, Frederic James Ramsey III, of 68 Florence Rd, Riverside, Connecticut 06878, USA.

The 1st baronet, Sir Douglas Alexander (son of Andrew Alexander, of Errol, Perthshire and Hamilton, Canada), was for many years Pres of The Singer Manufacturing Co, of New York.

ALEXANDER (UK) 1945, of Sundridge Park, co Kent

Sir CHARLES GUNDRY ALEXANDER, 2nd *Baronet*, *b* 5 May 1923; *s* his father *Sir* FRANK SAMUEL, 1959; *ed* Bishop's Stortford Coll, and St John's Coll, Camb (BA 1943, MA 1947); Lieut RN (ret); Master Merchant Taylors' Co 1981, Prime Warden Shipwrights' Co 1983-84: *m* 1st, 1944, Mary Neale, only child of late Stanley Robert Richardson, of Maple Lawn, Lyndhurst, Hants; 2ndly, 1979, Eileen Ann, da of Gordon Stewart, of Inveresk, Finchampstead, and has issue by 1st *m*.

Arms – Barry wavy on ten azure and argent a lion rampant gules holding a trident erect or, on a chief of the second three lymphads sable with pennons flying gules. Crest – On a bundle of sticks fessewise banded or, a cock proper collared gold.
Residence – Hollytree Farmhouse, N Cadbury, Yeovil, Somerset BA22 7DD.
Club – RAC.

SON LIVING (By 1st marriage)

RICHARD (Wealden Hall, Pilgrims Way, Detling, nr Maidstone, Kent ME14 3JY), *b* 1 Sept 1947; *ed* Bishop's Stortford Coll; MIPR; Liveryman of Merchant Taylors' Co, Freeman of City of London: *m* 1971, Lesley Jane, da of Frederick William Jordan, of Bishop's Stortford, and has issue living, Edward Samuel, *b* 1974, — James Gundry, *b* 1977.

DAUGHTER LIVING (By 1st marriage)

Jennifer, *b* 1949.

Always watchful

BROTHER LIVING

John Edward, *b* 1924; late Lieut RNVR: *m* 1953, Maureen Dickson, and has issue living, Jonathan Charles, *b* 1957, — Catherine, *b* 1954. *Residence* – Dene Court, Oldfield Drive, Heswall, Wirral, Cheshire.

SEMPER VIGILANS

SISTERS LIVING

Elizabeth Jane, *b* 1927: *m* 1949, Lieut-Col Peter Walter Swinton Boult, TD, and has issue living, Geoffrey Pattisson, *b* 1957, — Rosanne Margaret, *b* 1950, — Alison Judith, *b* 1955. *Residence* – Little Holt, Bull Lane, Chislehurst, Kent BR7 6HX. —— Margaret Mary, *b* 1929: *m* 1951, Neville Manwaring Wells and has issue living, Michael Edward Alexander, *b* 1956, — Martin Charles Stanley, *b* 1959, — Frances Mary, *b* 1954. *Residence* – Durant Hollies, Hookwood Park, Limpsfield, Surrey RH8 0DO.

The 1st baronet, Sir Frank Samuel Alexander (son of Edward Alexander, of Highgate, N) was a shipowner and shipbroker, and was Lord Mayor of London 1944-5.

CABLE-ALEXANDER (UK) 1809, of the City of Dublin.

Sir PATRICK DESMOND WILLIAM CABLE-ALEXANDER, 8th *Baronet*; *b* 19 April 1936; *s* his father, *Sir* DESMOND WILLIAM LIONEL, 1988; *ed* Downside, and RMA Sandhurst; late Lt-Col Royal Scots Drag Gds (Carabiniers and Greys); Bursar and Clerk to the Council Lancing Coll 1984-98; Dir of Administration, Inst of Optometry since 1999: *m* 1st, 1961 (*m diss* 1976), Diana Frances, eldest da of late Col Paul Heberden Rogers, of Bushey, Herts; 2ndly, 1976, Jane Mary, da of Anthony Arthur Gough Lewis, MD, FRCP, of Budleigh Salterton, and has issue by 1st and 2nd *m*.

Arms – Per pale argent and sable a chevron, and in base a crescent counterchanged; on a canton azure a harp or, in the sinister chief point a mullet of the last. **Crest** – An armed arm embowed holding a sword proper, charged on the wrist with a mullet or.
Address – Windrush House, Hoe Court, Lancing, W Sussex BN15 0QX.

Per mare, per terras
By sea and land

SON LIVING (*By 2nd marriage*)

FERGUS WILLIAM ANTONY *b* 19 June 1981.

DAUGHTERS LIVING (*By 1st marriage*)

Melanie Jane, *b* 1963; has issue living (by 1st Earl of Snowdon, GCVO), Jasper William Oliver CABLE ALEXANDER, *b* 1998. —— Louise Fenella, *b* 1967: *m* 1995, Massimo A. Reina, elder son of G. Reina, of Milan.

HALF-SISTERS LIVING

Jacqueline (11 Holmbush Rd, Putney, SW15 3LE), *b* 1942: *m* 1962, Dillon Godfrey Welchman, who *d* 1998, and has issue living, James Dillon, *b* 1969; *ed* Sherborne, and Reading Univ: *m* 1998, Nicola McKeag, — Sara Dawn, *b* 1964. *m* 1990, Gregory Sebastian Porter, and has issue living, William Edward *b* 1992, Archie Jocelyn *b* 1997, Jake Rollo *b* (twin) 1997. —— Susan (Shepherds, Golden Square, Petworth, Sussex), *b* 1948: *m* 1970, Richard Humphrey Hardwicke, and has issue living, Humphrey Richard *b* 1978, — Caroline Amelia, *b* 1977.

HALF-UNCLE LIVING (*son of 6th baronet by 2nd marriage*)

Nigel William ALEXANDER, *b* 1925; *ed* Haileybury; Maj (ret) Grenadier Guards; 1939-45 War: *m* 1964, Anne, da of Bernard Ambrose Wheatley, of Stolford, Somerset, and has issue living, Hugh William, *b* 1967; *ed* Haileybury, — Charlotte Anne, *b* 1971. *Residence* – Rose Cottage, Underhill Lane, Lower Bourne, Farnham, Surrey GU10 3NF.

WIDOW LIVING OF SEVENTH BARONET

MARGARET MABEL (*Margaret, Lady Cable-Alexander*), da of late John Leopold Burnett, of Dublin: *m* 1942, as his 2nd wife, Sir Desmond William Lionel Cable-Alexander, 7th Bt, who *d* 1988. *Address* – 1 Denne Park House, Horsham, W Sussex.

COLLATERAL BRANCHES LIVING

Grandchildren of late Richard Alexander-Shaw, son of late William John Alexander-Shaw (who had assumed the additional surname of Shaw 1846), 2nd son of 1st baronet:—
Issue of late Godfrey William ALEXANDER, *b* 1861, *d* 1903, having discontinued the surname of Shaw: *m* 1890, Alice Maude, da of James Priestley, of Bankfield, Taylor Hill, Huddersfield:—
Kathleen, *b* 1892. *Residence* –

Issue of late Charles Henry ALEXANDER, b 1866, d 1898: m 1890, Susie Macauly, da of Robert Alexander, of Harwich, Kent, Canada:—
Robert Godfrey, b 1894. *Residence* –

Of this family the Earls of Caledon are a branch. John Alexander (el son of Capt Andrew Alexander, of Ballyclose, who was attainted in 1689) had three sons (1) John, ancestor of the Alexanders of Milford, co Carlow, (2) Nathaniel, ancestor of the Earls of Caledon and Earls Alexander of Tunis, (3) William, ancestor of William Alexander, 1st baronet, who was Lord Mayor of Dublin. The 2nd baronet was a Director of the Bank of Ireland, and the 3rd baronet was Attorney-General to HM King Edward VII, when Prince of Wales, and a Member of the Council of HRH. Sir Desmond William Lionel Cable-Alexander, 7th Bt, assumed by deed poll 1931 the additional surname of Cable-Alexander in lieu of his patronymic.

HAGART-ALEXANDER (UK) 1886, of Ballochmyle, co Ayr

Perseverance conquers. Without fear

Sir CLAUD HAGART-ALEXANDER, 3rd *Baronet*, son of late Wilfred Archibald Alexander, 2nd son of 2nd baronet; b 6 Jan 1927; s his grandfather Sir CLAUD, 1945; ed Sherborne, and Corpus Christi Coll, Camb (BA); Vice-Lord-Lieut Ayrshire and Arran 1983-98; JP; additional surname of Hagart recognized by decree of Lord Lyon 1948; a DL for Ayr: m 1959, Hilda Etain, yr da of late Miles Malcolm Acheson, late Chinese Maritime Customs Ser (D St Albans, colls), and has issue.

𝕬rms – Quarterly: 1st and 4th, per pale argent and sable, a chevron between a fleur-de-lys in chief and a crescent in base all counterchanged, within a bordure parted per pale gules and or, *Alexander*; 2nd, per bend azure and argent, in chief a star of sixteen points or, and in base another star of as many points of the first, on a bend sable a lion passant of the second between two crosses moline of the third, *Hagart*; 3rd, gules, two straight swords in saltire, points downwards, proper, hilted and pommelled or, between two fleur-de-lys in chief and base of the second and two mullets in the flanks argent, *McCaul*. 𝕮rest – 1st, an elephant passant proper, *Alexander*; 2nd, a lion rampant, proper, *Hagart*.
Seat – Kingencleuch House, Mauchline, Ayrshire KA5 5JL. *Club* – New (Edinburgh).

SONS LIVING

CLAUD, b 5 Nov 1963; ed Trin Coll, Glenalmond, and Glasgow Univ (BSc): m 1994, Elaine Susan, only da of Vincent Park, of Winnipeg, Manitoba, Canada, and has issue living, Claud Miles, b 28 Sept 1998. *Residence* – 3820 West 17th Av, Vancouver, BC, Canada V6S IA4. —— Boyd John, b 1966; ed Trin Coll, Glenalmond, and Liverpool Univ: m 1995, Cynthia Lacambra Ayala, da of José Ayala, by his wife Tita Lacambra, and has issue living, Tala Elizabeth Ayala, b 1996.

DAUGHTERS LIVING

Helenora Etain, b 1960: m 1983, Carl C. Smith, and has issue living, Christon Claud William, b 1987, — Aidan Boyd Angus, b 1988. —— Anna Joanna Elizabeth, b 1961: m 1984, Michael C. L. Adam, son of C. L. Adam, of Somerset House, Somerset Rd, Wimbledon, and has issue living, James Robert, b 1991, — Charlotte Etain, b 1989, — Elizabeth Rose, b 1998.

SISTER LIVING

Penelope Marion Acheson (*Lady Head*) b 1924: m 1967, as his second wife, Sir Francis David Somerville Head, 5th Bt.

COLLATERAL BRANCH LIVING

Issue of late Claud Alexander, 3rd son of 2nd baronet, b 1897; d 1976: m 1st 1928, Maude, who d 1936, da of Lt-Col J. Oswald Clazey, of Lamorva, Falmouth; 2ndly 1949, Peggy, formerly wife of late Bernard Lawrence Silley, and da of Ewart Raby le Mare, of Birchington, Kent:—
(By 1st m) John Oswald Claud, CB, OBE, b 1936; Maj-Gen R Signals; OBE (Mil) 1974, CB (Mil) 1991: m 1962, Mary, el da of Col Derek Grant Birkett, OBE, RA, and has issue living, Liza Jane, b 1964, — Sharon Louise, b 1968.

The 1st baronet, Maj-Gen Sir Claud Alexander (son of Boyd Alexander, of Ballochmyle and Southbar, co Ayr), served in Crimea 1854-5 and was MP for S Ayrshire (C) 1874-85.

ALISON (UK) 1852 (Extinct 1970)

Sir FREDERICK BLACK ALISON, 5th and last *Baronet*.

DAUGHTER LIVING OF FIFTH BARONET

Phoebe Ann, *b* 1926: *m* 1947, Leslie Thomas Allen, of Down Cottage, Lamberhurst Down, Lamberhurst, Kent, and has issue living, Richard Thomas, *b* 1948, — Bruce Harry, *b* 1950, — David Frederick, *b* 1953, — Peter Robert, *b* 1961.

HAVELOCK-ALLAN (UK) 1858, of Lucknow

Faithfully

He bears the cross bravely

Sir ANTHONY JAMES ALLAN HAVELOCK-ALLAN, 4th *Baronet*; *b* 28 Feb 1904; *s* his brother, *Sir* HENRY RALPH MORETON, 1975; *ed* Charterhouse, and in Switzerland; a Film Producer: *m* 1st, 1939 (*m diss* 1952), Valerie Babette Louise (the film actress Valerie Hobson), who *d* 1998, da of late Cdr Robert Gordon Hobson, RN; 2ndly, 1979, Maria Theresa Consuela (Sara), da of late Carlos Ruiz de Villafranca, formerly Spanish Ambassador to Chile and to Brazil, and has had issue by 1st *m*.

𝕬rms – Quarterly, 1st and 4th sable, a cross potent quarter pierced or, charged with four guttes de sang; in chief two lions heads erased of the second, all within a bordure engrailed erminois; a canton ermine, *Allan*; 2nd and 3rd, vert, a castle double-turreted argent between two fleurs-de-lys in chief, and a cross-crosslet fitchée in base or, *Havelock*. 𝕮rest – 1st, a demi-lion rampant argent, ducally crowned gules, charged on the shoulder with a cross-crosslet fitchée sable, holding in the dexter paw a cross potent or, supporting in the sinister a rudder of the second; 2nd, a lion rampant gules, semée of ermine spots, charged on the shoulder with a castle argent, sustaining a Danish battleaxe proper.
Address – c/o Lloyds Bank Ltd, 14 Berkeley Sq, W1. *Clubs* – Boodle's, and RAC.

SONS LIVING AND DECEASED (*By 1st marriage*)

†Simon Anthony Henry, *b* 1944; *d* 1991. —— (ANTHONY) MARK DAVID, *b* 4 April 1951; *ed* Eton, Durham Univ (BA), and Trin Coll, Camb (LLB); Bar Inner Temple 1974 (Master of the Bench 1995), QC 1993, Assistant Recorder SE Circuit 1993-97, since when Recorder: *m* 1st, 1976 (*m diss* 1984), Lucy Clare, da of late Alexander Plantagenet Mitchell-Innes, of Kitchers, Albury, Herts; 2ndly, 1986, Alison Lee Caroline, da of late Leslie Francis Foster, and has issue living (by 2nd *m*), Henry Caspar Francis, *b* 6 Oct 1994, — Miranda Antonia Louise, *b* 1993, — Hannah Marie Josephine, *b* 1997. *Residence* – 38 West Sq, SE11 4SP.

HALF-BROTHER LIVING

Gervaise George Michael, *b* 1921: *m* 1946, Rhoda, da of Thomas Beard, of Swansea, and has issue living, Thomas Allan Spencer, *b* 1949, — Louise Charlotte, *b* 1954: *m* 1976, Stephen J. Reeves, and has issue living, Lydia Chloe *b* 1980, Naomi Lucy *b* 1983. *Residence* – 3c Storemore, Dilton Marsh, Westbury, Glos.

HALF-SISTERS LIVING

Diana Constance (50 Belfield Rd, Pembury, Tunbridge Wells, Kent TN2 4HL): *m* 1939, Evelyn Francis Scott, who *d* 1981, and has issue living, Angus Allan Lindsay, *b* 1940, — Julian Peter Francis, *b* 1946, — David Nigel, *b* 1947, — Mark Michael, *b* 1950, — Ralph Neil Allan, *b* 1958, — Nina Alison Margaret, *b* 1941, — Elaine Ruth, *b* 1953. — Nancy Stella: *m* 1948, Maj Patrick Thorvald Auchmuty Musters, DFC, RA, of 4 Spring Close, Market Overton, Oakham, Leics LE15 7PT, and has issue living, Patrick Havelock Auchmuty (34 Overcliff, Manor Rd, Westcliff-on-Sea, Essex SS0 7SE), *b* 1952: *m* 1991, Mrs Lavinia Stephanie Hurst, da of late James Edward Moore, — Fiona Havelock Auchmuty (63 Gipsy Lane, Norwich, Norfolk), *b* 1948, — Gillian Havelock Auchmuty, *b* (twin) 1952: *m* 1980, John A. Armstrong, of 6 Fir Tree Lane, Swinford, Lutterworth, Warwicks, — Nicola Havelock Auchmuty, *b* 1954: *m* 1978, Patrick M. I. Day, of 16 Glebe Rd, W Perry, Huntingdon, Cambs.

COLLATERAL BRANCHES LIVING

Granddaughter of George Eric Havelock, yr son of Capt Joshua HAVELOCK, next brother of 1st Bt (who was in special remainder to the Baronetcy):—
Issue of late Eric Henry Edwardes Havelock, CB, CBE, *b* 1891, *d* 1974: *m* 1st, 1919, Christina Ramsay Scott, who *d* 1958, da of late Alexander Moodie, of Edinburgh; 2ndly, 1962, Eileen, who *d* 1972, da of late Col John W. H. Potts, RHA, and widow of Maj-Gen Walter Reginald Paul, CBE:—
(By 1st *m*) Elizabeth Kerr, *b* 1920: *m* 1946, Konstanty Kosciuszko, of Apart 2C, 1196 Eastern Parkway, Brooklyn 11213, New York, USA, and has issue living, Stefan Henry, *b* 1959.

Granddaughters of late George Broadfoot HAVELOCK, yst brother of 1st baronet:—
Issue of late Major Beresford Arthur Jardine Havelock (only son), 2nd Batn attached 7th Ser Batn Prince of Wales's (N Staffordshire Regt), *b* 1889, *ka* at Baku Sept 1918 (despatches): *m* (March) 1916, Kathleen Margaret (who *d* 1962, having *m* 2ndly, 1921, Col Daniel Frederick Bartlett, MBE, Indian Army), da of Sydney Smith, formerly Dep Inspector-Gen of Police, Punjab:—
Patricia Margaret Helen, *b* (Dec) 1916. —— Beres Aileen, *b* (*posthumous*) Feb 1919.

Maj-Gen Sir Henry Havelock, KCB, father of the 1st baronet, distinguished himself by his unparalleled march from Allahabad to Cawnpore and Lucknow, which latter place he held with astonishing bravery against the rebels for two months. A patent of baronetcy in his favour was granted 26 Nov 1857, but as he died two days prior to the date thereof, the honour was extended to his son, Henry Marshman, with special remainder, in default of his issue male, to his father's issue. Lieut-Gen Sir Henry Marshman Havelock, VC, GCB, 1st baronet, Col-in-Ch Roy Irish Regt, who also served with distinction during the Indian Mutiny, assumed by Roy licence 1880 the additional surname of Allan, and sat as MP for Sunderland (*L*) 1874-81, and for Durham, S-E Div (LU) 1885-92 and 1895-97, when he was murdered by Afridis in the Khyber Pass having *m* 1865, Lady Alice Moreton, who *d* 1922, 2nd da of 2nd Earl of Ducie. Sir Henry Spencer Moreton Havelock-Allan, 2nd baronet, was Parliamentary Private Sec to Under-Sec of State for India (Hon E. S. Montagu, MP) 1910-14, and sat as MP for Durham Co, Bishop Auckland Div (*L*) 1910-18. He served during European War 1916-18 as Major 17th Lancashire Fusiliers (wounded).

ALLEN (UK) 1933, of Marlow, co Buckingham (Extinct 1939)

Sir FRANCIS RAYMOND ALLEN, 2nd and last *Baronet*.

DAUGHTER LIVING OF FIRST BARONET

Violet Parkinson, *b* 1903: *m* 1st, 1924, Alfred Francis Hope Baldry; 2ndly, 1942, William Fisher-Luttrelle, and has issue living, (by 1st *m*) Felicia, *b* 1927, — Ann, *b* 1931.

WIDOW LIVING OF SECOND BARONET

ALTHEA JOAN (BLACK), da of Owen Leonard Hanks, of Wallasey Bay, Essex: *m* 2ndly, 1935, Sir Francis Raymond Allen, 2nd baronet, who *d* 1939, when the title became ext; 3rdly, 1941, Capt Dennis L. Bennett, Staffordshire Yeo, who was *ka* 1942; 4thly, 1945, Lieut-Col Oliver Charles Berger, Roy Scots Greys, of 19 Warwick Sq, SW1, and has issue living (by 4th *m*), one son and one da.

ALLEYNE (GB) 1769, of Four Hills, Barbados
(Name pronounced "Alleen")

Rev Sir JOHN OLPHERTS CAMPBELL ALLEYNE, 5th *Baronet; b* 18 Jan 1928; *s* his father, *Capt Sir* JOHN MEYNELL, DSO, DSC, RN, 1983; *ed* Eton, and Jesus Coll, Camb (MA); ordained 1955, Rector of Weeke, Winchester, 1975-93 (ret): *m* 1968, Honor Emily Margaret, el da of late William Albert Irwin, of Linkview Park, Upper Malone, Belfast, and has issue.

Arms – Per chevron gules and ermine in chief two lions heads erased or. Crest – Out of a ducal coronet a horse's head argent.
Residence – 2 Ash Grove, Guildford, Surrey GU2 5UT.

SON LIVING

RICHARD MEYNELL, *b* 23 June 1972.

DAUGHTER LIVING

Clare Emma Gila, *b* 1969: *m* 1995, Thierry Praud, son of Claude Praud, of La Roche sur Yon, France.

SISTERS LIVING

Let not your own interests move you but rather the wishes of the public

Eileen Violet, *b* 1923. —— Rosemary, *b* 1925: *m* (6 Dec) 1954, John Perry, who *d* (10 Dec) 1954. *Residence* – Greenacres, Minstead, Lyndhurst, Hants.

Sir John Gay, the 1st baronet, represented St Andrew's in the Barbados House of Assembly 1757-67, and was Speaker of the House 1767-97; he had two sisters, one married the 1st Earl of Radnor, and the other, Sir Charles Knowles, 1st baronet.

HEATHCOAT-AMORY (UK) 1874, of Knightshayes Court, Tiverton, Devon

Sir IAN HEATHCOAT-AMORY, 6th *Baronet; b* 3 Feb 1942; *s* his father, *Lt-Col Sir* WILLIAM, DSO, 1982; *ed* Eton, a DL and JP for Devon: *m* 1972, (Frances) Louise, da of late (Jocelyn Francis) Brian Pomeroy (*see* V Harberton, colls), and has issue.

Arms – Quarterly: 1st and 4th argent, two bars gules; on a bend engrailed with plain cottises sable, two annulets of the field, *Amory;* 2nd and 3rd, vert, three piles, one reversed in base between the others issuant from the chief, each charged with a pomme, thereon a cross of the second, *Heathcoat.* Crest – 1st, the battlements of a tower or, therefrom issuant a talbot's head azure charged with two annulets fessewise, and interlaced gold, *Amory;* 2nd, upon a mount vert, between two roses springing from the same gules, stalked and leaved proper, a pomme charged with a cross or, *Heathcoat.*
Residence – Calverleigh Court, Tiverton, Devon EX16 8BB.

SONS LIVING

WILLIAM FRANCIS, *b* 19 July 1975. —— Harry James, *b* 1977. —— Patrick Thomas, *b* 1979. —— Benjamin David, *b* 1983.

BROTHER LIVING

Charles William, *b* 1945; *ed* Eton; Capt R Green Jackets: *m* 1st, 1977, Harmony Joanna, yr da of Malcolm Charles Alastair Lyell; 2ndly, 1988 (*m diss* 1991), Hon Angela Jane, eldest da of 4th Baron Borwick, MC; 3rdly, 1991, Mrs Diana Elizabeth Mann, and has issue living (by 1st *m*), Simon Charles, *b* 1982, — Toby Derick, *b* 1985. *Residence* – Meethe Barton, S Molton, N Devon EX36 4JA.

SISTERS LIVING

Diana Chrystel, *b* 1938: *m* 1962, Peter Allan Sichel, who *d* 1998, of Château d'Angludet 33460, Cantanac, France, and has issue living, Allan Gordon, *b* 1962, — James William, *b* 1963, — Charles Edward, *b* 1963 (twin), — Benjamin Pierre, *b* 1966, — David Mark, *b* 1968, — Rebecca, *b* 1978. —— Catherine Elizabeth, *b* 1945 (twin): *m* 1st, 1967 (*m diss* 1975), Michael Godfrey Melvin Groves; 2ndly, 1977, David Alan Drummond Cavender, of The Manor House, Dowlish Wake, Ilminster, Som, and has issue living (by 1st *m*), Alistair Michael William, *b* 1968, — Henry Grenville Havelock, *b* 1971.

COLLATERAL BRANCHES LIVING

Issue of late Brigadier Roderick Heathcoat-Amory, MC, 4th son of 2nd baronet, *b* 1907, *d* 1998: *m* 1947, Sonia Myrtle (Allington Grange, nr Chippenham, Wilts), da of late Commodore Edward Conyngham Denison, MVO, RN (*see* B Londesborough colls), and widow of Maj Edgar Fitzgerald Heathcoat-Amory (infra):—

Rt Hon David Philip, MP (12 Lower Addison Gdns, W14), *b* 1949; *ed* Eton, and Ch Ch, Oxford; Treas HM Household (Dep Chief Whip) 1992-93, since when Min of State for Foreign and Commonwealth Affairs 1993-94, Min of State and Paymaster Gen 1994-96; MP (*C*) Wells since 1983, PC 1996: *m* 1978, Linda Margaret Legh, yr da of Alec Desmond Adams, of The Old Rectory, Winchfield, Hants, and has issue living, John, *b* 1980, — Matthew, *b* 1982, — Florence, *b* 1988. —— Bridget Alexandra (*Lady Beck*), *b* 1952: *m* 1st, 1984, Michael Roger Lewis Cockerell, eldest son of Prof Hugh A.L. Cockerell; 2ndly, 1991, as his 2nd wife, Sir (Edgar) Philip Beck, of Pylle Manor, Shepton Mallet, Som, and has issue living (by 1st *m*), Eliza Sonia, *b* 1985, — Alice Fanny, *b* 1987.

Grandchildren of late Lieut-Col Harry William Ludovic Heathcoat Heathcoat-Amory (infra):—
Issue of late Richard Frank Heathcoat-Amory, *b* 1903 *d* 1957: *m* 1938, Hon Margaret Irene Gaenor Scott-Ellis (Hele Manor, Exebridge, Dulverton, Som TA22 9RN), da of 8th Baron Howard de Walden:—
(Ian) Mark (Hele Manor, Dulverton, Somerset), *b* 1941; *ed* Eton, and Ch Ch, Oxford: *m* 1982, Charlotte Elizabeth, da of (Doulrish) Evelyn Louis Joll, of Flat 3, 42 Tregunter Rd, SW10 9LQ, and has issue living, Evelyn Caroline, *b* 1985, — Olivia Rachel, *b* 1988, — Katharine Eleanor, *b* 1991. ——Evelyn Helen (*Lady Jacomb*), *b* 1939: *m* 1960, Sir Martin Wakefield Jacomb, and has issue living, Matthew Barnabas Wakefield, *b* 1963, — Thomas Richard (The Malt House, Chilton, Oxon), *b* 1964: *m* 1988, Philippa A., yst da of Frederick Thomas Winter, CBE, of Uplands, Lambourn, Berks, and has issue living, Tara *b* 1989, Saffron *b* 1992, — Emma Félise, *b* 1961: *m* 1988, Simon Jock Bruce, and has issue (*see* E Elgin and Kincardine, colls). ——Rachel Belinda (Saddlers, Croscombe, Wells, Somerset), *b* 1946: *m* 1973 (*m diss* 1986), Christopher Joseph Ryan, and has issue living, Jessica Siobhan Elizabeth, *b* 1976, — Margherita, *b* 1978.

Issue of late Lieut-Col Harry William Ludovic Heathcoat Heathcoat-Amory, 3rd son of 1st baronet, *b* 1870; *d* 1945: *m* 1st, 1898, Evelyn Mary, who *d* 1929, da of late Edward James Stanley (E Derby, colls); 2ndly, 1931, Marjorie Una, who *d* 1973, da of Rev Edgar Astley Milne, R of Compton Valence, Dorset, and widow of E. P. Gundry, of Chilfrome, Dorchester:—
(By 1st *m*) Mary Millicent, *b* 1907: *m* 1930, Capt Adam Trevor Smail, 11th Hussars, and has issue living, Simon Trevor (Melcombe Newton Farm, Melcombe Bingham, Dorchester), *b* 1934; *ed* Eton; late Major 11th Hussars: *m* 1960, Margaret, da of late Maj Hon Arthur Bernard John Grenfell (*see* B Grenfell, colls), and has issue living, Tom Patrick *b* 1964, Lucy Jane *b* 1962. *Residence* – Melcombe Newton Farm, Melcombe Bingham, Dorchester, Dorset.

Grandchildren of late Major Ludovic Heathcoat-Amory, 5th son of 1st baronet:—
Issue of late Major Edgar Fitzgerald Heathcoat-Amory, Roy Devon Yeo, *b* 1917, *ka* in Normandy 1944: *m* 1940, Sonia Myrtle (who *m* 2ndly, 1947, Brigadier Roderick Heathcoat-Amory, MC, The Royals (ante), who *d* 1998), only da of Commodore Edward Conyngham Denison, MVO, RN (*see* B Londesborough, colls):—
Michael FitzGerald (Chevithorne Barton, Tiverton, Devon), *b* 1941; *ed* Eton, and Ch Ch, Oxford; High Sheriff Devon 1985-86: *m* 1st, 1965 (*m diss* 1970), Harriet Mary Sheila, da of late Lt-Gen Sir Archibald Edward Nye, GSCI, GCMG, GCIE, KCB, KBE, MC (*see* E Ranfurly, colls, 1985 Edn); 2ndly, 1975, (Sarah) Arabella Marjorie, da of late Raimund von Hofmannsthal (*see* M Anglesey, 1980 Edn), and formerly wife of Piers von Westenholz, and has issue living, (by 1st *m*) Edward Fitzgerald, *b* 1967; *ed* Eton and Bristol Univ: *m* 1994, Alice M.R., elder da of David Paget Thomson, of Little Stoke House, Wallingford, Oxon, — (by 2nd *m*) Lucy Sonia Elizabeth, *b* 1977, — Jessica Diana Mary, *b* 1979. ——Amanda Mary (*Countess Cairns*) (Bolehyde Manor, Allington, Chippenham, Wilts), *b* (*posthumous*) 1944: *m* 1964, 6th Earl Cairns.

The 1st baronet, Sir John, maternal grandson of John Heathcoat, MP, of Bolham, Devon, was partner J. Heathcoat & Co, Lace Manufacturers; MP for Tiverton (*Lib*) 1868-85; assumed by Roy Licence the additional surname and arms of Heathcoat, and was *cr* a *Baronet* 1874. The 4th baronet, *Sir* DERICK, KG, GCMG, TD, PC, Chancellor of the Exchequer 1958-60, British High Commr in Canada 1961-63, was *cr* VISCOUNT AMORY, of Tiverton, co Devon; *dunm* 1981, when the Peerage became *ext*.

ANSON (UK) 1831, of Birch Hall, Lancashire

Never despair

Sir PETER ANSON, CB, 7th *Baronet, b* 31 July 1924; *s* his father, *Sir* EDWARD REYNELL, 1951; *ed* RNC Dartmouth; CEng, FIEE; High Sheriff Surrey 1993, DL 1993; Rear Adm (ret); Comdg Officer, HMS *Alert* 1957-58, on Staff of RN Tactical Sch 1959-61, Comdg Officer, HMS *Broadsword* 1961-62, Dep Dir, Weapons Radio (Naval), Min of Defence 1963-65, and Dir 1965-66, Comdg HMS *Naiad* and Capt (D) Londonderry Sqdn 1966-68, and Comdg HMS *Mercury*, and Capt HM Signal Sch 1968-70, Cdr Naval Forces Gulf 1970-72 and Assist Ch Defence Staff (Sigs) 1972-74; SW Pacific 1941-45 (prisoner); Chm Marconi Space Systems Ltd 1985-91; Man Dir Marconi Space Systems Ltd 1984; Divisional Man Satellites Marconi Space and Defence Systems Ltd 1977; Assist Marketing Dir Marconi Space and Defence Systems Ltd 1975; Chm UK Industrial Space Cttee 1980-82; CB (Mil) 1974: *m* 1955, Elizabeth Audrey, DBE, da of late Rear Adm Sir (Charles) Philip Clarke, KBE, CB, DSO, and has issue.

Arms – Argent, three bendlets engrailed gules, a crescent for difference. **Crest** – Out of a ducal coronet or, a spear's head proper.
Residence – Rosefield, 81 Boundstone Rd, Rowledge, Farnham, Surrey GU10 4AT.

SONS LIVING

PHILIP ROLAND (34 Martello Rd, Eastbourne, E Sussex BN22 7SS), *b* 4 Oct 1957; *ed* Charterhouse, and Chelsea Coll, London (BPharm 1979); MR PharmS 1980; Chm SE England Region of Royal Pharmaceutical Soc 1996-98. —— Hugo William, *b* 1962: *m* 1986, Sharon E., da of L. J. Gardner, of Palmers Green, London.

DAUGHTERS LIVING

Louisa Frances, *b* 1956: *m* 1st, 1978 (*m diss* 1985), Robert W. A. Cuthill; 2ndly, 1994, Dr Michael Barnsley. —— Sarah Elizabeth, *b* 1966: *m* 1992, Robert A. van Lieshout, only son of J.A. van Lieshout, of Helmond, The Netherlands.

BROTHER LIVING

Sir John, KCB, *b* 1930; *ed* Winchester, and Magdalene Coll, Camb (MA); 2nd Permanent Sec HM Treasury 1987-90; CB (Civil) 1980, KCB (Civil) 1990: *m* 1957, Myrica, da of late Dr H. Fergie-Woods, and has issue living, Christopher Edward, *b* 1958; MA, PhD: *m* 1986, Susan Melanie, PhD, da of R. Robinson, of Cleveleys, Lancs, and has issue living, Thomas Anthony *b* 1987, Matthew David *b* 1990, Joshua Daniel *b* 1993, — Timothy John, *b* 1967, — Rachel Mary, *b* 1961; BA: *m* 1984, Michael John Snelson, son of D. L. Snelson, of Handforth, Cheshire, and has issue living, William Lawrence *b* 1991, Katherine Louise *b* 1989, — Elizabeth Margaret, *b* 1968.

The 1st baronet, a younger brother of the 1st Viscount Anson, and uncle of the 1st Earl of Lichfield, greatly distinguished himself during the Peninsular War. The 2nd baronet was killed in a railway accident at Wigan, 2 August 1873. The 3rd baronet, Rt Hon Sir William Reynell, PC, was Warden of All Souls' Coll, Oxford 1881-1914, Vice-Chancellor, Oxford Univ 1898-9, Parliamentary Sec to Board of Education 1902-5, MP for Oxford Univ (LU) 1899-1914, and a Trustee of National Portrait Gallery and of British Museum. The 4th baronet, Sir Denis George William, was drowned in the Thames July 1914, shortly after his succession to the Baronetcy. The 5th baronet, Sir John Henry Algernon, Lieut RN; *d* on active service 1918. The 6th baronet, Sir Edward Reynell served in RN during European War 1915-19, and as Lieut-Col RA during European War 1939-45.

ANSTRUTHER OF THAT ILK (NS) 1694, of Balcaskie, and (NS) 1700 of Anstruther, Fife

Sir RALPH HUGO ANSTRUTHER, GCVO, MC, 7th *Baronet* of 1st and 12th of 2nd creation, son of late Capt Robert Edward Anstruther, MC, only son of 6th baronet; *b* 13 June 1921; *s* his grandfather, *Col Sir* RALPH WILLIAM, 1934, and his cousin, *Sir* WINDHAM ERIC FRANCIS CARMICHAEL-ANSTRUTHER OF CARMICHAEL AND OF ANSTRUTHER, 1980; *ed* Eton, and at Magdalene Coll, Camb (BA 1940); is a Member of the Queen's Body Guard for Scotland (Roy Co of Archers), a DL of Fife and Caithness, and formerly Major Coldstream Guards; Equerry to HM Queen Elizabeth The Queen Mother since 1959 and Treasurer since 1961; Assist Private Sec 1959-64; Hereditary Carver to the Sovereign, and a Master of the Royal Household in Scotland; 1939-45 War (wounded, MC), Malaya 1948-50 (despatches); CVO 1967, KCVO 1976, GCVO 1992.

Arms – Argent, three piles sable, above the shield, from which is pendent by an orange-tawny ribbon the appropriate badge of a Baronet of Nova Scotia, is placed a chapeau gulse furred ermine thereon a helmet with mantling sable doubled argent and issuant from a crest-coronet of four strawberry leaves (three visible) or is set for crest two arms in armour holding a pole-axe with both hands gauntleted proper. Motto – Periissem ni Periissem. Supporters – Two falcons with wings expanded proper, beaked and membered gules, belled and jessed or.
Seats – Balcaskie, Pittenweem, Fife; Watten, Caithness.

COLLATERAL BRANCHES LIVING

Grandchildren of late Henry Torrens Anstruther, 2nd son of 5th baronet:—
Issue of late Douglas Tollemache Anstruther, *b* 1893, *d* 1956: *m* 1st, 1914 (*m diss* 1924), Enid who *d* 1964, da of late Lord George Granville Campbell (D Argyll, colls); 2ndly, 1925, Evelyn Mabel, who *d* 1981, da of Sir John Wormald, KBE:—
(By 1st *m*) IAN FIFE CAMPBELL (Estate Office, Barlavington, Petworth, Sussex GU28 0LG; Brooks's Club), *b* 11 May 1922; *ed* Eton and New Coll, Oxford; an author; Capt late R Corps of Signals; a Member of the Queen's Body Guard for Scotland (Roy Co of Archers); 1939-45 War with Argyll and Sutherland Highlanders, Signals and Intelligence Corps: *m* 1st, 1951 (*m diss* 1963), Honor, el da of late Capt Gerald Blake; 2ndly, 1963, Susan Margaret Walker, da of H. St. J. B. Paten, and has issue living, (by 1st *m*) Emily Kate Campbell, *b* 1953, — (by 2nd *m*) Sebastian Paten Campbell, *b* 1962, — Tobias Alexander Campbell, *b* 1968, — Rachel Whittome Campbell, *b* 1965, — Harriet Joan Campbell, *b* 1967: *m* 1991, Hamish H. A. Summers, of 14 Onslow Mews W, S Kensington, SW7 3AF, eldest son of Tony Summers, of Adelaide, Australia, and has issue living, Celestia Nell Campbell *b* 1993, — Eleanor Thurloe Campbell, *b* 1971. —— (Janet) Finetta Campbell (Westwood, Bucklebury Alley, Cold Ash, Newbury, Berks RG16 9NN), *b* 1920: *m* 1st, 1945 (*m diss* 1959), Rev William Pritchard Cole, Chap to Forces; 2ndly, 1968 (*m diss* 1983), Clive Ernest Baker, and has issue living, (by 1st *m*) Michael Henry Campbell, *b* 1945, — Janet Barbara Campbell, *b* 1947.

Grandchildren of late Adm Robert Hamilton Anstruther, CMG, 3rd son of 5th baronet:—
Issue of late Col Philip Noel Anstruther, DSO, MC, *b* 1891, *d* 1960: *m* 1st, 1920 (*m diss* 1931), Mary Hope who *d* 1963, da of Harold Chaloner Lewin, of Birchdale, Bromley, Kent; 2ndly, 1937, Mary Were, of New Zealand; 3rdly, 1952, Mrs Marion Secretan, da of late Capt I. Gregor MacGregor, RNR:—
(By 1st *m*) Robert Lewin, *b* 1924; *ed* Eastbourne Coll; is a FRICS: *m* 1950, Rosemary Nathalie, only da of Com (E.) Guy Ernest Williamson, MBE, RN, and has issue living, Peter Robert, *b* 1955: *m* 1981 (*m diss* 1984), Joanna Mary, da of Ken Herring, OBE, and has issue living, Charlotte Daisy *b* 1982, — Catherine Jane, *b* 1951: *m* 1981, Robert Adrian Emerson, and has issue living, Nicolas *b* 1980, Joseph *b* 1983, — Sally Elizabeth, *b* 1958: *m* 1st, 1978, James Trevor Reader; 2ndly, 1984, John Michael Smith, and has issue living (by 1st *m*), Mark Richard James *b* 1981, Rebecca Claire *b* 1979, (by 2nd *m*) Victoria Wendy *b* 1984. *Residence* – Windy Ridge, Peartree Lane, Dymchurch, Romney Marsh, Kent. —— Jean Mary (The Little House, 2E Southlands Grove, Bromley, Kent BR1 2DQ), *b* 1921: *m* 1951, Fl-Lt Robert (Robin) Owen Blackall, RAF, who *d* 1952.

Grandchildren of late Lieut-Col Robert Hamilton Lloyd-Anstruther, son of late Col James Hamilton Lloyd-Anstruther, son of late Brig-Gen Robert Anstruther, el son of 3rd baronet:—
Issue of late Sir Fitzroy Hamilton ANSTRUTHER-GOUGH-CALTHORPE, Bt, *b* 1872, *d* 1957, who was *cr* a *Baronet* 1929 (see that title).

Granddaughters of late Lt-Col William Anstruther-Gray, of Kilmany, Cupar, Fife, and of Carntyne, Lanarks, 3rd son of Col John Anstruther-Thomson, of Charleton, co Fife, elder son of John Anstruther-Thomson, of Charleton, co Fife, eldest son of Col John Anstruther, 3rd son of 2nd baronet:—
Issue of late William John St Clair ANSTRUTHER-GRAY, MC, PC (*Baron Kilmany*), *b* 1905, *d* 1985; *cr* a *Baronet* 1956, and *Baron Kilmany* (Life Baron) 1966: *m* 1934, Monica Helen, OBE, who *d* 1985, da of late Geoffrey Lambton (*see* E Durham, colls, 1985 Edn):—
Hon Diana Mary, *b* 1936; DL Fife 1992: *m* 1959, James Charles Macnab of Macnab (The Macnab), of Leuchars Castle Farmhouse, Leuchars, St Andrews, Fife KY16 0EY, and has issue living, James William Archibald (Macnab of Macnab, yr), *b* 1963: *m* 1994, Dr Jane Louise, da of late Dr David Mackintosh, of Exmouth, Devon, — Geoffrey Charles, *b* 1965: *m* 1998, Catriona, yr da of John Alexander Campbell, of Achiltibuie, Ross-shire, — Virginia Mary, *b* 1960: *m* 1986, Richard Laurence Oliphant Fyffe, elder son of late Laurence Fyffe, MC, JP, DL, of Corsindae, Sauchen, Aberdeenshire, and has issue living Alice Catherine *b* 1989, Emma Cicely *b* 1992, — Katharine Monica, *b* 1968: *m* 1998, Christopher C. Cox, yr son of Stephen Cox, of N Walsham, Norfolk. —— *Hon* Jane Caroline, *b* 1943: *m* 1st 1962 (*m diss* 1992), Hon

George Anthony Weir; 2ndly, 1992, F. Graham Gillies, who *d* 1992, and has issue (by 1st *m*) (*see* V Weir). *Residence* – Kilmany, Cupar, Fife KY15 4QW.

The 1st baronet of Balcaskie, Sir Robert Anstruther (third son of Sir Philip Anstruther) purchased Balcaskie in 1698. The 5th Baronet was Lord-Lieut of co Fife and sat as MP for co Fife (*L*) 1864-80, and for St Andrews District of Burghs 1885-6. The 6th Baronet was also Lord-Lieut of co Fife. The 1st baronet of Anstruther, Sir John Anstruther, son of Sir William Anstruther, eldest son of Sir Philip Anstruther (ante), was MP for county of Fife, and was created a baronet with remainder to heirs male 6 Jan 1700.

Anstruther-Gough-Calthorpe, see Calthorpe.

ANTROBUS (UK) 1815, of Antrobus, Cheshire

Mindful of God, grateful to friends

Sir EDWARD PHILIP ANTROBUS, 8th *Baronet*; *b* 28 Sept 1938; *s* his father, Sir PHILIP COUTTS, 1995; *ed* Witwatersrand Univ (BSc Min Eng), and Magdalene Coll, Camb (MA): *m* 1st, 1966, Janet Sarah Elizabeth, who *d* 1990, da of Philip Walter Sceales, of Johannesburg; 2ndly, 1996, Rozanne Penelope, da of Neville Simpson, formerly of Durban, and has issue by 1st *m*.

Arms – Lozengy or and azure, on a pale gules three estoiles of the first. Crest – Issuing out of rays proper an unicorn's head couped argent, horned and maned or, gorged with a leaf of laurel proper. Supporters – Two horses proper.
Address – 54A 3rd Av, Parktown North, Johannesburg, S Africa.

SON LIVING (*By 1st marriage*)

FRANCIS EDWARD SCEALES, *b* 24 Oct 1972; *ed* St Andrew's Coll, Grahamstown, and Cape Town Univ (BSc).

DAUGHTERS LIVING (*By 1st marriage*)

Barbara Joanna, *b* 1968: *m* 1998, Simon van der Veen, and has issue living, Elizabeth Martha, *b* 1998 . —— Sarah Diana, *b* 1970.

BROTHER LIVING

Michael Ronald, *b* 1939; Dip of Agric (S Africa): *m* 1968, Sandra, da of Jurgens Hans Moolman, of Middleton, Cape Prov, and has issue living, Philip Michael, *b* 1973; *ed* St Andrew's Coll, Grahamstown, — Cherie Joann, *b* 1969, — Elizabeth Ruth, *b* 1971. *Address* – PO Box 433, Cradock 5880, S Africa.

SISTER LIVING

Patricia Jennifer, *b* 1948: *m* 1971, Maj Michael George Rodgers Montgomery, late RE, and has issue living, Charles George Philip, *b* 1978; *ed* Wellington Coll, — Geraldine Claire Margaret, *b* 1977. *Address* – Tumbling Bay, Church St, Amesbury, Wilts SP4 7EU.

AUNTS LIVING (*sisters of 7th baronet*)

Ida Dorothy, *b* 1909; 1939-45 War in S African Mil Nursing Ser: *m* 1st, 1937 (*m diss* 1940), Frank Thomas Hayes, who *d* 1972, of Cathcart, Cape Prov; 2ndly, 1944, Cyril Embleton Hilton Barber, who *d* 1985, and has had issue (by 1st *m*), Heather Ann (18 Somerset Place, Port Alfred, 6170 Cape Prov, S Africa), *b* 1938: *m* 1963, Leonard Erle Twentyman-Jones, who *d* 1995, and has issue living, Leonard Hilton *b* 1965: *m* 1992, Mrs Tammy Lyn Boraman Crabtree (and has issue living, Frank Hilton Boraman *b* 1992), Lee-Ann *b* 1964, Julie *b* 1968: *m* 1991, John Howard Kinsley (and has issue living, Jordan Howard *b* 1997, Michaela Amy *b* 1994), — (by 2nd *m*), Charles Geoffrey Hilton, *b* 1047; *d* 1070, Valerie May Hilton (9 Bedford St, Grahamstown, Cape Prov 6140), *b* 1948; *m* 1974 (*m diss* 19—), William Gerald Sieberhagen, and has issue living, Hilton John *b* 1978; *ed* St Andrew's Coll, Grahamstown. *Residence* – 9 Bedford St, Grahamstown, 6139 Eastern Prov, Africa. —— Mary Shakerley, *b* 1913: *m* 1937, Edward Mounsey Gilfillan, JP, and has issue living, Edward Crawfurd, *b* 1940: *m* 1968, Ruth-Mary, da of Herbert James McJannet, and has issue living, Edward Hugh *b* 1970, Ross Mounsey *b* 1974, Claire Mary *b* 1972, — Philip Mounsey, *b* 1950; Dr Vet Sc: *m* 1980, Helen, da of Graham Kinsey, and has issue living, Edward Mounsey *b* 1985, David Graham *b* 1993, Caitlin Mary *b* 1987, Anthea Doretta *b* 1990, — Camilla Mary, *b* 1938: *m* 1967, Henry Gurney Gush (formerly Goesche), and has issue living, Giles Joseph Gurney *b* 1968, Andrew Edward Gurney *b* 1970, — Jocelyn May, *b* 1948; Matron-in-Ch Libertas Hosp, Goodwood, Cape

Town: *m* 1978, Christiaan Visser, and has issue living, Richard *b* 1982, Christine *b* (twin) 1982. *Residence* – Conway Farm, PO Conway Station, Cape Prov, S Africa.

WIDOW LIVING OF SEVENTH BARONET

ESMÉ FLORENCE BAYES (*Dowager Lady Antrobus*), da of Dudley Charles Windsor, and widow of Frank Herbert Mawer: *m* 1991, as his 3rd wife, Sir Philip Coutts Antrobus, 7th Bt, who *d* 1995. *Residence* – Elizabeth Gdns, Howick, Natal, S Africa.

COLLATERAL BRANCHES LIVING

Grandchildren of late Geoffrey Edward Antrobus, 2nd son of late John Coutts Antrobus (infra):—
Issue of late Crawfurd Ralph Antrobus (yr brother of 7th Bt), *b* 1915, *d* 1996: *m* 1943, Sheila (PO Box 390, Grahamstown, 6140 S Africa), da of late Ven Archdeacon Alfred Edward McKenzie:—
Geoffrey Gordon (5 South St, Grahamstown, 6140 S Africa), *b* 1944; *ed* Natal Univ (MSc Agric), and Rhodes Univ (PhD); Registrar (Academic) to Fort Hare Univ 1988-90, Prof of Economics Rhodes Univ, Grahamstown since 1991: *m* 1973, Margaret Elizabeth, da of late Roy Nettleton Gordon, and has issue living, Charles Crawfurd, *b* 1982, — Richard Roy, *b* (twin) 1982, — Helen Catherine, *b* 1976: *m* 1998, Michael James Pfister, son of Dr Peter John von Solms Pfister, — Shirley Jean, *b* 1977. —— Margaret Jean (Oriel House, Rhodes Univ, Grahamstown, 6140 S Africa), *b* 1947: *m* 1969 (*m diss* 1984), John Rodney Baker, and has issue living, John Andrew, *b* 1971, — Bruce Stephen, *b* 1975, — Carol Lynne, *b* 1973.

Granddaughters of late Ralph Edmund Antrobus (infra):—
Issue of late Geoffrey John Antrobus, *b* 1904, *d* 1990: *m* 1st, (Jan) 1938, Mary Dorothea Van der Byl, who *d* 1950; 2ndly, 1953, Antonia Marie (BLEW), who *d* 1994, da of late William H. Carlin, of Johannesburg, S Africa:—
(By 1st *m*) Prunella Mary, *b* (Oct) 1938: *m* 1961, David Burt, of Silton, Peaslake, Surrey, and has issue living, Lyndon Oliver Antrobus, *b* 1965, — Nicola Katherine, *b* 1962. —— Chloe Louise, *b* 1943: *m* 1969, Alan Douglas Saunders, of Gordon Heights, Constantia, Cape Town, S Africa, and has issue living, Thandi Antonia, *b* 1973, — Lucy, *b* 1975.

Grandchildren of John Coutts Antrobus (nephew of 2nd baronet):—
Issue of late Ralph Edmund Antrobus, *b* 1871, *d* 1927: *m* 1901, Millicent, who *d* 1937, da of late Edward Lindsey De Morgan:—
Edmund Shakerley Alexander (20A Sherwood Rd, Forest Town, Johannesburg 2193, S Africa), *b* 1919; *ed* Magdalene Coll, Camb (BA 1946), and at McGill Univ, Montreal (MSc 1949, PhD 1955); 1939-45 War as Capt RA: *m* 1947, Shelagh Elizabeth Rich, and has issue living, (Edmund) Bayard (6 Dunkeld Rd, Talbot Woods, Bournemouth), *b* 1949: *m* 1978, Gillian Van Hasselt, and has issue living, Sara Kate *b* 1988, Lucy Jane *b* 1989, Olivia Sage *b* 1991, — Bryan Ralph (95 Kerry Rd, Parkview, Johannesburg), *b* 1951: *m* 1982, Rosemary Logie, and has had issue, Nicholas Hugh *b* 1986, Caroline Elizabeth *b* 1984; *d* 1994, Megan Elizabeth *b* 1996, — Christopher Adrian (51 Rothesay Av, Craighall Park, Johannesburg), *b* 1952: *m* 1979, Ann Tuffin, and has issue living, Kyra Liza *b* 1984, Jacinta Leigh-Ann *b* 1986, — Robin Clive (28 Broadbent Loop, Leeming, Perth, W Australia 6155), *b* 1954: *m* 1982, Theresa Susan, da of Arthur Allenby Noble, and has issue living, Courtney Lynne *b* 1990.

Issue of late Rev Jocelyn James Antrobus, *b* 1876, *d* 1953: *m* 1915, Justine Mary Louisa, who *d* 1964, da of late Maj William Affleck King (Duckworth-King, Bt, colls):—
Mary Elizabeth (16 Prospect Place, Camden Rd, Bath), *b* 1918.

Grandson of Walter Guy Antrobus (infra):—
Issue of late Robert Michael Antrobus, *b* 1910, *d* 1961: *m* 1st, 1938 (*m diss* 1948), Janet Lyle Holmes, da of late Neil Mackay, of Seapoint, Cape Town, S Africa; 2ndly, 1959, Peggy, da of Douglas Graham, and widow of Donald Halley:—
(By 1st *m*) Norman Hugh (17 Plover St, Horizon, Extension, 1 Roodeport, Transvaal), *b* 1940: *m* 1963, Barbara Gwen, da of E. J. M. Gravitt, of Pietermaritzburg, and has issue living, Stephen Craig, *b* 1965, — Liane Mary, *b* 1966.

Grandsons of late John Coutts Antrobus (ante):—
Issue of late Walter Guy Antrobus, *b* 1879, *d* 1963: *m* 1907, Kathleen Frances, da of late Brig-Gen Arthur Broadwood, CVO (E Clanwilliam, colls):—
Henry Lindsay (PO Box 428 Umtentweni, Natal 4235), *b* 1916; *ed* Witwatersrand Univ; an AMICE: *m* 1943, Mary Lammie, da of Thomas Howie, of Wankie, Zimbabwe and has issue living, Ronald James, *b* 1950; *ed* Onesdepoort Univ (BVSc): *m* 1984, Merle Petersen, and has issue living, Micah Lindsay *b* 1988, Carol Lee *b* 1986, — Rosemary Lindsay, *b* 1947; *ed* Natal Univ (BSc) and Cape Town Univ (MBA), — Helen Kathleen, *b* 1951; *ed* Natal Univ (BA Hons, BEd): *m* 1976, Kenneth Edward Hall, of 10 Abelia Rd, Kloof 3610, S Africa, and has issue living, Isla Lindsay *b* 1983, Iona Rosemary *b* 1987. —— Dennis Ronald, *b* 1920; *ed* Witwatersrand Univ (BSc 1949): *m* 1950, Audrey Eleanor, da of William James McGill, of Rustenberg, and has issue living, Dennis Mark, *b* 1956, Sally Elizabeth, *b* 1952.

Issue of late Lt-Col Ronald Henry Antrobus, MC, DL, *b* 1891, *d* 1980: *m* 1921, Muriel Kathleen, who *d* 1980, da of late Richard Henry Gosling, of Hawthorn Hill, Bracknell, Berks (Dyer, Bt), and widow of Capt Henry Miles Chetwynd-Stapylton (*see* V Chetwynd, colls, 1916 Edn):—
John Ronald Lindsay (The School House, 18 School Lane, Eaton, Congleton, Cheshire CW12 2NG), *b* 1926; *ed* Eton, Magdalene Coll, Camb (MA), and Trin Coll, Oxford; late Lt Duke of Wellington's Regt, and 8th R Irish Hussars; Palestine 1947-48 as Lt 17th/21st Lancers: *m* 1st, 1952 (*m diss* 1960), Ann, el da of late Cdr Denys Royds Brocklebank, RN, of Longbridge House, Warminster, Wilts (*see* E Crawford and Balcarres, colls, 1985 Edn); 2ndly, 1961 (*m diss* 1966), Margaret Jane, only child of late Dr J. H. Penman, of Eskbank, Midlothian; 3rdly, 1966, Rochelle Christine, yr da of late Theodore William Candee, of Pasadena, Cal, USA, and has issue living, (by 1st *m*) Nigel John Lindsay (Grey Wall, Ship St, East Grinstead, W Sussex), *b* 1953; *ed* Michael Hall Sch, Forest Row, — James Hugh Lindsay, *b* 1954; *ed* London Univ (Charing Cross Hosp Med Sch); BSc, MB BS, FRCA: *m* 1983, Elisabeth Anne, yr da of Bryan Jarman Wright, of

Norwich, Norfolk, and has issue living, Philip Edward b 1987, Lucy Elizabeth b 1989, — (by 3rd m) Richard Henry Lindsay, b 1967; ed Keele Univ (BA), — Charles Edward Lindsay, b 1968; ed Brighton Univ (BEng 1997), — Rosemary Caroline Lindsay, b 1969; ed Salford Univ (BA 1997), — Jane Elizabeth Lindsay, b 1972, — Catherine Mary Lindsay, b 1975.

This Baronetcy was conferred upon Edmund Antrobus, of Antrobus Hall, Antrobus Village, Cheshire, with special remainder to his nephews Edmund (who s as 2nd Bt) and Gibbs Crawfurd (ancestor of 7th Bt).

ARBUTHNOT (UK) 1823, of Edinburgh

INNOCENT AND TRUE

Sir KEITH ROBERT CHARLES ARBUTHNOT, 8th *Baronet; b* 23 Sept 1951; *s* his father, *Capt Sir* HUGH FITZGERALD, 1983, *ed* Wellington, and Edinburgh Univ: *m* 1982, Anne R., yr da of late Brig Peter Moore, of Hastings Hill House, Churchill, Oxon, and has issue.

𝔄rms – Azure, a crescent between three mullets, two and one, argent; the whole within a bordure or, charged with three boars' heads, couped gules. 𝔠rest – A peacock's head proper. 𝔖upporters – *Dexter*, a wyvern vert vomiting flames proper; *sinister*, a greyhound argent, collared and line reflexed over the back gules.
Seat – Mount Ulston, Jedburgh, Roxburghshire. *Residence* – Whitebridge, Peebles, Peebleshire.

SONS LIVING

ROBERT HUGH PETER, b 2 March 1986. ⸻ Patrick William Martin, b 1987.

DAUGHTER LIVING

Alice Elizabeth Mary, b 1990.

BROTHER LIVING

David William Patrick, b 1953; ed Wellington: m 1988, Diana, only da of John Yeomans, of Hill House, Baughurst, Hants, and has issue living, Phoebe Elizabeth, b 1988, — Rosanna Mary, b 1989. *Residence* – Hamilton Stables, Compton, nr Newbury, Berks RG16 6QJ.

SISTER LIVING

Christian Aline, b 1950: m 1973, (Geoffrey) John Morley (*see* V Hood, colls, 1995 Edn), and has issue living, William Everard Hugh, b 1980, — Aline Elizabeth Georgina, b 1974, — Emily Alice, b 1977. *Residence* – Mount Ulston, Jedburgh, Roxburghshire.

WIDOW LIVING OF SEVENTH BARONET

JULIA GRACE (*Julia, Lady Arbuthnot*), only da of late Lt-Col Frederick Gerard Peake, CMG, CBE, of Hawkslee, St Boswells, Roxburghshire, and formerly wife of — Grant: m 1977, as his 2nd wife, Capt Sir Hugh Fitzgerald Arbuthnot, 7th Bt, who d 1983.

COLLATERAL BRANCHES LIVING

Branch from 3rd son of 2nd baronet

Grandchildren of late Henry FitzGerald Arbuthnot, son of late Rev Robert Keith Arbuthnot, 3rd son of 2nd baronet:—
Issue of late Hugh FitzGerald Arbuthnot, b 1903, d 1990: m 1928, Kathleen Phyllis (Peggy), who d 1982, da of late Reginald Walter Sheppard, of Looe:—
Robert Ian FitzGerald (Robin), b 1933; ed Haileybury; 2nd Lieut Royal Warwicks Regt; d of gunshot wounds while serving in Korea, 1953. ⸻ Patrick Stephen FitzGerald (The Litten, Grimsdells Lane, Amersham, Bucks), b 1936; ed Haileybury: m 1967, Jennifer Anne, da of late Sidney George Roe, and has issue living, Simon Charles FitzGerald, b 1969. ⸻ Rosemary Elizabeth FitzGerald, b 1930; ed Headington Sch, Oxford, and Bristol Univ (BA): m 1957, William Allen Humpherson, FRCO, BDS, LRAM, and has issue living, Robert William, b 1958, — Michael Hugh, b 1962, — Edward Allen, b 1970, — Susan Linley, b 1960.

Branch from 2nd son of 1st baronet

Grandchildren of late Maj John Bernard Arbuthnot, MVO, eldest son of late Col George Arbuthnot, 2nd son of late John Alves Arbuthnot, 2nd son of 1st baronet:—
Issue of late David George Arbuthnot, b 1905, d 1985: m 1st, 1933 (m diss 1946), Hon Elizabeth Dorothy Kemeys-Tynte, later Baroness Wharton, who d 1974; 2ndly, 1946, Barbara Margherita, who d 1974, da of Francis Chiappini, JP, of Wynberg, Cape Province, S Africa, and widow of Percy Seymour Douglas-Hamilton (see D Hamilton, colls):—
(By 1st m) (See Bs Wharton).

Issue of late Group Capt Terence John Arbuthnot, RAF, b 1906, d 1995: m 1937, Karin Gunborg, who d 1983, da of Carl Adolph Sundgren, of Hudiksvall, Sweden:—
(John Sten) Robert (Flat 6, 86 Redcliffe Gdns, SW10), b 1941; ed Sherborne: m 1st, 1971 (m diss 1982), Elizabeth Marjorie, da of Sir (Charles) Henry Plumb (later Baron Plumb); 2ndly, 1984, Swee Lien Ong, da of Boon Bah Ong, of Pentaling Jaya, W Malaysia, and has issue living (by 2nd m), James Robert Yu-Ming, b 1984, — Jennifer Mei-Chen, b 1987. — Susan Christine, b 1939: m 1970, B. John Minchin, who d 1987, and has issue living, Karin Christine, b 1972, — Joanna Lesley, b 1975. —— Diana Karin, b 1942: m 1963, Geert Holger Sonderhoff, of 316 Stevens Drive, W Vancouver, BC, Canada, and has issue living, Terence Sven, b 1965, — Stefan Andrew, b 1967.

Issue of late Cmdr Bernard Kieran Charles Arbuthnot, DSC, RN, b 1909, d 1975: m 1939, Rosemary Harold, who d 1978, da of late Lt-Col Harold Thompson, DSO, Royal Scots Fus:—
Shirley, b 1949: m 1970, Nigel Murray, of Myrtle Grove, Youghal, co Cork, and has issue living, Simon Peregrine Gauvain, b 1974, — Iona Louise Arbuthnot, b 1972. ——Penelope Anne, b 1953: m 1983, Michael Drake Stewart, of Stokestown, New Ross, co Wexford, and has issue living, Kerry (spelling changed to Keri 1995) Blake (a da), b 1987.

Branch from 3rd son of 1st baronet

Grandson of late Adm Sir Geoffrey Schomberg Arbuthnot, KCB, DSO (infra):—
Issue of late Michael Geoffrey Henderson Arbuthnot, b 1919, d 1967: m 1948, (Nicole) Patricia (5 Egerton Place, SW3 2EF), da of late Lt-Col Richard Leslie Halliburton Collins, of Thurston House, Bury St Edmunds:—
Peter Geoffrey (4 Great Western Terrace, Glasgow G12 0UP), b 1950; ed Stowe, and Trin Coll, Camb: m 1979, Belinda, el da of Herbert Terry-Engell, of Guernsey, CI, and has issue living, James Nicholas, b 1982, — Harriet Emily b 1984.

Granddaughter of late Adm Charles Ramsay Arbuthnot, 2nd son of late George Clerk Arbuthnot, 3rd son of 1st baronet:—
Issue of late Adm Sir Geoffrey Schomberg Arbuthnot, KCB, DSO, b 1885, d 1957: m 1913, Jessie Marguerite, who d 1947, 2nd da of late William Henderson, of Berkley House, Frome:—
Mary Marguerite, b 1914: m 1934, Lt-Col Walter Stuart Augustus Clough-Taylor, late RWF (E Castle Stewart), who d 1988, and has issue living, Juliet Mary, b 1935: m 1st, 1961 (m diss 19—), Timothy Charles Austin Horn; 2ndly, 1978, Colin Malcolm Paul, of Yew Tree Cottage, Halland, Lewes, Sussex BN8 6PW, and has issue living (by 1st m), Francis William Austin b 1962, Charlotte Mary b 1965.

Grandchildren of late James Arbuthnot, 3rd son of late George Clerk Arbuthnot (ante):—
Issue of late (George) Ramsay Arbuthnot, b 1880, d 1932: m 1910, Rose Anna Branson, who d 1973:—
George Ramsay (56 Wimborne Close, Bransholme, Hull), b 1930: m 1950, Sheelah Margaret Inchbold, and has issue living, Graham Stewart, b 1952; ed Salthouse High Sch, — Glynis Kathleen, b 1954: m 1977 (m diss 1988), John Campbell, and has issue living, Jamie John b 1980, Zoe b 1978, — Colleen, b 1964: m 1984, Philip Dolan, and has issue living, Kelly Arbuthnot b 1986, Lynsey Caroline Arbuthnot b 1988, — Alison Georgina, b 1968. ——Ivy, b 1913: m 1931, (William Charles) Norman Chilvers, who d 1986, of 52 Graham Av, Hull, and has had issue, Raymond Dennis, b 1932; d 1994, — David, b 1937, — Michael Charles, b 1949, — Malcolm Roy, b 1954, — Betty Doreen, b 1934, — Joyce, b 1936, — Joan Mary, b 1944, — Audrey Lyn, b 1952. ——Queenie Steward, b 1923: m 1941, Lesley Fox, and has issue living, Norman, b 1942, — Raymond, b 1948, — Sylvia, b 1953.

Branch from 4th son of 1st baronet

Grandchildren of late Lt-Col Archibald Hugh Arbuthnot (infra):—
Issue of late Lt-Cdr Archibald Hugh Gough Arbuthnot, RN, b 1900; d 1959: m 1st, 1935 (m diss 1954), Molly Irene Frances Weeks; 2ndly, 1955, (Emma) Mary, da of late Rev Gilbert Ambrose Bell, MA:—
(By 2nd m) Viola Jane, b 1957.

Issue of late Maj Patrick Charles Arbuthnot, b 1902, d 1988: m 1952, Evelyn Margaret (Quay Head, Sampford Peverell, Tiverton, Devon EX16 7BS), da of late George Robert Crawford, of Leamington:—
Patrick Hugh Alexander (41 Merrivale Square, Oxford OX2 6QX), b 1954; ed Blundell's, and Sidney Sussex Coll, Camb: m 1986, Susan Elizabeth, da of John Frederick Shaw, of Auckland, NZ, and has issue living, Charles Alexander, b 1990, — Robert Hugh, b 1991, — Roseanna Louise, b 1997. ——Colin Hugh David, b 1957; ed Blundell's, and Sidney Sussex Coll, Camb.

Issue of late Ernest Douglas Arbuthnot, b 1905, d 1984: m 1939, (Eveline) Mary (10 Vicar St, Wymondham, Norfolk), da of late Harold Morgan, of Worksop, Notts:—
Antony Hugh Gough, b 1948; ed Blundell's: m 1974, Frances, da of S/Ldr F. W. Williamson, of Garveston, Norfolk, and has issue living, Rupert, b 1981, — Emily Kate, b 1974. ——Robin Douglas, b 1951; ed Blundell's: m 1979, Elizabeth Ann, da of F. C. Palmer, of Yarmouth, Norfolk, and has issue living, Kitty Ann, b 1980, — Amy Elizabeth, b 1984.

—— Ann Faith, *b* 1941; JP, BA, MB, BS, MRC (Psych): *m* 1966, Raymond Barker, of 77 Dacre Park, SE13 5BX, and has issue living, Kate Abigail, *b* 1973, — Lucy Grace, *b* 1975.

Grandchildren of late Maj Archibald Ernest Arbuthnot, 3rd son of late Archibald Francis Arbuthnot, 4th son of 1st baronet:—
Issue of late Lt-Col Archibald Hugh Arbuthnot, *b* 1874, *d* 1957: *m* 1st, 1900, Gertrude, who *d* 1918, da of late Rev Frederick Charles Green, V of Denmead, Hants; 2ndly 1920, Marjory, who *d* 1975, da of late Rev Howard Beech, formerly R of Barlavington and Burton-with-Coates, Sussex:—
(By 1st *m*) Sheila Gertrude Tollemache, *b* 1917; 1939-45 War as Subaltern, ATS: *m* 1942, Maj Robert (Roy) Dunlop, MBE, Derbyshire Yeo, who *d* 1991, of Meadow Cottage, Aldingbourne, nr Chichester, W Sussex, and has issue living, Robert Andrew (Alding Farm, Aldingbourne, nr Chichester, Sussex), *b* 1948: *m* 1985, Catherine Jennifer Ewart, and has issue living, Robert James *b* 1987, Archibald Montgomery *b* 1994, Letitia Annabel *b* 1989, — Caroline Jane, *b* 1944: *m* 1973, James Lawrence Monro, MB BS, FRCS, of Rolle House, East Tytherley, nr Salisbury, Wilts, and has issue living, Charles Reed *b* 1975, Andrew James *b* 1981, Rosanne Elspeth *b* 1978, — Elspeth Marilyn (44 Tivoli St, Cheltenham, Glos), *b* 1951; MB BS, DA, DRCOG. —— (By 2nd *m*) Faith Deborah Etrenne (Quoins, Pound Place, Petworth, W Sussex GU28 0DZ), *b* 1921; 1939-45 War as Subaltern, ATS: *m* 1948, Edmund O'Donnel Colley Grattan, FRCS, late Colonial Med Ser, Kenya, who *d* 1985, and has issue living, Howard Colley Arnout Hugh, *b* 1949; *ed* Wellington Coll, — Clive Edmund Hume (Downham Lodge Farmhouse, Barnham Broom Rd, Wymondham, Norfolk NR18 0RS), *b* 1953; *ed* Wellington Coll, and King's Coll, Camb; MRCP: *m* 1980, Diana Mary, da of late Lt-Cdr William John Prowse, RN, and has issue living, Amanda Mary Winifred *b* 1983, Harriet Lucy *b* 1988, Abigail Frances *b* 1991, Claudia Etrenne *b* 1994, — Sarah Faith Madalyn, *b* 1950: *m* 1981, Iain Charles Mackie, ARICS, of Beggearn Huish Manor, Beggearn Huish, nr Watchet, Som TA23 0LZ, and has had issue, Alistair Graeme *b* 1983, Neil Edmund *b* 1986, Ewan James Stuart *b* and *d* 1988, Edward James Stephen *b* 1991, — Clare Winifred Melissa (20 Rowan Close, Sonning Common, Berks RG4 9LD), *b* 1956.

Issue of late Capt Ernest Kennaway Arbuthnot, DSO, RN (ret), *b* 1876 *d* 1945: *m* 1st, 1910, Edith Elizabeth (the actress Miss Evie Greene), who *d* 1917, da of Richard Bentley Greene, formerly of Parnholt, Laburnum Grove, Portsmouth; 2ndly, 1920, Gladys who *d* 1946, da of late William Butland Mann, of Downe, Broadhampton, S Devon:—
(By 2nd *m*) †John Keith, OBE, RN (23 Bowfell Rd, W6 9HE; 11 Ivry St, Ipswich, Suffolk IP1 3QP; Naval and Military Club), *b* 1927; Lt-Cdr RN (ret); 1939-45 War; Korea 1951 and 1954; OBE (Mil) 1967: *m* 1949, Susan Philippa, only da of Kenneth Petrie Letts, of Tickerage Mill, Blackboys, Sussex, and *d* 1998, having had issue, Richard Keith (87 Haverhill Rd, SW12), *b* 1950: *m* 1st, 1978 (*m diss* 1980), Jacqueline Hazel, da of George William White; 2ndly, 1984, Anne L. Pitman, — Charles Petrie, *b* 1959: *m* 1991, Penelope Jane, only da of J.F.J. Dickinson, of Kirby-le-Soken, Essex, and has issue living, Emily Jane *b* 1997, Rose Philippa *b* 1999, — Sally Anne, *b* 1954: *m* 1st, 1972 (*m diss* 1978), Richard Dumbrell-Howie; 2ndly, 1983, Brian Bovie, of Flat 3, Arndale, Anglesea Rd, Kingston, Surrey, — (Philippa) Jane, *b* 1961; WPC Chelsea Police Station; *k* in IRA bomb attack nr Harrods, 1983. —— Peter Kennaway (Winstons, Fieldgate Close, Monks Gate, Horsham, Sussex), *b* 1930; Lt RN (ret); Korea 1952: *m* 1957, Mia, el da of late Maj Percy Montagu Nevile, of Skelbrooke, Yorks, and has issue living, Matthew Kennaway, *b* 1959: *m* 1998, Glynis, 3rd da of Derek William Baines, of Milcombe, Oxon, — Mr and Mrs Peter K. Arbuthnot also have two adopted das, Katherine Jane, *b* 1964: *m* 1st, 1987 (*m diss* 1992), Keith Robert Howe, yst son of F. J. Howe, of Newcastle-upon-Tyne; 2ndly, 1998, Richard William Huddlestone, eldest son of William John Huddlestone, of Ashington, W Sussex, and has issue living (by 2nd *m*), Daniel Peter *b* 1999, — Emma Mary, *b* 1966: *m* 1992, Nigel S. Dent, of 25 Monks Walk, Beeding, Steyning, W Sussex, son of late C. R. Dent, of Steyning, W Sussex, and has issue living, Cassandra Mia *b* 1994.

Grandchildren of late Robert George Arbuthnot, 4th son of late Archibald Francis Arbuthnot (ante):—
Issue of late Capt Robert Wemyss Muir Arbuthnot, MC, *b* 1889, *d* 1962: *m* 1915, Mary, who *d* 1986, elder da of Norman Coghill, of Almington Hall, Market Drayton:—
Rev Andrew Robert Coghill, *b* 1926; *ed* Eton; 1939-45 War as Capt Scots Guards (wounded), Chm Arbuthnot Latham Holdings Ltd 1974-81; Dir Sun Alliance and Lon Insurance 1970-91; ordained a Priest 1975, Lon Healing Mission: *m* 1952, Mrs Audrey Eileen Dutton-Barker, da of Denys Billinghurst Johnson, MC, of Midhurst, Sussex, and has issue living, Charles Robert Denys (17 Frewin Rd, SW18 3LR), *b* 1956; *ed* Eton, and Camb Univ (MA): *m* 1985, Jennifer Rosemary, da of C. T. Arden-White, of West Lodge, 5 West Drive, Ferring, Worthing, W Sussex, and has issue living, Alexander Barnabas David *b* 1993, Kezia Louise *b* 1987, Johanna Rachel *b* 1989, — Caroline Rose, *b* 1954: *m* 1st, 1977 (*m diss* 1988), Paul J. Francis Clusker; 2ndly, 1988, Andrew Geuter, and has issue living (by 1st *m*), Rowan *b* 1978, Jade *b* 1980, Sacha *b* 1984, (by 2nd husband) Christian *b* 1986, Samuel *b* 1990. *Residence* – Monksfield House, Tilford, nr Farnham, Surrey. —— Juliet Mary Gough, *b* 1917: *m* 1939, Guy Marsden Halsey, TD, who *d* 1990 (*see* Halsey, Bt, colls). *Residence* – Whitehouse Farm, Gaddesden Row, nr Hemel Hempstead, Herts HP2 6HG.

This family is a branch of the Lairds of Arbuthnot, who have held lands in Kincardineshire from about 1160. The 1st baronet, Sir William, Lord Provost of Edinburgh in 1822, entertained George IV to a public banquet in that city, and was created a baronet by the King in person, the patent, however bearing date 1823. The 4th baronet, Rear-Adm Sir Robert Keith Arbuthnot, KCB, MVO, was *ka* at the battle of Jutland 1916 (despatches, posthumous KCB). The 5th baronet, Brig-Gen Sir Dalrymple Arbuthnot, CMG, DSO, served in S Africa 1900-1901, and in European War 1914-18 (CMG, DSO). The 6th baronet, Major Sir Robert Dalrymple, 24th Lancers, was *ka* in Normandy 1944.

ARBUTHNOT (UK) 1964, of Kittybrewster, Aberdeen

Praising God

Sir WILLIAM REIERSON ARBUTHNOT, 2nd *Baronet*; *b* 2 Sept 1950; *s* his father, *Sir* JOHN SINCLAIR-WEMYSS, MBE, TD, 1992; *ed* Eton; employed with Arbuthnot Latham Holdings Ltd 1970-76; Joynson-Hicks & Co, Solicitors 1978-81; Underwriting Member of Lloyd's; Dir ALM since 1997, Dep Chm High Premium Group since 1995; Liveryman of Worshipful Co of Grocers.

Arms – Azure, a crescent between three mullets argent, a bordure gules charged with two escallops in chief and a buck's head cabossed or in base, and in centre chief (overlapping bordure) an inescutcheon argent. **Crest** – A peacock's head and neck proper, accompanied on either side by a spray of strawberry leaves vert, each flowered of a cinquefoil Argent. *Residences* – 14 Ashburn Gdns, SW7 4DG; 37 Cathcart Rd, SW10 9JG.

DAUGHTER LIVING (*by Dr Tanya Bowyer Bower, yr da of late Michael Bowyer Bower*)

(Thomasina) Lucy Arbuthnot BOWYER BOWER, *b* 1998.

BROTHER LIVING

Rt Hon JAMES NORWICH, MP, *b* 4 Aug 1952; *ed* Eton, and Trin Coll, Camb (MA); Bar Inner Temple 1975 and Lincoln's Inn 1977; Min of State for Defence Procurement, Min of Defence 1995-97; Opposition Chief Whip since 1997; MP (C) for Wanstead and Woodford 1987-97, and for NE Hants since 1997; *cr* PC 1998: *m* 1984, Emma Louise, da of (John) Michael Broadbent, of 87 Rosebank, Holyport Rd, SW6, and has issue living, Alexander Broadbent, *b* 1986, — Katherine Rose Joste, *b* 1989, — Eleanor Sophie Duff, *b* 1992, — Alice Tempest Wemyss, *b* 1998.

SISTERS LIVING

Elizabeth Mary, *b* 1947; *ed* St Mary's Sch, Calne, and Kent Univ (BA). ⸺ Louise Victoria, *b* 1954; *ed* St Mary's Sch, Calne, and Exeter Univ (LLB); Solicitor: *m* 1984, David Bernard Lancaster, Solicitor, of Beech House, Ramsdell, Tadley RG26 5PR, only son of late Maj Bernard Thomas Lancaster, of Salisbury, Wilts, and has issue living, Rachel Alice, *b* 1985, — Rebecca Saskia, *b* 1987, — Tamara Louise, *b* 1988. ⸺ Alison Jane, *b* 1957; *ed* Benenden, and New Hall, Camb (MA); Solicitor.

WIDOW LIVING OF FIRST BARONET

(MARGARET) JEAN (*Lady Arbuthnot*), yr da of late (Alexander) Gordon Duff: *m* 1943, Sir John Sinclair-Wemyss Arbuthnot, 1st Bt, MBE, TD, who *d* 1992. *Residence* – 7 Fairholt St, SW7 1EG.

The 1st baronet, Sir John Sinclair-Wemyss Arbuthnot, MBE, TD (el son of Maj Kenneth Wyndham Arbuthnot, Seaforth Highlanders, and grandson of William Reierson Arbuthnot, 5th son of George Arbuthnot of Elderslie, brother of Sir William Arbuthnot, 1st Bt (*cr* 1823)), was MP (C) for Dover Div of Kent 1950-64, a Church Commr for England 1962-77, and a Member of Church Assembly and Gen Synod of Church of England 1955-75.

ARCHDALE (UK) 1928, of Riversdale, co Fermanagh

Sir EDWARD FOLMER ARCHDALE, DSC, RN, 3rd *Baronet*; *b* 8 Sept 1921; *s* his father, *Vice Adm Sir* (NICHOLAS) EDWARD, CBE, 1955; *ed* Copthorne Sch, and RNC Dartmouth; served WW II; Capt RN (ret); 1939-45 War (despatches, DSC): *m* 1954 (*m diss* 1978), Elizabeth Ann Stewart, da of late Maj-Gen Wilfrid Boyd Fellowes Lukis, CBE, RM, and has had issue.

Arms – Quarterly 1st and 4th, azure, a chevron ermine between three talbots passant or, *Archdale*; 2nd, or, a chevron sable, *Mervyn*; 3rd quarterly, 1st and 4th azure, three fleurs-de-lis or; 2nd and 3rd gules, three gem rings gold, all within a bordure or, charged with a tressure flory, gules, in the centre point an inescutcheon argent charged with a tilting spear and sword saltireways, points upwards proper, *Montgomery*. **Crest** – Out of a ducal crest coronet or, an heraldic tiger's head argent, maned, tufted and armed sable. **Motto** – Data Fata Secuta.
Residence – ......

Follow the destiny allotted

SON LIVING

NICHOLAS EDWARD, *b* 2 Dec 1965.

DAUGHTERS LIVING AND DECEASED

Annabel Frances, *b* 1956; *d* 1996. —— Lucinda Grace, *b* 1958: *m* 1991, Targino Luedy Kalid Filho, and has issue living, Sibylla Archdale, *b* 1993.

COLLATERAL BRANCHES LIVING

Issue of late William Porter Palgrave Archdale, CBE, 2nd son of 1st baronet, *b* 1883, *d* 1956: *m* 1918, Alice Edith Palgrave, who *d* 1963, da of late Capt Charles Alexander Price Chetwynd-Talbot (E Shrewsbury, colls):—
Mervyn Talbot, *b* 1924; DL Tyrone 1974, High Sheriff Tyrone 1985: *m* 1951, Aureole Helen, da of late Rev Canon Robert Hamilton Whelan, and has issue living, Peter Mervyn, Lt Cmdr RN; *b* 1953: *m* 1976, Caroline Anne, da of N. R. C. Griffin, and has issue living, Jonathan Talbot *b* 1982, Kathryn Emma *b* 1984, — Geraldine Angel, *b* 1952. *Residence* – The Cottage Farm, Knockmoyle, Omagh, co Tyrone.

Issue of late Lt-Col Audley Quintin Archdale, RHA, 3rd son of 1st baronet, *b* 1886, *d* 1978: *m* 1922, Mary Edith Haigh, who *d* 1987, da of Oliver Bury, MICE, JP, of 7 Vale Av, Chelsea, SW3:—
Rosemary, *b* 1923: *m* 1949, William Anthony Twiston Davies, who *d* 1989, of The Mynde, Much Dewchurch, Hereford, and has issue living, Audley William (Mynde Park, Much Dewchurch, Hereford HR2 8DN), *b* 1950; *ed* Radley: *m* 1985, Hon Caroline Mary Elaine Harbord-Hamond, da of 11th Baron Suffield, MC, and has issue living, Thomas Audley *b* 1994, Antonia Rose *b* 1987, Sophie Louise *b* 1990, Zoë Caroline *b* 1992, — Nigel Anthony (Grange Hill Farm, Naunton, Cheltenham, Glos), *b* 1957; *ed* Radley: *m* 1st 1981 (*m diss* 1987), Hon Sara Emma Hamilton-Russell, who *d* 1989, da of 10th Viscount Boyne; 2ndly, 1988, Catherine B., yst da of John Farey, of Bredon's Norton, nr Tewkesbury, and has issue living (by 2nd *m*), Sam *b* 1992, William *b* 1994, —— Alexandra Rosemary, *b* 1954: *m* 1986, Robin L.F. Burgess, of Hall Flatt, Scaleby, Carlisle, Cumbria, elder son of late Sir John Lawie Burgess, OBE, TD, JP, DL, of The Limes, Cavendish Terrace, Carlisle, and has issue living, James *b* 1994, Rose Charlotte *b* 1987, Catherine *b* 1989, Rachel *b* 1992, —— Penelope Auriol, *b* 1959: *m* 1982, Giles H. Mounsey-Heysham, of Castletown House, Rockcliffe, Carlisle, Cumbria, son of late Maj R. H. G. Mounsey-Heysham, and has issue living, Toby *b* 1984, Benjamin *b* 1986, Rory *b* 1989, Anna *b* 1991. —— Judith Penelope, *b* 1924. —— Anne Alicia, MBE, *b* 1928; MBE (Civil) 1973.

Issue of late Capt Humphrys Archdale, DSC, RN, yst son of 1st baronet; *b* 1896; *d* 1972: *m* 1944, Mary Katherine, who *d* 1975, da of late Robert Leslie Gilbert:—
Gilbert Humphrys, *b* 1947; *ed* Tonbridge: *m* 1984, Susan Anne, elder da of Dennis John Boyles, of Enton, Surrey, and has issue living, Thomas Robert Humphrys, *b* 1988, — Peter Charles Alexander, *b* 1991. *Residence* – Shaftesbury, Dorset.

The 1st baronet, the Rt Hon Sir Edward Mervyn Archdale (el son of Nicholas Montgomery Archdale, of Crock na Crieve, co Fermanagh), was MP for N Div of Fermanagh (*U*) 1898-1903 and 1916-22, and a Member of House of Commons of N Ireland 1921-37. He was first Min of Agriculture, N Ireland 1921-33, and of Commerce 1921-5. The 2nd baronet, Vice-Adm Sir Nicholas Edward Archdale, CBE, served during European War 1914-18 Comdg Submarine Flotillas, and was Senior Naval Officer, Copenhagen 1920.

ARMSTRONG (UK) 1841 of Gallen Priory, King's County

Lt-Col Sir CHRISTOPHER JOHN EDMUND STUART ARMSTRONG, MBE, 7th *Baronet*; *b* 15 Jan 1940; *s* his father *Sir* ANDREW CLARENCE FRANCIS, 1997; *ed* Ampleforth, and RMA; Lt-Col RLC; MBE 1979: *m* 1972, Georgina Elizabeth Carey, 2nd da of Lt-Col W. G. Lewis, of Hayling Island, Hants, and has issue.

Arms – Quarterly: 1st and 4th argent, issuing from the sinister a dexter arm embowed habited gules grasping the trunk of an oak-tree eradicated and broken at the top proper (Armstrong); 2nd and 3rd argent, two ravens hanging paleways sable suspended from an arrow gules headed and feathered proper piercing both their heads fessways (Murdoch). **Crests** – 1 (Armstrong), an arm in armour embowed the hand grasping the broken trunk of an oak-tree, all proper; 2 (Murdoch), a raven rising sable pierced through the breast by an arrow as in the arms. **Mottoes** – Invictus maneo (below), Omnia pro bono (over 2nd crest).
Residence – Sheepridge House, Lordswood Lane, Chilworth, Southampton SO16 7JG.

I am still unconquered

SONS LIVING

CHARLES ANDREW, *b* 1973. —— James Hugo, *b* 1974. —— Sam Edward, *b* 1986.

DAUGHTER LIVING

Victoria Jane, *b* 1980.

UNCLE LIVING

Edmund Charles Mark, *b* 1914; *ed* St Edmund's Ware, and St John's Coll, Camb (BA 1935); 1939-45 War as Lt (S) RNR; civil servant MoD (ret 1977); assumed by deed poll 1945 the christian names of Edmund Charles Mark in lieu of Edmund Clarence Charles: *m* 1st, 1939 (*m diss* 1949), Patricia Phyllis Vassall, da of late Edward Robert Vassall Adams, of Horn's Cross, Devon; 2ndly, 1951, Dorice, who *d* 1983, da of late William Harold Austin, of White Cottage, Marlow, Bucks, and has issue living (by 2nd *m*), Mark Simon Warneford (20 Boulevard Princesse Charlotte, MC 98000, Monte Carlo), *b* 1954; *ed* The Royal Naval Sch, Tal Handaq, Malta, Univ of Kent at Canterbury, and Sorbonne (BA 1977); with Sotheby's, Monaco: *m* 1992, Roselyne Jeanne Thérèse, da of Roberto Moro, of Cavalaire-sur-Mer, Var, France, and has issue living, Alexander Edmund Roberto *b* 1994, Anne-Victoire Emily *b* 1993, —— Sean Andrew (Free Hill House, Westbury-sub-Mendip, Somerset BA5 1HJ), *b* (triplet) 1954; *ed* The Royal Naval Sch, Tal Handaq, Malta, and Bristol Univ (BSc 1976, MBA 1993); Co Dir, —— Patrick Austin (15 Lower Beadon, Merriott, Som), *b* (triplet) 1954; *ed* The Royal Naval Sch, Tal Handaq, Malta, and Merrist Wood Agric Coll, Surrey; horticulturalist. *Residence* – Free Hill House, Westbury-sub-Mendip, Somerset BA5 1HJ.

COLLATERAL BRANCHES LIVING

Granddaughter of late Andrew Charles Armstrong, 3rd son of 1st baronet:—
Issue of late John Andrew Armstrong, *b* 1892, *d* 1974: *m* 1935, Pauline who *d* 1983, da of late Maj C. O. N. Williams, of Pulborough, Sussex:—
Jill Sara, *b* 1937: *m* 1958, Capt Alexander Bayly Maxwell-Hyslop, 17th/21st Lancers (ret) of Black Barn Farm, Leigh, Sherborne, Dorset, and has issue living, Lucinda Francis (Coach House Cottage, Chilfrome, Dorchester, Dorset), *b* 1959: *m* 1985 (*m diss* 1992), Charles John Moubray, son of John Michael Moubray, of Ridlington House, Rutland, and has issue living, James Alexander John *b* 1987, —— Zara Belinda, *b* 1962: *m* 1988, Lt-Col James Pollock, OBE, Irish Gds, son of Brig J. P. O'H. Pollock, MBE, DL, of Upper Froyle, Hants.

Granddaughters of late Montagu Fullerton Armstrong, 5th son of 1st baronet:—
Issue of late Jack Proby Armstrong, *b* 1878, *d* 1953: *m* 1912, Maria Dominga Alvarenga, who *d* 1988, da of John Molina:—
Martha Florence (PO Box 3019, Warrenton, VA 20188-1719, USA), *b* 1920: *m* 1st, 1944 (*m diss* 1956), Elmer Page Madsen; 2ndly, 1958, James W. Thornton, who *d* 1983, of Coventry Estates, Bealeton, Virginia 22712, USA, son of late Sir Henry Worth Thornton, KBE.

Issue of late Frederick Edmund John Armstrong, *b* 1889, *d* (on active ser N-W Frontier of India) 1919: *m* 1915, Stella, who *d* 1966, el da of J. R. Morgan, late of Portmore, Weymouth:—
Beatrice, *b* 1916: *m* 1937, Com Edric Guy Philip Bromfield Knapton, DSC, RN, of Wimborne, Dorset, and has issue living, Guy Augustus Bromfield (Av des Bouleaux 4B, 1310 La Hulpe, Belgium), *b* 1940: *ed* Downside, and Pembroke Coll, Camb: *m* 1966, Catherine Margaret Ffoulkes, da of late Francis Herbert Walker, of Gt Ayton, N Yorks, and has issue living, Philip Guy Bromfield *b* 1971, Claire Stella Mary *b* 1969, —— Julian Richard Anthony (Christchurch, NZ), *b* 1954: *m* 1991, Jacqueline Robin, da of late Jack Gordon Brookes, of Auckland, NZ, and has had issue, Autumn (a da) *b* and *d* 1993, Gemma Rose *b* 1994, —— Vanessa Josephine Stella KNAPTON DE BLANCO (Plaza San Clemente 1, 07712 San Clemente, Mahon, Menorca, Spain), *b* 1944: *m* 1971 (*m diss* 1997), Antonio Blanco Pons, and has issue living, Antonio *b* 1973, Alfonso *b* 1975, Beatriz *b* 1982, —— Marie Victoria Gwendolyn (17 Brainsmead, Cuckfield, W Sussex RH17 5EY), *b* 1947: *m* 1980 (*m diss* 1987), John Rutland Cowen; has issue living, Henry TOWNES *b* 1990, Alice TOWNES *b* 1986, Emily TOWNES *b* 1988, —— Louise Elizabeth Teresa, *b* 1956: *m* 1995, Alessandro Mario Augusto Rastello, of Via Pomba 7, Turin 10123, Italy.

Granddaughter of late Charles Nesbitt Frederic Armstrong, 6th son of 1st baronet:—
Issue of late George Nesbitt Armstrong, *b* 1883, *d* 1971: *m* 1st, 1906 (*m diss* 1908), Phoebe Georgina Frances Ruby, who *d* 1939, only da of Col Jocelyn Otway; 2ndly, 1913, Evelyn Mary, who *d* 1973, da of late Michael Doyle, of Brisbane:—
(By 2nd *m*) Helen Pamela Fullerton (Melba) (*Pamela, Baroness Vestey*) (Coombe Cottage, Coldstream, Vic, Aust), *b* 1918; raised to the rank of a Baron's widow 1955: *m* 1939, Capt Hon William Howarth Vestey, Scots Gds, who was *ka* in Italy 1944, only son of 2nd Baron Vestey.

This family was anciently settled on the Scottish Border, and John Armstrong, Laird of Gilnockie Hall, Eskdale, the most famous leader of the warlike clans that made frequent inroads into the northern counties of England, was, with many of his retainers, executed on the orders of King James V of Scotland about 1530. Andrew Armstrong, his descendant, and ancestor of the present family, migrated to Ireland early in the 17th century, and settled in co Fermanagh; he greatly distinguished himself in the army of Charles I. Capt Sir Andrew H. Armstrong, 3rd Bt, was High Sheriff of King's co 1914.

ARMSTRONG (UK) 1892, of London (Extinct 1944)

Sir FRANCIS PHILIP ARMSTRONG, OBE, 3rd and last *Baronet*

WIDOW LIVING OF SECOND BARONET

MILLICENT (*Lady Armstrong*), da of late Adolph Leopold Ortlepp, of Graaff Reinert, Cape Province, S Africa: *m* 1925, as his second wife, Sir George Elliot Armstrong, CMG, 2nd baronet, who *d* 1940.

ARMYTAGE (GB) 1738, of Kirklees, Yorkshire

Always ready

Sir (JOHN) MARTIN ARMYTAGE, 9th *Baronet*; *b* 26 Feb 1933; *s* his father, *Capt Sir* JOHN LIONEL, 1983; *ed* Eton, and Worcester Coll, Oxford.

Arms – Gules, a lion's head erased between three cross-crosslets argent. **Crest** – A dexter arm embowed couped at the shoulder habited or, the cuff argent, holding in the hand proper a staff gules, headed and pointed or.
Seat – Kirklees Park, Brighouse, Yorks. *Residence* – 5 St James Place, Cheltenham, Glos.

SISTER LIVING

Ann, *b* 1928: *m* 1st, 1948 (*m diss* 1960), Francis Richard Anson, who *d* 1989 (*see* E Lichfield, colls); 2ndly, 1962 (*m diss* 1971), Philip John Warburton-Lee; 3rdly, 1972, as his 2nd wife, Maj David Henry Fetherstonhaugh, Coldm Gds, who *d* 1994, and has issue living, (by 1st *m*) (*see* E Lichfield, colls), — (by 2nd *m*), John Henry Bernard, *b* 1965; Maj Welsh Gds: *m* 1996, Louie, eldest da of late Tim Macpherson, of Walcote Grange, Lincs. *Residence* – Blacksmith Cottage, Little Compton, Moreton-in-Marsh, Glos.

HALF-SISTER LIVING (*Daughter of 8th baronet by 2nd marriage*)

Christina Mary, *b* 1952: *m* 1980, Richard Cornish, of 12 Market St, Bradford on Avon, Wilts.

MOTHER LIVING

Evelyn Mary Jessamine, da of late Edward Herbert Fox (Arbuthnot, Bt, *cr* 1823, colls), of Adbury Park, Hants : *m* 1st, 1927 (*m diss* 1946), Capt John Lionel Armytage (later Sir John Armytage, 8th Bt), who *d* 1983; 2ndly, 1946 (*m diss* 1950), Capt John Samuel Pontifex Cooper; 3rdly, 1950, Lt-Col John Warwick Tainton Wooldridge, who *d* 1973; 4thly, 1980, her 2nd husband, Capt John Samuel Pontifex Cooper. *Residence* – Thompson's Hill, Sherston, Malmesbury, Wilts.

WIDOW LIVING OF EIGHTH BARONET

(MARIA) MARGARETE (*Lady Armytage*), da of Paul Hugo Tenhaeff, of Bruenen, Niederhein: *m* 1949, as his second wife, Capt Sir John Lionel Armytage, 8th Bt, who *d* 1983. *Residence* – Kirklees Park, Brighouse, York.

COLLATERAL BRANCHES LIVING

Issue of late Rear-Adm Reginald William Armytage, GC, CBE, yr son of 7th baronet, *b* 1903, *d* 1984: *m* 1928, Sylvia Beatrice, who *d* 1996, da of Lt-Col Charles Russell Staveley-Staveley, of Pamflete, Holbeton, Plymouth:—
DAVID GEORGE, CBE (Sharcott Manor, Pewsey, Wilts), *b* 4 Sept 1929; Capt RN; comdg HMS *Minerva* 1968-70, Defence Policy Staff 1970-72, and Naval Assistant to First Sea Lord 1972-74, commanded 7th Frigate Sqdn 1976-77, commanded Standing Naval Force Atlantic 1980-81; ADC 1981; CBE (Mil) 1981: *m* 1954, Countess Antonia Cosima, el da of Count Cosimo Diodono de Bosdari (*see* Walker-Okeover, Bt, 1985 Edn), and has issue living, Hugh Anthony, *b* 6 Aug 1955, — Charles David (26 Cicada Rd, SW18), *b* 1962: *m* 1987, Katharine Alexandra, yr da of Dr Anthony Cooper Sudell Bloomer, of London W2, and has issue living, Harry Charles George *b* 1992, Alexander Hugh Edward *b* 1995, — Davina Jane, *b* 1956: *m* 1977, Lt-Col David Martin Chappel, 4th/7th R Dragoon Guards, who *d* 1990, and has issue living, William David George *b* 1987, Rupert Henry Edward *b* 1989, Jeremy David Hugh *b* 1990. —— Maurice John Reginald (Maplehurst, Staplehurst, Tonbridge, Kent), *b* 1932: *m* 1956, Brioni Katharine, da of Gerald Wellington Williams (*see* D Northumberland, colls, 1985 Edn), and has issue living, Lucinda Jane Brioni, *b* 1959: *m* 1983, Maj Mark Andrew Tilden Hibbert-Hingston, Coldstream Guards, elder son of Andrew Donovan Huntly Hibbert-Hingston (*see* E Denbigh and Desmond, colls, 1976, Edn) and has issue living, Jonathan *b* 1985, Nicholas *b* 1988, James *b* 1989, Edwina *b* 1986, Joy *b* 1991, — Nicola Susan Katharine, *b* (twin) 1959: *m* 1981, Maj Richard Bowen Woosnam, 15th/19th King's R Hus, of Birch Farm, Great Edstone, Kirkbymoorside, York, elder son of Charles Woosnam, and has issue living, David Ralph William *b* 1983, Katharine Patricia Mary *b* 1985, — Jane Annette, *b* 1962. —— Roderick Charles (Nelson House, East Ilsely, Berks), *b* 1934: *m* 1961, Susan, who *d* 1996, da of Maj Reginald T. Whitehead, of Abergavenny, and has issue living, Marcus David, *b* 1964, — Gaye, *b* 1965.

Grandchildren of late John Hawksworth Armytage, 2nd son of 6th baronet:—
Issue of late Walter John Armytage, *b* 1913, *d* 1980: *m* 1st, 1947 (*m diss* 1958), Frances Mary Daphne, only da of late Thomas Grant Fletcher, of Ardmulchan, Navan, co Meath, and formerly wife of Philip Alwyn Lucas; 2ndly, 1959, Marion Elizabeth, who *d* 1986, only child of late Maj David Mitchell Anderson, DL, LLD, of Creevy Rocks, Saintfield, co Down, and widow of Edward John Wakefield d'Arcy;—
(By 1st *m*) Julian Ralph Fitzroy (18 Lowndes Sq, SW1), *b* 1948; *ed* Milton Abbey: *m* 1st, 1973 (*m diss* 1982), Laura, da of late Capt Ian Galloway; 2ndly, 1983, Julia, da of Lawrence George Buchanan, and has issue living (by 2nd *m*), Georgina Caroline, *b* 1986, — Edwina Frederica, *b* 1992. —— Clare Frances Elizabeth ARMYTAGE, *b* 1950: *m* 1973 (*m diss* 1983), Jonathan E. Clarke. —— (By 2nd *m*) Diana Marion, *b* 1960: *m* 1996, (William) Harry Smith, of Savernake Forest, Wilts, and has issue living, Elizabeth Clare, *b* 1998, — Katherine Sophia, *b* (twin)1998.

This family is descended (according to a pedigree attested by Sir Henry St George, Norroy King of Arms) from John Armytage, of Wrigbowls, Lincolnshire, *temp* King Stephen. Two branches of the family at different times have been created baronets. Brig-Gen Sir George Ayscough Armytage, CMG, DSO, 7th baronet, served in European War 1914-18 as Brig-Gen Comdg an Inf Brig, DSO, CMG.

ARNOTT (UK) 1896, of Woodlands, St Anne, Shandon, co Cork

Sir ALEXANDER JOHN MAXWELL ARNOTT, 6th *Baronet*; *b* 18 Sept 1975; *s* his father, *Sir* JOHN ROBERT ALEXANDER, 1981.

Arms – Per chevron argent and azure, in chief two mullets and in base a crescent, all counterchanged, on a chief of the second three mullets of the first. **Crest** – On a rock a tower proper, therefrom a pennant of one point flying to the sinister azure. *Residence* – 11 Palmerston Rd, Dublin.

BROTHER LIVING

ANDREW JOHN ERIC, *b* 20 June 1978.

UNCLE LIVING (Son of 4th baronet)

Prof Eric John (Trottsford Farm, Headley, Hants; Kildare St and Garrick Clubs), *b* 1929; *ed* Harrow, and Trin Coll, Dublin (MB and BCh, FRCS): *m* 1960, Veronica Mary, only da of late Capt Arvid Langué Querfeld von der Seedeck, of West Green Cottage, Hartley Wintney, Hants, and has issue living, Stephen John, *b* 1962: *m* 1989, Katherine Jane Keep, eldest da of Colin Thompson, of The Old House, Sutton Veny, Wilts, and has issue living, Oliver Timothy John *b* 1990, Lara Georgina Emma *b* 1992, Isabella Anastasia *b* 1996, — Robert Lauriston John, *b* 1971, — Tatiana Amelia, *b* 1963: *m* 1986, Nicholas Paul Whishaw, eldest son of Michael Whishaw, of Anaheim Hills, California, USA, and has issue living, Timothy Alexander *b* 1988, Natasha *b* 1990, Tilesa *b* 1994.

Speratum et completum

Hoped for and realized

WIDOW LIVING OF FIFTH BARONET

ANN MARGARET (*Lady Arnott*) (11 Palmerston Rd, Dublin), da of late Terence Alphonsus Farrelly, of Kilcar, co Cavan: *m* 1974, Sir John Robert Alexander Arnott, 5th Baronet, who *d* 1981.

COLLATERAL BRANCHES LIVING

Grandchildren of late John Frederic Arnott, MC (infra):—
Issue of late Lt-Cdr (John) Anthony Arnott, RNVR, FRICS, *b* 1921, *d* 1980: *m* 1944, Jean Barbara (changed to Jill Benedicta by deed poll 1989) (Devon Cottage, Bourton, Dorset), da of late Charles Lovett Gill, of Odiham, Hants:—
John David (100 Richmond Rd, Bristol BS6 5ER), *b* 1947; *ed* Cheltenham Coll, Birmingham Univ and Liverpool Univ (BA): *m* 1971, Jennifer Mary Dooley, and has issue living, John Andrew, *b* 1974, — Myles Anthony, *b* 1980. —— (Ann Margaret) Amabel, *b* 1945: *m* 1st, 1969, Robert Hughes; 2ndly, 1981, Peter Bolton, of 7 Silver St, Wells, Som BA5 1UN and has issue living (by 2nd *m*), Gabriel Peter, *b* 1982, — Mary Christabel, *b* 1985.

Granddaughter of late David Taylor Arnott, 2nd son of 1st baronet:—
Issue of late John Frederic Arnott, MC, *b* 1892, *d* 1967: *m* 1919, Phyllis, who *d* 1967, da of James Cundell:—
Patricia Ruth (3 Uigshadder, by Portree, I of Skye), *b* 1920: *m* 1961, Evrard Burke (formerly Bourque), who *d* 1964.

Grandchildren of Sir John Alexander Arnott, 2nd Bt, JP, DL:—
Issue of late Maj Thomas John Arnott, *b* 1899, *d* 1979: *m* 1927, Lettice Mary, who *d* 1986, da of late Lt-Col Charles Montagu Crompton-Roberts, of Drybridge, Monmouth (Greenwell, Bt):—
Peter John (38 Braemar, Kersfield Rd, SW15; *Club* – Army and Navy), *b* 1929; late Lt 15th/19th Hussars. —— Guy (12/500 Marine Parade, Biggera Waters, Queensland 4216, Australia; *Club* – United Service, Brisbane), *b* 1932; late Lt 15th/19th Hussars: *m* 1963, Diana, who *d* 1982, da of D. Staines, of Wahroonga, Queensland. —— Caroline, *b* 1934.

The 1st baronet, Sir John Arnott (son of John Arnott, of Auchtermuchty, Fifeshire), was a noted philanthropist and largely connected with many Irish industries, and sat as MP for Kinsale (L) 1859-63.

ARTHUR (UK) 1841, of Upper Canada

Sir STEPHEN JOHN ARTHUR, 6th *Baronet*; *b* 1 July 1953; *s* his father, Sir BASIL MALCOLM, 1985; *ed* Timaru Boys' High Sch, *m* 1978 (*m diss* 19—), Carolyn Margaret, da of Burnie Lawrence Diamond, of Cairns, Queensland, Australia, and has issue

ᴀrms – Or, on a chevron azure between two clarions in chief gules and a kangaroo sejant in base proper, two swords the points upwards also proper, points and hilts of the first; on a chief of the third a horse courant argent. ℭrest – In front of two swords in saltire proper, pommels and hilts or, a pelican in her piety sable, the nest or.
Residence – Timaru, New Zealand.

Stet fortuna domûs

May the fortune of the house stand

SON LIVING

BENJAMIN NATHAN, *b* 27 March 1979.

DAUGHTERS LIVING

Amanda, *b* 1975. —— Melanie, *b* 1976.

SISTERS LIVING

Marylin Jane, *b* 1950: *m* 1972, W.B.M. Keeman, of Pohutukawa Drive, Howick, Auckland, NZ, and has issue living, Zane Basil Cornelius, *b* 1974, — Kris William Reginald, *b* 1981, — Lauriely Elizabeth Wanda, *b* 1976. —— Cheryl Dawn, *b* 1951: *m* 1971, G.L. Blanchard, of 1RD Springbrook, Timaru, NZ.

AUNTS LIVING (*Daughters of 4th baronet*)

Helen Fay, *b* 1931: *m* 1st, 1949 (*m diss* 1981), Morton King; 2ndly, 1982, Peter William Caird, of 8RD Waimate, S Canterbury, NZ, and has issue living (by 1st *m*), Donald Malcolm, *b* 1950, — Peter Morton, *b* 1955, — Yvonne Jane, *b* 1951, — Maree Fay, *b* 1960. —— Maureen Beatrice, *b* 1933: *m* 1st, 1953 (*m diss* 1972), James Warren Patterson; 2ndly, 1976,

James Wright McLauchlan, and has issue living (by 1st *m*), Warren John, *b* 1954, — James Bartley, *b* 1956, — Desmond Bruce, *b* 1965, — Moira Fay, *b* 1957, — Rosana Mae, *b* 1961. —— Elizabeth Adele, *b* 1948: *m* 1972, Lindsay Gerald Dawkins, and has issue living, Hayden Gerald, *b* 1977, — Leah Janette, *b* 1973.

WIDOWS LIVING OF FOURTH AND FIFTH BARONETS

DORIS FAY (*Dowager Lady Arthur*), da of Joseph Wooding, JP, of Woodland Grange, Woodbury, and Geraldine, S Canterbury, New Zealand: *m* 1928, Sir George Malcolm Arthur, 4th Bt, who *d* 1949. *Residence* – ......

SANDRA COLLEEN (*Lady Arthur*), da of William Boaz, of Whangarei, New Zealand: *m* 1983, as his 2nd wife, Sir Basil Malcolm Arthur, 5th Bt, who *d* 1985. *Residence* – 6 Ellerton Way, Karori, Wellington, New Zealand.

MOTHER LIVING

Elizabeth Rita, da of Alan Mervyn Wells, of Wakefield, Nelson, New Zealand: *m* (Jan) 1950 (*m diss* 1983), as his 1st wife, Sir Basil Malcolm Arthur, 5th Bt, who *d* 1985.

COLLATERAL BRANCHES LIVING

Grandsons of late George Frederick Neale Arthur (infra):—
Issue of late Maj George Leonard Arthur, *b* 1908, *d* (29 March) 1997: *m* 1936, Gladys Raina, who *d* (23 Nov) 1997, da of George Percy Farr, JP, of Bedford, Cape Prov, S Africa:—
†Leonard Compton, *b* 1942; *d* 1956. —— Gavyn Farr (2 Harcourt Buildings, Temple, EC4Y 9DB), *b* 1951; *ed* Harrow, and Ch Ch, Oxford (MA); Bar Middle Temple 1975; Alderman, City of London 1991, Sheriff, City of London 1998.

Grandson of late George Arthur, son of late Col Edward Penfold Arthur, Bombay CS, 4th son of 1st baronet:—
Issue of late George Frederick Neale Arthur; *b* 1878, *d* 1939: *m* 1905, Edith Lavender, who *d* 1966, da of late J. H. Taylor:—
Archibald John, *b* 1909; last heard of in 1951. *Residence* –

Grandchildren of late Rev John Sigismund Arthur, MC (infra):—
Issue of late Capt Leonard John Henry Arthur, RAMC (TA), *b* 1926, *d* 1983: *m* 1954, Hon Janet Stella Brain (Royal Oak Cottage, Church Broughton, Derby), da of 1st Baron Brain:—
Robert Leonard Sigismund (18 Keston Rd, SE15 4JB), *b* 1955: *m* 1997, Anne Caroline, da of Christopher Lawrence Hampton, and has issue living, Jamie Lawrence, *b* 1999. —— Linet Stella, *b* 1956. —— Tansy Amy Anne, *b* 1959. —— Elaine Fay, *b* 1961. —— Hazel Jane, *b* 1964. —— Ruth Gilly, *b* 1966.

Grandchildren of late Sigismund Raynor Arthur, eldest son of late John Raynor Arthur (infra):—
Issue of late Rev John Sigismund Arthur, MC, *b* 1894, *d* 1974: *m* 1925, Constance Amy Farquhar, who *d* 1980, da of Joseph Sladen, late ICS:—
Flora Jessamine Mary, *b* 1928; MA Oxon: *m* 1954, Charles Edward Elliott, BM, BCh, of 35 Cook St, Northgate, Brisbane, Qld, and has issue living, Charles John Peter (Lot 4, Arthy's Rd, Cooran, Qld 4569; PO Box 161, Pomona, Qld), *b* 1955: *m* 1982, Elizabeth Mary, da of Denley Keeling, and has issue living, Charles Leonard George *b* 1983, James Edward *b* 1984, Henry Robert *b* 1988, Georgina Mary-Jane *b* 1990, — John Michael (104 Cavendish St, Nundah, Brisbane, Qld 4012), *b* 1956: *m* 1986, Barbara Jane, da of Bernard Russell Arthur Stuart, and has issue living, Conor Stuart *b* 1992, Caitlin Elaine *b* 1988, Sally Brenda *b* 1990, — Thomas George (3791 West 3rd Av, Vancouver, BC, Canada), *b* 1958: *m* 1982, Gwenneth Mary, da of John Stanley Shaw, and has issue living, Tristan *b* 1989, Reece *b* 1991, Tyne Rebecca *b* 1993, — Mary Jessamine, *b* 1960: *m* 1990, Lee Cameron Thompson, and has issue living, Eliot George *b* 1991, Rachel Rebecca *b* 1993, — Lucy Jane, *b* 1972. —— Rose Eleanor, *b* 1931; MA Oxon: *m* 1961, Rev Canon Edward Longman, of 16 Coleshill St, Sutton Coldfield, W Midlands B72 1SH, and has issue living, Harold John, *b* 1962; MA Cantab: *m* 1989, Alison Louise, da of Col William E.I. Armstrong, and has issue living, Margaret Amy Armstrong *b* 1994, — Peter George, *b* 1965: *m* 1994, Melanie Joy, da of late Terry James Pitcher, — George Roland, *b* 1969; BSc, — Anna Frances, *b* 1963; MA (Oxon). —— Cecil Lucy Sylvia, *b* 1939: *m* 1980, Richard Denis Vooght, of 14 Kingsdown Parade, Bristol 6, and has issue living, Jenny Madeleine Rose, *b* 1981, — Abigail Katharine Amy, *b* 1983.

Issue of late Sir (Oswald) Raynor Arthur, KCMG, CVO, *b* 1905, *d* 1973: *m* 1935, Mary Elizabeth, MBE, who *d* 1994, da of late Rt Hon Sir Cecil Arthur Spring Rice, GCMG, GCVO (see B Monteagle of Brandon, colls):—
Thomas Sigismund Raynor (Burwash Glebe, Etchingham, Sussex), *b* 1940; *ed* Eton, and Oriel Coll, Oxford (MA): *m* 1966, Angela Susan Clare, da of late Lt-Col Roland T. W. MacLeod, of Weston, Dunsyre, Lanark, and has issue living, George Raynor Macleod, *b* 1969, — Juliet Caroline, *b* 1966, — Valentine Bridget, *b* 1968: *m* 1991, J. Hugo S. Akerman, of Moat Farm House, Whiston, Northants, eldest son of John Akerman, of 42 Temperley Rd, SW12, and has issue living, Mungo Henry Strange *b* 1995, Somerset James MacLeod *b* 1997, Valentine Cosima *b* 1994, — Alexandra Maxine, *b* 1973. —— Caroline Anne Florence, *b* 1937; MA Oxon: *m* 1972, Courtney Kenny, of 14 Grange Grove, N1, and has issue living, Courtney Arthur Francis, *b* 1983.

Grandson of late John Raynor Arthur, 6th son of 1st baronet:—
Issue of late Major Edmond John Arthur, *b* 1873, *d* 1953: *m* 1921, Kathleen Emily Isabel Ada, who *d* 1987, da of George Penn Simkins:—
George Henry Edmond, *b* 1927: *m* 1950, Kathleen, da of Frederick Joseph Bow, of Sea Mills, Bristol, and has issue living, Robert George, *b* 1950: *m* 1969, Janice Margaret, da of Gerald Poolman, of 266 Tavy House, Plymouth, and has issue living, Niel Robert *b* 1970, Kieron Gerald *b* 1970.

This family migrated from Cornwall to Plymouth early in the 18th century. The 1st baronet, Lieut-Gen Right Hon Sir George Arthur, KCH, DCL, Col of the 50th Foot, was knighted in 1837. He was successively Governor of Honduras, Van Diemen's Land, Upper Canada, and Bombay and Provisional Gov-Gen of India 1846. The 3rd baronet, Capt Sir George Compton Archibald Arthur, MVO, was Private Sec of State for War. The 5th baronet, Sir Basil Malcolm Arthur, who served as MP for Timaru, NZ for 23 years, was Min of Transport and Min in Charge of State Insurance Office, NZ, and Speaker of New Zealand House of Representatives 1984-85.

ASHBURNHAM (E) 1661, of Broomham, Sussex

Will God, and I shall

†*Sir* DENNY REGINALD ASHBURNHAM, 12th *Baronet*: *b* 24 March 1916; *s* his father, *Sir* FLEETWOOD, 1953; is Capt S Staffordshire Regt, and a co-heir to Barony of Grandison: *m* 1946, Mary Frances, da of Major Robert Pascoe Mair, of Wick, Udimore, Sussex, and has had issue. The 12th baronet *d* 21 June 1999.

Arms – Gules, a fesse between six mullets argent. Crest – Out of a ducal coronet or an ash-tree proper.
Residence – Little Broomham, Church Lane, Guestling, Hastings, E Sussex TN35 4HS.

GRANDCHILDREN LIVING

Issue of late John Anchitel Fleetwood Ashburnham, *b* 1951, *d* 1981: *m* 1975, Corinne A. (who *m* 2ndly, 1982, John Philip Merricks, of The Manor, Icklesham, Winchelsea, E Sussex), da of D. W. J. O'Brien, of Amerique, Castle St, Winchelsea, E Sussex:—
JAMES FLEETWOOD, *b* 17 Dec 1979. —— Henrietta Mary, *b* 1981.

DAUGHTERS LIVING

Frances, *b* 1947: *m* 1973, Robert Charles Taylor, of Summerhayes, Pett, Hastings, E Sussex, and has issue living, Robert Denny, *b* 1982, — Ellen Frances, *b* 1979. —— Honor Rosemary, *b* 1949: *m* 1981, Frank Cooke, of Broomhill Farm, Camber, Rye, E Sussex, and has issue living, Matthew John, *b* 1983, — Lucy Frances, *b* 1981, — Alice Mary, *b* 1985.

SISTER LIVING

Honor Elfrida, *b* 1920: *m* 1951, Ernest James Boorman.

This family, which takes its name from Ashburnham (originally written Esseburnham), in Sussex, is of great antiquity. This line derives from Richard of Broomham, 2nd son of Thomas Ashburnham, *temp* Henry VI. The el son John was ancestor of the Earls of Ashburnham (ext 1924). Sir Denny Ashburnham, 1st baronet, was MP for Hastings, and Victualler of the Navy. The 2nd baronet was Chamberlain of the Exchequer and MP for Hastings; the 4th baronet was Bishop of Chichester: and the 7th baronet was Chancellor and Prebendary of Chichester. Sir Anchitel Piers, 9th baronet, assumed by Roy licence 1899 the additional surname of Clement.

ASKE (UK) 1922, of Aughton, East Riding of Yorkshire.

Rev Sir CONAN ASKE, 2nd *Baronet*; *b* 22 April 1912; *s* his father *Sir* ROBERT WILLIAM, LLD QC, 1954; *ed* Rugby, and Balliol Coll, Oxford (MA): *m* 1st, 1948, Vera, who *d* 1960, yr da of late George Rowbotham, of Iffley, Oxford, and formerly wife of Roland Faulkner; 2ndly, 1965, Rebecca, who *d* 1996, yr da of late Hugh Fraser Grant, of Wick, Caithness.

ᴀrms – Argent, a martlet sable between two bars azure, each charged with as many cross-crosslets of the first. ᴄrest – In front of a Saracen's head proper wreathed around the temples argent and azure, two roses argent.
Residence – 167 Malvern Rd, Worcester, WR2 4NN.

SISTER LIVING

Margaret, *b* 1910: *m* 1936, Richard Adolphe Charles Du Vivier, CBE, who *d* 1998, of 45 Chatsworth Rd, Ealing, W5, and has had issue, (Charles) Richard, *b* 1938; *ed* Malvern, and King's Coll, Camb; *d* 1992, — Hugh Michael (43 Britannia Rd, SW6 2HJ), *b* 1945; *ed* Malvern, and Trin Coll, Dublin: *m* 1969, Jacqueline Sarah, da of Harry Reginald Albert de Belleroche, of 38 De Vere Gdns, W8, and has issue living, Juliet Amy *b* 1979, Katherine Lucy Sarah *b* 1984, — Carol Anne, *b* 1941: *m* 1st, 1963 (*m diss* 1969), Bearnard O'Riain, of Dun Laoghaire, co Dublin; 2ndly, 1978, Lt-Col Allan Joseph Shaw, of 28 La Roche Drive, Humewood, 6001 Port Elizabeth, S Africa, and has issue living (by 1st *m*), Manus Justin *b* 1966, Natasha Celina *b* 1963, (by 2nd *m*) Nicholas Simon Dominic *b* 1978, Simon Philip Benedict *b* 1982, — Nicola Jill, *b* 1953: *m* 1975, Gordon Walter Prosser, of 7 Hooley Range, Heaton Moor Rd, Stockport, Cheshire SK4 4HU, and has issue living, Alexander Marcos *b* 1978, Hugh Angus *b* 1980, Giles Henry James *b* 1983, Edward Hamish Neal *b* 1987.

COLLATERAL BRANCH LIVING

Issue of late Robert Edward Aske, yr son of 1st baronet, *b* 1915, *d* 1999: *m* 1940, Joan Bingham (45 Holland Rd, W14), only da of late Capt Eric Bingham Ackerley, of White Lodge, Cobham, Surrey:—
ROBERT JOHN BINGHAM (5 Bicton Place, Exeter EX1 2PF), *b* 12 March 1941; *ed* King's Sch, Canterbury.

The 1st baronet, Sir Robert William Aske, TD, LLD, QC (son of late Edward Aske, of Hull), was Dep Sheriff of Hull 1906-8, and sat as MP for Newcastle-upon-Tyne E Div (*Lib*) 1923-24, and 1929-45.

Assheton-Smith (Duff-Assheton-Smith), see Duff.

ASTLEY (UK) 1821, of Everleigh, Wiltshire (Extinct 1994)

Sir FRANCIS JACOB DUGDALE ASTLEY, 6th and last *Baronet*.

DAUGHTER LIVING OF SIXTH BARONET

Bridget Mary, *b* 1939: *m* 1960, Capt John Pollock Maxwell, R Tank Regt, of Matsudana Lodge, Diomed Drive, Great Barton, Suffolk IP31 2TF, and has issue living, Robert Astley Kennedy, *b* 1962: *m* 1998, Kimberley Anne, da of J. Timothy Ryan, of Sun Valley, Idaho, USA, — Simon Harrison, *b* 1965: *m* 1998, Isabella Mary, da of David Babington Hill, of Elmdon, Essex.

SISTER LIVING OF FIFTH BARONET

Pamela Irene ASTLEY-CORBETT, *b* 1919: *m* 1951, Archibald Thomas Dunn, who *d* 1977, and has issue living, Thomas Astley (Chateau Rousseland, 18800 Villabon, France), *b* 1952: *m* 1984, Jane Margaret Dudley, da of late John Guy Dudley Parsons, and has issue living, Archibald Guy Astley *b* 1985, Frederick William Francis *b* 1986, Henry Thomas

George *b* 1988, Theodore Hugo James *b* 1992, Augustine Quentin Matthias *b* 1993, Sarah Jane Frances *b* 1996, — Archibald John Hugh (Moat Hall, Layham, nr Ipswich, Suffolk), *b* 1955: *m* 1987, Allison Adams, da of Morton Hutchinson Clark, of 608 Linkhorn Drive, Virginia Beach, Virginia, USA, and has issue living, William Francis Corbett *b* 1990, Anna Katherine Harrison *b* 1992, — Marcia Mary, *b* 1953: *m* 1975, Justin Francis Quintus Fenwick, and has issue (*see* B Lilford, colls), — Susannah Madeline Sara, *b* 1956, — Katherine Elizabeth Corisande, *b* 1962. *Residence* – Moat Hall, Layham, Ipswich IP7 5RB.

Aubrey-Fletcher, see Fletcher.

AUSTIN (UK) 1894, of Red Hill, Castleford, West Riding of York.

Trust in God and He will give strength

Sir ANTHONY LEONARD AUSTIN, 6th *Baronet, b* 30 Sept 1930; *s* his brother, *Sir* MICHAEL TRESCAWEN, 1995; *ed* Downside: *m* 1st, 1956 (*m diss* 1966), Mary Annette, da of Richard Kelly, of Greenogue, Kilsallaghan, co Dublin; 2ndly, 1967, Aileen Morrison Hall, da of William Hall Stewart, and has issue by 1st and 2nd *m*.

𝔄rms – Gules, eight mullets three, three and two argent, within a border dovetailed or, charged with four thistles slipped and leaved proper. Crest – A dexter arm embowed in fesse, couped at the shoulder, vested or, cuff indented ermine, the hand proper grasping a cross botony fitchée gules, resting on the arm a mullet of the last. *Residence* – Stanbury Manor, Morwenstow, Bude, Cornwall EX23 9JQ.

SONS LIVING (*By 1st marriage*)

PETER JOHN, *b* 29 July 1958: *ed* Belmont Abbey: *m* 1988, Jane Clare, da of Peter W. Dracup, of Broadaford, Widecombe in the Moor, Newton Abbot, Devon. *Residence* – Ladymead, Green Lane, Haytor, Newton Abbot, Devon TQ13 9RB. —— Nicholas Michael James, *b* 1960; *ed* Oratory Sch, and RMA Sandhurst: *m* 1996, Susan Margaret, da of John Sarjeant, of Toronto, Canada. *Residence* – 146 Snowdon Av, Toronto, Ontario, Canada M4N 1S2.

DAUGHTERS LIVING (*By 1st marriage*)

Caroline Dorothy, *b* 1957: *m* 1991, Peter Victor Hobbs, and has issue living, Richard Anthony, *b* 1996, — Alice Mary, *b* 1994. *Residence* – Chapel Amble, Wood Lane, Beech Hill, nr Reading, Berks RG7 2BE.

(*By 2nd marriage*)

Rebecca Dorothy Mary, *b* 1968: *m* 1997, Guy P. Allman, yr son of Ray Allman, of Far Poden, Honeybourne, Worcs.

DAUGHTERS LIVING OF FIFTH BARONET

Mary, *b* 1951: *m* 1981, John Orchard. *Residence* – Mill-Roy, Budleigh Salterton, Devon. —— Jane, *b* 1954. *Residence* – Goldburn, Okehampton, Devon EX20 3BD. —— Susan (Station House, Ballivor, co Meath), *b* 1956: *m* 1978, Antony Farrell, and has issue living, Sean Patrick, *b* 1982, — Bridget Aoife, *b* 1980.

WIDOWS LIVING OF THIRD, FOURTH AND FIFTH BARONETS

RHODA NOREEN (*Mrs John B. F. Austin*, preferred style), da of late Herbert Lloyd Pinches, of Eastbourne, and widow of Col Charles Vincent Douglas Rose: *m* 1960, as his 2nd wife, Sir John Byron Fraser Austin, 3rd Bt, who *d* 1981. *Residence* – ......

MARY HELEN (*Mrs M. H. Austin*, preferred style), da of Francis Henry Arthur Joseph Farrell, of Miltown, co Meath: *m* 1958, as his 2nd wife, Sir William Ronald Austin, 4th Bt, who *d* 1989. *Residence* – ......

BRIDGET DOROTHEA PATRICIA (*Dowager Lady Austin*), da of late Francis Henry Arthur Joseph Farrell (ante): *m* 1951, Sir Michael Trescawen Austin, 5th Bt, who *d* 1995. *Residence* – Goldburn, Okehampton, Devon EX20 3BD.

COLLATERAL BRANCH LIVING

Issue of late John Standish Thomas Joseph Austin, 2nd son of 1st baronet, *b* 1875, *d* 1941: *m* 1908, Gwendolyne Aubrey Beverley, who *d* 1959, da of late Capt Beverley Robinson, of Hyde Lodge Winchester:—

John Standish Beverley, *b* 1909; *ed* Ampleforth, and Downside. *Residence* – 33 Muncaster Gate, Malton Rd, York.
—— Janetta Agnes Gwendolyne, *b* 1912.

The 1st baronet, Sir John Austin, sat as MP for Osgoldcross Div of E Part of W Riding of Yorkshire (*L*) 1886-1906.

AYKROYD (UK) 1920, of Lightcliffe, West Riding of co of York

Victory in truth

Sir WILLIAM MILES AYKROYD, MC, 3rd *Baronet*; *b* 24 Aug 1923; *s* his father, *Sir* ALFRED HAMMOND, 1965.

Arms – Azure, on a chevron ermine between three stags' heads erased or, as many crosses couped sable. **Crest** – In front of a stag's head erased and gorged with a wreath of oak proper, two crosses as in the arms.
Residence – Buckland Newton Place, Dorchester, Dorset.

COLLATERAL BRANCHES LIVING

Issue of late Col Harold Hammond Aykroyd, OBE, MC, TD, DL, 2nd son of 1st baronet, *b* 1896, *d* 1974: *m* 1st, 1926 (*m diss* 1938), Nina Marguerite, da of late Edward J. Hulse, of Oakdene Duffield Rd, Derby; 2ndly, 1941, Kathleen Ellen (The Glebe House, Aldborough, Boroughbridge, N Yorks), el da of late Harry Tyrrell-Gray, FRCS:—

(By 1st *m*) Susan, *b* 1931: *m* 1st, 1951 (*m diss* 1958), John Kenneth Benney, RE; 2ndly, 1967, Christopher John Day, and *d* 1995, leaving issue, (by 1st *m*) Cecilia Anne, *b* 1952. —— Sally Mary (The Old Cottage, High St, Whixley, York), *b* 1934: *m* 1960, Christopher Boyd Stoddart, who *d* 1984, and has issue living, Mark Harold Boyd, *b* 1966: *m* 1990, Suzanna Baynard, and has issue living, Tom Lawrence Boyd *b* 1993, — Margaret Jane, *b* 1962: *m* 1987, Steven Bentley, and has issue living, Christopher Alan *b* 1990, Tobias Frank *b* 1993. —— (By 2nd *m*) Harriet Louisa, *b* 1951: *m* 1977, John Flinders Highley, of Lawrence House, Studley Roger, Ripon, N Yorks, and has issue living, Samuel Thomas George, *b* 1981, — Henry William Charles, *b* 1985.

Issue of late Col George Hammond Aykroyd, TD, yst son of 1st baronet, *b* 1900, *d* 1972: *m* 1924, Margaret Roberts, who *d* 1981, da of Sir Frederic Alfred Aykroyd, 1st Bt, *cr* 1929:—
MICHAEL DAVID (The Homestead, Killinghall, Harrogate, Yorks), *b* 14 June 1928: *m* 1952, Oenone Gillian Diana, da of Donald George Cowling, MBE, of Leeds, and has issue living, Henry Robert George (Cushnie, Auchterless, Turriff, Aberdeen), *b* 1954: *m* 1975, Lucy Merlin, da of late Col Jack Houghton Brown, and has issue living, George Jack *b* 1977, Bertie Thomas *b* 1983, Emma Rachel *b* 1978, Kate *b* 1989, Rose *b* (twin) 1989, — Annabel Mary Diana, *b* 1956: *m* 1979, Robin Guy Graham, and has issue (*see* Graham, Bt, *cr* 1662), — Sarah Jane, *b* 1960: *m* 1985, Guy Matthew Davis, son of James Davis, of The Garden Flat, Sharedeloes Park, Bucks, — Susannah Margaret, *b* 1964. —— †(John) Richard, *b* 1934: *m* 1st, 1963 (*m diss* 1974), Catherine Marthe, el da of George Vettier, of La Hulottière, Yvré, L'Evéque (Sarthe), France; 2ndly, 1974, Lavinia Mary, da of late Patrick Thomas Beasley (*see* E Wilton, 1990 Edn), and formerly wife of Confrey A. Phillips, and *d* 1997, leaving issue (by 1st *m*) Bettina Dominique, *b* (Nov) 1963, — (by 2nd *m*), Serena Mary, *b* 1976, — Clare Lavinia, *b* 1978. —— David Peter (Sweethills, Nun Monkton, York), *b* 1937: *m* 1958, (Lydia) Huldine, yr da of Richard Beamish, of Castlelyons, co Cork, and has had issue, †Nicholas William, *b* 1962; *d* 1989, as a result of a motor accident in Ireland, — Amanda Huldine, *b* 1960, — Emily Sorrel, *b* 1970: *m* 1996, Luke Thomas Fenwicke-Clennell (*see* Blackett, Bt), — Matilda Rose, *b* 1978. —— Patricia Jean, *b* 1925.

The 1st baronet, Sir William Henry Aykroyd (son of Alfred Aykroyd, of Oakwood, Manningham, Yorkshire), was a Director of T. F. Firth & Sons, Ltd, of Brighouse, and High Sheriff for W Riding of Yorkshire 1926.

AYKROYD (UK) 1929, of Birstwith Hall, Hampsthwaite, co York

Victory in truth

Sir JAMES ALEXANDER FREDERIC AYKROYD, 3rd *Baronet*; eldest son of late Bertram Aykroyd, 3rd son of 1st baronet; *b* 6 Sept 1943; *s* his uncle, *Sir* CECIL WILLIAM, 1993; *ed* Eton, Aix-en-Provence Univ, and Madrid Univ; is patron of the living of Hampsthwaite: *m* 1973, Jennifer, da of late Frederick William Marshall, MB, BS, DA (Eng), of 3 Penylan Av, Porthcawl, Glam, and has issue.

Arms – Azure, on a chevron ermine between three stags' heads erased or, as many crosses patonce sable. **Crest** – In front of a stag's head erased and gorged with a chaplet of oak proper, two crosses as in the arms.
Seat – Birstwith Hall, near Harrogate, N Yorks HG3 2JW. *Residence* – 15 Highbury Crescent, N5 1RS.

DAUGHTERS LIVING

Gemma Jane, *b* 1976. —— Victoria Louise, *b* 1977.

HALF-BROTHERS LIVING AND DECEASED

†Jeremy Charles, *b* 1950; *d* 1982. —— TOBY NIGEL BERTRAM, *b* 13 Nov 1955; *ed* Eton, and St Catharine's Coll, Camb (MA). *Residence* – 37 Pembridge Villas, W11 3EP.

SISTER LIVING

Jean Margaret Elizabeth (The Old Vicarage, Moreton Pinkney, Daventry, Northants NN11 6SJ), *b* 1940: *m* 1st, 1962 (*m diss* 1972), Michael Frederick David Morley, who *d* 1998; 2ndly, 1984, Col Timothy John Seymour Eastwood, RA, and has issue living (by 1st *m*), Harry Michael Charles (71 Musard Rd, W6 8NR), *b* 1965: *m* 1996, Katherine Susan, yr da of Christopher John Jellicoe Balfour (*see* E Jellicoe, colls), —— Edward James Cecil, *b* 1967.

HALF-SISTER LIVING

Rachel, *b* 1952: *m* 1981, Charles Patrick Helmore, of Wyndham Cottage, Rogate, nr Petersfield, Hants GU31 5BL, and has issue living, Max David Charles, *b* 1984, —— Caspar William, *b* 1987.

MOTHER LIVING

Margot, DBE (*Dame Margot Smith*), da of late Leonard Graham-Brown, MC, FRCS, of 82 Portland Place, W1: *m* 1st, 1938 (*m diss* 1947), as his 1st wife, Bertram Aykroyd, who *d* 1983, yst son of 1st baronet; 2ndly, 1947, Roy Smith MC, TD, who *d* 1983. *Residence* – Howden Lodge, Spennithorne, Leyburn, N Yorkshire DL8 5PR.

STEPMOTHER LIVING

Catalina, da of late Henry Marchington, of Hope Green, Adlington, Cheshire: *m* 1949, as his 2nd wife, Bertram Aykroyd, who *d* 1983, yst son of 1st baronet. *Residence* – Houghtons, East Harting, Petersfield, Hants GU31 5LU.

COLLATERAL BRANCH LIVING

Issue of late Frederic Howard Aykroyd, 2nd son of 1st baronet, *b* 1907, *d* 1978: *m* 1932, (Ruth) Joan, who *d* 1992, da of Carlton Oldfield, of Moor Hall, Harewood, Yorks:—
Mary Elisabeth Wendy Carlton, *b* 1934: *m* 1st, 1955 (*m diss* 1980), Nigel David Sykes Porter; 2ndly, 1989, William Richard Whitwell, of The Old Vicarage, Whorlton, Barnard Castle, co Durham. —— Joanna Jane, *b* 1937: *m* 1960, Christopher Jonathan Pumphrey, TD, DL, of Bolam West Houses, Middleton, Morpeth, Northumberland, and has issue living, Edward Jonathan Lawrence, *b* 1963, —— Andrew Charles, *b* 1965: *m* 1991, Juliet Evelyn, yr da of John Harold Booth Blackett (*see* Blackett, Bt, colls), and has issue living, Oliver Jonathan *b* 1997, Kate Annabel *b* 1995, —— (Sara) Rose, *b* 1062: *m* 1987, Nicholas Walter Alexander, eldest son of Cyril Alexander, of Woodside, Dollar, Clackmannanshire, and has issue living, Christopher James Turnbull *b* 1991, John Michael *b* 1998, Lucy Kate *b* 1990, Clare Rose *b* 1994. —— Victoria Margaret, *b* 1939: *m* 1962, Robin Fleming, of Barton Abbey, Steeple Aston, Oxon, and has issue living, Philip, *b* 1965: *m* 1997, Jane M. A., da of Richard Carter, of Gt Baddow, Essex, and has issue living, Robert *b* 1998, —— Rory David, *b* 1968, —— Joanna Kate, *b* 1963: *m* 1997, James King, yst son of Jack King, of Little Shelford, Cambridge.

The 1st baronet, Sir Frederic Alfred Aykroyd (son of William Edward Aykroyd, of Ashdown, Apperley Bridge, Yorks, uncle of Sir William Henry Aykroyd 1st baronet (*cr* 1920)), was a Merchant and High Sheriff of Yorkshire 1941-42.

AYLMER (I) 1622, of Donadea, co Kildare

Sir RICHARD JOHN AYLMER, 16th *Baronet*; *b* 23 April 1937; *s* his father, *Sir* FENTON GERALD, 1987: *m* 1962, Lise, da of Paul Emile Demers, of Montreal, and has issue.

Arms – Argent, a cross sable between four Cornish choughs proper. Crest – A Cornish chough proper rising out of a ducal coronet or.
Residence – ......

SON LIVING

FENTON PAUL, *b* 31 Oct 1965; *ed* Selwin House Sch, and Concordia Univ: *m* 19—, Pina, da of Mrs Velia Mastromonaco.

DAUGHTER LIVING

Genevieve, *b* 1963.

SISTER LIVING

Rosalind Alice, *b* 1941: *m* 1st 1965 (*m diss* 1973), Michael Neal Dennis White, of Victoria, BC; 2ndly 1977, Milton Cameron, of 2197 Queen's Av, W Vancouver, BC V7V 2Y1, Canada, and has two adopted children, Michael Aylmer CAMERON, *b* 1968, — Anna Rosalind CAMERON, *b* 1970.

COLLATERAL BRANCHES LIVING

Grandson of late Capt John Evans-Freke Aylmer, 2nd son of 11th baronet:—
Issue of late Rear-Adm Henry Evans-Freke Aylmer, CBE, *b* 1878, *d* 1933: *m* 1910, Edith Winifred, who *d* 1952, da of late Vet-Col Sir Francis Duck, KCB, FRCVS:—
John Francis, *b* 1910; late RAF. *Residence* –

Granddaughters of late Rev William Josiah Aylmer, 3rd son of 7th baronet:—
Issue of late William Henry Aylmer, *b* 1833, *d* 1882: *m* 1st, 1861, Henrietta, who *d* 18-, da of Dr Martin; 2ndly, 1874, Elizabeth, who *d* 1936, da of late Dr Gordon, of Sydney, N S Wales:—
(By 2nd *m*) Blanche Emily. —— Ida Mildred. —— Madge Irene. —— Muriel Lilian.

Granddaughters of late William Henry Aylmer (ante):—
Issue of late Percy Gordon Aylmer, *b* 1865, *d* 1923: *m* 1888, Eliza Anne, who *d* 1951, da of late William Haddon:—
Inez Amy (c/o Holy Spirit Convent, Brisbane, Qld, Aust), *b* 1895: *m* 1921, Cyril Frederick Mullins, who *d* 1965. —— Muriel Eileen (75 Wyralla Av, Epping, NSW), *b* 1907.

Grandchildren of late Percy Gordon Aylmer (ante):—
Issue of late Arthur William Aylmer, *b* 1899, *d* 1964: *m* 1924, Daisy, da of William Goodall of Firthcliffe, NY:—
Constance Elizabeth, *b* 1931: *m* 1953, Charles T. Brown, and has issue living.

Issue of late Justin Kenneth Aylmer, *b* 1893, *d* 1951: *m* 1918, Winifred Clare Mullins:—
Francis Gordon, *b* 1919: *m* 19-, Dura Marion Onus, of Inverell, NS Wales, and has issue living, Michael, *b* 19-, — Peter, *b* 19-, — Anthony, *b* 19-, — Marion Dura, *b* 19-. —— Ernest Austin (Clement Terr, Christie's Beach, St Lawrence, Australia), *b* 1921: *m* 1943, Jean Elsie, da of late James Alfred Walker, of Earlwood, NS Wales, and has issue living, David Ernest, *b* 1945, — Philip Kenneth Raymond, *b* 1952, — James Raymond, *b* 1953, — Margaret Jean, *b* 1944, — Irene Clare, *b* 1950. —— Kenneth Richard, *b* 1922: *m* 1952, Trudy, da of W. Everingham. —— Bruce William, *b* 1927: *m* 19-, Elizabeth Law, and has issue living, Robert, *b* 19-, — Barbara, *b* 19-. —— Marjorie Irene, *b* 1924: *m* 1946, John Michael McGann, and has issue living, Beverley Gay, *b* 1948, — Lynette Joy, *b* 1951, — Jeanette Ellen, *b* 1953.

Issue of late Frederick Gordon Aylmer, *b* 1900, *d* 1954: *m* 1940, Alma Elton (48 Maxim St, West Ryde, Sydney, NSW 2114, Australia):—
Carolyn Ann, *b* 1946; BSc, BA: *m* 1970, Ronald Bucholtz, of 48 Maxim St, W Ryde, NSW 2114, Australia. —— Margaret Susan, *b* 1948: *m* 1969, Alan Robert Underwood, 3 James Rd, Brooklyn, NSW 2083, Australia, and has issue living, Julie, *b* 1975, — Fiona, *b* 1978.

The Aylmers are found in the cos of Dublin and Kildare in the 13th century, and John Aylmer got the Manor of Lyons, co Kildare, about 1400 by *m* with Helen Tyrrell. The present representative of the Lyons, or Elder Branch, is Gerald Valentine Aylmer. Sir Gerald Aylmer, Knt, *cr* a Baronet 1621-2 (founder of the Donadea branch of the family), was third son of Richard Aylmer, of Lyons, co Kildare (temp 1509-1559). The 13th baronet, Sir Fenton John Aylmer, VC, KCB, was a Lieut-Gen in the Army.

BACKHOUSE (UK) 1901, of Uplands, Darlington, co Durham, and The Rookery, Middleton Tyas, North Riding of Yorkshire.

Sir JONATHAN ROGER BACKHOUSE, 4th *Baronet*, *b* 30 Dec 1939; *s* his father, *Major Sir* JOHN EDMUND, MC, 1944; *ed* Ampleforth, and Brasenose Coll, Oxford; formerly a Dir of W. H. Freeman and Co, Ltd, publishers: *m* 1997, Sarah Ann, only da of J. A. Stott, of Cromer, Norfolk and has issue.

🙰rmɔ – Per saltire or and azure, a saltire engrailed ermine between two roses in pale gules barbed and seeded proper, and as many passion crosses in fesse of the first. **Crest** – In front of a rock proper thereon an eagle desplayed vert holding in each claw a passion cross or, a serpent on its back, the tail nowed, also proper.

DAUGHTER LIVING

Eleanor Jane Stott, *b* 1998.

BROTHER LIVING

Confido in Deo
I trust in God

OLIVER RICHARD, FCA, Member Securities Inst, *b* 18 July 1941; *ed* Ampleforth, and RMA Sandhurst: *m* 1970, Gillian Irene, only da of L. W. Lincoln, of Northwood, Middx, and has an adopted son and an adopted da. *Residence* – Highcroft, 141 Quickley Lane, Chorleywood, Rickmansworth, Herts WD3 5PD.

SISTERS LIVING

Jenifer Ann, *b* 1938: *m* 1959, Arthur Wreford Reed, who *d* 1989, and has issue living, Dominic Wreford, *b* 1962: *m* 1998, Julia Ponomarenko, — Rupert Wreford, *b* 1964, — Catherine Anna, *b* 1960, — Suzanne Belinda, *b* 1961: *m* 19—, Guido Giulio Lombardo, of 65 Clapham Common West Side, SW4 9AU, and has issue living, Giacomo Willoughby *b* 1996, Isabella Ivana *b* (twin) 1996. *Residence* – Flat 4, 69 Charlwood St, SW1V 4PG. ⸻ Judith Mary, *b* (*posthumous*) 1945: *m* 1st, 1967 (*m diss* 1971), Garth Bentley Gibson; 2ndly, 1973, Filippo Lo Giudice, of Via di S Eufemia II, 00187 Rome, Italy, and has issue living (by 2nd *m*), Barbaro, *b* 1982, — Barbara, *b* 1975, — Francesca, *b* 1987.

AUNT LIVING (*Sister of 3rd baronet*)

Joan Margaret, *b* 1920: *m* 1944, Lt Archibald Norman Macpherson, RN (ret), and has issue living, Allan Alisdair (53 Culmstock Rd, SW11 6LY), *b* 1951, — Angus John (Honeymans Farm, Longwood Estate, nr Owslebury, Winchester, Hants SO21 1LB), *b* 1953: *m* 1982, Anne Louise Felicity Barford, and has issue living, William Archibald *b* 1988, Eloise Isobel *b* 1985, Myrtle Maud *b* 1991, — Susan Margaret, *b* 1947: *m* 1973, Maj Harry Alexander Desmond Buchanan, MC, late Gren Gds, of Keepers, Totford, nr Alresford, Hants SO24 9TJ, and has issue living, Harry Alexander *b* 1980. *Residence* – 5 Little Hayes Lane, Itchen Abbas, Winchester, Hants SO21 1XA.

WIDOW LIVING OF THIRD BARONET

JEAN MARIE FRANCES, only child of late Lt-Col Gavin Robert Vernon Hume-Gore, MC: *m* 1st, 1937, Major Sir John Edmund Backhouse, 3rd Bt, MC, RA, who was *ka* 1944; 2ndly, 1953 (*m diss* 1966), (William) Nicol Gray, CMG, DSO, KPM, who *d* 1988; 3rdly, 1970, Norman Renshaw Sharpe, of Twinpines Orchard, Ohaeawai RD 2, Kaikohe, Bay of Islands, NZ.

COLLATERAL BRANCHES LIVING

Issue of late Richard Miles Backhouse, brother of 3rd baronet, *b* 1911, *d* 1969: *m* 1st, 1948 (*m diss* 1951), Angela Mary, da of late Peter Haig-Thomas (*see* E Normanton, 1970 Edn), and widow of Capt Richard Dudley Melchior Gurowski, Scots Guards; 2ndly, 1951, Edeltraud Margaretha (73 Divinity Rd, Oxford OX4 1LH), da of Hofrat Dr Hans Perz of Vienna:—
(By 2nd *m*) Louise Maria Theodora, *b* 1955: *m* 1984, Lt-Col Jonathan Arthur Francis Howard, King's Royal Hus (PWO), and has issue (*see* E Carlisle, colls). ⸻ Julia Maria Florence, *b* 1956: *m* 1990, Paul Cameron Taylor, of 41 Hambalt Rd, SW4 9EQ, son of late J. A. Taylor, of Westbourne, Bournemouth, and has issue living, Maximilian John, *b* 1993, — John Richard, *b* 1998, — Marie-Louise Florence May, *b* 1992.

Grandchildren of late Lt-Col Miles Roland Charles Backhouse, DSO, TD, yst son of 1st baronet:—
Issue of late Major Roger Trelawny Backhouse, RRC, *b* 1905, *d* 1977: *m* 1938, Beatrice Ada Janet (Penny Cottage, Crakehall, Bedale, N Yorks), da of late Capt Hedleigh St George Bond, R Canadian Engineers, of Toronto, Canada:—
Jane Trelawny, *b* 1939: *m* 1st, 1962 (*m diss* 1982), Michael Lake Coghlan; 2ndly, 1982, Duncan Irwin Eyre, of Silvester Cottage, Hudswell, Richmond, N Yorkshire, and has issue living (by 1st *m*), Henry Trelawny Lake, *b* 1964: *m* 1998, Samantha Jane Gibbs, — Benjamin Patrick Lake, *b* 1970: *m* 1997, Elizabeth Mowatt, of Brisbane, Australia, — Jane Louise Lake, *b* 1962: *m* 1994, Stevan Caldwell, of Sydney, Australia, and has issue living, Amy Elizabeth *b* 1994, Mary Beatrice *b* 1997, — Serena Mary Lake, *b* 1969: *m* 1996, Thomas Montgomery, and has issue living, Jack Thomas *b* 1996, Phoebe Jane *b* 1998. ⸻ Avery St George, *b* 1941: *m* 1st 1963 (*m diss* 1973), Colin Frohawk Burrell; 2ndly 1978, Jeremy James Fraser, of Stutton Vale Farm, Tattingstone, Ipswich, Suffolk, and has issue living (by 1st *m*), Oliver Roy St George BACKHOUSE, *b* 1966; assumed surname of Backhouse in lieu of his patronymic by deed poll 1990, — Katharine Victoria, *b* 1964: *m* 1989, Peter John Bowring, and has issue living, Oscar Peter James *b* 1989, — (by 2nd *m*) Juliet Avery Virginia, *b* 1980. ⸻ Elizabeth Esté, *b* 1943: *m* 1969, Angus Hugh Fraser, who *d* 1994, of Hornton Hall, Banbury,

Oxon, and has issue living, Sophie Lavinia, b 1971: m 1999, Simon W. T. Barber, son of Gerald Barber, of Ludgrove, Wokingham, Berks, — Camilla Elizabeth, b 1973, — Emma Caroline, b 1977.

Issue of late Jonathan Backhouse, b 1907, d 1993: m 1934, Alice Joan, who d 1984, da of Brig Gen Charles Richard Woodroffe, CMG, CVO, CBE:—
David Miles (South Farm, Fairford, Glos GL7 3PN), b 1939; ed Eton: m 1969, Sophia Ann, da of late Col C.H.S. Townsend, and has issue living, Benjamin Jonathan, b 1974, — Cilla Gael, b 1972. —— William (Layer Marney Wick, Colchester, Essex CO5 9UT), b 1942; ed Eton: m 1971, Deborah Jane, da of late Lt-Col Hon David Edward Hely-Hutchinson (see E Donoughmore), and has issue living, Timothy James, b 1981, — Harriet Diana, b 1975, — Tessa Louise, b 1977. —— Joanna (Hawkins Farm, Monk, Eleigh Tye, Ipswich, Suffolk IP7 7JW), b 1936: m 1956, Jeremy James Norris Wyatt, who d 1988, only son of late Sir Myles Dermot Norris Wyatt, CBE, and has issue living, Thomas, b 1967, — Sarah, b 1957, — Nell Victoria, b 1959, — Carina Mary, b 1963.

Issue of late Maj Wilfred Jasper Backhouse, MBE, b 1913, d 1980: m 1946, Nancy Catherine, who d 1994, da of Lindsay Edward Bury, CBE, and widow of David Haig-Thomas:—
Joseph Lindsay, b 1953. —— Mary, b 1947: m 1973, Angus Bancroft, of Water Farm, Raydon, Hadleigh, Suffolk, and has issue living, William Harry, b 1978, — Anna Charlotte, b 1975. —— Hannah Margaret, b 1948: m 1968, Robert Braeme Skepper, of Ferry Farm, Sudbourne, Woodbridge, Suffolk, and has had issue, Jonathan b 1971, — Jane, b 1969, — Georgina, b 1976, d 1986, — Poppy, b 1988.

The 1st baronet, Sir Jonathan Edmund Backhouse (el son of late Edmund Backhouse, JP, of Trebah, Falmouth), was a DL and JP for N Riding of Yorkshire and co Durham. The 2nd baronet, Sir Edmund Trelawny, was Professor, Peking Univ 1902-13, and subsequently Professor of Chinese, King's Coll, London. The 3rd baronet, Maj Sir John Edmund Backhouse, MC, RA, was ka 1944.

BACON, First (E) 1611, of Redgrave, Suffolk; Second (E) 1627, of Mildenhall, Suffolk

Moderation is stable

Sir NICHOLAS HICKMAN PONSONBY BACON (*Premier Baronet of England*), 14th Baronet of Redgrave, and 15th Baronet of Mildenhall; b 17 May 1953; s his father, *Lt-Col Sir* EDMUND CASTELL, KG, KBE, TD, 1982; ed Eton, and Dundee Univ (MA); a Page of Honour to HM 1966-69; Barrister-at-law (Gray's Inn 1978); DL Norfolk 1998: m 1981, Susan Henrietta, da of Raymond Dinnis, of Delaware Farm, Edenbridge, Kent, and has issue.

𝕬rms – Gules, on a chief argent, two mullets pierced sable. 𝕮rest – A boar passant ermine.
Residence – Raveningham Hall, Norwich.

SONS LIVING

HENRY HICKMAN, b 23 April 1984. —— Edmund, b 1986. —— Nathaniel, b 1989. —— Thomas Castell, b 1992.

SISTERS LIVING

Lavinia Winifred, b 1939; a Trustee of Nat Galleries of Scotland 1986-98: m 1972, Stephen Cokayne Gibbs, of Dougarie, Isle of Arran (see B Aldenham and Hunsdon of Hunsdon, colls). —— Elizabeth Albinia, b 1944: m 1971, Ronald James Bremner Hoare, of Roydon Hall, Diss, Norfolk IP22 3XL, and has issue living, Jocelyn Charles Stewart, b 1974, — Selina Albinia, b 1976, — Nicola Clare, b 1977. —— Sarah (*Lady Nicholson*), b 1947: m 1970, Sir Paul Douglas Nicholson, of Quarry Hill, Brancepeth, co Durham, and has issue (see Lawson Tancred, Bt).

AUNT LIVING (*Daughter of 12th baronet*)

Katharine Mary, b 1906: m 1930, John Fowell Buxton, who d 1970 (see Buxton, Bt colls). *Residence* – Newhouse Farm, Wareside, Ware, Herts.

WIDOW LIVING OF THIRTEENTH BARONET

PRISCILLA DORA (*Priscilla, Lady Bacon*), DL (Orchards, Raveningham, Norwich NR14 6NS), da of Col Sir Charles Edward Ponsonby, 1st Bt TD: m 1936, Lt-Col Sir Edmund Castell Bacon, 13th Bt, KG, KBE, TD, who d 1982.

COLLATERAL BRANCHES LIVING

Issue of late Thomas Walter Bacon, 4th son of 10th baronet of Redgrave and 11th baronet of

Mildenhall, *b* 1863, *d* 1950: *m* 1901, Edith Mary, who *d* 1950, da of late Alexander Samuel Leslie Melville (E Leven and Melville, colls):—
Anthony Walter, *b* 1902; *ed* Eton, and Trin Coll, Camb (BA 1923); formerly Flight-Lieut Auxiliary Air Force: *m* 1941, Lola Mary, who *d* 1998, da of late Charles Stanley Martin, of Dowlais, Glamorgan, and has issue living, Christopher Nicholas (Boundary Farm, Framsden, Stowmarket, Suffolk), *b* 1945; *ed* Eton: *m* 1977, Margaret Anne, yst da of late John Walker Craig, of Terrace House, Earl Soham, Woodbridge, Suffolk, and has issue living, Nathaniel John *b* 1978, Catharine Anne *b* 1979. *Residence* – Crag Pit House, Aldeburgh, Suffolk.

Grandchildren of late Thomas Walter Bacon (ante):—
Issue of late Francis Thomas Bacon, OBE, FRS, *b* 1904, *d* 1992: *m* 1934, Barbara Winifred (Trees, 34 High St, Little Shelford, Cambridge CB2 5ES), da of late Godfrey Papillon, of Barrasford, Northumberland:—
Edward Thomas Godfrey (17 Abingdon Court, Abingdon Villas, W8), *b* 1939; *ed* Eton, and Fitzwilliam House, Camb (BA): *m* 1980, Angelina Mary, da of late Alphonse Morhange, and has issue living, Francis Edward Alphonse, *b* 1982, — Veronica Elizabeth, *b* 1984. —— (Elizabeth) Daphne, *b* 1935: *m* 1958, Giles Arthur Vivian-Neal, of Welbeck House, Brooke, Norfolk, and has issue living, Henry Arthur, *b* 1963, — James Francis, *b* 1968, — Gina Rosemary, *b* 1960, — Marianne Clare, *b* 1961.

Issue of late Christopher Henry Bacon, *b* 1906, *d* 1956: *m* 1940, Diana Sybil Richmond, who *d* 1995, da of late Frederick Richmond Brown (*see* Brown, Bt, 1995 Edn):—
Richard Anthony (Devondale, Beh's Lane, Uralba Rd, Alstonville, NSW 2477, Australia) *b* 1943: *m* 1973, Doreen Nan, da of John Keillar, and has issue living, Georgina Louise, *b* 1974, — Philippa Jane, *b* 1977. ——Timothy Roger (Ramsden Farm, Stone-cum-Ebony, nr Tenterden, Kent TN30 7JB) *b* 1947: *m* 1985, Marylyn Rowan Ogilvie, twin da of late Arthur Grant, of Trecarrell, St Just in Roseland, Cornwall, and has issue living, Rosalind Sarah, *b* 1987, — Laura Charlotte, *b* 1988. —— Elizabeth Anne, *b* 1942: *m* 1971, Pierre Bartlett (Leeswood Hall, Mold, Clwyd), and has issue living, Nicholas Michael, *b* 1972, — Andrew Christopher, *b* 1977, — Suzannah Louise, *b* 1973.

Granddaughters of late Capt Francis Rimington Bacon (infra):—
Issue of late Roger David Coats Bacon, *b* 1922, *d* 1998: *m* 1947, Phyllis Eleanor Claire (2 Caledon Rd, Parkstone, Poole, Dorset BH14 9NN), da of late Roland Oliver, of Hong Kong:—
Sarah, *b* 1948: *m* 1972, Roger William D'Alton, and has issue living, Matthew Roger, *b* 1975, — Rebecca Claire, *b* 1974, — Gemma Elizabeth, *b* 1979. ——Fiona Jane Oliver, *b* 1950: *m* 1972, John Franklin Dubsky of 78 Sussex Drive, Beaconsfield, Quebec, Canada, and has issue living, Jason Peter, *b* 1981, — Jonathan Edmund, *b* 1986. ——Veronica Claire, *b* 1953: *m* 1985, George K. Dragonas, and has issue living, Sandy George, *b* 1986, — Stephanie Veronica, *b* 1989. —— Diana Mary, *b* 1958. ——Jennifer, *b* 1963: *m* 1986, Kevin Charles Croucher, and has issue living, Benjamin Charles, *b* 1988, — Hannah Michelle, *b* 1986.

Grandson of late Rev Reginald Cazalet Bacon, son of late Rev Francis Bacon, son of late Nicholas Bacon, 2nd son of 8th baronet of Redgrave and 9th baronet of Mildenhall, *b* 1861:—
Issue of late Capt Francis Rimington Bacon, *b* 1891, *d* 1947: *m* 1919, Winifred Marie, who *d* 1973, da of late Col George Henry Brook Coats, CB, of 5 Powis Sq, Brighton:—
Anthony Peter Coats (10 Buccleuch Rd, Branksome Park, Poole, Dorset BH13 6LE), *b* 1924; *ed* Downside, and Trin Coll, Camb; MB, BChir, MD, FRCP: *m* 1947, Helen, da of Harold Jaques, of Legram's Lane, Bradford, and has issue living, Hugh Francis (Les Ruettes Farm, Le Gron, St Saviour, Guernsey GY7 9FT, CI), *b* 1952; *ed* Downside, Trin Coll, Camb (MA), and St Thomas's Hosp Med Sch, London (MB, BChir), DO, FRCPS, FRCOphth: *m* 1977, Tania Margaret Mary, da of Douglas Charles Frank Smart, of Clarendon Av, Trowbridge, Wilts, and has issue living, Thomas Hugh *b* 1981, Joanna Mary *b* 1979, Marina Tania *b* 1983, Susannah Helen *b* 1992, — Peter Jaques (Poplar House Farm, Snainton, nr Scarborough, N. Yorks YO13 9BA), *b* 1953; *ed* Downside, and St Thomas's Hosp Med Sch (MB, BS, MRCP, FRCS): *m* 1977, Susan Baird, da of David Montague Rowse, of Clapper Hill, Ramsdell, Basingstoke, Hants, and has issue living, Nicholas David *b* 1980, George Anthony Hugh *b* 1986, Diana Mary Louise *b* 1982, Annabel Jane Elizabeth *b* 1984, — Annette Susan, *b* 1959: *m* 1995, Paul Henry Rosen, of Rupert's Bell, Bell Lane, Henley upon Thames, Oxon, and has issue living, Harry Samuel *b* 1996, Oliver Calman *b* 1998, — Patricia Margaret, *b* 1962: *m* 1988, Paul Kelly, of The Coach House, Little Gaddesden, Berkhamsted, Herts HP4 1PE, and has issue living, Frederick George Bacon *b* 1997, Hugh Nicholas Bacon *b* 1998.

This family is descended from Sir Nicholas Bacon (Lord Keeper of the Great Seal to Queen Elizabeth I), who was father of that great luminary of science Sir Francis Bacon, born 1561. Sir Nicholas' el son Sir Nicholas was the first person to receive a Baronetcy. Sir Hickman Beckett, 12th Bt, was a JP and DL for Lincolnshire (High Sheriff 1887), and a County Alderman for Lindsey Div of Lincolnshire (Chm 1914-24). Sir Edmund Castell, 13th Bt, KG, KBE, TD, was Lord Lieut for Norfolk 1949-78, a Dir Lloyds Bank Ltd 1949-73, Pro-Chancellor of Univ of E Anglia 1969-73, High Steward of Norwich Cathedral 1956-79, and of Gt Yarmouth 1968-82, a Church Commr 1955-63, Chm British Sugar Corpn 1957-68, and Chm Economic Development Cttee of Agric 1966-71; served NW Europe 1944 (despatches OBE).

BADDELEY (UK) 1922, of Lakefield, Parish of St Mary Stoke Newington, co London

In thee, O Lord, I trust

Sir JOHN WOLSEY BERESFORD BADDELEY, 4th *Baronet*; *b* 27 Jan 1938; *s* his father *Sir* JOHN BERESFORD, 1979; *ed* Bradfield: *m* 1st, 1962 (*m diss* 1992), Sara Rosalind, da of late Colin Crofts, of Scarborough; 2ndly, 1998, Mrs Carol F. Quinlan (*née* Greenham), and has issue by 1st *m*.

Arms – Argent, a sword erect between two crosses couped gules, on a chief of the last a hind trippant between two garbs or. **Crest** – An arm couped and erect, vested azure, cuff argent, the hand holding an open book buckled and clasped proper between two crosses as in the arms.
Residence – Springwood, Sandgate Lane, Storrington, W Sussex.

DAUGHTERS LIVING (*By 1st marriage*)

Sara Alexandra, *b* 1964: *m* 1989, Andrew C. E. Turner, elder son of D. E. Turner, of W Chiltington, Sussex; has issue living, Peter Andrew John Baddeley, *b* 1982, — Matthew Charles, *b* 1991, — Lucinda Clare, *b* 1993. —— Anna Victoria, *b* 1965: *m* 1992, Brian A. Chambers, eldest son of D. B. Chambers, of Rutherglen, Victoria, Australia, and has issue living, William John, *b* 1993, — Thomas Donald, *b* 1995, — Eleanor Rosalind Margaret, *b* 1998. —— Emma Elisabeth, *b* 1972.

SISTERS LIVING

Susan Catherine, *b* 1932: *m* 1956, Anthony Philip Harris, of Corner Cottage, Middle St, Petworth, W Sussex, and has issue living, Ian Robert Beresford, *b* 1958: *m* 1988, Rosie, da of Rotin Tebaki, of Gizo, Solomon Is, and has issue living, William Atoia Beresford *b* 1992, Emily Kirika *b* 1989, Lucy Teromita *b* 1993, — Michael Anthony, *b* 1959: *m* 1988, Joanna Mary, da of Rear Adm Peter Nicholas Marsden, of Lucerne, Niton, IoW, and has issue living, Thomas Wolsey *b* 1991, Henry Beresford *b* 1993, Edward Holman *b* 1996, Milly Rose *b* 1999, — David John Tindall, *b* 1961: *m* 1989, Deborah L. M., da of late R. H. Green, of Ludlow, Shropshire, and has issue living, Robert Anthony *b* 1991, Isabelle Margaret *b* 1990, — Peter Wolsey, *b* 1964: *m* 1989, Amelia Angela, da of Nigel Azis, of Cokes Barn, West Burton, Pulborough, W Sussex, and has issue living, Jack Wolsey *b* 1991, Nicholas Peter *b* 1993, — Andrew Charles, *b* 1966, — Lucinda Jane, *b* 1963: *m* 1991, Andre Jon Neumann, son of R. Neumann, of Wellington, NZ, and has issue living, Benjamin Charles *b* 1993, Fergus Guy *b* 1997, Alexandra Rose *b* 1999. —— Shirley Anne, *b* 1934: *m* 1956, Alan Richard Anthony Grout-Smith, and has issue living, John Alan Beresford, *b* 1962, — Nicola Susan, *b* 1958, — Sally Caroline, *b* 1960. *Residence* – Saddlers, Church Lane, Bury, W Sussex.

COLLATERAL BRANCHES LIVING

Issue of late Mark Baddeley, 2nd son of 1st baronet, *b* 1871, *d* 1930: *m* 1918, Mabel Annie, who *d* 1988, da of John Frederick Trigg:—
MARK DAVID, *b* 12 May 1921; *ed* Cliftonville Coll. —— Mabel Joyce: *m* 1948, Henri Charles Buellet, who *d* 1979, and has issue living, Marc Charles, *b* 1955, — Patrick François, *b* 1963, — Anne Louise Marie, *b* 1953, — Henriette Oya, *b* 1954. *Residence* – Residence Etoile, 3 rue Vernet, 78150 Le Chesnay, France.

Issue of late Bernard Beresford Baddeley, 3rd son of 1st baronet, *b* 1876, *d* 1956: *m* 1900, Ethel Emily, who *d* 1955, da of Sir David Burnett, 1st Bt:—
†Allan Beresford, *b* 1909; *ed* Christ's Coll, Camb (BA 1931, MA 1936); formerly Capt RE: *m* 1945, Dorothy Ronwen, da of late H. J. Head, of Highlands, Wych Cross, Sussex, and *d* 1999, leaving issue, Paul Allan, *b* 1948: *m* 1977, Lesley, da of R. G. Springett, and has issue living, Thomas Sands *b* 1978, Samuel Joseph *b* 1980, — John Burnett, *b* 1951, — Rozanne Mary, *b* 1946: *m* 1973, Ashley Beeby, and has issue living, Morgan Douglas *b* 1978, Joshua John *b* 1981.

The 1st baronet, Sir John James, head of the firm of Baddeley Bros, wholesale stationers, etc, of 19 and 20, Moor Lane, EC2, was Sheriff of City of London 1908-09 and Lord Mayor 1921-22. The 2nd baronet, Sir (John) William Baddeley, was Managing Director of the firm of Baddeley Bros, Ltd, and Alderman (Cripplegate Ward) for City of London, and Master of Stationers' and Newspapermakers' Co 1937. The 3rd baronet, Sir John Beresford Baddeley, was Managing Director of Baddeley Bros, Ltd.

BAGGE (UK) 1867, of Stradsett Hall, Norfolk

Sir (JOHN) JEREMY PICTON BAGGE, 7th *Baronet*; *b* 21 June 1945; *s* his father, *Maj Sir* JOHN ALFRED PICTON, ED, 1990; *ed* Eton; DL Norfolk 1996; FCA; Councillor King's Lynn and W Norfolk Borough Council since 1981; Freeman City of London: *m* 1979, Sarah Margaret Phipps, da of late Maj James Shelley Phipps Armstrong (*see* Smith, Bt, *cr* 1947, 1990 Edn), and has issue.

Arms – Lozengy paly bendy, argent and gules, two flaunches or, on a chief of the last an annulet between two cinquefoils of the second. **Crest** – A pair of wings addorsed or, semée of annulets gules.
Seat – Stradsett Hall, King's Lynn, Norfolk PE33 9HA. *Club* – Boodle's.

SONS LIVING

ALFRED JAMES JOHN, *b* 1 July 1980. —— Albert Daniel Bracewell, *b* 1985.

DAUGHTER LIVING

Alexandra Mary Pleasance, *b* 1982.

BROTHERS LIVING

(Alfred) James Stephen, *b* 1952; *ed* Eton; Blues & Royals; ADC to Gov S Australia 1975-77; Bar-at-law Lincoln's Inn 1979-93, since when Partner, Norton Rose, Solicitors: *m* 1981, Victoria Imogen, elder da of Michael Andrew Lyndon Skeggs, of Oakhall, Cornhill-on-Tweed, Northumberland, and has issue living, Edwina Rose, *b* 1985. —— Thomas Philip (Hall Farm, Irnham, Grantham, Lincs NG33 4JD), *b* 1955; *ed* Eton, RMA Sandhurst, and RAC Cirencester; FRICS; Blues & Royals; ADC to GOC 4 Armd Div 1977-78; ptnr Strutt & Parker 1987.

SISTERS LIVING

My hope is in God

Christabel Rosamund (Windlesham Park, Windlesham, Surrey GU20 6AT), *b* 1940; High Sheriff Greater London 1990: *m* 1st, 1963, James Hinton Scott (*see* V Downe, 1962 Edn), who *d* 1988; 2ndly, 1990, as his 2nd wife, Peter Dimmock, CVO, OBE, and has issue living (by 1st *m*), Anthony Craufurd, *b* 1964; *ed* Charterhouse, and RMA Sandhurst, Capt The Blues and Royals: *m* 1st, 1996 (*m diss* 1998), Sara Jane, yr da of Col Robert Christie Stewart, CBE, TD (*see* B Cochrane of Cults, colls); 2ndly, 1999, Diana Lasswell, only da of Charles William Brocklebank (*see* Brocklebank, Bt, colls), — Lucinda Ruth, *b* 1966, — Sara Rosamund, *b* 1968: *m* 1995, Ivor Warren Ernst Engel, son of late Ernst Emil Otto Engel. —— Rosaleen Pleasance, *b* 1947: *m* 1972, Maj Jonathan James Buxton, of 62 Endlesham Rd, SW12, and has issue (*see* Buxton, Bt, colls). —— Elizabeth Mary Frances, *b* 1949: *m* 1981, Dean Rasheed, of Arkaba Station, Hawker, S Australia 5434, and has issue living, Edward James, *b* 1985, — Lucy Elizabeth, *b* 1983.

COLLATERAL BRANCH LIVING

Issue of late Major Henry Percy Bagge, MC, yst son of 3rd baronet, *b* 1879, *d* 1942: *m* 1928, Marjorie Aubrey, who *d* 1951, da of late Com Alexander Young Crawshay Mainwaring Spearman (Spearman, Bt, colls):—
Mary Pleasance (7 Stack House, Cundy St, SW1), *b* 1929; *ed* Newnham Coll, Camb (BA): *m* 1952 (*m diss* 1973), Amir Feridun Garakani.

The 1st baronet, Sir William Bagge (son of late Thomas Philip Bagge, JP, DL, of Stradsett, and Islington, Norfolk), sat as MP for West Norfolk (C) 1837-57 and 1865-80. The 6th baronet, Sir John Alfred Picton Bagge, ED, Maj Inns of Court Regt, was High Sheriff and DL Norfolk, and Chm W Norfolk Dist Council.

BAILEY (UK) 1919, of Cradock, Province of Cape of Good Hope, Union of South Africa

Virtue is my fortress

Sir Derrick Thomas Louis Bailey, DFC, 3rd *Baronet*; *b* 15 Aug 1918; *s* his half-brother, *Sir* John Milner, 1946; *ed* Winchester, and Ch Ch, Oxford; Capt S African Air Force; formerly 2nd Lieut S African Irish; European War 1939-45 (DFC): *m* 1st, 1946 (*m diss* 19—), (Katherine) Nancy, who *d* 1998, da of late Robert Stormonth Darling, of Rosebank, Kelso, Scotland; 2ndly, 1980 (*m diss* 1990), Mrs Jean Roscoe, and has issue by 1st *m*.

Arms – Argent, on a fesse between three martlets gules a bezant between two sprigs of mimosa proper. Crest – A demi-female figure with arms extended proper habited azure, round the neck a ruff, and trimmed at the collar, cuffs and shoulders argent, holding in the dexter hand a castle or, and in the sinister a sprig of mimosa also proper.
Seat – Bluestones, Alderney, CI.

SONS LIVING (*By 1st marriage*)

John Richard (67 Darley Rd, Randwick, NSW 2031, Australia), *b* 11 June 1947; *ed* Winchester, and Christ's Coll: *m* 1977, Philippa Jane, only da of John Sherwin Mervyn Pearson Gregory, of Monnington House, Monnington-on-Wye, Hereford, and has issue living, James Edward, *b* 7 Sept 1983, — Michael Abe, *b* 1987, — Anna, *b* 1980. —— Thomas Noel (Lower Brinsop Court Farm, Hereford HR4 7AZ), *b* 1948; *ed* Bradfield: *m* 1987, Penelope Jane, da of F. B. Aggas, of Kibworth, Leics, and has issue living, Peter Robert, *b* 1988, — Charles Richard, *b* 1990, — Jack Frederick, *b* 1994. —— William Abe (Poortje Stud, PO Box 83, Colesberg 5980, Cape Prov, S Africa), *b* 1950; *ed* Winchester: *m* 1982, Nikki, formerly wife of — Riley, and da of late Vernon Langerman, of Cape Town, and has issue living, David Moir, *b* 1983, — Camilla, *b* 1985. —— Patrick James (Upton Court, Upton Bishop, Ross-on-Wye, Hereford HR9 7UN), *b* 1959; *ed* Bradfield: *m* 1st, 1983 (*m diss* 1986), Hon Lucy Jane Hamilton-Russell, yst da of 10th Viscount Boyne; 2ndly, 1990, Sarah E., yr da of Brian J. Hammond, of White Leas, Sopworth, Chippenham, Wilts, and has issue living (by 2nd *m*), Edward William Abe, *b* (twin) 1997, — Jemima Jane, *b* 1994, — Lucinda Mary, *b* (twin) 1994, — Annabel Lettice, *b* 1997.

DAUGHTER LIVING (*By 1st marriage*)

Patricia Rosemary, *b* 1951: *m* 1986, Anthony Howard Collins, of Llantellen, Skenfrith, Gwent, son of Michael Collins, of W Grinstead, Sussex, and has issue living, Edward, *b* 1989, — Sam, *b* 1991, — Tara, *b* 1987.

BROTHER LIVING

James Richard Abe, DFC, *b* 1919 *ed* Winchester, and Ch Ch, Oxford, formerly Squadron Leader RAF, Vol Reserve; European War 1939-45 (DFC): *m* 1st, 1958 (*m diss* 1963), Gillian Mary, who *d* 19—, da of John Kilgour Parker, of Cape Town, S Africa; 2ndly, 1964, Barbara (Taylor), da of Harry Epstein, of Johannesburg, and has had issue, (by 1st *m*) Jonathan Alcuin Abe, *b* 1959, — (by 2nd *m*) Alaric James Abe, *b* 1965, *d* 1986, — Prospero James Thomas, *b* 1969. *Address* – PO 226, Bryanston, Transvaal.

SISTER LIVING

Noreen Helen Rosemary, *b* 1921: *m* 1st, 1941, W/Cdr Peter Anker-Simmons, DFC, RAF, who *d* 1947; 2ndly, 1947 (*m diss* 1951), Count Peter Christian Raben-Levetzau, who *d* 1969, and has had issue, (by 1st *m*) Richard James (Manutsa Farm, PO Box 84, Hoedspruit, Eastern Transvaal), *b* 1944: *m* 1981 (*m diss* 1982), — , and has issue living, Justin Rorke James *b* 1982, — (Noreen) Starr, *b* 1941: *m* 1st, 1967 (*m diss* 1975), as his 2nd wife, Sir Vivyan Edward Naylor-Leyland, 3rd Bt, who *d* 1987; 2ndly, 1986, Philip Thomas Harper, of Tchinga, Postman Suite 19, P Bag X15, Hermanus, 7200, S Africa, — (by 2nd *m*) Paul Michael (*Count Raben-Levetzau*), *b* 1949, — Alexandra Louise, *b* 1948; *d* 1984. *Residences* – L'Ermitage, rue de Soeurs, Vineuil, St Firmin, 60500 Chantilly, France; 94 Pretoria Av, Atholl, Johannesburg, S Africa.

The 1st baronet, Sir Abe Bailey, KCMG (son of Hon Thomas Bailey, of Queenstown, S Africa), was engaged in Farming in Cape Colony, and a Company Director; implicated in Jameson Raid (sentenced to two years' imprisonment and fined £2,000); S African War 1899-1902 as an Intelligence Officer, and Major Gorringe's Flying Column; S-W Africa 1914-15 as Major and DAQMG Union Forces; in 1908 raised and equipped at own expense 200 Inf and 100 Mounted Inf to quell Zululand Rebellion in Natal; had Corps of Sharpshooters in Flanders during European War 1914-18; a Member of House of Assembly, Union of S Africa 1910-24; a MLA of Cape Colony and of Transvaal (Whip in both Parliaments).

BAILLIE (UK) 1823, of Polkemmet, Linlithgowshire

It shines in the dark

Sir GAWAINE GEORGE HOPE BAILLIE, 7th *Baronet*; *b* 8 March 1934; *s* his father, Sir ADRIAN WILLIAM MAXWELL, 1947; *ed* Eton, and Camb Univ: *m* 1966, Mrs Lucile Margot Gardner, da of Senator Louis P. Beaubien, and has issue.

ᴬrms – Azure, nine mullets, three, three, two, and one or within a bordure counter-nebulée argent and sable. ᴄrest – Issuant out of clouds proper an estoile or. ˢupporters – Two lions guardant argent.
Residence – Freechase, Warninglid, Sussex RH17 5SZ.

SON LIVING

ADRIAN LOUIS, *b* 26 March 1973.

DAUGHTER LIVING

Liza Katharine, *b* 1969.

The father of the 1st baronet was a Lord of Session (Lord Polkemmet). Sir William, 2nd baronet, sat as MP for Linlithgowshire (*C*) 1845-7. The 5th baronet, Sir Gawaine George Stuart Baillie, Lieut 2nd Dragoons, was *ka* 1914. The 6th baronet, Sir Adrian William Maxwell Baillie, sat as MP for Linlithgowshire (*C*) 1931-5, and for Tonbridge Div of Kent 1937-45.

BAIRD (NS) 1695, of Saughton Hall, Edinburghshire

By strength and valour

Sir (JAMES) ANDREW GARDINER BAIRD, 11th *Baronet*; *b* 2 May 1946; *s* his father, *Capt Sir* JAMES RICHARD GARDINER, MC; 1997; *ed* Eton: *m* 1984 (*m diss* 1988), Jean Margaret, da of Brig Sir Ian Liddell Jardine, 4th Bt, OBE, MC, and has issue.

ᴬrms – Gules, a sanglier passant or; on a canton ermine a sword pale-wise proper. ᴄrest – A boar's head erased or.
Residence – ......

SON LIVING

ALEXANDER, *b* 28 May 1986.

BROTHER LIVING

(William) Julian Gardiner, *b* 1947; *ed* Milton Abbey: *m* 1984, Nichola Bridget Halsall, da of Lt-Col Cecil West, OBE, of Hythe, Kent, and has issue living, William Rupert Gardiner, *b* 1995, — James Toby Gardiner, *b* 1998. *Residence* – 7 Bettridge Rd, SW6 3QB.

SISTER LIVING

Lavinia Mary Arabella, *b* 1951. *Residence* – School House, Upper Clatford, Andover, Hants SP11 7QW.

WIDOW LIVING OF TENTH BARONET

MABEL ANN (GAY) TEMPEST (*Lady Baird*), da of A. Algernon Gill, of Toronto, Canada: *m* 1941, Capt Sir James Richard Gardiner Baird, 10th Bt, MC, who *d* 1997. *Residence* – Bab Essalam, 55 Route de la Village, Marshan, Tangier, Morocco.

COLLATERAL BRANCHES LIVING

Issue of late William Henry Gardiner Baird, yr brother of 10th baronet, *b* 1914, *d* 1989. *m* 1st, 1946 (*m diss* 1966), Helen Mary, eldest da of late Rev Canon Edward Charles Rich, of 31 Yeoman's Row, SW3; 2ndly, 1966, C. Gwendolyn (Flat 71, The Cloisters, Pegasus Grange, White House Rd, Oxford OX1 4OO), da of late James Smart, OBE, of Ottawa:—
(By 1st *m*) Mervyn Edward Hozier (22 The Terrace, Sunninghill, nr Ascot, Berks SL5 9NH), *b* 1947; *ed* Milton Abbey: *m* 1970, Isobel Frances, only da of late Stewart Winzor, of Adelaide, S Australia, and has issue living, James Edward Hozier, *b* 1976, — Mirella Frances Hozier, *b* 1973. ——— Roderick Frank Gardiner, *b* 1955; *ed* The Elliot Sch, Putney: *m* 1985, Julia Mary, elder da of Gerald Barry, WS, of Haddington, E Lothian, and has issue living, Arabella Elizabeth Gardiner, *b* 1987. ——— Judith Mary Gardiner, *b* 1951: *m* 1974, David Ashworth Sydney Phillips Cosby, of Ballycreen House, Aughrim, co Wicklow, 3rd son of late Maj Errold Ashworth Sydney Cosby, of Stradbally Hall, co Leix, and has issue living, Alexander James Ashworth, *b* 1977, — Philip William Sydney, *b* 1980.

Descendants of late William Baird (el son of late William Baird, 2nd surviving son of 1st baronet), whose 2nd son David was *cr* a *Baronet* 1809 with special remainder to his el brother Robert:—
See Baird, Bt, *cr* 1809.

King Charles I issued a warrant creating James Baird, of Newbyth, co Haddington, Baron Devern, but he died before the patent passed the great seal. His el son, Sir John Baird, was a Lord of Session under the style of Lord Newbyth, and his son Sir William of Newbyth was *cr* a baronet (NS 1680, ext 1745). The 2nd son of James Baird of Newbyth, Robert of Saughton Hall, Midlothian, an Edinburgh merchant, was *cr* a baronet with remainder to heirs male of the body. Sir William Baird, 5th baronet, *m* 1750, Frances, da of the celebrated Col James Gardiner, of Bankton, who was *k* at the battle of Prestonpans 1745.

BAIRD (UK) 1809, of Newbyth, Haddingtonshire

By strength and valour

Sir DAVID CHARLES BAIRD, 5th *Baronet*, son of late William Arthur Baird, 2nd son of 3rd baronet; *b* 6 July 1912; *s* his uncle, Sir DAVID, MVO, 1941; *ed* Eton, and Cambridge Univ.

Arms – Gules, in chief within an increscent an estoile of eight points argent; in base a boar passant or; on a canton ermine a sword erect proper, pommel and hilt gold. Crest – 1st, a Mameluke mounted on a horse, and holding in his dexter hand a scimitar all proper; 2nd, a boar's head erased or. *Residence* – Novar, Barrhill Rd, Dalbeattie, Kirkcudbrightshire DG5.

SISTER LIVING

Hersey Ellen, *b* 1916: *m* 1939 (*m diss* 1959), Maj Lachlan Gordon-Duff, Gordon Highlanders, and has issue living, Simon Lachlan (Lodge Farm, Stowood, nr Beckley, Oxon OX3 9SR), *b* 1942; Maj Scots Gds: *m* 1990, Mrs Caroline Edith Mary Craig, elder da of late Col Charles Neil Howard, MC late Black Watch (*see* E Denbigh, colls), — Robert Andrew (Glebe House, Stobo, Peebleshire), *b* 1945: *m* 1973, Mrs Caroline Orby Robarts, da of Maj Robert Clifton Gascoigne (*see* Munro, Bt, *cr* 1634, colls), and has issue living, Hersey Diana *b* 1973, Philippa Sophie *b* 1976. *Residence* – Spring Cottage, Hardgate, Castle Douglas, Kirkcudbrightshire.

COLLATERAL BRANCHES LIVING

Issue of late Robert Walter Stuart Baird, yr brother of 5th baronet, *b* 1914, *d* 1989: *m* 1st, 1938 (*m diss* 1960), Maxine Christine, only da of Rupert Darrell, of New York, USA; 2ndly, 1960, Maria Florine Viscart (39 Grand Rue, Geneva 1204, Switzerland):—
(By 1st *m*) CHARLES WILLIAM STUART (12 Falstaff St, Sunnybank Hills, Brisbane, Qld 4109, Australia), *b* 8 June 1939; *ed* in Switzerland: *m* 1965, Jane Joanna, da of late Brig A. Darley Bridge, and has issue living, Tara Francesca Stuart, *b* 1970, — Senta Louise Stuart, *b* 1973, — Petra Helen Stuart, *b* 1975. —— (By 2nd *m*) Frances, *b* 1960: *m* 1981 (*m diss* 1994), Jean Luc Bollack, and has issue living, William Jean Luc Stephen Stuart, *b* 1984, — Floria Frances Stuart, *b* 1981.

Grandchildren of late Robert George Baird, son of late Robert Henry Baird, son of late Capt Wynne Baird, RN, brother of 2nd baronet:—
Issue of late Maj Robert Douglas Baird, MC, *b* 1893, *d* 1969: *m* 1926 Alice Patience, who *d* 1995, da of late Cecil Gordon Crawley, CBE, of 19 Cranley Place, SW7:—
Dawn, *b* 1927: *m* 1968, as his 2nd wife, Geoffrey Haig Loyd, MBE, of Remenham House, Ocle Pychard, Hereford (*see* Oakeley, Bt, 1985 Edn).

Issue of late Maj George Henry William Baird, *b* 1903, *d* 1992: *m* (Jan) 1931, Catherine Augusta, who *d* 1986, da of late Capt Francis William Forester (Milbank, Bt):—
†Angus George David, *b* 1934; *ed* Eton: *m* 1961, Fiona Elizabeth Hildred (Hartsfield House, Westland Green, Little Hadham, Ware, Herts SG11 2AJ), da of John Sholto Fitzpatrick Cooke, CBE, and *d* 1996, leaving issue, Andrew James, *b* 1970, — Nicola Laura, *b* 1964, — Eliza Caroline, *b* 1967. —— Diana Catherine, *b* (Dec) 1931: *m* 1953, Julian Charles Lewis Jenkinson, of Folly Faunts House, Goldhanger, Maldon, Essex, and has issue (*see* Jenkinson, Bt, colls).

The 1st baronet, Rt Hon Sir David Baird, GCB, PC (2nd son of late William Baird, el son of late William Baird, 2nd surviving son of Sir Robert Baird, 1st Bt (*cr* 1695)), was a distinguished military commander, and was *cr* a baronet with special remainder to the heirs male of his brother, Robert. At the capture of Seringapatam he headed the storming party, and as Commander-in-Chief he captured the Cape of Good Hope. In the battle of Corunna he lost an arm. On his death without issue in 1847, he was succeeded under the special remainder by his nephew, David. This family is a junior branch of Baird, baronet of Saughton Hall, to whose title the present Baronet of Newbyth is in remainder. The 3rd baronet, Sir David, served in the Crimea, and in the Indian Mutiny.

BAKER (UK) 1802, of Wembley (Extinct 1959)

Sir RANDOLF LITTLEHALES BAKER, DSO, 4th and last *Baronet*.

DAUGHTER LIVING OF FOURTH BARONET

Selina Littlehales (Ranston, Blandford, Dorset), *b* 1925: *m* 1955, Major William Harry Gibson Fleming, JP, DL, RA (ret), who *d* 1981, and has issue living, James Randolf (Smugglers Mead, Stepleton, Blandford, Dorset), *b* 1958: *m* 1986, Fiona Lucy, da of Robert Don, of Elmham House, Dereham, Norfolk, and has issue living, Hector *b* 1987, William Robert *b* 1989, Olivia Rose *b* 1992, — Anthea Margaret, *b* 1956.

SHERSTON-BAKER (GB) 1796, of Dunstable House, Richmond, Surrey.

Sir ROBERT GEORGE HUMPHREY SHERSTON-BAKER, 7th *Baronet*; *b* 3 April 1951; *s* his father, *Sir* HUMPHREY DODINGTON BENEDICT SHERSTON, 1990: *m* 1991, Vanessa R. A., yst da of C. E. A. Baird, of Grouville, Jersey, CI, and has issue.

Arms – Argent, a saltire sable charged with five escallops erminois, on a chief azure a lion passant of the third, armed and langued gules. **Crest** – A demi-lion rampant per fesse indented, erminois and pean, holding in the paws an escallop argent charged with an ermine spot.
Residence – Wealden House, North Elham, Kent CT4 6UY.

SON LIVING

DAVID ARBUTHNOT GEORGE, *b* 24 Nov 1992.

DAUGHTER LIVING

Fideri coticula crux
The cross is the test of faith

Amy Margaret, *b* 1994.

SISTERS LIVING

Margaret Elizabeth, *b* 1939: *m* 1st, 1969 (*m diss* 1973), Peter Leggatt, son late Harry Leggatt, and of Mrs Gerald Cobb, of Meonstoke, Hants; 2ndly, 1978, Nicholas Lechmere Spaulding Kirkbride, of 6/1801 S Flagler Drive, West Palm Beach, Florida 33401, USA. —— Sarah Loraine, *b* 1940: *m* 1963, Christopher Charles Jervis Johnson-Ferguson, 2nd son of Lt-Col Sir Neil Edward Johnson-Ferguson, 3rd Bt, TD, and has issue. *Residence* The Old House, Staverton, nr Daventry, Northants NN1 6JA. —— Jane Magdalen, *b* 1948: *m* 1978, Quentin Randolph Johnson, of Ayleswade Farm, Biddenden, Kent TN27 8LE, and has issue living, Jasper Ronald Paul *b* 1986, — Mae, *b* 1982, — Edwina Alice, *b* (twin) 1986.

COLLATERAL BRANCHES LIVING

Issue of late John Dunstan Sherston BAKER, 2nd son of 4th baronet, *b* 1882, *d* 1940: *m* 1915, Anna Josephine, who *d* 1952, da of late Alexander Wood, FSA:—
Peter SHERSTON-BAKER, MC (3D Sheen Gate Gdns, SW14), *b* 1918: *ed* Downside; Maj (ret) RA; a Queen's Messenger 1964-77; 1939-45 War (despatches, MC): *m* 1947, Elizabeth, da of late Walter Hugh Barham, of 1 Camden Park, Tunbridge Wells, and has issue living, Veronica (108 Cranbrook Rd, Chiswick, W4 2LJ), *b* 1948: *m* 1969 (*m diss* 1989), Christopher Carlton Fulton, son of late F. J. A. Fulton, of Nelson, NZ, and has issue living, Guy Charles Jeffreys *b* 1970, Robyn Frances Jeffreys *b* 1973, — Josephine *b* 1950: *m* 1975, John Gordon Chambers, of 26 Shalstone Rd, SW14, son of late Norman Henry Chambers, of 24 Liverpool Rd, St Albans, Herts, and has issue living, Oliver Henry Sherston *b* 1979, — Gabrielle, *b* 1954: *m* 1977, Geoffrey Tuff of 21 Redwood Drive, Writtle, Chelmsford, Essex CM1 3LY, son of late Col Charles Reginald Tuff, and has issue living, Rebecca *b* 1981, Alice *b* 1983.

This family was settled in the west of England several centuries before the creation of the baronetcy. The 1st baronet received a baronetcy for raising and maintaining for King George III a troop of 600 horse styled "The Richmond Rangers", and the 4th Bt was many years Recorder of Barnstaple and Bideford and a County Court Judge. The 5th Baronet, Sir Dodington George Richard Sherston, Lieut-Col (ret) IMS, assumed by deed poll 1923 (recorded at Heralds' College) the additional surname of Sherston.

Baker-Wilbraham, see Wilbraham.

BALFOUR (UK) 1911, of Albury Lodge, Albury, Hertfordshire (Extinct 1929)

Sir ROBERT BALFOUR, 1st and last *Baronet*.

GRANDDAUGHTER LIVING OF FIRST BARONET

(Issue of late Alexander Balfour, el son of 1st baronet, *b* 1882, *d* 1923: *m* 1910, Ruth Frances, who *d* 1940, da of late John D. Macfarland, banker, of Lincoln, Nebraska, USA) — Margaret, *b* 1917: *m* 1948, John B. Ashbrook, and has issue living, Susan Margaret, *b* 1950: *m* 1973, F. V. Casselman, of Mass, USA, — Katherine Jessie, *b* 1955. *Residence* – Wrango Hall, Denham Village, Bucks.

BALL (UK) 1911, of Merrion Square, City of Dublin, and Killybegs, co Donegal

Sir CHARLES IRWIN BALL, 4th *Baronet*; *b* 12 Jan 1924; *s* his father, *Sir* NIGEL GRESLEY, 1978; *ed* Sherborne; a Chartered Accountant: *m* 1st, 1950 (*m diss* 1983), Alison Mary, da of late Lt-Col Percy Holman Bentley, MBE, MC, of Farnham, Surrey; 2ndly, 1994, Christine Trilby Knowles and has issue by 1st *m*.

Arms – Argent, on a chevron gules between three fireballs proper a galley with one mast, sail furled, pennant flottant in stern of the first. Crest – An arm vambraced embowed argent, charged with two ogresses, the hand proper grasping a fireball as in the arms.
  Residence – Killybegs, Eddystone Rd, Thurlestone, Kingsbridge, Devon TQ7 3NU

SONS LIVING (*By 1st marriage*)

RICHARD BENTLEY (Evenshade, Sandown Rd, Esher, Surrey KT10 9TT), *b* 29 Jan 1953; *ed* Sherborne, and Leicester Univ; ACA: *m* 1991, Beverley Ann, da of late Bertram Joffre Wright, and has issue living, Anna Frances, *b* 1996.

DAUGHTER LIVING (*By 1st marriage*)

Diana Margaret (56 Barrons Way, Comberton, Cambridge), *b* 1955.

SISTER LIVING

Valerie Margaret, *b* 1929: *m* 1953, Christopher Elliott Winn, and has issue living, David Elliott (219 Hempstead Rd, Hempstead, nr Gillingham, Kent), *b* 1958: *m* 1988, Esther Maria Lewis, and has issue living, Catherine Elizabeth *b* 1988, Stephanie Fay *b* 1991, — Joanna Margaret, *b* 1955: *m* 1979, Anthony Oliver Bay Green, of Oak Cottage, Hill House Hill, Liphook, Hants, and has issue living, Barnaby Oliver Bay *b* 1983, Samantha Margaret Bay *b* 1981, Susannah Katharine Bay *b* 1986, — Fiona Anne, *b* 1957: *m* 1985, Charles Christopher Carter Brett, of St Swithun's Gate, Kingsgate Rd, Winchester, Hants, and has issue living, Luisa Annabel Carter *b* 1987, Claudia Alessandra Isabel *b* 1990. *Residence* – 8 Broadlands Court, Kew Gardens Rd, Richmond, Surrey.

COLLATERAL BRANCHES LIVING

Issue of late Ronald Herbert Ball, yr son of 3rd baronet, *b* 1925, *d* 1995: *m* 1st, 1950, Pamela Mary, who *d* 1969, da of late John Morton, of Hunningham Grange, Warwicks; 2ndly, 1970 (*m diss* 1980), Mrs Diana Joy Maitland, da of late Lt-Col James Pridham, of 54 Elm Park House, Fulham Rd, SW10:—
(By 1st *m*) Christopher Nigel Morton (31 Waterlip Cottage, Cranmore, Shepton Mallet, Som BA4 4RN), *b* 1951: *m* 1974, Melanie, da of Col David James Fenner, of 1 Riverside Cottage, Lyme Regis, Dorset, and has issue living, Peter Jonathan, *b* 1981, — Amelia Kate, *b* 1983. ——— Jonathan Gresley (The Headlands, Luntley, nr Pembridge, Hereford HR6 9EJ), *b* 1956: *m* 1981, Molly, da of late Christopher Major, and has issue living, Christopher James, *b* 1984, — Katherine Elizabeth, *b* 1987, — Joanna Rachel, *b* (twin) 1987. ——— Rupert Valentine (Smugglers Bar, Parque Don José, Costa del Silencio, Arona, Tenerife, Spain), *b* 1958: *m* 1981, Christine, da of Cliff Hampson, of 46 Hereford Rd, Blackburn, Lancs, and has issue living, James Irwin Hampson, *b* 1992, — Emma Frances, *b* 1983. ——— Susan Mary (24 Beach Av, S Golden Beach, NSW 2483, Australia) *b* 1953: *m* 1979 (*m diss* 1981), Steven Rhead Allen.

Issue of late Ivan Hellicar Ball, 4th son of 1st baronet, *b* 1894, *d* 1963: *m* 1929, Dorothy, who *d* 1992, da of late Charles E. Gill:—
Ursula Pamela Joyce, *b* 1930: *m* 1959, Herbert John Lewis, of Strath Isla, Wothorpe Drift, Stamford, Lincs, and has issue living, Peter John, *b* 1961, — Joanna Mary, *b* 1964, — Sarah Catherine, *b* 1966. —— Dorothy Lucia Anne (2 Abbots Way, Neston, S Wirral, Cheshire L64 3SU), *b* 1933.

The 1st baronet, Sir Charles Bent Ball, MD, FRCSI, was Hon Surg to King Edward VII in Ireland 1904-10 and to King George V 1910-16. The 2nd baronet, Sir (Charles) Arthur Kinahan Ball, MD, was appointed Regius Professor of Surgery, Dublin Univ 1933.

HARMOOD-BANNER (UK) 1924, of Liverpool, co Lancaster (Extinct 1990)

Sir GEORGE KNOWLES HARMOOD-BANNER, 3rd and last *Baronet*.

DAUGHTERS LIVING OF THIRD BARONET

Susan, *b* 1951: *m* 1999, Alexander William Richard Cameron, FCA. *Residence* – 40 Barons Court Rd, W14 9DT. —— Gillian, *b* 1953: *m* 1981, John Richard Taylor-Medhurst, and has issue living, (John) Tim Banner, *b* 1982, — James Richard Banner, *b* 1984, — Henry Bruce Banner, *b* 1987, — Peter George Banner, *b* 1989. *Residence* – Greenbanks, Cranbrook Rd, Hawkhurst, Kent TN18 5EF.

SISTER LIVING OF THIRD BARONET

Elizabeth, *b* 1908: *m* 1931, Ronald Percy Crawshaw, and has issue living, James Robert Harwood, *b* 1947; *ed* Repton, — Joanna Eve, *b* 1934, — Cordelia Anne, *b* 1937: *m* 19—, —, Courtney, of The Old Rectory, New Church, Romney Marsh, Kent TN29 0DZ. *Residence* – ......

WIDOW LIVING OF THIRD BARONET

ROSEMARY JANE (*Lady Harmood-Banner*), da of Col Maurice Lawrence Treston, CBE: *m* 1947, Sir George Knowles Harmood-Banner, 3rd Bt, who *d* 1990, when the title became ext. *Residence* – 10 Foxmore St, SW11.

BANNERMAN (NS) 1682, of Elsick, Kincardineshire

For my country

Sir DAVID GORDON BANNERMAN, OBE, 15th *Baronet*; *b* 18 Aug 1935; *s* his brother, *Sir* ALEXANDER PATRICK, 1989; *ed* Gordonstoun, and New Coll, Oxford (MA); late 2nd Lieut Queen's Own Cameron Highlanders; HMOCS (Tanzania) 1960-63; Min of Defence 1963-97; OBE 1976: *m* 1960, Mary Prudence, elder da of Rev Philip Frank Ardagh-Walter, V of Woolton Hill, Hants, and has issue.

Arms – Gules, a banner displayed argent, thereon a canton azure charged with St Andrew's cross of the second, as the badge of Scotland. **Crest** – A demiman in armour holding in his right hand a sword proper. **Supporters** – Two armed men proper.
Residence – 3 St George's Rd, St Margaret's, Twickenham, Middx.

DAUGHTERS LIVING

Clare Naomi, *b* 1961: *m* 1991, Michael Angus O'Neill, only son of Shane O'Neill, of Betchton, Cheshire, and has issue living, Alexander Constantine, *b* 1996, — Hector Harry, *b* 1998, — Constance Isobel, *b* 1994. —— Margot Charlotte, *b* 1962. —— Arabella Rose, *b* 1965. —— Clodagh Isobel Rose, *b* 1975.

SISTERS LIVING

Ruth Mary Charlotte (Gatcombe House, Little Hempston, Totnes, Devon), *b* 1937: *m* 1958, Michael Joseph Orgill Massey, MA, MB, BChir, MFOM, who *d* 1989, and has issue living, Jonathan David, *b* 1962; BEng (Hons), — William Michael, *b* 1964, — James Richard, *b* 1966, — Alexander Mary, *b* 1959; MB BS, — Charlotte Elizabeth, *b* 1960; MB BS. —— Janet Elizabeth Naomi, *b* (twin) 1937; ARCM 1959: *m* 1966, Warren Jackson, MA, of 117 Longhurst Lane, Mellor, Stockport, Cheshire, and has issue living, Catherine Elizabeth, *b* 1967; BA 1989, — Ruth Helen Isobel, *b* 1969.

DAUGHTER LIVING OF ELEVENTH BARONET

Eve Mary, *b* 1921: *m* 1951, (Thomas) Cecil (Leyburn) Symmes, who *d* 1991, of 39 Karu Crescent, Waikanae, NZ 6454, and has issue living, Howard Alexander (5 Connaught Terrace, Wellington, NZ), *b* 1954: *m* 1989, Jane Williams, and has issue living, Kirk Thomas *b* 1992, Hilary Mary *b* 1994, — George Weymouth (5 Thatcher Crescent, Crofton Downs, Wellington, NZ), *b* 1956: *m* 1989, Veronica Anne Challies, and has issue living, Andrew Gordon *b* 1998, Rose Laura *b* 1994.

WIDOW LIVING OF THIRTEENTH BARONET

BARBARA CHARLOTTE (*Dowager Lady Bannerman*), da of late Lt-Col Alec Cameron, OBE, IMS, of Southwold, Suffolk: *m* 1932, Lt-Col Sir Donald Arthur Gordon Bannerman, 13th Bt, who *d* (16 Sept) 1989. *Residence* – Cecil Court, 2 Priory Rd, Kew, Richmond, Surrey TW9 3DG.

WIDOW LIVING OF FOURTEENTH BARONET

JOAN MARY (*Joan, Lady Bannerman*), da of late John Henry Wilcox, of Tadcaster, Yorks: *m* 1977, Sir Alexander Patrick Bannerman, 14th Bt, who *d* (21 Nov) 1989. *Residence* – 73 New Causeway, Reigate, Surrey RH2 7PP.

COLLATERAL BRANCHES LIVING

       Granddaughter of late Edward Mordaunt Bannerman (infra):—
       Issue of late Com Bertrand Bannerman, DSO, *b* 1883, *d* 1954: *m* (April) 1909, Vera, who *d* 1976, da of Edward Stuart:—
Sheila Christina (*Lady Walsham*), *b* (Dec) 1909: *m* 1936, Rear-Adm Sir John Scarlett Warren Walsham, 4th Bt, CB, OBE, who *d* 1992. *Residence* – 19 Beckford Close, Tisbury, Wilts.

       Granddaughter of late Mordaunt Francis Bannerman, 8th son of late Edward Mordaunt Bannerman, 6th son of Patrick Wilson Bannerman, 2nd son of Charles Bannerman, 2nd brother of 6th baronet:—
       Issue of late Nigel Mordaunt Bannerman, LRCP, MRCS, *b* 1943, *d* 1975: *m* 1971, Jane Alison, el da of Paul Taylor, of Milford, Godalming, Surrey:—
Henrietta Jane, *b* 1973.

    The ancestors of this family were hereditary banner-bearers to the kings of Scotland. The baronetcy was conferred by Charles II upon Sir Alexander Bannerman for "his constant loyalty during the Rebellion, and the heavy calamities he had suffered on that account." The 3rd baronet raised a regiment, and was with it at the battle of Culloden. His son, the 4th baronet, sold the Elsick estate for a nominal price, having been threatened with forfeiture on account of his father's and his own alleged participation in the rebellion of 1745. A portion of the Elsick estate was repurchased by 9th baronet, and passed on his death to his da, the wife of the 10th Earl of Southesk. Sir Arthur D'Arcy Gordon Bannerman, KCVO, CIE, 12th Bt, was Resident, Kashmir 1917-21, and Gentleman-Usher to HM King George V 1928-36. Lt-Col Sir Donald Arthur Gordon Bannerman, 13th Bt, Queen's Own Cameron Highlanders 1918-48, wrote *A Short Family Family History* and *Random Recollections*, and was a Housemaster at Gordonstoun 1948-52 and Fettes 1952-69.

BARBER (UK) 1960, of Greasley, co Nottingham

Sir (THOMAS) DAVID BARBER, 3rd *Baronet; b* 18 Nov 1937; *s* his father, *Col Sir* WILLIAM FRANCIS, TD, 1995; *ed* Eton, and Trin Coll, Camb (MA); late 2nd Lieut RA 1957-58: *m* 1st, 1972 (*m diss* 1975), Amanda Mary, da of Frank Rabone, of Beacon Barn Farm, Coton, Milwich, Staffs, and widow of Maj Michael Healing, Gren Gds; 2ndly, 1978, Mrs Jeannine Mary Boyle, da of Capt Timothy John Gurney, Coldstream Gds (*see* De Bathe, Bt, ext), and has issue by 1st and 2nd *m.*

Arms – Ermine, two chevronels, between three fleurs-de-lys gules a bordure embattled also gules. Crest – In front of two swords in saltire points upward proper hilts and pomels or, a bull's head erased also proper.
Residence – Windrush House, Inkpen, Hungerford, Berks RG17 9QY.

SONS LIVING (*By 1st marriage*)

THOMAS EDWARD, *b* 14 March 1973; *ed* Eton, and St Aidan's Coll, Durham (BA 1995).

(*By 2nd marriage*)

William Samuel Timothy, *b* 1982.

DAUGHTER LIVING (*By 2nd marriage*)

Sarah Emily, *b* 1981.

SISTER LIVING

Diana Mary, *b* 1939: *m* 1965 (*m diss* 1990), Nicholas Bache Barlow Davie-Thornhill (*see* Barlow, Bt, *cr* 1907, 1976 Edn), and has issue living, John Philip Bache (Hinderclay Hall, Diss, Norfolk), *b* 1966; *ed* Bloxham, and RAC Cirencester: *m* 1998, Rebecca Ann, eldest da of F. H. C. Podger, of Winchester, Hants, — Adrian George Barber, *b* 1968; *ed* Eton, RAC Cirencester, and Glagow Univ. *Residence* – Gunhill Place, S Green, Southwold, Suffolk.

AUNTS LIVING (*Daughters of 1st baronet*)

Beatrice Naomi (The Manse, Moor Green, Newthorpe, Notts), *b* 1911: *m* 1939, Flight Lieut Charles David Stewart, RAF, who was *ka* 1940. —— Honor (Limehurst, Halam Rd, Southwell, Notts), *b* 1914: *m* 1947, Cdr Noel Hunt, RNVR (ret), who *d* 1974.

COLLATERAL BRANCH LIVING

Issue of late Thomas Cecil Barber, el son of 1st baronet, *b* 1903, *d* 1930: *m* 1928, Joyce Mary (Albury Park, Albury, nr Guildford, Surrey) (who *m* 2ndly, 1933 (*m diss* 1948), Col John Sydney North FitzGerald, CVO, MBE, MC, who *d* 1976 (*see* By North, colls); 3rdly, 1948, Lt-Col Arthur Frederick Reginald Wiggins, who *d* 1961; Mrs Wiggins subsequently assumed the surname of HANBURY *ca* 1975/76), da of late Dr Edward Williams Hedley, MBE, of The Cottage, Thursley, Surrey:—
Susan, *b* 1930: *m* 1st, 1951 (*m diss* 1965), Ian Hope Johnstone; 2ndly, 1968, David Day, who *d* 1970, and has issue living, (by 1st *m*), Robin (26 Kelvedon Rd, SW6 7BW), *b* 1956, — Rosanna (7 Woodmancote, Cirencester, Glos GL7 7ED), *b* 1958: *m* 1982 (*m diss* 19—), Andrew Hugh Hope, and has issue living Oliver *b* 1989, Clara Harriet *b* 1984.

The 1st baronet, Col Sir (Thomas) Philip Barber, DSO, TD (son of late Thomas Barber, of Lamb Close, Greasley, Notts), was Hon Col S Notts Hussars Yeo, High Sheriff of Notts 1907, a Councillor of Notts Co Council 1898-1925, and Alderman 1925-61 (Chm 1931-45), and Pro-Chancellor of Nottingham Univ 1955-61.

BARBOUR (UK) 1943, of Hilden, co Antrim (Extinct 1951)

Right Hon Sir JOHN MILNE BARBOUR, 1st and last *Baronet.*

DAUGHTER LIVING OF FIRST BARONET

Elizabeth Law Milne, *b* 1910: *m* 1st, 1941, Hugh Chapman MacLean, who *d* 1945; 2ndly, 1954, Robin Young Paton, MB, FRCS, who *d* 1974. *Residences* – Gorse Hill Manor, Gorse Hill Rd, Virginia Water, Surrey; 9 Astell St, SW3.

BARCLAY (NS) 1668, of Pierston, Ayrshire

The cross of Christ is our crown

Sir COLVILLE HERBERT SANFORD BARCLAY, 14th *Baronet*, el son of late Rt Hon Sir Colville Adrian de Rune Barclay, KCMG, 3rd son of 11th baronet; *b* 7 May 1913; *s* his uncle, *Sir* ROBERT CECIL DE BELZIM, 1930; *ed* Eton, and Trin Coll, Oxford (BA 1935, MA 1946); was a 3rd Sec in Diplo Ser 1938-41; European War 1939-45 as Lieut-Com RNVR: *m* 1949, Rosamond Grant Renton, da of late Dr Walter Armstrong Elliott, and has issue.

𝕬rms – Azure, a chevron between three crosses patée or. 𝕮rest – A sword erect proper, hilted and pommelled or.
Residence – 23 High St, Broughton, Stockbridge, Hants SO20 8AE.

SONS LIVING

ROBERT COLRAINE (Av Lineu de P. Machado 1005/COB, Jardim Botanico, 22470-040 Rio de Janeiro, Brazil), *b* 12 Feb 1950; *ed* Eton, and E Anglia Univ; FCA: *m* 1980 (*m diss* 1986), Lucília, da of Carlos Saboia de Albuquerque, of Ipanema, Rio de Janeiro, Brazil and has issue living Henry William Saboia, *b* 16 Jan 1982, — Caroline Saboia, *b* 1983. —— Alistair James Elliott, *b* 1952. —— (Colville) Edwin Ward (Watts Farm, River Lane, Watersfield, Pulborough, W Sussex RH20 1NG), *b* 1956; *ed* Charterhouse, and Aberdeen Univ: *m* 1992, Fiona M., da of late Robin Bell, of Coopers Green, Uckfield, Sussex, and has issue living, Frederick Colville Beresford *b* 1993.

BROTHERS LIVING

Cecil Edward Sanford (44 Church St, Eye, Suffolk IP23 7BD) *b* 1914: *ed* Eton, and Magdalen Coll, Oxford (BA): *m* 1st, 1939 (*m diss* 1957), Yvonne Eleanor Mutch, who *d* 1995, da of Sir William Edward Leonard Shenton; 2ndly 1958, Marcia Isobel Mary, da of late John Horatio Macoun, and has issue living, (by 2nd *m*) Melanie Sarita, *b* 1958: *m* 1985, Roger William Stephen Hale, and has issue living, John William Sanford *b* 1988, Harriet Sarita *b* 1989, Isobel Helena *b* 1996. —— Robert Charles Sanford (Green Bank South, Grundisburgh, nr Woodbridge, Suffolk IP13 6TD), *b* 1918; *ed* Eton, and Magdalen Coll, Oxford, formerly Maj Intelligence Corps; a JP, and a Chevalier of Legion of Honour; Croix de Guerre: *m* 1st, 1941 (*m diss* 1964), Camilla, who *d* 1997, da of Sir George Menteth Boughey, 9th Bt, CBE; 2ndly, 1964, Alice Molly, who *d* 1985, da of late Sydney Blackman, and has issue living (by 1st *m*) Peter John (8 Broomhill Rd, SW18), *b* 1941: *m* 1964 (*m diss* 1973), Angela Mary, da of Harold Francis Blackborow, and has issue living, Alasdair James *b* 1968, Piers David *b* 1972, — Michael George (Frostland Farm, Newchurch, Romney Marsh, Kent), *b* 1945: *m* 1973, Susan, da of James Thompson, and has issue living, Philippa *b* 1973, Sacha *b* 1976, — Jonathan Robert (The Old Vicarage, Stoke Holy Cross, Norwich, NR14 8AB), *b* 1947: *m* 1969, Clare Amabel, da of late Capt Philip Cecil Langdon Yorke, OBE, RN (*see* E Hardwicke, colls), and has issue living, Timothy Robert *b* 1984, Emily Rose *b* 1976, — Christopher Richard (29 Bicester Rd, Richmond, Surrey), *b* 1949: *m* 1986, Linda Anne, da of Joseph Redshaw, and has issue living, Leonora Sophie *b* 1989, Chloe Imogen *b* 1989.

COLLATERAL BRANCHES LIVING

Granddaughter of late William Malo de Rune Barclay (*b* 1871, *d* 1917), 3rd son of William Malo de Rune Barclay (infra):—
Issue of late Leslie William Hamilton de Rune Barclay, MBE, *b* 1899, *d* 1983: *m* 1927, Mabel Dobson Freene:—
Beverley Lesley Lorraine (2 Danmark Court, Buderim, Queensland 4556, Australia), *b* 1936; *ed* Sydney Church of England Gram Sch for Girls.

Granddaughter of late William Malo de Rune Barclay, 3rd son of 10th baronet:—
Issue of late Aubrey Henri de Rune Barclay, *b* 1880, *d* 1950: *m* 1903, Alice Anne, who *d* 1969, el da of Sir Edward Osborne Gibbes, 3rd Bt:—
Betty Theodosia: *m* 1936, Russell Gellatly, of 3 Harbour St, Wollongong 2500, NSW, and has issue living, Peter Russell, *b* 1947: *m* 1967, Marilyn Fay, el da of Peter Fletcher, of Dural, NSW, — Susan Alice (50 Grace Av, French's Forest, NSW), *b* 1939: *m* 1961, Roy Lancaster Lucena, who *d* 1975, and has issue living, Peter Blair Lancaster *b* 1964, Karen Jane *b* 1962, Belinda Maree *b* 1969.

Grandchildren of Frederick Arthur d'Epinay Barclay, 4th son of late William Malo de Rune Barclay (ante):—
Issue of late William Cradock de Rune Barclay, NZ Forces, *b* 1906, *d* 1992: *m* 1943, Frances Berenice Aplin:—
Elizabeth Beauchamp, *b* 1945: *m* 1967, Anthony Leatherbarrow, of 14B Stephen St, Upper Hutt, NZ, and has issue living, Clifford Beau, *b* 1975, — Catherine Anne, *b* 1972.

Issue of late Capt Beauchamp d'Epinay Barclay, RAMC, *b* 1911; *ka* Hong Kong 1941: *m* 1935, Margaret Katharine (who *m* 2ndly, 1945, Ian Rutherford, of 38 Michie Street, Roslyn, Dunedin, New Zealand), da of late James Begg, of Dunedin, New Zealand:—
James Fergus (Cruachan, RD1 Miller's Flat, Central Otago, NZ), *b* 1940: *m* 1964, Sally Elizabeth, da of Hugh Stuart Fleming, MB, ChB, of Hove, Sussex, and has issue living, Andrew James, *b* 1967, — Hamish Beauchamp, *b* 1969, — Fiona Jane, *b* 1972. —— Margaret Elizabeth, *b* 1936: *m* 1958, John Michael Gibbs, MB, ChB, FFARCS, FFARACS, of 150 Hackthorne Rd, Christchurch 2, NZ, and has issue living, David Douglas, *b* 1966, — Margaret Jennifer, *b* 1959, — Hilary Eva, *b* 1961, — Helen Dorothy, *b* 1970. —— Frances Beauchamp, *b* 1938: *m* 1966, Robert Campbell, MICE, MIStructE, of 3 Over Place, Knutsford, Ches WA16 8NN, and has issue living, James Robert, *b* 1968, — Alastair John, *b* 1969, — Margaret Elizabeth, *b* 1966.

Issue of late Capt Leslie George de Rune Barclay, son of late Henry Torrens de Rune Barclay, 4th son of 10th baronet, *b* 1870, *d* 1965: *m* 1926, Dorothea, who *d* 1971, el da of Rev Charles Herbert Griffith:—
Ninian de Rune (111 St Helens Rd, Hastings, E Sussex), *b* 1927: *m* 1971, Aileen Margaret, who *d* 1987, el da of late Maj Hayes, and has issue living, Robert David, *b* 1972, — Anna Marie, *b* 1974. —— Michael George (4539 Donald Av, San Diego, Cal 92117, USA), *b* 1932, late RAF: *m* 1953, Agnes Joy, yr da of A. Batehup, of Northiam, Sussex, and has issue living, Wendy Margaret, *b* 1954, — Beverley Ann, *b* 1959.

The ancestors of this family were of distinction in Ayrshire in the 12th century. The 8th baronet, who had been officially employed on the Continent, fell into the hands of the French, 1798. He was closely confined in the Temple, and twice tried by a Military Commission on account of a mission he was supposed to have filled at the Hague 1796-8. He was each time acquitted, and in November 1799 was released and sent by cartel to England by the special order of Bonaparte.

BARING (UK) 1911, of Nubia House, Northwood, Isle of Wight

By uprightness and labour

Rosalind Mary Blanche, *b* 1986.

Sir JOHN FRANCIS BARING, 3rd *Baronet*, 2nd son of late Capt Raymond Alexander Baring, yr son of 1st baronet; *b* 21 May 1947; *s* his uncle, *Maj Sir* CHARLES CHRISTIAN, 1990; *ed* Eton, RAC Cirencester, and LSE: *m* 1971, Elizabeth, yr da of late Robert David Henle Pillitz, of Juramento 3437, Buenos Aires, Argentina, and has issue.

Arms – Azure, a fesse or, in chief a bear's head couped proper, muzzled and ringed of the second. **Crest** – A mullet erminois, two of the points resting on the pinions of a pair of wings conjoined and elevated argent.
Residence – 89 June Rd, N Salem, New York, NY 10560-0322, USA.

SONS LIVING

JULIAN ALEXANDER DAVID, *b* 10 Feb 1975. —— James Francis, *b* 1984.

DAUGHTER LIVING

Andrea Hermione, *b* 1977.

BROTHER LIVING

(Andrew) Michael (Godfrey) (Ravenscourt House, Ravenscourt Park, W6), *b* 1949; *ed* Eton, and — Coll, Oxford: *m* 1976, Anstice Mary Blanche, da of late Alfred George Cardale, of Newbury, Berks, and has issue living, Alexander Francis, *b* 1978, — Edward George, *b* 1980, — Andrew Thomas, *b* 1983, —

SISTER LIVING

Ann Hermione, *b* 1941; *ed* Southampton Univ (PhD 1990), Fellow St Hilda's Coll, Oxford 1994: *m* 1963, Alistair John Buchanan, of Hill Barn, Gt Bedwyn, Marlborough, Wilts, son of John James Buchanan, of 67 Chester Sq, SW3, and has issue living, Catherine Anne Louise, *b* 1965, — Teresa Margaret, *b* 1967: *m* 1995, Vladko Fras, elder son of late V. Fras, of Zagreb, Croatia, — Helen Hermione, *b* 1973.

COLLATERAL BRANCH LIVING

Granddaughters of late Capt Raymond Alexander Baring, yr son of 1st baronet:—
Issue of late Charles Peter Baring, *b* 1909, *d* 1987: *m* 1st, 1964 (*m diss* 1974), Sarah, yr da of late Lt-Col William Gill Withycombe, of Providence House, Sutton, Thirsk, N Yorks; 2ndly, 1976, Susannah Jane (31 Grantley St, Shelton, Shrewsbury SY3 5LA), da of Dr William Ezra Smith, of Bashaw, Alberta, Canada:—
(By 1st *m*) Arabella, *b* 1965. —— Henrietta, *b* 1966. —— (By 2nd *m*) Gabriella Louise, *b* 1977. —— Olivia, *b* 1980.

Sir Godfrey Baring, KBE, 1st Bt, son of late Lieut-Gen Charles Baring (*see* B Northbrook, colls), was Chm of co Council for Isle of Wight, an Alderman of London co Council 1920-22, Parliamentary Private Sec (unpaid) to Under-Sec of State for the Colonies 1908, and to Pres of Board of Education 1911, and sat as MP for Isle of Wight (*L*) 1906-1910, and N-W or Barnstaple Div of Devonshire 1911-18. Major Sir Charles Christian, 2nd Bt, JP, DL, was a Member of Cttee of Management of Board of Visitors, HM Prison, Parkhurst.

BARLOW (UK) 1803, of Fort William, Bengal

Love peace

First of all things be thou pious

Sir CHRISTOPHER HILARO BARLOW, 7th *Baronet*; *b* 1 Dec 1929; *s* his father, *Wing-Com Sir* RICHARD HUGH, AFC, RAF, 1946; *ed* Eton, and McGill Univ, Montreal (BArch): *m* 1952, Jacqueline Claire de Marigny, el da of John Edmund Audley, of Chester, and has issue.

𝖆rms – Argent, on a chevron engrailed gules between three cross-crosslets fitchée azure, two lions passant counter-passant supporting an eastern crown or, in chief between the two cross-crosslets a branch of olive and another of palm in saltire proper. 𝕮rest – Out of an eastern crown or a demi-lion argent, the paws supporting a cross-crosslet as in the arms, issuing from the crown on the dexter side of the lion a branch of olive and on the sinister another of palm both proper. 𝖘upporters – On either side an angel proper, vested argent, zoned and on the head an eastern crown or; the dexter holding in the exterior hand a balance or, and in the other a book proper, the sinister bearing in the exterior hand an olive branch, and in the other an escroll proper.
Residence – 18 Winter Av, St John's, Newfoundland, Canada A1A 1T3.

SON LIVING

CRISPIAN JOHN EDMUND AUDLEY, *b* 20 April 1958; sometime Inspector R Hong Kong Police: *m* 1981, Anne Wai Ching Siu, and has issue living, Jennifer Claire Audley, *b* 1990. *Residence* – 22 Milford Rd, Plumstead, Cape Town 7800, S Africa.

DAUGHTERS LIVING

Persephone Claire, *b* 1953: *m* 1975, Robert Eric Booth, of The Timbers, Church Rd, Kettleburgh, Woodbridge, Suffolk IP13 7LE, and has issue living, Katherine Claire, *b* 1982, — Sophie Elizabeth Barlow, *b* 1986. —— Caroline Claire, *b* 1960: *m* 1986, James Cass Jordan, of 11813 Silent Valley Lane, Gaithersburg, Maryland, USA.

BROTHERS LIVING

David Peter, *b* 1931; *ed* Eton, and Peterhouse, Camb: *m* 1958, Mary June Emmerton, of Victoria, British Columbia, and has issue living, Peter Stephen, *b* 1961, — Richard Owen, *b* 1963, — Rosemary Sylvia Mary, *b* 1968. *Residence* – 1335 Franklin Terr, Victoria, BC, V8S 1C8. —— Anthony Donald (33 Cleevelands Drive, Cheltenham, Glos GL50 4QD), *b* 1935; *ed* Stowe: *m* 1st, 1962 (*m diss* 1972), Ginette Burki, of Courrendlin, Switzerland; 2ndly, 1973, Patricia Jennifer Bond, of Geneva, Switzerland, and has issue living (by 2nd wife), Nicholas Hugh, *b* 1973.

SISTER LIVING

Lucinda Mary, *b* 1941: *m* 1962, Edward James Chubb, of Blackbird Cottage, Woodside Lane, King's Stanley, Stonehouse, Glos, and has issue living, Richard John, *b* 1963, — William Maurice (Rosetree Cottage, 1 Nelmes Rd, London Rd, Charlton Kings, Glos GL5 2YX), *b* 1969: *m* 1996, Sarah Louise Jeffery.

WIDOW LIVING OF SIXTH BARONET

Rosamund Sylvia de la Fontain, da of late Francis Swithin Braithwaite Anderton: *m* 1st, 1928, Wing-Com Sir Richard Hugh Barlow, 6th Bt, AFC, RAF, who *d* 1946; 2ndly, 1950, Rev Leonard Haslett Morrison, MA, Bar-at-law, who *d* 1985. *Residence* – Laurel Cottage, Parracombe, Barnstaple, N Devon EX31 4QQ.

Sir George Hilaro Barlow, GCB, the 1st baronet, was a Member of the Council of Bengal, Provisional Governor-General of India 1805-7, and Governor of Madras 1807-13. The 2nd baronet was a Judge of the Supreme Court of Calcutta. Sir Morison, the 3rd baronet, who was in the 7th Hussars and 9th Lancers, served during the Indian Mutiny (medal with clasp for Lucknow). The 4th baronet, Sir Richard, was a Member of the Legislative Council of Madras and Chm of Madras Harbour Trust. The 5th baronet, Col Sir Hilaro William Wellesley, CB, CMG, was 11 years Sup of Roy Laboratory, Woolwich, SE, and was subsequently in Min of Munitions. The 6th baronet, Wing-Com Sir Richard Hugh, AFC, served in European War 1939-45 (AFC).

BARLOW (UK) 1902, of Wimpole Street, St Marylebone, co London

I will renew my youth like the eagle

Sir THOMAS ERASMUS BARLOW, DSC, RN, 3rd *Baronet*; *b* 23 Jan 1914; *s* his father, *Sir* (JAMES) ALAN (NOEL), GCB, KBE, 1968; *ed* Winchester; Hon DLitt Sussex 1997; Capt RN (ret); 1939-45 War (DSC); DL Bucks 1976: *m* 1955, Isabel, da of late Thomas Munn Body, MRCS, LRCP, of Middlesbrough, and has issue.

Arms – Argent, on a pile sable between two torches erect in base fired proper, an eagle displayed with two heads of the field. Crest – In front of a staff erect entwined by a serpent proper, an eagle's neck erased with two heads argent, thereon a rose gules.
Residence – 45 Shepherds Hill, N6 5QJ. *Clubs* – Athenaeum, Savile.

SONS LIVING

JAMES ALAN *b* 10 July, 1956, *ed* Highgate, and Manchester Univ (BSc); metallurgist. —— Philip Thomas, *b* 1960.

DAUGHTERS LIVING

Monica Ann *b* 1958. —— Teresa Mary, *b* 1963.

BROTHERS LIVING

Erasmus Darwin (Elbrook House, Ashwell, Baldock, Herts), *b* 1915; *ed* Marlborough, and Trin Coll, Camb (MA, MB, BChir); MRCS England, LRCP London; DPM; FRC Psych; late Sen Lecturer and Consultant in Psychiatry, St Thomas's Hosp; a Dir of Group Investors, Ltd; Dir CIC Investment Holdings Ltd; Chm Bath Inst of Medical Engineering from 1975: *m* 1938, Brigit Ursula Hope, da of late Ladbroke Black, and has issue living, Thomae Jeremy Erasmus (20 Leverton St, NW5 2PI), *b* 1939; MA, ARCM: *m* 1962 (*m diss* 1994), Jane, da of Bernard Hollowood, and has issue living, Josiah Bernard *b* 1973, and three adopted children, Mark Thomas Duncan *b* 1967, Thomas Daniel *b* 1972, Deborah Marian Susan *b* 1970, — Camilla Ruth, *b* 1942: *m* 1st, 1965 (*m diss* 1973), Martin Christopher Mitcheson, MB, BChir, DPM; 2ndly, 1974, (Stuart) Anthony Whitworth-Jones, Dir-Gen Glyndebourne Festival Opera, of 81 St Augustine's Rd, NW1 9RR, and has issue living, (by 1st *m*) Luke Thomas *b* 1966, Amy Brigit *b* 1967, (by 2nd *m*) Eleanor Gwen *b* 1975, — (Gillian) Phyllida, *b* 1944; Head of Sculpture, Slade Sch of Fine Art: *m* 1966, Fabian Peake, son of late Mervyn Peake, the writer, and has issue living, Edward *b* 1981, Lewis *b* 1981 (twin), Florence *b* 1973, Clover *b* 1975, Tabitha *b* 1978. —— Andrew Dalmahoy, *b* 1916; *ed* Eastbourne Coll, and Trin Coll, Camb (MA, MB and BChir); MRCP, London: *m* 1951, Yvonne Tanner, and has issue living, Martin Thomas, *b* 1953, — Claire, *b* 1954. *Residence* – 10 Wimpole St, W1M 7AB. —— Horace Basil, FRS (Trin Coll, Camb), *b* 1921; *ed* Winchester, Trin Coll, Camb (MB and BCir) and Harvard Univ, USA (MD); Fellow of Trin Coll, Camb, 1950-54, of King's Coll, Camb 1954-64, and Prof of Physiology, Berkeley Univ, Calif, USA 1964-73, since when Prof of Physiology, Camb Univ: *m* 1st, 1954 (*m diss* 1970), Ruth Chattie, da of Dr Myer Salaman, 2ndly, 1980, Elisabeth Miranda, da of J. Weston Smith, of Hampstead, and has issue living, (by 1st *m*) Rebecca Nora, *b* 1956, — Natasha Helen, *b* 1958, — Naomi Jane, *b* 1962, — Emily Anne, *b* 1967, — (by 2nd *m*) Oscar Hugh, *b* 1986, — Ida Lucy, *b* 1988, — Pepita Elisabeth, *b* 1990.

SISTER LIVING

Hilda Horatia, *b* 1919: *m* 1944, John Hunter Padel, BA, MB, BS, DPM, and has issue living, Oliver James, *b* 1948, — Felix John, *b* 1955, — Adam Frederick, *b* 1958, — Ruth Sophia, *b* 1946, — Nicola Mary, *b* 1951. *Residence* – 16 Staverton Rd, Oxford, OX2 6XJ.

COLLATERAL BRANCHES LIVING

Granchildren of late Sir Thomas Dalmahoy Barlow, GBE (infra):—
Issue of late Basil Stephen Barlow, *b* 1918, *d* 1991: *m* 1st, 1940 (*m diss* 1950), Harriette Alice, da of late His Honour Judge (Robert) Peel, OBE, KC (*see* Worsley-Taylor, Bt (ext)) 2ndly, 1950, Gerda Theresia Zaar Ferrari da Grado (Stancombe Park, Dursley, Glos), da of late Prof Dr Zaar, of Graz, Austria:—
(By 2nd *m*) Nicholas Dalmahoy, *b* 1951; *ed* Eton. —— Maria-Theresa BARLOW, *b* 1953; has resumed her maiden name: *m* 1977 (*m diss* 1996), Martin William Llewellyn, and has issue living, Harry Owen, *b* 1982, — Thomas Edge, *b* 1986. —— (Esther) Alexandra, *b* 1956: *m* 1998, Matthew Manning.

Issue of late Sir Thomas Dalmahoy Barlow, GBE, 2nd son of 1st baronet, *b* 1883, *d* 1964: *m* 1911, Esther Sophia, JP, who *d* 1956, da of Henry Gaselee:—
Theodora Gertrude (Flat 76, Hurlingham Court, Ranelagh Gdns, SW6), *b* 1912: *m* 1936 (*m diss* 1951), Carl Winter, who *d* 1966, and has issue living, Robert Stephen, *b* 1939, — John Barlow, *b* 1944, — Caroline Helen, *b* 1942.

The 1st baronet, Sir Thomas Barlow, KCVO, MD, FRCP, FRS (son of late James Barlow, JP, of Greenthorne, Edgworth), Physician Extraor to Victoria 1899-1901, Edward VII and George V, Physician to the Households of Queen Victoria 1897-1901 and King Edward VII, 1901-10 and George V 1910-36. The 2nd Bt Sir (James) Alan Noel Barlow, GCB, KBE, was 2nd Sec to Treasury 1942, and Chm of Nat Gallery 1948-55. He donated his collections of Persian pottery to the Ashmolean 1953, and Chinese porcelain to Univ of Sussex 1967.

BARLOW (UK) 1907, of Bradwall Hall, Sandbach, co Chester

QUI·NON·PROFICIT DEFICIT

Sir JOHN KEMP BARLOW, 3rd *Baronet*; *b* 22 April 1934; *s* his father, *Sir* JOHN DENMAN, 1986; *ed* Winchester, and Trin Coll, Camb (BA 1956); Chm Thomas Barlow & Bro Ltd, and Majedie Investment plc: *m* 1st, 1962 (*m diss* 1998), Susan, elder da of late Col Sir Andrew Marshal Horsbrugh-Porter, 3rd Bt, DSO; 2ndly, 1998, Mrs Pauline Windsor, da of Richard Meyrick Bancroft, and has issue by 1st *m*.

Arms – Per pale ermine and gules, three chevrons counter-changed, over all two lions combatant or. Crest – A lion sejant affrontée or holding erect in the forepaws a cross-crosslet fitchee gules.
Clubs – Brooks's, Jockey, City of London.

SONS LIVING

(JOHN) WILLIAM MARSHALL (Herbert House, Warfield, Berks RG42 6EE), *b* 12 March 1964; *ed* Eton, and Liverpool Univ: *m* 1991, Sarah Hilary, da of John Nobes, of Windsor, Berks, and has issue living, John William Oakley, *b* 4 April 1993, — Henry James Marshall, *b* 1995. —— (Thomas) David Bradwall (Moat Manor, Kingston Blount, Oxon OX9 4RZ), *b* (Jan) 1966; *ed* Eton, and Manchester Univ: *m* 1993, Melissa Emily, only da of Anthony Andrew Ward Kimpton, of Tarrington, Herefords (*see* B Hazlerigg, 1990 Edn), and has issue living, Thomas Arthur Sinnott, *b* 1998, — Olivia Emily, *b* 1996. —— (Andrew) Michael Kemp, *b* (Dec) 1966; *ed* Harrow: *m* 1997, Veronica Mary, yr da of Andrew Robert Fowell Buxton (*see* Buxton, Bt; colls). —— Charles James Bulkeley, *b* 1970: *m* 1998, Michelle C., da of Michael Tory, of Hemsworth, Witchampton, Dorset.

BROTHERS LIVING

George Bradwall (Bradwall Manor, Sandbach, Ches), *b* 1938; *ed* Radley: *m* 1967, Daphne Anne, da of Henry R. Birtwistle, of Gt Dudland, Sawley, Clitheroe, Lancs, and has issue living, Jeremy George Read, *b* 1968: *m* 1995, Miranda J., yst da of Gerald Parton, of Duddon, Cheshire, and has issue living, William George Read *b* 1996, Antonia Jane Ascroft *b* 1998, — Edward Bradwall, *b* 1972, — Deborah Jane Kemp, *b* 1970: *m* 1994, John G. McD. Simpson, of Huxley Lane Farm, Huxley, Chester, elder son of Nigel Simpson, of Tockington, Bristol, and has issue living, Lucy Victoria Kemp *b* 1997. —— Mark Henry Denman (Waldridge Manor, Stockwell Lane, Meadle, Aylesbury) *b* (twin) 1938; *ed* Radley: *m* 1968, Rosemary Alexandra, da of late J. Alan Bell, of Anglesey, and has issue living, Andrew Mark Egerton, *b* 1972: *m* 1997, Sarah L., yst da of Ray Chambers, of Wettenhall, Ches, — Camilla Frances, *b* 1970: *m* 1994, Alexander J. Wakeley, elder son of Martin Wakeley, and has issue living, Benjamin John Denman *b* 1998.

SISTER LIVING

Jennifer Beatrice, *b* 1932; has issue living, Sacha Jane Anna, *b* 1971; *ed* Yehudi Menuhin Sch, and USC Los Angeles. *Residence* – Flat 3, 9 Kensington Park Gdns, W11.

COLLATERAL BRANCH LIVING

Issue of late Thomas Bradwall Barlow, yr son of 1st baronet, *b* 1900, *d* 1988: *m* 1943, Elizabeth Margaret, who *d* 1988, da of late Hon Bertrand Sackville-West (*see* B Sackville):—
Henry Sackville, OBE (PO Box 10139, 50704 Kuala Lumpur, Malaysia), *b* 1944; *ed* Eton, and Trin Coll, Camb (MA); FCA; OBE 1989. —— Anna Elizabeth (Thornby House, Northampton), *b* 1949.

The first baronet, Sir John Emmott, was senior partner in the firms of Thomas Barlow and Brother of London and Manchester, and Barlow and Co of Calcutta, Shanghai, Singapore, and Kuala Lumpur (Federated Malay States), and sat as MP for Frome Div of Somerset (*L*) 1892-5, and 1896 to 1918.

BARNEWALL (I) 1623, of Crickstown Castle, Meath

Sir REGINALD ROBERT BARNEWALL, 13th *Baronet*; *b* 1 Oct 1924; *s* his father, *Sir* REGINALD JOHN, 1961 *ed* Xavier Coll, Melbourne; 1939-45 War with Royal Australian Engineers AIF in S-W Pacific: *m* 1st, 1946, Elsie Muriel, who *d* 1962, da of Thomas Matthews Frederick, of Brisbane, Queensland; 2ndly, 1962, Maureen Ellen, da of William Daly, of S Caulfield, Victoria, and has issue by 1st and 2nd *m*.

Arms – Ermine, a bordure engrailed gules. **Crest** – From a plume of five ostrich feathers, or, gules, azure, vert, and argent, a falcon rising of the last. *Residence* – Innisfree House, Normandie Court, Mount Tamborine, Queensland 4272, Australia.

SONS LIVING (*By 2nd marriage*)

PETER JOSEPH, *b* 26 Oct 1963; *ed* St Joseph's Coll, Nudgee, and Queensland Univ (B Agric Sc Econ); Lieut 2nd/14th Light Horse QMI, Royal Australian Armoured Corps, since 1982: *m* 1988, Kathryn Jane, da of Hugh Carroll, of Brisbane, Queensland, and has issue living, Christopher Patrick, *b* 3 June 1995, Richard Joseph, *b* 1997, — Jessica Rose, *b* 1992. *Residence* – 26 Tirrabella St, Carina Heights, Queensland 4152, Australia.

DAUGHTERS LIVING (*By 1st marriage*)

Mary Catherine, *b* 1947: *m* 1979, Peter Lynch, of Toowoomba, Queensland. — Frances Patricia, *b* 1948: *m* 1969, Michael Curley, of Brisbane, Queensland. — Margaret Anne, *b* 1952.

I had rather die than be disgraced

COLLATERAL BRANCHES LIVING

Granchildren of late Arthur Walter Aylmer Barnewall (infra):—
Issue of late Alfred Reginald Barnewall, *b* 1921, *d* 1979: *m* 1950, Daisy Mabel, da of late Charles Newman:—
Graeme David, *b* 1957: *m* 1987, Lindy Jean, da of James Donaldson, and has issue living, Samantha Kate, *b* 1994. *Residence* – 20 Lachlan Court, Sunbury, Victoria 3429, Australia. — Ronald William, *b* 1960: *m* 1986, Susan Jennifer, da of Raymond Welsford. *Residence* – 1 Wootton Court, Melton South, Victoria 3338, Australia. — Michael James, *b* 1962: *m* 1988, Glenda Michelle, da of Michael Condon. *Residence* – 2 Bishop Place, W Melton, Victoria 3337, Australia, and has issue living, Jessica Kate, *b* 1990, — Sarah Jane, *b* 1992. — Kaye Lorraine, *b* 1951. — Margaret Anne, *b* 1953. — Sandra Maree, *b* 1970.

Issue of late Arthur Walter Aylmer Barnewall, 2nd son of 11th baronet, *b* 1890, *d* 1961: *m* 1921, Hilda, da of Thomas Triffit:—
John Robert (50 Anderson St, Euroa, Victoria 3666, Australia), *b* 1922: *m* 1950, Joan Catherine, da of.late Shadrack Allen, and has issue living, John Robert, *b* 1952: *m* 1981, Jennifer Hooper, and has issue living, Ann Louise *b* 1986, Laura Mary *b* 1989, — Kieran Gerard, *b* 1958. — Anthony Brian, *b* 1960. — Mark Raymond, *b* 1961. — Eileen Mary, *b* 1951, — Catherine Frances, *b* 1955, — Clare Therese, *b* 1970. — Henry Marcus Joseph (56 Elizabeth Drive, Rosebud, Victoria 3939, Australia), *b* 1924: *m* 1976, Barbara Ruth Mary, da of late Reginald Lindsley, and widow of John Douglas Bayes. — Kevin Arthur (3 Rosamond Cres, Doncaster E. Victoria 3109, Australia) , *b* 1925: *m* 1949, Marjorie Joyce, da of Charles Body, and has had issue, Ross David, *b* 1950: *m* 1973, Dianne Robyn (17 Landale Av, Croydon, Vic 3136), da of Victor Jordan (formerly Vitto Giordano), and *d* 1989, leaving issue, David Mathew *b* 1973, Daniel Leigh *b* 1976, Benjamin Scott *b* 1978, — Murray Charles (Hennessy St, Port Campbell, Vic 3269), *b* 1954: *m* 1976, Lesley Christine, da of Ronald O'Brien, and has issue living, Brooke *b* 1978, Lisa *b* 1979, — Kevin Bruce, *b* 1956, — Dianne Maree, *b* 1952: *m* 1970, Michael John Primmer, of 4 Morrison St, Colac, Vic 3250, son of Roy Charles Primmer, and has issue living, Michael John *b* 1976, Matthew Scott *b* (twin) 1976, Leanne Maree *b* 1971 Jacqueline Louise *b* 1972, — Debra Michelle, *b* 1962: *m* 1984, Robert James Phibbs, of 15 Olympus Drive, Croydon, Vic 3136, son of Mervyn John Phibbs, and has issue living, Cody James *b* 1990, Loran Michelle *b* 1988. — Patrick Thomas (74 Yuillc St, Frankston, Victoria 3199, Australia), *b* 1928: *m* 1947, Mavis Leone, da of Charles Cooper, and has had issue, Dennis John, *b* 1948; RAN, served Vietnam War with HMAS *Brisbane*; *d* 1971, — Suzanne Elizabeth, *b* and *d* 1952, — Annette Lynne, *b* 1954: *m* 1973, Wayne Peterson, and has issue living, Dennis Norman *b* 1980, Amanda Patricia *b* 1976.

Granddaughter of late Alfred George Barnewall (infra):—
Issue of late Patrick Joseph Barnewall, JP, *b* 1915, *d* 1980: *m* 1949, Daphne Mavis (c/o Postmaster, Tootool, NSW, Australia), da of Charles Turner Lockhart:—
Naomi Patricia, *b* 1955.

Issue of late Alfred George Barnewall, half-brother of 11th baronet, *b* 1880, *d* 1952: *m* 1915, Sarah, da of J. Footter, of Violet Town, Victoria, Australia:—
John Robert, *b* 1917: *m* 1946, Marietza Elizabeth, da of Henry James O'Rourke, of Tullamore, NSW, and has issue living, John Jeffrey, *b* 1951: *m* 1976, Frances Erica, da of Eric Ernest Virieux, of Glen Garry, Tasmania, and has issue living, Ricky John *b* 1984, Tammie Elizabeth *b* 1980, Alison Louise *b* 1983, — Marietza Anne, *b* 1947, — Linda Mary, *b* 1955, — Dorothea Laree, *b* 1959. *Residence* – 52 Glenrae Terrace, Urangan, Queensland 4655, Australia — Francis Richard, *b* 1922; 1939-45 War with AIF in SW Pacific: *m* 1951, Margaret Mary, da of L. Lyons, of Euchuca, Victoria, Australia, and has issue living, Brian Francis, *b* 1956: *m* 1981, Judith Diane, da of late Thomas Bowland, of Whitemark, Flinders Island, Tasmania, and has issue living, Holly Renae *b* 1985, Rhianna Kate *b* 1987, — Kerry Teresa, *b* 1952, — Dianne Margaret, *b* 1953. *Residence* – Whitemark, Flinders Island, Tasmania. — Terrence James (53 Seignior St, Junee, NSW 2663, Australia), *b* 1935: *m* 1st, 1957, Laurene, da of Robert Smith, of Junee; 2ndly, 1978, Marie Patricia, da of Fredric Davies, of Sydney, and formerly wife of John Layton, and has issue living, (by 1st *m*) Judith Margaret, *b* 1959: *m* 1st, 1979, Warren Wright; 2ndly, 1995, Mark Reginald Small, and has issue living (by 1st *m*), Daniel Leigh *b* 1981, Nathan Warren *b* 1983, (by 2nd husband), Zachary Terrence, *b* 1991, — Teena Merrie, *b* 1965; Nurse, Canberra ACT.

Descendants of Robert Barnewall, who settled in America 1840, and Benjamin, who went to Australia (uncles of 11th baronet), and Samuel Barnewall and William Barnewall (great-uncles of 11th baronet), who both emigrated to America.

This family, the name of which was originally de Berneval, is of great antiquity. Sir Michael de Berneval, who landed on the coast of Cork before 1170, was the first of the family who settled in Ireland. The 2nd baronet suffered severely during the Cromwellian usurpation; and of the extensive possessions then wrested from him, he obtained, after the re-establishment of the monarchy, only his castle and 2000 acres of land. The 3rd baronet was MP for Meath 1689-90. Sir George, 4th Bt (a descendant of the 2nd son of the 1st Bt), established his right to this title in 1744; his cousin, Thomas, however, did not assume it, and it remained dormant from 1790 until 1821, when the succession of Sir Robert, 8th Bt, was registered at the Ulster Office, Dublin.

BARRAN (UK) 1895, of Chapel Allerton Hall, Chapel Allerton, West Riding of co York, and of Queen's Gate, St Mary Abbots, Kensington, co London

The love of country

Sir JOHN NAPOLEON RUTHVEN BARRAN, 4th *Baronet: b 14 Feb 1934; s his father,* Sir JOHN LEIGHTON, 1974; in remainder to Lordship of Ruthven of Freeland; *ed* Winchester; late Lt 5th R Inniskilling Dragoon Gds; served British High Commission Ottawa 1964-67; Head of Videotex Services, COI: *m* 1965, Jane Margaret, da of late Sir Stanley George Hooker, CBE, of Orchard Hill, Milbury Heath, Wotton-under-Edge (*see* B Bradbury, 1985 Edn), and has issue.

ᷓrms – Per saltire gules and sable, a bear passant or, muzzled of the second, between two mascles palewise of the third. ᷓrest – In front of a tower gules charged with three mascles intertwined palewise, a lion's jamb fessewise erased or. *Residences* – 17 St Leonard's Terr, SW3; The Hermitage, East Bergholt, Suffolk.

SON LIVING

JOHN RUTHVEN, *b* 10 Nov 1971.

DAUGHTER LIVING

Susannah Margaret, *b* 1981.

UNCLE LIVING (*Son of 2nd baronet*)

Sir David Haven, *b* 1912; *ed* Winchester, and Trin Coll, Camb (BA); Pres, Asiatic Petroleum Corpn (NY) 1958-61; Chm of Shell Transport and Trading Co Ltd 1966-72, Midland and International Banks, Midland Bank 1980-82, *cr* Knt 1971: *m* 1944, Jane Lechmere, da of late Nicholas Lechmere Cunningham Macaskie, QC, and has had issue, †Tristram Cosmo, *b* 1945: *m* 1973, Miranda Clare (The 'oldall, Brent Eleigh, Sudbury, Suffolk CO10 9NP), yst da of Maj Sir Robert Crichton Mitchell Cotts, 3rd Bt, and *d* 1992 in a motor accident, leaving issue, Ferdinand Roc *b* 1974, Giuseppe Maria *b* 1978, Petra Sely *b* 1975, — Julian Mark Lechmere (Welham Farm, Shepton Montague, Castle Cary, Som), *b* 1947: *m* 1st, 1970, Mary, da of Sir Edward Wilder Playfair, KCB; 2ndly, 1986, Diana, da of late Cosmo de Bosdari, and has issue living (by 1st *m*), Leo David *b* 1973, Laurence Edward *b* 1977, Tabitha Jane *b* 1972, (by 2nd *m*) Cosmo Ralph *b* 1990, Milo Xavier *b* 1996, Hugh Sebastian *b* (twin) 1996, Emily Dolores *b* 1988, — Marius Peregrine Lechmere (64 St Marks Rd, W10 6NN), *b* 1949: *m* 1972, Veronica Teresa, da of Prof Alphonsus Ligouri d'Abreu, CBE, of Ford House, Coughton, Alcester, Warwicks (Throckmorton, Bt), and has issue living, Perdita Elizabeth *b* 1972, Lorna Marina *b* 1974, Phoebe Alice *b* 1981, Amy Louise *b* 1984, — Adrian Stuart Lechmere, *b* 1959, — Jane Francesca, *b* 1950: *m* 1980, Philip Anthony Francis Scoones, of 199 Goldhawk Rd, W12, only son of Dr Francis Scoones, of Abbotsbury Rd, W14, and has issue living, Benedict Boniface Nicholas *b* 1983, Eleanor Jane *b* 1981, — Lalage Margarita, *b* 1957: *m* 1996, Stephen J. Reeve-Tucker, 4th son of late Lt-Col T. S. W. Reeve-Tucker, of Perrystone Towers, Ross-on-Wye, and has issue living, Scarlett Grace Haven *b* 1998, — Calista Maria Lechmere, *b* 1960: *m* 1986, William Walrond Lucy, of 10 Grace's Rd, SE5, only son of Maj D.P.V. Lucy, of The Chantry, Ilminster, Som, and has issue living, Tancred Edmund Walrond *b* 1992, Laetitia Alice Haven *b* 1989. *Residences* – 36 Kensington Sq, W8 5HP; Brent Eleigh Hall, Sudbury, Suffolk CO10 9NP. *Club* – River (New York).

COLLATERAL BRANCHES LIVING

Issue of late Edward Nicholson Barran, 2nd son of 2nd baronet, *b* 1910, *d* 1994: *m* 1st, 1940 (*m diss* 1953), Daphne Margaret, who *d* 1987, only da of late Herbert William Bird, of Norther, Cranleigh, Surrey; 2ndly, 1955, Patricia Helen (Ackworth Grange, Pontefract, W Yorks), eldest da of late Alexander Granville Blake, ICS, of Kennilworth Cottage, Ascot, Berks:—
(By 1st *m*) Nicholas Dudley Edward (17046 Parthenia, North Ridge, CA 91325-3216, USA), *b* 1942; *ed* Harrow, and Univ of Calif (BSc 1967): *m* 1964, Feliksa, da of Feliks Pabilionis, of Omaha, Nebraska, and previously of Kaunas, Lithuania, and has issue living, Antony Nicholas, *b* 1967, — Daniel Nicholas, *b* 1968. —— Stephen William Edward (37 Parklands Rd, SW16), *b* 1954; *ed* Winchester, and Trin Coll, Camb. —— Alice Daphne Margarita, *b* 1946: *m* 1975, Giovanni-Battista Luigi Dalle Nogare, of 16 Prospect Rd, Bulleen, Victoria 3105, Australia, and has issue living, Adriano Gino, *b* 1977, — Damiano Edward, *b* 1979. —— (By 2nd *m*) Charles Patrick Edward (Sunnyside, 47 Hathill Rd, Blackheath, NSW 2785, Australia), *b* 1955: *m* 19—, Deborah, da of Robert Henville. —— Frances Margarita, *b* 1958: *m* 1979, John de Moraville,

of Frethorne House, Wantage, Oxon, and has issue living, George Maximilian, *b* 1985, — Henry John, *b* 1987, — Edward Humphrey, *b* 1989.

Grandchildren of late Philip Austyn Barran (infra):—
Issue of late Arthur Haworth Barran, *b* 1911, *d* 1991: *m* 1945, Rosa, da of late John Russell Greenwood, of The Oval, Tranmere Park, Guiseley, Yorks:—
Jonathan Haworth (13 Tumene Drive, Owhata, Rotorua, NZ), *b* 1946; *ed* Badingham Coll: *m* 1973, Lindsey Margaret, da of late Clifford Bruce Ward, and has issue living, Alastair Haworth, *b* 1973, — Rachael Louise, *b* 1976. —— Helen Margaret, *b* 1949; *d* 1953. —— (Elizabeth) Claire, *b* 1954: *m* 1977, David George Glendinning, who *d* 1992, and has issue living, Richard David Peter, *b* 1981, — Hamish Donald, *b* 1986, — Thomas John, *b* 1990, — Sophie Rosa, *b* 1984.

Issue of late Philip Austyn Barran, yr brother of 2nd baronet, *b* 1876, *d* 1953: *m* 1908, Dorothy Currer, who *d* 1956, only da of late Arthur Currer Briggs, of Leeds:—
Donald Austyn Nicholson, MB, BChir, MRCS, LRCP, FRSM, *b* 1922; *ed* Repton, and Trin Coll, Camb (MB and BChir, MA); FFARCS and FRSM. *Residence* - 3 Gt Western Terr, Glasgow, W2. —— Dorothy Stella Margaret, *b* 1919: *m* 1943, Joseph William Sloan Allison, CA, and has issue living, Joseph Philip Sloan (4 Raeburn St, Edinburgh 4), *b* 1944: *m* 1976, Caroline Margaret, da of late James Roxburgh Paton, of Gullane, and has issue living, James Austyn Sloan *b* 1978, Gerard Joseph Roxburgh *b* 1982, Peter William Donald *b* 1987, Catherine Margaret Elaine *b* 1980, — Judith Stella Elaine, *b* 1948: *m* 1968, Cdr Simon Hugh Stone, RN, of 120 Divinity Rd, Oxford, and has issue living, Charlotte Anne *b* 1972, Harriet Jane *b* 1974, — Dorothy Lucy Louise, *b* 1951. *Residence* - The Cottage, Longbarn, Cardross, Dunbartonshire.

Grandchildren of late Alfred Barran, 4th son of 1st baronet:—
Issue of late Richard Wharton Barran, *b* 1905, *d* 1961: *m* 1936, Marie Eileen, who *d* 1995, da of late George Crabbe, of Ceylon:—
Valerie Anne Heather, *b* 1941: *m* 1977, Malcolm Gordon Chase, FCA (Byways, 12 Kent Rd, Fleet, Hants GU13 9AH), and has issue living, Jennifer Marianne Alison, *b* 1978, — Sarah Elizabeth Lucy, *b* 1979.

Issue of late George Fletcher Barran, MB, BCh, *b* 1908, *d* 1983: *m* 1936, Clare Mary Elizabeth, who *d* 1998, da of Albert Dudley, of London:—
George Wharton (Rose Farm, East Ruston, Norfolk), *b* 1939; *ed* Douai Sch: *m* 1st, 1967, Sue Russell; 2ndly, 1984, Sally Elizabeth, da of David Charles Jeffcott Mansfield, of Suffolk, and has issue living, (by 1st *m*) Nicholas George, *b* 1968, — (by 2nd *m*) George Arthur Mansfield, *b* 1985, — Elizabeth Margery, *b* 1986. —— Richard Martin, *b* 1941; *ed* Douai Sch. —— Hugh Paull (1 Church Walk, N Petherton, Som TA6 6SE), *b* 1943; *ed* Douai Sch: *m* 1973, Anthea Janet, da of late Rowland W. Baker-Beall, of Beer, Devon, and has issue living, Rowland Paull, *b* 1974, — Alice Matilda, *b* 1978. —— Rosemary Clare, *b* 1947: *m* 1974, Capt Rae Tugwell, RA, and has issue living, David Alexander Barran, *b* 1978, — Laura Clare, *b* 1976.

Granddaughters of late Henry Barran, 5th son of 1st baronet:—
Issue of late Henry Vernon Flower Barran, *b* 1894, *d* 1943: *m* 1921, Cicely, who *d* 1985, da of late Vice-Adm Francis Wade Caulfeild, CBE (*see* V Charlemont, colls):—
Mary Rosalie, *b* 1922: *m* 1963, Antony Giles Heron, of Bank House, Glaisdale, Whitby, Yorks. —— Elfrida Cicely, *b* 1929: *m* 1957, Martin Bennett Cordeaux, of 15 Lee Rd, Lincoln LN2 4BJ, and has issue living, Charles Nicholas (136 Victoria Av, Kingston-upon-Hull), *b* 1958: *m* 1987, Margaret Elizabeth, da of William M. A. Davidson, of Hopeman, Elgin, Moray, and has issue living, Michael Robert *b* 1992, Heather Claire *b* 1988, — Elizabeth Katharine, *b* 1961, — Cicely Jane, *b* 1964. —— Selina Elizabeth, *b* 1934: *m* 1960, Michael Stanley Makower, of Gogar House, Blairlogie, by Stirling (*see* V Chetwynd, colls). —— Christabel Lucy, *b* 1939.

Grandchildren of late Sir Rowland (Hirst) Barran, 6th son of 1st baronet:—
Issue of late Capt Hugh Bradley Barran, MC, *b* 1889, *d* 1975: *m* 1917, Estelle, da of late Frank Lockhart Cox, of 85 Cadogan Gdns, SW3:—
Hugh Rowland Murray (Robin) (Hildenley, Malton, Yorks), *b* 1929: *m* 1957, Diana Buttercup, da of late Eric Geoffrey Dawnay (*see* V Downe, colls), and has issue living, Patrick Robin, *b* 1959: *m* 1989, Miranda Jane, da of Christopher John Spence, of Chieveley Manor, Newbury, Berks (*see* Ropner, Bt, *cr* 1952), and has issue living, Hugo Jeremy *b* 1993, Daisy Charlotte *b* 1991, Camilla Violet *b* 1997, — Nicholas Eric Hugh (Lodge Cottage, Barton-le-Willows, York YO6 7PD), *b* 1964: *m* 1990, Emma Louise Moya, only da of Robert George Gee (*see* E Shrewsbury, colls), and has issue living, Toby Nicholas Hugh *b* 1991, Hebe Elisabeth Blair *b* 1993, — Annabelle Clare, *b* 1960: *m* 1989, Edward B. McMullan, of 16 Acfold St, SW6 2AL son of Alan McMullan, of Fixby, Huddersfield, W Yorks, and has issue living, Alexander William Hugh *b* 1991, James Guy Harry *b* 1996, Poppy Victoria Ines *b* 1992, — Verena April, *b* 1968: *m* 1993, William A. Ritson, son of Capt Tim W. Ritson, of Ebnal Grange, Malpas, Cheshire, and has issue living, Harry William *b* 1997, Alice India Emma *b* 1995. —— Jean Lockhart, *b* 1919. —— Elspeth Estelle, *b* 1921. —— Ann Lockhart, *b* 1930: *m* 1950, Maj John Francis Leetham Robinson, MC, 12th R Lancers, of The Normans, Bilbrough, York, and has issue living, Hugh Andrew Leetham (Sandwith Lodge, Bilbrough, York), *b* 1955: *m* 1st, 1980 (*m diss* 19—), Amanda Jane Menage; 2ndly, 1997, Fiona Bell, and has issue living (by 1st *m*), Oliver Leetham *b* 1981, Georgina *b* 198-, — Marion Lockhart (*Hon Mrs Michael Bourne*), *b* 1951: *m* 1985, Hon Michael Kemp Bourne, of 50 Bradbourne St, Fulham, SW6, son of late Baron Bourne, GCB, KBE, CMG (Life Baron), — Caroline Mary, *b* 1957: *m* 1987, John Edwards, of 26 Summerfield Av, Queens Park, NW6, and has issue living, Thomas *b* 1991, Kate *b* 1990, — Joanna Susan, *b* 1961: *m* 1982, Capt Martin James Butterfield Drake, Duke of Wellington's Regt, of 98 The Mount, York, and has issue living, James *b* 1988, Lucie *b* 1985.

The 1st baronet, Sir John Barran, who was founder of the firm of John Barran and Sons merchants, of Leeds, sat as MP for Leeds (*L*) 1876-85, and for Yorkshire, W Riding, E Part Otley Div 1886-95. The 2nd baronet, Sir John Nicholson Barran, was Parliamentary Private Sec to Rt Hon H. H. Asquith MP, and sat as MP for Hawick Dist (*L*) 1909-18.

Barrett-Lennard, see Lennard.

BARRINGTON (UK) 1831, of Limerick.

The same while I live

Sir ALEXANDER FITZWILLIAM CROKER BARRINGTON, 7th *Baronet; b* 19 Nov 1909; *s* his brother, *Sir* CHARLES BACON, 1980; *ed* Shrewsbury and Ch Ch Oxford; served 1939-45 War as Capt (Japanese POW); Publisher.

Arms – Argent, three chevronels gules and a label of three points vert, on a canton of the second, a trefoil slipped or. Crest – Out of a crown vallery or a hermit's bust with a cowl vested paly argent and gules.
Residence – Rush Court, Shillingford Rd, Wallingford, Oxon OX10 8LL.

DAUGHTERS LIVING OF SIXTH BARONET

Victoria Elizabeth Josephine, *b* 1940. —— (Diana) Mary-Rose BARRINGTON, *b* 1946; resumed her maiden name: *m* 1968 (*m diss* 1998), Thomas Manuel, and has issue living, Jessica Barrington, *b* 1977.

COLLATERAL BRANCHES LIVING

Grandchildren of late John Frederick Barrington, DSO, yst son of late Col Joseph Thomas Barrington, elder son of Daniel Barrington, 2nd son of 1st baronet:—
Issue of late Major John William Barrington, *b* 1917, *d* 1999: *m* 1st, 1949, Annie, who *d* 1985, da of Florian Wetten, of Coire, Switzerland; 2ndly, 1986, Evelyn Carol Paterson (PO Box 894, Invermere, BC, Canada V0A 1K0), da of late Oscar Broten, of Oslo, Norway:—
(By 1st *m*) BENJAMIN (44 Cherovan Drive SW, Calgary, Alberta, Canada T2P 2P1), *b* 23 Jan 1950: *m* 1980, Carola Christel Mogck, and has issue living, Patrick Benjamin, *b* 1988, — Marisa Christel, *b* 1982. —— Reto, *b* 1953: *m* 1976, Shelley Ann Lapham, and has issue living, Lauren Anne, *b* 1984, — Amy, *b* 1986. —— Annette (No 708, 3130 66th Av SW, Calgary, Alberta, Canada T3E 5K8), *b* 1951: *m* 1984 (*m diss* 1995), David Clinkett, and has issue living, Nicole, *b* 1985, — Claire, *b* 1987.

Issue of late Major Peter Malet Barrington, MC, TD, *b* 1920, *d* 1999: *m* 1945, Joan Warren (Thorn Cottage, The Green, Chiddingfold, Godalming, Surrey GU13 4TU), da of Col Guy Warren Meade, DSO, MC:—
Charles Peter (The Lodge, Great Bealings, nr Woodbridge, Suffolk IP13 6NW), *b* 1946; *ed* Wellington Coll; ACA 1970: *m* 1969, Ann Elizabeth, da of Harold Bertram Foster, and has issue living, Elizabeth Ann (13 Sinclair Rd, W14 0NS), *b* 1973. —— Michael, *b* 1951.

Grandchildren of late Richard Irving Williams Barrington, son of late Capt Richard Williams Barrington, HEICS, yr son of Daniel Barrington (ante):—
Issue of late Major Laurence Hew Williams Barrington, *b* 1928, *d* 1998: *m* 1st, 1950 (*m diss* 1968), (Patricia) Anne Isabella, da of Ralph Whitson; 2ndly, 1968, Merle Aurelia (Church End House, Great Rollright, Chipping Norton, Oxon), da of Sir Leonard Ropner, 1st Bt, MC, TD (*cr* 1952), and formerly wife of Christopher John Spence:—
(By 1st *m*) Rupert Hew Williams (Dillay Farm, Bisley, Stroud, Glos), *b* 1963: *m* 1991, (Ann) Olivia, elder da of Nicholas Ronald Nutting (*see* Nutting, Bt, colls), and has issue living, Dominic Hew Williams, *b* 1994, — Edward Alexander, *b* 1997. —— Serena Henrietta Williams, *b* 1956: *m* 1977, Adrian Michael Campbell Underwood, of 757 Wandsworth Rd, SW8, and has issue living, Charles Edward Thomas, *b* 1982, — Katherine Anne, *b* 1984. —— (By 2nd *m*) Shaun Richard Williams *b* 1969.

This family claims to be descended from Odo du Barentin, who came to England with the Conqueror. Fifteenth in descent from Odo, who received grants of land in Essex, and became custodian of Hatfield forest, was Sir Francis Barrington, of Barrington Hall, Essex, created a baronet, 1611. This title became extinct, upon the death of the 10th baronet, in 1833; but prior thereto (1831) a baronetcy had been conferred upon a yr branch, Sir Joseph Barrington, of Limerick, who, with his sons, founded the Limerick Hospital and Infirmary, an institution incorporated by Act of Parliament.

BARROW (UK) 1835, of Ulverstone, Lancashire

Little suffices

Sir RICHARD JOHN UNIACKE BARROW, 6th *Baronet; b* 2 Aug 1933; *s* his father, *Major Sir* WILFRID JOHN WILSON CROKER, 1960; *ed* Beaumont; Capt (ret) Irish Gds; joined Internat Computers and Tabulators, Ltd 1960: *m* 1961 (*m diss* 1974), Alison Kate, yr da of late Capt Russell Grenfell, RN (ret), and has issue.

ẞrms – Sable, two swords in saltire points upwards argent, pommels and hilts or between three fleurs-de-lis, one in chief and two in flanche, an anchor erect in base of the last. Crest – On a mount vert a squirrel sejant cracking a nut all proper, charged on the shoulder with an anchor.

SON LIVING

ANTHONY JOHN GRENFELL, *b* 24 May 1962; *ed* Dulwich, and Edinburgh Univ (MA): *m* 1990 (*m diss* 1996), Rebecca Mary Long; has issue living, Bryony Helen Ann Lambert, *b* 1996. *Residence* – 73 Chase Side, Enfield EN2 6NL.

DAUGHTERS LIVING

Nony Mary Louise, *b* 1963: *m* 1992, Simon Alastair Hugh Kerr-Smiley, of North Lodge, Preston Candover, Hants RG25 2EN, and has issue (*see* Smiley, Bt, colls). —— Frances Teresa Catherine, *b* 1971.

SISTERS LIVING

Rosamond Mary Geraldine, *b* 1927: *m* 1956, George Myles Sterling, and has issue living, Myles Patrick, *b* 1958, —— Andrew David, *b* 1963, —— Natalie Rosamond *b* 1960. *Residence* – Castletown, Coolbawn, Nenagh, co Tipperary. —— Ann Patricia, *b* 1951 (*m diss* 1960), Maj Anthony Richard Carr, and has issue living, Julian Anthony Robie, *b* 1955. *Residence* – Fellover, St Breward, nr Bodmin, Cornwall. —— Angela Mary Philippa, *b* 1940: *m* 1968, Geoffrey Swaine, who *d* 1991, and has issue living, Jonathon David, *b* 1971, —— Mary Angela, *b* 1972. *Residence* – 9 Oaktree Close, Ealing, W5.

AUNT LIVING (*Daughter of 4th baronet*)

Mildred Mary Winifred, *b* 1901: *m* 1st, 1922, Edward Stanhope Benbow Rowe, who *d* 1941; 2ndly, 1949, Gerard Dun, and has issue living, (by 1st *m*) John, *b* 1930, —— Anthony, *b* 1934, —— Ursula, *b* 1923, —— Joscelyn, *b* 1925. *Residence* – Wellington Terrace Home for Senior Citizens, PO Box 7070, Elora, Ontario, Canada N0B 1F0.

COLLATERAL BRANCHES LIVING

Issue of late Alfred Francis Lendon Barrow, 3rd son of 4th baronet, *b* 1904, *d* 1989: *m* 1933, Ruth (13 The Lindens, Gt Austins, Farnham, Surrey GU9 8LA), only da of William Sydney Milsum:—
John Lendon (31 Lingfield Av, Torkington Park, Hazel Grove, Cheshire), *b* 1934. *m* 1961, Maureen Ann, da of Alfred Stanley Gover, and has issue living, Paul Lendon, *b* 1966, —— Nicola Mary, *b* 1963. —— Anthony Francis (Street Farm, Tilford, Surrey), *b* 1937: *m* 1962, Alexa, da of Raleigh Ashlin Skelton, and has issue living, Kevin Mark, *b* 1963, —— Katharine Laura, *b* 1965. —— Simon William (Oratory School, Woodcote, Reading, Berks), *b* 1942: *m* 1977, Brenda Cora, da of Dermot Ernest Kelly, and has issue living, Julian Alexander Dermot, *b* 1981, —— Jennifer Ann, *b* 1979. —— Susanne Mary, *b* 1946: *m* 1st, 1972 (*m diss* 1983), Patrick Hugh Walker-Taylor; 2ndly, 1987, Charles D'Arcy, of Norreys, Heath Lane, Crondall, Farnham, Surrey, and has issue living, (by 1st *m*) Timothy Patrick, *b* 1974, —— Alice Mary, *b* 1976, —— Sally Anne, *b* 1981. —— Catherine Ruth, *b* 1950: *m* 1976, Christopher John Price, of 9 Tilney Close, Alton, Hants, and has issue living, Robert Christopher, *b* 1981, —— Sarah Kate, *b* 1978.

Issue of late Edward Joseph Merriman Barrow, 4th son of 4th baronet, *b* 1912, *d* 1988: *m* 1938, Mary Ellen (12 West Hermitage, Belle View, Shrewsbury, Shropshire), da of John William Allen, of Shrewsbury:—
Timothy John, *b* 1946; BVSC; MRCVS: *m* 1969, Fiona, da of Eric Lord, of Croydon, Surrey. —— Diana Margaret (5 Thurston Close, Grestun Manor, Abingdon, Oxon OX14 5RD), *b* 1938: *m* 1st, 1963 (*m diss* 1979), Peter McConnell; 2ndly, 1980, Geoffrey Lindsay Clarke, ACIOB, who *d* 1998, and has issue living (by 1st *m*), Simon John (34 Anna Pavlova Close, Abingdon, Oxon OX14 1TE), *b* 1969: *m* 1995, Pippa Hardy, and has issue living, Laura *b* 1998, —— Julie Mary, *b* 1967: *m* 1987, William Alexander Humphries, of 56 Hermitage Rd, Abingdon, Oxon OX14 5RP, and has issue living, Edward Simon Alexander *b* 1992, Emma Diana Lindsay *b* 1988, —— Sarah Frances, *b* 1971. —— Marylin Elizabeth Emily, *b* 1944: *m* 1970, John Richard Butler, FSVA, of Rope Walk Cottage, Lyth Hill, Shrewsbury, and has issue living, Jane Mary, *b* 1972.

The 1st baronet, Sir John Barrow, for many years Secretary to the Admiralty, and Founder of the Royal Geographical Society, was highly distinguished as an author, a traveller, and a meritorious public servant, to whose memory a monumental tower, 100 feet high, was erected by public subscription on the Hoad Hill, Ulverston, his birthplace. The 2nd baronet was Chief Clerk at the Colonial Office and Secretary and Registrar of the Order of St Michael and St George, of which he was a Companion. The 3rd baronet, Sir John Croker Barrow, was a Bar-at-Law of Lincoln's Inn, and a JP for Kent. The 4th baronet, Sir Francis Laurence John Barrow, was an architect and ornithologist

BARRY (UK) 1899, of St Leonard's Hill, Clewer, Berks, and Keiss Castle Wick, Caithness-shire

Sir (LAURENCE) EDWARD ANTHONY TRESS BARRY, 5th *Baronet*; *b* 1 Nov 1939; *s* his father, *Maj Sir* RUPERT RODNEY FRANCIS TRESS, MBE, 1977; *ed* Haileybury; Capt Grenadier Guards 1958-64; Lord of the Manors of Ockwells and Lillibrooke, Berks, and Baron de Barry of Portugal: *m* 1st, 1968 (*m diss* 1991), Fenella, da of Mrs Hilda Hoult of Knutsford, Cheshire; 2ndly, 1992, Elizabeth Jill, da of Geoffery Bradley, of Fishtoft, Boston, and has issue by 1st *m*.

Arms – Azure, two lions passant guardant or.
Residence – 4 The Gables, Argos Hill, Rotherfield, E Sussex TN6 3QJ.

SON LIVING (*By 1st marriage*)

WILLIAM RUPERT PHILIP TRESS, *b* 13 Dec 1973.

DAUGHTER LIVING (*By 1st marriage*)

Alexandra Diana Frances Louise, *b* 1977.

HALF-BROTHERS LIVING

Timothy Rupert Francis Tress (Le Carroi de Bonchamp, 37240 Ligueil, Indre et Loire, France), *b* 1952, late Capt RMP: *m* 1977, Valerie, yst da of Mrs M. D. M. Reid, of Otterburn, Northumberland, and has issue living, Victoria Louise Frances Tress, *b* 1982, — Georgina Alicia Frances Tress, *b* 1985, — Henrietta Elizabeth Frances Tress, *b* 1990. —— Nicholas Mark Francis Tress (The Kennels, Lenacre St, Eastwell, Ashford, Kent), *b* 1957: *m* 1985, Fiona Mary, yr da of late John Rankin, QC, of Prospect House, Boughton, Faversham, Kent, and has issue living, Lucy Arabella Francis Tress, *b* 1987, — Katharine Rose Francis Tress, *b* 1989. —— Jonathan Rodney Francis Tress, *b* 1960.

SISTER LIVING

Amorel Madeleine Frances Tress, *b* 1936: *m* 1959, Maj Peter Miles Lambert, Gren Gds (*see* D Wellington, colls, 1995 Edn), and has issue living, Peter Tobin, *b* 1966, — Annabel Madeleine Jane, *b* 1960: *m* 1992, Jonathan Reinier Manuel, of 64 Ridgway Place, Wimbledon, SW19, and has issue living, Olivia Victoria Greta *b* 1993, Venetia Elizabeth Emily *b* 1995, — Miranda Caroline Tress, *b* 1962. *Residence* – Half Moon House, Rectory St, Halesworth, Suffolk IP19 8AF.

HALF-SISTERS LIVING

Tara Caroline Frances Tress, *b* 1954: *m* 1977, (Fokko) Peter Anthony Kortlang, of The Duck Farm Cottage, Sandy Hurst Lane, Ashford, Kent, and has issue living, Piers Anthony Fokko Tress, *b* 1978, — Christian Rupert Fokko Tress, *b* 1988, — Lavinia Cordelia Frances Tress, *b* 1982, — Venetia Sophia Frances Tress, *b* 1984. —— Xandra Georgina Frances Tress, *b* 1962: *m* 1996, Maj Simon J. Cox, RA, elder son of J. C. Cox, of Burrington, Devon.

AUNT LIVING (*Daughter of 3rd baronet*)

Sheila Yvonne Elizabeth Doris, *b* 1915: *m* 1941, Col John Loftus Carter, RM (M Ely, colls), of 56 The High St, Charing, nr Ashford, Kent, and has issue living, Brian Loftus, OBE (13 Testcombe Rd, Alverstoke, Gosport, Hants), *b* 1945; Col RM; OBE 1989: *m* 1st, 1969 (*m diss* 1971), Caroline Jane Halsey; 2ndly, 1973, Eva Jorunn Berglund, of Horten, Norway, and has issue living, (by 1st *m*) Andrew Charles Loftus *b* 1971, (by 2nd *m*) Anneli Victoria Solveig *b* 1980, — Sally Elizabeth, *b* 1943: *m* 1970, David William Mearns Gow (The Oak House, Church Lane, Aldington, Kent), and has issue living, William Hugh Mearns *b* 1971, Amanda Elizabeth Mearns *b* 1973.

GREAT-AUNT LIVING (*Daughter of 2nd baronet*)

Margaret Colquhoun (Abbey Mews, Amesbury, Wilts), *b* 1894; 1914-18 War in VAD Jan 1917 to Dec 1918 (two medals): *m* 1919, Capt James Clifton Colquhoun, MBE, formerly Highland LI, and has issue living, James Barry, *b* 1931, — William Baliol, *b* 1934, — Elizabeth, *b* 1924, — Margaret, *b* 1927.

WIDOW LIVING OF FOURTH BARONET

SHEILA GEORGINA VERONICA (*Sheila, Lady Barry*) (Brisley Rise, Willesborough Lees, Ashford, Kent), da of late Maj George Joseph Francis White, MBE, of Ashford, Kent: *m* 1951, as his 2nd wife, Maj Sir Rupert Rodney Francis Tress Barry, 4th Bt, MBE, who *d* 1977.

COLLATERAL BRANCHES LIVING

Grandchildren of late William James Barry (infra):—
Issue of late Lt-Col Gerald Barry, MC, *b* 1896, *d* 1977: *m* 1923, Lady Margaret Pleydell-Bouverie, da of 6th Earl of Radnor:—
Richard John (Hampton Fields, nr Cirencester, Glos), *b* 1938: *m* 1965, Jillian Frances, da of Lt-Col A. L. Novis, MC, of Fryern House, Storrington, Sussex, and has issue living, James Tress, *b* 1967, — Anthony Gerald, *b* 1969, — Bridget Margaret, *b* 1973. —— Anne (*Marchioness of Aberdeen and Temair*), *b* 1924: *m* 1950, 6th Marquess of Aberdeen and Temair. —— Diana, *b* 1927: *m* 1st, 1951 (*m diss* 1959), Kenneth Robert Motion; 2ndly, 1959 (*m diss* 1984), Nathaniel Edward Carwardine Sherwood, who *d* 1998, and has issue living, (by 1st *m*) Richard Peter (Badcocks, Easthorpe, Colchester, Essex), *b* 1954: *m* 1983, Jacqueline Mary, da of Michael Huson Morris, and has issue living, Jake Robert *b* 1986, Alice Victoria *b* 1985, Rosie Elizabeth *b* 1993, — Sarah, *b* 1955: *m* 1st, 1980 (*m diss* 1984), Guy Patrick Hemsley Smith; 2ndly, 1993, John Stuart Edwards, of 62a Brightwell Crescent, SW17 9AE, and has issue living (by 2nd husband), Georgie Arabella *b* 1992, Jessie Harriet *b* 1994, — (by 2nd *m*) David Gerald, *b* 1960. —— Patricia Helen, *b* 1932: *m* 1958, Peregrine Michael Hungerford Pollen (*see* Pollen Bt colls). —— Gillian Margaret, *b* 1934: *m* 1953 (*m diss* 1964), Edward Alexander Martin, and *d* 1972, leaving issue, Alexander, *b* 1956, — Margaret, *b* 1957: *m* 1995 (Timothy) James Sainsbury, elder son of Rt Hon Sir Timothy Alan Davan Sainsbury, and has issue (*see* B Sainsbury), — Helena, *b* 1960: *m* 1993, Peter N. D. Barrowcliff, son of Dr Derek F. Barrowcliff, of Warwick, and has issue living, Alexander John Peter *b* 1996, Arthur Digby Marmaduke *b* 1998, Matilda Margaret *b* 1994, — Georgina, *b* 1961: *m* 19—, Ben Lutyens, and has issue living, Emily *b* 19—, Katie *b* 19—. —— Pamela Rosemary, *b* (twin) 1938: *m* 1966, Colin Vyvyan Peterson, of Balldown Farmhouse, Sparsholt, Hants, son of late Sir Maurice Drummond Peterson, GCMG, and has issue living, Andrew Drummond, *b* 1967, — Thomas Richard, *b* 1970, — Helen Margaret, *b* 1969, — Alice Diana, *b* 1974.

Issue of late Cmdr Hubert Wyndham Barry, RN (ret), *b* 1898, *d* 1992: *m* 1936, Violet Agatha, who *d* 1994, da of Sir Edward Archibald Ruggles-Brise, 1st Bt, MC, TD, MP:—
William Edward (12 Kensington Park Mews, W11; Malhouse Farmhouse, Manningford Abbots, Pewsey, Wilts), *b* 1938; *ed* Eton, and Trin Coll, Camb: *m* 1965, Juliet Alexandra Sarah, da of James Herbert Lonsdale Musker (*see* E Lauderdale, colls), and has issue living, Catherine Jane, *b* 1968; *ed* St Paul's Girls' Sch, Durham Univ (MSc), and Imperial Coll (MSc). —— James Hubert, *b* 1947; *ed* Eton. —— Rosemary, *b* 1939: *m* 1963, Alastair Pinckard Leslie, TD, late Capt RSF (*see* E Rothes). —— Susan (*Baroness Glenarthur*), *b* 1945: *m* 1969, 4th Baron Glenarthur.

Issue of late William James Barry, 4th son of 1st baronet, *b* 1864, *d* 1952, *m* 1896, Lady Grace Murray, MBE, who *d* 1960, da of 7th Earl of Dunmore:—
Nancy Elizabeth, *b* 1910: *m* 1935, (George) Nigel Capel Cure, TD, DL, JP, and has issue living, (George) Ronald (Blake Hall, Ongar, Essex), *b* 1936: *m* 1st, 1968, Caroline, who *d* 1986, only da of Giles Yarnton Mills, of Puys sur Dieppe, France; 2ndly, 1995, Mrs Isabella Margaret Ruth Doble, da of late Col William Henry Whitbread, TD, and has issue living (by 1st *m*), three sons, — Michael, *b* 1947, — Sarah Virginia (*Hon Mrs Thomas R. Lindsay*), *b* 1938: *m* 1961, Hon Thomas Richard Lindsay, of The Old Rectory, Ashmore, Salisbury, Wilts SP5 5AG (*see* E Crawford). *Residence* – Ashlings, Moreton Rd, Ongar, Essex.

Issue of late Col Stanley Leonard Barry, CMG, CBE, DSO, MVO, late 10th Hussars, 5th son of 1st baronet, *b* 1873, *d* 1943: *m* 1st, 1906, Hannah Mary, who *d* 1924, el da of James Hainsworth, of 34 Phillimore Gardens, W8, and formerly wife of Col W. MacGeorge, 6th Dragoon Guards; 2ndly, 1927, Laline Annette, who *d* 1969, da of late William Harvey Astell, JP, DL (sometime Lt Grenadier Guards), of Woodbury Hall, Sandy, Beds, and widow of Lt-Col Arthur Preston Hohler, DSO (V Gort):—
(By 1st *m*) Jeanne Irene (*Hon Mrs James A. G. McDonnell*), *b* 1915: *m* 1939, Hon James Angus Grey McDonnell (*see* E Antrim). *Residences* – Hoebridge Cottage, Balls Cross, Petworth, Sussex; 36 Farley Court, Melbury Rd, W14.

The 1st baronet, Sir Francis Tress Barry, was descended from Richard Barry, of Eynsham, Oxon, temp 1476, and the family arms were recorded by Lawrence Barry, of Hampton Gay Manor, Oxon, at the Visitations of Oxfordshire in 1566 and 1574, identical with those recorded for Sir Robert Barry, of Stanton Barry, Bucks, temp Edward I; Sir Francis was *cr* Baron de Barry in Portugal 1876, sat as MP for Windsor (C) 1890-1906, and was Consul-Gen in Great Britain for Ecuador. The 2nd baronet, Sir Edward Arthur Barry, was High Sheriff of Berks in 1907, and Lieut-Col Berks Yeo.

BARTLETT (UK) 1913, of Hardington-Mandeville, Somerset

With fortitude and fidelity

Sir ANDREW ALAN BARTLETT, 5th *Baronet; b* 26 May 1973; *s* his father, *Sir* JOHN HARDINGTON DAVID, 1998.

Arms – Argent, two barrulets dancettée between in chief two cinquefoils and in base a crescent issuant therefrom a cross formée fitchée, all azure. Crest – A demi eagle displayed azure, winged or, supporting with the beak a pennon of the first, charged with the arms.
Residence – Hardington House, Ermyn Way, Leatherhead, Surrey KT22 8TN.

BROTHER LIVING

STEPHEN MARK, 5 July 1975.

HALF-SISTER LIVING (*daughter of 4th baronet by 1st marriage*)

Nichola Jane, *b* 1969: *m* 1995, Robert Mack, of 104 Swan Lane, Whetstone, N20, and has issue living, Zoe Catherina, *b* 1999.

UNCLES LIVING

Simon Hardington (Cobweb Cottage, 23 Lower Town, Sampford Peverell, Devon EX16 7BJ), *b* 1940; *ed* St Peter's, Guildford: *m* 1967 (*m diss* 1972), Antoinette Lois, da of Gaston Charpentier, and has issue living, Rebecca Rosamund, *b* 1969. —— Christopher Mandeville (1 Redlands Bank Cottages, Mid Holmwood, Dorking, Surrey RH5 4ES), *b* 1942; *ed* St Peter's, Guildford: *m* 1966, Brenda June, da of Eric Thorne, of Beech Cottage, Coneyhurst Lane, Ewhurst, Surrey, and has issue living, Paul David *b* 1968; *ed* —, — Sarah Jane, *b* 1972.

DAUGHTERS LIVING OF SECOND BARONET

Julia Jane, *b* 1937: *m* 1966, John Atkinson, and has had issue, Thomasina Kate, *b* 1967: *m* 1998, Simon Nicholas Brown, — Teresa Mary, *b* 1968, — Cressida Jane Elizabeth, *b* 1971; *d* 1994. *Residence* – 12 Brookside, Cambridge CB2 1JE. —— Lucy Mary le Breton, *b* 1941: *m* 1969, as his 2nd wife, Adrian Alexander Bridgewater (*see* B Vivian, 1985 Edn), and has issue living, Benjamin Hardington, *b* 1979, — Nancy le Breton, *b* 1971: *m* 1999, Richard J. F. Batty, yr son of Peter Batty, of Kingston, Surrey, — Daisy Maud, *b* 1973. *Residence* – Manor Farm, Gt Eversden, Cambs. —— Annabel Kate, *b* 1945: *m* 1988, as his 2nd wife, Anthony David McCall, and has issue living, Hardington Alexander William, *b* 1988. *Residence* – 214 West 17th St, Apt PHC, New York, NY 10011-5347, USA.

WIDOW LIVING OF THIRD BARONET

JEANNE MARGARET ESTHER (*Jeanne, Lady Bartlett*), da of Charles William Brewer, of St John's Wood: *m* 1982, as his 3rd wife, Lt-Col Sir (Henry) David Hardington Bartlett, 3rd Bt, who *d* 1989. *Residence* – Brockley Place, Brockley, Bury St Edmunds, Suffolk IP29 4AG.

WIDOW LIVING OF FOURTH BARONET

ELIZABETH JOYCE (*Lady Bartlett*), da of late George Thomas Raine, of Kingston-upon-Thames, Surrey: *m* 1971, as his 2nd wife, Sir John Hardington David Bartlett, 4th Bt, who *d* 1998. *Residence* – Hardington House, Ermyn Way, Leatherhead, Surrey KT22 8TN.

COLLATERAL BRANCHES LIVING

Issue of late Eric Oscar Bartlett, 4th son of 1st baronet, *b* 1882, *d* 1968: *m* 1907, Irene, who *d* 19—, da of late Lawrence Alport, of 100 Lexham Gdns, W.:—
Mary Augusta, *b* 1911: *m* 1st, 1934, Fl-Lt Roy James Oliphant Bartlett, RAF, who *d* 1936; 2ndly, 1941, Group Capt James Douglas Ferrier Bruce, RAF, and has issue living, (by 1st *m*) Peter Howard Oliphant (*posthumous*), *b* 1937, — Jill Rose Alyne Charlotte, *b* (Dec) 1934: *m* 1955, Stuart Bollam, and has issue living, Miles Stuart *b* 1957, Kim Pauline, *b* 1956, — (by 2nd *m*) Mhairi Christina Deborah *b* 1945.

Issue of late Maj Norman Edwin Bartlett, yst son of 1st baronet, *b* 1888, *d* 1972: *m* 1st, 1917 (*m diss* 1928), Mary Adelaide Leslie, who *d* 1981, da of Norman R. Foster, of 47 Murray Rd, Wimbledon SW; 2ndly, 1928, Sheila Barton, who *d* 1993, da of Mrs Hill, of 11 Bentinck Terr, SW8:—
(By 1st *m*) Norman Alaric, RN (Lonesome Pine, Bickenhall, Taunton, Som), *b* 1920; Lt-Cdr and Pilot, Flying Branch, RN (ret); 1939-45 War (despatches): *m* 1945, Mary Paterson Waugh, and has issue living, Michael Alaric, *b* 1946: *m* 1st, 1967, Sheila Taylor, 2ndly, 1983, Linda Ireson, and has issue living (by 1st *m*), Colin *b* 1967, Glen *b* 1971, (by 2nd *m*) Andrew *b* 1984, Gary *b* 1986, — Carol Anne, *b* 1948: *m* 1985, Harry Page. —— Hazel Leslie (21 Garstons, Bathford, Avon BA1 7TE), *b* 1922: *m* 1st, 1947, George Edward Short, who *d* 1962; 2ndly, 1966, Philip John Elwood, who *d* 1979, and has had issue (by 1st *m*), Edward Louis, *b* 1949; *d* 1967, — Jennifer Anne, *b* 1947: *m* 1st 1964 (*m diss* 19—), James William Price; 2ndly, 1978, Vivian Leslie Stuart Stokes, and has issue living (by 1st *m*), Hamish Dudley *b* 1965, — Angela Jill, *b* 1948: *m* 1970 (*m diss* 19—), Brian K. Rogers, and has issue living, Thomas Edward George *b* 1977, Jamie Alexander Francis Forgan *b* 1988, Tiffany Roberta Kate *b* 1974, — Catherine Leslie, *b* 1952: *m* 1st, 1977 (*m diss* 19—), Mark Hoy; 2ndly, 1987, Alan Jones, and has issue living (by 2nd *m*), Nicola Suzanne *b* 1988, Elizabeth Leslie *b* 1991.

—— (By 2nd *m*) Derek (Fiveways, Jigs Lane North, Warfield, Bracknell, Berks RG42 3DH), *b* 1930; late Maj The Life Guards: *m* 1956, Joan Patricia, da of late Robert Joshua Breyfogle, and has issue living, Peter Mandeville (Colorado, USA), *b* 1960; *ed* Eton, and William & Mary Coll, Virginia, USA: *m* 1992, Suzanne Eva Marie, da of Göran Sture Stache, of Sweden, and USA, and has issue living, Alexander Mandeville *b* 1995, Nicholas Hugo Hardington *b* 1998, Emma Mariel *b* 1993, —— Robert Hardington (Cherry Orchard Farm, Lower South Wraxall, nr Bradford-on-Avon, Wilts BA15 2RU; Leander Club), *b* 1965; *ed* Eton, George Washington Univ, USA, and RAC Cirencester: *m* 1992, Susannah Morag Christine, elder da of John Angus Maclean, of Bath, and has issue living, Catriona Mya Mandeville *b* 1993, Albany Flora Maisie Mandeville *b* 1997, —— Jonica Mary Mandeville, *b* 1958: *m* 1994, Gerard Ian Fox, of Hobdens, Mayfield, E Sussex. —— Edwina, *b* 1933: *m* 1956, Esmond Dunn Boldero, late Capt LG, of Gyles Croft, Bellingdon, Chesham, Bucks, and has issue living, Jonathan Dunn, *b* 1958; Capt LG, —— Alexandra, *b* 1964: *m* 1988, (Nicholas) Rory Tapner, of 13 Woodstock Rd, W4 1DS and has issue living, Frederick James *b* 1990, Anna Violet *b* 1992, Rose Edwina *b* 1995, —— Louisa, *b* 1966: *m* 1999, James Richard Powell-Tuck.

Sir Herbert Henry Bartlett, 1st Bt, was many years Chm of Perry and Co (Bow) Limited, contractors, and was one of the principal contractors involved in the construction of Tower Bridge, Bakerloo Underground, Waterloo Station, and other notable buildings. He founded the Bartlett Sch of Architecture, part of Univ Coll London, was a Freeman of the City of London, and a Member Pattenmakers' Co (Master three times).

BARTTELOT (UK) 1875, of Stopham, Sussex
(Name pronounced "Bartlot")

In good time

Sir BRIAN WALTER DE STOPHAM BARTTELOT, OBE, 5th *Baronet*; *b* 17 July 1941; *s* his father, *Brigadier Sir* WALTER DE STOPHAM, DSO 1944; *ed* Eton; Col Coldstream Guards (ret 1992); is patron of two livings; DL W Sussex 1988, High Sheriff 1997; Equerry to HM 1970-72; OBE (Mil) 1983; Mil Sec to Maj-Gen Commanding London District and Household Divn 1978-80; Commanding officer 1st Bn Coldstream Guards 1982-85; Regt Lt-Col commanding Coldstream Guards 1987-92; Col Foot Guards 1989-92; Member HM Body Guard of The Hon Corps of Gentlemen at Arms since 1993; Chm Exec Cttee Standing Council of the Baronetage since 1996; Liveryman of Gunmakers' Co 1980: *m* 1969, Hon (Mary Angela) Fiona Weld Forester, yst da of late 7th Baron Forester, and has issue.

Arms – Quarterly, 1st and 4th sable, three sinister gloves pendent argent, tasselled or, *Barttelot*; 2nd and 3rd quarterly, per fesse argent and gules, four crescents counterchanged, *Stopham*. Crest – 1st, a swan couchant wings endorsed argent; 2nd, a castle with three turrents sable.
Seat – Stopham House, Pulborough, Sussex. *Residence* – Stopham Park, Pulborough, Sussex RH20 1DY. *Clubs* – Cavalry and Guards', Pratt's, Farmers'.

DAUGHTERS LIVING

Isabel Emily, *b* 1971: *m* 1997, Luke T. M. Sanders, son of Andrew Sanders, of Hempstead, Essex, and has issue living, Benedict Brian, *b* 1999. —— Sophie Rosalind, *b* 1973. —— Ursulina May, *b* 1978. —— Emma Amelia, *b* 1981.

BROTHER LIVING

ROBIN RAVENSCROFT (Targrove, Fittleworth, Sussex), *b* 15 Dec 1943; *ed* Seaford Coll, and Perth Univ, W Aust: *m* 1987, Teresa, elder da of late Kenneth Greenlees, and has issue living, Hugo Ravenscroft, *b* 7 April 1990, —— Emily Rose, *b* 1988.

COLLATERAL BRANCH LIVING

Issue of late Lt-Col William Frederick Geoffrey Nelson Barttelot, RE, yr son of 3rd baronet, *b* 1905, *d* 1996: *m* 1930, Jane Elizabeth, who *d* 1990, only da of late Daniel Stirling, of Santiago, Chile:—
Richard James Stuart Walter, *b* 1932; *ed* Wellington Coll. *Residence* – 4 Heron's Rye, Pulborough, W Sussex. —— Elizabeth Georgiana Margaret, *b* 1933: *m* 1st, 1955 (*m diss* 1973), James Drury Edward Kelly, Essex Regt; 2ndly, 1973, Nigel John Petrie Mermagen, and has issue living (by 1st *m*), Thomas James Barttelot, *b* 1956: *m* 1981 (*m diss* 1986), Sarah Jane St Clair Weir, and has issue living, Louis Frederick Charles *b* 1986, —— Rose Jane Elizabeth, *b* 1958: *m* 1984, John Charles Harding, and has issue living, Minnie Apphia Rose *b* 1990, Patience Elizabeth Ann *b* 1992. *Residence* – Richmond House, 61 High St, Chard, Som

Issue of late Lieut-Com Nigel Kenneth Walter Barttelot, RN, 2nd son of 2nd baronet, *b* 1883, *ka* 1914: *m* 1906, Dorothy Maud (who *d* 1961, having *m* 2ndly, 1923, as his 2nd wife, Vice-Adm Sir Frank Forrester Rose, KCB, DSO, who *d* 1955), el da of late Frederick Aldcroft Kay:—
James Nigel Walter, *b* 1911; Cdr RN (ret): *m* 1st, 1936, Rachel Mildred, who *d* 1964, da of Raymond Courage, of Edgcote, Banbury; 2ndly, 1965, Sara Patricia, who *d* 1998, da of late Lt-Col Herbert Valentine Ravenscroft, and widow of Brig Sir Walter de Stopham Barttelot, 4th Bt, DSO, and' has issue living, (by 1st *m*) Nigel Michael Anthony (Longcroft,

Martin, Notts), *b* 1941: *m* 1971, Serena, da of F. W. Brett, of The Little Cottage, Hurst, Twyford, Berks, and has issue living, Piers Nigel Edward *b* 1976, Sasha Rachel *b* 1972, Olivia Henrietta *b* 1974, Hannah *b* 1981, — David James Raymond (49 Grandison Rd, SW11), *b* 1946; Liveryman Armourers' and Brasiers' Co 1980: *m* 1st, 1973 (*m diss* 1980), Lucinda Jane, who *d* 1997, da of late Cdr G. R. Callingham, RN (ret); 2ndly, 1983, Charmian, elder da of late Cdr John S. Kerans, DSO, RN (ret), of 44 Gordons Way, Oxted, Surrey, — Carol Rachel Mildred (Altyre House, Gt Horkesley, Colchester, Essex CO6 4AB), *b* 1938: *m* 1st, 1961 (*m diss* 1988), Torquil Robin Armour Macmillan; 2ndly, 1998, Christopher O. A. Bindloss, and has issue living (by 1st *m*), James Armour *b* 1965: *m* 1986, Susan Margaret Falle (and has issue living, Joshua *b* 1990, Benedict *b* 1993, Sophie Charlotte *b* 1987), Andrew Giles *b* 1968, Timothy Iain *b* 1969: *m* 1996, Kirsty Rawlings (and has issue living, Ella *b* 1997), Lucinda Jane Carol *b* 1963: *m* 1989, John Brezak (and has issue living, Tiffany *b* 1992, Audrey *b* 1994, Zoe *b* 1997). *Residence* – Crowpits, Stopham, Pulborough, Sussex RH20 1ED.

John Barttelot, who *d* 1428, acquired Stopham in the right of his wife Joan, da and co-heir of William de Stopham. The Rt Hon Sir Walter Barttelot, CB, PC, 1st baronet, sat as MP for W Sussex (*C*) 1860-85, and for Sussex, NW, or Horsham, Div 1885-93. Capt Sir Walter Barttelot, 2nd baronet, was *ka* 1900, while Comdg 2nd Vol Bn R Sussex Regt. The 3rd baronet, Sir Walter Balfour Barttelot, DSO, Major and Brevet Lieut-Col Coldstream Guards, was *k* during European War while Mil Attaché at Teheran (Croix de Guerre). The 4th baronet, Brigadier Sir Walter de Stopham Barttelot, DSO, late Coldstream Guards, was *ka* in France 1944, while comdg 4 Gds Tank Bde.

BARWICK (UK) 1912, of Ashbrooke Grange, Borough of Sunderland (Extinct 1979)

Sir RICHARD LLEWELLYN BARWICK, 3rd, and last *Baronet*.

DAUGHTERS LIVING OF THIRD BARONET (*by 1st wife Valerie Maud, who d 1989, da of Robert Jeremiah Skelton, of Nairobi, Kenya*)

Rozanne Valerie, *b* 1950: *m* 1970, Alan Michael Bulmer, of Coombe Cross House, East Meon, Petersfield, Hants, and has issue living, Caroline Valerie, *b* 1974, — Rozalind Margot, *b* 1978. —— Sandra-Anne (The New Inn, Coln St Aldwyns, nr Cirencester, Glos GL7 5AN), *b* 1952; MD 1986: *m* 1st 1971 (*m diss* 1986), Timothy George Wheaton Heycock; 2ndly, 1989, Brian Antony Evans, son of late Evan Stanley Evans, CBE, FRCS, and has issue living (by 1st *m*), Tobias George Francis, *b* 1974, — Nathalie Louise Katharine, *b* 1976. —— Victoria Maud Lorraine, *b* 1961: *m* 1994, Andrew Kenneth Wallis, of Lower Farm, Ramsden, Chipping Norton, Oxon OX7 3AZ, son of Francis Wallis, and has issue living, Georgina Alice, *b* 1994.

COLLATERAL BRANCH LIVING

Issue of late George Short Barwick, 2nd son of 1st baronet, *b* 1879, *d* 1937: *m* 1913, Marianne, who *d* 1975, da of late William Marshall, of Davenham, Ches:—
Diana Marianne, *b* 1917: *m* 1st, 1945 (*m diss* 1955), Lieut John Louis Arnott Bowles, RN; 2ndly, 1959, Gerald Leopold Wiener, OBE, of 45 Edwardes Sq, W8, and has issue living, (by 1st *m*) (George) Anthony John (Holmhead, Corsock, Castle Douglas, Kirkcudbrightshire DG7 3DT), *b* 1946: *m* 1979, (Joan) Miranda Mary, 2nd da of Maj Julius Arthur Sheffield Neave, CBE (*see* Neave, Bt, colls), and has issue living, Richard Anthony Julius *b* 1981, Humphrey John Edward *b* 1984, Georgina Helen Diana *b* 1987, — Sarah Margaret Diana, *b* 1949: *m* 1991, Henry Christopher Bennett, of The Shrubbery, Linton, Cambs (*see* Bazley, Bt), and has issue living, Jonathan Ronald Sebastian *b* 1991.

BATES (UK) 1880, of Bellefield, co Lancaster

Labore et virtue

By labour and virtue

Sir GEOFFREY VOLTELIN BATES, MC, 5th *Baronet*, son of late Major Cecil Robert Bates, DSO, MC, 3rd son of 2nd baronet; *b* 2 Oct 1921; *s* his uncle *Sir* PERCY ELLY, GBE, 1946; *ed* Radley; Capt (ret) 8th Hussars, and Maj (ret) Cheshire Yeo; High Sheriff of Flintshire 1969; 1939-45 War (MC): *m* 1st, 1945, Kitty, who *d* 1956, da of Ernest Kendall-Lane, of Saskatchewan, Canada; 2ndly, 1957, Hon Olivia Gwyneth Zoë Fitz Roy, who *d* 1969, da of 2nd Viscount Daventry; 3rdly, 1971, Juliet Eleanor Hugolyn Whitelocke-Winter, widow of Edward Colin Winter, and da of late Cdr G Whitelocke, RN, and has issue by 1st and 2nd *m*.

Arms – Argent, on a fesse azure a quatrefoil between two fleurs-de-lys argent, between in chief two quatrefoils azure, and in base a fleur-de-lys of the same. Crest – A stag's head erased azure, attired or, transfixed by two arrows crosswise of the second, and charged on the neck with two quatrefoils in pale or.
Residence – Gyrn Castle, Llanasa, Holywell, Flintshire CH8 9BG.

SONS LIVING *(By 1st marriage)*

EDWARD ROBERT, *b* 4 July 1946; *ed* Gordonstoun. *Residence* – Cae Dai, Denbigh, N Wales LL16 4SU. —— Richard Geoffrey, *b* 1948: *m* 1st, 1971, Diana Margaret Rankin, who *d* 1990; 2ndly, 1994 (*m* annulled 19—), Diana M. P., yr da of Michael Pridham, of Pudleston, Herefords, and has issue living (by 1st *m*), James Geoffrey, *b* 14 March 1985, — Margot Zoe, *b* 1976, — Nichola Sarah, *b* 1979. *Residence* – Pirates House, Bowen Bay, Bowen Island, BC, Canada VON 1G0.

DAUGHTER LIVING *(By 2nd marriage)*

Celina Zoë, *b* 1958: *m* 1992 (*m diss* 1998), Timothy M. Radcliffe, only son of R. J. Radliffe, of Bodedern, Anglesey, and has issue living, Olivia Philippa Zoë, *b* 1993.

COLLATERAL BRANCHES LIVING

Issue of late Col Denis Haughton Bates, MC, TD, 5th son of 2nd baronet, *b* 1886, *d* 1959: *m* 1922, Aline Mary, who *d* 1974, da of Edward T. Crook, of Woodlands Hall, Bridgnorth:—
Philip Edward, VRD (2 Squirrels Cottages, Poles Lane, Woodside, Lymington, Hants S041 8AD) *b* 1925; *ed* Shrewsbury; Maj (ret) RM Force VR; 1943-45 War: *m* 1952, Mary Patricia Carol, da of Lt Col Clive Vincent Mobcrly-Bell, OBE, and has issue living, Hugh Percy (Hathaway House, Lower Pennington Lane, Lymington, Hants), *b* 1953: *m* 1977, Angela Roberta Wall, and has issue living, James Edward *b* 1984, Kathryn Ann *b* 1981, — Denis Moberly (Wisteria Cottage, Minstead, Lyndhurst, Hants SO4 7FX), *b* 1954: *m* 1979, Hilary Mackay, and has issue living, Alastair Martin *b* 1987, Jennifer Jane *b* 1985, — Patricia Mary, *b* 1956: *m* 1978, Dr Anthony Yates, of Yate's Place, Lot 5 Minsterly Rd, Denmark 6333, W, Australia, and has issue living, Colin Robert *b* 1979, Robert Mark *b* 1981, Christopher John *b* 1983, William Anthony *b* 1987, — Carol Elisabeth, *b* 1957: *m* 1981, Brian Hedley Thomas, of Bracken Dene, 17 Clifton Rd, Parkstone, Poole, Dorset, and has issue living, Sophie Patricia *b* 1983, Nicola Hedley *b* 1985. —— Denise Elisabeth, *b* 1928: *m* 1958, Rev Canon Thomas Michael Rylands, and has issue living, Thomas Gordon, *b* 1959; *ed* Shrewsbury, and Univ of Birmingham (BSc): *m* 1985, Jane Lesley, da of Alan Goode, and has issue living, Thomas Christopher *b* 1987, Peter Michael *b* 1993, Louise Victoria *b* 1989, — *Rev* Mark James, *b* 1961; *ed* St Hild and St Bede Coll, Durham (BA): *m* 1986, Rev Amanda, da of Peter Craig Byrom, OBE, and has issue living, Samuel George Ambrose *b* 1990, Frances Elisabeth *b* 1988, — Alison Joane, *b* 1963; *ed* Moreton Hall, and City and Guilds Coll of Art. *Residence* – Haughton Thorn, nr Tarporley, Cheshire CW6 9RN.

Issue of late Lieut-Col Austin Graves Bates, DSO, MC, 6th son of 2nd baronet, *b* 1891, *d* 1961: *m* 1920, Jean Christian Marguerite, who *d* 1982, da of Col James Hunter, of Anton's Hill, Coldstream, Berwickshire:—
Jeremy Dickson (Hornshaw House, 47 Mount Harry Rd, Sevenoaks, Kent TN13 3TN), *b* 1932; *ed* London Univ (BSc 1955): *m* 1978, Elizabeth Marjorie, da of late H. W. Rudd, of High Pines, Woodend Drive, Sunninghill, Ascot, Berks, and has issue living, Thomas James Dickson, *b* 1980, — Sarah Marjorie, *b* 1981. —— Martin Graves (17 Queen's Gate Place, SW7 5NY), *b* 1935; *ed* St Edmund Hall, Oxford (BA); late Queen's Own Cameron Highlanders: *m* 1965, Susan Myfanwy Prudence, da of Capt Robert Edward Dudley Ryder, VC, RN (*see* E Harrowby, colls), and has issue living, Oliver Robert Hunter, *b* 1969, — Susannah Hilaré Myfanwy, *b* 1970.

Issue of late Maurice Halifax Bates, Lt RA, 7th son of 2nd baronet, *b* 1898, *d* 1925: *m* 1922, May Frances (who *d* 1969, having *m* 2ndly, 1927, Brig Ralph Emerson Pickering, CBE, late Queen's Roy Regt, who *d* 1962), da of late Sir Edward Arthur Henry Blunt, KCIE, OBE (Blunt, Bt colls):—
Ann Maurice, *b* (*posthumous*) 1925. *Residence* – ......

Granddaughter of late Sydney Eggers Bates, 3rd son of 1st baronet:—
Issue of late Col Arthur Sydney Bates, DSO, TD, *b* 1879, *d* 1958: *m* 1905, Mary da Costa, who *d* 1962, da of late Lieut-Col Charles Robert Crosse, CMG, MVO, formerly Roy W Kent Regt:—
Anne Mary (Beech House, Wootton St Lawrence, Basingstoke, Hants), *b* 1915: *m* 1939, Lt-Col John Oliver-Bellasis, DSO, JP, DL, Royal Fusiliers, who *d* 1979, and has issue living, Charles Arthur John (The Old Rectory, Boxford, nr Newbury, Berks RG20 8DR), *b* 1940; *ed* Winchester, and Royal Agric Coll, Cirencester; FRICS; MRAC: *m* 1972, Julia Elizabeth, da of Lt Cdr John Errol Manners, DSC, RN (ret), of Laurel House, Great Cheverell, Devizes, Wilts, and has issue living, John Edward *b* 1976, Richard Charles *b* 1977, Clare Elizabeth *b* 1974, — Hugh Richard, *b* 1945; *ed* Winchester, and RMA; Maj WG (ret 1977); FRAgS: *m* 1971, Daphne Phoebe, yr da of Arthur Christopher Parsons (*see* E Rosse, colls),

and has issue living, Joanna Gwenda *b* 1975, Nicola Mary *b* 1978. *Residence* – Wootton House, Wootton St Lawrence, Basingstoke, Hants RG23 8PE.

The 1st baronet, Sir Edward, was MP for Plymouth (C) 1871-80 and 1885-92. The 4th baronet Sir Percy Elly, GBE, was Chm of Cunard Steamship Co, Ltd, and of Cunard-White Star Ltd.

BATES (UK) 1937, of Magherabuoy, co Londonderry

Sir RICHARD DAWSON HOULT BATES, 3rd *Baronet*; *b* 12 May 1956; *s* his father, *Sir* (JOHN) DAWSON, MC, 1998; *ed* Winchester Coll, Durham Univ.
Residence – Ballabeg Cottage, Grenaby, Ballasalla, Isle of Man IM9 3BA.

BROTHER LIVING

CHARLES JOSEPH DILL, *b* 25 April 1959: *m* 1984, Suzanne C., yr da of David Beaumont, of Much Hadham, Hertfordshire, and has issue living, Patrick Charles Beaumont, *b* 1990, — Oliver James Beaumont, *b* 1993, — Claudia Jane, *b* 1988. *Residence* – Old Manor Farm, Balscote, nr Banbury, Oxon OX15 6JJ.

SISTER LIVING

Drusilla Mary Cynthia, *b* 1954: *m* 1983, Gervase Belfield, of Garth House, Lankhills Rd, Winchester, Hants, eldest son of late Eversley Belfield, of Beauchamp, Sark, CI, and has issue living, Felix Swithun Theodore, *b* 1995, — Laura Daisy, *b* 1987, — Matilda May, *b* 1992.

WIDOW LIVING OF SECOND BARONET

MARY MURRAY (*Lady Bates*), da of late Lt-Col Joseph Murray Hoult, RA, of Norton Place, Lincoln: *m* 1953, Sir (John) Dawson Bates, 2nd Bt, who *d* 1998. *Residence* – Butleigh House, Glastonbury, Som BA6 8SU.

The 1st baronet, Rt Hon Sir (Richard) Dawson Bates, OBE (son of late Richard Dawson Bates, solicitor, of Belfast), was Min for Home Affairs, N Ireland 1921-43.

BATHO (UK) 1928, of Frinton, Essex

Sir PETER GHISLAIN BATHO, 3rd *Baronet*; *b* 9 Dec 1939; *s* his father, *Lt-Col Sir* MAURICE BENJAMIN, 1990; *ed* Ampleforth; Co Councillor Suffolk 1989-93: *m* 1966, Lucille Mary, da of late Wilfrid Francis Williamson, of The White House, Saxmundham, Suffolk, and has issue.

Arms – Gules, on a fess argent two castles of the first, over all a sword in pale point upwards proper. Crest – A dragon sejant or gorged with a mural crown gules, and holding in the dexter claw a sword as in the arms.
Residence – Park Farm, Saxmundham, Suffolk IP17 1DQ.

Neither do I hesitate at trifles

SONS LIVING

RUPERT SEBASTIAN GHISLAIN (4 Hedgerow Cottages, Gosbeck, Ipswich, Suffolk IP6 9SD), *b* 26 Oct 1967; *ed* St Joseph's Coll, Ipswich, and Harper Adams Agric Coll: *m* 1995, Jo-Anne Louise, elder da of Rodney Frank Hellawell, of Kesgrave, Suffolk. —— Alexander Francis Ghislain (10 Archway Cottages, Leiston, Suffolk IP16 4AR), *b* 1970: *m* 1994, Zoe Elizabeth, eldest da of Nigel J. Miller, of Aldeburgh, Suffolk, and has issue living, George Alexander Ghislain, *b* 1997, — Bethany Frances Ghislaine, *b* 1996. —— Hugh Charles Ghislain, *b* 1973; *ed* Univ Coll, London (BSc Hons).

BROTHER LIVING

Richard Ghislain (Carlton, Marden, Hereford HR1 3ES), b 1941; ed Ampleforth, and Wye Coll, London Univ (BSc): m 1970, Georgina Catherine Ann Gwynne, da of late William Reginald Gwynne Chadwick, of Abergavenny, Gwent, and has issue living, Charles William Ghislain, b 1971; ed Belmont Abbey, — Sarah Catherine Ghislaine, b 1974.

SISTERS LIVING

Anne Madelaine Bessie Ghislaine, b 1938: m 1964, Stephen Robert Morgan Oliver, of St Briavels, Wetherden, Stowmarket, Suffolk, and has issue living, Felix Benjamin Morgan, b 1966, — Alban Geoffrey Morgan, b 1968, — Damian Paul Morgan, b 1970, — Justin Edmund Morgan, b 1978. —— Jacqueline Ghislaine, b 1947: m 1987, Ian David Bruce-Jones, of Little Garth, The Street, Walberswick, Southwold, Suffolk IP18 6UH, son of late Douglas Bruce-Jones, of Warlingham, Surrey.

The 1st baronet, Sir Charles Albert Batho (son of late William Smith Batho, of Highgate, N), was an Alderman of City of London (Aldgate Ward) 1921-38, Sheriff 1925-6, and Lord Mayor 1927-8. The 2nd baronet, Lt-Col Sir Maurice Benjamin Batho, was Regional Advisor on Cereals Collection to Min of Finance, Iran, 1944, and Dept Dir of Rice Procurement, Bengal, 1945.

HERVEY-BATHURST (UK) 1818, of Lainston, Hants
(Name pronounced "Harvy-Bathurst")

Hold thy faith

Sir (FREDERICK) JOHN CHARLES GORDON HERVEY-BATHURST, 7th Baronet; b 23 April 1934; s his father, Capt Sir FREDERICK PETER METHUEN, 1995; ed Eton, and Trin Coll, Camb (BA 1957); Lieut Gren Gds (Res); sometime Dir Lazard Bros & Co Ltd: m 1957, Caroline Myrtle, only da of Sir William Randle Starkey, 2nd Bt, and has issue.

Arms – Quarterly, 1st and 4th, sable, two bars ermine, and in chief three crosses-patée or, a crescent for difference, Bathurst; 2nd and 3rd, gules, on a bend argent three trefoils vert, a martlet for difference, Hervey. Crest – 1st, a dexter arm embowed in armour proper, grasping a spiked club or, Bathurst; 2nd, an ounce passant sable, bezantee ducally gorged and chained or, in the paw a trefoil slipped vert, Hervey.

SON LIVING

FREDERICK WILLIAM JOHN, b 18 Sept 1965; ed Harrow, and Buckingham Univ: m 1991, Annabel Peta, yr da of Donald Warburg, of Zurich, and has issue living, Frederick Benjamin Guy, b 9 March 1998, — Eleanor Maryse, b 1995.

DAUGHTERS LIVING

Louisa Caroline (Lady Portal), b 1959: m 1982, Sir Jonathan Francis Portal, 6th Bt, and has issue (see that family). Residence – Burley Wood, Ashe, Basingstoke, Hants RG25 3AG. —— Sophia Selina Irene, b 1961: m 1982, Henry Nicholas Almroth Colthurst, yst son of Sir Richard La Touche Colthurst, 9th Bt, and has issue (see that family). Residence – 1 Wandle Rd, SW17 7DL.

SISTER LIVING

Selina Anthea Maureen, b 1936: m 1st, 1959 (m diss 1989), Brig Peter Gerald Sandeman Tower, CBE, who d 1996 (see Butler, Bt, cr 1628, 1943 Edn); 2ndly, 1990, (Oswald) Henry Chaldecott (see Worsley-Taylor, Bt, 1959 Edn), and has issue living (by 1st m), William John (Wellington Cottage, Longbridge Deverill, nr Warminster, Wilts BA12 7DR), b 1963; ed Harrow; Maj Coldstream Gds: m 1995, Emma Maria, da of William Joseph Hall, of Castle Espie House, co Down, — Nicola Jane, b 1961: m 1987, Richard Derek Crosthwaite, of 25 Lavender Gdns, SW11 1DH, yr son of late Tudor Derek Crosthwaite. Residence – Lauristina Cottage, Lower Inkpen, Hungerford, Berks RG17 9DP.

MOTHER LIVING

Maureen Gladys Diana, eldest da of late Charles Wilfred Gordon, of Boveridge Park, Cranborne, Salisbury: m 1st, 1933 (m diss 1956), as his 1st wife, Capt Sir Frederick Peter Methuen Hervey-Bathurst, 6th Bt, who d 1995; 2ndly, 1966, as his 3rd wife, Charles Ryves Maxwell Eley, OBE, of E Bergholt Place, Suffolk, who d 1983. Residence – Flat 6, 13 Wetherby Gdns, SW5 0JW.

COLLATERAL BRANCHES LIVING

Issue of late Major Benjamin Alexander Frederick Hervey-Bathurst, OBE, 2nd son of 5th baronet, *b* 1920, *d* 1997: *m* 1st, 1947, Hon Elizabeth Violet Virginia Somers Cocks, who *d* 1986, only child of 6th Baron Somers; 2ndly, 1992, Mrs Anne Pollak (Hillend House, Eastnor, Ledbury, Herefords), only da of late Rev Thomas Vernon Garnier, OBE, and formerly wife of Robert Pollak, of Burtons Farm, Ledbury, Herefords:—
(By 1st *m*) James Felton Somers (Eastnor Castle, Ledbury, Herefords) *b* 1949; *ed* Eton, and Trin Coll, Camb (BA 1971): *m* 1982, Hon Sarah Rachel Peake, 2nd da of 2nd Viscount Ingleby, and has issue living, Imogen Elizabeth Somers, *b* 1986, — Isabella Katherine Somers, *b* 1990, — Nancy Rose Somers, *b* 1995. —— George Arthur Somers (29 Collingham Gdns, SW5; Hillend House, Eastnor, Ledbury, Herefords), *b* 1952; *ed* Eton.

Grandchildren of late Capt Sidney Lionel Paston-Cooper, son of Lt-Col Lionel Paston-Cooper (who assumed the name of Paston-Cooper by R Licence 1905), 2nd son of 3rd baronet, *b* 1887, *d* 1934: *m* 1927, Ermyntrude Mary, who *d* 1936, da of Henry Caley, of Hovingham, Yorks:—
Issue of late Astley Cecil Hervey PASTON-COOPER, *b* 1929; *d* 1978: *m* 1950, Jean Louise, da of Lawrence Dickinson, of 8 Dorset Avenue, Welling, Kent:—
Lionel Lawrence Hervey, *b* 1951: *m* 1987, Edwina Jane, da of F. Ward Smith, of Wave Crest, Whitstable, Kent, and has issue living, Thomas Astley Ward, *b* 1993. *Residence* – 33 St Mark's Rd, Teddington, Middx. —— Sally Anne, *b* 1953.

The 1st baronet, Sir Felton Elwell Hervey, was a grandson of late Hon Felton Hervey, 7th son of 1st Earl of Bristol (*see* M Bristol), and was ADC to the Duke of Wellington after Waterloo. He assumed in 1801 the additional surname and arms of Bathurst, and on his death without issue in 1819, he was succeeded, under special remainder, by his next brother, Sir Frederick Anne Hervey-Bathurst, 2nd Bt. Lt-Col Sir Frederick, 4th baronet, sat as MP for S Wilts (*C*) 1861-5. Major Sir Frederick Edward William, 5th Bt, DSO, Grenadier Guards, served in Egyptian Campaign 1898, S Africa 1900, and European War 1914-18 (DSO).

BAYNES (UK) 1801, of Harefield Place, Middlesex

Rage supplies arms

Sir JOHN CHRISTOPHER MALCOLM BAYNES, 7th *Baronet*; *b* 24 April 1928; *s* his father, *Sir* RORY MALCOLM STUART, 1979; *ed* Sedbergh Sch, RMA Sandhurst, and Edinburgh Univ (MSc); late Lt-Col Queen's Own Highlanders, served in The Cameronians (Scottish Rifles) 1948 until disbandment 1968; Malaya 1950-53 (despatches): *m* 1955, Shirley Maxwell, only da of late Robert Allan Dodds, of Foxbury, Lesbury, Alnwick, and has issue.

Arms – Sable, a shin-bone in fesse surmounted of another in pale argent; on a canton of the last, a vulture proper. **Crest** – A cubit arm vested, azure, cuffed erminois, the hand holding a jaw-bone argent. **Supporters** – Two savages wreathed with holly about the head and waist, carrying clubs over their exterior shoulders all proper.
Residence – Talwrn Bach, Llanfyllin, Powys SY22 5LQ. *Club* – Army & Navy.

SONS LIVING

CHRISTOPHER RORY, *b* 11 May 1956: *m* 1992, Sandra Finuala Merriman, and has issue living, Alasdair William Merriman, *b* 1993, — Fergus Joseph Malcolm, *b* 1996. *Residence* – Greywalls, High St, Findon, W Sussex. —— Timothy Peter (Muirton of Drumlochy, Blairgowrie PH10 6TD), *b* 1957: *m* 1986, Estelle Anne Gabrielle, elder da of late Nicholas John Dennys Parry de Winton, of Llangattock House, Penpergwm, Abergavenny, Gwent, and has issue living, Rory Nicholas Aimery, *b* 1992, — Adam John Stuart, *b* 1994. —— Simon Robert Maurice (154 Campden Hill Rd, W8 7AS), *b* 1960: *m* 1992, Margaret Anne Mary, yr da of late Sydney Boag, of Boar's Hill, Oxford. —— William John Walter, *b* 1966.

COLLATERAL BRANCH LIVING

Grandson of late Edward Neil Baynes, yst son of 3rd baronet:—
Issue of late Edward Stuart Augustus Baynes, OBE, *b* 1889, *d* 1972: *m* 1918, Helen Mary (32 Avondale Cres, Killiney, co Dublin), da of G. Meredith, of Epsom, and widow of J. S. White:—
Anthony Edward George (School Hill, Little Minster, Minster Lovell, Oxon), *b* 1921; Artist; 1939-45 War as Sub-Lt RNVR.

The 1st baronet, Sir Christopher, was the son of William Baynes (a Gentleman of the Privy Chamber to George II and George III), of Harefield Place, Middlesex, and Kilburn Hall, Yorkshire, descended from the old Yorkshire family of Bayne; Sir Christopher served in Royal Horse Guards 1781-8, and in 1796 was Major-Commandant of the Uxbridge Gentlemen and Yeomanry Cavalry, which corps he helped to raise; he was also a DL for Middlesex.

BAZLEY (UK) 1869, of Hatherop, co Gloucester

Sir (THOMAS JOHN) SEBASTIAN BAZLEY, 4th *Baronet*; *b* 31 August 1948; *s* his father, *Sir* THOMAS STAFFORD, 1997; *ed* St Christopher Sch, Letchworth.

𝕬rms – Per pale azure and sable, a bee volant or between three fleurs-de-lis argent. 𝕮rest – A cubit arm erect proper charged with a bee volant or, the hand holding a chapeau gules, turned up gold; the whole between two branches of oak vert.

BROTHERS LIVING

ANTHONY MARTIN CHRISTOPHER, *b* 23 Feb 1958. —— John Francis Alexander, *b* 1961.

SISTERS LIVING

Catherine Elisabet Annemarie, *b* 1950. —— Virginia Isabella Marged, *b* 1953.

WIDOW LIVING OF THIRD BARONET

CARMEN (*Lady Bazley*), only da of James Tulla, of 11 Stanley Gdns, W11: *m* 1945, Sir Thomas Stafford Bazley, 3rd Bt, who *d* 1997.

Consider the end

COLLATERAL BRANCH LIVING

Granddaughter of late Gardner Sebastian Bazley, only son of 2nd baronet (ante):—
Issue of late Anthony Gardner Bazley, *b* 1911, *d* 1937: *m* 1934, Anne (*Baroness Howard of Penrith*) (who *m* 2ndly, 1944, 2nd Baron Howard of Penrith), da of late John Beaumont Hotham (*see* B Hotham, colls):—
Susan Antonia (Dean Farm, Coln St Aldwyn, Cirencester, Glos GL7 5AX), *b* 1937: *m* 1st, 1958 (*m diss* 1970), Peter Humphrey Alexander Van Oss (*see* E Waldegrave, 1947 Edn); 2ndly, 1970 (*m diss* 1984), William John Vicary, and has issue living (by 1st *m*), Mark Peter Anthony, *b* 1959: *m* 1985, Caroline Elizabeth, da of Ian Maxwell Scoggins, of High Thicket, Dockenfield, nr Farnham, Surrey, and has issue living, Emily Atalanta *b* 1988, Francesca Camilla *b* 1989, Octavia Rose *b* 1994, — Anthony Tom Francis, *b* 1961, — Juliet Anne Favell (twin), *b* 1961: *m* 1991, Robert Gwyn Palmer, only child of late John Gwyn Palmer, of Treboeth, W Glam, and has issue living, Xanthe Hope *b* 1995, Syrie Favell *b* 1997, — Katharine Susanna, *b* 1964: *m* 1999, Iain Charles Lochnell Campbell (*see* D Argyll, colls), — (by 2nd *m*) William Sebastian, *b* 1973.

The 1st baronct sat as MP for Manchester (*L*) 1858-80, and the 2nd baronet was High Sheriff of Gloucestershire 1874.

BEAUCHAMP (UK) 1911, of Grosvenor Place, City of Westminister (Extinct 1976)

Sir BROGRAVE CAMPBELL BEAUCHAMP, 2nd and last *Baronet*.

DAUGHTER LIVING OF SECOND BARONET

Patricia Evelyn, *b* 1925: *m* 1949, Maj Michael William Thomas Leatham, who *d* 1992, and has issue living, Simon Anthony Michael, *b* 1951: *m* 1973, Cristiana Elisabeth, da of Dr Carl Uvo Stein, of Hindenburgstrasse 31, Oldenburg, Germany, and has issue living, Anthony Michael *b* 1977, Nicholas James Edward *b* 1981, — Edward Arthur Martyn (19 Inner Park Rd, Wimbledon SW19), *b* 1953: *m* 1975, Elizabeth Scarlet, da of Charles Hardwick, of Hampshire Hunt Cottage, Ropley, and has issue living, Alexander Charles Edward *b* 1982, Evelyn Elizabeth *b* 1980. *Residence* – King's Moor, Sunningdale, Berks.

PROCTOR-BEAUCHAMP (GB) 1745, of Langley Park, Norfolk
(Name pronounced "Proctor-Beecham")

Always faithful

Sir CHRISTOPHER RADSTOCK PROCTOR-BEAUCHAMP, 9th *Baronet*; *b* 30 Jan 1935; *s* his father, *Rev Sir* IVOR CUTHBERT, MB, BCh, 1971; *ed* Rugby, and Trin Coll, Camb (MA): *m* 1965, Rosalind Emily Margot, da of Gerald Percival Wainwright, of 135 Marina, St Leonard's-on-Sea, and has issue.

𝔄rms – Argent, a chevron between three martlets sable 𝔠rest – On a mount vert, a greyhound sejant argent, spotted brown, collared or.
Residence – The Coach House, 4 Balfour Mews, Sidmouth, Devon EX10 8XL.

SONS LIVING

CHARLES BARCLAY, *b* 7 July 1969: *m* 1996, Harriet A. V., elder da of Anthony Meacock, of W Hoathly, W Sussex, and has issue living, Henry Montagu *b* 20 May 1999. —— Robert Ivor, *b* 1971: *m* 1998, Kate L., elder da of Rodney Hutchinson, of Tunbridge Wells, Kent.

DAUGHTER LIVING

Rosalind Caroline, *b* 1967.

BROTHER LIVING

Rev Anthony Hazlerigg (The Rectory, 18 Thorpe Rd, Kirby Cross, Frinton-on-Sea, Essex CO13 0LT), *b* 1940; *ed* Monkton Combe Sch and Trin Coll, Camb (MA); MICE; ordained 1975: *m* 1965, Anne Elise, da of late Rev Thomas Hewitt, V of St George's, Worthing, and has issue living, Guy James (81 Saxon Way, Willingham, Cambridge CB4 5UR), *b* 1967: *m* 1992, Hilda Catherine, da of R. H. Craig, of Campbeltown, Argyll and has issue living, Angus Robert *b* 1997, Finlay Thomas *b* 1998, Lucy Claire *b* 1994, — Julian Thomas, *b* 1968, — Claire Alexandra, *b* 1970: *m* 1996, Mark R. O'Donoghue, elder son of R. W. O'Donoghue, of Woking, Surrey.

SISTER LIVING

Rosemary Jean, *b* 1936: *m* 1964, Thomas Henry Geake, MA, AMIMechE, and has issue living, William Beauchamp, *b* 1968, — Elisabeth Marjorie, *b* 1965, — Helen Mary, *b* 1967.

UNCLE LIVING (*Son of 7th baronet*)

Basil Ralph, *b* 1906; *ed* Marlborough, and Toronto Univ (Diploma in Agriculture 1932): *m* 1st, 1932 (*m diss* 1957), Joan, who *d* 1998, da of Tom Storey; 2ndly, 1957, Diana, da of late Lt-Col Bernard H Elliott, RA, of Goring House, North Woodchester, nr Stroud, Gloucestershire, and, has had issue, (by 1st *m*) †Nicholas, *b* 1935; FRHS, FPWI: *m* 1964, Pauline (26 Howard St, Thatto Heath, St Helens, Lancs WA10 3RG), da of Jacob de Mos, of Hook of Holland, and *d* 1998, leaving issue, Alison de Mos *b* 1965, Sarah Jane *b* 1966, Victoria Isobel *b* 1967, — Carol Margot, *b* 1933: *m* 1958, Claude de Pina D. Swain, of 29 Springhead, Tunbridge Wells, Kent TN2 3NY, and has issue living, Charles de Pina Beauchamp *b* 1959: *m* 1984, Caroline Kerr, da of Alexander Alfred Stuart, of Holly House, Manor Lane, Gerrards Cross SL9 7NJ (and has issue living, Charles Douglas Stuart *b* 1988, Victoria Caroline *b* 1989, Alexandra Phillida *b* 1997, Lucinda Charlotte *b* 1999), Claudia Fenella *b* 1961: *m* 1983, Richard William Pettifer, son of W/Cdr John Kenyon Pettifer, RAF, of Paddock House, Little London, Whitchurch, Aylesbury, Bucks HP22 4LE (and has issue living, Julian Richard *b* 1987, William Gregory *b* 1989, Felix George *b* 1991, Miranda Imogen Hilary *b* 1995), — Elisabeth Waldegrave (Flat 3, Croft Rd, Willesborough, Ashford, Kent TN24 8AZ), *b* 1934, — (by 2nd *m*) Sophie Joy (43 Richmond Av, Islington N1 0MB), *b* 1958. *Residence* – Penhwyr, Dinas Cross, Newport, Dyfed SA42 0UQ.

COLLATERAL BRANCHES LIVING

Granddaughter of late Sir Edward Beauchamp (2nd son of late Rev William Henry Beauchamp, 2nd son of 3rd baronet), who was *cr* a *Baronet* 1911.
See Beauchamp, Bt, *cr* 1911. Ext 1976.

Grandchildren of Reginald Percy Beauchamp (infra):—
Issue of late Percy Tremayne Beauchamp, *b* 1908, *d* 1959: *m* 1935, Eileen Alice, who *d* 1964, da of Arthur Edward Croft:—
Anthony Tremayne (5A Walton St, Prospect, Launceston 7250, Tasmania), *b* 1937: *m* 1961, Nancy Ann, da of Mark Vincent Jones, of Muddy Creek, Tas, and has issue living, Christopher Tremayne, *b* 1964: *m* 1995, Lynn Mathews, and has issue living, Robert Tremayne *b* 1998, — Mark Andrew, *b* 1972: *m* 19—, Vanessa Randall, and has issue living, Bradley *b* 1996, Jordan *b* 1998, Rosina *b* 1995, — Wendy Ann, *b* 1965: *m* 1984, Allan Gregory Mason. —— Suzanne Elizabeth, *b* 1946.

Grandchildren of late Robert Beauchamp, 3rd son of 3rd baronet:—
Issue of late Reginald Percy Beauchamp, *b* 1873, *d* 1944: *m* 1904, Malvina Blanche Natalie, who *d* 1967, da of Jonathan Purdy Plummer:—

Geoffrey Frank (El-Retiro, Rosevears, W Tamar, Tasmania), *b* 1914: *m* 1950, Dorothy Vernon, who *d* 1970, da of Vernon Thomas Lewis, of 9 Hilda Cres, Hawthorne, Vic, and has issue living, Pamela Nerida, *b* 1952. —— Nerida Nadine (El-Retiro, Rosevears, W Tamar, Tasmania) *b* 1916: *m* 1935 (*m diss* 1943), Ronald Breadalbane Postle.

        Grandsons of late Edward Hayes Beauchamp, eldest son of late Capt Edward Halhed Beauchamp, RN, 3rd son of George Edward Beauchamp (infra):—
        Issue of late Edward Guy Beauchamp, *b* 1885, *d* 1966: *m* 1918, Louise France Caroline, da of late A. T. Haultain, of Napier, NZ:—
Trevor Haultain, *b* 1919; Capt 2nd NZEF; 1939-45 War in S-W Pacific and Italy: *m* 1952 Beryl Irene, da of Herbert Maxwell, of Otorahanga, King Country, NZ, and has issue living, Robin Max, *b* 1953, — Christine, *b* 1960.

        Issue of late Herbert Rolf Haultain Beauchamp, DCM, *b* 1890, *d* 1968: *m* 1st 1918 Ida, who *d* 1952, da of late John Stevenson, of Naumai, Wanganui, NZ; 2ndly 1955, Mary Joyce, who *d* 1979, da of late Capt James Stevenson Hempton, of Dunedin, NZ.
(By 1st *m*) John Proctor (91 Deep Creek Rd, Torbay, Auckland 10, NZ), *b* 1923; 1939-45 War with New Zealand Forces: *m* 1947, Barbara, da of Oliver Coupland, of 18 Grey St, Wanganui, NZ, and has issue living, Warwick Rolf, *b* 1952: *m* 1974, Jan, da of Lester Wintere, of Parr Terr, Milford, NZ, — Michael Douglas, *b* 1957: *m* 1978, Laura Ann, da of Rev Campbell Nicol, of Milton, South Otago, NZ, and has issue living, Christopher David *b* 1979, Robin Anthony Nicol *b* 1985, — Bruce Proctor *b* 1963, — Margaret Anne, *b* 1947: *m* 1st, 1966, Colin Daniel Mayes; 2ndly, 1974, Stewart Rankin, and has issue living (by 2nd *m*), Douglas John *b* 1978, — Jane Allison, *b* 1950: *m* 1974, Alan Stewart Davis, — Elizabeth Claire, *b* 1956: *m* 1974, Peter David Anderson.

        Grandchildren of late Herbert Lloyd Beauchamp, 2nd son of Capt Edward Halhed Beauchamp, RN, 3rd son of George Edward Beauchamp, 2nd son of 2nd baronet:—
        Issue of late Hugh Edward Beauchamp, *b* 1886, *d* 1962: *m* 1st, 1907, Grace Ethel, da of F. Quistorf, of Santa Cruz, California, USA; 2ndly, 19—, Tekla, who *d* 19—, da of Carl Viborg, of Stockholm, Sweden:—
(By 1st *m*) Dorothy Margaret, *b* 1909: *m* 1931, Harry Eugene Lennon.

        Issue of late Herbert Cecil Beauchamp, *b* 1888, *d* 1969: *m* 1913, Dora, who *d* 1968, da of H. Dohrmann, of Reinbeck, Iowa:—
†David Dohrmann, *b* 1916; F/O Air Transport Command, US Army Air Corps: *m* 1941, Jean Anita (830 Overhill Drive, Redding, Cal, USA 96001), da of Wade Greening Moores, of Redding, Cal, USA, and *d* 1998, leaving issue, Mark David Beauchamp, *b* 1952: *m* 1st, 1980 (*m diss* 1987), Carla Jenoyce Norton, of Redding, Cal, USA; 2ndly, 1988, Ellen Paris, of Santa Monica, Cal, USA, and has issue living (by 2nd *m*), Rebecca Sim *b* 1998, — Sarah Caroline, *b* 1954: *m* 1988, Harry Holverson, of Arcata, Cal, USA, and has issue living, Elizabeth Jean *b* 1989.

        Granddaughter of late Henry Champion Beauchamp, yst son of late George Edward Beauchamp (ante):—
        Issue of late James Lloyd Hobart Beauchamp, *b* 1862, *d* 1927: *m* 1891, Maria Radford Knight, da of late Augustus George Stead:—
Maria Georgiana, *b* 1892: *m* 1928, Robert Desmond Carruthers, and has issue living, Marie Lucy Beauchamp, *b* 1930.

        Grandchildren of late Capt Willoughby George Beauchamp, eldest son of Willoughby James Beauchamp, 4th son of Henry William Johnson Beauchamp, el son of William Henry Beauchamp, 3rd son of 1st baronet:—
        Issue of late Capt Willoughby Greaves Beauchamp, CBE, VRD, Ceylon, RNVR, *b* 1890, *d* 1960: *m* 1912, Kathleen Alice, who *d* 1983, da of late Dr W. B. Benison, of King's Heath, Worcestershire:—
(Kathleen) Patricia (Rooftops, 19 Church St, Wiveliscombe, Taunton, Som TA4 2LR), *b* 1913; formerly Junior Com ATS: *m* 1947, Alfred Thomas Morant, who *d* 1987, and has issue living, Willoughby Vivian Paul (520 Rue Le Bouvier, 76160 St Martin du Vivier, France), *b* 1950: *m* 1st, 1975 (*m diss* 1995), Monica Oates; 2ndly, 19—, Marie, da of Jean Roda, and has issue living (by 2nd *m*), Marc Alfred Roger *b* 1996, Simon Paul *b* 1998, — Julian Philip, *b* 1953: *m* 1977, Jane Peppard, and has issue living, Timothy Charles *b* 1982, Donna Kathleen *b* 1979, — Auriol Ann Melicent, *b* 1948: *m* 1975, Ottavio Croze, of 592B Dorsoduro, 30123 Venice, Italy, who *d* 1993, and has issue living, Ottavio Alfred *b* 1976, Cristina *b* 1979. —— Elaine Joyce, *b* 1916: *m* 1st, 1936 (*m diss* 1954), Edward Gordon Windus; 2ndly, 1955, Anthony Edward Davy Windus, who *d* 1989, and *d* 1996, leaving issue (by 1st *m*) Michael Edward Beauchamp, *b* 1937: *m* 1st, 1965 (*m diss* 1971), Evelyn Vera Pugh; 2ndly, 1990, Paola Elaine Ozkizil, and has issue living (by 1st *m*), Dirk Edward Beauchamp *b* 1966: *m* 1993, Isobel Mary Chisholm, Fiona Elaine Beauchamp *b* 1968: *m* 1992, James David McAllister (and has issue living, Hamish James *b* 1994), — Stefanie Gail Elaine, *b* 1940: *m* 1959, Robin Outram, of PO Box 797, Kilifi, Kenya, and has issue living, Stephen Jeremy *b* 1960: *m* 1992, Colleen Carr-Hartley (and has issue living, Ryan Carl *b* 1993, Oliver Stephen *b* 1996), Christopher James *b* 1961: *m* 1989, Helen Lewis (and has issue living, Joshua Martin *b* 1990, Anthony James Willoughby *b* 1992, Sam Harry *b* 1996), Suzanne Nicola Gail *b* 1963: *m* 1988, Gordon Russell St Amond Millar (and has issue living, Craig Russell St Amond *b* 1990, Kaila Gail Belinda *b* 1991, Cheza Elaine *b* 1998). —— Barbara Meredith, *b* 1923: *m* 1943, Ronald Arthur Lushington, late Maj Indian Army, who *d* 1996, and has issue living, Christopher Saxton, *b* 1947: *m* 1982, Maria Gabriella Quatrochchi, and has issue living, Shaun Robert *b* 1983, Kaley Nicola *b* 1986, Daniella *b* 1991, — Madeleine Dawn, *b* 1945: *m* 1972, Raynes Lloyd Sherewell, of Meadowend, Bryanston, S Africa, and has issue living, Francis Lloyd *b* 1975, Isla Madeleine *b* 1977.

        Issue of late Com Harold Charles Beauchamp, Roy Indian Navy, *b* 1891, *d* 1942: *m* 1918, Olive, who *d* 1983, da of Maurice Smelt Duke, MRCS, of 272 Kennington Park Rd, SE:—
Peter Clare (31 Langham Gdns, W13 8PY), *b* 1928; *ed* Cheltenham; served RAFVR and TAVR (2nd Regt HAC); FRSA. —— Betty (Elisabeth), *b* 1922. *m* 1946, James Paten Cooper, late Maj King's African Rifles, and has issue living, Charles James Beauchamp Douglas, *b* 1954: *m* 1985, Anne Nicholson, — Caroline Elisabeth Beauchamp Paten, *b* 1949: *m* 1977, Richard Barton, and has issue living, Ashley Douglas *b* 1982, Hannah Olive *b* 1979, — Rosemary Deborah Beauchamp, *b* 1951: *m* 1991, Philip Ashbourn, and has issue living, Rose Emily *b* 1992. *Residence* - 18 Clarence Hill, Dartmouth, Devon.

        Issue of late Cdr Lawrence King Beauchamp, RN, *b* 1900, *d* 1966: *m* 1924, Helen Mary Victoria who *d* 1996, da of late Robert Edward Stuart, solicitor, of Gannicox, Stroud, Glos:—

Julian Lawrence Stuart (Springfield House, Nunney, Frome, Som BA11 4LG) *b* 1928; MNI, Assoc RINA; Cdr RN; *ed* Kelly Coll: *m* 1st, 1951 (*m diss* 1966), Jennifer, who *d* 1978, da of late Harry George Parkes, of Wolverhampton; 2ndly, 1968, Isobel Mary, who *d* 1992, da of late Thomas Layfield, of Beckenham, and widow of Cdr Peter Angus Fickling, RN; 3rdly, 1994, Felicity Daphne Dorina, da of late Maj-Gen Robert Cotton Money, CB, MC, and widow of Gerard Galloway Riddick, and has issue living (by 1st *m*), Timothy Christopher Julian, *b* 1952; *ed* Kelly Coll, Birmingham Univ, and London Univ; BSocS, MA: *m* 1977, Anna Maria Magdalena, da of Henryk Zukowski, of Warsaw, Poland, and has issue living, John Christopher Michael *b* 1981, — Caroline Susan, *b* 1954: *m* 1st, 1977, Graeme Stanley Thomson Gibson, who *d* 1978; 2ndly, 1979, G. Stephen W. Woods, of Greystones, Le Mont de Rozel, St Martin, Jersey CI, and has issue living (by 2nd *m*), (Gerald) Alexander William *b* 1981, Georgina Rozelle *b* 1982, — (by 2nd *m*) Fenella Jane Isobel, *b* 1970; BA: *m* 1998, Joshua E. P. Fitch, 3rd son of Colin Digby Thomas Fitch, of The Coach House, Royston, Herts. —— Daphne Helen Stuart, *b* 1932.

Grandson of late Henry King Beauchamp, 2nd son of late Willoughby James Beauchamp (ante):—
Issue of late Brig Henry Rex Beauchamp, OBE, late RAPC, and Royal Leicestershire Regt, *b* 1906, *d* 1991: *m* 1st, 1937 (*m diss* 1947), Moira Helen, da of late G. H. Normand, of Edinburgh; 2ndly, 1954, Mrs Elizabeth Margaret Dobson (Oakfields, 20 Buckstone Close, Everton, Lymington, Hants), da of A. H. Ford-Moore, of Salisbury:—
(By 1st *m*) David Fitzgerald, *b* 1940; *ed* Uppingham, and Trin Coll, Oxford: *m* 1971, Victoria-Mary, da of James Clark, of Conn, USA, and has issue living, Gillian Alexandra, *b* 1973, — Catriona Clare, *b* 1974, — Tanya Catherine, *b* 1976.

Grandson of late Willoughby James Beauchamp (ante):—
Issue of late Vernon Francis Beauchamp, *b* 1869, *d* 1949: *m* 1897, Amy, who *d* 1948, da of late William Henry Herbert, of Great Missenden, Bucks:—
Lucien Willoughby, *b* 1903: *m* 1937, Nancy Knight, da of Bradford Richards, and has issue living, Peter Willoughby, *b* 1943: *m* 1970, Stacy Ann, da of Joseph Maurice Scanlon, of Middleboro', Mass, — Sandra, *b* 1945. *Residence* – 1 Lyman St, Westborough, Mass 01581, USA.

Grandson of late Vernon Francis Beauchamp (ante):—
Issue of late Alan Charles Douglas Beauchamp, *b* 1901, *d* 1976: *m* 1944, Olga, da of late W. K. Rhodes:—
Hugh Alan Vernon, *b* 1945.

Sir William Beauchamp-Proctor, 1st Bt (grandson of Ephraim Beauchamp of White Hall, Tottenham, Middx, citizen and mason of London); was MP for Middlesex 1747-68 which latter name he added by Act of Parliament in compliance with the terms of the will of his maternal uncle, George Proctor of Langley Park, Norfolk. The 4th Bt assumed by Roy licence 1852 the surname of Proctor-Beauchamp in lieu of Beauchamp-Proctor. The 6th Bt, Col Sir Horace George, CB Norfolk Regt, was *ka* 1915. The Rev Sir Montagu Harry Proctor-Beauchamp, 7th Bt, was a Missionary in China 1885-1936.

BEAUMONT (E) 1661, of Stoughton Grange, Leicestershire.

Exalted, not elated

Sir GEORGE HOWLAND FRANCIS BEAUMONT, 12th *Baronet*; *b* 24 Sept 1924; *s* his father, Sir GEORGE ARTHUR HAMILTON, 1933; *ed* Stowe; formerly Warrant Officer Australian Army; N-W Europe 1944-45 with Coldstream Guards, and as Lieut 60th Rifles: *m* 1st, 1949 (*m diss* 1951), Barbara, da of William Singleton; 2ndly, 1963 (*m diss* 1986), Henrietta Anne, da of late Dr Arthur Weymouth, and has issue by 2nd *m*.

𝔄rms – Azure, semée of fleurs-de-lis, a lion rampant or. 𝔠rest – On a chapeau azure, semée of fleurs-de-lis and turned up ermine, a lion passant or.
Residence – Stretton House, Stretton-on-Fosse, nr Moreton-in-Marsh, Glos GL56 9SB.

DAUGHTERS LIVING (*By 2nd marriage*)

Georgina Brienne Arabella BEAUMONT-FAY, *b* 1967: *m* 1994, Patrick Thomas Fay, yr son of John Fay, of Adderbury, Oxon. —— Francesca Renée Henrietta BEAUMONT-CLARKE, *b* (twin) 1967: *m* 1993, John William Storey Clarke, of 18 Kotara Place, Korora, NSW 2450, Australia, only son of Ernest W. S. Clarke, of Glasgow, and has issue living, Douglas William George, *b* 1994, — Eleanor Isabella Victoria *b* 1996.

This family is descended in a direct paternal line from John de Brienne, King of Jerusalem and Emperor of Constantinople. His 2nd son, Louis, *m* Agnes, heiress of Beaumont, in France, and their sons took the name of Beaumont. Henry, the 4th son of Louis and 2nd Lord Beaumont, married Eleanor, 5th daughter of Henry Plantagenet, Earl of Lancaster, grandson of King Henry III. On the death of William, 2nd Viscount Beaumont, the el branch became extinct in the male line (*see* D Norfolk). A younger branch (descended from Thomas Beaumont, second son of 4th Baron Beaumont) settled at Cole Orton, *temp* Edward IV, of which was Nicholas Beaumont, who died 1585, leaving, besides other issue, two sons: (1) Sir Henry, whose son, Sir Thomas, was created a baronet in 1619, and Viscount Beaumont, of Swords, Dublin, in 1622, which titles became extinct on the death of the 3rd viscount, in 1702; (2) Sir Thomas, of

Stoughton, grandfather of Sir Thomas, the 1st baronet, from whom is descended the present baronet. Sir Thomas, 1st Bt, was MP for Leicestershire, and Sir Henry, 2nd Bt, was also MP for Leicestershire 1679-87. Sir George, 4th Bt, represented Leicester in Parliament 1702-37, and the 7th Bt, Sir George Howland, sat for Beeralston 1790-96.

WRIXON-BECHER (UK) 1831, of Ballygiblin, Cork

He lives twice who lives well

Sir WILLIAM FANE WRIXON-BECHER, MC, 5th *Baronet*; *b* 7 Sept 1915; *s* his father, *Sir* EUSTACE WILLIAM WINDHAM, 1934; *ed* Harrow, and Magdalene Coll, Camb (BA); is Lieut and temporary Major Rifle Brig (Supplementary Reserve); European War 1939-45 in Middle East and Italy (twice wounded, MC); Lloyd's Underwriter 1950: *m* 1st, 1946 (*m diss* 1960), Hon (Ursula) Vanda Maud (BRIDGEWATER), who *d* 1984, 2nd da of 4th Baron Vivian; 2ndly, 1960, Yvonne Margaret (MOSTYN), yst da of Arthur Stuart Johnson, JP, of Henshall Hall, Congleton, Cheshire, and has issue by 1st *m*.

Arms – Vair, argent and gules, on a cantoon or a stag's head couped sable.
Crest – Out of a ducal coronet or, a demi-lion ermine gorged with a plain collar vair.
Residence – 13 Montpelier Crescent, Brighton, E Sussex BN1 3JF. *Clubs* – MCC, Royal Green Jackets, I Zingari (Secretary 1952-92).

SON LIVING (*By 1st marriage*)

JOHN WILLIAM MICHAEL (28 Atherton St, SW11 2JE; *Clubs* – White's, MCC, I Zingari, Swinley Forest Golf, Royal St George's Golf, BFSS), *b* 29 Sept 1950; *ed* Harrow, and Univ of Neuchâtel; Lloyd's 1971-87, Wise Speke Financial Services 1987-93, since when Financial Consultant HSBC Gibbs Ltd, etc; Member of Lloyd's.

DAUGHTER LIVING (*By 1st marriage*)

Susannah Elizabeth, *b* 1948: *m* 1st, 1970, Gordon M. A. P. Whitson, who *d* 1974; 2ndly 1975, Timothy William Jackson (Forth Lodge, Hill Rd, Gullane, East Lothian), and has had issue (by 1st *m*) James Alexander, *b* 1973 — (by 2nd *m*), William Harry, *b* 1978, — Lucy Alexandra Esther, *b* 1983, *d* 1984.

SISTERS LIVING

Sheila, *b* 1913. —— Rosemary, *b* 1914: *m* 1938 (*m diss* 1948), Cyril Jeremy Taylor Watson, who *d* 1974, and has issue living, Ann Maree, *b* 1939, — Joy Rosemary, *b* 1941, — Susan Brenda, *b* 1942: *m* 1963, Simon George Barff, MICE, and has issue living, Patrick George *b* 1966, Katharine Jane *b* 1968. *Residence* – Ashways, Stogumber, Taunton, Som.

The 1st baronet, Sir William Wrixon, MP for Mallow, assumed by Roy licence in 1831, his mother's maiden name of Becher. She was Mary, da of John Townsend Becher of Annisgrove, co Cork, and sister and heir of Henry Becher of Creagh. Their ancestor, Fane Becher, was granted lands in co Cork 1588.

BECKETT (UK) 1921, of Kirkdale Manor, Nawton, N Riding of Yorkshire

To benefit the State

Sir MARTYN GERVASE BECKETT, MC, 2nd *Baronet*; *b* 6 Nov 1918; *s* his father, *Hon Sir* (WILLIAM) GERVASE, 1937; *ed* Eton and Trin Coll, Camb (BA); RIBA; Capt Welsh Guards; 1939-45 War (MC): *m* 1941, Hon Priscilla Léonie Helen Brett, da of 3rd Viscount Esher, and has issue.

Arms – Gules, a fesse between three boars' heads couped erminois, a crescent for difference. Crest – A boar's head couped or, pierced by a cross patée fitchée erect gules.
Residences – 3 St Alban's Grove, W8 5PN; Kirkdale Farm, Nawton, Yorks.

SONS LIVING

RICHARD GERVASE (33 Groveway, SW9), *b* 27 March 1944; *ed* Eton; QC 1988: *m* 1976, Elizabeth Ann, da of Maj (Charles) Hugo Waterhouse (*see* D Marlborough, 1990 Edn), and has issue living, Walter Gervase, *b* 16 Jan 1987; Page of Honour to HM since 1998, — Willa Marjorie, *b* 1977, — Molly Rachel, *b* 1979, — Catherine Rose, *b* 1983. —— Jeremy Rupert (Kirkdale Manor Farm, Nawton, Kirkbymoorside, Yorks), *b* 1952: *m* 1978, Perdita Rosemary, yst da of late Capt Hugo Francis Guy Charteris, MC (*see* E Wemyss, colls), and has had issue, Joseph Hugo, *b* 1980, — Matthew Martyn, *b* 1984, *d* 1985, — William Slingsby, *b* 1987, — Lorna Elizabeth, *b* 1982.

DAUGHTER LIVING

Lucy Caroline, *b* 1942: *m* 1st, 1962 (*m diss* 1969), Adrian Whitfield; 2ndly, 1970, John Warrack, of Beck House, Rievaulx, nr Helmsley, York, and has issue living (by 1st *m*) Teresa, *b* 1963, — Emily, *b* 1965, — (by 2nd *m*), Benedict John, *b* 1971, — Christopher Martyn, *b* 1974.

HALF-SISTER LIVING

Ann Prunella (Flat 21, 27 Onslow Sq, SW7), *b* 1907: *m* 1936, Harry Bathurst Norman, GM, MD, who *d* 1966, and has issue living, Paul Bathurst (Brundon Hall, Sudbury, Suffolk), *b* 1937: *m* 1960, Susan Mary, yr da of Charles Orbell, of The Hermitage, Clare, Suffolk, and has issue living, Hal Charles *b* 1969, Arabella Harriet Bathurst *b* 1961, Teresa Prunella *b* 1963, Deborah Mary *b* 1966, — Harriet Rose, *b* 1939, — Deirdre Nell, *b* 1946: *m* 1st, 1964 (*m diss* 1970), Luciano Billi, of Florence; 2ndly, 1971, Nicholas Paul Beresford-Jones, of The Sett, Leavenheath, Colchester, Essex, and has issue (by 1st *m*) Selina Elizabeth *b* 1964: *m* 1987, Timothy Charles Kleingeld (and has issue living, Oliver Max *b* 1992, Lydia Mary *b* 1994), (by 2nd *m*), Alexandra Juliet *b* 1973.

The 1st baronet, Hon Sir (William) Gervase Beckett (2nd son of late William Beckett-Denison, and brother of 2nd Baron Grimthorpe), was Principal Proprietor and Editor-in-Ch of *Saturday Review*, and MP for Whitby Div of N Riding of Yorkshire (C) 1906-18, for Scarborough and Whitby Div thereof 1918-22, and for N Div of Leeds 1923-9.

PASTON-BEDINGFELD (E) 1661, of Oxburgh, Norfolk

Despising earthly things I look only towards the sun

Sir EDMUND GEORGE FELIX PASTON-BEDINGFELD, 9th *Baronet*; *b* 2 June 1915; *s* his father, *Sir* HENRY EDWARD, 1941; *ed* Oratory Sch, and New Coll, Oxford; is a co-heir to Barony of Grandison, and Major Welsh Guards; European War 1939-45 (wounded, despatches); Freeman City of London, and Liveryman of the Bowyers' Company; Pres Suffolk Heraldry Soc 1993: *m* 1st, 1942 (*m diss* 1953), Joan Lynette, who *d* 1965, da of Edgar G. Rees, of Llwyneithin, Llanelly; 2ndly, 1957, Agnes Kathleen Susan Anne Danos, who *d* 1974, da of late Miklos Gluck, of Budapest, Hungary; 3rdly, 1975, Mrs Peggy Hannaford-Hill, who *d* 1991, of Fort Victoria, Zimbabwe; 4thly, 1992, Mrs Sheila Riddell, eldest da of late John Douglas, of Edinburgh, and has issue by 1st *m*.

Arms – Quarterly, 1st and 4th, ermine, an eagle displayed gules, *Bedingfeld*; 2nd and 3rd, argent, six fleurs-de-lis, three, two, and one azure, a chief indented or, *Paston*. Crests – 1st, an eagle displayed or, *Bedingfeld*; 2nd, a griffin sejant wings elevated or gorged with a collar gules, therefrom a line held in the beak and terminating in a ring of the last, *Paston*. Badges – A fetter the thong gules edged and studded and with buckles at both ends chained together gold, *Bedingfeld*; a loop of chain or, *Paston*.
Seat – Oxburgh Hall, King's Lynn, Norfolk. *Residence* – The Old Stables, Great Barton, Bury St Edmunds, Suffolk IP31 3RZ.

SON LIVING (*By 1st marriage*)

HENRY EDGAR (Oxburgh Hall, King's Lynn, Norfolk PE33 9PS; College of Arms, Queen Victoria St, EC4V 4BT; *Club* – Boodle's), *b* 7 Dec 1943; *ed* Ampleforth; Chartered Surveyor; Rouge Croix Pursuivant of Arms 1983, York Herald of Arms 1993; Kt of Sovereign Mil Order of Malta; Freeman City of London and Liveryman of the Scriveners' and Bowyers' Cos; Vice-Pres of the Norfolk Heraldry Soc and of the Cambridge Univ Heraldic and Genealogical Soc: *m* 1968, Mary da of late Brig Robert Denis Ambrose, CIE, OBE, MC, and has issue living, Richard Edmund Ambrose, *b* 8 Feb 1975; *ed* Ampleforth, and Manchester Univ (BA), — Thomas Henry, *b* 1976; *ed* Ampleforth, and Bath Univ (BSc Hons), — Katherine Mary, *b* 1969; *ed* St Mary's, Camb, and Bath Univ (BSc Hons, BArch), — Charlotte Alexandra, *b* 1971; *ed* St Mary's, Camb, and Univ of Westminster (BA).

DAUGHTER LIVING (*By 1st marriage*)

Alexandra Winifred Mary, *b* 1947: *m* 1st, 1970 (*m diss* 1977), J. Michael Yearsley; 2ndly, 1978, Jack Pemberton, and has issue living (by 1st *m*), Simon, *b* 1973, — Nicola, *b* 1971, — Jennifer, *b* 1976, — (by 2nd *m*) Benjamin, *b* 1981, — Joseph, *b* 1983, — Grace, *b* 1985.

SISTER LIVING

Frances Mary Teresa, *b* 1919: *m* 1st, 1949, Frank Douglas Playford, who *d* 1956; 2ndly, 1957, Maitland Maitland-Nimmo, who *d* 1977; 3rdly, 1978, Philip James Greathead, who *d* 1997, and has issue living (by 2nd *m*), Adam Peter, *b* 1960: *m* 1989, Sandra Cavalieri, and has issue living, Roberto *b* 1991, Tamara *b* 1993, Jacqueline *b* 1995, — Mariella, *b* 1958: *m* 1981, Rodney Vincent Norman, and has issue living, Natasha Felicity *b* 1982, Sarah Frances *b* 1984. *Residence* – C31 Larmenier Village, Vredehoek, Cape Town 8001, S Africa.

COLLATERAL BRANCH LIVING

Issue of late Francis Augustus Bedingfeld, 6th son of 7th baronet, *b* 1874, *d* 1950: *m* 1926, Dorothy
Mary Hooker, who *d* 1932:—
Rev Richard Francis (Padre Pio Mission, P.O. Harding 4680, Natal, S Africa), *b* 1930; consecrated Bishop in irregular orders 1987.

This family took its name from Bedingfield, Suffolk, where they settled in 11th cent. Edmund Bedingfeld (*d* 1451) acquired the lordship of Oxburgh on marriage with Margaret, sister and co-heir of Sir Thomas Tuddenham. During the civil wars Sir Henry Bedingfeld, Knt, besides being imprisoned in the Tower, lost £47,194 18s 8d in the King's cause. His son claimed this amount of Charles II, but that monarch, being unable to pay the money, created him a baronet. The 6th baronet assumed, in 1830, by Royal Licence, the additional surname and arms of Paston, having married Margaret Anne, da and heir of Edward Paston of Appleton, Norfolk, and Horton, Glos.

BEECHAM (UK) 1914, of Ewanville, Huyton, co Palatine of Lancaster

Nothing without labour

Sir JOHN STRATFORD ROLAND BEECHAM, 4th *Baronet*; *b* 21 April 1940; *s* his father, *Sir* ADRIAN, 1982; *ed* Winchester, and Queen's Coll, Oxford.

𝕬rms – Per fesse gules and sable, a fesse nebuly plain cotised, in chief an escallop between two martlets and the like in base all or. 𝕮rest – A swan's head erased argent, beaked gules, holding an escallop and between two escallops or.

BROTHER LIVING

ROBERT ADRIAN *b* 6 Jan 1942; *ed* Winchester, and Clare Coll, Camb: *m* 1969, Daphne Mattinson, and has issue living, Michael John, *b* 1972, — Judith Mary, *b* 1970.

SISTER LIVING

Jane (Longdon Manor, Shipston-on-Stour), *b* 1945: *m* 1969, Frederick Charles Brabyn, and has issue living, Adrian Alexander Benjamin, *b* 1972, — Lowdy (a da), *b* 1978.

WIDOW LIVING OF SECOND BARONET

SHIRLEY JEAN (*Lady Beecham*) (Denton House, Denton, Harleston, Norfolk IP20 0AA), da of Albert George Hudson, of 69 Oakwood Pk Rd, N14: *m* 1959, as his 3rd wife, Sir Thomas Beecham, 2nd Bt, CH, who *d* 1961.

COLLATERAL BRANCHES LIVING

Issue of late Thomas Welles Beecham, yr son of 2nd baronet, *b* 1909, *d* 1988: *m* 1937, Mozelle, who *d* 1988, da of Edward Cairn:—
Thomas Richard, *b* 1944. —— Henry John (Tidmington Lodge, Tidmington, Shipston-on-Stour, Warwicks), *b* 1947; *ed* Winchester: *m* 1978, Carola Fiona, da of Charles Ring, of The Green, Puddletown, Dorset. —— Ann Margaret, *b* 1949: *m* 1978, Charles Hoste Hetherington, of Yew Tree, Donhead St Mary, nr Shaftesbury, Dorset, and has issue living, Peter Hoste, *b* 1980, — John Gabriel, *b* 1982, — Rebecca Claire, *b* 1984, — Emma Sarah Elizabeth, *b* 1992. —— Elizabeth Marion, *b* (twin) 1949: *m* 1st, 1969 (*m diss* 1977), Andrew George Birtwell; 2ndly, 1987, Christopher Hall, of Hundalee Cottars Farm, by Jedburgh, Roxburghshire TD8 6PA, and has issue living, (by 1st *m*) Emily Jane, *b* 1970, — (by 2nd *m*) Madeline Thomasina, *b* 1988.

Granddaughter of late Henry Beecham, 2nd son of 1st baronet:—
Issue of late Maj Joseph Michael Beecham, MBA, RA, *b* 1917, *d* 1994: *m* 1939, Sylvia (C7 Shirley Towers, Vane Hill Rd, Torquay, Devon TQ1 2BY), only child of late Frank B. Nathan, of 14 Charleville Mansions, W14:—
Valerie Anne, *b* 1941: *m* 1st, 1960, John Keenan, MB, BChir, son of late James Keenan; 2ndly, 1978, Julian Allan, of 22 Westgate Terrace, SW10 9BJ, son of late Maj Alexander William Allan, and has issue living (by 1st *m*), Lucinda Jane, *b* 1964, — Katharine Victoria, *b* 1968.

Issue of late (Henry Robert) Derrick Beecham, 2nd son of late Henry Beecham (ante), *b* 1921, *d* 1988: *m* 1st, 1943, (*m diss* 1949), Annie Ellen, da of late Thomas John King; 2ndly, 1951, Sheila (28 Grove Park Gardens, W4), da of Bertram John Martin, of Bushey Heath, Herts:—
(By 1st *m*) Jasmine Heather, *b* 1944: *m* 1963, David George Heaps, of Benington Bury, Walkern Rd, Benington, Herts SG2 7LN, and has issue living, Daniel Blue, *b* 1974, — Judith Ann, *b* 1971. —— Priscilla Rosamunde, *b* 1947: *m* 1982, Wilfred Staples. —— Susan Jane *b* 1949; adopted 1950 by W. A. Whithear, whose surname she assumed: *m* 1969 (*m diss* 1985), Roland Vaughan, and has issue living, Rhianon Jane, *b* 1969.

Issue of late Paul Beecham, 3rd son of Henry Beecham (ante), *b* 1923, *d* 1985: *m* 1952, Mary, who *d* 1990, da of William Arthur, of Pill Lawn, Barnstaple, Devon:—
†William Henry Mark, *b* 1954; *d* 1990. —— Hugh Joseph (Middle Meadow, Ilmington, nr Shipston-on-Stour, Warwicks), *b* 1957: *m* 1990, Rachel Nelson, and has issue living, Celia Mary, *b* 1992, — Eve Angelina, *b* 1995. —— Matthew Arthur (Lace Cottage, 3 Newton Lane, Turvey, Beds MK43 8HA), *b* 1965: *m* 1995, Sarah HARRISON, da of Peter Brameld, of St Mary's House, 108 Westgate, Southwell, Notts, and has issue living, Eleanor Mary, *b* 1999. —— Sarah Caroline, *b* 1953: *m* 1st, 1971, Kevin Pigott, who *d* 1974; 2ndly, 1981, Graham Jonathan Howard, of Bratch House, Station Rd, Chipping Campden, Glos, and has issue living, (by 1st *m*) Dominic Kingsley, *b* 1972, — (by 2nd *m*) Freya Helewise, *b* 1982. —— Hannah Charlotte, *b* 1956: *m* 1989, John O'Mahony, of 8 Wolstonbury Rd, Hove, E Sussex BN3 6EJ, son of late Joseph O'Mahony, and has issue living, Callum Paul Joseph, *b* 1993, — Catherine Holly Amber, *b* 1990. —— Emma Ruth BEECHAM (1 Coldicote Farm Cottage, Evenlode, Moreton-in-Marsh, Glos), *b* 1960; has resumed her maiden name: *m* 1977 (*m diss* 1992), Peter Lloyd Edmondson, and has issue living, Richard Thomas Lloyd, *b* 1980, — Josephine Alice Mary, *b* 1978.

Issue of late Christopher Beecham, 4th son of Henry Beecham (ante) *b* 1925, *d* 1970: *m* 1951, Kathleen Elizabeth, da of Maj Bertie Orme Collis, of Pinner, Middx:—
Philip Henry Orme, *b* 1962: *m* 1st, 1983 (*m diss* 1988), Suzanne, da of William Wright, of London; 2ndly, 1997, Sandra Williams. —— Diana Mary, *b* 1953: *m* 1974, John Heap, of Southampton, Hants, and has issue living, Richard Jérémie, *b* 1997, — Jessica Amy, *b* 1989. —— Honor June, *b* 1955: *m* 1984, Michael William Johnson, of Lichfield, Staffs. —— Jennifer Kate, *b* 1957: *m* 1986, Peter Cook, of Faversham, Kent. —— Penelope Carol BEECHAM, *b* 1960; resumed her maiden name: *m* 1984 (*m diss* 1994), Philip William Gray. —— Sally Helen, *b* 1965: *m* 1998, Alan Williams.

The 1st baronet, Sir Joseph Beecham, was the well-known pill manufacturer, of St Helens, a Director of A. and F. Pears (Limited), and Mayor of St Helens 1899-1900, and 1910-11-12. The 2nd baronet, *Sir* Thomas Beecham, CH, the well-known Musical Conductor, was knighted in 1916.

BEEVOR (GB) 1784, of Hethel, Norfolk

*Gentle in manner, but vigorous
in deed*

Sir THOMAS AGNEW BEEVOR, 7th *Baronet*; *b* 6 Jan 1929; *s* his father, *Com Sir* THOMAS LUBBOCK, RN, 1943; *ed* Eton, and Magdalene Coll, Camb: *m* 1st 1957 (*m diss* 1965), Barbara Clare, yst da of Capt Robert Lionel Brooke Cunliffe, CBE, RN (ret) (*see* Cunliffe Bt, colls); 2ndly, 1966 (*m diss* 1975), Carola, da of His Honour Judge Jesse Basil Herbert, MC, QC (*see* B Rea, 1985 Edn); 3rdly, 1976, Mrs Sally Elisabeth Bouwens, only da of Edward Madoc, of White Hall, Saham Toney, Thetford, Norfolk, and has issue by 1st *m*.

Arms – Per pale or and argent, on a chief indented sable, three lions rampant of the first. **Crest** – A beaver passant proper.
Residence – Hargham Hall, Norwich.

SON LIVING (*By 1st marriage*)

(THOMAS) HUGH CUNLIFFE, *b* 1 Oct 1962; *ed* Radley, Pembroke Coll, Camb, and RAC Cirencester: *m* 1988, Charlotte Louise, eldest da of Keith Ernest Harvey, of Nuthall, Nottingham, and has issue living, Thomas William Harvey, *b* 15 April 1990, — Joshua Peter Hugh, *b* 1992, — Georgina Emily Clare, *b* 1995.

DAUGHTERS LIVING (*By 1st marriage*)

Bridget Anastasia, *b* 1958: *m* 1984, Matthew J. LeF. Porteous, FRCS, eldest son of John Porteous, of London W11, and has issue living, Samuel Thomas Le Fanu, *b* 1986, — Tancred John Octavian, *b* 1988, — Anastasia Catherine Lucie, *b* 1991, — Elizabeth Clare Mary, *b* 1993. —— Juliana Clare, *b* 1960: *m* 1988, Dr Roderick Peter Ross Marrs, son of Alan Ross Marrs, of Watchet, Somerset, and has issue living, Adam, *b* 1990.

SISTERS LIVING

Ina Margaret Anastasia, *b* 1920: *m* 1942, Capt John Lewis, RA, and has issue living, Peter John Elliott, *b* 1943, — William Beevor, *b* 1948, — Judith Margaret Anne, *b* 1946. —— Jocelyn Mary (*Lady Warner*), *b* 1927: *m* 1949, Sir (Edward Courtenay) Henry Warner, 3rd Bt. *Residence* – The Grove, Great Baddow, Essex. —— Christian Chevallier, *b* 1934: *m* 1959, George Habib Homsi.

COLLATERAL BRANCHES LIVING

Granddaughter of late Ralph Jermy Beevor, 3rd son of 4th baronet:—
Issue of late Ralph Branthwayt Beevor, *b* 1895, *d* 1970: *m* 1921, Phyllis Margaret Ashburner, who *d* 1972, da of Henry Oliver Minty:—
Ruth Margaret, *b* 1929: *m* 1956, Dennis Frederick Outwin, of 17 Buxton Av, Gorleston, Gt Yarmouth, Norolk NR31 6HG, and has issue living, Christopher Dennis, *b* 1960, — Daphne Margaret, *b* 1958: *m* 1984 (*m diss* 1994), John Albert Benford, and has issue living, Abigail Jane *b* 1987, — Wendy Ruth, *b* 1964: *m* 1991, Dr David John Ekbery, and has issue living, Benjamin William *b* 1995, Robert James *b* 1998, Harriet Louise *b* 1994.

Grandchildren of late Rowland Beevor, 6th son of 4th Baronet:—
Issue of late Lt-Col Cecil Thomas Ashworth Beevor, OBE, TD, *b* 1898, *d* 1989: *m* 1925, Violet Babington, who *d* 1985, da of Edward Babington Lenton, of Ivy House, Fritton, Gt Yarmouth, Norfolk:—
Elizabeth Bridget Babington, *b* 1928: *m* 1952, John Clifford Painter, of Myrobalan, Upton, Norfolk, and has issue living, Stephen Langman, *b* 1956, — Hilary Joanna, *b* 1953, — Philippa Jane, *b* 1961.

Issue of late Miles Beevor, *b* 1900, *d* 1994: *m* 1st, 1924, Margaret Florence, who *d* 1934, da of late Algernon John Frederick Platt, of Barnby Manor, Newark-on-Trent; 2ndly, 1935, Sybil, who *d* 1991, only da of late Lt-Col John Babington Gilliat, DSO, of The Manor House, Welwyn, Herts:—
(By 1st *m*) John Rowland (104 Defoe House, Barbican, EC2), *b* 1930; *ed* Winchester, and Ch Ch, Oxford (BA); FCA: *m* 1955, Fenella Sybil, da of late Brig John Gordon Bedford-Roberts, CBE, and has issue living, Timothy James, *b* 1957, — Justin Miles, *b* 1961: *m* 1990, Isobel Rose, of Cambridge, — Catrina Margaret, *b* 1958: *m* 1989, Robert MacLean Mull, only son of Arthur Mull, of Whitwell House, Huntingdon, and has issue living, Ishbel Mary *b* 1990, Olivia *b* 1992. —— (By 2nd *m*) Antony Romer (20 Radipole Rd, SW6 5DL), *b* 1940; *ed* Winchester, and New Coll, Oxford (BA); solicitor 1966: *m* 1970, Cecilia, da of late John G. Hopton, and has issue living, Mark Andrew Antony, *b* 1975, — Karen Louise, *b* 1974. —— Ronald Hugh (35 Fairfax Rd, Bellevue Hill, NSW 2023, Australia), *b* 1947; *ed* Winchester, and Worcester Coll, Oxford (BA): *m* 1st, 1972 (*m diss* 1977), Sabina Margaret Anne, da of Harman Joseph Gerard Grisewood, CBE; 2ndly, 1981, Fiona Mary, da of John Francis Partridge, of Toragay, Sollas, N Uist, and has issue living (by 2nd *m*), Harriet Clare, *b* 1984. —— Helen, *b* 1943: *m* 1966, Norman Jonathon Dudley Foster, of Badger Farmhouse, Badger, Wolverhampton WV6 7JS, and has issue living, Peter, *b* 1972, — Charlotte Anne, *b* 1967: *m* 1994, David Ian Bruce, of Beckbury, Shropshire, and has issue living, Thomas Martin Jonathon *b* 1997, — Caroline Jane, *b* 1968: *m* 1996, Alexander Maximilian John Michaelis, of Rycote Park, Oxford, and has issue living, Zachary John *b* 1998, — Elizabeth Amy, *b* 1970.

Sir Thomas Beevor, 1st Baronet (son of Thomas Beevor, of Norwich), was a great agriculturalist. The 6th Baronet, Cdr Sir Thomas Lubbock, RN, was *ka* 1943.

BEIT (UK) 1924, of Tewin Water, Tewin, co Hertford (Extinct 1994)

Sir ALFRED LANE BEIT, 2nd and last *Baronet*.

WIDOW LIVING OF SECOND BARONET

CLEMENTINE MABELL KITTY (*Lady Beit*), da of late Maj Hon Clement Bertram Ogilvy Mitford, DSO (*see* B Redesdale, colls): *m* 1939, Sir Alfred Lane Beit, 2nd Bt, who *d* 1994. *Residences* – Russborough, Blessington, co Wicklow; 2 The Little Boltons, SW10.

BELL (UK) 1885, of Rounton Grange, co York, and of Washington Hall, co Durham

Sir JOHN LOWTHIAN BELL, 5th *Baronet*; *b* 14 June 1960; *s* his father, *Sir* HUGH FRANCIS, 1970; *ed* Glenalmond, and Royal Agric Coll, Cirencester: *m* 1985, Venetia Mary Frances, 2nd da of J. A. Perry, of Taunton, Som, and has issue.

Arms – Argent on a fesse azure, between three hawks' lures of the second, as many hawks' bells of the first. **Crest** – A hawk or, holding in its beak a hawk's lure azure, and resting its dexter claw on a sun in splendour or.
Seat – Arncliffe Hall, Ingleby Cross, Northallerton, Yorks.

SON LIVING

JOHN HUGH, *b* 29 July 1988.

DAUGHTER LIVING

Sophia Amelia Bridget, *b* 1990.

BROTHERS LIVING

David Hugh, *b* 1961. —— Andrew Mark, *b* 1963. —— Thomas Hugh, *b* 1964.

Perseverance

PERSEVERANTIA

WIDOW LIVING OF FOURTH BARONET

MARY, MB, ChB (The Hollins, E Rounton, Northallerton, Yorks DL6 2LG); D Obst RCOG; a JP for Yorks, da of late George Howson, MC, of The Hyde, Hambleden, Bucks: *m* 1st, 1959, as his 2nd wife, Sir Hugh Francis Bell, 4th Bt, who *d* 1970; 2ndly, 1991, as his 2nd wife, Prof Dominick Stuart Graham, MC, late Maj RA (*see* Graham, Bt, *cr* 1629, colls).

The 1st baronet, Sir Lowthian Bell, an Ironmaster and Coal-owner, sat as MP for Hartlepool (*L*) 1875-80. The 2nd baronet, Sir (Thomas) Hugh, was Lord-Lieut for N Riding of York 1906-31, and Pres Iron and Steel Institute 1907-10. The 3rd baronet, Sir Maurice Hugh Lowthian Bell, CMG, TD, was Col Yorkshire Regt, and served in S Africa 1900-1901, and in European War 1914-19 (CMG).

MORRISON-BELL (UK) 1905, of Otterburn Hall, Elsdon, Northumberland

Perseverance

Sir WILLIAM HOLLIN DAYRELL MORRISON-BELL, 4th *Baronet; b* 21 June 1956; *s* his father, *Capt Sir* CHARLES REGINALD FRANCIS 1967; *ed* Eton, and St Edmund Hall, Oxford: *m* 1984, Cynthia Hélène Marie, yr da of Teddy White, of Château d'Oex, Switzerland, and has issue.

ᴀrms – Quarterly, 1st and 4th, sable, on a fesse ermine between three bells argent, a falcon close between two crescents of the field; 2nd and 3rd, argent, on a fesse azure between three Moors' heads couped at the neck proper, the turbans vert turned up argent, three roses or. ᴄrest – 1st, a falcon close proper, belled and jessed or, holding in the beak a bell argent; 2nd, in front of a Moor's head couped at the shoulders as in the arms three roses gules.
Seat – Highgreen, Tarset, Northumberland. *Residence –* 106 Bishop's Rd, SW6 7AR.

SON LIVING

THOMAS CHARLES EDWARD, *b* 13 Feb 1985.

DAUGHTER LIVING

Emily Prudence Colette, *b* 1997.

BROTHER LIVING

Julian Francis Tarret, *b* 1959: *m* 1st, 1984, Penelope Josephine, da of late Lt-Col Richard Ian Griffith Taylor, DSO, MC, JP, DL, of Chipchase Castle, Wark-on-Tyne, Northumberland (*see* By Buckland, 1973-74 Edn), and formerly wife of Robert John Elkington (*see* B Wolverton, 1970 Edn); 2ndly, 1991, Karenina A., da of Nigel O'Flaherty, of Glenlion, Cabinteely, Dublin 18, and has issue living (by 1st *m*), Charles Richard Francis, *b* 17 Nov 1986, — (by 2nd *m*) Francis William Doyle, *b* 1995, — Alice Ursula Grace, *b* 1992.

AUNTS LIVING (*Daughters of 2nd baronet*)

Kathleen Frances, TD *b* 1906; a JP and an Hon Alderman for Northumberland (formerly Alderman); formerly Senior Com ATS. *Residence –* Charlton, Tarset, Northumberland. —— Veronica Frances, *b* 1911: *m* 1942, John Jerome Stonborough, formerly Maj Canadian Army, and has issue living, Jerome Claude, *b* 1943; *ed* Stowe, — John Tarret Christian, *b* 1948; *ed* Gordonstoun: *m* 1987, Jane, only da of Louis Berger, and widow of Charles Tallents, and has issue living, Eloise Charlotte India *b* 1988, — Margaret Isabella, *b* 1944; *ed* Benenden. *Residence –* Glendon, Corfe Mullen, Wimborne, Dorset BH21 3HB.

WIDOW LIVING OF THIRD BARONET

PRUDENCE CAROLINE (70 Doneraile St, SW6), only da of late Lt-Col Wyndham Dayrell Davies, 60th Rifles (ret): *m* 1st, 1955, Sir Charles Reginald Francis Morrison-Bell, 3rd Bt, who *d* 1967; 2ndly, 1969, Peter Gillbanks.

COLLATERAL BRANCHES LIVING

Issue of late (Arthur) Clive Morrison-Bell (2nd son of 1st baronet), who was *cr* a *Baronet* 1923:—
See Morrison-Bell, Bt, *cr* 1923 (ext).

Issue of late Ernest Fitzroy Morrison-Bell, OBE, 3rd son of 1st baronet, *b* 1871, *d* 1960: *m* 1902, Maud Evelyn, who *d* 1960, da of late Lieut-Col Frank Henry, JP, formerly 9th Lancers, of Elmestree, Tetbury, Gloucestershire:—
Louise Monica (The Harroways, Shop Lane, East Lavant, Chichester, W Sussex PO18 0BA), *b* 1903: *m* 1929, Col Cecil Everard Montague Grenville-Grey, CBE, late KRRC, who *d* 1973, and has issue living, Wilfrid Ernest, *b* 1930: *m* 1963, Edith Dlamini, and has issue living, Wilfrid Jonathan *b* 1964, Peter Thulani *b* 1967, Susan Thandi *b* (twin) 1964, — Susan Monica (*Duchess of Richmond and Gordon*), *b* 1932: *m* 1951, 10th Duke of Richmond and Gordon, and has issue (see that title). —— Claire Wilhelmina Maud, *b* 1907: *m* 1928, Maj Robert Moubray, formerly 16th Lancers, who *d* 1961, and has issue living, John Robert Fitzroy (Glencairn, Castlegate, Jedburgh, Roxburghshire TD8 6BD), *b* 1945: *m* 1972 (*m diss* 1990), Patricia Maeve MacLeod, and has issue living, Belinda Mary Claire *b* 1973, — Evelyn Mary (*Duchess of Sutherland*), *b* 1929: *m* 1979, 6th Duke of Sutherland, — Anne Catherine Wilhelmina (Alebank House, Ancrum, Jedburgh, Roxburghshire), *b* 1931, — Gillian Claire (*Lady Boughey*), *b* 1933: *m* 1976, Sir Richard James Boughey, 10th Bt, who *d* 1978. *Residence –* The Glebe House, Maxton, St Boswells, Roxburghshire. —— Mary Ernestine, *b* 1910; formerly Sen Com ATS: *m* 1946, Brig Geoffrey William Goschen, DSO, MC, late RHA, who *d* 1988, and has issue living, John Henry, *b* 1949, — Mary (10B Downfield Rd, Clifton, Bristol BS8 2JT), *b* 1948: *m* 1973, David Robson Moore, who *d* 1987, and has issue living, Nathaniel James William *b* 1974, Roxanne Diana *b* 1977. *Residence –* 2 Close Gdns, Tetbury, Glos GL8 8DO.

Issue of late Lieut-Col Eustace Widdrington Morrison-Bell, 4th son of 1st baronet, *b* 1874, *d* 1947: *m* 1914, Hon Harriet Margaret Hepburn-Stuart-Forbes-Trefusis, who *d* 1975, da of 20th Baron Clinton:—
Pamela Elizabeth, *b* 1918. —— Sylvia Morwenna, *b* 1922: *m* 1941, Maj Arthur Thomas Chamberlayne, R Fusiliers, and has issue living, Michael Thomas, LVO (Lower Hearn, Headley, Hants), *b* 1943; *ed* Wellington Coll; FCA 1968; LVO 1997. *Residence –* Clouds Garden Lodge, East Knoyle, Salisbury, Wilts.

The 1st baronet, Sir Charles William Bell, assumed by Roy Licence 1905 the additional surname and arms of Morrison. The 2nd baronet, Sir Claude William Hedley Morrison-Bell, sometime Capt Argyll and Sutherland Highlanders, served on N-W Frontier of India 1897-8 and during European War 1914-18.

MORRISON-BELL (UK) 1923, of Harpford, co Devon (Extinct 1956)

Sir (ARTHUR) CLIVE MORRISON-BELL, 1st and last *Baronet*.

DAUGHTERS LIVING OF FIRST BARONET

Shelagh Jocelyn (*Lady Campbell*), *b* 1913: *m* 1st, 1943 (*m diss* 1951), William Cooper Moore; 2ndly, 1968, as his 2nd wife, Sir Ralph Abercromby Campbell, who *d* 1989, and has issue living (by 1st *m*), David Anson Clive (373 Marion St, Denver, Colorado 80218, USA), *b* 1944: *m* 1978, Christiane Hyde, da of Casper Citron, of New York, NY, USA, and has issue living, Cornelia Wingfield *b* 1986. —— Patricia Louisa *b* 1919: *m* 1st, 1941 (*m diss* 1956), Maj John Nevile Wake Gwynne, RA, who *d* 1981 (Wake, Bt); 2ndly, 1968, Henry Michael Barclay, of Hanworth Hall, Norfolk, and has issue living (by 1st *m*), Nevile Martin (7 Campden Hill Mansions, Edge St, W8), *b* 1941; *ed* Eton, and Trin Coll, Oxford: *m* 1st, 1972, Charlotte, da of late Sir Cyril Hugh Kleinwort (*see* Kleinwort Bt, colls) and formerly wife of Richard Lawrence Baillieu; 2ndly, 1983, Frederica Rosana Gale Lennox, and has issue living (by 1st *m*), Chloe Patricia *b* 1973, — Jessica Violet, *b* 1944: *m* 1st, 1966, Charles Cospatrick Douglas-Home, who *d* 1985 (*see* B Home of the Hirsel, colls); 2ndly, 1993, Rodney Leach.

GRATTAN-BELLEW (UK) 1838, of Mount Bellew, co Galway

Sir HENRY CHARLES GRATTAN-BELLEW, 5th *Baronet*; *b* 12 May 1933; *s* his father, *Lieut-Col Sir* CHARLES CHRISTOPHER, MC, 1948; *ed* Ampleforth; was Assist Dist Commr Kenya Police Reserve 1953-4, and Dist Officer, Kenya Administration 1954-55; journalist, radio and TV broadcaster, publisher; Dir of several Cos: *m* 1st, 1956 (*m diss* 1966), Naomi, formerly wife of Herbert Ellis, and da of late Dr Charles Cyril Morgan, of Chester; 2ndly, 1967 (*m diss* 1974), Gillian Hulley; 3rdly, 1978, Elzabe Amy, only da of Henry Gilbert Body, of Utrecht, Natal, and widow of J. B. Westerveld, of Pretoria, and has issue by 2nd *m*.

Arms – Quarterly, 1st and 4th sable, fretty or, a crescent argent or difference, *Bellew*; 2nd and 3rd, per saltire sable and ermine over all a lion rampant or, *Grattan*. Crests – 1st, an arm embowed in armour proper, charged with a crescent for difference, grasping in the hand a sword proper, pommel and hilt or, *Bellew*; 2nd, a dove proper, holding in its dexter claw a sceptre and standing on a barrel or, *Grattan*.
Residence – Sandford Park, PO Box 7, Bergville, Natal 3350, S Africa.

Tout d'en haut

All from above

SON LIVING (*By 2nd marriage*)

PATRICK CHARLES, *b* 7 Dec 1971.

DAUGHTER LIVING (*By 2nd marriage*)

Deirdre Sophia, *b* 1967.

SISTER LIVING

Deirdre Maureen, *b* 1924: *m* 1946, Gerard Kiernan, and has issue living, Charles Dominick, *b* 1947, — Henry Gerard, *b* 1952, — Valerie Maureen, *b* 1946, — Maureen Gabriel, *b* 1949, — Dawn Vivien, *b* 1956. *Residence* – 35 Priory Grove, Stillorgan, Dublin.

COLLATERAL BRANCHES LIVING

Issue of late Thomas Henry Grattan-Bellew, 4th son of 3rd baronet, *b* 1901, *d* 1967: *m* 1933, Bettina Idrone Dorothy, who *d* 1995, el da of late Maj John Edward Blake Loftus, of Mount Loftus, co Kilkenny:—
Patrick Edward (472 Edison Av, Ottawa, Ontario, Canada K2A 1T9), *b* 1934; *ed* Univ Coll, Dublin (BSc), and McGill Univ, Canada (MSc); PhD Camb; a mineralogist: *m* 1980, Elly Bollegraaf-Dwinger, da of late Nathan Gruner, and step-da of late Ernst Bollegraaf. —— Idrone Pauline Mary, *b* 1936: *m* 1964, Roger William Brittain, of 90 Broxash Rd, SW11 DAB, and has issue living, William Henry Grattan, *b* 1965, — Charles Francis, *b* 1966, — James Nicholas, *b* 1971, — Georgina Mary Idrone, *b* 1968.

Issue of late Sir Arthur John Grattan-Bellew, CMG, QC, 5th and yst son of 3rd baronet, *b* 1903, *d* 1985: *m* 1931, Winifred Mary, who *d* 1979, da of Edmond R. Mahony, of Kilinan, Kilchreest, co Galway:—
(Arthur Henry) Bertram (Hole Farm, Gt Waldingfield, nr Sudbury, Suffolk), *b* 1937; *ed* Downside; 2nd Lieut late 8th Hussars; Jt Master of the Galway Blazers: *m* 1961, Georgina Madeleine Mary, da of Sir George Edward Mordaunt Milner, 9th Bt, and has issue living, Charles Henry Mordaunt, *b* 1964, — Sophie Rose, *b* 1962: *m* 1995, David George Oliver, of 689 Fulham Rd, SW6 5UJ, son of George Oliver, of Eungai Creek, NSW, and has issue living, Edward George Mordaunt *b* 1996, Cosmo Patrick Valentine *b* 1999. —— Gillian Barbara, *b* 1934: *m* 1967, Peter Haggard Lyster, of Little Chishill Manor, Cambs, and has issue living, Thomas Henry, *b* 1971, — Grania Mary, *b* 1968, — Anna Gillian, *b* 1969.

The 1st baronet was fourth in descent from Michael Bellew of Mount Bellew, a descendant of Christopher Bellew, brother of Sir Patrick Bellew, 1st baronet (*cr* 1688) (*see* B Bellew). The father of the 3rd baronet assumed by Roy licence the additional surname and arms of Grattan. The 4th baronet, Sir Charles Christopher, MC, was Lieut-Col King's Roy Rifle Corps (Reserve).

BELLINGHAM (GB) 1796, of Castle Bellingham, co Louth
(Name pronounced "Bellinjum")

So it is

A friend to a friend

†*Sir* NOEL PETER ROGER BELLINGHAM, 7th *Baronet* (of 2nd creation), *b* 4 Sept 1943; *s* his father, *Sir* ROGER CARROLL PATRICK STEPHEN, MB, ChB, DA, 1973; *ed* Lindisfarne Coll: *m* 1977, Jane, da of Edwin William Taylor, of Willow Close, White Hall Rd, Sale, Cheshire. The 7th baronet *d* 7 July 1999.

Arms – Argent, three bugle horns sable, stringed gules and garnished or. **Crest** – A buck's head couped or.
Seat – Castle Bellingham, co Louth. **Residence** – 20 Davenport Park Rd, Davenport, Stockport, Cheshire SK2 6JS.

BROTHER LIVING

ANTHONY EDWARD NORMAN, *b* 24 March 1947; *ed* Rossall; Headhunter: *m* 1991, Denise Marie, da of Henry Calvin Moity, of 29476 Anner Rd, Picayune, Mississippi, USA, and has issue living, William Alexander Noel Henry, *b* 19 Aug 1991. *Residence* – ......

WIDOW LIVING OF SIXTH BARONET

MARY (*Mary, Lady Bellingham*), da of late William Norman: *m* 1941, Sir Roger Carroll Patrick Stephen Bellingham, 6th Bt, MB, ChB, DA, who *d* 1973.

COLLATERAL BRANCHES LIVING

Grandchildren of late Maj Sydney Edwin Bellingham, el son of late Lt-Col William Johnston Bellingham, 5th son of 2nd baronet:—
Issue of late Major Alan Mure Bellingham, MC, *b* 1881; *d* 1946: *m* 1st, 1914 (*m diss* 1930) Beatrix Laura, who *d* 1962, da of late John Henry Harrison, ICS; 2ndly, 1930, Mabel Theodora Lucy, who *d* 1981, da of Theodore Seton Dury, Ch Master, Supreme Court, and formerly wife of Nestor Seppings Tirard:—
(By 1st *m*) Beatrix Pamela BELLINGHAM-KIGGELL, *b* 1918; assumed the surname of Bellingham-Kiggell by deed poll 1970: *m* 1st, 1938 (*m diss* 1945), Ronald Arthur Cleave; 2ndly, 1947 (*m diss* 1962), John Chatterton Coysgarne Sim, and has issue living, (by 1st *m*) Zenia Sophia SIM, *b* 1938; assumed by deed poll 1948 the name of Sim in lieu of her patronymic, — (by 2nd *m*) Carol Ann, *b* 1950. —— (By 2nd *m*) Patrick Alan Sydney (22 Willow View, Straightway Head, Whimple, Devon), *b* 1936; *ed* Christ's Hosp: *m* 1st, 1958 (*m diss* 1981), Elizabeth Mary, da of late Harold Hall Bagnall, of Westerham, Kent; 2ndly, 1981 (*m diss* 1990), Elizabeth Mary, da of Maj Stanislas Lis, Polish Army, and widow of Arnold Derrick Workman; 3rdly, 1991, Brenda Mary Nixon, formerly wife of Jack Hal Nixon, and has issue living (by 1st *m*), Alan Hall (96 Ross St, Cambridge CB1 3BU), *b* 1960; *ed* Christ's Hosp, and St Catharine's Coll, Camb: *m* 1984 (*m diss* 1991), Anne Crick, — Dorcas Elizabeth, *b* 1962: *m* 1st, 1984 (*m diss* 1994), Richard Puczynski; 2ndly, 1994, Tom Harold Glasgow III, of Florida, USA, — Isobel Marie, *b* (twin) 1962: *m* 1982, Philip Morgan, and has issue living, Charles Henry *b* 1986, Purdey Ashley *b* 1988, — (by 2nd *m*) Jasper Guy Patrick, *b* 1981, — Katharine Lucy Rose, *b* 1985. —— Brigid Alaine, *b* 1933: *m* 1st, 1954 (*m diss* 1969), Brian Deakin: 2ndly, 1970 (*m diss* 1978), Richard Barham; 3rdly, 1978, Dr Gene Don Smith, who *d* 1985, of 2795 Teller St, Lakewood, Colorado 80215, USA, and has issue living (by 1st *m*), Charles Rupert Deakin BARHAM (14 Drury St, Hill End, Qld 4101, Australia), *b* 1956; legally adopted by stepfather 1972 and assumed surname of Barham; patronymic retained as a forename: *m* 1985, Cheryl Robyn Pearce, and has issue living, Courtney Rebecca *b* 1993, — Timothy Graham DEAKIN (14 Nearco St, Fig Tree Pocket, Qld 4068, Australia), *b* 1959: *m* 1985, Leith Perkins, and has issue living, Kiera Adele *b* 1991, — Helena Judith DEAKIN (19599 E Belleview Place, Aurora, Colorado 80015, USA), *b* 1958; has issue living, Jessica Renee *b* 1990.

Grandchildren of late Thomas Eudo Bellingham (infra):—
Issue of late William Eudo Bellingham, b (Dec) 1882, d 1954: m 1906, Louisa Bertha, who d 1935, da of William
Arthur Krick, of Chicago, USA:—
William Arthur Eudo (2810 Merrimac Blvd, Toledo, Ohio 43606, USA), b 1909: m 1932, Myrna Arlene, da of Edwin T.
Netser, and has issue living, William Edwin (4506 Shadow Glen Drive, Colorado Springs, CO 80909, USA), b 1938: m
1959, Renee Anne, da of Wayne McGrew, and has issue living, William Keith (2915 Haystack Drive, Colorado Springs,
CO 80922, USA), b 1967: m 1990, Clara Margi Hutchinson (and has issue living, William Clifton b 1992), Catherine Anne
b 1971, — Kay Arlene, b 1934: m 1st, 1959 (m diss 1989), Thomas Huntington Taylor; 2ndly, 1993, Lewis Saxby, of 5565
Citation Rd, Toledo, Ohio 43606, USA, and has had issue, Thomas Huntington b 1959; d 1993, Jane Arlene b 1961: m
1994, Peter Elfers, of 777 N Macqueston Pky, Mt Vernon, NY 10552, USA, — Jean Carolyn, b 1941: m 1967, Patrick
James Johnson, of 3534, Edgevale, Toledo, Ohio 43606, USA, and has two adopted children, Jonathan Patrick b 1971,
Jodi Jean b 1973, — Linda Anne, b 1944: m 1970, Richard Henry Allardyce, of 11606 Helmont Drive, Oakton, VA 22124,
USA, and has issue living, Julie Anne b 1976, Julie Anne b 1979, — Gwen Francis, b 1946: m 1970, Richard
Osenbaugh, of 3543 Robin, Toledo, Ohio 43623, USA. ——— †Frederick Richard, b 1923: m 1st, 1944 (m diss 1947), Mary
Winifred, da of Cary C. Winans; 2ndly, 1951, Elizabeth Hayes; 3rdly, 1958, Geraldine Helen Hermanson (140 N Hilltop
Drive, Titusville, Florida 32796-2529, USA), and d 1990, leaving, (by 1st m) Patricia, b 1945, — Kathleen, b 1947, — (by
2nd m) Michelle, b 1952, — (by 3rd m) Timothy Shane, b 1959: m 1985, Leslie Anne Fritz, and has issue living, Shane
Patrick b 1989, Brian Lewis b 1992. ——— Louise Hazel, b 1913: m 1932, Conrad Edward Nelson, and has issue living,
Constance Paulette, b 1944: m (March) 1963, Thomas Neil Nelson, of 2711 East First St, Marina Terrace, Ft Myers, FL
33901, USA, and has issue living, Rodney Kirk b (Nov) 1963, — Ryan Jay, b 1973.

Issue of late John Stuart Bellingham, b 1889, d 1965: m 1937, Doreen, who d 1974, da of late Edward O'Brien,
of Ambleside, Westmorland:—
Roger Graham (13 Ridgeway Close, Lightwater, Surrey GU18 5XU) b 1939: m 1965, Pauline, da of David Rankine, and
has issue living, Alan Graham, b 1966: m 1991, June Rose, da of Harry Doran, and has issue living, Tara Pauline Doran
b 1994, — John Terrance, b 1969: m 1995, Hazel Katherine, only da of Harding Derek Spencer, of Wey Farm, Dargle, S
Africa, and has issue living, Kate Charlotte b 1998.

Grandchildren of late William Stewart Bellingham, son of late John Bellingham, brother of 2nd
baronet:—
Issue of late Thomas Eudo Bellingham, b 1849, d 1923: m (March) 1882, Grace, who d 1905, da of late Rev W.
Harkness, MA, of Athea, co Limerick:—
Thomas Francis Gordon, b 1885: m 1918, Iva Abigail, da of A. E. Bridge, and has issue living Stewart (Bawlf, Alberta,
Canada), b 1921: m 19—, and has issue living, Roger b 19—, a da b 19—, — William Milton, b 1922, — Stephen
Ramsay (Calgary, Alberta, Canada), b 1924: m 19—, and has issue living. Residence – Bawlf, Alberta, Canada.
——— Hazel, b 1887: m 1915, Charles Wundabaldt Christen, who d 1961, and has issue living, Charles Patrick Harkness b
1918: m 1946, Virginia Beane, and has issue living, Charles Patrick b 1947, Julia Hazel b 1949, Christina Helen b 1953,
— John Wundabaldt, b 1923: m 1943, Theresa Lucille Lovich, and has issue living, John Charles b 1946, Steven William
b 1948, Daniel Thomas b 1952, David Paul b 1953, Patricia Terese b 1944, — Hazel Mary b 1924: m 1st, 1943, Albert
Jackson; 2ndly, 1946, Lawrence Robert Hanstein, of Staunton, Illinois, USA, and has issue living, (by 1st m) Anthony Lee
b 1945, (by 2nd m) Laurence Robert b 1948, David b 1953, Mary Lynn b 1951.

Grandson of late Arthur D'Arcy Bellingham, 5th son of William Stewart Bellingham (ante):—
Issue of late Lt-Col Arthur Stuart Bellingham, b 1893, d 1969: m 1923, Jean (Glencara, Ballynacargy, co West-
meath; Salar Lodge, Leenane, co Galway; The Cliffs, Howth, co Dublin), da of Andrew Arthur, of Rosemount,
Ayrshire:—
John Stuart (5 rue Paul-Louis-Courier, F75007 Paris, France), b 1929; ed Eton, and Magdalene Coll, Camb (BA): m 1989,
Fiona Aileen, elder da of Sir Peter Walter James Nugent, 5th Bt (cr 1831).

Grandchildren of late Lt-Col Arthur Stuart Bellingham (ante):—
Issue of late (Arthur) Henry Bellingham, Lieut, Leicestershire Yeo, b 1926, d 1959: m 1953, June Marion
Cloudesley, of Congham Lodge, Hillington, King's Lynn, who m 2ndly, 1962, Col Ian Bruce Baillie, Life Gds,
who d 1978 (see B Burton, colls), da of Arthur Cloudesley Smith, FRCS:—
Henry Campbell, MP, b 1955; ed Eton, and Magdalene Coll, Cambridge (BA 1977); Barrister-at-Law, Middle Temple
1978; MP for Norfolk North West (C) since 1983: m 1993, Emma Louise, da of Peter John Henry Whiteley (see E
Guilford). ——— Elizabeth Alison, b 1956: m 1989, Richard Charles Rowley, only son of Sir Charles Robert Rowley, 7th
Bt.

This ancient family derives its name from Bellingham-in-Tyndale, Northumberland. William de Bellingham was Sheriff of
Tyndale 1279. Robert of Bellingham, temp Henry V, m Elizabeth, da of Sir Richard Tunstall, KG. His el son, Sir Henry
was cr Knt Banneret at Battle of Wakefield 1460, whose son, Sir Robert, was similarly honoured at Battle of Stoke 1487.
The present family descends from Alan of Levens, Westmorland, 8th son of Robert (ante). Alan's gt-grandson, Robert,
settled in Ireland and was father of (i) Sir Daniel of Dubber, co Dublin, Lord Mayor of Dublin, who was cr a Bt of Ireland 1687 (title ext 1699), and (ii) Henry of Gernonstown (later called Castle Bellingham) co Louth. Henry served as
Cornet in a Regt of Cavalry raised in the north for suppressing the Irish rebellion. By his wife, Lucy Sibthorpe, he was
father of Col Thomas who raised a Regt of Cavalry and served with William III, where he acted as his guide during the
march from Dundalk to the Boyne. After that battle he accompanied the King to Duleek. In consequence, James II's
army destroyed Castle Bellingham by fire. His grandson, Alan of Castle Bellingham, m 1738, Alice, da of co-heir of the
Rev Hans Montgomery of Grey Abbey, co Down. Alan's 4th son, Sir William, was in 1796 cr a Bt of GB with remainder
to the heirs male of the body of his father, and was MP for Reigate and Private Sec to Pitt. He was s by his nephew, Sir
Alan (el son of Alan, el brother of 1st Bt) 1826. Sir (Alan) Henry, 4th Bt was MP for co Louth and Private Chamberlain
to Popes Pius IX, Leo XIII and Pius X. Brig-Gen Sir Edward Henry Charles Patrick, CMG, DSO, late R Scots, was a
Senator of the Irish Free State 1925-56.

BENN (UK) 1914, of The Old Knoll, Metropolitan Borough of Lewisham

By God's favour

Ann, *b* 1996.

Sir (JAMES) JONATHAN BENN, 4th *Baronet*, *b* 27 July 1933; *s* his father, *Sir* JOHN ANDREWS, 1984; *ed* Harrow, and Clare Coll, Camb (BA 1957, MA 1961); Dir Reedpack Ltd 1988-90, Chm and Chief exec, Reed Paper and Board (UK) Ltd 1976-90, and Chm SCA Pension Trustees Ltd 1990-98, Pres, British Paper and Board Industries Federation 1985-87: *m* 1960, Jennifer Mary, eldest da of late Dr Wilfred Vivian Howells, OBE, of The Ferns, Clun, Shropshire, and has issue.

Arms – Argent, two barrulets indented gules, between in chief as many dragons' heads erased and in base a pencil and a pen in saltire proper, tied with a lace azure, pendent therefrom a torteau, charged with a figure "1914" or. **Crest** – On a rock a spear erect proper, flowing therefrom a pennon azure, charged with the word "Onward", letters or.
Residence – Fielden Lodge, Tonbridge Rd, Ightham, nr Sevenoaks, Kent TN15 9AN.

SON LIVING

ROBERT ERNEST (ROBIN) (15 Northumberland St, Edinburgh EH3 6LL), *b* 17 Oct 1963; *ed* Judd Sch, Tonbridge, and Corpus Christi Coll, Camb (BA 1985, MA 1989); ACA 1989, FCA 1999; Principal Deloitte & Touche, Edinburgh: *m* 1985, Sheila Margaret, 2nd da of Dr Alastair Macleod Blain, of Braco Lodge, Elgin, Moray, and has issue living, Alastair Frederick, *b* 28 Feb 1995, — Catriona Jennifer, *b* 1997.

DAUGHTER LIVING

Juliet Clare, *b* 1966: *m* 1993, Simon M. Erridge, yr son of Francis Erridge, of Goldhanger, Essex, and has issue living, Thomas Christopher, *b* 1999, — Alison

BROTHER LIVING

Timothy John, *b* 1936; *ed* Harrow, Princeton Univ, and Clare Coll, Camb (MA); Lt Scots Guards; formerly Chm and Man Dir of Benn Bros Ltd; Chm Timothy Benn Publishing Ltd, Bouverie Publishing Co Ltd, South Eastern Magazines Ltd, Buckley Press Ltd, Henry Greenwood & Co Ltd, Stone & Cox (Publications) Ltd, Dalesman Publishing Co Ltd: *m* 1st, 1959 (*m diss* 1973), Valerie Hamlyn, yr da of late Capt P.H.W. Davie; 2ndly, 1973, Mrs Susan Elizabeth Hardingham, only da of George Hodges; 3rdly, 1982, Christina Grace Townsend, da of late W. R. Hughes, and has issue living (by 1st *m*), Peter Quentin, *b* 1961, — William Justin, *b* 1964: *m* 1994, Isabelle F., yst da of John Anthony Bloxridge, of Bosco Grande, Tuscany, and has issue living, Chiara Carlotta Hamlyn *b* 1998, — Thomas Hamlyn, *b* 1967: *m* 1988, Yvette, yr da of G. B. Wilson, of Buckfastleigh, Devon, and has issue living, Louella *b* 1986, Charlotte *b* 1989, Jemima Jaye *b* 1993.

SISTERS LIVING

Susan Paschal, *b* 1930: *m* 1952, Michael Graeme Compton, of Michaelmas Lodge, Limpsfield, Surrey, and has issue living, Josephine, *b* 1953, — Ann, *b* 1956. —— Christina Frances, *b* 1948: *m* 1976 (*m diss* 19—), J. Andrew R. Wilton, and has issue living, Henry, *b* 1979. —— Marigold Margaret, *b* 1950.

UNCLE LIVING (*son of 2nd baronet*)

Edward Glanvill, *b* 1905; *ed* Harrow, and Clare Coll, Camb; Pres of Benn Bros Ltd; Major E Surrey Regt: *m* 1931, Beatrice Catherine, MBE, da of late Claude Newbald, of Lyndhurst, Wallington, Surrey, and has issue living, James Glanvill, *b* 1944: *m* 1st, 1967, Judith, da of late W. II. McMinn, of 15 Ingram House, Hampton Wick, Surrey; 2ndly, 1973, Susan May, da of late Vivian G. Beardsell, of Yellow Flat, Borde Hill, Haywards Heath, W Sussex; 3rdly, 1990, Claire Stephanie, da of Eric Baverstock, of 4 Bealings Close, Southampton Hants, and has issue living (by 2nd *m*) Peter Glanvill *b* 1974, Alistair James *b* 1975, Suzanna Victoria *b* 1979, — Elizabeth, *b* 1936: *m* 1961, Kenneth Charles Stewart Young, of Old Rectory, Buckland, nr Aylesbury, Bucks, and has had issue, Catherine Ann *b* 1962, Miranda *b* 1964, *d* 1988. *Residence* – Crescent Cottage, Aldeburgh, Suffolk IP15 5HW.

AUNT LIVING (*daughter of 2nd baronet*)

Elizabeth, *b* 1907: *m* 1935, Paul Alfred Shinkman, who *d* 1975, and has issue living, Paul Glanvill (617 Shady Lawn Rd, Chapel Hill, NC 27514, USA), *b* 1936; *ed* Landon Sch, Harvard Coll (BA), Univ of Michigan (MA, PhD): *m* 1969, Judith Kay, da of F. E. Barnett, of Charlotte, NC, USA, — Christopher Joseph (5607 Wood Way, Bethesda, Maryland 20816, USA) *b* 1940; *ed* St Albans Sch, Thiel Coll (BA), Westminster Coll (MA), Univ of Pittsburgh (PhD): *m* 1965, Marsha Ann, el da of Marshall Axel Friberg, of Jamestown, NY, and has issue living, Matthew Christopher *b* 1972, Elizabeth Ann *b* 1975, — Bernard Francis (5600 Wood Way, Sumner, Bethesda, Maryland 20816, USA), *b* 1943; *ed* St Mark's Sch, Dartmouth Coll (BA): *m* 1974, Gillian Claire, yr da of Daniel Crawley, of London, SE, and has issue living, Paul Daniel *b* 1983, Claire Amelia *b* 1980. *Residence* – 3040, Dent Pl, NW, Georgetown, Wash, DC 20007, USA.

WIDOW LIVING OF THIRD BARONET

Hon URSULA HELEN ALERS HANKEY (*Hon Lady Benn*), da of 1st Baron Hankey: *m* 1929, Sir John Andrews Benn, 3rd Bt, who *d* 1984. *Residence* – 15 The Waldrons, Oast Rd, Hurst Green, Oxted, Surrey RH8 9DY.

COLLATERAL BRANCHES LIVING

Issue of late Capt Frederick Christopher Benn, 3rd son of 2nd baronet, *b* 1912, *ka* 1941: *m* 1937, Phyllis, who *d* 1990, da of late E. M. Preston, of Slaugham Park, Sussex:—
Oliver Preston, *b* 1938; *ed* Eton, and Clare Coll, Camb; 2nd Lieut Intelligence Corps; Bar Middle Temple 1970: *m* 1st, 1970, Clarissa Dorothy Jeannette, da of Guillermo Sergio Santa Cruz y Zerrano, of Weybridge, Surrey; 2ndly, 1996, Tran da Thao, yr da of Tran van Trong, and Mrs Le Thi Nhi, of Ho Chin Minh City, Vietnam, and has issue living (by 1st *m*), Belinda Alice Irene, *b* 1970: *m* 1993, Timothy Francis Farnfield (*see* Wigram, Bt, colls).

Issue living of late Rt Hon (William) Wedgwood Benn, DSO, DFC, PC (2nd son of 1st baronet), who was *cr* Viscount Stansgate 1942 (*see* that title).

The 1st baronet, Sir John Williams Benn, Chm of Benn Brothers (Limited), publishers, was a Member of London County Council 1889-1922 (Chm 1904-5), and sat as MP for St George's Div of Tower Hamlets (*L*) 1892-95, and for Devonport 1904-10. The 2nd baronet, Sir Ernest John Pickstone Benn, CBE, was a Director (sometime Chm) of Benn Bros Ltd, of Ernest Benn Ltd, and of United Kingdom Provident Institution, Pres of So of Individualists, and High Sheriff of co London 1932. The 3rd baronet, Sir John Andrews Benn, was Chm United Kingdom Provident Inst 1951-69, and Chm of English-Speaking Union of the Commonwealth 1969-72.

BENNETT (UK) 1929, of Kirklington, co Nottingham

To serve the King

Sir RONALD WILFRID MURDOCH BENNETT, 3rd *Baronet*, *b* 25 March 1930; *s* his father, *Sir* (CHARLES) WILFRID, TD, 1952; *ed* Wellington, and Trin Coll, Oxford: *m* 1st, 1953, Audrey Rose-Marie Patricia, only da of Maj A. L. J. H. Aubépin, of co Mayo; 2ndly, 1968, Anne, da of late Leslie George Tooker, and has issue by 1st *m*.

Arms – Gules, a cross moline between three demi-lions rampant or. **Crest** – In front of a lion rampant gules charged on the shoulder with a cross moline argent, a scaling ladder fessewise or.
Residence – Rue St Jean 10, CH-1260, Nyon, Switzerland.

DAUGHTERS LIVING (*By 1st marriage*)

Anne-Marie Julia, *b* 1954: *m* 1973, Stephen Hickman. —— Georgina Marion, *b* 1956.

SISTER LIVING

Anne, MBE, *b* 1928; MBE (Civil) 1996: *m* 1st, 1961, Gerald Norman Fox-Edwards; 2ndly, 1974, Conrad Lyddon Voss-Bark, of Lyd Cottage, Leat Rd, Lifton, Devon, and has issue living (by 1st *m*), Adam, *b* 1962, — Jane, *b* 1964.

HALF-UNCLE LIVING (*Son of 1st baronet by 2nd marriage*)

Peter, *b* 1938; *ed* Charterhouse, and Pembroke Coll, Camb: *m* 1966, Monique Christine, el da of Amade Monsempès, of St Maur, Des Fossès, Seine, France.

AUNT LIVING (*Daughter of 1st baronet by 1st marriage*)

Audrey, *b* 1904: *m* 1928, Douglas Haultain Phillips, son of Hon Sir William Watkin Phillips, and has issue living, Susan, *b* 1929: *m* 1954, Timothy Ernle Gilpin (By Ernle, 1958 Edn), and has issue living, Joanna Clare *b* 1955, Henrietta Haultain *b* 1957, — Caroline Louise, *b* 1931.

WIDOW LIVING OF FIRST BARONET

LEOPOLDINE (*Dowager Lady Bennett*), da of Leopold Armata, of Vienna: *m* 1938, as his 2nd wife, Sir Albert James Bennett, 1st Bt, who *d* 1945.

COLLATERAL BRANCHES LIVING

Grandchildren of late Frank Carlton Bennett, 2nd son of 1st baronet:—
Issue of late Michael Bennett, *b* 1924, *d* 1987: *m* 1952, Janet Hazel Margaret (Flat 70, Albert Hall Mansions, SW7), da of Brig Edward Joseph Todhunter, TD, JP, of The Glebe House, Great Bedwyn, nr Marlborough, Wilts:—
MARK EDWARD FRANCIS, *b* 5 April 1960. —— Caroline Mariella Carleton, *b* 1954. —— Victoria Serena, *b* 1957.

Issue of late David Bennett, *b* 1927, *d* 1988: *m* 1959, Hilary Sheridan (The Gate House, Wing, Leighton Buzzard, Beds), da of Bernard F. Clarke:—
Algernon James, *b* 1962. —— Sarah Elizabeth, *b* 1967.

Sir Albert James Bennett, 1st baronet (son of late Edward Bennett), sat as MP for Mansfield Div of Notts (*L*) 1922-3, and for Central Div of Nottingham (*U*) 1924-30. Sir (Charles) Wilfrid Bennett, TD, 2nd baronet, was Lieut-Col Notts Yeo (Sherwood Rangers), and a Metropolitan Magistrate 1946-52.

Beresford-Peirse, see Peirse.

BERNARD (UK) 1954, of Snakemoor, co Southampton

Sir DALLAS EDMUND BERNARD, 2nd *Baronet*; *b* 14 Dec 1926; *s* his father, *Sir* DALLAS GERALD MERCER, 1975; *ed* Eton, and Corpus Christi Coll, Oxford (MA); Chm Thames Trust Ltd 1983-86, Nat & Foreign Securities Trust Ltd 1982-86; Dir Italian Internat Bank plc; Dir Morgan Grenfell & Co Ltd 1964-79; Member Monopolies and Mergers Commn 1973-79: *m* 1st, 1959 (*m diss* 1979), Sheila Mary, el da of Arthur Gordon Robey; 2ndly, 1979, Mrs Monica J. Montford, da of late James Edward Hudson, and has had issue by 1st and 2nd *m*.

Arms – Sable, two greyhounds rampant and addorsed argent in chief as many stags' heads caboshed or. **Crest** – Issuant from a circlet of bezants, a demi bear sable, muzzled or.
Residence – 106 Cheyne Walk, SW10 0DG.

DAUGHTERS LIVING AND DECEASED (*By 1st marriage*)

Juliet Mary, *b* 1961; *d* 1998. —— Alicia Elizabeth, *b* 1964: *m* 1999, William James Micklethwait (*see* D Norfolk, colls). —— Sarah Jane, *b* 1968: *m* 1998, Matthew Boulton, yst son of John Boulton, of Richmond, Surrey.

(*By 2nd marriage*)

Olivia Louise, *b* 1981.

SISTER LIVING

Margaret Anne, *b* 1929; *ed* Southover Manor, Lewes; has resumed the surname of Cleverly: *m* 1st, 1952 (*m diss* 1974), William Geoffrey Cleverly, MB, BS; 2ndly, 1975 (*m diss* 1980), Charles Bevan Meeres.

Sir Dallas Gerald Mercer Bernard, 1st Bt, son of Edmund Bowen Bernard, JP, of Snakemoor, Botley, Hants, was Man Dir of Jardine Matheson & Co, Ltd, 1922-28, Dep Gov of Bank of England 1949-54 and Chm of Courtaulds Ltd, 1962-64.

BERNEY (E) 1620, of Parkehall in Redham, Norfolk

Nothing rashly nor with fear

Sir JULIAN REEDHAM STUART BERNEY, 11th *Baronet*, only son of late John Reedham Erskine Berney, Lieut R Norfolk Regt, only son of 10th baronet; *b* (*posthumous*) 26 Sept 1952; *s* his grandfather, *Sir* THOMAS REEDHAM, MC, 1975; *ed* Wellington, and NE London Polytechnic; FRICS: *m* 1976, Sheena Mary, yr da of Ralph Day, of The Coach House, Hill House Park, Maldon, Essex, and has issue.

𝔄rms – Quarterly gules and azure, a cross engrailed ermine. 𝔠rest – A garb argent.
Residence – Reeds House, 40 London Rd, Maldon, Essex CM9 6HE.

SONS LIVING

WILLIAM REEDHAM JOHN, *b* 29 June 1980. —— Hugo Ralph, *b* 1987.

DAUGHTER LIVING

Jessica Mary, *b* 1982.

HALF-AUNT LIVING (*Daughter of 10th baronet by 1st marriage*)

Estelle Elaine, *b* 1922: *m* 1st, 1940, Maj Kenneth William Bols, Indian Army, who was *ka* in Italy 1944 (Strickland-Constable, Bt, colls); 2ndly, 1946, Lt-Col Mark Frederic Strutt, MC, RHA (TA) (*see* B Rayleigh, colls), and has issue living, (by 1st *m*) Andrew Nevile David, *b* 1943; Maj late The Blues and Royals; Queen's Messenger 1989: *m* 1st, 1971, Sally Jane, only da of ACM Sir John Alexander Carlisle Aiken, KCB; 2ndly, 1980, Mrs Anne Hard, yst da of J. A. Meade, of London, — Erica Sarah *b* 1941: *m* 1st, 1966 (*m diss* 1990), Nigel Frederick Burch; 2ndly, 1996, Malcolm Reason White, — (by 2nd *m*) (*see* B Rayleigh, colls). *Residence* – Crix, Hatfield Peverel, Essex.

AUNTS LIVING (*Daughters of 10th baronet by 2nd marriage*)

Elizabeth Ann (Claydon House, Clare Rd, Hundon, Suffolk CO10 8DL), *b* 1927: *m* 1952 (*m diss* 1960), Allan E Shepherd. —— Claire, *b* 1933: *m* 1st, 1956 (*m diss* 19——), Lt Jeremy Michael Lynch, RN; 2ndly, 1992, Prof Richard Christie, of 11 Harman Rd, Claremont, 7690 Cape Town, S Africa, and has issue living (by 1st *m*), Lewis Reedham, *b* 1967, — Nicole, *b* 1958, — Tania, *b* 1962.

MOTHER LIVING

Hon Jean Davina Stuart (*Hon Mrs Ritchie*) (Tannachie, Findhorn, Forres, Moray 1V36 0YJ), da of 1st Viscount Stuart of Findhorn: *m* 1st, 1951, John Reedham Erskine Berney, Lieut R Norfolk Regt, who was *ka* Korea 1952; 2ndly, 1954, Percy William Jesson; 3rdly, 1985, Michael D. Ritchie.

COLLATERAL BRANCHES LIVING

Granddaughters of late John Hanson Berney (infra):—
Issue of late Hugh Barton Berney, MB, ChB, *b* 1902, *d* 1977: *m* 1931, Lillian Irene, who *d* 1977, da of Robert William Grigor, of Blenheim, NZ:—
Helen, *b* (Nov) 1931: *m* 1955 Rev Edward Maurice Dashfield, of 53 Miro St, Masterton, NZ, and has issue living, Philip Berney, *b* 1958, — James Gilbert, *b* 1961, — Prudence Ann, *b* 1956. —— Janet Douglas, *b* 1935; BA (1955): *m* 1960, Terence Daniel O'Leary, CMG, and has issue living, John Terence, *b* 1960, — Daniel Hugh (twin), *b* 1960, — Helen Fiona, *b* 1964.

Issue of late Sinclair Henry Hanson Berney *b* 1906, *d* 1967: *m* 1936, Barbara May, da of late Andrew Roby Bloxam, of Christchurch, NZ:—
Jenifer May, *b* 1965: *m* 1965, David Kennedy Logan, of 94 Titoki St, Lansdowne, Masterton, NZ, and has issue living, John Berney Kennedy, *b* 1968, — Helen Margaret, *b* 1966: *m* 1998, David Walter Herron, of Mosgiel, Otago, NZ, — Robyn Elizabeth, *b* 1971. —— Diana Margaret, *b* (twin) 1938: *m* 1st, 1962 (*m diss* 1983), John Allan D. Burnett; 2ndly, 1997, Arthur Neill Cooper, of Grovely, 126A West St, Greytown 5953, S Wairarapa, NZ, and has issue living (by 1st *m*), Andrew John Hanson, *b* 1971, — Margaret Jane, *b* 1967: *m* 1994, Stephen David Daltrey, of Eastbourne, Surrey, and has issue living, Georgia May *b* 1999.

Issue of late John Hanson Berney, 3rd son of 9th baronet, *b* 1868, *d* 1959: *m* 1900, Margaret, who *d* 1948, da of Sinclair George, of New Zealand:—
John Reedham (PO Box 25, Rawene, Northland, NZ), *b* 1911: *m* 1937, Joyce, da of Donald Bennett, and has issue living, John Reedham Donald, *b* 1944: *m* 1975, Noralyne Maxine, da of G. Reid, of Hawaii, and has issue living, Gareth Elijah *b* 1977, Nalani Kalua *b* 1976, Juana Marguerite *b* 1979, — Richard Warwick, *b* 1946, — Jocelyn Margaret, *b* 1938: *m* 1960, Thomas William Burgess, of Sydney, Australia, and has issue living, Matthew Sinclair *b* 1966, Janette Joyce *b* 1961, — Juliet Alice, *b* 1953. —— Margaret Lorraine, *b* 1914: *m* 1937, Harold Arthur Roland Dunderdale, of Edinburgh, and has issue living, Francis John Berney, *b* 1939, — David Bruce, *b* 1942, — Antonia Margaret, *b* 1944. —— Barbara Dorothy, *b* (twin with Richard Bruce, AFC, AmDFC, DFM, RAF 1939-45 War (despatches); *k* in flying accident 1948) 1916: *m* 1942, Melvin Cooper Armstrong, of 15 College Av, Christchurch 5, S Island, NZ, and has issue living, David Warwick, *b* 1946, — Richard Thomas, *b* 1948, — Philippa Jane, *b* 1943.

Issue of late Alexander David Berney, 7th son of 9th baronet, *b* 1877, *d* 1942: *m* 1924, Alice, who *d* 1939, da of A. J. Moore, of Lowestoft:—
Olive Maud, *b* 1925: *m* 1st, 19—, Paul Rafoth, of USA; 2ndly, 19—, Rolf Merton, of Fiddler's Roost, Knapton Estate, Smith-Parish 3-06, Bermuda.

The Berneys, claiming to be of Norse origin, were seated at Berney, near Walsingham, Norfolk, at the time of the Norman Conquest. It is further claimed that they are one of the three families who settled in England before the Conquest and have never wanted a male heir. The 1st baronet, Sir Richard Berney, was Sheriff of Norfolk 1622, and the 4th baronet was Sheriff of Norwich 1762.

SHARP BETHUNE (NS) 1683, of Scotscraig, co Fife (extinct 1997)

Sir ALEXANDER MAITLAND SHARP BETHUNE, 10th and last *Baronet; d* 1997.

DAUGHTER LIVING OF TENTH BARONET

Lucy Elizabeth, *b* 1959.

WIDOW LIVING OF TENTH BARONET

(Ruth) Mary (*Lady Sharp Bethune*), da of James Hurst Hayes, of Marden House, East Harting, Sussex: *m* 1955, Sir Alexander Maitland Sharp Bethune, 10th and last Bt, who *d* 1997. *Residence* – 21 Victoria Grove, W8 5RW.

EVANS-BEVAN (UK) 1958, of Cadoxton-juxta, Neath, co Glamorgan

Sir MARTYN EVAN EVANS-BEVAN, 2nd Baronet; *b* 1 April 1932; *s* his father, *Sir* DAVID MARTYN, 1973; *ed* Uppingham; High Sheriff of Breconshire 1967-68; Freeman of City of London; Liveryman of Worshipful Co of Farmers: *m* 1957, Jennifer Jane Marion, da of Robert Hugh Stevens, of Lady Arbour, Eardisley, Herefordshire, and has issue.

Arms – Argent, three boars' heads couped sable on a chief gules a demi lion rampant erased or between two castles of the field. Crest – Issuing from the battlements of a tower argent a demi lion rampant or gorged with a collar gules holding between the paws a boar's head as in the Arms.
Residence – Felin-Newydd, Llande Falle, Brecon, Powys. *Club* – Carlton.

SONS LIVING

DAVID GAWAIN, *b* 16 Sept 1961: *m* 1987, Philippa Alice, yst da of Patrick Sweeney, of East Moors, Helmsley, N. Yorks, and has issue living, Patric David, *b* 9 Feb 1994, — Robert Alexander, *b* 1998, — Alice Laura, *b* 1989. —— Richard Martyn, *b* 1963. —— Thomas Rhydian, *b* 1966. —— Huw Evan, *b* 1971.

SISTER LIVING

Marigold Evans (*Countess of Rothes*), *b* 1934: *m* 1955, 21st Earl of Rothes. *Residence* – Tanglewood, West Tytherley, Salisbury.

WIDOW LIVING OF FIRST BARONET

EIRA WINIFRED (*Eira, Lady Evans-Bevan*) (Spring Valley, St Ouen, Jersey), el da of late Sidney Archibald Glanley, 2nd son of late Rev David Lloyd Glanley, MA: *m* 1929, Sir David Martyn Evans-Bevan, 1st Bt, who *d* 1973.

BIBBY (UK) 1959, of Tarporley, co Palatine of Chester

Sir DEREK JAMES BIBBY, MC, 2nd *Baronet, b* 29 June 1922; *s* his father, *Sir* (ARTHUR) HAROLD, 1986; *ed* Rugby, and Trin Coll, Oxford (MA 1941); DL for Cheshire 1987; Pres Bibby Line Group Ltd; 1939-45 War as Capt RA (wounded, MC): *m* 1961, Christine Maud, da of late Rt Rev Frank Jackson Okell, Bishop of Stockport, and has issue.

𝔄rms – Azure a saltire parted and fretty argent surmounted in fesse pointby a lion rampant pean between two escallops in pale and as many mullets of six points in fesse of the second. ℭrest – Upon a plate a cubit arm erect holding a sword in bend sinister proper pomel and hilt or.
Residence – Willaston Grange, Hadlow Rd, Willaston, Norton, Cheshire CH64 2UN.

SONS LIVING

MICHAEL JAMES, *b* 2 Aug 1963; *ed* Rugby, and Oxford Univ; CA: *m* 1994, Beverley L., only da of Donald Graham, of Wallsend, Tyne & Wear, and has issue living, Alexander James, *b* 24 Aug 1997, — Christopher Graham, *b* (twin) 1997. —— Geoffrey Frank Harold, *b* 1965; *ed* Rugby, and Exeter Univ: *m* 1994, Sarah, eldest da of Frederick Robinson, of Huntington, Cheshire, and has issue living, Charles James, *b* 1995, — Kate Tamara, *b* 1998. —— Peter John, *b* 1969; *ed* Rugby, and Manchester Univ. —— David Richard, *b* 1970; *ed* Rugby, and Bath Univ: *m* 1998, Nicola Jane, yst da of Michael Williams, of Tidworth, Hants, and has issue living, Chloe Laura, *b* 1998.

DAUGHTER LIVING

Jennifer Margaret, *b* 1962; *ed* Howells, and Oxford Univ; CA: *m* 1995, Peter J. Smith, son of late Graham Smith, of Knutsford, Cheshire, and has issue living, Alice Louise, *b* 1996, — Lucinda Victoria, *b* 1998.

SISTERS LIVING

Patricia Mary, *b* 1921; *m* 1st, 1944 (*m diss* 1956), Ronald Stuart Kinsey; 2ndly, 1962, Iain Hall Brookes Macdonald, who *d* 1990, and has issue living (by 1st *m*), Anne Quenelda Stuart, *b* 1947; *m* 1972, Julian Ralph Avery, of Bardown, Stonegate, Wadhurst, E Sussex TN5 7EL, — Hilary Jane Stuart, *b* 1951: *m* 1983, Simon Francis Reed, of 62 Streathbourne Rd, SW17. *Residence* – 100 Old Church St, SW3 6EP. —— Joan Elizabeth, *b* 1926; *m* 1st, 1951, Major Reginald Francis Foster, Indian Army, who *d* 1974; 2ndly, 1985 (*m diss* 1987), Clifford Haines, and has issue living (by 1st *m*), Rachel Frances, *b* 1955; *m* 1977 (*m diss* 1990), Gp-Capt Ian Thomas Nicoll, RAF. *Residence* – 20A Thorney Crescent, Morgans Walk, SW11 3TT. —— Anne Marjorie, *b* 1928: *m* 1st, 1951, Lt-Col John Hamilton Palairet, who *d* 1969; 2ndly, 1976 (*m diss* 1980), Denis Justin Beattie, and has issue living (by 1st *m*), Sarah Lillias, *b* 1953: *m* 1977, Christopher Neston Ord Capper, of Chedglow Manor, Crudwell, Malmesbury, Wilts SN16 9EZ, — Joanna Vivian, *b* 1955: *m* 1979, Jeremy William Hicks, of Gaskells Farmhouse, Winstone, nr Cirencester, Glos GL7 7JZ, — Ailsa Jane, *b* 1957: *m* 1980, Lt-Col Stephen John Duyland Bush, OBE, RM, of Cockspur Thorns, Berwick St James, nr Salisbury, Wilts SP3 4TS. *Residence* – 102 Walton St, SW3 2JJ.

The 1st baronet, Sir (Arthur) Harold Bibby, DSO, who was Snr Partner in the firm of Bibby Bros & Co 1935-73 and Chm of Bibby Line Ltd 1935-69, was a DL for Cheshire and High Sheriff 1934-35.

BIDDULPH (E) 1664, of Westcombe, Kent

Sir IAN D'OLIER BIDDULPH, 11th *Baronet*; *b* 28 Feb 1940; *s* his father, *Sir* STUART ROYDEN, 1986: *m* 1967, Margaret Eleanor, only da of late John Gablonski, of Oxley, Brisbane, and has issue.

𝔞rms – Vert, an eagle displayed argent. 𝔠rest – A wolf rampant argent, wounded on the shoulder proper.
Address – Fernway Pty Ltd, Mail Service 23, Mt Walker, via Rosewood, Queensland 4340, Australia.

SON LIVING

PAUL WILLIAM, *b* 30 Oct 1967.

DAUGHTERS LIVING

Julie Denise, *b* 1969. —— Roslyn Mary, *b* 1971.

SISTERS LIVING

Wendy Margaret, *b* 1946: *m* 1966, Huan Donald John Fraser, of 10 El Rancho St, Daisy Hill, Qld 4127, and has issue living, Stuart Donald John, *b* 1974, — Gina Margaret, *b* 1969, — Jodie Maree, *b* 1972. —— Mary Estelle, *b* 1947: *m* 1968, Ian Sutherland, of Edward St, Tambo, Qld 4478, and has issue living, Timothy Andrew, *b* 1969, — Lee-Anne, *b* 1970.

COLLATERAL BRANCHES LIVING

Issue of late Malcolm Francis Biddulph, son of 9th baronet, *b* 1910, *d* 1983: *m* 1936, Inez Margaret, who *d* 1978, da of James Donnelly, of Longreach, Qld, Australia:—
Peter Michael (Blackall St, Dingo, Qld 4702, Australia), *b* 1939: *m* 1963, Beverley Marie, who *d* 1987, only da of late Wilson Story, of St George's Heights, Sydney, NSW, and has issue living, Michael Andrew, *b* 1964: *m* 1989, Tamara, yst da of Thomas Kelly, of Charleville, Qld, — Sean Gregory, *b* 1970, — Craig, *b* 1973, — Mark Sterling, *b* 1975, — Anne Marie, *b* 1971. —— David Francis (Blackall Motel, Blackall, Qld, Australia), *b* 1942: *m* 1968, Doreen Power, and has issue living, Dennis, *b* 1980, — Sally, *b* 1973. —— Janice Claire, *b* 1937: *m* 1958 (*m diss* 1978), Lionel Garth Moody, and has issue living, Peter, *b* 1969, — Alison Marie, *b* 1959: *m* 1980, Michael Stally, — Tanya Claire, *b* 1962, — Fiona Margaret, *b* 1963.

Descendants, if any, of late Francis Henry Biddulph (who was *b* 1839, and left issue a son), uncle of 9th baronet.

Descendants, if any, of late Charles Biddulph (who left issue, one son), 2nd son of late John Burnet Biddulph (*b* 1796), 5th son of late Simon Biddulph (infra), and great-uncle of 9th baronet.

Grandchildren of late William Burnett Biddulph (infra):—
Issue of late Ernest William Biddulph, *b* 1889, *d* 1963. *m* 1939, Anna Brando;—
William Burnett (Moria, 158 Heerenstraat, Vryheid 3100, Natal, S Africa), *b* 1930: *m* 1955, Helena Hendrina Naude, and has issue living, Erlo William Burnett, *b* 1965, — Zelda, *b* 1956: *m* 1979, Manus Andreas Louw, and has issue living, Hermanus Andreas *b* 1984, — Janène, *b* 1962: *m* 1981, Wilm Kempden Smalberger, and has issue living, Chantel *b* 1983, — Bernadine, *b* 1974. —— Magdalena Suzanna *b* 1944: *m* 1964, Raymond Fraser Morris, of 109 South St, Vryheid, Natal, and has issue living, Wayne William, *b* 1966, — Delainie Anne, *b* 1970, — Rochell *b* 1979.

Grandchildren of late Ernest Walstrand Biddulph, 3rd son of late John Burnet Biddulph (*b* 1796), 5th son of late Simon Biddulph, great-grandfather of the 9th baronet:—
Issue of late William Burnett Biddulph, *b* 1859, *d* 1946: *m* 18—, Florentia Magdalena, who *d* 1947, da of late James Brookes, of Farm, Welgelegen, Van Reenen, Orange Free State:—
Joseph Gilbert, *b* 1891: *m* 1921, Anna Struwig, and has issue living, William Burnett, *b* 1925: *m* 1951, Hester Botha, and has issue living, Joseph Gilbert *b* 1955, Wilma *b* 1953, Annalise *b* 1955, Brenda *b* 1956, — Catherina, *b* 1922: *m* 1943, Hans Jurie Vosloo, Box 36, Sandspruit, Transvaal, and has issue living, George Sebastiaan *b* 1944, Joseph Gilbert *b* 1950, Anna Margaretta *b* 1955, — Florentina, *b* 1923: *m* 1944, Willem Pieter Van Breda, of Sandspruit, Transvaal, and has issue living, Frederic Charles *b* 1946, Joseph Gilbert *b* 1948, Willem Pieter *b* 1952, Burnett *b* 1956, — Anna, *b* 1930: *m* 1950, Desmond Stokes, and has issue living, William *b* 1951, Joseph *b* 1954, Ann *b* 1952, Nellie *b* 1958, Margaret *b* 1959, Desiree *b* 1962, — Josephine, *b* 1936: *m* 1955, Hilbert Austin Glad, of 14 Marais St, Heidelberg, Transvaal, and has issue living, Hilbert Pierre *b* 1958, Joseph Alfred *b* 1959. —— Alphonso Charles, *b* 1896. —— Henry William, *b* 1898: *m* 1925, Johanna Elizabeth Francisca Struwig, and has issue living, William Burnett (PO 160, Volksrust, Transvaal), *b* 1927: *m* 1955, Maria Susanna Johanna Swanepoel, of Estcourt, Natal, and has issue living, Henry William, *b* 1956, Eleanor Burnett *b* 1959. —— Jacobus Cornelius, *b* 1899: *m* 1930, Miemie Van Reenen, and has issue living, William Burnett, *b* 1939: *m* 1960, Gesina Van Aswegen, and has issue living, Reenen Jacobus *b* 1961, — Elizabeth Susanna, *b* 1932: *m* 1954, Hendrick Van Zyl, of 30a, Dan Piernaar Rd, Volksrust, Transvaal, and has issue living, Susan Mari *b* 1959. —— Simon Thomas, *b* 1911: *m* 1947, Mrs Jacoba Wilhelmina Dannhauser, da of Matheus Willemse. —— Catherine Maude, *b* 1903. —— Maria Elizabeth, *b* 1909: *m* 1929, Tiberius Neser, and has issue living, Florentina Magdalena, *b* 1930: *m* 1953, Roy Goldhill, of 18 St David's Rd, East London, Cape Prov, S Africa, and has issue living, David Roy *b* 1958. —— Violet Maud, *b* 1915: *m* 1939, Hendrik Sebastiaan Kriek, and has issue living, Sebastian William, *b* 1949.

Issue of late Alphonso Biddulph, *b* 1860, *d* 19—: *m* 1887, Catharina Magdalene Hendrica, da of late Joseph Brookes (ante):—
Ernest Walstrand, *b* 1888. —— Joseph Cornelis, *b* 1889: *m* 1924, Anna Maria Grobler, and has issue living, Anna Maria, *b* 1927. —— Henry Stephen, *b* 1892. —— Bertie William, *b* 1893. —— Edward Charles, *b* 1897. —— Alphonso Gilbert, *b* 1904. —— Violet Catherine, *b* 1895. —— Florence Emma Roselin, *b* 1907.

Descendants, if any, of late Thomas Burnet Biddulph, 5th son of late John Burnet Biddulph (*b* 1796) (ante).

SELBY-BIGGE (UK) 1919, of King's Sutton, co Northampton (Extinct 1973)

Sir JOHN AMHERST SELBY-BIGGE, OBE, 2nd and last *Baronet*.

DAUGHTERS LIVING OF SECOND BARONET

Lydia Jane, *b* 1920: *m* 1941 (*m diss* 1946), Gabriel Morand. —— Cornelia Diana, *b* 1922: *m* 1947, Hugh Max Bowden, of Stager Rd, Babinda, Queensland 4861, Australia, and has issue living, Anna Melissa Radclyffe, *b* 1954, — Joanna Katherine Radclyffe, *b* 1963. —— Mary Elizabeth, *b* 1924: *m* 1st, 1951, John Sheals Pratt, MD, who *d* 1956; 2ndly, 1967, Group Capt Richard Irwin Knight Edwards, DFC, AFC, RAF (ret), who *d* 1967.

BIRD (UK) 1922, of Solihull, co Warwick

Success is the reward of endeavour

Sir RICHARD GEOFFREY CHAPMAN BIRD, 4th *Baronet*; *b* 3 Nov 1935; *s* his father *Sir* DONALD GEOFFREY, 1963; *ed* Beaumont: *m* 1st, 1957, Gillian Frances, who *d* 1966, da of Bernard Haggett, of Solihull; 2ndly, 1968, Helen Patricia, only da of Frank Beaumont, of Pontefract, and has issue by 1st and 2nd *m*.

Arms – Vert, on a pale or two popinjays of the field, on a chief ermine three garbs of the second. Crest – A garb as in the arms between two roses per pale gules and argent, leaved and slipped proper.
Residence – 39 Ashleigh Rd, Solihull, W Midlands B91 1AF.

SONS LIVING (*By 1st marriage*)

JOHN ANDREW, *b* 19 Jan 1964. —— Mark Richard, *b* 1965.

DAUGHTERS LIVING (*By 1st marriage*)

Cecilia Mary, *b* 1957. —— Frances Bernadette, *b* 1959. —— Brigitte Ann, *b* 1960. —— Rowena Clare, *b* 1962.

(*by 2nd marriage*)

Catherine Veronica, *b* 1970. —— Denise Helen, *b* 1972.

BROTHER LIVING

Peter Donald Chapman, *b* 1938; *ed* Beaumont: *m* 1962, Vera Mary, da of Albert Seymour, of Northfield, and has issue living, Anthony Donald, *b* 1964, — Christopher Robert, *b* 1967. *Residence* – The Gables, Whitecroft Rd, Bream, nr Lydney, Glos.

SISTER LIVING

Elizabeth Anne, *b* 1931: *m* 1955, John Rodney Wilford Brigg, and has had issue, David Lockwood John *b* 1956: *m* 1982, Carolyn Froy, and *d* 1989, leaving issue, Joanna Louise *b* 1986, — Michael James, *b* 1957; B Chir 1982, MB 1983: *m* 1991, Fiona Anne Wheatcroft, and has issue living, Emma Charlotte *b* 1992, — Peter Donald, (*b* (twin) 1957; MB BS 1980: *m* 1986, Lynne Goulden, and has issue living, William James *b* 1987, Thomas David *b* 1989, Aimée Eleanore Beatrice *b* 1992. *Residence* – The Soundings, Bosham Hoe, Chichester P018 8ET.

AUNT LIVING

Eleanore Marshall, b 1915: m 1932, Vernon Harms-Cooke, who d 1987, and has issue living, Sylvia HARMS-COOKE (Monks Meadow, Winchcombe, Glos GL54 5PA), b 1934; has resumed her maiden name: m 1959, Peter John Smith, and has issue living, Nigel Peter b 1961, Charles Francis b 1963, Christabel b 1964, — Annalova (Monks Meadow, Winchcombe, Glos GL54 5PA), b 1936: m 1953, David Stanley Faber, who d 1981, and has issue living, Geoffrey David b 1961, Rosanne b 1955, Colleen b 1957, Anita b 1959, — Geoffrena, b 1938: m 1959, Lt-Col James William Beachus (ret), HQ Rhine Garrison BFPO 140, and has issue living, Timothy James b 1962, Simon Jeremy b 1964, Justin b 1968, Lucinda b 1961, Tanya b 1966, — Eleanore, b 1940: m 1964, James Thomas Askew, and has issue living, Christopher Robert James b 1972, Mark William b 1974, — Carol, b 1941: m 1st, 1962, John Edmund Davies; 2ndly, 1990, Kenneth Rose, of 6 Bibsworth Av, Broadway, Worcs, and has issue living (by 1st m), Anthony William Gordon b 1968, Tracey Anne b 1971. Residence – Monks Meadow, Winchcombe, Glos GL54 5PA.

DAUGHTER LIVING OF SECOND BARONET

Pamela Stephanie Helen EVANS, b 1909; assumed by deed poll 1974 the surname of Evans: m 1st, 1934 (m diss 1946), Reginald William Bell; 2ndly, 1952 (m diss 1973), Vicomte Alain de Mauduit de Kervern, and has issue living, (by 1st m) Robert Reginald, b 1935, — Thomas Randal, b 1937, — William Andrew, b 1940, — (by 2nd m) Françoise Hélène, b 1952. Residence – Mille Fiori, 20217 St Florent, France.

Sir Alfred Frederic Bird, 1st Bt (cr a Knt 1920, nominated a Baronet 1 Jan 1922, d Feb 1922), was Chm of Alfred Bird and Sons (Limited), Manufacturing Chemists, and sat as MP for W Div of Wolverhampton (CoU) Jan 1910 to Feb 1922. Sir Robert Bland Bird, KBE, 2nd baronet, was Chm of Alfred Bird & Sons, and sat as MP for W Div of Wolverhampton (C) 1922-29, and 1931-45.

BIRKIN (UK) 1905, of Ruddington Grange, Ruddington, Notts

Prepared for peace and war

Sir JOHN CHRISTIAN WILLIAM BIRKIN, 6th *Baronet*, b 1 July 1953; s his father, Sir CHARLES LLOYD, 1985; ed Eton, Trin Coll, Dublin, and at London Film Sch; Freelance TV Producer and Director: m 1994, Emma Louise, da of Roger Leonard Gage, of Chantry House, Aveton Gifford, nr Kingsbridge, Devon, and has issue.

Arms – Argent, a cross raguly couped vert between in the 1st and 4th quarters, a bee volant, and in the 2nd and 3rd a birch tree eradicated proper. Crest – A scorpion erect proper.
Residence – Place Barton, Ashton, Exeter EX6 7QP.

SON LIVING

BENJAMIN CHARLES, b 4 Nov 1995.

SISTERS LIVING

Jennifer Claire Eleanor, b 1941: m 1971, Charles de Clermont, and has issue living, Araminta, b 19—. — Amanda Jane Averill, b 1943; has issue living, Luke TOYNE, b 1979.

COLLATERAL BRANCHES LIVING

Issue of late Major Philip Austen Birkin, OBE, 5th son of 1st baronet, b 1869, d 1951: m 1900, Frances Emily who d 1953, 2nd da of Joseph Littlewood, JP, of the Park, Nottingham:—
Frances Marjorie, b 1905: m 1st, 1928, Duncan William Grant, who d 1933; 2ndly, 1938, Douglas Charles Lockwood. Residence – La Adela, Vivorata, Argentina.

Grandchildren of late Maj Harry Laurence Birkin, TD, 6th and yst son of 1st baronet:—
Issue of late Hon Air Commodore (James) Michael Birkin, CB, DSO, OBE, DFC, AFC, b 1912, d 1985: m 1st, 1956 (m diss 1977), Antonia, da of late Lt-Col A.F. Stanley-Clarke; 2ndly, 1980, Susan (The Boathouse, Ashlake, Fishbourne, I of Wight), da of late Edward Mitchell, of Wellington, Shropshire:—
(By 1st m) James Francis Richard, b 1957. — Abigail Victoria Ann, b 1959; has issue living, Antony David James BIRKIN, b 1996, — George Alexander Michael BIRKIN, b 1998.

Issue of late Lt-Cdr David Leslie Birkin, DSC, b 1914, d 1991: m 1943, Judy Mary (Judy Campbell, the actress) (21 Old Church St, SW3), da of late John Arthur Gamble, OBE (J. A. Campbell):—
Andrew Timothy, b 1945; ed Harrow; author of *The Lost Boys*; has recognised issue living, David Tristan BIRKIN, b 1977, — Alexander Kingdom BIRKIN, b 1980, — Edmund (Ned) Xavier BIRKIN, b 1985. — Jane Mallory, b 1946; actress: m 1965 (m diss 1968), John Barry, composer, and has issue living, Kate, b 1967; has issue living (by Pascal de Kermadec, who d 1992), Roman b 1987, — (by Serge Gainsbourg, who d 1991), Charlotte GAINSBOURG, b 1971; actress; has issue living (by Yvan Attal), Ben b 1997, — (by Jacques Doillon), Lou DOILLON, b 1982. — Linda Mary Deborah, b 1950: m 1978, Michael Charles William Norreys Jephson, of Hawthorn Lodge, Bushy Park, Teddington, Middx, and has issue living, Henry Denham Robert Arthur, b 1983, — George Mounteney David Aubrey, b 1984, — Jack Norreys William Orlando, b 1988.

The 1st baronet, Sir Thomas Isaac Birkin (son of Richard Birkin, JP, of Aspley Hall, Nottingham), was a Director of Great Northern Railway Co, and of Mercantile Steamship Co, and High Sheriff of Notts 1892. The 2nd baronet, Sir Thomas Stanley Birkin, was High Sheriff for Notts 1915. The 3rd baronet, Sir Henry Ralph Birkin, was a well-known Racing Motorist, and holder of several records.

BIRKMYRE (UK) 1921, of Dalmunzie, co Perth

Advance

Sir ARCHIBALD BIRKMYRE, 3nd *Baronet*; *b* 12 Feb 1923; *s* his father, *Sir* HENRY, 1992; *ed* Radley; Burma 1942-45 as Capt RA; Memb London Stock Exchange 1960-88: *m* 1953, Gillian Mary, only da of late Eric Mytton Downes, OBE, of Dorndon House, Hurst, Berks and has issue.

𝕬rms – Per chevron argent and sable, in chief two eagles heads erased and in base a thistle leaved and slipped all proper. 𝕮rest – In front of a rising sun proper an eagle displayed sable.
Residence – The Old Presbytery, Buckland, Faringdon, Oxon SN7 8QW. *Clubs* – Boodle's, Huntercombe Golf, M.C.C.

SON LIVING

JAMES, *b* 29 Feb 1956; *ed* Radley: *m* 1990, Leslie Amanda, elder da of Dr Richard Lyon, of Seal Beach, California, USA, and has issue living, Alexander, *b* 24 May 1991. *Residence* – Ashmore Green Cottage, Ashmore Green, Berks RG16 9EY.

DAUGHTERS LIVING

Alison Mary (*Baroness De Ramsey*), *b* 1954: *m* 1984, as his 2nd wife, 4th Baron De Ramsey, and has issue (*see* B De Ramsey). *Residence* – Abbots Ripton Hall, Huntingdon, Cambs. —— Serena Jane, *b* 1960: *m* 1988, Hugo Edward Stainton Jackson, yr son of Sir (John) Edward Jackson, KCMG, of 17 Paulton's Sq, SW3, and has issue living, George Edward Stainton, *b* 1990, — Thomas Archie Stainton, *b* 1994, — James Hugo Stainton, *b* 1996. *Address* – c/o Sir Edward Jackson, KCMG, 17 Paulton's Sq, SW3.

SISTER LIVING

Jane Henrietta, *b* 1929: *m* 1952, Major Robert Evelyn Russell Smallwood, of Finches, Pembury, Kent TN2 4BA, and has issue living, Rosemary Jane, *b* 1954: *m* 1977, Andrew Peter Geoffrey Holmes, of 51 Doneraile St, SW6 6EW, — Susan Caroline, *b* 1957: *m* 1979, Peter Richard Vivian Houston (*see* B Swansea), of Fair Dawn, Packhorse Lane, South Stoke, Bath BA2 7DJ.

COLLATERAL BRANCH LIVING

　　　Issue of late Archy Birkmyre, yr son of 1st baronet, *b* 1904, *d* 1992: *m* 1940, Doreen (Dalchonzie Lower Cottage, by Comrie, Perthshire PH6 2LB), only child of late Robert Barclay, of Kilbirnie, Ayrshire:—
David, *b* 1941; *ed* Trinity Coll, Glenalmond: *m* 1976, Mrs Margot Rogerson, da of late William Rogerson, of Rothesay, Isle of Bute, and has issue living, Rebecca, *b* 1978. —— Adelaide (*Lady Borthwick*), *b* 1945: *m* 1974, 24th Lord Borthwick, of Crookston, Heriot, Midlothian, and has issue (*see* L Borthwick).

The 1st baronet, Sir Archibald Birkmyre, CBE (son of late Henry Birkmyre, of Port Glasgow), was knighted 1917, and was senior partner in the firm of Birkmyre Bros, merchants, of Calcutta.

BLACK (UK) 1922, of Midgham, co Berks

Not the cross, but the light

Sir (ROBERT) DAVID BLACK, 3rd *Baronet, b* 29 March 1929; *s* his father *Sir* ROBERT ANDREW STRANSHAM, 1979; *ed* Eton; Maj (ret) R Horse Guards; late Maj Berks and Westminster Dragoons (TA), and Berks Territorials (TAVR III); Vice-Chm (Berkshire) Eastern Wessex TAVRA 1985-92; Hon Col 94 (Berkshire Yeomanry) Signal Sqdn (V) 1988-98; DL Caithness 1991; High Sheriff Oxfordshire 1993; Joint MFH Garth and S Berks Hunt: *m* 1st, 1953 (*m diss* 1972), Rosemary Diana, da of Sir Rupert John Hardy, 4th Bt; 2ndly, 1973 (Dorothy) Maureen, yst da of Maj Charles Robert Eustace Radclyffe, and widow of Alan Roger Douglas Pilkington, and has had issue by 1st *m.*

𝔄rms – Argent, a saltire sable between two crescents in pale and as many mullets in fesse gules, on a chief of the second three trefoils slipped of the field. 𝔄rest – Issuant out of a cloud a demi-lion rampant proper, charged on the shoulder with a trefoil vert and holding in the paws a fylfot sable.
Residences – Beech Farm House, Woodcote, Reading, Berks RG8 0PX; Shurrery Lodge, Shebster, Thurso, Caithness. *Clubs* – Cavalry and Guards', Fly Fishers'.

DAUGHTERS LIVING AND DECEASED (*By 1st marriage*)

Diana Sarah, *b* 1955: *m* 1979, Mark Robert Newton, of The Old Rectory, Church Langton, Leics, and has issue living, William David Rupert, *b* 1989, — James Robert George, *b* 1993. —— Fiona Caroline, *b* 1957: *m* (May) 1982, Christopher E. J. Jerram, only son of late Col Edward Jenner Jerram, MC, of Poplars Farm, Evenlode, nr Moreton-in-Marsh, Glos, and *d* (Dec) 1982. —— Joanna Rosemary Violet, *b* 1966: *m* 1991, Christopher Robert Caspar Wild, yr son of Robert Wild, of Slade Farm, Ockham, Surrey, and has issue living, Maximilian Robert David, *b* 1995, — Luke Christopher Rupert, *b* 1997.

The 1st baronet, Sir Robert James Black, was Chm of Mercantile Bank of India, and a Director of Shell Transport Co (Limited).

BLACKETT (E) 1673, of Newcastle, Northumberland

We will labour in hope

Sir HUGH FRANCIS BLACKETT, 12th *Baronet; b* 11 Feb 1955; *s* his father, *Maj Sir* FRANCIS HUGH, 1995; *ed* Eton: *m* 1982, Anna Margaret, yr da of James St George Coldwell, of Somerton, Oxon, and has issue.

𝔄rms – Argent, on a chevron between three mullets pierced sable three escallops of the field.
Seat – Halton Castle, Corbridge, Northumberland.

SON LIVING

HENRY DOUGLAS, *b* 2 Feb 1992.

DAUGHTERS LIVING

Amelia, *b* 1984. —— Isabella, *b* 1986. —— Flora, *b* 1988.

BROTHER LIVING

Marcus Henry, *b* 1961; *ed* Harrow. *Residence* – 11 Waverley Rd, Liverpool L17 8TY.

SISTERS LIVING

Angela Frances, *b* 1951: *m* 1979, Ewan Follett Bell (*see* B Wyfold, 1980 Edn), and has issue living, Archibald, *b* 1981, — Caspar Francis, *b* 1989, — Georgia Elizabeth, *b* 1983. *Residence* – Easter Coul, Auchterarder, Perthshire. —— Charlotte Elizabeth, *b* 1952; has issue living, Theophania Eve BLACKETT OGRAM, *b* 1990. *Residence* – 30A Mount Ephraim Rd, SW16.

DAUGHTERS LIVING OF NINTH BARONET

Caroline Ann, *b* 1936: *m* 1957, Capt (Geoffrey Thomas) Warren Fenwicke-Clennell, late 11th Hussars, of Kirk Hammerton House, York YO26 8DD, and has issue living, Nicholas (Deans Hall, Little Maplestead, Halstead, Essex C09 2RT), *b* 1959: *m* 1984, Susan Elizabeth, da of Peter Roy Herbert Gould, of Little Barn, Gt Chesterford, Saffron Walden, Essex, and has issue living, Oliver Edward *b* 1986, Toby *b* 1988, Antonia Ursula *b* 1991, — Luke Thomas (75 Rodenhurst Rd, SW4 8AF), *b* 1961: *m* 1996, Emily Sorrel, yr da of David Peter Aykroyd (*see* Aykroyd, Bt, *cr* 1920, colls), and has issue living, Sorrel May *b* 1998, — Katharine Mary, *b* 1963: *m* 1989, James Richard Boughey, yr son of late Sir Richard James Boughey, 10th Bt. ——Lucinda Mary (*Lady Peto*), *b* 1940: *m* 1st, 1964 (*m diss* 1971), Ewan Iain Macleod Hilleary; 2ndly, 1971, Sir Michael Henry Basil Peto, 4th Bt, and has issue living (by 1st *m*), Iain Douglas, *b* 1965, — (by 2nd *m*) (*see* Peto, Bt, *cr* 1927).

WIDOWS LIVING OF TENTH AND ELEVENTH BARONETS

DAPHNE LAING (*Dowager Lady Blackett*), da of late Maj Guy Laing Bradley, TD, of Bridge End House, Hexham: *m* 1964, as his 2nd wife, Sir George William Blackett, 10th Bt, who *d* 1994. *Residence* – ......

Mrs JOAN CHOWDRY (*Joan, Lady Blackett*): *m* 1985, as his 2nd wife, Maj Sir Francis Hugh Blackett, 11th Bt, who *d* 1995.

COLLATERAL BRANCHES LIVING

Issue of late Maj Rupert Henry Blackett, DLI (ret), yst son of 8th baronet, *b* 1911, *d* 1992: *m* 1941, Mrs Felicity Mary Audley Clapton (Errington Hill Head, Hexham, Northumberland), da of late Lt-Col William Alfred Scudamore Smith:—
Piers Rupert, *b* 1941; *ed* Univ of Cape Town Med Sch (MB, ChB). *Residence* – –. —— (Rose) Miranda, *b* 1944: *m* 1975 (*m diss* 19—), Merlin Pearson-Rogers, and has issue living, Jack Rupert, *b* 1977. *Residence* – —

Grandson of late Harold Blackett, el son of late John Charles Blackett, RN, 4th son of 5th baronet:—
Issue of late Henry Beaumont Blackett, *b* 1886, *d* 1964: *m* 1916, Evelyn Nora Mary, who *d* 1966, da of J. Booth Lazenby, of Newcastle-on-Tyne:—
John Harold Booth (Seven Stars House, Whalton, Morpeth, Northumberland NE61 3XA. *Club* – Cavalry and Guards'), *b* 1923; *ed* Radley; 1939-45 War as Lieut 15th/19th King's Roy Hussars: *m* 1953, Veronica Heath Stuart, da of Henry Tegner, of Whalton, Northumberland, and has issue living, (John) Simon (Clunie Cottage, Braemar, Aberdeenshire AB35 5XQ), *b* 1954; *ed* Radley: *m* 1987, Hon Geva Charlotte Caroline Winn, only da of 5th Baron St Oswald, and has issue living, (Helena) Charlotte Rose *b* 1988, (Camilla Harriet) Eve *b* 1989, Letitia *b* 1991, Annabel *b* 1993, — Rupert Beaumont (Merle Cottage, 89 High St, Westerham, Kent), *b* 1957; *ed* Radley: *m* 1984, Hendrika Theresa, da of Wilhelmus Marinus Bouwman, of Utrecht, Netherlands, and has issue living, James Henry *b* 1988, William Luke *b* 1994, Rebecca Anne *b* 1985, Kate Elizabeth *b* 1990, Lucy Georgia *b* (twin) 1994, — Caroline Rose, *b* 1960: *m* 1987, Robert Murray-Brown, yst son of late Lt-Col C. R. Murray-Brown, DSO, and of Lady Loyd, of Aldeburgh, Suffolk, and has issue living, Francis William *b* 1994, John Frederick Jerome *b* 1996, — Juliet Evelyn, *b* 1965: *m* 1991, Andrew Charles Pumphrey (*see* Aykroyd, Bt, *cr* 1929, colls).

Granddaughter of John Charles Blackett, RN (ante):—
Issue of late Adm Henry Blackett, CBE, *b* 1867, *d* 1952: *m* 1906, Hon Pamela Mary Fisher, who *d* 1949, yst da of 1st Baron Fisher:—
Pamela, *b* 1911: *m* 1957, Clifford Henry Bray, who *d* 1980. *Residence* – 8 Homedrive House, 95/97 The Drive, Hove, Sussex BN3 6GE.

The 1st baronet, Sir William Blackett (son of William Blackett, of Hoppyland, co Durham), was MP for Newcastle-upon-Tyne 1673-80. The 2nd baronet, Sir Edward, was MP for Newcastle-upon-Tyne, and an Alderman and sometime Mayor of that borough. Sir Hugh Douglas Blackett, 8th baronet, was High Sheriff of Northumberland 1914; Sir Charles Douglas Blackett, 9th baronet, was High Sheriff of Northumberland 1953; Maj Sir Francis Hugh Blackett, 11th baronet, *m* 1st, 1950, Mrs Elizabeth Eily Barrie, who *d* 1982, da of late Howard Dennison, of Valparaiso, Chile.

BLAIR (UK) 1945, of Harrow Weald, co Middlesex (Extinct 1962)

Sir REGINALD BLAIR, 1st and last *Baronet*.

GRANDDAUGHTER LIVING OF FIRST BARONET

(Issue of late Capt Malcolm Reginald Blair, Roy Fusiliers, el son of 1st baronet, *b* 1906, *ka* in France 1940: *m* 1936, Sheila Pasmore), Jenny Mabel, *b* 1937: *m* 1st, 1957 (*m diss* 19—), Robert Alan Cumming Greenleas; 2ndly, 19—, Peter Trier, of Alderwood House, Greenham Common, Newbury, Berks.

ADOPTIVE GRANDSON OF FIRST BARONET

Adopted son of late Walter MacLellan Blair, 2nd Lieut Royal Fusiliers, 3rd and yst son of 1st baronet, *b* 1913, *d* on active service 1941: *m* 1937, Mrs Margaret (Madge) Assheton Smith (who *d* 1966, having *m* 3rdly, 1949, Douglas Patrick Motion), da of late Cyril Assheton Luckman, and formerly wife of Hugh Ernest Assheton Smith:—

Michael Cyril Assheton BLAIR (4 The Almshouses, Church Hill, Hurst, nr Reading, Berks RG10 0SL), *b* 1936; *ed* Harrow: *m* 1st, 1962 (*m diss* 1976), Tessa Annette, da of John Derek Fowler; 2ndly, 1992, Anna Mary Louise, da of John Gordon Fraser, of 2 Ash Lane, Winsford, Som, and has issue living (by 1st *m*), Nicholas Derek Assheton, *b* 1963, — Timothy Michael Assheton, *b* 1964, — Christopher John Assheton, *b* 1964.

DAUGHTER LIVING OF FIRST BARONET

Mary Lile Wieland, *b* 1910: *m* 1937, Lieut-Com G. Vernon W. Harrison, RN, who was *ka* 1941, and has issue living, Peter Reginald Wallace, *b* 1939.

HUNTER BLAIR (GB) 1786, of Dunskey

Vigilance, strength, pleasure

Sir EDWARD THOMAS HUNTER BLAIR, 8th *Baronet*, *b* 15 Dec 1920; *s* his father, *Sir* JAMES 1985; *ed* Eton, and Balliol Coll, Oxford; 1939-45 War with KOYLI; Member of Kirkcudbrightshire Co Council 1970-71; *m* 1956, Norma, who *d* 1972, el da of late Walter Sidney Harris, and has an adopted son and da.

𝔄rms – Quarterly: 1st, argent, a chevron gules between three bugles vert, vested and stringed of the second, *Hunter*; 2nd, argent, on a chevron gules between three cross-crosslets fitchée sable a fleur-de-lis or, within a double tressure flory counterflory of the second, *Kennedy* of Culzean; 3rd, argent, on a saltire sable eight mascles of the field, in chief a star sable eight mascles of the field, in chief a star gules, Blair; 4th argent, a shake-fork sable, and in chief a rose gules, surmounted of a mullet of the field, *Cunninghame of Brownhill*. 𝔠rest – A stag's head cabossed proper. 𝔖upporters – *Dexter*, a dog of chase salient argent; *Sinister*, an antelope springing proper, gorged with an open crown and a chain hanging thereat or.
Residence – Parton House, Castle Douglas, Kirkcudbrightshire DG7 3NB.

ADOPTED SON LIVING

Alan Walter, *b* 1961.

ADOPTED DAUGHTER LIVING

Helen Cecilia, *b* 1963: *m* 1985, L.B. (James) Watson, 2nd son of Peter Watson, of 17 Adams Rd, Cambridge, and has issue living, Emily Ann, *b* 1989, — Natasha Jean, *b* 1991.

BROTHER LIVING

JAMES, *b* 18 March 1926; *ed* Eton, and Balliol Coll, Oxford; formerly Lt Scots Guards; a DL for Ayrshire. *Residence* – Blairquhan Castle, Maybole, Ayrshire.

COLLATERAL BRANCHES LIVING

Issue of late Com Gaspard Patrick Hunter Blair, RN, 2nd son of 6th baronet, *b* 1895, *ka* 1941; *m* 1929, Sophie (who *d* 1968, having *m* 2ndly, 1945, as his 2nd wife, Rear Adm Robert Cathcart Kemble Lambert, DSO, who *d* 1950), el da of late Prince Alexis Koudacheff:—

Francis, *b* 1930; formerly Sub-Lieut RNVR: *m* 1957, Joyce, da of Cdr James Graham, OBE, RN, and has issue living, Patrick David, *b* 1958, — Michael Francis, *b* 1959, — Alexander John, *b* 1974, — Caroline Mary, *b* 1963. *Residence* – Marbrack, Carsphairn, Castle Douglas, Kirkcudbrightsire. ⸻ Katherine Isabel, *b* 1933; *ed* Oxford Univ (MA); BA London 1958 *m* 1960, Michael R. Stidworthy, of The Old Rectory, Caldecote, Cambridge, and has issue living, John Damian, *b* 1967, — Alexander Luke, *b* 1969, — Xenia Mary Gabriel, *b* 1961, — Imogen Theresa, *b* 1963.

Grandchildren of late Major Reginald Stanley Hunter Blair, MBE, 7th son of 4th baronet:—
Issue of late Lt-Col David Walter Hunter Blair, *b* 1894, *d* 1961: *m* 1st, 1919 (*m diss* 1941), Barbara, who *d* 1965, da of late George Cameron Norman: 2ndly, 1941, Hughe Thelma, who *d* 1972, da of late Capt H. E. Reid, R. Scots, and widow of Maj J. W. Williams, 2nd Punjab Regt; she *m* 3rdly, 1965, Adm Sir Walter Thomas Couchman, KCB, CVO, DSO, OBE, of Tandymead, Bromeswell, nr Woodbridge, Suffolk:—
(By 1st *m*) John David (34 Orange Grove Drive, Box 269, Harare, Zimbabwe), *b* 1925; *ed* Eton: *m* 1st, 1952 (*m diss* 1978), Jennifer Mary, only da of Leslie Hamilton Gault; 2ndly, 1988, Edwina Margaret, da of late James Done, of Harare, Zimbabwe, and has issue living (by 1st *m*), Thomas (The Mount, Brightling, nr Robertsbridge, E Sussex), *b* 1957: *m* 1986, Caroline (Pol), only da of D. Unwin, of Coventry, Warwicks, and of Mrs D. M. Bee, of St John, Jersey, and has issue living, Jack David Hamilton *b* 1989, Charlie *b* 1997, Sophie *b* 1991, — Jane, *b* 1956: *m* 1st, 1982 (*m diss* 1986), William Scott Hutton; 2ndly, 1990, Max Wolf, and has issue living (by 1st *m*), Oliver David *b* 1982, Louis Philip *b* 1985, (by 2nd *m*) Gabriella Ilse *b* 1990, Cordelia Iris *b* 1992, — Sophie, *b* 1960: *m* 1984, Philip John McCann, el son of Ian McCann, of Oak Park, Melbourne, and has issue living, Alexander *b* 1989, Rebecca *b* 1986, Georgia *b* 1990. —— (By 2nd *m*) Neil Malcolm, *b* 1944; late Gordon Highlanders; a Buddhist Monk in Thailand. —— (By 1st *m*) Aline Rosemary, *b* 1921: *m* 1st, 1944 (*m diss* 1949), Lt-Col David Theodor Dobie, DSO, formerly Parachute Regt; 2ndly, 1949 (*m diss* 1965), as his 2nd wife, Maj Hugh Cam Hobhouse, N Somerset Yeo (*see* Hobhouse, Bt); 3rdly, 1965, John Alastair Livingston Timpson, MC, late Maj Scots Gds, who *d* 1997, of 19 Ashcombe Court, Ilminster, Som TA19 0ED.

Issue of late Cmdr Ronald Hunter Blair, DSC, RN, *b* 1898, *d* 1968: *m* 1929, Nancye Murry, who *d* 1998, aged 90, da of late W. B. Colbeck, of Auckland, NZ:—
Alister (8 The Belvedere, Burnham-on-Crouch, Essex CM0 8AW), *b* 1930; *ed* Wellington Coll; Lt-Cdr RN (ret); Korea 1952-53: *m* 1st, 1958 (*m diss* 1975), Jennifer Shirley, el da of Rev Basil William Greenup, of Rock, Cornwall; 2ndly, 1976 (*m diss* 1994), Susan, yr da of late Lewis Rhodes Billinghurst, of Burnham-on-Crouch, Essex, and has issue living, (by 1st *m*) Nicholas Patrick Alister (9 The Drive, Worthing, Sussex), *b* 1959. —— Reginald Stuart (Fiddlers Hall, Charlestown, Fife KY11 3ER), *b* 1942; late Lt Gordon Highlanders: *m* 1968, Jennifer Marjorie, el da of Jack Paley Yorke, and has issue living, Camilla Louise, *b* 1970, — Antonia Claire, *b* 1972. —— Ronald Patrick (Fiddlers Hall, Charlestown, Fife KY11 3ER), *b* 1944; MBA: *m* 1972, Mary Fitzhugh, da of William T. Stewart, Jr, of Far Hills, New Jersey, USA, and has issue living, James Stewart, *b* 1974, — a son, *b* 1977. —— Julia HUNTER BLAIR (409 E 9th St, Davis, CA 95616, USA), *b* 1932; has resumed her maiden name: *m* 1st, 1958, Charles Maitland Zane; 2ndly, 1966, Arnold J. Bauer, and has issue living, (by 1st *m*) Lucy Sarah Mackenzie, *b* 1960, — (by 2nd *m*) Rebecca Penelope, *b* 1968. —— Elizabeth Mary (twin) (34 Beltran Rd, SW6 3AJ), *b* 1944; has issue living (by 3rd Baron Spens), William Ronald Patrick SPENS, *b* 1983.

Sir James Hunter Blair, 1st baronet was MP and Lord Provost of Edinburgh, and a partner in the banking house of Sir William Forbes and Co. He was 2nd son of John Hunter of Mainholm and Brownhill, Ayrshire, yr son of James Hunter of Abbotshill, Ayrshire, an estate granted to his ancestor James Hunter by charter 1569. The 1st Bt added the name of Blair about 1774, having *m* 1770, Jean, sister and heir of David Blair, and only da of John Blair of Dunskey, Wigtownshire by Anne Kennedy, sister and co-heir of 10th Earl of Cassillis. The 5th baronet, Rt Rev Sir David Oswald, was Abbot of Fort Augustus Dunfermline and Private Chamberlain to Pope Leo XIII.

BLAKE (I) 1622, of Menlough, Galway

Sir (THOMAS) RICHARD VALENTINE BLAKE, 17th *Baronet; b* 7 Jan 1942; *s* his father, *Sir* ULICK TEMPLE, 1963; *ed* Bradfield: *m* 1st, 1976, Jacqueline, da of late Desmond E. Daroux, and formerly wife of Peter Alers Hankey; 2ndly, 1982 (*m diss* 1986), Bertice Reading, singer, who *d* 1991, formerly wife of Eddie Meyer; 3rdly, 1991, Wendy, da of late Edward William Gough, of Richmond, Surrey, and widow of Anthony Ronald Roberts.

Arms – Argent, a fret gules. Crest – A tiger-cat passant guardant proper.
Residences – Old Janes, River, nr Petworth, W Sussex GU28 9AY; Chateau de Mappe, Route de Carces, 83510 Lorgues, Var, France.

COLLATERAL BRANCHES LIVING

Virtus sola nobilitas

Virtue alone ennobles

Grandchildren of late Major Cecil Bruce Blake (infra):—
Issue of late Major Charles Anthony Howell Bruce Blake, Roy Ulster Rifles, *b* 1911, *ka* in Korea 1951: *m* 1948, Elspeth (who *m* 2ndly, 1961, Patrick Michael Gardner, MBE, who *d* 1980), da of late Lt-Col A. M. Arnott:—
ANTHONY TEILO BRUCE (Woodlands, Higher Lane, Lymm, Cheshire WA13 0AZ), *b* (*posthumous*) 5 May 1951; *ed* Wellington Coll: *m* 1988, Geraldine, da of Cecil Shnaps, of Cape Town, S Africa, and has issue living, Charles Valentine Bruce, *b* 1994, — Sarah Elizabeth Bruce, *b* 1990, — Rachal Louise Bruce *b* 1991. —— Caroline Bruce, *b* 1949.

Issue of late Valentine John Bruce Blake, *b* 1914, *d* 1993: *m* 1950, Carla Maria Aida Wrinch-Schulz (Carnival, Spikle, Conna, co Cork), of Gardens, Cape Town, S Africa:—
Jonathan Luttrell (53 Sellick Drive, Croydon, Victoria 3136, Australia), *b* 1953: *m* 1977, Eleanora Mostert, of Holland, and has issue living, Suzanne May, *b* 1978, — Tonya Carla, *b* 1982, — Rachel Marie, *b* 1984. —— Kerry Valentine (Kolumbus Strasse 19, 8000 Munich 90, Germany), *b* 1963. —— Rosalie Julianne, *b* 1951: *m* 1977, Kevin Byrne, of Tollgate, Church St, Milnthorpe, Cumbria, and has issue living, Anna Louise, *b* 1981, — Philippa Elizabeth, *b* 1984. —— Noelle Claire Louise, *b* 1959.

Granddaughters of late Surg-Maj Walter Blake, 2nd son of late Walter Blake, grandson of 10th baronet:—
Issue of late Maj Cecil Bruce Blake, *b* 1880, *d* 1937: *m* 1909, Effie, who *d* 1969, da of S. Earnshaw Howell, JP:—
Elinor Joyce, *b* 1910: *m* 1933, Cyril Hall Green, and has issue living, Jeremy Dominic Blake (Ballyvolane House, Castlelyons, co Cork) *b* 1934: *m* 1965, Gabriel Meredith, only da of Ian James Wishaw Benson, of Tim's House, Ballyvolane, Castlelyons, Co Cork, and has issue living, Justin Toby *b* 1969, Sebastian Dominic *b* 1971: *m* 1995, Philippa Jane, da of John Edward King, of Bridlington, E Yorks (and has issue living, Sasha Clare *b* 1999), Adam Matthew *b* 1973, — Celia Elinor Vadyn, *b* 1936: *m* 1958, Edward John Mansel Hugh Frampton Child-Villiers, and has issue (*see* E Jersey, colls). —— Patricia Honora, *b* 1919: *m* 1st, 1942 (*m diss* 1951), Samuel Francis Hewitt Haughton, MB, BCh; 2ndly, 1957, Joseph Gerald Caulfield Kirby-Turner, who *d* 1961 (B Kilmaine, colls), and has issue living, (by 2nd *m*) Belinda Shiralee Anne, *b* 1959: *m* 1990, Jehanbaz Ali Khan, — Sharon Briar Rose, *b* 1960: *m* 1987, David Andrew Wallace, of Springfield House, Ballacolla, Abbeyleix, co Laois, 2nd son of Bruce Wallace, of Fruitlawn, Abbeyleix, and has issue living, Timothy Caulfield Daniel *b* 1991, Victoria Kirby *b* 1989.

Grandchildren of late Valentine Joseph Blake, 3rd son of late Valentine O'Connor Blake, yr son of late Maurice Blake, grandson of Maurice Blake (*d* 1789), grandson of John Blake, 4th son of 3rd baronet:—
Issue of late Lt-Col Arthur Maurice Joseph Blake, MC, LRCP, LRCS, *b* 1884, *d* 1974: *m* 1938, Barbara, who *d* 1994, only da of Raymond Stephenson, of Cranford, Stillorgan Rd, Dublin:—
Martin Joseph (Castlewood House, Durrow, co Leix), *b* 1952. —— Anne Meriel Josephine, *b* 1939: *m* 1964, Patrick Leonard, of Edmondstown Park, Dublin 16, and has issue living, John Arthur (Sean), *b* 1967, — Jeremy Charles, *b* 1973, — Dominic Stephen, *b* 1975, — Natasha Veronica, *b* 1965. —— Erica Mary Josephine, *b* 1940: *m* 1966, Bernard H. C. Corbally, of Gilspear, Kilmacanogue, co Wicklow, and has issue living, Simon Herbert Arthur, *b* 1967, — Colin George Eric, *b* 1968, — Ruth Ida Mary, *b* 1974, — Linda Clare Cecilia, *b* 1977.

Issue of late Gerald Joseph Blake, *b* 1896, *d* 1971: *m* 1943, Anne Josephine Deegan (54 Edmonscote, Cleveland Rd, Ealing, W13 8AJ):—
Valentine (13a Woodville Gdns, Ealing, W5 5LG), *b* 1945: *m* 1971, Madelene, only da of J. Andrews, of Perivale, Middx, and has issue living, Victoria Helen Josephine, *b* 1982. —— Gerald (14 Haven Lane, Ealing, W5 2HN), *b* 1947: *m* 1968, Elaine Thomas, of Baglan, Glamorgan, and has issue living, Gervase (227 Balmoral Drive, Hayes, Middx UB4 0AA), *b* 1969: *m* 1993, Angela Bennett, and has issue living, James Edward *b* 1997, — Emma Josephine, *b* 1972: *m* 1997, Adrian Dolan, of 82 Park Lane, Hayes, Middx UB4 8AE. —— Arthur (10 Haven Lane, Ealing, W5 2HN), *b* 1950; has issue living, Charlotte Anne Josephine, *b* 1983.

The founder of this family is said to have accompanied King John to Ireland in 1185. The 1st baronet, Sir Valentine Blake, was Mayor of Galway borough 1611 and 1630. The 6th baronet, Sir Walter, was the first Catholic gentleman of any distinction who joined William III; he maintained and clothed a regiment at his own expense.

BLAKE (GB) 1772, of Langham, Suffolk (Extinct 1975)

Cdr Sir CUTHBERT PATRICK BLAKE, DSO, RN, 6th and last *Baronet*.

DAUGHTER LIVING OF SIXTH BARONET

Veronica Anstace, *b* 1919; late 2nd Officer WRNS: *m* 1942, Maj Hugh Gilson-Taylor, Suffolk Regt, who *d* 1984, and has issue living, Christopher Gilson, *b* 1943: *m* 1st, 1969 (*m diss* 1981), Patricia Anne, da of Ismay Emanuel, of London, W6; 2ndly, 1987, Luise Daemen, of Zürich, Switzerland, and has issue living (by 1st *m*), Andrew Blake *b* 1972, David Patrick *b* 1975, — Anstace Felicity, *b* 1949: *m* 1971, Gilbert William Peter Wright, and has issue living, Jonathan William Blake *b* 1972, James Robert *b* 1974. *Residence* – 3 Peddars Court, Long Melford, Sudbury, Suffolk CO10 9ST.

BLAKE (UK) 1907, of Tillmouth Park, Cornhill, co Northumberland

RESURGAM

I shall rise again

Sir (FRANCIS) MICHAEL BLAKE, 3rd *Baronet*; *b* 11 July 1943; *s* his father, *Sir* (FRANCIS) EDWARD COLQUHOUN, 1950; *ed* Rugby: *m* 1968, Joan Ashbridge, only da of Frederic Cecil Ashbridge Miller, of Ramsay Lodge, Kelso, and has issue.

Arms – Per chevron argent and sable, a chevron per chevron in chief two garbs and in base a frette all countercharged. **Crest** – A morion proper, thereon a martlet argent, holding in the beak a sprig of barley sable.
Residence – The Dower House, Tillmouth Park, Cornhill-on-Tweed, Northumberland TD12 4UR.

SONS LIVING

FRANCIS JULIAN, *b* 17 Feb 1971. —— Nicholas Winston, *b* 1974.

HALF-SISTER LIVING

Caroline Anne Honey, *b* 1948: *m* 1975, Adam Henville Simonds, who *d* 1989, of 31 Lauder Rd, Edinburgh EH9 2JG, and has issue living, Alasdair David Henville, *b* 1977, — Kim Shona, *b* 1980.

WIDOW LIVING OF SECOND BARONET

DOREEN MAUD, da of late James Bertram Sample, of Stoneleigh, Hexham-on-Tyne, Northumberland: *m* 1st, 1947, as his 2nd wife, Sir (Francis) Edward Colquhoun Blake, 2nd Bt, who *d* 1950; 2ndly, 1961, Wing Cmdr John Francis Grey, DSO, DFC, RAF, who *d* 1964. *Residence* – Oxendean Burn, Cornhill-on-Tweed, Northumberland TD12 4UW.

COLLATERAL BRANCH LIVING

Issue of late Patrick Delaval Blake, yr son of 1st baronet, *b* 1904, *d* 1961: *m* 1st, 1927 (*m diss* 1944), Phyllis, da of W. Lee Ellison, of Chester; 2ndly, 1944, Mrs Ruby Holdsworth, who *m* 3rdly, 1973, W. E. Sweet, and *d ca* 1983:—
(By 1st *m*) Ian Francis (Nibelungengasse 1, A-1010 Vienna, Austria), *b* 1929; Lt-Cdr RN: *m* 1st, 1954 (*m diss* 1977), Frances Jillian, da of W. T. Barton of Shepherd's Hurst, Outwood, Surrey; 2ndly, 1979, Elisabeth Maria Aloisia Theresia, da of Univ Prof Dr Gustav Ortner, of Vienna, Austria, and has issue living, (by 1st *m*) Philip Ian, *b* 1955: *m* 1989, Rebecca, da of Rev Bernard Marshall, — Carol Patricia, *b* 1957: *m* 1st, 1980 (*m diss* 1982), Clive Richardson; 2ndly, 1986, Hugh Campbell, and has issue living (by 2nd *m*), Emma Mary Scott *b* 1987, Charlotte Fiona *b* 1989, Sarah Victoria *b* 1992. —— Mary Douglas, *b* 1931: *m* 1965, Dr Peter Branson, Oaklands Cottage, Wray Common, Reigate, Surrey, and has an adopted son and da, Adam Robert, *b* 1969, — Sara Jane, *b* 1972.

The 1st baronet, Sir Francis Douglas Blake, CB (son of late Francis Blake, of Tillmouth Park, Northumberland) sat as MP for Berwick-on-Tweed Div of Northumberland (*Co L*) 1916-22. The 2nd Baronet, Sir Francis Edward Colquhoun Blake, was Capt RA (TA Reserve), and served in European War 1914-18 and European War 1939-45.

BLAKER (UK) 1919, of Brighton, Sussex.

Sir JOHN BLAKER, 3rd *Baronet*; *b* 22 March 1935; *s* his father, *Maj Sir* REGINALD TD, 1975: *m* 1st, 1960 (*m diss* 1965), Catherine Ann, da of late Francis John Anselon Thorold (*see* Thorold, Bt, colls); 2ndly, 1968, Elizabeth Katharine, da of Col John Tinsley Russell, DSO.

Arms – Ermine three chevronelles, in chief two towers sable. **Crest** – A horse's head sable, charged with three chevronelles argent.
Residence – Stantons Farm, East Chiltington, nr Lewes, Sussex.

SISTER LIVING

Anne, *b* 1932: *m* 1953, Edmund Crosby Cockburn, and has issue living, Crosby Bay, *b* 1956, — Crosby Kim, *b* 1958, — Georgina Gay, *b* 1954. *Residence* – Glebe Farm, Shuckburgh, Daventry, Northants.

The 1st baronet, Sir John George Blaker, OBE, was Mayor of Brighton 1895-9.

BLAKISTON (GB) 1763, of the City of London

(Name usually pronounced "Blackiston")

Sir FERGUSON ARTHUR JAMES BLAKISTON, 9th *Baronet*; *s* his father, *Sir* (ARTHUR) NORMAN HUNTER, 1977; *b* 19 Feb 1963; *ed* Lincoln Coll, NZ, Auckland Inst of Technology, and NZ Inst of Business Studies: *m* 1993, Linda Jane, da of late Robert John Key, farmer, of Queenstown, NZ, and has issue.

𝕬rms – Argent, two barsgules, in chief three cocks of the last. 𝕮rest – A cock gules.
Residence – Cortington, 8 Waihi Terrace, Geraldine, S Canterbury, NZ.

DAUGHTER LIVING

Lydia Mary Ann, *b* 1996.

BROTHER LIVING

(NORMAN) JOHN BALFOUR, *b* 7 April 1964: *m* (14 May) 1997, Rhonda Maree Hart, and has issue living, Nicholas James Balfour, *b* 1995, — Lucy Anne Polly, *b* (5 Oct) 1997. *Residence* – 29 Colemans Rd, Springlands, Blenheim, NZ.

WIDOW LIVING OF SEVENTH BARONET

ANN HOPE PERCIVAL (*Ann, Lady Blakiston*) (42A Corton, Warminster, Wilts), da of late Purcell Cooke Jeans, of Cortington Grange, Warminster, Wilts: *m* 1954, as his 2nd wife, Sir Arthur Frederick Blakiston, 7th Bt, MC, who *d* 1974.

COLLATERAL BRANCHES LIVING

Grandchildren of late Charles Robert Blakiston, 5th son of 3rd baronet, *b* 1825, *d* 1898: *m* 1858, Mary Anna, who *d* 1924, da of late Most Rev Henry John Chitty Harper, DD, sometime Bishop of Christchurch, and Primate of New Zealand:—
Issue of late Charles Douglas Blakiston, *b* 1868 *d* 1950: *m* 1908, Ethel Anne, who *d* 1967, da of late John Henley Whishaw, of Featherston, NZ:—
Charles Michael Hardy, *b* 1919: *m* 1945, Nancy, da of Charles E. Holmes, of Wellington, New Zealand, and has issue living, David Holmes (Bruce Rd, PO Box 1039, Levin, NZ), *b* 1946: *m* 1982, Susan Margaret, da of Maj-Gen Robin Hugh Ferguson Holloway, CB, CBE, of Waikanae, NZ, and has issue living, Matthew Robin *b* 1983, — Roger Charles (15 Rue Maurice, Herzog, Magenta, New Caledonia), *b* 1948: *m* 1st, 1975 (*m diss* 1991), Victoria Jane, da of Peter L. Marshall, of Taoroa, Taihape, NZ; 2ndly, 1993, Francoise Vallino, and has issue living (by 1st *m*), Charles Rupert Hardy *b* 1976, Samuel James *b* 1980, Alice *b* 1977, (by 2nd *m*) Isaura *b* 1993, — Simon Michael (12 Highbury Crescent, Highbury, Wellington, NZ), *b* 1952: *m* 1981, Nell, da of Michael Pouajen, of Bipi Island, Papua New Guinea, and has issue living, Manu Sangak *b* 1983. *Residence* – NZ. —— Barbara Helen Joan: *m* 1st, 1940, Henry Frank Seymour, who was *ka* 1941; 2ndly, 1945, Allan Frederick Palairet, who *d* 1990, of 7/107 Walker Rd, Point Chevalier, Auckland, NZ, and has issue living (by 1st *m*) Nicholas Charles (Wensleydale Station, Private Bag, Gisborne, NZ), *b* 1941: *m* 1966, Patricia Anne Ingram, of Auckland, and has issue living, Howard Frank *b* 1970, Patrick James *b* 1974, Andrea June *b* 1972, — (by 2nd *m*) Anthea Gay, *b* 1949: *m* 1973, Noel Morris Kershaw, of Koeko, Moutere, Nelson, NZ, — Penelope Sue, *b* 1955: *m* 1974, Lindsay Graeme Everingham, of Lot 1, Meryla St, Couridjah, NSW 2571, Australia, and has issue living, Nicholas James *b* 1975, Malika *b* 1978.

Grandchildren of late John Rochfort Blakiston, son of Maj John Blakiston, 27th Regt, 2nd son of 2nd baronet:—
Issue of late John Francis Blakiston, CIE, *b* 1882, *d* 1965: *m* 1st, 1918 (*m diss* 1930), Paula, da of late E. Allen Howard, Bar-at-law; 2ndly, 1937, Margaret Dora, who *d* 1991, el da of Rev G. A. Ward-Jackson, R of Rousham, with Lower Heyford, Oxford:—
(By 2nd *m*) John Alan Cubitt (Grove House, Lydiard Millicent, nr Swindon, Wilts SN5 9LP), *b* 1938; Lt-Col 13th/18th R Hus: *m* 1975, Sally Anne, da of Lt-Col John David Logan Dickson, MC, RHA (*see* E Westmorland, colls), and has issue living, John William Matthew, *b* 1982, — Caroline Mary, *b* 1979, — Emma Elizabeth, *b* 1981. —— Susan Anne Margaret, *b* 1940. —— Jane Mary Dora Helen, *b* 1944: *m* 1st, 1968 (*m diss* 1978), Richard Parker; 2ndly, 1991, Edward Peter Jonathan Darmady, of Teviot Cottage, Tyninghame, nr Dunbar EH42 1XL, and has issue living (by 1st *m*) Nycolas Sebastian Robert Blakiston, *b* 1970, — Venetia Clare Rosalind, *b* 1969.

Grandchildren of late Capt Richard Blakiston-Houston, son of late Capt John Blakiston-Houston, eldest son of late Richard Bayly Blakiston-Houston (who assumed by Royal Licence 1843 the additional surname of Houston), 5th son of 2nd baronet:—
Issue of late Col John Matthew Blakiston-Houston, DL, *b* 1898, *d* 1984: *m* 1931, Lettice Arden, who *d* 1982, da of Henry Gervas Stobart, of Thornton Hall, Thornton-le-Dale, Yorkshire:—
Richard Patrick (Beltrim Castle, Gortin, co Tyrone; Roddens, Ballywater, co Down), *b* 1948; *ed* Eton, and RAC, Cirencester; ARICS 1972; JP and DL co Down and High Sheriff 1989: *m* 1988, Lucinda Mary Lavinia, da of Lt Cdr Theodore Bernard Peregrine Hubbard, RN (ret), of Thurston Croft, Thurston, Bury St Edmunds, Suffolk (*see* Norfolk, D), and has issue living, Jack Peregrine, *b* 1989, — Christopher George, *b* 1991, — Harry Charles, *b* 1996, — Michael Peter, *b* 1998. — Leticia Sadhbh Miriam, *b* 1993, — Felicia Grace Lilian, *b* 1994. —— Mary Bridget, *b* 1932: *m* 1956, Gavin Rowan Hamilton, of The Horse Mill, Stenton, Dunbar, E Lothian, and has issue living, James (Hamish) John, *b* 1961: *m* 1990, Venetia E., da of John Carter, of High Holms, Steel, Hexham, Northumberland, and has issue living, Frederick John *b* 1993, Tamara Mary-Ann *b* 1995, — Patrick Gawaine, *b* 1964, — Catherine Nicola Blanche, *b* 1957: *m* 1987, Bartholomew Evan Eric Smith, and has issue (*see* E Northesk, colls). —— Anne (*Lady Hallifax*), *b* 1934: *m* 1962, Adm Sir David John Hallifax, KCB, KCVO, KBE, RN (*see* Hughes, Bt, *cr* 1773 1972-73 Edn), who *d* 1992, of The Brew

House, Englefield, Reading, Berks RG7 5EN, and has had issue, Thomas Ronald, b 1965, — Matthew William Hughes, b 1967; ed Edinburgh Univ; drowned in a boating accident 1989, — Louisa Kate, b 1964: m 1993, Hugo Roderick Charles Burnand, of 3 Garden Mews, Linden Gdns, W2 4HF, son of Peter Vere Burnand, and has issue living, Fergus Matthew Christian b 1994, Lily Susan Hallifax b 1996, Una Peta Rose b 1998. —— Prudence, b 1936: m 1964, John Archibald Douglas-Menzies, of Mounteagle, Fearn, Ross-shire, and has issue living, John William, b 1966, — Andrew Edward, b 1968, — James, b 1970. —— Elizabeth, b 1939: m 1973, Michael Geoffrey Minton Haines, of 82A Mortimer Rd, N1, and has issue living, Francis Christopher Minton, b 1975, — Richard Walter Minton, b 1977, — Rosaline Marion Minton, b 1979. —— Patience Victoria, b 1944: m 1979, Ron Long, of Twiglees, Boreland, Dumfriesshire, and has issue living, Joshua, b 1975, — Daniel, b 1977.

        Grandsons of late Ralph Blakiston, eldest son of late John Richard Blakiston, son of late Rev Peyton Blakiston, MD, FRS, 6th son of 2nd baronet:—
    Issue of late Rev Robert Ralph Christian Blakiston, b 1890, d 1983: m 1929, Winifred Muriel, who d 1988, yr da of late John Frost, of Ripley, Derbys:—
John Robert, b 1931; ed Haileybury: m 1960, Carol Helen, yst da of John C. Durham, of Anniswood, Warninglid, Sussex, and has issue living, Michèle Anne, b 1964, — Rachel Jane, b 1966. Residence – Wood Sorrel Cottage, Nutley, Sussex.

        Issue of late John Horace Blakiston, b 1897, d 1982: m 1928, Winifred Kathleen Maybank, who d 1988, da of Archie William Webb, of Banstead, Surrey:—
David, b 1934; ed Haileybury, and Loughborough Coll (BSc, MIMechE, CEng): m 1962, Joanna Averil, da of Cecil Green, of Kingsthorpe, Northampton, and has issue living, John, b 1967; BCom, ACMA, ACA: m 1995, Elizabeth Nina Edith, da of Andrew Palmer, of Havant, Hants, and has issue living, Josephine Ann b 1997, — Anne, b 1970; BA, BTS: m 1998, David Emile Claude Le Tiec, of Monbazon, France, — Carol Clare, b 1972; BA. Residence – Tara, 65 Curley Hill Rd, Lightwater, Surrey GU18 5YH.

        Grandsons of late Matthew Folliott Blakiston, son of late Rev Peyton Blakiston, MD, FRS (ante):—
    Issue of late Rochfort Folliott Blakiston, b 1860, d 1949: m 1st, 1907, Ellen Kate, who d 1929, only da of late George Greenleaf, of Great George Street, Westminster, SW; 2ndly, 1930, Elizabeth Lilian Diana, who d 1976, el da of Rev David Jones, V of Goodwick, Pembrokeshire:—
(By 2nd m) Digby Rochfort David (Yet y Gors, Seleddau, Fishguard, Dyfed), b 1931: late Lt RN: m 1959, Dorothea Irene Louise Walser, and has issue living, Matthew Simon Rochfort, b 1964, — Louise, b 1961: m 198-, Andrew P. M. Jenkins, of Gelliwernfawr, Felindre, nr Swansea, yr son of Dr John Richard Everett Jenkins, of Michaelston-le-Pit, S Glamorgan, — Caroline, b 1962. —— Michael Peyton Folliott (90 York Mansions, Prince of Wales Drive, SW11) b 1933; ed Trin Coll, Oxford (MA); m 1973, Mrs Fanny Marie Francis, el da of Henri Roquette, of Lille, France.

    This is a branch of the family of Blakiston, of Blakiston, co Durham, in which two baronetcies were conferred in 1615 and 1642, expiring respectively in 1619 and 1713. The 1st baronet of the present creation was Sheriff of London 1753, and Lord Mayor 1760.

BLANE (UK) 1812, of Blanefield, Ayrshire (Extinct 1916)

Com Sir CHARLES RODNEY BLANE, RN, 4th and last Baronet.

DAUGHTER LIVING OF FOURTH BARONET

Helen Mary, b 1913: m 1940, William Robert Tomkinson, TD, late Capt Middx Regt, who d 1980, and has issue living, Robert Charles (Home Farm, Wappenham, nr Towcester, Northants), b 1941: m 1968, Joanna Sally Hastings, and has issue living, James Robert b 1970, Simon William b 1972, — David Edward (Stonecrop, Rectory Lane, Buckland, Betchworth, Surrey RH3 7BL), b 1945: m 1976 (m diss 1993), Catherine Jane Monica Austen, da of late Lt-Col Austen Bertram Knight, MC, of Pamber End, Basingstoke, Hants, and has issue living, Elizabeth Helen Beatrice b 1978, Catherine Amy Mary b 1980, — Virginia Susan, b 1943: m 1964, Maj-Gen Andrew Evans, late 5th R Inniskilling Dragoon Gds, and has issue living, Lucinda Emma Katherine b 1967, Alexandra Louise Harriet b 1969, — Diana Helena (twin), b 1943: m 1969, David Rainald Lewthwaite, and has issue living (see Lewthwaite, Bt). Residence – Stonecrop, Rectory Lane, Buckland, Betchworth, Surrey.

BLENNERHASSETT (UK) 1809, of Blennerville, co Kerry

Sir (MARMADUKE) ADRIAN FRANCIS WILLIAM BLENNERHASSETT, 7th *Baronet*; *b* 25 May 1940; *s* his father, *Lieut Sir* MARMADUKE CHARLES HENRY JOSEPH CASIMIR, RNVR, 1940; *ed* McGill Univ, Imperial Coll, London (MSc) and Cranfield Business Sch (MBA): *m* 1972, Carolyn Margaret, da of late Gilbert Brown, and has issue.

𝔄rms – Gules, a chevron ermine between three dolphins embowed argent. 𝔠rest – A wolf sejant proper.
Residence – 54 Staveley Rd, Chiswick, W4 3ES.

SON LIVING

CHARLES HENRY MARMADUKE, *b* 18 July 1975.

DAUGHTER LIVING

Celina Mary Charlotte, *b* 1973.

COLLATERAL BRANCHES LIVING

Grandchildren of late Capt William Lewis Rowland Paul Sebastian Blennerhassett, DSO, OBE, yst son of 4th baronet:—
Issue of late Maj (Casimir Paul Francis) Rowland Blennerhassett, *b* 1911, *d* 1993: *m* 1945, Elizabeth Charlotte Josephine, who *d* 1995, da of late Com Gregory Stapleton, RN (*see* D Norfolk, colls), and widow of Maj Francis John Angus Skeet:—
John Rowland, *b* 1952. —— Rosanna Frances, *b* 1946.

Fortune helps the brave

Granddaughter of late Rowland Ponsonby Blennerhassett, son of late Richard Francis Blennerhassett, son of late Rowland Blennerhassett, 4th son of 1st baronet:—
Issue of late Richard Francis Ponsonby Blennerhassett, *b* 1879, *d* 1938: *m* 1914, Silvia, who *d* 1957, only da of late Frederic W. H. Myers, of Leckhampton, Cambridge:—
Diana Mary Ponsonby, *b* 1916: *m* 1939, Richard John Moreton Goold-Adams, CBE, who *d* 1995, only son of late Maj Sir Hamilton Goold-Adams, GCMG, CB. *Residence* – 33 Great Pulteney St, Bath, Avon BA2 4BX.

The ancestors of this family were long seated in Cumberland, and took their name from the township of Blennerhassett in that co. Members of the family represented Carlisle in nearly every Parliament from Richard II to James I, and later frequently represented either Kerry co or the borough of Tralee. Robert Blennerhassett settled in co Kerry in the reign of James I. The 4th baronet, Rt Hon Sir Rowland, sat as MP for Galway (*L*) 1865-74, and for co Kerry 1880-85. The 5th baronet, Sir Arthur Charles Francis Bernard, held various positions in the Indian Civil Service ending as JP for the Central Provinces. He *d* 1915. The 6th baronet, Lieut Sir Marmaduke Charles Henry Joseph Casimir was *ka* 25 May 1940 serving in HMS *Greyhound* at Dunkirk.

BLOIS (E) 1686, of Grundisburgh Hall, Suffolk
(Name pronounced "Bloyss")

Sir CHARLES NICHOLAS GERVASE BLOIS, 11th *Baronet*: *b* 25 Dec 1939; *s* his father, *Capt Sir* GERVASE RALPH EDMUND, MC, 1968; *ed* Harrow and Trin Coll, Dublin: *m* 1967, Celia Helen Mary, only da of late Cyril George Francis Pritchett, CBE, of Mayfield, and has issue.

𝔄rms – Gules, a bend vair between two fleurs-de-lis argent. 𝔠rest – A gauntlet proper holding a fleur-de-lis argent.
Residence – Red House, Westleton, Saxmundham, Suffolk.

SON LIVING

ANDREW CHARLES DAVID, *b* 7 Feb 1971.

Je me fie en Dieu
I trust in God

DAUGHTER LIVING

Helen Janet, *b* 1974.

BROTHER LIVING

Rodney John Derek (Hill Farm, Yoxford, Suffolk), b 1941; ed Harrow; High Sheriff Suffolk 1989: m 1968 (m diss 1992), Lady (Elizabeth) Caroline (Elinor Evelyn) Giffard, da of 3rd Earl of Halsbury, and has issue living, Camilla Frances Elizabeth, b 1970, — Susanna Gillian Caroline, b 1972: m 1997, Christopher J. Lye, yr son of Raymond Lye, of Enstone, Oxon.

SISTER LIVING

Gillian Frances Audrey (Foxcote Grange, Andoversford, Cheltenham, Glos), b 1943: m 1st, 1965 (m diss 1970), Hugh Christopher Riddle; 2ndly, 1975, Gilbert John Chalk (see E Shrewsbury, colls), and has issue living, (by 2nd m) Alexander John Gervase, b 1976, — Christopher Harry Gilbert, b 1985, — Nicola Elizabeth, b 1978.

AUNT LIVING (Daughter of 9th baronet)

Christian Frances (Stanhope, Yoxford, Suffolk), b 1902: m 1st, 1928 (m diss 1940), Edward Archibald Fraser Harding; 2ndly, 1940 (m diss 1955), Geoffrey Henry Cecil Bing, QC, who d 1977, and has issue living, (by 2nd m) Inigo Geoffrey, b 1944, — Richard, b 1946.

COLLATERAL BRANCHES LIVING

Grandchildren of late Maj Eardley Steuart Brooke, TD (3rd son of 8th baronet), who assumed by Royal licence 1931 for himself and his issue the surname and arms of Brooke in lieu of his patronymic:—
Issue of late Thomas Eardley Blois Brooke, b 1918, d 1986: m 1948, Joy Mary (Cresborough, Rhos, Haverfordwest, Pembrokeshire), only da of Maj-Gen Robert Stedman Lewis, CB, OBE:—
Thomas Robin Eardley BLOIS-BROOKE (Cresborough, Rhos, Haverfordwest, Pembrokeshire), b 1951; ed Wellington: m 1978, Philippa de Courcy, da of John Fryer, and has issue living, Thomas Eardley, b 1982, — Edward Charles, b 1984. — Jennifer Mary, b 1949: m 1980, Guy William Meakin Farmiloe, of Heatherbank, Sheepsetting Lane, Heathfield, E Sussex TN21 0UY, yr son of late Leslie Farmiloe, MC, and has issue living, Toby Nicholas, b 1987. — Elizabeth Anne, b 1953: m 1986, Michael John Read, of 17 The Winery, Regents Bridge Gdns, SW8 1JR, elder son of T. H. Read, of Northlands, Fishbourne, Chichester, Sussex, and has issue living, Harry Thomas, b 1987, — Alice Louise, b 1990.

Issue of late Lt-Cmdr Michael Steuart Blois-Brooke, RD, RNR, b 1919, d 1995; resumed by deed poll 1953 the surname of Blois in addition to and before that of Brooke: m 1949, Mary (Cherry) (St Austin's House, Curtis Lane, Sheringham, Norfolk), yr da of Cecil Harvey Mead, of Oak House, Crawley Down, Sussex:—
Mark Harvey BLOIS-BROOKE (St Austin's House, Curtis Lane, Sheringham, Norfolk NR26 8DE), b 1954; ed Felsted: m 1997, Amanda Caroline Wade, and has issue living, Henry Michael, b 1999. — Susan Penelope, b 1950: m 1973, Nigel Robert Clifford (PO Box 190, George Town, Grand Cayman, Cayman Is), and has issue living, Joanna Mary, b 1976, — Louise Rosemary, b 1979. — Diana Mary, b 1959.

Issue of late Robert John Brooke, BL, b 1923, d 1963: m 1949, Ann Hamerton Gordon (St Aidan's, Morebattle, Kelso), el da of late Capt Francis Gordon Troup, of Dunbennan:—
Alastair John BLOIS-BROOKE (Pen Hay, Bevington, nr Berkeley, Glos), b 1950: m 1989, Julia, da of J. A. Burgess, of Bristol, and has issue living, Alexander David, b 1991, — Christopher John, b 1993. — Ian Steuart BLOIS, b 1953: m 1991, Clare, da of late Peter Champkin, of Sussex, and has issue living, Katharine Ann, b 1993. — (Katharine) Margaret, b 1961: m 1989, Ian W. Thomson, of 27 Gawler Crescent, Deakin, ACT 2600, Australia, 2nd son of late Lewis Thomson, of Canberra, Australia, and has issue living, Robert Lewis, b 1994, — Amy Blois b 1991, — Elizabeth Ann, b 1996, — and has an adopted da, Jessica Louise, b 1987.

Granddaughters of late Lieut-Col Dudley George Blois, DSO, RFA (infra):—
Issue of late Wing Com John Dudley Blois, RAF Regt (late Major Irish Guards), b 1915, d 1954: m 1948, Elizabeth Catharine, who d 1993, da of Rear-Adm Sir Wellwood George Courtenay Maxwell, KBE, CMG (B Chesham):—
(Elizabeth) Frances Moyra (6 St Augustine's Mansions, Bloomburg St, SW1V 2RG), b 1949. — Sarah Jane, b 1951: m 1982, Miles Tobias (Toby) Ward, of Church Farm, E Woodhay, nr Newbury, Berks RG20 0AL, yr son of late P. T. Ward, and of Mrs Mark Chaytor, of Aston Towers, Coal Aston, Derbys, and has issue living, Lomax Blois, b 1984, — Sam Philip, b 1986, — Thomas Dudley, b 1990.

Issue of late Lieut-Col Dudley George Blois, DSO, RFA, 5th son of 8th baronet, b 1875, ka 1916: m 1914, Georgiana Isabella Frances, who d 1967, da of late Adm Sir Compton Edward Domvile, GCB, GCVO (Peel, Bt, cr 1800, colls):—
Jane Elizabeth Georgiana Joan (26 Manchester St, WIM 5PG), b 1916; formerly 3rd Officer WRNS.

Issue of late Rev Gervase Vanneck Blois, yst son of 8th baronet, b 1881, d 1961: m 1914, Hon Hester Murray Pakington, who d 1973, da of 3rd Baron Hampton:—
Anthony Gervase, DFC, b 1918; ed Wellington Coll, and Phillips Acad, Andover, Mass, USA; formerly Flight-Lieut, RAF Vol Reserve: m 1957, Ivy Tucker, who d 1983, da of William Charles Bell. Residence – 19 Bilton Rd, Rugby. — David Pakington, b 1923; Capt MN: m 1951, Joan, da of late Capt L. R. Brock, and has issue living, Michael David Stuart (PO Box 595, 2149 Riverclub, Republic of South Africa), b 1955: m 1983, Heather, da of James W. Davidson, of Buccleuch, nr Johannesburg, S Africa, and has issue living, Stuart Murray b 1992, Fiona Claire b 1994, — Angela Claire, b 1958: m 1982, Steven Russell Tuhey, of 2 River Lane, Randalls Road, Leatherhead, Surrey. Residence – 34 Strawberry Vale, Twickenham, Middx, TW1 4RU. — Evelyn Hester (Baroness MacLeod of Borve), b 1915; cr Baroness MacLeod of Borve (Life Baroness) 1971 (see that title). — Elizabeth Mary, b 1921; formerly Subaltern ATS: m 1953, Francis George

Smith, of 8681, Shepherd Way, Delta, British Columbia, Canada, and has issue living, Fiona Elizabeth, *b* 1956, — Gillian Hester, *b* 1958, — Jennifer Margaret, *b* 1962.

Grandchildren of late Lt-Col William Thornhill Blois, brother of 8th baronet:—
Issue of late Ernest Pierrepoint Blois, *b* 1880, *d* 1950: *m* 1990, Lilian Emily, who *d* 1918, da of Joseph William Moore, and formerly wife of Herbert William Oakeley (*see* Oakeley, Bt, Colls, 1931 Edn):—
†Trevor Galfridus, *b* 1904; bloodstock agent: *m* 1943, Mrs Diana Kathleen Mary Horton, who *d* 1950, da of Cornelius Horton, and formerly wife of Samuel Bach, and *d* 1992. —— Esmé Ernestine, *b* 1901: *m* 1st, 1924, William Farquhar Healey; 2ndly, 19—, ... Windle, and has issue living (by 1st *m*), Daphne (adopted by Mr and Mrs Noel Burton Spurway 1930, and renamed Rosemary Yvonne Spurway), *b* 1926: *m* 1951, Alfred Donald Gilbert, of 34 Meeting House Lane, Balsall Common, Warws CV7 7FX, son of Neville Wallace Gilbert, and has issue living, Stephen Donald Spurway (The Pentre, Trefonen, Oswestry, Shropshire SY10 9EE) *b* 1953: *m* 1979, Helen Nicola Harben (and has issue living, Sarah Diana *b* 1982, Kate Gwenda *b* 1984), Deborah Mary *b* 1958: *m* 1st, 1981 (*m diss* 1992), David Simon Mumby; 2ndly, 1996, Christopher William Frank Smith (and has issue living, (by 1st *m*) Oliver William *b* 1989, Hannah Mary *b* (twin) 1989, (by 2nd *m*) Callie Louise *b* 1998). —— Agnes Mary (Stella), *b* 1903: *m* 1928, Reginald Calvert Empson, son of Frederick James Empson, and *d* 1982. —— Fanny Susan (also known as Raymonde Margaret), *b* 1911; *d unm* 1968. —— Nancy Avril, *b* 1917; *d unm* 1947.

Issue, if any, of late Basil Frederic Blois, *b* 1881, *d* 1929: *m* 19—, Kathleen, who *d* 1922, da of Robert Overall:—

Issue, if any, of Geoffrey Stephen Blois, *b* 1884, *d* 1955:—

Galfridus de Blois held lands in Walpole, Suffolk, *temp* Richard I. The family resided at Norton, Suffolk, till *temp* King Henry VII, and at Grundisburgh Hall, Suffolk. They removed in 1693 to Cockfield Hall, which was in possession of a member of the Blois family until it was sold ca 1997.

BLOMEFIELD (UK) 1807, of Attleborough, co Norfolk

Sir (THOMAS) CHARLES (PEREGRINE) BLOMEFIELD 6th *Baronet*, *b* 24 July 1948; *s* his father, *Lt-Cdr Sir* THOMAS EDWARD PEREGRINE, 1984; *ed* Wellington, and Mansfield Coll, Oxon; is a Co Dir: *m* 1975, Georgina Geraldine, da of late Cdr Charles Over, RN, of Lugger End, Portscatho, Cornwall, and has issue.

Arms – Sable, on a chevron argent a branch of laurel between two bomb shells fired proper; and on a canton or, a spear's head imbrued proper. **Crest** – Issuant from a mural crown argent a demi-heraldic tiger azure, armed and tufted or, collared argent, and holding a sword broken in the middle proper. *Address* – c/o Bank of Scotland, 38 Threadneedle St, EC3.

SON LIVING

THOMAS WILLIAM PEREGRINE, *b* 16 July 1983.

DAUGHTERS LIVING

Emma Georgina, *b* 1980. —— Harriet Elizabeth, *b* 1986.

WIDOW LIVING OF FIFTH BARONET

GINETTE (*Ginette, Lady Blomefield*), formerly wife of George Harting, and da of late Dr Raphael Massart, of 15 Boulevard des Invalides, Paris: *m* 1947, Lt-Cdr Sir Thomas Edward Peregrine Blomefield, 5th Bt, RNVR, who *d* 1984.

COLLATERAL BRANCHES LIVING

Grandson of late Lt-Col Wilmot Blomefield, OBE, RE (infra):—
Issue of late His Honour Judge Peregrine Maitland Blomefield, *b* 1917, *d* 1988: *m* 1941, Angela Catherine, who *d* 1998, yst da of late Maj Geoffrey Hugh Shenley Crofton:—
Adam Peregrine Horatio, *b* 1946; *ed* Renton, and Trin Coll, Oxford: *m* 1st, 1970 (*m diss* 1976), Esther Margaret, da of Vaughan Lewis, of Swansea; 2ndly, 1981, Gertraud Elisabeth, da of Heinrich Tophinke, of Mörnsheim, and has issue living, (by 1st wife) Anna Claudia, *b* 1972, — (by 2nd wife) Georges Peregrine, *b* 1982, — Nora Katharina, *b* 1976. *Residence* – Chaussée de Namur 73, B-1315 Incourt, Belgium.

Issue of late Lieut-Col Wilmot Blomefield, OBE, RE, yst son of 4th baronet, *b* 1878, *d* 1926: *m* 1907, Jessie Leila, who *d* 1976, only da of late William A. Hodges, JP, of East Bridgeford, Notts:—

Rosemary Eardley (*Lady Hayman*), *b* 1914: *m* 1942, Sir Peter Telford Hayman, KCMG, CVO, MBE, who *d* 1992, of No 3 Cherry Tree Close, Stoke Row, Henley-on-Thames, Oxon RG9 5RD, and has issue living, Christopher Wilmot Arden, *b* 1947: *m* 1979, Joanna, da of James O'Reilly, of Ballyfaskin, Ballylanders, co Limerick, and has issue living, Daniel Peter James *b* 1980, Oliver Christopher *b* 1995, Emily Rosemary Annabel *b* 1997, — Virginia Rosemary, *b* 1944: *m* 1974, Michael Jerrold Philipson, and has issue living, Stephen Ralph Peter *b* 1977, Claire Leila *b* 1980.

Grandson of late Edward Hugh Blomefield, MVO, son of Rev Samuel Edward Blomefield, 3rd son of 2nd baronet:—
   Issue of late Allan Herbert Blomefield, *b* 1891; *d* 1978: *m* 1935, Olive Nesfield Cookson, who *d* 1980:—
Roger Stanley (41 Forresters Rd, Burbage, Hinckley), *b* 1937; LBIPP, AMPA: *m* 1959, Eve Kathleen Bartlett, and has issue living Adrian Paul, *b* 1964: *m* 1994, Roseann Kane, — Dawn Lesley, *b* 1960.

Granddaughters of late Lawrence Woodyeare Blomefield (infra):—
   Issue of late John Woodyeare Blomefield, *b* 1903, *d* 1967: *m* 1927, Dorothea Mae, who *d* 1981, da of A. Farr:—
Anne Shirley (5 Loerie Mews, Loerie Lane, Beacon Bay, E London 5241, S Africa), *b* 1927: *m* 1st, 1947 (*m diss* 1966), Pieter Barendse Botha Van Gend; 2ndly, 1969, Cecil James Meyers, who *d* 1992, and has issue living, (by 1st *m*) Nardi Anne, *b* 1949: *m* 1971, William Henry Raubenheimer, — Cornelia Mae, *b* 1952; *m* 1983, Terence Anthony Carroll, and has issue living, Byron Terence Anthony *b* 1986, — (by 2nd *m*) Donovan James, *b* 1972. —— Elizabeth Jill (31 Leadwood Place, Beacon Bay, E London 5241, S Africa), *b* 1931: *m* 1st, 1954, John Charsley Meyer, who *d* 1979; 2ndly, 1989 (*m diss* 1990), David Edward Hugh Davies, and has issue living (by 1st *m*), Mark William, *b* 1955: *m* 1977, Noël Lynn Cotton, and has issue living, Lindi Elaine *b* 1979, Julie Elizabeth *b* 1981, Kristy Lynn *b* 1983, — Bruce Woodyeare, *b* 1957, — Colin John, *b* 1959: *m* 1982, Rosemary Anne Seeney, and has issue living, Ross John *b* 1984, James Colin *b* 1987.

Granddaughter of late Rev John Blomefield, 4th son of 2nd baronet:—
   Issue of late Lawrence Woodyeare Blomefield, *b* 1870, *d* 1956: *m* 1899, Celia Nora, who *d* 1961, da of late A. B. Caldwell:—
Frances Celia, *b* 1901: *m* 1922, Dr Arnold Klosser van Niekerk, dental surgeon (S Africa), who *d* 1976, and has issue living, Olive Joan (PO Box 15, Kidds Beach 5264, S Africa), *b* 1926: *m* 1947, Kenneth Louis Clur, who *d* 1994, and has issue living, Robert Louis *b* 1955: *m* 1978, Cheryl Lynn Randall (and has issue living, Greggory Louis *b* 1981, Tarryn Lynn *b* 1985), Linda Ann *b* 1947: *m* 1967, Christian John Flemmer, who *d* 1994 (and has issue living, Wendy Ann *b* 1970: *m* 1994, Anton van Bergen [and has issue living, Graham John *b* 1997, Robyn Ann *b* 1995], Caryn Ann *b* 1976: *m* 1997, Grant Leuthardt [and has issue living Bridget Ann *b* 1998], Angela *b* 1978), Beverley Louise *b* 1952: *m* 1978, Richard Charles Bishop (and has issue living, Russell Alan *b* 1984, Kristi-Lee *b* 1981), — Valerie Ellen (17 Greenfields, Pinewood Rd, Rondebosch, Cape 7700, S Africa), *b* 1928: *m* 1948, Garth Cox Latimer, who *d* 1966, and has issue living, Dean Andrew *b* 1949: *m* 1979 (*m diss* 1987), Susan Coetzee (and has issue living, Tamara Anne *b* 1980, Caralyn Grace *b* 1982), Michael Garth *b* 1951: *m* 1977, Jacqueline Barbara Forbes (and has issue living, Gareth Ross *b* 1982, Kerry-Anne *b* 1984), Alan John *b* 1953: *m* 1977, Anne Muriel Sabberton (and has had issue, Gregg *b* 1983 *d* 1986, Brennan John *b* 1987, Peta Anne *b* 1981).

Grandchildren of late Charles Allan Blomefield, eldest son of late Rev Charles David Blomefield, 6th son of 2nd baronet:—
   Issue of late Allan Arthur Blomefield, late Prin English Medium Sch, Lichtenburg, Transvaal, *b* 1903, *d* 1985: *m* 1st, 1930 (*m diss* ca 1944), Dorothy Jane, who *d* 1982, da of A. Thorne Adams; 2ndly, ca 1945, Eileen Ethel Hinwood Jones, who *d* 1966; 3rdly, 1969, Rosalie Isabel Margaret Murray (*née* Law), who *d* 1991:—
(By 1st *m*)†John Peregrine, *b* 1937; *d* 1941. —— Justine (PO Box 915-617 Faerie Glen, Pretoria 0043, S Africa), *b* 1931: *m* 1955, Errol Malcolm Armstrong, who *d* 1992, and has issue living, Eamon Collison, *b* 1963: *m* 1991, Wendy Fitzhenry, and has issue living, Emily Jane *b* 1994, Charlotte Jean *b* 1996, — Fergus Fitzgerald, *b* 1965, — Amanda Lee, *b* 1960. —— Jennifer Ann, *b* 1934: *m* 1957, John Steele Chalsty, of 24 Taylor Rd, Short Hills, NJ 07078, USA, and has issue living, Susan, *b* 1957: *m* 1982, John Hamlin Neely, and has issue living, John Harrison *b* 1987, Timothy Allan *b* 1990, Meghan Chalsty *b* 1989, — Deborah, *b* 1959. —— (By 2nd *m*) Halcyone Rosalind (12 Lowen Place, Stirling, Perth, W Australia 6021), *b* 1949: *m* 1973 (*m diss* 1988), Brian Bennett, and has issue living, Gavin Douglas, *b* 1975, — Heather Leigh, *b* 1977.

   Issue of late Loftus Charles Blomefield, *b* 1905, *d* 1981: *m* 1937, Una Innes (214 Zwartkop Rd, Pietermaritzburg, Natal 3201, S Africa), da of J. A. Munro:—
John Alan (214 Zwartkop Rd, Pietermaritzburg, Natal, S Africa), *b* 1942: *m* 1967, Norma Ann, el da of B. A. R. Schefermann, and has issue living, Peter Annand, *b* 1970, — Monica Ann, *b* 1968. —— Thomas Loftus (24 Harewood Av, Helderberg Estate, Somerset West, Cape Province, S Africa), *b* 1944; *ed* Univ of Natal (MSc Agric 1968): *m* 1980, Pamela Anne, 2nd da of Dr J. T. Sonnenberg, and has issue living, Stephen Lyle, *b* 1989, — Jessica Rosanne, *b* 1986. —— Margaret Otway (11 Moyeni Park, Gillitts, 3610 Kwazulu-Natal, S Africa), *b* 1938: *m* 1962, Allan John Nicol, who *d* 1993, and has issue living, Deborah Margaret, *b* 1968: *m* 1991, Wayne André Smit, and has issue living, Michaela Heather Dersley *b* 1996, — Jacqueline Jennifer, *b* 1970: *m* 1992, Murray John Eden Kirkwood.

   The 1st baronet, Maj-Gen Sir Thomas, commanded the Artillery in the expedition to Copenhagen 1807. The 4th Baronet, Sir Thomas Wilmot Peregrine, acted as Private Sec to Successive Pres of Board of Trade (Baron Stanley of Preston, and Sir Michael Hicks-Beach, Bt), and was Assist Sec to Board of Trade (Finance Depart) 1901-8.

LYNCH-BLOSSE (I) 1622, of Galway

Sir RICHARD HELY LYNCH-BLOSSE, 17th *Baronet, b* 26 Aug 1953: *s* his father, *Sir* DAVID EDWARD, 1971; *ed* Welwyn Garden City, and R Free Hosp (Univ of London); MRCS, LRCP 1978; MB, BS 1979; DRCOG 1983; MRCGP 1984; Capt RAMC: *m* 1976 *(m diss* 1999), Cara Lynne, only da of George Longmore Sutherland, of St Ives, Cambs, and has issue.

Arms – Azure, a chevron between three trefoils slipped or. *Crest* – A lynx passant coward argent.
Residence – The Surgery, Clifton Hampden, Oxfordshire OX14 3EL.

DAUGHTERS LIVING

Katherine Helen, *b* 1983. ―― Hannah Victoria, *b* 1985.

SISTERS LIVING

Caroline Susan, *b* 1951: *m* 1st, 1978 *(m diss* 1984), Christopher Elliot Stuart, only son of late Anthony Stuart, of Birstall, Leics; 2ndly, 1987 *(m diss* 1994), Steven Rollnick, of 67 Conway Rd, Cardiff CF11 9NW, and has issue living, (by 1st *m*) Josephine Rachel Blosse, *b* 1979, ― (by 2nd *m*) Jacob Julian, *b* 1987. ―― Bridget Ruth, *b* 1958: *m* 19―, Peter James Barry, of Rotorua, NZ, and has issue living, Charlie James Bloss, *b* 1994.

AUNT LIVING *(Sister of 16th baronet)*

Neither rashly nor timidly

Sylvia Diana, *b (posthumous)* 1928: *m* 1958, Maj Robert Basil Sullivan-Tailyour, late Worcestershire & Sherwood Foresters Regt, of The Curate's Egg, Dymocks Lane, Sutton Veny, Warminster, Wilts, and has issue living, James Robert, *b* 1960, ― Sarah Jane, *b* 1963.

DAUGHTER LIVING OF FIFTEENTH BARONET

Susan Frances (Hawthorn Cottage, Ridgeway, nr Frome, Somerset BA11 4NU), *b* 1917; 1939-45 War with WAAF: *m* 1942, Wing-Cdr Brian Robert Noble, RAF (ret), who *d* 1990, and has issue living, Nigel Brian, OBE (24 Wadham Close, Shepperton, Middx TW17 9HT), *b* 1947; Lt-Col RAPC (ret); OBE (Mil) 1991: *m* 1974, Diana Mary Fogg, and has issue living, James Colin *b* 1975, Charles Christopher *b* 1977, ― Elizabeth Hilary, *b* 1945: *m* 1st, 1974, Richard Charles Perry; 2ndly, 1985, Anthony Allom, of Hawthorns, Ridgeway, nr Frome, Som BA11 4NU, and has issue living (by 1st *m*), Charles Edward Bruce *b* 1978, Katherine Jane Susannah *b* 1979.

DAUGHTER LIVING OF THIRTEENTH BARONET *(By 2nd marriage)*

Frances Clodagh, *b* 1936: *m* 1960, Paul Richard Nevell, and has issue living, Christopher Paul *b* 1965, ― James Robert, *b* 1968.

WIDOW LIVING OF SIXTEENTH BARONET

ELIZABETH *(Elizabeth, Lady Lynch-Blosse)*, da of late Thomas Harold Payne, of Welwyn Garden City: *m* 1950, Sir David Edward Lynch-Blosse, 16th Bt, who *d* 1971.

COLLATERAL BRANCHES LIVING

Grandson of late Capt Edward Falconer Lynch-Blosse, uncle of 13th baronet, and son of late Very Rev Henry Lynch-Blosse, Dean of Llandaff, 2nd son of 8th baronet:—
Issue of late Maj Cecil Eagles Lynch-Blosse; *b* 1890; *d* 1966: *m* 1st, 1915 *(m diss* 1940), Dorothy Delahaize, who *d* 1962, da of late Rev John Delahaize Ouvry R of Haydon, Sherborne; 2ndly, 1943, his cousin, Violet Emily, who *d* 1976, da of late Francis Traherne Lynch-Blosse:—
(By 1st *m*) (ERIC) HUGH, OBE (17 Queens Acre, Newnham, Glos GL14 1DJ); *b* 30 July 1917; *ed* Blundell's, and RAF Coll; Group Capt RAF (ret); OBE (Mil) 1952: *m* 1946, Jean Evelyn, da of late Cdr Andrew Robertson Hair, RD, RNR, of Edinburgh, and has had issue, David Ian, *b* 14 Jan 1950; *ed* Blundells: *m* 1st, 1984, Mrs Barbara Susan McLaughlin, who *d* 1985; 2ndly, 1989, Nadine, da of John Baddeley, and has issue living (by 2nd *m*) Oliver Daniel *b* 12 Nov 1989, Jessica Hannah *b* 1992, ― Valerie Jean, *b* 1947: *m* 1974, Irvine Cormack, of Fieldridge, Broombarn Lane, Great Missenden, Bucks, and has issue, ― Fiona Carol, *b* 1955, *d* 19―.

Grandchildren of late Maj Cecil Eagles Lynch-Blosse (ante):—
Issue of late Anthony Cecil Lynch-Blosse, *b* 1919, *d* 1991: *m* 1st, 1942 *(m diss* 1946), Margaret, da of late Maj-Gen David Graeme Ridgeway, CB, DSO, of Kenya; 2ndly, 1948, Marjorie Elizabeth (PO Box 1602, Lunenburg, Nova Scotia B0J 2C0, Canada), da of late James Joseph William Morris, of Portland, Maine, USA:—
(By 2nd *m*) Michael Anthony (18 Clear Springs Court, Sugar Land, Texas 77479, USA), *b* 1950: *m* 1977, Barbara Lorraine, da of late Jack Haberthur, of St Augustine, Florida, USA, and has issue living, Danielle Bryann, *b* 1981, ― Shannon Elizabeth, *b* 1983, ― Heather Michelle, *b* 1985, ― Brittany Noel, *b* 1989. ―― Sean James (PO Box 1602,

Lunenburg, Nova Scotia B0J 2C0, Canada), *b* 1960; has issue living, Sean James SANTIAGO, *b* 1984. ——— Sharon Delahaize, *b* (twin) 1960: *m* 1997, Robert James Rueter, of 8 Green Tree Lane, Dover, New Jersey 07801, USA.

　　　Issue of late George Robert Lynch-Blosse, *b* 1895, *d* 1976: *m* 1929, Lucy Myra, who *d* 1988, da of Bertram
　　　Adams, of Auckland, NZ:—
Robert Edward (3/70-76 Fernhill Way, Browns Bay, Auckland, NZ), *b* 1932: *m* 1954, Alannah Marie, da of John Donald Graham Drought, and has issue living, Robert Mark, *b* 1955; has issue living, Reyhan Samual *b* 1986, Sahra Ji *b* 1983, Hannah Letita *b* 1989, — Brendon Scott, *b* 1960, — Jennifer Sue, *b* 1957. ——— Gerald Bertram (11 Stour St, Oamaru, NZ), *b* 1936: *m* 1st, 1966 (*m diss* 19—), Moira Jean, da of R. B. Johns, of Auckland, NZ; 2ndly, 1990, Jenny Lesley Thompson, and has issue living, (by 1st *m*) Craig Allan, *b* 1967, — Blair Robert, *b* 1974, — Catharine Mary, *b* 1970, — Joanne Maree, *b* 1972. ——— Timothy Richard (31A Coldham Crescent, St Johns Park, Auckland, NZ), *b* 1939; Snr Police Sgt (ret): *m* 1962, Joan, da of Richard Wittington, of Auckland, and has issue living, Stephen John, *b* 1964: *m* 1994, Karin Faye, da of Neil Gallagher, of Whangarei, NZ, and has issue living, Mitchell Rhys *b* 1998, Deana Patricia *b* 1995, — David Paul (21 Sail Terrace, Heathridge, Perth 6027, W Aust), *b* 1966; has issue living, Marshall Harvey LYNCH-BLOSSE *b* 1995. ——— †Andrew John (7 Catherine St, Onehunga, Auckland, NZ), *b* 1946: *m* 1968, Janice Marie, da of E. Swinburne, and *d* 19—, leaving issue, Christopher Andrew, *b* 1972, — Timothy Nigel, *b* 1974.

　　　The family of Lynch is of great antiquity in Connaught, being among the earliest settlers who were denominated the "Tribes of Galway". Sir Henry Lynch, 1st Bt, and Sir Robuck (Robert) Lynch, 2nd Bt, successively sat as MP for Galway. The 2nd Baronet was Mayor of Galway 1638. Sir Henry Lynch, 3rd Bt, was a Baron of the Exchequer in Ireland 1686. Sir Robert, 6th Bt, assumed the additional surname of Blosse, having *m* 1749, Elizabeth, da and heir of Francis Barker, and heir of Tobias Blosse, of Little Belstead, Suffolk.

BLOUNT (E) 1642, of Sodington, Worcestershire
(Name pronounced "Blunt")

Sir WALTER EDWARD ALPIN (JASPER) BLOUNT, DSC, 12th *Baronet*; *b* 31 Oct 1917; *s* his father *Sir* EDWARD ROBERT, 1978; *ed* Beaumont Coll, and Sidney Sussex Coll, Camb (MA 1943); solicitor; farmer; Lt RNVR; 1939-45 War (DSC and two Bars): *m* 1954, Eileen Audrey, only da of late Hugh Blasson Carritt, and has issue.

𝕬rms – Barry nebulée of six or and sable. 𝕮rest – An armed foot in the sun.
Residences – Regent House, Seaview, IOW PO34 5EX; Tilkhurst, Imberhorne Lane, E Grinstead, Sussex RH19 1TY.

DAUGHTER LIVING

Nicola Jane Eileen, *b* 1955: *m* 1990, Charles Foster Glanville, son of John Foster Glanville, DSC, of Emsworth, Hants, and has issue living, Edward Foster Blount, *b* 1992, — Robert Alexander Charles, *b* 1993, — Oliver William John, *b* 1995.

Lux tua via mea
Thy light, my path

SISTER LIVING

Diana Apollonia, *b* 1916. *Residence* – South Heathercombe, nr Manaton, Newton Abbot, Devon TQ13 9XE.

　　　The 1st baronet suffered for his loyalty during the civil war, and was long imprisoned, first at Oxford, and afterwards in the Tower. Sir Walter Kirkham Blount, 3rd Bt, was Sheriff of Worcestershire 1687-8, and Sir Edward, 8th Bt, was High Sheriff of the same county in 1835.

BLUNDEN (I) 1766, of Castle Blunden, Kilkenny

We must yield to love

Sir PHILIP OVERINGTON BLUNDEN, 7th *Baronet*, *b* 27 Jan 1922; *s* his brother, *Lt-Cdr Sir* WILLIAM, RN, 1985; *ed* Repton; World War II 1942-45 with RN: *m* 1945, Jeanette Francesca Alexandra (WRNS), eldest da of Capt D. Macdonald, RNR, of Portree, Isle of Skye, and has issue.

Arms – Quarterly: 1st and 4th argent, ten billets four, three, two, and one, sable; 2nd and 3rd, or a lion passant-guardant per pale gules and sable. Crests – 1st, a demi-lion rampant per fesse sable and argent, armed and langued gules; 2nd, a griffin sergeant vert, armed, winged and beaked or.
Residence – The Grove, Castletown, Celbridge, co Kildare.

SONS LIVING

HUBERT CHISHOLM, *b* 9 Aug 1948; *ed* Avoca Sch, Blackrock; 1st Bn Irish Guards: *m* 1975, Allish O'Brien, and has issue living, Edmond, *b* 31 July 1982, — Amelia, *b* 1977. —— John Maurice Patrick, *b* 1955.

DAUGHTER LIVING

Marguerite Eugenie, *b* 1967.

DAUGHTERS LIVING OF SIXTH BARONET

Sarah Vanessa, *b* 1946: *m* 1970, John Edward Spencer Perceval Maxwell, of Moore Hill, Tallow, co Waterford, son of Edward Perceval Maxwell, of Ballyclement, Tallow, co Waterford. — Grizelda Jane, *b* 1948. —— Caroline Susan (twin), *b* 1948. —— Rowena Mary Phillida, *b* 1952: *m* 1985, Andrew Gillies Macbain, of Cranagh Castle, Templemore, co Tipperary. —— Elizabeth Anne, *b* 1955: *m* 1985, Nicholas Bryan Marshall, of 2 Suhle St, Edmonton, Queensland 4869, Australia, elder son of Bryan Marshall, of Compton House, Compton, Berks. —— Fiona Christine, *b* 1958: *m* 1990, John Flscher MacGovern, of 140 Chestnut St, Weston, MA 02193-1560, USA.

WIDOW LIVING OF SIXTH BARONET

PAMELA MARY (*Pamela, Lady Blunden*), da of late John Purser, of Merton House, Dublin 6; formerly 2nd Officer WRNS: *m* 1945, Lt-Cdr Sir William Blunden, 6th Bt, RN, who *d* 1985. *Residence* – Castle Blunden, Kilkenny.

COLLATERAL BRANCH LIVING

Issue of late Eric Overington Blunden, yr son of 4th baronet, *b* 1892, *d* 1969: *m* 1918, Bridget Constable, who *d* 1980, da of late Henry George Constable Curtis:—

Josephine Bridget Annette, *b* 1926: *m* 1947, Col George Vicary Kenyon, CBE, TD, DL, who *d* 1990, of Highfields Lodge, Ware, Herts, and Pier View, Dunmore East, co Waterford, and has issue living, Robin George Blunden, *b* 1950; *ed* Charterhouse: *m* 1984, Marcia Joan, da of Hon Mr Justice John T. Ludeke, of Sydney, NSW, Australia, — Crispin Simon Vicary, *b* 1955; *ed* Charterhouse: *m* 1983, Carolyn Isabel, da of Collingwood Peter Drinkwater, of Sacombe, Ware, Herts, and Bradden, Isle of Man, — Rowena Josette Caroline, *b* 1953.

The 1st baronet was MP for Kilkenny and a distinguished member of the Irish Bar. Sir William Blunden, MB, 4th Bt, was High Sheriff of co Kilkenny 1904, and *d* 25 Oct 1923, only three days prior to his son and successor, Sir John, 5th Bt.

BLUNT (GB) 1720, of London

Thy light is my life

Sir DAVID RICHARD REGINALD HARVEY BLUNT, 12th *Baronet*; *b* 8 Nov 1938; *s* his father, *Sir* RICHARD DAVID HARVEY, 1975: *m* 1969, Sonia Tudor Rosemary, da of late Albert Edward Day, and has issue.

Arms – Per pale or and sable, barry nebuly of six counterchanged. **Crest** – Issuing out of clouds a sun in splendour charged with an eye issuing tears, all proper.
Residence – 74 Kirkstall Rd, SW2 4HF.

DAUGHTER LIVING

Davina Angela Rosemary, *b* 1972.

HALF-SISTERS LIVING

Georgina Lavinia, *b* 1945: *m* 1981, Martin Frederick Trotter, yr son of late Maj Frederick Liddell Trotter, JP, of Mells Park, Frome, Somerset, and has issue living, James Martin, *b* 1982, — Camilla Julia Margaret, *b* 1983. *Residence* – Winterwell Farm, Northleach, Glos. —— Caroline Margaret *b* 1947.

AUNT LIVING

Cecily Maud Helen, *b* 1910: *m* 1934, Robin Aymer Whitworth, who *d* 1996, of 9 Richmond Rd, Oxford OX1 2JJ, son of late Geoffrey Arundel Whitworth, CBE, FRSL, and has issue living, Anna Maureen Cecily, *b* 1945.

COLLATERAL BRANCHES LIVING

Issue of late Charles William Lockhart Blunt, 3rd son of 8th baronet, *b* 1882, *d* 1958: *m* 1913, Lilian, who *d* 1958, da of late C. Calcutt, of Goudhurst, Kent:—
ROBIN ANTHONY (15 York House, Turk's Row, SW3; 14 Allée du Château, 31770 Colomiers, France) *b* 23 Nov 1926; *ed* Wellington Coll, CEng, MIMechE: *m* 1st, 1949 (*m diss* 1962), Sheila Stuart, da of C. Stuart Brindley; 2ndly, 1962, June Elizabeth, da of Charles Wigginton, of The Park, Duffield, and has issue living (by 1st *m*) Jonathan Stuart, *b* 1955, — (by 2nd *m*) Mark Charles, *b* 1963.

Issue of late Henry Wilfrid Blunt, yst son of 8th baronet, *b* 1887, *d* 1957, *m* 1915, Maud Etta, da of late J. Hyde:—
Gabrielle Hilda, *b* 1919: *m* 1st, 1941 (*m diss* 1950), Capt Tony Thawnton, 3rd King's Own Hussars; 2ndly, 1955 (*m diss* 1972), Julian Bond, and has issue living, (by 1st *m*) Paul John Anthony BOND, *b* 1946, adopted 1955 by his stepfather, Julian Bond, whose surname he assumed; has issue living (by Jenny Desmond), Laurence Jack *b* 1983, Alice Pearl Sweetpea *b* 1981, — Nicholas Peter BOND, *b* 1947; adopted 1955 by his stepfather, whose surname he assumed; W/Cdr RAF & RNZAF (ret 1994): *m* 1970, Diane Christine Edwards, and has issue living, Karen Kirsten *b* 1972, Alexis Alison *b* 1977, — (by 2nd *m*) Stella Mary, *b* 1956. *Residence* – 3 Gingerbread Lane, Hawkhurst, Kent.

Grandson of late Sir Edward Arthur Henry Blunt, KCIE, OBE, elder son of late Capt Francis Theophilus Blunt (infra):—
Issue of late Lt-Col John Edward Chicheley Blunt, RA, *b* 1907, *d* 1988: *m* 1936, Margaret, who *d* 1998, da of R. Whiteley, of Heath, Wakefield:—
John Michael Chicheley (Birdforth, Terrington, York YO60 6PZ), *b* 1937; Major RA: *m* 1964, Pauline Susan, da of M. Oliver, of Market Harborough, and has issue living, James William, *b* 1969; *ed* Canford, and Portsmouth (BA), — Richard Michael, *b* 1971; *ed* Canford, RMA Sandhurst, and RMCS Shrivenham (BEng Hons); Capt RE.

Grandchildren of late Capt Francis Theophilus Blunt, 2nd son of the Rev Edward Powlett Blunt, yr son of late James Blunt, el son of Walter Blunt, 5th son of 2nd baronet:—
Issue of late Right Rev Bishop Alfred Walter Frank Blunt, DD, formerly Bishop of Bradford, *b* 1879, *d* 1957: *m* 1909, Margaret Catherine, who *d* 1963, el da of Lieut-Col Joshua Duke, formerly Indian Med Ser:—
David Alfred Chicheley, *b* 1915: *m* 1940, Dorothy Brailsford Booth, and has issue living, Peter Robin Chicheley (Home Farm, Newburgh, Coxwold, York), *b* 1946: *m* 1st, 1969, Angela Shirley, who *d* 1992, da of late Arthur Benjamin Drane, MA, of 33 Simbalk Lane, Bishopthorpe, York; 2ndly, 1993, Jane Clough, and has issue living (by 1st *m*), Michael Peter Chicheley *b* 1975, Jenny Elizabeth *b* 1972, — Patricia Anne Brailsford, *b* 1941: *m* 1967, Timothy Steuart Hallam Piper, of 4 St Nicholas Rd, Copmanthorpe, York, son of late Donald Piper, and has issue living, Richard David Steuart *b* 1969: *m* 1998, Elaine Burleigh, Nicholas James Steuart *b* 1970, James William Steuart *b* 1976, Sarah Catherine Brailsford *b* 1982. *Residence* – 7 The Coppice, Bishopthorpe, York. —— Margaret Dorothy, *b* 1913: *m* 1936, Rudolf Paul Gerard Kirchem, and has issue living, Michael Hans Edward, *b* 1937: *m* 1965 (*m diss* 1976), Jean Miriam McKenna, and has issue living, Michael John Geoffrey *b* 1966, Catherine Marina *b* 1967, — Elisabeth Jane, *b* 1940: *m* 1971, David George Cross, of 25 Cité Joseph Bech, Gonderange, Luxembourg, and has issue living, Andrew David Jonathan *b* 1973, Geoffrey Mark Timothy *b* 1974, Nicholas Edward Benjamin *b* 1976, — Anthony Peter Francis, *b* 1953. *Residence* – Adlington Lodge, Albury Rd, Burwood Park, Walton on Thames, Surrey.

Granddaughter of late Col Conrad Edward Grant Blunt, CBE, DSO, eldest son of late Maj-Gen Grant Blunt, RE, 3rd and yst son of Rev Edward Powlett Blunt (ante):—
Issue of late Hugh Clavell Blunt, *b* 1908, *d* (May) 1986: *m* 1939, Elizabeth Marjorie, who *d* (Sept) 1986, only da of W. S. Campbell:—

Susan Pamela BLUNT, *b* 1940; has retained her maiden name: *m* 1992, Brian James Clayden, and has issue living, Kay Meredith BLUNT-CLAYDEN (a son), *b* 1981. *Residence* – 751 Eden Place, W Vancouver, BC, Canada.

Grandsons of late Maj-Gen Grant Blunt, RE, 3rd and yst son of Rev Edward Powlett Blunt (ante):—
    Issue of late Arthur Powlett Blunt, CMG, *b* 1883; *d* 1946: *m* 1919 (*m diss* 1937), Winifred Grace, who *d* 1988, da of Dr W. H. Fawcett, of Bournemouth:—
Grant Anthony Clavell (12 Warwick Drive, SW15), *b* 1920; *ed* Bradfield; ACIS; Capt RM (ret); 1939-45 War: *m* 1942, June Dorothy, da of J. C. Liddle, and has issue living, Alistair Clavell, *b* 1946; *ed* Bradfield, Essex Univ (BA), and Heriot Watt Univ, Edinburgh (MSc): *m* 1st, 1973 (*m diss* 1980), Elizabeth Harden; 2ndly, 19—, Ida, da of Col Estioko, of Quezon City, Philippines, and has issue living (by 2nd *m*), Joachim Estioko Grant *b* 1982, Thomas Paul *b* 1985, — Gene Carol, *b* 1943; *ed* Cheltenham Ladies' Coll and Bedford Coll, London (BSc): *m* 1967, Bertrand Edouard Doger de Speville, of 55, The Avenue, Richmond, Surrey, and has issue living, Guy Rollo *b* 1971; *ed* Ampleforth, and R Holloway & Bedford New Coll, London (BSc), Claire Anne Maude *b* 1974. ——— Evelyn Powlett Clavell, RD (45 Uplands Court, Tallai, Queensland 4213, Australia) *b* 1924; Lt-Cdr RNR, 1939-45 War with RNVR: *m* 1956, Patricia, da of Col William Joseph Gaunt Beach, MBE, and has issue living, Jonathan Andrew Clavell, *b* 1959: *m* 1997, Sara Jane, da of J. C. D. Mill, FRCS, and has issue living, Katherine May *b* 1998, — Sarah Virginia Clavell, *b* 1957; has issue living, Elizabeth Marie *b* 1983, — Philippa Mary Clavell, *b* 1960: *m* 1987, Steven Peter Hunt, and has issue living, Rebecca *b* 1988, Raechel *b* 1993.

Descendants of late Lt-Col Edward Walter MACKENZIE (who assumed the additional surname of Mackenzie 1905, but subsequently discontinued the use of the surname Blunt), cl son of Maj-Gen Charles Harris Blunt, CB, 4th son of Edward Walter Blunt, 3rd son of Walter Blunt (ante): *m* 1899, Sibell Lilian, Countess of Cromartie, who *d* 1962 (*see* E Cromartie).

Grandchildren of late Col Arthur Blunt, 6th son of late Edward Walter Blunt (ante):—
    Issue of late Arthur Wharton Blunt, *b* 1866, *d* 1939: *m* 1906, Mary, who *d* 1936, da of Col Arthur Edward Ward, formerly Roy Welch Fusiliers:—
Joyce Cautley, *b* 1921: *m* 1946, Peter J. Presnail, of 210 Coromandel Parade, Coromandel Valley, S Aust 5051, and has issue living, Richard, *b* 1947: *m* 1975, Marilyn Rowan, and has issue living, Catharine Louise *b* 1980, Elizabeth Anne *b* 1982, — Shirley, *b* 1951: *m* 1972, Jeremy Cuthbertson, and has issue living, Dayle Deanne Shirley *b* 1986, — Hazel, *b* 1954: *m* 1990, Leon Marshall.

    Issue of late Hugh Roper Blunt, *b* 1874, *d* 1931: *m* 1915, Agnes Sara, who *d* 1948, da of Charles Gray, of Waiohika, Gisborne, New Zealand:—
†Michael Hugh, *b* 1920: *m* 1958, Susanne Mary, who *d* 1983, da of Lawson Field, of Gisborne, NZ, and *d* 1983, leaving issue, Gerald Hugh Lawson (63 Barnard St, Wadestown, Wellington, NZ), *b* 1959: *m* 1990, Emma Tamsin Harcourt, da of Phillip Armes, of Hurstpierpoint, W Sussex, and has issue living, Isabella Rose Henrietta *b* 1992. ——— Richard Mark (9 Highbridge Way, Karrinyup, Western Australia 6018), *b* 1924; late Lt RN: *m* 1st, 1952 (*m diss* 1963), Adrien Seldon Truss; 2ndly, 1965, Patricia Eileen, da of Walter Stanley Lee, of Perth, W Aust, and has issue living, (by 1st *m*), Teresa June, *b* 1953, — (by 2nd *m*) David Mark, *b* 1967, — Georgia Alison, *b* 1969.

    Issue of late Lieut-Col Allan St John Blunt, DSO, *b* 1880, *d* 1931: *m* 1914, Doris Elizabeth, who *d* 1948, da of late John G. Stephen, of Douglas, Isle of Man:—
Elizabeth Shirley, *b* 1923: *m* 1944, Harry Batten Poustie, DSC, RD, and has issue living, John David, *b* 1948: *m* 1981, Sandra Mason, — Michael Ian, *b* 1954: *m* 1977, Coral Purton, and has issue living, Simon Ian William *b* 1978, James Michael *b* 1981, Elizabeth Claire *b* 1979, Rosemary *b* 1984, — Richard Hugh, *b* 1965: *m* 1989, Sandra Cording, — Charles Christopher (twin), *b* 1965: *m* 1993, Heather Pinner, — Vivienne Mary *b* 1951: *m* 1974, Leslie Keast, and has issue living, Christopher John *b* 1978, Deborah Jane *b* 1977, Katherine Louise *b* 1983, — Louise Caroline, *b* 1964: *m* 1991, Gary Castleton, and has issue living, Joshua Allan *b* 1993. *Residence* – Little Fairstowe, Ashburton Rd, Bovey Tracey, Devon.

According to the pedigree on record at the College of Arms, Sir John, 1st baronet, was the fourth child of Thomas Blunt, of Rochester, Kent, Thomas, "shoemaker and baptist", was baptized at St Nicholas, Rochester, 24 July 1665, and was buried at St Nicholas, Rochester, 28 March 1703, his father having been John Blunt, of St Sepulchre's, London, "upholder." In 1732 the Court of Chivalry summoned and fined the 1st Bt for using without right the arms of Sir Charles Blount, Lord Mountjoy, Earl of Devonshire: he appealed from the sentence, and a day was appointed for hearing his appeal, but he died before any further proceedings took place, and the officially recorded arms of the family are as described above. The 4th baronet sat as MP for Lewes (*L*) 1832-7, and Capt Sir John Harvey Blunt, 8th Bt, Roy Dublin Fusiliers, served throughout the Indian Mutiny.

CRAWLEY-BOEVEY (GB) 1784, of Highgrove, Gloucestershire
(Name pronounced "Crawley-Boovey")

To be, rather than seem to be

Sir THOMAS MICHAEL BLAKE CRAWLEY-BOEVEY, 8th *Baronet*; *b* 29 Sept 1928; *s* his father, *Sir* LAUNCELOT VALENTINE HYDE, 1968; *ed* Wellington Coll, and St John's Coll, Camb (MA); late 2nd Lt Durham LI; Editor of *Which?* 1976-81: *m* 1957, Laura, who *d* 1979, el da of late Jan Pouwels Coelingh, of The Hague, Holland, and has issue.

ᴀrms – Erminois, on a fesse azure between three cranes proper a saltire couped between two cross-crosslets fitchée or, on a chief ermine a bend gules, charged with three guttes-d'or between two martlets sable. Crest – A mount vert thereon a crane proper gorged with a collar or, holding in his dexter claw a saltire couped on the last.
Residence – Trebanau, Cilycwm, Llandovery, Dyfed SA20 0HP.

SONS LIVING

THOMAS HYDE, *b* 26 June 1958. —— William Walstan, *b* 1960.

BROTHER LIVING

Anthony Francis d'Auvergne (4 Station Rd, Lydney, Glos), *b* 1932; *ed* RNC Dartmouth: *m* 1968 (*m diss* 1976), Gertrud, da of late Dr Johannes Felix Potrykus, of Soerabaya, Java.

COLLATERAL BRANCHES LIVING

Grandson of late Capt Edward Martin Crawley-Boevey, 2nd son of 5th baronet:—
Issue of late Richard Martin Crawley-Boevey, *b* 1908; *d* 1977: *m* 1945, Gladys Frances Farrer Young, who *d* 1955:—
Timothy Martin, *b* 1949: *m* 1975, Agnes Avelene Peché, and has issue living, Richard Martin, *b* 1979, — Karin, *b* 1976. *Residence* – 38 Balfour Rd, Pinetown, Natal 3610, S Africa 3610.

Issue of late Rev Canon Arthur Curtis Crawley-Boevey, 3rd son of 5th baronet, *b* 1874, *d* 1965: *m* 1906, Evelyn Rosalie, who *d* 1962, da of late Robert Carnegie, of Terenure, co Dublin:—
Rev Robert Arthur (3 St Michaels Close, Urchfont, Devizes, Wilts), *b* 1912; *ed* Hertford Coll, Oxford (MA): *m* 1947, Josephine, da of late Joseph Howard, of Evenlode House, Moreton-in-Marsh, Glos, and has issue living, David Alexander (Lewins, Shurlock Row, nr Reading, Berks RG10 0PR), *b* 1948: *m* 1977, Isabelle Frances Lee, da of late Donald Eyre, of Torquay, and has issue living, Catherine Rosanna *b* 1979, Sarah Frances *b* 1982, Julia Alexandra *b* 1985, — Peter Robert (25 Elizabeth St, Mentone 3194, Victoria, Australia), *b* 1957: *m* 1991, Joanne Margaret, da of Ian Kurrle, of Somers, Australia, and has issue living, Robert Ian, *b* 1993, Natasha Margaret *b* 1996, Rachel Josephine *b* 1998, — Juliet Ann, *b* 1950: *m* 1975, Andrew Dean, of St Margarets, Willand Rd, Cullompton, Devon EX15 1AP, and has issue living, Kelvin John *b* 1985, Jamie Lee *b* 1986. —— Nancy Albinia (Sceapea, Sheepy Magna, Atherstone, Warwickshire), *b* 1910. —— Marjorie Evelyn, *b* 1916. —— Elizabeth Jocosa, *b* 1918; *ed* Girton Coll, Camb.

Grandchildren of late Maj Martin Crawley-Boevey, DSO, MC, Duke of Cornwall's LI, only son of late Arthur William Crawley-Boevey, 6th son of 4th baronet:—
Issue of late Maj Antony Crawley-Boevey, MBE, 17/21st Lancers, *b* 1921, *d* 1996: *m* 1st, 1950 (*m diss* 1957), Cynthia Louise, who *d* 1988, da of late William Hugh Neville Bagot, of Haut du Mont, La Haule, Jersey; 2ndly, 1960, Josephine Beryl (Sunny Cottage, Piddletrenthide, Dorchester, Dorset DT2 7QX), only child of Lt-Col Nathaniel Henry Kindersley:—
(By 1st *m*) Susan Elizabeth Mary, *b* 1951: *m* 1980, Dr Peter Laurence Stanley Hard, of Upper Street House, Pulborough, W Sussex RH20 1AF, eldest son of Lt-Col L. F. Hard, MBE, MC of Shaftesbury, Dorset, and has issue living, Georgina Susan, *b* 1981, — Emily Alice, *b* 1984. —— (By 2nd *m*) Martin Henry, *b* 1963: *m* 1998, Elizabeth Anne, da of Capt Michael Edward Southgate, CBE, RN (Ret), of Applegates, Burton Bradstock, Dorset, and has issue living, Benjamin Antony *b* 1998. —— Simon Antony, *b* 1967. —— Katherine Lucy, *b* 1964: *m* 1991, Nicholas J. Walters, of White House Farm, Holnest, Sherborne, Dorset DT9 6HX, elder son of Dr P. J. R. Walters, of Clifden, co Galway, and has issue living, James Patrick *b* 1998, Charlotte Lucy, *b* 1994, — Rebecca Sophie, *b* 1997.

Grandchildren of late Octavius Charles Crawley-Boevey (infra):—
Issue of late Santiago Carlos Crawley-Boevey, *b* 1872, *d* 1913: *m* 18—, a da of Alamos Cuadra, of Valparaiso, Chile:—
Charles, *b* 1897. —— Marie, *b* 1899.

Issue of late Octavius Charles Crawley-Boevey, 7th son of 4th baronet, *b* 1846, *d* 1897: *m* 1871, Maria Francisca, da of Bernardino Murga, Judge of the Corte Superior, Arequipa, Peru:—
Edward Maximo, *b* 1875. —— Mary Isabel, *b* 1878: *m* 1904, Frederico de la Fuenta, and has issue living, Frederico Francisco, *b* 1906, — Hilda Carmela, *b* 1911. —— Rose Agnes, *b* 1880. —— Lilian Maude Antonia, *b* 1882. —— Leonor Octavia, *b* 1884. —— Blanche Josephine, *b* 1889: *m* 1910, Gerald Bingham (M Sligo, colls, 1912 Edn), and has issue living, Norah Frances, *b* 1912, — Dorothy Blanche, *b* 1913, — Eileen Gertrude, *b* 1915, — Elizabeth Hilda, *b* 1918. —— Ella Margaret, *b* 1894. —— Hilda Ines, *b* 1896.

Grandchildren of late Thomas William Crawley, el son of late Rev Thomas William Crawley (infra):—

Issue of late Thomas Charles Rochfort Crawley, *b* 1882, *d* 1963: *m* 1914, Margaret (71 Duke St, Dryden, Ontario, Canada), da of Charles McKerrow, MB of Workington, Cumberland:—
Thomas Bryson (PO Box 546, Mount Albert, Ontario, Canada, LOG 1MO), *b* 1918: *m* 1947, Christina, only da of H. Vollweiter, of Toronto, Canada, and has issue living, Thomas Henry (5c Randolph Rd, W9 1AN), *b* 1958: *m* 1998, Louise, da of Peter Ashton, — Christopher John, *b* 1963, — Gilda Carolyn, *b* 1951, — Carla Susan, *b* 1953, — Lisa Marlene, *b* 1956. —— James Bryan (139 Kingston Row, Winnipeg, Manitoba R2M 0S7, Canada), *b* 1921: *m* 1964, Edith Janice Doreen, da of Charles Player Halls, of Regina, Sask, Canada, and has issue living, Devin Charles Bryan, *b* 1968: *m* 1993 (*m diss* 19—), Heather Cullen. —— Margery, *b* 1915.

Issue of late Rev Canon John Lloyd Crawley, *b* 1884, *d* 1951: *m* 1921, Marion, who *d* 1961, da of Charles McKerrow, MB:—
Rev John Lloyd Rochfort (Cove, Tarbert, Argyll PA29 6SX), *b* 1922; V of St Anthony's, Newcastle 1953-59, V of Longhoughton and R of Howick 1959-69, and Master of St Thomas the Martyr, Newcastle, and Chap Newcastle Univ 1969-74, R of Cockermouth 1974-86: *m* 1947, Isabell, da of late William Robson, of Reaveley Powburn, Alnwick, and has issue living, *Professor* Michael John (22 Blake Grove Rd, Sheffield S6 3JX), *b* 1949; PhD; DIC: *m* 1971, Greer Anne, only da of George Williams, of New London, Conn, USA. —— Margaret, *b* 1924: *m* 1946, Maj William Vivian Dickinson, MBE, RA, who *d* 1994, and has issue living, John (16 Conduit Rd, Sheffield), *b* 1948: *m* 1st, 1970 (*m diss* 1973), Dianne Warby; 2ndly, 1981, Christine Gregory, — Michael (16a Horsebrook Park, Calne, Wilts SN11 8EY), *b* 1955: *m* 1982, Rachel Garson, and has issue living, Samuel Caradoc *b* 1985, Hannah Beatrice *b* 1987, Eleanor Grace *b* 1990, Phoebe Rose *b* (twin) 1990, — Richard, *b* 1960: *m* 1999, Kathryn, only da of Richard Moore, of W Falloden, Northumberland, — *Rev* Susan (St Johns Vicarage, 23 Housley Park, Chapeltown, Sheffield S35 2UE) *b* 1949; ordained priest 1994; Vicar St John's Church, Chapeltown: *m* 1971 (*m diss* 1974), Kenneth Hope.

Grandchildren of Rev Thomas William Crawley, son of late Rev John Lloyd Crawley, 2nd son of 2nd baronet:—
Issue of late Lt-Col George Burridge Crawley, *b* 1858, *d* 1932: *m* 1st, 1882 (*m diss* 1887), Kate Ouseley, da of late Surg-Maj Henry Sherlock; 2ndly, 1892, Adelaide, who *d* 1946, da of late Charles Bell Syer:—
(By 1st *m*) George Ouseley, *b* 1883.

Issue of late Charles Purrier Crawley, *b* 1859, *d* 1896: *m* 18 , Emily Kent, da of late Hooper:—
Charles Robert Thomas Edmund, *b* 1880. —— Noel George, *b* 1888. —— Albinia, *b* 19—. —— Hannah Dorothy, *b* 1887.

Grandson of late Charles James Crawley, only son of late Rev Charles Yonge Crawley, son of late Rev Charles Crawley, 3rd son of 2nd baronet:—
Issue of late (Charles) Alan Crawley, *b* 1887, *d* 1975: *m* 1915, Jean Nairn (830 Sayward Rd, Vic, BC, Canada), only child of David Horn, of Winnipeg:—
(Charles) David (1757 N Stanley Av, Los Angeles, Calif 90046, USA), *b* 1916; *ed* BC Univ (BA); 1939-45 War as F/O RCAF: *m* 1st, 1942 (*m diss* 1960), Lois Kathleen, only da of Francis Ritchie, of Vancouver, BC; 2ndly, 1965, Dorothy Fern Fried, of Los Angeles, Calif, and has issue living (by 1st *m*) (Charles) Peter (c/o 830 Sayward Rd, Victoria, BC, Canada V8Y 1R4), *b* 1943: *m* 1st, 1963 (*m diss* 1971), Carole Cavalier, of Los Angeles, Calif; 2ndly, 1987, Janet Lesley King, of Vic, BC, Canada, and has issue living (by 1st *m*), Theresa Lynn *b* 1963, Brandi Michelle *b* 1969, Trista *b* 1971, — (Christopher) David (25 Howe St, Victoria, BC, Canada V8V 4K2), *b* 1947: *m* 1st, 1972 (*m diss* 1977), Erin McMartin, of Sidney, BC, Canada; 2ndly, 1980 Victoria Jean Miller, of Ottawa, Canada, and has issue living (by 1st *m*), Aleta *b* 1974 (by 2nd *m*) Jennifer Michelle *b* 1982, — (by 2nd *m*) Andrew, *b* 1973.

Grandson of late William Savage Crawley, son of late Rev William Crawley, 5th son of 2nd baronet:—
Issue of late William Evelyn Maddock Crawley, *b* 1859, *d* 1926: *m* 1st, 1894, Fanny Gertrude, who *d* 1911, da of late Arthur Wellesley Critchley; 2ndly, 1913, Harriet Gladys, da of late Robert Chambres Chambres:—
(By 2nd *m*) Evelyn Myres Chambres, *b* 1914.

The 1st baronet, Sir Charles Barrow, sat as MP for Gloucester 1751-89; his patent of baronetcy was made with remainder to his kinsman, Thomas Crawley-Boevey, grandson of Thomas Crawley, who, on inheriting Flaxley Abbey 1726, took the additional surname of Boevey; the 6th baronet, Sir Francis Hyde, and the 7th baronet, Sir Launcelot Valentine Hyde, were Verderers of the Forest of Dean.

BOILEAU (UK) 1838, of Tacolnestone Hall, Norfolk

Sir GUY FRANCIS BOILEAU, 8th *Baronet*; *b* 23 Feb 1935; *s* his father, *Sir* EDMOND CHARLES, 1980; *ed* Xavier Coll, Melbourne, and RMC Duntroon, Aust; Lt-Col; Observer, UN Mil Observer Gp in India and Pakistan 1959-60; Instructor, Aust Army Training Team, Vietnam 1963-64, attached US Dept of Defence, Washington, DC 1966-68; Security Adviser, Dept of the Administrator, Territory of Papua - New Guinea 1970-71; Comdg Officer, Army Intelligence Centre 1972-74; Directing Staff (Instructor), Aust Staff Coll 1975-76: *m* 1962, Judith Frances, da of Senator George Conrad Hannan, of Glen Iris, and Canberra, and has issue.

𝔄rms – Azure, a castle triple towered or, masoned sable, and in base a crescent of the second. ℭrest – A pelican in her piety proper charged on the breast with a saltire couped gules.
Residence – 14, Faircroft Av, Glen Iris, Victoria 3146, Australia.

DE·TOUT·MON·CŒUR

With all my heart

SONS LIVING

NICOLAS EDMOND GEORGE, *b* 17 Nov 1964. —— Christopher Guy, *b* 1969.

DAUGHTERS LIVING

Simone Teresa, *b* 1963. —— Caroline Virginia, *b* 1968. —— Antonia Josephine, *b* 1975.

BROTHER LIVING

Peter Linden (22 Sheffield St, Corinda, Qld 4075, Aust), *b* 1937: *m* 1967, Claudia, da of Alan Edward Mills, of Wanganui, NZ, and has issue living, Dominic Peter, *b* 1968, — James Edward, *b* 1971, — Simon Charles, *b* 1975.

DAUGHTERS LIVING OF SIXTH BARONET (*By 1st marriage*)

Prudence Despréaux, *b* 1925: *m* 1954, Anthony Harvey, of 138 Napoleon St, Eltham, Victoria 3764, Australia, and has issue living, Georgia, *b* 1955, — Tracey, *b* 1958. —— Angela Mary, *b* 1927: *m* 1949, John Stewart Milne, of 240 Wattle Tree Rd, E Malvern, Victoria, Australia, and has issue living, Anthony Stewart, *b* 1950, — Virginia, *b* 1951, — Sarah, *b* 1952, — Jane, *b* 1954, — Lisa, *b* 1956, — Elizabeth, *b* 1967, — Melanie, *b* 1967.

(*By 2nd marriage*)

Madelon Mary, *b* 1945: *m* 1970, Geoffrey George Foletta, of Woburn, Willowmarvin Rd, Kilmore, Victoria, Aust, and has issue living, Gregory George, *b* 1972, — Samuel Geoffrey, *b* 1976, — Hamish, *b* 1978, — Monique Louise, *b* 1974. —— Elizabeth Ann, *b* 1948: *m* 1974, Simon John File, of Buckajo, Oakwood, Via Inverell, NSW, Aust, and has issue living, Simon Charles, *b* 1977, — Trinity, *b* 1975, — Melody, *b* 1976. —— Mary Anne, *b* 1953: *m* 1976, John Yeager Pye, of PO Box 854, Civic Square, ACT 2608, Australia, and has issue living, Benjamin Joseph, *b* 1977, — Angus John, *b* 1978, — William James Boileau, *b* 1984, — Elizabeth Catherine, *b* 1987.

COLLATERAL BRANCH LIVING

Issue of late Patrick Etienne Boileau, 3rd son of 5th baronet, *b* 1912, *d* 1986: *m* 1940, Jean Frances, da of John Jordan Moore:—
Michael Donald, *b* 1949. —— Patricia Ann, *b* 1943.

Grandchildren of late Edmond Boileau, brother of 5th baronet:—
Issue, if any, of late Maurice Boileau, *b* 1904, *d* 19—.
Issue, if any, of late Eric Boileau, *b* 1906, *d* 19—.

This baronet is descended in an unbroken line from Etienne Boileau, Baron de Castelnau and St Croix (Province of Languedoc), who, in 1250, on the departure of Louis IX for the Holy Land, was appointed during his absence, Governor of Paris, and 1st Grand Provost of France. He drew up the first Municipal Code, which is still used. His descendant, Charles Boileau, Baron of Castelnau and St Croix, fled to England at the Revocation of the Edict of Nantes.

BOLES (UK) 1922, of Bishop's Lydeard, Somerset

Sir JEREMY JOHN FORTESCUE BOLES, 3rd *Baronet*; *b* 9 Jan 1932; *s* his father, *Capt Sir* GERALD FORTESCUE, 1945; *ed* Stowe: *m* 1st, 1955 (*m diss* 1970), Dorothy Jane, yr da of James Alexander Worswick, of Enmore, Som; 2ndly, 1970 (*m diss* 1981), Elisabeth Gildroy, yr da of Edward Phillip Shaw, of Englefield Green, Surrey, and widow of Oliver Simon Willis Fleming; 3rdly, 1982, Marigold, eldest da of Donald Frank Seckington, of Clevedon, Avon, and widow of Laurence Frederick Aspey, and has issue by 1st and 2nd *m*.

Arms – Azure, on a fesse ermine, between three standing bowls argent, out of each a boar's head or, a portcullis also or. **Crest** – In front of a rising sun or a demi-boar azure, pierced in the left shoulder by an arrow proper.

SONS LIVING (*By 1st marriage*)

RICHARD FORTESCUE (3 Orchard Close, Lower Cross, Clearwell, Coleford, Glos GL16 8LX), *b* 12 Dec 1958: *m* 1990, Allison Beverley, da of Brian MacDonald, and has issue living, James Alexander Fortescue, *b* 25 May 1993, — Samantha Jane, *b* 1996. —— David Hastings Fortescue, *b* 1967.

DAUGHTERS LIVING (*By 1st marriage*)

As I do to thee so will I do to others

Sarah Jane, *b* 1956: *m* 1986, Paul Bird, and has issue living, Simon Callum, *b* 1990, — Georgina Jane, *b* 1988.

(*By 2nd marriage*)

Jessica Blanche Mary, *b* 1971.

The 1st baronet, Lieut-Col Sir Dennis Fortescue Boles, CBE (son of late Rev James Thomas Boles, of Ryll Court, Exmouth, and Moyge, co Cork), was MP for W, or Wellington, Div of Somerset (C) 1911-18, and for Taunton Div of Somerset 1918-21. The 2nd baronet, Capt Sir Gerald Fortescue, 17th/21st Lancers, *d* on active ser 1945.

BONHAM (UK) 1852

Sir ANTONY LIONEL THOMAS BONHAM, 4th *Baronet*; *b* 21 Oct 1916; *s* his father, *Major Sir* ERIC HENRY, CVO, 1937; *ed* Eton, and RMC Sandhurst; Major (ret) Royal Scots Greys; a DL of Glos: *m* 1944, Felicity, only da of late Col Frank Lionel Pardoe, DSO, of Bartonbury, Cirencester, and has issue.

Arms – Sable, a chevron nebulée between three crosses patée fitchée at the foot argent; on a canton of the last a squirrel sejant gules. **Crest** – A mermaid holding in the dexter hand a wreath of coral and in the sinister a mirror proper. *Residence* – Ash House, Ampney Crucis, Cirencester, Glos GL7 5RY.

SONS LIVING

(GEORGE) MARTIN ANTONY (69 Kirkstall Rd, SW2 4HE. *Club* – RAC), *b* 18 Feb 1945; *ed* Eton, and Aston Univ, Birmingham: *m* 1979 (*m diss* 1992), Nenon Baillieu, el da of Robert Ruttan Wilson, of Durford Knoll, Petersfield, Hants (*see* Bs Berners, colls), and has issue living, Michael Francis, *b* 24 May 1980, — Lucie Nenon, *b* 1982, — Camilla Felicity, *b* 1984, — Sarah Yvette, *b* 1987. —— Simon Philip (Rectory House, Ogbourne St George, nr Marlborough, Wilts), *b* 1947: *m* 1977, Elizabeth Ann, yr da of late Robert Ducas, of Saratoga Springs, NY, and has issue living, Zoe Virginia, *b* 1979, — Sophie Jean, *b* 1982. —— Timothy Eric, *b* 1952: *m* 1978, Hester Suzette, yst da of Sir James Arnold Stacey Cleminson, MC, DL, of Loddon Hall, Hales, Norfolk, and has issue living, Emma Claire *b* 1981, — Georgina Sarah *b* 1983.

To be, rather than to seem to be

The 1st baronet, Sir Samuel George Bonham, KCB (son of Capt George Bonham, HEICS, a descendant of Sir John Bonham, of Stanway Hall, Essex), was Gov of Straits Settlements 1837-47, and Gov and Com-in-Ch at Hong Kong, and Ch Superintendent of British Trade in China 1847-53. The 2nd baronet, Sir George Francis, was Envoy Extraor and Min Plen to Serbia 1900-1903, and to Swiss Confederation 1905-9. The 3rd baronet, Sir Eric Henry, CVO, was Comptroller of the Household to HRH Prince Arthur of Connaught 1913-26.

BONSOR (UK) 1925, of Kingswood, Epsom, Surrey

Every good thing is the gift of God

Sir NICHOLAS COSMO BONSOR, 4th *Baronet; b* 9 Dec 1942; *s* his father, *Maj Sir* BRYAN COSMO, MC, TD, 1977; *ed* Eton, and Keble Coll, Oxford (MA); Bar Inner Temple 1967; late R Bucks Yeo; MP for Nantwich 1979-83, and for Upminster 1983-97; Min of State, Foreign and Commonwealth Office 1995-97: *m* 1969, Hon Nadine Marisa Lampson, da of 2nd Baron Killearn, and has issue.

Arms – Per fesse azure and argent, a pale counterchanged, three lions' heads erased or, on a chief also or three roses gules, barbed and seeded proper. Crest – A wolf passant sable, collared and chained gold, resting the dexter fore-paw on a rose as in the arms.
Seat – Liscombe Park, Leighton Buzzard, Beds LU7 0JN. *Residence* – 2 Waldegrave Court, Upminster, Essex.

SONS LIVING

(ALEXANDER) COSMO, *b* 8 Sept 1976. —— James Charles, *b* 1983.

DAUGHTERS LIVING

Sacha Henrietta, *b* 1974. —— Elizabeth Nadine, *b* 1987. —— Mary Catherine, *b* (twin) 1987.

BROTHER LIVING

Richard Angus, *b* 1947; *ed* Eton, and Keble Coll, Oxford (BA): *m* 1971, Susan Anne, da of Flight-Lieut David Henry Lewis Wigan, RAFVR (*see* By Tweedmouth), and has issue living, — Rupert James, *b* 1974, — Edward Richard, *b* 1976, — Clare Lucinda, *b* 1981. *Residences* – 61 Hartington Rd, W4; Cliddesden Down House, Basingstoke, Hants RG25 2JD.

UNCLE LIVING (*Son of 2nd baronet*)

David Victor, MC, *b* 1918; *ed* Eton; Major late Grenadier Guards; European War 1939-45 (MC): *m* 1945, Sheila Valerie, who *d* 1995, da of Maj-Gen Sir Miles William Arthur Peel Graham, KBE, CB, MC (*see* E Lovelace, 1973-74 Edn), and has issue living, Anthony Miles, *b* 1948: *m* 1980, Frances Elizabeth, only da of David Lindsay Bankes, of 32 Holroyd Rd, SW15 6LN, and has issue living, Miles *b* 1984, Sophie *b* 1982, Laura *b* 1988, — Neil Reginald David (9 Second Av, SW14 8QF), *b* 1950: *m* 1992, Sophie B., da of Col Frederick Walter James, TD, DL, of Hopstone, Claverley, nr Wolverhampton, — Caroline Sheila, *b* 1946: *m* 1st, 1974 (*m diss* 1996), Bruce Hodges; 2ndly, 1999, Henry Francis Coke (*see* E Leicester, colls), and has issue living (by 1st *m*), Camilla Ellen *b* 1978, Katharine Alexandra *b* 1980.

AUNT LIVING (*Daughter of 2nd baronet*)

Daphne Marion, *b* 1924: *m* 1st, 1944, Clyde Euan Miles Graham, Flying Officer RAF, who was *ka* 1944 (*see* E Peel, colls, 1956 Edn); 2ndly, 1948, Alexander David Stewart, MBE, TD, who *d* 1985 (*see* E Galloway, colls). *Residence* – North Green, Kelsale, Saxmundham, Suffolk.

COLLATERAL BRANCH LIVING

Issue of late Robert Cecil Bonsor, MC, 3rd son of 1st baronet, *b* 1880, *d* 1932: *m* 1922, Enid, da of S. Lawrence:—
Michael Cosmo, *b* 1926; *ed* Eton; Lieut Gren Gds 1944-47: *m* 1951, Ann Marie, da of Marcus Wallenberg, and has issue living, Robert Angus Cosmo (3923 Green Look Court, Fairfax, Virginia 23033, USA), *b* 1963: *m* 1989, Kasandra Noel, yst da of Dr Joseph Patton, of Great Falls, Virginia, USA, — Celia Jane, *b* 1954: *m* 1983, Nigel Douglas Pilkington, of 11 Chester Sq, SW1, yst son of Maj Thomas Douglas Pilkington, JP, of Hyde Mill, Stow-on-the-Wold, Glos, and has issue living, Emma Douglas *b* 1985, Tessa Douglas *b* 1987, — Charlotte Serena *b* 1956: *m* 1980, Christopher J. Milln, of Kelvedon Hall, Kelvedon, Colchester, Essex, elder son of John Milln, of Frogmorton House, Greywell, Hants, and has issue living, Frederick John *b* 1985, Louise Emma *b* 1983, Kristina Rose *b* 1995, — Camilla Ann (22 Queen's Gate Terrace, SW7), *b* 1961. —— Ann Elizabeth, *b* 1923.

The 1st baronet, Sir (Henry) Cosmo Orme Bonsor, sat as MP for Surrey, NE, or Wimbledon, SW, Div (*C*) 1885-1900, and was sometime a Director of the Bank of England. The 2nd baronet, Sir Reginald, was Major Surrey Yeo, Chm of John Dickinson & Co, Ltd, of Apsley Mills, Hemel Hempstead, and High Sheriff of Bucks, 1940-41.

BOORD (UK) 1896, of Wakehurst Place, Ardingly, Sussex
(Name pronounced "Board")

By integrity and industry

Sir NICOLAS JOHN CHARLES BOORD, 4th *Baronet*, *b* 10 June 1936; *s* his father, *Sqdn-Ldr Sir* RICHARD WILLIAM, 1975; *ed* Eton, Sorbonne, Societa Dante Alighieri (Italy), and Univ of Santander (Spain): *m* 1st, 1960 (*m diss* 1965), Francoise, da of Giuseppe Tempra; 2ndly, 1965, Françoise Renée, da of Marcel Clovis Mouret, of 69, Traverse de Carthage, 13 Marseilles 8.

Arms – Per fesse azure and gules, a goat's head erased within an orle of eight martlets argent. Crest – A goat argent, guttee de poix, resting the dexter leg on an escutcheon gules, charged with a martlet of the first.
Residence – 61 Traverse le Mée, 13009-Marseilles, France.

BROTHER LIVING

ANTONY ANDREW (Darch House, Stogursey, Bridgwater, Som), *b* 21 May 1938; *ed* Charterhouse: *m* 1960, Anna Christina von Krogh, and has issue living, Andrew Richard, *b* 1962, — Tamsin Katrina, *b* 1961.

MOTHER LIVING

Yvonne Swingler, only da of late Joseph Arthur Hubert Bird: *m* 1933, (*m diss* 1944), Sqdn-Ldr Sir Richard William Boord, 3rd Bt, who *d* 1975.

The 1st baronet, Sir (Thomas) William Boord (el son of Joseph Boord, JP, of Harefield Grove, Uxbridge), was a partner in the firm of Boord and Son, distillers, and a Director of London and Provincial Bank Limited, and sat as MP for Greenwich (C) 1873-95.

BOOTH (UK) 1916, of Allerton Beeches, City of Liverpool

Neither rashly nor timidly

Sir DOUGLAS ALLEN BOOTH, 3rd *Baronet*; *b* 2 Dec 1949; *s* his father, *Sir* PHILIP, 1960; Television and Film Writer; *ed* Beverley Hill High Sch, and Harvard Univ (BA): *m* 1991, Yolanda Marcela Scantlebury, and has issue.

Arms – Per pale and per chevron argent, ermine, and sable, in chief two boars' heads erased and erect of the last and in base a like boar's head of the first. Crest – A rose gules, barbed, seeded and encircled by two olive branches proper, thereon a lion passant argent.
Residence – 22933 Portage Circle Drive, Topanga, CA 90290, USA.

DAUGHTER LIVING

Zahra Jessica, *b* 1993.

BROTHER LIVING

DEREK BLAKE, *b* 7 April 1953; *ed* Hampshire Coll, and Univ of California (BA): *m* 1981, Elizabeth Dreisbach, and has issue living, Colin, *b* 1982, — Rachel, *b* 1986.

WIDOW LIVING OF SECOND BARONET

ETHEL, da of Joseph Greenfield, of New York, USA; has resumed surname of Booth: *m* 1st, 1948, as his 2nd wife, Sir Philip Booth, 2nd baronet, who *d* 1960; 2ndly, 1962 (*m diss* 1965), Prof Winston R. Weisman, PhD. *Residence* – 11687 Montana Av, Los Angeles, Calif 90049, USA.

COLLATERAL BRANCHES LIVING

Grandchildren of late Edmund Booth (infra):—
Issue of late Anthony Edmund Booth, FRCS, *b* 1934, *d* 1996: *m* 1st, 1957, Margaret Helen Elizabeth, only child of late Maj A. B. Miller; 2ndly, 1969, Susan Ailsa Letitia, da of late Lieut R. O'Neill Roe, RN; 3rdly, 1989, Mrs Janet Margaret Ward, da of late Rev G. Argyle:—
(By 1st *m*) Edmund Stuart, *b* 1960. —— Sam Andrew, *b* 1962. —— Adam Piper, *b* 1963. —— (By 2nd *m*) Harriet Ailsa, *b* 1971. —— Emily Charlotte, *b* 1973.

Issue of late Edmund Booth, yr son of 1st baronet, *b* 1908, *d* 1985: *m* 1933, Henrietta Mary, who *d* 1987, 4th da of late Sir Charles Stewart Addis, KCMG, of Woodside, Frant, Sussex:—
Martin Butler (22 Worts Causeway, Cambridge), *b* 1936; *ed* Gordonstoun, and King's Coll, Camb (MA, PhD): *m* 1968, Margaret Hilary, MB BS, da of Clifford Birch, of The Old Orchard, Skelton, York, and has issue living, Emma Jane Mary, *b* 1971, — Caroline Rachel, *b* 1973. —— Philip Addis (4 Ventnor Place, Nether Edge, Sheffield S7 1LA), *b* 1946; *ed* King's Coll Sch, Wimbledon, and King's Coll, Camb (MA, PhD). —— Edmund Dwight (11 Buckingham Rd, S Woodford, E18 2NH), *b* 1948; *ed* King's Coll Sch, Wimbledon, and King's Coll, Camb (MA, CEng, FIStructE): *m* 1983, Sheena Jean, da of late Ralph Laing Collison, of Loughton, Essex. —— (Mary) Rachel, *b* 1939; *ed* Cranbourne Chase

Sch: *m* 1967, James William Bruce Douglas, BM, BCh, of 6 Bellgate Mews, NW5 1SW, and has issue living, Ned, *b* 1972, — Catherine, *b* 1970.

The 1st baronet, Sir Alfred Allen (son of late Alfred Booth, JP, of Liverpool) was a director of Alfred Booth & Co, Ltd, and sometime chairman of Cunard Steamship Co, Ltd.

GORE-BOOTH (I) 1760, of Artarman, Sligo

Genti aequus utrique

Just to either line

Sir JOSSLYN HENRY ROBERT GORE-BOOTH, 9th *Baronet*; *b* 5 Oct 1950: *s* his father, *Capt Sir* ANGUS JOSSLYN, 1996; *ed* Eton, Balliol Coll, Oxford (BA), and INSEAD (MBA): *m* 1980, Jane Mary, only da of Rt Hon Sir (James) Roualeyn Hovell-Thurlow-Cumming-Bruce (*see* B Thurlow), and has issue.

Arms – Quarterly of six: 1st quarterly, 1st and 4th, argent three boars heads couped and erect sable; 2nd and 3rd, gules, a fesse between three cross-crosslets or; 2nd, argent, on a fesse sable three bezants; 3rd, argent a lion's head erased between three crescents gules; 4th, gules three cinquefoils argent; 5th, gules on a bend or, three martlets; 6th, checky azure and argent a fesse gules. **Crest** – 1st, a lion passant pean, the dexter forepaw resting on a chaplet of roses proper, *Booth*; 2nd, a wolf rampant argent ducally gorged or, *Gore*. **Mottoes** – over **First Crest** – "Quod ero spero" (*I hope for what I shall be*); over **Second Crest** – "In hoc signo vinces" (*Under this sign thou shalt conquer*). **Seat** – Lissadell, co Sligo. *Residence* – Selaby Hall, Gainford, Darlington, co Durham DL2 3HF. *Clubs* – Brooks's.

DAUGHTERS LIVING

Mary Georgina, *b* 1985. —— Caroline Sarah, *b* 1987.

SISTER LIVING

(Georgina Clara Rosaleen) Eirenice GORE-BOOTH, *b* 1949; has resumed her maiden name: *m* 1970 (*m diss* 1981), Clive Abercromby Blomfield-Smith, only son of Brig D. C. Blomfield-Smith, MBE, and has issue living, Edward Abercromby, *b* 1973; *ed* Wellington Coll, — Olivia Rosemary, *b* 1976. *Residence* – Zetland House, Staindrop, Darlington, co Durham DL2 3JS.

MOTHER LIVING

Hon Rosemary Myra Vane, only da of 10th Baron Barnard, CMG, OBE, MC, TD: *m* 1948 (*m diss* 1954), Capt Angus Josslyn Gore-Booth (later 8th Bt), who *d* 1996.

COLLATERAL BRANCHES LIVING

Grandchildren of late Mordaunt Gore-Booth, yr son of 5th baronet:—
Issue of late Paul Henry Gore-Booth, GCMG, KCVO (*Baron Gore-Booth*), *b* 1909, *d* 1984 (*cr* a Life Baron 1969): *m* 1940, Patricia Mary (*Baroness Gore-Booth*) (152 Rivermead Court, Ranelagh Gdns, SW6 3SF), da of late Montague Ellerton, of Yokohama, Japan:—
Hon Sir DAVID ALWYN, KCMG, KCVO (27 Wetherby Mansions, SW5 9BH. *Clubs* – MCC, Travellers', Hurlingham, Garrick), *b* 15 May 1943; *ed* Eton, and Ch Ch, Oxford (MA); HM Amb to Saudi Arabia 1993-96, High Commr to Republic of India 1996-98; Special Adviser to Chm HSBC Holdings plc since 1999; CMG 1990, KCMG 1997, KCVO 1997: *m* 1st, 1964 (*m diss* 1970), Jillian Sarah, yr da of James Wyatt Valpy; 2ndly, 1977, Mrs Mary Elizabeth Janet Gambetta, only da of late Sir David Francis Muirhead, KCMG, CVO (*see* Hollenden, B, 1990 Edn), and has issue living (by 1st *m*), Paul Wyatt Julian, *b* 1968. —— *Hon* Christopher Hugh, *b* (twin) 1943; *ed* Eton, and Durham Univ: *m* 1st, 1979 (*m diss* 1988), Mrs Jolanta Maria Nicholls, only da of late Dr L. S. Bernacinski; 2ndly, 1993, Mrs Annette Sheila Melli, da of late Joseph Rose, and has issue living (by 1st *m*), Oliver Lucian Ralph, *b* 1980. —— *Hon* Celia Mary, *b* 1946; *ed* Downe House, and London Acad of Music and Dramatic Art: *m* 1983, Douglas George Gill, of 7 St John's Park Mansions, Pemberton Gdns, N19 5RT, and *d* 1992, leaving issue, Fionn Paul, *b* 1984. —— *Hon* Joanna Rosamond Georgina, *b* 1954; *ed* Sherborne Sch, and New Hall, Camb (MA): *m* 1978, Paul Richard Teverson, and has issue living, Richard Hugh, *b* 1984, — Peter Henry, *b* 1991, — Cathryn Frances, *b* 1986.

Issue of late Colum Robert Gore-Booth, *b* 1913, *d* 1959: *m* 1st, 1939, Joan Yvonne Ballard, adopted da of Rev C. W. Chastel de Boinville; 2ndly, 1947, Mary (who *m* 2ndly, 1971, Michael William McLean Barker, who *d* 1982), da of late Edward Paget Scholfield, JP, of Sandhall, Howden, York (D Northumberland, colls):—
(By 2nd *m*) Francis Peter, *b* 1948. —— (Nicholas) Justin, *b* 1952: *m* 1982, Patricia Roberts, and has issue living, Jane, *b* 1984, — Helen, *b* 1986, — Sarah, *b* 1988. —— Susan Caroline, *b* 1950: *m* 1973, Ashley Casie-Chitty, who *d* 1982.

This family has a common origin with the Earl of Arran, Earl Temple of Stowe, Baron Harlech, and Gore Bt (cr 1622). Nathaniel Gore, father of Sir Booth Gore, 1st baronet, m 1711, Lettice, da and heir of Humphrey Booth, of Dublin. Sir Robert Newcomen Gore, 3rd baronet, assumed by Roy licence 1804, the additional surname and arms of Booth.

BOOTHBY (E) 1660, of Broadlow Ash, Derbyshire

The death of Christ is to me the death of death

Sir BROOKE CHARLES BOOTHBY, 16th *Baronet*; *b* 6 April 1949; *s* his father, *Sir* HUGO ROBERT BROOKE, 1986; *ed* Eton, and Trin Coll, Camb: *m* 1976, Georgiana Alexandra, da of late Sir John Wriothesley Russell, GCVO, CMG (*see* D Bedford, colls), and has issue.

𝕬rms – Argent, on a canton sable a lion's jamb erased erect or. 𝕮rest – A lion's jamb as in the arms.
Residence – Fonmon Castle, Barry, South Glamorgan, CF62 3ZN.

DAUGHTERS LIVING

Aliki Ann Charlotte, *b* 1977. —— Francesca Rafela Marina, *b* 1983.

SISTERS LIVING

Penelope Ann, *b* 1939: *m* 1959 (*m diss* 1965), Cdr Timothy Hale, RN, and has issue living, Veronica Ann Leslie, *b* 1960. —— Caroline Serena, *b* 1941: *m* 1st 1962 (*m diss* 1972), Ifor Lewis; 2ndly 1977, Richard Hugh Parry, of Manton Weir Farm, Manton, Marlborough, and has issue living (by 1st *m*), Vivienne Serena, *b* 1966, — Carina Cecilia, *b* 1969, — (by 2nd *m*) James Hugo, *b* 1981.

AUNT LIVING (*Daughter of 14th Baronet*)

Serena Margaret, *b* 1914: *m* 1958, Herbert Charles Richards Homfray, who *d* 1960. *Residence* – Church House, Penllyn, Cowbridge, Glamorgan.

COLLATERAL BRANCHES LIVING

Grandsons of late George Boothby (*b* 1867) (infra):—
Issue of late George William Bernard Boothby, *b* 1917, *d* 1972: *m* 1942, Avril Alice, who *d* 1993, da of John Edward Innell:—
GEORGE WILLIAM (Ivy Wall House, Back Lane, Batcombe, Shepton Mallet, Somerset), *b* 18 June 1948; Capt Merchant Navy: *m* 1977, Sally Louisa Thomas, and has issue living, Jane Penelope, *b* 1979, — Fenella Susan, *b* 1981, — Imogen Roberta, *b* 1982. —— Richard Charles Brooke (Garth, Gwernogle, Carmarthen SA32 7RN), *b* 1955; *ed* Barry Boys' Comprehensive Sch, Manchester Univ (MusB), and Salzburg Mozarteum; musician: *m* 1992, Fiona Clare, da of Peter Padfield, and has issue living, Maximillian Brooke, *b* 1995, — Megan Miranda, *b* 1998.

Granddaughters of late Com George William Boothby, son of late Rev Brooke Boothby, 2nd son of 7th baronet:—
Issue of late George Boothby, *b* 1867, *d* 1921: *m* 1904, Mabel Gertrude, who *d* 1961, da of Bernard Flanagan:—
Violet Dora, *b* 1908: *m* 1935, Ernest Victor Evans, of 11 Birch Grove, Barry, S Glam CF6 8SX, and has issue living, Geoffrey Boothby (44 Greenfield Rd, Brunton Park, Gosforth, Newcastle-upon-Tyne), *b* 1937; MSc, PhD: *m* 1964, Elizabeth Jane Furneaux Friend, and has issue living, Michael Meredith *b* 1965: *m* 1998, Elizabeth Ann Goss, Susan Sian *b* 1967. —— Edna Frances, *b* 1910: *m* 1940, Ronald George Henry Steele, and has issue living, Elizabeth Penelope *b* 1944. —— *Residence* – Rangeworthy, 3 West Town Drive, Brislington, Bristol.

Granddaughters of late Capt William Osbert Boothby, CVO, CB, RN, 2nd son of late Rev Evelyn Boothby (infra):—
Issue of late Maj Christopher Evelyn Boothby, RM, *b* 1912, *d* 1991: *m* 1940, Pamela Gertrude (26 Cwrt Deri, Heol-y-Felin, Rhiwbina, Cardiff CF4 6JB), da of late Frederick Lewis Heriot-Maitland (*see* E Lauderdale, colls):—
Marilyn Susan, *b* and *d* 1942. —— Marilyn Susan, *b* 1944: *m* 1967, Stanley LeBlanc, of 2301 Oakwood Drive, Carrollton, Texas 75006, USA, and has issue living, James Boothby, *b* 1971, — Sarah Maria, *b* 1968: *m* 1993, Pat Mullens. —— Diana Mary, *b* 1948: *m* 1969, John Michael Spiller, of 3 Clos Brynderi, Rhiwbina, Cardiff, S Wales, and has issue living, Nicholas Michael, *b* 1979, — Christina Ruth, *b* 1976.

Grandchildren of late Basil Tanfield Beridge Boothby, yst son of late Rev Evelyn Boothby, 2nd son of Rev Charles Boothby, 3rd son of 7th baronet:—
Issue of late (Evelyn) Basil Boothby, CMG, *b* 1910, *d* 1990: *m* 1946, Susan Penelope (23 Holland Park Av, W11), da of late Brig Gen Hon Arthur Melland Asquith, DSO (*see* E Oxford and Asquith, colls):—
John Joseph (19 Frithville Gdns, W12), *b* 1947; *ed* St Lawrence Coll, Ramsgate, and London Univ: *m* 1982, Isabel Rose, eldest da of John Paget Chancellor (*see* B Hylton), and has issue living, Roland Arthur, *b* 1984, — Francis George, *b*

1987, — Dolores Ann, *b* 1992. ——†Philip Sebastian, *b* 1952; *d* 1974. ——Henry Alexander (Stag Park Farm, Petworth, W Sussex), *b* 1955 *ed* Westminster Sch, London Univ, and Trin Coll, Dublin, MB, BCh, LRCP: *m* 1992, Laura Frances Albinia, elder da of Richard St Clair de la Mare (*see* M Normanby, colls). ——Emily Albertine, *b* 1948: *m* 1967, Piers Paul Read, writer, of 50 Portland Rd, W11 4LG, son of late Sir Herbert Edward Read, DSO, MC, and has issue living, Albert Nathaniel, *b* 1970, — William Edward, *b* 1978, — Martha Mariana, *b* 1972, — Beatrice Mary, *b* 1981.

Grandson of late Rev Walter Ralph Jebb Boothby, 3rd son of Col Basil Charles Boothby (infra):—
Issue of late Basil Frederick Boothby, MBE, *b* 1904, *d* 1984: *m* 1934, Dorothy Marian, who *d* 1990, da of Frank Gould, of Ryde, I of Wight, and Calcutta:—
Christopher Brooke (St Nicholas, Hollow Rd, Bury St Edmunds, Suffolk IP32 7AU), *b* 1938; *ed* Lancing; MRCP London, MRCS, FRCP England; Consultant Paediatrician, W Suffolk Hosp; Hon Clinical Assist, Hosp for Sick Children, Gt Ormond St; Mem of Gen Nursing Council for England and Wales 1978-83: *m* 1969, Anne Barrow Dalston, of Torcross, Devon, and has issue living, Hugo Thomas Brooke, *b* 1972; BA, — William Jebb Dalston, *b* (twin) 1972; BSc, — Margaret Elizabeth Prescott, *b* 1974; MB ChB.

Grandsons of late Capt Evelyn Leonard Beridge Boothby, DSO, RN, 5th son of late Col Basil Charles Boothby, 4th son of late Rev Charles Boothby, 3rd son of 7th baronet:—
Issue of late Walter Evelyn Brooke Boothby, *b* 1927, *d* 1994: *m* 1st, 1951 (*m diss* 1974), Yvonne, da of J. S. Capewell, of Harlesden, NW; 2ndly, 1974, Catharine Jane (40 Calmore Gdns, Totton, Southampton), da of Ralph Forrester Stobart, of Newton Farm, Tregony, Cornwall:—
(By 1st *m*) Martin William (Green Gardens, Block 3 No 24, Jakarta, Barat, W Java, Indonesia), *b* 1953: *m* 1st, 1982 (*m diss* 1993), Stephanie Anne, da of H. G. Mills, of Portstuart, co Londonderry; 2ndly, 1996, Martha, da of ......, and has had issue, (by 1st *m*) Bryn, *b* 1982, *d* 1999, — Tara, *b* 1980, — (by 2nd *m*) Samantha Maharani, *b* 1997. ——Bruce Michael (23 Ashfield Green, Yateley, Hants GU46 6AL), *b* 1959: *m* 1984, Trudy Frith, da of Kenneth Frith Williams, of Sunbury, Middx, and has issue living, Reef Alan Frith, *b* 1998, — Blu Evelyn Brooke (a da), *b* 1995.

A baronetcy was conferred, in 1644, upon Henry Boothby, of Claytor Close; but, though the creation received the signmanual of Charles I, it did not pass the Great Seal, by reason of the confusion of the civil wars. At the Restoration his only son, William Boothby, of Broadlow Ash, Derbyshire, was *cr* a Baronet *de novo* by Charles II, with the date of 1660. Ashbourne Hall, Derbyshire, the seat of the family for 200 years, was sold in 1846, in accordance with the will of the 9th baronet. The 10th baronet, Sir Brooke, was in Diplo Ser, and the 11th, Sir Charles Francis, was Lieut N Mayo Mil.

BOREEL (E) 1645, of Amsterdam, Holland
(Name pronounced "Borale")

Jonkheer Sir FRANCIS DAVID BOREEL, 13th *Baronet*; *b* 14 June 1926; *s* his father *Jonkheer Sir* ALFRED, 1964, *ed* Univ of Utrecht: *m* 1964, Suzanne, da of Willy Campagne, of Paris, and has issue.

𝕬rms – Argent, on a chevron between three bugle horns sable, two whips thonged proper, on a chief gules a lion passant guardant or. 𝕾upporters – On clouds two angels proper, vested argent. *Residence* – Kapellstraat 25, 4351 AL Veere, Netherlands.

DAUGHTERS LIVING

Reiniera Adriana, *b* 1965. ——Christina Wilhelmina, *b* 1966. ——Titia Florence, *b* 1973.

COLLATERAL BRANCHES LIVING

Granddaughters of late Jonkheer William Walter Astor Boreel, son of late Jonkheer Francis Robert Boreel, son of Lt-Gen William Francis Boreel, 3rd son of 7th baronet:—
Issue of late Jonkheer Robert John Ralph Boreel, *b* 1867, *d* 1904: *m* 1891, Edith Margaret, who *d* 1933 (having *m* 2ndly, 1905, Jacob Pieter Crommelin), da of Philo Ives, of Hartford, Connecticut, USA:—
Helen Barbara Isabella (c/o Nat Westminster Bank, 96-97 Strand, WC2), *b* 1894: *m* 1921 (*m diss* 1944), Ralph Clarmont Skrine Stevenson, CMG (*cr* KCMG 1946 and GCMG 1949), who *d* 1977, and has issue living, Mark Boreel, *b* 1924. ——(Edith) Wendela Dorothy, *b* 1896; Asso R Soc Painter Etchers: *m* 1924, Leslie George Wylde, late Lt Canterbury Regt (NZ Forces), who *d* 1935, and has issue living, James Paxton de Eglesfield, *b* 1927. *Residence* –

Grandchildren of late Jonkheer James Lucas Boreel (infra):—
Issue of late Jonkheer Gerard Lucas Cornelis Boreel, *b* 1913, *d* 1970: *m* 1943, Virginia Rae, who *d* 1972, da of Frank Gervin Bright, of New York:—
STEPHAN GERARD (Elzenoord 30, 8172 AZ Vaassen, Netherlands), *b* 9 Feb 1945: *m* Francien P. Kooijman, and has issue living, Jacob Lucas Cornelis, *b* 29 Sept 1974. ——Maurits (Wieselseweg 102, 7345 CC Apeldoorn, Netherlands), *b* 1946: *m* 1971, Tilde Anna Eisma, and has issue living, Gerard Lucas, *b* 1973, — Joris Siebrand, *b* 1975, — Maurits Willem, *b* 1981. ——Joan (Grentelsweg 70, 7345 CR Wenum Wiesel, Netherlands) *b* 1949.

Grandchildren of late Jonkheer Gerard Salomon Boreel, 2nd son of Jonkheer Jacob Otto Bernard Boreel, yr son of Jonkheer Lucas Boreel, 4th son of 7th baronet:—
Issue of late Jonkheer James Lucas Boreel, *b* 1883, *d* 1939: *m* 1911, Baroness Adriana Sophia, who *d* 1958, da of Baron Maurits van Randwijck:—
Maurits (Oude Kleefsebaan 217, 6572 AM Bergen Dal, Netherlands), *b* 1914: *m* 1942 (*m diss* 1980), Antoinette Crommelin, and has issue living, Lucas Jacob (Beekmansdalseweg 9 6522 KC, Nijmegen, Netherlands), *b* 1945: *m* 1st 1966 (*m diss* 1975), Henriette van Teunenbroek; 2ndly 1978, Angeline Marie Sassen, and has issue living (by 1st *m*), Elsa-Bertha *b* 1967: *m* 1992, Emile R. Lemoine, of USA, Esther Nanette *b* 1970, (by 2nd *m*) Sophie Mechteld *b* 1980, Maeke Willemijn *b* 1982, — Paul Marinus (Rembrandtlaan 22, 3941 CH Doorn, Netherlands), *b* 1949: 19—, Simone C. Bouwman, and has issue living, David Gustaaf *b* 1979, Thomas Arthur *b* 1982, — Willem (Beerse 112, 3961 HE Wijk bij Duurstende, Netherlands), *b* 1952: *m* 1978 (*m diss* 1983), Louis G. Peizel, and has issue living, Robert Jan *b* 1981, — Jacoba Francina, *b* 1943: *m* 1968, Arnold Hendrick Tieleman. —— Henriette, *b* 1917: *m* 1947, Dirk J. G. Buurman, of Hulkesteinflat, Utrechtseweg 145/101, 6812 AB Arnhem, Netherlands.

Issue of late Jonkheer Hugo Boreel, *b* 1884, *d* 1962: *m* 1930, Baroness Emilie Henriette Adele, who *d* 1970, da of Baron Cornelis Jan van Tuyll van Serooskerken:—
Lucas Gerard (Eikenhorstlaan, 19, 2245 BC Wassenaar, Netherlands), *b* 1931: *m* 1960, Marie Louise, da of Pierre van Son. —— Cornelis Jan (Pieter de Hooghlaan 23, 3723 GR Bilthoven, Netherlands) *b* 1932; Sec Boreel Foundation: *m* 1959, Claudine Wilhelmina Woltera, da of Willem Jan Royaards, and has issue living, Robert Jan Willem, *b* 1960: *m* 1993, Sigrid, da of S. Karsten, — Lucas Wolter, *b* 1966: *m* 1994, Jacqueline Nelly, da of H.A.G. Hofman, — Claudine Emilie Amarante, *b* 1963: *m* 1992, H.M. Hinloopen. —— Geert Frans (Bruggenbosch, Blikkenweg 15, 7391 NA Twello, Netherlands) *b* 1934: *m* 1958, Henriette Nancy Leopoldine, da of Jonkheer B W. F. van Riemsdijk, and has issue living, Hugo Geert (Van Wijkplein 3, 2101 EL Heemstede, Netherlands), *b* 1959: *m* 1986, Alice Marie, da of William Schwartz, and has issue living, Lucas William Geert *b* 1994, Frédérique Pauline *b* 1996, — Barthold Willem Lucas (Berkenlaan 33, Zeist, Netherlands), *b* 1960: *m* 1992, Petra Martine, da of Pieter Arie de Ruiter, and has issue living, Daan Floris *b* 1993, Maud Martine Emilie *b* 1995, — Pauline Danielle (Van Der Woertstraat 5, 2597 PJ The Hague, Netherlands), *b* 1964: *m* 1995, Godfried Nicolaas Jnsinger, who *d* 1997.

Granddaughter of late Jonkheer Jacob Otto Bernard Boreel, 5th son of late Jonkheer Jacob Otto Bernard Boreel (ante):—
Issue of late Jonkheer Marius Willem Boreel, *b* 1856, *d* 1905: *m* 1886, Cornelia, who *d* 1939, da of late Jonkheer Theodor Prins van Westdorpe, of Haarlem, Netherlands:—
Catharina Margaretha, *b* 1891: *m* 1918, Henri Louis van Eeghen, who *d* 1977. *Residence* – Noordhout, Driebergen, Netherlands.

Grandchildren of late Jonkheer Hendrik Etienne Gustave Boreel (infra):—
Issue of late Jonkheer Jacob Gerard Joseph Boreel, *b* 1891, *d* 1945: *m* 1914, Charlotte Susanna (Hanenburglaan 198, The Hague), da of Eduard Manuel:—
Henri Etienne Gustave (Pyrolalaan 80, 2554 HG, The Hague, Netherlands), *b* 1915: *m* 1949, Hendrika Catharina Allegonda, da of Ferdinand Karel August Luder, and has issue living, Henri Etienne Gustave (Pr Beatrixlaan 104, 2741 DJ Waddixveen, Netherlands), *b* 1952: *m* 1990, Janneke van der Gaag, — Jacqueline Marguérite Charlotte, *b* 1950, — Margot Jeanne Françoise, *b* 1955, — Jacqueline Louise, *b* 1918: *m* 1943, Jan Arbouw, of Sportlaan 466, The Hague, Netherlands.

Issue of late Jonkheer Willem Boreel, *b* 1893, *d* 1973: *m* 1915, Clasine Justine Cornelie, da of Willem Anton Van Andel:—
Robert Hugo, *b* 1919; Maj-Gen Dutch Army: *m* 1939, Marie Louise Colette, da of Wilhelmus Jacobus Antonius Van der Valk, and has issue living, Paul, *b* 1947: *m* 1968, Martha Deirdre de Graaf, and has issue living, Daphne Cherette *b* 1968, Cynthia Jasmine *b* 1970, — Ernst Boudewijn, *b* 1948, — Maud, *b* 1941: *m* 1964, Frederik Racke. —— Paul René, *b* 1922: *m* 1946, Audrey, da of Arthur James Ritchie, and has issue living, Robert Willem, *b* 1947, — Helen Elisabeth, *b* 1948: *m* 1970, Wayne McKell. —— Jeanne Marie Josephine, *b* 1916: *m* 1939, Hendrick Dirk Buurman, who *d* 1989, of Brussels, Belgium.

Grandchildren of late Jonkheer Hendrick Etienne Gustave Boreel, son of late Jonkheer Theodoor Gustaaf Victor Boreel, son of late Jacob Boreel (*b* 1777), son of late Jacob Boreel (*b* 1746), next brother of 7th baronet:—
Issue of late Jonkheer Alfred Boreel, *b* 1894, *d* 1979: *m* 1st, 1920 (*m diss* 1953), Marie Francoise, who *d* 19—, da of Frederick Hendrik de Bruine; 2ndly, 1955, Raden Dalia Mingsih, who *d* 19—:—
(By 1st wife) Jacob Alfred, MD (Brikkenweg 3, 7475 RE, Netherlands), *b* 1932: *m* 1st, 1959 (*m diss* 1982), Albertine, da of Jan Willem Cornelis De Vletter; 2ndly, 1984, Martine van Leeuwen, and has issue living (by 1st *m*), Jacob Jan, *b* 1960, — David Tibor, *b* 1962, — Michiel (van Dalenlaan 10, 2082 VG Santpooer-Ouid, Netherlands), *b* 1963: *m* 1988, Carla Louise van Gorselan, and has issue living, Daniel Willem *b* 1989. —— Eleanore, *b* 1920: *m* 1951, Cornelis Ian Reindert Phaff. —— Ilse Anetta Jacoba, *b* 1924: *m* 1951, Gustaf Adolf Cordesius, of Vlierboomstraat 614, The Hague, Netherlands. —— (By 2nd wife) David Dradjat, *b* 1959. —— Yvonne Annette, *b* 1953.

Granddaughters of late Jonkheer Johan Jacob Boreel, 2nd son of Jonkheer Theodoor Gustaaf Victor Boreel (ante):—
Issue of late Jonkheer Willem Boreel, CBE, Capt R Netherlands Navy, *b* 1895; *d* 1977: *m* 1923, Ernestina Augusta Maria, da of Prof Dr Hajo Brugmans:—
Maria Augusta, *b* 1924: *m* 1953, Cornelis Christiaan van Saarloos, MD, who *d* 1988. —— Sophia Fredrika, *b* 1927: *m* 1958, Dr Mario Mancosu.

Grandchildren of late Jonkheer Victor Eduard Anthon Boreel, 3rd son of Jonkheer Theodoor Gustaaf Victor Boreel (ante):—
Issue of late Jonkheer Willem Boreel, *b* 1898, *d* 1981: *m* 1926, Elizabeth Johanna Maria Peman (96 Paulinastraat, The Hague, Netherlands), da of Dr Adriaan Marinus Kakebeeke:—
†Victor Eduard, *b* 1928: *m* 1955, Gijsberta, da of Dirk Nicolaas Verschoor, and *d* 1992, leaving issue, Willem Hendrik

Dirk, *b* 1956: *m* 1983 (*m diss* 19—) Bernadette Maria Larsen, and has issue living, Adriënne Maria Saskia *b* 1988, — Victor Cornelis, *b* 1959, — Barbara Saskia, *b* 1961: *m* 1992, Pieter van der Meulen.

Issue of late Jonkheer Eduard Boreel, *b* 1901, *d* 1967: *m* 1st (*m diss* 1946), Karin Elisabeth, who *d* 1992, da of Jonkheer Maximiliaan Jacob Theodor van de Poll; 2nd, 1950, Maria Luisa Marques (Rua Ribeiro Sanches 21-3, Lisbon, Portugal), da of Dr José Santos Gouveia:—
(By 1st *m*) Victor Charles (Brusselsesteenweg 177, 3080 Tervuren, Belgium), *b* 1932: *m* 1957, Béatrice Marie Louise Andrée, da of Jonkheer Paul Marie Camille Frédéric de Kerckhove dit van der Varent and has issue living, Frederik Eduard Paul (Messchaertstraat 2, 1077 WS Amsterdam, Holland), *b* 1958: *m* 1991, Reiniera M., da of Baron Wilprand van Pallandt, and has issue living, Emelie Béatrice Wilhelmina *b* 1996 Charlotte Felicia Christine *b* 1999, — Christine Ghislaine Béatrice Karin *b* 1957. —— Maximiliaan Willem Felix (Brouillaud, 24300 Nontron, France), *b* 1935: *m* 1962, Meta Dorothea Ludmilla, da of René André Rost Onnes, and has issue living, Ghislaine Cornélie Carine, *b* 1963: *m* 1988 (*m diss* 1997), Thomas Crema, of Georgetown, Washington, DC, USA, — Eugénie Renée *b* 1965: *m* 1990, Willem Bos, of Cologny, Geneva, Switzerland. —— Karin Ghislaine Johanna (47 Av Herbert Hoover, 1030 Brussels) *b* 1940.

The 1st baronet, an envoy to England, was knighted by King James I in 1619, and it is related that he received from King Charles II on 28 June 1653, a Royal Warrant as a Baron of England. The 9th baronet was a Member of the Upper House of Representatives in the Netherlands, and was several times President of the Second Chamber of the States-General, and Gov of North Holland. The 10th Baronet, was Gentleman of the Privy Chamber to the King of the Netherlands and subsequently Chamberlain to the Queen of the Netherlands.

BORTHWICK (UK) 1908, of Whitburgh, Humbie, Co Haddington

Sir JOHN THOMAS BORTHWICK, MBE, 3rd *Baronet*, only son of late Hon James Alexander Borthwick, 2nd son of 1st Bt; *b* 5 Dec 1917, *s* to baronetcy on death of his uncle, 1st and last Baron Whitburgh, 1967; *ed* Eton, and Trin Coll, Oxford; late Maj Rifle Brig (TA); MBE (Mil) 1945: *m* 1st, 1939 (*m diss* 1961), Irene, who *d* 1978, only child of Joseph Heller, of 2 Buckingham Place, SW1; 2ndly, 1962, Irene, da of late Leo Fink, of 26 Rue Franqueville, Paris XVI, and has issue living by 1st and 2nd *m*.

Arms – Argent, a cinque foil sable, on a chief invected of the last two cinquefoils of the first. **Crest** – A staff raguly fessewise sable, thereon a blackamoor's head in profile couped proper.
Residence – 41 Mizzentop, Warwick, Bermuda.

SONS LIVING (*By 1st marriage*)

ANTONY THOMAS, *b* 12 Feb 1941; *ed* Eton: *m* 1st, 1966, Gillian Deirdre Broke, twin da of Nigel Vere Broke Thurston, RN; 2ndly, 1985, Jenny, eldest da of George Lanning, and has issue living (by 1st *m*), Matthew Thomas Thurston, *b* 1968, — Suzanna Claire Irene, *b* 1970, — Camilla Fay Broke, *b* 1973. —— Peter Richard John (Australia), *b* 1943: *m* 1970, Helen, yr da of T. C. Vogel, of Cudgewa, Vic, Aust, and has issue living, Linton, *b* 1977, — Maya Irene, *b* 1975, — Iona Christine, *b* 1980. —— Patrick James Joseph (33 Crockford Place, Bracknell) *b* 1945: *m* 1st, 1969, Amanda Rosemary, yr da of R. G. A. Wells, of Lines End, Winchelsea, Sussex; 2ndly 1978 (*m diss* 1992), Sally Anne, da of Geoffrey Chase Gardener, and has issue living, (by 1st *m*) Alexander, *b* 1971, — (by 2nd *m*) Edward James Chase, *b* 1980, — Timothy Geoffrey Chase, *b* 1984, — Sophie Irene L. Chase, *b* 1979, — Annabelle Evangeline M. Chase, *b* 1983.

(*By 2nd marriage*)

Mark George Alexander, *b* 1962: *m* 1988, Maria Cornejo. —— John Kelly Leo, *b* 1965: *m* 1999, Blair Kampmann, and has issue living, Bibi Chiarra, *b* 1991, — Jo Kelly, *b* 1997.

COLLATERAL BRANCHES LIVING

Issue of late Hon William Borthwick, 3rd son of 1st baronet, and brother of 1st Baron Whitburgh, *b* 1879, *d* 1956: *m* 1909, Ruth Margery, who *d* 1971, only da of late Jason Rigby, MICE, of Wimbledon, SW:—
(Elinor) Valerie, *b* 1915: *m* 1940, Maj Robert William Augustus Fane, MBE, RA, who *d* 1989, and has issue (*see* E Westmorland, colls). *Residence* – Hoo Lodge, Hoo, Woodbridge, Suffolk IP13 7QJ. —— Margaret Ruth, *b* 1926: *m* 1949, Henry Neville Hemsley, and has issue living, John Neville, *b* 1956: *m* 1984, Nicole Irene, da of Rudolph Hans Walter, of Zürich, and has issue living, Ralph Neville *b* 1985, Philip John *b* 1989, Timo Sean *b* 1992, Colette Irene *b* 1987, — Oliver Charles, *b* 1960: *m* 1992, Deborah Simone Michelle Warr, and has issue living, Lily Simone *b* 1999, — Clare Margaret, *b* 1953: *m* 1980, Charles Edward Spencer Atkins, and has issue living, Edward Oliver *b* 1982, Nicholas Charles *b* 1985, Matthew Spencer *b* 1988, Katherine Margaret Lucy *b* 1992, — Patricia Mary, *b* 1964: *m* 1990, Giles Henry Matthew Martin, and has issue living, Christopher Giles *b* 1994. *Residence* – Langham Lodge, Oakham, Rutland.

Grandchildren of late Hon William Borthwick (ante):—
Issue of late (William) Jason Maxwell Borthwick, DSC, *b* 1910, *d* 1998: *m* 1937, Elizabeth Cleveland, who *d* 1978, da of late Herbert Elworthy, of Timaru, NZ:—
Alister Jason (Deepdale Farm, Burnham Deepdale, King's Lynn, Norfolk), *b* 1945: *m* 1970, Verily Anne, da of Albert Augur East, and has issue living, Jason Matthew *b* 1971, — Fiona Anne, *b* 1974, — Anna Elizabeth, *b* 1981. —— Josephine Cleveland, *b* 1939: *m* 1960, John James Luddington (Millhouse, Brancaster, King's Lynn, Norfolk PE31 8AQ), and has issue living, Peter William, *b* 1966, — Julia Ruth, *b* 1961: *m* 1st, 1983, Mark Eustace Landon; 2ndly, 1995, Barry Lang, — Mary Elizabeth, *b* 1963: *m* 1989, Nigel Anthony Ward, and has issue living, Harry John *b* 1993, Megan Amy *b* 1995. —— Rosalind Cleveland, *b* 1942: *m* 1968, Robert Andrew Spedding, of The Manor, Sampford Spiney, Horrabridge, Devon, and has issue living, Harry George William, *b* 1973, — Joanne Elizabeth *b* 1970. —— Celia Cleveland, *b* 1947. *Clubs* – United University, Royal Thames Yacht.

Issue of late Brian Thomas Borthwick, *b* 1920, *d* 1989: *m* 1946, Jennifer Ruth, JP (Manor Farm Lodge, Brancaster, King's Lynn, Norfolk PE31 8AU), da of Maj Evelyn Ronald Moncrieff Fryer, MC, Gren Gds, of Selborne, Hants (*see* E Peel, colls, 1985 Edn):—
Simon William Frederick (36 Kenilworth Rd, W5), *b* 1950: *m* 1974, Bozena, da of Alfons Edward Podwojski, of Poland, and has issue living, Michael Edward Waclaw, *b* 1977, — Ian Philip Miroslaw, *b* 1979, — William Martin Stanislaw, *b* 1981, — Alexander Thomas Zdzilaw, *b* 1983. —— Nicholas James, *b* 1953: *m* 1981, Peng-Chin, da of Lával Li Kwong In, of Mauritius, and has issue living, Anthony Timothy William, *b* 1984. —— Charles Thomas, *b* 1955: *m* 1984, Jayne Alexandra, only da of Donald Cooke, of Warmington, Peterborough, and has issue living, Maximilian Thomas, *b* 1985, — Anna Georgina, *b* 1987. —— Timothy Michael, *b* 1958: 1st, *m* 1987, Justin, yr da of Jerry Rosenholtz, of Chicago, USA; 2ndly, 1998, Jenny, eldest da of Reginald Lees, of S Africa, and has issue living, Sophie Clementine, *b* 1999. —— Sara Marjorie, *b* 1951.

Grandchildren of late Hon Malcolm Algernon Borthwick (infra):—
Issue of late Lt-Col Algernon Malcolm Borthwick, MC, TD, *b* 1907, *d* 1975: *m* 1935, Edith Wylde, who *d* 1975, da of James Stanley Addison, of Wethersfield Place, Essex:—
Malcolm (Heriot, Midlothian), *b* 1938: *m* 1966, Dorothy Mary Prudence, 2nd da of Alan M. Barker, of Salisbury, and has issue living, Benedict, *b* 1971, — Sophie Alexander, *b* 1967, — Kate Cecile, *b* 1969. —— Winifred Letitia (*Lady Tumim*), OBE, *b* 1936; Trustee Nat Portrait Gallery 1992-99; OBE (Civil) 1992: *m* 1962, His Honour Sir Stephen Tumim, formerly HM Ch Inspector of Prisons and has issue living, Matilda Edith, *b* 1963, — Emma Renée, *b* 1964, — Olivia, *b* 1968. —— Lucilla Blanche, *b* 1942: *m* 1960 (*m diss* 1977), Hon Samuel James Butler (*see* B Butler of Saffron Walden).

Issue of late Patrick John Borthwick, *b* 1908, *d* 1994: *m* 1931, Nancy Hope, who *d* 1984, da of Guy C. Williams, of Te Parae, Masterton, NZ:—
Thomas Malcolm (Rocklands, Redesdale, Vic 3444, Australia), *b* 1933; *ed* Harrow: *m* 1957, Wendy Alison, da of late Linden Wood, of N Adelaide, and has issue living, Thomas Linden, *b* 1958; *ed* Melbourne Gram Sch: *m* 19—, Margaret Mary, da of late Edward Ferncliffe Bartley, and has issue living, Lachlan Thomas *b* 1991, Charles Patrick *b* 1993, — Angus Patrick, *b* 1959; *ed* Geelong Gram Sch: *m* 1985, Jane Amanda Louise, da of late Robin Ninian Paisley, and has issue living, William James *b* 1988, Harry Robert *b* 1991, — Nigel, *b* 1963; *ed* Scotch Coll: *m* 1994, Susan Valentia, da of Christopher James Stafford Morris. —— Robin John (Te Whanga RD4, Masterton, NZ), *b* 1938: *m* 19—, Robin Gay McGregor, and has issue living, Patrick Andrew, *b* 1967, — Shamus James, *b* 1969, — Belinda Hope, *b* 1965. —— Hamish Charles (Dakabin, McDonalds Rd, Palmwoods, Qld 4555, Australia), *b* 1940; *ed* Christ's Coll, NZ: *m* 1965, Anne Florence, eldest da of Edward Dixon Cameron, of Teebah, Hannaford, Qld, and has issue living, Geoffrey Robert, *b* 1966, — Andrew Hamish, *b* 1968: *m* 1991, Cindy-Anne, yst da of James Lawson Storey, of Mooloolaba, Qld, — James Patrick, *b* 1971: *m* 1994, Karen Maree, eldest da of Noel Garth Hooper, of Buderim, Qld, — Fiona Anne Jeane, *b* 1969. —— Patricia Mary, *b* 1936: *m* 1956, Michael Dillon Bell, of Olivers Rd, RD6, Masterton, NZ, and has issue living, Henry Dillon (Ngaiana, Masterton, NZ), *b* 1957; *ed* Christ's Coll, NZ: *m* 1986, Rebecca Anne Lawrence, and has issue living, James Harry Dillon *b* 1995, Amelia Anne *b* 1988, Emma Mary *b* 1990, — Johnathan Dillon, *b* 1960: *m* 1990, Lady Lilias Catriona Maighearad Graham, da of 7th Duke of Montrose, and has issue living, Charles Michael Dillon *b* 1993, Eleanor Caroline *b* 1994, — Sarah, *b* 1959: *m* 1982, Roger Broughton, of Pohatu, Masterton, NZ, and has issue living, Thomas George *b* 1986, Belinda Mary *b* 1985, Rosie Amanda *b* 1989, — Nicola Mary, *b* 1962: *m* 1989, Marcus Yardley Wilkins, of 14 Eleventh Av, Tauranga, NZ, and has issue living, Marcus George *b* 1991, Patrick James *b* 1993, Guy Michael *b* 1995, Anna Mary *b* 1998.

Issue of late Hon Malcolm Algernon Borthwick, yst son of 1st baronet, and brother of 1st Baron Whitburgh, *b* 1881, *d* 1941: *m* 1905, Blanche Buckland, who *d* 1965, da of Henry Thomson Gorrie, of Auckland, NZ:—
Letitia Blanche, *b* 1913: *m* 1st, 1934, Capt Michael Valentine Paul Fleming, who *d* of wounds while a pow 1940 (Rose, Bt, *cr* 1874, colls); 2ndly, 1945, James Currie Thomson, MBE, TD, JP, DL, late Lt-Col Queen's Own Cameron Highlanders, and has had issue (by 1st *m*), Valentine Patrick (Stonewall Park, Edenbridge, Kent), *b* 1935: *m* 1963, Elizabeth Helen, only da of late Hon Sir Geoffrey Cokayne Gibbs, KCMG (*see* B Aldenham, colls), and has issue living, Matthew Valentine (Great Woodland Farm, Lyminge, Kent) *b* 1964: *m* 1989, Caroline Mary, yst da of John Joseph Buxton, of Horsey Hall, Gt Yarmouth, Norfolk (*see* Buxton, Bt, colls) (and has issue living, Hannah Elizabeth *b* 1992, Victoria Mary *b* 1994, Matilda *b* 1997), Harry Geoffrey *b* 1966, Rupert Michael *b* 1969, Thomas Mungo *b* 1971, — Christopher Michael (Briff Farm, Bucklebury Common, nr Reading, Berks) *b* 1937: *m* 1975, Judy, da of Lt-Col Godfrey Jeans, of Broadchalke, Wilts, and has issue living, Lucy *b* 1976, Nicola *b* 1977, — David Algernon, *b* 1938: *m* 1967, Jocelyn Ishabel Ann (who *m* 2ndly, 1978, as his 2nd wife, John Edmund Kincaid Floyd *see* Floyd, Bt), da of late Sir John MacLeod, TD, late Queen's Own Highlanders (*see* B Dulverton, colls, 1995 Edn), and *d* 1975, leaving issue, Lara Kate *b* (Jan) 1968: *m* 1998, Anthony John Buxton (*see* Buxton, Bt, colls), Annabel Theodora *b* (Dec) 1968: *m* 1997, Rupert Noris, Katrina Jane *b* 1971, — Gillian, *b* 1940: *m* 1966, Nigel Colin Newbery, of Barbon, Kirkby Lonsdale, via Carnforth, Cumbria, and has issue living, Alexander Douglas *b* 1970, Georgina Blanche *b* 1967, Beatrice Laura *b* 1968, — (by 2nd *m*) James Borthwick (Mains of Cairnies, Glenalmond, Perthshire), *b* 1946: *m* 1970, Maureen Angela, yr da of W. G. Scott, of Forres, and has issue living, James Angus Wilfred *b* 1972, Tanya Hilda *b* 1974, — Clare Nell (*Hon Mrs Robin C. Denison-Pender*) *b* (twin) 1946: *m* 1966, Hon Robin Charles Denison-Pender, of Jessups, Mark Beech, Edenbridge, Kent (*see* B Pender), and has issue (see that title).

Sir Thomas Borthwick, 1st Bt, *b* 1835, son of Thomas Borthwick of Edinburgh; was Chm and Snr partner of Thos Borthwick & Sons (Ltd), Colonial Merchants; was nominated a peer June 1912, but *d* July 1912, before the patent passed the Great Seal. His widow Letitia Mary, da of Thomas Banks, received Roy licence Feb 1913 to use the title of *Baroness Whitburgh* Dec 1912; she *d* 1935. Their son Sir Thomas Banks, 2nd Bt, was cr *Baron Whitburgh* Dec 1912; he *d* 1967, when the Barony became ext, and the Baronetcy passed to his nephew, Sir John Thomas, 3rd Bt.

BOSSOM (UK) 1953, of Maidstone, Kent

Hon Sir CLIVE BOSSOM, 2nd *Baronet*; *b* 4 Feb 1918; *s* his father ALFRED CHARLES, Baron Bossom (Life Baron), in his baronetcy 1965; *ed* Eton; Maj (ret) The Buffs; Master of Grocers' Co 1979; FRSA; a Co Councillor for Kent 1949-52; formerly Internat Pres of Internat Social Service (ISS); formerly Pres BARC and Anglo-Netherlands Soc; Pres Anglo-Belgian Soc, Iran Soc, and Vice-Pres d'honneur Federation International de l'Automobile (FIA); Almoner Order of St John; Chm of Europ Assistance, Ltd 1971-88, of Ex-Ser War Disabled Help Dept 1973-88, of RAC 1975-78, of RAC Motor Sports Council 1975-82; Council of R Geographical Soc 1971-77; Council of Royal Soc of Arts 1969-72; PPS to Joint Parl Secs to Min of Pensions and Nat Insurance 1960-62, to Sec of State for Air 1962-64, and to Home Sec 1970-72; MP for Leominster (*C*) 1959-74; KStJ; Kt Cdr Order of Orange Nassau (Netherlands); Cdr Order of Crown of Belgium; Cdr of Order of Leopold II of Belgium; Order of Homayoun (Iran): *m* 1951, Lady Barbara Joan North, el sister of 9th Earl of Guilford, and has issue.

Arms – Gules a representation of a steel building column and three floor girders with wind bracing projecting therefrom to the sinister or, on a chief of the second an antique lamp inflamed sable between on the dexter a rose gules barbed proper, and on the sinister a thistle leaved and slipped also proper. **Crest** – Upon a mount vert an oak tree fructed charged with an eye irradiated proper.
Residence – 97 Cadogan Lane, SW1X 9DU. *Clubs* – Carlton, RAC.

SONS LIVING

BRUCE CHARLES (Overbury Court, nr Tewkesbury, Glos GL20 7NP), *b* 22 Aug 1952; *ed* Eton, Coll of Estate Management, and Harvard Business Sch; FRICS: *m* 1985, Penelope Jane, only child of late Edward (Ruby) Holland-Martin, of Overbury Court, nr Tewkesbury, Glos, and has issue living, George Edward Martin, *b* 21 Feb 1992, — Rosanna Emily, *b* 1986, — Amanda Lucy, *b* 1988. —— Andrew Clive, *b* 1954: *m* 1997, Amza Walbrook, only da of Lloyd Amza Horton, of Florida and Pennsylvania, USA. —— James Edward, *b* 1962.

DAUGHTER LIVING

Arabella Emily, *b* 1968.

COLLATERAL BRANCH LIVING

Issue of late Doric Bossom, yr son of Life Baron and 1st Baronet, *b* 1922, *d* 1959: *m* 1949, June (Flat 2, 28 Sloane Court East, SW3 4TG) (who *m* 2ndly, 1967, Maj Kenneth Arnold Gibbs Crawley, TD, who *d* 1988, *see* Crawley-Boevey, Bt, colls, 1968 Edn), el da of V. B. Longworth, of Port Elizabeth, S Africa:—
Doric Alfred Howard, *b* (*posthumous*) 1960: *m* 1986, Sara J., only da of Lt-Col Derek Vaughan, and has issue living, Theo Doric Alfred, *b* 1988, — Caspar Luke Sebastian, *b* 1991, — Barnaby David Vaughan, *b* 1995. *Residence* – 9 Rumbold Rd, SW6 2JA.

Alfred Charles Bossom, son of Alfred Henry Bossom, of Holloway, London, was MP for Maidstone (*C*) 1931-59, and was *cr* a baronet 1953, and *Baron Bossom*, of Maidstone, co Kent (Life Baron) 1960.

Bosville Macdonald, see Macdonald.

HOUSTOUN-BOSWALL (UK) 1836
(Name pronounced "Hoostun-Boswall")

Sir (THOMAS) ALFORD HOUSTOUN-BOSWALL, 8th *Baronet*, *b* 23 May 1947; *s* his father, *Sir* THOMAS, 1982: *m* 1971 (*m diss* 1996), Eliana Michele, da of Dr John Pearse, of New York, and has issue.

Arms – Not recorded at Lyon Office.
Residences – 18 rue Basse, Biot 06410, France; 11 East 73rd St, New York, NY10021, USA.

SON LIVING

ALEXANDER ALFORD, *b* 16 Sept 1972.

DAUGHTER LIVING

Julia Glencora, *b* 1979.

SISTER LIVING

Amber Georgina, *b* 1946: *m* 1969, Alan Moore, of 14 Stafford Terrace, W8, and has issue living, Thomas James, *b* 1980, — Georgina, *b* 1972, — Chloe, *b* 1977.

HALF-SISTER LIVING

Sophie, *b* 1973.

UNCLE LIVING (*Son of 6th baronet*)

Alistair, *b* 1931. *Residence* –

DAUGHTERS LIVING OF FIFTH BARONET

Pamela Nanine, *b* 1916: *m* 1938, William Oliver Calvert, who *d* 1959, and has issue living, Ian Arbuckle, *b* 1939, — George William, *b* 1951, — Susan Arbuckle, *b* 1942. —— Patricia Mary, *b* 1917: *m* 1939, Maj Leslie Le Mottee, late RA, and has issue living, Judith Christina, *b* 1942, — Pamela Mary, *b* 1947. *Residence* – 34 Kingsway, Ewell, Surrey. —— Elizabeth Flora, *b* 1923: *m* 1941, Anthony Hawker, MC, formerly Maj RA, and has issue living, Nicholas George James, *b* 1942, — Victoria Jane, *b* 1956. *Residence* –

DAUGHTER LIVING OF FOURTH BARONET

Elizabeth Phœbe, *b* 1915: *m* 1940 (*m diss* 1956), Major John Alastair Livingston Timpson, MC, Scots Guards, who *d* 1997, and has issue living, Nicholas George Lawrence (Ardington Croft, Wantage, Oxon), *b* 1941: *m* 1972, Lady Selina Catherine Meade, el da of 6th Earl of Clanwilliam, and has issue living, Lawrence Rupert John *b* 1974, Catherine Selina Alexandra *b* 1979, — Rupert Alastair Hugh, *b* 1945: *m* 1980, Anne, eldest da of H. Meigh, of Ash House, Cheltenham, — Gerard Brian Sebastian, *b* 1946: *m* 1972, Siobhan Anne Southwell, da of Maurice Fitzgerald, of Hill Place, Haywards Heath, Sussex, — Veronica Naomi Livingston (*Veronica, Countess Peel*), *b* 1950: *m* 1973 (*m diss* 1987), 3rd Earl Peel.

MOTHER LIVING

Margaret (*Margaret, Lady Houstoun-Boswall*), da of George Bullen-Smith, of Squirrels, Arlington, Sussex: *m* 1945 (*m diss* 1970), Sir Thomas Houstoun-Boswall, 7th Bt, who *d* 1982. *Residence* – 8 College Rd, Eastbourne.

WIDOW LIVING OF SEVENTH BARONET

ANNE-LUCIE (*Anne-Lucie, Lady Houstoun-Boswall*), da of Pierre Naquet: *m* 1971, as his 2nd wife, Sir Thomas Houstoun-Boswall, 7th Bt, who *d* 1982.

COLLATERAL BRANCH LIVING

Granddaughter of late Alfred Houstoun Boswall, 5th son of 2nd baronet:—
Issue of late Capt Charles Houstoun-Boswall, R Scots Greys, b 1894; d 1946: m 1935, Marguerite Yvonne
Savage, da of Herbert Pritchard, of Toronto, Canada, and Nassau, Bahamas:—
Jane Carolyn, b 1936: m 1957, John Clyfford Trevor, and has issue living, Mark Clyfford Houstoun, b 1961: m 1985, Elise
Thayer, eldest da of David Green, of West Hayes, Rockbourne, Hants, and has issue living, Alexander John Houstoun b
1990, Natasha Thayer Houstoun b 1992, — Richard Charles Houstoun, b 1969, — Carolyn Elizabeth, b 1959: m 1989,
Patrick Lahiff, and has issue living, Max Alexander Patrick b 1989, Jack William Oliver b 1991, — Emma Cecil, b 1963:
m 1991, David Blake, and has issue living, Rory Dominic David b 1993. Residence – Northborough Manor, Peterborough,
Cambs PE6 9BJ.

This baronet is male heir and representative of the ancient family of the Houstouns of Cotrioch hereditary baillees and
justiciaries of the Barony of Busbie, Wigtownshire, and of Calderhall, Midlothian. Gen Sir William Houstoun, GCB, 1st
Baronet, was a Gen in the Army. The 2nd baronet, Col in Grenadier Guards, assumed in 1847 the additional surname of
Boswall on his marriage with Euphemia, daughter of Thomas Boswall, of Blackadder. The 3rd baronet was Capt
Grenadier Guards and Convener of Berwickshire. The 4th baronet, Capt Sir George Reginald, Grenadier Guards, was
killed in action 1915. The 5th Baronet, Capt Sir (Thomas) Randolph Houstoun-Boswall served in Royal Scots, and d 1953.
His son and heir, George Cleeton Houstoun-Boswall, Lt Royal Scots, was killed on active ser at Hong Kong, 1941. The
6th baronet, Maj Sir Gordon Houstoun-Boswall, 1st Life Guards (whose father, Col Thomas Alford Houstoun-Boswall-
Preston, assumed by Roy licence in 1886 the additional surname of Preston) discontinued the surname of Preston 1953.

BOUGHEY (GB) 1798, of Newcastle-under-Lyme, Staffordshire
(Name pronounced "Boey")

Neither to seek nor to despise distinction

Sir JOHN GEORGE FLETCHER BOUGHEY, 11th *Baronet*; b
12 Aug 1959; s his father *Sir* RICHARD JAMES, 1978; ed
Eton, and Univ of Zimbabwe.

Arms – Quarterly: 1st and 4th, sable, a cross wavy erminois
between four plates, each charged with an arrow in bend sable of
the first, *Fletcher*; 2nd and 3rd, argent, three bucks' heads erased
and affrontée ermines, *Boughey*. **Crests** – 1st, a plate charged with
a pheon per pale ermine and sable; 2nd, out of an eastern crown
gold the points alternate or and argent, a buck's head ermines,
attired and collared of the first.
Residence – Vern Leaze, Calne, Wilts SN11 0NB.

BROTHER LIVING

JAMES RICHARD (The Manor House, Piddletrenthide, Dorchester,
Dorset DT2 7QX), b 29 Aug 1960; ed Eton, and RAC Cirencester:
m 1989, Katharine Mary, only da of Capt (Geoffrey Thomas)
Warren Fenwicke-Clennell (see Blackett, Bt), and has issue living,
George Richard Douglas, b 27 March 1992, — William James, b
1995, — Victoria Rose, b 1990, — Charlotte Emily Venetia, b
1998.

SISTERS LIVING

Julia Mary, b 1952: m 1973, Peregrine James Chadwyck-Healey, of
Vern Leaze, Calne, Wilts (see Chadwyck-Healey, Bt).
—— Rosalind Jane, b 1954: m 1st, 1978, Richard Herbert Dennis
Steele; 2ndly, 1994, Antony Penrose, of Burgh Hill House,
Chiddingly, Lewes, Sussex BN8 6JF. —— Clare Anne (Chestnut
Cottage, Stubhampton, Blandford, Dorset), b 1957.

AUNTS LIVING (Daughters of 9th baronet)

(Mary) Hermia, b 1914: m 1935, Robert Hugh Priestley, of Oakley Manor, Basingstoke. —— Anne, b 1922: m 1946,
(James) Roddy Huff, Lieut US Army, and has issue living, James David (88 Whitehead Rd, Buford, Georgia, USA), b
1947, — Elizabeth Anne (109 Winsome Lane, Chapel Hill, N Carolina 27516, USA), b 1949: m 1971, David M. Rooks III,
and has issue living, Kathryn Elizabeth b 1979, Adrienne Emily b 1982, — Celia, b 1958: m 1983, Michael Mark
Mattingly, of 25 Red Oak Drive, Lititz, Pennsylvania 17543, USA, and has issue living, Emma Caitlin b 1986, Chloë
Elizabeth b 1989.

MOTHER LIVING

Davina Julia (Baroness Loch), da of late FitzHerbert Wright (see V Powerscourt, 1990 Edn): m 1st, 1950 (m diss 1975),
Sir Richard James Boughey, 10th Bt, DL, JP, who d 1978; 2ndly, 1979, as his 2nd wife, 4th Baron Loch, MC, who d
1991. Residence – The Cobbles, Shillingstone, Blandford, Dorset DT11 0SF, and Lochluichart, by Garve, Ross-shire IV23
2PZ.

WIDOW LIVING OF TENTH BARONET

GILLIAN CLAIRE (*Lady Boughey*) (Alebank House, Ancrum, Jedburgh, Roxburghshire TD8 6XH), yst da of late Maj Robert Moubray, DL, late 16th Lancers (*see* Morrison-Bell, Bt): *m* 1976, as his 2nd wife, Sir Richard James Boughey, 10th Bt, JP, DL, who *d* 1978.

COLLATERAL BRANCH LIVING

Grandson of late William Fenton Fletcher Boughey, 4th son of 2nd baronet:—
Issue of late Com Alfred Fletcher COPLESTONE-BOUGHEY, RN, *b* 1883, *ka* during battle of Jutland 1916, having assumed by deed poll 1910 the surname of Coplestone before that of Boughey: *m* 1910, Mary Cliffe, who *d* 1955, da of late Frederick Coplestone, CBE, JP, of Richmond Hill, Chester:—
John Fenton, *b* 1912; *ed* Shrewsbury, and Brasenose Coll, Oxford (BA 1934); Bar Inner Temple 1935; Judge of Co Courts 1969: *m* 1944, Gilian Beatrice, da of late Hugh Alfred Counsell, of Appleby, Westmorland, and has issue living, William Fenton (Ebworthy, Manaton, Devon TQ13 9UL), *b* 1947; *ed* Winchester, Brasenose Coll, Oxford (MA), and Kings Coll, London (LLM): *m* 1978, Clare Louise, only da of late Lester B. Wilson, and has issue living, Robert Fenton *b* 1984, Katharine Elizabeth *b* 1987, — Mary, *b* 1946. *Residence* – 82 Oakley St, SW3. *Club* – Athenæum.

Sir Thomas Fletcher, 1st Bt, was High Sheriff of Staffordshire 1783 and 1789. The 2nd baronet (MP for Staffordshire 1820-22) assumed by sign-manual 1805 the surname of Boughey, in lieu of his patronymic. The 3rd baronet, Sir Thomas Fletcher Fenton, was High Sheriff of Staffordshire 1832, and the 4th baronet, Sir Thomas Fletcher, was also High Sheriff of that county 1898. The 5th baronet, Sir George, was R of Forton 1863-1908, and the 7th, Sir Robert, V of Betley. Sir George Menteth, CBE, 9th baronet, was Under-Sec to Govt of Punjab 1912-13, and sometime Principal Clerk, Med Ser Div, Min of Pensions.

ROUSE-BOUGHTON, First (E) 1641, of Lawford Parva, Warwickshire; Second (GB) 1791, of Rouse Lench, Worcestershire (Extinct 1963)

Sir EDWARD HOTHAM ROUSE-BOUGHTON, 13th and last *Baronet* of Lawford, and 5th and last of Rouse Lench.

WIDOW LIVING OF THIRTEENTH BARONET

ELIZABETH (*Lady Rouse-Boughton*) (Dickens Cottage, Seagrove Bay, Seaview, Isle of Wight), da of late E. W. Hathaway Hunter, and widow of Geoffrey Swaffer: *m* 1948, as his 2nd wife, Maj Sir Edward Hotham Rouse-Boughton, 13th baronet, who *d* 1963, when the title became ext.

BOULTON (UK) 1905, of Copped Hall, Totteridge, Herts (Extinct 1996)

Sir (HAROLD HUGH) CHRISTIAN BOULTON, 4th and last *Baronet*

DAUGHTER LIVING OF THIRD BARONET

Marie Louise, *b* 1921: *m* 1948, James Russell Smith, and has issue living, Carlton Michael, *b* 1949, — Duncan Rumsey, *b* (twin) 1949, — Marie Louise, *b* 1952. *Residence* – 83 Bryant St, Buffalo, New York 14209, USA.

BOULTON (UK) 1944, of Braxted Park, co Essex

Sir WILLIAM WHYTEHEAD BOULTON, CBE, TD, 3rd *Baronet*; *b* 21 June 1912; *s* his brother, *Maj Sir* EDWARD JOHN, 1982; *ed* Eton, and Trin Coll, Camb (BA honours 1934); Bar Inner Temple 1936; served 1939-45 War in Middle East 1939-44, Staff Coll Camberley 1944, served with Allied Command in Germany 1945-50; Hon Lt-Col RHA Essex Yeo (TA); Sec to General Council of the Bar 1950-74, and to the Senate of the Inns of Court and the Bar 1974-75; CBE (Civil) 1958, Kt 1975: *m* 1944, (Margaret) Elizabeth, only da of late Brig Henry Noel Alexander Hunter, DSO, and has issue.

Arms – Argent on a bend engrailed couped gules three leopards' faces or. Crest – Upon a holly bush fructed a falcon rising proper, belled or. *Residence* – The Quarters House, Alresford, Colchester, Essex.

SON LIVING

JOHN GIBSON, *b* 18 Dec 1946; *ed* Stowe.

DAUGHTERS LIVING

Julia Rosalind, *b* 1945: *m* 1965, Anthony John Nevill Russell, of Elm House, Elmdon, Saffron Walden, Essex, and has issue living, William Jonathan, *b* 1968, — Jennifer Rosalind, *b* 1969. —— Susan Elizabeth, *b* 1949: *m* 1985, Roger Donald Harrison, of The Pink House, Hedgerley Close, Cambridge CB3 0EW, yr son of Robert Harrison, of Stratford-upon-Avon, and has issue living, Alexander Barnaby, *b* 1986, — Rupert Michael, *b* 1988.

Sir William Whytehead Boulton, 1st Bt (son of William Whytehead Boulton, JP, of Beverley, Yorkshire), was Govt Whip, and a Junior Lord of the Treasury 1940-42, and Vice-Chamberlain of HM's Household 1942-4, and sat as MP for Central Div of Sheffield (C) 1931-45.

BOWATER (UK) 1914, of Hill Crest, Borough of Croydon

Sir JOHN VANSITTART BOWATER, 4th *Baronet*; *b* 6 April 1918, son of late Capt Victor Spencer Bowater, 3rd son of 1st baronet; *s* his uncle, *Sir* (THOMAS) DUDLEY (BLENNERHASSETT), 1972: *m* 1943, Joan Kathleen, who *d* 1982, da of late Wilfrid Ernest Henry Scullard, of Boscombe, and has issue.

Arms – Argent, on an inescutcheon sable between eight martlets in orle gules a crescent of the field. *Residence* – 214 Runnymede Av, Bearwood, Bournemouth, BH11 9SP.

SON LIVING

MICHAEL PATRICK (The Anchorage, Quay West, Minehead, Som), *b* 18 July 1949: *m* 1968, Alison, da of Edward Wall, of Knowle, and has issue living, Suzanne, *b* 1969, — Juliette, *b* 1972, — Jennifer, *b* 1973, — Katherine, *b* 1980.

DAUGHTER LIVING

Penelope Ann, *b* 1954: *m* 1973, Martin Doughty, son of Geoffrey Doughty, of 16 Victoria Rd, Acocks Green, Birmingham B27 7YA, and has issue living, Samantha, *b* 1976, — Hannah, *b* 1978, — Laura, *b* 1982.

DAUGHTERS LIVING OF SECOND BARONET

Daphne Audrey, *b* 1919. —— Rowena Maud, *b* 1926.

Sir (Thomas) Vansittart Bowater, 1st Bt (son of William Vansittart Bowater, of Bury Hall, Lower Edmonton, N), was an Alderman of the City of London 1907-38, Lord Mayor 1913-14, and MP 1924-38.

BOWATER (UK) 1939, of Friston, Suffolk

Sir EUAN DAVID VANSITTART BOWATER, 3rd *Baronet*; *b* 9 Sept 1935; *s* his father, *Sir* NOEL VANSITTART, GBE, MC, 1984; *ed* Eton, and Trin Coll, Camb: *m* 1964, Susan Mary Humphrey, da of A. R. O. Slater, FCA, and has issue.

𝔄rms – Argent, an orle of eight martlets gules on an inescutcheon sable a crescent of the field. ℭrest – A rainbow issuant from water proper.

SONS LIVING

MORAY DAVID VANSITTART, *b* 24 April 1967: *m* 1993, Mandana Firoozan, and has issue living, Juliet, *b* 1990, — Persia, *b* 1996. —— Lucien Ross Thomas, *b* 1973.

DAUGHTERS LIVING

Jackie, *b* 1965: *m* 1997, Andrew Edward Browne, son of Mrs Hazel Browne, of Paignton, Devon, and has issue living, Alexander, *b* 1999. —— Alexis, *b* 1969.

SISTERS LIVING

Anne Patricia, *b* 1925: *m* 1954, Group Capt Randolph Stuart Mills, DFC, RAF, and has issue living, Philip Stuart, *b* 1956, — William Stuart, *b* 1957. —— Jane Gillian, *b* 1930: *m* 1953, Christopher William Restarick Beeson, and has issue living, Mark, *b* 1954, — Peter, *b* 1956, — David, *b* 1957, — Oona, *b* 1960. *Residence* – Ford Farm, Manaton, Devon.

COLLATERAL BRANCH LIVING

Issue of late Lt-Col Sir Ian Frank Bowater, GBE, DSO, TD, Lord Mayor of London 1969-70, yr son of 1st baronet, *b* 1904; *d* 1982: *m* 1927, Hon Ursula Margaret Dawson (38 Burton Court, Franklin's Row, SW3 4SZ), da of 1st Viscount Dawson of Penn:—
Michael Ian Vansittart (16 Rocky Point Rd, Rowayton, Conn 06853, USA), *b* 1934; *ed* Eton; Maj (ret) Scots Gds; Head of Communications Bowater Corpn: *m* 1960, Camilla Caroline, el da of Air Commodore Whitney Willard Straight, CBE, MC, DFC (*see* E Winchilsea), and has issue living, Arabella Charlotte, *b* 1961: *m* 1990, Carl W. Wend, jr, son of Carl Wend, of White Plains, New York, — Katherine Elizabeth, *b* 1963: *m* 1988, Mark Beaumont, son of Michael Beaumont, and has issue living, James *b* 1990, Emma Camilla *b* 1992, — Caroline Mary, *b* 1964, — Sophie Melissa, *b* 1970. —— Susan Vansittart, *b* 1929: *m* 1956, George Crofton Addison Doughty, of 60 Clonmel Rd, SW6 5BJ, son of late Sir Charles Doughty, QC, and has issue living, Caroline Susan, *b* 1958, and an adopted son, John Addison, *b* 1961. —— Charlotte Mary, *b* 1937: *m* 1st, 1961, (Denis) Anthony Russell, who *d* 1966 (*see* Russell, Bt, colls, *cr* 1916); 2ndly, 1970, J. Watcyn Lewis, of 66 Clifton Hill, NW8 0JT, and has issue living (by 1st *m*) (*see* Russell, Bt, colls, *cr* 1916) (by 2nd *m*), Damian Watcyn, *b* 1971, — Gareth Hugh Bowater, *b* 1973.

The 1st baronet, Major Sir Frank Henry Bowater, TD (son of William Vansittart Bowater, of Bury Hall, Lower Edmonton, N, and brother of Sir (Thomas) Vansittart Bowater, 1st Bt (*cr* 1914)), sometime Major RFA, was a Paper Maker and a Lieut and Alderman of the City of London (Sheriff 1929-30, Lord Mayor 1938-9). Sir Noël Vansittart Bowater, GBE, MC, 2nd Bt, was Alderman of the City of London 1944-70, and Lord Mayor 1953-54.

BOWDEN (UK) 1915, of City of Nottingham

With faith and hope

Sir FRANK HOUSTON BOWDEN, 3rd *Baronet*; *b* 10 Aug 1909; *s* his father, *Sir* HAROLD, GBE, 1960; *ed* Rugby, and Merton Coll, Oxford (BA 1931, MA 1953); assumed the additional forename of Houston 1960; formerly Lieut (*S*) RNVR; 1939-45 War: *m* 1st, 1934 (*m diss* 1936), Marie José Stiénon de Messey, only da of Charles Stiénon, of Paris, and Comtesse Laure de Messey; 2ndly, 1937, Lydia Eveline, who *d* 1981, da of Jean Manolovici, of Bucharest, Roumania; 3rdly, 1989, Oriol Annette Mary, only da of Charles Hooper Bath, of London, and has had issue by 1st and 2nd *m*.

Arms – Quarterly, sable and or, over all a bow in bend of the second, between two cycle wheels charged in the centre with a winged foot, couped at the ankle, all proper. **Crest** – A heron's head erased at the neck proper, gorged with a mural crown gold.
Clubs – White's, Royal Thames Yacht.

SONS LIVING AND DECEASED

(By 1st marriage)

NICHOLAS RICHARD (4 Hensting Farm Cottages, Hensting Lane, Fishers Pond, Eastleigh, Hants S05 7HH), *b* 13 Aug 1935; *ed* Millfield.

(By 2nd marriage)

†Adrian Harold Houston, *b* 1938; *ed* Radley, and Merton Coll, Oxford (MA); assumed the additional forename of Houston 1960: *m* 1968, Marjorie Walter (33 Grosvenor Sq, W1X 9LL), da of John Dozier Gordan, of New York City, USA, and *d* 1995, leaving issue, Alexander Gordan, *b* 1972, — Richard Waring Baylor, *b* 1979, — Stephanie Florence, *b* 1975. —— Aubrey Francis Houston (The Old Vicarage, Winkfield, Windsor, Berks; *Clubs* – Brooks's, and Pratt's), *b* 1940; *ed* Eton, and Merton Coll, Oxford (MA); assumed the additional forename of Houston 1960: *m* 1969, Mary Julia, da of David Richard Colville (*see* V Colville of Culross, colls), and has had issue, James Edward Houston, *b* 1975, *d* 1994, — Victoria Houston, *b* 1973. —— Gregory Andrew Houston (Bucknell Manor, Bicester, Oxfordshire; White's Club), *b* 1948; *ed* Eton, and Mansfield Coll, Oxford (MA); assumed the additional forename of Houston 1960: *m* 1978, Michaela, da of Sir John Figgess, KBE, CMG, and has issue living, Charles John Houston, *b* 1986, — Alexandra Frances Houston, *b* 1981, — Georgina Houston, *b* 1983.

SISTER LIVING

Ruth, *b* 1911: *m* 1st, 1932 (*m diss* 1947), Christopher Bourchier Wrey, who *d* 1976 (*see* Wrey, Bt, colls); 2ndly, 1947, Ernest Wittmann, who *d* 1995. *Residence* – Flat 3, Hale House, 34 de Vere Gdns, W8.

Sir Frank Bowden, 1st Bt, was Founder, Chm, Managing Director, and Principal Owner of Sturmey-Archer Gears (Limited), and of Raleigh Cycle Co (Limited). Sir Harold Bowden, GBE, 2nd Bt was Pres of Raleigh Industries Ltd, Chm of Council of British Olympic Assocn 1931, and High Sheriff of Notts 1933.

BOWEN (UK) 1921, of Colworth, co Bedford

Audaces fortuna juvat

Fortune favours the brave

Sir MARK EDWARD MORTIMER BOWEN, 5th *Baronet*; *b* 17 Oct 1958; *s* his father, *Sir* THOMAS FREDERIC CHARLES, 1989; *ed* Wellington Coll: *m* 1983, Kerry Tessa, da of Michael John Moriarty, of The Grey House, Links Rd, Worthing, Sussex, and has issue.

Arms – Azure, a lion rampant within an orle, all within four roses or and as many bezants alternately. Crest – A lion sejant proper holding in the dexter paw a Bowen knot argent.
Residence – 14 Pendarves Rd, West Wimbledon, SW20 8TS.

SON LIVING

GEORGE EDWARD MICHAEL, *b* 27 Dec 1987.

DAUGHTER LIVING

Grace Francesca *b* 1989.

SISTERS LIVING

Julia Rosemary (13 Barnet Close, Yeovil, Som), *b* 1950: *m* 1970 (*m diss* 1983), Lt-Cdr Robert Andrew Fewings, RN, and has had issue, Paul Stuart, *b* 1973; *d* 1993, — James Andrew Murray, *b* 1977. —— Margot Claire, *b* 1952: *m* 1974, Malcolm Ivison Kirkpatrick, of 70 Netherby Park, Weybridge, Surrey, and has issue living, Joanna Claire, *b* 1978, — Verity Juliet Elizabeth, *b* 1986.

WIDOW LIVING OF FOURTH BARONET

JILL CLAUDE MURRAY (*Jill, Lady Bowen*), da of Cyril Lloyd Evans, of Prestea, Ghana, W Africa: *m* 1947, Sir Thomas Frederic Charles Bowen, 4th Bt, who *d* 1989. *Residence* – 30 Central Lodge, Pegasus Court, Hants GU13 8SX.

COLLATERAL BRANCH LIVING

Issue of late Harold Cedric Bowen, yr son of 1st baronet, *b* 1896, *d* 1959: *m* 1921, Vera Donnet, who *d* 1967:—

Nicholas Edward (Apartado 249, 07840 Sta Eulalia del Rio, Ibiza, Spain), *b* 1923; *ed* Harrow; is Wing-Cdr RAF (ret); served in World War II; Mil and Air Attaché at Oslo 1968-71: *m* 1944, Evelyn, da of late Edward Batty, and has issue living, Michael Edward, *b* 1944; *ed* Harrow: *m* 1968, Gillian Margaret, da of Col B. R. D. Garside, MC, and has issue living, Nicola Emma *b* 1969, Victoria Margaret *b* 1972, Anabel Elizabeth *b* 1974, — Christopher Anthony Richard (71 Bolingbroke Grove, SW11), *b* 1947; *ed* Harrow: *m* 1975, Mary Olivia, da of Alexander Walcot Stewart, and has issue living, Robert Alexander Edward *b* 1978, Katherine Olivia *b* 1976, Clare Rowena *b* 1982. —— Clarissa, *b* 1929: *m* 1954, Mervyn Heald, QC, of Colhook Lodge, Ebernoe, Petworth, Sussex, son of Rt Hon Sir Lionel Frederick Heald, QC, MP, and has issue living, Robert Lionel, *b* 1974, — Henrietta Sara, *b* 1955: *m* 1981, Adam Curtis, of 15 Cloudesley Sq, N1 0HT, and has issue living, James Nathaniel *b* 1990, Sophie Clarissa *b* 1986, — Annabel Clare, *b* 1957: *m* 1989, Timothy Peter Smith, of The Stables, Headfoldswood, Loxwood, W Sussex RH14 0SX, and has issue living, Harrison Oscar *b* 1990, Ottoline Amelia *b* 1994, — Julia Elizabeth (Glenternie, Manor Valley, Peebles), *b* 1959: *m* 1979 (*m diss* 1998), Charles Stewart Prescot, and has issue living, Nicholas Hugh *b* 1980, Rupert James *b* 1985, Alexandra Constance *b* 1990.

Sir Albert Edward Bowen, 1st Bt (son of Edward Bowen, of Hanley), was Pres of Buenos Aires Great Southern Railway Co, and of many Cos in City of London. Major Sir Edward Crowther Bowen, 2nd Bt, 6th Inniskilling Dragoons, served during European War 1914-18 (MC). Sir John Edward Mortimer Bowen, 3rd Bt, was *k* in a motor racing accident 1939.

BOWLBY (UK) 1923, of Manchester Square, Borough of St Marylebone

Yield not to adversity

Sir RICHARD PEREGRINE LONGSTAFF BOWLBY, 3rd *Baronet*, elder son of late Lt-Col (Edward) John Mostyn Bowlby, CBE, MD, 2nd son of 1st baronet; *b* 11 Aug 1941; *s* his uncle, *Sir* ANTHONY HUGH MOSTYN, 1993; *ed* Dauntsey's Sch: *m* 1963, Xenia, only da of late Roderick Paul Agnew Garrett, of 28 Southwood Lane, N6, and has issue.

𝔄rms − Per fesse sable and argent, a pale with three hinds' heads erased two and one, and as many annulets one and two all counterchanged. ℭrest − Three annulets interlaced one and two or, between two thorn branches proper. *Residence* − Boundary House, Wyldes Close, NW11 7JB.

SON LIVING

BENJAMIN, *b* 2 Nov 1966; *ed* King Alfred Sch: *m* 1992, Mylanna Sophia, elder da of Michael Case Colyer, of Harlech, Gwynedd, and has issue living, Roderick Peter, *b* 18 July 1996, — Alexander John, *b* 1998. *Residence* − Rose Tree Cottage, 29 High St, Graveley, Cambs PE18 9PL.

DAUGHTER LIVING

Sophia, *b* 1969.

BROTHER LIVING

Robert John Mostyn, *b* 1948; *ed* Grenville Coll. *Residence* − Wyldes Close Corner, Wyldes Close, Hampstead Way, NW11 7JB.

SISTERS LIVING

Mary Hamilton Victoria Ignatia, *b* 1939: *m* 1st, 1964 (*m diss* 1980), Capt Timothy Richard Holbrook Dawson, RE; 2ndly, 1980, Anthony Gatling, of White Lodge, Berwick St James, Salisbury, Wilts, and has issue living (by 1st *m*), Guy Philip Richard, *b* 1965; *ed* John Masefield Gram Sch, and City Univ, — Patrick Timothy John, *b* 1969; *ed* Solihull Sch, and Univ Coll London: *m* 1993, Anna, da of Rev Canon Richard Kingsbury, of The Rectory, Church Lane, Caversham, Reading. —— Pia Rose Whitworth, *b* 1945: *m* 1968, Carlos Duran, of 70 Northway, NW11, and has issue living, Xohan, *b* 1968; *ed* Oak Lodge, — Xavier, *b* 1973; *ed* King Alfred Sch, — Xulia Tareixa, *b* 1978.

DAUGHTERS LIVING OF SECOND BARONET

Anthea, *b* 1930: *m* 1956, Jolyon Dromgoole, of 13 Gladstone St, SE1 6EY, and has issue living, Emma, *b* 1957, — Julia, *b* 1961, — Rose, *b* 1964, — Susanna, *b* (triplet) 1964, — Belinda, *b* (triplet) 1964. —— Sophia, *b* 1945.

DAUGHTER LIVING OF FIRST BARONET

Dorothy Evelyn Mostyn (*Lady Phelps Brown*), *b* 1910: *m* 1932, Sir Ernest Henry Phelps Brown, MBE, FBA, who *d* 1994, late Professor of Economics, London Univ, and sometime Fellow of New Coll, Oxford, and has issue living, Nicholas Anthony Phelps, *b* 1936; *ed* Trinity Hall, Cambridge, — Thomas Henry Phelps, *b* 1948; *ed* New College, Oxford, — Juliet Virginia Phelps, *b* 1934; *ed* Newnham College, Cambridge: *m* 1964, Keith Hopkins, Professor of Ancient History, University of Cambridge. *Residence* − 16 Bradmore Rd, Oxford.

MOTHER LIVING

Ursula, 3rd da of Tom George Longstaff, MD: *m* 1938, Lt-Col (Edward) John Mostyn Bowlby, CBE, MD, 2nd son of 1st baronet, who *d* 1990. *Residence* − Wyldes Close Corner, Hampstead Way, NW11.

The 1st baronet, Sir Anthony Alfred Bowlby, KCB, KCMG, KCVO, FRCS (Pres Coll of Surgs 1920-23), was Surg to Royal Household 1904-10, and an Hon Surg to HM 1910-29, and served in S African War 1899-1900 in charge of Portland Hospital (despatches, medal, CMG), and during European War 1914-19 as Maj-Gen Army Med Ser, and as Advisory Consulting Surg to British Forces in France (American DSM).

BOWMAN (UK) 1884, of Holmbury St Mary, co Surrey

We conquered formerly with these arms

Sir PAUL HUMPHREY ARMYTAGE BOWMAN, 5th *Baronet*, only son of late Maj Humphrey Ernest Bowman, CMG, CBE, eldest son of late John Frederick Bowman, 2nd son of 1st baronet; *b* 10 August 1921; *s* his kinsman, *Sir* JOHN PAGET, 1994; *ed* Eton; sometime Maj Coldstream Guards; Dir Hill Samuel & Co Ltd 1962-78: *m* 1st, 1943 (*m diss* 1947), Felicité Anne Araminta, da of Sir Harold Alfred MacMichael, GCMG, DSO (*see* E Leven and Melville, colls, 1946 Edn); 2ndly, 1947 (*m diss* 1974), Gabrielle May, da of Thomas Hapgood Hudson, of Sydney, Australia, and formerly wife of Lt-Col Walter Currie, US Army; 3rdly, 1974, Elizabeth Deirdre, who *d* 1993, yr da of late Bruce R. Campbell, of Goorianawa, NSW, and formerly wife of Maj-Gen Thomas Bell Lindsay Churchill, CB, CBE, MC, and has issue by 2nd *m*.

Arms – Or, on a chevron between three bows stringed palewise gules, two lions combatant of the first between as many escallops argent. **Crest** – Upon a mount vert the stump of a tree proper, around the upper part a belt sable, and pendant therefrom, on the dexter side, a quiver gules filled with arrows argent. *Residence* – 3/414 Edgecliff Rd, Woollahra, NSW 2025, Australia. *Clubs* – White's, Royal Corinthian Yacht, and The Brook (NY).

DAUGHTER LIVING (By 2nd marriage)

Amanda Caroline, *b* 1947: *m* 19—, David Levy, and has issue living. *Residence* – 4 Spring House, Sterlington, New York 10974, USA.

SISTER LIVING

Cynthia Pamela Mary (*Lady Macdonald*), *b* 1918: *m* 1st, 1943 (*m diss* 1969), Rear Adm Josef Czeslaw Bartosik, CB, DSC, RN; 2ndly, 1980, Vice Adm Sir Roderick Douglas Macdonald, KBE, of Ollach, Braes, Isle of Skye, and has issue living (by 1st *m*), Jan Josef, *b* 1946; *ed* Downside: *m* 1978, Lesley Anne, da of Dr John Meehan, of Forest Mere, Liphook, Hants, and has issue living, James *b* 1980, Lucy Olivia *b* 1983, — Conrad Josef (Sam) (4 Beauclerc Rd, W6), *b* 1948: *m* 1978, Claudia, da of Maj Thomas Pitman, MC, of Cliffe Lodge, Leyburn, Yorks, and has issue living, Luke *b* 1982, Daniel *b* 1985, Humphrey *b* 1989, — Matthew Timothy (9 Lansdowne Crescent, Cheltenham, Glos), *b* 1954: *m* 1980, Catherine, da of late John McDonnell, of Dundalk, co Louth, and has issue living, Robert *b* 1982, — Kristina Cynthia (Norton, Worcs), *b* 1945: *m* 1969, Christopher Thomasson, of Somerton Castle, nr Lincoln, and has issue living, Thomas *b* 1970, Charles *b* 1976, Sophy *b* 1969, Clare *b* 1977.

DAUGHTER LIVING OF FOURTH BARONET (by 1st marriage)

Rachel Elinor, *b* 1938; SRN: *m* 1967, Gerald William Wensley Clarkson, of Manor Farm House, Ryme Intrinseca, Sherborne, Dorset DT9 6JX (*see* Lane, Bt, ext, 1976 Edn), and has issue living, James Hugo Wensley, *b* 1970, — Alexandra Juliet Cajetana, *b* 1974: *m* 1997, Angus John Mayhew, and has issue living, Rosalyn Cajetana Honeysuckle *b* 1998.

WIDOW LIVING OF FOURTH BARONET

CHRISTIAN (*Lady Bowman*), yst da of Col Sir Arthur Grant of Monymusk, 10th Bt, CBE, DSO, and widow of John Gordon Ogston Miller: *m* 1993, as his 3rd wife, Sir John Paget Bowman, 4th Bt, who *d* 1994. *Residence* – The Walled Garden, Chamberlain St, Wells, Som BA5 2PE.

COLLATERAL BRANCHES LIVING

Granddaughters of late John Frederick Bowman, 2nd son of 1st baronet:—
Issue of late Clive Frederick Bowman, MC, *b* 1884, *d* 1972: *m* 1920, Erica Violet, who *d* 1972, da of late Col Robert George Wardlaw-Ramsay, DL (B Magheramorne, colls):—
Erica Rosemary, *b* 1921: *m* 1948, Douglas Burch Law, formerly Maj Seaforth Highlanders, of Redfriars, E Linton, E Lothian EH40 3DS, and has issue living, Nicholas Simon, *b* 1954; *ed* Wellington Coll: *m* 1979, Virginia Halliday, and has issue living, Hamish *b* 1982, Sarah Catherine *b* 1980, — James Christopher, *b* 1956; *ed* Wellington Coll. —— Dorothea Vivien, *b* 1924; a Nun of Order of the Sacred Heart.

Granddaughter of late Rev Arthur Gerald Bowman, 3rd son of 1st baronet:—
Issue of late Arthur William Bowman, London Regt, *b* 1887, *ka* 1918: *m* 1911, Elinor Marion (who *d* 1957, having *m* 2ndly, 1925, Humphrey Ernest Bowman, CMG, CBE (*ante*)), da of late Rev Charles Conybeare, R of Tichborne, Hants:—
Barbara Paget, *b* 1912: *m* 1932, Wing-Com Douglas Sender, RAF (ret), who *d* 1987, and has issue living, Michael Conybeare (4 Rivermount Gdns, Portsmouth Rd, Guildford, Surrey), *b* 1933; *ed* Wellington Coll: *m* 1962 (*m diss* 1984), Judith Olivia Hedley, and has issue living, Richard Paget *b* 1964, — Katherine Elizabeth *b* 1966, — Penelope Markland, *b* 1936: *m* 1959, Lt-Col Anthony John Carter Wells, RA (ret), RAA (ret), of Wirrabara, Devon Rd, Exeter, NSW 2579, Australia, and has issue living, Pandora Markland *b* 1965: *m* 1991, Gregory John Bailey (and has issue living, Samantha Markland JOBBINS WELLS *b* 1986, Jasmine BAILEY *b* 1993), — Joanna Paget, *b* 1953: *m* 1982, Christopher John Askham, of

10 Frogmore Village, St Albans, Herts, and has issue living, Jonathan Piers *b* 1986. *Residence* – L'Espine, Millbrook, Jersey.

The 1st baronet was an eminent ophthalmic surgeon. Sir W. Paget Bowman, 2nd Bt, was many years Registrar of the Corporation of the Sons of the Clergy. The Rev Sir Paget Mervyn Bowman, 3rd Bt, was R of Shere, Rural Dean of Cranleigh and Surrogate 1919-50.

BOWMAN (UK) 1961, of Killingworth, co Northumberland (Extinct 1990)

Sir GEORGE BOWMAN, 2nd and last *Baronet*.

DAUGHTERS LIVING OF SECOND BARONET

Julie Victoria, *b* 1961. —— Louise Janet, *b* 1963. —— Claire Elizabeth, *b* 1965.

WIDOW LIVING OF SECOND BARONET

OLIVE (*Lady Bowman*), da of — Case, of South Shields: *m* 1960, Sir George Bowman, 2nd Bt, who *d* 1990. *Residence* – Parkside, Killingworth Drive, Killingworth Station, Newcastle 12.

Bowyer (Bowyer-Smyth), see Smyth.

BOYCE (UK) 1952, of Badgeworth, co Gloucester

Sir ROBERT CHARLES LESLIE BOYCE, 3rd *Baronet*, *b* 2 May 1962; *s* his father, *Sir* RICHARD (LESLIE), 1968; *ed* Cheltenham, Salford Univ (BSc), and Nottingham Univ (BMedSc, BM, BS); FRCS Ed; Ophthalmologist: *m* 1985, Fiona Margaret, 2nd da of John Savage, of Whitmore Park, Coventry, and has issue.

Arms – Or on a chevron gules an open book proper edges and clasps of the first on a chief of the second a portcullis chained also of the first between two swords erect also proper pomels and hilts gold. Crest – A demi lion gules grasping in the dexter paw a pen or.

SON LIVING

THOMAS LESLIE, *b* 3 Sept 1993.

DAUGHTER LIVING

Amelia Moira, *b* 1996.

SISTER LIVING

Sarah Jane Leslie, *b* 1960

DO IT WITH THY MIGHT

UNCLE LIVING (*Son of 1st baronet*)

John Leslie (182 Huntingdale Rd, Mt Waverley, Victoria 3149, Aust), *b* 1934: *m* 1st, 1957 (*m diss* 1975), Finola Mary, da of late James Patrick Maxwell, of Bansha, co Tipperary; 2ndly, 1980, Fusako, da of Yonesaku Ishibashi, of Sinagawa-ku, Tokyo, Japan, and has issue living, (by 1st *m*) Richard Allen, *b* 1968, — Elizabeth Jane Leslie, *b* 1958, — Evelyn Mary, *b* 1961, — Suzanne Caroline, *b* 1963, — (by 2nd *m*) Miyo Maybery, *b* 1981, — Kyoko Jacqueline, *b* 1983.

WIDOW LIVING OF SECOND BARONET

JACQUELINE ANNE, only da of Roland A. Hill, of Chipping Norton, Oxon: *m* 1st, 1958, Sir Richard (Leslie) Boyce, 2nd Bt, who *d* 1968; 2ndly, 1974, Christopher Richard Boyce-Dennis.

COLLATERAL BRANCH LIVING

Issue of late Charles Francis Leslie Boyce, late Maj 5th Bn Glos Regt (TA), yst son of 1st baronet, *b* 1936, *d* 1985: *m* 1963, Elizabeth (1 Upton Grove Cottages, Tetbury Upton, Tetbury, Glos), only da of William Todd, of 130 Meadoway, Bishop's Cleeve, Cheltenham:—
Edward Neal Leslie, *b* 1965. —— Phillp William James, *b* 1971. —— Kathryn Maybery, *b* 1966: *m* 1990, Alistair Cone, and has issue living, Megan Louise, *b* 1993, — Victoria Claire Alexandra, *b* 1973.

The 1st baronet Sir (Harold) Leslie Boyce, KBE (son of Charles Macleay Boyce, of Sydney, NSW), was Sheriff of Gloucester 1941-2, and Lord Mayor of London 1951-2, and sat as MP for Gloucester (C) 1929-45.

BOYD (UK) 1916, of Howth House, Howth, co Dublin

I trust

Sir ALEXANDER WALTER BOYD, 3rd *Baronet*, son of late Major Cecil Anderson Boyd, MC, MD, late RAMC, 2nd son of 1st baronet; *b* 16 June 1934; *s* his uncle, *Sir* WALTER HERBERT, 1948: *m* 1958, Molly Madeline, da of late Ernest Arthur Rendell, of RR3 Vernon, British Columbia, and has issue.

Arms – Azure, a fesse chequy argent and gules between three estoiles or. **Crest** – Out of a crest coronet or charged, with three ermine spots, a dexter hand erect having the two last fingers turned in and the rest pointing upwards proper.
Residence – ......

SONS LIVING

IAN WALTER RENDELL, *b* 14 March 1964: *m* 1986, Lee-Ann Dillon, and has issue living, Kyle Robert Rendell *b* 1987, — Cameron Rendell Ian, *b* 1991, — Dawson Alexander Cecil, *b* 1992. —— Robert Alexander Rendell, *b* 1966.

DAUGHTERS LIVING

Heather Lynn, *b* 1959: *m* 1st, 1986 (*m diss* 1992), Francis J. McAnally; 2ndly, 19—, Peter E. McLennan, and has issue living (by 1st *m*), Matthew Alexander, *b* 1986, — Erin Christine, *b* 1989. —— Susan Christine, *b* 1961· *m* 1985 (*m diss* 1990), Paul H. Saarinen, and has issue living, Tory (son), *b* 1988, — Melissa Jenna, *b* 1990. —— Sandra Molly, *b* 1967: *m* 1992, Eric A. Bay.

HALF-SISTERS LIVING

Deirdre Anna, *b* 1925: *m* 1944, Walter V. Dunham, of 532 11th St, New Westminster, BC, Canada, and has issue living, David, *b* 1964, — Ruth Aideen, *b* 1946, — Patricia Ann, *b* 1948, — Beverley Jean, *b* 1951, — Mary Elizabeth, *b* 1953. —— Aideen Gwendolyn, *b* 1926: *m* 1947, Robert Laird Russell, of 3022 S 253rd St, Kent, Washington, USA, and has issue living, Heather Joanne, *b* 1959. —— Ruth Mary, *b* 1927: *m* 1951, Anthony Weisgarber, and has issue living, Kathleen Mary *b* 1957, — Tracy Ann *b* 1962. *Residence* – 1154, Tolmie Av, Victoria, BC.

COLLATERAL BRANCHES LIVING

Grandson of late Lieut-Col Henry Alexander Boyd (infra):—
Issue of late Major Ronald Walter Boyd MC, Roy Ulster Rifles, *b* 1914, *ka* 1944; *m* 1939, Virginia (Courthay, 47

Gatton Rd, Reigate, Surrey RH2 0HJ) (who *m* 2ndly 1949), Humphrey Allen Walter, ERD who *d* 1979, da of late John Freeman, of Bexleyheath, Kent:—
Nigel Cecil John, *b* 1943; *ed* Seaford.

Issue of late Lieut-Col Henry Alexander Boyd, CMG, DSO, 3rd son of 1st baronet, *b* 1877, *d* 1943: *m* 1908, Moya, who *d* 1959, da of late John Shaw Exham, JP, of Worlington, Suffolk:—
Heather, *b* 1910.

Issue of late Robert Reginald Boyd, yst son of 1st baronet, *b* 1880, *d* 1959: *m* 1922, Agnes Maria Dorothea, who *d* 1964, da of late Lt-Col Charles Harrison, of Ross, Herefordshire:—
Walter Michael Stewart (3 Glenarm Court, Flagstaff Hill 5159, S Australia) *b* 1924: *m* 1951, Janet Brown, and has issue living, Nicholas Michael (20 Kenny Drive, Duncraig, W Australia 6023), *b* 1954: *m* (and has issue), — Jonathan Peter, *b* 1956, — Emma Jane, *b* 1960. —— Robert Stanley, CB (Great Beere, North Tawton, Devon EX20 2BR), *b* 1927; *ed* Wellington Coll, and Trin Coll, Dublin (BA, LLB); Bar-at-law, Inner Temple, 1954; Solicitor of Inland Revenue 1979-86; CB 1982: *m* 1965, Ann, who *d* 1999, da of late Daniel Hopkin, MC, MP.

The 1st baronet, the Rt Hon Sir Walter Boyd, PC, LLD, was successively Receiver Judge for Ireland, a Judge of the Court of Bankruptcy in Ireland, and one of the Justices of the High Court of Justice in Ireland. The 2nd baronet, Sir Walter Herbert Boyd, KC, was Ch Registrar of Bankruptcy (Ireland) 1912-37.

BOYLE (UK) 1904, of Ockham, Salehurst, Sussex

GOD'S PROVIDENCE IS MY INHERITANCE

Sir STEPHEN GURNEY BOYLE, 5th *Baronet*; *b* 15 Jan 1962; *s* his father, *Sir* RICHARD GURNEY, 1983.

Arms – Per bend raguly gules and argent, two staves raguly in bend counterchanged. **Crest** – In front of a lion's head couped argent, a staff fessewise gules.
Address – 19 Gibb Croft, Harlow, Essex CM18 7JL.

BROTHERS LIVING

MICHAEL DESMOND, *b* 16 Sept 1963. —— Roger Edward Bartholemew, *b* 1966.

AUNT LIVING (*Daughter of 2nd baronet*)

Ann Constance Beatrice, *b* 1926: *m* 1948, Jack Brunner Gold (Brunner, Bt), and has issue living, Jason, *b* 1950; *ed* St Paul's: *m* 1972, Ann Elizabeth Stewart, and has issue living, Matthew Guy *b* 1981, James Alexander *b* 1991, — Georgina Beatrice, *b* 1952: *m* 1981, Kenneth Neil Burney Dunlop, and has issue living, Kenneth Edward George *b* 1984, Richard Nicholas *b* 1985. *Residence* – 123 St George's Rd, SE1.

MOTHER LIVING

Elizabeth Ann, yr da of Norman Dennes, of Middle Green, Poulshot, Devizes, Wilts: *m* 1961 (*m diss* 1974), Richard Gurney Boyle (later Sir Richard Boyle, 4th Bt), who *d* 1983. *Residence* – 44 Old Orchard, Harlow, Essex.

The 1st baronet, Sir Edward, KC, a Dir of London and India Docks and the Imperial Life Office, sat as MP for Taunton (*C*) 1906-9. The 2nd baronet, Sir Edward, was a JP for Sussex (High Sheriff 1927), acting British High Commr for Serbia 1915, and Chm Balkan Cttee 1924-45. He *d* 1945. The 3rd baronet, Sir Edward, CH, PC, was Min of Educ 1962-64, and Min of State Educ and Science April-Oct 1964, MP for Handsworth Div of Birmingham (*C*) 1950-70, Vice-Chancellor of Leeds Univ 1970-81, Chm Top Salaries Review Body 1971-81, and was *cr Baron Boyle of Handsworth*, of Salehurst, co Sussex (Life Baron) 1970. He *d* 1981.

BRADFORD (UK) 1902, of South Audley Street, City of Westminster, co London

(*Sir*) EDWARD ALEXANDER SLADE BRADFORD, 5th *Baronet*; *b* (*posthumous*) 18 June 1952; *s* his half-brother, *Sir* JOHN RIDLEY EVELYN, 1954, but does not use the title.

Arms – Argent, on a fesse embattled counter-embattled between three mural crowns sable, as many stags' heads erased or. Crest – A stag's head erased or, charged on the neck with a mural crown, and suspended from the mouth a bugle horn stringed sable.
Residence – ......

HALF-SISTER LIVING

Alison Rose, *b* 1939: *m* 1957 (*m diss* 1993), James Ronald Creighton Adams, and has issue living, John Evelyn Creighton, *b* 1959, — Bradford Michael, *b* 1965. *Residence* – Marylands Farm, 549 Rose Ave, New Haven, Indiana 46774, USA.

COLLATERAL BRANCHES LIVING

Humani nihil alienum

Nothing concerning man is indifferent to me

Issue of late Capt Donald Clifton Bradford, youngest son of 2nd baronet, *b* 1914, *d* 1998: *m* 1949, Constance Mary (The Barns, Tapnell, Yarmouth, IOW PO41 0YJ), da of late C. J. Morgan, of Glyncorrwg, S Wales:—
Susan Jane, *b* 1950: *m* 1975, Richard Rogers, of 5 Buntings, Gilbert White Way, Alton, Hants, and has issue living, Jonathan, *b* 1984, — Jennifer Mary, *b* 1981. —— Joanna Mary Louise, *b* 1957: *m* 1994, Graham Richards, of Upper Branstone, Chale, nr Ventnor, IOW, and has issue living, Stephanie, *b* 1995, — Josceline, *b* 1997.

Grandchildren of late Lt-Col Edward Austen Bradford, DSO (*infra*):—
Issue of late Brig Berenger Colborne Bradford, DSO, MBE, MC, Black Watch, *b* 1912, *d* 1996: *m* 1951, Susan (Kincardine, Kincardine O'Neil, Aberdeenshire), yr da of late Col Arthur Hanning Vaughan-Lee, of Dillington Park, Ilminster, Som:—
ROBERT BERENGER PICKERING (Holestone Lodge, Pool O'Muckart, Clackmannanshire), *b* 12 Aug 1952: *ed* Eton. —— Andrew Edward Hanning (Kincardine, Kincardine O'Neil, Aberdeenshire), *b* 1955; *ed* Eton, and Aberdeen Univ (BSc); Member Queen's Body Guard for Scotland (Royal Company of Archers): *m* 1978, Nicola Barbara, da of late David Philip Symthe, and has issue living, a son, *b* 1980, — a da, *b* 1988, — a da, *b* 1982. —— Ronald James Knight, *b* 1958; *ed* Eton, and Aberdeen Univ (BSc); Lt-Col The Black Watch (Royal Highland Regt): served NI (despatches): *m* 1986, Katherine Ferguson, yr da of Sir Ian Denholm, CBE, of Newton of Belltrees, Lochwinnoch, Renfrewshire, and has issue living, Victoria Jane Ferguson, *b* 1989, — Kirstin Elizabeth Hardy, *b* 1992. —— Margaret Jane, *b* 1953: *ed* Glasgow Univ (BMus): *m* 1982, Robert Hamilton Gladstone of Capenoch, of Capenoch, Thornhill, Dumfries-shire, and has issue living, John Berenger, *b* 1983, — Harry William, *b* (twin) 1983, — Catharine Susan, *b* 1986.

Issue of late Lt-Col Edward Austen Bradford, DSO, yst son of 1st baronet, *b* 1879, *d* 1958: *m* 1908, Margaret Louisa, who *d* 1972, da of late Herbert Carey Hardy, of Danehurst, Sussex:—
Diana Elizabeth, *b* 1919: *m* 1941, Rupert P. Shervington, late Capt RE, and has issue living, Evelyn Arthur, *b* 1942; BA, Trin Coll, Dublin, — Diana Clare, *b* 1943, — Caroline Faith, *b* 1954. *Residence* – The Villa Ware, Ware Lane, Lyme Regis, Dorset DT7 3EJ.

The 1st baronet, Col Sir Edward Ridley Colborne, was Commr of Police of the Metropolis 1890-1903. The 2nd baronet, Col Sir Evelyn Ridley Bradford, Comdg 2nd Batn Seaforth Highlanders (Ross-shire Buffs, Duke of Albany's), was *ka* 1914. The 3rd baronet, Sir Edward Montagu Andrew, was Major The Cameronians. The 4th baronet, Sir John Ridley Evelyn, was *k* in a tractor accident 1954.

BRADY (UK) 1869, of Hazelbrook, co Dublin, Ireland (Extinct 1927)

Sir WILLIAM LONGFIELD BRADY, 4th and last *Baronet*.

DAUGHTER LIVING OF FOURTH BARONET

Ethne Florence, *b* 1902.

DAUGHTER LIVING OF THIRD BARONET

Jessie Elizabeth Maziere *b* 1901.

BRICKWOOD (UK) 1927, of Portsmouth

NIL·ARDUUM

Nothing arduous

Sir BASIL GREAME BRICKWOOD, 3rd *Baronet*; *b* 21 May 1923; *s* his half-brother, *Sir* RUPERT REDVERS, 1974; *ed* King Edward's Gram Sch, Stratford, and Clifton; served with RAF 1940-46: *m* 1st, 1947, Betty Cooper; 2ndly, 1956, Shirley Anne, da of Richard Wallace Brown, and has issue by 2nd *m*.

Arms – Argent a pale checky azure and or between two oak trees couped vert on a chief gules three ears of barley slipped and leaved of the third and a sprig of hop slipped and leaved proper in saltire between two billets gold. **Crest** – A demi savage wreathed about the temples with a chaplet of oak holding in the dexter hand a sprig of hop slipped and leaved proper and resting the sinister hand upon a billet or.
Club – RAF.

DAUGHTERS LIVING (*By 2nd marriage*)

Tessa Anne, *b* 1959: *m* 1991, Roger Frederick Norgrove, and has issue living, Oliver Nicholas Richard, *b* 1992, — Abigail Anne, *b* 1993. —— Gail Anne BRICKWOOD, *b* 1963; has resumed her maiden name: *m* 1984 (*m diss* 19—), Michael Horsnell, elder son of R.N. Horsnell, of Thorvington, Essex.

DAUGHTERS LIVING OF SECOND BARONET

Sally (Neale), *b* 1933: *m* 1956, Nigel William Seville Yonge, of Homefields, Bulls Lane, Cowfold, Sussex, and has issue living, William Jonathan Michael, *b* 1961, — Andrew James Neale (Paybank House, Church St, Bentworth, Alton, Hants GU34 5RD), *b* 1964: *m* 1990, Katherine Olivia, da of John Valentine McCulloch Jameson, OBE, and has issue living, Jack William Alexander *b* 1995, Philippa Mary *b* 1997, — Susannah Mary, *b* 1957: *m* 19—, Nicholas Broome, of 26 Larkspur Terr, Jesmond, Newcastle-upon-Tyne NE2 2DU, and has issue living, Phoebe *b* 1990, Ionie *b* 1993, — Annabel Mary (29 Adelaide Grove, W12 0JU), *b* 1959; has issue living (by Mark Dudek), Matthew DUDEK *b* 1994. —— Ann Neale, *b* 1934: *m* 1st, 1959, John Colin Caldecott Bauer; 2ndly, 1986, Peter A. Van den Bergh, and has issue living (by 1st *m*), John William, *b* 1960: *m* 1989, Clare Jennet, and has issue living, George *b* 1992, Katie *b* 1990, — Nicola Anne, *b* 1962: *m* 1989, Graham Brooks, and has issue living, Benjamin *b* 1991, Hannah *b* 1995, Serina *b* 1997.

The 1st baronet, Sir John Brickwood, was Chm and Managing Director of Brickwood & Co Ltd, brewers, of Portsmouth, and sometime Chm of Portsmouth Chamber of Commerce.

BRINCKMAN (UK) 1831, of Burton or Monk Bretton, Yorkshire

PERSEVERANDO

By persevering

Sir THEODORE GEORGE RODERICK BRINCKMAN, 6th *Baronet*; *b* 20 March 1932; *s* his father, *Sir* RODERICK NAPOLEON, DSO, MC, 1985; *ed* Millfield, Trin Coll Sch, Port Hope, Ontario, Ch Ch, Oxford, and Trin Coll, Toronto Univ; publisher and antiquarian bookseller: *m* 1st, 1958 (*m diss* 1983), Helen Mary Anne, da of late Arnold Elliot Cook, of Toronto, Canada; 2ndly, 1983, Hon Greta Sheira Bernadette Grant-Ferris, da of Baron Harvington, PC (Life Baron) (extinct), and formerly wife of (i) John Frederick Edward Trehearne, and (ii) Christopher Mark Henry Murray, and has issue by 1st *m*.

Arms – Quarterly: 1st and 4th, argent, three hills azure, for Brinckman; 2nd and 3rd, ermine, two eagles displayed in chief gules, and a lion rampant in base proper collared and a chain therefrom reflexed over the back or, for Broadhead. **Crest** – A pair of wings quarterly argent and azure.
Residence – Monk Bretton, Barnsley, Cirencester, Glos GL7 5EJ. *Club* – White's, University (Toronto).

SONS LIVING (*By 1st marriage*)

THEODORE JONATHAN, *b* 19 Feb 1960; *ed* Lakefield College Sch, Ontario, Yale Univ (BA), and Columbia Graduate Sch of Journalism (MSc) (4012 SE 27th St, Portland, Oregon 97202, USA). —— (Roderick) Nicholas, *b* 1964; *ed* Lakefield College Sch, Ontario, Univ of Toronto (BA), and Univ of Victoria Law Sch (LLB) (54 Astley Av, Toronto, Ontario M4W 3B4, Canada).

DAUGHTER LIVING (*By 1st marriage*)

Sophia Theresa (74 Abdale Rd, W12 7EU), *b* 1963; *ed* Bishop's College Sch, Quebec.

BROTHER LIVING

John Francis (191 St George St, Toronto, Ontario, Canada M5R 2M6), *b* 1933: *m* 1st, 1963 (*m diss* 1973), Susan Jennefer, da of Peter Woodburn Blaylock, of Toad's Tooting, Ile Bizard, Quebec, Canada; 2ndly, 1983 (*m diss* 1988), Eve Napier, da of Clifford Murray, of Huntington, Quebec, Canada, and has issue living, (by 1st *m*) Adam Blaylock, *b* 1965: *m* 1993, Eva, da of Antonio Balsells, of Espluga Calba, Lerida, Catalunya, — Theodora Southam, *b* 1966: *m* 1992, James Smith, son of James Smith, of Braintree, Essex, and has issue living, James Montgomery BRINCKMAN-SMITH *b* 1993, — (by 2nd *m*) John Christian Napoleon, *b* 1985, — and further issue (by Kerry, da of Thomas Bingham, of Victoria, BC), Nigel Thomas Bingham, *b* 1988.

HALF SISTER LIVING

Theadora Elizabeth, *b* 1944: *m* 1st, 1964 (*m diss* 1976), Gerard Francis Campbell (*see* B Harlech); 2ndly, 1978, Dennis Cordell Lavarack, and has issue living, (by 1st *m*) (*see* B Harlech), — (by 2nd *m*) Milo Napoleon, *b* 1978, — Emerald Clare, *b* 1981. *Residence* – 491 Fulham Rd, SW6.

COLLATERAL BRANCH LIVING

Granddaughter of late William Henry Brinckman, son of William Edward Brinckman, RN, 3rd son of 1st baronet:—
Issue of late William Brian Brinckman, *b* 1904, *d* 1975: *m* 1937, Marjorie, da of late John Ashbrook Hughes:—
Hilary Anne, *b* 1937.

The 1st baronet whose patronymic was Broadhead, in 1842 resumed for himself and issue by Roy licence, the family name of Brinckman. He sat as MP for Yarmouth 1820-26. Sir Theodore, 2nd Baronet, sat as MP for Canterbury (*L*) 1868-74. Sir Theodore Francis, CB, 3rd Baronet, was Hon Col The Buffs and sometime Lieut-Col London Regt. Sir Theodore Ernest Warren, 4th baronet, was Major 1st Life Guards. The 5th baronet, Sir Roderick Napoleon, DSO, MC, was Col Grenadier Guards and ADC to Gov-Gen and C-in-C, Canada, and to Gov of Victoria, and was Ch of Staff, Mil Mission to Moscow 1944-45 and Head of Liaison Mission to Netherlands 1945.

BRISCO (GB) 1782, of Crofton Place, Cumberland

Sir CAMPBELL HOWARD BRISCO, 9th *Baronet*, son of late Gilfred Rimington Brisco, grandson of 3rd baronet; *b* 11 Dec 1944; *s* his cousin, Sir DONALD GILFRID, 1995: *m* 1969, Kaye Janette, da of Ewan William McFadzien, of 15 Russell St, Winton, Southland, NZ, and has issue.

𝕬rms – Argent, three greyhounds courant in pale sable. 𝕮rest – A greyhound courant sable seizing a hare proper.
Residence – 134 Park St, Winton, Southland, NZ.

SONS LIVING

KENT RIMINGTON *b* 24 Sept 1972; Marine Mechanic RNZN. —— Shannon Gregory, *b* 1974; *ed* Otago Univ, Dunedin.

DAUGHTER LIVING

Rebecca Kaye, *b* 1978.

SISTER LIVING

Rosemary Robyn, *b* 1943: *m* 1966, Peter Collin Neale, of 169 Delmonte Place, PO Box 4026, Copacabana, NSW 2251, Australia, and has issue living, Adam Hylton, *b* 1968.

DAUGHTERS LIVING OF EIGHTH BARONET

Take with a grateful hand

Barbara Ann, *b* 1946: *m* 1983, William Ian Wilson, of Lot 56 Melaleuca Drive, Lamb Island, Queensland 4184, Australia. —— Penny Christine (19 Delhi Rd, Napier, NZ) *b* 1949. —— Jill Kathleen, *b* 1952: *m* 1974, Wayne George Brunton, of 97 Awanui St, New Plymouth, NZ.

DAUGHTERS LIVING OF SEVENTH BARONET

Joan Elsie, *b* 1923: *m* 1952, F. J. A. McTague, of 33 Kennedy Rd, Napier, Hawke's Bay, New Zealand, and has issue living, Robert Howard, *b* 1953, — Richard Patrick, *b* 1957, — Steven Francis, *b* 1965. —— Oriel Patricia, *b* 1926: *m* 1st, 1950 (*m diss* 1974), James C. Waldren; 2ndly, 1975, Lt-Col Reginald Henry Spicer, MC, who *d* 19—, and has issue living, (by 1st *m*) Murray David, *b* 1951, — Christine Lesley, *b* 1953. *Residence* – 2/211 Windsor Av, Hastings, Hawke's Bay, NZ.

WIDOW LIVING OF EIGHTH BARONET

IRENE (*Dowager Lady Brisco*), only da of Henry John Gage, of Ermine Park, Brockworth, Glos: *m* 1945, Sir Donald Gilfrid Brisco, 8th Bt, who *d* 1995. *Residence* – 27a Chambers St, PO Box 8165, Havelock North, Hawkes Bay, NZ.

Sir John Brisco, 1st Bt of Crofton, was grandson of John Brisco of Crofton, descended from Isold Brisco of Brisco, who acquired the Manors of Crofton, Whinnow, and Dundraw, in right of his wife, Margaret, da of Sir John Crofton, and was great-grandson of Robert Brisco, of Brisco, Cumberland. The 5th baronet Sir Hylton Ralph Brisco, was drowned at sea on a voyage to Bombay 1922: he *m* 1st, 1904 (*m diss* 1915), Lilian Mabel, da of late James King; 2ndly, 1916, Grace *m diss* 1921, da of late Henry Vaughan.

BRISCOE (UK) 1910, of Bourn Hall, Bourn, co Cambridge

Sir JOHN GEOFFREY JAMES BRISCOE, 6th *Baronet*; *b* (*posthumous*) 4 Nov 1994; *s* his father, *Sir* (JOHN) JAMES, 1994.

Arms – Argent, two greyhounds courant sable, on a chief arched of the last two roses of the first, barbed and seeded proper. **Crest** – Upon a mount of heather proper a greyhound courant paly of twelve argent and sable. *Residence* – Hall Barn, Swainsthorpe, Norwich, Norfolk NR14 8QA.

SISTER LIVING

Amanda Mary Louise, *b* 1993.

UNCLE LIVING (*son of 4th baronet*)

EDWARD HOME, *b* 27 March 1955; *ed* Ampleforth: *m* 1st, 1979 (*m diss* 1987), Anne Mary, da of late Peter Vincent Lister, of Great Missenden, Bucks; 2ndly, 1994, Sandy Elizabeth King, 2nd da of Victor Lloyd, of Oxford, and has issue living (by 1st *m*), Guy Home Sebastian, *b* 12 Feb 1983, — Fay D'Arcy, *b* 1981. *Residence* – Ambury Farm, Barnard Gate, Oxon OX8 6XE.

AUNT LIVING (*daughter of 4th baronet*)

Diana Clare, *b* 1949. *Residence* – 124 Cholmley Gdns, Fortune Green Rd, NW6 1AA.

I perform and persevere

GREAT UNCLE LIVING (*son of 3rd baronet*)

Richard Kynaston, *b* 1914; *ed* Charterhouse, and Balliol Coll, Oxford (BA 1936, MA 1947); ACA 1940; FCA 1960; European War 1940-45 as Capt RA: *m* 1951, Margaret Hamilton, da of Sir Hugh Mallinson Rigby, 1st Bt, KCVO, FRCS. *Residence* – 12 Rosemary Court, Church Rd, Haslemere, Surrey GU27 1BH.

WIDOW LIVING OF FIFTH BARONET

FELICITY MARY (*Lady Briscoe*), eldest da of David Melville Watkinson, of Gowthorpe Manor, Swardeston, Norwich: *m* 1985, Sir (John) James Briscoe, 5th Bt, who *d* as the result of a motor accident (2 July) 1994. *Residence* – Hall Barn, Swainsthorpe, Norwich, Norfolk NR14 8QA.

COLLATERAL BRANCHES LIVING

Grandchildren of late Hugh Kynaston Briscoe, CSI, CIE (infra):—
   Issue of late John Arthur Briscoe, *b* 1925, *d* 1983: *m* 1955, Hilary Mary (who *m* 2ndly, 1990, John Willis, of 10 Bridgewater Close, Little Gaddesden, Berkhamsted, Herts HP4 1PX), da of late S. K. Shaw, of Eastbourne:—
Neil David, *b* 1956: *m* 1981, Bryony Virginia Jane, da of Sqdn Ldr Clifford Basil Warwick-Spaul, of St Vincents, Tilstock, Shropshire, and has issue living, Jenny Elise, *b* 1989, — Peta Jayne, *b* 1992, — Ella Aisling, *b* 1996. —— Andrew Mark, *b* 1960: *m* 1990, Clare Montgomery. —— Lindsay Ann, *b* 1958: *m* 1983, Timothy John Fell, of The Grange, Grange Lane, N Kelsey, Lincs LN7 6EZ.

Issue of late Hugh Kynaston Briscoe, CSI, CIE, yst son of 1st baronet, *b* 1879, *d* 1956: *m* 1919, Noel, who *d* 1971, da of late John E. Worrall, of Oxton, Birkenhead:—
Ellen Kathleen, *b* 1920: *m* 1945, Maj Anthony Stanley Purcell Jeans, TD, Wilts Regt, and has issue living, Michael Anthony Purcell, *b* 1947: *m* 1975, Christine Anne Woodley, — Jennifer Rosemary Ellen, *b* 1950: *m* 1982, Maj Peter McComas, RA. *Residence* – 35 Elizabeth Court, Crane Bridge Rd, Salisbury, Wilts SP2 7UX.

Sir John James Briscoe, 1st baronet, was High Sheriff of Cambridgeshire 1888. Sir (John) Charlton Briscoe, MD, FRCP, 3rd baronet, was a Consulting Physician to King's Coll Hospital and to Evelina Hospital for Sick Children.

RUGGLES-BRISE (UK) 1935, of Spains Hall, Finchingfield, Essex

Sir JOHN ARCHIBALD RUGGLES-BRISE, CB, OBE, TD, 2nd *Baronet*; *b* 13 June 1908; *s* his father, *Col Sir* EDWARD ARCHIBALD, MC, TD, MP, 1942; *ed* Eton; is a JP for Essex, a Freeman of Chelmsford, a former Gov of Felsted and Chigwell Schs, a KStJ, an Underwriting Member of Lloyd's, appointed Lord-Lt of Essex 1958, and Pro Chancellor of Essex Univ 1963-74; Pres Country Landowners Assocn 1958-59, and Game Fair; Chm of Standing Council of the Baronetage 1958-63 and a Church Commr 1959-65; formerly Hon Col 459th Mixed Heavy Anti-Aircraft Regt RA (TA); 1939-45 War (OBE); OBE (Mil) 1945, CB (Civil) 1958.

𝕬rms – Quarterly, 1st and 4th, gules, a cross between four mascles argent, all within a bordure sable, charged with eight quatrefoils of the second, *Brise*; 2nd and 3rd, argent, on a chevron gules, between three roses of the second, barbed, seeded, leaved and slipped proper, as many estoiles or, *Ruggles*. 𝕮rest – 1st, a demi-crocodile sable, *Brise*; 2nd, in front of twelve arrows in saltire proper, heads outwards, a tower or, inflamed proper, *Ruggles*.
Seat – Spains Hall, Finchingfield, Braintree, Essex CM7 4PF. *Club* – Carlton.

BROTHER LIVING

GUY EDWARD, TD, *b* 15 June 1914; *ed* Eton; late Capt Essex Yeo; a DL of Essex; High Sheriff 1967-68; a Member of London Stock Exchange; Consultant of Brewin Dolphin & Co (Stockbrokers) and Vice-Chm Riding for the Disabled Trust; 1939-45 War in N Africa (prisoner (Italy), escaped): *m* 1st, 1940, Elizabeth, who *d* 1988, only da of late James Knox, of Smithstone House, Kilwinning, Ayrshire; 2ndly, 1994, Christine Margaret Fothergill-Spencer, only da of late Lt John A. Fothergill, and has issue living (by 1st *m*), Timothy Edward, *b* 1945; *ed* Eton: *m* 1975, Rosemary E., yr da of J. S. Craig, of 1 Buckland Court, 37 Belsize Park, NW3 4EB, and has issue living, Archibald Edward *b* 1979, Charles Evelyn *b* 1983, Iain *b* 1989, Olivia Agnes *b* 1977, Felicity Rose *b* 1984, — James Rupert, *b* 1947; *ed* Eton, — Samuel Guy (Mill House, Little Bardfield, Essex), *b* 1956; *ed* Stowe: *m* 1979, Katharine Margaret, only da of late Brig Richard John Bishop, MBE, MC, RA (ret) (*see* V Thurso, colls), and has issue living, Edward James *b* 1985, Camilla Jane *b* 1983. *Residences* – Pitkeathly, Cole End Lane, Wimbish, Essex CB10 2UT; Ledgowan Lodge, Achnasheen, Wester Ross. *Club* – City of London.

The 1st baronet, Col Sir Edward Archibald Ruggles-Brise, MC, TD (son of Archibald Weyland Ruggles-Brise, JP, DL, of Spains Hall, Finchingfield, Essex), was Lieut-Col and Brevet Col late 104th (Essex Yeo) Brig, RA (TA), Vice-Lieut for Essex, and MP for Maldon Div of Essex (C) 1922-3 and 1924-42.

BROADBENT (UK) 1893, of Brook Street, co London, and Longwood, Yorkshire

Sir ANDREW GEORGE BROADBENT, 5th *Baronet*, *b* 26 Jan 1963; *s* his father, *Sir* GEORGE WALTER, AFC, 1992; *ed* Monkton Combe; late Capt The Prince of Wales's Own Regt of Yorkshire.

𝕬rms – Per pale ermine and azure, a fesse nebulée counter-changed, in the dexter chief quarter a caduceus erect proper. 𝕮rest – In front of a pheon the staff rompée, a serpent nowed, all proper.
Resides in Notts.

SISTER LIVING

Ione Charlotte Elizabeth, *b* 1967.

UNCLE LIVING (*brother of 4th baronet*)

ROBERT JOHN DENDY, *b* 4 Nov 1938; *ed* Stamford Sch; FRICS. *Residence* – 19 Aplin Way, Lightwater, Surrey GU18 5TT.

àiem'aqiesèteim

To excel always

WIDOWS LIVING OF THIRD AND FOURTH BARONETS

MIRANDA (*Miranda, Lady Broadbent*), 2nd da of late Donald George Pilcher-Clark, of Port St Mary, IoM: *m* 1982, as his second wife, Sir William Francis Broadbent, 3rd Bt, who *d* 1987. *Residence* –

VALERIE ANNE (*Lady Broadbent*), only da of (Cecil) Frank Ward, of York: *m* 1962, Sir George Walter Broadbent, AFC, 4th Bt, who *d* 1992. *Address* – c/o Lloyd's Bank, 2 Pavement, York YO1 2NE.

COLLATERAL BRANCH LIVING

Grandchildren of late Maj Walter Broadbent, MD, FRCP, 3rd son of 1st baronet:—
Issue of late Hubert William Lonsdale Broadbent, MB, *b* 1908, *d* 1988: *m* 1934, Marjorie, da of late Sir Arthur
Kirwan Agar, Ch Justice of British Honduras:—
Graham Agar (Blacketts End, Chalfont Lane, Chorleywood, Herts WD3 5PP), *b* 1938; *ed* Charterhouse, and Pembroke
Coll, Camb (BA): *m* 1964, (Valerie) Suzanne, elder da of Charles Edward Henry Mytton, of Hampstead Garden Suburb,
NW11, and has issue living, Charles Richard (54 Carnation Drive, Winkfield Row, Berks RG42 7QT), *b* 1968; *ed* High-
gate, and Kent Univ: *m* 1995, Angela Jane, da of Edmund Parker, of Willington, Durham, and has issue living, Emily
Marie *b* 1997, — Philip David, *b* 1972, — Juliet Fiona, *b* 1977. ——Judith Anne, *b* 1935: *m* 1960, Robin Scoones, of
Bessells Cottage, Iwerne Courtenay, Blandford Forum, Dorset, and has issue living, Ian Christopher, *b* 1962, — Simon
Richard, *b* 1964, — Timothy Graham, *b* 1967.

Sir William H. Broadbent, KCVO, MD, FRCP, hon LLD, FRS, 1st Bt, son of John Broadbent, was an eminent consulting
Physician and Physician-in-Ord to Queen Victoria, King Edward VII and the Prince of Wales. Sir John Francis Harpin
Broadbent, MD, FRCP, MRCS, 2nd Bt, was Consulting Physician to St Mary's Hospital, London Fever Hospital, and
King Edward VII Sanatorium, Midhurst.

BROCKLEBANK (UK) 1885, of Greenlands, co Cumberland and Springwood, co Lancaster

God send grace

Sir AUBREY THOMAS BROCKLEBANK, 6th *Baronet*; *b* 29 Jan 1952; *s* his
father, *Maj Sir* JOHN MONTAGUE, TD, 1974; *ed* Eton, and Univ Coll,
Durham (BSc): *m* 1st, 1979 (*m diss* 1990), Anna-Marie, da of Dr
William Dunnet, of Heroncroft, Woldingham, Surrey; 2ndly, 1997,
Hazel, yr da of Brian Roden, of Wellingborough, Northants, and has
issue by 1st *m*.

꿈rms – Argent, three brocks proper, each on a mount vert; on a chief azure as
many escallops of the first. Crest – On an anchor fessewise sable, a cock argent,
combed and wattled gules, and charged on the shoulder with an escallop of the
first.
Residence – 120 Gloucester Terrace, W2 6HP. *Club* – Brooks's.

SONS LIVING (*By 1st marriage*)

AUBREY WILLIAM THOMAS, *b* 15 Dec 1980. ——Hamish John, *b* 1987.

WIDOW LIVING OF FIFTH BARONET

PAMELA SUE (*Dowager Lady Brocklebank*), da of late William Harold Pierce, OBE, of
Bidston, Cheshire, and formerly wife of Maj Leslie Forshaw-Wilson: *m* 1950, Maj Sir
John Montague Brocklebank, TD, 5th Bt, who *d* 1974.

COLLATERAL BRANCHES LIVING

Grandchildren of late Major John Jasper Brocklebank, DSO, 2nd son of 2nd baronet:—
Issue of late Lt-Cdr John Maurice Brocklebank, RNVR, *b* 1917, *ka* 1945: *m* 1944, Evelyn Margaret, who *d* 1985,
da of Gordon Pyper, and widow of T. L. Stephenson, 2nd Lieut:—
John Daniel (7 Kitson Rd, Barnes, SW13 9HJ), *b* (*posthumous*) 1945; *ed* Eton, and Keble Coll, Oxford: *m* 1971, Donna
Jean, da of Maj Clixby Fitzwilliams, of Hazeldene, Healing, nr Grimsby, and has issue living, Daniel Maurice, *b* 1975; *ed*
Radley, and Brasenose Coll, Oxford, — Edward John, *b* 1982.

Issue of late Thomas Gordon Brocklebank, *b* 1921, *d* 1992: *m* 1st, 1952, Gillian Chester, who *d* 1966, da of late
William Francis Cardew, of Lanteglos, Eiffel Flats, S Rhodesia; 2ndly, 1970, Mrs Edith Josephine Abbott, (9
Swan Mews, Wendover, Bucks HP22 6EZ), da of late William Geoffry Ward, and widow of Neville Wells
Abbott:—
(By 1st *m*) Robin John (Budleigh, Rue Cauchez, St Martins, Guernsey GY4 6PE, CI), *b* 1954: *m* 1983, Susan Elizabeth
Coverdale, da of late Capt John Robert Hawkins Wilson, of Ruwa, Zimbabwe, and has issue living, Nicholas Gordon, *b*
1985, — Fiona Jane, *b* 1986. ——Geoffrey Cardew, *b* 1959: *m* 1993, Diana, da of Diederik Johannes Vorster, of S Africa.
——Christopher Philip, *b* 1963. ——Anne Frances, *b* 1962: *m* 1992, Andrew David Wildblood, of 6 Henshaw Way,
Yarnfield, Stone, Staffs ST15 0TY, son of late Norman Creyke Wildblood, of Kiddlestich, Uttoxeter, Staffs, and has issue
living, David George, *b* 1995, — Charles Jasper, *b* (triplet) 1995, — Louise Margaret, *b* (triplet) 1995.

Granddaughters of late Robert Allport Brocklebank, 3rd son of 2nd baronet:—
Issue of late Lt-Cmdr Oliver Brocklebank, RN, *b* 1908, *d* 1978: *m* 1st, 1931, Diana, who *d* 1994, da of late Col
Wilford Boteler, DSO, RA; 2ndly, 1947, Marjorie Joan, who *d* 1998, da of late Horace Snowling, of Gt
Yarmouth:—
(By 2nd *m*) Alison Philippa, *b* 1948: *m* 1978, Michael Thurgood, of Carrickmore, Gt Salkeld, nr Penrith, Cumbria CA11

9NA. —— Elizabeth Joanna (Redbourne, 205 Lowestoft Rd, Gorleston-on-Sea, Norfolk NR31 6SX), *b* 1950. —— Edwina Jane (Meadowland, 203 Lowestoft Rd, Gorleston-on-Sea, Norfolk NR31 6SX), *b* 1952.

Grandchildren of late Rev Charles Henry Brocklebank, 4th son of 1st baronet:—
Issue of late Charles Gerald Brocklebank, MC, *b* 1893, *d* 1940: *m* 1925, Beatrice Gresley, who *d* 1992, da of late Falconer Madan:—
Charles William (Giffords Hall, Stoke-by-Nayland, Suffolk; 17 Grosvenor Sq, W1X 9LD), *b* 1930; *ed* Eton, and Ch Ch Oxford: *m* 1965, Marcia Andrea, da of late Arthur Early, of Kalamazoo, Michigan, USA, and has issue living, James Gerald Arthur, *b* 1970: *m* 1999, Baroness Felicia, yst da of Baron van Pallandt van Westervoort, of The Netherlands, — William Falconer, *b* 1976, — Diana Lasswell, *b* 1968: *m* 1999, Anthony Craufurd Scott (*see* Bagge, Bt, colls). —— Mary, *b* 1926: *m* 1948, Michael Guy Molesworth Bevan, who *d* 1992 (*see* V Molesworth, 1931 Edn), and has issue living, Roger Anthony Briscoe, *b* 1951; *ed* Eton: *m* 1st, 1980 (*m diss* 198-), Marion Casey, da of Theodore Donahue, of Litchfield, Connecticut, USA; 2ndly, 1994, Beverly D. Anastopolis, — William George Briscoe (Longstowe Hall, Longstowe, nr Cambridge), *b* 1958: *m* 1985, Annabel Jane, da of William Bertram Weatherall, of Shorndown, Mursley, Bucks (*see* Russell, Bt, *cr* 1916, colls), and has issue living, George Michael Briscoe *b* 1988, Lucy Clare *b* 1990, Victoria Mary *b* 1993, — James Edward Briscoe (Bulby Hall, Bulby, Lincs), *b* 1960: *m* 1986, Susan Fiona, da of Victor Parker, of Appleton, Cheshire, — Penelope Anne, *b* 1955: *m* 1982, Geoffrey Thomas Carwardine Probert, of Grounds Farm, Hook Norton, Banbury, Oxon, son of Lt-Col Richard Harlackenden Probert, OBE, DL, of Bevills, Bures, Suffolk, and has issue living, Thomas Henry Carwardine *b* 1985, Jack Michael Harlackenden *b* 1993, Rebecca Mary *b* 1988, Isobel Loveday *b* 1991. *Residence* – Longstowe Hall, Longstowe, nr Cambridge CB3 7UH. —— Ann, *b* 1928.

The 1st baronet, Sir Thomas, was son of Wilson Fisher, of Keekle, Whitehaven; assumed in 1845, by Royal licence the surname of Brocklebank, on succeeding to the estate of his maternal uncle Thomas Brocklebank, of Greenlands, Cumberland, and was High Sheriff of Cumberland 1864. The 2nd baronet was High Sheriff of Lancashire 1908, and the 3rd baronet, Sir Aubrey (Chm of Thomas and John Brocklebank (Limited), and a Director of Suez Canal Co, Cunard Steamship Co (Limited), and other cos), was High Sheriff of Cumberland 1921.

BRODIE (UK) 1834, of Boxford, Suffolk

Sir (BENJAMIN) DAVID ROSS BRODIE, 5th *Baronet*; *b* 29 May 1925; *s* his father, *Sir* BENJAMIN COLLINS, MC, 1971; *ed* Eton; late Royal Signals: *m* 1956 (*m diss* 19—), Ludmilla Maria, da of August Adamer, and has issue.

𝔄rms – Azure, on a chevron between three mullets argent, three civic wreaths vert. 𝔈rest – A dexter cubit arm erect, holding a civic wreath as in the arms with three arrows, one in fesse and two in saltire points towards the dexter argent.

SON LIVING

ALAN ROSS, *b* 7 July 1960: *m* 1993, Jutta Maria, da of Alfred Johann Herrmann, of Habsburger Str, Murg, Germany.

DAUGHTER LIVING

Sonja Mary, *b* 19—: *m* 19—, C...... Fairhead, of 51 Westbourne Av, Emsworth, Chichester, W Sussex.

SISTER LIVING

Angela Mary, *b* 1933; *ed* St Andrews Univ (MA). *Residence* – Betchworth Lodge, Betchworth, Surrey.

COLLATERAL BRANCH LIVING

Issue of late Colin Alexander Brodie, QC, yr son of 4th baronet, *b* 1929, *d* 1999: *m* 1955, Julia Anne Irene (2 Stone Buildings, Lincoln's Inn, WC2A 3XB), da of late Norman E. Wates, of Elmore, Chipstead, Surrey:—
Christian Norman, *b* 1957: *m ca* 1981, Geraldine Jones, and has issue living, James Alexander, *b ca* 1985, — Benjamin Christian, *b ca* 1988, — Hugo William, *b ca* 1990. —— Alexander Colin (Squires Farm, Coldharbour, Dorking, Surrey RH4 3UJ), *b* 1959: *m* 1993, Meredith, only da of R. G. Bloore, of Orange, NSW, Australia, and has issue living, Tom, *b* 1996, — Jack, *b* 1998.

Grandson of late Capt Edgar Waldegrave Brodie, 3rd son of late Rev William Brodie, 2nd son of 1st baronet:—
Issue of late Capt Malcolm William O'Callaghan Brodie, *b* 1887, *d* 1966: *m* 1st, 1922, Phyllis Gwavas, who *d* 1940, da of Henry Tredenham Fitzherbert Carlyon; 2ndly, 1948, Sybil Barbara, da of late Henry Shearburn Clark, of Fenhill, Hawke's Bay, NZ:—
(By 1st *m*) Mark Donald Carlyon William (36 Oregon Drive, Taupo, NZ), *b* 1928: *m* 1955, Patricia Isobel, who *d* 1995, only child, of Judge Arnold Admiral Whitehead, of NZ, and has issue living, Malcolm Robert, *b* 1956: *m* 1988, Kimba

Jane Alexander, and has issue living, Thomas William Alexander *b* 1990, Anna-Kate *b* 1991, — Douglas William, *b* 1958, — Christopher Mark, *b* 1961: *m* 1996, Janet Smith, — Philip John Edgar (c/o Te-Mata Estate Winery, PO Box 8335, Havelock North, Hawkes Bay, NZ), *b* 1964: *m* 1995, Leanne Marie Corbishley Anderson, and has issue living, Benjamin James *b* 1996.

The 1st baronet, Sir Benjamin Collins Brodie, DCL, FRS, a distinguished surgeon, was Pres of Roy Soc, Serjeant-Surgeon to King William IV, and to Queen Victoria, and first Surgeon-in-Ordinary to late Prince Consort: the 2nd baronet was Waynflete Professor of Chemistry, Oxford Univ, and the 3rd baronet was High Sheriff for Surrey 1912.

BROMHEAD (UK) 1806, of Thurlby, Lincolnshire
(Name pronounced "Brumhead")

By concord property is
increased

Sir JOHN DESMOND GONVILLE BROMHEAD, 6th *Baronet*; *b* 21 Dec 1943; *s* his father, *Col Sir* BENJAMIN DENIS GONVILLE, OBE, 1981; *ed* Wellington Coll, and privately.

Arms – Azure, on a bend argent, between two leopards' faces or, a mural crown gules, between two fleurs-de-lis sable. **Crest** – Out of a mural crown gules, an unicorn's head argent, armed or, in the mouth a rose gules, slipped and leaved proper.

SISTERS LIVING

Diana Jane Gonville, *b* 1940: *m* 1966, Dr Paul Sherwood, of 2 Devonshire Place, W1, and has issue living, Robin Paul Austen, *b* 1969, — Julian George, *b* 1974. —— Anne Kathleen Gonville, *b* 1942: *m* 1965 (*m diss* 1998), Robin James German, of Thurlby Hall, Lincoln, and has issue living, Patrick Benjamin James, *b* 1967, — Robin Piers Gonville, *b* 1969, — Alexander Henry Bromhead, *b* 1971.

WIDOW LIVING OF FIFTH BARONET

NANCY MARY (*Lady Bromhead*) (Thurlby Hall, Lincoln), da of late Thomas Seon Lough, of Buenos Aires, Argentina: *m* 1938, Col Sir Benjamin Denis Gonville Bromhead, 5th Bt, OBE, who *d* 1981.

COLLATERAL BRANCHES LIVING

Grandchildren of late Maj Edward Gonville Bromhead, el son of 4th baronet:—
Issue of late Lt-Col Edmund de Gonville Hosking Bromhead, *b* 1903, *d* 1976: *m* 1938, Joan, who *d* 1997, da of late Brig Sir Henry Lawrence Scott, CB, DSO, MC:—
JOHN EDMUND DE GONVILLE (Duiker House, Fencott, Islip, Oxford), *b* 10 Oct 1939; *ed* St Andrew's Coll, Grahamstown, S Africa, and RAF Coll, Cranwell; Capt British Airways: *m* 1965, Janet Frances, da of Henry Brotherton, of Moreton-in-Marsh, Glos, and has issue living, Alistair John de Gonville, *b* 1969, — Amanda-Jane de Gonville, *b* 1965. —— David de Gonville, CBE, LVO, *b* 1944; *ed* St Andrew's, S Africa, and RMA; Lt-Col R Regt of Wales, Brig 1991; Gen Ser Medal (Clasps), S Arabia and NI; Equerry to HRH The Prince of Wales 1982-84; Freeman of the Bezirk of Wilmersdorf 1993; LVO 1984, OBE (Mil) 1988, CBE (Mil) 1994: *m* 1970, Susan, da of Cdr Richard Furley Fyson, DSC, JP, RN, and has issue living, James Henry de Gonville, *b* 1974, — Annabel Suzanne de Gonville, *b* 1973, — Antonia Diana de Gonville, *b* 1978. —— Jacqueline Anne Gonville, *b* 1942: *m* 1971, James Boonzaier (7 Ngaio Rd, Kelburn, Wellington 5, NZ), and has issue living, Ann Maria Gonville, *b* 1977, — Julia Gonville, *b* 1979.

Issue of late Major Benjamin Gonville Bromhead, 2nd son of 4th baronet, *b* 1876, *d* 1939: *m* 1912, Edith Maud, who *d* 1975, da of late Lt-Col R. C. Andrews, Indian Army:—
Kathleen Constance, *b* 1915: *m* 1941, Lt-Col Cyril Frederick Hembrough Walter, Indian Army, of 5 St Mary's Close, Chitterne, Warminster, Wilts, and has issue living, Jonathan, *b* 1944.

Anthony Bromhead of Wheatley, Notts, supported Charles I and was killed at Newark. His el son Benjamin purchased Thurlby and Bassingham manors, Lincs and *d* 1702. Bordman Bromhead of Thurlby *m* 1756, Frances, da and heir of William Gonville, last male heir of family whose ancestor, Edmund de Gonville founded Gonville Hall (now Gonville and Caius Coll), Camb, 1348. Their son, Lt-Gen Sir Gonville Bromhead, was the 1st baronet.

BROMLEY (GB) 1757, of East Stoke, Nottinghamshire

Sir RUPERT CHARLES BROMLEY, 10th *Baronet; b* 2 April 1936; *s* his father, *Maj Sir* RUPERT HOWE, MC, 1966; *ed* Michaelhouse, Natal, Rhodes Univ, and Ch Ch, Oxford; Bar Inner Temple 1959: *m* 1962, Priscilla Hazel, da of late Maj Howard Bourne, HAC, and has issue.

Arms – Quarterly, per fesse indented gules and or. **Crest** – a pheasant sitting proper.
Residence – PO Box 249, Rivonia 2128, Gauteng, S Africa.

SONS LIVING

CHARLES HOWARD, *b* 31 July 1963: *m* 1998, Marie, 2nd da of W. J. Taylor, of Knysna, S Africa, and has issue living, Robert Charles, *b* 12 Feb 1999. —— Philip Anthony, *b* 1964: *m* 1994, Carole Frances, yr da of Gerard Damp, of Malmesbury, CP, S Africa. —— Henry Walford, *b* 1970.

BROTHER LIVING

Maurice David (50/1 Tambon Sanna Maeng, Amphur Sansai, Chiangmai 50200, Thailand), *b* 1941: *m* 1st, 1965 (*m diss* 1984), Heather Mary Estcourt-Cutter; 2ndly, 1985, Renita Lopez Amador, and has issue living (by 1st *m*), Caroline Margaret, *b* 1966: *m* 19—, George Francisco Ramirez de Arellano (88 St Martin St, Valle Verde 1, Pasig, M Manila, Philippines), and has issue living, Patricia Teresa *b* 1993, Jacquelyn Nichole *b* 1995, — Jennifer Mary, *b* 1968: *m* 19—, Albert Choco Aguirre, and has issue living, Colin Michael Smith *b* 1991, Agustus Albert *b* 1993, — (by 2nd *m*) Robert Howe, *b* 1986.

Think firmly

PENSEZ FORTE

DAUGHTER LIVING OF EIGHTH BARONET

Elizabeth Mary (*Lady Collins*), *b* 1919: *m* 1st, 1940, 6th Baron Sudeley, who was *ka* 1941; 2ndly, 1965, Maj Sir Arthur James Robert Collins, KCVO, of Kirkman Bank, Knaresborough, N Yorks HG5 9BT.

The 1st baronet, Sir George Smith, married Mary Howe, great-granddaughter of Prince Rupert. Lord Carrington is descended from a yr brother of the first baronet. Sir George Bromley, 2nd Bt, assumed by sign-manual in 1778, the name of Bromley in lieu of his patronymic. Sir Robert Bromley, 6th Bt, was Administrator of St Kitts and Nevis. Sir Maurice Bromley-Wilson, 7th Bt was High Sheriff of Westmorland 1901, and assumed by Roy licence 1897 the additional surname and arms of Wilson. Rear-Adm Sir Arthur Bromley, KCMG, KCVO, 8th baronet, was a Gentleman Usher to HM 1927-61, and Ceremonial and Reception Sec, Dominion and Colonial Office 1931-53.

BROOKE (E) 1662, of Norton Priory, Cheshire

Sir RICHARD DAVID CHRISTOPHER BROOKE, 11th *Baronet; b* 23 Oct 1938; *s* his father, *Sir* RICHARD NEVILLE, 1997; *ed* Eton; *m* 1st, 1963 (*m diss* 1978), Carola Marion, el da of Sir Robert Erskine Hill, 2nd Bt; 2ndly, 1979, Lucinda, only da of John Frederick Voelcker, of Happy Hill, Lidgetton, Natal, and formerly wife of William Barlow, and has issue by 1st *m*.

Arms – Or, a cross engrailed per pale gules and sable. **Crest** – A brock, or badger, passant proper.
Residence – The Manor House, Cholderton, Salisbury, Wilts SP4 0DW.

SONS LIVING (*By 1st marriage*)

(RICHARD) CHRISTOPHER *b* 10 July 1966; *m* 1995, Sophie L., elder da of Michael Scott, of Sutton-cum-Lound, Notts, and has issue living, Tabitha Elizabeth, *b* 1996. —— Edward Marcus, *b* 1970: *m* 1995, Catherine J., only da of Peter Richard Corbett, of Dene House, Bluley, St Mary Bourne, Hants, and has issue living, Thomas Michael, *b* 1998.

BROTHER LIVING

Piers Leighton (37 Yeomans Row, SW3), *b* 1940; *ed* Eton: *m* 1967, Susan, da of John Davenport, of New York City, and has issue living, Sebastian Piers, *b* 1974,

—— Arabella Elinor, *b* 1973.

FASTE WITHOUT FRAUDE

WIDOW LIVING OF TENTH BARONET

JEAN EVISON (*Jean, Lady Brooke*), da of late Lt-Col Arthur Cecil Corfe, DSO, and formerly wife of Sir Nicolas John Cheetham, KCMG; *m* 1960, as his 2nd wife, Sir Richard Brooke, 10th Bt, who *d* 1997. *Residence* – 34 Sloane Court West, Flat 14, SW3 4TB.

COLLATERAL BRANCHES LIVING

Grandchildren of late Victor Alexander Brooke, 4th son of 7th baronet:—
Issue of late Victor James Brooke, *b* 1899, *d* 1976: *m* 1927, Doris Isabella, who *d* 1971, da of late John Bull Ware:—
Bladen James (107 Hillvue Rd, Tamworth, NSW 2340, Australia), *b* 1928; a JP; Alderman, Tamworth City Council 1987-: *m* 1958, Adeline Ruth, da of Kenneth Field Clemson, JP, of Wyndella, Collarenebri, NSW, and has issue living, Daron James Clemson, *b* 1964: *m* 1992, Cherelle Kay, da of Phillip Corbett, of Sydney, and has issue living, Morgan Alexander *b* 1995, — Kim Anabel, *b* 1959: *m* 1980, John Francis Mannion, JP, of 7 Mataro Av, Muswellbrook, NSW 2333, Australia, eldest son of William Mannion, of Tamworth, NSW, and has issue living, Elissa Jane *b* 1982, Rebekah Anne *b* 1983, — Anthea Kay, *b* 1960: *m* 1989, Scott Robert Hamilton, of 13 Marshall Rd, Dundas, NSW 2117, Australia, only son of William Robert Hamilton, of Melbourne, and has issue living, Luke Bladen William *b* 1994, Samantha Nichole Brooke *b* 1990.

Issue of late Reginald Marcus Brooke, *b* 1905, *d* 1980: *m* 1st, 1927, Beth Allender, who *d* 1957, da of Andrew John Telfer; 2ndly, 19—, Dulcie Louise (11 Hill St, Port Macquarie, NSW, Australia), da of late Joseph Arnold, of George St, Inverell, NSW:—
(By 1st *m*) Peter Brabazon (40 Sullaroop St, Duffy, ACT 2611, Australia), *b* 1929; is a JP: *m* 1954, Beverley Elizabeth, only da of Francis William George Vincent, of 14 Virginia St, N Wollongong, NSW, and has issue living, Victor Garry, *b* 1956. —— Donald John (Brisbane, Queensland, Australia), *b* 1932. —— Lynton Marcus (21 Maxwell Brown Drive, Southport, Queensland, Australia), *b* 1933: *m* 1st, 1956 (*m diss* 1960), Wendy Vida, only da of late David Arthur Kenneth Miller, of 84 Midson Rd, Epping; 2ndly, 196-, Eileen Adele, da of William Henry Humphreys, of 5 Linda St, Sherwood, Queensland, and has issue living, (by 2nd *m*) Stephen Mark, *b* 1963, — Lynda Kay, *b* 1961, *m* 1st, 19—, Stephen Williams; 2ndly, 19—, Allan Hector McEwan McKay, and has issue living, (by 1st *m*) Danielle Anita Virginia *b* 1981, — Stacey Ann, *b* (twin) 1963. —— Richard Michael, *b* 1937: *m* 1959, Lena Hazel Maureen Childs, and has issue living, Richard George, *b* 1968, — Louise Kate, *b* 1965. —— Pamela Elizabeth, *b* 1935: *m* 1st, 1953 (*m diss* 19—), Anthony John Glasgow; 2ndly, 1962, Grahame Vance Baillie, of 24 Kennedy St, Appin, NSW, Australia, and has issue living, (by 1st *m*) Peter John, *b* 1954: *m* 1972, Carol Anne Gilliver, and has issue living, Malcolm Ian BAILLIE *b* 1981, Cathryn Jane BAILLIE *b* 1978, Rebecca Anne BAILLIE *b* 1980, — Denise Beth, *b* 1957: *m* 1988, Geoffrey John Reeve-Parker, and has issue living, Camilla Brooke *b* 1982, Parissa *b* 1986, — Ruth Elizabeth, *b* 1959.

The 1st baronet, Sir Henry Brooke, was four times appointed Sheriff of Cheshire by the Parliamentarians. The 2nd baronet, Sir Richard, was Sheriff of the same co 1667. The 3rd baronet, Sir Thomas, was Gov of Chester Castle during the greater part of Queen Anne's reign.

BROOKE (UK) 1903, of Summerton, Castleknock, co Dublin

Glory, the end

Sir FRANCIS GEORGE WINDHAM BROOKE, 4th *Baronet*; *b* 15 Oct 1963; *s* his father, *Maj Sir* GEORGE CECIL FRANCIS, MBE, 1982; *ed* Eton, and Edinburgh Univ (MA): *m* 1989, Hon Katharine Elizabeth Hussey, only da of Baron Hussey of North Bradley (Life Baron), and has issue.

𝕬rms – Or, a cross engrailed per pale gules and sable, in dexter canton a crescent of the second, and in sinister canton a martlet of the third, for difference. 𝕮rest – A badger passant proper, charged with a crescent and a martlet gules.
Residence – 65 Sterndale Rd, W14 0HU. *Club* – White's, Turf.

SON LIVING

GEORGE FRANCIS GEOFFREY, *b* 10 Sept 1991.

DAUGHTERS LIVING

Olivia Nancy, *b* 1994. —— Sarah Mary, *b* 1996.

SISTER LIVING

Emma Nancy, *b* 1965: *m* 1993, Charles C. Thompson, only son of S/Ldr James Thompson, of Mijas, Spain, and has issue living, a son, *b* 1995. *Residence* – 28 Irene Rd, SW6 4AP.

WIDOW LIVING OF THIRD BARONET

Lady MELISSA EVA CAROLINE WYNDHAM-QUIN (*Lady Melissa Brooke*), el da of 6th Earl of Dunraven and Mount-Earl: *m* 1959, Maj Sir George Cecil Francis Brooke, MBE, 3rd Bt, who *d* 1982. *Residence* – Glenbevan, Croom, co Limerick.

COLLATERAL BRANCHES LIVING

Issue of late George Brooke, Lt Irish Gds, el son of 1st baronet, *b* 1877, *ka* 1914: *m* 1907, Nina, who *d* 1970, da of late Rt Hon Lord Arthur William Hill (M Downshire, colls):—
Nancy Myra, *b* 1911: *m* 1st, 1931 (*m diss* 1934), John Hollingworth Roberts; 2ndly, 1941, Capt Charles Michael Stratton, who *d* 1991, of Moss Cottage, 48 High St, Croughton, Brackley, Northants, and has issue living, (by 2nd *m*) Patrick Michael (5 Maple Close, Alresford, Hants SO24 9JF), *b* 1945: *m* 1992, Miriam, da of David Anderson, of 3 Pine Walk, Liss Forest, Liss, Hants, and has issue living, Luke Nicholas *b* 1994, Adam Neil *b* 1996, — Juliet Nina, *b* 1942: *m* 1973, John William Clark-Maxwell, of Speddoch, Dumfries-shire, and has issue living, James Michael Gilchrist *b* 1975; assumed the addl forename of Gilchrist by deed poll 1990, Alice Louise *b* 1979.

Issue of late Capt John Brooke, DSC, RN (ret), 6th son of 1st baronet, *b* 1887, *d* 1974: *m* 1918, Margaret Winifred, MBE, only da of late Col Francis Tothill, RA, of Roseneath, Fareham:—
Geoffrey Arthur George, DSC, (Beech House, Balcombe, Sussex RH17 6PS), *b* 1920; *ed* RNC, Dartmouth; Lt-Cdr RN (ret); 1939-45 War in Europe and Far East (DSC, Atlantic Star, Mediterranean star, Pacific star): *m* 1956, Venetia Mabel, only da of late Capt Hon Oswald Wykeham Cornwallis, OBE, RN (ret) (*see* B Cornwallis, colls), and has issue living, Caroline Jane, *b* 1957: *m* 1989 (*m diss* 1992), Barry Rudolf, of Santa Fé, New Mexico, — Venetia Anne Margaret, *b* 1959, — Georgina Emily Rose, *b* 1963: *m* 1st, 1986, Lanto Millington Synge, eldest son of late John Samuel Synge, of Mill Grange, Ballinglen, co Wicklow; 2ndly, 1993, Michael Paul Boulter Bochmann, of The Barns, Ford, Glos, son of late Martin Paul Bochmann.

Issue of late Basil Gerald Brooke, 7th son of 1st baronet, *b* 1894, *d* 1969: *m* 1919, Essex Vere, who *d* 1996, aged 105, da of late Charles Vere Gunning, CB, CMG, 7th Bt:—
Henry Arthur Gunning, MC (23 Halsey St, SW3; Cavalry and Guards' Club), *b* 1923; *ed* Winchester; Col 16th/5th The Queens R Lancers 1980-85; Lt-Col Comdg 16th/5th The Queens R Lancers 1966-69; 1939-45 War in Tunisia and Italy (MC).

This family is a branch of the family of Viscount Brookeborough (of Colebrooke, co Fermanagh). The 1st baronet, Sir George Frederick was a Director (sometime Gov) of the Bank of Ireland, over 50 years head of the late firm of George F. Brooke and Son, wine merchants, of Dublin, and High Sheriff for co Wexford 1882, and for co Dublin 1898.

BROOKE (UK) 1919, of Almondbury, West Riding of Yorkshire

Sir ALISTAIR WESTON BROOKE, 4th *Baronet*; *b* 12 Sept 1947; *s* his father, *Maj Sir* JOHN WESTON, 1983; *ed* Repton, and RAC Cirencester: *m* 1982, Susan Mary, only da of Barry Griffiths, of Church House, Norton, Powys, and has issue.

Arms – Argent, a cross nebulée per pale gules and sable, in the first and fourth quarters a boar's head erased of the last. Crest – In front of a sword erect, the blade entwined by two serpents respecting each other proper, a boar's head erased sable.
Seat – Fearn Lodge, Ardgay, Ross-shire.
Residence – Wootton Farm, Pencombe, Hereford.

DAUGHTER LIVING

Lorna Rosemary Weston, *b* 1983.

BROTHER LIVING

CHARLES WESTON (Midfearn, Ardgay, Ross-shire IV24 3DL) *b* 27 Jan 1951; *ed* Repton: *m* 1984, Tanya Elizabeth, da of Antony Thelwell Maurice, of Lloran, Robertson, NSW, Australia, and has issue living, John Weston, *b* 23 Feb 1992, — Nicola Margery, *b* 1985, — Emily Grace, *b* 1988.

AUNTS LIVING (*Daughters of 2nd baronet*)

Elizabeth Jean, *b* 1910: *m* 1939, Lt-Cdr Malcolm Buist, RN, who *d* 1965, and has issue living, Elizabeth Mary, *b* 1944: *m* 19—, — Jane Christine, *b* 1947.
—— Hazel Mary, *b* 1918: *m* 1942, Maj John Alexander Lochore, Seaforth Highlanders, who was *ka* 1944, son of Sir James Lochore, and has issue living, Hamish John (Burgie House, Forres, Moray), *b* 1943; late Capt R Scots Greys; DL Moray 19—: *m* 1970, Pollyann Elise, da of Lt-Col Hon David Edward Hely-Hutchinson (*see* E Donoughmore), and has issue living, Alexander David *b* 1971, Hugh Mark *b* 1974, Clare Hermione *b* 1977, — Fiona Margery, *b* 1945: *m* 1971, Lt-Cdr Ian Patrick Forbes Meiklejohn, RN, of Forres, Moray, and has issue living, James Forbes *b* 1976, Clodagh Kirsteen *b* 1974. *Residence* – Blervie, by Forres, Moray.

Sir John Arthur Brooke, 1st baronet, was a Director of John Brooke and Sons (Limited), of Armitage Bridge, Huddersfield, a JP, and Chm York House of Laymen, Maj Sir John Weston Brooke, 3rd Bt, was a JP and DL for Ross-shire.

BROOKSBANK (UK) 1919, of Healaugh Manor, Healaugh, West Riding of Yorkshire

Sir (EDWARD) NICHOLAS BROOKSBANK, 3rd *Baronet*; *b* 4 Oct 1944; *s* his father, *Lt-Col Sir* (EDWARD) WILLIAM, TD, JP, DL 1983; *ed* Eton; Capt The Blues and Royals: *m* 1970, Hon Emma Myrtle Mary Anne Wood, only da of Baron Holderness, PC (Life Baron), and has issue.

𝕬rms – Azure, two bars wavy argent within a bordure or. 𝕮rest – A white hart's head couped proper, attired or, accolled with two bars wavy azure. *Seat* – Ryton Grange, Malton, N Yorks.

SON LIVING

FLORIAN TOM CHARLES, *b* 9 Aug 1982.

DAUGHTER LIVING

Victoria Mary Grania, *b* 1985.

WIDOW LIVING OF SECOND BARONET

ANN (*Ann, Lady Brooksbank*), da of Lt-Col Thomas Claud Clitherow, DSO, of Hotham Hall, Brough, Yorks: *m* 1943, Lt-Col Sir Edward William Brooksbank, 2nd Bt, who *d* 1983. *Residence* – Menethorpe Hall, Malton, N Yorkshire.

COLLATERAL BRANCH LIVING

Issue of late Lt-Col Edward York Brooksbank, 2nd son of 1st baronet, *b* 1888; *d* 1935: *m* 1912, Hazel, who *d* 1968, da of late Henry Brockholes Thomas, of Scaftworth Hall, Yorks:—
Stamp Godfrey (45 Cedar Lodge, Lythe Hill Park, Haslemere, Surrey), *b* 1922; *ed* Eton; 1939-45 War with Coldstream Gds: *m* 1st, 1942, Celia Dorothy, who *d* 1996, da of late Maj Hon Sir John Spencer Coke, KCVO (*see* E Leicester, colls, 1995 Edn); 2ndly, 1996, Mrs Pauline E. Harrington, da of late Walter Leslie Burt, of Steyning, W Sussex, and has issue living (by 1st *m*), David William, *b* 1946; *ed* Eton: *m* 1972, Vanessa, el da of late Kenneth A. Whittome, and has issue living, Scott William *b* 1976, Charles Henry *b* 1979, Anna Louise *b* 1984, — George Edward Hugh, *b* 1949; *ed* Eton: *m* 1985, Nicola, yr da of Michael Newton, of Balcombe, Sussex, and has issue living, Jack *b* 1986, Thomas *b* 1988. —— Diana Hazel, *b* 1914: *m* 1st, 1936, Robert Froude Norton, who *d* 1966; 2ndly, 1972, George Milford-Cottam, of Barn Acre, Stream Rd, Upton, Didcot, Oxon OX11 9JG. —— Crystal Elizabeth, *b* 1924: *m* 1st, 1946 (*m diss* 1960), Henry Desmond Verner Pakenham, CBE (*see* E Longford, colls); 2ndly, 1960, Ivor George Salmond, OBE, who *d* 1981; 3rdly, 19—, Vere Tweedie, of West Green Cottage, West Green Common, Hartley Wintney, Hook, Hants RG27 8JF, and has issue living (by 1st *m*) (*see* E Longford, colls), — (by 2nd *m*), Felicity Diana, *b* 1962: *m* 1990, Christopher Edward Delaval Stonehill, of 44 Westover Rd, Wandsworth, SW18 2RH, and has issue living, Edward Ivor Christopher *b* 1994, Rupert David Thoroton *b* 1996, Lydia Cressida *b* 1999.

The 1st baronet, Sir Edward Clitherow Brooksbank (son of late Edward Brooksbank of Healaugh Manor, Tadcaster, and Newton House, Whitby), was Chm of Barkston Ash Conservative Assoc for over 40 years.

BROUGHTON (E) 1660, of Broughton, Staffordshire
(Name pronounced "Brawton")

Sir DAVID DELVES BROUGHTON, 13th *Baronet; b* 7 May 1942; son of late Lt Cdr Peter John Delves Broughton, RN (by his 1st wife, Nancy Rosemary, who *d* 1960, da of late J. E. Paterson), only son of late Lt-Col Geoffrey Delves Broughton, OBE, yr son of late Lt-Col Delves Broughton, only son of late Rev Delves Broughton, 2nd son of 8th baronet; *s* his kinsman, *Sir* EVELYN DELVES, 1993; craftsman: *m* 1969, Diane, who *d* 19—, da of Ronald Lindsay Nicol, of Victoria, Australia; has issue.

𝕬rms – Argent, two bars gules, on a canton of the second a cross of the field.
𝕮rest – A sea-dog's head couped gules, finned argent.
Residence – 31 Mayfield Court, Sandy, Beds SG19 1NF.

DAUGHTER LIVING (*by Hildegard Weitzel*)

Jennifer Zoë WEITZEL, *b* 1977.

HALF-BROTHER LIVING

GEOFFREY DELVES (140 Claremore Av, Scarborough, Ontario, Canada M1N 3S4), *b* 1962: *m* 1986, Karen Louise, da of Samuel Wright, of Toronto, Ontario, and has issue living, Peter Thomas Delves, *b* 16 Aug 1991, — Christopher James Delves, *b* 1997, — Kathryn Louise Delves, *b* 1988, — Jennifer Anne Delves, *b* 1989.

HALF-SISTERS LIVING

Susan Delves, *b* 1950: *m* 1970, Clyde Charles Victor Dimmell, of 60 Manning Cres, Newmarket, Ontario, Canada, and has issue living, Scott Peter, *b* 1971, — Christopher Jason, *b* 1977, — Mark Clyde, *b* 1978, — Jason Geoffrey, *b* 1979. —— Patricia Delves, *b* 1953: *m* 1982, William Henry Mair. —— Shelagh Delves (5 Rosehill Ave No 502, Toronto, Ontario, Canada), *b* 1959.

AUNTS DECEASED (*daughters of late Lt-Col Geoffrey Delves Broughton, OBE, Welch Regt*)

Elizabeth Jane Delves, *b* 1918: *m* 1st, 1940, Lieut Bernard Willoughby, RN, who *d* on active ser 1942 (*see* B Middleton, colls, 1942 Edn); 2ndly, 1943, S/Ldr Anthony Pim, RAF, who was *k* in action 1945; 3rdly, 1948, Kenneth Phillips, who *d* 1950; 4thly, Capt (Arthur Bernard) Bruce Clark, RN, of The Lorne, 57 Newland, Sherborne, Dorset DT9 3JG, and *d* 1992, leaving issue (by 2nd *m*), Rosemary Jane Delves, *b* 1943: *m* 1966, Lt-Cmdr William John Henry Eustace, RN (ret), of Ferney Hill, Coombe Green, Birtsmorton, nr Malvern, Worcs WR13 6AN, — (by 4th *m*), Michael Anthony (11 Bristow Rd, Hounslow, Middx TW3 1UP), *b* 1952; *ed* Clifton, and Bristol Univ: *m* 1983 (*m diss* 1986), Sharon, da of William Jones. —— Ann Joan Delves, *b* 1922: *m* 1st, 1942 (*m diss* 1943), Frederick P. Lansdell, Lieut RA; 2ndly, 1959, Arthur Kent, and *d* 1991, leaving issue (by 1st *m*), Brian *b* 1942, — (by 2nd *m*), Bruce, *b* 1960, — David, *b* (twin) 1960, — Andrew, *b* 1964, — Elizabeth, *b* 1962.

DAUGHTERS LIVING OF TWELFTH BARONET

Isabella Delves, *b* 1958; *ed* Heathfield, and Columbia Univ, New York; Fashion Editor and Director (*American Vogue, The Tatler, British Vogue, The Sunday Times*); Memb Rare Breeds Soc, and Farming Wildlife Advisory Group (Glos Branch): *m* 1st, 1981 (*m diss* 1983), Nicholas Taylor, of USA; 2ndly, 1989, Detmar Hamilton Lorenz Arthur Blow (*see* B Tollemache, colls), of 5 Theed St, SE1 8ST, and Hilles, Edge, Stroud, Glos GL6 6NW. —— Julia Helen Delves, *b* 1961. —— Lavinia Mary Delves, *b* 1965: *m* 1st, 1985, Douglas Gerald Dawes, who *d* 1989, yst son of Cdr Michael Dawes, RN; 2ndly, 1992, as his 2nd wife, Harry George Vivian Verney (*see* Verney, Bt, *cr* 1818, colls), of The Old Forge, Ewen, Cirencester, Glos, and has issue living (by 1st *m*), Frederick Evelyn, *b* 1988, — Rosamond Esmé, *b* 1985, — (by 2nd *m*) (*see* Verney, Bt, *cr* 1818, colls).

DAUGHTER LIVING OF ELEVENTH BARONET

Rosamond (*Lady Lovat*), *b* 1917: *m* 1938, Brig 15th Lord Lovat, DSO, MC, TD, who *d* 1995. *Residence* – Balblair House, Beauly, Inverness-shire.

STEPMOTHER LIVING

Evelyn Gunn (6061 Yonge St, Suite 1504, Willowdale, Ontario, Canada), da of late J. G. Sutherland: *m* 1948, as his 2nd wife, Lt Cdr Peter John Delves Broughton, RN, who *d* 1963.

WIDOW LIVING OF TWELFTH BARONET

RONA (*Dowager Lady Delves Broughton*), da of Ernest Clifford Johns, of Wargrave, and formerly wife of Donald Ian Crammond; Member of Ruling Council of Lloyd's of London 1991-97 and since 1999, Member of Regulatory Board 1993-98: *m* 1974, as his 3rd wife, Sir Evelyn Delves Broughton, 12th Bt, who *d* 1993. *Residences* – 37 Kensington Square, W8; Doddington Park, Nantwich, Cheshire.

COLLATERAL BRANCHES LIVING

Grandsons of late Vernon Delves Broughton, eldest son of late Rev Thomas Delves Broughton, elder son of late Thomas Delves Broughton, 3rd son of 6th baronet:—
Issue of late Vernon Warburton Delves Broughton, *b* 1864, *d* 1936: *m* 1899, Frangiski, who *d* 1957, da of late Epamenondas da Ponte, of Cephalonia, Greece:—
James Epamenondas, *b* 1916; BScEng: *m* 1st, 1945, Iris Evelyn Grace, who *d* 1959, da of late Joseph Jameson, of Wembley; 2ndly, 1962, Jean Margaret, da of late Arthur Williams, of Caerleon, Wales, and has issue living (by 1st *m*), Roger Vernon (Plas Cottage, Llanarmon-yn-Ial, Mold, Clwyd), *b* 1949, — Evelyn Rosemary, *b* 1947: *m* 1975, Anthony Dacres Symes, of 10 Hanover St, Bath, Avon, and has issue living, David Matthew Trenchard *b* 1976, Anna Louisa Trenchard *b* 1979, — (by 2nd *m*) Nicolas Charles Warburton, *b* 1969: *m* 1997, Emma, da of late Pawel Antoni Botor, of Bath, — Sonia Francesca, *b* 1967: *m* 1992, Alistair McLay, and has issue living, Fiona Margaret *b* 1989, Shona Catherine *b* 1992. *Residence* – Moynes Court, Mathern, Chepstow, Mon NP16 6HZ. —— Paul Nicholas, *b* 1916 (twin): *m* 1948, Joyce, who *d* 1984, da of late Eric Francis Duckham, and has issue living, Jonathan (The Dairy House, Ryme Intrinseca, Yetminster, Dorset DT9 6JX), *b* 1949: *m* 1972, Susan Elizabeth, da of Donald Marston, of 12 Donstan Rd, Highbridge, Som, and has issue living, Alexander Paul *b* 1981, Kathryne Alice *b* 1978, Anne Elizabeth *b* 1984. *Residence* – 1 College View, Fore St, Kingswear, Devon.

Grandson of late Brig Theodore Delves Broughton (infra):—
Issue of late Brian Charles Delves Broughton, *b* 1903, *d* 1976: *m* 1931, Margaret Gwenda, who *d* 1991, da of late Edmund Law:—
Rev Simon Brian Hugo (Christ Church Vicarage, 3 Christ Church Rd, Northampton), *b* 1933; *ed* Marlborough, and Exeter Coll, Oxford (MA): *m* 1971, Tin Tin Mar Marcia Patricia, da of U Ni, of Burma, and has issue living, Philip Andrew, *b* 1972; 2nd Queen's Chorister of St George's Chapel, Windsor, 1981, Head Chorister 1985; *ed* Eton (scholar), and New Coll, Oxford.

Granddaughter of late Cdr Cecil Delves Broughton, RN, 3rd son of late Rev Thomas Delves Broughton (ante):—
Issue of late Brigadier Theodore Delves Broughton, *b* 1872, *d* 1944: *m* 1st, 1897, Marion Julia, who *d* 1905, da of late Charles Augustus Theodore Bouwens; 2ndly, 1908, Eva Joanna, who *d* 1959, el da of Col John Warre Sill (Sutton, Bt colls):—
(By 1st *m*) Diana Sill, *b* 1920.

Granddaughters of late Col John Delves Broughton, son of late Gen William Edward Delves Broughton, yr son of late Thomas Delves Broughton (ante):—
Issue of late Brian Delves Broughton, *b* 1879, *d* 1926: *m* 1912, Elizabeth Annie, da of H. K. Osborn, of Lady-smith, Natal:—
Cecilia Dorothy, *b* 1913: *m* 1938, Major Guise Montgomery Foxton Beaumont, ED, and has issue living, Michael Foxton (9 Leicester St, Grahamstown, Cape, S Africa), *b* 1939: *m* 1966, Marion Egerton, da of B. E. B. White, of Glen Cliff, Bedford, Cape, S Africa, and has issue living, Warrick Foxton *b* 1967, Bruce Egerton *b* 1969, — Keith Alan (PO Box 152, Alice 5700, S Africa), *b* 1945: *m* 1969, Lynda Jean, yst da of C. W. Giles, of Pietermaritzburg, Natal, and has issue living, Gavin Guise *b* 1970, Stephen John *b* 1972. *Address* – Brookshaw Home, Box 454, Grahamstown, Cape, S Africa. —— Joan Christine, *b* 1916: *m* 1942, Leonard Newnham Malyon, who *d* 1983, and has issue living, Rodney Charles, *b* 1956, — Sandra Ellen, *b* 1944: *m* 1st, 1969, Sinclair Stanley Blunden, who *d* (April) 1980; 2ndly, (Oct) 1980, Herbert Graham Roslyn Smith, and has issue living, (by 1st *m*) Merle Iris *b* 1970, Fiona Joan *b* 1973, Lynda Joy *b* 1975.

Granddaughters of late Capt Henry Douglas Delves Walthall, OBE, 3rd son of late Edward Walthall Delves Walthall, only son of late Edward Delves Broughton, son of late Edward Delves Broughton, 5th son of 6th baronet:—
Issue of late Capt Leigh Edward Delves WALTHALL, CBE, DSC, RN, *b* 1914, *d* 1996: *m* 1951, Dorothy Margaret (Hill House Farm, Sapperton, Cirencester, Glos), elder da of late Hugh Robert Leonard, of Ladywalk, Heronsgate, Herts:—
Fiona Ann, *b* 1953. —— Louisa Delves, *b* 1956: *m* 1977, Lt-Col Rodney Crisp, OBE, Intelligence Corps, and has issue living, Dominic John, *b* 1981, — Charles Edward Delves, *b* 1986, — Joanna Margaret Delves, *b* 1984. —— Theodora Serena Delves, *b* 1959: *m* 1990, David Ian Jones.

The annals of this old Staffordshire family extend to *temp* Henry VI. Thomas Broughton, who *d* in 1648, was fined 3200*l* by the sequestrators, for his loyalty to King Charles I. His eldest son Brian was *cr* a baronet by King Charles II, immediately after the Restoration, in recognition of his support for the Royalist cause. Sir Brian Broughton 3rd Bt, was MP for Newcastle 1715-24. He *m* 1710, Elizabeth, only da and sole heir of Sir Thomas Delves, 3rd Bt, of Doddington, co Chester. The 4th baronet, their son, who *s* also to the Doddington Estates in Cheshire, assumed the additional name of Delves, in compliance with the terms of his grandfather's will. The 6th Bt was High Sheriff of Staffordshire in 1740, and the 9th in 1859.

BROUN (NS) 1686, of Colstoun, Haddingtonshire.

Sir WILLIAM WINDSOR BROUN, 13th *Baronet*, son of late William Arthur Broun, 2nd son of 10th baronet; *b* 11 July 1917; *s* his cousin, *Sir* LIONEL JOHN LAW, 1995; Vice Pres Scottish Australian Heritage Council; FCA (Australia); 1939-45 War as Lieut AIF: *m* 1952, D'Hrie, da of Frank R. King, of Bingara, NSW, and has issue.

Arms – Gules, a chevron between three fleurs-de-lis or. **Crest** – A lion rampant gules, holding in the dexter forepaw a fleur-de-lis and in the sinister a rose both or.
Residence – 12 Tamarisk Gdns, 2 Reed St, Cremorne, NSW 2090, Australia.

DAUGHTERS LIVING

D'Hrie Sheree, *b* 1956; *ed* Univ of NSW: *m* 1988, Rev Zachary Veron, and has issue living, Désirée D'Hrie Marie, *b* 1991, — Anne Grace, *b* 1993, — Larissa Victoria, *b* 1995. *Residence* – 24 Prospect Street, Carlton, NSW 2218, Australia. —— Rani Beverley, *b* 1959; *ed* Sydney Univ: *m* 1985, Richard Patrick Morrison, and has issue living, Silas Patrick Broun, *b* 1987, — Jasper William, *b* 1989, — Isaac Richard, *b* 1991, — Savannah Rose, *b* 1994. *Residence* – 10 George St, Greenwich, NSW 2065, Australia.

BROTHERS LIVING AND DECEASED

Let majesty flourish

HULANCE HADDINGTON (462 Pittwater Rd, N Manly 2100, NSW), *b* 10 March 1919; 1939-45 War as Sergeant Pilot RAAF, Middle East 1940-42: *m* 1947, Joy Maud, who *d* 1996, da of Alfred Leslie Stack, of Mosman, NSW, and has issue living, Wayne Hercules (7 Hasey Rd, Kenthurst, NSW 2154, Australia), *b* 1952; *ed* Sydney Gram Sch; formerly Lieut 5 Bn RAR: *m* 1976, Anna Marie Paolucci, and has issue living, Richard Haddington *b* 1984, Samantha Louise *b* 1981, — Robyn Joy, *b* 1948; *ed* Sydney Univ: *m* 1974, Cedric Hoare, and has issue living, Timothy James *b* 1976, Jeremy Lachlan *b* 1981, Nicole Suzanne *b* 1978, — Julie Christine, *b* 1955; *ed* Univ of NSW: *m* 1978, William Lyons, and has issue living, Tamara Suzanne *b* 1982, Eleanor Amy *b* 1985, Georgia Anne *b* 1988. —— †Lionel McIntyre, *b* 1921; 1939-45 War with RAAF: *m* 1955, Shirley, who *d* 1990, da of A. L. Stack (ante) and *d* 1990, leaving issue, Walter Leslie (Mount Monopoly, Uralla, NSW 2358, Australia), *b* 1961; *ed* Sydney Univ, — Steven McIntyre (Invergowrie West, Invergowrie, NSW 2350, Australia), *b* 1963; *ed* New England Univ: *m* 1992, Helen McRae-Smith, and has had issue, George McRae McIntyre *b* 1994, †Henry *b* and *d* 1996, Oliver Murray *b* 1998, — Lucinda Maree, *b* 1957; *ed* Sydney Univ: *m* 1981, Russell Anthony Aboud, MB, and has issue living, Angus Alfred McIntyre *b* 1985, Annabelle Louise *b* 1988, Jacqueline Lucinda *b* 1994. —— John Hercules August (5 Daniel Keane Crescent, Gunnedah, NSW 2380), *b* 1923: *m* 1st, 1953, Patricia Johnson; 2ndly, 1962, Margaret, da of Reginald Chapman, of Dubbo, NSW, and has issue living, (by 1st *m*) Richard, *b* 1954, — (by 2nd *m*) Tracy Lee, *b* 1963, — Phoebe Margaret, *b* 1968: *m* 1992, Andrew Beniac, and has issue living, George Joseph August *b* 1994.

COLLATERAL BRANCHES LIVING

Issue of late Reginald Augustus Broun, 3rd son of 10th baronet, *b* 1878, *d* 1948: *m* 1910, Alice Maude, who *d* 1983, da of W. B. Wilkinson, of Mosman, NSW:—
Reginald William Wilkinson, *b* 1912. *Residence* – Dalblair, Gunnedah, NSW. —— Noël Marian, *b* 1918: *m* 1944, Charles Edward Robinson, of Southernwood, 15 Cambridge St, Mooroolbark, Victoria, Aust 3138, and has issue living, Bernard James, *b* 1946: *m* 1968, Annie Kernihan, and has issue living, Nicole Marie *b* 1973, Emma Jane *b* 1975.

Grandchildren of late David Limond Broun (infra):—
Issue of late William James Broun, *b* 1882, *d* 1963: *m* 1st, 1914, Miriam Rheta, da of Sidney T. Peryman, of Mosman, Sydney, NSW; 2ndly, 1947, Dorothea Esther, who *d* 1968, da of David A. Strahley, of Sandy Knowe, Inverell, NSW:—
(By 1st *m*) William James Peryman (6 Epacris Av, Forestville, NSW 2087), *b* 1922; *ed* Sydney Univ (BE); formerly Lt RAN: *m* 1956, Penelope Jane, da of late W. T. H. Horn, of Canberra, and has issue living, William James Harvey *b* 1958: *m* 1980, Margaret Anne, da of late A. W. Quinn, of Roseville, NSW, and has issue living, William James Christopher *b* 1983, Jacqueline Ann *b* 1986, — Anthony Fraser Cameron, *b* 1960. — Malcolm David (61 Greenwich Rd, Greenwich, NSW 2065), *b* 1935; *ed* Sydney Univ (BA, LLB); Bar NSW 1959, QC 1982; accorded the honour of Cyfaill y Celtaidd, Celtic Council of Australia: *m* 1st, 1962 (*m diss* 1971), Janet Patricia, da of late Allan Douglas Edwards; 2ndly, 1972, Wendy Sue, da of W. J. Hannelly, and has issue living, (by 1st *m*) Alexander Alan Hercules, *b* 1965: *m* 1998, Lynne, da of W. J. Christoffels, of Cape Town, SA, — Charlotte Doriam, *b* 1963: *m* 1st, 1989 (*m diss* 1996), Olivier Jean Jacques Eugene dit Rochesson, son of Jacques Eugene dit Rochesson, of Clamecy, France; 2ndly, 1997, Arthur Simpson, and has issue living, (by 2nd *m*) Brigitte *b* 1997, Sophie Amelia, *b* 1969, — (by 2nd *m*) Nicholas Malcolm, *b* 1975, Virginia Barbara *b* 1976. —— Wilga Joan, *b* 1917: *m* 1937, Ian Cecil de Courcy Dutton, of 59 Barraba St, Manilla, NSW 2346, and has issue living, Ian Herbert, *b* 1941: *m* 1963, Irene Elizabeth Mary Archer, and has issue living, Anthony Ian de Courcy *b* 1970: *m* 1st, 1992 (*m diss* 1998), Donna Michelle Sharpe; 2ndly, 1998, Claudine Helen Pepperall (and has issue living, (by 1st *m*) Joshua Robert *b* 1990, Jade Louise *b* 1993), Michael Leslie de Courcy *b* 1974, Jennifer de Courcy *b* 1966: *m* 1990, David Peter Porter (and has issue living, Teagan Emma *b* 1992), — Peter James, *b* 1952: *m* 1975, Judith Margaret Atherton, and has issue living, Grant Peter de Courcy *b* 1977, Peter Jaye de Courcy *b* 1979, Thomas Arthur de Courcy *b* 1984, Lee Jane de Courcy *b* 1976, Emma Joan *b* 1987, — Christopher Cecil, *b* 1955: *m* 1978, Vicki Janelle Beard, and has issue living, Casey John de Courcy *b* 1980, Rachael Maree de Courcy *b* 1982, Melanie Louise de Courcy *b* 1984, — Anne Wilga, *b* 1938: *m* 1957, William Arthur Jones, and has issue living, Wayne William Dutton *b* 1968: *m* 1980, Kerry Therese Weaver (and has issue living, Scott Jeremy *b* 1983, Tara Leigh *b* 1986), Robert Hugh Dutton *b* 1967: *m* 19—, Cherl Anne Miller (and has issue living, Alex William *b* 1993, Taylah Marie *b* 1990), Debra Anne Dutton *b* 1959: *m* 1979, David John Oliphant (and has issue living, Joshua Luke *b* 1983, Beau Jacob *b* 1985, Zoe Aleesha *b* 1981), Rebekah Letitia Dutton *b* 1970: *m* 1996, Michael Chapman (and has issue living, Michaela Letitia *b* 1998), — Melissa Judith, *b* 1945: *m* 1969, Kenneth Beresford Abberfield, and has issue living, Derk Beresford *b* 1973, Natalie Terese *b* 1969: *m* 1997, Barnaby Thomas Joyce (and has issue living, Bridgette Marie *b* 1996, Julia Frances *b* 1998), Stephanie Maree *b* 1971: *m* 1993, Thomas Andrew Ryan (and has issue living, Fergus James *b* 1997, Charles Bartolomew *b* 1998), — Pauline, *b* 1946: *m* 1st, 1967 (*m diss* 1974), David Ross Medway; 2ndly, 1974 (*m diss* 1990), John

Allan Phoo; 3rdly, 19—, John Malcolm Young, and has issue living, (by 1st *m*) Shayne David *b* 1968, Allyn Ross *b* 1969: *m* 1990 Stephanie Thomas, Jarrod Barrington *b* 1971: *m* 1997, Maree Ainsworth, (by 2nd *m*) Jayson John *b* 1975: *m* 1999, Kim Diane Hardy, Matthew James *b* 1983, Suzanne Lillian *b* 1976, — Miriam Lillian, *b* 1953: *m* 1st, 1975 (*m diss* 1983), Paul Christopher Thomas; 2ndly, 19—, Petrus Johannas Hendricus Valks, and has issue living (by 1st *m*), Darren Paul de Courcy Dutton *b* 1975, (by 2nd *m*), Myram Petrus de Courcy Dutton *b* 1985, Ashley Ian de Courcy Dutton *b* 1987, Lysander Maurhys de Courcy Dutton *b* 1990. —— Mario Rheta, OAM (Orroroo, RMB 266, Moore Creek, Tamworth, NSW, Australia), *b* 1918: OAM 1986: *m* 1st, 1943 (*m diss* 1970), Capt Maxwell Charles Halliday, AIF, DDS, MDS; 2ndly, 1970, Hon Mr Justice (Martin Francis) Hardie, who *d* 1974, and has issue living, (by 1st *m*) Miriam Victoria, *b* 1948: *m* 1973, Adam Cowper Hudson, BE, BSc, of 14 McRae Place, Turramurra, NSW 2074, Australia, and has issue living, David Adam Halliday *b* 1976, Emma Victoria Gillett *b* 1978, Alice Rheta Broun *b* 1980, — Catherine Eleanor Broun, *b* 1952: *m* 1973, Philip MacArthur Brown, of Subiaco, Walcha, NSW 2354, Australia, and has issue living, Hamish Ross MacArthur *b* 1980. —— Dorothy Lenglen (Orroroo, RMB 266, Moore Creek, Tamworth, NSW 2340), *b* 1919: *m* 1947 (*m diss* 1975), Walter Woods, NSW, and has issue living, Michael William Frank (Tregarthen, Dunoon Rd, Tamworth, NSW, Australia), *b* 1954: *m* 1983, Helen Lynette Trythall, and has issue living, Timothy Michael *b* 1989, Jessica Margaret *b* 1992, — Adam Lindsay Broun, *b* 1956, — Justin Thomas, *b* 1957; has issue living (by Nicola Griffin), Ashlea GRIFFIN WOODS *b* 1986, — Margarita Henry, *b* 1959, — Sara Dorothy Broun, *b* 1962; has issue living (by Glenn Atkinson), Caitlin Hayley *b* 1993. —— June Joy, *b* 1921; *ed* NSW Univ (BA): *m* 1949, Ross Abbott Hayes, MB, BS, FRCPA, FRCPath, JP, of 98 Balfour Rd, Rose Bay, NSW 2029, and has had issue, Clive Broun Abbott (1 Genders Av, Burwood, NSW), *b* 1950: *m* 1985, Jennifer Anne McLean, and has issue living, Rebecca McLean *b* 1987, Michaela McLean *b* 1990, — Jamie Abbott Broun (66 Boticelli St, Fig Tree Pocket, Qld 4069), *b* 1953: *m* 1986, Ellen Armstrong, and has issue living, Ryan Armstrong *b* 1987, Taylor Broun *b* 1991, Dakoda *b* 1992, — David Broun Abbott (17 Kaboda St, Dover Heights, NSW), *b* 1954: *m* 1981, Jackie Ann Ryba, and has issue living, Kobe Ryba *b* 1984, Billi Ryba *b* 1987, Zoe Ryba *b* 1992, — Matthew George Broun, *b* 1964; *d* 1987.

Descendants of Peter Nicholas Broun (1797-1846), Colonial Sec, of Swan River (who adopted the ancient spelling of his surname in lieu of Brown 1844), 2nd son of William Broun (1769-1831), 2nd son of 6th baronet:—

Grandchildren of late Frederick Richard Boyd Broun, eldest son (by 1st *m*) of late James William Broun (1831-1897), 2nd son of Peter Nicholas Broun (ante):—
Issue of late Alexander Bruce Broun, *b* 1897, *d* 1968: *m* 1927, Gwendoline Elsie Macnish, who *d* 1992:—
Peter Boyd (34 Sydenham Rd, Doubleview, W Australia 6018), *b* 1928: *m* 1958, Pauline Anita Cliffen, and has issue living, Clive James (53 Hensman St, S Perth 6151), *b* 1960: *m* 1989, Colleen Gail Walter, — Julie Anne, *b* 1962: *m* 1992, Paul Dunleavy Hanvey, of 4 St Thomas Loop, Iluka, W Australia 6028. —— Frederick Boyd (29 Mippi St, Halls Head, W Australia 6210), *b* 1933: *m* 1959, Patricia Thompson, and has issue living, Mark Ian (25 Tallering Heights, Woodvale, W Australia 6026), *b* 1961: *m* 1990, Juliana Maria Peres, — Ross David (4B Castle Rock Turn, Joondalup, W Australia 6919), *b* 1965: *m* 1994, Selina Zoe Parker, — Karen Patricia, *b* 1970. —— James Boyd (PO Box 1881, Palmerston, NT 0830), *b* 1936. —— Rosemary Gwen (12 The Arcade, Doubleview, W Australia 6018), *b* 1930.

Issue of late Raymond Broun, *b* 1908, *d* 1983: *m* 1939, Helen Daly, who *d* 1992:—
Donald John (11 Lewton Rd, Mt Waverley, Melbourne, Vic 3149, Australia), *b* 1940. —— Ross Frederick (13 Wendover Court, Mt Waverley, Melbourne, Vic 3149, Australia), *b* 1942: *m* 1966, Helen Stanton, and has issue living, Michael Francis, *b* 1967, — Simon Ross, *b* 1971, — Elizabeth Jane, *b* 1968, — Kate Helene, *b* 1975. —— Mary Louise, *b* 1951: *m* 1974, Denis John O'Halloran, of 18 Bradstreet Rd, Mt Waverley, Vic 3149, Australia, and has issue living, Claire Louise, *b* 1976, — Emma Brigid, *b* 1978, — Lisa Madeline, *b* 1978.

Grandchildren of late James William Broun, 2nd son (by 1st *m*) of late James William Broun (1831-1897) (ante):—
Issue of late William Broun, *b* 1904, *d* 1986: *m* 1928, Jocelyn Compton (29 Chatsworth Terrace, Claremont, W Australia 6010):—
James Nicholas (Forest View, Beverley, W Australia 6304), *b* 1929: *m* 1953, Barbara Paterson, and has issue living, Simon (Southbourne, Beverley, W Australia 6304), *b* 1954: *m* 1982, Jenny Delandgrafft, and has issue living, Andrew *b* 1985, Clare *b* 1983, Louise *b* 1988, — James (Chocolate Hills, Beverley, W Australia 6304), *b* 1957: *m* 1987, Jill Learmonth Finch, — Robert (25 Dunbar Rd, Claremont, W Australia 6010), *b* 1958: *m* 1985, Deborah Jill de Burgh, and has issue living, Peter *b* 1993, Amelia *b* 1988, Alice *b* 1991, — Katherine Sarah, *b* 1967.

Issue of late Peter Clifton Broun, *b* 1913, *d* 1963: *m* 1936, Phyllis St Clair McManus:—
Michael James (39 Heytesbury Rd, Subiaco, W Australia 6008), *b* 1940; has issue living, Jake Michael Ginnivan, *b* 1986. —— Jocelyn Patricia, *b* 1945: *m* 1975, John Brian Devine, of 26 Grainger Drive, Mt Claremont, W Australia 6010, and has issue living, Alistair Scott, *b* 1976, — Matthew James, *b* 1982.

Grandchildren of late Frank Tyndall Broun (infra):—
Issue of late William Owen Tyndall Broun, *b* 1906, *d* 1980: *m* 1926, Brenda Burgess, who *d* 1985:—
Dulcie Margaret, *b* 1927: *m* 1950, Robert Charles Zehnder, of 51B Ednah St, Como, W Australia 6162, and has issue living, Gregory Robert, *b* 1952: *m* 1978, Julia Wood, and has issue living, Claire Rosemary *b* 1982, Jane Alice *b* 1984, — Scott Charles, *b* 1955: *m* 1992, Susan Knight, and has issue living, Samuel Charles *b* 1995, Hayley Rose *b* 1999. —— Jacquelin Fay, *b* 1929: *m* 1951, Kevin Wisely Shepheard, of 9 Buxton Rd, Wembley Downs, W Australia 6019, and has had issue, Richard Wisely, *b* 1954, — Mark Broun, *b* and *d* 1964, — Erica Helen, *b* 1953: *m* 1975, Michael Patrick Howe, and has issue living, Jemma Jane *b* 1976. —— Helen Patricia, *b* 1934: *m* 1st, 1955, Derek Colin Briggs, who *d* 1992; 2ndly, 1993, Peter Henry Brown, of 76 The Promenade, Mt Pleasant, W Australia 6153, and has issue living (by 1st *m*), Clifford, *b* 1955: *m* 1979, Dalveen Edward, and has issue living, Kallan Thomas *b* 1984, Rhiannon Patricia *b* 1983, Nerissa Josephine *b* 1987, — Peter, *b* 1959: *m* 1st, 1981, Lorraine Langman; 2ndly, 1995, Charmaine Marrett, and has issue living (by 1st *m*), Adam Peter *b* 1983, Nicholas Kenneth *b* 1986, Emma Lorae *b* 1988, — Ian, *b* 1966.

Issue of late Frank Marmion Tyndall Broun, *b* 1911, *d* 1990: *m* 1st, 1938, Doreen McKellar, who *d* 1958; 2ndly, 1959, Phyllis Audas:—
(By 1st *m*) Delia Alexandra (PO Box 173, Blackheath, NSW 2785, Australia), *b* 1940. —— Sandra Claudia, *b* 1944: *m*

1st, 1964, Graham Edward Giles; 2ndly, 1989, Colin McGrath, of 15 Riley Rd, Mundaring, W Australia 6073, and has issue living (by 1st *m*), Bronwyn Doreen, *b* 1965, — Belinda Jane, *b* 1969, — Samantha Faye, *b* 1972.

Grandchildren of late James William Broun (1831-1897), 2nd son of Peter Nicholas Broun (1797-1846) (ante):—
Issue of late Frank Tyndall Broun, *b* 1876, *d* 1930: *m* 1903, Constance May Sewell, who *d* 1969:—
Richard Tyndall (Box 76, Beverley, W Australia 6304), *b* 1920: *m* 1946, Thelma Iolanthe Caporn, and has issue living, Paul Richard Tyndall (Waterhatch, Beverley, W Australia 6304), *b* 1954: *m* 1992, Annette Helene Friebel, and has issue living, Cameron Paul *b* 1996, Nicola Ann *b* 1994, — Georgina Marianne, *b* 1956: *m* 1980, Robert Solomon, of 24 Tennyson Av, Halls Head, Mandurah, W Australia 6210, and has issue living, William Alexander Monger *b* 1989. —— May Constance, *b* 1903: *m* 1938, Ernest McKeand, of 2/12 Star St, Sandy Bay, Tas 7005, and has issue living, David Edwin (10 Eurella Av, Sandy Bay, Tas 7005), *b* 1940, — Ross Tyndall (3 Uralla Place, Wahroonga, NSW 2076), *b* 1945. —— Gwennyth Amelia, *b* 1918: *m* 1945, Philip William Atkins, of Unit 225 Ocean Gdns, 60 Kalinda Drive, City Beach, W Australia 6015, and has issue living, Robert Philip (21 Hartung St, Mundaring, W Australia 6073), *b* 1951: *m* 1975, Janet Roberts, — Michael William (28 Owston St, Mosman Park, W Australia), *b* 1954: *m* 1975, Susan Busby, and has issue living, Matthew Stuart *b* 1978, Emily Louise *b* 1980, Lucy Katherine *b* 1983, — Kenneth James (4 Bantry Rd, Floreat, W Australia 6014), *b* 1956: *m* 1981, Noeline Elias, and has issue living, Timothy James *b* 1985, Katherine Jane *b* 1983.

Issue of late Norman Wilfred Broun (only son by 2nd *m*), *b* 1891, *d* 1976: *m* 1916, Lillian Henrietta Nicholson, who *d* 1979:—
†Mervyn Leake, *b* 1917: *m* 1941, Claudia Venetia Fyfe, who *d* 1992, and *d* 1981, having had issue, Margot Venetia, *b* 1945; *k* in an air crash 1972, — Suzette Anne (Mondweg 5/1/11, 1140 Vienna, Austria), *b* 1947: *m* 1st, 1968 (*m diss* 1976), Michael Hobden; 2ndly 1977 (*m diss* 1987), Peter Franc, and has issue living (by 2nd *m*), Katharina Ann *b* 1982, — Leonie Marion, *b* 1953: *m* 1st, 1976 (*m diss* 1991), Joseph Frank Mihaly; 2ndly, 1992, Stephen Andrew Paterson, of 2 Sheppard Way, Marmion, W Australia 6020, and has issue living (by 1st *m*), Kelly Margot *b* 1981, Chantelle Suzette *b* 1983, Donna Louse *b* (twin) 1983, (by 2nd *m*), Mitchell David *b* 1994, Stacey Christine *b* 1992. —— Allan McBryde (3 Bunthorne Court, Duncraig, W Australia 6023), *b* 1924: *m* 1948, Brenda Johnston, and has issue living, Allan Norman (51 Ripley Way, Duncraig, W Australia 6023), *b* 1948: *m* 1972, Judith Anne Tondut, and has issue living, Daryl Allan *b* 1976, Louise Jane *b* 1980, — Colin Gregory (43/44 Janet St, Safety Bay, W Australia 6169), *b* 1952: *m* 1979, Kyme Michelle Hooson, and has issue living, Dale Gregory *b* 1979, Leigh Nicholas *b* 1985, Crystal Michelle *b* 1982, — Jeffrey Cameron (5 Truslove Way, Duncraig, W Australia 6023), *b* 1956: *m* 1980, Robyn Clare Gibb, and has issue living, Tyson Cameron *b* 1987, Sophie Clare *b* 1985, — Janet Maree, *b* 1964: *m* 1988, Christopher Burnham Crossley, of 12 Balmain St, Kingsley, W Australia 6026, and has issue living, Lachlan Ray Mond *b* 1995, Tristan Liam *b* 1998.

Granddaughter of late Richard M'Bryde Broun, son of late William Broun (ante):—
Issue of late Capt William Luke Broun (P & O Co's Ser), *b* 1850, *d* 1935: *m* 1st, 1886, Harriet Louisa, who *d* 1906, da of late William Boodle, solicitor, of Cheltenham; 2ndly, 1909, Alice Glen, who *d* 1959, widow of Charles Wilson, of Melbourne, Australia:—
(By 2nd *m*) Edith Elizabeth McBryde, *b* 1911: *m* 1940, Douglas Matthew Duder Raper, who *d* 1981, and has issue living, Rosemary Elizabeth Broun, *b* 1949: *m* 1972, George Antony Alexander Johnson, and has issue living, Matthew Alexander *b* 1979, Antony Christopher *b* 1983, Elizabeth Alice *b* 1977, — Sarah Christian Broun, *b* 1952: *m* 1983, Keith Raphael Briffa, and has issue living, Amy Katherine Raper *b* 1984, Kirsten Fay Broun *b* 1986.

This family claims descent from Walter le Brun, a warrior who came to Scotland from France about 1073, supported the cause of King Malcolm III and obtained the baronies of Colstoun in Haddingtonshire and Gamilshiels in Berwickshire. In 1116 he was a witness to an inquisition of the possessions of the Church of Glasgow. In 1248 Philip le Brun witnessed a charter by Sir Roger de Mowbray to Matthew, ancestor of the Lairds of Moncrief. Prior to 1267, Sir David Broun, Baron of Colstoun, knighted by King Alexander III, married the daughter of Sir Hugo de Gifford, Baron of Yester, the wizard warrior described in Sir Walter Scott's "Marmion". As they were proceeding to the church, Sir Hugo stopped the bridal procession beneath a pear tree and, plucking one of the pears, gave it to his daughter, saying that so long as the gift was preserved, good fortune would never desert her or her descendants, but if harm should come to it misfortune would surely follow. It became renowned as the "Colstoun Pear". In about 1513, George Broun, 12th Laird of Colstoun, married Marion Hay, daughter of John, 2nd Lord Hay of Yester, ancestor of the Marquess of Tweeddale. Sir Patrick Broun of Colstoun, Sheriff-Depute of Edinburgh 1670-1681, Commissioner of Supply, was created a Baronet of Nova Scotia 16 Feb 1686. Sir George Broun, the 2nd Baronet, married Lady Elizabeth Mackenzie (daughter of George, 1st Earl of Cromartie) who, succumbing to temptation, bit a piece out of the Colstoun Pear. In accordance with the wizard's warning, misfortunes gathered. Sir George suffered losses and was obliged to sell Colstoun to his brother Robert, who subsequently was drowned with his two sons when their coach overturned while crossing a swollen river. His estates were inherited by his eldest daughter Jean, who married a cousin Charles Broun of Cleghornie. On Sir George's death in 1718 without issue the baronetcy was assumed by his cousin George Broun as 3rd Baronet. The pear minus the bite is still preserved in a silver box at Colstoun and even when shorn of its superstitious surroundings is, nevertheless, a wonderful vegetable curiosity.

BROWN (UK) 1863, of Richmond Hill

There is unity among brothers

EST CONCORDIA FRATRUM

Sir GEORGE FRANCIS RICHMOND BROWN, 5th *Baronet*; *b* 3 Feb 1938; *s* his father, *Lt-Col Sir* CHARLES FREDERICK RICHMOND, TD, 1995; *ed* Eton; late Maj Welsh Guards; Extra Equerry to HRH The Duke of Edinburgh 1961-63, and ADC to Gov of Queensland 1963-65: *m* 1978, Philippa Jane, da of late Capt Edward Joseph Willcox, and has issue.

Arms – Quarterly; 1st and 4th, gules, a chevron or between two bears' paws erased in chief argent, and, four hands conjoined in saltire of the second in base; on a chief engrailed gold, an eagle displayed sable, *Brown*; 2nd and 3rd, argent a chevron nebuly sable between two moorhens close in chief proper and a fleur-de-lys in base azure, *Luxmoore*. **Crest** – A bear's paw erased argent, issuant out of a wreath of oak vert, holding a sinister hand proper.
Residence – Mas de Sudre, 81600 Gaillac, France. *Club* – Pratt's.

SONS LIVING

SAM GEORGE RICHMOND, *b* 27 Dec 1979; *ed* in France. —— Harry Richmond, *b* 1982. —— Edward Richmond, *b* 1987.

SISTERS LIVING

Jennifer Richmond, *b* 1934. —— (Elizabeth) Maud Richmond, *b* 1943: *m* 1970, Guy M. A. Crawford, and has issue living, George, *b* 1974, — Alice, *b* 1975. *Residence* – St Blanes, Dunblane, Perthshire.

COLLATERAL BRANCHES LIVING

Granddaughters of late Col James Clifton Brown (infra):—
Issue of late Brig-Gen Howard Clifton Brown, *b* 1868; *d* 1946: *m* 1903, Mary Eirene, who *d* 1951, da of late Hon Sir Henry Edward Agincourt Hodges, a Puisne Judge of Supreme Court, Melbourne:—
Katharine Clifton, *b* 1917: *m* 1946, Ion Hunter Touchet Garnett-Orme, CBE, who *d* 1991. *Residence* – Cheriton Cottage, Cheriton, Alresford, Hants. —— Margaret Eirene Clifton (*Margaret, Baroness Amherst of Hackney*), *b* 1921: *m* 1939, 3rd Baron Amherst of Hackney, CBE, who *d* 1980. *Residence* – 138 Cranmer Court, Sloane Av, SW3.

Issue of late Douglas Clifton Brown, *b* 1879, *d* 1958 *cr Viscount Ruffside* 1951 (see that title):—

Grandchildren of late Edward Clifton Clifton-Brown (assumed additional surname of Clifton by deed poll 1923), 2nd son of late Col James Clifton Brown (ante):—
Issue of late Lt-Col Geoffrey Benedict Clifton-Brown, *b* 1899, *d* 1983: *m* 1927, Robina Margaret Hill, who *d* 1978, da of late Rowland Sutton (*see* Sutton, Bt, colls):—
Edward Geoffrey (14 St James Gdns, W11; W Bradley House, Glastonbury, Som), *b* 1928: *m* 1st, 1953 (*m diss* 1958), Jillian Mary, da of David Walkinshaw, of Bishopton, Half Moon Hall, Haslemere; 2ndly, 1960, Sarah Simonetta, yr da of Roger Herbert Frances, OBE, of 7 Clarendon Close, W2, and has issue living (by 1st *m*), James Benedict *b* 1956: *m* 1980, Priscilla Sarah, da of Sir John Valentine Jardine Paterson, of North Bavant, Warminster, Wilts, and has issue living, a son *b* 1985, Laura *b* 1987, — Margaret Joanna, *b* 1957, — (by 2nd *m*), Louisa, *b* 1961: *m* 1991, Alexander Penrose Gordon Cumming, son of Sir William Gordon Gordon Cumming, 6th Bt, — Sarah, *b* 1964. —— Robert Lawrence (Little Bradley House, nr Haverhill, Suffolk), *b* 1929: *m* 1952, Florence Elizabeth Lindsay, el da of Ronald Arthur Vestey (*see* Vestey, Bt), and has issue living, Geoffrey Robert, *b* 1953: *m* 1979, Alexandra Mary, yr da of W/Cdr Denis Peto-Shepherd, of Great Durnford, Wilts, and has issue living, Jacqueline Florence *b* 1983, — (Ronald) Colin, *b* 1963: *m* 1987, Emily Joan, yr da of Laver John Morgan Oliver, of Bury St Edmunds, Suffolk, and has issue living, George *b* 1992, Charles Laver *b* 1997, Archie Ralph *b* 1999, Isabelle *b* 1993. — Jane Elizabeth, *b* 1954: *m* 1978, Mark Corner Bailey, son of Leonard Corner Bailey, of Brinkley, Cambs, and has issue living, Peter Robert Corner *b* 1983, a son *b* 1993, Rosemary Catherine *b* 1980, Florence *b* 1989, — Angela Florence, *b* 1956: *m* 1984, Timothy Sills, of Whites Farm, Helions Bumpstead, Haverhill, Suffolk, and has issue living, James *b* 1987, Robert Marett *b* 1990, Michael *b* 1993.

Issue of late Maj Anthony George Clifton-Brown, TD, *b* 1903, *d* 1984: *m* 1st, 1930, Delia Charlotte Gordon, who *d* 1947, da of late George Edward Wade, sculptor; 2ndly, 1949, Phyllis Adrienne (Bridget), who *d* 1977, da of late Francis Harvey, of Kyle, co Wexford, and formerly wife of late Capt Alexander McGowan McCulloch, RN:—
(By 1st *m*) Georgiana Elmira, *b* 1934: *m* 1962, Prof Anthony Charles Bailey, LLM, Barrister-at-law, of 6/129 The Parade, Ascot Vale, Victoria 3032, Australia, son of Hugh Somerville Bailey, of Hampstead, NW, and has issue living, Edward Hugh Clifton (58 Bank St, Ascot Vale, Victoria 3032), *b* 1966, — Jane Delia, *b* 1964: *m* 1990, Robin Arthur Wellesley Redgrave, of 7 Westbrook Close, Oakley, Basingstoke, Hants RG23 7HW, yr son of Maj-Gen Sir Roy Redgrave, KBE, MC, of Chelsea, SW, and has issue living, Thomas Roy Philip *b* 1993, Catherine Georgiana Wellesley *b* 1995, — Felicity Caroline, *b* 1970: *m* 1994, Mark Julian Lewis, of 135 Maribyrnong Rd, Ascot Vale, Victoria 3032, son of Hywel Lewis, of Bribie Is, Queensland, and has issue living, Julia Elizabeth *b* 1997. —— Mora Delia, *b* 1936: *m* 1957, John Norman Abell, of Whittonditch House, Ramsbury, nr Marlborough, Wilts SN8 2PZ, son of late Sir George Edmond Brackenbury Abell, KCIE, OBE, and has issue living, Martin George, *b* 1962, — Antony Philip Norman (18 Tunley Rd, SW17 7QJ), *b* 1964: *m* 1996, Alexandra Louise, da of Benita Burbidge, of Albury Farmhouse, Tiddington, Oxon, and has issue living, Athena Madeleine *b* 1998, — Sarah Elizabeth, *b* 1959: *m* 1984, William Mark Evans, of 60 Portland Rd, W11, and has issue living, Matthew George *b* 1987, Michael Timothy *b* 1990, Jonathan *b* 1996, Stephanie Susan *b* 1988. —— Julia Mary, *b* 1942: *m* 1985, Brian Edward Leaver, of PO Box 596, Maitland, NSW 2320, Australia.

Grandchildren of late Col James Clifton Brown, second son of late Alexander Brown, el son of 1st baronet:—

Issue of late Capt Cedric Clifton Brown, b 1887, d 1968: m 1938, Mary Aymee Lilian, OBE, who d 1980, da of late Rev John A. Labouchere:—

Peter Cedric Clifton (Ballinamona, Cashel, co Tipperary), b 1939: m 1968, Petronelle, yr da of S. L. Grubb, of Beechmount, Fethard, co Tipperary, and has issue living, John Cedric Clifton, b 1970, — Louis Peter Clifton, b 1971, — Henry Samuel Clifton, b 1974. —— Anthony John Clifton (Perces, Greenstead Green, Halstead, Essex CO9 1RB), b 1942; m 1st, 1967 (m diss 1988), Françoise, da of M. Mooser, of Neuchâtel, Switzerland; 2ndly, 1989, Veronica Jane, eldest da of late Reginald Eric Stevens, of Willingdon, Eastbourne, E Sussex, and has issue living (by 1st m), Douglas Alexandre Clifton b 1968, — Philippe Anthony Clifton, b 1975. —— Ursula Mary Clifton, b 1941.

Descendants of late Alexander Hargreaves Brown (3rd son of late Alexander Brown, el son of 1st baronet), who was cr a Baronet 1903:—

See Pigott-Brown, Bt.

Sir William Brown, 1st baronet, an eminent merchant in Liverpool and New York, sat as MP for South Lancashire 1846-59, and was High Sheriff of Lancashire 1863. He established the mercantile firm of Brown, Shipley, and Co, Liverpool, and founded, in 1860, the Public Library and Museum in William Brown Street, Liverpool, at a cost of £42,000, and for that and other services to Liverpool he was created a baronet. The 2nd baronet was High Sheriff of Northamptonshire 1873.

PIGOTT-BROWN (UK) 1903, of Broome Hall, Capel, Surrey

There is unity among brothers

Sir WILLIAM BRIAN PIGOTT-BROWN, 3rd *Baronet, b* 20 Jan 1941; *s* his father, *Sir* JOHN HARGREAVES, 1942; *ed* Eton.

Arms – Quarterly, 1st and 4th gules, a chevron or between two bears' paws erased in chief argent, and four hands conjoined in saltire of the second in base; a chief engrailed of the last thereon an eagle displayed sable (for distinction), in the honour point a cross-crosslet of the third, *Brown*; 2nd and 3rd ermine, three fusils conjoined in fesse sable, *Pigott.* Crest – Issuant out of a wreath of oak vert a bear's paw erect argent, holding a sinister hand couped at the wrist proper.
Residence – 47 Eaton Mews North, SW1X 8LL.

AUNT LIVING (daughter of 1st baronet)

Joan Terrell Hargreaves (*Lady Prideaux*), b 1911: m 1934, Col Sir John Francis Prideaux, OBE, DL, who d 1993, and has issue living, Christopher John (Doddershall Park, Aylesbury; Brooks's Club), b 1936; ed Eton: m 1959, Celia, only da of Sir Peter Averell Daniell, TD, DL, of Glebe House, Buckland, Surrey, and has issue living, David John b 1962: m 1989, Sally M., da of Ian Liddell, of Sheering, Essex, and of Mrs Colin Carter, of Ousden, Suffolk (and has issue living, Thomas b 1992), Charles Christopher b 1966: m 1998, Barbara H. V., elder da of Andrei Hoogeweegen, of Sandridge Park, Wilts, Lavinia Marion b 1961: m 1st, 1981, Barry J. Cameron, of Western Australia; 2ndly, 1992, Allan Gilfillan (Sam) Mainds and has issue (by 2nd m), Polly b 1994, — Michael Charles Terrell (Selehurst, Lower Beeding, Horsham, Sussex), b 1950; ed Eton, and Trin Coll, Camb: m 1975, Mrs Susan H. Monsarrat, da of late Peto Bennett, of La Haute, Fliquet, Jersey, and has issue living, John Peto b 1979, Laura Hargreaves b 1976, — Editha Anne, b 1940: m 1968, Alaster Templeton of The Old Rectory, Whatfield, nr Ipswich, Suffolk, and has issue living, Katherine Elizabeth b 1968, Jane Celia b 1970. *Residence* – Rallywood, Ockley, Surrey.

WIDOW LIVING OF SECOND BARONET

HELEN VIOLA EGERTON, only da of late Maj Gilbert Francis Egerton-Cotton (*see* V Combermere, colls): m 1st, 1940, Capt Sir John Hargreaves Pigott-Brown, Coldstream Guards, 2nd Baronet, who was ka 1942; 2ndly, 1948, Capt Charles Raymond Radclyffe, late Roy Scots Greys. *Residence* – Lew, Oxfordshire.

COLLATERAL BRANCH LIVING

Issue of late Walter Hargreaves BROWN, 2nd son of 1st baronet, b 1881, d 1936: m 1913, Alberta Laura who m 2ndly, 1937, Alexander Innes, MC (Innes, Bt, cr 1620, colls), da of late Capt Guy Mainwaring, RN:—

Susan Henrietta Hargreaves, b 1914: m 1935, Curtis Delmar-Morgan, DSC, RNVR, who d 1987, of Eadens Wedge, East Meon, Petersfield, Hants, and has issue living, Michael Walter (Oak Tree Farm, Newtown, Fareham, Hants PO17 6LJ), b 1936: m 1962, Marjorie, da of John Kennedy Logan, and has issue living, Benjamin John b 1966, Katharine Susan b 1968, Alexandra Jane b 1971, — Jeremy Hugh, b 1941: m 1st, 1966, Nicolie Jane, da of Howard Eden Smith; 2ndly, 1978, Mary E., da of R. J. Hope, of Cookham Dean, Berks, and has issue living, (by 1st m) Piers Jonathan b 1974, Frances Jane b 1971, (by 2nd m) Alexander Curtis b 1981, Alice Clodagh b 1984, — (Dorothy) Sarah, b 1956: m 1979, Peter S. Cooper, and has issue living, Robert James *b* 1989, Elizabeth Anne *b* 1987. —— Margaret Hargreaves, *b* 1917: *m* 1st, 1938, Robert Graham Fletcher, who *d* 1960; 2ndly, 1961, Alexander Ronan Nelson, who *d* 1997, and has issue living, (by 1st *m*) Alastair Robert Leslie, *b* 1941; *ed* Eton: *m* 1965, Maria Lucia Simoes, and has issue living, Robin Simoes *b* 1972, Monica Simoes *b* 1966, Katia Simoes *b* 1967, — Charles Hugh (Ardlussa, Isle of Jura, Argyll), *b* 1946; *ed* Eton: *m* 1970, Rose Noreen Nugent Sherlock, and has issue living, Andrew Charles *b* 1972, Catriona Rose *b* 1973, Elizabeth Noreen *b* 1976, — Ronald James (Easter Lennieston, Thornhill, by Stirling FK8 3QP), *b* 1948; *ed* Eton: *m* 1974, Damaris Hunne- man, and has issue living, Ewan James *b* 1978, Robert Gordon *b* 1980, — Fiona Margaret, *b* 1939, — Katharine Har- greaves, *b* 1953: *m* 1977, Douglas Johnson, and has issue living, Fiona Mary *b* 1977, Helen Margaret *b* 1979. *Residence* – Muckairn, Taynuilt, Argyll.

The 1st baronet, Sir Alexander Hargreaves Brown (*see* Brown, Bt, *cr* 1863, colls), sat as MP for Wenlock (8) 1868-85, and for Mid or Wellington, Div of Shropshire (LU) 1885-1906. His el son Capt Gordon Hargreaves Brown was *ka* 1914. He *m* 1910, Edith Ivy, el da and co-heir of Adm William Harvey Pigott of Doddershall Park, Bucks who in 1925 assumed the additional surname and arms of Pigott for herself and her issue. Their son, Capt Sir John Hargreaves Pigott-Brown, 2nd Bt Coldstream Guards, was *ka* 1942.

Browne (Cave-Browne-Cave), see Cave.

BROWNRIGG (UK) 1816

Virescat vulnere virtus

Valour strengthens from a wound

Sir NICHOLAS GAWEN BROWNRIGG, 5th *Baronet*, son of late Gawen Egremont Brownrigg, 2nd and only surviving son of 4th baronet; *b* 22 Dec 1932; *s* his grandfather, *Rear-Adm Sir* DOUGLAS EGREMONT ROBERT, CB, 1939: *m* 1st, 1959 (*m diss* 1965), Linda Louise, da of Jonathan B. Lovelace, of Beverly Hills, California, USA; 2ndly, 1971, Valerie Ann, da of Julian A. Arden, of Livonia, Michigan, USA, and has issue by 1st *m*.

Arms – Argent, between three crescents gules, a lion rampant-guardant sable holding in the dexter fore-paw a sword proper, hilt or, thereon a serpent entwined vert; and for augmentation, on a chief embattled of the last, a representation of the sceptre of the King of Kandy or, and of the banner of the said King, being gules within a bordure with a ray of the sun issuing from each angle a lion passant holding a sword in saltire, the whole ensigned with a representation of the crown of Kandy. **Crests** – 1st, augmentation, a demi-Kandian proper holding in the dexter hand a sword and in the sinister the crown of Kandy; 2nd, out of a mural crown or, a sword erect in pale proper, hilt or, thereon a serpent entwined vert. *Address* – PO Box 548, Ukiah, Calif 95482, USA.

SON LIVING (*By 1st marriage*)

MICHAEL GAWEN (c/o US Dept of State, 2100 C St NW, Washington, DC 20520, USA), *b* 11 Oct 1961; US Foreign Service 1985—: *m* 19—, (Dr) Margaret Dillon, da of Dr Clay Burchell, and has issue living, Nicholas James, *b* 7 July 1993.

DAUGHTER LIVING (*By 1st marriage*)

Sylvia Alderyn, *b* 1964.

MOTHER LIVING

Baroness Lucia, da of late Baron Victor von Borosini, of 1270, Mesa Rd, San Marino 9, California, USA: *m* 1st, 1931 (*m diss* 1936), Gawen Egremont Brownrigg (ante), who *d* 1938; 2ndly, 1936 (*m diss* 1941), John Burnham; 3rdly, 1941 (*m diss* 1957), Com Edmund Lyford Engel, US Naval Reserve; 4thly, 19—, Harry Albert Batten, who *d* 1966. *Residence* – 207 Griegos Rd, NE, Albuquerque, New Mexico 87107-4002, USA.

The 1st baronet, Sir Robert Brownrigg, GCB (son of Henry Brownrigg, of Rockingham, co Wicklow), was a Gen in the Army, and Col 9th Foot. The 4th baronet, Sir Douglas Egremont Robert, CB, was a Rear-Adm RN.

BRUCE (NS) 1628, of Stenhouse, Stirlingshire

We have been

FUIMUS

DO·WELL·AND·DOUBT·NOT·

Sir (FRANCIS) MICHAEL IAN BRUCE, 12th *Baronet*; *b* 3 April 1926; *s* his father, *Sir* MICHAEL WILLIAM SELBY, 1957; discontinued use of his Christian name of Francis; US Marine Corps, Amphibious Forces, and Fleet Marines Force 1943-46 (Solomons, Bismarck Archipeligo, and Philippines Campaigns); Member of Sqdn A, 7th Regt NY 1948 (ret); Master's Ticket 1968; Pres Newport Sailing Club and Academy of Sail, Newport Beach since 1978, Pres American Maritime Co since 1981: *m* 1st, 1947 (*m diss* 1957), Barbara Stevens, da of Francis J. Lynch; 2ndly, 1961 (*m diss* 1963), Frances Keegan; 3rdly, 1966 (*m diss* 1975), Marilyn Anne, da of Carter Mullaly; 4thly, Patricia Gail, da of Frederich Root; 5thly, 1994, Alessandro Conforto, MD, and has issue by 1st *m*.

Arms – Or, a saltire and chief gules, in the dexter canton an escutcheon argent charged with a chief sable. *Crest* – On a cap of dignity an arm from the shoulder couped fessewise holding a sceptre ensigned on the point with an open crown as that worn by Robert I of Scotland. *Supporters* – *Dexter*, a knight in armour the vizor open and a plume of feathers in his helmet holding a sceptre in his right hand all proper; *sinister*, a lion rampant azure armed and langued gules, crowned with the crown of Robert I, and gorged with that of David II, chained with an antique chain or.
Address – 3424 Via Oporto #204, Newport Beach, California 92663, USA; *Clubs* – Balboa Bay, Newport Beach, and The Vikings of Orange, Newport Beach.

SONS LIVING (*By 1st marriage*)

MICHAEL IAN RICHARD *b* 10 Dec 1950. —— Robert Dudley, *b* 1952.

HALF-BROTHER LIVING

Michael David Lennon, *b* 1948.

HALF-SISTER LIVING

Corinna Mary Constance, *b* 1940.

WIDOW LIVING OF ELEVENTH BARONET

MARGARET HELEN (*Margaret, Lady Bruce*), da of late Sir Arthur Lennon Binns, CBE, MC; late Section Officer, WAAF: *m* 1946, as his fourth wife, Sir Michael William Selby Bruce, 11th Bt, who *d* 1957. *Residence* – —

COLLATERAL BRANCHES LIVING

Issue of late William Nigel Ernle Bruce, yr son of 10th baronet, *b* 1895, *d* 1953: *m* 1921, Violet Pauline, who *d* 1970, da of the late Col Willington Shelton, of Bruree, co Limerick:—
Pauline Margaret, *b* 1922: *m* 1946, Wing-Com Geoffrey Page, DSO, DFC, RAF (ret), and has issue living, Nigel Geoffrey, *b* 1953, — Jamie Douglas, *b* 1958, — Pauline Shelley, *b* 1948.

Grandchildren of late Capt Arthur Neil Bruce, son of late William Cuningham Bruce, 2nd son of 7th baronet:—
Issue of late William Cuningham Bruce, *b* 1866, *d* 1924: *m* 1897, Ellen, da of John Scott:—
Robert Neil, *b* 1904. —— William Cuningham, *b* 1907. —— Colin Cadell, *b* 1914. —— Corinna Joan, *b* 1916. —— Lornas Dorothy, *b* 1910.

Granddaughter of late Robert Cathcart Bruce, MD, 3rd son of late Maj-Gen Alexander James Bruce, el son of late Alexander Fairlie Bruce (*b* 1799), 3rd son of 7th baronet:—
Issue of late Robert Cathcart Bruce, *b* 1898, *d* 1966: *m* 1927, Christian Adeline, who *d* 1990, da of late William Henderson, of Berkley House, Frome:—
Fairlie Cathcart, *b* 1928: *m* 1951, Charles William Hutton, BArch FRIBA, who *d* 1995, of Brook House, Sampford Brett, Taunton, Som TA4 4LE, and has issue living, Fairlie Elizabeth, *b* 1952: *m* 1977, Philip Julian Moore, MSc FRICS, of 108 Kennington Rd, SE11 0EH, and has issue living, Alastair Philip *b* 1980, Dominic William *b* 1983, — Julia Frances (2 Dray

Cottages, Horton Kirby, Kent DA4 9DA), *b* 1954; has issue by Darrell Martin Whittaker, Luke Hutton WHITTAKER *b* 1981, Tom Hutton WHITTAKER *b* 1983, — Anina Mary (37 St James's Square, Bath, N Somerset BA1 2TT), *b* 1955; has issue by Martin Bruce Robertson, Walter Douglas HUTTON *b* 1982, Zoë Bruce HUTTON *b* 1979, Rose Matilda HUTTON *b* 1986.

Grandchildren of late Alexander Fairlie Bruce, *b* 1857, son of George Cadell Bruce, 2nd son of Alexander Fairlie Bruce, *b* 1799 (ante):—
Issue of late Lt-Cdr Alan Cathcart Fairlie Bruce, RN, *b* 1894, *d* 1927: *m* 1919, Barbara Clarributt, who *d* 1992, da of E. Clarributt Skinner:—
Colin Michael Fairlie (Airth House, South Drive, Littleton, Winchester, Hants SO22 6PY), *b* 1925; *ed* Christ's Hospital, and Oxford (MA) and Edinburgh Univs; World Bank, Washington DC 1965-84; part-time economic development consultant; Far East, 1943-45 as Sub-Lt RNVR: *m* 1st, 1946, Patricia Mary Platt, who *d* 1997; 2ndly, 1963, Georgina Morrison Baker, and has issue living, (by 1st *m*) Timothy Michael Fairlie (430 E Bruce Av, Dayton, Ohio 45405, USA), *b* 1948: *m* 1978, Kate Ella Armpriester, — Alan Simon Fairlie (415 Evergreen Rd (No 41E), Bolinas, Cal 94924, USA), *b* 1950; *ed* Kingston Polytechnic (Dip Arch); RIBA; Vice-Pres Stone Marraccinni and Patterson, San Francisco: *m* 1973, Mary Jean Alstad, and has issue living, Abigail Emily Fairlie *b* 1969, Sarah Alison Fairlie *b* 1981, — Jonathan Neil Fairlie (33 Henley Rd, Iffley, Oxford), *b* 1958: *m* 1982, Carrie Marie Gomm, and has issue living, Joshua Thomas Fairlie *b* 1983, Lauren Fairlie *b* 1980, Sian Katie Fairlie *b* 1981, Jessica Maeze Fairlie *b* 1986, — Lindsay Madeleine Fairlie, *b* 1953: *m* 1970, Barry Shapland, of Dene Cliff, Palace House Rd, Hebden Bridge, W Yorks, and has issue living, Fionn *b* 1972, Ruari *b* 1983, Megan *b* 1976, — Jenny Catriona Fairlie, *b* 1960; *ed* Nottingham Univ: *m* 1986, Andrew Harker, of Tankard Cottage, Tankard Lane, Ramsbury, Marlborough, Wilts GN8 2PJ, and has issue living, Thomas Alexander *b* 1991, Patrick James Brook *b* 1998, Grace Catriona *b* 1993, Anatesse Kate *b* 1995, — (by 2nd *m*) Fiona Elspeth (9 The Green, Sutton Courtenay, Oxon OX14 4AE), *b* 1965. ⸺ John Alan Fairlie (Beechbrook, 16 ½ Colebrook St, Winchester, Hants SO23 9LH), *b* 1926; *ed* Christ's Hosp, and Oxford Univ; Personnel Mgr, R Dutch Shell Group of Cos 1948-84; Far East 1945-47 as Lieut, RA: *m* 1950, Joyce Edna Soffe, and has issue living, Iain Alasdair Fairlie, *b* 1954; *ed* Camb Univ (BA), and R Coll of Art (Dip in Film Making); has issue living, David Malcolm BRUCE *b* 1993, Hannah Eileen Jones BRUCE *b* 1987, Alexandra Kathleen Jones BRUCE *b* 1991, — Andrew Stuart Cathcart (14 Hastings Close, Polegate, E Sussex), *b* (twin) 1954; *ed* Manchester Polytechnic (BA), and Bristol Polytechnic (Dip in Personnel Admin): *m* 1988, Maureen Lesley Hull, — Alison Jean, *b* 1951: *m* 1977, Paul Richard Moore, of Triffeny, 13a Stoney Lane, Winchester, Hants, and has issue living, Jonathan Paul Bruce *b* 1980, Nicola Jane Bruce *b* 1982. ⸺ Barbara Jean, *b* 1921: *m* 1941, Col Robert John Augustine Hornby, OBE (ret), E Surrey Regt, of 38A The Broadwalk, Imperial Square, Cheltenham, Glos GL50 1QG, and has issue living, Vivien Sheena (*Deaconess Hon Mrs Edward F. Northcote*) (27 Shaftesbury Hall, St George's Place, Cheltenham, Glos GL50 3PP), *b* 1942: *m* 1963 (*m diss* 1980), Hon Edward Frederic Northcote, TD (*see* E Iddesleigh), — Louise Panette, *b* 1947: *m* 1967, Kenneth Dudley Johns Bootes-Johns, of GPO Box 4701, Sydney, NSW 2001, Australia.

Grandchildren of late Col Elliott Armstrong Bruce, 7th son of late Alexander Fairlie Bruce, *b* 1799 (ante):—
Issue of late Lieut-Col Malcolm Edward Lloyd Bruce, Indian Army, *b* 1872, *d* 1952: *m* 1903, Clementina Blyth, who *d* 1958, yst da of late W. F. B. Dalzel, MD, Surg-Major Bengal Army:—
Elizabeth Mary Dalzel (twin), *b* 1910: *m* 1933, Neville Eugene Govett, who *d* 1972, and has issue living, Bryan, *b* 1934, — Richard, *b* 1937, — Robert John, *b* 1944.

Issue of late Elliott Henry Rochfort Bruce, *b* 1874, *d* 1933: *m* 1905, Frances Maude, who *d* 1949, da of A. McDonald:—
Elliott McDonald, *b* 1906; *m* 1932, Kathleen, da of G. Clarke, and has issue living, Michael, *b* 1939, — Josephine, *b* 1945, — Heather, *b* 1949. *Residence* – Launceston, Tasmania. ⸺ Malcolm Alexander, *b* 1913: *m* 1942 (*m diss* 19—), Doris Gwynnith, and has issue living, Donald Malcolm, *b* 1944, — Geoffrey, *b* 1946, — Richard, *b* (twin) 1946. ⸺ Beryl Brenda *b* 1919: *m* 1947, Herbert Winston Eaton, and has issue living, Geoffrey Winston, *b* 1949, — Linda Christine, *b* 1952.

Grandchildren of late Michael McCubbin Bruce, 8th son of Alexander Fairlie Bruce, *b* 1799 (ante):—
Issue of late Robert Cathcart Bruce, *b* 1878, *d* 1968: *m* 1916, Emma Dolores, who *d* 1983, da of late John Croce:—
Vivian Richard, MB, FRCGP (Lindavanally, 25A George Douglas Drive, Ryedale, Dumfries DG2 7ES), *b* 1919: *m* 1st, 1942, Norah Maeve Yates, who *d* 1960; 2ndly, 1962 (*m diss* 1983), Bernadette Yates; 3rdly, 1983, Valerie Florence May Bruce, da of late Nelson Fitzroy Baylis, and has issue living, (by 1st *m*) Robert James, OBE (Ahmibah Farm Estate, No 4 The Polo Centre, London Rd, Sunninghill, Ascot, Berks SL5 7SE), *b* 1946; Maj RM (ret): *m* 1969, Elizabeth Jane Moira, da of late David Clement Burgess, and has issue living, Robert David Cathcart *b* 1977, James Hubert William *b* 1985, (Elizabeth) Maeve (5 Heron Place, Hermes Rd, Oxford OX2 7QR) *b* 1970: *m* 1991 (*m diss* 1997), Adrian Bruce-Purchase (formerly Purchase) (and has issue living, Jake Hamilton *b* 1993), (Laura) Christian *b* 1971, — Michael Alexander (Welshmill Lodge, Welshmill Rd, Frome, Somerset BA11 2LA), *b* 1949; FCA: *m* 1983, Patricia Sheila, da of late Col Peter Johnson, OBE, and has issue living, Alexander Peter *b* 1987, David *b* 1990, Natasha *b* 1985, Diana *b* (twin) 1990, — Richard Hubert (17 Danvers Rd, Mountsorrel, Loughborough, Leics LE12 7JG), *b* 1956, — (by 2nd *m*) Paul Cathcart (26 Templars Close, Wheatley, Oxford OX33 1PA), *b* 1963; BSc: *m* 1989, Louise, da of late Hari Ratan Ker (and has issue living, Hamish Benjamin *b* 1995, Hannah Amy *b* 1992), — Angus Peter (Cross Keys, Lower Bristol Rd, Clutton, Bristol BS39 5PB), *b* 1964: *m* 1st, 1990 (*m diss* 1993), Jennifer Tatum; 2ndly, 1995, Paola Eleanora, da of Sante Zanetti, and has issue living (by 2nd *m*), Emma Frances *b* 1996, Isabel Bernadette *b* 1998, — Joseph Douglas (3 Julian Rd, Ludlow, Salop SY8 1HA), *b* 1970.

Issue of late Charles Kerr Bruce, *b* 1880, *d* 1955: *m* 1928, Lily, who *d* 1959, da of Charles Leonard:—
Ian Robert (Weston Down Cottage, Micheldever, Winchester, Hants SO21 3AQ), *b* 1931: *m* 1st, 1956 (*m diss* 1980), Dorothy Evelyn Knight; 2ndly, 1994 (*m diss* 1995), Elisabeth Joan, da of late Col Harry Lacy, and widow of Richard Swanwick, and has issue living (by 1st *m*), Anne, *b* 1960: *m* 1st, 1985 (*m diss* 1989), Simon Eadie; 2ndly, 1996, Nicholas Charles Simpson Green, of East Stoke Farmhouse, Stoke Charity, Hants SO21 3PL, and has issue living, (by 2nd *m*) Charles Alexander *b* 1996, — Caroline Jane, *b* 1963: *m* 1989, Mark Spedding, of The Stables, Water Lane, Hawkhurst, Kent TN18 5AY, and has issue living, Max Edward Mark *b* 1992, George Alexander Mark *b* 1996. ⸺ Margaret, *b* 1930: *m* 1956, Norman Terence Whight, of The Cherries, 15 Fairfield Way, Hildenborough, Kent, and has had issue, Charles Bruce, *b* 1963; *d* 1980, — Fiona Margaret, *b* 1960. ⸺ Audrey Mary, *b* 1935; *m* 1958, George David James Morgan, of 16 Heslop Rd, SW12 8EG, and has issue living, Christopher David, *b* 1962, — Felicity Claire, *b* 1960.

Grandchildren of late Robert Perry Bruce, 9th and yst son of late Alexander Fairlie Bruce (ante):—

Issue of late Michael Macaulay Bruce, *b* 1904, *d* 1964: *m* 1937, Louise Françoise (62 Bolton Rd, Windsor, Berks), da of Prof Van der Pot, of the Netherlands:—
Robert William (Am-Bermar, Jaggers Lane, Hathersage, Hope Valley S32 1AZ), *b* 1940: *m* 1964, Jennifer Patricia Guilfoyle Brown, and has issue living, Michael Gregory Macaulay, *b* 1968, — Rosalind Ellen Macaulay, *b* 1966, — Miranda Jane Macaulay, *b* 1970. —— Michael Zachary (62 Bolton Rd, Windsor, Berks), *b* 1951: *m* 1981, Ellen Katharina, da of Siegbert Oscar Leuthold, of Switzerland, and has issue living, Edgar, *b* 1989, — Catherine, *b* 1984, — Leanne, *b* 1986. —— Mary Louise, *b* 1938: *m* 1961, Colin Hugh Prince, of 19 Alexandra Rd, Kingston upon Thames, and has issue living, Hamish Robin John, *b* 1966, — Anna Louise, *b* 1964. —— Vanessa Bertha Jane, *b* 1942: *m* 1968, Christopher Ryle, of Green Cottage, Park Rd, Chipping Camden, Glos GL55 6EB, and has issue living, Deborah Louise, *b* 1968, — Xanthe Sarah, *b* 1969, — Octavia Georgina, *b* 1979. —— Barbara Lucy, *b* 1945: *m* 1969, Paul Lewis Henderson, of The Beeches, 279 High St, Boston Spa, W Yorkshire LS23 6AL, and has issue living, James, *b* 1974, — Barnaby, *b* 1981, — Juliet, *b* 1972.

Issue of late Edward Macaulay Bruce, *b* 1908, *d* 1986: *m* 1939, Nancy Elinor (Horseshoe Cottage, Arlington, Bibury, Glos), yr da of late Lt-Col F.G.C. Humfrey, late 12th Bengal Cav:—
David Nigel Macaulay (15 St Helena Rd, Bristol BS6 7NR), *b* 1947; *ed* Gresham's Sch, St Andrew's Univ (MA), and Edinburgh Univ (MPhil); Lecturer at Bristol Polytechnic: *m* 1972, Diana, da of Cluny Dale, and has issue living, James, *b* 1974, — Rebecca, *b* 1977. —— Elizabeth Mary, *b* 1942: *m* 1966 (*m diss* 1978), Dirk Detert, PhD, and has issue living, Niels Bruce, *b* 1970, — Jan Bruce, *b* 1974.

Grandchildren of late Eric Henry Stuart Bruce, only son of late Gen Michael Bruce, grandson of late Patrick Craufurd Bruce, 5th son of 6th baronet:—
Issue of late Brigadier Ian Robert Craufurd George Mary Bruce, DSO, MBE, *b* 1890, *d* 1956: *m* 1926, Joan Mary, who *d* 1991, da of late Lt-Col Rowland Charles Feilding, DSO (*see* E Denbigh, colls):—
Anne Mary, *b* 1927: *m* 1953, Nicholas Patrick Reyntiens, and has issue living, Dominick Percival Ian (5 Craster Rd, SW2), *b* 1957; dancer and actor: *m* 1988, Caroline Sophie, yr da of William Adrian Liddell (*see* B Ravensworth, colls), — John Patrick Martin, *b* 1964, — Edith Mary Isabel, *b* 1954, — Lucy Mary Anne, *b* 1959: *m* 1982, Nicholas Durnan, of Compton Farmhouse, Compton Durville, S Petherton, Som TA13 5ET, and has issue living, Sophie Belle *b* 1984, Grace Louise *b* 1987. *Residences* – Ilford Bridges Farm, Close Stocklinch, Ilminster, Som. —— Janet Mary, *b* 1928: *m* 1950, Peter Michaeljohn Ward, and has issue living, Jonathan Francis Bruce (2 Olive Hill, Wyck Rissington, Cheltenham, Glos GL54 2PW), *b* 1954: *m* 1979, Sarah Elizabeth Sophia, da of Maj Mark Winton Slane Fleming, 10th R Hus (*see* By Emmet of Amberley), and has issue living, Christopher Luke *b* 1980, Hugh Basil *b* 1982, — Robert Richard Craufurd *b* 1959: *m* 1996, Angeline Malaba, — Edmund Giles William (Dovecote Barn, Maltkiln Farm, Stretton Underfosse, Rugby CV23 0PE), *b* 1962: *m* 1991, Gillian Elizabeth McCord, — Damian Peter Michael, *b* 1966, — Clare Dorothy, *b* 1951: *m* 1976, Christopher James Thomson, of 28 Gordonbrock Rd, SE4, and has issue living, Edmund Christopher *b* 1985, Lucy Stephanie *b* 1981, — Catharine Joan, *b* 1952: *m* 1983, Henry Swift Thompson, Jr, of 11 Douglas Crescent, Edinburgh, and has issue living, James Edwin Jerome *b* 1987, Emma Joan Douglas *b* 1985, Joanna Janet Henrietta *b* 1991, — Magdalen Mary, *b* 1955: *m* 1989, Axel Howarth Goodbody, of 2 First Av, Bath BA2 3NW, and has issue living, Brendan Christian *b* 1987, Rowland Benedict *b* 1993, Laura Brigid *b* 1990, — Hester Janet Teresa, *b* 1964: *m* 1992, James Alastair Innes, of 7 Wardie Crescent, Trinity, Edinburgh EH5 1AF, and has issue living, Hamish Ian *b* 1997, Ailsa Helen *b* 1994, Mairi Catriona *b* (twin) 1994. *Residence* – Waterdell House, Croxley Green, Herts WD3 3JH. —— Helen Mary, *b* 1929: *m* 1st, 1956 (*m diss* 1980), Stephen Edward Francis Bally, who *d* 198—; 2ndly, 1983, Edward Todd, of 55 Tallai Rd, Mudgeeraba, Queensland 4213, Australia, and has issue living, (by 1st *m*) Ian Stephen Edward (59 Gibson St, Ayr 4807, Australia), *b* 1959: *m* 1983, Mrs Kay Louise Moffitt (née Lewis), and has issue living, Sarah Ann Frances *b* 1992, and has adopted his stepchildren, Mark William *b* 1976, Tabitha Louise *b* 1978, and Jodie Marie *b* (twin) 1978, — Alexander St John, *b* 1963: *m* 1st, 1993 (*m diss* 1998), Kay Therese Halley; 2ndly, (Nov) 1998, Elisita Agosto Guillen, and has issue living, (by 2nd wife) Samantha Mary *b* (May) 1998, — David Anthony, *b* 1968, — Louise Frances Joan (Maleny, Australia), *b* 1957: *m* 1977 (*m diss* 1987), David Bain, and has issue living, Aaron Ian *b* 1987, Madonna *b* 1976, Michelle *b* 1978; has further issue, Madelain Marie *b* 1994. —— Eynor Mary (Hillside Farm, Salisbury Rd, Shaftesbury, Dorset SP7 8BX), *b* 1933: *m* 1957, Alfred Edwin Bell, who *d* 1987, and has issue living, Christopher Michael Ian (32 Alderney St, SW1V 4EU), *b* 1958, — Julian Sebastian, *b* 1962: *m* 1989, Justin Chappell Day, and has issue living, Tatiana *b* 1994, — Theodore Richard John, *b* 1972. —— Philena Mary Edith (Flat 4, 36 Russell Rd, W14 8HT), *b* 1949.

This family is a cadet branch of the Bruces of Clackmannan, from whom the Earls of Elgin also derive their descent. Sir William Bruce, who was created a baronet with remainder to his heirs male whatsoever, was a yr son of William son and heir of Sir Alexander Bruce of Airth, 6th in descent from Sir Edward Bruce of Airth, yr son of the second Sir Robert Bruce of Clackmannan, who *d* before 1406.

Bruce-Gardner, see Gardner.

BRUNNER (UK) 1895, of Druids Cross, Little Woolton, Lancashire; Winnington Old Hall, Winnington, Cheshire; and Ennismore Gardens, Westminster, co London

If thou art wise, drink

Sir JOHN HENRY KILIAN BRUNNER, 4th *Baronet*; *b* 1 June 1927; *s* his father, *Sir* FELIX JOHN MORGAN, 1982, but his name does not appear on the Official Roll of the Baronetage; *ed* Eton, and Trin Coll, Oxford; formerly Lieut RA: *m* 1955, Jasmine Cicely, da of late John Wardrop-Moore (Erskine, Bt, *cr* 1821, colls), and has issue.

ᴁrms – Gules, a fountain playing proper, charged on the basin with a rose gules, in chief two mullets of six points or. ℭrest – In front of a wing erect gules, a fountain as in the arms.
Residence – 138 Victoria Av, Dalkeith, W Australia 6009.

SONS LIVING

NICHOLAS FELIX MINTURN, *b* 16 Jan 1960. —— (Mark) Jonathan Irving, *b* 1962.

DAUGHTER LIVING

Claire Eliza, *b* 1958.

BROTHERS LIVING

(Timothy) Barnabas Hans, *b* 1932; *ed* Eton, and Trin Coll, Oxford; formerly Lt Irish Gds: *m* 1960, Helen Ursula, da of Norris Marshall, of 17 Oxford Rd, Teddington, Middx, and has issue living, Jacob Sebastian, *b* 1961, — Conrad Orlando, *b* 1966: *m* 19—, (Helen) Cecily, 3rd da of Edward Victor Gatacre, of Vorden, The Netherlands (*see* Paget, Bt, *cr* 1886, 1995 Edn), — Francesca Laura, *b* 1963, — Imogen Charlotte, *b* 1965. *Residence* – Greys Court, Henley-on-Thames, Oxon RG9 4PG. —— Hugo Laurence Joseph, *b* 1935; *ed* Eton, and Trin Coll, Oxford; High Sheriff Oxfordshire 1988, DL 1994, and Lord Lieut since 1996: *m* 1967, Mary Rose Catherine, da of late Arthur Joseph Lawrence Pollen (*see* Pollen, Bt, colls), and has issue living, Joseph Gabriel, *b* 1967, — Samuel Felix, *b* 1972, — Magnus Gregory Nathaniel, *b* 1974, — Philip James Daniel, *b* 1977, — Francis John Michael, *b* 1982, — Isabel Mary, *b* 1969. *Residence* – 26 Norham Rd, Oxford OX2 6SF.

WIDOW LIVING OF THIRD BARONET

DOROTHEA ELIZABETH (*Elizabeth, Lady Brunner*), OBE, JP, da of late Henry Brodribb Irving: *m* 1926, Sir Felix John Morgan Brunner, 3rd Bt, who *d* 1982. *Residence* – Greys Court, Henley-on-Thames, Oxon RG9 4PG.

COLLATERAL BRANCHES LIVING

Issue of late Daniel Felix Brodribb Brunner, 3rd son of 3rd baronet, *b* 1933, *d* 1976: *m* 1959, Helen Elizabeth, of Clayhill, Stoke Row, Henley-on-Thames, Oxon (who *m* 2ndly, 1981, Douglas Mitchell), only da of James Alan Price, FRCP, of Heaton, Bradford:—
Rupert James Brodribb, *b* 1961. —— Piers Daniel Carlyle, *b* 1967. —— Rachel Elizabeth, *b* 1962: *m* 1983, Raymond Talbot, of Malvern, Worcs. —— Lucy Charlotte, *b* 1964: *m* 1992, James R. Anderson, son of Robin Anderson, of Quainton, Bucks.

Grandchildren of late Harold Roscoe Brunner, 3rd son of 1st baronet:—
Issue of late Anthony Brunner, *b* 1901; assumed by deed poll 1919 the christian name of Anthony in lieu of his baptismal names of Egbert Sidney Houston; *d* 1970: *m* 1934, Amy Phyllis Ivy (Felicity) Whittaker, who *d* 1994:—
†John Kilian Houston *b* 1934, *d* 1995; *ed* Cheltenham; author and poet: *m* 1st, 1958, Marjorie Rosamond, who *d* 1986, only da of late Edwin Charles Sauer; 2ndly, 1991, Tan Li Yi (The Square House, Palmer St, South Petherton, Som TA13 5DB), 3rd da of late Tan Quan, of Guangzhou, Guangdong, China. —— Verena Hilda May, *b* 1937; MA, and Dip Ed Edinburgh: *m* 1967, Arthur Edward William Thornton, of 24 Mannerston Holdings, Linlithgow, W Lothian, and has issue living, Amabel Celia, *b* 1976, — Felicity May, *b* 1977.

Issue of late Wing-Cdr Oswald Patrick O'Brien Brunner, RAF, *b* 1908, *d* 1966: *m* 1933, Mary Elaine, who *d* 1998, da of late Richard Howlett, of Ambassadors' Court, St James's Palace, SW1:—
Mary Elizabeth April, *b* 1936: *m* 1961, David Arthur Steuart Gladstone, CMG, of 2 Mountfort Terr, Barnsbury, N1 1JJ, and has issue living, Patrick, *b* 1969, — Perdita *b* 1965: *m* 198-, Mark Williams, of 21A Barnsbury Terrace, N1, and has issue living, Christopher James *b* 1989.

The 1st baronet, Rt Hon Sir John Tomlinson Brunner, PC, was second son of Rev John Brunner, a native of Zurich, and proprietor of Mere Bank Sch, Everton, Liverpool; he founded Brunner Mond and Co (Limited), alkali manufacturers, of Northwich, Cheshire, and gave new building and land for the Witton Gram Sch, Northwich; subscribed liberally to Liverpool Univ (besides endowing Chairs of Economic Science, Physical Chemistry and Egyptology); also donated to the Nantwich, Winsford, and Middlewich Public Libraries, and in July, 1885, presented to the town of Northwich a Public Library (rebuilt in 1909); gave Village Halls to several villages, and "Guildhalls" to Runcorn and Winsford; sat as MP for Cheshire, Northwich Div (*L*) 1885-6, when he was defeated; re-elected 1887, and sat until 1910. The 2nd baronet, Sir John Fowler Brunner (who discontinued by deed poll a third christian name of Leece), was a Director of Brunner, Mond and Co (Limited), and of Madeley Collieries (Limited), and sat as MP for Lancashire (SW), Leigh Div (*L*) Jan 1906 to Jan 1910, for Cheshire, Northwich Div Jan 1910 to Nov 1918, and for Southport Dec 1923 to Oct 1924.

BRUNTON (UK) 1908, of Stratford Place, St Marylebone.

*The incitement of glory is the
torch of the mind*

God is our refuge and strength

Sir (EDWARD FRANCIS) LAUDER BRUNTON, 3rd *Baronet*; *b* 10 Nov 1916; *s* his father, *Sir* (JAMES) STOPFORD (LAUDER), 1943; *ed* Trin Coll Sch, Port Hope, at Bryanston Sch, and McGill Univ (BSc MD and CM); Hon Attending Physician, R Victoria Hosp Montreal, a Fellow of International Soc of Hematology, and of American Coll of Physicians; 1940-45 War as Capt R Canadian Army Med Corps: *m* 1946, Marjorie Grant, only da of David Sclater Lewis, MSc, MD, FRCP (Canada), of Montreal, and has issue.

Arms – Or, a caduceus sable on a chief azure three pallets argent. *Crest* – On a mount vert, a beacon fired between two sprigs of laurel proper. *Address* – PO Box 140, Guysborough, Nova Scotia, Canada BOH 1N0.

SON LIVING

JAMES LAUDER, *b* 24 Sept 1947; *ed* Bishops Coll Sch, Montreal and McGill Univ (BSc 1968, MDCM 1972); MD, FRCP (Canada); Prof of Medicine Toronto Univ, Head Divn of Infectious Diseases, Dept of Medicine, Univ of Toronto, Microbiologist in Chief, The Toronto Hosp, Toronto: *m* 1st, 1967 (*m diss* 1983), Susan Elizabeth, da of Charles Hons; 2ndly, 1984, Beverly Anne Freedman, and has issue living (by 1st *m*), Douglas Lauder, *b* 1968, — Jennifer Anne, *b* 1971, — (by 2nd *m*) Robert James, *b* 1987. *Residence* – 7 Blaine Drive, Don Mills, Ont M3B 2G3, Canada.

DAUGHTER LIVING

Nancy Elizabeth, *b* 1949: *m* 1977, Ian Willson.

SISTER LIVING

Ethel Alice Bonsall (117 Old S River Rd, Antigonish, Nova Scotia, Canada), *b* 1918: *m* 1942, Ralph Hoskins.

The 1st baronet, Sir (Thomas) Lauder Brunton, MD, DSc, FRS, FRCP, LLD, was an eminent Consulting Physician. The 2nd baronet, Sir (James) Stopford (Lauder) Brunton, was a Mining Geologist.

Buchan-Hepburn, see Hepburn.

BUCHANAN (UK) 1878, of Dunburgh, Stirlingshire.

Never conquered

Sir ANDREW GEORGE BUCHANAN, 5th *Baronet*; *b* 21 July 1937; *s* his father, *Sir* CHARLES JAMES, 1984; *ed* Eton, Trin Coll, Camb, and Wye Coll, London Univ; late 2nd Lieut Coldstream Gds; farmer, Chartered Surveyor and Co Dir; High Sheriff Notts 1976, DL 1985, and Lord Lieut 1991; Chm Bd of Visitors, HM Prison, Ranby 1983: *m* 1966, Belinda Jane Virginia (JP Notts 1980-92, and DL 1998), da of Donald Colquhoun Maclean, of Thurloe Sq, SW7, and widow of Gresham Neilus Vaughan (*see* D Sutherland, colls, 1990 Edn), and has issue.

Arms – Or, a lion rampant sable between two otters' heads erased in chief proper and a cinque-foil in base of the second, all within a double tressure flory counter flory of the last. Crest – An armed dexter hand holding a cap of dignity purpure, the facings ermine. Supporters – *Dexter*, a falcon wings elevated and addorsed proper, belled and beaked or; *sinister*, a gryphon sable; each charged on the breast with two branches of laurel conjoined or.
Residence – Hodsock Priory, Blyth, Worksop, Notts S81 0TY.

SON LIVING

GEORGE CHARLES MELLISH, *b* 27 Jan 1975.

DAUGHTER LIVING

Laura Evelyn, *b* 1967: *m* 1992, A. James Mayes, yr son of Brig Andrew Mayes, of Chelsea, SW3, and has issue living, Hugo Charles, *b* 1995, — Angus Alexander, *b* 1999.

BROTHER LIVING

Hugh Charles Stanley (Home Farmhouse, Pusey, Faringdon, Oxon), *b* 1942; *ed* Eton, and McGill Univ, Canada; solicitor; Member of Oxfordshire CC 1985-89: *m* 1969, Nony Caroline Vatcher, da of Lt-Col John Johnston Dingwall, DSO, of Lyford Grange, Lyford, Oxon (*see* V Galway, colls, 1985 Edn), and has issue living, James Iain Stanley, *b* 1974, — Clarissa Victoria Rosamund, *b* 1972, — Arabella Patricia Dingwall, *b* 1981.

SISTERS LIVING

Georgina Mary Gabrielle, *b* (Dec) 1932: *m* 1966, Michael Denzil Grierson Clayton, of 6 Cobden Cres, Edinburgh, who *d* 1991, and has issue living, Roger Lancelot, *b* 1969, — Harriet Beatrix Evelyn, *b* 1971. —— Constance Carolyn, *b* 1934: *m* 1961, Hugh John Alexander Lindsay, of The Old Rectory, Litton Cheney, nr Dorchester, Dorset DT2 9AH (*see* E Crawford).

This family descends from Archibald Buchanan of Auchintorlie, Dunbartonshire (a cadet of Buchanan of Leny), whose yst son Andrew was grandfather of the 1st baronet, Rt Hon Sir Andrew Buchanan, successively Ambassador at Berlin, St Petersburg and Vienna. The 4th baronet, Sir Charles James, was High Sheriff of Notts 1962 and County Commr for Notts of Boy Scouts Assocn 1949-62.

Buchanan-Jardine, see Jardine.

LEITH-BUCHANAN (GB) 1775, of Burgh St Peter, Norfolk

Sir CHARLES ALEXANDER JAMES LEITH-BUCHANAN, 7th *Baronet*; only son of late John Wellesley Macdonald Leith-Buchanan, el son of James Macdonald Buchanan Leith-Buchanan, 3rd son of 4th baronet, *b* 1 Sept 1939; *s* his kinsman, *Sir* GEORGE HECTOR MACDONALD, 1973, but his name does not appear on the Official Roll of the Baronetage; Pres United Business Machines Inc since 1978: *m* 1st, 1962 (*m diss* 1987), Marianne, da of Col Earle Wellington Kelly; 2ndly 1988, Janice J. Jenkins, and has issue by 1st *m*.

Arms – Quarterly: 1st and 4th or, a cross-crosslet fitchée sable, between three crescents in chief and as many fusils in base gules; 2nd, or, a lion rampant sable, in the dexter forepaw a heart gules within a double tressure flory counterflory of the second, all within, a bordure compony argent and azure; 3rd, counter-quartered, 1st argent, a lion rampant gules, 2nd or, a hand couped at the wrist holding a cross crosslet fitchée gules, 3rd, per fesse or and vert in chief a lymphad sable and in base a salmon naiant argent; 4th argent an oak tree eradicated proper charged with an eagle displayed or, all within a bordure invected gules. Crest – 1st, a cross-crosslet as in the arms, and, a dexter hand erect proper couped below the wrist, holding a dagger of the last, hilt and pommel or.
Residence – 9527 Possum Hollow Drive, Delaplane, Va 22025, USA.

SON LIVING (*By 1st marriage*)

GORDON KELLY McNICOL, *b* 18 Oct 1974.

DAUGHTER LIVING (*By 1st marriage*)

Mary Elizabeth, *b* 1964.

AUNT LIVING

Jean Isobel Barbara (645 Chelsea Cloisters, SW3), *b* 1911.

STEPMOTHER LIVING

Isabel Sim (Floyd, Scargil, Berwick, Vic, Aust), da of late A. W. Fraser, of Birchwood, Inverness; *m* 1948, as his 2nd wife, John Wellesley Macdonald Leith-Buchanan (ante), who *d* 1956.

COLLATERAL BRANCHES LIVING

Granddaughter of late Charles John Leith-Buchanan (infra):—
Issue of late Thomas Wellesley Macdonald Leith-Buchanan, *b* 1907, *d* 1967: *m* 1932, Mary C. (100 Sulphur Springs Rd, Ancaster, Ont, Canada), da of late Allan J. Cameron, Bar-at-law, of Halifax, Nova Scotia:—
Eleanor Clare, *b* 1935: *m* 1955, William Hugh Shaw, and has issue living

Issue of late Charles John Leith-Buchanan, 4th son of 4th baronet, *b* 1875, *d* 1948: *m* 1905, Mary Eleanor, who *d* 1946, da of William Farmer, of Ancaster, Ontario, Canada:—
Mary Elizabeth Warburton, *b* 1911. *Residence* – —

The family, of considerable antiquity in Scotland, is in direct descent from William Leith, Provost of Aberdeen 1350. The 1st baronet, Sir Alexander Leith, was Lieut-Col 88th Foot; his father was killed while commanding artillery at siege of Havannah, 1763. The 3rd baronet, Sir Alexander Wellesley William Leith, *m* Jemima, da of Hector Macdonald Buchanan, and their son, Sir George Hector, 4th baronet assumed the additional surname of Buchanan 1877.

Buckworth-Herne-Soame, see Soame.

WILLIAMS-BULKELEY (E) 1661, of Penrhyn, Caernarvonshire

Sir RICHARD THOMAS WILLIAMS-BULKELEY, 14th *Baronet, b* 25 May 1939; *s* his father, *Lt-Col Sir* RICHARD HARRY DAVID, TD, 1992; *ed* Eton; Capt Welsh Gds 1963; High Sheriff Gwynedd 1993, DL 1998; FRICS: *m* 1964, Sarah Susan, elder da of late Rt Hon Lord Justice (Sir Henry Josceline) Phillimore, OBE, and has issue.

𝔄rms – Quarterly: 1st and 4th, sable a chevron between three bulls' heads cabossed argent; a canton ermine, *Bulkeley;* 2nd and 3rd, gules, a chevron ermine between three men's heads couped in profile proper, *Williams.* ℭrest – 1st, out of a ducal coronet a bull's head argent, horned or, charged with a cheron sable; 2nd, a stag's head cabossed argent.
Seat – Baron Hill, Beaumaris, Anglesey. *Residence* – Red Hill, Beaumaris, Anglesey LL58 8YS.

SONS LIVING

RICHARD HUGH, *b* 8 July 1968; *ed* Eton, and Reading Univ (BSc); Capt Welsh Guards: *m* 1995, Jacqueline Ann, elder da of David Edwards, of Kenn, Devon, and has issue living, Richard David Harry, *b* 26 April 1996, — Oliver Huw, *b* 1998. —— Harry David, *b* (twin) 1968; *ed* Eton, and Manchester Univ (BA).

DAUGHTER LIVING

Victoria Mary, *b* 1973; *ed* St Mary's, Wantage, and Univ of W of England (BA).

BROTHER LIVING

Michael (Rhiwlas, Pentraeth, Anglesey LL75 8YG), *b* 1943; *ed* Eton; Lt Welsh Gds: *m* 1968, Ellen-Marie, eldest da of late Leif Falkum-Hansen, of Oslo, Norway, and has issue living, James, *b* 1970; *ed* Rugby, and Reading Univ (BSc): *m* 1997, Marie-Louise, elder da of Robert J. Troup, of Sunningdale, Berks, — David Haakon, *b* 1973; *ed* Eton.

COLLATERAL BRANCH LIVING

Granddaughter of late Maj Arthur Wellesley Williams, 3rd son of 9th baronet:—
Issue of late Rupert Owain Glendwr Williams, *b* 1886, *d* 1939: *m* 1899, Marion Winkworth, who *d* 1937, only child of late Henry Hammond, of Duncton, Sussex:—
Sylvia Mary *b* 1905.

This family descends in the male line, as did the House of Tudor, from Ednyfed Vychan, Chief Minister of Llywelyn the Great. William ap Griffith, of Cochwillan, Caernarvonshire, 10th in descent, assisted Henry VII at Bosworth. His son William Williams was the first to adopt that surname. His great-great-grandson, Sir Griffith Williams, of Penrhyn (nephew of John Williams, Archbishop of York), was *cr* a baronet by Cromwell 1658 and by Charles II 1661. Sir Richard Bulkeley Williams, 10th Bt, assumed the additional surname of Bulkeley in 1826 on succeeding to the estates of Viscount Bulkeley.

BULL (UK) 1922, of Hammersmith, co London

Sir SIMEON GEORGE BULL, 4th *Baronet*; *b* 1 Aug 1934; *s* his father, *Sir* GEORGE, 1986; *ed* Eton, Innsbruck, and Paris; admitted a solicitor 1959; sr partner in the legal firm of Bull & Bull, 199 Piccadilly, W1; Hon Solicitor to Standing Council of the Baronetage: *m* 1961, Annick Elisabeth Renee Genevieve, yr da of late Louis Bresson, of Chateau des Masselins, Chandai, Orne, France, and has issue.

Arms – Sable, three astronomical signs of Taurus or. Crest – A bull's head cabossed sable, charged on the forehead with the sign of the Taurus as in the arms.
Residences – Oakwood, Island Rd, Sturry, Kent; Pen Enez, Tréméoc, Finistère, France. *Club* – Royal Thames Yacht, MCC.

SON LIVING

STEPHEN LOUIS, *b* 5 April 1966; *ed* Downside, and Slough Coll of Computer Technology.

DAUGHTERS LIVING

Jacqueline-Hester, *b* 1964. ——— Sophia Ann, *b* 1971.

SISTER LIVING

Charlotte Sophia, *b* 1938; *ed* Roedean, and at Emma Willard Sch, New York: *m* 1964, Christopher Adney Walter Gibbons, of 4 Hammersmith Terr, W6, son of late Adney Walter Gibbons, and has issue living, Sybil Jemima, *b* 1965, ——— (Georgina) Loveday, *b* 1967: *m* 1995, Charlie P. Gaynor, son of John Gaynor, of Hermanus, S Africa.

UNCLE LIVING (*son of 1st baronet*)

Anthony, CBE, *b* 1908; *ed* Gresham Sch, Holt, and Magdalene Coll, Camb (MA); Col late RE; Transport Consultant; Vice-Chm of London Transport Exec 1965-71 (Pres of Inst of Transport 1960-70), and a CStJ; Transport Div Control Commr for Germany (British Element), Berlin 1945-46; 1939-45 War (American Bronze Star); OBE (Mil) 1944, CBE (Civil) 1968: *m* 1946, Barbara, who *d* 1947, da of Peter Donovan, of Great Banks, Rye, Sussex, and has issue living, Caroline (*Lady Chichester-Clark*), *b* 1947: *m* 1974, as his 2nd wife, Sir Robert Chichester-Clark (M Donegall, colls), and has issue living, Adam Tamniarn *b* 1975, Thomas Finn *b* 1976. *Residence* – 35 Clareville Grove, SW7 5AU. *Club* – United Oxford and Cambridge Univ.

The 1st baronet, Rt Hon Sir William (James) Bull, FSA, was senior partner in the firm of Bull & Bull, solicitors, of 3 Stone Buildings, Lincoln's Inn, WC, and King Street, Hammersmith, W, a Director of Equity and Law Life Assurance Co, and of Siemens, Ltd, Pres of Council of Roy Albert Hall, Hon Solicitor to League of Mercy, and to Roy So of St George, first Hon Freeman of Hammersmith, and Maltravers Herald of Arms Extraor; sat as MP for Hammersmith (*C*) 1900-1918, and for S Div thereof 1918-29, and was Parliamentary Private Sec to Rt Hon W. H. Long, MP (afterwards Viscount Long of Wraxall) 1902-21. The 2nd baronet, Flight-Lieut Sir Stephen John, RAF Vol Reserve, partner in the firm of Bull & Bull was *ka* in Java 1942.

BULLOCK (UK) 1954, of Crosby, co Palatine of Lancaster (Extinct 1966)

Sir (HAROLD) MALCOLM BULLOCK, MBE, 1st and last *Baronet*.

DAUGHTER LIVING OF FIRST BARONET

Priscilla Victoria; Dir of Newbury racecourse; *b* 1920: *m* 1947, Peter Robin Hood Hastings Bass, who *d* 1964 (*see* E Huntingdon, colls). *Residence* – Well's Head House, Kingsclere, nr Newbury, Berks. *Club* – Jockey.

BUNBURY (E) 1681, of Stanney Hall, Cheshire

To be rather than to seem

Sir MICHAEL WILLIAM BUNBURY, 13th *Baronet, b* 29 Dec 1946; *s* his father, *Sir* (JOHN) WILLIAM NAPIER, 1985; *ed* Eton, and Trin Coll, Camb (MA); appointed to the Council of the Duchy of Lancaster 1993: *m* 1976, Caroline Anne, da of Col Anthony Derek Swift Mangnall, OBE, and has issue.

Arms – Argent, on a bend sable three chess-rooks of the field. **Crest** – Two swords saltire-wise through the mouth of a leopard's face or, the blades proper, hilted and pommelled gold.
Residence – Naunton Hall, Rendlesham, Woodbridge, Suffolk IP12 2RD.

SONS LIVING

HENRY MICHAEL NAPIER, *b* 4 March 1980. —— Edward Peter, *b* 1986.

DAUGHTER LIVING

Katherine Rosemary, *b* 1978.

BROTHERS LIVING AND DECEASED

†Charles Thomas, *b* 1950; *ed* Radley, and RAC, Cirencester: *m* 1st, 1971 (*m diss* 1985), Sarah Elizabeth, eldest da of William D. Hancock, of Sherborne Hall, King's Lynn, Norfolk; 2ndly, 1986, Amanda Carol (22 Balham Park Rd, SW12 8DU), yr da of John Richard Daniel Green (*see* B Bicester), and *d* 1997, leaving issue (by 1st *m*), Emma Sarah, *b* 1973, — Rebecca Louise, *b* 1974, — Venetia Alice, *b* 1978, — (by 2nd *m*) James William Rufus, *b* 1989, — Dominic John Frederick, *b* 1990, — Augusta Jane, *b* 1991. —— Christopher Henry, *b* (twin) 1950; *ed* Radley: *m* 1988, Mrs Amanda M. B. Greenwell, elder da of H. E. R. Stewart, MC, of Paulton's Sq, SW3, and formerly wife of Timothy Smallwood.
Residence – 5 The Benthills, Thorpness, Suffolk.

AUNT LIVING (*Daughter of 11th baronet*)

Margaret Elinor, *b* 1918: *m* 1945, Lt-Col James Michael Heigham Royce Tomkin, MC, DL, 5th R Inniskilling Dragoon Gds, of Red House, Wissett, Halesworth, Suffolk, and has issue living, Alastair Peter Royce, *b* 1949, — Richard James Royce, *b* 1951, — Caroline Susan (*Hon Mrs David Brougham*), *b* 1947: *m* 1st, 1967 (*m diss* 1976), Julian Dixon, of Grantham, Lincs; 2ndly, 1977, Hon David Peter Brougham (*see* B Brougham and Vaux).

WIDOW LIVING OF TWELFTH BARONET

MARGARET PAMELA (*Pamela, Lady Bunbury*), da of late Thomas Alexander Sutton (*see* Sutton, Bt, colls): *m* 1940, Sir (John) William Napier Bunbury, 12th Bt, who *d* 1985.

COLLATERAL BRANCHES LIVING

Grandchildren of late Lt-Col Gerald Bruce St Pierre Bunbury, IA, eldest son of Lt-Col William St Pierre Bunbury, 3rd and yst son of late Col Henry William St Pierre Bunbury, CB, 3rd son of 7th baronet:—
Issue of late Brig Francis Ramsay St Pierre Bunbury, CBE, DSO, *b* 1910, *d* 1990: *m* 1933, Elizabeth Pamela Somers, who *d* 1969, da of late Francis Reginald Liscombe, of Lansoar House, Lansoar, Monmouthshire:—
Charles Napier St Pierre, MBE (Creeting Lodge, Creeting St Mary, Ipswich, Suffolk IP6 8PH), *b* 1941; *ed* Rugby; late Maj Duke of Wellington's Regt; MBE (Mil) 1974: *m* 1977, Veronica Evelyn, only da of Capt Peter Evelyn Fanshawe, CBE, DSC, RN (*see* E Lindsay and Abingdon, colls), and has issue living, William Francis St Pierre, *b* 1982, — Victoria Elizabeth St Pierre, *b* 1979. —— Ann Geraldine St Pierre, *b* 1934: *m* 1978, Roland Ernest Bird, CBE, of 505 Duncan House, Dolphin Square, SW1V 3PP.

Grandson of late Lt-Col William St Pierre Bunbury (*ante*):—
Issue of late Brig Noel Louis St Pierre Bunbury, DSO, *b* 1890, *d* 1971: *m* 1923, Iris Graham, who *d* 1965, da of James Baird Whitelaw, of N Berwick:—
David St Pierre (1 Hazelwood Rd, Hale, Cheshire), *b* 1926; *ed* Imperial Coll of Science and Tech, London (PhD, BSc).

This family traces its origin to a yr branch of the Norman house of St Pierre. From Hugh Lupus, second Norman Earl of Chester, the family obtained the manor of Bunbury in Cheshire. David de Bunbury, 7th in descent from St Pierre, acquired by marriage, *temp* Edward III, the lordship of Stanney, which the family possessed until 1859. 11th in descent from David de Bunbury was Sir Thomas, the 1st baronet. The 6th baronet, Sir Thomas Charles, was forty-three years MP for Suffolk. The 7th baronet, Lieut-Gen Sir Henry Edward, KCB, sat as MP for Suffolk, and was Under-Sec of State for War 1809-16. Sir Edward Herbert Bunbury, 9th baronet, was MP for Bury St Edmunds (*L*) 1847-52.

RICHARDSON-BUNBURY (I) 1787, of Augher, co Tyrone

Virtue appears like an oak

Lt Cmdr *Sir* (RICHARD DAVID) MICHAEL RICHARDSON-BUNBURY, RN, 5th *Baronet*, el son of late Richard Richardson-Bunbury, 2nd son of late Moutray Frederic Richardson-Bunbury, 2nd son of late William Richardson-Bunbury, 2nd son of 2nd baronet; *b* 27 Oct 1927; *ed* RNC, Dartmouth; *s* his kinsman, *Sir* MERVYN WILLIAM, 1953: *m* 1961, Jane Louise, da of late Col Alfred William Pulverman, IA, and has had issue.

Arms – Quarterly: 1st and 4th, ermine, a chess-rook between two leopards' faces in bend between two bendlets sable, *Bunbury*; 2nd and 3rd, azure, on a fesse argent between an ancient ship the sails furled in chief, and in base a bull's head couped or, a saltire gules, *Richardson*. **Crests** – 1st, in front of a tree proper on a mount vert a leopard's face, paly of six argent and sable, transfixed by two arrows in saltire also proper; 2nd, a lion rampant ermine, in the mouth a trefoil slipped vert, between the fore-paws a torteaux charged with a cross-crosslet or.
Residence – Upper House, Crowcombe, Taunton, Som TA4 4AG.

SONS LIVING AND DECEASED

†Roger Michael, *b* 1962; *ed* Sherborne, and Manchester Univ (BA); *d unm* 1994. ——— THOMAS WILLIAM, *b* 4 Aug 1965; *ed* Millfield, and Durham Univ (BA); Solicitor 1989.

BROTHER LIVING

Roger Hugh Moutray (Fonthill Cottages, Lewannick, Launceston, Cornwall PL15 7QE), *b* 1934; Capt RN: *m* 1965, Carol Irene, da of F. J. H. Arnold, of 10 The Beeches, Bramley, Guildford, and has issue living, Robert Moutray, *b* 1968, — David, *b* 1972, — Judith Mervyn, *b* 1967, — Elizabeth (twin), *b* 1972.

SISTERS LIVING

Margaret Delves, *b* 1931; SRN: *m* 1966, James Harvey Woolliams, of Fairview, Pilgrim's Way, Boughton Aluph, Ashford, Kent TN25 4JD, and has issue living, Richard Frank, *b* 1968. ——— Angela Mervyn (132 Cambridge St, SW1V 4QF), *b* 1946; BA.

COLLATERAL BRANCHES LIVING

Grandsons of late Moutray Frederic Richardson-Bunbury (infra):—
Issue of late James Richardson-Bunbury, *b* 1901, *d* 1970: *m* 1938, Betty Winifred, who *d* 1984, da of late Col Roger Gordon Thomson, CMG, DSO (Broughton, Bt, colls, 1976 Edn):—
Patrick James (PO Box 31, Burswood, W Australia 6100) *b* 1939; *ed* Millfield. ——— William Hedley (Unit 13, 12 Convoy St, Maylands, W Aust 6051), *b* 1940; *ed* King's Sch, Bruton, and Durham Univ (BA); MACE; DipEd: *m* 1964, Jennifer Anne, da of late L. D. Syer, of Folkestone, and has issue living, Alison Claire, *b* 1969, — Katherine Anne, *b* 1971. ——— Andrew (104 Hydethorpe Rd, SW12 0JB), *b* 1943; *ed* Millfield, and Keble Coll, Oxford (MA), DipEd (Makerere Univ, Uganda), CQSW: *m* 1976, Christine, da of late J. A. Halley, of Workington, Cumberland, and has issue living, Daniel Christian, *b* 1981, — Rebecca, *b* 1980.

Grandchildren of late William Richardson-Bunbury, 2nd son of 2nd baronet:—
Issue of late Moutray Frederic Richardson-Bunbury, *b* 1865, *d* 1917: *m* 1896, Mary Capel Vines, who *d* 1949:—
Issue of late Archibald Edward Richardson-Bunbury, *b* 1868, *d* 1937: *m* 1909, Vida Muriel, who *d* 1967, da of late Arthur Heppingstone:—
†Archibald Vernon, *b* 1916: *m* 1939, Iris Jensen who *d* 1998, and *d* 1993, leaving issue, Edward Vernon, *b* 1941, — Richard Archibald, *b* 1943, — Dorothy Margaret, *b* 1940, — Wendy Muriel, *b* 1944, — Patricia Iris, *b* 1946, — Doreen Jennifer, *b* 1948. ——— Dorothy Emelie, *b* 1911: *m* 1st, 1932, Robert Edward Drake Brockman; 2ndly, 1940, Wilfrid Gordon Johnston, and has issue living (by 1st *m*), Mervyn Molloy JOHNSTON (Chapman Hill, via Busselton, W Australia 6280), *b* 1935; has assumed the surname of Johnston in lieu of his patronymic, — (by 2nd *m*) Elizabeth Margaret, *b* 1941: *m* 1962, Anthony Hedley Copeland, of 14 Geographe Bay Rd, Busselton, WA 6280, and has issue living, Michael Gordon *b* 1963: *m* 1990, Jane Georgina McGregor (and has issue living, James Stuart *b* 1996, Georgiana Elizabeth *b* 1993), Anthony James *b* 1965: *m* 1990, Michelle Robin Fitzgerald (and has issue living, John Anthony *b* 1994, Ellen Louise *b* 1993), — Judith Bunbury, *b* 1942: *m* 1966, Hubert van Helden, of 62 Stanley St, Nedlands, W Australia 6009, and has issue living, Nicholas *b* 1966, Vincent *b* 1971, and an adopted da, Caroline *b* 1970, — Margaret Bunbury, *b* 1944: *m* 1965, Peter Shugg, of 88 Florence Rd, Nedlands, W Australia 6009, and has issue living, Sabina Jane *b* 1967, Vanessa Amelia *b* 1970, — Vida Bunbury (Augusta, W Australia 6290), *b* 1948: *m* 19—, —, Hart, — Robin Bunbury (Nedlands, W Australia 6009), *b* 19—: *m* 19—, Gregory Kane. *Residence* – 49 Clifton St, Nedlands 6009, W Australia.

This family was originally Scottish; they became possessed of the Castle of Augher, in Tyrone by the marriage of Archibald Richardson with the da of Sir James Erskine. Sir James, the 2nd baronet in 1822, assumed his aunt's name of Bunbury.

BURBIDGE (UK) 1916, of Littleton Park, co Middlesex

Sir HERBERT DUDLEY BURBIDGE, 5th *Baronet*, only son of Herbert Edward Burbidge, 2nd son of 1st baronet; *b* 13 Nov 1904; *s* his kinsman, *Sir* JOHN RICHARD WOODMAN, 1974; *ed* Univ Sch, Victoria, BC, Canada: *m* 1933, Ruby, who *d* 1994, da of Charles Ethelbert Taylor, of The Willows, Comox, Vancouver 1, BC, and has issue.

Arms – Argent, a chevron sable between in chief two gads proper and in base an unicorn of the second. **Crest** – A stag's scalp, between the attires a boar's head erased and erect, all proper.
Residence – 3809 W 24th Av, Vancouver, BC V65 1LD, Canada.

SON LIVING

PETER DUDLEY (3809 West 24th Av, Vancouver, BC, Canada), *b* 20 June 1942: *m* 1967, Peggy Marilyn, da of Kenneth Anderson, of Ladner, BC, and has issue living, John Peter, *b* 1975, — Kathleen Jean, *b* 1973.

ADOPTED DAUGHTER LIVING OF FOURTH BARONET

Alexandra Louise, *b* 1970: *m* 1996, Antony P. N. Abell, yr son John Abell, of Ramsbury, Wilts, and has issue living, Athena Madeleine, *b* 1997.

Labour conquers all things

DAUGHTER LIVING OF THIRD BARONET

Susan Woodman, *b* 1927: *m* 1949, Michael Deric Lloyd Pearson, and has issue living, Robert Lloyd, *b* 1954, — Teresa Ann, *b* 1951, — Kate Alexandra, *b* 1959. *Residence* – Coach Hill Cottage, Coach Hill Lane, Burley St, Ringwood, Hants BH24 4HL.

WIDOW LIVING OF FOURTH BARONET

BENITA ROXANE (*Lady Burbidge*) (Albury Farmhouse, Draycot, Tiddington, Oxon OX9 2LX), da of late Adrian Willem Mosselmans, of Ascot, Berks: *m* 1956, Sir John Richard Woodman Burbidge, 4th baronet, who *d* 1974.

The 1st baronet, Sir Richard Burbidge, was Managing Director of Harrods (Limited), of Knightsbridge, SW, Joint Managing Director of Harrods (Buenos Aires) Limited, Chm of Dickins and Jones (Limited), a Director of Hudson's Bay Co, and a Member of Advisory Board of Ministry of Munitions.

BURDETT (E) 1665, of Burthwaite, Yorkshire

Sir SAVILE AYLMER BURDETT, 11th *Baronet*; *b* 24 Sept 1931; *s* his father, *Sir* HENRY AYLMER, MC, 1943; *ed* Wellington Coll, and at Imperial Coll, London; late temporary Sub-Lieut (E) RNVR: *m* 1962, June Elizabeth Campbell, only da of late Dr James Mackay Rutherford, of Westside, Knowl Hill, Woking, Surrey, and has issue.

Arms – Paly of six argent and sable, on a bend gules three martlets or. **Crest** – On a tower argent a martlet with wings displayed or.

SON LIVING

CRISPIN PETER, *b* 8 Feb 1967: *m* 1988, Julia Winifred Gresham, yr da of John Gresham Copeland, of Church Lawton, Cheshire.

DAUGHTER LIVING

Felicity Susan, *b* 1963.

SISTER LIVING

Jennifer Joyce, *b* 1934: *m* 1st, 1952, Marian Stachowiak; 2ndly, 1970, Gordon Skinner; 3rdly, 19—, Donald Wise, and has issue living (by 1st *m*), Nicholas John, *b* 1959, — Martin Allen, *b* 1961, Sarah Margaret, *b* 1957. *Residence* – 304 Bexhill Rd, St Leonards-on-Sea, Sussex.

DAUGHTER LIVING OF EIGHTH BARONET

Constance Hay BURDETT (7 Kensington Heights, Campden Hill Rd, W8 7BA), *b* 1908; resumed her maiden name of Burdett for herself and her issue 1953: *m* 1938 (*m diss* 1952), Albert Charles Blau, Swiss Diplo Ser, and has issue living, Charles Albert BURDETT (Roncal 7, 28002 Madrid, Spain) *b* 1942: *m* 1977, Christina L, da of Jost E. von Kursell, and has issue living, Charles Nicholas Wentworth *b* 1978, Andrew James Hay *b* 1983, Alexandra Christina Coutts *b* 1981, — John Coventry BURDETT (11 Lawn Crescent, Kew, Surrey), *b* 1945: *m* 1970, Judith Lisle Folkes, and has issue living, Edward Charles Coventry *b* 1974, Camilla Rose Sanderson *b* 1984.

COLLATERAL BRANCH LIVING

      Grandchildren of late Lt-Col Ernest Wyndham Burdett, DSO, MC, yst son of late Rev William Jerome Burdett, yr son of 6th baronet:—
      Issue of late Lt-Cdr Arlingham Jerome D'Arcy Burdett, RN, *b* 1922, *d* 1995: *m* 1948, Elizabeth Alix (Birch Piece, Milland, Liphook, Hants GU30 7NA), el da of late Sir Charles Holditch Bristow, CIE:—
Jeremy Francis D'Arcy, *b* 1951: *m* 1976, Jacqueline Elizabeth Mary, da of late Ian Corner, and has issue living, Daniel Ian Jerome, *b* 1997, — Lucy Joanna, *b* 1979, — Jenny Alix, *b* 1983. —— Richard Wyndham, *b* 1962; Lt-Cdr RN: *m* 1994, Annmarie Margaret, da of late James Wellwood, of Dunfermline, Fife, and has had issue, †Mathew, *b* and *d* 1996. —— Susan Priscilla, *b* 1949: *m* 1973, John Patrick Manley, of The Beeches, Bunny, Nottingham NG11 6QA, and has had issue, Robert George, *b* and *d* 1980, — Edward John, *b* 1981, — Anna Louise, *b* 1976, — Katherine Elizabeth, *b* 1984. —— Marion Elizabeth, *b* 1953.

Sir Francis, 1st Bt, was son of Francis Burdett, of Burthwaite, co York.

BURKE (I) 1797, of Marble Hill, Galway

One king, one faith, one law

Sir JAMES STANLEY GILBERT BURKE, 9th *Baronet*: *b* 1 July 1956; *s* his father, Sir THOMAS STANLEY, 1989: *m* 1980, Laura, da of Domingo Branzuela, of Catmon, Cebu, Philippines, and has issue.

Arms – Erminois, a cross gules; in the first quarter a lion rampant sable. **Crest** – A cat-a-mountain sejeant-guardant proper, collared and chained or.
Residence – Lindenbergstrasse 231, CH-5618 Bettwil, Switzerland.

SON LIVING

MARTIN JAMES, *b* 22 July 1980.

DAUGHTER LIVING

Catherine Elisabeth, *b* 1982.

SISTER LIVING

Caroline Elizabeth, *b* 1959.

COLLATERAL BRANCHES LIVING

      Grandson of late Henry Ulick Burke, only son of late Ulick Ralph Burke, elder son of late Charles Granby Burke, 2nd son of 2nd baronet:—
      Issue of late Lt-Col Ulick Richard Samuel Burke, *b* 1907, *d* 1963: *m* 1930, Cynthia (Glenhurst Manor, Bournemouth, Dorset BH4 8BB), da of H. Darling:—
Jeremy Ulick (Malvern, 11 Ham Meadow, Marnhull, Sturminster Newton, Dorset DT10 1LR), *b* 1931; *ed* Univ Coll, NW; CEng, FICE, FIArb: *m* 1st, 1954 (*m diss* 1962), Anne, el da of J. E. Chinneck, of Berkhamsted, Herts; 2ndly, 1963, Prudence Mary, da of H. P. Stride, of Milbury Heath, Glos, and has issue living (by 1st *m*), Ulick Simon, *b* 1957, — (by 2nd *m*) Ulick Jacquelyn, *b* 1964: *m* 1995, James Robert Shepherd, of Ampthill, Beds, and has issue living, Matthew James *b* 1997, Christopher Stephen *b* 1998, — Ulick Karen, *b* 1966: *m* 1995, Robert John Rose, of Wareham, Dorset, and has issue living, Harry Robert *b* 1997, Jennifer Karen *b* 1996.

      Grandson of late Capt James Henry Thomas Burke, CB, RN, son of Maj Gen James Henry Burke, 3rd son of 2nd baronet:—
      Issue of late James Howe Campbell Ulick Burke, *b* 1880, *d* 1946: *m* 1st, 1912 (*m diss* 1928), Lilian Maud, da of William John Whenmouth; 2ndly, 1930, Annie Amelia Granville, of 6, Churchfield Rd, Ealing, W13:—
(By 2nd *m*) James Ulick Hubert, *b* 1932. *Residence* – 6 Churchfield Rd, Ealing, W13.

Sir Thomas, 1st Bt, raised a Regt of Foot at his own expense during the Napoleonic Wars. The 2nd baronet was Vice-Lieut for co Galway (High Sheriff 1838), and sat as MP there for 1830-32. The 3rd baronet was also MP for co Galway 1847-65.

BURNETT (NS) 1626, of Leys, Kincardineshire (Dormant 1959)

Sir ALEXANDER EDWIN BURNETT OF LEYS, OBE, 14th *Baronet*, *d* 9 May 1959.

COLLATERAL BRANCH LIVING

Descendants of late Alexander Burnett (2nd son of 6th baronet), who assumed the surname and arms of Ramsay by Roy licence, and was *cr* a *Baronet* 1806:—
Of whom *Sir* ALEXANDER WILLIAM BURNETT RAMSAY, 7th *Baronet*, *b* 4 Aug 1938, is presumed heir to this Baronetcy.

The lands of Leys are held under a charter from Robert Bruce, dated 1324. The 1st baronet, Sir Thomas Burnett, though a Covenanter, was much trusted by Charles I, and was a friend of the great Marquess of Montrose. He was uncle of the famous Dr Gilbert Burnet, Bishop of Salisbury. The son of the 6th baronet, who assumed the name of Ramsay, was created a baronet 1806. The 12th baronet, Col Sir Thomas Burnett, RA, was Lord-Lieut and Convener for co of Kincardine. The 13th baronet, Maj-Gen Sir Thomas Lauderdale Gilbert Burnett, CB, CMG, DSO, was Brigadier of Queen's Body Guard for Scotland (Roy Co of Archers), Vice-Lieut of Kincardineshire, and Col of the Gordon Highlanders, and commanded the 14th, 153rd and 8th Inf Brigs and 51st (Highland) Div (TA).

BURNETT (UK) 1913, of Selborne House, County Borough of Croydon

Firmness in dangers

DAVID HUMPHERY BURNETT, MBE, TD, 3rd *Baronet*; *b* 27 Jan 1918; *s* his father, *Col Sir* LESLIE TREW, CBE, TD, 1955; *ed* Harrow, and St John's Coll, Camb (MA): FRICS, FLS; a Lt of City of London, Dir of The Proprietors of Hay's Wharf Ltd 1950-80 (Chm 1965-80), Guardian Royal Exchange Assurance 1967-88, a Member of Port of London Authority 1962-75 and Chm of S London Botanical Inst 1964-80; Chm of The London Wharfingers Assocn 1964-71; Master of Co of Watermen and Lightermen 1964, and of Girdlers' Co 1970; late Maj RA (TA) 1939-45 War in France, Africa, Sicily, and Italy (despatches, MBE); MBE (Mil) 1945: *m* 1948 Geraldine Elizabeth Mortimer, da of late Sir Godfrey Arthur Fisher, KCMG, and has issue.

Arms – Per chevron or and sable, two holly leaves in chief vert, in base a hunting horn of the first, stringed argent. *Crest* – Issuing from flames a branch of holly erect proper.
Residences – Tandridge Hall, nr Oxted, Surrey RH8 9NJ; Tillmouth Park, Cornhill-on-Tweed, Northumberland. *Club* – Turf.

SONS LIVING

CHARLES DAVID (25 Marloes Rd, W8 6LG), *b* 18 May 1951; *ed* Harrow, and Lincoln Coll, Oxford: *m* 1989 (*m diss* 199—), Victoria Joan, elder da of James Simpson, of Rye, Sussex, and has issue living, Roberta Elizabeth, *b* 1992. —— John Godfrey, *b* 1954; *ed* Harrow.

BROTHER LIVING

Richard Leslie, *b* 1932; *ed* Eton, and King's Coll, Camb; LRAM 1952, ARCM 1952; formerly 2nd Lt R Leicester Regt: *m* 1969, Katrina Eveline, only da of W. Graeme Hendrey, of Snatts Hill, Bletchingley, Surrey. *Residences* – 51 Frant Rd, Tunbridge Wells, Kent; Finchcocks, Goudhurst, Kent.

SISTER LIVING

Nancy, *b* 1926: *m* 1st, 1948 (*m diss* 1960), Ian Alastair Sinclair; 2ndly, 1972, Prof A. H. Gerrard, of Leyswood, Groombridge, Sussex, and has issue living, (by 1st *m*), Guy, *b* 1951, — Josephine Anne, *b* 1949, — Karen Lesley, *b* 1954.

Sir David, 1st baronet, was Lord Mayor of London 1912-13. Sir Leslie Trew, CBE, TD, 2nd baronet, was Hon Col 460th Heavy Anti-Aircraft Regt RA (TA), and Master of Coopers Co 1947.

BURNEY (UK) 1921, of Preston House, Preston Candover, co Southampton.

What is done honourably is right

Sir CECIL DENNISTON BURNEY, 3rd *Baronet*; *b* 8 Jan 1923; *s* his father, *Cdr Sir* (CHARLES) DENNISTOUN, CMG, 1968; *ed* Eton, and Trin Coll, Camb; Chm Hampton Trust plc 1975-87; Chm JMD Group plc 1986-92; a MLC, N Rhodesia 1959-64, and an MP for Zambia 1964-68; RNVR 1942-45: *m* 1957, Hazel Marguerite, yr da of late Thurman Coleman, of Weymouth, and formerly wife of Trevor de Hamel, and has issue.

Arms – Azure, a pale argent two bars counter-embattled counterchanged between in chief and in base a fountain proper. Crest – Out of a naval crown gold a bull's head azure, armed or.
Addresses – PO Box 32037, Lusaka, Zambia; 5 Lyall St, SW1X 8DW.

SONS LIVING

NIGEL DENNISTOUN, *b* 6 Sept 1959; *ed* Eton, and Trinity Coll, Cambridge: *m* 1992, Lucy Vanessa, yst da of Robert Anthony Brooks, of Chelsea, SW3, and has issue living, Max Dennistoun, *b* 15 Sept 1994, — Otto James Cecil, *b* 1995. *Residence* – Springhill House, Springhill Rd, Begbroke, Oxon OX5 1RX. —— Philip Julian Gerard, *b* 1961; *ed* Eton, and Christ Church, Oxford: *m* 1999, Francesca Louise, only da of Roydon John Tucker, of Highgate. *Residence* – 58 Bradbourne St, SW6 3TE.

The 1st baronet, Adm of the Fleet Sir Cecil Burney, GCB, GCMG, was 2nd in Command of Grand Fleet at battle of Jutland 1916 and 2nd Sea Lord 1916-1917. The 2nd baronet, Cdr Sir (Charles) Dennistoun Burney, CMG, RN, was inventor of Explosive Paravane and Protector Paravane during the 1914-18 War.

BURRARD (GB) 1769, of Walhampton, Hampshire (Extinct 1965)

DAUGHTER LIVING OF EIGHTH BARONET

Elizabeth Geraldine (Colwin, Rouge Huis Av, St Peter Port, Guernsey, CI), *b* 1927.

BURRELL (GB) 1774, of Valentine House, Essex.

Per fluctus ad oram

Through the waves to the shore

Castle, Horsham, W Sussex RH13 8LJ.

Sir (JOHN) RAYMOND BURRELL, 9th *Baronet*; *b* 20 Feb 1934; *s* his father, *Lt-Col Sir* WALTER RAYMOND, CBE, TD, DL, 1985; *ed* Eton: *m* 1st, 1959 (*m diss* 1971), Rowena Frances, da of late Michael H. Pearce; 2ndly, 1971, Margot Lucy, da of F.E. Thatcher, of Sydney, NSW, and has issue by 1st and 2nd *m*.

Arms – Vert, three plain shields argent, each having a bordure engrailed or.
Seat – Knepp Castle, Horsham, West Sussex RH13 8LJ. *Residence* – 14 Rosemont Av, Woollahra, Sydney, NSW 2025, Australia.

SON LIVING (*By 1st marriage*)

CHARLES RAYMOND, *b* 27 Aug 1962; *ed* Millfield, and RAC Cirencester: *m* 1993, Isabella Elizabeth Nancy, elder adopted da of Michael Lambert Tree (*see* D Devonshire), and has issue living, Edward Lambert, *b* 10 Oct 1996, — Nancy Catherine, *b* 1995. *Residence* – Knepp

(*by 2nd marriage*)

Andrew John, *b* 1974.

DAUGHTER LIVING (By 2nd marriage)

Catherine Anne Lucy, b 1977.

BROTHER LIVING

Mark William (Bakers Farm, Shipley, West Sussex RH13 7JJ; 43A Reeves Mews, W1Y 3PA), b 1937; ed Eton, and Pembroke Coll, Camb (BA): m 1966, Mrs Margot Rosemary Munro, yr da of Westray Pearce, of Killara, NSW, and has issue living, William Westray, b 1967; ed Eton: m 1994, Celia Ann, only da of late Peter Shelmerdine, of Toorak, Melbourne, Australia, and has issue living, Coco Camellia b 1998, — Anthony Merrik, b 1969; ed Eton: m 1998, Lady Louise Iona Campbell, only da of 12th Duke of Argyll, — Sophia Judith, b 1974.

SISTERS LIVING

Penelope Anne, b 1932: m 1953, John Richard Greenwood, DL, of Stone Hall, Balcombe, W Sussex RH17 6QN, and has issue living, John Simon, b 1955; ed Eton, — James Anthony, b 1959; ed Millfield: m 1985, (Julia) Anne, yr da of late Edward Maynard Denny, and has issue living, Jennifer Adelaide b 1987, — (Anne) Lucinda, b 1957: m 1994, Maj Patrick James Auchinleck Darling, The Light Dragoons, of Caradoc, Sellack, Ross-on-Wye, Herefs HR9 6LS, son of late Lt Cdr Gerald Ralph Auchinleck Darling, RD, QC, of Crevenagh, Omagh, co Tyrone, and has issue living, Etheldreda Anne Auchinleck b 1997, — Fiona Mary, b 1962: m 1987, Charles John Martin, 3rd son of Cyril Patrick John Martin, and has issue living, Michael George b 1990, Charlotte Emma b 1988, Susanna Tara b 1993. —— Julia Mary Rona, b (twin) 1934: m 1953, Jeremy Fox Eric Smith, DL, of The Old Rectory, Slaugham, Haywards Heath, W Sussex RH17 6AG, and has issue living, Julian Raymond Eric (Balcombe House, W Sussex RH17 6PB), b 1956; ed Eton, and New Coll, Oxford: m 1982, Caroline Fiona, elder da of W/Cdr Gordon Leonard Sinclair, DFC (see E Fortescue), and has issue living, Oliver George Eric b 1983, Henry Thomas Eric b 1986, Lucy Alexandra b 1984, — Hugo Jeremy Eric (Ley Farm House, Dullingham, Newmarket, Suffolk CB8 9XG), b 1957; ed Eton, and Exeter Univ: m 1992, Sophie Diana, da of Jeffrey Hernu, and has issue living, Milo Thomas Eric b 1996, Arabella Diana b 1994, Lettice Helen b 1998, — Dione Angela (Countess of Verulam), b 1954: m 1976, 7th Earl of Verulam, and has issue (see E Verulam), — Sarah Helen, b 1962: m 1987, Ashley Charles Preston, of The Mill House, Gibbons Mill, The Haven, Billingshurst, W Sussex RH14 9BL, and has issue living, Frederick Charles Fox b 1989, Rupert Merrik Arthur b 1993.

UNCLE LIVING (son of 7th baronet by 1st marriage)

Peter Eustace, CBE (Long Hill, Moulton Rd, Newmarket, Suffolk CB8 8QG), b 1905; ed Eton; formerly Squdn Ldr, RAF; Dir of National Stud 1937-71; 1940-44 War Sqdn Ldr RAF; CBE (Civil) 1957: m 1st, 1929 (m diss 1940), Margaret Edith Pamela, da of late Lt-Col Stephen Hungerford Pollen, CMG (see Pollen, Bt, colls); 2ndly, 1971, Mrs Constance P. Mellon, of Ligonier, Pa, USA, and has issue living (by 1st m), Merrik Kay (Casa del Hilario, Yaiza, Lanzarote, Canary Islands), b 1937; ed Harrow; m 1st, 1960 (m diss 1968), Julian Sarah, el da of David Hugo Burr; 2ndly, 1968, Molli Cecily Lalla, da of late Stanley Cooke, of Knysna, Cape, South Africa, and has issue living (by 1st m), Peter b 1963.

HALF-AUNT LIVING (daughter of 7th baronet by 2nd marriage)

Etheldreda Josephine (Dreda, Baroness Tryon), b 1909: m 1939, 2nd Baron Tryon, who d 1976. Residence – Church Farm, Great Durnford, Salisbury SP4 6AZ.

COLLATERAL BRANCH LIVING

Issue of late Peter Timothy Burrell, late Lieut RN, el son of Peter Eustace Burrell, CBE (ante), b 1930, d 1975: m 1955, Patricia Clarice Marion, who d 1999, da of Capt Arthur Thomas Thompson, of Morcott, Rutland, and formerly wife of Ralph John Hamilton Pollock (see Pollock Bt, colls):—
Nicola Pamela Jane, b 1957: m 1989, James Donald McGregor Reevely, yr son of Desmond Reevely, of Mill Corner, W Chiltington, Sussex, and has issue living, Timothy James McGregor, b 1997, — Lucy Elizabeth Constance, b 1991.

The first baronet was Sir Charles Raymond, who was created with remainder to his son-in-law, William Burrell, who succeeded as 2nd baronet. The 3rd baronet sat as MP for Shoreham (C) 1806-62, and at the time of his death was "father" of the House of Commons. The 4th baronet was also MP for Shoreham (C) 1862-76, and the 5th baronet sat as MP for New Shoreham (C) 1876-85, Lieut-Col Sir Merrik Raymond Burrell, CBE, 7th Bt, was High Sheriff of Sussex 1918, and Pres of Roy Agricultural Soc of England 1936, and served in S Africa 1900-01, and during European War 1914-19 as Lieut-Col (CBE). Lt-Col Sir Walter Raymond Burrell, CBE, TD, 8th Bt, was Chm CLA, Pres Royal Agric Soc of England, an Alderman W Sussex CC, and DL W Sussex, served 1939-45 War with Surrey & Sussex Yeo.

BUTCHER (UK) 1960, of Holland, co Lincoln (Extinct 1966)

Sir HERBERT WALTER BUTCHER, MP, 1st and last *Baronet*.

DAUGHTERS LIVING OF FIRST BARONET

Joy Daphne, *b* 1936: *m* 1956, Jonathan Payn Fellows-Smith, of 30 Tandridge Drive, Orpington, Kent BR6 8BZ, and has issue living, Richard Jonathan, *b* 1957: *m* 1983, Collette Middleton, — Charles Herbert, *b* (twin) 1957, — James William, *b* 1958. —— Pauline Mary, *b* 1938: *m* 1960, John Embleton Cardwell, of 12 Woodcote Park Av, Purley, Surrey, and has issue living, David Anthony, *b* 1963, — William John, *b* 1968, — Caroline Mary, *b* 1961: *m* 1988, Richard Charles Geary, — Jane Elizabeth, *b* 1967. —— Elisabeth Clare, *b* 1944: *m* 1966, John Alun Kelvin-Davies, of 133 Fishpool St, St Albans, Herts, AL3 4RY, and has issue living, Claire Elisabeth, *b* 1967: *m* 1994, Simon Godwin, and has issue living, Emily Rebecca *b* 1998, — Holly Ann *b* 1969: *m* 1997, Charles Wordie.

BUTLER (I) 1628, of Cloughgrenan, co Carlow, Ireland.

As I find

Sir RICHARD PIERCE BUTLER, 13th *Baronet*; *b* 22 July 1940; *s* his father, *Col Sir* THOMAS PIERCE, CVO, DSO, OBE, 1994; *ed* Eton, New York Univ, and Inst of Chartered Accountants in England and Wales; MBA, FCA: *m* 1965, Diana, da of Col Stephen John Borg of The Palms, St Julians, Malta, and has issue.

𝕬𝖗𝖒𝖘 – Or, a chief indented azure, a bordure indented ermine. 𝕮𝖗𝖊𝖘𝖙 – Out of a ducal coronet or, a plume of five ostrich feathers therefrom a falcon rising argent.
Seat – Ballin Temple, Ardattin, co Carlow.

SONS LIVING

THOMAS PIERCE, *b* 9 Oct 1966; *ed* Eton, and Univs of Pennsylvania and Lausanne; MBA, BSc: *m* 1993, (Lucinda) Pamela, eldest da of Edward Joseph Murphy, of Ste Foy, Quebec, Canada, and has issue living, Tymandra, *b* 19—, — Antonia, *b* 1996. *Address* – 60 Conduit St, Hong Kong. —— Stephen Patrick, *b* 1968; *ed* Eton, and Univ of E Anglia (BSc). —— Rupert Dudley, *b* 1971.

SISTERS LIVING

Caroline Rosemary, *b* 1939: *m* 1958, Maj-Gen Richard Charles Keightley, CB, 5th Roy Inskilling Dragoon Guards, of Kennels Cottage, Tarrant Gunville, Dorset, el son of late Gen Sir Charles Frederic Keightley, GCB, GBE, DSO, and has issue living, Charlotte Joan, *b* 1961: *m* 1985, Howard Stephen Buchanan Jenkinson, of The Rectory, Willey, Broseley, Shropshire TF12 5JJ, elder son of Barry Jenkinson, of Chetton Grange, Bridgnorth, Shropshire, and has issue living, Alistair Charles Buchanan *b* 1988, William Howard Thomas *b* 1990, Benjamin Christopher Patrick *b* 1994, Sophia Elizabeth Rosemary *b* 1992, — Arabella Caroline, *b* 1962: *m* 1989, Peter J. O'Connell, of Australia, eldest son of T. O'Connell, of Dorset, — Victoria Rosemary, *b* 1965. —— Virginia Pamela Liège, *b* 1949: *m* 1970, Capt Michael Cunningham, The Queen's Own Hussars, of Dolhyfryd, Denbigh, Clwyd, and has issue living, Charles Alexander Clunie, *b* 1978, — Rupert Jasper Clunie, *b* 1984, — Sophia Louisa Caroline, *b* 1973, — Henrietta Maria Charlotte, *b* 1975.

AUNT LIVING (*Daughter of 11th baronet*)

Joan, *b* 1908: *m* 1943, Robert Nigel Bright Brunt, CBE, who *d* 1982, and has issue living, Nicholas John Pierce (118 Elm Grove Rd, Barnes, SW13 0BS), *b* 1946; *ed* Marlborough; Lt-Col Royal Fusiliers: *m* 1977, Jennifer May Charlotte Boon, — Nigel Richard Pierce (Mildmay House, Twyford, Winchester, Hants SO21 1NT), *b* 1948; *ed* Harrow; JP NW Hants 1996, — Rosemary Helen, *b* 1944; *ed* Lady Eleanor Holles Sch, and King's Coll, London Univ (BA): *m* 1971, Rev Anthony Broughton Hawley, MA, of The Rectory, Mill Lane, Kirkby, Liverpool L32 2AX. *Residence* – The Lodge, Cox's Hill, Twyford, Winchester, Hants WO21 1PQ.

COLLATERAL BRANCHES LIVING

Grandchildren of late Hans Pierce Butler (*infra*):—
    Issue of late Richard Pierce Butler, *b* 1911, *d* 1976: *m* 1st, 1933, Vida McDonald, who *d* 1968; 2ndly, 1970, Elsa Butler (now Lee) (196 Plainsview, Regina, Sask, Canada SR3 6LZ):—
(By 1st *m*) Arthur Hans Pierce (Erickson, Manitoba, Canada), *b* 1934: *m* 1955, Elsie Elaine Laycock, and has issue living, Walter Richard Pierce (Site 3, Box 124, RR3, Brandon, Manitoba, Canada), *b* 1964: *m* 1st, 1989 (*m diss* 19—), Leah Jane Findlater; 2ndly, 1998, Kathryn Graham, — Kerrie Lee, *b* 1966. —— Kathleen Enid Selena, *b* 1935: *m* 1956, John Francis Lochhead, of Basswood, Manitoba, Canada, and has issue living, Richard Francis, *b* 1959: *m* 1982, Judy Loucks, and has issue living, Andrew Francis *b* 1990, Catherine Jean *b* 1985, — George Walter, *b* 1967, — Phyllis Marie, *b* 1961: *m* 1986, John Adam Land, and has issue living, Dylan Adam *b* 1993, Nicole Marie *b* 1989. —— Sheila Margaret Eva, *b* 1939: *m* 1958, John Richard Fawcett (Box 515, Swan River, Manitoba, Canada) and *d* 1984, leaving issue, Cherylyn Sheila, *b* 1961: *m* 1980, Dennis Watts, and has issue living, Jeremy Steven *b* 1983, Amanda Marie *b* 1981, —

Kimberly Dawn, *b* 1963: *m* 1983, Dennis Napady, and has issue living, Stephanie Eva Rose *b* 1984, Lynette Dennisa *b* 1986, Raylene Johnelle *b* 1991, Tamara *b* 1993, — Lorilee Faye, *b* 1967: *m* 1988, Curtiss Barrett, and has issue living, Tyler Richard Joseph *b* 1991, Taran John *b* 1993.

Grandchildren of late Richard Pierce Butler, 2nd son of 9th baronet:—
Issue of late Hans Pierce Butler, *b* 1880, *d* 1940: *m* 1st, 1908, Agnes Lenore, who *d* 1931, da of late William Edward Spurstow Moulson, of Solsgirth, Manitoba; 2ndly, 1932, Maude Addison, who *d* 1973:—
(By 1st *m*) John Edward (Youngstown, Alberta), *b* 1916: *m* 1940, Kathleen Wilson, and has issue living, Walter, *b* 1941: *m* 1968, Elaine Prowse, and has issue living, Karen *b* 1974, Susan *b* 1977, — Melvin *b* 1943: *m* 1970, Patricia Bolduc, and has issue living, Val *b* 1970, Melvin *b* 1973, — Donald, *b* 1945: *m* 19—, — , and has issue living, Ryan *b* 1981, Lynn *b* 1966, Tami *b* 1973, and an adopted da, Mandy *b* 1972, — Gordon, *b* 1949: *m* 1st, 19—, — ; 2ndly, 1985, Lee Ann Johnston, and has issue living (by 1st *m*), Curt *b* 1976, Kim *b* 1974, (by 2nd *m*) Matthew *b* 1986, Timothy *b* 1988. —— Arthur Cecil (Box 26D, RR2 Winnipeg, Manitoba, R3C 2E6), *b* 1919: *m* 1st, 1942, Joan Goodings, who *d* 1951; 2ndly, 1956, Isabelle Panting, and has issue living, (by 1st *m*) Leslie Grant, *b* 1947, — Barbara, *b* 1944: *m* 1964, Gary McRindle, and has issue living, Joan Louise *b* 1965, Judy Lynn *b* 1970, — (by 2nd *m*) James Arthur George, *b* 1957, — Thomas David, *b* 1964, — Valerie Louise, *b* 1960: *m* 1981, James Roger Merkl, and has issue living, James Roger *b* 1983, Ashley Dawn Valene *b* 1987, Selina Alynn *b* 1993. —— William Hans (Foxwarren, Manitoba), *b* 1922: *m* 1943, Betty Atwell, and has issue living, Alan David, *b* 1944: *m* 1965, Linda Stewart, and has issue living, David Pearce *b* 1969: *m* 1992, Kirstine Miller, Mark *b* 1978, Tanis Dawn *b* 1975, — Garth Charles, *b* 1946: *m* 1966, Gwenyth Dodge, and has issue living, William Neal *b* 1969: *m* 1992, Bonnie Allen (and has issue living, Brendan 1989, Nicole Randi *b* 1992), Kathleen Audrey *b* 1967, — William Grant, *b* 1957: *m* 1978, Mary Dalton, and has issue living, Jeremy Hans *b* 1987, Cory Grant *b* 1990. —— Charles Edwin (Solsgirth, Manitoba), *b* 1926: *m* 1948, Marian McKay, and has issue living, Morley, *b* 1951: *m* 1973, Lexie Hodgson, and has issue living, Jared Chane *b* 1977, Mandie Leigh *b* 1975, Shanda *b* 1984, — Barry, *b* 1953: *m* 1974, Karen Pizzey, and has issue living, Jack Heath *b* 1976, Vicki Lynn *b* 1978, Charla Ann *b* 1979, Kari Dayle *b* 1981. —— Sidney Clarence (Dugald, Manitoba), *b* 1928: *m* 1952, Joan Murray. —— (By 2nd *m*) Home Pierce (Box 1, Site 25, RR8, Calgary, Alberta, Canada T2J 2T9), *b* 1939: *m* 1962, Robin Carol Boaden, and has issue living, Robert Pierce, *b* 1967, — Katy-Jo, *b* 1964. —— (By 1st *m*) Agnes Gertrude, *b* 1913: *m* 1932, Walter Taylor, of 3262, Clive Av, Vancouver, BC, and has issue living, William, *b* 1942, — Constance Lena, *b* 1934: *m* 1952, Mike Rooney. —— Eva Constance, *b* 1915: *m* 1936, Walter McTavish, and has issue living, Walter Lloyd, *b* 1936, — Corinne Gertrude, *b* 1938: *m* 1957, Edward James Perrin, — Selina Elsie, *b* 1944, — Wynona May, *b* 1952. —— (By 2nd *m*) France Kathleen Marina, *b* 1935: *m* 1956, Garry Neil Chaloner, and has issue living, Neil Garry, *b* 1962, — Susan Leslee Anne, *b* 1960. —— Brenwyn Maude, *b* 1937: *m* 19—, — Klassen, of 414, 7 Av NW, Calgary, Alberta T2N 0Y7, Canada.

Grandchildren of late Frederick Francis Baron Butler (infra):—
Issue of late Reginald Percy BUTLER-FITZGERALD, *b* 1896, *d* 1983, having assumed by authority of Ch Herald of Ireland 1946, the additional surname and arms of FitzGerald, and discontinued by deed poll 1946 the christian name of FitzGerald: *m* 1930, Muriel, who *d* 1971, yst da of F. J. B. Martin, of New Farm, Brisbane, Queensland:—
Frederick FitzGerald (PO Box 6054, Gold Coast Mail Centre, Queensland 4217, Australia), *b* 1933. —— Geraldine BUTLER-FITZGERALD (17 Enderley Av, Clayfield, Brisbane, Queensland 4011, Australia), *b* 1946; resumed her maiden name 1990: *m* 1972 (*m diss* 1988), John Conoplia, and has issue living, Rebecca Frances, *b* 1973, — Jessica Jane, *b* 1976.

Grandchildren of late Capt Henry William Paget Butler, 4th son of 8th baronet:—
Issue of late Frederick Francis Baron Butler, *b* 1861, *d* 1926: *m* 1891, Bertha Florence, who *d* 1928, da of late P. J. Dunne, of Rockhampton, Queensland:—
Mabel Florence, *b* 1905. *Residence* – Unit 39, Roselin Court, Payneham Rd, Joslin, 5070 Adelaide, S Australia.

Issue of late Thomas Percy Butler, *b* 1862, *d* 1933: *m* 1st 1905, Harriette Gwendoline, who *d* 1931, da of late Col John Henry Graham Smyth, CMG (E Mount Cashell, ext); 2ndly, 1932, Rosabel May, who *d* 1954, only da of Capt Charles Walker, 21st Fusiliers, and widow of Sir George Beresford Butler, of Island View, Clifden, co Galway:—
(By 1st *m*) Tyssen Desmond, *b* 1906; Major (retired) Roy Welch Fusiliers: *m* 1940, Dorothy, da of George Saltonstall West, of Chestnut Hill, Massachusetts, USA, and has issue living, George Tyssen (True Farm, Holderness, New Hampshire 03245, USA), *b* 1943; *ed* Groton Sch Massachusetts, and Univ of N Carolina; film producer, director and author: *m* 1970 (*m diss* 19—), Mary Victoria Leiter, and has issue living, Desmond Oates *b* 1972, Tyssen West *b* 1975, — Richard Percy (300 McKinstry Rd, Gardiner, NY 12525, USA): *b* 1944: *m* 1968, Florence, da of late Frank Lyman, and has issue living, James Paget *b* 1979, Chanda Anne *b* 1972.
Address – True Farm, Holderness, New Hampshire 03245, USA

Granddaughter of late James Butler, 4th son of 7th baronet:—
Issue of late Beauchamp Charles Butler, *b* 1865, *d* 1919: *m* 1896, Elizabeth (who *m* 2ndly, 19—, — Hamilton), da of late T. Findlay Muirhead, of Durban, Natal:—
Eileen Doris, *b* 1901: *m* 19—, — Jones, and has issue living, a son, *b* 19—. *Residence* – Repson Rd, Durban, Natal.

Grandchildren of late Capt John Bayford Butler, RN, el son of Capt Charles George Butler, RN, 5th son of 7th baronet:—
Issue of late Francis Algernon Butler, *b* 1878, *d* 1935: *m* 1909, Dorothy Jean, da of late Douglas James Chester, of Bedford:—
Doreen Marjorie, *b* 1912: *m* 1st, 1932, Frank Clear, of Victoria, BC, who *d* 1989; 2ndly, 1945, Charles Emil Burgess, of Victoria, BC, who *d* 1971; 3rdly, 1955, Lawrence George Alexander, of Victoria, BC, who *d* 1990, and *d* 1976, leaving issue (by 1st *m*), Donald Lloyd Francis (Maple Ridge, BC, Canada), *b* 1937: *m* 1956, Anne Dolores Barne, and has issue living, Raymond Lloyd *b* 1957, Charles Patrick *b* 1958, Sharon Ann *b* 1966, — Marjorie Butler, *b* 1932: *m* 1951, Raymond Marquette, RCAF, of Fourth St, Nanaimo, BC, Canada, and has issue living, Gregory Dean *b* 1953, Matthew Perry *b* 1958, Kevin Anthony *b* 1960, Christopher Adam *b* 1964, — Barbara Joan, *b* 1934: *m* 1957, Denis Joseph Beaulac, of Fernie, BC, Canada, and has issue living, Michael Brian *b* 1951, Joseph Denis *b* 1958, Daniel Mark *b* 1962, Delvina Marie *b* 1959, Doreen Marie *b* (twin) 1959, Jacqueline Marie *b* 1960, Joni Marie *b* 19—, — Frances Rhoda, *b* 1935: *m* 1954, Kenneth Roy Suddaby, of Brentwood Bay, BC, Canada, and has issue living, Michelle Lynn *b* 1962, Liana Marie *b* 1965, — (by 2nd *m*) Helaine Charlotte, *b* 1944: *m* 1st, 19—, Kenneth Donald Charters; 2ndly, 1987, Lisle Darwin Frank, of Westholme, BC, Canada, and has issue living (by 1st *m*), Wayne Kenneth *b* 1964, Douglas Allan *b* 1965, Debra Lynn *b* 1962. —— Eileen Mary Paget, *b* 1914; 1939-45 War with CWAC in UK, Holland and France 1940-44; *dunm* 1979.

—— Vivienne Frances, *b* 1920: *m* 1939, Sidney Bryan Beswick, of 411-1433 Faircliff Lane, Victoria, BC, Canada V8S 3J6, and has issue living, Kenneth Bryan (216 Linden Av, Victoria, BC), *b* 1941: *m* 19—, Sonja Georgette, da of George Yakimovich, of Victoria, BC, and has issue living, Gary Bryan *b* 1966, Laura Sonja *b* 1970, —— Gary Chester (24 Fairway Drive, Spruce Grove, Alberta), *b* 1954: *m* 1976, Laura Rose, da of Gordon Barne, of Port Alberni, BC, and has issue living, Bryan Samuel Butler *b* 1981.

Issue of late Humphrey Charles Butler, *b* 1880, *d* 1969: *m* 1st 1904, Emily Laura, who *d* 1916, da of late Alexander J. Baxter; 2ndly, 1918, Helen Howard, who *d* 1919; 3rdly, 1920, Sheila Gertrude Edith, da of late William Bernard Blackwell:—
(By 1st *m*) †Humphrey de Bohun Bayford, *b* 1904; *ed* Haileybury, and Stanford Univ (AB 1928): *m* 1930, Mildred, who *d* 1986, da of late William Erskine Duncan, of Oroville, Cal, USA, and *d* 1991, leaving issue, Bayford Duncan (6350 Butler Circle, Penryn, CA 95663, USA), *b* 1938, *ed* Stanford Univ (AB); MS Agric Econ of Univ of California at Davis 1962: *m* 1964 (*m diss* 1986), Nancy, da of James F. Grandin, and has issue living, Bayford Duncan *b* 1965, James Devereux *b* 1969, Cortlandt Pierce *b* 1974. —— (by 3rd *m*) †Greville Humphrey, *b* 1921; *ka* 1945. —— Anthony Bernard, *b* 1929; Maj RTR (ret): *m* 1st, 1969 (*m diss* 1972), Amanda McBlain, da of Lt-Col W McBlain Stephen; 2ndly, 1973, Mrs Harriet Eileen Harland.

Grandchildren of late Lt-Col Charles Walter Butler, OBE, son of late William Charles Butler, 2nd son of Capt Charles George Butler, RN (ante):—
Issue of late Maj Richard Shirley Butler, Gloucestershire Regt, *b* 1907, *d* 1988: *m* 1940, Auriol Lilian Evelyn (Long Ham House, Cornwood, S Devon), da of late Rev A. R. Biddle, of Temple Hill, East Budleigh, Devon:—
Patrick James Richard, *b* 1944; *ed* Wellington, and Auckland Univ, NZ. —— Penelope Eve BUTLER BROOKE (Southwood Hayes, Chilmark, Salisbury, Wilts), *b* 1942; *ed* Ruskin Sch of Drawing and Fine Art: *m* 1968 (*m diss* 1988), Lt-Col Thomas Christopher Peter Brooke, IG, and has issue living, James Richard Henry Ormonde, *b* 1972; *ed* Eton, and Newcastle Univ.

Issue of late Brig Walter George Ormonde Butler, DSO, MC, *b* 1917, *d* 1967: *m* 1945, Pamela Winsome Muriel (who *m* 2ndly, 1970, Brig Cuthbert Grafton Moore, OBE, of Patches, On the Green, Amport, Andover) da of Dr Sidney Owen, of Isleworth, Middlesex:—
David Simon Ormonde (Britty Hill Cottage, Britty Hill, Elstead, Surrey), *b* 1947: *m* 1971, Vivienne Claire, el da of Cdr R. P. FitzGerald, RN, of Petworth, Sussex, and has issue living, Toby George Ormonde, *b* 1974, —— Alice Chia, *b* 1979.

Grandchildren of late James Thomas Butler, grandson of William Paul Butler, 4th son of 5th baronet:—
Issue of late Somerset Edward Molyneux Butler, LRCSI, LRCPI, *b* 1867, *d* 1914: *m* 1902, Elise Jessie, who *d* 1942, only child of Reginald Bearcroft:—
Margaret Elise, *b* 1902: *m* 1928, Maj Philip Anderson, A & SH, who *d* 1968, and has issue living, Oliver George Bearcroft (Orchard Farm, Kirkmichael, Ayrshire), *b* 1943; Reserve A & SH: *m* 1969, Phillipa Kate, da of late Maj C. L. Stephenson, and has issue living, Philip George *b* 1970, Emily Mary *b* 1971, Nancy Rose *b* 1983. *Residence* – Orchard Farm, Maybole, Ayrshire.

Grandchildren of late Charles Richard Butler, eldest son of late James Thomas Butler (ante):—
Issue of late Group-Capt James Humphrey Butler, RAF, *b* 1897, *d* 1979: *m* 1st, 1925, Marguerite Kathleen Louise, who *d* 1938, da of John Hale, of Donaghcloney House, Donaghcloney, co Down; 2ndly, 1939, Freda, who *d* 1993, da of F. E. Peto, of Pietermaritzburg, S Africa:—
(By 1st *m*) Charles Humphrey John (11210 Thomlar Drive, Fairfax Station, VA 22039, USA), *b* 1927; *ed* Wellington, and Univ of Virginia (AB); Lt-Col US Army Reserve: *m* 1957, Elizabeth Ann, who *d* 1990, da of Harry F. Mett, of Schenectady, NY, and has issue living, Bradford Frederick, *b* 1962; *ed* Univ of Oregon (BS 1984); Capt US Army Reserve: *m* 1992, Kim Kyong Oh, of S Korea. —— (By 2nd *m*) Barbara Ann Somerset, *b* 1941; late 2nd Officer WRNS: *m* 1971, Godwin Scerri, of Malta, and has issue living, Fiona Somerset Paula, *b* 1973, — Eleanor Margaret Louise, *b* 1978. —— Isobel Louise (13 Northcote Rd, St Margaret's, Twickenham, Middx), *b* 1945.

Issue of late Edward Walter Charles Butler, *b* 1900, *d* 1988: *m* 1939, Iris Courtenay, da of late Rev G. Moriarty, R of Erganagh, co Tyrone:—
Walter Richard Courtenay (160 Drum Rd, Cookstown, co Tyrone), *b* 1944; late 3rd Officer, Blue Funnel Line: *m* 19—, Alexandra McQueen, and has issue living, Gavin, *b* 1980. — Corrin, *b* 1982, — Ewan, *b* 1984. —— Maeve Geraldine Audley, *b* 1940: *m* 1964, Rt Rev Brian Desmond Anthony Hannon, Bishop of Clogher since 1986, of The See House, Fivemiletown, co Tyrone, and has issue living, Desmond Pierce O'Brian, *b* 1965, — Brendan Gerald, *b* 1968, — Edward Neil Anthony, *b* 1970.

Issue of late Lieut-Col Beauchamp Henry Butler, DSO, Roy Inniskilling Fusiliers, *b* 1902, *ka* 1943: *m* 1938, Vera May (who *d* 1986, having *m* 2ndly 1946, Major Charles Patrick Fitzgerald, who *d* 1996, of Turlough Park, Castlebar, co Mayo), da of late Maj William Stewart, MC, JP, of Daisy Hill, Clogher, co Tyrone:—
Michael Henry, *b* 1939; formerly in Roy Signals. —— Patrick Beauchamp Rupert (Breaffy, Castlebar, co Mayo), *b* 1943: *m* 1982, Deirdre Anne, da of late Very Rev John Ernest Leeman, Dean of Killala, and has issue living, Andrew John Beauchamp, *b* 1990, — Nicola Ann Leeman, *b* 1985, — Susannah May Frances, *b* 1987.

The 1st baronet, Sir Thomas Butler, High Sheriff and MP for co Carlow, was the natural son of Hon Sir Edmund Butler, 2nd son of 9th Earl of Ormonde. Lieut-Col Sir Richard Pierce Butler, OBE, 11th baronet, was High Sheriff of co Carlow 1905, and served in S African War 1901-2, and in European War 1914-19 (despatches twice, OBE).

BUTLER (UK) 1922, of Old Park, Devizes, Wilts.

Sir (REGINALD) MICHAEL THOMAS BUTLER, QC, 3rd *Baronet*; *b* 22 April 1928; *s* his father, *Sir* (REGINALD) THOMAS, 1959; *ed* Brentwood Coll, Victoria, BC, Univ of BC (BA), and Osgoode Hall Sch of Law, Toronto; Bar and Solicitor Ontario 1954 and BC 1967; QC 1967: *m* 1st, 1952 (*m diss* 1967), Marja Margaret Elizabeth, only da of late Ewen H. McLean, of Toronto; 2ndly, 1968 (*m diss* 1974), Mrs Barbara Anne Hogan, da of late Kevin Cahill, of Dublin, and has issue by 1st *m*.

Arms – Azure, three covered cups in pale between two flaunches or, each charged with a cross-crosslet sable. Crest – A demi-horse sable, charged on the shoulder with a covered cup and resting the sinister hoof upon a cross-crosslet or.
Residence – Old Park Cottage, 634 Avalon Rd, Victoria, BC V8V 1N7, Canada.

SONS LIVING (*By 1st marriage*)

(REGINALD) RICHARD MICHAEL, *b* 3 Oct 1953: *m* 1st, 1982 (*m diss* 1998), Dale Karen, only da of Frederick William Piner, of Vancouver, BC; 2ndly, 1999, Penelope Joy, da of Frederick Lipsack, of Campbell River, BC, and has issue living, (by 1st *m*) (Reginald) Paul, *b* 26 June 1988, — Andrew, *b* 1991, — Nicholas, *b* 1993. —— Geoffrey MacLean, *b* 1956. —— Thomas David, *b* 1960.

ADOPTED SON LIVING (*son of Sir Michael's second wife by her previous marriage*)

Patrick Colman, *b* 1958 (adopted 1971).

BROTHER LIVING

Peter Woods, *b* 1933; QC: *m* 1959, Lucia Harris, and has issue living, Hugh, *b* 1960, — James, *b* 1965, — Thomas, *b* 1963, Andrea, *b* 1961, — Theresa, *b* 1967. *Residence* – Vancouver, British Columbia.

BUTLER (UK) 1926, of Edgbaston co Warwick (Extinct 1939)

Sir WILLIAM WATERS BUTLER, 1st and last *Baronet*.

COLLATERAL BRANCH LIVING

Issue of late William Owen Butler, only son of 1st baronet, *b* 1898, *d* 1935: *m* 1922, Beatrice Eileen (who *d* 1970, having *m* 2ndly, 1939 (*m diss* 1950), Lt-Com Clive Gordon Trencham, RN (ret), who *d* 1982), da of Thomas Charles Byrne:—
Patricia Ann, *b* 1924: *m* 1947, Peter Henry Murray Yeo, and has issue living, Christopher David, *b* 1948, — Sally Ann, *b* 1950, — Murray Clare, *b* 1953. —— Teresa Jill, *b* 1928: *m* 1951 (*m diss* 1974), Robert Arthur Young, who *d* 1977, and has issue living, Robert Mark, *b* 1951, — Sarah Caroline, *b* 1954. —— Genevieve Owen, *b* (*posthumous*) 1935: *m* 1970 (*m diss* 1972), William McQueen. *Residence* – 27261 Sunset Blvd East, Lathrup Village, Michigan 48076, USA.

BUTT (UK) 1929, of Westminster, co London (Extinct 1999)

Sir (ALFRED) KENNETH DUDLEY BUTT, 2nd and last *Baronet*.

Arms – Argent, on a chevron engrailed gules between in chief two torteaux and in base a trefoil slipped vert, with a portcullis chained or. Crest – A lion sejant proper gorged with a collar gemelle or, and supporting with the dexter fore paw a spear, the head fracted and dependent also proper.

WIDOW LIVING OF FIRST BARONET

WILHELMINE (Vilma) (*Viscountess Harberton*) (2 Brock Terrace, St Peter Port, Guernsey), da of late Heinrich Wahl: *m* 1st, 1960, as his second wife, Sir Alfred Butt, 1st Bt, who *d* 1962; 2ndly, 1978, 10th Viscount Harberton.

WIDOW LIVING OF SECOND BARONET

MARIE JOSEPHINE (*Lady Butt*), da of late John Bain, of Wadhurst, and widow of Lt-Col Ivor Watkins Birts: *m* 1948, as his second wife, Sir (Alfred) Kenneth Dudley Butt, 2nd Bt, who *d* 1999.

I am what I am

Sir Alfred Butt, 1st Bt, son of F. Butt, of Hampshire, was Director of Rationing, Min of Food 1917-18, Chm and Managing Dir, Theatre Royal, Drury Lane 1925-31, and MP for Wandsworth (Balham and Tooting Div) (*U*) 1922-36.

BUXTON (UK) 1840, of Belfield, Dorset

Sir JOCELYN CHARLES RODEN BUXTON, VRD, 7th *Baronet*, elder son of late Capt Roden Henry Victor Buxton, CBE, RN, 2nd son of 4th baronet; *b* 8 Aug 1924; *s* his cousin, *Sir* THOMAS FOWELL VICTOR, 1996; Lt-Cmdr RNVR, 1939-45 War (despatches), Korea 1953, VRD, 1972: *m* 1960, Ann Frances, da of Frank Smitherman, MBE, HM Foreign Ser, and has issue.

Arms – Argent, a lion rampant tail elevated and turned over the head sable, between two mullets of the second. Crest – A buck's head couped gules, attired or, gorged with a collar of the last, therefrom pendent an escutcheon argent, charged with an African's head sable. Supporters – *Dexter*, an African sable, wreathed about the head and loins vert; *sinister*, a buck gules, attired or.
Residence – Rodwell House, Loddon, Norwich, Norfolk. *Club* – Norfolk.

DAUGHTERS LIVING

Frances Dorothy, *b* 1960: *m* 1st, 1981 (*m diss* 1989), Oliver P...... St John, eldest son of late Lt-Col Charles Arthur Roland Langshaw St John, of Glebe Manor, Havant; 2ndly, 1989, Henry Ellis Jones-Davies, son of Col T. E. Jones-Davies, JP, DL, of Erwlon, Nantgaredig, Carmarthen, and has issue living (by 2nd *m*), Edward Owain Ellis, *b* 1991, — Thomas Llywelyn Ellis, *b* 1993. *Residence* – Erwlon, Nantgaredig Carmarthen. —— Harriet Lucy (*Hon Mrs Michael Dalrymple*), *b* 1962: *m* 1991, Hon Michael Colin Dalrymple, yst son of 13th Earl of Stair, KCVO, MBE, and has issue (*see* E Stair). *Residence* – Cranstoun Riddel, Oxenfoord, Midlothian. —— Caroline Sarah, *b* 1964: *m* 1987, Nicholas Michael Jarrett, son of Lt-Col Michael Jarrett, of Wellow, Hants, and has issue living, James Nicholas, *b* 1995, — Arthur Jocelyn, *b* 1999. *Residence* – Westhill, Salisbury Rd, Broughton, Hants.

BROTHER LIVING

GERARD ST JOHN RODEN, *b* 28 Sept 1927; Lt-Cmdr RN, 1944-45 War; OStJ: *m* 1954, Judith Averil, da of late Hon Angus Dudley Campbell, CBE (*see* B Colgrain, colls), and has issue living, Crispin Charles Gerard (16A Harwood Rd, SW6 4PH; Osborne House, Trunch, nr N Walsham, Norfolk NR28 0PX. *Club* – Puffins (Edinburgh)), *b* 1958; *ed* Eton, — Charlotte Anne Gerard (Hill Farm, Neatishead, Norwich, Norfolk NR12 8YE), *b* 1955: *m* 1981, Sardar Mandhir Singh Sethi, son of Sardar Mehar Singh Sethi, of Chandigarh, India, and has two das, Selina Sangeeta Kaur *b* 1984, Hermione Sukjeevan Kaur *b* 1988, — Laura Joan Gerard (50 Rue Crulaincourt, Paris 75018, France), *b* 1961. *Residence* – Pitteadie House, Kirkcaldy, Fife KY2 5UN. *Clubs* – Naval and Military, Puffins (Edinburgh).

B 182   DEBRETT'S ILLUSTRATED BARONETAGE

SISTERS LIVING

Anne Frances Roden (*Hon Mrs Thomas Hazlerigg*), *b* 1920: *m* 1st, 1945 (*m diss* 1978), Henry Winterstein Gillespie, MD; 2ndly, 1979, Hon Thomas Heron Hazlerigg (*see* B Hazlerigg), who *d* 1998, and has issue living (by 1st *m*), Nicola Henrietta St John GILLESPIE (Bolwick Hall, Marsham, Norfolk), *b* 1946; has resumed her maiden name: *m* 1st, 1965 (*m diss* 1969), Charles Rupert Raw; 2ndly, 1975 (*m diss* 1978), John Latimer Smith, and has issue living, Richenda Anne Latimer GILLESPIE *b* 1976, Dalila Nerissa Claire GILLESPIE *b* 1982, — Richenda Antoinette de Winterstein, *b* 1949. *Residence* – Caflida, Klosters, Switzerland. ——— Elisabeth Lucy Roden (21 Millbrook Close, Child Okeford, Blandford Forum, Dorset DT11 8HA), *b* 1922: *m* 1951, Maj Thomas Arnett Hughes-Ross, MBE, RCT, who *d* 1981, and has issue living, Timothy Arnett Ross (Coombe Down Farm, Charisworth, Blandford Forum, Dorset DT11 9AL), *b* 1954: *m* 1985, Sally Anne, da of Peter Michael Roe, of E Stoke, Dorset, and has three children, Thomas Ashley James *b* 1987, Hannah May *b* 1990, Elisabeth Lauren *b* 1993, — Joanna Elisabeth Ross, *b* 1952: *m* 1973, Anver Jamal Rizvi, of Honeysuckle Cottage, Woodcutts, Salisbury, Wilts SP5 5RT, and has issue living, Tamara Elisabeth Shamsa *b* 1982, Carina Lucy Parveen *b* 1985, — Penelope Jane Ross, *b* 1956. *Residence* – 21 Millbrook Close, Childe Okeford, Blandford Forum, Dorset DT11 8HA. ——— Phyllida Dorothy Roden, *b* 1932: *m* 1959, her kinsman, Ronald Carlile Buxton, and has issue (see colls, infra). *Residences* – 67 Ashley Gdns, SW1; Kimberley Hall, Wymondham, Norfolk.

DAUGHTER LIVING OF FIFTH BARONET

Montagu Lucy, *b* 1927: *m* 1965, John Harold Rose, who *d* 1996. *Residence* – 3 Wyndham Gdns, Wallingford, Oxon OX10 9AU.

STEPMOTHER LIVING

Hilda, MBE, da of late Charles Alfred Meadows, of Rainham, Kent: *m* 1957, as his 2nd wife, Capt Roden Henry Victor Buxton, CBE, RN, who *d* 1970. *Residence* – Rodwell Cottage, Loddon, Norfolk.

COLLATERAL BRANCHES LIVING

Branch from 3rd son of 4th Baronet:—

Issue of late Maj Clarence Edward Victor Buxton, MC, 3rd son of 4th baronet, *b* 1892, *d* 1967: *m* 1st, 1917 (*m diss* 19—) Mary Aline, MBE, who *d* 1954, da of Lt-Col Frederic Ewart Bradshaw, DSO; 2ndly, 1945, Mrs Mavis Jean Fox (Kinuni (PO Box 17), Vipingo, Kenya Coast), da of Walter Bromhead:— (By 1st *m*) Maurice (Braishfield Lodge, Romsey, Hants S051 0PS), *b* 1919; Capt Coldm Gds; 1939-45 War: *m* 1st, 1941 (*m diss* 1978), Alison Mary, da of L. L. Savill, of Comenden Manor, Cranbrook; 2ndly, 1979, Susan Whiteway, da of A. H. Alexander, of Guernsey, CI. ——— †Rupert (PO Box 950, Mutari, Zimbabwe), *b* 1923; 1939-45 War as Lt RNVR: *m* 1st, 1949 (*m diss* 1968), Frances Ann, da of Prof Frank Debenham, OBE, of Cambridge; 2ndly, 1972, Betty Webb, of S Africa, and *d* 1994, having had issue (by 1st *m*), Jonathan, *b* 1950: *m* 1st, 1975 (*m diss* 1984), Susan Elizabeth, da of late James Elgie Lloyd; 2ndly, 1990, Susan Elizabeth, da of Ronald Charles Williamson, of Little Harrowden, Northants, and has issue living (by 1st *m*), Nicholas Rupert *b* 1982, Emma Louise *b* 1978, — †Terence Rupert, *b* 1952; *d* 1970, — Paul Stephen, *b* 1954: *m* 1980, Patricia Jane, da of Claude Alexander Rockhill, of Durban, S Africa, and has issue living, Terence Anthony *b* 1981, Quinton Stephen Andrew *b* 1992, Gwendoline Jill *b* 1983, — Colin, *b* 1957: *m* 1992, Michelle, da of Louw Burmeister, of Cape Town, S Africa, and has issue living, Kayley Lorraine Lempriere *b* 1998, — (by 2nd *m*) Sarah Jane, *b* 1976. ——— Gwendolen, *b* 1921: *m* 1960, Terence Leland Bowles, who *d* 1968, of 53 Silverwood Drive, Laverstock, Salisbury, Wilts SP1 1SQ, and has issue living, Katherine *b* 1963. ——— Rosemary, *b* 1927: *m* 1955, Francis Henry Alastair Julian Lochrane, of 2 Lochside Cottage, Inverinan, by Taynuilt, Argyll. ——— (By 2nd *m*) Rowena Clarence, *b* 1945: *m* 1st, 1970 (*m diss* 1978), Colin Woods; 2ndly, 1984, Fredrik Louis Tauber, of 125 Cheryl Drive, Hendersonville, TN 37075, USA. ——— Carissa Clarence, *b* 1946: *m* 1974, Peter Ray Nightingale (62/63 Severnhampton, Cheltenham, Glos), and has issue living, Edward Clarence, *b* 1976, — Rosalind Lucy, *b* 1978, — Eva Helen Charis, *b* 1980, — Rosemary Victoria Catherine, *b* 1983, — Rowena Nell, *b* 1989.

Branches from yr sons of 3rd baronet:—

Issue of late Rt Hon Noel Edward NOEL-BUXTON (2nd son of 3rd baronet), who was *cr Baron Noel-Buxton* 1930 (*see* that title).

Issue of late Charles Roden Buxton, 3rd son of 3rd baronet, *b* 1875, *d* 1942: *m* 1904, Dorothy Frances, who *d* 1963, da of late Arthur Trevor Jebb, of Ellesmere, Salop:— David Roden (Old Ellwoods, 55 Bridleway, Grantchester, Cambs CB3 9NY), *b* 1910; ed Trin Coll, Camb (MA); *m* 1st, 1939 (*m diss* 1948), Annelore, who *d* 1988, da of H. Albers; 2ndly, 1950, Mary Violet, da of late Denis Alfred Jex Buxton (infra), and has had issue (by 1st *m*) Roden Arnold (15 Henleaze Gdns, Bristol BS9 4HH) *b* 1942; ed St Christopher Sch, and Trin Coll, Camb (MA); DArch; RIBA: *m* 1971, Linda Jane, da of Richard Miller, MVO, of Bromley, Kent, and has issue living, Samuel Roden *b* 1972, Oliver Silas *b* 1976, — (by 2nd *m*) Charles Benedict, *b* 1958: *m* 1985, Caroline Mavis Beadle, and has issue living, Toby Finbarr *b* 1990, Richard Ronan *b* 1992, Martin Patrick Mingulay *b* 1994, — James Andrew Denis, *b* 1964, — Elizabeth Eglantyne, *b* 1951: *m* 1976, John Waterfield, and *d* 1985, — Richenda Mary, *b* 1953: *m* 1987, Michael Desmond Tennyson Barley, Walnut Tree Cottage, 61 Fowlmere Rd, Heydon, nr Royston, Herts SG8 8PZ, 2nd son of late J. H. T. Barley, of Tunbridge Wells, Kent, and has issue living, Max John Roden *b* 1989, Orlando Hugh Buxton *b* (twin) 1989, Joshua Bernard Tennyson *b* 1990, — Francesca, *b* 1956.

Issue of late Leland William Wilberforce Buxton, yst son of 3rd baronet, *b* 1884, *d* 1967: *m* 1912, Ada Mary, who *d* 1979, el da of the Rev Thomas Henry Royal Oakes, BD, formerly R of Thurgarton, Norwich:—

Aubrey Leland Oakes, MC, *b* 1918; *cr Baron Buxton of Alsa* 1977 (see that title). ———— Diana Elizabeth, *b* 1915: *m* 1939, Cdr Adrian James Dent, RN, of Quarr Acre, Brighton Rd, Sway, Hants, son of Sir Francis Henry Dent, CVO, and has issue living, Simon Adrian (Am Steinberg 59, 8031 Steinebach, Germany), *b* 1949: *m* 1972 (*m diss* 1985), Brigitte Englehart, and has issue living, Clara *b* 1973, — Jeremy Francis (2 Keble House, Manor Fields, Putney SW15 3LS), *b* 1952: *m* 1971 (*m diss* 1988), Penelope Linton, and has issue living, Simon Timothy *b* 1971, Jason Paul *b* 1973, — Gladys Henrietta (Meadow Thatch, Mount Pleasant, Sway, Hants SO41 8LS), *b* 1940: *m* 1963 (*m diss* 1989), Simon Aidan Reynolds, and has issue living, Augustine Francis *b* 1964, Thomas Becket *b* 1968, Sophie Elizabeth *b* 1965, — Janet Sylvia, *b* 1947: *m* 1976, Maj Michael Robjohn, MBE, Royal Irish Fusiliers, of Ramley Cottage, Ramley Rd, Pennington, Lymington, Hants SO41 8LH, and has issue living, Benjamin James *b* 1983, Molly Fionnuala *b* 1978, Diana Bryony *b* 1979. ———— Mary Judith, *b* 1922; formerly in ATS: *m* 1st, 1942, Philip Arthur Leo Gompertz, Lt RA, who was *ka* 1942; 2ndly, 1945, Maj Clement Wynter Lister, RA (ret), of Walnut Corner, Orford, Woodbridge, Suffolk, and has had issue, (by 2nd *m*) Patrick Thomas Buxton, *b* 1948, *d* 1989, — Philippa Judith (22 Belitha Villas, N1 1PD), *b* 1946; MA (RCA): *m* 1971 (*m diss* 1980), David John Lloyd Watkins, MA.

Branches from 2nd son of 2nd Baronet:—

Grandchildren of late Edward Gurney Buxton (infra):—
Issue of late Lt-Col Desmond Gurney Buxton, *b* 1898, *d* 1987: *m* 1930, Rachel Mary, who *d* 1994, da of late Lt-Col Arthur Francis Morse, of Coltishall Mead, Norwich:—
Andrew Edward (Hoveton Hall, Hoveton, Norfolk NR12 8RJ), *b* 1935; *ed* Eton, and Magdalene Coll, Camb (MA); High Sheriff Norfolk 1998: *m* 1967, Barbara Anne, da of late Cyril Gascoigne Lloyd (*see* Preston, Bt, 1980 Edn), and has issue living, Harry Desmond Gascoigne, *b* 1972, — Laura Catherine, *b* 1968: *m* 1996, Charles Robert Erith, eldest son of Robert Felix Erith, TD, of Lamarsh, Essex, and has issue living, Jemima Barbara *b* 1997, — Nicola Rachel Anne, *b* 1971. ———— James Desmond (23 Murrayfield Rd, Edinburgh EH12 6EP), *b* 1947; *ed* Eton, and Magdalene Coll, Camb (MA): *m* 1975, Annabella, yst da of late Douglas Collins, of Gt Missenden, Bucks (*see* Backhouse, Bt, colls, 1980 Edn), and has issue living, Jasper Francis, *b* 1979, — Oliver Desmond, *b* 1980. ———— Annabel Audrey, *b* 1938: *m* 1979, Iain Francis Wauchope Buchan, of 144 Bronsart Rd, SW6 6AB, yr son of late H. F. W. W. Buchan. ———— Rosalinde Rachel, *b* 1939: *m* 1965, John Raoul Wilmot Stansfeld, JP, DL, of Dunninald, Montrose, Angus (*see* Eardley-Wilmot, Bt, colls, 1995 Edn), and has issue living, Edward John Buxton, *b* 1966: *m* 1996, Mary Katharine Margaret, da of Robert Graham Langton Brackenbury, and has issue living, Harold John Maryons *b* 1998, Katharine Elizabeth *b* 1997. ———— Robert George Wilmot, *b* 1967, — Nicholas Desmond Morse, *b* 1972. ———— Elizabeth Laura, *b* 1941: *m* 1962, Rev William Lister Archibald Pryor, of Elm Tree Cottage, Summer Fields, Oxford, 2nd son of late Rev Archibald Selwyn Pryor, of The Rectory, Upper Broughton, Leics, and has issue living, Alexander Timothy William, *b* 1968, — Hugh William Arthur, *b* 1974, — Victoria Elizabeth, *b* 1965.

Granddaughter of late Samuel Gurney Buxton, 2nd son of 2nd baronet:—
Issue of late Edward Gurney Buxton, *b* 1865, *d* 1929: *m* 1895, Laura, MBE, who *d* 1957, da of late John Gurney:—
Monica, *b* 1916: *m* 1937, Maj Robert Henry Calvert, Middx Yeo, of Picts House, Horsham, Sussex (Cholmeley, Bt), who *d* 1987, and has issue living, Monica Julia (*Lady Blewitt*), *b* 1939: *m* 1st, 1964, Maj John Dominic Morrogh Bernard, Irish Gds, who *d* 1968; 2ndly, 1969, Maj Sir Shane Gabriel Basil Blewitt, GCVO, IG, of South Corner, Duncton, Petworth, Sussex, and has issue living, (by 1st *m*) Alexander Dominic Calvert *b* 1966, Katherine Mary *b* 1965: *m* 1994, Keith Bryant, son of Keith Bryant, of Borden, Kent (and has issue living, William Thomas *b* 1998, Susannah Mary *b* (twin) 1998), (by 2nd *m*) Piers Shane Basil Calvert *b* 1972, Davina Henrietta *b* 1970: *m* 1998, Maj Hume Richard Webb Jones, Roy Green Jackets (*see* E Romney, colls), — Diana *b* 1941: *m* 1981, Richard Makepeace Martineau, of The Lawn, Walsham-le-Willows, Bury St Edmunds, Suffolk, — Patricia Rohays, *b* 1943: *m* 1968, Michael Charles Richardson, of St Vincents, Addington, W Malling, Kent, and has issue living, Mark Jonathan *b* 1969, Lucinda Patricia *b* 1971, Anna Monica *b* 1973, — Georgina Sophia, *b* 1949: *m* 1973, John Richard Hull Moore, of Woodlands Farm, Nuthurst, Horsham, Sussex, and has issue living, Alexander John Calvert *b* 1975, Marianne Sophia *b* 1978, Sophie Diana *b* 1980.

Grandchildren of late Edward Gurney Buxton (ante):—
Issue of late Hubert Edward Buxton, *b* 1901, *d* 1973: *m* 1932 (*m diss* 1948), Anne Hawise Colleton, da of of late Col Arthur Hautayne Bowring, RFA (*see* Colleton Bt. ext, 1980 Edn):—
Robert Hugh (45 Merthyr Terrace, SW13 8DL), *b* 1933; *ed* Eton: *m* 1st, 1963 (*m diss* 1972), Helen Loveday, el da of D. M. R. Piesse, of St Helena; 2ndly, 1973 (*m diss* 1991), Mrs Judith Serena Lourenço, da of John Richard Rumsey; 3rdly, 1992, Mrs Anne Gamble, da of late Antony McCormick, of Sunning House, Sunningdale, Berks, and has issue living (by 1st *m*), David Colleton, *b* 1964, — Henry Gurney, *b* 1966, — (by 2nd *m*), Jonathan Hugh, *b* 1978. ———— Sara Carolyn Colleton *b* 1937: *m* 1964, Peter James Foot (RMB 1073, Porongurup Rd, Mount Barker, W Aust 6324), and has issue living, Lorna Alice, *b* 1965, — Elizabeth Angela, *b* 1967.

Issue of late Mervyn Buxton, Lieut RAPC, *b* 1903, *d* (on active service) 1944: *m* 1932, Carmela Mary Beatrice, who *d* 1989, da of George Herbert Lyon:—
Simon Lyon (104 Cameron St, Edgecliff, NSW), *b* 1935; *ed* Wellington Coll, and at Magdalene Coll, Camb (BA): *m* 1971, Janet Susan, da of Haille Paine, of Bowral, NSW, and has issue living, Thomas Lyon, *b* 1973, — Bennington Haille, *b* 1975. ———— Ian Lyon (12 Grand Parade, Tynemouth, Tyne & Wear, NE30 4JS), *b* 1937; *ed* Wellington Coll, and Glasgow Univ (BSc, PhD); CEng; Reader in Marine Transport, Newcastle Univ; author of *Big Gun Monitors*, *Cargo Access Equipment for Merchant Ships*, and *Metal Industries*: *m* 1966 Jean Mary, da of late William Cochrane, of E Lothian, and has issue living, Keith Mervyn Lyon, *b* 1974; *ed* Leeds Univ (BEng); Flying Officer RAF, — Fiona Anne, *b* 1969; *ed* Sheffield Hallam Univ (BSc).

Issue of Mark Buxton, *b* 1909, *d* 1972: *m* 1949, Penelope Ann Cecil (8 Walker Av, W Perth, W Aust), da of Edmund C. Clifton, of Perth, W Aust, and widow of P/O O. K. Fisher, RAF.—
Jeremy Clifton Gurney, *b* 1952; *ed* Ch Ch Gram Sch, Perth, and Univ of W Aust (BA 1974, MA 1977).

Granddaughters of late Samuel Gurney Buxton, 2nd son of 2nd baronet:—
Issue of late Capt Richard Gurney Buxton, *b* 1887, *d* 1972: *m* 1914, Mary Primrose, who *d* 1972, da of late Maj Anthony Stephen Ralli, 12th Lancers:—

Pamela Chloe (Wiveton Hall, Holt, Norfolk, and 25 Wellington Sq, SW3), *b* 1915: *m* 1948, Michael Desmond MacCarthy, who *d* 1973, and has issue living, Desmond James, *b* 1956: *m* 1993, Hon Christina Anne Loder, da of 3rd Baron Wakehurst, and has issue living, Edmund Michael *b* 1995, Isabel Inge *b* 1997, — Mary Lisa, *b* 1950. —— (Marian) Camilla, *b* 1919: *m* 1947, Maj Richard Peyton, RHA, who *d* 1998, of Leaside, South St, Hinton St George, Ilminster, Som, and has issue living, Robin Derek, *b* 1950, — Nigel Richard, *b* 1951.

Branches from 3rd son of 2nd Baronet:—

Grandchildren of late Gerald Buxton, el son of Edward North Buxton, 3rd son of 2nd Baronet:—
Issue of late Lieut-Col Edward North Buxton, MC, *b* 1894, *d* 1957: *m* 1st, 1924, Hon Sibyl O'Neill, MBE, who *d* 1946, sister of 3rd Baron O'Neill; 2ndly, 1951, Daphne Rosemary, who *d* 1996, da of late Lieut H. N. Munro, RNVR, of Rushall, Diss:—
(By 1st *m*) Mark Gerald Edward North (Coppice, Spreyton, Crediton, Devon EX17 5AL), *b* 1929; *ed* Harrow, and Trin Coll, Camb (BA 1952): *m* 1962, Leucha Daphne Mary, yr da of late Col Sir Edward Courtney Thomas Warner, DSO, MC, 2nd Bt, and has issue living, Edward North (70 Palace Gardens Terrace, W8 4RR), *b* 1963; *ed* Harrow, and Edinburgh Univ (BSc 1985): *m* 1992, Fiona Helen, elder da of E. Nicholas Shaw, of Sheriffston, Elgin, Moray, and has issue living, James Nicholas Edward North *b* 1996, — Terence Mark (57 Ovington St, SW3 2JA) *b* 1965. —— Morna Annabel, *b* 1926: *m* 1951, Clive Ernest Arkle, MB, ChB, who *d* 1991, and has issue living, Alexander Edward Buxton, *b* 1953, — Alwyn Gerald Buxton, *b* 1957, — Bridget Ayliffe Buxton, *b* 1955, — Ann Daphne Buxton, *b* 1959: *m* 1988, Stephen Derek Pitts of New Manor Farmhouse, 24 Priory Rd, Manton, Oakham, Rutland LE15 8ST, and has issue living, Rosemary Angharad Arkle *b* 1994, Georgina Morna Arkle *b* 1997. *Residence* – Bryn-y-Pin, Ty'n-y-Groes, Conwy, Gwynedd.

Grandchildren of late Edward North Buxton (ante):—
Issue of late Maj Anthony Buxton, DSO, *b* 1881, *d* 1970: *m* 1926, Mary Philomena, who *d* 1953, da of late Hon Bernard Constable-Maxwell (D Norfolk, colls):—
John Joseph (Horsey Hall, Gt Yarmouth, Norfolk) *b* 1927; *ed* Ampleforth, and Trin Coll, Camb (BA); DL Norfolk 1989: *m* 1958, Bridget, only da of Charles de Bunsen (*see* Buxton, Bt, 1953 Edn), and has issue living, Robin Anthony, *b* 1963: *m* 199—, S. P. d'A. (Zanna), da of late Stuart McCarthy, and of Mrs Donald Birts, of Hill Deverill, Wilts, and has issue living, Kate *b* 1996, Emma *b* 1998, — Jane Mary, *b* 1959: *m* 1986, Timothy James Sheldon, of Spexhall Hall, Halesworth, Suffolk, yst son of Rev J. G. Sheldon, and has issue living, Bridie *b* 1988, Minna *b* 1989, Louisa Margaret *b* 1992, — Clare Margaret, *b* 1960: *m* 1993, Theodore Thomas More Agnew, 5th son of Stephen William Agnew, of Outton, Norfolk (*see* Agnew, Bt (*cr* 1895)), and has issue (*see* that title), — Caroline Mary, *b* 1965: *m* 1989, Matthew Valentine Fleming, and has issue (*see* Borthwick, Bt, colls). —— Elizabeth Mary, *b* 1926: *m* 1951, Jurat Michael Walter Bonn, who *d* 1997, of Oaklands, St Peters, Jersey, and has issue living, Simon Michael Joseph, *b* 1953: *m* 1981, Melissa Ann, da of Lt-Col Daniel Patrick Cadoux-Hudson, of Brighton, and has issue living, Edward Simon Daniel *b* 1982, Hugh Michael Leo *b* 1984, Harry Joseph Anthony *b* 1986, Laura *b* 1988, — Sara Mary Philomena, *b* 1952: *m* 1978, Charles George Lacy Hulbert-Powell (*see* E St Leven), — Mary Elizabeth, *b* 1956, — Theresa Mary, *b* 1959. —— Jean Mary, *b* 1930: *m* 1956, Christopher Richard Miles, of Court Lodge Farm, Bletchingly, Surrey (*see* Greenwell, Bt). —— Judith Mary (Sister Mary Pia, IBVM) (47 Fitzjohns Av, NW3 6PG), *b* 1932; is a Nun.

Branch from 7th son of 2nd Baronet:—

Grandson of late Hugh Forster Buxton (2nd son of Francis William Buxton, 7th and yst son of 2nd baronet):—
Issue of late Philip Olaf Buxton, JP, *b* 1906, *d* 1978: *m* 1934, Ruth Christian, JP, who *d* 1976, da of late Aubrey Trevor Lawrence, MBE, KC (Lawrence Bt, *cr* 1867, colls):—
Hugh Lawrence (Widford Manor, Widford, Burford, Oxon, OX18 4DU); *b* 1936; *ed* Eton, and Ch Ch Oxford; JP: *m* 1965, Elizabeth Caroline Tilden Whitelocke, da of late D. A. Abernethy, MA, BM, BCh, FRCS, MRCOG, of Bampton, Oxon, and has issue living, Guy Lawrence, *b* 1969, — Belinda Ruth, *b* 1967, — Anne Caroline, *b* 1975.

Branches from eldest son of 2nd son of 1st baronet:—

Grandchildren of late Henry Fowell Buxton, eldest son of late John Henry Buxton, eldest son of late Thomas Fowell Buxton, 2nd son of 1st baronet:—
Issue of late John Fowell Buxton, *b* 1902, *d* 1970: *m* 1930, Katharine Mary (Newhouse Farm, Wareside, Ware, Herts), da of Sir Nicholas Henry Bacon, 13th Bt:—
Henry Alexander Fowell (Mardocks Mill, Wareside, Ware, Herts SG12 7QN), *b* 1937; *ed* Eton; High Sheriff Herts 1992, DL 1993: *m* 1964, Victoria, only da of (Edward John) Ronald Bennett, of Hartwell Farm, Cirencester (*see* Bazley, Bt, 1995 Edn), and has issue living, Nicholas Fowell, *b* 1966: *m* 1994, Henrietta Louise, eldest da of Richard Wilson Jewson, of Dades Farm, Barnham Broom, Norfolk, and has issue living, Edward Arthur Fowell *b* 1996, Thomas *b* 1997, — Anthony John, *b* 1968: *m* 1998, Lara Kate, eldest da of late David Algernon Fleming (*see* Borthwick, Bt, colls), — Katharine Louise, *b* 1971. —— Bridget Jane (*Hon Mrs Reuben Pleydell-Bouverie*), *b* 1931: *m* 1956, Hon Reuben Pleydell-Bouverie (*see* E Radnor). —— Anna Katharine, *b* 1934: *m* 1965, George Watkin Myrddin-Evans, of Church House, Llandefalle, Llyswen, Powys, and has issue living, David Guildhaume, *b* 1967. —— Penelope Mary Albinia, *b* 1939; JP: *m* 1966, Richard Christopher Naylor (*see* Holt, Bt, *cr* 1935, 1985 Edn), and has issue living, Thomas Murray, *b* 1967, — Harriet Albinia, *b* 1970. —— Elizabeth Priscilla, *b* 1947: *m* 1976, Maj Thomas Tudor Riversdale Lort-Phillips, Gren Gds, and has issue living, Hugh Thomas, *b* 1981, — Frances Katharine, *b* 1977, — Anna Elizabeth, *b* (twin) 1977. —— Teresa Constance, *b* (twin) 1947: *m* 1996, (John) Patrick Latta, yr son of late J. D. Latta, and *d* 1998.

Issue of late Maj Robert James Buxton, MB BChir, MRCS, LRCP, DOMS, *b* 1908, *d* 1968: *m* 1935, Lilla Mary Alyson, who *d* 1979, da of C. E. Pumphrey, of W Bitchfield, Belsay, Northumberland:—
James Anthony Fowell (Galhampton Manor, Yeovil, Som), *b* 1948; *ed* Harrow, and Trin Coll, Camb (MA); Bar Inner Temple 1971, disbarred at own request 1983; admitted a solicitor of the supreme court 1984: *m* 1975, Margaret Elizabeth, only da of late Adm Hon Sir Guy Herbrand Edward Russell, GBE, KCB, DSO (*see* B Ampthill, colls), and has issue living, Edward Guy Fowell, *b* 1978, — Charles Robert James, *b* 1986, — Harriet Faith Alyson, *b* 1976, — Meriel Lavinia Margaret, *b* 1980. —— Richard Moberly (40 Clarendon St, Cambridge CB1 1JX), *b* 1953; *ed* Harrow, Trin Coll, Camb (BA, MA), and Yale Univ (Master of Environmental Studies); Solicitor 1978: *m* 1979, Julia Grace, da of

Commodore Frank Dudley Elcock RCN (ret), of Ottawa, Ontario Canada, and has issue living, David Mark Reford, b 1983, — Simon Cosmo Robert, b 1985, — Elinor Grace Alyson, b 1988. —— Victoria Mary Rose, b 1937: m 1958, David James Faulkner, Maj Irish Gds, who d 1993 (see D Buccleuch, colls). —— Lavinia Hermione (Lady Thorpe) (Brook Cottage, St Agnes, Cornwall TR5 0PT), b 1938: m 1966 (m diss 1989), Rt Hon Lord Justice (Sir Mathew Alexander) Thorpe, and has issue living, Gervase James Doncaster, b 1967, — Alexander Lambert, b 1969, — Marcus Somerled, b 1971. —— Lettice Katharine, b 1941. —— Rosamond Mary Alyson, b (twin) 1948: m 1977, Rt Rev Anthony C. Foottit, Bishop of Lynn, of The Old Vicarage, Castle Acre, King's Lynn, Norfolk PE32 2AA, and has issue living, James Hugh Percival, b 1978, — Caroline Mary Alyson, b 1980, — Georgina Rose b 1983.

Issue of late Capt Joseph Gurney Fowell Buxton, Grenadier Guards, b 1913, ka 1943: m 1938, Elizabeth Langley (who m 2ndly, 1946, Alexander Ludovic Grant, who d 1986, of Marbury Hall, Whitchurch, Shropshire), da of late Major Robert Barbour, of Bolesworth Castle, Tattenhall, Chester:—
Andrew Robert Fowell (Bentley Park, Ipswich, Suffolk), b 1939; ed Winchester, and Pembroke Coll, Oxford (BA); late 2nd Lt Grenadier Guards: m 1965, Jane Margery, only da of late Lt-Col John Peter Grant of Rothiemurchus, MBE (see Cs of Dysart), and has issue living, Tessa Rose, b 1966: m 1993, Athanasios Deriziotis, son of Eustache Deriziotis, of Glyfada, Athens, and has issue living, Anthony Eustace b 1996, Theodore Andrew b (twin) b 1996, — Veronica Mary, b 1970: m 1997, (Andrew) Michael Kemp Barlow, 3rd son of Sir John Kemp Barlow, 3rd Bt (cr 1907). —— Joseph William Henry (8 Acfold Rd, SW6 2AL), b 1943; ed Harrow; Capt Gren Gds: m 1st, 1972, Sarah Louise, who d 1974, el da of Lt-Col Richard Patrick Pilkington Smyly, MC, of Eaton Garden House, Eccleston, Chester; 2ndly, 1981, Ann, da of Paul Boggis-Rolfe, of Martens House, Willow Lane, Wargrave-on-Thames, Berks, and has issue living (by 2nd m), William Paul, b 1983, — Robert Alexander, b 1984, — Laura Elizabeth Verena, b 1990. —— Meriel Rose, b 1940; Extra Lady in Waiting to HRH Princess Alexandra, the Hon Lady Ogilvy: m 1st, 1964, Robert Ivan Kenyon-Slaney, who d 1984, and has issue (see B Kenyon, colls); 2ndly, 1985, Peter Maurice Afia, of 7 Douro Place, W8 5PH.

Issue of late Lt-Cdr Michael Auriol Buxton, RNVR, b 1914, d 1990: m 1938, Elizabeth Edith Millicent (Rose Cottage, Gayton, King's Lynn, Norfolk PE32 1PI), yr da of late Capt Robert Hamond Arthur Elwes, RASC, of Congham House, King's Lynn:—
Gervase Michael (22 Chipstead St, SW3), b 1939; ed Harrow, and Trin Coll, Camb; late 2nd Lieut Royal Scots Greys: m 1965, Susan Margaret, da of late Malcolm McKenzie, of 40 Hans Place, SW1, and has issue living, Matthew Thomas Gervase, b 1967, — Jocelyn David, b 1972, — Lucy Jane, b 1966: m 1998, Lt-Col Jonathan D. Gray, Argyll and Sutherland Highlanders, only son of Ronald Gray, of Colinton Village, Edinburgh, — Caragh Susan, b 1969. —— Christopher Robert (Mulberry House, Little Wilbraham, Cambridge CB1 5LE), b 1940; ed Harrow; FRICS: m 1st, 1965 (m diss 1970), Judy Frances, eldest da of Gordon Hollingsworth Dixon, of Somerton House, Winkfield Row, Berks; 2ndly, 1973, Priscilla, da of Maj John Gardner, and has issue living (by 1st m), Timothy James, b 1967, — Richard Anthony, b (twin) 1967: m 1997, Anna-Louise, yst da of late Brian Reilly, of Henley-on-Thames, Oxon, and has issue living, Daniel Thomas b 1999, — (by 2nd m) Edward Robert, b 1977, — Thomas Michael, b 1980, — Alexandra Mary, b 1975. —— Jonathan James (62 Endlesham Rd, SW12), b 1943; ed Harrow; Maj late 17th/21st Lancers: m 1972, Rosaleen Pleasance, da of late Sir John Alfred Picton Bagge, 6th Bt, and has issue living, Georgina Elizabeth, b 1973, — Victoria Rose, b 1975, — Rosaleen Poppy, b 1979. —— Charles Joseph, b 1951; ed Harrow; Lt-Col 17th/21st Lancers: m 1978, Veronica Juliet Mary, yr da of Francis David Paterson-Morgan, of Hospital of St Cross, Winchester, Hants, and has issue living, Leonie Carinna Rose, b 1979, — Katriona Topaz Mary, b 1985, — Sophie, b 1990.

Grandchildren of late John Henry Buxton, el son of late Thomas Fowell Buxton (ante):—
Issue of late Rev Leonard Buxton, b 1877, d 1946; m 1903, Kathleen, who d 1958, da of late Capt John Digby Wingfield-Digby, of Coleshill Park, Warwickshire, and Sherborne Castle, Dorset:—
Rev Edmund Digby (Pilgrims, 10 Pound Hill, Alresford, Hants, SO24 9BW), b 1908; ed Charterhouse, and Trinity Coll, Camb (MA): m 1940, Katharine Monsarrat, el da of late John Arthur Hargreaves, of Neston, Cheshire, and has issue living, Rev Edmund Francis (362 Franklin Rd, Kings Norton, Birmingham B30 1NE), b 1942; ed Sherborne, Trin Coll, Camb, (MA), Birmingham Univ (DPS), and Sheffield Univ (Master of Min in Theology): m 1969, Jane Mary, only da of Rev Arthur Leslie Jones, of Upwey Rectory, Weymouth, and has issue living, Nicholas Andrew b 1972, Thomas Mark b 1974, Asha Theresa b 1976 (adopted 1979), — Antony Leonard (36 Portland Rd, Summertown, Oxford OX2 7EY), b 1950; ed Sherborne, and Trin Coll, Camb: m 1977, Heather Morwenna Marie, da of Surg Rear-Adm Leslie Bartlett Osborne, and has issue living, Laura Rose b 1978, — Mary Ethel, b 1944: m 1972, David James Grundy, MB, BS, FRCS (Oak Cottage, Winsor Rd, Winsor, Southampton SO40 2HP), and has issue living, Katharine Mary b 1973, Joanna Lucy b 1976, — Lucy Jane, b 1947. —— Kenneth Leonard, FRCS, LRCP, DTM&H (The Old Vicarage, Moulsford, Wallingford, Oxon OX10 9JB), 1909; ed Charterhouse, and at Trin Coll, Camb (Exhibitioner, BA 1930, MA 1935): m 1935, Agnes Josephine, who d 1999, da of late Rev Dr Tom Bragg, V of Christ Church, Lowestoft, and has issue living, Paul Kenneth (Old Inzievar House, by Dunfermline, Fife KY12 8HA), b 1936; ed Trin Coll, Camb (MA, MB, BChir, FRCP Ed): m 1962, Heather Clive, da of Lt-Col J. C. Edlmann, of Tattenhall, Chester, and has issue living, Jonathan Charles Fowell (Ivydown House, Malshanger, Oakley, Basingstoke, Hants RG23 7ES) b 1965; ed Shrewsbury, and Pembroke Coll, Oxford. m 1990, Victoria J. H., da of late Seth Bottom, of Killuney, Armagh (and has issue living, Thaddeus Alexander b 1996), Joanna Rachel b 1967; MB BS: m 1994, Lt-Col E. Francis Hobbs, Gren Gds, eldest son of late R. F. Hobbs, of Alton, Hants, (and has issue living, (Richard) Frederick Michael b 1997, Isobel Josephine b 1995), — Andrew Wakefield (Red Oaks, Henfield, E Sussex), b 1939, — Angela Josephine, b 1944: m 1974, Simon Christopher Edward Kendall, of Cumbers, Liss, Hants, GU33 7LL, and has issue living, Benjamin Edward Buxton b 1976, Matthew Simon Digby b 1979, Andrew Christopher Barclay b 1984, — Susanna Rachel, b 1945: m 1969, Terry William Walter Hookway, of Oakleigh House, 4, Wallingford Rd, Goring-on-Thames RG8 0AH, and has issue living, John Leonard Walter b 1973: m 1998, Heather Dawn, eldest da of Derek Underwood, Timothy Kenneth Walter b 1983, Peter Francis Walter b 1984, Rachel Lucy b 1975. —— Daniel Richard (240 Devonport Rd, Tauranga, NZ), b 1913; ed Bryanston, and Trin Coll, Camb; m 1940, Josephine Burdekin, and has issue living, Timothy Richard Blake (308 Fencourt Rd, RD1, Cambridge, NZ), b 1942: m 1964, Juliette Gaye, da of late C. W. L. Jex-Blake, of RD2, Whitianga, NZ, and has issue living, Darren Richard Blake b 1966, Shane Laurence Blake (11 Hulme Place, Cambridge, NZ), b 1968: m 1994, Regina Yuet Mei, da of late Mark Yuen Song Wong, of Kuala Lumpur, and has issue living, Blake Mark Chee-Meng b 1995, Jaeden Laurence Chee-Kan b 1997, — David Adrian Leonard (35 Silverdale Rd, Hamilton, NZ), b 1945; ed Massey Univ, NZ (BSc Ag): m 1970, Lynley Anne, da of late J. O'Connor, of 10 Mere Mere St, Timaru, NZ, and has issue living, Adrian David b 1973, Bruce John b 1975, Greig Daniel b 1978. —— Kathleen Hannah (Brackenlea, Shawford, Winchester, Hants SO21 2AG), b 1905.

Grandson of late John Henry Buxton (ante):—
Issue of late Rev Arthur Buxton, b 1882, d 1958: m 1908, Esmé Caroline, who d 1971, da of late Col Francis William Pixley, VD, DL, JP, FSA, of Wooburn House, Wooburn, Bucks:—
Nigel Arthur, MB, BChir, MRCS, LRCP (Eagle Lake Rd, South River, Ontario, Canada P0A 1X0), b 1909; ed Harrow, and Trin Coll, Camb (BA), LMCC; 1939-45 War as Capt RAMC: m 1948, Elmira, MD, da of late William Richli, MD, of Mariposa, Cal, USA, and has issue living, David Edson (32201 Ne Dial Rd, Camas, Wash 98607, USA), b 1949: m 1974,

Terri, da of Gerald Snyder, of Oregon, USA, and has issue living, Daniel Elliot *b* 1976, Douglas Edward *b* 1979, — John Arthur, *b* 1950; MD, FACS (Fellow American Coll of Surgs): *m* 1983, Susan, da of Paul Smith, of Pennsylvania, USA, and has issue living, Ashley *b* 1987, Sara *b* 1985, — Louise Elizabeth, *b* 1952; Dr of Health Science: *m* 1978, Kimber Schneider, MD, Certified Ophthalmologist, and has issue living, Jonathan *b* 1982, Richard *b* 1985.

Branches from 3rd son of 2nd son of 1st Baronet

Grandchildren of late Major Geoffrey Charles Buxton, TD, el son of late Geoffrey Fowell Buxton, CB, 3rd son of Thomas Fowell Buxton, 2nd son of 1st baronet:—
Issue of late Major Peter Stapleton Buxton, Leicestershire Yeo, *b* 1904, *ka* 1944: *m* 1934, Julia Victoria (Mansion House, Gainford, Darlington, co Durham), da of late Claude Edward Pease:—
James Geoffrey Pease (Springfield Farm, Smeeton Westerby, Leics LE8 0QW), *b* 1939; *ed* Eton, and Trin Coll, Camb: *m* 1970, Meriel Jessica, da of late Maj Denis Cowen, of E Farndon Manor, Market Harborough, and has issue living, Hugh David, *b* 1975, — Rose Emma, *b* 1973. —— Anne Victoria, *b* 1936: *m* 1959, Robin Slingsby Pease, of Hill House, Gainford, co Durham, and has issue living, Peter Charles Gordon, *b* 1965, — Victoria Julia Diana, *b* 1962: *m* 1994, Stephen John Fordham, 2nd son of late John Rupert Fordham, of Milton House, Kilmalcolm, Renfrewshire, and has issue living, John Finn Slingsby *b* 1998, Poppy *b* 19—, — Annabel Primrose Robin, *b* 1971.

Granddaughters of Geoffrey Fowell Buxton, CB (ante):—
Issue of late Maj Ivor Buxton, DSO, TD, *b* 1884, *d* 1969: *m* 1918, Phyllis Dorothy, who *d* 1976, da of late Col Hugh Gurney Barclay, CVO, of Colney Hall, Norwich, and widow of Henry Cecil Johnson, DSO:—
Nancy, *b* 1919; *m* 1st, 1940, Lt-Col John Noel Ronald Loveday, 16th/5th Lancers, who was *ka* 1944; 2ndly, 1947, Maj John Hallifax Weller Poley, MC, of Boxted Hall, Bury St Edmunds, who *d* 1976, and has issue living, (by 1st *m*) Tessa, *b* 1942: *m* 1972, Andrew Henry Scott, and has issue living, Archie John *b* 1973, Daniel Ian *b* 1974, Tobina Fiona *b* 1977, Laura Nancy *b* 1979, — (by 2nd *m*) Richard Hallifax (Keeper's Cottage, Boxted, Bury St Edmunds, Suffolk IP29 4LN), *b* 1949: *m* 1st, 1970 (*m diss* 1991), Sarah Francesca, el da of John Valentine Gosling, of The Claw, Brushford, Dulverton, Som; 2ndly, 1992, Isobel Muriel, da of Maj Douglas Wade Reader, of Halvergate House, Halvergate, Norfolk, and has issue living (by 1st *m*), Guy Hallifax *b* 1975, Katherine Francesca *b* 1973, Annabelle Rose *b* 1980, (by 2nd *m*) Hugh Thomas *b* 1994, Bridget Grace *b* 1995, — Nicholas Toby, *b* 1950: *m* 1992, P. Sue Bond. —— Felicity Mary (*Lady Blacker*), *b* 1921: *m* 1st, 1942, Maj John Rew, who was *ka* 1943; 2ndly, 1947, Gen Sir Cecil Hugh Blacker, GCB, OBE, MC, of Cowpasture Farm, Hook Norton, Banbury, and has issue living (by 2nd *m*), Terence, *b* 1948; *ed* Wellington Coll, and Trin Coll, Camb; author: *m* 1975, Hon Caroline Susan Dean Soper, da of Baron Soper (Life Baron), and has issue living, Alexander *b* 1977, Alice *b* 1979, — Philip, *b* 1949; Sculptor, and former Nat Hunt Jockey: *m* 1979, Susan, da of late Colin Davies, of Oakgrove, Chepstow, and has issue living, Daniel *b* 1982, Stephanie *b* 1984.

Granddaughters of late Com Bernard Buxton, DSO, 2nd son of Geoffrey Fowell Buxton, CB (ante):—
Issue of late Group-Capt Geoffrey Mungo Buxton, OBE, RAF, *b* 1906, *d* 1979: *m* 1929, Horatia Mary (Wiveton Green, Holt, Norfolk), da of late Adm Sir William Wordsworth Fisher, GCB, GCVO:—
Carolyn Viola, *b* 1934. —— Juliet Horatia, *b* 1937. —— Rose Vivian, *b* 1951.

Granddaughter of late Com Bernard Buxton, DSO (ante):—
Issue of late Major Samuel Luckyn Buxton, MC, 17th/21st Lancers, *b* 1914, *ka* Italy 1944: *m* 1941, Pamela Mary (who *m* 2ndly, 1946, Baron Buxton of Alsa, MC (Life Baron) (ante), and *d* 1983), da of Sir Henry Ralph Stanley Birkin, 3rd Bt:—
Christina Hermione, *b* 1944: *m* 1967, John David Millard Barnes, of The Craig, Balmaclellan, Kirkcudbrightshire DG7 3QR, and has issue living, Amanda Mary, *b* 1968, — Sarah Hermione, *b* 1970.

Branches from 4th son of 2nd son of 1st Baronet:—

Grandchildren of late Patrick Alfred Buxton, CMG, FRS, MRCS, LRCP, el son of Alfred Fowell Buxton, 4th son of Thomas Fowell Buxton (ante):—
Issue of late Martin Patrick Buxton, *b* 1920, *d* 1966: *m* 1949, Jacqueline Marcelle, who *d* 1968, da of Percival James Stokes:—
James Patrick, *b* 1957: *m* 1993, Liane Frances Jones, and has issue living, Angharad Grace Jones, *b* 1993. —— Eleanor Ruth *b* 1950: *m* 1970, Paul Hudson Stanford, and has issue living, Richard, *b* 1975. —— Rachel Phyllida, *b* 1952: *m* 1973, Leslie William Huson, and has issue living, Thomas Patrick, *b* 1977, — Ruth Huson *b* 1980. —— Alice Richenda, *b* 1954: *m* 1974, Charles Walsh, and has issue living, Patrick, *b* 1982, — Brendan, *b* 1990, — Katherine, *b* 1987.

Issue of late Fl-Lt Andrew Patrick Buxton, DFC, late RAF, *b* 1923, *d* 1952: *m* 1949, Kathleen Audrey (who *m* 2ndly, 1955, Martin Francis Wood, of The Manor House, Little Wittenham, Oxon), da of late Rev J. H. Stanfield, of Seaton, Devon:—
Robin David, *b* 1950: *m* 1986, Elizabeth Holmes, and has issue living, Andrew, *b* 1986, — Christopher, *b* 1992. —— Sarah Margaret, *b* 1951.

Grandchildren of late Alfred Fowell Buxton (ante):—
Issue of late Patrick Alfred Buxton, CMG, FRS, MRCS, LRCP, *b* 1892, *d* 1955: *m* 1917, Muryell Gladys, who *d* 1989, da of late Rev Hon William Talbot Rice (*see* B Dynevor, coll):—
Helen Muryell, *b* 1925; *ed* Camb Univ (BA 1948): *m* 1948, Arthur Robert Donald Wright, OBE, and has issue living, Simon Nicholas, *b* 1949: *m* 1989, Margaret Woodliff, — Patrick Stephen, *b* 1951: has issue living, Edward Fenton *b* 1985, Nicholas Patrick *b* 1987, Richard *b* 1990, — Hannah Elizabeth, *b* 1953: *m* 1994, Ian Peter Downie, FRCS, and has issue living, James *b* 1997, Eleanor *b* 1995, — Charlotte Helen, *b* 1956: *m* 1979, George Reynolds Cannon, who *d* 1992, of Denver, Colorado, USA, and has issue living, Patrick George *b* 1984, Samuel Claude *b* 1986, — Lesley Rachel, *b* 1961: *m* 1993, Nicholas Knight, who *d* 1993. *Residence* – Mill Barn, Coulston, Westbury, Wilts. —— Rachel Katharine, *b* 1930; *ed* Camb Univ (BA 1951): *m* 1st, 1952, Christopher Herzig, CBE, who *d* 1993; 2ndly, 1996, Prof Peter Gray, Master of Gonville and Caius Coll, Camb, and has issue living (by 1st *m*), Stephen Christopher, *b* 1954: *m* 1977, Anita, da of Johan

Mostert, of Pretoria, S Africa, and has issue living, Austin Jarred *b* 1989, Richenda Grace *b* 1986, — Francis Patrick, *b* 1955: *m* 1980, Petra, da of Prof Ambrose Rogers, of Univ Coll, London, and has issue living, Anthony *b* 1990, Robert *b* 1992, — Edmund Martin, *b* 1958: *m* 1990, Ana Novaković, and has issue living, Thomas Dusan *b* 1990, James *b* 1995, Katherine Novaković *b* 1993, — Hugh John *b* 1961: *m* 1992, Isabel Oriane Clare, eldest da of Maj Count Charles John de Salis, DL, and has issue (*see* Ly Herries of Terregles, colls), — Harriet Elizabeth, *b* 1963: *m* 1995, Peter Carty, and has issue living, Samuel Christopher *b* 1995, Eleanor *b* 1996. *Residence* – Gonville and Caius Coll, Cambridge. —— Lucy Bertha (*Lady Chandler*), *b* 1932; *ed* Camb Univ (BA 1954): *m* 1955, Sir Geoffrey Chandler, CBE, and has issue living, Hilary Jane, *b* 1957: *m* 1981, James A. Otter, son of John Otter, of Pilton, Northants, and has issue living, Thomas Geoffrey *b* 1983, Nicholas *b* 1990, Susannah *b* 1987, — Sarah Elizabeth, *b* 1959: *m* 1st, 1991 (*m diss* 1996), Richard A. Armstrong, eldest son of Dr Alan Armstrong, of Bladon, Oxon; 2ndly, 19—, Dr Alan Cowley, of Ellington, The Park, Northampton, and has issue living, (by 1st *m*) Holly *b* 1994, — Clare Marjorie, *b* 1961: *m* 1991, John Walker, of Ranfold Barn, Slinfold, W Sussex RH13 7RL, — Susan Ann (9 Maude Rd, Camberwell, SE5 8NY), *b* 1964. *Residence* – 46 Hyde Vale, Greenwich, SE10 8HP.

Issue of late Denis Alfred Jex Buxton, *b* 1895, *d* 1964: *m* 1923, Emily Mary, who *d* 1970, da of late William Hollins (B Sherwood):—

Paul William Jex (Castle House, Chipping Ongar, Essex; *Club* – Brooks's), *b* 1925; *ed* Rugby, and Balliol Coll, Oxford (MA); formerly Capt Coldm Gds; Diplo Ser 1950-71; banking 1972-74; NI Office since 1974, Assist Under-Sec of State 1981-85; NW Europe 1945 (wounded): *m* 1st, 1950 (*m diss* 1971), Katharine, who *d* 1977, da of Sir Hubert Hull, CBE; 2ndly, 1971, Hon Margaret Evelyn Bridges, da of 1st Baron Bridges, and formerly wife of Trevor Henry Aston, and has issue living (by 1st *m*), Charles Hubert Jex *b* 1951: *m* 1976, Cecile Moss, and has issue living, Sam *b* 1977, Amy *b* 1980, — Tobias Richard Valentine, *b* 1953; has issue living, Oliver *b* 1982, Xavier *b* 1990, Yvo *b* (twin) 1990, — Mary Katharine, *b* 1956; has issue living, Joe GRACE *b* 1993, — (by 2nd *m*) Sophia Frances, *b* 1972, — Hero Elizabeth, *b* 1974. —— Mary Violet, *b* 1924: *m* 1950, as his second wife, David Roden Buxton (ante). —— Elizabeth Rosalind (89 Brian Av, Norwich NR1 2PD), *b* 1929: *m* 1953 (*m diss* 1964), Tristram Yelin, who *d* 1982, and has issue living, Francis North Hunter Buxton, *b* 1957, — Cecilia Mary, *b* 1954, — Natasha Vera *b* 1959.

Branches from youngest son of 2nd son of 1st Baronet:—

Granddaughter of late Thomas Fowell Buxton (infra):—
Issue of late Rev Barclay Fowell Buxton, *b* 1860, *d* 1946: *m* 1886, Margaret Maria Amelia, who *d* 1947, da of late William Railton, of 65, Onslow Square, SW:—
Rachel Jane, *b* 1905. *Residence* – Wayside, Stanway, Colchester Essex.

Grandchildren of late Rev Barclay Fowell Buxton, 5th son of late Thomas Fowell Buxton, 2nd son of 1st baronet:—
Issue of late Capt Murray Barclay Buxton, MC, *b* 1889, *ka* 1940: *m* 1920, Janet Mary Muriel, who *d* 1942, da of Sir (Edward) Hildred Carlile, CBE, 1st Bt:—
Ronald Carlile, *b* 1923; *ed* Eton, and Trin Coll, Camb (MA); formerly Capt REME, is a Co Dir; MP for Leyton (*C*) 1965-66: *m* 1959, Phyllida Dorothy Roden, yr da of late Capt Roden Henry Victor Buxton, CBE, RN (ante), and has issue living, Peter Hildred, *b* 1960: *m* 1987, Eleanor Charlotte, da of Richard Anthony Brooke Winch, of Swannington Manor, Norfolk, and has issue living, Freddie Mark *b* 1995, Laura Juliet *b* 1990, — Robert Victor, *b* 1964: *m* 1996, Iona Louise, da of Michael Spens, of Wormiston, Fife, and has issue living, Dorian North *b* 1999, — Camilla Janet St John *b* (twin) 1960: *m* 1st, 1992, Edward Thomas Baxter; 2ndly, 1997, (George) Dominic Mackintosh Warre (*see* D Devonshire, 1973-74 Edn), of Tullibardine House, Auchterarder, Perthshire PH3 1JX, and has issue living (by 2nd *m*), Rupert Antony Mackintosh *b* 1998, — Vanessa Anne Carlile, *b* 1962. *Residences* – 67 Ashley Gdns, SW1; Kimberley Hall, Wymondham, Norfolk.

Issue of late Alfred Barclay Buxton, *b* 1891, *ka* 1940: *m* 1916, Edith Mary Crossley, who *d* 1977, da of C. T. Studd, formerly of 17 Highland Rd, Upper Norwood, SE:—
Susan Studd (*Lady Wood*), MBE, *b* 1918; MBE (Civil) 1990: *m* 1943, Sir (Arthur) Michael Wood, CBE, MB, BS, FRCS, who *d* 1987, Founder and Dir Gen AMREF ("The Flying Doctor"), and has issue living, Mark Lionel, *b* 1945, — Hugo Charles, *b* 1948, — Janet Mary, *b* 1946, — Katrina Susan, *b* 1951. *Address* – Box 24277, Nairobi, Kenya.

Issue of late Barclay Godfrey Buxton, MBE, MC, *b* 1895, *d* 1986: *m* 1922, Dorothea Reader, who *d* 1967, yr da of late Reader Harris, KC, of Clapham, SW:—
Christopher Godfrey Reader, OBE, *b* 1929; *ed* Charterhouse, and Trin Coll, Camb (MA); Master of Business Admin Dartmouth Coll, USA, 1955; OBE (Civil) 1982: *m* 1964 (*m diss* 1969), Margaret Isabel, yr da of Lt-Col H. B. Watkins, of Knighton, Radnorshire. *Residences* – Kirtlington Park, Oxon; 61 Harcourt Terr, SW10 9JP. —— Joanna Margaret Reader, MBE, *b* 1927; *ed* Sherborne Sch for Girls, and Edinburgh Univ; Market Research Consultant; MBE (Civil) 1993. *Residence* – 21A Porchester Terr, W2.

The family of Buxton were seated for nearly three centuries at Coggeshall, Essex. The 1st baronet, Sir Thomas Fowell Buxton, MP for Weymouth (*L*) 1820-36, was distinguished for his exertions for the abolition of slavery and reform of the penal code. The 2nd baronet, Sir Edward North, was MP for S Essex 1847-52 and E Norfolk 1857-58 (*L*). The 3rd baronet, Sir Thomas Fowell, GCMG, sometime a partner in the firm of Truman, Hanbury and Co, sat as MP for Lyme Regis (*L*) 1865-8, and was Gov of S Australia 1895-8. The 4th baronet was High Sheriff of Essex 1905. The 5th baronet was High Sheriff of Essex 1928.

BUZZARD (UK) 1929, of Munstead Grange, Godalming, co Surrey

Be what you seem to be

Sir ANTHONY FARQUHAR BUZZARD, 3rd *Baronet; b* 28 June 1935; *s* his father *Rear-Adm Sir* ANTHONY WASS, CB, DSO, OBE, 1972; *ed* Charterhouse, Ch Ch, Oxford (MA), Ambassador Coll, Pasadena, Cal (BA), and Bethany Theological Coll (MA Th); ARCM; freelance educational Consultant and Tutor; Lecturer, Atlanta Bible Coll, Georgia, USA: *m* 1970, Barbara Jean, da of Gordon Earl Arnold, of Mendon, Michigan, USA, and has issue.

𝕬rms – Per chevron azure and argent, in chief two covered cups of the second and in base a rod of Æsculapius proper. €rest – Rising from clouds an eagle proper, gorged with an Eastern crown or.
Address – 185 Summerville Drive, Brooks, Georgia 30205, USA.

DAUGHTERS LIVING

Sarah Jane *b* 1971. ——— Claire Judith *b* 1974. ——— Heather Elizabeth, *b* 1988.

BROTHER LIVING

TIMOTHY MACDONNELL (Kennel Cottage, Lindfield, Haywards Heath, Sussex, RH16 2QN), *b* 28 Jan 1939; a LRAM and a Graduate of Roy Schs of Music: *m* 1970, Jennifer Mary, da of late Peter Patching, and has issue living, Jonathan Mark, *b* 1977, ——— Rachel Mary, *b* 1974.

SISTER LIVING

Gillian Margaret, *b* 1944; BSc: *m* 1979, William John Oates Blenkinsop, of 46 Melrose Rd, SW18 1LY.

AUNT LIVING (*Daughter of 1st baronet*)

Isabel May, *b* 1910: *m* 1933, Cdr Herbert William Acworth, RN, who *d* 1987, and has issue living, William Farquhar, *b* 1934: *m* 1964, Susan Henrietta, yr da of late Capt Roddie Casement, OBE, RN, (*see* Greenwell, Bt), and has issue living, William Bernard *b* 1965: *m* 1993, Julia Beale, James Michael *b* 1966, Anna Claire *b* 1970, ——— Adam Buzzard, *b* 1943, ——— Susan Esmé, *b* 1936, ——— Jane Marion, *b* 1941.

COLLATERAL BRANCH LIVING

Issue of late Surg-Lt-Cdr Edward Miller Buzzard, FRCP, RNVR, yr son of 1st baronet, *b* 1909, *d* 1976: *m* 1937, Sylvia Bevan (The Barn, Oakley Park, Frilford Heath, Abingdon, Oxon), da of late John William Fordham of Hughenden, Loughborough Rd, Leicester:—
†David, *b* 1950; *d* 1985. ——— Sarah Bevan, *b* 1941: *m* 1962, Michael William Leishman Gear, of Moons Well, Bournes Green, nr Stroud, Glos GL6 7NL, and has issue living, Susan Anne Buzzard, *b* 1965: *m* 1991, George Patrick Walker, ——— Nicola Leishman, *b* 1967: *m* 1997, Adrian Farrow. ——— Judith Miller, *b* 1944: *m* 1968, Sydney Guy Anthony Scammell, of 5 Courtfield, 1 Castlebar Hill, W5, and has issue living, Anthony Charles Miller, *b* 1974, ——— Louise Jane, *b* 1975. ——— Sylvia Anne, *b* 1947: *m* 1973, Rupert Grenside Bowen, of 83 Montholme Rd, Battersea, SW11, and has issue living, Miranda Juanita, *b* 1975, ——— Henrietta Alice, *b* 1977:

The 1st baronet, Sir (Edward) Farquhar Buzzard (son of late Thomas Buzzard, MD, FRCP, of 74 Grosvenor St, W1), was Physician Extraor, to HM 1924-32, Physician-in-Ord 1932-6, and an Extra Physician 1937-45.

BYASS (UK) 1926, of Port Talbot, co Glamorgan (extinct 1976)

Sir GEOFFREY ROBERT SIDNEY BYASS, TD, 2nd and last *Baronet.*

DAUGHTERS LIVING OF SECOND BARONET

Gillian Mary, *b* 1921: *m* 1948, Kenneth Mackenzie Knight, of 22 Oaklea Court, High St, Hartfield, E Sussex, and has issue living, Nigel Geoffrey Roy, *b* 1950, ——— Simon Gerald, *b* 1953. ——— Daphne Caroline, *b* 1925: *m* 1st, 1949, Capt Ian Guy Mathews, Duke of Cornwall's LI; 2ndly, 1962, Lt-Col William Roland Lawson, of Court Mews, Newnham Bridge, Tenbury Wells, Worcs, and has issue living, (by 1st *m*) Caroline, *b* 1951: *m* 1972, ——— Belinda, *b* 1952: *m* 1973. ——— Pamela Julia, *b* 1926: *m* 1953, Arthur David Veall, of Merry Hall, Newbridge on Wye, Powys, and has issue living, Robert John, *b* 1955, ——— Christopher Toby, *b* 1956, ——— Ivan, *b* 1964, ——— Julia Diana, *b* 1958. ——— Rosemary Valentine

(Sydney, NSW, Australia), *b* 1933: *m* 1959, Kenneth Michael Bond Wright, who *d* 1982, and has issue living, Sarah Caroline, *b* 1960. — Charlotte Mary, *b* 1962. —— Ursula Marian, *b* 1940: *m* 1963, John Patrick Dornton, who *d* 1998, of Stonewell House, Duck St, Churchill Green, Bristol, and has issue living, Charles Geoffrey, *b* 1964, — Elizabeth Henrietta, *b* 1967, — Susannah Marian, *b* 1971.

Cable-Alexander, see Alexander.

CAHN (UK) 1934, of Stanford-upon-Soar, co Nottingham

They are able who believe they can

Sir ALBERT JONAS CAHN, 2nd *Baronet*; *b* 27 June 1924; *s* his father, Sir JULIEN, 1944; *ed* Harrow: *m* 1948, Malka, da of late Reuben Bluestone, and has issue.

𝔄rms – Gules, a cross raguly ermine between in the second and third quarters a fleur-de-lis or. 𝔠rest – In front of a fox's head erased two branches of willow in saltire proper.
Seat – Stanford Hall, Loughborough. *Residence* – 6 Fairacres, Roehampton Lane, SW15.

SONS LIVING

JULIEN MICHAEL (1 Court Hope Villas, Wimbledon, SW19), *b* 15 Jan 1951; *ed* Harrow: *m* 1987, Marilynne Janelle, da of Frank Owen Blyth, and has issue living, Benjamin Albert, *b* 28 Feb 1988, — Jessie Laura, *b* 1976. —— Edward John (55 Kyrle Rd, SW11), *b* 1959; *ed* King's Coll, UMIST: *m* 1996, Ana Clara, da of Carlos Cruz, and has issue living, Luca Jonas, *b* 1998, — Gabriella Rosa, *b* 1996.

DAUGHTERS LIVING

Madeleine Jane (52 Cascade Av, N10), *b* 1949: *m* 1st, 1979 (*m diss* 1987), Richard Albert Smith; 2ndly, 1997, David Thomas Waller, and has issue living (by 1st *m*), Charles Joseph, *b* 1982, — Mariza Joanna Phyllis, *b* 1980. —— Valerie Janet, *b* 1954: *m* 1982, Peregrine Kenneth Oughton Crosthwaite, of 30 Larpent Av, SW15 6UU, and has issue living, Nicholas Anthony, *b* 1985, — Thomas William, *b* 1986, — Sally-Anne Claire, *b* 1989.

BROTHER LIVING

Richard Ian (Crispa, Bashurst Copse, Itchingfield, Horsham, Sussex), *b* 1927: *m* 1964, Marietta da of Joseph Seidler.

The 1st baronet, Sir Julien Cahn (son of Albert Cahn), was Master of Burton Hunt 1926-35; of Woodland Pytchley Foxhounds 1935-7, and of Fernie's Foxhounds 1937-9, and sponsored and captained many cricket teams on tours abroad.

CAIN (UK) 1920, of Wargrave Manor, co Berkshire (Extinct 1969)

Sir ERNEST CAIN, 2nd and last *Baronet*.

DAUGHTERS LIVING OF SECOND BARONET

Joan, *b* (twin) 1925: *m* 1952, Ian Merrick Cuthbertson Hill, OBE, and has issue living, Christopher Michael Ian, *b* 1957, — Susan Elizabeth, *b* 1955: *m* 1979, Norman Allen Bradley. *Residence* – Windsor House, Gotham, Cranborne, Wimborne, Dorset BH21 5QY. —— Vivien Elizabeth WILSON, *b* 1932; has resumed her former married name: *m* 1st, 1954 (*m diss* 1959), Charles William Munro Wilson; 2ndly, 1961 (*m diss* 1966), Baron Pierre Cervello, and has issue living, (by 1st *m*) Amanda Louise, *b* 1956. *Residence* – Mais de Pan, Les Stes Maries de la Mer, 13460 Camargue, France.

ANSTRUTHER-GOUGH-CALTHORPE (UK) 1929, of Elvetham Hall, Elvetham, co Southampton

The same way but by different steps

Sir EUAN HAMILTON ANSTRUTHER-GOUGH-CALTHORPE, 3rd *Baronet*, *b* 22 June 1966, son of late Niall Hamilton Anstruther-Gough-Calthorpe; *s* his grandfather, *Brig Sir* RICHARD HAMILTON, CBE, 1985; *ed* Harrow, and RAC, Cirencester.

Arms – Quarterly: 1st and 4th checky or and azure, a fesse ermine, and (for distinction) a canton ermine, *Calthorpe*; 2nd, gules, on a fesse argent, between three boars' heads couped or, a lion passant azure, and (for distinction) a canton ermine, *Gough*; 3rd, argent, three piles issuing from the chief sable, *Anstruther*. Crests – 1st, a boar's head couped erect argent, charged (for distinction) with an ermine spot azure, *Calthorpe*; 2nd, a boar's head couped argent, pierced through the check with a broken spear gules, and charged (for distinction) with an ermine spot azure, *Gough*; 3rd, two arms in armour holding in the gauntlet a battle-axe all proper, *Anstruther*.

SISTER LIVING

Lara Nancy Don, *b* 1968.

UNCLE LIVING *(Son of 2nd baronet)*

JOHN AUSTEN (Shroner Wood, Martyr Worthy, Winchester, Hants), *b* 14 July 1947; *ed* Harrow: *m* 1st, 1977 (*m diss* 1986), Lady Mary Gaye Georgiana Lorna Curzon, da of 5th Earl Howe, and formerly wife of late (Kevin) Esmond (Peter) Cooper-Key (*see* V Rothermere); 2ndly, 1987, Vanessa Mary Theresa, yst da of Lt Cdr Theodore Bernard Peregrine Hubbard, RN (*see* D Norfolk), and formerly wife of David St Vincent Llewellyn (*see* Llewellyn, Bt, *cr* 1922), and has issue living (by 1st *m*), Jacobi Richard Penn, *b* 1983, — Georgiana Moireach Gay, *b* 1978, — Isabella Amaryllis Charlotte, *b* 1980, — (by 2nd *m*) Gabriella Zanna Vanessa, *b* 1989, — Octavia Elsa, *b* 1991.

GREAT-AUNTS LIVING *(Daughters of 1st baronet)*

Frances Jean, *b* 1910: *m* 1942, His Honour Judge (Frank Alleyne) Stockdale, el son of late Sir Frank Arthur Stockdale, GCMG, CBE, and has had issue, James Arthur FitzRoy (Moons Mill, Tinkers Lane, Hadlow Down, E Sussex), *b* 1948; *ed* Eton, and Southampton Univ (LLB); Bar Gray's Inn 1972: *m* 1974, Jane Mary Gabriel, el da of William Hazzard, and has issue living, John Francis *b* 1978, Kathryn Jane *b* 1980, Philippa Rachel *b* 1982, Elinor Victoria *b* 1985, — Sarah Victoria, *b* 1943: *m* 1965, Christopher N. A. Castleman, and *d* 1979, leaving issue, Jonathan William *b* 1971, Amanda Lucy *b* 1967, — Frances Jane, *b* 1946: *m* 1967, Charles J. Deacon, of 9 Dinorbin, 79/81 Woodcote Rd, Wallington, Surrey, and has issue living, Julian Mark *b* 1972, Rebecca *b* 1970. *Residence* – Victoria Place, Monmouth, Gwent NP5 3BR. —— Barbara (*Barbara, Baroness Luke*), *b* 1911: *m* 1932, 2nd Baron Luke, who *d* 1996. *Residence* – Odell Castle, Bedfordshire, MK43 7BB.

MOTHER LIVING

Martha Rodman (*Lady Nicholson*), da of Col Stuart Warren Don, of 5 Orchard Court, Portman Sq, W2: *m* 1st, 1964, Niall Hamilton Anstruther-Gough-Calthorpe, who *d* 1970, eldest son of 2nd baronet; 2ndly, 1975, Sir Charles Christian Nicholson, 3rd Bt (*cr* 1912).

Sir FitzRoy Hamilton Anstruther-Gough-Calthorpe, 1st Bt (el son of late Lieut-Col Robert Hamilton Lloyd-Anstruther (Anstruther, Bt, colls)), assumed by Roy Licence 1910, the surname and arms of Anstruther only; also later by Roy Licence 1910, for himself and issue the surnames of Gough-Calthorpe in addition to, and after that of Anstruther, and the Arms of Gough and Calthorpe quartered with those of Anstruther, having *m* 1898, Hon Rachel Gough-Calthorpe, who *d* 1951, el da and co-heir of 6th Baron Calthorpe.

CAMPBELL (NS) 1628, of Auchinbreck

Sir ROBIN AUCHINBRECK CAMPBELL, 15th *Baronet, b* 7 June 1922; *s* his father, *Sir* LOUIS HAMILTON, 1970; *ed* Eton; late Lt (A) RNVR; sheep farmer: *m* 1st, 1948, Rosemary (Sally), who *d* 1978, da of Ashley Dean, of Christchurch, NZ; 2ndly, 1978, Elizabeth Mary, da of Sir Arthur Colegate, MP (Worsley, Bt), and formerly wife of Richard Wellesley Gunston (*see* Gunston, Bt), and has issue by 1st *m*.

Arms – Gyronny of eight or and sable, and a bordure checky ermine and purpure. Crest – A dexter hand proper holding a spur or.
Residence – 287A Waikawa Rd, Picton, NZ. *Clubs* – Christchurch (NZ), and Bembridge Sailing.

SON LIVING (*By 1st marriage*)

LOUIS AUCHINBRECK, *b* 17 Jan 1953: *m* 1976, Fiona Mary St Clair, da of Gordon King, of Middlehill, Marlborough, NZ, and has issue living, Lucinda Louise, *b* 1982, — Charlotte Virginia, *b* 1985.

DAUGHTERS LIVING (*By 1st marriage*)

Rosemary Fiona, *b* 1955. ——Sophia Louise, *b* 1960: *m* 1984, Philip Michael Darcey Pinniger, son of late T. K. Pinniger, of Hunters, Lincoln's Inn, and has issue living, Angus, *b* 1989, — Rhiannon Louise, *b* 1986.

COLLATERAL BRANCH LIVING

Descendants of late Patrick Campbell, of Stuck, co Bute, brother of late Rev Duncan Campbell, V of Kilfinnan, great-great-great-grandfather of 8th baronet:—

Grandchildren of late Sir Archibald Young Gipps Campbell, KCIE, CSI, CBE, VD (infra):—
Issue of late Lt-Col Archibald Hugh Campbell, R Sigs, *b* 1914, *d* 1981: *m* 1940, Mary Alison (24 Langside Drive, Comrie, Perthshire PH6 2HR), da of late Lt-Col Herbert Nugent Young, DSO, R Inniskilling Fus:—
Archibald James (2 Parrs Head Mews, George Lane, Rochester, Kent ME1 1NP), *b* 1943: *m* 1976, Lorna Isobel, da of John Scott, of Elderslie, Renfrewshire, and has issue living, Archibald Malcolm Scott, *b* 1979, — Ewan Anton Hugh, *b* 1983, — Iona Lanor, *b* 1980, — Isla Rowena, *b* 1985. ——Alison Margaret, *b* 1941: *m* 1966, Robert John Michael, of 6 Swanston Field, Whitchurch-on-Thames, Reading, Berks RG8 7HP, and has issue living, Anthony Richard, *b* 1967, — Geraint Philip, *b* 1977, — Isobel Margaret, *b* 1969. ——Christian Jean Mary, *b* 1948.

Grandsons of late Archibald Samuels Campbell, great-great-great-grandson and heir male of late Rev Patrick Campbell, of Torblaren, and grandson and heir male of late Patrick Campbell, of Stuck, co Bute (ante):—
Issue of late Sir Archibald Young Gipps Campbell, KCIE, CSI, CBE, VD, *b* 1872, *d* 1957: *m* 1910, Frances Irene, who *d* 1967, da of late Rev Henry Savill Young, of Mallard's Court, Stokenchurch, Oxfordshire (Young, Bt, *cr* 1769, colls):—
Colin Alan George (The Old Manse, Lochgair, by Lochgilphead, Argyll PA31 8SB), *b* 1917: Capt (ret) Black Watch, late Foreign Ser: *m* 1st, 1945 (*m diss* 1961), Mary Cosser, da of late Ramsay Young; 2ndly, 1966, Joanna Frances, da of late George Falconer Ball, MC, and has issue living, (by 1st *m*) Mary Irene Young, *b* 1946: *m* 1973, Patrick Barwise, of No 6 Grange House, Highbury Grange, N5 2QD, and has issue living, Alexander Mark Colin *b* 1976, Katharine Mary *b* 1979, — Claire Elizabeth, *b* 1949. *m* 1983, Michael Anthony Bastian, of 10 Riverside, Swallowfields, Totnes, Devon TQ9 5JB, — Fiona Penelope, *b* 1955: *m* 1980, Lt-Cdr Peter Langford Rice, RN, of Oak Lodge, Laverstock Park, Laverstock, Salisbury, Wilts SP1 1QJ, and has issue living, Eleanor Young Rowley Campbell *b* 1985, Alice Camilla Campbell *b* 1987. —— †Niall Patrick, *b* 1925; Lt (ret) RE: *m* 1st, 1953 (*m diss* 1965), Gillian Margaret Elizabeth, da of Arthur John Morris; 2ndly, 1967, Peta Caroline (Westbrook, 5 Leadhall Crescent, Harrogate HG2 9NG), da of William Kelso Paul, and *d* 1988, leaving issue, (by 1st *m*) Sarah Caroline, *b* 1954: *m* 1985, David Thomas Woodward, of Rookery Cottage, Clay Lane, Marton-over-Winsford, Cheshire, and has issue living, Lucy Elizabeth Campbell *b* 1988, Stephanie Jane Campbell *b* 1990, — Julia Anne, *b* 1956: *m* 1980 (*m diss* 1995), David Jon Slym, and has issue living, Jessica Elizabeth *b* 1982, Katherine Margaret *b* 1985, — (by 2nd *m*) James William Patrick, *b* 1968, — Malcolm Niall Kelso *b* 1978, — Rebecca Louise, *b* 1971.

This baronetcy was conferred upon Sir Dugald Campbell, Knight, with remainder to his heirs male whatsoever. Upon the death of the 6th baronet in 1812, Dugald Campbell, of Kildalloig, Day-Keeper of the Great Seal in Ireland, is said to have become *de jure* 7th baronet, but not to have assumed the title, and the baronetcy remained dormant until 1841, when it was claimed by Dugald Campbell's heir, John Eyton Campbell, of Killdalloig, who proved himself heir to the title, and was subsequently recognized as 8th baronet *de facto*.

CAMPBELL (NS) 1668 (about), of Aberuchill, Perthshire

Victory follows the brave

Sir JAMES ALEXANDER MOFFAT BAIN CAMPBELL, 9th *Baronet*; *b* 23 Sept 1956; *s* his father, *Sir* COLIN MOFFAT 1997; *ed* Stowe; Capt Scots Gds: *m* 1993, Carola Jane, yr da of George Denman (*see* B Denman), and has issue.

Arms – Quarterly: 1st and 4th, gyronny of eight or and sable; 2nd, argent, a lymphad with her oars in action sable; 3rd, or a fesse checky argent and azure; all within a bordure ermine. **Crest** – A lion guardant gules crowned with laurel and holding in his dexter paw a sword proper, hilted and pommelled or, and in the sinister a dag, or Highland pistol. **Supporters** – Two bloodhounds guardant, proper, collared and leashed or.
Residence – Kilbryde Castle, Dunblane, Perthshire FK15 9NF.

DAUGHTERS LIVING

Catherine Janet Denman, *b* 1994. —— May Alexandra Landale, *b* 1996.

BROTHER LIVING

JOHN ALISTAIR CHICHESTER, *b* 1960; *ed* Fettes: *m* 1987 (*m diss* 19—), Carole Lesley, yr da of Geoffrey Knowles, of Cornton, Stirling, and has issue living, Louise, *b* 19—.

UNCLE LIVING

Alistair Bromley, OBE, *b* 1927; *ed* Tonbridge; Vice-Chm Countryside Commn for Scotland 1972-81, since when Member of Scottish Land Court; OBE (Civil) 1976: *m* 1952, Rosemary, da of late J. Lindsay Pullar of Glenfarg House, by Perth, and has issue living, Christopher John, *b* 1954, — Caroline Margaret, *b* 1956: *m* 1980, Andrew J. Fraser, son of late John C. Fraser, and has issue living, John Campbell *b* 1987, Alice Margaret *b* 1986, Rosamund Mary *b* 1990, — Colina Mary, *b* 1964: *m* 1989, Jonathan Humphrey, son of David Humphrey. *Residence* – Grainston Farm, Kilbryde, Dunblane, Perthshire, FK15 9NF.

WIDOW LIVING OF EIGHTH BARONET

MARY ANNE CHICHESTER (*Mary, Lady Campbell*), da of late Brig George Alexander Bain, OBE (see M Donegall, colls, 1990 Edn): *m* 1952, Sir Colin Moffat Campbell, 8th Bt, who *d* 1997. *Residence* – Kilbryde Castle, Dunblane, Perthshire FK15 9NF.

COLLATERAL BRANCHES LIVING

Granddaughter of late Alexander Bulwer Campbell (infra):—
Issue of late Alexander Colin le Grand Campbell, *b* 1898, *d* 1980: *m* 1922, Mavis Macdonald, who *d* 1937:—
Janet Glenn, *b* 1926: *m* 1953, Neil Lester, of 551 South Titirangi Rd, Auckland 7, NZ, and has issue living, Mark Robert Alexander, *b* 1954.

Grandson of late Alexander le Grand Campbell, 2nd son of 4th baronet:—
Issue of late Alexander Bulwer Campbell, *b* 1855, *d* 1938: *m* 1894, Maude, da of J. Knight:—
Clyde Coldstream, *b* 1904; Solicitor, Auckland, NZ: *m* 1st, 1936, Mary Fisher; 2ndly, 1943, Eleanor Laura Curnow, of Auckland, who *d* 1982 and has issue living, (by 2nd *m*) Alexander Edward Lindsay, *b* 1948: *m* 1977, Mary Lesley Griffin, and has issue living, Elizabeth Mary *b* 1978, Joanna Margaret *b* 1980, Kathryn Laura *b* 1982, — Margaret Alison, *b* 1945.

Grandsons of late Col George Frederick Colin Campbell, CMG, VD, 2nd son of late Alexander le Grand Campbell (ante):—
Issue of late Capt Alan le Grand Campbell, *b* 1896, *d* 1960: *m* 1928, Barbara Alison, da of late James Marchbanks of Wellington, NZ:—
John Graham Colin, *b* 1929: *m* 1957, Anna Margaret, da of late Bertram Kay, of Fulham, London, and has issue, Alexander James le Grand, *b* 1958, — Robert Neil, *b* 1960. —— Donald James (Campbell St, Karori, Wellington, NZ), *b* 1930; ANZIA: *m* 1963, Barbara Mary, da of Frank Grear, of Nelson, NZ.

Granddaughter of late William Hunter Campbell, yr son of late Robert Stuart Campbell (*b* 1815), yst son of William Campbell, WS, 4th son of 3rd baronet:—
Issue of late Robert Stuart Campbell, *b* 1873, *d* 1958: *m* 1903, Annie, who *d* 1960, da of John Holloway:—
Annie Elizabeth, *b* 1906: *m* 1928, Andrew B. Straughan, who *d* 1987, of 126 Park St, Goderich, Ont N7A IK8, Canada, and has issue living, Benson Robert James, *b* 1929: *m* 1950, Catherine La Verdiere, and has issue living, Stephen Benson *b* 1960, Heather Victoria *b* 1970, — Martin Kalmor, *b* 1931: *m* 1952, Noreen Fuller, and has issue living, Martin Wayne *b* 1953: *m* 1991, Nancy Ann Walters (and has issue living, Justin Kaleb *b* 1992), Michael James *b* 1955: *m* 1986, Heather de Penier (and has issue living, Alexander John *b* 1988, Scott James *b* (twin) 1988, Nicholas *b* 1992), Brian Alexander *b* 1960: *m* 1986, Grechten Ball (and has issue living, Sarah Nicole *b* 1991), Martha Noreen *b* 1962: *m* 1987, Robert Marcel Girard (and has issue living, Laura Alexandra Noreen *b* 1992), — Donald Ivan, *b* 1934: *m* 1951, Lois Freeman, and has issue living, Donald Kenneth *b* 1957: *m* 1977, Anita Bourdeau (and has issue living, Jefferey *b* 1980, Lori Ann *b* 1978), Linda Elizabeth *b* 1951: *m* 1973, Donald Johnston (and has issue living, Mark *b* 1978, Alecia *b* 1980), Barbara Louise *b*

1959: *m* 1978, Philip Petre (and has issue living, Michael *b* 1980), — William Stuart, *b* 1936: *m* 1960, Victoria La Verdiere, and has issue living, William Glenn *b* 1967, Cynthia Catherine *b* 1962, Nancy Carol *b* 1963, — Clayton Lyal, *b* 1936: *m* 1st, 1963, — ; 2ndly, 1982, Donna Gibson, and has issue living, (by 1st *m*) Clayton Lyal *b* 1964, Sean Andrew *b* 1966, (by 2nd *m* adopted) James *b* 1986, — Roy Campbell, *b* 1940: *m* 1966, Irene Phillips, and has issue living, Cameron Alexander *b* 1967, Allyson Elizabeth *b* 1970, Christine Lydia *b* 1972, — John Arnold Clark, *b* 1944: *m* 1964, Marion Sutherland, and has issue living, David Joseph *b* 1965, Susan Anne *b* 1967, — David Glenn, *b* 1946: *m* 1969, Katharine Huff, and has issue living, John Andrew *b* 1973, Jeffrey David *b* 1975, Sarah Katharine *b* 1977.

Grandchildren of late Robert Stuart Campbell (ante):—
Issue of late Robert Edmund Hunter Campbell, *b* 1904, *d* 1980 (matriculated arms as Campbell of Bellsyde, Ont, with Lyon Court 1964): *m* 1st, 1930, Minerva, who *d* 1955, da of W. J. Finlay; 2ndly, 1964, Marjorie, who *d* 1997, da of Frank Preston:—
(By 1st *m*) Charles Robert, JP (Box 907, Seaforth, Ont N0K 1W0, Canada), *b* 1943: *m* 1964, Margaret Jane, da of late Charles E. Campbell, and has issue living, James Robert, *b* 1965: *m* 1989, Catherine T. Kelly and has issue living, James Hunter Fergus *b* 1990, Haden Connor *b* 1992, Colin Robert *b* 1993, Kiernyn Kelly *b* 1997, — Barry Charles, *b* 1966, — Christine, *b* 1969: *m* 1992, Donald William Bruxer, and has issue living, Dylan Robert *b* 1993, Logan Donald Louis *b* 1995, Isaac Christopher *b* 1997. —— Grace Anne Pauline, *b* 1933: *m* 1952, Frederick McGee, of Box 154, Wingham, Ontario N0G 2W0, Canada, and has issue living, Robert William John, *b* 1953: *m* 1975, Brenda Joanne Maize, and has issue living, Jonathan Robert *b* 1983, David James *b* 1984, Heather Joanne *b* 1978, — Ronald Frederick, *b* 1958: *m* 1979, Susan Mae Harrison, and has issue living, Christopher Ronald *b* 1986, Candace Mae *b* 1981, — Janet Grace *b* 1955: *m* 1977, Kenneth Russell MacAdams, and has issue living, Darryl Kenneth *b* 1978, Kevin Robert *b* 1981.

Issue of late William John Campbell, *b* 1875, *d* 1963: *m* 1901, Mary Hutton, who *d* 1933—
John, *b* 1916: *m* 1946, Muriel Mackay, and has issue living, Robert, *b* 1956, — Linda M., *b* 1951. —— Jean B., *b* 1905, *d* 1987.

Issue of late George Alexander Campbell, *b* 1882, *d* 1967: *m* 1st, 1906, Jennie Hutton; 2ndly, 1925 Flossie Saunders, who *d* 1960:—
(By 1st *m*) John Hunter (Blyth, Ontario, Canada) *b* 1914: *m* 1st, 1935, Margaret Gillies; 2ndly, 1945, Frances Rosetta Gillies, and has issue living (by 1st *m*) Harold John Linklater, *b* 1935: *m* 1957, Rose-Marie Whitfield, and has issue living, John Lewis *b* 1957, Scott Harold *b* 1970, Sherri Lou *b* 1959, — Ronald Keith, *b* 1939: *m* 19—, Elizabeth Mary Oliver, and has issue living, Ronald Thomas *b* 1970, William Paul *b* 1972, — Gail, *b* 1941: *m* 1959, Kenneth Nekon Paterson, and has issue living, (by 2nd *m*) Danny, *b* 1948, Mary Barbara, *b* 1946: *m* 1967, Douglas Ross Howson, and has issue living, Douglas Jeffrey, *b* 1969, Sherri Lynn, *b* 1972. —— Harold Alexander (Blyth, Ontario, Canada), *b* 1919: *m* 1939, Adeline Isabel Cardiff, and has issue living, William John, *b* 1939: *m* 1958, Diana Teresa Wozniak, and has issue living, Curtis William *b* 1961: *m* 1978, Tammy Kerr (and has issue living, Daniel William *b* 1986, Lisa Marie *b* 1985), Randall Steven Harold *b* 1962: *m* 1986, Elizabeth Heath, Lorie Diana Catherine *b* 1959: *m* 1st, 1979, Kevin Faber; 2ndly, 1988, Mark Fischer (and has issue living, (by 1st *m*) Kristopher Kevin *b* 1981, Jacqueline Lorie *b* 1983, (by 2nd *m*) Natasha Danielle *b* 1988), Suzanne Adeline *b* 1969, — Dwight Alexander, *b* 1941: *m* 1960, Lyla Joan Marie Johnston, and has issue living, Grant Dwight *b* 1961: *m* 1985, Elaine Jobe, Charlene Marie *b* 1960: *m* 1987, Gary Carpenter (and has issue living, Matthew Garrison Campbell *b* 1987), Sharon Rebecca Jane *b* 1967, — Nancy Lee, *b* 1942: *m* 1965, John Michael Pawitch, and has issue living, Michael Alexander, *b* 1972, Mark Andrew, *b* 1975, — Frances Elizabeth, *b* 1961: *m* 1984, Steven Roy Bearss, and has issue living, Candice Elizabeth *b* 1985, Amanda Jane *b* 1987. —— Mary Haugh, *b* 1909: *m* 1928, Edgar McMichael, who *d* 1978, and has issue living, Alice Isobel, *b* 1933: *m* 1956, Robert Morrison, who *d* 1966, and has issue living, Bruce Edward *b* 1963. —— (By 2nd *m*) Stuart Edgar, *b* 1934: *m* 1963, Shirley Lee, who *d* 1988, and has issue living, Denise, *b* 1964, Karen Ann, *b* 1967. —— Margaret Lillian Christine, *b* 1927: *m* 1954, John Toth, and has issue living, James John, *b* 1954. —— Ina May, *b* 1929: *m* 1962, Herbert Stephen. —— Florence Alexandra, *b* 1930: *m* 1965, Ronald Dolmage.

The 1st baronet, a Lord of Justiciary in Scotland, under the title of Lord Aberuchill, was a Privy Councillor, and sat as MP for Perthshire 1690-1702. He lost £17,201 (Scots), from the Highland army under Lord Dundee, and though an Act of Parliament granting him compensation was passed, he did not receive the money. The original patent or baronetcy is lost, and the actual date when it was conferred is not known. Sir Colin Moffat Campbell, 8th Bt, MC, was Chm James Finlay & Co, tea merchants, Chm Tea Board of Kenya, and thrice Chm E African Tea Trade Assocn; he restored the family seat, Kilbryde Castle, Dunblane.

CAMPBELL (UK) 1808, of Succoth, Dunbartonshire

Labour overcomes everything

Sir ILAY MARK CAMPBELL OF SUCCOTH, 7th *Baronet*; *b* 29 May 1927; *s* his father, *Capt Sir* GEORGE ILAY, 1967; *ed* Eton, and Ch Ch, Oxford (MA); Scottish Agent for Christie, Manson & Woods 1968-73, Joint Agent 1973-78; Chm Christie's & Edmistons Ltd (Christie's, Scotland) 1978-96; Pres of Assocn for Protection of Rural Scotland 1978-90; Member of Gardens Cttee, National Trust for Scotland since 1994; Convener Church of Scotland Cttee for Artistic Matters 1987-91; Trustee, Tree Register of the British Isles since 1988; Memb Historic Council for Scotland 1989-98; Chm Church Buildings Renewal Trust 1995-98; Hon Vice Pres Scotlands Garden Scheme since 1983; Dir High Craigton Farming Co, Trustee Crarae Gardens Charitable Trust: *m* 1961, Margaret Minette Rohais, only da of late James Alasdair Anderson of Tullichewan (*see* E Halsbury, 1995 Edn), and has issue.

ᴁrms – Quarterly; 1st and 4th, gyronny of eight engrailed or and sable; 2nd and 3rd azure, a lion rampant argent, within a bordure counter-compony argent and azure. *Wallace of Elderslie.* ᴄrest – A camel's head couped proper; ᴤupporters – *Dexter*, a lion rampant guardant proper; *sinister*, a savage wreathed about the temples and loins with oak leaves, all proper.
Residence – Crarae Lodge, by Inveraray, Argyll PA32 8YA. *Club* – Turf.

DAUGHTERS LIVING

Cecilia Margaret Lucy, *b* 1963: *m* 1988, Capt Malcolm Gregor Charles MacGregor, yr of MacGregor, elder son of Brig Sir Gregor MacGregor of MacGregor, 6th Bt. —— Candida Harriett Rohais, *b* 1964: *m* 1991, Gerard Joseph Rafferty, elder son of Richard Byrne Rafferty, of Bellshill, Lanarks, and has issue living, Ruaraidh Ilay Byrne, *b* 1993, — Fintan Campbell, *b* 1997.

  Sir Ilay Campbell, 1st baronet, was Lord President of Court of Session, with the title of Lord Succoth; and the 2nd baronet Sir Archibald was a Lord of Session 1809-24, with the same designation. The 1st baronet's mother, Helen, who *d* 1767, was the only da and heir of John Wallace of Elderslie.

CAMPBELL (UK) 1815

Sir LACHLAN PHILIP KEMEYS CAMPBELL, 6th *Baronet*; *b* 9 Oct 1958; *s* his father, *Col Sir* GUY THEOPHILUS HALSWELL, OBE, MC, 1993; *ed* Lyceé Français, Temple Grove, Eton, and RMA Sandhurst; late RGJ, served N Ireland, Queen Victoria's Rifles (TA): *m* 1986, Harriet Jane Sarah, only da of late Frank Edward Jex Girling, of West Malvern, Worcs, and has issue.

ᴁrms – Quarterly: 1st and 4th, gyronny of eight or and sable; 2nd, argent, a lymphad, sails furled and oars in action sable, with a flag and pennants flying gules; 3rd, or, a fesse checky azure and argent, all within a bordure embattled ermine. ᴄrest – A boar's head arrachée or.
Residence – 32 Malwood Rd, SW12. *Clubs* – Army and Navy, MCC, London Scottish, The Royal Green Jackets.

SONS LIVING

ARCHIBALD EDWARD FITZGERALD, *b* 13 June 1990. —— Ivo David Orlando, *b* 1997.

DAUGHTER LIVING

Georgia Charlotte Clementine, *b* 1995.

BROTHER LIVING

Rory Charles FitzGerald (Flat C, 103 Gloucester Rd, SW7 4SF), *b* 1961; *ed* Lycée Français, Temple Grove, Amersham Art Coll, and Royal Coll of Music; actor: *m* 1st, 1985 (*m diss* 1991), Angela Victoria, da of late Victor Orman Phillis, of Pacific Highway, Killara, NSW, Australia; 2ndly, 1997, Brigitte, da of Kaspar Wolfensberger, of Zurich, and has issue living (by 2nd *m*), Olivia Isabella Marie *b* 1998.

WIDOW LIVING OF FIFTH BARONET

ELIZABETH WILLS-WEBBER (*Elizabeth, Lady Campbell*), formerly wife of D. H. Parker; actress as Lizbeth Webb: *m* 1956, Col Sir Guy Theophilus Halswell Campbell, 5th Bt, OBE, MC, who *d* 1993. *Residence* – 18 Lansdown Terrace, Malvern Rd, Cheltenham, Glos GL50 2JT.

COLLATERAL BRANCHES LIVING

Issue of late Col John Archibald Campbell, yst son of 3rd baronet, *b* 1898, *d* 1974: *m* 1st, 1925 (*m diss* 1940), Dorothy, da of late John Field, of Perthi, Ruthin; 2ndly, 1944 (*m diss* 1963), Elizabeth, da of Renard Pearth, of Pittsburgh, USA:—
(By 1st *m*) Colin Guy Napier (23 Lansdowne Gdns, SW8; White's and Puffins Clubs), *b* 1930; Capt late KRRC: *m* 1st, 1965 (*m diss* 1981), Mrs Lucy Barnett Smith, da of James A. Barnett, of Bel Air, Cal, USA, and formerly wife of Clifford Smith, Jr; 2ndly, 1987, Charmian Rachel, formerly wife of Archibald Hugh Stirling, yr of Keir (*see* Stirling-Maxwell, Bt), and yr da of late Col Lord George Francis John Montagu Douglas Scott (*see* D Buccleuch, colls), and has issue living (by 1st *m*), Georgina Dorothy, *b* 1969, — Tessa Sylvia, *b* 1971. —— (By 2nd *m*) (Henrietta) Nina Sylvia, *b* 1945: *m* 1971, Andrew Guy Louis de Chappuis Konig, of 6 Molyneux St, W1, and has issue living.

Grandchildren of late Charles James Napier Campbell, 3rd son of 2nd baronet.—
Issue of late Major Edward Fitzgerald Campbell, *b* 1890, *d* 1950: *m* 1915, Agnes Catherine, who *d* 1977, da of late Henry Templer Prior, Master of Supreme Court:—
Charles Colin (Woolpit Farm, Ewhurst, Cranleigh, Surrey), *b* 1923; *ed* Loretto, and Pembroke Coll, Camb (Foundation Scholar) (MA); 1939-45 War as Lt RE: *m* 1970, Julia Margaret Rachel, da of Anthony Smithson Russell, and has issue living, James Charles Anthony, *b* 1971, — Lucy Catherine Isabel, *b* 1974. —— Geraldine Mary (11 Culverwell Gdns, Winchester, Hants), *b* 1917: *m* 1941, Maj Neville Glyn Williams, MC, Indian Army, who was *ka* in Burma 1945, and has issue living, Fiona Glyn, *b* 1944: *m* 1963, Julian John Hamling Smith, of Bishopsway, Twyford, nr Winchester, Hants SO21 1NY, and has issue living, Colin Nigel Neville *b* 1965; *ed* Winchester, Emma Mary Glyn *b* 1968: *m* 1996, Robert William Middleton Brook. —— Frances Margaret, *b* 1919: *m* 1954, Denys Newell Pitts Squarey, who *d* 1983. *Residence* – Brigge House, Broughton, Stockbridge, Hants.

Grandson of late Ion Douglas FitzGerald Campbell, 8th son of 2nd baronet:—
Issue of late Major Ion Edward FitzGerald Campbell, Duke of Cornwall's LI, *b* 1897, *d* (April) 1936: *m* 1933, Evelyn Julia (who *d* 1992, having *m* 2ndly, 1952, as his second wife, the 11th Earl of Southesk, KCVO, who *d* 1992), da of Lieut-Col Arthur Peere Williams-Freeman, DSO, OBE:—
Ion Edward FitzGerald (Feathercombe, Hambledon, Godalming, Surrey GU8 4DP), *b* (*posthumous*), (May) 1936: *m* 1963, Muriel Elisabeth, da of late Brig Leslie Frederick Ethelbert Wieler, CB, CBE, and has issue living, John Edward FitzGerald, *b* 1964: *m* 1990, Patricia, da of James O'Brien, and has issue living, Christopher *b* 1995, Laura *b* 1992, Naomi *b* 1998, — Leslie James FitzGerald, *b* 1965: *m* 1995, Christine Laurens, and has issue living, Thomas *b* 1996, — Robert Christopher FitzGerald, *b* 1967, — Peter Michael FitzGerald, *b* 1972.

Issue of late George Theophilus Campbell, 9th son of 2nd baronet, *b* 1872, *d* 1924: *m* 1917, Winifred Edna Boyd, da of late James FitzGibbon Black, of Montreal:—
Elspeth Griselda Theophila, *b* 1919: *m* 1946, Robin John Patrick Flynn, MC, DFC, and has issue living, Michael George Alexander Robin Fitzgerald Campbell, *b* 1949, — Reidy Georgina Campbell, *b* 1948.

Granddaughter of late Capt Frederic Augustus Campbell, 4th son of 1st baronet:—
Issue of late John St Clair CAMPBELL-BRABAZON, OBE, *b* 1865, *d* 1942, having assumed by Roy licence 1923 the additional surname of Brabazon: *m* 1900, Caroline Leavett, of Mayford Lodge, Mayford, Woking:—
Geraldine, *b* 1904: *m* 1928, Brigadier Edward Hamilton Grant, late Argyll and Sutherland Highlanders, and has issue living, Rosemary Ann, *b* 1930: *m* 1st, 1952 (*m diss* 1959), William Whitehead; 2ndly, 1961, Francis Buck.

The 1st baronet, Sir Guy Campbell, CB (el son of late Lieut-Gen Colin Campbell, Lieut-Gov of Gibraltar 1809-14), was a Maj-Gen in the Army, and Col of the 3rd West India Regiment; served with distinction throughout the Peninsular war and at Waterloo. The 2nd baronet, Sir Edward FitzGerald, Col 60th Rifles, served with distinction in the Punjab campaign 1848 and through the Indian Mutiny campaign 1857-8. The 3rd baronet, Sir Guy Theophilus, was Lieut-Col 60th Rifles and served in Afghan War 1878-80. The 4th baronet, Sir Guy Colin, was Major 60th Rifles, and served in European Wars 1914-19 and 1941-45. The 5th baronet, Col Sir Guy Theophilus Halswell, OBE, MC, served KOYLI, 60th Rifles, Camel Corps, Sudan Defence Force, and commanded Kenya Regt 1952-56, European War 1939-45 (wounded, MC), OBE (Mil) 1954.

CAMPBELL (UK) 1831, of Barcaldine and Glenure, Argyllshire

I am prepared

PARATUS SUM

Sir NIALL ALEXANDER HAMILTON CAMPBELL, 8th *Baronet*; *b* 7 Jan 1925; *s* his father *Sir* IAN VINCENT HAMILTON, CB 1978; *ed* Cheltenham, and Corpus Christi Coll, Oxford; Hereditary Keeper of Barcaldine Castle; Bar Inner Temple 1951; 1939-45 War as Lt RM; Assist Sec, St Mary's Hosp, Paddington 1955-60, Sec W Middx Hosp, Isleworth 1960, and Dep House Gov, London Clinic 1960-68, since when Sec to Board of Management, Royal Home and Hosp for Incurables, Putney: *m* 1st, 1949 (*m diss* 1956), Patricia Mary, da of R. Turner; 2ndly, 1957, Norma Joyce, da of W. N. Wiggin, of Albrighton, and has had issue by 2nd *m*.

Arms – Quarterly: 1st, gyronny of eight or and sable, *Campbell*; on a canton argent a bend sable, between a unicorn's head in chief and a cross-crosslet fitchée in base gules, *Dennistoun*; 2nd, or, a fesse checky azure and argent, *Stewart of Lorn*; 3rd argent, a lymphad, sails furled and oars in action sable, *Lorne*; 4th gyronny of eight or and sable, *Campbell*; on a canton gules two bars, or *Cameron of Lochiel*; the whole within a bordure quarterly or and sable. **Crest** – A Highlander fully armed and equipped, having a claymore in the dexter hand and on the sinister arm a target or. **Supporters** – *Dexter*, a leopard; *sinister*, a stag — all proper.
Seat – Barcaldine Castle, Ledaig, Argyllshire. *Residence* – The Old Mill, Milltown, Muddiford, Barnstaple EX31 1DX.

SONS LIVING (*By 2nd marriage*)

RODERICK DUNCAN HAMILTON (Barcaldine Castle, Ledaig, by Oban, Argyll PA37 1QS), *b* 24 Feb 1961: *m* 1989, Jean Caroline, da of Laurence Bicknell, of Tom's Hill, Lobb, Braunton, Devon, and has issue living, Kate Emily Dennistoun, *b* 1990, — Anna Iona Hamilton, *b* 1993. —— Angus Charles Dundas, *b* 1967.

DAUGHTERS LIVING AND DECEASED (*By 2nd marriage*)

Fiona Madeline Hamilton, *b* 1958: *m* 19—, Philip Rogers, and *d* 1997. —— Lucy Catriona Margaret, *b* (twin) 1967.

COLLATERAL BRANCH LIVING

Issue of late Richard Henry Dennistoun Campbell, yr brother of 7th baronet, *b* 1901, *d* 1978: *m* 1936, Kathleen Adair, who *d* 1993, yst da of late Richard Fallowes Dunn, of Wolverhampton:—
Lorne Mary Dennistoun, *b* 1939: *m* 1971, Heinrich Richard Gerlinger, of Stanislaus Gasse 4/5, 1030 Vienna, Austria, and has issue living, Bianca Agnes Adair, *b* 1973, — Francesca Lorne, *b* 1977. —— Elizabeth Gay Adair, *b* 1942: *m* 1973, Alun Morse Davies, of 92 Ifield Rd, SW10 9AX, and has issue living, Hugh Timothy Hamilton, *b* 1978, — Serena Gwendolen Adair, *b* 1974.

Granddaughter of late Maj-Gen John Peter William Campbell, 3rd son of 1st baronet:—
Issue of late Gerald Edward Lyon Campbell, *b* 1863, *d* 1902: *m* 1886, Sybil (who *d* 1958, having *m* 2ndly, 1911, Com Wentworth Vernon Cole, formerly RN), da of Maj-Gen Thomas Ross Church, CIE:—
Mary Hamilton, *b* 1888: *m* 1915, Alfred Thomas Duncan Anderson, who *d* 1949, and has issue living, Ian Duncan Hamilton, *b* 1916, — Alec Vernon *b* 1921.

This family is descended from Patrick Campbell, of Innerzeldies, legitimated son of Sir Duncan Campbell, 1st baronet of Glenorchy, ancestor of the Earls of Breadalbane (a branch of the Ducal House of Argyll). Sir Duncan Campbell of Barcaldine, 1st Bt, was Capt Scots Fusilier Guards, and served at Copenhagen, Walcheren, and the Peninsula. He *m* 1815, Elizabeth Dreghorn, da of John Dennistoun of Dennistoun, Dunbartonshire. Sir Alexander, 2nd Bt, was Sergeant-at-Arms in Queen Victoria's Household. The 3rd Bt, Sir Duncan Alexander Dundas, CVO, was Gentleman Usher of the Green Rod 1884-95, and Sec to Order of the Thistle 1895-1926. The 4th baronet, Sir Alexander William Dennistoun Campbell, was Col Indian Army. The 5th baronet, Sir Duncan John Alfred Campbell, was sometime a Dist Judge in Central India, and Acting Commr in Burma and Central Provinces, India. The 6th baronet, Sir (Francis) Eric Dennistoun Campbell was Capt S Lancs Regt and served in 1914-18 War Afghan War 1919. The 7th baronet, Sir Ian Vincent Hamilton Campbell, CB, was Private Sec to Ch of Air Staff 1926-27 and to Permanent Sec of Air Min 1927-30, and Assist Private Sec to successive Secs of State for Air 1930-34, Prin Air Min 1939, and Assist Under-Sec of State 1945-55.

CAMPBELL (UK) 1913, with precedence of 1804, of Ardnamurchan, Argyllshire

Sir BRUCE COLIN PATRICK CAMPBELL, 3rd *Baronet* (*cr* 1913) (but his name has not appeared on the Official Roll of Baronets); *b* 2 July 1904; *s* his father, *Lieut-Col Sir* JOHN BRUCE STUART, DSO, 1943; *ed* Edinburgh Acad; no information concerning this baronet has been received since 1943.

Arms – Not recorded in Lyon Register.

SISTER LIVING

Marjorie Ethelle (Flat E2, Queen Alexandra's Court, St Mary's Rd, Wimbledon, SW19), *b* 1911: *m* 1938, Malcolm Melville, who *d* 1942, and has issue living, Pamela Elaine Marguerite, *b* 1940: *m* 1st, 1959, Richard Crockett Knox; 2ndly, 1984, Dolph Warren Zink, of Apt 32 Mayfair, 3 Park Av, Crawley, Western Australia 6009, and has issue living (by 1st *m*), Andrew Melville *b* 1961: *m* 1988, Joy Gibbs (and has issue living, James Charles Richard *b* 1993, Isabel Clare *b* 1990), Fiona Heather *b* 1964: *m* 1994, Peter Anthony Sarich (and has issue living, Karl Knox Anthony *b* 1995, Aaron Ralph Knox *b* 1997), — Heather Jacqueline Malcom *b* 1942: *m* 1971, Richard Norton Orlando Kingsbury, of Hamsell Farm, Eridge, Sussex (*see* B Brabourne, colls, 1980 Edn), and has issue living, Nicholas James Melville *b* 1971, Benjamin Francis Knatchbull *b* 1978.

  Donald Campbell was created a Baronet of Nova Scotia 1628, and resigned his dignity into the King's hands on 28 Aug 1643, for a new enfeoffment of it and the lands annexed, in favour of his nephew and heirs male. Upon the decease of Donald, his nephew (George) did not, however, claim the title, neither did the three next succeeding heirs, but about 1790 John Campbell, great-great-grandson of George Campbell (ante) resumed the title as 6th baronet, being followed in turn by his son John, Lieut-Guv of St Vincent's 1845-53, and his grandson, Maj-Gen John William Campbell, CB (who served in Crimean Campaign 1855, in China Campaign 1860 and in Afghan War 1879-80), whose claim, however, to be placed on the Roll of Baronets in right of the 1628 creation was not recognized, but upon whom a new Baronetcy of the United Kingdom was conferred in Nov 1913, with special precedence as above-mentioned. The 2nd baronet *d* (whilst a prisoner in Palembang Camp, Sumatra) 1943.

CAMPBELL (UK) 1939, of Airds Bay, co Argyll, and Bromley, co Kent (Extinct 1954)

Sir CHARLES DUNCAN MACNAIR CAMPBELL, 2nd and last *Baronet*.

DAUGHTER LIVING OF FIRST BARONET

Elspeth Ada *b* 1919: *m* 1940, Lawrence William Orchard, of Flat 2, Chanters, West St, Marlow, Bucks SL7 2BS, and has issue living, William Henslow (Corners, Jordans Lane, Jordans, Beaconsfield, Bucks HP9 2SU), *b* 1947: *m* 1st, 1973 (*m diss* 1988), Susan Jane Field; 2ndly, 1990, Mrs Susan Davidson, and has issue living (by 1st *m*), Dominic Henslow *b* 1976, Edward William *b* 1978, Alexander Peter *b* 1980, — Laurence Augustine, *b* 1950: *m* 1986, Lucinda Mary Emrys-Roberts, and has issue living, Peter Augustine *b* 1990, Benedict William *b* 1994, Philip Edmund *b* 1996, Rosalind Ann *b* 1988, — Anthony Edward, *b* 1962, — Gillian Mary, *b* 1941, — Sarah Elspeth, *b* 1942: *m* 1967, Norman Hampel, of Two Oaks, Slade Oak lane, Denham, Bucks, and has issue living, Simon Mark, *b* 1968, John Laurence *b* 1969, Angus James *b* 1973, Nicola Jane *b* 1971, — Wendy Frances, *b* 1944.

  Sir Edward Taswell Campbell of Airds Bay, 1st Bt, was MP for Camberwell NW Div 1924-29, and for Bromley, Kent 1930-45; PPS to Lord Privy Seal 1940-43. His eldest son, Sir (Charles) Duncan McNair Campbell of Airds Bay, 2nd Bt, *dsp* 1954 (when the baronetcy became ext), and his only remaining son, Gillian Lorne Campbell, DFC, Fl Lieut RAFVR, was *ka* 1942. Sir Edward's eldest da, Frances Henriette (ante) *s* her brother as Representor of the family of Campbell of Airds Bay, and her yr son, Michael McNeil Campbell of Airds Bay, was officially recognised by the Lord Lyon as her Representor 1954, when he matriculated the arms.

COCKBURN-CAMPBELL (UK) 1821, of Gartsford, Ross-shire
(Name pronounced "Coburn-Campbell")

WITHOUT FEAR

Sir THOMAS COCKBURN-CAMPBELL, 6th *Baronet; b* 8 Dec 1918; *s* his father, *Sir* ALEXANDER THOMAS, 1935; *ed* Church of England Gram Sch, Melbourne, Australia; author of *Land of Lots of Time: m* 1st, 1944 (*m diss* 1981), Josephine Zoi, el da of Harold Douglas Forward, of Cunjardine, W Australia; 2ndly, 1982 (*m diss* 1990), Janice Laraine, yst da of William John Pascoe, of Bundoora, Victoria, and has issue by 1st *m.*

Arms – Quarterly 1st and 4th: quarterly, i and iv gyronny of eight or and sable, *Campbell*; ii, argent, a galley or lymphad sails furled, oars in action sable; iii, or, a fesse checky azure and argent, over all a chief argent charged with a rock proper superscribed "Gibraltar," between two medals for Seringapatam and Talavera; 2nd and 3rd, quarterly, i and iv, argent, an ostrich feather ensigned with an Imperial crown proper, between three cocks, two and one, gules; ii and iii, six mascles three two and one or, *Cockburn.* Crest – 1st, a dexter hand holding a scimitar all proper, *Campbell.*
Residence – 21 Cardwell St, York, 6302 W Australia.

SON LIVING (*By 1st marriage*)

ALEXANDER THOMAS (11 Templetonia Retreat, Livingston Estate, Canning Vale 6155, W Australia), *b* 16 March 1945: *m* 1969, Kerry Anne, el da of late Sgt K. Johnson, of Mt Hawthorne, W Aust, and has issue living, Thomas Justin, *b* 10 Feb 1974, — Felicity Ann, *b* 1981.

BROTHER LIVING

Alexander Bruce (90 Evans St, Shenton Park, W Australia), *b* 1923; Leading Aircraftman, Roy Australian Air Force; S-W Pacific 1944-45: *m* 1951, Beryl, da of William Elder, of Shenton Park, W Australia, and has issue living, Susan Peta, *b* 1954, — Nola Gay, *b* 1957, — Judith Ann, *b* 1961, — Alison Lee, *b* 1964.

Lieut-Gen Sir Alexander Campbell, 1st Bt, Col of 80th Regiment, greatly distinguished himself at Seringapatam, also in the Peninsula, 1809-11, where he commanded a division of the British Army. He was created a baronet 1815, and in 1821 obtained a new patent, which extended the limitation to the male issue of his daughter Olympia (Mrs Cockburn), and afterwards to the male issue of his daughter Isabella Charlotte (Lady Malcolm), which is now extinct. The 2nd baronet assumed in 1824 the additional surname of Campbell. Sir Thomas, 4th baronet, was Pres of Legislative Council of W Australia.

HOME-PURVES-HUME-CAMPBELL (NS) 1665, of Purves Hall, Berwickshire (Dormant or Extinct 1960)

Sir JOHN HOME-PURVES-HUME-CAMPBELL, 8th and last *Baronet.*

DAUGHTERS LIVING OF EIGHTH BARONET

Mabel Jane, *b* 1905. —— Elsie Barbara *b* 1907: *m* 1st, 1928 (*m diss* 1940), Donovan Storr Allom; 2ndly, 1954, George Moxon Cook, and has issue living (by 1st *m*), Michael Donovan (Railway Cottage, Black Mountain, NSW 365, Australia), *b* 1930; *ed* Wellington Coll, and Trin Coll, Camb, — Bridget Barbara, *b* 1935, — Sheila Ann, *b* 1938.

Campbell-Orde, see Orde.

CARDEN (I) 1787, of Templemore, Tipperary

With faith and love

FIDE·ET·AMORE

Sir JOHN CRAVEN CARDEN, 7th Baronet; *b* 11 March 1926; *s* his father, *Sir* JOHN VALENTINE, MBE, 1935; *ed* Eton: *m* 1947, Isabel Georgette, yst da of late Robert de Hart, and has issue.

Arms – Argent, a mascle gules between three pheons sable. Crest – A pheon sable. *Address* – PO Box 66, 35-39 Colomberie, St Helier, Jersey, Channel Isles JE4 8PZ. *Club* – White's.

DAUGHTER LIVING

Isabel Mary, *b* 1952. *Address* – 142 East 71st St, Apt 5D, NY 10021, USA.

COLLATERAL BRANCH LIVING

Grandsons of late Major Henry Charles Carden, DSO, 2nd son of 4th baronet:—
Issue of late Rev Canon Henry Craven Carden, *b* 1882, *d* 1964: *m* 1913, Olive, who *d* 1966, da of late Rev Canon C. V. Gorton:—
DERRICK CHARLES, CMG (17 The King's House, Peninsula Sq, Winchester, Hants SO23 8GJ), *b* 31 Oct 1921; *ed* Marlborough and Ch Ch, Oxford, in Sudan Political Ser 1942-54; entered HM's Dip Ser 1954; HM Political Agent, Qatar, Persian Gulf 1955-58, Oriental Sec, British Embassy, Tripoli, Libya 1958-62, at Foreign Office, 1962-64 Head of Chancery, Cairo 1964-65, Consul-Gen, Muscat 1965-69, and Dir Middle East Centre of Arab Studies 1969-73, since when Ambassador to Yemen Arab Republic 1973-76; Visiting Fellow Inst of Development Studies Sussex Univ 1977, since when Ambassador to Sudan; a JP; CMG 1974: *m* 1952, Elizabeth Anne, da of late Capt Alfred Spalding Russell, DSO, RN, and has issue living, John Craven (38 Somerstown, Chichester, Sussex), *b* 1953: *m* 1983, Celia Howitt, and has issue living, Patrick John Cameron *b* 1988, — Peter James Charles, *b* 1958, — Elisabeth Louise, *b* 1956, — Clare Margaret, *b* 1961.

Issue of late John Humphrey Carden, *b* 1886, *d* 1957: *m* 1923, Eileen Winifred Bourke, who *d* 1996, da of late Lieut-Col Thomas Patrick Shannon, RASC:—
Patrick Henry, *b* 1928; Trin House Pilotage Ser: *m* 1951, Rosalie Alice, da of late Rev Canon S. W. Groom, formerly V of Holy Trinity, Lamorbey, Sidcup, and has issue living, Derek Edward Trevor, *b* 1952: *m* 1977, Amanda Mary Smyllie, and has issue living Toby James *b* 1980, Philip Paul *b* 1983, Oliver Mark *b* 1987, — Nigel John Patrick, *b* 1954, — Roger Michael Colin, *b* 1956: *m* 1989, Helena Louise Davis, and has issue living, Harry Grahame Patrick *b* 1997, Katy Louise *b* 1993. *Residence* – The Old Rectory, 91 Windmill St, Gravesend, Kent. —— †Michael Humphrey *b* 1929, *d* 1995; late Capt Worcestershire Regt.

Issue of late Frederick Richard Carden, 3rd son of 4th baronet, *b* 1856, *d* 1935: *m* 1885, Miriam, da of — Beale:—
Richard Craven, *b* 1893. —— Selwyn, *b* 18—. —— Rodney, *b* 18—. —— Geoffrey, *b* 18—. —— Helen Mary: *m* 1912, Herbert Roger. —— Pattie: *m* 1915, D. A. Morrell.

Issue of late Capt Coldstream James Carden, 4th son of 4th baronet, *b* 1857, *d* 1925: *m* 1891, Rose Margaret Ponton, yst da of late David Johnstone, of Croy Shandon, Dunbartonshire:—
Eileen Margaret, *b* 1893: *m* 1919, Brig Thomas Dix Perkin, DL, KSLI, who *d* 1961, and *d* 1984.

Grandson of late Lieut-Col Henry Westenra Carden (infra):—
Issue of late Bernard Westenra Carden, *b* 1887, *d* 1951: *m* 1923, Gwendoline, who *d* 1980, da of Joseph Price, of Leamington:—
Patrick Westenra, *b* 1928; *ed* Univ of Wales (BSc 1951): *m* 1955, Janet Hilda, da of William Stickland, of Cambridge, and has issue living, David Westenra, *b* 1957: *m* 1984, Jane Leslie Clough, and has issue living, Benjamin Westenra *b* 1989, Timothy Peter *b* 1992, — Trevor Courtenay (129 Haliburton Rd, Twickenham, Middx TW1 1PE) *b* 1959: *m* 1995, Daniela, da of Joseph Mamo, of Sliema, Malta, and has issue living, Alexandra Elena *b* 1996, Nicola Courtenay *b* 1999, — Angela, *b* 1961: *m* 1985, Keith West, and has issue living, Christopher William *b* 1990, Heather Carol *b* 1992, — Carol Mary, *b* 1967: *m* 1994, Charles William Taylor, son of Stuart Taylor, of Oakham, Rutland, and has issue living, Jonathan Stuart *b* 1996, Ross William *b* 1998. *Residence* – Sandy Top, 174 Station Rd, Fordingbridge, Hants SP6 1DS.

Granddaughters of late Rev Arthur Carden, 3rd son of 3rd baronet:—
Issue of late Lieut-Col Henry Westenra Carden, *b* 1857, *d* 1928: *m* 1st, 1886, Emily Elphinstone, who *d* 1918, da of late Rev William Courtenay Clack, R of Moretonhampstead, Devon; 2ndly, 1919, Beatrice, who *d* 1944, da of Peter Sharp, formerly of Cannock, Stafford:—
Muriel Elphinstone, *b* 1899: *m* 1924, Charles Pelham Thursby, who *d* 1977, and has issue living, Hugh James, *b* 1931. *Residence* – The Bungalow, Clive, Salop. —— Christina Annette (205, 7720-108th St, Edmonton, Alberta, Canada), *b* 1900: *m* 1924, John Elliot Weir, who *d* 1976, and has issue living, Charles Henry (14003-75th Av, Edmonton, Alberta, Canada T5R 2Y5), *b* 1925; MSc, DLS, PEng: *m* 1949, Kathleen McLellan, and has issue living, Douglas Charles *b* 1953, Wendy Kathleen *b* 1954, Sandra Christina *b* 1957, — Carden Fraser (14 Atlanta Cres, Calgary, Alberta, Canada), *b* 1927: *m* 1950, Freda Irene McCoy, and has issue living, Carlene Ann *b* 1061: *m* 1072, Ronald Joseph Bourassa (and has issue living, Jeffery Alexander *b* 1976, Ronalee Jo-Ann *b* 1974, Danielle Lynn Patricia *b* 1975), Marion *b* 1954: *m* 1973, Carmon Marshall Woodworth (and has issue living, Collin Matthew *b* 1976, Carl Alexander *b* 1978), Patti *b* 1961: *m* 1984, David Mitchell Dennis.

This family, originally of Lincolnshire, settled at Templemore, co Tipperary, about 1650.

CARDEN (UK) 1887, of Wimpole Street, Middlesex, and of Molesey, Surrey

Sir CHRISTOPHER ROBERT CARDEN, 5th *Baronet, b* 24 Nov 1946; *s* his father, *Sir* HENRY CRISTOPHER, OBE, 1993, but his name does not appear on the Official Roll of the Baronetage; *ed* Eton, and Aberdeen Univ (BSc Forestry): *m* 1st, 1972 (*m diss* 1979), Sainimere Rokotuibau, of Suva, Fiji; 2ndly, 1981, Clarita Peralta, of Manila, Philippines.

Arms – Per pale sable and gules, a staff sling in bend between four pheons saltirewise, all argent. Crest – On a fasces fessewise or, a wolf's head erased sable, pierced in the neck with an arrow bendwise or, point downwards gold, embrued proper.
Address – Casilla 1341, Santa Cruz, Bolivia.

SISTER LIVING

Melinda Jane, *b* 1950: *m* 1975, Andrew James Wilson, of Glenfall Stables, Ham, Charlton Kings, Cheltenham, Glos, son of late Capt G. A. J. Wilson, of Ballyburn, Castledermot, co Kildare, and has issue living, Fiona Jane, *b* 1981, — Sarah Bobby, *b* 1984.

MOTHER LIVING

Jane St Clare, da of late Lt-Col Thomas Edward St Clare Daniell, OBE, MC: *m* 1st, 1943 (*m diss* 1961), as his 1st wife, Sir Henry Christopher Carden, 4th Bt, OBE, who *d* 1993; 2ndly, 1962, Maj Thomas Douglas Pilkington of Reay, of Hyde Mill, Stow-on-the-Wold, Cheltenham, Glos.

COLLATERAL BRANCH LIVING

With faith and love

Granddaughter of late Alexander James Carden, 3rd son of 1st baronet:—
Issue of late Henry Carden, *b* 1872, *d* 1948: *m* 1st, 1894, Martha Vinnineda, who *d* 1918, da of Ernst Tronson of Romsdalen, Norway; 2ndly, 1919, Mildred Kedge, who *d* 1946:—
(By 1st *m*) Florence Lillian, *b* 1895: *m* 1924, Brigadier Francisco Rabia Muñoz, Mexican Army. *Residence* – Antonio Maura, 181 Col Moderna, Mexico, DF.

The 1st baronet, Sir Robert Walter Carden (sometime MP for Barnstaple) was Lord Mayor of London 1857, and an Alderman 1849-88. The 2nd baronet was High Sheriff of Hants 1891. The 3rd baronet was High Sheriff of Hants, 1922.

CAREW (E) 1661, of Haccombe, Devonshire

Sir RIVERS VERAIN CAREW, 11th *Baronet; b* 17 Oct 1935; *s* his father, *Sir* THOMAS PALK, 1976; *ed* St Columba's Coll, co Dublin, and Dublin Univ (BA-gric(Hort), MA); author of *Figures out of Mist*: *m* 1st, 1968 (*m diss* 1991), Susan Babington, da of late Harold Babington Hill, of London; 2ndly, 1992, Siobhán, 2nd da of late Críostóir Seán Mac Cárthaigh, of Cork, and has issue by 1st *m*.

Arms – Or, three lions passant in pale sable. Crest – A main-mast, the round top set off with palisadoes or, a demi-lion issuant thereout sable.
Residence – Cherry Bounds, Hicks Lane, Girton, Cambridge CB3 0JS.

SON LIVING (By 1st marriage)

GERALD DE REDVERS, *b* 24 May 1975.

Nil conscire sibi

Conscious of no guilt

DAUGHTERS LIVING (By 1st marriage)

Marcella Tamsin, *b* 1970. —— Marina Lys, *b* 1972. —— Miranda Rose, *b* (twin) 1973.

SISTER LIVING

Oenone Venetia, *b* 1929: *m* 1957, John O'Sullivan, of 17 Brighton Av, Rathgar, Dublin 6, and has issue living, Rowan John Amadeus, *b* 19—, — Kilda Mary Venetia *b* 19—, — Marney Darrell Owen, *b* 19—.

HALF-SISTER LIVING

Zia (23 Hill Lands, Wargrave, Berks), *b* 1914; 1939-42 War with WAAF: *m* 1939, Maj Hugh Richard Stirling, RA, who *d* on active service 1944, and has issue living, Anthony Carew (High Wood, Green Lane, Ellisfield, nr Basingstoke, Hants), *b* 1942; *ed* Pangbourne Nautical Coll: *m* 1968, Geraldine Erica, yst da of Fl Lt Walter Frank Barker, of Wargrave, — Valerie Frances, *b* 1943: *m* 1969, Jeremy Hamilton Lightly, and has issue living, Yvonne Susan *b* 1970, Nicola Jane *b* 1973.

COLLATERAL BRANCHES LIVING

Grandson of late Col Peter Fitzwilliam Carew, late Suffolk Regt, elder son of Rev Henry William Carew, eldest son of Thomas Carew, of Rattery, Devon, 3rd son of 7th baronet:—
Issue of late Capt John Mohun Carew, MC, 3rd Gurkha Rifles, *b* 1921, *d* 1980: *m* 1950, Barbara Joan Stewart, who *d* 1993, da of Maj Arthur Neil Stewart Roberts, OBE, and widow of Maj Richard Henry Baird Shakespear:—
Nicolas John Stewart, *b* 1952. *Residence* – 20 Samian Place, Binfield, Berks RG42 4BX.

Grandchildren of late Com Alfred Curtis Carew, RN, 2nd son of Thomas Carew, of Rattery, Devon (ante):—
Issue of late Thomas Alfred Curtis Carew, *b* 1895, *d* 1970: *m* 1921, Christina, who *d* 1991, da of John Hanna:—
Patrick Henry Curtis, CD (1070 Sunnyside Rd, Kelowna, BC, Canada VIZ 2N8), *b* 1931; *ed* Trafalgar Sch, Nelson, and Kelowna Senior High Sch; Brig-Gen late R Canadian Dragoons; Korea 1952-53 (two medals); NW Europe 1959-63; Cyprus 1966; NW Europe 1970-72: *m* 1954, Norma Diane, da of Claude Rupert Methune Willcox, of Vancouver, BC, and has issue living, Janice Lynn CAREW, *b* 1956; resumed maiden name: *m* 1983 (*m diss* 1993), Andrew Kowal, — Dana Elizabeth, *b* 1958; has an adopted da, Myken Diane Dancia Dawn *b* 1996, — Suzanne Marie CAREW, *b* 1961; resumed maiden name 1993: *m* 1986 (*m diss* 1992), David Paul Williams. —— Verona Lorraine, *b* 1922: *m* 1945, Allan Cameron Barton, who *d* 1987, of Boucherie Rd, Westbank, BC, Canada, and has issue living, Thomas Allan, *b* 1946, — Gerald Patrick, *b* 1948, — Donald Bruce, *b* 1956. —— Dorothy Joan, *b* 1926: *m* 1948, Charles Henry Pfyffer von Altishofen (3910 Suncrest Court, Kelowna, BC, Canada, V1W 4E8), and has issue living, Charles Russell, *b* 1950, — Richard Louis, *b* 1956, — Christine Marie, *b* 1951, — Alice Jerryl, *b* 1955.

Issue of late Nicholas John Carew, *b* 1904, *d* 1974: *m* 1930, Miken Viola, da of late George Borg:—
Elizabeth Shirley Diane, *b* 1931: *m* 1953, Arthur Le Page, and has issue living.

Granddaughter of late Thomas Carew, of Rattery, Devon, 3rd son of 7th baronet:—
Issue of late Com Alfred Curtis Carew, RN, *b* 1847, *d* 1927: *m* 1893, Susannah, who *d* 1939, da of late Edmund Grantham:—
Dorothy Susannah, *b* 1894: *m* 1932, Hugh Fraser Cunningham.

Granddaughter of late Charles Robert Sydenham Carew (infra):—
Issue of late Capt Peter Gawen Carew, *b* 1894, *d* 1966: *m* 1927, Ruth, who *d* 1983, da of Arthur Chamberlain, JP, of Rackenford Manor, Tiverton:—
Nicola CAREW (*Lady Kennard*), *b* 1930; resumed in 1968 the surname of Carew until her remarriage: *m* 1st, 1950 (*m diss* 1968), Charles Louis Breitmeyer, solicitor; 2ndly, 1985, Lt-Col Sir George Arnold Ford Kennard, 3rd Bt, and has issue living (by 1st *m*), Hugo Charles BREITMEYER (The Stables, Warnicombe, Tiverton, Devon EX16 4PP), *b* 1951: *m* 1986, Diana Margaret, elder da of Michael Harold Wrigley, OBE, of Ganton, Yorks, and has issue living, Alice Holway *b* 1988, Eleanor Audrey *b* 1991, — Peter Alan CAREW (Warnicombe House, Tiverton, Devon EX16 4PP), *b* 1953; assumed 1970 the surname of Carew: *m* 1984, Laura Lang, elder da of Esmond Gerahty, of West Farm, Owermoigne, Dorset, and has had issue, Finn Rivers Alexander *b* 1985, Ivo Antony Gawen *b* 1989, Edmund Walter Otho *b* 1998, Oriole Rose Estelle *b* 1987, Stella *b* and *d* 1996, — Henry John CAREW (Overlands, Tiverton, Devon), *b* 1957; assumed 1970 the surname of Carew: *m* 1976 (*m diss* 1997), Louise Star, yr da of Roger Francis Mortimer, by his wife, Cynthia Sydney, yst da of late Maj Henry Denison Pender, DSO, OBE, MC (yr brother of 1st Baron Pender), and has issue living, Benjamin Charles Henry *b* 1985, Rowan Alexander *b* 1987, Frederick Lawrence *b* 1994, Rebecca Louise *b* 1978, — Geoffrey Nicholas CAREW (Private Bag 295A, Harare, Zimbabwe), *b* 1962; assumed 1970 the surname of Carew: *m* 1987, Maxine, da of Douglas Robson, of Cote, Eskdalemuir, nr Langton, Dumfriesshire, and has issue living, Thomas Mohun *b* 1990, Sophy Bloodaxe *b* 1992, Tarka Nichola *b* 1994. *Residence* – Gogwell, Tiverton, Devon EX16 4PP.

Granddaughter of late Rev Robert Baker Carew, son of late Rev Thomas Carew, 3rd son of 6th baronet:—
Issue of late Charles Robert Sydenham Carew, *b* 1853; *d* 1939: *m* 1891, Muriel Mary Heathcoat, who *d* 1939, da of Sir John Heathcoat Heathcoat-Amory, 1st Bt:—
Nancy, *b* 1899.

The family of Carew is of great antiquity in Devon and Cornwall, and claims a common descent with the Dukes of Leinster and Earls of Plymouth from Walter Fitz-Other, who was Castellan of Windsor 1078. For several generations the heads of the family are described as Barons of Carew and Idrone, but none of them sat in Parliament with the exception of Nicholas de Carew, who subscribed to the celebrated Barons' letter to the Pope in 1300, and from his second son the present family is descended in a direct line.

Carew Pole, see Pole.

CARLILE (UK) 1917, of Ponsbourne, co Hertford (Extinct 1942)

Sir (EDWARD) HILDRED CARLILE, CBE, TD, 1st and last *Baronet*.

DAUGHTER LIVING OF FIRST BARONET

Eleanor Cicely: *m* 1927, Rev Thomas Vyner Southey, who *d* 1928, V of Ponsbourne.

GIBSON-CRAIG-CARMICHAEL (NS) 1702, of Keirhill, co Edinburgh, and (UK) 1831, of Riccarton, Midlothian

Live to God, and you shall live

Sir DAVID PETER WILLIAM GIBSON-CRAIG-CARMICHAEL, 15th *Baronet* of Keirhill, and 8th *Baronet* of Riccarton; *b* 21 July 1946; *s* his father *Sir* (ARCHIBALD HENRY) WILLIAM, 1969; *ed* Queen's Univ, Kingston, Canada (BSc): *m* 1973, Patricia, da of Marcos Skarnic, of Santiago, Chile, and has issue.

ᴀrms – Quarterly: 1st and 4th, ermine, on a fesse sable three crescents argent, *Craig*; 2nd and 3rd, gules, three keys fesseways in pale, wards downwards or, *Gibson*. Crest – A knight on horseback in full armour, his right hand grasping a broken tilting spear shivered all proper. Supporters – Dexter, a man in armour holding in exterior hand a spear all proper; sinister, a war-horse argent, saddled and bridled proper.
Residence – Quintas, Nova Lima, Brazil.

SON LIVING

PETER WILLIAM, *b* 29 Dec 1975.

DAUGHTER LIVING

Margaret Anne, *b* 1977.

BROTHERS LIVING

Alasdair John, *b* 1948: *m* 1973, Irene, da of Bruno Haverbeck, of Santiago, Chile. —— Andrew Charles, *b* 1952.

SISTER LIVING

Susan Ann, *b* 1949: *m* 1970, her cousin, Richard John Darling (infra), and has issue living, Christopher John, *b* 1971, — Nicholas Patrick, *b* 1973.

AUNTS LIVING (*Daughters of 13th baronet*)

Emily Edith, *b* 1915. —— Kathleen Joan, *b* 1919: *m* 1940, Charles Taylor Darling, of Universidad Nacional de Tucuman, Argentina, and has issue living, Anthony Robin, *b* 1941, — Richard John, *b* 1944: *m* 1970, his cousin, Susan Ann, only da of Sir Archibald William Gibson-Craig-Carmichael, 14th Bt, and has issue (ante), — Judith Ann, *b* 1946.

COLLATERAL BRANCH LIVING   *(In remainder to the Nova Scotia (cr 1702) Baronetcy only)*

Grandson of late James Whitaker Gibson, son of late William Charles Gibson, CMG, a descendant of
Alexander Gibson of Durie, brother of 1st baronet:—
Issue of late William James Carmichael Gibson, *b* 1883, *d* 1955: *m* 1918, Maude, da of Roger Buston:—
John Carmichael, *b* 1919. *Residence* – ......

Sir James, 1st Bt (*cr* 1831), was second son of William Gibson (B Carmichael, colls), and assumed the additional
surname of Craig 1818. The 2nd baronet, Rt Hon Sir William, PC, sat as MP for Edinburghshire (*L*) 1837-41, and for
Edinburgh city 1841-52, and was Lord Clerk Register and Keeper of the Signet of Scotland 1862-78. Sir James, 3rd Bt,
was Brigadier Roy Co of Archers (King's Body Guard for Scotland). The 4th Bt, Sir Archibald Charles Gibson-Craig,
Lieut Highland LI, was *ka* 1914 (despatches). The Nova Scotia Baronetcy (*cr* 1702) was conferred upon Thomas Gibson,
son of Sir John Gibson of Pentland and Addistone, with remainder to his heirs male whatsoever, and the 6th baronet
(John) of this creation assumed the additional surname of Carmichael succeeding under the entail of Skirling, Peeblesshire, while Sir Thomas David 11th Bt, was *cr* Baron Carmichael 1912. In 1914, Capt Henry Thomas Gibson-Craig *s* his
brother as 5th Bt of Riccarton, and in Jan 1926, his kinsman, the 1st Baron Carmichael, in the NS Baronetcy (*cr* 1702)
of Keirhill; *d* 1926, having assumed the additional surname of Carmichael.

Carmichael-Anstruther, see Anstruther.

RIVETT-CARNAC (UK) 1836, of Derby

Thus they go to Heaven

Rev Sir (THOMAS) NICHOLAS RIVETT-CARNAC, 8th *Baronet*, son of late
Vice-Adm James William Rivett-Carnac, CB, CBE, DSC, 2nd son of
6th baronet; *b* 3 June 1927: *s* his uncle, *Sir* HENRY GEORGE CRABBE,
1972; *ed* Marlborough; late Capt Scots Gds; Malaya 1950
(despatches); V of St Mark's, Kennington Oval, SE11 1972-89, Rural
Dean of Lambeth (Southwark) 1978-82, Hon Canon of Southwark
Cathedral since 1980: *m* 1977, Susan Marigold MacTier, yr da of late
C. Harold Copeland.

Arms – Quarterly, argent and azure, two swords in saltire proper between three
mullets, one in chief and two in fesse, and a crescent in base counterchanged. **Crest**
– a sword erect pommel and hilt or, issuing from a crescent ermine, the internal
part gules.
Address – The Haven, Sandhurst Lane, Little Common, Bexhill-on-Sea, E Sussex
TN39 4RH.

BROTHER LIVING

MILES JAMES (The Manor House, Martyr Worthy, Winchester SO21 1DY), *b* 7 Feb
1933; *ed* RNC Dartmouth; Cdr RN; High Sheriff Hants 1995, DL 1996; Far East Fleet
Patrols and Borneo Territories 1964-65 (despatches); Man Dir Baring Bros & Co
Ltd: *m* 1958, April Sally, da of late Maj Arthur Andrew Sidney Villar, of 48 Lowndes
Sq, SW1, and has issue living, Jonathan James, *b* 1962, — Simon Miles, *b* 1966: *m*
19—, Sarah J., yst da of Ian Petrie, of Strathardle, Perthshire, and has issue living,
Geordie James *b* 1999, — Lucinda Jane (*Hon Mrs Valentine Guinness*), *b* 1960: *m*
1986, Hon Valentine Guy Bryan Guinness, 2nd son of 3rd Baron Moyne.

SISTER LIVING

Isla Carolyn (*Baroness Abinger*), *b* 1925: *m* 1957, 8th Baron Abinger, of Sheepcote House, Castle Hedingham, Essex CO9
3HA, and has issue.

AUNT LIVING *(daughter of 6th baronet)*

Aileen Mary (15A Kensington Mansions, Trebovir Rd, Earls Court, SW5), *b* 1908: *m* 1945, Edward F. Wakeford, who *d*
1973.

COLLATERAL BRANCHES LIVING

Issue of late Maj John Temple Rivett-Carnac, late The Duke of Wellington's Regt, yst son of 6th baronet, b 1906, d 1991/2: m 1st, 1941 (m diss 1951), Sarah Winifred (7 Main Rd, Farrarmere, Benoni 1500, S Africa) (who m 2ndly, 1978, Capt Lancelot Charles Henry Hope, who d 1978), only da of Wilfred Herbert Eglin, of Trimmingham, Halifax, W Yorks; 2ndly, 1951, Vivienne Mary Fairchild, who d 1979:—
(By 1st m) (John) Clive (49 Dalbini Drive, Mulbarton, Johannesburg 2091, S Africa), b 1944. —— Rosemary Jane, b 1943: m 1972, John Drysdale Gilchrist, of 4b Bright St, Western Extension, Benoni, S Africa, and has issue living, David Matthew, b 1976, — George Robert, b 1979.

Grandson of late William John Rivett-Carnac, 2nd son of 1st baronet:—
Issue of late Col Percy Temple Rivett-Carnac (brother of 6th baronet), b 1852, d 1932: m 1898, Alice, who d 1928, da of late Maj Sidney Herbert, of Pietermaritzburg, S Africa:—
Percival Sydney, b 1904: m 1950, Joan, da of late Jeffery Waddington, and has issue living, Jeremy Charles Percy (4400 Telegraph Rd, Cowichan Bay, BC, Canada), b 1954: m 1981, Monique Madeleine Marie Faivre, and has issue living, Paul Fabien Alexander b 1981, Gabriel Gérard Faivre b 1984, — Sahlaa, b 1952: m 1973, Robert Morris, of 42 Dunham Cres, Aurora, Ontario, Canada L4G 2V4, and has issue living, Jeffery Luke b 1981, Jay Matthew b 1985, — Gai (adopted da), b 1957: m 1979 (m diss 1984), Ian James.

Granddaughter of late Wilfred Theodore Rivett-Carnac, yst brother of 6th baronet, b 1864, d 1929: m 18— (m diss 19—), Alice, da of late John Southam, and widow of — Wells:—
Issue of late Peter Rivett-Carnac, b 1900, d 1948: m 1944, Grace Kilgore, who d 1979, of Traynor, Saskatchewan, Canada:—
Eleanor Grace, b 1946: m 1968, Peter Johnston, of RR1 Barrie, Ontario, Canada L4M 4Y8, and has issue living, Christina, b 1969, — Cheri Lyn (adopted da), b 1976.

Grandchildren of late Vernon Charles Rivett-Carnac, son (by 1st m) of late Charles James Rivett-Carnac (infra):—
Issue of late Nelson Charles Rivett-Carnac, b 1906, d 1979: m 1932, Bertha Ella Inez Litt, who d 1978:—
Cleone Patricia (Finistere, 254 Te Awa Av, Napier, New Zealand), b 1933. —— Lynette Marion (66 Glengarry Rd, Glen Eden, Auckland, New Zealand), b 1934: m 1st, 1956 (m diss 1972), John Lathom Croft; 2ndly, 1985, William Glen Douglas, and has issue living, (by 1st m) Meesha Briggette Lathom, b 1957: m 1st, 1978 (m diss 1996), Renmark Darby; 2ndly, 1996, James Neville Waite. —— Robin Genevieve (18 Carnell St, Napier, NZ), b 1939: m 1st, 1957 (m diss 1986), Alfred Edward Symon; 2ndly, 1986, John Miller Mercer, who d 1988, and has issue living, (by 1st m) Christopher Robin St Clair, b 1957, — Caroline Jane Fitzalan, b 1962, — Sarah Diana Fitzalan, b 1963.

Issue of late Maurice Vernon Rivett-Carnac, b 1910, d 1964: m 1934, Merlene Clare Crosby (24 Churchill St, Whangarei, New Zealand):—
Paul Charles (152 Flower St, Northgate 4013, Brisbane, Queensland, Australia), b 1945: m 1965, Valerie Kay Anderson, and has issue living, Natalie Eve, b 1969, — Lisa Marie, b 1971. —— Marie Anne, b 1938: m 1957, Clive Palmer, of PO Box 29, Hikurangi, North Island, New Zealand, and has issue living, Michael Brett, b 1959, — Gregory John, b 1960, — Victoria Ann, b (twin) 1960, — Jacqueline Ellen, b 1965. —— Dianne Adele, b 1943: m 19—, David Lambdin, and has issue living, Shayne, b 1963. —— Christine Verna, b 1941: m 1972, Wayne Wilson Ridgley, of New Zealand, and has issue living, Cory, b 1975, — Dionne, b 1973, — Vicky, b 1978.

Grandchildren (by 2nd m) of late Charles James Rivett-Carnac, eldest son of late Charles Forbes Rivett-Carnac, 3rd son of 1st baronet:—
Issue of late Douglas Charles Mahisra Rivett-Carnac, OBE, b 1907, d 1989: m 1946, Barbara Joyce (The Chilterns, Woodgreen, Fordingbridge, Hants), da of late A. R. Pratt:—
Christopher Charles (Heathermoor, Hale Purlieu, Fordingbridge, Hants), b 1947: m 1974, Sara Catherine, da of late Dr R. J. C. Hutchinson, and has issue living, Thomas Charles, b 1977, — Alexander John, b 1980, — Michael James, b 1983, — Louise Claire, b 1976. —— John Benedict (Lion House, 23 Onslow Rd, Richmond, Surrey), b 1949: m 1975, Mary Rose, da of Col K. A. P. Fergusson, and has issue living, Charles John Fergus, b 1991, — Sophie Caroline, b 1979, — Francesca Jane, b 1982, — Alice Josephine, b 1984. —— Michael Francis, b 1950: m 1984, Robert Grace, only da of W/ Cdr R. O. Mearns Jones, of 22 Parkview Close, Charlton Hill, Andover, Hants, and has issue living, Philippa Jane Mearns, b 1988.

Issue of late Lt-Col Charles Francis Rivett-Carnac, Indian Army, b 1909, d 1958: m 1936, Lorna, Evelyn Pemberton, who d 1993, da of late B. Darling:—
Jacqueline Anne, b 1937: m 1957, David Lindsay Millar, OBE, of Bepton Lodge, Bepton, nr Midhurst, W Sussex, and has issue living, Guy McIntyre, b 1959: m 1983, Kim Lorraine, da of Philip Birch, and has issue living, Katherine Forbes b 1981, — Mark Charles Forbes, b 1961: m 1987, Anna Jo, da of W/Cdr A. MacKinnon, and has issue living, Rory James McIntyre b 1989, Angus David Forbes b 1993, Charlotte Mary Louise b 1990, — Nicholas Lindsay (35 Tunley Rd, SW17 7QH) b 1962: m 1989, Karen Elizabeth, da of Dr Hugh McLean, and has issue living, Henry James Forbes b 1993.

Issue of late Louis Charles Wykeham Rivett-Carnac, b 1912, d 1985: m 1939, Alice, who d 1976, da of late J. Docherty:—
Clive Anthony Charles (16 Springwater Mill, Bassetsbury Lane, High Wycombe, Bucks), b 1940: m 1971, Marilyn, da of H. C. Wilkes, and has issue living, James, b 1976, — John Daniel, b 1979. —— Louis Charles James (Anchor Cottage, The Holway, Winterton-on-Sea, Gt Yarmouth, Norfolk), b 1942: m 1968 (m diss 1983), Ann Elsey, and has issue living, Paul Antony, b 1969, — Andrew Justin, b 1970. —— Timothy Charles (1 Julian Rd, Folkestone, Kent), b 1949: ed Aston Univ (BSc hons): m 1st, 1977 (m diss 1983), Virginia Trust; 2ndly, 1984, Michelle Jefferies, and has issue living (by 1st m), Tristan, b 1978, — James Michael, b 1980, — Charlotte Louise, b 1977, — (by 2nd m) Sebastian Louis, b 1984, — Nicholas, b 1987. —— Nichola Frances, b 1947: m 1st, 1967 (m diss 1981), Robin Wentworth Mason; 2ndly, 1983, Ernest Dare, of 19 Ashby Drive, Rushden, Northants, and has issue living (by 1st m), Toby Wentworth, b 1970, — Christopher Wentworth, b 1971.

Grandchildren of late John Thurlow Rivett-Carnac, 2nd son of Charles Forbes Rivett-Carnac (ante):—
Issue of late Lt-Col John Claude Thurlow Rivett-Carnac, MC, KPM, *b* 1888, *d* 1975: *m* 1st, 1923, Ola Jane, who *d* 1953, da of S. Wilson, of Maine, USA; 2ndly, 1953, Hon Evelyn Hope Balfour, who *d* 1967, da of 1st Baron Riverdale, and widow of Gp Capt Eustace Jack Linton Hope, AFC, RAF:—
(By 1st *m*) Sheila Veronica Mary, *b* 1927: *m* 1st, 1954 (*m diss* 1969), John Coleman Averill; 2ndly, 1969, Alfred Edwin Valentine, who *d* 1981, and has issue living (by 1st *m*), John Miles Rochford, *b* 1958 *m* 1984, Torill Peele, — Andrew Clive Rochford, *b* 1960, — Catherine Veronica, *b* 1955: *m* 1979, George Braoudakis, and has issue living, Emmanuel John *b* 1985, Georgina Virginia *b* 1982, Elizabeth Lucy *b* (twin) 1985, — Elizabeth Jane Rochford, *b* 1957: *m* 1980, Andrew Barrett, and has issue living, two das. —— (By 2nd *m*) John Charles Malcolm (27 Pilgrims Lane, Bugbrooke, Northants NN7 3PJ), *b* 1955: *m* 1984, Carol Ann Hedley, and has issue living, Amanda *b* 1986, Tamara *b* 1989.

Issue of late Lt-Col Herbert Gordon Rivett-Carnac, Indian Army, *b* 1892, *d* 1962: *m* 1925, Cushla Margarette, who *d* 1974, da of Lt-Col Robert Southey Pottinger:—
Eric Gordon, *b* 1926. —— John Southey, *b* 1929.

Issue of late Edward Charles Rivett-Carnac, *b* 1901, *d* 1980: *m* 1st, 1932, Mary Dillon, who *d* 1970, da of Col Francis Bethel Ware, DSO, VD, of London, Ontario; 2ndly, 1975, Ora-Lee (206-1035 Belmont Av, Victoria, BC, Canada V8S 3TS), who *m* 3rdly, 1984, Dan Eckley, who *d* 1996, da of late Harry Edward Tharsing, of Berkeley, Cal, USA, and widow of Capt R. A. Pennington, OBE, RCNVR:—
(By 1st *m*) Beverley Ann (1746 Garnet Rd, Victoria, BC, Canada V8P 3E1), *b* 1933: *m* 1954 (*m diss* 1968), A. F. Griffin, and has issue living, Brenda Gayle, *b* 1956: *m* 1995, Dr Bruce T. Yoneda, FRCS (C), and has issue living, Cameron Charles Benjiro *b* 1998, Taryn Frances Toshie *b* 1995.

Grandson of late Harry Morland Rivett-Carnac, 3rd son of late Charles Forbes Rivett-Carnac (ante):—
Issue of late Charles Walter Rivett-Carnac, *b* 1893, *d* 1930: *m* 1920, Freda Gertrude, who *d* 1959, da of late Frederick Hean Roger, of Melbourne, Australia:—
Gordon Seymour (200 Lawrence Rd, Mt Waverley, Victoria 3149, Australia), *b* 1925: *m* 1949, Marian Propert, da of Robert Newman Scott, of Melbourne, and has issue living, Susan Marian, *b* 1956: *m* 1980, John Gardiner Manning, of 14 Delany Av, Bright, Victoria 3741, Australia, and has issue living, Benjamin John Garry *b* 1982, Andrew Stephen *b* 1987, Emma Suzanne *b* 1985, Meaghan Kate *b* 1990, — Penelope Berril (10 Leena Court, Warranwood, Victoria 3134, Australia), *b* 1961.

Grandson of Gordon Seymour Rivett-Carnac (ante):—
Issue of late Garry Seymour Rivett-Carnac, *b* 1950, *d* 1979: *m* 1974, Jane Baker (Victoria, Australia):—
Scott Harry, *b* 1978.

Grandchildren of late Charles Walter Rivett-Carnac (ante):—
Issue of late Roger Arnott James Rivett-Carnac, *b* 1927, *d* 1967: *m* 1947, Lorna Isabel (who *m* 2ndly, 19—, Raymond Ernest Merrett, of 10 Cunliffe Rd, Killara, NSW 2071, Australia), da of late John Hamilton-Dee:—
Peter William (8 Oxford St, Newtown, NSW 2042, Australia), *b* 1955: BAppSc. —— Lana Kay, *b* 1949: *m* 1968, Ronald John Ernest Russell, of 34 Porlock Way, Karrinyup, W Australia 6018, and has issue living, Glenn John, *b* 1971, — Joanne Jeanette, *b* 1973, — Sharon Jane, *b* 1974. —— Jeanette Anne, *b* 1953: *m* 1978, David Keith Gordon Milne, of 13 Daintrey St, Fairlight, NSW 2094, Australia, and has issue living, Lisa, *b* 1980, — Tanya Judith Kay, *b* 1983.

The 1st baronet was Chairman of the East India Co 1836-37 and 1837-38; MP for Sandwich, 1938-39 and Governor of Bombay 1839-41. His father, James Rivett, of HEICS (Bombay), assumed by Royal Warrant in 1801 the additional surname of Carnac. The 2nd baronet sat as MP for Lymington (C) 1852-60. The 4th baronet, Sir Claud James, having been missing for many years, an order was issued in the Chancery Div of 11 March 1924, presuming his death as having occurred 31 Dec 1909. Sir William Percival, 5th Bt, *d* 21 March 1924. The 6th baronet, the Rev Sir George Clennell (sometime R of Woldingham), was son of William John Rivett-Carnac, 2nd son of 1st Bt.

CARY (UK) 1955, of Withington, co Lancaster

Sir ROGER HUGH CARY, 2nd *Baronet*; *b* 8 Jan 1926; *s* his father, *Sir* ROBERT ARCHIBALD, 1979; *ed* Eton, and New Coll, Oxford (BA Modern History 1949); Lt Grenadier Gds (Reserve), and an Asso of Roy Historical Soc; was Documentary Producer BBC 1950-56 and Talks Assist, European Ser, 1956-58, Dep Editor *The Listener* 1958-61, Management Training Organiser, BBC 1961-66, Snr Assist Secretariat BBC 1966-74, Special Assist Public Affairs BBC 1974-77, Special Assist to Man Dir BBC TV 1977-83, Chief Assist to the Secretary, BBC 1982-83, Chief Assist to Dir of Programmes TV 1983-86, since when a Consultant to Dir Gen; Sec Central Music Advisory Cttee BBC 1966-77 and 1983; a Trustee of Kedleston since 1988: *m* 1st, 1948 (*m diss* 1951), Marilda, who *d* 1996, da of late Maj Philip Pearson-Gregory, MC; 2ndly, 1953, Ann Helen Katharine, el da of Hugh Blair Brenan, OBE, former Assist Sec Roy Hosp, SW1, and has issue by 1st and 2nd marriages.

Arms – Argent, on a bend cotised sable three roses of the field barbed and seeded proper in-sinister chief a cinquefoil gules. Crest – A swan, wings elevated and addorsed proper between two cinquefoils gules.
Residence – 23 Bath Rd, Chiswick, W4 1LJ. *Clubs* – Pratt's, First Guards.

SONS LIVING (*By 2nd marriage*)

NICOLAS ROBERT HUGH (78 Severalls Av, Chesham, Bucks HP5 3EL), *b* 7 April 1955; *ed* St Paul's, and London Univ (BA): *m* 1st, 1979 (*m diss* 1991), Pauline Jean, da of Dr Thomas Ian Boyd, MB, ChB; 2ndly, 1994, Lesley Anne, da of John Henry Gilham, of Kelvedon Common, Essex, and has issue living (by 1st *m*), Alexander Robert, *b* 27 Nov 1981, — Nathaniel Ian, *b* 1983, — Peter Edward Blair, *b* 1988, — (by 2nd *m*), Matthew Nicholas John, *b* 1999. —— (Roger) Nathaniel Blair (153 Caxton End, Bourn, Cambs CB3 7ST), *b* 1957: *m* 1st, 1978 (*m diss* 1994), Tesney Vera, da of Jasper Partington; 2ndly, 19—, Sally Ann, da of Maurice Taylor, of Spalding, Lincs, and has issue living (by 1st *m*), Jonathan Nicolas Partington, *b* 1985, — Robert, *b* 1990, — Sara, *b* 1989, — (by 2nd *m*) Alice *b* 1997.

DAUGHTERS LIVING (*By 1st marriage*)

(By 1st *m*) Marcia Susan, *b* 1949; BA; landscape painter: *m* 1971, Hon Robin Gibson-Watt, DL, of Gelligarn, Llandrindod Wells, Powys LD1 6EY, and has issue living (*see* B Gibson-Watt).

(*By 2nd marriage*)

Charlotte Rhoda Rosamond, *b* 1960: *m* 1982, David Mayou, son of Simeon Mayou, and has issue living, George, *b* 1984, — Jack, *b* 1986, — Joseph Edward, *b* 1987, — Joshua, *b* 1989.

CASSEL (UK) 1920, of Lincoln's Inn, City of London

Let justice be done

Sir HAROLD FELIX CASSEL, TD, QC *(His Honour Sir Harold Cassel, Bt, TD, QC)* 3rd *Baronet, b* 8 Nov 1916; *s* his brother, *Sir* FRANCIS EDWARD, 1969; *ed* Stowe, and Corpus Christi Coll Oxford; Bar Lincoln's Inn 1946; QC 1970; Recorder of Gt Yarmouth 1968-72; Recorder of Crown Court 1972-76, Circuit Judge 1976-88; 1939-45 War, as Capt RA: *m* 1st, 1940 *(m diss* 1963) Ione Jean, da of late Capt Evelyn Hugh Barclay (B Somerleyton); 2ndly, 1963, Mrs Eileen Elfrida Smedley, da of James Rider Faulkner, and has issue by 1st *m*.

𝕬rms – Per fesse embattled azure and gules, in chief a pair of scales or between two swords points upwards, pommels and hilts of the third and in base a portcullis also of the third. 𝕮rest – A lion rampant gules, resting the dexter paw on a mill-rind gold. *Residence* – 49 Lennox Gdns, SW1.

SONS LIVING *(By 1st marriage)*

TIMOTHY FELIX HAROLD (Studdridge Farm, Stokenchurch, Bucks), *b* 30 April 1942; *ed* Eton; Bar Lincoln's Inn 1965; QC 1988: *m* 1st, 1971 *(m diss* 1977), Mrs Jenifer Samuel, da of Kenneth Bridge Puckle; 2ndly, 1979, Ann *(Baroness Mallalieu)* (Life Baroness), only da of late Sir (Joseph Percival) William Mallalieu and has issue living (by 1st *m*) Alexander James Felix, *b* 25 May 1974, — Natalia Hermione, *b* 1972, — (by 2nd *m*) *Hon* Bathsheba Anna, *b* 1981, — *Hon* Cosima Ione Harriet, *b* 1984. ——Jeremy James, *b* 1950: *m* 1982, Vivien Helen, da of John David Hayter, of Dolivers Farm, Holwell, Sherborne, Dorset, and has issue living, Hugo Timothy, *b* 1982, — Felix, *b* 1988, — Chlöe Sieglinde, *b* 1984. ——Evelyn Martin, *b* 1952.

DAUGHTER LIVING *(By 1st marriage)*

Miranda Phyllis, *b* 1946: *m* 1980, Ronald Ryer, of USA, and has issue living, Sarah Elizabeth Jean, *b* 1979.

SISTER LIVING

Josephine Helen, *b* (twin) 1916: *m* 1939, Griffith Cresswell Evans Pugh, BM, BCh, and has issue living, David Sheridan Griffith (Hatching Green House, Harpenden, Herts), *b* 1940, — Simon Francis (10 Coniger Rd, SW6), *b* 1945, — Oliver Lewis Evans (28 Redan St, W14), *b* 1955, — Harriet Veronica, *b* 1946: *m* 1974, James Tuckey, of 95 Elgin Cres, W11 2JF and has issue living, Venetia *b* 1978, Elizabeth *b* 1979, Rose *b* 1981. *Residence* – Hatching Green House, Hatching Green, Harpenden, Herts.

The Rt Hon Sir Felix Cassel, QC, 1st Bt (son of M. S. Cassel, of 2 Orme Sq, W), was Pres of Management Cttee of Cassel Hosp for Functional Nervous Disorders, a Member of Council of King Edward VII Sanatorium, Midhurst, and Chm of Trustees of Cassel Education Trust, Judge Advocate-Gen 1916-34, and MP for St Pancras, W (C) 1910-16.

CAVE (UK) 1896 of Cleve Hill, Mangotsfield, co Gloucester; Sidbury Manor, Sidbury, co Devon; and Stoneleigh House, Clifton, Bristol

Cave
Beware

Sir JOHN CHARLES CAVE, 5th *Baronet; b* 8 Sept 1958; *s* his father, *Sir* CHARLES EDWARD COLERIDGE, 1997; *ed* Eton, and RAC Cirencester; *m* 1984, Carey Diana, elder da of John Lloyd, of Coombeland, Cadeleigh, Tiverton, Devon, and has issue.

𝕬rms – Azure, fretty argent, on a fesse or a greyhound courant sable, collared of the second, a bordure of the third pelletée. 𝕮rest – A daisy-flower slipped proper, a greyhound's head issuant therefrom per pale argent and sable, guttée counterchanged. *Seat* – Sidbury Manor, Sidmouth, Devon. *Residence* – Sidbury Manor, Sidmouth, Devon EX10 0QE.

SONS LIVING

GEORGE CHARLES *b* 8 Sept 1987. ——William Alexander, *b* 1992.

DAUGHTER LIVING

Alice Elizabeth, *b* 1989.

BROTHERS LIVING

Nicholas Stephen (Bishops Court, Fluxton, Ottery St Mary, Devon EX11 1RJ), *b* 1961: *m* 1991, Alexandra Frances Elizabeth, eldest da of late Simon Hicks, of Battersea, SW11, and has issue living, Frederick Stephen, *b* 1995, — Harriet Patricia, *b* (twin) 1995, — Louisa Elizabeth, *b* 1996. ——Thomas Henry, *b* 1964. ——Richard Hugh, *b* 1967: *m* 1996,

Emily Jane, eldest da of Algernon Eustace Hugh Heber-Percy (*see* D Northumberland, colls), and has issue living, Olivia Jane, *b* 1997.

AUNT LIVING (*daughter of 3rd baronet*)

Daphne Frances, *b* 1930. *Residence* – Greenhead, Sidbury, Devon.

WIDOW LIVING OF FOURTH BARONET

MARY ELIZABETH (*Elizabeth, Lady Cave*), da of late John Francis Gore, CVO TD, (*see* E Arran, colls): *m* 1957, Sir Charles Edward Coleridge Cave, 4th Bt, who *d* 1997. *Residence* – Court Hall, Sidbury, Sidmouth, Devon EX10 0RS.

COLLATERAL BRANCH LIVING

Granddaughters of late Maj Arthur Stephen Cave, 4th son of 1st baronet:—
Issue of late Ronald Arthur Cave, *b* 1910, *d* 1964: *m* 1936, Audrey Oenone (Ramblers, Holford, Somerset), da of Dr Francis Child, formerly of Penlee, Weybridge:—
Diana Ann, *b* 1938: *m* 1957, Charles Thoburn Maxwell II, and has issue living, Bruce Maxwell, *b* 1959, — Steven Maxwell, *b* 1961, — Brandon Maxwell, *b* 1964. —— Sylvia Margaret, *b* 1944: *m* 1992, Richard Antony Hackney.

This family is probably a branch of the Caves of Yorkshire and Leicestershire, but their recorded pedigree commences with John Cave of Leigh Sinton, co Worcester, *temp* 15th century, who was ancestor of Sir Richard Cave, Kt, a distinguished General *k* at Naseby, and also of John Cave (great-grandfather of 1st baronet), founder of the Cave bank at Bristol. The arms, which have been confirmed three times by the Heralds' College, were originally granted in the reign of Henry VII. The 1st baronet, Sir Charles Daniel, was a Director of Union of London and Smith's Bank (Limited), and the 2nd baronet, Sir Charles Henry, was High Sheriff of Devon 1926.

CAVE-BROWNE-CAVE (E)1641, of Stanford, Northamptonshire

Beware

Sir ROBERT CAVE-BROWNE-CAVE, 16th *Baronet*; *b* 8 June 1929; *s* his father, *Sir* CLEMENT CHARLES, 1945; *ed* St George's Sch, Vancouver, Univ Sch, Victoria, and British Columbia Univ: is Pres of Cave & Co Ltd: *m* 1st, 1954 (*m diss* 1975), Lois Shirley, da of John Chalmers Huggard, of Winnipeg, Canada; 2ndly, 1977, Joan Shirley, da of Dr Kenneth Ashe Peacock, of W Vancouver, BC, and has issue by 1st *m*.

Arms – Quarterly: 1st and 4th, azure, fretty argent, *Cave*; 2nd and 3rd, azure, a chevron between three escallops or, a bordure engrailed gules, *Browne*. Crest – 1st, a greyhound courant sable, collared argent; 2nd, a stork, proper, winged and gorged with a ducal crown or, beaked and membered gules.
Residence – 20901-83 Av, RR11, Langley, British Columbia V3A 6Y3, Canada.

SON LIVING (*By 1st marriage*)

JOHN ROBERT CHARLES, *b* 22 June 1957,

DAUGHTER LIVING (*By 1st marriage*)

Lisé Irene, *b* 1955.

WIDOW LIVING OF FIFTEENTH BARONET

DOROTHEA PLEWMAN (*Dorothea, Lady Cave-Browne-Cave*), da of Robert Greene Dwen, of Chicago, USA: *m* 1923, Sir Clement Charles Cave-Browne-Cave, 15th Bt, who *d* 1945.

COLLATERAL BRANCHES LIVING

Grandchildren of late Rev Fitzherbert Astley Cave-Browne-Cave, son of late Rev William Astley Cave-Browne-Cave, 2nd son of 9th baronet:—
Issue of late Cecil Beckwith Cave-Browne-Cave, *b* 1871, *d* 1953: *m* 1st, 1896, Sara Eleanor, who *d* 1928, da of late John W. Nicholson, of St John, New Brunswick; 2ndly, 1929, Edith Beatrice, who *d* 1948, da of Alfred Evans, JP formerly of Chesham Bois, Bucks:—

(By 2nd *m*) Penelope Margaret Cecil (c/o Barclays Bank Ltd, 31 Avenue de la Costa, Monaco 98000), *b* 1931: *m* 1965, Timothy Fitzgerald ffrench-Mullen, who *d* 1982, and has issue living, Candetta Lydia Cecil, *b* 1966: *m* 1994, Mark Burnyeat, of Ramsdale House, Mattingley, nr Hook, Hants, and has issue living, Henry Timothy William *b* 1998, — Tara Eve Siobhan, *b* 1970. ——— Catherine Priscilla Astley, *b* 1937: *m* 1958 (*m diss* 19—), David Bates, and has issue living, Joanna Catherine, *b* 1959.

        Issue of late Courtney Priestley Edwards Cave-Browne-Cave, *b* 1890, *d* 1961: *m* 1915, Helen Freda, who *d* 1955, only da of A. J. Cable, of Epping, Essex:—
Paul Astley *b* 1917; Publisher and Editor of *Hampshire*, the county magazine (established 1960); formerly Capt Gen List; a JP for Southampton: *m* 1940, Joan, da of late Thomas Norman Jones, JP, of Rhyl, N Wales, and has issue living, Paul, *b* 1954; *ed* Manchester Univ (BA): *m* 1979, Jane, da of late Maj J. Reeves, of St Austell, Cornwall, — Jane, *b* 1943; *ed* Birmingham Univ (BSc): *m* 1980, Eugene Versluysen, of 1539 T St NW, Washington DC, USA, — Adrienne, *b* 1947; BA (Cantab): *m* 1968, Clifford Burrows, who *d* 1970, — Sarah, *b* 1959; *ed* London Univ (BA), and Durham Univ (MA): *m* 1983, James Chiriyankandath, and has issue living, Joseph *b* 1988, Sathyan Paul *b* 1992. ——— Lyndon Fraser, *b* 1923; *ed* Liverpool Univ; Dip Arch (Liverpool), M Phil (Warwick), FSA: *m* 1952, Betty, only da of Walter Rush, of Dinnington, Yorks, and has issue living, Anthony John (9 Preseli Close, Meadow Vale, Risca, Gwent NP1 6RQ), *b* 1952; LLB, London: *m* 1980, Susan Margaret, da of K. G. L. Chalk, of Leamington Spa, Warwickshire, and has issue living, Edmund Jonathan *b* 1981, Melissa Betty *b* 1983, — *Rev* Bernard James William (97 Barton Rd, Lancaster) *b* 1954; MA (Cantab); Chap Prison Service: *m* 1977, Rosalind, GRNCM, LRAM, only da of Col Oliver Robert Corbett, ERD, and has issue living, James William *b* 1979, Lucy Marie *b* 1983. *Residence* – 24 Portland St, Leamington Spa, CV32 5EY. ——— Anthony, DSO (Cheney Longville, Craven Arms, Shropshire SY7 8DR), *b* 1925; *ed* Birmingham Sch of Architecture; an ARIBA; Burma 1945 as Capt S Wales Borderers (DSO), Sumatra 1945-46 as Intelligence Officer, 4th Indian Inf Bde, 26th Indian Div; DSO 1945: *m* 1957, Dinah Ann, da of J. W. Mitchell, of Longville, Much Wenlock, Salop, and has had issue, Genille Anthony, *b* 1959, *d* 1977, — Courtney Peter, *b* 1961: *m* 1988, Rachel Sarah, da of Brian Fish, of Ettington, Warwicks, and has issue living, Jack Priestley *b* 1994, Amy Ann *b* 1995, — Jonathan Lyndon, *b* 1962, — William Astley, *b* 1967: *m* 1988, Lorraine Katharine, da of Philip Wood, of Leamington Spa, Warwicks, and has issue living, Alexandra Grace *b* 1990, Isabella Poppy *b* 1995, Verity Jade *b* 1997. ——— Bernard Adrian *b* 1926; 1939-45 War as Lt, Middx Regt, Palestine 1946-47: *m* 1961 (*m diss* 1975), Ann, da of late Richard George William Pritchard, JP, of Roddis House, Wellesbourne, Warwick, and has issue living, Richard Ambrose, *b* 1962, — Rowland Fraser (358 Scott St Upper, St Catharines, Ontario, Canada L2N 1J5), *b* 1966; Pres Horticulturally Yours Inc: *m* 1995, Charlene Ruth, da of Gordon Minor, of Dunnsville, Ontario, Canada, and has issue living, Paige Beverley *b* 1997, — Helen Ann, *b* 1963: *m* 1991, Rui Manual Martins, of 114 Ellerslie, Willowdale, Ontario, Canada M2N 1X8, and has issue living, Kyle Anthony *b* 1992, Aidan Lindon *b* 1998. *Address* – 49 Sunvale Crescent S.E., Calgary, Alberta, Canada T2X 2S7.

        Grandsons of late Edward Johnson Cave-Browne-Cave, elder son of late Rev John Walker Cave-Brown-Cave, eldest son of late Thomas Cave-Brown-Cave (infra):—
        Issue of late Edward Jordayne Cave-Browne-Cave, *b* 1885, *d* 1970: *m* 1910, Jane Ella, who *d* 1968, da of late Joseph Hilton Cant, of Appleby:—
Genille Hilton Jordayne, *b* 1912; *ed* BC Univ (MA), and Massachusetts Inst. of Tech (PhD); Prof of Chemistry, McGill Univ, Montreal: *m* 1944, Mary Margaret Elizabeth, da of Lt-Col Robert Henry Palmer, DSO (*see* Palmer, Bt, *cr* 1660, colls). ——— Wilmot Wyamarus, *b* 1915: *m* 1969, Janet Kyle, da of late Thomas Peddie, MA.

        Grandson of late William Cave-Browne-Cave, 2nd son of late Thomas Cave-Browne-Cave, 3rd son of 9th baronet:—
        Issue of late Stretton Cave-Browne-Cave, *b* 1878, *d* 1961: *m* 1907, Ethel Milbro, who *d* 1943, da of late W. H. B. Higgin-Birket, of Birket Houses, Lancashire:—
Glen Myles LEVERING, *b* 1910; *ed* Winchester; is an Aeronautical Engineer; assumed the name of Glen Myles Levering in lieu of Myles Verney Cave-Browne-Cave 1944: *m* 1936 (*m diss* 1943), Christina Elizabeth, da of late Wilfred Bentley, of Inglewood, Huddersfield, and Westward Ho!, Windermere.

        Grandchildren of late Stretton Cave-Browne-Cave (ante):—
        Issue of late Bryan William Cave-Browne-Cave, OBE, *b* 1915, *d* 1980: *m* 1947, Margaret Royston, MBE, who *d* 1978, da of late Alfred Cooke, of Gorse Hill, Linton, Wetherby, Yorks:—
Myles Alfred (c/o Denton Hall, 5 Chancery Lane, EC4), *b* 1949; *ed* Rugby, and St Edmund Hall, Oxford (MA); Solicitor 1974: *m* 1986, Sally Jayne, da of Geoffrey Lilley, of 15 King's Av, Higham Ferrers, Northants, and has issue living, Sam, *b* 1990. ——— Claire Birket, *b* 1948: *m* 1970, Stuart William Brown, of Church Farm, Ratley, nr Banbury, Oxon, and has issue living, Matthew Myles Antony, *b* 1980, — Laura Margaret Zoë, *b* 1977. ——— Elise Margaret, *b* 1952: *m* 1972, Franz Friedrich Nadenau, of 52391 Vettweiss-Gladbach, Petrusstrasse 52, Germany. and has issue living, Stephan, *b* 1974.

        Grandchildren of late Sir Thomas Cave-Browne-Cave, CB, 3rd son of late Thomas Cave-Browne-Cave (ante):—
        Issue of late Wing-Cdr Thomas Reginald Cave-Browne-Cave, CBE, RAF, *b* 1885, *d* 1969: *m* 1st, 1918, Marjorie Gwynne, who *d* 1969, da of late Albert Wright; 2ndly, 1929, Elsie May, who *d* 1991, da of late James Ricks:—
(By 1st *m*) Thomas Milton (The Old Rectory, Clatworthy, Wiveliscombe, Taunton TA4 2EQ), *b* 1926: *m* 1964, Anne, da of Ralph P. Symons, of Truro, and has issue living, Thomas Edward, *b* 1968, — Janet Mary *b* 1965; BSc Manchester and London. ——— Gillian Mary, *b* 1923; BSc London.

        Grandchildren of late Frank Wyamarus Cave-Browne-Cave (*b* 1844), 6th son of late Thomas Cave-Browne-Cave (ante):—
        Issue of late Frank Wyamarus Cave-Browne-Cave, *b* 1886, *d* 1942: *m* 1926, Kathleen, who *d* 1983, da of late John Douglas de Fenzi:—
Norman John, *b* 1927: *m* 1st, 1952 (*m diss* 1957), Eveline Fay, who *d* 1989, yr da of late John Stanley Hill; 2ndly, 1957, Margaret Dobbs, da of late John Stanley Maw, and has issue living, (by 1st *m*) Peter Stanley, *b* 1955: *m* 1987, Caroline Anne, eldest da of Gerald Smith, of Alfriston, Sussex, and has issue living, Thomas Edward *b* 1991, Lucy Fay *b* 1989, — and two adopted das Helen, *b* 1966: *m* 1997, Marc Joseph Hatch, son of Joseph Hatch, and has issue living, Oliver John *b* 1997, Rosie Ellen *b* 1994, — Joanna *b* 1967: *m* 1992 (*m diss* 1996), Andrew J. Pearce, son of J. Pearce, of Prestbury, Cheltenham. *Residence* – Trefeddian Hotel, Aberdovey, Gwynedd. ——— Anne Molly, *b* 1929: *m* 1952, Selwyn W. Hill, who *d* 1993, and has issue living, Anthony Wootton (129 Swanshurst Lane, Moseley, Birmingham B13 0AS), *b* 1966: *m* 1st, 1987 (*m diss* 1991), Sarah Raybould; 2ndly, 1993, B. Happy, da of Dr Mehta, of Wolverhampton, and has issue living (by 2nd *m*), Aaron Selwyn Wootton *b* 1993, Madeleine Anne *b* 1996, — Frances Anne, *b* 1954: *m* 1st, 1988, John A. R. Shipp,

who *d* 1995; 2ndly, 1998, Ian Hickman, of 7 Lower Court, Pennal, Machynlleth, Powys SY20 9LA, — Judith Wootton, *b* 1955: *m* 1996, Anthony Rowe, of 18 Newmarket Close, Stratford-upon-Avon CV37 9FT, and has issue living, Jessica Mary *b* 1977, — Stacey Wootton (da) (Oak Cottage, Coton Hill, Shrewsbury SY1 2DZ), *b* 1961: has issue living, Edward Selwyn Dodwell *b* 1994, Lily Rebecca Dodwell *b* 1991.

Granddaughters of late Maj-Gen William Cave-Browne, CBE, DSO, MC (infra):—
Issue of late Brig John Raban Cave-Browne, MC, *b* 1917, *d* 1989: *m* 1940, Ulrica Ellen (The Walled Garden, Wonersh, Guilford, Surrey), da of late Maj Frank Paget-Hoblyn:—
Susan Margaret, *b* 1942: *m* 1969, Richard Laybourne Perry, of Coppers Cottage, Kimpton, Andover, Hants SP11 8NU, and has issue living, Nicholas Charles Laybourne, *b* 1972, — Camilla Margaret, *b* 1970: *m* 1998, James Philip Tregelles Stephens. ——— Ulrica Sarah, *b* 1946: *m* 1969, Patrick Lawrence Gargrave Covernton, and has issue living, Natasha Louise, *b* 1973, — Charlotte Sophia, *b* 1975.

Grandchildren of Edward Raban Cave-Browne, CSI, yst son of Lt-Col Edward Cave-Browne, 4th brother of 9th baronet:—
Issue of late Maj-Gen William Cave-Browne, CBE, DSO, MC, *b* 1884, *d* 1967: *m* 1916, Muriel, who *d* 1971, da of J. W. Wainwright, AMICE:—
Caroline Jane (Keepers, Plaistow Rd, Dunsfold, Surrey GU8 4PF), *b* 1926: *m* 1948, Derek Marten Brightman, DSC, who *d* 1995, of Keepers, Dunsfold, Surrey, and has issue living, Christopher Marten, *b* 1949: *m* 1976, Lindsey Elizabeth Nicholson, — Jeremy Richard, *b* 1951: *m* 1993, Sarah Leachman, — Elizabeth Jane, *b* 1953: *m* 1984, Clive Halls, — Nicola Anne, *b* 1959: *m* 1983, Brian Walker.

Issue of late Major Horace Cave-Browne, Indian Army, *b* 1886, *d* 1960: *m* 1920, Alice Rose, who *d* 1972, da of late Col P. A. Weir, Indian Med Ser:—
Patrick Norman Rose (150 Greenbank Rd, Edinburgh, EH10 5RN), *b* 1926; *ed* Charterhouse; Maj late N Rhodesia Regt and late Seaforth Highlanders; Orientation and Mobility Instructor, Roy Blind Sch, Edinburgh: *m* 1956, Mary Davy, da of late Lt-Col M. F. D. Cobbold, Indian Army, and has issue living, Margaret Alison, *b* 1959: *m* 1981, Alan McLellan Millar, of Milton Eonan, 4 Kilallan Av, Bridge of Weir, Renfrewshire, and has issue living, Robert Ewan McLellan *b* 1987, Stuart Alexander Cave *b* 1989, — Ann Mary, *b* 1961: *m* 1994, Gerald Reginald Clark, of 51 Cliffe Rd, Gonerby Hill Foot, Grantham, Lincs, and has issue living, Keith Charles Cave *b* 1995, Kenna Mary Rose *b* 1997. ——— Alison Barbara Rose *b* 1932; *ed* R Sch for Daughters of Officers of the Army, Bath; served WRNS: *m* 1954, Maj Robin John Ronald Campbell, Queen's Own Highlanders (Seaforth and Camerons) (*see* E Cawdor, colls). *Residence* – Kinrara, Aviemore, Inverness-shire PH22 1QA.

According to a pedigree collected and certified by the Garter King of Arms, 1632, this family is derived from Jordan de Cave, who inherited the Lordships of North and South Cave, co York, 1068. Sir Thomas Cave, 1st baronet, was, during the civil war, a strenuous supporter of his sovereign. The 2nd baronet was MP for Coventry, and the 3rd and 7th baronets each sat as MP for Leicestershire. The 3rd baronet, Sir Thomas Cave, of Stanford Hall, *m* Hon Margaret Verney, a descendant of the 1st Baron Braye. Sarah Otway-Cave, of Stanford Hall, only da of Sir Thomas, became Baroness Braye on the termination of the abeyance in 1839, and was great great great grandmother of the present peeress. John, father of the 9th baronet, assumed the name of Browne by Act of Parliament 1752, his mother having been an heiress of that name, and Sir William 9th baronet assumed the additional surname of Cave by Roy licence 1839. The 12th baronet, Rev Sir Genille, sometime engaged in ranching, and served in Boxer Expedition, in Spanish-American War 1898-99 and during 1914-18 War; afterwards a Min in Wesleyan Methodist Church in America; took Holy Orders in Church of England 1920, and became R of Londesborough, Yorkshire. The 13th baronet, Sir Reginald Ambrose, was Capt RN, and served at Bombardment of Alexandria 1882.

CAYLEY (E) 1661, of Brompton, Yorkshire

Sir DIGBY WILLIAM DAVID CAYLEY, 11th *Baronet*; son of late Lt-Cdr William Arthur Seton Cayley, 2nd son of late Digby Leonard Arthur Cayley (infra); *b* 3 June 1944; *s* his kinsman, Maj Sir KENELM HENRY ERNEST, 1967; *ed* Malvern, and Downing Coll, Camb (MA): *m* 1st, 1969 (*m diss* 1987), Christine Mary, only da of late Derek Francis Gaunt, of Ilkley, Yorks; 2ndly, 1993, Cathryn M., elder da of Brian Russell, of Gosport, Hants, and has issue by 1st and 2nd *m*.

Arms – Quarterly argent and sable, a bend gules charged with three mullets of the first. *Crest* – A demi-lion rampant or charged with a bend gules, thereon three mullets argent, in the paws a battleaxe argent, helved gules.
Residence – Heylyns, 70A Bath St, Abingdon, Oxon OX14 1EB.

Callide sed honeste

With skill but with honour

SONS LIVING (*By 2nd marriage*)

THOMAS THEODORE WILLIAM, *b* 17 Feb 1997. —— George Edward Digby, *b* 1999.

DAUGHTERS LIVING (*By 1st marriage*)

Emma Jane, *b* 1974. —— Catherine Mary, *b* 1975.

SISTER LIVING

Josephine Beatrice Seton, *b* (twin) 1944: *m* 1968, Giacomo Bertolini, of Via Bergognone 27, Milan, Italy.

DAUGHTERS LIVING OF TENTH BARONET

Angela Elizabeth (Brompton, Scarborough, Yorks), *b* 1930, *m* 1950 (*m diss* 1959), as his 1st wife, Sir Robert John Frank, 3rd Bt, who *d* 1987. —— Susan Dorothy Marie Gabrielle (*Lady Lawson-Tancred*), *b* 1934: *m* 1st, 1955 (*m diss* 1977), Maldwin Andrew Cyril Drummond (*see* E Perth colls); 2ndly, 1978, Sir Henry Lawson-Tancred, 10th Bt. *Residence* – Aldborough Manor, Boroughbridge, Yorks. —— Virginia Anne (*Hon Lady Storey*), *b* 1936: *m* 1961, Hon Sir Richard Storey, 2nd Bt, CBE, DL, of Settrington House, Malton, Yorks, and Zetland House, Marloes Rd, W8. —— Belinda Jane, *b* 1940: *m* 1962, Mark Singleton Evans, of Manor House, Brompton-by-Sawdon, Scarborough, Yorks, and has issue living, Arthur Nicolas Singleton Cayley, *b* 1963, — Alexander Kenelm Singleton Cayley, *b* 1970, — Amanda Elizabeth Singleton Cayley, *b* 1966: *m* 1990, Damien Peter Adam Doyle McCrystal, son of Cal C. McCrystal, of Totteridge Lane, N20, and has issue living, Kit Charles *b* 1997, Jemima Cayley, *b* 1995. —— April Mary, *b* 1945: *m* 1969, Thomas Vernon Partridge, of Fen Farm, Fen Lane, Ditchingham, Norfolk NR35 2DL, and has issue living, William Kenelm Thomas, *b* 1972, — Annabel Elizabeth Diana *b* 1974. —— Alison Rose, *b* (twin) 1945: *m* 1972, Patrick Dermot Maloney, of The Green, Brompton-by-Sawdon, Scarborough, Yorks, and has issue living, Elizabeth Mary, *b* 1974: *m* 1999, Mark Rigby, son of David Rigby, of Formby, Liverpool, — Caroline Rose, *b* 1979, — Katharine Olivia, *b* 1976. —— Joanna Storm (*Baroness Grey of Codnor*), *b* 1947: *m* 1974, 6th Baron Grey of Codnor, and has issue (see that title). *Residence* – High Legh House, Knutsford, Cheshire WA16 0QR.

COLLATERAL BRANCHES LIVING

Branch from 2nd son of 7th baronet

Granddaughter of late Digby Leonard Arthur Cayley (grandfather of 11th baronet), cl son of Digby Cayley (*b* 1834), 2nd son of 7th baronet:—
Issue of late Maj Digby Coddington Cayley, *b* 1895, *d* 1965: *m* 1924, Beatrice Elizabeth Eleanora, who *d* 1996, da of Robert Charles Campbell-Renton, of Lamberton, and Mordington, Berwick-on-Tweed:—
Katherine Sonia (*Sonia, Baroness ffrench*), *b* 1926: *m* 1954, 7th Baron ffrench, who *d* 1986. —— Amanda Beatrice, *b* 1938.

Grandchildren of late Adm George Cuthbert Cayley, CB, 2nd son of Digby Cayley (*b* 1834) (ante):—
Issue of late Capt Charles Paul Cuthbert Cayley, RE, *b* 1906, *d* on active service 1945: *m* 1939, Cassandra Rosamond Elaine (who *d* 1989, having *m* 2ndly, 1946, John Sarginson, who *d* 1972), da of Sir Digby Algernon Hall Legard, 13th Bt:—
George Paul (Applegarth, Brewers Green, Roydon, Diss, Norfolk IP22 3SD), *b* 1940; *ed* Felsted: *m* 1967, Shirley Southwell, da of Frank Woodward Petford, of Kirby Cane, Norfolk, and has issue living, Paul Alistair, *b* 1971, — Kevin George, *b* 1974. —— Sarah Philadelphia, *b* 1943.

Granddaughter of late Digby Cayley (*b* 1834) (ante):—
Issue of late Capt Harry Francis Cayley, DSO, RN, *b* 1873, *d* 1954: *m* 1900, Margery, who *d* 1901, da of Sir Thomas George Freake, 2nd Bt:—
Alexandra Margery Eileen, *b* 1901: *m* 1928, Lt-Cdr Arthur Frank Armitage, RN (ret), and has issue living, Mark Cecil Christopher, *b* 1937, — Diana Eileen, *b* 1932: *m* 1956, John Trevor Lewis, of Gosport House, Laugharne, Carmarthenshire.

Branch from 3rd son of 7th baronet

Granddaughter of late Rev Reginald Arthur Cayley, 3rd son of 7th baronet:—
Issue of late Capt Edmund Henry George Cayley, *b* 1870, *d* 1945: *m* 1st, 1898, Marie Olga, who *d* 1910, da of Otto Martin, of Valparaiso, Chile; 2ndly, 1914, Laura Eugénie Beatrice, who *d* 1949, da of late George Fox:—
Evelyn Olga Vivienne, *b* 1899: *m* 1923, Wilhelm Wilkendorf, of Quilpue, and has issue living, Heinz Ferdinand Otto (of Quilpue, Chile), *b* 1927: *m* 1958, Ursula Wilckens, of Valparaiso, Chile, and has issue living, Richard *b* 1959, Astrid *b* 1960, — Harold Christian (Casilla 3070, Santiago, Chile), *b* 1934: *m* 1966, Senta Schwarzenberg, of Santiago, and has issue living, Robert Christian *b* 1970, Stephan Alfred (twin) *b* 1970, Helga Veronica *b* 1968.

Granddaughters of late Capt Edmund Henry George Cayley (ante):—
Issue of late Squadron Leader Damyon Edmund Martin Cayley, *b* 1909, *d* 1957: *m* 1944, Mary Ann, who *d* 1973, da of Stephen Taylor, of Sheffield:—
Barbara Ann, *b* 1945: *m* 1962, Victor Mason, and has issue living, Michael Shaun, *b* 1965, — Deborah Anne, *b* 1963. — Patricia Janis, *b* 1948: *m* 19—.

Branch from 4th son of 1st baronet

Grandsons of late Rev Edward Cartwright Cayley, DD (infra):—
Issue of late Arthur Bowen Cayley, *b* 1898, *d* 1973: *m* 1921, Katherine Vanderwerken, who *d* 1973, da of Peleg Howland, of Toronto:—
Edward Cartwright, *b* 1922: *ed* Trin Coll Sch, Port Hope, and Toronto Univ (BA); MA Columbia Univ; Lt-Cdr RCNVR; late Assist Headmaster of Holderness Sch; 1939-45 War: *m* 1st, 1944 (*m diss* 1956), Margaret Noble, of Mansfield, Notts; 2ndly, 1956, Catherine Norma, da of late Alexander Stuart, of Eganville, Ont, and has issue living (by 1st *m*), David Cartwright, *b* 1946, — Susan Margaret, *b* 1948, — Catherine Jane, *b* 1952. —— Peleg Howland (Glen Lea, High Pitfold, Hindhead, Surrey), *b* 1924: *ed* The Grove, Lakefield, Ont; Capt RCN (ret): *m* 1st, 1945 (*m diss* 1953), Freda Rosemary, da of Alfred Cotter, of 8 Cherryhill, Beechlands, Belfast; 2ndly, 1955, Patricia Challinor, da of late Dr John C. Poole, of Craig Allen, Lettermore, Argyll, and has issue living, (by 1st *m*) Jennifer Margaret (501 Addison Av, Ottawa, Ontario, Canada), *b* 1947: *m* 19— (*m diss* 19—), Alastair Sweeney, — (by 2nd *m*) John Howland (1 Grove End House, 150 Highgate Rd, NW5), *b* 1956: *m* 1st, 1977 (*m diss* 1983), Ivy Wetzelberger; 2ndly, 1983 (*m diss* 1995), Bronwyn Borrow, and has issue living (by 1st *m*), Johannes Arthur *b* 1977, and further issue (by Dr Harriet Evans), Rebecca Katherine EVANS CAYLEY *b* 1990, Gabriel Irena EVANS CAYLEY *b* 1994, — Richard Arthur, *b* 1960: *m* 1990, Anne Young, and has issue living, John Peter *b* 1994, Megan Louise *b* 1992, — Christopher Peter (11 Oakfield St, Tivoli, Cheltenham, Glos GL50 2UJ), *b* 1966: *m* 1993, Fiona H., yst da of Robert Carr, of Morpeth, Northumberland, and has issue living, Catriona Emily *b* 1997, Madeleine Elizabeth *b* 1999.

Granddaughter of late Rev John D'Arcy Cayley, el son of William Cayley, MP, 2nd son of John Cayley, *b* 1761, el son of John Cayley, *b* 1730, 2nd son of Cornelius Cayley, *b* 1692, 5th son of Cornelius Cayley, 4th son of 1st baronet:—
Issue of late Rev Edward Cartwright Cayley, DD, *b* 1864, *d* 1921: *m* 1895, Alice, who *d* 1951, da of late Rev A. J. Broughall, formerly R of St Stephen's, Toronto:—
Ray D'Arcy, *b* 1912: *m* 1947, William Ramsay Osler of 800 Bardsey Lane, Saanichton BC, Canada V8M 1S4.

Grandchildren of late William Cayley, MP (ante):—
Issue of late Francis Cayley, *b* 1845, *d* 1909: *m* 1874, Jane Isabel, who *d* 1920, da of late Henry Easton, Collector of Customs, of Cobourg, Ontario:—
William Henry, *b* 1881. —— Emma Robinson, *b* 1876. —— Adelaide Mary, *b* 1877: *m* 19—, R. H. Strickland. —— Muriel Isabel, *b* 1879: *m* 19—, Jay Scholefield. *Residence –*

Grandchildren of late Claud Thornton Cayley, son of late John Cayley (*b* 1816) (infra):—
Issue of late Claud D'Arcy Cayley, *b* 1882, *d* 1948: *m* 1917, Lilian Gertrude, who *d* 1943, da of R. Hall of Retford, Notts:—
Robert Edward Digby, *b* 1918: *m* 1942, Mary Robson. *Residence –*

Issue of late Capt Edward St Quenton Cayley, *b* 1887, *d* 1941: *m* 1916, Sybil Frances, who *d* 1975, da of late Rev Joseph Alfred Halloran, of The Old Parsonage, Ospringe, Faversham:—
Patricia St Quentin, *b* 1922: *m* 1948, Anthony Bruce Askew, who *d* 1980, and has issue living, Rory Anthony Rank (Beara Farm, Romansleigh, S Molton, Devon EX36 4JR), *b* 1949: *m* 1978, Susan Mary Hargreave, da of late Maj Charles Edward Hargreave Mawson (*see* Every, Bt, colls), and has issue living, Henrietta Charlotte Rank *b* 1980, Georgina Anne Rank *b* 1982, — Cleone St Quentin, *b* 1952: *m* 1977, Maxim Hastings Pengelley, of Lywood House, Ardingly, W Sussex, and has issue living, Tristan Anthony Hastings *b* 1979, Venetia St Quentin *b* 1982. *Residence –* Birches Farm, Isfield, Uckfield, E Sussex.

Issue of late Charles Knightley Cayley, *b* 1888, *d* 1916: *m* 1915, Alice Leach, of S Africa, who *d* 1956:—
Alice Knightley, *b* 1916: *m* 1940, Christian John Rosslee, SAAF 1939-45 War, Capt SA Airways (ret), of Walton Rd, St Francis Bay, S Africa and has issue living, Jean Knightley, *b* 1944: *m* 1966 (*m diss* 1974), Edmund Nixon, and has issue living, Vanessa Jane *b* 1970, Andrea Knightley *b* 1973, — Gael Iris, *b* 1946: *m* 1971 (*m diss* 1981), Uwe Neke, and has issue living, Kirsten Sima *b* 1972, Justine Cayley *b* 1973.

Granddaughter of late John Cayley (*b* 1816), 4th son of late John Cayley (*b* 1761) (ante):—
Issue of late Francis Osmund Cayley, *b* 1856, *d* 1921: *m* 1882, Marion Louisa, who *d* 1943, da of Sir James Lukin Robinson, 2nd Bt:—
Marjorie Gordon, *b* 1897: *m* 1925, John William Gamble Boyd, and has issue living, John William Gamble *b* 1929; RCAF — Philip Cayley, *b* 1932: RCAF, — Peter Beverley, *b* 1935. *Residence –* Toronto, Canada.

Grandchildren of late Hugh Charles Cayley, only son of late Sir Richard Cayley, 3rd son of late Edward
Cayley (b 1782) (infra):—
Issue of late Capt Richard Wilkins Cayley, late REME, b 1902, d 1991: m 1935, Joan Harvey, who d 1990, da of
late Dr E. Harvey Sutcliff, of Torrington, N Devon:—
William Richard (2 Meadow Rd, Corn Meadow Lane, Claines, Worcs), b 1944; ed Taunton Sch: m 1972, Mary Elizabeth,
da of George Arthur Baillie, of The Riggs, Midlem, Selkirk, and has issue living, Alexander Richard, b 1973, — Arthur
Edward, b (twin) 1973, — Lucy Claire Christina, b 1984. —— Mary Catherine, b 1938: m 1963, Richard John Wood, of
Ashlar, Hilton, Blandford, Dorset, and has had issue, James Julian, b 1965: m 1992 (m diss 1999), Samantha, da of Stuart
Schofield, of Cove, Farnborough, Hants, — Jonathan Mark, b 1968, d 1999. —— Janet Rose, b 1940: m 1965, Barry
Keith Palmer, of The Poppies, 20 Queen's Drive, Great Malvern, Worcs, and has issue living, Daniel Barry, b 1970, —
Louise Jane, b 1967: m 1992, — Eleanor Mary, b 1969.

Grandchildren of late Cyril Henry Cayley, MD, son of late Dep-Surg-Gen Henry Cayley, CMG, FRCS,
4th son of late Edward Cayley (b 1782), only son of Edward Cayley (b 1733), 3rd son of Cornelius
Cayley (b 1692) (ante):—
Issue of late Henry Douglas Cayley, OBE, b 1904, d 1991: m 1940, Nora Innes (63 Beluga St, Mount Eliza,
Victoria, Australia), da of late Maj Nigel Paton, of Covehithe, Wrentham, Suffolk:—
Neil Henry (7 Cooleena Rd, Elanora Heights, Sydney, NSW, Australia), b 1943; ARICS, FVLE; Dir Cayleys Pty Ltd,
Property Consultants: m 1970, Julie, da of A. L. Bowen, of Melbourne, Australia, and has issue living, Henry James (Lot
154, Walker St, Sawyers Valley, Perth, W Australia 6074), b 1972: m 1997, Melissa, da of L. Bowman, of Perth, W
Australia, — Victoria Anne, b 1971: m 1993 (m diss 1994), Patrick Andrew Dare. —— Innes Margaret, b 1941: m 1971,
Terence John Benson, and has issue living, Andrew Douglas, b 1973, — Mark David, b 1975. —— Lindsay Mary, b
1948: m 1970, Ian Leslie James, and has issue living, Alison Mary, b 1980, — Kirsty Innes, b 1982.

Granddaughter of Maj-Gen Douglas Edward Cayley, CB, CMG, 3rd son of late Dep-Surg-Gen Henry
Cayley, CMG, FRCS (ante):—
Issue of late Com Richard Douglas Cayley, DSO, RN, b 1907, d on active ser 1943: m 1933, Nancy (who m
2ndly, 1943, Herbert Samuel Gild, FRCS), yr da of Edward Coutts, of Sweffling, Fleet, Hants:—
Jennifer Jane, b 1934: m 1st, 1956, Sqdn-Ldr Arthur Christopher Doggett, RAF (see B Horder, 1968 Edn); 2ndly, 1989,
Capt Nicholas John Barker, CBE, RN (Capt HMS Endurance 1980-82), who d 1997, and has issue living (by 1st m),
Antonia Clare, b 1958, — Jessica, b 1963: m 1990, Major James Cushnir, Royal Scots Dragoon Guards, and has issue
living, Toby Edward b 1993, Louisa Jennifer b 1997.

Grandson of late Bernard Cayley (infra):—
Issue of late William Bernard Cayley, b 1907, d 1963: m 1935, Bronwen, who d 1976, da of R. C. Young, of
Yanco, NS Wales:—
John William Douglas (Hamilton, Victoria, Aust), b 1938; ed Geelong Gram Sch, Victoria, and Melbourne Univ (BSc
agriculture): m 1964, Glenys Robertson, da of W. R. Wilson, of Newcastle-upon-Tyne, and has issue living, Ross Andrew,
b 1965; ed Hamilton Coll, Victoria, and Melbourne Univ (BSc), — Fiona Bronwen Robertson, b 1968; ed Hamilton Coll,
Victoria, Melbourne Univ (BA), New Hall, Camb (M Phil), and Jesus Coll, Camb (PhD): m 1996, Jacobus Marinus Frans
Zachariasse, PhD, MA (Cantab), of Leiden, Zuid-Holland, The Netherlands, yr son of Dr J. A. Zachariasse, of
Veenendaal, The Netherlands.

Granddaughter of late Dep-Surg-Gen Henry Cayley, CMG, FRCS (ante):—
Issue of late Bernard Cayley, b 1871, d 1914: m 1904, Gertrude Mary, who d 1942, da of J. C. Large:—
Agnes Mary (53 Cobham Rd, Fetcham, Leatherhead, Surrey), b 1906: m 1926, Maj Charles Fraser Raper, late Indian
Army, 3rd Madras Regt, 6th Rajputana Rifles, who d 1965, and has issue living, John James, b 1927, — Charles Richard,
b 1929.

Grandchildren of late Rear Adm Henry Priaulx Cayley, R Australian Navy, 6th and yst son of Dep-Surg-
Gen Henry Cayley, CMG, FRCS (ante):—
Issue of late Henry Francis Cayley, b 1910, d 1981: m 1940, Marea (44A Shirley Rd, Wollstoncraft, Sydney,
NSW), da of Colin Borthwick, of Sydney:—
Charles Francis, b 1943. —— Susan Aneva Mary, b 1947. —— Mary Lorraine, b 1950.

Grandchildren of late Arthur Cayley, 6th son of late Edward Cayley, b 1782 (ante):—
Issue of late Osbert Arthur Cayley, b 1869, d 1947: m 1910, Dorothy, who d 1942, da of late Rev George
Herbert Lewis (Indian Ecclesiastical Establishment, ret), of Allandale, Burnham, Somerset:—
Forde Everard de Wend, MBE, MD, FRCP, b 1915; formerly Capt RAMC; 1939-45 War in Far East (prisoner, MBE);
MBE (Mil) 1946: m 1941, Eileen Lilian, who d 1997, da of late Arthur C. Dalton, and has issue living (Arthur) Charles
Digby (17 Conolly Rd, W7), b 1946; ed Brighton Coll, and Middx Hosp; MB, BS, FRCP: m 1969, Jeanette Ann, MSc,
MB, BS, MFFP, da of late G. Avery, of Plymouth, and has issue living, George Cornelius Forde b 1971; ed Aberystwyth
Univ (LLM), Adam Charles Francis b 1975; ed Exeter Univ (BSc Hons), Seth Marcus Hugo b 1980, — Michael Forde
(13 Grove Rd, East Molesey, Surrey) b 1950; ed Brighton Coll, and St John's Coll, Oxford (MA): m 1987, Jennifer, MA,
MB, BS, da of late Patrick Lytle, of Southsea. —— Frances Dorothy, b 1912: m 1941, S. A. Yates, who d 1977. Residence
– 33 Kenilworth Rd, Ealing, W5.

The Sire de Cailly (or Cayley), from Cailly in Normandy, was one of the followers of William the Conqueror, and is
celebrated in the Roman de Rou. His descendants were settled in Norfolk for three centuries, when the chief
representative of the family removed to Yorkshire, where his descendants have since remained. The 1st baronet, Sir
William Cayley, was knighted by Charles I, and created a baronet by Charles II, for his services in the Civil War. He m
Dorothy, daughter of Sir William St Quintin, of Harpham, a lineal descendant of Joan, daughter of Edward I. The 6th
baronet, Sir George, was a pioneer of aviation. In 1804 he made a successful model glider, and in 1809 a full sized glider
which he flew with ballast in lieu of a pilot. In 1852 he launched the first man-carrying glider. The 9th baronet, Sir
George Everard Arthur, Capt Roy Defence Corps, d on active service 1917.

CAYZER (UK)1904, of Gartmore, co Perth

Cautiously but fearlessly

Sir JAMES ARTHUR CAYZER, 5th Baronet; *b* 15 Nov 1931; *s* his brother, *Sir* NIGEL JOHN, 1943; *ed* Eton.

ᴀrms – Party per chevron azure and argent, in chief two fleurs-de-lis or, and in base an ancient ship with three masts, sails furled sable, colours flying gules; a chief invected of the third thereon three estoiles of the first. ℭrest – A sea-lion erect proper, holding in the dexter paw a fleur-de-lis, and supporting with the sinister an estoile, both or.
Seat – Kinpurnie Castle, Newtyle, Angus PH12 8TW. *Club* – Carlton.

SISTERS LIVING

Deva, *b* 1923: *m* 1946, Lieut-Com John Studholme Brownrigg, DSC, RN, who *d* 1971, only son of late Adm Sir (Henry John) Studholme Brownrigg, KBE, CB, DSO, and has issue living, Henry John Studholme, *b* 1961: *m* 1985, Sally Anne, da of late Barry Jepson, and has issue living, Jonathan Studholme *b* 1990, Sarah Louise *b* 1988. *Residence* – 2 The Court, Ridgeway Lane, Lymington, Hants SO41 9NR. —— Angela, *b* 1926: *m* 1950, Anthony Malcolm Galliers-Pratt, CBE, who *d* 1998, and has issue living, Rupert Anthony (Mawley Hall, Cleobury Mortimer, Worcs DY14 8PN), *b* 1951: *m* 1973, Alexandra Mary, da of Maj Hugh Rose, DL, of Buriton House, Buriton, nr Petersfield, and has issue living, George Anthony *b* 1979, Frederick Hugh *b* 1981, Isabella Eileen *b* 1985, Alexandra Georgina Angela *b* 1988, — Nigel Kenneth CAYZER (Thriepley House, Lundie, Angus), *b* 1954; assumed surname of Cayzer by deed poll 1982: *m* 1986, Henrietta Caroline Rose, yr da of late Sir Richard Tatton-Sykes, 7th Bt, and has issue living, Arthur James Richard *b* 1988, John Nigel *b* 1996, Virginia Angela *b* 1990, Angelica Eileen Rose *b* 1992, — Anthony Charles (60 Rutland Gate, SW7 1PJ), *b* 1958. *Residence* – The Priest's House, Mawley Hall, Cleobury Mortimer, Worcs DY14 8PN.

AUNT LIVING (*daughter of 2nd baronet*)

Iris Cecilie, *b* 1905: *m* 1938 (*m diss* 1968), Duncan Alistair McKellar, and has had issue, Heather Joy, *b* 1943: *m* 1965, Kenneth Leonard Hyman, and *d* 19—, leaving issue, Jeanne Cecile *b* 1966, Tara Penelope *b* 1968.

COLLATERAL BRANCHES LIVING

Issue of late Sir Herbert Robin Cayzer, 5th son of 1st baronet, who was *cr Baron Rotherwick* 1939 (see that title), of whom (Herbert) Robin, 3rd Baron Rotherwick, *b* 12 March 1954; is *hp* to this baronetcy.

The 1st baronet, Sir Charles Cayzer, was head of the firm of Cayzer, Irvine and Co (Limited), steamship owners, of London, Liverpool, Manchester, and Glasgow, and sat as MP for Barrow-in-Furness (C) 1892 to 1906. The 3rd baronet, Sir Charles William Cayzer, was MP for Cheshire, City of Chester Div (C) 1922-40, and a Member of Roy Co of Archers (King's Body Guard for Scotland): *m* 1919, Beatrice Eileen, OBE, who *d* 1981, elder da of late James Meakin, of Westwood Manor, Staffs, by his wife, late Emma Beatrice (Countess Sondes), da of Percy Hale Wallace, of Muckamore Abbey, co Antrim. The 4th baronet, Sir Nigel John Cayzer, Lieut Scots Guards, was *ka* in Italy 1943.

CHADWICK (UK) 1935, of Bidston, co Palatine of Chester

Honour is purity

Sir Joshua Kenneth Burton Chadwick, 3rd *Baronet*; *b* 1 Feb 1954; *s* his father, *Sir* Robert Peter, 1983.

Arms – Azure, on water in base barry wavy argent and vert an ancient ship or sail set and banner flying at the stern of the second, each charged with a martlet of the first, at the masthead a pennon gules fimbriated argent, in chief a lion passant between two mullets of the last. Crest – Or and azure a demi-sea horse proper gorged with a naval crown and holding between the fins a portcullis chained or.
Residence – 3/1933 Gold Coast, Highway, Burleigh Heads, Qld 4220, Australia.

SISTER LIVING

Wendy Lorraine, *b* 1951: *m* 1978, Andrew Haig Palmer, of Blackberry Patch, Bealey Rd, Honanata RD2, Darfield, Canterbury, NZ.

HALF-SISTERS LIVING

Diana, *b* 1938: *m* 1965, Andrew William Neilson Gemmill, of 18 Lyndhurst St, Richmond, Melbourne, Victoria 3121, Australia, and has issue living, Tristan John, *b* 1967, — Giles William, *b* 1968, — Lucinda Harriet, *b* 1972. —— Sally Virginia, *b* 1940, *m* 1961, Grahame Robert Hadwen, of Stradbroke Towers, 2-90 Goodwin St, Kangaroo Point, Brisbane, Queensland 4169, Australia, and has issue living, Michael Robert, *b* 1970, — Debbie Anne, *b* 1963, — Susan Jane, *b* 1965.

AUNT LIVING *(Daughter of 1st baronet)*

Gwynfa Burton, *b* 1906: *m* 1935 (*m diss* 1955), George D'Arcy Edmondson, CMG, CVO, OBE. *Residence* – 40 Ovington Street, SW3.

WIDOW LIVING OF SECOND BARONET

(Beryl) Joan (*Lady Burton-Chadwick*), da of Stanley Frederick James Brailsford: *m* 1950, as his second wife, Sir Robert Peter Burton Chadwick, 2nd Bt, who *d* 1983. *Address* – 10 Marquet Place, Tairoa 2853, New Zealand.

The 1st baronet, Sir Robert Burton Burton-Chadwick (el son of Joseph Chadwick, of Liverpool), assumed by deed poll 1936, the additional surname of Burton; was head of the firm of Chadwick & Askew, shipowners, of Liverpool and London, and Parliamentary Sec to the Board of Trade 1924-28. He sat as MP for Barrow-in-Furness (C) 1918-22 and for Wallasey 1922-31.

Chadwyck-Healey, see Healey.

CHAMBERLAIN (UK) 1828 of London (Extinct 1980)

Sir Henry Wilmot Chamberlain, 5th and last *Baronet*.

COLLATERAL BRANCH LIVING

Granddaughter of late Lt-Cdr Henry Chamberlain, RN, 2nd son of late Rear-Adm William Charles Chamberlain, 3rd son of 1st baronet:—
Issue of late Capt Neville Grahame Chamberlain, *b* 1896, *d* 1945: *m* 1927, Edna Claire, who *d* 1951, da of John Spence-Nicol, of Wellington, New Zealand:—
Pamela Barbara, *b* 1928: *m* 1950, Peter James Pound, and has issue living, William Grahame, *b* 1951, — Toby James, *b* 1954, — Hugo Giles Barclay *b* 1957. *Residence* – ......

Champion de Crespigny, see de Crespigny.

CHANCE (UK) 1900, of Grand Avenue, Hove, co Sussex

Sir (GEORGE) JEREMY FFOLLIOTT CHANCE, 4th *Baronet*, *b* 24 Feb 1926; *s* his father, *Sir* ROGER JAMES FERGUSON, 1987; *ed* Gordonstoun, and Ch Ch, Oxford (MA); late RNVR; formerly a Dir of Massey-Ferguson Ltd, Coventry: *m* 1950, his cousin, Cecilia Mary Elizabeth, da of late Sir (William) Hugh Stobart Chance, CBE (infra), and has issue.

Arms – Gules, a saltire vair between two fleurs-de-lis in pale and as many towers in fesse argent. Crest – A demi-lion rampant gules, semée of annulets or, holding between the paws a sword erect entwined by a wreath of oak all proper.
Residence – Hafod-y-Bryn, Criccieth, Gwynedd LL52 0AH.

Deo non fortuna

Through God, not by chance

SONS LIVING

(JOHN) SEBASTIAN, *b* 2 Oct 1954; *ed* Dartington Hall, and Stourbridge Coll of Art (BA): *m* 1977, Victoria Mary, da of Denis McClean, of Newcastle-upon-Tyne, and has issue living, Thomas Hugh Jeremy, *b* 14 May 1983, — Michael John Ferguson, *b* 1987, — Madeleine Katharine Eustacia, *b* 1981. —— Roger William Tobias (Toby), *b* 1960; *ed* Eton, and Fitzwilliam Coll, Camb (BA): *m* 1996, Katy, da of Peter Surgison, of Johannesburg.

DAUGHTERS LIVING

Victoria Katherine Elizabeth, *b* 1952. —— Helena Mary ffolliott, *b* 1957: *m* 1979, John Christopher (Toby) Beaufoy, elder son of Harold Beaufoy, of 76 High St, Kenilworth, Warwicks, and has issue living, William Tobias Roland, *b* 1986, — Joanna Mary Constance, *b* 1988.

SISTER LIVING

Teresa Margaret, *b* 1930: *m* 1955, George Gilbert Kennedy, DFC, of Cashelnagor, Gortahork, co Donegal, and has issue living, Seamus Michael ffolliott, *b* 1963, — Miles Thomas Pitt, *b* 1965.

COLLATERAL BRANCH LIVING

Grandchildren of late George Ferguson Chance, 2nd son of 1st Baronet:—
Issue of late Sir (William) Hugh Stobart Chance, CBE, *b* 1896; *d* 1981: *m* 1st, 1926 (*m diss* 1961), Cynthia May, who *d* 1998, da of late Maj Addison Francis Baker Cresswell, of Cresswell and Harehope, Northumberland; 2ndly, 1961, Rachel, who *d* 1998, having *m* 3rdly, 1983, Lt-Col Thomas Argyll Robertson, who *d* 1994, of Box Farmhouse, Birlingham, Pershore, Worcs, da of late Lt Cyril Henry Cameron, RHA, of Tasmania, and formerly wife of James W. Carr:—
(By 1st *m*) (William) John Ferguson (630 Essenwood Rd, Berea, Durban 4001, S Africa), *b* 1929: *m* 1st, 1951, Elizabeth Kathleen, da of Victor J. S. Crookes, of Chartwell, Umzinto, Natal; 2ndly, 1989 (*m diss* 1992), Mrs Ingrid Bonnet, *née* von Christierson; 3rdly, 1996, Mrs Patricia (Paddy) Stewart Fowlis, and has issue living (by 1st *m*), Christopher John Hugh (Shepley, Gingindhlovu 3800, S Africa), *b* 1952: *m* 1976, Merilyn Koller, and has issue living, Justin William Timmins *b* 1988, Lara Elizabeth *b* 1978, Sarah Jean *b* 1982, — James William Frederick (c/o Tomahawk Citrus Estate, PO Malelane 1320, S Africa), *b* 1953: *m* 1978, Tessa Stretton-Barry, and has issue living, David James Victor *b* 1981, Philippa Ann *b* 1979, Camilla Jane *b* 1985, — Richard George Ferguson (260 Ridge Rd, Durban 4000, S Africa), *b* 1956: *m* 1987, Nicola Anne Butcher, and has issue living, Michael John William *b* 1989, Natasha Anne *b* 1991, Samantha Jane *b* 1996, — Sarah Elizabeth (31 Linden Rd, Durban 4000, S Africa), *b* 1960. —— Hugh Nicholas (103 Mountain View Av, Santa Cruz, California 95062 3611, USA), *b* 1940: *m* 1st, 1963 (*m diss* 1977), Caroline Susan, da of Patrick Edward Michael Holmes, of Stourton House, Stourbridge, Worcs; 2ndly, 1990 (*m diss* 1995), Mrs Rose E. Baldwin, elder da of — Heft, of Winsconsin, USA, and has issue living (by 1st *m*), Timothy William Holmes, *b* 1966, — Henry Charles Hugh, *b* 1969, — Lucy Emma, *b* 1971. —— (Kathleen) Idonea Cresswell (Laramie, Taymount, Stanley, Perth PH1 4QG), *b* 1927: *m* 1st 1948 (*m diss* 1956), William Henry Dunamace Heaton-Armstrong, son of Sir John Dunamace Heaton-Armstrong, MVO; 2ndly, 1956 (*m diss* 1965), Lt-Cdr John Timothy Fetherston-Dilke, CBE, RN (ret); 3rdly, 1965 (*m diss* 1975), Colin Frederick Rogers, LDS, RCS; 4thly, 1992 (*m diss* 1998), Martin Joseph Crossley, and has issue living (by 1st *m*), Anthony Eustace John (34 Gironde Rd, SW6 7DZ), *b* 1950; *ed* Ampleforth, and Bristol Univ; Bar-at-law, Grays Inn 1973: *m* 1st, 1973, Susan Margaret, da of Ian Peter Allnut, of Karen Cottage Boulters Lane, Maidenhead, Berks; 2ndly, 1982, Anne Frances, da of Mrs E. E. M. Robigo, and formerly wife of Marcus Hugh Lecky, and has issue living (by 2nd *m*), John William *b* 1983, Eleanor Katharine *b* 1985, Celestine Anne *b* 1988, — Mary Suzanne Bertha, *b* 1949: *m* 1977, John Beresford-Iles, of 18 Cooba St, Canterbury, Vic 3126, Australia, and has issue living, James Geoffrey *b* 1964: *m* 1990, Andrea Lorraine Stuart, Penelope Jane *b* 1966, — Bridget Cynthia HEATON-ARMSTRONG (504 Lockington Rd, RD2, Katikati, NZ), *b* 1952 (has issue, Morgan Lei, a da, *b* 1973): *m* 1st, 1982 (*m diss* 1991), Michael Roger David Dansey; 2ndly, 1997, Bill Hensley, and has further issue (by 1st *m*), Katherine Marie Bridget *b* 1984, Georgina Michaela Celestine *b* 1986, — Rachael Catherine (60 Gaskarth Rd, SW12 9NL), *b* 1954: has issue living, Theodore *b* 1997, — (by 2nd *m*), Timothy Hugh (14 Walsingham Place, SW4 9RR), *b* 1958. — Miranda Catherine, *b* 1956: *m* 1985, William Murray Lindsay (*see* E Mansfield, colls, 1990 Edn), of Taymount Mains, Stanley, Perthshire, and has issue living, Alicia Flora *b* 1987, Harriet Idonea *b* (twin) 1987. —— Cecilia Mary Elizabeth (*Lady Chance*), *b* 1928: *m* 1950, her cousin, Sir (George) Jeremy ffolliott Chance, 4th Bt (ante). —— Bridget Nicola (Willow Cottage, Kingsland, Herefordshire, HR6 9RU), *b* 1931: *m*

1963, Rt Rev John Richard Gordon Eastaugh, sometime Bishop of Hereford, who *d* 1990, and has issue living, James Gordon Mark, *b* 1964: *m* 1994, Philippa Jane Skeates, and has issue living, Samuel John Timothy *b* 1997, — Edward John Hugh, *b* 1970, — Katharine Elizabeth Sophia, *b* 1967.

The 1st baronet was for many years head of the firm of Chance Bros and Co (manufacturers of dioptric illuminating apparatus for lighthouses, etc) of Smethwick and Oldbury, near Birmingham.

CHAPMAN (UK) 1958, of Cleadon, co Durham

Gently but firmly

Sir DAVID ROBERT MACGOWAN CHAPMAN, 3rd *Baronet*; *b* 16 Dec 1941; *s* his father *Col Sir* ROBERT (ROBIN) MACGOWAN, CBE, TD, 1987; *ed* Marlborough, Grenoble Univ, and McGill Univ, Montreal (BCom); High Sheriff Tyne and Wear 1993; DL Tyne and Wear 1997; a Dir Northern Rock plc since 1994, and Wise Speke Ltd, Stock and Share Brokers, Newcastle-upon-Tyne 1987-99; Chm Northern Unit of Stock Exchange 1988-91, and Northumbria Coalition Against Crime since 1995; North East Pres The Securities Assoc since 1993, and Cresstale Ltd since 1999; Memb The Greenbury Cttee 1995, Council of the Stock Exchange 1979-88, and Council of Durham Univ since 1997; Dir The Shrievalty Assoc since 1999: *m* 1965, Maria Elizabeth de Gosztonyi-Zsolnay, da of Dr Nicholas de Mattyasovszky-Zsolnay, of Pecs, Hungary, and has issue.

Arms – Per chevron argent and gules a crescent counterchanged in dexter chief a portcullis chained sable over all in pale a sword point downwards proper pommel and hilt or. Crest – Issuant from a wreath of oak proper a dexter arm embowed vested gules cuffed argent grasping in the hand a harpoon also proper.
Residence – Westmount, 14 West Park Rd, Cleadon, Sunderland, Tyne and Wear SR6 7RR. *Club* – Northern Counties.

SON LIVING

MICHAEL NICHOLAS, *b* 21 May 1969; *ed* Univ of Ottawa (BA), and Univ of East Anglia (MA): *m* 1998, Eszter Marta, yst da of Dr Attila Perlényi, of Budapest.

DAUGHTER LIVING

Christina Elisabeth, *b* 1970.

BROTHER LIVING

Peter Stuart (62 Lansdowne Rd, W11 2LR) *b* 1944; *ed* Marlborough, the Sorbonne, and Trin Coll, Camb (MA), and LSE (MSc); Dir Chapman Hendy Associates: *m* 1972, Joan, da of late R. S. V. Hewitt, of Middle Barton, Oxon, and has issue living, Christopher Edward, *b* 1974; *ed* Bristol Univ (BA), and Camb Univ (MA), — Victoria Rose, *b* 1977, — Katherine Rebecca, *b* 1980, — Rachel Emily, *b* 1981.

SISTER LIVING

Elizabeth Mary, *b* 1946; *ed* Benenden, St Aidan's Coll, Durham, and Columbia Univ, New York (Phi Beta Kappa): *m* 1967, Dr Mark Ivan Levy, of 126 Corte Madera Av, Mill Valley, Cal 94941, USA, and has issue living, Noah, *b* 1970, — Gabriel, *b* 1972.

WIDOW LIVING OF SECOND BARONET

BARBARA MAY, MBE (*Barbara Lady Chapman*), da of Hubert Tonks, of Ceylon, MBE (civil) 1998: *m* 1941, Col Sir Robert (Robin) Macgowan Chapman, 2nd Bt, CBE, TD, who *d* 1987. *Residence* – Pinfold House, Cleadon, Sunderland, Tyne and Wear SR6 7RR.

COLLATERAL BRANCH LIVING

Issue of late Henry James Nicholas Chapman, yr son of 1st baronet, *b* 1914, *d* 1991: *m* 1950, Anne Barbara, who *d* 1998, da of late Sir William Dawson Croft, KCB, KBE, CIE, CVO:—
Caroline Anne, *b* 1955: *m* 1985 (*m diss* 1992), Christopher John Steane, and has issue living, Sebastian James David, *b* 1986, — Isobel Sarah, *b* 1988. *Residence* – 32 Lilyville Rd, SW6 5DW.

Sir Robert Chapman, CB, CMG, CBE, DSO, TD, son of Henry Chapman, JP of Westoe, S Shields, was a Chartered Accountant, MP for Houghton-le-Spring Div of co Durham (C) 1931-35, Sheriff of co Durham 1940-41, and Vice Lord-Lieut for co Durham. Sir Robin Chapman, 2nd Bt, was a ptnr Chapman, Hilton and Dunford, of S Shields, a consultant with Spicer and Pegler, Chm James Hogg & Sons (N Shields) Ltd, etc; Vice Lord Lieut for Co Tyne and Wear 1974-84.

CHAYTOR (UK) 1831, of Croft, Yorkshire, and Witton Castle, Durham

Sir GEORGE REGINALD CHAYTOR, 8th *Baronet*; *b* 28 Oct 1912, son of late William Richard Carter Chaytor, el son of Reginald Clervaux Chaytor, yr son of 2nd baronet; *s* his kinsman, *Sir* WILLIAM HENRY CLERVAUX, 1976, but his name does not appear on the Offical Roll of the Baronetage; patron (alternatively) of Witton-le-Wear V: *m* 1970 (*m diss* 19—), Mrs Elsie Magdeline Rogers.

Arms – Per bend dancettée argent and azure, four quartrefoils two and two bendwise counter-changed. **Crest** – A buck's head couped lozengy argent and sable, attired or, in the mouth a trefoil slipped vert.
Residence – 103-9372 Fletcher Av, Chilliwack, BC, Canada.

SISTERS LIVING

Florine May, *b* 1920: *m* 1951, Edwin John Dauncey, of 2288 Le Clair Drive, Coquitlam, BC, Canada, and has issue living, Darwin Ross, *b* 1953, — Dale Allen, *b* 1956, — Douglas Edwin, *b* 1960. ——— Doreen Isabelle, *b* (twin) 1920: *m* 1941, Herbert William Scott, who *d* 1994, and has issue living, Edward William (6896 Winnifred Place, Saanichton, BC, Canada V05 1M0), *b* 1946; has issue living, Christopher William *b* 1989, — Beverley Ann (B6520 Bella Vista Drive, Victoria, BC, Canada V8Z 6Y4), *b* 1949.

DAUGHTER LIVING OF SEVENTH BARONET

Fortune wills it

(Carol) Miranda (24 Cruden St, N1), *b* 1948.

WIDOW LIVING OF SEVENTH BARONET

PATRICIA NORA (*Patricia, Lady Chaytor*), da of Loftus Joseph McCaffry, and formerly wife of George Walkley Alderman: *m* 1947, Sir William Henry Clervaux Chaytor, 7th Bt, who *d* 1976.

COLLATERAL BRANCHES LIVING

Grandchildren of late Reginald Clervaux Chaytor, yst son of 2nd baronet:—
Issue of late Herbert Archibald Chaytor, *b* 1884, *d* 1979: *m* 1911, Effie Bell, who *d* 1976, da of William Smith:—
†(Herbert) Gordon, *b* 1922: *m* 1947, Mary Alice (1899 Deborah Drive, Duncan, BC, Canada V9L 5A5), da of Thomas Craven, and *d* 1992, leaving issue, BRUCE GORDON (2785 Sooke Rd, Victoria, BC, Canada V9C 2P7), *b* 31 July 1949: *m* 1969 (*m diss* 1978), Rosemary Lea, da of Reid Stephen, of Lake Cowichan, and has issue living, John Gordon *b* 17 Jan 1973, Sharon Kathleen *b* 1969, — Kenneth Reginald (4689 Anderson Rd, Camp 32, RR1, Bowser, BC, Canada V0R 1G0), *b* 1952: *m* 1st, 1973 (*m diss* 1993), Susan Shroetter, of Toronto, Ont; 2ndly, 1993, Warunee, da of Gon Ruanyai, of Thailand, and has issue living (by 1st *m*) Wisteria Willow *b* 1974, Naomi Sage *b* 1976, (by 2nd *m*) Aleah *b* 1995, — Robert David, *b* 1958. ——— Dorothy May (406-1010 MacKenzie Av, Victoria, BC, V8X 4B2, Canada), *b* 1912: *m* 1936, George Walter Blewett, who *d* 19—.

Issue of late Perley Edgar Chaytor, *b* 1886, *d* 1939: *m* 1907, Dora May Lodge:—
Jean Pearl, *b* 1908: *m* 19—, John H. Sutherland. ——— Rita Alberta, *b* 1909: *m* 1936, Donald S. Cowan, of 1368 Duncan Dr, Delta, BC, Canada V4L 1R4, and has issue living, Donald R., *b* 1943: *m* 1966, Louise, da of late Robert Coltart, and has issue living, Steven M. *b* 1971, Michael L. *b* 1975, Andrea E. *b* 1973, — Barbara L., *b* 1941: *m* 1963, Ken Matsuzaki, son of I. Matsuzaki, of Delta, BC, and has issue living, Dean Scott *b* 1972, Dana Jane *b* 1970. ——— Audrey, *b* 1913: *m* 19—, George S. Laing, of 1657, East 62nd Ave, Vancouver, BC, Canada V5P 2K8.

Grandchildren of late Alfred Henry Chaytor, KC (infra):—
Issue of late (Alfred) Drewett Chaytor, *b* 1901, *d* 1977: *m* 1929, Rachel Elizabeth, who *d* 1997, da of late Rev Canon William Hartley Carnegie, Sub-Dean of Westminster Abbey, and Chap to Speaker of House of Commons:—
William Drewett (Old Spa Farm, Croft, Darlington), *b* 1937: *m* 1964, Susan Philippa, el da of James Lawrence Bunting Ansell, MRCS, LRCP, and has issue living, Clervaux James, *b* 1967, — Nicholas John Drewett, *b* 1976, — Katharine

Elizabeth, *b* 1970: *m* 1994, Trevor A. H. Norris (now Chaytor-Norris), of Croft Hall, Croft, Darlington, eldest son of Hugh Norris, of Somerton, Som, and has issue living, George Drewett *b* 1997, Rosie Arabella *b* 1999. —— Elizabeth, *b* 1934: *m* 1959, Lt David Henry Ashwin, of Hill Farm, Dedham, Colchester, and has issue living, Philip David, *b* 1960, — Henry William, *b* 1962, — Rachel Elizabeth, *b* 1964. —— Jane, *b* 1935: *m* 1st, 1966, John Richard Evelyn Atkinson, who *d* 1973; 2ndly, 1976, John A. C. Watherston, of 39 Sutherland St, SW1, and has issue living (by 1st *m*), Richard Matthew Clervaux, *b* 1968, — Harriet Rachel *b* 1972, — (by 2nd *m*), Charles Crispin, *b* 1977. —— Susannah Albinia, *b* 1939: *m* 1st, 1971, Hon Edward Lawies Jackson, who *d* 1982, son of 3rd Baron Allerton; 2ndly, 1997, John Walter Douglas Ewart, CBE, DL, of Astrop Park, Northants.

Issue of late Lt-Col Edward Drewett Chaytor, MC, *b* 1913, *d* 1999: *m* 1938, Mary Monica, who *d* 1987, only da of late Rev Canon Thomas John Woodall, of The Close, Salisbury:—
Richard Clervaux (Stonington, Maine, USA), *b* 1939; *ed* King's Sch, Bruton: *m* 1983, Janet, da of Irving D. Miller, of Malboro, USA, and has issue living, Alexandra Clare, *b* 1986. —— Michael Clervaux, *b* 1944; *ed* King's Sch, Bruton.

Granddaughter of late John Clervaux Chaytor (*b* 1836), eldest son of late John Clervaux Chaytor (*b* 1806), 2nd son of 1st baronet:—
Issue of late Alfred Henry Chaytor, KC, *b* 1869, *d* 1931: *m* 1899, Dorothy Elizabeth, who *d* 1960, eldest da of Harry Percy Burrell:—
Dorothy Anne, *b* 1912: *m* 1937, George Egerton Lambert Manley, and has issue living, Robert John Lambert (11010 Maria Rosa Way, Cupertino, CA 95014, USA), *b* 1938, — Christopher Michael, *b* 1948, — Peter George, *b* 1949: *m* 1975, Elaine Mary, only da of John Bernard Dancer, MRCS, LRCP, and has issue living, Matthew Peter *b* 1987, Jennifer Daughne Emma *b* 1978, Anna Sarah *b* 1985, — Jessica Helen, *b* 1940: *m* 1968, Charles James Mansfield, of PO Box 127, Roma, Qld 4455, son of Hon Sir Alan James Mansfield, KCMG, KCVO, and has issue living, Anthony Roderick *b* 1969, David William *b* 1970. *Residence* – 11 Bonnets Lane, Wareham, Dorset BH20 4HB.

Granddaughters of late Col Lawrence Clervaux Chaytor, MC, VD (infra):—
Issue of late John Lawrence Clervaux Chaytor, *b* 1926, *d* 1976: *m* 1954, Susan Ruth (Apt 3, 40 Andover St, Merivale, Christchurch, NZ), da of George M. Turrell, of Banks Peninsula, Canterbury, NZ:—
Sarah Frances Clervaux Cox-Chaytor, *b* 1956: *m* 1989, Philip Graham Cox, of 80B Landscape Rd, Mt Eden, Auckland, NZ, and has issue living, Peter John, *b* 1995, — Katherine Lousie, *b* 1993. —— Miranda Jane Clervaux Chaytor (Aysgarth, Marshlands, RD3, Blenheim, NZ), *b* 1958; has resumed her maiden name: *m* 198— (*m diss* 19—), Christopher Prosser; has issue (by Jonathan Waddy), Isabel Juliet, *b* 1998. —— Frances Alexandra Clervaux (45 Muller Rd, Blenheim, NZ), *b* 1961.

Grandchildren of late John Clervaux Chaytor (*b* 1836) (ante):—
Issue of late Col Lawrence Clervaux Chaytor, MC, VD, New Zealand Mounted Rifles, *b* 1892, *d* 1954: *m* 1920, Dorothy Mary Bullen, who *d* 1983, da of late John Robert Bullen Tripe:—
Anthony David Clervaux (Marshlands, Marlborough, NZ), *b* 1934. —— Jocelyn Dorothy Clervaux, *b* 1921: *m* 1947, Michael Fearon Hall, and has issue living, Michael Timothy Chaytor, *b* 1949, — Annabel Rose, *b* 1954, — Georgina Miranda Mary, *b* 1959. *Residence* – Pendeen RD2, Darfield, Hororata, New Zealand.

Issue of late Col John Clervaux Chaytor, RA, *b* 1896, *d* 1957: *m* 1930, Olive Mary, who *d* 1957, da of Col Reginald Brittan, DSO, OBE, of Failand Hill, Failand, Somerset:—
Pamela June (Castle Hill Cottage, Eyke, Woodbridge, Suffolk IP12 2QF), *b* 1934: *m* 1959, Capt Henry Raymond Harvey Fooks, who *d* 1996, son of Sir Raymond Hatherell Fooks, CBE, of Reves Hall Farm, Eyke, Suffolk, and has issue living, Caroline Mary (78 Tennyson St, SW8 3SX), *b* 1961, — Serena Alice, *b* 1963: *m* 1993, Graeme Weston Elliot Murray, of Goodlands Farm, Raydon, Ipswich, Suffolk IP7 5LQ, son of Alexander Elliot Murray, and has issue living, James Alexander Elliot *b* 1994, Isobel Alice Elliot *b* 1996, — Sarah Clervaux, *b* 1965: *m* 1993, Jonathan de Hoghton Dumergue Veale, of Hempland Barn, Eyke, Woodbridge, Suffolk IP12 2QE, elder son of Dr Michael Henry Dumergue Veale, and has issue living, Edward Henry Charles *b* 1996, Georgina Anabel Chaytor *b* 1998. —— Jennifer Margaret (Oak Farm, Gwehelog, Usk, Mon) *b* 1936: *m* 1st, 1959 (*m diss* 1985), Thomas Barrington Cubitt, of Forbury House, Kintbury, Berks; 2ndly, 1985, (Edward) Martin Dean, who *d* 1985, son of Col Frank Longueville Dean, and has issue living, (by 1st *m*) Annabelle Jane (52 Canterbury St, Lyttelton, Canterbury, NZ), *b* 1964: *m* 1995, John Robert Watson Newell, son of Jack Newell, of Rangiora, nr Christchurch, NZ, — Alicia Mary, *b* 1965: *m* 1992, Christopher Edward Howard Guinness, of Park Farm House, Redenham Park, Andover, Hants SP11 9AQ, elder son of Lt-Cdr Sir Howard Christian Sheldon Guinness, VRD, RNR, and has issue living, James Edward Chaytor *b* 1997, Tatiana Emily *b* 1995, — Miranda Louise, *b* 1967: *m* 1996, Alexander R. B. Shaw, of Penthouse, Building No 8, 10 Underwood Row, N1 7LQ, only son of late Peter Shaw, of Nairobi, and of Mrs Donald Factor, of London, — Sophia Henrietta, *b* 1968: *m* 1997, (John) Casper J. Yeoward, of Glenwood, Wrexham Rd, Pulford, Chester CH4 9DG, yr son of Richard Yeoward, of Pulford, Chester, — Natasha Isabelle, *b* 1976.

Grandchildren of late Arthur Chaytor, 2nd son of John Clervaux Chaytor, *b* 1806 (ante):—
Issue of late Arthur Cuthbert Chaytor, *b* 1873, *d* 1948: *m* 1908, Linda, who *d* 1971, da of Charles Martin, of Stoke, Nelson, New Zealand:—
Jack Martin (29b Didsbury Drive, Waihi Beach, Waihi, NZ), *b* 1913: *m* 1937, Ida Kathleen da of E. A. Russell, and has two children, Warren John, *b* 19—: *m* 19—, Susan Mary Rohl, and has issue living, Melanie Elizabeth *b* 19—, Kathryn Alanna *b* 19—, — Lynne Marie, *b* 19—: *m* 19—, Clifton Hallam, and has issue living, Richard Wayne *b* 19—, Donna Adele *b* 19—, Kathryn Marie *b* 19—.

Issue of late Capt Frank Clervaux Chaytor, *b* 1884, *d* 1962: *m* 1922, Alice, who *d* 1983, da of John Hill, of Winslow:—
Joan Clervaux, *b* 1925: *m* 1952, Ian McKelvie Bull, and has issue living, Mary Clare, *b* 1953, — Susan Alice, *b* 1958.

The 1st baronet of the *cr* 1831 was descended from Henry Chaytor, brother of Sir William Chaytor (*cr* 1671). He and the 2nd baronet sat in Parliament for Sunderland and Durham respectively. Christopher Chaytor, Surveyor-Gen to Queen Elizabeth I, obtained a grant of arms in 1571. He married Elizabeth, sole heiress of the Clervaux family, which had owned estates at Croft since 1246. William Chaytor, grandson of Christopher Chaytor, was *cr* a Baronet 1671 (title ext 1721). The 4th baronet was High Sheriff of co Durham 1902.

CHETWYND (GB) 1795, of Brocton Hall, Staffordshire

QUOD·DEUS·VULT·FIET

What God wills, let it be done

Sir ARTHUR RALPH TALBOT CHETWYND, 8th *Baronet*, son of late William Ralph Talbot Chetwynd, MC, brother of 7th baronet; *s* his uncle, *Sir* (ARTHUR HENRY) TALBOT, OBE, MC, 1972; *b* 28 Oct 1913; *ed* Vernon Prep Sch, Vernon, BC, and Provincial Normal Sch; Dir Remedial Gymnastics BC Workman's Compensation Board 1942; Ch Instructor Med Reconditioning RCAF 1943-45; Associate in Physical and Health Ed, Univ of Toronto, and Publicity Officer Univ of Toronto Athletic Assocn 1946-52; Chm Chetwynd Films Ltd, Toronto, Canada since 1977; Pres Brocton Hall Communications Ltd, Toronto, Canada: *m* 1940, Marjory May MacDonald, el da of late Robert Bruce Lang, of Vancouver, BC, and has issue.

Arms – Quarterly, 1st and 4th, azure a chevron between three mullets or; 2nd and 3rd argent, two gules.
Residences – 117 King St East, Apt 3, Coburg, Ontario K9A 1L2; The Carib, Holetown, St James, Barbados, WI. *Clubs* – Naval and Military, Empire (Canada; Past Pres), Royal Canadian Yacht.

SONS LIVING

ROBIN JOHN TALBOT, *b* 21 Aug 1941: *m* 1967, Heather Helen, el da of George Lothian, of Baie D'Urfe, Quebec, and has issue living, Peter James Talbot, *b* 1973, — Kimberly Anne, *b* 1971. —— (William) Richard Talbot (1090 Sycamore Cres, Oshawa, Ont L1G 6S7, Canada), *b* 1946: *m* 1971, Patricia Anne, da of late Geoffrey Senior, of Manchester, and has issue living, Hugh Geoffrey Talbot, *b* 1973, — Brian William Talbot, *b* 1977.

COLLATERAL BRANCHES LIVING

Granddaughters of late Charles Chetwynd, 3rd and yst son of late Maj William Fawkener Chetwynd, 2nd son of 1st baronet:—
Issue of late Charles William George Chetwynd, *b* 1894, *d* 1975: *m* 1st, 1914 (*m diss* 1932), Olive Mary, who *d* 1980, yr da of J. Hall, of Huntingdon; 2ndly, 1932, Kathleen M. Langworthy; 3rdly, 19—, Mary Elizabeth, who *d* 1996, da of Arthur Griffiths, JP, of Worcester:—
(By 1st *m*) Rhona Mary, *b* 1916: *m* 1940, Philip Graham Stacey Brinson, of Byways, Church Lane, Horton, Ilminster, Som, and has issue living, John Philip (Barton Lodge, Poundisford, Taunton, Som TA3 7AF), *b* 1948: *m* 1975, Jayne Lesley Neale, and has issue living, Michael John *b* 1986, Kerrie Jayne *b* 1976, Nicola Helen *b* 1983. —— (By 3rd *m*) (Valerie) Elizabeth, *b* 1940: *m* 1st, 1961, Rupert Carrington; 2ndly, 1978, Lt-Col Mark F. Murray, RM, of Wall Hills, Thornbury, Bromyard, Hereford HR7 4NW, and has issue living (by 1st *m*), Lucy Jane, *b* 1964: *m* 1995, John Charles Baldwin, of Old Stone Cottage, Hermitage Rd, E Grinstead, Sussex, — Rosemary Ann, *b* 1966: *m* 1992, Andreas Valencia, of San Clemente, California, USA, and has issue living, Emma Elizabeth *b* 1998.

Grandsons of late Charles William George Chetwynd (ante):—
Issue of late Basil Charles Fawkener Chetwynd, *b* 1915, *d* 1980: *m* 1944, Margaret Joan, who *d* 1992, da of late George Ernest Welch:—
Paul Ernest Fawkener (Greenacres, Charlton Rd, Creech Heathfield, Taunton, Somerset), *b* 1945: *m* 1972, Shirley Evelyn, el da of Raymond Godfrey Manuel, of Creech Heathfield, and has issue living, Karen Lynne, *b* 1975, — Wendy Caroline, *b* 1977. —— Raymond Charles Fawkener (Westlake, Cockpit Rd, Great Kingshill, nr High Wycombe, Bucks), *b* 1950: *m* 1974, Susan Jane, el da of John Kershaw, of Taunton, Som, and has issue living, Joanne Louise, *b* 1978, — Rebecca Claire, *b* 1978 (twin), — Sarah Jane, *b* 1982.

Sir Philip Chetwynd, 2nd son of Sir John Chetwynd of Chetwynd, Salop (*d c* 1240), whose family was of great antiquity in that co, obtained Ingestre, Staffs, by marriage with Isabella, da and heir of Sir Adam de Mytton. Their descendant, Sir William Chetwynd of Ingestre (*d* 1547), had issue, Thomas of Ingestre (*d* 1555) and Anthony of Ridge, Staffs, grandfather of the 1st, 2nd and 3rd Viscounts Chetwynd, who inherited Ingestre. Thomas of Ingestre (*d* 1555) was grandfather of John Chetwynd of Ingestre (*d* 1592), whose 4th son, Thomas of Rugeley, Staffs (*d* 1633), was ancestor of the Chetwynds of Brocton in that co. Sir George Chetwynd 1st Bt, was 5th in descent from Thomas (*d* 1633). The 1st baronet, many years Clerk to the Privy Council, received knighthood in 1787, and the 2nd sat as MP for Stafford. Sir George Chetwynd 4th Bt, was High Sheriff of Warwickshire 1875.

CHEYNE (UK) 1908, of Leagarth, Fetlar, and North Yell, co Zetland
(Name pronounced "Chain")

He conquers by patience

Sir JOSEPH LISTER WATSON CHEYNE, OBE, 3rd *Baronet*; *b* 10 Oct 1914; *s* his father, *Col Sir* JOSEPH LISTER, MC, 1957; *ed* Stowe, and Corpus Christi Coll, Camb; 2nd Sec (Information) British Embassy, Rome 1968-70, 1st Sec 1970-73; 1st Sec (Information) 1973-76; curator, Keats-Shelley Memorial House, Rome 1976-90; European War 1939-45 as Major, Queen's Westminsters, KRRC; OBE (Civil) 1976: *m* 1st, 1938 (*m diss* 1955), Mary Mort, who *d* 1959, da of Vice-Adm John Derwent Allen, CB; 2ndly, 1955, Cicely, da of Thomas Metcalfe, of Padiham, Lancashire, and has issue by 1st and 2nd marriages.

Arms – Azure, on a bend between six crosses patée fitchée argent an oak tree eradicated proper, fructed or. **Crest** – A cross patée fitchée argent.
Residences – The Haa, Gloup, N Yell, Shetland; Leagarth, Fetlar, Shetland.

SONS LIVING (*By 1st marriage*)

PATRICK JOHN LISTER (37 Chapel Lane, Hale Barns, Altrincham, Cheshire WA15 0AG), *b* 2 July 1941: *ed* Lancing: *m* 1968, Helen Louise Trevor, yr da of Louis Smith, of Marine Lodge, 25 Driftwood Gardens, Southsea, Hants PO4 9ND, and has issue living, Louis Richard Patrick Lister, *b* 25 March 1971, — Elizabeth Henrietta Louise, *b* 1969, — Mary Catherine Fleur, *b* 1974, — Caroline Victoria Alice, *b* 1979.

(*By 2nd marriage*)

John Joseph Peter (La Vignaccia, Via Del Bandino 6, Pergine Val D'Arno, Arezzo, Italy), *b* 1956: *m* 1980, Emma, 2nd da of late Luciano Sestini, of Arezzo, Italy, and has issue living, Edward William Watson, *b* 1980. —— James Andrew Watson (140 Viale Regina Margherita, Roma, Italy), *b* 1957; *ed* Stowe: *m* 1984, Frederica Elda Cristina, yr da of Paolo Napolitani, of Rome, and has issue living, William Giovanni Joseph Watson, *b* 1986, — Victoria Emma Watson, *b* 1991.

DAUGHTERS LIVING (*By 1st marriage*)

Ann Caroline Lister, *b* 1939: *m* 1961, Lt-Col Ronald Eric Croll Adam, Queen's Own Highlanders. *Residence* – Coombe House, Sharnden, Mayfield, E Sussex TN20 6QA.

(*By 2nd marriage*)

Helen Margaret Watson, *b* 1959: *m* 1989, Rinaldo G M Rinaldi (Piazza San Salvatore in Lauro 13, Roma, Italy), elder son of late Avv Francesco Rinaldi, and has issue living, Cecilia, *b* 1992.

BROTHER LIVING

Andrew Watson, *b* 1921; *ed* Stowe, and Loughborough Coll, Leicester; late Capt RE, and a FICE; Burma 1941-45, NW Europe 1945 (despatches): *m* 1946, Joyce, da of Conway Stanton, of Kensington, SW10. *Residence* – 49 Hurlingham Court, Ranelagh Gdns, SW6.

COLLATERAL BRANCHES LIVING

Issue of late Brig William Watson Cheyne, DSO, OBE, 2nd son of 2nd baronet, *b* 1920, *d* 1970: *m* 1946, Laurel Audrey (12 Crondace Rd, SW6), da of late Lt-Gen Sir Balfour Oliphant Hutchison, KBE, CB (*see* Jervis-White-Jervis, Bt (ext), colls, 1990 Edn):—
Julian Lister Hutchison, *b* 1947. —— David Watson (19 Ladbroke Gdns, W11 2PT), *b* 1948; *ed* Stowe and Trin Coll, Camb (BA): *m* 1978, (Judith) Gay McAuslane, el da of David Anstruther Passey, of The Hall, Kirkby Fleetham, Northallerton, Yorks, and has issue living, Alexander William David, *b* 1980, — Rory Alistair Watson, *b* 1984, — Rupert Valentine Hutchinson, *b* 1989. —— (William) Gerald (32 Ringmer Av, SW6), *b* 1950; *ed* Stowe, and Trin Coll, Camb (BA): *m* 1978 (*m diss* 1984), Clare Rosdew, da of Stamford Robert Francis Vanderstegen-Drake, of The Old Tannery, Ecchinswell, Newbury, Berks (*see* Mowbray, Bt), and has issue living, Katherine Clare, *b* 1980. —— Bridget Nelita, *b* 1955: *m* 1984, Richard Patrick Lanyon, of 16 Dryburgh Rd, SW15, eldest son of Major Patrick Lanyon, of The Great House, Timberscombe, Minehead, Somerset, and has issue living, William Patrick, *b* 1988, — Frances Alice, *b* 1986, — Alexandra Polly, *b* 1990.

Grandchildren of late William Hunter Watson Cheyne, MB, MRCS, LRCP (infra):—
Issue of late George Watson Cheyne, *b* 1929, *d* 1996: *m* 1964, (Alison) Diana Muir (The Priory, Monk Sherborne, Basingstoke, Hants), da of C. Muir Jones, of Hawarden, Chester:—
Piers William Watson (147 Grace Church St, Rye, NY 10580, USA), *b* 1965; *ed* Radley, and Bristol Univ (BA): *m* 1994, Anne, eldest da of Jean-Louis Richard, of St Germain-en-Laye, France, and has issue living, Hugo Edward Watson, *b* 1997. —— Phyllida Alison, *b* 1968; *ed* Downe House, and Trinity Hall, Camb (MA, MPhil); Bar Inner Temple 1992. —— Catriona Helen, *b* 1971; *ed* Wycombe Abbey; architect.

Issue of late William Hunter Watson Cheyne, MB, MRCS, LRCP, 2nd son of 1st baronet, b 1889, d 1957: m 1923, Grizel, who d 1975, da of I. F. Bayley, formerly of Halls, East Lothian:—
(Janet) Mary Watson (*Baroness Cochrane of Cults*), b 1931: m 1956, 4th Baron Cochrane of Cults. *Residence* – Cults, Cupar, Fife.

The 1st baronet, Sir (William) Watson Cheyne, KCMG, CB, FRCS, FRS, an eminent surgeon, and Pres of Roy Coll of Surgs, was Lord-Lieut of Orkney and Shetland 1919-30, and sat as MP for Edinburgh and St Andrews Univ (*C*) 1917-18 and for Edinburgh St Andrews, Glasgow, and Aberdeen Univs (*Co U*) 1918-22. The 2nd baronet, Sir Joseph Lister Cheyne, MC, was Col Comdg 16/5th Lancers.

CHICHESTER (E) 1641, of Raleigh, Devonshire

Sir (EDWARD) JOHN CHICHESTER, 11th *Baronet*; b 14 April 1916; s his father, *Com Sir*EDWARD GEORGE, RN (ret), 1940; *ed* Radley, and RMC Sandhurst; late Capt Roy Scots Fusiliers; is patron of one living; was King's Foreign Service Messenger 1947-50, and with Imperial Chemical Industries Ltd 1950-60; European War 1939-45 with Roy Scots Fusiliers, and as Lieut RNVR: m 1950, Hon Anne Rachel Pearl Douglas-Scott-Montagu, da of 2nd Baron Montagu of Beaulieu, and widow of Major Howel Joseph Moore-Gwyn, Welsh Guards, and has had issue.

Arms – Checky or and gules, a chief vair. Crest – A heron rising with an eel in its beak proper.
Address – Battramsley Lodge, Boldre, Lymington, Hants SO41 8PT.

SONS LIVING

JAMES HENRY EDWARD, b 15 Oct 1951; *ed* Eton: m 1990, (Margaret) Anne, only da of late Maj John Walkelyne Chandos-Pole, JP, DL, of Radbourne Hall, Derbys, and has issue living, Edward John Chandos-Pole, b 27 July 1991, — Charles James, b 1992. —— Julian John Raleigh, b 1963: m 1994, Holly J. B., yr da of Capt John Holliday Bingham Hartley, of SW1, and of Mrs Keith Martin, of Chittoe, Wilts, and has issue living, Linus, b 1997, — Silvi, b 1998.

Ferme en foy

Firm in faith

DAUGHTERS LIVING AND DECEASED

Coral Anne, b 1954: m 1977, Christopher Angus McEwen, MICE, of Aldhams, Bromley Rd, Lawford, Manningtree, Essex CO11 2NE, and has issue living, Rosanna Clare, b 1981, — Alexia Catherine, b 1982, — Sabrina Caroline, b 1988. —— Georgina Caroline, b 1955: m 1985, Christopher J. Leyland, of Greymare Farm, Belford, Northumberland NE70 7PG, son of late John Christopher Michael Leyland (*see* Cotterell, Bt, 1944 Edn), and has issue living, Benjamin John, b 1994, — Emma Rose, b 1989. —— Mary Rose, b 1957: m 1978, as his 2nd wife, Greville Patrick Charles Howard (*see* E Suffolk and Berkshire, colls), and d 1980.

SISTER LIVING

Mary, b 1917: m 1941, Cdr John Blakeley Russell, DSC, RN (ret), of 37 Horne Rd, Ilfracombe, N Devon EX34 8HD, and has issue living, Christopher John, b 1954, — Hermione Anne GOACHER (17 Gloucester St, SW1V 2DB), b 1942: m 1962, Robin Labron Johnson, and has issue living, Nicolas Patrick Amyas Labron b 1963, Tristan Alexander Labron b 1965, — Cherry Rose, b 1952: m 1977, Wing Cdr Andrew Renshaw, RAF, of UK MODSAP, Khamis Mushayt, BFPO 633, and has issue (*see* Renshaw, Bt).

COLLATERAL BRANCHES LIVING

Issue of late Marcus Beresford Chichester, yst son of 9th baronet, b 1896, d 1985: m 1925, Myra Brownrigg, who d 1985, yst da of late Maj Harvey Brownrigg Jay:—
Imogen Ann (Crawley Lodge, Yarcombe, Honiton, Devon), b 1926: m 1948, Maj Arthur John Digby Hamilton, Scots Gds, who d 1980 (*see* Fairlie-Cunninghame, Bt, 1964 Edn), and has issue living, Philip Arthur Marcus, b 1949, — Edward Digby Hamilton, b 1953, — James John, b 1959. — Thomas Patrick, b (twin) 1959. — Kate Antonia, b 1950: m 1st, 1972 (*m diss* 1979), Robin John Salt, who d 1997; 2ndly, 1981, Simon Peter Dewhurst, of The Old Vicarage, Bickley, Malpas, Cheshire, and has issue living (by 1st *m*), Thomas Bertram b 1972, Antonia Jane b 1974 (by 2nd *m*), Patrick Digby b 1983, Frederick Olivier b 1989. —— Jane Catherine, b 1929: m 1957, Roger Longrigg, of Orchard House, Crookham, Hants, and has issue living, Laura Jane, b 1958, — Frances Angelica, b 1961, — Clare Selina, b 1963.

Grandchildren of late George Chichester, 6th son of 8th baronet:—
Issue of late Group Capt Patrick George Chichester, OBE, RAF, b 1901, d 1983: m 1931, Gladys Evelyn Vesta Clemency, who d 1977, da of William Carnegie Barnes, of Hayne Manor, Lewdown, Devon:—
Jeremy Patrick (Hawthorn Cottage, Congresbury, Som BS19 5BE), b 1932: m 1956, Kathleen Anne, only da of William George Lloyd, of Nashley House, Weston-super-Mare, Som, and has issue living, Mark Arlington Raleigh (The Lodge, Hayne Manor, Lewdown, nr Okehampton, Devon), b 1957: Cdr RN: m 1984, Adrienne Valmai, yr da of Douglas Henry Cook, of Sutherland Drive, Hutton, Avon, and has issue living, Amelia Henrietta Frances Lily b 1989, Alicia Vesta Anne b 1991, — Matthew Patrick Lloyd, b 1966: m 1997, Jill Katharine, yst da of David Allen, of Bierton, Bucks, and has issue

living, Talitha Georgiana Lloyd *b* 1999, — Miranda Frances Louise, *b* 1962: *m* 1987, Trevor D. Jones, son of K. H. Jones, of Tenterden, Kent, and has issue living, Hugo George Herm *b* 1993, Oscar Joseph Lloyd *b* 1996. —— Patricia Gladys Clemency, *b* 1939: *m* 1963, Anthony Arthur Greves Quinton, MD, and has issue living, Lucinda Clemency, *b* 1965. —— Caroline Sandra Pietre Katrina, *b* 1944: *m* 1970, Rear Adm Michael George Temple Harris, RN, and has issue (*see* B Harris, colls). —— Clarissa Evelyn Georgette, *b* 1948: *m* 1972, Keith James Keating, of Cloncurry, W Qld, Aust, and has issue living, Simon Keith, *b* 1979, — Melissa Evelyn, *b* 1973, — Georgina Naomi, *b* 1974.

Grandson of late Rev Charles Chichester, 7th son of 8th baronet:—
Issue of late Sir Francis Charles Chichester, KBE, *b* 1901, *d* 1972: *m* 1st, 1923, Muriel Eileen, who *d* 1929, da of late M. F. Blakiston; 2ndly, 1937, Sheila Mary, who *d* 1989, da of late Gerald Craven, of Belle Eau Park, Notts:—
(By 2nd *m*) Giles Bryan (9 St James's Pl, SW1), *b* 1946; *ed* Ch Ch, Oxford: *m* 1979, Virginia, yst da of late Edwin Ansell, and has issue living, George Arthur Francis, *b* 1981, — Charles Edward Orlando, *b* 1990, — Jessica Mary, *b* 1984.

This family took its name from Chichester Sussex. On the marriage of Thomasine Raleigh with John Chichester in 1384 this family settled at Raleigh, Devon. Sir Roger Chichester was knighted by the king at the siege of Calais, and afterwards served at Poitiers. The 9th baronet, Rear-Adm Sir Edward Chichester, was a Naval ADC to HM Queen Victoria and HM King Edward VII 1899-1902.

CHILD (UK) 1868, of Newfield, and of Stallington Hall, Staffordshire and of Glen Losset, co Argyll (Extinct 1958)

Sir (SMITH) HILL CHILD, GCVO, CB, CMG, DSO, 2nd and last *Baronet*.

DAUGHTER LIVING OF SECOND BARONET

Mary Cornelia, *b* 1933: *m* 1959, Henry Charles Whitbread, who *d* 1993, and has issue living, Caroline Mary, *b* 1960· *m* 1986, Major (Jonathan) Peter Wikeley, RA, of Hill View Farm, Brickyard Lane, Corfe Mullen, Dorset BH21 3RJ, 3rd son of Sqdn/Ldr J. D. Wikeley, of Gillingham, Dorset, and has issue living, Rosalyn Elizabeth *b* 1990, — Flora Joscelyne, *b* 1962, — Angela Helen, *b* 1965. *Residence* – Haymans Farm, Plaistow, Billingshurst, W Sussex RH14 0PQ.

CHILD (UK) 1919, of Bromley Palace, Bromley, Kent

Sir (COLES JOHN) JEREMY CHILD, 3rd *Baronet*; *b* 20 Sept 1944: *s* his father, *Sir* (COLES) JOHN, 1971; *ed* Eton, and Poitiers Univ; actor: *m* 1st, 1971 (*m diss* 1976), Deborah Jane, da of Henry Percival Snelling; 2ndly, 1978 (*m diss* 1987), Jan, yst da of Bernard Todd, of Kingston upon Thames; 3rdly, 1987, Elizabeth (Libby), yst da of Rev Grenville Morgan, of Canterbury, Kent, and has issue (by 1st, 2nd and 3rd *m*).

Arms – Per chevron azure and gules, on a chevron engrailed ermine between three eagles close argent a fylfot sable. **Crest** – An eagle, wings expanded argent charged on the breast with a fylfot sable, holding in the beak by its neck a serpent entwined round the body vert.
Residence – The Farm House, Warren Farm, Rectory Rd, Streatley on Thames, Berks RG8 9QE.

To imitate rather than to envy

SONS LIVING (By 2nd marriage)

(COLES JOHN) ALEXANDER, *b* 10 May 1982.

(by 3rd marriage)

Patrick Grenville, *b* 1991.

DAUGHTERS LIVING (By 1st marriage)

(Honor) Melissa, *b* 1973.

(by 2nd marriage)

Leonora, *b* 1980.

(by 3rd marriage)

Eliza Caroline, *b* 1989.

SISTERS LIVING

Deirdre Kathleen, *b* 1934: *m* 1959, Antony Edward Woodall, of Hill House, Great Hormead, Buntingford, Herts (Crawley-Boevey, Bt, colls), and has issue living, James Henry, *b* 1960, — Andrew Hugh, *b* 1963; actor: *m* 1990, Jane Mary Ashton, and has issue living, Gabriel Sanderson *b* 1992, Leo Vincent *b* 1996, Constance Rose *b* 1991, — Edward Antony John, *b* 1967: *m* 1997, Amanda Pritchett, and has issue living, Chester *b* 1999. —— Honor Diana, *b* 1936: *m* 1st, 1959, Capt Noel Hardwick Matterson, late R Dragoons, who *d* 1982; 2ndly, 1985, Robin Patrick Fremantle (*see* E Cottesloe, colls), and has issue living (by 1st *m*), Charles John Hardwick *b* 1960: *m* 1987, Elizabeth Caroline McGregor Moffat, — Justin George Hardwick, *b* 1962, — Nicholas Noel Hardwick, *b* 1963: *m* 1992, Georgia Cadwaladr, — Dominic Graham Hardwick, *b* 1965: *m* 1992, Camilla Mary Roche.

Sir Coles Child, 1st Bt, was son of Coles William John Child, JP, DL, of Bromley, Kent. The latter's great-great-grandfather John Child, of Yaxley, Hunts (*d* 1743): *m* Isabella, da of William Coles, of London.

CHINUBHAI (UK) 1913, of Shahpur, Ahmedabad, India

Sir UDAYAN CHINUBHAI, 3rd *Baronet*; *b* 29 July 1929; *s* his father, *Sir* CHINUBHAI MADHOWLAL RUNCHORELAL, 1990: *m* 1953, Muneera Khodadad, da of Khodadad Mancherjee Fozdar, of Bombay, and has issue.

Arms – Azure, in base on water a lotus flower leaved proper, issuant from the dexter chief a sun in splendour or. **Crest** – An elephant proper, resting the dexter fore-foot on an escutcheon argent, charged with a lotus flower proper.
Residence – Shantikunj, Shahibag, Ahmedabad 380 004, India.

SON LIVING

PRASHANT, *b* 15 Dec 1955: *m* 1978, Swati Rushikesh, da of Rushikesh Janakray Mehta, of Ahmedabad, and has issue living, Abha (a da), *b* 1980, — Gayatri (a da), *b* 1981, — Roshni (a da), *b* 1988.

DAUGHTERS LIVING

Radhika, *b* 1954. —— Prasann, *b* 1960: *m* 1982, Arvind Surendra Kumar Somany, of Soma House, Ellis Bridge, Ahmedabad. —— Aradhana, *b* 1963.

BROTHERS LIVING

Kirtidev (Chinunath Mahader, nr Police Stadium, Shahibag, Ahmedabad 380 004, India), *b* 1932: *m* 1967, Meera Ratilal, da of Ratilal Tribhovandas Nanavati, of Surat, India. —— Achyut (Balantyne Haveli, Three Gates, Ahmedabad 380 004, India), *b* 1941: *m* 1967, Uttara Vilochan, da of Vilochan Keshavlal Dhruva, of Bombay, and has issue living, Aneesh (a son), *b* 1969.

AUNT LIVING (*daughter of 1st baronet*)

Vasumati, *b* 1913: *m* 1937, Yashodhar Narmadashankar Mehta, Bar-at-law.

Sir Chinubhai Madhowlal Runchorelal, 1st Bt (first Hindu baronet to be created), was a cotton manufacturer of Ahmedabad and an MLC; he contributed largely to educational schemes in India.

CHITTY (UK) 1924, of The Temple

Sir THOMAS WILLES CHITTY, 3rd *Baronet; b* 2 March 1926; *s* his father, *Sir* (THOMAS) HENRY WILLES, 1955; *ed* Winchester, and Univ Coll, Oxford: *m* 1951, Susan Elspeth Russel, da of late Rudolph Glossop, and has issue.
Residence – Bow Cottage, West Hoathly, West Sussex RH19 4QF.

SON LIVING

ANDREW EDWARD WILLES, *b* 20 Nov 1953.

DAUGHTERS LIVING

Cordelia Anne, *b* 1955. —— Miranda Jane, *b* 1967. —— Jessica Susan, *b* 1971.

BROTHERS LIVING

Michael Willes, *b* 1929: *m* 1954, Janet Leonora, da of W. A. Messenger, of Forest Down, Pyrford, Woking, and has issue living, Sebastian William, *b* 1958, — Anne-Marie, *b* 1966. *Residence* – Leonora Cottage, Mithian, St Agnes, Cornwall. —— John Henry Willes (38 Riddlesdown Avenue, Purley, Surrey CR8 1JJ), *b* 1932; late Lt RA: *m* 1968, Diana Mary, da of G. D. B. Dear, of Coulsdon, Surrey, and has issue living, Antonia Mary Willes, *b* 1970, — Louise Elizabeth Willes, *b* 1973.

COLLATERAL BRANCH LIVING

Issue of late Robert Michael Willes Chitty, 2nd son of 1st baronet, *b* 1893, *d* 1970: *m* 1922, Norah A., da of W. Cooke, of Toronto:—
Thomas Michael Willes Chitty, *b* 1930: *m* 1952, Edith Jeremy Weir, of Toronto, and has issue living, Robert Arthur, *b* 1953, — Diana, *b* 1956, — Susan Elizabeth *b* 1957. —— Norah Elizabeth, *b* 1926: *m* 1958, Ross Alexander Wilson and has issue living, Lesley, *b* 1959.

The 1st baronet, Sir Thomas Willes Chitty, KC (son of Thomas Edward Chitty), was a Master of Supreme Court 1901-20, and Senior Master of Supreme Court and King's Remembrancer 1920-26. The 2nd baronet, Sir (Thomas) Henry Willes Chitty, wsa a Bar-at-law of Inner Temple.

CHOLMELEY (UK) 1806, of Easton, Lincolnshire
(Name pronounced "Chumly")

Sir (HUGH JOHN) FREDERICK (SEBASTIAN) CHOLMELEY, 7th *Baronet; b* 3 Jan 1968; *s* his father, *Sir* MONTAGUE JOHN 1998; *ed* Eton, and RAC; ARICS: *m* 1993, Ursula Ann, eldest da of Sir Hugh Peter Derwyn Bennett, QC, of Highbrook, Ardingly, Sussex, and has issue.

𝔄rms – Gules, two helmets in chief proper, and a garb in base or; a mullet for difference ℭrest – A garb or.
Seat - Easton Hall, Grantham. *Residence* - The Dower House, Easton, Grantham, Lincs NG33 5AP.

SON LIVING

MONTAGUE HUGH PETER, *b* 19 May 1997.

SISTERS LIVING

Camilla, *b* 1962: *m* 1982, William Murdoch, eldest son of Andrew Murdoch, of Parsonage Farm, Hurstbourne Tarrant, Andover, Hants, and has issue living, Andrew William, *b* 1991, — John Oliver, *b* 1994. —— Davina, *b* 1964: *m* 1985, Nicholas Morgan, and has issue living, Peter, *b* 1986, — James, *b* 1990.

WIDOW LIVING OF SIXTH BARONET

JULIET AURIOL SALLY (*Sal, Lady Cholmeley*), yst da of Maj-Gen Sir (Eustace) John Blois Nelson, KCVO, CB, DSO, MC (*see* D Grafton), and sister of Baroness Arlington: *m* 1960, Sir Montague John Cholmeley, 6th Bt, who *d* 1998. *Residence* - Church Farm, Burton le Coggles, Grantham, Lincs.

This family is a younger branch of the noble house of Cholmondeley. Henry Cholmeley, of Burton Coggles, settled in Lincolnshire in the 16th century, and from him the present baronet is descended in a direct line. The 1st baronet was MP for Grantham 1820-26, and the 2nd baronet sat for many years successively as MP for Grantham and Lincolnshire North (L). The 4th baronet, Capt Sir Montague Aubrey Rowley Cholmeley, Grenadier Guards, was *ka* Dec 1914.

CHRISTISON (UK) 1871, of Moray Place, Edinburgh (Extinct 1993)

Sir (ALEXANDER FRANK) PHILIP CHRISTISON, GBE, CB, DSO, MC, 4th and last *Baronet,* who *d* 21 Dec 1993, aged 100.

DAUGHTERS LIVING OF FOURTH BARONET (*By 1st marriage*)

Alison Ann, *b* 1924; formerly Junior Com WAC (India): *m* 1945, Capt Denis Clode James, Roy Indian Army Ser Corps, of 83 Branksome Gdns, City Beach, Perth, W Aust, and has issue living, Michael Christison, *b* 1947: *m* 19—, Nancy Connors, of Colorado, USA, and has issue living, Michael Christison, *b* 19—, Alison Ann *b* 19—, Clare *b* 19—, — Philip Christison, *b* 1949: *m* 19—, Marilyn Runciman, and has issue living, Rachel *b* 19—, Catherine Heather *b* 19—, — Jane Alison, *b* 1946: *m* 19—, David Morrell, and has issue living, Rupert *b* 19—, Sebastian *b* 19—, Caroline *b* 19—, — Kandy Ann, *b* 1953: *m* 1974, Barnard Clarkson, and has issue living, Thomas James Drummond *b* 1978, James Drummond *b* 1981. — Fiona CHRISTISON, *b* 1932: *m* 1954 (*m diss* 1977), Peter Thomson McLintock (*see* McLintock, Bt).

CLARK (UK) 1883, of Cavendish Square, co Middlesex (Extinct 1979)

Sir ANDREW EDMUND JAMES CLARK, MBE, MC, QC, 3rd and last *Baronet*.

DAUGHTERS LIVING OF THIRD BARONET (*By 2nd marriage*)

Jennifer Jane, *b* 1934; Bar Inner Temple 1955: *m* 1956, John Bertrand Worsley, of Furlong House, Hurstpierpoint, Sussex BN6 9QA (*see* B Napier of Magdala, colls, 1980 Edn), and has issue living, James Jonathan, *b* 1957: *m* 1987, Marion Coratte, and has issue living, Arthur Richard Jacques *b* 1988, Edward Andrew Stanimir *b* 1989, Eleanor Morgan *b* 1994, — Harriet Laura, *b* 1960: *m* 1986, Mark Thornycroft Vernon, and has issue (*see* Vernon, Bt, colls), — Alison Margaret, *b* 1963: *m* 1st, 1992 (*m diss* 1997), Christian Holstein; 2ndly, 1997, Alistair McIntosh, and has had issue (by 1st *m*), Jacob Sebastian *b* 1993, *d* 1998, (by 2nd *m*) Mabel Jane *b* 1999, — Victoria Mary, *b* 1966: *m* 1996, Kevin Smith. — Susan Mary, *b* 1936; Bar Inner Temple 1957: *m* 1958, Ian Malcolm Maxwell Scott, who *d* 1993, and has issue (*see* Constable-Maxwell-Scott, Bt, *cr* 1642).

CLARK (UK) 1886, of Melville Crescent, Edinburgh

In God I trust

Sir FRANCIS DRAKE CLARK, 5th *Baronet*; *b* 16 July 1924; *s* his brother, *Sir* JOHN DOUGLAS, 1991; *ed* Edinburgh Academy; served 1939-45 War with RN: *m* 1958, Mary, who *d* 1994, yr da of late John Alban Andrews, MC, FRCS, and has issue.

𝕬rms – Azure, a fesse or between a castle triple towered argent masoned sable in chief, and a crescent of the second in base. 𝕮rest – A demi-lion rampant azure, holding in his dexter paw a battleaxe proper.
Residence – Woodend Cottages, Burgh-next-Aylsham, Norfolk NR11 6TS.

SON LIVING

EDWARD DRAKE, *b* 27 April 1966; *ed* Westminster, and St Andrews Univ.

SISTER LIVING

Laura Moubray, *b* 1916: *m* 1940, Maj Hugh Mackinlay Renwick, RAC (ret), who *d* 1991, of Greenacres, 49 Gogarbank, Edinburgh 12, and has issue living, William Norman Hugh, *b* 1950; *ed* Melville Coll, Edinburgh: *m* 1970 (*m diss* 1982), Patricia Jamieson, and has issue living, George Martin *b* 1970, Paul William *b* 1974, — Diana Elizabeth, *b* 1942: *m* 1st, 1967 (*m diss* 1972), Allan Miller Duthie; 2ndly, 1972, David Richardson, of Carlesgill, Langholm, Dumfriesshire, and has issue living (by 2nd *m*), Susan Carolyn, *b* 1975, — Cynthia Caroline, *b* 1947.

WIDOW LIVING OF FOURTH BARONET

ANNE (*Dowager Lady Clark*), da of late Angus Gordon, of Beauly, Inverness-shire, and widow of William Swan, of Edinburgh: *m* 1969, Sir John Douglas Clark, 4th Bt, who *d* 1991. *Residence* – 52 Ormidale Terrace, Edinburgh 12.

COLLATERAL BRANCHES LIVING

Issue of late Brig Henry James Douglas Clark, MC, 2nd son of 2nd Bt, *b* 1888, *d* 1978: *m* 1915, Isobel, who *d* 1969, da of Lt-Col Wentworth Forbes, of Glcbc House, Brackley:—
Wentworth Douglas (Jesus Hospital, High St, Bray, Bucks), *b* 1916; Lt-Col Argyll and Sutherland Highlanders (ret); 1939-45 War (wounded): *m* 1st, 1948, Florence Mary, who *d* 1987, da of late Duncan Richard Ricketts, and formerly wife of Alexander Addis Leslie; 2ndly, 19—, Margaret Baker, and has issue living (by 1st *m*), (Wentworth Mary) Carolyn, *b* 1949· *m* 1st, 1973 (*m diss*), Gp/Capt Peter Butt, RAF; 2ndly, 1992, Richard Northcote, and has issue living (by 1st *m*), Susannah Jane *b* 1974, Annabel Laura Mary *b* 1988.

Issue of late John Maurice Clark, MBE, yst son of 2nd baronet, *b* 1903, *d* 1995: *m* 1933, Winnie Stratton, who *d* 1996, da of late Dr Campbell Highet:—
†Ian Campbell Clark, *b* 1937; Lieut RM; served Cyprus, Aden, Borneo and Sarawak: *m* 1962, Melita (who *m* 2ndly, 1971 (*m diss* 1979), Anthony Hurst), only da of late Ivor G. Powell, of Woking, Surrey, and was *ka* Sarawak 1966 (despatches posthumously) leaving issue, Timothy Ian Hugh, *b* (*posthumous*) 1966. —— Hugh Lothian, *b* 1939; Lt-Col (sometime comdg) Argyll and Sutherland Highlanders (ret): *m* 1967, Deborah Mary Ann, da of Col William Innes Moberly, CBE, and has issue living, Hugo Ian Moberly, *b* 1970; Capt Argyll and Sutherland Highlanders, — Harry James Lothian, *b* 1972; Capt Argyll and Sutherland Highlanders, — Benedict John Innes, *b* 1975, — Luke Edward Campbell, *b* 1979. —— Hamish Douglas, *b* 1945; Maj Argyll and Sutherland Highlanders (ret); despatches Aden 1967: *m* 1969, Wendy Ann Macdonald, only da of Ian M. Harper, of Redlairdston, Buchlyvie, Stirlingshire, and has issue living, Ian Nicholas Harper, *b* 1971, — Mark James Macdonald, *b* 1974.

Grandchildren of late Lt-Col Thomas George Clark, TD, 2nd son of 1st baronet:—
Issue of late Capt Thomas George Clark, *b* 1895, *d* 1986: *m* 1921, Mary Hall, who *d* 1987, da of late Thomas Aldcorn, of Johannesburg, S Africa:—
Thomas George Ramsay Davidson (Tyneford House, Ford, Midlothian), *b* 1922; a Chartered Accountant, and former Dir T & T Clark, publishers; 1939-45 War with RAF: *m* 1956, Sheila Campbell, da of Herbert Campbell Brown, of Littleacre, Strathkinnes Rd, St Andrews, Fife, and has issue living, Thomas George Nigel, *b* 1965, — Karen Ramsay, *b* (twin) 1959: *m* 1985, Christopher John Heaton-Armstrong, eldest son of Capt Thomas Michael Robert Heaton-Armstrong, of Couligarton, Aberfoyle, Perth, and has issue living, Gabrielle Louise *b* 1991, — Gillian Davidson, *b* 1962. —— Wendy Margaret, *b* 1935: *m* 1968, George Gordon Brown, Maj (ret) 9/12th R Lancers; Barrister, of Kingshot, Edward Rd, St Cross, Winchester, Hants, and has issue living, Richard Gordon, *b* 1973, — Melanie Ann, *b* 1969.

Sir Thomas Clark, 1st baronet (many years senior partner in the publishing firm of T and T Clark of Edinburgh), was Lord Provost of Edinburgh 1885-8. Sir John Maurice Clark, 2nd Bt, MBE, VD, DL (sometime senior partner in the publishing firm of T and T Clark), was Chm Scottish Life Assurance Co (Limited), and Col (sometime Comdg) 7th Batn, Roy Scots. Sir Thomas Clark, 3rd Bt, DL, was sometime snr ptnr in publishing firm T. & T. Clark, Hon Col The Forth Heavy Regt, RA, and Chm TAAVA Scotland 1955-65.

CLARK (UK) 1917, of Dunlambert, City of Belfast

FREE·FOR·A·BLAST

Sir JONATHAN DOUGLAS CLARK, 5th *Baronet*; *b* 9 Oct 1947; *s* his father, *Maj Sir* COLIN DOUGLAS, MC, 1995; *ed* Eton; late Capt Royal Green Jackets: *m* 1971, Susan Joy, da of Brig Thomas Ian Gordon Gray, and has issue.

Arms – Barry wavy of four argent and azure, a galley with sail set and flags flying all or, on a chief of the second a thistle slipped with two leaves, between two roses of the third. Crest – A demi huntsman proper, vested azure, blowing a horn or. *Residence* – Somerset House, Threapwood, Malpas, Cheshire SY14 7AW.

SON LIVING

GEORGE SIMON GRAY, *b* 3 Oct 1975; *ed* Shrewsbury.

DAUGHTERS LIVING

Polly Caroline, *b* 1973. —— Tessa Louise, *b* 1978.

SISTERS LIVING

Sarah Louise, *b* 1949: *m* 1975, Michael Alan de Cheveley Kohler, of 16a Marlborough Rd, Richmond, Surrey, TW10 6JR, and has issue living, Rosalie de Cheveley, *b* 1979, — Mirabel Margaret Macadam, *b* 1982, — Katharine Isobel Lesoipa, *b* 1985. —— Gillian Margaret Ann, *b* 1957: *m* 1987, Roger Dixon Spain, of The Old Hall, Whitecross Lane, Tilney All Saints, King's Lynn, Norfolk PE34 4SR.

UNCLE LIVING (*son of 2nd baronet*)

Peter Aubrey, *b* 1927; *ed* Campbell Coll, Belfast: *m* 1951, Rosemary Frazer, da of T. Frazer Mackie, of Guincho, Helen's Bay, co Down, and has issue living, Richard Henry Frazer (4 Beechfield Drive, Bangor, co Down BT19 7ZW), *b* 1952: *m* 1977, Hazel Yvonne Elizabeth, da of Edmund Irvine Smith, of Ellenvine, Craigavad, co Down, and has issue living, Linda Helen *b* 1978, Fiona Elizabeth *b* 1980, — Michael Peter George (Grendon, Sinclair St, Helensburgh, Dunbartonshire G84 9AT), *b* 1955: *m* 1976, Sandra Muriel Jane Foster, da of Martin Reid-Foster, of Flagpoint, Campbell St, Helensburgh, and has issue living, Paul Michael Frazer *b* 1978, Jamie Stewart *b* 1979, Garry Martin *b* 1982, Katie Jane *b* 1984. *Residence* – Cillenamara, Ringhaddy, Killinchy, co Down.

DAUGHTER LIVING OF THIRD BARONET

Elizabeth Frances Catherine, *b* 1960: *m* 1981, Nicholas James Reid, late Royal Green Jackets, and has issue living, Henry George Donald, *b* 1984, — Georgina Charlotte Elizabeth, *b* 1987. *Residence* – Overbury Hall, Layham, Hadleigh, Suffolk IP7 5RP.

WIDOW LIVING OF THIRD BARONET

NANCY CATHERINE (*Dowager Lady Clark*), da of George Wallis Newport Clark, of Upperlands, co Londonderry: *m* 1949, Sir George Anthony Clark, 3rd Bt, who *d* 1991. *Residence* – Tullykilty, Ballygowan, co Down.

WIDOW LIVING OF FOURTH BARONET

MARGARET COLEMAN (*Margaret, Lady Clark*), yst da of late Maj-Gen Sir Charlton Watson Spinks, KBE, DSO, and widow of Maj Guy William Going Threlfall, MC, 8th Hussars: *m* 2ndly, 1946, Maj Sir Colin Douglas Clark, 4th Bt, MC, who *d* 1995. *Residence* – Flaxpool House, Crowcombe, Taunton, Som TA4 4AW.

The 1st baronet, Sir George Smith Clark (son of James Clark, of Paisley), was MP for N Div of Belfast (C) 1907-10, and a Member of Senate of N Ireland 1925-34. The 2nd baronet, Sir George Ernest Clark, was High Sheriff of co Antrim 1940, and of co Down 1941. The 3rd baronet, Sir George Anthony Clark, was High Sheriff of co Antrim 1954, a Senator N Ireland 1951-69, a DL Belfast, Grand Master of Grand Orange Lodge of Ireland 1957-68, and Imperial Grand Master of Imperial Grand Orange Council of the World 1961-63; MP for Dock Div of Belfast (U) in Parliament of N Ireland 1938-45.

STEWART-CLARK (UK) 1918, of Dundas, West Lothian

Sir JOHN (JACK) STEWART-CLARK, 3rd *Baronet*; *b* 17 Sept 1929; *s* his father, *Sir* STEWART, 1971; *ed* Eton, and Balliol Coll, Oxford; AMP Harvard Business Sch; late Lt Coldm Gds; Member of Queen's Body Guard for Scotland (Roy Co of Archers); Man Dir of J & P Coats, Pakistan, Ltd 1961-67, of J A Carp's Garenfabrieken, Helmond, Holland, 1967-70, and Philips Electrical, Ltd, London 1971-75, and Pye of Cambridge, Ltd 1974-79; elected rep to European Parliament for E Sussex 1979-94, and for E Sussex and Kent South 1994-99; Vice-Pres European Parliament 1991-97: *m* 1958, Lydia Frederika, da of Jonkheer James William Loudon, of Valkenswaard, Netherlands, and has issue.

Arms – Sable, a fesse chequy argent and azure, between a crescent or in chief, a boar's head couped of the last, armed and langued of the third in base, a bordure ermine for difference. **Crest** – An anchor cabled gules.
Residence – Dundas Castle, South Queensferry, Edinburgh EH30 9SP. *Club* – White's.

SON LIVING

ALEXANDER DUDLEY (28 Fairfield St, SW18 1DW), *b* 21 Nov 1960; *ed* Worth Abbey.

DAUGHTERS LIVING

Daphne Beatrix Felicia, *b* 1959: *m* 1997, Nicholas Stephenson, el son of Michael Stephenson, of Shrewsbury, Shropshire, and has issue living, Chiara *b* 1986. —— Nadia Marie Anne, *b* 1963: *m* 1990, Patrick J. Waterfield, yr son of Jolyon Waterfield, of Edge Grove, Aldenham, Herts, and has issue living, Natasha Sophie, *b* 1993, —— Elena Grace, *b* (twin) 1993, —— Emily Rose, *b* 1998. —— Zarina Gabrielle, *b* 1965. —— Natalie Frederika Louise, *b* 1969.

SISTER LIVING

(Sara) Norina Marie, *b* 1932: *m* 1961, Col Patrick Thomas Salvin Bowlby, TD, of Caythorpe Hall, Caythorpe, Grantham, Lincs, and has issue living, Anthony Adrian Francis Salvin, *b* 1962: *m* 1988, Camilla Victoria, only da of James Cookson, of Sticklepark, Yarlington, Wincanton, Som, and has issue living, James *b* 1993, Archie *b* 1995, —— Michael Stewart Salvin, *b* 1964: *m* 1987, Amanda Jane Harvey, and has issue living, Thomas Edward Salvin *b* 1988, —— Jack William Salvin, *b* 1996, —— Karina Jane Maria Minette Salvin, *b* 1968.

The 1st baronet, Sir John, was a Director of Clark and Co (Limited), and assumed the additional surname of Stewart 1909.

CLARKE (UK) 1831, of Dunham Lodge, Norfolk

Sir (CHARLES MANSFIELD) TOBIAS CLARKE, 6th *Baronet; b* 8 Sept 1939; *s* his father, *Sir* HUMPHREY ORME, 1973; adopted the additional christian name of Tobias 1962; *ed* Eton, Ch Ch Oxford (MA), Sorbonne, and NY Univ, Graduate Business Sch; Vice-Pres London Branch of Bankers Trust Co, New York; Member Exec Cttee The Pilgrims since 1998: *m* 1st, 1971 (*m diss* 1979), Charlotte, elder da of late Roderick Walter, of 12 Stanford Court, Cornwall Gdns, SW7; 2ndly, 1984, Teresa Lorraine Aphrodite, elder da of late Somerset Struben de Chair, of St Osyth's Priory, St Osyth, Essex, and has issue by 2nd *m*.

Arms – Ermine, on a bend cotised gules, three swans argent between three annulets sable. Crest – A mount vert, thereon a lark wings elevated or, in the beak an ear of wheat proper, the dexter claw resting on an annulet as in the arms.
Residences – 80 Campden Hill Rd, W8 7AA; The Church House, Bibury, Glos.
Clubs – Boodle's, Pratt's, Jockey (Paris), The Brook (New York), Racquet and Tennis (New York), Pilgrims.

SON LIVING (*By 2nd marriage*)

(CHARLES) LAWRENCE SOMERSET, *b* 12 March 1990.

DAUGHTERS LIVING (*By 2nd marriage*)

Theodora Roosevelt, *b* 1985. —— Augusta Elfrida, *b* 1987.

UNCLE LIVING (*Son of 4th baronet*)

Charles Frederick Orme, *b* (twin) 1909; *ed* Eton, and Ch Ch, Oxford: *m* 1942, Sylvia Vera, da of late Leo Kaelin, of Einsiedeln, Switzerland, and has issue living, William Oliver (13 Pembridge Gdns, W2 4EA), *b* 1943; *ed* Gordonstoun, and Trin Coll, Dublin: *m* 1981, Elizabeth, da of John Ivimy, and has issue living, Frederick William Michael *b* 1982, Percival John Theodore *b* 1983, Maximilian Tobias Ivimy *b* 1986, — Katharine Sybil CLARKE (Mühletobelstrasse 24, 9400 Rorschach, Switzerland), *b* 1950; resumed her maiden name: *m* 1981 (*m* annulled 1991), Michael Pearl. *Residence* – Weltpoststrasse 18/032, 3015 Bern, Switzerland.

COLLATERAL BRANCHES LIVING

Issue of late Orme Roosevelt Clarke, yr son of 5th baronet, *b* 1947, *d* 1992: *m* 1st, 1971 (*m diss* 1989), Joanna Valentine, da of late John Barkley Schuster, TD (*see* B Wyfold); 2ndly, 1991, Christine V. (41 Kensington Place, W8), da of J. G. O'Flaherty, of Melbourne, Australia:—
(By 1st *m*) Nicholas Orme, *b* 1976. —— (By 2nd *m*) Alexander, *b* 1992.

Grandsons of late William Peter Dunham Clarke, OBE, el son of late William Alexander Clarke (infra):—
Issue of late Peter Ethelston Clarke, *b* 1916, *d* 1975: *m* 1940, Isabel Helen, da of Philip Elton Longmore, CBE:—
Peter Alexander, *b* 1941; *ed* Eton, and Trin Coll, Camb: *m* 1967, Lilah Victoria Mary, da of John Forrester, of Ardnacross, Isle of Mull, and has issue living, Paul Sebastian, *b* 1971, — Timothy Forrester, *b* 1975. — Robert Theodore, *b* 1983. —— John Elton, *b* 1948; *ed* Eton, and Kent Univ: *m* 1979, Caroline Anne Bannatyne, da of Edward Michael Courage, and has issue living, Edward Peter, *b* 1985, — Helena Margaret, *b* 1981.

Grandchildren of late William Alexander Clarke (3rd son of 2nd baronet):—
Issue of late Paul Humphrey Clarke, MC, *b* 1891, *d* 1946: *m* 1927, Joyce Chicheley, who *d* 1934, da of late Richard Chicheley Plowden:—
Humphrey (124 Off Lane, Gladstone, Queensland 4680, Australia), *b* 1929. —— Barbara (10/16 Telopea St, Telopea Gdns, Labrador, Queensland 4215, Australia), *b* 1928: *m* 1951 (*m diss* 1973), Anthony Lucien Noon Arlaud, and has issue living, Anthony Stephen (Beim Grünen Jäger 21, 20359 Hamburg, Germany), *b* 1953, — David Paul (120 Hankinson Rd, Charminster, Bournemouth, Dorset BH9 1HK), *b* 1955: *m* 1981, Hilary Dawn, da of John Goldsworthy Palmer, and has issue living, Jonathan Paul *b* 1996, Kimberly Rose *b* 1992, — Christopher John (Møllehavevej 12, Ramløse, 3200 Helsing, Denmark), *b* 1961; *ed* Queensland Inst of Technology (BB Comn): *m* 1st, 1984 (*m diss* 1990) Mette Slej, da of Villy Bertlesen; 2ndly, 1996, Hannah Kristine Lind, and has issue living (by 2nd *m*), Maria Lind *b* 1996, Sara Lind *b* 1999.

Granddaughters of late Paul Humphrey Clarke, MC (ante):—
Issue of late Paul Ivor Clarke, *b* 1931, *d* 1977: *m* 1963, Angela Mary (Elgon, Tilsmore Rd, Heathfield, E Sussex), da of late Thomas George Cleaver:—
Fiona Mary, *b* 1964. —— Rosemary Ann, *b* 1965.

The 1st baronet, Sir Charles Mansfield Clarke, was Physician to Queen Adelaide. The 3rd baronet, Gen Sir Charles Mansfield Clarke, GCB, GCVO, served on Taptee River with 57th Regt 1858, in New Zealand Wars 1861 and 1863-6, in Zulu Campaign 1879 (despatches, medal with clasp, CB), and in Basutoland 1880-81 (medal with two clasps), and was Gov of Malta and in command of troops there 1903-7.

CLARKE (UK) 1882, of Rupertswood, Colony of Victoria

Seeking the sign in the wool

Sir RUPERT WILLIAM JOHN CLARKE, MBE, 3rd *Baronet*; *b* 5 Nov 1919; *s* his father, *Sir* RUPERT TURNER HAVELOCK, 1926; *ed* Eton, and Magdalen Coll, Oxford (MA), Hon Fellow Trinity Coll, Melbourne; FAIM; Maj Irish Guards, Consul-Gen for Monaco in Melbourne, Chm P & O Australia Ltd until 1992; Pres Royal Humane Soc of Australasia Inc; Member Board of Howard Florey Inst (Melbourne); ADC (later PA) to Com-in-Ch, Middle East 1942-43; N Africa 1942-43 (MBE), Italy 1943-45 (despatches); MBE (Mil) 1943, Chev Légion d'Honneur (France), Offr Order of Léopold (Belgium), Order of the Grimaldi (Monaco): *m* 1947, Kathleen Grant, da of Peter Grant Hay, of Toorak, Victoria, Aust, and has issue.

Arms – Or, two bars azure between four escallops, three in chief and one in base gules; two flaunches of the second. Crest – In front of a dexter arm embowed in armour, the hand in a gauntlet proper holding an arrow in bend sinister or, flighted argent, three escallops also or.
Residences – Richmond House, 56 Avoca St, S Yarra, Australia 3141; Bolinda Vale, Clarkefield, 3430 Victoria, Australia. *Clubs* – Cavalry and Guards', Lansdowne, Australian, Athenæum, Melbourne (Victoria), Union (Sydney), Queensland (Brisbane).

SONS LIVING

RUPERT GRANT ALEXANDER, *b* 12 Dec 1947; *ed* Melbourne Univ (LLB): *m* 1978, Susannah, da of Sir (Richard) Robert Law-Smith, and has issue living, Rupert Robert William, *b* 24 June 1981, — Samantha Kathleen, *b* 1980, — Joanna Georgina, *b* 1983. ——— Peter Robert Justin John, *b* 1955; *ed* Melbourne Univ (B Com): *m* 1983, Andrea, da of Joshua Pitt, and has issue living, William Peter Norman Grant, *b* 1986, — Alexandra Kathleen, *b* 1984.

DAUGHTER LIVING

Vanessa Margaret, *b* 1952: *m* 1975, Roden David Cutler, son of Sir Arthur Roden Cutler, VC, AK, KCMG, KCVO, KStJ, CBE, and has issue living, Jonathan Roden Rupert David, *b* 1981, — Richard William Grant Clarke, *b* 1983, — James Robert Oliver David, *b* 1986, — Christina Annabelle Kate, *b* 1988.

SISTER LIVING

Elizabeth Elsie Faith, *b* 1924: *m* 1952, Willoughby Alfred Lake, who *d* 1986, and has issue (*see* Lake, Bt). *Residence* – Ashleigh, Much Hadham, Herts.

COLLATERAL BRANCHES LIVING

Issue of late Hon William Lionel Russell Clarke, 3rd son of 1st baronet, *b* 1876, *d* 1954: *m* 1908, Florence Douglas, who *d* 1961, da of late Col Henry Douglas Mackenzie (Mackenzie, Bt, *cr* 1673, colls):—
(*Hon*) Michael Alastair, *b* 1915; *ed* Harrow, and New Coll, Oxford (BCL, MA); 1939-45 War as Lieut Australian Imperial Force; a MLC, Victoria: *m* 1948, Helen Rosalind, da of Essington Lewis, CH, and has issue living, Andrea Rosalind, *b* 1950, — Louise Merilyn, *b* 1953, — Rosemary Janet, *b* 1956. *Residence* – 82 Mathoura Rd, Toorak, Victoria, Australia. ——— Janet Marjorie Nina, *b* 1911: *m* 1941, Capt Henry Armstrong Hammond, 5th Light Horse, AIF, of Swift St, Murrumburrah, NSW, and has issue living, Russell Rupert, *b* 1945: *m* 1973, Cheryl Gay, da of W. R. Harvey.

Grandchildren of late Hon Sir Francis Grenville Clark (infra):—
Issue of late William Antony Francis Clarke, *b* 1908, *d* 1953: *m* 1939, Jessie Deakin, da of Herbert Robinson Brookes:—
Francis Brookes, *b* 1940: *m* 1st, 1969 (*m diss* 1976), Jacqueline, da of Graham Crossley; 2ndly, Vivica Spens, and has issue living, Antony Graham, *b* 1970. ——— William Severn, *b* 1945; BA, BSc, MBA. ——— Janet Deakin, *b* 1942; *ed* Melbourne Univ (Dip OT): *m* 1970, Robert Stirling Hogarth-Scott, of 6 Selbourne Rd, Toorak, Victoria, Aust, and has issue living. ——— Barbary Cotton, *b* 1950; *ed* Melbourne Univ (BA).

Issue of late Colin Grenville Clarke, *b* 1914, *d* 1962: *m* 1943, Elizabeth Lennox, da of Norman Lennox Speirs:—
Jason William, *b* 1952. ——— Sally Miranda, *b* 1949.

Issue of late Hon Sir Francis Grenville Clarke, KBE, 5th son of 1st baronet, *b* 1879, *d* 1955: *m* 1901, Nina Ellis, who *d* 1948, da of Thomas Cotton, banker, of Melbourne:—
Patricia Kathleen, *b* 1906: *m* 1939, Sqdn Ldr Raymond Vincent O'Byrne, who *d* 1973.

Grandchildren of late Lt-Col Reginald Hastings Clarke, 6th son of 1st baronet:—
Issue of late Reginald Clive Nevil Clarke, *b* 1910, *d* 1964: *m* 1935, Elizabeth Macpherson, who *d* 1965:—

Robin, *b* 1935: *m* 1958, Prunella, da of Wilfred Weigall, of Cobden, Vic, Australia, and has issue living, Anthony Clive, *b* 1963, — Sara Elizabeth, *b* 1965. —— Lucilla (Ernestine), *b* 1937.

This family was settled at Weston Zoyland, Somerset since the beginning of the 18th century. The Hon William John Turner Clarke, father of 1st baronet, settled in Australia in 1829. The 1st baronet, Hon Sir William John Clarke, was many years engaged in pastoral pursuits in Victoria and was a MLC there.

Clarke-Jervoise, see Jervoise.

CLAY (UK) 1841, of Fulwell Lodge, Middlesex

Per orbem

Throughout the world

Sir RICHARD HENRY CLAY, 7th *Baronet*, *b* 2 June 1940; *s* his father, *Sir* HENRY FELIX, 1985; *ed* Eton; *m* 1963, Alison Mary, only da of late Dr James Gordon Fife, of Summer Hill, Alde House Drive, Aldeburgh, Suffolk, and has issue.

𝕬rms – Argent, a chevron engrailed paly of eight sable and or between three trefoils of the second. Crest – Two wings argent each charged with a chevron engrailed between three trefoils slipped sable.
Residence – The Copse, Shiplate Rd, Bleadon, Som BS24 0NX.

SONS LIVING

CHARLES RICHARD, *b* 18 Dec 1965; *ed* Manor Sch, Cambridge, and Univ of E Anglia (BA). —— Thomas Henry, *b* 1967; *ed* Manor Sch, Cambridge. —— James Felix, *b* 1969; *ed* Manor Sch, Cambridge, and York Univ (BA).

DAUGHTERS LIVING

Virginia Rachel, *b* 1964: *m* 1988, Robin P. Taylor, of Elton Farm, Elton, Ludlow, Shropshire SY8 2HQ, yst son of late Richard Taylor, of Grange Farm, Bourn, Cambs, and has issue living, Richard James, *b* 1993, — Timothy Robin *b* 1998, — Megan Catherine, *b* 1992. —— Catherine Victoria, *b* 1971; *ed* Bath Univ (BA).

SISTERS LIVING

Jenny Elizabeth (31 The Terrace, Aldeburgh, Suffolk), *b* 1936: *m* 1959 (*m diss* 1975), Oswyn Murray, MA, only surv son of late (Malcolm) Patrick Murray, CB, and has issue living, James Augustus Henry, *b* 1961, — Octavia, *b* 1965. —— Sarah Richenda, *b* 1938: *m* 1979, Frederic Henry Wise, of 9 Market Cross Place, Aldeburgh, Suffolk.

COLLATERAL BRANCH LIVING

Issue of late Anthony George Hobhouse Clay, yr son of 5th baronet, *b* 1914; *d* 1997: *m* 1st, 1938 (*m diss* 1959), Elizabeth Alice, who *d* 1996, da of Sir Gilbert Charles Upcott, KCB; 2ndly, 1960, Patricia Barbara, who *d* 1967, da of late Archibald Foulcher, of West Wickham, Kent; 3rdly, 1971, Pamela Joan, da of late Edward Farley Oaten, of Walton-on-Thames:—
(By 1st *m*) Christopher George Anthony (6 Berkeley Rd, Bristol, 6), *b* 1940: *m* 1973, Diana, da of Edward Hippolyte Joseph Burbidge, and has issue living, Felix Temple, *b* 1974, — Francis Benjamin, *b* 1976, — Caroline Emily, *b* 1978. —— (By 2nd *m*) Timothy Paul, *b* 1961.

This family descends from the Clays of Crich, co Derby. George Clay, of Cambridge, who married Elizabeth, daughter of Felix Calvert, of Ferneaux Pelham, in 1670, was great-grandfather of George Clay, born 1757, who for upwards of half a century was extensively engaged in London as a merchant and shipowner, and his son, William, created a baronet, was MP for the Tower Hamlets 1832-57, Secretary of the Board of Control 1839-41, and author of numerous works on Joint Stock Banking, Banks of Issue, the Currency, etc.

CLAYTON (GB) 1732, of Marden Park, Surrey

QUID LEONE FORTIUS

What is braver than the lion

Sir DAVID ROBERT CLAYTON, 12th *Baronet*; *b* 12 Dec 1936; *s* his father, *Sir* ARTHUR HAROLD, DSC, 1985; *ed* HMS Conway, and Sir John Cass Coll, London; Capt MN; Dir Oceanic Liners (UK) Ltd since 1989: *m* 1971, Julia Louise, da of late Charles Henry Redfearn, and has issue.

𝕬rms – Argent, a cross sable between four pellets. 𝕮rest – A leopard's paw erased and erect argent, grasping a pellet. 𝕾econd 𝕸otto – Virtus in actione consistit (*Virtue consists in action*).
Residence – Rock House, Kingswear, Devon TQ6 0BX.

SONS LIVING

ROBERT PHILIP, *b* 8 July 1975. ―― John Richard, *b* 1978.

SISTER LIVING

Ann, *b* 1933. *m* 1st, 1951 (*m diss* 1977), Alfred Plews; 2ndly, 1978, John Hawksely Martin.

DAUGHTER LIVING OF EIGHTH BARONET

Cynthia Anne, *b* 1914; 1939-45 War as Section Officer WAAF: *m* 1949, as his second wife, Walter Gerald Cloete Graham, CBE, who *d* 1995, and has two adopted children, Alan Richard, *b* 1956, ―― Harriet Jane, *b* 1954: *m* 1986, Fulvio Richetto. *Residence* – Knabbs Farmhouse, Fletching, Uckfield, Sussex TN22 3SX.

WIDOW LIVING OF ELEVENTH BARONET

DIANA KATHERINE MARY (*Diana, Lady Clayton*), only child of late Capt Charles Alverey Grazebrook, 60th Rifles, and formerly wife of (i) Peter Neve, and (ii) ―― Bircham: *m* 1965, as his 4th wife, Sir Arthur Harold Clayton, 11th Bt, DSC, who *d* 1985. *Residence* – Colonsay, Kingswear, Devon.

COLLATERAL BRANCHES LIVING

Issue of late FitzRoy Richard Henry Clayton, yr son of 10th baronet, *b* 1907, *d* 1989: *m* 1st, 1930, Morwen, who *d* 1941, da of Judge Fedor Andrew Satow (V Chilston); 2ndly, 1944, Moira Consuelo, who *d* 1971, da of Philip Fidelis Ryan, of Ceylon; 3rdly, 1973, (Phyllis) Margaret (108A Alderney St, SW1V 4EZ), da of late Reginald James Tindal, of Wirral, Cheshire, and widow of Sydney James Pullan, of Lillington Manor, Leamington Spa:—
(By 1st *m*) Barry Drew Satow (Tyringham Gateway, Newport Pagnell, Bucks MK16 9EX), *b* 1935.

Grandchildren (by 2nd *m*) of late FitzRoy Richard Henry Clayton (ante):—
Issue of late Roderick John Clayton, *b* 1945, *d* 1980: *m* 1968, Diana Melissa (who *m* 2ndly, 1985, Rupert Uvedale Corbett) (24 Duke's Av, Chiswick, W4 2AE), yr da of late Sir (Horace) Alan Walker, of Eaton Place, SW1:—
Patrick Justin FitzRoy, *b* 1970. ―― Louisa Jane, *b* 1972: *m* 1997, Jean-Luc Deiches, son of Lucien Deiches, of Monte Carlo, and has issue living, Roddy James, *b* 1998.

Grandson of late Lieut-Col Sir FitzRoy Augustus Talbot Clayton, KCVO, son of late Rev Augustus Philip Clayton, 5th son of 4th baronet:—
Issue of late Capt Cecil Fraser Talbot Clayton, *b* 1880, *d* 1940: *m* 1st, 1909 (*m diss* 1918), Kathleen Agnes, who *d* 1969, da of late Lieut-Col William E. Bradish-Ellames, of Manor House, Little Marlow; 2ndly, 1918, Alice, who *d* 1957, da of late John T. Hatton, JP:—
(By 2nd *m*) †Gilbert Talbot Hatton, *b* 1920; European War 1943-5 in RAF Vol Reserve; *d* 1999.

Grandsons of Col Emilius Clayton (*b* 1841), eldest son of Capt Emilius Clayton (*b* 1803), eldest son of Lt-Col George Clayton, 2nd son (by 2nd *m*) of William Clayton, 2nd son of 1st baronet:—
Issue of late Lt-Col Emilius Clayton, OBE, *b* 1884, *d* 1967: *m* 1915, Irene Dorothy Constance, who *d* 1971, da of late Col T. E. Strong, Indian Army:—
†Michael Thomas Emilius, CB, OBE, *b* 1917; attached Min of Defence 1939-1977; OBE (Civil) 1958, CB (Civil) 1976: *m* 1942, Mary Margery, who *d* 1994, el da of late Dr J. Roberts Pate, of Oxford, and *d* 1995, leaving issue, Amanda Rosemary, *b* 1949; *ed* Reading Univ (BA, PhD): *m* 1976, Peter Hobson, MA, of The Headmaster's House, Charterhouse, Godalming, Surrey GU7 2DE. ―― Anthony Hugh Le Quesne, TD (April Cottage, 43 Ford Lane, Lower Bourne, Farnham, Surrey GU10 4SF), *b* 1928; MA and PhD, St Andrews Univ; FSA, Scot; Chevalier dans l'Ordre des Palmes Académiques 1908; Lt Col Intelligence Corps (TAVR); Kenya Civil Ser 1952-65, since when Sen Lect, RMA, Sandhurst: *m* 1973, Judith Mary, da of P. L. Blackstone, of Rhu, Dunbarton, and has issue living, Robert Anthony Emilius, *b* 1976; *ed* Edinburgh Univ (BSc), ―― Penelope Fleur, *b* 1977; *ed* Nottingham Univ (BSc).

Grandchildren of late Lieut-Col Henry Edward Gilbert Clayton (infra):—
Issue of late Henry Hubert Clayton, *b* 1906, *d* 1989: *m* 1944, Isobel May, who *d* 1990, da of W. G. Winters, of Pembroke, Ontario, Canada:—

William Edward (14007-23A Av, Surrey, BC V4A 9V3, Canada), *b* 1945: *m* 1967, Sharon Joan, da of Kenneth Campbell, of Edmonton, Alberta, and has issue living, Stacey Anne, *b* 1972, — Susan Amanda, *b* 1975. —— Florence Nancy Thackray, *b* 1947: *m* 1971 (*m diss* 1997), Erik van Veenen, and has issue living, Hendrick Hubert Clayton, *b* 1982, — Vanessa *b* 1977, — Erica Maegan, *b* 1979.

Granddaughter of late Major Sir Edward Gilbert Clayton, CB, el son of late Maj-Gen Henry Clayton, 2nd son of Lt-Col George Clayton (ante):—
Issue of late Lieut-Col Henry Edward Gilbert Clayton, *b* 1867, *d* 1947: *m* 1900, Huberta, da of Capt Hubert Grenfell, RN, formerly of Alverstoke, Hants:—
Grace Cynthia Maude (Headquarters Rd, RR4, Courtenay, BC V9N 7J3, Canada), *b* 1909: *m* 1934, Philip Hennell Amsden, formerly RN, who *d* 1992, and has issue living, Michael Phillip, *b* 1935: *m* 1958, Lorna Ryder, and has issue living, Brian *b* 1964: *m* 1993, Sharon Johnson (and has issue living, Natasha Elizabeth *b* 1994, Rachel *b* 1997), Lisa Maria *b* 1959: *m* 1989, Robert Mallony (and has issue living, Erin *b* 1990, Connor Michael *b* 1992, Stephen Padrack *b* 1995), Sheryl Louise *b* 1961: *m* 1985, John McCall (and has issue living, Kyle Alexander *b* 1988, Thomas Michael *b* 1990), Susan Maureen *b* 1962, Julia Jane *b* 1968: *m* 1992, Gino Celebre (and has issue living, Jordan Robert *b* 1993), — Harry Linton, *b* 1938: *m* 1965, Josephine Venebles, and has issue living, Sarah *b* 1974, — Stephen Oliver, *b* 1944: *m* 1968, Janet Ives, and has issue living, Jessica Ann *b* 1975, Jacquline Cynthia *b* 1978, — Robin Petite, *b* 1941: *m* 1966 (*m diss* 1972), Allen Cripps, and has issue living, Cynthia *b* 1968.

Sir William Clayton, MP, the 1st baronet (*cr* 1732), was a nephew of Sir Robert Clayton, Knight, Lord Mayor of London 1679. The 2nd, 3rd and 4th baronets were also Members of Parliament, and the 5th baronet, Gen Sir William Robert, KCB, a distinguished Waterloo officer, sat as MP for Great Marlow (*L*) 1831-42. The 6th Baronet was High Sheriff for co Bucks 1876, and at his death the title devolved upon his kinsman Sir Gilbert Augustus Clayton-East, 3rd Baronet of Hall Place, whose immediate ancestor was William East, of Hall Place, Berks, created a baronet in 1766, which title became extinct 1828. His nephew, the 1st baronet of the 2nd creation (1838), of Hall Place, Sir East George Clayton-East, was 2nd son of Sir William Clayton, 4th baronet (*cr* 1838), and nephew of Sir Gilbert East, the last baronet of the 1st creation. The 2nd baronet took the surnames of Gilbert-East and the arms of East for his life only by Roy licence 1839. The 7th baronet, Sir Gilbert Augustus Clayton-East, *s* his father 1866 in the Baronetcy *cr* 1838 as 3rd Bt, and his kinsman, Sir William Robert Clayton 1914 in the Baronetcy *cr* 1732 as 7th Bt, having resumed in 1870 the name and arms of Clayton-East in lieu of Gilbert-East. Sir Robert Alan Clayton-East-Clayton, 9th Bt of Marden and 5th Bt of Hall Place, assumed by deed poll 1932 the surnames of Clayton-East-Clayton in lieu of Clayton-East, and *d* Sept 1932, when the Baronetcy of Hall Place became ext, and the baronetcy of Marden Park devolved on his kinsman, Sir Harold Philip Dudley Clayton, 10th Bt.

CLERK (NS) 1679, of Penicuik, Edinburgh
(Name pronounced "Clark")

Victory loves care

Sir JOHN DUTTON CLERK, CBE, VRD, 10th *Baronet*: *b* 30 Jan 1917; *s* his father, *Sir* GEORGE JAMES ROBERT, 1943; *ed* Stowe; Commodore RNR (ret); FRSE; a JP for Midlothian since 1955, Vice-Lieut 1965-72, Lord-Lieut 1972-92; Lieutenant Queen's Body Guard for Scotland (Royal Company of Archers); CBE (Mil) 1966: *m* 1944, Evelyn Elizabeth, da of late W. Robertson, and has issue.

Arms – Or, a fesse checky azure and argent between two crescents in chief gules, and a boar's head couped in base sable. Crest – A demi-huntsman winding a horn proper. Supporters – *Dexter*, a naked man wreathed about the middle with oak, in the dexter hand a bow, over his shoulder a quiver of arrows, and the skin of a wild beast hanging behind his back all proper; *sinister*, A druid priest with flowing beard proper, vested and hooded argent, holding in the sinister hand an oak-branch acorned vert.
Seat – Penicuik House, Penicuik, Midlothian EH26 9LA.

SONS LIVING

ROBERT MAXWELL, OBE (Penicuik House, Penicuik, Midlothian EH26 9LA), *b* 3 April 1945; *ed* Winchester, and London Univ (BSc Agric); OBE 1995; DL Midlothian 1995; FRICS; Member Queen's Body Guard for Scotland (Royal Company of Archers): *m* 1970, Felicity Faye, yr da of George Collins, of Grayshott House, Bampton, Oxford, and has issue living, George Napier, *b* 1975, — Edward James, *b* 1986, — Julia Elizabeth, *b* 1973. —— Piers Edward John (Newport House, Weston-under-Lizard, Shifnal, Shropshire TF11 8JT), *b* 1955; *ed* Winchester, and Aberdeen Univ (BLE); ARICS: *m* 1983, Lucy Ann, only da of Michael Hewens, of Crookham Manor, Thatcham, Berks, and has issue living, William James, *b* 1987, — Iona Mary, *b* 1985.

DAUGHTERS LIVING

Aymée Lavinia, *b* 1947: *m* 1969, George Robin Paget Ferguson (High Sheriff Bristol 1996), of 5 Windsor Terr, Clifton, Bristol, and has issue living, John Spencer Guy *b* 1974, — Alice Rose, *b* 1971: *m* 1997, Mark Collins, — Corinna May, *b* 1979. —— Honor Elizabeth, *b* 1957.

SISTER LIVING

Aymée Lavender, *b* 1907; radionic therapist: *m* 1928, Col Alan Vincent Gandar Dower, TD, DL, 2nd Dragoon Guards, who *d* 1980, and has issue living, Natalie Gay Stuart, *b* 1931. *Residence* – Swinbrook Cottage, Swinbrook, Oxon.

COLLATERAL BRANCHES LIVING

Granddaughters of late George Edward Clerk, MD, CM (*b* 1877), el son of late George Edward Clerk (*b* 1850) (infra):—
Issue of late Sydney Percy Clerk, *b* 1912, *d* 1953: *m* 1938, Thérèse Marie Céline, da of Louis St Laurent:—
Michelle Marie Madeleine (7491-22e Av, Montreal, Quebec, Canada H2A 2H7), *b* 1940: *m* 1st, 1959, André Bruneau; 2ndly, 1984, Jean-Claude Brunelle, and has issue living, (by 1st *m*) Sylvie, *b* 1960: *m* 1985, Sylvain Paradis (33 des Vétérans, Boucherville, Quebec, Canada J4B 2V3), and has had issue, Cédric *b* 1997, Annie *b* and *d* 1990, Chloé *b* 1993, Dominique *b* 1996. —— Hélène, *b* 1943: *m* 1970, Michel Plante, and has issue living, Isabelle, *b* 1971, — Martine, *b* 1973, — Julie, *b* 1977.

Issue of late Joseph Harry Clerk, *b* 1914, *d* 19—: *m* 1950, Alberta Therese, da of Armand Drouin:—
Irene Gail, *b* 1952.

Grandson of late George Edward Clerk, *b* 1850, el son of late George Edward Clerk (*b* 1815), 2nd son of 6th baronet:—
Issue of late Abel Clerk, *b* 1897, *d* 1964: *m* 1927, Cecile, da of R. Poisson:—
André Arthur (10430, Meunier St, Ahuntsic, Montreal, Canada), *b* 1929: *m* 1955, Claire, da of Armand Charbonneau, and has issue living, Georges (6694 rue Galarneau, Laval, Quebec, Canada H7L 4J2), *b* 1958: *m* 1988, Marie-Claude, da of Jean Lussier, and has issue living, François-Liam *b* 1995, Julie *b* 1992, — Benoit (1601 rue Louis-Alphonse-Venne, Montreal, Quebec, Canada H2C 3J7), *b* 1962; has issue living, Charlotte *b* 1997, — Bruno (857 av McEachran, Outremont, Quebec, Canada H2V 3C9), *b* 1964, — Micheline (700 rue Fleury W, Montreal, Quebec, Canada H3L 1W3), *b* 1956.

Grandchildren of late Edmund Antoine Clerk, 4th son of late George Edward Clerk (*b* 1815) (ante):—
Issue of late Walter Charles Clerk, *b* 1891, *d* 1937: *m* 1st, 1915, Jeanne Beauchamp, who *d* 1920; 2ndly, 1922, Gabrielle Beauchamp:—
(By 1st *m*) Françoise, *b* 1917: *m* 1943, Pierre R. Gendron, DSC, Sub-Lieut Roy Canadian Naval Vol Reserve, who *d* 1983. —— Marguerite, *b* 1919: *m* 1943, Jacques de Tonnancour. —— (By 2nd *m*) George *b* 1925: *m* 1950, Lucette C. Barbeau, and has issue living, Patrice, *b* 1964, — Philippe, *b* 1959, — Josée, *b* 1952, — Michelle, *b* 1953, — Danie, *b* 1957. *Residence* – . —— Robert, *b* 1926. —— Suzanne, *b* 1924.

Issue of late Henry Clerk, *b* 1896, *d* 19—: *m* 1918, Liliane Payette:—
Gérard, *b* 1919: Capt Canadian Army: *m* 1949, Lucille McCaughan, and has issue living, Joanne, *b* 1955. —— Jacques, *b* 1922; P/O RCAF: *m* 19—, Rejane Gauvin. —— Raymonde, *b* 1918: *m* 1940, Paul Fortin, and has issue living, Micheline, *b* 1941, — Monique, *b* 1943.

Grandchildren of late Alexander Marie Joseph Clerk (infra):—
Issue of late Edouard Clerk, *b* 1889, *d* 1982: *m* 1917, Fernande, who *d* 1969, da of late Dr Ernest Choquette, MCL, of Quebec:—
Michel (390 Chemin des Patriotes North, St Hilaire, Quebec, Canada J3H 3H6), *b* 1920; MCom 1943: *m* 1952, Monique Martineau, and has had issue, Philippe, *b* 1953, — Cyril, *b* 1954, — Emmanuel, *b* 1960, — Catherine, *b* 1957; *d* 1987, — Sophie, *b* 1964; *d* 1987. —— Marc (31 Fielding East Hill, PO Box 1158, Lac Brome, Quebec, Canada J0E 1V0), *b* 1923; writer: *m* 1949, Gabrielle, PhD (Emeritus Prof Montreal Univ), da of Raymond Brunet, OBE, of Hull, Quebec, and has issue living, David (250 Greene Av #6, St Lambert, Quebec, Canada J4P 1T2), *b* 1952: *m* 1982, Carmen Picard, — Nathalie, *b* 1950: *m* 1982, André Lamalice (RR#1, Chelsea, Quebec, Canada J0X 1N0), and has issue living, Maxime *b* 1983, Olivier *b* 1985, Julien *b* 1987. —— †Stephan, *b* 1926; QC: *m* 1954, Thérèse, da of Maurice Saint-Jacques, of St-Hyacinthe, Quebec, and *d* 1989, having had issue, Eric Fraser (1261 La Mancha Av, Coral Gables, Florida, USA), *b* 1955: *m* 1982, Ileana Balladares Diez, and has issue living, Christina *b* 1993, — †Nicolas Edouard, *b* 1957; *d* 1976, — Jean (209 Chemin des Patriotes South, St Hilaire, Quebec, Canada J3H 3H6), *b* (twin) 1957. —— Pierre (70 Grand St, New York, NY 10013, USA), *b* 1928; painter: *m* 1953, Adriana Bertolini, and has issue living, Jessica, *b* 1954.

Issue of late Paul Clerk, *b* 1890, *d* 1960: *m* 1927, Alice Gascon, who *d* 1947:—
†Paul, *b* 1930; *d* 1997: *m* 1975, Vivian Winsor. —— Françoise, *b* 1928: *m* 1952, Léon O. Des Lauriers, SBStJ, of 1105 rue Doguire, St Laurent, Quebec, Canada H4L 1M1, and has issue living, Francois, *b* 1959, — Nathalie, *b* 1962: *m* 1989, Alain Barrette, and has issue living, Nicolas *b* 1990, Amelie *b* 1993, —— Andrée (132 Blvd Deguire, St Laurent, Quebec, Canada H4N 1P4), *b* 1933: *m* 1955, René Beaucage, who *d* 1991, and has issue living, Michel, *b* 1956, — Dominique, *b* 1959, — Edith, *b* 1962.

Issue of late Maurice Clerk, *b* 1893, *d* 1926: *m* 1926, Marguerite Lajoie:—
Louise, *b* 1926: *m* 1948, Léopold Brégent.

Grandchildren of late George Edward Clerk (*b* 1815) (ante):—
Issue of late Alexander Marie Joseph Clerk, *b* 1861, *d* 1932: *m* 1888, Blanche Gelinas, who *d* 1942:—
Bernard, *b* 1902. —— Yvette, *b* 1912: *m* 1937, Jacques Trépanier, LLD, journalist, of 1000 rue Rockland, apt 918, Outremont, Quebec H2V 4P5, and has issue living, Francois, *b* 1938, — Maurice, *b* 1942, — Helene, *b* 1945, — Josette, *b* 1946, — Micheline, *b* 1947.

Issue of late Jean Pio Robert Clerk, *b* 1870, *d* 1932: *m* 1898, Marie Alma, da of late Hon Senator L. O. David:—
†Jacques Donald, *b* 1904: *m* 1927, Elizabeth Labrecque, who *d* 1987, and *d* 1967, leaving issue, †Robert, *b* 1929, *d* 1970, — Gilles, *b* 1931, — Jacques, *b* 1935, — Lise, *b* 1928, — Janine, *b* 1933. —— Louis Phillippe Duncan, *b* 1907: *m* 1936, Gabrielle, da of the Hon G. C. Simond, and has issue living, Henri, *b* 1941, — Michelle, *b* 1937. —— Jean Elton, *b* 1919. —— Jeanne Isabella, *b* 1899: *m* 19—, Theodore Fautoux, and has issue living, Pierre, *b* 1928, — Louise, *b* 1927. —— Camille Gertrude, *b* 1902.

Grandsons of late Major Edward Clerk, 7th son of 6th baronet:—
Issue of late William Henry Clerk, *b* 1867, *d* 1915: *m* 1906, Sarah Cecilia Reeves, who *d* 1954:—
Edward, *b* 1907: *m* 1940, Dora Appleby, and has issue living, Edward Peter, *b* 1941. —— William Robert, *b* (twin) 1907.

Grandchildren of late Arthur Stanley Clerk (infra):—
Issue of late Charles Beverley Clerk, *b* 1904, *d* 1983: *m* 1925, Angela Herbin, who *d* 1969:—
Alexander Simpson (109 Bonivista Av, New Minas, Nova Scotia, Canada B4N 3M2), *b* 1930: *m* 1953, Shirley Evangeline, da of Robert S. Cook, of Kentville, Nova Scotia, and has issue living, Charles Alexander (PO Box 206 Truro, Nova Scotia, Canada B2N 5C1), *b* 1954: *m* 1987, Friedel Moser, — Thomas Richard (802-2 St SW, High River, Alberta, Canada T1V 1A3), *b* 1956: *m* 1980, Kimberley Denhartog, and has issue living, Courtney Ruth *b* 1980, Kendra Ann *b* 1983, — Katharine Lois (1383 Princess Crescent, Coldbrook, Nova Scotia, Canada B43 1B2), *b* 1958: *m* 1980, Peter Charles Cooper, and has issue living, Christopher Allan *b* 1984, Jason Alexander *b* 1986, Elizabeth Katherine *b* 1988, — Susan Bernice (7A Byron Crescent, Dartmouth, Nova Scotia, Canada B2X 1L7), *b* 1961: *m* 1986, Mark Stuart Hersey, and has issue living, Justin Robert *b* 1986, Benjamin Stuart *b* 1988, Angela Faye *b* 1985, — Faye Marie (43 Greg Rd, Greenfield, Nova Scotia, Canada B2N 5BZ), *b* 1965: *m* 19—, Doug Hounsell. —— Mary Beverley (265 Nichols Rd, Kentville, Nova Scotia, Canada) *b* 1954, William Stevens, who *d* 1979, and has issue living, William Charles, *b* 1954, — Marylynne Margaret, *b* 1958: *m* 1980, Michael Carl Middelkoop, of Halifax, Nova Scotia, and has issue living, Adam Jason *b* 1986, Stephanie Anne *b* 1983.

Granddaughter of late Col Alexander Clerk, 8th son of 6th baronet:—
Issue of late Arthur Stanley Clerk, *b* 1864, *d* 1948: *m* 1897, Edith Maud, who *d* 1955, da of late C. E. Sheffield, of Nova Scotia:—
Dorothy Evangeline, *b* 1902: *m* 1926, Arthur Merlin, who *d* 1983, of 82 Broadway Av, Apt 1, Toronto, M4P 1T7, Ont, and has issue living, Marilyn, *b* 1928: *m* 1st, 19— (*m diss* 1967), Kenneth Arthur Wynne; 2ndly, 1967, Richard Arthur Kirby, of 244 Armour Blvd, N York, Ontario M3H 1N2, Canada, and has issue living, (by 1st *m*) Kenneth Arthur *b* 1955: *m* 1983, Barbara Anne Jame, Derrick Andrew *b* 1957: *m* 1988, Brenda Lee Crack.

The family is descended from John Clerk, distinguished for his loyalty and attachment to the party of Mary Stuart. His great-grandson, John was created a baronet by Charles II. The 2nd baronet was a Baron of the Exchequer of Scotland 1707-55. The 6th baronet, a Privy Councillor, was MP for Edinburghshire (C) 1818-32 and 1835-7, for Stamford 1838-47, and for Dover 1847-52, and during his political career, held office in several administrations. Sir George Douglas, 8th Bt, was Lieut-Col in the Army, and a Commr of Supply for cos Midlothian and Peebles.

CLERKE (E) 1660, of Hitcham, Buckinghamshire
(Name pronounced "Clark")

Sir JOHN EDWARD LONGUEVILLE CLERKE, 12th *Baronet*, son of late Francis William Talbot Clerke, Lieut Coldstream Guards (*ka* 1916), el son of 11th baronet; *b* 29 Oct 1913; *s* his grandfather, *Sir* WILLIAM FRANCIS, 1930; *ed* Eton, and Magdalene Coll, Camb (BA 1934); is Capt Reserve of Officers Roy Wilts Yeo (TA); FCA (1948) (ret): *m* 1948 (*m diss* 1986), Mary, da of late Lieut-Col Ivor Reginald Beviss Bond, OBE, MC, of Prosperity, Natal, S Africa, and has issue.

Arms – Argent, on a bend gules between three pellets as many swans of the field; on a sinister canton azure a demi-ram salient of the first, and in chief two fleurs-de-lis or, over all a baton trunked. **Crest** – A ram's head couped proper.
Residence – 48 Savernake Av, Melksham, Wilts SN12 7HD.

SON LIVING

FRANCIS LUDLOW LONGUEVILLE (12 Barmbeck Av, Newlands 7700, Cape, S Africa), *b* 25 Jan 1953; *ed* Diocesan Coll, Cape Town, Stellenbosch Univ (BA), and Witwatersrand Univ (LLB): *m* 1982, Vanessa Anne, only da of late Charles Cosman Citron, of 506 Fortuna Beach Rd, Mouille Point, Cape Town, S Africa, and has issue living, William Francis Talbot, *b* 1987, — Camilla Frances, *b* 1984.

DAUGHTERS LIVING

Albinia Jennifer, *b* 1949. —— Teresa Mary, *b* 1951: *m* 1982, Michael Cyprian Waller-Bridge, of 62 Creffield Rd, W3 9PS (*see* Grayson, Bt, 1980 Edn), and has issue living, Jasper Cyprian, *b* 1987, — Isobel Nocline, *b* 1984, — Phoebe Mary, *h* 1985.

COLLATERAL BRANCH LIVING

Grandchildren of late Francis William Talbot Clerke, elder son of 11th baronet:—
Issue of late G/Capt Rupert Francis Henry Clerke, DFC, RAF *b* 1916, *d* 1988: *m* 1st, 1945 (*m diss* 1972), Ann Jocelyn, da of late M. J. Tosswill; 2ndly, 1975, Pamela Emily, da of late F. H. Bayliss:—
(By 1st *m*) Robert William, *h* 1952; *ed* Eton. —— Nicola Frances, *b* 1950: *m* 1975, Alan Wynter Robinson, of Remenham House, The Street, Whiteparish, nr Salisbury, Wilts, and has issue living, James Wynter, *b* 1978, — Simon Francis, *b* 1983.

The first person named in the pedigree of this family (some members of which were benefactors to Magdalen College, Oxford) is Richard Clerke, of Willoughby, *temp* Henry VI. From him is descended in the 4th generation, Sir John Clerke, who, at the battle of Spurs, 1513, took the Duke of Longueville prisoner, and for that signal service received from Henry VIII a grant of the canton of honourable augmentation, still borne in the family arms. The 9th baronet served in the 52nd Regt at Waterloo.

CLIFFORD (UK) 1887, of Flaxbourne, Marlborough, New Zealand

Sir ROGER JOSEPH GERRARD CLIFFORD, 7th *Baronet*; *b* 5 June 1936; *s* his father, *Sir* ROGER CHARLES JOSEPH GERRARD, 1982; *ed* Beaumont: *m* 1968, Joanna Theresa, da of Cyril James Ward (*see* Ward, Bt, *cr* 1911), and has issue.

Arms – Checky or and azure, a fesse gules. **Crest** – Out of a ducal coronet or, a wyvern rising gules.
Address – 135 Totara St, Christchurch 4, NZ.

DAUGHTERS LIVING

Angela Mary Jane, *b* 1971. —— Annabel Mary Louise *b* 1973.

Semper paratus
Always ready

BROTHER LIVING

CHARLES JOSEPH, *b* (twin) 5 June 1936: *m* 1983, Sally Madeline, da of William Hartgill Pennefather Green. *Residence* – 2/44 Wairarapa Terr, Fendalton, Christchurch, NZ.

SISTER LIVING

Elizabeth Mary Jane, *b* 1938: *m* 1972, Godfrey Matthew Goodson, of 7A Blondell Way, Heretaunga, Wellington, NZ, and has issue living, Charles Godfrey, *b* 1974, — Catherine Cecilia Mary, *b* 1973.

COLLATERAL BRANCH LIVING

Granddaughter of late Charles William Clifford JP, 3rd son of 1st baronet:—
Issue of late Capt George Gilbert Joseph Clifford, *b* 1893, *ka* 1940: *m* 1925, Alcie Mary (*Alcie Mary, Lady Clifford*) (52 Onslow Sq, SW7 3NX); granted 1958, the same style, title, place, and precedence as if her late husband had survived and succeeded to the title, da of J. J. Calder, of Ardargie, Perthshire:—
Anne Caroline, *b* 1926. *Residence* – 52 Onslow Sq, SW7 3NX.

The 1st Baronet, Sir Charles, el son of George Lambert Clifford (5th son of the Hon Thomas Clifford, 2nd son of 3rd Baron Clifford of Chudleigh), was Speaker of the House of Representatives NZ 1853-60.

BRUCE-CLIFTON (UK) 1804, of Downhill, Londonderry

Sir HERVEY JAMES HUGH BRUCE-CLIFTON, 7th *Baronet*; *b* 4 Sept 1952; *s* his father, *Sir* HERVEY JOHN WILLIAM BRUCE, 1971; *ed* Eton; late Maj Gren Gds; assumed the additional surname and arms of Clifton by Royal Licence 1997, upon *s* to the estates of his kinsman, Lt-Col Peter Thomas Clifton, CVO, DSO: *m* 1st, 1979 (*m diss* 1990), Charlotte Sara Jane, el da of John Temple Gore, of Bridgefoot, Spedham, Midhurst, W Sussex (*see* E Eglinton, 1990 Edn); 2ndly, 1992, J. M. (Anna), yst da of Frank Pope, of Tavistock, Devon, and has issue (by 1st and 2nd *m*).

Arms – Not available at the time of going to press.
Address – PO Box 19, Van Reenen 3372, Natal, S Africa. *Club* – Cavalry and Guards'.

SONS LIVING (*By 1st marriage*)

HERVEY HAMISH PETER, *b* 20 Nov 1986.

(*By 2nd marriage*)

Louis William Sinclair, *b* 1993. —— Alasdair Robert Chandos, *b* 1995.

DAUGHTER LIVING (*By 1st marriage*)

Laura Crista, *b* 1984.

SISTER LIVING

Lauretta Chinty, *b* 1950: *m* 1st, 1971, David Ralph Foster Harbord, Capt 15th/19th King's Royal Hussars, who *d* 1974 (*see* B Suffield, colls); 2ndly, 1978, Nicholas Charles Wetherill Ridley, elder son of Harold Ridley, of 53 Harley St, W1. *Address* – Swinstead Hall, Swinstead, nr Grantham, Lincs NG33 4PH.

COLLATERAL BRANCHES LIVING

Issue of late Ronald Cecil Juckes Bruce, yr son of 5th baronet, *b* 1921, *d* 19—: *m* 1960, Jean, da of Lewis James William Murfitt:—
Alan James, *b* 1964.

Granddaughters of late Lt-Col Percy Robert CLIFTON, CMG, DSO, TD, 2nd son of 4th baronet; assumed by Royal Licence 1919 the surname and arms of Clifton in lieu of his patronymic:—
Issue of late Lt-Col Peter Thomas CLIFTON, CVO, DSO, *b* 1911, *d* 1996: *m* 1st, 1934 (*m* annulled 1936), Ursula Sybil, who *d* 1989, da of late Sir Edward Hussey Packe, KBE (By Colebrooke); 2ndly, 1948, Patricia Mary Adela, DStJ (Dummer House, Dummer, Basingstoke, Hants), da of late Maj James Miller Gibson Watt, of Doldowlod, co Radnor, and widow of Maj Robert Nevill Cobbold, Welsh Gds (M Abergavenny, colls):—

(By 2nd *m*) Georgina Anne, *b* 1949: *m* 1st, 1967, Hon Richard Francis Gerard Wrottesley, who *d* 1970, 2nd son of 5th Baron Wrottesley; 2ndly, 1982, Lt-Col Jonathan Lovett Seddon-Brown, Scots Gds, and has issue (by 1st *m*) (*see* B Wrottesley). *Residence* – The Coach House, Dauntsey, Chippenham, Wilts SN15 4HP. —— Rose Amelia (*Hon Mrs Mark W. Vestey*), *b* 1952: *m* 1975, Hon Mark William Vestey, and has issue (*see* B Vestey). *Residence* – Foxcote Manor, Andoversford, Glos.

Issue of late Henry James Bruce, CMG, MVO, 4th son of 4th baronet, *b* 1880, *d* 1951: *m* 1915, Tamara Karsavina (the ballerina), who *d* 1978, da of M. Karsavin, of Petrograd, Russia:—
Nikita, *b* 1916: *m* 1st 1940 (*m diss* 1946), Kay (Kay Bannerman, actress and dramatic author), who *d* 1991, da of Capt Robert G. Bannerman; 2ndly, 1957, Dorothy Mary Norah Mostyn, da of William Mostyn Bell, and has issue living (by 2nd *m*), Nicholas Henry William, *b* 1960, — Caroline Mary Tamara, *b* 1958: *m* 1984, Keith Douglas Crampton, son of Douglas Crampton, and has issue living, James Nicholas Douglas *b* 1992. *Residence* – 38 Longfield Drive, Amersham, Bucks.

Grandchildren of late Rev Robert Douglas Bruce, eldest son of late Rev Canon Lloyd Stewart Bruce, 4th son of 2nd baronet:—
Issue of late Dr Nigel Patrick Bruce, BM, BCh, *b* 1905, *d* 19—: *m* 1934, Audrey Patricia Villiers, only child of late Rev Owen Samuel Edward Clarendon, V of Iffley, Oxford:—
Clare, *b* 1935: *m* 1956 (*m diss* 1972), Peter Colpoys Paley Johnson (later Sir Peter Johnson, 7th Bt, *cr* 1755), and has issue. *Residence* – ......

Issue of late Rev Michael Bruce, *b* 1908, *d* 1968: *m* 1935, Jean Stuart who *d* 1996, da of late Ian Campbell, LRCP, LRCS, of 11 Herford Rd, Harrogate:—
Robert John (19 Grange Rd, Edinburgh, EH9 1UQ), *b* 1936. —— Elspeth Mary, *b* 1942: *m* 1965, Stuart Semple, MB, ChB, of Mounthooly, Winchburgh, Broxburn, W Lothian, EH52 6PY, and has issue living, Jean, *b* 1968, — Sheila, *b* 1970, — Mairi, *b* 1971, Elspeth, *b* 1975.

Grandchildren of late Rev Canon Lloyd Stewart Bruce (ante):—
Issue of late Rev Francis Rosslyn Courtenay Bruce, DD, *b* 1871, *d* 1956: *m* 1908, Rachel, who *d* 1971, el da of late Richard Hanbury Joseph Gurney, JP, DL (Buxton, Bt):—
†Merlin, OBE, *b* 1909; Cdr RN (ret); 1939-45 War; Korea 1950-52 (despatches); Councillor Hemel Hempstead RDC 1961-70; OBE (Mil) 1959: *m* 1933, Marjorie Joan, who *d* 1991, only da of late William Hitchcock, of Kettlewells Farm, St Albans, and *d* 1999, having had issue, †Euslin, *b* 1933; late Sub-Lt RN: *m* 1957, Enid Pedley (Flat 3, 10 Grove Av, Tunbridge Wells, Kent TN1 1UT), and *d* 1997 leaving issue, Quinton Rosslyn *b* 1959, Roderick Hulme (19 Ashford Rd, Hastings, E Sussex TN34 2HA) *b* 1962: *m* 1997, Mrs Rebecca Mary Christina Long, da of Richard Hanlow, of co Donegal (and has issue living, Zivan *b* 1997), Damian Trispen *b* 1970, Jeremy Larick *b* 1974, Nicola Jane *b* 1958, Caroline Fiona *b* 1964: *m* 1999, David Aitken (and has issue living, Felix Alexander *b* 1999), — Rollo (Cobblers Cottage, Foscot, Chipping Norton, Oxon), *b* 1939; *ed* St Catharine's Coll, Camb (BA): *m* 1965, Katharine Margaret, da of Ronald Hill, of Princethorpe, Warwicks, and has issue living, Rory James *b* 1968 (has issue living, Jack Merlin *b* 1993), Lucy Helen *b* 1966: *m* 1995, Warren Squire (and has issue living, Toby Montague *b* 1996, Bertie Peregrine *b* 1998). —— Erroll, *b* 1913; Cdr RN (ret): *m* 1939, Silvia Daphne, only da of late Col C. R. Sylvester Bradley, and has issue living, Peregrine (Pilgrims, Broadmead, Sway, Lymington, Hants), *b* 1940; late Capt R Signals: *m* 1974, Fiona Anne, da of Gp Capt Reginald Bryson Wardman, OBE, AFC, and has issue living, Rachel *b* 1974, Anna *b* 1976, — Peter (Kestrel Cottage, Shirley Holmes, Lymington, Hants; *Club* - Royal Yacht Sqdn), *b* 1941, Cdr RN, — Rosamund, *b* 1943: *m* 1st, 1962, Terence Patrick Griffin; 2ndly, 1978, Jeremy Alan Holmes, MA, MB, BCh, MRCP, FRCPsych, of The Old Rectory, Stoke Rivers, Devon, and has issue living, (by 1st *m*) Benedict James *b* 1963, Polly Bridget *b* 1966 (has issue living, Marcus *b* 1991, Rosy *b* 1986, Zenta Esther *b* 1987), Matilda Victoria *b* 1968, Flora Rhalou *b* 1972, (by 2nd *m*) Joshua Thomas Cecil *b* 1983, — Errollyn, *b* 1950: *m* 19—, Richard Charles Lindley, MA, DPhil, of Hainworth, Keighley, W Yorkshire, and has issue living, Samuel James *b* 1977, Joseph Galen *b* 1983, Emma Rosamund *b* 1978, — Chloe Siola, *b* 1965. *Residence* – Lofts, Lower Pennington, Lymington, Hants. —— Verily, *b* 1915: *m* 1st, 1940, Capt Donald Clive Anderson, late Indian Army, who *d* 1957; 2ndly, 1971, Paul Edward Paget, CVO, FSA, FRIBA, of The Gatehouse, Templewood, Northrepps, Cromer, Norfolk (*see* Paget, Bt, colls, *cr* 1871), and has issue living, (by 1st *m*) Edward (Templewood, Northrepps, Cromer, Norfolk) *b* 1948: *m* 1973, Mrs Christina Bolt, yr da of F. G. Raymond, and has issue living, Evelyn *b* 1973, Beatrice *b* 1978, — Marian, *b* 1941: *m* 1964, James Haldane O'Hare, of Woodview, Frogshall, Northrepps, Cromer, Norfolk NR27 0LJ, and has issue living, Justin *b* 1966: *m* 1991, Janet Robb, of Whale Beach, Sydney, Australia (and has issue living, Lillian Robb *b* 1994, Elspeth Haldane *b* 1997), Christina *b* 1965: *m* 1989, Simon Gerredd Evans, of Sally Beans House, Northrepps, Norfolk (and has issue living, Botticelli Verily Boadicea *b* 1990, Piranesi Vita Lolita *b* 1992), Eloise *b* 1970, — Rachel, *b* 1943: *m* 1965, Prof David Henry Bradby, MA, PhD, of Lower Damsels, Northrepps, Norfolk, and 27a Whitcomb St, WC2, and has issue living, Lawrence *b* 1968, Donald *b* 1973, Hannah *b* 1966, and an adopted son, Nguyen Thanh Sang *b* 1970 (adopted 1980), — Janie, *b* 1952: *m* 1971, Charles Lockwood Hampton, of 80 Temple Rd, Temple Cowley, Oxford OX4 2EZ, and has issue living, Orlando Francis Alexander *b* 1975: *m* 1999, Claire Rachel Purdham, Joseph Barnaby *b* 1978, Daisy Maya *b* 1973, and an adopted da, Pamela Nyabadza *b* 1978, — Alexandra (21 Humberstone Rd, Cambridge), *b* 1953; MA (Cantab): *m* 1st, 1972 (*m diss* 1989), Michael Holgreaves Allerhand; 2ndly, 1993, Gray Innis Walker, yr son of Rev Colin Walker, and has issue living (by 1st *m*), Taffeta Annie *b* 1976, Rhalou Gladys *b* 1979. —— Lorema, *b* 1920: *m* 1942, Alan Wilfrid Gough Goolden, MB, BS, MRCP, FRCR, and has issue living, Adrian French, *b* 1945: *m* 1st, 1971 (*m diss* 1979), Penelope, da of John Godber; 2ndly, 19—, Sally, da of Malcolm Lower, MB, and has issue living (by 1st *m*), Jack Malago *b* 1973, Amy Apple Louise *b* 1976, Rosemary Alice *b* 1978, (by 2nd *m*) Leo Samson *b* 1989, — Robin Massey, *b* 1948: *m* 1976, Mrs Madelaine Mulholland, da of George Nation, and has issue living, Oliver Nation *b* 1978, Rachel Bruce *b* 1980. *Residence* – 31 West St, Osney Island, Oxford.

Issue of late Capt Wilfred Montagu Bruce, CBE, RD, RNR, *b* 1874, *d* 1953: *m* 1913, Hon Dorothy Florence Boot, who *d* 1980, da of 1st Baron Trent:—
Nancy Jessica, *b* 1915: *m* 1940, Adriano Guarnieri, who *d* 1983, and has issue living, Giovanni Bruce, *b* 1947: *m* 1973, Cristina Ongania, and has issue living, Gaia *b* 1973, Valentina *b* 1978, Isotta *b* 1982, — Antonio Wilfrid, *b* 1949: *m* 1981, Anna Lisa Sacerdoti, and has issue living, Matteo *b* 1981, Ambra *b* 1983, — Andrea, *b* 1953: *m* 1981, Luisa Gamba, and has issue living, Lorenzo *b* 1983, Matilde *b* 1981, — Francesca Flora, *b* 1941: *m* 1968, Giuliano Ferrari Bravo, PhD (Cantab), and has issue living, Nicolo *b* 1968, Jacopo *b* 1970, Martino *b* 1974. *Residences* – via Principe 71, Ronca de Treviso, Italy; Les Pommiers, Millbrook, Jersey, CI.

Grandchildren of late Arthur Bonnycastle Dalrymple Bruce (infra):—

Issue of late Arthur Blair Dalrymple Bruce, *b* 1924, *d* 1985, having assumed the name of Arthur in lieu of his first christian name of Frederick: *m* 1951, Patricia (258 S Taylor Mills Drive, Richmond Hill, Ontario, Canada), da of late Richard Raymond Jarvis, of Ottawa:—
Richard Neale Dalrymple, *b* 1954. —— Susan Elizabeth, *b* 1955: *m* 1984, Jefferson Scott Reade, and has issue living, Shannon Kathleen, *b* 1986, — Kirstin Alexandra, *b* 1988.

Granddaughter of late Henry Barnard Dalrymple Bruce, el son of late Lt-Col Henry Stewart Beresford Bruce (infra):—
Issue of late Arthur Bonnycastle Dalrymple Bruce, *b* 1890, *d* 1934: *m* 1916, Marguerite Heloise, who *d* 1976, da of Frederick Edward Neale, of Chatham, New Brunswick:—
Heloise Patricia, *b* 1918: *m* 1945, Capt Robert John McLaughlin, Toronto Scottish Regt, who *d* 1949, and has issue living, Robert Bruce (900 Gulf Blvd, apt 303, Indian Rocks Beach, Florida 33785, USA), *b* (*posthumous*) 1949: *m* 1991, Sandra Catherine, da of Norman John Thorpe, of Chapeltown, Sheffield, Yorks. *Residence* – 900 Gulf Blvd, apt 303, Indian Rocks Beach, Florida 33785, USA.

Granddaughters of late Arthur James Henry Bruce (infra):—
Issue of late Arthur Michael Edward Bruce, *b* 1938, *d* 1993: *m* 1st, 1962 (*m diss* 19—), Holly, da of Carl Cunningham, of Toronto; 2ndly, 1993, (Dorothy) Ferne Lancaster (2003-415 Greenview Av, Ottawa, Ont, Canada):—
(By 1st *m*) Wendy Raina, *b* 1968. —— Susan Ann, *b* 1969.

Grandchildren of late Arthur Hill Nunn Bruce, 2nd son of late Lt-Col Henry Stewart Beresford Bruce, eldest son of late Adm Sir Henry William Bruce, 3rd son of 1st baronet:—
Issue of late Arthur James Henry Bruce, *b* 1901, *d* 1992: *m* 1931, Gladys, da of Edward Bearinger, of Waterloo, Ont:—
Patricia Mary Jane, *b* 1934: *m* 1956, Robert Arthur Davey, of 64 Lockhart Rd, Collingwood, Ont, Canada L9Y 2L3, and has issue living, Robert Bruce, *b* 1958 (has issue living, Ryan *b* 1992), — Steven Michael, *b* 1967: *m* 1990, Linda Diane Godwin, — Susan Patricia, *b* 1960, — Karen Elizabeth, *b* 1962: *m* 1993, Gregory Willison, and has issue living, Brendan Gregory Bruce *b* 1993.

Issue of late Reginald Alexander Steen Bruce, *b* 1904, *d* 1993: *m* 1933, Marie, da of George Albert Blouin, of Ottawa, Ont:—
Robert Arthur Stewart (71 Torcastle Way, Kanata, Ontario K2L 2Y7, Canada), *b* 1936: *m* 1963, Karen, da of James Dunn, of Old Chelsea, Quebec, and has issue living, Reginald Arthur Spencer, *b* 1964, — Alexander James Robert, *b* 1967, — D'Arcy Stewart Anthony, *b* 1968, — Justin Martin Maynard, *b* 1971. —— Marie Elizabeth Claire, *b* 1934: *m* 1956, Frederick Reginald Anfossie, of 2771 Salina St, Ottawa, Ont, Canada K2B 6P8, and has issue living, Frederick Bruce, *b* 1957: *m* 19—, Maryann Helen, da of Andrew Stasko, of Odessa, Ont, and has issue living, Frederick Andrew *b* 1985, Matthew Alexander *b* 1990, Mackenzie Elizabeth Irene *b* 1992, — Christine Elodie, *b* 1959, — Janet Marie, *b* 1961: *m* 1988, Michael Ernest Peiffer, and has issue living, Emily Claire *b* 1989, Katherine Marie *b* 1991, — Heather Claire, *b* 1963, — Margo Elizabeth, *b* 1968. —— Sandra Margo Ann, *b* 1938: *m* 1960, Grant Pereigo McDonald, of 16 Tadonssac Drive, Aylmer, Quebec, J9J 1G2, Canada, and has issue living, Reginald Albert Stroud, *b* 1962, — Robert Bruce Reid, *b* 1963: *m* 1995, Josee Marie Pierrette, da of Robert Lebrun, of Gatineau, Quebec, Canada, and has issue living, Steven Alexander Grant *b* 1993, Lea Christine Margo *b* 1995, — Adam Alfred Grant, *b* 1964; has issue living, (by Marie Jean Joanne Durham) Jake Adam Michael *b* 1994, Breanna Lois Diana *b* 1999, — John Arthur Steen, *b* 1968: *m* 1997, Kathryn Marie Claire, da of Craig Gaston, of Aylmer, Quebec, Canada, and has issue living, Nicholas Craig Grant *b* 1998.

Issue of late Stewart Frederick Dundonald Bruce, *b* 1905; *d* 1982: *m* 1940, Kathleen Edna (513 Westminster Av, Ottawa, Ontario, Canada), da of Charles Cooke, of Ottawa:—
Nona Frances Evelyn, *b* 1944: *m* 1970, John Douglas Argue, of 19 Maplehill Way, Nepean, Canada, and has issue living, Bruce Dugan, *b* 1975, — Sally, *b* 1973. —— Joan Kathleen Susan BRUCE-NIBOGIE, *b* 1946: *m* 1972, Walter William Nibogie, of PO Box 69, Victoria St, Metcalfe, Ontario K0A 2P0, and has issue living, Jeremy Ryan Bruce, *b* 1977, — Krista Kathleen Andra, *b* 1975. —— Nancy Elizabeth Ann, *b* 1949: *m* 1975, Myles Julien Kowalyshen, and has issue living, Bryan Mikael, *b* 1977, — Kara Anne, *b* 1979.

Issue of late Allan Ernest Hill Bruce, *b* 1907, *d* 1973: *m* 1930 (*m diss* 1946), Maria Ann, da of Elidore Sauvé, of Ottawa, Canada:—
Allan Alexander Dundonald (18 Lynhar Rd, Nepean, Ontario K2H 6L9), *b* 1931: *m* 1956, Patricia Anne Leeks, and has issue living, Stewart Allan Robert, *b* 1957, — Steven Christopher David, *b* 1961, — Donald Andrew James, *b* 1964: *m* 1988, Deborah Lynn Boright, and has issue living, Jessica Dawn *b* 1989. —— Hervey William Beresford (5 Ashford Drive, Ottawa, Ont, Canada), *b* 1932: *m* 1966, Molly Margaret MacLaurin, and has issue living, Cameron Allan Beresford, *b* 1972, and two adopted sons, Todd Roy, *b* 1961, — Scott Rodrick, *b* 1962. —— Marie Lorraine Caroline, *b* 1934: *m* 1957, Patrick Francis Timlin, of 78 Harris Place, Ottawa, Ont, K2G 2P8, Canada, and has issue living, Michael Allan, *b* 1961, — Robert Patrick, *b* 1966, — Brenda Marion, *b* 1958.

Granddaughter of late Lt-Col Henry Stewart Beresford Bruce (ante):—
Issue of late Col Stewart Armit Macdonald Bruce, *b* 1858, *d* 1937: *m* 1891, Helen, da of late John McGregor, of Balmenach, Cromdale, Morayshire:—
Jean Mariette Isabel Otway, *b* 1892: *m* 1916 (*m diss* 1932), Cyril Gordon Taylor.

Granddaughter of late Reginald Archibald Kenneth Bruce, 7th son of late Lt-Col Henry Stewart Beresford Bruce (ante):—
Issue of late Capt William Reginald Richard Stewart Bruce, Irish Guards, *b* 1910, *ka* 1944: *m* 1934, Mirabel Melville Gray (who *d* 1994, having *m* 2ndly 1946, James Mitchell Hawkes, who *d* 1979), da of J. D. Walker, of Balgownie Lodge, Aberdeenshire:—
Mirabel Hermione, *b* 1941: *m* 1st, 1964 (*m diss* 1972), Alan Hamill, MN; 2ndly, 1974, James Garry Simpson of Aberdeen and Brazil, and has issue living (by 2nd *m*), James Alexander Bruce, *b* 1975. *Residence* – 7 Racecourse Rd, Stanley, Falklands Is.

Granddaughter of late Rear-Adm James Minchin Bruce, son of late Adm Sir Henry William Bruce, KCB, 3rd son of 1st baronet:—
Issue of late James Minchin Bruce, *b* 1859, *d* 19—: *m* 1888, Ethelwynne, da of the Rev James Powell:—
Minnie, *b* 1889. *Residence* –

Granddaughter of late Major Stewart Hervey Bruce, son of late Lieut-Col Stewart Craufurd Bruce, 4th son of 1st baronet:—
Issue of late Rev Stewart Alexander Bruce, *b* 1870, *d* 1956: *m* 1911, Ada Frances who *d* 1945, da of late Dr R. E. MacDowell:—
Maire Frances Patricia, *b* 1913: *m* 1939, Sqdn-Ldr Reginald Maurice Cracknell, MBE, late RAFVR, who *d* 1970, and has issue living, Andrew Alexander Leon, *b* 1943, — Peter Bruce, *b* 1947. *Residence* – 4 Ashcroft, Cedar Drive, Hatch End, Middx.

The Bruces of Downhill, Londonderry, descend from Patrick Bruce of Newton, yr brother of Sir William Bruce of Stenhouse, 1st baronet (*cr* 1628). Sir Henry Harvey Bruce, 1st baronet, was 5th in descent from him. The only brother of the 1st baronet of this creation, Sir Stewart Bruce, also received a patent of baronetcy in 1812 (extinct 1841). The Rt Hon Sir Henry Hervey Bruce, PC, 3rd Bt, was Lieut and Custos Rotulorum for Londonderry (High Sheriff 1846), and sat as MP for Coleraine (*C*) 1862-74 and 1880-85. The 4th baronet was High Sheriff of co Londonderry 1903.

COATES (UK) 1921, of Haypark, City of Belfast

Sir DAVID CHARLTON FREDERICK COATES, 3rd *Baronet*; *b* 16 Feb 1948; *s* his father, *Brig Sir* FREDERICK GREGORY LINDSAY, 1994; *ed* Millfield: *m* 1973, Christine Helen, da of Lewis F. Marshall, of Ely, Cambs, and has issue.

Arms – Gules, a chevron cotised argent, on a chief ermine two bells or; on an escutcheon of pretence, quarterly, 1st and 4th argent, a fir tree growing out of a mount in base vert surmounted by a sword in bend supporting a crown in the dexter canton proper, and in chief and base, a lion's head erased armed and langued gules; 2nd and 3rd gules, three bears' heads couped argent, muzzled sable. **Crest** – A cock statant, wings closed, gules.
Residence – 30 Hauxton Rd, Little Shelford, Cambs CB2 5HJ.

SONS LIVING

JAMES GREGORY DAVID, *b* 12 March 1977. —— Robert Lewis Edward, *b* 1980.

SISTERS LIVING

Elizabeth Sara Ann, *b* 1941: *m* 1964, Maj Carol James Hay Gurney, 2nd Green Jackets (ret) (High Sheriff Suffolk 1993, DL 1995), of Higham Lodge, Higham, Stratford St Mary, Suffolk, and has issue living, Christopher Hay *b* 1968, — Sara Catherine, *b* 1965: *m* 1990, Rupert Lyle Charles Eley, son of Oliver John Maxwell Eley, of East Bergholt Place, Suffolk, and has issue living, Cuthbert Oliver Edmund *b* 1997. —— Moira Louise, *b* 1945: *m* 1967, Anthony Hunt, of 74 Lynn St, Swaffham, Norfolk, and has issue living, Nigel David Anthony Howard, *b* 1968, — Michael William Richard, *b* 1971, — Jonathan Andrew Frederick *b* 1974.

AUNT LIVING (*daughter of 1st baronet*)

Jean Ann Dorothy (610 Bridlespur Lane, Earlysville, VA 22936, USA), *b* 1919: *m* 1938, Thomas Roland Lecky Sinclair, who *d* 1991, son of late Capt Sir Kenneth Duncan Lecky Sinclair, DL, RNR, and has issue living, Francis David Nicholas (RTI, Box 196, Earlysville, VA 22936, USA), *b* 1940: *m* 1st, 1963 (*m diss* 1966), Peggy Elizabeth Biller; 2ndly, 1984, Mary Virginia Otto, and has issue living, (by 2nd *m*) Thomas William Patrick *b* 1985, Frederick Duncan Andrew *b* 1990, — Kenneth Richard Coates (1204 Colonial Way, Charleston, W Virginia, USA) *b* 1946: *m* 1972, Marion Evans Jefferds, of W Virginia, USA, and has issue living, Joseph Jefferds *b* 1975, Elizabeth Young *b* 1973, Catherine Coates *b* 1978, — Eleanor Margaret, *b* 1943: *m* 1st, 1962 (*m diss* 1981), Walter Roger Shope, Lt-Col US Army; 2ndly, 1986, James Edwin Lewis, of 635 Chatas Court, Lake Mary, Florida 32746, USA, and *d* 1996, having had issue, (by 1st *m*) Thomas Roger *b* 1968: *m* 1992, Lisa Ann Crandall (and has issue living, Zachary *b* 1995, Brett *b* 1997), Jean Marie *b* 1964: *m* 1996, Scott Cottrill (and has issue living, Melissa Jean *b* 1998).

WIDOW LIVING OF SECOND BARONET

JOAN NUGENT (*Joan, Lady Coates*), da of late Maj-Gen Sir Charlton Watson Spinks, KBE, DSO: *m* 1940, Brig Sir Frederick Gregory Lindsay Coates, 2nd Bt, who *d* 1994. *Residence* – Launchfield House, Bryantspuddle, Dorset DT2 7HN.

The 1st baronet, Sir William Frederick Coates, JP, DL (son of David Lindsay Coates, JP, of Clonallon, Belfast), was senior partner in William F. Coates & Co., stockbrokers, of Belfast, High Sheriff of Belfast 1906, Lord Mayor of Belfast 1920, 1921, 1922, 1929, and 1930, High Sheriff of co Antrim 1931, a Freeman of City of Belfast, and first Member of the Senate of N Ireland. The 2nd baronet, Brig Sir Frederick Gregory Lindsay, was with Min of Supply 1947-53, Col Gen Staff, War Office and Min of Defence 1961-66, and Dir Munitions, Defence Research and Development Staff, Assist Mil Attaché, Washington, USA 1966-69.

MILNES COATES (UK) 1911, of Helperby Hall, Helperby, North Riding of Yorkshire

While I breathe I will struggle

Professor Sir ANTHONY ROBERT MILNES COATES, 4th *Baronet*; *b* 8 Dec 1948; *s* his father, *Lt-Col Sir* ROBERT EDWARD JAMES CLIVE, DSO, 1982; *ed* Eton, and St Thomas's Hosp; BSc, MBBS, MRCS, FRCP, FRCPath, MD; Professor and Chm Dept of Medical Microbiology, St George's Hospital Medical Sch, London: *m* 1978, Harriet Ann, yr da of Raymond Burton, of The Old Rectory, Slingsby, York, and has issue.

Arms – Per fesse or and argent, three pallets sable, two flaunches gules, the dexter charged with a rose of the second, barbed and seeded proper, and the sinister with a lion passant also of the second. Crest – Upon a rock proper, a cock or, charged on the breast with a quatrefoil gules, and resting the dexter leg on an escarbuncle argent.
Residences – Helperby Hall, Helperby, York; Hereford Cottage, 135 Gloucester Rd, SW7 4TH.

SON LIVING

THOMAS, *b* 19 Nov 1986.

DAUGHTERS LIVING

Sara, *b* 1981. —— Sophie, *b* 1984.

SISTER LIVING

Mary Freda, *b* 1947: *ed* St Mary's, Wantage, Univ Hall, Buckland, and Sheffield Univ (BA, CQSW); a JP: *m* 1977, Peter Gordon Brodrick, of 25 Wandle Rd, SW17 7DL, and has issue living, Robert Cumberland, *b* 1983, —— Frances Celia, *b* 1979, — Emma Charlotte, *b* 1981.

AUNTS LIVING *(Daughters of 2nd baronet)*

Bridget Sibyl, *b* 1910; Lady-in-Waiting to HRH The Princess Royal 1953-63: *m* 1st, 1931 (*m diss* 1944), Harold David Cuthbert, Scots Gds, who *d* 1959; 2ndly, 1962, Seton Hedley Dearden, MBE, who *d* 1989 of Hill House, W Witton, Leyburn, N Yorks, and has issue living, (by 1st *m*) (John) Aidan (Beaufront Castle, Hexham), *b* 1934: *m* 1975 (*m diss* 19—), Lady Victoria Lucy Diana Percy, 2nd da of 10th Duke of Northumberland, KG, TD, PC, and has issue living, David Hugh *b* 1987, Alice Rose *b* 1978, Lucy Caroline *b* 1982, — Belinda Jane Elizabeth (*Hon Mrs Matthew Beaumont*), *b* 1932: *m* 1973, as his 2nd wife, Hon Matthew Henry Beaumont, of Bearl House, Stocksfield, Northumberland NE43 7AJ (*see* V Allendale), — Caroline Alice Celia CUTHBERT (42 Eland Rd, SW11), *b* 1940; has resumed her maiden name: *m* 1985 (*m diss* 1992), Jonathan Mark Hamilton Priaulx Raban. —— Elizabeth Hermione, *b* 1914: *m* 1937, William Barclay Harris, QC, of Moatlands, E Grinstead, Sussex, and 29 Barkston Gdns, SW5, and has issue living, Jonathan William (9 Lower Addison Gdns, W14), *b* 1940: *m* 1966, Nabila, da of Fares Sarofim Bey, OBE, of Minia and Cairo, — Jessica Elizabeth, *b* 1938: *m* 1973, Peter Tcherepnine, of 1192 Park Av, New York, NY, USA, — Hermione Mary, *b* 1942: *m* 1982, Marc Karlin, who *d* 1999.

WIDOW LIVING OF THIRD BARONET

Lady (ETHEL) PATRICIA HARE (*Lady Patricia Milnes Coates*), da of 4th Earl of Listowel, and widow of Lt-Col Charles Thomas Milnes Gaskell, Coldm Gds (E Ranfurly): *m* 1945, Lt-Col Sir Robert Edward James Clive Milnes Coates, DSO, 3rd Bt, who *d* 1982.

The 1st baronet, Sir Edward Feetham Coates (a member of the firm of Coates, Son and Co, stockbrokers, of Gresham St, EC), MP for Lewisham (C) 1903-18, and W Lewisham 1918-21. Sir Edward Clive Coates, 2nd Bt, who *m* 1906, Lady Celia Hermione Crewe-Milnes, da of 1st and last Marquess of Crewe, assumed by deed poll 1946 the surname of Milnes-Coates.

COATS (UK) 1905, of Auchendrane, Maybole, co Ayr

Sir ALASTAIR FRANCIS STUART COATS, 4th *Baronet*; *b* 18 Nov 1921; *s* his father, *Lt-Col Sir* JAMES STUART, MC, 1966; *ed* Eton; Capt late Coldstream Guards: *m* 1947, Lukyn, da of Capt Charles Gordon, and has issue.

Arms – Or, three mascles sable, a chief engrailed azure, semée-de-lis of the field. **Crest** – A stag's head erased proper, charged on the neck with an escarbuncle or.
Residence – Birchwood House, Durford Wood, Petersfield, Hants GU31 5AW.

SON LIVING

ALEXANDER JAMES, *b* 6 July 1951; *ed* Eton: *m* 1999, Clara, da of Ernesto Abril de Vivero, of Lima, Peru. *Residence* – 5 Bina Gdns, SW5 0LD.

DAUGHTER LIVING

Sarah Mary (49 Kenilworth Av, SW19), *b* 1948: *m* 1st, 1972 (*m diss* 1976), William Humble David Jeremy, Viscount Ednam, el son of 4th Earl of Dudley; 2ndly, 1976 (*m diss* 1999), Archibald David Sampson Lloyd (Keane, Bt), and has issue living (by 2nd *m*), Katherine Mary, *b* 1978, — Amy Constance, *b* 1981.

BROTHER LIVING

Ivor Paul, *b* 1923; late Lieut 12th Lancers: *m* 1959, Gay, da of Dr Charles Pinckney, and has issue living, Dominic Peter, *b* 1962, — James Charles, *b* 1964, — Emma Lucinda, *b* 1960, — Sophie Louise, *b* 1966. *Residence* – 110c Victoria Rise, SW4 0NW.

With a faithful heart

COLLATERAL BRANCH LIVING

Issue of late Alfred Mainwaring Coats, 2nd son of 1st baronet, *b* 1869, *d* 1942: *m* 1895, Elizabeth, who *d* 1940, da of late Morris Barnewall, of Flushing, Long Island, USA:—
Elizabeth Barnewall, *b* 1902: *m* 19— (*m diss* 1938), Kenneth McCall, and has issue living.

The first baronet, Sir James Coats (a Director J. and P. Coats (Limited), sewing cotton manufacturers of Ferguslie Thread Works, Paisley), was el son of Sir Peter Coats, of Auchendrane, Ayrshire, who was el surviving son of late James Coats, of Paisley, and el brother of late Thomas Coats, of Ferguslie and Maxwellton (*see* B Glentanar and Glen-Coats, Bt). The second baronet, Sir Stuart Auchincloss Coats, was Private Chamberlain of Sword and Cape to Popes Pius X, Benedict XV, Pius XI and Pius XII, and sat as MP for Wimbledon (*C*) 1916-18, and for E Div of Surrey 1918-22.

GLEN-COATS (UK) 1894, of Ferguslie Park, Paisley, co Renfrew (Extinct 1954)

Sir THOMAS COATS GLEN GLEN-COATS, 2nd and last *Baronet*.

COLLATERAL BRANCH LIVING

Issue of late Alexander Harold Glen-Coats, 2nd son of 1st Baronet, *b* 1883, *d* 1933: *m* 1924, Elizabeth Millar, who *d* 1969, da of late Thomas Greenlees, of Newark, Paisley:—
(Margaret) Elizabeth (Home Farm, Hindon, Salisbury), *b* 1928. —— (Winifred) Lettice (Underhill, E Knoyle, Salisbury), *b* 1929; a JP of Wilts.

COCHRANE (UK) 1903, of Woodbrook, Old Connaught, Bray, co Wicklow, Lisgar Castle, Bailieborough, co Cavan, and Kildare Street, City of Dublin

By virtue and labour

Sir (HENRY) MARC SURSOCK COCHRANE, 4th Baronet, *b* 23 Oct 1946; *s* his father, *Maj Sir* DESMOND ORIEL ALASTAIR GEORGE WESTON, 1979; *ed* Eton, and Trin Coll, Dublin (MA); Hon Irish Consul General in Lebanon 1979-84; Dir Hambros Bank Ltd 1979-85, Dir GT Management plc since 1986: Trustee Chester Beatty Library and Gallery of Oriental Art, Dublin: *m* 1969, Hala, 2nd da of Fouad Mahmoud Bey es-Said, of Beirut, Lebanon, and has issue.

Arms – Azure, on chevron engrailed argent, between in chief two boars' heads erased or, and in base a sun in splendour of the last, a thistle proper between two trefoils slipped vert. Crest – In front of two tilting-spears in saltire a bay horse passant all proper.

SONS LIVING

ALEXANDER DESMOND SURSOCK, *b* 7 May 1973. —— Patrick Talal, *b* 1976.

DAUGHTER LIVING

Faiza Maria Rosebud, *b* 1971.

BROTHERS LIVING

Alfred Marie Stanislas Sursock, *b* 1948: *ed* Eton, and Univ of Rome (DrArch, MSDI). —— Roderick Inigo Marie Sursock, *b* 1952; *ed* Le Rosay, and American Univ of Beirut.

SISTER LIVING

Isabelle Maria Elsa Sursock, *b* 1962: *m* 1987, Count Gregorio Riccardi, son of late Count Roberto Riccardi, and Sra Giulio Pascucci-Righi.

AUNT LIVING (*Daughter of 2nd baronet*)

Elizabeth Margaret, *b* 1915: *m* 1939, Robert Elsworth Steen, MD, FRCPI, who *d* 1981, and has issue living, David Michael Cochrane Elsworth, *b* 1945; *ed* Eton, and Oriel Coll, Oxford (MA); FCA: *m* 1971, Rosemary Florence, el da of Maj William Bellingham Denis Dobbs, R Ulster Rifles (ret), (*see* B Vestey, colls), and has issue living, Peter Robert Denis Elsworth, *b* 1977, Jane Elizabeth Norah *b* 1973: *m* 1999, Dr Guy Deutscher, PhD, of St John's Coll, Cambridge, Lucy Alannah Rosemary *b* 1975, Rosalie Frances Elsworth (twin) *b* 1977, — Sarah Fiola Elsworth, *b* 1942: *m* 1975, Capt Lewis Dixon-Brown, RM (ret), only son of late Brig Cecil Thomas Dixon-Brown, OBE, RM (*k* on active ser 1942), and has issue living, Elizabeth-Olga Cochrane *b* 1977, Cecily Anne Cochrane *b* 1979, Nicola Frances Cochrane *b* 1982. *Residence* – Elstow, Foxrock, co Dublin.

HALF-AUNT LIVING (*Daughter of 2nd baronet*)

Jan Asa Helen Grahame, *b* 1939.

WIDOW LIVING OF THIRD BARONET

YVONNE (*Yvonne, Lady Cochrane*) (Palais Sursock, Rue Sursock, Beirut, Lebanon), only child of late Alfred Bey Sursock, of Beirut, Lebanon: *m* 1946, Maj Sir Desmond Oriel Alastair George Weston Cochrane, 3rd Bt, who *d* 1979.

The 1st baronet, Sir Henry Cochrane, was Governing Director of Cantrell and Cochrane (Limited) mineral water manufacturers, of Dublin, and an Alderman of that City for over 25 years. Sir Ernest Cecil, 2nd Bt, was an Hon Gentleman-in-Waiting to the Lord-Lieut of Ireland 1908-09, and a dramatist (author of *A Matter of Fact* and *Monica*).

COCKBURN (NS) 1671, of That Ilk
(Name pronounced "Coburn")

He arises with a song

Sir JOHN ELLIOT COCKBURN, 12th *Baronet*; *b* 7 Dec 1925; *s* his father, *Lieut-Col Sir* JOHN BRYDGES, DSO, 1949; *ed* RNC Dartmouth, and RAC Cirencester: *m* 1949, Glory Patricia, el da of late Nigel Tudway Mullings, of Snitterfield, Stratford-on-Avon, and has issue.

𝕬rms – Quarterly: 1st and 4th argent, three cocks gules, *Cockburn*: 2nd and 3rd, gules, six mascles or, three, two and one, *Weapont*; all within a bordure vert. ℭrest – A cock crowing proper.
Residence – 48 Frewin Rd, SW18 3LP. *Club* – Naval and Military.

SONS LIVING

CHARLES CHRISTOPHER, *b* 19 Nov 1950; *ed* Emanuel Sch, City of London Poly (BA) and Garnett Coll: *m* 1st, 1978, Beverly J., only da of B. Stangroom, of Richmond, Surrey; 2ndly, 1985, Margaret Ruth, da of Samuel Esmond Bell, of 18 Portland Dr, Bury Green, Cheshunt, Herts, and has issue living (by 2nd *m*), Christopher Samuel Alexander, *b* 24 March 1986, — William James John, *b* 1996,   Charlotte Elspeth Catherine, *b* (twin) 1986. *Residence* – West Dene House, 84 Medstead Rd, Beech, nr Alton, Hants GU34 4AE. —— James Chandos, *b* 1952. —— Jonathan McQueen, *b* 1956.

DAUGHTERS LIVING

Julia Georgina, *b* 1954. —— Catherine Isabel, *b* (twin) 1956: *m* 1982, Stephen Edward Keal.

SISTER LIVING

Frances Isabel, *b* 1921.

COLLATERAL BRANCHES LIVING

Watchful and bold

Granddaughters of late Col George William Cockburn, 4th son of 7th baronet:—
Issue of late Charles Edward Stuart Cockburn, *b* 1867, *d* 1917: *m* 1894, Lilian, who *d* 1943, da of Sir Morton Edward Manningham-Buller, 2nd Bt:—
Rosalind, MBE; MBE (Civil) 1962: *m* 1921, Cdr Guy Darracott Millar, RN (ret), who *d* 1940. *Residence* –

Issue of late Donald Graham Cockburn (twin), *b* 1872, *d* 1938: *m* 1st, 1915, Dorothy Agnes, who *d* 1916, da of Lewis Evans; 2ndly, 1922, Nora, who *d* 1947, el da of G. Walton, and widow of H. D. Douglas:—
(By 1st *m*) Edith Penelope, *b* 1916.

Alexander de Cockburn, ancestor of this family, was Heritable Usher of the White Rod 1373 and later Keeper of the Great Seal of Scotland. Sir James Cockburn of that Ilk, 1st Bt, purchased from his cousin Sir Archibald Cockburn, 4th Bt (whose title became dormant 1880) the lands of Langton, Berwickshire, and office of Usher.

Cockburn-Campbell, see Campbell.

CODRINGTON (GB) 1721, of Dodington, Gloucestershire

Face to the enemy

VULTUS·IN·HOSTEM

Sir WILLIAM ALEXANDER CODRINGTON, 8th *Baronet*; *b* 5 July 1934; *s* his father, *Lieut-Com Sir* WILLIAM RICHARD 1961; *ed* St Andrew Coll, S Africa, and S African Naval Coll; Dir World-Wide Shipping Agency Ltd, Hong Kong; ret 1998.

Arms – Argent, a fesse embattled counter-embattled sable fretty gules between three lions passant of the third. **Crest** – Not recorded at College of Arms. *Residence* – 75 Backchurch Lane, E1 1LQ.

BROTHERS LIVING

GILES PETER (Shutters, 2031 Intercoastal Drive, Fort Lauderdale, Florida 33305, USA), *b* 28 Oct 1943: *m* 1989, Shirley Linda Duke, and has issue living, Christopher Harry, *b* 1988, — Daniel Peter, *b* 1993, — Michele Anne, *b* 1990. —— Andrew Richard (5 Cambridge News, Kingsley, Perth, Western Australia 6026, Australia), *b* 1947; Capt: *m* 1975, Claire Marie Agnes Frichot, of Mahé, Seychelles, and has issue living, Adrian Richard, *b* 1981, — Estelle Louise, *b* 1985.

SISTER LIVING

Sally Ann, *b* 1939: *m* 1962, Philip John Francis Collingwood, of 51 Longcroft Lane, Welwyn Garden City, Herts, and has issue living, Richard Francis, *b* 1964, — Sophia Catherine Mary, *b* 1963: *m* 1989, Julian Thomas Rowe, — Charlotte Mary, *b* 1966.

MOTHER LIVING

Joan Kathleen Birelli, el da of Percy E. Nicholas: *m* 1933 (*m diss* 1952), Lieut-Com Sir William Richard Codrington, 7th Bt, who *d* 1961.

COLLATERAL BRANCHES LIVING

Issue of late Frank Christopher Codrington, yr son of 6th baronet, *b* 1908, *d* 1992: *m* 1933, Monica Bawn, who *d* 1983, eldest da of Sir James Philip Reynolds, 1st Bt, DSO, MP:—
Christopher Michael, *b* 1937; *ed* St Andrew's Coll, Grahamstown, S Africa: *m* 1972, Christine Beatrice, eldest da of Lt-Col Max Emil Bürki, of Château Surpierre, Switzerland, and has issue living, Rosalind Bawn, *b* 1974, — Emily Jane, *b* 1977.

Issue of late Gerald William Henry Codrington (son of late Christopher William Codrington, MP, grandson of late Edward Codrington (infra)), who was *cr* a *Baronet* 1876:—
See Codrington, Bt, *cr* 1876.

Grandchildren of late Lt-Gen Sir Alfred Edward Codrington, GCVO, KCB, yr son of late Gen Sir William John Codrington, GCB, MP, 2nd son of late Adm Sir Edward Codrington, GCB, 3rd son of late Edward Codrington, 4th son of 1st baronet:—
Issue of late Col Sir Geoffrey Ronald Codrington, KCVO, CB, CMG, DSO, OBE, TD, *b* 1888, *d* 1973: *m* 1923, Cecilia Mary, who *d* 1979, da of late Ernest James Wythes, CBE (Thorold, Bt):—
Michael Christopher Alfred (159 Church Green, Broughton Giffard, Melksham, Wilts SN12 8PS), *b* 1926; late Maj 16th/5th Lancers: *m* 1st, 1953 (*m diss* 1986), Irene Margaret, who *d* 1994, da of late Col Mark Edward Makgill-Crichton-Maitland, CVO, DSO (*see* E Lauderdale, colls); 2ndly, 1986, Alma Patricia, who *d* 1997, widow of Norman G. Batcheller, and da of late Patrick Sheridan, and has issue living (by 1st *m*), Camilla Ann (*Comtesse de Rochambeau*), *b* 1957: *m* 1993, Eric, Comte de Rochambeau, of 790 Ten Rod Rd, N Kingstown, Rhode Is 02852, USA, and has issue living, John Donatien Lacroix de Vimeur *b* 1996, — Bridget Margaret (116 Portland Rd, W11), *b* 1958: *m* 1st, 1979, George Daniel Rossiter, who *d* 1984; 2ndly, 1990, Ross O'N. Witherow, and has issue living, (by 1st *m*) Peter Goodman *b* 1983, (by 2nd *m*), Thomas Edward *b* 1991, — Katherine Alice, *b* 1965. —— James Geoffrey (Lyde Barn, Lower Lyde, Herefordshire), *b* 1935: *m* 1961, Lorraine, el da of R. G. A. Wells, of Stable Cottage, Winchelsea, E Sussex, and has issue living, Richard Melville, *b* 1962, — Charles Sebastian, *b* 1964: *m* 1995, Sarah Juliet, yr da of late Michael Style, of Broadway, Worcs, and has issue living, Benjamin Michael *b* 1997, — Annabelle Cecilia, *b* 1967: *m* 1991, Graham P. Sylvester, of Polsoe Manor, Roanhighlanes, Truro, Cornwall, only son of Dr Derek Sylvester, of Almondsbury Field, Lower Almondsbury, Bristol, and has issue living, Thomas James Hogarth *b* 1994, Nicholas Alexander Hogarth *b* 1996. —— Mary Alice (*Hon Mrs Robert T. Boscawen*), *b* 1924; a JP of co London: *m* 1949, Rt Hon Robert Thomas Boscawen, MC (*see* V Falmouth). —— Emma Cecilia (West Lodge, Wilton, Salisbury), *b* 1930.

Issue of late Capt William Melville Codrington, CMG, MC, *b* 1892, *d* 1963: *m* 1935, Katharine Theodosia (The Cottage, Hambleton, Oakham, Rutland) (who *m* 2ndly, 1968, Edward Kirkpatrick, who *d* 1972), da of John Houston Sinclair, CMG, CBE (Cockburn, Bt, colls):—
Jane Evelyn, *b* 1937: *m* 1961, Richard Miles Micklethwait, of Preston Hall, Oakham (*see* D Norfolk, colls). —— Teresa Anne, *b* 1944: *m* 1979, John Stuart Wheeler (*see* Gibbons, Bt, 1990 Edn), of Dane Street House, Chilham, nr Canterbury, Kent CT4 8ER, and has issue living, Sarah Rose, *b* 1980, — Jacquetta Lydia, *b* 1981, — Charlotte Mary, *b* 1985.

The 2nd baronet, who died 1792, disinherited his son, Sir William, 3rd Bt, and bequeathed his estates to his nephew, Christopher Bethell-Codrington, whose grandson was *cr* a baronet 1876.

CODRINGTON (UK) 1876, of Dodington, Gloucestershire

Sir SIMON FRANCIS BETHELL CODRINGTON, 3rd *Baronet*; *b* 14 Aug 1923; *s* his father *Sir* CHRISTOPHER WILLIAM GERALD HENRY, 1979; *ed* Eton; formerly Major Coldstream Guards; European War 1942-5 in Italy: *m* 1st, 1947 (*m diss* 1959), Joanne, da of John William Molineaux, of Rock Castle, Kilmacsimon, co Cork, and widow of William Humphrey Austin Thompson; 2ndly, 1959 (*m diss* 1979), Pamela Joy Halliday, da of Major George Walter Bentley Wise, MBE; 3rdly, 1980 (*m diss* 1987), Mrs Sarah Gwynne Gaze (*née* Pennell); 4thly, 1989, Shirley Ann, da of Percival Lionel Davis, and has issue living by 2nd *m*.

Arms – Argent, a fesse embattled counter-embattled sable fretty gules between three lions passant of the third. Crest – Issuant from a coronet composed of four roses set upon a rim or a dragon's head gules between two dragon's wings per fesse or and azure.
Seat – Dodington Park, Chipping Sodbury, Gloucestershire. *Residence* – Bean Cottage, Dodington, Chipping Sodbury, Bristol BS17 6SF.
Club – Cavalry and Guards'.

IMMERSABILIS·EST·VERA·VIRTUS

True virtue is imperishable

SONS LIVING (*By 2nd marriage*)

CHRISTOPHER GEORGE WAYNE (The Old Hundred, Tormarton, Badminton, Avon), *b* 20 Feb 1960; *ed* Millfield, and RAC Cirencester : *m* 1991, Noelle Lynn, da of Dale Wilford Leverson, of Houston, Texas, USA, and of Mrs Genell K. Benner, of Xenia, Ohio, and has issue living, Alexander Edward Kristoffer, *b* 9 Nov 1993, — Cecilia Elizabeth Lillian, *b* 1996. —— Bethell, *b* 1961. —— Hugo John, *b* 1964: *m* 1992, Antonia Hannah Beaufort, eldest da of Andrew McCullough, of Windsor, Berks, and has issue living, Charlie, *b* 1996.

This family is a younger branch of the Codringtons, baronets, of Dodington, creation 1721. The Codringtons have been established in Gloucestershire since *temp* Henry IV. The 1st Bt was Sir Gerald William Henry Codrington, son of late Christopher William Henry Codrington, MP (*see* Codrington, Bt, *cr* 1721, colls).

COGHILL (GB) 1778, of Coghill, Yorkshire

Sir EGERTON JAMES NEVILL TOBIAS (TOBY) COGHILL, 8th *Baronet*; *b* 26 March 1930; *s* his father, *Sir* JOSCELYN AMBROSE CRAMER, RNVR, 1983; *ed* Gordonstoun, and Pembroke Coll, Camb (MA): *m* 1958, Gabriel Nancy, da of late Maj Dudley Claud Douglas Ryder (*see* E Harrowby, colls), and has issue.

Arms – Quarterly: 1st and 4th ermine a chevron between three cocks gules, *Coghill*: 2nd and 3rd, gules, on a chevron argent three pellets, a chief indented of the second. Crest – On a mount vert a cock gules charged on the breast with a bezant.
Residence – Sourden, Rothes, Morayshire AB38 7AE.

SON LIVING

PATRICK KENDAL FARLEY, *b* 3 Nov 1960.

DAUGHTER LIVING

Elizabeth Louisa Gay, *b* 1962: *m* 1999, Dr Charles J. Easmon, of 26 Gowrie Rd, SW11.

SISTER LIVING

NON·DORMIT·QVI·CUSTODIT

He does not sleep who keeps guard

Faith Patricia Elizabeth, *b* 1928: *m* 1955, James Leslie Garson, of Hill Farm, Elsfield, Oxford OX3 9SW, and has issue living, Jeremy James, *b* 1961, — Elizabeth Lucy, *b* 1956, — Rachel Margaret, *b* 1958: *m* 1982, Michael Dickinson, and has issue living, Samuel Caradoc *b* 1985, Hannah Beatrice *b* 1987, Phoebe Rose *b* 1990, Eleanor Grace, *b* (twin) 1990, — Isobel Laura, *b* 1968: *m* 1992, Tobias Andrew Baxter, and has issue living, Joshua James *b* 1994, Isaac Jeremy *b* 1996.

HALF-SISTERS LIVING AND DECEASED

Bridget Olivia Françoise, *b* 1949. —— Jocelyn Edith Louise, *b* 1952, *d* 1983: *m* 1972, Stephen George Thomas, of 135 Sommerville Rd, Ashley Down, Bristol. —— Deborah Katharine Hildegarde, *b* 1954: *m* 1987, Alan Nye, of 35 Nevil Rd, Bishopston, Bristol, and has issue living, Alistair William James, *b* 1989, — Lucy Elizabeth Katherine, *b* 1991.

COLLATERAL BRANCHES LIVING

Grandchildren of late Claude Plunket Coghill, 4th son of 4th baronet:—
Issue of late Joscelyn Kendal Bushe Coghill, *b* 1893 *d* 1959: *m* 1925, Maud Evelyn, da of late Leslie Phillips Filder, of Crawley, Sussex:—
John Kendal Plunket, OBE, *b* 1929; *ed* Sherborne, and RMA Sandhurst; late Lt-Col RAOC; OBE (Civil) 1990: *m* 1951, Diana Mary, da of late Frederick Charles Callen, of Tanganyika, and has issue living, Michèle Mary, *b* 1957: *m* 1988, Julian David Sinclair Lyon, of 4 East Meads, Onslow Village, Guildford, Surrey GU2 5SP, 2nd son of Stewart Lyon, of Guildford, and has issue living, Georgina Mary Coghill *b* 1991, — Amanda Patricia, *b* 1960: *m* 1985, Stephen John Lowcock Downing, of 22, Bowood Rd, SW11, and has issue living, Thomas Peter *b* 1989, Katherine Louise *b* 1991, — Samantha Jane, *b* 1967: *m* 1990, Peter James Wilken. —— Sheila Mary, *b* 1926: *m* 1952, David Polwhele Cooper, and has issue living, Shaun David Coghill, *b* 1956, — Sally Muara Coghill, *b* 1954, — Julie Rosalyn Coghill, *b* 1965, — Lucinda Jane Coghill, *b* 1966. *Residence* – Pine Trees, 3 Ferguson Av, Greendale, Harare, Zimbabwe.

The 1st baronet, Sir John Cramer, LLD, of Coghill Hall, Knaresborough (grandson of Oliver Cramer, of Ballyfoile, co Kilkenny, and his wife Hester, sister of Rt Hon Marmaduke Coghill, Chancellor of the Exchequer, Ireland), succeeded to the family estates of his cousin Hester, da and heiress of James Coghill, LLD, and widow of 1st Earl of Charleville, and assumed by roy licence the additional surname of Coghill 1774/5. His successor Sir John Thomas Coghill, 2nd Bt, and his brother and successor, Sir Josiah Coghill Coghill, 3rd Bt, assumed by Roy licence the surname of Coghill only in 1807 and 1817 respectively. The 4th baronet was High Sheriff of co Dublin in 1859, and was *s* by his second son as 5th Bt, the el, Nevill Josiah Aylmer Coghill, VC, Lieut 24th Regt, having been killed while saving the Colours of his regt at the battle of Isandhlwana 22 Jan 1879. Sir Egerton Coghill, 5th Bt, *s* 1905; landscape painter (studied Barbizon School, Paris); DL co Cork. His eldest son, Sir Patrick Coghill, 6th Bt, *s* 1921, served in both European Wars with distinction, the Arab Legion, in Turkey and Iraq; DL Hertfordshire. His brother, Sir Joscelyn Coghill, 7th Bt, *s* 1981, *d* 1983.

WALEY-COHEN (UK) 1961, of Honeymead, co Somerset

Sir STEPHEN HARRY WALEY-COHEN, 2nd *Baronet*; *b* 22 June 1946; *s* his father, *Sir* BERNARD NATHANIEL, 1991; *ed* Eton, and Magdalene Coll, Camb (MA); Financial journalist *Daily Mail* 1968-73, Editor *Money Mail Handbook* 1973 and 1974; Dir Euromoney Publications Ltd 1969-77, Publisher Euromoney 1977-83; Chief Executive Maybox Group plc 1984-89; Gov of Wellesley House Sch; Man Dir Victoria Palace, Vaudeville and Savoy Theatres and of Mousetrap Productions Ltd, Dir S. M. Theatre Ltd, Society of London Theatre, and Exeter Preferred Capital Investment Trust plc; Chm Policy Portfolio plc, Willis Faber and Dumas (Agencies) Ltd, Portsmouth and Sunderland Newspapers plc; Chm Jewish Colonisation Assocn; Chm UK Executive Cttee, British American Project for the Successor Generation; Trustee The Theatres Trust since 1998: *m* 1st, 1972 (*m diss* 1986), Pamela Elizabeth, yr da of J. E. Doniger, of Knutsford, Cheshire; 2ndly, 1986, Josephine Burnett, yr da of late Duncan M. Spencer, of Bedford, New York, and has issue by 1st and 2nd *m*.

Arms – Quarterly, 1st and 4th argent, on a chevron gules cottised azure, between in chief two roses of the second barbed and seeded proper, and in base a buck's head couped also proper, three annulets or, *Cohen*; 2nd and 3rd, argent a chevron azure cottised sable between in chief two eagles displayed of the last and in base on a mount vert a hind trippant proper, *Waley*. **Crest** – 1st, a buck's head couped argent, attired or, holding in the mouth a rose slipped gules, the neck encircled by a wreath of oak proper between four barrulets gules, *Cohen*; 2nd, out of a bush of fern a hind's head proper in the mouth a rose argent stalked and leaved also proper, *Waley*.
Residence – 1 Wallingford Ave, W10 6QA. *Club* – Garrick.

SONS LIVING (By 1st marriage)

LIONEL ROBERT, *b* 7 Aug 1974; *ed* Eton, and Bath Univ. —— Jack David, *b* 1979; *ed* Eton, and St John's Coll, Oxford.

DAUGHTERS LIVING (*By 1st marriage*)

Harriet Ann, *b* 1976; *ed* Wycombe Abbey, St Paul's Girls' Sch, and Univ Coll, London.

(*By 2nd marriage*)

Tamsin Alice, *b* 1986. —— Freya Charlotte, *b* 1989.

BROTHER LIVING

Robert Bernard (18 Gilston Rd, SW10 9SR; *Clubs* – Boodle's, Jockey and Queen's), *b* 1948; *ed* Eton; Exec at Christie, Manson & Woods Ltd 1969-81, Gen Man in USA 1970-73; Ch Exec Alliance Imaging Inc 1983-88; Ch Exec Alliance Medical Ltd since 1989; elected Jockey Club 1983, Dep Senior Steward since 1998; Board Memb, Countryside Alliance since 1998: *m* 1975, Hon Felicity Ann Samuel, da of 3rd Viscount Bearsted, and has issue living, Marcus Richard, *b* 1977, — Sam Bernard, *b* 1982, — Thomas Andrew, *b* 1984, — Jessica Suzanna, *b* 1979.

SISTERS LIVING

Rosalind Alice, *b* 1945; *ed* Cranborne Chase Sch: *m* 1966, Philip Ralph Burdon, of 140 Straven Rd, Christchurch, NZ, and has issue living, Miranda Ruth, *b* 1970, — Rebecca Joyce, *b* 1972, — Josephine Virginia, *b* 1975. —— (Eleanor) Joanna, *b* 1952; *ed* Cranborne Chase Sch, and Girton Coll, Camb (MA): *m* 1977, Keith Bradoc Gallant, and has issue living, Christopher Edward Bernard (Kit), *b* 1988, — Isobel Claire, *b* 1993.

WIDOW LIVING OF FIRST BARONET

Hon JOYCE CONSTANCE INA NATHAN, MA, JP (*Hon Lady Waley-Cohen*), only da of 1st Baron Nathan: *m* 1943, Sir Bernard Nathaniel Waley-Cohen, 1st Bt, who *d* 1991.

The 1st baronet, Sir Bernard Nathaniel Waley-Cohen (el son of Sir Robert Waley Cohen, KBE, who *d* 1952, of Caen Wood Towers, Highgate, N6, and Honeymead, Simonsbath, Somerset) assumed by deed poll 1950 his final forename as an additional surname. An Underwriting Member of Lloyd's he served as Alderman of City of London 1949-84, Sheriff of City of London 1955-56, and Lord Mayor of London 1960-61.

COLFOX (UK) 1939, of Symondsbury, co Dorset

Light, Law, Liberty

Sir (WILLIAM) JOHN COLFOX, 2nd *Baronet*; *b* 25 April 1924; *s* his father, *Sir* (WILLIAM) PHILIP, MC, 1966; *ed* Eton; a JP for Dorset; High Sheriff 1969; DL 1977; 1939-45 War as Lt RNVR: *m* 1962, Frederica Loveday, da of Adm Sir Victor Alexander Charles Crutchley, VC, KCB, DSC, DL, of Mappercombe Manor, Bridport, Dorset, and has issue.

𝔄rms – Sable, three spinning-cogs erect and in fesse or, on chief argent, as many fox-heads couped at the neck gules. 𝔠rest – A fox proper, charged on the body with two fleurs-de-lys in fesse sable, and resting the sinister paw on a fleur-de-lys gules. *Residence* – Symondsbury House, Bridport, Dorset DT6 6HB.

SONS LIVING

PHILIP JOHN (Mill Lane, Symondsbury, Dorset DT6 6HB), *b* 27 Dec 1962; *ed* Eton: *m* 19—, Julia R., yr da of Geoffrey St George Schomberg, of Durfort, France, and Mrs H. D. Lyon, of Dallington, Sussex, and has issue living, Alice, *b* 1993, — Lilly, *b* (twin) 1993, — Mary Rose (Mamie), *b* 1997. —— Edward Timothy, *b* 1969.

DAUGHTERS LIVING

Victoria Mary, *b* 1964: *m* 1996, Fergus Byrne, son of late James J. Byrne, of Kilcullen, co Kildare, and has issue living, Ismay Scarlet, *b* 1996, — Isla Frederica, *b* 1999, — Tara Loveday, *b* (twin) 1999. —— Charlotte Ismay Joan, *b* 1966: *m* 1987, Capt James William Harwood Daniel, WG, of Antrim Farm, Broadoak, Bridport, Dorset, eldest son of Col John Robert Austen Daniel, of Chideock Court, Bridport, Dorset, and has issue living, John James Colfox, *b* 1998, — Olivia Mary Frederica, *b* 1988, — Ismay Henrietta (Hettie) Loveday, *b* 1991, — Posy, *b* 1995. —— Constance Ruth, *b* 1971.

SISTERS LIVING

Susan Helen Frances, *b* 1929: *m* 1950, William Henry Batten, and has issue living, David Henry Cary, *b* 1952: *m* 1981, Sarah Bagnell, — Michael John, *b* 1960: *m* 1984, Joanna Winslade, and has issue living, two sons and one da, — Tessa Mary, *b* 1954: *m* 1976, John Mackenzie-Green, and has issue living, two sons and one da, — Bridget Caroline, *b* 1955: *m* 1978, Angus Handasyde Dick, and has issue living, two sons and one da. *Residence* – Church Farm, Ryme Intrinsica, Dorset. ——— Bridget Alice, *b* 1931: *m* 1st, 1958, Lt-Col Peter Amyand Brenton Wickham, late RA, who *d* 1967; 2ndly, 1968, Alexander David Evelyn Mure, JP, of Pevington Farm, Pluckley, Kent TN27 0PF, and has issue living (by 1st *m*), Anthony John Macarthur, *b* 1960: *m* 1994, Georgina Dimity Cumberland-Brown, and has issue living, Adelaide *b* 1997, — Mark Andrew, *b* 1962: *m* 1991, Corinne Lynne Barker, and has issue living, William Peter Mure *b* 1993, Charlotte Alice *b* 1994, — Tania Catherine, *b* 1959: *m* 1998, Ezeddine Hamdi, and has issue living, Alexander Ezeddine Hamdi Wickham *b* 1998.

COLLETT (UK) 1934, of Bridge Ward in the City of London

Sir IAN SEYMOUR COLLETT, 3rd *Baronet*; *b* 5 Oct 1953; *s* his grandfather, *Sir* HENRY SEYMOUR, 1971; *ed* Lancing Coll; a Freeman of City of London: *m* 1982, Philippa J., only da of James R. I. Hawkins, of Preston St Mary, Suffolk.

𝕬rms – Azure, on a chevron couped or between three hinds trippant proper, collared of the second, an arch sable, between two open books, also proper. 𝕮rest – A demi-hind proper, collared or, resting the sinister foot on an escutcheon gold, charged with a maul sable.
Residence – Low Farm, Dog Lane, Bedfield, Woodbridge, Suffolk IP13 7EQ.

SON LIVING

ANTHONY SEYMOUR, *b* 1984.

DAUGHTER LIVING

Georgina, *b* 1986.

SISTER LIVING

Joanna Ruth, *b* 1956; a Freeman of City of London: *m* 1st, 1984, Nigel E. Wicks, eldest son of Malcolm E. Wicks, of Peterborough; 2ndly, 1998, Thomas E. S. Lynch, who *d* 1998, and has issue living (by 1st *m*), Jennifer Ruth, *b* 1989, — Katharine Sheila, *b* 1994. *Club* – Hurlingham.

UNCLE LIVING (*Son of 2nd baronet*)

Sir Christopher, GBE, *b* 1931; *ed* Harrow and Emmanuel Coll, Camb (MA); Capt RA (TA); a FCA, a Freeman of City of London, a Liveryman of Glovers' Co (Master 1981-82), a Liveryman of Chartered Accountants' Co, and a Liveryman of Haberdashers' Co; Common Councilman 1973-79; Alderman 1979, Sheriff 1985, Lord Mayor of City of London 1988; *cr* GBE 1988: *m* 1959, Christine Anne, da of late Oswald Hardy Griffiths, of Nunthorpe, Yorks, and has issue living, Alastair John Calvert (77 Faraday Rd, Wimbledon, SW19), *b* 1961: *m* 1992, Tiana J., only da of Anthony Peck, of Kingston upon Thames, Surrey, and has issue living, Aidan Anthony Calvert *b* 1995, Edmund *b* 1996. — Angus Christopher Calvert, *b* 1964, — Alexandra Louise Calvert, *b* 1972. *Residence* – Broomholm, Langholm, Dumfriesshire DG13 0LJ.

AUNT LIVING (*Daughter of 2nd baronet*)

Margaret Ruth, MBE (Mardle House, Wangford, nr Beccles, Suffolk), *b* 1922; AIMA, JP, a Freeman of City of London: *m* 1950, Col George Victor Nudd Chadd, OBE, TD, JP, DL, who *d* 1997, and has issue living, Richard Jonathan (Ditchingham Cottage, Ditchingham, nr Bungay, Suffolk), *b* 1953; (MA Oxon); Notary Public: *m* 1977, Jane, da of Dr William Ayles, of Edinburgh, and has issue living, Hugo George William *b* 1987, Emma Louise Mary *b* 1981, Caroline Lavinia Rose *b* 1983, — Nicholas Martyn Philip (Brampton Grove, Brampton, nr Beccles, Suffolk), *b* 1958; Freeman City of London; Liveryman Farriers' Co: *m* 1987, Amelia Catherine, da of Timothy Sallitt, of France, and has issue living, Edward George Alexander *b* 1991, Rollo Nicholas William *b* 1995, Eleanor Alice *b* 1993.

MOTHER LIVING

Sheila Joan (*Lady Miskin*), only da of late Harold Scott, of Inverleith Gdns, Edinburgh; a Freeman of City of London: *m* 1st, 1951, David Seymour Collett, who *d* 1962, el son of 2nd baronet; 2ndly, 1980, as his 2nd wife, Sir James William Miskin, QC, who *d* 1993, late Recorder of London. *Residence* – 62 Rivermead Court, Ranelagh Gdns, SW6 3RY.

COLLATERAL BRANCHES LIVING

Issue of late Richard Ionn Collett, 4th son of 1st baronet, *b* 1901, *d* 1993: *m* 1926, Helen Alice, who *d* 1992, da of late Harry Hayns:—
Norman Ionn (1380 Carlton Drive, RR#1, Cobble Hill, Vancouver, BC, Canada V0R 1L0), *b* 1927; *ed* Ipswich Sch, Perse Sch, Cambridge, and HMS Conway: *m* 1954, Ethne Maureen, da of Samuel Chadwick, and has issue living, Kevin Samuel Richard, *b* 1955, — Norman Michael, *b* 1959, — Helen Margaret, *b* 1962. —— James Masterman (Owl's Hoot, 23 Bramley Av, Coulsdon, Surrey CR3 2DS), *b* 1930; *ed* Ipswich Sch, Perse Sch, Cambridge, and Bishop's Stortford Coll: *m* 1962, Rosalind Mary, da of John Humphrey Lane, of Meldreth, Woodcote Av, Wallington, Surrey, and has issue living, Lucinda Mary, *b* 1963: *m* 1987, Colin M. Ayles, of 80 St Andrew's Rd, Coulsdon, Surrey, and has issue living, Matthew James *b* 1992. —— †Richard Patrick, *b* 1932; *ed* Ipswich Sch, Perse Sch, Cambridge, and Bishop's Stortford Coll; Capt RE (TA): *m* 1958, Gillian Anne (7 Broughton Rd, Ipswich, Suffolk IP1 3QR), da of Alfred James Remes, and *d* 1982, leaving issue, Jane Louise, *b* 1960, — Johanna Mary, *b* 1962. —— Henry Alexander (Mill Farm House, Blythburgh, Suffolk), *b* 1944; *ed* Bishop's Stortford Coll; ACA; a Freeman of City of London; a Liveryman of Distillers' Co: *m* 1969, Joy Eileen, da of Rev Ross McPherson Heard, of Hatch Beauchamp Rectory, Taunton, Somerset, and has issue living, Christian Tom, *b* 1972, — Ross Tobias, *b* 1973.

Issue of late John Collison Collett, 5th son of 1st baronet, *b* 1903, *d* 1956: *m* 1928, Ethel Ruth, who *d* 1985, da of late Benjamin A. Glanvill:—
John Brian Glanvill, *b* 1929: *m* 1959, Phyllis Ivy Sybil Kiddy, and has issue living, Robert Glanvill (15 Mill Rise, Holbrook, Ipswich, Suffolk IP9 2QH), *b* 1961: *m* 1997, Caroline Elizabeth, da of Alan Whyte, of Leigh, Worcester, and of Dubai, and has issue living, Rachel Louise *b* 1998. — John Charles, *b* 1969, — Helen Mary, *b* 1960: *m* 1990, John Charles Remfry, of 1 Highbarn Hall Cottages, Greenstead Green, Halstead, Essex, son of late Harold Charles Remfry, C Eng, of Harlow, Essex, and has issue living, Catherine Amelia *b* 1991, Elizabeth Alice *b* 1993. *Residence* – Shimmens Pightle, Dennington Rd, Framlingham, Suffolk. —— Peter Glanvill, *b* 1933: *m* 1st, 1959, Cecilia Judith, who *d* 1966, da of Gerald Eliot Meysey Bromley-Martin; 2ndly, 1973, Mary Jean, da of Leonard George Truelove, and has issue living, (by 1st *m*) Gerard Henry Glanvill (11 Clarence Rd, Stansted, Essex), *b* 1961: *m* 1989, Nicola May Marie, da of William Robson, and has issue living, Charles Henry *b* 1992, Sally Elizabeth *b* 1990, — Thomas John Eliot, *b* 1962, — Alexander Peter Glanvill, *b* 1965, — Nicola Mary, *b* 1959, — (by 2nd *m*) Rebecca Mary, *b* 1974, — Anna Catherine, *b* 1976. *Residence* – Stable End, Windhill, Bishop's Stortford, Herts CM23 2ND. —— Sheila Mary *b* 1931: *m* 1955, (John) Donald Sewell, and has issue living, David John Elliott, *b* 1956, — *Rev* Andrew William, *b* 1961: *m* 1985, Julie Harrison, and has issue living, Rachel Ruth *b* 1987, Charlotte Alison *b* 1989, Hannah Louise *b* 1993, — Michael James, *b* 1967: *m* 1994, Rebecca Elizabeth Mary Treays, and has issue living, William Herbert *b* 1999, Imogen Mary *b* 1995, — Jean Mary, *b* 1958: *m* 1995, Richard Coake, and has issue living, Benjamin Donald *b* 1997, Alexander Jack *b* (twin) 1997. *Residence* – Windward, 72 North Rd, Southwold, Suffolk IP18 6BH. —— Diana, *b* 1940: *m* 1st, 1959 (*m diss* 1969), Thomas Joseph Henighan; 2ndly, 1971, Robert Hugh MacDonald (Box 204, N Gower, Ontario, Canada), and has issue living (by 1st *m*), Stephen Patrick Glanvill, *b* 1960, — Phoebe Clare, *b* 1964.

Issue of late David Brooke Collett, 7th son of 1st baronet, *b* 1907, *d* 1998: *m* 1933, (Mary) Cecily Beatrice, FCA (3 Buckenham Court, Southwold Suffolk), da of late Hugh C. Aston:—
Anthony Hugh (7 Drayton Close, Fetcham Park, Leatherhead, Surrey KT22 9EZ), *b* 1936; MA Camb; CEng; FICE; a Freeman of City of London: *m* 1962, Christine Ann Little, and has issue living, Gail Christine, *b* 1964: *m* 1993, Robert Dean, — Clare Elizabeth, *b* 1967: *m* 1993, Guy W. Williams, — June Alison, *b* 1969. —— Elizabeth Anne, *b* 1934; Freeman of City of London: *m* 1957, David Luard Boult, of Mariners, Southwold, Suffolk and has issue living, David Mark, *b* 1960; MA Cantab: *m* 1997, Sally Anne, da of Trevor White, of Maldon, Essex, — Edward William, *b* 1963, — Nicola Anne Louise, *b* 1958: *m* 1989, Clive William Huish, son of George Huish, of Ottery St Mary, Devon, and has issue living, William George Brooke *b* 1993. —— Bridget Mary, *b* 1945: *m* 1981, James David Blackburn, of Railroad Mills Rd, Pittsford, NY, USA, and has issue living, David Peter, *b* 1986, — Barbara Ann (adopted), *b* 1972: *m* 1997, Thomas Sadowski, and has issue living, Lydia *b* 1998.

Issue of late Roger Collett, yst son of 1st baronet, *b* 1909, *d* 1972: *m* 1934 (*m diss* 19—), Doreen Frances Alvie, da of late Sydney Platt:—
Roger James (8 Vanbrugh Fields, Blackheath, SE3 7TZ), *b* 1942; *ed* Ellesmere Coll: *m* 1966 Valerie Doreen, da of late Prof Cyril George Beasley, and has issue living, Christopher James, *b* 1973, — Nicola Valerie, *b* 1971. —— Susan Marjory, *b* 1939: *m* 1960, James Stafford Coombe, of Glenmore, Church Lane, Chipstead, Surrey, and has issue living, Andrew James Grant, *b* 1964, — John Edward, *b* 1979, — Caroline Jane, *b* 1961, — Edwina Gay, *b* 1963, — Georgina Susan, *b* 1974, — Genevieve Frances, *b* 1983.

The 1st baronet, Sir Charles Henry Collett (son of Henry John Richard Collett, JP of The Hall, Peasenhall, Suffolk), was a Common Councilman of the City of London 1912-27, an Alderman 1927-38, Sheriff 1932-3, and Lord Mayor 1933-4.

COLMAN (UK) 1907, of Gatton Park, Gatton, Surrey

Sir MICHAEL JEREMIAH COLMAN, 3rd *Baronet*; *b* 7 July 1928; *s* his father, *Sir* JEREMIAH 1961; *ed* Eton; Capt Queen's Own Yorks Yeo (RARO); Chm of Reckitt & Colman plc 1986-95; 1st Church Estates Commissioner 1993-99; Dir of Reckitt & Colman Ltd and Foreign & Colonial Private Equity Trust plc; Pres R Warrant Holders Assocn 1984; Associate of Trin House and Member of Lighthouse Board since 1985, Younger Brother 1994; Member of the Court of Skinners' Co 1985-94; Member of Gen Council and Finance Cttee of King Edward's Hospital Fund for London; Special Trustee, St Mary's Hospital, Paddington: *m* 1955, Judith Jean Wallop, da of late Vice Adm Sir Peveril Barton Reibey Wallop William-Powlett, KCB, KCMG, CBE, DSO (*see* E Portsmouth, colls), and has issue.

Arms – Ermine, on a pale rayonée or, between two crosses flory sable, a lion rampant gules. Crest – In front of two wings argent, each charged with an estoile azure, a rock proper, thereon a caltrap or. Badge – Issuant through an antique crown or, a greyhound's head proper.
Residence – Malshanger, Basingstoke, Hants RG23 7EY.

Quick enough if well enough

SONS LIVING

JEREMIAH MICHAEL POWLETT, *b* 23 Jan 1958; *ed* Eton, and Univ of Leicester (LLB): *m* 1981, Susan Elizabeth, yr da of John Henry Britland, of 15 Straylands Grove, York, and has issue living, Joseph Jeremiah, *b* 31 Oct 1988, — Nathaniel James, *b* 1990, — Jacob Robert John, *b* 1996, — Eleanor Mary, *b* 1985. —— John Powlett, *b* 1962.

DAUGHTERS LIVING

Olivia Helena Judith, *b* 1956: *m* 1979, Rev Canon Patrick John Whitworth, yr son of Maj-Gen Reginald Henry Whitworth, CB, CBE, of Abbey House Farm, Goosey, Wantage, Oxon, and has issue living, David John William, *b* 1990, — Emma Rachel, *b* 1982, — Louisa Judith, *b* 1984, — Sophia Rose, *b* 1987. —— Victoria Rose, *b* 1960: *m* 1988, Rev Matthew S. Persson, of 41 Marloes Rd, W8 6LA, elder son of Rt Rev William Michael Dermot Persson, Bishop of Doncaster, and has issue living, Augustus William, *b* 1990, — Bartholomew Jo, *b* 1993. —— Alice Mary *b* 1965: *m* 1994, Timothy A. C. Page, of Lower Dunge Farm, West Ashton, Trowbridge, Wilts BA14 6AX, eldest son of Col (John Patrick) Anthony Page, of Croft House, Brackley, and has issue living, Thomas Joseph Dalziel, *b* 1995, — Natasha Phoebe Anastasia, *b* 1998.

BROTHER LIVING

Oliver James, *b* 1933: *m* 1967, Hon Cynthia Makins, twin da of 1st Baron Sherfield, and has issue living, Thomas James, *b* 1969, — Camilla Mary, *b* 1972. *Residence* – 7 Tor Gardens, W8 7AB.

SISTER LIVING

Gillian Veronica, *b* 1926.

The 1st baronet, Sir Jeremiah Colman (son of Jeremiah Colman, of Carshalton Park, Surrey), was Chm of J. & J. Colman Ltd, manufacturers, of Norwich and London, and a Lieut for City of London.

COLQUHOUN (GB) 1786, of Luss, Dumbarton
(Name pronounced "Cohoon")

If I can

Sir IVAR IAIN COLQUHOUN OF LUSS, 8th *Baronet*; *b* 4 Jan 1916; *s* his father, *Lt-Col Sir* IAIN, KT, DSO, LLD, 1948; *ed* Eton; is Chief of the Clan Colquhoun, and Capt Gren Gds, DL and JP of Dunbartonshire and Hon Sheriff Substitute: *m* 1943, Kathleen, 2nd da of late Walter Atholl Duncan, of 53 Cadogan Sq, SW1, and has issue.

Arms – Argent, a saltire engrailed sable. Crest – A hart's head couped gules, attired argent. Supporters – Two ratch-hounds argent, collared sable.
Seat – Camstraddan, Luss, Dunbartonshire G83 8NX. *Clubs* – White's, Puffin's, Royal Ocean Racing.

SON LIVING

MALCOLM RORY (74 Nightingale Lane, SW12 8NR; White's and Turf Clubs), *b* 20 Dec 1947; *ed* Eton, and London Univ: *m* 1st, 1978 (*m diss* 1983), Susan, el da of Stewart W. Timmerman, of Harrisburg, Penn, USA; 2ndly, 1989, Katharine A. H., eldest da of A. C. Mears, of Canberra, Australia, and has issue living (by 1st *m*), Patrick John, *b* 17 Dec 1980, — (by 2nd *m*) Fergus Alexander Mears, *b* 1991, — Georgina Iona Helena, *b* 1993.

DAUGHTER LIVING

Iona Mary (*Duchess of Argyll*), *b* 1945: *m* 1964, 12th Duke of Argyll. *Residence* – Inveraray Castle, Argyll.

SISTERS LIVING

Fiona Bryde (*Fiona, Countess of Arran*), *b* 1918: *m* 1937, 8th Earl of Arran, who *d* 1983. *Residence* – Pimlico House, Hemel Hempstead, Herts. —— Robina (*Robina, Lady Wigan*), *b* 1923; sometime in WRNS: *m* 1950, Capt Sir Alan Lewis Wigan, 5th Bt, who *d* 1996. —— Frances Mary, *b* 1925.

COLLATERAL BRANCH LIVING

Issue of late Donald Colquhoun, yr son of 7th baronet, *b* 1920, *d* 1992: *m* 1946, Josephine Griselda (Valadie, Marminiac, 46250 Cazals, Lot, France), only da of late Charles Wilfrid Janson, of 16 Wilton Crescent, SW1:—
James (1043 Jefferson Av, W Vancouver, BC V7T 2A6, Canada), *b* 1947; *ed* Gordonstoun: *m* 1986, Margaret Susan, da of late Dr John Leishman, and has issue living Michael James, *b* 1989, — Steffany Susan, *b* 1993. —— Iain, *b* 1949; *ed* Gordonstoun. —— Catherine Mary, *b* 1958: *m* 1982, James Hyde Forshall, of Mourlane, Marminiac, 46250 Cazals, Lot, France, and has had issue, Rose Alexandra, *b* 1982, — Romilly Louise, *b* 1984; *d* 1999, — Beatrice Isabella, *b* 1992, — Flora Hyde, *b* 1998.

The earliest surname under which the family of Colquhoun is traced is that of Kilpatrick. Sir John Colquhoun of Luss, 14th in descent from Umphridus de Kilpatrick (*temp* Alexander II), was created a baronet of Nova Scotia by Charles I. Sir Humphrey Colquhoun, 3rd Bt, in 1704 resigned his Baronetcy to the Crown, and obtained a new patent with the old precedency, but with the remainder to his son-in-law James Grant, (who on succeeding to the Baronetcy assumed the surname of Colquhoun, but resumed that of Grant in 1719) and the heirs male of his marriage with Sir Humphrey's da (*see* E Seafield). In 1786 James, 4th son of the above mentioned James Grant, was *cr* a Baronet of Great Britain. The 3rd baronet (*cr* 1786), sat as MP for Dunbartonshire in 1802; and Sir James, the 4th baronet (who *m* 1843, Jane, 2nd da of Sir Robert Abercromby, 5th Bt, of Birkenbog, co Banff), was Lord-Lieut of Dunbartonshire, and MP (*L*) therefor 1837-41. Sir James, 5th Bt, was also Lord-Lieut of Dunbartonshire 1887-1907. Lieut-Col Sir Iain Colquhoun, KT, DSO, LLD, Scots Guards, was Lord-Lieut of Dunbartonshire, Lord High Commr for Church of Scotland 1932, 1940, and 1941, and Lord Rector of Glasgow Univ 1934.

COLT (E) 1694, of St James's-in-the-Fields Liberty of Westminster, Middlesex

He conquers who endures

Sir EDWARD WILLIAM DUTTON COLT, 10th *Baronet*, son of late Major John Rochfort Colt, North Staffordshire Regt, half-brother of 9th baronet; *b* 22 Sept 1936; *s* his uncle *Sir* HENRY ARCHER, DSO, MC 1951; *ed* Douai; MB BS, London: FRCP; FACP; Associate Clinical Prof of Medicine, Columbia Univ, and Associate Attending Physician St. Luke's Hosp, New York, NY 10025: *m* 1st, 1966 (*m diss* 1972), Jane Caroline, da of James Histed Lewis, of 12 Pont Céard, Versoix, Geneva, and Washington, DC; 2ndly, 1979, Suzanne Nelson (*née* Knickerbocker), and has had issue by 2nd *m*.

Arms – Argent, a fesse between three colts courant sable. **Crest** – A colt passant or.
Residence – 12 E 88th St, New York, NY 10128, USA.

SON DECEASED (*By 2nd marriage*)

Tristan Charles Edward, *b* 27 June 1983; *d* 19 May 1992.

DAUGHTER LIVING (*By 2nd marriage*)

Angela Cecily, *b* 1979.

SISTER LIVING

Joan Margaret Roper, *b* 1932.

The pedigree of this family commences with Thomas Colt, of Carlisle; his son, Thomas Colt, of Essex and Suffolk (Keeper of the Rolls of Chancery in Ireland, and a Privy Councillor to King Edward IV), was father of John Colt, whose da Joan (or Jane) was 1st wife of Sir Thomas More, Lord Chancellor of England. From him descended George Colt (son of Sir Henry Colt, Knt, who was son of George Colt, High Sheriff of Suffolk 1587, and great-grandson of Sir George Colt, Knt); he was father of the 1st baronet, Sir Henry Dutton Colt, Adj to Prince Rupert, Ensign of the Yeoman of the Guard, and MP for Westminster *temp* William III and Anne. His brother, John Dutton Colt, was MP for Leominster, and his brother, Sir William Dutton Colt, Knt, was Master of the Horse to Prince Rupert, and Envoy at the Courts of Hanover and Dresden.

COLTHURST (I) 1744, of Ardrum, co Cork

Justum et tenacem

Just and firm of purpose

Sir RICHARD LA TOUCHE COLTHURST, 9th *Baronet*; *b* 14 Aug 1928; *s* his father, *Sir* RICHARD ST JOHN JEFFERYES, 1955; *ed* Harrow, and Peterhouse, Camb (MA); Member Dendrology Society; Organiser of Blarney Castle International Three Day Annual Event since 1992; a Liveryman of Grocers' Co: *m* 1953, Janet Georgina, da of late Leonard Almroth Wilson-Wright, of Coolcarrigan, co Kildare, and has issue.

Arms – Argent, on a fesse azure between three colts courant sable, as many trefoils slipped or. **Crest** – A colt statant sable.
Seats – Blarney Castle, co Cork; Ardrum, Inniscarra, co Cork. *Clubs* – MCC, Pitt (Camb), Hawks' (Camb), I Zingari, Cork County CC.

SONS LIVING

CHARLES ST JOHN (Turret Farm, Blarney, co Cork; MCC, and RIAC (Dublin) Clubs), *b* 21 May 1955; *ed* Eton, Magdalene Coll, Camb (MA), and Univ Coll, Dublin; Solicitor, Cork: *m* 1987, Nora Mary, da of Mortimer Kelleher, of Dooniskey, Lissarda, co Cork, and has issue living, John Conway La Touche, *b* 13 Oct 1988, — Charlotte Louisa Margaret, *b* 1990, — Isabel Janet Denys *b* 1991, — Olivia Mary Penelope, *b* 1995. —— James Richard (Balsdon Farmhouse, Folly Rd, Inkpen, Hungerford, Berks RG17 9DH; Leander, MCC); *b* 1957; *ed* Eton, and St Thomas's Med Sch, London Univ (BSc MB BS) 1982, FRCS (Edin) 1985; MBA (Brunel) 1992, MFHom 1995; inventor, medical consultant: *m* 1990, Dominique G., elder da of Gale Coles, of Little Streele, Framfield, E Sussex, and has issue living, Leah Alexandra, *b* 1994, — Cicely Rachel, *b* 1997. —— Henry Nicholas Almroth (Asserton House, Berwick St James, Salisbury, Wilts SP3 4TZ; MCC, Pitt (Camb)), *b* 1959; *ed* Eton, and Christ's Coll, Camb (MA): *m* 1982, Sophia Selina Irene, yr da of Sir (Frederick) John Charles Gordon Hervey-Bathurst, 7th Bt, and has issue living, Edward Henry John, *b* 1986, — Harriet Sophia, *b* 1984, — Caroline Georgina, *b* 1991.

DAUGHTER LIVING

Georgina Margaret, b 1961; Organiser of Blarney Castle International Three Day Annual Event since 1992; author of *Fighting Back* (1990).

BROTHER LIVING

George Silver Oliver Annesley, b 1931; ed Harrow, and Trin Coll, Camb (MA); late 2nd Lt Life Gds; Member of London Stock Exchange, Partner de Zoete and Bevan 1961-81, Liveryman Goldsmiths' Co, Member of Court of Common Council (Broad St Ward) 1976-80: m 1st, 1959 (m diss 1966), Hon Elizabeth Sophia Sidney, el da of 1st Viscount De L'Isle, VC, KG, GCMG, GCVO; 2ndly, 1968, Caroline Romaine, da of late Cdr Anthony Boyce Combe (see Farquhar, Bt, colls, 1990 Edn), and has issue living, (by 1st m) Shaunagh Anne Henrietta (*Hon Mrs Crispin Money-Coutts*), b 1961: m 1st, 1980 (m diss 1990), Thomas Peter William Heneage (see E Morton, colls); 2ndly, 1995, Hon Crispin James Alan Nevill Money-Coutts, elder son of 8th Baron Latymer, — (by 2nd m) Romaine Louisa, b 1969, — Rowena Barbara, b 1971. *Residence* – Le Bourg, 16450 Beaulieu-sur-Sonnette, St Claud, Charente, France. *Clubs* – Turf, Pratt's, MCC, I Zingari.

HALF-SISTER LIVING (*Daughter of 8th Baronet by 1st marriage*)

Shournagh Dorothy, b 1914: m 1937, Robert Tristram Combe, Lt Coldm Gds, who d of wounds received in action at Dunkirk 1940, and has issue living, Richard Tristram (Earnshill, Hambridge, Langport, Som), b 1938; ed Eton; Capt Coldm Gds; Underwriting Member of Lloyds; a JP: m 1985, Mrs Bridgett Anne Glide, da of late Charles Fleetwood Crombie, of South Hillside, Strete, Dartmouth, Devon, — Henry Cecil, b 1940: m 1st, 1968, Gillian Margaret, who d 1973, da of late Ralph Hancock, of Port Elizabeth, S Africa; 2ndly, 1975 (m diss 1992), Ingerise Andersen, and has issue living, (by 1st m) Nicholas Hamilton b 1969; Dip Eng; Leighton Engineering Ltd, Tsing Yi Island, Hong Kong, (by 2nd m) Kirstina Louise b 1977, Andrea Shournagh Margrethe b 1979. *Residence* – Hundry Lodge, Hambridge, nr Langport, Som.

The 1st baronet, Sir John Colthurst (el son of John Colthurst, of Ardrum and Ballyandy) was MP for Doneraile 1751-60, for Youghal 1761-8, and for Castle Martyr 1769-75. Sir John Conway Colthurst, 2nd Bt, d of wounds received in a duel 1787. Sir Nicholas Colthurst, 3rd Bt, was MP for Johnstown, Longford 1783-90, and for Castle Martyr 1791-5, and High Sheriff, co Cork 1788. Sir Nicholas Conway Colthurst, 4th Bt, was MP for the City of Cork 1812-29. Sir George Conway Colthurst, 5th Bt, was MP for Kinsale (L) 1863-74 and High Sheriff, co Cork 1850. Sir George St John Colthurst, 6th Bt, was High Sheriff, co Cork 1884; ADC to Lord Lieut of Ireland. Sir George Oliver Colthurst, 7th Bt, served in 1914-19 War as Capt Special Cav, South Irish Horse (Croix de Guerre). Sir Richard St John Jefferyes Colthurst, 8th Bt, was Capt London Regt 1914-19 and High Sheriff of co Dublin 1920-21.

Colyer-Fergusson, see Fergusson.

CONANT (UK) 1954, of Lyndon, co Rutland.

It shall be given to him who tries

Sir JOHN ERNEST MICHAEL CONANT, 2nd *Baronet*; b 24 April 1923; s his father Sir ROGER JOHN EDWARD, CVO, 1973; ed Eton, and Corpus Christi Coll, Camb (BA); High Sheriff of Rutland 1960: m 1st, 1950, Periwinkle Elizabeth, who d 1985, elder da of late Dudley Thorp, of Brothers House, Kimbolton, Hunts; 2ndly, 1992, Mrs (Mary) Clare Attwater, yr da of William E. Madden, of Petersfield, Hants, and has issue by 1st m.

Arms – Per saltire gules and azure billetée or. **Crest** – A stag proper the dexter foreleg resting on a shield gules billetée or.
Residence – Periwinkle Cottage, Lyndon, Oakham, Rutland.

SONS LIVING (*By 1st marriage*)

(SIMON) EDWARD CHRISTOPHER, b 13 Oct 1958; ed Eton, and RAC Cirencester. — William John Nathaniel, b 1970.

DAUGHTERS LIVING (*By 1st marriage*)

Fiona Elizabeth, b 1955: m 1987, Jonathan P. N. Driver, elder son of R. M. Driver, of Warren Bay, Watchet, Somerset, and has issue living, Alexander Edward, b 1990. — Melanie Lucinda, b 1961: m 1986, Richard Alastair Firmston-Williams, son of late Gordon Firmston-Williams, and has issue living, Hamish Alastair, b 1991, — Jessica Alice, b 1989, — Emily Periwinkle, b 1994.

BROTHERS LIVING

Guy Timothy Geoffrey, b 1924; ed Stowe, and RAC Cirencester; formerly Fl Lt RAF; JP and DL Northants, High Sheriff 1969: m 1st, 1953 (m diss 19—), Elizabeth, da of late A. T. Handley, I of Wight; 2ndly, 1981, Davina Huntley, el da of late Sir Guy Hope Holland, 3rd Bt, and has issue living (by 1st m), Rupert Edward Geoffrey, b 1964: m 1993, Kathryn

Jean, 4th da of Harold Miller, of Bridgend, Glam, — Sheena Lorraine, *b* 1954, — Elizabeth Jane, *b* 1955, — Diana Juliet, *b* 1960: *m* 1985, Peter S. McMahon, 2nd son of R. F. McMahon, of Australia, — (by 2nd *m*) Melissa Sothern, *b* 1984. *Residence* – Bulwick Park, nr Corby, Northants. —— Charles Richard, *b* 1929; *ed* Eton: *m* 1958, Katherine Anne Ross, da of Hubert George Anthony Ross-Wilson, of Gaddesby, Leics, and has issue living, Caroline-Rose, *b* 1959: *m* 1988, Timothy John Hawkins, of 35 Nansen Rd, SW11, yr son of late Lt-Col Tony Hawkins, OBE, of Chelsea, SW10, and has issue living, William Anthony Charles Horatio *b* 1992, Charlotte Lucy *b* 1990, — Francesca Louise, *b* 1962: *m* 1986, Philip Henry Kendall, of Apethorpe Lodge, Apethorpe, nr Peterborough, Northants PE8 5DE, and has issue living, Josephine Louise *b* 1988, Claudia Daphne *b* 1991. *Residence* – Fishponds Cottage, Deene Rd, Harringworth, nr Corby, Northants NN17 3AB.

CONGREVE (UK) 1927, of Congreve, co Stafford (Extinct 1941)

Com Sir GEOFFREY CECIL CONGREVE, DSO, RN, 1st and last *Baronet*; *ka* 1941.

DAUGHTERS LIVING OF FIRST BARONET

Anne Henrietta, *b* 1923: *m* 1944, Richard M. T. Tyler, formerly Capt RE, and has issue living, (John) Christian Congreve, *b* 1945: *m* 1st, 1968 (*m diss* 1984), Kathryn Cornelia, da of late George Rader, of Old Red Hill Rd, Dauphin, Penn, USA; 2ndly, 1987, Ciaran Anne Magdalene (the actress Ciaran Madden), da of late James George Madden, of Glebe House, Tollesbury, Essex, and has issue living (by 1st *m*) Frederick Christian Townsend *b* 1975, Elisabeth Helen Madeleine *b* 1977, Madeleine Amelia Congreve *b* 1981, — (Richard Henry) Felix (12 Brandlehow Rd, SW15 2ED), *b* 1954, — Camilla Madeleine Mary, *b* 1946: *m* 1969, John Michael Antony Dinkel, who *d* 1991, of 14 Victoria Rd, Brighton, Sussex BN1 3FS, and has issue living, Cosima Lucy *b* 1971, Sophie Alexandra *b* 1975, — Amelia Henrietta Rose (10 Albany Rd, Montpelier, Bristol BS6 5LH), *b* 1950: *m* 1968 (*m diss* 1981), Mark Walter Fletcher (*see* B Mottistone), and has issue living, Benjamin Charles *b* 1971, Ellen Maisie Madeleine *b* 1973, Rose Athalie RANDLES *b* 1981. *Residence* – Brachamfield House, Burstock, Beaminster, Dorset. —— Marygold Elizabeth, *b* 1926: *m* 1953, Maj Ian Stafford Alexander, Roy Irish Fusiliers (ret), and has issue living, Maria Congreve, *b* 1959; resumed her maiden name 1987: *m* 1983 1st, (*m diss* 1985), James Richard Anthony Bamford; 2ndly, 1989, as his 3rd wife, Maj Raymond Alexander Carnegie (*see* D Fife, colls). *Residence* – Castle Bank, Stowe by Chartley, Stafford. —— Carola, *b* 1929: *m* 1948 (*m diss* 1959), John Horatio Gordon Shephard, formerly Capt Gren Gds, who *d* 1993, and has issue living, Thomas Horatio Congreve (Claigan Farmhouse, Dunvegan, Isle of Skye), *b* 1949: *m* 1971, Hon Mary Anna Shaw, 2nd da of late Baron Kilbrandon, PC (Life Baron), and has issue living, Samuel *b* 1973, Edward Congreve *b* 1975, Francis *b* 1977, Christian *b* 1985, Josephine *b* 1981, — Henry John (20 Lots Rd, SW10 0QF), *b* 1955. *Residence* – 20 Lots Rd, SW10.

STRICKLAND-CONSTABLE (E) 1641, of Boynton, Yorkshire

To the will of God

Sir FREDERIC STRICKLAND-CONSTABLE, 12th *Baronet*; *b* 21 Oct 1944; *s* his father, *Lt-Cdr Sir* ROBERT FREDERICK, RNVR, 1994; *ed* Westminster, Corpus Christi Coll, Camb (BA), and London Business Sch (MSc): *m* 1982, Pauline Margaret, da of ..... Harding, of ......, and has issue.

Arms – Quarterly: 1st and 4th, gules and vair a bend or, *Constable*; 2nd and 3rd, gules a chevron or, between three crosses-pattée argent on a canton ermine a buck's head erased and attired sable, *Strickland*. Crest – 1st, a ship, sails furled, all or. *Constable*; 2nd, a turkey cock in his pride proper, *Strickland*. *Address* – Estate Office, Old Maltongate, Malton, York YO17 0EG.

SON LIVING

CHARLES, *b* 10 Oct 1985.

DAUGHTER LIVING

Rose, *b* 1983.

BROTHER LIVING

John Robert Francis, *b* 1949; *ed* Bryanston, Slade Sch of Fine Art, and London Univ (Higher Dip in Fine Art): *m* 1971, Christine, da of D...... W...... Roberts, of St Paul's Cray, Kent, and has issue living, Thomas Robert, *b* 1976; *ed* ......, — Louisa Emma, *b* 1979. *Residence* – Combe Wood, Brasted, Westerham, Kent.

SISTERS LIVING

Miranda, *b* 1938; *ed* London Univ (BA). *Residence* – .... ——Elizabeth Diana, *b* 1940; *ed* Royal Coll of Music (ARCM), and Staatliche Hochschüle für Musik, Cologne: *m* 1972, John Maxwell Fairley, BSc, and has issue living, Lucy Fiona, *b* 1974, — Alice Susannah, *b* 1977. *Residence* – ......

WIDOW LIVING OF ELEVENTH BARONET

LETTICE (*Lettice, Lady Strickland-Constable*), yst da of late Maj Frederic Strickland (see colls, infra): *m* 1936, as his 2nd wife, her 2nd cousin, Lt-Cdr Sir Robert Frederick Strickland-Constable, 11th Bt, RNVR, who *d* 1994. *Residence* – 3 Chart Lane, Brasted, Westerham, Kent.

COLLATERAL BRANCHES LIVING

Issue of late Major Frederic Strickland, 2nd son of 8th baronet, *b* 1867, *d* 1934: *m* 1903, Mary Beatrix, who *d* 1965, da of late Sir John Isaac Thornycroft, LLD, FRS:—
Lettice (*Lettice, Lady Strickland-Constable*), *b* 1913: *m* 1936, as his 2nd wife, Sir Robert Frederick Strickland-Constable, 11th Bt, RNVR, who *d* 1994.

Grandsons of late Walter Richard Strickland (who assumed by deed poll 1886 the surname of Cholmley, but continued to use the surname of Strickland), son of Rev Nathaniel Constantine Strickland, 6th son of 6th baronet:—
Issue of late Gerald Constantine Strickland, MM, *b* 1888, *d* 1962: *m* 1st, 1910 (*m diss* 1921), Mary, da of John Hampton, of Pretoria; 2ndly, 1922, Magdalene, da of Peter Hünten, of Pretoria, S Africa:—
(By 1st *m*) †Gerald John, *b* 1911; *ed* Rand Univ: *m* 1940, Patricia, who *d* 1988, da of Archibald Edward Benson, of Pretoria, and *d* 1993, leaving issue, John, *b* 1950, — Margaret Julia Patricia, *b* 1942: *m* 1978, Hubert Henri Malherbe, of 12105 S Hidden Valley, Club Drive, Sandy, Utah 84092, USA.

Issue of late Arthur William Strickland, *b* 1890, *d* 1970: *m* 1918, Violet May, who *d* 1956, da of Edward S. Margerum, of Merrylands, W Aust:—
Stanley Arthur (28 Cavendish Rd, New Malden, Surrey KT3 6DH), *b* 1920: *m* 1952, Eileen Mary, da of late Patrick Henry Keeley, of Surbiton and has issue living, Janet Frances, *b* 1960. —— John Edward (56 Chertsey Drive, N Cheam, Surrey) *b* 1923: *m* 1953, Rose Ena, da of late George Thomas William Greenfield, of N Cheam, Surrey, and has issue living, Christopher Graham, *b* 1962: *m* 1986, Tracey Susan, da of Charles Alec Lang, of Abbey Wood, London, and has issue living, Charlie *b* 1990, Lauren *b* 1986, — Susan Carol, *b* 1960: *m* 1977, Trevor Fisher, of Carshalton, Surrey, and has issue living, Alan David *b* 1977, Liam Steven *b* 1991, Natalie Alison *b* 1979, — Alison Ruth, *b* 1966: *m* 1989, Frederick Charles Wakelin, of Shepperton, Middx, and has issue living, Charlotte Rose *b* 1990, Rachel Louise *b* 1992.

Granddaughters of late Hugh Strickland, 2nd son of late Rev Nathaniel Constantine Strickland, 6th son of 6th baronet:—
Issue of late Nathaniel Lewis Hugh Strickland, *b* 1899, *d* 1954: *m* 1923, Unity Margaret, who *d* 1975, da of late Arthur Birch:—
Mavis Rae, *b* 1929: *m* 1952, Eric Richard Earl, of 7 Lombardy Drive, Berkhamsted. —— Mary Joy, *b* (twin) 1929: *m* 1952, George Arthur Jones, of Hayley House, Main St, Brancaster, N Norfolk. —— Margaret Anne, *b* 1932: *m* 1st, 1953 (*m diss* 1977), Lionel Wood; 2ndly, 1977, Dr Israel Kessel, who *d* 1985, of The Stables, Little Common, Stanmore, Middx.

Grandchildren of late Robert Strickland, elder son of Walter Strickland, eldest son of George Strickland, 2nd son of 5th baronet:—
Issue of late Claude Francis Strickland, CIE, *b* 1881, *d* 1962: *m* 1915, Dorothy Lisa, who *d* 1972, da of late G. A. Branson, MD, of Dandaraga, Riddell, Victoria, Australia:—
Patricia Elizabeth Mary (19 Sumner Court, Sumner Rd, Farnham, Surrey), *b* 1916: *m* 1941, Col Arthur Vyvyan Denton, Loyal Regt, who *d* 1987, and has issue living, Amanda Elizabeth Ann Vyvyan, *b* 1943: *m* 1968, David Frederick James Leathers (*see* V Leathers), — Joanna Mary Vyvyan (6 Brunswick St, Bath), *b* 1946: *m* 1974 (*m diss* 1986), Martyn Frederick Laurence, and has issue living, Ashton Aynsley (a son) *b* 1980, Alice Joanna *b* 1976. —— Frances Pamela Ann, *b* 1919: *m* 1st, 1942, Anthony William Vivian, RAF Vol Reserve, who was *ka* in Mediterranean 1942; 2ndly, 1946, Capt Anthony James Parr, of Old Dove House, Kingbourne Green, Harpenden, Herts, and has issue living, (by 2nd *m*) Francis Nicholas, *b* 1949: *m* 1974, Sakiko Fukuda, — Laetitia Mary, *b* 1948: *m* 1970, William Logan Jack, of Huntington Court, Kington, Herefords, and has issue living, Robert Logan *b* 1977, Rosemary Ann *b* 1979.

Issue of late Cecil Eustace Strickland, BSc, *b* 1889, *d* 1981: *m* 1st, 1923 (*m diss* 1942), Dorothy Enid, 2nd da of Edward Stocker, of Blackheath, SW; 2ndly, 1949, Galatea, da of Costas Patzatzis, of Cairo:—
(By 1st *m*) Martin Robert Cecil (4 Irene Rd, Rondesbosch, Cape, S Africa), *b* 1927; BSc, MIEE: *m* 1953, Judith Melvia, da of Cecil Kerr, and has issue living, Walter Robert Cecil, *b* 1954: *m* 1980, Christine Clark, and has issue living, James Robert *b* 1984, Natalie Judith *b* 1982, Kyle Rhoana *b* 1989, — Hugh Edward, *b* 1955: *m* 1984, Bridget Newmarch, and has issue living, Charles Robert *b* 1987, Evelyn Judith *b* 1985, — Kenneth William, *b* 1959, — Alexander David, *b* 1965. —— Walter Nicholas, *b* 1930; PhD: *m* 1st, 1956 (*m diss* 1964), Margaret Brown, of Dunoon, Argyll; 2ndly, 1968, Marie, da of Lynn Shields, of Salt Lake City, and has issue living, (by 1st *m*) Gina Elizabeth, *b* 1963, — (by 2nd *m*) Robert Nicholas, *b* 1971. —— Jessica Helen, *b* 1951: *m* 19—, Philip Lissaman, of Marlborough, NZ, and has issue living, Bridget, *b* 1979, — Claire, *b* 1982, — Sandra, *b* 1983.

Issue of late Clement Cyprian Strickland, *b* 1892, *d* 1943: *m* 1920, Violet Isobel, who *d* 1983, da of late Meyrick Edward Selby-Lowndes, JP, of Mursley Grange, Winslow, Bucks:—
Rev Paul Clement Lowndes (The Anchorage, 4 Albany Gdns East, Clacton-on-Sea, Essex CO15 6HW), *b* 1921: *m* 1st, 1950, Emily Hartley, of Pontefract; 2ndly, 1986, Ruth Elizabeth, da of late Harold Kingston Harwood, of Harrow, Middx, and has had issue (by 1st *m*), †Walter Francis Lowndes, *b* 1953; *ed* St John's, Leatherhead; *d* 1970, — Janet Elizabeth, *b* 1951; assumed by Statutory Declaration 1986 the surname of STRICKLAND-MILLER: *m* 1979, Allan James Miller, of The Old Manor, Naughton, nr Ipswich, Suffolk IP7 7BY, and has issue living, Oliver Thomas Lowndes *b* 1985, William Edward Lowndes *b* 1987, — Mary Isobel, *b* 1961.

Granddaughter of late Walter Kennedy Strickland, son of late Charles Strickland, son of late George Strickland (ante):—
Issue of late Com Charles Walter Campbell Strickland, RN, *b* 1873, *d* 1918: *m* 1909, Constance Margaret Lorn Campbell (who *d* 1959, having *m* 2ndly, 1928, Benjamin Charles Apps), da of late Major F. W. Campbell, RHA:—
Katarin Jarrard Campbell, *b* 1914: *m* 1938, John Evan Privett, of Priory Cottage, Naish, East Coker, Yeovil, Som, and has issue living, John Hugh Charles, *b* 1939: *m* 1971, Jane Dilys Rowland Macqueen, and has issue living, Jonathan Edward Macqueen *b* 1972, Rowland Alexander Charles *b* 1978, Guy Frederick Andrew *b* 1981, Philada Jane *b* 1974, — Robin Jarrard Campbell, *b* 1940: *m* 1964, Penelope Lisbeth Bate, and has issue living, James Jarrard Campbell *b* 1966, Edward Tobias *b* 1970, Kathryn Louise *b* 1968, — Alan Frederick, *b* 1943: *m* 1st, 1975 (*m diss* 19—), Carolin Graham Fawcett; 2ndly, 1981, Jenny Maria Miller, and has issue living (by 2nd *m*), Imogen Frances *b* 1981, Alice Rose *b* 1987, — Christina Katarin *b* 1946: *m* 1984, Cedric Thomas Sandford, and has issue living, Anna Elizabeth *b* 1990.

Granddaughters of late Algernon Henry Peter Strickland, son of late Algernon Augustine de Lille Strickland (infra):—
Issue of late Algernon Walter Strickland, *b* 1891, *d* 1938: *m* 1915, Lady Mary Charteris, who *d* 1991 (having *m* 2ndly, 1943, Major John George Lyon, RA), da of 11th Earl of Wemyss:—
Pamela Sabina, *b* 1921: *m* 1947, Maj Henry Benjamin Van der Gucht, MC, late R Northumberland Fusiliers, and has issue living, Guy Tristam, *b* 1951, — Hugo Charles, *b* 1956: *m* 1992, Sarah Alvina CAPLIN THOMAS, da of T. G. Thomas, of Hatfield Heath, Essex, — Juliet Clare, *b* 1948: *m* 1972, Julian Jan Ivor de Haan, and has issue (*see* E Plymouth colls). *Residence* - Apperley Court, Gloucester. —— Sara Ann Mary (*Lady Carr*), *b* 1926: *m* 1950, Prof Sir (Albert) Raymond Maillard Carr, late Warden of St Anthony's Coll, Oxford, of Burch, N Molton, N Devon, and has issue living, Adam Henry Maillard, *b* 1951, — Matthew Xavier Maillard (4 Perham Rd, W14), *b* 1953; portrait painter: *m* 1988, Lady Anne Mary Somerset, only da of 11th Duke of Beaufort, and has issue living, Eleanor *b* 1992, — Alexander Rallion Charles, *b* 1958, — Laura Selina Madeline, *b* 1954: *m* 1978, Richard Edmond Barrowclough, and has issue (*see* E Limerick, colls). *Residence* – Pyncombe Farm, Wiveliscombe, Som.

Grandchildren of late Claud Hugh Strickland, 4th and yst son of Algernon Augustine de Lille Strickland, elder son of Augustine Edmund Christopher Strickland (infra):—
Issue of late Walter Claud Strickland, *b* 1896; *d* 1982: *m* 1st, 1932 (*m diss* 1946), Charmian Louise, only child of Lt-Col Harold Cazenove Hessey, of Bethersden, Kent; 2ndly, 1954, Mary Julianne, el da of late Wilfred Henry Kellam-Harris, of Putney, SW:—
(By 2nd *m*) Walter Hugh Jeremy, *b* 1960.

Issue of late Hugh Baring Strickland, *b* 1899, *d* 1972: *m* 1954, Pauline (Ventonvaise, Callestick, Truro), da of P. Wood, of Shaldon, Devon:—
Christopher Claud Hugh, *b* 1955. —— Sarah Janet, *b* 1962.

Grandchildren of late Walter Cecil Strickland, son of late Augustine Edmund Christopher Strickland, 4th son of late George Strickland, 2nd son of 5th baronet:—
Issue of late Dudley Herbert Cecil Strickland, *b* 1860, *d* 1953: *m* 1901, Margaret, who *d* 19—, da of Edwin J. Gilbert, of San Bernadino, California, USA:—
Arthur Cecil, *b* 1902. —— Violet St Leger: *m* 19—, — Frederick Segrist.

Issue of late Cecil St Leger Strickland, b 1876, d 1929: m 1903, Lucy Estes, who d 1968, da of late Henry Edward Smithes, of Mount Pleasant, Kansas, USA:—
Joan, b 1908: m 1933, Maj George Vilett Rolleston, Worcestershire Regt (Supplementary Reserve), and has issue living, George Lancelot St Leger, MBE, b 1939; Capt Coldstream Guards; MBE (Mil) 1969; FO1969; 2nd Sec Baghdad 1971, 1st Sec Yemen 1972, Counsellor Yemen 1978, Saudi-Arabia 1981-86 and Algeria 1992-94 (ret): m 1976, Claude-Annie, da of N. J. Cointet, of Paris and Beirut, and has issue living, James George Andrew Lancelot b 1982, Natalia Lucy b 1980. Residence – Holetown House, Sampford Spiney, Yelverton, S Devon PL20 6LF.

The 1st baronet, Sir William Strickland, was summoned to Cromwell's House of Peers as Lord Strickland. The 3rd baronet was a distinguished MP during the reigns of William III, Anne and George I, and the 4th baronet was a Lord of the Treasury and Secretary for War temp George II. The 7th baronet assumed, in 1865, by royal permission, the surname of Cholmley for himself and those of his heirs male who may succeed to the Cholmley estates. He m 1818, Mary, da and heir of Rev Charles Constable of Wassand, Yorks. Sir Walter William Strickland, 9th Bt, became a Czechoslovakian citizen and did not use the title.

Constable-Maxwell-Scott, see Scott.

COOK (UK) 1886, of Richmond, Surrey

Esse quam videri

To be rather than to seem

Sir CHRISTOPHER WYMONDHAM RAYNER HERBERT COOK, 5th *Baronet*; b 24 March 1938; ed King's Sch, Canterbury; late RAF; s his father, Sir FRANCIS FERDINAND MAURICE, 1978; Co Dir since 1979; Dir Diamond Guarantees Ltd 1980-91: m 1st, 1958 (m diss 1975), Malina, da of Aster Gunasekera, and formerly wife of Cyril Wettasinghe, of Ceylon; 2ndly, 1975, Margaret, da of late John Murray, and formerly wife of Ronald Miller, and has issue living by 1st and 2nd m.

Arms – Gules, a rose argent barbed and seeded proper between three crescents of the second, a chief vaire. Crest – Issuant from a chaplet of roses gules a dexter arm embowed proper, holding in the hand a mullet of six points or between two branches of oak vert. Residence – La Fosse Equierre, Bouillon Rd, St Andrews, Guernsey, CI.

SONS LIVING (By 1st marriage)

RICHARD HERBERT ASTER MAURICE, b 30 June 1959: m 1996, Corinne Solange Andrée, da of René Daniel Dayras, of 6 rue Ogier de Baulny, 77120 Coulommiers, France, and has issue living, Ella Solange Lorraine, b 1996. Address – #10 JLN 1/87D, Persiaran Syed Putra 1, 50460 KL, Malaysia.

(By 2nd marriage)

Alexander James Frederick, b 1980.

DAUGHTERS LIVING (By 1st marriage)

Priscilla Melina, b 1968: m 1995, Daniel Bitton, of 15 Gt Saling, Wickford, Essex SS11 8XH.

(By 2nd marriage)

Caroline Emma, b 1978.

HALF-SISTER LIVING (Daughter of 4th baronet by 6th marriage)

Cleone Willa Johanne Vera Rosemary, b 1952: m 1st, 1970 (m diss 1983), Peter Wilson; 2ndly, 1986, Michael Robert Hendry, of 64 Heigham Rd, Norwich NR2 3AU, and has issue living, (by 1st m) Stuart Francis James, b 1971, — Catherine Jane Brenda Rachael, b 1972, — (by 2nd m) Simon Michael, b 1986.

WIDOW LIVING OF FOURTH BARONET

BRIDGET BRENDA (*Brenda, Lady Cook*), da of late Thomas David Lynch, and formerly wife of late Capt John Barclay Polland, RNVR: *m* 1956, as his 7th wife, Sir Francis Ferdinand Maurice Cook, 4th Bt, FRSA, who *d* 1978. *Residence* – Le Coin, La Haule, St Aubin, Jersey JE3 8BE, CI.

COLLATERAL BRANCH LIVING

Grandson of late Wyndham Francis Cook, 2nd son of 1st baronet:—
Issue of late Humphrey Wyndham Cook, *b* 1893, *d* 1978: *m* 1st, 1926 (*m diss* 1934), Gillian, da of late Frederick William Hedderley, of Oxford; 2ndly, 1941, Anne Beattie Blakeley, who *d* 197-, da of late John Moffett, of Ballynnhinch, N Ireland:—
(By 1st *m*) William Wyndham Humphrey, *b* 1928.

The 1st baronet, Sir Francis Cook (son of late William Cook, of Roydon Hall, Kent), was *cr Visconde de Monserrate*, of Cintra, Portugal, and was founder and donor of Queen Alexandra's House (an institution for lady art students), Kensington Gore, and a well-known collector of works of art. Sir Frederick Lucas, 2nd Bt, was head of the firm of Cook, Son and Co, warehousemen and Shippers, of St Paul's Churchyard, EC, and SAT as MP for Lambeth, Kennington Div (*C*) 1895 to 1906. Sir Herbert Frederick, 3rd Bt, Bar-at-law, was a Trustee of National Gallery 1923-30, and National Portrait Gallery 1916-30, and author of Giorgione, and Reviews & Appreciations and other publications.

COOKE (E) 1661, of Wheatley Hall, Yorkshire

Sir DAVID WILLIAM PERCEVAL COOKE, 12th *Baronet*, *b* 28 April 1935; *s* his father, *Sir* CHARLES ARTHUR JOHN, 1978; *ed* Wellington, RMA Sandhurst, and Open Univ (BA 1983); Col RCT; FCIT, FBIM, AMInstTA, AssocRAeS: *m* 1959, Margaret Frances, da of late Herbert Skinner, of Knutsford, Ches, and has issue.

𝕬rms – Or, a chevron gules between two lions passant-guardant sable. 𝕮rest – Out of a mural crown argent, a demi-lion guardant issuant as in the arms gorged with a ducal coronet or.

DAUGHTERS LIVING

Sara Elisabeth Mary, *b* 1960: *m* 1984, Darren P. Grosvenor of 47 Bellamy Close, Eggbuckland, Plymouth, Devon PL56 5LG, and has issue living. —— Louise Diana Margaret COOKE, *b* 1962; has resumed her maiden name: *m* 1986 (*m diss* 1988), Michael Moriarty. —— Catherine Faith Maria, *b* 1968: *m* 19—, Matthew Blakstad, of 1B St Saviour's Rd, Brixton, SW2 5HP.

SISTER LIVING

Amanda Norah Mildred, FRES, *b* 1939: *m* 1st, 1964 (*m diss* 1970), David Old; 2ndly 1975, Robert W. Watson, FAIA, FCIS, FFAA, FBAA, FCommA, FRES, who *d* 1982, and has issue living (by 1st *m*), Amanda Mary Perceval, *b* 1966. *Residence* – 15 Bilton Grove Av, Harrogate, N Yorks.

HALF-AUNT LIVING (*daughter of 10th baronet by 2nd marriage*)

Elizabeth Hera, *b* 1928: *m* 1968, Group Capt Cecil Edgar Arthur Garton, OBE, RAF (ret), of Quinta da Boa Vista, Funchal, Madeira, and has issue living, Patrick William, *b* 1969, — Dorothy Margaret, *b* 1970.

COLLATERAL BRANCHES LIVING

Branch from elder son of 10th baronet

Issue of late William Francis Henry Cooke, elder son of 10th baronet, *b* 1903, *dvp* 1950: *m* 1946, Irene Mary (who *d* 1981, having *m* 3rdly, 1953, Arthur Patrick Herbert), da of Thomas Perronet Thompson, and widow of Capt O. Bellingham-Smith:—

Patricia Irene Mildred, *b* 1949: *m* 1st, 1968 (*m diss* 1975), John Robert Struthers; 2ndly, 1976, John Walter Smith, of 90 Manor Rd, Marston Moretaine, Beds MK43 0PD, and has issue living (by 1st *m*), Patrick Francis John Robert, *b* 1971.

Branch from younger son of 9th baronet

Granddaughter of late Arthur Gordon Wyatt Cooke, yr son of 9th baronet:—
Issue of late William Bryan Cooke, *b* 1909, *d* 1974: *m* 1959, Marion June, yr da of late Maj Mervyn Hampden Corsellis:—
Marion Nathalie COOKE, *b* 1960; MA 1983, MA 1987, PhD 1990; Assist Prof, English Dept, McGill Univ; retained surname of Cooke after marriage: *m* 1984, Samuel Altman, LLB, MBA, of Toronto, Ontario, Canada, and has issue living Jordan Saul Cooke ALTMAN, *b* 1988, — Bryan Jeremy ALTMAN, *b* 1990, — Simon Zev ALTMAN, *b* 1993.

Branch from 2nd son of 3rd baronet

Grandchildren of late George Bryan Cooke-Yarborough, eldest son of George Cooke-Yarborough (*b* 1794), eldest son of John Cooke-Yarborough (*b* 1765), grandson of George Cooke, 2nd son of 3rd baronet:—
Issue of late George Eustace Cooke-Yarborough, *b* 1876, *d* 1938: *m* 1914, Daphne Isabel (who *m* 2ndly, 1950, Capt Tadeusz Mincer, who *d* 1969, and *d* 1984), yr da of Henry Cordy Wrinch of Ipswich:—
EDMUND HARRY, *b* 25 Dec 1918; *ed* Canford Sch, Ch Ch Oxford (BA 1944, MA 1944); FInstP, FEng, FIEE; formerly Dep Ch Scientist UK Atomic Energy Authority (ret): *m* 1952, Anthea Katharine, da of John Alexander Dixon, of King Charles Cottage, Colden Common, nr Winchester, and has issue living, Anthony Edmund (Barton House, Middle Barton, Chipping Norton, Oxon OX7 7DH), *b* 1956; *ed* Eton, and Gonville and Caius Coll, Camb (MA): *m* 1990, Joanna S., da of Anthony Northrop, of Felgate Farm, Ashfield-cum-Thorpe, Stowmarket, Suffolk, and has issue living, George Edmund *b* 1991, Eliza Flora *b* 1993, — Jane Anthea, *b* 1958: *m* 1986, Giles Vicat, of Woodbine Cottage, Bucknell, Bicester, Oxon OX6 9RS, elder son of Alan Vicat, of Shoreham-by-Sea, Sussex, and has issue living, Felix *b* 1989, Theodore *b* 1993. *Residence* – Lincoln Lodge, Longworth, nr Abingdon, Oxon OX13 5DU.

Grandchildren of late Capt Orfeur Frederick Cooke-Yarborough (infra):—
Issue of late Bryan Orfeur Eustace Cooke-Yarborough, *b* 1907, *d* 1987: *m* 1938, Ellen (Nellie) Martha, who *d* 1974, da of late John Myers, of Mount Silinda, Zimbabwe:—
Edmund Orfeur (160 Marimba Rd, Matsheumhlope, Bulawayo), *b* 1940: *m* 1966, Jennifer Anne, da of Lt-Col John Winterton Scott, and has issue living, David Jon Orfeur, *b* 1970, — Nichola Joan, *b* 1966: *m* 1987, Roderick Young. —— Rosemary Anne, *b* 1945: *m* 1966, Rodney Franklin Buckley, of 60A Padfield Rd, Pinetown 3600, Natal, and has issue living, Craige Franklin, *b* 1970, — Samantha Anne, *b* 1974. —— Susan Mary, *b* 1951: *m* 1973, Jacobus Petrus van Lelyveld, and has issue living, Darren Richard, *b* 1974, — Tracy Lee, *b* 1977, — Sherryl Lyn, *b* 1979.

Issue of late Thomas Nicholas Cooke-Yarborough, *b* 1910, *d* 1991: *m* 1940, Elizabeth Thomson (6 Westbury Court, Hedge End, Southampton), da of late William Gilmore, of Edinburgh:—
Nicholas Michael, *b* 1941: *m* 1967, Sheila, da of R. Symonds, of Southampton, and has issue living, Sarah Louise, *b* 1969: *m* 1995, Stephen John Searle, of 51 Firs Drive, Hedge End, Southampton SO30 4QQ, and has issue living, Harrison Thomas *b* 1998, — Claire Elizabeth, *b* 1972.

Grandchildren of late George Bryan Cooke-Yarborough (ante):—
Issue of late Capt Orfeur Frederick Cooke-Yarborough, *b* 1878, *d* 1965: *m* 1906, Anne (Nancy) Henrietta Lucy, who *d* 1965, el da of late Rev William Wyatt, R of Broughton Brigg, Lincs:—
Nancy Penelope Mary (Spicers, Newtown, Heytesbury, Warminster, Wilts BA12 0HN), *b* 1912: *m* 1939, Lt-Col George Michael Donaldson Wingate, RA, who *d* 1977, and has issue living, Elizabeth Anne, *b* 1940, — Sarah Penelope, *b* 1944: *m* 1964, Lt Michael R. R. Peever, RN, who *d* 1982, and has issue living, Richard Charles *b* 1971. —— Orfeur Henrietta Rosemary, *b* 1918; formerly in ATS: *m* 1944, Maj William Victor Smith, Lancs Yeo, of March Wall, King's Drive North, Caldy, Wirral, Ches L48 1LL, and has issue living, Richard Orfeur Bateson (12 Thurstaston Rd, Irby, Wirral), *b* 1949: *m* 1984, Vivien Dovey, — Rosemary Julia, *b* 1945: *m* 1972, John Brian Cheshire, of 14 Maes-y-Llan, Llanfairtalhaiarn, Flintshire, and has issue living, Melissa Rosemary Jean *b* 1972, Alkana Susan *b* 1978.

Issue of late Humfrey Charles Cooke-Yarborough, *b* 1880, *d* 1955: *m* 1911, Honor Lake, who *d* 1977, da of late Col Henry Lake Wells, CIE, RE:—
†Michael Humfrey, *b* 1915; an architect: *m* 1942, Pamela, who *d* 1996, da of late Sir John Baldwin, KCMG, CB, and *d* 1995, leaving issue, Ann (36 Rue de Chabrol, 75010 Paris), *b* 1944: *m* 1967, Alain Paul René Nérot, and has issue living, Alex *b* 1975, Lucie *b* 1974, — Penelope *b* 1946: *m* 1974, George Roger Frank Wallbridge, of The Chapel, Sandon, Buntingford, Herts SG9 0QJ. —— Steven Sandford, *b* 1919; an Engineer; formerly Capt RE: *m* 1941, Evelyn, da of late Charles Buccleuch Scott, of Trinidad, and has issue living, Christopher (6802 SW 64th Av S, Miami, FL 33143, USA), *b* 1949, — Nicholas (5000 SE 8th St, Ocala, FL 34471, USA), *b* 1952: *m* 1983, Tina, da of Marco Sierra, of Miami, Florida, and has issue living, Michael Charles *b* 1988, Stephanie Marie *b* 1986. *Residence* – 3555 Crystal Court, Miami, Florida 33133, USA. —— Eustace, *b* 1921; an Industrial Designer: *m* 1981, Patricia Marion Gardiner. *Residence* – Spring House, Priors Way, Aldeburgh, Suffolk.

Granddaughter of late Alfred Cooke-Yarborough, 2nd son of George Cooke-Yarborough (*b* 1701) (ante):—
Issue of late Randall Francis Cooke-Yarborough, *b* 1883, *d* 1980: *m* 1917, Norma, who *d* 1970, da of George Downes, of Opara, Hokianga, NZ:—
Pauline, *b* 1923: *m* 1947, Raymond Leslie Gerrard Rogers, of Nilgris, S India, and has issue living, Sandra Frances, *b* 1946, — Diana Leslie, *b* 1948.

Grandchildren of late Richard Cooke-Yarborough (*b* 1851), 2nd son of Richard Cooke-Yarborough (*b* 1805), 2nd son of John Cooke-Yarborough (*b* 1765) (ante):—
Issue of late Francis Michael Cooke-Yarborough, *b* 1904, *d* 1970: *m* 1933, Mary, who *d* 1965, da of late Everett L. Hudson, of Newcastle-upon-Tyne:—
Richard Everett (2 Ramsay Av, W Pymble, NSW 2073, Australia), *b* 1935; BSc (Honours) 1961, FAIAS 1983: *m* 1960, Sheila Margaret, da of late John Hugill, of Strathnaver, Walton, Brampton, Cumberland, and has issue living, Helena Margaret, *b* 1960; BSc (Hons): *m* 1983, John Robert Croker, of 17 Constitution Rd, Dulwich Hill, NSW, — Claire Mary, *b* 1963, — Ruth Meryl *b* 1967. ——— Jean Christine, *b* 1937: *m* 1960, Alan Keith Martin, BSc, PhD, of Dalmore, Greenhead, Mauchline, Ayrshire, and has issue living, Colin Seath, *b* 1962, — Patricia Anne, *b* 1964, — Christine Fiona, *b* 1966, — Mary Kay, *b* 1967. ——— Mary Elizabeth *b* 1942: *m* 1965, Robert Alexander Porteous, of 65 Lyncroft Gdns, Hounslow, Middx, and has issue living, Alexander Michael, *b* 1967 — Robert James, *b* 1968.

Branch from 7th son of 3rd baronet

Grandsons of late Charles Edward Cooke, 2nd son of late Capt Bryan William Darwin Cooke, 2nd son of late Bryan William Darwin Cooke (*b* 1764), only son of late Bryan Cooke, 2nd son of late John Cooke, 7th son of 3rd baronet:—
Issue of late Capt Arthur Charles Darwin Cooke, *b* 1876, *d* 1963: *m* 1913, Muriel, who *d* 1958, el da of late Leonard Brownlow Horrocks:—
David Charles Darwin (175 Victoria Av, Remuera, Auckland, New Zealand), *b* 1917; Lt, New Zealand Forces; 1939-45 War: *m* 1944, Phyllis Edith, da of late Capt Arthur Henry Prosser, OBE, and has issue living, Richard Charles Darwin, *b* 1947: *m* 1972, Dorothy Jane, da of late Eric George Woollams, — Elizabeth Angela Darwin, *b* 1948: *m* 1970, Martin John Beattie, LLB, of 184 Popes Rd, Manurewa, Auckland, NZ, and has issue living, James Brian David *b* 1976, Rosemary Ann *b* 1971, Amanda Jane *b* 1973.

Issue of late Philip Bryan Cooke, *b* 1886, *d* 1968: *m* 1st, 1909, Florence Alma, who *d* 1950, da of James Leamy, of Vancouver, BC; 2ndly, 1951, Katharine, who *d* 1963, da of David Walter Price, of Westerley, Rhode Island, USA:—
(By 1st *m*) Bryan Edward, *b* 1910: Maj AIF (Reserve); 1939-45 War/prisoner: *m* 1st, 1933 (*m diss* 1945), Margaret Ida, who *d* 1965, da of late Walter Hiskens, of Melbourne; 2ndly, 1946, June Mary, da of late Arthur Tregea, of Sydney, and has issue living (by 1st *m*) Robin May (Ganamead, Rocks Crossing, via Mt George, 2424 NSW, Australia), *b* 1936: *m* 1st, 1956 (*m diss* 1960), Michael Threlfall; 2ndly, 1961 (*m diss* 1983), Bruce Arthur Rickard, and has issue living (by 1st *m*) Philip *b* 1957, (by 2nd *m*) Samuel Bruce *b* 1962, James Arthur *b* 1963, Nicholas Lancelot *b* 1965, — (by 2nd *m*), Elizabeth Alice, *b* 1948: *m* 1st 1966 (*m diss* 1979), John Curley; 2ndly, 1980, Robert Michael Drury, of 5 Crampton Court, West Lakes, Adelaide 5021, S Aust, and has issue living (by 1st *m*), Louise Alice *b* 1967, Amanda June *b* 1970, Penelope Anne *b* 1971, (by 2nd *m*) Kathleen Bethal *b* 1981.

Grandson of late Lancelot Darwin Cooke (infra):—
Issue of late Charles Bryan Cooke, *b* 1925, *d* 1975: *m* 1952, Vajira Wijesinghe Kannangara (Ramanathan Hall, Peradeniya, Sri Lanka):—
Arjuna Bryan, *b* 1953; BSc (Eng) (Sri Lanka), AMIE (Sri Lanka), AMIEE (Lond): *m* 1990, Ramyamala Dhana Lakshmie Gunawardane, and has issue living, Uppalawanna Manju Edith, *b* 1992. *Residence* – 21/9 Polhengoda Gdns, Colombo 5, Sri Lanka.

Granddaughter of late Rev Charles Herbert Cooke (infra):—
Issue of late Lancelot Darwin Cooke, *b* 1891, *d* 1975: *m* 1922, Edith Euphemia Catherine, assumed the forename of Halimah in lieu of Edith Euphemia Catherine by deed poll 19—, da of late Maj Allan Ewen Grant, IMS:—
Sheila Beatrice (6630 Linda Vista Rd, Apt 3, San Diego, Ca 92111, USA), *b* 1923: *m* 1943, Lt-Col John A Nelson, Med Corp, US Army, who *d* 1963, and has issue living, James Darwin, *b* 1946. — Lance Edward, *b* 1947. — Richard Crosby, *b* 1949: *m* 1973, Nancy Mack, and has issue living, Colin Douglas *b* 1981, Dael Byrony *b* 1978.

Granddaughters of late Rev Charles Cooke, 4th son of late Bryan William Darwin Cooke (*b* 1764) (ante):—
Issue of late Rev Charles Herbert Cooke, *b* 1862, *d* 1946: *m* 1890, Ida Beatrice, who *d* 1941, da of late Rev G. F. A. Armstrong, R of Lorum, co Carlow:—
Marjorie Sheila (PO Box 86, Triangle, Zimbabwe): *m* 19—, Thomas Murray MacDougal, OBE, MC. ——— Betty Mary: *m* 1929, Louis Dennis Martin, and has issue living, Patrick Graeme, *b* 1930.

Branch from 2nd son of 2nd baronet

Grandchildren of late Maj Philip Tatton Davies-Cooke, OBE, el son of late Maj Philip Bryan Davies-Cooke, el son of late Philip Davies-Cooke, great grandson of late Henry Cooke 2nd son of 2nd baronet:—
Issue of late Col Philip Ralph Davies-Cooke, CB, TD, *b* 1896, *d* 1974: *m* 1924, Kathleen Mabel, OBE, who *d* 1994, da of late William Hugh Davies-Cooke (*see* Cooke, Bt, colls, 1995 Edn):—
(Philip) Peter DAVIES-COOKE (Gwysaney Hall, Mold, Flintshire CH7 6PA), *b* 1925; late Capt 1st R Dragoons: *m* 1st, 1957, Jane, who *d* 1981, da of Edmund George Coryton (Carew, Bt, colls); 2ndly, 1985, Mrs Zinnia Mary Arfwedson (CHARLTON), elder da of late Col Reggie Hodgkinson, of Shennington House, Stratford upon Avon, and has issue living (by 1st *m*), Richard Piers, *b* 1960: *m* 1986, Sarah Jane, eldest da of John Latham, of Caldecott Hall, Farndon, nr Chester, and has issue living, James Portland *b* 1988, Sophie Jane *b* 1989, Clara Louise *b* 1995, — Paul Bryan, *b* 1962, — Michael Anthony, *b* 1965: *m* 1993, Helen Marie, da of Eric Roberts, of Nercwys, Flintshire. ——— David Ralph DAVIES-COOKE (25 Barkston Gdns, SW5), *b* 1930; late Capt R Welch Fus: *m* 1955, Henrietta Sarah Angénis, da of Edward Jan Hoos (*see* B Brownlow, 1990 Edn), and has issue living, Philip Rupert Hugh, *b* 1960: *m* 1995, Chiena, da of Dr Yoshiharu Hiruta, of Ashiya, Japan, — Nicola Sarah Angénis, *b* 1958: *m* 1988, Ian William Reed, of Colpa, Gilgandra, NSW 2827, Australia, yr son of D. C. Reed, of Wirral, Molong, NSW, and has issue living, Hugh William Bryan *b* 1994, Emma Sarah Annabel *b* 1989, Alice Bronwyn Diana *b* 1991. ——— Philippa Marjorie, *b* 1938: *m* 1961, William George Antony Warde-Norbury

(High Sheriff S Yorks 1996), late Coldm Gds, of Hooton Pagnell Hall, Doncaster, S Yorks, son of Harold George Warde-Norbury, and has had issue, Mark William Antony, *b* 1962, — Alistair George, *b* 1966; *d* 1999.

Issue of late Capt Richard Anthony Davies-Cooke *b* 1909, *d* 1962: *m* 1934, Berys who *d* 1966, da of late T. Fanning-Evans, of Plas Cadnant, Menai Bridge, Anglesey:—
Doris Caroline, *b* 1935: *m* 1971 (*m diss* 1991), Arthur Henry Grant, and has issue living, Arthur Paul, *b* 1972.

Grandson of late Bryan Davies Poole; assumed by R Lic 1907 the surname of Poole in lieu of Cooke; eldest son of Col Bryan George Davies-Cooke, 2nd son of Philip Davies-Cooke (ante):—
Issue of late Capt Bryan Cudworth Halsted Poole, RWF, *b* 1892, *d* 1971; *m* 1925, Eleanor Margaret Lawson, who *d* 1948, da of Rt Hon Sir Adrian Knox, KCMG, KC, LLB.
Adrian Bryan POOLE (Dellawong, Box 279, Wellington 2820, NSW, Australia; *Clubs* – Union Sydney, Royal Sydney Golf), *b* 1927: *m* 1957, Philippa, da of Judge Adrian Herbert Curlewis, CVO, CBE and has issue living, Adrian Peter, *b* 1958, — Bryan David Edward, *b* 1964, — Belinda Margaret, *b* 1960, — Susan Philippa, *b* 1962.

This family was settled in the vicinity of Doncaster. Laurence Cooke, Prior of Doncaster 1536-38, was executed at Tyburn 1540 for denying the King's Supremacy. Sir George Cooke of Wheatley, Yorks, 1st Bt, was great-grandson of the prior's brother William. He received his baronetcy for his father's and his services for the Royal cause in the Civil War, with remainder to his next brother, Henry, who *s* as 2nd Bt 1683, and rebuilt Wheatley Hall.

COOPER (UK) 1821, of Gadebridge, Hertfordshire

Sir PATRICK GRAHAM ASTLEY COOPER, 6th *Baronet*, el son of late Col Clifton Graham Astley Cooper, DSO, RA, 3rd son of late Major Loftus Lewis Astley Cooper, 8th son of 2nd baronet; *b* 4 Aug 1918; *s* his kinsman, *Sir* HENRY LOVICK, 1959; *ed* Marlborough; formerly Senior Assist Land Commr, Min of Agriculture and Fisheries: *m* 1942, Audrey Anne, yr da of late Major Jervoise Collas, Mil Knight of Windsor, and has issue.

Arms – Vert, a fesse embattled or between two pheons in chief, and as many thigh-bones saltirewise in base argent. Crest – Out of a mural crown argent, a demi-spear erect proper, fringed or, pointed argent, and surmounted by two palm-branches in saltire vert.
Residence – The White Cottage, 3 Townside, Haddenham, Aylesbury, Bucks HP7 8BG.

SON LIVING

ALEXANDER PASTON ASTLEY (8 Berkshire Close, Leigh-on-Sea, Essex SS9 4RT), *b* 1 Feb 1943: *m* 1974, Minnie Margaret, da of late Charles Harrison.

DAUGHTERS LIVING

Nothing is great that is not good

Patricia Ann, *b* 1950; *ed* Malvern Girls' Coll, and E Anglia Univ: *m* 1979, Michael Robert Snodin, of 58 Leyborne Park, Kew, Richmond, Surrey, and has issue living, Oliver Karl Astley, *b* 1985. —— Helena Rosalind Collette, *b* 1958: *m* 1982, Jonathan David Holford, and has issue living, Graham Richard Desmond, *b* 1984, — Diana Sophia, *b* 1986.

COLLATERAL BRANCHES LIVING

Grandchildren of late Capt Albert Beauchamp Astley Cooper, 9th son of 2nd baronet:—
Issue of late Lieut-Col Geoffrey Beauchamp Astley Cooper, OBE, *b* 1884, *d* 1948: *m* 1st, 1911, Gladys Mary, who *d* 1912, da of Lieut-Col Orbell Henry Oakes of Nowton Court, Bury St Edmunds; 2ndly, 1914, Louisa Maude, who *d* 1972, da of late I. W. H. White, of West Lea, Meanwood, Leeds:—
(By 2nd *m*) Gerald Nigel Astley, *b* 1916; *ed* Wellington Coll; Maj (ret) 1st R Green Jackets: *m* 1st, 1941 (*m diss* 1945), Mary Constance, da of late Capt Basil Hamilton Piercy, RN (ret) (B Forteviot); 2ndly, 1951, Joan Ryland, da of Dr Bernard Wall, of Coleshill, Warwickshire, and has issue living, (by 1st *m*) Juliet Jane, *b* 1942: *m* 1964, Peter Robert Bellfield, of The Old Rectory, Clopton, Woodbridge, Suffolk IP13 6QB, and has issue living, Robert James Astley *b* 1965; *ed* Framlingham Coll; Lt-Cdr RN: *m* 1994, Zoë, da of Capt Thomas Le Marchand, RN, of Hasketon, Woodbridge, Suffolk (and has issue living, Eleanor Charlotte *b* 1997), Charles Peter *b* 1969; *ed* Uppingham, Edward Jonathan *b* 1972; *ed* Uppingham, — (by 2nd *m*) Desmond Beauchamp (36 Darwin Court, Gloucester Av, NW1), *b* 1955; *ed* Wellington Coll (Scholar), and St Peter's Coll, Oxford: *m* 1984, Randa, da of Dr Joseph Yammine, and has issue living, Kimball *b* 1986, Joseph *b* (twin) 1986, — Felicity Ann, *b* 1961; *ed* Royal Sch, Bath, and Durham Univ: *m* 1981, Maj-Gen Anthony David Pigott, CBE, twin son of Lt-Col P. J. Pigott, of Bexhill-on-Sea, and has issue living, James Anthony Alexander *b* 1991, Matthew Thomas Michael *b* 1992, Anna Louisa *b* 1984. *Residence* – Five Bells Cottage, Hessett, nr Bury St Edmunds.
—— Rosemary Anne, *b* 1920: *m* 1946, Lt-Col Peter Jarrett Lewis, The Buffs, who *d* 1983, and has issue living, Virginia Rosemary (*Lady Cordy-Simpson*), *b* 1949: *m* 1974, Lt-Gen Sir Roderick Alexander Cordy-Simpson, KBE, CB, Light Dragoons, and has issue living, Angus John *b* 1978, Zoë Finovola *b* 1976. *Residence* – Thedwastre White House, Thurston, Bury St Edmunds, Suffolk IP31 3QY.

Granddaughters of late Clement Astley Paston Cooper, 10th son of 2nd baronet:—
Issue of late Stephen Clement Paston Cooper, *b* 1885, *d* 1935: *m* 1915, Florence Gertrude Taylor, who *d* 1966:—
Diana Susan, *b* 1919: *m* 1st, 1939 (*m diss* 1967), Com Cecil John Grenfell, RN (ret) (E Cavan, colls); 2ndly, 1969, Clive
Walter Edwin Windsor-Richards, of Golf Lodge, Steepways, Hindhead, Surrey, GU26 6PQ, and has issue living (by 1st
m), John Stephen (58 Heath Rd, Petersfield, Hants) *b* 1940; Capt RN: *m* 1967, Stephanie Ann, da of Capt James
Marigold, RN, and has issue living, James Christopher *b* 1969, Nicholas Ian *b* (twin) 1969, Alastair Mark *b* 1974, —
Richard Francis, *b* 1944: *m* 19—, Jennifer, da of —, — Michael Gerrard *b* 1947, — Sally Angela *b* (twin) 1947: *m* 1980,
Francis Robert Gugen, and has issue living, Lucy Francesca *b* 1981. ——— Pamela Jane (Cheyne Lodge, Brook Rd,
Wormley, Godalming, Surrey), *b* 1921: *m* 1966 (*m diss* 1974), Lt-Cdr John Woolven Anderton, VRD, RNVR (ret).

The 1st baronet, Sir Astley Paston Cooper (5th son of late Rev Samuel Cooper, DD, R of Great Yarmouth, Yelverton,
and Morley), and was an eminent Surg. He was created a Baronet with special remainder, in default of male issue, to
his nephew, Astley Paston Cooper (3rd son of his el brother, the Rev Samuel Lovick Cooper, R of Ingoldsthorpe and
Barton, Norfolk), by whom he was *s*.

COOPER (UK) 1863, of Woollahra, New South Wales

Sir WILLIAM DANIEL CHARLES COOPER, 6th *Baronet*; *b* 5 March 1955; *s* his
father, *Maj Sir* CHARLES ERIC DANIEL, 1984: *m* 1988, Julia Nicholson.

Arms – Azure, a chevron engrailed between two lions passant in chief and a star of eight
points in base or. **Crest** – A lion sejant or, collared azure, supporting with the dexter paw a
lance erect proper, and suspended therefrom by a chain or an escutcheon also azure
charged with a star as in the arms.
Residence – 1 Victoria Cottages, Andover Rd, Micheldever Station, Winchester, Hants S021
3AX.

BROTHER LIVING

GEORGE JOHN (Blanche House, Turkdean, Cheltenham, Glos GL54 3NX), *b* 28 June 1956; *ed*
Harrow.

Perseverantia omnia
vincit

*Perseverance conquers
all things*

COLLATERAL BRANCHES LIVING

Grandchildren of late Arthur Hamilton Cooper, 2nd son of 3rd baronet:—
Issue of late Geoffrey Mervyn Cooper, *b* 1916, *d* 1984: *m* 1st, 1941 (*m diss* 1956),
Elise Marie, da of late George McGregor Richmond, of Balnacraig, Perthshire;
2ndly, 1957 (*m diss* 1967), Jean Margaret, da of William Ross-Brown, of Durban,
Natal; 3rdly, 1967 (*m diss* 19—), Jean Mellor, da of late Cdr J. W. W. M. Standring, RN, and of Mrs Guy Wilson —:—
(By 1st *m*) Marie Frances Richmond (*Hon Mrs Robert Eliot*), *b* 1942: a JP of Cornwall: *m* 1st, 1979, A.R. Lusk, of
Comrie, Perthshire, who *d* 1981; 2ndly, 1983, Hon (Montagu) Robert (Vere) Eliot (*see* E St Germans), who *d* 1994.

Issue of late Robert Henry Cooper, *b* 1922, *d* 1994: *m* 1946, Teri (The Down House, Blandford St Mary,
Blandford Forum, Dorset), elder da of Emin Agolli Doshishti, by his wife HH Princess Adilé Zogu, sister of HM
late King Zog of Albania:—
William Jeremy Daniel (Middle Farm House, Down House Estate, Blandford Forum, Dorset DT11 0HG), *b* 1951; *ed*
Eton: *m* 1975, Teresa Margaret, da of late Ralph Ernest Bamford, of Frogmore, Winterbourne Whitchurch, Blandford
Forum, Dorset, and has issue living, Daniel Alexander Westrow, *b* 1982, — Richard Gregory Christopher, *b* 1984, —
Samuel Robert Paul, *b* 1988. ——— Westrow Gerald Alan (Garden Cottage, Down House Estate, Blandford Forum, Dorset
DT11 9AD), *b* 1956: *m* 1986, Helen Margaret, da of George William Stokes, of 25 Greencourt Gdns, Croydon, and has
issue living, George Westrow Alexander, *b* 1991, — Katherine Teri Helen, *b* 1988.

The 1st baronet, Sir Daniel, GCMG, was the first Speaker of Legislative Assembly of NS Wales 1856-60.

COOPER (UK) 1905, of Shenstone Court, Shenstone, co Stafford

Complete things attempted

Sir RICHARD POWELL COOPER, 5th *Baronet*; *b* 13 April 1934; *s* his father, *Sir* FRANCIS ASHMOLE, 1987; *ed* Marlborough: *m* 1957, Angela Marjorie, elder da of Eric Wilson, of Norton-on-Tees, Durham, and has issue.

Arms – Ermine, on a pile argent three martlets sable, and on a chief gules two boars' heads couped or. Crest – Between two sprigs of holly erect a lion's jamb grasping in the paw a like sprig in bend sinister, all proper.
Residence – Lower Farm, Chedington, Beaminster, Dorset DT8 3HY. *Clubs* – Bucks and Carlton.

SON LIVING

RICHARD ADRIAN, *b* 21 Aug 1960; *ed* Millfield: *m* 1994, Mrs Belinda Buchanan, da of late William Potter, of Jersey, CI.

DAUGHTERS LIVING

Jane Alice, *b* 1958. —— Belinda Gay, *b* 1963.

SISTERS LIVING

Jacqueline Margaret, *b* 1939: *m* 1962, Peter Desmond Flaherty, of Glen Cottage, Butlers Dene Rd, Woldingham, Surrey, and has issue living, Andrew Niall *b* 1970, — Sally Clodagh, *b* 1963, — Sheena Mary, *b* 1964, — Julia Siobhan, *b* 1966. —— Dione Frances, *b* 1944: *m* 1970, Christopher Bruce Jones, of Ashmole, RD Manurewa, Auckland, NZ.

WIDOW LIVING OF FOURTH BARONET

DOROTHY FRANCES HENDRIKA (*Dowager Lady Cooper*), da of late Emile Deen, of Berkhamsted Hill, Herts: *m* 1933, Sir Francis Ashmole Cooper, 4th Bt, who *d* 1987. *Residence* – Mas Folie, 320 Route de la Madeleine, 06140 Tourrettes S/Loup, France.

The 1st baronet, Sir Richard Powell, was Vice-Pres of Council of Royal Agricultural Soc, and High Sheriff of Staffordshire 1901, and the 2nd baronet was a JP for Herts, and sat as MP for Walsall (C) 1910-22.

COOTE (I) 1621, of Castle Cuffe, Queen's County, Ireland

Cost what it may

Truth conquers

Sir CHRISTOPHER JOHN COOTE, 15th *Baronet*; *b* 22 Sept 1928; *s* his father *Rear Adm Sir* JOHN RALPH, CB, CBE, DSC, 1978; *ed* Winchester, and Ch Ch Oxford (MA); late Lieut 17th/21st Lancers; Coffee and Tea Merchant: *m* 1952, Anne Georgiana, yr da of late Lt-Col Donald James Handford, RA (Bs D'Arcy de Knayth, colls), and has issue.

Arms – Argent, a chevron sable between three coots close proper. Crest – A coot proper.
Residence – Monkton House, Broughton Gifford, Mclksham, Wilts SN12 8PA.

SON LIVING

NICHOLAS PATRICK, *b* 28 July 1953; *ed* Winchester: *m* 1980, Mona Rebecca, da of late Moushegh Bedelian, and has issue living, Rory Alasdair, *b* 3 April 1987, — Eleanor Marianne, *b* 1984.

DAUGHTER LIVING

Vanessa Jean, *b* 1955; *ed* Southampton Univ (BSc), Camborne Sch of Mines (MSc), and Univ Coll, London (PhD), FGS, MIMM.

BROTHER LIVING

Terence Eyre (Rushmoor, The Warren, Radlett, Herts WD7 7DU), *b* 1933; *ed* Winchester: *m* 1976, Jennifer, only da of late H. B. Cumming, of Duncal Farm, Bulawayo, Zimbabwe, and has issue living, Jonathan Eyre, *b* 1977, — Sarah Jane *b* 1980.

COLLATERAL BRANCHES LIVING

Issue of late John Methuen Coote, OBE, 2nd son of 12th baronet, *b* 1878, *d* 1967: *m* 1912, Leonora Wray who *d* 1969, da of late John Townsend Trench, of Kenmare (B Ashtown, colls):—

Joanna Frances (Gins, Beaulieu, Hants) *b* 1913; 1939-45 War 1st Officer WRNS; HM Diplo Ser 1948-73. —— Diana Jean, MBE, *b* 1914; N-W Europe 1944-45 as Senior Cdr ATS; MBE (Mil) 1946: *m* 1946, Edmund Luxmoore, who *d* 1997, of Glenspean, Inverness-shire, and Staindrop Hall, Staindrop, co Durham DL2 3NH, and has issue living, Michael John, *b* 1948: *m* 1st, 1973 (*m diss* 1988), Margaret Rosemary, da of Surg-Cdr John Graham More-Nisbett RN, of The Drum, Gilmerton, Edinburgh; 2ndly, 1988, Ann Dalrymple-Smith, and has issue living (by 1st *m*), Andrew Aylmer *b* 1976, James Francis *b* 1979, — Richard Aylmer, *b* 1955: *m* 1994, Samantha Emmerich, and has issue living, Alasdair William *b* 1997, — Elizabeth Jean, *b* 1950: *m* 1st, 1976 (*m diss* 1987), Geoffrey Wells Abbott, of Harare, Zimbabwe; 2ndly 1987, Alexander Lindsay Macdonald, of Ardslignish, Glenborrodale, Ardnamurchan, Argyll PH36 4JG, and has issue living, (by 1st *m*) Jessica *b* 1980, Lucy *b* 1983.

Issue of late Com Bernard Trotter Coote, OBE, 3rd son of 12th baronet, *b* 1880, *d* 1955: *m* 1907, Grace Harriet, who *d* 1958, el da of late Very Rev John Joseph Robinson, DD (B Avebury):—
Michael Henry (13 Laurelton, Bushy Park Rd, Rathgar, Dublin 6), *b* 1913; *ed* Woking Gram Sch: *m* 1st, 1939, Barbara Netterville, who *d* 1987, da of late Richard Netterville Eaton, of Roslyn Churchtown, Dundrum, co Dublin; 2ndly, 1987, Joan May, da of late W. W. G. Stevenson, of Cowper Drive, Dublin 6, and has issue living, (by 1st *m*) David Brian (Slieve Thoul, Brittas, co Dublin), *b* 1942: *m* 1968, Elizabeth Joy, da of late A. P. Brooks, of Dublin, and has issue living, Susan Barbara *b* 1972, Linda Elizabeth *b* 1975, — Deirdre Joan, *b* 1940: *m* 1973, Sean Rowsome, of Ballintober, Hollywood, co Wicklow, — Sheila Anne (2 Wellhead Lane, Westbury, Wilts), *b* 1946: *m* 1968, Maj Patrick Brian Hemming Robeson, 6th Queen Elizabeth's Own Gurkha Rifles, and has issue living, Simon Michael Hemming *b* 1970: *m* 1999, Kirsty Jane, da of Thomas Swan, of Bedburn, co Durham, Nicholas Andrew Hemming *b* 1973: *m* 1999, Pippa Anne, da of Paul Hartley, of 23 Blandford Close, NZ, Philippa Charlotte Hemming *b* 1969, — Jennifer Hazel, *b* 1949: *m* 1969, Peter Stuart Todd, of Monastery, Enniskerry, co Wicklow, and has issue living, Sam Stuart *b* 1981, Sarah Stuart *b* 1972, Jane Stuart *b* 1974, and an adopted da, Cathy *b* 1976. —— *Rt Rev* Roderic Norman, DD (Friday Woods, Stoke Rd, Cobham, Surrey KT11 3AS), *b* 1915; *ed* Woking Gram Sch, and Trin Coll, Dublin (MA, DD); Bishop of Gambia and the Rio Pongas 1951-57, Bishop of Fulham 1957-66, Bishop of Colchester 1966-87; Archdeacon of Colchester 1969-72: *m* 1964, Erica Lynette, da of late Rev Eric G. Shrubbs, MBE, R of Lawshall, Suffolk, and has issue living, Patrick Shrubbs, *b* 1972, — Antoinette Alexandra, *b* 1965: *m* 1995, Dean Richard Buckley, of 9 Dedham Court, Stalin Rd, Colchester, Essex, and has issue living, Carl Roderick *b* 1997, — Bernadette Sophie, *b* 1966.

Granddaughters of late Com Bernard Trotter Coote, OBE, RN (ante):—
Issue of late G/Capt Rev Denis Ivor Coote, CBE, *b* 1908, *d* 1985: *m* 1st, 1933, Olive Sheelagh (late Fl Officer WAAF), who *d* 1978, only da of late Hugh Crompton Bishoff, of Woodhayes, Woodlands, Woking, Surrey; 2ndly, 1979, Mary, who *d* 1997, da of William McDonough, of Newcastle upon Tyne:—
(By 1st *m*) Caragh Mary, *b* 1949: *m* 1st, 1973 (*m diss* 1983), Patrick O'Fáoláin; 2ndly, 1984, Gerald Harford, and has issue living (by 1st *m*), Tamsin Emilie, *b* 1973.

Issue of late W-Cmdr Patric Bernard Coote, RAF, *b* 1910, *d* (presumed *ka*) 1941: *m* 1935, Muriel, who *d* 1995, da of late Maj-Gen Alexander Montagu Spears Elsmie, CB, CMG:—
Susan Brigid, *b* 1939: *m* 1970, Geoffrey Maurice Young, of 78 Harpenden Rd, St Albans, Herts AL3 6DA, and has issue living, Michael Patrick, *b* 1971: *m* 1998, Nicola Howard, — Catherine Ann, *b* 1974.

Issue of late W/Cmdr Brian Philip Coote, MC, RAF, *b* 1919, *d* 1997: *m* 1949, Elizabeth Helen (The Mount, Wroxham, Norfolk Broads), da of late W. J. Rutt, of Trimley St Mary, Suffolk:—
Grace Elizabeth, *b* 1956: *m* 1984, Ian Arthur Bagster, of Bozen Green, Braughing, Herts.

Grandson of late Charles Chenevix Coote, OBE (infra):—
Issue of late Maj Mervyn Charles Coote, RE, *b* 1913, *d* 1985: *m* 1949, Inger Dahl (30 Ettrick Lodge, The Grove, Gosforth, Newcastle-upon-Tyne), da of Dahl Sorensen, of Copenhagen, Denmark:—
Peter Mervyn Dahl (332 Maple Avenue, Oakville, Ontario, Canada), *b* 1950; BA, BArch (Hons), ARIBA: *m* 1976, Ann Patricia, da of William John Taylor, and has issue living, Joanna Louise, *b* 1980, — Sophie Alexandra, *b* 1984, — Charlotte, *b* 1993.

Issue of late Charles Chenevix Coote, OBE, 4th son of 12th baronet, *b* 1884, *d* 1944: *m* 1908, Alice Maud, who *d* 1948, only da of late Most Rev John Baptist Crozier, DD, Archbishop of Armagh, and Primate of All Ireland:—
Dermot Chenevix, OBE, RN (21 Carlton Court, Wells, Som BA5 1SF), *b* 1915; Cdr (ret) 1939-45 War, Operations in Madagascar (despatches); OBE (Mil) 1967: *m* 1945, Dorothy Oliver, 2nd Officer WRNS, who *d* 1999, and has issue living, Christopher Chenevix, *b* 1946; Lt-Cdr RN (ret): *m* 1971, Cheryl, da of William Bridge, and has issue living, James Chenevix *b* 1971, Timothy Charles *b* 1973, — Richard Anthony, *b* 1950; BSc: *m* 1974, Lynne, da of Sydney Matthews, and has issue living, Christopher Neil *b* 1977, William Richard *b* 1987, Emma Louise *b* 1980. —— Patricia Aileen, *b* 1919; formerly Section Officer WAAF, and attached RAF Delegation, Washington; USA: *m* 1943, Air Commodore Nelles Woods Timmerman, DSO, DFC, RCAF, and has issue living, Mark, *b* 1945, — Peter, *b* 1950, — Nicola Mary, *b* 1952: *m* 1979, Eric Jean Pierre Maillé, and has issue living, Victor Alfred *b* 1993, Dominique Patricia *b* 1986. *Address* – House 407, 55 Waterford Drive, Weston, Ont M9R 2N7, Canada.

Issue of late Arthur Philip Coote, JP, 5th son of 12th baronet, *b* 1887, *d* 1954: *m* 1918, Margaretta, who *d* 1977, da of late Albert Leslie Wright (B Fitzwalter, colls):—
Stephen Arthur (Pippins, Ardforton, Wigmore, Shropshire SY7 0NF), *b* 1925; *ed* Repton, Selwyn Coll Camb, and Roy Agric Coll Cirencester; formerly Lt Rifle Bde: *m* 1951, Sheila Mary Healey, and has issue living, Michael Philip John (55 Mid Lavant, Chichester, W Sussex PO18 0BL), *b* 1952: *m* 1st, 1978 (*m diss* 1997), Barbara Jean, da of Darrell Cecil Phipps, of Hill View, Brascombe, Devon; 2ndly, 1998, Juliet Mary, da of Rear Adm Edmund Shackleton Jeremy Larken, DSO, RN, of Hawarden, Flintshire, and has issue living (by 1st *m*), Samuel Jack *b* 1980, Thomas Michael James *b* 1982, Ellen Jean *b* 1984, and also issue (by Karen Alexandra Newbery), Daniel Joseph Coote NEWBERY *b* 1976, — Nicholas Anthony (20A New Quebec St, W1H 7DE), *b* 1955, — Peter Richard (17 Poyner Rd, Ludlow, Shropshire SY8 1QT), *b* 1965: *m* 1996, Sharon Ann, da of Cyril Thomas Mytton, of Churchill House, Ludlow, Shropshire, and has issue living, Amber Danielle *b* 1993. —— Bridget (Brickfield Cottage, Brickfield Lane, Walhampton, Lymington, Hants SO41 5RD), *b* 1924: *m* 1959, Capt Reginald Fife Whinney, DSC, RN, who *d* 1992, Walhampton Hill, Lymington, Hants, and has issue

living, Alison Bridget, *b* 1963: *m* 1991, Jonathan West, of Petersfield, Hants GU32 3NE, and has issue living, Bede Robert Fife *b* 1992, Fritha Anne *b* 1995.

Grandchildren of late Com John Pemberton Plumptre Coote, 3rd son of 11th baronet:
Issue of late Lieut-Col Mervyn Chidley Coote, *b* 1885; *d* 1950: *m* 1915 Cecil Maud Vera, who *d* 1989, da of late Maj-Gen Cecil William Park, CB:—
Chidley (Emano St, Nelson, New Zealand), *b* 1918: *m* 1954, Mavis Ellen Thompson. —— Eleanor Patricia, *b* 1916: *m* 1940, James Chilton Francis Hayter, of Rocklands, Golden Bay, Nelson, NZ, and has had issue, Stephen James, *b* 1945, *d* 1987. —— Maureen Joyce, *b* 1923: *m* 1963, Samuel Nicholson, of 93 Coronation Rd, Morrinsville, Waikato, NZ, and has issue living, Ian Andrew, *b* 1964. —— Rosemary Cecilia, *b* 1929: *m* 1951, Joseph Trevor Clark, of Kakenga Rd, Stoke, Nelson, NZ, and has issue living, Anthony Joseph, *b* 1952: *m* 1979, Cushla Kerr, and has issue living, Benjamin Joseph *b* 1981, Anna Louise *b* 1984, — Peter Andrew, *b* 1954, — Geoffrey Robert, *b* 1956, — Jeremy John, *b* 1961.

Grandchildren of late Cecil Henry Coote, 5th son of 11th baronet:—
Issue of late John Cecil Coote, M.M. *b* 1889, *d* 1937: *m* 1915, Edith Blechynden, who *d* 1976:—
John Robin, *b* 1916; European War 1939-45 as Major 20th New Zealand Armoured Regt: *m* 1947, Anna May McDonald, and has had issue, John McDonald (Damian Grove, Lower Hutt, NZ), *b* 1949; Lieut RNZAC: *m* 1976, Stephanie Buchanan, and has issue living, Jack Buchanan *b* 1980, Evan Blechynden *b* 1985, Anna Doloughan *b* 1982, — Isobel Anne, *b* 1950: *m* 1978, Mark Rodger Taylor, of Havelock N, NZ, — Alison May, *b* 1954, *d* 1975, — Ann Cecile, *b* 1956: *m* 1979, Dr Duncan Bull, of Erin, Ontario, Canada, and has issue living, Alexandra Alison *b* 1981, Ainsley Frances *b* 1984. *Residence* – 88 Valley, Wakefield, New Zealand. —— †Peter Chidley, *b* 1921; formerly Flying Officer Roy New Zealand Air Force: *m* 1942, Nancy Bower Playter, who *d* 1997, and *d* 1990, leaving issue, Robin Maxwell (Clifton, Takaka, NZ), *b* 1943: *m* 1st, 1968 (*m diss* 1987), Jacqueline Phillippa Elliott; 2ndly, 1991, Glennis Susan Hinch. —— Richard Eyre, *b* 1929: Korea 1950-52 as Capt New Zealand Forces: *m* 1953, Janet Patricia Armatage Holmes, and has issue living, Stephen Richard, *b* 1955: *m* 1978, Judith Goff, and has issue living, Logan Eyre *b* 1981, Tyler Lesley *b* 1982, Emma Jane *b* 1984, — David Eyre, *b* 1959: Warrant Officer US Army: *m* 1979, Jody Susan Bishop, — Jonathan Robert, *b* 1966: *m* 1995, Karina Nadine Meyer, and has issue living, Zach Robert *b* 1988, Hanna Eve *b* 1995, — Sarah Patricia, *b* 1965: has issue living, Joshua John *b* 1995. *Residence* – Ballyfin, 25 Enner Glynn Rd, Nelson, NZ. —— Edith Jane, *b* 1919: *m* 1953, Ralph Armatage Holmes, and has issue living, Marion Jane, *b* 1954.

Issue of late Frederick Stanley Coote, OBE, *b* 1896; *d* 1967: *m* 1920, Edith Farquharson Crowe, who *d* 1985:—
†John Oldham, *b* 1921; Capt RN (ret); 1939-45 War: *m* 1944, Sylvia (47 Caversham St, SW3), el da of late Rear-Adm J. L. Syson, and *d* 1993, leaving issue, Judith Sylvia, *b* 1945: *m* 19—, — Angela Mary, *b* 1947, — Belinda Jane, *b* 1953.

Issue of late Eric Royds Methuen Coote, *b* 1902, *d* 1974: *m* 1932, Patricia Vercoe, who *d* 1993 :—
Philip Arthur Cecil (Mountrath, 26 Mount St, Nelson, NZ), *b* 1935: *m* 1957, Gabrielle Alice Goodman, and has issue living, John Anthony Royds (St Arnaud, Nelson, NZ), *b* 1959: *m* 1992, Kris Vollebregt, and has issue living, Jack Eric *b* 1992, Wilbur Anthony *b* 1994, Emile Philip *b* 1998, — Richard Philip, *b* 1964, — Timothy Philip (twin), *b* 1964, — Thomas Stanley Eyre, *b* 1967, — Catherine Alice, *b* 1958, — Bridget Ann, *b* 1961: *m* 1990, Lloyd James Harwood, and has issue living, George Sebastian *b* 1994, Amelia Alice *b* 1993, Lucy Helen *b* 1996. —— Robert Malcolm (Mountrath, 23 Browallia Cres, Loftus 2232, Sydney, NSW), *b* 1947: *m* 1971, Rhondda Beverly Kenny, of Sydney, NSW, and has issue living, Justin Russell Royds, *b* 1977, — Deborah Michelle, *b* 1974. —— Jennifer Margaret, *b* 1933: *m* 1959, Arthur Edward Maskill, and has issue living, Patricia Ann, *b* 1960, — Margaret Kaye, *b* 1961, — Virginia Robyn, *b* 1964, — Diana Mary, *b* 1965.

Granddaughters of late Charles Purdon Coote, son of late Charles Purdon Coote, son of late Capt Robert Carr Coote, brother of 9th baronet:—
Issue of late Major Charles Robert Purdon Coote, *b* 1875, *d* 1954: *m* 1933, Noel Margaret Jephson (Durham House, Balsham, Cambs CB1 6EZ), da of late Lt-Col Ernest Henry Denne Stracey (*see* Stracey, Bt colls):—
Nicola Harriette (*Baroness Clinton*), *b* 1937; High Sheriff Devon 1998, DL 1999: *m* 1959, 22nd Baron Clinton. —— Margaret Lydia Faith, *b* 1939: *m* 1966, Colin Patrick Annesley Martin Hill (*see* E Annesley, colls, 1995 Edn), of 260 Snowden Lane, Princeton, New Jersey 08540, USA, and has issue living, Sebastian Martin Coote (975 Prospect Park West, Apt 2c, Brooklyn, NY 11215, USA), *b* 1967: *m* 1998, Margaret Warne Heher, — Brendan Colin Charles (3303 South Dearborn St, Seattle, Washington 98144, USA), *b* 1970: *m* 1997, Sophia Procter, and has issue living, Annabelle Marie *b* 1999, — Orlando William Eyre, *b* 1980, — Cordelia Diana Margaret, *b* 1978. —— Caroline Anne, *b* 1940: *m* 1963, Baron Lambert Frederick Casijn van Till, Royal Netherlands Navy (ret), of Fortlaan 1, Bussum, Holland, and has issue living, Rupert Maurice Casijn, *b* 1967, — Edward Nicholaas Frederick, *b* 1972, — Lydia Julie, *b* 1964, — Vanessa Caroline, *b* 1976. —— Rosamond Aileen, *b* 1943: *m* 1965, Timothy Hetherington Earle Bulwer-Long, 15th/19th King's R Hussars (ret), Lodge Farm, Higham, Bury St Edmunds, Suffolk IP28 6NJ, and has issue living, Lucy Wiggett, *b* 1966, — Charlotte Louise, *b* 1968, — Harriet Elizabeth, *b* 1977, — Laura Rose, *b* 1979. —— Mary Patricia, *b* 1945.

Sir Charles Coote, 1st Bt, Provost-Marshal and Vice-President of the Province of Connaught, greatly distinguished himself at the relief of Birr, 1642. The 2nd baronet was created in 1661, Earl of Mountrath, in the peerage of Ireland, when the baronetcy merged in the peerage. The 7th earl and 8th baronet, having no heir, obtained in 1800 a new creation, that of Baron Castle Coote, with special remainder, which title became extinct in 1827, when the baronetcy reverted to the great-great-grandson of the 2nd son of 1st baronet. Rear Adm Sir John Ralph Coote, CB, CBE, DSC, 14th Bt, was Dept Dir of Naval Ordnance (Material) and Ch Ordnance Engineer Officer 1955-8.

COPE (E) 1611, of Hanwell, Oxfordshire (Dormant or Extinct 1972)

Sir MORDAUNT LECKONBY COPE, 16th and last *Baronet*.

WIDOW LIVING OF FIFTEENTH BARONET

ANGELA ROSE ELIZABETH (*Lady Thomas*), da of late James Alfred Snarey Wright, AFC, FDS, RCS: *m* 1st, 1956, Sir Anthony Mohun Leckonby Cope, 15th Bt, who *d* 1966; 2ndly, 1967, Rt Hon Lord Justice (Sir Swinton Barclay) Thomas, of 36 Sheffield Terr, W8.

CORBET (UK) 1808, of Moreton Corbet, Shropshire (Extinct 1996)

Sir JOHN VINCENT CORBET, MBE, 7th and last *Baronet*.

SISTER LIVING OF SEVENTH BARONET

Helen Anne Evelyn, *b* 1913: *m* 1946, John Dennis Russell, who *d* 1973, and has issue living, Christopher Corbet CORBET (Preston Hall, Preston Brockhurst, Shrewsbury, Shropshire SY4 5QA), *b* 1949; assumed the surname of Corbet in lieu of his patronymic, and was granted the arms of Corbet by Royal Licence 5 March 1997: *m* 1979, Leila Elizabeth, el da of Maj Charles John Richard Errington, of 18 Porthill Rd, Shrewsbury, Shropshire SY3 8SE, and has issue living, Richard Corbet *b* 1981, Catriona Corbet *b* 1980, Alice Ella *b* 1983, — Georgina Anne (*Lady Craufurd*), *b* 1947: *m* 1987, as his 2nd wife, Sir Robert James Craufurd, 9th Bt. *Residence* – East Grove, Grove Rd, Lymington, Hants SO41 3RF.

CORNWALL (UK) 1918, of Holcombe Burnell, co Devon (Extinct 1962)

Sir REGINALD EDWIN CORNWALL, 2nd and last *Baronet*.

DAUGHTER LIVING OF FIRST BARONET

Laura Ellen.

CORRY (UK) 1885, of Dunraven, co Antrim

Sir WILLIAM JAMES CORRY, 4th *Baronet*; *b* 1 Aug 1924; *s* his father, *Sir* JAMES PEROWNE IVO MYLES, 1987; *ed* RNC Dartmouth; Lt Cdr RN (ret): *m* 1945, Diana Pamela Mary, only da of late Lt-Col James Burne Lapsley, MC, IMS, and has issue.

Arms – Gules, a saltire engrailed argent, between in chief, a rose of the last, in fesse two thistles slipped proper, and in base a trefoil slipped or. Crest – A cock combed and wattled proper, and charged on the breast with a trefoil slipped vert.
Residence – East Hillerton House, Hillerton Cross, Bow, Crediton, Devon EX17 5AD

Vigilans et audax

Watchful and bold

SONS LIVING

JAMES MICHAEL, *b* 3 Oct 1946; *ed* Downside: *m* 1973, Sheridan Lorraine, da of Arthur Peter Ashbourne, of Crowland, Peterborough, and has issue living, William James Alexander, *b* 7 Dec 1981, — Robert Philip John, *b* 1984, — Christopher Myles Anthony, *b* 1987. *Residence* – Aronskelkweg 40, 2241 WC Wassenaar, The Netherlands. —— Timothy William (18 Beeches Rd, SW17 7LZ), *b* 1948; *ed* Downside; Lt-Col RGJ: *m* 1971, Bridget Isabella, da of Sydney Litherland, of Tenerife, Canary Is, and has issue living, Edward Charles, *b* 1976, — Georgina Katharine, *b* 1974, — Charlotte Louise, *b* 1981. —— Nicholas John (Rose Cottage, Mill Lane, W Ashling, Chichester, W Sussex PO18 8EA), *b* 1958; *ed* Downside. —— Simon Miles (Rose Cottage, Mill Lane, W Ashling, Chichester, W Sussex PO18 8EA), *b* 1961; *ed* Downside; Lt Cdr RN.

DAUGHTERS LIVING

Jane Susannah, *b* 1949: *m* 1976, John Anthony Grant-Brown Redman, of Rothiemurchus Lodge, 32 Glenmore Rd, Minehead, Som TA24 5BH, only son of late Henry Gordon Redman, OBE, of Brockenhurst, Hants, and has issue living, Angus Richard William, *b* 1986. —— Patricia Diana, *b* 1956: *m* 1987, Mark Hassall, of 2 Esher Rd, E Molesey, Surrey KT8 0AA, only son of late M. Hassall, of Woodbank House, Teddesley Rd, Penkridge, Staffs, and has issue living, Oliver Jamie Bowen, *b* 1990, — George Frederick, *b* 1997, — Rebecca Holly, *b* (twin) 1990.

HALF-SISTER LIVING *(daughter of 3rd baronet by 2nd marriage)*

Amanda Jane, *b* 1947: *m* 1972, Hamlyn Gordon Jones, MA, PhD, FIHort, and has issue living, Katherine Myleta Gordon, *b* 1974, — Julia Patricia Gordon, *b* 1976.

WIDOW LIVING OF THIRD BARONET

CYNTHIA MARJORIE PATRICIA (*Dowager Lady Corry*), widow of Capt David Alexander Polson, Seaforth Highlanders, and da of late Capt Frederick Henry Mahony, The Cheshire Regt, and of late Mrs Francis Bliss, of Santa Barbara, Calif, USA: *m* 1946, as his 2nd wife, Sir James Perowne Ivo Myles Corry, 3rd Bt, who *d* 1987. *Residence* – Dunraven, Fauvic, Jersey, CI.

This family emigrated from Dumfriess-shire to co Down early in the 17th century. The 1st baronet sat as MP for Belfast (C) 1874-85, and for Mid Armagh Div 1886-91 Armagh co. The 2nd baronet, Sir William, was a Director of Cunard Steamship Co, Ltd. The 3rd baronet, Sir James Perowne Ivo Myles, was Secretary and a Director of Port Line Ltd, and Vice-President of King George's Fund for Sailors, The Royal Alfred Merchant Seamen's Society and the Royal Merchant Navy School.

CORY (UK) 1919, of Coryton, Whitchurch, co Glamorgan

One heart, one way

Sir (CLINTON CHARLES) DONALD CORY, 5th *Baronet*; *b* 13 Sept 1937; *s* his father, *Sqdn-Ldr Sir* CLINTON JAMES DONALD, 1991; *ed* Brighton Coll, and abroad.

Arms – Argent, a saltire between two quatrefoils in pale sable, on a chief azure a griffin's head erased between two quatrefoils or. **Crest** – In front of a griffin's head erased or between two wings per pale of the last and gules three quatrefoils sable.
Residence – 18 Cloisters Rd, Letchworth, Herts SG6 3JS.

AUNTS LIVING (*daughters of 2nd baronet*)

Valerie (*Lady Gane*), *b* 1905: *m* 1st, 1928 (*m diss* 1948), Walter Pidcock Woolland, who *d* 1949; 2ndly, 1954, as his 2nd wife, Sir Irving Blanchard Gane, KCVO, who *d* 1972, and has had issue, (by 1st *m*), David Anthony Walter *b* 1929: *m* 1955, Zilia Annie Cooper (Dickamoor, Ramsbury, Marlborough, Wilts SN8 2HG), and *d* 1997, leaving issue, Terrence David Charles *b* 1958, Paul Richard Anthony *b* 1960, — Peter Donald Cory, *b* 1931. *Residence* – Sandaig, Knoydart by Mallaig, Inverness-shire PH41 4PL. —— Diana Ethel Muriel, *b* 1918: *m* 1943, Maj Andrew Lyell, DFC, RA, late Dorset Yeo, and has issue living, Vivien Diana, *b* 1944, — Clementina Lindsay, *b* 1949. *Residence* – Wester Auchleuchrie, Forfar, Angus DD8 3TU.

WIDOW LIVING OF FOURTH BARONET

MARY (*Lady Cory*), only da of Arthur Douglas Hunt, MD, ChB, of Park Grange, Duffield Rd, Derby: *m* 1935, Sqdn-Ldr Sir Clinton James Donald Cory, 4th Bt, RAFVR, who *d* 1991. *Residence* – 18 Cloisters Rd, Letchworth, Herts SG6 3JS.

The 1st baronet, Sir (James) Herbert Cory (a Director of John Cory & Sons, Ltd, shipowners), was High Sheriff for Glamorgan 1913, and MP for Cardiff Dist (*C*) Nov 1915 to Nov 1918, and S Div thereof Dec 1918 to Nov 1923.

Cory-Wright, see Wright.

COTTER (I) 1763, of Rockforest, Cork

While I breathe I hope

Sir DELAVAL JAMES ALFRED COTTER, DSO, 6th *Baronet*; *b* 29 April 1911; *s* his father, *Sir* JAMES LAURENCE, 1924; *ed* Malvern, and RMC Sandhurst; Lieut-Col (ret) 13th/18th Roy Hussars; N-W Europe 1944-45 (DSO); DSO 1944: *m* 1st, 1943 (*m diss* 1949), Roma, only da of Adrian Rome, of Dalswinton Lodge, Salisbury, S Rhodesia, and widow of Squadron-Leader Kenneth A. Kerr MacEwen, RAF; 2ndly, 1952, Eveline Mary, who *d* 1991, da of late Evelyn John Mardon, of Halsway Manor, Crowcombe, Somerset, and widow of Lieut-Col John Frederick Paterson, OBE, RHA, and has issue by 1st *m*.

Arms – Quarterly: 1st and 4th, argent a chevron gules between three serpents proper, *Cotter*; 2nd and 3rd, azure, a fesse between a fleur-de-lis in chief and a mullet in base or, *Rogerson*. **Crest** – A dexter arm embowed, armed and grasping a dart, all proper.
Residence – Greenlines, Iwerne Courtney, Blandford, Dorset DT11 8QR. *Club* – Army and Navy.

DAUGHTERS LIVING (*By 1st marriage*)

Sarah Gay Lisette, *b* 1944: *m* 1976, Michel Vigneron, of 4 Villa DuFresne, 75016, Paris. —— Charnisay Ann, *b* 1946: *m* 1971, Capt Charles Anthony Hugh Gwyn, Scots Gds, of Tyninghame House, Tyninghame, E Lothian, and has issue living, Simon, *b* 1979, — Victoria, *b* 1972, — Rebecca, *b* 1975, — Jessica, *b* 1977.

COLLATERAL BRANCHES LIVING

Branch from 2nd son of 5th baronet

Issue of late Laurence Stopford Llewelyn Cotter, 2nd son of 5th baronet, *b* 1912, *ka* 1943: *m* 1935, Grace Mary (who *d* 1992, having *m* 2ndly, 1945, Lt-Col Geoffrey Rittson-Thomas, late Manchester Regt, who *d* 1975), da of late Ivor Downing, of Beverley, Llanishen, Cardiff:—
PATRICK LAURENCE DELAVAL (Beara Farmhouse, Bishops Tauton, Barnstaple, N Devon), *b* 21 Nov 1941; *ed* Blundell's, and Roy Agric Coll, Cirencester: *m* 1967, Janet, da of late George Potter, of Goldthorne, Barnstaple, and has issue living, Julius Laurence George, *b* 1968, — Jemima Grace Mary, *b* 1970, — Jessica Lucy Kathleen, *b* 1972. —— Peta Natalie *b* 1935: *m* 1st, 1963 (*m diss* 1972), George Derek Wilson; 2ndly, 1991, Surg Capt Nicholas G. B. Hersey, of Appletrees, Great Churchway, Plymstock, Devon PL9 8JY, and has issue living (by 1st *m*), Paul Sean, *b* 1964: *m* 1991, Helen Jane Atkins, and has issue living, James Alexander *b* 1994, Kieran Andrew *b* 1996, — William Robin, *b* 1966, — Adam Edward, *b* 1969, — Charlotte Emma, *b* 1971. —— Primrose Anne, *b* 1939: *m* 1st, 1960 (*m diss* 1967), Richard Hugh Nicholas Creswell, 2ndly, 1968 (*m diss* 1969), Henry George Herbert, Viscount Throwley (later 5th Earl Sondes), who *d* 1996; 3rdly, 1976, Charles Denys Burnett-Hitchcock, of Old Court, 26 The Strand, Topsham, Exeter, Devon, and has issue living, (by 1st *m*) Belinda Jane, *b* 1960: *m* 1986 (*m diss* 1996), James Roger Glinn Eaton, — Robin Amanda, *b* 1962: *m* 1994, Jean Marc Faure; has issue living, Joshua Robin CRESWELL *b* 1986, — (by 3rd *m*) Jacob Nicholas, *b* 1978.

Branch from brother of 5th baronet

Issue of late Thomas Lombard Cotter, brother of 5th baronet, *b* 1888, *d* 1923, *m* 1912, Victoria Jean Robertson, who *d* 1923:—
Bettine, *b* 1920: *m* 1st, 1943, J. Harrison Owen, RAAF, who was *ka* 1943; 2ndly, 1946 (*m diss* 1956), Wing-Com Richard C. Cresswell, DFC, RAAF; 3rdly, 1956, Group-Capt Alan Graham Douglas, CBE, MC, RAF Regt, who *d* 1995.

Branch from eldest son of 4th son of 1st baronet

Grandchildren of late Col George Sackville Cotter, CB, son of late Rev James Laurence Cotter, LLD (infra):—
Issue of late James Laurence Cotter, *b* 1839, *d* 1889: *m* 1868, Frances, da of Capt Ironside:—
George Sackville, *b* 1870. —— Wemyss M'Kenzie Osborne, *b* 1872. —— Henry Martin Stuart, *b* 1873. —— Oliver Wendell Holmes, *b* 1879. —— Agnes Mary. —— Evadne Kilgour. —— Ada Margaret. —— Katherine. —— Anne Winifred.

Grandchildren of late James Laurence Cotter (ante):—
Issue of late Arthur Douglas Cotter, *b* 1878, *d* 1918: *m* 1904, Marion Church Solmes:—
James Guthrie Sackville, *b* 1906: *m* 19—, and has issue living. —— George Clinton Solmes, *b* 1905: *m* 19—, and has issue living. —— Frances Marion Louise, *b* 1908: *m* 1926, Alexander Nicholson Salisbury, who *d* 19—, and has issue living, Virginia Puella, *b* 1927: *m* 19— Lloyd Fieley, and has issue living, a son, *b* 19—, a da, *b* 19—, a da *b* 19—.

Granddaughter of the Rev William Henry Cotter, LLD (infra):—
Issue of late Capt George Edmund Sackville Cotter, *b* 1882, *d* on active ser 1917: *m* 1914, Beatrice Mary Grove (who *m* 2ndly, 1921, Brig John Keily Gordon, DSO, RHA, and *d* 1981), da of Com Hans Thomas Fell White, JP, late RN, of Springfort Hall, Mallow, co Cork:—
Benita May, *b* 1915: *m* 1st, 1936, Major Arthur William Granville Dobbie, RE, who was *ka* 1944, el son of Lt-Gen Sir William George Shedden Dobbie, GCMG, KCB, DSO; 2ndly, 1950, Major Derek Wrey Savile, RA, who *d* 1992, and has issue living, (by 1st *m*) William Ian Cotter, *b* 1939; Brig RE, — (by 2nd *m*) George Keith Wrey, *b* 1951: *m* 1987, Philippa Mary, elder da of Brian Dudgeon, of Broadfield, Guildford, and has issue living, Joshua Andrew Keith *b* 1990, Samuel Christopher *b* 1992, Hannah Elizabeth *b* 1989.

Granddaughter of late Rev James Laurence Cotter, LLD, el son of late Rev George Sackville Cotter, 4th son of 1st baronet;—
Issue of late Rev William Henry Cotter, LLD, *b* 1844, *d* 1931: *m* 1st, 1878, Catherine Letitia, who *d* 1894, da of late George Stawell, of Crobeg, co Cork; 2ndly, 1896, Eva, who *d* 1903, da of J. T. Sikes, of Elmvale, co Cork, and Kincora, Ceylon:—
(By 2nd *m*) Eva Maude (Little Kenbank, Dalry, Castle Douglas, Kirkcudbrightshire), *b* 1901: *m* 1921, Lt-Col Alexander Patrick Cathcart Hannay, OBE, MC, Queen's Own Cameron Highlanders (also Sqdn-Ldr RAF), who *d* 1977, and has issue living, Patrick Victor Cathcart (16 via Privata Cieli, La Spezia, Italy), *b* 1923; MA, PhD: *m* 1st, 1943, Maria Benita Rosalia Greco, who *d* 1944; 2ndly, 1948, Elvira Teodora Facchetti, who *d* 1964; 3rdly, 1965, Mrs Iride Giuseppina Antonietta Ercolini, who *d* 1986, — Timothy John, *b* 1929, Fl-Lt RAF: *m* 1st, 1956 (*m diss* 1974), Judith Butler; 2ndly, 1974, Linda Jess Elizabeth Callan, of Edinburgh, and has issue living, (by 1st *m*) Patrick George *b* 1958: *m* 1988, Urasa, da of Aim Sanasen, of Bangkok, Thailand (and has issue living, Pimon *b* 1991, Tim *b* 1993), William Victor Bladworth *b* 1963, (by 2nd *m*) Neil Lennox Cotter *b* 1976, Timothy Alexander *b* 1977.

Branch from 2nd son of 4th son of 1st baronet

Grandson of late James Laurence Sackville Cotter, 3rd son of late George Sackville Cotter (*b* 1829), eldest son of Col George Sackville Cotter (*b* 1783), 2nd son of Rev George Sackville Cotter, 4th son of 1st baronet:—
Issue of late James Laurence Cotter, *b* 1900, *d* 1960: *m* 1924, Anna, da of R. Harris, of Penna, USA:—

James Laurence, *b* 1925; Lt-Cdr US Navy (ret): *m* 1st, 1950 (*m diss* 1972), G. Cerra; 2ndly, 1972, Mariruth Reed, and has issue living (by 1st *m*), Thomas J., *b* 1954: *m* 1977, Karen Jones, and has issue living, Thomas J. *b* 1979, Matthew R. *b* 1981, — Gwendolyn A., *b* 1957. *Residence* – 5562 Zieger Rd, Verona, PA 15147, USA.

Grandsons of late William Crofts Cotter, 2nd son of late Col George Sackville Cotter (*b* 1783) (ante):—
Issue of late James Laurence Cotter, *b* 18—, *d* 1943: *m* 1916, Jane, who *d* 19—, da of William Blyth, of Edinburgh:—
Laurence Meldrum, *b* 1917. *Residence* – Meadow Creek, Alberta, Canada. ——— James Lawrence *b* 1919; European War 1942-5 with Roy Canadian Army Ser Corps: *m* 1948, Phyllis, da of Frank Peters, of Claresholm, Alberta, Canada, and has issue living, Garry Laurence, *b* 1953, — Marlane Phyllis, *b* 1957, — Karen Jean, *b* 1959. *Address* – Box 473, Claresholm, Alberta, Canada. ——— Blyth Sackville, *b* 1921.

Branch from 4th son of 4th son of 1st baronet

Grandchildren of late Joseph Henry Cotter (infra):—
Issue of late Charles Henry Cotter, *b* 1898, *d* 1976: *m* 1924, Louise da of late John Wesley Ray, of Miami, Manitoba, Canada:—
Charles Roy Henry (584 Victoria Av, Belleville, Ont), *b* 1927: *m* 1953, Gertrude Elizabeth, da of Hugh V. McCann, of Ottawa, and has issue living, Joseph Henry, *b* 1957, — Patricia Ann, *b* 1954, — Mary Elizabeth, *b* 1960, — Barbara Jane, *b* 1963, — Catherine Louise, *b* 1965. ——— John Raymond (338 Hartviksen St, Port Arthur, Ont), *b* 1929: *m* 1957, Vivienne Margaret, da of Henry A. Patton, of 4 Cotesbach Rd, Clapton, E5, and has issue living, Stephen Henry, *b* 1960, — Karen Louise, *b* 1959, — Susan Margaret, *b* 1961. ——— Marjorie Ethel, *b* 1930: *m* 1954, John Durward Johnson, of RR No 5, Truro, Nova Scotia, and has issue living, David Robert, *b* 1955, — Eric Charles, *b* 1957, — Bruce Allan, *b* 1958, — John Andrew, *b* 1965, — Susan Elizabeth, *b* 1961.

Issue of late Walter Richard Cotter, *b* 1902, *d* 1971: *m* 1923, Lois, da of George Benton King, of Camas, Washington, USA:—
Eugene Richard (210E 8th South, Springville, Utah, USA), *b* 1924: *m* 1947, Mary Agnes, da of Robert Ramsey, of Tempe, Arizona, USA, and has issue living, Charles Eugene, *b* 1952, — Neil Edward, *b* 1957, — Jennifer Marie, *b* 1954. ——— George Henry, *b* 1926: *m* 1st, 1949 (*m diss* 19—), Barbara Gene, da of Glenn Maxwell, of Richmond, Cal, USA; 2ndly, 1971, Judith Kay, da of Rex Clark, of Indianapolis, Indiana, USA, and has issue living, (by 1st *m*) Walter Richard, *b* 1953, — Kevin George, *b* 1966.

Grandchildren of late Rev Richard Henry Cotter, 5th son of late Rev Joseph Rogerson Cotter (*b* 1790), 4th son of late Rev George Sackville Cotter, 4th son of 1st baronet:—
Issue of late Joseph Henry Cotter, *b* 1867, *d* 1937: *m* 1896, Ethel Mary, who *d* 1960, da of late Surg-Maj Samuel Kyle Cotter, MD (infra):—
Lilian Muriel Edith, *b* 1910. *Residence* – 602-1976 Portage Av, Winnipeg, Manitoba, Canada R3J 0J8.

Issue of late Joseph Rogerson Cotter, *b* 1869, *d* 1957: *m* 1913, Ellen Harriet, who *d* 1948, da of late Surg-Maj Samuel Kyle Cotter, MD:—
Joan Jamieson, *b* 1916; *ed* Trin Coll, Dublin (BA); late Subaltern ATS: *m* 1944, Henry Haskins Ferrell, Junior, MD, late Capt US Army Med Corps, and has issue living, Henry Haskins (III), MD, *b* 1951: *m* 1984 (*m diss* 1987), Anne Elizabeth Edmunds, — Leslie Cotter (a da), *b* 1949: *m* 1974, José Manuel Kauffmann, and has issue living, Alejandro José *b* 1980, Ana Elena *b* 1982, — Joan Pinson, *b* 1954. *Residence* – 511 Cathedral Drive, Alexandria, Virginia, 22314, USA.

Issue of late Alexander McCaul Cotter, *b* 1871, *d* 1929: *m* 1896, Mildred Bertha Eveline, who *d* 1925, da of George Edwards:—
Felix Alexander, *b* 1900: *m* 1929, Ella Elenor Christopherson, of Brock, Sask, and has issue living, William Leroy, *b* 1935, — Bernice Eveline, *b* 1930. ——— Louis Stephen (RR2, Mannville, Alberta, T0B 2W0, Canada), *b* 1913; 1939-45 War with Canadian Army: *m* 1941, Elizabeth Ellen, da of Harry Thomas, of Mannville, Alberta, Canada, and has had issue, †Gavin Bryson, *b* 1947: *m* 1972 (*m diss* 1988), Rita Maureen, da of Allan McDonell, of St Albert, Alberta, Canada, and *d* 1998, leaving issue, Tyler Bryce *b* 1975, Kelly Shannon *b* 1978, — Arlene Berna, *b* 1942: *m* 1968, Dr Richard Ellis Danziger, Capt USNR, of 3211 Erie St, San Diego, California 92117, USA, and has issue living, Derek Scott *b* 1972, Kathryn Erin *b* 1975. ——— Florence Mildred, *b* 1906: *m* 1929, William James Shury, and has issue living, David William, *b* 1930; *ed* Sask Univ (LLB): *m* 1956, Jane Miller, and has issue living, William Brent Cotter *b* 1963, Debra Elizabeth *b* 1956, — Garry Clair, *b* 1938: *m* 1960, Claudia Fradette, and has issue living, Brian Keith *b* 1963, Todd Kevin *b* 1964, — Harold Lloyd, *b* 1942: *m* 1961, Alice Hartman, and has issue living, Dale Lloyd *b* 1962, Kyle Damon *b* 1971, — Terrance James, *b* 1944: *m* 1965, Mary, da of Doyle Edwards, of Saskatoon, and has issue living, Gregory Doyle *b* 1970, Sandra Lynn *b* 1966, Laurie Ann *b* 1971, — Donaline Elizabeth *b* 1932: *m* 1955, Harold Jones, and has issue living, Glenn Harold *b* 1960, — Evelyn Mildred, *b* 1933, is a Sch Teacher: *m* 1955, Donald MacKenzie, of 959 Herbert Rd, Richmond, BC, Canada, and has issue living, Janice *b* 1957, Valerie *b* 1958, Wendy *b* 1963.

Grandson of late Alexander McCaul Cotter (ante):—
Issue of late Lloyd George Cotter, *b* 1916, *d* 1968: *m* 1945, Iris May Webb (2300 E Valley Parkway #109, Escondido, CA 92027, USA), who *m* 2ndly, 1970, Charles Rogerson Cotter, who *d* 1983 (*see* Cotter, Bt, colls, 1980 Edn):—
Burney Thomas (2382 Anora Drive, Abbotsford, BC, Canada V2S 5P8), *b* 1946: *m* 1969, Rosemarie, da of Michael Koroluk, Geraldton, Ont, Canada, and has issue living, Kevin Michael, *b* 1980, — Christine Michelle, *b* 1975, — Shari Diane, *b* 1977, — Bonnie Mildred, *b* (twin) 1946: *m* 1972, Paul Halagaza, and has issue living, Mark Leonard, *b* 1975.

Grandchildren of late Rev Richard Henry Cotter (ante):—
Issue of late Gerald de Purcell Cotter, *b* 1881, *d* 1941: *m* 1917, Rosalind, who *d* 1961, da of James Billington Coughtrie, formerly of Hong Kong:—

Hilary James Coughtrie (38 Jill's Court, Barrie, Ontario L4M 4L7, Canada), *b* 1918; *ed* Westminster, and at Pembroke Coll, Oxford (MA): Lt (ret) RN; late ADC to Gov-Gen of British Somaliland: *m* 1957, Patricia Kathleen Angela Mary Esther, only da of late James Doyne, of Castlerickard, co Meath, and has issue living, Godwin Arthur, *b* (Jan) 1959; *ed* Univ of Toronto (BSc), — Hilary Patrick, *b* (Dec) 1959; *ed* Univ of Toronto (BSc), — Marcian Gerald, *b* 1962, — Rosalind Catherine, *b* 1958; *ed* Magdalen Coll, New Hampshire, USA (BA): *m* 1983, Brian David Pouliot, and has issue living, Dominic John Pio *b* 1984, Thomas Aquinas *b* 1986, Benedict Joseph-Marie *b* 1988, Francis Joseph-Marie *b* 1990, Jerome Joseph-Marie *b* 1994, Monique Marie *b* 1992, — Rebecca Claire, *b* 1961; *ed* Univ of Toronto, and Toronto York Univ (BA, BSc); SRN, — Mary Jane Frances, *b* 1963; SRN: *m* 1993, Ogden Michael Forbes, — Rowena Josephine, *b* 1964; SRN, — Rachel Anne Monica, *b* 1967; SRN. ——Arthur Gerald Purcell, MB, *b* 1924; *ed* Westminster, Oxford Univ, and Trin Coll, Dublin; late Capt RE: *m* 1959, Isabel Adams, of Gortin, co Tyrone, and has issue living, Colin Arthur, *b* 1961, — Lynda Marie, *b* 1962. ——Angela Mary Purcell (Tally Ho House, Castletownshend, co Cork), *b* 1921: *m* 1st, 1951, Ulick O'Connor Milborne-Swinnerton-Pilkington, who *d* 1979 (*see* Milborne-Swinnerton-Pilkington, Bt); 2ndly, 1981, Cdr Edward Alfred Eborall, RNVR, FIEE, who *d* 1992, and has issue living by 1st *m*.

Grandchildren of late Duncan Donald Darrock Cotter, 6th Regt, 8th son of late Rev Joseph Rogerson Cotter (*b* 1790) (ante):—
Issue of late Major Arundel John Plunkett Cotter, US Army, *b* 1883, *d* 1952: *m* 1911, Emma Stothard, da of William Robert Carter:—
Arundel, *b* 1912; Lieut-Col US Army; European War 1939-45: *m* 1st, 1942 (*m diss* 1952), Madelyn, da of Forest Mitchell; 2ndly, 19—, Gabrielle Pauline, da of Harry Tarter, of Washington, DC, and has issue living, (by 1st *m*) Arundel, *b* 1944, — (by 2nd *m*) Harry Bruce, *b* 1955, — Robert Darrock, *b* 1956. ——Joyce, *b* 1914; *ed* Connecticut Coll for Women (BS 19—): *m* 1948, Lieut-Col George Kern, US Army.

Issue of late Harry Norman Cotter, DDS, *b* 1885, *d* 1960: *m* 1912, Rose Isabel, who *d* 1975, da of Henri Malabre, of Kingston, Jamaica:—
Harry Norman Rogerson (533 Driftwood Rd, North Palm Beach, Florida, 33403, USA), *b* 1922; *ed* Cornell Univ (ME 1948): Lt, US Marine Corps (Reserve); 1939-45 War: *m* 1950, Beverly Jane, da of Alfred Edmund Hayes, and has issue living, Thomas Joseph, *b* 1952, — Anthony John, *b* 1962, — Patrick Hayes, *b* 1963, — Lark Ellen, *b* 1951, — Noreen Ann, *b* 1954, — Andrea Jane, *b* 1955. ——Margaret Charlotte, *b* 1917: *m* 1942, Cæsar Leopold Pitassy, LLB, of 11 Hidden Green Lane, Larchmont, New York, USA, and has issue living, Richard Norman *b* 1943.

Grandchildren of late Harry Norman Cotter DDS (ante):—
Issue of late Richard Duncan Rogerson, *b* 1922, *d* 1976: *m* 1949, Mary Theresa (5333 Ravensworth Rd, N Springfield, Virginia, USA), da of late James J. Kellcher:—
Richard Duncan, *b* 1950. ——Michael Patrick, *b* 1952. ——Peter James, *b* 1953. ——David Henry, *b* 1955. —— Matthew, *b* 1961. ——Eileen Mary, *b* 1956. ——Elizabeth Ann, *b* 1960.

Grandchildren of late Surg-Major Samuel Kyle Cotter, MD, yst son of late Rev Joseph Rogerson Cotter (*b* 1790) (ante):—
Issue of late Major Raymond Kyle Cotter, MC, Indian Army (ret); *b* 1889, *d* 1948: *m* 1914, Beryl Jessie Macdonald, who *d* 1972, da of late Charles Macdonald Wintle, Sup Frontier Police, India:—
Derek Raymond Kyle (18 Castleton Close, Mannamead, Plymouth, Devon PLE 5AE), *b* 1916: *m* 1st, 1938, Daphne Cushion who *d* 1963; 2ndly, 1968, Amelia Helena, da of late Maurice Walsh, of Cleveland, Ohio, USA, and has issue living, (by 1st *m*) Anthony Derek, *b* 1941, — Merril Victoria, *b* 1942, — Carolyn, *b* 1948, — (by 2nd *m*) Nicholas Paul, *b* 1970. ——Kathleen Beryl Kyle (Susan), (87 Dartford Rd, Sevenoaks, Kent), *b* 1915: *m* 1st, 1933 (*m diss* 1942), Reginald Barnes Elwin, ICS; 2ndly, 1942, Major Denis Erskine Ward, Roy Tank Regt (V Bangor, colls), who was *ka* 1945; 3rdly, 1946, her former husband, Reginald Barnes Elwin, ICS, who *d* 1961; 4thly, 1978, Stanley Chapman, and has issue living, (by 3rd *m*) David Michael Harrison, *b* 1948, — Peter John Ashton, *b* 1950, — (by 1st *m*) Verity Anne, *b* 1934: *m* 1959, Terry Nicholas Blows, of 58 Channel View Rd, Campbells Bay, Auckland 10, NZ, and has issue.

This family was seated in co Cork prior to the fifteenth century. Sir James Cotter of Anngrove, co Cork, was C-in-C of James II's forces in Cos Cork, Limerick and Kerry. His son, James Cotter, executed in 1720, was father of Sir James Cotter of Rockforest, Co Cork, 1st Bt, who was MP for Askeaton in the Irish Parliament. In 1874, Ludlow Cotter, son and heir of 4th Bt, was the last to receive a knighthood as a privilege of the Order under the second Letters Patent. He *dvp* 1882.

COTTERELL (UK) 1805, of Garnons, Herefordshire

I did not seize it, I recovered it

Sir JOHN HENRY GEERS COTTERELL, 6th *Baronet*; *b* 8 May 1935; *s* his father, *Lt-Col Sir* RICHARD CHARLES GEERS, CBE, TD, 1978; *ed* Eton, and RMC Sandhurst; Capt Royal Horse Guards; Vice Lord-Lieut Herefords 1998: *m* 1959, (Vanda) Alexandra (Clare), MBE (High Sheriff Hereford and Worcester 1992), da of Maj Philip Alexander Clement Bridgewater (*see* B Vivian, 1985 Edn), and has issue.

Arms – Quarterly or and argent, a cross engrailed per pale sable and gules, in the second quarter two escallops, and in the third one, all of the third; over all a bend also sable. Crest – An arm in armour embowed proper, garnished or, the hand gauntleted also proper, resting on an escutcheon argent, charged with a talbot's head erased sable, collared and lined or.
Residence – Downshill House, Bishopstone, Hereford HR4 7JT. *Club* – White's.

SONS LIVING

HENRY RICHARD GEERS (Garnons, Hereford HR4 7JU), *b* 22 Aug 1961: *m* 1986, Carolyn Suzanne, formerly Extra Lady in Waiting to HRH The Duchess of York, elder da of John Moore Beckwith-Smith, of Maybanks Manor, Rudgwick, Sussex, and has issue living, Richard John Geers *b* 1 May 1990, — George Dominic Geers, *b* 1994, — Poppy, *b* 1988. —— James Alexander Geers (Fairview, Maunsell Gamage, Hereford), *b* 1964: *m* 1991, Maria C. B., da of W. F. McManus, of Bryngwyn Close, Hereford, and has issue living, William John Geers, *b* 1992. —— David George Geers, *b* 1968.

DAUGHTER LIVING

Camilla Jane, *b* 1963: *m* 1993, Mark James Kenneth Houldsworth (*see* E Morton, colls, 1963 Edn), and has issue living, Archie James Ian, *b* 1998, — Letty Katherine, *b* 1996. *Address* – c/o Nomad Safaris, Arusha, Tanzania.

BROTHER LIVING

Thomas Richard Geers, *b* 1939; *ed* Eton: *m* 1966, Caroline Wan-Cheng, who *d* 1991, elder da of Foong Chong. *Residence* – The Salmon, Bridge Sollars, Hereford.

SISTERS LIVING

Rose Evelyn, *b* 1932: *m* 1954 (*m diss* 1976), Charles Eric Alexander Hambro (*cr Baron Hambro*, Life Baron 1994). *Residence* – Barton House, Guiting Power, nr Cheltenham, Glos. —— Anne Lettice (*Lady Sinclair*), *b* 1933: *m* 1968, 17th Lord Sinclair. *Residence* – Knocknalling, Dalry, Kircudbrightshire.

Col Sir John Geers, 1st Baronet, sat as MP for Herefordshire 1804-31; his grandfather, John Brooks, of Broadway, assumed the surname and arms of Cotterell, by Roy licence. The 3rd baronet was MP for Herefordshire 1857-9, and the 4th baronet was Lord-Lieut of Herefordshire 1904-33 (High Sheriff 1897).

COTTS (UK) 1921, of Coldharbour Wood, Rogate, Sussex

Forward trusting in God

Sir RICHARD CRICHTON MITCHELL COTTS, 4th *Baronet*; *b* 26 July 1946; *s* his father, *Maj Sir* ROBERT CRICHTON MITCHELL, 1995; *ed* Oratory Sch.

Arms – Azure, on a chevron between in chief two lions rampant and in base a representation of the Southern Cross, three lymphads sable. Crest – A quadriga or.
Address – 3 Coastguard Cottages, Shingle St, Woodbridge, Suffolk IP12 3BG.

BROTHER LIVING

HAMISH WILLIAM ANTHONY MITCHELL, *b* 15 Sept 1951; *ed* Ampleforth: *m* 1995, Merlyn Mattiuzzo, and has issue living, Celandine, *b* 1996. *Residence* – 3 Coastguard Cottages, Shingle St, Woodbridge, Suffolk IP12 3BG.

SISTERS LIVING

Susannah Marie-Josephe Mitchell, *b* 1945: *m* 1971, John Davies, of Cheshire, and has issue living, Justin, *b* 1981. *Residence* – 6 Barrack Lane, Lower Ufford, nr Woodbridge, Suffolk IP13 6DT. —— Miranda Clare Mitchell, *b* 1948: *m* 1973, Tristram Cosmo Barran, who *d* 1992, in a motor accident, and has issue (*see* Barran, Bt). *Residence* – 5 Rayner Court, Bamborough Gdns, W12 8QJ

The name of this family was originally spelt Coutts. The 1st baronet, Sir William Dingwall Mitchell Cotts, KBE (son of late William Cotts, of Sanquhar, Dumfries-shire), was head of the firm of Mitchell Cotts and Co, of London, and of allied firms in S Africa and elsewhere (merchants, colliery proprietors, and steamship owners), and sat as MP for Western Isles (NL) 1922-23. Sir (William) Campbell Mitchell-Cotts, 2nd baronet, an actor, assumed by deed poll 1932 the additional surname of Mitchell.

COUPER (UK) 1841
(Name pronounced "Cooper")

By valour

Sir (ROBERT) NICHOLAS OLIVER COUPER, 6th *Baronet*; *b* 9 Oct 1945; *s* his father, *Maj Sir* GEORGE ROBERT CECIL, 1975; *ed* Eton, and RMA Sandhurst; late Capt Blues and Royals: *m* 1st, 1972 (*m diss* 1986), Kirsten Henrietta, da of late Maj George Burrell MacKean, JP, DL, of Loughanmore, Dunadry, co Antrim (*see* E Donoughmore, colls); 2ndly, 1991, Katrina Frances, da of Sir (Charles) Michael Walker, GCMG, of W Chiltington, W Sussex, and has issue by 1st *m*.

Arms – Or, a chevron gules charged with another ermine, between three laurel-leaves slipped vert. Crest – Out of a mural coronet argent, a hand holding a garland proper.
Residences – Annery Barton, Monkleigh, Bideford, N Devon; 79 Devonshire Rd, W4 2HU. *Club* – Cavalry and Guards'.

SON LIVING (*By 1st marriage*)

JAMES GEORGE, *b* 27 Oct 1977.

DAUGHTER LIVING (*By 1st marriage*)

Caroline Doune, *b* 1979.

SISTER LIVING

Jennifer Susan Amanda, *b* (twin) 1945.

COLLATERAL BRANCHES LIVING

Grandchildren of late James Robert Couper, 4th son of 2nd Bt:—
Issue of late Maj John Every Couper, MBE, *b* 1900, *d* 1966: *m* 1928, Katherine Audrey Mary, who *d* 1987, da of late William Ross Alexander, of Cupar, Fife:—
Jonathan Every, *b* 1931; *ed* Douai.

Issue of late Capt Jem Ramsay Couper, 27th Lancers, *b* 1904, *d* 1979: *m* 1940, Aileen Jessie, da of late Thomas Robert Lamb Abbott:—
Francis Jem, *b* 1946; *ed* Marlborough. —— Caroline, *b* 1941: *m* 1968, Enrique Avendano, of 6405 30 De Agosto, FCNDFS, Prov de Buenos Aires, Argentina, and has issue living, Diego, *b* 1970, — Enrique Maria, *b* 1977, — Cecilia Maria, *b* 1969.

Granddaughter of late Gen James Kempt Couper, 2nd son of 1st baronet:—
Issue of late William Lemprière Couper, *b* 1874, *d* 1926: *m* 1919, Isabel Hodgson, who *d* 1968, having *m* 2ndly, 1952, Arthur Alfred Hitch, who *d* 1965:—
Cara Jocelyn Mary (45540 Spruce Drive, Sardis, British Columbia), *b* 1921: *m* 1952, Verne Barrett Dickey, who *d* 1984, and has issue living, William Miles, *b* 1955: *m* 1992, Tulia Carranza, and has issue living, Matthew Verne *b* 1993, Christopher Miles *b* 1996, — Roy Couper, *b* 1957, — Alan Verne, *b* 1960, — Mary Isabel, *b* 1953: *m* 1974, M. Borden, and has issue living, Jeffrey Wayne *b* 1975, Lisa Marie *b* 1977: *m* 1997, Robert Slack (and has issue living, Alisha Marie *b* 1997).

Col Sir George, CB, KH, 1st Bt, Capt 92nd Regt at Copenhagen; served throughout Peninsular War (medal with five clasps); was Mil Sec to Sir James Kempt in Canada, and subsequently to Lord Durham; afterwards Comptroller of Household and Equerry to HRH the Duchess of Kent. The 2nd baronet, Sir George Ebenezer Wilson Couper, KCSI, CB, CIE, of the HEICS, was present at the siege of Lucknow as ADC to Sir Henry Lawrence and Sir John Inglis, subsequently becoming Gov of N-W Provinces, India. Sir Guy Couper, 4th Bt, *d* 1975, when the baronetcy passed to Maj Sir George Robert Cecil Couper, 5th Bt, el son of James Robert Couper, 4th son of 2nd Bt.

Cowell-Stepney, see Stepney.

Cradock-Hartopp, see Hartopp.

Craig (Gibson-Craig-Carmichael), see Carmichael.

CRAUFURD (GB) 1781, of Kilbirney, North Britain

Sir ROBERT JAMES CRAUFURD, 9th *Baronet*; *b* 18 March 1937; *s* his father, *Sir* JAMES GREGAN, 1970; *ed* Harrow, and Univ Coll, Oxford (MA); Member of London Stock Exchange: *m* 1st, 1964 (*m diss* 1987), Catherine Penelope, yr da of late Capt Horatio Westmacott, RN; 2ndly, 1987, Georgina Anne, da of late John Dennis Russell (*see* Corbet Bt), and has issue (by 1st *m*).

Arms – Argent, two tilting spears in saltire proper between four ermine spots sable, a bordure chequy gules and of the field. Crest – An ermine proper. *Residence* – East Grove, Grove Rd, Lymington, Hants SO41 3RF.

DAUGHTERS LIVING (*By 1st marriage*)

Caroline Anne (17 New Ground Rd, Aldbury, Tring, Herts HP23 5RQ), *b* 1965. —— Penelope Jane (15 New Ground Rd, Aldbury, Tring, Herts HP23 5RQ), *b* 1967. —— Veronica Mary, *b* 1969.

SISTERS LIVING

Jane Elizabeth, *b* 1932: *m* 1st, 1960 (*m diss* 1979), Maj Michael Cumby Spurrier, late DLI; 2ndly, 1979, John Robson Hoyle, of 12 Linkfield, W Molesey, Surrey KT8 1SD. —— Margaret Ruth (9 Winston Rd, N16 9LU), *b* 1934: *m* 1962 (*m diss* 1989), John Peter Hudson, and has issue living, Alexander Matthew HUDSON CRAUFURD, *b* 1965; *ed* Edinburgh Univ (BA); assumed the surname of Craufurd in addition to that of Hudson by Deed Poll, — Emma Caroline, *b* 1963, — Erica, *b* 1968.

Distinction without a stain

DAUGHTERS LIVING OF SEVENTH BARONET

Isolda Vereker, *b* 1912: *m* 1945, Maj James Robertson Clement, and has issue living, James Robert Alexander, *b* 1949, — Helen Alexa Caroline, *b* 1950. —— Cynthia (53 Carey Court, Resthaven, 139 Goldcreek Rd, Brookfield, Queensland 4069, Australia), *b* 1917: *m* 1st, 1944, Jacques Pinkasfeld, who *d* 1963; 2ndly, 1972, Lt-Col Albert Francis Lamb, who *d* 1981, and has issue living (by 1st *m*), Peter Charles, *b* 1950, — Rosemary, *b* 1952.

COLLATERAL BRANCH LIVING

Granddaughters of late Capt Henry Robert Craufurd, grandson of Maj-Gen Robert Craufurd, 3rd son of 1st baronet:—
Issue of late Col Robert Quentin Craufurd, DSO, *b* 1880, *d* 1943: *m* 1st, 1909, Mildred Mary, who *d* 1929, da of late Rt Hon William Kenny, a Judge of High Court in Ireland, of Marlfield, Cabinteely, co Dublin; 2ndly, 1931, Muriel Frances, who *d* 1969, da of late George Edward Darroch, of 40 Stanhope Gdns, SW, and Braidley, Canford Cliffs, Dorset:—
(By 1st *m*) Dorothy Mary, *b* 1910; a Nun. —— Mildred Heather Mary, *b* 1916.

This family descends from John who possessed the Northern part of the Barony of Crawford 1153. His son, Sir Reginald de Craufurd, *m* Margaret, da and heir of James de Loudoun, and his descendants inherited the lands of Loudoun which passed to Susan, da and heir of Sir Reginald Craufurd executed by the English at Carlisle 1307. She *m* Sir Duncan Campbell of Reidcastle, from whom descend the Earls of Loudoun. Sir Alexander Craufurd, 1st Bt, was 11th in descent from Archibald Craufurd of Previck and Thirdpart, living 1401, 2nd son of Thomas of Auchenames, great-grandson of Hugh, yr brother of Sir Reginald.

CRAVEN (UK) 1942, of Crowhurst, co Surrey (Extinct 1946)

Sir DEREK WORTHINGTON CLUNES CRAVEN, 2nd and last *Baronet*.

DAUGHTER LIVING OF SECOND BARONET

Jennifer Anne, *b* (*posthumous*) 1946.

Crawley-Boevey, see Boevey.

Crespigny, see de Crespigny.

CRISP (UK) 1913, of Bungay, Suffolk

Sir (JOHN) PETER CRISP, 4th *Baronet*; *b* 19 May 1925; *s* his father, *Sir* JOHN WILSON, 1950; *ed* Westminster: *m* 1954, Judith Mary, who *d* 1998, yst da of late Herbert Edward Gillett, FRICS, of Marlborough, Wilts, and niece of Sir Harold Gillett, 1st Bt, MC, and has issue.

Arms – Paly of four ermine and gules, on a chevron or five horseshoes sable. Crest – A camelopard sejant or, gorged with a collar with chain reflexed over the back gules, supporting with the dexter foreleg an oar of the Royal State Barge proper.
Residence – Crabtree Cottage, Drungewick Lane, Loxwood, Billingshurst, W Sussex RH14 0RP.

SONS LIVING

JOHN CHARLES, *b* 10 Dec 1955: *m* 1992, Mary Jo, eldest da of Dr Daniel J. MacAuley, of Belfast, and has issue living, George Peter Daniel, *b* 17 Sept 1993. —— Michael Peter, *b* 1957: *m* 1988, Pauline Sarah, only da of Sydney Gold, of Pinner, Middx, and has issue living, Alexander Samuel, *b* 1990, — Joshua Peter, *b* 1993. —— Charles Frank, *b* 1960: *m* 1992, Susan Jennifer, elder da of Deryck Scrase, of Rudgwick, W Sussex, and has issue living, Frederick, *b* 1993, — Henry James, *b* 1995, — William, *b* 1997.

DAUGHTER LIVING

Catherine Mary, *b* 1962.

The 1st baronet, Sir Frank Crisp (son of John Shalders Crisp, of Bramfield, Suffolk), was senior partner in the legal firm of Ashurst, Morris, Crisp & Co, of

Deeds not words

17 Throgmorton Avenue, EC.

CRITCHETT (UK) 1908, of Harley Street, Borough of St Marylebone

Sir IAN GEORGE LORRAINE CRITCHETT, 3rd *Baronet*; *b* 9 Dec 1920; *s* his father, *Sir* (GEORGE) MONTAGUE, MVO, 1941; *ed* Harrow, and Clare Coll, Camb (BA 1942); formerly Flight-Lieut RAF Vol Reserve; entered Foreign Office 1948; was 3rd Sec (Commercial) in Vienna 1950-51, 2nd Sec (Commercial) in Bucharest 1951-53, 2nd Sec in Cairo 1956; 1st Sec, later Counsellor, FCO 1962 (ret 1980): *m* 1st, 1948, Paulette Mary Lorraine, who *d* 1962, da of late Col Henry Brabazon Humfrey, formerly Indian Army; 2ndly, 1964, Jocelyn Daphne Margret, el da of late Cdr Christopher Mildmay Hall, of Higher Boswarva, Penzance (*see* Broughton, Bt, 1980 Edn), and has issue by 2nd *m*.

Arms – Azure, a fire chest argent, flames proper, between three crickets or. Crest – A starling in front of an iris flowered proper.
Residence – Uplands Lodge, Pains Hill, Limpsfield, Surrey RH8 0RF.

SON LIVING (*By 2nd marriage*)

CHARLES GEORGE MONTAGUE, *b* 2 April 1965.

DAUGHTER LIVING (*By 2nd marriage*)

Xanthe Clare Lorraine, *b* 1968: *m* 1997, Richard Stephen Lindsay, and has issue (*see* E Crawford, colls).

Follow right

The 1st baronet, Sir (George) Anderson Critchett, KCVO, was a KGStJ, Pres of Ophthalmological Soc 1899-1900, and Surg-Oculist to King Edward VII 1901-10, and to King George V 1910-18, and Surg-Oculist-in-Ord to King George V 1918-25, and the 2nd baronet, Sir (George) Montague Critchett, MVO, was in Lord Chamberlain's Office, St James's Palace 1912-41.

CROFT (E) 1671, of Croft Castle, Herefordshire

To be rather than to seem

Sir OWEN GLENDOWER CROFT, 14th *Baronet*; *b* 26 April 1932; *s* his father, *Sir* BERNARD HUGH DENMAN, 1984: *m* 1959, Sally Patricia, da of Dr Thomas Montagu Mansfield, of Brisbane, Qld, and has issue.

𝔄rms – Quarterly per fesse indented azure and argent; in the 1st quarter a lion passant guardant or. ℭrests – 1st, a lion passant guardant argent; 2nd, a wyvern sable vulned in the side gules.
Residence – Salisbury Court, Uralla 2358, NSW, Australia.

SON LIVING

THOMAS JASPER (PO Box 140, Beechworth, Vic 3747, Australia), *b* 3 Nov 1962; *ed* The Armidale Sch, Armidale, and Darling Downs Inst (Assoc Dip Mech Eng): *m* 1989, Catherine Fiona, da of Graham William White. *Residence* – Haldon, Havelock Rd, Beechworth, Vic 3747, Australia.

DAUGHTERS LIVING

Patricia Alice, *b* 1960: *m* 1993, Peter James Rasmussen. —— Georgiana, *b* 1964.

BROTHERS LIVING

Hugh Fiennes Denman (Callemondah, Duri, NSW 2344, Aust), *b* 1942: *m* 1972, June Alison Cairnes, da of late John Wauch Johnston, of Straban, Walcha, NSW, and has issue living, Edwina Alexandra Cairnes, *b* 1974, — Katrina Alison Cairnes, *b* 1976, — Philippa Ann Cairnes, *b* 1977, — Lucinda Anna Cairnes, *b* 1983. —— Bernard John (Westview, PO Box 253, Guyra, NSW 2365, Australia), *b* 1943: *m* 1977, Janet Madeleine, da of Lloyd Alfred Streader, of Melbourne, Vic, and has issue living, David William, *b* 1977, — Ian Archer, *b* 1981, — Briony Elizabeth, *b* 1979, — Alice Madeleine, *b* 1985.

SISTER LIVING

Camilla, *b* 1947.

UNCLE LIVING (*Son of 12th baronet*)

Herbert Frederick, *b* 1906: *m* 1932, Marjorie Valmai, who *d* 1990, da of R. Evans, and has issue living, Peter Herbert (Wongalee, Uralla, NSW 2358), *b* 1933: *m* 1965, Ann, da of late L. G. Carpenter, of Toll-Bar, Cooma, NSW, and has issue living, Guy Herbert *b* 1966, — Andrew Peter (Rossmore, Burren Junction, NSW 2386) *b* 1968: *m* 1994, Sally, da of M. J. Holcombe, of Burren Junction, NSW (and has issue living, Lyndon Murray *b* 1996), — Robert Ryland (P.O. Box 1586, Armidale, NSW 2350, Australia), *b* 1937: *m* 1966, Helen, da of late D. J. Fraser, and has issue living, Quentin Stewart, *b* 1967, Carlisle Robert *b* 1974: *m* 1998, Peta Jane, da of R. Bissett, of Ballarat, Victoria, Australia, Sinclair Fraser *b* 1976, — James Philip (P.O. Box 266, Uralla NSW 2358), *b* 1950: *m* 1972, Elaine, da of late S. K. Wall, of Cowra, and has issue living, Michael James *b* 1977, Rowena Jane *b* 1974: *m* 1997, Simon Scott (and has issue living, Gryffin Robert James *b* 1998, Miranda Jane *b* 1999), — Shirley Anne *b* 1934: *m* 1954, David Gill, of 3 Buckingham Drive, Pottsville Beach, NSW 2489, Australia, and has issue living, Michael David (7 Gigas Court, Rochedale, Queensland 4123, Australia) *b* 1957: *m* 1982, Kim Elizabeth, da of late R. R. Crutcher, of Wee Waa, NSW (and has issue living, Nichole May *b* 1986, Samantha Jane *b* 1992), Philippa Shirley *b* 1955: *m* 1975, James Douglas Page, of Boolneringbar, Copmanhurst, NSW, Australia (and has issue living, Robert James *b* 1975, Rachelle Philippa *b* 1978, Jacqueline Frances *b* 1982), Katrina Anne *b* 1958: *m* 1988, John Douglas Kerrison, of P.O. Box 1107, Kingscliff, NSW 2487, Australia (and has issue living, Dean Andrew *b* 1993, Anna Maree *b* 1991). *Residence* – Bareena, Uralla, NSW 2358, Australia.

COLLATERAL BRANCHES LIVING

Branches from yr sons of 12th baronet

Issue of late Frederick James Croft, 3rd son of 12th baronet, *b* 1909, *d* 1993: *m* 1943, Barbara (Lugwardine, Barraba, NSW 2347, Australia), da of Howard Carter, of Barraba, NSW:—
Edward Hugh Wynford, *b* 1944: *m* 1969, Jennifer Mary, da of Thomas James Stirton, of Armoobilla, Cheepie, Qld, and has issue living, Edward James Wynford, *b* 1971, — Andrew John Wynford *b* 1974, — Amanda Jane, *b* 1978, — Lucinda Jennifer, *b* 1981.

Issue of late Archer John Croft, yst son of 12th baronet, *b* 1913, *d* 1971: *m* 1939, Marcie Issell Heathfield, who *d* 1976, da of late Clifton Hazlewood Eliott (*see* Eliott, Bt, colls).
Antony John (Vale St, Tamworth, NSW 2340, Australia), *b* 1940: *m* 1st, 1966 (*m diss* 1978), Kathleen Francis, yr da of R. F. Kelsall; 2ndly, 1978, Lyndall Forrest Warby; 3rdly, 1987, Gliss Holbrook, and has issue living (by 1st *m*), Michael John, *b* 1967, — Tania Jane, *b* 1968. —— David Archer (12 Hambledon Hill Rd, Singleton, NSW, Australia), *b* 1946: *m* 1971, Violeta, only child of V. Deikus, of 6 Albert St, Cabramatta, NSW, and has issue living, Justin Damian, *b* 1973, — Nathan David, *b* 1975, — Rebecca Lee *b* 1978. —— Stephen Hugh, *b* 1953: *m* 1981, Debra Maree Meredith, and has issue living, Emma Jane, *b* 1986, — Katherine Jane, *b* 1988.

Branches from yr sons of 9th baronet

Grandson of late Brig-Gen William Denman Croft, CB, CMG, DSO (infra):—
Issue of late Capt William Owen Glendower Croft, Indian Army, *b* 1913, *d* 1946: *m* 1944, Margaret, da of late Major Tobin, Indian Army:—
Richard Owen Glendower (Barnesfield, South St, Boughton, Faversham, Kent), *b* 1944; *ed* Kent Univ; Lt 1st Bn Cameronians (Scottish Rifles): *m* 1967, Elizabeth Jillian Allen, and has issue living, James Owen, *b* 1972, — Emma Kate, *b* 1974.

Issue of late Brig-Gen William Denman Croft, CB, CMG, DSO, 4th son of 9th baronet, *b* 1879, *d* 1968: *m* 1912, Esmé, who *d* 1977, da of Sir Arthur Edwin Sutton, 7th Bt:—
Rev John Armentieres, MC (Vine House, The Common, Wincanton, Som; Army and Navy Club), *b* 1915; *ed* Stowe; Maj (ret) RA; late Indian Army; V of Gwinear 1960-70; NW Frontier 1935 (despatches), Burma 1944 (wounded, MC): *m* 1948, Sheila Kathleen, da of late Maj J. A. Ford, of Pengreep, Cornwall, and has issue living, Edmund Hugh Glendower, *b* 1954, — Patricia Lucy, *b* 1951: *m* 1973, Lt-Col Robert Rowe, R Irish Rangers, and has issue living, Victoria Lucy *b* 1977, Harriet Alice *b* 1979. —— Violet Lorna, *b* 1917: *m* 1942, Lt-Cdr Thomas Charteris Black, RNVR, and has issue living, Peter Michael, *b* 1952, — Jane Margaret, *b* 1943, — Susan Mary, *b* 1945. —— Angela Desiree, *b* 1923: *m* 1st, 1955, Roland Grievson, who *d* 1974; 2ndly, 1984, Walter Carlson.

Issue of late Jasper Brodie Croft, 6th son of 9th baronet; *b* 1884; *d* 1950: *m* 1907, Catherine Harriett, who *d* 1975, da of F. G. Taylor, of Terrible Vale, NSW:—
Jasper Thomas (50 Sandstone Crescent, Lennox Head 2478, NSW, Australia), *b* 1924; Fl Lt RAAF; JP: *m* 1948, Editha Deirdre, da of late George Mansfield Westgarth, of Scone, NSW and has issue living, Jasper David (c/o NSW Agriculture & Fisheries, Wagga Wagga, NSW, Australia); *b* 1949; BA, MSc; JP: *m* 1977, Frances Ellen, da of Francis Hamilton, of Condobolin, and has issue living, Jasper Brett Frank *b* 1983, Amanda Kate *b* 1980, — Bettina Kay, *b* 1951: *m* 1973, David Peter Leslie, of Beverley, Nevertire, NSW, and has issue living, Victoria Jodi *b* 1976, Kristy Peta *b* 1987, — Kerrie Leigh (a da) *b* 1954. —— Kitty McLeod (Unit 49/45 Cook St, St David's Retirement Village, Forestville, NSW), *b* 1908: *m* 1938, Peter Assheton, who *d* 1970, and has had issue, Pedir Raif Orme, *b* 1941: *m* 1972, Nancy Shaw, of Sydney, NSW, and *d* 1992, leaving issue, Olwen Annaliese *b* 1975, — Rowena Tydwr, *b* 1939: *m* 1966, Zbyszek Lisak, of Lorne House, Kingsland, Herefordshire HR6 9RU, and has issue living, Tamara *b* 1967, Nadya *b* 1968. —— Isabel McLeod, *b* 1911: *m* 1945, Bassett Fredrick Care, of 16 Beaumetz St, Sandgate 4017, Qld, and has issue living, Frederick McLeod, *b* 1948: *m* 1969, Jennifer Dianne, da of late Arthur Silas Faulk, and has issue living, Thomas Lachlan *b* 1986, Amanda *b* 1970, Sally *b* 1972. —— Marjorie McLeod, *b* 1912: *m* 1943, Cecil Gordon Lowe, RAAF, of 32 North Rd, Woodridge, Qld, and has issue living, Benjamin John, *b* 1944: *m* 1st, 1962 (*m diss* 1975), Gloria Daphne, da of W. Williams, of W Aust; 2ndly, 1979, Patricia Lee Florian, and has issue living, (by 1st *m*) Dallas Gordon *b* 1969, (by 2nd *m*) Jason McLeod *b* 1979, — William James, *b* 1951: *m* 1974, Caroline, da of Kenneth Watson, and has issue living, Daniel William *b* 1975, Drummond Murray *b* 1978, Benjamin Gordon *b* 1979, — Catherine Jane, *b* 1947: *m* 1969, Brian Finnigan, of 65 Ashton St, Kingston, Qld, and has issue living, Matthew Brian *b* 1977, David Joseph *b* 1980, Joanne Maree *b* 1973, Anna *b* 1987, — Susanne Barbara, *b* 1950: *m* 1971, Kenneth Murray, of Tieri, Qld, and has issue living, Rachel Susanne *b* 1977, Deanne Gai *b* 1978, Alaina Alexandrea *b* 1981, — Elizabeth, *b* 1953: *m* 1975, Peter Anthony Ware, of Qld, and has issue living, Jodie Alisha *b* 1980, Melissa Jane *b* 1983, — Mary-Anne *b* 1955: *m* 1977, Denis Townsend, of Qld, and has issue living, Shane Andrew *b* 1980, Timothy Neil *b* 1983. —— Enid Barbara McLeod, *b* 1915: *m* 1959, Maj George Hyde, AIF, who *d* 1975. —— Nancy Perena McLeod, *b* 1921: *m* 1950, Eric W. Adams, of Balnabeen, Silver Leigh Rd, Kingsthorpe, Qld 4400, Australia.

Branch from 3rd son of 6th baronet

Grandchildren of late Lieut-Col Richard Page Croft, elder son of late Richard Benyon Croft, son of late Rev Richard Croft, 3rd son of 6th baronet:—
Issue of late Major Richard Arthur Fitzroy Page Croft, *b* 1910, *d* 1998: *m* 1st, 1939 (*m diss* 1956), Felice Amy (Peggy) McClymont; 2ndly, 1956, Daphne Frye, who *d* 1978; 3rdly, 1981, Maria Isabel (The Round House, Ware, Herts SG12 7PR), *née* De Eguidazu, and formerly wife of Count Aymon de Roussy de Sales:—
(By 1st *m*) Richard Nicholas Page, *b* 1941: *m* 1st, 1967, Teresa Mary, who *d* 1971, da of late Donald Jewell, of Burry Port, Carmarthenshire, and formerly wife of Sverré Wilberg, of Frederikstadt, Norway; 2ndly, 1973 (*m diss* 1989), Bruna Campesato; 3rdly, 1992, Maria (Polly) Beziers. —— Hugo Douglas Page (Castlebury, Bakers End, Ware, Herts), *b* 1944: *m* 1st, 1969 (*m diss* 1998), Dawn Pryde; 2ndly, 1998, Gwyneth Maud Wynn-Jones, and has issue living (by 1st *m*), Richard Page, *b* 1973, — Edward Page, *b* 1976, — James Craggs Page, *b* 1979, — Arabella, *b* 1971. —— Miriam Anne Page, *b* 1948: *m* 1974, Piers Rogers, of Timber Hall Cottage, Cold Christmas, Ware, Herts, and has issue living, Samuel Bennett, *b* 1978, — Scarlett Alice *b* 1980.

Issue of late Rt Hon Sir Henry Page Croft, CMG, TD, 1st Bt (*cr* 1924), who was *cr Baron Croft* 1940 (see that title)

Jasper de Croft came from Normandy 1066. Croft Castle, built 1200, was sold about 1765, having descended from father to son for more than 700 years (but was bought back by the Trustees for the 11th Bt in 1924, and is now the property of the National Trust). Members of the family represented Herefordshire in sixteen Parliaments between 1297 and 1874. Sir John Croft of Croft Castle *m* Janet, da of Owen Glendower. The father of the first baronet was Bishop of Hereford.

The 10th baronet, Sir Herbert Archer Croft, Capt Herefordshire Regt, was *ka* 1915. The 11th baronet, Sir James Herbert Croft, Capt No 1 Commando Special Ser Batn, was *k* on active ser 1941.

CROFT (UK) 1818, of Cowling Hall, Yorkshire

To be rather than to seem

Sir THOMAS STEPHEN HUTTON CROFT, 6th *Baronet*; *b* 12 June 1959; *s* his father, *Maj Sir* JOHN ARCHIBALD RADCLIFFE, 1990; *ed* King's Sch, Canterbury, Univ Coll, London (BSc), and Royal Coll of Art (MA); Architect.

Arms – Quarterly per fesse indented or and gules, in the first quarter a lion passant-guardant of the second. **Crest** – A lion passant guardant per pale, indented gules and erminois, the dexter fore paw resting on a shield argent charged with a star of the Order of the Tower and Sword. **Supporters** – Dexter, a lion guardant or, gorged with a wreath of laurel vert, therefrom pendent an escutcheon gules, charged with a tower or; sinister, a bull sable, horned crined hoofed and gorged with a wreath of laurel or, therefrom pendent an escutcheon argent, charged with the star of the Order of the Tower and Sword.
Residence – Flat 3, 17 Hatton St, NW8 8PL.

UNCLE LIVING (*brother of 5th baronet*)

CYRIL BERNARD, *b* 6 June 1918; late Lieut The Buffs: *m* 1st, 1957, Sheila Maisie, who *d* 1979, da of Henry Clark Cox, of Whitstable, Kent; 2ndly, 1980, Anne Heather Newbatt, da of Howard Cormack Bessant, and has issue living (by 1st *m*), Diana Louise, *b* 1959: *m* 1988, Neil Frederick Crumbie. — Wendy Jane, *b* 1961. *Residence* – Rayham Meadow, Rayham Rd, Whitstable, Kent CT5 3DZ.

WIDOW LIVING OF FIFTH BARONET

LUCY ELIZABETH (*Lady Croft*), Lieut ATS, Hon Col WRAC (TA), da of late Maj William Dallas Loney Jupp, OBE, of Stafford: *m* 1953, Maj Sir John Archibald Radcliffe Croft, 5th Bt, who *d* 1990. *Residence* – The Barn House, Rayham Rd, Whitstable, Kent CT5 3DZ.

This family is of common origin with the Crofts of Herefordshire, and the Crofts of Stillington Hall, Yorks. Sir John Croft, 1st Bt, a Portuguese Commr, Knt of the Portuguese Order of the Tower and Sword, and Baron da Serra da Estrella in Portugal, did considerable service in the Peninsular war by risking his life to obtain information for the Duke of Wellington, and in distributing the British Parliamentary grant of £100,000 for relieving the Portuguese, and was Hon Chargé d'Affaires at Lisbon 1815.

CROFTON (UK) 1801, of Mohill, Leitrim

God gives the increase

(*Sir*) HUGH DENIS CROFTON, 8th *Baronet*; *b* 10 April 1937; *s* his half-nephew, *Sir* (HUGH) PATRICK SIMON, 1987, but does not use the title; *ed* Eton, Worcester Coll, Oxford (BA), and Bristol Univ (BA).

ᴀrms – Per pale indented or and azure, a lion passant-guardant counterchanged, a crescent for difference. ℭrest – Seven ears of wheat, on one stalk proper.

BROTHER LIVING

EDWARD MORGAN, *b* 26 July 1945; *ed* Eton, and RMA; Maj Coldstream Gds (ret 1986); One of HM's Body Guard of Hon Corps of Gentlemen-at-Arms since 1996: *m* 1977, Emma Victoria Mildred, only da of Sir Henry George Massy Dashwood, 8th Bt (*cr* 1684), and has issue living, Henry Morgan, *b* 1979, — George Edward, *b* 1981. *Residence* – Marchwood Lodge, Rake, Liss, Hants GU33 7PG.

DAUGHTER LIVING OF SEVENTH BARONET

Atalanta Chloe Majken, *b* 1969.

WIDOW LIVING OF SIXTH BARONET

MARGARET AMELIA (*Margaret, Lady Crofton*), da of late Judge Morris Dallett, of Philadelphia, USA: *m* 1933, as his 3rd wife, Lt-Col Sir Morgan George Crofton, DSO, 6th Bt, who *d* 1958. *Residence* – 34 Rhinefield Close, Brockenhurst, Hants SO42 7SU.

WIDOW LIVING OF SEVENTH BARONET

LENE (*Lady Crofton*), da of Kai Augustinus, of Copenhagen, and of Mrs R. Tonnesen, of Port Elizabeth, S Africa, and formerly wife of Michael Eddowes: *m* 1967, Sir (Hugh) Patrick Simon Crofton, 7th Bt, who *d* 1987. *Residence* – Foxleys Farm, Holyport, nr Maidenhead, Berks.

MOTHER LIVING OF SEVENTH BARONET

Rosalie, da of late John Lever Tillotson, of Bidston Court, Cheshire: *m* 1st, 1934 (*m diss* 1941), Maj Morgan George Crofton, who *d* 1947; 2ndly, 1947, Lt-Col George St Vigor J. Vigor, OBE, late Welsh Gds, who *d* 1979. *Residence* – 27 Park St, Windsor, Berks.

COLLATERAL BRANCHES LIVING

Granddaughters of late Lt-Gen James Crofton, 3rd son of Capt Morgan Crofton, RN, el son of Morgan Crofton, 3rd son of 1st baronet:—
   Issue of late Charles D'Arcy Crofton, *b* 1879, *d* 1955: *m* 1910, Mary Helen Elizabeth, who *d* 1960, da of H. G. Gearing, formerly of Tea Hill, Coonoor, Nilgris, S India:—
Beatrice Barrett, *b* 1915: *m* 1938, Brig Anthony John le Grand Jacob, MBE, late RE, and has issue living, John (Model Farm, North End, nr Henley-on-Thames, Oxon RG9 6LJ), *b* 1940, — Rupert (53 Park Rd, Staple Hill, Bristol BS16 5LQ), *b* 1948: *m* 1986, Lynne, da of Thomas Raymond White, and has issue living, Thomas Alexander *b* 1989, Claudia Harriet *b* 1992, — Rosemary JACOB (PK 118, 48300 Fethiye, Turkey), *b* 1944: has resumed her maiden name: *m* 19— (*m diss* 19   ), and has issue living, Timon Montague JACOB *b* 1970, — Alice (10 Millfield Close, Saxmundham, Suffolk IP17 1XH), *b* 1950.

   Issue of late John Hutchinson Crofton, MB, MRCS, *b* 1883, *d* 1953: *m* 1914, Alice, who *d* 1943, da of late Arthur Charles Humphreys-Owen, MP, of Glansevern, Montgomeryshire:—
Anne Dorothy, *b* 1915. *Address* – The Cottage, Higherland, nr Callington, Cornwall PL17 8LD.

Grandchildren of late Rev Henry Woodward Crofton, 2nd son of Rev William Morgan Crofton, 2nd son of Morgan Crofton, 3rd son of 1st baronet:—
   Issue of late Maj Geoffrey Hugh Schenley Crofton, late Suffolk Regt, *b* 1881, *d* 1955: *m* 1908, Monica, who *d* 1977, da of late A. W. Hall, of Barton Abbey, Steeple Aston:—
Henry Horatio, *b* 1910; Capt W Yorks Regt. —— Monica Melesina Nem, *b* 1915. —— Angela Catherine, *b* 1917.

Grandson of late Maj Charles Woodward Crofton, yr son of late Rev Henry Woodward Crofton (ante):—
   Issue of late Maj Hugh Charles Henry Crofton, RA, *b* 1915, *d* 1986: *m* 1949, Margery (Rock House, Hudswell, Richmond, N Yorks), da of late Thomas Summerson, of Sunderland:—
John Hugh (6 Silver St, Reeth, Richmond, N Yorks), *b* 1954; *ed* Giggleswick Sch: *m* 1981, Martha June, da of William Thomas Holbert, of 435 Bluebird Lane, Delray Beach, Fla 33445, USA, and has issue living, Emma Zoe, *b* 1983, — Chloe Alexandra, *b* 1986.

Grandchildren of late Francis Blake Crofton, 5th son of Rev William Crofton (ante):—
Issue of late Arthur Molesworth Crofton, *b* 1874, *d* 1945: *m* 1897, Gwendolin Forrest, who *d* 1950, of Quebec, Canada:—

Brian Forrest (409 Kent St, Whitby, Ontario, Canada), *b* 1905: *m* 1930, Violet, da of Thomas Janes, R Canadian Mounted Police (Marine Section), and has issue living, Ralph Janes, *b* 1931: *m* 1954, Marcella, da of James Billard, and has issue living, Ralph Kevin *b* 1958, Heather Cavelle *b* 1956: *m* 1979, Jeffery Mitchell (and has issue living, Alicia Violet *b* 1982), — Ross Blake, *b* 1935: *m* 1961, Claire, da of Frederick Burke, and has issue living, Sandra Jane *b* 1962, Karen Eileen *b* 1964, — Brian Eric, *b* 1944: *m* 1970, Helen, da of James Seto, and has issue living, Brian James *b* 1971, David Andrew *b* 1973, — Gwendolyn Patricia, *b* 1939: *m* 1965, Harvey Thompson, and has issue living, Paul Gregory *b* 1970, David Harvey *b* 1975, — Edith Jane, *b* 1941: *m* 1966, Gary Carman Jones, and has issue living, Jeffery Carman Blake *b* 1973, — Brenda Faye, *b* 1943: *m* 1965, Clive Orville Garlow Denyke, and has issue living, Sean Forrest *b* 1968, Arthur Anslem *b* 1972. —— Henry Desmond, *b* 1907: *m* 1st, 1937, Frances Veron Borgeest, who *d* 1942; 2ndly, 1951, Marie Jeanne, da of Joseph Muloin, and widow of Sqn-Ldr Oliver J. Gaboury, RCAF. —— Charles Patrick, *b* 1913: *m* 1943, Catherine Kennedy, and has issue living, David Ian, *b* 1944, — Arthur Blake, *b* 1946, — Alan, *b* 1953, — Terence, *b* (twin) 1953, — Catherine Patricia, *b* 1948, — Joan, *b* 1949. —— Francis Terence, *b* 1915; is an organist.

Sir Morgan Crofton, 1st Bt of Mohill, co Leitrim, was 5th in descent from Henry Crofton of Mohill, yst son of Henry Crofton of Ballymurry (*d* 1643), el son of Edward Crofton of Ballymurry (*d* 1627). The father of the 4th baronet Col Hugh Denis Crofton (who commanded 20th Regt at Alma and was wounded at Inkerman) was accidentally shot by a soldier of the 32nd Foot, at Preston, September 15th, 1861, while commanding the Depôt Battalion; and it is a singular circumstance that the same bullet killed the Adjutant of the Battalion (Capt J. Hanham), who was also heir to a baronetcy. Lieut-Col Sir Morgan George Crofton, DSO, 2nd Life Guards, 6th Bt, served in S Africa 1899-1902 (severely wounded at relief of Ladysmith), 1914-18 War (DSO), and in 1939-45 War. The 6th baronet's eldest son, Maj Morgan George Crofton, *dvp* 1947, having *m* 1st, 1934 (*m diss* 1940), Rosalie (who *m* 2ndly, 1947, Lt-Col George St Vigor J. Vigor, OBE, Welsh Gds, who *d* 1979), da of late John Lever Tillotson, of Bidston Court, Cheshire, and had issue an only child, Sir Hugh Patrick Simon Crofton, 7th Bt, who *d* in a motor accident 1987.

CROFTON (UK) 1838, of Longford House, Sligo

Sir MALBY STURGES CROFTON, 5th *Baronet* (but his name does not, at time of going to press, appear on the Official Roll of Baronets); *b* 11 Jan 1923; *s* his father, *Major Sir* (MALBY RICHARD) HENRY, DSO, 1962; *ed* Eton and Trin Coll, Camb; Member of London Stock Exchange since 1957; member of Kensington Borough Council since 1962 (Leader since 1968); GLC 1970-73 and since 1977; 1941-45 War as Capt Life Gds in Middle East and Italy: *m* 1st 1961 (*m diss* 1966), Elizabeth Madeline Nina, el da of late Maj Rhys Clavel Mansel (*see* Mansel, Bt, colls); 2ndly, 1998, Sally, da of late Maj George Henley Eden, TD, RA (*see* B Auckland, colls).

Arms – Per pale indented or and azure, a lion passant-guardant counterchanged.
Crest – Seven ears of wheat on one stalk proper.
Seat – Longford House, co Sligo. *Residence* – 12 Caithness Rd, W14.

SISTER LIVING

Beatrix Katharine, *b* 1921; formerly Junior Com ATS. *Residence* – 2 Caithness Rd, W14.

AUNT LIVING (*Daughter of 3rd baronet*)

Dorothy. *Address* – Arva, Upper Glenageary Rd, Glenageary, co Dublin.

God gives the increase   ### COLLATERAL BRANCHES LIVING

Grandchildren of late Col Malby Edward Crofton, 3rd son of 2nd baronet:—
Issue of late Col Malby Crofton, DSO, *b* 1881; *d* 1948: *m* 1911, Sarah Dorothy Beatrice, JP, who *d* 1976, da of late Col William Frederick Noel, formerly RE (E Gainsborough, colls):—
(Ursula) Doryne (Elizabeth), *b* 1921; European War 1939-45 in Middle East (Africa Star); Section Officer WAAF: *m* 1951, William Robert Castle Cleary, RIBA, son of late Sir William Castle Cleary, KBE, CB. *Residence* – 64 Pelham Court, Fulham Rd, SW3.

Issue of late Brig Roger Crofton, CIE, MC, *b* 1888, *d* 1972: *m* 1st, 1914, Stella Clifton, who *d* 1916, da of late Judge Thomas Gilbert Carver, KC; 2ndly, 1921, Dorothy Frances, who *d* 1953, da of Col Henry Melville Hatchell, DSO, formerly R Irish Regt; 3rdly, 1954, Agnes Marjorie, who *d* 1982, aged 100, da of Samuel Osborn, and widow of (1) Capt Cyril Oswald Denman-Jubb, Duke of Wellington's Regt, and (2) John Johnston May:—
(By 2nd *m*) (HENRY EDWARD) MELVILLE, MBE (Haldon, St Giles Hill, Winchester, SO23 8JH), *b* 15 Aug 1931; *ed* Hilton Coll, Natal, and Trin Coll, Camb (BA Eng); formerly Prin Admin Officer, HM Overseas Civil Ser, MBE (Civil) 1970: *m* 1955, Mary Brigid, twin da of late Gerald K. Riddle, of Buttercombe, Newton Abbot, and has issue living, Julian Malby, *b* 6 Nov 1958: *m* 1989, Hilary, da of Thomas James Twort, of 35 Sompting Av, Worthing, Sussex, and has issue living, William Robert Malby *b* 5 Jan 1996, Edward James *b* 1998, Harriet Sophie *b* 1992, — Nigel Melville, *b* 1964: *m* 1996, Kate E., da of D. J. Spark, of Awliscombe, Devon, — Nicola Dorothy, *b* 1961: *m* 1990, Julian D. P. George, elder son of John George, of Wick House, East End, Fairford, Glos GL7 7AP, and has issue living, Henry Dacre Malby *b* 1994.

In 1661 a baronetcy was conferred upon Sir Edward Crofton of the Mote, co Roscommon (*d* 1675), grandson of Edward Crofton of Ballymurry, co Roscommon (*d* 1627); it became extinct on the death of the 5th baronet in 1780, and a new baronetcy was granted in 1838 to Sir James Crofton of Longford House, co Sligo, descended from Thomas Crofton, uncle of 1st Bt, and subsequent to 1780 the senior male line of Croftons in Ireland.

CROSS (UK) 1941, of Bolton-le-Moors, co Lancaster (Extinct 1968)

Rt Hon Sir RONALD HIBBERT CROSS, KCMG, KCVO, 1st and last *Baronet*.

DAUGHTERS LIVING OF FIRST BARONET

Angela Louise Vereker (*Hon Mrs Neil D. Campbell*), *b* 1925: *m* 1951, Hon Neil Donald Campbell, DSC, son of 2nd Baron Colgrain. *Residence* – Yorks Hill Farm, Ide Hill, Sevenoaks, Kent. —— Susanna Carolyn, *b* 1938: *m* 1966, Francis Trajan Sacheverell Sitwell (*see* Sitwell, Bt). *Residence* – Weston Hall, Towcester, Northants. —— Karina Mary, *b* 1942: *m* 1965, Maj Sean Michael Barton, 22nd Cheshire Regt. *Residence* – Bakers Mill Farmhouse, Mosterton, Beaminster, Dorset.

CROSSLEY (UK) 1909, of Glenfield, Dunham Massey, co Chester

I believe and love

Sir NICHOLAS JOHN CROSSLEY, 4th *Baronet*; *b* 10 Dec 1962; *s* his father, *Sir* CHRISTOPHER JOHN, 1989.

Arms – Azure, a chevron between in chief two Tau crosses and in base a hind statant. **Crest** – A hind's head couped or, holding in the mouth a Tau cross azure. *Residence* – 331 Penn St #1, El Segundo, CA 90245, USA.

BROTHER LIVING

JULIAN CHARLES, *b* 11 Dec 1964.

WIDOWS LIVING OF SECOND AND THIRD BARONETS

ELIZABETH JOYCE (*Elizabeth, Lady Crossley*), da of late Enoch Shenton, of Boxmoor, Herts: *m* 1954, as his second wife, Sir Kenneth Irwin Crossley, 2nd Bt, who *d* 1957. *Residence* – The Old Bakery, Milton Lilbourne, Pewsey, Wilts SN9 5LQ.
LESLEY A. (*Lady Crossley*), el da of late Dr K. A. J. Chamberlain: *m* 1977, as his second wife, Sir Christopher John Crossley, 3rd Bt, who *d* 1989.

STEP-GRANDMOTHER LIVING

Marjorie (WINTERBOTTOM), da of late John Gilley: *m* 2ndly, 1932, as his second wife, Lieut-Com Nigel John Crossley, RN who was *ka* 1939; 3rdly, 1957, as his second wife, Capt Richard William Ravenhill, CBE, DSC, RN.

MOTHER LIVING

Carolyne Louise Grey (*Carolyne, Lady Crossley*), da of late Leslie Grey Sykes, of Sandbanks, Dorset: *m* 1959 (*m diss* 1969), as his first wife, Sir Christopher John Crossley, 3rd Bt, who *d* 1989.

COLLATERAL BRANCHES LIVING

Issue of late Anthony Crommelin Crossley, MP, only son of 2nd baronet, *b* 1903, *d* 1939: *m* 1927, Clare (12a Selwood Place, SW7; Brankelow Folly, Whitchurch, Shropshire), da of late Brig Alan Fortescue Thomson, DSO:—
Penelope Georgina (*Penelope, Countess of Lindsay*) *b* 1928: *m* 1st, 1951 (*m diss* 1969), Maj Henry Ronald Burn Callander, MC, who *d* 1999; 2ndly, 1969, 15th Earl of Lindsay, who *d* 1989, and has issue living (by 1st *m*), Sarah Alexandra Mary, *b* 1952: *m* 1993, Peter Thomas Beckett, of Combermere Abbey, Whitchurch, Shropshire SY13 4AJ, eldest son of late Thomas Beckett, and of Mrs John Armitage, of Hall O'Coole, Cheshire, and has issue living, Peregrine Thomas Archie *b* 1996, — Victoria, *b* 1954: *m* 1993, as his 2nd wife, (Morland Herbert) Julian Agnew, and has issue (*see* Agnew, Bt, *or* 1895, colls). — Emma Georgina (Gigi), *b* 1959: *m* 1992, William Henry Salomon, only son of Sir Walter Hans Salomon and has issue living, Alexander David Henry *b* 1996, Bettina Charlotte Helene *b* 1994. *Residences* – Lindsay Lodge, Combermere, Whitchurch, Shropshire SY13 4AY. —— (Virginia Charlotte) Theresa, *b* 1936: *m* 1st, 1956 (*m diss* 1973), Alain R. E. Camu, of Brussels; 2ndly, 1973, Marchese Francesco d'Ayala Valva, and has had issue (by 1st *m*), Adrien Bonaventure, *b* 1957: *m* 1989, Melanie J., eldest da of Roger Worboys, of Putney, and has issue living, Julian *b* 1994, Anthony *b* 1997, Helena Claire *b* 1991, — Francois Henri, *b* 1958: *d* 1990, — Nicholas Pascal, *b* 1961: *m* 1991, Mrs Rebecca Compton, only da of Sir Alan Lewis Wigan, 5th Bt, and has issue living, Marguérite *b* 1993, — Virginie

Charlotte, *b* 1959: *m* 1986, Napier Anthony Sturt Marten, and has issue (*see* By Alington), — (by 2nd *m*) Tancredi Simone, *b* 1975, — Sebastino Vittorio, *b* 1978. *Residences* – 12 Selwood Place, SW7; Camporempoli, Pietrafitta, Castellina in Chianti, Tuscany, Italy.

Grandchildren of late Eric Crossley, 2nd son of 1st baronet:—
Issue of late Michael Nicholson Crossley, *b* 1912, *d* 1987: *m* 1st, 1940 (*m diss* 1945) Doreen Maud, only da of George Tibbitt; 2ndly, 1957, Sylvia, who *d* 1975, only da of late Cdr P. A. Heyder, RN; 3rdly, 1977, Moyra Louisa Margaret (*née* Hewitt) (Loughrigg, Box 379, White River, E Transvaal, SA), widow of Maj-Gen Theodore Henry Birkbeck:—
(By 2nd *m*) Sloan Nicholas, *b* 1958. —— Claudia Bettine, *b* 1959. —— Alison Michele, *b* 1964.

The 1st baronet, Sir William John Crossley (son of Major Francis Crossley, of Glenburn, co Antrim, descended from the Crossleys of Scaitcliffe, Todmorden), a Director of Manchester Ship Canal, and Chm of Crossley Bros (Limited), of Manchester, sat as MP for Altrincham Div of Cheshire (*L*) 1906-10. The 2nd baronet, Sir Kenneth Irwin Crossley, JP, was High Sheriff of Cheshire 1919.

Culme-Seymour, see Seymour.

GORDON CUMMING (UK) 1804, of Altyre, Forres

Sir WILLIAM GORDON GORDON CUMMING, 6th *Baronet*; *b* 19 June 1928; *s* his father, *Major Sir* ALEXANDER PENROSE, MC, 1939; *ed* Eton; late Lieut Roy Scots Greys: *m* 1st, 1953 (*m diss* 1972), Elisabeth, da of late Maj-Gen Sir (William) Robert Norris Hinde, KBE, CB, DSO; 2ndly, 1972 (*m diss* 1976), Lady Pauline Anne Illingworth, sister of 13th Earl of Seafield, and formerly wife of James Henry Harcourt Illingworth; 3rdly, 1989, Sheila Bates, and has issue by 1st *m*.

Arms – Azure, three garbs or. *Crest* – A lion rampant or holding in his dexter paw a dagger proper. *Motto* – Courage. *Supporters* – Two horses argent.
Seat – Altyre, nr Forres, Morayshire.

SON LIVING (By 1st marriage)

ALEXANDER PENROSE (ALASTAIR), *b* 15 April 1954: *m* 1991, Louisa, elder da of Edward Geoffrey Clifton Brown (*see* Brown, Bt, colls), and has issue living, William, *b* 4 April 1993, — Kit, *b* 1998, — Sophie, *b* 1995. *Residence* – Wardend House, Altyre, nr Forres, Morayshire.

DAUGHTERS LIVING (By 1st marriage)

Sarah, *b* 1955: *m* 1990 as his 2nd wife, Dominic Walter Langlands Pearse, of Holwell Downs Farm, Burford, Oxon OX8 4JX, and has issue (*see* B Fitzwalter, colls). —— Charlotte, *b* 1958: *m* 1984, Michael Edwards, son of John Edwards, of Darnaconnar, Barrhill, Girvan, Ayrshire. —— Henrietta, *b* 1959: *m* 1988, Donald Statham, son of D. E. S. Statham.

SISTERS LIVING

Cecily Josephine (*Countess Lloyd George of Dwyfor*) (Glenogil, by Forfar, Angus; The Hall, Freshford, Bath; 47 Burton Court, SW3), *b* 1925: *m* 1st, 1957, as his 2nd wife, 2nd Earl of Woolton, who *d* 1969; 2ndly, 1969 (*m diss* 1974), 3rd Baron Forres, who *d* 1978; 3rdly, 1982, as his 2nd wife, 3rd Earl Lloyd George of Dwyfor. —— Philippa, *b* 1933: *m* 1955, David Archibald Innes (*see* V Downe, colls, 1985 Edn), and has issue living, Guy Archibald, *b* 1956: *m* 1998, Catriona H., yr da of Alec Simpson, of Berrima, NSW, Australia, and has issue living, Elizabeth *b* 1998, — John Hugh, *b* 1959: *m* 1988, Deborah Jane, da of Rev W. A. G. Buxton (and has issue), — Davina Evelyn, *b* 1957: *m* 1989, Wojciech Markiewicz, and has issue living, William David *b* 1991. *Residences* – Hensill House, Hawkhurst, Kent; Titsey Place, Oxted, Surrey.

COLLATERAL BRANCHES LIVING

Issue of late Michael Willoughby Gordon Cumming, 3rd son of 4th baronet, *b* 1901, *d* 1979: *m* 1st, 1923 (*m diss* 1943), Rachel Jean, who *d* 1968, da of late Col John Anstruther Thomson (Anstruther, Bt, colls); 2ndly, 1943, (Shirley) Barbara, who *d* 1996, da of late Torben Laub, of Rush Court, Wallingford, Berks:—
(By 2nd *m*) (Priscilla) Jane, *b* 1950: *m* 1991, Edwin F. Osborn, son of late Rev Reginald Osborn, of Freeland, Oxford. *Residence* – 98 Southmoor Rd, Oxford OX2 6RB. —— Catherine Rose, *b* 1952: *m* 1972, Desmond Fforde, of Highcroft, Church Place, Rodborough, nr Stroud, Glos.

Issue of late Lt Cdr Roualeyn Geoffrey Gordon Cumming, RN, 2nd son of 4th baronet, *b* 1895, *d* 1928: *m* 1923, Mary Violet Katharine (who *m* 2ndly, 1929 (*m diss* 1939), John S. Newall; 3rdly, 1941 (*m diss* 1948), Geoffrey Hugh Wilkinson, and *d* 1984), da of late Capt W. M. Marter:—
Alexander Roualeyn, CMG, CVO (Woodstock, West Way, Chichester, Sussex), *b* 1924; Group Capt (ret) RAF; Assist Sec, Dept of Trade and Industry; *cr* CVO 1970, CMG 1977: *m* 1st, 1965, Beryl Joyce MacNaughton, who *d* 1973, da of late Naughton Dunn; 2ndly, 1974, Elizabeth Patricia, who *d* 1983, da of Travers Robert Blackley, CMG, CBE, of Gurrane, Fermoy, co Cork; 3rdly, 1999, Rosalind Diane Lynch Jones, formerly of Embankment Gdns, Chelsea, da of late Henry Milton Jones, and has issue living, (by 1st *m*) Ann Penrose, *b* 1968, — (by 2nd *m*) Mary Elizabeth, *b* 1975.

Grandson of late Henry William Grant Gordon Cumming, elder son of late Henry Gordon Cumming, 3rd son of 2nd baronet:—
Issue of late Cdr Henry Ronald Gordon Cumming, OBE, RN, *b* 1893, *d* 1971: *m* 1927, Lorna Isabelle, who *d* 1974, da of Ernest W. Morey, of Johannesburg:—
Rev Henry Ian (Bay Cottage, Brookside, Runcton, Chichester, Sussex PO20 6PX), *b* 1928: *m* 1955, Janet Elizabeth Latimer Cleave, and has issue living, Jane Evelyn, *b* 1957: *m* 1994, Guy Richard Hadland, — Joanna Mary, *b* 1959: *m* 1988, Christopher Morris, and has issue living, James *b* 1993, Julia *b* 1990, — Lucille Clare (*Hon Mrs Charles Thellusson*), *b* 1962: *m* 1988, Hon Charles William Brooke Thellusson, son of 8th Baron Rendlesham, and has issue (see that title), — Deborah Diana, *b* 1965: *m* 1991, Andrew Woodward.

The Cumyn or Cumming family settled in Scotland in the reign of David I. Richard Comyn, of Northallerton received grants of lands in Roxburghshire. John Comyn, of Badenoch, chief of this family, married Eleanor, sister of King John Balliol, by which marriage Sir John of Badenoch "Red Cumyn" was a competitor for the kingdom of Scotland. Robert Cumming, of Altyre, Forres, chief of the family, who bore undifferenced arms, married Lucy, da of Sir Ludovic Gordon of Gordonstoun, and his great-grandson Sir Alexander Cumming, 1st Bt, took the name of Gordon Cumming on *s* to the estates of Gordon of Gordonstoun.

CUNARD (UK) 1859, of Bush Hill, Middlesex (Extinct 1989)

Capt Sir GUY ALICK CUNARD, 7th and last *Baronet*.

COLLATERAL BRANCH LIVING

Granddaughter of late William Cunard, 2nd son of 1st baronet:—
Issue of late Cyril Grant Cunard, *b* 1867, *d* 1914: *m* 1896, Beatrice Rhoda, who *d* 1945 (having *m* 2ndly, 1918, Capt Walter H. Curran, Canadian Mil Forces, who *d* 1931), da of late George Louis Monck Gibbs (Elton, Bt):—
Virginia Beatrice, OBE (Flat 12 River House, The Terrace, Barnes, SW13), *b* 1912; is a CStJ; MBE (Civil) 1946, OBE (Civil) 1956: *m* 1963, Judge John Harcourt Barrington, TD, who *d* 1973.

CUNINGHAME (NS) 1672, of Corsehill, Ayrshire

Sir JOHN CHRISTOPHER FOGGO MONTGOMERY CUNINGHAME, 12th *Baronet*; *b* 24 July 1935; *s* his brother, *Sir* WILLIAM ANDREW MALCOLM MARTIN OLIPHANT, 1959; *ed* Fettes Coll, and Worcester Coll, Oxford; late Lieut Rifle Brig; Dir Ryobi Lawn & Garden Ltd, Purolite International Ltd, Bedford Capital Financial Corp, and other companies: *m* 1964, Laura Violet, da of Sir Godfrey Nicholson, 1st Bt (*cr* 1958), and has issue.

Arms – Argent, a shake-fork sable, a crescent for difference. Crest – A unicorn's head erased, proper.
Residence – The Old Rectory, Brightwalton, Newbury, Berks RG16 0BL. *Clubs* – Boodle's, Pratt's.

DAUGHTERS LIVING

Christian Elizabeth, *b* 1967. —— Georgiana Rose, *b* 1969. —— Elizabeth Clara, 1971.

WIDOW LIVING OF ELEVENTH BARONET

SARA CAROLYN (*Lady Fergusson*), da of late Brig-Gen Lord Esmé Charles Gordon Lennox, KCVO, CMG, DSO (*see* D Richmond and Gordon, colls): *m* 1st, 1956, Sir William Andrew Malcolm Martin Oliphant Montgomery Cuninghame, 11th Bt, who *d* 1959: 2ndly, 1959, Sir Ewen Alastair John Fergusson, GCMG, GCVO, son of Sir Ewen Macgregor Field Fergusson. *Address* – c/o Coutts & Co, 440 Strand, WC2R 0QS.

This family descends from Andrew Cuninghame, 1st of Corsehill, 2nd son of 4th Earl of Glencairn (dormant 1796), to whom the baronet is probably next in line.

FAIRLIE-CUNINGHAME (NS) 1630, of Robertland, Ayrshire

By fortitude　　　*I am prepared*

Sir WILLIAM HENRY FAIRLIE-CUNINGHAME, 16th *Baronet*; *b* 1 Oct 1930; *s* his father, Sir WILLIAM ALAN, 1981: *m* 1972, Janet Menzies, da of late Roy Menzies Saddington, and has issue.

Arms – Quarterly, 1st and 4th argent, a shake-fork between a bugle-horn in chief and two castles in base sable, *Cuninghame*; 2nd and 3rd, or, a lion rampant and in chief three stars gules, *Fairlie*. Crests – 1st, a unicorn's head proper, armed or, *Cuninghame*; 2nd, a lion's head or, *Fairlie*. Supporters – Two knights in complete armour, holding in their exterior hands batons or.
Residence – 29A Orinoco Street, Pymble, NSW 2073, Australia.

SON LIVING

(WILLIAM) ROBERT HENRY, *b* 11 July 1974.

UNCLE LIVING (*Son of 13th baronet*)

John Hastings, *b* 1899; Bachelor of Architecture, Sydney Univ; Lt (ret) Austn Forces: *m* 1934, Margaret, who *d* 1981, da of Charles Woodhill, of NSW, and has issue living, David Hastings (47 Cremorne Rd, Cremorne, Sydney, NSW), *b* 1937: *m* 1963, Susan Gai, da of Henry White, of Coolah, NSW, and has issue living, Charles Hastings *b* 1966, Annabel *b* 1964, — Peter (9 Austinmer St, Austinmer, NSW), *b* 1939: *m* 1972 (*m diss* 1992), Felicity Helen, da of Douglas Service, of Sydney, and has issue living, Samuel John *b* 1976, Georgina Mary *b* 1979, — Elisabeth, *b* 1941: *m* 1st, 1962 (*m diss* 1972), William Leslie Murray Robson; 2ndly, 1974, Peter Thomas Glanville, who *d* 1975, and has issue living, (by 1st *m*) Andrew Fairlie Murray *b* 1963, Hamish Hastings Murray *b* 1965, — Georgina Jane *b* 1947: *m* 1972, Christopher Harrold Martin, of Norfolk, Cassilis, NSW, and has issue living, Jonathan Hastings *b* 1977, Toby *b* 1980, Amber *b* 1979. *Residence* – Kanandah, 21 Douro St, Mudgee, NSW 2850, Australia.

AUNT LIVING (*Daughter of 13th baronet*)

Amabel Marguerite, *b* 1901: *m* 1933, Alick Scott Osborne, who *d* 1957, and has issue living, William Fairlie Cuninghame, *b* 1934: *m* 1964, Janet Stewart Stevenson, and has issue living, Alick Stevenson, *b* 1968, Stewart William *b* 1970, Susan Margaret *b* 1967, — Andrew Hastings, *b* 1937: *m* 1st, 1966, Barbara Constance Heron, who *d* 1973; 2ndly, 1974, Judith Nancy Pope, and has issue living, (by 1st *m*) Phillip Scott *b* 1967, Eleanor Marguerite *b* 1969, — Mary Macartney, *b* 1933: *m* 1959, John William Laurie, of 40 Kenthurst Rd, St Ives, NSW, and has issue living, William Alick Osborne *b*

1963, Margaret Kathleen *b* 1961, Sarah Elisabeth (twin) *b* 1963, Georgina Mary *b* 1969. *Residence* – 18 Park Av, Gordon 2072, NSW.

DAUGHTERS LIVING OF FOURTEENTH BARONET

Margaret Alice (43 Honeyton St, Seaton, S Australia): *m* 1946, Stanley C. Wood, who *d* 1971, and has issue living, Harold Anthony, *b* 1948, — Norma Margaret, *b* 1947: *m* 1968, George Millar Knight, of 23 Fairfax Av, Millswood, S Australia, and has issue living, Peter Stanley *b* 1972, Robert Reginald *b* 1981, Helen Margaret *b* 1973, Elizabeth Georgie *b* 1983, — Janice Alice, *b* 1952: *m* 1970, Edward James, of 17 Tereva Cres, Mulgrave, Victoria, Australia, and has issue living, Simon Stanley *b* 1976, David Matthew *b* 1979, Julie Alice *b* 1971, Karen Linda *b* 1973. —— Ann (53 Parni Place, Frenchs Forrest, NSW 2086, Australia), *b* 19—: *m* 1955, Arlie William Vout, who *d* 1985. —— Patricia: *m* 1960, Peter Goddard Sheldon, of 9B Henley St, Lane Cove, Sydney, NSW 2066, and has issue living, Robert Stewart (34 Manning Rd, Double Bay, NSW 2028, Australia), *b* 1961: *m* 1992, Sharon Susan Armstrong, and has issue living, Alec Stewart Armstrong *b* 1998, — Antony Stewart (53 Parni Place, Frenchs Forrest, NSW 2086, Australia), *b* 1966, — Jane Stewart, *b* 1963: *m* 1995, Dermot Michael Crowley, of 199 Farr St, Rockdale, NSW 2216, Australia.

COLLATERAL BRANCHES LIVING

Granddaughters of late Charles Rawdon Cuningham (infra):—
Issue of late Eric de Burgh Cuningham, *b* 1900, *d* 1946: *m* 1934, Betty Maurice, who *d* 1999, having *m* 2ndly, 1952, Henry William Hardess Waller, who *d* 1961; 3rdly, 1969, Michael Alexander Addison Kirkpatrick, who *d* 1991, da of late Mrs M. Barton, of Leura, NSW:—
Anthea *b* 1936: *m* 1959, Michael Havelock Marchbank, of 43 Memorial Av, St Ives, NSW 2075, Australia, and has issue living, Jonathan Havelock, *b* 1964, — Joanna Cuningham, *b* 1960, — Katharine Jane, *b* 1962. —— Rhonwen CUNINGHAM, *b* 1943; has resumed her maiden name: *m* 1971 (*m diss* 1981), Jack Aylward Mooney, and has issue living, Sean Aylward Michael, *b* 1972.

Issue of late Archibald Loudoun Cuningham, Australian Imperial Force, *b* 1905, *ka* Malayan Campaign 1942: *m* 1936, Nancy Maurice (who *d* 1994, having *m* 2ndly, 1946, Robin Ellison Cuningham (infra), who *d* 1984), da of late Mrs M. Barton, of Leura, NS Wales:—
Nancy Robin, *b* 1939: *m* 1964, Peter Edwin Bell (285a Durham St, Bathurst, NSW 2795, Australia), and has issue living, Alastair Christian Loudoun (36 Holland St, Tamworth, NSW 2340), *b* 1967: *m* 1992, Anastasia Louise Lord, — Belinda Jane, *b* 1965: *m* 1994, Terrence John Betts, of 5 Dalley St, Goulburn, NSW 2580, — Fairlie Louise, *b* 1972: *m* 1996, Ronald Eugene Long, of 25339 Via Viejo, Lake Forest, CA 92630, USA, and has issue living, Tyler Ryan *b* 1999.

Issue of late Robin Ellison Cuningham, *b* (twin) 1905, *d* 1984: *m* 1946, Nancy Maurice, who *d* 1994, widow of his twin brother Archibald Loudoun Cuningham (ante):—
Georgine Ellison, *b* 1951: *m* 1975, Robert Ranald Mackay, of Tinagroo, Scone, NSW, Australia, and has issue living, Robert Gordon, *b* 1983.

Grandson of late Charles Rawdon Cuningham, brother of 13th baronet:—
Issue of late Alister Gordon Cuningham, *b* 1902, *d* 1997: *m* 1948, Catherine Ida, da of late Hugh Rule, of Rockhampton:—
Robert Gordon (5 Wondsworth Rd, Surrey Hills, Victoria 3127, Australia), *b* 1953: *m* 1983, Christine Anne, da of Dr William Goldwin Gray, of Markdale, Ontario, Canada, and has issue living, William Gordon Gray, *b* 1991, — David Robert Gray, *b* 1997, — Emily Marguerite, *b* 1985, — Joanna Christine Mary, *b* 1986, — Jane Fairlie, *b* 1988.

Grandchildren of late John Fairlie Cuningham, 3rd son of late Surg-Gen James Macnabb Cuningham, CSI, MD, 5th son of late Maj William Cuningham (infra):—
Issue of late John Henry Cuningham, *b* 1898, *d* 1969: *m* 1924, Kathleen, MB, BS, da of late Prof T. E. Clouston, DD:—
James Fairlie Boyd (9/167 Victoria St, Kings Cross, NSW 2011, Australia), *b* 1932.

Issue of late Donald Macrae Cuningham, *b* 1905, *d* 1981: *m* 1929, Rose Eleanor, who *d* 1985, da of late Samuel Wilde Witts:—
John Fairlie (10 Edward St, Woollahra, NSW 2025, Australia), *b* 1943. —— Florence Ann, *b* 1933: *m* 1957, David Jones, BVSc (PO Box 7183, Lismore Heights, NSW 2480, Australia).

Grandchildren of late William Glencairn Cuninghame, only son of late Lt-Col Francis George Glencairn Cuningham (infra):—
Issue of late Anthony Glencairn Cuninghame, *b* 1935, *d* 1982: *m* 1961, Pamela Rosemary (Stones, Uffcott, Broad Hinton, Swindon, Wilts SN4 9NB), da of late Robert Horton, of The Manor, Broad Hinton, Wilts:—
Andrew Glencairn, *b* 1965; has issue living (by Mandy Penelope James), Niamh Shannon CUNINGHAME, *b* 1998. —— Sally Helen, *b* 1962; has issue living (by Marcus Reeve), Samantha Claire REEVE, *b* 1997. —— Clair Elizabeth, *b* 1964: *m* 1991, Martin Brian Anstice, son of Malcolm Anstice, of Huish Episcopi, Somerset, and has issue living, Henry James, *b* 1994, — Elizabeth Grace, *b* 1997.

Granddaughter of late Francis Goode Cuningham, 7th son of late Maj William Cuningham, only son of late Alexander Cuningham, 2nd son of 5th baronet:—
Issue of late Lieut-Col Francis George Glencairn Cuningham (who adopted the spelling of Cuninghame 19—), *b* 1880, *d* 1956: *m* 1912, Violet Jessie, who *d* 1957, da of Capt Phipps Hornby, Rifle Brig (Prince Consort's Own):—

Carol Jean (The Lodge, N Cheriton, Templecombe, Som), *b* 1915: *m* 1950, John Douglas Philip Watney, who *d* 1976, and has issue living, Guy Charles Glencairn, *b* 1954: *m* 1980 (*m diss ca* 1988), Mary Jane, el da of Sqdn Ldr John Sands, RAF, of Ramsey, Isle of Man, and has issue living, Juan *b* 1986.

This family is descended from the Hon William Cunningham (1st of Craigends), 2nd son of the 1st Earl of Glencairn, by the Hon William's 2nd *m* in 1499 with Dame Marion Auchinleck. The 1st baronet, Master of the Works to James VI of Scotland, was created a baronet, with remainder to heirs male whatsoever. At the death of his nephew, Sir David Cuninghame, 4th baronet, the title remained dormant until assumed by William Cuninghame, on being served heir in 1778, to his great-great-grandfather, Sir David Cuninghame, of Robertland, who was grandfather of the 1st baronet. The 5th baronet *m* Margaret, da of William Fairlie of Fairlie, co Ayr, to whose estate he succeeded. The 6th baronet assumed the additional surname of Fairlie, and the 8th received a grant of supporters to himself and his heirs male succeeding him in the baronetcy. The 13th baronet, Sir William Edward, assumed by deed poll 1912, the surname of Fairlie-Cuninghame in lieu of his patronymic Cuningham.

CUNLIFFE (GB) 1759, of Liverpool, Lancashire

Faithfully

Sir DAVID ELLIS CUNLIFFE, 9th *Baronet*, *b* 29 Oct 1957: *s* his father, *Sir* CYRIL HENLEY, 1969; *ed* St Alban's Gram Sch: *m* 1983, Linda Carol, da of John Sidney Batchelor, of 4 Kingcroft Rd, Harpenden, Herts.

𝔄rms – Sable, three conies courant argent, two and one. 𝔠rest – A greyhound sejant argent, collared sable.
Residence – Sunnyside, Burnthouse Lane, Needham, Harleston, Norfolk IP20 9LN.

DAUGHTERS LIVING

Emma Mary, *b* 1986. —— Katherine Alice, *b* 1990. —— Bridget Carol, *b* 1991.

BROTHER LIVING

ANDREW MARK *b* 17 April 1959: *m* 1980, Janice Elizabeth, da of Ronald William Kyle, and has issue living, Mark Ellis, *b* 1982, — Sarah Nicolette, *b* 1984, — Danielle Juliette *b* 1989, — Rachael Eileen Margaret *b* 1992.

SISTER LIVING

Susan Nicolette, *b* (twin) 1959.

WIDOW LIVING OF EIGHTH BARONET

EILEEN M. (17 Gurney Court Rd, St Albans), da of Frederick William Parkins, and widow of Charles Clifford, of Walton-on-Thames: *m* 2ndly, 1956, Sir Cyril Henley Cunliffe, 8th Bt, who *d* 1969; 3rdly, 1970, Frederick Henry Moore, who *d* 1987.

COLLATERAL BRANCHES LIVING

Grandchildren of late William Lockhart Cunliffe (infra):—
Issue of late Lt-Col Bruce Fergusson Cunliffe, *b* 1925, *d* 1989: *m* 1947, Joanne (481 State St, Portsmouth, NH, USA), da of Richard Holbrook, of Keene, NH, USA:—
Taylor Fergusson, *b* 1950. —— Orinda, *b* 1949: *m* 1970, Edward Andrew Jerue, of 53 Western Av, Westfield, MA 01085, USA, late Capt US Marine Corps, and has issue living, Tristan Aubrey, *b* 1975, — Brook Kai, *b* 1977, — Seth Orion, *b* 1979, — Summer Alia, *b* 1974. —— Catherine Suthers, *b* 1956: *m* 1978, Lawrence Samuel Muller, of Tallahassee, Florida, USA, and has issue living, Randi Michelle *b* 1981.

Grandchildren of late Col Ernest William Cunliffe, son of late David Cunliffe, BCS, 3rd son of 4th baronet:—
Issue of late William Lockhart Cunliffe, *b* 1902, *d* 1982: *m* 1923, Maude Ethel, who *d* 1983, da of Henry Suthers, of New York, USA:—
Stuart Owen (17 Squassick Rd, West Springfield, Mass, USA), *b* 1931; *ed* Kimball Union Acad, Meriden, New Hampshire; sometime in US Marine Corps: *m* 1957, Mary, da of David Beglund, of Albany, New York, USA, and has issue living, Fred Owen *b* 1958, David William *b* 1960, — Lorna Margaret, *b* 1929: *m* 1949, Amos Webster Gile, of Wyeth Rd Circle, W Lebanon, NH, USA, and has issue living, John Lockhart *b* 1952, Joanne Lorna *b* 1951: *m* 1972, Svein Michaelsen, of Bergen, Norway, Pamela Jean *b* 1954. —— Colin Fergusson (Torlundy, 71 Windermere Rd, SW16) *b* 1909; 1939-45 War with Gren Gds and as Maj N Staffordshire Regt: *m* 1st, 1934, Muriel Constance Gore, who *d* 1953; 2ndly, 1954, Sally Marion Mackay. —— Sonia, *b* 1911: *m* 1st, 1935 (*m diss* 1948), Frank Shaw; 2ndly, 1948, Eric Skead, and has issue living, (by 1st *m*) Sandra, *b* 1936, — (by 2nd *m*) Howard, *b* 1949.

Granddaughter of late Capt Ellis Brooke Cunliffe, el son of Ellis Watkin Cunliffe, 3rd son of 3rd baronet:—
Issue of late William Noel Cunliffe, *b* 1877, *d* 1933: *m* 1910, Nellie Phyllis, who *d* 1976, da of Sir John Aird, 2nd Bt:—

Gundred (3 West Halkin St, SW1), *b* 1913: *m* 1937, Mervyn Cunliffe-Fraser, who *d* 1996, and has issue living, Valerie, *b* 1942: *m* 1972, Mark Treanor Thomasin-Foster, of Moulsham Hall, Great Leighs, Essex, and has issue living, Nicholai Charles *b* 1975, Christopher William *b* 1976, David James *b* 1979.

Grandchildren of late Brooke Stewart Cunliffe, only son of Brooke Cunliffe (*b* 1815), elder son (by 1st *m*) of Brooke Cunliffe (*b* 1790) (infra):—
Issue of late Capt Brooke Foster Gordon Cunliffe, Scottish Horse Yeo, *b* 1889, *d* 1981: *m* 1921, Catherine Hay, who *d* 1962, da of Col H. R. Peake:—
Brooke Malcolm, *b* 1928; Supt, Rhodesian Police (ret). —— Diana Hay (50 Corstorphine Hill Gdns, Edinburgh), *b* 1923.

Grandchildren of late Col Foster Lionel Cunliffe, son of late Brooke Cunliffe (*b* 1790), 4th son of 3rd baronet:—
Issue of late Capt Robert Lionel Brooke Cunliffe, CBE, RN, *b* 1895, *d* 1990: *m* 1st, 1926, Barbara Eleanor, who *d* 1970, da of Col Harry Cooper, of Pakenham Lodge, Pakenham, Suffolk; 2ndly, 1971, Christina, who *d* 1989, da of Rev Canon Sydney Cooper:—
(By 1st *m*) Bridget Eleanor, *b* 1927: *m* 1957, Hugh Rosslyn Inigo Sackville-West, MC, of Knole, Sevenoaks, Kent (*see* B Sackville). —— Nicolette Anne, *b* 1929: *m* 1954, Robert Charles Cotton (*see* V Combermere, colls). —— Barbara Clare, *b* 1936: *m* 1957 (*m diss* 1965), Sir Thomas Agnew Beevor, 7th Bt.

Sir Ellis Cunliffe 1st Bt, MP for Liverpool (*d* 1767), descended from a yr branch of the Cunliffes of Hollins, Lancs. Sir Robert Henry Cunliffe, 4th baronet, a General in the Bengal Army received the honour of knighthood. The 6th baronet, Major Sir Foster Hugh Egerton Cunliffe, Rifle Brig (Prince Consort's Own), was *ka* 1916.

Cunliffe-Owen, see Owen.

CUNNINGHAM (UK) 1963, of Crookedstone, Killead, co Antrim (Extinct 1976)

Sir (SAMUEL) KNOX CUNNINGHAM, QC, 1st and last *Baronet*.

WIDOW LIVING OF FIRST BARONET

DOROTHY ENID (*Lady Cunningham*), a JP; da of late Edwin Riley, of Bilston, Staffs: *m* 1935, Sir (Samuel) Knox Cunningham, QC, 1st Bt, who *d* 1976, when the title became ext.

DICK-CUNYNGHAM, First (NS) 1669, Cunyngham of Lambrughtoun, co Ayr; Second (NS) 1707, Dick, of Prestonfield, Edinburgh (Extinct 1941)

Major Sir (COLIN) KEITH DICK-CUNYNGHAM, 9th of 1st and 11th of 2nd creation and last *Baronet*; (*ka* 1941).

COLLATERAL BRANCH LIVING

Issue of late Maj-Gen James Keith Dick-Cunyngham, CB, CMG, DSO, 3rd son of 7th and 9th baronet, *b* 1877, *d* 1935: *m* 1905, Alice Daisy, who *d* 1963, da of late Lieut-Col Sir Harold Arthur Deane, KCSI:—

Janet Mary DICK-CUNYNGHAM, *b* 1917, resumed her maiden surname 1963: *m* 1940 (*m diss* 1960), Capt Roderick Francis Oliver, Roy Horse Guards, (Grant-Suttie, Bt, colls), and has issue living, Caroline Stephanie, MBE *b* 1944; MBE (Civil) 1975: *m* 1st, 1965 (*m diss* 1967), Nicholas Kilmaine de Courcy-Ireland; 2ndly, 1987, Charles Cousins, — Georgina Mary *b* 1946: *m* 1977, Robert Kilgore, of Sunnyvale, California. *Residence* –

CUNYNGHAME (NS) 1702, of Milncraig, Ayrshire

Sir ANDREW DAVID FRANCIS CUNYNGHAME, 12th *Baronet*; *b* 25 Dec 1942; *s* his father, *Sir* (HENRY) DAVID ST LEGER BROOKE SELWYN, 1978; *ed* Eton; FCA: *m* 1st, 1972, Harriet Ann, da of Charles Thomas Dupont, of Montreal, Canada; 2ndly, 1989, Isabella, da of late Edward Everett Watts, Jr, and has issue by 1st *m*.

𝕬rms – Argent, a shake-fork sable between three fleurs-de-lis azure. 𝕮rest – A unicorn argent, unguled maned and armed or, lying on a mount vert. 𝕾upporters – *Dexter*, a knight in armour holding in his exterior hand a spear; *sinister*, a knight in the disguise of a countryman with a bonnet habited azure his thighs armed proper, and in his sinister hand a corn fork in pale of the last.
Residences – 17 Vicarage Gdns, W8 4AH; The School House, Williamscot, Banbury, Oxon. *Club* – Brooks's.

DAUGHTERS LIVING (*By 1st marriage*)

Ann Marie Albinia, *b* 1978. —— Tania Albinia Pamela Jean, *b* 1983.

BROTHERS LIVING

JOHN PHILIP HENRY MICHAEL SELWYN, (26D Belgrave Rd, SW1V 1RG), *b* 9 Sept 1944; *ed* Eton: *m* 1981, Marjatta, 2nd da of Martti Markus, of Muhos, Finland, and has issue living, Alexander David Martti, *b* 1985, — Niina Kaarina, *b* 1983. —— Arthur James Augustus (Grange Farm, Grange Lane, Alvechurch, Worcs B48 7DJ), *b* 1951; *ed* Westminster: *m* 1977, Rachel-Claire, el da of Guy Baines, FRCS, of Cattespoole, Tardebigge, Worcs, and has issue living, Richard George Arthur Selwyn, *b* 1980, — Edward David Lyulph, *b* 1983.

COLLATERAL BRANCHES LIVING

Issue of late Ian Francis Rowland Selwyn Cunynghame, yr son of 10th baronet, *b* 1910, *d* 1988: *m* 1st, 1938, Cicely Mary, who *d* 1945, elder da of late Francis Chaytor Starkey; 2ndly, 1947, Eugénie Beatrice Gwendolen, who *d* 1962, da of late James Howard Allport, and widow of Rear Adm John Uniacke Penrose-Fitzgerald, CB:—
(By 1st *m*) Michael Ian Francis Starkey (Dury Stores, N Nesting, Shetland), *b* 1945; *ed* Chilton Cantelo House, Yeovil: *m* 1970, Penelope Mary, yr da of Allan Mortimer, of Ballinger, Bucks, and has issue living, Ian Michael, *b* 1979, — Daisy Albinia, *b* 1981. —— Sarah Albinia Starkey, *b* 1940: *m* 1964, Feico Jan Leemhuis, of 429 Lansdowne Av, Westmount, Quebec Prov, Canada, and has issue living, Adrian Samuel, *b* 1969, — Ian, *b* 1971 (adopted son), — Cicely Toosje, *b* 1974. —— Caroline Mary Albinia Starkey, *b* 1943: *m* 1968, Barry John Lloyd, of 31 Ridgemount, Guildford, Surrey, and has issue living, Hannah Cicely, *b* 1973, — Leila Kate, *b* 1975. —— (By 2nd *m*) Moira Janet Albinia Allport, *b* 1947: *m* 1969, Konstantin Andreevich Stramentov, of Gurrington House, Woodland, nr Ashburton, Devon, and of Rhicarn, Lochinver, Sutherland, and has issue living, Bruce Sergei Cunynghame, *b* 1977, — Andrew Nikita Cunynghame, *b* 1979, — Alexandra Jane Cunynghame, *b* 1973, — Darya Esme Cunynghame, *b* 1983.

Issue of late Stuart Cunynghame, yr son of 9th baronet; *b* 1874, *d* 1962: *m* 1915, Helen Dorothy, who *d* 1944, da of late Rev A. Holland Taylor, DD:—
Colin Kenneth, *b* 1918; Maj late Indian Army. —— David Francis (British Airways, PO Box 4756, Durban, S Africa), *b* 1920; Capt late Indian Army; Airline Sales Representative, BOAC: *m* 1st, 1947 (*m diss* 1957), Ruth Armitage, da of late Walter Patrick Murray; 2ndly, 1964 (*m diss* 1975), Renate Maria Dietrich; 3rdly, 1984, Leslie Stokoe (*née* Anderson), and has issue living, (by 1st *m*) Diana Patricia, *b* 1950, — (by 2nd *m*) Christopher Daniel, *b* 1966, — Deborah Avril, *b* 1968.

Grandson of late James Robertson Thurlow Cunynghame, 4th son of 8th baronet:—
Issue of late Francis Thurlow Hardinge Cunynghame, *b* 1880, *d* 1940: *m* 1909, Frances Anne, who *d* 1954, da of Nicholas Murnane, of Brisbane:—
Frank Vincent, *b* 1910: *m* 1949, Mary Hennessy, and has issue living, Helen Anne, *b* 1949, — Diane Frances, *b* 1952, — Jennifer Anne, *b* 1955, — Frances Mary, *b* 1957. *Residence* – 18 Serpentine Parade, Vaucluse, Sydney, NS Wales.

Grandson of late Arthur Hardinge David Cunynghame, son of late Gen Sir Arthur Augustus Thurlow Cunynghame, GCB, 5th son of 5th baronet:—
Issue of late Maj David Hardinge Cunynghame, *b* 1897, *d* 1986: *m* 1934, Ruth Ilon Ismay Mary, da of Rev A.E. Phillips:—

Francis Arthur David Anthony, *b* 1935.

This family is a yr branch of the Earls of Glencairn (dormant since 1796), claiming descent from 2nd son of 1st Earl (*d* 1488). The 1st baronet, Sir David Cunynghame of Milncraig, co Ayr, a distinguished lawyer, and an eloquent member of the Scottish Parliament, was *cr* a Baronet with remainder to his "heirs male in perpetuum." The 10th baronet, Sir Percy Francis, OBE, in Sarawak Civil Ser 1886-1909, was Lieut-Col Middlesex Regt, and served in European War 1914-18 (despatches).

CURRIE (UK) 1847

Largs

Sir DONALD SCOTT CURRIE, 7th *Baronet*, *b* 16 Jan 1930; *s* his uncle, *Sir* ALICK BRADLEY, 1987, but no name has been entered on the Official Roll of the Baronetage since death of 5th Bt in 1978: *m* 1st, 1948 (*m diss* 1951), Charlotte, da of Charles Johnston, of Mesa, Arizona, USA; 2ndly, 1952, Barbara Lee, who *d* 1993, da of A. P. Garnier, of Calif, USA; 3rdly, 1994, Mrs Barbara Lou Lebsack, da of Joshua I. Fenn, of Kansas, and has had issue by 1st and 2nd *m*.

ᴀrms – Gules, a saltire couped argent, in the centre chief point a rose of the last barbed and seeded proper. ℭrest – A cock proper, resting its foot upon a rose argent, barbed and seeded proper.
Residence – 8152 WCR 34, Platteville, Colorado 80651, USA.

SONS LIVING AND DECEASED (*By 1st marriage*)

Donald Mark, *b* 1949: *m* 1st, 1969 (*m diss* 1969), Gloria, da of A. Price, of Calif, USA; 2ndly, 1969 (*m diss* 1971), Inga Mae, da of — Rouse, of —, and *d* 1994.

(*by 2nd marriage*)

GARY DWAYNE (Box 116, Vona, Colorado, USA), *b* 26 Sept 1953: *m* 1970, Wilma Kathleen, da of Tom Wyatt, of Colorado, USA, and has issue living, Bradley Wayne, *b* 1973, — Brandy Sue, *b* 1971.

DAUGHTERS LIVING (*By 1st marriage*)

Julia Ann, *b* 1950: *m* 1969, Eugene R. Gangaware, USAF, and has issue living, Elizabeth Ann, *b* 1970, — Tiffany Sue, *b* 1974, — Wendy Opal, *b* 1976, — Jeanette Mae, *b* 1978. *Residence* – . —— Janet Sue, *b* (twin) 1950: *m* 1st, 1970 (*m diss* 1970), Jack D. Hawkins, of Idaho, USA; 2ndly, 1973, Robert Eugene Buck, of Box 644, Odessa, Nebraska 68681, USA, and has issue living, (by 2nd *m*), Todd Allen, *b* 1973, — Terry Lee, *b* 1975.

(*by 2nd marriage*)

Tina Marie, *b* 1955: *m* 1974 (*m diss* 1992), Ricky Lee Linneman, of Gillette, Wyoming, USA, and has issue living, Shawn Michael, *b* 1976, — Tye Rae (a son), *b* 1985, — and an adopted da, Shayne Michelle, *b* 1973. *Residence* – .... —— Kathren Evelyn, *b* 1959: *m* 1973, Earl Avara, and has issue living, Scott William, *b* 1979, — Jennifer Marie, *b* 1981. *Residence* – ......

BROTHERS LIVING

James Davidson (15603 Espola Rd, Poway, Calif 92604, USA), *b* 1932: *m* 1956, Olga Mary, da of Miguel Otero, of Tampa, Flar, USA, and has issue living, Lila Jane, *b* 1957: *m* 1979, Justin Chase Estep, and has issue living, Crystal Lila, *b* 1980. —— George Robert, *b* 1943: *m* 1st, 1962 (*m diss* 1972), Lucy Lavonne, da of S. A. Gilliam, of Charlotte, N Carolina, USA; 2ndly, 19—, Judith, da of — Hoffman, of —, and has issue living (by 1st *m*), Michael Todd, *b* 1963, — Richard Eric, *b* 1967. *Residence* – 3631 Columbia Av, Palmdale, Calif 93550, USA.

SISTER LIVING OF SIXTH BARONET

Annie Flora, *b* 1897: *m* 1920, Clinton B. Fiske Harsh, who *d* 1974, and has issue living, George Clinton (Box 134, Cliff, New Mexico, USA), *b* 1920: *m* 1948, Julia Cecelia, da of Mathew John Retmiller, of Utica, Michigan, and has issue living, Rhett Mathew *b* 1954: *m* 1980, Cinde Lu Ball, of Mesa, Arizona (and has issue living, Mathew Clinton *b* 1980, Joshua Lee *b* 1983, Jason Earl *b* 1985), Diane Elizabeth *b* 1949: *m* 1st, 1968 (*m diss* 1971), Charles D. Mannino; 2ndly, 1971 (*m diss* 1983), Tamás Elemér Belá Kokovay (and has issue living, (by 1st *m*) Meridee Francis *b* 1968, (by 2nd *m*) Stephen Tamás *b* 1981, Estike *b* 1975, Erzsebet *b* (twin) 1975, Julia Etelka *b* 1979, (and further issue) Clinton George *b* 1991), —

Robert Currie (1916, Yucca Drive, Silver City, New Mexico, 88061, USA), *b* 1922: *m* 1948, Majorie Ruth, da of James E. Shean, of Silver City, New Mexico, and has issue living, Mathis Brayton *b* 1955: *m* 1975, Leona Rae, da of James Dudley Messer, of New Mexico (and has issue living, Brayton Bradley *b* 1978, Robert Cole *b* 1981), Alice Anne Thadia *b* 1949, June Margil *b* 1950: *m* 1975, James Monroe Foster, of New Mexico, USA, Alexis Mary *b* 1958, Cecily Louise *b* 1960: *m* 1984, Lt-Cdr Julio Jesus Gutierrez, US Navy, — Glenn Ray, *b* 1925: *m* 1949, Jeanne, da of Theophilus M. Prator, of New Orleans, Louisiana, USA, and has issue living, Glenn Ray *b* 1958: *m* 1982, Cheryl Ann Harty, Sandra *b* 1951: *m* 1977, Davis Carea Dixon, of New Orleans, Louisiana, USA (and has issue living, Katherine Jean *b* 1982), Christine Elizabeth *b* 1954, Nancy Jeanne *b* 1956.

COLLATERAL BRANCHES LIVING

Issue of late Percy George Colin Currie, 3rd son of 2nd baronet, *b* 1857, *d* 1932: *m* 1885, Agnes Grace Johnstone, da of late Charles Paterson, of Dumfries:—
Muriel Helen, *b* 1887: *m* 1911, Edgar Green, formerly Indian Telegraph Depart, and has issue living, Richard Colin, *b* 1914, — Agnes Muriel Rachel, *b* 1915, — Margaret Suzanne, *b* 1919. ──── Ethel Lilian Adelaide, *b* 1893.

Granddaughters of late Maj-Gen Fendall Currie, 6th son of 1st baronet:—
Issue of late Fendall James Pears Currie, *b* 1867, *d* 1946: *m* 1890, Christina, da of David Anderson:—
Veda Mary Fendall, *b* 1891: *m* 1922, Thomas Scott MacMillan of 83 Creyke Rd, Ilaen, Christchurch 4, NZ, and has issue living, Mary Christina, *b* 1924, — Elizabeth Scott, *b* 1925.

Issue of late Lieut-Col Ivor Bertram Fendall Currie, DSO, *b* 1872, *d* 1924: *m* 1906, May Constance, who *d* 1937, da of late F.-M. Sir George Stuart White, VC, GCB, OM, GCSI, GCMG, GCIE, GCVO, LLD:—
Sylvia Constance, *b* 1910: *m* 1937, Nigel George Kingsford Burgess, and has issue living, Anthony Malcolm Kingsford, *b* 1941, — Simon George Fendall, *b* 1945. *Residence* – 52 Cornwall Gdns, SW7.

Grandson of late Rivers Grenfell Currie, 8th son of 1st baronet:—
Issue of late Maj Disney Rivers Currie, MC, *b* 1894, *d* 1964: *m* 1919, Ethel Jeanette Bryce, who *d* 1981, da of Arnold Bryce Smith:—
Frederick Disney Rivers (Whitehayes, 93 Church St, Willingdon, Eastbourne), *b* 1921; Burma, 1943 as Capt Roy Scots (wounded): *m* 1949, Jean Alison, da of Lionel Westropp Jardine, CIE (*see* Jardine, Bt, *cr* 1916), and has issue living, Peter Frederick Rivers (85 Bouverie Rd, N16) *b* 1950: *m* 1973, Mary Rose Veronica, da of E. J. Goodman, and has had issue, Philip Simon Rivers, *b* 1977, Francis William Mordaunt *b* and *d* 1980, Morag Claire Rowan *b* 1981, Morna Agne Claire Laksmi *b* 1988, — Jennifer Jean, *b* 1953: *m* 1st, 1972 (*m diss* 19—), Alan Sayers; 2ndly, 19—, Jeffrey R. Smith, and has issue living (by 1st *m*), Jonathan Alan *b* 1974, — Daniel William *b* 1976, — Fiona Alexandra (134 Wannock Lane, Lower Willingdon, E Sussex), *b* 1958.

This family came from Duns, Berwickshire. William Currie, who *d* 1781, became a London banker. His grandson, Sir Frederick Currie, 1st Bt, was successively Foreign Secretary to the Indian Governmnent, a Member of the Supreme Council in India, a member of the Court of Directors of the HEICS, and one of the Home Council in London.

Currimboy, Sir Mahomed, see Ebrahim, Sir Currimboy.

CURTIS (UK) 1802, of Cullands Grove, Middlesex

We conquer step by step

Sir WILLIAM PETER CURTIS, 7th *Baronet, b* 9 April 1935; *s* his father, *Sir* PETER, 1976; *ed* Winchester, Trin Coll, Oxford (MA) and R Agric Coll, Cirencester; late 16/5th Lancers.

Arms – Paly of six or and azure, a fesse checky argent and sable, on a canton gules a dragon's wing erect of the third, in base a sword proper, pommel and hilt of the first, surmounting a key in saltire of the second. **Crest** – A ram's head couped argent, surmounted by two branches of oak in saltire proper. *Residence* – Oak Lodge, Bank St, Bishop's Waltham, Hants S03 1AN.

SISTERS LIVING

Rosemary Antonia Joan, *b* 1943: *m* 1966, John Clarkson Spink, of Poplars Farm, Rotherwick, Basingstoke, Hants RG27 9BH, and has issue living, Jonathan Peter Charles *b* 1976, — Timothy Mark Christopher, *b* 1981, — Annabel Louise, *b* 1970. —— Fiona Mary, *b* 1946: *m* 1968, Anthony David Findon Littlejohn, of Lythe Farm, Steep, Petersfield, Hants, and has issue living, — Patrick David, *b* 1979, — Ruth Hermione, *b* 1971, — Georgina Clare, *b* 1973.

DAUGHTER LIVING OF FIFTH BARONET

Winifred Lotus, *b* 1904: *m* 1927, Capt Alan Walter Dolby, who *d* 1943, sometime R Berks Regt, and has issue living, John Horatio Curtis (Highway Cottage, Whitchurch, Pangbourne, Berks RG8 7DD), *b* 1928; *ed* St Paul's Sch: *m* 1959, Anthea Louise Whitamore, and has issue living, Timothy William Curtis *b* 1964, Caroline Lurleen Curtis, *b* 1960, — Robert Francis (11 Oldfield Rd, Bath BA2 3ND), *b* 1933; *ed* Christ's Hosp Sch; was Master Mariner Merchant Navy: *m* 1st, 1960 (*m diss* 1967), Jean Patricia, da of Sidney Clark; 2ndly, 1981, Priscilla Jane, da of late Percy Ridley, OBE, DSC, Bengal Pilot Ser, and has issue living, (by 1st *m*) Simon Francis Curtis (520 Athlone Av, Ottawa, Canada) *b* 1962: *m* 1989, Faye Tough (and has issue living, Alan Curtis *b* 1989), Louise Wynett *b* 1964: *m* 1985, Richard Kracher, of 2208-133A Av, Edmonton, Alberta T5A HJ9, Canada (and has issue living, James Richard *b* 1992, Holly Louise *b* 1989, Christina Ellen *b* 1990). *Address* – Rush Court, Shillingford Rd, Wallingford, Oxon.

WIDOW LIVING OF SIXTH BARONET

JOAN MARGARET (*Lady Curtis*), (Oak Lodge, Bishop's Waltham, Hants), da of late Reginald Nicholson (E Waldegrave): *m* 1934, Sir Peter Curtis, 6th Bt, who *d* 1976.

COLLATERAL BRANCHES LIVING

Branch from younger brother of 6th baronet

Grandchildren of late Edward Beaumont Cotton Curtis, 2nd son of late William Cotton Curtis, el son of late George Lear Curtis, 2nd son of 2nd baronet:—
Issue of late Gerald Edward Curtis, *b* 1909, *d* 1975: *m* 1939, Philippa, who *d* 1975, da of late Capt Philip Clayton Alcock, JP, DL, of Overton Lodge, Ludlow:—
EDWARD PHILIP (Lower Court, Bitterley, Ludlow, Shropshire SY8 3HP), *b* 25 June 1940; *ed* Bradfield, and RMA; Maj 16/5th Lancers (ret); stockbroker: *m* 1978, Catherine Mary, da of Henry J. Armstrong, of Christchurch, NZ, and has issue living, George Edward, *b* 31 Oct 1980, — Patrick James, *b* 1986, — Henrietta Rose, *b* 1979, — Clementine Zita, *b* 1983. —— Sonia Mary, *b* 1944: *m* 1971 (*m diss* 1976), Charles Hamilton Ewart, of Sydney, Australia, and has issue living, Gabrielle Alice Anne, *b* 1972.

Branch from uncle of 6th baronet

Grandchildren of late William Cotton Curtis, el son of late George Lear Curtis, 2nd son of 2nd baronet:—
Issue of late Lieut-Col Hubert Montagu Cotton Curtis, DSO, *b* 1876, *d* 1948: *m* 1st, 1915 (*m diss* 1929), Lilian, who *d* 1931, da of late Louis Watson, of Brighton, and widow of Alfred Broadwood; 2ndly, 1929, Marcella Olive Penrose Robinson, who *d* 1969:—
(By 2nd *m*) William Richard (The Old Rectory, Mill Hill, Weston Colville, nr Cambridge CB1 5NY), *b* 1933, *ed* Eton: *m* 1961, Janice Clare, da of William Yates Duckworth, of Garstang, Lancs, and has issue living, William Giles (54 Mysore Rd, SW11 5SB), *b* 1962; *ed* Ampleforth, and RMA Sandhurst; commn'd 13th/18th Hussars 1985, — Mark Edward, *b* 1964, — Timothy David, *b* 1968, — Anna Clare, *b* 1963. —— Hilda Lucy Penrose (7 Lyston Lane, Long Melford, Suffolk), *b* 1930: *m* 1955 (*m diss* 1968), Charles Henry Anderson, Capt R Inniskilling Fus, and has issue living, Lucie Rose (98 Holland Rd, W14 8BD), *b* 1956: has issue living (by Giuseppe de Gregorio, of Capri), Pietro Lucia DE GREGORIO *b* 1997, — Arabella Joan Louisa, *b* 1960, — Caroline Rebecca, *b* 1961.

Branch from great-uncle of 6th baronet

Grandchildren of late Rear-Adm Arthur Cecil Curtis, 2nd son of late George Lear Curtis, 2nd son of 2nd baronet:—
Issue of late Brig Arthur Drury Curtis, b 1888, d 1950: m 1st, 1915, Margery May, who d 1943, el da of Robert Barlow, of Bombay; 2ndly, 1946, Evelyn Muriel, who d 1951, da of Murray Simmons, of Whitton, Middlesex:—
(By 1st m) (Arthur) Derek Edward, MC, b 1917; ed ISC, RMA Woolwich, and St Catharine's Coll, Camb (BA 1939, MA 1960); Lt-Col RE (ret); European War 1939-45 in France (MC): m 1943, Katherine Mary, da of late Thomas Hadfield, of Sheffield, and has issue living, (Arthur) Richard Edward (Stable House, 10 Sambourne Rd, Warminster, Wilts BA12 8LJ; Army and Navy Club), b 1947; Capt RA (ret); ed Haileybury, and RMA Sandhurst: m 1983, Georgina Carolyn, da of James Michael Arnott, of Woodmylne, of Bailey Cottage, Old Bursledon, Hants, and has issue living, Harriet Arabella b 1986, Imogen Elizabeth b 1988, Florence Helena b 1990, — Katherine Margaret, b 1944: m 1969, Lt-Col M. A. Langdon, RM, of Worth Cottage, Worth, Wookey, Wells, Som BA5 1LW, and has issue living, Julian Charles Anthony b 1972, Mathilda Mary b 1974, Eliza Katherine b 1979. Residence – Oak Covert, Kingsley Av, Camberley, Surrey, GU15 2NA. Club – Royal Commonwealth Society. —— Joan Mary Lavie, b 1916: m 1940, Col Edward Raymond Lewis, CBE, of Worcester Cottage, Beaufort West, Bath, and has issue living, — Robert Edward Curtis, b 1941, — Penelope Alison, b 1947.

Granddaughter of late Brig Arthur Drury Curtis (ante):—
Issue of late Lt-Col Robert Cecil Curtis, RA, b 1922, d 1992: m 1952, Pamela Margaret (Yew Tree, Little Coxwell, Faringdon, Oxon SN7 7LP), da of late Oliver S. Sedgwick, of Chislehurst, Kent:—
Carol Frances Margaret, b 1956: m 1979, Maj Rowland Charles John Woollven, BSc, FRGS, RE, and has issue living, Virginia Alexandra Frances, b 1989.

Grandchildren of late Rear-Adm Arthur Cecil Curtis (ante):—
Issue of late Capt Cecil Montagu Drury Curtis, OBE, b 1889, d 1966: m 1933, Rosa Marion (3 Church Close, Evercreech, Somerset), da of late R. H. Woodley:—
Christopher Francis, b 1939; BA, Oxford; PhD, Edinburgh: m 1970, Jill Pickup, PhD. —— Hazel Rosemary, b 1934: m 1960, Sidney Edward Smith, of 8 Blunts Wood Rd, Haywards Heath, Sussex, and d 1993, leaving David Edward, b 1965, — Rosalind Margaret, b 1961, — Alison Claire, b 1963, — Stephanie Jane, 1968.

Issue of late Francis Augustus Drury Curtis, b 1891, d 1927: m 1916, Gwendolen Angelo Taylour, who d 1961, da of late Edwin Taylour English, of Toronto, Canada:—
Ada Harriette Drury, b 1918: m 1958, John Bernard Scowcroft, Ch Engineer, Merchant Navy, who d 1989, and has issue living, Sarah Jane (Still Waters, 148 Durnford St, Plymouth, Devon), b 1960. Residence – The Manse Residential Home, Cargoll Rd, St Newlyn East, Cornwall.

Branch, if any, from 4th son of 2nd baronet

Descendants, if any, of late Augustus John Curtis, 4th son of 2nd baronet (whose son Maj Augustus Frederick Curtis b 1840, left issue three sons).

Branch from 3rd son of 1st baronet

Granddaughter of late Lieut-Gen William Frederick Curtis, el son of late Timothy Abraham Curtis, 3rd son of 1st baronet:—
Issue of late Col William Frederick de Hubbenet Curtis, b 1842, d 1906: m 1880, Mary Owen, who d 1934, da of late John Ward Nicholls, Sec of Greenwich Hospital:—
Joceline Sophia Lilian: m 1925, Paul Stutfield. Residence –

Grandchildren of late Capt George Arthur Hamilton Curtis, RAN, el son of late Col James Charles Curtis (infra):—
Issue of late Cecil Arthur Hamilton Curtis, b 1895, d 1970: m 1929, Constance May, who d 1968, da of Aubrey E. Webb, of Melbourne, Aust:—
Geoffrey Cecil Hamilton (Tigh-na-Ceard, Mt Cotton Rd, Capalaba, Qld), b 1932: m 1960, Barbara Ellen, da of Peter Angus, of Newmarket, Brisbane, Qld, and has issue living, Fiona Madeline Hamilton, b 1962, — Helen Mary Hamilton, b 1964. —— Anne Eleanor Hamilton, b 1935.

Grandchildren of late Col James Charles Curtis, son of late Timothy Abraham Curtis (ante):—
Issue of late Alfred William Hamilton Curtis, b 1864, d 1918: m 1901, Euphemia Hilda McClung, da of William A. C. Reynolds, and widow of Henry Cooperthwaite:—
James Alfred Percy Hamilton, b 1907; Lt 2nd Bn Rocky Mountain Rangers (ret): m 1939, Barbara Milsom, da of Frank Weldon Russell, of Dartmouth, Nova Scotia, and has issue living, James Russell Hamilton (650 Beachview Drive, N Vancouver, BC, Canada, VFG 1R1), b 1941; B Com (UBC), MBA (SFU): m 1966, Marion Eileen, BEd, da of George B. Moore, of Vancouver, BC, and has issue living, James David Hamilton, b 1974, Russell Andrew Hamilton b 1975, — Alfred William Hamilton, b 1945: m 1971, Barbara Joan, da of Benjamin Earl Tompkins, of Terrace, BC, and has issue living, James William Hamilton b 1973. —— Grace Anna Delicia Florence Hamilton, b 1903: m 1923, Laurie E. Wiren, and has issue living, John b 1930, — James, b 1934, — Margaret, b 1926, — Leonore, b 1928. —— Margaret Euphemia Cecilia Hamilton b 1909: m 1940, Lloyd E. Kindleysides.

Branch from 4th son of 1st baronet

Grandchildren of late Col Charles Herbert Curtis, el son of late Charles William Curtis, el son of Charles Berwick Curtis, 4th son of 1st baronet:—
Issue of late Maj Timothy Herbert William Curtis, b 1882, d 1966: m (Jan) 1913, Edith Marjorie, who d 1968, da of late F. Aldcroft Kay:—
Pamela Kay, b (Oct) 1913; sometime Junior Com ATS: m 1943, Maj John Howard Nickson, RA, of South Well, Marnhull, Dorset, and has issue living, Simon John Curtis, b 1945, — Jeremy David, b 1947, — Cecelia Anne, b 1953. —— Mary Kay, b 1917: m 1939, Col Alexander George Jeffrey Readman, DSO, R Scots Greys, of 15 Victoria Sq, SW1, and has issue living, Timothy Christopher George, b 1944, — Teresa Mary (Hon Mrs Christopher C. Lyttelton), b 1947: m 1973, Hon Christopher Charles Lyttelton (see V Cobham).

Issue of late Maj Philip Pinckney Curtis, MC, late 15th The King's Royal Hussars, b 1884, d 1974: m 1st, 1925 (m diss 1933), Hélène Ellinor Clare, da of late Capt Glen Kidston, 3rd Bn Black Watch; 2ndly, 1941, Marion, who d 1997, da of late George Berkeley Wilson, of Long Barn, Ringwood:—
(By 1st m) Cherry April Ellinor, b 1926: m 1949, Maj Terence Leslie Gossage, MBE, late KOYLI, of Flexford House, Sway, Lymington SO41 6DP, and has issue living, Philip Leslie, b 1951: m 1st, 1983 (m diss 1986), Deborah Ann Darrell; 2ndly, 1991, Nicola Jane, da of Sir Nigel Frederick Althaus, of Swallowcliffe, Wilts, and has issue living (by 2nd m), James Peter b 1993, Sophie Harriet b 1994, — Andrew Alexander, b 1963: m 1988, Jessica Lucy, da of late Cdr Gresham Vaughan, RN, and has issue living, Thomas Edmund Gresham b 1994, Henrietta Ellinor b 1993, — Julia April Ellinor, b 1954: m 1982, Christopher Jenkin, and has issue living, Annabel Louise b 1985, Camilla Rose b 1988. —— Alison Audrey Primrose, b 1928: m 1956, William Ashe Dymoke Windham, of Parc Gwynne, Glasbury-on-Wye, via Hereford HR3 5LL (see Bowyer Smyth, Bt, colls). —— (By 2nd m) Timothy Malise (Street Farmhouse, Vernham St, nr Andover, Hants SP11 0EL), b 1942; ed Eton, Trin Coll, Camb (BA), and Harvard Business Sch, USA (MBA): m 1st, 1968 (m diss 1982), Sally Elizabeth, da of Ambrose Stevens Higgins, of Bangor, Maine, USA; 2ndly, 1986, Cecilia Leueen, da of Maj Peter Brown, of Longworth, Oxon, and has issue living (by 1st m), Timothy George, b 1972, — Edward Ambrose, b (twin) 1972, — Katherine Pinckney, b 1970. —— Giles Philip (Walnut Tree Cottage, Upper Wootton, Basingstoke, Hants), b 1945; ed Eton, and St Andrews Univ (BSc): m 1971, Sarah Anne, eldest da of late Lt-Col Walter George Finney, TD, RA (TA) (see E Perth, colls, 1995 Edn), and has issue living, Rowena Mary, b 1972, — Arabella Jean, b 1975, — Camilla Sarah, b 1979, — Lavinia Frances, b 1982.

Granddaughters of late Thomas Reginald Curtis, 3rd son of late Charles William Curtis (ante):—
Issue of late Col William Patrick Stewart Curtis, OBE, b 1899, d 1965: m 1929, Margaret Pamela Adderley, who d 1979, da of Lt-Col H. Adderley Cradock:—
Jill Elizabeth, b 1930: m 1952, Frederick Michael Pelly (see Pelly, Bt). —— Dorcas Sara (Lady Ross), b 1932: m 1965, Lt-Gen Sir Robert Jeremy Ross, KCB, OBE (c/o Barclays Bank, 50 Jewry St, Winchester), and has issue living, Edward, b 1966, — Annabel, b 1968. —— Jocelyn Patricia, b 1936: m 1960, Mark Tress (19 Finlay Street, SW6 6HE), and has issue living, Oliver James Mark, b 1967, — Amanda, b 1961, — Camilla, b 1963. —— Victoria Anne Dorothea Adderley b 1939: m 1965, Denis Gamberoni, of 43 Chepstow Place, W2, and has issue living, Tobias Felix, b 1970, — Justine Louise, b 1964. —— Tessa Cecilia Evelyn, b 1943.

Grandchildren of late Charles William Curtis (ante):—
Issue of late Eustace Henry Curtis, b 1863, d 1948: m 1904, Laura, da of Alfred Ibbotson, of 45 Hill Street, Berkeley Square, W1:—
John Eustace, b 1910. —— Corina Laurel Mary, b 1908.

Grandchildren of late Col Edward George Curtis, CMG, 3rd son of late Maj-Gen Reginald Curtis, 3rd son of Charles Berwick Curtis (ante):—
Issue of late Lt-Col David Sacheverell Curtis, b 1913, d 1990: m 1st, 1935 (m diss 1945), Annora Beatrice, da of late Maj Frederick Rowland Williams-Wynn, CB (see Williams-Wynn, Bt, colls); 2ndly, 1948 (m diss 1957), Pamela Ruth, da of late Reginald Walter Preston; 3rdly, 1957, Monica Sarah (4 Odos Ploutarchou, Athens, Greece), da of late Mrs Nina Payne, of Athens:—
(By 1st m) Edward Peregrine Sacheverell (Oak House, The Green, Richmond, Surrey TW9 1NQ; Clubs – White's, MCC), b 1937; ed Stowe; late Lieut 8th Hussars: m 1970, Marie-Adèle, da of late Francis Le Baron Smoot, of George-town, Washington DC, and has issue living, Charles Edward Peregrine, b 1971; ed Eton, — William Francis Peregrine, b 1974; ed Eton, and Bristol Univ, — Robert Frederick Peregrine, b 1978; ed Stowe, and King's Coll, London, — Caroline Annora Adèle, b 1980; ed Godolphin and Latymer Sch. —— Hugh Frederick (58 The Vineyard, Richmond, Surrey. Clubs – White's, RTYC), b 1941; ed Stowe: m 1970, Maija Kaarina, da of Aulis Samuli Pyy, of Helsinki, and has issue living, Victoria Ann, b 1971; ed Westonbirt, St Paul's Girls' Sch, and Somerville Coll, Oxford (BA): m 1998, Jocelyn David Stanton Dare, of 57 Sinclair Rd, W14, son of Barry Dare, of Blockley, Glos, — Natasha Kaarina Helena, b 1973; ed Godolphin Latymer Sch, and Univ of Manchester (BA), — Annabel Mary, b 1981; ed Surbiton High Sch. —— (By 3rd m), Isabella Alexandra Nina, b 1959: m 1984 (m diss 1992), Goulven Courtaigne, son of Pierre Courtaigne, of Versailles, and has issue living, Emma Louise Marie, b 1985.

Granddaughter of late Spencer Henry Curtis, 5th son of Charles Berwick Curtis (ante):—
Issue of late Major Spencer Carey Curtis, TD, b 1865; d 1945: m 1902, Edith Mabel, who d 1931, da of late T. J. Eaton, of Malmesbury, Cape Colony:—
Sylvia Rosamond D'Urban Carey (Little Orchard, Buckham Thorns, Westerham, Kent), b 1908: m 1932, Thomas Mus-grave Pyke, OBE, TD, HM's Inspector of Schs (ret), who d 1992 and has issue living, Susan Musgrave, b 1935: m 1966, John Leo Monaghan (10 Wilton Close, Street, Somerset), and has issue living, David John b 1968, Benjamin Musgrave b 1970, — Anne Curtis, b 1939: m 1962, Dr John Ferens Turner, of The Old Vicarage, Church Rd, Combe Down, Bath, and has issue living, Edward Thomas b 1966, Sophia Jane b 1964, Jessica Charlotte b 1968.

Granddaughters of late Wilfred Henry Curtis, 2nd son of late Spencer Henry Curtis (ante):—
Issue of late Anthony Edmund Spencer Curtis, b 1906 d 1962: m 1931, M. Nancy, who d 1986, (who m 2ndly 1969, John Ormsby Chapple) only child of late R. Nesbit Taylor, of Meadow Bank, Epsom:—
Jean Anna, b 1933: m 1st, 1960 (m diss 1978), John Richard Aley; 2ndly, 1980, Brian James Humphreys, of Jalna, St Johns Rd, Crowborough, E Sussex TN6 1RT. —— Brenda Carey, b 1936: m 1st, 1960, William John Stickland Budd;

2ndly, 1979, Malcolm Cecil Upstone, of Waters Edge, Florida Rd, Ferring, Worthing, W Sussex, and has issue living (by 1st *m*), Duncan Spencer, *b* 1962, — Roger Alastair, *b* 1964, — Caroline Carey, *b* 1965.

Granddaughter of late Henry Downing Curtis, yst son of Charles Berwick Curtis (ante):—
Issue of late Vice-Adm Berwick Curtis, CB, CMG, DSO, *b* 1876, *d* 1965: *m* 1st, 1907, his cousin, Mildred Henrietta Constable, who *d* 1927, da of Frank John Constable Curtis; 2ndly, 1929, Violet Penelope Munro, who *d* 1973, da of late Robert J. B. Thomson, and widow of Lt-Cdr George Francis Cholmley, of Thorpe Bassett, Malton, Yorks:—
(By 1st *m*) Janet Henrietta (Marrett Cottage, Hoarwithy, Hereford), *b* 1908: *m* 1st, 1927 (*m diss* 1936), Com William Kenneth Ramsden Cross, RN, who was *ka* 1941; 2ndly, 1940 (*m diss* 1950), Major Arthur Christopher John Congreve, who *d* 1992; 3rdly, 1951, A. Russell Cowell, who *d* 1964, and has issue living, (by 1st *m*) Giles Berwick (Halfpenny House, Common Hill, Fownhope, Hereford), *b* 1928; Lt-Cdr RN (ret): *m* 1st, 1953 (*m diss* 1971), Sonia, da of E. Welsby Williams; 2ndly, 1971, Lavinia, da of Gp Capt P. C. Thomson, and has issue living (by 1st *m*), Piers William *b* 1955, Belinda Jane *b* 1954, — Henrietta Caroline, *b* 1931: *m* 1957, Christopher Jermyn Pratt, of Bothampstead House, Hampstead Norreys, Newbury (*see* M Bath, colls, 1969 Edn), and has issue living, Roderick Jermyn (Bussock Mayne Cottage, Snelsmore, Newbury, Berks) *b* 1959, James Berwick *b* 1963.

The 1st baronet was Lord Mayor of London 1794-5, and sat as MP for the City of London 1790-1820. He was offered a peerage, but declined the honour.

Cusack-Smith, see Smith.

DALRYMPLE (UK) 1887, of Newhailes, Midlothian (Extinct 1971)

Sir (CHARLES) MARK DALRYMPLE, 3rd and last *Baronet*.

WIDOW LIVING OF THIRD BARONET

Lady ANTONIA MARIAN AMY ISABEL STEWART (*Lady Antonia Dalrymple*) (Garden Cottage, Newhailes, Musselburgh, Midlothian), only da of 12th Earl of Galloway: *m* 1946, Sir (Charles) Mark Dalrymple, 3rd Bt, who *d* 1971, when the title became ext.

Dalrymple-Champneys, see Champneys.

Dalrymple-Hay, see Hay.

Dalrymple-White, see White.

ELPHINSTONE-DALRYMPLE (UK) 1828, of Horn, and Logie Elphinstone, Aberdeenshire
(Dormant or Extinct 1956)

Sir FRANCIS NAPIER ELPHINSTONE-DALRYMPLE, CBE, DSO, 7th *Baronet*; *d* 18 Dec 1956, and concerning the next heir, his kinsman, HEW DRUMMOND ELPHINSTONE-DALRYMPLE, no information is available. At the time of going to press no name appears on the Official Roll of Baronets in respect of this title.

DAUGHTER LIVING OF SEVENTH BARONET

Daphne Jean, *b* 1916: *m* 1938, Brig David Meynell, CBE, late Roy Irish Fusiliers, who *d* 1986, and has issue living, Timothy, *b* 1940; *ed* Bryanston, — Peter David, *b* 1945; *ed* Wellington, and RMA Sandhurst. *Residence* – 6 Elm Rd, Gt Stukeley, Huntingdon, Cambs, PE17 5AU

This family is descended from Hon Sir Hew Dalrymple, 3rd son of James, 1st Viscount Stair, sometime Lord President of the Court of Session, and also MP for North Berwick, who was created a baronet 1698 (*see* E Stair, colls). Francis Anstruther Elphinstone Dalrymple, 5th son of 1st baronet, left issue, Hew Drummond *b* 1857, and Francis Herbert, *b* 1862. If they left male issue, the senior in line would be heir to this Baronetcy.

HAMILTON-DALRYMPLE (NS) 1698, of North Berwick, Haddingtonshire

Sir HEW FLEETWOOD HAMILTON-DALRYMPLE, KCVO, 10th *Baronet*; *b* 9 April 1926; *s* his father, *Sir* HEW CLIFFORD, 1959; *ed* Ampleforth; Maj (ret) Gren Guards; Capt-Gen Queen's Body Guard for Scotland (Royal Company of Archers), and Gold Stick for Scotland since 1996, Adjt 1964-85, President of the Council 1988-96; DL E Lothian 1964, Vice-Lieut 1973, Lord Lieut 1986; Dir of Scottish & Newcastle Breweries 1967-86, Vice-Chm 1983-86, Chm Scottish American Investment Co 1985-91 (Dir since 1967-93), CVO 1974, KCVO 1985: *m* 1954, Lady Anne-Louise Mary Keppel, da of 9th Earl of Albemarle, MC, and has issue.

𝕬rms – Quarterly: 1st and 4th grand quarters or on a saltire azure between two water-bougets in flank sable, nine lozenges of the first, *Dalrymple*; 2nd and 3rd grand quarters, quarterly 1st and 4th gules, three cinquefoils, ermine; 2nd and 3rd, argent, a lymphad with sails furled sable, all within a bordure componée argent and azure, the first charged with hearts gules and the second with mullets argent, *Hamilton*. 𝕮rest – A rock proper. 𝕾upporters – *Dexter*, a lion guardant gules; *sinister*, a falcon proper. *Residence* – Leuchie, North Berwick, East Lothian. *Club* – Cavalry and Guards'.

SONS LIVING

HEW RICHARD, *b* 3 Sept 1955; *ed* Ampleforth, Corpus Christi Coll, Oxford (MA), Clare Hall, Camb (M Phil), and Lond Univ (MSc): *m* 1987, Jane Elizabeth, yr da of Lt-Col John Morris, of Leighterton, Glos, and has issue living, Hew John Lucian, *b* 28 Aug 1990, — Hero Cecilia, *b* 1989, — Theophania Mary Anne, *b* 1992, — Lydia Jane Diana Hamilton, *b* 1996. *Residence* – Blackdykes, North Berwick, E Lothian. —— *Rev Fr* John James, *b* 1957; *ed* Ampleforth, and Queen's Coll, Oxford; RC Priest. —— Robert George, *b* 1959; *ed* Ampleforth: *m* 1984, Anna Mary, only da of Maj David Gibson, of Bishopswood Grange, nr Ross-on-Wye, Herefordshire, and has issue living, David Fleetwood, *b* 1993, — Effie Charlotte, *b* 1986, — Sophia Louise, *b* 1988, — Honor Rose, *b* 1991. *Residence* – Bolton Old Manse, by Haddington, E Lothian. —— William Benedict, *b* 1965; *ed* Ampleforth, and Trin Coll, Camb: *m* 1991, Olivia Mary Juliet, 3rd da of Simon Joseph Fraser (*see* L Lovat, colls), and has issue living, Sam Hew Tantallon, *b* 1997, — Elizabeth Kashmir, *b* 1995. *Residence* – Page's Yard, Church St, Chiswick, W4.

SISTER LIVING

Elsie Margaret Mary, *b* 1922: *m* 1947, Major Martin Antony Gibbs, Coldstream Gds, who *d* 1994, and has issue living, Antony William Hew (The Home Farm, Darrow Gurney, Bristol), *b* 1947; *ed* Eton, and Worcester Coll, Oxford: *m* 1974, Lady Virginia Rous, da of 5th Earl of Stradbroke, and has issue living, Abram *b* 1976, William Martin *b* 1986, Mary *b* 1975, Emily-Anna *b* 1978, Elizabeth Rose *b* 1979, Margaret Blanche *b* 1988, — Mary Blanche *b* 1949; *ed* London Univ (BA): *m* 1971, Rupert Leander Pattle Ridge, son of late Maj Robert Vaughan Ridge, of Brockley, Som, and has issue living, Thomas Leander *b* 1972, Edward Francis *b* 1976, Marian Sophia *b* 1973, Adeline Dyce Albinia Rose *b* 1979, — Anstice Bridget, *b* 1951: *m* 1978, Anthony Richard Howard, and has two children (*see* B Howard of Penrith), — Cecily Ann Albinia, *b* 1952: *m* 1975, Robert Mathers, who was *k* in a traffic accident 1992, and has issue living, John Alexander

Joseph *b* 1978, Simon Martin *b* 1984, Ralph Michael *b* 1987, Alice Mary Albinia *b* 1976, Imogen Blanche *b* 1982, — Katharine Rose, *b* 1955, — Julian Margaret GIBBS (32 Northumberland Av, E12), *b* 1957; has retained her maiden name; *ed* Sussex Univ (BA): *m* 1986, Julian Alexander Stanley, son of Oliver Duncan Stanley, and has issue living, Isaac Martin *b* 1990, Madeline Leah *b* 1988, Elinor Katherine Eve *b* 1992, Albinia Sarah Beatrice *b* 1995. *Residence* – Sheldon Manor, Chippenham, Wilts.

COLLATERAL BRANCH LIVING

Descendants (if any) of Robert Dalrymple-Horn-Elphinstone (2nd son of Robert Dalrymple-Horn-Elphinstone, 3rd son of Hew Elphinstone, 2nd son of 1st baronet), who was *cr* a Baronet 1828:—
See Elphinstone-Dalrymple, Bt (dormant or ext).

The 1st baronet, Hon Sir Hew Dalrymple, 3rd son of 1st Viscount Stair, sat as MP for North Berwick in the Scotch Parliament, and was subsequently Lord President of Session, and one of the Commissioners appointed to arrange the Articles of Union. Sir Hew, the 2nd baronet, was MP for co Haddington, and King's Remembrancer in the Exchequer for Scotland. The 3rd baronet, Sir Hew, MP for Midlothian, assumed the additional surname of Hamilton, and the 4th baronet assumed the surname of Hamilton after Dalrymple (*see* E Stair, colls), while the 8th baronet assumed it before that of Dalrymple.

DALYELL (NS) 1685, of the Binns

(*Sir*) THOMAS (TAM) DALYELL OF THE BINNS, MP, 11th Baronet (established his claim in 1973, but does not use title); son of late Lt-Col Gordon Loch, CIE, DL, JP; *b* 9 Aug 1932; *s* his mother, (*Dame*) ELEANOR ISABEL (*de jure Baronetess*), who *d* 1972 (da of Sir James Bruce Wilkie-Dalyell, 9th Bt), who, with her husband, assumed the surname and arms of Dalyell of The Binns (officially recognized that year by Lord Lyon King of Arms); *ed* Eton, and King's Coll, Camb; Hon DSc Edinburgh 1994, Hon Dr City Univ London 1998; Dep Dir of Studies, Ship-School, Dunera, 1961-62, Sec of Labour Standing Conference on the Sciences 1962-64, PPS to Min of Housing of Local Govt 1964-66; PPS to Leader of House of Commons 1967-68, and to Sec of State for Social Security 1968-70; a Member of Public Accounts Cttee, House of Commons 1962-65, and of House of Commons Select Cttee on Science and Tech 1966-68; Chm of Parl Labour Party Foreign Affairs Group 1973, Vice-Chm of Parl Labour Party 1974; Member of European Parliament 1975-78, Vice-Chm of Sub-Cttee on Public Accounts of Budget Cttee 1975-78; a Member of Select Cttee of Scrutiny on European Legislation 1979-83; a Member of National Executive Committee, Labour Party 1986-87; Political Columnist of *New Scientist* since 1968, author of *Devolution: the End of Britain*; *The Case for Ship Schools* 1960; *Ship School Dunera* 1962; *One Man's Falklands* 1982; *Thatcher's Torpedo* 1983; *A Science Policy for Britain* 1983; *Misrule: How Mrs Thatcher deceived Parliament* 1987; *Dick Crossman: A Portrait* 1989; MP for W Lothian (*Lab*) since 1962: *m* 1963, Hon Kathleen Mary Agnes Wheatley, only da of Baron Wheatley (Life Baron), and has issue.

𝕬𝖗𝖒𝖘 – Quarterly, 1st and 4th, sable a naked man with his arms extended proper on a canton argent a sword and pistol disposed in saltire also proper for *Dalyell of the Binns*; 2nd, or a saltire engrailed sable between two swans proper naiant in lochs undy azure and argent and in chief point a mullet gules for difference for *Loch*; 3rd, or a bend chequy sable and argent betwixt three buckles azure for *Menteith of Auldcathie*. Over all an intra-escutcheonal additament of a Baronet of Nova Scotia. 𝕮𝖗𝖊𝖘𝖙 – A dexter arm issuant from the wreath the hand grasping a scimitar proper hilted and pommelled or. 𝕾𝖚𝖕𝖕𝖔𝖗𝖙𝖊𝖗𝖘 – Two lions sejant guardant gukes armed and langued azure each supporting with its inferior forepaw a pavilion pole sable with rosette and pennon spike garnished or, the pennon argent with forks of the same and sable is charged with a sword and pistol in saltire proper.
Residence – The Binns, Linlithgow EH49 7NA.

SON LIVING

GORDON WHEATLEY, *b* 26 Sept 1965: *m* 1990, Pamela, yr da of David Leslie, of Peebles.

DAUGHTER LIVING

Moira Eleanor, *b* 1968: *m* 1997, Ian Grant Shearer, yst son of late James Shearer, of Oxshott, Surrey.

COLLATERAL BRANCHES LIVING *(Males and Females in remainder)*

Descendants of George Falconar of Carlowrie, W Lothian, el son of Jane Stewart (who *m* David Falconar of Carlowrie and *d* 1837), da and heir of Magdalen (who *m* Robert Stewart of Binny, W Lothian), da of 3rd Bt:—

Granddaughter of late George Mercer Falconar-Stewart, 2nd son of George Falconar of Carlowrie (ante) (*see* L Falconer of Halkerton).

Grandchildren of late Helen Jane (who *m* John Monsey Collyer of Gimingham, Norfolk, and *d* 1919), yr da of George Falconar of Carlowrie (ante):—
Issue of late Brig-Gen John Johnston Collyer, CB, CMG, DSO, *b* 1870, *d* 1941: *m* 1903, Hilda Rochford, da of Michael Henry Quinn:—
†Freda Falconar, *b* 1906: *m* 1938, Donald Stewart, of 4 Chequers, Drama Street, Somerset West, Cape 7130, S Africa, and *d* 1989, leaving issue, Ian Patrick Collyer (Matepe Estate, Marandellas, Zimbabwe): *m* and has issue, two sons, — Neil D. Collyer (Kooringa Estate, PO Box Fingal, Tasmania, Australia): *m* and has issue, two das.

Issue of late Roger Messenger Monsey Collyer, *b* 1874, *d* 19—: *m* 1909, Maud Winifred, da of late Byron Noel:—
Helen Nova, *b* 1911. —— Elizabeth Maud, *b* 1913. —— Ruth Amy, *b* 1914. —— Winifred Noel, *b* 1918. —— Judith, *b* 1921.

This Baronetcy was created with a special remainder "to heirs male and of tailzie." The right of the 9th baronet, Sir James Bruce Wilkie-Dalyell of the Binns, to be placed on the Official Roll of the Baronetage was admitted by the Baronetage Committee of the Privy Council on 1 July 1914.

DARELL (GB) 1795, of Richmond Hill, Surrey

Sir JEFFREY LIONEL DARELL, MC, 8th *Baronet*, only son of late Col Guy Marsland Darell, MC, 3rd son of 5th Baronet; *b* 2 Oct 1919; *s* his cousin, *Sir* WILLIAM OSWALD, 1959; *ed* Eton, and RMC Sandhurst; High Sheriff of Norfolk 1985-86, Brig (ret) Coldstream Guards, and patron of one living commanded 1st Batn Coldstream Guards 1957-9, AAG, War Office 1959-61, Coll Comd, RMA Sandhurst 1961-64, Regimental Lt-Col Comdg Coldstream Guards 1964, and Comdg 56th (London) Inf Bde (TA) 1965-67; Vice-Pres of Regular Commns Board 1968-70, Comdt Mons Officer Cadet Sch 1970-72; ADC to HM 1973-74; Trustee and Memb of London Law Trust 1981-99; 1939-45 War (MC): *m* 1953, Bridget Mary, da of Maj Gen Sir Allan Henry Shafto Adair, 6th Bt, GCVO, CB, DSO, MC, and has issue.

𝕬rms – Azure, a lion rampant or ducally crowned argent. 𝕮rest – Out of a ducal coronet or a Saracen's head couped at the shoulders proper, bearded sable, wreathed about the temples or and azure, on his head a cap of the last fretty argent tasselled or, turned up ermine.
Residence – Denton Lodge, Harleston, Norfolk IP20 0AD. *Clubs* – Army and Navy, MCC (Life Memb).

SON LIVING

GUY JEFFREY ADAIR, *b* 8 June 1961; *ed* Eton, and RMA Sandhurst; Coldm Gds 1981-84; Dir Fenchurch Group Ltd since 1993; *m* 1988, (Justine) Samantha, da of Mr Justice T. Reynolds, of Quambi Place, Edgecliff, Sydney, Australia, and has issue living, Harry Thomas Adair, *b* 10 May 1995, — Sophia Elizabeth Alexandra, *b* 1989, — Amelia Flora Frances, *b* 1993. *Residence* – 5 Norland Sq, W11 4PX.

DAUGHTERS LIVING

Katherine Mary, *b* 1954: *m* 1977, (John) Richard Astor, and has issue (*see* B Astor of Hever, colls). —— Camilla Viola, *b* 1956: *m* 1983, Henry Robert Thomas Adeane, of Babraham, Cambridge, only son of late Charles Raymond Wyndham Adeane, and has issue living, Anthony Charles, *b* 1991, — Madeline Bridget, *b* 1987. *Residence* – 44 Sterndale Rd, W14 0HU.

SISTER LIVING

Cynthia Mary, *b* 1916: *m* 1940, Michael Webster Harrap, and has issue living, Simon Richard (Perryland, Bentley, Farnham, Surrey; 16 Kelso Place, W8 5QD), *b* 1941; *ed* Harrow: *m* 1969, Hon Diana Akers-Douglas, sister of 4th Viscount Chilston, and has issue living, Nicholas Guy *b* 1975, Louise Jane *b* 1971: *m* 1998, Dermot Daly, elder son of late James Daly (*see* Milborne-Swinnerton-Pilkington, Bt), Lara Sophie *b* 1979, — John Michael Darell (7 East Green, Bentley, Farnham, Surrey GU10 5JQ), *b* 1943; *ed* Harrow: *m* 1973, Elizabeth (Izzy) Helen Rodica, yr da of Radu Tilea (*see* E Carnarvon, colls, 1995 Edn), and has issue living, Peter Mark *b* 1975, Edward Michael *b* 1983, — Giles Thresher (Hill Farm, Bentley, Farnham, Surrey GU10 5HB), *b* 1948; *ed* Harrow: *m* 1981, Sona Sophia, elder da of late John Gladstone, TD, of Capenoch, Thornhill, Dumfriesshire, and has issue living, Richard Thresher *b* 1984, Gilbert William Frederick *b* 1987, Isla Marie *b* 1990. *Residence* – Marsh House, Bentley, nr Farnham, Surrey GU10 5JF.

The 1st baronet, Sir Lionel Darell, sat as MP for Lyme Regis 1780-84, and for Heydon 1784-1802. The 2nd baronet, Sir Harry Verelst Darell, was extensively engaged in commerce in Bengal. Sir Lionel Darell, 5th Baronet, was High Sheriff of Gloucestershire 1887. The 6th baronet, Col Sir Lionel Edward Darell, DSO, 1st Life Guards, was a Co Councillor, Co Alderman, and High Sheriff of Gloucestershire 1924, and Hon Col 5th Batn Gloucestershire Regt 1936.

DASHWOOD (E) 1684, of Kirtlington Park, Oxfordshire

Nothing is inaccessible to virtue

Sir RICHARD JAMES DASHWOOD, 9th *Baronet*; *b* 14 Feb 1950; *s* his father, Sir HENRY GEORGE MASSY, 1972; *ed* Eton; Lt 14th/20th Kings Hussars; T & AVR 1973: *m* 1984 (*m diss* 1993), Kathryn Ann, elder da of Frank Mahon, of Barretts Farm, Eastbury, Newbury, Berks, and has issue.

Arms – Argent, on a fesse double cotised gules three gryphous' heads erased or. Crest – A griffin's head erminois, erased gules. Supporters – On either side a male gryphon argent, gorged with a collar flory counterflory gules.
Residence – Ledwell Cottage, Sandford St Martin, Oxon, OX7 7AN. *Club* – Boodle's.

SON LIVING

FREDERICK GEORGE MAHON, *b* 29 Jan 1988.

SISTER LIVING

Emma Victoria Mildred, *b* 1955: *m* 1977, Maj Edward Morgan Crofton, and has issue (*see* Crofton, Bt, *cr* 1801). *Residence* – Marchwood Lodge, Rake, Liss, Hants GU33 7PG.

COLLATERAL BRANCHES LIVING

Issue of late Arthur Paul Dashwood, OBE, 3rd son of 6th baronet, *b* 1882, *d* 1964: *m* 1919, Edmeé Elizabeth Monica (E. M. Delafield, novelist), who *d* 1943, da of late Count Henry Philip Ducarel de la Pasture:—
Rosamund Margaret, *b* 1923: *m* 1948, Leslie Harold Truelove, MRCP, late RNZAF, and has issue living, Paul Alexander, *b* 1948, — Leslie Simon, *b* 1950, — Patrick, *b* 1955, — Michael Andrew, *b* 1961.

Grandchildren of late Alexander Thomas Dashwood, elder son of Alexander John Dashwood, eldest son of Lt-Col Alexander Wilton Dashwood, yr son of Thomas Dashwood, EICS:—
Issue of late Alexander John Dashwood, *b* 1905, *d* 1979: *m* 1947, Mary Whitburn (3 Ladwill Sq, Ashburton, nr Newton Abbot, Devon), da of late Reginald Frank Thorne, of Southborough, nr Tunbridge Wells:—
Alexander Thomas Whitburn (9 Bradley Rd, Mannamead, Plymouth, Devon), *b* 1950: *m* 1977, Christine Ellen, da of Walter Lewis Badge, of 20 Ocean View Rd, Bude, Cornwall, and has issue living, Benjamin Alexander John, *b* 1979. —— Jeremy Charles Whitburn, *b* 1957. —— Sophia Ann Whitburn, *b* 1954.

Grandchildren of late George Lionel Dashwood, yst son of Lt-Col Alexander Wilton Dashwood (ante):—
Issue of late Sir Henry Thomas Alexander Dashwood, *b* 1878, *d* 1959: *m* 1909, Norah Creina Bruce, who *d* 1948, da of Henry Arthur Whately, of Midford Castle, Bath:—
Robert Henry Nevile, *b* 1921; *ed* Harrow, and Magdalene Coll, Camb (BA 1942, MA 1946); formerly Capt RA; is a JP, DL and High Sheriff (1980) for Northants: *m* 1959, Ruth Mary, da of Dr W. B. R. Monteith, of Purston Manor, Brackley, Northants, and has issue living, David Henry William, *b* 1960: *m* 1994, Katherine E., da of Walter Connies-Laing, of Cyncoed, Cardiff, and has issue living, Henry Charles Napier *b* 1995, Sophia Ruth Elizabeth *b* 1998, — (Ian) Bruce Robert (Grounds Farm, Hockliffe, Leighton Buzzard, Beds), *b* 1962: *m* 1997, Janet C., yr da of P. Broadhead, of Fridaythorpe, Yorks, and has issue living, Harriet Kathleen *b* 1999. *Residence* – Farthinghoe Lodge Farm, Farthinghoe,

Brackley, Northants. ——Norah Creina Frances, *b* 1910: *m* 1958, William Nell. *Residence* – The Farm House, Farthinghoe, Brackley, Northants NN13 5NY.

Grandchildren of late Maj Claude Burrard Lewes Dashwood, 2nd son of late Rev Robert Lewes Dashwood, grandson of late Samuel Francis Dashwood, great-grandson of Richard Dashwood, of Ledwell, co Oxon, 3rd son of 1st baronet:—
Issue of late Capt Robert Armand Lewes Dashwood, *b* 1916, *d* 1986: *m* 1938, Peggy Violet, who *d* 1963, only da of Herbert Reeves, of Bournmouth:—
Ian Burrard Lewes (Camelot, 1 Groeneveld Rd, Rondebosch 7700, Cape, S Africa), *b* 1947: *m* 1968, Marlene Dolores, el da of Pieter Kruger, of Sea Point, Cape, and has issue living, Paul Burrard Lewes, *b* 1972, — Annemarie, *b* 1969. —— Anne, *b* 1956.

Granddaughter of late Rev Robert Lewes Dashwood (ante):—
Issue of late Capt Sidney Lewes Dashwood, MBE, *b* 1882, *d* 1966: *m* 1922, Joan, who *d* 1963, da of Sir Sidney Gerald Burrard, 7th Bt, KCSI, FRS:—
Mary Edith Burrard, *b* 1923: *m* 1946, John Harry Walrond Simmons, MBE, who *d* 1994, and has issue living, Geoffrey Philip, *b* 1952: *m* 1976, Wendy Jean, da of Maurice Aylen, of Barton-on-Sea, and has issue living, Heather Julie *b* 1988, — Roland Paul, *b* 1957; has issue living, Georgina Louise *b* 1994, — Rosemary Jane KEANE, *b* 1949; assumed surname of Keane by deed poll 19—; has issue living, Michael Francis *b* 1975, Rebecca Sairn *b* 1972: *m* 1998, Damien Timmer, — Pamela Anne, *b* 1959: *m* 1998, Kenneth Edward Milner. *Residence* – 24 Lovelace Close, Abingdon, Oxon OX14 1XW.

Descendants of Richard Dashwood, of Cockley Cley, Norfolk, 2nd son of Alderman George Dashwood, of Hackney, Middlesex, and brother of 1st Bt, who are in special remainder to the Baronetcy:—

Grandchildren of late Charles Horace Pettus Dashwood, el son of Rev Charles John Dashwood, R. of Billingford, Norfolk (*d* 1890), 4th in descent from Richard Dashwood, of Cockley Cley (ante):—
Issue of late Horace Raikes Dashwood, of Caldecott Hall, Fritton, Suffolk, *b* 1885, *d* 1967: *m* 1912, Jessie Nina, who *d* 1978, da of late Walter Cassels, of Buenos Aires, Argentina:—
John Horace Cassels (2 The Mariners, 44 Sea Rd, Milford-on-Sea, Hants), *b* 1913; Maj (ret) RASC: *m* 1941, Elizabeth Christina FitzGibbon, and has issue living, Elizabeth Patricia, *b* 1942, — Annette Diana, *b* 1947, MB BS, MRCPsych: *m* 1975, Peter Anthony Goulden (Beechings, Water St, Hampstead Norreys, Newbury, Berks, RG18 0SB), and has issue living, Michael John Toby *b* 1979, Nicholas James *b* 1981, — Rosemarie, *b* 1950. —— Donald Cassels (Long Acre, Cley, Holt, Norfolk), *b* 1914: *m* 1941, Rachel, da of Rev James Mortimer La Fontaine McAnally, formerly R of Hethersett, Norfolk, and has issue living, Timothy James (43 Wood Lane, Fleet, Hants), *b* 1947; *ed* Marlborough, King's Coll, Camb (scholar), and Trin Coll, Oxford: *m* 1983, Katherine Ruth, da of late John Oliver Harris, of Epsom, Auckland, NZ, and has issue living, Peter James Oliver *b* 1985, Anne Jennifer Raven *b* 1987, — Margaret Jessie, *b* 1942: *m* 1983, Neil Douglas Sconce, of 11 Cromer Villas Rd, SW18 1PH, only son of late Maj Douglas Sconce, and has issue living, Francisca Barbara *b* 1985. —— Elizabeth Cassels, *b* 1916: *m* 1st, 1941, Antony Josiah Boek Gimson, who was *ka* 1942; 2ndly, 1944, Owen Lloyd Davies, of 16 Olivedale Court, Toowoomba, Qld 4350, Australia, and has had issue (by 1st *m*), Josiah Jeremy Dashwood Boek, *b* 1942; *d* 19—, — (by 2nd *m*), Elizabeth Anne, *b* 19—.

Issue of late Richard Raikes Dashwood, *b* 1890, *d* 1967: *m* 1918, Rachel Mary Windham, da of late Rev Alfred Charles Lowth, R. of Colden Common, Winchester:—
Roland Pettus (formerly Argentina; The Haven, Drillham, Qld 4424, Australia), *b* 1922; *ed* Marlborough: *m* 1st, 1946, Helen Theresia, da of late Leslie Armitage, of La Mimosa, Buena Esperanza, Argentina; 2ndly, 1990, Jean Carol, da of late Eric Dack, of Scotland and Argentina, and has issue living, (by 1st *m*) John Richard, *b* 1959, — Alan Roland, *b* 1960, — Paul Charles, *b* 1962, — Ray James, *b* 1964. —— Jean Mary, *b* 1919: *m* 1941, her cousin, John Stuart Michael Dashwood (infra). —— Edith Rachel, *b* 1920: *m* 1949, Ian McCulloch, who *d* 1971. —— Molly Frances, *b* 1925: *m* 1946, George Locke Smiles, of Beta Gamma, Ombu, Argentina, and has issue living, Dorothy June, *b* 1957.

Grandchildren of late Edmund Samuel Dashwood, surg, 2nd son of Rev Charles John Dashwood, R. of Billingford, Norfolk (*d* 1890) (ante):—
Issue of late John Rawdon Dashwood, *b* 1889, *d* 1961: *m* 1918, Marian, who *d* 1965, da of Robert Kohlhoff Clark, tea-planter, of Ceylon:—
John Stuart Michael (10 Curtis St, Toowoomba, Qld, 4350, Australia), *b* 1917: *m* 1941, his cousin, Jean Mary, da of late Richard Raikes Dashwood (ante), and has issue living, Geoffrey Richard (27 rue de l'Etang de la Tour, 78120 Rambouillet, France), *b* 1942: *m* 1966, Eliane Michèle, da of Kleber Barrassé, of Colombes, Seine, France, and has issue living, Sophie Michèle *b* 1968, Valerie Mary *b* 1971, Annabel Anne *b* 1973, — Oliver Michael, *b* 1947; schoolmaster at Toowoomba Gram Sch: *m* 1983, Ann, da of Joseph Waxman, of Merricks North, Vic, Australia, and has issue living, Robert Michael *b* 1983, Timothy Kester Paul *b* 1985. —— Mary Elizabeth Anne (18 Crofton Lane, Hill Head, Fareham, Hants, PO14 3LP), *b* 1921: *m* 1942, Lt-Cdr Patrick Hugh Moss, RN, who *d* 1989, and has issue living, Nigel Patrick Stringer (Henhurst Lodge, Beare Green Rd, Ockley, Dorking, Surrey), *b* 1946: *m* 1971, Linda, da of Reginald Alfred Baillie, of 26 Green Lane, Copnor, Portsmouth, and has issue living, James Robert *b* 1975, Jonathan Mark *b* 1977, — Jane Elizabeth Moss (14 Maizemore Walk, Lee-on-the-Solent, Hants), *b* 1943; has resumed her maiden name by deed poll: *m* 1st, 1969 (*m diss* 1974), Roger Sowerby; 2ndly, 1976 (*m diss* 1980), Brian James Maby; 3rdly, 1982 (*m diss* 1987), John Paul Ceresole.

Descendants of late Henry Dashwood, MP, grandson of Lt-Col George Dashwood (who assumed the surname and arms of Peyton, and was *cr* a *Baronet* 1776), brother of 1st baronet (The male line, now ext, was in special remainder to the Baronetcy.)
See Peyton, Bt, (ext).

Alderman George Dashwood, of London, undertook, with others, to farm the whole revenue of the kingdom of Ireland *temp* Charles II. He afterwards, with others, farmed the whole revenues of excise and hearth money in England, and was a commissioner of Revenue till his death in 1682. A patent of baronetcy was granted to him, but as he did not take it out, his widow was given the precedence of a baronet's widow, while a new patent of baronetcy was granted to his son with special remainder, in default of male issue, to the male descendants of his father. The 1st baronet of this creation was MP for Banbury, the 2nd was MP for Oxfordshire, and the 3rd MP for Woodstock. Alderman Francis Dashwood, of London, elder brother of Alderman George Dashwood (ante), was father of Sir Francis Dashwood, 1st baronet, of West Wycombe.

DASHWOOD (GB) 1707, of West Wycombe, Buckinghamshire

For the Great Charter

Sir FRANCIS JOHN VERNON HEREWARD DASHWOOD, 11th *Baronet*, and Premier Baronet of Great Britain; *b* 7 Aug 1925; *s* his father, Sir JOHN LINDSAY, CVO, 1966; *ed* Eton, Ch Ch, Oxford (MA) and Henry Fellow at Harvard Business Sch; a Member of Lloyd's; a Co Councillor of Bucks 1951-52; High Sheriff of Bucks 1976; author of *The Dashwoods of West Wycombe* 1987: *m* 1st, 1957, Victoria Ann Elizabeth Gwynne, who *d* 1976, only da of late Maj John Frederick Foley, Baron de Rutzen, Welsh Guards (Foley-Philipps, Bt); 2ndly, 1977, Marcella Teresa Guglielmina Maria, da of Marcellino Scarafina, formerly wife of Giuseppe Sportoletti Baduel, and widow of Jack Frye, CBE, and has issue by 1st *m*.

𝕬rms – Argent, on a fesse double cotised gules, three griffins' heads erased or. 𝕮rest – A griffin's head erased per fesse, erminois and gules. *Residence* – Sawmill House, West Wycombe, High Wycombe, Bucks. *Club* – White's.

SON LIVING (*By 1st marriage*)

EDWARD JOHN FRANCIS, *b* 25 Sept 1964; *ed* Eton, and Reading Univ (BSc); ARICS: *m* 1989, Lucinda Nell, only da of Gerrard Herman Francis Miesegaes, of Upperton Farmhouse, Upperton, Petworth, W Sussex, and has issue living, George Francis, *b* 17 June 1992, — Robert Edward, *b* 1993, — Victoria Lucinda, *b* 1991. *Residence* – West Wycombe Park, Bucks.

DAUGHTERS LIVING (*By 1st marriage*)

Emily Jane, *b* 1958: *m* 1981, Charles William Lennox Naper (*see* Valentia colls, 1973/4 Edn), and has issue living, Nicholas, *b* 1984, — Edward, *b* 1986, — John, *b* 1990. —— Georgina Helen, *b* 1960: *m* 1991, Charles Humphrey Joseph Weld, and has issue (*see* L Lovat, colls). —— Caroline Sarah, *b* 1962: *m* 1997, Michael John Wade, only son of Peter Wade, of Sutton Green, Surrey, and has issue living, Alexander Francis Neville, *b* 1998.

BROTHER LIVING

John (27 Matham Rd, East Molesey, Surrey), *b* 1929; *ed* Eton, and Ch Ch, Oxford: *m* 1st, 1959 (*m diss* 1964), Susan Boyter Duncombe, el da of Maj Ernest Duncombe Shafto, of Little Beamishe, Aldeburgh, Suffolk; 2ndly, 1965, Harriet Louise, el da of J. P. Spencer, of Norbury Park, Mickleham, Surrey, and has issue living (by 2nd *m*), Thomas *b* 1973, — Rebecca Louise, *b* 1971: *m* 1996, Sean Keith Westrope, son of Keith Lesley Westrope, of Mundesley, Norfolk.

SISTER LIVING

Maud Helen Sarah (*Baroness Aberdare*), *b* 1924: *m* 1946, 4th Baron Aberdare, of 32 Elthiron Rd, SW6.

The Dashwoods were established in NE Dorset in early Tudor times, and Henry Dashwode is named in the Subsidy for Tarrant Gunville 1524/5 and the muster 1539. In the person of Robert Dashwood, son of Thomas Dashwood of Tarrant Monkton next Tarrant Gunville, the senior line of the family moved after 1575 to Stogumber in Somerset where the said Robert Dashwood (*d* 1610) was the ancestor of the Baronets line. The 1st baronet was knighted 1702, and sat as MP for Winchilsea. The 2nd baronet became 8th Baron LeDespencer in right of his mother, and was successively head of the War Office, Chancellor of the Exchequer, and Postmaster-General. He died without male issue, and the barony fell in abeyance. The 3rd baronet — who was half-brother to the 2nd baronet — assumed the additional surname of King. Sir John Dashwood, 4th Bt, who *d* 1849, was fifth in descent from Ann Agar, sister of John Milton, the poet, and sat as MP for Wycombe 1796-31. The 5th baronet sat as MP for Bucks (*L*) 1832-7, and for Wycombe 1837-62.

DAVID (UK) 1911, of Bombay (Extinct 1964)

Sir PERCIVAL VICTOR DAVID EZEKIEL DAVID, 2nd and last *Baronet*.

DAUGHTER LIVING OF SECOND BARONET

Katherine Viola Monica, *b* 1914: *m* 1952, William Frederick Taylor. *Residence* – 35 Monkridge, Haslemere Rd, Crouch End Hill, N8.

FERGUSON DAVIE (UK) 1847, of Creedy, Devonshire

Sir JOHN FERGUSON DAVIE, 7th *Baronet*, only son of late Edward Cruger Ferguson Davie, 4th son of 3rd baronet; *b* 1 May 1906; *s* his kinsman, *Sir* ANTONY FRANCIS, 1997; *ed* Winchester: *m* 1942, (Joan) Zoe Charlotte, who *d* 1987, da of late Raymond Hoole, of Vancouver, BC, and has issue.

Arms – Quarterly; 1st and 4th, argent, a chevron sable between three mullets pierced gules; 2nd and 3rd, azure, three cinquefoils or, upon a chief of the last a lion passant, gules. Crests – 1st, a pascal lamb reguardant argent; 2nd, a kingfisher wings elevated proper, in the beak a branch of olive vert fructed or.
Address – c/o Coutts & Co, 1 Cadogan Place, SW1X 9PX.

SONS LIVING

MICHAEL, *b* 10 Jan 1944; *ed* St Edward's Sch, Oxford: *m* 1968 (*m diss* 1992), (Margaret) Jean, only da of late Douglas John Macbeth, of Bowden, Ches, and has had issue, †James Michael, *b* 1970; *d* 1988. *Residence* – 63 Hillgate Place, SW12 9ES. —— Julian Anthony, *b* 1950; *ed* Uppingham: *m* 1976, Louise, da of John Marsden, of Huttons Ambo, York, and has issue living, Charles John, *b* 1978; *ed* Wellington Coll, — John Robert, *b* 1981; *ed* Wellington Coll, — William Edward, *b* 1986. *Residence* – Rue Aux Fleurs 26, 1380 Ohain, Belgium.

COLLATERAL BRANCHES LIVING

Under the auspices of Christ

Grandchildren of late Henry Herrick Ferguson Davie (*b* 1869) (infra):—
Issue of late Henry Herrick Ferguson Davie, *b* 1894, *d* 1952: *m* 1919, Julia Victoria, da of John Stokes, of London:—
Henry Herrick (1420, Washington Avenue, Severn, Baltimore, Maryland, USA), *b* 1920: *m* 1st, 1941 (*m diss* 1943), Joyce Sanders, of Brooklyn, Baltimore, USA; 2ndly, 1951, Anna Marie, da of Bender Clarke, of Gambrillo, Maryland, USA, and has issue living, (by 1st *m*) Henry Herrick, *b* 194—, — (by 2nd *m*) Anna Louise, *b* 1952.

Issue of late Charles Francis Ferguson Davie, *b* 1898, *d* 1967: *m* 1924, Alice Clarke, who *d* 1968, da of Henry Newman, of Potterne, Wilts:—
Muriel Frances, *b* 1926: *m* 1st, 1948 (*m diss* 1952), Basil Anthony King; 2ndly, 1952, Bernard, William Pearce, of 1003 Harbour View, Victoria Embankment, Durban, S Africa, and has issue living (by 2nd *m*), Michael Stephen, *b* 1953: *m* 1st, 1975 (*m diss* 1977), Judith Melanie McClelland; 2ndly, 1979, Carol Ann Ebelthite, and has issue living (by 2nd *m*), Clinton Noel *b* 1990, Megan Bernardine *b* 1980, Mandy *b* 1985, Tamsin *b* 1988, — Geoffrey Mark, *b* 1956: *m* 1981, Belinda Ryall, of Natal, and has issue living, Raymond *b* 1984, Bronwyn Muriel *b* 1983, — Robert Andrew, *b* 1959: *m* 1st, 1980 (*m diss* 1988), Odette Jean-Jacques; 2ndly, 1992, Beverley Ann Smith, and has issue living (by 1st *m*), Dylan Bradley *b* 1983, Lloyd *b* 1985.

Grandchildren of late Capt William Carey Ferguson Davie (infra):—
Issue of late William George Michael Ferguson Davie, *b* 1923, *d* 1973: *m* 1953, Margaret Mary (Wendy), da of late Capt William J. Fowler:—
Christopher Mark, *b* 1956: *m* 1st, 1976 (*m diss* 1982), Wendy K., da of John McGillivray, of Castlegar, BC, Canada; 2ndly, 1984, Joanne Elma, da of David James Thomas, QC. —— Deirdre Ann, *b* 1955: *m* 1977 (*m diss* 1988), Herbert J. Markgraf, of Kelowna, BC, Canada. —— Jean Elizabeth, *b* 1961: *m* 1986, Gordon Richard Boothe, of Summerland, BC.

Granddaughter of late Henry Herrick Ferguson Davie (*b* 1869), 2nd son of late Rev Charles Robert Ferguson Davie, 4th son of 1st baronet:—
Issue of late Capt William Carey Ferguson Davie, *b* 1900, *d* 1974: *m* 1922, Katherine, who *d* 1986, da of late William Robertson Kay, of Sutton, co Dublin:—
Jean Anne, *b* 1932: *m* 1956, George Hellyer-Crawford, and has issue living, Anne Katherine, *b* 1959: *m* 1984, Thomas P. O'Reilly, of Tullamore, Co Offaly, and has issue living, Nanci Jean *b* 1994, — Alison Jane, *b* 1963.

Frances Juliana Davie (only surviving sister of Sir John Davie, 9th baronet (*cr* 1641), and niece and heiress of Sir Humphrey Phineas Davie, 10th and last baronet, who *d* 1846): *m* 1823, Gen Henry Robert Ferguson. In the following year the baronetcy was revived in favour of Gen Ferguson, who had assumed by Roy licence 1846 the additional surname and arms of Davie after his patronymic.

d'Avigdor-Goldsmid, see Goldsmid.

DAVIS (UK) 1946, of Barrington Hall, co Cambridge

Sir JOHN GILBERT DAVIS, 3rd *Baronet*; *b* 17 Aug 1936; *s* his father, *Sir* GILBERT, 1973; *ed* Oundle, and RNC Dartmouth: *m* 1960, Elizabeth Margaret, el da of Robert Smith Turnbull, of Falkirk, and has issue.

Arms – Quarterly; 1st and 4th, per saltire sable and argent, two pierced mullets or in pale and a dexter and sinister dragon's wing in fesse gules, *Davis*; 2nd and 3rd, per fesse embattled gules and argent in chief three castles or, *Terrett*. **Crest** – In front of a spear erect the shaft couped argent, and in front of a vol of dragon's wings three pierced mullets as in the arms.
Residence – 5 York Ridge Rd, Willowdale, Ontario M2P 1R8, Canada.

SON LIVING

RICHARD CHARLES, *b* 11 April 1970.

DAUGHTERS LIVING

Wendy Elizabeth, *b* 1962. —— Linda Mary, *b* 1964.

SISTER LIVING

Ann, *b* 1931: *m* 1956 (*m diss* 1976), John Robert Whatley, and has issue living, Alison Jane, *b* 1959. *Residence* – Chestnut Tree, Wildcroft Wood, Gasden Lane, Witley, Surrey.

AUNT LIVING (*Daughter of 1st baronet*)

Margaret, *b* 1904: *m* 1935, Col Ernest O. A. Singer, RAMC, who *d* 1957. *Residence* – 119 Barkston Gardens, SW5.

The 1st baronet, Sir (Arthur) Charles Davis (son of George John Davis), formerly of Stone Castle, Greenhithe, Kent, was an Underwriting Member of Lloyd's, High Sheriff of Kent 1934-5, and Lord Mayor of London 1945-46.

Davis-Goff, see Goff.

DAVSON (UK) 1927, of Berbice, British Guiana

Sir CHRISTOPHER MICHAEL EDWARD DAVSON, 3rd *Baronet*; *b* 26 May 1927; *s* his brother *Sir* ANTHONY GEOFFREY LEO SIMON GLYN, 1998; *ed* Eton; late Capt Welsh Gds; FCA; Liveryman of Musicians' Co, and Freeman of City of London; *m* 1st, 1962 (*m diss* 1972), Evelyn Mary, only da of late James Wardrop; 2ndly, 1975, Kate, da of Ludo Foster, of Greatham Manor, Pulborough, Sussex, and has issue by 1st *m*.

Arms – First and fourth; argent, on a chevron sable between two stags lodged gules attired of the second in chief, and a representation of the sailing ship Santa Maria proper in base, three pheons inverted or: second and third; argent, an eagle displayed with two heads sable guttée d'or. **Crest** – A dove proper gorged with an antique crown or, standing upon a branch of oak fructed proper.
Residence – 4 Mermaid St, Rye, Sussex TN31 7ET.

SON LIVING (*By 1st marriage*)

GEORGE TRENCHARD SIMON, *b* 5 June 1964; *ed* Eton, and Magdalen Coll, Oxford. *Residence* – 34 Dean Court Rd, Cumnor Hill, Oxford OX2 9XD.

DAUGHTERS LIVING AND DECEASED OF SECOND BARONET

Caroline Mary GLYN, *b* 1947; novelist; *d* 1981. —— Victoria Anne GLYN, *b* 1951; Bar Inner Temple 1978.

WIDOW LIVING OF SECOND BARONET

Steadfast in faith

SUSAN ELEANOR (*Lady Glyn*), da of Lieut-Col Sir Rhys Rhys Williams, DSO, QC, 1st Bt; Bar Inner Temple 1950; *m* 1946, Sir Anthony Geoffrey Leo Simon Glyn, 2nd Bt, who *d* 1998. *Residence* – Marina Baie des Anges, Appt Ducal U-03, F-06270 Villeneuve-Loubet, Alpes Maritimes, France.

The 1st baronet, Sir Edward Rae Davson, KCMG (son of late Sir Henry Katz Davson, a Member of Court of Policy, British Guiana), was a Past Chm of Federation of Chambers of Commerce of British Empire, and a Member of Imperial Economic Cttee, Colonial Development Advisory Cttee, and Empire Marketing Board. He *m* 1921, Margot Elinor, OBE, da of Clayton Louis Glyn and his wife Elinor Sutherland (the novelist Elinor Glyn). The 2nd baronet, Sir Geoffrey Leo Simon Davson, novelist, biographer and travel writer, assumed by deed poll 1957 the surname of Glyn in lieu of his patronymic and the additional forename of Anthony.

DAWSON (UK) 1920, of Edgwarebury, co Middlesex

Sir HUGH MICHAEL TREVOR DAWSON, 4th *Baronet*; *b* 28 March 1956; *s* his father, *Maj Sir* (HUGH HALLIDAY) TREVOR, 1983.

Arms – Azure, on a chevron ermine between three bird bolts argent a rose gules, slipped and leaved between two daws respectant proper. **Crest** – Out of a naval crown or a daw proper.
Residence – 11 Burton Court, Franklin's Row, SW3.

BROTHER LIVING

NICHOLAS ANTONY TREVOR, *b* 17 Aug 1957.

AUNTS LIVING (*Daughters of 2nd baronet*)

Avice Louise Trevor (Kames Lodge, Duns, Berwickshire), *b* 1923: *m* 1942 (*m diss* 1964), Maj Edwyn Inigo Lloyd Mostyn, MC, Scots Guards, who *d* 1978 (see B Mostyn, colls). —— Patricia Elinor Trevor, *b* (twin) 1923: *m* 1st, 1943 (*m diss* 1953), Maj Raymond Alexander Carnegie, late Scots Guards (see E Southesk); 2ndly, 1953, John Maxwell Menzies, and has issue living, (by 1st *m*) (see E Southesk), — (by 2nd *m*) Miranda Jane, *b* 1954: *m* 1979, Dermot Julian Jenkinson (see Jenkinson Bt, colls), — Sarah Jane, *b* 1955: *m* 1st, 1980 (*m diss* 19——), Nigel Rawlence; 2ndly, 1994, Charles Coppin Speke, and has issue living (by 2nd *m*), Alexander John Hanning *b* 1995, Savannah Rose *b* (twin) 1995, Sienna Clayre *b* 1997, — Cynthia Emma, *b* 1958: *m* 1984, Ian C.L. Harrison, and has issue living, Maxwell James Guy *b* 1988, Charlotte Cynthia Anne *b* 1986, Tamara Gabrielle Louise *b* 1992, — Katherine Patricia, *b* 1960: *m* 1996, Simon Hugh Slater, and has issue living, Flora Clementine *b* 1996, Rose Jane *b* 1998. *Residence* – Kames, Duns, Berwickshire.

Deeds not words

WIDOW LIVING OF THIRD BARONET

CAROLINE JANE (*Lady Dawson*) (11 Burton Court, Franklin's Row, SW3), only da of William Antony Acton (*see* V Cowdray, colls): *m* 1955, Maj Sir (Hugh Halliday) Trevor Dawson, 3rd Bt, who *d* 1983.

The 1st baronet, Com Sir (Arthur) Trevor Dawson, RN (son of late Hugh Dawson, Bar-at-law), was a Director and Sup of Ordnance of Vickers, Ltd, Chm of their Armament and Shipbuilding Management Board, and Vice-Principal of Council of Imperial Soc of Knights Bachelor.

DAWSON (UK) 1929, of Appleton Roebuck, co York (Extinct 1974)

(*Sir*) LAWRENCE SAVILLE DAWSON, 2nd and last *Baronet*.

DAUGHTER LIVING OF SECOND BARONET

Barbara Jane, *b* 1940.

WIDOW LIVING OF SECOND BARONET

RUTH M., da of late John Smith Baxter, of Harrogate; *m* 1971, as his 2nd wife, (Sir) Lawrence Saville Dawson, 2nd baronet (but did not use title), who *d* 1974, when the title became ext. *Residence* – Oldholme, Gorey Hill, Jersey, CI.

DE BATHE (UK) 1801, of Kingstown Cashel, co Meath (Extinct 1941)

Sir CHRISTOPHER ALBERT DE BATHE, RAF Vol Reserve, 6th and last *Baronet*; *ka* 1941.

DAUGHTER LIVING OF SIXTH BARONET

Charlotte Louise, *b* 1934: *m* 1967, Arthur Cyril Bryan, of 16 Drayton Gdns, SW10.

HALF-SISTER LIVING OF SIXTH BARONET

Bridget, *b* 1922: *m* 1942, Capt Timothy John Gurney, Coldstream Guards, and has issue living, Christopher, *b* 1950: *m* 1986, Linda Harvey, — Jeannine Mary (*Lady Barber*), *b* 1943: *m* 1st, 1964 (*m diss* 1978), John Richard Boyle (*see* E Cork, colls); *m* 2ndly, 1978, as his 2nd wife, Sir (Thomas) David Barber, 3rd Bt, of Windrush House, Inkpen, Berks, — Lucinda Marjorie (*Baroness Hothfield*) *b* 1946: *m* 1st, 1965 (*m diss* 1972), Capt Graham Morison Vere Nicoll, Welsh Guards (*see* Madden, Bt), 2ndly, 1975, 6th Baron Hothfield, of Drybeck Hall, Appleby-in-Westmorland, Cumbria. *Residence* – Maidshot, Great Hormead, Buntingford, Herts.

DEBENHAM (UK) 1931, of Bladen, co Dorset

Sir GILBERT RIDLEY DEBENHAM, 3rd *Baronet*, *b* 28 June 1906; *s* his brother, *Sir* PIERS KENRICK, 1964; *ed* Eton, and Trin Coll, Camb (BChir): *m* 1935, Violet Mary (Mollie), who *d* 1994, el da of late His Honour Judge (George Herbert) Higgins, and has had issue.

𝔄rms – Sable, a bend cottised between two crescents or. ℭrest – In front of a garb or, a sickle erect proper, the blade pointing to the sinister.
Residence – Tonerspuddle Farm, Dorchester, Dorset DT2 7JA.

GRANDCHILDREN LIVING

Issue of late George Andrew Debenham, eldest son of 3rd baronet, *b* 1938, *d* 1991: *m* 1969, Penelope Jane, da of John David Armishaw Carter:—
THOMAS ADAM, *b* 28 Feb 1971. —— (Anna) Rose, *b* 1972.

SONS LIVING

William Michael, *b* 1940; *ed* Bryanston, and Trin Coll, Camb (BA); MSC: *m* 1974, Gunnel Birgitta, da of Holger Elis Valfrid Holmgren, and has issue living, Oliver William, *b* 1976, — Martin Ellis, *b* 1980. —— Paul Edward, *b* 1942; *ed* Bryanston, and Trin Coll, Camb (BA, MB, BChir); MRCP: *m* 1968, Jennifer Mary, MB, ChB, da of late G. W. Rees, and has issue living, Edward James, *b* 1970, — Michael John, *b* 1973, — Clare Elizabeth, *b* 1977.

DAUGHTER LIVING

Virginia Mary, *b* 1936: *m* 1st, 1960 (*m diss* 1982), Graham Leslie Nicol; 2ndly, 1982, Nigel Denison Purchon, FLS, of 54 Gondar Gdns, NW6, and has issue living (by 1st *m*), Stephen Leslie, *b* 1961: *m* 1986, Judith, eldest da of Norman Farmer (and has issue), — Alan Leslie, *b* 1966: *m* 1994, Othaylat, da of Seif-el Din Suliman (and has issue), — Lucy Jean, *b* 1963: *m* 1994, Behrouz Shomali (and has issue).

SISTER LIVING

Cecil Audrey, *b* 1906: *m* 1953, Charles Robert Bielby, who *d* 1967.

DAUGHTERS LIVING OF SECOND BARONET

Caroline Susan (*Baroness Neill of Bladen*), *b* 1930: *m* 1954, Baron Neill of Bladen, QC (Life Baron), and has had issue (see that title). *Residence* – 8 Milborne Grove, SW10. —— Anne Charlotte, *b* 1932: *m* 1962, Peter Muir Horsfield, QC, of 24 Liverpool Rd, Kingston Hill, Surrey, and has issue living, Andrew Piers, *b* 1963: *m* 1991 Gigi, yr da of Dr Yvon Carignan, of Basking Ridge, NJ, USA, — Charles Peter, *b* 1964, — Thomas Martin, *b* 1966.

COLLATERAL BRANCH LIVING

Issue of late Martin Ridley Debenham, yst son of 1st baronet, *b* 1909, *d* 1977: *m* 1937, Beatrice Sydney (Dairy House, Affpuddle, Dorset), da of late Ven Harry Sydney Radcliffe: –
James Martin Robert (Fast Farm, Affpuddle, Dorchester, Dorset, DT2 7HH), *b* 1951: *m* 1982, Jean Veronica, da of late Maj Royston Eric Acres, MBE, and has issue living, Bosworth Ridley Oriol Acres, *b* 1982, — Branwell George Kenrick Acres, *b* 1985, — Bathsheba Alice Maisie Acres, *b* 1989. —— Susanna Elizabeth, *b* 1943: *m* 1964, Alexander Surtees Chancellor (see Paget, Bt, *cr* 1886, 1995 Edn), and has issue living, Elizabeth Beatrice, *b* 1964: *m* 1990, Alexander Evelyn Michael Waugh, and has issue (see E Onslow), — Cecilia Mary, *b* 1966.

The 1st baronet, Sir Ernest Ridley Debenham (son of late Frank Debenham, of Fitzjohns Avenue, Hampstead, NW3), was Chm of Debenhams, Ltd.

CHAMPION DE CRESPIGNY (UK) 1805, of Champion Lodge, Essex (Extinct 1952)
(Name pronounced "Champion de Crepiny")

Sir VIVIAN TYRELL CHAMPION DE CRESPIGNY, OBE, 8th and last *Baronet*.

DAUGHTER LIVING OF EIGHTH BARONET

FLEUR (Mount Pleasant Farm, Bexhill-on-Sea, Sussex), *b* 1937; resumed the surname of Champion de Crespigny by deed poll until remarriage: *m* 1st, 1967 (*m diss* 1975), John William Gordon-Harris; 2ndly, 1997, Michael Horley, and has issue living (by 1st *m*), William, *b* 1970, — Victoria Fleur, *b* 1972.

MALLABY-DEELEY (UK) 1922, of Mitcham Court, co Surrey (Extinct 1962)

Sir ANTHONY MEYRICK MALLABY-DEELEY, 3rd and last *Baronet*.

DAUGHTER DECEASED OF SECOND BARONET

Valerie Constance, *b* 1928: *m* 1947, Michael Peter Heaslett, who *d* 1998, and *d* 1993, leaving issue, Ingrid Ursula, *b* 1952: *m* 19—, Raymond Stevens, and has issue living, Patrick *b* 1981, Douglas *b* 1983, — Ilsa Kirsten, *b* 1954: *m* 19—, Keith Ferraro, who *d* 19—, — Helga Karen, *b* 1955: *m* 19—, Terence Price, — Sigrid Anna, *b* 1959: *m* 1980, Stephen John Cull, of Inglenook, Five Ashes, Mayfield, Sussex TN20 6HY, and has issue living, a son *b* 1990.

DE HOGHTON (E) 1611, of Hoghton Tower, Lancashire
(Name pronounced "de Horton")

In spite of wrong

Sir (RICHARD) BERNARD (CUTHBERT) DE HOGHTON, 14th *Baronet*; *b* 26 Jan 1945; *s* his half-brother, *Sir* (HENRY PHILIP) ANTHONY (MARY), 1978; *ed* Ampleforth, McGill Univ, Montreal (BA) and Birmingham Univ (MA): *m* 1974, Rosanna Stella Virginia, da of Terzo Buratti, of Florence, Italy, and has issue.

𝕬rms – Sable, three bars argent. 𝕮rest – A bull passant, argent, ears, tips of the horns, mane, hoofs, and points of tail, sable. 𝕾upporters – Two bulls argent.
Seat – Hoghton Tower, Hoghton, Preston, Lancashire PR5 0SH.
Town Residence – 22 St Maur Rd, SW6 4DP.

SON LIVING

THOMAS JAMES DANIEL ADAM, *b* 11 April 1980.

DAUGHTER LIVING

Elena Susannah Isabella, *b* 1976.

WIDOW LIVING OF TWELFTH BARONET

PHILOMENA, da of late Herbert Simmons, of Walton-le-Dale, Lancashire: *m* 1st, 1944, as his 2nd wife, Sir Cuthbert de Hoghton, 12th baronet, who *d* 1958; 2ndly, 1960, Richard Grahame Adams, JP, formerly of HM Colonial Admin Ser, N Nigeria, who *d* 1985. *Residence* – Dower House, Bourton on the Water, Cheltenham, Glos.

This baronetcy is 5th in precedence of the Roll of the Baronets, but as the 2nd, 3rd, and 4th creations are borne by Earls, it ranks immediately after the Premier baronetcy of Bacon. The property of Hoghton has been in the family since *temp* King Stephen. Members of the family were sheriffs of the county from the 13th century and knights of the shire representing Lancashire from the 14th century. Sir Richard de Hoghton held the office of Chief Steward 1399-1422. Following the Earls of Derby, they are the second oldest Freemen of Preston. The 1st baronet, Sir Richard Hoghton, MP for Lancs, entertained King James I for several days at Hoghton Tower. The 2nd baronet, Sir Gilbert, MP for Lancs, was Gentleman of the Bedchamber to King Charles I, and a Royalist leader. The 3rd and 4th baronets represented Lancs in Parliament, and the 5th, 6th and 7th baronets each sat as MP for Preston. The 8th baronet assumed the additional surname of Bold, and the 9th baronet resumed in 1862 by Roy licence the ancient surname of de Hoghton.

DE LA BERE (UK) 1953, of Crowborough, co Sussex

Sir CAMERON DE LA BERE, 2nd *Baronet; s* his father, *Sir* RUPERT 1978; *b* 12 Feb 1933; *ed* Tonbridge and abroad: *m* 1964, Clairemonde, only da of late Casimir Kaufmann, of 26 Avenue William Favre, Geneva, Switzerland, and has issue.

Arms – Argent on a fesse between three crescents sable a lizard of the field. **Crest** – Issuant from an ancient crown or, a plume of five ostrich feathers argent charged with a ladybird proper.
Residence – 1 Avenue Theodore Flournoy, 1207 Geneva, Switzerland.

DAUGHTER LIVING

Réjane, *b* 1965: *m* 19—, Michel Lacoste, and has issue living, Victoria, *b* 19—.

BROTHER LIVING

ADRIAN, *b* 17 Sept 1939.

SISTERS LIVING

Valerie, *b* 1923. —— Camilla (6 Quarry Hill, Sevenoaks, Kent), *b* 1926: *m* 1953 (*m diss* 1959), Louis Georges Bourcier, and has issue living, Andrew Charles, *b* 1954, —— Yolande (twin), *b* 1954.

Sir Rupert De la Bère, KCVO, 1st Bt, son of Reginald De la Bère, was Lord Mayor of London 1952-53, *m* 1919, Marguerite, who *d* 1969, da of Lt-Col Sir John Humphery; *d* 1978.

DE LA RUE (UK) 1898, of Cadogan Square, Chelsea, co London
(Name pronounced "Dellarue")

Sir ANDREW GEORGE ILAY DE LA RUE, 4th *Baronet; b* 3 Feb 1946; *s* his father, *Sir* ERIC VINCENT, 1989; *ed* Millfield: *m* 1984, Tessa Ann, elder da of David Dobson, of Stragglethorpe Grange, Lincoln, and has issue.

Arms – Or, three bars gules each charged with as many estoiles of the first, in chief an increscent and a decrescent of the second. **Crest** – Between two olive branches vert a cauldron gules, fired and issuant therefrom a snake nowed proper.
Residences – Stragglethorpe Grange, Brant Broughton, Lincs; 21 Atherton St, SW11.

SONS LIVING

EDWARD WALTER HENRY, *b* 25 Nov 1986. —— Harry William, *b* 1989.

BROTHER LIVING

John Vincent Francis, *b* 1953; *ed* Eton: *m* 1994, Barbara Catherine, only da of Joseph B. Sainton, of Sylvania, Ohio, USA. *Residence* – Longfield House, Rusper, Horsham, W Sussex RH12 4RB.

HALF-BROTHER LIVING

Seek the truth

Vincent St George, *b* 1965; *ed* Stowe.

WIDOW LIVING OF THIRD BARONET

CHRISTINE (*Christine, Lady de la Rue*), da of Kurt Schellin, MD, of Greenwich, Conn, USA: *m* 1964, as his 2nd wife, Sir Eric Vincent de la Rue, 3rd Bt, who *d* 1989. *Residence* – Ayton Castle, Eymouth, Berwickshire TD14 5RD.

COLLATERAL BRANCHES LIVING

Issue of late Ian Hector de la Rue, 3rd son of 2nd baronet, *b* 1910, *d* 1991: *m* 1936, Violet Bertha, who *d* 1983, da of Thomas Despard Bridges:—

Anthony St Vincent (Chichindwe, 322 Ard-na-Lea Close, Glen Lorne, Harare, Zimbabwe), *b* 1947; *ed* Peterhouse Sch, Zimbabwe: *m* 1st, 1971 (*m diss* 1985), Ann Wyndham, da of Frederic Roberts Blair, of Lloyds Neck, Long Island, NY; 2ndly, 1986, Merry, da of Lt-Col Sir Edward Hugh Dudley Thompson, MBE, TD, of Culland Hall, Brailsford, Derby, and has issue living (by 1st *m*) Thomas Edward, *b* 1973; *ed* Peterhouse Sch, Zimbabwe, and RMA Sandhurst, — Michael Alexander, *b* 1975; *ed* Peterhouse Sch, Zimbabwe, — Diana Alexandra, *b* 1982, — (by 2nd *m*) Justine Andrea, *b* 1987.

> Issue of late Stuart Andros de la Rue, 3rd son of 1st baronet, *b* 1883, *d* 1927: *m* 1912, Margaret Griselda (who *d* 1987, having *m* 2ndly, 1928, Air-Marshal Sir Bertine Entwisle Sutton, KBE, CB, DSO, MC, who *d* 1946), da of late Alexander Dundas Ogilvy Wedderburn, KC (*see* Ogilvy-Wedderburn, Bt, colls):—

Wedderburn Anthony, *b* 1914: *m* 1st, 1937, Jean Roberts; 2ndly, 1948, Marjorie Holland (MARSH), da of William Holland Harris.

Sir Thomas, 1st Bt, was many years Chm of Thomas de la Rue and Co, Limited.

de MONTMORENCY (I) 1631, of Knockagh, co Tipperary

Sir ARNOLD GEOFFROY DE MONTMORENCY, 19th *Baronet*; *b* 27 July 1908; *s* his cousin, *Sir* REGINALD D'ALTON LODGE, 1979; *ed* Westminster, and Peterhouse, Camb (LLB, MA); Bar Middle Temple 1932; 1939-45 War as Maj RASC: *m* 1949 (*m* annulled 1953) and re-married 1972, Nettie Hay, da of late William Anderson, of Morayshire.

Arms – Or, a cross gules, between four eaglets displayed azure. Crest – A peacock in his pride, proper.
Club – National Liberal.

DIEU AYDE

This baronetcy was granted to John Morres, of Knockagh, in 1631, and on the death of Sir Nicholas, 8th Bt, in 1796, the title devolved upon the 2nd Viscount Mountmorres. In 1815 the 3rd Viscount, and Lt-Col Reymond Hervey Morres, ancestor of the present baronet, resumed by Roy licence the surname of de Montmorency. In 1951, on the death of the 7th Viscount Mountmorres (also 7th Baron), the Viscountcy and the Barony became ext and the Baronetcy passed to his kinsman, Sir (Hervey) Angus de Montmorency, OBE, who *s* as 16th baronet. The 17th Baronet, Sir Miles, was a member of R Soc of British Artists, painter of portraits for National War Records.

DENNY (I) 1782, of Castle Moyle, Kerry

The harvest also shall be mine

Sturminster Newton, Dorset.

Sir ANTHONY CONINGHAM DE WALTHAM DENNY, 8th *Baronet*; *b* 22 April 1925; *s* his father, *Rev Sir* HENRY LYTTELTON LYSTER, 1953; *ed* Clayesmore, Anglo French Art Centre, and Regent St Polytechnic School of Architecture; FRSA, MCSD; a Designer, Partner in firm of Verity and Beverley, Architects and Designers; an Hereditary Free-man of Cork; 1943-45 War with RAF in Middle East: *m* 1949, Anne Catherine, elder da of late Samuel Beverley, FRIBA, and has issue.

Arms – Gules, a saltire argent between twelve cross-crosslets or. Crest – A cubit arm vested azure, turned up argent, holding in the hand proper five wheat-ears or. *Residence* – The Priest's House, Muchelney, Langport, Somerset TA10 0DQ.

SONS LIVING

PIERS ANTHONY DE WALTHAM, *b* 14 March 1954; *ed* King Alfred Sch, and Westfield Coll, Lond Univ: *m* 1987, Ella Jane, only da of Peter P. Huhne, of SW5, and has issue living, Matilda Ann, *b* 1988, — Isabel Margaret, *b* 1990. *Residence* – Gilletts Farm, James Lane, Yarcombe, Devon. —— Thomas Francis Coningham, *b* 1956; *ed* King Alfred Sch, and Edinburgh Coll of Art: *m* 1985, Benita Jane, yr da of late Sq-Ldr Simon Hugh Kevill-Davies, RAF (*see* Lees, Bt, *cr* 1897), and has issue living, Madeline Anne, *b* 1987. *Residence* – Lower Cross Cottage, Hinton St Mary,

ADOPTED DAUGHTER LIVING

Sophy Elinor Sisophanh, *b* 1974; *ed* Univ of West of England: *m* 1998, Harvey Layzell, son of Peter Layzell, and has issue living, Jemima Elizabeth, *b* 1998. *Residence* – The Yellow House, Pound Rd, Horton, Ilminster, Som TA19 9QU.

BROTHERS LIVING

Barry Francis Lyttelton, LVO (Tudor House, Broadwindsor, Dorset DT8 3QP), *b* 1928; *ed* Clayesmore, and RMA Sandhurst; Maj RA (ret); formerly in Queen's Royal Regt, and Cadet Indian Army; FCO 1962-89, Counsellor (ret); LVO, 1979; Commander Order of St Olav (Norway) 1981: *m* 1st, 1951 (*m diss* 1968), Mrs Gertrude Tamara Crofton, da of late Henry Carnet Jex, of Hong Kong; 2ndly, 1969, Anne Rosemary Jordon, da of Col James Frederick White, MC, late Warwicks Fus, of Claypit Hall, Foxearth, Suffolk, and has issue living (by 1st *m*), James Barry Lyster (9 Burlington Rd, Muswell Hill, N10 1NJ), *b* 1958: *m* 1979, Susan Elizabeth, da of Derek Scholfield, of Dummer, Hants, and has issue living, Thomas James Lyttleton *b* 1988, — Shelagh Joan Lyttelton (Honey), *b* 1959: *m* 1989, Paul Nigel Wickman, son of Guy Wickman, of Reigate, Surrey, and has issue living, Edward Guy Denny *b* 1991, Eleanor Katherine Denny *b* 1994, — (by 2nd *m*) Emma Harriet Lyttelton, *b* 1970. —— Edward Maurice FitzGerald (Robyn) (Unit 4B, 20/30 Wilds Rents, SE1 4QG), *b* 1930; *ed* Clayesmore, and Royal Coll of Art; ARCA 1957: *m* 1953 (*m diss* 1975), Anna Rose Frances, da of late Geoffrey Teasdale, of London; 2ndly, 1995, Marjorie May, da of George Abéla, of Cahors, France, and has issue living (by 1st *m*), Dominic Charles Fitzgerald (4 Lawrence Mansions, Lordship Place, SW3), *b* 1963, — Edward Drouet Coningham, *b* 1975, — Lucy Anna Dando (5 Malvern Buildings, Fairfield Park, Bath), *b* 1966; has issue living, Charles Hendrix David DENNY *b* 1984. —— Richard William Geoffrey (Foxcote Court, Moreton-in-Marsh, Glos GL56 0NJ), *b* 1940: *m* 1st, 1961 (*m diss* 1978), Andrée Suzanne Louise, el da of Marcel Louis Parrot, of 210 Rue de Rivoli, Paris; 2ndly, 1984, Linda May, da of Maximillian Magnun, of Calcutta, India, and formerly wife of William Jones, and has issue living (by 1st *m*), Lyster Richard Henry, *b* 1961: *m* 1990, Sheena Anderson, and has issue living, Thomas Lyster Anderson *b* 1988, Jessica Caroline Lucy *b* 1991, — Walter Victor Marcel (7 Willow Cottages, Kew, Surrey TW9 3AT), *b* 1963: *m* 1990, Lorna Caroline, elder da of Maurice Statham, of Aylesbury, Bucks, and has issue living, Archibald Walter Statham *b* 1997, Ottilie Rose Statham *b* 1995, — Giles Anthony William (92 Darwin Rd, W5), *b* 1964: *m* 1995, Anne Louise, yst da of Theo Charles Gallegos, of Ealing, W5, and has issue living, Hill Richard Charles *b* 1997, — Julius André Geoffrey (15 Clarence Rd, Kew, Surrey TW9 3NL), *b* 1966: *m* 1993, Elizabeth-Anne, only da of John Henry Smith, of Stockbridge, Hants.

COLLATERAL BRANCHES LIVING

Granddaughters of late Lt-Col Richard Denny, 7th son of Rev Henry Denny (infra):—
Issue of late Maj (Richard) Brougham Denny, *b* 1889, *d* 1967: *m* 1st, 1928 (*m diss* 1963), Sybil Nina, who *d* 1977, da of late Francis N. Evans-Freke; 2ndly, 1967, Edith Winifred, da of late G. F. Winstone, of Worcester:—
Diana Brougham, *b* 1930: *m* 1960, Ronald Herbert Macintosh, CEng, AMIME, MRINA, of 77 Oriel Av, Tawa, Wellington, NZ, and has two adopted das, Claire Diana *b* 1965: *m* 1st, 1985 (*m diss* 1988), Steven Charles Marshall; 2ndly, 1988, Peter John Ball, of 17 Lake Apex Drive, Gatton, Queensland, Australia, and has issue living (by 1st *m*), Kylie Deanna *b* 1987, (by 2nd *m*) Benjamin Peter *b* 1989, — Fiona Juliet, *b* 1966: *m* 1993, Nyoman Putra Abriawan, of Bali, Indonesia. —— Juliet Oldfield, *b* 1932: *m* 1952, Peter Walter Taylor, ARSM, PhD, FGS, of The Chipping Croft, Tetbury, Glos GL8 8EY, and has issue living, Christopher Richard de Courcy, *b* 1957, — Caroline Mary Louise, *b* 1954: *m* 1988, Douglas Wagstaff, MA, and has issue living, James Douglas *b* 1989, Adam *b* 1990, — Catherine Jane, *b* 1961: *m* 1988, Anthony Nicholas Dickinson, and has issue living, Piers Anthony Brougham *b* 1993.

Granddaughters of late Edmund Barry Denny, 9th son of late Rev Henry Denny, 3rd son of 3rd baronet:—
Issue of Henry Allen Maynard Denny, *b* 1887, *d* 19—: *m* 1st, 1926, Kathleen Mary, da of late W. W. Goddard, of Stroud, Gloucestershire; 2ndly, 1950, Elsi Margaret, da of late R. O. Williams, and widow of J. Ryall:—
(By 1st *m*) Norah Peta, *b* 1928: *m* 1949, Robert Addison King, and has issue living, Keith Allan (Banff, Alta) *b* 1951: *m* 1974, Heather Ann, da of late William Farquharson, — Kathy Diane *b* 1953, — Rachel Ann *b* 1955. —— Kathleen Wendy Elizabeth, *b* 1930: *m* 1st, 1952 (*m diss* 1963), James Palmer Lee; 2ndly, 1964, William Ernest Smith, and has issue living (by 1st *m*), Randall *b* 1953, — Teresa *b* 1955: *m* 1975, Michael Farup, of Salt Spring Island, BC and has issue living, Jodie Lee *b* 1975.

Issue of late Capt Thomas Hamilton Denny, MBE, Indian Army, *b* 1893, *d* 1959: *m* 1920, Muriel Mary, who *d* 1974, da of late Edward Doncaster, of Silk Willoughby, Sleaford:—
Pamela Diana, *b* 1924: *m* 1952 (*m diss* 1969), Anthony Miles Denny, and has issue living, Patrick Jonathan Hamilton, *b* 1956: *m* 1981, Bridget Anne Meneer, and has issue living, Samuel Patrick *b* 1988, Lucy Anne *b* 1982, Kate Joanna *b* 1985, — Caroline Peta, *b* 1955: *m* 1st, 1982 (*m diss* 1983), Errol Currie; 2ndly, 1986, Kevin Clive Arthur Hollyoak, and has issue living (by 2nd *m*), Rory Clive Anthony *b* 1987, Liam Cam *b* 1992. *Residence* – Daphne Cottage, 55 High Street, Aldeburgh, Suffolk IP15 5AU.

Grandson of late Arthur de Courcy MacGillycuddy Denny, 4th son of late Edmund Barry Denny (ante):—
Issue of late Maynard de Courcy Barry Denny, *b* 1927, *d* 1993: *m* 1966, Christine Mary, da of Walters S. Browne, of Ipswich:—
Anthony de Courcy Edmund, *b* 1973. *Residence* – Willow House, Lower St, Stratford St Mary, Colchester, Essex CO7 6JS.

Grandchildren of late Ven Anthony Denny, 4th son of 3rd baronet:—
Issue of late George Herbert Denny, *b* 1851, *d* 1937: *m* 1876, Ellen, who *d* 1937, da of N. Jarvis:—
Edward Jarvis, *b* 1879: *m* 1903, Clara Elizabeth, da of August Will, and has issue living, Ellen Elizabeth, *b* 19—, — Catharine Antoinette, *b* 19—. —— Anthony George, *b* 1882: *m* 1910, Mathilda Henrietta, da of C. Dargeloh. —— Catharine Magill: *m* 1900, Curtis L. Sleeper. *Residence* –

Granddaughters of late Edward Coningsby Denny (infra):—
Issue of late William Coningsby Denny, *b* 1867, *d* 1935: *m* 1892, Rose Elizabeth, who *d* 1947, da of late Joseph Ingram, of Wellington Square, Hastings:—
Marjorie Ethel, *b* 1896. *Residence* – Tralee, 54 Privett Rd, Alverstoke, Gosport, Hants.

Issue of late Charles Edward Denny, *b* 1875, *d* 1946: *m* 1902, Alice, who *d* 1965, da of Samuel Grantham Baker, of Brighton:—
Letitia Ivy Coningsby, *b* 1904: *m* 1940, Woolmore Stewart Duncan. *Residence* – Bowersbury, Bowers Heath, Harpenden, Herts. ——— Ethel Mildred Coningsby, *b* 1907: *m* 1933, Sydney Walter Stubbs, and has issue living, Brian Maurice Denny, *b* 1936, — Colin Anthony, *b* 1939, — Richard Ivan, *b* 1949. ——— Kathleen Mary Coningsby, *b* 1910: *m* 1936, Joseph Harry Smith, and has issue living, Peter Nigel Coningsby (19 Redding Drive, Amersham, Bucks), *b* 1948: *m* 1978, Susan Spriggs, and has issue living, Oliver James Coningsby *b* 1980, Victoria Clare Coningsby *b* 1982, — Kathleen Hazel Coningsby, *b* 1940: *m* 1964 (*m diss* 1979), Peter James Guile, and has issue living, Christopher James *b* 1968, Moyra Elizabeth *b* 1970, — Yvonne Coningsby, *b* 1944: *m* 1965, Stanley Ritter, of Tophams, Brays Lane, Hyde Heath, Bucks, and has issue living, Martin Neill *b* 1976, Michelle Clare *b* 1973. *Residence* – Inchkeith, 54 Swakeleys Drive, Ickenham, Middlesex. ——— Geraldine Coningsby, *b* 1917: *m* 1939, Stanley Robson Clarke, and has issue living, Barry Ian Charles, *b* 1946, — Diana Susan, *b* 1948. *Residence* – 44 Swakeleys Drive, Ickenham, Middlesex.

Grandsons of late William Denny, 5th son of 3rd baronet:—
Issue of late Edward Coningsby Denny *b* 1839, *d* 1888: *m* 1863, Louisa Mary, who *d* 1916, da of late Augustus Callaway, of Rogate, Sussex:—
Horace, *b* 1877: *m* 1904, Mabel, da of Adm Arthur de Bellin, late Roy Italian Navy, and has issue living, John, *b* 19—, — a da, *b* 19—, — a da, *b* 19—. *Residence* –

Issue of late Henry Arthur Denny, Lieut RFA, *b* 1841, *d* 1888: *m* 1870, Emma Florence, who *d* 1886, da of late A. Denny, JP of Rockfield, Tramore:—
Frederick Wootton, *b* 1881; formerly Lieut Duke of Edinburgh's (Wiltshire Regt): *m* 1913, Rose, da of Charles T. G. Bright, of Toronto, and widow of — Cramp, and has issue living, Shirley Geraldine, *b* 1915. *Residence* –

Granddaughter of late Lieut Alfred Edward Denny, RN, son of late William Denny (ante):—
Issue of late Major William Alfred Charles Denny, OBE, *b* 1871, *d* 1934: *m* 1st, 1896, Lucy Florence, who *d* 1931, only da of late Maj-Gen Herbert Coningham, of 32 Vernon Terrace, Brighton; 2ndly, 1933, Beatrice Mary Louisa, who *d* 1942, only child of late Alfred Boydell Golborne, of Chester, and widow of his cousin, Edmund Henry Denny:—
(By 1st *m*) Eileen Mary Diana, *b* 1903: *m* 1933, William Samuel Sandes Boxwell, who *d* 1961.

Sir Robert Denny, Knt, was MP for Cambridgeshire 1391-3, and Lieut of the Duke of Bedford, Constable of England, at the time of the siege of Rouen. His descendant, Sir Edmond Denny (son of William Denny, of Cheshunt — High Sheriff of Herts 1480), King's Remembrancer to Henry VII, and a Baron of the Exchequer, was father of Rt Hon Sir Anthony Denny, PC, MP, Chief Gentleman of the Privy Chamber and Groom of the Stole to Henry VIII, the only Gentleman who dared to inform the King of his approaching end, and received from him a pair of gloves (which still exists) worked with pearls; he was constituted an Executor of Henry VIII, and one of the Guardians of Edward VI. His grandson, Sir Edward Denny, was created Lord Denny de Waltham 1604, and Earl of Norwich 1626. The present family is descended from Sir Edward Denny, Knight Banneret, MP (a yr son of Rt Hon Sir Anthony Denny), who, being Governor of Kerry and Desmond, Gentleman of the Privy Chamber to Queen Elizabeth, and Com under Adm Howard, etc, received a grant of the Seignory of Dennyvale and Castlemore, co Kerry, with the Desmonds' chief castle of Tralee, in 1587, as a reward for his naval and military services. For successive generations the family provided representatives for Tralee and co Kerry in Parliament. Sir Barry, 2nd Bt, was about to be raised to the peerage when he was killed in a duel 1794. Sir Cecil Edward Denny, 6th Bt (sometime Archivist and Keeper of Records of Govt of Alberta, and historian of that Province), founded Calgary (Alberta). There is no such place as "Castle Moyle," which is an error in the patent of Baronetcy for Castle More, ie "the great castle" of Tralee. The Rev Sir Henry Lyttelton Lyster Denny, 7th Bt, was V of Winslow-cum-Shipton 1916-18, R of Horsted Keynes 1918-20, V of St Mark's, Myddelton Square, EC, and Fellow of Sion Coll 1920-25, R of Wickham 1925-30, R of Abinger, Surrey 1930-36, and R and V of Burwash 1938-52.

DENNY (UK) 1913, of Dumbarton, co Dunbarton

Brave and kind

Sir CHARLES ALISTAIR MAURICE DENNY, 4th *Baronet*; *b* 7 Oct 1950; *s* his father, *Sir* ALISTAIR MAURICE ARCHIBALD, 1995; *ed* Wellington Coll, and Edinburgh Univ: *m* 1981, Belinda Mary, yr da of James Patrick McDonald, of Dublin, and has issue.

Arms – Azure, three suns in their splendour in chief or, and in the honour point a martlet of the last for difference. Crest – A dexter hand erect, pointing with two fingers at a sun in his splendour, all proper.
Residence – East Winchet, Winchet Hill, Goudhurst, Kent TN17 1JX. *Club* – Royal and Ancient Golf.

SON LIVING

PATRICK CHARLES ALISTAIR, *b* 2 Jan 1985.

DAUGHTER LIVING

Georgina Mary, *b* 1989.

BROTHERS LIVING AND DECEASED

†Nigel Peter, *b* 1952; *ed* Wellington Coll; *d* 1977. —— Mark Richard Leslie, *b* 1955; *ed* Wellington Coll; MB BS (Lond) 1978: *m* 1983, Junemary, 2nd da of Robert Edward Jameson, of Durban, S Africa, and has issue living, James William Leslie, *b* 1986, — Michael John Leslie, *b* 1991, — Suzannah Caroline, *b* 1988. *Residence* – White Gables, Forest Green Rd, Fifield, Berks SL6 2NR.

UNCLE LIVING (*son of 2nd baronet*)

Graham Royse, *b* 1927; *ed* Marlborough, and King's Coll, Camb. *Residence* – Ash Cottage, Balfron Rd, Killearn, Glasgow G63 9NJ.

AUNTS LIVING (*daughters of 2nd baronet*)

Rosamund Margaret, *b* 1917: *m* 1941, Lieut Col John Malcolm Thorpe Churchill, DSO, MC, Seaforth Highlanders, who *d* 1996, and has issue living, Malcolm John Leslie (51 Gloucester Court, Kew Rd, Richmond, Surrey TW9 3EA), *b* 1942; *ed* Wellington Coll, and Woodberry Forest, Virginia, USA, — Rodney Alistair Gladstone (28 Nightingale Rd, Hampton, Middx TW12 3HX), *b* 1947; *ed* Wellington Coll: *m* 1st, 1973, Susan L. Dicker; 2ndly, 1993, Angela Gay Bickford, and has issue living (by 1st *m*), James Alistair Gladstone *b* 1977. *Residence* – Sunhill House, Mayford, near Woking, Surrey. —— Patricia Leslie, *b* 1931. *m* 1952, Thomas Dunlop Bruce Jones, MC, of House on the Hill, Dunblane, Perthshire (*see* Dunlop Bt, 1972-73 Edn), and has issue living, Veronica Margaret, *b* 1953, — Victoria Leslie, *b* 1956, — Claire Patricia, *b* 1958, — Juliet Mary, *b* 1966.

WIDOW LIVING OF THIRD BARONET

ELIZABETH HUNT (*Dowager Lady Denny*), da of Major Sir (Ernest) Guy Richard Lloyd, 1st Bt, DSO (*cr* 1960): *m* 1949, Sir Alistair Maurice Archibald Denny, 3rd Bt, who *d* 1995. *Residence* – Crombie Cottage, Abercrombie, Anstruther, Fife KY10 2DE.

The 1st baronet, Sir Archibald Denny, LLD (son of Peter Denny, of Helenslee, Dumbarton), was a Naval Architect and a Director of William Denny & Bros Ltd, shipbuilders and engineers, of Dumbarton. The 2nd baronet, Sir Maurice Edward Denny, KBE, was Pres of William Denny & Bros, Ltd, Chm of Air Registration Board, and Pres of Institute of Marine Engineers 1935-6, and of Junior Institution of Engineers 1943-4.

DERING (E) 1627, of Surrenden Dering, Kent (Extinct 1975)

Sir RUPERT ANTHONY YEA DERING, 12th and last *Baronet*.

DAUGHTER LIVING OF TWELFTH BARONET

Susan Helen, *b* 1941: *m* 1967, Henry John Fredman, and has issue living, Jenny Annabelle, *b* 1968.

WIDOW LIVING OF TWELFTH BARONET

BETTY BRIDGETT (*Lady Dering*) (Bellings, Midhurst, Sussex), only da of late Lt-Col Vere Powys Druce, of Rose Cottage, Charminster, Dorset: *m* 1940, Lt-Col Sir Rupert Anthony Yea Dering, 12th Bt, who *d* 1975, when the title became ext.

COLLATERAL BRANCH LIVING

Granddaughter of late Lt-Col Edgar William Wallace Dering, son of late Cholmeley Charles William Dering, 2nd son of 7th baronet:—
Issue of late Cdr Claud Lacy Yea Dering, DSO, RN, *b* 1885, *d* 1943: *m* 1915, Winifred, who *d* 1941, da of Edmund Gellibrand, of Petrograd:—
Enid Deborah Claud (11 Welbeck Court, Addison Bridge Place, W14), *b* 1922: *m* 1942 (*m diss* 1965), Robin Craig Guthrie, portrait painter, and has issue living, Linnet Marion, *b* 1946.

DES VŒUX (I) 1787, of Indiaville, Queen's County (Extinct 1944)

Lieut-Col Sir WILLIAM RICHARD DE BACQUENCOURT DES VŒUX, 9th and last *Baronet*; *ka* in Holland 1944.

DAUGHTERS LIVING OF NINTH BARONET

Mary Elizabeth, *b* 1940: *m* 1967, Jeremy John Aird, of Quarry Wood Cottage, Burghclere, Newbury, Berks, and has issue (*see* Aird, Bt, colls). —— (Patricia) Jane, *b* 1941: *m* 1965, Penrhyn Charles Benjamin Pockney, of West Court, Inkpen, Hungerford, Berks RG17 9DP, and has issue living, Richard Penrhyn, *b* 1968: *m* 1998, Antoinette Elizabeth, da of Anthony Arthur Vivian Sharp, — James Charles, *b* 1969. —— Dorothy Susan, *b* 1944: *m* 1973, Lt-Cdr John David Caldecott, RN, of Ladle Hill House, Old Burghclere, Newbury, Berks, and has issue living, Edward Randolph, *b* 1976, — Jane Cynthia, *b* 1974, — Laura Cicely, *b* 1978, — Alice Selina, *b* 1978 (twin).

DE TRAFFORD (UK) 1841, of Trafford Park, Lancashire

Sir DERMOT HUMPHREY DE TRAFFORD, VRD, 6th *Baronet*; *b* 19 Jan 1925; *s* his father, *Sir* RUDOLPH EDGAR FRANCIS, OBE, 1983; *ed* Harrow, and Ch Ch, Oxford (MA): *m* 1st, 1948 (*m diss* 1973), Patricia Mary, only da of late Francis Mycroft Beeley, of Long Crumples, nr Alton, Hants; 2ndly, 1974, Xandra Carandini, only da of Lt-Col Geoffrey Trollope Lee, and formerly wife of Roderick Walter, and has issue by 1st *m*.

𝕬rms – Argent, a griffin segreant gules. 𝕮rest – A thrasher proper, his hat and coat per pale argent and gules, sleeves counterchanged, breeches and stockings of the 2nd and 3rd, his flail of the 1st.
Residences – The Old Vicarage, Appleshaw, Hants SP11 9BH; 1 Roper's Orchard, SW3 5AX. *Clubs* – White's, Roy Ocean Racing.

SONS LIVING (By 1st marriage)

JOHN HUMPHREY (30 Norland Sq, W11 4PU; Royal Ocean Racing Club), *b* 12 Sept 1950; *ed* Ampleforth, and Bristol Univ (BSc): *m* 1975, Anne, da of Jacques Faure de Pebeyre, and has issue living, Alexander Humphrey, *b* 28 June 1978, — Isabel June, *b* 1980. —— Edmund Francis, *b* 1952; *ed* Worth, and Ch Ch, Oxford. —— Gerard Thomas Joseph (63 Eccleston Sq Mews, SW1), *b* 1968; *ed* Harrow, and Ch Ch, Oxford: *m* 1998, Susan, da of Ian Evans, of Johannesburg, S Africa.

DAUGHTERS LIVING (By 1st marriage)

Mary Annette (85 Peel St, W8), *b* 1949. —— Elizabeth Eugenie, *b* 1951: *m* 1975, John Augustin Langdon, of 50 Chepstow Rd, W2, and has issue living, Tobias Hector, *b* 1985, — Frederick George, *b* 1989. —— Patricia Clare, *b* 1955: *m* 1975, (Patrick) William Uvedale Corbett, and has issue living, Edmund Uvedale, *b* 1983, — Laura, *b* 1985. —— Victoria Mary, *b* 1958: *m* 1983, Andrew Roberts, and has issue living, Mark Lonsdale, *b* 1985, — Katherine, *b* 1987. —— (Cynthia) June Bernadette, *b* 1959: *m* 1990, Nicholas C. Kirkman, and has issue living, Christopher Chevalier, *b* 1991, — James Alexander, *b* 1994. —— (Antonia) Lucy Octavia, *b* 1966: *m* 1994, David Carotti, and has issue living, Thomas Raymond Barton, *b* 1997.

DAUGHTERS LIVING OF FOURTH BARONET

Mary (*Lady Bowes-Lyon*) (Beltingham House, Bardon Mill, Hexham, Northumberland), *b* 1920: *m* 1941, Maj-Gen Sir Francis James Cecil Bowes-Lyon, KCVO, CB, OBE, MC, who *d* 1977 (*see* E Strathmore, colls). —— Violet (*Lady Aitken*), *b* 1926: *m* 1951, as his 3rd wife, Group Capt Sir (John William) Maxwell Aitken, DSO, DFC, 2nd Bt (who *s* as 2nd Baron Beaverbrook 1964, but disclaimed this peerage that year), who *d* 1985. *Residence* – Mickleham Downs House, Dorking, Surrey. —— Catherine, *b* 1928: *m* 1952, Fulke Thomas Tyndall Walwyn, CVO, who *d* 1991, and has issue living, Jane, *b* 1957. *Residence* – Saxon House Stables, Lambourn, Berks.

COLLATERAL BRANCH LIVING

Grandchildren of late Charles Edmund de Trafford, 2nd son of 2nd baronet:—
Issue of late Capt Hubert Edmund Francis de Trafford, *b* 1893, *d* 1974: *m* 1927, Hon Cecilia, who *d* 1982, da of 1st Baron Strickland (ext), and 6th Count Della Catena (Maltese Nobility):—
Gerald Edmund Hubert (Villa Bologna, Attard, Malta GC), *b* 1929; *ed* McGill Univ (BA), and Oxford Univ; a Knt of Sovereign Mil Order of Malta: *m* 1971, (Helena Catherina) Charlotte, only da of Herman Sybrand Hallo, former Ambassador of the Netherlands, of 27 Verdala St George's Dragonara, Malta, and has issue living, Jasper Peter Paul Sybrand, *b* 1975, — Aloisia Cecilia Mary, *b* 1973. —— Anthony Charles Everard (Apricot Cottage, Upper Slaughter, Cheltenham, Gos GL54 2JQ), *b* 1935: *m* 1966, Gabrielle Frances, da of Maj Ronald Edward Boone, of Rockcliffe House, Upper Slaughter, Glos. —— †Hubert George Joseph, *b* 1937: *m* 1st, 1966 (*m diss* 1973), Christine Elizabeth, only da of Lt-Cdr Maurice Sydney Adams, RN (ret); 2ndly 1975, Mary Kate Willis (Ta Majsiet, Tal Balal, B'Kara, Malta), da of late Lt-Col Edward C. A. Willis Fleming, and *d* 1993, leaving issue (by 1st *m*), Rachel Samantha, *b* 1967: *m* 1991, Bengt G. Sjöberg, of Tjurgränd 4, 175 45 Järfalla, Stockholm, Sweden, and has issue living Rebecca Linnéa Christine *b* 1993, Matilda Emma Cecilia *b* 1995, — Martha Christine Joanna, *b* 1969, — (by 2nd *m*) John Oliver George, *b* 1976, — George Jonathon Augustus, *b* 1980, — Fleur Cecilia Kate, *b* 1978. —— Elizabeth Clare Hilda Melita (*Lady Turner*) (Compton, Lower Farm Rd, Effingham, Surrey), *b* 1932: *m* 1963, Adm Sir Arthur Francis Turner, KCB, DSC, who *d* 1991, and has issue living, Francis Christopher Neale, *b* 1966: *m* 1992 Rebecca Jane Thompson, and has issue living, Jack Francis George *b* 1995, — Michael Paul Charles, *b* 1969.

The knightly family of Trafford of Trafford, Lancs can be traced in the male line to the 12th century. Sir Thomas Joseph Trafford, 1st Bt in 1842 received a Roy licence to resume the original name of de Trafford. Sir Humphrey, 4th Bt owner and breeder of racehorses, and was a snr steward of the Jockey Club 1936 and 1942-53. Sir Rudolph, 5th Bt, was Chm Atlas Assurance and Philip Hill Higginson and Elliott-Automation.

DEVITT (UK) 1916, of Chelsea, co London

Sir JAMES HUGH THOMAS DEVITT, 3rd *Baronet*; *b* 18 Sept 1956; *s* his father, *Lt-Col Sir* THOMAS GORDON, 1995; *ed* Sherborne, and Corpus Christi Coll, Camb (MA); ARICS: *m* 1985, Susan Carol, elder da of Dr (Adrian) Michael Campbell Duffus, of Woodhouse Farm, Thelbridge, Credition, Devon, and has issue.

Arms – Per pale gules and azure a bascule argent, chained or, in chief a fountain. **Crest** – A merman azure, pointing with the index finger of the dexter hand and holding in the sinister hand a rudder gold.
Residence – The Old Rectory, Ford Lane, Alresford, Colchester, Essex C07 8AX.

SONS LIVING

JACK THOMAS MICHAEL, *b* 29 July 1988. —— William James Alexander, *b* 1990.

DAUGHTER LIVING

Gemma Florence, *b* 1987.

SISTER LIVING

Angela Susan, *b* 1954: *m* 1979, Iain Cardean Spottiswoode Morpeth, elder son of Sir Douglas Spottiswoode Morpeth, TD, of Shamley Green, Surrey, and has issue living, Richard Douglas Gordon, *b* 1985, — Duncan Hugh Sinclair, *b* 1987, — James Rutherford Thomas, *b* 1992, — Catherine Louise Nicholl, *b* 1990. *Residence* – 32 Alleyn Rd, Dulwich, SE21 8AL.

HALF-SISTERS LIVING (*daughters of 2nd baronet by 2nd marriage*)

Georgina Jane (*Hon Mrs Nigel G. Parker*), *b* 1937: *m* 1965, Hon Nigel Geoffrey Parker, and has issue (*see* E Morley). *Residence* – Combe Lane Farm, Wormley, Godalming, Surrey. —— Stephanie Gordon, *b* 1942: *m* 1966, Col (James Norman) Dudley Lucas, late The Royal Scots (The Royal Regt), and has issue living, Timothy James Stephen, *b* 1968; *ed* Wellington Coll; Capt late Scots Gds, — Chloe Henrietta, *b* 1967: *m* 1998, Adrian Mark Jones. *Residence* – Becketts, Chilmark, Salisbury, Wilts.

WIDOW LIVING OF SECOND BARONET

JANET LILIAN (*Janet, Lady Devitt*), only da of late Col Hugh Sidney Ellis, CBE, MC: *m* 1953, as his 3rd wife, Lt-Col Sir Thomas Gordon Devitt, 2nd Bt, who *d* 1995. *Residence* – 5 Rembrandt Close, Holbein Place, SW1W 8HS.

COLLATERAL BRANCHES LIVING

Grandchildren of late Howson Foulger Devitt (infra):—
Issue of late Howson Charles Devitt, OBE, late W/Cmdr RAF, *b* 1909, *d* 1996: *m* 1939, Elisabeth Carola (Gat-e-Whing, Andreas, I of Man), da of Edward George Fairholme, OBE, of Burke's Corner, Beaconsfield:—
Richard Howson (The Dower House, Nettlecombe, Williton, Som TA4 4HS), *b* 1940; *ed* Nautical Coll, Pangbourne, and Trin Hall, Camb (MA): *m* 1992, his cousin, Mrs Lucy Clare Hulme, yst da of Edward Michael Harrison (infra). —— Carola Waveney, *b* 1942: *m* 1962, Peter John Laidlaw Jenkins, of Kuala Lumpur, Malaysia, and of Pages, Shalford, Braintree, Essex, and has issue living, Mark Alan Laidlaw, *b* 1964, — Carola Rosemary, *b* 1965, — Tamsin Elisabeth, *b* 1970.

Issue of late W/Cmdr Peter Kenneth Devitt, RAF, *b* 1911, *d* 1997: *m* 1st, 1935 (*m diss* 1950), Eunice Stephanie (Forge Cottage, East Hill House, Liss, Hants GU33 7RR), yst da of late Sir Charles Sheriton Swan; 2ndly, 1950 (*m diss* 1953), Joan Elizabeth, da of late T. Forbes Robertson, of Santa Barbara, Calif, USA; 3rdly, 1953 (*m diss* 1965), his 1st wife, Eunice Stephanie (ante):—
(By 1st *m*) Jeremy Peter (2 Chelfham Barton Cottages, Chelfham, Barnstaple, N Devon EX31 4RP), *b* 1937; *ed* Sherborne; Cmdr RN (ret): *m* 1961, Elspeth, eldest da of Brig William Edward Guest, MBE, of The Old Coach House, Lizard, Cornwall, and has issue living, Mark Edward Peter, *b* 1962, — Simon Charles Guest, *b* 1964, — Nicholas Jeremy James, *b* 1968, — Timothy William Guy, *b* (twin) 1968: *m* 1996, Vanessa A., yst da of late Cranley Pickford, of Southsea, Hants. —— Lorna Stephanie, *b* 1942: *m* 1963, Geoffrey Glynn-Jones, of Leat House, Sowton Village, Exeter, Devon EX52 2AD, and has issue living, Timothy Patrick, *b* 1965, — Lavinia Mary, *b* 1969. —— Jacquetta Anne (10 Leconfield Av, Barnes, SW13 0LD), *b* 1946: *m* 1st, 1968 (*m diss* 1974), Christopher David Legge; 2ndly, 1976 (*m diss* 1987), Robert Patrick Pease, and has issue living (by 2nd *m*), Tanya Jacquetta, *b* 1977, — Sophie Claire, *b* 1980. —— Vivien Gay, *b* 1948.

Issue of late Howson Foulger Devitt, 2nd son of 1st baronet, *b* 1869, *d* 1949: *m* 1908, Winifred Lina, who *d* 1972, el da of late Richard Woollcombe, of Starmead, Wokingham, Berks:—
Ursula Helen, *b* 1912: *m* 1935, Maj Michael Alastair Spencer-Nairn, Fife and Forfar Yeo (TA) (*see* Spencer-Nairn, Bt). —— Sheila Winifred (twin), *b* 1912: *m* 1936, Edward Michael Harrison, who *d* 1993, and has issue living, Hugh Michael James (Ringcombe Farm, West Anstey, S Molton, Devon EX36 3NZ), *b* 1942: *m* 1st, 1968 (*m diss* 1974), Joanna Mary, da of late Col W. R. Healing, of Budleigh Salterton; 2ndly, 1974, Stephanie Christine, el da of the Rev Peter Haslewood Shaw, of Greatworth, Northants, and has issue living, (by 1st *m*) James Edward *b* 1969, (by 2nd *m*) Camilla Rose *b* 1975, Zoë Grace *b* 1977. — Juliet Mary, *b* 1937: *m* 1964, Tuckerman Moss, PhD, of 67 Alta Vista, Orinda, Ca, USA, and has issue living, Michael Duval *b* 1965, Jeremy Gilbert *b* 1968, Rebecca Alice (twin) *b* 1968, — Lucy Clare, *b* 1950: *m* 1st, 1971, Paul Robert Hulme; 2ndly, 1992, her cousin, Richard Howson Devitt (ante) and has issue living (by 1st *m*), Richard Jeremy *b* 1973, Emma Catherine *b* 1971.

Grandchildren of late Herbert Pye-Smith Devitt, MRCS, LRCP, 3rd son of 1st baronet:—
Issue of late Maj Philip Eyre Devitt, *b* 1907, *d* 1992: *m* 1947, Patricia Melicent (Whydown Lodge, Little Common, Bexhill-on-Sea, Sussex), eldest da of late Walter Edward Leslie, of Tarbert, co Kerry:—
Desmond Philip, *b* 1950: *ed* Sherborne. —— Ann Patricia, *b* 1954.

Issue of late (Herbert) Lionel Devitt, *b* 1910; *d* 1964: *m* 1st, 1939 (*m diss* 1948), (Myfanwy Rina) Doreen, da of late Alwyn H. Holman; 2ndly, 1949 (*m diss* 1954), Sheila Mary da of Edmond Ironside Bremner; 3rdly, 1954, Fleur Traherne Thomas (11B Bina Gdns, SW6):—
(By 1st *m*) Michael Wyn (Farmhill Manor, Braddan, I of Man), *b* 1943: *m* 1967, Susan Gundreda de Warrenne, only child of Walter Kingsley Brett, and has issue living, Roland, *b* 1972, — Madeleine, *b* 1969. —— Judith Anne Mary, *b* 1940: *m* 1963, Edward David Beresford Tebbs, and has issue living, Andrew, *b* 1971, — Lucy, *b* 1965, — Amanda, *b* 1967.

Issue of late John Desmond Devitt, MRCS, LRCP, *b* 1917, *d* 1973: *m* 1957, Pamela Ruth, da of late Leonard Bruce Foot, of Egbury, Hants:—
Timothy John Herbert, *b* 1958. —— Jonathan Stephen, *b* 1960: *m* 1992, Maria Soledad Fidalgo Suarez, and has issue living, Calum John, *b* 1993, — Elena, *b* 1995, — Ines, *b* 1998, — Lydia, *b* 1998. —— (Andrew) James (59 Hill Top Rd, Paddock, Huddersfield, W Yorks), *b* 1962.

Issue of late Philip Henry Devitt, yst son of 1st baronet (*cr* 1916), who was *cr* a *Baronet* 1931:—
See Devitt, Bt, *cr* 1931 (ext).

Sir Thomas Lane Devitt, 1st Bt (sometime senior partner in the firm of Devitt and Moore, and Pres of Chamber of Shipping of the United Kingdom 1890, and of Institute of Marine Engineers 1913-14), was one of the Managers of the Orient Line from its foundation, Pres of the Shipping Federation 1890 to 1923 (also Chm 1890-1914), Chm of Lloyd's Register of Shipping 1911-22, and Founder of the Nautical Coll, Pangbourne. His grandson, Lt-Col Sir Thomas Gordon Devitt, 2nd Bt, *b* 1902, was Senior Ptnr Devitt and Moore, sometime Chm National Service for Seafarers and a Gov Sherborne Sch; he *m* 1st, 1930 (*m diss* 1936), Joan Mary, da of late Charles Reginald Freemantle, of Hayes Barton, Pyrford, Surrey; 2ndly, 1937 (*m diss* 1953), Lydia Mary, who *d* (2 May) 1995, da of late Edward Milligen Beloe, of King's Lynn, Norfolk; 3rdly, 1953, Janet Lilian, only da of late Col Hugh Sidney Ellis, CBE, MC; *d* (23 Dec) 1995.

DEVITT (UK) 1931, of Pangbourne, Berks (Extinct 1947)

Sir PHILIP HENRY DEVITT, 1st and last *Baronet*.

DAUGHTERS LIVING OF FIRST BARONET

Theodora Joan, *b* 1919. —— Elizabeth Anne (*Lady Koelle*). *b* 1921: *m* 1948, as his 2nd wife, Vice-Adm Sir Harry Philpot Koelle, KCB, who *d* 1980, and has issue living, Victoria Anne, *b* 1949: *m* 1980, Andrew James Carter, and has issue living, Philip Harry *b* 1976, Jack Edward *b* 1981, Timothy Robert *b* 1985, — Philippa June, *b* 1951: *m* 1979, Hugo C. Woolley and has issue living, Giles Thomas *b* 1984, Emily Anne *b* 1981. *Residence* – Pippins, Long Burton, Sherborne, Dorset. —— Bridget Helen, *b* (twin) 1931: *m* 1952, Oliver Michael Robin Greenwood, who *d* 1992, late Capt Coldstream Guards, and has issue living, Simon Nelson, *b* 1954: *m* 1984, Sara A. Johnston, — Christopher Philip, *b* 1957: *m* 1988, Tara Simonis, — James William Dickon, *b* 1974, — Nicola Jane, *b* 1954: *m* 1979, Robert C. Atkinson. *Residence* – Tyn y Waen, Glasfryn, Corwen, Clwyd.

DEWEY (UK) 1917, of South Hill Wood, Bromley, Kent

The wise man is strong

Sir ANTHONY HUGH DEWEY, 3rd *Baronet*, el son of late Major Hugh Grahame Dewey, MC, el son of 2nd Baronet; *b* 31 July 1921; *s* his grandfather, *Rev Sir* STANLEY DAWS, 1948; *ed* Wellington Coll, and Roy Agric Coll Cirencester, is a JP for Somerset; European War 1940-45 as Capt RA and Major N Somerset Yeo: *m* 1949, Sylvia Jacqueline Rosamund, da of late John Ross MacMahon, MB, CM, of Branksome Manor, Bournemouth, and has issue.

𝕬rms – 1st and 4th per fesse sable and, or, three cinquefoils between two barrulets between three dragons' heads erased counterchanged, in each of their mouths a sword in bend proper, pommels and hilts of the second, *Dewey*; 2nd and 3rd sable, a griffin segreant ermine, armed or, the wings erminois, a bordure compony argent and gules, *Ballard*. 𝕮rest – A dragon's head erased sable, holding in the mouth, a sword in bend proper, pommel and hilt or, betwee two dragons' wings of the last, on each a bend of the first, charged with a cinquefoil of the third.
Residence – The Rag, Galhampton, Yeovil, Somerset BA22 7AH. *Club* – Army and Navy.

SONS LIVING

RUPERT GRAHAME, *b* 29 March 1953; solicitor: *m* 1978, Suzanne Rosemary, da of late Andrew Lusk, of Fordie, Comrie, Perthshire, and has issue living, Thomas Andrew, *b* 27 Jan 1982, — Oliver Nicholas, *b* 1984, — Laura Kate, *b* 1988. *Residence* – Church Farm House, Wellow, Bath BA2 8QS. —— Charles Ross, *b* 1960: *m* 19—, Melinda R., da of late Peter Marriott, and has issue living. Fabian Peter Christopher, *b* 1993, — Isobel Hope, *b* 1995. *Residence* – Manor Cottage, Egford, Frome, Som BA11 3JQ.

DAUGHTERS LIVING

Delia Mary, *b* 1951: *m* 1977, Nicholas John Wingfield-Digby, of Lanwades, Moulton, Newmarket, Suffolk CB8 8QS, 2nd son of late Rev Canon Stephen Basil Wingfield-Digby, MBE, of The Vicarage, Sherborne, Dorset, and has issue living, James Anthony, *b* 1988, — Emily Clare, *b* 1981, — Julia Mary, *b* 1985. —— Carola Jane, *b* 1955: *m* 1981, Robert Hiles Sutton, son of John Ormerod Sutton, of The Old Schoolhouse, Tichborne, Hants, and has issue living, Patrick William, *b* 1984, — Jonathan David Ormerod, *b* 1990, — Joanna Kate, *b* 1987. —— Angela Rosamund, *b* 1957: *m* 1992, Ivan Hicks, and has issue living, Miles Anthony, *b* 1992, — Alice Rosamund, *b* 1986, — Lydia Jane, *b* 1987.

COLLATERAL BRANCHES LIVING

Grandchildren of late Maj Hugh Grahame Dewey, MC, el son of 2nd baronet:—
Issue of late Maj Michael Grahame Dewey, *b* 1928, *d* 1973: *m* 1954, Anne Cecilia (Warden Grange, Chipping Warden, Banbury, Oxon), da of late Brig Edward Thomas Arthur George Boylan, CBE, DSO, MC (*see* O'Brien, Bt, 1980 Edn):—
Philippa Mary, *b* 1955: *m* 1980, Stephen William George Neel, of Langleys Farm, Charlton, Malmesbury, Wiltshire, and has issue living, George, *b* 1983, — Henry William, *b* 1988, — Jessica Anais, *b* 1985. —— Amanda Julia, *b* 1957: *m* 1978, Col Richard Neville Brayley Quicke, Light Dragoons, and has issue living, Edward James, *b* 1983, — Michael Charles, *b* 1985, — Thomas William, *b* 1987, — Jonathan Alexander, *b* 1992.

Issue of late Norman Strafford Dewey, MC, 2nd son of 2nd baronet, *b* 1896, *d* 1985: *m* 1925, Ursula Marguerite, who *d* 1994, da of late H.D.D. Barman, of Helensburgh:—
Thomas Norman (4 Beadon Rd, Bromley, Kent BR2 9AT), *b* 1926; *ed* Radley, Pembroke Coll, Camb (MA), and Brunel Univ (MTech); CEng; MIEE, MIMechE: *m* 1964, Janet Mary, da of late B.C. Baxter, of Enfield, Middlesex, and has issue living, Stephen Thomas, *b* 1965; *ed* Brighton Coll, and Sheffield Univ (B Eng, PhD): *m* 1992, Elizabeth Ann, da of J. Cartledge, of Sheffield, and has issue living, Adam Meredith *b* 1998, — Claire Margaret, *b* 1966; *ed* Bromley High Sch, and City of London Univ (BA): *m* 1994, Timothy Michael Corum, and has issue living, Miles Julius *b* 1998. ——— David Lewis (Happs Edge, 60 Box Lane, Bovingdon, Herts), *b* 1927; *ed* Radley, and Pembroke Coll, Camb (MA); PhD London 1953: *m* 1960, Jacqueline Anne, da of late L.F. Curtis, of Dartford, Kent, and has issue living, Nigel Lewis (6 Home Farm Court, Bovingdon, Herts), *b* 1967: *m* 1998, Annette, da of Colin Davis, of Kings Langley, Herts, and has issue living, Katherine Anne *b* 1998, — Fiona Jane, *b* 1961: *m* 1989, Andre Mook, of Douw van der Kraplaan 23, 2252 Bt Voorschoten, Netherlands, and has issue living, Christopher Benjamin *b* 1992, Emily Louise *b* 1994, — Helen Gay, *b* 1964: *m* 1988, Ross Andrew Heath, of 201 Peet Rd, Roleystone 6111, Perth, Australia, and has issue living, David Russell *b* 1993, James Michael *b* 1994. ——— Martin Ross (Terra Cotta, Llandevaud, nr Newport, NP6 2AE), *b* 1933; *ed* Radley: *m* 1964, Barbara, who *d* 1990, da of late David Sharp, of Wokingham, and has issue living, Ross Meredith (31 Mill Crescent, Southam, Warwicks CV33 0LL), *b* 1966: *m* 1st, 1994 (*m diss* 1998), Vita, da of G. Arena, of Ventimiglia di Sicilia; 2ndly, 1999, Emma Louise, da of J. Bousfield, of Stockton, Rugby. ——— Olive Rosemary, *b* 1931; BSc London 1955: *m* 1962, Peter Gordon Hiam Wilson, of Holywater House, Rembrandt Way, Bury St Edmunds, Suffolk IP33 2LR, and has had two children, Alan Richard Hiam, *b* 1964; *d* 1997, — Carol Tania, *b* 1966: *m* 1st, 1987 (*m diss* 1991), Adam Edward Grainger Simpson; 2ndly, 1994, Gary Bushnell.

Issue of late Thomas Lewis Dewey, 3rd son of 2nd baronet, *b* 1900, *d* 1951: *m* 1936, Josephine Mary Sadler (who *d* 1998, having *m* 2ndly, 1957, Andrew Mackenzie Ross, MD, DLO, of Cherry Tree Cottage, Nether Compton, Sherborne, Dorset), da of Joseph Sadler Stockton, of Whitely Woods, Sheffield:—
Rev Peter Lewis, *b* 1938; *ed* Lancing: *m* 1977, Hilary Elizabeth, da of late George Dudley Ricketts, and has issue living, Alexander Peter, *b* 1986, — Ana Maria Elizabeth, *b* 1985. *Residence* – St Laurence's Rectory, Newington Rd, Ramsgate, Kent CT11 0QT. ——— Jennifer Ann, *b* 1937: *m* 1966, Lt-Col David Younger, Queen's Own Hussars, of Ravenswood, Melrose, Roxburghshire, and has issue living, William Grahame Ralph, *b* 1970, — James David, *b* 1972, — Catherine Belinda, *b* 1967.

Issue of late Dr Theodore Stanley Dewey, 4th son of 2nd baronet, *b* 1902, *d* 1978: *m* 1929, Monica, who *d* 1996, da of Vincent Daniel, of Coppings, Leigh, Kent:—
Timothy Hugh (The Cottage, Kelston, Bath), *b* 1935: *ed* Ampleforth: *m* 1962, Margaret Mia, da of late Dr T. R. D. Aubrey, of Bitton, Glos, and has issue living, Adrian Charles (24 Ashburnham Rd, Tonbridge, Kent TN10 3DU), *b* 1963: *m* 1992, Jane Genevieve, da of Charles Patrick Byrne, of Honeysuckle, Scarborough Drive, Minster, I of Sheppey, Kent, and has issue living, Charles Theodore *b* 1996, — Annabel Mary, *b* 1965: *m* 1987, Peter Vernon Mosse, of 18 Park Rd, Lower Weston, Bath BA1 3EE, only son of late Richard Kemble Mosse, of Bromyard, Herefords, and has issue living, Jack Kemble *b* 1989, Lucy Kemble *b* 1992, Camilla Rose *b* 1995, — Laura Rose, *b* 1967, — Jessica Mia, *b* 1968. ——— Amanda Jane, *b* 1931: *m* 1st, 1956 (*m diss* 1966), John Robin Millner; 2ndly, 1966, Peter Michael Lloyd Wenham, who *d* 1992, of Gt Cozens, Fanhams Hall Rd, Ware, Herts SG12 7PU, and has issue living (by 1st *m*), Julian John (22 White Hart Lane, Barnes, SW13), *b* 1958; has issue living, Keely Samantha *b* 1986, — Piers Theodore (14 Meluca Crescent, Hornsey Heights, Sydney, NSW 2077, Australia), *b* 1960: *m* 1993, Andrea, da of Dennis Jones, and has issue living, Bede Havard *b* 1986, Jaiden *b* 1989, Cael Theodore *b* 1993, — Giles William (Flat 7, 8 Hatherley Rd, Kew) *b* 1961, — (by 2nd *m*), Susanna Jane, *b* 1964; has issue living, Fenella Amy *b* 1986, — Arabella Monica, *b* 1966: *m* 1992, Christopher Simpkin, of 33 Seymour Rd, Wimbledon SW19 5JL, and has issue living, Florence Elaine *b* 1994, Jessica Jenifer *b* 1996. ——— Caroline Mary, *b* 1938: *m* 1961, Julian Reginald Brinton Clist, MBE, of The Yard House, Gt Witley, Worcs WR6 6JS, and has issue living, Sophia Anne Brinton (6B Carlton Vale, Maida Vale, NW6 5EE), *b* 1963: *m* 1999, Jonathan M. Jackson, — Samantha Gëbrielle Brinton, *b* 1964: *m* 1992, Andrew M. Coates, of 46 Beechcroft Manor, Weybridge, Surrey KT13 9NZ, and has issue living, Alexander Luke Brinton *b* 1996, Matthew Dominic Brinton *b* 1998, — Imogen Cecilia Brinton, *b* 1969. ——— Corinne Rose, *b* (twin) 1938: *m* 1960, (Stanley) Keith Knowles, of 37 Castelnau, Barnes, SW13, and has issue living, Tobias Sebastian (7 Oldfield Rd, Acton, W4), *b* 1961, — Hugh Stanley Keith (149 Castelnau, Barnes, SW13), *b* 1962: *m* 1989, Georgina Anne, who *d* 1998, eldest da of Capt Anthony John Maxse, and has issue (*see* B Berkeley, colls), — Benedict Caradoc, *b* 1968: *m* 1998, Gillian Rona, only da of Hugh Fergus Kerr, of Perth, Australia, — Miranda Vivian, *b* 1964: *m* 1991, Philip James Thompson, of Carer Pujol 29, Alaro, Mallorca, and has issue living, William James Islwyn *b* 1999, Angelica Rose *b* 1993, Isabella Corinne *b* 1995.

Grandson of late Marshall Dewey, yr son of 1st baronet:—
Issue of late Sidney Maurice Dewey, *b* 1902, *d* 1968: *m* 1931, Dorothy Catherine Holt, who *d* 1968:—
Anthony Guy, *b* 1932; *ed* Repton: *m* 1968, Mrs Caroline Rose Hardie, da of late L. M. Hanbury-Bateman, and has issue living, Martin Guy, *b* 1969, — Nicholas George, *b* 1971.

Sir Thomas Charles Dewey, 1st Bt, was Pres of Prudential Assurance Co. The Rev Sir Stanley Daws Dewey, 2nd Bt, was Preb of Exeter Cathedral 1935-43, and High Sheriff of Devon 1945.

TENNYSON-d'EYNCOURT (UK) 1930, of Carter's Corner Farm, Parish of Herstmonceux, co Sussex

Sir MARK GERVAIS TENNYSON-D'EYNCOURT, 5th *Baronet*; *b* 12 March 1967; *s* his father, *Sir* GILES GERVAIS, 1989; *ed* Charterhouse, and Kingston Polytechnic (BA); fashion designer; Freeman City of London 1989.

Nothing rashly

Forward

Arms – Quarterly: 1st and 4th, azure, a fesse dancettée between ten billets, four and six or, *d'Eyncourt*; 2nd and 3rd, gules, three leopards' faces or, jessant-de-lis azure, over all a bend of the last, *Tennyson*. **Crests** – 1st,a lion passant guardant argent, on the head a crown of fleur-de-lis or, the dexter fore-paw supporting a shield charged with the arms of *d'Eyncourt*; 2nd, a dexter arm in armour, the hand in a gauntlet or, grasping a broken tilting spear, enfiled with a garland of laurel proper, *Tennyson*.

WIDOW LIVING OF SECOND BARONET

VINNIE LORRAINE (*Vinnie, Lady Tennyson-d'Eyncourt*) (Catalino Pueblo, 2556 Avenida Maria, Tucson, Arizona 85718, USA), da of late Andrew Pearson, of Minneapolis, USA, and widow of Robert J. O'Donnell: *m* 1964, as his 2nd wife, Sir (Eustace) Gervais Tennyson-d'Eyncourt, 2nd Bt, who *d* 1971.

WIDOW LIVING OF THIRD BARONET

NORAH (*Norah, Lady Tennyson-d'Eyncourt*), da of late Thomas Gill, of Sheffield, Yorks: *m* 1977, as his 3rd wife, Sir (John) Jeremy Eustace Tennyson-d'Eyncourt, 3rd Bt, who *d* 1988. *Residence* – Bayons House, Hinton St George, Somerset TA17 8RX.

WIDOW LIVING OF FOURTH BARONET

JUANITA (*Lady Tennyson d'Eyncourt*), da of late Fortunato Borromeo: *m* 1966, Sir Giles Gervais Tennyson d'Eyncourt, 4th Bt, who *d* 1989. *Residence* – 22 Novello St, Parson's Green, SW6 4JB.

The 1st baronet, Sir Eustace Henry William Tennyson-d'Eyncourt, KCB, FRS, DSc, LLD (son of late Louis Charles Tennyson-d'Eyncourt, of Bayons Manor, Market Rasen), was a Naval Architect, Director of Naval Construction, Admiralty, and Principal Technical Adviser 1912-23, and Head of the Landships Committee which designed and produced the first tanks.

Dick-Cunyngham, see Cunyngham.

Dick-Lauder, see Lauder.

DILKE (UK) 1862, of Sloane Street, Chelsea

Leo inimicis amicis
columba

Sir CHARLES JOHN WENTWORTH DILKE, 6th *Baronet*; *b* 21 Feb 1937; *s* his father, *Sir* JOHN FISHER WENTWORTH, 1998; *ed* Winchester, and King's Coll, Camb (BA); Provost 1981-87, London Oratory, SW7.

𝕬rms – Quarterly of nine: 1st, gules, a lion rampant per pale argent and or; 2nd, argent, a mullet gules; 3rd, sable a chevron between three leopards' faces or; 4th, argent, a cross grady throughout sable; 5th, paly or six argent and gules a bend counterchanged; 6th, gules, on a bend argent three escallops azure; 7th, paly of six argent and sable on a bend gules, three mullets argent; 8th, quarterly: or and gules on a bend sable, between two fretts or, three escallops of the first; 9th, ermine two chevrons sable. 𝕮rest – A dove proper. *Residence* – The Oratory, SW7 2RP.

BROTHER LIVING

TIMOTHY FISHER WENTWORTH, *b* 1 Aug 1938; *ed* Winchester, and New Coll, Oxford (MA); BM, BCh; FRCP London; *m* 1965, his cousin, Caroline Sophia, da of late Christopher Wentworth Dilke (infra), and has issue living, Felix Wentworth, *b* 1967, — Rosemary Frances, *b* 1970. *Residence* – 15 Wemyss Rd, SE3 0TG.

MOTHER LIVING

Sheila, only da of late Sir William Seeds, KCMG: *m* 1st, 1934 (*m diss* 1949), as his 1st wife, Sir John Fisher Wentworth Dilke, 5th Bt, who *d* 1998; 2ndly, 1949 (*m diss* 19—), John C. Phipps; has assumed the surname of KNAPP. *Residence* – 48 Peace St, Denmark 6333, W Australia.

WIDOW LIVING OF FIFTH BARONET

IRIS EVELYN (*Lady Dilke*), only da of late Ernest Clark: *m* 1951, as his 2nd wife, Sir John Fisher Wentworth Dilke, 5th Bt, who *d* 1998. *Residence* – Ludpits, Etchingham, E Sussex TN19 7DB.

COLLATERAL BRANCHES LIVING

Issue of late Michael Clifford Wentworth Dilke, 2nd son of 4th baronet, *b* 1909, *d* 1944: *m* 1940, Rosemary Blanche, who *d* 1974, da of Capt Sir Thomas Herbert Cochrane Troubridge, 4th Bt, and widow of Capt Roderick Kilgour Mackenzie, yr, of Kincraig:—
Lucilla Rose *b* 1941: *m* 1970, Gareth Ulric van den Bogaerde, of 42 Bennerley Rd, Wandsworth, SW11, and has issue living, Ulric Michael Amadeus Landrover, *b* 1970, — Alice Rosemary Patience Lucilla, *b* 1973.

Issue of late Christopher Wentworth Dilke, novelist, 3rd son of 4th baronet, *b* 1913, *d* 1987: *m* 1939, Alice Mary (Valehouse Farm, Whitchurch Canonicorum, Bridport, Dorset DT6 6RP), da of late Hon James William Best (*see* B Wynford, colls):—
Fisher William Wentworth (142 Iffley Rd, W6), *b* 1948; *ed* Westminster, Sussex Univ and Camb Univ (PhD): *m* 1985, Diana Madelaine, da of Dr Raymond John Adie, and has issue living, Thomas Wentworth, *b* 1991, — Stella Maye, *b* 1987, — Athene Elizabeth, *b* 1988. —— Caroline Sophia, *b* 1940: *m* 1965, her cousin, Timothy Fisher Wentworth Dilke, and has issue (ante). —— Annabel Mary (23 Lynette Av, SW4), *b* 1942: *m* 1975, Georgi Markov, who was assassinated 1978, and has issue living, Alexandra Raina, *b* 1976. —— Lucy Catherine, *b* 1952; *ed* York Univ (MA): *m* 1975, Anthony Charles Pinney (*see* B Norton, 1960 Edn), of Egremont Farm, Payhembury, Devon, and has issue living, Samuel Charles, *b* 1980, Nathaniel Henry *b* 1994, — Katharine Elizabeth, *b* 1979.

The 1st baronet took a prominent part in the International Exhibitions of 1851 and 1862, and sat as MP for Wallingford (*L*) 1865-8. The 2nd baronet, Rt Hon Sir Charles Wentworth Dilke, was Under-Sec for Foreign Affairs 1880-82, and Pres of Local Govt Board 1882-5, and sat as MP for Chelsea (*L*) 1868-86, and for Forest of Dean Div of Gloucestershire 1892-1911.

DILLON (UK) 1801, of Lismullen, Meath (Extinct 1982)

WIDOW LIVING OF EIGHTH BARONET

(ELIA) SYNOLDA AUGUSTA (*Lady Dillon*), only da of late Cecil Butler Cholmondeley Clarke, of The Hermitage, Holycross, co Tipperary (*see* B Hemphill, 1925 Edn): *m* 1947, Sir Robert William Charlier Dillon, 8th Bt (a Baron of the Holy Roman Empire, *cr* 1782), who *d* 1982, when the title became *ext*.

Dillwyn-Venables-Llewelyn, see Llewelyn.

DIXIE (E) 1660, of Market Bosworth, Leicestershire (Dormant or Extinct 1975)

Sir (ALEXANDER ARCHIBALD DOUGLAS) WOLSTAN DIXIE, 13th *Baronet, d* 1975. A possible heir to the baronetcy may exist among the descendants (if any) of Capt Richard Thomas Dixie, brother of the 6th, 7th and 9th baronets, or of Beaumont or John Dixie, brothers of the 3rd baronet, or of Henry Dixie, yr son of the 1st baronet.

DAUGHTERS LIVING OF THIRTEENTH BARONET (*By 2nd marriage*)

Eleanor Barbara Lindsay (Bosworth Park, Leics), *b* 1952: *m* 1983 (*m diss* 1986), Scott M. Mellor, of USA; has issue living (by William H. Wood, of USA), Emma Louise Olivia DIXIE-WOOD, *b* 1988. —— Caroline Mary Jane, *b* 1960: *m* 1989, Andrew Davies; has issue living, Charles Wolstan DAVIES, *b* 1983; legally adopted by his stepfather 1990, — Abigail Charlotte, *b* 1990, — Polly Elizabeth, *b* 1992. *Residence* – Shellbrook House Farm, Ashby de la Zouche, Leics.

WIDOW LIVING OF THIRTEENTH BARONET

DOROTHY PENELOPE (*Lady Dixie*) (Market Bosworth, Leics), da of E. King-Kirkman: *m* 1950, as his 2nd wife, Sir (Alexander Archibald Douglas) Wolstan Dixie, 13th Bt, who *d* 1975, when the title became dormant or ext.

This family was settled at Bosworth *temp* Queen Elizabeth I. Sir Wolstan Dixie, 1st baronet, received his warrant of baronetcy from Charles I, for his activity and zealousness in the royal cause, however, through the confusion of the times, the patent was not taken out until 1660, in which year Sir Wolstan was Sheriff of Leicestershire.

DIXON (UK) 1919, of Astle, Chelford, co Palatine of Chester

Manners maketh man

Sir JONATHAN MARK DIXON, 4th *Baronet*, son of late Capt Nigel Dixon, OBE, RN, yr son of 2nd baronet; *b* 1 Sept 1949; *s* his uncle, *Capt Sir* JOHN GEORGE, 1990; *ed* Winchester, and University Coll, Oxford (BA 1972, MA 1987): *m* 1978, Patricia Margaret, da of James Baird Smith, and has issue.

Arms – Gules, a fleur-de-lis or, on a chief argent three ermine spots sable. Crest – A demi-lion rampant gules-holding between the paws a fylfot or. *Residence* – 19 Clyde Rd, Redland, Bristol BS6 6RJ.

SONS LIVING

MARK EDWARD, *b* 29 June 1982. —— Timothy Nigel, *b* 1987.

DAUGHTER LIVING

Katherine Anne, *b* 1980.

DAUGHTER LIVING OF THIRD BARONET

Mary Jane, *b* 1951: *m* 1976, Olav Alexander Ek, and has issue living, Christian Alexander, *b* 1982, — Stefan Alexander, *b* 1985. *Residence* – Blijdensteinlaan 11, 1217 PD, Hilversum, The Netherlands.

AUNT LIVING (*daughter of second baronet*)

Beryl, *b* 1916. *Residence* – Marley House, Winfrith Newburgh, nr Dorchester, Dorset.

MOTHER LIVING

Margaret Josephine, da of late Maurice John Collett, of Aston Lodge, Malvern Wells, Worcs: *m* 1948, Capt Nigel Dixon, RN, who *d* 1978. *Residence* – 3 Abbots Quay, Wareham, Dorset.

Sir George Dixon, 1st Bt, was High Sheriff for Cheshire 1881.

DODDS (UK) 1964, of West Chiltington, co Sussex.

Sir RALPH JORDAN DODDS, 2nd *Baronet*; *b* 25 March 1928, *s* his father, *Sir* (EDWARD) CHARLES, MVO, 1973; *ed* Winchester, and RMA Sandhurst; late Capt 13/18th Hussars; an Underwriting Member of Lloyd's since 1964: *m* 1954, Marion, da of late Sir Daniel Thomas Davies, KCVO, and has issue.

Arms – Azure issuant from a chief argent and out of a sunburst a dexter hand proper between two crabs heads downward argent each transfixed by a sword or on the chief a steer's head and caboshed sable armed gold between two capons proper. Crest – A demi woman affronty proper vested azure holding an open book proper inscribed with the chemical formula for stilboestrol sable. *Residence* – 49 Sussex Square, W.2. *Clubs* – Cavalry and Guards', and Hurlingham.

DAUGHTERS LIVING

Caroline, *b* 1956: *m* 1st, 1981, James George Ball; 2ndly, 1987, David Pegg. —— Arabella, *b* 1961: *m* 1982, Maj Philip Henry Marmion Dymoke, WG (*see* E Westmorland, colls), and has issue (see that title).

The 1st baronet, Sir (Edward) Charles Dodds, MVO, son of Ralph Edward Dodds, of Darlington, and London, was Pres Roy Coll of Physicians 1962-66.

SMITH-DODSWORTH (GB) 1784, of Newland Park and Thornton Watlass, Yorkshire

Sir JOHN CHRISTOPHER SMITH-DODSWORTH, 8th *Baronet*; *b* 4 March 1935; *s* his father, *Sir* CLAUDE MATTHEW, 1940; *ed* Ampleforth: *m* 1st, 1961 (*m diss* 1971), Margaret Anne, da of Alfred Jones, of Pludds, Gloucestershire; 2ndly, 1972, Margaret Theresa, who *d* 1990, da of Henry Grey, of Auckland, NZ; 3rdly, 1991, Lolita, da of Romeo Pulante, of Laur, Nueva Ecija, Philippines, and has issue by 1st, 2nd and 3rd *m*.

Arms – Quarterly: 1st and 4th, argent, a bend engrailed sable between three annulets gules, *Dodsworth*; 2nd and 3rd, per saltire argent and sable two trefoils slipped in pale gules, *Smith*. **Crest** – 1st, a dexter cubic arm in chain mail or, the hand proper grasping a broken tilting spear or, embrued gules, *Dodsworth*; 2nd, out of a ducal coronet or, a boar's head couped at the neck azure, crined and tusked or, *Smith*.
Seat – Thornton Watlass Hall, Ripon, Yorks. *Residence* – Driving Creek, Coromandel, NZ.

Pro lege senatu que rege
*Govern in accordance
with law and parliament*

SONS LIVING (*By 1st marriage*)

DAVID JOHN, *b* 23 Oct 1963; *ed* Ampleforth: *m* 1996, Elizabeth Anne, da of Gerald Michael Brady, of Bordercot, Baldersby, N Yorks. *Residence* – Thornton Watlass Hall, Ripon, Yorks.

(*By 2nd marriage*)

Daniel Leui'i, *b* 1974.

(*By 3rd marriage*)

John Joseph, *b* 1995.

DAUGHTERS LIVING (*By 1st marriage*)

Cyrilla Denise, *b* 1962.

(*By 3rd marriage*)

Joanna Marie, *b* 1993.

SISTERS LIVING

Mary Cyrilla, *b* 1933: *m* 1978 (*m diss* 1993), Gresham Clacy, of Arizona, USA. —— Julia Agnes, *b* 1938: *m* 1963, Brian Maccelari, of Johannesburg, S Africa, and has issue living, Douglas Charles Dodsworth, *b* 1965, — Jeremy Christopher Dodsworth (twin), *b* 1965, — Mary Frances Dodsworth, *b* 1963, — Angela Josephine Dodsworth, *b* 1969.

The 1st baronet, Sir John Silvester Smith (son of John Smith, of Newland Hall, Yorkshire), married the sister and heiress of Frederick Dodsworth, of Thornton Watlass, whose surname their children assumed. Thomas Dodsworth, of Dodworth, W Riding, co York, Receiver to Henry, 3rd Lord Fitzhugh, KG, acquired the Thornton Watlass estate in 1415 by marriage with Agnes, da and heiress of Hugh Thoresby, Ch Capt of Richmondshire, and niece of John Thoresby, Cardinal St Praxis, Archbishop of York, and Chancellor of England, who built the Choir of York Cathedral. Of this family was Sir Edward Dodsworth, Comy-Gen to the Army of the Parliament, and Roger Dodsworth, the famous Yorkshire antiquary. Besides the families of Silvester, Dodsworth and Thoresby the Smiths of Newland represent Howarth of Howarth, co Lancashire, founded by Osbert Howarth, Master of the Buckhounds to Henry II, and Blayney, Barons Blayney, of Monaghan, which peerage *cr* 1621, became extinct in 1874. This family is lineally descended from Lionel, Duke of Clarence, third son of Edward III, through Mortimer, Percy, Clifford, Conyers, D'Arcy, Stapylton and Dodsworth. Also, from Elizabeth, yst da of King Edward I and Eleanor of Castile, through de Bohun, Butler, Talbot, Bowes and Hutton.

DOMVILLE (UK) 1814, of St Albans, Hertfordshire (Extinct 1981)

Lieut-Com Sir (Gerald) Guy Domville, RN, 7th and last *Baronet*; *d* 1981.

DAUGHTERS LIVING OF SIXTH BARONET

Anne Juliet, *b* 1923; sometime Section Officer WAAF: *m* 1943 (*m diss* 1959), Walter Siner, 1st Lieut USA Air Force, and has issue living, Guy Domville, *b* 1947, — Anne Catherine, *b* 1945. *Residence* – The Bothy, Compton, near Guildford, Surrey. ——— Rosemary Gervaise, *b* 1924: *m* 1955 (*m diss* 1979), Rev Wolfgang Müller, and has issue living, Harald Martin Domville, *b* 1956, — Mark Bernhard Domville, *b* (twin) 1956, — Steven Rufus Domville, *b* 1959.

Don-Wauchope, see Wauchope.

DORMAN (UK) 1923, of Nunthorpe, co York

Valour in difficulties

Sir PHILIP HENRY KEPPEL DORMAN, 4th *Baronet*, only son of late Richard Dorman, 2nd but only surviving son of late Arthur John Dorman, yst son of 1st baronet; *b* 19 May 1954; *s* his cousin, *Lt-Col Sir* CHARLES GEOFFREY, MC, 1996; *ed* Marlborough, and St Andrews Univ; Tax Accountant; Life Protector Dorman Museum, Middlesbrough: *m* 1st, 1982 (*m diss* 1992), Myriam Jeanne Georgette Bay; 2ndly, 1996, Sheena Alexandra Faro, and has issue by 1st *m*.

Arms – Argent, two bars azure, each charged with as many roses of the field, barbed and seeded proper, over all a lozenge sable charged with a lion's head erased or. **Crest** – Upon a rock proper, a lion's paw erased sable, grasping a spear in bend sinister proper.
Residence – Belmont House, St George's Lane, Hurstpierpoint, W Sussex BN6 9QX. *Club* – MCC.

DAUGHTER LIVING (*By 1st marriage*)

Megan Bay Keppel, *b* 1984.

SISTER LIVING

Jane Elizabeth Keppel, *b* 1950; MB BS, LRCP, MRCS, DRCOG: *m* 1977, Michael John Orr, and has issue living, Katherine Jane Keppel, *b* 1981, — Mary Elizabeth Keppel, *b* 1983, — Lucy Caroline Keppel, *b* 1984. *Residence* – Selhurst, 119 Gordon Rd, Camberley, Surrey GU15 2JQ.

DAUGHTER LIVING OF THIRD BARONET

Eve Constance, *b* 1962; has issue living (by Stephen John Dredge), Kean Dorman DREDGE, *b* 1989, — (by Stephen Richards), Patrick Dorman RICHARDS, *b* 1996. *Residence* – La Plenelière, St Pierre du Chemin, 85120 La Chataigneraie, Vendée, France.

MOTHER LIVING

(Lilian) Diana Keppel, da of late Dr Henry Edward Barrett, of 33 Holland Park, W11 (*see* E Albemarle, colls, 1916 Edn): *m* 1947, Richard Dorman, late Capt Green Howards, who *d* 1976. *Residence* – 14 Fitzjohn Court, Hassocks, W Sussex BN6 8QP.

The 1st baronet, Sir Arthur John Dorman, KBE, was Founder and Chm of Dorman, Long & Co Ltd, of Middlesbrough. The 2nd, Sir Bedford Lockwood Dorman, CBE, was Dep Chm of N Riding of Yorkshire Quarter Sessions, and Chm of N Riding of Yorkshire War Agricultural Executive Committee.

Doughty-Tichborne, see Tichborne.

DOUGLAS (UK) 1831, of Glenbervie, Kincardine

Sir SHOLTO COURTENAY MACKENZIE DOUGLAS, MC, 5th and last *Baronet*: *d* 1986 (his name never having appeared on the Official Roll of Baronets).

DAUGHTERS LIVING OF FIFTH BARONET

Jean Mackenzie, *b* 1930: *m* 1956 (*m diss* 1968), Capt Brian Joseph Craig, late R Signals, and has issue living, Alastair James Mackenzie, *b* 1960, — Duncan Quinnell Mackenzie *b* 1963. *Residence* – 18 Portland Av, Hove, Sussex BN3 5NG. —— Lorna Inga Mackenzie, *b* 1932: *m* 1st, 1955 (*m diss* 1972), James Neil Maclay; 2ndly, 1973, Capt John Edward Homewood, of Trees, Higher Broad Oak Rd, West Hill, Devon EX11 1XJ, and has issue living (by 1st *m*), Mary Christine, *b* 1955.

DOYLE (UK) 1828 (Extinct 1987)

Sir JOHN FRANCIS REGINALD WILLIAM HASTINGS DOYLE, 5th and last *Baronet*; *d* 1987.

DAUGHTER LIVING OF FIFTH BARONET

Sylvia Yolande, *b* 1948. *Residence* – Burnt House Cottage, Bargains Lane, Little Markle, Ledbury, Hereford and Worcester.

D'OYLY (E) 1663, of Shottisham, Norfolk

Do no ill, quoth Doyle

Sir NIGEL HADLEY MILLER D'OYLY, *b* 6 July 1914; *s* his half-brother, *Sir* JOHN ROCHFORT, 1986; *ed* Radley, and RMC Sandhurst; formerly Maj R Scots; served 1939-45 War in Hong Kong, France, War Office: *m* 1939, Dolores, who *d* 1971, da of Robert H. Gregory, of New Lodge, Crowhurst, Sussex, and has issue.

𝕬rms – Gules, three bucks' heads cabossed argent. 𝕮rest – Out of a ducal coronet or, two wings, erect sable bezantée, between which and resting on the strawberry leaf of the coronet an estoile of six points argent. *Residence* – New Lodge, Crowhurst, nr Battle, E Sussex TN33 9AB.

SON LIVING

HADLEY GREGORY, *b* 29 May 1956; *ed* Milton Abbey: *m* 1st, 1978 (*m diss* 1982), Margaret Mary Dent; 2ndly, 1991, Annette Frances Elizabeth, yst da of Maj Michael White, of Farnham Royal, Bucks, and has issue living (by 2nd *m*), India Dolores, *b* 1992. *Residence* – Flat B, 37 New North Rd, Islington, N1 6JB.

DAUGHTERS LIVING

Carol Dolores, *b* 1942: *m* 1st, 1961 (*m diss* 1966), Robert Macvarish; 2ndly, 1968, Charles Pearce, and has issue living (by 1st *m*), Simon, *b* 1962, — Robyn, *b* 1964, — (by 2nd *m*) Carl, *b* 1970. *Residence* – New Lodge, Crowhurst, nr Battle, Sussex. —— Sherry Angela (Woodcote, Crowhurst, nr Battle, Sussex), *b* 1946: *m* 1st, 1969 (*m diss* 1981), Charles Coxsedge; 2ndly, 19—, R..... Mumford, and has issue living (by 1st *m*), Benjamin John, *b* 1975, — Hannah Ruth, *b* 1974.

DAUGHTERS LIVING OF THIRTEENTH BARONET

Jill Rochfort, *b* 1931: *m* 1952, George Creighton, of 31 Jalan Kampong Chantek, Singapore, 588612, and has issue living, Glen John, *b* 1953: *m* 1976 (*m diss* 1990), Catherine Heffernan and has issue living, Chay George *b* 1982, Keir James (twin) *b* 1982, Maxine Leah *b* 1970, — Ian Robert, *b* 1960: *m* 1988 (*m diss* 1991), Alexandra Mary Poxon, — Linden Gay, *b* 1954: *m* 1974, Rolf Evans, and has issue living, Scott Jamie *b* 1977, Jacey Samantha *b* 1979. —— Ann Hastings, *b* 1936: *m* 1959, Thomas Hepburn James, of Lambs Farm, Tanyard Lane, Danehill, East Sussex, RH17 7JN, and has issue living, Shona Ann, *b* 1960: *m* 1986 (*m diss* 1994), Simon James Robert Thomas, — Karen Hepburn, *b* 1964: *m* 1987 (*m diss* 1997), David Leslie Ashby, — Tiffany Carterette, *b* 1965: *m* 1991, Shaun Dudley Sizen.

COLLATERAL BRANCH LIVING

        Issue of late Edward Halliday D'Oyly, son of 10th baronet, *b* 1865, *d* 1957: *m* 1891, Laura, who *d* 19—,
        da of Herbert George Yatman, formerly of Studley, Wimborne Rd, Bournemouth:—
Mary Edith, *b* 1892. —— Mildred Dorothea, *b* 1893.

Robert d'Ouilly, who came over with William the Conqueror, and was Baron of Hocknorton, in Oxfordshire, in 1071-2, built and fortified Oxford Castle, and was made Constable of Oxford. The 3rd Baron of Hocknorton founded the Abbey of Oseney on an island in the Isis. This family descends from Sir Henry D'Oyly of Pondhall, Sheriff of Suffolk, who *d* 1564. The 1st baronet, Sir William D'Oyly, MP for Norfolk and Yarmouth, a partisan of the royal cause, was knighted, and subsequently created a baronet. Sir William D'Oyly, 2nd baronet, a Teller of the Exchequer, was knighted during the lifetime of his father. Sir John Hadley D'Oyly, 6th baronet, Collector of Calcutta and of the twenty-four Pergunnahs, sat as MP for Ipswich during the trial of his friend Warren Hastings. Sir Charles D'Oyly, 7th Baronet, HEICS, was a distinguished amateur artist. Maj-Gen Sir Charles Walters D'Oyly, 9th baronet, Bengal Army, served in Gwallor Campaign and Indian Campaign 1857.

DRUGHORN (UK) 1922, of Ifield Hall, Ifield, Sussex (Extinct 1943)

Sir JOHN FREDERICK DRUGHORN, 1st and last *Baronet*.

DAUGHTERS LIVING OF FIRST BARONET

Lucienne Frederique, *b* 1893: *m* 1914, Dacre de Jersey Crondace, AIMM, CE, who *d* 1977, and has issue living, John Michael Dacre (Dacredale, Borrowdale, Harare, Zimbabwe) *b* 1928: *m* 1952, Heather Margaret Gilmour, and has issue living, Alistair Michael Dacre *b* 1965, Rosmairi Heather *b* 1954, Caroline Jean *b* 1958, Janette Alison *b* 1962, — William Ian *b* 1931: *m* 1956, Marilyn Patricia Jones, and has issue living, Peter George *b* 1965, Mark Andrew *b* 1969, Deborah Lucienne *b* 1961, — David Brian *b* 1932: *m* 1972, Grace Lily Logan, — Elizabeth Lucienne *b* 1915: *m* 1945, Robert Cherer Smith, of End of Kingsmead Rd, PO Borrowdale, Harare, Zimbabwe, and has issue living, Gareth *b* 1953, Deryn *b* 1946: *m* 1966, Michael James Read, Beulah Joy *b* 1949: *m* 1971, Graham McGuiness, — Margaret Frederique, *b* 1916: *m* 1939, Gerald Alfred O'Reilly, and has issue living, Gerald James *b* 1940: *m* 1966, Marie Fitzgibben, Kevin *b* 1945: *m* 1966, Wendy Bailey, Patrick *b* 1948: *m* 1972, Jennifer Barnard, Anne Bernice *b* 1942: *m* 1970, Manuel Tavares, — Eileen Mary, *b* 1917: *m* 1940, Keith Alistaire Forbes, and has issue living, Brian Alistaire *b* 1942: *m* 1966, Shaughn Watson, Nigel *b* 1950, Jacqueline *b* 1953, — Pamela Denise, *b* 1919: *m* 1942, Lawrence Stanley Rix, and has issue living, Jeremy *b* 1952, Graham *b* 1954, Allan *b* 1957, Molly *b* 1947: *m* 1967, Robin Booth, Patricia *b* 1950: *m* 19—, Michael Toronyi. *Residence* – Dacredale, Borrowdale, Harare, Zimbabwe. —— Maud Frederica, *b* 1897: *m* 1926, Lionel James Berry, BSc, ARIC, and has issue living, Joyce Ann, *b* 1928: *m* 1951, Ronald Lynch, and has issue living, Michael *b* 1953, James *b* 1956, Susan *b* 1958, — Susan Elizabeth Wendy, *b* 1932; ARCM, LRAM.

COLLATERAL BRANCH LIVING

        Issue of late John Frederic Drughorn, son of 1st baronet, *b* 1887, *d* 1919: *m* 1914, Marie Elizabeth, who
        d 1943, da of George Newport:—
Marie Frederica Elizabeth, *b* 1915: *m* 1945, Charles F. Hudson.

DRYDEN (GB) 1733, of Ambrosden, Oxfordshire; and 1795, of Canons Ashby, North-amptonshire

Sir JOHN STEPHEN GYLES DRYDEN, 11th *Baronet* of 1st and 8th of 2nd creation; *b* 26 Sept 1943; *s* his father, *Sir* NOEL PERCY HUGH, 1970; *ed* The Oratory Sch: *m* 1970, Diana Constance, da of Cyril Tomlinson, of Highland Park, Wellington, NZ, and has issue.

Arms – Azure, a lion rampant, and in chief a sphere between two estoiles or. Crest – A demi-lion sustaining in his right paw a sphere as in the arms. *Address* – Spinners, Fairwarp, Uckfield, East Sussex TN22 3BE.

SON LIVING

JOHN FREDERICK SIMON, *b* 26 May 1976; *ed* Worth.

DAUGHTER LIVING

Caroline Diana Rosamund, *b* 1980.

AUNT LIVING

Evelyn Kate Mary, *b* 1909: *m* 1931, Brig Gerald Ernest Thubron, DSO, OBE, N Stafford Regt, who *d* 1992, and has had issue, Colin Gerald Dryden, *b* 1939; *ed* Eton; FRSL; writer (won Hawthornden Prize for Literature 1987), — Carol Sheena, *b* 1937; *d* 1959, — and an adopted da, Sarah Elizabeth, *b* 1963. *Residence* – Pheasant's Hatch, Piltdown, Sussex.

Sir Erasmus Dryden, Sheriff of Northamptonshire, was created a baronet 1619. One of his grandsons was John Dryden, the celebrated poet. The title became extinct at the death of the 7th baronet in 1770, when the estates devolved upon his niece, who married John Turner, 2nd son of Sir Edward Turner, 2nd baronet of Ambrosden. Mr Turner in 1791 assumed by sign-manual the surname and arms of Dryden only, was knighted 1793, and created a baronet 1795. The 4th baronet, of creation 1795, in 1874 succeeded, as 7th baronet, to the Turner baronetcy, creation 1733.

DUCKWORTH (UK) 1909, of Grosvenor Place, City of Westminster

Sir EDWARD RICHARD DYCE DUCKWORTH, 4th *Baronet*; *b* 13 July 1943; *s* his father, *Sir* RICHARD DYCE, 1997; *ed* Marlborough, and Cranfield: *m* 1976, Patricia, only da of Thomas Cahill, of Datchet, Berks, and has issue.

Arms – Argent: on a chevron engrailed azure, between two leopards' faces in chief and a garb in base sable, three crosses patée or. Crest – Upon a mount between two palm branches vert, a garb fesseways or charged with two crosses patée in fesse, and surmounted by a duck sable. *Residence* – Holly Cottage, Moreton Paddox, Warwick CV35 9BU.

SON LIVING

JAMES DYCE, *b* 1984.

DAUGHTER LIVING

Helen Dyce, *b* 1987.

BROTHER LIVING

Anthony George Dyce, *b* 1946: *m* 1974, Geraldine, da of Kevin Broderick, of 118 Mount Merrion Ave, Blackrock, co Dublin, and has issue living, Nathaniel James Dyce, *b* 1977.

Perseverance

COLLATERAL BRANCH LIVING

Issue of late Capt Arthur Dyce Duckworth, RN, 3rd son of 1st Bt, *b* 1896, *d* 1973: *m* 1927, Grace Ella Mary, who *d* 1993, da of late Edmund Lionel Pontifex, of Bishopscourt, Broadwater Down, Tunbridge Wells:—
Geoffrey Loraine Dyce, CBE (Weir Cottage, Bickton, Fordingbridge, Hants SP6 2HA), *b* 1930; *ed* Stowe; Brig late RTR; ADC to HM 1982-85, CBE (Mil) 1977: *m* 1961, Philippa Ann, da of Sir (Edward) Percy Rugg, and has issue living, Jeremy Dyce, *b* 1963: *m* 1997, Christabel Elizabeth Ffynone (Kitty), da of Arthur Nicholas Graeme Fordham, of Dolgoch, Brongest, Newcastle Emlyn, Cardiganshire, — Juliet Ann, *b* 1964: *m* 1992 Christopher Brian Davidson Smith, and has issue living, Francesca Elizabeth *b* 1994, Isabella Louise *b* 1995, Emily Alice *b* (twin) 1995.

The 1st baronet, Sir Dyce Duckworth, MD, LLD, was an eminent physician, Treasurer, Roy Coll of Physicians 1884-1923, Pres of Clinical Soc of London 1891-3, and Hon Physician to King Edward VII, when Prince of Wales 1890-1901. The 2nd baronet, Sir Edward Dyce was a Puisne Judge of High Court of Burma 1924-27.

Duckworth-King, see King.

DU CROS (UK) 1916, of Canons, Middlesex

Sir CLAUDE PHILIP ARTHUR MALLET DU CROS, 3rd *Baronet*; *b* 27 Dec 1922; *s* his father, *Capt Sir* PHILIP HARVEY, 1975, formerly Capt WG: *m* 1st, 1953 (*m diss* 1974), Christine Nancy, who *d* 1988, da of late F. E. Bennett, of Spilsby, Lincs, and formerly wife of George Tordoff; 2ndly, 1974 (*m diss* 1982), Margaret Roy, da of late Roland James Frater, of Gosforth, Northumberland, and has issue by 1st *m*.

Arms – Quarterly; 1st vert, a greyhound courant argent in chief a crescent or; 2nd azure, an eastern crown or; 3rd azure, within the horns of a crescent a heart in chief argent; 4th azure, a saltire or, and on an escutcheon argent, a rose gules, stalked and leaved vert. **Crest** – Out of an eastern crown or, a demi greyhound sable.
Residence – Longmeadow, Ballaugh Glen, Ramsey, I of Man. *Clubs* – Carlton, Guards'.

SON LIVING (*By 1st marriage*)

JULIAN CLAUDE ARTHUR MALLET, *b* 23 April 1955; *ed* Eton: *m* 1984, Patricia M., only da of Gerald A. Wyatt, of Littlefield School, Liphook, Hants, and has issue living, Alexander Julian Mallet, *b* 25 Aug 1990, — Henrietta Mary, *b* 1988.

SISTERS LIVING

Edome Dita Mallet (Quita Pena, Hinton St George, Somerset), *b* 1924. —— Primrose Millicent Elaine Mallet, *b* 1938; assumed by deed poll the surname MALLET-HARRIS upon marriage; FLS, the botanical artist: *m* 1978, James Gordon Shute Harris, of Mallet Court, Curry Mallet Somerset (*see* B Airedale, 1995 Edn).

The 1st baronet, Sir Arthur du Cros (son of late (William) Harvey du Cros, JP, formerly MP for Hastings), was Founder and sometime Chm and Pres of Dunlop Rubber Co Ltd, and Founder, with his father, of Pneumatic Tyre Industry, a Pioneer of Rubber Growing Industry, and a Founder of Junior Imperial League, and first Chm of its Committee. He initiated Motor Ambulance Movement during European War 1914-19, and sat as MP for Hastings (*C*) 1908-18, and for Clapham Div of Wandsworth 1918-22.

Dudley-Williams, see Williams.

Duff-Gordon, see Gordon.

DUGDALE (UK) 1936, of Merevale and Blyth, co Warwick

PESTIS · PATRIÆ · PIGRITES

Sloth is the plague of one's country

Sir WILLIAM STRATFORD DUGDALE, CBE, MC, 2nd *Baronet*; *b* 29 March 1922; *s* his father, *Sir* WILLIAM FRANCIS STRATFORD, 1965; *ed* Eton, and Balliol Coll, Oxford; a JP and DL of Warwicks (High Sheriff 1971-72); Solicitor 1949; 1939-45 War as Capt Grenadier Gds in N Africa and Italy (despatches, MC); Chm Nat Water Council 1982-83; CBE (1982): *m* 1st, 1952, Lady Belinda Pleydell-Bouverie, who *d* 1961, da of 7th Earl of Radnor; 2ndly, 1967, Cecilia Mary, da of Sir William Malcolm Mount, 2nd Bt, and has issue by 1st and 2nd *m*.

Arms – Quarterly; 1st and 4th argent a cross moline gules, charged in the centre with a Garter King of Arms, coronet or, and in the 1st quarter a torteau; 2nd and 3rd, barry of ten argent and azure, over all a lion rampant gules. Crest – A Griffin's head, wings endorsed or, gorged with a coronet as in the arms.
Seat – Merevale Hall, Atherstone, Warwickshire.
Residences – Blyth Hall, Coleshill, Birmingham; 24 Bryanston Mews West, W1H 7FR. Clubs – White's, Brooks's, Jockey.

SONS LIVING (By 1st marriage)

(WILLIAM) MATTHEW (STRATFORD), *b* 22 Feb 1959: *m* 1990, Paige Sullivan, da of late Thomas Haines Dudley Perkins, and has issue living, William Stratford, *b* 15 Aug 1992, — Nathaniel Francis Stratford, *b* 1996, — Clementine Alexandra Louise, *b* 1991, — Fernanda Elizabeth Grace, *b* 1994. *Residence* – Merevale Hall, Atherstone, Warwicks CV9 2HG.

(By 2nd marriage)

Thomas Joshua Stratford, *b* 1974.

DAUGHTERS LIVING (By 1st marriage)

Laura, *b* 1953: *m* 1986 (*m diss* 1998), Hon Arthur Grey Hazlerigg, only son of 2nd Baron Hazlerigg, and has issue (see that title). —— Matilda, *b* 1955. *m* 1989, Marcus May, son of Col R. K. May, of Cairn House, Warwick Bridge, Carlisle, Cumbria. —— Charlotte (*Hon Mrs Gerard Noel*), *b* (twin) 1955: *m* 1985, Hon Gerard Edward Joseph Noel, 2nd son of 5th Earl of Gainsborough, and has issue (see that title).

(By 2nd marriage)

Adelaide Margaret Victoria Jane, *b* 1970.

SISTERS LIVING

Susan: *m* 1950, Timothy Neil Hughes-Onslow, of 32 Godfrey St, SW3 (*see* E Onslow, colls), who *d* 1995, and has issue (see that title). —— Judith Margaret: *m* 1952, Maj John Evelyn Shirley, KRRC (ret), of Ettington Park, Stratford-on-Avon (*see* E Ferrers, colls), and has issue (see that title).

COLLATERAL BRANCH LIVING

Issue of late Sir John Robert Stratford Dugdale, yr son of 1st baronet, *b* 1923, *d* 1994: *m* 1956, Kathryn Edith Helen (*Lady Dugdale*), DCVO (Tickwood Hall, Much Wenlock, Shropshire TF13 6NZ), da of late Rt Hon Oliver Frederick George Stanley, MC, MP (*see* E Derby, colls):—
Edward Stratford, *b* 1959. —— Henry Stratford (122 St Stephen's Av, W12), *b* 1963: *m* 1991, Adi Litia Cakobau Mara, da of the President of Fiji and Paramount Chief of Lau, and of Adi Lady Lala Mara, Paramount Chief of Rewa, and has issue living, Michael, *b* 1993, — a da, *b* 1996. —— Elizabeth Alice, *b* 1957. —— Mary, *b* 1961.

The present baronet is descended from Sir William Dugdale, Garter King of Arms 1677-86, and author of *Monasticon Anglicanum* and *Baronage of England*, who *d* 1686. Richard Geast, maternal nephew of John Dugdale of Blyth, Mowbray Herald Extraordinary, having inherited Blyth Hall, assumed by Royal Licence 1799 the surname and arms of Dugdale. His wife, Penelope Bate, was the el da of co-heir of Francis Stratford of Merevale Hall, Warwicks, which was inherited by their son, Dugdale Stratford Dugdale, great-grandfather of 1st baronet.

DUNBAR (NS) 1694, of Mochrum, Wigtownshire

Sir JAMES MICHAEL DUNBAR, 14th *Baronet*; *b* 17 Jan 1950; *s* his father, *Sir* JEAN IVOR, 1993; Col USAF: *m* 1st, 1978 (*m diss* 1989), Margaret Marie, da of Albert Jacobs; 2ndly, 1989, Margaret Elizabeth, da of Gordon Talbot, and has issue by 1st and 2nd *m*.

Arms – Gules, a lion rampant argent, armed and langued azure, within a bordure of the second charged with eight roses of the first, barbed and seeded vert, in a dexter canton argent a saltire azure, surmounted of an inescutcheon charged with a lion rampant gules within a double tressure flory counterflory gules. Crest – A horse's head argent, bridled and reined gules. Supporters – Two white doves imperially crowned proper.
Seat – Mochrum Park, Kirkcowan, Wigtownshire. *Address* – 86 Medical Group, PSC #2, Box 7047, APO AE 09012.

SONS LIVING (*By 1st marriage*)

MICHAEL JOSPEH, *b* 5 July 1980. —— David Scott, *b* 1983.

DAUGHTERS LIVING (*By 1st marriage*)

Stacy Beth, *b* 1985.

(*By 2nd marriage*)

Cassandra Talbot, *b* 1991.

BROTHER LIVING

Dennis William, *b* 1952: *m* 1980, Claire Maria, da of late Kenneth A. Kruemmel, Sr, and has issue living, Dawn Michele, *b* 1981. *Residence* – 510 Oakwood Station Rd, Glen Burnie, Maryland 21061, USA.

SISTER LIVING

Anne Marie, *b* 1946: *m* 19—, ... Bickauskas. *Residence* – 1427 St Christopher Court, Edgewood, Maryland 21040, USA.

HALF-UNCLES LIVING (*sons of 12th baronet by 2nd marriage*)

Rowland Adrian (1 Sandhurst Av, Cullercoats, Tyne and Wear), *b* 1934: late US Med Corps: *m* 1957, Janet Lockhart, da of George Heron, of Newton Stewart, Wigtownshire, and has issue living, Mary Naomi, *b* 1958: *m* 1983, Edward Thomas Lisle, and has issue living, Scott *b* 1988, Sarah Elizabeth *b* 1985, Joanna Marie *b* 1986, — Sylvia Katharine, *b* 1960: *m* 1984, Derek Graham, and has issue living, Ross Christopher *b* 1985, David Adrian *b* 1989, Laura Marie *b* 1987, — Shonna Janet, *b* 1962. —— Donald Robert (51 Judith Av, Knodishall, Saxmundham, Suffolk), *b* 1936; formerly Senior Master Sgt US AF, and US Army Med Corps: *m* 1st, 1957, Marie F., da of Douglas Allen, of Newtown Stewart, Wigtownshire; 2ndly, 1963, Susan Elizabeth May, da of William Radden Gates, and has issue living (by 1st *m*), Allan William, *b* 1958, — Roseanne, *b* 1960, — (by 2nd *m*), David Wayne, *b* 1966, — Linda Carol, *b* 1969.

DAUGHTERS LIVING OF ELEVENTH BARONET

Joyce Marguerite, *b* 1912. —— Vida Mary, *b* 1916. *Residence* – 69 Grandison Rd, Battersea, SW11.

MOTHER LIVING

Rose Jeanne, da of Henry William Hertsch: *m* 1944 (*m diss* 1979), as his 1st wife, Sir Jean Ivor Dunbar, 13th Bt, who *d* 1993. *Residence* – 4426 Black Rock Rd #9, Hampstead, Maryland 21074, USA.

COLLATERAL BRANCHES LIVING

Issue of late William Uthred Dunbar, brother of 12th baronet, *b* 1902, *d* 19—: *m* 1924, Theresa Rose Della, who *d* 19—, da of Jerome Cole:—
William Thomas, *b* 1925: *m* 19—.

Grandsons of late Richard Taylor Dunbar, el son of Lt-Col Thomas Clement Dunbar, 4th son of James Dunbar, yr son of 5th baronet:—

Issue of late Lt-Col William Henry George Dunbar of Kilkonzie, OBE, TD, *b* 1893 (legitimated in terms of Legitimation (Scotland) Act 1968, and in remainder to baronetcy); unsuccessfully petitioned Lord Lyon to *s* to baronetcy 1984; author of *Dunbars' 1000 Years*; *d* 1987: *m* 1st, 1917, Stella Kathleen, who *d* 1941 as the result of enemy action, da of Henry Underdown, of Dover; 2ndly, 1941, Joan Marguerite, who *d* 1966, da of Capt Sydney Church Leopard, TD, RAMC, of Eastbourne, Midhurst, Sussex; 3rdly 1967, Irene Mary (St Benedicts, 22/23 St George's Terrace, Herne Bay, Kent CT6 8RF), da of Charles Edwin Frith, of Weeley, Essex:—

(By 1st *m*) Graham William DUNBAR OF KILKONZIE, *b* 1920: *m* 1955, Alice Louise, da of Joseph Lollee (otherwise Zoller), of Stolzenberg, Uzwil, St Gallen, Switzerland, and has issue living, Andrew William, Younger of Kilkonzie (Dorfstrasse 19, 4222 Zwingen, Basel, Switzerland), *b* 1961; BSc, — Janet Marjorie (Moosmühle Strasse 20, 9112 Schachen, Herisau, Switzerland), *b* 1964: *m* 1998, Mauritzio De Cet, and has issue living, Oliver William *b* 1998. *Residence* – 4 Gibbs Close, Cheshunt, Herts EN8 9RX.

Issue of late Richard John Victor Michael Dunbar, *b* 1897 (legitimated in terms of Legitimation (Scotland) Act 1968, and in remainder to baronetcy), *d* 1983: *m* 1932, Daffodil Helen (Beechbrook, The Holt, Hare Hatch, Wargrave, Berks RG10 9SA), only da of late Rev Eardley Wilmot Michell, V of Bolney, Sussex:—

Gavin Cospatric Michell, RD (Summer Place, Loddon Drive, Wargrave, Berks RG10 8HH) *b* 1936; *ed* St Catharine's Coll, Camb (MA); Cdr RNR: *m* 1960, Jean, only da of Dr Roy Kemball Price, of Hove, Sussex, and has issue living, Emma Claire, *b* 1961: *m* 1988, James Harrison, and has issue living, Henry Douglas *b* 1995, Molly Rachel *b* 1998, — Katrina Michelle, *b* 1964, — Lisa Carol, *b* 1966: *m* 1996, Andrew Hosie. —— David Randolph Michell, FCA, (The Hermitage, 193 Lower Rd, Great Bookham, Surrey), *b* 1938: *m* 1965, Brenda, yr da of Maurice W. Mitchell, of Ashstead, Surrey, and has issue living, James Stuart Michell, *b* 1967, — Struan Gordon David, *b* 1970.

The present baronet is descended from the Dunbars, the ancient Earls of March and Moray, and is the lineal male representative of the heritable Sheriffs of Elgin and Forres, and chief of that name. Alexander Dunbar, Younger of Conzie, obtained Mochrum by marriage in 1564. The 1st Baronet had a Charter, under the great seal, of the lands and barony of Mochrum in 1677, and was *cr* a Baronet with a grant of supporters on his coat of arms. The 3rd baronet was Judge-Advocate for Scotland. Sir William, 7th baronet, sat as MP for Wigton Burghs (*L*) 1857-65, was successively a Lord of the Treasury, Keeper of the Privy Seal to HRH the Prince of Wales, Keeper of the Great Seal to HRH in Scotland, one of the Council to HRH, and Comptroller-Gen of the Exchequer, and Auditor-Gen of Public Accounts. The 9th baronet, Sir William Cospatrick Dunbar, CB, was Assist Under-Sec for Scotland 1885-1902, and Registrar-Gen for England and Wales 1902-9. The 10th baronet, Sir James George Hawker Rowland, *d* 23 Jan 1953, and the 11th baronet, Sir Richard Sutherland, *d* 25 Jan 1953. Sir Jean Ivor, 13th Bt, was Sgt Mountain Engrs, USA Army, and *d* Aug 1993.

DUNBAR (NS) 1698, of Durn, Banffshire

Spes dabic auxilium

Hope will give aid

Sir DRUMMOND COSPATRICK NINIAN DUNBAR, MC, 9th *Baronet*; *b* 9 May 1917; *s* his father, Sir GEORGE ALEXANDER DRUMMOND, 1949; *ed* Radley, and Worcester Coll, Oxford (BA 1938); Major (ret) Black Watch; European War 1939-45 in Middle East, N Africa, Sicily, and Normandy (twice wounded, MC): *m* 1957, Sheila Barbara Mary, da of John Berkeley de Fonblanque, and has issue.

Arms – Quarterly; 1st and 4th, gules, a lion rampant within a bordure argent, charged with eight roses of the first barbed and seeded vert; 2nd and 3rd, or, three cushions within the royal tressure gules, all within a bordure nebuly, quartered azure and gules. Crest – Two sprigs of laurel in saltire proper. *Residence* – Town Hill, Westmount, Jersey, CI. *Club* – RAC.

SON LIVING

ROBERT DRUMMOND COSPATRICK, Younger of Durn, *b* 17 June 1958; *ed* Harrow, and Ch Ch, Oxford: *m* 1994, Sarah, da of Robert Brooks, of Hattingley, Hants, and has issue living, Alexander William Drummond, *b* 1 March 1995. *Residence* – 32 Westover Rd, SW18 2RQ.

COLLATERAL BRANCHES LIVING

Grandchildren of late Hugh Stephen Dunbar, 3rd son of 7th baronet:—
Issue of late Uthred Ninian Vere Dunbar, *b* 1910, *d* 1977: *m* 1942, Susan Kathleen, da of Arthur George Thompson:—
Stephen Bruce, *b* 1949. —— Eleanor Lynne, *b* 1947.

Issue of late William Hancorn Vere Dunbar *b* 1912, *d* 1984: *m* 1936, Dorothy Christobel, da of James Smith Gow:—
Coral Lisette, *b* 1939: *m* 1964, Henry William Walker, and has issue living, Gordon Henry *b* 1965.

Issue of late Aldred Cospatrick Dunbar, *b* 1916, *d* 1971: *m* 1940, Isidoris Elliott, who *d* 1986, da of Maj William Harrison:—
Raymond Robert, *b* 1943.

Issue of late Robert Fyfe Dunbar, *b* 1920, *d* 1991: *m* 1941, Eileen May (33 Julia Rd, Overport, Durban, Natal, S Africa), da of Frederick Locke:—
George Drummond, *b* 1957: *m* 1990, Lydia, da of Gawie Grobbelaar, and has issue living, Merissa Anne, *b* 1992. —— Beverley Anne, *b* 1946: *m* 1974, John Derek Walters, who *d* 1992. —— Gail Elizabeth *b* 1953: *m* 1976, Patrick Murphy. —— Dianne Roberta, *b* 1959: *m* 1991, Peter Riddle, of 7 Gadge Close, Thame, Oxon, and has issue living, Robert Adam, *b* 1992.

Issue of late Patrick Martin Borlase Dunbar, 4th son of 7th baronet, *b* 1884, *d* 1925: *m* 1924, Mary who *d* 1983, el da of late Claude F. Shoolbred, of Greenstead Hall, Halstead, Essex:—
Patricia Martin *b* (*posthumous*) 1926: *m* 1951, William Harold Groves, and has issue living, Martin Westley, *b* 1960, — James Arthur, *b* 1967. *Residence* – 2 Cumberland Av, Vandia Grove, Randburg, Johannesburg, Transvaal, S Africa.

This family is lineally descended from James, 4th Earl of Moray, by Isabel Innes, and so from John, 1st Earl of Moray (3rd creation 1371-3), who *m* Marjorie, da of Robert II, King of Scots (first of the Stewart Kings), and was brother of George, 10th Earl of Dunbar and uncle of 11th and last of the ancient Earls of Dunbar, whose line was founded by Gospatric, Earl of Northumberland (see following article), grandson of Elgitha, da of Ethelred II, King of England. The Baronetcy was created with remainder to the heirs male of the body of the grantee and their heirs male for ever.

DUNBAR (NS) 1700, of Northfield, Moray

Vigilance strengthens hope

Sir ARCHIBALD RANULPH DUNBAR, 11th *Baronet*; *b* 8 Aug 1927; *s* his father, *Maj Sir* (ARCHIBALD) EDWARD, MC, 1969; *ed* Wellington, Pembroke Coll, Camb, and Imp Coll of Tropical Agric, Trinidad; late Agric Officer, Uganda Civil Ser, and HMOCS: *m* 1974, Amelia Millar Sommerville, da of late Horace Campbell Davidson, of 10 Forth View Cres, Currie, Midlothian, and has issue.

Arms – Quarterly: 1st and 4th, gules, a lion rampant argent within a bordure of the last charged with eight roses of the field, *Dunbar*; 2nd and 3rd, or three cushions within the royal tressure gules, *Ranulph*; all within a bordure quartered azure and of the first. Crest – A dexter hand apaumée reaching at an astral crown proper.
Residence – The Old Manse, Duffus, Elgin IV30 2QD.

SON LIVING

EDWARD HORACE, *b* 18 March 1977.

DAUGHTERS LIVING

Harriet Sophie, *b* 1974. —— Stephanie Clare, *b* 1975.

BROTHER LIVING

Alexander Arbuthnott (Pitgaveny, Elgin, Moray), *b* 1929; *ed* Wellington Coll, and Pembroke Coll, Camb; Bar, Inner Temple, 1953: *m* 1965, Elizabeth Susannah, da of Rev Edward Denzil Chetwood Wright, of Brattleby House, Brattleby, Lincs (*see* Strickland-Constable, Bt, colls, 1985 Edn), and has issue living, Crinan James, *b* 1965, — Clodagh Rebecca Helen, *b* 1968.

This family is paternally descended in direct male line (through John Dunbar, Earl of Moray, by his wife, Marjorie, da of Robert II) from Gospatric, Earl of Northumberland (see preceding article) in right of his mother Ealdgyth, grandda of Ethelred II, King of England. He had from his cousin, Malcolm III, son of Duncan I, a grant of Dunbar in 1072. Earl Gospatric's father, Maldred, King of Cumbria, was younger brother of Duncan I, who became King of Scots in right of his mother, Bethoc, wife of Crinan the Thane (married *circa* 1000), el da and heir of Malcolm II, King of Scots. The 1st baronet, 4th Laird of Hempriggs, died without male issue, when the baronetcy (with remainder to his heirs male whatsoever) devolved upon his brother. The 3rd baronet *d* in 1763, and his cousin Alexander Dunbar of Northfield (descendant of the 2nd Laird of Hempriggs), was served heir-male, 1776 by the Lord Lyon, who directed him to continue the designation of Northfield.

DUNBAR (NS) 1706, of Hempriggs, Caithness-shire

SUB·SPE·

Sir RICHARD FRANCIS DUNBAR OF HEMPRIGGS, 9th *Baronet*; *b* 8 Jan 1945; *s* his mother, *Dame* MAUREEN DAISY HELEN, 1997; assumed the name of Dunbar of Hempriggs in lieu of Blake 1965; *ed* Charterhouse: *m* 1969, (Elizabeth Margaret) Jane, only da of George Lister, of Gloucester, and has issue.

𝕬rms – Quarterly: 1st gules, a lion rampant within a bordure argent, charged with eight roses of the field, *Dunbar*; 2nd, gules, three mullets or, a crescent of the last for difference, *Sutherland*; 3rd vert, on a fesse dancettée ermine between a buck's head cabossed in chief and two escallops in base or, a mullet of the first for difference, *Duff*; 4th, or, three cushions within a double tressure flory counter-flory gules. *Randolph*; all within a bordure vairy or and gules. 𝕮rest – A key and sword in saltire proper. 𝕾upporters – *Dexter*, a lion rampant argent; *sinister*, a savage man holding a baton over his shoulder proper.
Residences – 732 Crossway Rd, Burlingame, California 94010, USA; Reiss, Wick, Caithness.

DAUGHTERS LIVING

EMMA KATHERINE Dunbar of Hempriggs, yr, *b* 9 Nov 1977, — Fiona Blake, *b* 1981.

SISTER LIVING

Eleanor Margaret, *b* 1949: *m* 1st, 1973 (*m diss* 1987), David C. Eldridge; 2ndly, 1989, Michael Constable, and has issue living, (by 1st husband) Hannah Louise, *b* 1980, — (by 2nd husband) Thomas Matthew Dunbar, *b* 1987.

COLLATERAL BRANCHES LIVING *(Males and females in remainder)*

Grandchildren of Jessie Mona Duff (who *m* 1869, Rev Canon Courtenay Moore), da of *de jure* 5th Bt:—
Issue of late Harriet Emma Moore, *b* 1874, *d* 1957: *m* 1909, Lieut-Col Hubert Bernard Tonson Rye, DSO, who *d* 1950, formerly Roy Munster Fusiliers (Dancer, Bt):—
Eudo John TONSON RYE, *b* 1910; formerly Maj Duke of Cornwall's LI: *m* 1940, Rosemary Hilda, who *d* 1983, da of late Maj Guy Hughes, XIIth Bengal Cav, and has issue living, Rohaise Harriet Julia, *b* 1942: *m* 1966, Christopher Thomas-Everard, of Broford Farm, Dulverton, Som TA22 9JH, and has issue living, Guy Richard *b* 1969, Lucilla Damaris Mary *b* 1966: *m* 1993, Timothy John Coates Newman, of Hill Head, Chulmleigh, Devon EX18 7AL (and has issue living, Nathaniel Christopher Coates *b* 1994, Hector Bartholomew Edward *b* 1996, Amelia Bridget Rosemary *b* 1998), Adella Jessie Bridget *b* 1974, — Caroline Mary Georgina (11 Warren Rd, SW19 2HY), *b* 1947, — Amarylde Louise, *b* 1950: *m* 1972, Richard Peter Eliot, of Upcott House, Bishop's Hull, Taunton, Som TA4 1AQ, and of Munich, Germany, and has issue living, Peter David *b* 1974, James Edward *b* 1977.

Issue of late Jessie Louisa Rickard (who resumed that surname 1916), *b* 1876, *d* 1963: *m* 1st, 1901, Robert Dudley Innes Ackland, of Boulston, Pembrokeshire; 2ndly, 1908, Lieut-Col Victor George Howard Rickard, Roy Munster Fusiliers, who was *ka* 1915; 3rdly, 1916 (*m diss* 1935), Lieut-Col Tudor Fitzjohn, DSO (formerly Worcestershire Regt):—
(By 2nd marriage) †Justin Victor RICKARD, *b* 1913: *m* 1939, Joan (St Catherine's, 50 Edgarton Rd, Bembridge, I of Wight PO35 5RJ), da of late Alexander William Haig, of Henley-on-Thames, and *d* 19—, leaving issue, Alexander (St Catherine's, 50 Edgarton Rd, Bembridge, I of Wight PO35 5RJ), *b* 1944, — Catherine, *b* 1949, — Patricia, *b* 1955.

Granddaughter of late Douglas Garden Duff, OBE, yr son of late Gen Sir Beauchamp Duff, GCB, GCSI, KCVO, CIE, 2nd son of Garden William Duff, next brother of *de jure* 5th Bt:—
Issue of late Margaret Jean Duff, *b* 1919, *d* 1999. *m* 1st, 1943 (*m diss* 1947), René Dorval, of Montreal, Canada; 2ndly, 1957, Percy Mansfield Scaddan, who *d* 1994:—
(By 1st *m*) Marie Margaret Diane, *b* 1943: *m* 1964, Henry Robert Denholm Hallam, of 1 Badgers Close, Ashford, Middx, and has two children, Alison Jeanette, *b* 1966, — Paul Ian Douglas, *b* 1969.

Descendants of Louisa Alice Duff, da of Robert George Duff, brother of *de jure* 5th Bt, *b* 1853 *d* 1926: *m* 1876, 3rd Baron Vivian, who *d* 1893:—
See B Vivian.

Grandchildren of late Rev Canon Garden Llanoe Duff, son of late Col James Duff of Knockleith, yst brother of *de jure* 5th Bt:—
Issue of late Enid Blackburn Duff, *b* 1889, *d* 1971: *m* 1922, Rev Edward Archibald Forbes (*see* Stuart-Forbes, Bt, colls), who *d* 1929:—
See Stuart-Forbes, Bt, colls.

Grandchildren of late James Duff Duff (infra):—
Issue of late Maj-Gen Alan Colquhoun Duff, CB, OBE, MC, *b* 1896, *d* 1973: *m* 1935, Diana Frances (The Hope Residential Home, Brooklands Av, Cambridge CB2 2BQ), el da of late Col Richard Parry Crawley, DSO, OBE, MVO:—

James Richard Valentine DUFF (10 Groves Close, Bourne End, Bucks SL8 5JP), *b* 1941: *m* 1973, Helen Jolliffe, and has issue living, James Lindsey Alan, *b* 1975. ——Lindsay Margaret, *b* 1937: *m* 1st, 1959 (*m diss* 1972), Stephen Francis Robertson; 2ndly, 1972, Colin M. Carden, of South Mudge Farm, Ilton, Ilminster, Som TA19 9HL, and has issue living, (by 1st *m*) Patrick John, *b* 1962: *m* 1986, Alison Leisk, and has issue living, Sarah Robertson *b* 1987, — Penelope Ann *b* 1964; has issue living, Milo James Fox *b* 1997, Ella Rose Fox *b* 1994, — (by 2nd *m*) Charles Anthony, *b* 1973, — David Henry, *b* 1976. ——Christian Frances (12 Pine Tree Grove, Middleton St George, Darlington DL2 1AG), *b* 1942.

              Granddaughter of late Col James Duff of Knockleith, yst brother of *de jure* 5th Bt:—
         Issue of late James Duff Duff, *b* 1860, *d* 1940: *m* 1895, Laura Eleanor, da of Sir William Fitzwilliam Lenox-
              Conyngham, KCB:—
Hester Laura Elisabeth, *b* 1912. *Residence* – 12 Pine Tree Grove, Middleton St George, Darlington DL2 1AG.

              Grandson of late Adm Sir Alexander Ludovic Duff, GCB, GBE, KCVO, 4th son of Col James Duff of
              Knockleith (ante):—
         Issue of late Helen Douglas, *b* 1887, *d* 1978: *m* 1923, Lt-Cdr Edgar Dolphin, DSO, RN:—
Peter Western DOLPHIN (Stable Cottage, Speen Lane, Newbury, Berks RG14 1RJ), *b* 1924; Lt-Cdr RN (ret): *m* 1st, 1948 (*m diss* 1953), Anne Marion Galbraith; 2ndly, 1955, Margaret Sally, da of Cdr Patrick Rycroft Maurice, OBE, RN (ret), and has issue living (by 2nd *m*), Mark Patrick, *b* 1958: *m* 1983, Kirstie Leyland-Naylor, and has issue living, Tristan Ross *b* 1985, Kylie *b* 1987, — Jane Douglas, *b* 1957: *m* 1988, Anthony Julian Bellmont, and has issue living, Jack Robert *b* 1990, Thomas Patrick *b* 1992, — Sarah Katherine, *b* 1962: *m* 1986, Peter James McLaverty, and had issue living, Christopher *b* 1988, Robert *b* 1991.

              Grandsons of late Dorothy Alexandra Duff (*Lady James*), OBE, da of late Adm Sir Alexander Ludovic
              Duff, GCB, GBE, KCVO (ante):—
         Issue of late Capt Christopher Alexander James, RN, *b* 1916, *d* 1969: *m* 1938, Cynthia, who *d* 1971, da of late
              Douglas Swire (E Glasgow, colls):—
Julian Alexander Ludovic JAMES (The Lodge, St Aubyns, Rottingdean, Brighton, BN2 7GA), *b* 1939: *m* 1965, Hilary, da of Thomas Browne, of Puddletown, Dorset, and has issue living, Christopher Mark William, *b* 1967, — David Hugh Geoffrey, *b* 1969, — Andrew Michael Richard, *b* 1976. ——David Robin Millais JAMES DUFF (Yew House, Rectory Lane, Bramshott, Liphook, Hants), *b* 1945; assumed by deed poll, 1963, the additional surname of Duff after his patronymic: *m* 1st, 1970, Monica, da of Thomas Browne, of Puddletown, Dorset; 2ndly, 1988, Jayne, da of James Bryce, of Coupar Angus, Perthshire, and has issue living, (by 1st *m*) Rory Thomas, *b* 1978, — Fiona Louise, *b* 1971, — Tania Robin, *b* 1973, — Nicola Mary, *b* 1980, — (by 2nd *m*) Gardie William Beauchamp, *b* 1993, — Patrick Alexander *b* 1995. ——Simon Christopher JAMES (20 Delvino Rd, SW6), *b* 1946: *m* 1975, Anna Catherine, da of late Col William Burleigh Shine, of Englemere Lodge, Ascot, Berks.

              Grandson of late Rev Charles Edmund Duff, 5th son of late Col James Duff of Knockleith (ante):—
         Issue of late Capt Ian Archibald James Duff, MC, *b* 1895, *d* 1949: *m* 1916, Kathleen Frances, who *d* 1932, da of
              Patrick Vernon Chinnery Haldane:—
Patrick Charles DUFF, *b* 1920.

   This Nova Scotia Baronetcy was conferred with remainder to *heirs whatsoever*, ie, it can be and has been inherited through or by a female representative of the family. The 1st Bt, Hon James Sutherland, advocate, 2nd son of 2nd Lord Duffus *m* Elizabeth, da and ultimate heiress of Sir William Dunbar of Hempriggs, 1st Bt (*cr* 1700) (Dunbar, Bt, of Northfield) whose surname and arms he assumed. The 3rd Baronet assumed the title of Lord Duffus as heir male of the body and *d* 1843, leaving an only son, the 4th Baronet, who did not claim the Peerage title. After the death in 1875 of Sir George Dunbar, 4th Bt the male issue of the 1st Bt became ext, and the Baronetcy devolved on Capt (Sir) Benjamin Duff, *de jure* 5th Bt (son of his sister Louisa, who married, 1805, Garden Duff of Hatton, Aberdeenshire), but he did not prove his right to the title. Sir George Duff-Sutherland-Dunbar, grandson of the *de jure* 5th Bt, who assumed the additional surnames of Sutherland-Dunbar on succeeding to the Hempriggs and Ackergill estate, established his right as 6th Bt at Lyon Court 1899. His son Sir George Cospatrick Duff-Sutherland-Dunbar, 7th Bt, *d* 1963, and was *s* by Dame Maureen Daisy Helen Dunbar, granddaughter of Jessie Mona (who *m* 1869 Rev Canon Courtenay Moore), da of *de jure* 5th Bt and established her right as Baronetess at Lyon Court 1965. Dame Maureen *m* 1940, Leonard James Blake, who *d* 1989, sometime Dir of Music, Malvern Coll, and *d* 1997.

HOPE-DUNBAR (NS) 1664, of Baldoon

The more prepared, the more powerful

Sir DAVID HOPE-DUNBAR, 8th *Baronet*, *b* 13 July 1941; *s* his father, *Major Sir* BASIL DOUGLAS, 1961; *ed* Eton, and Roy Agric Coll, Cirencester; ARICS: *m* 1971, Kathleen Ruth, yr da of late J. Timothy Kenrick, of Birmingham, and has issue.

Arms – Quarterly, 1st, gules, a lion rampant argent, armed and langued azure, a bordure of the second charged with ten roses, of the field, barbed and seeded vert, *Dunbar*; 2nd, azure, on a chevron or between three bezants a bay leaf slipped veret, a mullet of the second in chief for difference, *Hope*; 3rd, argent, a man's heart imperially crowned proper, on a chief azure three mullets of the field, *Douglas*; 4th counter-quartered, 1st and 4th gules, three cinquefoils ermine, 2nd and 3rd, argent, a lymphad sails furled, sable, flagged gules, *Hamilton*. Crest – A horse's head couped argent, bridled gules. Supporters – Two lions rampant guardant argent, armed and langued gules, each holding in one of the forepaws a rose slipped proper.
Residence – Banks House, Kirkcudbright.

SON LIVING

CHARLES, *b* 11 March 1975.

DAUGHTERS LIVING

Philippa, *b* 1973. —— Juliet Antonia, *b* 1976.

COLLATERAL BRANCHES LIVING (*Males and females in remainder*)

Grandchildren of late Helen Jacqueline Hope (Mrs Alan Burns), MBE, sister of 6th baronet:—
Issue of late Lt-Col John Alan Burns, *b* 1905, *d* 1987: *m* 1944, Joyce Margaret (Fairfield, 9 Cole Rd, Bruton, Som), da of G. A. B. August, of Bedford:—
Felicity Margaret, *b* 1945: *m* 1974, Francis Michael Morton Peto, of Cowdenknowes Mains, Earlston, Berwickshire, and has issue (*see* Peto, Bt, *cr* 1855). —— Marion Jacqueline, *b* 1948: *m* 1968, Lt-Col Peter Guy Chamberlin, late Royal Green Jackets, of Drove House, Coombe Bissett, Salisbury, Wilts, and has issue living, Edward Alan, *b* 1974, — Lucinda Geraldine, *b* 1970, — Vanessa Louise, *b* 1977.

Issue of late Charles Hope Burns, *b* 1912, *d* 1958: *m* 1949, Barbara Delscey (16 Sinclair St, Milngavie, Glasgow), da of late Dr E. Macmillan, of Pretoria, S Africa:—
Geoffrey Douglas Charles, *b* 1954: *m* 1980, Celia, da of Guy Kynaston of Croxdalewood, Co Durham, and has issue living, Kirstin, *b* 1981, — Phebe, *b* 1985, — Shiona, *b* 1988. —— Delscey Hope, *b* 1951.

This baronetcy was granted to David Dunbar, of Baldoon, co Wigtown, in 1664, with remainder "provydit to his heirs male and tailzie." On the death of the grantee the baronetcy became dormant, and so remained until 1916, when Major Charles Dunbar Hope-Dunbar (*see* M Linlithgow, colls), grandson of Lady Isabella Ellen Hope, da of 5th Earl of Selkirk, and a descendant of Mary (who *m* Lord Basil Hamilton) grandda and sole heiress of the 1st Bt, in 1916, successfully proved his claim before the Baronetage Committee of the Privy Council to be placed on the Official Roll of Baronets as the 6th Baronet.

DUNCAN (UK) 1905, of Horsforth Hall, Guiseley, West Riding of Yorkshire (Extinct 1964)

Sir (CHARLES EDGAR) OLIVER DUNCAN, 3rd and last *Baronet*.

WIDOW LIVING OF THIRD BARONET

ETELKA DE VANGEL (*Lady Duncan*): *m* 1958, Sir (Charles Edgar) Oliver Duncan, 3rd baronet, who *d* 1964, when the title became ext.

DUNCAN (UK) 1957, of Jordanstone, co Perth (Extinct 1974)

Sir JAMES ALEXANDER LAWSON DUNCAN, 1st and last *Baronet*.

WIDOW LIVING OF FIRST BARONET

BEATRICE MARY MOORE (*Lady Duncan*) (Jordanston, by Alyth, Perthshire), da of Thomas Laurence O'Carroll, of Ballinvullen, co Cork, and widow of Maj Philip James Kington Blair-Oliphant, of Ardblair Castle, Perthshire: *m* 1966, as his 2nd wife, Sir James Alexander Lawson Duncan, 1st baronet, who *d* 1974, when the title became ext.

PAUNCEFORT-DUNCOMBE (UK) 1859, of Great Brickhill, Buckinghamshire

Non fecimus ipsi
*We have not done it
ourselves*

Sir PHILIP DIGBY PAUNCEFORT-DUNCOMBE, 4th *Baronet*; *b* 18 May 1927; *s* his father, *Maj Sir* EVERARD PHILIP DIGBY, DSO, 1971; *ed* Stowe; Maj (ret) late Gren Gds; DL of Bucks; Harbinger HM Body Guard of the Hon Corps of Gentlemen at Arms 1993-97: *m* 1951, Rachel Moyra, da of Maj Henry Gerald Aylmer (*see* B Aylmer, colls), and has issue.

Arms – Quarterly: 1st and 4th per chevron engrailed gules and argent three talbots' head erased counterchanged, a chief ermine, *Duncombe*; 2nd, gules, three lions rampant argent, *Pauncefort*; 3rd azure. Crest – 1st, out of a ducal coronet or a horse's leg sable, the shoe argent, charged with a cross-crosslet gold, *Duncombe*; 2nd, a lion rampant argent ducally crowned or, and charged on the shoulder with an escallop sable, *Pauncefort*.
Residence – Great Brickhill Manor, Milton Keynes, Bucks. *Club* – Cavalry and Guards'.

SON LIVING

DAVID PHILIP HENRY, *b* 21 May 1956; *ed* Gordonstoun, and RAC Cirencester: *m* 1987, Sarah Ann, elder da of late Reginald T. G. Battrum, and has issue living, Henry Digby, *b* 16 Dec 1988, — Laura Mary, *b* 1991. *Residence* – Westfield Farm, Gt Brickhill, Bletchley, Bucks MK17 9BG.

DAUGHTERS LIVING

Diana (The Grange, Gt Horwood, Milton Keynes, Bucks) *b* 1953: *m* 1974, Jeremy David Trevor West (*see* B Graves, colls, 1976 Edn), and has issue living, Edward, *b* 1984, — Katrina, *b* 1981. —— Charlotte, *b* 1967.

SISTER LIVING

Sophia, *b* 1925: *m* 1957, Archibald Evariste Yuill, JP, of 32 Eresby House, Rutland Gate, SW7 1BG, and has issue living, William George Henry, *b* 1961: *m* 1997, Nicola Anne Dowling.

The father of the 1st baronet, Philip Pauncefort, assumed by Roy licence, in 1804, the additional surname of Duncombe and *m* Lady Alicia Lambart, da of 7th Earl of Cavan.

DUNDAS (UK) 1898, of Arniston, Borthwick, Midlothian (Extinct 1970)

Sir THOMAS CALDERWOOD DUNDAS, MBE, 7th and last *Baronet*.

DAUGHTERS LIVING OF SEVENTH BARONET

Alice Kirsty (*Lady Pilkington*), *b* 1937: *m* 1960, Sir Antony Richard Pilkington (High Sheriff Cheshire 1996), of Crofton, Lodge, Kingsley, Cheshire, and has issue living, Jerome Antony Simon, *b* 1961, — David Christopher, *b* 1963, — Simon Benedict, *b* 1972, — Miranda Kirsty *b* 1966: *m* 1996, Christopher Mark Petheram, son of M. A. Petheram, of Wem, Shropshire, and has issue living, Jack Gabriel *b* 1998. —— Davina Margaret, *b* 1939: *m* 1966, Martin Charles Findlay, of Ledburn Manor, Leighton Buzzard, Beds (*see* E Dartmouth).

DAUGHTERS LIVING OF FOURTH BARONET

Althea Enid Philippa, *b* 1939: *m* 1972, Aedrian Bekker, of Arniston, Gorebridge, Midlothian, who *d* 1990, and has issue living, Kirsty Jean, *b* 1973, — Henrietta May, *b* 1975. —— Myfanwy Elizabeth Jean, *b* 1946; BA: *m* 1977, Mark Walker Baldwin, MSc, PhD, of 24 High St, Cleobury Mortimer, Kidderminster, Worcs, and has issue living, Samuel Philip Telford *b* 1978, — Patrick Charles Jeremy, *b* 1980, — Alexander Dundas Lancey, *b* 1983. —— Joanne Montgomerie, *b* 1949: *m* 1974, Richard Henry James Kerr-Wilson, MB, BChir, of 26 Moorend Rd, Leckhampton, Cheltenham, Glos, and has issue living, Alice Dundas, *b* 1977, — Héloïse Lucy, *b* 1979, — Catriona Olivia, *b* 1986.

DUNLOP (UK) 1916, of Woodbourne, co Renfrew

Deservedly

MERITO

Sir THOMAS DUNLOP, 3rd *Baronet*; *b* 11 April 1912; *s* his father, Sir THOMAS, 1963; *ed* Shrewsbury, and St John's Coll, Camb; Chartered Accountant, a partner in the firm of Thomas Dunlop & Sons, ship and insurance brokers, of 50 Wellington St, Glasgow, until firm ceased trading 1986; late Chm of Savings Bank of Glasgow; an OStJ; 1939-45 War as Maj Roy Signals: *m* 1947, (Adda Mary) Alison, da of late Thomas Arthur Smith, of Lindsaylands, Biggar, and has issue.

Arms – Argent, a double-headed eagle displayed gules, armed and membered azure; on a chief of the last, a three-masted galley under full sail proper, flagged of the second, at her stern the banner of Scotland, all between two garbs or. **Crest** – A dexter hand couped at the wrist, grasping a dagger all proper.
Residence – The Corrie, Kilmacolm, Renfrewshire PA13 4NY.

SON LIVING

THOMAS (Bredon Croft, Bredons Norton, Tewkesbury, Glos GL20 7HB), *b* 22 April 1951; *ed* Rugby, and Aberdeen Univ (BSc): *m* 1984, Eileen, elder da of late Alexander Henry Stevenson, of Hurlford, Ayrshire, and has issue living, Thomas, *b* 11 March 1990, — Nicola Mary, *b* 1987.

DAUGHTER LIVING

Jennifer Margaret, *b* 1948: *m* 1st, 1978 (*m diss* 1983), Rupert V. Bruce; 2ndly, 1983, David Johnson of High Gables, Thelwall, Warrington, and has issue (by 2nd *m*), James David, *b* 1992, — Charlotte Mary, 1991.

SISTER LIVING

Dorothy Frances, *b* 1921: *m* 1948, Ernest Forrester Fortune, MBE, TD, who *d* 1993, of Allanton, Elie, Fife, and has issue living, George Dunlop (PO Box 707, 07080 Palma, Mallorca, Spain), *b* 1953: *m* 1977, Patricia Elise, da of Eric Moore, of Cheadle, Lancs, — Susan Elizabeth, *b* 1949.

COLLATERAL BRANCHES LIVING

Issue of late Capt William Beckett Dunlop, RHA, yr son of 2nd baronet, *b* 1915, *d* 1970: *m* 1947, Charmian Katherine Chauncy (66 Novar Drive, Glasgow, G12), da of late Col Gavin Charteris Towers Speirs, of Hume, Bearsden, Dunbartonshire:—
Anthony Charles Beckett, *b* 1948; *ed* Rossall. —— Michael William Beckett, *b* 1951; *ed* Rugby. —— Simon Speirs Beckett, *b* 1955; *ed* Millfield.

Issue of late Peter Mitchell Dunlop, 2nd son of 1st baronet, *b* 1883, *d* 1962: *m* 1915, Florence Leathard, who *d* 1983, da of John Gardner Brewis:—
Mary Mitchell, *b* 1924: *m* 1963, Walter A. Bishop, who *d* 1983, of Larchfield, Old Rd, Buckland, Betchworth, Surrey.

Grandchildren of late Robert Jack Dunlop (infra):—
Issue of late George Teacher Dunlop, *b* 1923, *d* 1992: *m* 1950, Margaret Jane Schoelles (Torbarn, Milson, Kidderminster, Worcs):—

Nicholas George Teacher, *b* 1956: *m* 1978, Schuyler Ann, da of Robert V. Fullan, of Long Is, NY, USA, and has issue living, Angus George Teacher, *b* 1979, — Meghan Victoria, *b* 1982. —— Rosalie Anne, *b* 1951: *m* 1976, Irwin Andrew Jeremy Bidgood, of Horsehill House, Ribbesford, nr Bewdley, Worcs, and has issue living, Jonathan Mark, *b* 1979, — Jeremy Paul, *b* 1983, — Susanna Ruth, *b* 1986. —— Carolyn Jane, *b* 1954: *m* 1975, David Hugh Gordon-Brown, of 53403 Range Rd 274, Spruce Grove, Alberta, Canada, and has issue living, Andrew Timothy, *b* 1983, — Natasha Jane, *b* 1978, — Rowena Christine, *b* 1980. —— Philippa Christine, *b* 1961: *m* 1983, John Reginald Low, of Duneam Cottage, Burntisland, Fife, and has issue living, Hamish Reginald, *b* 1985, — Roderick James, *b* 1990, — Jennifer Ruth, *b* 1987. —— Sally Margaret, *b* 1963: *m* 1989, John Peter Ashmore, of The Old Farmhouse, Britwell Salome, Watlington, Oxon, and has issue living, Benjamin Peter George, *b* 1995, — Lara Elizabeth, *b* 1993.

Issue of late Robert Jack Dunlop, youngest son of 1st baronet, *b* 1891, *d* 1952: *m* 1918, Maude Rowena, who *d* 1988, da of late William C. Teacher, of Bellcairn, Cove, Dunbartonshire:—

Robert Jack, *b* 1927: *m* 1950, Dorothy Shirley Dixon, and has issue living, Robert Alastair (5 Temple Village, by Gorebridge, Midlothian), *b* 1951: *m* 1975, Jane Christian Rankin, and has issue living, Robert Michael *b* 1985, Tessa Elizabeth Jane *b* 1979, Alison Ruth *b* 1981, — Timothy Dixon (Woodside Cottage, Kirk Brae, Shandon, Dunbartonshire), *b* 1953: *m* 1979, Pauline Anne Paisley, and has issue living, Ross Timothy *b* 1983, Brodie Kenneth *b* 1980, Gavin Craig *b* 1989, — Andrew James (Midway House, Partridge Green, Horsham, W Sussex), *b* 1959: *m* 1991, Lucia Elizabeth Mary Campbell Murfitt, and has issue living, Catriona Dorothy *b* 1992, Rhiannon Frances *b* (twin) 1992, Isobel Anne *b* 1995, — Gillian Elizabeth, *b* 1956: *m* 1983, David James Conway, and has issue living, Christopher James *b* 1984, Kathryn Elizabeth *b* 1986. *Residence* – Glaiceriska Cottage, Appin, Argyll. —— Audrey Dorothy, *b* 1932: *m* 1952, Antony Leonard Cullen, MC, TD, and has issue living, Michael Robert Antony, *b* 1955: *m* 1991, Julie Cox, and has issue living, one son and one da, — Roderick Leonard Dunlop, *b* 1958: *m* 1983, Marianne Carlsen and has issue living, three sons, — John Hamish Charles, *b* 1965: *m* 1989, Susan Flowers, and has issue living, one son, and two das, — David Alastair Thomas, *b* 1971: *m* 1999, Emma Stent, — Rowena Gay, *b* 1959, — Audrey Hilary, *b* 1963: *m* 1989, John Grigg, and has issue living, two sons and one da. *Residence* – Leighon, Manaton, Newton Abbot, S Devon.

The 1st baronet, Sir Thomas Dunlop, GBE (son of Thomas Dunlop, of Glasgow), was head of the firm of Thomas Dunlop & Sons, shipowners and grain merchants, of Glasgow, and Lord Provost of Glasgow and Lord-Lieut of co of City of Glasgow 1914-17.

DUNN (UK) 1921, of Bathurst, Province of New Brunswick, Dominion of Canada (Extinct 1976)

Sir PHILIP GORDON DUNN, 2nd and last *Baronet*.

DAUGHTERS LIVING OF SECOND BARONET

Serena Mary (*Baroness Rothschild*), *b* 1934: *m* 1961, 4th Baron Rothschild, of 28 Warwick Av, W9, and Stowell Park, Marlborough, Wilts, and has issue. —— Nell Mary, *b* 1936; author of *Up The Junction, Poor Cow, Grandmothers*, etc: *m* 1957 (*m diss* 1979), Jeremy Christopher Sandford, and has issue living, Roc (Gometra House, Isle of Gometra, Ulva Ferry, Isle of Mull), *b* 1957; has issue living (by Cassia Sarah Jacoba, da of Michael Kidron, of 221 Portobello Rd, W11), Cato Philip SANDFORD *b* 1989, and further issue (by Carmen Daphne, da of late John Hall, of Dallas, Texas), Savannah Rosabelle Scarlet Ivy Hall SANDFORD 1998, — Reuben (11 Argyll Mansions, King's Rd, SW3 5ER), *b* 1964, — Jem (3 White Horse St, W1Y 7LA), *b* 1967.

DAUGHTER LIVING OF FIRST BARONET (*By 2nd marriage*)

Anne, *b* 1929; painter: *m* 1st, 1951 (*m diss* 1960), Michael Wishart, painter and writer, who *d* 1996; 2ndly, 1960 (*m diss* 1987), as his 2nd wife, Rodrigo Moynihan, CBE, the portrait painter, who *d* 1990, and has issue living (by 1st *m*), Francis Dominic (Lambesc, Aix-en-Provence, France), *b* 1951; ed Bryanston, and Slade Sch of Art; painter, and founder Co-ordination Associative Regional pour la Défense de l'Environment (CARDE) 1990: *m* 1982, Catherine, da of Jean Vormus, and has issue living, James Derek *b* 1982, Antonin Michael *b* 1988, — (by 2nd *m*) Daniel Henry, *b* 1959. *Residence* – 40 Avenue du Leman, Lausanne, Switzerland.

DUNNING (UK) 1930, of Beedinglee, Lower Beeding, Sussex

Sir SIMON WILLIAM PATRICK DUNNING, 3rd *Baronet*; *b* 14 Dec 1939; *s* his father, *Sir* WILLIAM LEONARD, 1961; *ed* Eton: *m* 1975, Frances Deirdre Morton, da of Maj Patrick William Morton Lancaster, of Wapsbourne Manor, Sheffield Park, Sussex, and formerly wife of Capt Nigel Edward Corbally Stourton (*see* B Mowbray, colls), and has issue.
Residence – Low Auchengillan, Blanefield, Glasgow, G63 9AU.

DAUGHTER LIVING

Mariota Kathleen Masika, *b* 1976.

The 1st baronet, Sir Leonard Dunning (son of late Simon Dunning, of Warwick Square, SW), was an Inspector of Constabulary at Home Office 1912-30.

Dunnington-Jefferson, see Jefferson.

DUNTZE (GB) 1774, of Tiverton, co Devon

Sir DANIEL EVANS DUNTZE, 9th *Baronet*; *b* 11 Aug 1960; *s* his father, *Sir* DANIEL EVANS, 1997; *ed* Univ of Missouri, St Louis.
Residence – 6811 University Drive 2E, St Louis, Missouri 63130, USA.

SISTERS LIVING

Jill Alison, *b* 1957: *m* 1988, Eugene Pfeiffer, and has issue living, William Thomas, *b* 1988, — Benjamin Carl, *b* 1991. *Residence* – 7827 Greensfelder Lane, University City, Mo, USA 63130. —— Dr Robin Evans, *b* 1959: *m* 1987, Dr Mark Wright, and has issue living, Thomas Walker, *b* 1991, — Jack McGee, *b* 1996. *Residence* – 8944 Powell, Brentwood, MO, USA 63144.

AUNT LIVING (*Sister of 8th baronet*)

Dorothy Jane, *b* 1923: *m* 1950, Hal Roach, and has issue living, Michael Todd (21322 Wilderness Drive, Mountain Brook, Alabama 35213, USA) *b* 1952: *m* 19— (*m diss* 19—), and has issue living, Chauncey Blane *b* 1979, — Scott Evans (3814 Old Leeds Rd, Mountain Brook, Alabama 35213, USA), *b* 1953: *m* 1978, Leigh Anne Sellers, and has issue living, Katie Elizabeth *b* 1979, Hillary Anne *b* 1981, — Brooke Normile (204 Fairmont Drive, Mountain Brook, Alabama 35213, USA), *b* 1955: *m* 1983, Susan Lynn Alford, and has issue living, Keegan Wade *b* 1984, Sarah Savannah *b* 1986, — Todd Douglas (1454 Linkwood Lane, Decatur, Georgia 30033, USA), *b* 1957: *m* 1986, Daisy Cleveland, and has issue living, Zachary Cleveland *b* 1987. *Residence* – 9 Woodhill Rd, Birmingham, Alabama 35213, USA.

DAUGHTER LIVING OF SIXTH BARONET

Elizabeth Joan, *b* 1944: *m* 1966, Nicholas Lowther James Grove, of Cliffe House, Forge Hill, Aldington, Ashford, Kent, and has issue living, Richard Nicholas Dougal, *b* 1970, — Iain Anthony Douglas, *b* 1973.

WIDOW LIVING OF SIXTH BARONET

NESTA (*Dowager Lady Duntze*), da of late Thomas Richard Pendrell Herbert, of Newport, Mon, and formerly wife of late Lt-Col Godfrey Ariel Evill: *m* 1966, as his 2nd wife, Sir George Edwin Douglas Duntze, 6th Bt, CMG, who *d* 1985.

WIDOW LIVING OF SEVENTH BARONET

EMILY ELLSWORTH (*Emily, Lady Duntze*), da of Elmer Ellsworth Harlow, of New Bedford, Mass: *m* 1935, Sir John Alexander Duntze, 7th Bt, who *d* 1987.

WIDOW LIVING OF EIGHTH BARONET

MARIETTA (*Lady Duntze*), da of Ferdinand Welsh, of St Louis, Missouri, USA: *m* 1954, Sir Daniel Evans Duntze, 8th Bt, who *d* 1997. *Residence* – 6811 University Drive 2E, St Louis, Missouri 63130, USA.

The 1st baronet, an eminent merchant of Exeter, was sometime MP for Tiverton. The 2nd baronet was Receiver-General of the taxes of the co of Devon. The 6th baronet, Sir George Edwin Douglas Duntze, CMG, was a Provincial Commr, Uganda.

DUPREE (UK) 1921, of Craneswater, Portsmouth, co Southampton

The world is my field

Sir PETER DUPREE, 5th *Baronet*; *b* 20 Feb 1924; *s* his father, *Capt Sir* VICTOR, 1976: *m* 1947, Joan, da of late Capt James Desborough Hunt.

Arms – Vert, on a bend between two calves passant or three mullets of the field. Crest – A lion sejant proper supporting with the dexter forepaw a flagstaff proper, flowing therefrom a banner vert, charged with a mullet or.
Residence – 15 Hayes Close, Chelmsford, Essex, CM2 0RN.

SISTER LIVING

Mary, *b* 1926: *m* 1948, George Dutton Gibb, CB, FDS, RCS, of Yenda, Haw Lane, Bledlow Ridge, High Wycombe, Bucks, and has issue living, Elizabeth, *b* 1951: *m* 1983, Peter Glen, of 10 Paddocks, Wendover, Aylesbury, Bucks.

HALF-AUNT LIVING (*Daughter of 1st baronet by 2nd marriage*)

Irene Amy Marion: *m* 1936, John Gerrard Brendan O'Hagan, Squadron-Leader RAF, of Upperton Cottage, Petworth, W Sussex, and has issue living, Timothy David Brendan (The Old Rectory, 1 Mill Hill Rd, Norwich, Norfolk), *b* 1945; *ed* Westminster, and Corpus Christi Coll, Oxford (BA, DPhil) *m* 1970, Jennifer Kaue, and has issue living, Gabrielle *b* 1973, Rachel *b* 1974, — Elizabeth Mary Marion, *b* 1936: *m* 1st, 1961 (*m diss* 19—), John Shelley Bevington; 2ndly, 19—, — Burton, of 239 Main Rd, Southbourne, Emsworth, Hants, and has issue living (by 1st *m*), Mark *b* 1963, Amanda *b* 1967, Catherine *b* 1968, — Jennifer Ann, *b* 1938: *m* 1962, Rear Adm Guy Francis Liardet, CB, CBE, RN, of Downs Cottage, Meonstoke, Hants, and has issue living, Patrick (63 Kingsley St, SW11 5LF) *b* 1965: *m* 1995, Sophie Louise, da of Christopher Peter Maynard Gomm, of Frating Lodge, Frating, nr Colchester (and has issue living, Frederick William *b* 1998), Frances *b* 1962, Sophie *b* 1969.

DAUGHTER LIVING OF THIRD BARONET

Mary Marcella Lucy: *m* 1941, Terence Patrick Lawrence, of Fawley Vicarage, Wantage, son of late Sir Walter Lawrence, JP, of Hyde Hall, Sawbridgeworth, and has issue.

COLLATERAL BRANCHES LIVING

Issue of late Eric Dupree, 4th son of 1st baronet, *b* 1895, *d* 1932: *m* 1928, Gwendoline Violet, who *d* 1993, da of Henry Harvey:—
Monica Mary (43b York Street, Broadstairs, Kent), *b* 1930: *m* 1954 (*m diss* 1974), Robin Gordon Hazlitt Morris, and has issue living, Anthony John David, *b* 1955, — John Richard Hazlitt, *b* 1958, — Andrew Quentin Dupree, *b* 1963. —— Barbara Jane (51 High Street, Broadstairs, Kent), *b* 1931: *m* 1st, 1954, Lt John Richard Haward, RN, who *d* 1956; 2ndly, 1957 (*m diss* 1967), Ronald Mitchell, and has issue living, (by 2nd *m*) Terence Roger Anstey, *b* 1957, — Robert Killian, *b* 1959, — Simon Paul Adam, *b* 1966.

Issue of late Lt-Cdr James Dupree, RNVR, 5th son of 1st baronet, *b* 1899, *d* 1972: *m* 1928, Mary Ethel Gillott, who *d* 1949, da of late T. W. Reid, and widow of A. Stuart Elsworth:—
(THOMAS WILLIAM JAMES) DAVID (Little Fircliff, Whitworth Rd, Darley Dale, nr Matlock), *b* 5 Feb 1930. —— Jennifer Rosemary Gillott, *b* 1933: *m* 1962, Roberto Lorenzo Mercadal, and has issue living, a son, *b* 19—, — a son, *b* 19—, — Maria-Victoria, *b* 1964, — a da, *b* 1975. *Residence* – Son Moix Blanc 16, Palma de Mallorca, Spain.

Issue of late Thomas William Dupree, 6th son of 1st baronet, *b* 1913, *d* 1995: *m* 1st, 1938 (*m diss* 1953),

Anne, yst da of late Sir Henry Getty Chilton, GCMG; 2ndly, 1953, Mrs Jacqueline Harari (Paradis Roc, Bloc D, Chemin de St Christophe, 06130 Grasse, France), da of Commendatore Leo Goldschmied:—
(By 1st *m*) Delia, *b* 1939: *m* 1962, Peter Guy, and has issue living, Dominic William, *b* 1963, — Susannah, *b* 1965. — Sarah Anne, *b* 1942: *m* 1977, Michael Wilkins, of 47 St John's Av, SW15 6AL, and has issue living, William Michael, *b* 1978, — Sarah Jeanne, *b* 1979.

Issue of late Capt John Rupert Dupree, 7th son of 1st baronet, *b* 1915, *d* 1965: *m* 1946, Ann Margaret Frances (who *d* 1996, having *m* 3rdly, 1965, Roger Thornycroft, DSC, who *d* 1983, son of late Sir John Edward Thornycroft, KBE; and 4thly, 1984, Col Stuart Warren Don, of 113 Dovehouse St, SW3), only da of late Lt-Col Robert George Barlow, Seaforth Highlanders (ret), and formerly wife of late Hon William Gladstone Bethell (*see* B Bethell):—
Michael John (Uphills House, Hampton, Wilts), *b* 1947: *m* 1982, Alexandra Columbia, da of Michael Anthony Telfer Smollett, and has issue living, Tamara, *b* 1985.

The 1st baronet Col Sir William Thomas Dupree, VD, TD (son of late William Dupree) was Mayor of Portsmouth 1901-3 and 1909-10 and Hon Col RFA. The 2nd baronet, Sir William was Chm and Managing Director of the Portsmouth and Brighton United Breweries, Ltd.

DURAND (UK) 1892, of Ruckley Grange, Salop
(Name pronounced "Du-rand")

Sir EDWARD ALAN CHRISTOPHER DAVID PERCY DURAND, 5th *Baronet*; *b* 21 Feb 1974; *s* his father, *Rev Sir* (HENRY MORTIMER) DICKON MARION ST GEORGE DURAND, 1992; *ed* St Columba's Coll, Dublin, Milltown Inst of Theology and Philosophy, and Univ of Ulster.

𝔄rms – Azure, five fusils conjoined in fesse within a bordure or; on a chief embattled of the last, a pair of manacles of the first. 𝔠rest – Over a rock proper, a crescent argent between two laurel branches or.
Residence – Lisnalurg House, Sligo.

BROTHER LIVING

DAVID MICHAEL DICKON PERCY *b* 6 June 1978; *ed* St Columba's Coll, Dublin.

SISTERS LIVING

Esperance en Dieu
Hope in God

Rachel Elizabeth Marion, *b* 1972; *ed* St Columba's Coll, Dublin, Heatherley Sch of Fine Art, London, and Nat Coll of Art and Design, Dublin. —— Madeleine Eleanor Marion, *b* 1980; *ed* St Columba's Coll, Dublin.

AUNT LIVING (*sister of 4th baronet*)

Elizabeth Pamela Marion, *b* 1932: *m* 1957, Maj George Naismith Bowden, Loyal Regt (ret), of Higher Shute Farm, Huish Champflower, Taunton, Somerset, and has two adopted children, Alexander Dickon Naismith, *b* 1971, — Veronica Mary Patricia, *b* 1968.

DAUGHTER LIVING OF THIRD BARONET

Patricia Marion, *b* 1925: *m* 1st, 1960, Wing-Cdr Howard Rex English Rumsey, who *d* 1964; 2ndly, 1969, Kenneth Alec James Booth, MBE, FILA, who *d* 1981, of Fletching Cottage, Fletching St, Mayfield, E Sussex TN20 6TN, and has issue living (by 1st *m*), Alan, *b* 1962, — Fiona Marion, *b* 1964.

WIDOW LIVING OF FOURTH BARONET

STELLA EVELYN (*The Rev Lady Durand*), el da of late Capt Christopher Carleton L'Estrange, of Lisnalurg, co Sligo: *m* 1971, Rev Sir (Henry Mortimer) Dickon Marion St George Durand, 4th Bt, who *d* 1992. *Residence* – Lisnalurg House, Sligo, Republic of Ireland.

Sir Edward Law Durand, 1st Bt, Resident in Nepal 1888-91 was el son of Maj-Gen Sir Henry Marion Durand, KCSI, CB, Lt-Gov of Punjab 1870, *m* 1880, Maude Ellen, who *d* 1953, da of Algernon Charles Heber-Percy (D Northumberland).

DURRANT (GB) 1784, of Scottow, Norfolk

Sir WILLIAM ALEXANDER ESTRIDGE DURRANT, 8th *Baronet*; *b* 26 Nov 1929; *s* his father, *Sir* WILLIAM HENRY ESTRIDGE, 1994; Capt late 12th/16th Hunter River Lancers; JP: *m* 1953, Dorothy, da of Ronal Croker, of Quirindi, NSW, and has issue.

Arms – Or, a cross-crosslet ermines between four ermine spots sable. Crest – A boar passant per fesse wavy argents and gules, bristled and tusked azure, and pierced through the body with a broken lance bendwise sable, point downwards, gold.
Residence – Red Hill, Nundle Rd, Nemingha, NSW 2340, Australia.

SON LIVING

DAVID ALEXANDER, *b* 1 July 1960; MES, BSc (Sydney); electrical engr: *m* 1989, Maria Lucia, da of Neil Leonard, of Raymond Terrace, NSW, and has issue living, Alexander Llewelyn Estridge, *b* 1990, — Dominic Acelin William, *b* 1992, — Ellery James Gaspard, *b* 1994. *Residence* – 1/12 Ormond Rd, Ormond, Victoria 3163, Australia.

DAUGHTER LIVING

Susan Elizabeth, *b* 1962. *Residence* – ......

SISTER LIVING

Beryl Elizabeth Wildbredt, *b* 1928: *m* 1952, Douglas James Weaving, and has issue living, John Laurence, *b* 1956, — Peter Douglas, *b* 1958, — Elizabeth Anne, *b* 1953. *Residence* – Unit 90, Taroola, 9 Batman Av, Shepparton, Victoria 3630, Australia.

A dishonouring stain is worse than death

COLLATERAL BRANCH LIVING

Issue of late Reginald Walter Estridge Durrant, yr son of 6th baronet, *b* 1905, *d* 1986: *m* 1937, Joy Minnie (42 Hayle St, St Ives, NSW 2075, Australia), da of William George Smith, of Manly, NSW, Australia:—
Beverley Joy, *b* 1938: *m* 1957, Stanley Ross Ackers, of 17 Apps Av, Turramurra, NSW, Australia, and has had issue, Geoffrey Ross, *b* 1965, *d* 1991, — Annette Ruth, *b* 1959, — Margaret Lynne, *b* 1963. —— Kaye Lorraine, *b* 1944: *m* 1966, Malcolm Harvey Bird, of 384 Bobbin Head Rd, Turramurra, NSW, Australia, and has issue living, Murray Scott, *b* 1969, — Julie Anne, *b* 1968.

This family was established in Rutland and Derbyshire. William Durrant, from whom the present baronet is in direct descent, migrated to Scottow, Norfolk, and *d* 1700. Sir Thomas, 1st baronet, was High Sheriff of Norfolk 1784.

DYER (E) 1678, of Tottenham, Middlesex

Sir (HENRY) PETER FRANCIS SWINNERTON DYER, KBE, FRS, 16th *Baronet*; *b* 2 Aug 1927; *s* his father, *Sir* LEONARD SCHROEDER SWINNERTON, 1975; *ed* Eton (Fellow 1981-96) and Trin Coll, Camb (Fellow 1955, Dean 1963-73); FRS (1967); Master of St Catharine's Coll, Camb 1973-83, Prof Maths Camb Univ 1971-88, lect 1960-71, Univ Lectr Camb Mathematical Lab 1960-67; Vice-Cllr 1979-81; Chm Cttee on Academic Organisation (Lond Univ) 1980-82; Visiting Prof, Harvard Univ 1971; Commonwealth Fund Fellow, Univ of Chicago 1954-55 and Research Fellow Trin Coll Camb 1950-54; Chm Univ Grants Cmmn 1983-89; Chief Executive, Univ Funding Council 1989-92; Chm Sec of State for National Heritage's Advisory Cttee, the Library and Information Sers Council 1992-96; KBE (1987): *m* 1983, Dr Harriet Crawford, elder da of late Rt Hon Sir Patrick Reginald Evelyn Browne, OBE, TD.

Arms – Or, a chief indented gules. Crest – Out of a ducal coronet or a goat's head argent, horned gold.
Residence – The Dower House, Thriplow, Cambs.

Unwilling to frighten, unacquainted with fear

SISTER LIVING

Anne Winifred Swinnerton, *b* 1932.

DAUGHTER LIVING OF TWELFTH BARONET

Jacqueline Christine Swinnerton, b (*posthumous*) 1918; late Asst Section Officer WAAF: *m* 1st, 1943 (*m diss* 1949), Colin E. C. Campbell; 2ndly, 1949, Col Vincent Paravicini, TD, who *d* 1989, and has issue living (by 1st and 2nd *m*).

COLLATERAL BRANCHES LIVING

Granddaughters of late Maj Richard Stewart Dyer-Bennet (infra):—
Issue of late Richard Dyer-Bennet, folk singer, b 1913, d 1991: *m* 1st, 1936 (*m diss* 1941), Elizabeth Hoar Pepper; 2ndly, 1942, Melvene Ipcar (Star Route 62 Box 29, Great Barrington, MA 01230, USA):—
(By 1st *m*) Ellen WOOD (7921 Millvale Rd, Chesterfield, VA 23832, USA), b 1937; has assumed her stepfather's surname. — Eunice, b 1939: *m* 1962, Hilary Roche Davis, of 11030 SW 42 Court, Davie, FL 33328, USA, and has issue living, Robert Hilary, b 1967, — Lance Bradshaw, b 1971, — Mary Ellen, b 1965: *m* 19—, Scott Vincent Smith. — (By 2nd *m*) Bonnie, b 1943. — Brooke (a da), b 1946.

Grandchildren of late Frederick Stewart Hotham DYER-BENNET (assumed additional surname of Bennet 1894), only son of late Maj Frederick Carr Swinnerton Dyer, 3rd son of 9th baronet:—
Issue of late Maj Richard Stewart Dyer-Bennet, b 1886, d 1983: *m* 1st, 1912 (*m diss* 1955), Miriam Wolcott, who d 1973, da of late Prof Edward Bull Clapp, of Univ of California, USA: 2ndly, 1956, Christina, who d 1999, da of late John Colbert, of Newcastle-upon-Tyne:—
(By 1st *m*) JOHN (907 Winona St, Northfield, Minn 55057, USA), b 17 April 1915; Emeritus Prof of Mathematics at Carleton Coll, Northfield, Minn: *m* 1951, Mary Abby, da of late George B. Randall, and has issue living, David, b 1954, — Barbara, b 1965. — Miriam (10 Ross St, Toronto, Ont, Canada M5T 1Z9), b 1922: *m* 1st, 1945 (*m diss* 1962), Thomas Timothy Crocker; 2ndly, 1963, Kenneth O. May, who d 1977, and has issue living (by 1st *m*), Steven, b 1949, — Thomas, b 1952, — Cedric, b 1954, — Edith, b 1947.

Grandchildren of late Maj Richard Stewart Dyer-Benet (ante):—
Issue of late Frederick Dyer-Benet, architect, b 1918, d 1991: *m* 1941, Patricia Esther Arndt (154 Hillcroft Way, Walnut Creek, CA 94596, USA):—
Oliver (5847 Sharpe Rd, Calistoga, CA 94515, USA), b 1945: *m* 1984, Linda Helen Specht, and has issue living, Colin Wesley, b 1988, Katherine Elise, b 1985. — John (425 42nd Ave, Oakland, CA 94609, USA), b 1947. — Cynthia (634 King St, Santa Rosa, CA, USA), b 1949: *m* 1983, David Karl Peoples.

Issue of late Christopher Dyer-Bennet, b 1920, d 1985: *m* 1st, 1945, Peggy Friedman; 2ndly, 1973, Mrs Anna Louise Erben Baumhoff:—
(By 1st *m*) Christopher, b 1946. — Matthew, b 1948. — Anne, b 1952.

Grandson of late Capt Stewart John Dyer, 4th son of 9th baronet, b 1842, d 1925: *m* 1873, Emily Mary Elizabeth, who d 1912, only child and heir of late Henry Edmund Bythesea, of Nettleton, Wilts.
Issue of late Major Stewart Barton Bythesea Dyer, DSO, 2nd Life Guards, b 1875, d 1917: *m* 1906, Mai (she *m* 2ndly, 1921), Baron A. Pontenani, who d 1937, da of late Capt S. L. Osborne, RN, of Shankling, Isle of Wight:—
Thomas Musgrave Swinnerton, b 1907; *ed* Oratory Sch, and St Catharine's Coll Camb, formerly Lieut The Buffs; European War 1939-44 in Middle East: *m* 1936 (*m diss* 1948), Violet Elizabeth, da of Ebenezer Cunningham.

Grandchildren of late Thomas Richard Dyer, son of late Capt Edward Dyer, son of late Edward Dyer, brother of 8th baronet:—
Issue of late Frederick Thomas Swinnerton Dyer, b 1898, d 1982: *m* 1927, Beatrice Henrietta, who d 1978, da of Charles John Davies:—
John Frederick (Holdens, Shipton Green, Itchenor, Chichester), b 1928; late Fl-Lt RAF: Sen Training Capt British Airways (ret): *m* 1950, Linda Mary, who d 1996, da of Thomas Rees James, and has issue living, Martin John Swinnerton, b 1955; *ed* Worcester Coll, Oxford (MA, DPhil), and King's Coll, Camb (MB, BChir); FRCP, FRCPath; Mere's Student, St John's Coll, Camb, 1987-90, Reader, Inst of Cancer Research; Louise Buchanan Fulbright Scholar, Stanford Univ, Calif, 1996: *m* 1982, Sally Ann, da of John Woodward of Torquay, and has issue living, Samuel John Swinnerton b 1987, Rebecca Ann Swinnerton b 1984, — Richard Kenneth Swinnerton, b 1960; *ed* Hadlow Coll: *m* 1991, Mary Finlay, da of Timothy William Palmer, of Cranbrook, Kent. — Julian Swinnerton (The Mews, Rystwood, Forest Row, East Sussex) b 1936; late PO RAF; Co Sec, Vickers Group of Cos; Assist Sec Vickers Ltd, 1973-94: *m* 1961, Patricia Newman, and has issue living, Jeremy Swinnerton, b 1964; *ed* Sheffield Hallam Univ (BA Hons), — Ann-Louise, b 1966. — Jean Anne, b 1931: *m* 1952, A.W. Gransden, who d 1996, of 23 Mavis Close, Ewell, Surrey, and has issue living, Jonathan Kim, b 1953: *m* 1980, Janice Ruth, da of William Smith of Beddington, Surrey, — Joanna Debra, b 1957.

Issue of late Hugh Swinnerton Dyer, ED, b 1902, d 1981: *m* 1933, Barbara Eileen Homewood:—
David Swinnerton (Apt 417, 371, S Ellesmere Av, Burnaby, BC), b 1934; with Dept of Attorney Gen (Sheriff Office): *m* 1971, Beverley, da of Robert W. Steep. — Patrick Swinnerton, b 1937; *ed* Haileybury: *m* 1st, 1960 (*m diss* 1970), Elizabeth Rule, da of late Air Marshal Sir Thomas Arthur Warne-Brown, KBE, CB, DSC; 2ndly, 1971, Angela Evelyn Caldicott, and has issue living, (by 1st *m*), Thaila Elisabeth Swinnerton b 1962, — Lucinda Jane Swinnerton b 1963, — Susannah (Zanna) K. Swinnerton, b 1966: *m* 1991, Stuart D. R. Bell, of 130 Fawe Park Rd, Putney, SW15, elder son of John Sydney Bell, of The Manor House, Overthorpe, Banbury, Oxfordshire.

Grandchildren of late Thomas Harry Dyer (infra):—
Issue of late John Arnold Swinnerton Dyer, b 1905, d 1971: *m* 1st, 1930, Theresa Sylvester, who d 1947, da of Henry Sylvester Stannard; 2ndly, 1949, Elizabeth Mahala, da of Edward Valentine Johnston, of Bedford:—
(By 1st *m*) Thomas John Swinnerton, b 1931. — (By 2nd *m*) Philip John, b 1952. — Linda Theresa, b 1950.

Granddaughters of late Frederick Campbell Spencer Dyer, 4th and yst son of late Capt Edward Dyer (ante):—
Issue of late Thomas Harry Dyer, *b* 1878, *d* 1937: *m* 1904, Kate, who *d* 1953, da of John Willis, of Harpenden, Herts:—
Nellie Jane Kathleen, *b* 1906; Proprietor of Nell Dyer's Hat Shop, William St, Dublin, for 21 years; emigrated to USA 1959; Private and Gen Hosp nurse (ret): *m* 1957, Francis Coyle, who *d* 1982, of Blackrock, co Dublin. *Residence* – 141 Healdsburg Av 13, Cloverdale, Calif 95425, USA. —— Patricia Swinnerton, *b* 1912: *m* 1940, John Eric Mackenzie, Staff Sergeant, Roy Corps of Signals, and has issue living, Alan Ronald, *b* 1946, — Valerie Jean, *b* 1950. *Residence* – 2 Greenville Rd, Stradbrook Rd, Blackrock, co Dublin.

Grandchildren of late Frank Stanley Dyer, 3rd son of late Frederick Campbell Spencer Dyer (ante):—
Issue of late Benjamin Stanley Dyer, *b* 1914, *d* 1993: *m* 1937, Lillian Averina (312-2315 Mills Rd, Sidney, BC, Canada V8L 5W6):—
Althea Dawn, *b* 1938: *m* 1st, 1956, Allan Francis Millin, who *d* 1983; 2ndly, 19—, Brian Baldwin, of 3925 Gordon Rd, Powell River, BC, Canada V8A 2T8, and has had issue (by 1st *m*), Montgomery Allan, *b* 1956, — Andrew Brian, *b* 1961, — Cynthia Dawn-Marie, *b* 1958; *d* 19—

Issue of late Frederick Douglas Dyer, *b* 1916, *d* 1984: *m* 1941, Myrtle Winifred Foster (5287 Parker Av, Victoria, BC, Canada V8Y 2N1):—
Barbara Louise (3159B Jackson St, Victoria, BC, Canada V8X 1E2), *b* 1942: *m* 1965 (*m diss* 1966), Derry Allan McDonnell. —— Carol Ann (Box M7, 741 Carter Rd, Bowen Island, BC, Canada V0N 1G0), *b* 1947: *m* 1967 (*m diss* 19—), Ronald Douglas Robb. —— Nancy May (3766 Seaton St, Victoria, BC, Canada V8Z 3W4), *b* 1957.

Sir William, 1st baronet, *m* Thomazine, only da and heir of Thomas Swinnerton, of Stanway Hall, Essex. Col Sir John Swinnerton, 6th baronet, was a Groom of the Bedchamber to the Prince of Wales (afterwards George IV). Lieut-Gen Sir Thomas Richard, 7th baronet, was Aide-de-Camp to Sir Ralph Abercromby in Egypt, and to Sir John Moore at Corunna. Com Sir Thomas Swinnerton, RN, 8th baronet, was present at numerous naval actions during the Peninsular war, and his brother, Lieut-Col Sir John, KCB, was present at Badajoz, Vittoria, St Sebastian, Pyrenees, Nievelle, Nive, Orthes, and Toulouse. The 10th baronet served in Crimean war, and was present at Sebastopol, both assaults on the Redan and the bombardment and surrender of Kimburne. The 12th baronet, Sir John Swinnerton Dyer, MC, Capt Scots Guards, was *ka* 1917. The 15th baronet, Sir Leonard Schroeder Swinnerton Dyer, was Chm, Shropshire Co Council 1969-72.

DYKE (E) 1677, of Horeham, Sussex

Prest a Faire

Ready to act

Sir DAVID WILLIAM HART DYKE, 10th *Baronet*; *b* 5 Jan 1955; *s* his father, *Sir* DEREK WILLIAM HART, 1987; *ed* Ryerson Polytechnical Inst; BAA; Exec Dir Dixie Magazine

𝕬rms – Or, three cinquefoils, sable. 𝕮rest – A cubit arm in armour, the hand in a gauntlet sable, garnished or, holding a cinquefoil slipped also sable.
Residence – 28 King St West, Apt 14B, Stoney Creek, Ont, Canada L8G 1H4.

SISTER LIVING

Diana Lynn, *b* 1957: *m* 1986, John Costello McDonald. *Residence* – 52 Evelyn St, Brantford, Ontario, Canada.

UNCLE LIVING (*son of 8th baronet*)

(OLIVER) GUY HART, *b* 9 Feb 1928; *ed* Univ of British Columbia (BSc) *m* 1974, Sarah Alexander Hart, yr da of late Com the Rev Eric Hart Dyke, RN (see colls infra), and has issue living, Thomas Guy, *b* 1976, — Anya Elizabeth, *b* 1978. *Seat* – Lullingstone Castle, Eynsford, Kent.

MOTHER LIVING

Dorothy, da of Thomas Ansley Moses, of Atlanta, Georgia, USA: *m* 1953 (*m diss* 1963), as his 1st wife, Sir Derek William Hart Dyke, 9th Bt, who *d* 1987.

COLLATERAL BRANCHES LIVING

Granddaughter of late Reginald Charles Hart Dyke, 4th son of 6th baronet:—
Issue of late Ashley Francis Hart Dyke, *b* 1899, *d* 1982: *m* 1940, Marie, da of Johan Voldengen, Lier, Norway:—
Margaretha Millicent Hart, *b* 1946: *m* 1st, 19— (*m diss* 1975), Gordon Stanton; 2ndly, 1978, James Derek Smith, and has issue living (by 1st *m*), Britt-Marie, *b* 1968, — Bridgitte Maja, *b* 1973. *Residence* – .

Granddaughter of late Thomas Dyke, eldest son of late Rev Thomas Hart Dyke, 2nd son of 5th baronet:—
Issue of late Col Percyvall Hart Dyke DSO, Indian Army, *b* 1872, *d* 1952: *m* 1900, Louisa Catherine, who *d* 1961, da of Adm John Halliday Cave, CB:—
Cicely Hart, *b* 1907: *m* 1936, Lt-Col John William Radclyffe Dugmore, KOYLI, who *d* 1992, and has issue living, William Radclyffe, *b* 1940: *m* 1974, Patricia Elizabeth, 2nd da of the late F. B. Jarvis, of Hen Ard, Morya Bychan, Gwynedd, and has issue living, Amy Tamsyn Elizabeth *b* 1976, Polly Louise *b* 1978, Daisy Catherine *b* 1983, — Janet Elvyn Catherine, *b* 1938: *m* 1964, John Peter Merrett, of Bank End, Plumgarth, Kendal, and has issue living, Peter William *b* 1965, Sophie Catherine *b* 1966, Nicola Mary *b* 1971. *Residence* – Storrs Hill, Windermere, Cumbria.

Grandchildren of late Col Percyvall Hart Dyke, DSO (ante):—
Issue of late Brig Trevor Hart Dyke, DSO, *b* 1905, *d* 1995: *m* 1st, 1933 (*m diss* 1965), Eileen Joyce, da of late John Herbert Niblock-Stuart, of Nairobi, Kenya; 2ndly, 1965, Mary Eliot, da of J. A. Roberts, of Brook Dean, Hope, Derbys, and widow of Maj David E. Lockwood:—
(By 1st *m*) Terence Percyvall Hart, *b* 1934; *ed* Marlborough; Capt The Royals: *m* 1964, Wanda Hermione Krystyna, only da of late Lt-Col Joseph Mostyn, (*see* Mostyn, Bt), and has issue living, Paul Percyvall Hart, *b* 1965, — James Terence Hart, *b* 1966. ——Jennifer Hart, *b* 1939: *m* 1967 (*m diss* 1979), Lt Oliver Nicholas Vaudrey, RN (ret), and has issue living, David Clough Percyvall, *b* 1969, — Annabel, *b* 1972.

Issue of late Com the Rev Eric Hart Dyke, RN, *b* 1906, *d* 1971: *m* 1935, Mary, da of late Robert Alexander (Shaw-Stewart, Bt, colls):—
David, CBE, LVO (Hambledon House, Hambledon, Hants, PO7 4RU), *b* 1938; *ed* St Lawrence Coll, Ramsgate and Britannia RNC; Capt RN; ADC to HM 1988-90; LVO 1980, CBE (Mil) 1990: *m* 1967, Diana Margaret, da of Sir William Henry Tucker Luce, GBE, KCMG, and has issue living, Miranda Katharine, *b* 1972, — Alice Louisa, *b* 1975. ——Jane Hart, *b* 1936: *m* 1959, David Charles Holland, ERD, of Little Tye, Upper Hartfield, East Sussex, and has issue living, Charles Thurstan, *b* 1962: *m* 1987, Rachel Margaret McCabe, and has issue living, Richard Oliver *b* 1994, Robert David *b* 1996, Catherine Jane *b* 1992, — Caroline Mary, *b* 1960: *m* 1983, Dr Stephen Cox, and has issue living, James Robert *b* 1986, Jonathan Richard Andrew *b* 1992, Rachel Elizabeth *b* 1988, — Clare Lucinda, *b* 1966: *m* 1996, David Jonathan Francis, and has issue living living, Constance Mary *b* 1998. ——Sarah Alexander Hart, *b* 1946: *m* 1974, (Oliver) Guy Hart Dyke (ante).

Grandson of late Rev Percival Hart Dyke, 2nd son of late Rev Thomas Hart Dyke (ante):—
Issue of late Robert Percyvall Hart Dyke, *b* 1864, *d* 1951: *m* 1908, Mary Harriette Theodore, who *d* 1974, da of late Rev John Shephard (sometime V of Eton), Hon Canon of Ch Ch, Oxford, of 33 Craven Hill Gardens, W:—
Michael Percyvall Hart (10 Goldney Av, Clifton, Bristol BS8 4RA), *b* 1909; *ed* Marlborough; Middle East 1940-45 as Major RASC; *m* 1955, Jean MacGlashan, who *d* 1992, and has issue living, Timothy Percyvall Hart, *b* 1959: *m* 1992, Kate, only da of late C.H.G. Proctor, of Teignmouth, Devon, — Jeremy Percyvall Hart, *b* 1963, — Jennifer Mary Hart, *b* 1956: *m* 1984, Stephen Jeffrey Peacock, yst son of F. G. Peacock, of Hitchin, Herts, and has issue living, Thomas Michael *b* 1990, Alice Felicity *b* 1987.

Grandsons of late Col Edward Hart Dyke, 2nd son of late Lt-Col John Dixon Dyke (infra):—
Issue of late Percyvall Hart Dyke, *b* 1902; *d* 1982: *m* 1931, Helen Leonora, who *d* 1985, da of Dr Philip Henry Welch MacAdam, JP, Colonial Med Ser, of British Guiana:—
Michael Percyvall Hart (Mahaicony, 37 St John's Rd, Farnham, Surrey), *b* 1932. ——Patrick Alan Hart (48 Abbots Ride, Farnham, Surrey), *b* 1938: *m* 1969, Elzbieta Izabella, da of Eugeniusz Lotocki, of Warsaw, and has issue living, James Paul, *b* 1972, — Stephen Peter, *b* 1975.

Granddaughters of late Lieut-Col John Dixon Dyke, 3rd son of 5th baronet:—
Issue of late Lieut-Col Frederick Hotham Dyke, *b* 1840, *d* 1934: *m* 1871, Emily, who *d* 1941, da of late Rev Charles Faunce Thorndike, of Villa Freeland, Trieste:—
Winifred Amy, *b* 1881: *m* 1911, Cyril Arthur Mileham, solicitor, and has issue living, Barbara Dera, *b* 1918: *m* 1936, Eric Adrian Milne, and has issue living, Adrian Edward *b* 1940, Ian Hugh Milne *b* 1950, Rosemary Faith *b* 1941: *m* 1966, Dr Christopher John Bretherton Hundleby, of 606 Forest Hills, Mowbray, Cape Town (and has issue living, Alison Mary *b* 1967). *Residence* – Bure Acre, Aylsham, Norfolk, NOR 07Y.

Issue of late Col George Hart Dyke, *b* 1847, *d* 1922: *m* 1895, Edith Louise, who *d* 1952, da of late Thomas William Kinder, Master of Mints of Hong Kong and Japan:—
Helen Sandra Millicent, *b* 1897: *m* 1920, Lieut-Col Esdaile Addison Burkitt Orr, MC, Roy Berkshire Regt, who *d* 1977, and has issue living, Elizabeth, *b* 1923: *m* 1947, William Edward Penlygon Moon, who *d* 1965, and has issue living, Sandra Anne *b* 1953. *Residence* – 2 St Peter St, Marlow, Bucks.

Sir Thomas Dyke, of Horeham, Sussex (whose father migrated from Cranbrook, Kent), *m* 1639, Catherine, da of Sir John Bramston, Lord Chief Justice of the King's Bench. His son Sir Thomas Dyke, 1st Bt was Commr of Public Accounts 1696. The 2nd baronet removed from Horeham to Lullingstone Castle, having married Anne, da and heir of Percival Hart of that place. Sir Percival Hart Dyke, 5th baronet, unsuccessfully claimed the Barony of Brayes, of which he was a co-heir through the Harts, 1836. The 7th baronet, Rt Hon Sir William Hart Dyke, sat as MP for W Kent (*C*) 1865-8 for Mid Kent 1868-85, and for Kent, Dartford Div 1885-1906, and was Sec to the Treasury 1874-80, Ch Sec for Ireland 1885-6, and Vice-Pres of Council on Education 1887-92.

Eardley-Wilmot, see Wilmot.

EARLE (UK) 1869, of Allerton Tower, Woolton, Lancashire

Preserve a medium

Sir (HARDMAN) GEORGE ALGERNON EARLE, 6th *Baronet*; *b* 4 Feb 1932; *s* his father, *Sir* HARDMAN ALEXANDER MORT, 1979; *ed* Eton: *m* 1967, Diana Gillian Bligh, da of late Col Frederick Ferris Bligh St George, CVO (*see* St George, Bt, colls), and has issue.

Arms – Argent, three pallets ermines. **Crest** – A lion's jamb erased sable, holding a harpoon argent.
Residence – Neopardy Mill, nr Crediton, Devon EX17 5EP. *Club* – Royal Yacht Sqdn.

SON LIVING

ROBERT GEORGE BLIGH, *b* 24 Jan 1970.

DAUGHTER LIVING

Katharine Susan, *b* 1968.

SISTER LIVING

Belinda Mary, *b* 1937: *m* 1st, 1959 (*m diss* 1968), Capt Patrick John Boteler Drury-Lowe, who *d* 1993 (*see* M Linlithgow, colls, 1990 Edn); 2ndly, 1973, Anthony David Arnold William Forbes, of Wakerley Manor, Oakham, Rutland (*see* B Faringdon, colls, 1980 Edn), and has issue living (by 1st *m*), Lucy Belinda, *b* 1961: *m* 1989, David Charles Palmer, and has issue living (*see* V Churchill), — Candida Dorothy, *b* 1963: *m* 1990, G. Piers Bracher, only son of Peter Bracher, of The Old Rectory, Ashford, Kent, and has issue living, Barnaby Alexander Patrick *b* 1993, Harvey Peter Garnett *b* 1995.

AUNT LIVING (*Daughter of 4th baronet*)

Myrtle Valentine, *b* 1911: *m* 1st, 1933 (*m diss* 1947), Robert Owen Symon; 2ndly, 1948, Sydney Vernon, who *d* 1961; 3rdly, 1962, Brig Maurice Robert Lonsdale, DSO, OBE, who *d* 1989, and has issue living, (by 1st *m*) Mairi Edith, *b* 1935.

COLLATERAL BRANCHES LIVING

Issue of late Charles Frederic Earle, 6th son of 2nd baronet; *b* 1867, *d* 1939; *m* 1911, Alice Adelaide, who *d* 1942, da of Henry Cleveland, and widow of Patrick Cumin Scott, MB, of Blackheath, SE:—
Evelyn Alice, *b* 1912. *Residence* – 18 Challoner Court, 224 Bromley Rd, Shortlands, Kent BR2 0AB. —— Josephine Noelle, *b* 1914: *m* 1941, Douglas Swinscow, DSc, MB, FLS, who *d* 1992, and has issue living. *Residence* – Everley, Monmouth St, Topsham, Exeter. —— Rosamond Cleveland, *b* 1918: *m* 1939, Rev Canon Eric Albert Metcalfe, who *d* 1984, of 14 Burnhill Rd, Beckenham, Kent, and has issue living.

Grandchildren of late Cecil Arthur Earle, el son of late Arthur Earle (infra):—
Issue of late Capt Guy Fife Earle, *b* 1891, *d* 1966: *m* 1st 1918 (*m diss* 1922), Isabel Bridget, who *d* 1971, da of late Andrew Greville Rouse-Boughton-Knight (Rouse-Boughton, Bt); 2ndly, 1924 (*m diss* 1928), Helen Alice who *d* 1967, da of late Ninian Lowis Elliott (E Minto, colls); 3rdly, 1935, Bridget Joan, who *d* 1993, da of late Peter Sherston, of Hill House, Templecombe, Som:—
(By 1st *m*) Audrey Bridget (Arnolds, Burnham Market, Kings Lynn), *b* 1920. —— (By 3rd *m*) Michael Guy (83 Fairview Av, Newtown, Vic 3220, Australia), *b* 1942; *ed* Harrow, and Roy Agric Coll, Cirencester: *m* 1969, Morrell Francis Armytage, el da of Sqdn Ldr John Robert Nassau Molesworth, DFC (*see* V Molesworth, colls), and has issue living, Guy Robert, *b* 1973, — Nicholas Molesworth, *b* 1980, — Amanda Morrell, *b* 1971. —— Susan Mary (Taponecco 45, Tavernelle (MS), 54010 Italy), *b* 1940: *m* 1978 (*m diss* 1996), Kenneth Searle, MBE, CMZS. —— Virginia Ida (Valley Barn, Colaton Raleigh, Sidmouth, Devon EX10 0JA), *b* 1945: *m* 1971 (*m diss* 1977), Frederick Jackson, and has issue living, Conrad Guy Frederick, *b* 1973.

Issue of late Brig Eric Greville Earle, DSO, *b* 1893, *d* 1965: *m* 1st, 1918 (*m diss* 1931), Noel, who *d* 1975, da of Capt Edward Downes-Martin, formerly of Killoskehane Castle, co Tipperary; 2ndly, 1931, Diana Mary, who *d* 1964, da of late Dr Vaughan Harley, of Walton Hall, Bletchley:—
(By 1st *m*) David Eric Martin, OBE (Shipways, Church Lane, Kington Langley, Chippenham, Wilts), *b* 1921; *ed* Stowe, and Ch Ch, Oxford; Col RA; Burma 1945; Palestine 1947-48; Cyprus 1955-56; OBE (Mil) 1969: *m* 1947, Betty Isobel Shield, and has issue living, Charles Henry Diccon (Riseholme, Seven Hills Rd, Cobham, Surrey), *b* 1951: *m* 1984, (Margorie) Lucy, da of Dr William Mervyn Jones, of Waunfawr, Aberystwyth, Dyfed, and has issue living, Guy Charles William *b* 1985, James Edward David *b* 1987, — George William Eric David (15 Castello Av, Putney, SW15), *b* 1953: *m* 1985, Clare, da of late Graeme Campbell Johnston, and has issue living, Graeme David Campbell *b* 1988, Andrew David Campbell *b* 1993, Rosemary Elizabeth Campbell *b* 1990, — Victoria Lilian Gay (Bank Top Cottage, Lazonby, Penrith, Cumbria CA10 1AJ), *b* 1952: *m* 1977 (*m diss* 1989), Richard Walter Sutcliffe, and has issue living, Diccon Thomas George *b* 1983, Sophie Isobel Susan *b* 1980, — Charlotte Mary, *b* 1959: *m* 1991, Anthony N. A'Hern, of Lantern Cottage, Lane End, Bucks, only son of Maj T. A'Hern, of Sherborne, Dorset, and has issue living, William David Anthony *b* 1993, Henry Thomas Edward *b* 1995. —— †Robin Denys Michael, OBE *b* 1922; *ed* Wellington Coll; formerly Lt Fleet Air Arm; SE Asia 1939-45, OBE 1942: *m* 1st, 1946 (*m diss* 1962), Rosemary, da of Maj F. A. Latter, of Birkdault, Lindfield; 2ndly, 1963 (*m diss* 19—), Anne da of late Capt Lawford; 3rdly, 1977, Ann —, who *d* 1999, and *d* 1990, leaving issue, (by 1st *m*) Toby Dick (Sunnyside, 54 Long Copse Lane, Emsworth, Hants PO10 7UR), *b* 1951: *m* 1981, Juliet Miranda, da of Basil Peredur Jones, of Constantine, Cornwall, and has had issue, †Robin *b* 1982, *d* 1984, Joshua Robin *b* 1984, Barnaby Dicken *b* 1988, — Penelope Jane, *b* 1947: *m* 1977, Kenneth Brunton Ward, of 54 Langham Rd, Teddington, Middx TW11 9HQ, son of James Alfred Ward, of Edinburgh, and has issue living, Gemma Kate *b* 1981, — Jemima Tamsin, *b* 1949: *m*

1st, 1970 (*m diss* 1985), Robert Arthur Meads, son of Arthur Meads; 2ndly, 1986, Roland Wooding, of 2 Little London, Silverstone, Northants NN12 8UP, son of George Clifford Wooding, and has had issue, (by 1st *m*) Nicholas John *b* 1972, Andrew David *b* 1975, *d* 1991, Caroline Elizabeth *b* 1977, (by 2nd *m*) David Richard *b* 1986, — Lucy Noel, *b* 1954: *m* 1st, 19— (*m diss* 19—), son of —; 2ndly, 19—, Stuart Willson, of Brewer's Cottage, Plymtree, nr Cullompton, Devon, son of — Willson. ——— Peter Noel Desmond (30 Hill Rise, Croxton, Thetford, Norfolk IP24 1LL), *b* 1923; *ed* Wellington Coll, and Ch Ch, Oxford (BA 1949, MA 1954); formerly Lt RNVR; Atlantic and S-E Asia 1939-45: *m* 1952, Shirley Hope, who *d* 1986, da of Wallace MacGregor, of Vancouver, British Columbia, and has issue living, Virginia Melanie, *b* 1963, and an adopted son and da, Robert Henry Matthew, *b* 1956, — Heather Anne, *b* 1958.

        Grandsons of late Arthur Earle, 4th son of 1st baronet:—
        Issue of late John Greville Earle, *b* 1869, *d* 1933: *m* 1920, Jacobina Reid, who *d* 1970, da of late James Clark, of Kilmarnock:—
John Arthur (21 via Udine, 34132 Trieste, Italy), *b* 1921; *ed* Winchester, and Trin Coll, Camb (BA 1948); European War 1939-45 in Middle East and Central Mediterranean as Capt Rifle Brig (wounded): *m* 1947, Anna Maria, da of late Maj-Gen Lorenzo Tiziani, Italian Army, of Trecenta, Italy, and has issue living, Lawrence Hardman (8 via Tor S Piero, Trieste, Italy), *b* 1948; *ed* Winchester, and Malta Univ (BA): *m* 1984, Rita Dougan, and has issue living, Mathew John *b* 1986, Martina Jacobina Paola *b* 1988, — Arabella Ida (14 via Machiavelli, Milan, Italy), *b* 1955: *m* 1996, Paul Lizioli, of Milan, Italy, and of Bombay, India. ——— William Hardman, *b* 1924; *ed* Winchester, and Trin Coll, Camb (BA 1945, MA 1954); S-E Asia 1945 as Capt RE: *m* 1958, Vera Charteris, who *d* 1992, da of Colin Black, of Fryars, West Chiltington, Sussex, and has issue living, Rupert Langton, *b* 1960; *ed* Winchester, and Trin Coll, Camb (BA), — Greville Hoare, *b* 1963; *ed* Winchester, and Edinburgh Univ, — (Alice) Jacobina, *b* 1970; *ed* Edinburgh Univ. *Residence* – The Walnuts, Beanacre, Melksham, Wiltshire. *Club* – United Oxford and Cambridge. ——— Richard Greville, *b* 1925; *ed* Winchester, and Trinity Coll, Camb (BA 1949, MA 1959); formerly Sub-Lt (A) RNVR, High Sheriff of Dorset 1983, DL Dorset 1984: *m* 1956, Joanna Mary (DL Dorset 1997), JP, da of Com H. K. B. Mitchell, CBE, JP, DL, RN (ret), of Folke Manor, Sherborne, Dorset, and has issue living, Elizabeth Mary, *b* 1957: *m* 1997, Geoffrey W. Kenton, son of Richard Kenton, of W Bexington, Dorset, — Susan Helen, *b* 1959: *m* 1993, Neil S. Ross, son of Leslie Ross, of Evesham, Worcs, and has issue living, Duncan *b* 1997, Fenella *b* 1995. *Residence* – Frankham Farm, Ryme Intrinseca, Sherborne, Dorset.

        Issue of late Lawrence Mathew Earle, *b* 1881, *d* 1968: *m* 1916, Helen Elizabeth Dunkin, who *d* 1963, da of late Capt Frederic Street, of Dulverton:—
Nigel Lawrence (5 Kite's Close, E Hunsbury, Northampton NN4 0QR), *b* 1926; *ed* Radley; 1944-45 War with R Armoured Corps: *m* 1951, Jean, da of late Dr Hugh McClintock, and has issue living, Brian Lawrence, *b* 1953, — Patrick Nigel, *b* 1958: *m* 1981, (Susan) Elizabeth, da of Capt David Kenneth Bawtree, RN, of Grant Rd, Farlington, Portsmouth, Hampshire, and has issue living, Guy *b* 1993, Amaryllis (Lily) Roxborough *b* 1991.

  This family was settled at Warrington in the 16th century, and in 1709 died John Earle (son of Gregory Earle), a principal inhabitant of the place. His son John settled in Liverpool, and was Mayor thereof 1709. His grandson, Thomas, Mayor of Liverpool 1787, was father of William, also Mayor of Liverpool in 1836, as well as of Sir Hardman, 1st baronet. Sir Henry, DSO, 3rd baronet, was Lieut-Col King's Own Yorkshire LI. Sir (Thomas) Algernon, TD, 4th baronet, was Lieut-Col sometime Comdg Lancashire Hussars.

EBRAHIM (UK) 1910, of Bombay

Sir MAHOMED CURRIMBHOY, 4th *Baronet*; previously styled *Sir* Currimbhoy Ebrahim; *b* 24 June 1935; *s* his father, *Sir* (HUSEINALI) CURRIMBHOY, 1952: *m* 1958, Dur-e-Mariam, da of Minuchehir Ahmed Nurudin Ahmed Ghulam Ally Nana, of Karachi, Sind, W Pakistan, and has issue.

Arms – Argent, in base on waves of the sea a Chinese junk sailing to the sinister, in chief also on waves two dhows sailing to the dexter all proper, and in chief per pale gules and or thereon a pale azure between a rose of the first and a lotus flower also proper, and charged with a mullet issuant from a crescent above five mullets in crescent also of the first. Crest – Above an Indian lily on water proper, a mullet radiated or.
Residence – F65/1 Block 4, KDA Scheme no 5, Clifton, Pakistan.

SONS LIVING

ZULFIQAR ALI, *b* 5 Aug 1960; *ed* Habib Public Sch, and DJ Science Coll: *m* 1984, Adila, da of Akhtar Halipota, and has issue living, Mustafa, *b* 22 Sept 1985. ——— Murtaza Ali, *b* 1963. ——— Raza Ali, *b* 1964.

DAUGHTER LIVING

Durre Najaf, *b* 1969.

God leading, nothing hurts

HALF SISTERS LIVING

Mumtaz, *b* 1922: *m* 1941, Ahmed Rahim Valimahomed Peermahomed. ——— Munira, *b* 1923: *m* 1941, Fazal Rahemtulla Maherali Chinoy, and has issue living, Nafeesa, *b* 19—.

GREAT-AUNTS LIVING (*Daughters of 1st baronet*)

Jenabai, *b* 1880: *m* 1896, Gulamhusein Ladhabhoy Ebrahim. —— Sherbanu, *b* 1882: *m* 1899, Gulamhusein Rehemtullah Khairaj. —— Labai, *b* 1883: *m* 1902, Abdullabhoy Gulamhusein Allana. —— Shireenbai, *b* 1888: *m* 1911, Rahin Vali Mahomed Pirmahomed. —— Khairubai (Khairunisha), *b* 1894: *m* 1916, Currimbhoy Nensey Khairaz. —— Mariumbai, *b* 1896: *m* 1916, Cassumali Subjeally. —— Sharifabai, *b* 1899: *m* 1921, Sulieman Rahimtulla Sayani. —— Khatijabai, *b* 1901: *m* 1923, Yusafali Moosabhoy Jaffer Pradham. *Residence* – Pabaney Villa, Warden Rd, Bombay, India.

WIDOW LIVING OF THIRD BARONET

ALHAJA AMINA KHANUM (*Alhaja, Lady Ebrahim*), da of Al-Qassamally Jairazbhoy, of Gulshanabad, Peddar Rd, Bombay: *m* 1926, as his second wife (*m diss* 1944), Sir (Huseinali) Currimbhoy Ebrahim, 3rd baronet, who *d* 1952, and whom she re-married 1949. *Residence* – .

COLLATERAL BRANCHES LIVING

Issue of late Sir Fazulbhoy Currimbhoy Ebrahim, CBE, 4th son of 1st baronet, *b* 1873, *d* 1970: *m* 1889, Sakinabai, who *d* 1930, da of late Datoobhoy Ebrahim, of Cutch Mandvi:—
Ahmedbhoy Fazulbhoy, *b* 1902: *m* 1923, Zarina, da of late Ahmedbhoy Currimbhoy Ebrahim (infra), and has issue living, Ariff, *b* 1926, — Niamat, *b* 1928. —— Mohamedali, *b* 1904. —— Gulamali, *b* 1905: *m* 1928, Hamida, da of late Rehemtullah Currimbhoy Ebrahim (infra). —— Hoosein, *b* 1911. —— Amir Ali, *b* 1913.

Granddaughter of late Ebrahim CURRIMBHOY (infra):—
Issue of late Allen CURRIMBHOY, *b* 1924, *d* 1960: *m* 1958, Pritee Misra:—
Alia *b* 1961.

Grandchildren of late Gulamhusein Currimbhoy Ebrahim (infra):—
Issue of late Ebrahim CURRIMBHOY, *b* 1897, *d* 1969: *m* 1923, Zarina, da of Ahmed Curmally Janmahomed:—
Zinet, *b* 1925. —— Asif Currimbhoy (43 Bakhtawar, 22 N Dabholkar Rd, Bombay 400 006, India), *b* 1928: *m* 1951, Suraiya Ismail, da of Ismailbhoy Currimbhoy Ebrahim (ante), and has issue living, Tabrik, *b* 1952: *m* 1979, Nelofar Hussain, and has issue living, Sharik, *b* 1980, — Tarek, *b* 1954, — Nahed, *b* 1959: *m* 1982, Amit Moitra, and has issue living, Tahzeeb *b* 1983, Tahini *b* 1991.

Issue of late Gulamhusein Currimbhoy Ebrahim, 5th son of 1st baronet, *b* 1879, *d* 1918: *m* 1896, Khanoobai, da of Datoobhoy Ebrahim, of Cutch Mandvi (ante):—
Ali Mahomed, *b* 1902. —— Aziz, *b* 1915. —— Ammeena, *b* 1896: *m* 1916, A. O. Jamal, of Calcutta.

Grandchildren of late Ahmedbhoy Currimbhoy Ebrahim (infra):—
Issue of late Hosseinali Ebrahim, *b* 1908, *d* 1968: *m* 1928, Nazli, da of late Rehemtullah Currimbhoy Ebrahim (infra):—
Semine, *b* 1929. —— a da, *b* 1933.

Issue of late Ahmedbhoy Currimbhoy Ebrahim, 6th son of 1st baronet, *b* 1885, *d* 1925: *m* 1902, Shireen, da of Dost Mahomed Allana, of Bombay:—
Habibbhoy, *b* 1910. —— Zarina, *b* 1904: *m* 1923, Ahmedbhoy Fazulbhoy Ebrahim (ante). *Residence* –

Issue of late Rehemtullah Currimbhoy Ebrahim, 7th son of 1st baronet, *b* 1887, *d* 1928: *m* 1908, Sakinabai, da of Jafferbhoy Ratansey, formerly of Bombay:—
Nazli, *b* 1909: *m* 1928, Hooseinali Ebrahim, who *d* 1968, (ante). —— Hamida, *b* 1912: *m* 1928, Gulamali Ebrahim (ante).

Issue of late Habibbhoy Currimbhoy Ebrahim, 8th son of 1st baronet, *b* 1889, *d* 1949: *m* 1913, Khatijabai, da of Nensey Khairaj, of Bombay:—
Nazim, *b* 1915: *m* 1941, Zarina, da of Ahmed S. Moloobhoy, of Bombay, and has issue living, Reisa, *b* 1944. —— Sultan, *b* 1921: *m* 1949, Munira, da of late Sir Fazal Ibrahim Rahimtoola, CIE, and has issue living, Habib, *b* 1950. —— Husem, *b* 1924. —— Aziz, *b* 1927. —— Munira, *b* 1926.

Issue of late Ismailbhoy Currimbhoy, 9th son of 1st baronet, *b* 1906, *d* 1975: *m* 1925, Zarina, da of Gulam Husain Sachedina:—
Aziz *b* 1927, — Suraiya Ismail, *b* 1929: *m* 1951 Asif Currimbhoy Ebrahim (ante).

Sir Currimbhoy Ebrahim, 1st Bt, was a leading member of the Khoja Community, and an opium, yarn, cotton, silk, tea, sugar, and cloth merchant of Bombay, Hong Kong, Kobe, Shanghai, and Calcutta; owned the Currimbhoy, the Mahomedbhoy, the Ebrahimbhoy Pabaney, the Fazulbhoy, the Crescent, the Indore Malwa United Mills, the Pearl Mills, and many other factories (ginning and pressing), and the Indian Bleaching, Dyeing, and Printing Works; established a Girl's Sch, a Madressa at Mandvi, the Curimbhoy Ebrahim Khoja Orphanage in Bombay, and Dharmsalas at Mandvi and Bhuj; gave large donations to Bombay New Museum Fund, for the new Science Sch for Bombay, and for Scholarships for Mahomedans. The 2nd baronet, Sir (Mahomedbhoy) Currimbhoy Ebrahim, was a partner in the firm of Currimbhoy Ebrahim and Sons. Each Baronet on succession assumes the name of the 1st Bt.

ECHLIN (I) 1721, of Dublin
(Name pronounced "Ecklin")

Sir NORMAN DAVID FENTON ECHLIN, 10th *Baronet*; *b* 1 Dec 1925; *s* his father, *Sir* JOHN FREDERICK, 1932; *ed* Masonic Boys' Sch, Clonskeagh, co Dublin; Capt (ret) Indian Army: *m* 1953, Mary Christine, only da of John Arthur, of Oswestry, Shropshire.

Arms – Quarterly, 1st and 4th or, an antique galley, sails furled sable, a forked pennon gules; 2nd and 3rd gules, a fesse chequey argent and azure, a chief of the last thereon a hound in full chase after a stag, both proper. **Crest** – A talbot passant proper.
Residence – Nartopa, Marina Av, Appley, Ryde, I of Wight.

Non sine praedâ

Not without prey

SISTER LIVING

Patricia Hazel, *b* 1928: *m* 1951, Fred Tiller, and has issue living, Fred, *b* 1966, — Hazel Jean, *b* 1952, — Heather Valerie, *b* 1956. *Residence* – 52A Lymington Rd, New Milton, Hants BH25 6PY.

AUNT LIVING

Aileen Alexandra: *m* 1919, John Atkinson, who *d* 1923.

The Echlin family is of ancient Scottish origin, and formerly possessed princely estates in Scotland, and also large domains in the counties of Kildare, Carlow, Dublin, Galway, and Mayo. Andrew Echlin, of Pittadro, Fifeshire, was Constable and Deputy-Gov of Edinburgh Castle during the siege of 1572. The Right Rev Dr Echlin, Bishop of Down and Connor, who *d* 1635, was great-grandfather of Sir Henry Echlin, Knight, a Baron of the Court of Exchequer in Ireland, who was created a baronet in 1721. The 2nd baronet sat as MP for Newry. The 3rd baronet dissipated the family estates. The 4th baronet was one of the gentlemen before whom Hamilton Ronan knelt in the Court of King's Bench to beg the King's pardon. The Kildare estates were dissipated by the 4th, 5th and 6th baronets. Sir Henry Frederick, 8th baronet, was sometime Landlord of The Cider House, Haddenham, Bucks, and Sir John Frederick, 9th baronet, was Sergeant in Roy Ulster Constabulary.

EDGE (UK) 1937 of Ribble Lodge, Lytham St Annes, co Lancaster

(*Sir*) WILLIAM EDGE, 3rd *Baronet*; *b* 5 Oct 1936; *s* his father, *Sir* KNOWLES, 1984, but his name does not appear on the Official Roll of the Baronetage, nor does he use the title; *ed* Shrewsbury, Trin Hall, Camb (MA), and Harvard Business Sch (MBA): *m* 1959, Avril Elizabeth, da of Harold Denson, and has issue.

Arms – Sable, an eagle displayed argent between four cinquefoils or. **Crest** – In front of a reindeer's head erased two rose sprigs in saltire proper flowered gules.
Residence – 66 Harrow Rd, Maidenhead, Berks.

SONS LIVING

EDWARD KNOWLES, *b* 6 June 1965. —— Martin William, *b* 1968.

DAUGHTERS LIVING

Christina Jane, *b* 1963 —— Susannah Clare, *b* 1971.

OFFICIO EGERE·NOLO

I do not wish to fail in my duty

The 1st baronet, Sir William Edge (son of late Sir Knowles Edge, of Great Marld, Smithills, Bolton), sat as MP for Bolton-le-Moors (*L*) 1916-18 and 1918-23, and for Leicestershire, Bosworth Div 1927-45, and was knighted in 1922.

EDMONSTONE (GB) 1774, of Duntreath, Stirlingshire.

Virtue adds to honour

Sir ARCHIBALD BRUCE CHARLES EDMONSTONE, 7th *Baronet*; *b* 3 Aug 1934; *s* his father, *Sir* ARCHIBALD CHARLES, 1954; *ed* Stowe: *m* 1st, 1957 (*m diss* 1967), Jane, el da of late Maj-Gen Edward Charles Colville, CB, DSO (*see* V Colville of Culross, colls); 2ndly, 1969, Juliet Elizabeth, da of Maj-Gen Cecil Martin Fothergill Deakin, CB, CBE (*see* Grant, Bt, *cr* 1705, 1980 Edn), and has issue by 1st and 2nd *m*.

𝕬rms – Or, an annulet gules, stoned azure, between three crescents of the second within a double tressure flory-counterflory of the second. 𝕮rest – Out of a crest-coronet of four strawberry leaves or, a swan's head and neck proper. 𝕾upporters – Two lions rampant gules.
Seat – Duntreath Castle, Blanefield, Stirlingshire G63 9AJ.

SONS LIVING (*By 1st marriage*)

ARCHIBALD EDWARD CHARLES, *b* 4 Feb 1961; *ed* Stowe, and RMA Sandhurst: *m* 1988, Ursula, eldest da of late Benjamin Worthington (*see* Howard-Lawson, Bt). *Residence* – 2A Rhodesia Rd, SW9 2EL. —— Nicholas William Mark, *b* 1964: *m* 1st, 1989, Mary M., da of Malcolm Hall, of Gibraltar Farm, Jersey, CI; 2ndly, 1994, Arabella Charlotte, da of Richard Johnsen, of Shalden Manor, Shalden, Hants (*see* Bowater, Bt, *cr* 1939, 1990 Edn), and has issue living (by 1st *m*), Emily Cari, *b* 1990, — (by 2nd *m*), Jack William Charles, *b* 1996, — Isabella May, *b* 1995.

(*By 2nd marriage*)

Dru Benjamin Marshall, *b* 1971.

DAUGHTERS LIVING (*By 1st marriage*)

Philippa Carolyn, *b* 1958: *m* 1983 (*m diss* 1994), Peter William Huntington, who *d* 1998, and has issue (*see* Palmer, Bt, *cr* 1886).

(*By 2nd marriage*)

Elyssa Juliet, *b* 1973.

SISTERS LIVING

Mary Bettine (*Lady McGrigor*), *b* 1927: *m* 1948, Capt Sir Charles Edward McGrigor, 5th Bt, late Rifle Brig. *Residence* – Upper Sonachan, by Dalmally, Argyll PA33 1BJ. —— Jane Fiona, *b* 1931: *m* 1st, 1950 (*m diss* 1975), Maj Sir (Andrew) Rupert John Buchanan-Jardine, 4th Bt, MC, Horse Gds; 2ndly, 1976, Hugh Alastair Cameron-Rose, who *d* 1994, of 25c Kelso Place, W8; and Hoopers Farm, Kings Somborne, Hants SO20 6QG. —— Susan Morag, *b* 1941: *m* 1964, Robert Keith Erskine, of 4 The Steadings, Walkmilton Farm, Linlithgow, nr Lothian EH49 7PU (*see* E Buchan, colls).

COLLATERAL BRANCH LIVING

Issue of late Cdr Edward St John Edmonstone, RN, yst son of 5th Bt, *b* 1901, *d* 1983: *m* 1936, Hon Alicia Evelyn Browne, who *d* 1992, da of 5th Baron Kilmaine:—
(William Henry) Neil (Barcombe Old Rectory, nr Lewes, Sussex; *Club* – Pratt's), *b* 1942; *ed* Eton; FCA: *m* 1994, Mrs Selma Patricia Deirdre Rees, da of late Sqdn-Ldr Finan O'Driscoll. —— (Helen) Antonia, *b* 1937: *m* 1960, Michael Edmund Hubert Gibbs, of 19 Caroline Place, W2 4AN (*see* Smith-Marriott, Bt, colls, 1973-74 Edn), and has issue living, Patrick Michael Evan (75 Arlington Rd, NW1 7ES), *b* 1962: *m* 1989, Catherine Barroll, and has issue living, Rufus *b* 1994, Clemency *b* 1992, — Edward Michael John, *b* 1964, — Adrian Michael Philip, *b* 1967, — Arabella Marina Clare, *b* 1969: *m* 1994, Quintin John Davies, of 36 Winfield House, Vicarage Crescent, SW11 3LN, son of late Thomas Davies, and has issue living, Hugh Alexander Evan *b* 1998.

This family is probably descended from an Edmundus of the powerful race of Seton, amid whose lands Edmonstone, the original family seat, is situated. Mary, da of King Robert III of Scotland, *m* (as her fourth husband) Sir William Edmonstone of Culloden, and to her and her husband the lands of Duntreath were granted in 1445. The 1st baronet, Sir Archibald, was eldest son of Archibald Edmonstone of Duntreath, and Red Hall, co Antrim, and sat as MP for Dunbartonshire and the Ayr and Irvine Burghs 1761-95; the 2nd and 4th baronets (Sir Charles and Adm Sir William, CB) were MP for Stirlingshire 1812-21 and 1874-80 respectively. Sir Archibald Edmonstone, CVO, 5th baronet, was a Groom-in-Waiting to King Edward VII 1907-10 and *d* (April) 1954. Sir Archibald Charles, 6th baronet was sometime an ADC to Gov of Madras and *d* (June) 1954.

EDWARDS (UK) 1866, of Pye Nest, Yorkshire

Sir CHRISTOPHER JOHN CHURCHILL EDWARDS, 5th *Baronet*; *b* 16 Aug 1941; *s* his father, *Sir* HENRY CHARLES SERRELL PRIESTLEY, 1963; *ed* Frensham Heights Sch, and Loughborough Coll: *m* 1972, Gladys Irene Vogelgesang, and has issue.

Arms – Azure, on a bend nebulée argent, cotised or, a fleur-de-lis between two martlets of the field. **Crest** – Out of a crown vallery or, a talbot's head argent, a semée-de-lis azure.
Residence – 11637 County Club Drive, Westminster, Colorado 80234, USA.

SONS LIVING

DAVID CHARLES PRIESTLEY, *b* 22 Feb 1974. ——— Ryan Matthew Churchill, *b* 1979.

Omne bonum Dei donum
Every good is the gift of God

BROTHER LIVING

Peter Henry, *b* 1944.

WIDOW LIVING OF FOURTH BARONET

DAPHNE MARJORY HILDA (*Daphne, Lady Edwards*) (24 Burntwood Grange Rd, Wandsworth Common, SW18), el da of William George Birt, of Kensington, W8; resumed her former married name of Edwards 1996: *m* 1st, 1935, as his 2nd wife, Sir Henry Charles Serrell Priestley Edwards, 4th baronet, who *d* 1963; 2ndly, 1972, Leonard Mallett, who *d* 1995.

The 1st baronet, Sir Henry Edwards, CB, Provincial Grand Master of Freemasons, W Riding, sat as MP for Halifax (*C*) 1847-52, and for Beverley 1857-68. The 3rd baronet, Sir John Henry Priestley Churchill Edwards, *d* on active ser 1942, whilst serving with Aust Forces.

Edwards-Moss, see Moss.

GREY EGERTON (E) 1617, of Egerton and Oulton, Cheshire

Sir (PHILIP) JOHN CALEDON GREY EGERTON, 15th *Baronet*, *b* 19 Oct 1920; *s* his father, *Sir* PHILIP REGINALD LE BELWARD, 1962; *ed* Eton; late Capt Welsh Guards; European War 1939-45, in N Africa and Italy: *m* 1st, 1952, Margaret Voase, who *d* 1971, el da of late Rowland Rank, of Aldwick Place, Aldwick, W Sussex, and widow of Sqdn Leader Robert Alexander Ullman, RAF; 2ndly, 1986, Frances Mary, da of late Col Robert Maximilian Rainey-Robinson, of Broadmayne, Dorset, and widow of Sqdn Leader William Dudley Williams, DFC, RAF.

Arms – Quarterly, 1st and 4th, argent, a lion rampant gules between three pheons sable. *Egerton*; 2nd and 3rd, barry of six argent and azure, a label of
I trust not in arms, but in valour   five points gules, *Grey*. **Crest** – 1st, three arrows, two in saltire argent, and one in pale, pointed downwards or, barbed and feathered sable, banded with a ribbon gules; 2nd, on a dexter glove argent, a falcon rising or. **Supporters** – *Dexter*, a lion argent ducally crowned or; *sinister*, a wyvern or; each gorged with a plain collar azure, and pendent therefrom an escutcheon gules charged with three pheons argent.
Address – Meadow House, W Stafford, Dorchester, Dorset DT2 8AQ.

COLLATERAL BRANCHES LIVING

Branch from 5th son of 9th baronet

Grandchildren of late F. M. Sir Charles Comyn Egerton, GCB, DSO, 3rd son of late Maj-Gen Caledon Richard Egerton, 5th son of 9th baronet:—
Issue of late Vice-Adm Wion de Malpas Egerton, DSO, *b* 1879, *ka* 1943: *m* 1913, Anita Adolphine, who *d* 1972, da of late A. R. David, of Eastfield, Grimsby:—
DAVID BOSWELL, CB, OBE, MC, *b* 24 July 1914; Maj-Gen (ret); late RA; FIMechE; Dir-Gen of Artillery, Min of Defence, 1964-67, Vice-Pres, and Sen Army Member of Ordnance Board 1967-69, and Pres 1969-70; Col Comdt RA; 1939-45 War (MC); OBE (Mil) 1956, CB (Mil) 1968: *m* 1946, Margaret Gillian, ARCM, da of late Rev Canon Charles Cuthbert Inge, of Streatley, Berks, and has issue living, William de Malpas (Northdown Farmhouse, Sutton Rd, Sutton Poyntz, Weymouth, Dorset), *b* 1949; *ed* Sherborne; MA Camb: *m* 1971, Ruth, only da of late Rev George Watson, of St Albans

Vicarage, Westcliff-on-Sea, and has issue living, Matthew Robert *b* 1977; *ed* Stanbridge Earls Sch, Richard John *b* 1980; *ed* Sherborne, — Charlotte Mary, *b* 1950; BA Oxford: *m* 1987, Stephen William Dixon, of 58 Abinger Av, Cheam, Surrey, son of Eric Dixon, of Windrush, Seaford, Sussex, and has issue living, John David William *b* 1988, Rose Margaret Elizabeth *b* 1991, — (Margaret) Caroline, *b* 1955; *ed* Oxford Univ (MA), and Lancaster Univ (MA): *m* 1984, Martin George White, BSc, FIA (2 Park Farm Rd, Kingston-upon-Thames, Surrey KT2 5TQ), son of late Alfred Walter White, of 66 Boxgrove Rd, Guildford, Surrey, and has issue living, Philip Martin *b* 1987, Robert Charles *b* 1989, Oliver Richard *b* 1992. *Residence* – Campion Cottage, Cheselbourne, Dorchester, Dorset; Army and Navy Club. —— Penelope, *b* 1919; formerly 2nd Officer WRNS: *m* 1955 (*m diss* 1967), Maj John Michael de Burgh Ibberson, late 16th/5th Lancers, and has issue living, Erika Mary, *b* 1956: *m* 1985, — and has issue living, Owen Robert *b* 1986, Inigo John *b* 1987. *Residence* – 38A High St, Puddletown, Dorset. —— Alison, *b* 1922; formerly 3rd Officer WRNS: *m* 1955, Lt-Col Richard Boutcher Gregory, RA (ret), and has issue living, Andrew Richard, *b* 1957; *ed* St John's Coll, Camb (MA 1981) Lt-Col RHA: *m* 1986, Sally Sheard, and has issue living, Rupert James *b* 1987, Charles Henry *b* 1990, — Jane Patricia, *b* 1960; BA: *m* 1989, Maj David Christopher Wicks, RLC, and has issue living, Toby Edward *b* 1991, Rebecca Mary *b* 1994. *Residence* – Rosslyn, Charmouth Rd, Lyme Regis, Dorset.

Grandson of late Sir Reginald Arthur Egerton, CB, 4th son of Maj-Gen Caledon Richard Egerton (ante):—
Issue of late Reginald Francis le Belward Egerton, *b* 1880, *d* 1927: *m* 1907, Elsie Lillian Rose Harris:—
Rowland le Belward (150 Font Blvd, Apt 7B, San Francisco, Calif 94132-2541, USA) *b* 1914: *m* 1st, 1945 (*m diss* 1948), Denise, da of late Capt Denis Hayes, MBE; 2ndly, 1966, Josephine Marie, who *d* 1986, da of Leonardo Passalacqua, of Boston, USA.

Branch from 3rd son of father of 8th and 9th baronets

Grandchildren of late John MARJORIBANKS-EGERTON, el son of late Philip Henry Egerton, ICS (infra):—
Issue of late Lt-Col John Louis Gerard Marjoribanks-Egerton, *b* 1901, *d* 1965: *m* 1936, (Cecilia Mary) Penelope, who *d* 1974, da of late Maj J. B. Barstow:—
John Caledon Richard, *b* 1940: *m* 1980, Helen Elizabeth, da of Frank Neville Hammond Dicks, of Amersham, Bucks, and has issue living, John Stephen, *b* 1981. *Residence* – Sneaton Hall, Sneaton, Whitby, Yorks. —— Mary Penelope Jane, *b* 1938, MA, Oxford, MSc, Alberta: *m* 1963, John L. Bannister, of 7 Mann St, Cottesloe, W Australia 6011, and has issue living, William John Egerton, *b* 1967, — Katharine Penelope, *b* 1964, — Caroline Nancy, *b* 1968. —— Sarah Cecilia Geraldine, *b* 1942; MA Oxon: *m* 1964, Charles B. Strouts, AMICE, and has issue living, Henry Gerard Egerton, *b* 1966, — Emma Louise Penelope, *b* 1968. —— Frances Mary Caroline, *b* 1948.

Issue of late Lt-Col Philip Morys Marjoribanks-Egerton, MBE, *b* 1903, *d* 1969: *m* 1933, Adeline Barbara, who *d* 1986, da of Maj Osborn Augustin Chambers (late R Warks Regt):—
Philippa Anne Mary (24 Wesley Av, Peverell, Plymouth PL3 4RA), *b* 1936: *m* 1st, 1959 (*m diss* 1976), Brian Edgar Ford; 2ndly, 1977, William Ernest Richards, who *d* 1978; 3rdly, 1979 (*m diss* 1984), Albin W. Piotr Szymusik, who *d* 1998, and has issue living (by 1st *m*), Martin Nicholas, *b* 1959 (adopted 1960); has issue living, one son and one da, — Philip Richard, *b* 1963, — Elizabeth Anne, *b* 1960; *ed* Plymouth Univ (BSc): *m* 1980, Steven Hodgkinson, and has issue living, John *b* 1984, Laura *b* 1988, — Sarah Jane, *b* 1964; BA (E London Poly), — Susan Lillian, *b* 1965: *m* 1998, Laurence Patrick Job, and has issue living, Patrick Terence Louis *b* 1998.

Grandchildren of late Philip Henry Egerton, ICS, son of late William Egerton, 3rd son of late Philip Egerton, father of 8th and 9th baronets:—
Issue of late Graham Egerton, *b* 1861, *d* 1922: *m* 1886, Julia Donegan, da of T. Easley, of Dickson Co, Tennessee, USA:—
William Graham, *b* 1896; with USA Air Force: *m* 19-, Rebecca Crenshaw White, of Kentucky, and has issue living, William Graham, *b* 19-, — John, *b* 19-, — a da, *b* 19-, — a da, *b* 19-. —— Philip Marjoribanks, *b* 1899; in US Dept of Agriculture; 1914-18 War with US Naval Air Force: *m* 19-, Susan Candler, of Corinth, Miss, USA.

Grandchildren of late William Egerton, ICS, son of late Philip Henry Egerton, ICS (ante):—
Issue of late William le Belward Egerton, ICS *b* 1901, *d* 1947: *m* 1931, Angela Doreen Loftus, who *d* 1973, da of late Brig-Gen Edward Humphry Bland, CB, CMG, RE (ret):—
Sir Stephen Loftus, KCMG (Brooks's Club), *b* 1932; *ed* Eton and Trin Coll, Camb; formerly 2nd Lt KRRC; entered HM Foreign Ser 1956; Private Sec to Under Sec of State for Foreign Affairs 1961-62, Oriental Sec at Baghdad 1963-67; Counsellor at British Embassy, Tripoli, 1972, and Head of Energy Depart FO 1973-77, HM Consul-Gen Rio de Janeiro 1977-80, HM Ambassador to Iraq 1980-82; Assist Under Sec of State FCO 1982-86, HM Ambassador to Saudi Arabia 1986-89, to Italy 1989-92, and to Albania (non-resident) 1992; Consultant to Enterprise Oil plc; CMG 1978, KCMG 1988: *m* 1958, Caroline, da of Maj Eustace Thomas Edward Cary-Elwes, TD, late R Norfolk Regt, of 5 Albion House, Bellamy Way, Poringland, Norfolk, and has issue living, William Luke le Belward, *b* 1966; *ed* Eton, and Trin Coll, Camb; entered Diplomatic Service 1988, 2nd Sec Moscow 1991-94, — Louisa Charlotte, *b* 1963; Associate Dir Lane Fox & Co, 35 Cadogan St, SW3. —— Susan Kirsteen, *b* 1936; *ed* Reading Univ (BA 1959); entered Diplomatic Ser 1960: *m* 1962, Jeremy Sandford Cohen, of Wiston Mill, Nayland, nr Colchester, Essex CO6 4LX, and has issue living, Thomas William Otway, *b* 1965; *ed* Leeds Univ (BA); risk manager, Swire Beverages, Nanjing, China, — Lucy Jane, *b* 1968; *ed* Bath Univ (BA); freelance photojournalist.

Grandson of late Sir Robert Eyles Egerton, KCSI, CIE, yst son of late William Egerton (ante):—
Issue of late Lieut-Col Charles Philip Egerton, *b* 1863, *d* 1943: *m* 1889, Lilian Isabel, who *d* 1950, da of Lieut-Gen Hugh Rose, Indian Army:—
Rowland Philip, *b* 1891: *m* 1918, Constance Alice, da of Edward Courtenay Pratt, of Montreal, and has issue living, Piers Brian Philip, *b* 1927: *m* 1948, Lorna, da of Lorne Green, of Ottawa, Canada, and has issue living, Brian Philip *b* 1949.

Grandchildren of late Lt-Col Charles Philip Egerton (ante):—
Issue of late Robert Charles Egerton, MIEE, *b* 1903, *d* 1969: *m* 1929, Mary Elizabeth Shaw, who *d* 1997, da of the Rev Charles Morris Trownsell, R of Gidleigh, Devon:—

†Julian Robert, *b* 1940; MSc, PhD: *m* 1967, Kay Lewis, da of George M. Stewart, of Pennant Hills, Sydney, NSW, and *d* 1997, leaving issue, Alexander Stewart, *b* 1977, — Julia Charlotte, *b* 1974. —— Una Mary (39 The Hartings, Flansham Park, Bognor Regis, W Sussex PO22 6QF), *b* 1939; MCSP: *m* 1963 (*m diss* 1981), Peter John Bayley Wassell, Hong Kong Police, and has issue living, Mark Peter, *b* 1966, — Amanda Claire, *b* 1969, — Victoria Jane, *b* 1970.

Branch from 7th son of father of 8th and 9th baronets

Grandchildren of late Piers Egerton-Warburton, only son of Rowland Eyles Egerton-Warburton, el son of Rev Rowland Egerton-Warburton, 7th son of Philip Egerton, father of 8th and 9th baronets:—
Issue of late Capt John Egerton-Warburton, Scots Guards, *b* 1883, *d* of wounds received in action 1915: *m* 1908, Hon Lettice Legh (who *d* 1968, having *m* 2ndly, 1919, Lt-Col John Dallas Waters, CB, DSO, who *d* 1967), da of 2nd Baron Newton:—
Elizabeth (*Elizabeth, Viscountess Ashbrook*), *b* 1911: *m* 1934, 10th Viscount Ashbrook, KCVO, MBE, who *d* 1995. *Residence* – Woodlands, Arley, Northwich, Cheshire. —— Priscilla, *b* (*posthumous*) 1915: *m* 1st, 1936, Major (William Matthew) Viscount Wolmer, who *d* on active ser 1942, el son of 3rd Earl of Selborne; 2ndly, 1948, 4th Baron Newton, who *d* 1992; 3rdly, 1994, Frederick Charles Horace Fryer (*see* E Peel, colls, 1985 Edn). *Residence* – Vernon Hill House, Bishop's Waltham, Hants.

Issue of late Col Geoffrey Egerton-Warburton, DSO, TD, *b* 1888, *d* 1961: *m* 1927, Hon Georgiana Mary Dormer, MBE, who *d* 1955, da of 14th Baron Dormer:—
Peter (Mulberry House, Bentworth, Hants GU34 5RB; 54 Princes Gate Mews, SW7 2RB), *b* 1933; *ed* Eton, and RMA; late Capt Coldm Gds: *m* 1st, 1955 (*m diss* 1958), Belinda Vera, da of late James R. A. Young, of Cowdrays, East Hendred, Berks; 2ndly, 1960 (*m diss* 1967) Sarah Jessica Norman, el da of Maj Willoughby Rollo Norman, Gren Gds (*see* Norman, Bt); 3rdly, 1969, Hon Marya Anne Noble, da of Baron Glenkinglas, and has issue living, (by 2nd *m*) Charles Piers, *b* 1961: *m* 1989, Fiona Clare, only da of Robin Desmond Bonham-Carter, and has issue living, Piers *b* 1992, Marcus *b* 1994, — James Willoughby *b* 1963: *m* 1st, 1993, Elizabeth Boughton, eldest da of Vincent Riggio, of Long Island, NY, USA; 2ndly, 1999, Anna Webb, da of Stanley DuBois Petter, Jr, — (by 3rd *m*), Christopher Geoffrey, *b* 1971, — Louisa Jane (twin), *b* 1971. —— Anne, *b* 1928: *m* 1954, His Hon James Eccles Malise Irvine (School House, Caulcott, Bicester, Oxon OX6 3NE), and has issue living, David Peter Gerard, *b* 1963; *ed* RAC Cirencester; BSc Buckingham; Lieut Gren Gds 1987-91 (Gulf War Medal), Maj 6 Royal (Northumberland) Regt Fus, — Susan Caroline Jane, *b* 1961. —— Jane, LVO (Crossways, Woodgreen, Fordingbridge, Hants), *b* 1931; Lady in Waiting to HRH Princess Alice, Duchess of Gloucester until 1984, since when an Extra Lady in Waiting; LVO 1983.

Grandchildren of late Rowland James Egerton-Warburton, 2nd son of Maj Peter Egerton-Warburton, CMG (infra):—
Issue of late John Egerton-Warburton, *b* 1873, *d* 1943: *m* 1913, Winifred Vaughan, of 131 Cambridge Terrace, Malvern, S Australia:—
Richard John, *b* 1916; Capt Australian Imperial Force (Reserve of Officers): *m* 1946, Audrey Doreen Roberts, of Melbourne, Victoria, Australia, and has issue living, Jill Rosalind, *b* 1948, — Elizabeth Jane, *b* 1952, — Bronwyn Grey, *b* 1954. —— Margaret, *b* 1919: *m* 1st, 1940, Lt Robert Paine, who was *ka* in New Guinea 1943; 2ndly, 1947, Maxwell Dunn, who *d* 1966, and has issue living, (by 1st *m*) Frances Margaret, *b* 1941.

Issue of late Peter Augustus Egerton-Warburton, *b* 1877, *d* 1944: *m* 1906, Ellen, who *d* 1949, da of W Fountain, of Saffron Walden:—
Elizabeth; is a Nursing Sister Australian Imperial Force: *m* 19-, Frank Mosey, of Anlaby, via Eudunda, S Australia 5374, Australia.

Issue of late Rowland Egerton-Warburton, *b* 1885, *d* 1963: *m* 1914, Isabel, who *d* 1957, da of W. F. Langdon, of Caulfield, Aust:—
Francis (42 Hortense St, Burwood, Vic, Aust), *b* 1917: *m* 1944, Joan, da of P. A. Ewing, of Bridgetown, W Aust, and has issue living, Anne, *b* 1945: *m* 1966, Herbert Timothy Lee-Steere, of Esperance, W Aust, and has issue living, Peter Timothy *b* 1968, Christopher Ian *b* 1969, Wendy Anne *b* 1972.

Granddaughters of late William Egerton-Warburton, 3rd son of Maj Peter Egerton-Warburton, CMG, 4th son of late Rev Rowland Egerton-Warburton (ante):—
Issue of late Richard Sandford Egerton Warburton, *b* 1880, *d* 1959: *m* 1908, Emily Meredith, who *d* 1965, da of Bayfield Moulden:—
Meredith (South Rd, Everard Park, S Australia), *b* 1913: *m* 1936, Donald Thomas Mitchell, who *d* 1994, and has issue living, Alan, *b* 1940, — Jean Meredith, *b* 1938, — Frances Egerton, *b* 1943. —— Alice Elizabeth Grey, *b* 1924: *m* 1947, Robert C. Bell, who *d* 1987, and has issue living, Hugh, *b* 1954, — Helen, *b* 1948, — Barbara, *b* 1950, — Judy, *b* 1952.

Grandchildren of late Richard Sandford Egerton-Warburton (ante):—
Issue of late Peter Bayfield Egerton-Warburton, *b* 1909, *d* 1997: *m* 1937, Roma Bailands Hosking, who *d* 1997, da of Frank Becker, of Adelaide, S Australia:—
Richard Francis (17A Macquarie Rd, Pymble, NSW 2073, Australia), *b* 1940: *m* 1966, Susan Elizabeth Chandler, of Perth, WA, and has issue living, Bayfield James, *b* 1970: *m* 1998, Emma Louise Bradshaw, — Matthew Robert, *b* 1973. —— Elizabeth Louise, *b* 1938: *m* 1962, Ian Wesley Giles, of 159 Gover St, N Adelaide, S Australia 5006, and has issue living, Benjamin Peter Wesley, *b* 1969, — Anna Louise, *b* 1963, — Sally Elizabeth, *b* 1964.

Issue of late Edward Howard Egerton-Warburton, *b* 1910, *d* 1974: *m* 1938, Margaret Newland, who *d* 1998.—
Peter Ridgeway (c/o Airfield Riding Centre, Boulder, W Aust 6432), *b* 1941: *m* 1966 (*m diss* 1993), Vanda Sue, da of J. B. Wood, of Bunbury, W Aust, and has issue living, David Peter, *b* 1967: *m* 1st, 1990 (*m diss* 1995), Gena Huck; 2ndly, 1997, Kathryn Lisa Ford, and has issue living (by 1st *m*), David William *b* 1989, — Edward James, *b* 1976, — Deanna Sue, *b* 1969, — Rosa Margaret, *b* 1972: *m* 1996, Brett Duthie, of Broome, WA, and has issue living, Max Harley *b* 1996. —— Ann, *b* 1946: *m* 1969, James William Clarke, of 21 Moreton Terrace, Dongara, W Aust 6525, and has issue living,

Benjamin James, *b* 1970: *m* 1990, Tara Hotham Jenkins, and has issue living, Jessica Elizabeth Ann *b* 1994, Sophie Jacqueline *b* 1998.

Issue of late William Arnold Egerton-Warburton, *b* 1918, *d* 1976: *m* 1940, Letty Dorian Parsons, who *d* 1977:—
Michael Philip (66 Yacka Rd, Seacliffe, S Aust), *b* 1948.

Grandchildren of late William Egerton-Warburton (ante):—
Issue of late Philip Egerton-Warburton, *b* 1882, *d* 1965: *m* 1912, Olive Rigarlsford, da of Alfred Palmer, late of Kapunda, S Australia:—
Patience Anne, *b* 1916. —— Cecily, *b* 1918.

Grandchildren of late George Grey Egerton-Warburton, eldest son of late George Edward Egerton-Warburton (infra):—
Issue of late Philip Grey Egerton-Warburton, *b* 1877, *d* 1954: *m* 1909, Verna Grace, who *d* 1939, da of S. J. Rowe, formerly of Perth, W Australia:—
Geoffrey Grey, *b* 1911: *m* (Jan) 1940, Marjorie Vere, da of late Nelson Hamilton-Taylor, of Mount Barker, W Australia, and has issue living, Arley Geoffrey (Gunngunnu, Frankland, W Aust), *b* (Dec) 1940, — Colin Yorke (Yeriminup, Frankland, W Aust), *b* 1947, — Ione Vere, *b* 1942, — Vivien Gay, *b* 1944, — Caroline Marjorie, *b* 1952. *Residence* – Yeriminup, Cranbrook, W Australia. —— Ronald Grey, *b* 1914: *m* 1937, Edith Mabel, da of G. J. A. Swiney, of Albany, and has issue living, Philip Alexander, *b* 1938: *m* 1st, 1968 (*m diss* 1984), Sheila, da of Donald La Claire, of Vancouver, BC, Canada; 2ndly, 1986, Pauline Anne Maxwell, and has issue living (by 1st *m*), John Alexander *b* 1973, Brooke Elizabeth *b* 1971, — Michael George (Mirinup, Frankland River, W Aust), *b* 1941: *m* 1966, Lois Elizabeth, da of H. O. Grimbly, of Attadale, Perth, W Aust, and has issue living, Antony Michael Grey *b* 1967, Grey Edward *b* 1972, Roland George *b* 1977, — David Ronald (Acacia Ridge, Frankland, W Aust), *b* 1945: *m* 1968, Margaret Elizabeth, who *d* 1998, da of A. E. Challenor, of Dandallup, W Aust, and has issue living, Joshua David *b* 1975, Blanche Elizabeth *b* 1971, Edwyna Margaret *b* 1974, — Jennifer Mary, *b* 1940: *m* 1964, John Mattiske, of Peppermint Grove, W Aust 6011, and has issue living Peter Rex *b* 1972, Marie Louise *b* 1966: *m* 1998, Derek Geoffrey Shaw, Philippa Jane *b* 1968, — Diana Margaret, *b* 1943: *m* 1972, Ivan Johnson, of Perth, W Aust, and has issue living, Daniel Slade *b* 1981, Joanna *b* 1974, Jennifer Lee *b* 1977. *Residence* – Lesmurdie, W Aust. —— Dorothy Antoinette, *b* 1909: *m* 1934, George Alexander Swiney, and has issue living, Wayne Haig Egerton, *b* 1935, — Graham Haig, *b* 1940. *Residence* – Franklands, Frankland River, W Aust.

Grandchildren of late Rowland Egerton-Warburton, 2nd son of late George Edward Egerton-Warburton, yst son of late Rev Rowland Egerton-Warburton (ante):—
Issue of late Philip Augustus Egerton-Warburton, *b* 1904, *d* 1981: *m* 1928 Alice Mary Price:—
Rowland (W Popanyinning, W Aust 6309), *b* 1928: *m* 1953, Laurel Gloria Ferguson, and has issue living, Graeme (RMB 212, W Pingelly, W Aust 6308), *b* 1954: *m* 1984, Raylene Holding, and has issue living, Peter *b* 1990, Emma *b* 1992, — Trevor, *b* 1958: *m* 19—(*m diss* 19—), Louise —, — Maxine, *b* 1955: *m* 1976, Gregory Beaton, and has issue living, Joseph Finlay *b* 1978, Donald Peter *b* 1980. —— Ross (RMB 228, W Pingelly, W Aust 6308), *b* 1931: *m* 1954, Wilma Joan Smoker, and has issue living, Dean Ross (RMB 255, W Pingelly, W Aust 6308), *b* 1961: *m* 1985, Diane Fay Roberts, and has issue living, Justin Roy *b* 1990, Troy Aron *b* 1994, Kristy Ann *b* 1992, — Evan Mark (RMB 230, W Pingelly, W Aust 6308), *b* 1966: *m* 1992, Roslyn Gail Cowcill, — Alison Joy, *b* 1955: *m* 1st, 1974 (*m diss* 19—), Bruce Edward Dowsett; 2ndly, 1991, Robert Kevin Lee, and has issue living (by 1st *m*), Ashley Michael *b* 1977, Narelle Marie *b* 1974, — Robyn Lois, *b* 1957: *m* 1976, Arthur Raymond Lines, and has issue living, Craig Phillip *b* 1979, Maree Karen *b* 1981, — Coral Janet, *b* 1960: *m* 1986, Robert Martin Miles, and has issue living, Jackson Ross *b* 1990, Alex Stephen *b* 1992, Eric Gregory *b* 1993. —— Philip (RMB 512, Williams, W Aust 6391, Australia), *b* 1934: *m* 1959, Georgina May, da of H.F.J. Higginson, of Kanandah, Pingelly, W Aust, and has issue living, Michael Philip, *b* 1959: *m* 1982, Jillian Steer, and has issue living, Benjamin Michael *b* 1986, Nicholas Jeremy *b* 1990, Rebecca Therese *b* 1985, Rachael Holly *b* 1988, — Brett Francis, *b* 1970: *m* 1992, Candice —, — Debra Suzanne, *b* 1961: *m* 1990, Peter Evelyn-Liardet, and has issue living, Christopher Luke EGERTON-WARBURTON *b* 1982, Jennifer Kate *b* 1992. —— Peter, *b* (twin) 1934.

Grandchildren of late Horace Egerton-Warburton, 3rd son of late George Edward Egerton-Warburton (ante):—
Issue of late John Le Belward Egerton-Warburton, *b* 1882, *d* 1949: *m* 1913, Blanche Josephine van Zuilecom, of Yeenyellup, Kojonup, W Australia:—
John (Box 20, Kojonup, W Aust 6395), *b* 1916: a farmer: *m* 1939, Celia Maltby, da of Alan Douglas Robinson, of Subiaco, Perth, W Aust, and has issue living, Quentin (Korellup, RMB 328, Kojonup 6395, W Aust), *b* 1942: *m* 1965, Mary Heath, da of J. W. Rowe, of Claremont, Perth, W Aust, and has issue living, David Grey *b* 1970: *m* 1997, Natalie Michelle, da of W. Coleman, of Wilgermar Estate, Katanning, WA 6317, Robert John Quentin *b* 1972, Megan Ann *b* 1967: *m* 1993, Bruce Alexander McCracken (and has issue living, Alexandra Mary *b* 1998), — Alan (Yeenyellup, Box 20, Kojonup, W Aust), *b* 1947: *m* 1971, Cynthia Margaret, da of C. D. Lee, of Royston Park, Kojonup, W Aust, and has issue living, George Thomas *b* 1988, Rachael Margaret *b* 1972, Emily Jane *b* 1974, Diana Elizabeth *b* 1976, — Celia Ruth, *b* 1940: *m* 1960, Anthony Randle Egerton-Warburton, (infra).

Issue of late Horace Grey Egerton-Warburton, *b* 1891, *d* 1956: *m* 1st, 1915, Ruth, who *d* 1918, da of Randle Egerton-Warburton (infra); 2ndly, 1920, Vera (St Werburgh's, Mount Barker, W Australia), da of Charles F. Lake, of Dandenong Rd, Malvern, Melbourne, Australia:—
(By 1st *m*) Mary Ruth, *b* 1916: *m* 1st, 1941, Edward Henry Finch, Roy Australian Air Force, who was *ka* 1943; 2ndly, 1946, Vernon Wells, Roy Australian Air Force, and has issue living, (by 1st *m*) Penelope, *b* 1942, — (by 2nd *m*) Grey Egerton, *b* 1947, — Peter Randell Scott, *b* 1950, — Diana Ruth, *b* 1948. *Residence* – . ——Joan, *b* 1918: *m* 1941, Henry Graham Johnson, Australian Imperial Force, and has issue living, Richard Grey *b* 1944, — Anthony Peter, *b* 1946. —— (By 2nd *m*) Edward Grey, *b* 1928: *m* 1960, Elizabeth, da of John Wade, of Perth, and has issue living, Grey Piers, *b* 1962: *m* 1992, Jennifer Anne, da of Dr P. Nash, of Mosman Park, Perth, W Aust, and has issue living, Angela Grace *b* 1993, — Robin, *b* 1967, — Rosemary, *b* 1961. —— Yexley Selina, *b* 1921: *m* 1946, Gordon Maitland-Roberts, Australian Imperial Force, and has issue living, Wade Maitland, *b* 1947, — Bruce Gordon, *b* 1950, — Helen Ena, *b* 1948. *Residence* – Chelsea, Moora, W Australia. —— Patricia Ann, *b* 1923: *m* (Jan) 1946, William Adolphus Chaffey, MLA, and has issue living, David Frank *b* 1957, Mary Ann *b* (Nov) 1946, — Elizabeth Patricia, *b* 1949. *Residence* – 119 Fitzroy Street, Tamworth, NS Wales. —— Ann Vera, *b* (twin) 1928: *m* 1952, Donald Charles Keir Collins, and has issue living, Bradford Keir, *b* 1958, — Scott Charles Egerton, *b* 1962, — Joanne Margaret, *b* 1953, — Jacqueline Anne, *b* 1955. *Residence* – 47 Martin Street, Mount Barker, W Australia. —— Helen Maud, *b* 1931: *m* 1957, John Halley Arnold, and has issue living, Richard John Halley, *b* 1960, — Brooke Egerton Halley, *b* 1962, — Amanda Jane, *b* 1958, — Michelle Tracey, *b* 1959.

Residence – Selsley Downs, Kojonup, W Australia. —— Carlene Alice, *b* (twin) 1931: *m* 1957, John Ronald Penn, and has issue living, Fiona Carlene, *b* 1958, — Sally Louise, *b* 1960. *Residence* – Parsons St, Mount Barker, W Australia.

Grandchildren of late Augustus Egerton-Warburton, 4th son of late George Edward Egerton-Warburton (ante):—
Issue of late Angus Egerton-Warburton, *b* 1889, *d* 1960: *m* 1925, Dorothy (RMB 406, Euretta, Kojonup, W Australia), da of John Weston, of Eastwood, Notts:—
†Brian Wayne, *b* 1933; *d* 19—. —— Ian Angus, *b* 1942: *m* 1965, Robin, da of Dr Robert Elphick, of Shenlon Park, and has issue living, Barney, *b* 1968, — Simone Elissa, *b* 1966. —— Joan Irma (South Parkfield, N Danalup, W Australia), *b* 1926: *m* 1st, 1950, Ross Bovell, who *d* 1950; 2ndly, 1955, John Griffin Money, who *d* 1962. —— Evelyn Isabel, *b* 1928: *m* 1953, Frank Devine, of Hillside, Frankland River, W Australia, and has issue living, Peter John, *b* 1954, — Christopher James, *b* 1956, Garry Matthew, *b* 1962, — Leonie Frances, *b* 1957. —— Margaret, *b* 1931. —— Dorothy June, *b* 1937: *m* 1961, John Kitto, of Nedlands, W Aust, and has issue living, Johnson Grey, *b* 1966, — Grantham Angus, *b* 1968.

Issue of late Reginald Hubert Egerton-Warburton, *b* 1894, *d* 1962: *m* 1925, Lena Mary Lambe:—
Rex (Woolareen, Kojonup, W Aust 6395), *b* 1928: *m* 1946, Muriel Faith Weise, and has issue living, Diane, *b* 1946: *m* 1968, John William Partridge, of Priory Park, Kojonup, W Aust, and has issue living, Craig John *b* 1969, Cindy Karen *b* 1968, — Denise EGERTON-WARBURTON, *b* 1947; has resumed her maiden name: *m* 1st, 1965, Kevin William Brown; 2ndly, 19— (*m diss* 19—), — Hall, of 40 Lower King Rd, Albany, W Aust 6330, Aust, and has issue living (by 1st *m*), Darrin Kevin *b* 1966, Gavin William *b* 1967, Byron Rex *b* 1971, — Maree, *b* 1953: *m* 1971, John James Matthews, and has issue living, Chad James *b* 1972, Damon John *b* 1974, Lisa Maree *b* 1979, — Dawn (Cherryton, Konjonup, W Aust), *b* 1926.

Grandchildren of late Randle Egerton-Warburton (infra):—
Issue of late Piers Edward Egerton-Warburton, *b* 1895, *d* 1961: *m* 1920, Winsome, who *d* 1971, da of John Ewing, MLC, of W Australia:—
Diana (2 Kite Court, Busselton, W Australia 6280), *b* 1924: *m* 1945, Julian B. Goyder, who *d* 1997, and has issue living, Piers Bruce, *b* 1950, — Melody Anne, *b* 1946, — Elizabeth, *b* 1947. —— Jenefer, *b* 1933: *m* 1956, Ian P. Johnston, of Dardanup, W Australia, and has issue living, Ian Justin, *b* 1958, — Julia, *b* 1956, — Andrea, *b* 1963, — Diana, *b* 1965. —— Angela (6 Mosman Terrace, Mosman Park, W Australia 6012), *b* 1941: *m* 1964, John Charles Roberts, and has issue living, Andrew Timothy, *b* 1966, — Timothy Andrew, *b* 1970, — Denby Emma, *b* 1976.

Issue of late George Grey Egerton-Warburton, *b* 1899, *d* 1975: *m* 1929, Ethel Vernon, da of Edmund Vernon Drake-Brockman, JP:—
Anthony Randle (Brackenhurst, Bridgetown, W Aust 6255), *b* 1935: *m* 1960, Celia Ruth, da of John Egerton-Warburton (ante), and has issue living, Randle, *b* 1963, — Nicholas, *b* 1966: *m* 1992, Ann Guthrie Bryson, and has issue living, Cordelia Ann *b* 1998, — Belinda Jane, *b* 1961: *m* 1984, Andrew John Viner, of 15 Mimosa Av, Mount Claremont, W Australia, and has issue living, Jack Randle *b* 1986, Fleur Ruth *b* 1988, Rosemary Jane *b* 1993, — Belinda Ruth, *b* 1967: *m* 1998, Peter Alfred Le Grice, and has issue living, Moses *b* 1999. —— Vernon Grey, *b* 1938: *m* 1970, Jeanny Vlahov, and has issue living, George, *b* 1971, — Anton, *b* 1972, — Virginia, *b* 1974. —— Dorothy Vernon, *b* 1929: *m* 1954, John Gordon Boyle, of 40 Tyrell St, Nedlands, 6009, W Aust, and has issue living, Angela Egerton, *b* 1955; *ed* Univ of Western Australia (BA, Dip Ed): *m* 1989, Anthony Francis Phillips, BA, M Phil, Dip Ed, and has issue living, Ariane Margaret Emerald *b* 1991, Genevieve Georgia Elizabeth *b* 1993, — Erica Egerton, *b* 1960; *ed* Univ of New South Wales (B L Arch): *m* 1987, Antony Luke Radunovich, B Mech Eng, and has issue living, Marcus John *b* 1989, Antony Michael *b* 1990, Miranda Adelaide *b* 1992. —— Fleur, *b* 1932: *m* 1956, John Aitken, of Hau Ora, Havelock North, Hawkes Bay, NZ, and has issue living, Timothy Murray (13c McMillan Place, Howick, Auckland, NZ), *b* 1957: *m* 1986, Susan Loffler, and has issue living, Richard George Murray *b* 1988, Andrew Robert *b* 1990, Michael Timothy *b* 1992, — Hamish Egerton (33 Perry St, Papanui, Christchurch, NZ), *b* 1960: *m* 1993, Susan Goodman, and has issue living, John Hamish Egerton *b* 1995, Fraser Grey Warburton *b* 1997, — Judith Jill, *b* 1962: *m* 1989, Bruce Thomas Wagg, of 27 Jordan Place, Masterton, NZ, and has issue living, Timothy Guy Thomas *b* 1991, Christopher George *b* 1994.

Granddaughter of late George Edward Egerton-Warburton (ante):—
Issue of late Randle Egerton-Warburton, *b* 1860, *d* 1938: *m* 1890, Eva, who *d* 1931, da of Edward Hester:—
Margaret Augusta, *b* 1903: *m* 1st, 1932, Robert Willgress, BSc, who *d* 1956; 2ndly, 1956, William Francis Dudley Allison, of Protea Rd, George, Cape Province, S Africa.

The House of Egerton, one of the most ancient and distinguished in Cheshire, traces its descent to William le Belward, who was Baron of Malpas under the Norman Earl Palatine of that county. David, great-grandson of William le Belward, took the name of Egerton from the Lordship of Egerton, which he had inherited; and from him, in a direct line, is descended the present baronet Sir Roland Egerton, 1st Bt, *m* Bridget, sister and co-heir of 15th Lord Grey de Wilton. The 7th Bt was created Earl of Wilton, with remainder to his maternal grandson, Hon Thomas Grosvenor. At his death in 1814 the baronetcy passed to his kinsman John Egerton of Oulton, descended from a yr son of 1st Bt. By Roy Warrant dated 30th June, 1825, King George IV granted to the Rev Sir Philip Egerton, 9th Bt, and all subsequent baronets on succeeding to the title the right to assume for themselves only the additional surname of Grey and the Arms and Supporters of Grey de Wilton. The 10th baronet sat as MP for Chester (C) 1830, for Cheshire West 1835-81. The 13th baronet, Rev Sir Brooke de Malpas Grey-Egerton, was R of Stoke-on-Terne, and Rural Dean of Hodnet 1901-13.

ELIOTT (NS) 1666, of Stobs, Roxburghshire

FORTITER ET RECTE

SOYEZ SAGE

Be wise

Sir CHARLES JOSEPH ALEXANDER ELIOTT OF STOBS, 12th *Baronet*: *b* 9 Jan 1937, eldest son of late Charles Rawdon Heathfield Eliott, son of Alexander Boswell Vassal Eliott, half-brother of 9th baronet; *s* his kinsman, *Sir* ARTHUR FRANCIS AUGUSTUS BOSWELL, 1989; *ed* St Joseph's Christian Brothers, Rockhampton, nr Brisbane: *m* 1959, Wendy Judith, da of Henry John Bailey, of Toowoomba, Qld, and has issue.

𝔄rms – Gules, on a bend or, a baton azure; in a dexter canton argent, a saltire azure surmounted of an inescutcheon or charged with a lion rampant within a double tressure flory counterflory gules, being the addition of Nova Scotia as a Baronet. Crest – A hand couped at the wrist in armour holding a cutlass in bend proper. Supporters – *Dexter*, a ram: *sinister*, a goat; both proper and gorged with a laurel branch vert, horned and hooved or.
Residence – 27 Cohoe St, Toowoomba, Qld 4350, Australia.

SON LIVING

RODNEY GILBERT CHARLES, *b* 1966: *m* 1988, Andrea Therese Saunders, and has issue living, Steven Charles, *b* 1990, — Cassandra Jane, *b* 1989.

DAUGHTERS LIVING

Elizabeth Jane, *b* 1960: *m* — Armanasco, and has issue living, Daniel Charles, *b* 19—, — Lindsay Clare, *b* 19—, — Kimberley Jane, *b* 1991. —— Jenny, *b* 1961: *m* — Land. —— Josephine Mary Anne, *b* 1963: *m* — Grofski, and has issue living, Ethan Joseph, *b* 1990, — Brigitte Kate, *b* 1992. —— Clare Melinda, *b* 1973.

BROTHERS LIVING

Keith Robert Vincent (65 Bunya St, Grunslopes, Brisbane, Qld 4120, Australia), *b* 1942: *m* 1965, Annette Mary Kijrgaard, and has issue living, Brett Robert, *b* 1966. —— Raymond Francis, *b* 1946.

SISTERS LIVING

Irene Gertrude, *b* 1930: *m* 1950, Peter Brown (PO Box 4, Yeppon, Qld, Australia). —— Myrtle Davies, *b* 1935. —— Bella Loraine, *b* 1939.

AUNTS LIVING

Gertrude May, *b* 1893: *m* 1929, Henry Wilson Mercer, of Evanston, via Ilfracombe, Qld, Australia. —— Constance Elizabeth, *b* 1894: *m* 19—, Clarence Quinn. —— Annabella Carmichael, *b* 1897: *m* 1927, James Bryson, of Denham Terrace, Rockhampton, Qld, Australia.

DAUGHTER LIVING OF ELEVENTH BARONET

Margaret Frances Boswell ELIOTT (*Mrs Margaret Eliott of Redheugh*), *b* 1948; recognised by Lord Lyon as Chief of the Eliott Clan 1991; resumed her maiden name: *m* 1974, Anthony E. B. Vaughan-Arbuckle, who *d* 1986; 2ndly, 1990, Christopher Powell Wilkins, and has issue living (by 1st *m*), Benjamin Robert, *b* 1978, — Kate Frances, *b* 1981. *Residence* – Redheugh, Newcastleton, Roxburghshire.

WIDOW LIVING OF ELEVENTH BARONET

FRANCES AILEEN (*Frances, Lady Eliott of Stobs*), eldest da of Sir Francis Kennedy McClean, AFC: *m* 1947, Sir Arthur Francis Augustus Boswell Eliot of Stobs, 11th Bt, who *d* 1989. *Residence* – Redheugh, Newcastleton, Roxburghshire.

MOTHER LIVING

Emma Elizabeth HARRIS: *m* 1925, Charles Rawdon Heathfield Eliott, who *d* 1972. *Residence* – 72 Derby St, Rockhampton, Qld, Australia.

COLLATERAL BRANCHES LIVING

Issue of late Clive John Eliott, *b* 1940, *d* 1971, brother of 12th baronet: *m* 1961, Estelle Maude Kelland:—
Bradley John, *b* 1962. —— Anthony Charles, *b* 1966. —— Dale Thomas, *b* 1969.

Grandson of late Gilbert William Henry Eliott, son of late Francis Willoughby Eliott (infra):—
Issue of late Gilbert William Eliott, *b* 1894, *d* 1961: *m* 1921, Lilian Mary, who *d* 1968, da of William Towle, of Nottingham, and widow of Neville Dalley:—
Gilbert Rowley Roxburgh (53 Epping Rd, Epping, NSW), *b* 1923; *ed* Sydney Univ (BDS); late F/Lt RAAF: *m* 1944, Helen Ross, yr da of A. H. Martin, MA, PhD, of Sydney, NSW, and has issue living, Gilbert William Heathfield, *b* 1961; BSc Sydney: *m* 1994, Rosemary Ann, da of Gerald J. Y. Mah, MB BS, FRCS (Edin), FRCS (Eng), of Newcastle, NSW, and has issue living, Gilbert Daniel Gerald *b* 1998, — Christine, *b* 1945; BSc New England, DipEd Sydney, BLArch NSW: *m* 1988, David Clark, of Beecroft, NSW, — Virginia Ruth, *b* 1947: *m* 1970 (*m diss* 1999), Mathias Faff, of Lake Cargelligo, NSW, and has issue living, Dieter *b* 1974, Heidi *b* 1970: *m* 1989, Michael Poyser, of Coonabarabran, NSW (and has issue living, Martin *b* 1993, Laurel *b* 1997, Rachel *b* 1999).

Grandchildren of late Francis Willoughby Eliott, son of late Gilbert Eliott, CMG, 3rd son of 6th baronet:—
Issue of late Edward Percy Eliott, *b* 1860, *d* 1931: *m* 1890, Annie, who *d* 1944, el da of John Connolly, of Gayndah, Queensland:—
Gilbert, *b* 1891: *m* 1929, Barbara, second da of late Charles Saddlier, of Gayndah, Queensland. —— Marjorie, *b* 1892: *m* 1938, Robert Livingston Boyd.

Grandsons of late Clifton Hazlewood Eliott (infra):—
Issue of late Francis Heathfield Eliott, *b* 1908, *d* 1970: *m* 1939, Florence Nell (Congi, Woolbrook, NSW), da of late O. B. Briggs:—
Graham Francis Heathfield (26 Kerferd St, Watson, ACT 2602), *b* 1941: *m* 1970, Karen Joyce, el da of Robert John Taylor, of Mt Druitt, NSW, and has issue living, Miles Francis Heathfield, *b* 1977, — Martyn Graham Heathfield, *b* 1979, — Tristan Robert Heathfield, *b* 1984, — Louise Karen Florence, *b* 1986. —— Geoffrey Osmer Heathfield (Congi, Woolbrook, NSW), *b* 1942: *m* 1974, Sally Green, of Moorabinda, Taroom, Qld, and has issue living, Mitchell Francis Heathfield, *b* 1978, Lachlan Edward Heathfield, *b* 1980.

Grandchildren of late Francis Willoughby Eliott (ante):—
Issue of late Clifton Hazlewood Eliott, *b* 1872, *d* 1938: *m* 1905, Mary Isabel, who *d* 1960, el da of the Rev R. W. Wilson, of Walcha, New England, NS Wales:—
Roger Clifton Heathfield (85 Oak St, Tamworth 2340, NSW), *b* 1909; late AIF: *m* 1st, 1942 (*m diss* 1947), Winifred Maud, only da of the Rev H. E. West, V of Tenterfield, NS Wales; 2ndly, 1948, Betty Muriel, el da of H. Williams, of Landsbrough, Queensland, and has issue living, (by 2nd *m*) Roger John (Bective Station, Tamworth, NSW 2340, Australia), *b* 1955: *m* 1980, Dianne Jennifer, yr da of William Henry Waugh, of Northbridge, NSW, and has issue living, Anika *b* 1982, — Robyn Jeannette, *b* 1949: *m* 1st, 1974 (*m diss* 1979), Jeffrey Alan Anderson; 2ndly, 1986, Bruce Raymond Melville, and has issue living, (by 1st *m*) Kris *b* 1975, (by 2nd *m*) James Raymond *b* 1988, Catherine Elizabet *b* 1990, — Wendy Sue, *b* 1954: *m* 1973, Alan John Hillier, of 54 Oak St, Tamworth, NSW 2340, and has issue living, Damian John *b* 1976, Brendan *b* 1978. —— Lyndsay Raine Heathfield, *b* 1919; in Australian Imperial Force: *m* 1949, Rosemary Margaret, yr da of Gordon W. Phillips, of 1 Carlos Rd, Artarmon, NS Wales, and has issue living, Andrew Clifton Heathfield (Greenwells, Walcha, NSW 2354), *b* 1954: *m* 1983, Melissa Helen, only da of Ronald A. Lee, of Armidale, NSW, and has issue living, Dougal Heathfield *b* 1987, Stuart Heathfield *b* 1988, Camilla Lee *b* 1994, Nichola Rose *b* 1995, — Gaeling Heathfield, *b* 1950: *m* 1997, Andrew Tosio, — Ruth Heathfield, *b* 1952: *m* 1975, Lawrence Smart, and has issue living, Timothy Gordon Bruce *b* 1978, Christopher David *b* 1980, Anita *b* 1976, Kathryn Elizabeth *b* 1984, — Rosemary Ann Heathfield, *b* 1956: *m* 1978, William Bernard Dowton, and has issue living, Belinda Jane *b* 1986, Alice Louise *b* 1989. *Residence* – Greenwells, Walcha, New England, NS Wales 2354. —— Dorothy Mary Heathfield (Dickinson Court, 32 Dickinson St, Charlestown, NSW 2290), *b* 1911: *m* 1933 (*m diss* 1957), Archibald John Kilpatrick, and has issue living, John Eliott, *b* 1936: *m* 1960, Janice Ellen Stidolph, and has issue living, Andrew John *b* 1966, Peter Gordon *b* 1972, Leanne Jane *b* 1962, Donna Louise, *b* 1963, — Owen Heathfield, *b* 1942: *m* 1963, Marie Maynard, and has issue living, Russell Owen *b* 1964, Alison Lyn *b* 1966: *m* 1988, James Sidney Chappell, — Jillian Mary (26 Ker St, Charlestown, NSW 2290), *b* 1934: *m* 1956, Allan John Stuart, who *d* 1984, and has had issue, Paul Andrew *b* 1960, *d* 1983, Michael John *b* 1961, David Allan *b* 1963, Anthony Mark *b* 1970.

Grandchildren of late Lt-Col Francis Augustus Heathfield Eliott, DSO (infra):—
Issue of late Heathfield George Henry Eliott, *b* 1897, *d* 1975: *m* 1922, Rhoda Isadora, who *d* 1990, da of Frederick William Augustus Daly:—
Ian Cecil Heathfield (PO Box 621, Howard Place, Cape 7450, S Africa; 17 Leerdam Rd, Bothasig 7441, CP, S Africa), *b* 1923; late Capt S African Engrs OC 106 Field Co attached to RAF in Italy, served World War II 1940-46; Consulting Engr: *m* 1st, 1945, Berenice Louise, who *d* 1994, da of George Joseph Washington; 2ndly, 1995, Millicent Mavis, da of late Abraham Ludwig Baxter, and widow of Basil Washington, and has issue living (by 1st *m*), Anthony John Heathfield, *b* 1949: *m* 1974, Sheila, da of John Kirkness, and has issue living, Taryn *b* 1979, Meghan *b* 1981, — Christopher Thomas Heathfield, *b* 1953. —— Ivor Keith Heathfield (300 Lister Rd, Rembrandt Park, 2192 Johannesburg, S Africa), *b* 1926: *m* 1962, Edythe Gloria, da of John Marshall Harrison, and has issue living, Graeme Allan (20D Margaret Av, Buccleuch, 2066 Sandton, S Africa), *b* 1964: *m* 1990, Lyndsay Ann, da of John Morrison Thomson, and has issue living, Gavin Sean *b* 1994, — Kevin John, *b* 1973, — Lynette, *b* 1963, — Alison Louise, *b* 1967: *m* 1990, John Morrison Thomson, of Midrand, S Africa, and has issue living, Tyrone Wesley *b* 1986, Tinita Natasha *b* 1990.

Issue of late Lt-Col Hugh Herbert Heathfield Eliott, OBE, TD, *b* 1903, *d* 1976: *m* 1927, Barbara, who *d* 1983, da of John Cullen Marsh, of Penge, SE:—
Ann Georgina Heathfield, *b* 1929: *m* 1954, William John Bullock, of The Mill Farm, Guarlford Rd, Malvern, Worcs WR14 3QP, son of William Edward Bullock, of The Mill Farm, Guarlford Rd, Malvern, and has issue living, Anthony John, *b* 1957: *m* 1985, Catherine Sally Greville Fox, and has issue living, James William Basil *b* 1989, Edward Adam Hugh *b*

1993, — Nigel Timothy, *b* 1960: *m* 1989, Susan Lindsay, da of late Kenneth Ellis, of Tal-y-Bont, Gwynedd, N Wales, and has issue living, Georgina Lindsay *b* 1997, Henrietta Emma *b* 1999.

Granddaughter of late Maj George Augustus Eliott, son of late Adm George Augustus Eliott, 5th son of 6th baronet:—
Issue of late Lieut-Col Francis Augustus Heathfield Eliott, DSO, *b* 1867, *d* 1937: *m* 1896, Evelyn Georgina Stirling, who *d* 1937, da of Richard William McDermott, of Dublin:—
Dymphna Helen Cynthia, *b* 1906: *m* 1930, John Richard Vernon, Nigerian Civil Ser (ret), who *d* 1984, and has issue living, Joanne Georgina Dymphna, *b* 1933: *m* 1953, Jorgen Lagoni, of Copenhagen, Denmark. *Residence* – 46 Rowans Park, Park, Lymington, Hants SO41 9GD.

The Eliotts or Elliots (then known as Elwalds or Ellots), are reputed to have come from Angus and settled as a clan in Liddesdale under grant of lands from Robert the Bruce, whose purpose was to strengthen the Scottish defences of the Middle March. Their chief built a tower on a bank overlooking Hermitage Water near its junction with the Liddel and was therafter known as Robert Ellot of Redheugh. His successors for several generations were Captains of Hermitage Castle. The Eliotts of Stobs are descended from Gilbert Ellot of Stobs, son of Robert Ellot, of Redheugh, and his wife, Jean Scott, known as "Gibbie wi' the gowden gartins," who bought Stobs in 1607 from the heirs-portioners of his step-father, Gavin Ellot of Stobs. The Elliots, Earls of Minto, are also descended from this first laird of Stobs. Gen George Augustus Eliott (Lord Heathfield) the famous defender of Gibraltar, was yst son of the 3rd baronet. Sir William Francis Eliott, 7th baronet: *m* 1826, Theresa, da of Sir Alexander Boswell, of Auchinleck, 1st Baronet, el son of James Boswell, biographer of Johnson, and sister and heir of Sir James Boswell, 2nd Baronet, who *d* 1857.

ELLIOTT (UK) 1917, of Limpsfield, Surrey

With others, for others

Sir CLIVE CHRISTOPHER HUGH ELLIOTT, 4th *Baronet b* 12 Aug 1945; *s* his father, *Sir* HUGH FRANCIS IVO, OBE, 1989; *ed* Bryanston, Univ Coll, Oxford (BA), and Cape Town Univ (DPhil); Research Officer, Cape Town Univ 1968-75; FAO/UN Project Mangr Chad 1975-78, Tanzania 1978-86, Kenya 1986-89; Agricultural Operations Division, Rome since 1989: *m* 1975, Marie-Thérèse, da of Johann Rüttimann, of Hohenrain, Switzerland, and has issue.

Arms – Argent, on a chevron sable between three bunches of grapes proper as many bezants. Crest – A garb purpure charged with a fleur-de-lis or.
Address – AGO, FAO, via della terme di Caracalla, 00100 Rome, Italy.

SONS LIVING

IVO ANTONY MORITZ, *b* 9 May 1978. —— Nicolas Johann Clive, *b* 1980.

SISTERS LIVING

Susan Elspeth, *b* 1940: *m* 1969, Lt-Col Timothy James Tedder, Gren Gds (c/o Westminster Bank, 96 Terminus Rd, Eastbourne), and has issue living, Zara Elizabeth *b* 1971: *m* 1997, Nigel George Hemmo Frend, — Laura, *b* 1974. —— Judith Margery, *b* 1942: *m* 1968, Erik Geissler, DPhil, and has issue living, — Stephen Francis, *b* 1975, — Beatrice Alison, *b* 1974, — Leonie Elizabeth Pauline, *b* 1978.

AUNTS LIVING (*Daughters of 2nd Baronet*)

Anne Carey *b* 1914; *ed* Lady Margaret Hall, Oxford (BA 1938): *m* 1939, John Thomson, late Capt RASC (The Knoll, Fulbrook, Burford, Oxon), and has issue living, Robert Hugh Gordon *b* 1947: *m* 1976, Rosalie Zoë Twitchin, and has issue living, Alix Rebecca *b* 1978, Camilla Rachel *b* 1981, — Andrew John, *b* 1949: *m* 1976 Alison Monica Berkley, and has issue living, Anna Marie *b* 1977, Pauline Clare *b* 1979, — Janet Carey, *b* 1941: *m* 1963, Keith Gilbert Robbins, and has issue living, Paul Gilbert John *b* 1965, Daniel Henry Keith *b* 1967, Adam Edward Ivo *b* 1972, Lucy Helen *b* 1970. —— Pauline Margery, *b* 1917; ARCM (Hon Fellow 1972).

WIDOW LIVING OF THIRD BARONET

ELIZABETH MARGARET (*Dowager Lady Elliott*), da of late Adolphus George Phillipson, of N Finchley, N12: *m* 1939, Sir Hugh Francis Ivo Elliott, 3rd Bt, OBE, who *d* 1989.

COLLATERAL BRANCH LIVING

Issue of late Thomas Anthony Keith Elliott, CMG, Ambassador to Israel, 2nd son of 2nd baronet, *b* 1921, *d* 1976: *m* 1951, Alethea Helen (1 Windrush, nr Burford, Oxon), el da of late Maj Alistair B. H. Richardson, King's Dragoon Gds (B Hotham, colls):—
Thomas Anthony William, *b* 1959: *m* 1986, Carolyn Smith, and has issue living, Anthony William Felix, *b* 1991, — Evelyn Alethea, *b* 1993. —— Victoria Carey, *b* 1952: *m* 1983, Frederick Dolan, and has issue living, Caitlin Emily, *b* 1987, — Alethea Cecilia, *b* 1990. —— Catherine Frances, *b* 1954: *m* 1982, George Cardona, and has issue living, Anthony, *b* 1985,

— Alexander, *b* 1988, — Natalie, *b* 1987. —— Anne Louisa, *b* 1956: *m* 1981, Jurek Bielecki, and has issue living, Anton Andrej, *b* 1984, — Kazimir, *b* 1986, — Lukas, *b* 1989, — Roman, *b* 1990, — Darius, *b* 1993.

The 1st baronet, Sir Thomas Henry Elliott, KCB (son of late Thomas Henry Elliott, of Rue Ruhmkorff, Paris), was Sec to Board of Agriculture and Fisheries 1892-1913, Dep Master and Comptroller of the Mint, and *ex-officio* Engraver of HM's Seals 1913-17. The 2nd baronet, Sir Ivo D'Oyly Elliott, was Under-Sec, Depart of Commerce and Industry, Govt of India 1916-19, Sec to Govt United Provinces, India 1926-31, and Financial Commr Mauritius 1931. The 3rd baronet, Sir Hugh Francis Ivo Eliott, OBE, served with the Tanganyika Administration 1937-61, Permanent Sec Ministry of Natural Resources 1958-61, Administrator of Tristan da Cunha 1950-52, and with the International Union for Conservation of Nature 1962-80, as Sec Gen 1964-66.

Ellis-Griffith, see Griffith.

ELPHINSTON (NS) 1701, of Logie, co Aberdeen

Not by strength but by valour

Sir JOHN ELPHINSTON OF GLACK, 11th *Baronet*, son of late Thomas George ELPHINSTON, 2nd son of *de jure* 9th baronet; *b* 12 Aug 1924; *s* his uncle, *Maj Sir* ALEXANDER LOGIE ELPHINSTONE, 1970; *ed* Repton, and Emmanuel Coll, Camb (BA); late Lt RM; retired land agent; claimant to dormant Baronetcy of Elphinstone (*cr* 1628), and feudal Barony of New Glasgow, Nova Scotia: *m* 1953, Margaret Doreen, da of late Edric Tasker, of Cheltenham, and has issue.

Arms – Argent, on a chevron sable between three boar's heads erased gules, armed and langued azure, an episcopal mitre of the first. **Crest** – A dexter hand proper holding a garb or.
Residence – Pilgrims, Churchfields, Sandiway, Northwich, Cheshire CW8 2JS.

SONS LIVING

ALEXANDER (High Banks, Sandy Lane, Brampford Speke, Exeter, Devon EX5 5HW), *b* 6 June 1955; *ed* Repton and St John's Coll, Durham Univ; solicitor: *m* 1986, Ruth Mary, elder da of Rev Robert Curtis Dunnett, of Edgbaston, Warwickshire, and has issue living, Daniel John, *b* 24 Sept 1989, — David Robert, *b* 1997, — Sarah Elisabeth, *b* 1992. —— Charles (West Water House, Edzell, Brechin, Angus), *b* 1958; *ed* Repton: *m* 1981, Lucy, da of Maj M. D. Reynolds, of Malton, N Yorks, and has issue living, William James, *b* 1986, — Thomas George, *b* 1988, — Mary Abigail, *b* 1984, — Charis Clare, *b* 1992. —— Andrew James, *b* 1961. —— William Robert, *b* 1963.

SISTER LIVING

Marjorie Mary, *b* 1915: *m* 1939, Maj-Gen Reginald Carteret de Mussenden Leathes, CB, MVO, OBE, RM, who *d* 1987, of Furthurhouse, Highbrook, Ardingly, Sussex, and has had issue, Rupert de Mussenden (West Barn, West St, Abbotsbury, Dorset DT3 4JT), *b* 1941: *m* 1967 (*m diss* 1998), Nicole Foucaud, and has issue living, Thomas de Mussenden *b* 1970, Isabelle de Mussenden *b* 1973, Francine de Mussenden *b* 1976, — Simon William de Mussenden, *b* 1948: *m* 1971, Belinda Haire, and has issue living, Timothy de Mussenden *b* 1978, Annabel de Mussenden *b* 1976, — *Rev* David Burlton de Mussenden, *b* 1949: *m* 1975, Mary Cross, and has issue living, Benjamin John de Mussenden *b* 1979, Miriam Frances de Mussenden *b* 1982, — Rosemary Sarah de Mussenden, *b* 1944: *m* 1976, Arthur Horsley, and *d* 1996.

COLLATERAL BRANCH LIVING

Grandchildren of late John William Robert Elphinstone, 3rd son of *de jure* 9th Baronet, *b* 1884, *d* 1949: *m* 1st, 1912 (*m diss* 1924), Vera Mary, da of Lloyd W. Griffith; 2ndly, 1924 (*m diss* 1931), Bettine Ariana, who *d* 1969, da of Sir William Michael Curtis, 4th Bt (*cr* 1802); 3rdly, 1938, Edna M. Nethersole:—
    Issue of late John Philip Elphinstone, *b* 1940, *d* 1981: *m* 1967, Beverley Madge (22 Adelaide Circle, Craigie, W Australia 6025), da of Ted Fischer:—
Colin Edward (Saul Lodge, Arlingham Rd, Saul, Glos), *b* 1967; *ed* Craigie State High Sch. —— Angela, *b* 1974.

On 30 Nov 1927, Alexander Logie Elphinstone (ante) proved his right (as 10th Bt) to this Baronetcy (*cr* with remainder to heirs-male whatsoever) before the Baronetage Committee of the Privy Council, being a direct descendant of Nicholas Elphinstone of Glack, a grandson of Sir Henry Elphinstone of Pittendreich (who *s* to the Elphinstone estates in Stirlingshire 1435) (*see* B Elphinstone), and cousin of Sir John Elphinstone, 4th Bt of Logie, since whose death in 1743 the title had remained dormant.

ELPHINSTONE (UK) 1816, of Sowerby, Cumberland

Always ready

Sir JOHN HOWARD MAIN ELPHINSTONE, 6th *Baronet*; *b* 25 Feb 1949; *s* his father, *Sir* (MAURICE) DOUGLAS WARBURTON, TD, 1995; *ed* Loretto: *m* 1990, Diane Barbara Quilliam, da of late Dr Brian Quilliam Callow, of Johannesburg.

Arms – Argent guttée de sang, on a chevron embattled sable between three boars' heads erased gules, two swords proper, pommels and hilts or. **Crest** – Out of a mural crown gules a demi-woman affrontée habited, and in the dexter hand a sword erect proper, pommel and hilt or, in the sinister an olive-branch vert.
Residence – Garden Cottage, 6 Amherst Rd, Sevenoaks, Kent TN13 3LS.

SISTER LIVING

Janet Christine Helen, *b* 1953; *ed* Manchester Univ (BA); MNIMH: *m* 1983, Kevin Grant, and has issue living, Ruari Jack Elphinstone, *b* 1991. *Residence* – 85 Woodlands Av, Wanstead, E11 3RB.

AUNT LIVING *(sister of 5th baronet)*

Norah Christine (97 Rennie's Mill Rd, St John's, Newfoundland, Canada A1B 2P1), *b* 1917; *ed* King's Coll, London, and King's Coll Hosp; MB BS, DCH, FRCP(C); Hon LLD Memorial Univ of Newfoundland 1987; Commemorative Medal for 125th Anniversary of Confedn of Canada 1992: *m* 1st, 1968, George Rex Renouf, who *d* 1971; 2ndly, 1973, William Joseph Browne, PC, QC, who *d* 1989.

DAUGHTERS LIVING OF FOURTH BARONET

Elizabeth Mary (16 The Mowbrays, Framlingham, nr Woodbridge, Suffolk IP13 9DC), *b* 1926: *m* 1952, Cmdr Giles Anthony St George Poole, RN (ret), who *d* 1986, and has issue living, Philip Anthony Howard, *b* 1955; *ed* Lancing, and Nottingham Univ (BSc); Lt-Col RE: *m* 1990, Katrina Mary Druce, da of AV-M Charles Stuart Moore, CB, OBE, of The Avenue, Crowthorne, Berks, and has issue living, Edward Anthony Charles *b* 1992, Lucy Mary Victoria *b* 1994, — Timothy Giles Elphinstone (75 Ravenslea Rd, SW12 8SL), *b* 1956; *ed* Lancing, and Pembroke Coll, Oxford (BA): *m* 1989, Cynthia, da of Walter Ellis Jones, Sr, of 930 Springer Drive, Griffin, Georgia 30223, USA, and has issue living, Giles William Alexander *b* 1995, Catherine Elizabeth Moffett *b* 1992, — Rosalind Kate Elizabeth, *b* 1961; *ed* St Michael's, Petworth, and St Andrews Univ (MA): *m* 1986, Stephen Norman Stuart Penrose, of Highfields, Seven Star Green, Eight Ash Green, nr Colchester, Essex CO6 3QB, and has issue living, Christopher Anthony Stuart *b* 1989, James Stuart Douglas *b* 1996, Alexandra Elizabeth Louise *b* 1991. —— Rosalind Constance, *b* 1930: *m* 1950, Robert William Atherstone (PO Box 10191, Linton Grange, Port Elizabeth 6015, S Africa), and has issue living, Howard Ian Damant, *b* 1954, — Anne Margaret Herschël, *b* 1950, — Rosemary Jane Herschël, *b* 1956, — Katherine Sarah Damant, *b* 1961, — Audrey Patricia Damant, *b* (twin) 1961.

WIDOW LIVING OF FIFTH BARONET

(HELEN) BARBARA (*Dowager Lady Elphinstone*), da of late George Ramsay Main, of Houghton, Kilmalcolm: *m* 1943, Maj Sir (Maurice) Douglas Warburton Elphinstone, 5th Bt, TD, who *d* 1995. *Residence* – 11 Scotby Green Steading, Scotby, Carlisle CA4 8EH.

COLLATERAL BRANCHES LIVING

Issue of late Rev Kenneth John Tristram Elphinstone (brother of 5th baronet), 3rd son of late Rev Canon Maurice Curteis Elphinstone, 4th son of 3rd baronet, *b* 1911, *d* 1980: *m* 1938, Felicity (who *m* 2ndly, 19—, Cmdr Eric Ford Schomberg Back, DSC, RN), 4th da of late His Honour Sir Gerald Berkeley Hurst, QC:—
Margaret Norah ELPHINSTONE (Flat 1L, 56 Queensborough Gdns, Glasgow G12 9TU), *b* 1948; *ed* St Mary's Coll, Durham (BA); has resumed her maiden name: *m* 1969 (*m diss* 1985), John David Button, M Phil, and has issue living, Rosalind Margaret, *b* 1972; has issue living, (by Tom Francis) Eve Catherine FRANCIS *b* 1999, — Catherine Joanna, *b* 1974.

Issue of late Rowland Henry Elphinstone, 4th son of late Rev Canon Maurice Curteis Elphinstone (ante), *b* 1915, *d* 1997: *m* 1954, Hester Frances, elder da of late Rev Charles Ravenscroft Bull, of the Vicarage, Milton Abbot, Devon:—
Henry Charles, *b* 1958; *ed* Grenville Coll. —— Mary Georgiana, MBE, *b* 1955; *ed* London Univ (MB BS); MBE (Civil) 1982. —— Constance Hester, *b* 1957; *ed* Leeds Univ; has issue living, Ruth Hester, *b* 1984.

This branch of the Elphinstones descends from Réné de Elphinstone, probably a descendant of Jock Elphinstone, a Member of Scots Guard in France 1494. Réné came to Scotland with Robert Stewart, Earl of Orkney, and *d* 1587. His yr son Robert was page to Prince Henry of Wales, son of James VI and I whose gt gt grandson, John Elphinstone, was Capt RN and Adm Russian Navy under Catherine *the Great*. His third and youngest son, Sir Howard, was the first baronet. He was a distinguished Peninsular veteran, and Col Comdt RE, and greatly distinguished himself at the capture of the Cape of Good Hope, in Egypt, and elsewhere. Sir Howard, 2nd baronet, sat as MP for Hastings (*L*) 1835-7, and for Lewes 1841-7.

Elphinstone-Dalrymple, see Dalrymple.

ELTON (GB) 1717, of Bristol

Sir CHARLES ABRAHAM GRIERSON ELTON, 11th *Baronet*; *b* 23 May 1953; *s* his father, *Sir* ARTHUR HALLAM RICE, 1973; *ed* Eton, and Reading Univ (BA 1976): *m* 1990, Lucy Lauris, da of late Lukas Heller, and of Mrs Caroline Garnham, and has issue.
Residences – Clevedon Court, Som BS21 6QU; 24 Maida Av, W2 1ST.

DAUGHTER LIVING

Lotte Caroline, *b* 1993.

SISTERS LIVING

Julia Margaret Hallam, *b* 1949. —— Rebecca Wiggin, *b* 1951: *m* 1984, L. Neal FitzSimons, of Kensington, Maryland, USA, son of late T.L. Fitz Simons and Mrs Wells N. Thompson.

COLLATERAL BRANCHES LIVING

Grandchildren of late Rev Henry George Tierney Elton, 5th son of 6th baronet:—
Issue of late Charles Henry Elton, *b* 1857, *d* 1929: *m* 1st, 1879, Emily Grace, da of late Thomas Christmas, 8th Hussars; 2ndly, 1897 (*m diss* 1927), Edith May, da of J. F. Ward, of Hallam House, Walmer, Port Elizabeth, S Africa:—
(By 2nd *m*) CHARLES TIERNEY HALLAM, *b* 1898: *m* 1924, Helen, who *d* 1963, da of late Capt Frederick Patrick Waud, Mercantile Marine, and has issue living, Heather Agnes Campbell, *b* 1928. —— Arthur Hallam (25 Sunny Rd, Glenhazel, Johannesburg, S Africa), *b* 1901: *m* 1926, Georgina, who *d* 1963, da of late A. W. Hemming, and has issue living, Anthony Charles Hallam, *b* 1942, — Rosemary Patricia, *b* 1930, — June Margaret, *b* 1933. —— Kathleen Patricia Hallam ELTON, *b* 1908; has resumed the surname of Elton in lieu of that of Baker: *m* 1940 (*m diss* 1947), Frank Baker. *Residence* – 58 Hurd St, Newton Park, Port Elizabeth, S Africa.

Grandchildren of late Hallam Edmund Arthur Elton, only son of Edmund Hallam Elton (infra):—
Issue of late Timothy Hallam Elton, *b* 1933, *d* 1978: *m* 1964, Linda Susan (Thaba 'Nchu, Box 1, Cashel, Zimbabwe), el da of Maj George Richard Paton Pollitt, of Makalanga, Mazoe, Zimbabwe (*see* B Heytesbury, colls, 1985 Edn):—
Simon Marwood Hallam, *b* 1965. —— Anthony Hallam, *b* 1966. —— Sarah Katharine, *b* 1970.

Granddaughter of late Rev Henry George Tierney Elton (ante):—
Issue of late Edmund Hallam Elton, *b* 1860, *d* 1925: *m* 1887, Ada Constance, da of J. H. Webbe, of Crown Lands Depart, Cape Town:—
Lily Avice Hallam, *b* 1896: *m* 1st, 1934 (*m diss* 1946), L. J. Lake; 2ndly, 1968, Henry Adrian Harington, who *d* 1969. *Address* – Apple, PO Magoebas Kloof, via Pietersburg, Transvaal, S Africa.

Grandchildren of late Com Frederick Elton, RN (infra):—
Issue of late Frederick Ernest Bayard Elton, *b* 1895, *d* 1976: *m* 1st 1914 (*m diss* 1925), Dorothy, da of Adm Thomas Young Greet, of Horsham; 2ndly, 1925 (*m diss* 19—), Vera Ida, da of Hugh Goldie, of Osborne Grange, Bournemouth; 3rdly, 1930, Katherine Mary (32 The Close, Harpenden, Herts), da of Arthur Hamilton Hackett:—
(By 1st *m*) Daphne, *b* 1917: *m* 1936, Derek Maxwell Sanderson (*see* Sanderson, Bt), who *d* 1983. —— Stephanie, *b* 1920: *m* 1947, Eden James Hungerford Morgan. —— (By 3rd *m*) John Arthur Bayard *b* 1940: *m* 1971, Jennifer Elizabeth, el da of William George Thomson, of 25 Mill Lane, Shoreham-by-Sea, and has issue living, James Edmund Bayard, *b* 1972, — Katherine Elizabeth, *b* 1975, — Juliet, *b* 1977.

Grandson of late Frederick Bayard Elton, son of Isaac Elton (*b* 1771), 2nd son of Isaac Elton (*b* 1739), great-grandson of Jacob Elton, 3rd son of 1st baronet:—
Issue of late Com Frederick Elton, RN, *b* 1854, *d* 1922: *m* 1893, Ernestine, who *d* 1951, da of late Ernest White, JP, of Beaudesert Estates, Logan River, Queensland:—
Cedric Edward Bayard, *b* 1904; Capt Roy Fusiliers: *m* 1930, Barbara Mary Parrott, and has issue living, Nicholas Edward Bayard, *b* 1931: *m* 1960, Eileen Dorothy, da of Arthur Preece, of Ross-on-Wye, and has issue living, Patrick Edward Bayard *b* 1966, Nicola Jane *b* 1961.

The 1st and 2nd baronets were successively Mayors of Bristol, and each sat as MP for that City. The 7th baronet sat as MP for Bath (*L*) 1857-9, and the 8th was High Sheriff of Somerset 1895.

ERRINGTON (UK) 1963, of Ness, in co Palatine of Chester

Sir GEOFFREY FREDERICK ERRINGTON, OBE, 2nd *Baronet*; *b* 15 Feb 1926; *s* his father, *Sir* ERIC, 1973; *ed* Rugby, and New Coll, Oxford; Col late King's Regt (ret 1975), GSO3 (Int) HQ 11 Armd Div 1950-52, GSO3 (Int) M13 (b) War Office 1955-57, Bde Maj 146 Inf Bde 1959-61, Coy Comd RMAS 1963-65, Mil Assist to Adjt-Gen 1965-67, CO 1st Bn King's Regt 1967-69, GSO1, 1 (BR)Corps 1969-71, Col GS HQ NW Dist 1971-74, Asst Adjt-Gen M1 (MOD) 1974-75; Col The King's Regt 1975-86; Dir of Personnel Services (Consultant), Brit Shipbuilders 1977-78; Bd Member Shipbuilding ITB 1977-78; Chm Man Cttee Kings and Manchester Regt's Assocn 1975-86, of Executive Appointments Ltd 1982-90; Member Kent Consumers Consultative Cttee, Southern Water Authority 1984-89; Chm Harefield Hosp NHS Trust 1991-98; Vice-Chm Association for the Prevention of Addiction 1991-94 (Chm 1994-98); Hon Dir Britain-Australia Soc since 1998; FRSA 1994; Liveryman, Broderers' Co, Coachmakers' and Coach Harness Makers' Co and Freeman (City of Lond) 1980; OBE (Civil) 1998: *m* 1955, Diana Kathleen Forbes, da of Edward Barry Davenport, of Edgbaston, and has issue.

ᚐrms – Or an open book clasped on a chief azure a spur rowel upwards between two portcullises chained or. Crest – A liver bird supporting with the dexter claw an oak sapling proper.
Residences – Stone Hill Farm, Sellindge, nr Ashford, Kent TN25 6AJ; 203a Gloucester Place, NW1. *Clubs* – Boodle's; United Oxford and Cambridge.

SONS LIVING

ROBIN DAVENPORT (68 Orbain Rd, SW6 7JY), *b* 1 July 1957; *ed* Eton. —— John Davenport (10 Dighton Rd, SW18), *b* 1959; *ed* Eton: *m* 1989, Prue, da of Brig Michael Lee, OBE, of Fulham, SW6, and has issue living, Isabel Jane Davenport, *b* 1993. —— Andrew Davenport (14 Nottingham Rd, SW17; Brooks's Club), *b* (twin) 1959; *ed* Eton; late Welsh Gds: *m* 1983 (*m diss* 1989), Georgina Sophie, yr da of Lt-Gen Sir Derek Boorman, KCB, of Goodnestone, Kent.

BROTHER LIVING

Stuart Grant, CBE (Earleywood Lodge, Ascot, Berks SL5 9JP), *b* 1929; *ed* Rugby, and Trin Coll, Oxford (MA); JP of Berks; CBE 1994: *m* 1954, Anne, yr da of A. Eric Baedeker, of Edgbaston, and has issue living, David Grant (47 Southdean Gdns, SW19), *b* 1957; *ed* Rugby: *m* 1982, Catherine Ann, yr da of Kenneth Neville, of Sydney, Australia, and has issue, Timothy Grant *b* 1983, Nicholas David *b* 1985, Frederick Charles *b* 1988, — Charles Stuart, *b* 1961; *ed* Rugby: *m* 1992, Nicole Cauverien, — Elizabeth Anne, *b* 1958: *m* 1983, Jaimie Coltart Corke, of Burltons, Donhead St Mary, Wilts, son of David Corke, of Lyndhurst, Hants, and has issue living, Milo Jaimie *b* 1991, Daisy Elizabeth *b* 1985, Imogen Sally *b* 1986, Ella Clementine *b* 1994.

SISTER LIVING

Anne Jacqueline (2 Willow Tree Close, Wickham Market, Suffolk IP13 0TB), *b* 1935; *ed* Wycombe Abbey; Community Relations Adviser, RAF Bentwaters 1963-85.

Sir Eric Errington, 1st Bt, was MP for Bootle (*C*) 1935-45 and Aldershot 1954-70.

ERSKINE (UK) 1821, of Cambo, Fife

Watchful and valiant

Sir (THOMAS) DAVID ERSKINE, 5th *Baronet*; *b* 31 July 1912; *s* his father, *Lieut-Col Sir* THOMAS WILFRID HARGREAVES JOHN, DSO, 1944; *ed* Eton, and Magdalene Coll, Camb (BA); Maj (ret) Indian Corps of Engineers; is a JP for co Fife; Vice-Lieut for co Fife 1982; Chm Fife CC 1970: *m* 1947, Ann, da of late Lieut-Col Neil Fraser-Tytler, DSO, TD, of Aldourie Castle, Inverness and has issue.

Arms – Quarterly, 1st and 4th, gules, an imperial crown within a double tressure flory counter-flory or; 2nd and 3rd argent, a pale sable; the whole within a bordure wavy ermine. **Crest** – On a garb fessewise or, banded azure, a cock wings elevated proper charged with a bendlet wavy sinister of the second.
Seat – Cambo House, Kingsbarns, Fife. *Residence* – Westnewhall, Kingsbarns, St Andrews, Fife.

SONS LIVING

(THOMAS) PETER NEIL (Cambo House, nr St Andrews, Fife KY16 8QD), *b* 28 March 1950; *ed* Eton, Birmingham Univ, and Edinburgh Univ: *m* 1972, Catherine, da of Col G. H. K. Hewlett, and has issue living, Thomas Struan, *b* 6 Feb 1977, — James Dunbar, *b* 1979, — Gillian Christian, *b* 1983, — Mary Caroline, *b* 1986. ▬▬ William (c/o ICARDA, PO Box 5466, Aleppo, Syria), *b* 1952; PhD; *m* 1st, 1973, Sarah Jane McElroy, el da of Charles William McElroy Pratt, MD, of Orwell Grange, Orwell, Royston, Herts; 2ndly, 1982, Mireille, da of late Georges Abdelnour, of Aleppo, Syria, and has issue living, (by 2nd *m*) Thomas Georges, *b* 1989, — Philip Neil, *b* 1991.

SISTERS LIVING

Diana Mildred, *b* 1915: *m* 1st, 1941, Major N. R. M. Skene, DSC, RM, who *d* on active ser 1942; 2ndly, 1945, David Grant Buxton TD, late Maj Middlesex Regt, and has issue living (by 2nd *m*) Andrew Ralph, *b* 1947: *m* 1979 (*m diss* 19—), Sally Higginbottom, — Lucinda Dierdre, *b* 1945: *m* 1973, Tudor Venn, and has issue living, 2 sons and 1 da. *Residence* – Cedar Gables, 15 Frenze Rd, Diss, Norfolk. ▬▬ Victoria Margaret, *b* 1919; formerly 2nd Officer WRNS. *Residence* – 41 Thurleigh Court, Nightingale Lane, SW12 8AS. ▬▬ Constance Gertrude, *b* 1921: *m* 1942, Maj Oliver Patch, DSO, DSC, RM, who *d* 1991, and has issue living, Janet Mary (58 Shelgate Rd, SW11), *b* 1945: *m* 1976 (*m diss* 1986), Simon Scott, — Olivia Cynthia (43 Cadogan Sq, SW1), *b* 1946: *m* 1st, 1972, Dimitri Tiomkin, who *d* 1979; 2ndly, 1988, James Alastair Sholto Douglas, son of Maj Henry James Sholto Douglas, late Scots Guards, of Hemingford Abbots, Huntingdon (*see* B Templewore, colls, 1959 Edn), — Emily Dorothea, *b* 1949: *m* 1st, 1980 (*m diss* 19—), Kenneth Page; 2ndly, 19—, Gavin Scott and has issue living (by 1st *m*) Harriet Constance Zenia *b* 1980, (by 2nd *m*) Tobias Oliver *b* 1986, — Diana Elizabeth, *b* 1953: *m* 1st, 1974 (*m diss* 1981), Stephen Sullivan; 2ndly, 1995, Lt-Col Terence Patrick McDowell, of Undercliffe Cottage, Donhead St Mary, Shaftesbury, Dorset SP7 9DG, — Penelope Margaret Christian, *b* 1957: *m* 1983, Gerald Olson, and has issue living, Nicholas Oliver *b* 1984, Natalie *b* 1986, Hannah *b* 1988. *Residence* – Conduit, Barkers Hill, Semley, Dorset SP7 9BJ. ▬▬ Harriet Katherine Lucinda, *b* 1924: *m* 1945, Lt-Cdr Hugh Doheny, Roy Canadian Naval VR, and has issue living, Hugh Erskine, *b* 1946: *m* 1987, Margaret Collins, — Penelope Ann, *b* 1949: *m* 1st, 1972 (*m diss* 1982), Ronald Carter; 2ndly, 1986, Mario Bousquet, of Mount Orford, Quebec, — Kathleen Janet, *b* 1951: *m* 1972, Brian Hanna, of Grandmere, Quebec, — Mary Harriet, *b* 1952, — Lucinda Margaret Ruth, *b* 1956: has issue, Mira Harriet Kathleen *b* 1992, — Victoria Diana, *b* 1960: *m* 1982, Brian Herring, of Lennoxville, Quebec, and has issue living, Charles Thomas *b* 1983, Margaret Lucinda *b* 1985, Mary Grace *b* 1988. *Residence* – 95 Moulton Hill, RR1, Lennoxville, Quebec Province J1M 2A2, Canada.

COLLATERAL BRANCHES LIVING

Grandchildren of late Sir James Malcolm Monteith Erskine, 2nd son of late Capt David Holland Erskine, 2nd son of 1st baronet:—
Issue of late Denys Malcolm Erskine, *b* 1903, *d* 1966: *m* 1923, Aleda Julia, who *d* 1971, da of E. C. Brownfield:—
Margaret Lucile (44 Rosedale Ct, Newcastle-on-Tyne), *b* 1927: *m* 1stly 1960, Anthony Colin Radclyffe, who *d* 1976; 2ndly, 1978, Kenneth Warner.

Issue of late Maj Sir Derek Quicke Erskine, *b* 1905, *d* 1977: *m* 1927 Elisabeth Mary Stretton (Riverside Paddocks, PO Box 14968, Nairobi, Kenya), da of late Maj Reginald Stretton Spurrier, King's Dragoon Gds:—
Francis David Monteith, MC (Sanctuary Farm, PO Box 244, Naivasha, Kenya), *b* 1929; Kenya 1954 (MC): *m* 1958 (*m diss* 1963), Marie-Claude Irene, da of late Roland M. A. Mange, of Kenya, and has issue living, Clive Patrick Monteith, *b* 1959: *m* 1985, Patrizia Pandora, da of Michele Loria, of Canino, Viterbo, Italy, and has issue living, Charlotte Irene *b* 1987, — Guy Francis, *b* 1961: *m* 1988, Juliet, da of John Dallas Amos, of Edinburgh, and has issue living, James Francis *b* 1989. ▬▬ Jane Petal, *b* 1928: *m* 1st, 1950 (*m diss* 1963), William Lee Harragin, son of late Sir Walter Harragin, CMG, QC; 2ndly, 1963 (*m diss* 1972), Robert William Young; 3rdly, 1973, David Wanric Allen (PO Box 14712, Nairobi, Kenya), and has issue living, (by 1st *m*) Mark Savile Austin, *b* 1956: *m* 1990, Patricia Walker, and has issue living, Daniel *b* 1992, Corinne Florence *b* 1994, — Vanessa Jane, *b* 1951: *m* 1977, Kirby McCaffrey, of Cedar Dr, Baltimore, Md, USA, and has issue living, James Flynn Cassius *b* 1980, — Robin Elisabeth, *b* 1953: *m* 1986, Peter Boone Hussey, and has issue living, Mary Victoria *b* 1988, Serwen *b* 1991, — Serena Claire, *b* 1959.

Issue of late Keith David Erskine, *b* 1907, *d* 1974: *m* 1st, 1936 (*m diss* 1940), Kathleen Diana, da of C. W. Kayser, of Eaton Hall, Retford; 2ndly, 1944, Audrey Skinner:—
(By 2nd *m*) Simon David, *b* 1953. ▬▬ Sarah Gay, *b* 1946: *m* 1967, Alex Ryan, and has issue living, Robert Keith, *b* 1973, — Audrey Mary, *b* 1970. ▬▬ Aleda Grace Elizabeth, *b* 1948. ▬▬ Fiona Margaret (*Lady Mottram*), *b* 1949: *m* 1971, Sir Richard Clive Mottram, KCB, and has issue living, Keith, *b* 1974, — David, *b* 1981, — Thomas, *b* 1985, —

Ruth, *b* 1977. —— Deborah Mary, *b* 1951: *m* 1974, David Langford Holt, and has issue living, Benjamin, *b* 1976, —— James (twin), *b* 1976, — Sara Maria, *b* 1978. —— Kathrina Jane, *b* 1956.

Issue of late James Monteith Erskine (twin), *b* 1907, *d* 1965: *m* 1931, Kathleen Brookes, who *d* 1991:—
David Monteith, *b* 1933; *ed* Camb Univ (MA); Solicitor 1960: *m* 1960, Tessa Victoria, da of Dr James Vernon, of Ascot, Berks, and has issue living, Dominic James Monteith, *b* 1962; has issue living, Daniel Jackson *b* 1991, — Malcolm David Vernon, *b* 1963, — Susan Eileen, *b* 1970. —— Shirley Monteith (twin), *b* 1933; *ed* Camb Univ (BA): *m* 1954, Barry Michael Clarke, of The Long House, Woodgreen, Hants, and has issue living, Thomas James Woodchurch, *b* 1958, — Eleanor Margaret, *b* 1962.

Sir David Erskine, 1st Bt, was a natural grandson of 9th Earl of Kellie. The 4th baronet, Sir Thomas Wilfred Hargreaves John Erskine, DSO, was Lieut-Col Queen's Own Cameron Highlanders, and served during European War 1914-16 (DSO).

Erskine-Hill, see Hill.

ESMONDE (I) 1629, of Ballynastragh, Wexford

Sir THOMAS FRANCIS GRATTAN ESMONDE, 17th Baronet , *b* 14 Oct 1960; *s* his father, *Sir* JOHN HENRY GRATTAN (*His Honour Judge Esmonde*), 1987; *ed* Sandford Park, and Trin Coll, Dublin; MD, MB, BCh, BAO (1984), MRCPI, MRCP (UK): *m* 1986, Pauline Loretto, 2nd da of James Vincent Kearns, and has issue.

Arms – Ermine, on a chief gules three mullets argent. Crest – Out of a mural crown a Saracen's head all proper.
Seat – Ballynastragh, Gorey, co Wexford. *Residence* – 6 Nutley Av, Donnybrook, Dublin 4.

SON LIVING

SEAN VINCENT GRATTAN, *b* 8 Jan 1989.

DAUGHTERS LIVING

Aisling Margaret Pamela Grattan, *b* 1991. —— Niamh Pauline Grattan, *b* 1996.

BROTHERS LIVING

Harold William Grattan, *b* 1964; *ed* Sandford Park, and Trin Coll, Dublin. —— Richard Anthony Grattan, *b* 1969; *ed* Sandford Park, and Trin Coll, Dublin.

Had rather die than be dishonoured

SISTERS LIVING

Karen Maria Grattan, *b* 1965. —— Lisa Marion Grattan, *b* 1968; *ed* Nat Univ, Dublin.

UNCLES LIVING (*Sons of 15th baronet*)

Bartholomew Thomas Grattan, *b* 1937; *ed* Glenstal Abbey. *Residence* – Ballynastragh, Gorey, co Wexford. —— Anthony James Grattan, *b* 1943; *ed* Glenstal, and Univ Coll, Dublin. *Residence* – St Oliver's, Coolbawn, co Tipperary.

AUNTS LIVING (*Daughters of 15th baronet*)

Alice Mary Grattan, *b* 1929; *ed* National Univ of Ireland (BSc 1951). *Residence* – 8 Palmerston Park, Dublin 6. —— Eithne Marion Grattan, *b* 1931; is a LRAM. *Residence* – Ballynastragh, Gorey, co Wexford. —— Anne Caroline Grattan, *b* 1940. *Residence* – Ballynastragh, Gorey, co Wexford.

HALF-GREAT-AUNT LIVING (*Half-sister of 15th Baronet*)

Mary Carmel, *b* 1912: *m* 1935, Dermot St John Gogarty, Flying Officer RAF Vol Reserve, of Nairobi, Kenya, and has issue living, Michael Dermot St John, *b* 1936.

WIDOW LIVING OF SIXTEENTH BARONET

PAMELA MARY (*Pamela, Lady Esmonde*), elder da of Dr Francis Stephen Bourke, FRCPI, MRIA: *m* 1957, Sir John Henry Grattan Esmonde, 17th Bt, who *d* 1987. *Residence* – 6 Nutley Av, Donnybrook, Dublin 4.

COLLATERAL BRANCHES LIVING

Grandchildren of late Capt John Joseph Esmonde, LRCSI, RAMC, 2nd son of James Esmonde, JP, DL, son of Com James Esmonde, RN, grandson of 7th Bt:—
Issue of late Owen James Esmonde (half-brother of 15th baronet), *b* 1905, *d* 1993: *m* 1938, Eira Margaret Antonia (Cloneen, Glendalough, co Wicklow), da of late George Henry Louis Mackenzie (*see* Mackenzie, Bt *cr* 1673, colls):—
Eugene Patrick Mackenzie (52 Enderley Rd, Clayfield, Brisbane, Queensland 4011, Australia), *b* 1942; *ed* RMC Duntroon, ACT, and Queensland Univ (BEcon); Lt-Col RAA (ret 1981); Man Dir Sharpe Group of Cos since 1982: *m* 1972, Jennifer Ann, da of Sir Frank Victor Sharpe, CMG, OBE, of Brisbane, and has issue living, Godfrey Christian, *b* 1980, — Eugene James, *b* 1983, — Grania Adelaide, *b* 1986. —— Deborah Anne Barbara, *b* 1939: *m* 1st, 1968 (*m diss* 1976), Dr Peter John Fraser Coutts; 2ndly, 1979, Kevin Clyde Scott, of Glendalough Park, Leongatha South, Vic 3953, Australia. —— Gillian Mary Antonia, *b* 1940: *m* 1963, Colin Leslie Rosewarne, of Hardigreen Park, Quirindi, NSW 2343, and has issue living, Andrew John, *b* 1964, — Liam Patrick, *b* 1974, — Allison Mary, *b* 1966, — Maria Patricia, *b* 1969. —— Vivienne Mary Patricia, *b* 1945: *m* 1970, (Charles) Timothy Cresswell, of Cilwych Farm, Bwlch, Powys, S Wales, and has issue living, Dominie Sidney, *b* 1973. —— Laragh Veronica Storm, *b* 1973. —— Rosemary Carolyn, *b* 1946: *m* 1966, Maj Robert Keith Peterswald, RAR (ret), of Salamanca, Battery Point, Hobart, Tasmania, and has issue living, Charlotte Antonia, *b* 1968, — Georgina Anne, *b* 1972.

Issue of late Capt John Witham Esmonde, OBE, DSC, RN (half-brother of 15th baronet), *b* 1907, *d* 1983: *m* 1940, Aileen (Ballyellis, Buttevant, co Cork), da of late Harold Harold-Barry, of Ballyvonare, co Cork:—
Peter Witham (PO Box 7978, Addis Ababa, Ethiopia), *b* 1945. —— Kevin Harold (Ballyellis, Buttevant, co Cork), *b* 1948. —— Helen Mary Karin, *b* 1950: *m* 1st, 1976, Paul Douglas Clark, of Toronto, Canada; 2ndly, 1985, Lt-Col Robert Charles Couldrey, 7th DEO Gurkha Rifles, of 80 Elms Crescent, SW4 8QX, only son of C. J. Couldrey, of Limpsfield Common, Oxted, Surrey, and has issue living (by 2nd *m*), David Witham James, *b* 1988, — Annabel Mary, *b* 1986.

Issue of late Maj Patrick Esmonde, MC, LRCP, LRCS (half-brother of 15th baronet), *b* 1914, *d* 1997: *m* 1943, (Norah), Marcia (88 St George's Sq, SW1V 3QX), da of William Cooper, of Malton, N Yorks:—
(Margaret) Shane, *b* 1944: *m* 1966, Col Peter Alexander Henderson, Cheshire Regt, of 48 Alderney St, SW1V 4EX, and has issue living, Dominic Patrick Alexander, *b* 1968, — Oliver Thomas Alexander, *b* 1971. —— Grania Mary, *b* 1947: *m* 1st, 1970 (*m diss* 1974), Denis Edward Chambers; 2ndly, 1975, (Ian Hugo) Loudon Greenlees, of Haymakers Farm, Waldron, E Sussex, and has issue living (by 1st *m*), Laragh Victoria, *b* 1971, — (by 2nd *m*), Rupert Hugo Loudon, *b* 1976, — Thomas Ian Esmonde, *b* 1985, — Camilla Shane, *b* 1978, — Daisy Thomasina, *b* 1987.

The Esmondes are descended from a family which was seated in co Wexford, and one of whose members was Bishop of Ferns in 1340, and another Bishop of Emly 1356. In the reign of Elizabeth I Sir Lawrence Esmond, abandoning the Roman Catholic faith, professed himself a Protestant, and was created Lord Esmond. He married a Roman Catholic lady, one of the O'Flaherties, Dynasts of Iar of Connaught, by whom he had a son. The mother, fearing that her child would be reared a Protestant, ran off with the boy, whom she brought up as a strict Catholic. By the statute of Kilkenny, the marriage was voidable in law. The son subsequently gained possession of the Wexford estate, and would probably have gained the peerage, but for the confusion wrought by civil war. He raised a troop of horse for the service of Charles I, and commanded a Regt in the Duke of Buckingham's expedition to Rochelle, on his return from which he was created a baronet in his father's lifetime. The 2nd baronet *m* Lucia Butler, niece of 1st Duke of Ormonde; his seat, Huntington Castle, co Carlow, was built by Lord Esmonde 1625, and named after the ancient seat of his ancestors in England. The 9th baronet, Right Hon Sir Thomas, sat as MP for Wexford (*L*) 1841-7, and the 10th baronet sat as MP for Waterford (*L*) 1852-76. The 11th baronet Sir Thomas Henry Grattan (sometime a Chamberlain to Vatican Household), sat as MP for S Div of Dublin co (*N*) 1885-92, tor W Kerry Div of co Kerry 1892-1900, and for N Wexford, Div of Wexford co 1900-18, and was a Senator of Irish Free State. The 12th baronet, Sir Osmond Thomas Grattan, was a Member of Parliament of Irish Free State 1923-7 and 1927-36. The 14th baronet, Sir John Lymbrick Esmonde, was a Bencher of King's Inns, Dublin, and Senior Counsel, and sat as MP for Tipperary, Co, N Tipperary Div (*N*) 1915-18. He was a Member of Dail Eireann 1937-44, and 1948-51. The 16th baronet, Sir John Henry Grattan Esmonde, bar King's Inn, Dublin 1950, who Senior Council 1971, and a Circuit Court Judge of W Circuit 1977-87.

ESPLEN (UK) 1921, of Hardres Court, Canterbury, Kent

Be faithful

(*Sir*) JOHN GRAHAM ESPLEN, 3rd *Baronet*; *b* 4 Aug 1932; *s* his father, *Sir* WILLIAM GRAHAM, 1989, but does not use the title; *ed* Harrow, and St Catharine's College, Cambridge (BA 1955): *m* 1956 (*m diss* 19—), Valerie Joan, yr da of Maj-Gen Albert Percy Lambooy, CB, OBE, and has issue.

ᴀrms – Sable, on a pile between two mascles or, a lymphad of the field. Crest – In front of a demi-eagle displayed sable charged on each wing with a mascle as in the arms, an anchor fessewise or.

SON LIVING

WILLIAM JOHN HARRY, *b* 24 Feb 1967: *m* 1996, Helen S., da of Dr D. Chesser, and of Mrs A. Self, of Surrey, and has issue living, Eleanor Jane, *b* 1998.

DAUGHTERS LIVING

Wendy Anne, *b* 1959. —— Fiona Mary, *b* 1960. —— Polly Caroline, *b* 1962.

The 1st baronet, Sir John Esplen, KBE (son of late William Esplen, of The Willows, Blundellsands), was sometime Senior Director of Esplen, Sons and Swainston (Limited), consulting engineers and naval architects, and Ch Technical Advisor to Min of Shipping during European War 1914-18.

EVANS (UK) 1920, of Wightwick, near Wolverhampton, co Stafford

With faith and virtue

Sir ANTHONY ADNEY EVANS, 2nd *Baronet*, *b* 5 Aug 1922; *s* his father, *Sir* WALTER HARRY, 1954; *ed* Shrewsbury, and Merton Coll Oxford: *m* 1st, 1948 (*m diss* 1957), Rita Beatrice, da of late Alfred David Kettle, of Souldern, Oxon, and formerly wife of Larry Rupert Kirsch; 2ndly, 1958, Sylvia Jean, and has issue.

ᴀrms – Gyronny of eight gules or, over all a lion passant, between two fleurs-de-lis in pale sable. Crest – In front of a wall embattled and masoned proper, a lion as in the arms.
Residence – Brook Cottage, Malborough, Combe, Devon.

SONS LIVING

Jeremy Joseph Anthony, *b* 1947. —— MARCUS A., *b* 19—.

DAUGHTER LIVING

—, *b* 19—.

SISTER LIVING

Diana Gillian Mary, *b* 1926: *m* 1st, 1948 (*m diss* 1954), Capt John Richard Pugh, RA; 2ndly, 1959, Alan Joseph Webber, who *d* 19—, and has issue living, (by 1st *m*) Vanessa Gillian WEBBER, *b* 1950; adopted 1959 by her step-father whose surname she assumed, — (by 2nd *m*) Daryl Adney, *b* 1960.

The 1st baronet Sir Walter Harry Evans (son of late Joseph Evans, JP, of The Lindens, Wolverhampton) was an hydraulic engineer, and a Co Councillor for Staffordshire.

EVANS (UK) 1963, of Rottingdean, co Sussex (Extinct 1983)

Sir (SIDNEY) HAROLD EVANS, CMG, OBE, 1st and last *Baronet*.

DAUGHTER LIVING OF FIRST AND LAST BARONET

Annabel Frances, *b* 1956.

WIDOW LIVING OF FIRST AND LAST BARONET

ELIZABETH (*Lady Evans*), da of William Jaffray, of Aberdeen: *m* 1945, Sir (Sidney) Harold Evans, CMG, OBE, 1st Bt, who *d* 1983. *Residence* – 1 Kipling Court, St Aubyns Mead, Rottingdean, Brighton, Sussex BN2 7JT.

Gwynne-Evans, see Evans-Tipping.

WORTHINGTON-EVANS (UK) 1916, of Colchester, Essex (Extinct 1971)

Sir (WILLIAM) SHIRLEY WORTHINGTON WORTHINGTON-EVANS, 2nd and last *Baronet*.

DAUGHTERS LIVING OF SECOND BARONET

Sarah MASON (17 The Gateways, Sprimont Place, SW3), *b* 1929: *m* 1st, 1957 (*m diss* 1971), Wing Cdr Hon Keith Alexander Henry Mason, DFC (later 3rd Baron Blackford), who *d* 1977; 2ndly, 1972, Eric Ivor Hopton; has resumed by deed poll her former married surname. —— Anne Louise (Annie-Lou), *b* 1934: *m* 1967 (*m diss* 1981), 2nd Baron Jeffreys. *Residence* – The Cottage, Willesley, Tetbury, Glos.

EVERARD (UK) 1911, of Randlestown, co Meath

Sir ROBIN CHARLES EVERARD, 4th *Baronet*, *b* 5 Oct 1939; *s* his father, *Lt-Col Sir* NUGENT HENRY, 1984; *ed* Harrow, and Sandhurst; management consultant: *m* 1963, Ariel Ingrid, eldest da of late Col Peter Cleasby-Thompson, MBE, MC, of Blackhill House, The Arms, Little Cressingham, Thetford, Norfolk, and has issue.

Arms – Argent, a fesse wavy between three estoile gules. Crest – A pelican in her piety proper.
Residence – Church Farm, Shelton, Long Stratton, Norfolk NR15 2SB.

SON LIVING

HENRY PETER CHARLES, *b* 6 Aug 1970; *ed* Gresham's Sch, Holt.

DAUGHTERS LIVING

Catherine Mary, *b* 1964: *m* 1994, Maj Timothy David Hyams, Royal Dragoon Gds, son of David Hyams, of Seer Green, Bucks, and has issue living, Oliver Charles David, *b* 1996, — Patrick John Henry, *b* 1997. —— Victoria Frances, *b* 1966.

SISTER LIVING

Susan Louise, *b* 1935: *m* 1957, Lieut-Col Henry George Dormer, RA, only son of H.J. Dormer, of Chilton Court, Sudbury, Suffolk, and has issue living, Sara Louise, *b* 1958, — Charlotte Rose, *b* 1962. *Residence* – Downside, Shortheath Rd, Farnham, Surrey.

Virtue consists in action

COLLATERAL BRANCH LIVING

Issue of late Matthias Richard Everard, 2nd son of 2nd baronet, *b* 1906, *d* 1949: *m* 1938, Maighréad Mary, who *d* 1973, da of Michael Joseph Macardle, of Miltown Grange, Castlebellingham:—
Patrick Matthias (White Mills, Castlebellingham, co Louth), *b* 1943: *m* 1968, Felicity Anne Brigid, da of late Brig Ralph Nevill Thicknesse, and has issue living, Anthony Matthias, *b* 1980, — Michael Ralph, *b* 1988, — Patricia Karen, *b* 1973, — Katherine Sophie, *b* 1982.

Sir Nugent Talbot Everard, 1st Bt (appointed High Sheriff of co Meath 1883, and HM's Lieut 1906), was a Senator of the Irish Free State 1922-8, and *d* 11 July 1929. Major Sir Richard William Everard, 2nd Bt, *d* 22 July 1929.

EVERY (E) 1641, of Egginton, Derbyshire

Every man to his own

Sir HENRY JOHN MICHAEL EVERY, 13th *Baronet*; *b* 6 April 1947; *s* his father *Sir* JOHN SIMON, 1988; *ed* Malvern; FCA; Partner Deloitte & Touche, Chartered Accountants, Birmingham; Memb Chartered Accountants' Co; Trustee National Memorial Arboretum since 1996; Patron Derby Heritage Devpt Trust since 1998; patron of one living: *m* 1974, Susan Mary, eldest da of Kenneth Beaton, JP, of East-shotte, Hartford, Cambs, and has issue.

𝕬rms – Erminois, two chevronels azure between two other gules. Crest – A demi-unicorn argent guttée-de-sang and crined or.
Seat – Egginton, Derby. *Residence* – Cothay, 26 Fishpond Lane, Egginton, Derbyshire DE65 6HJ.

SONS LIVING

EDWARD JAMES HENRY, *b* 3 July 1975. —— Jonathan Charles Hugo, *b* 1977. —— Nicholas John Simon, *b* 1981.

SISTERS LIVING

Celia Jane, *b* 1944: *m* 1st, 1965, Nicholas Charles Harcourt Stephens, who *d* 1984; 2ndly, 1990, Robin Christopher Moore, of The Old Rectory, Etwall, Derby, and has issue living (by 1st *m*), Jasper Roland Every, *b* 1972; *ed* Repton, and Univ of Wales (LLB), — Toby Oliver Every, *b* 1974; *ed* Repton, and Bristol Univ, — Candida Imogen Every, *b* 1969. —— Juliet Frances, *b* 1945: *m* 1964, John Coltman McCullagh, of Bramleys, Alleyns Lane, Cookham Dean, Berks, and has issue living, Andrew John (25 Rowan Rd, W6 7DT), *b* 1968; *ed* Eton and Exeter Coll, Oxford: *m* 1996, Kate Louise Riley, and has issue living, Thomas Andrew *b* 1997, Harry John *b* 1999, — Diana Mary, *b* 1965: *m* 1991, Donal Quigley, of 8 Shooters Hill Rd, Blackheath, SE3 7BD, and has issue living, Benedict John *b* 1994.

UNCLE LIVING (*son of 11th baronet*)

Charles Henry Sherard, *b* 1916; *ed* Harrow: *m* 1950 (*m diss* 1953), Deirdre Veronica, da of late Dr du Toit, of Johannesburg, S Africa, and has issue living, Vanessa Leila, *b* 1950: *m* 1974, Terrence William de Beer, of 17a Milton Rd, Westville N 3630, Natal, S Africa, and has issue living, Ryan Jeffery *b* 1978, Kelly Gillian *b* 1981. *Residence* – Casa Das Primas, Carvoeiro, Lagoa 8400, Algarve, Portugal.

AUNT LIVING (*daughter of 11th baronet*)

Leila Penelope, *b* 1911: *m* 1935, Maj Vivian Horrocks Ward, TD, 5th Bn Sherwood Foresters (TA), who *d* 1998, and has issue living, Peter Every (Pinfold, Pin Mill Lane, Chelmondiston, nr Ipswich, Suffolk), *b* 1938: *m* 1962, Rosalind Brereton, yr da of Giffard Page, of St Anne's, King George Av, King's Lynn, Norfolk, and has issue living, Rupert *b* 1969, Edward *b* 1970, — Simon Charles Vivian (The Dower House, Bulmer, Sudbury, Suffolk), *b* 1942; *ed* Shrewsbury, and Trin Coll, Camb (MA); Memb Securities Institute: *m* 1965, Myrtle Jillian Eileen, only da of late Thomas Roycroft East, of Dublin, and has issue living, Victoria Penelope Jane *b* 1969: *m* 1995, Matthew W. M. Doull, elder son of Adrian Doull, of Remaisnil, France, and of Mrs June Black, of Toronto, Canada, Antonia Lisa *b* 1971, Lucinda Fiona *b* 1971. *Residence* – Long Meadow House, Little Cornard, Sudbury, Suffolk.

WIDOW LIVING OF TWELFTH BARONET

JANET MARION (*Dowager Lady Every*), eldest da of late John Page, ARIBA, of Blakeney, Norfolk: *m* 1943, as his 2nd wife, Sir John Simon Every, 12th Bt, who *d* 1988. *Residence* – Egginton, Derby.

COLLATERAL BRANCHES LIVING

Grandsons (by 1st *m*) of late Capt Oswald Every, 75th Regt, brother of 10th baronet:—
Issue of late Edward Every, *b* 1865, *d* 19—: *m* 1902, Adeline, who *d* 1948, da of Ranson Smith:—
Edward Malcolm (102 Lincoln St, Brooklyn, Wisconsin, USA), *b* 1903: *m* 1934, Clarice Mildred, da of Elmer Doane, and has issue living, Thomas Owen, *b* 1938, — Barbara Ann, *b* 1942. —— Roderick Desmond, *b* 1904: *m* 1935, Carolyn Norma, da of Paul Tyler, and has issue living, Roderick Douglas, *b* 1936, — Lynn Gertrude, *b* 1943. —— Donovan Richmond (Evansville, Wisconsin, USA), *b* 1911: *m* 19—, Evelyn, da of Fred Rodd, and has issue living, Donovan Rodd, *b* 1941.

Grandson (by 2nd *m*) of late Capt Oswald Every (ante):—
Issue of late Francis William John Flower Every, *b* 1890, *d* 1979: *m* 1912, Mary Louisa, who *d* 1965, da of William John Murton:—
Christy Oswald (1 Combe Close, Axminster, Devon), *b* 1920: *m* 1948, Winifred Jessie, 2nd da of Luke Richards, and has issue living, Geoffrey Francis, *b* 1949: *m* 1971, Rosemarie, da of Otto Plec, of Borham Wood, — Stephen Victor (5 Loretto Rd, Axminster), *b* 1950: *m* 1975, Valerie Ena, da of late Peter Arthur Guest, of 25 Foxhill, Axminster, and has issue living, Caroline Amanda *b* 1980, Joanne Louise *b* 1982, Kathryn Frances *b* 1984, — Virginia Dawn, *b* 1953: *m* 1972, Alan Fry, of 2 Moor Fields, Colyton, Devon, — Katrina Mary, *b* 1957: *m* 1977, Michael Neale, of 35 Clive Rd, Colliers Wood, SW19, and has issue living, David Michael Ian *b* 1980, Laura Jane Alana *b* 1982.

Granddaughters of late Thomas Edward Every-Clayton, son of Lt-Col Edward Every-Clayton, 2nd son of 9th baronet:—
Issue of late Edward Every Every-Clayton, *b* 1867, *d* 1936: *m* 1st, 1892, Mary Fetherstonhaugh, who *d* 1905, da of Alexander Heylin, of Newcastle-upon-Tyne; 2ndly, 1907, Emily Mary, da of Arthur Edward Tooze, Bar-at-law:—
(By 1st *m*) Edith Margaret, *b* 1897. —— Ruth Fetherstonhaugh, *b* 1905.

Grandchildren of late Leopold Ernest Valentine Every-Clayton, MD, FRCS, 2nd son of late Thomas Edward Every-Clayton (ante):—
Issue of late Cecil Edward Every, *b* 1901; relinquished the surname of Clayton 1937; *d* 1974: *m* 1927, Viola, who *d* 1966, da of late Edward Ledger, of Hampstead, NW:—
Simon Flower (The White House, Crawley, Winchester SO21 2PR), *b* 1929: *m* 1956, Diana Mary Jennifer, da of late Cdr L. J. F. Howard-Mercer, RN, and has issue living, James Edward (8 The Glade, Sevenoaks, Kent TN13 3HD), *b* 1961: *m* 1988, Caroline Anne, da of John Frederick Mallett, and has issue living, Henry John Edward *b* 1996, Elizabeth Joanna *b* 1993, Alexandra Margaret *b* 1993, — Jennifer Ann, *b* 1958: *m* 1995, Phillip John Hopkins, and has issue living, David John *b* 1998, Rachel Ann *b* 1996, — Frances Elizabeth, *b* 1964: *m* 1990, William Thomas Pattisson, and has issue living, Frederick James *b* 1992, Mary Mia Charlotte *b* 1995, Louisa Bridget *b* 1997. —— Ann, *b* 1933.

Grandchildren of late George Frederick William Every-Clayton, 3rd son of late Thomas Edward Every-Clayton (ante):—
Issue of late Herbert Edward Every-Clayton, *b* 1892, *d* 1961: *m* 1913, Gwendolin Cox, who *d* 1931:—
Herbert Newbery, *b* 1917. —— Andrita Valentine, *b* 1919: *m* 1938, William Kenneth Franklin, and has issue living, Daniel William, *b* 1941: *m* 1965, Frances Yohradsky, and has issue living, William *b* 19—, — Christine Louise, *b* 1939: *m* 1961, Robert Toutant, and has issue living, Dianne Michelle *b* 1962, Jacqueline Marie *b* 1964.

Issue of late John Oswald Every-Clayton, DSC *b* 1898, *d* 1979: *m* 1925, Marie, da of William Lloyd, of Liverpool:—
George William, *b* 1929; *ed* Univ of BC: *m* 1950, Margot, da of William Forrest, of Victoria, BC.

Issue of late Thomas Edgar Every-Clayton, *b* 1899, *d* 1986: *m* 1943, Ellen May Hill:—
Wayne Thomas, *b* 1944: *m* 1974, Mary Hall, and has issue living, Patricia Mary, *b* 1975.

Grandchildren of late Thomas Edward Every-Clayton (ante):—
Issue of late George Frederick William Every-Clayton, *b* 1871, *d* 1928: *m* 1st, 1892, Sarah, who *d* 1912, da of William Whittaker; 2ndly, 1913, Evelyn May Yeates:—
(By 1st *m*) Frederick Harris, *b* 1906: *m* 1937, Ann Brown Morrison, and has issue living, Barbara Ann Gail, *b* 1939: *m* 19—, Donald Anderson, of Campbell River, BC, and has issue living, Nancy Janet *b* 1959, Cindy Donna *b* 1962. —— Arthur Eric Francis, *b* 1910: *m* 1948, Edna Beatrice Longley. —— Penelope Maud Valentine, *b* 1903: *m* 1934, George Anderson Churchill-Emery, who *d* 1941, and has issue living, Elizabeth Joy, *b* 1937: *m* 1955 (*m diss* 1978), Arthur Frederick Thompson, and has issue living, Gordon Anthony *b* 1958: *m* 1984, Kelly Charlton (and has issue living, Justin Joseph *b* 1985), Michael Arthur George *b* 1959: *m* 1988, Monica Rambie (and has issue living, Mack Ramsay *b* 1989, Fairleigh Taylor *b* 1976). —— Edith Minnie, *b* 1912: *m* 1943, Norton Hopkins, who *d* 1961.

Grandchildren of late Reginald Arthur Eric Every-Clayton (infra):—
Issue of late John Arthur Every-Clayton, *b* 1903, *d* 1969: *m* 1937, Martha Parker, who *d* 1988:—
Margaret Lois, *b* 1940: *m* 1st, 1959 (*m diss* 1976), Terry Lee Williams, attorney for Bank of America; 2ndly, 1976, William Smutz. *Address* – RR2, Box 481, Heber Springs, ARK 72543, USA.

Issue of late William Wilding Every-Clayton, *b* 1905, *d* 1993: *m* 1940, Joan Adelaide (51 Church Hill, Honiton, Devon), da of late Ronald John Bennett, of Exeter, Devon:—
(Henry) John (26 Dorian Rise, Melton Mowbray, Leics LE13 0TJ), *b* 1941: *m* 1963, Frances Anne Sangster, BA, of London, and has issue living, Catherine, *b* 1967, — Tessa, *b* 1969. —— Alan William (Beacon Down Cottage, Holcombe Burnell, Longdown, Exeter, Devon EX6 7SA), *b* 1945: *m* 1968, Myra Wynn Arthur, of Axminster, Devon, and has issue living, Richard William (9 Hansom Place, York YO31 8FJ), *b* 1971; BA: *m* 1997, Lindsay Jane Christopher, of Broadstone,

Poole, Dorset, — Anita Caroline, b 1973. —— †Robert Edward, b 1948; BA, FCA: m 1973, Karen Elizabeth Paine, BSc (Ashton House, St Mary Church, Cowbridge, S Glam), of Sidbury, Devon, and d 1994, leaving issue, Andrew John, b 1979, — Katherine Lucy, b 1982, — Elizabeth Claire, b 1984. —— David Stuart (37 Church Rd, Trull, Taunton, Som TA3 7LG), b 1955: m 1979, Angela Dawber, of Broadhembury, Devon, and has issue living, Christopher James, b 1985, — Helen Louise, b 1987. —— Pamela Nora Anne, b (twin) 1955: m 1st, 1981 (m diss 1989), Jeremy Peter Leeds; 2ndly, 1990, Ross Ian Darrah, of 18 Manuka Rd, Titirangi, Auckland, NZ, and has issue living (by 2nd m), Mitchell Robert, b 1994, — Christina Pamela, b 1991.

        Issue of late Thomas Edward Every-Clayton, b 1906, d 1991: m 1938, Irmgard Adele, who d 1982, da of late
        Arthur Jaekel, of Tallinn, Estonia:—
Glenn Thomas (Seminario Congregacional, Rua Arealva 19, Tejipió, 50,000 Recife, Brazil), b 1941; ed Kingston Gram Sch, and Christ's Coll, Camb (BA); BD, ALBC: m 1971, Joyce Elizabeth Winifred, el da of Hugh McKee, of Randalstown, co Antrim. —— Clive William (14a E Aubinaustraat, 1932 St Stevens-Woluwe, Belgium), b 1942; ed Kingston Gram Sch, and London Bible Coll (BD, ALBC): m 1970, Dorothy, da of Archibald M.O. Dobbie, of Dalry, Ayrshire, and has issue living, Mark Brian, b 1975, — Paul David Christian, b 1979, — Grace Esther Josette, b 1973, — Joy Claire Joanna, b 1977.

        Grandson of late Thomas Edward Every-Clayton (ante):—
        Issue of late Reginald Arthur Eric Every-Clayton, b 1874, d 1965: m 1902, Fanny, who d 1958, 3rd da of William
        Wilding, of Bolton, Lancashire:—
George Herbert (617 SW 21st Circle, Boynton Beach, Florida 33426, USA), b 1907; ed Rutgers Univ, BSc: m 1931, Jane Cecelia Welsh, who d 1981, of New Brunswick, New Jersey, USA, and has issue living, Donald George (Paseo de los Halcones 202, Mayorazgos de los Gigantes, Antizapan de Zaragoza, Edo de Mexico, Mexico), b 1935: m 1957, Celia Yolanda Garcia, of Mexico City, and has issue living, Geoffrey b 1961: m 1988, Andrea Garcia Puente, of Mexico City, Lisa b 1959: m 1983, Angelo Ceciarelli, of Mexico City, Jennifer b 1963: m 1979, Eduardo Ezquerro, of Mexico City (and has issue living, Pamela b 1980, Priscilla b 1985), Noreen b 1969, — Jon Arthur (438 Old Trail, Baltimore, Maryland 21212, USA), b 1938; Lieut Col, US Army Reserve; Vietnam 1966-67 (101st Airborne Div) and 1970-71; Bronze Star for Valour and Purple Heart for Wounds: m 1968 (m diss 1982), Janet Theresa Sabo, of Lakewood, New Jersey, and has issue living, Jon Ernest b 1970; Private, US Army Res, Janina Theresa b 1973, Malinda Jane b 1978, — June Moonyeen, b 1940: m 1969, Daniel Herbert Young III, of 419 Dumbarton Rd, Baltimore, Maryland 21212, USA, and has issue living, Jonathan Herbert b 1970, Heather Jane b 1972.

        Grandchildren of late Maj Charles Edward Every-Halsted (assumed by Royal licence 1886 the surname
        of Every-Halsted in lieu of Every-Clayton), 3rd son (but only son by 2nd m) of late Lt-Col Edward
        Every-Clayton, yr son of 9th baronet:—
        Issue of late Evelyn Stella Every-Halsted, b 1893, d 1969: m 1915, Col Arthur George Pardoe, RE (TF), who d
        1951:—
Arthur Anthony, b 1916; Lt RN; ka 1940. —— Charles Evelyn, b and d 1919. —— Sarah Stella, b 1920: m (March) 1944, Lt-Col Edward Robert Guy Ripley, King's Shropshire LI, who was ka in Normandy (June) 1944, and has issue (see Ripley, Bt, colls). —— Elizabeth Jane, b 1921: m 1952, Stanway Matthew Grafton Sprague, who d 1978, of Holiday Hall, Kington, Herefords, and has had issue, Jonathan Charles Grafton, b 1957; d 1979, — Susan Elizabeth Grafton, b 1954.

        Issue of late Mary Ruth Every-Halsted, b 1898, d 1991: m 1st, 1919 (m diss 1942), Capt Gerald Hargreave
        Mawson, MC, RE, who d 1964; 2ndly, 1951, Rev Henry William John Lancelot Reed Haywood, who d 1957:—
(By 1st m) Michael Gerald Hargreave, b 1921; ed Bedford Sch; Paymaster Midshipman RN; ka in sinking of HMS Neptune 1941. —— John Arthur Hargreave (Rte 1, Box 419C, Leon, W Virginia 25123, USA), b 1923; ed Bedford Sch; Capt Royal Signals (ret); served 1939-45 War: m 1st, 1947 (m diss 1961), Wenona, da of Neil Brown; 2ndly, 1962, Lois, da of Henry Pinson, and has issue living (by 1st m), Simon John Hargreave (863 Delaney St, Anchorage, Alaska 99501, USA), b 1952: m 1989, Ann, da of Nelson Walker, and has an adopted son, Douglas John Hargreave b 1996. —— Charles Edward Hargreave, b 1926; ed Bedford Sch; Maj Royal Signals, served 1939-45 War, and in Palestine 1945-48, and Malaya 1960: m 1st, 1951 (m diss 1962), Anne Mary, da of James Eastick; 2ndly, 1965, Iris May (Oaklands, 60 Kimbolton Rd, Bedford MK40 2NX), da of William Thomas Duthie, of Athy, co Kildare, and d 1994, leaving issue (by 1st m), Susan Mary Hargreave, b 1953: m 1978, Rory Anthony Rank Askew, and has issue (see Cayley, Bt, colls), — Rosemary Ann, b 1954: m 1st, 1975 (m diss 1989), John Langley Smith; 2ndly, 1989, Peter Jenkins, of Haslemere, Surrey, and has issue living (by 1st m), Peter b 1983, Elizabeth b 1982, (by 2nd m), James b 1991, Phillipa Mary b 1992, — (by 2nd m), Michael Charles HARGREAVE MAWSON (26A Russell Av, Bedford MK40 3TD), b 1967; ed Oundle; MCIPS: m 1992, Rachel Caroline, da of James Edward Young, and has issue living, Charles Henry Frederick b 1996, — Elizabeth Margaret Hargreave (74 Banbury Rd, Southam, Leamington Spa, Warwickshire CV33 0HJ), b 1969; ed Bedford High Sch, and Wye Coll, Lond (BSc), PhD. —— Richard James Hargreave, b 1928; d 1936. —— Mary Patricia Hargreave, b 1920: m 1949, James Surtees Phillpotts, MD, of Dublin, who d 1994, and d 1963, leaving issue, Ruth, b 1949: m 1st, 19— (m diss 19—), James McEwan; 2ndly, 19—, John Burke, and has issue living (by 1st m), Gregor b 1977, (by 2nd m), Claire b 1985.

Sir Simon Every, 1st Bt, originally of Chardstock, Dorset (who m Anne, da and co-heir Sir Henry Leigh, of Egginton, Derbyshire, and removed to that place), was a loyal supporter Charles I. Sir John Every, 4th Bt, Capt RN, served in cause of William III with distinction.

EWART (UK) 1887, of Glenmachan, Strandtown, co Down, and of Glenbank, Belfast, co Antrim

In cruce spero

In the cross I hope

Sir (WILLIAM) MICHAEL EWART, 7th *Baronet; b* 10 June 1953; *s* his father, *Sir* (WILLIAM) IVAN CECIL, DSC, 1995; *ed* Radley.

Arms – Or, three swords crossed, two in saltire and one in fesse, between in chief a cross-crosslet fitchée, and in base a dexter hand couped at the wrist gules. **Crest** – A hand erect gauntleted proper, holding a cross-crosslet fitchée gules.
Residence – Hill House, Hillsborough, co Down BT26 6AE.

SISTERS LIVING

Susan Eveleen, *b* 1950: *m* 1973, Colin Richard Cunningham, and has issue living, Katherine Pauline, *b* 1976, — Jennifer Alicia, *b* 1978. *Residence* – Tullycore, Killinchy, co Down BT23 6UA. —— Patricia Rébé, *b* 1951: *m* 1971, Jeremy James Clendinning Browne, and has issue living, Gordon Cawood Ivan, *b* 1977, — Anita Zaidee, *b* 1973. *Residence* – Claim Farm House, Manley, Frodsham, Cheshire WA6 6HT.

COLLATERAL BRANCH LIVING

Granddaughter of late Frederick William Ewart, 7th son of 1st baronet:—
Issue of late Maj Gerald Valentine Ewart, OBE, DL, *b* 1884, *d* 1936: *m* 1911, Annie Ruth (Pearl) (Clontagh Lodge, 31 Abbeyview, Crossgar, co Down), da of late Rev T. R. S. Collins, BD, Chap to the Archbishop of Dublin:—
Eileen Geraldine, *b* 1913: *m* 1939, Lieut-Com George Lennox Cotton, DSC, DL, RNVR, and has issue living, Caroline Mourne Lennox, *b* 1942: *m* 1965, Jeremy James Mackay-Lewis, of 27 Montpelier Sq, SW7, The Manor House, Kettlewell, Skipton, N Yorks, and of Clontagh House, Crossgar, co Down, and has issue living, Michael Charles *b* 1969, Peter Lennox *b* 1979, Mark James *b* 1983, Victoria Mourne *b* 1967, — Elizabeth Grania Lennox, *b* 1944: *m* 1967, David Graham Shillington, of Altafort, Skeagh Rd, Dromore, co Down, and has issue living, Thomas Gerard *b* 1972: *m* 1997, Polly Margaret, da of David Kennedy (and has issue living, Finnian David George *b* 1999), Christopher Gerald *b* 1978, Katherine Grania *b* 1969, Clare Mary Alice *b* 1981, — Kathleen Anne Lennox, *b* 1945: *m* 1969, John Francis Pope, of Watlington Hall, Watlington, Norfolk, and has issue living, Edward John *b* 1978, Georgina Julia *b* 1972: *m* 1997, James Edward Strutt (*see* B Belper, colls) Annabel Grania *b* 1974. *Residence* – Clontagh House, 35 Abbeyview Rd, Crossgar, co Down.

The 1st baronet, Sir William Ewart (son of late William Ewart, of Glenbank, near Belfast), was MP for Belfast (*C*) 1878-85, and for Belfast (N Div) 1885-89, and head of the firm of William Ewart & Son, Ltd, of Belfast. The 2nd Baronet, Sir William Quartus, was head of the firm of William Ewart & Son Ltd, of Belfast, and a KStJ. The 3rd baronet, Sir Robert Heard, was a Director of William Ewart & Son, Ltd, of Belfast. The 6th baronet, Sir (William) Ivan Cecil, DSC, was Chm William Ewart & Son Ltd, Linen Manufacturers, and Chm Ewart New Northern Ltd, Belfast.

ORR EWING (UK) 1886, of Ballikinrain, Stirlingshire, and Lennoxbank, co Dunbarton

Boldly

Sir RONALD ARCHIBALD ORR EWING, 5th *Baronet; b* 14 May 1912; *s* his father *Brig-Gen Sir* NORMAN ARCHIBALD ORR EWING, CB, DSO, 1960; *ed* Eton, and RMC Sandhurst; Maj (ret) Scots Guards; is a Member of Queen's Body Guard for Scotland (Roy Co of Archers), and a JP and a DL for Perthshire; 1939-45 War (prisoner): *m* 1938, Marion Hester, who *d* 1997, da of late Col Sir Donald Walter Cameron of Lochiel, KT, CMG (D Montrose), and has issue.

Arms – Argent, a chevron gules, issuant therefrom a banner of the second thereon in the first quarter the arms of St Andrew - viz, azure a saltire argent; between in chief two mullets gules and in base the sun in its splendour, the whole within a bordure indented gules charged with three martlets argent, two in chief and one in base. **Crest** – A demi-lion rampant gules holding in its dexter paw a mullet as in the arms.
Seat – Cardross, Kippen, Stirling FK8 3JY.

SONS LIVING

ARCHIBALD DONALD (18 Northumberland St, NE Lane, Edinburgh EH3 6LN; New (Edinburgh) and Pratt's Clubs), *b* 20 Dec 1938; *ed* Gordonstoun, and Trin Coll, Dublin (BA); a Member of Queen's Body Guard for Scotland (Roy Co of Archers): *m* 1st, 1965 (*m diss* 1972), Venetia Elizabeth, da of Maj Richard Turner; 2ndly, 1972, Nicola Jean-Anne, da of late Reginald Baron Black, of Brook House, Fovant, Salisbury, Wilts (*see* D Roxburghe, colls, 1995 Edn), and has issue living (by 2nd *m*), Alastair Frederick Archibald *b* 26 May 1982. —— Ronald James, *b* 1948; *ed* Gordonstoun, and Dundee Univ; LLB St Andrews.

DAUGHTERS LIVING

Janet Elizabeth, *b* 1940: *m* 1969, John Malcolm Wallace, of The Furnace, Ashburnham, Battle, Sussex, and has issue living, Jasper Simon, *b* 1973, — Jocelyn James *b* 1977, — Jemma Louise, *b* 1971. —— Fiona Marion, *b* 1946: *m* 1968, Adrian Peter Drewe, of Parsonage Farm House, Ticehurst, Wadhurst, E Sussex TN5 7DL, and has issue living, Jonathan James, *b* 1971, — Nicholas Robert Patrick, *b* 1982, — Anthony Adrian, *b* 1985.

SISTER LIVING

Jean Marjorie, *b* 1918: *m* 1941, Alexander Robert Webster, and has issue living, Robert Alexander, *b* 1942: *m* 1968, Margaret Elizabeth Mary, da of Gilbert Harrower, of Keith, Banffshire, and has issue living, Andrew Robert *b* 1970, Jill Margaret *b* 1973, — Yvonne Jean, *b* 1944: *m* 1st, 1965 (*m diss* 1969), Michael Montgomery; 2ndly, 1969, Leslie Murray, of Killinchy, Co Down, son of Morton Murray, and has issue living, (by 1st *m*) Alan Michael *b* 1966, Ian Aston *b* 1968, (by 2nd *m*) Laura Kay *b* 1972. *Residence* – 2A Leigh Court, Avonmore Rd, W Kensington, London W14 8RL.

COLLATERAL BRANCHES LIVING

Issue of late Dr Alan Lindsay Orr-Ewing, MC, yr son of 4th baronet, *b* 1915, *d* 1995: *m* 1945, Helen Isabelle (2125 Eddington Drive, No 109 Vancouver, BC V6L 3A9, Canada), da of late William Evans, of Toronto:—
Alexander Evans (3500 Willow St, Vancouver, BC, Canada), *b* 1947: *m* 1973, Louise Cantin, of Montreal, and has issue living, Simon Alan, *b* 1975, — Etienne Alec, *b* 1979. —— Isobel Laura (4712 Woodburn Court, W Vancouver, BC V7S 3B3, Canada), *b* 1954: *m* 1975, Robert Wain Reid, who *d* 1997, and has issue living, James William, *b* 1986, — Jennifer Laura, *b* 1987.

Grandson of late Capt John Orr Ewing, 4th son of 1st baronet:—
Issue of late Archibald Ian Orr Ewing, *b* 1884, *d* 1942: *m* 1911, Gertrude Bertha, who *d* 1974, da of late Charles Herman Runge, of Chilworthy House, Chard, Somerset:—
(Charles) Ian (*Baron Orr-Ewing*), OBE, *b* 1912; *cr* a Baronet 1963 and Baron Orr-Ewing 1971.

Grandchildren of late Charles Lindsay Orr Ewing, MP, 5th son of 1st baronet:—
Issue of late Sir Ian Leslie Orr Ewing, MP, *b* 1893, *d* 1958: *m* 1917, Helen Bridget, MBE, who *d* 1978, da of late Hon Henry Lloyd Gibbs (B Aldenham, colls):—
Anthea Helen (Thorn Falcon House, Taunton, Som), *b* 1917: *m* 1st, 1938, Major Wilfrid Michael Fox, Coldstream Guards, who *d* 1975; 2ndly, 1977, Edward John Ninien Lowes, elder son of Edward Lowes, and has issue living (by 1st *m*), Charles St Vigor, *b* 1941: *m* 1st, 1964 (*m diss* 1992), Charlotte Certhia, da of late Mervyn Jeffery Ingram, MB (*see* Ingram, Bt); 2ndly, 1994, Nicola Louise, da of Capt Edward de Lérisson Cazenove (*see* Kennedy, Bt), and formerly wife of Sir Charles Warren, 9th Bt, and has issue living (by 1st *m*), Laurence St Vigor *b* 1965: *m* 1995, Nancy A., yr da of John Basile, of Westchester, New York, Nina Jane *b* 1970, — (Helen) Mary (*Lady Stewart-Wilson*), *b* 1939: *m* 1962, Lt-Col Sir Blair Aubyn Stewart-Wilson, KCVO, Scots Gds, of The Old Brewery, N Curry, Taunton, Som, and has issue living, Alice Helen *b* 1963: *m* 1985, Jonathan Cecil Ian Young, only son of Capt H. R. C. Young, RN, of Petersfield, Hants (and has issue living, Archibald Blair Cecil *b* 1991, India Mary Katharine *b* 1988, Minnie Rose Alice *b* 1996), Sophia Mary *b* 1966: *m* 1991, A. Bruce McIntosh, eldest son of late Bob McIntosh, of Budleigh Salterton, Devon (and has issue living, Harry *b* 1999, Lily *b* 1993, Kitty *b* 1994, Tarn *b* 1995), Belinda Anthea *b* 1970: *m* 1997, William Anthony David St Lawrence Gethin (*see* Gethin, Bt, colls).

Issue of late Capt David Orr Ewing, DSO, RN, *b* 1900, *d* 1964: *m* 1930, Helen Mary Stuart, who *d* 1994, da of late Benjamin Noaks, of Bloemfontein, S Africa:—
Edward Stuart (Dunskey, Portpatrick, Stranraer, Wigtownshire), *b* 1931; Maj The Black Watch (ret); a DL of Wigtownshire, and Lord Lieut since 1989: *m* 1st, 1958 (*m diss* 1981), Fiona Anne Bowman, yr da of late Anthony Hobart Farquhar, of Hastingwood House, Harlow, Essex; 2ndly, 1981, Diana Mary, da of late William Smith Waters, OBE, of Greenfoot House, Raughton Head, Cumbria, and has issue living (by 1st *m*), Alastair Lindsay, *b* 1964, — Jane Helen *b* 1961: *m* 1991, Patrick Giles Gauntlett Dear, of Rutland Lodge, 83 Albert Bridge Rd, SW11, yr son of M. A. G. Dear, of Algarve, Portugal, and has issue living, Frederick Edward Gauntlett *b* 1993, Maxwell William Gauntlett *b* 1997, Arabella Mimi *b* 1995, — Victoria Susan *b* 1962. —— Charles David (Torhousemuir, Wigtown, Wigtownshire), *b* 1936; Lt Cdr, RN: *m* 1962, Bridget Juliet, da of Sir Thomas Astley Woolaston White, 5th Bt (*cr* 1802), and has issue living, David Robert, *b* 1964; The Black Watch (Royal Highland Regt): *m* 1992, Sally Katrine, elder da of Col R. S. B. Watson, of Edinburgh, and has issue living, Andrew Alexander *b* 1994, Hamish Thomas *b* 1997, — Robert Charles, *b* 1966: *m* 1996, Amani, yr da of M. Obeid, FRCS, of Harborne, Birmingham.

Sir Archibald Orr Ewing (7th son of late William Ewing, of Ardvullen House, Argyllshire, a merchant of Glasgow, and his wife Susan, da of John Orr, Provost of Paisley), 1st baronet, Dean of Faculties in Glasgow Univ, and an Ensign-Gen in Royal Co of Archers (HM's Body Guard for Scotland); MP for Dunbartonshire (*C*) 1868-92. Sir William, 2nd Bt, was a Member of Queen's Body Guard for Scotland (Royal Co of Archers). Brig-Gen Sir Norman Archibald Orr Ewing, 4th Bt, was a Lieut Queen's Body Guard for Scotland (Royal Co of Archers) and was Hon Col, 7th Bn Argyll and Sutherland Highlanders 1932-48.

FAGGE (E) 1660, of Wiston, Sussex

Safe if upright

Sir JOHN WILLIAM FREDERICK FAGGE, 11th *Baronet*, son of late William Archibald Theodore Fagge, 4th son of 8th Baronet; *b* 28 Sept 1910; *s* his uncle, *Sir* JOHN HARRY LEE, 1940; is a farmer: *m* 1940, Ivy Gertrude, who *d* 1992, da of William Edward Frier, of 15 Church Lane, Newington, Kent, and has issue.

ℬrms – Gules, two bends vaire. ℭrest – An ostrich with wings expanded argent, beaked, legged and ducally gorged or holding in the beak a horseshoe proper. *Residence* – 11 Forbes Rd, Faversham, Kent ME13 8QF.

SON LIVING

JOHN CHRISTOPHER, *b* 30 April 1942: *m* 1974, Evelyn Joy Golding.

DAUGHTER LIVING

Pauline Joy, *b* 1943.

SISTER LIVING

Gwendoline Beatrice May, *b* 1914.

DAUGHTER LIVING OF TENTH BARONET

Lucy Harriet Gertrude, *b* 1913. *Residence* – Boston, USA.

COLLATERAL BRANCH LIVING

Granddaughter of late Rev John Frederick Fagge, 4th son of 6th baronet:—
Issue of late Sarah Elizabeth Fagge, *d* 1947: *m* 1889, George Goldie, JP, who *d* 1904:—
Ethelreda Marie Teresa, *b* 1899: *m* 1936, Lawrence Henry Shattock, FRIBA (Knight of St Gregory). *Residence* – Little Wiston, Crescent Rd, Wimbledon, SW20.

The 1st baronet, Sir John Fagge (son of late John Fagge, of Brensett, Kent), sat as MP for Rye 1645-53, for Sussex 1654-9 and 1681-5, and for Steyning 1660-81 and 1685-1701, and was a Col in Parliamentary Army. He purchased the estate of Wiston, Sussex, from Dr Thomas Shirley, which passed from Sir Robert Fagge, 4th Bt to his sister Elizabeth who *m* 1743, Sir Charles Goring, 5th Bt.

FAIRBAIRN (UK 1869), of Ardwick, Lancashire

Always the same

Sir (JAMES) BROOKE FAIRBAIRN, 6th *Baronet*; *b* 10 Dec 1930; *s* his father, *Sir* WILLIAM ALBERT, 1972; *ed* Stowe: *m* 1st, 1960, Mary Russell, who *d* 1992, only da of late William Russell Scott, MB, ChB, FFARCS, of 59 Wyke Rd, Weymouth; 2ndly, 1997, Mrs Rosemary Anne Victoria Washbourn, da of late Edwin Henderson, of Lancs, and has issue (by 1st *m*).

ℬrms – Argent, on a chevron between three boars' heads couped gules three bezants. ℭrest – The sun in his meridian splendour or. *Residence* – Barkway House, Bury Rd, Newmarket, Suffolk, CB8 7BT.

SONS LIVING (By 1st marriage)

ROBERT WILLIAM, *b* 10 April 1965; *ed* King's Sch, Ely, and Durham Univ (BA): *m* 1990, Sarah Frances Colleypriest, elder da of Roger Griffin, of Malmesbury, Wilts, and has issue living, Jack Edmund Brooke, *b* 22 March 1995, — Luke William George, *b* 1997, — Imogen Mary Colleypriest, *b* 1993. —— George Edward, *b* 1969: *m* 1996, Lena Maria, da of Adolf Gstöttner, of Hamburg, Germany.

DAUGHTER LIVING (By 1st marriage)

Fiona Mary, *b* 1967: *m* 1996, Lt-Col James Henry Gordon, RGJ, only son of Graeme Gordon, of Kenmure Kennels, New Galloway, Kirkcudbrightshire.

BROTHER LIVING

(William) Andrew (Oulton House, Oulton, Stone, Staffs ST15 8UR), *b* 1934; *ed* Stowe; FCA: *m* 1961 (*m diss* 1998), Elspeth Alison, only da of late Robert Hally, of Brookfield, Barnham, W Sussex, and has issue living, James Andrew (82 Hambalt Rd, SW4 9EJ), *b* 1967: *m* 1994, Samantha Jane, only da of late David Harwicke, of The Paddocks, Hurst, Berks, and has issue living, Maddie Louise *b* 1998, — Nicola Christine, *b* 1962: *m* 1986, Dr Peter Gist, of 39 Hill Top,

Hampstead Garden Suburb, NW11 6ED, son of F. E. Gist, of Honiton, Devon, and has issue living, Duncan Edward *b* 1989, William Peter *b* 1995, Rosemary Eleanor *b* 1988, Philippa Helen *b* 1992, — Katharine Alison (29 Ingrams Close, Hersham, Surrey KT12 5JH), *b* 1964.

AUNTS LIVING (*Daughters of 4th baronet*)

Mildred Dorothy, *b* 1903. —— Constance Matilda, *b* 1908.

WIDOW LIVING OF FIFTH BARONET

CHRISTINE RENEE COTTON (*Dowager Lady Fairbairn*) (45 Williams Way, Radlett, Herts), da of late Rev Canon Robert William Croft, V of Kelvedon, Essex: *m* 1925, Sir William Albert Fairbairn, 5th Bt, who *d* 1972.

COLLATERAL BRANCHES LIVING

Grandchildren of late Rev William Murray Fairbairn, son of late William Andrew Fairbairn (infra):—
Issue of late Vice-Adm Bernard William Murray Fairbairn, CBE, *b* 1880, *d* 1960, *m* 1905, Alice Mary, who *d* 1970, only da of late William Phillipps, of Leigham Villas, Plymouth:—
†Alan Bernard Murray, MBE *b* 1906; *ed* Sherborne; Cdr RN (ret); 1939-45 War (despatches); MBE (1973): *m* 1943, Adeline Hilda, da of Lt-Col Edward Herbert Sweet, CMG, DSO, and *d* 1995, leaving issue, *Rev* John Alan, *b* 1946; *ed* Wellington Coll, and Trin Coll, Camb (MA 1972): *m* 1982, Susan Patricia, da of late Dr Charles Sergel, of Milford-on-Sea, and has issue living, Timothy John Charles *b* 1983, Katharine Mary *b* 1985. —— David Patrick, *b* 1919; *ed* Sherborne; CEng, MIMechE, FIMarE; Lt-Cdr RN (ret): *m* 1950, Margaret Winifred Ferrers (formerly 2nd Officer WRNS), da of late Ronald Ernest Ferrers Courage, of Redcross Dulverton, and has issue living, William David Murray (10 Caspar John Close, Hill Head, Fareham, Hants PO14 2DQ), *b* 1953; *ed* Radley, and Magdalene Coll, Camb (MA); Capt RN: *m* 1983, Rowena Katherine, da of Walter Angus Murray, of West Hill Court, Ottery St Mary, Devon, and has issue living, Oliver James Murray *b* 1987, Fiona Nina Katherine *b* 1992, — Anne Mary, *b* 1951; formerly Sister of the Society of St Margaret, St Saviour's Priory, Haggerston: *m* 1993, Harry Fox, of 11 Fisher's Close, Bushey, Herts WD2 2GY, and has issue living, Lucy Janet Rhoda *b* 1995. *Residence* – The Firs, Ryhall, Stamford, Lincolnshire PE9 4HF.

Issue of late Aubrey John Murray Fairbairn, *b* 1888, *d* 1961: *m* 1920, Adela, da of late Col T. A. Rawlins, of Clifton, Bristol, and Berrow, Somerset:—
Ian Aubrey, *b* 1927.

Grandsons of late William Andrew Fairbairn, 4th son of 1st baronet:—
Issue of late Edward Percy Fairbairn, *b* 1866, *d* 1931: *m* 1st, 1894, Mary, who *d* 1903, da of late John Sholto Douglas, of Tilquhillie, Kincardineshire; 2ndly, 1908, Constance, who *d* 1952, da of William Gaven Eden (B Henley, colls):—
(By 2nd *m*) George William, *b* 1911; formerly Capt RE; is an ARIBA: *m* 1940, Katharine Elizabeth, who *d* 1991, da of late Dr William Deane, of Waddington, Lincoln, and has issue living, Jacqueline Elizabeth, *b* 1948: *m* 1978, Luis Filipe Espadinha Fialho, of Casa Charrna, Albardeira, 8600 Lagos, Algarve, Portugal, son of late Pedro Manuel Fialho and Maria B. Espadinha, of Estoril, Portugal, and has issue living, Miguel Filipe Fairbairn *b* 1980, André Simon Fairbairn *b* 1984. —— Patrick Yelverton, *b* 1913; *ed* Charterhouse: *m* 1940, Dorothy Mary, who *d* 1986, da of late Lewis Henshaw, OBE, of Madras, and has issue living, Edward James (Applegarth, Bradfield, Berks), *b* 1950: *m* 1974, Fiona Catherine, da of Maj Malcolm Comrie Gray (*see* Jackson, Bt, *cr* 1902, colls) and has issue living, Miranda Sarah *b* 1976, Rosalind Nesta *b* 1979, — Judith Constance, *b* 1946: *m* 1970, His Honour Judge (Keith Anthony Delgado) Hornby, of 11 St Ann's Villas, W11, and has issue living, Jamie Alexander Fairbairn *b* 1976, Nicholas Thomas Fairbairn *b* 1980, Katya Eugenie *b* 1973.

Grandchildren of late William Fairbairn, son of late Rev Adam Henderson Fairbairn (infra):—
Issue of late Maj William Alan Thomas Fairbairn, TD, *b* 1908, *d* 1992: *m* 1944, Marian Ruth, da of late Capt W. T. Wyllie:—
Stephen Alan (Borgarholtsbraut 57, Kopavogur, Iceland), *b* 1947; *ed* Radley; Dip AD Bath Academy of Art: *m* 1970, Margaret Joelsdottir, and has issue living, Hilda, *b* 1973, — Sandra, *b* 1979. —— Susan Mary (Robin Cottage, Pauls Lane, Sway, Lymington, Hants), *b* 1953; *ed* Stonar: *m* 1974, Richard Ivor Sommerin, and has issue living, James Adrian, *b* 1974.

Grandchildren of late Maj David Alexander Fairbairn, OBE, Duke of Wellington's (W Riding) Regt, 6th son of late Rev Adam Henderson Fairbairn, 7th son of 1st baronet:—
Issue of late (Norman) David Nigel Fairbairn, *b* 1921, *d* 1997: *m* 1951, Mary Josephine (Mullins Mill, Donhead St Mary, Shaftesbury, Dorset SP7 9DS), da of Hector Hillaby, Bar-at-law, of 25 Gilston Rd, SW10:—
Jonathan David, *b* 1952: *m* 1981, Catherine Fursdon, and has issue living, Peter James, *b* 1983, — Susannah Mary, *b* 1986. —— Mark Benson Hector, *b* 1960: *m* 1990, A. Fiona, elder da of Cmdr Graham P. Stock, of Thornford, Dorset, and has issue living, David, *b* 1996, — Robert Graham, *b* 1998. —— Carol Evangeline Mary, *b* 1954. —— Alexandra Josephine Margaret, *b* 1957.

Sir William Fairbairn, 1st Bt, el surviving son of Andrew Fairbairn of Smailholm, Roxburghshire, was a celebrated engineer who was associated with Stephenson in erecting the tubular bridge across the Menai Straits 1848. He was a founder of the British Assocn for the Advancement of Science.

Fairfax (Ramsay-Fairfax-Lucy), see Lucy.

Fairlie-Cuninghame, see Cuninghame.

FALKINER (I) 1778, of Annemount, Cork
(Name pronounced "Fawkner")

Sir BENJAMIN SIMON PATRICK FALKINER, 10th *Baronet*; *b* 16 Jan 1962; *s* his father, *Sir* EDMOND CHARLES, 1997; *ed* Queen Elizabeth's Barnet: *m* 1998, Linda Louise Mason, and has issue.

Arms – Or, three falcons close proper, belled gules. Crest – A falcon's lure proper, between two wings azure.
Residence – 29 Glebeland, Hatfield, Herts AL10 8AA.

SON LIVING

Samuel James Matthew, *b* 1993.

DAUGHTER LIVING

Alice Katherine Sally, *b* 1996.

BROTHER LIVING

MATTHEW TERENCE, *b* 9 Jan 1964; *ed* Queen Elizabeth's, Barnet; has issue living (by Kim Dillon), William Charles, *b* 1995, — George Frederic, *b* 1997. *Residence* – 8 Sleapshyde Lane, Smallford, St Albans, Herts.

UNCLE LIVING (*son of 8th baronet*)

Henry Leslie Basil, *b* 1940; *ed* Downside: *m* 1967, (Dorothea) Angela, only da of Peter Wolfe-Taylor, of Chimneys, Ockham, Surrey, and has issue living, Tobias Peter Riggs, *b* 1972; *ed* Millfield, — Max Henry Wolfe, *b* 1974; *ed* Millfield. *Residence* – Dormer Cottage, Frensham, Surrey GU10 3AE.

AUNTS LIVING (*daughters of 8th baronet*)

Elizabeth Anne Thérèse (*Lady Hogg*), *b* 1929: *m* 1956, Sir Michael David Hogg, 8th Bt, and has issue (*see* Hogg, Bt). *Residence* – 19 Woodlands Rd, SW13. —— Maryclare, *b* 1934: *m* 1st, 1956 (*m diss* 1980), Noel John Taylor; 2ndly, 1991, Geoffrey Smith, and has issue living (by 1st *m*), Paul John, *b* 1957; *ed* Hereford Sch, — Mark Robert, *b* 1965, *ed* Hereford Sch: *m* 199-, Helen Elizabeth Jane Bennett, and has issue living Robert James *b* 1990, Emma Jane *b* 1992, — David James, *b* 1969; *ed* Hereford Sch: *m* 199-, Mandy Eileen Rogers, and has issue living, Ashley Paul *b* 1992, Thomas James *b* 1993, — Jane Clare, *b* 1961, — Sarah Kate, *b* 1971; has issue living, Lucy Jane *b* 1988. *Residence* – 22 Penny Plock, Madley, Herefords. —— Veronica Cicely, *b* 1935: *m* 1956, William David Brown, and has issue living, Adrian William, *b* 1958; *ed* Whitefriars Sch, Cheltenham: *m* 1996, Emily Maria, da of Peter James, of Enfield, Middx, — Edward David, MBE, *b* 1960; *ed* Whitefriars Sch, Cheltenham; MBE (Mil) 1990: *m* 1993, Ruth Mary, da of John Sandy, of Milford Surrey, and has issue living, Rosanna Honor Grace *b* 1996, Imogen Cicely Clare *b* 1998, — Rupert Duncan (Helsett Farm, Lesnewth, Boscastle, Cornwall), *b* 1963; *ed* Whitefriars Sch, Cheltenham: *m* 1997, Nina Karen, da of Peter William Talbot-Ponsonby (*see* E Shrewsbury, colls), — Dominic George Andrew, *b* 1966; *ed* Whitefriars Sch, Cheltenham. *Residence* – The Old Manse, Fownhope, Herefordshire.

MOTHER LIVING

Janet Iris, da of late Arthur Edward Bruce Darby, of The Park, Stoke Lacy, Bromyard, Herefords; *m* 1960 (*m diss* 1996), as his 1st wife, Sir Edmond Charles Falkiner, 9th Bt. *Residence* – 5 Park View Rd, Finchley, N3 2JB; 3 Springdale, Gorsley, Ross-on-Wye, Herefords HR9 7SU.

WIDOW LIVING OF NINTH BARONET

DIANA JEAN (*Dowager Lady Falkiner*), da of Percy Arthur Childs, of The New House, Wendover, Bucks: *m* (14 June) 1997, as his 2nd wife, Sir Edmond Charles Falkiner, 9th Bt, who was *k* in a motor accident in Northern Spain (20 Sept) 1997. *Residence* – Edgehill, The Parade, Monmouth, Mon NP25 3PA.

COLLATERAL BRANCH LIVING

Issue of late Maj Gervase Leslie Falkiner, 3rd and yst son of 7th baronet, *b* 1909, *d* 1988: *m* 1934, Rosemary Hastings (15 Glebelands, Merriott, Som), elder da of Herbert Smith, of Tower, Mold, Flintshire:—

Richard Gervase, *b* 1936; *ed* Ampleforth: *m* 1959, Gabrielle Mary, only da of Frank Woodgate, of Ledley House, Ebrington, Chipping Campden, Glos, and has issue living, Sebastian, *b* 1963, — Sophia Mary, *b* 1962. *Residences* – 38 Peel St, W8; Ledley House, Ebrington, Chipping Campden, Glos. —— Michael George Patrick, *b* 1940; *ed* Ampleforth: *m* 1970, Joanna Rosamund, eldest da of late (Walter) Peter Baxter (*see* V Hawarden), and has issue living, Caroline Helen, *b* 1972, — Emily Rosemary, *b* 1974. *Residence* – Downclose Stud, North Perrott, nr Crewkerne, Som.

Sir Riggs Falkiner, MP, 1st Bt of Annemount, co Cork, was great-grandson of Michael Falkiner of Brigart, Leeds, who settled in Ireland about 1651. Sir Charles Leslie Falkiner, 4th Bt, was Capt RN, and as Lieut in 1810 headed the "Shannon" main deck boarders at capture of American ship "Chesapeake" (promoted Com). His brother, Lt-Col Sir Samuel Edmund Falkiner, 5th Bt, served throughout the Peninsular war, was present at Talavera, Busaco, Salamanca, Ciudad Rodrigo, Fuentes d'Onore, and was wounded three times.

FARQUHAR (GB) 1796, of Cadogan House, Middlesex
(Name pronounced "Farkwer")

By mind and hand

Sir MICHAEL FITZROY HENRY FARQUHAR, 7th *Baronet*; *b* 29 June 1938; *s* his father, *Sir* PETER WALTER, OBE, DSO, 1986; *ed* Eton, and RAC Cirencester: *m* 1963, Veronica Geraldine, elder da of late Patrick Rowan Hornidge, of Helford Passage, Falmouth, Cornwall, and has issue.

Arms – Argent, a lion rampant sable between two sinister hands apaumée couped in chief gules, and a crescent in base azure. Crest – An eagle rising proper.
Residence – Manor Farm, West Kington, Chippenham, Wilts SN14 7JG.
Club – White's.

SONS LIVING

CHARLES WALTER FITZROY, *b* 21 Feb 1964; *ed* Stowe. *Address* — c/o Willis Faber (E.C.) Ltd, P.O. Box 10264, Manama, Bahrain. —— Edward Peter Henry, *b* 1966; *ed* Stowe, and RMA Sandhurst: *m* 1995, Nicola, only da of Michael John Christopher Stone, of Ozleworth Park, Wotton-under-Edge, Glos. *Residence* – 21 Newton Rd, W2 5JR.

BROTHERS LIVING

Anthony Charles, *b* 1942; *ed* Eton: *m* 1969, Elizabeth Jane, da of late Col Timothy M. Braithwaite, of Honey Cottage, Limpley Stoke, Bath, and has issue living, Alexandra Elizabeth, *b* 1971, — Annabelle Jean, *b* 1973, — Antonia Katharine, *b* 1977. *Residence* – St Gennys House, St Gennys, Bude, Cornwall EX23 0NW. —— Ian Walter, LVO, *b* 1945; *ed* Eton, and RMA Sandhurst; Capt Queen's Own Hussars; LVO 1972; Master Bicester & Warden Hill Hunt 1973, Jt Master, Beaufort Hunt 1985: *m* 1972, Pamela Jane, da of Charles L. Chafer, of Elleron Lodge, Pickering, Yorks, and has issue living, Emma Elizabeth, *b* 1977, — Victoria Rose, *b* 1979, — Rosanne Catherine, *b* 1983. *Residence* – Happylands, Doughton, Tetbury, Glos.

AUNT LIVING (*Daughter of 5th baronet*)

Ruth Violet Mary (*Ruth, Baroness Dulverton*), *b* 1910: *m* 1st, 1932 (*m diss* 1961), Major Richard Gennys Fanshawe, 16th/5th Lancers, who *d* 1988, son of Lieut-Gen Sir Edward Arthur Fanshawe, KCB; 2ndly, 1962, 2nd Baron Dulverton, who *d* 1992, and has issue living, (by 1st *m*) David Valentine, OBE (Ash House, St Mary Bourne, Andover, Hants SP11 6BG), *b* 1933; Col Gren Gds (ret); Clerk of the Cheque and Adjutant HM Body Guard Hon Corps of Gentlemen-at-Arms since 1998: *m* 1963, Sheila Christine, el da of Maj-Gen John Malcolm McNeill, CB, CBE, and has issue living, Angus Edward *b* 1965: *m* 1995, Marianna H. D. Anninos (and has issue living, Lucy Ruth *b* 1996, Elena Barbara *b* (twin) 1996), Robert Leighton *b* 1967; Capt Gren Gds: *m* 1992, Charlotte L. M. yr da of Hon Mr Justice (Sir Anthony Howell Meurig) Evans, RD, of Bucklers Hard, Hants (and has issue living, Alexander John *b* 1996, Rosanna Mary *b* 1998), William David *b* 1971, — Brian Edward (Manor Barn House, Nether Westcote, Chipping Norton, Oxon OX7 6SD), *b* 1936; Capt 9th/12th R Lancers: *m* 1960, Elizabeth, da of Geoffrey Pugh, of Temple Guiting House, Glos, and has issue living, James Robert (Pegasus Stables, Snailwell Rd, Newmarket, Suffolk) *b* 1961: *m* 1990, Jacqueline Mary Joan, da of late Geoffrey Cherry-Downes (and has issue living, Tom Frederick Anthony *b* 1997), Antony Geoffrey *b* 1964: *m* 1997, Hon Georgia Honor Margarethe Channon, da of Baron Kelvedon (Life Baron) (and has issue living, Oliver Hector Paul *b* 1999), Sarah Rose *b* 1967. *Residence* – Barnbrook Cottage, Milton Lilbourne, Pewsey, Wilts SN9 5LQ.

COLLATERAL BRANCHES LIVING

Issue of late Lt-Col Charles Richard Farquhar, MC, 2nd son of 5th baronet, b 1906 d 1980: m 1939, Dorothy Nancy, who d 1997, da of Maj James Gerald Thewlis Johnson, DSO (Alleyne, Bt):—
Daphne Violet, b 1945: m 1973, Terence John Pardoe, of North Hazelrigg, Chatton, Alnwick, Northumberland, and has issue living, Robert Charles, b 1977, — Amanda Susan, b 1975. ——— Angela Dorothy, b 1948: m 1977, Richard John Hassan Meade, OBE, and has issue living, James Richard, b 1981, — Harry Michael, b 1983, — Lucy Margaret b 1985.

Grandchildren of late Guy William John Farquhar (infra):—
Issue of late Capt Edward Vivian Farquhar, b 1929, d 1995: m 1st, 1956 (m diss 1983), Polly, yr da of late Adm of the Fleet Sir Philip Louis Vian, GCB, KBE, DSO; 2ndly, 1985, Careena (3 Ormond Av, Richmond, Surrey TW10 6TN), only da of William Thomas, of Hebron, Pembrokeshire:—
(By 1st m) Peter Christopher Edward (32 Briarwood Rd, SW4 9PX), b 1959: m 1st, 1986 (m diss 1992), Susan Jane, only da of Michael Williams, of Fairfield House, Pedmore, Worcs; 2ndly, 1992, Victoria Susannah, elder da of Brig Peter Collins, of Threapwood, The Maultway, Camberley, Surrey, and has issue living (by 2nd m), Edward Peter Grattan, b 1997, — Tatiana Elizabeth, b 1999. ——— Alastair Vian, b 1966. ——— Diana Susan, b 1961: m 1988, Nicholas David Morant, of Clenston Manor, Winterbourne Clenston, Blandford, Dorset, yst son of late Maj G. C. H. Morant, of Pigeon House Farm, Hatherden, Andover, Hants, and has issue living, Maximilian George Vian, b 1991, — Jack Edward Chearnley, b 1993, — Lara Patricia Polly, b 1996.

Grandchildren of late Grenville Frederick Richard Farquhar, 4th son of 3rd baronet:—
Issue of late Guy William John Farquhar, b 1899, d 1962: m 1928 (m diss 1947), Daphne Mary Christian, da of late Lieut-Col Vivian Henry, CB (Millbank, Bt):—
Peter Guy Powlett (17 Netheravon Rd, W4 2NA), b 1936: m 1st, 1961 (m diss 1973), Rosemary Anne Eaton, only da of Eaton Hammond; 2ndly, 1974, Carolyn, el da of Graham Robertson, of St Ives, NSW, and has had issue (by 1st m), Richard Charles, b 1962: m 1988, Emma de Hoghton, elder da of Jonathan Reeves, of Tewkesbury, Glos (see V Chelmsford, colls), and has issue living, Araminta Claire b 1990, Lydia Rose b 1994, — James Edward, b 1963: m 1991, Victoria, da of late Michael Clinton, of Sedgehill, near Shaftesbury, Dorset, — (by 2nd m), George Peter, b 1980, — Hugh Graham, b 1984, — Jane, b 1982, d 1983, — Alice Rose Jane, b 1987. ——— Antonia Daphne Diana, b 1932: m 1956, Antony Noel Gordon Leaf (Cleeve House, Ampney St Peter, Cirencester), late Lieut 15/19th Hussars, and has issue living, Guy Edmond James, b 1962; ed Harrow, Hertford Coll, Oxford, and RMA Sandhurst, late Capt 15/19th Hussars: m 1st, 1993 (m diss 1997), Noelle Browning, of California; 2ndly, 1998, Sally-Ann, da of Lt-Col Michael Scott, Scots Guards, — Anna Georgina, b 1958: m 1988, George Francis Windsor-Clive, and has issue (see E Plymouth).

Issue of late FitzRoy James Wilberforce Farquhar, OBE, 5th son of 3rd baronet, b 1858, d 1941: m 1884, Ada Mary, who d 1944, da of Sir John William Cradock-Hartopp, 4th baronet:—
Arthur Ronald, DSC, b 1888; became Com 1924, and Capt (ret) 1934, served 1914-18 War (wounded), 1939-45 War.

Grandson of late Ernest Farquhar, son of late Harvie Morton Farquhar, 2nd son of 2nd baronet:—
Issue of late Sir Harold Lister Farquhar, KCMG, MC, b 1894, d 1953: m 1917, Constance Audrey, who d 1963, da of late Hon Arthur Algernon Capell (E Essex, colls):—
Ian Rupert, b 1918; is Major Grenadier Guards: m 1944, Margaret Eugenie, da of late Francis John Gordon Borthwick, WS (see L Borthwick, colls), and has issue living, Francis Rupert, b 1952. Residence – Hamlyns, Chudleigh, S Devon. Clubs – White's, Pratt's.

Granddaughter of late Sir Harold Lister Farquhar, KCMG, MC (ante):—
Issue of late Adrian Farquhar, b 1924; d 1981: m 1955, Ann Elizabeth (Redlynch House, Salisbury), da of Edward John Johnston-Noad, of Paris:—
Annabel Cristina, b 1958: m 1983, Christopher Mark Yates, of 31 Lilyville Rd, SW6 5DP, son of T. Gordon Yates, of Covers, Lynchmere, W Sussex, and has issue living, Eden Mark Farquhar, b 1988, — Kieran Alexander Francis, b 1990.

Sir Robert Farquhar, Knt, of Munie, a yr son of the ancient family of Farquhar of Gilmilnscroft, was Deputy-Receiver of Scotland 1644, and Provost of Aberdeen 1646. His great-great-great nephew, Sir Walter, 1st baronet, was Physician to George IV when Prince Regent, and had a second son, Robert (first British Gov and Com-in-Ch of the Mauritius), who also was cr a Baronet in 1821 (ext 1924). The 5th baronet, Sir Walter Randolph Fitzroy Farquhar, Capt RFA, was ka 1918.

FARRINGTON (UK) 1818, of Blackheath, Kent

Sir HENRY FRANCIS COLDEN FARRINGTON, 7th *Baronet*; *b* 25 April 1914; *s* his father, *Sir* HENRY ANTHONY, 1944; *ed* Haileybury; Major (ret) late RA; Col (hon): *m* 1947, Anne, el da of late Major William Albert Gillam, DSO, Border Regt, and has issue.

𝔄rms – Ermine, on a chevron gules between three leopard's faces sable as many bombs or, fired proper. Crest – A dragon wings elevated tail nowed vert bezanty, gorged with a mural crown argent and a chain reflexed over the back or, the body charged with two caltraps fessewise of the last.
Residence – Higher Ford, Wiveliscombe, Taunton, Som, TA4 2RL.

SON LIVING

Le bon temps viendra
*There's a good time
coming*

HENRY WILLIAM (Castle, Wiveliscombe, Taunton, Somerset TA4 2TJ), *b* 27 March 1951; *ed* Haileybury, and RAC Cirencester; ARICS: *m* 1979, Diana Donne, ALI, yr da of Geoffrey Albert Broughton, of Impens, N Petherton, Som, and has issue living, Henry John Albert, *b* 4 Jan 1985, — Charles George Donne, *b* 1988.

DAUGHTER LIVING

Susan Maria (Tipnoller Cottage, Wiveliscombe, Taunton, Som, TA4 2RL), *b* 1949.

COLLATERAL BRANCHES LIVING

Grandchildren of late Alexander Farrington, 2nd son of 5th baronet:—
Issue of late Cmdr William Howard Farrington, RN, *b* 1907, *d* 1988: *m* 1934, Barbara, who *d* 1975, da of Herbert Smale, of 15 Harley St, W1:—
Andrew James (Bay Cottage, Wembury, Plymouth, Devon PL9 0HR), *b* 1942; *ed* Marlborough, and Birmingham Univ (BSc): *m* 1965, Susan Kathleen, BSc, da of late Ronald Hugh Wylsher Britton, MRCS, LRCP, of 10 Lane Head Close, Croyde Bay, Braunton, N. Devon, and has issue living, William James, *b* 1967, — Eleanor Kathleen, *b* 1970: *m* 1995, Simon Paul Merchant, and has issue living, Jacob William *b* 1998, — Alice Joanna, *b* 1973. —— Susan FARRINGTON (3 Cedar Close, Wokingham, Berks RG40 1EA), *b* 1937; has resumed her maiden name: *m* 1980 (*m diss* 1987), Ieuan Davies Williams. —— Jenifer, *b* 1938: *m* 1965, Maj Martin Rothery Sheldon, Royal Scots Greys (ret), of The Old Vicarage, Newtown, Wem, Shropshire SY4 5NU, and has issue living, Bryony Clare, *b* 1966: *m* 1994, Malcolm John, — Camilla Frances, *b* 1968, — Holly Samantha, *b* 1973. —— Angela, *b* 1941: *m* 1968, Andrew Arthur Rose, of Drimbuie, Kilchrenan, Taynuilt, Argyll PA35 1HF, and has issue living, David Andrew, *b* 1967: *m* 1995, Shuna Baillie, and has issue living, Anya May *b* 1997, — Susannah Angela, *b* 1968: *m* 1998, Gordon MacMillan, — Elizabeth Iona, *b* 1972

Issue of late John Marsden Farrington, yst son of 5th baronet, *b* 1874, *d* 1965: *m* 1917, Lynda May, who *d* 1981, da of George T. Simmonds, of Forest Hill, SE23:—
John Anthony (La Boudonniere, 35560 Bazouges La Perouse, Bretagne, France), *b* 1934; *ed* Eastbourne Coll: *m* 1958, Patricia Rose, da of John William Fowler, of Norwich, and has issue living, Charles Henry, *b* 1963; *ed* Shrewsbury: *m* 1990, Clair, el da of Francis Derek Rowland, and has issue living, Holly *b* 1992, Hannah *b* 1995, Lucy *b* 1998, — Richard John, *b* 1964; *ed* Shrewsbury: *m* 1993 (*m diss* 1994), Jasmine, da of Bill Pareira; has issue living (by Karen Rugg), Danielle *b* 1996.

Granddaughter of late Anthony Charles Farrington, MRCS, LRCPE 4th son of 4th baronet:—
Issue of late Charles Anthony Beevor Farrington, *b* 1873, *d* 1939: *m* 1908, Mabel, who *d* 1970, da of late George Hastings Rust D'Eye:—
Marjorie Joan Cicely (8 Naish Rd, Barton-on-Sea, New Milton, Hants BH25 7PU), *b* 1910.

Grandchildren of late George Edward Marshall Farrington, eldest son of late Francis John Farrington, 4th son of Rev Edward Holmes Farrington, 2nd son of 3rd baronet:—
Issue of late Marshall Francis William, *b* 1912, *d* 1986: *m* 1939, Christina Johanna (Crystal), who *d* 1992, da of late William John MacSeveney, of Nsoko, Swaziland:—
Alastair Edward, *b* 1946: *m* 1964, Nesta Eureka Minnie, and has issue living, Craig Grant, *b* 1965, — Alastair Ian, *b* 1969: *m* 1990 (*m diss* 1997), Julie Rene van Lingen, and has issue living, Kirsty, *b* 1991, and adopted children, Kennedy *b* 1982, Slade Alastair *b* 1984, Jaydee *b* 1987, Shaylee *b* 1987, — Charlene Debra, *b* 1966: *m* 1992, Mark Philip Schroder, and has issue living, Alexander Mark, *b* 1992, Michelle Simone *b* 1994, — Desire Marshall, *b* 1968: *m* 1994, Rory van Lingen, and has issue living, Astrid Leigh *b* 1995, Fawn *b* 1998. —— Graham William, *b* 1947: *m* 1970 (*m diss* 1978), Persis Eleanor Tozer. —— Ian Fraser, *b* 1948: *m* 1972, Daphne Grace Colling, and has issue living, Bradley Graham, *b* 1974, — Wayne Lewis, *b* 1977. —— Jacqueline Valerie, *b* 1941: *m* 1962, Leopold William Kenneth Ferreira, and *d* 1981.

Sir Anthony Farrington, 1st Bt of this creation, was a Gen in the Army, Director-Gen of RA and Field Train, and an Hon DCL, Oxford, and *m* 1766, Elizabeth, da of Alexander Colden, Lieut-Gov of New York. Sir Henry Anthony, 6th Bt, was Ch Conservator of Forests, Central Provinces India 1923-7.

Faudel-Phillips, see Phillips.

FAYRER (UK) 1896, of Devonshire Street, St Marylebone, co London
(Name pronounced "Fairer")

Sir JOHN LANG MACPHERSON FAYRER, 4th *Baronet*; *b* 18 Oct 1944; *s* his father, *Lt-Cdr Sir* JOSEPH HERBERT SPENS, DSC, RNVR, 1976; *ed* Edinburgh Acad, and Univ of Strathclyde.

𝔄rms – Argent, on a bend invected sable between in chief an Eastern crown gules and in base an esculapius proper enfiled with an Eastern crown of the third, three horseshoes or. 𝔈rest – In front of a sword erect, point upward proper, pommel and hilt or, a horseshoe or between two wings erect gules.
Residences – Overhailes, Haddington, E Lothian EH41 3SB; 9 Westfield St, Edinburgh.

WIDOW LIVING OF THIRD BARONET

NOREEN CHRISTIAN MAY (*Lady Fayrer*), (Overhailes, Haddington, E Lothian), only da of late Rev John Yuill Walker, of Innerleithen: *m* 1964, as his 3rd wife, Lt-Cdr Sir Joseph Herbert Spens Fayrer, 3rd Bt, DSC, RNVR, who *d* 1976.

Ne tentes aut perfice
*Do not attempt, or else
accomplish*

COLLATERAL BRANCH LIVING

Granddaughters of late Lt-Col Frederick Durand Stirling Fayrer, 6th son of 1st baronet:—
Issue of late Colin Robert Fayrer, *b* 1907, *d* 1983: *m* 1946, Evelyn Elinor May (Harbledown Lodge, Harbledown, Canterbury, Kent), da of late Thomas A. Carey, Ceylon Civil Ser:—
Anne Patricia (Dray Corner Barn, Headcorn, Kent), *b* 1947: *m* 1991, Roderick John McKellar. —— Wendy Elizabeth, *b* 1949: *m* 1974, David L. Allworthy, of Forest House, 99 Blean Common, Blean, Canterbury, Kent, and has issue living, James Jonathan Fayrer, *b* 1977, — Anna Elizabeth, *b* 1979.

The 1st baronet, Sir Joseph, was a FRCS, FRCP, an Hon Physician to HM Queen Victoria, and an Hon Physician (Mil) and Physician Extraordinary to HM King Edward VII; Gov of Wellington Coll, and many years Surg-Gen and Pres of Med Board at India Office.

FEILDEN (UK) 1846, of Feniscowles, Lancashire

Sir HENRY WEMYSS FEILDEN, 6th *Baronet*, elder son of late Col Wemyss Gawne Cunningham Feilden, CMG, 3rd son of 3rd baronet; *b* 1 Dec 1916; *s* his cousin, *Sir* WILLIAM MORTON BULLER, MC, 1976; *ed* Canford, and King's Coll London; 1939-45 War with RE; Civil Servant (ret): *m* 1943, Ethel May, da of late John Atkinson, of Annfield Plain, co Durham, and has issue.

𝔄rms – Argent, on a fesse cottised azure, between two martlets in chief and a rose in base gules, barbed and seeded proper, three lozenges or. 𝔈rest – A nuthatch perched upon a hazel-branch fructed, holding in its beak a rose gules, slipped proper. 𝔖econd 𝔈rest and 𝔐otto – A palm-tree weighted proper. "Crescit sub pondere virtus" (*Virtue grows under its imposed weight*).
Seat – Feniscowles, Lancashire. *Residence* – Littledene, Heathfield Rd, Burwash, Etchingham, E Sussex, TN19 7HN. *Club* – MCC.

SON LIVING

Henry Rudyard, *b* 26 Sept 1951; *ed* Kent Coll, Canterbury, and Bristol Univ (BVSc); MRCVS: *m* 1st, 1982 (*m diss* 1997), Anne, da of late William Frank Bonner Shepperd; 2ndly, 1998, Geraldine, da of Major Gerald Rayland Kendall, RA (ret), and has issue living (by 1st *m*), William Henry, *b* 5 April 1983. *Residence* – 340 Poole Rd, Branksome, Dorset BH12 1AW.

Honor is the reward of virtue

DAUGHTERS LIVING

Jennifer May, *b* 1944: *m* 1st, 1972 (*m diss* 1981), Philip Andrew Cooper; 2ndly, 1981, Graham Alexander Donald, of Dhoros Village, 4750 Limassol, Cyprus, and has issue living (by 1st *m*), Harry Edward, *b* 1975, — Paul Andrew, *b* 1978. —— Anne Margaret, *b* 1947: *m* 1970, William Hugh Stokoe, of Chantry Down, Echopit Rd, Guildford, Surrey GU1 3TN, and has issue living, Rupert William, *b* 1980, — Joanna Mary, *b* 1976.

BROTHER LIVING

Randle Richard (Chartridge, West St, Mayfield, E Sussex TN20 6DS), b 1923; ed Marlborough, Corpus Christi Coll, Camb (MA), and Cuddesdon Theo Coll, Bar Lincoln's Inn 1949; Curate of St Andrew's Moulsecoomb 1955-57, and of Steyning 1957-58, Tutor-Organiser for Workers' Educational Assocn, for NE Lancs, 1958-63, and HM Inspector of Schs, 1963-66; Assist Editor (Political Affairs) *Keesing's Contemporary Archives* 1967-81, and a Member Gen Synod of Ch of England 1970-80: m 1st, 1957, Leonora Mary, who d 1991, da of John Laurence Marshall, of Leicester; 2ndly, 1992, Eileen Hilda Braid.

COLLATERAL BRANCHES LIVING

            Issue of late Major Edward Leyland Cooke Feilden, OBE, 2nd son of 3rd baronet, b 1868, d 1921: m 1907, Hon Marjorie Graham Murray, who d 1967, da of 1st Viscount Dunedin:—
Esmè Mary Graham, b 1913: m 1935, George Richard Shaw, who d 1983, of Crossbank Hill, Hurworth-on-Tees, Darlington, and has issue living, Graham (West Bank, Kilmacolm, Renfrewshire PA13 4AY), b 1948: m 1972, Patricia Alexandra, da of William Brandon Veitch, and has issue living, William Graham b 1981, Katharine Alexandra b 1976, Philippa Jane b 1978; ed Newcastle Univ (BA Hons), — Angela Mary Graham (8 Narborough St, SW6 3AR), b 1936: m 1955 (m diss 1990), Air Commodore Anthony Walkinshaw Fraser, RAF, and has issue living, Robert Anthony Walkinshaw b 1963: m 1986 (m diss 1994), Kyoko Aoki, Amanda Evelyn (*Hon Mrs Timothy L. Buxton*) b 1956: m 1st, 1978 (m diss 1992), Mark Chaytor Dickinson (see Chaytor, Bt, 1990 Edn); 2ndly, 1994, Hon Timothy Leland Buxton (see B Buxton of Alsa) (and has issue living (by 1st m), Maximillian b 1981, Olivia Esme b 1983, Georgia Eve b 1987), Antonia Mary b 1959: m 1983, James Richard Michael Heard (and has issue living, William James b 1991, Samantha Mary b 1986, Rosie Anne, b 1988), Alexandra Esme b 1960: m 1986, Simon James Reid-Kay (and has issue living, Hamish George Strathern b 1989, Robert Simon b 1991, Angus Drummond b 1994), — Fiona Esme Gildroy, b 1942: m 1961, Maj Edward Fane Travers Gaffney, Welsh Guards (Guards' Club), of Crossbank Hill, Hurworth-on-Tees, co Durham, and has issue living, Edward William Bay Travers (2A Wyfold Rd, SW6 6SJ) b 1962: m 1988, Helen, da of Henry Ernest Tugwell, of Farleigh Lane, Barming, Maidstone, Kent (and has issue living, Frederick Henry Fane b 1992, Jack Erik b 1996), Richard Desmond Travers b 1963; Capt Welsh Gds, Adrian Tobias George Hannaford b 1972, Miranda Mary b 1967: m 1986, Christopher John Charles Legard, elder son of Sir Charles Thomas Legard, 15th Bt, and has issue (see that title), — Gelda Susan Marjorie Feilden, b 1947: m 1968, Robert Harding Churton, Maj 15th/19th King's R Hussars, of Skewsby House, Skewsby, York YO61 4SG, and has issue living, Thomas Edward Harding b 1972; ed Pembroke Coll, Camb (MA), FCA, David Richard Harding b 1975; ed St Catharine's Coll, Camb (BA Hons); Middle Temple.

            Issue of late Lt-Col Randle Montague Feilden, CBE, 4th son of 3rd baronet, b 1871, d 1965: m 1924, Rachel Mary Gordon, who d 1933, da of late Horace Gordon Lowe, of Truro:—
John Randle, b 1931. —— Fay Adah Rachel (The Sail Loft, Mulberry Quay, Falmouth, Cornwall TR11 3HD), b 1925; BA, PhD London, Dip Psych; lecturer and research worker London Univ 1962-82, since when Emeritus Reader in Clinical Psychology, London Univ; Founder and Dir Centre for Personal Construct Psychology since 1982: m 1st, 1948 (m diss 1955), Anthony John Fransella, RAF; 2ndly, 1968, John Royden Cole Hodson.

  This family has been settled near Blackburn, Lancashire, for more than four centuries. The 1st Baronet was MP for Blackburn (C) 1832-47.

Ferguson-Davie, see Davie.

JOHNSON-FERGUSON (UK) 1906, of Springkell, co Dumfries, Kenyon, Newchurch-in-Culcheth, co Palatine of Lancaster, and Wiston, co Lanark

Sir IAN EDWARD JOHNSON-FERGUSON, 4th *Baronet*: *b* 1 Feb 1932; *s* his father, Lt-Col *Sir* NEIL EDWARD, TD, 1992; *ed* Ampleforth, Trin Coll, Camb (BA), and Imperial Coll, London (DIC): *m* 1964, Rosemary Teresa, yr da of late Cecil John Whitehead, of The Old House, Crockham Hill, Edenbridge, and has issue.

𝕬rms – Quarterly, 1st and 4th per fesse indented gules and or a pale counterchanged, in chief two boars' heads couped of the second and in base a thistle slipped proper; 2nd and 3rd azure, on a pile or a lion statant of the first, on a chief azure, between two sprigs of oak slipped, a pale or, thereon a like sprig of oak, all counter-changed. 𝕮rest – 1st, in front of a thistle erect thereon a bee volant proper, a boar's head couped or; 2nd, between two oak branches erect proper, a lion statant per pale azure and or, holding in the mouth a sprig of oak also proper.
Residence – Copthall Place, Upper Clatford, Andover, Hants SP11 7LR.

SONS LIVING

MARK EDWARD, *b* 14 Aug 1965; *ed* Ampleforth and Trin Coll, Camb (MA); Major RE: *m* 1995, Dr Julia Catherine, da of T. D. Getley, of Wendover, Bucks, and has issue living, Emma Victoria, *b* 1998. —— Paul Duncan, *b* 1966, *ed* Ampleforth, and Keble Coll Oxford (MA); ACA: *m* 1990, Maria Barbara Antoinette, yst da of Prof Dr Karl-Heinz Menke, of Bonn, Germany, and has issue living, Cecilia Teresa Marie, *b* 1992, — Amelie, *b* 1995, — Lydia, *b* (twin) 1995. —— Simon Joseph, *b* 1967; *ed* Ampleforth, and Charing Cross Hosp, London; Maj RAMC: *m* 1998, Dr Helen J., yr da of Stuart Ferguson, of Romsey, Hants.

Know thyself

BROTHERS LIVING

Christopher Charles Jervis (The Old House, Staverton, nr Daventry, Northants NN1 6JA), *b* 1933; *ed* Ampleforth, and RMC Sandhurst; Lieut The Greys: *m* 1963, Sarah Loraine, 2nd da of Sir Humphrey Dodington Benedict Sherston Sherston-Baker, 6th Bt, and has issue living, Charles Patrick, *b* 1972, — Victoria Margaret, *b* 1965: *m* 19—, Tom Millar, — Katharine Jane, *b* 1966: *m* 1992 Keith Thompson, and has issue living, Jack *b* 1994, Benjamin Charles *b* 1996, — Lucy Mary, *b* 1974. —— Michael Herbert (Springkell, Eaglesfield, Dumfriess-shire), *b* 1934; *ed* Ampleforth; Capt Lowland Yeo; a JP for Dumfriess-shire: *m* 1963, Jennifer Mary, el da of Lt-Col Herbert Green, OBE, MC, of Manor House, Carlton Husthwaite, Thirsk, York, and has issue living, James Herbert, *b* 1963: *m* 19—, Rachel Alexandra, yr da of Peter Peddie, of Bannisters Farmhouse, Mattingley Green, Hants, and has issue living, Edward Herbert *b* 1998, Phoebe Charlotte *b* 1996, — Robert Charles, *b* 1969, — Sarah Catherine, *b* 1965, — Fiona Marion, *b* 1966: *m* 1993 James Patrick Hodson, and has issue (*see* Hodson, Bt), — Laura Rose, *b* 1967. —— Nicholas Swynfen, *b* 1938; *ed* Ampleforth: *m* 1st, 1963 (*m diss* 1975), Mabel, da of L— Dawson, of Plymouth; 2ndly, 1975 (*m diss* 1981), Maire, da of W— O'Reilly, of Dublin; 3rdly, 1984, Christina, da of Humberto Zambrano, of Ramos Arizpe, Mexico, and has issue living, (by 1st *m*) Alona Francesca, *b* 1964, — Karina Alicia, *b* 1966, — (by 2nd *m*) Ian Francis, *b* 1977, — Andrea Valerie, *b* 1975, — (by 3rd *m*) Alexander Edward, *b* 1985, — Christopher Andrew, *b* 1990, — Sophia Monica, *b* 1986.

COLLATERAL BRANCH LIVING

Issue of late Maj Brian Charles Johnson-Ferguson, TD, 2nd son of 2nd baronet, *b* 1908, *d* 1988: *m* 1947, Daphne Louie (Cloggers Cottage, Waterbeck, Lockerbie, Dumfriesshire), elder da of Brig Walter Andrew Stirling, DSO, MC, RA, of Polstead, Suffolk:—
Torquil Charles, *b* 1949; *ed* Stanbridge Earls: *m* 1980, Margaret, yr da of L. D. Finlay, of Ashgrove House, Hepscott, Morpeth, Northumberland, and has issue living, Ninian Charles, *b* 1983, — Iona, *b* 1981, — Ailsa Finlay, *b* 1988. —— †Denzil Crispin, *b* 1955; *ed* Charterhouse; *d* 1979. —— Merlin Louie, *b* 1950: *m* 1981, Peter James Dernie, of Kirtleton House, Waterbeck, Lockerbie, Dumfriesshire, son of late James Henry Dernie, of Preston, Lancs, and has issue living, Henry Crispin, *b* 1982, — Jemima Louie, *b* 1984, — Olivia Lucy, *b* 1986. —— Lorraine Giselle, *b* 1952: *m* 1975, Markus Luescher, and has issue living, Thomas, *b* 1978, — Callum, *b* 1982, — Ross, *b* 1987, — Kirsty, *b* 1980, — Nicola, *b* 1984.

The 1st baronet, Sir (Jabez) Edward (son of Jabez Johnson, JP, of Kenyon Hall, near Manchester), Chm of Jabez Johnson, Hodgkinson and Pearson (Limited), assumed by Roy licence 1881 the additional surname of Ferguson, and sat as MP for Mid, or Loughborough, Div of Leicestershire (*L*) 1885-6, and 1892-1900. The 2nd baronet, Sir Edward Alexander James Johnson-Ferguson, TD, was Lieut-Col and Brevet Col late Comdg Lanarkshire Yeo, and a Director of Tredegar Coal & Iron Co, Ltd.

FERGUSSON (NS) 1703, of Kilkerran, Ayrshire

Sweeter out of difficulties

That I may profit others

Sir CHARLES FERGUSSON, 9th *Baronet; b* 10 May 1931; *s* his father, *Sir* JAMES, FRSE, LLD, 1973; *ed* Eton: *m* 1961, Hon Amanda Mary Noel-Paton, da of Baron Ferrier (Life Baron), and has issue.

Arms – Azure, a buckle argent between three boars' heads couped or, in a dexter canton argent a saltire azure, surmounted of an inescutcheon or charged with a lion rampant within a double tressure flory counter-flory gules. Crest – A bee on a thistle proper. Supporters – Two gryphons or, armed and beaked gules.
Residence – Kilkerran, Maybole, Ayrshire KA19 7SJ.

SONS LIVING

ADAM, *b* 29 Dec 1962; Major Army Air Corps: *m* 1989, Jenifer Kirsty, yr da of Adam Thomson, of Ormiston, E Lothian, and has issue living, James, *b* 2 April 1996, — Samantha Kirsty *b* 1992, — Lucy Alice, *b* 1993. —— Joseph Victor, *b* 1965: *m* 1990, Emma Sarah Louise, yr da of (William) Martin Cracknell, of Freuchie, Fife, and has issue living, Oliver William, *b* 1993, — Flora Lucy, *b* 1995, — Louisa Katherine, *b* 1998.

BROTHER LIVING

Adam Dugdale (15 Warwick Gdns, W14 8PH) *b* 1932; *ed* Eton, and Trin Coll, Camb; Member European Parliament for West Strathclyde, 1979-84, Special Adviser, FCO 1985-89: *m* 1965, (Elizabeth Catherine) Penelope, da of late (Thomas) Peter Hughes, of Furneaux Pelham Hall, Herts, and has issue living, James, *b* 1966, — Marcus Francis, *b* 1972, — Petra Christian, *b* 1968: *m* 1997, Patrick Randal Gordon Cramsie, yr son of James Arthur Cramsie, of Lambourn, Berks, and has issue living, Hope Rose Penelope *b* 1999, — Lucy Josephine, *b* 1970.

SISTER LIVING

Alice Blanche Helen (*Baroness Renton of Mount Harry*), *b* 1934: *m* 1960, Baron Renton of Mount Harry, PC (Life Baron) and has issue (see that title).

COLLATERAL BRANCHES LIVING

Issue of late Rev Simon Charles David Fergusson, *b* 1907, *d* 1982, Lt-Col Argyll and Sutherland Highlanders, 2nd son of 7th baronet: *m* 1945, Auriole Kathleen (Alton Albany, Barr, Girvan, Ayrshire), da of late Com Sir Geoffrey Henry Hughes-Onslow, KBE, DSC, RN (*see* E Onslow, colls):—
Alexander Charles Onslow, *b* 1949; JP; MSP for Scotland South (*C*) since 1999: *m* 1974, Jane Merryn, da of G/Capt Bertram Barthold, OBE, RAF, of Langarth, St Merryn, Cornwall, and has issue living, Iain Alexander Onslow, *b* 1975, — Dougal George Onslow, *b* 1977, — Christopher David Onslow, *b* 1986. —— John Geoffrey Onslow (Old Nisthouse, Harray, Orkney Isles KW17 2LQ), *b* 1954: *m* 1979, Ann Caroline, yst da of G/Capt Bertram Barthold, OBE, RAF (ante), and has issue living, Catherine Alice, *b* 1982, — Joannah Ruth, *b* 1989. —— Henrietta Charity Onslow, *b* 1952.

Issue of late Brig Bernard Edward Fergusson (*Baron Ballantrae*), KT, GCMG, GCVO, DSO, OBE, yst son of 7th baronet, *b* 1911; *cr* Baron Ballantrae (Life Baron) 1972; *d* 1980: *m* 1950, Laura Margaret, who *d* 1979, da of late Lt-Col Arthur Morton Grenfell, DSO, TD (V Cobham, colls):—
(Hon) George Duncan (does not use courtesy title), *b* 1955: *m* 1981, Margaret Sheila, el da of Michael John Wookey, of Camberley, Surrey, and has issue living, Alexander Bernard Raukawa, *b* 1984, — Laura Margaret Huia, *b* 1982, — Alice Mary Marama, *b* 1986, — Elizabeth Sarah Tukino, *b* 1991.

Issue of late Adm Sir James Andrew Fergusson, KCB, KCMG, 2nd son of 6th baronet, *b* 1871, *d* 1942: *m* 1901, Githa Enid, who *d* 1964, da of late Thomas C. Williams, of Wellington, New Zealand:—
Margaret Edith, *b* 1903: *m* 1961, Ralph Beckett Scholfield, who *d* 1976, and *d* 1998. —— Augusta Susan, *b* 1904: *m* 1932, Capt George Francis Locke Marx, OBE, RN, who *d* 1965, and has issue living, Andrew John Locke (23A Nevern Sq, SW5 9PD), *b* 1933; Cdr RN: *m* 1st, 1963 (*m diss* 1979), Rosemary Evangeline, da of Christopher William Edward Collins, of The Old Rectory, Lackford, Bury St Edmunds; 2ndly, 1989, Amanda, da of Lt-Cdr Charles Reid, RAN, of Melbourne, Victoria, Australia, and has issue living (by 1st *m*), John William Francis *b* 1973, Caroline Elizabeth *b* 1964, Annabelle Mary *b* 1967: *m* 1996, Andrew Heap, son of Dr Derek Heap, of Bradford-on-Avon (and has issue living, Henry Robert *b* 1999), — David George Locke (43 Felden St, SW6), *b* 1936; Dir of John Rigby & Co: *m* 1975, Jill Morag, da of Bruce W. Dickie, of Whitehills, Abernyte, Perth, and has issue living, Francis Angus *b* 1981, Julian James *b* 1983.

Descendants of late Rt Hon Charles Dalrymple Fergusson (3rd son of 5th baronet), who assumed the surname and Arms of Dalrymple 1849, and was *cr* a *Baronet* 1887.
See Dalrymple, Bt.

Grandsons of late Robert Henry Duncan Fergusson (infra):—
Issue of late Robert Arthur George Fergusson, *b* 1878, *d* 1939: *m* 1912, Laura Gwendolen, who *d* 1962, da of late Arthur William English, of Wisbech, Cambridgeshire:—
Irwine Arthur (William Carey Court, 450 Bussen Highway, Busselton, W Australia 6280, Australia), *b* 1913; *ed* Fettes: *m* 1939, Pamela Vera, el da of Col P. R. Ayers, MC, of S Devon, and has issue living, Peter John Charles (Brookvale, La

Rue du Pont, St John, Jersey, CI JE3 4FF), *b* 1943: *m* 1st, 1966, Angela Star, da of late Capt W. H. Behenna, of Bitterne, Southampton; 2ndly, 1981, Anne Marie Ghislaine, yr da of late Maj Tom Brown, OBE, MC, Croix de Guerre, and has issue living (by 1st *m*), Sean James *b* 1973, Fiona Star *b* 1978, — Christopher Simon Arthur (3 Rosemary Lane, Scoriton, Devon TQ11 0JA), *b* 1949: *m* 1st, 1970, Susan Ann yst da of A. Probert, of Knowle, Bristol; 2ndly, 19—, Catherine Louise, yst da of J. Ratcliffe, of Fishguard, and has issue living (by 1st *m*), Charlotte *b* 1972, Harriett *b* 1974, — Valerie Ann, *b* 1941, — Sheena *b* 1958. —— Donald Andrew (4 St George's, Woolhope, Herefordshire HR1 4QR), *b* 1920; *ed* Fettes: *m* 1958, Patricia Dorothy, da of D. K. Orton, of Entebbe, Uganda, and has issue living, Colin Ivan Paul, *b* 1960: *m* 1989, Sheila Mary, yst da of M. Whalley, of Hereford, and has issue living, Laura Olivia *b* 1991, Alice Emily *b* 1994, — Martin Arthur, *b* 1963: *m* 1988, Angela Jayne, yst da of R. Cooper, of Portsmouth, and has issue living, Steven James, *b* 1991, Andrew Donald *b* 1992, — Heather Dorothy (twin), *b* 1963. —— Michael Ramsay (Box 959, Mutare, Zimbabwe), *b* 1922; *ed* Fettes, and Rhodes Univ, Grahamstown (BA 1948): *m* 1961, Joanna Rosalind, da of late H. Stratton, of Warminster, Wilts, and has issue living, Richard Anthony, *b* 1963.

Granddaughter of late Henry Duncan Fergusson, WS, 6th son of 4th baronet:—
    Issue of late Robert Henry Duncan Fergusson *b* 1849, *d* 1904: *m* 1877, Mabel Frances, who *d* 1930, da of late Robert Balfour Wardlaw-Ramsay, of Whitehall:—
Irene Hilda: *m* 19—, Douglas Langhorne, and has issue living. *Residence* – 313 Petersham Rd, Ham Common, Surrey.

Grandson of late Robert Dundas Octavius Fergusson, 8th son of 4th baronet:—
    Issue of late Robert Dundas Arthur Graham Fergusson, *b* 1851, *d* 1896: *m* 1877, Mary Rachel, who *d* 1923, da of late Francis Whitworth Russell (Russell, Bt, *cr* 1812, colls):—
A son, *b* 1880.

The 1st baronet was an eminent advocate. The 2nd baronet, sometime MP for Sutherland, was afterwards a Lord of Session (Lord Kilkerran). The 3rd baronet sat as MP for Ayrshire 1774-84 and 1790-96 and for Edinburgh 1784-9. He claimed in 1796 the Earldom of Glencairn (created 1488); the Lords decided that he had proved himself to be heir-general to Alexander, Earl of Glencairn, who died 1670, but had not proved his right to the Earldom. The 6th baronet, Rt Hon Sir James, GCSI, KCMG, CIE, PC, LLD, Grenadier Guards (*k* in Jamaica earthquake 1907), served in Crimean War (wounded at battle of Inkerman), sat as MP for Ayrshire 1854-7 and 1859-68, and for N-E Div of Manchester 1885-1906, and was under-Sec of State for India 1886-7, Under-Sec at Home Office 1867-8, Gov and Com-in-Ch of S Australia 1868-73, Gov of New Zealand 1873-5, and of Bombay 1880-85, Under-Sec of State for Foreign Affairs 1886-91, and Postmaster-Gen 1891-2. Sir Charles, GCB, GCMG, DSO, MVO, LLD, 7th baronet, was Gen in Army, Gov-Gen and Com-in-Ch, New Zealand 1924-30, Chm W Indies Closer Union Commn 1933, and Lord-lieut of Ayrshire 1937-50. Sir James, 8th Bt, author and historian; Keeper of the Records of Scotland 1949-69, and Lord-Lieut of Ayrshire 1969-73.

COLYER-FERGUSSON (UK) 1866, of Spitalhaugh, Peeblesshire

By strength and skill

Sir JAMES HERBERT HAMILTON COLYER-FERGUSSON, 4th *Baronet*, son of late Max Christian Hamilton Colyer-Fergusson, Capt RASC (*k* on active ser nr Ludgershall, 1940), el son of 3rd baronet; *b* 10 Jan 1917; *s* his grandfather, *Sir* THOMAS COLYER, 1951; *ed* Harrow and Balliol Coll, Oxford (BA 1939, MA 1945); formerly Capt The Buffs; 1939-45 War (prisoner 1940); Officer BR (ret).

Arms – Argent, a lion rampant azure armed and langued gules, on a chief engrailed of the last a mullet between two cinquefoils of the first. Crest – A dexter hand grasping a broken spear in bend sinister all proper.
Residence – Flat 8, 61 Onslow Square, SW7 3LS. *Club* – Naval and Military.

COLLATERAL BRANCH LIVING

Issue of late Sir Louis Forbes FERGUSSON, KCVO, 2nd son of 2nd baronet, *b* 1878, *d* 1962: *m* 1922, Elizabeth Frances Ethel, who *d* 1986, da of Seth Lewin, of Gt Bookham, Surrey:—
Christine Forbes, *b* 1934: *m* 1966, Charles Raymond Evans, MA, of 6 Fabyc House, Cumberland Rd, Kew, Surrey TW9 3HH.

The 1st baronet, Sir William LLD, FRS, a distinguished surgeon, was many years Sergeant-Surgeon to HM Queen Victoria. Sir James Ranken Fergusson, 2nd Bt, was Vice-Lieut for Peebleshire, and a Member of Roy Co of Archers (King's Body Guard for Scotland). Sir Thomas Colyer, 3rd Bt, was High Sheriff of Kent 1906, and assumed the additional surname of Colyer 1890.

FFOLKES, (GB) 1774, of Hillington, Norfolk
(Name pronounced "Foaks")

Sir ROBERT FRANCIS ALEXANDER, FFOLKES, OBE, 7th *Baronet*; *b* 2 Dec 1943; *s* his father, *Sir* (EDWARD JOHN) PATRICK BOSCHETTI, 1960; *ed* Stowe, and Christchurch, Oxford; with Save The Children Fund 1974-; OBE (Civil) 1990.

Arms – Per pale vert and gules, a fleur-de-lis argent. **Crest** – A dexter arm embowed vested per pale vert and gules, cuff ermine, holding in the hand a spear proper. *Residence* – Coast Guard House, Morston, Holt, Norfolk NR25 7BH.

SISTER LIVING

Sara Elizabeth, *b* 1946: *m* 1968, Maj Jocelyn James Rhys Wingfield, LI (*see* V Powerscourt, colls).

This family, in the person of Simon ffolkys, owned lands in Westley Waterless, Cambridgeshire, in 1486. Martin ffolkes, Pres of Roy and of Antiquarian Socs, inherited the Hovell estates in Norfolk through his mother, wife of Martin ffolkes, Attorney-Gen to Queen-Dowager of Charles II. The 5th baronet, the Rev Sir Francis Arthur Stanley, MVO, was an Hon Chap to Queen Victoria, a Chap-in-Ord to King Edward VII, and King George V, and a Chap to King Edward VIII and King George VI.

What will happen, will happen

TWISLETON-WYKEHAM-FIENNES (UK) 1916, of Banbury, co Oxford

Sir RANULPH TWISLETON-WYKEHAM-FIENNES, OBE, 3rd *Baronet*; *b* (*posthumous*) 7 March 1944; *s* his father, *Lieut-Col Sir* RANULPH, DSO, at birth; *ed* Eton; late Capt R Scots Greys; attached 22nd SAS Regt 1966, seconded SAF 1968; White Nile Hovercraft Expedition 1969; British Jostedals Glacier Expedition 1970; Scots Greys Headless Valley Expedition 1971; Vice-Pres World Expeditionary Assocn since 1974; North Greenland Jebel Shams Trials 1976; British North Pole Expedition 1977; first man, with Charles Burton, to reach both N and S Poles overland 1982 and first polar circumnavigation of the Earth 1979-82; led archaeological expedition which rediscovered the lost city of Ubar in Oman, 1992; led the Pentland South Pole Expedition 1992-93, achieving the first crossing of the Antarctic Continent unsupported, the longest unsupported polar journey in history; a Liveryman of Vintners' Co; author of *Talent for Trouble* 1970, *Icefall in Norway* and *The Headless Valley* 1972, *Where Soldiers Fear to Tread* 1975, *Hell on Ice* 1978, *Bothie the Polar Dog* (with his wife) 1985, *Living Dangerously* 1988, *The Feather Men* 1990, *Atlantis of the Sands* 1991, *Mind over Matter* 1993, *The Sett* 1998, and *Fit for Life* 1999; won one of Man of The Year Awards 1982 and led the Transglobe Circum-polar Expedition of 1979-82; OBE 1993, Dhofar Campaign Medal 1968,

Look for a brave spirit

Sultan's Bravery Medal 1970, Livingstones Gold Medal 1983, Gold Medal of the Explorers Club of New York 1983, Founders Medal R Geographical Soc 1984, Polar Medal 1987 (with bars for Arctic and Antarctica); Chm Offshore Abandonment Gp 1989: *m* 1970, Virginia Frances, Polar Medal 1987, da of late Thomas Pepper.

Arms – Quarterly, 1st and 4th azure, three lions rampant or, *Fiennes*; 2nd and 3rd argent, a chevron between three moles sable, *Twisleton*. **Crest** – 1st, a wolf sejant proper, gorged with a spiked collar, the line therefrom reflexed over

the back or, *Fiennes*; 2nd, an arm embowed, vested sable, cuffed argent, holding in the hand proper a mole spade or, headed and armed of the second.
Residence – Greenlands, Exford, Som TA24 7NU.

SISTERS LIVING

Susan Valerie, *b* 1933; *ed* Heathfield, Ascot and Cape Town Univ (BA 1951): *m* 1957, John Jervoise Fitzgerald Scott, Lt Col the Blues and Roys, and has issue living, Arabella Caroline, *b* 1959: *m* 1986, Francis D. Williams, — Venetia Lucy, *b* 1963. —— Celia Florence, *b* 1936; *ed* Trin Coll, Dublin (MB and BCh): *m* 1964, Dr Robert Savage Brown, of 4 Eagle Point Drive, Augusta, Georgia, USA, and has issue living, Anthony Newson *b* 1966; MD: *m* 1993, Sarah Halcyon, da of William Frantzich, and has issue living, Halcyon Eloise *b* 1998, — Deirdre Ann, *b* 1965: *m* 1987, James Evans Brabenec, and has issue living, James Jordan *b* 1993, Robert Tyler *b* 1995, Katherine Lee *b* 1998, — Nicola Lois, *b* 1969: *m* 1991, Keith Eric Schlechte, and has issue living, Alexandra Rose, *b* 1993, Elena Marie *b* 1996, Katrina Pauline *b* 1998. —— Gillian Audrey *b* 1938: *m* 1960, Timothy George Hoult, of Lower Octon Grange, Foxholes, Driffield, N Humberside, and has issue living, Andrew George, *b* 1966, — Rosalind Elfrida, *b* 1961, — Rachel Celia, *b* 1963.

WIDOW LIVING OF SECOND BARONET

AUDREY JOAN (*Audrey Lady Twisleton-Wykeham-Fiennes*), da of late Sir Percy Newson, 1st Bt; *ed* Heathfield, Ascot: *m* 1931, Lt-Col Sir Ranulph Twisleton-Wykeham-Fiennes, DSO, 2nd baronet, Roy Scots Greys, who *d* of wounds received in action in Italy 1943. *Residence* – Robins, Church Lane, Lodsworth, Sussex.

The 1st baronet, Hon Sir Eustace Edward Twisleton-Wykeham-Fiennes, 2nd son of 17th Baron Saye and Sele, was MP for Oxfordshire N, and Banbury Div (L) 1906-10 and 1910-18, and Gov and Com-in-Ch of Seychelles 1918-21, and of Leeward Islands 1921-9. The 2nd baronet Sir Ranulph, DSO, Lieut-Col Roy Scots Greys, *d* of wounds received in action in Italy 1943.

FINDLAY (UK) 1925, of Aberlour, co Banff (Extinct 1979)

Lt-Col *Sir* ROLAND LEWIS FINDLAY, 3rd and last *Baronet*.

DAUGHTER LIVING OF THIRD BARONET (*By 1st marriage*)

Barbara Jane (*Jane, Countess of Westmorland*) (The Old Vicarage, Badminton, Avon), *b* 1928: *m* 1950, 15th Earl of Westmorland, GCVO, who *d* 1993.

DAUGHTERS LIVING OF SECOND BARONET

Moira Juliet, *b* 1927: *m* 1951 (*m diss* 1984), Meyrick Adam Ovens, and has issue living, Michael John Meyrick (15 Criffel Av, SW2 4AY), *b* 1951; *ed* Sedbergh: *m* 1984 Sara Jane, elder da of John Robertson, and has issue living, John Henry Michael *b* 1989, — Charlotte Jean, *b* 1955: *m* 1975, Rupert Haydon White, of 78 Chelverton Rd, SW15 1RL, elder son of Major Simon Arnold Haydon White, of The Old Vicarage, Nether Wallop, Hants, and has issue living, Thomas Christopher *b* 1979; *ed* Eton, and Bristol Univ, Alexandra Charlotte *b* 1977; *ed* Sherborne Sch for Girls, and Durham Univ, Louisa Daisy, *b* 1983; *ed* Sherborne Sch for Girls. *Residence* – 15 Gayville Rd, SW11. —— Gillian, *b* 1930: *m* 1953, Maj-Gen John Myles (Robin) Brockbank, CBE, MC, DL, 9th/12th Royal Lancers, and has issue living, Henry John Findlay, *b* 1954; *ed* Eton, and Bristol Univ: *m* 1984, Serena, da of Capt John Macdonald-Buchanan, MC, of Cottesbrooke Hall, Northants (*see* By Woolavington, 1985 Edn), and has issue living, John *b* 1992, — Myles Robin, *b* 1958; *ed* Eton, and Ch Ch, Oxford: *m* 1989, Susanna J——, yr da of Sir John Drummond Milne, of Chilton House, Chilton Candover, Alresford, Hants, and has issue living, Harry John Myles *b* 1993, Joe Robin *b* 1997, Sophie Elizabeth *b* 1991, — Anthony Lionel, *b* 1960; *ed* Eton, and Ch Ch, Oxford: *m* 1997, Caroline Sarah, yr da of Capt Simon Hugh Walford, 17th/21st Lancers (*see* B Bellew), — Harriet Jane, *b* 1954: *m* 1977, Michael Robert McCalmont, of Winton House, Hampstead Norreys, Newbury, Berks RG18 0TF, yst son of late Maj Dermot Hugh Bingham McCalmont, MC, of Mount Juliet, Thomastown, co Kilkenny, and has issue living, Arthur James *b* 1984, Katherine Rose *b* 1981. *Residence* – Manor House, Steeple Langford, Salisbury.

WIDOWS LIVING OF SECOND AND THIRD BARONETS

LAURA HAWLEY ELSOM (*Laura, Lady Findlay*), da of late Percival Hawley, of Hull: *m* 1947, as his 2nd wife Sir (John) Edmund Ritchie Findlay, 2nd baronet, who *d* 1962. —— MARJORY MARY (*Lady Findlay*) (Lyddington, Uppingham, Leics), only da of late Hon Claud William Biddulph (*see* B Biddulph, colls), and formerly wife of Maj Philip Wilfred Cripps (who *d* 1965) : *m* 1964, as his 2nd wife, Lt-Col Sir Roland Lewis Findlay, 3rd baronet, who *d* 1979, when the title became *ext*.

COLLATERAL BRANCH LIVING

　　　　Issue of late Peter Findlay, 3rd son of 1st baronet, *b* 1910, *d* 1967: *m* 1933, Helen, who *d* 1965, da of
　　　　W. S. Brewer, of New York:—
Caroline Grace, *b* 1935: *m* 1st, 1956 (*m diss* 1962), Spencer William George Hooker; 2ndly, 1966, Wing-Cdr Lester
Francis Humphries, AFC, AFM, RAF (ret), of Twyford, Hants, and has issue living, (by 1st *m*) Philip Anthony, *b* 1957,
— Peter Neal Alan, *b* 1959, — (by 2nd *m*) Fiona Caroline, *b* 1968.

　　The 1st baronet, Sir John Ritchie Findlay, KBE, was proprietor of *The Scotsman*, Chm of Board of Trustees of National
Galleries of Scotland, and of National Housing Co, and Lord-Lieut of co Banff. Sir (John) Edmund Ritchie Findlayd, 2nd
Bt, was MP for Banffshire (*C*) 1935-45.

FINLAY (UK) 1964, of Epping, co Essex.

Sir DAVID RONALD JAMES BELL FINLAY, 2nd *Baronet*; *b* 16 Nov 1963; *s* his
father, Sir GRAEME BELL, 1st Bt, ERD, 1987; *ed* Marlborough, Grenoble
Univ and Bristol Univ: *m* 1998, Camilla, da of Peter Acheson, of
Castlecaulfield, co Tyrone.

Arms – Argent on a chevron azure between in chief two roses gules barbed and seeded
proper, and in base an estoile of eight points gules within two wings conjoined and erect
azure an ancient coronet or. **Crest** – In front of an oak tree fructed a whippet sejant proper
gorged with an ancient coronet pendent therefrom by the chains a portcullis azure.
Residences – Flat 8, Franchard, Albert St, St Helier, Jersey JE2 3YJ, CI.

SISTERS LIVING

Fiona Daphne Margaret Bell, *b* 1956. *Residence* – 18 Callcott Rd, NW6 7EA. —— Catrina
Mary Bell, *b* 1959: *m* 1984, Robin Nigel Cleave Knight Bruce, elder son of Nigel Knight
Bruce, of Crediton, Devon, and has issue living, Robert Evelyn Cleave, *b* 1993, — Siena-
Rose, *b* 1990, — Vita June, *b* 1992. *Residence* – The Sanctuary, Shobrooke, Crediton, Devon
EX17 1BG.

MOTHER LIVING

JUNE EVANGELINE (*June, Lady Finlay*), yr da of late Col Francis Collingwood Drake, OBE, MC, DL, 10th R Hussars, of
Mill Hurst, Harlow, Essex: *m* 1953, Sir Graeme Bell Finlay, 1st Bt, ERD, who *d* 1987. *Residence* – 45 Artesian Rd, W2
5DB.

FISON (UK) 1905, of Greenholme, Burley-in-Wharfedale, West Riding of Yorkshire

Sir (RICHARD) GUY FISON, DSC, 4th *Baronet*, *b* 9 Jan 1917; *s* his father, *Capt Sir* (WILLIAM) GUY, MC 1964; *ed* Eton, and New Coll, Oxford; 1939-45 War with RNVR (DSC): *m* 1952, Elyn, who *d* 1987, da of Mogens Hartmann, of Bordeaux, and formerly wife of Count Renaud Doria, and has issue.

𝔄rms – Per fesse azure and ermine, in chief three battle-axes argent, the staves or, and in base an heraldic tiger passant of the last. ℭrest – A demi-heraldic tiger or, collared gules, holding between the paws a shield argent, charged with a battle-axe sable.
Residence – Medwins, Odiham, Hants RG29 1NE.

SON LIVING

CHARLES WILLIAM, *b* 6 Feb 1954.

DAUGHTER LIVING

Isabelle Frances, *b* 1957.

BROTHER LIVING

John Michael, *b* 1920; *ed* Eton; 1939-45 War with RA. *Residence* – 9 de Walden St, W1.

Trust in God

The 1st baronet, Sir Frederick William, sat as MP for Doncaster Div, W Riding, Yorkshire (C) July 1895 to Jan 1906.

FITZGERALD (UK) 1880, of Valencia, co Kerry

Sir GEORGE PETER MAURICE FITZGERALD, MC (*The 23rd Knight of Kerry*), 5th *Baronet*; *b* 27 Feb, 1917; *s* his father, *Capt Sir* ARTHUR HENRY BRINSLEY, 1967; *ed* Harrow and RMC; Maj (ret) IG; Palestine 1938 (despatches), 1939-45 War in Italy (MC) 2nd in Command 1st Bn IG 1944; 2nd in Command 2nd Bn IG 1946: *m* 1939, Angela Dora, da of late Capt James Rankin Mitchell, of 2 Mansfield St, W1, and has issue.

𝔄rms – Ermine, a saltire gules; in centre point a cross pattée argent. ℭrest – A chevalier in complete armour on horseback at full speed, with his sword drawn and visor raised, proper; saddle gules, saddle-cloth or.
Residence – Colin's Farm House, 55 High St, Durrington, Salisbury, Wilts SP4 8AQ.

SON LIVING

ADRIAN JAMES ANDREW DENIS (16 Clareville St, SW7, and Lackaneask, Valentia Island, co Kerry; *Clubs* – Kildare St and University, and Pratt's), *b* 24 June 1940; *ed* Harrow; a Councillor Roy Borough of Kensington and Chelsea 1974, and Mayor 1984-85; Kt of Honour and Devotion of Sov. Mil. Order of Malta.

DAUGHTER LIVING

Rosanna, *b* 1945: *m* 1964, Count Richard Beaumont Melchior Gurowski (8th Count, Prussia, *cr* 1787) of North End House, Damerham, Fordingbridge, Hants, and has issue living, Iona, *b* 1967: *m* 1996, Oliver Forge, of 37 Devonshire Rd, W4; son of John Forge, and has issue living, Alexander Melchior *b* 1999, — Anya, *b* 1970.

My presence is victory

COLLATERAL BRANCHES LIVING

Grandsons of Robert John FitzGerald, 2nd son of 1st baronet:—
Issue of Lt-Col Peter Francis FitzGerald, DSO, *b* 1879, *d* 1968: *m* 1909, Baroness Adrienne de Geer, who *d* 1973, da of late Baron Gustave de Geer, of Zeist, Holland:—
(Peter) Desmond (Querns House, Cirencester, Gloucestershire; *Club* – Army and Navy), *b* 1910; Capt late R Tank Regt; Kt of Malta: *m* 1945, Elizabeth J. C. Norman, and has issue living, Anthony Desmond (*Club* - Kildare St and University), *b* 1953; *ed* Ampleforth; a Sloan Fell of London Business Sch: *m* 1986, Janine Heather, eldest da of A. R. Miller, of Badgers Hollow, Godalming, Surrey, and has issue living, Orlando Peter Desmond *b* 1989, — Caroline Rosemary, *b* 1946: *m* 1970, Maj Philip Statham, RA, of 10 Wyatts Drive, Thorpe Bay, Southend-on-Sea, Essex, and has issue living, Charles Reginald *b* 1971, Christopher Desmond *b* 1977, — Olivia Margaret GRAHAM (37 Cromwell Rd, SW7), *b* 1948, and has issue living, Alexandra Clare *b* 1974, — Louise Elizabeth, *b* 1951: *m* 1982, Richard John Burden, of 54 Emlyn Rd, W12 9TD, and has issue living, Jonathon Max Robert *b* 1986, Georgina Ann *b* 1983. —— Mervyn Robert Gustav (Pen Mill Cottage, Penselwood, Wincanton, Som), *b* 1911: *m* 1940, Hilary da of Percy Houghton Brown, LLD, and has issue living, Alastair Mervyn Malcolm (Red House Farm, Swallowcliffe, Salisbury, Wilts), *b* 1941: *m* 1964, Penelope Jane, el da of Lt-Col John Stewart Eyre, and has issue living, Colin John *b* 1970, Fiona Margaret *b* 1965: *m* 1996, Andrea Tiana, of Milan,

Italy, Katherine Lucy *b* 1967: *m* 1991, Richard Longbourne (and has issue living, Robert Alastair *b* 1995, Victoria Margaret *b* 1997), — Peter Robin (Pen Mill Farm, Penselwood, Wincanton, Som, and 48 Queen's Gate Terrace, SW8; Travellers' Club), *b* 1943; *ed* Canford, and Trin Coll, Oxford: *m* 1976, Sarah, da of John Christopher Dykes, of 31 Pembroke Gdns, W8, and has issue living, Alanna Clare Juliet *b* 1978, Miranda Jessica *b* 1980, Harriet Sarah Isabel *b* 1986, — Elizabeth Ann, *b* 1945: *m* 1969, Francis Mark Dineley, of Aubrey House, Aubrey Walk, W8, and Woodlands, Berwick St John, Shaftesbury, Dorset, and has issue living, Alexander Perin *b* 1973, Maria Frances *b* 1971.

Grandson of late Peter David FitzGerald, 3rd son of 1st baronet:—
    Issue of late Capt James Brinsley Peter FitzGerald, *b* 1894, *d* 1962: *m* 1924, Lady Moyra Marjorie Dawson-Damer, who *d* 1962, da of 5th Earl of Portarlington:—
Michael George Maurice (Gawcombe, Church Westcote, Oxford; South of Perth Yacht Club, and Farmers' Club), *b* 1925: *m* 1959, F. Ruth, da of Maj P. A. F. Spence, of Deddington Manor, Oxon, and has issue living, Peter Desmond Philip (Lansdowne Club) *b* 1961: *m* 1998, Camilla S., yr da of Russell Hanson, and of Mrs John Prescott, — Sarah Moyra, *b* 1962, — Ann Rachel (twin), *b* 1962: *m* 1989 Maj Timothy David Edward Morris (7th Gurkha Rifles) and has issue living, Christopher *b* 1991, Guy *b* 1993.

The title of Knight of Kerry was conferred upon his son Maurice by John Fitz Thomas FitzGerald, Lord of Decies and Desmond, by virtue of his royal seigniory as a Count Palatine, and his descendants have ever since been so styled in Acts of Parliament, patents under the Great Seal, and other legal documents. The 1st baronet was the 19th Knight of Kerry. The 2nd baronet, Capt Sir Maurice FitzGerald, CVO, served in Ashanti 1873-4 (several times mentioned in despatches, medal with clasp), and was an Extra Equerry to HRH the Duke of Connaught.

FITZGERALD (UK) 1903, of Geraldine Place, St Finn Barr, co Cork

A sea of trees

Rev (*Sir*) DANIEL PATRICK FITZGERALD, 4th *Baronet*; *b* 28 June 1916; *s* his brother, *Rev* (*Sir*) EDWARD THOMAS, 1988, but his name does not appear on the Official Roll of the Baronetage, nor does he use the title; a Roman Catholic Priest.

Arms – Ermine, on a saltire gules charged with two arrows saltirewise points downwards or, a chief arched of the second thereon a lymphan between two towers or. **Crest** – In front of three oak trees a knight mounted in full armour proper bearing on the sinister arm a shield argent charged with a civic crown gules.
Residence –

COLLATERAL BRANCH LIVING

    Issue of late Andrew FitzGerald, 4th son of 1st baronet, *b* 1885, *d* 1969: *m* 1916, Elizabeth Barry-Murphy, who *d* 1952:—
JOHN FINNBARR (Meadowlands, Wilton Rd, Cork), *b* 1918: *m* 1949, Margaret Hogg, and has issue living, Andrew Peter, *b* 1950, — Geraldine, *b* 1953. —— Andrew Joseph (60 Glenbrook Park, Rathfarnham, Dublin, 14), *b* 1922: *m* 1953, Patrica Clark, and has issue living, Paul Andrew, *b* 1966, — Anne, *b* 1955, — Helen, *b* 1959. —— Margaret Mary, *b* 1920.

    The 1st baronet, Sir Edward (son of Daniel FitzGerald, of Gurstmaurane, Iveleary, co Cork) was Lord Mayor of Cork, 1901, 1902 and 1903.

FITZHERBERT (GB) 1784, of Tissington, Derbyshire

Sir RICHARD RANULPH FITZHERBERT, 9th *Baronet*; *b* 2 Nov 1963; *s* his uncle, *Sir* JOHN RICHARD FREDERICK, 1989; *ed* Eton: *m* 1993, Caroline Louise, da of Maj Patrick Shuter, of Grangefield House, Tetbury, Glos, and has issue.

𝕬rms – Gules, three lions rampant or. 𝕮rest – A cubit arm in armour erect, the hand appearing clenched within the gauntlet all proper.
Seat – Tissington Hall, Ashbourne, Derbyshire DE6 1RA.

SON LIVING

FREDERICK DAVID, *b* 23 March 1995.

DAUGHTER LIVING

Francesca Norah, *b* 1998.

SISTERS LIVING

Selina Helen, *b* 1965. —— (Juliet) Sarah, *b* (twin) 1965: *m* 1992, Anthony J. Clay, of Lower House Farm, Nantyderry, Abergavenny, eldest son of Glynne Clay, of St Hilary, S Glamorgan, and has issue living, Henry Hastings, *b* 1996, — Posy Rose Charmian, *b* 1995. —— Lucy Hyacinthe, *b* 1967.

MOTHER LIVING

One (only) will I serve

Charmian Hyacinthe, yr da of late Samuel Ranulph Allsopp (*see* B Hindlip, colls): *m* 1962, Rev David Henry FitzHerbert, MC, yr brother of 8th baronet, who *d* 1976. *Residence* – Sycamore House, Tissington, Ashbourne, Derbys.

COLLATERAL BRANCHES LIVING

Grandchildren of late Arthur Richard FitzHerbert, son of late Lt-Col Richard Henry FitzHerbert, 2nd son of 3rd baronet:—
Issue of late Arthur Geoffry Marshall FitzHerbert, *b* 1882, *d* 1974: *m* 1908, Hilda Eunice, who *d* 1966, da of late W. Gray, of Marton, NZ:—
Arthur William (Tutaenui Rd, Marton, NZ), *b* 1922; 1939-45 War with RNZAF, and as Pilot Officer RAF: *m* 1952, Noeline Coral, da of Richard Kerkham, of Suva, Fiji, and has issue living, Arthur Gray, *b* 1954, — Madeline Grace, *b* 1953: *m* 1971 (*m diss* 1987), Barry Edward Fairburn, of Wanganui, NZ, and has issue living, Aaron Karl *b* 1972, Daniel Craig *b* 1974, Lisa Marie *b* 1975. —— Eileen Mildred, *b* 1919: *m* 1956, John Charles Shere, of Kahuterawa Rd, Palmerston North, NZ, and has an adopted son, Ian Geoffrey, *b* 1961: *m* 1984, Christine Gae Murcott, and has issue living, Caleb Charles David *b* 1992, Katie Elisabeth *b* 1985, Kelly Rose *b* 1989.

Issue of late Beresford Close FitzHerbert, *b* 1884, *d* 1969: *m* 1918, Gladys Ruby, who *d* 1985, da of John Owens, of Epsom, Auckland, NZ:—
Dorothy Grace, *b* 1920: *m* 1945, Robert William Smith, F/O RNZAF, and has issue living, Robert Phillip Beresford, *b* 1951, — Dorothy Christine, *b* 1946, — Pauline Beresford, *b* 1947, — Barbara Anne, *b* 1954. —— Ngaire Beresford (2/88 Riddell Rd, Glendowie 5, Auckland, NZ), *b* 1923: *m* 1950 (*m diss* 1972), John McRobert Calder, F/O RNZAF, and has issue living, John Beresford (232 Cook Dr, Whitianga, NZ), *b* 1953: *m* 1975 (*m diss* 1995), Christine Doreen Orange, and has issue living, Jude Anthony *b* 1976, Casey Beresford *b* 1988, Philippa Crystal *b* 1981, — Peter McRobert, *b* 1955: *m* 1st, 1980 (*m diss* 1991), Rosalind Mary Webb; 2ndly, 19—, Sandra Joy Welsh.

Grandchildren of late Herbert Haffenden FitzHerbert, el son of late Rev Alleyne FitzHerbert, 3rd son of 3rd baronet:—
Issue of late Egbert FitzHerbert, *b* 1863, *d* 1944: *m* 1st, 1891, Florence Grace, who *d* 1905, da of late Edward Gregory, of Feilding, New Zealand, 2ndly, 1912, Margaret, who *d* 1948, da of late Benjamin John Holloway, of Thame, Oxon, and widow of Charles Joseph Little, of Eldon Rd, Kensington, W:—
(By 1st *m*) John Alleyne, MC, *b* 1896; European War 1914-19 in France with 1st Australian Tunnelling Co (despatches, MC). —— †Herbert Haffenden, *b* 1905: *m* 1st, 1934 (*m diss* 1947), Stella Marguerite, da of late W. F. Seymour, of Auckland, NZ; 2ndly, 1947, Doris, da of late Gatland Gilberd, and *d* 1990, leaving issue (by 2nd *m*), Malcolm Haffenden (29 Gallway St, Windsor, Brisbane 4030, Australia), *b* 1947: *m* 1st, 1970 (*m diss* 1985), Christine Ballantine; 2ndly, 1985, Maureen Dawn, da of Gordon Howard Rosen, and has issue living (by 1st *m*), Jason Haffenden *b* 1971: *m* 1996, Melissa Ann, da of David James Couch (and has issue living, Blake David Haffenden *b* 1998), Paul Adrian *b* 1973: (has issue living by Katherine Therese, da of Len James Hooper, Joshua Paul *b* 1995, Danielle Therese *b* 1997), Craig Julian *b* 1976, — Kenneth Gregory (10 Mace Rd, Te Aroha, NZ), *b* 1951: *m* 1981, Peggy Denise, da of Lloyd Desmond Williams, and has issue living, Gavin Kenneth *b* 1981, Lance Gregory *b* 1983, Janet Denise *b* 1988, Deborah Holly *b* 1990, — Richard Alleyne (22a Thyra St, Dannevirke, NZ), *b* 1959: *m* 1981, Irene Anne, da of Murray Pearce, and has issue living, Daniel Alleyne *b* 1990, Melissa Anne *b* 1987, — Brenda Joan, *b* 1955: *m* 1975, Philip James Evison, of 16 Waihou Rd, Te Aroha, NZ, son of Arthur Cyril Evison, and has issue living, Angela *b* 1979, Tracie *b* 1980.

Grandchildren of late Horace FitzHerbert, 3rd son of late Herbert Haffenden FitzHerbert (ante):—
Issue of late Herbert FitzHerbert, *b* 1887, *d* 1958: *m* (Jan) 1915, Winifred, who *d* 1932, da of William Walpole:—
†William Michael, *b* (Nov) 1915: *m* 1947, Elsie Lillian, da of Charles Ogle, and *d* 1994, leaving issue, William Anthony (RD3 Hunterville, NZ), *b* 1950: *m* 1980, Gaylene Patricia, da of Phillip John Dawson, of Marton, and has issue living, Timothy William *b* 1982, Peter John *b* 1985, — Annette Margaret, *b* 1948: *m* 1968, Raymond Ernest Moss of RD7, Feilding, NZ, and has issue living, Helen Jane *b* 1970: *m* 1991, Hamish Andrew Williamson, Jo Ann, *b* 1972, Nicola Ann *b* 1978, — Jennifer Ann, *b* 1953: *m* 1st, 19— (*m diss* 19—), Gordon Bason; 2ndly, 19—, Nigel Bevin, and has issue living,

(by 1st *m*) Andrew Gordon *b* 1975, Anna Elise *b* 1970, Elizabeth Francis *b* 1985, (by 2nd *m*) Patrick *b* 1991, Emma (triplet) *b* 1991, Katie (triplet) *b* 1991. —— Mary Winifred, *b* 1917: *m* 1941, Raymond Windelborn. —— Eleanor Margaret, *b* 1919. *Residence* – 66 Brunswick St, Lower Hutt, New Zealand.

Issue of late Norman FitzHerbert, *b* 1889, *d* 1961: *m* 1919, Evelyn, who *d* 1992, da of late Robert M. Pemberton, CE, of Waikare, NZ:—
John Anthony (135 Tirau Rd, Putaruru, NZ), JP, ACA, *b* 1920: *m* 1st, 1942, Martha Betty, who *d* 1967, da of William George Hope; 2ndly, 1968, Gaynor Hudson, widow of Gordon Martin, of Hastings, NZ, and has issue living (by 1st *m*), David Anthony (10 Kurahaupo St, Orakei, Auckland 1005, NZ), *b* 1945; ACA: *m* 1st, 1969 (*m diss* 1998), Leith Alix Margaret, da of Clive A. Morton, of Auckland, NZ; 2ndly, 1999, Jeannette, da of Rolando A. Lee, of Quezon City, Philippines, and has issue living (by 1st *m*), Nicholas Anthony *b* 1975; BA, BCom, Jochen Richard *b* 1978, Matthew David *b* 1981, — Timothy John (Martins Bay, RD 2, Warkworth, NZ), *b* 1951: *m* 1974, Prudence Mary, da of T. W. Bush, of Auckland, NZ, and has issue living, Stephen John *b* 1984, Anna Elizabeth *b* 1979, Jane Prudence *b* 1981, — Catherine Mary, *b* 1947: *m* 1969, Gary Victor Sigley, of 12 Bannockburn Pl, Auckland 5, NZ, and has issue living, Michael Ainsley *b* 1974, Christina Evelyn *b* 1971, Haidee Margaret *b* 1979, — Margaret Alison, *b* 1952: *m* 1973, Robert Stephen Wickman, of 35 Western St, Matamata, NZ, and has issue living, John Stephen *b* 1983, Chloe Jennifer *b* 1986. —— Richard Gurden (4 Anderson St, Putaruru, NZ), *b* 1922.

Grandchildren of late Rev James FitzHerbert, 2nd son of late Rev Alleyne FitzHerbert (ante):—
Issue of late Humphrey Beresford FitzHerbert, *b* 1879, *d* 1951: *m* 1st, 1907, Kathleen, who *d* 1941, da of Charles Alexander, of Liverpool; 2ndly, 1941, Winifred Ivy Bing, who *d* 1962:—
(By 2nd *m*) Humphrey Bing Vivian (36 Westover Rd, Broadstairs, Kent CT10 3ES), *b* 1942: *m* 1971, Pamela Joan, da of James Sidney Pitt, of 7 Streete Court Rd, Westgate on Sea, Kent. —— Susan Eirene Angelina, *b* 1945: *m* 1st, 1964, Robert Viggo Jensen; 2ndly, 1974, Robert Coleman; 3rdly, 1986, John Poultney, of 2 Bethel Cottages, Laundry Rd, Minster, Ramsgate, Kent CT12 4HJ, and has issue living (by 1st *m*), Jetta Elva, *b* 1965; changed her name to Claire Coleman: *m* 1986, Mark Tourney, of 10 Prices Av, Cliftonville, Margate, Kent CT9 2NS, — (by 2nd *m*) Josephine, *b* 1975, — Gale, *b* 1977: *m* 1998, Simon Leigh, of 28 H. Jones Crescent, Goose Green Park, Aldershot GU11 2QH, and has issue living, Harrison *b* 1999.

Issue of late Capt Douglas Cecil FitzHerbert, *b* 1882, *d* 1933: *m* 1924, Daphne, who *d* 1979, da of late Henry Joseph Wigram (*see* Wigram, Bt, colls, 1980 Edn):—
(Alleyne) John, *b* 1931; *ed* Denstone; Capt Sherwood Rangers Yeo (TA) (ret): *m* 1959, Judith Mary, da of late Ernest T. Walker, and has issue living, (Amanda) Sara, *b* 1964; *ed* Oakham, and Swansea Univ (BSc). *Residence* – 3 The Green, Frieston, Grantham, Lincs NG32 3BZ.

Grandsons of late Godfrey White FitzHerbert (infra):—
Issue of late Henry FitzHerbert, *b* 1908, *d* 1960: *m* 1940, Betty (who *m* 2ndly, 19—, Robert Fulton), da of Arthur W. Barnley, of Kiriga Estate, Thika, Kenya:—
Henry Nicholas (4 Swallow St, Flamingo Vlei, Cape Town 7405, S Africa) *b* 1952: *m* 1st, 1975 (*m diss* 1982), Karin Schweiger; 2ndly, 198—, — and has issue living, (by 1st *m*) Stuart, *b* 198—, — Liesel Tanya FitzHerbert, *b* 1979. —— Simon John, *b* 1953.

Granddaughter of late John Knight FitzHerbert, 5th son of 3rd baronet:—
Issue of late Godfrey White FitzHerbert, *b* 1864, *d* 1939: *m* 1900, Anna Rachel, who *d* 1961, da of late Henry Alleyne Pile (Alleyne, Bt, colls):—
Judith Agnes (c/o Emmanuel Grammar School, Derwen Fawr Rd, Swansea), *b* 1914.

The 1st baronet was 9th in male descent from Nicholas, 2nd son of John FitzHerbert, of Somersal Herbert, whose ancestors possessed it from the beginning of the 13th century. Nicholas, died 1472, having acquired Tissington by his marriage with Margaret, da of Robert Fraunceys, of Foremark, and grand-da and co-heir of Sir Thomas Clinton (2nd son of 3rd Baron Clinton).

FLAVELLE (UK) 1917, of Toronto, Dominion of Canada (Extinct 1985)

Sir (JOSEPH) DAVID ELLSWORTH FLAVELLE, 3rd and last *Baronet*.

DAUGHTERS LIVING OF THIRD BARONET

Muriel Catherine, *b* 1944: *m* 1967, Rodger Henderson, of 242 Melrose Av, Toronto, Ontario M5M 1Z1, Canada, son of Peter Henderson, of Hamilton, Canada, and has issue living, Laura Katherine, *b* 1968, — Heather Anne, *b* 1971. —— Virginia Anne, *b* 1947: *m* 1970, Charles Arthur Millar, of 206 Arichat Rd, Oakville, Ontario, Canada, son of Charles Arthur Millar, of Mississauga, Ontario, and has issue living, Scott Arthur, *b* 1972, — Colin David, *b* 1976. —— Josephine Elizabeth, *b* 1950: *m* 1974, David Kenneth Martin, of 16 Meadowglade Crescent, Willowdale, Ontario, Canada, son of Dr Gordon Martin, of N York, Ontario, and has issue living, Christopher Flavelle, *b* 1979, — Andrew Flavelle, *b* 1983.

DAUGHTER LIVING OF SECOND BARONET

Clara Elizabeth, *b* 1918: *m* 1941, Gage Hayward Love, son of Harry Hayward Love, and has issue living, Gage Ellsworth, *b* 1942, — David Hayward, *b* 1946, — Peter Flavelle, *b* 1948, — William Geoffrey, *b* 1951.

WIDOW LIVING OF THIRD BARONET

MURIEL BARBARA (*Lady Flavelle*), da of David Reginald Morton: *m* 1942, Sir (Joseph) David Ellsworth Flavelle, 3rd Bt, who *d* 1985. *Residence* – 21490 Bay Village Dr, Fort Myers Beach, Florida 33931, USA.

AUBREY-FLETCHER (GB) 1782, of Clea Hall, Cumberland

Sir HENRY EGERTON AUBREY-FLETCHER, 8th *Baronet*; *b* 27 Nov 1945; *s* his father, *Sir* JOHN HENRY LANCELOT, 1992; *ed* Eton; High Sheriff Bucks 1995-96, DL Bucks 1997, Vice Lord-Lieut for Bucks since 1997: *m* 1976, (Sara) Roberta, da of late Maj Robert Buchanan, of Blackpark Cottage, Evanton, Ross-shire, and of late Mrs Ogden White, of Kiltinan Castle, co Tipperary, and has issue.

Arms – Quarterly: 1st and 4th, argent, a cross engrailed sable between four pellets each charged with a pheon argent, *Fletcher*; 2nd and 3rd azure, a chevron between three eagles' heads erased or, *Aubrey*. Crest – 1st, a horse's head argent, *Fletcher*; 2nd, an eagle's head erased or, *Aubrey*.
Address – Estate Office, Chilton, Aylesbury, Bucks HP18 9LR.

SONS LIVING

Martis, non cupidinis

Of war, not of love

JOHN ROBERT, *b* 20 June 1977. —— Thomas Egerton, *b* 1980. —— Harry Buchanan, *b* 1982.

UNCLES LIVING (*sons of 6th baronet*)

Lancelot Philip, *b* 1919; *ed* Eton; Capt (ret) Grenadier Gds; 1939-45 War (wounded, prisoner): *m* 1952, Audrey Muriel, who *d* 1993, only da of (Frederick) Ronald Oliver (*see* B Hindlip, colls, 1990 Edn), and has issue living, Mark Lancelot, *b* 1964; *ed* Harrow, — Jane Elizabeth, *b* 1961: *m* 1st, 1988 (*m diss* 1997), Jonathan Mark Davies; 2ndly, 1997, Desmond John Barron, of Rydal, Turners Hill Rd, Crawley Down, W Sussex RH10 4NW, and has issue living (by 1st *m*), James Robert *b* 1988, Katrina Elizabeth *b* 1991, Alexandra Sophie *b* 1993, (by 2nd *m*), Harry *b* 1997, Charlotte *b* (twin) 1997. *Residence* – Wychden, Chobham, Surrey. —— Edward Henry Lancelot (Stanford Hall, Lutterworth, Leics LE17 6DH), *b* 1930; *ed* Eton, and New Coll, Oxford; Lt-Col Gren Gds (ret); DL Northants: *m* 1st, 1953, Bridget Mary, who *d* 1977, el da of Brig Sir Henry Robert Kincaid Floyd, 5th Bt, CB, CBE; 2ndly, 1981, Hon Mary Penelope Verney-Cave (*Baroness Braye* in her own right), and has issue living (by 1st *m*), Richard Edward Henry, *b* 1954; *ed* Bradfield Coll, and RMA Sandhurst; Col late Gren Gds (despatches 1988): *m* 1980, Caroline Margaret Jolley, step da of Maj Henry Charles Blosse-Lynch, Irish Gds, of Headley, Newbury, Berks, and has issue living, George Richard Edward *b* 1985, — Patrick John Kincaid (Home Farm House, Ascott Park, Wing, Beds LU7 0PP), *b* 1955; *ed* Bradfield Coll, and RAC Cirencester: *m* 1977, Elizabeth Ann, el da of late Victor Sheerman, and has issue living, Rebecca Louise *b* 1981, Victoria Mary *b* 1982, — Gillian Mary, *b* 1958: *m* 1991, Miles Courtenay Ambler, yr son of Capt Quintin Ambler, of Little Orchard, Chapmanslade, Wilts, and has issue living, Henry Richard Edward *b* 1994, Camilla Mary *b* 1992.

WIDOW LIVING OF SIXTH BARONET

NANCY CECIL (*Nancy, Lady Aubrey-Fletcher*), da of Joseph Cecil Bull, and widow of Maj Charles Reynolds: *m* 1965, as his 2nd wife, Maj Sir Henry Lancelot Aubrey-Fletcher, 6th Bt, CVO, DSO, who *d* 1969. *Residence* – Barnfield, Delly End, Hailey, Witney, Oxon.

COLLATERAL BRANCHES LIVING

Issue of late Nigel Chilton Aubrey-Fletcher, 2nd son of 6th baronet, *b* 1914, *d* 1980: *m* 1942, Areta Mae (4 Monmouth Court, Church Lane, Lymington, Hants SO41 3RB), da of Frederick Lees, of Hamilton, Ont, Canada:—
Philip Nigel (9 Kings Satorn Rd, Lymington, Hants SO41 0QS), *b* 1941; *ed* Millfield: *m* 1969, Susan Anne, only da of Wing-Cdr M. L. Bathe, RAF (ret), and has issue living, Caroline Susan, *b* 1973, — Elizabeth Claire, *b* 1976. —— David Lancelot (Summer Lodge, 104 Western Rd, Tring, Herts H23 4BJ), *b* (twin) 1944; *ed* Millfield: *m* 1974, Carolyn Cochrane, only da of Kenneth F. Neale, of Beoley, Worcs, and has issue living, Sophie Rebecca, *b* 1976.

Issue of late John Lowther FLETCHER, 6th son of 3rd baronet, *b* 1851, *d* 1928: *m* 1893, Emily, who *d*
1937, da of late William Burkwood, and widow of Cecil H. Weston:—
Grace Vaughan, *b* 1891. —— Jacquetta May, *b* 1894: *m* 1919, Ronald G. Seaburne-May, Capt Sherwood Forresters, who
d 1940, and has issue living, Daphne, *b* 1923, — Jacquetta Jane, *b* 1929.

Henry Fletcher, of Cockermouth, entertained Mary, Queen of Scots, on her journey from Workington to Carlisle, 1568,
and presented her with robes of velvet, for which she returned him a letter of thanks. From him descended Sir Richard
Fletcher, whose son, Henry, was created a baronet, 1640. He raised a regiment for Charles I, and was slain at Rawton
Heath. The baronetcy expired with Sir Henry, 3rd baronet, who *d* a monk at Douay 1712. Sir Henry, 1st baronet of the
present creation, was a Cdr in Navy of HEICS; a distinguished Director of the East India Co, and MP for Cumberland
1768-1802. The 4th baronet, Rt Hon Sir Henry Aubrey-Fletcher, CB, sat as MP for Horsham (*C*) 1880-85, and for Lewes,
1885-1910. He was Parliamentary Groom-in-Waiting to Queen Victoria 1885-86, and assumed by Roy licence 1903 the
additional surname and arms of Aubrey. His brother Sir Lancelot, 5th baronet, also assumed by Roy licence 1910 this
additional surname and arms Maj Sir Henry Lancelot Aubrey-Fletcher, 6th baronet, was Lord Lieut of Bucks 1954-61,
and HM Lieut of Body Guard of Hon Corps of Gentlemen-at-Arms 1956-57.

FLOYD (UK) 1816

*Bearing patiently the dust and
the sun*

Sir GILES HENRY CHARLES FLOYD, 7th *Baronet*; *b* 27 Feb 1932; *s*
his father, *Lt-Col Sir* JOHN DUCKETT, TD, 1975; *ed* Eton; High
Sheriff of Rutland 1968; Chm Burghley Estate Farms Ltd: *m* 1st,
1954 (*m diss* 1978), Lady Gillian Moyra Katherine Cecil, da of 6th
Marquess of Exeter; 2ndly, 1985, Judy Sophia, formerly wife of
Thomas Ernest Lane, of Tickencote Hall, Stamford, and elder da
of William Leonard Tregoning, CBE, of Landue, Launceston,
Cornwall, and has issue by 1st *m*.

Arms – Sable, a lion rampant-reguardant argent, on a chief embattled or a
sword erect proper, pommel and hilt or, the blade passing through an eastern
crown gules, between two tigers' faces also proper. Crest – A lion rampant-
reguardant argent, murally crowned gules, bearing a flag (representing the
standard of Tippoo Sultan) flowing to the sinister proper.
Residence – Tinwell Manor, Stamford, Lincs. *Clubs* – Turf, and Farmers'.

SONS LIVING (By 1st marriage)

DAVID HENRY CECIL (Manor Farm, Bowerchalke, nr Salisbury, Wilts SP5 5BU), *b*
2 April 1956; *ed* Eton, and RMA Sandhurst; late 15/19th Hussars; ACA 1983,
FCA 1993; merchant banker: *m* 1981, Caroline Ann, da of John Henry Beckly,
of Manor Farm Cottage, Bowerchalke, Salisbury, Wilts, and has issue living,
Suzanna Mary Caroline, *b* 1983, — Claire Gillian Ann, *b* 1986. — Henry
Edward Cecil, *b* 1958: *m* 1994, Leonor, da of late Sergio Castillo, of Santiago de
Chile, and has issue living, Henry William, *b* 1994, — Daniela Sofia, *b* 1996.

BROTHER LIVING

John Edmund Kincaid, *b* 1936; *ed* Canford; late Capt 15th/19th Hussars; Founder and Chm Floyd Oil Participations plc
1979-88: *m* 1st, 1965 (*m diss* 1978), Victoria Jane, el da of late Richard N. Cannon, OBE, of Combe Place, Lewes; 2ndly,
1978, Jocelyn Ishabel Ann, widow of David Algernon Fleming (*see* Borthwick, Bt, colls), and 2nd da of late Sir John
MacLeod, TD, late Capt Queen's Own Cameron Highlanders, of Bunkers Hill, Farmington, Northleach, Glos (*see* B
Dulverton, colls, 1995 Edn), and has issue living (by 1st *m*), Clare Victoria, *b* 1966: *m* 1993, David Simon Townshend
Boscawen (*see* V Falmouth, colls), — Nicola Anne, *b* 1967: *m* 1996, Henry D. Pettifer, yr son of David Pettifer, —
Marina Jocelin, *b* 1971. *Residence* – 8 Riverpark Court, 22/23 Embankment Gdns, SW3 4LW.

COLLATERAL BRANCHES LIVING

Issue of late Lt-Col Charles Murray Floyd, OBE, RE, yst son of 4th baronet, *b* 1905, *d* 1971: *m* 1948,
Mary Elizabeth, OBE, JP, DL, who *d* 1996, only child of Robert Fleetwood Fuller, of Great Chalfield,
Melksham, Wilts, and widow of Lt-Col Patrick John Salvin Boyle, RSF (*see* E Glasgow, colls):—
Robert Charles (Great Chalfield, Melksham, Wilts; Turf and Beefsteak Clubs), *b* 1949; *ed* Eton, Keble Coll, Oxford, and
Pennsylvania Univ, USA; DL Wilts 1996: *m* 1977, Patricia Jan, yst da of Wing Cdr Timothy Ashmead Vigors, DFC, RAF,
of Coolmore, Fethard, co Tipperary, and has issue living, Charles Oliver, *b* 1978, — James Robert, *b* 1981, — Alexander
Edward, *b* 1987. —— Thomas Henry (Withey Place, Shalden, nr Alton, Hants), *b* 1951; *ed* Eton, and Univ Coll, Oxford:
m 1977, (Penelope) Sarah, el da of Sir James Cleminson, KBE, MC, DL, of Loddon Hall, nr Norwich, and has issue
living, Henry James, *b* 1979, — John, *b* 1981. —— William Duckett (71 rue Souveraine, 1050 Brussels, Belgium), *b* 1956;
ed Eton, and New Coll, Oxford: *m* 1989, Principessa Donna Vittoria Valeria, elder da of late Prince Raimondo Alliata di
Villafranca, of Palermo, Italy, and has issue living, Antony Edmond, *b* 1995, — Priscilla, *b* 1992.

Granddaughters of late Lt-Col Arthur Bowen Floyd, DSO, OBE, 2nd son of late Rev Charles Green-
wood Floyd, 4th son of 2nd baronet:—
Issue of late John Anthony Floyd, *b* 1923; Chm Christie's 1974-88; *d* 1998: *m* 1948, Margaret Louise
(Ecchinswell House, Newbury, Berks), da of Maj Hugo Rosselli:—
Elizabeth Joanna, *b* 1951. —— Caroline Philippa, *b* 1953: *m* 1984, Charles Henry Curzon Coaker, son of Maj-Gen Ronald
Coaker, of Daleacre House, Lockington, Derby, and has issue living, Henry John Curzon, *b* 1986, — Thomas James
Curzon, *b* 1987, — Molly Harriet, *b* 1990.

Issue of late Charles Ashburnham Floyd, 6th son of 2nd baronet, *b* 1838, *d* 1920: *m* 1867, Mary, who *d* 1907, da of George Pomeroy, of Exeter:—
Julia Miranda Laura: *m* 1926, as his 2nd wife, Col John Spottiswoode Purvis, CBE, late RE, who *d* 1927. —— Gertrude Frederica Mary Ashburnham.

    This family, of Welsh origin, was settled in Cheshire and Shrewsbury. Gen Sir John Floyd, 1st Bt, Col 8th Light Dragoons, distinguished himself in India as Col of 19th Light Dragoons, and was 2nd in command at the taking of Seringapatam, 1799, His daughter, Julia, *m* Sir Robert Peel the statesman. Brig Sir Henry Robert Kincaid Floyd, 5th Bt, CB, CBE, late 15th/19th Hussars (Col 1947-57) was Equerry to HRH the Duke of Gloucester 1927-28; BGS 8 Corps 1944, and Ch of Staff 8th Army 1944-45, Lord Lieut of Bucks 1961-68; HM Lieut of Body Guard of Hon Corps of Gentlemen-at-Arms 1966-68.

Foley-Philipps, see Philipps.

FORBES (NS) 1630, of Craigievar, Aberdeenshire

Sir JOHN ALEXANDER CUMNOCK FORBES OF CRAIGIEVAR, 12th *Baronet*, son (by 3rd *m*) of late Rear Adm Hon Arthur Lionel Ochoncar Forbes-Sempill, yst son of 17th Lord Sempill; *b* 29 Aug 1927; *s* his cousin, *Hon Sir* EWAN, 1991; *ed* Stowe; former Capt Seaforth Highlanders; JP Wigtown 1978: *m* 1st, 1956 (*m diss* 1963), Penelope Margaret Ann, only da of Arthur Gordon Grey-Pennington; 2ndly, 1966, Jane Carolyn, only da of Charles Gordon Evans, of Portpatrick, Wigtownshire.

Arms – Azure, a cross patée fitchee or between three bear's heads couped argent, muzzled gules. **Crest** – A cock proper. **Supporters** – *Dexter*. A knight in armour of the fifteenth century, armed at all points, leaving the beaver of his helmet up and leaning on a shield or, charged with a lion rampant gules armed and langued azure—within a double tressure flowered and counter-flowered with fleurs-de-lis of the second; *Sinister*, a bear argent, muzzled gules.
Residence – Benevean, Kendoon, St John's Town of Dalry, Castle Douglas, Kirkcudbrightshire DG7 3UB.

HALF-SISTER LIVING

Janet, *b* 1920; formerly Sergeant ATS: *m* 1958, Norman Walker, who *d* 1994, having assumed by deed poll 1958 the additional surname of Forbes before his patronymic, and has issue living, Iain, *b* 1960. *Residence* – The Post House, Midlem, Selkirk TD7 4QB.

WIDOW LIVING OF ELEVENTH BARONET

ISABELLA (*Hon Lady Forbes of Craigievar*), da of late Alec Mitchell, of Glenrinnes, Banffshire: *m* 1953, Hon Sir Ewan Forbes of Craigievar, 11th Bt, who *d* 1991.

COLLATERAL BRANCHES LIVING

Grandchildren of late Lt-Col James Ochoncar Forbes, yr son of late James Ochoncar Forbes of Corse, Lumphanan, Aberdeen, brother of 17th Lord Sempill:—
Issue of late Lt-Col Patrick Walter Forbes, OBE, *b* 1914, *d* 1979: *m* 1939, Margaret Hawthorne (Gardener's Cottage, Breda, Alford, Aberdeenshire AB3 8NN), da of Charles Hawthorne Lydall, of Brightling, Sussex:—
ANDREW IAIN OCHONCAR, *b* 28 Nov 1945; *ed* Trin Coll, Glenalmond, RMA Sandhurst, and St Catherine's Coll, Oxford (MA); Maj (ret) Gordon Highlanders. *Residence* – 12 Denham Green Place, Edinburgh EH5 3PB. —— Mhairi Margaret, *b* 1942. —— Shelagh Anne, *b* 1948.

Descendants of Duncan Forbes (who *m* 1852, Hon Sarah Forbes, sister of 17th Lord Sempill), el son of Alexander Forbes, 5th son of Duncan Forbes-Mitchell, 2nd son of 4th Bt:—
See L Sempill, colls.

Granddaughter of late Capt Arthur Newton Forbes-Gordon, el son of late Arthur Forbes-Gordon (infra):—

Issue of late Maj Arthur Dalrymple Forbes-Gordon of Langlee, Cameron Highlanders, *b* 1872, *d* 1931: *m* 1902, Dorothy Ione Helen, who *d* 1964, da of late Frederick Morton Eden (Eden, Bt, colls):—

Christian Dorothy ROYLE, *b* 1910; resumed the surname of Royle 1959: *m* 1st, 1934 (*m diss* 1938), Maj Frederick George Margaritus Grey, Highland LI; 2ndly, 1939, Maj John Popplewell Royle, Glider Pilot Regt, who was *ka* at Arnham 1944; 3rdly, 1950, Lt-Cdr John Charles Grattan, DSC, RN, and has issue living, (by 2nd *m*) Mark John Forbes, *b* 1941.

Grandson of late Capt William Balfour Forbes, AM, RN (infra):—

Issue of late Lt Arthur Walter Forbes, DSO, RN, *b* 1892, *d* lost at sea 1918: *m* 1917, Elizabeth (Eveline Betty), (who *d* 1961, having *m* 2ndly, 1919, Cdr John Gordon Aitchison, OBE, RN (Aitchison, Bt), who *d* 1964), da of late William Tudor Sutherland, of Skibo Castle, Sutherland:—

Arthur Michael Gerald Sutherland (*posthumous*) (11 Coxwell Ct, Cirencester, Glos GL7 2BQ), *b* 1918; *ed* Sherborne, and RMC Sandhurst; Maj (ret) King's Own Scottish Borderers; served World War II and Korea: *m* 1947, Phoebe Mabel, who *d* 1989, da of late Lt-Col Cyril Charles Johnson Barrett, CSI, CIE, and has issue living, Christine Helen, *b* 1949, — Lorna Betty May *b* 1952: *m* 1974, Martin John Guy Knights, MA, MB BS, MRCGP, DA, of Jenners Cottage, Poulton, Glos, and has issue living, Lucy Mary *b* 1980, Amelia May *b* 1981, Daisy Stella *b* 1987.

Grandson of late Arthur Forbes-Gordon, son of late Lt-Col Arthur Forbes, 5th son of 4th Bt:—

Issue of late Capt William Balfour Forbes, AM, RN, *b* 1845, *d* 1928: *m* 1889, Helen, who *d* 1958, da of late Capt Walter B. Persee, 90th Regt:—

William (Awosting, RD2 Hewitt, New Jersey 07421, USA), *b* 1905.

The Forbes of Craigievar, Aberdeenshire, descend from Patrick Forbes of Corse, 3rd son of 2nd Lord Forbes. Sir William Forbes of Craigievar, el son of William Forbes of Corse and nephew of Sir Arthur Forbes (*see* E Granard) was *cr* a *Baronet* of Nova Scotia with remainder to his heirs male 1630. He commanded a troop of horse in the Civil Wars, sat as MP for Aberdeen, and received a grant of 16,000 acres in New Brunswick. Sir William Forbes, 5th Bt, *m* 1780, the Hon Sarah Sempill, el da of the 12th Baron Sempill, and Sir William, 8th Bt (who *s* 1846), *s* as 17th Lord Sempill 1884, and assumed in 1885 the additional and principal surname of Sempill. On the death of 19th Lord Sempill 1965, the Lordship descended to his daughter (*see* Ly Sempill), and the baronetcy to his brother.

FORBES (UK) 1823, of Newe, Aberdeenshire.

They will attain a higher point, who strive at things the most exalted

Sir HAMISH STEWART FORBES, MBE, MC, 7th *Baronet*; *b* 15 Feb 1916; *s* his kinsman, Col Sir JOHN STEWART, DSO, 1984; *ed* Eton, Lawrenceville, USA, and SOAS London; Maj (ret) Welsh Gds; 1939-45 War (MC, prisoner after being captured at Dunkirk); MBE (Mil) 1945; KStJ: *m* 1st, 1945 (*m diss* 1981), Jacynthe Elizabeth Mary, da of late Eric Gordon Underwood; 2ndly, 1981, Mary Christine, MBE, da of late Ernest William Rigby, and has issue by 1st *m*.

𝔄rms – Quarterly: 1st and 4th azure, three bears' heads couped argent, muzzled gules, *Forbes*; 2nd and 3rd, azure, three cinquefoils argent, *Fraser*. ℭrest – A falcon rising proper. 𝔖upporters – Two bears argent, muzzled gules.
Residence – Newe, Strathdon, Aberdeenshire AB36 8TY. *Clubs* – Chelsea Arts; Turf.

SON LIVING (*By 1st marriage*)

JAMES THOMAS STEWART, *b* 28 May 1957; *ed* Eton, and Bristol Univ (BA): *m* 1986, Kerry Lynne, only da of Rev Lee Toms, of Sacramento, Calif, and has issue living, Theodora Christine, *b* 1989, — Katherine Elizabeth, *b* 1990. *Residence* – The Cottage, Hambleden, nr Henley, Oxon RG9 6RT.

DAUGHTERS LIVING (*By 1st marriage*)

(Caroline) Serena, *b* 1947: *m* 1984, E. Nicholas D. Herbert, only son of Ivor Herbert, of Bradenham, Bucks. —— Jane Henrietta Mary, *b* 1950: *m* 1976, Tarka Richard Bourke Leslie-King (*see* Leslie, Bt, colls, *cr* 1876, 1985 Edn), and has issue living, William, *b* 1981, — Olivia, *b* 1985. —— Christian Clare, *b* 1961: *m* 1988, Benjamin Victor Sheddon Scrimgeour, and has issue (*see* E Huntingdon, colls).

SISTERS LIVING

Mevagh (The Garage, 10A Edith Grove, SW10), *b* 1914: *m* 1948, Julius Joseph Alfred Horton, who *d* 1963. —— Juanita Ann Stewart (3 Eyot Green, Chiswick Mall, W4 2PT), *b* 1929: *m* 1st, 1949 (*m diss* 1954), Capt Anthony Maitland Steel, actor; 2ndly, 1961, Richard Currier Stickney, who *d* 1997, and has issue living (by 2nd *m*), Francis Robin Christopher (Culditch House, Gittisham, Honiton, Devon EX14 0AE), *b* 1962: *m* 1990, Lucy Anne, da of late Leonard H. R. Byng, of the Salutation, Sandwich, Kent (*see* E Moray), and has issue living, Jasper Oliver *b* 1994.

DAUGHTERS LIVING OF SIXTH BARONET

Bridget Rosemary Zilla, *b* 1935; JP, DL Aberdeenshire 1996: *m* 1962, Col Francis Mitchell Kent Tuck, RE, of Allargue, Corgarff, Strathdon, Aberdeenshire AB36 8YP, and has issue living, Rosemary Jean Winter, *b* 1963: *m* 1985, Adrian Jeremy Walker, of Upland House, Saxham St, Stowupland, nr Stowmarket, Suffolk, elder son of Sir Patrick Jeremy Walker, KCB, and has issue living, Thomas George Farquharson *b* 1987, Harry Charles Casby *b* 1995, Imogen Frances Katharine *b* 1989, Cecily Mary Elspeth *b* 1993, — Caroline Frances Stewart, *b* 1964: *m* 1993, Charles Denholm Ross Stewart, of 22c Sisters Av, SW11 5SR, yr son of David Ross Stewart, and has issue living, Kirsty Ellen Forbes *b* 1996, Lucy Emma Fraser *b* 1998, — Ellen Alexandra Farquharson, *b* 1968: *m* 1998, Hugh Francis Addison, son of Brig W. M. R. Addison, and has issue living, Katharine Frances *b* 1999. —— Elspeth Ann, *b* 1937; *ed* Aberdeen Univ (MA): *m* 1960, George Hardie, DA, of House of Newe, Strathdon, Aberdeenshire AB3 8TJ, and has issue living, Jonathan Forbes, *b* 1967, — Katharine Ann, *b* 1961: *m* 1990, David Billany, and has issue living, Ciaran Andrew *b* 1990, Roseanna Kirsten *b* 1992, — Ruth Mary, *b* 1964. —— Veronica Jean *b* 1938: *m* 1958, Edward Lancaster, DA, ARIBA, FRIAS, (31 McLeod Rd, Balloch, Inverness-shire), and has issue living, Alan Stewart, *b* 1961: *m* 1984 (*m diss* 1988), Sabine Wolniczak, and has issue living, Jonathan *b* 1984, Franziska *b* 1987, — Kevin Edward, *b* 1965: *m* 1991, Iona McGillivray, and has issue living, Hector John *b* 1996, Megan Janet *b* 1994, — Fiona Margaret, *b* 1958: *m* 1980, Robert Seymour, and has issue living, Duncan Robert *b* 1991, Hannah Frances *b* 1987. —— Margaret Xanthe Patricia, *b* 1940, MB, ChB, Aberdeen: *m* 1964, Prof James Colquhoun Petrie, MB, ChB, PRCP Ed, FRCP Ed, FRCP (Lond), FFPM of 126 Desswood Place, Aberdeen, and has issue living, John Ross, *b* 1965, — Mark Colquhoun, *b* 1969, — Rachel Xanthe Ann, *b* 1967, — Paula Jane, *b* 1970. —— Alison Stewart (99 Kinghorne St, Arbroath, Angus), *b* 1946: *m* 1968 (*m diss* 1981), T. Angus Ouchterlony, and has issue living, Peter Anthony Heathcote, *b* 1971, — James Angus Heathcote, *b* 1973, — Teresa Mary, *b* 1969.

COLLATERAL BRANCHES LIVING

Issue of late George Stewart Forbes, MRCVS, elder brother of 7th baronet, and eldest son (by 2nd *m*) of Lt-Col James Stewart Forbes, of Aslown, Aberdeenshire, only son of George Stewart, yr son of 3rd baronet, *b* 1911, *d* 1969: *m* 1st, 1938 (*m diss* 1949), Mrs Violet Mabel Doyle, da of Kenward Stuart Barker; 2ndly, 1949, Joan (Brindledown, Upper Lambourn, Berks), da of Frederick Turvey:—
(By 2nd *m*) Fiona Hay Lavens (Kingwood Stud, Lambourn, Newbury, Berks), *b* 1950: *m* 1st, 1970 (*m diss* 1992), Nicholas Ashmead Cliffe Vigors; 2ndly, 1995, Christian Marner, and has issue living (by 1st *m*), Charles Stewart Cliffe, *b* 1973, — Sarah Louise Rosemary, *b* 1974. —— Alison Feridah, *b* 1952: *m* 1973, John Albert King, Cottage Farm, Church Rd, Milton under Wychwood, Oxon and *d* 1983, leaving issue, James Stewart, *b* 1976, — Georgina Louise, *b* 1979. —— Teresa Frances Ida, *b* 1953: *m* 1978, Martin Gerard Byrne, of Murrulla Stud, Ashbrooke Rd, Wingen, NSW 2337, Australia, and has issue living, Simon Thomas, *b* 1988, — Clare Joan, *b* 1986. —— Joanna Grace, *b* 1955: *m* 1983, Alan Gerard Clarke, of 4 Bailey Av, Lane Cove, Sydney, NSW 2066, Australia, and has issue living, Owen Taylor Stewart, *b* 1987, — Mevagh Alison, *b* 1991. —— Sarah Georgina (9 Station Rd, Theale, Reading, Berks RG7 4AA), *b* 1967. —— Nicola Jane Stewart (5 Park Av, Palmers Green, N13 5PG), *b* 1969.

Issue of late Cdr Ian Dudley Stewart Forbes, DSC, RN, younger brother of 7th baronet, *b* 1919, *d* 1992: *m* 1st, 1950 (*m diss* 1960), Lady Penelope Anne Rous, da of 4th Earl of Stradbroke; 2ndly, 1961, Gunilla (Woodbine Cottage, Arthur's Place, Lockerbie, Dumfriesshire DG11 2EA), da of late Fritz Ryman, Swedish Army:—
(By 1st *m*) Charles Stewart, *b* 1956; *ed* Westminster, and Trin Coll, Oxford (MA, MSc): *m* 1989, Alison, da of Maj E. R. Payne. —— Catriona, *b* 1951: *m* 1981, Michael Neville Charles Bradley, of 17 Worfield St, SW11 4RB, son of Malcolm Bradley, of Lymington, Hants, and has issue living, Edward Benjamin Michael, *b* 1982; *ed* Harrow, — Belinda Daisy, *b* 1984; *ed* Downe House, — Henrietta, *b* 1989. —— Caroline Ianthe FORBES (53 St Dunstan's Rd, W6), *b* 1952; *ed* York Univ (BA); photographer: *m* 1977 (*m diss* 1982), Katsuhisa Sakai, and has issue living, Tyler Christopher Forbes, *b* 1978; *ed* Latymer Upper Sch.

Sir Charles Forbes, 1st Bt, merchant of Bombay, was in 1833 served heir male to 3rd Lord Forbes of Pitsligo (peerage attainted 1745) when Lord Lyon allowed him the Pitsligo arms and supporters, being descended from William Forbes of Daach and Newe, yr brother of Sir Alexander Forbes of Pitsligo (d c 1496, from whom 1st Lord Forbes of Pitsligo was 5th in descent) and gt grandson of Sir William Forbes of Kynnaldy (*d* 1446), next brother of 1st Lord Forbes.

STUART-FORBES (NS) 1626, of Pitsligo, and Monymusk, Aberdeenshire

NEC TIMIDE NEC TEMERE

ADVERSIS MAJOR PAR SECUNDIS

Greater than adversity, a match for prosperity

Sir WILLIAM DANIEL STUART-FORBES, 13th *Baronet; b* 21 Aug 1935; *s* his uncle, *Sir* CHARLES EDWARD, 1985: *m* 1956, Jannette, da of late Hori Toki George MacDonald, of Marlborough, NZ, and has issue.

𝔄rms – 1st and 4th, grand quarters, azure, on a chevron between three bears' heads couped argent, muzzled gules, a heart of the last; 2nd and 3rd, grand quarters, quarterly, 1st and 4th, azure, three bears' heads couped argent, muzzled gules; 2nd and 3rd, azure, three cinquefoils argent. 𝔈rest – Out of a baron's coronet a hand holding a scimitar all proper. 𝔖upporters – Two bears proper. *Residence* – 9 Churchill Street, Blenheim, Marlborough, New Zealand.

SONS LIVING

KENNETH CHARLES (Nukuhau, Taupo, NZ), *b* 26 Dec 1956: *m* 1981, Susan, da of Len Murray, of Taupo, NZ, and has issue living, Samuel Alexander Murray, *b* 21 Jan 1989, — Amy Dawn, *b* 1982, — Haylee Rachel, *b* 1985. ——Daniel Dawson, *b* 1962. —— Reginald MacDonald (26 Epping Place, Taupo, NZ), *b* 1964: *m* 1986, Heather, da of Phillip Jones, of Riverton, Invercargill, NZ.

DAUGHTERS LIVING

Catherine Florence, *b* 1958: *m* 1975, William Paraha, of 6a Arihia St, Taupo, NZ, and has issue living, William Bayden, *b* 1977, — Jayde Rebekah, *b* 1980. —— Eileen Jane, *b* 1960: *m* 1981, Neil Bertram Brown, of 57 North Rd, Kaitaia, NZ, and has issue living, Jessica Charlotte, *b* 1985, — Charlene Rachelle, *b* 1987.

SISTER LIVING

Avis Ilene, *b* 1932: *m* 1954, William Charles Russell, and has issue living, Stuart William, *b* 1961: *m* 1983, Laurette Dawn, da of John Cooper, of Newcastle, NSW, Australia, and has issue living, Gareth Stuart *b* 1986, Bryce Adrian *b* 1992, Lauren Renée *b* 1984, — Janice Kathyrn, *b* 1955: *m* 1981, Christopher Wayne Groube, of 20 St James Parade, Elsternwick, Vic, Australia, and has issue living, Nicolas James *b* 1986, Joshua Scott *b* 1989, — Diane Avis, *b* 1956: *m* 1987, (Norman) Allan Procter, and has issue living, Daniel William *b* 1989, Michael Forbes *b* 1992, — Susan Margaret, *b* 1958: *m* 1981, Alberto Juan Gutierrez, of 149 West St, S Hurstville, NSW 2221, Australia, and has issue living, Andrew Ryan *b* 1983, Kameron Blair *b* 1991, Bryoni Kate *b* 1989. *Address* – c/o 149 West St, S Hurstville, NSW 2221, Australia.

AUNT LIVING (*Daughter of 10th Baronet*)

Merlin (134a Muller Rd, Blenheim, Marlborough, NZ), *m* 1936, Ernest Edward Williams, who *d* 1974, and has issue living, Hugh Edward, *b* 1937: *m* 19—, Yvonne Carole, da of William Nott, of Marlborough, NZ, and has issue living, Daniel Isaac *b* 1965, Dale Lincoln *b* 1980, Carole Ann *b* 1965, — Lillian June, *b* 1938: *m* 1959, Anthony Laurence Roche Ryan, of Lochinvar, RD4, Blenheim, NZ, and has issue living, Christopher Michael *b* 1963, Edward Leo *b* 1965, Anthony John *b* 1974, Julia Felicia *b* 1960, Teresa Joan *b* 1961, Kathleen Patricia *b* 1962, Lucy Martha *b* 1969, Bernadette Maria *b* 1971, Michelle Joanne *b* 1972, — Barbara Joan (twin) (62 Howick Rd, Blenheim, Marlborough, NZ), *b* 1938: *m* 1957, James Laurence William Adams, who *d* 1982, and has issue living, Michael James David *b* 1962, Cheralee Merlin *b* 1958, Rose June *b* 1960, Karen Anne, *b* 1957: *m* 1979, Philip Walter McNabb, (17 Fyfe St, Blenheim, NZ).

MOTHER LIVING

Marjory, da of late Daniel Gilchrist, of Mahakipawa, NZ: *m* 1st, 1932, William Kenneth Stuart-Forbes, 3rd son of 10th baronet, who *d* 1946; 2ndly, 1951, Rayner Clifford Connolly, of 60 Hutcheson St, Blenheim, Marlborough, NZ.

COLLATERAL BRANCHES LIVING

Issue of late Reginald Alexander Stuart-Forbes, yst son of 10th baronet, *b* 1909, *d* 1974: *m* 1940, Florence Annie (who *m* 2ndly, 1986, Ross Sharpe), yr da of late Daniel Gilchrist, of Mahakipawa (ante):—
Dorothy Anne, *b* 1947: *m* 19—, Rex Smith, of 38 Bridge St, S Brighton, Christchurch, NZ, and has issue, Todd, *b* 1974. —— Marilyn, *b* 1951: *m* 1972, Alister James McAlpine, of Wairau Valley, RD1, Marlborough, NZ, and has issue living, Sarah, *b* 1978, — Emma, *b* 1981, — Katey, *b* 1985.

Issue of late William Forbes, 3rd son of 9th baronet, *b* 1876, *d* 1938: *m* 1906, Lillian Marian, who *d* 1959, da of late James Moore:—
Gwendoline Mary. *Residence* – 21 Elm Tree Ct, 123 Russell St, Palmerston North, New Zealand. —— Moya: *m* 1942, Owen Alfred Wiley, who *d* 1989, and has issue living, Andrew Owen, *b* 1943, — Kevin Francis, *b* 1944, — Paul Royson, *b* 1948, — Gordon John, *b* 1956. *Residence* – 9/18 Ada St, Palmerston North, New Zealand.

Grandson of late George Edward Forbes, 2nd son of George Forbes, 3rd son of 6th baronet:—
Issue of late Rev Canon Edward Archibald Forbes, *b* 1869, *d* 1929: *m* 1922, Enid Blackburn, who *d* 1971, da of late Rev Canon Garden Llanoe Duff (*see* Dunbar, Bt, *cr* 1706, colls):—
Andrew Garden Duff (Overskibo House, Dornoch, Sutherland IV25 3RQ), *b* 1925; *ed* Trin Coll, Glenalmond, at Wellington Coll, NZ, and Trin Coll, Camb (MA): *m* 1st, 1953 (*m diss* 1980), Alison, da of E. St Clair Wilson, of Wellington, New Zealand; 2ndly, 1989, Natalie Marion, da of late Lt-Col John Duguid Milne, OBE, of Ardmiddle, Turriff, Aberdeenshire, and has issue living (by 1st *m*), Alexander Duff (Druminnor Castle, Rhynie, Aberdeenshire), *b* 1955; *ed* Eton, and Trin Coll, Camb (MA), — Barbara Elizabeth (*Lady Grant of Monymusk*), *b* 1954: *m* 1982, Sir Archibald Grant of Monymusk, 13th Bt (*see* Grant, Bt, *cr* 1705), of House of Monymusk, Monymusk, Aberdeenshire, — Christian Margaret, *b* 1957: *m* 1985, Edward Maurice O'Morchoe, of Ashford, co Wicklow, yr son of late Maurice Gethin O'Morchoe, and has issue living, Frances Eileen *b* 1989, Patricia Christian *b* 1991, — Louisa Mary, *b* 1961: *m* 1985, Richard William Corbet Turnor, yr son of Maj Anthony Richard Turnor, CBE, of Foxley Manor, Malmesbury, Wilts (*see* Londesborough, B, 1980 Edn), and has issue living, William Michael Francis *b* 1988, Elizabeth *b* 1990, Rosalind Mary *b* 1993.

Grandchildren of late Cmdr Spencer Dundas Forbes, RN, yr son of late George Edward Forbes (ante):—
Issue of late Spencer Malcolm Edward Forbes, *b* 1917, *d* 1995: *m* 1st, 1940 (*m diss* 1947), Marie Teresa, da of Boleslaw Sulikowski, of Warsaw, Poland; 2ndly, 1954 (*m diss* 1980), Elizabeth Lechmere, da of late Sandys Stuart Macaskie, of Lustleigh, S Devon, and of late Mrs Raymond Windham de la Poer Beresford-Peirse:—
James Fergus Spencer, *b* 1956; *ed* Eton. —— Camilla Elizabeth (5 Kempson Rd, SW6 4PX), *b* 1958: *m* 1986 (*m diss* 1994), Ian E. Stewart, son of J. F. E. Stewart, of Whitehouse Farm, Warninglid, Sussex.

Grandchildren of late Capt Charles Hay Forbes, CBE, 2nd son of late Capt James Arthur Forbes, RN, 4th son of George Forbes (ante):—
Issue of late Lt-Cdr Reginald Arthur Forbes, RN (ret), *b* 1905, *d* 1975: *m* 1st, 1930 (*m diss* 1944), Margaret Evelyn, who *d* 1984, da of late Gideon Macpherson Rutherford (*see* Bs Willoughby de Eresby, colls); 2ndly, 1944, Joyce Charlotte Newton (Hammericks Rd, Blenheim, NZ):—
(By 1st *m*) James Hay (5708 Longfellow St, Riverdale, Maryland, USA), *b* 1931: *m* 1958, Helen Reddy, of Montreal, Canada, and has issue living, Peter Jonathan, *b* 1960, — Michael Todd, *b* 1963, — Susan Catherine, *b* 1959. —— Margaret Christine, *b* 1933: *m* 1959, John Jervis Murray Bankes, solicitor, of Tempus House, Hinton Ampner, Alresford, Hants, and has issue living, Henry Francis John, *b* 1966, — Caroline Margaret, *b* 1964: *m* 1993, Jonathan Piers Young, only son of Peter Alan George Young, of Chudleigh, Devon, and has issue living, Fergus George Jervis *b* 1996, Henrietta Margaret Evelyn *b* 1994. —— (By 2nd *m*) William Henry, *b* 1944.

Issue of late Lieut-Com John Hay Forbes, DSO, RN, *b* 1906, *d* on active ser 1940: *m* 1930, Edith Sheilah (who *d* 1951, having *m* 2ndly, 1943, as his 2nd wife, Lt-Col Hon Richard Martin Peter Preston, DSO, who *d* 1965, 2nd son of 14th Viscount Gormanston), da of late Reginald de Crecy Steel, of Walton-on-Thames:—
†Charles Hay, *b* 1931; a Tea Planter: *m* 1959, Juliet Rosalind Murray, and *d* 1998, leaving issue, John Hay, *b* 1960, — George Louis, *b* 1961, — Drostan Gerard, *b* 1962, — Sheila Emily, *b* 1963. —— Angus John Reginald (2967 Routt Circle, Lakewood, Colorado 80215, USA), *b* (*posthumous*) 1941: *m* 1st, 1962 (*m diss* 1973), Victoria Seward, of California, USA; 2ndly, 1989, Michelle Claudine Dewitt, of Denver, Colorado, USA, and has issue living (by 1st *m*), Richard Leland John, *b* 1965, — Caroline Lilah Jo, *b* 1963, — (by 2nd *m*) Ian Michael, *b* 1996, — Collette Barbara, *b* 1995, — Phoebe Fiona, *b* 1998. —— Fiona Eileen, *b* 1937: *m* 1st, 1961 (*m diss* 1976), Anthony Haig Morse; 2ndly, 1977, K. Anthony Ruddle, of Spring House, Ketton, Stamford, Lincs, and has issue living (by 1st *m*) Claire Emma, *b* 1962: *m* 1985, Martin George Wilson, of Chater Cottage, Aldgate, Ketton, Stamford, Lincs, son of Thomas Edward Wilson, of Beech House, Hambleton, Oakham, Rutland, Leics, and has issue living, George Anthony *b* 1986, Harriet Claire *b* 1988, Mariella Victoria *b* 1992, — Rachel Elizabeth, *b* 1965: *m* 1992 Nicholas John Curran, yr son of Peter Curran, of West Humble, Dorking.

Grandson of Capt James Arthur Forbes, RN (ante):—
Issue of late Air-Commodore James Louis Forbes, OBE, *b* 1880, *d* 1965: *m* 1919, Marjorie, da of Sir Thomas Putnam, and widow of Capt Philip Picot:—
James Alexander, *b* 1919; 1939-45 War as Maj Gordon Highlanders: *m* 1946, Susan Elizabeth, da of Maj-Gen Alan Hugh Hornby, CB, CBE, MC, and has issue living, Michael James, *b* 1949, — Caroline Susan, *b* 1952.

Sir William Forbes, of Monymusk, Aberdeenshire (4th in descent from Duncan Forbes of Corsindae, 2nd son of 2nd Lord Forbes) was *cr* a Baronet with remainder to heirs male whatsoever. Sir Charles Hay Hepburn Stuart-Forbes, 10th baronet assumed the additional surname of Stuart. Sir Walter Scott, in his Notes to "Marmion", speaking of Sir William, the 6th baronet, an Edinburgh banker, says: "He was unequalled, perhaps, in the degree of individual affection entertained for him by his friends, as well as in the general esteem and respect of Scotland at large". Sir William Forbes, 7th baronet, *m* 1797, Williamina Wishart, only child and heir of Sir John Belshes-Wishart, afterwards Stuart, 4th Bt of Fettercairn, who was descended in the maternal line from Stuart of Castlemilk. Sir John Stuart Hepburn Forbes, 8th baronet assumed the additional surname and arms of Hepburn. He was heir general of the last Lord Forbes of Pitsligo (his ancestor, the 4th Bt, having *m* Mary, da of the 3rd and sister of the 4th Lord). His only child *m* the 20th Baron Clinton, to whom the whole of the estates descended.

Forbes-Leith of Fyvie, see Leith of Fyvie.

FORD (UK) 1929, of Westerdunes, co of East Lothian

Sir ANDREW RUSSELL FORD, 3rd *Baronet*; *b* 29 June 1943; *s* his father, *Sir* HENRY RUSSELL, TD, JP, 1989; *ed* Winchester, New Coll, Oxford, Loughborough Coll of Education (DLC 1967) External BA London Univ, and External MA Birmingham Univ: *m* 1968, Penelope Anne, only da of late Harold Edmund Relph, of West Kirby, Wirral, and has issue.

Arms – Vert, a chevron between a dexter and a sinister wing in chief and in base a pyramid all or. Crest – A sphinx wings elevated, the head ensigned with a plume and supporting between the fore-paws a papyrus stalk flowered and leaved or.
Residence – 20 Coniston Rd, Chippenham, Wilts SN14 0PX.

SONS LIVING

TOBY RUSSELL, *b* 11 Jan 1973. —— David Andrew, *b* 1984.

DAUGHTER LIVING

Julia Mary, *b* 1970.

SISTERS LIVING

Jill Dorothy, *b* 1937. —— Alison Patricia, *b* 1946: *m* 1970, Robert M. Cowe, of Fountain Hall, Pencaitland, E Lothian EH34 5EY, and has issue living, Peter Henry McNab *b* 1972, — Ian Duncan McNab, *b* 1974, — Anne Louise, *b* 1978. —— Belinda Christine, *b* 1951: *m* 1974, Graeme P. C. McWilliam, of Bridge End Cottage, Ulpha, Broughton-in-Furness, Cumbria, and has issue living, Ralph Andrew Campbell, *b* 1984, — Alastair James, *b* 1992, — Amelia Mary, *b* 1976, — Louise Sarah, *b* 1979, — Dorothy Helen, *b* 1987.

AUNT LIVING *(daughter of 1st baronet)*

Marjorie Elaine (Apt 84, 1 Seabeach Av, Mona Vale, NSW 2103, Australia), *b* 1913: *m* 1941, Alan Murray, who *d* 1975, and has issue living, Peter Johnston (5 Tobruk Av, Balmain, NSW 2041, Australia), *b* 1943; *ed* Scots Coll, Sydney, and NSW Univ (BA Architecture); Master of Town and Country Planning, Sydney Univ: *m* 1967 (*m diss* 1987), Jennifer Lee, da of Harold Ambrose Terrey, of 5 Coolaroo Rd, Lane Cove, NSW, — Gillian Elaine (150 Green Point Drive, Green Point, via Forster, NSW 2428, Australia), *b* 1946: *m* 1967 (*m diss* 1978), Gary Richardson, and has issue living, Damien *b* 1971, Nathan *b* 1974, Heath *b* 1977, Kelly Ann *b* 1969.

COLLATERAL BRANCH LIVING

Issue of late Harold Frank Ford, yr son of 1st baronet, *b* 1915, *d* 1994: *m* 1948, Lucy Mary, da of late John Rudolph Wardlaw Burnet, KC, of Edinburgh:—
Patrick John (Tigerton, Menmuir, Brechin, Angus DD9 7RL), *b* 1952; *ed* Ampleforth, Magdalene Coll, Camb (MA), and Edinburgh Univ (LLB 1976); Solicitor, WS 1979. —— Claire Lucy, *b* 1949: *m* 1975, John W. Blair, and has issue living, Charles, *b* 1980, — Zepherine, *b* 1978, — Molly, *b* 1985. —— Harriet Mary, *b* 1955: *m* 1992, Mark James Cazalet, and has issue living, Felix James *b* 1994. —— Katharine Anne, *b* 1958: *m* 1989, Timothy Paul Cullinan, and has issue living, Finbar, *b* 1989, — Mungo, *b* 1991, — Bruno, *b* 1994.

The 1st baronet, Sir Patrick Johnston Ford (son of James Ford, of Edinburgh), sat as MP for Edinburgh, N Div (*U*) 1920-23, and 1924-35, and was a Junior Lord of the Treasury 1922-30.

ST CLAIR-FORD (GB) 1793, of Ember Court, Surrey

Sir JAMES ANSON ST CLAIR-FORD, 7th *Baronet; b* 16 March 1952; *s* his father, *Capt Sir* AUBREY, DSO, RN, 1991; *ed* Wellington, and Bristol Univ: *m* 1st, 1977 (*m diss* 1985), Jennifer Margaret, yr da of Commodore J. Robin Grindle, RN, of Drake House, Devonport; 2ndly, 1987, Mary Anne, elder da of His Honour late Judge (Nathaniel Robert) Blaker, QC, DL, of 2 Culver Rd, Winchester, Hants.

Arms – Per pale gules and or, two bends vaire; on a canton of the second a greyhound courant sable. Crest – A greyhound's head sable erased gules, muzzled or.
Residence – 161 Sheen Lane, SW14.

SISTER LIVING

Omnium rerum
vicissitudo
*All things are subject
to change*

Julia Mary, *b* 1954: *m* 1st, 1977 (*m diss* 1983), John E. Kerr; 2ndly, 1992, Patrick E. Hunter-Jones, son of Col Hugh Edward Hunter-Jones, CBE, MC, TD, of Church Farm, Langham, Essex, and has issue living (by 2nd *m*), Charles Alexander Aubrey, *b* 1995, — Lucy Clare, *b* 1994.

DAUGHTER LIVING OF FIFTH BARONET

Janetta Olive FORD, *b* 1925: *m* 1964, David Ryland Pullinger, of 16 Hollow Oak Rd, Stoborough, Wareham, Dorset BH20 5AH.

WIDOW LIVING OF SIXTH BARONET

ANNE (*Dowager Lady St Clair-Ford*), da of Harold Cecil Christopherson, of Penerley Lodge, Beaulieu, Hants: *m* 1945, Capt Sir Aubrey St Clair-Ford, 6th Bt, DSO, RN, who *d* 1991. *Residence* – West Winds, Woodgreen, Fordingbridge, Hants.

COLLATERAL BRANCHES LIVING

Issue of late Lt-Cdr Drummond St Clair-Ford, RN, and brother of 6th baronet, *b* 1907, *ka* 1943: *m* 1933, Norah Elizabeth (who *m* 2ndly, 1945, Rear-Adm Peter Noel Buckley, CB, DSO, who *d* 1988), da of Capt Charles James Astley Maberly, late 17th Lancers:—
COLIN ANSON (Honeysuckle Cottage, E Lambrook, S Petherton, Som TA13 5HW), *b* 19 April 1939: *m* 1964, Gillian Mary, da of Rear-Adm Peter Skelton, CB, and has issue living, Kate Mary, *b* 1967: *m* 1993, Jonathan Paul Weatherall, son of Ian Weatherall, of Purley, Surrey, and has issue living, Harry James *b* 1999, — Fiona Elizabeth, *b* 1969. —— Robin Sam (21 Claremont Crescent, Edinburgh EH1 26L), *b* 1941: *m* 1980 Alison F, yr da of late William Dickson, of Corsham, Wilts, and has issue living, William Sam, *b* 1982, — Peter James, *b* 1984. —— Elizabeth Jane, *b* 1937: *m* 1961, John Nigel Courtenay James, and has issue living, Simon, *b* 1966, — Annabel Clare, *b* 1964.

Issue of late Cdr Vernon John St Clair-Ford, MBE, RN, yst brother of 6th baronet, *b* 1918, *d* 1952: *m* 1947, Patricia Mary (who *m* 2ndly, 1954, Lt-Cdr Michael Ainsworth, RN, who *d* 1978, and 3rdly, 1984, Richard Patrick Beeny), da of late F. G. H. Bedford, of Petersfield, Hants:—
Timothy Bedford, *b* 1948: *m* 19—, Jennie Hemsley, and has issue living, Emma, *b* 1977, — Charlotte, *b* 1979. —— Gordon Sam, *b* 1950: *m* 1979, Hilary Jean, da of Maj H. Charlesworth, of Wokingham, Berks, and has issue living, Rufus, *b* 1980, — Joseph, *b* 1981, — Theresa, *b* 1984.

Grandchildren of late Rev Charles Primrose FORD, yst son of late Rev Charles Ford, 3rd son of 1st baronet:—
Issue of late Rev Roger Anson FORD, *b* 1878, *d* 1932: *m* 1916, Kathleen Orme, da of late Montague Torridge Morris, Colonial Civil Ser:—
Montague Patrick, *b* 1918; BSc, MRCVS; late Colonial Ser, N Nigeria: *m* 1st, 1951 (*m diss* 1967), Rosalind Elizabeth, da of Lt-Col Thomas Harold Barnes, of Castle Cary; 2ndly, 1969, Ivy Lillian Lowden, da of William Buckell, and has issue living (by 1st *m*), Sara Kathleen, *b* 1959. —— Charles Primrose (The Old Rectory, Skidbrooke, Louth, LN11 7DQ), *b* 1922, Fl Lt RAF (ret): *m* 1949, Margaret Watson, and has issue living, Victoria Primrose, *b* 1953. —— Dorothy Vernon, *b* 1930.

The 1st baronet was a Member of the Council in Barbados, and in 1790 sat as MP for Newcastle-under-Lyme. Capt St Clair Ford, yst son of 2nd Bt, and grandfather of the 6th Bt, assumed the additional surname of St Clair 1878.

Forestier-Walker, see Walker.

FORWOOD (UK) 1895, of The Priory, Gateacre, Childwall, co Palatine of Lancaster

Sir DUDLEY RICHARD FORWOOD, 3rd *Baronet*, *b* 6 June 1912; *s* his father, *Lieut-Col Sir* DUDLEY BAINES, CMG, 1961; *ed* Stowe; formerly Capt and temporary Major Scots Guards (Reserve); is an Underwriting Member of Lloyd's; Master of New Forest Buckhounds 1957-65; Hon Attaché British Legation, Vienna 1934-37, and Equerry to HRH the Duke of Windsor 1937-39; Chm New Forest Consultative Panel 1971-82, and Chm New Forest Agricultural Society 1964-82, Pres 1983; Chm of Crufts 1973-89, and Official Verderer of New Forest 1974-82; Trustee Kennel Club; Hon Dir Roy Agric Soc of England 1972-77, and Vice Pres since 1983: *m* 1952, Mary Gwendoline, who *d* 1999, formerly wife of (1) Inigo Brassey, Viscount Ratendone (later 2nd Marquess of Willingdon), (2) Frederick Robert Cullingford, and (3) Brig Donald Croft-Wilcock, and da of Basil S. Forster.

Fide virtue et labore
By faith, virtue and labour

Arms – Per fesse or and azure, in chief a cormorant sable, beaked and membered gules, between two fleurs-de-lis of the second, in base an ancient galley or, sail argent. **Crest** – Between two wings argent the battlements of a tower, thereon in front of a stag's head two hatchets in saltire all proper.
Residence – Uppacott, Bagnum, nr Ringwood, Hants BH24 3BZ.

ADOPTED STEPSON LIVING

Rodney Simon Dudley FORWOOD, *b* 1940; *ed* Malvern; late Capt Irish Gds: *m* 1964, Jennifer Jane Nelson (*Baroness Arlington* in her own right), and has issue (see that title). *Residence* – The New House, Rectory Gdns, Salisbury St, Shaftesbury, Dorset SP7 8EJ.

COLLATERAL BRANCHES LIVING

Issue of late Arthur Noel Forwood, 3rd son of 1st baronet *b* 1881, *d* 1959, *m* 1st, 1903 (*m diss* 1923), Evelyn Agnes, only da of W. Forrester Addie, JP; 2ndly, 1923, Hyacinth, da of late Henry Pollard, of Chester:—
(By 2nd *m*) PETER NOEL, *b* 15 Oct 1925; *ed* Radley; 1939-45 War with Welsh Guards: *m* 1950, Roy da of James Murphy, MBE, FRCS, LRCP, of Horsham, Sussex, and has issue living, Susan Noel, *b* 1951, — Diana Geraldine, *b* 1953: *m* 1980, Capt Edward Joshua Cooper, Irish Guards (ret), elder son of late Lt-Cmdr Edward Francis Patrick Cooper, RN, of Markree Castle, co Sligo (*see* B Castlemaine, colls, 1967 Edn), — Jane *b* 1954, — Joanna Baines, *b* 1956, — Caragh Vivien, *b* 1958, — Amanda Elizabeth, *b* 1963. *Residence* – Newhouse Farm, Shillinglee, Chiddingfold, Surrey. —— Enid, *b* 1924: *m* 1950, Herbert J. Wale, of Glebe Farm, W Haddon, Northampton, and has issue living, Robert Noel Cattell, *b* 1957, — Gerald Richard, *b* 1959, — Angela Mary, *b* 1954. —— Wendy Baines, *b* 1931.

The Rt Hon Sir Athur B. Forwood, 1st Bt, sat as MP for Lancashire (SW), Ormskirk Div (C) 1885-98, and was Sec to the Admirality 1886-92.

FOSTER (UK) 1838, of Norwich. (Extinct 1960)

Sir HENRY WILLIAM BERKELEY FOSTER, MC, 4th and last *Baronet*.

DAUGHTER LIVING OF FOURTH BARONET

Janet Elizabeth, *b* 1930.

FOSTER (UK) 1930, of Bloomsbury, co London

Sir JOHN (GREGORY) FOSTER, 3rd *Baronet*; *b* 26 Feb 1927; *s* his father, *Sir* THOMAS SAXBY GREGORY, 1957; *ed* Michaelhouse Coll, Natal, and Witwatersrand Univ (MB and BCh 1951); MRCP Edinburgh, FRCP, DIH London 1984; Physician; European War 1944-5 with S African Artillery: *m* 1956, Jean Millicent, da of late Elwin Watts, FRCSE, of Germiston, S Africa, and has issue.

Address – 7 Caledon St, PO Box 1325, George 6530, Cape Prov, S Africa. *Club* – Johannesburg Country.

SON LIVING

SAXBY GREGORY, *b* 3 Sept 1957: *m* 1989, Rowen Audrey, da of late Reginald Archibald Ford, of Durban, and has issue living, Thomas James Gregory, *b* 1 May 1991, — Robert John Gregory, *b* 1992.

DAUGHTERS LIVING

Deborah Jean Gregory, *b* 1959: *m* 19—, Steffen Zoutendijk, of 125 Wavecrest Av, Venice, Los Angeles, USA, and has issue living, Peter, *b* 1989. —— Carolyn Gregory, *b* 1962. —— Rosemary Gregory, *b* 1963.

COLLATERAL BRANCH LIVING

Issue of late Lewis Marshall Gregory Foster, yr son of 1st Baronet, *b* 1904, *d* 1970: *m* 1931, Margaret Amy (11 Vernon Close, Leamington Spa), da of Max Tillard, formerly of Johannesburg:—
Richard Tillard (PO Box 86, Southbroom, Natal, S Africa), *b* 1935: *m* 1st, 1964 (*m diss* 1973), Carola Margaret, da of Rev George Henry Talbot Roe, R of Wheathampstead, Herts; 2ndly, 1975, Mrs Winifred Moira Cameron, da of — Walker, and has issue living (by 1st *m*), Polly Tillard, *b* 1965, — Candy Tillard, *b* 1970. —— Eve Tillard, *b* 1932: *m* 1954, Donald Miller Croudace, of Woodcote Granary, Rouncil Lane, Kenilworth, Warwicks, and has issue living, Brigid Lucy, *b* 1959, — Charlotte Polly, *b* 1962.

The 1st baronet, Sir (Thomas) Gregory Foster (el son of late Thomas Gregory Foster, Bar-at-law), was Provost of Univ. Coll 1907-29, and Vice-Chancellor of Univ of London 1928-30.

FOULIS, (NS) 1634, of Colinton, Edinburgh
(Name pronounced "Fowls")

Ready with heart and hand

Sir IAN PRIMROSE LISTON FOULIS, 13th *Baronet*, son of late Lieut-Col James Alastair Liston Foulis, son of late Lieut-Col Archibald Primrose Liston Foulis, 4th son of 9th baronet; *b* 9 Aug 1937; *s* his kinsman *Sir* ARCHIBALD CHARLES, 1962; discontinued use of Liston as a surname, Lyon Court 1988.

Arms – Argent, three bay-leaves slipped vert. **Crest** – A dexter hand couped, holding a sword in pale, sustaining a wreath of laurel all proper.
Residences – Apdo de Correos 7, Portal 5-2-C, San Agustin de Guadalix, 28750 Madrid, Spain; Calle Universidad 28, Portal 2-5-D Jaca Huesca, Spain.

SISTERS LIVING

Simone Primrose, *b* 1934: *m* 1973, Geoffrey Richard Hall, of 7 Alexandra Rd, Dawlish, Devon EX7 9JT. —— Susan Thérèse Olga (Calle Mayor 3, Berdun, Huesca, Spain), *b* 1941; painter and illustrator: *m* 1st, 1962 (*m diss* 1974), Peter John Lely; 2ndly, 1976, José Luis Larraz (Casasus), and has issue living (by 1st *m*), Edward James Mountenay, *b* 1965, — Josephine Anne, *b* 1963, — (by 2nd *m*), Mark, *b* 1977, — James *b* 1978, — Sophie Anne, *b* 1986.

AUNT LIVING

Avril Primrose, *b* 1915: *m* 1946, Major Desmond Allhusen, late KRRC, who *d* 1977. *Residence* – Court Cottage, 62 High West St, Dorchester, Dorset.

COLLATERAL BRANCHES LIVING

Granddaughter of late James Foulis, MD, FRCPE, son of late John Foulis, MD 2nd son of 7th baronet:—
Issue of late Wilfrid Venour Foulis, *b* 1884, *d* 1951: *m* 1st 1909 (*m diss* 1923), Clara Millington, da of Alfred Dow, of King's Lynn; 2ndly, 1924, Ida, da of the Rev Joshua Brookes, Canon of Lahore:—
(By 2nd *m*) Ursula Patricia Carey, *b* 1926: *m* 1947 (*m diss* 1970), William Joseph Kiernan.

The Foulis (or de Feuilles) family originally owned land in Angus. William Foulis was Sec to King James I 1424, and Keeper of the Privy Seal 1427. His grandson, James Foulis, purchased Colinton 1519, and his descendant, Alexander Foulis of Colinton, co Edinburgh, was created a baronet with remainder to heirs male whatsoever. Sir James, the 2nd baronet, MP for Midlothian and a Privy Councillor, who was knighted during the lifetime of his father, was actively engaged in the wars in Scotland after the death of Charles I. He was, with his companions, the Earls of Leven, Crawford, and other gentlemen of rank, betrayed into the hands of the English, while attending a convention of Committee of Estates, at Alyth, in Angus. After the Restoration he was appointed Lord Justice Clerk, with the title of Lord Colinton. The 3rd baronet sat in the last Scottish Parliament 1706, and afterwards for Midlothian in the British Parliament. He was a Lord of Session and a Privy Councillor. On the death in 1825 of Sir James Foulis of Colinton, 6th Bt, the male line from the grantee and his father became ext, and the baronetcy passed to his 6th cousin and heir male, Sir James Foulis, 7th Bt, who was descended from George Foulis of Ravelston, uncle of the 1st Bt of Colinton. George's son, Sir John Foulis of Ravelston, was *cr* a Baronet in 1661, with remainder to heirs male of the body. The baronetcy of Ravelston was forfeited by Sir Archibald Primrose of Dunipace, 2nd Bt, for taking part in the rebellion of 1745, for which he was beheaded at Carlisle in 1746. The heir to this baronetcy, but for the attainder, is the Baronet of Colinton. Sir William Foulis of Colinton, 8th Bt (*cr* 1634), added the additional name of Liston, having *m* 1843, Henrietta Ramage Liston of Millburn Tower, great-niece and testamentary heir of Rt Hon Sir Robert Liston, GCB, HM Amb to USA.

FOWKE (UK) 1814, of Lowesby, Leicestershire.
(Name pronounced "Foke")

Arms are the guardians of peace

Sir DAVID FREDERICK GUSTAVUS FOWKE, 5th *Baronet*, only son of late Lt-Col Gerrard George Fowke, 2nd son of 3rd baronet; *b* 28 Aug 1950; *s* his uncle, *Sir* FREDERICK WOOLLASTON RAWDON, 1987; *ed* Cranbrook Sch, Sydney, and Sydney Univ (BA).

Arms – Vert, a fleur-de-lis argent. **Crest** – 1st, a dexter arm embowed, vested and cuffed argent, the hand proper grasping an arrow in bend sinister or, barbed and flighted silver; 2nd, an Indian goat's head erased vert, armed and eared argent. *Residence* – 1 Trafalgar Rd, Camberwell, Vic 3124, Australia.

SISTER LIVING

(Louise) Caroline Daphne, *b* 1948: *m* 1970 (*m diss* 1994), Bruce Theodore Davies, and has issue living, Gerrard Charles, *b* 1974. *Residence* – 30 Caroline St, Hawthorn East, Vic 2123, Australia.

DAUGHTERS LIVING OF FOURTH BARONET

Sarah Elizabeth (54 Orchard Av, Chichester, Sussex), *b* 1949: *m* 1989, Jon Robinson, and has issue living, Oliver, *b* 1980, — Kate, *b* 1981, — Alice, *b* 1990. —— Belinda Barbara, *b* 1955: *m* 1983, Richard Laban, of 53 Arcot Park, Sidmouth, Devon, and has issue living, Sam, *b* 1983, — Joe *b* 1985, — Lily, *b* 1986.

MOTHER LIVING

Daphne, da of Aristos Monasteriotis, of Corfu: *m* 1946, Lt-Col Gerard George Fowke, 2nd son of 3rd baronet, who *d* 1969. *Residence* – 1 Trafalgar Rd, Camberwell, Victoria 3124, Australia.

Sir Frederick Gustavus Fowke, 1st Bt, was son and heir of Lt-Gen Sir Thomas Fowke of Lowesby, Leics, Groom of the Bedchamber to the Duke of Cumberland.

FOWLER (UK) 1890, of Braemore, Ross-shire (Extinct 1933)

Rev Sir MONTAGUE FOWLER, 4th and last *Baronet*.

DAUGHTER LIVING OF FOURTH BARONET (*By 2nd marriage*)

Evelyn Denise (Cottrell House, High St, Angmering, W Sussex), *b* 1915: *m* 1st, 1936, Douglas Hamilton Watt, who *d* 1973; 2ndly, 1955, Lt-Col Alfred John Newling, CB, CBE, MVO, TD, who *d* 1957, and has issue living, (by 1st *m*) Donald George FOWLER-WATT (Brocks Hill, Walderton, nr Chichester, W Sussex PO18 9EA), *b* 1937; assumed the additional surname of Fowler 1956: *m* 1960, Sheila Mary Beynon, and has issue living, Andrew James *b* 1961: *m* 1993, Vivienne Hedges, Duncan John *b* 1963: *m* 1992, Karen Monger (and has issue living, Adam Sebastian *b* 1998, Laura Constance *b* 1996), Susanna Jane *b* 1969.

FOX (UK) 1924, of Liverpool, co Palatine of Lancaster (Extinct 1959)

Sir GIFFORD WHEATON GREY FOX, 2nd and last *Baronet.*

DAUGHTER LIVING OF SECOND BARONET (*By 1st marriage*)

Georgina Myra Albinia, *b* 1930; OStJ: *m* 1951, Patrick Tobias Telfer Smollett of Bonhill, MC, DL, KJStJ, Highland LI (ret), who *d* 1997, and has issue living, David Alexander Douglas Tobias, *b* 1953, — Gabrielle Georgiana, *b* 1960: *m* 1985, Robert Edmund John Boyle (*see* E Cork and Orrery, colls). *Residences* – Cameron, Alexandria, Dunbartonshire G83 8QZ; 9 Cleveland Row, SW1A 1DH.

DAUGHTER LIVING OF FIRST BARONET

Adeline Betty (*Lady Holman*)· *m* 1st, 1929 (*m diss* 1939), Capt Basil Holmsdale Allfrey, late 9th Lancers, who *d* 1981; 2ndly, 1940, as his 2nd wife, Sir Adrian Holman, KBE, CMG, MC, who *d* 1974, and has issue living (by 1st *m*) Anthony Rodney (c/o John Murray (Publishers) Ltd, 50 Albemarle St, W1X 4BD) *b* 1930: *m* 1st, 1955 (*m diss* 1974), Hon Julian Mary, da of late Baron Russell of Killowen (Life Baron); 2ndly, 1978, France de Brito e Cunha, da of Visconde de Pereira Machado, and has issue living (by 1st *m*), Charles Sebastian Holmsdale, *b* 1959, Arabel Mary *b* 1956, Georgiana Rose, *b* 1957, — Peter (67 Park Walk, SW10), *b* 1932: *m* 1st, 1962 (*m diss* 1975), Susanna Gabrielle, da of late Capt George Wareing Drewry Ormerod, RA; 2ndly, 1978, Clare Elizabeth Carder, and has issue living (by 1st *m*), Richard James Nugent *b* 1963: *m* 1990, Ellah Wakatama, Alexander Peter *b* 1965: *m* 1997, Martha Virginia, only da of Sir Adrian Christopher Swire (*see* M Northampton) (and has issue living, Jack Merlin Samuel *b* 1999), Candida Elizabeth *b* 1970 (by 2nd *m*), Margaux *b* 1979, Constance *b* 1981. *Residence* – Green Farm, Chalvington, Sussex.

WIDOW LIVING OF SECOND BARONET

Ludy MARIOTH CHRISTINA HAY (Forbes Lodge, Gifford, E Lothian), da of late Lt-Col Lord Edward Douglas John Hay, Gren Gds (*see* M Tweeddale), and formerly wife of Lt-Col George Richard Trotter, R Scots Greys (E Eglinton); resumed the surname of Hay 1971: *m* 2ndly, 1954, as his 2nd wife, Sq-Ldr Sir Gifford Wheaton Grey Fox, RAFVR, 2nd baronet, who *d* 1959, when the title became ext; 3rdly, 1963 (*m diss* 1971), Sir John Hastings James, KCVO, CB, who *d* 1980.

FRANK (UK) 1920, of Withyham, co Sussex

Sir (ROBERT) ANDREW FRANK, 4th *Baronet*; *b* 16 May 1964 *s* his father, *Sir* ROBERT JOHN, 1987; *ed* Eton; actor: *m* 1990, Zoë Alia, elder da of late S. A. Hasan, of Windsor, Berks.
Residence – Ruscombe End, Waltham St Lawrence, Reading, Berks RG10 0HE.

HALF-SISTERS LIVING (*Daughters of 3rd Bt by his 1st wife, Angela Elizabeth, eldest da of Sir Kenelm Henry Ernest Cayley, 10th Bt*)

Maria Elizabeth Jane, *b* 1952: *m* 1975, Vivian Murray Bairstow, and has issue living, George Robert, *b* 1987, — Katharine Selina, *b* 1982. *Residence* – Englewick, Englefield Green, Surrey. —— Katharine Lucy, *b* 1954: *m* 1976 (*m diss* 1998), Ian Forbes McCredie, OBE, son of John Henry McCredie, and has issue living, James Howard, *b* 1981, — Alexandra Elizabeth, *b* 1983.

The 1st baronet, Sir Howard George Frank, GBE, KCB, was senior partner in the firm of Knight, Frank, and Rutley, of 20 Hanover Square, W, 90 Princes Street, Edinburgh, and Ashford, Kent, a Director of Norwich Union Fire Insurance So, of Livett, Frank, and Son, of London and Southampton, and of Victoria and Albert Docks, and Director-Gen of Lands to War Office and Air Min and Min of Munitions 1917-22. The 2nd baronet, Sir Howard Frederick, Lieut Grenadier Guards, was *ka* 1944. The 3rd baronet, Sir Robert John, was F/O RAFVR and served in World War II.

Frankland-Payne-Gallwey, see Gallwey.

FRASER (UK) 1943, of Tain, co Ross

Deliverance and help

Sir IAIN MICHAEL FRASER, 3rd *Baronet*; *b* 27 June 1951; *s* his father, *Maj Sir* JAMES DAVID, 1997; *ed* Trin Coll Glenalmond, and Edinburgh Univ (BSc); Shipping Co Manager: *m* 1982 (*m diss* 1991), Sherylle Ann, da of Keith Gillespie, of Wellington, NZ, and has issue.

ᚠᚱᚿᛋ – Azure, three cinque foils argent, on a chief of the last three bears' heads couped of the field muzzled of the second. ᚲᚱᛖᛊᛏ – A buck's head erased proper.
Residence – 30/7 Elbe St, Edinburgh EH6 7HW.

SON LIVING

BENJAMIN, *b* 6 April 1986.

DAUGHTER LIVING

Joanna Karen, *b* 1983.

BROTHER LIVING

Christopher John, *b* 1954; has assumed the Tibetan name Wangchuk Dorji; *ed* Trin Coll, Glenalmond.

WIDOW LIVING OF SECOND BARONET

(EDITH) MAUREEN (*Lady Fraser*), da of late Rev John Reay, MC, of Bingham Rectory, Notts: *m* 1950, Maj Sir David Fraser, 2nd Bt, who *d* 1997. *Residence* – 2 Lennox St, Edinburgh EH4 1QA.

The 1st baronet, Sir John Fraser, KCVO, MC (son of James Fraser, of Tain, Ross-shire), was Hon Surg to HM in Scotland, Regius Professor of Clinical Surgery, Edinburgh Univ, and Surg, Edinburgh Roy Infirmary 1925-47, and Principal and Vice-Chancellor of Edinburgh Univ 1944-47. The 2nd baronet, Maj Sir James David Fraser, was Prof of Clinical Science in Surgery at Southampton Univ, formerly Senior Lecturer in Clinical Surgery, Edinburgh Univ Med Sch, and Pres Royal Coll of Surgeons, Edinburgh 1982-85.

FREAKE (UK) 1882, of Cromwell House, Kensington, and Fulwell Park, co Middlesex
(Extinct 1951)

Sir CHARLES ARLAND MAITLAND FREAKE, 4th and last *Baronet*.

DAUGHTER LIVING OF FOURTH BARONET

Sheila Winifred, *b* 1933: *m* 1957, John David O'Brien, who *d* 1980, son of Sir David Edmond O'Brien, 6th Bt.

FREDERICK (GB) 1723, of Burwood House, Surrey

Prudent simplicity blesses

Sir CHARLES BOSCAWEN FREDERICK, 10th *Baronet*; *b* 11 April 1919; *s* his father, *Lieut-Col Sir* EDWARD BOSCAWEN, CVO, 1956; *ed* Eton; Maj (ret) Gren Gds; a JP of Bucks; a Member Gen Commn of Income Tax since 1966, of Stock Exchange Council 1973-75 and Chm of Provincial Unit of Stock Exchange 1973-75; a Member of London Stock Exchange 1954-62; N Africa and Italy 1943-45 (despatches), Palestine 1946-47 (despatches), Malaya 1948-49, Egypt 1952-53: *m* 1949, Rosemary, el da of late Lt-Col Robert John Halkett Baddeley, MC, of Home Close, Donhead St Mary, Shaftesbury, and has issue.

Arms – Or, on a chief azure three doves argent. **Crest** – On a chapeau azure turned up ermine a dove as in the arms, holding in its beak an olive-branch proper.
Residence – 18 Esplanade, Fowey, Cornwall PL23 1HY.

SONS LIVING

CHRISTOPHER ST JOHN, *b* 28 June 1950: *m* 1990, Camilla Elizabeth, only da of Sir (Walter) Derek Gilbey, 3rd Bt, and has issue living, Benjamin St John, *b* 29 Dec 1991, — Amy Rose, *b* 1994. *Residence* – Home Farm, Batcombe, Shepton Mallet, Somerset BA4 6HF. —— James Boscawen, *b* 1963.

DAUGHTERS LIVING

Anne Rosemary, *b* 1952: *m* 1st, 1976, François Maurice; 2ndly, 1991, Miles Arthur Maitland French (*see* E Lauderdale, colls), of 70A Middle St, Brighton, Sussex, and has issue living (by 1st *m*), Thomas James, *b* 1977, — Nicholas Charles Roger, *b* 1979, — (by 2nd *m*) Raphaël Maitland, *b* 1994, — Naomi Hilda, *b* 1992, — Matilda Joan, *b* 1999. —— Jill Elizabeth, *b* 1956: *m* 1986, Stephen Douglas, of Los Angeles, California.

COLLATERAL BRANCHES LIVING

Grandchildren of late Henry Penrice Frederick, 2nd son of late George Septimus Frederick, 7th son of late Lt-Col Thomas Frederick, elder son of late Maj-Gen Marescoe Frederick, brother of 4th baronet:—
Issue of late Roger Frederick, *b* 1900, *d* 1991: *m* 1928, Nora Mary, who *d* 1977, da of Col Herbert Mansfield Whitehead, OBE, of The Grange, Penkridge, Staffs:—
Roger Mansfield (16 Orchard Close, Yealmpton, Plymouth PL8 2JQ), *b* 1930: *m* 1959, Valerie Anne, da of late S. A. Watts, and has issue living, Alan Marescoe, *b* 1960: *m* 1991, Joanne Bennison, and has issue living, Benjamin John *b* 1993, Laura Anne *b* 1992, — Jonathan Denley, *b* 1962, — Thomas Russell, *b* 1965: *m* 1988, Rae Jervis, and has issue living, Annie Rae *b* 1993, — Catherine Mary, *b* 1967. —— Rowena Mary, *b* 1935: *m* 1957, Lt-Col Ralph Plant, Royal Signals, yr son of N. J. Plant, of Thurnscoe, Yorks, and has issue living, Naomi Elizabeth, *b* 1958: *m* 1982, James Martin Ibbott, — Alison Mary, *b* 1959, — Nicola Ruth, *b* 1964, — Vanessa Jane, *b* 1965. —— Briony Margaret, *b* 1941: *m* 1960, G/Capt John Hamilton, RAF, of 1 Kestrel Cottage, East Knoyle, Wilts SP3 6AD, and has issue living, John Roger, *b* 1961, — David Nicholas, *b* 1963.

Grandchildren of late Ernest Prescott Frederick, 3rd son of late George Septimus Frederick (ante):—
Issue of late Capt John Cromwell Frederick, RN, *b* 1920, *d* 1974: *m* 1st, 1942 (*m diss* 1965), Mary Oliveria, da of late Rev Wynyard Warner, MC; 2ndly, 1966, Margaret Lilian (Woodview, Meavy, Yelverton, Devon), da of Richard Henry Dalbiac (B Sherwood):—
(By 1st *m*) John Peter, *b* 1945: *m* 1972, Janie Mary, da of Scott Gundersen, of NZ. —— Sarah Ann, *b* 1943.

Granddaughter of late George Septimus Frederick (ante):—
Issue of late Arthur Marescoe Frederick, *b* 1869, *d* 1963: *m* 1900, Petrona Elena, who *d* 1965, da of late C. J. F. Davie, of Montevideo:—
Louisa Carmen (c/o H. Frederick, Esq, PO Box 18952, Montevideo, 11500 Uruguay), *b* 1905: *m* 1934, W. J. H. Van Wijngaarden, who *d* 1964.

Grandchildren of late Arthur Marescoe Frederick (ante):—
Issue of late Arthur Roland Frederick, *b* 1901, *d* 1988: *m* 1930, Maria Esther, who *d* 1985, da of late Francisco Costa, of Montevideo:—
Richard Frank (Montevideo, Uruguay), *b* 1935: *m* 1960, Gloria, da of late Carlos Gracía Arocena, and has issue living, Ricardo, *b* 1963: *m* 1994, Marina, da of late J. Ferrari, — Odile Maria, *b* 1962: *m* 1983 (*m diss* 1991), H. Pérez Noble, — Madelón María, *b* 1965: *m* 1992, Alvaro Piñeirúa. —— Lilian Susan, *b* 1932: *m* 1959, Hugo Sapelli Mendez, who *d* 1988, of Montevideo, Uruguay.

Issue of late John Davie Geoffrey Frederick, *b* 1903, *d* 1975: *m* 1st, 1929, Maria Mercedes, who *d* 1950, da of late Luis Labadíe, of Montevideo, 2ndly, 1952, Elioa, da of late Juan Lotero:—
(By 1st *m*) John (Santa Rosa, Canelones, Uruguay), *b* 1930: *m* 1961, Marta Rosa, da of late Oscar Gulla, of Santa Rosa, Canelones, Uruguay, and has issue living, Carlos Alberto, *b* 1962: *m* 1985, Rosa, da of late F. Reggio, and has issue living, Carlos Nicolás *b* 1991, Fabiana Lorena *b* 1987, Lourdes Mercedes *b* 1993, — Rafael Daniel, *b* 1964: *m* 19—, Sonia, da of E. Baserga, and has issue living, Daniel *b* 1992, — Oscar Geoffrey, *b* 1966: *m* 19—, Melba, da of late J. Olivera, and has issue living, Luciana *b* 1992. —— Henry (PO Box 18952, Montevideo, Uruguay), *b* 1933: *m* 1958, Lia, da of

Julio Arocena Capurro, of Buenos Aires, Argentina, and has issue living, Henry Martin, *b* 1959: *m* 1992, Aurora, da of Dr Jaime Polto, and has issue living, Henry José *b* 1993, María de los Milagros *b* 1994, — Diego José, *b* 1962: *m* 1990, María Claudia, da of late Claudino Miguez, — Jamie Luis, *b* 1966, — Mercedes Inés, *b* 1961: *m* 1985 Ing. Marcelo Pittamiglio.

Grandchildren of late Edward Gurdon Frederick, MRCS, LRCP, 8th son of George Septimus Frederick (ante):—
     Issue of late Edward Vincent Frederick, *b* 1902, *d* 1969: *m* 1946, Joan Olive (80 Rodmell Av, Saltdean, Brighton, Sussex BN2 8PJ), da of late Albert Dunford, of Brighton:—
Christopher Hugh (c/o 80 Rodmell Ave, Saltdean, Brighton), *b* 1948; *ed* Embley Park, Romsey, Hants: *m* 1982 (*m diss* 1993), Mrs Diana Lesley Spiers, eldest da of late Leslie Kingham, of Coventry. —— Helen Mary, *b* 1947: *m* 1987, Brent Edwin Heath, of 441 Diehl Ave, San Leandro, CA 94577, USA, son of late Edwin C. Heath, of Phoenix, Arizona, USA. —— Auriol Rosalind (59B Camberwell Rd, SE5 0EZ), *b* 1952.

Granddaughter of late George Septimus Frederick (ante):—
     Issue of late Herbert Frederick, *b* 1874, *d* 1949: *m* 1900, Alice Louisa, who *d* 1943, da of late W. H. Priest, of HM's Civil Ser:—
Edith Nora, *b* 1901. *Residence* – 40 Rousham Rd, Eastville, Bristol, BS5 6XJ.

Sir John Frederick, Knight, a wealthy merchant, Lord Mayor of London 1662, and MP for that city 1663, was a munificent benefactor of Christ's Hospital, and, after the great fire of 1666, rebuilt the hall at a cost of £5,000. Sir John, the 1st baronet, was his grandson. The 5th baronet was for several years MP for Surrey. The 8th baronet, Sir Charles Edward St John Frederick, OBE, was High Sheriff of Northants 1934. The 9th baronet, Lieut-Col Sir Edward Boscawen Frederick, CVO, Roy Fusiliers (ret), was an Exon of King's Body Guard of Yeoman of the Guard 1925-37, and Ensign 1937-50.

FREEMAN (UK) 1945, of Murtle, co Aberdeen

Sir JAMES ROBIN FREEMAN, 3rd *Baronet*; *b* 21 July 1955; *s* his father, *Sir* (JOHN) KEITH NOEL, 1981.

or Freedom through Work

Arms – Per fesse azure and vair ancient, three fusils in chief and a crescent in base or, a bordure engrailed gules. **Crest** – A fusil or between two wings displayed azure.
Address – ......

SISTER LIVING

Katharine Noël, *b* 1950.

AUNT LIVING (*Daughter of 1st baronet*)

Bridget Anne Elizabeth, *b* 1920: *m* 1st, 1942 (*m diss* 1946), John Vernon Rob; 2ndly, 1954, Godfrey Henry Beese, of Church House, East Grafton, Marlborough, Wilts, and has issue living, (by 1st *m*) Joanna Elizabeth, *b* 1943, — (by 2nd *m*) Christopher David, *b* 1955, — Thomas Jolyon, *b* 1957, — Deborah Helen, *b* 1956, — Philippa Lucy, *b* 1960.

HALF-AUNTS LIVING

Joan Margaret, *b* 1936: *m* 1955, John Richard Bine Morgan-Grenville, who *d* 1994 (*see* Ly Kinloss). *Residence* – Upperton House, Petworth, Sussex. —— Susan Hilary Philippa, *b* 1939: *m* 1962, Robin Neill Lochnell Malcolm of Poltalloch, Chief of Clan Malcolm (MacCallum), of Duntrune Castle, Kilmartin, Argyll, and has issue living, Ian Rory, *b* 1963, — Andrew Neill, *b* 1965: *m* 1998, Victoria, only da of Christopher R. Marsden, of Penistone, Yorks, — Kirsty Elizabeth, *b* 1964, — Josephine Clare, *b* 1969.

WIDOW LIVING OF SECOND BARONET

PATRICIA DENISON (*Lady Freeman*) (c/o Royal Bank of Scotland, 32 St Giles, Oxford OX1 3ND), da of late Charles W. Thomas: *m* 1946, Sir (John) Keith Noel Freeman, 2nd Bt, who *d* 1981.

The 1st baronet, Air Ch Marshal Sir Wilfrid Rhodes Freeman, GCB, DSO, MC (3rd son of William Robert Freeman), commanded Headquarters, Transjordan and Palestine 1930-34; was Comdt Roy Air Force Staff Coll 1934-36; appointed Air Member of Research and Development on Air Council 1936 (also for Production 1938-40), and Vice-Ch of Air Staff 1940; Ch Executive, Min of Aircraft Production 1942-45. Sir (John) Keith Noel Freeman, 2nd Bt, was Chm and Man Dir Garmantex Ltd.

FRY (UK) 1894, of Woodburn, Blackwell, co Durham (Extinct 1987)

Sir FRANCIS WILFRID FRY, OBE, 5th and last *Baronet*.

DAUGHTER LIVING OF FOURTH BARONET

Margaret Jane (c/o Lloyds Bank plc, Packhorse Rd, Gerrards Cross, Bucks SL9 8PF), *b* 1928: *m* 1956 (*m diss* 1978), Arthur Keith Redway, MSc, and has issue living, Jeremy Nicholas Fry, *b* 1958; *ed* Roedean, and in Canada.

WIDOW LIVING OF FIFTH BARONET

ANNE PEASE (*Lady Fry*), JP, eldest da of late Kenneth Henry Wilson, OBE, JP, of Park Hall, Kidderminster, Worcs: *m* 1943, Sir Francis Wilfrid Fry, 5th Bt, OBE who *d* 1987. *Residence* – Cleveland Lodge, Gt Ayton, N Yorkshire TS9 6BT.

COLLATERAL BRANCH LIVING

Issue of late Walter Raymond Fry, 3rd son of 1st baronet, *b* 1870, *d* 1944: *m* 1897, Lilian, who *d* 1956, da of late M. Vallauri, Ch Dragoman to Turkish Embassy at St Petersburg:—
Eleanor Priscilla, *b* 1898: *m* 1923, Frank Edwin Ransome, who *d* 1959, and has issue living, Frank Fellows (RD5, Box 381D, Kincaid Rd, Boonton, NJ 07005, USA), *b* 1924: *m* 1950, Lois Pape, and has issue living, Steven *b* 1951, Patricia *b* 1954, — John Fry, *b* 1927: *m* 1950, Marjorie Ann Fisher, and has issue living, Blair E. *b* 1951, Meredith *b* 1970, Barbara F. *b* 1955, Sara Jane *b* 1958.

The 1st baronet, Sir Theodore Fry, FSA, JP, DL (yr brother of late Francis James Fry, of Cricket St Thomas Chard, father of Sir Geoffrey Storrs Fry, KCB, CVO, 1st Bt, *cr* 1929, ext 1960), was a Dir of Iron, Coal and Shipping cos, and MP for Darlington (*L*) 1880-95.

FRY (UK) 1929, of Oare, co Wilts (Extinct 1960)

Sir GEOFFREY STORRS FRY, KCB, CVO, 1st and last *Baronet*.

DAUGHTER LIVING OF FIRST BARONET

Ann Jennifer Evelyn Elizabeth (74 Bishops Mansions, Bishops Park Rd, SW6 6DY), *b* 1916: *m* 1st, 1942 (*m diss* 1947), Robert Vernon Heber-Percy (*see* D Northumberland, colls); 2ndly, 1949 (*m diss* 1985), Alan Ross, CBE, son of late John Brackenridge Ross, CBE, and has issue living (by 1st *m*) (*see* D Northumberland, colls), — (by 2nd *m*), Jonathan Timothy de Beaurepaire (286 Earls Court Rd, SW5 9AS), *b* 1953; *ed* Bryanston: *m* 1st, 1990, Diana Margaret Gort; 2ndly, 1998, Camilla Gabrielle, da of Alexander Shivarg (*see* B Egremont, colls).

FULLER (UK) 1910, of Neston Park, Corsham, Wiltshire

Sir JAMES HENRY FLEETWOOD FULLER, 4th *Baronet*; *b* 1 Nov 1970; *s* his father, *Maj Sir* JOHN WILLIAM FLEETWOOD, 1998; *ed* Milton Abbey; late Capt The Life Gds 1990-98.

Deo Duce Confido
I trust in God as my leader

Arms – Per pale nebuly azure and ermine two bars counterchanged, over all six martlets two, two, and two or. **Crest** – Issuant from a coronet flory or, a lion's head per pale nebuly azure and ermine. **Supporters** – *Dexter*, a lion reguardant proper; *sinister*, a wolf reguardant argent; each gorged with a collar or, pendant therefrom an escutcheon per pale nebuly azure and or, charged with six martlets counter-changed.
Seat – Neston Park, Corsham, Wilts SN13 9TG.

BROTHERS LIVING

ANDREW WILLIAM FLEETWOOD, 1 Dec 1972. —— Edward Richard Fleetwood, *b* 1977.

UNCLE LIVING (*son of 2nd baronet*)

Anthony Gerard Fleetwood, CBE (Little Chalfield Manor, Melksham, Wilts SN12 8NN; Bellvue House, Chiswick, W4) *b* 1940; *ed* Eton; late Lt The Life Guards; Lloyd's underwriter; Dir Fuller Smith and Turner plc since 1967 and Chm from 1982; Master of Brewers' Co 1986-87; Chm of Brewers' Society 1986-89; CBE 1990: *m* 1964, Julia Mary, el da of Lt-Col Eric Astley Cooper-Key, MBE, MC, of 25 Eaton Pl, SW1, and has issue living, William Gerard Fleetwood, *b* 1968, — Camilla Fleetwood, *b* 1966: *m* 1995, Allan Christensen, son of late Finn Christensen, of Copenhagen, and has issue living, Oliver Finn *b* 1998.

WIDOW LIVING OF SECOND BARONET

KATHERINE MARY (*Mary, Lady Fuller*) (Bay Tree Cottage, Chapel Lane, Neston, Corsham, Wilts SN13 9TD; Balmore, Cannich, Inverness), el da of late Douglas Leigh Spence, MC, BCh, MRCS, of Melksham, Wilts, and formerly wife of late E. H. Leventon: *m* 1966, as his 3rd wife Maj Sir (John) Gerard Henry Fleetwood Fuller, 2nd Bt, who *d* 1981.

WIDOW LIVING OF THIRD BARONET

LORNA MARIAN (*Lady Fuller*), only da of late F. Richard Kemp-Potter, of Hillside, Findon, Sussex: *m* 1968, Maj Sir John William Fleetwood Fuller, 3rd Bt, who *d* 1998. *Residence* – Neston Park, Corsham, Wilts SN13 9TG.

COLLATERAL BRANCH LIVING

Issue of late Lt-Col Christopher Herbert Fleetwood Fuller, TD, yr son of 1st baronet, *b* 1908, *d* 1976: *m* 1939, Susan, who *d* 1977, da of late Maj-Gen Sir Percival Otway Hambro, KBE, CB, CMG:—
Charles Christopher Fleetwood, *b* 1945; *ed* Winchester. —— Penelope Susanne Fleetwood, *b* 1942: *m* 1966, George Oliver Worsley, and has issue (*see* Worsley, Bt). —— Victoria Henrietta Fleetwood (*Lady Starkey*), *b* 1944: *m* 1966, Sir John Philip Starkey, 3rd Bt, and has issue (*see* Starkey, Bt). —— Georgina Jacintha Fleetwood, *b* 1951: *m* 1978, Reuben Charles Harford, of Ashcroft House, Kingscote, Tetbury, Glos, only son of Lt-Col Charles Evelyn Harford, and has issue living, Hugh Scandrett, *b* 1980, — Christopher Evelyn, *b* 1985, — Beatrice Louise *b* 1982, — Henrietta Mary, *b* 1987.

The 1st baronet, Sir John Michael Fleetwood, KCMG, was a Junior Lord of the Treasury (unpaid) 1906-7, Vice-Chamberlain of HM's Household 1907-11, and sat as MP for W, or Westbury, Div of Wilts (*L*) 1900-1911, and Gov of Victoria 1911-14.

Fuller-Acland-Hood, see Hood.

FURNESS (UK) 1913, of Tunstall Grange, West Hartlepool

Sir STEPHEN ROBERTS FURNESS, 3rd *Baronet*; *b* 10 Oct 1933; *s* his father, *Sir* CHRISTOPHER 1974; *ed* Charterhouse; Lt RN (ret); sporting artist (as Robin Furness); jt MFH Bedale Foxhounds 1979-87: *m* 1961, Mary, elder da of Jack Fitzroy Cann, of Newland, Cullompton, S Devon, and has issue.

Arms – Per saltire argent and or, a talbot, sejant sable, on a chief wavy gules three plates. Crest – Issuant from a wreath of cinquefoils vert, a bear's paw erect argent, charged with a torteaux, grasping a javelin in bend sinister sable, pendent therefrom by the straps proper two spurs or.
Residence – Stanhow Farm, Great Langton, N Yorks DL7 0TJ.

SON LIVING

MICHAEL FITZROY ROBERTS, *b* 12 Oct 1962; *ed* Sedbergh, and Askham Bryan Coll of Agric and Hort (HND); Farmer: *m* 1998, Katrine L, only da of Kenneth Oxtoby, of Bedale, N Yorks. *Residence* – Glebe Farm, S Otterington, Northallerton, N Yorks.

DAUGHTER LIVING

Serena Mary, *b* 1964: *m* 1991, Lieut Mark F. C. Searight, RM, yst son of late Maj M. P. C. Searight, of E Witton, N Yorks, and has issue living, Tristan Patrick Chamney, *b* 1995, — Kate Isabella, *b* 1992.

BROTHERS LIVING

Simon John (The Garden House, Netherbyres, Eyemouth, Berwickshire TD14 5SE; Army and Navy Club), *b* 1936; Lt-Col, Hon Col 1993, The LI; Comdg 5th Bn the LI (ret 1978); Deputy Col (Durham) The LI since 1989-93; a DL of Berwickshire since 1983, Vice Lord Lieut since 1990; *ed* Charterhouse, and RMA Sandhurst; Chm Nat Trust for Scotland's Garden Cttee. —— Colin Gerard (Cockerdale Farm, Coxwold, York), *b* 1939: *m* 1958, Margaret Grace, only da of Alfred J. Haddock, and has issue living, Francis Christopher, *b* 1963, — Fiona Elizabeth, *b* 1959. *m* 1987, Peter Alan Cloke, only son of Roland Cloke and has issue living, Andrew Philip *b* 1994, — Julia Margaret, *b* 1960, — Nicola Jane, *b* 1964.

SISTER LIVING

Patricia Flower (Whitehall, Old Cleeve, Minehead, Somerset TA24 6HU), *b* 1931: *m* 1960, Maj Paul Ian Craven Payne, late The Royal Scots (despatches), and has issue living, Brian Wyndham *b* 1961; *ed* Winchester and Bristol Univ; BSc; Dip L; Capt The King's Troop RHA 1988-91; Bar, Inner Temple, 1993: *m* 1992, Sally Jane, da of Garnet Thomas, of Ferwig, Dyfed, — Paul Frederick Craven, *b* 1964; *ed* Millfield, BA; ceramist: *m* 1989, Jennifer Anne, yst da of James Donald Douglas, of Tenerife.

COLLATERAL BRANCH LIVING

Issue of late Frank Wilson Furness, MBE, JP, yst son of 1st baronet, *b* 1906, *d* 1993: *m* 1949, Georgeana Anne (Knowle House, Kirby Knowle, Thirsk, N Yorkshire Y07 2JB), only da of Col Victor Alexander Henry Daly, OBE, MC, and widow of Alan Guthrie, Flying Officer RAF:—
John Wilson, *b* 1952; *ed* Wellington: *m* 1983, Grania Patricia, el da of John Brabazon Booth, of Darver Castle, Dundalk, co Louth, and has issue living, Christopher, *b* 1990, — Virginia, *b* 1987.

The 1st baronet, Sir Stephen Wilson, was Chm of Furness, Withy and Co (Limited), and sat as MP for Hartlepool (*L*) 1910-14.

FRANKLAND-PAYNE-GALLWEY (UK) 1812

I would rather die than be dishonoured

Sir PHILIP FRANKLAND-PAYNE-GALLWEY, 6th *Baronet*, only son of Lt-Col Lowry Philip Payne-Gallwey, OBE, MC, el son of Rev Francis Henry Payne-Gallwey, 4th son of Capt Philip Payne-Gallwey, yst son of 1st baronet; *b* 15 March 1935; *s* his kinsman *Sir* REGINALD FRANKLAND, 1964; *ed* Eton; late Lt 11th Hussars; Dir British Bloodstock Agency Ltd; assumed by Roy Licence 1966 the additional surname of Frankland before that of Payne and Gallwey.

Arms – Quarterly: 1st and 4th, per fesse or and gules, in chief an eagle displayed with two heads of the last, in base a bridge of three arches double towered argent, *Gallwey*; 2nd, gules, a fesse between two lions passant argent, *Payne*; 3rd, azure, a dolphin naiant or, on a chief of the last two saltires couped gules, *Frankland*. Crests – 1st, a cat-a-mountain passant guardant proper, gorged with a collar gemelle and charged on the body with a cross patée or, *Gallwey*; 2nd, a lion's jamb erased erect argent, holding the lower part of a tilting spear in bend sinister gules, *Payne*; 3rd, an anchor erect azure, stock or, the shank entwined by a dolphin hauriant argent, *Frankland*.
Residence – The Little House, Boxford, Newbury, Berks.

COLLATERAL BRANCH LIVING

Granddaughter of late Albert Philip Payne-Gallwey, yst son of 1st baronet:—
Issue of late Lt-Col Peter Payne-Gallwey, DSO, *b* 1906, *d* 1971: *m* 1953, Ann Josephine who *d* 1988, da of Roger John Kinloch Barber-Starkey (Legard, Bt, colls):—
Nicola, *b* 1955: *m* 1978, Henry George Fetherstonhaugh (*see* V Galway).

The 1st baronet, Gen Sir William Payne, yr half-brother of Ralph Payne, Lord Lavington (ext 1807), Gov of Leeward Islands, assumed by Roy licence 1814 the additional surname of Gallwey in compliance with will of Tobias Wall Gallwey of St Kitts, his maternal uncle. The 2nd baronet, Sir William Payne-Gallwey, sat as MP for Thirsk (*C*) 1851-80. The 3rd Bt, Sir Ralph William assumed by Roy licence 1914 for himself and issue the additional surname Frankland. The 4th baronet, Sir John Frankland-Payne-Gallwey assumed by Roy licence 1919 the additional surname of Frankland.

GAMBLE (UK) 1897, of Windlehurst, St Helens, Co Palatine of Lancashire

Vix ea nostra voco
I scarce call these things ours

Sir DAVID HUGH NORMAN GAMBLE, 6th *Baronet*; *b* 1 July 1966; *s* his father, *Sir* DAVID, 1984.

Arms – Or, on a pile gules between two trefoils slipped in base vert, a fleur-de-lis of the first, a chief ermine. Crest – On a mount between two trefoils slipped vert a stork argent, holding in the beak a rose gules, stalked, leaved, and slipped proper.
Residence – Keinton House, Keinton Mandeville, Somerton, Somerset TA11 4DX.

SISTERS LIVING

Caroline, *b* 1957. ——— Elinor Josephine, *b* 1961.

WIDOWS LIVING OF FOURTH AND FIFTH BARONETS

OLGA EVELYN (Wood End, Tregony, Truro, Cornwall), da of Robin Arthur Norman Gamble (infra): *m* 1st, 1965, as his 2nd wife, her cousin, Sir David Arthur Josias Gamble, 4th Bt, who *d* 1982; 2ndly, 1989, Anthony Poole, son of Frank Poole, of Leicester.
DAWN ADRIENNE (*Lady Gamble*) (Keinton House, Keinton Mandeville, Somerton, Som), da of late David Hugh Gittins, Pilot Officer, RAF, of The Manor House, W Hagley, Worcs: *m* 1956, Sir David Gamble, 5th Bt, who *d* 1984.

COLLATERAL BRANCHES LIVING

Issue of late Capt Robert Meredith Gamble, 2nd son of 3rd baronet, *b* 1909, *d* 1988: *m* 1st, 1931 (*m diss* 1940), Phyllis Mary, elder da of late Charles E. Bradbury; 2ndly, 1940, Diana Burnaby, who *d* 1977, da of late Walter Francis Drayson, AMICE, of Craven Hill, Lancaster Gate, W2:—

(By 2nd *m*) HUGH ROBERT GEORGE, *b* 3 March 1946: *m* 1989, Rebecca Jane, da of Lt Cdr David Gerald Odell, RN, of Sandpipers, Southampton Rd, Hythe, Havant, Hants, and has issue living, Tobias David Meredith, *b* 9 Aug 1998, — Emily Jessica Alice, *b* 1994. *Residence* – 34 Gallows Hill, Kings Langley, Watford, Herts WD4 8LU. —— Catherine Frances Dorothy, *b* 1940: *m* 1962, Anthony David Weguelin Bertram, of 20 Fraser Av, Caversham, Reading, Berks, and has issue living, Helen Diana Elizabeth, *b* 1965: *m* 1992, Stephen Thurgood, and has issue living, Alison Siân *b* 1994, Claire Tanya *b* 1997, — Isobel Catherine Joan, *b* 1966: *m* 1997, Paul Mrozowski, — Laura Margaret Louise, *b* 1970: *m* 1998, Richard Palmer, — Victoria Susannah Mary, *b* 1974: *m* 1998, Ian Hogg, and has issue living, Oliver Bertram Anthony *b* 1999. —— Sylvia Helen Jean (Cairnmore, Crianlarich, Perth FK20 8QS), *b* 1944: *m* 1967, John Alan Goodale, and has issue living, Benjamin John, *b* 1968: *m* 1995, Linley French, — Thomas Robert, *b* 1971. —— Rosemary Diana Margaret, *b* 1948: *m* 1967, Nicholas Rooker Roberts, of Park Lodge, Church Lane, Yapton-by Arundel, W Sussex BN18 0EH, and has issue living, Andrew Arthur Rooker, *b* 1970, — Eleanor Burnaby Rooker, *b* 1972, — Hannah Margaret Rooker, *b* 1976.

Issue of late John Christopher Gamble, 3rd son of 3rd baronet, *b* 1910, *d* 1989: *m* 1939 (*m diss* 1965), Pamela Margaret Grace, da of Arthur Grayhurst Hewat (Aylmer, Bt).
Antony Aylmer (Evandale, Tasmania, Australia), *b* 1941: *m* 1961, Julie Leslie, and has issue living, David Antony, *b* 1962: *m* 1982, Louise Bott, and has issue living, Christopher David *b* 1984, Dylan John *b* 1992, Hollie Louise *b* 1993, — Christine, *b* 1964, — Kathleen Doris, *b* 1967, — Jeanne, *b* 1971: *m* 1993, Andrew Pennington. —— Ann, *b* 1943: *m* 1962, David J. F. Bailey, RAN, of Perth, Tasmania.

Granddaughters of late John Arthur Gamble, 4th son of 2nd baronet, *b* 1883; *d* 1947: *m* 1910, Lilian Jane Emily who *d* 1913, da of late Rev Arthur Raggett Cole, of Hurstbourne Priors, Hants:—
Issue of late Robin Arthur Norman Gamble, *b* 1912; *d* 1981: *m* 1st, 1939, Emily Goodall, who *d* 1944; 2ndly, 1947, Muriel Maud (Overcreek, St Just-in-Roseland, Truro, Cornwall), da of late John Hale, of Knowsley, Lancs:—
(By 1st *m*) Elaine Lilian (Heathside, Jackmans Lane, St Johns, Woking, Surrey), *b* 1941: *m* 1970, Malcolm Charles Gubbins, who *d* 1987, and has issue living, Fiona, *b* 1981. —— Olga Evelyn, *b* 1944: *m* 1st, 1965, as his 2nd wife, her cousin, Sir David Arthur Josias Gamble, 4th Bt, who *d* 1982; 2ndly, 1989, Anthony Poole, son of Frank Poole, of Leicester. *Residence* – Wood End, Tregony, Truro, Cornwall.

Granddaughter (by 1st *m*) of David Gamble, 3rd son of 1st baronet (infra):—
Issue of late Lorentz Harry Gamble, *b* 1893, *d* 1968: *m* 1917, Annie Marian, who *d* 1972, da of F. T. Clarke, of Stony Stratford:—
Diana May (Bramble's Place, 6 Abbey Sq, Turvey, Beds), *b* 1920; formerly Jun Com ATS.

Grandchildren (by 2nd *m*) of David Gamble, 3rd son of 1st baronet (infra):—
Issue of late Graeme Neil, *b* 1904, *d* 1980: *m* 1936, Mary George (Coombe Cottage, Plainsfield, Over Stowey, Bridgwater, Som):—
Sheila Ann, *b* 1937: *m* 1959, James Bridley Douglas Bateman, of Lodmore Farm, E Harptree, Bristol, and has issue living, James Graeme Richard, *b* 1967, — William John Douglas, *b* 1974, — Angus Neil Cyril, *b* 1978, — Fiona Valerie, *b* 1964: *m* 1993, Mark Rule, — Sylvia Mary, *b* 1966, Rosalind Ann, *b* 1969. —— Judith Mary, *b* 1940: *m* 1962, Hagen Volken Dietrich Stöckl, and has issue living, Alexander Duncan Dietrich, *b* 1963, — Natasha Judith, *b* 1964. —— Jane Elizabeth, *b* 1943. —— Tessa Marion, *b* 1952: *m* 1976, Malcolm Paul Bennett of Summerstead House, Over Stowey, Bridgwater, Somerset TA5 1HA, and has issue living, Nicholas Paul, *b* 1984, — Jos Daniel Graeme, *b* 1986, — Fenella Heidi, *b* 1988.

Issue of late David Gamble, 3rd son of 1st baronet, *b* 1856, *d* 1933: *m* 1st, 1880, Josephine Henriette, who *d* 1899, da of Conrad von Dorner; 2ndly, 1901, Marion, who *d* 1955, da of Griffith Parsonage, of Australia:—
(By 2nd *m*) Alan Lionel, *b* 1905. *Residence* – 14 Lower Common South, Putney, SW15.

Grandchildren of late George Gamble, 4th son of 1st baronet:—
Issue, if any (by 2nd *m*) of late Charles Lancelot Gamble, *b* 1885, *d* 19—: *m* 1st, 1906 (*m diss* 1908), Zoë Armstrong; 2ndly, 1909.

Issue of late Henry Gamble, 6th son of 1st baronet, *b* 1868, *d* 1927: *m* 1895, Ethel, who *d* 1924, da of late Thomas Brewis:—
David Harry, *b* 1911: *m* 1949, May, who *d* 198-, only child of Olivier Swithenbank, JP, of Leeds. —— Winifred Kathleen, *b* 1899: *m* 1927, Fred Russell Roberts, who *d* 1953.

The 1st baronet, Sir David, KCB, was Mayor of St Helens 1868-70, 1882-3 and 1886-7, a pioneer of the Volunteer Movement, and first Hon Col (VD) 2nd Vol Batn Prince of Wales' Vols (S Lancashire Regt). The 2nd baronet, Sir Josias Christopher, was also Mayor of St Helens, 1888-9. The 3rd baronet, Sir David, was also Mayor of St Helens 1913-15. The 4th baronet, Sir David Arthur Josias, was Chm of Cirencester RDC, and served in Northern Province, Nigeria.

BRUCE-GARDNER (UK) 1945, of Frilford, co Berks

Sir ROBERT HENRY BRUCE-GARDNER, 3rd *Baronet*; *b* 10 June 1943; *s* his father, *Sir* DOUGLAS BRUCE, 1997; *ed* Uppingham, and Reading Univ; Dir Dept of Conservation and Technology, Courtauld Inst of Art: *m* 1979, Veronica Ann HAND OXBORROW, da of late Rev W. E. Hand, and has issue.

𝕬rms – Or, a saltire couped gules, charged with five bezants, on a chief of the second a bee volant proper between two roses argent, barbed and seeded also proper. 𝕮rest – In front of a miner's pick and gad in saltire a thistle leaved and slipped all proper.
Residence – 121 Brackenbury Rd, W6 0BQ. *Club* – Travellers'.

SONS LIVING

THOMAS EDMUND PETER, *b* 28 Jan 1982. —— Richard Tyndall Jowett, *b* 1983.

HALF-BROTHER LIVING

James Graham, *b* 1969.

SISTERS LIVING

By work and strength

Erica Judith, *b* 1941: *m* 1962, Paul H. Blackburn, of Cwm Meigan, Blaenffos, Boncath SA37 0JE, and has issue living, Richard Martin, *b* 1965: *m* 1991, Felicity Anne Sophia Jones, and has issue living, Thomas Alexander *b* 1997, Laura Jane *b* 1995, — Robert Paul, *b* 1967, — Katherine Mary, *b* 1963: *m* 1986, Guy Mark Larkin, and has issue living, Thea Gabriella *b* 1990, — Emma Louise (twin), *b* 1965: *m* 1st, 1984 (*m diss* 1988), Simon David Hamblin; 2ndly, 1990, Christopher Ernest Heard, and has issue living, (by 1st *m*) Kirsty Alexandra HEARD *b* 1985 (adopted by her step-father 1995), (by 2nd *m*) Jordan William *b* 1990, Rebecca Louise *b* 1991. —— Sarah Tanis, *b* 1952: *m* 1987, Richard William Towse, son of John Towse, of The Garth, Church Crescent, N3 1BG, and has issue living, Benjamin William, *b* 1988, — David James, *b* 1990, — Rachel Monica, *b* 1994.

HALF-SISTER LIVING

Joanna Margaret, *b* 1966; has issue living (by Peter John Richards), Ella Jane RICHARDS, *b* 1994. *Residence* – 2 Cleddon Cottages, Trellech, nr Monmouth NP5 4TP.

UNCLE LIVING

Bryan Charles, *b* 1924; *ed* Uppingham, and Trin Coll Camb (MA): *m* 1952, Helen Rosemary, da of late Digby B. Sowerby, of Kirmington House, nr Ulceby, Lincolnshire, and has issue living, Edwin Charles, *b* 1954, — Robin Digby (60 Cumberland St, SW1V 4LZ), *b* 1955: *m* 1987, Caroline Stuart, da of Peter S. Wright, of Thurlstone, Devon, — Stephen Bryan (Eaton Lodge, Pulford, Chester), *b* 1957: *m* 1990, Karen, yst da of Harry Spencer, of Mold, Clwyd, — Ian Douglas (Greenspot Farm, Oldmeldrum, Inverurie, Aberdeenshire AB51 0AG), *b* 1963: *m* 1990, Elisabeth (Beth) Mary, da of late R. D. White, and of Mrs D. H. McLellan, of Ollerton, Cheshire, and has issue living, Angus Ramsay *b* 1995, Rosannah Charlotte *b* 1992.

WIDOW LIVING OF SECOND BARONET

SHEILA JANE (*Sheila, Lady Bruce-Gardner*), da of late Roger Stilliard, of Henley-on-Thames, Oxon: *m* 1964, as his 2nd wife, Sir Douglas Bruce Bruce-Gardner, 2nd Bt, who *d* 1997. *Residence* – Stocklands, Lewstone, Ganarew, nr Monmouth NP5 3SS.

Sir Charles Bruce-Gardner, 1st Bt (son of late Henry Gardner, of Stanstead Lodge, SE23), was Industrial Advisor to the Gov of the Bank of England 1930-38, Chm Soc of British Aircraft Constructors 1938-43, Controller of Labour Allocation MAP 1943-44, Chief Executive for Industrial Conversion, Bd of Trade, 1944-46, Chm John Lysaght Ltd 1946-59, Dir GKN Ltd 1946-59, Dep Chm Steel Co of Wales 1946-60, Dir Consett Iron Co Ltd 1946-60, Vice-Chm Crompton Parkinson Ltd 1946-60, and Pres Iron and Steel Inst 1955-56.

GARTHWAITE (UK) 1919, of Durham

Sir (WILLIAM) MARK CHARLES GARTHWAITE, 3rd *Baronet*; *b* 4 Nov 1946; *s* his father *Sir* WILLIAM FRANCIS CUTHBERT, DSC, 1993; *ed* Gordonstoun, and Univ of Pennsylvania (BSc): *m* 1979, Victoria Lisette, da of Gen Sir Harry Tuzo, GCB, OBE, MC, of Heath Farm House, Fakenham, Norfolk, and formerly wife of Robert Henry Adolphus Hohler, and has issue.

𝔄rms – Azure, a cross between in the first and fourth quarters five ears of wheat banded, and in the second and third quarters a greyhound rampant, all or. ℭrest – In front of a capstan sable, garnished gold, and fleur-de-lis also gold. *Residence* – 3 Hazlewell Rd, SW15 6LU.

SON LIVING

WILLIAM TUZO, *b* 14 May 1982.

DAUGHTERS LIVING

Rosie Francesca, *b* 1980. ——— Jemima Victoria, *b* 1984.

HALF-BROTHERS LIVING

Cuique suum
To each his own

John William Philip (Matfield Oast, Chestnut Lane, Matfield, Tonbridge, Kent TN12 7JJ), *b* 1958: *m* 1983, Sarah Elizabeth, da of Rev Charles Anthony Maclea March, and has issue living, Joanna Rachel, *b* 1992, — Rebecca Elizabeth, *b* 1994. ——— Andrew William David, *b* 1962: *m* 19—, Georgina B., eldest da of Roger Hadlee, of Fairstead, Essex, and has issue living, Philip William Roger, *b* 1997, — Eleanor Kate Francesca, *b* 1996. ——— Simon William James (Ballingdon House, Gaddesden Row, Herts HP2 6HX), *b* (twin) 1962: *m* 1989, Caroline Sally, elder da of John Pigott, of Thrales End, Harpenden, Herts, and has issue living, James William John, *b* 1991, — George William Angus, *b* 1993.

HALF-UNCLE LIVING (*son of 1st baronet*)

Michael William Gladwin (c/o Barclays Bank, 68 Knightsbridge, SW1X 7NT), *b* 1937; *ed* Trinity College Sch, Ontario.

MOTHER LIVING

Patricia Beatrice Eden, da of the late Cdr Charles Eden Neate, RN, and widow of Cdr Barry Leonard, RN: *m* 1945 (*m diss* 1952), as his 2nd wife, Sir William Francis Cuthbert Garthwaite, 2nd Bt, DSC, who *d* 1993. *Residence* – The Old Rectory, Hawling, Glos.

WIDOW LIVING OF SECOND BARONET

PATRICIA MERRIEL (*Patricia, Lady Garthwaite*), only da of late Sir Philip d'Ambrumenil: *m* 1957, as his 3rd wife, Sir William Francis Cuthbert Garthwaite, 2nd Bt, DSC, who *d* 1993.

COLLATERAL BRANCH LIVING

Issue of late Anthony William Garthwaite, 2nd son of 1st baronet, *b* 1917, *d* 1972: *m* 1950, Hon Waveney Mancroft Samuel, who *d* 1986, da of 1st Baron Mancroft:—
Nicholas Anthony William Mancroft, *b* 1952: *m* 1982, Caroline C., da of Thomas Willbourne, of Thorney, Peterborough, and has issue living, Oliver Julian, *b* 1986, — Felix Sebastian, *b* 1987, — Piers Marcus, *b* 1990.

The 1st baronet, Sir William Garthwaite (son of William Garthwaite, of Staindrop, Durham), was a shipowner and was engaged in sugar planting. He rendered services in developing relations between Canada and France, and inaugurating direct line of shipping between those countries, and Special Ser to Admiralty in European Wars 1914-18 and 1939-45.

Gervis (Tapps-Gervis-Meyrick), see Meyrick.

GETHIN (I) 1665, of Gethinsgrott, Cork

Sir RICHARD JOSEPH ST LAWRENCE GETHIN, 10th *Baronet*; *b* 29 Sept 1949; *s* his father, *Lt-Col Sir* RICHARD PATRICK ST LAWRENCE 1988; *ed* Oratory Sch, RMA Sandhurst, and RMC of Science, Shrivenham; BSc (Civil Engrg), MSc; Maj RCT: *m* 1974, Jacqueline Torfrida, da of Cdr David Cox, RN, and has issue.

𝔄rms – Vert, a stag salient argent armed or. 𝔠rest – On a cap of dignity proper, a stag's head erased argent armed and ducally gorged or.

DAUGHTERS LIVING

Katherine Torfrida, *b* 1976. —— Rosanna Clare, *b* 1979. —— Belinda Jacqueline, *b* 1981.

SISTERS LIVING

Helen Mary Elizabeth, *b* 1947: *m* 1975, David Strachan, of 20 Pollock Esplanade, Woolgoolga, NSW 2456, Aust, and has issue living, Rachael Fara, *b* 1977, — Roxanne Emma, *b* 1979. —— Fara Mary Nicola, *b* 1948: *m* 1969, Michael Smee, and has issue living, Oliver Leo, *b* 1971. — Milo Henry, *b* 1973, — Leo Joseph, *b* 1976. —— Georgina Jennifer Mary, *b* 1952: *m* 1979, Daniel Meadows, of 7 St Dial's Close, Monmouth, Gwent NP5 4EE, and has issue living, Harry Daniel *b* 1980, — Luke Roland, *b* 1982, — Jack Richard, *b* 1987. —— Mary Valentine Harriet, *b* 1954: *m* 1978, Martin Philip Runnacles, and has issue living, Elizabeth Jane Fara, *b* 1982, — Sarah Caroline, *b* 1988.

AUNT LIVING (*daughter of 8th baronet*)

Norah Helen Catharine (2 Atwater Court, Lenham, Maidstone), *b* 1907: *m* 1938, James Andrew Paton Charles, who *d* 1979, and has issue living, Michael James Paton (85 Wylde Rd, Morley, Perth, W Australia), *b* 1939: *m* 1st, 1964 (*m diss* 1969), Barbara Elizabeth, da of A. M. Turner, of Strathfield, NSW; 2ndly, 1969, Maureen, da of J. Taylor, of Kiama, NSW, and has issue living, (by 2nd *m*) Julian Andrew Paton *b* 1973, Dominic *b* 1976, Timothy *b* 1979, — Edward William (Dacca, Bangladesh), *b* 1944; BSc Agric and Trop Dip Trinidad; MPhil: *m* 1973, Rosemarie, da of K. Kramer, of Winnipeg, Canada, and has issue living, Daniel *b* 1977, Andrew *b* 1980, Simon *b* 1984, Elizabeth Helen *b* 1975, — Elizabeth Ann, *b* (twin) 1944: *m* 1975 (*m diss* 1985), Clive Cromarty Bloom.

WIDOW LIVING OF NINTH BARONET

FARA (*Dowager Lady Gethin*); 2nd Officer WRNS, da of late Joseph Henry Bartlett: *m* 1946, Lt-Col Sir Richard Patrick St Lawrence Gethin, 9th Bt, who *d* 1988. *Residence* – 68 Emanuel House, 18 Rochester Row, SW1P 1BS.

COLLATERAL BRANCHES LIVING

Issue of late Lt-Col William Allan Tristram Gethin, MC, yr son of 8th baronet, *b* 1913, *d* 1997: *m* 1937, Nancy Ruth, who *d* 1999, only child of late Lt-Col H. G. MacGeorge, late RE, of Paignton:—
ANTHONY MICHAEL (Vale House, Loose, Maidstone, Kent) *b* 10 Jan 1939; *ed* Oundle, and Magdalene Coll, Camb (MA): *m* 1965, Vanse, yr da of late Col Cecil Disney Barlow, OBE, KSLI, and has issue living, Nicholas Richard Tristram (Lossenham Manor, Newenden, Kent), *b* 15 Dec 1965: *m* 1993, Tavia C. PARDOE-JONES, da of Ronald Jones, of Evander, Transvaal, and has issue living, Alistair Richard Tristram *b* 7 Jan 1999, Lydia Mary Christobelle *b* 1997, — William Anthony David St Lawrence, *b* 1970: *m* 1997, Belinda Anthea, yst da of Lt-Col Sir Blair Aubyn Stewart-Wilson, KCVO (see Orr-Ewing, Bt, colls), — Emma Kirstie, *b* 1968: *m* 1995, Robert V. Reid, eldest son of Hubert Reid, of Marton, Cheshire, and has issue living, Oliver Valentine *b* 1998. —— Patricia Jane (Rose Cottage, Loose, Maidstone, Kent), *b* 1944: *m* 1967 (*m diss* 1981), Malcolm Pringle, and has issue living, Richard Malcolm Andrew, *b* 1974, — Caroline Georgina, *b* 1970.

Grandchildren of late Lt-Col Frederick Durrant Scott Gethin (infra):—
Issue of late John Amory Forrest Gethin, *b* 1916, *d* 1965: *m* 1941, Barbara Damarel Cicely (Brae View, Wester Galcantray, Cawdor by Nairn), da of late Alan Robert Cecil Westlake, of Rowledge, Farnham, Surrey:—
Christopher John Forrest (Higher Pudsham, Buckland-in-the-Moor, South Devon TQ13 7HW) *b* 1945; *ed* Stowe, Magdalene Coll, Cambridge (MA), University of Sydney (MTCP), and Sch of Homoeopathy (Dip Hom): *m* 1983, Rebecca Mary, da of Benjamin Thomas Gibbins, of San Remo, Italy, and has issue living, Tobias John Forrest, *b* 1983. —— Nicholas Geoffrey Forrest (35 Claremont Rd, Teddington, Middx), *b* 1950; *ed* Stowe, Ch Ch, Oxford (MA), R Academy of Music (LRAM), and Hochschule Für Musik, Vienna: *m* 1993, Catherine, da of John Nelson, of Cardiff, and has issue living, Daniel Paul Forrest, *b* 1995, — Sebastian Christopher Forrest, *b* 1997. —— Stephen Amory Forrest (La Besse, 24620 Peyzac le Moustier, France), *b* (twin) 1950; *ed* Stowe, and Magdalene Coll, Camb (MA, Vet MB): *m* 1992, Christine, da of Hervé Fondecave, of Toulouse, France, and has issue living, Amory Lionel, *b* 1995. —— Elizabeth Amoret, *b* 1942: *m* 1965, Nicholas John du Cane Wilkinson, Lt-Cdr RN (ret), of Birkwood Cottage, Wester Brae of Cantray, Croy, Inverness-shire, and has issue living, Piers Nicholas, *b* 1973, — Samantha Karen, *b* 1967: *m* 1994, Matthew Godfrey-Faussett, yr son of Richard Godfrey-Faussett, of Badlesmere, Kent, and has issue living, Iona Elizabeth *b* 1997, — Claire Felicity, *b* 1968: *m* 1997, James Frank Lithgow, elder son of Sir William James Lithgow, 2nd Bt, and has issue living (see that title).

Issue of late Lieut-Col Frederick Durrant Scott Gethin, 2nd son of 7th baronet, *b* 1879, *d* 1959: *m* 1915, Margaret Cecilia, who *d* 1955, da of L. R. W. Forrest, of Beech Holme, Wimbledon Common, SW:—

Margaret Joan, *b* 1920. *Residence* – Coulmhor, Gollanfield, Inverness IV1 2QR.

Issue of late Percy Edward Lovell Gethin, yst son of 7th baronet, OBE, AFC, *b* 1884, *d* 1969: *m* 1918, Norah, who *d* 1960, da of James Norwood Stapledon:—
†Robert Hugh, *b* 1918; *ed* Stowe, and Corpus Christi Coll, Camb (MA); 1939-45 War with Intelligence Corps, and 1st Airborne Div: *m* 1946, Marjorie Gertrude (6 Montfort Fields, Kington, Herefords HR5 3AT), da of B. E. Elliott, and *d* 1999, leaving issue living, Rupert Mark Lovell (26 Morgan St, St Agnes, Bristol BS2 9LQ), *b* 1957; *ed* Manchester Univ (BA, MA, PhD): *m* 1997, Rita Elisabeth Maria, da of H. Langer, of Nordkirchen, Germany, and has issue living, Leonard Alexander Hugh *b* 1996, — Damaris Alicia Honor, *b* 1952; *ed* E Anglia Univ (BA); and Manchester Univ (MBA): *m* 1985, José Guillermo Albarrán, who *d* 1988, and has issue living, Isabel Grace *b* 1987. —— Percy Amorey Beaufort (60 Scotland Rd, Cambridge), *b* 1925; *ed* King's Sch, Canterbury; BA London: *m* 1st, 1948 (*m diss* 1972), Sylva, da of B. Olters, of Gothenburg, Sweden; 2ndly, 1972, Mieko, da of late Choji Suzuki, of Tokyo, Japan, and has issue living, (by 1st *m*) Terence Bertil Amorey (8 Elyne Rd, N4 4RA), *b* 1956; *ed* Imperial Coll, London Univ (BSc): *m* 1995, Rosemary Jane, da of Clifford Arthur Keer, of Leicester.

Grandchildren of late Percy Addison Hayward Gethin, el son of late William St Lawrence Gethin, 2nd son of late Capt Richard Gethin, son of 5th baronet:—
Issue of late Lieut-Col Percy St Lawrence Gethin, MBE, *b* 1889, *d* 1959: *m* 1913, Margery, who *d* 1968, da of late James J. Cleverly, of Walfish Bay, Cape Province, S Africa:—
Patrick St Lawrence Cleverly, *b* 1914; *ed* Cheltenham; Major (ret) Roy Inniskilling Fusiliers; European War 1939-42 (wounded): *m* 1940, Dagmar May, only child of late N. H. Daniell, of Race View, Coonoor, S India, and has issue living, Rowene Margaret, *b* 1944: *m* 1970, Salvador Rodriguez-Perez, of Namanga, Orchard Lane, E Hendred, Wantage, Oxon, OX12 8JW, and has issue living, Marcus Lawrence *b* 1974, Elaine Patricia (319 Beechgrove Drive, Scarborough, Ontario, Canada M1E 4A2), *b* 1946: *m* 1968, Paul Disbury Marsh, who *d* 1995, and has issue living, Jeremy Stephen *b* 1973, Nicola Clare *b* 1970. *Address* – 4 Orchard Close, Berry Lane, East Hanney, nr Wantage, Oxon OX12 0JD. —— Sheelagh Grace *b* 1923: *m* 1947, James Wilson Lindsay, CBE, of 22 Wellington Drive, Kingston 6, Jamaica, W1, and has issue living, Ian Gethin, *b* 1951: *m* 1978, Ann Bettany, and has issue living, Keri Gethin *b* 1986, Emma Alexandra *b* 1978.

Grandchildren of late Maj Randolph George Gethin, MBE (*infra*):—
Issue of late Maj Desmond Richard le Poer Gethin, *b* 1919, *d* 1984: *m* 1950, Susan Frances (who *m* 2ndly, 1988, Maj W. P. Mead, of 2 Harewood Green, Lymington, Hants SO41 0TZ), da of Brig F. Talbot Baines:—
Martin Anthony (Cnwc y Mortol, Letterston, Haverfordwest, Dyfed SA6Z 5XE), *b* 1952; *ed* St Columba's Coll, and Seale Hayne Coll: *m* 1978, Christine Ann, da of A.F. Bates, of Purley, Bognor Regis, Sussex, and has issue living, Robert Lawrence, *b* 1984, — Jared Desmond, *b* 1986. —— Deirdre Anne, *b* 1951.

Granddaughter of late Capt George Gethin, son of late Richard Gethin, grandson of late John Gethin, 2nd son of 3rd baronet:—
Issue of late Maj Randolph George Gethin, MBE, *b* 1871, *d* 1945: *m* 1911, Georgina Mary, who *d* 1956, da of late Rev George Beresford Power (Power, Bt, colls, *cr* 1836):—
Kathleen Beatrix (Rincurran, Ardbrack, Kinsale, co Cork), *b* 1912.

Grandsons of late Francis Reid Gethin, 2nd son of Richard Gethin (*ante*):—
Issue of late Capt Richard Gethin, *b* 1886, *d* 1976: *m* 1st, 1927 (*m diss* 1953), Mary Hunter, who *d* 1972, el da of Willoughby James Bond, of Farragh, co Longford; 2ndly, 1953, Winifred Louise (Registry Cottage, High St, Limpsfield, Surrey), da of Frank James Hall, of Edgbaston, Birmingham:—
(By 1st *m*) Richard Reid (6 Saxons Acre, Warminster, Wilts), *b* 1931: *m* 1980 (*m diss* 1994), Brenda Elizabeth, da of late Walter George Treadwell of Sidcup, Kent. —— Alexander Willoughby (Holly House, Orchehill Av, Gerrards Cross), *b* 1935; *ed* Jesus Coll, Camb (MA): *m* 1964, Patricia, yr da of Alfred Sweeney of Gerrards Cross, and has issue living, Alexandra Mary (2 Loris Rd, W6), *b* 1965; *ed* St John's Coll, Camb (MA), — Frances Sheilagh, *b* (twin) 1965; *ed* Downing Coll, Camb (MA): *m* 1991, Quintus R. C. L. Travis, of 26 Faroe Rd, W14, — Elizabeth Alice, *b* 1970.

Richard Gethin of Mallow, co Cork, *b* about 1615, was MP for Clonmell 1639-45, and Newton Limavady 1661-66. He received large grants of land from Charles II, upon the understanding that he should establish an English colony and erect manufactories. He received letters patent by which the lands of Cariglemleary were erected into a manor by the name of Gethinsgrott. The 1st wife of the 2nd baronet, Grace Norton, was remarkable for her talent and piety, and a monument to her memory is erected in Westminster Abbey. The 8th baronet, Col Sir Richard Walter St Lawrence Gethin, CMG, DSO, late RA, served in S Africa 1899-1901, and in 1914-18 War.

OSBORNE-GIBBES (GB) 1774, of Springhead, Barbados (Extinct 1940)

Sir PHILIP ARTHUR OSBORNE-GIBBES, 4th and last *Baronet*.

COLLATERAL BRANCH LIVING

Issue of late Philip Ernest Osborne-Gibbes, 7th son of 2nd baronet, *b* 1862, *d* 1934: *m* 1904: Dulcie, *b* 19—: *m* 1932, W. E. Bendrey, of Lakemba, Sydney, NSW, and has issue living, Michael, *b* 1938.

GIBBONS (GB) 1752, of Stanwell Place, Middlesex

It is more agreeable coming from a pious king

Sir WILLIAM EDWARD DORAN GIBBONS, 9th *Baronet*; *b* 13 Jan 1948; *s* his father, *Sir* JOHN EDWARD, 1982; *ed* Pangbourne, RNC Dartmouth, Bristol Univ (BSc), and Southampton Univ (MBA); JP South Westminster: *m* 1972, Patricia Geraldine, LLB, da of Roland Archer Howse, of Jersey, CI, and has issue.

𝕬rms – Gules, a lion rampant or debruised by a bend argent charged with a torteau between two crosses patée-fitchée sable. 𝕮rest – A lion's jamb erased and erect gules, charged with a bezant and holding a cross as in the arms.
Residence – 5 Yarborough Rd, Southsea, Hants P05 3DZ.

SON LIVING

CHARLES WILLIAM EDWIN, *b* 28 Jan 1983.

DAUGHTER LIVING

Joan Eleanor Maud, *b* 1980.

SISTERS LIVING

Charlotte Anne Wentworth, *b* 1939; a JP Avon: *m* 1963, Hylton Henry Bayntun-Coward (High Sheriff Avon 1993), of Dunkerton Grange, nr Bath, Somerset, and has issue living, Edward William George (Midford House, Bath, Somerset), *b* 1966: *m* 1995, Laura C., only da of Richard Banz, of Worplesdon, Surrey, and has issue living, Lily Ellen Georgia *b* 1998, — Jonathan Henry Alexander, *b* 1972, — Emma Louise Wentworth, *b* 1964: *m* 1998, Jetu Lalvani, son of Taru Lalvani, of Bombay, India, and has issue living, Coco Acacia Charlotte *b* 1999, — Polly Jane Constance, *b* 1970: *m* 1997, Edward W. G. Nicholson, yr son of Col David Nicholson, of Marlborough, and has issue living, Eve Kitty Charlotte *b* 1998. —— Jane *b* 1942: *m* 1966, Neville James Henry Grant, of 13 Glenluce Rd, Blackheath, SE3 7SD, and has issue living, Thomas Paul Wentworth, *b* 1969, — Alexander Hugh Wentworth, *b* 1973, — (by adoption) Tara Catherine, *b* 1975.

MOTHER LIVING

Mersa Wentworth, da of late Maj Edward Bayntun Grove Foster, of Warmwell, Dorset: *m* 1937 (*m diss* 1951), Sir John Edward Gibbons, 8th Bt, who *d* 1982. *Residence* – 30 Cornwallis Crescent, Clifton, Bristol B88 4PH.

COLLATERAL BRANCHES LIVING

Grandchildren of late Capt Frederick Gibbons, brother of 5th baronet:—
Issue of late Capt Frederick Kenrick Colquhoun Gibbons, RN, *b* 1865, *d* 1954: *m* 1895, Edith Kapiolani, who *d* 1959, da of late A. T. Atkinson, of Honolulu, Hawaii:—
Marjorie Kapiolani, *b* 1896: *m* 1925, Lieut-Col Pillans Scarth Whitehead, OBE, RA, and has issue living, Belinda Kapiolani, *b* 1929: *m* 1956, Archibald Peter Brown, and has issue living, Archibald Stephen *b* 1958, William Lambert *b* 1964, Isobel Clare *b* 1960, Judith Margaret *b* (twin) 1964. —— Nancy Alatau, *b* 1907: *m* 1939, Hugo Wilhelm Runfelt, and has issue living, Anne Marie, *b* 1941. *Residence* – Bastad, Sweden.

Grandchildren of late Robert Gibbons (*b* 1866), only son of late Rev Robert Gibbons, eldest son of late Robert Kenrick Gibbons (infra):—
Issue of late Com Robert Reginald Gibbons, OBE, RN, *b* 1894, *d* 1959: *m* 1st, 1922, Olive (*m diss* 1930), da of William Blane, CBE; 2ndly, 1930 (*m diss* 1939), Ellery, da of late Maj-Gen Sir Amyatt Hull, of Beacon Downe, nr Exeter; 3rdly, 1939, Joan Winifred, who *d* 1983, da of F. S. Paterson, of Southborough, Kent:—
(By 3rd *m*), Robert John, *b* 1944: *m* 1st, 1966 (*m diss* 1971), Pauline Elizabeth, da of Stanley Charles March, of 41 Deerswood Rd, West Green, Crawley, Sussex; 2ndly, 1973 (*m diss* 1980), Anne Marie, da of Charles Lundberg, of 19 Jeymer Drive, Greenford, Middx; 3rdly, 1986, Elizabeth Jean, da of late W/Cdr Norman Henry Carrier, of 16 Russell Hill, Purley, Surrey, and has issue living (by 3rd *m*), Pippa Christine, *b* 1987. —— Susan, *b* 1941: *m* 1959, Dennis Gordon Pollard, of 27 School Lane, Ashurstwood, E Grinstead, Sussex RH19 3QW, and has issue living, Peter Dennis (1 New Cottage, Homestall Rd, Ashurstwood, nr East Grinstead, Sussex), *b* 1964: *m* 1997, Mrs Janine Baldwin, — Lesley Susan, *b* 1960: *m* 1978, Edward John Hart, of 30 Stanmore Grove, Kirkstall, Leeds LS4 2RG, and has issue living, Jennifer Susan *b* 1979, — Janet May, *b* 1969: *m* 1989, Andrew Paul Brander, of 5 Betchley Close, East Grinstead, W Sussex, son of Anthony Brander, of 10 Garden Close, East Grinstead, and has issue living, Christopher Iain *b* 1993, Emma Louise *b* 1990.

Grandchildren of late Sir William Gibbons, KCB, yst son of Robert Kenrick Gibbons, 2nd son of Robert Gibbons, 4th son of 2nd baronet:—
Issue of late Sir William Kenrick Gibbons, CB, *b* 1876, *d* 1957: *m* 1915, Aileen Margaret Dale, who *d* 1969, da of George J. E. Trotter:—
Diana Maynard (Bernardene, The Green, Letchmore Heath, Watford, Herts), *b* 1916. —— Priscilla Doreen, *b* 1918. —— June Cecilia, *b* 1926.

Issue of late Lieut-Col Edward Stephen Gibbons, DSO, Duke of Cambridge's Own (Middlesex Regt), *b* 1883, *ka* 1918: *m* 1914, Annie Macgregor, who *d* 1968, da of late John Lyle, of Finnart House, Weybridge:—

Elisabeth Margaret, *b* 1915: *m* 1936, Lieut-Cdr John Edgar Burstall, RN, who *d* 1979, and has issue living, Mark Stephen, *b* 1945, — Elisabeth Ann, *b* 1937, — Gillian Margaret, *b* 1939. *Residence* – The Garden House, Orcheston, Salisbury, Wilts.

Grandson of late Lieut-Col Edward Stephen Gibbons, DSO (ante):—
Issue of late Lieut Cdr John William Gibbons, RN, *b* 1917, *d* 1993: *m* 1st, 1940 (*m diss* 1947), Alix, da of late Bertram Lenox-Simpson, of Forta Fayre, Havelet, Guernsey; 2ndly, 1964, Mrs Mary Lammin Stone (Flat 4, Lions Hall, St Swithun St, Winchester, Hants), yst da of late G. E. Woof:—
(By 1st *m*) Alan Clive, *b* 1941.

Granddaughter of late Lt-Col William Barton Gibbons, 3rd son of late Robert Gibbons (ante):—
Issue of late John Abel Gibbons, *b* 1854, *d* 1894: *m* 1884, Katharine Alice, who *d* 1937, da of Joseph Seymour Salaman, formerly of 143 Sutherland Avenue, W:—
Dorothy Margaret Maxwell: *m* 1914, John Brook (in Imperial Yeo during S African War, and as a Gunner in Canadian Field Artillery during European War), and has issue living, John Burbridge (1394 Mount Pleasant, Toronto, Canada), *b* 1914; is a Chemical Engineer: *m* 1940, Joanne Price, of Cleveland, Ohio, USA, and has issue living, David Jeremy *b* 1947, Calvin Price *b* 1955, Martha Lyn *b* 1944, — Philip Roy, DFC, *b* 1918; is Fl Lt Roy Canadian Air Force, and an Architect; 1939-45 War (DFC): *m* 1949, Sonia Dixon, of Bournemouth, and has issue living, Michael Brian *b* 1951, Gregory Laurence *b* 1953, Matthew Ian *b* 1959, Deborah Jane *b* 1955, Dinah Louise, *b* 1957, — June Rosemary, *b* 1920: *m* 1940, Charles H. Doty, of 49 Huntly St, Toronto, Canada, and has issue living, Stephen Charles *b* 1942, Susan Jane *b* 1944: *m* 19—, ... Jacobsen, of St Anne de Sorel, Quebec, Barbara Jane *b* 1949.

Grandchildren of late John Crookenden de Courcy Gibbons (infra):—
Issue of late John Hayton Gibbons, *b* 1909, *d* 1963: *m* 1945, Phyllis (who *m* 2ndly, 19—, Donald Sheehan, of 24 Springdale Rd, Killara, NSW 2071), da of ......:—
John William, *b* 1954. ——— Victoria Hayton, *b* 1948. ——— Elizabeth, *b* 1951.

Granddaughters of late Lieut-Col Frederick FitzRoy Gibbons, el son of late Lieut-Col William Barton Gibbons (ante):—
Issue of late John Crookenden de Courcy Gibbons, *b* 1874, *d* 1944: *m* 1907, Gladys Russell Jones, who *d* 1984:—
Marjorie Mary, *b* 1922: *m* 1944, Clive Stanley Willey, of 2901 Postgate Lane, Peabody, MA 01960-4746, USA, and has issue living, Lyn Gladys, *b* 1947, — Rae Marjorie, *b* (twin) 1947, — Sue Phillis, *b* 1951. *Residence* –

Issue of late Charles Coulthurst Gibbons, *b* 1884, *d* (April) 1926: *m* 1st, 19— (*m diss* 1923), Muriel Tidswell, who *d* 1949; 2ndly, 1924, Constance Winifred, who *d* 1976, da of David George Edward Wilkinson:—
(By 2nd *m*) Peta Jane Coulthurst (*posthumous*), *b* (Nov) 1926: *m* 1957, James William Edward Brown. *Residence* – Broadacres, 2 St John's Rise, Woking, Surrey.

Granddaughters of late Charles Kenrick Gibbons, 3rd son of late Lt-Col William Barton Gibbons (ante); *b* 1856, *d* 1918: *m* 1890, Emily Hinds, who *d* 1958, da of late Charles F Corbin, of The Beacon, Surbiton:—
Issue of late Charles William Kenrick Gibbons, *b* 1893, *d* 1969: *m* 1922, Winifred Maud Ethel, who *d* 1966, da of late George Eccles, of Mayaro, Trinidad:—
Rose Margaret Emily (80 Surbiton Hill Park, Surbiton), *b* 1926; late Lt QARANC.

Issue of late Edward John Kenrick, *b* 1900, *d* 1982; Town Clerk of Falmouth 1946-65: *m* 1938, Marguerite Leslie, who *d* 1977, da of late Nicholas Eyare Toke, of Penfillan House, Folkestone:—
Carol Leslie Kenrick (Hillside, Harlequin Lane, Crowborough, Sussex), *b* 1939.

The 1st baronet was Speaker of the House of Assembly, Barbados, and the 2nd baronet sat as MP for Wallingford. The 5th baronet was High Sheriff of Middlesex in 1891.

GIBSON (UK) 1926, of Great Warley, co Essex (Extinct 1997)

Rev Fr (Sir) DAVID GIBSON, 4th and last *Baronet*.

SISTER LIVING OF FOURTH BARONET

Joan Ingerid, *b* 1919: *m* 1942, Ronald Coad, of Trewhella, Cury, Helston, Cornwall.

GIBSON (UK) 1931, of Linconia, and of Faccombe, co Southampton

Rev Sir CHRISTOPHER HERBERT GIBSON, CP, 4th *Baronet; b* 17 July 1948; *s* his father, *Sir* CHRIST-OPHER HERBERT, 1994; ordained priest 1975.
Address – Santa Cruz 3150, 1228 Buenos Aires, Argentina.

SISTERS LIVING AND DECEASED

Penelope Lake, *b* 1946, *d* 1993. ——— Pamela Dorothy Madeleine, *b* 1950; MD: *m* 1973, Julio Cesar Muzio, and has issue living, Landon, *b* 1979, — André, *b* 1981, — Alejandro, *b* 1983, — Paula, *b* 1976. ——— Dawn, *b* 1953: *m* 1972, Daniel Carreras, of Apt 3-1026 Commercial Drive, Vancouver, BC V5L 3W9, Canada, and has issue living, Diego, *b* 1973, — Marie Noël, *b* 1975.

WIDOW LIVING OF THIRD BARONET

LILIAN LAKE (*Lady Gibson*), da of late Dr George Byron Young, of Colchester, Essex: *m* 1941, Sir Christopher Herbert Gibson, 3rd Bt, who *d* 1994.

COLLATERAL BRANCHES LIVING

Grandchildren of late Clement Herbert Gibson (infra):—
Issue of late Geoffrey Gibson, *b* 1934, *d* 1987: *m* 1964, Anne-Marie, who *d* 1998, da of late Martin de Selincourt:—
ROBERT HERBERT (Juncal 2174, 1er Piso "14", 1125, Buenos Aires, Argentina), *b* 21 Dec 1966: *m* 1992, Catherine Grace, da of Ernest William Pugh, and has issue living, William Barnaby Thomas, *b* 25 Oct 1997, — Flora Beatrice, *b* 1995. ——— Alexander Herbert, *b* 1973. ——— Clemency Rose, *b* 1968.

Issue of late Clement Herbert Gibson, 2nd son of 1st baronet, *b* 1900, *d* 1976: *m* 1933, Marjorie Julia who *d* 1982, da of late Robert Anderson:—
Clement Herbert (Westwell House, Rolvenden Rd, Tenterden, Kent TN30 6TT), *b* 1936: *m* 1966, Mrs Barbara Peel. ——— Thomas (Westwell Manor, Westwell, Burford, Oxon), *b* 1943: *m* 1966, Anthea Fiona Catherine, da of late Lt-Col G. A. Palmer, RE, and has issue living, Miles Cosmo Archdale, *b* 1968, — Sebastian Thomas Maximilian, *b* 1972, — Benjamin Hugh George, *b* 1973.

Issue of late Gerald Herbert Gibson, 3rd son of 1st baronet, *b* 1902, *d* 1951: *m* 1924, Ursula Marion Wilson, of San Martin 296, Buenos Aires, Argentina, da of late W. Greenwell-Robson:—
Roy Herbert, *b* 1933: *m* 1970, Georgina Odette, da of Santiago Even, and has issue living, Valerie, *b* 1971. ——— Diana Madeleine, *b* 1926.

Issue of late Cosmo Livingstone Herbert Gibson, yst son of 1st baronet, *b* 1904, *d* 1964: *m* 1937, Josephine Austin, da of James Austin Brown:—
Herbert, *b* 1938: *m* 1964, Margaret Jean, da of John Bruce Donald, and has issue living, James Bruce, *b* 1965, — Herbert Mark, *b* 1966, — Josephine Jean, *b* 1966, — Michel, *b* 1969, — Madeleine, *b* 1972. ——— Cosmo David, *b* 1944. ——— Noel Gerald *b* 1954. ——— David Hope, *b* 1956: *m* 1989, Maria Pia Cullen, and has issue living, Michael, *b* 1992, — Jennifer *b* 1990. ——— Yvonne, *b* 1939: *m* 1962, Baron Gaston Carlos Perkins Peers de Niewburgh, and has issue living, Thomas Gaston, *b* 1964: *m* 1993, Gianina, da of Nestor Koaper, and has issue living, Agustina *b* 1994, — Enrique Gaston, *b* 1968: *m* 1989, Soledad Bernal, and has issue living, Gaston Enrique *b* 1990, — Yvonne Cecilia, *b* 1967. ——— Roxana, *b* 1943: *m* 1963, Eduardo Francisco Pampillo, and has issue living, Francisco Severiano, *b* 1980, — Veronica Roxana, *b* 1963: *m* 1990, Aaron Hodari, and has issue living, Juana *b* 1991, — Edwina Alexandra, *b* 1965, — Victoria Patricia, *b* 1968: *m* 1988, Pablo Barbieri, and has issue living, Martin *b* 1989, Agustina *b* 1993, — Silvina Gloria, *b* 1975.

Sir Herbert Gibson, KBE, 1st Bt (son of Thomas Gibson, of Edinburgh), was a landowner and merchant in the Argentine Republic and Chm of Inter-Allied Commission for Purchase of Cereals in Argentina and Uruguay 1917-19. Sir Christopher Herbert, 3rd Bt, was Manager of Leach's Argentine Estates 1946-51, later a Design Draughtsman, Tea Plantation Manager, and Poultry Farmer.

Gibson-Craig-Carmichael, see Carmichael.

GILBEY (UK) 1893, of Elsenham Hall, Essex

Sir (WALTER) GAVIN GILBEY, 4th *Baronet*; *b* 14 April 1949; *s* his father, *Sir* (WALTER) DEREK, 1991; *ed* Eton: *m* 1st, 1980 (*m diss* 1984), Mary, da of late William E. E. Pacetti, of Florida, USA; 2ndly, 1984 (*m diss* 1992), Anna, da of Edmund Prosser, of Birmingham.

Arms – Gules, a fesse nebulèe or, in chief a horse rampant between two estoiles, and the like in base, all of the last. **Crest** – In front of a tower proper, issuant from the battlements thereof a dragon's head gules, a fleur-de-lis or, all between two ostrich feathers argent. *Residence* – Palm Beach, Florida, USA.

SISTER LIVING

Camilla Elizabeth, *b* 1953: *m* 1990, Christopher St John Frederick, elder son of Maj Sir Charles Boscawen Frederick, 10th Bt.

HALF GREAT-UNCLE LIVING (*Son of 2nd baronet*)

WALTER ANTHONY, Member of the House of Keys (Ballacallin Mooar, Crosby, Marown, Isle of Man), *b* 26 Feb 1935; assumed by deed poll 1958 the name of Walter Anthony in lieu of that of Anthony Walter: *m* 1964, Jenifer Mary, da of James Timothy Noel Price, of 98 Saddle Mews, Douglas, Isle of Man (O'Brien, Bt), and has issue living, Walter Anthony *b* 1966, — Caroline Anne, *b* 1967, — and an adopted da, Sarah Elizabeth, *b* 1969.

WIDOW LIVING OF THIRD BARONET

ELIZABETH MARY (*Dowager Lady Gilbey*), da of Col Keith Gordon Campbell, DSO, of Standen House, Newport, Isle of Wight: *m* 1948, Sir (Walter) Derek Gilbey, 3rd Bt, who *d* 1991. *Residence* – Little Paddock, The Street, Bury, W Sussex RH20 1PA.

COLLATERAL BRANCHES LIVING

Grandchildren of late Sebastian Walter Gilbey, el son of late Arthur Nockolds Gilbey, 2nd son of 1st baronet:–

Issue of late Arthur Sebastian Gilbey, *b* 1919, *d* 1964. *m* 1947 Jennifer Beryl (GOULD), who *d* 1991, da of late William Nigel Ernle Bruce (*see* Bruce, Bt, *cr* 1628, colls, 1990 Edn):–
Christopher Sebastian Bruce (The Coach House, Avonside, Fordingbridge, Hants SP6 2JT), *b* 1955; *ed* Harrow: *m* 1980, Medina, da of Sir Reginald Bennett, and has issue living, Jasper Sebastian Christopher, *b* 1981, — Sophie, *b* 1983. —— Patricia, *b* 1949: *m* 1972, Andrew Michael Talbot Millar (*see* Cockburn, Bt, colls, 1973-74 Edn), of Prospect House, N Stoke, Oxon OX10 6BL, and has issue living, Alexander Darracot, *b* 1976, — Olivia Rosalind, *b* 1977. —— Linda (*Hon Mrs Michael C. Gilbey*), *b* 1952: *m* 1971, Hon Michael Christopher Gilbey, of Pheasant's Ridge, Hambleden, Henley-on-Thames, Oxon RG9 6SD, and has issue living (*see* B Vaux of Harrowden).

Issue of late Capt Giles Milner Gilbey, MC, 12th R Lancers, *b* 1923, *d* 1983: *m* 1962, Diana Mary (RYERSON) (Flat 11, 53 Rutland Gate, SW7; Box 42, Colebrook, Conn 06021, USA), da of W. E. Melville-Cook, of Parkstone, Dorset:—
Lisa Maria, *b* 1965.

Issue of late Rupert Sydney Gilbey, yr son of late Arthur Nockolds Gilbey (ante), *b* 1900, *d* 1959: *m* 1927 Anne Penelope, who *d* 1970, da of late E. S. Prince:—
Simon Rupert, *b* 1929; *ed* Eton; formerly Capt 8th Hussars: *m* 1st, 1953 (*m diss* 1966), Chloë Rio, who *d* 1966, el da of late Col Christopher Rawlinson Cadge, of Ballygate House, Beccles, Suffolk; 2ndly, 1966, Mrs Sara Jane Twiston Davies, da of late Augustus Frederick Coryton, of Goleigh Farm House, Greatham, Hants, and has issue living, (by 1st *m*) Rupert John, *b* 1960: *m* 1996, Lisa Beddow, — Juliet Rio, *b* 1955: *m* 1979, John Michael Denison Bidwell, of Potman's Heath Cottage, Wittersham, Tenterden, Kent, and has issue living, James Denison *b* 1981, Patrick Simon *b* 1983, — Rachel Anne, *b* 1957: *m* 1981, Jonathan Dunn, of Wick Farm Oast, Udimore, nr Rye, Sussex TN31 6AH, el son of late A. A. Dunn, of 16 Pelham Place, SW7, and has issue, Thomas Alan *b* 1982, Imogen Chloë *b* 1985, Jessica Rose *b* 1988, — (by 2nd *m*) Lisa, *b* 1967: *m* 1997, Christopher Sandford. *Residence* – Dowgill Barn, Morland, Penrith, Cumbria. —— Sarah Anne *b* 1933: *m* 1953, Patrick Philip Bagshawe, and has issue living, Anthony William Newton, *b* 1956: *m* 1980, Alison Katrina, da of late John Auld Macdonald, and has had issue, Samuel Newton, *b* and *d* 1982, — Jasper Philip Adam, *b* 1960: *m* 1986, Chloë Mary Johnson, and has issue living, Samuel Oscar *b* 1986, Jessica Albinia *b* 1988, — Charlotte Anne, *b* 1954: *m* 1st, 1982 (*m diss* 1984), Stephen A. Buckle, son of late Lorne Buckle, of Ste Agathe des Monts, Quebec, Canada; 2ndly, 1989 (*m diss* 1991), Robert Bringhurst. *Residence* – Pond House, Meysey Hampton, Cirencester, Glos.

The 1st baronet, Sir Walter Gilbey, fifth son of late Henry Gilbey, of Bishop's Stortford, Herts, served in Pay Depart during Crimean War 1854-6; and was sometime Chm of W. & A. Gilbey, Ltd, wine merchants and distillers, of The Pantheon, Oxford Street, W; also a well-known Agriculturalist and Stock-breeder, and a Past Pres of Smithfield Club, of Hackney Horse So, of the Shire Horse So, Roy Agricultural So, and of Hunters' Improvement So. The 2nd baronet, Sir (Henry) Walter, was Chm of W. & A. Gilbey, Ltd, and a prominent figure in the horse-breeding and sporting worlds.

GILLETT (UK) 1959, of Bassishaw Ward, City of London

Truth conquers all things

Sir ROBIN DANVERS PENROSE GILLETT, GBE, RD, 2nd *Baronet*; *b* 9 Nov 1925; *s* his father, *Sir* (SYDNEY) HAROLD, MC, 1976; *ed* Nautical Coll, Pangbourne, and Hill Crest Sch; Hon DSc London 1976; 1943-45 Cadet with Canadian Pacific Steamships Ltd in Mediterranean and N Atlantic; Master Mariner 1951, Staff Comdr 1957; Elder Brother of Trinity House, Snr Warden of Hon Co of Master Mariners 1971 and Master 1979-80; Pres and FInstAM 1980-84, Vice-Pres 1985-94; Fellow and Founder Member of Nautical Inst; FInstD; KStJ; Common Councilman City of London 1965-69, Alderman 1969-96, Sheriff 1973-74, HM Lieut 1976, and Lord Mayor 1976-77; a Dir Wigham Poland Home Ltd, and Wigham Poland Management Sers Ltd 1965-86; Underwriting Member of Lloyd's; Dir St Katharine Haven Ltd 1979, Chm 1990-93; Pres National Waterways Transport Assocn 1979-83, RLSS UK Pres 1978-82, Dep Commonwealth Pres 1982-96; Vice-Pres of City of London Red Cross, Vice-Chm Port of London Authority 1979-84, Chm of Lord Mayor's Flood Relief Fund, and of Princess Victoria's Distress Fund, Vice-Pres of City Centre St John's Ambulance, Trustee of Nat Maritime Museum, and of St Paul's Cathedral Trust; Lay Vice Patron Missions to Seamen; Chm and a Gov of Pangbourne Coll 1978-92; Council of Royal Coll of Music, FRCM 1991; Vice-Pres KGFS since 1993; Hon Comdr RNR (RD 1965); Chm Maritime Volunteer Service Council since 1998; Gentleman Usher of the Purple Rod since 1985; Officer of the Order of Leopard of Zaire, Cdr of Order of Dannebrog of Denmark, Order of Johan Sedia Mahkota of Malaysia, Grand Cross of Municipal Order or Merit of Lima; Gold Medal of Administrative Management Soc (USA); GBE (Civil) 1976: *m* 1950, Elizabeth Marion Grace, who *d* 1997, el da of late John Findlay, JP, of Busby House, Lanarks, and has issue.

𝕬rms – In front of a ship's helm proper, an early nineteenth century waistcoat azure semée de lys and purfled or on a chief of the second between two estoiles a balance of the first. 𝕮rest – A grey horse's head and neck erased proper gorged with a coronet composed of six fleur-de-lys affixed to a circlet and chained or.
Residence – 4 Fairholt St, Knightsbridge, SW7 1EQ. *Clubs* – City Livery, Royal Yacht Squadron, Royal London Yacht Club (Commodore 1984-85), City Livery Yacht Club (Admiral), St Katherine Yacht Club (Admiral).

SONS LIVING

NICHOLAS DANVERS PENROSE (19 Woodland Court, Bishop Knoll, Sneyd Park, Bristol BS9 1NR; 220 Hermosa Av, #3, Hermosa Beach, CA 90254, USA), *b* 24 Sept 1955; *ed* Durlston Ct Sch, Pangbourne Coll, and Imperial Coll, London (BSc), ARCS, Dir Cargo Products, EG & G Astrophysics; Liveryman Worshipful Co of Coachmakers 1982: *m* 1987 (*m diss* 1997), Haylie, elder da of Dennis Brooks, of Abertawe, W Glam. —— Christopher John (3 Woolley St, Bradford on Avon, Wilts BA15 1AD) *b* 1958; *ed* Durlston Ct Sch, Pangbourne Coll, and King's Coll, Camb (MA), Roy Coll of Music, Nat Opera Studio 1982-83; Opera singer; Liveryman of Worshipful Co of Musicians 1981: *m* 1st, 1984 (*m diss* 1996), Julia A., yr da of late W. H. Holmes, of Tunbridge Wells, Kent; 2ndly, 1996, Lucy, yr da of H. Schaufer, of Arizona, USA, and has issue living, (by 1st *m*) Adam Holmes, *b* 1989, — Tessa Holmes, *b* 1987.

Sir (Sydney) Harold Gillett, MC, 1st Bt, son of William Henry Gillett, of Highgate, N6, was Lord Mayor of London 1958-59.

GILMOUR (UK) 1897, of Lundin and Montrave, Parishes of Largo and Scoonie, co Fife

Not the pen, but custom

Sir JOHN EDWARD GILMOUR, DSO, TD, 3rd *Baronet*; *b* 24 Oct 1912; *s* his father, *Rt Hon Sir* JOHN, GCVO, DSO, LLD, MP, 1940; *ed* Eton, and Trin Hall, Camb; Dundee Sch of Economics; Lt-Col Fife and Forfar Yeo 1947-51; Brevet Col 1952; Hon Col Highland Yeo RAC, TAVR 1971-75; JP and DL for Fife, Vice-Lieut 1979, and Lord-Lieut 1980-87; Lord High Commr to Gen Assembly of Church of Scotland 1982-83; Capt Queen's Body Guard for Scotland (R Co of Archers); NW Europe 1944-45 (wounded, DSO); MP for E Div of Fife (*C*) 1961-79, and Chm Conservative and Unionist Party in Scot 1965-67, DSO 1945: *m* 1941, Ursula Mabyn, da of late Frank Oliver Wills, of Cote Lodge, Westbury-on-Trym and has issue.

Arms – Argent, on a chevron between three trefoils slipped vert, as many bugle horns of the first. **Crest** – A hand fessewise couped at the wrist proper, holding a pen argent.
Seat – Montrave, Leven, Fife KY8 5NZ.

SONS LIVING

JOHN (Balcormo Mains, Leven, Fife KY8 5QF), *b* 15 July 1944; *ed* Eton, and North of Scotland Coll of Agriculture; Capt Fife and Forfar Yeo/Scottish Horse Sqdn, Hon Col Fife and Forfar Yeo/Scottish Horse (The Scottish Yeo) 1997; MFH (Fife) since 1972; DL for Fife 1988: *m* 1967, Valerie Jardine, da of late George Walker Russell, and has issue living, (John) Nicholas, *b* 1970: *m* 1996, Airin, yr da of Mr Thamrin, of Sulawesi, Indonesia, — Patrick George William, *b* 1980, — Corinna Valerie, *b* 1972: *m* 1998, Peter J. Vincent, yst son of R. W. Vincent, of Goulds Farm, Horsington, Som, — (Victoria) Juliet, *b* 1975. —— Andrew Frank (Pratis House, Leven, Fife), *b* 1947; *ed* Eton and West of Scotland Coll of Agric; Queens Body Guard for Scotland (Roy Co of Archers); Member of North East Fife District Council 1984-96; Chm Royal Smithfield Show 1998; JP 1984: *m* 1971, Mary Speirs, SSStJ, adopted da of late Sir Henry Campbell de la Poer Beresford-Peirse, CB, 5th Bt, and has issue living, Andrew Robert Campbell, *b* 1972, — David Edward, *b* 1974.

SISTER LIVING

Dame Anne Margaret, DBE, *b* 1909; Chm of Roy Free Hosp 1968-74; Vice-Chm of Exec Cttee BRCS (ret 1976), a Member Area Health Authority, Camden and Islington, of Council for Professions Supplementary to Medicine, and of Council of Florence Nightingale Hosp, Vice-Pres of Roy Coll of Nursing, and a DStJ; Dir and Commr for Middle East, British Red Cross and St John War Org 1943-45; CBE (Civil) 1945, DBE (Civil) 1957: *m* 1932, Lt-Cdr John Reginald Bryans, RN (ret), who *d* 1990, and has issue living, John Patrick Gilmour (Hatton, Leven, Fife), *b* 1933; Lt-Cdr RN (ret); FRGS: *m* 1st, 1959 (*m diss* 1970), Rosemary Ann, da of late Group Capt H. G. Wheeler, RAF; 2ndly, 1972, Patricia Mary, da of late W. A. MacPherson, and has issue living (by 1st *m*), Anthony James Gilmour *b* 1960, Edward John Gilmour *b* 1963, Robert Henry Charles *b* 1965, (by 2nd *m*) Lucy Anne *b* 1977. *Residence* – 25 Links Rd, Lundin Links, Leven, Fife KY8 6AT.

HALF-SISTER LIVING

Daphne Mary, *b* 1922: *m* 1943, Group Cap Everett Large Baudoux, DSO, DFC, RCAF (ret), and has had issue, Michael Alfred, *b* 1951: *m* 1984, Carol Anne Hingley, and has issue living, Katherine Anne *b* 1986, — Patricia Mary, *b* 1944: *m* 1966, Raymond Wayne Docker, and *d* 1987, leaving issue, Thomas Everett *b* 1970, Philip Ian *b* 1972, — Sharon Jane, *b* 1948: *m* 1974, J. Lewis MacKay, and has issue living, James Jeffrey *b* 1978, Amy Kathleen *b* 1976. *Residence* – Big Island, Merigomish, Nova Scotia.

COLLATERAL BRANCH LIVING

Issue of late Douglas Gilmour, 5th son of 1st baronet, *b* 1889, *ka* 1916: *m* 1910, Doris Hyacinth, who *d* 1977, da of late Charles Paget Hooker, of Cirencester, son of late Sir Joseph Dalton Hooker, OM, GCSI, CB:—
Doris Pamela Yvonne, *b* 1914: *m* 1940, Maj Philip Donald Howitt Marshall, late Middlesex Regt, of Bowhayes, Chetnole, Sherborne, Dorset DT9 6PE, and has issue living, Nicholas Charles Gilmour (Glanhonddu House, Llandefaelog Fach, Brecon, Powys), *b* 1950: *m* 1st, 1974 (*m diss* 1983), Rosemary Anne, da of late Maj W. J. Kingdom, RA; *m* 2ndly, 1988, Fiona Anne, elder da of Christopher Anthony William Leng (*see* Ly Herries of Terregles), and has issue living (by 1st *m*), Emily Sarah *b* 1978, Harriet *b* 1980, (by 2nd *m*) Douglas James Gilmour *b* 1990, Scarlett Josephine *b* 1992, — Sarah Gilmour, *b* 1948: *m* 1976, Christopher David Legge, of The Old House, Kingsclere, Newbury, Berks, and has issue living, Louisa Rebecca *b* 1977, Octavia Christina, *b* 1980, Henrietta, *b* 1984, — Teresa Gilmour, *b* 1953: *m* 1987, Michael Denison Gale Way, of Upper Park House, Upper Park Rd, Kingston, Surrey KT2 5LD, and has issue living, Henry Charles *b* 1990, Giles William Philip *b* 1994. —— Myrtle (The Grange, Thornford, Sherborne, Dorset), *b* 1915: *m* 1st, 1938, John William Hathorn, Flying Officer, RAF (Reserve), who *d* (killed in a flying accident whilst on active ser) 1940; 2ndly, 1940 (*m diss* 1949), Capt Cecil Horace Power Bellwood, Gloucestershire Regt; 3rdly, 1949 (*m diss* 1952), Col Patrick Curran Perfect, late KOSB; 4thly, 1901, Lt-Col Henry Mesnard (Tim) Bromilow.

Sir John Gilmour, 1st Bt (el son of Allan Gilmour, of Lundin and Montrave, Fife, and South Walton, Renfrewshire), was a JP and DL for co Fife. The 2nd Bt, the Rt Hon Sir John, GCVO, DSO, PC, sat as MP for Renfrewshire, E Div (*C*) 1910-18, and for Glasgow, Pollok Div 1918-40, and was Junior Lord of the Treasury 1921-2, Sec for Scotland 1924-6, Sec of State for Scotland 1926-9, Min of Agriculture and Fisheries 1931-32, Sec of State for Home Depart 1932-5, and Min of Shipping 1939-40.

GLADSTONE (UK) 1846, of Fasque and Balfour, Kincardineshire

By fidelity and valour

Sir (ERSKINE) WILLIAM GLADSTONE, KG, 7th *Baronet; b* 29 Oct 1925; *s* his father, (*Sir*) CHARLES ANDREW, 1968; *ed* Eton, and Ch Ch Oxford (MA); Hon LLD Liverpool 1998; Lord Lieut of Clwyd since 1985; Assist Master at Eton Coll 1951-61, and Headmaster of Lancing Coll 1961-69; Chief Scout of the UK and Overseas Branches 1972-82; 1939-45 War as Sub-Lt RNVR; KG 1999: *m* 1962, Rosamund Anne, da of late Maj Robert Alexander Hambro, and has issue.

Arms – Argent, a savage's head affrontée, distilling drops of blood and wreathed about the temples with holly proper within an orle fleury gules, all within eight martlets in orle sable. **Crest** – Issuant from a wreath of holly proper, a demi-griffin sable, supporting between the claws a sword, the blade enfiled by a wreath of oak also proper.
Residences – Hawarden Castle, Clwyd CH5 3PB; Fasque, Laurencekirk, Kincardineshire AB30 1DJ.

SONS LIVING

CHARLES ANGUS (Glen Dye, nr Banchory, Kincardineshire), *b* 11 April 1964; *ed* Eton, and Worcester College, Oxford: *m* 1988, Caroline M., only da of Sir Derek Morison David Thomas, KCMG, HM Amb to Italy, and has issue living, Jack William, *b* 28 July 1989, — India Kate, *b* 1991, — Tara Rosamund, *b* 1992, — Xanthe Flora Mali, *b* 1995, — Kinvara Rose, *b* 1997. —— Robert Nicolas, *b* 1968: *m* 1993, Nicola L., eldest da of Forbes Playfair, of Bale, Norfolk, and has issue living, Tom Archie Playfair, *b* 1995, — Rosie Lindsay, *b* 1993, — Kate Isla, *b* 1996.

DAUGHTER LIVING

Victoria Frances, *b* 1967: *m* 1991, Hugo C. Merison, son of Paul Merison, of Chiddingly, Sussex, and has issue living, William Hugh, *b* 1995, — Elinor Penelope, *b* 1994, — Dorothy Camilla, *b* 1998.

BROTHERS LIVING AND DECEASED

Peter (Fasque, Fettercairn, Laurencekirk, Kincardineshire), *b* 1928; *ed* Eton, and Ch Ch, Oxford (MA): *m* 1972, Jean Loveday, da of Allan Roy, of The Hawes, Ainsdale, Southport, and has issue living, Tom Xenophon, *b* 1973, — Allan Fergus, *b* 1978, — Cleodie Selina, *b* 1975. —— James Francis (West End, Hawarden Castle, Clwyd), *b* 1941; *ed* Eton, and Ch Ch, Oxford: *m* 1st, 1963, Janet Barbara, who *d* 1970, da of late Rudi Schumacher, of Kenya; 2ndly, 1972, Hon Josephine Jones, da of Baron Elwyn Jones (Life Baron), and has issue living (by 1st *m*), Melissa Janet, *b* 1970, — (by 2nd *m*) Andrew Elwyn, *b* 1974. —— †Andrew Victor, *b* 1945; *ed* Eton; FRICS: *m* 1975, Nicola Anne (Honeywick, Hadspen, Castle Cary, Somerset), da of late Lt-Col M. L. D. Skewes-Cox, of Uphill House, Ponsworthy, Devon, and *d* 1995, leaving issue, Isla Sophie, *b* 1979, — Clova Felicity, *b* 1982.

SISTERS LIVING

Penelope Anne, *b* 1930. —— Sara Helen, *b* 1943: *m* 1970, Philip John Young, of East End Farm, Ringstead, Hunstanton, Norfolk, and has issue living, James Edward, *b* 1971, — John Anthony, *b* 1974.

COLLATERAL BRANCH LIVING

Issue of late Capt Stephen Deiniol Gladstone, MC, brother of 5th and 6th baronets, *b* 1891, *d* 1965: *m* 1923, Mary St Clair, who *d* 1976, da of Lt-Col Charles Davidson, of Aboyne:—
Stephen Charles (13 Cliveden Rd, Wimbledon SW19 3RD), *b* 1924; *ed* Eton; late Lt Welsh Guards: *m* 1952, Susan Valerie, da of John Lindsay Guise, of Woodhaie, Cross in Hand, Heathfield, Sussex, and has had issue, †Stephen James, *b* 1955; *d* 1989, — Clare Elizabeth, *b* 1953: *m* 19—, Jack A. Abolins, of 19 Adkin Way, Wantage, Oxon, and has issue living, — Catherine Mary, *b* 1959, — Juliet Anne, *b* 1960: *m* 1985, Simon Keith Blows, of 19 Spencer Hill, SW19 4PA, and has issue living Daniel Lewis Gladstone *b* 1989, Michael Thomas Gladstone *b* 1991, Peter Stephen Gladstone *b* 1994, Sarah Madeleine Victoria *b* 1996, — Victoria Jane, *b* 1963. —— John Neville (Old Buckhurst, Mark Beech, Kent), *b* 1932; *ed* Eton: *m* 1959, Jane Gordon, da of late Maj-Gen Robert Alexander Stephen, CB, CBE, MD, ChM, FRCS, QHS, and has issue living, David Gordon William (74 Lavender Sweep, Battersea, SW11), *b* 1960, — Peter Robert John, *b* 1963: has issue living (by Jane Scott), Charlotte Emily GLADSTONE *b* 1998, — Claire Jane (8A Mandalay Rd, Clapham, SW4 9ED), *b* 1962. —— Mary Felicity, *b* 1926. —— Anne (7 Daisy Lane, SW6 3DD), *b* 1928: *m* 1957, Nigel John Robson, who *d* 1993, and has issue living, Andrew Stephen (Holford House, N Chailey, E Sussex BN8 4DT), *b* 1958: *m* 1982, Fiona, da of Jeremy Veasey, of Cinder Farm, N Chailey, Sussex, and has issue living, (Andrew) James *b* 1987, Gemma Anne *b* 1989, Sophie Felicity *b* 1992, — William Nigel, *b* 1960, — Hugo John, *b* 1962.

The 1st baronet assumed, by Roy licence, the surname of Gladstone in lieu of his patronymic Gladstones. Sir Thomas, 2nd Bt, sat as MP for Queensborough (C) 1830, for Portarlington 1832-5, for Leicester 1835-7, and for Ipswich 1842, and was Lord-Lieut of Kincardineshire. Sir John Evelyn, 4th Bt, was a JP and DL for Wilts (High Sheriff 1897). Rt Hon William Ewart Gladstone, Prime Min 1868-74, 1880-85, 1886 and 1892-94, was yst son of 1st baronet, and grandfather of 5th and 6th baronets.

Glen-Coats, see Coats.

GLYN (GB) 1759, of Ewell, Surrey, and (GB) 1800, of Gaunt's House

Sir RICHARD LINDSAY GLYN, 10th *Baronet*, of Ewell, and 6th *Baronet*, of Gaunt's House; *b* 3 Aug 1943; *s* his father, *Col Sir* RICHARD HAMILTON, OBE, TD, 1980; *ed* Eton; late 2nd Lt 1st Bn R Hampshire Regt: *m* 1970 (*m diss* 1979), Carolyn Ann, da of late Roy Frank Williams, of Pasadena, Calif, USA, and has issue.

𝔄rms – Argent, an eagle displayed with two heads sable guttée d'or, with a crescent for difference. Crest – An eagle's head erased sable, guttée d'or, holding in the beak an escallop argent.
Seat – Gaunt's House, Wimborne, Dorset.

SON LIVING

RICHARD RUFUS FRANCIS, *b* 8 Jan 1971.

DAUGHTER LIVING

Eliza Jane Rose, *b* 1975.

BROTHER LIVING

Jeremy George Trion (8 Guion Rd, SW6) *b* 1946; *ed* Eton.

Firm to my trust

SISTER LIVING

Amanda Jane, *b* 1940: *m* 1969, Lt-Col Charles John Holroyd, R Green Jackets (ret), of Providence Cottage, Chute Cadley, Andover, Hants and has issue (*see* E Cairns).

AUNT LIVING (*Daughter of 8th baronet*)

Philippa Ann (The River House, Tarrant Rushton, Blandford, Dorset), *b* 1915; MB and ChB Edinburgh 1946: *m* 1949, Andrew B. Swan, MB, ChB, FRCPE, BSc, who *d* 1998, and has issue living, Jeremy Michael, *b* 1952, — Jocelyn Ann, *b* 1956.

COLLATERAL BRANCHES LIVING

Issue of late Gerald Hugh Glyn, 2nd son of 8th baronet, *b* 1909, *d* 1981: *m* 1954, Philomena (22 Seaforth Lodge, Barnes High St, SW13), da of Denis O'Leary, of Macroom, Co Cork:—
Charles Gerald (94 Ashleigh Rd, SW14), *b* 1959. —— Lesley Maye, *b* 1955: *m* 1992, Ian M. Lorimer, yr son of Andrew Lorimer, of Amport, Hants. *Residence* – 2 Westwood Rd, Barnes, SW13.

Grandchildren of late Charles Robert Glyn, el son of Rev Charles Thomas Glyn, eldest son of late Col Thomas Glyn, 5th son of 1st baronet (*cr* 1759):—
Issue of late Charles Glyn, *b* 1878, *d* 1943: *m* 1912, Gwendolen, who *d* 1982, da of Charles Mills, of Riebeek House, Kenilworth, Cape Province, S Africa:—
Ronald St George, *b* 1913: *m* 1954, Marion Mevagh, da of Donald James Laing, of Kildrummy Farm, Rivonia, Johannesburg, and has issue living, Donald Charles St George, *b* 1954, — Patrick St George, *b* 1956, — Rowena May, *b* 1960, — Virginia Aitchison, *b* 1964. *Residence* – 10 St Andrew's St, Melrose, Johannesburg, S Africa. *Club* – Rand (Johannesburg). —— Kathleen Phillipa, *b* 1920: *m* 1st, 19—, Edward Charles Sawyer, who *d* 1946; 2ndly, 1962, Gordon

George Booth, of 10 Roosevelt Rd, Gillitts 3603, Natal, S Africa, and has issue living, (by 1st *m*) Charles Garth, *b* 1946, — Bruce Gavin, *b* 1948, — Amanda May, *b* 1953.

Grandchildren of late Charles Glyn (ante):—
Issue of late John St George Glyn, *b* 1916, *d* 1985: *m* 1958, Norma Baillie (Ballyrock, 81 Highway, Fish Hoek, Cape Town, S Africa), da of Hugo Orlando Bean, of Nakwela Farms, Mazabuka, Zambia:—
Patricia Jane St George, *b* 1959; *ed* Capetown Univ (BA). —— Shirley Gwendoline St George, *b* 1962; *ed* Capetown Univ (BSc, LLB).

Grandchildren of late Charles Robert Glyn (ante):—
Issue of late Douglas John Glyn, *b* 1883, *d* 1952: *m* 1926, Dorothy Margaret, who *d* 1962, da of late Alexander Gordon of Wynberg, Cape, S Africa.:—
William George Rutherford (PO Box 2310, Somerset W 7130, CP, S Africa), *b* 1927: *m* 1950, Lillamary, who *d* 1988, da of late I. W. Kretzen, and has issue living, Richard William Douglas (18 Moray Drive, Bryanston, Johannesburg, S Africa) *b* 1951; *ed* Natal Univ (BCom, LLB) and Trin Hall, Camb (LLB): *m* 1983, Mary Elizabeth, da of Robert Leonard Stanley, of 4 Moorside, Palmers Lane, Walberswick, Suffolk, — Brenda Margaret, *b* 1954; *ed* Natal Univ (BSc); CA (SA).

Issue of late Wilfrid Henry Glyn, *b* 1885, *d* 1967: *m* 1933, Petronella, who *d* 1975, da of late J. G. Strydom:—
Michael Robert Henry (The 49 Steps, 4 Gascoyne Street Observatory, Johannesburg, S Africa), *b* 1933: *m* 1960, Suzanne Ursula, da of late T. P. Lyons, and has issue living, Alister Michael, *b* 1965, — Jeremy Charles, *b* 1969, — Caroline Frances, *b* 1963.

Granddaughter of late Rev Charles Thomas Glyn, 2nd son of Thomas Christopher Glyn, 3rd son of 1st baronet (*cr* 1800):—
Issue of late Thomas Richard Glyn, *b* 1856, *d* 1937: *m* 1901, Florence Ann, who *d* 1928, da of late John Brownless, of Whorlton Grange, co Durham:—
Cicely May, *b* 1906: *m* 1931 (*m diss* 1947), John William Murray, MD, and has issue living, Caroline Glyn, *b* 1942.

Descendants of late George Carr Glyn (4th son of 1st baronet, *cr* 1800), who was *cr Baron Wolverton* 1869 (*see* that title).

(*In remainder to the Baronetcy of Ewell only*)

Grandchildren of late Capt Egerton John Glyn, son of late Clayton William Feake Glyn, son of late Rev Thomas Clayton Glyn, eldest son of late Col Thomas Glyn, 5th son of 1st baronet (*cr* 1759):—
Issue of late John Murray Egerton Glyn, *b* 1894, *d* 1936: *m* 1923, Iris Margaret, da of John P Lawton, of Mid Oaks, San Gabriel, Los Angeles, California, USA:—
John Murray Egerton, *b* 1926. —— Helena Margaret, *b* 1931.

Sir Richard, LLD, 1st baronet, a banker, was MP for London City, Lord Mayor of London 1758, and President of Bridewell and Bethlem Hospitals. His fourth son, Sir Richard Carr Glyn, Lord Mayor of London 1798, a banker in that City, and 2nd Pres of Bridewell and Bethlem Hospitals, was *cr* Baronet (GB), of Gaunt's House, Dorsetshire 1800. On the death of the 7th Baronet of Ewell in 1942, he was *s* by Sir Richard Fitzgerald Glyn, 4th Bt, DSO, of Gaunt's House, who was High Sheriff of Dorset 1927, and served in S Africa 1899-1902, and in European War 1914-18 (DSO).

Glyn, see Davson.

GODFREY (I) 1785, of Bushfield, co Kerry, Ireland (Extinct 1971)

Sir WILLIAM MAURICE GODFREY, 7th and last *Baronet*.

DAUGHTERS LIVING OF SEVENTH BARONET

Susan Mary, *b* 1934: *m* 1st, 1959, Anthony Dale Jones; 2ndly, 1993, Robert James Olive, of Deerswood, Leith Hill, Dorking, Surrey, and has issue living (by 1st *m*), Timothy Simon, *b* 1965, — Petrina Claire, *b* 1961, — Annabel Mary, *b* 1963. —— Bridget Jane (*Lady Dervaird*), *b* 1937: *m* 1960, John Murray (a Lord of Session as Lord Dervaird), of 4 Moray Pl, Edinburgh, EH3 6DS, and has issue living, Alexander Godfrey, *b* 1964, — William John, *b* 1965: *m* 1988, Hazel Margaret, da of Dr Charles Glennie, of Edinburgh, and has issue living, Charles William *b* 1993, Alexander James *b* 1995, Mary Jane *b* 1998, — David Gordon, *b* 1968. —— Iris Belinda, *b* 1939: *m* 1962, Robert Edward Jacob, of Digby Lock Cottage, Sallins, Naas, co Kildare, and has issue living, William Godfrey, *b* 1967, — Richard Thomas, *b* 1968: *m* 1997, Mairead, da of Dennis Crowley, of Cork, — Ann Caroline, *b* 1963: *m* 1994, John O'Brien, son of Timothy O'Brien, of Dublin, and has issue living, Daniel Timothy *b* 1997, — Sarah Margaret, *b* 1965: *m* 1992, Finbar John Drennan, son of Frank Drennan, of Cork, and has issue living, Rachel Sarah *b* 1997.

WIDOW LIVING OF SEVENTH BARONET

CAROLINE IRIS (*Lady Godfrey*) (Martins, The Forstal, Eridge, Tunbridge Wells, Kent), da of late Alban Robins, of Rusthall Grange, Tunbridge Wells: *m* 1933, Sir William Maurice Godfrey, 7th Bt, who *d* 1971, when the title became ext.

DAVIS-GOFF (UK) 1905, of Glenville, Parish of St Patrick's, co Waterford

Sir ROBERT WILLIAM DAVIS-GOFF, 4th *Baronet*, *b* 12 Sept 1955; *s* his father Sir ERNEST WILLIAM, 1980; *ed* Cheltenham Coll, *m* 1978, Nathalie Sheelagh, da of Terence Chadwick, of Lissen Hall, Swords, co Dublin.

Honesty is the best policy

Arms – Quarterly, 1st and 4th, azure, a chevron between two fleurs-de-lys in chief and a lion rampant in base or, a crescent for difference; 2nd and 3rd, per pale gules and argent, a chevron between three boars' heads couped, all counter-changed. **Crest** – A squirrel sejant argent.
Residences – Eairy Moar Farm, Glen Helen, I of Man; Lissen Hall, Swords, co Dublin.

SONS LIVING

WILLIAM NATHANIEL, *b* 20 April 1980. —— Henry Terence Chadwick, *b* 1986. —— James Sammy Chadwick, *b* 1989.

DAUGHTER LIVING

Sarah Chadwick, *b* 1982.

SISTERS LIVING

Annabel Claire, *b* 1942: *m* 19— (*m diss* 19—), Mike Nichols, of Bridgewater, Conn, USA, and has issue living, Max *b* 1973, Jenny *b* 1976. —— Julia Christian, *b* 1943: *m* 1968 (*m diss* 19—), John G. Barker, and has issue living, Christian Charles, *b* 1970, — Andrea Mary, *b* 1971. —— Alice Maria, *b* 1948: *m* 1969, Christopher Quarry, of The Olde House, Oad St, Borden, Sittingbourne, Kent, and has issue living, Andrew Simon, *b* 1973, — Suzanne Nichola, *b* 1975.

UNCLE LIVING (*Son of 2nd baronet*)

Charles Herbert, *b* 1908; *ed* Repton and Trin Coll, Camb.

AUNT LIVING (*Daughter of 2nd baronet*)

Doreen Christian, *b* 1905: *m* 1935, Major Michael Wentworth Beaumont, TD, who *d* 1958 (*see* V Allendale, colls).
Residence – Harristown House, Brannockstown, co Kildare.

Sir William G. Davis-Goff, 1st Bt, Sheriff of Waterford City 1869 and 1899, and High Sheriff of Waterford Co 1892, was a descendant of Rev Stephen Goffe, of Stanmer, Sussex (Fellow of Magdalen Coll, Oxford, *temp* 1595), whose son Stephen was Chaplain to Charles I. Sir Herbert, 2nd Bt, was High Sheriff of co Waterford 1914.

D'AVIGDOR-GOLDSMID (UK) 1934, of Somerhill, co Kent (Extinct 1987)

Maj-Gen Sir JAMES ARTHUR D'AVIGDOR-GOLDSMID, CB, OBE, MC, 3rd and last *Baronet.*

DAUGHTER LIVING OF SECOND BARONET

(Rosemary) Chloe, *b* 1945; High Sheriff Kent 1994: *m* 1969, (Anthony) James Moreton Teacher, of Hadlow Place, Kent TN11 0BW, and has issue (*see* Macnaghten, Bt, colls).

GOOCH (GB) 1746, of Benacre Hall, Suffolk.

Sir TIMOTHY ROBERT SHERLOCK GOOCH, 13th *Baronet*, MBE; *b* 7 Dec 1934; *s* his brother, *Sir* (RICHARD) JOHN SHERLOCK, 1999; *ed* Eton, and RMA Sandhurst; Major The Life Guards (ret); MBE (Mil) 1970; Member of HM Bodyguard of Hon Corps of Gentlemen at Arms since 1986: *m* 1963, Susan Barbara Christie, only da of late Maj-Gen Kenneth Christie Cooper, CB, DSO, OBE, of Donhead St Andrew, Wilts, and has issue.

𝕬rms – Per pale argent and sable a chevron between three talbots statant counterchanged; on a chief gules three leopards' faces or. 𝕮rest – A talbot statant per pale argent and sable. *Seat* – Benacre Hall, Beccles, Suffolk. *Residence* – The Cedars, Covehithe, Wrentham, Beccles, Suffolk NR34 73W. *Clubs* – White's, Cavalry and Guards'.

DAUGHTERS LIVING

Fide et virtute

By fidelity and valour

Lucinda, *b* 1970. —— Victoria, *b* 1974.

SISTER LIVING

Katharine Anne, *b* 1932: *m* 1967, Maj Andrew Patrick Forbes Napier, KStJ, DL, late Coldstream Gds, Member of HM Body Guard for Scotland (R Company of Archers), of Syleham Manor, nr Eye, Suffolk IP21 4LN (Royal Yacht Squadron, and Boodle's Clubs) (*see* B Essendon, 1970 Edn), and has issue living, James Frederick Brian, *b* 1968; *ed* Eton, and RMA Sandhurst; late Capt Coldstream Gds (Cavalry and Guards', and Boodle's Clubs): *m* 1998, Miranda Meriel, 2nd da of Christopher Michael Edward Talbot (*see* E Shrewsbury, colls), — Katharine Louisa, *b* 1969.

COLLATERAL BRANCHES LIVING

Issue of late Col Brian Sherlock Gooch, DSO, TD, 2nd son of 10th baronet, *b* 1904, *d* 1968: *m* 1935, Monica Mary, who *d* 1975, only child of Nathaniel Arthur Heywood, of Glevering Park, Wickham Market, Suffolk:—

ARTHUR BRIAN SHERLOCK HEYWOOD (Manor Farmhouse, Chitterne, Wilts BA12 0LG), *b* 1 June 1937; *ed* Eton; Brig Staff, comdg The Life Gds 1978-81: *m* 1963, Sarah Diana Rowena, JP, da of late Lt-Col John Francis George Perceval, of Templehouse, co Sligo, and has issue living, Rowena Elizabeth, *b* 1965, — Katherine Sarah, *b* 1967: *m* 1992, Edward J. Hawkings, son of late Peter Hawkings, of Greywell, Hants, and has issue living, James Arthur Edward *b* 1998, Georgina Sarah Daphne *b* 1995. —— Thomas Sherlock Heywood (Chantry House, Greens Norton, Towcester, Northants NN12 8BL), *b* 1943: *m* 1971, Elizabeth, da of late Brig Guy Arthur Eliot Peyton, OBE, of Bengal Manor, Greens Norton, Towcester, Northants, and has issue living, Robert Brian Sherlock, *b* 1976, — Caroline Elisabeth, *b* 1973: *m* 1998, Michael N. Kingsnorth, yr son of George Kingsnorth, of Wellingborough, Northants. —— (Mary) Elise (*Lady Quilter*), *b* 1940: *m* 1964, Sir Anthony Raymond Leopold Cuthbert Quilter, 4th Bt, of Sutton Hall, Woodbridge, Suffolk. —— Jennifer Isobel, *b* 1942: *m* 1965, Lt-Cdr John Marjoribanks Chevallier Guild, RN (who assumed the additional surname of CHEVALLIER before that of Guild by deed poll 1970), of Aspall Hall, Stowmarket, and has issue living, John Barrington Chevallier, *b* 1967: *m* 1997, Dale K., 2nd da of David Hosking, of Abbey Mill Farm, Dunkeswell Abbey, Devon, — Henry Chevallier, *b* 1968.

Issue of late Brig Richard Frank Sherlock Gooch, DSO, MC, yst son of 10th baronet, *b* 1906, *d* 1973: *m* 1939, Barbara Susan, who *d* 1981, da of late William Douro Hoare, CBE:—
Richard Edward Sherlock (10a Simla Crescent, Khandallah, Wellington NZ) *b* 1942: *m* 1st, 1967, Rosemary Hill; 2ndly 1981, Linda Kathleen, da of late John Caradus of Napier, NZ, and has issue living (by 1st *m*), Tobias Douro Sherlock, *b* 1969, — Theodore Frank Sherlock, *b* 1972.

Granddaughter of late Brig Richard Frank Sherlock Gooch, DSO, MC (ante):—
Issue of late William David Sherlock Gooch, *b* 1944, *d* 1978: *m* 1970, Anna Nicholls (30 Bridge St, Framlingham, Suffolk):—
Elisabeth Anne, *b* 1971.

The 1st baronet, Sir William, after serving gallantly in the wars of Queen Anne's reign, was appointed Lieut-Gov of Virginia. The 2nd baronet, Sir Thomas, was successively Bishop of Bristol, of Norwich, and of Ely. The 4th baronet, Sir Thomas, was High Sheriff of Suffolk 1785. The 5th and 6th baronets were each successively MP for that county.

GOOCH (UK) 1866, of Clewer Park, Berkshire.

Sir TREVOR SHERLOCK GOOCH, VRD, 5th *Baronet*, son of late Charles Trevor Gooch, 2nd son of Charles Fulthorpe Gooch, 2nd son of 1st baronet; *b* 15 June 1915; *s* his kinsman, *Sir* ROBERT DOUGLAS, 1989; *ed* Charterhouse; Fl-Lt RAFVR: *m* 1st, 1956, Denys Anne, who *d* 1976, only da of late Harold Victor Venables, of Edificio la Vileta, Camino Vecinal le Vileta 215, Palma de Mallorca, Baleares; 2ndly, 1978, Jean, da of late John Joseph Wright, and has issue by 1st *m*.

Arms – Per pale argent and sable, on a chevron between three talbots passant two escallops all counterchanged, on a chief engrailed gules a wheel between two leopards' faces or. Crest – A talbot per pale sable and argent gorged with a wreath of oak or, and resting the dexter foot on a gold wheel.
Residence – Jardin de la Rocque, Mont de la Rocque, St Aubin, Jersey, CI.

Fide et virtute
By fidelity and valour

SON LIVING (*By 1st marriage*)

MILES PETER, *b* 3 Feb 1963; *ed* Victoria Coll, Jersey, and Preston Poly Lancs (B Eng).

DAUGHTERS LIVING (*By 1st marriage*)

Beverly Jacqueline, *b* 1957: *m* 1st, 1981 (*m diss* 1988), Laurence Andrew Wilde; 2ndly, 1988, Bernard Charles Amy, of St John's Villa, 68 St John's Rd, St Helier, Jersey, CI, and has issue living (by 1st *m*), Samantha Ria AMY, *b* 1983; legally adopted by her stepfather 1991. —— Vanda Madeleine, *b* 1958. —— Yvonne Daryl, *b* 1961. —— Rowan Claire, *b* 1971.

DAUGHTER LIVING OF FOURTH BARONET (*By 2nd marriage*)

Gillian Daphne (Ball Hill Farm, Sampford Courtenay, nr Okehampton, Devon EX20 1SB), *b* 1931: *m* 1st, 1953 (*m diss* 1973), Guy Stephen Foster Wilkin; 2ndly, 1974, Kenneth George White, who *d* 1988, and has issue living, (by 1st *m*) Paul Guy Foster, *b* 1955: *m* 1978, Carolyn Noakes, and has issue living, Mathew Paul Foster *b* 1984, Samantha Ann Foster *b* 1982, — Mark Guy Foster (22 Denmark Rd, W13), *b* 1957.

COLLATERAL BRANCHES LIVING

Granddaughter of late Charles Fulthorpe Gooch, 2nd son of 1st baronet:—
Issue of late Eric Daniel Astwood Gooch, *b* 1886, *d* 1937: *m* 1910, Gwynedd, who *d* 1964, da of late Col George Brooke Meares (M Townshend, colls):—
Pamela Vivian, *b* 1911: *m* 1934, Robert Herbert Smidt Van Gelder, and has issue living Jacqueline, *b* 1935, — Pamela Gwynedd Marie, *b* 1946: *m* 1971, David Lawrence Jamison, of Westerland Stud, Graffham, Sussex, and has issue living, Antonia Alexandra *b* 1972, Melanie Pamela *b* 1976, Emma Laura *b* 1988, — Margaret, *b* 1950. *Residence* – Rodlease House, Boldre, near Lymington, Hants.

Grandchildren of late George Daniel Gooch, son of Alfred William Gooch, 3rd son of 1st baronet:—
Issue of late Major George Ernest Gooch, MBE, TD, *b* 1905, *d* 1958: *m* 1933, Jennifer Eve, who *d* 1981, da of late Brig-Gen Philip Maud, CMG, CBE:—
John Daniel, VRD, OStJ (The Schoolhouse, Oathlaw, Forfar, Angus), *b* 1935; *ed* Cheltenham Coll; FRICS: *m* 1972, Ann Patricia, da of David Miles Lubbock (*see* B Avebury, colls), and has issue living, Katherine Janita, *b* 1974, — Diana Veronica, *b* 1976. —— Peter David (1111 Skeena Place, Victoria, BC, Canada), *b* 1938; *ed* Cheltenham Coll; MSc: *m* 1965, Pamela Sarah, da of late Robert Hartley, and has had issue, Adam Daniel, *b* 1969, — Thomas Daniel, *b* 1970, — Fiona Louise, *b* 1972, *d* 1991. —— Belinda, *b* 1944: *m* 1984, Harry Merriam Ash, of 35 Essex Place, Newtown, PA 18940, USA, and has issue living, George Gooch *b* 1985.

The baronetcy was conferred upon Sir Daniel Gooch, who was Chm of the Great Western Railway 1865-89, for the services he rendered in promoting the successful submersion of the Atlantic Cables of 1865 and 1866.

GOODENOUGH (UK) 1943, of Broadwell and Filkins, co Oxford

Sir WILLIAM McLERNON GOODENOUGH, 3rd *Baronet*; *b* 5 Aug 1954; *s* his father, *Sir* RICHARD EDMUND, 1996; *ed* Stanbridge Earls: *m* 1982, Louise Elizabeth, da of Capt Michael Ortmans, LVO, RN, of 48 Bishops Rd, SW6, and has issue.

ᴂrms – Or a chevron gules between three guttes de sang. Crest – A demi-wolf proper holding between his paws an escallop argent.
Residence – The Old Rectory, Blickling, Norfolk NR11 6NF.

SON LIVING

SAMUEL WILLIAM HECTOR, *b* 11 June 1992.

DAUGHTERS LIVING

Sophie Julia, *b* 1986. —— Celia Isobel, *b* 1989.

SISTERS LIVING

Rosemary Louise, *b* 1952: *m* 1st, 1977, Frederick Charles le Roux; 2ndly, 1993, Patrick George MacGregor Masson, son of late Dr George Aird Masson, MD, FRCPE, and has issue living (by 1st *m*), Amy Elizabeth, *b* 1978, — Nancy Jane, *b* 1983. —— Joanna Jane, *b* 1958.

UNCLE LIVING (*son of 1st baronet*)

(Frederick) Roger, *b* 1927; *ed* Eton, and Magdalene Coll, Camb (MA); MA Oxon; FRSA; FCIB 1968; Local Dir of Barclays Bank, Oxford 1969-87; a Dir of Barclays Bank UK Management plc 1979-87, of Barclays plc 1985-89, of Barclays Bank plc 1979-89, of Barclays Bank International Ltd 1977-87, and Advisory Dir Barclays Bank Thames Valley Region 1988-89, a Curator of Oxford Univ Chest 1974-93, a Trustee of Nuffield Medical Benefaction and Nuffield Dominions Trust (Chm since 1987) since 1968 and since 1981 Chm of Nuffield Orthopaedic Trust (Trustee since 1978) and of Oxford and Dist Hosps Improvement and Development Fund 1982-88 (Trustee since 1968), a Gov of Shiplake Coll 1963-74 (Chm 1966-70), and of Wellington Coll 1968-74, and a Fellow of Linnean Soc (Member of Council 1968, Treas, 1970-75); High Sheriff of Oxfordshire 1987-88, DL Oxon 1989; Supernumerary Fell of Wolfson Coll, Oxford 1989-95, since when an Hon Fell; a patron of Anglo-Ghanaian Soc since 1991; Pres Oxfordshire Rural Community Council 1993-98; Gov London Goodenough Trust for Overseas Graduates since 1985; Trustee Radcliffe Medical Foundation 1987-98; RN 1946-48: *m* 1954, Marguerite June, only da of late David Forbes Mackintosh, of Bowling Green Cottage, Broadwell, nr Lechlade, Glos, and has issue living, David Frederick, *b* 1955; *ed* Clifton, and Grey Coll, Durham (BSc): *m* 1988, Nicola Dawn Foreman, and has issue living, Michael John Frederick *b* 1989, Mark William Anthony *b* 1991, — Annabel Margaret, *b* 1957; *ed* Lady Margaret Hall, Oxford (MA): *m* 1980, Col Paul Christopher Charles Molyneaux, RA, and has issue living, Harriet Frances Rose *b* 1986, Emma Flora Louise *b* 1989, — Victoria Frances, *b* 1961; *ed* Lady Margaret Hall, Oxford (MA): *m* 1989, David Richard Arden Bott, yr son of Dr Edward Bott, of Manor Fields, Moreton Morrell, Warwickshire, and has issue living, Patrick Edward Arden *b* 1991, Archie Frederick Arden *b* 1993. *Residence* – Broadwell Manor, Lechlade, Glos GL7 3QS. *Club* – Brooks's.

AUNT LIVING (*daughter of 1st baronet*)

Mary Dorothea, *b* 1940: *m* 1965, Capt John Alistair Ponsonby Forbes, late Coldstream Guards, of All Saints House, nr Axminster, Devonshire EX13 7LR, and has issue (*see* L Forbes, colls).

The 1st baronet, Sir William Macnamara Goodenough (son of late Frederick Craufurd Goodenough, of Filkins Hall, Lechlade), was Chm of Barclays Bank, of Nuffield Foundation, and of five other Nuffield Trusts, and Dep Steward of Oxford Univ.

GOODHART (UK) 1911, of Portland Place, St Marylebone, and Holtye, Sussex.

From God all things

Sir ROBERT ANTHONY GORDON GOODHART, 4th *Baronet*; *b* 15 Dec 1948; *s* his father, *Sir* JOHN GORDON, 1979; *ed* Rugby, and Lond Univ (Guy's Hosp) (MB, BS); MRCS, LRCP (1972), MRCGP (1976): *m* 1972, Kathleen Ellen, el da of late Rev Alexander Duncan MacRae, of 45 Laggan Rd, Inverness, and has issue.

Arms – Gules, a buck trippant argent, in chief two bees volant or, on a chief nebulée of the third a Cross of Lorraine of the field, between two eagles displayed sable. Crest – A beehive or between two bees with a rainbow terminating in clouds proper.
Residence – The Old Rectory, Netherbury, Bridport, Dorset DT6 5NB.

SONS LIVING

MARTIN ANDREW, *b* 9 Sept 1974. —— Iain Michael, *b* 1980.

DAUGHTERS LIVING

Kim Elaine, *b* 1977. —— Rachel Alice, *b* 1987.

SISTER LIVING

Anne Rosemary, *b* 1945: *m* 1969, John Oliver Soul, of Trevenevow, Crapstone Rd, Yelverton, Devon PL20 6BT, and has issue living, Nicholas John, *b* 1971, —— Sarah Victoria, *b* 1974.

AUNTS LIVING

Dorothy Joyce, *b* 1921 (Bayfield, Copp Hill Lane, Budleigh Salterton, Devon EX9 6DT). —— Alice Mary, RD (Bayfield, Copp Hill Lane, Budleigh Salterton, Devon EX9 6DT); *b* 1926; DL.

WIDOW LIVING OF THIRD BARONET

(MARGARET MARY) EILEEN (*Eileen, Lady Goodhart*) (Venn House, Lamerton, Tavistock, Devon PL19 8RX), da of late Morgan Morgan, of Cray, Breconshire: *m* 1944, Sir John Gordon Goodhart, MB, FRCGP, 3rd Bt, who *d* 1979.

The 1st baronet, Sir James Frederic Goodhart, MD, CM, FRCP (Hon LLD Aberdeen), was Consulting Physician to Guy's Hospital and to Evelina Hospital.

GOODSON (UK) 1922, of Waddeton Court, Parish of Stoke Gabriel, co Devon

Sir MARK WESTON LASSAM GOODSON, 3rd *Baronet*, son of late Maj Alan Richard Lassam Goodson, 2nd son of 1st baronet: *b* 12 Dec 1925; *s* his uncle, *Sir* ALFRED LASSAM, 1986; *ed* Radley, and Jesus Coll, Camb: *m* 1949, Barbara Mary Constantine, da of Surg-Capt Reginald Joseph McAuliffe Andrews, RN, of Crandel, Ferndown, Dorset, and has issue.

Arms – Ermine, on a chevron between three quatrefoils gules, leaved and slipped vert, as many garbs or. Crest – A wolf's head erased gules, collared and charged on the neck with a spur or.
Residence – Kilham, Mindrum, Northumberland TD12 4QS.

SON LIVING

ALAN REGINALD, *b* 15 May 1960; *ed* Ampleforth.

DAUGHTERS LIVING

Phylida Mary, *b* 1950: *m* 1973, Dr Timothy Freeman Wright, and has issue living, Matthew, *b* 1975, — Sacha, *b* 1977, — Tanya, *b* 1979, — Elisa, *b* 1981. —— Hilary Frances, *b* 1953. —— Christian Mary, *b* 1958: *m* 1983, Christopher Collins.

AUNT LIVING (*Daughter of first baronet*)

Kathleen Mary Lassam, *b* 1900; was Co Organizer WVS 1940-45; JP 1941-53: *m* 1920, Roy Neville Craig, MD, DPM, BS, MRCS, LRCP, and has issue living, David Neville, *b* 1924. *Residence* – The Old Parsonage, Wilmington, Honiton, Devon.

COLLATERAL BRANCH LIVING

Issue of late Hugh Lassam Goodson, OBE, 3rd and yst son of 1st baronet, *b* 1905, *d* 1985: *m* 1945, June Patricia (Waddeton Court, nr Brixham, S Devon TQ5 0EN), da of late Maj Joseph Charles Hunter, CBE, MC, DL, of Havikil Lodge, Scotton, Knaresborough:—
Alfred Lassam, *b* 1946: *m* 1st, 1970, Rosemary Anne Swales; 2ndly, 1989, Suzanne Harris, and has issue living, (by 1st *m*) Barnaby, *b* 1972, — Alfred, *b* 1974, — Amy, *b* 1977, — Polly, *b* 1979. —— Hugh Anthony Lassam (Waddeton Court, Brixham, S Devon TQ5 0EN; Royal Yacht Squadron, Royal Torbay Yacht Club, Royal Ocean Racing Club), *b* 1955; Chm of Devonshire Investment Estates; Rear Commodore of Royal Torbay Yacht Club 1988: *m* 1977, Jame Mary, da of Brian Kirley, of Southside, Cobham, Surrey, and has issue living, Hugo Matthew Lassam, *b* 1982. —— Sarah June, *b* 1947: *m* 1972, Guy Arthur Louis Cruwys, and has issue living, Robert, *b* 1976, — Emily, *b* 1974, — Mary, *b* 1978, — Belinda, *b* 1982. —— Penelope Jane, *b* 1948: *m* 1975, Capt Rhydian Peter Vaughan, and has issue living, Sholto, *b* 1977, — Orlando, *b* 1983, — Camilla, *b* 1980.

GOOLD (UK) 1801, of Old Court, Cork

Sir GEORGE WILLIAM GOOLD, 8th *Baronet*; *b* 25 March 1950; *s* his father, *Sir* GEORGE LEONARD, 1997: *m* 1973, Julie Ann, da of late Leonard Powell Crack, of Whyalla, S Aust, and has issue.

𝕬rms – Azure, on a fesse, or, between five goldfinches, three in chief and two in base proper, three mullets gules. 𝕮rest – A demi-lion rampant or.
Residence – 180 Hargrave St, Paddington, NSW 2021, Aust.

SONS LIVING

GEORGE LEONARD POWELL, *b* 1 Dec 1975. —— Jon, *b* 1977.

SISTERS LIVING

Deus mihi providebit

God will provide for me

Dianne Joy, *b* 1946: *m* 1968, Gary Neville Button, of 28 Mary Penfold Drive, Rosslyn Park, Adelaide, S Australia 5072, and has issue living, Darren Scott, *b* 1970: *m* 1994, Penelope Kocent, — Kelly Lou, *b* 1972. —— Georgina Susan, *b* 1948: *m* 1969, Malcolm Kennedy Sard, of 12 First St, Napperby, S Aust, and has issue living, Stephen Kennedy, *b* 1970, — Michael Leonard, *b* 1974. —— Michelle Julie, *b* 1956: *m* 1979, John Joseph O'Dwyer, and has issue living, Stuart Goold, *b* 1981, — Rachel Louise, *b* 1985, — Sarah Kate, *b* 1988, — Hannah Charlotte, *b* 1990. —— Louise Mary GOOLD, *b* 1962; has retained her maiden name: *m* 1st, 1987 (*m diss* 19—), Paul James Christie; 2ndly, 1999, Dennis Rankin Murray, of 28 Mary Penfold Drive, Rosslyn Park, S Australia 5072.

WIDOW LIVING OF SEVENTH BARONET

JOY CECELIA (*Joy, Lady Goold*), da of late William Percival Cutler, of Melbourne, Victoria: *m* 1945, Sir George Leonard Goold, 7th Bt, who *d* 1997. *Residence* – 60 Canterbury Rd, Victor Harbor, S Aust 5211.

This family was settled for many centuries in the county and city of Cork. William Gould was Mayor of Cork *temp* Henry VII. George Gould, of Old Court, changed the spelling of his surname from Gould to Goold. His son Henry Michael, at a critical moment, rendered material political and pecuniary services to the Government of George III, and his son Francis was created a baronet with remainder to the heirs male of the body of his father.

GORDON (NS) 1631, of Embo, Sutherlandshire (Dormant 1956)

Sir HOME SETON CHARLES MONTAGU GORDON, 12th *Baronet*; *d* 1956, and at the time of going to press no name appears on the Official Roll of Baronets in respect of this title.

COLLATERAL BRANCHES LIVING

Granddaughters of late John Richard Colin Gordon (infra):—
Issue of late Colin Ernest Sutherland Gordon, *b* 1907, *d* 1960: *m* 1940, Patricia Hayward, who *d* 1997 (having *m* 2ndly, 1963, Rev Kenneth Thomas Jenkins), da of late Harold Newbigin:—
Sarah Victoria, *b* 1944: *m* 1970, John Richard Bishop, and has issue living, Joseph Alexander Gordon, *b* 1978, — Andrew Gordon, *b* 1980. —— Dinah Jillian Hayward, *b* 1948: *m* 1970, Robert Neil Morrison, and has issue living, Colin Robert, *b* 1977, — Meagan Kate, *b* 1978, — Caroline Emma, *b* 1982.

Grandsons of late John Sutherland Gordon, son of Gilbert Gordon, of Woodlands, yr son of late Alexander Gordon in Dalcharn, great-grandson of late Hutcheon Gordon of Moy, yst brother of 1st baronet:—
Issue of late John Richard Colin Gordon, *b* 1868, *d* 1947: *m* 1906, Hilda, da of late Very Rev Ernest Sloman, Dean of St George's Cathedral, Georgetown, British Guiana:—
Michael Ian Newnham, *b* 1914; probable heir to Baronetcy; *ed* Charterhouse; formerly an Assist Commr of Police, Ghana: *m* 1944, Margaret Noreen, da of late Reginald Hubert Payne, and has issue living, Philip Michael Sutherland, *b* 1946, — Helen Elizabeth, *b* 1945: *m* 1982 (*m diss* 1986), Andrew John Tweedie, and has issue living, Alexandra Helen Rose *b* 1983, — Carol Margaret, *b* 1947: *m* 1980, Stuart Fraser Murray, and has issue living, William John Fraser *b* 1988, Holly Georgina Christian *b* 1981, Anna Florence Margaret *b* 1984. *Residence* – 11 Craven Rd, Reading.

Issue of late William James Sutherland Gordon, *b* 1870, *d* 1969: *m* 1906, Mabel N who *d* 1957, da of late J. J. Conner:—
Huntly Sutherland (487 Wanapum Drive, La Conner, Washington 98257, USA), *b* 1911: *m* 1936, Ann Elizabeth, da of Charles A. Parker, and has issue living, Huntly Sutherland (12453 Patricia Lane, Burlington, WA 98233, USA), *b* 1937: *m* 1st, 1968 (*m diss* 1983), Nancy Aiken; 2ndly, 1989, Sandra Gauntlett, and has issue living, (by 1st *m*) Ann Elizabeth *b* 1971, — Charles Cooper (945-88th Av NE, Bellevue, Washington 98004, USA), *b* 1944: *m* 1968, Margaret Mellor Stull, and has issue living, Huntly S. *b* 1975, Parker Stull *b* 1981 Cori Ann *b* 1973, — Josephine Ann, *b* 1941: *m* 1964, William Irven McCaughey, of 9829 NE 21st, Bellevue, Washington, and has issue living, Susan Elizabeth *b* 1966: *m* 1992, Todd Christopher Meadows, of 5674 SO Carie Lane, Freeland, WA 98249, USA (and has issue living, Connor James *b* 1998, Anne Elizabeth *b* 1996), Sally Ann *b* 1968: *m* 1994, Steven James Davey of 3143 NE 83rd, Seattle, WA 98115, USA.

This family descends from Adam Gordon, Dean of Caithness, 3rd son of 1st Earl of Huntly. His great grandson, Sir John Gordon of Embo, was the 1st baronet, created with remainder to heirs male whatsoever.

GORDON (NS) 1706, of Afton and Earlston, Kirkcudbrightshire.

The Lord will Provide
Dominus providebit

Sir ROBERT JAMES GORDON, 10th *Baronet*; *b* 17 Aug 1932; *s* his father, *Sir* John Charles Gordon, 1982; probably next in remainder to the Viscountcy of Kenmure and Lordship of Lochinvar (dormant since 1872): *m* 1976, Helen Julia Weston, da of late John Weston Perry, of Cammeray, NSW.

𝔄rms – Azure, a bezant between three boars' heads erased or and in a dexter chief a canton of a Baronet of Nova Scotia. ℭrest – A dexter hand grasping a sabre proper.
Residence – Earlstoun, Guyra, NSW 2365, Aust.

SISTER LIVING

Ann Gordon (183 Raglan St, Mosman, NSW 2088, Australia), *b* 1929: *m* 1953, Timothy Raymond Harry Savill, who *d* 1992, and has issue living, Joanna Mary Gordon, *b* 1956: *m* 1988, Giuliano Dambelli, son of Ilma Dambelli, of Brescia, Italy, and has issue living, Lily Rose *b* 19—, Milena *b* 19—, — Lisbeth Jane Gordon, *b* 1958: has issue living, Samson *b* 19—, Bruno *b* 19—, — Camilla Ann Gordon, *b* 1961: *m* 1990, Bruce MacInnes, and has issue living, Georgina *b* 19—, Bronte (da) *b* 19—, — Katherine Helen Gordon, *b* 1963: *m* 1996, Gregory Johnson, and has issue living, Annie *b* 19—.

The family were distinguished loyalists during the Rebellion. The 1st baronet, Col Sir William, Governor of Fort William, led the descent on the west coast of Scotland at the time that the Duke of Monmouth landed in the south of England. Sir Alexander, the 2nd baronet, celebrated in Scottish history, escaped to Holland after the battle of Bothwell Bridge, but was afterwards captured; during his absence he was found guilty, and sentenced to death and forfeiture of estates. On his capture it was decreed that the sentence should be put in force, but, after six years' imprisonment in Edinburgh Castle, he was released in 1689.

DUFF GORDON (UK) 1813, of Halkin, Ayrshire.

Sir ANDREW COSMO LEWIS DUFF GORDON, 8th *Baronet*; *b* 17 Oct 1933; *s* his father, *Sir* DOUGLAS FREDERICK, 1964; late Worcestershire and Cheshire Regt; Suez 1953-54: *m* 1st, 1967 (*m diss* 1975), Grania Mary, da of Fitzgerald Villiers-Stuart, of Dromana, Villierstown, co Waterford; 2ndly, 1975, Eveline Virginia, yst da of Samuel Soames, of Boxford House, Newbury, and has issue by 1st and 2nd *m*.

Arms – Quarterly, 1st and 4th, azure, three boars' heads couped or, armed proper and langued gules, within a double tressure flory counterflory interchangeably with thistles, roses and fleurs-de-lis of the second, *Gordon*; 2nd and 3rd, vert, a fess dancettee ermine between a buck's head cabossed in chief and two escallops in base, or *Duff*. **Crest** – *Dexter*, two arms from the shoulder naked holding a bow, and ready to let fly an arrow all proper. *Sinister*, a demi-lion holding in the dexter paw a sword erect proper, hilted and pommelled or, charged on the shoulder with a mullet argent. **Supporters** – *Dexter*, a savage wreathed about the head and middle with laurel, holding in the dexter hand the branch of a tree all proper. *Sinister*, a stage proper unguled and attired or gorged with a ducal coronet of the last and pending therefrom an inescutcheon charged with the following arms, vert a fess dancettee ermine between a buck's head cabossed in chief and two escallops in base or, the fees charged of a mullet argent.
Residences – Downton House, Walton, Presteigne, Radnorshire; 27 Cathcart Rd, SW10. *Club* – City University.

SONS LIVING (*By 1st marriage*)

COSMO HENRY VILLIERS, *b* 18 June 1968.

(*By 2nd marriage*)

William Andrew Lewis, *b* 1977. —— Thomas Francis Cornewall, *b* 1979. —— Frederick Samuel Douglas, *b* 1981.

AUNT LIVING (*Daughter of 6th baronet*)

Anne Maud, *b* 1903: *m* 1926, Richard S. de Q. Quincey, who *d* 1991. *Residence* – Blackaldern, Narberth, Pembrokeshire.

COLLATERAL BRANCH LIVING

Issue of late John Cornewall Duff-Gordon, MBE, 3rd son of Cosmo Lewis Cornewall, 2nd son of 3rd baronet, *b* 1869, *d* 1964: *m* 1920, Ruth Mary, who *d* 1977, da of C. F. Dodson:—
Cosmo John, *b* 1924. —— Alexander Mostyn, *b* 1927.

Sir James Duff, 1st Bt, of Hankin, Ayrshire, British Consul at Cadiz, was created a Bt with remainder to his maternal nephew. Sir William Duff-Gordon, 2nd Bt, was grandson of the 2nd Earl of Aberdeen (*see* M Aberdeen and Temair, colls).

SMITH-GORDON (UK) 1838.

By courage,   *My hope is*
not by craft   *in God*

SIR (LIONEL) ELDRED PETER SMITH-GORDON, 5th *Baronet*; *b* 7 May 1935; *s* his father, *Sir* LIONEL ELDRED POTTINGER, 1976; *ed* Eton and Trin Coll, Oxford: *m* 1962, Sandra Rosamund Ann, yr da of late Wing Cdr Walter Ronald Farley, DFC, and has issue.

Arms – Quarterly, 1st and 4th, per fesse azure and gules two barrulets engrailed ermine, between three boars' heads erased or, *Gordon*; 2nd and 3rd, argent on a bend cotissed between two unicorns' heads erased azure three lozenges or, a canton gules, thereon a sword erect proper, pommel and hilt gold the blade encircled by an eastern crown or, *Smith*. **Crest** – 1st, issuant from the battlements of a tower argent a stag's head affrontée proper, all between two palm-branches vert; 2nd *(for augmentation)*, a representation of the ornamental centre-piece of the service of plate all proper presented to the 1st baronet by his European and native friends at Bombay; 3rd, issuant out of an eastern crown or, a dexter arm embowed in armour entwined with a branch of laurel proper, the hand grasping a sword also proper, pommel and hilt gold.
Residence – 13 Shalcomb St, SW10.

SON LIVING

LIONEL GEORGE ELDRED, *b* 1 July 1964; *ed* Eton, Westfield Coll and King's Coll London: *m* 1993, Kumi, only da of Masashi Suzuki, of Urawa, Saitama, Japan, and has issue living, Lionel Henry Yuji, *b* 22 Dec 1998. *Residence* – Beverly Mai #09-37, 31 Tomlinson Rd, Singapore 247855.

DAUGHTER LIVING

Isobel Charlotte Laura, *b* 1966: *m* 1997, Thomas V. Magee, yst son of Hugh F. Magee, of Santa Rosa, California, USA, and has issue living, Benjamin Hugh, *b* 1998.

The 1st baronet, Gen Sir Lionel Smith, GCB, GCH, received his baronetcy for distinguished military services in the West Indies, and for carrying out the emancipation of the slaves in Jamaica, of which island he was Gov-Gen. He was subsequently Gov of Mauritius, where he died, and where a column is erected to his memory. Sir Lionel Eldred Smith, 2nd Bt, assumed by Roy licence 1868, the additional surname and arms of Gordon, his mother, Isabella Curwen, having been a da of Eldred Curwen Pottinger of Mount Pottinger, co Down, by Anne, da of Robert Gordon of Florida Manor, co Down.

Gordon-Cumming, see Cumming.

GORE (I) 1622, of Magherabegg, co Donegal.

Sir NIGEL HUGH ST GEORGE GORE, 14th *Baronet*, yr son of late St George Richard Gore, eldest son of late Frederick Dundas Corbet Gore, yr brother of 9th baronet; *b* 23 Dec 1922; *s* his nephew, *Sir* RICHARD RALPH ST GEORGE, 1993: *m* 1952, Beth Allison, da of R. W. Hooper, of Allawah, Tambo, Qld, and has issue.

Arms – Gules, a fesse argent between three cross-crosslets fitchée or. Crest – A wolf rampant argent, collared gules.
Residence – Hillhaven, Preston Rd, Hodgson Vale, Toowoomba, Qld 4352, Australia.

DAUGHTER LIVING

Seonaid Beth, *b* 1955.

Sola salus servire Deo

To serve God is the only Salvation

SISTERS LIVING

Phyllis Ruth St George (5 Chelsea Court, Toowoomba, Qld 4350, Australia), *b* 1912. —— Margaretta Leonie St George, *b* 1921: *m* 1958, John Henry Cory, of PO Box 607, Goondiwindi, Qld 4390, Australia, and has issue living, Alan Fitzroy, *b* 1961, — Janet Ruth, *b* 1959: *m* 1995, Anthony Peter Gorring, of Camiloroi, Pittsworth, Queensland 4356, Australia, and has issue living, Matthew John Thomas *b* 1997.

DAUGHTER LIVING OF ELEVENTH BARONET

Maxine Marjorie St George, *b* 1947: *m* 1968, Capt Timothy Basil Edward Eugster, Irish Gds, and has issue living, Maximilian Brian Michael, *b* 1969, — Alexandra Marcia Gabrielle, *b* 1971, — Julia Clare Elizabeth, *b* 1974.

DAUGHTERS LIVING OF TWELFTH BARONET

Annabel St George, *b* 1951: *m* 1989, Bruce Julian Knowles, of 18 Fairfax St, Red Hill, Qld 4059, Australia. —— Elizabeth St George, *b* 1952: *m* 1981, Patrick Hay Campbell, of RSD 385, Devonport, Tasmania 7310, Australia, and has issue living, Georgina Louise Gore, *b* 1989, — Claudia Jane Gore, *b* 1991. —— Juliet St George, *b* 1957: *m* 1982, David Sheridan Butler, of 31 Angus St, Goodwood, S Australia 5034, Australia.

WIDOW LIVING OF ELEVENTH BARONET

Irene Lamont, el da of Albert James Marshall, of Stranraer, Wigtownshire: *m* 1st, 1971, as his 3rd wife, Lt-Col Sir Ralph St George Brian Gore, 11th Bt, who *d* 1973; 2ndly, 1975, James Biggar, of Old House, Willards Hill, Etchingham, Surrey.

COLLATERAL BRANCHES LIVING

Grandchildren of late Frederick Dundas Corbet Gore, yr brother of 9th baronet:—
Issue of late Frederick Dundas Corbet Gore, *b* 1885, *d* 1964: *m* 1919, Ella Maud, who *d* 1967, da of Charles Sydney Jones, of Brisbane:—
DUNDAS CORBET (31 Ruskin Rowe, Avalon Beach, NSW 2107), *b* 20 April 1921; *ed* Sydney Univ (BEng); 1939-45 War as Flt-Lt RAAF. —— Hugh Frederick Corbet (7 Romney Rd, St Ives, NSW), *b* 1934: *m* 1963, Jennifer Mary, el da of Milton Gordon Copp, of Rose Bay, NSW, and has issue living, Timothy Milton Corbet, *b* 1969, — Penelope Mary Corbet, *b* 1965, — Virginia Louise, *b* 1967. —— Rosemary Ella Corbet, *b* 1920; 1939-45 War with AIF: *m* 1957, Nicholas George Knox Adams, of 36 The Circle, Bilgola Plateau, Sydney, NSW 2107, Australia, and has an adopted son, David Alexander Ian, *b* 1963. —— Barbara Corbet, *b* 1926.

Grandchildren of late Francis Arthur Gore, el son of late Rev William Francis Gore, yst son of late Rev Thomas Gore, brother of 7th baronet:—
Issue of late Francis William Baldock Gore, *b* 1873, *d* 1937: *m* 1920, Mary Isabel Kirsteen, who *d* 1986, da of late Francis Corbet-Singleton, formerly of Finchampstead, Berks:—
(Francis) St John Corbet, CBE (Grove Farm, Stoke-by-Nayland, Colchester, Essex C06 4SL), *b* 1921; *ed* Wellington Coll; Capt (ret) R Northumberland Fus; 1939-45 War: *m* 1st, 1951 (*m diss* 1975), Priscilla Margaret, da of Cecil Harmsworth King; 2ndly, 1981, Lady Mary Sophia, yst da of 3rd Earl of Selborne, and widow of Maj Hon (Thomas) Anthony Edward Towneley Strachey (*see* B O'Hagan), and has issue living, (by 1st *m*) William Ralph St John (Pencarrow Farm, Advent, Camelford, Cornwall PL32 9RZ), *b* 1956: *m* 1984, (Mary) Susan, yst da of late Edmund Arthur Collingridge, of Kentigern, Hunter's Hill, Sydney, Australia, and has issue living, Ralph St John Edmund *b* 1985, Alice Catharine Mary *b* 1988, — Catharine Harriet Cecilia, *b* 1954: *m* 1977, Richard Edward Geoffrey Gayner, and has issue living, John Robert Haydon *b* 1983, William Richard Francis *b* 1986. —— Alan Charles Corbet, *b* 1926; *ed* Wellington Coll: *m* 1953, Ann Sabine, da of W. D. K. Thellusson, of Disley, Gloucestershire, and has issue living, Francis Charles Storar, *b* 1957, — Thomas Corbet, *b* 1960: *m* 1989, Skye Gyngell, and has issue living, Holly *b* 1989. *Residence* – Grandcourt Farm, East Winch, King's Lynn, Norfolk.

Issue of late Cyril Gerard Gore, *b* 1876, *d* 1954: *m* 1911, Gladys Marie Howard, who *d* 1974, da of Allan A. Spowers, Surveyor-Gen of Queensland:—
Leonie Frances, *b* 1918: *m* 1st, 1938, Hugh John Walsh; 2ndly, 1956, Shane Page, and has issue living, (by 1st *m*) Joanna Leonie, *b* 1939: *m* 1959, Mervyn Fitzhenry, and has issue living, William Hugh Shaun *b* 1961, Brendan Mervyn *b* 1964,

Shamus Terence *b* 1968, Bridgit Madeline *b* 1963, — Emlyn Anna, *b* 1942: *m* 1960, John Thompson, and has issue living, Simon Patrick *b* 1963, Leonie Helen *b* 1961.

Grandchildren of late Cyril Gerard Gore (ante):—
  Issue of late Francis Arthur Gore, *b* 1921, *d* 1987: *m* 1947, Lenore (who *m* 2ndly, 1980, Richard John Lewis, of 4/136 Macquarie St, St Lucia, Brisbane 4067, Australia), da of Leonard Lee, of Queensland, Australia:—
Simon Gerard (Mail Service 422, Clifton, Queensland, Australia), *b* 1955: *m* 1979, Leone Christine, da of H. Beck, of Queensland, and has issue living, Richard Anthony, *b* 1984, — Adam William, *b* 1986, — Francis Arthur Douglas, *b* 1991, — Elizabeth Leone Amanda, *b* 1994. ── Leonie Christine, *b* 1948: *m* 1st, 1972, James Cruden; 2ndly, 1985, Jean-Marie Alain Simart, and has issue living, (by 2nd *m*) Thomas Elliot, *b* 1987, — Clélia Aurélia, *b* 1990. ── Amanda Lenore GORE, *b* 1954: *m* 1979 (*m diss* 1981), Robert John Lyttleton Turner, son of Roland Turner, of Tasmania.

Grandson of late William Wyndham Gore, eldest son of late Lieut Robert William Gore, RN (infra):—
  Issue of late Lt-Col Thomas Gerard Gore, DSO, OBE, *b* 1907, *d* 1965: *m* 1933, Mrs Barbara Young:—
Gerard Anthony St George (Box 27128, Sunnyside, Pretoria, S Africa), *b* 1936; *ed* Radley; late Cyprus Police; Lieut 60th Rifles (KRRC) and Capt S African Infantry (Res): *m* 1st, 1957 (*m diss* 1973), Wendy, da of late Mrs C. V. Rippon, of Umkomaas, Natal; 2ndly, 1975 (*m diss* 1985), Velma, da of Capt McKinnon, of 4A Le Grand Rue, Grouville, Jersey, CI, and Baroness von Puttkamer; 3rdly, 1986, Felicity Ann, da of Kathleen Ferreira, of Sydenham, Johannesburg, and has issue living, (by 1st *m*) Sean Ralph St George, *b* 1961, — Nicole Holly St George, *b* 1965.

Grandchildren of late Lieut Robert William Gore, RN, 3rd son of late Rev William Francis Gore (ante):—
  Issue of late St George Arthur Gore, *b* 1886, *d* 1970: *m* 1st, 1914 (*m diss* 1954), Muriel Mary, da of John Broughton, Surveyor-Gen of NSW; 2ndly, 1954, Mildred Prudence, who *d* 1979, da of late Charles James Vyner, MRCVS, of London:—
†Thomas William St George, *b* 1915: *m* 1945, Jane Nichols, who *d* 1968, only da of Samuel Bennett, of W Aust, and widow of Lt Donald Stewart Fletcher, RAA, and *d* 1999, leaving issue, Donald Stewart St George (8 Eunson Av, Northcote, Victoria 3070, Australia), *b* 1952. ── Patrick St George (Homeleigh, O'Connell, NSW), *b* 1921: *m* 1948, Coralie May, da of Mark Reuben Venn, of Tas, and has issue living, Robert Ralph St George (Box 157, Savage River, Tas), *b* 1949: *m* 1978, Prudence (DAVIS) da of Kenneth A. McKercher Burnie of Tas, and has issue living, William Robert Kenneth St George, *b* 1978, — Jonathan Ian St George, *b* 1953, — Peter Simon St George (3 Hasluck Place, Bathurst, NSW), *b* 1955: *m* 1979, Sylvia Joyce, da of Cyril Gardiner of Vittoria, NSW, and has issue living, Stephen Gregory St George *b* 1981.

Grandchildren of late Brig-Gen Robert Clement Gore, CB, CMG, only son of late Nathaniel Gore, 6th son of late Col William Gore, MP, son of late Rt Rev William Gore, Bishop of Limerick, eldest son of late Very Rev William Gore, Dean of Down, yr son of 3rd baronet:—
  Issue of late Brig Adrian Clements Gore, DSO, *b* 1900, *d* 1990: *m* 1927, Enid Aimée, who *d* 1997, da of late John Jameson Cairnes:—
Toby Clements (Monks Alley, Binfield, Bracknell, Berks; 94 Smith St, SW3), *b* (Dec) 1927; Maj Rifle Bde; High Sheriff Berks 1993: *m* 1959, (Isolde) Marian, who *d* 1996, yr da of late Edward H. Macintosh, of Rebeg, Kirkhill, Invernessshire, and has had issue, Fiona Marian, *b* 1960: *m* 1987, Irvine J. Maccabe, 2nd son of Jeffrey J. Maccabe, of Dulwich Village, — Juliet Carolyn, *b* 1962: *m* 1994, Charles M. Simpson, son of Robin Simpson, QC, of Kensington, and of Lady Webster, of Bratton, Wilts, — Tessa Jane, *b* 1967; *d* 1994, in Thailand, — Stephanie Serena, *b* 1969; has issue living (by Rory Sweet), a da *b* 1997. ── Dinah Priscilla, *b* 1930: *m* 1958, Lt-Col (John) Richard (Seymour) Besly, Gren Guards, and has issue living, Adrian Thomas, *b* 1963: *m* 1998, Sarah Powys Maurice, — Michael John, *b* 1966: *m* 1998, Bonnie Blumenthal, of Chicago, USA, — Emma Belinda, *b* 1958: *m* 1984, Keith Warner, — Lucinda Mary, *b* 1960: *m* 1991, John Anthony Watt Torrance, — Sara-Jane Beatrice, *b* 1964. ── Belinda Beatrice (*Lady Milbank*), *b* 1940: *m* 1970, Sir Anthony Frederick Milbank, 5th Bt, and has issue (*see that title*).

Descendants of late Arthur Gore (2nd son of 1st baronet), who was *cr* a *Baronet* 1662 (*see* E Arran).

Sir Paul, or Poule, Gore, 1st Bt, Capt of Horse (brother of Sir John Gore, Lord Mayor of London 1624, ancestor of Earl Temple of Stowe), was granted lands in co Donegal in the reign of Elizabeth I which he designated Manor Gore. From his 2nd son Sir Arthur descended the Earls of Arran and from his 4th son Sir Francis, Gore of Lissadill baronets (now Gore-Booth). The 3rd baronet was a Privy Councillor and Custos Rotulorum of co Limerick. The 4th baronet, a Privy Councillor, was MP for co Donegal, Chancellor of the Exchequer, and afterwards Speaker of the House of Commons in Ireland. The 5th baronet sat as MP for co Donegal; and the 6th baronet, a distinguished military officer, was, after representing Donegal co in Parliament, created Baron Gore (1764), Viscount Belleisle (1768), and Earl of Ross (1771), and died without surviving male issue. Sir Ralph Gore, 10th Bt, was elected Commodore of Roy Yacht Squadron 1947, Pres of Yachting Assocn 1945, and of Roy Yachting Assocn 1953.

Gore-Booth, see Booth.

GORING (E) 1678 (with precedency of 1627), of Highden, Sussex.

Renascentur

They will rise again

Sir WILLIAM BURTON NIGEL GORING, 13th *Baronet*; son of late Major Frederick Yelverton Goring, 6th son of 11th baronet; *b* 21 June 1933; *s* his uncle, *Sir* FORSTER GURNEY, 1956; *ed* Wellington Coll; late Lieut 1st Roy Sussex Regt: *m* 1st, 1960 (*m diss* 1993), Hon Caroline Thellusson, el da of 8th Baron Rendlesham; 2ndly, 1993, Mrs Judith Rachel Walton Morison, who *d* 1995, da of Rev (Raymond) John Walton Morris, OBE, of Shaftesbury, and formerly wife of Thomas Richard Atkin Morison, QC (later Hon Mr Justice Morison); 3rdly, 1998, Mrs Stephanie H. Bullock, da of George Carter.

Arms – Argent, a chevron between three annulets gules. **Crest** – A lion rampant-guardant sable.

COLLATERAL BRANCHES LIVING

Issue of late Lt-Cdr Edward Yelverton Combe Goring, RN, yr brother of 13th baronet, *b* 1936, *d* 1991: *m* 1969 (*m diss* 1990), Daphne Christine Seller: —
Elizabeth Christine, *b* 1970. —— Joanna Margaret, *b* 1972.

Issue of late Craven Charles Goring, 3rd son of 11th baronet, *b* 1881, *d* 1952: *m* 1908, Mary Elizabeth, da of John Conlon, of Roscommon:—
Beryl Elizabeth (Castle Farm, Bridgwater Rd, Bristol 3, Somerset BS13 8AF), *b* 1909: *m* 1930, George Frederick Thawley, who *d* 1958, and has issue living, Peter Frederick (Castle Farm, Bridgwater Rd, Bristol 3, Somerset BS13 8AF), *b* 1940: *m* 1966 (*m diss* 1980), Christine Mary, da of Charles Henry Jones Payne, and has issue living, Nicholas *b* 1971, Lisa *b* 1969.

Grandchildren of late Charles Goring, eldest son of late Rev John Goring, yr son of late Charles Goring (*b* 1744) (infra):—
Issue of late John Goring, CBE, TD, DL, *b* 1907, *d* 1990: *m* 1947, Lady Hersey Margaret, who *d* 1993, da of 8th Earl of Glasgow, and widow of Cdr Hon John Montagu Granville Waldegrave, DSC, RN (*see* By Radstock, ext):—
RICHARD HARRY (Findon Park House, Findon, W Sussex), *b* 10 Sept 1949; *ed* Eton; High Sheriff W Sussex 1993, DL 1995: *m* 1972, Penelope Ann, da of J. K. Broadbent, of Coppull Farm, Stanford, Cape, S Africa, and has issue living, Richard John, *b* 1978, — Charles, *b* 1980, — Dominic James David, *b* 1989, — Eloise Isabella, *b* 1974, — Catherine Clare, *b* 1975, — Gabrielle Mary, *b* 1991. —— John James (Upper Buncton, Wiston, Steyning, W Sussex), *b* 1953: *m* 1982, Maxine Jane, yr da of ACM Sir David Evans, GCB, CBE, CBIM, of Milton House, Little Milton, Oxon, and has issue living, Jasper David George, *b* 1986, — India Catherine, *b* 1984, — Elizabeth Iona, *b* 1989, — Francesca Mary Hyacinth, *b* 1992. —— (Corinna) Jane GORING (2 Barclay Rd, SW6 1EH), *b* 1948; resumed her maiden name 1998: *m* 1969 (*m diss* 1989), Nigel Vere Nicoll, and has issue living, Adam Nigel, *b* 1972, — Rory Raymond, *b* 1978, — Zoe Gabrielle, *b* 1971, — Corinna Mary, *b* 1980. —— Anne Elizabeth (Linkylea Cottages, Gifford, East Lothian), *b* 1951; has issue living, Nicola Bonny Goring SQUAIR, *b* 1981, — Flora Hersey Goring SQUAIR, *b* 1984.

Granddaughters of late Lt-Col Harold Goring, IA (infra):—
Issue of late Brian Hamilton Goring, MBE, *b* 1935, *d* 1989: *m* 1958, Prudence Mary (Lowerwood House, New Lane, Billingshurst, W Sussex RH14 9DS), da of George Baker, of Dickhurst, Lurgashall, Sussex:—
Alice Lucinda, *b* 1959: *m* 1984, Dominique Bouilliez, of Lille, France, and has issue living, Georges Brian Ferdinand Goring, *b* 1985, — William Philippe Xavier Goring, *b* 1987, — Esme Eleanor Joan Goring, *b* 1983. —— Sya Charlotte, *b* 1964: *m* 1993, Marcus Henry Robert Elwes, of Elder Farm, Grimston, Norfolk, eldest son of Henry Arthur Elwes, of Congham, Norfolk, and has issue living, Cosmo Brian Henry, *b* 1996, — Millicent Lettice Susan Mary Primrose, *b* 1994. —— Lydia Mary, *b* 1965.

Grandson of late Maj Alan Goring, 3rd son of late Rev John Goring, yr son of late Charles Goring (*b* 1744), 2nd son of 5th baronet:—
Issue of late Lt-Col Harold Goring, IA, *b* 1903, *d* 1990: *m* 1st, 1929, Mary Frances Eleanor (Kaisar-i-Hind medal), who *d* 1975, da of late Capt Hamilton Augustus Woodruffe, of Garsington, Oxon; 2ndly, 1975, (Joan) Henrietta Radcliffe, da of late Spencer Domett Secretan, of Swaynes, Rudgwick, Sussex:—
(By 1st *m*) George (Holland House, Warnham, W Sussex), *b* 1937; *ed* Cheltenham, and Millfield; Maj The Queen's Regt (ret): *m* 1969 (*m diss* 1987), Nicola Jean, da of William Ian Gordon, of Rye, Sussex, and has issue living, Michael, *b* 1974, — Fiona Mary, *b* 1972.

Henry Goring, of Highden, Sussex, succeeded Feb 1679-80 as 2nd Bt (by virtue of the special remainder in the patent of 1678), Sir James Bowyer, 3rd Bt, of Leighthorne, Sussex (yr son of Sir Thomas Bowyer, *cr* a baronet 23 July 1627), surrendered by fine his patent and was granted a new patent dated 18 May 1678, for life with remainder after his death to Henry Goring, of Highden, Sussex (ante), and the heirs male of his body, with precedence of the former patent of 23 July 1627. The Goring family is of great antiquity in Sussex, and John Goring was MP for Sussex 1467. A member of the family was created Baron Goring 1628, and Earl of Norwich 1644, titles that became extinct on the death of the 2nd Earl (*cr* 1644) in March 1672. The 2nd baronet was MP for Sussex 1660, for Steyning 1661-79, and again for Sussex 1685-7; the 4th baronet, Col 31st Foot, was MP for Horsham 1707-8, Steyning 1708-15, and again for Horsham 1715, and the 6th baronet was MP for Shoreham 1790-6; the 7th baronet was High Sheriff of Sussex, 1827, and the 8th baronet sat as MP for Shoreham 1832-41. The 12th baronet, Sir Forster Gurney Goring, was appointed a Capt of Invalids, Roy Hospital, Chelsea 1912.

GOSCHEN (UK) 1916, of Beacon Lodge, Highcliffe, co Southampton.

For peace

Sir EDWARD CHRISTIAN GOSCHEN, DSO, 3rd *Baronet*; *b* 2 Sept 1913; *s* his father, *Sir* EDWARD HENRY, 1933; *ed* Eton and Trin Coll, Oxford; dep Chm of Stock Exchange Cncl 1963-71, C with War Graves commissioner since 1977, European War 1939-45 in Italy as Major Tower Hamlets Rifles, Rifle Brig (TA) (DSO); DSO 1944: *m* 1946, Cynthia, JP, da of late Rt Hon Sir Alexander George Montagu Cadogan, OM, GCMG, KCB, PC (*see* E Cadogan, colls), and has issue.

Arms – Argent, a human heart gules flamant and transfixed by an arrow bendwise point upwards proper. Crest – Upon an arrow fessewise the point to the dexter a dove wings endorsed, all proper.
Residence – Lower Farmhouse, Hampstead Norreys, Berks.

SON LIVING

(EDWARD) ALEXANDER (Pixton Stables, Dulverton, Taunton, Somerset TA22 9HW) *b* 13 March 1949; *ed* Eton: *m* 1976, Louise Annette, da of Lt-Col Ronald Fulton Lucas Chance, MC, KRRC (*see* E Kintore), and has issue living, Charlotte Leila, *b* 1982.

DAUGHTER LIVING

Caroline Clare, *b* 1950: *m* 1989, Jonathan Mendham.

COLLATERAL BRANCHES LIVING

Grandchildren of late George Gerard Goschen (infra):—
Issue of late David Bernard Goschen, *b* 1931, *d* 1980: *m* 1954, Angela (Oakwood Cottages, High Routham, Bury St Edmunds, Suffolk), only da of James Macnabb:—
Sebastien Bernard, *b* 1959, —— Chrysoula Angela, *b* 1955. —— Mariora Vivienne, *b* 1957.

Issue of late George Gerard Goschen, yr son of 1st baronet, *b* 1887, *d* 1953: *m* 1930, Vivienne, who *d* 1957, da of late Bernard de Watteville:—
Tana Mary, *b* 1932: *m* 1962, John Alais Fletcher, and has issue living, Mark Alais, *b* 1963: *m* 1996, Samantha, da of Sir Mark Aubrey Weinberg, — Miranda Clare, *b* 1964: *m* 1993, Toby Hawkins, — Katherine Alice, *b* 1966: *m* 1995, Dr Sanjay Singh Yadav, — Alexandra Sophia, *b* 1970: *m* 1997, Vito Morawetz. *Residence* – Dolphin Cottage, 68 Altwood Rd, Maidenhead, Berks SL6 4PZ.

The 1st baronet, Rt Hon Sir (William) Edward Goschen, GCB, GCMG, GCVO, was Envoy Extraor, and Min Plen at Belgrade and Copenhagen 1898-1905, Ambassador Extraor and Min Plen at Vienna and Berlin 1905-14, and Gentleman Usher to the Sword of State 1919-24. Sir Edward Henry Goschen, 2nd Bt, was sometime Controller of Secretariat, Egyptian Min of Finance.

Gough (Anstruther-Gough-Calthorpe), see Calthorpe.

GOULDING (UK) 1904, Millicent, Clane, co Kildare, and Roebuck Hill, Dundrum, co Dublin.

Sir (WILLIAM) LINGARD WALTER GOULDING, 4th *Baronet*; *b* 11 July 1940; *s* his father, *Sir* (WILLIAM) BASIL, 1982, but his name does not appear on the Official Roll of the Baronetage; *ed* Winchester, and Trin Coll, Dublin; Headmaster, Headfort Preparatory Sch, co Meath.

Arms – Per bend or and argent, a gryphon segreant within an orle of martlets sable. Crest – A dexter hand apaumée and couped at the wrist, encircled with a chaplet of oak leaves bendwise, and transfixed with an arrow bend sinisterwise, all proper.

Seat – Ballyrusheen, co Cork. *Address* – Dargle Cottage, Enniskerry, Co Wicklow, Eire.

BROTHERS LIVING

TIMOTHY ADAM, *b* 15 May 1945; *ed* Winchester: *m* 1971, Patricia Mohan, of Dublin. ——Hamilton Paddy, *b* 1947; *ed* Winchester, and Trin Coll, Dublin; First Officer, Aer Lingus: *m* 1970, Yvonne Denise, el da of S. V. Holmes Thompson, of Tir-Owen, Viewfort Park, Dunmurry, co Antrim.

UNCLE LIVING (*son of 2nd baronet*)

Ossian, *b* 1913: *m* 1st, 1936 (*m diss* 1943), Felice Martell, of Montreal, Canada; 2ndly, 1943 (*m diss* 1962), Yasu Elisabeth Katherine, da of Lennart Tham, of Husqvarna, Sweden; 3rdly, 1962, Margaret Angela, who *d* 1988, da of late Frank Chadwick, of Eastbourne, Sussex, and has issue living, (by 1st *m*) Lynn *b* 1937: *m* 1st, 1958, Richard Edgeson Cathcart, Lt RN; 2ndly, 1966, Ken Irwin; 3rdly, 19—, Al Hinderleiter, — (by 2nd *m*) Richard Michael George, *b* 1951: *m* 1979, Hon Caroline Laurence Patricia Cavendish, elder da of 7th Baron Waterpark, and has issue living, William Roderick Ossian *b* 1983, Laura Yasuko Danielle *b* 1986, — Carola Nesta Katherine, *b* 1946: *m* 1972, Giovanni Vincenzo Geddes da Filicaia, of Florence, Italy, and has issue living, Lisa *b* 1976, Bianca *b* 1979, — Sara Elizabeth Louise, *b* 1947: *m* 1975, Claude François de Senarclens, and has issue living, Olivier George *b* 1977, Christophe Bernard *b* 1979, Charles Lionel *b* 1983. *Residence* – Route Vieux Mont, Longuevilliers, 62630 Etaples, France.

AUNT LIVING (*Daughter of 1st baronet*)

Kathleen: *m* 1912, Capt Maurice Falkine Dennis, formerly Seaforth Highlanders, who *d* 1960. *Residence* – Batlyngmede, Cannon Hill, Maidenhead.

WIDOW LIVING OF THIRD BARONET

Hon VALERIE HAMILTON MONCKTON (*Hon Lady Goulding*) (Dargle Cottage, Enniskerry, co Wicklow), only da of 1st Viscount Monckton of Brenchley: *m* 1939, Sir William Basil Goulding, 3rd Bt, who *d* 1982.

GRAAFF (UK) 1911, of Cape Town, Cape of Good Hope Province of Union of South Africa.

The Creator favours the just

Sir DE VILLIERS GRAAFF, MBE, 2nd *Baronet*: *b* 8 Dec 1913; *s* his father, *Sir* DAVID PIETER DE VILLIERS, 1931; *ed* Cape Town Univ (BA 1932), and Magdalen Coll, Oxford (BA 1935, MA 1944); BCL 1936; Hon LLD Rhodes Univ 1969; Bar Inner Temple 1937; Advocate of Supreme Court of S Africa 1938; a Member of House of Assembly of Union of S Africa 1948-77; Leader of United Party 1956-77, since when Life Pres of New Republic Party; Dir of Graaffs' Trust; 1939-45 War with S African Defence Force (prisoner, MBE); MBE (Mil) 1947; DMS (South Africa 1978): *m* 1939, Helena le Roux, da of Frederick Carel Marthinus Voigt, of Claremont, Cape Province, S Africa, and has issue.

𝔄rms – Argent, a Paschal Lamb proper, on a chief azure five stars of the first (representing the constellation of the Southern Cross). 𝔠rest – In front of three spades erect in pale, a dexter arm embowed in armour, the hand holding a scimitar, all proper. 𝔖upporters – *Dexter*, a Boer farmer supporting with the exterior hand a rifle *sinister*, a Cape miner supporting with the exterior hand a pickaxe, both proper.
Address – PO Box 1609, Cape Town 8000, S Africa.

SONS LIVING

DAVID DE VILLIERS (Box 1, Hex River, Cape, South Africa), *b* 3 May 1940; *ed* Diocesan Coll, S Africa, Stellenbosch Univ (BSc Agric), Grenoble Univ, and Magdalen Coll, Oxford (BA); Dir of Graaffs' Trust; Fruit Farmer: *m* 1969, Sally, da of Robin Williams and has issue living, de Villiers, *b* 16 July 1970, — Robert, *b* 1974, — David John, *b* 1977, — Leeza, *b* 1973. ——Johann Frederick de Villiers, *b* 1946.

DAUGHTER LIVING

Genée de Villiers, *b* 1948.

BROTHER LIVING

Johannes de Villiers, *b* 1928; *ed* Cape Town Univ, and St John's Coll, Camb (Fellow 1951): *m* 1951, Lilian Clare, da of George Paget Thomson, and has issue living, Pieter Johannes, *b* 1958, — Janet Kathleen, *b* 1954, — Teresa Clare, *b* 1955, — Anna Louise, *b* (twin) 1955, — Monica Suzanne, *b* 1960, — Linda Elaine, *b* 1966. *Residence* – Morgenrood Rd, Kenilworth, Cape Province, S Africa.

The 1st baronet, Hon Sir David Pieter de Villiers Graaff, was Mayor of Cape Town 1892-2, Min without portfolio, Cape Colony 1908-10, Min of Public Works, Posts, and Telegraphs of Union of South Africa 1910-12, again Min without portfolio 1912-3, and Min of Finance 1915-6; acted as High Commr for S Africa in London 1914.

GRACE (GB) 1795, of Minchenden House, co Middlesex. (Extinct 1977)

Sir RAYMOND EUSTACE GRACE, 6th and last *Baronet*.

DAUGHTER LIVING OF FIFTH BARONET

Mary Lillian, *b* 1912: *m* 1st, 1940 (*m diss* 1969), Maj Paul McConnell, Ches Regt (ret); 2ndly, 1969, Lt-Col Clive O'Neill Wallis (ret) E Surreys, MC, JP, of 50 Bosman Drive, Windlesham, Berks.

COLLATERAL BRANCH LIVING

Granddaughter of late Col Sheffield Hamilton-Grace (nephew of 2nd baronet):—
Issue of late Major Raymond Sheffield Hamilton-Grace, *b* 1881, *ka* 1915: *m* 1912, Gladys, CBE, who *d* 1978 (having *m* 2ndly, 1919, Col Joseph Benskin, DSO, OBE, who *d* 1953), da of Michael Paul Grace, of 40 Belgrave Square, SW:—
Anne Veronica, *b* 1914; European War 1939-45 as Flight Officer WAAF (despatches): *m* 1948, Com William Frances Roderick Segrave, DSC, RN (ret), who *d* 1974, and has had issue, Raymond Roderick Grace, *b* 1951; *d* 1956, — Nicholas John Paul, *b* 1953; *d* 1977, — Roderick Alan Neil (21 Clarendon Gdns, Little Venice, W9 1AZ), *b* 1956; *ed* Ampleforth; has issue living (by Hilary Greene), Alexander Nicholas *b* 1985, Laurence Francis *b* (twin) 1985, — Elisa Mary (5 Kensington Park Gdns, W11), *b* 1949; writer, author of *The Diary of a Breast* (1995), *Ten Men* (1997), etc: *m* 1981 (*m diss* 1992), Andrew Barrow, and has issue living, Nicholas *b* 1983, Lauretta *b* 1981. *Residence* – Camelot, Ringles Cross, Uckfield, E Sussex.

GRAHAM (E) 1629, of Esk, Cumberland

Sir RALPH STUART GRAHAM, 14th *Baronet*; *b* 5 Nov 1950; *s* his father, *Sir* RALPH WOLFE, 1988, but no name has been entered on the Official Roll of the Baronetage since death of 12th Bt in 1975; *ed* Hofstra Univ: *m* 1st, 1972, Roxanne, who *d* 1978, da of Mrs Lovette Gurzan, of Elmont, Long Island, New York; 2ndly, 1979, Deena Louise, da of William Robert Vandergrift, of 2963 Nemesis, Waukegan, Illinois, USA.

Arms – Quarterly: 1st and 4th, or, on a chief sable three escallops of the first, *Graham*; 2nd and 3rd, or, a fesse checky argent and azure in chief a chevron gules, *Stuart*. Crest – Two wings addorsed or.
Residence – 7429 Highway 70, Apt 270, Nashville, Tennessee 37221-1732, USA.

ADOPTED SON LIVING

Gabriel Lawrence, *b* 1974: *m* 19—, Jennifer Lynn, and has issue living, Taylor Addison (a son), *b* 1993.

BROTHER LIVING

ROBERT BRUCE, *b* 14 Nov 1953: *m* 1974, Denise, da of T. Juranich, of Floral Park, Long Island, NY, and has issue living, Brian Robert, *b* 19 March 1979, — Stephen Ralph, *b* 1981.

DAUGHTERS LIVING OF TWELFTH BARONET

Lynne Elizabeth, *b* 1937: *m* 1959, Robert Jager, of 110 Elward Av, West Islip, Long Island, New York, and has issue living, Marie Lynne, *b* 1960, — Cindy Kay, *b* 1961. —— Dana Stuart, *b* 1940: *m* 1961, Robert Brust, of 2501 Rutler St, Bellmore, Long Island, New York, and has issue living, Robert George, *b* 1961, — William Edward, *b* 1965, — Elizabeth Lynne, *b* 1971.

DAUGHTER LIVING OF ELEVENTH BARONET

Jessie Louise (Apt 12G, 9000, Shore Rd, West Brooklyn, NY 11209, USA), *b* 1907: *m* 1936, Robert S. Bolton, who *d* 1944.

WIDOWS LIVING OF TWELFTH AND THIRTEENTH BARONETS

ELIZABETH ANN (*Elizabeth, Lady Graham*) (45 Aster Av, North Merrick, Long Island, New York, USA), da of John Gerken, of St Albans, Long Island, USA: *m* 1932, Sir Montrose Stuart Graham, 12th Bt, who *d* 1975.
GERALDINE (*Geraldine, Lady Graham*) (134 Leisureville Blvd, Baynton Beach, FL 33426, USA), da of Austin Velour, of Brooklyn, New York, USA: *m* 1949, as his 2nd wife, Sir Ralph Wolfe Graham, 13th Bt, who *d* 1988.

COLLATERAL BRANCHES LIVING

Issue of late Robert Vernon Graham, 3rd son of 10th baronet, *b* 1883, *d* 1943: *m* 1904, Charlotte Elizabeth, who *d* 1938, da of late Gilbert Baldwin Smith of Brooklyn, USA:—
Mildred Jane Elizabeth, *b* 1916; *m* 1st, 1942 (*m diss* 1953), William E. Young, RM; 2ndly, 1965 F. W. Rementer, and has issue living, (by 1st *m*) William Ernest (Box 436, Millheim, Pa 16854, USA), *b* 1944; late US Navy, a doctor: *m* 1976, Marylou, da of Charles Matz, of Ohio, and has issue living, Jonathan *b* 1984, Gretchen *b* 1983.

Grandchildren of late Robert Vernon Graham (ante):—
Issue of late James Robert Stuart Graham, *b* 1907, *d* 1960: *m* 1929, Agnes, who *d* 1976, da of late Dennis Harvey, of Brooklyn, USA:—
Roberta Naomi, *b* 1930: *m* 1957, James Joseph Munson, of 10710 Shore Front Pkwy, Far Rockaway, New York 11694-2637, USA, and has issue living, James, *b* 1958, — John, *b* 1959, — Joseph, *b* 1964, — Marilyn, *b* 1963. —— Joan Charlotte, *b* 1933: *m* 1958, Herbert John Nichol, of Merrick, NY, USA, and has issue living, Robert, *b* 1959, — Stephen, *b* 1970, — Catherine, *b* 1962, — Linda, *b* 1967, — Susan, *b* 1972.

Issue of late Howard George William Graham, *b* 1910, *d* 1957: *m* 1938, Madelyn, da of Joseph Fitzsimmons, of Archbold, Pennsylvania, USA:—
Charlotte Elizabeth, *b* 1940: *m* 1960, Daniel Coradi, and has issue living, Robert, *b* 1961, — Kenneth, *b* 1963, — Andrew, *b* 1965, — Cregg, *b* 1973.

Issue of late Douglas Duncan Graham, *b* 1912, *d* 1984; *m* 1st, 1937 (*m diss* 1948), Harriet, da of Thomas Lloyd, of Brooklyn, USA; 2ndly, 1948, Sally, who *d* 1988, da of Thomas Gale, of Southampton, Long Island, USA:—
(By 1st *m*) Harriet Mable, *b* 1938. —— (By 2nd *m*) James Robert (3557 Princeton Drive S, Wantagh, NY 11793, USA), *b* 1952. —— Roland E. (1428 Bellmore Av, N Bellmore, NY 11710-5540, USA), *b* 1954. —— Brenda Gail (196 Egret

Circle, W Palm Beach, Florida 33413-2141, USA), *b* 1949: *m* 1981, Robert F. Beatus, son of late Herman Beatus, of New York, NY.

Issue of late George Edward Graham, yst son of 10th baronet, *b* 1890, *d* 1969: *m* 1912, Florence Ethel, who *d* 1979, da of late George Alfred Milne, of Brooklyn, New York:—
George Edward (329, Benton St, Orlando, Fla 32809, USA), *b* 1920; Lt-Col USAF (ret): *m* 1945, Jean Myra MacRury, and has issue living, Stuart George, *b* 1949, — Leslie Jean, *b* 1951. ⸺ Dorothy, *b* 1917: *m* 1938, Ralph Alfred Hassler, and has issue living, Donald Evan, *b* 1950, — Laura Jean, *b* 1948, — Judith Ann, *b* 1953.

Granddaughter of late Lieut-Col Frederick Graham, el son of Maj-Gen Stuart Frederick Graham (infra):—
Issue of late Stuart Menteith Graham, *b* 1886, *d* 1957: *m* 1919, Leonore (Mollie) da of late Capt Morrish, Rifle Brig:—
Marjorie Barbara Stuart, *b* 1921: *m* 1963, David Sherwin Walker.

Grandchildren of late Maj-Gen Stuart Frederick Graham, 5th son of 8th baronet:—
Issue of late Major William Bannatyne Graham, *b* 1858, *d* 1897: *m* 1884, Mary Beatrice, who *d* 1941, da of late Rev E. H. Hansell, R of East Illsley, Berks:—
Edward William Harold, *b* 1888; formerly in Eastern Extension Telegraph Co, Cocos Keeling Islands; European War 1916-18 in Italy. ⸺ Mary Dorothy: *m* 1916, Wilfrid Saunders, formerly India Education Dept.

Issue of late Malcolm Macleod Graham, *b* 1872, *d* 19—: *m* 1896, Leopoldine (Buenos Aires, Argentine Republic), da of Mark Gallacher, of Rosario, Argentine Republic:—
Richard Walter Malcolm, *b* 1903: *m* 19—. ⸺ Oswald Charles, *b* 1906. ⸺ Agnes Beatrice, *b* 1897: *m* 19—, Jack Maclaughlin.

Descendants of late James Graham (2nd son of late Rev Robert Graham, DD, 2nd son of late Very Rev William Graham, DD 3rd son of 2nd baronet), who was *cr* a *Baronet* 1783:—
See Graham, Bt *cr* 1783.

Grandchildren of late Major Fergus Graham, son of late Rev William Paley Graham, son of late Rev Fergus Graham, LLD, 4th son of late Rev Robert Graham (ante):—
Issue of late Col Fergus Reginald Winsford Graham, DSO, MC, *b* 1884, *d* 1961: *m* 1915, Egeria Marion Spottiswood, who *d* 1973, da of Vice-Adm Casper Joseph Baker, formerly of Oaklands, Petherton, Somerset:—
Dominick Stuart, MC (The Hollins, East Rounton, Northallerton, N Yorkshire), *b* 1920; Maj (ret) RA; PhD; Prof of History, Univ of New Brunswick; 1939-45 War (wounded twice, despatches, MC): *m* 1st, 1947, Valerie Mary, da of late Farleigh H. Greig, of Fleet, Hant; 2ndly, 1991, Mary, widow of Sir Hugh Francis Bell, 4th Bt, and da of late George Howson, MC, of The Hyde, Hambledon, Bucks, and has issue living (by 1st *m*), Anita Caroline, *b* 1949, — Patricia Robin, *b* 1952. ⸺ Caroline Egeria Malise, *b* 1929: *m* 1952, Col Thomas Wemyss Muir, Queen's Dragoon Guards (ret), and has issue living, James Fergus Wemyss, *b* 1963: *m* 1998, Diana Catherine, da of Julien Courtauld, of Spencers, Gt Yeldham, Essex (*see* L Napier and Ettrick, colls, 1980 Edn), — Elizabeth Anne, *b* 1955: *m* 1979, Brig Sebastian John Lechmere Roberts, OBE, Irish Gds, of Turner's Chapel, Weaveland Rd, Tisbury, Wilts SP3 6HJ, — Sarah Jane, *b* 1957: *m* 1986, Colin George Climie, — Alexandra Caroline, *b* 1959: *m* 1978, Nicholas Leese. *Residence* – Torquhan, Stow, Midlothian.

The 1st baronet, Sir Richard Graham (son of Fergus Graham), was a Gentleman of the Horse to Charles I, and distinguished himself at the battle of Edgehill. The 3rd baronet, Sir Richard, was *cr Viscount Preston* (peerage of Scotland) 1680, was British Ambassador to France and sometime a Sec of State to James II; after the Revolution he was condemned for high treason, but was subsequently pardoned. The Baronetcy remained merged in the Viscountcy until the death of the 3rd Viscount in 1739, when it devolved upon his kinsman, Rev Sir William, 6th Bt.

GRAHAM 1662, of Norton Conyers, Yorkshire

Sir JAMES BELLINGHAM GRAHAM, 11th *Baronet*; *b* 8 Oct 1940; *s* his father, *Wing-Com Sir* RICHARD BELLINGHAM, OBE, RAFVR, 1982; *ed* Eton, and Ch Ch: *m* 1986, Halina, yr da of late Major Wiktor Grubert, of Putney, London.

𝕬rms – Quarterly: 1st and 4th or, of a chief sable three escallops of the field, *Graham*; 2nd and 3rd, or, a fesse checky argent and azure in chief a chevronel gules, *Stuart*; in the centre of the quarters a crescent of the last; all within a border engrailed of the third. 𝕮rest – Two wings addorsed or.
Seat – Norton Conyers, Melmerby, nr Ripon, N Yorks HG4 5EQ. *Address* – 3 Glebe Rd, Bedford MK40 2PL.

BROTHER LIVING

JEREMY RICHARD (Badger Bank, Norton Conyers, Ripon, N Yorks), *b* 23 Jan 1949; *ed* Eton: *m* 1976, Judith, da of Gerard McCann, of Castle House, Aldborough, Boroughbridge, Yorks, and has issue living, Samuel Reginald, *b* 1979, — Edward Richard, *b* 1985, — Sophia Harriet, *b* 1977.

COLLATERAL BRANCHES LIVING

Issue of late Maj Alastair Graham, MC, 2nd son of 9th baronet, *b* 1915, *d* 1975: *m* 1942, Gundreda Margaret, da of late J. L. Graham Jones, MB, of Bockhampton House, Dorchester, Dorset:—
Caroline Susan, *b* 1943: *m* 1990, Robert H. Richheimer, only son of late Robert C. Richheimer, of La Jolla, California. —— Priscilla Ann (*Hon Mrs R. Nicholas Crossley*), *b* (twin) 1948: *m* 1st, 1968, Maj Peter Norman Bingham Kennedy, TD, DL, of Doonholm, Ayr; 2ndly, 1995, as his 2nd wife, Hon (Richard) Nicholas Crossley (*see* B Somerleyton), and has issue living (by 1st *m*), Sara Margaret, *b* 1971, — Annabel Deborah, *b* 1973, — Caroline Anne, *b* 1980, — Rosanna Jane, *b* 1982.

Issue of late Jeremy Frank Graham, yst son of 9th baronet, *b* 1926, *d* 1992: *m* 1950, Susan May (Plaster Pitts, Ripon, Yorks), 2nd da of late Col Sir Thomas Eustace-Smith, CBE, TD, of Barton Hall, Darlington:—
Robin Guy, *b* 1953: *m* 1979, Annabel Mary Diana, el da of Michael David Aykroyd (*see* Aykroyd, Bt *cr* 1920), and has issue living, Andrew Guy Bellingham, *b* 1981, — Rory Michael, *b* 1984, — Jonathan Richard, *b* 1997. —— Nigel Ronald, *b* 1957: *m* 1982, Henrietta Jane Fane, da of Maj Jerome De Salis, of Bourne House, E Woodhay, Newbury, Berks (*see* B Monk Bretton, 1995 Edn), and has an adopted son, Thomas Guy, *b* 1995. —— (Elizabeth) Jacoba, *b* 1951: *m* 1971, Capt Christopher Russell Oldham, R Hussars (ret), of 78 Paxton Rd, W4 2QX, and has issue living, Justin Russell, *b* 1974, — Mark Russell, *b* 1977.

The 1st baronet of Norton Conyers, received his baronetcy from Charles II, 1662, for services rendered to the Restoration. He was the 2nd son of Sir Richard Graham, 1st Bt (*cr* 1629), of Esk, the distinguished Royalist and Gentleman of the Horse to King Charles I, and fought at Edgehill and Marston Moor. The 9th Bt, Major Sir (Reginald) Guy, DSO, served in S Africa 1899-1902 and in European War 1914-19 (DSO). The 10th Bt, Sir Richard was Chm of Yorkshire TV from 1968-82.

GRAHAM (GB 1783), of Netherby, Cumberland

Sir JAMES FERGUS SURTEES GRAHAM, 7th *Baronet*; *b* 29 July 1946; *s* his father, *Major Sir* CHARLES SPENCER RICHARD, 1997; *ed* Milton Abbey: *m* 1975, Serena Jane, yr da of Major Ronald Frank Kershaw (*see* E Lindsey and Abingdon, colls), and has issue.

𝕬rms – Quarterly: 1st and 4th or, on a chief sable three escallops of the field, *Graham*; 2nd and 3rd or, a fesse checky argent and azure in chief a chevronel gules, *Stuart*; in the centre of the quarters a crescent of the last; all within a bordure engrailed azure. 𝕮rest – Two wings addorsed or.
Property - Netherby, Longtown, Cumbria. *Residence* – The Tower, Kirkandrews-on-Esk, Longtown, Cumbria CA6 5NF.

SON LIVING

ROBERT CHARLES THOMAS, *b* 19 July 1985.

DAUGHTERS LIVING

Catherine Mary, *b* 1978. ——— Iona Susan Alice, *b* 1980.

BROTHER LIVING

Malise Charles Richard, *b* 1948; *ed* Milton Abbey: *m* 1974, Hon Pamela Winifred Whitelaw, da of 1st Viscount Whitelaw, CH, MC, and has issue living, Arabella Mary Susan, *b* 1975, — Georgina Carol Cecilia, *b* 1977, — Laura Meliora Winifred, *b* 1981, — Victoria Malise Samantha, *b* 1985. *Residence* – The Cottage, Sproxton, Melton Mowbray, Leics LE14 4QS.

SISTER LIVING

Susanna Anne Mary, *b* 1951.

WIDOW LIVING OF SIXTH BARONET

(ISABEL) SUSAN ANNE (*Susan, Lady Graham*), only da of Major Robert Lambton Surtees, OBE: *m* 1944, Major Sir Charles Spencer Richard Graham, 6th Bt, who *d* 1997. *Residence* – Crofthead, Longtown, Cumbria CA6 5PA.

COLLATERAL BRANCHES LIVING

Grandchildren of late (Richard) Preston Graham-Vivian, MVO, MC (infra):—
Issue of late Henry Richard Graham-Vivian, JP, DL, *b* 1923, *d* 1993: *m* 1955, Rosemary (Bosahan, Manaccan, Helston, Cornwall), only da of Col Giffard Loftus Tyringham:—
Richard John, *b* 1957: *m* 1993, Christine Trippeau. ——— Lavinia, *b* 1959: *m* 1996, Gregory J. Powles, and has issue living, Rupert Pendarves *b* 1998.

Issue of late (Richard) Preston GRAHAM-VIVIAN, MVO, MC, 2nd son of 4th baronet (who assumed by Royal Licence 1929 the additional surname of Vivian), Windsor Herald 1947-66, Norroy and Ulster King of Arms 1966-72, *b* 1896, *d* 1979: *m* 1921, Audrey Emily, who *d* 1986, da of late Maj Henry Wyndham Vivian (*see* B Swansea, colls):—
Catherine Maude (Ludgates, Nutbourne, Pulborough), *b* 1926: *m* 1947, Lt-Col John Peter Thomson-Glover, MC, 9th/12th Royal Lancers, who *d* 1968, and has issue living, Michael William (20 Crondace Rd, SW6), *b* 1948; *ed* Wellington, and Trin Coll, Camb (BA): *m* 1974, Katherine, da of John David Summers, and has issue living, James Antony *b* 1988, Peter David *b* (twin) 1988, Sarah Emily *b* 1977, Rebecca Evelyn *b* 1979, Rachel Caroline *b* 1981, — (Peter) James, *b* 1953; *ed* Wellington; FCA: *m* 1982, Veronica Harrison, and has issue living, Edward *b* 1984, Rosie Catherine *b* 1990, — Caroline Veronica, *b* 1950.

Grandson of late Rev Malise Reginald Graham, 2nd son of 2nd baronet:—
Issue of late Reginald Graham, *b* 1867, *d* 1908: *m* 1897, Helen Dacia, da of G. S. Herck, of St Petersburg:—
Ernest Reginald, *b* 1898.

This family is descended from Very Rev William Graham, DD, 4th son of Sir George Graham, 2nd Bt, of Esk (*cr* 1629). The 2nd baronet of Netherby, Sir James, GBE, PC, an eminent statesman, sat as MP successively for Hull, East Cumberland, Carlisle, Pembroke, Dorchester, and Ripon, and filled various high offices of State.

GRAHAM 1906, of Larbert House, Larbert and Househill, Dunipace, co Stirling

Forget not

Sir JOHN ALEXANDER NOBLE GRAHAM, GCMG, 4th *Baronet*; *b* 15 July 1926; *s* his father, *Lt-Col Sir* JOHN REGINALD NOBLE, VC, OBE, 1980; *ed* Eton, and Trin Coll, Camb; Lt Gren Gds, Palestine 1946-47; entered Foreign Service 1950, 3rd Sec Bahrain 1951-52, Kuwait 1952-53, and Amman 1953-54, Assist Private Sec to Foreign Sec 1954-57, Second (later First) Sec Belgrade 1957-60, First Sec and Consul Benghazi 1960-61, FO 1961-66, Counsellor Kuwait 1966-69, Prin Private Sec to Foreign Sec 1969-72, Head of Chancery, Washington 1972-74, and Ambassador to Iraq 1974-77, Dep Under-Sec FC0 1977-78 and 1980-81; HM Amb to Iran 1979-80; UK Permanent Rep N Atlantic Council, Brussels 1982-86; Dir The Ditchley Foundation 1987-92; Registrar of the Most Distinguished Order of St Michael and St George since 1987; CMG 1972, KCMG 1979, GCMG 1985: *m* 1st, 1956, Marygold Ellinor Gabrielle, who *d* 1991, da of late Lt-Col Clive Grantham Austin, RHA, JP, DL (E Scarbrough); 2ndly, 1992, Jane, widow of Christopher Howells, and has issue living by 1st *m*.

Arms – Or, on a chief invected ermine three escallops of the first. Crest – A falcon proper, beaked and armed or, killing a stork argent armed gules.
Residence – Salisbury Place, Church St, Shipton under Wychwood, Chipping Norton, Oxon OX7 6BP. *Club* – Army and Navy.

SONS LIVING *(By 1st marriage)*

ANDREW JOHN NOBLE, MBE, *b* 21 Oct 1956; *ed* Eton, and Trin Coll Camb; Col late Argyll and Sutherland Highlanders; MBE (Mil) 1993; Member Queen's Body Guard for Scotland (Royal Company of Archers) 1998: *m* 1984, Susan Mary Bridget, da of Rear Adm John Patrick Bruce O'Riordan, CBE, RN (ret), of Nether Cray, Laurieston, Kirkcudbrightshire, and has issue living, James Patrick Noble, *b* 15 March 1990, — Katharine Rose, *b* 1986, — Louisa Christian, *b* 1988, — Isabella Alice, *b* 1993. *Clubs* – MCC, RGS. —— George Reginald Clive, *b* 1958; *ed* Eton, and Trin Coll, Camb; journalist: *m* 1988, Carol A., da of Julian Madison, of Cleveland, Ohio, USA, and has issue living, John Reginald Austin, *b* 1992, — Julian, *b* 1995.

DAUGHTER LIVING *(By 1st marriage)*

Christian Rachel, *b* 1961: *m* 1985, Dr Matthew Scott Dryden, elder son of W.S. Dryden, of Great Gaddesden, Herts, and has issue living, Alexander William Scott, *b* 1988, — Thomas Andrew, *b* 1992, — Gabriella Josephine, *b* 1990, — Iona Clare, *b* 1994.

SISTER LIVING

Lesley, *b* 1921: *m* 1945, Jock Wykeham Strang Steel, who *d* 1991, 2nd son of Sir Samuel Strang Steel, 1st Bt, and has issue (*see* Steel, Bt). *Residence* – Haydean, Haddington, East Lothian EH41 4HN.

COLLATERAL BRANCH LIVING

Grandsons of late Sir (John) Frederick Noble Graham, 2nd Bt:—
Issue of late Maj-Gen Frederick Clarence Campbell Graham, CB, DSO, late Argyll and Sutherland Highlanders, *b* 1908, *d* 1988: *m* 1936, Phyllis Mary, who *d* 1997, da of late Maj-Gen Hugh Francis Edward MacMahon, CB, CSI, CBE, MC:—
Colin Hugh Campbell, TD (Mackeanston House, Doune, Perthshire. *Club* – RPGS (Perth)), *b* 1940; *ed* Eton; late Capt 51st Highland Volunteers (TAVR); Memb Queen's Body Guard for Scotland (Royal Company of Archers) since 1983; a Dir Grahams (Oporto) Ltd 1963-67, Export Exec Macdonald and Muir Ltd, Leith, 1978-91: *m* 1st, 1963 (*m diss* 1985), Joanna (Jan) Kathleen, da of late David Chancellor, of Pencaitland, E Lothian; 2ndly, 1986, Fiona Jacqueline Richmond, da of late John Michael Richmond Paton, of Hay Park, Stow, Borders, and has issue living, (by 1st *m*) William Frederick Chancellor, *b* 1963: *m* 1989, Victoria L., eldest da of John Beasley, of Shrewsbury, and has issue living, Frederick Sebastian Chancellor *b* 1994, Alice Elizabeth *b* 1991, — David Campbell, *b* 1969, — Suzanna Lucy, *b* 1967: *m* 1997, Charles E. D'Oyly, eldest son of Nigell D'Oyly, of Albury, Herts, — (by 2nd *m*) Rory Michael Alexander, *b* 1988, — Neil Alasdair Richmond, *b* 1991. —— †Ewan Alastair MacMahon, *b* 1944; *ed* Eton; Lt-Col Argyll and Sutherland Highlanders; Member Queen's Bodyguard for Scotland (Royal Company of Archers): *m* 1st, 1967 (*m diss* 1982), Sara Diones, da of late Maj-Gen Reginald Geoffrey Stirling Hobbs, CB, DSO, OBE; 2ndly, 1982, Sarah Rose (c/o Lloyds Bank, Cox's & King's Branch, 6 Pall Mall, SW1), da of late Cdr David Enderby Blunt, RN, and *d* 1996, leaving issue (by 1st *m*), Calum James MacMahon, *b* 1970, — Fergus Hugh Stirling, *b* 1973. —— (Kenneth) James (Home Idover Farm, Dauntsey, nr Chippenham, Wilts), *b* 1947; *ed* Eton, and Northwestern Univ, Chicago; late 2nd Lieut Argyll and Sutherland High-landers; Exec Digital Equipment Corpn: *m* 1972, Victoria Margaret Anne, yst da of late Maj Andrew Stirling Home Drummond Moray, of Easter Ross, Comrie, Perthshire, and has issue living, Magnus James, *b* 1974, — Nina Louise, *b* 1976.

This family is a cadet branch of Graham of Tamrawer, descended from Graham of Auchincloich, nr Kilsyth, Stirlingshire, who derive from John, 3rd son of Sir David Graham (d *c* 1376), ancestor of Dukes of Montrose. The 1st baronet, Sir John Hatt Noble Graham was a member of the firm of William Graham and Co, merchants, of 400

Cathedral St, Glasgow, and of Grahams Co (London), East India merchants. The 2nd baronet was Chm of Glasgow Chamber of Commerce.

GRAHAM (UK) 1964, of Dromore, co Down

Sir JOHN MOODIE GRAHAM, 2nd *Baronet*; *b* 3rd April 1938; *s* his father, *Sir* CLARENCE JOHNSTON, 1966; *ed* Trin Coll, Glenalmond, and Queen's Univ, Belfast (BSc); Pres of N Ireland Leukaemia Research Fund: *m* 1970 (*m diss* 1982), Valerie Rosemary, da of late Frank Gill, of 5 Greenview Park, Belfast 9, and has issue.
Residence – Portofino, 77 South Birch Rd 11D, Fort Lauderdale, Florida 33316, USA.

DAUGHTERS LIVING

Suzanne Margaret, *b* 1971. —— Alyson Rosemary, *b* 1974. —— Lucy Christina, *b* 1978.

Sir Clarence Johnston Graham, 1st Bt, was Chm of Standing Cttee, Ulster Unionist Council 1947-63, and a Dir of John Graham (Dromore) Ltd, Engineering Contractors.

GRANT (NS) 1688, of Dalvey

Te favente virebo

Under thy favour will I flourish

Sir PATRICK ALEXANDER BENEDICT GRANT, 14th *Baronet*; *b* 5 Feb 1953; *s* his father, *Sir* DUNCAN ALEXANDER, 1961; *ed* Abbey Sch, Fort Augustus and Glasgow Univ (LLB); Chm and Man Dir of Grants of Dalvey Ltd, Queen's Award for Exports 1992; Chieftain of Clan Donnachy: *m* 1981, Carolyn Elizabeth, MB, ChB, da of John Highet, MA, DPhil, of 319 Albert Drive, Glasgow, and has issue.

Arms – Gules, three antique crowns or within a bordure engrailed of the last with the Baronets' badge of Nova Scotia in the dexter canton. **Crest** – The trunk of an oak-tree sprouting out some leaves with the sun shining thereon all proper. **Supporters** – *Dexter*, a highlander; *sinister*, a negro proper.
Residence – Tomintoul House, Flichity, Farr, Inverness-shire IV1 2XD.

SONS LIVING

DUNCAN ARCHIBALD LUDOVIC, *b* 19 April 1982. —— Neil Patrick, *b* 1983.

BROTHERS LIVING

Denzil Mohun Bede (Drinkstone House, Drinkstone, Bury St Edmunds, Suffolk IP80 9TG), *b* 1955; *ed* Abbey Sch, Fort Augustus, and W Dean Coll, Chichester (BA); Man Dir of Suffolk Fine Arts Ltd: *m* 1977, Nicola, da of A. J. Savill, of Godalming, Surrey, and has issue living, Alexandra, *b* 1978, — Diana *b* 1983, — Charlotte *b* 1986. —— Drostan John (34 Morehampton Rd, Dublin 4), *b* 1956; BE, MBA: *m* 1986, Celia Gabriella, elder da of Gerald Mattei, of Malta, and has issue living, Antonia Maria, *b* 1987, — Christina Andrea, *b* 1989.

SISTERS LIVING

Fiona Mary Julia, *b* 1950: *m* 1966, Christopher Kanthack St John Bird, of The Mill House, Bulmer Rd, Sudbury, Suffolk, and has issue living, Christopher Kenelm Anthony, *b* 1967, — Theodore Denzil Drostan, *b* 1971, — Penelope Frances Julia, *b* 1968. —— Maria Teresa, *b* 1951: *m* 1968, Ramon Anthony Cooke, BE, CEng, MIEI, and has issue living, Jessica Fiona, *b* 1969.

AUNT LIVING (*Sister of 13th baronet*)

Diana Mary, *b* 1931; *ed* St Leonard's Sch, and London (BA 1954) Univ: *m* 1954, Jean-Pierre Dalcher, and has issue living, Claude Francis, *b* 1957, — Derrick Albert Alexander, *b* 1959: *m* 1987, Anne Parel, and has issue living, Samuel *b* 1991,

Philippe *b* 1996, Sarah *b* 1988, Rachel *b* 1993, — Anne, *b* 1956: *m* 1995, Daniel Venditti. *Residence* – Chemin des Patouriaux, Villette, 1603 Grandvaux, Vaud, Switzerland.

COLLATERAL BRANCH LIVING

Issue of late Percy Frere Grant, MB, 4th son of 10th baronet, *b* 1869, *d* 1909: *m* (Feb) 1905, Theodora, who *d* 1938, da of J. H. Goodrich:—
Winifred Anne St John, *b* (Nov) 1905; *ed* Cape Town Univ (BA): *m* 1930, Gerard Anthony Thomson, of 55 Kings Way, Warner Beach S Coast, Natal 4125. ——— Susan Ursula (10 Westerford Rd, Newlands, Cape, S Africa), *b* 1907: *m* 1930, Christian Arnold Wahl, who *d* 1967.

This baronetcy was conferred with remainder to heirs male whatsoever, and on the death of the 1st baronet without issue in 1695, the title remained unassumed until Patrick Grant, of Inverladinen, a distant relative, was served heir male general to the 1st baronet in 1752, *s* as 4th baronet and *d* in his 101st year in 1755. The 8th baronet, MP, for Cambridge, was Chairman of Committees in Parliament 1826-30, a member of the Board of Control 1835, and subsequently, a Commissioner for Auditing the Public Accounts. The 10th baronet was Principal and Vice-Chancellor of Edinburgh University 1868-84. The 11th baronet was Regius Professor of Public Law and of the Law of Nature and Nations in Edinburgh Univ 1890-1922. The 12th baronet was Foreign Sec to Gov of India 1914-19, and Ch Commr N-W Frontier Province 1919-21.

GRANT (NS) 1705, of Monymusk, co Aberdeen

Sir ARCHIBALD GRANT OF MONYMUSK, 13th *Baronet*, *b* 2 Sept 1954; *s* his father, *Capt Sir* FRANCIS CULLEN, 1966; *ed* Trinity Coll, Glenalmond, and RAC Cirencester (Dip Farm Mgmnt): *m* 1982, Barbara Elizabeth, el da of Andrew Garden Duff Forbes, of Over-skibo House, Dornoch, Sutherland (*see* Stuart-Forbes, Bt, colls), and has issue.

𝕬rms – Gules, three antique crowns or, within a border ermine. 𝕮rest – A Bible expanded proper. 𝕾upporters – Two Angels proper, wings or.
Seat – House of Monymusk, Monymusk, Aberdeenshire.

DAUGHTERS LIVING

Christian Mariot, *b* 1986. ——— Catriona Elizabeth, *b* 1988.

BROTHERS LIVING

FRANCIS TOLLEMACHE, *b* 18 Dec 1955: *m* 1993, Virginia Elizabeth, da of R. Scott Russell, of E Hanney, Oxon, and has issue living, Alexander William, *b* 28 Nov 1996, — Elizabeth Charlotte, *b* 1994. *Residence* – Kingston House, Kingston Bagpuize, Oxon. ——— Duncan John Cullen, *b* 1957: *m* 1985, Maureen Cecilia, only da of Thomas Innes of Learney (*see* Innes, Bt, *cr* 1628), and has issue living, Robert Francis, *b* 1985, — Thomas William, *b* 1988, — Henry Douglas, *b* 1991, — Alasdair John, *b* 1997.

SISTERS LIVING

Catriona Charmiane, *b* 1959; *ed* Univ Coll, London (BSc Hons): *m* 1996, Christopher J. Blackwell, elder son of Prof D. E. Blackwell, of Oxford. ——— Sarah Jean, *b* 1961.

AUNTS LIVING (*Daughters of 10th baronet*)

Catherine Jean (*Lady Legge-Bourke*) (121 Dovehouse St, SW3 6JZ), *b* 1917: *m* 1938, Maj Sir Edward Alexander Henry Legge-Bourke, KBE, MP, DL, Royal Horse Gds, who *d* 1973, and has issue (*see* E Dartmouth, colls). ——— Christian (*Lady Bowman*) (The Walled Garden, Chamberlain St, Wells, Som BA5 2PE), *b* 1920: *m* 1st, 1942 (*m diss* 1951), Michael Fife William Angas, Gren Gds, who *d* 1983; 2ndly, 1953, John Gordon Ogston Miller, who *d* 1992; 3rdly, 1993, as his 3rd wife, Sir John Paget Bowman, 4th Bt, who *d* 1994, and has issue living, (by 1st *m*) Auburn Carolyn Catherine, *b* 1945; has issue living (by Thomas Murray Donnelly), Catherine Grace DONNELLY *b* 1982, — Cherill Melmere, *b* 1947: *m* 1966 (*m diss* 1974), Charles Heckstall, of Virginia, USA, and has issue living, Cyprian Carolus *b* 1967, and further issue (by Richard Philip Glyn Hughes), David William HUGHES *b* 1975, Freya Rhonwen HUGHES *b* (twin) 1975.

DAUGHTERS LIVING OF ELEVENTH BARONET (and of Baroness Tweedsmuir of Belhelvie)

Hon Joanna Catherine, *b* 1935: *m* 1954 (*m diss* 1966), Dominick Jones, son of Sir (George) Roderick Jones, KBE, and has issue living, Romily Arthur, *b* 1956. —— *Hon* (Margaret) Anne GRANT (24 Amity Grove, SW20 0LJ), *b* 1937; *ed* Lady Margaret Hall, Oxford (MA); has resumed her maiden name: *m* 1965 (*m diss* 1983), Nicholas Mangriotis, of Athens, Greece, and has issue living, Paraskevas, *b* 1971, — Arthuros, *b* 1974.

WIDOW LIVING OF TWELFTH BARONET

JEAN MARGHERITA (*Jean, Baroness Tweedsmuir*), da of late Capt Humphrey Douglas Tollemache, RN (*see* B Tollemache, colls): *m* 1st, 1953, Capt Sir Francis Cullen Grant of Monymusk, 12th Bt, who *d* 1966; 2ndly, 1980, as his 2nd wife, 2nd Baron Tweedsmuir, CBE, CD, who *d* 1996. *Residence* – Flat 2 The White House, 24 Dirleton Av, N Berwick, E Lothian EH39 4BQ.

This family is a branch of the noble house of Grant (Earls of Seafield). Archibald Grant of Ballentomb, progenitor of this line was 4th son of James Grant, 3rd of Freuchie (now Castle Grant), who *d* 1553. The 1st baronet, Sir Francis (Lord Cullen, a Senator of the College of Justice and 4th in descent from Archibald) was seated at Cullen when he was created a baronet by Queen Anne, but shortly after purchased the estate of Monymusk and sold Cullen. The 2nd baronet, Sir Archibald, carried out extensive agric reforms and tree planting. The 10th baronet, Col Sir Arthur Grant, CBE, DSO, served in S Africa 1899-1902, and during 1914-18 War (severely wounded). The 11th baronet, Maj Sir Arthur Lindsay Grant, Grenadier Guards, was *ka* 1944 (despatches). The 12th baronet, Capt Sir Francis Cullen Grant, RE served in Normandy campaign (despatches).

MACPHERSON-GRANT (UK) 1838, of Ballindalloch, Elgin (Extinct 1983)

Maj Sir EWAN GEORGE MACPHERSON-GRANT, 6th and last *Baronet*.

DAUGHTER LIVING OF SIXTH BARONET

Clare Nancy, *b* 1944; DL Banffshire: *m* 1967, Oliver Henry Russell, of Ballindalloch Castle, Banffshire, son of late Adm Hon Sir Guy Herbrand Edward Russell, GBE, KCB, DSO, and has issue (*see* B Ampthill, colls).

COLLATERAL BRANCH LIVING

Issue of late Alastair Macpherson-Grant, 3rd son of 3rd baronet, *b* 1874, *d* 1949: *m* 1904, Hester Charlotte, who *d* 1945, da of late Arthur C. Kennard, of 17 Eaton Place, SW:—
Anne Frances, *b* 1914: *m* 1939, Lt-Col William D. Keown-Boyd, CVO, OBE, 60th Rifles, and has issue living, Alexander (5D Stewarts House, Sycamore Av, Chandlers Ford, Hants SO53 5RW), *b* 1949, — Jennifer (La Colomera, Arans, Ordino, Principat d'Andorra), *b* 1942. *Residence* – The Dower House, Headbourne Worthy, Winchester, Hants SO23 7JG.

Grant-Suttie, see Suttie.

Grattan-Bellew, see Bellew

GRAY (UK) 1917, of Tunstall Manor, Hart, co Durham.

Sir WILLIAM HUME GRAY, 3rd *Baronet*, only son of late William Talbot Gray, el son of 2nd baronet; *b* 26 July 1955; *s* his grandfather, *Sir* WILLIAM, 1978; *ed* Eton, and Polytechnic of Central Lond; High Sheriff Durham 1998: *m* 1984 (*m diss* 1998), Catherine, yst da of late John Naylor, of The Mill House, Bramley, Hants, and of Mrs Richard Jerram, of Trevanson, Wadebridge, Cornwall, and has issue.

ᶅrms – Barry of six argent and azure, a lion rampant gules, on a chief of the second two lymphads or. Crest – An anchor or in front of and supported by two lions jambs erased gules.
Seat – Eggleston Hall, Eggleston, Barnard Castle, co Durham.

SON LIVING

WILLIAM JOHN CRESSWELL, *b* 24 Aug 1986.

DAUGHTERS LIVING

Octavia, *b* 1987. —— Clementine, *b* 1990.

SISTERS LIVING

Victoria Eyre *b* 1958: *m* 1980, Nicholas David Barclay Straker, of Sough Hill, Caldwell, Darlington, co Durham, 2nd son of late Hugh Charles Straker, of Gaucin, Spain, and has issue living, Sam, *b* 1991, — Jacquetta, *b* 1984, — Chloë, *b* 1986, — Selina, *b* 1998. —— Emma, *b* 1962.

UNCLE LIVING (*Son of 2nd baronet*)

Nicholas Anthony, *b* 1934: *m* 1956, Amanda, only da of late H. W. Edwards, of Ashmore Green, Newbury, Berks, and has issue living, Daisy, *b* 1970.

MOTHER LIVING

Rosemarie Hume (The Cottage, Eggleston Hall, Eggleston, Barnard Castle, co Durham), da of late Air Commodore Charles Elliott-Smith: *m* 1954, William Talbot Gray, el son of 2nd Bt, who *d* 1971.

The 1st baronet, Sir William Cresswell Gray, Chm of the firm of William Gray and Co Limited, and a Member of *Lloyds Register* Committee, founded the S Durham Steel and Iron Co Limited 1889.

GRAYSON (UK) 1922, of Ravenspoint, Co Anglesey

Sir JEREMY BRIAN VINCENT GRAYSON, 5th *Baronet*, son of late Brian Harrington Grayson, 3rd son of 1st baronet; *b* 30 Jan 1933; *s* his uncle, *Sir* RUPERT STANLEY HARRINGTON, 1991; *ed* Downside: *m* 1958, Sara Mary, da of late C. F. Upton, of Monte Carlo, and has issue.

ᶅrms – Sable, on a fesse between a portcullis in chief and a lymphad in base or, two ravens of the first. Crest – In front of a rising sun or, a tower proper, issuant therefrom a demi-lion sable resting between the paws a spur gold.
Residence – 54 Bucharest Rd, SW18 3AR.

SONS LIVING

SIMON JEREMY, *b* 12 July 1959. —— Paul Francis, *b* 1965. —— Mark Christopher, *b* 1968.

DAUGHTERS LIVING AND DECEASED

Caroline Mary, *b* 1961. —— Anna Katherine, *b* 1962: *m* 1991, Christopher William Turner, and has issue living, Max Harrington, *b* 1990, — Sam Christopher, *b* 1993. —— Mary, *b* and *d* 1964. —— Lucy Kate, *b* 1970.

SISTER LIVING

Virtue is the safest tower

Jane Angela, *b* 1931.

HALF-SISTER LIVING

Alicia Lorraine, *b* 1953: *m* 1973, Clive Trevor Thorne Rogers, of 70 Wattleton Rd, Beaconsfield, Bucks HP9 1RY, and has issue living, Timothy Piers Thorne, *b* 1981, — Sophie Claire Thorne, *b* 1977.

UNCLE LIVING (*son of 1st baronet*)

Ambrose Desmond Harrington (Saumarez Park Manor, Route de Saumarez, Catel, Guernsey, CI), *b* 1913; formerly a King's Foreign Ser Messenger: *m* 1966, Lilian, who *d* 1995, da of Gerald Westwood Potter, of Park Gates, Eastbourne and widow of Dr Lydiard Wilson.

AUNT LIVING (*daughter of 1st baronet*)

Meryl Lorraine Harrington, *b* 1909. *Residence* – 18 Barney St, Newport, Rhode Island 02840, USA.

MOTHER LIVING

Sofia, 4th da of late George Buchanan, Commercial Counsellor at Chilean Embassy, London, of 7 Addison Rd, W14: *m* 1930 (*m diss* 1946), as his 1st wife, Brian Harrington Grayson, who *d* 1989, 3rd son of 1st baronet. *Residence* – —

STEPMOTHER LIVING

Ruth, da of late Oscar Louis Anders, of Littlethorpe Hall, Ripon, and formerly wife of Edwin Bernhard Gange: *m* 1949, as his 2nd wife, Brian Harrington Grayson, who *d* 1989, 3rd son of 1st baronet. *Residence* – Summerfield, 67 Lewes Rd, Ditchling, Hassocks, Sussex BN6 8TY.

WIDOWS LIVING OF THIRD AND FOURTH BARONETS

DOROTHY VERA (VICKI) HOARE (*Vicki, Lady Grayson*), da of Charles Serrell, of Hoylake, Cheshire: *m* 1946, as his 2nd wife, Sir Ronald Henry Rudyard Grayson, 3rd Bt, who *d* 1987. *Residence* – 5 Cheero Point Rd, Cheero Point, NSW, Australia.
VARI COLETTE (*Vari, Lady Grayson*), da of Maj Henry O'Shea, late IA and Royal Dublin Fus, of Cork: *m* 1950, as his 2nd wife, Sir Rupert Stanley Harrington Grayson, 4th Bt, who *d* 1991. *Residence* – PO Box 626, Indiantown, Florida 34956, USA.

COLLATERAL BRANCH LIVING

Issue of late Col Tristram Hugh Harrington Grayson, OBE, IG 4th son of 1st baronet, *b* 1902, *d* 1984: *m* 1928, Barbara, who *d* 1974, da of Morgan Ignatius Finucane, MRCS, JP, Bar-at-law, of 10 Ashley Pl, SW1:—
Patrick Tristram Finucane (3 Rosenau Crescent, SW11 4RY; *Clubs* – White's, Special Forces), *b* 1942; *ed* Downside, and RMA Sandhurst; Maj late IG; Dir Defence Systems Ltd 1983-86; Man Dir and Dep Chm Kroll Associates 1986-94; Man Dir Ciex Ltd 1994-96; Chm CDR International since 1996; Non-Exec Dir ArmorGroup since 1998: *m* 1965 (*m diss* 1989), Vivienne Mary, da of Hector Rowcliffe Munro, of Javea, Alicante, Spain, and has issue living, Mark Patrick Munro, *b* 1974; *ed* Eton, and RMA Sandhurst; Lt IG 1997. — Louise Mary Munro, *b* 1968: *m* 1998, David J. Minchin, elder son of Peter Minchin, — Nikki Kathryn Munro, *b* 1970. —— Mary Dora Finucane (Caleb's Cottage, St Ippolyts, Hitchin, Herts SG4 7PE), *b* 1931: *m* 1958, John Owen Blaksley, who *d* 1982, and has issue living, John Patrick, *b* 1959, — Richard Edmund, *b* 1961: *m* 1990, Sally-Anne, da of Dr John Deller, and has issue living, Thomas Percival *b* 1992, Alice Anastasia *b* 1993. —— Angela Mary Finucane, *b* 1934: *m* 1955, Michael John Drummond-Brady, Maj late The Queen's Regt, Member of HM Body Guard of Hon Corps Gentlemen at Arms, of Keepers Lodge, Great Chart, Ashford, Kent TN26 1JX, and has issue living, Simon Michael Grayson, *b* 1955: *m* 1988, Nicola, da of Peter Fletcher, — Mark Frederick Grayson, *b* 1957; BA: *m* 1984, Susie, da of Nicholas Fair, and has issue living, Frederick Mark *b* 1987, Lucy Elizabeth *b* 1989, — Emma Angela Grayson, *b* 1962.

Issue of late Godfrey Ramsay Harrington Grayson, 6th son of 1st baronet, *b* (twin) 1913, *d* 1998: *m* 1939, Ida, who *d* 1995, da of late Sextus Hassing, of Frederica, Denmark:—
Simon Anthony (F. C. Sainz de Robles 25 (512), 28035 Madrid, Spain), *b* 1952: *m* 19—, Teresa Casaseca. —— Karen Grethe Maria (PO Box 1375, Kengray 2100, Johannesburg, S Africa), *b* 1940: *m* 1st, 1960 (*m diss* —), Colin Ross; 2ndly, 19— (*m diss* 19—), Derek Stilwell, and has issue living, (by 1st *m*) Nicholas, *b* 1962, — James, *b* 19—, — (by 2nd *m*) Darren, *b* 19—, — Fiona, *b* 19—. —— Lila Marianna, *b* 1945: *m* 1st, 1966 (*m diss* 1983), Colin Michael Creswell, son of late Sir Michael Justin Creswell, KCMG; 2ndly, 1985, Philippe Bassett, of 20 Garricks Island, Hampton, Middx TW12 2EW, and has issue living, (by 1st *m*) Mark Colin, *b* 1972, — Tonya Elizabeth, *b* 1974. —— Lorna Theresa, *b* 1948: *m* 1972, Vicente Romero, of Paseo de Los Andes 3, 28761 Soto de Vinuelas Tres Cantos, Madrid, Spain, and has issue living, Miguel, *b* 1984.

The 1st baronet, Sir Henry Mulleneux Grayson, KBE (son of Henry Holdrege Grayson, JP, of Liverpool) was Lieut-Col RM, a Director of several Shipping and Shipbuilding Cos, and High Sheriff of Anglesey 1917-18, and sat as MP for W Div of Birkenhead (*Co U*) 1918-22.

GREEN (UK) 1886, of Wakefield, Yorkshire, and Ken Hill, Norfolk

Sir SIMON LYCETT GREEN, TD, 5th *Baronet*; *b* 11 July 1912; *s* his brother, *Maj Sir* (EDWARD) STEPHEN, CBE, 1996; *ed* Eton, and Magdalene Coll, Camb (MA); DL W Riding of Yorkshire 1952, JP Wakefield 1959; Lt-Col comdg Yorkshire Dragoons Yeo 1947-51; served 1939-45 War; TD 1947; Chm Green's Economiser Group Ltd 1956-83: *m* 1st, 1935 (*m diss* 1971), Gladys, eldest da of late Arthur Ranicar, of Springfield, Wigan; 2ndly, 1971, Mary, da of late George Ramsden, of Dale House, Wakefield, and has issue by 1st *m*.

Arms – Vert, guttee d'eau, three stags trippant or, in fesse two roses argent. **Crest** – In front of a mount vert thereon a stag trippant or, collared vert, three roses argent. *Residence* – Cliff Bank, N Rigton, Leeds LS17 0BZ.

DAUGHTER LIVING (By 1st marriage)

Waste not

Diana Rose Frances, *b* 1935: *m* 1964, Capt Ronald Eden Wallace, of Mounsey Farm, Dulverton, Som TA22 9QE (*see* Lindsay-Hogg, Bt, 1980 Edn), and has issue living, David Lycett (Rock Farm, Hetton, Skipton, N Yorks BD23 6LR), *b* 1967; *ed* Milton Abbey, and RAC Cirencester: *m* 1991, Emma Lisa, elder da of Stephen Roger Freegard, of Langbar, N Yorks, and has issue living, Lawrence Theodore Lycett *b* 1997, Miranda Ophelia Lycett *b* 1993.

DAUGHTER LIVING OF FOURTH BARONET

Livia Lycett, *b* 1937: *m* 1961, Robert Edmond Buscall, JP, DL (High Sheriff Norfolk 1993), and has living, Harry Charles, *b* 1963; *ed* Ampleforth, and Magdalene Coll, Camb: *m* 1989, Kathryn Adrianna, da of Edward William Hill, of Farnham Royal, Bucks, and has issue living, Dominic *b* 1992, Nicholas Edmond *b* 1994, — Patrick Edward, *b* 1965; *ed* Ampleforth, and Bristol Univ: *m* 1996, Sarah E., elder da of Adrian Walter Hamilton, QC, of Holland Park, W8, and has issue living, Fergus Adrian *b* 1998. *Residence* – Carbrooke Hall, Thetford, Norfolk.

COLLATERAL BRANCHES LIVING

Grandchildren of late Cmdr David Lycett Green, RN (infra):—
Issue of late Richard David Rafe Lycett Green, *b* 1925, *d* 1969: *m* 1st, 1948 (*m diss* 1956) (Marie) Patricia, who *d* 1995, da of Michael Maguire, of Melbourne, Australia, and widow of Capt Hon Peter Rudyard Aitken, Royal Fus (*see* B Beaverbrook); 2ndly, 1958, Margaret Alison, da of Maj Geoffrey Denis Lock, MBE, MC, of Rainbow Wood, Bath, and formerly wife of Yan Kai-Nielsen:—
(By 1st *m*) EDWARD PATRICK LYCETT (Lower Broadmeadow, Hardwicke, Hay-on-Wye, Herefs HR3 5TA), *b* 14 Oct 1950; *ed* Stowe: *m* 1st, 1971 (*m diss* 1975), Corden Sarah, da of C. B. Stretton Wilson, of Stratford-on-Avon; 2ndly, 1977, Annette Patricia Josephine, da of Oswald Patrick John Rochfort, of Broad Marston, Warwicks, and has issue living, (by 2nd *m*) Charlotte Rose, *b* 1979, — Alice Josephine, *b* 1983. —— Mary Angela (Moo Barton, Petton Cross, Shillingford, Tiverton, Devon), *b* 1949.

Issue of late Cmdr David Cecil Lycett Green, RN, 2nd son of 2nd baronet, *b* 1892, *d* 1960: *m* 1st, 1923 (*m diss* 1944), Angela, who *d* 1992, yst da of late Edward Hubert Courage, of Kirkby-Fleetham Hall, Bedale; 2ndly, 1948, Margaret Dora Helen, who *d* 1988 (having *m* 3rdly, 1970 (*m diss* 1978), Alec Pilkington), da of Lt-Col Henry Ross, CIE, OBE, and formerly wife of Col Thomas Cromwell Williamson, DSO:—
(By 1st *m*) Rupert William Lycett (The Mill House, Uffington, Faringdon, Oxon), *b* 1938; late 2nd Lt Royal Armoured Corps: *m* 1963, Candida Rose, da of late Sir John Betjeman, CBE (*see* B Chetwode, 1985 Edn), and has issue living, David Lycett, *b* 1975; *ed* Eton, — John Peregrine Lycett, *b* 1978; *ed* Eton, — Lucy Rose Lycett, *b* 1964: *m* 1988, Alexander Evelyn Giles Ward (*see* E Dudley), — Imogen Rose, *b* 1966: *m* 1993, Augustus Jack Christie, 2nd son of Sir George William Langham Christie, DL, of Glyndebourne, E Sussex, and has issue living, Jackson *b* 1996, Romulus *b* (twin) 1996, — Endellion Rose, *b* 1969: *m* 1998, Robert W. Nagel, son of Sidney Nagel, of Highgate, and has issue living, Grace Tulane *b* 1998. —— Catherine Auriol Lycett, *b* 1935: *m* 1st, 1967, Raja Ranbir Singh; 2ndly, 1981, Patrick Field Till, and has issue living, (by 1st *m*), Xenia, *b* 1968, — Tamara, *b* 1970, — Alexia, *b* 1972.

Sir Edward Green, 1st Bt (el son of Edward Green, of Wakefield); Capt 1st W Yorkshire Yeo; sat as MP for Wakefield (C) 1874 (but was unseated) and July 1885 to July 1892 (when he resigned). Sir Edward Arthur Lycett Green, TD, 3rd Bt, was Lieut-Col and Brevet Col Yorkshire Dragoons, Yeo. Sir Edward Stephen Lycett Green, CBE, 4th Bt, was JP, DL and High Sheriff Norfolk, Chm E Anglian Hosp Board, and formerly Maj RA.

GREEN (UK) 1901, of Belsize Park Gardens, Hampstead, co London (Extinct 1959)

Sir GEORGE ARTHUR HAYDN GREEN, 4th and last *Baronet.*

DAUGHTER LIVING OF SECOND BARONET

Evelyn Kate, *b* 1905.

Green-Price, see Price.

GREENAWAY (UK) 1933, of Coombe, co Surrey

Either do not attempt, or complete

Sir JOHN MICHAEL BURDICK GREENAWAY, 3rd *Baronet*; *b* 9 Aug 1944; *s* his father, *Sir* DEREK BURDICK, CBE, TD, 1994; *ed* Harrow; Lieut Life Guards 1965-70; a Dir Daniel Greenaway & Sons Ltd 1970-79: *m* 1982, Susan Margaret, da of Henry Birch, of Lion House, Tattenhall, Cheshire, and has issue.

Arms – Quarterly: 1 and 4, gules, a chevron between in chief two covered cups and in base a closed book clasps downwards or, *Greenaway*; 2 and 3, vert an ancient ship with three masts sails set or, between four seagulls clooc proper, *Burdick.* **Crest** – A griffin's head erased or, semée of roses gules, barbed and seeded proper, suspended from the beak an annulet gold.
Residence – Lois Weedon House, Weedon Lois, Towcester, Northants NN12 8PJ.

SON LIVING

THOMAS EDWARD BURDICK *b* 3 April 1985.

DAUGHTER LIVING

Camilla Helen, *b* 1983.

SISTER LIVING

Anne Jennifer, *b* 1939: *m* 1969 (*m diss* 1995), Capt David Patrick Lewis Hewson, Blues and Royals (*see* B Merthyr, 1963 Edn), and has issue living, George Patrick David, *b* 1980, — Annabel Mary, *b* 1971, — Clare Louise, *b* 1973. *Residence* – 103 Abbotsbury Rd, W14.

AUNT LIVING (*daughter of 1st baronet*)

Doreen Lydie, *b* 1908; a JP: *m* 1936, Harold Francis Ralph Sturge, who *d* 1993, and has issue living, Martin Greenaway (3 Lower Camden Place, Bath), *b* 1938, — Simon Harold (Lyndhurst, Woodhouse Lane, Holmbury St Mary, Surrey), *b* 1940: *m* 1st 1967, Hilary Barbara Highet; 2ndly, 1982, Sheila Anne Jean Longsdale, and has issue living (by 1st *m*), Charles Campbell *b* 1969, Alexander James *b* 1972.

WIDOW LIVING OF SECOND BARONET

SHEILA BEATRICE (*Sheila, Lady Greenaway*), only da of late Richard Cyril Lockett, of 58 Cadogan Place, SW1: *m* 1937, Sir Derek Burdick Greenaway, 2nd Bt, CBE, TD, who *d* 1994. *Residence* – Dunmore, Four Elms, Edenbridge, Kent TN8 6NE.

COLLATERAL BRANCH LIVING

Issue of late Capt Alan Pearce Greenaway, JP, yr son of 1st baronet, *b* 1913, *d* 1994: *m* 1948, Patricia Frances, who *d* 1982, da of Sir Frederick Michael Wells, 1st Bt (*cr* 1948):—
Michael Philip (Criplands, Lindfield, W Sussex), *b* 1949; *ed* Harrow: *m* 1978, Alison Robyn, da of Geoffrey Douglas Cohen, and has issue living, Daniel Pearce, *b* 1981, — Hannah Kate, *b* 1980, — Rebecca Lucy, *b* 1984. —— Susan Mary (The Doone, Byfleet Rd, Cobham, Surrey), *b* 1952: *m* 1973, Alexander Andrew Campbell Cruickshank, who *d* 1998, and has issue living, David Alexander, *b* 1976, — Benjamin Andrew, *b* 1982, — Sarah Frances Louise, *b* 1974.

The 1st baronet, Sir Percy Walter Greenaway (son of Daniel Greenaway, Dep of City of London), was Chm of Daniel Greenaway & Sons, Ltd, printers and stationers, and of other Cos, a Member of Court of Common Council of of City of London (Alderman 1923, Senior Sheriff 1931-2, and Lord Mayor 1932-3), and Master of Stationers' and Newspaper Makers' Co, 1932 (re-elected 1933), and Treasurer 1951; Sir Derek Burdick Greenaway, 2nd Bt, CBE, TD, was Pres Daniel Greenaway & Son Ltd, printers, JP and DL Kent, and Master Stationers' & Newspaper Markers' Co 1974-75.

GREENWELL (UK) 1906, of Marden Park, Godstone, co Surrey, and Greenwell, Wolsingham, co Durham

I become green

Sir EDWARD BERNARD GREENWELL, 4th *Baronet*, *b* 10 June 1948; *s* his father, *Capt Sir* PETER MCCLINTOCK, TD, DL, 1978; *ed* Eton, Notts Univ (BSc), and Cranfield Inst of Technology (MBA), DL of Suffolk 1988: *m* 1974, Sarah Louise, yr da of late Lt-Col Philip Maitland Gore-Anley, of Sculthorpe House, Fakenham, Norfolk, and has issue.

ᴀrms – Or, two bars azure between three ducal coronets gules. ℭrest – A stork statant proper, beaked and legged gules, gorged with a wreath of laurel vert.
Seat – Greenwell, co Durham. *Residence* – Gedgrave Hall, Woodbridge, Suffolk IP12 2BX. *Club* – Turf.

SON LIVING

ALEXANDER BERNARD PETER, *b* 11 May 1987.

DAUGHTERS LIVING

Belinda Clayre, *b* 1977. —— Lucy Rose, *b* 1979. —— Daisy Julia, *b* 1983.

BROTHER LIVING

James Peter (Boyton House, Boyton, Woodbridge, Suffolk IP12 3LH), *b* 1950; *ed* Eton; late Maj The Blues & Royals: *m* 1979, Serena Jane, yr da of Maj Hon Colin James Dalrymple (*see* E Stair), and has issue living, Andrew Peter, *b* 1983, —— Davina Louise, *b* 1984.

SISTER LIVING

Julia Henrietta, *b* 1946: *m* 1970, Alexander Richard Trotter, DL, of Charterhall, Duns, Berwickshire, and has issue living, Henry Peter, *b* 1972, — Edward John, *b* 1973, — Rupert James, *b* 1977.

AUNTS LIVING (*Daughters of 2nd baronet*)

Elisabeth Kathleen, *b* 1908: *m* 1931, Capt Roddie Casement, OBE, RN, who *d* 1987, and has issue living, Michael Bernard, OBE (Dene Cottage, West Harting, Petersfield, Hants), *b* 1933; *ed* Winchester; Cdr RN: *m* 1956, Christina Rose, 3rd da of Capt John Cassilis Maclean, RN, and has issue living, William Rory John *b* 1961: *m* 1989, Rachel, yst da of late John Berry (and has issue living, Samuel Frederick Constantine *b* 1998, Daisy *b* 1992, Rosanna Isobel *b* 1994), Rachel Christina *b* 1957: *m* 1985, Charles James Middleton, of 6 Brandreth Rd, SW17 8ER, elder son of Brig R. C. Middleton, of Gannets, Tolleshunt D'Arcy, Essex (and has issue living, Oliver Charles *b* 1995, Jemima Louise Mary *b* 1988, Imogen Ayesha *b* 1991), Flora Susan (*Hon Mrs Henry L. A. Hood*) *b* 1959: *m* 1991, Hon Henry Lyttelton Alexander Hood, eldest son of 7th Viscount Hood (and has issue (*see* V Hood)), — Patrick John (122 Mansfield Rd, NW3 2JB), *b* 1935; *ed* Winchester, and Trin Coll, Camb (MA): *m* 1966, Margaret Rose, da of Anthony George Lloyd, and formerly wife of Peter Jens McCowen, and has issue living, Hanna *b* 1968, Isabella *b* 1970, — Elisabeth Ann, *b* 1942: *m* 1963, Anthony John Howard, of Drove Cottage, Newbridge, Cadnam, Southampton, and has issue living, Tom Peter *b* 1967, Kate Elisabeth *b* 1965: *m* 1990, Stuart Judd (and has issue living, George William *b* 1993), Emma *b* (twin) 1967, — Susan Henrietta, *b* 1944: *m* 1964, William Farquhar Acworth, of Little Hidden Farm, Hungerford, Berks, and has issue (*see* Buzzard, Bt). —— Anna Margaret (60 Oxford Gdns, W10) *b* 1913: *m* 1st, 1940, Sir James Henderson-Stewart, MP, 1st Bt, who *d* 1961; 2ndly, 1965, Geoffrey Walford Wilks, CBE, TD, who *d* 1987. —— Ruth Veronica, *b* 1916: *m* 1st, 1936, William Reginald Colquhoun, TD, who *d* 1971; 2ndly, 1972, Peter Birchall, of Cotswold Farm, Cirencester, and has issue living (by 1st *m*) William Patrick (2 Thornton Close, Girton, Cambridge CB3 0NQ), *b* 1939: *m* 1971, Frances Elspeth, only da of late Archibald Cameron, and has issue living, Anna Elizabeth *b* 1973: *m* 1997, Matthew R. J. Purver, eldest son of Richard Purver, Rhona Frances *b* 1978, — Alastair Peter, *b* 1941: *m* 1977, Elisabeth, el da of late Capt Geoffrey Stanning, DSO, RN, of Mildenhall House, Mildenhall, Marlborough, and has issue living, Andrew John *b* 1983, Mary Louise *b* 1979, — John Humphrey (Brooke House, Frocester, nr Stonehouse, Glos GL10 3TE), *b* 1943: *m* 1969, Susan Elizabeth, el da of Maj Michael Warren Ingram, OBE, of The Manor House, South Cerney, Cirencester, and has issue (*see* Ingram, Bt), — Neil Robert (Glenborrodale House, Ardnamurchan, Argyll), *b* 1947: *m* 1974, Rosemary Elizabeth, da of late Archibald Colville (*see* Gibson-Craig-Carmichael, Bt, 1995 Edn), and has issue living, William Alexander *b* 1976, Nicholas Peter *b* 1978, Robert *b* 1983, Hamish Patrick *b* 1985, — Anna Margaret, *b* 1946: *m* 1968, Nigel Guthrie McNair Scott, of 1 Edwardes Sq, W8 (*see* V Camrose, 1995 Edn), and has issue living, Robert William *b* 1970: *m* 1997, Maurette R., only da of late John Norris, and of Mrs Walter Berryman, Alastair Nigel *b* 1972, David Ronald *b* 1973, Benjamin Guthrie *b* 1976.

WIDOW LIVING OF THIRD BARONET

(JEAN) HENRIETTA ROSE, twin da of Peter Haig-Thomas (see E Normanton, 1970 Edn): m 1st, 1940, Capt Sir Peter McClintock Greenwell, 3rd Bt, who d 1978; 2ndly, 1985, Hugh Kenneth Haig, of Butley Abbey Farm, Woodbridge, Suffolk.

COLLATERAL BRANCHES LIVING

Grandchildren of late Maj Aynsley Eyre Greenwell (infra):—
Issue of late Lt-Cdr Whitfield Ava Aynsley Greenwell RNVR, b 1907, d 1977: m 1935, Violet Rosemary Evelyn (Shermanbury Place, Shermanbury, nr Horsham, Sussex), da of Frederick Charles Turner, CIE, of The Little Place, Lyme Regis, Dorset:—
William Maxwell Walpole, b 1942, ed Harrow, and RAC Cirencester. —— Eve Jennifer GREENWELL, b 1939; has resumed her maiden name: m 1974 (m diss 1981), Anthony Murly-Gotto, and has issue living, Antonia Mary Eve Alexandra, b 1975.

Issue of late Lt-Cdr Ivor Desmond Greenwell, RNVR, b 1911, d 1993: m 1939, Diana, who d 1991, da of Maj John Simeon Ward, The Rifle Bde:—
Jane Elizabeth, b 1954. —— Mary Claire, b (twin)1954.

Grandchildren of late Maj Aynsley Eyre Greenwell, 2nd son of 1st baronet:—
Issue of late Basil Evelyn Greenwell, b 1915, d 1990: m 1st, 1948 (m diss 1952), Phyllis Joyce, da of late K. L. Weatherall Pepper, of Lewes, Sussex; 2ndly, 1955, Sarah (Tanners, River, Petworth, Sussex GU28 9AY), da of late Capt Hon Walter Seymour Carson, RN (By Carson, ext):—
(By 2nd m) Simon Lloyd (Tanners, River, Petworth, Sussex GU28 9AY), b 1956: m 1986, Caroline Posner, and has issue living, Thomas Basil, b 1990, — Louise, b 1986, — Emma, b 1989. —— †Giles Henry, b 1957, d 1990. —— Joanna Beatrice Taswell, b 1962: m 1986, Rupert Clevely, and has issue living, Coco Samantha Millicent, b 1990, — India Sarah Taswell, b 1991, — Montana Imogen Louise, b 1998. —— Virginia Annette, b 1965.

Issue of late Walpole Edward Greenwell, b 1920, d 1992: m 1963 (m diss 1972), Mrs Rosemary Heather Bunn, yr da of late John Pares-Wilson, of Little Shelford, and of Lady Daniels, and formerly wife of Douglas Henry David Bunn:—
Rupert John Walpole, b 1964.

Issue of late Geoffrey Eyre Greenwell, yst son of 1st baronet, b 1894, d 1949: m 1922, Mildred who d 1970, da of late J. Evans, of Norwood, SE:—
John Evelyn (East Field, Henfold Hill, Beare Green, Dorking, Surrey) b 1924; ed King's Sch, Canterbury; 1939-45 with RAFVR: m 1956, Frances Valerie Anne, da of late Marnix Cremer, of Lovelocks, Horley, and has issue living, Andrew John, b 1959, — Jane Frances, b 1963.

Sir Walpole Lloyd Greenwell, 1st Bt (2nd son of late Walpole Eyre Greenwell), was High Sheriff of Surrey 1903. The Greenwell family was seated at Greenwell in the parish of Wolsingham, co Durham, from a very early period and Gulielmus Presbyter and his son James de Grenewelle are mentioned as holding land there in 1183 in the Bolden Book. A connected pedigree can be traced from John de Grenwell, of Park Yate in Wolsingham, who d before 13 Jan 1391.

GRESLEY (E) 1611, of Drakelowe, Derbyshire (Extinct 1976)

Sir WILLIAM FRANCIS GRESLEY, 13th, and last Baronet.

WIDOW LIVING OF THIRTEENTH BARONET

ADA MARY (Lady Gresley) (59A Grand Av, Southbourne, Bournemouth), da of late George Miller: m 1924, Sir William Francis Gresley, 13th Bt, who d 1976, when the title became ext.

COLLATERAL BRANCH LIVING

Issue of late Nigel Morewood Gresley, el brother of 13th baronet, b 1892, d 1966: m 1921, Mary Mansfield, who d 1989, da of late R. M. Hobill:—
Mary Penelope (The Old Lodge, 92 Alumhurst Rd, Bournemouth, Dorset), b 1928: m 1959, Brian Stacy Warham Rigby-Hall, who d 1981, and has issue living, Robert Gresley (St Margarets, Twickenham, Middx), b 1965; ed Canford, and

Portsmouth Univ: *m* 1989, Siobhan Claire Mary, da of Colin Stewart Field, of Canford Park, Dorset, and has issue living, William Gresley *b* 1995, Victoria Mary *b* 1997. — Frances Margaret, *b* 1968: *m* 1995, Robert Moore, of Rushford Warren, Mudeford, Dorset, and has issue living, Robert *b* 1996, Eleanor Mary *b* 1997.

Grey (cr 1711), see Lambert (cr 1711).

GREY (UK) 1814, of Fallodon, Northumberland

To serve the king with good will

Sir ANTHONY DYSART GREY, 7th *Baronet*; *b* 19 Oct 1949; *s* his grandfather, *Sir* ROBIN EDWARD DYSART, 1974; *ed* Guildford Grammar Sch Perth; late Man, Fibre Glass Div Bel Art Corpn; Inspector Dept of Industrial Affairs, Govt W Aust: *m* 1st, 1970 (*m diss* 19—), Donna, da of Donald Daniels, of 60 Park Lane, W1; 2ndly, 1993, Alison Turner, and has issue by 2nd *m*.

Arms – Gules, a lion rampant within a bordure engrailed argent, a mullet for difference. Crest – A scaling ladder in bend sinister or, hooked and pointed sable.
Residence – —

SON LIVING

THOMAS JASPER, *b* 30 April 1998.

DAUGHTERS LIVING (*By 2nd marriage*)

Matilda Jessie, *b* 1994. —— Lucinda Jane, *b* 1996.

MOTHER LIVING

Nancy (86 Kingsway Gdns, 38 King's Park Rd, Perth, W Aust 6005), da of late Francis John Meagher, of Winning Station, W Aust: *m* 1946, Edward Elton Grey, who *d* 1962, only son of Sir Robin Edward Dysart Grey, 6th Bt.

The 1st baronet, Hon Sir George Grey, was third son of the 1st Earl Grey; the 2nd baronet, Rt Hon Sir George, GCB, PC, sat as MP for Devonport (*L*) 1832-47, for Northumberland North 1847-52, and for Morpeth 1853-74; was Sec of State for Home Department 1846-52, 1855-8 and 1861-6, Sec of State for the Colonies 1854-5, and Chancellor of the Duchy of Lancaster 1841 and 1859-61; the 3rd baronet, Rt Hon Sir Edward, KG, sat as MP, for Berwick-on-Tweed (*L*) 1885-1916, and was Under-Sec of State for Foreign Affairs 1892-95, and Sec of State for Foreign Affairs 1905-15, and Ambassador to USA (on special mission) 1919; *cr Viscount Grey of Fallodon*, co Northumberland 1916 (ext 1933).

Grey Egerton, see Egerton.

GRIERSON (NS) 1685, of Lag, Dumfriesshire

Safer by this

HOC·SECURIOR

Sir MICHAEL JOHN BEWES GRIERSON, 12th *Baronet*, only son of late Lt-Col Alexander George William Grierson, RM (ret), 2nd son of 9th baronet; *b* 24 July 1921; *s* his cousin, Sir RICHARD DOUGLAS, 1987; *ed* St Edmund's Sch, Canterbury: *m* 1971, Valerie Anne, da of late Russell Wright, of Gidea Park, Essex, and has issue.

Arms – Gules, on a fesse or, between three fetterlocks argent a mullet azure. **Crest** – A lock as in the arms.
Residence – 40C Palace Rd, Streatham Hill, SW2 3NJ.

DAUGHTER LIVING

Sarah Anne, *b* 1973.

SISTER LIVING

Pamela Violet, *b* 1925: *m* 1955, Richard Wallace Vernon, and has issue (*see* Vernon, Bt, colls). *Residence* – Park Lodge, 46 Park Rd, Aldeburgh, Suffolk IP15 5EU.

COLLATERAL BRANCH LIVING

Issue of late Frederick Vedast Grierson, Lieut King's Own Scottish Borderers, yst son of 9th baronet, *b* 1888, *d* 1922: *m* 1909, Frederica, who *d* 1941, da of Arthur Frederick Skipp, of Cheltenham:—
Lorna Mary Sheila: *m* 1941 (*m diss* 1951), Carl Berger.

This family claim descent from Gilbert, yr son of Malcolm MacGregor of MacGregor (*d* 1374). Sir Robert Grierson, Knight, of Lag, who sat as MP for Dumfries 1678-86, was created a baronet with remainder to heirs male whatsoever. He was a great persecutor of the Covenantors, and presided at the trial and execution of two women known as the Wigtown Martyrs who refused to take the abjuration oath. He was "Sir Robert Redgauntlet" of Wandering Willie's tale in Sir Walter Scott's *Redgauntlet*. Sir Gilbert Grierson, 4th baronet, joined the Jacobite Rising 1715.

NORTON-GRIFFITHS (UK) 1922, of Wonham, Betchworth, co Surrey

For King and Empire

PRO REGE ET IMPERIO

Sir JOHN NORTON-GRIFFITHS, 3rd *Baronet*; *b* 4 Oct 1938; *s* his father, *Maj Sir* PETER, 1983; *ed* Eton; late Sub-Lieut RN; ACA: *m* 1964, Marilyn Margaret, elder da of Norman Grimley, of S Blundellsands, Liverpool.

Arms – 1st and 4th, sable, a flaming sword erect between two griffins combatant or, *Griffiths*; 2nd and 3rd argent, on a fesse raguly between two fleur-de-lis azure, a fleur-de-lis between two crescents or, *Norton*. **Crest** – 1st, a demi-lion rampant gules, grasping in the paws a flaming sword erect, *Griffiths*; 2ndly, a dexter gauntlet closed sable between two ostrich feathers argent, *Norton*. **Supporters** – *Dexter*, a Colonial soldier in the uniform of a trooper of the Second Regiment King Edward's Horse, resting the exterior hand upon a terrestrial globe in frame environed with a meridian; *sinister*, a labourer holding in the exterior hand a Jack-hammer drill all proper.
Address – P.O. Box 396, Rutland, Vermont 05702, USA.

BROTHER LIVING

MICHAEL (Box 24532, Nairobi, Kenya; 47 Campden Hill Towers, W11 3QP), *b* 11 Jan 1941; *ed* Eton, and Keble Coll, Oxford (DPhil, Zoology); Ecologist, Serengeti Research Inst 1960-73; Man Dir of EcoSystems Ltd, Nairobi, Kenya 1977-87, Head Eastern Sahel Unit, World Conservation Union, 1988; Consultant to Global Environment Monitoring System of the United Nations Environment Programme 1989-92; Visiting Research Fell, Centre for Social and Economic Research on the Global Environment, Univ Coll, London since 1993: *m* 1965, Ann, only da of late Group Capt Blair Alexander Fraser, RAF, of 12 Mount Beacon, Lansdown, Bath (E Dundonald, colls), and has issue living, Alastair, *b* 23 Feb 1976.

SISTER LIVING

Anne, *b* 1936: *m* 1956 (*m diss ca* 1984), Richard Hathaway Morgan, and has issue living, Kathryn, *b* 1957, — Christina, *b* 1958, — Pascale, *b* 1960. *Residence* – Le Tertre, 61360 Montgaudry, France.

COLLATERAL BRANCH LIVING

Issue of late Capt Michael Norton-Griffiths, RE, 2nd son of 1st baronet, *b* 1908, *ka* 1940: *m* 1936, Mrs Elizabeth Gertrude Colclough, who *d* 1988, having *m* 3rdly, 1946, George Paul Minchin Woodward, of New Jersey, USA, and 4thly, 1954, Ralph Arthur Hubbard, who *d* 1983 (*see* B Addington, colls), yr da of late Stephen Cozens, of Mackney Manor, Wallingford, Berks:—
Johanna, *b* 1936: *m* 1969, Keith Martin Butt, MA, Vet MB (Cantab), MRCVS, and has issue living, Jason Martin, *b* 1972, — Ben Michael, *b* 1979, — Martha, *b* 1971.

The 1st Baronet, Lieut-Col Sir John Norton-Griffiths, KCB, DSO (son of late John Griffiths, of Brecon), assumed by deed poll 1917, the additional surname of Norton, and was Governing Director of Sir John Norton-Griffiths & Co, Ltd, public works contractors and engineers: served in S African War, first in Colonial Div, and afterwards as Capt and Adj Lord Roberts's Body Guard, Headquarter Staff, and in European War 1914-16 when he raised a Special Cav Regt, subsequently being on Staff of Engineer-in-Ch to organize and start Tunnelling Cos RE, and went on special mission to Roumania for destruction of oil wells and corn stores (despatches thrice, DSO): MP for Wednesbury (C) Jan 1910 to Nov 1918, and for Central Div of Wandsworth Dec 1918 to Oct 1924. Maj Sir Peter Norton-Griffiths, 2nd Bt, Bar Inner Temple, Mil Attaché Madrid 1941-42, was Man Dir Belgian Shell Co, SA 1953-60.

GROTRIAN (UK) 1934, of Leighton Buzzard, co Bedford

By courage and faith

Sir (PHILIP) CHRISTIAN BRENT GROTRIAN, 3rd *Baronet*, only son of late S/Ldr Robert Philip Brent Grotrian, RAF, yst son of 1st baronet; *b* 26 March 1935; *s* his uncle, Sir JOHN APPELBE BRENT, 1984; *ed* Eton, and Trin Coll, Toronto: *m* 1st, 1960, Anne Isabel, da of Robert Sieger Whyte, of Toronto; 2ndly, 1979, Sarah Frances, da of Reginald Harry Gale, of Montreal, and has issue.

Arms – Gules, a wyvern or, in chief two roses argent, barbed and seeded proper.
Crest – A wyvern or, resting the dexter leg upon a rose argent, barbed and seeded proper.
Residence – RR3, Mansfield, Ontario LON 1MO.

SONS LIVING (*By 1st marriage*)

(PHILIP) TIMOTHY ADAM BRENT, *b* 9 April 1962. *Residence* – 28 Bishop St, Toronto, Ontario, Canada M5R 1N2.

(*By 2nd marriage*)

John Hugh Brent, *b* 1982.

DAUGHTER LIVING (*By 2nd marriage*)

Frances Elizabeth, *b* 1980.

HALF-SISTER LIVING

Jane Felicity, *b* 1942: *m* 1964, Peter Lewis Andrews, of Old Timbers, Shere Rd, W Horsley, Surrey, and has issue living, Philip Kenneth, *b* 1964: *m* 1987, Caroline Jane, da of Raymond Woodcock, of Wivenhoe, Essex and has issue living, Lucy Jane *b* 1991, Emily Sarah *b* 1993, — Sarah Jane, *b* 1967: *m* 1st, 1993 (*m diss* 199—), Nicholas James Hughes, son of David Hughes, of Woldingham, Surrey; 2ndly, 1995, Darren Robert William Houghton, son of Robert Houghton, of Sutton Coldfield, West Midlands, and his issue living (by 2nd *m*), Jack *b* 1996.

DAUGHTER LIVING OF FIRST BARONET

Lilian Désirée, *b* 1914. *Residence* – 10 New Yatt Rd, Witney, Oxon.

MOTHER LIVING

Elizabeth Mary, only da of late Maj John Hardy-Wrigley: *m* 1st, 1931 (*m diss* 1940), as his 1st wife, S/Ldr Robert Philip Brent Grotrian (yst son of 1st Baronet), who *d* on active ser in the Far East 1945; 2ndly, 1947, William Percy George, late US Foreign Service, who *d* 1955, and has further issue. *Residence* – 17 Hogarth Rd, Hove, Sussex BN3 5RH.

COLLATERAL BRANCH LIVING

Issue of late Major Charles Herbert Brent Grotrian, TD, BCL, JP, RA (TA), el son of 1st baronet, *b* 1902, *ka* Burma 1944: *m* 1936, Aileen Georgina, who *d* 1987, only da of late George Ernest Etlinger:—
Charlotte Elizabeth (17 Hogarth Rd, Hove, Sussex BN3 5RH), *b* 1941.

The 1st baronet, Sir Herbert Brent Grotrian, KC, DL, BCL (2nd son of Frederick Brent Grotrian, MP), was Recorder of Scarborough 1918-46, sat as MP for S-W Div of Kingston-upon-Hull (*C*) 1924-29, and was High Sheriff of Bedfordshire 1931.

GROVE (UK) 1874, of Ferne, Wiltshire

Sir CHARLES GERALD GROVE, 5th *Baronet*; *b* 10 Dec 1929; *s* his brother, *Sir* WALTER FELIPE PHILIP, 1974, but no name has been entered on the Official Roll of the Baronetage since death of 3rd Bt in 1962.

𝕬rms – Ermine, on a chevron engrailed gules; three scallops, the centre one or, the others argent. Crest – A talbot statant sable, collared argent. *Residence* – USA.

BROTHER LIVING

HAROLD THOMAS, *b* 6 Dec 1930.

MOTHER LIVING

Elena, da of late Felipe Crosthwaite: *m* 1926 (*m diss* Mexico 1933), Walter Peel Grove, who *d* 1944.

Neither above nor below

This family claims descent from John Grove, who settled in Wilts from Bucks. *temp* Henry VI, William Grove, MP for Shaftesbury, who died 1582, purchased Ferne in 1563 and Sedghill in 1582. Sir Thomas Fraser Grove, 1st Bt, was MP for S Wilts (*L*) 1865-74, and for Wilts S, or Wilton, Div 1885-92.

GUINNESS (UK) 1867, of Ashford, co Galway

My hope is in God

Sir KENELM ERNEST LEE GUINNESS, 4th *Baronet*, son of late Kenelm Edward Lee Guinness, MBE, RNVR, 2nd son of late Capt Benjamin Lee Guinness, 2nd son of 1st baronet; *b* 13 Dec 1928; *s* his uncle, Sir ALGERNON ARTHUR ST LAWRENCE LEE, 1954; *ed* Eton, and Mass Institute of Technology, USA; Engineer with International Bank for Reconstruction and Development (World Bank) 1954-75 and Consulting Engineer, late 2nd Lieut Roy Horse Guards: *m* 1961, Mrs Jane Nevin Dickson, and has issue.

𝕬rms – Quarterly: 1st and 4th per saltire gules and azure, a lion rampant or, on a chief ermine a dexter hand couped at the wrist of the first, *Guinness*: 2nd and 3rd argent, on a fesse between three crescents sable a trefoil slipped or, *Lee*. Crests – 1st, a boar passant, quarterly or and gules; 2nd, on a pillar argent, encircled by a ducal coronet or, an eagle preying on a bird's leg erased proper. Supporters – On either side a stag gules, attired and gorged with a collar gemmel or, pendant therefrom by a chain gold an escutcheon, the dexter charged with the arms of Guinness, and the sinister with those of Lee. (The supporters in the arms were granted to Sir Benjamin Lee Guinness, 1st baronet, and his heirs male, upon whom the dignity of a baronet may descend, as a special mark of favour for the public spirit and munificent liberality manifested by him in the restoration of St Patrick's Cathedral, Dublin).
Residence – Rich Neck, Claiborne, Maryland 21624, USA. *Clubs* – Cavalry and Guards', Household Division Yacht.

SONS LIVING

KENELM EDWARD LEE, *b* 30 Jan 1962. —— Sean St Lawrence Lee, *b* 1966: *m* 1997, Christine Black.

SISTER LIVING

Geraldine St Lawrence, *b* 1930: *m* 1956, Mikhael Essayan, QC, and has issue living, Martin Sarkis, *b* 1959, — Joanna Consuelo, *b* 1958. *Residence* – 6 Chelsea Sq, SW3.

DAUGHTER LIVING OF THIRD BARONET

Susan (Shoonan) Rosemary Lee, *b* 1931: *m* 1st, 1953 (*m diss* 1956), Samuel Charles Gillchrest; 2ndly, 1958, Keith Rawlings Hall, and has issue living, (by 2nd *m*) Simon Patrick Rawlings, *b* 1959, — Timothy Mark Lee, *b* 1967, — Susan Felicity, *b* 1960, — Jennifer Margaret, *b* 1963.

Sir Benjamin Lee Guinness, MP, LLD, 1st Bt, sat as MP for Dublin City (*C*) 1865-8, and at his own cost restored the Cathedral of St Patrick, Dublin. His el son, Sir Edward, 2nd Bt, sat as MP for Dublin (*C*) 1868-9 and 1874-80, when he was *cr Baron Ardilaun*, of Ashford, co Galway (peerage of United Kingdom), which Barony became ext at his death in 1915.

GUISE (GB) 1783, of Highnam Court, Gloucestershire
(Name pronounced "Gyze")

The more honest, the more safe

Sir JOHN GRANT GUISE, 7th *Baronet*; *b* 15 Dec 1927; *s* his father, *Sir* ANSELM WILLIAM EDWARD, 1970; *ed* Winchester, and RMC Sandhurst; Capt (ret) Queen's Own Hussars; patron of one living: *m* 1992, Sally H. M., da of late Cmdr H. G. C. Stevens, RN.

Arms – Gules, seven lozenges conjoined vaire, three, three, and one, on a canton or a mullet of six points pierced sable. **Crest** – Out of a ducal coronet or a swan wings elevated argent, gorged with a ducal crown and chain over the back or. **Supporters** – (to descend with the baronetcy)—*Dexter*, a swan with wings endorsed argent crusilly and langued gules, beaked and membered sable, collared and chained or; *sinister*, a bear sable, billetty, collared and chained or, langued and armed gules.
Seat – Elmore Court, nr Gloucester GL2 3NT. *Club* – Turf.

BROTHER LIVING

CHRISTOPHER JAMES (Easton Town Farm, Sherston, Malmesbury, Wilts; 106 Claxton Grove, W6), *b* 10 July 1930; *ed* Stowe: *m* 1969, Mrs Carole Hoskins Benson, elder da of Jack Hoskins Master, of The Dower House, Crawley, Winchester, Hants, and formerly wife of Charles Edward Riou Benson, and has issue living, Anselm Mark, *b* 1971: *m* 1997, Hannah L., yst da of John L. Bruce, of Sculthorpe House, Sculthorpe, Norfolk, — Ruth Victoria Margaret, *b* 1972.

SISTER LIVING

Philippa Margaret, *b* 1926: *m* 1950, Maj Alastair Hugh Joseph Fraser, MC, Lovat Scouts (*see* L Lovat, colls), who *d* 1986. *Residence* – Moniack Castle, Kirkhill, Inverness-shire.

COLLATERAL BRANCHES LIVING

Grandchildren of late Lt-Cdr Jack Francis Vernon Guise (*infra*):—
Issue of late John Nicholas Guise, *b* 1920, *d* 1981: *m* 1st, 1946 (*m diss* 196-), Valerie, da of Ronald Parker, of Warrie Station, W Aust; 2ndly 196-, Beverley, who *d* 1982, da of James Parker, of Maida Vale, W Aust:—
(By 1st *m*) Anthony John, *b* 1951. —— Nikki, *b* 1952, *d* 1998. —— Judith Anne, *b* 1955. —— (By 2nd *m*) James Nicholas, *b* 1969.

Issue of late Christopher Rivett Guise, *b* 1921, *d* 1991: *m* 1948, Marion Strang:—
Christopher John (8 Stevens St, High Wycombe, WA 6057, Australia), *b* 1949: *m* 1969, Daphne Jean, only da of Edgar Mackie, of Kalgoorlie, WA, and has issue living, David Johnathan, *b* 1977, — Diane Elizabeth, *b* 1974. —— Georgina Elizabeth, *b* 1951: *m* 1st, 1968 (*m diss* 19—), Peter Dowding; 2ndly, 1988, Marian Zupan, of Bassendean, WA, and has issue living (by 1st *m*). —— Penelope Jane, *b* 1955: *m* 1971, Ljubo Tolj, of 3 Salisbury Rd, Rivervale, WA 6103, Australia, and has issue living.

Issue of late Reginald Ireland Guise, *b* 1923, *d* 1978: *m* 1951, Gladys Constance (15 McLintock Way, Karrinyup, W Aust 6018), only da of late Robert Alexander Baxter, of Cunderdin, W Aust:—
Larry Steven, *b* 1958: *m* 1984, Susan, only da of Peter Gunning of 10 Bulimba Rd, Nedlands, W Aust 6009, and has issue living, Megan Isabella, *b* 1987, — Simone Renée, *b* 1989, — Caitlin Ruth, *b* 1992. —— Neil Reginald, *b* 1960: *m* 1984, Amanda Frances, el da of Michael Seabrook, of Roleystone, W Aust, and has issue living, Samuel Benjamin, *b* 1996, — Holly Rebecca, *b* 1992, — Abby Juliette, *b* 1998. —— David Nigel, *b* 1970. —— Wendy Nola, *b* 1954.

Grandchildren of late Rivett Francis Guise, 2nd son of late Francis Edward Guise, 3rd son of 3rd baronet:—
Issue of late Lt-Cdr Jack Francis Vernon Guise, *b* 1882, *d* 1964: *m* 1917, Catherine Renée, who *d* 1970, da of late Gilbert Ireland-Blackburn, of Bristol:—
Marguerite Renee, *b* 1918: *m* 19—, Ralph James Lang, of 288 Summer Lakes Parade, Ballajura, WA 6066, Aust, and has issue living. —— Diana Mary, *b* 1925: *m* 19—, Graham Johnson, who *d* 1992, of 2 Gabor Rd, Wattle Grove 6107, W Aust, and has issue living. —— Tacy Avena, *b* 1927: *m* 1st, 19— (*m diss* 19—), Thomas Turbett; 2ndly, 19—, Bernard Kelly, of 23 Kooham Way, Balga 6061, W Aust, and has issue living, (by 1st *m*), —, (by 2nd *m*), —. —— Georgina Frances, *b* 1930: *m* 19—, Jack Pritchard, and has issue living.

Issue of late Capt Francis Edward Boissier Guise, *b* 1892, *d* 1970: *m* 1st, 1914, Ethel Mary, who *d* 1943, da of Edward Valentine Holme; 2ndly, 1944, Gertrude Joyce (10 Harrow Rd, Brislington, Bristol 4), da of E. F. Taylor, of Kingswood, Bristol:—
(By 2nd *m*) Christopher Francis (4 Blackthorn Close, Marford, nr Wrexham, Clwyd LL12 8LB), *b* 1945; late RN: *m* 1973, Gwynneth Hancock, of Bristol, and has issue living, Nicola, *b* 1974, — Rhian *b* (twin) 1974. —— Penelope Catherine, *b* 1946: *m* 1966, Nigel Wilkinson, of 2 Melford Gdns, Old Kempshott Lane, Basingstoke, Hants, and has issue living, Simon, *b* 1970, — Nicholas, *b* 1972. —— Elizabeth Anne, *b* 1950: *m* 1973, David Richard Fynn, of 50 Littledean, Yate, nr Bristol, and has issue living, Colin Richard, *b* 1980, — Deborah Caroline, *b* 1982. —— Rosemary Caroline, *b* 1954: *m* 1979, Michael Anthony Hills, of Cain Valley Hotel, High St, Llanfyllin, Powys SY22 5AQ, and has issue living, Jennifer Claire, *b* 1983.

Issue of late Lieut-Col John William Guise, *b* 1894, *d* 1963: *m* 1924 (*m diss* 1937), Dorothy Alma, da of Theodore Hewitt English:—
Patricia Frederica, *b* 1929.

Issue of late Christopher Probyn Guise, *b* 1899, *d* 1965: *m* 1st, 1931 (*m diss* 1956), Hope, who *d* 1983, da of late F. G. P. Neison, of Lahore; 2ndly, 1959 (*m diss* 1963), Catherine Elizabeth de Villiers:—
(By 1st *m*) Anselm Neison (21 Motukaraka Point, Grays Rd, Pauatahanui, RD1, Porirua 6221, nr Wellington, New Zealand), *b* 1935: *m* 1959, Eileen Mary, da of Col Patrick Henry Cummins, IMS (ret) (*see* E Lauderdale, colls, 1985 Edn), and has issue living, Edward William, *b* 1962, — Christopher Patrick, *b* 1973, — Laura Joan, *b* 1960: *m* 1984, Wing Cmdr William John Sommer, RNZAF (ret), of 45 Victory Crescent, Tawa, NZ, and has issue living, Michael Patrick *b* 1990, Scott Douglas *b* 1997, Jamie Richard Sommer *b* (twin) 1997, — Susan Mary, *b* 1965: *m* 1986, Owen Philip Bieleski, of 9 Jan Higgins, Howick, Auckland, NZ, and has issue living, David Owen *b* 1989, Andrew Craig *b* 1993, Linda Jean *b* 1995. —— John Francis, *b* 1947. —— Dinah Gabrielle (Crebor Cottage, Dunmere, Bodmin, Cornwall), *b* 1936: *m* 1957, Peter Maunder, who *d* 1988.

Issue of late Rivett Arthur Guise, *b* 1902, *d* 1965: *m* 1924, Beatrice Geraldine who *d* 1979, da of late Edward Charles Rudge, of Abbey Manor, Evesham:—
Peter Rivett John (Highnam, 4 Cae Castell, Builth Wells, Powys), *b* 1928: *m* 1953, Morfydd Meredydd, da of late Lewis Morris, of St Harman, Rhayader. —— Sheila Mae COLLIS-RUDGE (Sandpiper's, Northfield Av, Shiplake, Henley-on-Thames, Oxon RG9 3PD), *b* 1925: assumed the surname of Collis-Rudge by Deed Poll 1992: *m* 1st, 1952, Francis Brian Collis, who *d* 1987; 2ndly, 1996, Edward Charles Rudge, eldest son of late John Edward Rudge, of Atley Manor, Evesham, and has issue living (by 1st *m*), David Brian (8 Ashcroft Close, Caversham Heights, Reading, Berks RG4 7NU), *b* 1954: *m* 1978, Kerry Alison Elizabeth, da of Derek Alfred Preece, of Little Oak, Chiltern Rd, Peppard Common, Henley-on-Thames, and has issue living, Oliver Thomas Richard Rivett *b* 1985, Elizabeth Louisa Mae *b* 1982, — Simon Christopher (10 Borderside, Yateley, Hants), *b* 1957: *m* 1983, Jane Constance Hutchins, da of Trevor Thomas Farmiloe, of 4 Longridge Close, Reading, Berks, and has issue living, Max Christopher *b* 1985.

Granddaughter of late Francis Edward Guise (ante):—
Issue of late John Wright Guise, *b* 1855, *d* 1916: *m* 1st, 1884, Helen Edith, who *d* 1885, da of His Honour Judge Sumner, of Hempsted Court, Gloucester; 2ndly, 1888, Charlotte, who *d* 1931, da of Edwin Crawshay:—
(By 2nd *m*) Lesa Frances, *b* 1893: *m* 1920, Capt Kingsmill Foster Manley Power, MC, Gloucestershire Regt Reserve, who *d* 1963, and has issue living, Manley Anselm, *b* 1920, — Charlotte Lesa, *b* 1922.

Granddaughter of late Rev Vernon Lane Guise, son of late Rev Vernon George Guise, 4th son of 3rd baronet:—
Issue of late Maj Vernon Robert Guise, OBE, MC, *b* 1885, *d* 1939: *m* 1919, Nadine Alice, who *d* 1977, da of late Andrew Charles Armstrong (Armstrong, Bt, *cr* 1841, colls):—
Veronica Louise, *b* 1921: *m* 1946, Alan Falconer, FRCS, Surg-Lieut-Com RN, and has issue living, John Hedley, *b* 1951, — Alastair, *b* 1955, — Jennifer Anne, *b* 1947, — Catherine Scott, *b* 1949. *Residence* – 71 Alexander Park Rd, Muswell Hill, N10.

In 1262 Nicholas de Gyse (having *m* a near relative of Sir John de Burgh, el son of Hubert, Earl of Kent) received in right of his wife the manor and lordship of Elmore in Gloucestershire. Sir Anselm de Gyse, son of Nicholas, received (temp 1274) a confirmation of this manor by a further grant (still in possession of the family), and assumed the de Burgh arms, differenced by a canton. His descendant, Christopher Guise, el son of William Guise, of Elmore (Sheriff of Gloucestershire 1647), was *cr* a Baronet 1661, which Baronetcy became ext at the death of the 5th baronet in April 1783; but eight months after, in Dec 1783, his cousin and heir male, John Guise (of the younger branch), of Highnam Court, co Gloucester, great-grandson of Henry Guise, a younger son of William Guise, of Elmore (ante), yr brother of 1st Baronet of 1st creation, was also *cr* a Baronet. The 2nd baronet (of the 2nd creation) sat as MP for Gloucestershire.

Gen Sir John Guise, 3rd Bt, GCB, was granted supporters to descend to heirs male of the body on succession to the baronetcy 1863, and the 4th and 5th Baronets were High Sheriffs of Gloucestershire.

GULL (UK) 1872, of Brook Street

Without God labour is in vain

Sir RUPERT WILLIAM CAMERON GULL, 5th *Baronet*; *b* 14 July 1954; *s* his father *Sir* MICHAEL SWINNERTON CAMERON, 1989; *ed* Diocesan Coll, Cape Town, and Cape Town Univ; *m* 1980, Gillian Lee, da of Robert Howard Gordon MacFarlaine, and has issue.

Arms – Azure, a serpent nowed or between three seagulls proper; a canton ermine, thereon an ostrich feather argent, quilled or, enfiled by the coronet which encircles the plume of the Prince of Wales, gold. Crests – 1st, a lion passant guardant or, supporting with his dexter forepaw an escutcheon azure, thereon an ostrich feather argent, quilled or, enfiled with a coronet as in the canton; 2nd, two arms embowed, vested azure, cuffs argent, the hands proper holding a torch or fired proper.
Residence – Harcourt Rd, Claremont, Cape Town, S Africa.

DAUGHTERS LIVING

Victoria Yvonne, *b* 1984. —— Katie Alexandra, *b* 1986. —— Olivia, *b* 1993.

SISTER LIVING

Katherine Dona Mary, *b* 1951: *m* 19—, — and has issue living.

AUNT LIVING (*Daughter of 3rd baronet*)

Pamela Dona Anne, *b* 1922: *m* 1946, Col Alistair James Strang Martin, CBE, Queen's Own Highlanders (ret), who *d* 1992, and has issue living, Christopher Thomas, *b* 1948, — Michael Richard Alistair, *b* 1953.

GREAT-AUNT LIVING (*Daughter of 2nd baronet*)

Rosemary Violet, *b* 1912: *m* 1954, Maj R. S. Schreiber who *d* 1978, late Coldm Gds. *Residence* – Campsea Ashe House, Woodbridge, Suffolk.

WIDOW LIVING OF FOURTH BARONET

MARGARETHA CATHERINA JOHANNA (*Dowager Lady Gull*), da of late Charles Henry Adrian Pentz, of Cape Town: *m* 19—, as his 2nd wife, Sir Michael Swinnerton Cameron Gull, 4th Bt, who *d* 1989. *Residence* – Wedgeport, Bertha Av, Newlands, Cape Town, S Africa.

COLLATERAL BRANCH LIVING

Issue of late John Evelyn Gull, yst son of 2nd baronet, *b* 1914, *d* 1997: *m* 1957, Margaret Colquhoun (Trowley Hill Farm, Flamstead, St Albans, Herts AL3 8DZ), da of late Capel Berger, of Hatfield, Herts:—
ANGUS WILLIAM JOHN, *b* 24 Dec 1963: *m* 1988, Jacqueline Mary, da of Gerald Edgar Ford. —— And two adopted children, Mark Capel James, *b* 1962: *m* 1963, Lene Tang Rasmussen, of Aarhus, Denmark. —— Lucinda Jane Evelyn, *b* 1961: *m* 1983, Doko Gorov, of Macedonia, and has issue living.

This baronetcy was conferred on William Withey Gull, MD, an eminent Physician (subsequently Physician in Ordinary to HM Queen Victoria), in recognition of services rendered to HRH Albert Edward, Prince of Wales, during his severe illness in the winter of 1871; and HM Queen Victoria also, in 1872, granted the canton as an augmentation to the arms. The 2nd baronet, Sir (William) Cameron, sat as MP for Devonshire N-W Div (LU) 1895-1900.

GUNNING (GB) 1778, of Eltham, Kent

He rules alone with impartial sway

Sir CHARLES THEODORE GUNNING, 9th *Baronet; b* 19 June 1935; *s* his father, *Sir* ROBERT CHARLES GUNNING, 1989; *ed* Canadian Mil Coll, RNEC (Plymouth), and Tech Univ of Nova Scotia; BEng, CEng, AIMIMechE, AMIMarE; late Lt Cdr RCN; senior consultant, Eyretechnics Ltd (Ottawa); Vice-Chm RCS Nat Council in Canada since 1980: *m* 1st, 1969 (*m diss* 1982), Sarah, da of Col Patrick Arthur Eaton, of 121 Hadlow Rd, Tonbridge, Kent; 2ndly, 1989, Linda, da of Theodore Kachmar, of Montreal, and has issue by 1st *m.*

Arms – Gules, on a fesse erminois between three doves argent, as many crosses formée per pale gules and azure. **Crest** – A dove holding in its dexter claw a caduceus proper.
Residence – 2940 McCarthy Rd, Ottawa, Ontario K1V 8K6, Canada.

DAUGHTER LIVING (*By 1st marriage*)

Caroline Anne, *b* 1971.

BROTHERS LIVING

JOHN ROBERT, *b* 17 Sept 1944: *m* 1969, Alina Tylicki, and has issue living, Derek John Robert, *b* 1972, — Kevin Philip, *b* 1976, — Lori-Ann, *b* 1969. ——— Joseph Jeremy, *b* 1946: *m* 1968, June Smith, and has issue living, Diana Elizabeth, *b* 1968, — Theressa Kathleen, *b* 1971, — Michelle Wendy, *b* 1973. ——— David Laurence (Alberta, Canada), *b* 1948: *m* 1978, Claudette Dubois, and has issue living, Leslie Anita, *b* 1978, — Kristina Jaclyn, *b* 1980. ——— Henry Michael (Bourtreebush House, Cammach Moor, nr Stonehaven, Aberdeenshire), *b* 1949: *m* 1970, Rita Bruneau, and has issue living, Holly Michelle, *b* 1970, — Melanie Dawn, *b* 1975. ——— Bernard Christopher (47 Helene Av, Dartmouth, Nova Scotia B2X 1G5, Canada), *b* 1951; Land Surveyor: *m* 1979, Elizabeth McLaughlin. ——— George Peter (Box 6626, Peace River, Alberta T8S 1S4, Canada), *b* 1953; apiarist: *m* 1974, Pauline Maud Karpiak, and has issue living, George Bryce, *b* 1975, — Angela Marion, *b* 1977. ——— Anthony Andrew Simon (2536 Victor St, Victoria, Canada V8R 409), *b* 1955: *m* 1986, Darelle Wilson, has issue living, Dylan Charles Wilson, *b* 1986, — and an adopted son, John Robert Wilson *b* 1982.

SISTERS LIVING

Iseult Sara, *b* 1936: *m* 1970 (*m diss* 1977), Klaus Krey, and has issue living, Andrew Lee, *b* 1974, — Suzanne Nicole, *b* 1972. ——— Elaine Beatrice, *b* 1939: *m* 1958, Arnold Nelson Jones (Box 772, High Prairie, Alberta, Canada), and has issue living, Michael Robert, *b* 1959, — Charles Mark, *b* 1960, — George Marion, *b* 1961, — Bruce Gordon, *b* 1963: *m* 1984, Kathleen Margaret Barnes , — Christopher John Peter, *b* 1971, — Kathryn Ann, *b* 1967.

WIDOW LIVING OF EIGHTH BARONET

HELEN NANCY (*Ann, Lady Gunning*) (Box 6602, Peace River, Alberta T8S 1S4, Canada), da of late Vice Adm Sir Theodore John Hallett, KBE, CB: *m* 1934, Sir Robert Charles Gunning, 8th Bt, who *d* 1989.

COLLATERAL BRANCHES LIVING

Granddaughter of late Col George Hamilton Gunning, DSO, uncle of 8th baronet:—
Issue of late Major Jack Hamilton Gunning, Indian Army, *b* 1907, *d* 1956: *m* 1st, 1938, Judith Clowes, who *d* 1942, da of late Capt Norton Clowes Castle, Roy Irish Regt; 2ndly, 1951, Kathleen Irene, who *d* 1993, da of P. W. A. Wilson, of Shirley, Surrey:—
(By 1st *m*) Cherry Hamilton (9 Linkfield, East Molesey, Surrey KT8 9SD), *b* 1939: *m* 1962, John Benjamin Lionel Underwood, Maj (ret) King's Own Roy Border Regt, and has issue living, Michael John Benjamin, *b* 1966: *m* 1995, Joanne Foster, and has issue living, Oliver Francis *b* 1994, Louis Hamilton *b* 1995, — Catherine Louise, *b* 1964: *m* 1992, Mark George Beatty, and has issue living, Benjamin George *b* 1994, Samuel George *b* 1996, Emily Catherine *b* 1999, — Jennifer Elizabeth, *b* 1967.

Granddaughters of late Brig-Gen Orlando George Gunning, CMG, DSO, 2nd son of late Col John Campbell Gunning (infra):—
Issue of late Sir (Orlando) Peter Gunning, CMG, *b* 1908, *d* 1964: *m* 1940, Patricia Mary (42 Upper Cheyne Row, SW3), da of late Capt Dermot O'Connor, MC:—
Susan Mary, *b* 1944. ——— Diana Rosemary *b* 1947. *m* 1971, Patrick Durnford, of Stoney Down, Corfe Mullen, Dorset, and has issue living, Richard Peter Henry, *b* 1974, — James Edward, *b* 1976, — Nicholas John, *b* 1980, — Clare Susannah, *b* 1978.

Grandson of late Col John Campbell Gunning, son of late Maj John Gunning, 6th son of 2nd baronet:—
Issue of late Capt Henry Ross Gunning, *b* 1879, *d* 1951: *m* 1st, 1904, Charlotte Henrietta, who *d* 1908, da of late Anthony Harley Bacon; 2ndly, 1914, Violet Gwendoline, who *d* 1973, da of late Robert Cubitt:—
(By 2nd *m*) Richard Ross, *b* 1928: *m* 1951, Hilda, da of John Ronald Staniforth, and has issue living, Christopher John Ross (151 West 17th Av, Vancouver, BC V5Y 1Z7, Canada), *b* 1955 and has issue living, Jennifer Christina *b* 1976, Tasha Joy *b* 1997, — Timothy Robin (41832 Majuba Hill Rd, Chilliwack, BC V2R 5G9, Canada), *b* 1959 and has issue living, Brodie Adam *b* 1982, — Heather Jean, *b* 1954: *m* 1997, Gordon J. Langson, of 2060 White Birch Rd, Sidney, BC, Canada. *Residence* – 58-901 Kentwood Lane, Victoria, BC, Canada.

The 1st baronet was successively Minister Plenipotentiary at the Courts of Berlin and St Petersburg and the 2nd baronet was successively MP for Wigan (1800-1802), Hastings (1802-6), and East Grinstead (1812-18). Sir Robert, 3rd Bt, sat as MP for Northampton 1830-31, and was High Sheriff of Northamptonshire 1841-2, and Sir Henry, 4th Bt, was successively R of Knockyn, Incumbent of Horton, and R of Wigan, and Rural Dean. The 7th baronet, Brig-Gen Sir Charles Vere Gunning, CB, CMG, served in S Africa 1900-02 and during European War 1914-18 (despatches twice).

GUNSTON (UK) 1938, of Wickwar, co Gloucester

Sir JOHN WELLESLEY GUNSTON, 3rd *Baronet*; *b* 25 July 1962; *s* his father, *Sir* RICHARD WELLESLEY, 1991; *ed* Harrow, and RMA Sandhurst: *m* 1990 (*m diss* 1998), Rosalind Gordon, yst da of Edward Gordon Eliott, of Bower's Mill House, nr Guildford, Surrey, and has issue.

Arms – Not exemplified at time of going to press.

SON LIVING

RICHARD ST GEORGE, *b* 3 July 1992.

HALF-SISTER LIVING (*daughter of 2nd baronet and 1st wife, Elizabeth Mary, eldest da of Sir Arthur Colegate, MP*)

Caroline Jane, *b* 1950: *m* 1971, Jonathan Robert Felton Peel, and has issue living, Edmund Robert Felton, *b* 1979, — Victoria Mary, *b* 1972, — Lucy Caroline, *b* 1975. *Residence* – 12 Mallinson Rd, SW11 1BP.

MOTHER LIVING

JOAN ELIZABETH MARIE, only da of late Reginald Forde, of Inanda, Johannesburg, S Africa, and formerly wife of H. B. Coldicott: *m* 1959 (*m diss* 19—), as his 2nd wife, Sir Richard Wellesley Gunston, 2nd Bt, who *d* 1991. *Residence* – 15 Riverside Mews, off Fagan St, Somerset West 7130, Cape Province, S Africa.

WIDOW LIVING OF SECOND BARONET

VERONICA ELIZABETH (*Veronica, Lady Gunston*), da of Maj — Haynes, and widow of Capt Vivian Graham Loyd: *m* 1976, as his 3rd wife, Sir Richard Wellesley Gunston, 2nd Bt, who *d* 1991. *Residence* – The Arboretum, Tidebrook, Wadhurst, E Sussex TN5 6NY.

The 1st baronet, Sir Derrick Wellesley Gunston, MC, yr son of Maj Bernard Hamilton Gunston (*see* D Wellington, colls, 1953 Edn), was MP for Thornbury Div of Glos 1924-45, served as Parliamentary Priv Sec to Min of Health 1926-29, to Chancellor of the Exchequer 1931-36, and to Jt Under-Sec of State for War 1940-42, and was a Member of Parliamentary Mission to Newfoundland 1943.

GUNTER 1901, of Wetherby Grange, Collingham, West Riding of Yorkshire (Extinct 1980)

Lt-Cdr *Sir* RONALD VERNON GUNTER, RNVR, 3rd and last *Baronet*; *d* 1980.

DAUGHTERS LIVING OF THIRD BARONET

(By 1st *m*) Hazel Ursula Anne, *b* 1927: *m* 1948, Kjell Christian Andresen, and has issue living, Peter Christian Gunter, *b* 1952, — Hazel Anne Christine Gunter, *b* 1955. *Residence* – Endsleigh, Crossway, Walton-on-Thames, Surrey. —— Jane Hilda Clara, *b* 1929: *m* 1950, Harry Ian Lee-Duncan and has had issue, Linda-Jane Victoria Gunter (8 Willow Walk, Cambridge CB1 1LA), *b* 1952, — Diana Charlotte Gunter, *b* 1954; *d* 1988, — Alexandra Karen Gunter, *b* 1959. *Residence* – Byways, Shells Lane, Colyford, Devon EX24 6QE.

GUTHRIE (UK) 1936, of Brent Eleigh Hall, co Suffolk

Sir MALCOLM CONNOP GUTHRIE, 3rd *Baronet*; *b* 16 Dec 1942; *s* his father, *Sir* GILES CONNOP MCEACHARN, OBE, DSC, 1979; *ed* Millfield: *m* 1967, Victoria, da of late Douglas Willcock, and has issue.

Arms – Per chevron argent and azure, in chief two eagles displayed of the second, and in base a lymphad with oars and sails furled of the first, pennons flying gules. **Crest** – A cubit arm in armour proper, charged with two crosses patée fitchée in pale azure, holding in the hand proper a grenade sable, fired also proper.
Residence – Brent Eleigh, Belbroughton, Stourbridge, Worcs DY9 0DW.

SON LIVING

GILES MALCOLM WELCOME, *b* 16 Oct 1972; *ed* Shrewsbury.

DAUGHTER LIVING

Islay Mary Welcome, *b* 1968.

AUNT LIVING (*Daughter of 1st baronet*)

Diana Mary, *b* 1919.

WIDOW LIVING OF SECOND BARONET

RHONA (*Rhona, Lady Guthrie*) (Les Vaux, Rozel, St Martin, Jersey JE3 6AJ), only da of late Frederic Stileman of Bombay: *m* 1939, Sir Giles Connop McEacharn Guthrie, OBE, DSC, 2nd Bt, who *d* 1979.

COLLATERAL BRANCH LIVING

Issue of late Alastair Peter Guthrie, 3rd but yst surv son of 2nd Bt, *b* 1944, *d* 1986: *m* 1966, Elizabeth (Stanley Mill, Chippenham, Wilts), yr da of late Valentin Schaposchnikoff:—
Alexander Valentine Connop, *b* 1966. —— Barnaby Giles, *b* 1969.

The 1st Baronet, Sir Connop Thirlwall Robert Guthrie, KBE, was a financier and a director of public companies. In 1914-18 War he was Capt Grenadier Guards (wounded), a Special Representative in USA of Min of Shipping 1916-19, and a Member of USA Govt Shipping Control Cttee 1918-19. In 1939-45 he was Head of Security Div of British Security Co-ordination in W Hemisphere 1941-5, and an Hon Air Commodore Auxiliary Air Force. The 2nd baronet, Sir Giles Connop McEacharn Guthrie, OBE, DSC, served in 1939-45 War in Fleet Air Arm as fighter and test pilot (Lt-Cdr RNVR 1943); Man Dir of Brown Shipley & Co Ltd, Dir of Prudential Assurance Co Ltd, Chm and Ch Exec of BOAC, Dir of BEA and Chm of Air Transport Insurance Ltd.

Gwynne-Evans, see Evans.

Hagart-Alexander, see Alexander.

Haggerston, see Constable-Maxwell-Scott, Bt (cr 1642).

HALL (NS) 1687, of Dunglass, Haddingtonshire

Sir DOUGLAS BASIL HALL, KCMG, 14th *Baronet*; *b* 1 Feb 1909; *s* his brother, Sir NEVILLE REYNOLDS, 1978; *ed* Radley, and Keble Coll, Oxford (MA); JP of Devon, and a Member of Police Authority for Devon and Cornwall 1971-79; entered Overseas Civil Ser as a Cadet, N Rhodesia 1930; Dist Officer 1932-50, Sen Dist Officer 1950-53, Provincial Commr 1953, Admin Sec 1955-56, Sec for Native Affairs 1956, and Gov and C-in-C of Somaliland Protectorate 1959-60; CMG 1958, KCMG 1959: *m* 1933, Rachel Marion, who *d* 1990, da of late Maj Ernest Gartside-Tippinge, RA, and has issue.

Arms – Azure, a chevron argent between three cranes' heads erased at the necks or, and on an inescutcheon or charged of a lion rampant gules within a double tressure flory counterflory of the last. Crest – A stork sitting on a mount in a watching posture proper.
Residence – Barnford, Ringmore, nr Kingsbridge, Devon TQ7 4HL.

SON LIVING

JOHN DOUGLAS HOSTE (Brook Mill, Buckfastleigh, S Devon TQ11 0HL), *b* 7 Jan 1945; *ed* Dover Coll, Gonville and Caius Coll, Camb (BA), and Southampton Univ (Cert Ed); Vice Principal (Academic) Dartington Coll of Art: *m* 1972, Angela Margaret, da of George Keys, of 2 Barnsfield Lane, Buckfastleigh, S Devon, and has issue living, Thomas James, *b* 10 Dec 1975, — Bernard Neville, *b* 1979.

DAUGHTERS LIVING

Marion, *b* 1940; *ed* Trin Coll, Dublin (MA): *m* 1965, John Francis Fuller-Sessions, MA, of Orchard Farm, Parwich, nr Ashbourne, Derbys DE6 1QB, and has issue living, Nicholas Francis Blair, *b* 1974, — Sara, *b* 1969. —— Ruth, *b* 1942: *m* 1963, Anthony Bernard Cragg (PO Box 1274, Umhlanga Rocks, Natal, S Africa 4320), and has issue living, Stephen Browning, *b* 1966: *m* 1998, Jenny-Lynn Frazer, — Christopher Douglas, *b* 1968, — Timothy Hugh, *b* 1970: *m* 1996, Philipa Ann Thompson, — Ann Louise, *b* 1965: *m* 1992, Christopher Charles Peter Latham, and has issue living, Alfred Michael, *b* 1992, — Joseph Anthony, *b* 1996, — Oliver Douglas, *b* 1998, — Emily Rachel, *b* 1993.

DAUGHTERS LIVING OF TWELFTH BARONET

Mary Jane Rosamond, *b* 1922; 1939-45 as 3rd Officer WRNS: *m* 1946, Mark Peter Whitlock, of 3 Ramm's Court, Wells-next-the-Sea, Norfolk NR23 1JN, and has issue living, John Mark, *b* 1955, — Paul Mark, *b* 1957, — Martin Mark, *b* 1959, — Mary Louise, *b* 1947, — Jane Frances Mary, *b* 1949. —— Elizabeth Katharine Marion, *b* 1925; *ed* Edinburgh Univ (BSc); MRCVS: *m* 1949, Oliphant Fairburn Jackson, PhD, MRCVS, who *d* 1991, of Little Stagenhoe, Horningtoft, Dereham, Norfolk NR20 5ED, and has issue living, James Ellis, *b* 1959; MRCP FRCR: *m* 1989, Mary Elizabeth Roddie, MRCP FRCP, and has issue living, Jonathan Ian Fairburn *b* 1992, Thomas Anthony Douglas *b* 1993, Alastair Kenneth Wilson *b* 1998, — Anthony Oliphant, *b* 1961; MB BS DA (UK): *m* 1995, Wendy Etherton, and has issue living, Rebecca Joy *b* 1996, — Rosemary Frances, *b* 1955: *m* 1980, Nicholas John Wintle, and has issue living, Timothy James *b* 1985. —— Teresa Madeleine, *b* 1930: *m* 1952, Herbert Norman Constantine, of Laskill, Hawnby, York, and has issue living, Robert Francis, *b* 1953, — Nigel Loudon, *b* 1954, — Neville Egerton, *b* 1959: *m* 1990, Karen, only da of Mrs J. Tushingham, of Bamber Bridge, Lancs, — Serena Mary, *b* 1963: *m* 19—, Stephen M. Rainbow, 2nd son of W/Cdr E. Rainbow, of Thorp Arch, Yorks, and has issue living, Emily Laura Francesca *b* 1992, Jessica Louise Sorrell *b* 1994, Harriet Jayne Kezia *b* 1997.

WIDOW LIVING OF THIRTEENTH BARONET

DOROTHY MAUD (*Dorothy, Lady Hall*) (Ash Cottage, Ash, Dartmouth, S Devon), da of late William Lawrence Jones: *m* 1957, Sir Neville Reynolds Hall, 13th baronet, who *d* 1978.

Sir James Hall, 4th baronet, MP for St Michael's, was President of the Royal Society of Edinburgh. Sir Martin Julian Hall, OBE, 10th baronet, was Director of Food Section, Min of Munitions during 1914-19 War, and Ch Reconstruction Officer for Scotland, Min of Labour.

HALL (UK) 1919, of Burton Park, Sussex

Sir JOHN BERNARD HALL, 3rd *Baronet*; *b* 20 March 1932; *s* his father, *Lieut-Col Sir* DOUGLAS MONTGOMERY BERNARD, DSO, 1962; *ed* Eton, and Trin Coll, Oxford (MA); Lt R Fus (RARO); Lord of Manor of Burton; formerly Chm The Nikko Bank (UK) plc; Liveryman and Member of Court of Assistants, Clothworkers' Co (Prime Assistant 1998-99); Memb St Alban's Diocesan Synod and Diocesan Finance Board: *m* 1st, 1957, Delia Mary, who *d* 1997, da of late Lt-Col James Archibald Innes, DSO (*see* V Downe, colls, 1985 Edn); 2ndly, 1998, Mrs Diana (Danzie) Ravenshear, da of late Surg-Cmdr E. R. Sorley, and of Mrs John Dove, of Levington, Suffolk, and widow of Peter A. Ravenshear, and has issue by 1st *m*.

Arms – Vert, on a fesse or, between in chief a cross-crosslet fitchée between two talbots' heads erased argent collared and ringed gules, and in base a like talbot's head, three escallops sable. **Crest** – A talbot's head erased sable, ears argent, gorged with a chaplet or, garnished with roses gules, between two cross-crosslets fitchée or.
Residences – Penrose House, Patmore Heath, Albury, Ware, Herts SG11 2LT; Inver House, Lochinver, Lairg, Sutherland IV27 4LJ.

In Deo Fides

Trust in God

SON LIVING (*By 1st marriage*)

DAVID BERNARD *b* 12 May 1961; *ed* Eton, and York Univ. *Residence* – Long Crumples, Alton, Hants GU34 4DP.

DAUGHTERS LIVING (*By 1st marriage*)

Caroline Evelyn, *b* 1959; *ed* Cobham Hall, and Durham Univ: *m* 1995, Martin F. Dixon-Ward, only son of Frank Dixon-Ward, CBE, of Beckenham, Kent, and has issue living, a son, *b* 19—, — a da, *b* 19—. —— Julia Nancy, *b* 1965; *ed* Cobham Hall, and Edinburgh Univ.

The 1st baronet, Sir Douglas Bernard Hall (son of late Bernard Hall, JP, first Mayor of City of Liverpool, of Villa Mariposa, Cannes, France), sat as MP for Isle of Wight (*C*) Jan 1910 to Oct 1922 and was High Sheriff of Sussex 1907.

HALL (UK) 1923, of Grafham, co Surrey

Sir (FREDERICK) JOHN (FRANK) HALL, 3rd *Baronet*; *b* 14 Aug 1931; *s* his father, *Sir* FREDERICK HENRY, 1949; *ed* Bryanston; Partner, KPMG Peat Marwick 1987-93; Dir Thomson McLintock Associates 1976-87; founded KPMG Career Consultancy Services 1983, ret 1993; Sr Manager McLintock Mann & Whinney Murray 1969-76, The Nestlé Co Ltd 1965-69; Group Personnel Manager Findus Ltd 1967-69; Nestlé UK Head Office Training and Development Manager 1965-67; Personnel Manager Johnson Wax Ltd 1963-65, Personnel Officer The Nestlé Co Ltd 1959-63, Personnel Manager Universal Pattern & Precision Engrg Co Ltd 1955-59; Dir Roffey Park Institute 1978-90 (Chm 1985-87, Vice-Chm 1983-85): *m* 1st, 1956 (*m diss* 1960), Felicity Anne, da of late Edward Rivers-Fletcher, of Norwich; 2ndly, 1961 (*m diss* 1967), Patricia Ann, da of late Douglas Atkinson, of Greystead, Longlands Rd, Carlisle; 3rdly, 1967, re-married his 1st wife, Felicity Anne (ante), and has issue by 2nd and 3rd *m*.

Arms – Sable, a cross moline between in the first and fourth quarters a talbot's head erased and in the second and third a chaplet of oak or. **Crest** – A demi-griffin sable holding between the claws a portcullis or.
Residence – Carradale, 29 Embercourt Rd, Thames Ditton, Surrey, KT7 0LH.

DAUGHTERS LIVING (*By 2nd marriage*)

Nicola Jane, *b* 1962: *m* 1998, Michael Ian Gale, yr son of late Ian George Gale, of Surrey, and has issue living, Francesca Lucy, *b* 1999. —— Samantha Mary, *b* 1965.

(By 3rd marriage)

Antonia Anne, *b* 1970: *m* 1998, Philippe Robert Calame, elder son of Henri Calame, of Geneva, Switzerland. —— Victoria Joy, *b* 1973.

BROTHER LIVING

DAVID CHRISTOPHER, *b* 30 Dec 1937: *m* 1st, 1962 (*m diss* 1987), Irene, da of William Duncan, of 2 Tollohill Pl, Kincorth, Aberdeen; 2ndly, 19—, Annie Madelaine Renée Olivier, adopted da of late Bottemanne Raould, of Thieusies-Lez Soignies (Mons), Belgium, and has issue living (by 1st *m*), John Christopher, *b* 22 May 1965, — Olwen Evelyn, *b* 1967. *Residence* – 22 Buckstone Row, Edinburgh EH10 6TP.

SISTER LIVING

Olwen Mary Primrose, *b* 1928: *m* 1st, 1958 (*m diss* 1977), Carlyle Herbert Peter Gardner (*see* B Blyth, 1944 Edn), who *d* 1992; 2ndly, 1977, James Alexander Macrae, and has issue living (by 1st *m*), Alan Frederick Peter (PO Box 95044, 546 Swanson Rd, Swanson, Auckland 8, NZ), *b* 1952: *m* 1st, 1972 (*m diss* 1993), Pamela Susan Wheal; 2ndly, 1994, Christine Penelope Metcalf, and has issue living (by 1st *m*), Geoffrey Alan Peter *b* 1973, Nicola Susan *b* 1975, — Marcus Hillier Clive, *b* 1958, — Crispin John Stuart Hyde, *b* 1961, — Jonathan Carlyle Heiko, *b* 1963, — Jason Peter Alan, *b* 1965, — Matthew Reginald Saul, *b* 1968, — Merrily Mary Susan, *b* 1955: *m* 1986, Anthony Willis, — Josephine Juliet, *b* 1956: *m* 1978 (*m diss* 1993), Jonathan Peter Matich, — Susannah Mary Ann, *b* 1962. *Residence* – 3 Nandina Place, Kaiapoi, N Canterbury, NZ.

The 1st baronet, Sir Frederick Hall, KBE, DSO, Chm and Managing Director of Mercantile Marine Finance Corporation Ltd, and a Member of Lloyd's and the Baltic Exchange, sat as MP for Dulwich Div of Camberwell (C) 1910-32.

HALSEY (UK) 1920, of Gaddesden, co Hertford

The spoken word cannot be recalled

Rev Sir JOHN WALTER BROOKE HALSEY (*Rev Brother John Halsey*), 4th *Baronet*; *b* 26 Dec 1933; *s* his father, *Capt Sir* THOMAS EDGAR, DSO, RN, 1970; *ed* Eton and Magdalene Coll, Camb (BA).

𝕬rms – Argent, on a pile sable three griffins' heads erased of the field. 𝕮rest – A dexter cubit arm proper, habited gules, the cuff argent, holding a griffin's claw erased or.
Residence – The Fraternity, 23 Manse Rd, Roslin, Midlothian EH25 9LF.

SISTER LIVING

Margaret Anne, *b* 1938: *m* 1961, John Farnon, of Old Bell House, Market Lavington, Devizes, and has issue living, Jennifer Anne, *b* 1962, — Nicola Jane, *b* 1964, — Alison Sarah, *b* 1966.

AUNTS LIVING (*Daughters of 2nd baronet*)

Agatha: *m* 1942 (*m diss* 1976) Alan Edmondson Bainbridge, and has issue living, Thomas Howard, *b* 1943: *m* 1977, Isabel Frances Collins, — Andrew Halsey, *b* 1944: *m* 1973, Helen Brown, and has issue living, Alexander James *b* 19—, Elizabeth Anne *b* 19—, — David James Macalpine, *b* 1950: *m* 1974, Judith Roslyn Manley, and has issue living, Fiona *b* 1979, Megan *b* 19—, — Patricia Mary, *b* 1946: *m* 1976, John Bruce McBride, — Jean Vivien, *b* 1955. —— Evelyn Cecilia: *m* 1944, Brig Frederick Manus De Butts, CMG, OBE, DL, late SCLI, of Church Cottage, Hoggeston, Buckingham, and has issue living, David Frederick, *b* 1950: *m* 1977, Barbara Elizabeth Scott Hooper, and has issue living, Richard Frederick *b* 1978, Michael McCrea *b* 1980, Lucy Katherine *b* 1983, — Caroline Mary, *b* 1952: *m* 1974, Anthony Hugh Bond, and has issue living, Jonathan James Hugh *b* 1977, Rupert Charles *b* 1980, Victoria Jane *b* 1984.

COLLATERAL BRANCHES LIVING

Issue of late Lt-Cdr William Edmund Halsey, RN, yr son of 2nd baronet, *b* 1903, *d* 1986: *m* 1931, Barbara Dorothea, who *d* 1993, da of late Charles Lindsay Orr Ewing, MP (*see* Orr Ewing, Bt, colls):—
Bridget, *b* 1934: *m* 1958, Edward Alfred Heycock of Sunnyside, Moniaive, Thornhill, Dumfriesshire DG3 4HR, elder surv son of Morris Sadler Heycock, MC, and has issue living, Susan Mary, *b* 1959: *m* 1990, William Kennedy McConnel (*see* Montagu-Pollock, Bt, colls), — Caroline Bridget, *b* 1961, — Jennifer Lucy, *b* 1966.

Grandsons of late Rev Canon Frederick Halsey (*infra*):—
Issue of late Lt-Col Guy Marsden Halsey, TD, JP, *b* 1908, *d* 1990: *m* 1939, Juliet Mary Gough (Whitehouse Farm, Gaddesden Row, Hemel Hempstead, Herts HP2 6HG), da of late Capt Robert Wemyss Muir Arbuthnot, MC (*see* Arbuthnot, Bt, colls):—

NICHOLAS GUY, TD (The Golden Parsonage, Gaddesden Row, Hemel Hempstead, Herts HP2 6HG; *Club* – Brooks's), *b* 14 June 1948; *ed* Eton, and RAC Cirencester; Maj RGJ(V); High Sheriff Herts 1995, DL 1998; FRICS: *m* 1976, Viola Georgina Juliet, da of Maj George Thorne, MC, DL, ERD (*see* B Peel), of Blounts Farm, Sonning Common, Reading, Berks, and has issue living, Guy Francis Johnston, *b* 1981. —— Robert Frederick, *b* 1950; *ed* Eton, and RAC Cirencester; FCA: *m* 1976, Elizabeth Virginia, da of John Holman, and has issue living, Daniel John, *b* 1978, — Samuel Treve, *b* 1983.

Issue of late Rev Canon Frederick Halsey, 3rd son of 1st baronet, *b* 1870, *d* 1952: *m* 1901, Audrey Katharine, who *d* 1969, da of late Lt-Col William Marsden, of Cedar Court, Farnham:—
Katharine Audrey (7 Chestnut Close, Potten End, Berkhamsted, Herts). —— Barbara (Old House Cottage, Combe, Oxon): *m* 1961, John Parr Curgenven, who *d* 1982, el son of late Sir Arthur Joseph Curgenven.

Issue of late Adm Sir Lionel Halsey, GCMG, GCVO, KCIE, CB, 4th son of 1st baronet, *b* 1872, *d* 1949: *m* 1905, Morwenna, who *d* 1959, da of Major Bevil Granville, of Wellesbourne Hall, Warwick:—
Joan, *b* 1910; is a JP for Herts: *m* 1933, George Lockhart Wood, who *d* 1959, and has issue living, John Lockhart (The Hoo, Gt Gaddesden, Hemel Hempstead), *b* 1935: *m* 1963, Rosemary Sonia Despard, da of Richard Graham Hensley Hopkins, and has issue living, George Edmund Richard, *b* 1966: *m* 1993, Caroline T., yr da of Rev Canon Anthony Johnson, of Semley, Wilts, Kirstin Rebecca *b* 1968, — Lionel David (Manor Farm, Milcombe, Banbury, Oxon), *b* 1938; Lt-Col Welsh Gds (ret); Extra Equerry to HRH the Duke of Edinburgh 1965-67: *m* 1960, Belinda Mary, da of late Gilbert Graham Balfour (*see* Halsey, Bt, 1990 Edn), and has issue living, James Lionel Norman *b* 1963, Sarah Morwenna *b* 1961, Alexandra Louise *b* 1965, — Richard George (Markham House, Badminton, Avon), *b* 1939: *m* 1963, Penelope Gay, da of Lt-Col John Bertie Harris Daniel, MBE, MC, and has issue living, Andrew John *b* 1966: *m* 1991, Rachel Claire Morris (and has issue living, Angus Richard *b* 1993, Elinor Claire *b* 1991), Emma Ruth *b* 1965, — Edmund Michael (The Old Rectory, Holwell, Hitchin, Herts), *b* 1943: *m* 1971, Elizabeth Anne, da of Sqd-Ldr Robert Roland Patrick Fisher, RAF (ret) and has issue living, Sarah Georgina *b* 1974, Ann Louise *b* 1977, — Ruth Mary, *b* 1945: *m* 1973, James Henry Wood Ritchie, of Drissaig House, Lochavich, by Taynuilt, Argyll, and has issue living, Fiona Mary *b* 1975, Margaret Jean *b* 1976. *Residence* – The Old Schoolhouse, Whipsnade, Dunstable, Beds. —— Ruth, *b* 1915. *Residence* – Parsonage Piece, Whipsnade, Dunstable, Beds.

This family is descended from John Halsey of Great Gaddesden, Herts, who was living 1512. The 1st Baronet Rt Hon Sir (Thomas) Frederick Halsey (son of Thomas Plumer Halsey, MP) sat as MP for Herts (*C*) 1874-85, and for W Herts 1885-1906 and *d* 1927.

HAMBLING (UK) 1924, of Yoxford, co Suffolk

Discern and decide

Sir (HERBERT) HUGH HAMBLING, 3rd *Baronet*, *b* 3 Aug 1919; *s* his father, *Sir* (HERBERT) GUY (MUSGRAVE), 1966; *ed* Eton; late Flt-Lt RAF; formerly in BOAC, Montreal; 1939-45 War: *m* 1st, 1950, Anne Page, who *d* 1990, da of late Judge Hugo Edmund Oswald, of Seattle, USA; 2ndly, 1991, Helen Seymour, elder da of Donald Mackinnon, of Marida Yallock, Victoria, Australia, and widow of David Maitland Gavin, of Clabon Mews, SW3, and has issue by 1st *m*.

𝕬rms – Argent, a sword erect sable between two flaunches azure, each charged with a hank of cotton of the field. 𝕮rest – A falcon supporting with the dexter claw a distaff proper, and charged on the body with a bezant.
Seat = Rookery Park, Yoxford, Suffolk. *Address* – 1219 Evergreen Point Rd, Medina, Washington 98039, USA.

SON LIVING (*By 1st marriage*)

(HERBERT) PETER HUGH, *b* 6 Sept 1953; *ed* Univ of Washington (BSc); Co-founder and Ch Operating Officer Digital Control (Inc), WA: *m* 1st, 1982 (*m diss* 1989), Jan Elizabeth, da of Stanton Frederick, Jr, of Seattle, Washington; 2ndly, 1991, Lorayn Louise, da of Frank Joseph Koson, and has issue living (by 2nd *m*), Colin Hugh, *b* 1991, — Austin Peter, *b* 1993, — Mitchell Peter, *b* 1998. *Residence* – 2108 92nd Avenue NE, Bellevue, WA 98004, USA.

SISTER LIVING

Margherita, *b* 1912: *m* 1937, Fl-Lt Maurice Hare, who *d* 1993, yst son of Maj-Gen Sir Steuart Welwood Hare, KCMG, CB, and has issue living, David Steuart (23 Vale Rd, Claygate, Esher, Surrey), *b* 1942: *m* 1st, 1969 (*m diss* 1983), Julie, da of Walter Pierre Courtauld; 2ndly, 1986, Pippa, only da of R.I. McDonald, and has issue living (by 1st *m*), Lucas Welwood Bruno *b* 1971, Samuel James *b* 1974, Fergus Lincoln *b* 1977, (by 2nd *m*) Poppy Helen *b* 1988. — Robin Gordon (Fordley Hall, Middleton, Saxmundham, Suffolk), *b* 1944: *m* 1st, 1973 (*m diss* 1987), Caroline Mary, da of Edward Felix Mason, and formerly wife of William Oscar Watson; 2ndly, 1989, Margaret Julia, da of Leo William Ritchie, and previously wife of (i) Mark Leigh Scorer, and (ii) John Stewart Bassett, and has issue living (by 1st *m*), Reuben Edward Hare *b* 1975, Rachel Veronica *b* 1978, — Philippa, *b* 1938: *m* 1st, 1959 (*m diss* 1965), Timothy Peckover Burrill; 2ndly, 1967, Simon Pierre Courtauld, of The Close, Pewsey, Wilts SN9 5DB, and has issue living (by 1st *m*), Rebecca Nina *b* 1961, (by 2nd *m*) Kim Guy Augustine *b* 1973, Leila Alice *b* 1975. *Residence* – The Cottage, Rookery Park, Yoxford, Suffolk.

The 1st baronet, Sir (Henry) Herbert Hambling, son of Lt-Col William James Hambling, JP, of Dunstable, Bedford, was Dep Chm of Barclays Bank (Limited), of Barclays Bank (France) (Limited), Barclays Bank (Dominion, Colonial and Overseas), and of Barclays Bank SAI, first Gov Director of Imperial Airways Ltd, 1924-30 (formed as a result of report presented by Hambling Committee of which he was Chm), and a Director of North British and Mercantile Insurance Co, and of Ocean Marine Insurance Co (Limited); Financial Member of Min of Munitions during European War 1914-19 (Knt): *m* 1st, 1882, Thirza, who *d* 1891, da of William George Twigg, solicitor, of Dublin; 2ndly, 1893, Isabella Mary, who *d* 1916, da of Frederick Brown, of Clapham; *d* 1932.

HAMILTON (NS) 1646, of Silvertonhill, Lanarkshire

Sir (ROBERT CHARLES) RICHARD CARADOC HAMILTON, 9th *Baronet*; *b* 8 Sept 1911; *s* his father, *Major Sir* ROBERT CARADOC, 1959; *ed* Charterhouse, and St Peter's Coll, Oxford: *m* 1952, Elizabeth Vidal, da of late Sir William Pell Barton, KCIE, CSI, and has issue.

Arms – Gules, a gillie flower stemmed and leaved proper between three cinquefoils ermine, all within a bordure or. Crest – A horse's head and neck couped argent, maned or.
Residence – The Old Rectory, Walton, Warwick CV35 9HX.

SON LIVING

ANDREW CARADOC, *b* 23 Sept 1953; *ed* Charterhouse, and St Peter's Coll, Oxford (MA): *m* 1984, Anthea Jane, da of late Frank Huntingford, of Hindhead, Surrey, and has issue living, Alice, *b* 1986, — Harriet, *b* 1989, — Imogen Rose, *b* 1993.

DAUGHTERS LIVING

Susanna Eve, *b* 1956: *m* 1990, Richard Andrew Freeman, yr son of late Harold Freeman, of Piddinghoe, E Sussex, and has issue living, Frederick Archie Hamilton, *b* 1997, — Gabriella Eve Hamilton, *b* 1993. ———— Sophia Louisa, *b* 1964. ———— Penelope Katherine, *b* 1966: *m* 1989, Trevor Wells, son of William Wells, of Brighton, and has issue living, Jack Oliver, *b* 1999, — Anna Elizabeth, *b* 1996.

COLLATERAL BRANCHES LIVING

Grandsons of late Frank Hamilton (infra):—
Issue of late Ian Frank Howden Hamilton, *b* 1916, *d* 1982: *m* 1950, Zelma, who *d* 1997, da of Laurence Theodore Snyman, of Ermelo, S Africa:—
Paul Howden (The Red House, 24 New St, St Dunstan's, Canterbury, Kent CT2 8AU), *b* 1951: *m* 1980, Elizabeth Anne Harrison, and has issue living, Alexandra Isabel, *b* 1983, — Annabelle Kate, *b* 1985. ———— Mark Howden (PO Box 1130, Sun Valley 7975, Cape Town, S Africa), *b* 1955: *m* 1983, Sally Anne Macklin, and has issue living, Guy Howden, *b* 1991. ———— Warwick Howden (PO Box 412136, Craighall, Gauteng 2024, S Africa), *b* 1959: *m* 1990, Jacqueline, da of Frederick Arthur Smith, of Lyon House, Lynsted, Kent.

Issue of late Frank Hamilton, 2nd son of 7th baronet, *b* 1878, *d* 1934: *m* 1913, Mary Elizabeth, who *d* 1961, da of late John Williams Batterham, MB, FRCS, of St Leonards-on-Sea:—
Joan Mary Hamilton, *b* 1915: *m* 1941, Stanley Abbott Silson, and has issue living, Ian Frank, *b* 1943: *m* 1976 (*m diss* 19—), Barbara Thompson, — Raymond Robert Hamilton, *b* 1946, — Simon Hatchard, *b* 1957: *m* 1982, Sophia Stallbom, — Mary Elizabeth Joy, *b* 1952: *m* 1983, David Anthony Rocke, FRCP (UK), FFA (SA), of 12 Pearson Rd, Everton 3610, Natal, S Africa. *Residence* – 15 Fairydene Village, 18 Stapleton Rd, Sarnia 3610, S Africa.

Granddaughter of late Frederic Howden Faulconer Hamilton (infra):—
Issue of late Howden McMinn Hamilton, *b* 1900, *d* 1988: *m* 1935, Patricia Campbell, who *d* 19—, only child of Matthew Currie, of Ayr:—
Gloria Constance Barbara, *b* 1937: *m* 1956, Edward Watson, and has issue living, Andrew Charles Howden (Keathbank Cottage, Balmoral Rd, Blairgowrie, Perthshire), *b* 1958: *m* 1990, Susan Jean, da of Peter Findlay, of W Yorks. *Residence* – Frog Cottage, 69 Perth St, Blairgowrie, Perthshire.

Grandsons of late Howden Anson Philip Hamilton, el son of Capt Frederick William Hamilton, 3rd son of 5th baronet:—
Issue of late Frederic Howden Faulconer Hamilton, *b* 1877, *d* 1959: *m* 1st, 1899, Jessie Jean, who *d* 1929, elder da of late W. McMinn; 2ndly, 1930, Beatrice Agnes, who *d* 1955, only da of late Samuel Banfield of Exeter:—
(By 1st *m*) Frederic William Seymour (42995 Adams Rd, RR1 Sardis, BC VOX 170, Canada) *b* 1906: *m* 1930, Florence Maud, who *d* 1982, da of George John Saby, of Cambridgeshire, and has issue living, Kathleen Anita, *b* 1931, — Barbara Joanne, *b* 1933: *m* 1955, Oscar Mitchell Taylor, of Delta, BC, Canada, and has issue living, Keith Donald *b* 1958: *m* 1979, Penny Dawn Millar (and has issue living, Allan Keith *b* 1981, Carl Brian *b* 1984, Stephanie Anne Mary *b* 1987), Colleen Susan *b* 1956: *m* 1978, Vincent James Lee, of Perth, Australia (and has issue living, Dennis James *b* 1981, Vanessa Joanne *b* 1983, Deborah Janette *b* 1987).

Issue of late Capt Henry Rudston STUART-HAMILTON, Gordon Highlanders (who assumed by deed poll 1920, the additional surname of Stuart), *b* 1883, *d* 1962: *m* 1920, Mabel Mary, who *d* 1968, el da of late Rev Edmund Milnes Ellerbeck:—
Donald Maclaren (The Shooting Greens, Potarch, Banchory AB31 4BL), *b* 1926; *ed* Harrow, and King's Coll, Camb (MA); Capt The Black Watch (TA); MIMSM: *m* 1956, Jill, MSAOT, yr da of late Lt-Col David Guy Porteous, OBE, JP, of

St Cyrus, Angus, and has issue living, Clova Claire Ducarol, *b* 1959: *m* 1988, Michael Andrew Stinton, of 92 Walton St, Oxford OX2 6EB, — Alison Fenella, *b* 1967.

           Granddaughter of late Lieut-Col Henry Charles Hamilton, son of late Henry Charles Hamilton, CSI, 4th son of 5th baronet:—
           Issue of late Charles Norman Maclean Hamilton, *b* 1885, *d* 1957: *m* 1926, Molly Eileen, who *d* 1986, da of late D. Crowe, MB, of Melfield, Blackrock, co Dublin:—
Anne Maclean, *b* 1927. *Residence* – 24 Oakleigh Court, Station Rd West, Oxted, Surrey RH8 9EY.

    This is the nearest branch of the Ducal House next to the great family of Abercorn, descending from Alexander Hamilton of Silvertonhill, brother of 1st Lord Hamilton. Sir Robert Hamilton, 1st Bt, a steady loyalist, was a favourite of Charles I; his patent of baronetcy was not, however, recorded in the General Register owing to the then confusion and distraction of the country.

HAMILTON, First Creation (GB) 1776, of Marlborough House, Hampshire Second Creation (UK) 1819, of Trebinshun House, Brecknockshire

Virtue is the only nobility

Sola nobilitas virtus

Sir EDWARD SYDNEY HAMILTON, 7th *Baronet* of 1st, and 5th *Baronet* of 2nd creation; *b* 14 April 1925; *s* his father, *Sir* (THOMAS) SYDNEY PERCEVAL, 1966; *ed* Canford; late RE.

Arms – Quarterly: 1st and 4th, gules, three cinquefoils pierced ermine, 2nd and 3rd, argent, a lymphad with her sails furled sable. **Crest** – Out of a ducal coronet or, an oak-tree proper fructed of the first and penetrated transversely in the main stem by a frame-saw proper, the frame also of the first, and the blade inscribed with the word "Through." *Residence* – The Cottage, Fordwater Rd, East Lavant, W Sussex PO18 0AL.

    Capt Sir John Hamilton, RN, 1st Bt of Trebinshun, grandson of William Hamilton (one of the five "Kentish Petitioners" in 1701), brother of 6th Earl of Abercorn, distinguished himself at the Siege of Quebec 1775. Adm Sir Edward Joseph Hamilton, younger son of 1st Bt (*cr* 1776) was *cr* a Bt of Marlborough House, Hants, 1819. Sir Edward Archibald Hamilton, 2nd Bt (*cr* 1819), *s* in 1892 as 4th Bt (*cr* 1776).

HAMILTON (UK) 1937, of Ilford, co Essex (extinct 1992)

Sir PATRICK GEORGE HAMILTON, 2nd and last *Baronet*.

WIDOW LIVING OF SECOND BARONET

WINIFRED MARY (PIX), CBE, MA (*Lady Hamilton*), only da of late Hammond Beaconsfield Jenkins, of Maddings, Had-stock, and formerly wife of Prof John Richard Nicholas Stone, CBE: *m* 1941, Sir Patrick George Hamilton, 2nd Bt, who *d* 1992. *Residence* – 43 Lancaster Close, St Petersburgh Place, W2 4JZ.

Hamilton-Dalrymple, see Dalrymple.

STIRLING-HAMILTON (NS) 1673, of Preston, Haddingtonshire

For my country

Sir MALCOLM WILLIAM BRUCE STIRLING-HAMILTON, 14th *Baronet*; *b* 6 Aug 1979; *s* his father, *Sir* BRUCE, 1989; *ed* Stowe.

Arms – Gules, three cinquefoils within a bordure argent. **Crest** – An armed man from the middle brandishing a sword aloft proper.
Residence – Narborough Hall, Narborough, King's Lynn, Norfolk PE32 1TE.

SISTERS LIVING

Georgina Claire, *b* 1970. ——— Iona Stephanie, *b* 1985.

AUNTS LIVING (*daughters of 12th baronet*)

Joanna Eileen, *b* 1930: *m* 1955, Lt-Col Ian Kroyer MacKinnon of MacKinnon, Queen's Own Highlanders (Seaforth and Camerons). *Residence* – Little Breck House, 4 Trenchard Crescent, Watton, Norfolk IP25 6HR. ——— Eila Mary, *b* 1939: *m* 1st, 1959, Lt Timothy Martin Woodford, RN, who *d* 1966 (*see* Crofton, Bt, *cr* 1801, colls; 1976 Edn); 2ndly, 1967, George Rudolf Wratislaw Walker, MA, and has issue living, (by 1st *m*) Charlotte Amanda, *b* 1960: *m* 1981, Capt Charles Rodney Style, RN (*see* Style, Bt, colls), — Amanda Caroline, *b* 1962, — (by 2nd *m*) Harriet Nicola, *b* 1970: *m* 1993, Julian Pemberton-Pigott, Lieut Royal Logistic Corps, — Emily Mary, *b* 1972: *m* 1996, Xavier Paturel. *Residence* – 16 Town Close, Dartmouth, Devon TQ6 9ES.

WIDOW LIVING OF THIRTEEENTH BARONET

STEPHANIE, el da of late William Campbell, LRCP, LRCS, of Alloway, Ayr: *m* 1st, 1968, Sir Bruce Stirling-Hamilton, 13th Bt, who *d* 1989; 2ndly, 1990, Anthony Cole Tinsley, of Narborough Hall, Narborough, King's Lynn, Norfolk PE32 1TE.

COLLATERAL BRANCHES LIVING

Grandchildren of late William Stirling Hamilton, eldest son of late Hubert Hamilton, 2nd son of 9th baronet:—
     Issue of late Robert William Hamilton, *b* 1905, *d* 1995: *m* 1935, Eileen Hetty, who *d* 1997, eldest da of late Francis Goldworth Lowick:—
Rev ANDREW ROBERT (16 Cranston Close, Reigate, Surrey), *b* 5 Sept 1937; *ed* New Coll, Oxford (MA); FCA: *m* 1972, Josephine Mary, da of Reginald Sargant. ——— William Alexander Hubert (92 Woodwarde Rd, SE22 8UT), *b* 1941; *ed* Trin Coll, Camb (MA): *m* 1966, Cecilia Louise Somerville, da of late Maj Charles Erling Bernard Catt (*see* Somerville, Bt (ext), 1973-74 Edn), and has issue living, Alexander James Erling, *b* 1967; Maj Light Dragoons: *m* 19—, Angelika Ilse, da of Wolfgang Oehrl, of Oldenburg, Germany, — Anna Cecilia Louise, *b* 1969. ——— Thomas, *b* 1952; *ed* Magdalen Coll, Oxford (BA): *m* 1st, 1978, Cornelia, da of Willy Brüllmann, of Zuben, Switzerland; 2ndly, 1991, Sally Lisa, da of late Donald Charles McArthur, and has issue living (by 2nd *m*), Robert Louis, *b* 1993. ——— Penelope Frances, *b* 1936: *m* 1st, 1960 (*m* annulled 1985), Maj Robert Alan Mountcastle Seeger, MC, RM (ret); 2ndly, 1989, Lt-Col Brereton Robert Fairclough, MC, TD, S Lancs Regt (ret), of Garden Cottage, Aldersey Park, Handley, Chester CH3 9ED, and has issue living (by 1st *m*), Frances Clare, *b* 1965: *m* 1994 (*m* annulled 1996), Avard Warren Kaleoaloha Pereira, and has issue living, Kaela Kalawai Penelle *b* 1994, — Katharine Anne, *b* 1966. ——— Katharine Jane Patricia (Haskers, Westleton, Saxmundham, Suffolk IP17 3AP), *b* 1955; *ed* Camberwell Art Coll, and Royal Coll of Art (BA): *m* 1987, Bernard Francis Purcell, and has issue living, George Alexander *b* 1992, Stephanie Jane *b* 1990.

     Grandchildren of late Lt-Col William Gavin Hamilton (infra):—
     Issue of late Capt John William Stirling Hamilton, MC, *b* 1919, *d* 1959: *m* 1945, Kathleen Dorothea, da of John Alexander Thomson, MBE, of Tordarroch, Helensburgh:—
Alastair Colin Stirling (Tillyfourie Farm, Monymusk, Aberdeenshire), *b* 1954: *m* 1979, Miranda Louise, da of Jeffrey Watson Boughey, of Whitehills Farm, Monymusk, and has issue living, Rory Colin Stirling, *b* 1980, — James Alexander, *b* 1982, — Thomas Daniel, *b* 1986. ——— Alison Lesley, *b* 1947: *m* 1970, Nicholas Parsons, of Ballindarroch, Aldourie, Inverness IV1 2DL, and has issue living, Alexander Colin, *b* 1973, — Claudia Katherine, *b* 1974. ——— Daphne Helen, *b* 1950: *m* 1980, Michael Murray, of Kilmahumaig, Crinan, Argyll, and has issue living, William, *b* 19—, — Nina, *b* 19—.

     Grandchildren of late Thomas Hamilton, MD, FRCS, 3rd son of 9th baronet:—
     Issue of late Lieut-Col William Gavin Hamilton, *b* 1874, *d* 1937: *m* 1st, 1908, Louise, who *d* 1914, da of late Alison Cunningham, of Peterborough; 2ndly, 1916, Helen, who *d* 1950, da of late Dugald Stewart Macphee, of Glasgow:—
(By 2nd *m*) Alastair Gavin, DSC (Dunmar, Tighnabroaich, Argyll PA21 2EA), *b* 1922; Lt Cdr RN (ret); 1939-45 War (DSC): *m* 1956, Gillian Bomford, and has had issue, Jock, *b* 1960, — Gail, *b* 1958: *m* 1986, Patrick J. Dempsey, and *d* 1993, leaving issue, Harry John *b* 1991, Katherine Phoebe *b* 1988, — Katharine, *b* 1964: *m* 1989, R. Martin Pender, and has issue living, Patrick Iago *b* 1992. ——— Margaret Audrey, *b* 1918; is 2nd Officer WRNS; 1939-45 War: *m* 1946, Charles Ian Turcan, of Oxey Barn, Woodside, Lymington, Hants, and has issue living, Gavin Charles, *b* 1948, — Alan Ronald Hamilton, *b* 1952: *m* 1985, Gillian Hart, and has issue living, Mathew *b* 1987, Sarah *b* 1989, — Lydia Helen, *b* 1950: *m* 1978, Nicholas Hampton Oldham Clough, of 159 Maldon Rd, Colchester, Essex, and has issue living, Anthony Oldham *b* 1984, David James *b* 1988, Charlotte Emma *b* 1981.

     This family descends from Sir John Hamilton of Fingalton, yr brother of Sir David Hamilton of Cadzow (*dc* 1392) ancestor of Duke of Hamilton. Sir William Hamilton, 1st Bt, was *cr* a Baronet with remainder to his heirs male whatsoever. On the death of Sir Robert, 2nd Bt 1701, the baronetcy passed to his kinsman Sir Robert of Airdrie, 5th in descent from John who was killed at Flodden 1513, yr brother of Robert of Preston, ancestor of 1st Bt, but the baronetcy was not re-assumed until 1834 by Sir William *de jure*, 9th Bt, who had been served heir male to the 2nd Br 1816. He was Prof of Logic and Metaphysics at Edinburgh Univ. Gen Sir William, CB, 10th Bt assumed by deed poll, in

1889, the additional surname of Stirling, his grandmother Elizabeth being a da of William Stirling of Drumpellier, whose son established in 1818 representation of the family of Stirling of Cadder.

HAMMICK (UK) 1834, of Cavendish Square, London

To be praised by one already praised

Sir STEPHEN GEORGE HAMMICK, 5th *Baronet b* 27 Dec 1926; *s* his father, *Sir* GEORGE FREDERICK, 1964; *ed* Stowe, and RAC Cirencester; High Sheriff of Dorset (1981), DL 1989: *m* 1953, Gillian Elizabeth, yr da of late Maj Pierre Elliot Inchbald, MC (*see* Bingham, Bt, 1985 Edn), and has issue.

Arms – Paly of four or and vert, a bordure ermine charged with seven hurts, on a chief azure a lion passant argent. Crest – A demi-lion per pale or and vert holding an escarbuncle gold.
Residence – Badgers, Wraxall, Dorchester, Dorset DT2 0HN.

SONS LIVING

PAUL ST VINCENT (Butterfly Cottage, Lower Wraxall, Dorchester, Dorset), *b* 1 Jan 1955; *ed* Sherborne: *m* 1984, Judith Mary, da of Ralph Ernest Reynolds, of Lorien, Grange Rd, Wareham, Dorset. —— Jeremy Charles, *b* 1956.

DAUGHTER LIVING

Wendy Jane, *b* 1960: *m* 1990, Bob Koster, of Albrecht Thaerlaan 47, 3571EE Utrecht, Holland, son of late Jacob Koster, and has issue living, a son, *b* 1991, — a da, *b* 1992.

COLLATERAL BRANCHES LIVING

Issue of late Rear-Adm Alexander Robert Hammick, brother of 4th baronet *b* 1887, *d* 1969: *m* 1918, Nancy, who *d* 1964, el da of D. Ross-Johnson:—
Anne Felicity (The Old House, Lodsworth, Sussex), *b* 1919.

Issue of late Capt Stephen Frederick Hammick (Oxfordshire and Bucks LI) only son of 3rd baronet, *b* 1871, *d* of wounds received in action 1916: *m* 1906, Muriel Katharine, who *d* 1924, da of Capt Andrew Hamilton Russell, formerly 58th Regt of The Heath House, Petersfield, Hants:—
Penelope Katherine, MB, BS (46 Castle Rd, Salisbury), *b* 1910.

Grandchildren of late Stephen Hammick, 3rd son of 2nd baronet.—
Issue of late Maj St Vincent Frederick Hammick, *b* 1886, *d* 1976: *m* 1919, Annie Caroline Massingberd, who *d* 1978, da of late Aubone Aldrich Pyke, of The Hermitage, Netley Abbey:—
Stephen Aubone, DSC, *b* 1922; Cdr RN; 1939-45 War (DSC, despatches twice): *m* 1943, Mary Elizabeth, da of John Laurence Westmacott (*see* Hamilton-Spencer-Smith, Bt, colls, 1980 Edn), and has issue living, Stephen Timothy John, *b* 1946: *m* 1969, Raymonde, da of Maj Eugene I. J. Carson, of S Africa, and has issue living, Bryone Catherine Annie *b* 1978, — Susan Patricia, *b* 1945: *m* 1973, Henry James Craven Smith, of Tettenhall, Wolverhampton, and has issue living, Henry Stapleton *b* 1975, Jane Rachel Anne *b* 1977. —— Mary Désirée Massingberd, *b* 1930: *m* 1953, Colin Edward Foster, and has issue living, Michael Colin, *b* 1954, — Christopher John, *b* 1956, — Caroline Antonia, *b* 1957. —— Adrianne Elaine Patricia, *b* 1937: *m* 1964, Vincent George Jarvis Ball, and has issue living, Anthony St Vincent, *b* 1965, — Stephen Jarvis, *b* 1967, — David Jonathan, *b* 1971.

Granddaughters of late Maj St Vincent Frederick Hammick (ante):—
Issue of late Lt-Cdr Aubone St Vincent Hammick, RN, *b* 1925, *d* 1992: *m* 1948, Cynthia Florence Katharine, da of William George Shiell (*see* B Airedale, 1972-73 Edn):—
Marion, *b* 1949: *m* 1967, Ian Donald Pickett, FCII, and has issue living, Melissa Juliette, *b* 1967, — Eleanor Theresa, *b* (twin) 1967. —— Imogen Katherine, *b* 1952: *m* 1st, 1972, John Blandford; 2ndly, 1977, David Megginson, and has issue living (by 2nd *m*), Edward *b* 1985, Katherine Rose *b* 1980. —— Miranda Jane, *b* 1958; BA; has issue living (by Jonathan Parkinson), Martha Louise *b* 1993.

Grandchildren of late Sir Murray Hammick, KCSI, CIE, 7th son of 2nd baronet:—
Issue of late Maj Henry Alexander Hammick, OBE, MC, *b* 1890, *d* 1968: *m* 1919, Mabel Emily (May), who *d* 1990, da of Sir Philip Edward Pilditch, MP, 1st Bt:—
Henry Edgar Murray (9 Newenham Rd, Lymington, Hants), *b* 1919; late Lt RNVR: 1939-45 War: *m* 1949, Eleanor Macleod, da of Cdr Patrick Bruce Lawder, RN, and has issue living, Elizabeth Helen Macleod, *b* 1951: *m* 1992, Mark William Scott, and has issue living, Chloë Eleanor *b* 1992, — Anne Olivia Mary, *b* 1953. —— †Charles Cyril Willmott *b* 1927; late Maj Gren Guards: *m* 1st, 1953 (*m diss* 1959), Mary Rose, only da of late Col Walter Hugh Crichton, CIE; 2ndly, 1961, Georgina (writer, Georgina Hammick), da of late Maj-Gen George Douglas Gordon Heyman, CB, CBE; 3rdly, 1984, Carol Elspeth (Waterston Manor, Dorchester, Dorset DT2 7SP), da of late Brig Richard Montagu Villiers, DSO (*see* F Clarendon, colls), and formerly wife of Gerald Charles Mordaunt (*see* Mordaunt, Bt, colls), and *d* 1990, leaving issue (by 1st *m*), Piers St Vincent Charles, *b* 1954,   Charlotte Emily Dorothea, *b* 1955: *m* 1985 (*m diss* 1987), Michael P. Dennis, and has issue living, Oliver Charles Frederick *b* 1986, — (by 2nd *m*) Thomas Henry Heyman St Vincent, *b* 1963: *m* 1996, Martha Theis, and has issue living, Charles Michael *b* 1997, Isabella Grace Lilius *b* 1999, — Katherine Emily Amanda, *b* 1965: *m* 19—, Duncan K. Cargill, son of Alan Cargill, of The Old Hall, Knapton, Norfolk, and of Mrs James McBurney, of Cranleigh House, Thorpeness, Suffolk, and has issue living, Eliza Rose Horatia *b* 1997, — Rose Sophia, *b* 1970. —— Alexander Philip (The Priory, Woodbury, Exeter), *b* 1928: *m* 1954, Pamela Mary, da of C.

Prosper-Liston, of Penang, and has issue living, Murray Philip St Leger, *b* 1957; late Capt 14th/20th King's Hussars: *m* 1984, Alexandra-Carolin, yr da of C. H. Preuss, of Buckholz, Hamburg, and has issue living, Alexander Charles Frederick Prosper Love *b* 1988, Philip Henry Murray St Vincent Love *b* 1990, Catherine Edwardina Pamela Mary Love *b* 1993, — Melinda Mary, *b* 1955: *m* 1981, Richard Guy Hilliard, only son of late R. G. Hilliard, and has issue living, Alexandra Cary *b* 1985, Georgina Mary *b* 1988, — Victoria Rosanne, *b* 1958: *m* 1982, Capt John Gale, and has issue living, Emily Caroline *b* 1984, Amanda Catherine *b* 1987, — Nicola May, *b* 1961: *m* 1989, Anthony Alexander de Nouaille Rudge, elder son of Anthony Rudge, of Church Farm, Churchover, Warwicks, and has issue living, Alexander William Edward Findlay de Nouaille *b* 1992, Serena Mary Kate Felizarda *b* 1991, Felicity *b* 1995. ——— Anthea Elizabeth Eve, *b* 1922: *m* 1949, Dennis John Dale Shepherd, and has issue living, Justin Philip William, *b* 1952, — Miranda Dorothy Emila, *b* 1950, — Zoë Alexandra Denise, *b* 1954, — Isobel Anthea, *b* 1956, — Melissa May, *b* 1966.

Sir Stephen Love Hammick, FRCS, 1st baronet (el son of Stephen Hammick, Alderman of Plymouth), was an eminent surgeon and physician, and 1st Surg of RN Hospital, Plymouth. The 3rd baronet, Sir St Vincent Alexander Hammick, served in New Zealand War 1864-5 (medal, and specially mentioned).

Hamond-Græme, see Græme.

HANHAM (E) 1667, of Wimborne, Dorsetshire

Sir MICHAEL WILLIAM HANHAM, DFC, 12th *Baronet*, *b* 31 Oct 1922; only son of Patrick John Hanham, yst son of Col Phelips Brooke Hanham, brother of 9th baronet; *s* his kinsman, *Sir* HENRY PHELIPS, 1973; *ed* Winchester; 1939-45 War as Fl-Lt RAFVR (DFC): *m* 1954, Margaret Jane, only da of late Wing-Cdr Harold Thomas, RAF, of Marine Court, St Leonards-on-Sea, and has issue.

ᴁrms – Quarterly, or and gules, on a bend sable three crosses paté fitchée of the first. Crest – A griffin's head erased, beaked sable.
Residence – Deans Court, Wimborne, Dorset BH21 1EE.

SON LIVING

WILLIAM JOHN EDWARD, *b* 4 Sept 1957; *ed* Winchester, and Courtauld Inst of Art (BA): *m* 1st, 1982 (*m diss* 1986), Elizabeth Ann, yr da of Paul Keyworth, of Farnham, Surrey; 2ndly, 1996, Jennifer T., da of Harold Sebag-Montefiore, of Kensington. *Residence* – 48 Lexham Gdns, W8 5JA.

DAUGHTER LIVING

Victoria Jane, *b* 1955: *m* 1987, David L. Gross, son of Dr Joseph Gross, of Chippaqua, New York, and has issue living, Hugo Augustus William, *b* 1989, — Dulcie Harriet Jane, *b* 1992.

To be, rather than to seem

Sir John Alexander Hanham, 9th baronet, and his son Sir John Ludlow Hanham, 10th baronet, were Apparitors-Gen of Province and Diocese of Canterbury.

HANMER (GB) 1774, of Hanmer, Flintshire

Keep fast honour

GARDE·L'HONNEUR

Sir JOHN WYNDHAM EDWARD HANMER, 8th *Baronet*; *b* 27 Sept 1928; *s* his father, *Lt-Col Sir* (GRIFFIN WYNDHAM) EDWARD, 1977; *ed* Eton; Capt (ret) R Dagoons; a JP for Clwyd, High Sheriff 1977, and DL 1978: *m* 1954, Audrey Melissa, el da of late Maj Arthur Christopher John Congreve, of Westering, Yeoman's Lane, Newtown, Newbury, Berks, and has issue.

𝔄rms – Argent, two lions passant guardant azure. 𝔠rest – On a chapeau azure turned up ermine a lion sejeant guardant argent.
Residence – The Mere House, Hanmer, Whitchurch, Shropshire SY13 3DG.

SONS LIVING

(WYNDHAM RICHARD) GUY, *b* 27 Nov 1955; *ed* Wellington Coll; late Blues and Royals: *m* 1986, Elizabeth A., yr da of Neil Taylor, of Frampton-on-Severn, Glos, and has issue living, Thomas Wyndham William, *b* 10 May 1989, — George Hugh Richard, *b* 1992, — Alicia Marina, *b* 1994. *Residence* – The Stables, Bettisfield Park, Whitchurch, Shropshire SY13 2JZ. — Edward Hugh, *b* 1957; *ed* Wellington Coll; Capt late Blues and Royals.

SISTERS LIVING

Joan Essex, *b* 1922. — Pamela Aileen (*Pamela, Lady Wilson*), *b* 1923: *m* 1947, Capt Sir Thomas Douglas Wilson, 4th Bt, MC, who *d* 1984. *Residence* – Lillingstone Lovell Manor, Bucks. — Evelyn Mary, *b* 1926.

COLLATERAL BRANCHES LIVING

Grandchildren of late John Hanmer, 2nd son of Rev Henry Hanmer, brother of 3rd and 4th baronets:—
Issue of late Group Capt Henry Ivan Hanmer, DFC, RAF, *b* 1893, *d* 1984: *m* 1st, 1937, Margaret Florence Mary, who *d* 1947, only da of late Rev Henry Kennth Warrand, of Westhorpe Hall, Southwell, Notts; 2ndly, 1954, Lady Frances Jane Cole (1 Church Way, Grendon, Northampton), da of 5th Earl of Enniskillen:—
(By 1st *m*) John Henry Warrand (Stubbins Farm, Stubbins Lane, Southwell, Notts), *b* 1938; Capt 17th/21st Lancers (ret); High Sheriff of Notts (1981): *m* 1964 (*m diss* 1989), Penelope Clare, da of Sir Denis Le Marchant, 5th Bt, and has issue living, Thomas Stephen, *b* 1971, — Isabel Jane, *b* 1965, — Harriet Mary, *b* 1969: *m* 1996, Michael J. Worthington, only son of Col John Worthington, of Wiveliscombe, Som. — William Richard, *b* 1945: *m* 1976, Maria Paula Vianna, of Sao Paulo, Brazil, and has issue living, Daniel Henry Vianna, *b* 1981, — Alexander Richard Vianna, *b* 1983. — Flora Elizabeth, *b* 1939: *m* 1967, Frederick John Sasse, who *d* 1994, of Hendy, Afonwen, Mold, Clwyd, and has issue living, Stephen John, *b* 1968, — Matthew Alexander, *b* 1974, — David Edward Jeremy, *b* 1979, — Selina Margaret (*Hon Mrs Edward J. F. Penny*), *b* 1970: *m* 1996, Hon Edward James Frederick Penny, yst son of 3rd Viscount Marchwood, and has issue (see that title). — (By 2nd *m*) †Thomas Edward Trevor, *b* 1956; *d* 1980.

Issue of late William Francis Busby Hanmer, *b* 1899, *d* 1980: *m* 1st, 1927, Margaret, who *d* 1967, da of Archibald Cameron Norman, of The Rookery, Bromley Common (Wake, Bt, colls); 2ndly, 19—, Bethia Ann (now known as Nancy Whaley) (4 Chelmscote Mansions, 171 Baines Av, Harare, Zimbabwe; PO Box HG 607, Highlands, Harare), da of late Joseph Condy, of Umtali:—
(By 1st *m*) †John Anthony, *b* 1928: *m* 1st, 1952 (*m diss* 1973), Margaret May, da of I. G. Morrison, of Cape Town; 2ndly, 1973, Dale Berenice (Mitsasa, PO Box 3076, Paulington, Mutare, Zimbabwe), da of late J. A. Dickinson, of Johannesburg, S Africa, and *d* (26 Oct) 1994, having had issue (by 1st *m*), †Quentin William, *b* 1952: *m* 1976, Colleen (Minto Farm, PO Box 136, Bindura, Zimbabwe), da of C. Campbell-Morrison, of Mutare, and *d* (26 Sept) 1994, leaving issue, Luke Ashton *b* 1984, Kim Louise *b* 1980, Cheryl Anne *b* 1982, — Andrew Ian, *b* 1958, — Deborah Anne, *b* 1954: *m* 1974, Muller Maas (PO Box 55, Kasane, Botswana), — (by 2nd *m*), Julia Mary, *b* 1976. — Richard Norman Montagu (Edmonton, Alberta, Canada), *b* 1937, BSc, Cape Town, AMSAIMechE, PEng, MEIC: *m* 1st, 1963, Joyce Catherine, who *d* 1973, da of late Ernest Philpot, of Beckenham, Kent; 2ndly, 1974, Mrs Myrna Dorothy Tanner, da of late A. G. Plumb, of Bulawayo, and has issue living (by 1st *m*), Anthony David, *b* 1967, — Gillian Margaret, *b* 1964: *m* 1985, Way Choy, of Edmonton, Albert, Canada, and has issue living, Jessica Joyce *b* 1987, Vanessa Mei Lei *b* 1992. — Phoebe Margaret, *b* 1931; Community of St Mary the Virgin, Wantage, Berks. — Janet Virginia (24 Pine St, Buderim, Qld 4556, Australia), *b* 1932: *m* 1971, Charles George Davis Sutherland, who *d* 1995, and has issue living, George Francis Hanmer (16 Bernhard St, Paddington, Qld 4064, Australia), *b* 1972; *ed* Queensland Univ (BEng): *m* 1998, Katie Louise Devitt. — Catherine Yvonne, *b* 1936: *m* 1958, Keith Allen, of Old Presthayes, Eccliffe, Gillingham, Dorset SP8 5RE, and has issue living, John Hanmer, *b* 1958: *m* 1984, Jane Louise Ward-Lee, of Greenfield Hall, Laleham, Middx, and has issue living, Hayley Claire *b* 1986, Olivia Catherine *b* 1988, — Charles William, *b* 1960: *m* 1985, Helen Frances Jones, of Holt, Clwyd, and has issue living, Joanna Rachel *b* 1988, Catherine Rebecca *b* 1992, — Stephen Guy, *b* 1963: *m* 1988, Giselle Victoria Margaret Becker, of Shepperton, Middx, and has issue living, Guy Robert *b* 1990, Georgia Giselle *b* 1993, Phoebe Claire *b* 1997, — Caroline Elizabeth, *b* 1965: *m* 1991, Craig James Allan, PhD, of Winnipeg, Manitoba, Canada, and has issue living, Genevieve Catherine Armande *b* 1994, Skye Elizabeth *b* 1996.

Grandchildren of late Rev Hugh Hanmer, 6th son of Rev Henry Hanmer (ante):—
Issue of late Robert Hugh Hanmer, OBE, MC, *b* 1895, *d* 1971: *m* 1922, Mary Helen, who *d* 1945, da of late Nathaniel Spens:—
Hugh Niel (Fontevrault, Letcombe Regis, Wantage, Oxon OX12 9JP), *b* 1926: *m* 1953, Diana, da of Robert Hurst, of Lustleigh, Devon, and has issue living, Robert David (15c Brussels Rd, SW11 2AF), *b* 1957: *m* 1989, Isabel, da of John de Meur, of Sydney, NSW, and has issue living, Freddie *b* 1996, Daisy *b* 1994, Emily *b* 1995, — Lucia Caroline (Dr), *b* 1956.

Issue of late Lt-Col Arthur Richard Hanmer, MBE, TD, *b* 1899, *d* 1976: *m* 1929, Violet Millicent, who *d* 1968, da of late Maj William John Corbett-Winder, of Vaynor Park, Berriew, Powys:—

John Richard Lyon, *b* 1940; *ed* Eton: *m* 1979, Gillian Mary, yr da of George Herbert Smith, of Aldfield Farm, East Hendred, Wantage, Oxon. —— Sara Elizabeth, *b* 1938: *m* 1973, Charles Henry Wroughton Michell, of 10 Wandon Rd, SW6 2JF (*see* Carden, Bt, *cr* 1887, 1976 Edn), and has issue living, Samuel Richard Alfred, *b* 1979; *ed* Eton.

Issue of late Brig John Michael Hanmer, DSO, OBE, *b* 1907, *d* 1977: *m* 1934, Esther, who *d* 1995, da of Reginald Black, DL, JP, of Prees Hall, Whitchurch, Shropshire:—
Michael David Adam (The Old Granary, Gt Wilbraham, Cambridge) *b* 1935; *ed* Stowe and Clare Coll, Camb (BA): *m* 1964, Judy Carol, yr da of Cecil Jack Fairchild, of Tunbridge Wells, and has issue living, Clare Lucinda, *b* 1965; *ed* Clare Coll, Camb (BA), — Julia Caroline, *b* 1968; *ed* Brasenose Coll, Oxford (BA): *m* 1997, Trevor Sturmy, son of Roy Sturmy, of Stockport, Ches. —— *Rev Canon* Richard John (52 The Close, Norwich), *b* 1938; *ed* Winchester, and Peterhouse, Camb (MA): *m* 1972, Sheila, da of Robert King, of Tettenhall, Wolverhampton, and has issue living, Jonathan James, *b* 1974, — Adam Robert, *b* 1976, — Frances Rachel, *b* 1982.

Grandsons of late Brig John Michael Hanmer, DSO, OBE (ante):—
Issue of late Henry Hanmer, *b* 1943, *d* 1989: *m* 1972, Cristina Beatriz (who *m* 2ndly, 1991, José Oliveri-Biagiani, who *d* 1998, of Av Gral Santander 1782, Apt 202, Carrasco, Montevideo, Uruguay), da of Prof Hector D'Elia, of 21 de Setiembre 3122, Montevideo, Uruguay:—
Edward John, *b* 1974; *ed* Yale Univ (BA). —— Stephen Patrick, *b* 1975; *ed* Yale Univ (BA).

Granddaughter of late George Hanmer, only son of late Humphrey Hanmer, 3rd son of late Rev John Hanmer, 3rd son of 2nd baronet:—
Issue of late Humphrey George Hanmer, *b* 1886, *d* 1936: *m* 1st 1914 (*m diss* 1924), Beatrice Winnifred, da of late George Sumpter, of Oamaru, New Zealand; 2ndly, 1925, Muriel Emma, who *d* 1985, da of George Henry Bostock, of Staunton Springs, W Australia:—
(By 2nd *m*) Elizabeth Muriel, *b* 1929: *m* 1951, Arthur Cecil John Coates, who *d* 1958, and has issue living, David John (8 Weldon Way, City Beach, 6015 Perth, W Australia), *b* 1953: *m* 1983, Julie Howard, and has issue living, Christopher Michael *b* 1985, Ellen Margaret *b* 1987, — Anne Muriel, *b* 1955: *m* 1991, Barry Daniel Rick, of Newdegate, W Australia, and has issue living, Harry Daniel *b* 1993, Kate Elizabeth *b* 1996. *Residence* – Unit 3, 109 Weaponess Rd, Wembley Downs, Perth 6019, W Australia.

Grandson of late Thomas Hanmer, son of late William Hanmer, 6th son of 2nd baronet:—
Issue of late Thomas William Hanmer, *b* 1868, *d* 1950: *m* 1911, Ivy Mira Frances, who *d* 1965, only da of late Charles John Dodd, of The Belfry, Uckfield, Sussex:—
Nicholas Brian, MBE (Westholme West, Cumberland St, Woodbridge, Suffolk), *b* 1921; Maj (ret) R Sussex Regt; formerly Sen Dist Commr, Colonial Ser; MBE (Civil) 1960: *m* 1st, 1944, Felicity Mary, who *d* 1969, only da of Frank William Sly, of Bruton; 2ndly, 1970, Betty May, who *d* 1999, da of Harry Smith, of Sudbury Hill, and has issue living (by 1st *m*), David Nicholas Frank (Buckland, Slapton, Kingsbridge, Devon), *b* 1944; Maj Parachute Regt (ret): *m* 1st, 1968 (*m diss* 1977), Susan, da of George Inverarity, DFC, of Brighton; 2ndly, 1978, Sarah, da of Dr Roger Blackney, of Kirkham, Babbacombe, Torquay, Devon, and has had issue (by 1st *m*), †Guy David *b* 1971; *d* 1989, Emma Jane *b* 1969: *m* 1996, Andrew Kenneth Gibbs, son of Kenneth Gibbs, of Winchmore Hill, Middx, a da *b* 1973, — Oliver William, *b* 1955: *m* 1st, 1977 (*m diss* 1989), Christine Ann, da of Jeffrey Benjamin Woodin, of North Walsham, Norfolk; 2ndly, 1994, Melinda Lee, da of Colin Zweck, of Henty, NSW, and has issue living (by 1st *m*), Gavin Edward *b* 1982, Claire Louise *b* 1980, — Jill Elizabeth (PO Box 80, Coolum Beach, Qld 4573, Australia), *b* 1951: *m* 1st, 1978 (*m diss* 1981), Iain Murray; 2ndly, 1981 (*m diss* 1995), Christopher Kenneth Peachey, only son of late Kenneth Cavalier Peachey, of Sydney, Australia.

Grandson of late Lt-Col Lambert Alfred Graham Hanmer, DSO, IA, elder son of late Rear-Adm John Graham Job Hanmer (infra):—
Issue of late Lt-Col Richard Graham Hanmer, *b* 1906, *d* 1986: *m* 1939, Helen (Forbury Farm, Kimbolton, Leominster, Herefordshire), yst da of late Dr A.W. Campbell, of Sydney, NSW, Australia:—
David Graham (Yew Tree Cottage, Kimbolton, Leominster, Herefordshire; Cavalry Club), *b* 1940; *ed* Wellington Coll; late Capt R Dragoons: *m* 1st, 1968 (*m diss* 1984), Susan Evelyn, da of Brig I.M. Christie; 2ndly, 1988, Beryl, da of Joseph Henry White, and has issue living (by 1st *m*), Piers Christie Graham, *b* 1971, — Eugenie Claire, *b* 1973.

Grandchildren of late Rear-Adm John Graham Job Hanmer, son of late Capt Job Thomas Syer Hanmer, RN, son of late Capt Job Hanmer, RN, 2nd son of 1st baronet:—
Issue of late Thomas Walden Hanmer, *b* 1875, *d* 1949: *m* 1903, Ida, who *d* 1961, 2nd da of A. Whitby Simpson, of Armidale, NS Wales:—
John Walden, ED, *b* 1915; is a JP; 1939-45 War with 6th Australian Div (pow); Greek Medal 1979: *m* 1949, Jean Eileen Davies, el da of Arthur Archibald Sterling Nixon, of Claremont, Oaklands, NS Wales, and has issue living, Ruth Madeleine, *b* 1950, — Jean Anne, *b* 1955, — Patricia Margaret, *b* 1957. *Residence* – Claremont, Oaklands, nr Corowa, NS Wales. *Clubs* – Royal Sydney Golf, and Imperial Service (Sydney). —— Helen Walden (20 Bertha Rd, Cremorne, Sydney, NSW. *Clubs* – Royal Sydney Golf, and Queen's), *b* 1903: *m* 1958, Ernest Charles Stumm, who *d* 1974.

This family is of considerable antiquity in Flintshire. Sir John de Hanmer, of Hanmer, was Constable of Carnarvon Castle *temp* Edward I. His great-grandson, Sir Jenkin Hanmer, joined Owen Glendower in his rebellion against Henry IV, and was killed at the battle of Shrewsbury in 1403. The 1st baronet (*cr* 1774), Sir Walden, MP for Sunbury in two Parliaments, was 15th in descent from Sir John de Hanmer. The 3rd baronet sat as MP for Shrewsbury (*L*) 1832-37, for Hull 1841-47, and for Flint 1847-72, when he was created Baron Hanmer; he died *sp* in 1881, when the Peerage became extinct, and the Baronetcy reverted to his brother. The 6th Baronet was High Sheriff of Flintshire 1902. There was an earlier Baronetcy (*cr* 1620) in the Hanmer family, which became ext in 1746.

HANSON (UK) 1887, of Bryanston Square, co Middlesex (Extinct 1996)

Sir ANTHONY (LESLIE OSWALD) DOMINIC SEAN HANSON, 4th and last *Baronet*.

DAUGHTER LIVING OF FOURTH BARONET

Charlotte, *b* 1971.

WIDOW LIVING OF FOURTH BARONET

DENISE JANE (*Lady Hanson*), da of Richard S. Rolph, BEM, of Stoke-sub-Hamdon: *m* 1964, Sir Anthony (Leslie Oswald) Dominic Sean Hanson, 4th Bt, who *d* 1996. *Residence* – Woodland Cottage, Woodland, Ashburton, Devon.

COLLATERAL BRANCH LIVING

Issue of late Sir Francis Stanhope Hanson, 2nd son of 1st baronet, *b* 1868, *d* 1910: *m* 1897, Pearl Norcott (who *d* 1960, having *m* 2ndly, 1926, Maj Henry Noel Winter, late Roy Fusiliers, who *d* 1952), da of late Charles Albert Winter, JP, of 33 Hyde Park Sq, W:—
Violet Gwendoline Pearl, *b* 1899: *m* 1st 1919 (*m diss* 1923), William Bullivant; 2ndly, 1924 (*m diss* 1944), Capt Donald Selfe Leonard Gregson, formerly Indian Cav; 3rdly, 1946 (*m diss* 1949), John Roland Adams, QC. *Residence* – Little Gubbions, Great Leighs, Chelmsford, Essex.

The 1st baronet, Sir Reginald, was Lord Mayor of London 1886-7, and sat as MP for City of London (*C*) 1891-1900.

HANSON (UK) 1918, of Fowey, Cornwall

Sir (CHARLES) RUPERT PATRICK HANSON, 4th *Baronet*; *b* 25 June 1945; *s* his father, *Capt Sir* (CHARLES) JOHN, 1996; *ed* Eton, and Central London Polytechnic; HM Inspector of Taxes: *m* 1977, Wanda, da of Don Arturo Larrain, of Santiago, Chile, and has issue.

Arms – Argent, three lions rampant in chevron between as many mascles azure. **Crest** – A lion rampant azure, holding in the dexter forepaw an antler or, and resting the sinister paw upon two mascles fesseways and interlaced of the last. *Residence* – 125 Ditchling Rd, Brighton, E Sussex BN1 4SE.

SON LIVING

ALEXIS CHARLES, *b* 25 March 1978; *ed* Brighton Coll.

SISTER LIVING

Bridget Clare, *b* 1948: *m* 1969, Michael Grahame Cloete Graham-Cloete, and has issue living, James Montrose Stuart, *b* 1975, — Hermione Clare, *b* 1977.

MOTHER LIVING

Patricia Helen, only child of late Adm Sir (Eric James) Patrick Brind, GBE, KCB: *m* 1st, 1944 (*m diss* 1968), as his 1st wife, Sir (Charles) John Hanson, 3rd Bt, who *d* 1996; 2ndly, 1968 (*m diss* 1986), Philip Louis Miéville. *Residence* – Windlesham Manor, Hurtis Hill, Crowborough, E Sussex TN6 3AA.

SEMPER PARARE.

To be ready always

WIDOW LIVING OF THIRD BARONET

(VIOLET) HELEN (*Dowager Lady Hanson*), da of late Charles Ormonde Trew, and formerly wife of Capt Philip Cecil Landon Yorke, OBE, RN (*see* E Hardwicke, colls): *m* 1968, as his 2nd wife, Sir (Charles) John Hanson, 3rd Bt, who *d* 1996. *Residence* – 11 Osborne Court, Lime Tree Rd, Norwich, Norfolk NR2 2NN.

The 1st baronet, Sir Charles Augustin Hanson (a partner in the firm of Coates, Son & Co, stockbrokers, of 99 Gresham Street, EC), was Lord Mayor of London 1917-18, and sat as MP for S-E, or Bodmin, Div of Cornwall (*U*) 1916-22. The 2nd baronet, Sir Charles Edwin Bourne Hanson, was a partner in the firm of Coates, Son & Co, stockbrokers, of 99 Gresham Street, EC2, Major Duke of Wellington's Regt, and High Sheriff of Cornwall 1939.

HARDY (UK) 1876, of Dunstall Hall, co Stafford

Armed with faith bold

Sir RICHARD CHARLES CHANDOS HARDY, 5th *Baronet*; *b* 6 Feb 1945; *s* his father, *Lt-Col Sir* RUPERT JOHN, 1997; *ed* Eton: *m* 1972, Venetia Anne, only da of late Kenelm Simon Digby Wingfield Digby, TD, DL, of Sherborne Castle, Sherborne, Dorset, and has issue.

𝕬rms – Argent, on a bend invected plain cotised gules, three catherine wheels or; on a chief of the second as many leopards' faces of the third. 𝕮rest – A dexter arm embowed in armour proper, garnished or, entwined by a branch of oak vert, charged with two catherine wheels, the one above, the other below the elbow gules, the hand grasping a dragon's head erased proper.
Residence – Springfield House, Gillingham, Dorset SP8 5RD. *Club* – Turf.

DAUGHTERS LIVING

Arabella Venetia Jane, *b* 1976. —— Jacquetta Anne, *b* 1977. —— Georgina Charlotte, *b* 1982. —— Henrietta Alicia Diana, *b* 1986.

SISTER LIVING

Rosemary Diana, *b* 1931: *m* 1953 (*m diss* 1972), Robert David Black (later Sir Robert Black, 3rd Bt), and has had issue (see that title). *Residence* – Redmoor Lodge, Guilsborough Rd, W Haddon, Northants NN6 7AD.

WIDOW LIVING OF FOURTH BARONET

Hon DIANA JOAN ALLSOPP (*Hon Lady Hardy*), da of 3rd Baron Hindlip: *m* 1930, Lt-Col Sir Rupert John Hardy, 4th Bt, who *d* 1997. *Residence* – Gullivers Lodge, Guilsborough, Northampton NN6 8RB.

COLLATERAL BRANCHES LIVING

Issue of late Lt-Col Hugh Bertram Hardy, yr son of Sir Bertram Hardy, 3rd Bt, *b* 1907, *d* 1988: *m* 1933, Joan Stella Gwendolyn, da of Charles Hammond Dracott, and formerly wife of James Alexander Guthrie:—
Audrey Elizabeth Una, *b* 1936: *m* 1965, Charles Frederick Backhouse (c/o Bank of Montreal, Calgary, Alberta, Canada), and has issue living, David Hugh, *b* 1971, — Isabelle Joan, *b* 1969.

Grandchildren of late Rt Hon Laurence Hardy, 4th son of 1st baronet:—
Issue of late Maj Arthur Evelyn Hardy, *b* 1893, *d* 1986: *m* 1918, Nancy Marion, who *d* 1983, da of late Horace George Devas, formerly of Nizels, Hildenborough, Kent (*see* E Cawdor, colls, 1924 Edn):—
†Gerald Alan, *b* April 1926: *m* 1953, Carolyn, da of late Maj-Gen Arthur Charles Tarver Evanson, CB, MC, and *d* 1999, leaving issue, Sarah, *b* 1957: *m* 1972, William John Hurley, of Pedlinge Farm, Hythe, Kent, and has issue living, Kathryn Jane *b* 1985, Susannah Evelyn *b* 1988, Lucinda Barbara *b* 1990, — Jane, *b* 1958. *Residence* – Sandling Park, Hythe, Kent.
—— Ruth, *b* 1919; a JP for Kent: *m* 1940, Col Charles Reginald Tuff, Buffs, DL (ret), and has issue living, Timothy Charles, *b* 1947; *ed* Eton, and Dalhousie Univ, Halifax, Nova Scotia, — Geoffrey, *b* 1954; *ed* Eton, — Prunella Primrose, *b* 1942. *Residence* – Hogs Green, Sandling, Hythe, Kent.

Issue of late Maurice John Hardy, MBE, *b* 1902, *d* 1993: *m* 1926, Rosalie Kathleen, who *d* 1979, da of late Brig-Gen Tyrell Other William Champion de Crespigny (*see* Champion de Crespigny, Bt, ext, 1976 Edn):—
†Christopher John, *b* 1928; *ed* Eton; *d unm* 1974. —— Jane (Fox Hollow, Sandhurst Lane, Rolvenden, nr Cranbrook, Kent), *b* 1931: *m* 1955, Peter Leonard Eckersley, who *d* 1988, and has issue living, Peter David Charles (Woolscott House, nr Rugby, Warws CV23 8DB), *b* 1957: *m* 1987, Juliet Emma Margaret, da of Derek Graham Blundell Knight of Little Dane, Biddenden, Ashford, Kent, and has issue living, Peter Maurice Percival *b* 1989, Cliantha Florence Beatrice *b* 1991, Evangeline Violet Margaret *b* 1993, — Clare Arabella, *b* 1960: *m* 1981, David Richard Stapylton Fairbank (*see* V Chetwynd, colls), and has issue living, Thomas David Peter *b* 1984, Arabella Clare Mary *b* 1987, — Suzanne Jane, *b* 1962: *m* 1982, Charles Roderick Roberts, of Gosden Heath, Lodsworth, Petworth, W Sussex, and has issue living, Edward Alan Christopher *b* 1987, Samantha Rosalie *b* 1986. *Residence* – Peasmarsh Place, nr Rye, E Sussex.

Sir John, 1st baronet, sat as MP for Midhurst (*C*) 1859, for Dartmouth 1860-68, and for S Warwickshire 1868-74. Sir Bertram, 3rd baronet was High Sheriff of Staffordshire 1925.

HARE (UK) 1818, of Stow Hall, Norfolk

Sir PHILIP LEIGH HARE, 6th *Baronet; b* 13 Oct 1922; son of late Edward Philip Leigh Hare, youngest son of 2nd baronet; *s* his kinsman, *Sir* THOMAS, 1993; *ed* privately: *m* 1950, Anne Lisle, 2nd da of Maj Geoffrey Nicholson, CBE, MC (E Annesley, colls), and has issue.

𝔄rms – Gules two bars or, a chief indented of the last. 𝔠rest – A demi-lion rampant argent, gorged with a ducal coronet or.
Residence – The Nettings, Hook Norton, Banbury, Oxon OX15 5NP.

SON LIVING

NICHOLAS PATRICK (Manor Farm, Culkerton, nr Tetbury, Glos GL8 8SS), *b* 27 Aug 1955; *ed* Bryanston: *m* 1982, Caroline Keith, da of Terence Playfair Keith Allan, of Elsted Green, nr Midhurst, W Sussex, and has issue living, Thomas, *b* 7 Aug 1986, — Robert *b* 1987.

Non videri sed esse
Not to seem, but to be

DAUGHTER LIVING

Louisa Kathleen, *b* (twin) 1955: *m* 1981 (*m diss* 1988), Benson Whittle, of Utah, USA, and has issue living, Charlotte, *b* 1981.

HALF-SISTER LIVING

Elizabeth Mildred Leigh (4 Old Museum Court, Haslemere, Surrey GU27 2JR), *b* 1915.

DAUGHTER LIVING OF THIRD BARONET

Joan Muriel Leigh (Redmount, Old Totnes Rd, Buckfastleigh, Devon TQ11 0BY), *b* 1905.

DAUGHTERS LIVING OF FOURTH BARONET

(By 1st wife, Doreen Pleasance Anna, eldest da of late Maj Sir Richard Ludwig Bagge, DSO)

Jean Bridget (11 Lady Jane Court, Cavendish Av, Cambridge), *b* 1929: *m* 1st, 1949 (*m diss* 1957), Nigel E. Beard; 2ndly, 1957 (*m diss* 1971), Richard John Wallis, son of late Leonard John Wallis, of Merton Park, SW19, and has issue living, (by 1st *m*) Jeremy Nigel Thomas, *b* 1953, — Laraine Susan, *b* 1950, — (by 2nd *m*) Robin John, *b* 1961.

(By 2nd wife, Natalie Alexandria Elizabeth Julia, only child of late Capt Baron Oscar Gerard de Langué; m 2ndly, 1980, Edward Keith Dipple, who d 1984, of 82 Swan Court, Flood St, SW3 5RU)

Angela Florence Natalie, *b* 1948: *m* 1971, Terence Ronald Duke, son of late Maj Ronald Duke, of Dalkeith, W Australia, and has issue living, Simon Ronald, *b* 1976, — Penelope Jane Deirdre, *b* 1974. —— Lorna Lillianne Katrina (127 Mornington Crescent, Cranford, Hounslow, Middx TW5 9SU), *b* 1957: *m* 1975 (*m diss* 19—), Michael Page, and has issue living, David, *b* 1976, — Jonathan, *b* 1980, — Andrew, *b* 1981, — Thomas, *b* 1982, — Samuel, *b* 1986, — Alfred, *b* 1988, — Rebecca, *b* 1985, — Rosemarie, *b* 1992.

(By 3rd wife, Barbara Mary Theodora (Ann), infra)

Mary Ann, *b* 1961: *m* 1993, Anthony Jacklin, of The Rowans, 14 Rowley Rd, Boston, Lincs PE21 6JE, and has issue.

DAUGHTERS LIVING OF FIFTH BARONET

Lucy Rose, *b* 1962. —— Elizabeth Florence, *b* 1964: *m* 1992, William Nicholas Esse, son of late David Charles Scott Esse, of Horsley, Glos, and has issue living, Barnaby Samuel Hare, *b* 1993, — Otto Thomas Hare, *b* 1995, — Tristan William Hare, *b* 1996, — Pollyanna Ophella Hare, *b* 1998.

WIDOWS LIVING OF FOURTH AND FIFTH BARONETS

BARBARA MARY THEODORA (ANN) (*Ann, Lady Hare*) (Stow Bardolph, King's Kynn, Norfolk), yst da of late Joseph Arthur Walton: *m* 1960, as his 3rd wife, Maj Sir Ralph Leigh Hare, 4th Bt, who *d* 1976.

Lady ROSE AMANDA BLIGH (*Lady Rose Hare*) (Stow Bardolph, King's Lynn, Norfolk PE34 3HU), 2nd da of 9th Earl of Darnley: *m* 1961, Sir Thomas Hare, 5th Bt, who *d* 1993.

Sir Nicholas Hare, twice Speaker of the House of Commons and sometime Master of the Rolls (a Commissioner to execute the Office of Lord Chancellor and Keeper of the Great Seal 1555), purchased Stow Bardolph in 1553. His great-great-great-nephew Ralph Hare (son of Sir John Hare, Knt) was *cr* 1st Baronet of Stow Bardolph in 1641. Mary, second da of his son Sir Thomas Hare, 2nd Bt (*cr* 1641), and sister and eventual co-heiress of the 5th Bt (at whose death in 1764 the Baronetcy became ext), married Thomas Leigh, of London, son of Edward Leigh, of Iver, Bucks (will proved 1689) and in common descent with the Stoneleigh Abbey family, from the Leighs of Cheshire. Her grandson, Thomas Leigh, who succeeded to Stow Bardolph (son of Thomas Leigh, of Iver, Bucks), served with distinction in the American war, assumed in 1791 by Act of Parliament the surname of Hare in lieu of his patronymic of Leigh, and was *cr* a Baronet in 1818, becoming Sir Thomas Hare, 1st Bt. The 2nd baronet was Capt 2nd Life Guards, while the 3rd was Lieut 2nd Life Guards, and High Sheriff of Norfolk 1906.

HARFORD (UK) 1934, of Falcondale, co Cardigan

Inter utrumque tene

Hold between the two

Sir (JOHN) TIMOTHY HARFORD, 3rd *Baronet*; *b* 6 July 1932; *s* his father, Lt-Col *Sir* GEORGE ARTHUR, OBE, 1967; *ed* Harrow, Worcester Coll, Oxford, and Harvard Business Sch: *m* 1962, Carolyn Jane, only da of late Brig Guy John de Wette Mullens, OBE, of North House, Weyhill, Andover, and has issue.

𝕬rms – Sable, two bendlets argent between three cross-crosslets fitchée in pale of the last. 𝕮rest – In front of flames issuant therefrom a phœnix proper, two cross-crosslets fitchée in saltire argent.
Residence – South House, South Littleton, Evesham, Worcs.

SONS LIVING

MARK JOHN (6 Redcliffe Square, SW10 9JZ), *b* 6 Aug 1964: *m* 1999, Louise R., da of Robert Langford, of Tadworth, Surrey. —— Simon Guy, *b* 1966.

DAUGHTER LIVING

Clare Elisabeth, *b* 1963: *m* 1989, Nicholas Clatworthy, yr son of late Peter Clatworthy, of Bayswater, and has issue living, Guy Peter, *b* 1992, — Laura Jane, *b* 1995.

BROTHER LIVING

Piers Scandrett (Church Farm, Great Somerford, Chippenham, Wilts), *b* 1937; *ed* Eton, and Worcester Coll, Oxford: *m* 1st, 1961 (*m diss* 1972), Hyacinthe Cecilia, da of Lt-Col Nigel Walter Hoare, OBE, TD (*see* Portal, Bt, colls); 2ndly, 1975, Patricia Jane, da of Air Commodore Patrick Burnett, and has issue living (by 1st *m*), Henry Scandrett (Pease Bay Manor, Bodden Town, Grand Cayman, BWI), *b* 1963: *m* 1994, Eliza, 2nd da of Richard Strachan, and has issue living, Alexander Scandrett *b* 1995, Carina Frances *b* 1996, — Charlotte Anstice, *b* 1965, — (by 2nd *m*) William Patrick, *b* 1976.

SISTER LIVING

Robina Elspeth, *b* 1934: *m* 1956, Jeremy Christopher Glyn, who *d* 1984, and has issue (*see* B Wolverton, colls). *Residence* – Upton Farm, Upton, Andover, Hants SP11 0JS.

The 1st baronet, Major Sir John Charles Harford (son of late John Battersby Harford, of Falcondale, co Cardigan, and of Blaise Castle, Henbury, Bristol) was created a baronet June 1934, and *d* July 1934.

HARINGTON (E) 1611, of Ridlington, Rutland

Sir NICHOLAS JOHN HARINGTON, 14th *Baronet*, elder son of late His Honour Judge (John Charles Dundas) Harington, QC, yr son of 12th baronet; *b* 14 May 1942; *s* his uncle, *Sir* RICHARD DUNDAS, 1981; *ed* Eton, and Ch Ch, Oxford (MA).

𝕬rms – Sable, a fret argent. 𝕮rest – A lion's head erased or, langued and collared gules, buckled of the first.
Residences – 16 Weltje Rd, W6 9TG; Ring'o Bells, Whitbourne, Worcester WR6 5RT.

BROTHER LIVING

DAVID RICHARD (7 Vale Grove, W3 7QP), *b* 25 June 1944; *ed* Westminster, and Ch Ch, Oxford: *m* 1983, Deborah Jane, eldest da of Maurice William Catesby, MC, of Long Compton, Warwicks, and has issue living, John Catesby, *b* 7 Jan 1984, — Christopher, *b* 1986.

SISTER LIVING

Susan Alexandra, *b* 1948: *m* 1977, Anis Nacrour, of 18 Montague Rd, W7 3PQ, and has issue living, Aurélien-Antoine John Mourad, *b* 1985, — Alexandre Philippe, *b* 1988, — Laurent Francois, *b* 1989.

With a firm knot

COLLATERAL BRANCHES LIVING

Grandchildren of late Rev Charles Harington, 2nd son of 11th baronet:—
Issue of late Sir Charles Robert Harington, KBE, *b* 1897, *d* 1972: *m* 1923, Jessie McCririe, who *d* 1975, da of Rev James Craig, of The Manse, Kirkpatrick-Durham, Kirkcudbright:—
Michael (69 Waterford Rd, SW6 2DT), *b* 1924; *ed* Trin Hall, Camb (MA), and Univ Coll Hosp Medical Sch; MB, BChir, FRCP: *m* 1958, Marta Rosenfeld, and has issue living, Robert Michael, *b* 1963; *ed* Trin Coll, Oxford (DPhil): *m* 1988, Pamela, da of P. Nadash, of Columbia, Maryland, USA, — Amanda, *b* 1967; *ed* St Paul's Girls' Sch, and St John's Coll, Camb; Bar Inner Temple 1989. —— Alison Mary, *b* 1927; MB, BChir: *m* 1952, Derek Raymond Bangham, MB, BS, FRCP, of 4 Crown Close, Highwood Hill, NW7, and has issue living, Charles Richard Mark, *b* 1955; BM, BCH, MRCP, PhD, MRCPath: *m* 1990, Jocelyne Marie Ragody Hughes, PhD, and has issue living, George Richard Derek *b* 1991, Madeleine Edith *b* 1993, Florence Clara Jocelyne *b* 1997, — Humphrey Bernard, *b* 1957: *m* 1980, Elizabeth Mary Stafford Baker, and has issue living, Charles Stafford *b* 1987, Guy Nicholas *b* 1992, Olivia Charlotte *b* 1989, — Celia Elizabeth, *b* 1954; MB, ChB, DRCOG: *m* 1995, David Charles Lowe, — Jessica Frances, *b* 1961: *m* 1990, John Graham Lawrence, and has issue living, Anna Mary *b* 1996. —— Margaret Jane (43 Upton Lovell, Warminster, Wilts), *b* 1931.

Granddaughters of His Honour Judge Edward Harington (infra):—
Issue of late (Edward Henry) Vernon Harington, *b* 1907, *d* (26 Dec) 1995: *m* 1st, 1937 (*m diss* 1949), Mary Elizabeth, who *d* (24 April) 1995, only surv da of late Louis Edwin William Egerton (*see* M Hertford, colls, 1971 Edn); 2ndly, 1950, (Mary) Johanna Jean, JP (16 Lower Mill St, Ludlow, Shropshire), only da of late Lt-Col Ralph George Snead Cox, MC:—
(By 1st *m*) (Victoria) Jane, *b* 1941: *m* 1973, Sidney Morgan Whitteridge, VRD, MRCS, LRCP, of Inverlael Lodge, Loch Broom, by Ullapool, Ross-shire, and has issue living, Ashley Edward John, *b* 1976, — Mary Ruth, *b* 1974. —— (By 2nd *m*) (Marie) Louisa, *b* 1951: *m* 1979, Robin Pagan Taylor, of The Pulpits, Little Hereford, Shropshire SY4 4AU, and has issue living, William Vernon, *b* 1980, — Philip Edward, *b* 1984. —— Susan Anne Jean, *b* 1953: *m* 1984, David Robert Geoffrey Scott, of Upper Hamnish Farm, Leominster, Herefords, and has issue living, Edwina Alexandra, *b* 1985, — Sophie Amelia, *b* 1987.

Issue of late His Honour Judge Edward Harington, 3rd son of 11th baronet, *b* 1863, *d* 1937: *m* 1906, Louisa Muriel, who *d* 1963, only da of late Herbert C. Erskine Vernon:—
Kenneth Douglas Evelyn Herbert, *b* 1911; *ed* Stowe Sch; Bar Inner Temple 1952; Hon Attaché, British Legation, Stockholm 1930-32; a JP and Acting Dep Chm of Quarter Sessions in Greater London 1966-67, a Metropolitan Magistrate 1967-84; 1939-45 War, Maj Coldm Gds: *m* 1st, 1939, Lady Cecilia Bowes-Lyon, who *d* 1947, da of 15th Earl of Strathmore; 2ndly, 1950, Maureen Helen, who *d* 1992, da of late Brig-Gen Sir Robert (Chaine Alexander) McCalmont, KCVO, CBE, DSO, and has issue living (by 2nd *m*), Michael Kenneth (Bakers Cottage, Great Rissington, Cheltenham, Glos GL54 2LP), *b* 1951; *ed* Eton and Ch Ch, Oxford; Bar Inner Temple 1974, Recorder 1998: *m* 1984, Deirdre Christine Kehoe, and has issue living, Robert John Michael *b* 1988, Charlotte Mary Ann *b* 1985, Caroline Lucy Christine *b* 1991, — Jonathan Edward McCalmont (Barnwell Lodge Farm, Lilford, nr Oundle, Northants PE8 5SB), *b* 1955; *ed* Eton; 2nd Lt Coldm Gds: *m* 1st, 1983 (*m diss* 1986), Lucinda Margaret, only da of Maj William Lloyd (John) Baxendale (*see* E Fortescue); 2ndly, 1989, Susan Antonia, yst da of Anthony Walter Fenwick, of Eaton Grange, Eaton, nr Grantham, Lincs, and has issue living (by 2nd *m*), Antonia Lucy Diana *b* 1991, Katherine Rose Caroline *b* 1994. *Residence* – Bakers Cottage, Great Rissington, Cheltenham, Glos GL54 2LP.

Grandchildren of late Brig-Gen John Harington, CB, CMG, DSO (infra):—
Issue of late Maj John Temple Harington, DSO, MBE, *b* 1909, *d* 1983: *m* 1946, Catherine, who *d* 1997, da of late Lt-Col Donald Cameron, of Fordon, The Nile, Tasmania:—
Richard Donald John (Wester Balduon, Ardroon, Alness, Ross and Cromarty), *b* 1948: *ed* Winchester, and Hertford Coll, Oxford: *m* 1974, Jane Pickin, da of Peter Wellburn Bayliss, of Burcher Court, Titley, Kington, Herefordshire, and has issue living, Alastair Peter John, *b* 1983, — Lucy Aline, *b* 1979, — Miranda Jane, *b* 1980. —— Serena Catherine Lucy, *b* 1947: *m* 1971, Julian G. Barrow, of 33 Tite St, SW3, and has issue living, Cecilia Margaret, *b* 1975, — Eugenie Catherine, *b* 1977. —— Cecilia Aline, *b* 1953: *m* 1994, Jacques Richard, of 60 rue Doudeauville, 75018 Paris, France.

Issue of late Brig-Gen John Harington, CB, CMG, DSO, 5th son of 11th baronet, b 1873, d 1943: m 1908, Lady Frances Aline Temple-Gore-Langton who d 1952, da of 4th Earl Temple, of Stowe:—
Aline Lucy (*Hon Mrs Walter Keppel*), b 1918: m 1941, Lt-Com Hon Walter Arnold Crispian Keppel, DSC, RN (*see* E Albemarle). *Residence* – Little Barton House, Meonstoke, Hants SO32 3NT.

Granddaughter of late Arthur CHAMPERNOWNE, son of Henry Champernowne, el son of Arthur Champernowne (infra):—
Issue of late Arthur Melville CHAMPERNOWNE, b 1871, d 1946: m 1907, Helen Iris, who d 1950, el da of Lieut-Col Herbert John Ouchterlony Walker, late RA, formerly of Leeford, Budleigh Salterton:—
Katharine Iris (Parnham's Farm, Melbury Abbas, Shaftesbury, Dorset), b 1912: m 1949, Wing-Cdr Adrian Henry Paull, AFC, who d 1965, and has issue living, Angela Iris Constance, b 1951.

Grandson of late Rev Richard CHAMPERNOWNE, son of late Arthur CHAMPERNOWNE (who assumed the surname and arms of Champernowne 1774), son of late Rev Richard Harington, 2nd son of 6th baronet:—
Issue of late Francis Gawayne CHAMPERNOWNE, b 1866, d 1921: m 1911, Isabel Mary, who d 1969, da of late George Burvill Rashleigh, Bar-at-law, of Riseley, Horton-Kirby, Dartford and 5 Stone Buildings, Lincoln's Inn, WC (E Darnley):—
David Gawen, b 1912; *ed* Winchester, and King's Coll, Camb (Fellow 1937-48); a Fellow of Trin Coll, Camb; Prof of Statistics, Oxford Univ 1948-59; Prof of Economics & Statistics, Camb Univ 1970-78: m 1948, Wilhelmina Barbara Maria, da of late Petrus Ludovicus Dullaert, of Zutphen, Holland, and has issue living, Arthur Francis, b 1949. — Richard Peter, b 1953: m 1986, Jackie, da of Bill Wills, of Petersfield, Hants. *Residence* – 25 Worts Causeway, Cambridge, CB1 4RJ.

John, son of Robert de Haverington, of Haverington (now Harington), Cumberland, was one of the barons summoned to Parliament by Edward II. His lineal descendant, Sir John Harington of Exton, co Rutland, brother of the 1st baronet, and tutor to the Princess Elizabeth, daughter of James I, was created Baron Harington, which title became extinct on the death of the 2nd baron. Sir James, 3rd baronet, one of the Judges commissioned (but only attended one day and did not sign the death warrant) to try Charles I, was, by an Act of 13 Car II, nevertheless excepted at the Restoration out of the general acts of indemnity, and with Lord Monson, Sir Henry Fieldings, and others subjected to personal degradation from his honours and rendered personally incapable of bearing arms or title of dignity (but the penalty did not forfeit the honours or attaint the blood). Sir Richard, 11th Bt, was a Metropolitan Police Magistrate 1871-2, and a Judge of County Courts 1872-1905. Sir Richard, 12th Bt, was a Puisne Judge of High Court, Calcutta 1899-1913.

STAFFORD-KING-HARMAN (UK) 1914, of Rockingham, co Roscommon (Extinct 1987)

Lt-Col Sir CECIL WILLIAM FRANCIS STAFFORD-KING-HARMAN, 2nd and last *Baronet*.

DAUGHTER LIVING OF SECOND BARONET

Cicely Joan (*Lady Dunn*), b 1918: m 1943, 1st, Capt George Heffernan Dennehy, late Irish Guards, who d 1990, 2nd son of late George Heffernan Dennehy, of Ballymanus, Stradbally, Queen's Co; 2ndly, 1997, as his 2nd wife, Rt Hon Sir Robin Horace Walford Dunn, MC, and has issue living (by 1st m), Rosemary Anne b 1944: m 1964, Charles Ralph Nicolas Tindal, of Ballyloughan, Bruckless, co Donegal, eldest son of G/Capt Nicolas Henry Joseph Tindal, RAF (ret), of Ballyloughan, and has issue living, Nicolas Henry Charles b 1965, Richard Mark b 1968, Matthew Thomas b 1973, Katherine Mary b 1966 Emma Caroline b 1970, Victoria Jacqueline Frances b 1971, Lucy Josephine b 1977, — Sarah Elizabeth DENNEHY, b 1949; has resumed her maiden surname: m 1970 (m diss 1990), Don Leopoldo de Bolivar Torres, of Seville, and has issue living, Isabel b 1970, Alexandra Rose b 1974, — Mary Katharine DENNEHY, b 1951; has resumed her maiden surname: m 1st, 1977 (m diss 1984), David Starkie; 2ndly, 1984 (m diss 1993), Joseph Jenkins, of Grove City, Pennsylvania, USA, and has issue living, (by 1st m) Lauryn Hannah b 1978, (by 2nd m) Cayli Sunrise b 1984, Orion b 1985, — Caroline Jean, b 1954: m 1975 (m diss 1979), Stuart Anthony Reed; 2ndly, 1982, Heribert Ernst Schiansky, of Kailasa, Minsterley, Shrewsbury, Shropshire, and has issue living (by 2nd husband), Jethro Felix b 1983, Holly Eve b 1980, Frances Maria b 1990. *Residence* – Lynch Mead, Allerford, Minehead, Somerset TA24 8HJ.

COLLATERAL BRANCH LIVING

Issue of late Capt Edward Charles Stafford-King-Harman, Irish Guards, el son of 1st baronet, b 1891, ka 1914, having assumed by Roy licence 1900 the additional surname of King-Harman: m 1914, Olive (who m 2ndly, 1921, Wilfred Stuart Atherstone Hales Pakenham Mahon (d 1980), and d 1981), only da of late Capt Henry Pakenham Mahon (*see* E Longford, colls):—
Lettice Mary (*Lady Fitzpatrick*) (*posthumous*), b 1915: m 1st, 1935 (m diss 1971), Col Robert Humphrey Lomer, MBE, Gren Gds, who d 1991; 2ndly, 1975, Maj George Henry Errington, MC, late 10th Hussars, who d 1989; 3rdly, 1998, Gen Sir Desmond Fitzpatrick, GCB GCVO, DSO, MBE, MC, of Belmont, Otley, Ipswich, Suffolk IP6 9PF, and has issue living (by 1st m), Caroline Mary, b 1937: m 1st, 1957 (m diss 1964), Maj Patrick Haselden Wood, late 11th Hussars; 2ndly, 1964, Maj Neil Gordon Ramsay, Scots Gds, of St Anns, Alyth, Perthshire, and has issue living (by 2nd m), Melanie Mary b 1966: m 1990, John J. M. St John, yst son of Lt-Col Charles A. R. L. St John, of Glebe Manor, Havant, Hants (and has issue living, William b 1995, Celia b 1997, Lily Joy Eliza b 1998), and an adopted da, Victoria Anne b 1968: m 1994, Christopher Peter Theobald, yr son of G. P. Theobald, of Tower Hill, Gomshall, Surrey, and has issue living, Iona Mary

b 1997, Camilla Kate *b* 1998, — Lavinia Rohays (184 Latymer Court, Hammersmith Rd, W6 7JQ), *b* 1939: *m* 1968 (*m diss* 1973), Cdr Harry James Startin, RN.

Harmood-Banner, see Banner.

HARMSWORTH (UK) 1922, of Freshwater Grove, Parish of Shipley, co Sussex

Sir HILDEBRAND HAROLD HARMSWORTH, 3rd *Baronet*; *b* 5 June 1931; *s* his father *Sir* HILDEBRAND ALFRED BERESFORD, 1977; *ed* Harrow, and Trin Coll, Dublin: *m* 1960, Gillian Andrea, only da of William John Lewis, of Tetbury, Glos, and has issue.

Arms – Azure, two rolls of paper in saltire or, banded in the centre gules, between four bees volant of the second. **Crest** – Issuant out of a coronet composed of three roses set upon a rim or, a cubit arm erect, the hand grasping a roll of paper fessewise proper.
Residence – Ewlyn Villa, 42 Leckhampton Rd, Cheltenham GL53 0BB.

SON LIVING

HILDEBRAND ESMOND MILES, *b* 1 Sept 1964; *ed* Dean Close Sch, and Crewe and Alsager Coll: *m* 1988, Ruth Denise, da of Dennis Miles, of Cheltenham, and has issue living, Hildebrand Darcy Laurence, *b* 16 July 1994, — Alice Katherine Elspeth, *b* 1990, — Grace Hester Elaine, *b* 1991. *Residence* – 14 Miles Rd, Epsom, Surrey KT19 9AD.

DAUGHTERS LIVING

Claire Elen Mary, *b* 1961. ——— Kirsten Elizabeth Ashley, *b* 1963.

SISTER LIVING

Bene · qui · sedulo

He who acts diligently acts well

Ingeborg Kathleen Elen, *b* 1926: *m* 1951, Capt Thomas James Johnson, RA, who *d* 1963, and has issue living, Ingeborg Caroline Kathleen Elen, *b* 1952, — Melissa Eugenie Ingeborg Thomasine, *b* 1954, — Atalanta Kathleen Ingeborg Elen, *b* 1962: *m* 1989, Raymond Clive Wright, and has issue living, Alfred Thomas Hildebrand *b* 1997. *Residence* – Chiffley Grange, Staplefield, Sussex.

WIDOW LIVING OF SECOND BARONET

ELEN (*Elen, Lady Harmsworth*) (Aucassin, Le Vallon, St Clair, Le Lavandou, France), da of Nicolaj Billenstein, of Randers, Denmark: *m* 1925, Sir Hildebrand Alfred Beresford Harmsworth, 2nd Bt, who *d* 1977.

COLLATERAL BRANCH LIVING

Issue of late (Chamberlain) Michael Hildebrand Harmsworth, 3rd son of 1st baronet, *b* 1903, *d* 1955: *m* 1st, 1931, Barbara Irene, who *d* 1941, da of Henry Savile Dean; 2ndly, 1945, Lucette Charlotte, only da of Jean Riché, of Paris:—
(By 2nd *m*) John Hildebrand, *b* 1949. ——— Charles Hildebrand, *b* 1951. ——— (By 1st *m*) Josephine Angela, *b* 1932. ——— Melanie Barbara, *b* 1934.

Sir Hildebrand Harmsworth, 1st Bt (son of late Alfred Harmsworth, Bar-at-law), was a younger brother of the 1st Viscount Northcliffe (ext), and the 1st Viscount Rothermere; edited *New Liberal Review* 1901-4, and was sometime Proprietor of *The Globe*.

HARRIS (UK) 1932, of Bethnal Green, co London

Sir JACK (WOLFRED) ASHFORD HARRIS, 2nd *Baronet, b* 23 July 1906; *s* his father, *Rt Hon Sir* PERCY ALFRED HARRIS, 1952; *ed* Shrewsbury, and Trin Hall, Camb (BA 19—); sometime Pres of Wellington Chamber of Commerce; European War 1939-45 with New Zealand Forces: *m* 1933, Patricia, da of Arthur P. Penman, of Wahroonga, near Sydney, NS Wales, and has issue.
Residence – Te Rama, Waikanae, near Wellington, New Zealand. *Clubs* – Royal Automobile, Wellington (New Zealand).

SONS LIVING

CHRISTOPHER JOHN ASHFORD, *b* 26 Aug 1934: *m* 1957, Anna, da of F. de Malmanche, of Auckland, New Zealand, and has issue living, Andrew Frederick Ashford, *b* 1958: *m* 1990, Terena Ann, da of ......, and has issue living, Madeleine Ann *b* 1992, — Charlotte Anna, *b* 1960, — Phoebe Jane Ashford, *b* 1963. *Residence* – 21 Anne St, Wadestown, Wellington, NZ. *Clubs* – Wellington, Royal Port Nicholson Yacht. ——— Paul Percy Ashford (28 Middlehead Rd, Mosman, NSW, Australia), *b* 1945: *m* 1969, Gail, da of late Arthur Stewart, of Manchester, and has issue living, Mark Percy, *b* 1970, Nicholas, *b* 1978, Samuel *b* 1980, Sophie, *b* 1973.

DAUGHTER LIVING

Margaret, *b* 1939.

BROTHER LIVING

Thomas Nicholas Robinson, *b* 1908; *ed* King's Sch, Burton, and Trin Hall, Camb; is Lieut RNVR: *m* 1942, Lucille, only child of D. H. Jonas, and has issue living, Antony Guy David Bloxham, *b* 1943.

The 1st baronet, Rt Hon Sir Percy Alfred Harris (son of Wolf Harris, of 197 Queen's Gate, SW), was MP for S (or Harborough) Div of Leicestershire 1916-18, and for S-W Div of Bethnal Green 1922-45, and was Ch Liberal Whip 1935-45.

HARRIS (UK) 1953, of Chepping Wycombe, Bucks (Extinct 1996)

Sir ANTHONY TRAVERS KYRLE HARRIS, 2nd and last *Baronet.*

DAUGHTERS LIVING OF FIRST BARONET (*by 1st marriage*)

Marigold Patricia (Amesbury Abbey, Amesbury, Wilts), *b* 1920: *m* 1946, Robert William Armitage, TD, who *d* 1978, and has issue living, Rupert Dudley (71 York Mansions, Prince of Wales Drive, SW11 4BW), *b* 1947; *ed* Eton: *m* 1976, Venetia, da of Anthony Greville-Bell, of 20 Sumner Place, SW7, and has issue living, Edward James *b* 1979, Katherine Rose *b* 1981, — Peter James (47 Swanage Rd, SW18 2DZ), *b* 1950; *ed* Eton, and Camb Univ: *m* 1974, Flavia Margaret Guthrie, da of Mark Phillips, and has issue living, Remeny Tanya Iona *b* 1972. ——— Rosemary Jeanne (33 Cheyne Court, Flood St, SW3 5TR), *b* 1923.

(*by 2nd marriage*)

Jacqueline Jill (*Hon Mrs Nicholas Assheton*), *b* 1939: *m* 1960, Hon Nicholas Assheton, and has issue (*see* B Clitheroe). *Residence* – 15 Hammersmith Terrace, W6 9TS.

HARRISON (UK) 1922, of Eaglescliffe, co Durham

While I breathe, I hope

Sir (ROBERT) COLIN HARRISON, 4th *Baronet*; *b* 25 May 1938; *s* his brother, *Sir* (JOHN) WYNDHAM, 1955; *ed* Radley, and St John's Coll, Camb: *m* 1963, Maureen Marie, da of late E. Leonard Chiverton, and has issue.

Arms – Per chevron azure and or, in chief two demi-lions rampant of the second and in base a lymphad sable. Crest – Upon a fernbrake a falcon rising proper, belled and charged upon the sinister wing with a fleur-de-lis or.
Residence – Stearsby Hall, Stearsby, York YO61 4SA.

SON LIVING

JOHN WYNDHAM FOWLER, *b* 14 Dec 1972.

DAUGHTERS LIVING

Rachel Deborah, *b* 1966: *m* 1991, Alistair G. Waddell, elder son of W. Waddell, of 4 Eglinton Drive, Troon, Ayrshire, and has issue living, Isabella Skye, *b* 1999. *Residence* – Hong Kong. —— Claire Grace, *b* 1974.

SISTER LIVING

Judith May *b* 1935: *m* 1962, Paul Standing, and has issue living, Christopher Hugh, *b* 1965, — Jane Kathleen, *b* 1963.

The 1st baronet, Sir John Harrison (son of John Harrison, of Stockton-on-Tees), was Mayor of Stockton 1903, 1906, 1916, 1917, and 1918.

HARRISON (UK) 1961, of Bugbrooke, co Northampton

Sir MICHAEL JAMES HARWOOD HARRISON, 2nd *Baronet*; *b* 28 March 1936; *s* his father, *Sir* (JAMES) HARWOOD, 1980; *ed* Rugby; JP 1993; a Member of Lloyd's 1964-96, and of Council of Sail Training Assocn, Vice-Pres of Assocn of Combined Youth Clubs; a Liveryman Mercers' Company (Master 1986-87), and a Freeman of City of London; Chm Berrite Ltd: *m* 1967, (Rosamund) Louise, da of late Edward Buxton Clive, of Swanmore Lodge, Swanmore, Southampton, and has issue.
Residence – 35 Paulton's Sq, SW3. *Clubs* – MCC, Boodle's, Royal Harwich Yacht.

SONS LIVING

EDWIN MICHAEL HARWOOD, *b* 29 May 1981. —— Tristan John, *b* 1986.

DAUGHTERS LIVING

(Auriol) Davina, *b* 1968: *m* 1998, (Alexander) Benet Paul Hornby Northcote, yr son of Hon Edward Frederick Northcote, TD (*see* E Iddesleigh). —— Priscilla Caroline, *b* 1971.

SISTER LIVING

Joanna Kathleen *b* 1939: *m* 1966, William Ashton Sanders, of Nine Chimney House, Balsham, Cambridge CB1 6ES, and has issue living, James William Ashton, *b* 1968.

The 1st baronet, Sir (James) Harwood Harrison, TD, MP (son of Rev Ernest Wivelsfield Harrison, of Bugbrooke, Northampton), was Brevet-Col 4th Suffolk Regt (TA); Assist Govt Whip 1954-56, Lord Commr of the Treasury 1956-59, Comptroller of HM Household 1959-61, Chm Select Sub Cttee on Defence and Overseas Affairs 1971-79; also MP (*C*) for Eye Div of Suffolk 1951-79.

CRADOCK-HARTOPP (GB) 1796, of Freathby, Leicestershire

Lt-Cmdr Sir KENNETH ALSTON CRADOCK-HARTOPP, MBE, DSC, RN, 10th *Baronet*, only son of late Maj Louis Montague Cradock-Hartopp, yst son of late Col Edmund Charles Cradock-Hartopp, yr son of 3rd baronet; *b* 26 Feb 1918; *s* his cousin, *Maj Sir* JOHN EDMUND, TD, 1996; Lt-Cmdr RN (ret); served 1939-45 War and in Korea (cmd'd HMNZ frigate *Taupo* 1951-52), DSC 1952, Legion of Merit (USA) 1953; Assoc Member Inst of Management; MBE (Mil) 1946, FRGS 1949: *m* 1942, Gwendolyn Amy Lilian, da of late Capt Victor Crowther Upton, Malay States Guides, of Taiping, Malaya, and has issue.

Arms – Quarterly: 1st and 4th, sable, a chevron argent between three otters passant argent, *Hartopp*; 2nd and 3rd, per saltire gules and argent crusily, three boars' heads two and one, couped counterchanged, *Cradock*. Crest – Out of a ducal coronet or a pelican argent vulning herself proper, *Hartopp*.
Residence – Keepers, Yeovilton, Yeovil, Som BA22 8EX.

DAUGHTER LIVING

Christina, *b* 1948: *m* 1977, as his 2nd wife, Thomas Montagu Hickman, and has issue (*see* Hickman, Bt, colls). *Residence* – 60 Acre Lane, SW2 5SP.

SISTER LIVING

Virginia Anne, *b* 1922: *m* 1952, Michael Henry Tindall Carter, who *d* 1995, son of Arthur Herbert Carter, and has issue living, Christopher Henry James (Park Farm Deeping St Nicholas, Lincs PE11 3BJ), *b* 1953; *ed* Uppingham: *m* 1980, Jane Anne, da of Dr Brian Hardie, of Ledbury, Herefords, and Newcastle, NSW, Australia, and has issue living, Sophie Louise *b* 1987, — Geraldine Anne, *b* 1956: *m* 1st, 1985 (*m diss* 1991), Bruce Gordon Scott Coles; 2ndly, 1994, William Sam Fletcher, of Pulvertoft Hall, Gedney, Lincs, and has issue living (by 1st *m*), Alexander Henry Rufus Scott *b* 1987, James Edward Rupert Scott *b* 1989, (by 2nd *m*), Charles William Louis *b* 1996, — Paula Margaret, *b* 1962. *Residence* – Dormer Cottage, Long Sutton, Lincs PE12 9RG.

DAUGHTERS LIVING OF NINTH BARONET

Melinda Anne, *b* 1954: *m* 1984, Murray Lewis, only son of late Rev Raymond Lewis, of E Dean, E Sussex, and has issue living, Jonathan Murray, *b* 1988, — Katherine Anne, *b* 1990. *Residence* – 11 Clevedon Rd, Tilehurst, Reading, Berks RG31 6RL. —— Nicola Jane, *b* 1957. —— Joanna Elizabeth, *b* 1960: *m* 1985, Michael Victor Charter, 2nd son of Victor Noël Charter, of Chelmsford, Essex, and has issue living, Thomas Michael, *b* 1994, — Nicola Bryany, *b* 1996. *Residence* – 1 Tricklebanks, Catterall Hall Lane, nr Garstang, Lancs PR3 0PA.

WIDOW LIVING OF NINTH BARONET

PRUDENCE (*Prudence, Lady Cradock-Hartopp*), 2nd da of late Sir Frederick William Leith-Ross, GCMG, KCB: *m* 1953, Maj Sir John Edmund Cradock-Hartopp, 9th Bt, TD, who *d* 1996. *Residence* – The Cottage, 27 Wool Rd, Wimbledon Common, SW20 0HN.

Edward Hartopp, MP for Leicestershire, was created a baronet 1619, and the baronetcy became extinct 1762, on the death, without male issue, of Sir John, 4th baronet, whose granddaughter and heiress, Anne Hurlock, married 1777, Edmund Bunney, of The Newark, Leicester, who assumed the surnames of Cradock-Hartopp, and was created a baronet 1796. Sir Charles William Everard Cradock-Hartopp, 6th Bt, was a 1st Sec in Diplo Ser.

HARTWELL (UK) 1805, of Dale Hall, Essex

Sir (FRANCIS) ANTHONY CHARLES PETER HARTWELL, 6th *Baronet*; *b* 1 June 1940; *s* his father, *Sir* BRODRICK WILLIAM CHARLES ELWIN, 1993; *ed* Thames Nautical Training Coll, HMS *Worcester*, Cadet RNR, Cadet P & OSN Co, Navigation Officer; Univ of Southampton (Sch of Navigation), Master Mariner 1971; Merchant Navy 1958-75; MRIN, MNI, MCIT; Port Management, Marine Surveyor and Consultant: *m* 1968 (*m diss* 1989), Barbara Phyllis Rae, da of late Henry Rae Green, of Sydney, NSW, Aust, and has issue.

Arms – Sable, a buck's head cabossed argent, attired or, between the attires a cross patée-fitchée of the last; in chief a lion passant guardant per pale of the second and third; on a canton ermine two bars per pale azure and gules. **Crest** – On a mount vert within seven pales or, the second and fifth charged with a spear-head argent imbrued proper, a hart lodged argent, the dexter foot on a well of the last, and in the mouth a sprig of oak vert. *Residence* – Trevean, Highlands Rd, Barton-on-Sea, Hampshire BH25 7BL.

Sorte suā contentus

Contented with his lot

SON LIVING

TIMOTHY PETER MICHAEL CHARLES, *b* 8 July 1970; *ed* Allhallows Sch, and Nene Univ, Northampton.

COLLATERAL BRANCHES LIVING

Grandchildren (by 2nd *m*) of late Maj-Gen John Redmond Hartwell, CB, DSO (infra):—
Issue of late Cmdr Barry Benton Hartwell, RN, *b* 1933, *d* 1992; *m* 1st, 1956 (*m diss* 1968), Lois Maureen, yst da of Eric C. Bratt, of Bexhill-on-Sea, Sussex; 2ndly, 1970, Elizabeth Linley (Burnigill, Fettercairn, Kincardineshire AB30 1XX), yst da of Linley Underwood, of Linden House, Countesthorpe, Leics:—
(By 1st *m*) Karen Fiona, *b* 1961: *m* 1987, Nicholas Paul Baker, of The Dower House, Longwood, Owlesbury, Winchester, and has issue living, Charles Nicholas Midelton, *b* 1993, — Rosanna Isabella Jane, *b* 1988, — Francesca Louise, *b* 1990. —— (By 2nd *m*) Jonathan Barry, *b* 1975. —— Charlotte Linley, *b* 1973.

Granddaughter of late Sydney Charles Elphinstone Hartwell, 3rd son of 2nd baronet:—
Issue of late Maj-Gen John Redmond Hartwell, CB, DSO, *b* 1887, *d* 1970: *m* 1st, 1911 (*m diss* 1921), Nina Oliver, who *d* 19—, da of late Gen George Francis William St John, CB, RA; 2ndly, 1929, Hazel Hay, who *d* 1945, da of late Sir John Benton, KCIE, and widow of Capt R. C. C. Liston, IA; 3rdly, 1946, Edith Elizabeth, da of late F. W. Frosdyke:—
(By 1st *m*) Diana Marion, *b* 1912: *m* 1st, 1934, Lt-Col Sidney Clive Blaber, RA, who was *ka* Belgium 1944; 2ndly, 1951, Stephen Terrell, OBE, TD, QC, of 59 Brooksby St, Islington, N1 1EX, and has issue living (by 1st *m*), Marcus Oliver (2 Greatwood Cottages, Marley Lane, Battle, E Sussex), *b* 1942: *m* 1971, Susan Ingrid Neustrup Potts, and has issue living, Christopher Paul *b* 1984, Lucy Annabelle *b* 1980, — Carol Ann (21 Ripplevale Grove, Islington, N1), *b* 1940: *m* 1973, Charles Bruce Nairn, and has issue (*see* Nairn, Bt), — (by 2nd *m*), Peter, *b* 1951, — Paul, *b* 1953.

Issue of late Frederick Edward Hartwell, youngest son of 2nd baronet, *b* 1857, *d* 19—: *m* 1881, Susan Mary Ann, da of William Green, of Wannamboor, Victoria, Australia:—
Frederick Sydney, *b* 1886. —— Broderick William, *b* 1889. —— John Malcolm, *b* 1903. —— George Rollen, *b* 1905. —— Ada Wilhelmina, *b* 1887. —— Frances Mary Ann, *b* 1895. —— Julia Sarah, *b* 1901. —— May Alicia, *b* 1908.

Capt Humphrey Hartwell received grants of land in co Limerick and Kings co 1666. The 1st baronet Adm Sir Francis John Hartwell, was Col Deptford and Woolwich Volunteers, and Director of Greenwich Hospital.

HARVEY (UK) 1933, of Threadneedle Street, City of London

Professor (*Sir*) CHARLES RICHARD MUSGRAVE HARVEY, 3rd *Baronet*; 7 April 1937; *s* his father, *Sir* RICHARD MUSGRAVE, 1978, but does not use title; *ed* Marlborough, and Pembroke Coll, Camb; Professorial Fellow Sussex Univ Inst of Development Studies: *m* 1967, Celia Vivien, da of George Henry Hodson, and has issue.

SON LIVING

PAUL RICHARD, *b* 2 June 1971.

DAUGHTER LIVING

Tamara Catherine, *b* 1977.

SISTER LIVING

Joanna Musgrave, *b* 1934: *m* 1958, Angus Donald Macintyre, Fellow of Magdalen Coll, Oxford, who *d* 1994, and has issue living, Benedict Richard Pierce, *b* 1963: *m* 1993, Katherine A., da of Douglas Muir, of Dalmuir, Glasgow, and has issue living, Angus Barnaby *b* 1995, Finnian Alexander *b* 1997, — Magnus William Lachlan, *b* 1971, — Katherine Cressida Eve, *b* 1962.

AUNTS LIVING *(daughters of 1st baronet)*

Ruth Musgrave (945 Arlington Av, Berkeley, Calif), *b* 1902: *m* 1930 (*m diss* 1953), George MacGowan Harper, and has issue living, Jane Alison, *b* 1932: *m* 1959, Lt-Col Justus Michael Molitor Lenschau, US Army, who *d* 1993, and has issue living, James Gabriel Molitor, *b* 1961: *m* 1989, Angelina Renee, da of Mrs Shirley Huddleston Royer, of Memphis, Tenn, USA (and has issue living, Alexandra *b* 1993), Katherine Jane *b* 1964. —— Eleanor Paget Musgrave, *b* 1905: *m* 1930, Edward Kent Haliburton Karslake (Darell, Bt, colls), who *d* 1988, and has issue living, Antony Edward Kent (Nymet St George House, George Nympton, S Molton, Devon), *b* 1932; Brig late Royal Green Jackets: *m* 1956, June Pauline, el da of Henry William Harris Eastwood, and has issue living, John Burgess (3 Montolieu Gdns, W15) *b* 1956: *m* 1983, Naomi Celia, eldest da of Rt Hon Sir Timothy Hugh Francis Raison, (Cunard, Bt, colls), of Hillbreak, Brill, Bucks (and has issue living, Samuel Kent *b* 1990, Matthew William *b* 1997, Eleanor Veldes *b* 1985, Clare Laura, *b* 1988), William Edward Kent (109 Hopton Rd, SW16) *b* 1963: *m* 1989, Sarah Ann, da of William G. Hynard, of Violets Lane, Furneux Pelham, Buntingford, Herts (and has issue living, Emma Kate *b* 1992, Lucy Olivia *b* 1995, Alice Charlotte *b* 1998), Caroline Sarah *b* 1960: *m* 1989, Luis Talavera Corona, son of late Agustin Talavera Becerril, of Mexico City (and has issue living, Thomas *b* 1990, Alexander *b* 1992, Dominic *b* 1996), Henrietta Sarah *b* 1965: *m* 1993, James B. Forsyth, son of James Forsyth, of Bamburgh, Northumberland (and has issue living, Rory James *b* 1997, Rebecca Anne *b* 1995), — Sophia Susan (14 Duke St, S Molton, N Devon), *b* 1935: *m* 1964 (*m diss* 1983), Donald Watkins Brown, and has issue living, Stephen Scott *b* 1969, Geoffrey Mark *b* 1972, Bridget Joan *b* 1967, — Mary Leonora, *b* 1944: *m* 1966, Andrew Nicholas Dakin Goodhart, of 35 Mount Park Rd, W5, and has issue living, Gavin John *b* 1976, Rachel Mary *b* 1970, Catherine Jervis Ruth *b* 1973. *Residence* – 13 Duke St, South Molton, N Devon.

The 1st baronet, Sir Ernest Musgrave Harvey, KBE (son of late Rev Charles Musgrave Harvey, V of Hillingdon, Middlesex, and Preb of St Paul's) was a Director and Dep Gov of Bank of England.

Harvie-Watt, see Watt.

Havelock-Allan, see Allan.

HAWKEY (UK) 1945, of Woodford, co Essex (Extinct 1975)

Sir ROGER PRYCE HAWKEY, 2nd and last *Baronet*.

DAUGHTER LIVING OF SECOND BARONET

Sarah Elizabeth, *b* 1934: *m* 1960, William de Vallières Frith, Chevalier de l'Ordre du Merite Agricole (1968), Chevalier de L'Ordre National du Mérite (1976), and Chevalier de la Légion d'Honneur (1992), of Lizards Leap, Warwick, Bermuda, and has issue living, William Roger, *b* 1963, — Benjamin James, *b* 1964: *m* 1996, Michele, only da of George Poole, of Langshott, Horley, Surrey, — Carter Andrew, *b* 1970.

HAWKINS (GB) 1778, of Kelston, Somersetshire

PRO DEO ET REGE

For God and the king

Sir RICHARD CÆSAR HAWKINS, 9th *Baronet*; *b* 29 Dec 1958; *s* his brother, *Sir* HOWARD CÆSAR, 1999; *ed* Hilton Coll, Natal, and Witwatersrand Univ; CA: *m* 1992, Ernestine Ehrensperger, and has issue.

Arms – Argent, on a saltire engrailed sable a quatrefoil between four fleurs-de-lis or. **Crest** – On a mount vert a hind lodged or, the dexter forefoot resting on a gunstone.
Residence – 29 York Av, Craighall Park, Johannesburg, S Africa. *Address* – PO Box 410838, Craighall Park 2024, Johannesburg, S Africa.

SON LIVING

JONATHAN CÆSAR, *b* 23 June 1992.

SISTERS LIVING

Carrol Lee, *b* 1953: *m* 1985, Francis David Durand, and has issue living, James Matthew, *b* 1986, — Jessica Frances, *b* 1989. *Residence* – 32 13th Av, Parktown North, Johannesburg 2193, S Africa. — Kathryn Ann, *b* 1954: *m* 1974 (*m diss* 19—), Stephano Belluigi, and has issue living, Shawn Stephano, *b* 1975, — Gina Julia, *b* 1979. *Address* – PO Box 787234, Sandton 2146, S Africa. —— Helena Julia, *b* 1963: *m* 1986, William Kay, 2nd son of late Wilfrid Kay, of Droitwich, Worcs, and has issue living, Anthony Wilfrid, *b* 1990, — Natacha Katherine, *b* 1988. *Residence* – La Maison du Portier, Rue de la Garenne, Trinity, Jersey JE3 5FE.

AUNT LIVING (*daughter of 6th baronet*)

Joy Blanche, *b* 1921: *m* 1st, 1944, John Stobart Longworth; 2ndly, 1977, James Sloane Hume Maxwell, of 12 Heathrow, 6th Rd, Hyde Park, Sandton 2196, S Africa, and has issue living (by 1st *m*), Humphry John (6 Ethel Rd, Claremont 7708, S Africa), *b* 1945: *m* 1st, 1972, Lynne Edward; 2ndly, 1994, Jennifer Aberdein, and has issue living, (by 1st *m*) Grant Edward *b* 1974, Kevin John *b* 1977, Julia Claire *b* 1979, — Veronica Anne LONGWORTH (Esmoreitschouw 49, 2726 KJ Zoetermeer, The Netherlands), *b* 1951; has resumed her maiden surname: *m* 1987 (*m diss* 1998), ..., and has issue living, David Harry *b* 1987.

WIDOW LIVING OF SEVENTH BARONET

ANITA (*Anita, Lady Hawkins*), da of Charles H. Funkey, of Michigan, USA: *m* 1952, Sir Humphry Villiers Caesar Hawkins, 7th Bt, who *d* 1993. *Address* – PO Box 52340, Saxonwold, 2132, Johannesburg, S Africa.

COLLATERAL BRANCHES LIVING

Grandchildren of late Arthur Cæsar Hawkins, 7th son of 3rd baronet:—
Issue of late Percy Cæsar Hawkins, *b* 1863, *d* 19—: *m* 18—, Catherine Ripkin, who *d* 1937:—
Rupert Cæsar, *b* 1901. —— Oscar Cæsar, *b* 1908: *m* 19—, Zella Bunn, and has issue living, John Michael Cæsar, *b* 19—, — Patrick Cæsar, *b* 19—. —— Percy Cæsar, *b* 1910. —— Julia Louisa, *b* 19—. —— Kathleen Laura, *b* 19—. —— Cecelia Margaret, *b* 19—. —— Adeline Daisy, *b* 19—.

Issue of late Cyril Cæsar Hawkins, *b* 1878, *d* 1955: *m* 1909, Lulu, who *d* 1955, da of W. H. E. During:—
Marie, *b* 1910. *Residence* – Johannesburg, S Africa.

Grandchildren of late Reginald Hawkins, 2nd son of late Rev Henry Annesley Hawkins (infra):—
Issue of late Lieut-Col Eustace Fellowes Sinclair Hawkins, DSO, OBE, RASC, *b* 1881, *d* 1954: *m* 1908, Patience, da of Capt J. Henderson, late 12th Lancers:—
Patrick Reginald Cæsar, *b* 1918. —— Honour Marie Marguerite, *b* 1913.

Grandchildren of late Rev Henry Annesley Hawkins, yr son of the Rev Charles Hawkins, eldest son of Serjeant-Surgeon Charles Hawkins 4th son of 1st baronet:—
Issue of late Arthur Cockburn Hawkins, *b* 1852, *d* 19—: *m* 1883, Agnes, da of H. Carmichael:—
Henry Cecil Carmichael, *b* 1884: *m* 1907, Winnifred, da of John Robinson, and has issue living, Cecil Arthur Robinson, *b* 1908, — Harold Percy, *b* 1909, — Winnifred Agnes Ruth, *b* 1910. —— Arthur Charles, *b* 1885. —— Reginald Cæsar, *b* 1890. —— Agnes Isabel, *b* 1889. —— Frances Kathleen, *b* 1892.

Granddaughter of late Cdr Caesar Hugh Hawkins, RN, elder son of late Rev Charles James Hawkins, elder son of late Rev Charles Hawkins (ante):—
Issue of late Caesar Hugh George Wills Hawkins, *b* (*posthumous*) 1889, *d* 1947: *m* 1st, 1914 (*m diss* 1926), Margaret Edith, who *d* 1980, da of late James Shaw Robertson, of The Vache, Chalfont St Giles; 2ndly, 1930, Diodata (who *d* 1991, having *m* 2ndly, 1948 (*m diss* 1956), Archibald Laurence Lyall, who *d* 1964, and 3rdly, 19—, Marco Lucic-Roki, of Venice), da of late Count Bernhard Caboga, of Dubrovnik, Ragusa:—

(By 1st *m*) Margaret Elizabeth Anne, *b* 1917: *m* 1st, 1940, Lieut Hilliard Baxley Wilson, USNR, who *d* 1961; 2ndly, 1967, James Rowland Lowe, who *d* 1969, and *d* 1986, leaving issue (by 1st *m*), Penelope Jane, *b* 1944: *m* 1st, 1972 (*m diss* 19—), Michael McClure; 2ndly, 19—, Charles Giorgi. *Residence* – 947 Green St, San Francisco, Calif 94133, USA.

       Granddaughter of late Cæsar Hugh George Wills Hawkins (ante):—
   Issue of late Lieut Cæsar Charles Hawkins, DSC, RN, *b* 1915, *d* on active ser 1940: *m* 1937, Mary Redwood Vachell (who *m* 2ndly, 1945, Desmond John Dudley Torrens, MBE, MB, late Lieut-Col RAMC, and *d* 1962), da of Edmund Hann:—
Alice Penelope, *b* 1938: *m* 1961, Robin Audley Clinton Vivian, B92 Res Amiral, Marina Baie des Anges 06270, Villeneuve-Loubet, France (*see* B Vivian, colls).

       Granddaughter of late Edward Caesar Hawkins, son of late Caesar Richard Hawkins, son of late Rev Edward Hawkins, DD, el son of late Rev Edward Hawkins, 5th son of 1st baronet:—
   Issue of late Cdr Richard Pennell Caesar Hawkins, RN, *b* 1899, *d* 1990: *m* 1st, 1929 (*m diss* 1952), Enid Helen, who *d* 1983, da of Rev John Warren Corbould-Warren, Rector of Caistor with Markshall; 2ndly, 1964, Mary Constance Emily (Shelton Hall, Long Stratton, Norfolk), da of Rev Frank Percy Law, Rector of Shelton, Norfolk:—
(By 1st *m*), Diana Elizabeth, *b* 1930: *m* 1953, Anthony Pott.

       Grandson of late Rev Robert Hawkins, 4th son of late Rev Edward Hawkins (ante):—
   Issue of late Col Herbert Pennell Hawkins, CBE, *b* 1859, *d* 1940: *m* 1910, Hester Vera, who *d* 1972, da of Fleetwood Rynd, formerly of Mount Armstrong, co Kildare:—
Gerald Francis Cæsar (Newton Orchard, Pound Lane, Whitestone, Exeter EX4 2LJ), *b* 1912; *ed* Eton, and Oxford Univ (BM and BCh), MRCS England and LRCP London; 1939-45 War as Maj RAMC: *m* 1940, Patricia Enid Lambart, da of Maj Alexander George Lambart Sladen, MC, of Crabtree Furlong, Haddenham, Bucks, and has issue living, Julia Margaret, *b* 1946: *m* 1971, Ilgvars Spruntulis, of 3 Brookleigh Av, Heavitree, Exeter, Devon, and has issue living, Ben *b* 1979, Liza Mia *b* 1975.

The 1st baronet, Sir Cæsar Hawkins (son of late Cæsar Hawkins), was Serjeant-Surg to George II and George III.

HAWLEY (GB) 1795, of Leybourne Grange, Kent

(*Sir*) Henry Nicholas Hawley, 8th *Baronet*; *b* 26 Nov 1939; *s* his father, *Maj Sir* David Henry, 1988, but his name does not appear on the Official Roll of the Baronetage, nor does he use the title; *ed* Stowe.

𝕬rms – Vert, a saltire engrailed or. ℭrest – A dexter arm in armour proper, garnished or, holding in the hand a spear in bend sinister, point downwards, also proper.
Residence – No Man's Friend, New York, Lincoln LN4 4YE.

SISTERS LIVING

Margaret Serena, *b* 1946. *Residence* – 49 Watling Crescent, Handbridge, Chester CH4 7HD.
—— Penelope Marion, *b* 1948: *m* 1971, Richard M. Mansell-Jones. *Residence* – 66-67 The Bromptons, SW3.

HAWORTH (UK) 1911, of Dunham Massey, co Chester

Sir PHILIP HAWORTH, 3rd *Baronet*; *b* 17 Jan 1927; *s* his father, *Sir* (ARTHUR) GEOFFREY, 1987; *ed* Dauntseys, and Reading Univ (BSc 1948): *m* 1951, Joan Helen, da of late Stanley Percival Clark, of Ipswich, and has issue.

Arms – Azure, on a bend between two stags' heads couped or, as many garbs gules. Crest – Issuant out of grass proper a stag's head gules arme and collared with a chain or.
Residence – Free Green Farm, Over Peover, Knutsford, Cheshire WA16 9QX.

SONS LIVING

CHRISTOPHER, *b* 6 Nov 1951; *ed* Rugby, and Reading Univ (BSc); ARICS: *m* 1994, Mrs Susan Rachel Dent, da of David Ives, of Tunbridge Wells, Kent, and widow of Jonathan Dent, and has issue living, Oliver Jonathan Christopher, *b* 20 Oct 1996, — Annabelle Lucy Alice, *b* 1998. *Residence* – Applegates, Queens Rd, Crowborough TN6 1PX. —— Mark, *b* 1956; *ed* Rugby. —— Simon Nicholas, *b* 1961; *ed* Rugby, and Reading Univ. —— Adam Ewart, *b* 1964; *ed* Rugby, and Magdalene Coll, Camb.

DAUGHTER LIVING

Penelope Jane, *b* 1953; *ed* Sheffield Univ.

BROTHER LIVING

Jeremy Geoffrey, *b* 1931; *ed* Dauntseys, and New Coll, Oxford. *Residence* – The Bog Farm, Minsterley, Shropshire.

SISTERS LIVING

Jennefer, *b* 1928: *m* 1952, Herbert Hilton Minnis, and has issue living, Sterling Herbert, *b* 1953, — Russell Harold, *b* 1954, — Quentin Geoffrey, *b* 1963, — Royan Alexander, *b* 1974, — Jedda Alison, *b* 1957, — Sonya Jennefer, *b* 1960. *Address* – PO Box 1720, Nassau, Bahamas. —— Alison, *b* 1934: *m* 1958, Richard Crosfield Godlee, of The Grange, Clay Lane, Handforth, Wilmslow, Ches, and has issue living, Deborah Claire, *b* 1961, — Sarah Haworth, *b* 1965.

The 1st baronet, Sir Arthur Adlington Haworth (son of late Abraham Haworth, JP, of Bowdon, Cheshire), sat as MP for S Div of Manchester (*L*) 1906-12, and was a Junior Lord of the Treasury Feb to March 1912.

HAY (NS) 1635, of Smithfield, and Haystoun, Peeblesshire (Dormant 1966)

Sir BACHE MCEVERS ATHOLE HAY, 11th *Baronet*; *d* 1966, and at time of going to press no name appears on the Official Roll of Baronets in respect of this title.

COLLATERAL BRANCHES LIVING

Issue of late Capt Robert Athole Hay, elder brother of 11th baronet, *b* 1890, *d* 1939: *m* 1914, Margaret, who *d* 1928, da of late Richard Heywood Heywood Jones, of Badsworth Hall, York:—
Sarah Dorothea, *b* 1924: *m* 1946, David Rimington Tetley, of Brawby Park, Malton, N Yorks, and has issue living, Christopher Michael (Manor Farm, Little Habton, N Yorks), *b* 1948; *ed* Harrow; Capt 16th/5th Lancers: *m* 1972, Camilla Ann Molyneux Linton, da of late Maj-Gen Gerald Patrick Linton Weston, CB, CBE, DSO, of N Warnborough, Hants, and has issue living, Hugo Donald *b* 1975, Robin David *b* 1977, Charlotte Rose *b* 1979, Fiona Myfanwy *b* 1982, — Catherine Jane (49 Acacia Gdns, Bathpool, Taunton, Somerset), *b* 1950: *m* 1973 (*m diss* 1982), James Kimber McGavin, and has issue living, Joseph Sule Eric *b* 1974, Emma Simone *b* 1976, and further issue (by Francis Deas), Briar Dawn Annu *b* 1979.

Descendants of John, 3rd Lord Hay of Yester, great-great-uncle of 1st baronet, of whom the Marquess of Tweeddale is the presumed heir to the baronetcy.

The 1st baronet was an Esquire of the body of James VI. With his patent of baronetcy he received 16,000 acres of land in Nova Scotia. The 3rd baronet inherited only the title, which on his death, in 1683, became dormant. In 1762 James Hay, MD, claimed and assumed the baronetcy, was served heir to his great-great-grandfather, John Hay of King-smeadows — a younger brother of the grandfather of the 1st baronet — by a jury assembled at Perth 1805, and subsequently, in 1806, matriculated arms as a baronet in the Lyon Office.

HAY (NS) 1663, of Park, Wigtownshire

Sir JOHN ERROLL AUDLEY HAY OF PARK, 11th *Baronet*; *b* 3 Dec 1935; *s* his father, *Sir* ARTHUR THOMAS ERROLL, ISO, 1993; *ed* Gordonstoun, and St Andrew's Univ (MA 1960).

𝕬rms – Argent, three escutcheons gules and in chief an ox-yoke fesseways proper.

The present baronet is senior male representative of Sir Gilbert Hay, of Dronlaw, 2nd son of Sir Thomas Hay, of Erroll, Constable of Scotland. By the marriage of Sir John Hay, 7th Bt of Park, with Sarah Beresford Cossins (da of John Cossins by Hon Elizabeth Susannah Thicknesse Tuchet, da of 19th Baron Audley), his descendants are in remainder to the Barony of Audley.

HAY (NS) 1703, of Alderston

Sir RONALD FREDERICK HAMILTON HAY, 12th *Baronet*; *b* 1941; *s* his father, *Sir* RONALD NELSON, 1988: *m* 1978, Kathleen, da of John Thake, and has issue.

𝕬rms – Quarterly: 1st and 4th, azure, three fraises, *Fraser*; 2nd and 3rd, gules, three bars ermine, *Gifford of Yester*, over all, upon an escutcheon of pretence argent three escutcheons gules, in the centre a key fesseways wards downwards sable, *Hay*. 𝕮rest – A goat's head erased, argent, armed or.
Residence – Aspendale, Victoria 3195, Australia.

SONS LIVING

ALEXANDER JAMES, *b* 1979. ——— Anthony Ronald, *b* 1984.

DAUGHTER LIVING

Spare Nought

Sarah Jane, *b* 1981.

SISTER LIVING

Pamela Rosemary, *b* 1945: *m* 1972, Michael Edward Finnegan, and has issue living, Mark Andrew, *b* 1977, — Jodie Dawn, *b* 1980.

AUNTS LIVING

Lucy, *b* 1901. ——— Thelma Violet, *b* 1914: *m* 1938, Frank Coulton, and has issue living. *Residence* – Unit 38, Gleneaon, 207 Forest Way, Belrose, NSW 2085, Australia.

WIDOW LIVING OF ELEVENTH BARONET

RITA (*Rita, Lady Hay*), da of John Munyard: *m* 1940, Sir Ronald Nelson Hay, 11th Bt, who *d* 1988. *Residence* – 17 Murrumbeena Crescent, Murrumbeena, Victoria 3163, Australia.

COLLATERAL BRANCHES LIVING

Issue of late Howard Augustus Hay, 4th son of 6th baronet, *b* 1828, *d* 1884: *m* 1853, Sarah, who *d* 1902, da of Henry Harris, of Bitterne, Southampton:—
Douglas Hector, *b* 1869: *m* 1896, Amy Margaret, da of Alexander Jansen, formerly of Ridgway, Ontario, Canada, and has issue living, Douglas Howard Jerome, *b* 1898, — Thelma Arline, *b* 1903. —— Jane Sophia Louisa: *m* 1902, William Watts, and has issue living, Ernest Hay, *b* 1904.

Grandchildren of late James Shaw Hay (infra):—
Issue of late Conran Ker Hay, *b* 1882, *d* 1958: *m* 1908, Grace, who *d* 1960, da of Thomas B. Horsfield, of Manchester:—
Alexander Horsfield (Westtown School, Westtown, Pa, USA 19395), *b* 1912; MA; a Sch Teacher: *m* 1st, 1939, Bernice Louise, who *d* 1968, da of Walter C. Woodward, of Richmond, Indiana, USA; 2ndly, 1969, Agnes Marshall, da of George Ferguson Finnie, of Glasgow, and has issue living (by 1st *m*), Conran Alexander, *b* 1946, — Thomas Carlton, *b* 1951, — Arminal Elizabeth, *b* 1943. —— Gordon Conran (689 Westmount Hill's Drive, London, Ont, Canada), *b* 1919, MEd, Prof Emeritus: *m* 1943, Elizabeth Jean, da of Edward Henry Stevenson, of Renfrew, Ont, Canada, and has issue living, Stuart Gordon, *b* 1946; MSc: *m* 1975, Christiane Morisset, of St Michel, Quebec, and has issue living, Gregoire Alexander *b* 1976, — Alexander Edward, *b* 1949; PhD: *m* 1984, Jocelyne Hellou, of Montreal, and has issue living, Philip Conran *b* 1988, Natasha Bronwen *b* 1986, — Elizabeth Grace, *b* 1951; BA: *m* 1985, Mark Fried, of Swampscott, Mass, USA, and has issue living, Ben Angus *b* 1988, Sochi Bess *b* 1985, — Jean Anne, *b* 1957; BMus: *m* 1989, Ignatius Solis, of Mexico City, and has issue living, Carlos Andreas *b* 1990.

Issue of late Thomas Corlett Hay, VD, *b* 1883, *d* 1952: *m* 1930, Muriel, da of the Rev Charles Harry Dant, R of Babcary, Taunton:—
Pamela Jane, *b* 1931: *m* 1956, John G. Ewing, and has issue living, James Johanathan, *b* 1965, — Masindi Jane, *b* 1958, — Katherine Winifred Anne, *b* 1963. —— Bettine Muriel, *b* 1932; a SRN: *m* 1962, René Bouganon, of Johannesburg.

Granddaughter of late Alexander Murray Hay, el son of late Capt John Hay, half-brother of 5th baronet:—
Issue of late James Shaw Hay, *b* 1850, *d* 1908: *m* 1st, 1880, Charlotte Anne, da of William Corlett, of Ramsey, Isle of Man; 2ndly, 1889, Arminal Walmsley, da of James Scotson, of Liverpool:—
(By 2nd *m*) Muriel Scotston, *b* 1891: *m* 1921, Georges Louis Bard.

Grandchildren of late Loraine Macdonald Hay (infra):—
Issue of late Sydney Bertram Macdonald Hay, *b* 1918, *d* 1981: *m* 1945, Joan Reis:—
Phillip Michael Macdonald, *b* 1946. —— Roger Macdonald, *b* 1948. —— Aubrey Andrew Macdonald, *b* 1949. —— Edmund Macdonald, *b* 1954. —— Anthony Macdonald, *b* 1956. —— Ann Maureen, *b* 1951. —— Kathleen, *b* 1953.

Grandchildren of late Loraine Geddes Hay, 3rd son of late Lt-Col Thomas Pasley Hay, 3rd son of late Capt John Hay (ante):—
Issue of late Loraine Macdonald Hay, *b* 1883, *d* 1961: *m* 1917, Mequeline Eugenie Hamel-Smith, who *d* 1978:—
Mary Mildred, *b* 1924: *m* 1948, Aldred Mitchell, and has issue living, Alfred Bernard, *b* 1950, — William Joseph, *b* 1958, — Bernadette Mary, *b* 1949: *m* 1969, Michael David Diaz, and has issue living, Pamela Bernadette *b* 1970, — Denise Mequeline, *b* 1951: *m* 19—, John A. C. Forster, and has issue living, Andrew Donald *b* 1969, — Nanette Celine, *b* 1954, — Susan Marie, *b* 1955, — Sidney Debra, *b* 1959.

Issue of late James Carrington Hay, *b* 1888, *d* 1961: *m* 1921, Maria Cynthia Fifi, who *d* 1956:—
Ranald Louis (Canada), *b* 1925; *ed* St Francis Xavier Univ (BSc), and McGill Univ (BEng), PEng Ont: *m* 1955, Lorraine Marianné, da of late Frederick John Fecteau, of Toronto, and has issue living, Ranald Joseph, *b* 1956, — Dominic Louis, *b* 1958, — Cynthia Maria, *b* 1959, — Genevieve Anne, *b* 1960, — Marianne Noel, *b* 1962, — Laurie Elizabeth, *b* 1965. —— Donald Joseph (Smart St, St Augustine, Trinidad), *b* 1927: *m* 1955, Lola Sue Martin, and has issue living, Donald Roger Paul, *b* 1956; *ed* Kent State Univ, Ohio, USA (BSc Architecture), and Wisconsin Univ, Milwaukee (Masters in Architecture and Urban Planning): *m* 1982, Maureen Ellen Baker, of Cleveland, Ohio, — Bruce Victor Joseph, *b* 1959; *ed* W Indies Univ, Trinidad (BSc Eng), — Christopher Michael Charles, *b* 1967, — Paula Emily Rebecca, *b* 1966.

Grandchildren of late Maj-Gen Woulfe Hay, son of late Lieut-Col Thomas Pasley Hay (ante):—
Issue of late Alexander Hay, *b* 1872, *d* 1923: *m* 1909, Kathleen, da of late Gordon Styles Hare, of Croydon:—
James Woulfe, *b* 1910: *m* 1933, Edith Mary, da of Arthur Henry Myrton, of Johannesburg, S Africa, and has issue living, Bertha Lillian, *b* 1934, — Hilda Rose, *b* 1937. —— William Henry Ker, *b* 1912: *m* 1938, Violet Mary, da of late Harold Mortimer, of Manchester, and has issue living, Lynette Florence, *b* 1939, — Evadne Felicity, *b* 1943, — Merilyn Wendy, *b* 1951. *Residence* – Summer Place, 4 Sunbird St, Elspark, Elsburg, Transvaal, S Africa.

Descendants of late Thomas Hay (Lord Huntingdon, a Scottish Lord of Session), grandfather of 5th baronet:—

Grandchildren of late William Montgomery Hay, son of late Capt Henry Hird Hay, 5th Dragoon Guards, great-grandson of late Thomas Hay (ante):—
Issue of late Vincent Henry Hay, *b* 1889, *d* 1949: *m* 1915, Edicel Bassett, who *d* 1959:—
Wayne W., *b* 1918: *m* 1942, Harriet Johnson, and has issue living, Michael William, *b* 1943, — Robert Wayne, *b* 1950, — Ronald Patrick, *b* 1957, — Barbara Ann, *b* 1945, — Becky Ann, *b* 1948, — Jacquelline Marie, *b* 1953, — Catherine Marie, *b* 1960. —— Helen Francis, *b* 1922: *m* 1946, Richard Connell, and has issue living, Thomas Richard, *b* 1949, — Timothy Peter Joseph, *b* 1959, — Mary Theresa Louise, *b* 1947, — Mary Catherine, *b* 1952, — Mary Anita, *b* 1954, — Mary Jennifer, *b* 1956, — Mary Elizabeth, *b* 1958.

Granddaughter of late Capt Henry Hird Hay, 5th Dragoon Guards (ante):—
Issue of late Vincent Henry Fulford Hay, *b* 1868, *d* 1936: *m* 1905, Olive Ellen, da of Thomas John Richards, of Liskeard, Cornwall:—
Majorie Letitia, *b* 1907: *m* 1937, Frederick Guy Darvall, banker, and has issue living, Diana Hay, *b* 1938. *Address* – c/o National Bank of Australasia Ltd, Jandowaae, Queensland.

This family, anciently seated at Huntingdon, E Lothian, and at Mordington and Thornydykes Berwickshire, is descended in direct line from the old House of Lockerwort and Yester, whose progenitor was William de Haya (cup bearer to Malcolm IV and William the Lion), who *d* 1170. Sir John Hay, 1st baronet (el son of Thomas Hay, of Alderston, E Lothian (lineally descended from Sir Edmond Hay, of Linplum (*v* 1429-49), younger brother of Sir David Hay, of Yester (*v* 1475), ancestor of the Marquesses of Tweeddale)), was *cr* a Baronet with remainder to heirs male forever. The 8th Baronet, Sir William Henry, a housepainter by trade, *d* in Australia in 1927, and was *s* by his brother, Sir Edward Hamilton, who *d* 1936, without proving his succession or using the title.

DALRYMPLE-HAY (GB) 1798, of Park Place, Wigtownshire

Sir JAMES BRIAN DALRYMPLE-HAY, 6th *Baronet*, son of late Lieut-Col Brian George Rowland Dalrymple-Hay, son of late George Houston Dalrymple-Hay, son of late Col George James Dalrymple-Hay, 2nd son of 2nd baronet; *b* 19 Jan 1928; *s* his kinsman, Sir CHARLES JOHN, CVO, 1952; *ed* Blundell's; sometime Lieut RM: *m* 1958, Helen Sylvia, da of late Stephen Herbert Card, of Reigate, Surrey, and has issue.

Arms – Quarterly: 1st and 4th, or, on a saltire azure nine lozenges of the field, all within a bordure gules; 2nd and 3rd, argent, three escutcheons gules in chief on ox yoke lying fess-ways proper. Crests – 1st, a rock per pale azure and or; 2nd, between two piles or issuant from the torse a falcon proper, charged on the breast with an escutcheon gules. Supporters – Two volunteers belonging to the Corps of Wigton in their uniforms of the year 1800 all proper.
Residence – The Red House, Church St, Warnham, Horsham, W Sussex RH12 3QW.

DAUGHTERS LIVING

Fiona Louise, *b* 1963: *m* 1993, Richard M. Norcross, only son of Donald Norcross, of Churchdown, Glos, and has issue living, Rylan Daniel, *b* 1995, — Briony Laura, *b* 1996. —— Charlotte Ann, *b* 1966. —— Lucie Helen, *b* 1969.

BROTHERS LIVING

JOHN HUGH (Little Meadow, Forty Green Rd, Knotty Green, Beaconsfield, Bucks HP9 1XL), *b* 16 Dec 1929; *ed* Blundell's Sch; sometime Capt R Scots Fusiliers: *m* 1962, Jennifer Phyllis Roberta, da of late Brig Robert Johnston, CBE, and has issue living, Malcolm John Robert, *b* 1966. —— Ronald George Inglis (Glenluce, Lee's Gully Rd, Tetoro RD4, Waiuku, Auckland, NZ), *b* 1933; *ed* Blundell's Sch: *m* 1973, Anne Valerie, da of Bernard James Dawson, and has issue living, Russell James, *b* 1977.

HALF-BROTHER LIVING

Christopher Hamish (Klein Constantia, PO Box 160, Letsitele, 0885, N Transvaal), *b* 1941: *m* 1968, Margaret Linda Smith, and has issue living, Hamish Ian, *b* 1971, — Amanda Jane, *b* 1975.

COLLATERAL BRANCHES LIVING

Granddaughter of late Col George Houston Dalrymple-Hay, 5th and yst son of late Col George James Darlymple-Hay, 2nd son of 2nd baronet:—
Issue of late Lt-Col Hugh Brereton Dalrymple-Hay, DSO, IA, *b* 1900, *d* 1987: *m* 1939, Gwendyth Margaret (who *m* 2ndly, 1994, — Blake, of 1a Moorfield Rd, Woodbridge, Suffolk), da of late Lt-Col Norman L. Callard:—
Janet Margaret, *b* 1941: *m* 1963 (*m diss* 1986), Anthony David Stericker, only son of J. A. Stericker and has issue living, Johanna Margaret, *b* 1966, — Sophia Harriett, *b* 1968, — Lucinda Jean, *b* 1969. *Residence* – Brownings, Pytches Rd, Woodbridge, Suffolk.

Granddaughter of late Lt-Col Stair Francis Barton Dalrymple-Hay, yst son of late Col George James Dalrymple-Hay (ante):—
Issue of late Com Christopher Montague Vernon Francis Dalrymple-Hay, DSC, RN, b 1896; d on active ser 1944: m 1st, 1919 (m diss 1929), Mary Teresa, who d 1977, yr twin da of late Lt-Col Edward Henry Joseph Mostyn (Mostyn, Bt, colls); 2ndly, 1929, Helen Violet, da of H. K. Grierson, formerly of Castle Douglas:—
(By 1st m) Mary Cecily Edith Teresa, b 1920: m 1947, John Walter Ferlex Lloyd-Johnes.

Granddaughter of late Houston Stewart Dalrymple-Hay, 3rd son of 2nd baronet:—
Issue of late James Stewart Dalrymple-Hay, b 1860, d 1931: m 1886, Emily, da of William Irving:—
Mary Grace (Glenluce, Woy Woy, NSW), b 1888.

Grandchildren of late Richard Tycho Dalrymple Hay, 2nd son of late Houston Stewart Dalrymple-Hay (ante):—
Issue of late Charles Stewart Dalrymple-Hay, MC, b 1891, d 1972: m 1922, Barbara (22 Amaroo Pl, Yass, NSW), da of late Warwick Chambers, of Sydney, NSW:—
John Warwick (Glen Luce, Free Selectors Rd, RMB 337A Fox Ground, NSW 2534) b 1928; author and lecturer: m 1953, Barbara Deidre, da of M. Moir, of Canberra, and has issue living, Heather Nan, b 1954, — Ann Louise, b 1956. —— Ann, b 1924; 1939-45 War with WRANS: m 1947, David Thompson, stockbroker, of 41 Bundabah Av, St Ives, Sydney, NSW.

Grandchildren of late Houston Stewart Dalrymple-Hay (ante):—
Issue of late Claude Thomas Hugh Vans Dalrymple-Hay, b 1865, d 1953: m 1898 (m diss 1921), Belle, who d 1967, da of Frank Wheelhouse:—
†Houston Francis Wilfred, b 1907, d 1985: m 1st, 1938 (m diss 1943), Marie Hawke; 2ndly, 1967, Olive May, da of late John Jacob Worner. Residence – 5/55 King Street, Wollstonecraft, NSW 2065, Australia. —— Isobel Ellen Ruby b 1904: m 1924, Arthur John Peverley Hall, LLB, who d 1975 and has issue living, Isobel Wendy Anne, b 1928: m 19—, Andrew Erickson, of 78 Lord St, Laurieston, NSW 2443, Australia.

Issue of late Houston Stewart Dalrymple-Hay, b 1871, d 1956: m 1906, Daisy Annie, who d 1928, da of David Davis, of Christchurch, New Zealand:—
Houston Stewart, b 1909; formerly Capt 2nd Australian Imperial Force: m 1942, Peggy Fitzmaurice, who d 1982, da of Argyle Charles Charleston Loftus, of Brighton, Victoria, and has issue living, Charles Stewart, b 1949, — Helene Fitzmaurice, b 1951: m 1975, Christopher James Bell, of 181 Rymans Rd, Eltham North, Vic 3095, and has issue living, Simon Christopher b 1981, James Stewart b 1983. Residence – 3/15 Prince Albert St, Mosman, NSW 2088. —— Barbara (of 4 Howell Av, Lane Cove, Sydney, NS Wales), b 1913: m 1938, Charles John Newhill Leleu, OBE, formerly Roy Australian Air Force, who d 1961, and has issue living, John Stewart Newhill, b 1939, — Antonia Blanche Newhill, b 1945: m 1971, Melchor Puig Scribani, of Caracas, Venezuela, now of 38 Lady St, Mt Colan, NSW, and has issue living, Damian Antonio b 1972, Natalia Daniela b 1975. —— Nancy Stair, b 1915: m 1940, Frank Lawrence Fletcher, and has issue living, James Lawrence, b 1941, — Susan Stair b 1945: m 1970, Peter Brian Barton Pollock, of 26 Ryeburn Av, E Hawthorn, Victoria, NSW, and has issue living, Peter James b 1972, Simon Stewart b 1974, Robert Lawrence b 1978, — Josephine Daisy, b 1948: m 1972, Timothy Martin Harpur, of 22 Suffolk Av, Collaroy, NSW, and has issue living, Richard Sydney Frank b 1978, Sophic Irene b 1974, Elizabeth Nancy (twin) b 1974. Residence – 6 Beauty Point Rd, Beauty Point, NSW. —— Elizabeth Mary, b 1921: m 1947, Roy Charles Cooper, CBE, who d 1998, and has issue living, Peter Charles b 1951: m 1984, Catherine Black, and has issue living, Elizabeth Marie b 1985, Zoe Catherine b 1987, — Donald Stewart, b 1957: m 1987, Heather-Mary, — Sally Victoria, b 1948: m 1st, 1969 (m diss 19—) Douglas Sturrock; 2ndly, 19—, Reginald Marsh, and has issue living, (by 1st m) Angus John b 1973, Kate Elizabeth b 1975. Residence – Unit 12, Coronation Towers, 24 Dunmore Terr, Auchenflower, Qld 4066, Australia.

The 1st baronet, Col Sir John Dalrymple, of Dunragit, Wigtownshire, married the daughter of Sir Thomas Hay, 3rd Bt, of Park, on inheriting whose estates in 1794 he assumed by Roy licence the name of Hay. The 3rd baronet, Adm Rt Hon Sir John Charles, sat as MP for Wakefield (C) 1862-65, for Stamford 1866-80, and for Wigton Burghs 1880-85. The 5th baronet, Sir Charles John Dalrymple-Hay, CVO, was a Clerk in Foreign Office 1887-95, and in Privy Council Office 1895-1928.

HEAD (UK) 1838, of Rochester, Kent

STUDY QUIET

Sir FRANCIS DAVID SOMERVILLE HEAD, 5th *Baronet*; *b* 17 Oct 1916; *s* his father, *Sir* ROBERT POLLOCK SOMERVILLE 1924; *ed* Eton, and Peterhouse, Camb (BA 1937); Major (ret) Queen's Own Cameron Highlanders; 1939-45 War: *m* 1st, 1950 (*m diss* 1965), Susan Patricia, da of late Arthur Douglas Ramsay, OBE (*see* Ramsay, Bt, *cr* 1806, colls); 2ndly, 1967, Penelope Marion Acheson, da of late Wilfrid Archibald Alexander (*see* Hagart-Alexander, Bt) and has issue by 1st *m*.

Arms – Argent, a chevron ermines between three unicorns, heads couped sable. Crest – A unicorn's head, couped ermine.
Residence – 63 Chantry View Rd, Guildford, Surrey GU1 3XU. *Club* – Naval and Military.

SON LIVING (*By 1st marriage*)

RICHARD DOUGLAS SOMERVILLE, *b* 16 Jan 1951; *ed* Eton, Magdalene Coll, Camb (BA), and Bristol Poly (BA): *m* 1991 (*m diss* 1998), Edwina, da of late Edward Mansell, of Underwood, Notts.

DAUGHTER LIVING (*By 1st marriage*)

Diana Mary Frances, *b* 1954; BA: *m* 1983, Michael Robert Parkin, only son of F. R. Parkin, of Pittenween, Fife, and has issue living, Zuleika Florence Rosa, *b* 1988.

BROTHER LIVING

John Kenelm Somerville, *b* 1918; *ed* Wellington Coll, and at Oriel Coll, Oxford (MA); BEd Calgary; 1939-45 War, with RAMC and Intelligence Corps: *m* 1942, Lilah Doreen Prittie Wingfield, da of late Lt-Col Samuel James Chatterton Prittie Perry, FRCS (V Powerscourt, colls), and has issue living, Patrick John Somerville (1406-20 Avenue N, Lethbridge, Alberta, Canada; 2ndly, 1995, Joan Fay, da of late Ezekiel A. Crawford, of Taber, Alberta, and has issue living, (by 1st *m*) Kathleen Patricia *b* 1974: *m* 1996, Neil Jesske, of 437 Vancouver Av NW, Saskatoon, Sask, Canada, Sheila Nadine *b* 1979, — David Charles Somerville (2627-49 A Street, Edmonton, Alberta T6L 3X2), *b* 1949: *m* 1978, Constance Faye, da of Clifford Schowalter, of Edmonton, Alberta, and has issue living, Phillip Arthur Somerville *b* 1983, Graeme Douglas Somerville *b* 1986, Alana Christina *b* 1991, — Sarah Grace Edith, *b* 1947: *m* 1972, Ronald James Zezulka, of 331 Queensland Rd SE, Calgary T2J 3S4, Alberta, Canada, and has issue living, Michael John Jaroslav *b* 1977, — Angela Lilah Mary (twin) *b* 1949: *m* 1973, Joseph Andrew Panter, of Box 242, Clyde, Alberta T0G 0PO, Canada, and has issue living, David James *b* 1974: *m* 1997, Christina, da of Karl Beiwart, of Edmonton, Alberta, Jennifer Anne *b* 1979. *Residence* – 123 First St NW, Medicine Hat, Alberta T1A 6H2, Canada.

SISTER LIVING

Angela Grace Mary *b* 1922: *m* 1941, Henry Paddison Granlund, DSC, who *d* 1993, late Lt RNVR, and has issue living, Hew Richard Paddison (7 Bell Hill Ridge, Petersfield, Hants GU32 2DZ), *b* 1943: BA, CDipAF; Lt-Cdr RN: *m* 1977, Gillian Hazel, da of Rev Canon J. J. Cresswell, of Eastleach, Turville, Glos, and has issue living, Charles Richard Alexander *b* 1979, Angus Gordon Howard *b* 1981, — Karen Mary, *b* 1945: *m* 1981, Jeremy Patrick New, of 3 Bythorn St, SW9, — Margaret Jane, *b* 1950: *m* 1st, 1973 (*m diss* 1977), Anthony Hewett-Hicks; 2ndly, 1988, Christopher Ian Peters, of 1 Dunkirk Bank, Amberley, Stroud, Glos GL5 5AX, and has issue living, George Duncan *b* 1990. *Residence* – Little Weekhayne, Southleigh, Colyton, Devon EX13 6JA.

COLLATERAL BRANCH LIVING

Granddaughters of George Burges Digby Head, yr son of 3rd baronet:—
Issue of late Com Robert Digby Head, DSC, RN, *b* 1917, *d* 1956: *m* 1946, Lorraine, ARRC (Balgay, 21 Dewlands Way, Verwood, Dorset BH31 6JN), who *m* 2ndly, 1967 (*m diss* 1973), William Gerard Fallon, da of late Townley Walter Dowding, of Dolphin Sq, SW1:—
Pauline Anne (Brick Cottage, Gorsely, Ross-on-Wye, Herefords), *b* 1948: *m* 1991, Graham D'Arcy. —— Linda Mary, *b* 1951: *m* 1st, 1971 (*m diss* 1976), Paul Richard Wilder; 2ndly, 1978 (*m diss* 1980), Stephen Robert Whitby; 3rdly, 1982, Michael Benjamin Bobak, of 11 Berkeley Pl, Wimbledon, SW19 4NN and has issue living (by 1st *m*), Robert James, *b* 1972, — (by 3rd *m*) Danielle Anne, *b* 1982.

The 1st baronet, Right Hon Sir Francis Bond Head, KCH, PC (grandson of Moses Mendes, of Old Buckenham, Norfolk, and London, who *m* Anna Gabriella, 2nd da and co-heir of Rev Sir Francis Head, 4th Bt, of The Hermitage, Kent (*ext*), and whose surname her heirs of the body were authorised to assume by Roy licence 1770), was Lieut-Gov of Upper Canada 1835-38.

CHADWYCK-HEALEY (UK) 1919, of Wyphurst, Cranleigh, co Surrey, and New Place, Luccombe, Somerset.

Believe in me

Sir CHARLES EDWARD CHADWYCK-HEALEY, 5th *Baronet*; *b* 13 May 1940; *s* his father, *Lt-Col Sir* CHARLES ARTHUR, OBE, TD, 1986; *ed* Eton, and Trin Coll, Oxford (MA 1968): *m* 1967, Angela Mary, eldest da of late John Metson, of Brook End, Little Dunmow, Essex, and has issue.

Arms – 1st and 4th gules, four fusils engrailed and conjoined in bend, ermine between two lilies leaved and slipped proper, *Healey*; 2nd and 3rd gules, an anchor cabled within an orle argent, charged with eight martlets of the field (*Chadwyck*). Crest – 1st, in front of four fusils engrailed and conjoined fessewise ermine a lily as in the arms, *Healey*; 2nd, a talbot's head gules, charged on the neck with an escutcheon argent, thereon a martlet as in the arms, *Chadwyck*.
Residence – Manor Farm, Bassingbourn, Cambs SG8 5NX.

SON LIVING

EDWARD ALEXANDER, *b* 2 June 1972: *m* 1999, Denise Suzanne, eldest da of C. Osborne, of 65 Falkenham Rise, Basildon, Essex SS14 2JF.

DAUGHTERS LIVING

Catherine, *b* 1970. —— Faith, *b* 1977.

BROTHERS LIVING

Nicholas Gerald (39 Fairlawn Av, W4 5EF), *b* 1946; *ed* Eton: *m* 1978, Alison Jill, only da of Dr. N. Stevens, of Morris House, Fishmarket St, Thaxted, Essex, and has issue living, Gerald Norton, *b* 1979, — Cherry Kathleen, *b* 1980. —— Peregrine James (Vern Leaze, Calne, Wilts), *b* 1950; *ed* Eton: *m* 1973, Julia Mary, el da of Sir Richard James Boughey, 10th Bt, and has issue living, Oliver Peregrine, *b* 1982, — Alice Rachel, *b* 1977, — Rose Henrietta, *b* 1980.

SISTERS LIVING

Philippa Harriet (15 Lena Gdns, W6 7PY), *b* 1943: *m* 1974 (*m diss* 1987), her cousin, Jeremy Michael Lubbock (*see* B Avebury, colls). —— Serena Margaret, *b* 1948: *m* 1971, Jeremy D. Nickson, of Mount Pleasant House, Great Shefford, Newbury, Berks, and has issue living, George Howard, *b* 1977, — Francesca Verena, *b* 1975, — Theresa Viola, *b* 1980.

COLLATERAL BRANCH LIVING

Issue of late Oliver Nowell Chadwyck-Healey, 3rd son of 1st baronet, *b* 1886, *d* 1960: *m* 1916, Gwendoline Mary, who *d* 1979, da of Major Hugh Charrington, of Hill Cottage, Taplow, Bucks:—
John Hugh, *b* 1922; *ed* Eton; formerly Capt Rifle Brig; N Africa, and Italy 1943-5 (wounded). *Residence* – 9d Thistle Grove, SW10 9RR. —— Patience Mary, *b* 1917; late Junior Com ATS: *m* 1946, Lieut-Col Peter St George Hereward Maxwell, MC, HLI, who *d* 1997, and has issue living, Philip Hugh (72 Leathwaite Rd, SW11 3RT), *b* 1947: *m* 1976, Anne Briar, da of late W/Cmdr Frederick Nairn Royle-Bantoft, and has issue living, Rory Nairn *b* 1977, Andrew Philip *b* 1978, — Ian Peter (Sydney, NSW, Australia), *b* 1949: *m* 1971, Elizabeth Weddell, and has issue living, Peter Ross *b* 1982, Catherine Elisabeth *b* 1980, — Gillian Mary, *b* 1954: *m* 1980, Hamish John Corbet Clifton, and has issue living, Thomas Wykeham *b* 1983, Alastair Maxwell *b* 1985, Louise Venetia *b* 1988, — Penelope Frances, *b* 1956: *m* 1993, David Andrew Smart, of Sandton, Leighton Rd, Northall, Dunstable, Beds LU6 2HA, and has issue living, James Alexander *b* 1994, Sophie Victoria *b* 1996. *Residence* – 1 Thames Bank, Thames Rd, Goring-on-Thames, Oxon RG8 9AH.

The 1st baronet, Sir Charles Edward Heley Chadwyck Chadwyck-Healey, KCB, KC, Hon Capt RNR, was Chm Admiralty Vol Committee 1903-14, commanded a Hospital Ship during European War 1915-18, and was *cr* a baronet for valuable service on Admiralty Transport Arbitration Board. The 2nd baronet Sir Gerald Edward Chadwyck-Healey, CBE, was Director of Materials and Priority, Admiralty 1918.

HEATHCOTE (GB) 1733, of Hursley, Hampshire
(Name pronounced "Hethcut")

Et Dieu mon appui

And God my help

Sir MICHAEL PERRYMAN HEATHCOTE, 11th *Baronet*, *b* 7 Aug 1927; *s* his father, *Sir* LEONARD VYVYAN, 1963; *ed* Winchester, and Clare Coll, Camb; late 2nd Lieut 9th Lancers; in remainder to the Earldom of Macclesfield: *m* 1956, Victoria, el da of Com James Edward Rickards Wilford, RD, RNR, of Ackland Cottage, Shirley Holms, Lymington, Hants, and has issue.

𝕬rms – Ermine, three pomels each charged with a cross or. 𝕮rest – On a mural crown azure, a pomey charged with a cross or between two wings displayed ermine. 𝕾econd 𝕸otto – "Deus prosperat justos" (*God prospers the just*).
Residence – Warborne Farm, Boldre, Lymington, Hants S041 5QD.

SONS LIVING

TIMOTHY GILBERT, *b* 25 May 1957. —— George Benjamin, *b* 1965.

DAUGHTER LIVING

(Harriet) Louise, *b* 1962: *m* 1982, Richard J. Rouse, of Sea Cottage, Westfield Rd, Lymington, Hants only son of Lt-Cdr P. J. Rouse, RN (ret), of Tarnaut House, Tiptoe, Hants.

SISTER LIVING

Pamela Mary, *b* 1923: *m* 1945, (John) Gilbert Jones, of Walnut Tree Cottage, Harkstead, Ipswich, Suffolk, and has issue living, Richard Edmund, MBE, *b* 1947 (c/o Glasgow Univ, Glasgow): *m* 1987, Euphemia Photos, and has issue living, Alexander Xenophon *b* 1988, Michael Andronicus *b* 1991, Simon Maximian *b* 1993, — Rosemary Anne, *b* 1948: *m* 1975, T. J. Aston, of Rose Cottage, Pear Tree Green, Brockhampton, Heref HR1 4SA, and has issue living, Emma Meriel May *b* 1979.

COLLATERAL BRANCHES LIVING *(All male line in special remainder to Earldom of Macclesfield)*

Branch from youngest son of father of 9th and 10th baronets

Granddaughter of late Rev Gilbert Vyvyan Heathcote, father of 9th and 10th baronets:—
Issue of late William Charles Perceval Heathcote, *b* 1867, *d* 1937: *m* 1921, Ruth, who *d* 1950, da of late Arthur Malcolm Heathcote (infra):—
Anne, *b* 1923: *m* 1945, Baron Diederic W. van Lynden, late Ambassador Netherlands Foreign Ser, who *d* 1990, of Lange Voorhout, 48 The Hague, and has issue living, Jan Willem Alexander, *b* 1948, — Carel Diederic Aernout, *b* 1954, — Carola, *b* 1947: *m* 1969, Jonkheer A. G. Beelaerts van Blokland.

Grandchildren of late Reginald St Alban Heathcote, DM, FRCP, yst son of late Rev Gilbert Vyvyan Heathcote (ante):—
Issue of late Anthony Giles Salvin Heathcote, CD, *b* 1919, *d* 1970: *m* 1953, Kathleen Joan (276 McKee Av, Willowdale, Ont, Canada), only da of H. Dawson, of Burton-on-Trent, Staffs:—
William Reginald Salvin, *b* 1955. —— Andrew Henry Salvin, *b* 1962. —— Jean Viola, *b* 1954. —— Catherine Dawson, *b* 1959. —— Ann Elisabeth, *b* 1960. —— Ruth Margaret, *b* 1963.

Branch from 6th son of 5th baronet

Grandchildren of late James Shirley Heathcote, eldest son of late Arthur Malcolm Heathcote, 6th son of 5th baronet:—
Issue of late Martin Shirley Heathcote, *b* 1914, *d* 1992: *m* 1948, Mary Gertrude, da of Dr H. H. Nowland, of Sydney, NSW:—
Richard Desmond (Warrawong, Tambar Springs, NSW), *b* 1950: *m* 1973, Carmel, da of William Montgomery, of Ganalgang, Trangie, NSW, and has had issue, James Martin, *b* 1974, — Samuel William, *b* 1978, — Benjamin Richard, *b* 1990, — Sophie Louise, *b* 1976, — Amy Patricia, *b* 1982; *d* 1984. —— Pamela Shirley, *b* 1949: *m* 1971, Gasper Rey i de Grief. —— Ann Margaret, *b* 1956.

Branch from 3rd son of 3rd baronet

Grandchildren of late Capt Arthur Cleveland Heathcote, RN, son of late Adm Edmund Heathcote, son of late Rev Samuel Heathcote, 3rd son of 3rd baronet:—
Issue of late Maj Eustace Cleveland Heathcote, RM, *b* 1895, *d* 1976: *m* 1926, Marie Macmurrough Teresa, who *d* 1977, da of late J. J. Kavanagh:—
Michael Edmund (Hursley Cottage, Dockenfield, nr Farnham, Surrey), *b* 1931; Capt RM (ret): *m* 1959, Jean, el da of D. J. V. Hamilton-Miller, of Shrewsbury House, Ditton Hill, Surrey, and has issue living, Kathryn Gay, *b* 1961: *m* 1987, Christopher David McDonald Cann, son of G. D. T. Cann, of Cardiff, — Georgina Anne (twin), *b* 1961: *m* 1986, (Alfred Joseph Gerard Robert) Alain Rey, of Beau-Bassin, Mauritius, son of Jacques Robert Rey, of Beau-Bassin, Mauritius, and

has issue living, Olivier Michael Robert *b* 1987, — Jenny Louise, *b* 1964: *m* 1996, Markus James Fischer, son of Fritz Hans Otto Fischer, of Wollongong, Australia. —— Valerie, *b* 1929; late 2nd Officer WRNS.

Branch from 4th son of 3rd baronet

Granddaughter of late Charles Heathcote (*b* 1833), 5th son of William Lovell Heathcote, el son of Adm Sir Henry Heathcote, 4th son of 3rd baronet:—
Issue of late Frederick Lovell Heathcote, *b* 1875, *d* 1968: *m* 1901, Mimmie Ethel Ziervogel, who *d* 1938:—
Joan, *b* 1910: *m* 1938, Maurice E. Wilmot, who *d* 1986, and has issue living, Chester George, *b* 1948, — Felicity Mary, *b* 1940: *m* 1964, John St Laurence Beaufort, and has issue living, Sandra *b* 1966. *Address* – Box 69, Kenton-on-Sea 6191, S Africa.

Grandchildren of late Frederick Lovell Heathcote (ante):—
Issue of late Geoffrey Charles Heathcote, *b* 1906, *d* 1988: *m* 1939, Megan Edith Pugh-Jones (Crestwood, PO Box 7160, Newton Park 6055, Port Elizabeth, S Africa):—
Charles William (Crestwood, PO Box 7160, Newton Park 6055, Port Elizabeth, S Africa), *b* 1942: *m* 1967, Hester Cornelia de Lange, and has issue living, Charles Geoffrey, *b* 1981, — Karen Sarah, *b* 1968, — Lucille Megan, *b* 1970, — Dianne May, *b* 1972, — Marian Louise, *b* 1976. —— Warwick Geoffrey, *b* 1946: *m* 1969, Helena Louisa Marais, and has had issue, †Geoffrey Charles Lovell, *b* 1973, *d* 1994, — Elizabeth Anne, *b* 1970, — Caroline Louise, *b* 1987. —— Gerard Lovell, *b* 1951: *m* 1975, Laura Glen HUGHES (*née* Anderson), and has issue living, Caleb Geoffrey Lovell, *b* 1994, — Olivia Megan, *b* 1980, — Carmen Joy, *b* 1982. —— Eleanor May, *b* 1948: *m* 1968, Lysle Horace Wilmot, and has issue living, Mark Lysle, *b* 1969, — David Geoffrey, *b* 1972, — Suzanne Megan, *b* 1969, — Michelle May, *b* 1978.

Issue of late Albert Ziervogel Heathcote, *b* 1909, *d* 1977: *m* 1943, Doreen Oke Thomas (Glenfield, PO Box 7071, Newton Park, Port Elizabeth, S Africa):—
Frederick Malcolm (PO Box 7071, Port Elizabeth, S Africa), *b* 1944: *m* 1972, Elenor Fourie, and has issue living, Frederick Henry, *b* 1973, — Llewellyn Malcolm, *b* 1975. —— Albert Dennisson (PO Box 252, Humansdorp, S Africa), *b* 1946: *m* 1969, Elizabeth Stoutjesdyk, and has issue living, Yvonne Sharon, *b* 1970, — Carol Lisé, *b* 1973, — Lynne Denise, *b* 1976, — Hellen Delia, *b* 1980. —— Richard John (PO Box 252, Humansdorp, S Africa), *b* 1948: *m* 1969, Finette van Gend, and has issue living, Charmaine Sunette, *b* 1969, — Richelle Doreen, *b* 1970, — Teresé Finette, *b* 1975, — Jacqueline Melodé, *b* 1978. —— Hilary Oke, *b* 1950: *m* 1975 (*m diss* 1979), William Kirkman Allen, and has issue living, Wilfred Gavin, *b* 1976.

Grandchildren of late Charles William Heathcote (infra):—
Issue of late Frederick Lennox, Heathcote, *b* 1903, *d* 1969: *m* 1932, Mildred Walkenshaw Shaw, who *d* 1974:—
Leon Geoffrey (PO Box 998, Gweru, Zimbabwe), *b* 1934: *m* 1957, Gillian Jean Lawson, and has issue living, Frederick Garth (PO Box 809, Gweru, Zimbabwe), *b* 1958, — Mark Andrew, *b* 1962, — Jean Pamela, *b* 1960: *m* 1980, Glendyn Stephen Delamere Thompson (PO Box 633, Gweru, Zimbabwe), and has issue living, Bruce Glen *b* 1988, Shay Jean *b* 1983, Donna Caron *b* 1985. —— Roy (5 Farthing Hill, PO Borrowdale, Harare, Zimbabwe), *b* 1938: *m* 1965, Gillian Helen Dalling, and has issue living, Paul Roy (PO Box BW732, Borrowdale, Harare, Zimbabwe), *b* 1972: *m* 1998, Kim Eugenie Stander, — Amanda Kim, *b* 1968. —— Frederick Noel, *b* 1945: *m* 1967, Catherine Caryln Barry, and has issue living, Clive Noel (PO Marondera, Zimbabwe), *b* 1968, — Wayne Douglas, *b* 1972, — Kelly, *b* 1980. —— Stella Lenore, *b* 1933: *m* 1950, Bruce John Humpage, of 3 Canary Close, Avondale, Harare, Zimbabwe, and has issue living, Denise Marie, *b* 1953: *m* 1971, John Sealy, and has issue living, Gail *b* 1971, Leigh-Anne *b* 1974, — Carol Gail, *b* 1955: *m* 1974, Neville Thompson. —— Colleen, *b* 1936: *m* 1954, Errol Dennis Roberts (PO Box 598, Gweru, Zimbabwe), and has issue living, Cheryl Gail, *b* 1955: *m* 1979, Stephan William Cloete, and has issue living, Barry James *b* 1980, Ashley *b* 1983, — Melody Gaynor, *b* 1957: *m* 1984, Roland Francis Woods, and has issue living, Craig Dennis *b* 1988, Wendy Frances *b* 1986, — Fiona Gaylin, *b* 1958: *m* 1981, Bryan Matthew Rabie, and has issue living, Robert Matthew *b* 1985, Tracey-Lee *b* 1982, — Beverley Colleen, *b* 1959: *m* 1978, Anthony Kreft, and has issue living, Sean Anthony *b* 1982, Nicolette Colleen, *b* 1980. —— Cleone, *b* 1942: *m* 1963, Rodney E. M. Roberts, of Gweru, Zimbabwe, and has issue living, Shane Gavin, *b* 1965, — Felicity Ann, *b* 1967.

Grandchildren of late Charles Heathcote (*b* 1833) (ante):—
Issue of late Charles William Heathcote, *b* 1877, *d* 1918: *m* 1st, 19—, Sophie Kichner, who *d* 1910; 2ndly, 1911, Nellie van Heerden, who *d* 1918:—
(By 1st *m*) Millicent Pearl, *b* 1908: *m* 1937, Harry Dale, and has issue living, Margaret Ann *b* 1939: *m* 1st, 1960 (*m diss* 1962), Peter Reynecke; 2ndly, 1963, Michael Herbert Smit, and has issue living (by 1st *m*) Millicent Sharon *b* 1961, (by 2nd *m*) Steve Carl *b* 1967, Irene Tessa *b* 1965, Fiona Ann *b* 1969. —— (By 2nd *m*) Kathleen Mary, *b* 1912: *m* 1933, Rev Martin Luther Janse van Rensburg, and has issue living, Luther Calvyn *b* 1935: *m* 1959, Anne Elizabeth Nieuwoudt, and has issue living, Johanna Maria *b* 1960, — Marleen, *b* 1938: *m* 1960, Johannes Daniel Nieuwoudt, of Hoopstad, Orange Free State, S Africa. —— Emma Ida May, *b* 1915: *m* 1937, Jacobus Wessel Janses van Rensburg, and has issue living, Jacobus Hendrikus, *b* 1938, — Martin Luther, *b* 1946, — Jacobus Wessel, *b* 1949, — Kathleen Mary, *b* 1943, — Alida Jacoba, *b* 1949.

Issue of late Fitzroy Hamilton Heathcote, *b* 1881, *d* 1938: *m* 1903, Edith Beamish, who *d* 1947:—
Grace Sybil Beamish, *b* 1904: *m* 1930, Norman Sharwood, and has issue living, Norma Dorothy, *b* 1931: *m* 1954, Tristan McGibbon Maynier, c/o Standard Bank, Queenstown, S Africa, and has issue living, Derek *b* 1959, Nicolette *b* 1956: *m* 1980, Matthew Haxton Millar Guiney (and has issue living, Jacquelyn Martha *b* 1981, Gillian Norma *b* 1983). —— Ida Beamish, *b* 1906: *m* 1932, William Leslie Lyddon Farrant, c/o Box 375, Pretoria, S Africa, and has issue living, Leslie Heathcote, *b* 1935: *m* 1961, Antoinette du Toit, — David Heathcote (c/o Box 375, Pretoria, S Africa) *b* 1937. —— Winifred Beamish, *b* 1917: *m* 1st, 1935, John Rennie, who was *ka* 1942; 2ndly, 1944, Patrick Dairmid Dolan, who *d* 1981; 3rdly, 1994, John Radforth Mountjoy, of 48 Douglas Av, Craighall, 2196 Johannesburg, S Africa, and has issue living (by 1st *m*), Myrle Allison, *b* 1938: *m* 1963, Paul de Vere Noaké, of 49 Douglas Av, Craighall, Johannesburg, S Africa, and has issue living, John de Vere *b* 1964, Susan *b* 1966, — (by 2nd *m*) Elizabeth Ann, *b* 1945: *m* 1965, Alan Tucker, of 9 Government Rd, Beauty Point, 2088 Mosman, Sydney, NSW, Australia, and has issue living, Robert Kidger *b* 1967, James Kidger *b* 1969, George Kidger *b* 1971, Ian Kidger *b* 1973.

Issue of late Cecil Heathcote, *b* 1883, *d* 1918: *m* 1911, Engela Starr, who *d* 1941 (having *m* 2ndly, 1930, Maurice Meek, formerly of PO Willoughby's Siding, Zimbabwe), el da of Ambrose George Campbell Shaw:— Cecil Starr, *b* 1912: *m* 1935, Norah Edith, da of Walter James, and has issue living, Janet Mary, *b* 1949: *m* 1976, John Marshall, of E London, S Africa, and has issue living, Andrew Keith *b* 1983, Pamela Susan *b* 1979. —— Ambrose Carl Starr (Village House, PO Esigodini, Zimbabwe), *b* 1915: *m* 1940, Dorothy, yr da of W. B. Richards, of Fort Victoria, Zimbabwe, and has issue living, David Starr (6 Ada Attwell Rd, Ilanda, Bulawayo, Zimbabwe), *b* 1952, — Sylvia Starr, *b* 1956: *m* 1979, Michael Basil Gibbons, of 39 Stanley Rd, Irene 1675, S Africa, and has issue living, Richard Michael *b* 1985, Lara Kathryn *b* 1983. —— Mary Lesley Starr, *b* 1913: *m* 1937, Harry Edward Smith. *Residence* – Stanhope Farm, Somabula, Zimbabwe.

Issue of late Albert Jerrold Heathcote, *b* 1887, *d* 1964: *m* 1st, 1914 (*m diss* 19—), Dorothy Twycross; 2ndly, 1945, Mrs Muriel Korsten, who *d* 1961, and has issue:— (By 1st *m*) William Jerrold, *b* 1915: *m* 1959, Johanna Hofmeyr. —— John Albert, *b* 1916; formerly Sergt, Union Defence Force, S Africa: *m* 1944, Mrs Rosemary Hilda Beresford Carter, da of Oswald Beresford Lonsdale, and has issue living, Charles John Beresford, *b* 1948: *m* 1978, Anna Krystyna, da of Jerzy Rafal Cywinski, — Phyllis May Beresford, *b* 1945: *m* 1968, Lawrence A. Green, — Rosemary Alice Beresford, *b* 1953. —— George Twycross (Stutterheim, E Cape, S Africa), *b* 1918: *m* 1943, Elizabeth Mary Allport, and has issue living, Michael John, *b* 1954, — Dorothy Ann, *b* 1955.

Grandchildren of Cecil Starr Heathcote (ante):— Issue of late Maj Cecil Walter Heathcote, *b* 1936, *d* 1984: *m* 1st, 1955, Sylvia Ann Boyd Varty, who *d* 1959; 2ndly, 1961 (*m diss* 1978), Jennifer Gaie Brinsley; 3rdly, 1981, Hendrika Albertha Roos (née Kotze) (Northcliff, Johannesburg, S Africa):— (By 1st *m*) Susan Norah, *b* 1958: *m* 1980, Terrence André Mangnall, of Harare, Zimbabwe, and has issue living, Mark John, *b* 1982, — Paul Ian, *b* 1985. —— (By 2nd *m*) Debbie Gaie, *b* 1962: *m* 1983, Lionel Victor Moore, and has issue living, Rory Victor, *b* 1984, — Kerry Gaie, *b* 1986. —— Carol Jean, *b* 1964: *m* 1983, Graham Peter Rattey, of Mafikeng, Bophuthatswana, and has issue living, Kai Mark, *b* 1985. —— Linda Heidi, *b* 1971.

Descendants, if any, of late Henry Gage Heathcote (*b* 1877), son of late Henry Heathcote, youngest son of late William Lovell Heathcote (ante).

Descendants, if any, of late Clifford Heathcote (*b* 18—), son of late Henry Heathcote, youngest son of late William Lovell Heathcote (ante).

Grandchildren of late Gage Charles Heathcote, son of Lieut George Gage Heathcote, RN, son of late Adm Sir Henry Heathcote (ante):— Issue (if any) of late Edward Munro Heathcote, *b* 1882. Issue of late William Heathcote, Lieut SA Cavaliers, *b* 1884, *d* 1961: *m* 19—, Helena Cathrina Faure, who *d* 1985:— William Charles (Box 439, Keetmanshoop, SW Africa), *b* 1929: *m* 1955, Connie Danie van Niekerk, and has had issue, William, *b* 1958: *m* 1984, Annemarie van Zyl, and has issue living, Damien *b* 1991, William Charles *b* 1995, Elizmarie *b* 1988, — Conrad, *b* 1960 *d* 1985, — Raymond, *b* 1964: *m* 1992, Thelma Galloway, and has issue living, Gillian *b* 1996, Nicola *b* 1998. —— Maria Wilhelmina, *b* 1919: *m* 1940, Norman Charles Venables, of Lushington Park, PO Kidds Beach, East London, S Africa, and has issue living, Keith Norman, *b* 1942: *m* 1965, Yvonne Valerie Flugel, and has issue living, Bevan Keith *b* 1972, Sandra Lee *b* 1966: *m* 1991, John James Ward (and has issue living, Jay Cameron *b* 1989, Ryan *b* 1992), Terri-Ann *b* 1969, — Peter Kevin, *b* 1956: *m* 1978, Janet Edith Ewers, and has issue living, Wesly *b* 1981, Dal *b* 1983, — Bernadette, *b* 1945: *m* 1966, Johan Martinus Els, and has issue living, Hank *b* 1969, Dominique *b* 1968. —— Thora, *b* 1922: *m* 19—, William Herbert van Schoor (PO Box 2013, Johannesburg, S Africa), and has issue living, Denise Thora, *b* 1944: *m* 1965, Alva Felix Walter Oldknow, of 39 The Willows, 4th Av, Florida, Transvaal, — Marlene Diedré, *b* 1948: *m* 1969, Lukas Matthee Auó. —— Maureen Cathrine, *b* 1937: *m* 1961, Petrus Jacobus Alwyn van der Merwe, and has issue living, Petrus, *b* 1962, — Rudolph, *b* 1965, — Marina, *b* 1966.

Branch from 4th son of 2nd baronet

Granddaughter of late Thomas Jenkyns Heathcote, el son of late Rev Thomas Heathcote, son of late Samuel Heathcote, 4th son of 2nd baronet:— Issue of late George Wadham Bruce Heathcote, OBE, *b* 1868, *d* 1944: *m* 1895, Mary, da of Mark Bate:— Grace Mary, *b* 1896: *m* 1923, Thomas B. Randall.

Granddaughter of late John Cuthbert Heathcote, son of late Rev Samuel John Heathcote, 2nd son of late Rev Thomas Heathcote (ante):— Issue of late Lt-Col John Robert Campbell Heathcote, *b* 1879: *d* 1947: *m* 1st, 1898 (*m diss* 1920), Margaret McClellan; 2ndly, 1920, Mary Gertrude, da of late Oscar Brandt:— (By 1st *m*) Evelyn Marie, *b* 1899.

The 1st baronet, Sir William, MP for Southampton and Buckingham, *m* Elizabeth, only da of the 1st Earl of Macclesfield (Lord Chancellor), to whose peerages Sir William's heir is in remainder. The 3rd baronet was MP for Hampshire; the 4th baronet, also MP (C) for Hants, assumed the additional surname of Freeman. The 5th baronet, Rt Hon Sir William, DCL, sat as MP for Hampshire (C) 1826-32, for N Hampshire 1837-49, and for Oxford University 1854-68. The 9th baronet, Rt Rev Sir Francis, DD, was Bishop of New Westminster, British Columbia, 1941-50.

HEATHCOTE (GB) 1733, of London

Sir GILBERT SIMON HEATHCOTE, CBE, 9th *Baronet*, only son of Lt-Col Robert Evelyn Manners Heathcote, DSO, R Scots and later RA, only son of Capt Robert Heathcote, only son of Capt George Augustus Frederick Heathcote, LG, el son of Robert Heathcote, 3rd son of baronet, *b* 21 Sept 1913; *s* his kinsman, (GILBERT) JAMES HEATHCOTE-DRUMMOND-WILLOUGHBY, 3rd and last Earl of Ancaster and 8th Baronet, in his baronetcy, 1983; *ed* Eton; Brig (ret) RA; CRA 50th Div 1960-62, Ch of Staff, Middle East Command 1962-64, and Brig RA Scottish Command 1964-66; 1939-45 War in N-W Europe; MBE (Mil) 1945, CBE (Mil) 1964: *m* 1st, 1939 (*m diss* 1984), Patricia Margaret, da of Brig James Travers Leslie, MC; 2ndly, 1984, Ann, da of W/Cdr J. A. Hatton, and widow of Brig James Frederick Charles Mellor, DSO, OBE, and has issue by 1st *m*.

Arms – Ermine, three pomeys, each charged with a cross or. **Crest** – On a mural crown azure, a pomey as in the arms, between two wings displayed ermine.
Property — Manton, Oakham, Leics. *Residence* – The Coach House, Tillington, Petworth, W Sussex GU28 0RA. *Clubs* – Garrick, Army and Navy.

SON LIVING (By 1st marriage)

MARK SIMON ROBERT, OBE, *b* 1 March 1941; *ed* Eton, and Magdalene Coll, Camb (BA); P & O Orient Lines, Foreign and Commonwealth Office, BPAmoco Plc; OBE (Civil) 1988: *m* 1975, Susan, da of late Lt-Col George Ashley, The Cameronians (Scottish Rifles), of Rosamundford, Aylesbeare, Devon, and has issue living, Alastair Robert, *b* 18 Aug 1977, — Nicholas Alexander, *b* 1979. *Address* – c/o Upton Dean, Upton, nr Andover, Hants.

DAUGHTER LIVING (By 1st marriage)

Joanna, *b* 1947.

SISTER LIVING

Evelyn Suzanne Valhalla, *b* 1917: *m* 1st, 1938 (*m diss* 1952), Henry Lester Louis Morriss, who *d* 1963; 2ndly, 1952, Robert John Colling, who *d* 1981, and has issue living (by 1st *m*), Hugo Henry, *b* 1939; *ed* Downside, and Univ Coll, Oxford: *m* 1967, Marie Diston, da of David Scull, of Philadelphia, USA, — Amanda Mary, *b* 1942: *m* 1965, Cosimo Prantera, and has issue living, Sophie *b* 1965, Costanza *b* 1967.

HALF-SISTER LIVING

Diana Nesta (Somerby House Farm, Somerby, Leics), *b* 1923: *m* 1953, Michael James Mellows, who *d* 1974, and has issue living, Anna Caroline, *b* 1954: *m* 1982, Edward Henry Garnier, and has issue (*see* B Walsingham), — Julia Dominica, *b* 1956: *m* 1992, William John Newlands Moore, — Antonia Philippa, *b* 1960.

COLLATERAL BRANCHES LIVING

Grandson of late Rev Thomas Heathcote, 2nd son of late Robert Heathcote, 3rd son of 3rd baronet:—
Issue of late William Lionel Heathcote, *b* 1874, *d* 1961: *m* 1919, Alice Mabel, who *d* 1972, da of late Rev John Dand Todd, R of Newton Folkingham:—
Gilbert Michael, *b* 1924: *m* 1953, Dorothy, da of H. W. Pratchett, and has issue living, Jane Michele, *b* 1954: *m* 1980, Russell Curtis, eldest son of A. Curtis, of New Malden, Surrey, — Amanda Joy, *b* 1959: *m* 1984, Graham Denny Girling, of 55 Radnor Rd, Harrow, Middx, yr son of D. Girling, of Kingsbury, NW9, — and an adopted da, Annabel Dorothy, *b* 1967. *Residence* – Janda Cote, 8 Armand Close, Nascot Wood, Watford, Herts.

Grandsons of late John Moyer Heathcote, el son of late John Heathcote, MP (*b* 1834), son of late John Moyer Heathcote, grandson of 2nd baronet:—
Issue of late Arthur Ridley Heathcote, *b* 1877; *d* 1951: *m* 1909, Margaret Georgina, who *d* 1944, only surviving da of late Horace Broke, of Gladwyns, Essex:—
John Horace Broke, *b* 1910; *ed* Eton, and Trin Coll, Camb (BA 1932): *m* 1949, Dorelle Geraldine, da of late Lt-Col Gerald Dominic Rice, DSO, of Fermoy, co Cork, and has issue living, Miranda Lydia, *b* 1950: *m* 1973, Guy Anthony Belcher, of 6 Connaught Sq, W2, son of Anthony George Belcher, of Chiddingfold, Surrey, and has issue living, Tara *b* 1977, — Venetia Catherine, *b* 1951: *m* 1982, Nicholas Annesley Marler Thompson, of Maxgate, George Rd, Kingston-upon-Thames, el son of Sir Richard Hilton Marler Thompson, 1st Bt, and has issue (*see* Thompson, Bt, cr 1963). *Residence* – Maxgate, George Rd, Kingston-upon-Thames, Surrey KT2 7NR. —— Norman Richard, *b* 1914; *ed* Eton, and Trin Coll, Camb: *m* 1946, Margaret Enid, da of Alan Keith Burnett, of Durban, S Africa, and has issue living, Richard John, *b* 1951, — Katherine Louise, *b* 1952, — Diana Elizabeth (twin), *b* 1952. *Address* – c/o Rhodesia House, 429 Strand, WC2.

Sir GILBERT HEATHCOTE, KB, MP in four Parliaments, Lord Mayor of London 1711 and one of the originators of the Bank of England; *cr* a Baronet 1733; *d* 1733; *s* by his son *Sir* JOHN, 2nd Bt; was MP for Grantham 1715-22, and for Bodmin 1733-4; *d* 1759; *s* by his son *Sir* GILBERT, 3rd Bt, MP for Shaftesbury; *d* 1785; *s* by his son *Sir* GILBERT, 4th Bt; was MP for Lincolnshire 1796-1802 and 1806, and for Rutland (*L*) 1812-41; *d* 1851; *s* by his son *Sir* GILBERT JOHN, 5th Bt, *b* 16 Jan 1795; sat as MP for Boston (*L*) 1820-31. Lincolnshire South 1832-41 and Rutland 1841-6: was Lord-Lieut of Lincolnshire: *cr Baron Aveland* (peerage of UK) 1856: *m* 1827, Hon Clementina Elizabeth, in her own right Baroness Willoughby de Eresby, da of 19th Baron Willoughby de Eresby; *d* 1867; *s* by his son GILBERT HENRY, 2nd Baron and 6th Baronet, who *s* as 24th Baron Willoughby de Eresby 1888, and was *cr Earl of Ancaster* (Peerage of UK) 1892. On the death in 1983 of his grandson, (GILBERT) JAMES, 3rd Earl of Ancaster, 4th Baron Aveland, 26th Baron Willoughby de Eresby and 8th Baronet (of London), the first two peerages became extinct, the Barony of Willoughby de Eresby passed to his daughter (see that title), and the Baronetcy to his kinsman, *Brig Sir* GILBERT SIMON HEATHCOTE, CBE, descendant of Robert Heathcote, 3rd son of 3rd Baronet.

HENNIKER-HEATON (UK) 1912, of Mundarrah Towers, Sydney, Australia

There is light in letters

Sir YVO ROBERT HENNIKER-HEATON, 4th *Baronet*; *b* 24 April 1954; *s* his father, *Wing-Cdr Sir* (JOHN VICTOR) PEREGRINE, 1971; memb NW Leics Dist Cncl; MIIA: *m* 1978, Freda, da of Brian Jones, of The Hollies, Broughton Astley, Leics, and has issue.

Arms – Argent on a bend sable three bulls, heads couped of the first, over all on an escutcheon of pretence, quarterly of six; 1st, vert, three escutcheons argent, each charged with a bordure engrailed or, *Burrell*; 2nd, argent, three battering rams fesseways in pale proper headed and garnished azure, *Bertie*; 3rd, or, fretty azure, *Willoughby*; 4th, vert, three eagles displayed fesseways or, *Owen Gwynedd*; 5th, gyronny of eight or and sable, *Campbell*; 6th, per pale sable and gules, on a cross between four fleurs-de-lys argent, five pheons azure, *Banks*. **Crest** – Out of a crest coronet gules, a bull's head argent.
Residence – 7 Brendon Way, Ashby de la Zouch, Leics LE6 5EW.

SON LIVING

ALASTAIR JOHN, *b* 1990.

DAUGHTER LIVING

Julia Sermonda, *b* 1987.

SISTER LIVING

Priscilla Margaret, *b* 1949: *m* 1976, Iain James Saddler Mann, and has issue living, Alison Catriona, *b* 1977, — Jessamy Roberta, *b* 1980.

HALF SISTER LIVING

Anthea Jennifer, *b* 1934.

WIDOW LIVING OF THIRD BARONET

MARGARET PATRICIA (*Margaret, Lady Henniker Heaton*), da of late Lt Percy Wright, Canadian Mounted Rifles: *m* 1948, as his 2nd wife, Wing-Cdr Sir (John Victor) Peregrine Henniker Heaton, 3rd Bt, who *d* 1971.

COLLATERAL BRANCHES LIVING

Issue of late Maj Clement Algernon Charles Henniker-Heaton, yst son of 2nd Bt, *b* 1909, *d* 1983: *m* 1940, Marjorie (Clevemede, Goring-on-Thames, Reading), da of William E. Speight, of Bournemouth:— John Lindsey (Northwoods House, Northwoods, Winterbourne, Bristol BS36 1RS), *b* 1946; *ed* Wellington, and Emmanuel Coll, Camb (MA): *m* 1970, Elisabeth Gladwell, and has issue living, Anthony James, *b* 1974, — Robert Piers, *b* 1978. ——Charles Peter (Brussels, Belgium), *b* 1956; *ed* Eton: *m* 1989, Julia A., da of Derek Johnson, of Much Hadham, Herts, and has issue living, Alexander James Peter, *b* 1992, — Toby Anthony, *b* 1994. —— Hilary Rose, *b* 1948: *m* 1976, Edward Holloway, and has issue living, Nicholas Henniker, *b* 1977, — William David, *b* 1980, — Rachel Sermonda, *b* 1983, — Charlotte Anne (twin), *b* 1983.

Issue of late Sir Herbert Henniker Heaton, KCMG, 3rd son of 1st baronet, *b* 1880, *d* 1961: *m* 1st, 1909, Susan Angèle Phœbe, who *d* 1922, da of late Lindsey Talbot-Crosbie of Ardfert Abbey, Ardfert, co Kerry; 2ndly, 1926, (Helena) Iris, who *d* 1927, da of late Sir Henry Edward McCallum, GCMG; 3rdly, 1947, Gladys Meta, who *d* 1962, da of late Col Claud Francis, and widow of Col George Going, S Staffordshire Regt:— (By 1st *m*) Dermot Wynne (2 Manor Gdns, Kingskerswell, Devon TQ12 5HF), *b* 1922: *m* 1956, Joan Townsend, who *d* 1997, and has issue living, Colin Edward Richard, *b* 1956, — Keith Patrick, *b* 1962. —— (By 2nd *m*) Christopher Robin, *b* 1927; late Nigerian Civil Ser: *m* 1st, 1952 (*m diss* 1967), Elizabeth da of H. Curtis, MD, of Bermuda; 2ndly, 1967, Estelle Patricia, who *d* 1986, da of Samuel John Newing, of Cheshunt, Herts, and *d* 1990, leaving issue, (by 1st *m*) Elizabeth Anne, *b* 1954: *m* 1974, Anthony James Walter, and has issue living, Aaron James *b* 1976, Rebecca Elizabeth *b* 1980. —— (By 1st *m*) Rose Phoebe Anne (Beaufort House, Beaufort, co Kerry), *b* 1914: *m* 1945, Maj Norman Keith Cameron, Coldm Gds, who *d* 1971, and has had issue, Alastair, *b* 1951, *d* 1989 in the Falkland Is, — Donald, *b* 1953: *m* 1987, Rachel Wendy Fell, and has issue living, Katherine *b* 1991, Eleanor *b* 1995, — Jane, *b* 1950, — Susan (22a Mandalay Rd, SW4 9EE), *b* 1956. —— Priscilla Angèle Moira, *b* 1916: *m* 1940, Walter Theodore Ballantyne, who *d* 1971, and has issue living, Priscilla Sarah Anne, *b* 1943: *m* 1968 (*m diss* 1998), Sven Gahlin, of 7 Eastville, Bath BA1 6QN, and has issue living, Adam Hugo *b* 1972, Lucia Karin *b* 1970: *m* 1995, Richard Huw Evans (and has issue living, Dexter Anthony *b* 1999).

Issue of late Capt Arthur Henniker-Heaton, RN, 4th son of 1st baronet, *b* 1883, *d* 1965: *m* 1913, Vera Isabel, who *d* 1965, da of late Hamilton Atherley:—
Michael Hamilton Henniker, *b* 1914: 1939-45 War as Maj R. Signals: *m* 1st, 1937; 2ndly, 1956, Brenda (MILLER), da of Morrison Davies; 3rdly, 1957, Elizabeth Catherine, FLA, da of Maurice Budgett.

Grandchildren of late Capt Arthur Henniker-Heaton, RN (ante):—
Issue of late Lt-Cdr Robin James Henniker-Heaton, RNVR, *b* 1915, *d* 1985: *m* 1st, 1951, Sylvia Elizabeth, yr da of Julian Charles Grumbar, MBE; 2ndly, 1958, Barbara (15 South Cliff, Eastbourne, Sussex), da of William Newman Ayres:—
(By 2nd *m*) Anthony, *b* 1958. —— Sally, *b* 1961.

The 1st baronet, Sir John Henniker Heaton, introduced a motion in House of Commons (1886) for Universal Ocean Penny Postage, and was instrumental in carrying a large number of postal reforms, and especially in reducing Postal Rates to India and Australia 1890, and Penny Postage to America 1908; carried Imperial Postage Resolution 1898, and sat as MP for Canterbury (C) 1885 to 1910. The 2nd baronet, Sir John, assumed the surname of Henniker Heaton.

Henderson-Stewart, see Stewart.

HENNIKER (UK) 1813, of Newton Hall, Essex

DEUS

MAJOR COLUMNA

God is the greatest support

Sir ADRIAN CHANDOS HENNIKER, 9th *Baronet*; *b* 18 Oct 1946; *s* his father, Brig Sir MARK CHANDOS AUBERON, CBE, DSO, MC, 1991; *ed* Marlborough: *m* 1971, Ann, da of Stuart Britton, of Malvern House, Fairwater Rd, Llandaff, Cardiff, and has issue.

Arms – Or, on a chevron gules between two crescents in chief, and in base an escallop azure, three estoiles argent. **Crest** – An escallop or, charged with an estoile gules.
Residence – The Coach House, Llwyndu, Abergavenny, Gwent.

DAUGHTERS LIVING

Victoria Louise, *b* 1976. —— Holly Georgina, *b* (twin) 1976.

SISTER LIVING

Fiona Jane (5 Picton Close, Crundale, Haverfordwest, Pembrokeshire), *b* 1951: *m* 1977 (*m diss* 1997), Peter Jan Milewski, M Chir, FRCS, and has issue living, Andrew Mark Jan, *b* 1982, — Henry Bish Chandos, *b* 1984, — Lucy Amina Kathleen, *b* 1984, — Anna Denys Olive, *b* 1987.

DAUGHTERS LIVING OF SIXTH BARONET

Beryl Inger HENNIKER-HUGHAN, *b* 1904. —— Alison Frances HENNIKER-HUGHAN, *b* 1910: *m* 1936 (*m diss* 1947), John Gladstone (E Shrewsbury, colls).

The Hon Sir Brydges Trecothick Henniker, 1st baronet, was yst son of 1st Baron Henniker, he sat as MP for Kildare in the last Irish Parliament, the 4th baronet was Private Sec to Local Govt Board 1877-80, and Registrar-Gen of Births, Deaths, and Marriages 1880-1900. The 6th baronet, Adm Sir Arthur John Henniker-Hughan, CB, assumed the additional surname of Hughan 1896, and served during European War 1914-16 with Grand Fleet (1914-15 star); was Adm Sup-

Devonport Dockyard 1916-19, and sat as MP for Galloway (*U*) 1924-5. The 7th baronet, Lieut-Col Sir Robert John Aldborough Henniker, MC, served in European War 1914-18 (MC), and in European War 1940-45.

HENRY (UK) 1923, of Cahore, co Londonderry

Sir PATRICK DENIS HENRY, 3rd *Baronet*, only son of late Denis Valentine Henry, yr son of 1st baronet; *b* 20 Dec 1957; *s* his uncle, *Sir* JAMES HOLMES, CMG, MC, TD, 1997; *ed* Corpus Christi Coll, Oxford: *m* 1997, Georgina, da of Arthur Dennis Ravenscroft, of Formby, Greater Merseyside. *Residence* – The Mount, Cleavesty Lane, E Keswick, Leeds LS17 9EZ. *Club* – Blackburn Rovers.

SISTERS LIVING

Jessica Ellen, *b* 1960: *m* 1988 (*m diss* 1998), Ian Beech, of 1 Park Av, Bridgwater, Som TA6 7EE. —— Martha Olive (307 Revidge Rd, Blackburn, Lancs BB1 8DF), *b* 1961.

DAUGHTERS LIVING OF SECOND BARONET (*By 2nd marriage*)

Teresa Violet, *b* (Nov) 1949: *m* 1982, Gordon Stewart, of 7 Vanbrugh Fields, Blackheath, SE3, and has issue living, Edmund James, *b* 1985, — Roland Valentine *b* 1988. —— Christina Mary, *b* 1951: *m* 1979, Peter William Irving Ingram, and has issue (*see* Ingram, Bt, colls). —— Rosemary Jane, *b* 1955: *m* 1990, Peter Winckley, of 24 Elleray Rd, Teddington, Middx TW11 0HG, son of John Winckley, of E. Aberthaw, S Glam, and has issue living, James Christopher, *b* 1994, — Mark John, *b* 1997.

AUNTS LIVING (*daughters of 1st baronet*)

Denise Olive, MB, BS, MRCS, LRCP (7 Morley Rd, Farnham, Surrey). —— Lorna Mary (7 Morley Rd, Farnham, Surrey).

WIDOW LIVING OF SECOND BARONET

(CHRISTINA) HILARY (*Hilary, Lady Henry*), da of late Sir Hugh Oliver Holmes, KBE, CMG, MC, QC, and widow of Lt-Cdr Christopher Hayward Wells, RN (*see* Wells, Bt, *cr* 1944, colls): *m* 1949, as his 2nd wife, Sir James Holmes Henry, 2nd Bt, CMG, MC, TD, who *d* 1997. *Residence* – 24 Seymour Rd, Hampton Hill, Middx.

The 1st baronet, Rt Hon Sir Denis Stanislaus Henry, LLD, sat as MP for S Div of Londonderry co (*CoU*) 1916-21, and was Solicitor-Gen for Ireland 1918-19, Attorney-Gen 1919-21, and Lord Ch Justice of N Ireland 1921-5. The 2nd baronet, Sir James Holmes Henry, CMG, MC, TD, Bar Inner Temple 1934, was Solicitor Gen 1952 and Attorney-Gen Cyprus 1956, QC Tanganyika 1953, Cyprus 1957.

BUCHAN-HEPBURN (UK) 1815, of Smeaton Hepburn, Haddingtonshire
(Name pronounced "Bukkan-Hebburn")

DOMUM · ANTIQUAM · REDINTEGRARE

To restore an ancient house

Sir (JOHN) ALASTAIR TRANT KIDD BUCHAN-HEPBURN OF SMEATON HEPBURN, 7th *Baronet; b* 27 June 1931; son of late John Trant Buchan-Hepburn, son of late Capt John Buchan-Hepburn, eldest son of John Buchan-Hepburn of Clune, co Fife, 2nd son of 2nd Bt; *s* his kinsman (3rd cousin), *Sir* NINIAN BUCHAN ARCHIBALD JOHN, 1992; *ed* Charterhouse, St Andrews Univ, and RMA Sandhurst; Capt (ret) late 1st King's Dragoon Gds; attached Household Cav 1953, attached Swiss Cav 1954, was ADC to GOC Malaya 1955-57; Member Baronets' Trust, and Member St Andrews Preservation Trust: *m* 1957, Georgina Elizabeth, SRN, only da of late Oswald Morris Turner, MC, of Armathwaite, Cumberland, and has issue.

Arms – Quarterly: 1st and 4th, gules, on a chevron argent a rose between two lions rampant of the first, *Hepburn*; 2nd, argent, three lions, heads erased gules, *Buchan*; 3rd, argent an anchor in bend azure, on a chief of the last three cranes or, *Beck*. Crests – 1st, a horse argent, furnished gules, tied to a yew tree proper, over it the motto "Keep tryst", 2nd, the sun in the dexter chief with a sunflower in full blow open to it proper, over it the motto "Non inferiora secutus" (*Not having followed mean pursuits*). Supporters – Dexter, a lion, gules; *sinister*, a heron with an eel in its beak proper. *Residence* – Chagford, 60 Argyle St, St Andrews, Fife KY16 9BU. *Club* – Royal and Ancient Golf Club of St Andrews.

SON LIVING

(JOHN) CHRISTOPHER ALASTAIR (18 Queen's Terrace, St Andrews, Fife KY16 9QF), *b* 9 March 1963; *ed* Cheltenham Coll, and Univ of Portsmouth (BA, DipArch); Principal Officer Performance Unit, Dundee City Council since 1994: *m* 1990, Andrea, da of Kenneth Frederick Unwin, of Elmview, Ryarsh, Kent, and has issue living, (John) James Christopher Thomas, *b* 1 Dec 1992, — Henry Robert, *b* 1997, — Charlotte Mary, *b* 1998.

DAUGHTERS LIVING

Caroline Georgina, *b* 1958; *ed* Gray's Sch of Art, Aberdeen (BA): *m* 1987, Andrew William Pollard Thomson, of Ardgowan, 37 Deeview Rd South, Cults, Aberdeen AB15 9NA, son of Dr William Pow Thomson, of Edinburgh, and has issue living, Hamish Andrew Buchan, *b* 1993. —— Sarah Elizabeth, *b* 1960; *ed* Univ Coll of N Wales, Bangor (BA): *m* 1988, David Arthur Cox, of Kettins House, Kettins, Blairgowrie, Perthshire PH13 9JL, only son of late Arthur Maurice Cox, and has issue living, Nicholas David Maurice, *b* 1990, — Frederick Alastair, *b* 1992. —— Louise Mary, *b* 1966; *ed* Dollar Acad: *m* 1989, (Alexander) David Stewart Kinnear, of New Easter Delfour, Alvie Estate, Kincraig, by Kingussie, Inverness-shire PH21 1ND, only son of late Alexander Norman Stewart Kinnear, of Druimore, Findhorn, Moray, and has issue living, (Alexander) Christopher Stewart *b* 1995, — Joanna Georgina Stewart, *b* 1998.

SISTER LIVING

Elizabeth Agnes Joyce, *b* 1933; *ed* St Leonard's Sch, St Andrews, and St Andrews Univ (MB and ChB 1956): *m* 1957, James Archibald Scott, CB, LVO, FRSE, of 38 Queen's Cres, Edinburgh EH9 2BA, and has issue living, Thomas James Buchan (35 Tennyson Rd, Harpenden, Herts AL5 4BD), *b* 1962; *ed* Edinburgh Acad, and Durham Univ (LLB): *m* 1993, Sally Patricia Mary Broadbridge, and has issue living, James Elliot Buchan *b* 1994, George Frederick Buchan *b* 1995, Patrick Edward Buchan *b* 1997, — Robert Alastair Howie (51 Cramond Road N, Edinburgh EH4 6NQ), *b* 1964; *ed* Edinburgh Acad, and St Thomas' Hosp, London (MB BS); FRCOphth, FRCSEd, Consultant Ophthalmic Surg Princess Alexandra Eye Pavilion Edinburgh; Sqdn-Ldr RAF: *m* 1991, Dr Minakshi Gupta, and has issue living, David Kishen Howie *b* 1994, Hamish Robert Rai *b* 1996, Ruchika Elizabeth *b* 1998, — Hector Michael Hepburn (3 Craiglockhart Av, Edinburgh EH14 1DG), *b* 1969; *ed* Edinburgh Acad, Royal Scottish Acad of Music and Drama, Glasgow, and New England Conservatory, Boston; Leader Saltire Quartet: *m* 1996, Shinobu Miki, and has issue living, Shona Miki *b* 19—, — Rachel Elizabeth Frances, *b* 1960; *ed* St George's Sch, Edinburgh, Royal Northern Coll of Music, Manchester; Repetiteur Royal Ballet: *m* 1986, François Louis Rive, of 16 Station Rd, Winchmore Hill, N21 3RB, and has issue living, Louis James Kenneth *b* 1989, Angus Alec François *b* 1994, Alec Scott Francis *b* 1996.

SISTER LIVING OF SIXTH BARONET

Primrose Eda, *b* 1917; European war 1939-45 in First Aid Nursing Yeo: *m* 1949, Major Ulick Edmund Burke Roche, S Wales Borderers (*see* B Fermoy, colls), who *d* 1990. *Residence* – Ynysfor, Penrhyndeudraeth, Gwynedd Ll48 6BJ.

WIDOW LIVING OF SIXTH BARONET

(MARY) ANGELA (*Dowager Lady Buchan-Hepburn*), da of late Thomas Ian Scott, of Balfunning, Balfron, Stirlingshire, formerly wife of John Miller Richard, and widow of Jack Walch Lyne: *m* 1991, as his 2nd wife, Sir Ninian Buchan Archibald John Buchan-Hepburn of Smeaton Hepburn, 6th Bt, who *d* 1992. *Residence* – Kailzie, by Peebles, Tweeddale EH45 9HT.

This family descends from the Buchans, lairds of Auchmacoy, Aberdeenshire, who claim descent from the Celtic Mormaers and Earls of Buchan. The 13th laird was recognised in 1792 as Chief of the name of Buchan. The lands of Alexander were erected into a barony 1598. His 2nd son, George, was ancestor of John Buchan of Letham, East Lothian, whose 1st wife, Elizabeth (*d* 1742) was sister and heir of George Hepburn of Smeaton Hepburn, East Lothian. Their son and heir George in 1764 *s* his maternal uncle as heir of line of Hepburn of Smeaton Hepburn and to that barony, and was recognized in the name and arms of Buchan-Hepburn. He was Advocate 1763, Judge of Admiralty Court 1790-1 and Baron of the Exchequer, Scotland 1800-14. On retirement he was *cr* a Baronet in 1815.

The Hepburns of Smeaton Hepburn descended from Adam 3rd son of Sir Patrick Hepburn of Waughton and Luffness to whom his father granted these lands in 1538. The Hepburns of Waughton descended from Sir Patrick of Waughton, uncle of Sir Patrick Hepburn of Hailes, who was *cr* Lord Hailes 1452/3. The 2nd Lord Hailes was in 1482 *cr* Earl of Bothwell, but both dignities were forfeited 1567 on attainder of James 4th Earl (and 1st Duke of Orkney), 3rd husband of Mary, Queen of Scots. He *d* without legitimate issue 1578.

Herne (Buckworth-Herne-Soame), see Soame.

Heron (Heron-Maxwell), see Maxwell.

Hervey-Bathurst, see Bathurst.

HEWETT (UK) 1813, of Nether Seale, Leicestershire

Seek nothing beyond your sphere

Sir PETER JOHN SMITHSON HEWETT, MM, 6th *Baronet*; *b* 27 June 1931; *s* his father, Sir JOHN GEORGE, MC, 1990; *ed* Bradfield Coll, and Jesus Coll, Camb (BA); Bar Gray's Inn 1954: *m* 1958, Jennifer Ann Cooper, only child of late Emrys Thomas Jones, OBE, of Nairobi, Kenya, and has issue.

𝕬rms – Gules, on a chevron embattled argent, between three owls of the second, each crowned with an eastern coronet or, as many bombs fired proper. 𝕮rest – Out of a mural crown or, the stump of an oak-tree with branches, thereon a hawk proper gorged with an eastern coronet, belled gold. 𝕾upporters – *Dexter*, a tiger proper gorged with an eastern crown or; *sinister*, a buffalo charged on the shoulder with a trefoil slipped, all proper. *Address* – PO Box 15669, Nairobi, Kenya.

SONS LIVING

RICHARD MARK JOHN, *b* 15 Nov 1958; *ed* Bradfield, and Jesus Coll, Camb (BSc). *Residence* – 118 Lovibonds Av, Orpington, Kent BR6 8EN. —— David Patrick John, *b* 1968; *ed* Bradfield, Reading Univ (BSc), and St Hugh's Coll, Oxford (MSc): *m* 1997, Kate Suzanne Elizabeth Ormand, and has issue living, Hector Alexander, *b* 1999. *Address* – PO Box 117, Tanga, Tanzania.

DAUGHTER LIVING

Joanna Yuilleen, *b* 1960: *m* 1993, Patrick Fitzgerald Blundell, elder son of Maj Alan F. Blundell, of Gooseberry Hill, W Australia, and has issue living, Michael Benjamin Patrick, *b* 1995, — Juliet Jennifer, *b* 1998. *Residence* – 10 Robinson Rd, Darlington, W Australia 6070.

BROTHER LIVING

Richard Harald, *b* 1933; *ed* Gordonstoun: *m* 1959, Bridget Elizabeth Anne, only da of late Alistair John Kirkman Finlay, and has had issue, Anthony John Finlay, *b* 1962; *d* 1982, — Julia Caroline, *b* 1960: *m* 1984, Michael Hyde-Duder, of Nairobi, Kenya, and has issue living, James Hyde *b* 1986, Ross Finlay Hyde *b* 1997, Siana Nicole *b* 1985. *Residence* – Nairobi, Kenya.

COLLATERAL BRANCHES LIVING

Issue of late George Nele Hewett, yst son of 4th baronet, *b* 1901, *d* 1972: *m* 1931, Margaret Skaife (Vitré, Coldash, Newbury), da of G. T. Denis de Vitré:—
Denis Nele, *b* 1932; Lt RN (ret). *Address* – PO Box 246 Keri Keri, Bay of Islands, NZ. —— Jeremy Patrick Nele (78: 6616 Alii Drive, Kailua Kona, 96740 Hawaii), *b* 1935: *m* 1963, Norma Shirley Garnett Smith, and has issue living, Geoffrey Alexander, *b* 1966, — Harald Randall Marsh, *b* 1969, — Kari Denise, *b* 1964.

Grandchildren of late Capt Charles William Hewett, RN, 2nd son of late Frank William Hewett, 2nd son of 2nd baronet:—
Issue of late Brig William George Hewett, OBE, MC, *b* 1894, *d* 1973: *m* 1st, 1922 (*m diss* 1931), Louise Susan, da of late Francis R. Wolfe; 2ndly, 1932, Beatrice, who *d* 1961, da of late Lt-Col James Francis Donegan, CB:—
(By 1st *m*) Richard William, *b* 1923; Maj RA (ret); Malaya 1953 (despatches); Chm and Man Dir The Readers Digest UK; Dir International Operations Readers Digest USA since 1986: *m* 1954, Rosemary, yr da of Basil Cridland, MC, TD, of Fernhurst, Sussex, and has issue living, Vanessa Annabel, *b* 1957: *m* 1995, John D. Church, yst son of late Lt-Col James Cunningham Church, MC, and of late Mrs Jocelyn Hambro, — Virginia Carolyn Rose, *b* 1960: *m* 1985, Dominic Marius Dennis Anthony Wheatley, of 64 Orbain Rd, SW6 7JY, elder son of Dennis Anthony Marius Thomas Wheatley, of Ridgway Gdns, Wimbledon, SW19, and has issue living, a son *b* 1991, Charlotte Rose *b* 1989. —— (By 2nd *m*) Sarah Margaret Arianwen, *b* 1942.

Issue of late Capt George Stuart Hewett, CBE, Roy Indian Navy, *b* 1863, *d* 1937: *m* 1899, Maude Mary Brind, who *d* 1958, da of Surg-Gen Henry Kendall, formerly Army Med Depart:—
Neale Brind Stuart (9 Egmont Rd, Ngongotaha, NZ), *b* 1906; Cdr (ret) Roy Indian Navy Reserve; a JP of NZ: *m* 1930, Thecla Edana, who *d* 1993, yst da of A. J. Davis, and has issue living, Neale John Patrick (PO Box 357 Seven Hills, NSW 2147, Australia), BEM, *b* 1931; *ed* Ampleforth; ACA; Kenya 1953 (BEM): *m* 1960 (*m* annulled 198—), Felicity Anne, da of late B. H. Kerby, and has issue living, Matthew Patrick George *b* 1969, Merri Bernard Neale *b* 1961, Felicity Sheena *b* 1963, Anita Noreen *b* 1967, — George Andrew Kendall, *b* 1942: *m* 1967, Sharon Rose, yst da of W. Souster, of Takapuna, Auckland, NZ, and has issue living, Jason Conrad Neale *b* 1969, Brind Nicholas Andrew *b* 1974, — Jeanne Marie Thecla, *b* 1933: *m* 1955, Alan Dever, of Glenbrook Station, c/o Putorino PO, Hawkes Bay, NZ, and Tiromaunga, Puketapu Po, Hawkes Bay, NZ, and has issue living, Neale Alan Kendall *b* 1958, Alan Guy *b* 1961, Wendy Janet Thecla *b* 1956, Penelope Jeanne *b* 1959, Catherine Adelaide *b* 1967.

Gen Right Hon Sir George GCB, 1st baronet, was Col 61st Regt, and C-in-C of the Forces in India, in Ireland. The 2nd baronet, a Col in the Army, was a distinguished Officer in Peninsular War.

HEWITT (UK) 1921, of Barnsley, West Riding, co Yorkshire

Always the same

Sir NICHOLAS CHARLES JOSEPH HEWITT, 3rd *Baronet*; *b* 12 Nov 1947; *s* his father *Maj Sir* JOSEPH, 1973: *m* 1969, Pamela Margaret, only da of Geoffrey J. M. Hunt, TD, of Broadacres, Scalby, Scarborough, and has issue.

Arms – Sable, a chevron in chief three owls or. **Crest** – Upon the battlements of a tower argent an owl proper.
Residence – Colswayn House, Huttons Ambo, York YO6 7HJ.

SONS LIVING

CHARLES EDWARD JAMES, *b* 15 Nov 1970. —— Michael Joseph, *b* 1973: *m* 1998, Lucinda F., da of Martin Dawson-Brown, of Low Askew, N Yorks.

DAUGHTER LIVING

Victoria Alexandra Margaret, *b* 1978.

BROTHER LIVING

Timothy George, *b* 1950.

SISTER LIVING

Elizabeth Margaret, *b* 1945.

WIDOW LIVING OF SECOND BARONET

MARGUERITE (*Marguerite, Lady Hewitt*) (Lebberston Hall, nr Scarborough), da of Charles Burgess, of Deepdene, Filey: *m* 1940, Maj Sir Joseph Hewitt, 2nd Bt, who *d* 1973.

HEYGATE (UK) 1831, of Southend, Essex
(Name pronounced "Haygate")

Boulogne et Cadiz
Boulogne and Cadiz

Sir RICHARD JOHN GAGE HEYGATE, 6th *Baronet*; *b* 30 Jan 1940; *s* his brother, *Sir* GEORGE LLOYD, 1991; *ed* Repton, and Balliol Coll, Oxford: *m* 1st, 1968 (*m diss* 1972), Carol Rosemary, da of late Cdr Richard Michell, RN, of Leith House, Amberley, Surrey; 2ndly, 1974 (*m diss* 1988), Jong-Ja Hyun, da of In Suk, of Seoul; 3rdly, 1988, Susan Fiona, da of late Robert Buckley, of Cobblers Cottage, Peasmarsh, E Sussex, and has issue by 2nd and 3rd *m*.

Arms – Gules, two bars argent, on a bend or, a torteau between two leopards' faces azure. **Crest** – A wolf's head erased gules.
Residence – 29 Rossetti Gdns Mansions, Flood St, SW3 5QX.

SONS LIVING (*by 3rd marriage*)

FREDERICK CARYSFORT GAGE, *b* 28 June 1988. —— Robert George Liam, *b* 1991.

DAUGHTER LIVING (*by 2nd marriage*)

Eun-Hee Isobella Gage, *b* 1977.

DAUGHTERS LIVING OF FIFTH BARONET

Joanna, *b* 1977. —— Catherine, *b* (twin) 1977.

WIDOW LIVING OF FIFTH BARONET

HILDEGARD MATHILDE (*Dowager Lady Heygate*), da of August Anton Kleinjohann, of Wildstrasse 69, Duisburg, Germany: *m* 1960, Sir George Lloyd Heygate, 5th Bt, who *d* 1991. *Residence* – Willow Grange, Wissett, Halesworth, Suffolk.

COLLATERAL BRANCHES LIVING

Granddaughters of late Maj William Howley Beaumont Heygate, son of late William Unwin Heygate, 2nd son of 1st baronet:—
Issue of late Lieut-Col Gerald Heygate, DSO, RFA, *b* 1882, *d* 1954: *m* 1916, Cynthia, who *d* 1963, da of C. Darley, of Thorne:—
Felicity Cynthia June, *b* 1926: *m* 1950, Lt-Cdr Charles Owen, DSC, RN (ret), of Flat 31, 15 Portman Sq, W1, and has issue living, Rupert Charles (91 Cambridge St, SW1) *b* 1956: *m* 1988, Astrid Bigbie, and has issue living, Charles William *b* 1990, Henry Beaumont *b* 1991, — Caroline Angela, *b* 1954: *m* 1983, James Richard Dunsmuir Knox, of Martnaham Lodge, by Ayr, Ayrshire, and has issue living, Bryce William Dunsmuir *b* 1992, Constance Felicity Rose *b* (twin) 1992.

Issue of late Maj Lionel Clement Heygate, *b* 1893, *d* 1947: *m* 1st, 1918, Janet Leigh, who *d* 1923, only da of late Richard Jeston Ogle, of Christchurch, NZ; 2ndly, 1935 (*m diss* 1943), Yvonne Sylvia, da of late W. F. Tyler:—
(By 1st *m*) Diana Juliet Beaumont (61 Campana Rd, SW6 4AT), *b* 1920: *m* 1946, Lt-Col John Francis Rush, RASC, who *d* 1992, and has issue living, Charles Burlison OGLE-RUSH, *b* 1947; *ed* Uppingham; assumed by deed poll 1968 the surname of Ogle-Rush: *m* 1977, Melanie Elizabeth Roche, da of Austin Hasslacher, of Bowler's Farm, Dockenfield, Farnham, Surrey, and has issue living, Michael Pellew Roche *b* 1980, Sophie Elizabeth *b* 1982, — Diana Louise OGLE-RUSH, *b* 1949; assumed by deed poll 19— the surname of Ogle-Rush in lieu of Bailey: *m* 1972 (*m diss* 1977), Michael Bailey. —— (By 2nd *m*) Marilyn Jennifer, *b* 1938: *m* 1966, John Brigg Charles Fountaine, of Moor Farm, Great Bircham, King's Lynn, Norfolk PE31 6QP, yr son of Adm Charles Andrew Fountaine, CB, of Narford Hall, King's Lynn, Norfolk, and has issue living, Alexandra Juliet Catherine, *b* 1973, — Auriole Diana Eleanor, *b* 1975.

Granddaughters of late Major Edward Nicholas Heygate, 3rd son of 1st baronet:—
Issue of late Capt Richard Lionel Heygate, *b* 1859, *d* 1926: *m* 1895, Eleanor Mary Gwenllian, who *d* 1958, da of late Edward James Evans:—
Mary Ursula, *b* 1896: *m* 1930, Capt Eustace King-King, formerly Queen's R Regt, who *d* 1975, and has issue living, Edward Michael, *b* 1931; *ed* Stowe. *Residence* – . —— Gladys Henrietta, *b* 1898: *m* 1st, 1924, Major Brereton Rigby, who *d* 1931; 2ndly, 1934, Richard Thomas, and has issue living, (by 1st *m*) Richard Arthur, *b* 1926: *m* 1950, Margaret Stocker, and has issue living, Janice Anita *b* 1951, Yvonne Linda *b* 1953, — Walter Oswald, *b* 1931, — (by 2nd *m*) Harold Mostyn, *b* 1936: *m* 1960, Kathleen Ada Hughes, and has issue living, Richard Edward *b* 1963, Roger Harold *b* 1970, Elizabeth Mary *b* 1960. *Residence* – Buckland, Docklow, Leominster, Hereford.

The 1st baronet was Lord Mayor of London 1822, City Chamberlain 1843-4, and MP for Sudbury in two Parliaments. Thomas Heygate, of Hayes, was Provost Marshal General under the Earl of Essex at the capture of Cadiz; his father held the same position in the Army, and was present before St Quintin; he was afterwards Provost Marshal in Scotland. Nicholas Heygate, the celebrated collector of curious books and writings, was of this family. Sir Frederick, 2nd baronet, was MP for co Londonderry (C) 1859-74, and the 3rd baronet, Sir Frederick Gage, was Parliamentary Under-Sec to Lord-Lieut of Ireland 1887-8. Sir John, 4th baronet, was a journalist and novelist, his first wife, Hon Evelyn Gardner, was formerly wife of Evelyn Waugh, the celebrated author. He *m* 2ndly, 1936 (*m diss* 1947), Gwyneth Eliot (who *d* 1994, having *m* 2ndly, 19— (*m diss* 1967), Arthur Donaldson, DSO), da of late John Eliot Howard Lloyd.

HEYWOOD (UK) 1838, of Claremont, Lancashire

Sir PETER HEYWOOD, 6th *Baronet*; *b* 10 Dec 1947; *s* his father, *Sir* OLIVER KERR, 1992; *ed* Bryanston, and Keble Coll, Oxford (BA 1969): *m* 1970, Jacqueline Anne, da of Sir Robert Frederick Hunt, CBE, of Maple House, Withington, Glos, and has issue.

Arms – Argent, three torteaux in bend between two bendlets gules; on a canton of the last a cross-patée or. Crest – On a mount vert the trunk of a tree with two branches sprouting therefrom and entwined with ivy, thereon a falcon wings displayed all proper. *Residence* – 64 Newbridge Rd, Weston, Bath, Avon BA1 3LA.

DAUGHTERS LIVING

Vanessa Jane, *b* 1975. —— Annabel Sarah, *b* 1976.

BROTHERS LIVING

Alte volo

I fly high

MICHAEL (Kings Acre, Leys Rd, Tostock, Bury St Edmunds, Suffolk), *b* (twin) 10 Dec 1947; *ed* Bryanston, and Keble Coll, Oxford (BA 1969): *m* 1972, Carolyn Awdry, da of late Ian Joseph Greig, and has issue living, Daniel Oliver, *b* 1979, Katie May, *b* 1977. —— James Philip, *b* 1951; *ed* Bryanston: *m* 1978, Alizen, da of Reginald Merryweather, FRCS, of Painswick, Glos, and has issue living, Jack Theyre, *b* 1981, — Barnabas Timothy, *b* 1985, — Lucy, *b* 1979.

AUNT LIVING (*sister of 5th baronet*)

Joan Margaret, *b* 1919: *m* 1950, John Marsden Preston, of Boxhanger Cottage, Box, Stroud, Glos, and has issue living, Nicolas, *b* 1952; *ed* Lycée Français, London.

WIDOW LIVING OF FIFTH BARONET

DENISE (*Dowager Lady Heywood*), yr da of late Jocelyn William Godefroi, MVO, and formerly wife of Hon David Montague de Burgh Kenworthy (later 11th Baron Strabolgi): *m* 1947, Sir Oliver Kerr Heywood, 5th Bt, who *d* 1992. *Residence* – Ilsom House, Tetbury, Glos.

COLLATERAL BRANCHES LIVING

Granddaughters of late Lt-Col Gerald Graham Percival Heywood, TD, yst son of 2nd baronet:—
Issue of late Graham Scudamore Percival Heywood, *b* 1903, *d* 1985: *m* 1937, Valerie, who *d* 1992, da of Lt-Col Railton Wyatt, of Locks Heath, Hants:—
Susan Mary, *b* 1938: *m* 1961, John Michael Knight, of Oakwood, Itchen Abbas, Winchester, Hants, SO21 1AX, and has issue living, Timothy John, *b* 1963: *m* 1991, Lynda Marie, da of Keith Seymour, of Bradford, Yorks, and has issue living, Thomas Daniel *b* 1997, Catherine Louise *b* 1994, — Nicola Susan, *b* 1962: *m* 1989, Glenn Allan Royall, of Ulladulla, NSW, Australia, and has issue living, Lachlan Allan *b* 1992, Jack Duncan *b* 1995, Charlotte Louise *b* 1991, — Deborah Ann, *b* 1965, — Bridget Julia, *b* 1970. —— Veronica Anne, *b* 1942.

Grandchildren of late Henry Arthur Heywood, eldest son of late Rev Henry Robinson Heywood, 5th son of 1st baronet:—
Issue of late Geoffrey Henry Heywood, CBE, *b* 1903, *d* 1986: *m* 1931, Magdeleine Jeanne Georgette Marie, who *d* 1987, yr da of late Jean Herpin, of Paris:—
Claude Geoffrey (1626 Verling Av, Saanichton, BC V8M 1W8, Canada), *b* 1933; *ed* Repton, and Gonville and Caius Coll, Camb (MA); late Lt RA; HM Overseas Civil Service, Kenya 1957-62; Dep Min of Labour, Prov of BC 1989-96: *m* 1960, Anne Helen, da of late Theron Wilding-Davies, of Fayre Ways Stud Farm, Dorstone, Herefordshire, and has issue living, James Claude, *b* 1962: *m* 1995, Susan Anne Amesbury, and has issue living, Thomas James *b* 1998, — Peter Geoffrey, *b* 1965: *m* 1989, Heather Joan, elder da of Barry Gill, of Brentwood Bay, BC, and has issue living, David Geoffrey *b* 1996, Erin Heather *b* 1994, — Sarah Anne, *b* 1963: *m* 1991, Colin Derek Ewart, elder son of Hampton Ewart, of co Armagh, and has issue living, Annie Magdeleine *b* 1993, Lucy Rose *b* 1996. —— Claire Margaret, *b* 1938: *m* 1st, 1961 (*m diss* 1968), Mark Hugh Learoyd Piercy; 2ndly, 1973, Alexander Campbell Newton Ferguson, of Bernisdale, Hook Heath, Woking, Surrey GU22 0LE, and has issue living (by 1st *m*), Giles Hugh Scott, *b* 1966: *m* 1994, Camilla Anne, eldest da of Giles Sim, of Littles Farmhouse, Shalford Green, Braintree, Essex, and has issue living, Matthew Giles Torridon *b* 1998, — Emma Magdeleine, *b* 1963: *m* 1989, Edward Vincent Knox, of Godalming, Surrey, and has issue living, Amy Claire *b* 1994.

Issue of late Rev Charles Richard Heywood, *b* 1908, *d* 1979: *m* 1939, Alice Ruth (Thornhill House, Church Lane, Great Longstone, W Bakewell, Derbys), da of Dr W. Henry Dobie, of Chester:—
Richard Henry Norman (42 Clarkfield, Mill End, Rickmansworth, Herts), *b* 1946; *ed* Workshop Coll; formerly Sec Gen Jaycees Internat; MIMS, MICFM: *m* 1971 (*m diss* 1987), Melody Dawn, el da of Col J. A. H. Nicholson, of Quinton, Bamford, Sheffield, and has issue living, Tamsin Melody, *b* 1975, — Nicola Dawn, *b* 1977. —— Margaret Anne, *b* 1950.

Grandchildren of late Charles Christopher Heywood, MB, MRCS, MRCP, 4th son of late Rev Henry Robinson Heywood (ante):—
Issue of late Very Rev Hugh Christopher Lempriere Heywood, *b* 1896, *d* 1987: *m* 1920, Margaret Marion, who *d* 1982, da of late Herbert Vizard, of Whitepost House, Redhill, Surrey:—
Peter (2 Dalemoor Gdns, Aspley Park Drive, Nottingham NG8 3EB), *b* 1922; *ed* Haileybury, and Gonville and Caius Coll, Camb (MA); formerly Capt Oxford and Bucks LI; Headmaster of William Sharp Comprehensive Sch, Nottingham 1968-87. —— Ann Rosemary, *b* 1930: *m* 1954, Thomas Strachan James, of The Mill House, 32 Mill Lane, Linton, Cambridge CB1 6JY, and has issue living, Christopher William, *b* 1955, — Timothy Robert, *b* 1956, — Pamela Susan, *b* 1961.

Issue of late Alan Lempriere Heywood, *b* 1899, *d* 1960: *m* 1925, Constance, who *d* 1988, da of Mrs Frederick Swales, of Simla:—
Denys Guy Lempriere (Deddington Manor, Deddington, Oxford), *b* 1926; *ed* Denstone and Caius Coll, Camb; Gp Capt RAF; commanded No 94 (F) Sqdn, and No 617 Sqdn (Dambusters) (ret); Bursar Tudor Hall Sch, Banbury 1977-88: *m* 1957, Elizabeth Ann, da of late J. Jeffrey Baker, of Windyridge, Altwood, Rd, Maidenhead, and has issue living, Robin Guy, *b* 1958: *m* 1984, Mitchiko, da of John Cole, of Deddington, — Simon John, *b* 1966: *m* 1992, Alison, da of Garry Cook, of Adderbury, Oxon, — Annabel Jane, *b* 1961, — Carol Elizabeth, *b* 1962: *m* 1992, Charles Skinner, of Winchester. —— Adrian Christopher Lempriere (c/o The Willows, Sandown Park, Tunbridge Wells, Kent), *b* 1928; *ed* Denstone, and Selwyn Coll, Camb (MA); formerly 2nd Lt RA: *m* 1962, Patricia Mollie Gardner, da of Guy Goulden, of 16 Grange Rd, Eastbourne, and has issue living, Christopher Lempriere, *b* 1962: *m* 1991, Lisa Mary Buckley, of Oldham, Lancs, — Guy Lempriere, *b* 1965: *m* 1993, Tracy Jane McCormack,of Melbourne, Australia, and has issue living, Sascha Lauren *b* 1996, Innes Lauren *b* 1998.

Issue of late Basil Lempriere Heywood, *b* 1903, *d* 1989: *m* 1930, Phyllis Miriam, who *d* 1997, da of late John Orchard, Bar-at-Law, of Haigh Moor, Topsham, Exeter:—
John Basil Sumner (6 Pheasant Field, Hale, Liverpool L24 5SD), *b* 1933; CEng, MIEE. —— Christopher Richard (Rozel, Ditchling Rd, Haywards Heath, W Sussex RH17 7RF), *b* 1949: *m* 1971, Susan Rosa, da of Thomas William Howarth, of Tynwald, The Moorings, Preston Brook, Runcorn, Cheshire, and has issue living, Christopher David, *b* 1979, — Nicola Jane, *b* 1974. —— Diana Ruth EVANS (31 Howard Av, Lymm, Ches WA13 9EH), *b* 1937; has resumed her former married name: *m* 1st, 1963, Michael John Evans, who *d* 1988; 2ndly, 1991 (*m diss* 1995), Brian Victor Woodcock, and has issue living (by 1st *m*), Andrew Michael (1 Highway Cottages, E Stratton, Winchester SO321 3DP), *b* 1964; *ed* Girton Coll, Camb (BA): *m* 1993, Sheelagh Marie Jones, and has issue living, Elliot Xavier *b* 1997, Effie Elizabeth *b* 1994, — Christopher Philip, *b* 1966, — Jennifer Lesley, *b* 1968: *m* 1996, Martin Gordon Croxford, and has issue living, Michael Peter *b* 1998.

Grandchildren of late Rt Rev Bernard Oliver Francis Heywood, DD, yst son of late Rev Henry Robinson Heywood (ante):—

Issue of late Michael Henry Lempriere Heywood, *b* 1900, *d* 1990: *m* 1941, Marjorie (The Hollies, Barningham, Richmond, Yorks), da of C. B. Wood, of High Green, Sheffield:—
Charles Michael Lempriere, *b* 1942: *m* 1963, Robina Anne Pattison, and has issue living, Benjamin Michael Lempriere, *b* 1971, — Lucy Catherine Adamson, *b* 1977. —— Peter Bernard Martin, *b* 1946. —— David Mark, *b* 1947. —— Margaret Adamson, *b* 1944.

Issue of late Oliver Martin Heywood, *b* 1904, *d* 1982: *m* 1946, Eileen Maud (Virginia Cottage, Church Rd, Rotherfield, E Sussex), da of late Dr Martin Liebert, of Beckenham, Kent:—
Timothy David Lempriere (PO Box 26425, Abu Dhabi, United Emirates), *b* 1948; *ed* Haileybury: *m* 1st, 1972 (*m diss* 1986), Kathleen Ellen, da of J. L. Waldman, of Caracas; 2ndly, 1986, Jane, da of late Julian Sherrard, of Tunbridge Wells, Kent, and has issue living (by 1st *m*), Benjamin Michael, *b* 1973, — Nicholas Anthony, *b* 1976, — (by 2nd *m*) Sophie Henrietta, *b* 1986, — Jessica Jane, *b* 1989, — Joanna Clare, *b* (twin)1989. —— Jonathan Martin (Scripp, Foxhunt Green, Waldron, E Sussex), *b* (twin) 1948; *ed* Haileybury: *m* 1982, Elizabeth Mary, da of Thomas Wilks, of Laggan, Isle of Islay, Argyll, and has issue living, Thomas Martin, *b* 1985, — Emma Caroline, *b* 1983, — Kate Elizabeth Bridget, *b* 1993.

Issue of late Francis Melville Heywood, *b* 1908, *d* 1995: *m* 1937, Dorothea Kathleen, who *d* 1983, da of Sir Basil Edgar Mayhew, KBE:—
Susan Frances (9 Residence des Canadiens, Puys, 76370 Neuville les Dieppe, Seine Maritime, France), *b* 1939: *m* 1965 (*m diss* 1984), Jean Marc Duquesne, and has issue living, Marc Dominic, *b* 1966, — Benjamin Piers, *b* 1969, — Sebastian Paul, *b* 1972. —— Janion Lempriere (Bruce Rd RD5, Te Awamutu, NZ) *b* 1947; BSc London; MB, BS, MRCS, LRCP: *m* 1972, Robert John LeQuesne, MB, BS, MRCS, LRCP, and has issue living, Nicholas Robert Paget, *b* 1981, — Katherine Amy, *b* 1977, — Rebecca Janion, *b* 1978.

The 1st baronet, an eminent banker of Manchester, led the Reform Agitation in Lancashire, and sat as MP for that county in the Parliament preceding the passing of the Reform Bill of 1832. His yst brother, James Heywood, FRS, who *d* 1897, sat as MP for North Lancashire (*L*) in the Parliaments of 1847 and 1852. The 2nd baronet was High Sheriff of Lancashire 1851. The 3rd baronet was High Sheriff of Derbyshire 1899. The 4th baronet, Lieut-Col Sir (Graham) Percival, CB, DSO, TD, TA (ret), served in European War 1914-18 (DSO).

HICKMAN (UK) 1903, of Wightwick, Tettenhall, Staffordshire

By fire and sword

Sir (RICHARD) GLENN HICKMAN, 4th *Baronet*; *b* 12 April 1949; *s* his father, *Sir* (ALFRED) HOWARD WHITBY, 1979; *ed* Eton: *m* 1981, Heather Mary Elizabeth, da of Dr James Moffett, of Westlecot Manor, Swindon, Wilts, and has issue.

Arms – Party per saltire sable and or, two leopards' faces jessant-de-lis in pale and as many fleur-de-lis in fesse, all counterchanged. Crest – A Phœnix issuing out of flames, transfixed through the mouth by a tilting spear palewise proper, each wing charged with two annulets erect and interlaced or.
Residence – Manor Farm House, Liddington, Wilts SN4 0HD. *Club* – Turf.

SONS LIVING

CHARLES PATRICK ALFRED, *b* 5 May 1983. —— Edward William George, *b* 1990.

DAUGHTER LIVING

Elizabeth Margaret Ruth, *b* 1985.

UNCLE LIVING (*son of 2nd baronet*)

Patrick Nelson (Hale Park, Fordingbridge, Hants; 65 Onslow Gdns, SW7; *Club* – White's), *b* 1921; F/L RAFVR (ret); a Freeman of City of London, and a Liveryman of Fishmongers' Co: *m* 1st, 1944 (*m diss* 1950), Leontine Mariette (Marylena), da of Capt James Allan Dyson Perrins, MC and bar, JP, late Welsh Guards; 2ndly, 1953 (Margaret) Gail, da of Col Cassell Ryan St Aubyn, 60th Rifles of 34 Rue de la Faisanderie, Paris XVI, and has issue living, (by 1st *m*) (Patrick) Rupert COTTRELL (Stable Cottages, Great Meadows, Castletown, I of Man; *Clubs* – Boodle's, R Yacht Sqdn, Beefsteak, Jockey Club Rooms), *b* 1945; assumed by deed poll 1953 the surname of Cottrell in lieu of his patronymic; *ed* Gordonstoun: *m* 1st, 1968 (*m diss* 1989), Claire, el da of late Lt-Col James Gray Round, OBE, JP, DL; 2ndly, 1989, Anne, only da of late Arthur Ralph Holbrook, of Mahon House, Cropwell Butler, Notts, and has issue living (by 1st *m*), Nicholas Rupert Round *b* 1970, Jessica Victoria *b* 1974, — Rozanna Mariette, *b* 1946; assumed by deed poll 1953 the surname of Cottrell in lieu of her patronymic: *m* 1969, Michael John Hardy Hammond, and has issue living, James David Hardy *b* 1972, Matthew Charles Perrins *b* 1975, — (by 2nd *m*) (Patrick) Sloan, *b* 1955: *m* 1993, Candida R. d'Ombrain, da of Dr Roderick William Grant (*see* By Ardilaun, colls, 1944 Edn), — Vivien Anne, *b* 1957: *m* 1983, Edmund B. MacDonald, jr, of 88 West Clay Park, San Francisco 94121, California, USA, son of Edmund B. MacDonald, of San Francisco, and has issue living, Angus Nelson *b* 1987, Kenneth *b* 1996, Fiona *b* 1990.

WIDOW LIVING OF SECOND BARONET

NANCY BERYL (*Beryl, Lady Hickman*), da of late Capt Trevor George Morse-Evans, JP, Barrister-at-law (Inner Temple), MA (Cantab), MFH: *m* 1940, as his 2nd wife, Sir Alfred Edward Hickman, 2nd baronet, who *d* 1947. *Residence* – Holmbush House, Faygate, nr Horsham, W Sussex.

COLLATERAL BRANCHES LIVING

Granddaughters of late Alfred William Hickman, el son of 1st baronet:—
Issue of late Lieut-Col Arthur Hickman, *b* 1891, *d* 1959; *m* 1914, Dorothy Gwendolen, RRC, who *d* 1957, da of late Edward Charles Rudge, JP, DL, of Abbey Manor, Evesham:—
Christine Gwen, TD, *b* 1920; late Major WRAC (TA). —— Pamela Jill, *b* 1921; formerly Subaltern ATS. *Residence* – 308A Barkham Rd, Wokingham, Berks.

Grandchildren of late Brig-Gen Thomas Edgecombe Hickman, CB, DSO, 4th son of 1st baronet:—
Issue of late Capt Thomas Alfred Kenneth Hickman, *b* 1912; *ka* 1940: *m* 1936, Leila Philippa, of Holme Cottage, Church St, Nunnington, York YO6 5US (who *m* 2ndly, 1945, Major Eric Inman Scott, MC, who *d* 1967), el da of Lt-Col Montagu Martindale Parry-Jones, MC (*d* 1969), Roy Fusiliers (Borrowes, Bt):—
Thomas Montagu (60 Acre Lane, SW2 5SP), *b* 1940; *ed* Eton; Major (ret) The Life Gds: *m* 1st, 1967 (*m diss* 1974), Lieselotte Brandstetter, of Vienna; 2ndly, 1977, Christina, da of Lt-Cdr Sir Kenneth Alston Cradock-Hartopp, 10th Bt, MBE, DSC, RN (ret) (*see* Cradock-Hartopp, Bt, colls), and has issue living (by 1st *m*), Thomas Michael, *b* 1972; *ed* Eton, Univ Coll London, and St Bartholomew's; MB BS, BSc, — Lucinda Ann, *b* 1970: *m* 1991, Anthony Kenneth Noel Terry, eldest son of Peter Noel Leetham Terry, of Cherry Hill, Brandsby, York, and has issue living, Anna Catriona *b* 1994, Emily Constance *b* 1996, — (by 2nd *m*), Alexander Kenneth, *b* 1980, — Louise Amy, *b* 1978. —— Mary Elizabeth, *b* 1937: *m* 1st, 1962 (*m diss* 1975), Timothy Haworth, son of late Maj Philip Knight Haworth, MC, of Filey, N Yorks; 2ndly, 1975, Richard Malise Graham, of Cedar Hill, Roscrea, co Tipperary, and has issue living (by 2nd *m*), Lileth Rosamund Anne, *b* 1975, — Ruth Leila Margaret, *b* 1977.

Grandchildren of late Edward Hickman, 5th son of 1st baronet:—
Issue of late Maj Charles Edward Hickman, *b* 1890, *d* 1963: *m* 1st, 1915, Edith Barbara, who *d* 1915, da of late Frank Spencer, JP, of Egerton, Harrow-on-the-Hill; 2ndly, 1921, Dorothy, who *d* 1966, da of late W. Deans Forster, of Ponteland, Newcastle-upon-Tyne:—
(By 2nd *m*) David Michael Roy (Tower House, West Castle St, Bridgnorth, Shropshire), *b* 1930: *m* 1st, 1959 (*m diss* 1967), Eileen Elizabeth, yr da of late Brian Robert Boyd, of Belfast; 2ndly, 1978, Valerie Beatrice, el da of Frank Victor Collins, of Wolverhampton, and has issue living (by 1st *m*), Charles John, *b* 1960: *m* 1st, 1985 (*m diss* 1990), Vivienne Jeffery; 2ndly, 1993, Sarah Louise, eldest da of Derek Bidwell, of Stratford-upon-Avon, and has issue living (by 1st *m*), Lucy Ciaran *b* 1986, (by 2nd *m*), James Patrick Alfred *b* 1994, Aidan Richard Edward *b* 1998, — Timothy Robert (Whey Farm, Umberleigh, Devon), *b* 1964: *m* 1990, Vanessa Caroline, eldest da of Lt-Col R. A. Latchford, of Düsseldorf, Germany, and has issue living, Camilla Beatrice *b* 1990, Holly Olivia *b* 1994, Harriet Lucy *b* 1998, — Peter Richard (twin), *b* 1964. —— Catherine Elaine, *b* 1926: *m* 1st, 1949, Giles Reid Walker, who *d* 1951 (*see* Walker-Okeover, Bt, colls); 2ndly, 1955, Patrick Campbell Hall, who *d* 1998, of Cae Grugog, Trearddur Bay, Holyhead, Anglesey LL65 2UD, and has issue living (by 1st *m*) (*see* Walker-Okeover, Bt, colls), — (by 2nd *m*) Andrew Campbell, *b* 1957.

Issue of late Wilfred Haden Hickman, *b* 1892, *d* 1973: *m* 1915, Kathleen Mary Stuart, who *d* 1978, da of Edward Noel Nason, MD, of Nuneaton:—
†Denis Stewart, MC, *b* 1918; late Capt RASC; 1939-45 War in Italy (MC, 1939-41 Africa and Italy stars, prisoner): *m* 1st, 1947 (*m diss* 1964), Peggy Barbara (McALPINE), who *d* 19—, da of late John Ernest Sanders, of Gresford; 2ndly, 1965, Jean (8 Old Forge Close, Bledington, Chipping Norton, Oxford OX7 6XW), da of A. Urwin, of Tynemouth, and *d* 1995, leaving issue, (by 2nd *m*) Tara Jane, *b* 1966: *m* 1991, Ian Potter, of Bozeat, Northants, and has issue living, Elliot Keith *b* 1993, — Rona Stuart, *b* 1967: *m* 1993, Mark Stuart-Bourne, of Haddenham, Bucks, and has issue living, Edward *b* 1984, Louis Denis *b* 1995, Annabel *b* 1997, — Anya Lucy, *b* 1969: *m* 1996, Adam Beatty, of London. —— Christopher Wolf Arden (Barnhill, Naunton, Stow-on-the-Wold, Glos), *b* 1925; 1939-45 War with RASC: *m* 1949, Daphne Esther, da of John Alec Clift, and has issue living, Rachael, *b* 1951: *m* 1979, Peter Austin, of Ludbridge Mill, East Hendred, Wantage, Oxfordshire OX12 8LN, and has issue living, William Michael *b* 1980, James Peter *b* 1983, Claire Poppy Rosina *b* 1986, — Rosemary, *b* 1953, — Gillian, *b* 1955, — Joanna, *b* 1964. —— Rona Kathleen, *b* 1921; 1939-45 War with WRNS: *m* 1943, Reginald Alfred Reardon Smith, and has issue living, Christopher John Harry Reardon (139 Learg St, Coolum, Queensland, Australia), *b* 1946: *m* 1967, Frances Barnes, and has issue living, David Harry Reardon *b* 1978, Paula Maria *b* 1967, Tina Georgina *b* 1971, — William Jeremy Reardon (Winnipeg, Manitoba, Canada), *b* 1949: *m* 1st, 19— (*m diss* 19—), Margaret Harrap; 2ndly, 19—, Judith —, — Anthea Kathleen, *b* 1944: *m* 1st, 1967 (*m diss* 19—), Michael Monks; 2ndly, 19—, Richard Holborow, of Tetbury, Glos, and has issue living (by 1st *m*), Emma Kathrine *b* 1969, — Janice Caroline, *b* 1953: *m* 1979, Antony Collins, and has issue living, Timothy Gerald *b* 1980, Sarah Jocelyn *b* 1983.

Grandchildren of late Victor Emanuel Hickman, 6th son of 1st baronet:—
Issue of late Cdr Geoffrey Victor Hickman, DSC, RN, *b* 1890, *d* 1975: *m* 1st, 1914, Josephine Helen, who *d* 1933, da of Lt-Col Walter Reginald Fox, formerly RA; 2ndly, Gwendoline Dorothy Miell:—
(By 1st *m*) Hugh Geoffrey, *b* 1916; 1939-45 War as Lt S Staffs, Regt. —— Geraldyne Rosemary Margaret, *b* 1917: *m* 1946, Richard Wiltshire, of 4 Claverdon Close, Solihull, and has issue living, Hugh Richard, *b* 1947: *m* 1970, Barbara Gwenyth Price, and has issue.

Issue of late John Owen Hickman, 7th son of 1st baronet, *b* 1870, *d* 1949: *m* 1903, Nancy Viola, who *d* 1963, da of Harry Barlow:—
Michael Ranulf (The Acorn, Bovingdon, Herts), *b* 1922; *ed* Wellington Coll, and Trin Hall, Camb; Bar Middle Temple 1949; formerly Fl-Lt RAFVR; appointed a Circuit Court Judge 1974: *m* 1943, Diana, da of Col D. C. H. Richardson, 10th Hussars, and has issue living, Peter Derek, *b* 1951: *m* 1974, (Hilary) Clare, da of Don Sadler, of Gwelo, Zimbabwe, and has issue living, Richard Ranulf *b* 1977, Adam Derek *b* 1980, — Susan Marilyn, *b* 1948: *m* 1972, Aris Alexander Pierre Zarpanely, of 2 Old Dock Close, Kew Green, Surrey, and has issue living, Petros Alexander *b* 1975, Rene Diana *b* 1977. —— Angela Mary, *b* 1924: *m* 1st, 1943, Charles Gordon Richards, who was *ka* 1943; 2ndly, 1948, William Freshwater, who *d* 1989, and has issue living (by 2nd *m*), Michael David Latimer, *b* 1950, — Martin Walter James, *b* 1958, — Jane Elizabeth Mary, *b* 1948, — Christine Ellen Nancy, *b* 1962. *Residence* – Chaiya, Ball Hill, Newbury, Berks.

Grandchildren of late John Owen Hickman (ante):—
Issue of late John Barlow Hickman, *b* 1904, *d* 1932: *m* 1925, Joan, who *d* 1995, da of late Kyrle Chatfield Hankinson, of Eden Mount, Tunbridge Wells:—

John Kyrle, CMG (Ivy Bank, Oare, nr Marlborough), *b* 1927; *ed* Tonbridge, and Trin Hall, Camb (BA), Diplo Ser; CMG 1977: *m* 1956, Jennifer, da of Reginald Kendall Love, and has issue living, Matthew John Kyrle, *b* 1964: *m* 1994, Andrea F., da of late D. J. P. Hudson, and of Sra Adriana Kimber, of Santiago, Chile, and has issue living, Sebastian John Matthew *b* 1995, Thomas David Kyrle *b* 1997, Nicholas Andrew Owen *b* 1999, — Andrew Giles Lovell, *b* 1966, — Catherine Lucy, *b* 1960: *m* 1987, Tom Owen Edmunds, of 15 Glengall Rd, SE15, son of David Owen Edmunds, and has issue living, Luke Lovell David *b* 1995. —— Richard Malim (6/72 Shackleton Circuit, Mawson, ACT 2607, Australia), *b* 1930; *ed* Tonbridge, and Pembroke Coll, Camb (MA); *m* 1st, 1962 (*m diss* 1985), Judy Penelope Sylvia, da of late Brig Charles Douglas Armstrong, CBE, DSO, MC; 2ndly, 1993, Maureen Louise, da of late Patrick Dillon Walsh, of Sydney, NSW, and has issue living, Marcus Sebastian Charles (Fir Cottage, Backsideans, Wargrave, Berks), *b* 1963; *ed* Sydney Univ (BEc), and Cranfield Univ (MBA): *m* 1997, Joanna, da of Dr Gareth Davies, of Cardiff, and has issue living, Sebastian Henry Morris *b* 1997, — Jonathan Edward Barlow, *b* 1964: *m* 1992, Eva, da of Jan Suchovsky, of Womboin, NSW, and has issue living, Joshua Jan Nathaniel *b* 1996. —— Dinah (Hilvern, 56290 St Gonnery, Brittany, France), *b* 1929: *m* 1953, John Frederick Saunders, and has issue living, Richard Neville, *b* 1955, — Joanna Elizabeth, *b* 1958.

The 1st baronet, Sir Alfred Hickman, Chm of Alfred Hickman (Limited), sat as MP for Wolverhampton (*C*) 1885-6, and 1892-1906.

HILL (I) 1779 of Brook Hall, Londonderry

Sir JOHN ALFRED ROWLEY HILL, 11th *Baronet*; *b* 29 Feb 1940; *s* his half-brother, *Maj Sir* RICHARD GEORGE ROWLEY, MBE, 1992: *m* 1966 (*m diss* 1981), Diana Anne, da of Donald Wilfred Walker, of Blaby, Leicester, and has two adopted children.

𝕬rms – Sable, a chevron erminois between three leopards' faces argent. 𝕮rest – A talbot's head couped sable, guttés d'eau, collared gules, studded and ringed or.
Residence – 12 Ledbury Close, Oadby Grange, Leicester LE2 3PN.

ADOPTED SON LIVING

James Richard Rowley, *b* 1974.

ADOPTED DAUGHTER LIVING

Samantha Rowley, *b* 1976.

SISTER LIVING

Margaret Anne Rowley, *b* 1942: *m* 1st, 1962 (*m diss* 1970), Rodney Michael Saunders; 2ndly, 1973, John Godfrey Phillips. *Residence* – 472 Uppingham Rd, Leicester.

DAUGHTERS LIVING OF TENTH BARONET (by his 2nd wife, Zoreen Joy Macpherson, only da of late Norman Warburton Tippett, and widow of Andrew David Wilson Marshall)

Attempt not, or accomplish

Charlotte Mary Rowley, *b* 1976; *ed* Fettes, and Aberdeen Univ. —— Georgina Emma Rowley, *b* 1977; *ed* Fettes.

COLLATERAL BRANCHES LIVING

Grandchildren of late Rowley John Hill (infra), son of Marcus Hill, el son of Capt Rowley John Hill, 2nd son of Rev John Beresford Hill, 2nd son of 1st baronet:—
Issue of late Leslie Thomas Hill, *b* 1897, *d* 1958: *m* 1920, Irene Howlett:—
Joan Maria *b* 1925: *m* 1945, Leslie Bailey, and has issue living, Kenneth Leslie, *b* 1946, — Cheryl Larraine, *b* 1948. —— Dorothy Irene, *b* 1928: *m* 1947, Herbert Alfred Morley, and has issue living, Christopher John, *b* 1950, — Carol Anne, *b* 1948.

Issue of late Claude Adam James Hill, *b* 1901, *d* 1991: *m* 1928, Ruby Alice (8 Lancaster Rd, Mooroolbark, Vic, Aust), da of Robert Mallett:—
ALLAN CLAUDE JAMES (18/20 Havelock St, Lawrence, NSW 2460, Aust), *b* 10 Feb 1936: *m* 1970 (*m diss* 1978), Rachel ST JUST, da of Geoffrey Filsell, and has issue living, Marcus Adam James, *b* 22 Aug 1974; has issue living (by Narelle Catherine Byrne), Braedy Adam HILL *b* 1996, Keanan Marcus Leo HILL *b* 1998, — Sonya Rachel Anne, *b* 1972: *m* 1995 (*m diss* 1996), Ian Scott Thomson, and has issue living, Ian Clarence James *b* 1994, Natasha Dawn Anne *b* 1993. —— Joyce Patricia, *b* 1933: *m* 1951, Geoffrey Paul, of 8 Lancaster Rd, Mooroolbark, Vic, Aust, and has issue living, Allan Geoffrey, *b* 1952, — Cheryl Therese, *b* 1955: *m* 1987, Andrew Rhodes, of 112 Chirnside St, West Footscray, Vic, Aust, and has issue living, Gene Paul *b* 1987.

Issue of late Marcus George Hill, *b* 1904, *d* 1993: *m* 1929, Lydia May Liddle:—
†George Frederick, *b* 1930: *m* 1951, Jean Craggel, and *d* 1991, having had issue, Anthony Rowland, *b* 1961, — Debra, *b* 1964, — Sallyanne, *b* 1966; *d* 1989. —— Kevin Leslie (49 Fraser St, Sunshine, Vic 3020), *b* 1935: *m* 1959, Wendy Chandler, and has issue living, Mark, *b* 1961: *m* 1986, Caryn Geddes, and has issue living, Joshua Mark *b* 1992, — Paul, *b* 1964: *m* 1989, Tina-Jane Pinchen, and has issue living, Jason Paul *b* 1996. —— Patricia Miriam, *b* 1932: *m* 1954, Rolf

Ludviksen, of 26 Poole St, Deer Park, Vic 3023, and has issue living, John Kenneth (75 Tarella Drive, Kealba, Vic 3021), *b* 1955: *m* 19—, Tracey Ruth, da of John McLoone, and has issue living, Michael John *b* 1991, — Brett, *b* 1972, — Leanne Michelle (16 Locke St, Essendon, Vic 3040), *b* 1959: *m* 1977 (*m diss* 1983), Allan Borg, and has issue living, Melinda Amy *b* 1979. —— Dawn Anne, *b* 1939: *m* 1963, John Justin, of 7 Bellair Av, Glenroy, Vic 3046, and has issue living, Kenneth, *b* 1964, — Darren, *b* 1966, — Glen *b* 1971.

Issue of late Cyril Edward Hill, *b* 1908, *d* 1988: *m* 1931, Mary Elizabeth (Unit 16/2, High Field Rd, Canterbury, Vic 3126, Aust), da of Francis Tinker:—
James Rowland Edward (Lot 7, 9 Arnold St, Kilsyth, Melbourne, Vic, Aust), *b* 1943: *m* 1969, Lynette Jean, da of — Berry, and has issue living, Jason James *b* 1972, — Christophe Eric, *b* 1974. —— Janice Ann, *b* 1940: *m* 1962, Ronald Arthur Haynes, of 39 Sandy St, Nunawading, Vic 3131, Aust, and has issue living, Diane Mary, *b* 1964, — Michelle Lucy, *b* 1966, — Joanne Lisa, *b* 1969: *m* 1990, Carl Gittins, of 4/34 Oak St, Seymour, Vic 3660, Aust, — Belinda Jane, *b* 1975. —— Elizabeth Dianna, *b* 1945: *m* 1967, Constantine Politis, of 16 Russell Av, Mooroolbank, Vic, Aust, and has issue living, Andrew Edward, *b* 1973, — Jeannette Ann, *b* 1969, — Debra Lee, *b* 1971.

Grandchildren of late Marcus Hill (ante):—
Issue of late Rowley John Hill, *b* 1873, *d* 1960: *m* 1896, Anne Elizabeth Morrow, who *d* 1912:—
Albert John, *b* 1912: *m* 1935, Annie Melba, da of Edgar William Johnstone.

Issue of late James Henry Sale Hill, *b* 1885, *d* 1954: *m* 1910, Ethyl May Woodbury, who *d* 1967, of Wangaratta, Victoria:—
Roy Ernest (Rau St, Albury, NSW, Australia), *b* 1914: *m* 1935, Phyllis Jean Allen, of Ringwood, Victoria, and has issue living, Lorres Ann, *b* 1938: *m* 19—, Robert E. Johnson, of Launceston, Tasmania, and has issue living, Antony *b* 1964, David *b* 1970, Elizabeth *b* 1966. —— James Herbert (Rau St, Albury, NSW), *b* 1912: *m* 1936, Charlotte Ethel Bastion. —— Olive May, *b* 1915: *m* 1933, Allan Klinberg.

Issue of late Philip Ernest Hill, *b* 1887, *d* 1960: *m* 1913, Hilda Maria Ambrosina Cooper, who *d* 1966:—
Stanley George (27 Summerhill Av, E Malvern, Melbourne 3145, Vic, Aust), *b* 1935: *m* 1964, Patricia Ann McLellan, and has had issue, †Philip William Adrian, *b* 1966; *d* 1974, — Paul Timothy, *b* 1968, — Michael John, *b* 1975, — Catherine Elizabeth, *b* 1979. —— Philis May, *b* 1917: *m* 1938, George Lewis Robinson, of 49 Hardy Av, Wagga Wagga, NSW, and has issue living, Helen, *b* 1940: *m* 1960, —, — Shirley, *b* 1942: *m* 1962 —, — Dawn, *b* 1950, — Maree, *b* 1956. —— Thelma Rose, *b* 19—: *m* 19—, Ronald Charles Wheeler, and has issue living, Garry, *b* 19—, — Robert, *b* 19—, — Janet, *b* 19—.

Grandchildren of late Marcus Henry Sale Hill (infra):—
Issue of late Wilfred Henry Hill, *b* 1906, *d* 1972: *m* 1936, Thelma Mattingly:—
Robert Maxwell (17 Walker Crescent, Gore, Southland, NZ), *b* 1938: *m* 1962, Wendy Cross, and has issue living, Christopher, *b* 19—, — Robyn, *b* 1962, — Julie, *b* 1965. —— Lesley Robin Gael, *b* 1949: *m* 1st, 1966, Gavan McEntee; 2ndly, 19—, Allan Rush, of RD1, Winton, Southland, NZ, and has issue living, (by 1st *m*) Gavan Chayne, *b* 1966, — Brett Owen, *b* 1968, — Stephen Robert, *b* 1969. —— Dawn Adeline, *b* 1937: *m* 1963, Raymond Wilkins, and has issue living Lionel David, *b* 1964, — Deborah Margery, *b* 1967, — Dionne Beryl, *b* 1970.

Issue of late Henry George Hill, *b* 1909, *d* 1988: *m* 1940, Eileen Webb:—
Harold Alexander, *b* 1941: *m* 1st, 19— (*m diss* 19—), Fay Ogarman; 2ndly, 19— (*m diss* 19—), Cynthia Joan Letherland. —— Francis John, *b* (twin) 1941: *m* 1963, Margaret —, and has issue living, David John, *b* 1986, Joanne —, and has issue living, Cheryl Maree *b* 1987, — Brett Christopher, *b* 1966, — Yvonne Clare, *b* 1970. —— Owen Patrick, *b* 1943. —— Mervyn George, *b* 1945: *m* 1967, Janet Murgatroyd, and has issue living, Aaron Mervyn, *b* 1967, — Adrian Bevan, *b* 1974, — Leanne Marie, *b* 1968, — Deborah Anne, *b* 1970. —— Michael David, *b* 19—: *m* 1974, Robyn —, and has issue living, Allan Paul, *b* 1981, — Jocelyn, *b* 1979. —— Sharon Joy, *b* 1947: *m* 1966, David Dick, and has issue living, Steven Kidmond, *b* 1968, — Tracey Joy, *b* 1969. —— Angela Fay, *b* 19—: *m* 1975, Ian Page, and has issue living, Steven, *b* 1979, — Anita, *b* 1981. —— Eileen Christine, *b* 19—: has issue living, Tania Marie, *b* 1974.

Issue of late Edward Albert Hill, *b* 1911, *d* 1995: *m* 1935, Jessie Margaret McWilliam, who *d* 1988, da of Robert Wilson, of Whakatane, NZ:—
Edward Wilson Sale (Matata Rd, Awakaponga, Whakatane, NZ), *b* 1936: *m* 1969, Elaine Mary Striger, and has had issue, †Paul Edward, *b* 1972; *d* 1995, — Kim Pamela, *b* 1970, — Jacqueline, *b* 1971: *m* 1993, Jason Barrett, — Cindy Lea, *b* 1977. —— Robert George (Manawahe Rd, RD4, Whakatane, NZ), *b* 1940: *m* 19—, Zita Noelene Howell, and has issue living, Darryn Robert, *b* 1965: *m* 19—, Kim Teresa Wilson, and has issue living, Jared Robert *b* 1990, Jacob Anthony *b* 1997, Shayna-lee Jessie *b* 1988, — Martin Anthony, *b* 1966: *m* 19—, Holly Rodgers, and has issue living, Ethan Piripi *b* 1990, Martin Rugby *b* 1992, Priscilla Marie *b* 1988, Jason Kane, *b* 1972; has issue living, Ricky Dean *b* 1992, Aaron Davies *b* 1996, Courtney Gina *b* 1994, Jayden Troy *b* 1995, — Catherine Rose, *b* 1961: *m* 19—, Merritt John Winter, and has issue living, Michael Joseph *b* 1993, Kylee Ngahuia *b* 1980, Stephanie Louise *b* 1988, Nicole Ashlee *b* 1992, — Gina, *b* and *d* 1963, — Alana Marie, *b* 1970: *m* 19—, Roger Michael Hunter and has issue living, Michael Kane, *b* 1998, Samantha Jade *b* 1996. —— Leonard James (43 South St, Ulladulla, NSW 2539, Aust), *b* 1943: *m* 1st, 1965 (*m diss* 19—), Christine Webster; 2ndly, 19—, Deborah Anne Armstrong, and has issue living (by 1st *m*), Susan Mary, *b* 1965, — (by 2nd *m*), Arron James, *b* 1993, — Jessica Rene, *b* 1992. —— Marwyn Albert (10 Rata Av, Edgecumbe, NZ), *b* 1955: *m* 19—, Hana Venus, da of Aubrey John Rogers, of Whakatane, NZ, and has issue living, Ray Charles Edward Harawae Tarei McWill, *b* 1997, — Jessie Agnes Rangiteataura Wilson, *b* 1996. —— Margaret Elizabeth, *b* 1938.

Grandchildren of late George Henry Hill, 3rd son of Capt Rowley John Hill (ante):—
Issue of late Marcus Henry Sale Hill, *b* 1870, *d* 1946: *m* 1903, Emma Frances, da of Henry Kenton, of Lower Harbour, Port Chalmers, New Zealand:—
Russell Sale, *b* 1913: *m* 1945, Pearl Iris, da of Lewis Septimus Civil, of Pukekohe, NZ, and has issue living, Marie June, *b* 1946: *m* 1968, David Ivor Jones, of Manawahe Rd, Matata, Whakatane, NZ, and has issue living, Glenn David *b* 1969, Justine Joanne *b* 1971, — Carolyn Lesley, *b* 1947: *m* 1982, Gerry McGillicuddy (B Eng), of Mongonui, Northland, NZ. —— †Ernie Parker *b* 1916: *m* 1946, Jessie May Court (Deborah Bay, Port Chalmers, NZ), of Waimate, S Canterbury, NZ, and *d* 1992, leaving issue, Malcolm Ross (398 Churchill Rd, Judea, Tauranga, NZ), *b* 1947: *m* 19— (*m diss* 19—),

Clare McAlley, and has issue living Sarah-Jane Frances *b* 1978, Rebecca Ailsa *b* 1981, — Donald Graeme, *b* 1962, — Janice Audrey, *b* 1950: *m* 1st, 1970 (*m diss* 19—), Lindsay Wilson; 2ndly, 1974, Neville Billington, of 40 Stone St, Mornington, Dunedin, NZ, and has issue living, (by 1st *m*) Jocelyn Anne *b* 1971, Deborah Kaye *b* 1973, (by 2nd *m*) Philip John *b* 1975, Craig Neville *b* 1978, — Nellie May, *b* 1952: *m* 1976 (*m diss* 19—), Stephen Rayston, and has issue living, Michael Alexander *b* 1979, — Barbara Ann, *b* 1959: has issue living, Kelly Marie *b* 1978. —— Thelma Alice (9 Islington St, Te Aroka, N Island, NZ), *b* 1920: *m* 1940, Walter James McLay, who *d* 1986, and has issue living, Ernest James, *b* 1941: *m* 1961, Sylvia May Rolf, and has issue living, Stephen James *b* 1962: *m* 1984, Linda Quigley (and has issue living, Christopher James *b* 1988), Kenneth Stuart *b* 1963: *m* 1987, Sarah Ash, Peter Ernest *b* 1967, Donna Ann *b* 1964, — Douglas Stuart, *b* 1942: *m* 1969, Carol Jean Grice, and has issue living, Jason Stuart Marshall *b* 1971, Scott Douglas *b* (twin) 1971, Katrina Maree *b* 1969, — Alastair David, *b* 1946: *m* 1980 Bronwen Roger, and has issue living, Joanne Beth *b* 1981, Heather Ruth *b* 1983, Rebecca Lois *b* 1986, — Trevor Sale, *b* 1947: *m* 1982, Carol Cunningham, — Norman Walter, *b* 1951: *m* 1982, Sandra Grubber, and has issue living, Bradley Walter *b* 1984, Jonathan David *b* 1986, — Ian Murray, *b* 1956: *m* 1984, Fiona Mary Lowery, and has issue living, James Murray *b* 1987, — Sheryl Joy, *b* 1949: *m* 19—, Hugh Kay Sueistrup, and has issue living, Shawn Kay *b* 1971, Darrell Boyes *b* 1974, Kassandra Joy *b* 1972. —— Dorothy Loraine (12 Argyle Av, Palmerston N, NZ), *b* 1924: *m* 1956 (*m diss* 19—), James Barclay, and has issue living, Bruce Lindsay, *b* 1957: *m* 1977, Pauline Joy Adams, of Palmerston N, NZ, and has issue living, Patrick Allan *b* 1978, Kevin Philip *b* 1981, — Christopher Warren, *b* 1958. — Sandra Kaye, *b* 1961: *m* 1979, Stewart James Wallis, of Camden, NSW, and has issue living, Joleen Lisa Wallis *b* 1979, Logan James *b* 1981.

　　　　　　Grandsons living of late Marcus Henry Sale Hill (ante):—
　　　　　　Issue of late Leonard Graham Hill (twin), *b* 1911, *ka* 1942: *m* 1935, Christina Agnes Allan Wilson, of Section 3, Awakaponga, RD Whakatane, New Zealand:—
Graham Robert Marcus (Corner of Pakeha and Mar Sts, Matata, Bay of Plenty, NZ), *b* 1936: *m* 1958, Shirley Whan, of Sydney, Australia, and has issue living, Michael Peter John, *b* (Jan) 1960, — Leonard Graham, *b* (Dec) 1960, — Warren Stephan, *b* 1962, — Stanley Norman, *b* 1963, — Deborah Joy, *b* 1964. —— Allan Henry (19 Appleby Rise, Whakatane, NZ), *b* 1938: *m* 1959, Raewyn Alice Smith, of Whakatane, New Zealand, and has issue living, Douglas Allan, *b* 1960: *m* 1986, Linda Duncum, of Rotorua, NZ, — Gordon France, *b* 1962: *m* 1990, Deborah D. Hunter, of Rotorua, NZ, and has issue living, Rory Nathan *b* 1991, Krystal Moira *b* 1984, — Rowley Wilson, *b* 1964: *m* 1993, Sharon Naylor, of Warwick, Qld, — Murray Richard, *b* 1967: *m* 1991, Leah Longdon, of Rotorua, NZ.

　　　　　　Grandchildren of late George Henry Hill (ante):—
　　　　　　Issue of late George Rowley Sale Hill, *b* 1874, *d* 1936: *m* 1899, Elizabeth Attfield, who *d* 1941:—
Three sons. —— Five daughters.

　　　　　　Issue of late Louis Hill, *b* 1878, *d* 19—: *m* 19—, Elizabeth Walker, who *d* 19—:—
Two sons and a daughter.

　　　　　　Issue of late Percy Graham Hill, *b* 1883, *d* 1953: *m* 1905, Mary Ellen Wilson:—
George Arthur Graham, *b* 1905: *m* 1931, Kathleen Geary, who *d* 1998, and has issue living, David Graham (RD6, Makarewa, Southland, NZ), *b* 1931, — †Douglas George, *b* 1933; *d* 1941, — Donald Percival, *b* 1937: *m* 1956, Elaine Agnes Batt, and has issue living, David Charles *b* 1960: *m* 1979, Barbara Mary Leonard (and has issue living, Roger Donald *b* 1980, Timothy Allan *b* 1983, Adam David *b* 1988), Lindsay George *b* 1967, Kathleen Mary *b* 1954: *m* 1976, Graham Rex Sycamore (and has issue living, Stephen David *b* 1979, Shane Bevin *b* 1983, Jamic Rex *b* 1985), Marion Elaine *b* 1964: *m* 1981, Lyall Gillett (and has issue living, Shaun Lyall *b* 1986, Emma Jane *b* 1983), Deborah Anne *b* and *d* 1967, — Russell George, *b* 1942: *m* 1967, Margaret Anne Robertson, and has issue living, Gary Russell *b* 1971, Bronwyn Anne *b* 1969, — Douglas John, *b* 1943: *m* 1973, Kathleen Gail Henderson, and has issue living, Christopher John *b* 1977, Kevin James *b* 1980, — Valerie Mae, *b* 1946: *m* 1967, Deo Datt Sharma, and has issue living, Indria Dati *b* 1973, Sarita Devi *b* 1977, Pranetta Devi *b* 1979, Rachael Anne, *b* 1981. —— Helen Caroline (c/o Takitimu Home, 110 Conyers St, Invercargill, NZ), *b* 1910: *m* 1927, William Robert Lewis, who *d* 1981. and has issue living, William Leonard (17 Keldon Av, Rangiora, Canterbury, New Zealand), *b* 1932: *m* 1956, Jeanette McGregor, and has issue living, Bruce David *b* 1958: *m* 1985 Anne Marie Glendening (and has issue living, Scott William *b* 1988, Todd Robert *b* 1990), Donald James *b* 1959: *m* 1981, Nicola Ann Dennison (and has issue living, Bradley Donald *b* 1984, Janelle Nicola *b* 1989), Rodney William *b* 1961: *m* 1987, Heather Woods (and has issue living, Mark William *b* 1992, Emma Lee *b* 1992), Susan Gaye *b* 1960: *m* 1984, George Paul Hastings (and has issue living, Bonnie Lewis *b* 1990), — Mary Catherine, *b* 1928: *m* 1952, Maxwell Maurice Murphy, of 49 Peel St, Westport, New Zealand, and has issue living, Brian William *b* 1955: *m* 1981, Kathryn Margaret Peick, of Westport, NZ (and has issue living, Thomas Brian *b* 1988, Jacinta Kathryn *b* 1985, Emma Grace *b* 1992), Anthony Maxwell *b* 1958: *m* 1981, Marcia Dianne Tipping (and has issue living, Samuel Maurice *b* 1982, Andrew William *b* 1984, James Anthony *b* 1992, Rebekah May *b* 1988), Patrick Thomas *b* 1961: *m* 1988, Cathy Ann Talbot (and has issue living, Cody Allan *b* 1993, Teagan Rae *b* 1990, Brandon Maxwell *b* 1994), Helen Margaret *b* 1954: *m* 1973, Anthony John Robertson, (and has issue living, Blair Anthony *b* 1979, Glen Francis *b* 1981, Mia Catherine *b* 1985), Gloria Mary *b* 1957: *m* 1983, Bernard John Hutchinson (and has had issue, Maxwell Connell *b* 1997, Caitlan Rose *b* and *d* 1995, Hannah Louise *b* 1992), Kathleen Ann *b* 1963: *m* 1986, Andrew Robin Hobern (and has issue living, Michael Andrew *b* 1994, Sean Maxwell *b* 1994, Clare Alyce *b* 1992), Julie Maureen *b* 1964, — Vera Joy, *b* 1930: *m* 1954, John J. Walsh, of Menzies Ferry No. 1 RD, Edendale, Southland, NZ, and has had issue, Angela Mary *b* 1956: *m* 1979, Russell Caldwell (and has issue living, Hayden James *b* 1983, Kieran John *b* 1985, Ryan Gerrad *b* 1987, Nadia Lauren *b* 1981, Olivia Leah *b* 1989), Jillian Caroline *b* 1960, *d* 1986, Maree Jane *b* 1962: *m* 1983, Maurice John Crawford, of Waghorn's Rd, RD Waharoa, Matamata, New Zealand (and has issue living, Matthew John *b* 1984, Braden Walsh *b* 1991, Krystal Jillian *b* 1987, Jordyn Deanna *b* 1992), Leanne Ruth *b* 1966: *m* 1987, Ross McLeod (and has had issue, Daniel Ross *b* and *d* 1984), Denise Louise *b* 1968: *m* 1990, David Dunlop (and has issue living, Jeremy Ross *b* 1992, Cameron John *b* 1994, Hadlee Daniel *b* 1996), — Lorna Ellen, *b* 1939: *m* 1958, John Desmond Wright, of 49 Tees St, Oamaru, NZ, and has issue living, Darrell John (106A Eden St, Oamaru, NZ) *b* 1959: *m* 1982, Carol Margaret Blair (and has issue living, Christopher John *b* 1988, Michelle Leigh *b* 1987), Graham Norman *b* 1960, Paul Robert *b* 1961, — Dawn Margaret, *b* 1942: *m* 1961, Stuart Gray, of 61 Forth St, Mataura, Southland, NZ, and has issue living, David Andrew *b* 1962: *m* 1st, 1990 (*m diss* 19—), Karen Ann Marie Puru; 2ndly, 19— (*m diss* 19—), Sonya Fraser (and has issue living (by 1st *m*), Graham William *b* 1991), Julie Margaret Irene *b* 1964: *m* 1986, Nigel John Blackler (and has issue living, Holly Margaret *b* 1988), — Sonia Carol, *b* 1947: *m* 1965, Alexander George Kelly, of 476 Racecourse, Invercargill, Southland, NZ, and has issue living, Allan Peter *b* 1966: *m* 1992, Donna Kathryn McLellan (and has issue living, Josha William *b* 1996, Nathan Peter *b* 1998, Lauren Margaret *b* 1994), Katrina May *b* 1969: *m* 1990, Logan Maxwell (and has issue living, Benjamin George *b* 1996, Kate Hannah *b* 1994).

The 1st baronet, Sir Hugh Hill (son of late Rowley Hill, MP), was MP for Londonderry. The 2nd baronet, a Privy Councillor, sat as MP for city and co of Derry 1795-1830; he was successively Clerk of the Irish House of Commons,

Vice-Treasurer of Ireland, Governor of the Island of St Vincent, and Governor of Trinidad. The 4th baronet, Major Sir John Hill, served throughout the Indian Mutiny with Bengal Light Cav. The first ancestor of this family, originally of Buckinghamshire, was Treasurer of Ireland under Oliver Cromwell.

HILL (UK) 1916, of Bradford

Sir JAMES FREDERICK HILL, 4th *Baronet*; *b* 5 Dec 1943; *s* his father, *Sir* JAMES, 1976; *ed* Wrekin Coll, and Bradford Univ; DL W Yorks 1994: *m* 1966, Sandra Elizabeth, da of late J. C Ingram, of Summerfield, S Parade, Ilkley, W Yorks, and has issue.

𝕬rms – Or, on a fesse between three leopards' faces sable, as many roses leaved and seeded proper. 𝕮rest – Upon a rock charged with two roses as in the arms a merino ram statant proper.
Residence – Roseville, Moor Lane, Menston, Ilkley, W Yorks LS29 6AP.

SON LIVING

JAMES LAURENCE INGRAM, *b* 22 Sept 1973.

DAUGHTERS LIVING

Juliet Clare, *b* 1969: *m* 1st, 1989 (*m diss* 1996), James Christopher Kaberry, elder son of Hon Sir Christopher Donald Kaberry, 2nd Bt; 2ndly, 1996, Richard Murton, and has issue (by 1st *m*) (*see* B Kaberry). —— Georgina Margaret, *b* 1971. —— Josephine Valerie, *b* 1976.

SISTERS LIVING

Anita Joan, *b* 1931: *m* 1953, Michael John Riley, who *d* 1988, and has issue living, Peter James Wynne, *b* 1956, — Christopher John, *b* 1960, — Wendy Jeanne, *b* 1954. —— Ellen Barbara, *b* 1936: *m* 1960, Edward Norman Robson, of Braeside, Trebetherick, Wadebridge, Cornwall, and has issue living, Susan Joy, *b* 1960, — Jacqueline Ann, *b* 1963, — Penelope Jane, *b* 1967. —— Florence Margaret (twin) (Windsor Mews, Windsor Rd, Vincent, E London, S Africa), *b* 1943: *m* 1965 (*m diss* 19——), Terence John Coombs, and has issue living, Tessa Annette, *b* 1965, — Linda Margaret, *b* 1967, — Tracey Elizabeth, *b* 1973.

Attempt not, or else accomplish

WIDOW LIVING OF THIRD BARONET

MARJORY, JP (*Marjory, Lady Hill*) (Brea House, Trebetherick, Wadebridge, Cornwall), da of late Frank Croft, of Brocka, Lindale, Grange-over-Sands: *m* 1930, Sir James Hill, 3rd Bt, who *d* 1976.

COLLATERAL BRANCH LIVING

Issue of late Arthur James Hill, el son of 1st baronet, *b* 1876, *d* 1935: *m* 1898, Eleanor Beatrice Hindle, who *d* 1975, da of late Thomas Duxbury, FCS, AMICE, of Temple Moyle, Darwen:—
Noeline Etrenne (*Lady Aarvold*), *b* 1909: *m* 1934, His Honour Judge (Sir Carl Douglas) Aarvold, OBE, TD, DL, JP, Recorder of London (ret), who *d* 1991, and has issue living, Christopher Olaf, *b* 1943: *m* 1981, Sandi Gazzard, and has issue living, Tobias Carl *b* 1981, Dominic Ralph Ole *b* 1983, Camilla Louise *b* 1984, — James Hillary, *b* 1946: *m* 1976, Dr Jillian Stanley Jones, and has issue living, Daniel Alexander *b* 1977, Thomas William *b* 1982, Eleanor Pippin *b* 1980, — John Merriman, *b* 1947: *m* 1976, Elizabeth Rumball, of Johannesburg, S Africa, and has issue living, Robert John Douglas *b* 1978, Angus David Merriman *b* 1981, Douglas Henry Eric *b* 1984. *Residence* – Coach House, Crabtree Lane, Westhumble, Dorking.

The 1st baronet, Sir James Hill (son of late William Hill, of Harden, Bingley, Yorkshire), was head of the firm of Sir James Hill & Sons, wool merchants (which he founded in 1890), and sat as MP for Central Div of Bradford (*L*) 1916-18.

ERSKINE-HILL (UK) 1945, of Quothquhan, co Lanark

Sir (ALEXANDER) ROGER ERSKINE-HILL, 3rd *Baronet*; *b* 15 Aug 1949; *s* his father, *Sir* ROBERT, 1989; *ed* Eton, and Aberdeen Univ (LLB): *m* 1984 (*m diss* 1994), Sarah Anne Sydenham, elder da of late Dr Richard John Sydenham Clarke, and has issue.

Arms – Quarterly: 1st grand quarter, azure, a hill argent, charged with two pens, points downwards in saltire, quills or, feathers sable, in chief the sun in his splendour, *Hill*, 2nd grand quarter, counterquarterd, 1st and 4th, argent, on a pale sable, a cross-crosslet fitches or, *Erskine of Shielfield*; 2nd, azure, a bend between two cross-crosslets fitchees or, *Mar*, 3rd, or, on a bend azure three mascles of the field, and in the sinister chief a round buckle of the second, *Haliburton*; all within a bordure per pale azure and sable, a canton or charged with a fleur-de-lys of the second, for difference; 3rd grand quarter, counterquartered, 1st argent, on a mount in base a lion rampant vert, on a chief of the second a crescent between two mullets or, *Halcro*; 2nd, or a fesse chequy azure and argent, a border gules charged with eight round buckles of the first, *Stewart of Barscube*; 3rd, or, on a bend gules, three buckles of the first, *Bonkyll* of that ilk; 4th, argent a heart purpure ensigned with an imperial crown proper, on a chief gules, three pallets or, *Keith of Galston*; 4th grand quarter, argent, a lion rampant, azure, armed and langued gules, on a chief of the second, an elephant's head, cabossed of the first, tusked or, accompanied by two lymphads of the first under full sail proper, *Galloway*. Crest – 1st, a stag's head couped proper, attired sable, 2nd, a dexter arm from the elbow, couped proper, the hand grasping a cross-crosslet fitchee or.

SON LIVING

ROBERT BENJAMIN, *b* 6 Aug 1986.

DAUGHTER LIVING

Kirsty Rose, *b* 1985.

BROTHER LIVING

Henry James, *b* 1953; *ed* Eton: *m* 1979 (*m diss* 1998), Gwen Carolyn, da of Ian Russell Chalmers. *Residence* – Bangkok, Thailand.

SISTERS LIVING

Carola Marion, *b* 1943: *m* 1st, 1963 (*m diss* 1978), Sir Richard David Christopher Brooke, 11 Bt (*see* Brooke Bt, *cr* 1662); 2ndly, 1981, as his 3rd wife, Robin Andrew Stormonth Darling, of Balvarran, Enochdhu, Blairgowrie, Perthshire PH10 7PA. —— Alison, *b* 1945: *m* 1966, John Selby North Lewis, of Walwick Hall, Humshaugh, Hexham, Northumberland, and has issue living, Selby James (Colwell South Farm, Hexham, Northumberland), *b* 1968: *m* 1994, Emma Clare, yr da of Richard Denis de Vitre Gaisford, and has issue living, Jack Selby *b* 1996, Polly Emma *b* 1998, — Harriet Alison, *b* 1970, — Rebecca Elspeth, *b* 1975, — Hannah Margaret, *b* 1979.

AUNT LIVING (*daughter of 1st baronet*)

Jean Halcro, *b* 1928: *m* 1st, 1950, Derek John Seth-Smith, who *d* 1964; 2ndly, 1972, George Henry Smith-Wright, who *d* 1998, and has issue living (by 1st *m*), Frederick Alexander, *b* 1963: *m* 1992, Kathryn R., eldest da of Comdt Barry O'Sullivan, of Naas, co Kildare, and has issue living, Jack Alexander *b* 1994, Ellen *b* 1996, — Kay Christian, *b* 1951: *m* 1981, Charles W. King, of 12 Hambalt Rd, SW4, yr son of Col C. W. King, of Cutham Hill House, Bagenden, Cirencester, Glos, and has issue living, Henry Charles James *b* 1983, Laura Christian *b* (twin) 1983, Alice Jane *b* 1987, — Rosemary Jean, *b* 1954: *m* 1977, Maj Peter F. S. Gwatkin, Welsh Gds, of Shustoke Hall, Shustoke, Warwicks B46 2RJ, son of late John Stapleton Gwatkin, and has issue living, Frederick John Stapleton *b* 1983, Amy Jean Stapleton *b* 1980, Martha Elspeth Stapleton *b* 1986, Hannah Rosemary Theophila Stapleton *b* 1990, — (Mary) Jane, *b* 1957: *m* 1984, William Lee Rothery, son of late George W. Rothery, and has issue living, Charles Alexander *b* 1987, Arthur George *b* 1992, Rosemary Anne *b* 1985. *Residence* – 34 Moore St, SW3 2QW.

WIDOW LIVING OF SECOND BARONET

CHRISTINE ALISON (*Lady Erskine-Hill*); ARCM 1970; only da of late Capt Henry James Johnstone, RN, of Alva (*see* Johnstone, Bt, colls): *m* 1942, Sir Robert Erskine-Hill, 2nd Bt, who *d* 1989. *Residence* – Harelea House, Libberton, Carnwath, Lanarkshire ML11 8LX.

COLLATERAL BRANCH LIVING

Issue of late John Colville Erskine-Hill, DSC, VRD, yr son of 1st baronet, *b* 1921, *d* 1984: *m* 1959, Myra Elizabeth (Hoopoe House, Maytham Rd, Rolvenden Layne, Cranbrook, Kent TN17 4NP), da of late Cdr Richard Homewood, RN:—
Mark Colville, *b* 1960: *m* 1992, Lucy Diana Elspeth, da of D. B. Hulme, of Reigate, Surrey, and has issue living, David, *b* 1996, — Alice, *b* 1993. —— David John, *b* 1962.

The 1st baronet, Sir Alexander Galloway Erskine-Hill, KC (son of Robert Alexander Hill) was a Director of London & NE Railway and sat as MP for N Div of Edinburgh (*U*) 1935-45. Sir Robert, 2nd Bt, was Chm The Life Assocn of Scotland Ltd 1960-85, and ptnr Chiene & Tait, CA, Edinburgh 1946-80.

Hill-Wood, see Wood.

HOARE (I) 1784, of Annabella, Cork

The hour approaches

Sir TIMOTHY EDWARD CHARLES HOARE, OBE, 8th *Baronet*; *b* 11 Nov 1934; *s* his father, *Maj Sir* EDWARD O'BRYEN, 1969; *ed* Radley, Worcester Coll, Oxford (MA), and London Univ (MA); Dir Careerplan Ltd since 1970, Dir New Metals & Chemicals since 1966, Dir World Vision UK 1983-95, Memb General Synod since 1970, Crown Appointments Commn 1987-92, Church and State Commn 1970; Memb Council St John's Coll, Durham since 1995; sometime 60th Rifles (Nat Service Commn); OBE (Civil) 1996: *m* 1969, Felicity Anne, da of late Peter Boddington, JP, of Stratford-upon-Avon, and has issue.

Arms – Sable, a double-headed eagle displayed within a bordure engrailed argent. Crest – A deer's head and neck proper, erased argent.
Residence – 10 Belitha Villas, Barnsbury, N1 1PD.

SON LIVING

CHARLES JAMES, *b* 15 March 1971.

DAUGHTERS LIVING

Louisa Hope, *b* 1972. —— Kate Annabella, *b* (twin) 1972: *m* 1997, Philip A. Chitty, elder son of Anthony Chitty, of Brighton.

SISTER LIVING

Catherine Mary, *b* 1937: *m* 1963, David James Clark, and has issue living, David Noah, *b* 1966, — Ezra David, *b* 1968, — Abel David, *b* 1971, — Hester Catherine, *b* 1973. *Residence* – 37 Thornhill Rd, N1.

COLLATERAL BRANCHES LIVING

Grandchildren of late John Hoare (infra):—
Issue of late James O'Bryen Hoare, *b* 1910, *d* 1967: *m* (Jan) 1941, Helen Dorey Hardie, who *d* 1991:—
Richard James O'Bryen (242 Hurstmere Rd, Takapuna, Auckland, NZ), *b* 1947: *m* 1971, Sally Ann, da of John Cornwell, of Northcote Auckland, NZ, and has issue living, David O'Bryen, *b* 1974, — Matthew James, *b* 1976, — Rosemary Jane, *b* 1978. —— Stewart John (27 Morvern Rd, Mt Eden, Auckland, NZ), *b* 1949: *m* 1976, Marcelle, da of Elie Bitoun, of Fez, Morocco, and has issue living, Andrew James *b* 1982. —— Janet O'Bryen, *b* (Nov) 1941: *m* 1965, William Frank Richardson, of 45 St Leonard's Rd, Mt Eden, Auckland 4, NZ, and has issue living, Michael George, *b* 1970, — Diana Helen, *b* 1967.

Issue of late John Leslie Hoare, *b* 1919, *d* 1991: *m* 1945, Maxine Heaslip:—
Susan Elizabeth, *b* 1946: *m* 1970, Michael Clifford Quinnell, of Closeburn, Brisbane, Qld, and has issue living, Mark Alexander, *b* 1976. —— Jane Victoria, *b* 1950: *m* 1977, Marion Lester Woods, of Salt Lake City, Utah, USA, and has issue living, Clare Marcello, *b* 1980, — Caroline Elizabeth, *b* 1983, — Hannah Victoria, *b* 1987.

Granddaughters of late Rev James O'Bryen Dott Richard Hoare, el son of Joseph James Parish Hoare, 3rd son of 3rd baronet:—
Issue of late John Hoare, *b* 1874, *d* 1954: *m* 1904, Margaret Jane Leversedge, who *d* 1959:—

Margaret Alice, *b* 1912: *m* 1943, Jack Steane Comport, who *d* 1961, and has issue living, Stephen (15 The Grange, E Malvern, Vic), *b* 1944: *m* 1st, 1966 (*m diss* 1972), Mary Boyd Thomson; 2ndly, 1973, Gillian Elizabeth Sinton, and has issue living (by 2nd *m*), David John *b* 1980, Michael Douglas *b* 1982. *Residence* – 28 Latimer St, Holland Park, Qld. —— Molly Gertrude, *b* 1913: *m* 1942, Patrick Shine, who *d* 1985, and has issue living, John (2 Mayfield Av, Woolwich, NSW), *b* 1946 (Prof): *m* 1969, Kathleen Mary Morgan, and has issue living, Michael Patrick *b* 1972, Rebecca Kathleen *b* 1970, — Richard (30 Farnell St, Boronia Park, NSW), *b* 1950: *m* 1978, Terri Sue Griffith, of Penn, USA, and has issue living, James Macquarie *b* 1982, Benjamin Griffith *b* 1984, — Judith Mary (62 Hamilton St, Lane Cove, NSW), *b* 1948: *m* 1971, Joseph Ohana, of Beersheba, Israel, and has issue living, David Patrick Yaniv *b* 1978, Yael Simma *b* 1973. *Residence* – 59 Sofala Av, Lane Cove, NSW.

      Granddaughter of late Cyril Bertie Edward Hoare, son of late Edward Senior Hoare, 7th son of late Joseph James Parish Hoare (ante):—
      Issue of late Wing-Com Bertie Rex O'Bryen Hoare, DSO, DFC, *b* 1912, *d* 1947: *m* 1945, Lucy, who *d* 1970, da of Richard Nimmo Watson, of Harrogate:—
Rosemary Verity O'Bryen (*posthumous*), *b* 1947: *m* 1977, Nicholas Russell (Box 14357, Nairobi, Kenya), and has issue living, Samantha O'Bryen, *b* 1980, — Alexis Lucy O'Bryen, *b* 1986.

      Grandson of late Edward Hoare, son of late Rev Thomas Hoare, 3rd son of 2nd baronet:—
      Issue of late William Wallis Hoare, MD, FRCS, LRCP, *b* 1871, *d* 19—: *m* 1903, Kathleen Mary Bolton, of Ascot, Brisbane, Queensland:—
Edward Bryan, *b* 1905.

      Granddaughters of late Edward Wallis Hoare, FRCVS (infra):—
      Issue of late Edward William Wallis Hoare, *b* 1902, *d* 1966: *m* 1936, Elizabeth, who *d* 1977, da of late Angus Baillie, of Glasgow:—
Elizabeth McLean (Redcliffe, 1a Sinclair Drive, Helensburgh, Dunbartonshire G84 9BB), *b* 1937. —— Barbara, *b* 1948: *m* 1st, 1979 (*m diss* 1984), Geoffrey Goddin; 2ndly, 1987, Paul Green, of 10 Ranelagh Drive North, Grassendale, Liverpool L19 9DS, and has issue living, (by 1st *m*) Alastair William, *b* 1979.

      Granddaughter of late Capt William Jesse Hoare, son of late Rev Thomas Hoare (ante):—
      Issue of late Edward Wallis Hoare, FRCVS, *b* 1863, *d* 1920: *m* 1899, Emily, who *d* 1961, da of late Henry Lindsay Helen, of Dublin:—
Viola Cecilia, *b* 1913: *m* 1939, Richard Roberts Gorsuch, and has issue living, Diarmind Roberts, *b* 1941: *m* 1970, Jane, el da of Arthur Stanley Peacock of Vancouver, — Terence Richard, *b* 1947: *m* 1969, Patricia, da of Arthur Stanley Peacock, of Vancouver, — Deirdre Cecilia, *b* 1943: *m* 1970, Michel le Bell, — Maeve Emily, *b* 1946: *m* 1972, Keith Harrison, of Ch Ch, NZ. *Address* – PO Box 2936 Invermere, BC, Canada V0A 1K0.

  The 1st baronet, Sir Joseph, MP for Askeaton in the Irish House of Commons, was many years Advising Counsel at Dublin Castle. It has been represented that he lived in *three centuries* — viz, from 25 Dec 1699, to 24 Dec 1801. Recent researches, however, show that he was born on 25 Dec 1707, and died on 24 Dec 1801. At the age of 93 he attended in his place in Parliament to vote against the Union. Sir Edward, the 2nd baronet, sat as MP for Carlow 1769-76.

HOARE (GB) 1786, of Barn Elms, Surrey

Sir PETER RICHARD DAVID HOARE, 8th *Baronet*, *b* 22 March 1932; *s* his father, *Sir* PETER WILLIAM, 1973; *ed* Eton: *m* 1st, 1961 (*m diss* 1967), Jane, only da of late Daniel Orme, of Bulleigh Barton, Ipplepen, S Devon; 2ndly, 1978 (*m diss* 1982), Katrin Alexa, da of late Erwin Bernstiel, and formerly wife of Sir Michael Robin Adderley Hodson, Bt; 3rdly, 1983, Angela Francesca de la Sierra, yr da of late Fidel Fernando Ayarza, of Santiago, Chile.

Arms – Sable, an eagle displayed with two heads argent, charged on the breast with an ermine spot, a bordure engrailed of the second. **Crest** – An eagle's head and neck erased argent charged with an ermine spot.
Address – c/o Hoare & Co, 37 Fleet St, EC4.

In ardua
For arduous undertakings

BROTHER LIVING

DAVID JOHN (Luscombe Castle, Dawlish, S Devon), *b* 8 Oct 1935; *ed* Eton: *m* 1st, 1965, Mary Vanessa, yst da of Peter Cardew, of Westhanger, Cleeve, Bristol; 2ndly, 1984, Mrs Virginia Victoria Labes, da of Michael Menzies, of Long Island, NY, and formerly wife of Claus Labes, and has issue living (by 1st *m*), Simon Merrick, *b* 1967.

COLLATERAL BRANCHES LIVING

Granddaughter of late Peter Merrik Hoare, grandfather of 7th baronet:—
Issue of late Lennox Merrik Noel Colt Hoare, b 1871, d 1924: m 1895, Evelyn Augusta, who d 1952, da of late
Thomas Gerard, of Claughton, near Birkenhead, Cheshire:—
Alda Evelyn, b 1905: m 1929, Brig Henry Anthony Lampen Shewell, OBE, late RE, who d 1974, and has issue living,
John Michael Henry (The Lindens, Hutton Rd, Ash Vale, Aldershot, Hants GU12 5EY), b 1931; Maj ACC (ret): m 1959,
Alison Averil Jones, and has issue living, Christopher John Henry b 1961, Anthony Martin Edward b 1962, — Alda Mary
b 1933: m 1962, John Charles Allday Mousley, of Norleigh House, Widecombe-in-the-Moor, Newton Abbot, Devon TQ13
7TF, and has issue living, Peter John Hunter (Boundary Cottage, Knaphill, Surrey) b 1963: m 1991, Jacqueline Frances
Shelbourne (and has issue living, Thomas Barnabas Hunter b 1996, Joseph Peter Clifford b 1998), Claire Alda Louisa b
1964: m 1987, Lt-Col Neil Guy Trepess Polley, Kings Royal Hussars, of Grantsfield, Kimbolton, Herefordshire, and has
issue living, Lucy Alda Elspeth b 1991, Alicia Charlotte Oenone b 1994. Residence – Bramble Down, Denbury, Devon.

Grandchildren of late Charles Arthur Richard Hoare, son of late Peter Richard Hoare (b 1803), son of
Peter Richard Hoare, 5th son of 1st baronet:—
Issue of late Wilfrid Arthur Richard Hoare, b 1876, d 1971: m 1915, Helen Adria, da of late Col Harry Hepenstall
Rose Heath, CB:—
Richard Michael St George, b 1918: m 1947, Gladys Margaret Tysack, and has issue living, Richard Charles, b 1947: m
19—, Helen, da of —, and has issue living, Michael John b 19—, — Nigel, b 1949, — John Michael, b 1950.
—— Jacquetta Adria Margaret (Sorley Farm, Kingsbridge, S Devon), b 1916: m 1st, 1940 (m diss 1946), Terence Stafford,
Lt RAPC; 2ndly, 1946, Dudley Fisher, who d 19—, and has issue living, (by 1st m) Rebecca, b 19—: m 19—, —, and has
issue living, Bridget b 19—, — (by 2nd m) Noel Hugh, b 1949, — Philipa Jacquetta (twin), b 1949, — Heather Sophia, b
1953.

Issue of late Reginald Arthur Hoare, b 1878, ka 1918: m 1909, Una Mildred, who d 1951, da of Thomas C.
Williams, of Wellington, New Zealand:—
Reginald Merrick (Blue Cottage, Lower Froyle, nr Alton, Hants) b 1918: m 1st, 1950, Barbara Jean, who d 1984, da of
Francis John Buckland (B Melchett); 2ndly, 1984, Meriel Karen, da of late Michael Gold, and has issue living (by 1st
m), Charles Mark (24 Niton St, SW6), b 1961: m 1984, Morag White, — Paul Reginald Richard, b 1963, — Diana
Charlotte, b 1956: m 1978, William Taunton, of 27 Longburton, nr Sherborne, Dorset, and has issue living, Mathew
William b 1984, Rebecca Charlotte b 1982, — Clare Githa, b 1958.

Issue of late Ralph Francis Hoare, b 1881, d 1956: m 1906, Katherine Hallen, who d 1969, da of R. J. Sumner
Drinkwater, of Northbrook, Orillia, Ontario, Canada:—
Eric Reginald, b 1918: m 1949, Rosemary Brodie Hallowell, da of late Francis Vickerman Lumb, and has issue living,
Geoffrey Charles Brodie (Apt 302, 2256 Brunswick St, Vancouver, BC, Canada V5T 3L7), b 1953, — Richard Sumner
Anthony, b 1955, — Wendy Pamela Brodie (1304 73rd Av SW, Calgary, Alberta, Canada T2V 0S1), b 1961: m 1989,
Gerald Timothy Griffin, son of James Griffin, of Edmonton, Alberta. Residence – Salus House, West Sechelt, BC, Canada.
—— Peter Richard (204 Park St, Orillia, Ontario, Canada), b 1920: m 1960, Beverley Jean, da of Arthur Frederick Hessel,
and has issue living, Barbara Lynne, b 1965: m 1992, James Arthur Orell, son of F. Arthur Orell, of Toronto, and has
issue living, Conner James b 1997, — Deborah Katherine Jean, b 1969: m 19—, Jeffrey Brian John Richardson, son of
Brian John Richardson, of Pickering, Ont. —— Margaret Katherine Dorothy (Apt 310-South, 412 Muskoka Rd, Orillia,
Ontario L3V 6M5, Canada), b 1907: m 1938, William Stephens Gill, who d 1951, son of Dr William Craw Gill, of Cleve-
land, Ohio, USA, and has issue living, Peter William (Edgewood Farm, RR2, Orillia, Ontario, Canada), b 1939: m 1967,
Angela Patricia, da of Ernest D. Gillezeau, of St Vincent, WI, and has issue living, Jeremy David Hallen b 1968, Nicholas
Anton Stephens b 1971, — Ralph John David (42 Andrea Cres, Orillia, Ontario L3V 6W5, Canada), b 1947: m 1976,
Marlene Elsie, da of Hugh Doyle, of Orillia, Ontario, and has issue living, Trevor William Hugh b 1981, Ryan David b
1984, — Margaret Natalie Katherine, b 1944: m 1965, Bruce Teague Budd, of 10534 26th Av, Edmonton, Alberta T6J
4B9, Canada, son of Luther H. Budd, of Montreal, Quebec, and has issue living, Teague William Garth b 1971, Donicka
Anne Evelyn b 1966, Tehranna Margaret Katherine b 1969. —— Natalie Kathleen Grove, b 1915. Residence – Apt 310-
South, 412 Old Muskoka Rd, Orillia, Ontario, Canada.

The 1st baronet's father was Lord Mayor of London 1745. Sir Henry Ainslie Hoare, 5th Bt, was MP for Windsor (L)
1865-6 and for Chelsea 1868-74.

HOARE (UK) 1962, of Fleet Street, City of London (Extinct 1986)

Sir FREDERICK ALFRED HOARE, 1st and last Baronet.

DAUGHTERS LIVING OF FIRST BARONET (by 1st marriage)

Mary Rose, b 1944. —— Marinella, b 1952: m 1988, Jeremy Alfred Franks, son of Jack Franks, of 71 Portland Place,
W1, and has issue living, Alexei, b 1988, — Mary Cleo I., b 1989. Residence – 100 Eaton Place, SW1.

HOBART (UK) 1914, of Langdown, co Southampton
(Name pronounced "Hub'bert")

Sir JOHN VERE HOBART, 4th *Baronet*; *b* 9 April 1945; *s* his father *Lieut-Cdr Sir* ROBERT HAMPDEN, 1988; is *hp* to Earldom of Buckinghamshire: *m* 1980, Kate, only da of late George Henry Iddles, of Cowes, I of Wight, and has issue.

Arms – Quarterly, 1st, sable, an estoile of six rays or between two flaunches ermine, *Hobart*; 2nd, argent, a saltire gules between four eagles displayed azure, *Hampden*; 3rd, argent, three battering-rams fessewise in pale proper, armed and garnished azure, *Bertie*; 4th, quarterly, gules and or, in the first quarter a mullet argent, *Vere*. Crest – A bull statant per pale sable and gules bezanté, in his nose a ring or.
Residence – Shore End, Queen's Rd, Cowes, Isle of Wight.

SONS LIVING

GEORGE HAMPDEN, *b* 10 June 1982. ———— James Henry Miles, *b* 1986.

BROTHERS LIVING

Robert Henry (12 Brunswick Gdns, W8), *b* 1948; *ed* Harrow: *m* 1976, Una Mary Diana, da of late Archibald Henry Parker (*see* E Macclesfield, colls), and has issue living, Sophie Camilla, *b* 1978, — Jessica, *b* 1980. ———— Anthony Hampden, *b* 1956: *m* 1985, Katherine Anne, 3rd da of Robert Noel Willis Fleming, of Acorn House, St Helens, Isle of Wight, and has issue living, Charles Hampden, *b* 1986.

The giver makes the gift valuable

SISTER LIVING

Penelope Diana, *b* 1954: *m* 1979, Robert Maunsell Hunter-Jones, son of Michael Hunter-Jones, of Burmington House, Shipston-on-Stour, Warwicks.

WIDOW LIVING OF THIRD BARONET

CAROLINE FLEUR (*Dowager Lady Hobart*), yr da of late Col Henry Monckton Vatcher, MC, of Valeran, St Brelade's, Jersey, widow of 11th Duke of Leeds, and formerly wife of Peter Hendrick Peregrine Hoos (*see* B Brownlow): *m* 1975, as his 2nd wife, Lt-Cdr Sir Robert Hampden Hobart, 3rd Bt, who *d* 1988. *Residence* – The Boat House, Cowes, I of Wight.

The 1st baronet, Sir Robert Henry Hobart, KCVO, CB (el son of late Very Rev Hon Henry Lewis Hobart, DD, Dean of Windsor and Wolverhampton) (E Buckinghamshire, colls), was Private Sec to Sec of State for War, Postmaster-Gen, Ch Sec for Ireland, and Sec of State for India 1863-74 and 1889-95, and to four Secs for Scotland 1886-7 and 1892-5, Sec for Coronation of King Edward VII 1902, Gold Staff Officer at Coronation of King George 1911, MP for Hampshire, New Forest Div (*L*) Jan 1906 to Jan 1910, and Official Verderer of the New Forest 1907-27. The 2nd baronet, Sir (Claud) Vere Cavendish Hobart, DSO, OBE, was Major Grenadier Guards, and Lieut-Col Hampshire Regt, and was Gold Staff Officer at Coronations of King Edward VII and King George V.

HOBHOUSE (UK) 1812, of Broughton-Gifford, Bradford-on-Avon, and of Monkton Farleigh, Wiltshire

The hope of a better life

Sir CHARLES JOHN SPINNEY HOBHOUSE, 7th *Baronet*; *b* 27 Oct 1962; *s* his father, *Sir* CHARLES CHISHOLM, TD, 1991; *ed* Eton: *m* 1993 (*m diss* 1997), Katrina, da of late Maj-Gen Sir Denzil Macarthur-Onslow, CBE, DSO, ED (*see* E Onslow, colls).

Arms – Per pale azure and gules, three crescents, two and one, argent, issuing therefrom as many estoiles irradiated or. Crest – Out of a mural crown per pale azure and gules, a crescent and estoile as in the arms.
Residence – The Manor, Monkton Farleigh, Bradford-on-Avon, Wilts BA15 2QE.

UNCLE LIVING (*son of 5th baronet*)

JOHN SPENCER, AFC, *b* 15 Nov 1910; *ed* Eton, and — Coll, Oxford; formerly Squadron Leader RAF: *m* 1940, Mary, who *d* 1991, yr da of late Llewelyn Roberts, MD, of Porthcawl. *Residence* – Farleigh Court, Farleigh, Hungerford, nr Bath, Avon.

AUNT LIVING (*daughter of 5th baronet*)

Audrey, *b* 1912: *m* 1934 (*m diss* 1952), Maj-Gen Cecil Llewellyn Firbank, CB, CBE, DSO, late Somerset LI, who *d* 1985, and has issue living, Simon Christopher, *b* 1937: *m* 1962 (*m diss* 1988), Caroline Anne, only da of late Lt-Col J. T. C. Howard, of East Pennard, Shepton Mallet, Som, and has issue two sons and one da. *Residence* – Old Mill, Bourton, Gillingham, Dorset.

WIDOW LIVING OF SIXTH BARONET

ELSPETH JEAN (*Dowager Lady Hobhouse*), yr da of late Thomas George Spinney, of Mazagan, Morocco: *m* 1959, as his 2nd wife, Sir Charles Chisholm Hobhouse, 6th Bt, TD, who *d* 1991. *Residence* – South Wing, The Manor, Monkton Farleigh, Bradford-on-Avon, Wilts BA15 2QE.

COLLATERAL BRANCHES LIVING

Issue of late Benjamin Arthur Hobhouse, 3rd son of 5th baronet, *b* 1914, *d* 1970: *m* 1942, Valerie Cuthbertson, who *d* 1990, da of late Dr John Cuthbertson Walker, of Barnwell, Troon, Ayrshire;—
John Cam (13/11 College Lane, Gibraltar), *b* 1947: *m* 1971 (*m diss* 1982), Mary Angela Deakins, da of Arthur George Newton, and has issue living, a da, *b* 19—, — a da, *b* 19—. —— Carol Ann, *b* 1943: *m* 1964, George Rogers, of 35 Sunnyhill Rd, Salisbury, Wilts, and has issue living, Bruce Andrew, *b* 1967.

Issue of late Maj Hugh Cam Hobhouse, 4th and yst son of 5th baronet, *b* 1917, *d* 1987: *m* 1st, 1939 (*m diss* 1947), Diana, yr da of Philip George; 2ndly, 1949 (*m diss* 1965), Aline Rosemary, formerly wife of Lt-Col David Theodor Dobie, DSO, and only da of Lt-Col David Walter Hunter Blair (*see* Hunter Blair, Bt, colls); 3rdly, 1965, Judy Margaret (1 Pullen's Orchard, Church Lane, W Pennard, Som), da of late John Denis Tisdall, of Butcombe, Som:—
(By 1st *m*) Mark Cam (Wood Court, Ashill, Ilminster, Som TA19 9NR), *b* 1940; *ed* Eton; Lieut RAC: *m* 1975, Stephanie, da of late Capt K. E. Buxton, and has issue living, Benjamin Alexander Cam, *b* 1977, — Matthew Jack *b* 1979. —— (By 2nd *m*) James Charles (18 Upper Park Rd, Kingston-upon-Thames, Surrey KT2 5LD), *b* 1951; *ed* Millfield: *m* 1974, Sarah, da of David Sladen, and has issue living, Rebecca Sarah, *b* 1980, — Nicola, *b* 1984. —— Martin Hugh John (Quarley Wood House, Grateley, nr Andover, Hants SP11 8LF), *b* 1955; *ed* Eton: *m* 1981, Julia Isobel, da of Dr David Andrew Young Craib, of Ruxley, Hankham, Pevensey, E Sussex, and has issue living, Hugh James, *b* 1984, — Alexander David, *b* 1986, — George Cam, *b* 1991, — Katharine Ann, *b* 1993. —— Julia Mary, *b* 1956: *m* 1985, Henry G. Buckmaster, of The Roses, Twinstead, Sudbury, Suffolk CO10 7NB, son of late Richard Guy Buckmaster, of Radway, Warwicks, and has issue living, (Eleanor) Rose, *b* 1986, — Camellia Aline, *b* 1988, — Lily Henrietta, *b* 1990. —— (By 3rd *m*) Sophie Victoria, *b* 1967: *m* 1995, (Robert) Peter Ridsdale, of Wrayton Hall, Wrayton, Carnforth, Lancs LA6 2QU, son of late Arthur Ridsdale, of Leeds, and has issue living, Charlotte Louise, *b* 1996, — Olivia Rose, *b* 1997.

Sir Benjamin Hobhouse, 1st Bt, descended from the Hobhouses of Minehead, Somerset, was MP for Bletchingley 1797, for Grampound 1802, and for Hendon 1806-18, and Ch Sec, Board of Control, India 1801-03, and 1806-07. Rt Hon Sir John Cam Hobhouse, 2nd baronet, created Baron Broughton 1851, was one of the poet Byron's most intimate friends. He was MP for Westminster 1820-33, for Nottingham 1838-47, and Harwich 1849-51; Secretary for War 1832-3, Secretary for Ireland 1833, Chief Commissioner of Woods and Forests 1834, President of the Board of Control 1835-41 and 1846-51, and author of several important works. He died 1869, when the barony became extinct, and the baronetcy passed to his nephew, Sir Charles Parry Hobhouse. The 4th baronet, Rt Hon Sir Charles Edward Henry Hobhouse, TD, sat as MP for Wilts, E or Devizes Div (*L*) 1892-95, and for Bristol, E Div 1900-1918, and was Church Estate Commr 1906-7. Under-Sec of State for India 1907-8, Financial Sec to Treasury 1908-11, Chancellor of Duchy of Lancaster 1911-14, and Postmaster-Gen 1914-15.

HODGE (UK) 1921, of Chipstead, co Kent

Sir ANDREW ROWLAND HODGE, 3rd *Baronet*; *b* 4 Dec 1968; *s* his father, *Sir* JOHN ROWLAND, MBE, 1995; *ed* ......

Arms – Sable, an eagle wings addorsed and inverted or between three crescents argent. **Crest** – An eagle as in the arms supporting with the dexter claw an increscent argent and looking at the rays of the sun issuant from clouds proper. *Residence* – ......

Glory the reward of virtue

SISTER LIVING

Louise Vivienne, *b* 1970. Resides in Freeport, Bahamas.

HALF-SISTERS LIVING (*daughters of 2nd baronet by 2nd wife, Joan, only da of late Sydney Foster Wilson*)

Wendy Madeleine, *b* 1941: *m* 1st, 1962 (*m diss* 1971), Michael Dennis Whiting, who *d* 1995; 2ndly, 1973, John Edward Aitken Kidd, of Holders House, St James, Barbados, W Indies, and Suite 1809, 745 Fifth Av, New York, NY, USA (*see* B Beaverbrook, 1985 Edn), and has issue living (by 1st *m*), Nicholas D'Arcy, *b* 1962; *ed* Lancing, — Deborah Joanna, *b* 1964, — (by 2nd *m*), Jack Edward *b* 1973; *ed* Harrow, — Iemma Madeleine, *b* 1974, — Jodie Elizabeth, *b* 1978. —— Sally Joan, *b* 1943. —— Vicki Alexandra, *b* 1946: *m* 1969, George Ian Alexander Heath, who *d* 1996.

AUNT LIVING (*daughter of 1st baronet*)

Vivien Rosemary, *b* 1911: *m* 1st, 1930 (*m diss* 19—), St John Legh Clowes, who *d* 1951 (*see* B Clanmorris, 1919 Edn); 2ndly, 1941, Hugh Gordon Murton-Neale, who *d* 1987, and has issue living (by 1st *m*), Timothy Legh (The Oasts, Budds Lane, Wittersham, Tenterden, Kent; 10 Shepherd St, W1), *b* 1932; *ed* Wellington Coll: *m* 1st, 1955 (*m diss* 1965), Rosemary Patricia, da of late Clarence Parker, of Church House Farm, Etchingham, Sussex; 2ndly, 1988, Mrs Ah W. Benson, da of late A. K. Lim, and has had issue (by 1st wife), Matthew Herrick Legh *b* 1956, Mark Timothy Hugh *b* 1958; *d* 1974, Tamsin Rosemary Laura *b* 1959: *m* 1988, Christopher Edward Scott Walsby, of Flora Cottage, Lower Green, Wimbish, Essex CB10 2XH (and has issue living, James Mark *b* 1990, Madelaine Anne *b* 1992), (by 2nd wife), Jonathan Lim *b* 1990, Susan Lim *b* 1984, — Susan Carol (Box 146, Shelburne, Ontario, Canada L0N 1S0), *b* 1935: *m* 1st, 1957, Francis Timothy Parker, who *d* 1990, son of late Clarence Parker (ante); 2ndly, 1996, Andrew John Osyany, son of Bela Osyany, and has issue living (by 1st *m*), Justin Hugh *b* 1960, Sophie Louise *b* 1965: *m* 1989, Geoffrey Kitchen (and has issue living, Zachary Timothy *b* 1993, Conor Geoffrey *b* 1995, Charles Parker *b* 1997, Justin Michael *b* 1997). *Residence* – 14 Cedar Court, Woodbury Lane, Tenterden, Kent TN30 6JH.

WIDOW LIVING OF SECOND BARONET

VIVIENNE (*Lady Hodge*), da of Alfred Knightley, of Norwood, Middx: *m* 1967, as his 4th wife, Sir John Rowland Hodge, 2nd Bt, MBE, who *d* 1995.

COLLATERAL BRANCH LIVING

Issue of late Peter Rowland Hodge, yr son of 1st baronet, *b* 1915, *d* 1982: *m* 1st, 1940 (*m diss* 1945), Mia, da of late Capt Sir (Albert) Noel Campbell Macklin, of Fairmile, Cobham, Surrey; 2ndly, 1951, Margaret Norma (Clifford Lodge, High St, Hurstpierpoint, Sussex BN6 9PX), da of Harold Plow, of Broadway, Barnton, Cheshire:—
(By 2nd *m*) Jacqueline Jane (Copyhold Cottage, Lock Lane, Partridge Green, Horsham, W Sussex RH13 8EF), *b* 1954: *m* 1991, Richard A. D. Jesse, and has issue living, Lawrence Rowland, *b* 1992, — Alexander Peter, *b* 1995, — Ellena Joy, *b* 1995. —— Bridgitte Michele, *b* 1956: *m* 1989, Patrick L. Field, of 2 Corner Cottage, Brighton Rd, Shermanbury, W Sussex.

The 1st baronet, Sir Rowland Frederic William Hodge (son of John Rowland Hodge), was a Shipbuilder and Chm of Eltringhams, Ltd of Quay-on-Tyne, Northumberland. Sir John Rowland Hodge, 2nd Bt, MBE, was Lt-Cdr RNVR, and formerly Lieut Oxfordshire and Bucks LI, served European War 1939-40.

HODSON (I) 1787, of Holybrooke House, Wicklow

Peace and love

Sir MICHAEL ROBIN ADDERLEY HODSON, 6th *Baronet*; *b* 5 March 1932; *s* his father, *Maj Sir* EDMOND ADAIR, DSO, 1972; *ed* Eton; Capt (ret) Scots Gds: *m* 1st, 1963 (*m diss* 1978), Katrin Alexa, da of late Erwin Bernstiel, of St Andrew's House, St Andrew's Major, Dinas Powis, Glam; 2ndly, 1978, Catherine, da of John Henry Seymour, of Wimpole St, W1, and formerly wife of Ralph Denne, and has issue by 1st *m*.

Arms – Sable, a chevron between three martlet, or. Crest – A dove close azure, beaked and membered or, holding in her beak an olive-branch proper.
Residence – The White House, Awbridge, Romsey, Hants S051 0HF.

DAUGHTERS LIVING (*By 1st marriage*)

Tania Elizabeth, *b* 1965: *m* 1994, Maj Guy H. J. Deacon, 1st The Queen's Dragoon Gds, son of Lt-Col J. W. Deacon, of Amesbury, Wilts, and has issue living, Wilfred Michael Hodson *b* 1998. —— Alexa Adderley, *b* 1966: *m* 1990, Christopher Michael Chambers, son of W. M. Chambers, of Chipping Camden, Glos, and has issue living, Lara Adderley, *b* 1992, — Gemma Marlis, *b* 1994, — Anna Isabel, *b* 1998. —— Jane Katrina, *b* 1970.

BROTHER LIVING

PATRICK RICHARD (Shipton Slade Farm, Woodstock, Oxford OX7 1QQ) *b* 27 Nov 1934; *ed* Eton; Capt (ret) Rifle Bde; *m* 1961, June, only da of late Herbert Michael Shepherd-Cross, of The Old Rectory, Brandsby, Yorks, and has issue living, Mark Adair (52 Orbain Rd, SW6), *b* 1964: *m* 1991, Kathleen (Kate) Mary Florence, only da of late William Rippon Bissill (*see* B Nunburnholme), and has issue living, Edward Charles Adair *b* 1998, Charlotte Adderley *b* 1996, — James Patrick, *b* 1966: *m* 1993, Fiona Marion, 2nd da of Michael Herbert Johnson-Ferguson (*see* Johnson-Ferguson, Bt), and has issue living, George Patrick *b* 1996, Flora Anne *b* 1998, — Rupert Edward, *b* 1972.

COLLATERAL BRANCH LIVING

Granddaughters of late Richard Edmond Hodson, 3rd son of 3rd baronet:—
Issue of late Gilbert Stanley Hodson, *b* 1895, *d* 1972: *m* 1948, Felicity Margaretta, who *d* 1995, yr da of late Lt-Col Hon Claud Patrick Brabazon, OBE (*see* E Meath, colls):—
Kathleen Margaret, *b* 1949: *m* 1980, Charles Gerald Dalby, and has issue (*see* Smiley, Bt). *Residence* – Dalbie House, Castle Donington, Derbys DE14 2PP. —— Marion Felicity, *b* 1951: *m* 1989, Bruce Swanhuyser, of White Salmon, Washington, USA, and has issue living, Robin Adair, *b* 1990, — Emma Paige, *b* 1993.

Sir Robert Hodson, 1st baronet, was descended in direct line from the Rev John Hodson, who belonged to a family long settled at Houghton, Staffordshire, and who assisted in the escape of King Charles I from Oxford in 1646. After the Restoration, Dr Hodson was successively Dean of Clogher and Bishop of Elphin; he *d* 1686.

HOGG (UK) 1846, of Upper Grosvenor Street, co Middlesex

Glory gives strength

Sir MICHAEL DAVID HOGG, 8th *Baronet*; *b* 19 Aug 1925; *s* his father, *Maj Sir* ARTHUR RAMSAY, MBE, 1995; *ed* Sherborne, and Ch Ch, Oxford (BA 1950, MA 1953); Journalist *The Daily Telegraph* 1951-87 (Assistant Ed 1976); European War 1943-45, as Capt Grenadier Gds: *m* 1956, Elizabeth Anne Thérèse, eldest da of Sir Terence Edmond Patrick Falkiner, 8th Bt, and has issue.

Arms – Argent, three boars' heads erased azure, langued gules, between two flaunches of the second, each charged with a crescent of the field. **Crest** – Out of an eastern crown argent, an oak-tree fructed proper, and pendent therefrom an escutcheon azure charged with a dexter arm embowed in armour, the hand grasping an arrow in bend sinister, the point downwards also proper.
Residence – 19 Woodlands Rd, Barnes, SW13 0JZ.

SONS LIVING

PIERS MICHAEL JAMES (54 Loveday Rd, W13 9JX), *b* 25 April 1957; *ed* St Paul's Sch: *m* 1982 (*m diss* 1996), Vivien, yr da of Dr Philip Holman, of 3 Atwood Av, Kew, Surrey, and has issue living, James Edward, *b* 11 Sept 1985, — Sarah Alice, *b* 1988. —— Adam Charles (23 Gibbon Rd, Kingston-upon-Thames, Surrey), *b* 1958; *ed* St Paul's Sch: *m* 1987, Alison Pauline, da of Nicholas Selby, of 45 Gwendolen Av, Putney, SW15, and has issue living, Daniel Richard, *b* 1988. — Madeleine Victoria, *b* 1989. —— Oliver John (9 Idlecombe Rd, SW17), *b* 1961; *ed* Shene Gram Sch, and Colchester Inst.

BROTHERS LIVING

Mark Arthur Philip (7 Quadrangle House, St Peter's Rd, Wolvercote, Oxford OX2 8BN), *b* 1928; *ed* Sherborne, and Ch Ch, Oxford (BA 1949, BSc 1950, MA 1953): *m* 1st, 1955 (*m diss* 1977), Jennifer Mary, da of late Michael Farrer Spurrell, of Greenhayes, Reigate, Surrey; 2ndly, 1977, Jane Margaret, da of late Rev Alan James Sutherland Symon, and formerly wife of David R. Lawrence, and has issue living (by 1st *m*), Stephen Mark (3 Wivelsfield Rd, Haywards Heath, W Sussex RH16 4EF), *b* 1960: *ed* Sherborne, and Bristol Univ: *m* 1986, Deborah, elder da of Cyril Skipworth, of 42 Charnock View Rd, Sheffield S12 3HJ, and has issue living, Charlotte Katharine *b* 1988, — Philippa Mary (36 Alexandria Rd, W13 0NR), *b* 1956: *m* 1979 (*m diss* 1995), Jeremy James Leon, 2nd son of late Arthur Jesse Douglas Leon, of 87 Three Bridges Rd, Crawley, Sussex, and has issue living, Frances Clare *b* 1983 Nicola Robyn *b* 1987, — Sally Elizabeth, *b* 1958: *m* 1985, Simon Mark Hamling, of Rowena, Bridge, Constantine, Falmouth, Cornwall TR11 5AL, son of late Norman Arthur Hamling, and has issue living, Edmund Arthur *b* 1994, William Bryher *b* (twin) 1994, — Nicola Frances, *b* 1962. —— Simon Charles (Meadow Cottage, Church St, Beckley, Oxford OX3 9UT), *b* 1936.

SISTER LIVING

Anthea Aileen, *b* (twin) 1936: *m* 1957, Iain Stewart Gordon Carmichael, of Harracott House, Harracott, nr Barnstaple, Devon EX31 3JT, son of late Col D.R. Gordon Carmichael, of Powntley Copse, nr Alton, Hants, and has had issue, Donald Malcolm, *b* 1961; *d* 1984, — Alison Fiona (34 Chantry Rd, Chessington, Surrey KT9 1JP), *b* 1958: *m* 1982 (*m diss* 1995), Nigel Justin Llewelyn-Price, son of G.F. Price, — Victoria Anthea *b* 1966: *m* 1989, Giles Eric Gordon Brown, of Fairlawn House, Fairlawn, Chestfield, Whitstable, Kent CB5 3JZ, elder son of Barry R. Cooper, and has issue living, Callum James *b* 1997, Emily Megan *b* 1991.

COLLATERAL BRANCHES LIVING

Grandchildren of late Quintin Hogg, 7th son of 1st baronet:—
Issue of late Rt Hon Sir Douglas McGarel Hogg (*Viscount Hailsham*), *b* 1872; *cr Viscount Hailsham* 1929 (*see* B Hailsham of St Marylebonc).

Issue of late Sir Malcolm Nicholson Hogg, *b* 1883, *d* 1948: *m* 1910, Lorna (who *m* 2ndly Com N. B. Deare (dec), and *d* 1978), da of late Sir Frank Clement Offley Beaman, sometime a Puisne Judge of High Court of Judicature, Bombay:—
†Sir John Nicholson, TD *b* 1912; *ed* Eton, and Balliol Coll, Oxford; Dep Chm of Williams & Glyn's plc, 1970-83, and of Gallaher, Ltd 1964-78, Chm of Banque Francaise de Credit International Ltd 1972-83, and a Dir of Prudential Corpn plc 1964-85, The R Bank of Scotland Group plc 1965-82, and Honeywell, Ltd 1972-80; Sheriff of co London 1960, a Fellow of Eton 1951-70, and Chm of Abu Dhabi Investment Board 1967-75; Chm Export Guarantees Advisory Council 1962-67, and a Member of Commonwealth War Graves Commn 1958-64; 1939-45 War as Maj KRRC ((TA) in Greece, Crete, W Desert, N Africa and NW Europe): *m* 1948, Barbara Elisabeth, who *d* 1998, da of Capt Arden Franklyn, of New Place, Shedfield, Hants, and widow of Brig Viscount Garmoyle, DSO, late Rifle Bde, el son of 4th Earl Cairns, and *d* 1999, leaving issue, Malcolm David Nicholson (Lanterns, Mapledurham, Basingstoke RG25 2LU), *b* 1949: *m* 1975, Mary Clare, only da of late Maj Richard Francis Preedy, RE, and has issue living, Richard John Nicholson *b* 1982, Lucy Mary Arden *b* 1977, Alice Emily Geraldine *b* 1979, — Susan Elisabeth, *b* 1954: *m* 1980, Jeremy A. J. F. Burnett Rae, of The Ponts Cottage, S Moreton, Didcot, Oxon OX11 9AG, and has issue living, Henry Oliver *b* 1985, Charles Frederick *b* 1986, Emma Louise *b* 1983.

The 1st baronet, Rt Hon Sir James Weir Hogg, Registrar of the Supreme Court of Judicature and Vice-Admiralty Court, Calcutta 1815-33, was twice elected Chm of E India Co and sat as MP for Beverley (*C*) 1834-47 and for Honiton 1847-57. The 2nd baronet, Sir James Macnaghten, KCB, was Chm of Metropolitan Board of Works 1870-89, and was MP for Bath

(C) 1865-8, for Truro 1871-85, and for Middlesex, Hornsey Div, 1885-7, when he was *cr Baron Magheramorne*, having in 1877 assumed the additional surname of McGarel. The Barony of Magheramorne became ext in 1957 on the death of 4th Baron and 5th baronet.

LINDSAY-HOGG (UK) 1905, of Rotherfield Hall, Rotherfield, Sussex

†*Sir* EDWARD WILLIAM LINDSAY-HOGG, 4th *Baronet*, yr son of late William Lindsay Hogg, only son of 1st baronet; *b* 23 May 1910; *s* his nephew, *Sir* WILLIAM LINDSAY, 1987; *ed* Eton: *m* 1st, 1936 (*m diss* 1946), Geraldine Mary (the actress and producer Geraldine Fitzgerald), da of late Edward Martin Fitzgerald, of Greystones, co Wicklow; 2ndly, 1957, Kathleen Mary, widow of Capt Maurice Cadill, MC, and da of James Cooney, of Carrick-on-Suir, co Tipperary, and has issue by 1st *m*. Sir Edward Lindsay-Hogg *d* 18 June 1999.

Arms – Per pale indented vert and azure, on a bend or three boars' heads couped sable. **Crest** – Issuant out of a mural crown argent a boar's head erect sable holding in the mouth a sprig of oak fructed proper.
Residence –

SON LIVING (*By 1st marriage*)

MICHAEL EDWARD, *b* 5 May 1940; film dir: *m* 1967 (*m diss* 1971), Lucy Mary, only da of Donald Davies, of Enniskerry, co Wicklow.

DAUGHTER LIVING OF THIRD BARONET

Sarah Frances, *b* 1961: *m* 1982, Simon John Gatliff, and has had issue, George Auben, *b* 1990; *d* 1991, — John William, *b* 1994, — Rosie Frances, *b* 1988.

WIDOW LIVING OF THIRD BARONET

MARIE TERESA (*Marie, Lady Lindsay-Hogg*), writer, da of late John Foster, of St Helen's, Lancs, and formerly wife of Dr P. V. Aldiss, of Norfolk: *m* 1987, as his 2nd wife, Sir William Lindsay-Hogg, 3rd Bt, who *d* 1987.

The 1st baronet, Sir Lindsay Hogg, assumed by Roy licence 1906, the additional surname of Lindsay, and sat as MP for S, or Eastbourne, Div of Sussex (C) Oct 1900 to Jan 1906.

HOLCROFT (UK) 1921, of Eaton Mascott, Berrington, co Salop

Constant and faithful

Sir PETER GEORGE CULCHETH HOLCROFT, 3rd *Baronet*; *b* 29 April 1931; *s* his father, *Sir* REGINALD CULCHETH HOLCROFT, TD, 1978; High Sheriff Shropshire 1969-70, JP 1976: *m* 1956 (*m diss* 1987), Rosemary Rachel, da of late Capt George Nevill Deas, 8th Hussars (M Anglesey, colls), and has issue living.

Arms – Argent, a cross engrailed between in the 1st and 4th quarters an eagle wings elevated sable, preying upon an infant proper, swaddled gules, banded or. Crest – Upon a log lopped proper, a raven sable holding, in the dexter paw a sword erect, also proper.
Residence – Berrington House, Berrington, Shrewsbury.

SONS LIVING

CHARLES ANTHONY CULCHETH, *b* 22 Oct 1959: *m* 1986, Mrs Elizabeth Carter, yr da of late John Raper, of Four Crosses, Powys, and has issue living, Toby David Culcheth, *b* 5 Feb 1990, — Samara Elisabeth, *b* 1988. —— Thomas Marcus Culcheth, *b* 1967: *m* 1997, Camilla L., yr da of Brian Marr, of Sutton Scotney, Hants. —— Alexander James Culcheth, *b* 1969: 1997, Amy I., elder da of Dr Duncan Stewart, of Hove, E Sussex.

DAUGHTER LIVING

Tania Melanie, *b* 1961.

BROTHER LIVING

Michael William Culcheth (Wrentnall House, Pulverbatch, Shrewsbury, Shropshire SY5 8ED), *b* 1935; *ed* Radley; Lt-Cdr RN (ret): *m* 1968 (*m diss* 1978), Amanda Victoria, da of Wing-Cdr Ian Roy Cardew Macpherson, DFC, AFC, of Winterbourne Abbas, Dorset.

SISTERS LIVING

Ann Cherida, *b* 1929: *m* 1952, John Dewé Neville Lake (*see* Walsham, Bt, colls, 1990 Edn), and has issue living, Christopher John Neville (Jasmine Cottage, School Lane, Stadhampton, Oxon OX9 7TR), *b* 1954: *m* 1978, Jacqueline Maria Harris, and has issue living, Henry Christopher Neville *b* 1990, Sarah Jane Victoria *b* 1988, — Timothy Michael David (Edlins, Aston Upthorpe, Oxon OX11 9EF), *b* 1955: *m* 1984, Natalie Anne Isard, and has issue living, Alice Florence Lucy *b* 1989, Harriet Alexandra Daisy *b* 1992. —— Mary Virginia, *b* 1939: *m* 1960, Maj William Kemp Trotter, 11th Hussars, and has issue living, James William Dale (Bell House Farm, Staindrop, Darlington, co Durham DL2 3PA), *b* 1964: *m* 19—, Nicola, eldest da of Vivian Mahaffy, and has issue living, George Frederic Kemp *b* 1998, Hebe Florence *b* 1994, Lavinia Alathea (Minna) *b* 19—, — Henry Edward Dale (23 Sisters Av, SW11 5SR), *b* 1966, — Philip George Dale (43C Wandsworth Common Northside, SW18 2ST), *b* 1969: *m* 1998, Louise, only da of late R. C. Hall, and of Mrs John Hammond, of Cirencester, Glos, — Victoria Mary, *b* 1962: *m* 1989, Maj Nicholas J. Thomas, The Queen's Own Hussars, son of Maj T. J. Thomas, of Hey House, Heytesbury, Wilts, and has issue living, Ivo James *b* 1994, Letitia Mary *b* 1992. *Residence* – The Deanery, Staindrop, co Durham.

COLLATERAL BRANCH LIVING

Issue of late John Culcheth Holcroft, Lieut 3rd Co London Yeo, 3rd son of 1st baronet, *b* 1905, *ka* 1941: *m* 1932, Beatrice Mathewson, who *d* 1985, da of late George F. Feathers:—
Timothy Gilbert Culcheth, *b* 1934; *ed* Radley; Capt (ret) 11th Hussars; JP: *m* 1st, 1958, Joanna Eve, who *d* 1983, da of Adm Sir Stuart Sumner Bonham-Carter, KCB, CVO, DSO; 2ndly, 1982, Mrs Charmian Joy Nicholson, only da of late Maj Harcourt Michael Scudamore Gold, MC, of W Stratton House, Winchester, Hants (*see* Trent, By), and has issue living (by 1st *m*), Alexandra Jane, *b* 1962: *m* 1986, Andrew Fion Bethune Norman, only child of late Alexander Vesey Bethune Norman, Master of the Armouries, HM Tower of London, and has issue living, Angus James Bethune *b* 1996, Natasha Isobel *b* 1992, — Caroline Joanna, *b* 1966: *m* 1993, Charles J. D. Todhunter, of 81 The Chase, SW4 0NR, only son of Michael John Benjamin Todhunter, of The Old Rectory, Farnborough, nr Wantage, Oxon. —— Tania, *b* 19—: *m* 1956, Mark Richard Geoffrey Cory-Wright, of Tilhill House, Tilford, Surrey, and has issue (*see* Cory-Wright, Bt).

The 1st baronet, Sir George Harry Holcroft (son of late William Holcroft, JP, of Prescot House, Stourbridge), was Chm of Littleton Collieries (Limited), High Sheriff of Staffordshire 1913-14, and rendered notable sers to Birmingham Univ.

HOLDEN (UK) 1893, of Oakwoth House, Keighley, Yorkshire

Sir EDWARD HOLDEN, 6th *Baronet*; *b* 8 Oct 1916; *s* his father, *Sir* ISAAC HOLDEN, 1962; *ed* Leys Sch, Christ's Coll Camb, and St Thomas's Hosp; MRCS England and LRCP London 1942; DA England 1945, Fellow of Faculty of Anæsthetists 1958: *m* 1942, Frances Joan, el da of John Spark, JP, of Ludlow, Stockton-on-Tees.

Arms – Or, a chief azure, over all a bend nebulée between two roses gules. Crest – Issuant from a chaplet of oak vert, an eagle's head erased or, gorged with a collar gemel azure.
Residence – 40 South End, Osmotherly, Northallerton, N Yorks DL6 3BL.

BROTHER LIVING

PAUL, *b* 3 March 1923: *m* 1950, Vivien Mary, yst da of late Hedley Broxholme Oldham, of Allesley, Coventry, and has issue living, Michael Peter (1 Greenways, Pembroke Rd, Woking, Surrey GU22 7D4), *b* 19 June 1956: *m* 1990, Irene, da of Cyril Salmon, of 107 Sandringham Rd, Worcester Park, and has issue living, Stephanie Louise *b* 1992, Natasha Jade *b* 1995, — Judith Margaret, *b* 1952: *m* 1st, 1974 (*m diss* 1979), Robert Forrest; 2ndly, 1986, Joseph Francis Michael Tumelty, of 15 Henwick Hall Av, Ramsbottom, Bury, Lancs BL0 97M, and has issue living (by 2nd *m*), Nuala Ruth *b* 1986, Carla Susan *b* 1989, — Susan Diana, *b* 1953: *m* 1976, Damien Gerard Aked, of 31 Jefferson Drive, Rainham, Kent ME8 0PB, and has issue living, Jody *b* 1981, Kristie *b* 1983. *Residence* – Glenside, Rowhills, Heath End, Farnham, Surrey GU9 9AU.

SISTERS LIVING

Ruth, *b* 1915. —— Helen, *b* 1918: *m* 1947, William Herbert Chapman, MB, ChB, of 6 Jennifer Way, Rossmoyne, W Aust 6155, and has issue living, Andrew, *b* 1948, — Richard Holden, *b* 1953, — Bridget, *b* 1950: *m* 1971, Peter Herbert Stone, — Anne, *b* 1957. —— Janet, *b* 1920: *m* 1946, Capt George Richmond Aagaard Welsh, RAOC, of 12 Bylands, White Rose Lane, Woking, Surrey, and has issue living, Geoffrey Peter, *b* 1948, — Raymond Michael, *b* 1949, — Malcolm Nigel, *b* 1950.

COLLATERAL BRANCH LIVING

Grandchildren of late Peter Wood Holden, 2nd son of Edward Holden, 2nd son of 1st baronet:—
Issue of late Duncan Holden, *b* 1907, *d* 1985: *m* 1930, Helen, da of Kinross White, of Hawkes Bay, NZ:—
Peter Ritson (Forest Gate, Onga Onga, Hawkes Bay, NZ), *b* 1933: *m* 1958, Juliet, da of Keith de Castro, of Christchurch, NZ, and has issue living, Duncan Dudley *b* 1963, Matthew Keith *b* 1967, Deborah Elizabeth *b* 1959, Caroline Jane *b* 1961, — Diana Margaret, *b* 1930: *m* 1955, John Morris Williams, and has issue living, Michael *b* 1956, — Philip *b* 1960, — Fiona *b* 1958, — Jennifer *b* 1961.

The 1st baronet, Sir Isaac Holden (son of Isaac Holden, of Gunends, Alston, Cumberland), was senior partner in the firm of Isaac Holden and Sons, Wool combers, of Alston Works, Bradford, and sat as MP for Knaresborough (*L*) 1865-68, for Yorkshire, W Riding, N Div 1882-85, and for Yorkshire, W Riding, N Part, Keighley Div 1885-95. The 2nd baronet, Sir Angus Holden sat as MP for Bradford, E Div (*L*) 1885-86, and for Yorkshire, E Riding, Buckrose Div, 1892-1900, and was *cr Baron Holden*, of Alston, co Cumberland (peerage of United Kingdom) 1908. In 1951, on the death of the 3rd Baron Holden, the peerage became ext, but the baronetcy passed to his cousin, Sir Isaac Holden (nephew of 1st Baron Holden), who succeeded as 5th baronet.

HOLDEN (UK) 1919, of The Firs, Leigh, co Lancaster

Sir JOHN DAVID HOLDEN, 4th *Baronet*, only son of late David George Holden, el son of 3rd baronet; *b* 16 Dec 1967; *s* his grandfather, *Sir* GEORGE, 1976: *m* 1987, Suzanne Cummings, of York, and has issue.

Arms – Sable, on a pale ermine between two chevrons or a covered cup of the last. **Crest** – In front of a rising sun in its splendour or, a moorcock sable, jelloped and wattled gules.
Residence – 13 Sterne Av, Tang Hall, York YO3 0TF.

Deo omnia debeo

I owe all things to God

DAUGHTERS LIVING

Abigail Suzanne, *b* 1988. —— Samantha Jo, *b* 1990.

UNCLE LIVING (*son of 3rd baronet*)

BRIAN PETER JOHN, *b* 12 April 1944: *m* 1984, Bernardette Anne Lopez, da of George Gerard O'Malley, of Manchester.

AUNTS LIVING (*daughters of 3rd baronet*)

Patricia Margaret Anne, *b* 1942; *m* 1963, David Coates Mitchell, of Lynden Royd, 60 Scott Lane West, Riddlesden, Keighley, Yorks, and has issue living, Kieron (25 Falsgrave Av, Fagley, Bradford, W Yorks), *b* 1970: *m* 1991, —, and has issue living, James Declan *b* 1992, Kyle Patrick *b* 1993, Sophie Louise *b* 1995, — Deborah, *b* 1964: *m* 1989, David John Petty, of 45 Airedale Rd, Undercliffe, Bradford, W Yorks. —— Deirdre Rosemary, *b* 1949: *m* 1969, David Marsh, and has issue living, Andrew David, *b* 1974, — Christopher George, *b* 1986, — Nicola Catherine *b* 1972; MB, ChB: *m* 1998, Andrew James Cox, BSc, MB, ChB.

GREAT-UNCLE LIVING (*son of 2nd baronet*)

James Temple (22 Lambs Rd, Thornton, Blackpool, Lancs), *b* 1922: *m* 1st, 1948 (*m diss* 1956), Olive, da of Henry Thompson Kirby; 2ndly, 1957, Golda Bracey, da of Clifford Shirley, and has issue living (by 1st *m*), Peter James, *b* 1954, — Jacqueline Peta, *b* 1950 — (by 2nd *m*), Carl Temple, *b* 1963; LLB: *m* 1992, Caroline Anne, da of Stanley Gould, of Llanferres, and has issue living, James Joseph *b* 1997.

GREAT-AUNT LIVING (*daughter of 2nd baronet*)

Margaret, *b* 1916: *m* 1942, Maj E. R. Webster, R Corps of Signals, of Green Banks, Beechwood Lane, Culcheth, nr Warrington, Cheshire, and has issue living, Pamela Pixie Anne (Glen House, Upper Rochestown, Co Cork), *b* 1946: *m* 1970, Timothy Joseph Cahill, FRCS, who *d* 1988, and has issue living, Timothy Joseph *b* 1977, Bryan Anthony Ernest *b* 1979, Jeremy James *b* 1981, Joanne Amanda *b* 1971, Rachael Louise *b* 1972, — Carol Yvonne Margaret, *b* 1949: *m* 1973, Kenneth G. Wilcock, and has issue living, Ian Michael *b* 1977, James Richard *b* 1982, Jennifer Louise *b* 1975.

MOTHER LIVING

Nancy, da of H. W. D. Marwood, of Bodnor House, Whenby, York: *m* 1964, David George Holden (ante), who *d* 1971, el son of 3rd baronet.

COLLATERAL BRANCHES LIVING

Issue of late Christopher William Holden, 2nd son of 3rd baronet, *b* 1940, *d* 1968: *m* 1965, June (who *m* 2ndly, 1970, Barry Hargreaves Beaumont, of Thornlea House, Souttergate, Hedon, E Yorks), da of Stephen Carrington:—
Sara, *b* (*posthumous*) 1968.

Issue of late John Holden, 2nd son of 2nd baronet, *b* 1918, *d* 1985: *m* 1940, Margaret Lois, who *d* 1985, da of Ivan Sharpe, of Southport:—
Robin John (Tall Trees, Barry Rise, Bowdon, Altrincham, Cheshire), *b* 1942; *ed* Oundle; FCA; Pres Manchester Soc of Chartered Accountants 1984; Dir and Hon Treas Manchester Chamber of Commerce and Industry 1983-93: *m* 1964, Margaret Susan, da of G. I. Rushton, of Birkdale, and has issue living, Richard Ingham, *b* 1966, — Jonathan Robin, *b* 1969. —— Anthony Ivan (c/o Rogers Coleridge White, 20 Powis Mews, W11 1JN), *b* 1947; *ed* Oundle, and Merton Coll, Oxford (MA); biographer: *m* 1st, 1971 (*m diss* 1988), Amanda Juliet, MA, LGSM, LRAM, ARCM, da of Sir Harold Brian Seymour Warren, MRCS, LRCP, of 94 Oakley St, SW3; 2ndly, 1990, Cynthia BLAKE, da of Mrs George Blake, of Brookline, Mass, USA, and has issue living (by 1st *m*), Samuel Ivan, *b* 1975, — Joseph Anthony, *b* 1977, — Benjamin John, *b* 1070.

Grandchildren of late Arthur Holden, 4th son of 1st baronet:—
Issue of late Henry David Holden, *b* 1922, *d* 1980: *m* 1947, Marjorie (Anglezarke, Belmont Rd, Penn, Wolverhampton), da of T. A. Brown, of Astley Bridge, Bolton:—

David Lawrence (Bobbins, 4 Marsh Way, Catshill, Bromsgrove, Worcs B61 0JD), *b* 1948: *m* 1971, Sharon Joyce, da of A. C. W. Mobbs, of Perton, and has issue living, Robert Arthur, *b* 1972, — Emma Jane, *b* 1974. —— Andrew Charles (Cote Leasowe, Heath House Lane, Codsall, Wolverhampton), *b* 1949: *m* 1972, Susan, da of J. W. Dicken, of Bilston. —— William John (Knights Close, Penkridge, Staffs), *b* 1953: *m* 1975, Patricia Joan, da of R. C. Knight, of Wolverhampton. —— Madeline Julie, *b* 1967: *m* 1989, David Raymond Haynes, of 5 Ayrton Close, Perton, Wolverhampton, and has issue living, Lauren Victoria, *b* 1991, Evelyn Grace *b* 1994.

Issue of late John Holden, 5th and yst son of 1st baronet, *b* 1900, *d* 1977: *m* 1925, Rita, da of H. Walton, of Reedley, Burnley:—
Derek John (5 Greystoke Court, 41 Albemarle Rd, Beckenham, Kent BR3 2HL), *b* 1927: *m* 1951, Patricia Kathleen, da of F. Mansfield, of Heaton Moor, and has issue living, Richard John, *b* 1960: *m* 1982, Atie, da of G. Nieuwenhuis, of Durban N, S Africa, — Elizabeth Anne, *b* 1955. —— Norman Michael (7 Trafford Av, Westville, Durban, S Africa), *b* 1928: *m* 1957, Enid N, da of M. Smith, of Adelaide, S Aust, and has issue living, Christopher Derek, *b* 1959, — Peter James, *b* 1960. —— Gillian Nancy, *b* 1935: *m* 1964, Dennis George Edwin Cox, of Highlands, Berden, Bishop's Stortford, and has issue living, Gordon Michael, *b* 1967, — Julia Alison, *b* 1965.

Sir John Henry Holden, 1st Bt (son of John Holden), was twice Mayor of Leigh, Lancashire. The 2nd baronet, Sir George, was also twice Mayor of Leigh.

HOLDER (UK) 1898, of Pitmaston, Moseley, Worcestershire

Nisi Dominus frustra

It is in vain without the Lord

Sir (JOHN) HENRY HOLDER, 4th *Baronet*; *b* 12 March 1928; *s* his father, *Sir* JOHN ERIC DUNCAN, 1986; *ed* Eton, and Birmingham Univ (Dip in Malting and Brewing): *m* 1960, Catharine Harrison, who *d* 1994, yr da of late Leonard Baker, of Stone Lane, Kinver, nr Stourbridge, Worcs, and has issue.

𝕬rms – Per pale indented or and gules three chevronels ermine, in chief two trefoils slipped and countercharged. 𝕮rest – On the battlements of a tower per pale or and argent, charged with a cross gules, a lion sejant per pale indented azure and of the third supporting with the dexter paw an anchor argent.
Residence – Connaught Cottage, The Fairstead, Cley next the Sea, Holt, Norfolk NR25 7RJ.

SONS LIVING

NIGEL JOHN CHARLES, *b* 6 May 1962; *ed* Wisbech Gram Sch, and The Isle Coll, Wisbech. —— Hugo Richard, *b* (twin) 1962: *m* 1991, Barbara, only da of Walter Plenk, of Sperberstrasse 42, 81827 Munich, Germany, and has issue living, Alexander John, *b* 1993, — Stephanie Jasmin, *b* 1994.

DAUGHTER LIVING

Bridget Georgina, *b* 1964: *m* 1991, Christopher L. T. Davis, only son of L. F. Davis, of Burrough Green, Newmarket, Suffolk, and has issue living, Thomas Henry Frederick, *b* 1993.

SISTERS LIVING

Anthea Josephine, *b* 1930: *m* 1961, Peter Wilbraham Swayne, yr son of Philip Coney Swayne, of Higher Down, Over Stowey, Somerset. —— Meryl Evelyn, *b* 1936.

WIDOW LIVING OF THIRD BARONET

MARJORIE EMILY (*Marjorie, Lady Holder*), da of late Frank Reynolds Markham, of Cape Town and of London: *m* 1971, as his 2nd wife, Sir John Eric Duncan Holder, 3rd Bt (MA Oxon), who *d* 1986. *Residence* – Clare Park, Crondall, Farnham, Surrey GU10 5DT.

COLLATERAL BRANCHES LIVING

Granddaughters of late Alfred Ernest Holder (infra):—
Issue of late Lt-Col Charles Frederic Chavasse Holder, RA, *b* 1910, *d* 1989: *m* 1951, Margaret (Balsam House, Wincanton, Som BA9 9HT), yst da of A. E. Wrigley, of Gaines, Whitbourne, Worcs:—
Lucy Margaret, *b* 1953: *m* 1987, David B. Badham-Thornhill, of Holton House, Wincanton, Som, son of Maj D. G. B. Badham-Thornhill, of Cheltenham, and has had issue, Thomas Charles George, *b* 1989, — Edward David, *b* 1993, — Mark Frederick, *b* 1995, — Ruth Elizabeth, *b* and *d* 1991, — Helen Lucy, *b* (twin) 1991. —— Judith Mary, *b* 1954.

Issue of late Alfred Ernest Holder, 3rd son of 1st baronet, *b* 1879, *d* 1963: *m* 1909, Gwendoline Louisa Ryland, who *d* 1976, da of late Sir Thomas Chavasse, MD, of The Linthurst Hill, Barnt Green, Worcs:—

Gwendoline Mary Chavasse, *b* 1913: *m* 1943, Lawry Knight, of 59 Victoria Rd, Topsham, Exeter, and has issue living, William, *b* 1945, — Caroline, *b* 1944. —— Phyllis Margaret Chavasse, *b* 1918: *m* 1st, 1956 (*m diss* 1967), as his 2nd wife, William Raymond John Evelyn Whateley, now Balfour (*see* Page-Wood, Bt, colls); 2ndly, 1967, Lt-Col Matthew Wakefield Drury Evelyn Wood (*see* Page-Wood, Bt, colls, 1985 Edn).

HOLDERNESS (UK) 1920, of Tadworth, co Surrey

Sir MARTIN WILLIAM HOLDERNESS, 4th *Baronet*; *b* 24 May 1957; *s* his father, Sir RICHARD WILLIAM, 1998; *ed* Bradfield Coll; CA, MSFA: *m* 1984, Elizabeth D., da of Dr William Dickson Thornton, MD, of Belfast, and has issue.
Residence – 16 Jennings Rd, St Albans, Herts AL1 4NT.

SON LIVING

MATTHEW WILLIAM THORNTON, *b* 23 May 1990.

DAUGHTER LIVING

Tessa Elizabeth Mary, *b* 1992.

BROTHER LIVING

Andrew James, *b* 1962; LLB: *m* 1989, Charlotte E. M., elder da of Frederick Michael Broadbent, of Maddington Manor, Shrewton, Wilts, and has issue living, Edward Thomas James, *b* 1995, — Henrietta Emily Alice, *b* 1993. *Residence* – Birch House, High Street, Bramley, Surrey GU5 0HS.

SISTER LIVING

Jane Carleton, *b* 1955: *m* 1976, Richard David Bruce Pailthorpe, only son of Dr D. B. Pailthorpe, of Raughmere Drive, Lavant, Chichester, W Sussex, and has issue living, Nicholas Richard Bruce, *b* 1980, — Victoria Emma Carleton, *b* 1983. *Residence* – The Chase, Charlton, Chichester, W Sussex.

AUNT LIVING (*daughter of 2nd baronet*)

Margaret Carleton, *b* 1929; MB, ChB Edinburgh 1954; FFARCS: *m* 1965, William Frederick Walter Southwood, MD, MCh, FRCS, of 1 Aldwick Av, Bognor Regis, W Sussex, and has issue living, Robert William, *b* 1966, — John Carleton, *b* 1967.

WIDOW LIVING OF THIRD BARONET

PAMELA (*Pamela, Lady Holderness*), da of late Eric Chapman, CBE: *m* 1953, Sir Richard William Holderness, 3rd Bt, who *d* 1998. *Residence* – 1 Tollhouse Close, Chichester, W Sussex PO19 1SE.

The 1st baronet, Sir Thomas William Holderness, GCB, KCSI (son of late John William Holderness, of Liverpool), was sometime Permanent Under-Sec of State for India.

HOLLAND (UK) 1917, of Westwell Manor, co Oxford (Extinct 1997)

Capt Sir GUY HOPE HOLLAND, 3rd and last *Baronet*.

DAUGHTERS LIVING OF THIRD BARONET

Davina Huntly, *b* 1946: *m* 1981, Guy Timothy Geoffrey Conant, DL, JP, of Bulwick Park, Corby, Northants, 2nd son of late Sir Roger Conant, 1st Bt, CVO, and has issue (*see* Conant, Bt). —— Georgiana, *b* 1951: *m* 1979, Nicholas Antony Norman Stuart Robertson, of The Old Rectory, Thorpe Malsor, Kettering, Northants, son of Antony Stuart Robertson, CBE, and has issue living, Ralph Edmund Sothern Stuart, *b* 1982, — Guy Sothern Antony, *b* 1985.

DAUGHTERS LIVING OF SECOND BARONET

Jennifer Lisabeth Gwynllyn, *b* 1940. —— Claerwen Belinda, *b* 1942.

WIDOW LIVING OF SECOND BARONET

ELISABETH HILDA MARGARET (*Elisabeth, Lady Holland*) (Dderw, Rhayader Powys), only child of Thomas Francis Vaughan Prickard, CVO, CA, FRICS, of Dderw, Rhayader, Powys: *m* 1937, Sir Jim Sothern Holland, 2nd Bt, who *d* 1981.

WIDOW LIVING OF THIRD BARONET

JOAN MARIANNE (*Baroness Mowbray, Segrave and Stourton*), only surv child of late Capt Herbert Edmund Street, 20th Hussars: *m* 1st, 1945, Capt Sir Guy Hope Holland, 3rd Bt, who *d* 1997, when the title became extinct; 2ndly, 1999, as his 2nd wife, 26th Baron Mowbray, Segrave and Stourton, CBE. *Residences* – 23 Warwick Sq, SW1; Marcus, by Forfar, Angus.

HOLLINS (UK) 1907, of Greyfriars, Broughton, co Palatine of Lancaster (Extinct 1963)

Sir FRANK HUBERT HOLLINS, 3rd and last *Baronet.*

COLLATERAL BRANCHES LIVING

Issue of late Philip Leslie Hollins, 3rd son of 1st baronet, *b* 1878, *d* 1933: *m* 1919, Doris Mary, who *d* 1969, da of Charles Arthur Abraham (Parker, Bt *cr* 1681):—

Anne, *b* 1923: *m* 1st, 1947 (*m diss* 1951), Brig Percy de Courcy Jones, King's Shropshire LI; 2ndly, 1953, Peter Robert Gibson, of 15 Warren Hill Rd, Woodbridge, Suffolk, and has issue living, (by 1st *m*) Nigel Anthony de Courcy, *b* 1948: *m* 1982, Jane Wilson, of Ulverston, Lancs, — (by 2nd *m*) Christopher Robert, *b* 1956: *m* 1980, Margaret Ruth, da of John Anthony Salt, — Philip James, *b* 1959: *m* 1984, Linda, da of John Todd, of Ipswich, Suffolk, — Julia Elizabeth, *b* 1954: *m* 1982, Dr John Stanger, son of Dr Robin Stanger, of Burlesdon, Hants.

Issue of late John Chard Humphrey Lancelot Hollins, 4th son of 1st baronet, *b* 1890, *d* 1938: *m* 1914, Ruth, who *d* 1977, da of late John Keil Tullis, of Glasgow:—

Ruth Jean (Gelston, Dawson Lane, Whittle le Woods, Chorley, Lancs), *b* 1928.

HOME (NS) 1671, of Blackadder, co Berwick
(Name pronounced "Hume")

Look to the end

Sir WILLIAM DUNDAS HOME, 14th *Baronet*; son of late John Home, elder son of 13th baronet; *b* 19 Feb 1968; *s* his grandfather, *Sir* DAVID GEORGE, 1992; *ed* Cranbrook Sch, Sydney: *m* 1995, Dominique Meryl, da of Sydney Fischer, OBE, and has issue.

Arms – Quarterly; 1st, azure on a chevron argent three roses gules, *Blackadder*, 2nd, vert, a lion rampant argent langued and armed gules, *Home*; 3rd, argent, three popinjays, vert beaked and limbed gules, *Pepdie*; 4th, argent, a cross engrailed azure, *Sinclair*. Crest – An adder sable in pale, holding in its mouth a rose gules, leaved and stalked vert. Supporters – *Dexter*, an otter; *sinister*, a falcon, both proper.
Residence – 53 York Rd, Queen's Park, NSW 2022, Australia. *Club* - Royal Sydney Golf.

SON LIVING

THOMAS JOHN, *b* 24 Nov 1996.

DAUGHTER LIVING

Petra Sydney, *b* 1998.

SISTER LIVING

Georgina Helen (142 Tachbrook St, SW1V 2NE), *b* 1969; *ed* Ascham Sch, Sydney.

UNCLE LIVING (*son of 13th baronet*)

Patrick, *b* 1941; *ed* Harrow: *m* 1984, Catherine Mary, yr da of James McLaren Henderson, of Spittalrigg, Haddington, E Lothian, and has issue living, David McLaren, *b* 6 March 1993, — Janet, *b* 1986. *Residence* – Winterfield, North Berwick, E Lothian EH39 4LY. *Clubs* – Royal and Ancient, The Hon Co of Edinburgh Golfers.

AUNT LIVING (*daughter of 13th baronet*)

Hermione (*Lady Malcolm*), *b* 1934; *ed* Lady Margaret Hall, Oxford (BA); a JP for Inner London 1971-84: *m* 1959, Sir David Peter Michael Malcolm, 11th Bt, of Whiteholm, Gullane, E Lothian EH31 2BD.

MOTHER LIVING

Nancy Helen (*Lady Gorton*), elder da of Harry Greenlaw Elliott, of Perth, W Australia, and widow of Cdr Ian Macgregor, RAN: *m* 2ndly, 1966, John Home, who *d* 1988, elder son of Sir David George Home, 13th Bt; 3rdly, 1993, Rt Hon Sir John Grey Gorton, GCMG, AC, CH. *Residence* – 32 Parsley Rd, Vaucluse, NSW 2030, Australia.

The Homes of Blackadder descend from John, 4th son of Sir David Home of Wedderburn, who fell at Flodden 1513, whose sons present there were known as the "Seven Spears of Wedderburn." John Home of East Blackadder *m* 1518, Beatrix, el da and co-parcener of Robert Blackadder of that Ilk. On the failure of descendants of her yr sister who *m* Robert Home, another of the "the Spears," the whole barony passed to this family. The Homes of Wedderburn descend from Sir David Home (living 1453), yr son of Sir Thomas Home of that Ilk, ancestor of the Earls of Home. Sir John Home, 5th in descent from John of Easter Blackadder, was *cr* a baronet with remainder to heirs male of his body. Sir George Home, 7th baronet, was Vice-Adm of the Blue. The 10th baronet in 1878 assumed the additional surname of Speirs.

Home-Purves-Hume-Campbell, see Campbell.

HONYWOOD (E) 1660, of Evington, Kent

Sir FILMER COURTENAY WILLIAM HONYWOOD, 11th *Baronet*: *b* 20 May 1930; *s* his father, *Col Sir* WILLIAM WYNNE, MC, 1982; *ed* Downside, RMA Sandhurst, and RAC Cirencester (MRAC Diploma); FRICS; late 3rd Carabiniers (Prince of Wales' Dragoon Gds); farmer 1954-64 (Suffolk County Dairy Herd Production Awards 1955 and 1956); joined Agric Land Service, MAFF, Maidstone 1964; Assist Land Commr 1966; Surveyor Cockermouth, Cumbria 1973-74; Sr Lands Officer SE Region Central Electricity Generating Board 1974-78, Regional Surveyor and Valuer 1978-88; Part-time Senior Valuer, Inland Revenue Valuation Service, Folkestone 1989-90; Agricultural Compensation and Restoration Consultant to UK Nirex Ltd 1988-89; Land Agency Consultant, Nuclear Electric plc 1993-94; Examiner in Agric, Incorporated Soc of Estates and Wayleaves Officers 1989-95, and Soc of Surveying Technicians 1996-97: *m* 1956, Elizabeth Margaret Mary Cynthia, who *d* 1996, 2nd da of late Sir Alastair George Lionel Joseph Miller, 6th Bt (*cr* 1788), and has issue.

𝔄rms – Argent, a chevron between three hawks' heads erased azure beaked or.
𝔄rest – A wolf's head couped ermine.
Residence – Greenway Forstal Farmhouse, Hollingbourne, Maidstone, Kent ME17 1QA.

OMNE·BONUM·DESUPER

Every good thing is from above

SONS LIVING

RUPERT ANTHONY PAGAN, *b* 2 March 1957: *m* 1992, Wendy, da of Thomas Young, of Carshalton, and has issue living, Samuel Thomas Courtenay, *b* 1996. —— Simon Joseph (182 Annie St, New Farm, Queensland 4005, Australia), *b* 1958; BA, Grad Dip Landscape Architecture, MRTPI, MRAPI, AAILA.

DAUGHTERS LIVING

Mary Caroline, *b* 1961; SRN, SCM: *m* 1992, Christopher Bear, of 904 Nassassalga Rd, RR7, Belleville, Ontario K8N 4Z7, Canada, yr son of Eric Bear of Gedling, Notts, and has issue living, Edward James, *b* 1994. —— Judith Mary Frances, *b* 1964: *m* 1999, Paul William Baker, of 1 Primrose Drive, Ditton, Aylesford, Kent ME20 6EG, only son of Maurice Baker, of Ditton, Kent.

SISTERS LIVING

Rosamund Iseulte Mary, *b* 1924; 1939-45 War with WRNS: *m* 1947, Paul Anthony Prior, late Lt RNVR, and has issue living, Jacqueline Mary, *b* 1950; *ed* Sussex Univ (BSc), London (PhD): *m* 1972, Timothy Charles Feline, PhD, and has issue living, William James *b* 1979, David Charles *b* 1981, Eleanor Ruth *b* 1983, — Helen Catherine, *b* 1953; SRN, SRCN: *m* 1976, Aribert Wolframm, and has issue living, Thomas *b* 1980, Martin Hawtayne *b* 1982, Yvonne Bianca *b* 1978, — Sarah Jane, *b* 1956: *m* 1975 (*m diss* 19—), Leslie Howe, — Emma Charlotte Claudia, *b* 1962; NNEB. *Residence* – La Croix Parens, 30500 Courry, France. —— Zaidée Maud Elsie, *b* 1926; SRN, SCM, Edinburgh: *m* 1954, Lt-Cdr Douglas Inglefield Haywood, RN, and has issue living, Richard Douglas, *b* 1964; BA: *m* 1986, Malika Dukali, and has issue living, Daniel Douglas *b* 1994, Karima Frances *b* 1986, Aisha Zaidée *b* 1992, — Elizabeth Zaidée, *b* 1955; BSc, PhD, — Katherine Mary, *b* 1962; SRN: *m* 1989, Derek Moore, and has issue living, André John *b* 1997, — Patricia Anne, *b* 1967; DCRR, DMU. *Residence* – Downgate Cottage, N Petherwin, Launceston, Cornwall PL15 8LR.

COLLATERAL BRANCH LIVING

Grandchildren of late Guy Honywood, 8th son of 7th baronet:—
Issue of late Thomas Guy Honywood, *b* 1903, *d* 1968: *m* 1st, 19—, —; 2ndly, 1931, Anne Gertrude Molloy:—
(By 2nd *m*) Barry (28 Church St, Riverstone, NSW 2765, Australia), *b* 1932: *m* 19—, Anne —, who *d* 1996, and has issue living, Michael, *b* 19—, — Matthew, *b* 19—. —— Bernadette Margaret, *b* 1936: *m* 1960, Nepia Tauri Maniapoto, RNZA Regt Korean War, of 44 Wharenui Rd, Rotorua, NZ, and has issue living, Maru John, *b* 1967; BMS, — Moana Maree, *b* 1961; LLB: *m* 19—, William Wakatere Jackson, of 44 Tamaki Av, Otahuhu, Auckland, NZ, and has issue living, Kimiora Hikurangi Elijah *b* 1990, — Katarina Mae, *b* 1962: *m* 19—, Warren Ruru Morgan, of 290 Old Taupo Rd, Rotorua, NZ, and has issue living, Nepia Thomas *b* 1986, Katarina Aroha *b* 1991, — Niki Ann, *b* 1964, — Keri Lee, *b* 1965: *m* 19—, David Cheer, of 141 Tavistock Rd, Waipukurau, NZ, — Lisa Aroha, *b* 1969; BEd.

The 1st baronet was Sir Edward Honywood (son of late Sir John Honywood, High Sheriff of Kent 1607-9). Sir John Honywood, 4th baronet, was MP for Steyning 1784-5 and 1788-90, for Canterbury 1790-1802, and for Honiton 1802-6. Sir John William Honywood, 8th baronet, was an Alderman of Kent County Council.

HOOD (UK) 1922, of Wimbledon, co Surrey

Sir HAROLD JOSEPH HOOD, TD, 2nd *Baronet*; *b* 23 Jan 1916; *s* his father, *Sir* JOSEPH, 1931; *ed* Downside; is Lieut RA (TA); a Dir of Catholic Herald Ltd; appointed Editor of *The Catholic Who's Who* 1952; a Knt of St Gregory the Great (Knt Cdr 1978, Knt Grand Cross 1987), and Knt of Magistral Grace, Sovereign Mil Order of Malta 1986: *m* 1946, Hon Ferelith Rosemary Florence Kenworthy, da of 10th Baron Strabolgi, and has issue.

Arms – Argent, on a mount vert an oak tree fructed proper, a chief sable, thereon a bow stringed also proper. **Crest** – A demi-stag proper resting the sinister foot on a fret or.
Residence – 31 Avenue Rd, St John's Wood, NW8 6BS. *Clubs* – MCC, RAC.

SONS LIVING

JOHN JOSEPH HAROLD, *b* 27 Aug 1952. —— Basil Gervase Francis Gerard, *b* 1955.

DAUGHTERS LIVING

Josepha Ferelith Emma Margaret-Mary, *b* 1953: *m* 1981, Ian Murray, eldest son of Sir Donald Murray, KCVO, CMG, late HM Amb to Sweden, and has issue living, Andrew Duncan Culverwell, *b* 1985, — Alasdair Angus Culverwell, *b* 1987, — Kirstie Iona Culverwell, *b* 1990. —— Margaret Marie Elizabeth Felicia, *b* 1965: *m* 1990, Michael Gresslin, son of Heinz Gresslin, of Badenweiler, Germany.

COLLATERAL BRANCH LIVING

Issue of late Robin Adrian Hood, yst son of 1st baronet, *b* 1924, *d* 1993: *m* 1949, Miriam Teresa, who *d* 1991, yr da of late Don Humberto Blanco-Fombona:—
Simon Joseph Paul Blanco (4 Bedford Rd, Bedford Park, Chiswick W4 1JJ), *b* 1951: *m* 1st, 1979 (*m diss* 1989), Josette Elian, only da of Jean Baumgartner, of Montchoisi 55, Lausanne, Switzerland; 2ndly, 1990 (*m diss* 1991), Judith M., only da of D. W. Prickett, of Kingston Hill, Surrey; 3rdly, 1996, Charlotte, only da of Dr J. Leahy-Taylor, and has issue living (by 1st *m*), Victoria Alexandra, *b* 1984, — (by 3rd *m*), Natasha Lara Leahy Isabel, *b* 1996. —— Martin Joseph Blanco (now *Dom James Hood*, OSB) (Downside Abbey, Stratton-on-the-Fosse, Somerset) *b* 1953; *ed* Downside. —— Bernadette Marie Blanco, *b* (twin) 1953. —— Anne-Marie Elena Kathleen Blanco, *b* 1957: *m* 1979, Nicholas Edward True, CBE, of 114 Palewell Park, SW14 8JH, son of late Edward T. True, of W Bridgford, and has issue living, James Alexios Edward, *b* 1981, — Thomas-Leo Richard, *b* 1984, — Sophia Miriam Marie-Louise Blanco, *b* 1992.

The 1st baronet, Sir Joseph Hood, a solicitor, sometime a Dep Chm British American Tobacco Co Ltd, sat as MP for Wimbledon (*U*) 1918-24, and was Mayor of Wimbledon 1930-31.

FULLER-ACLAND-HOOD (UK) 1806 of Hartington, co Derby, and 1809, of St Audries, co Somerset (Extinct 1990)

Sir (ALEXANDER) WILLIAM FULLER-ACLAND-HOOD, 8th Baronet of Hartington and 6th Baronet of St Audries; last *Baronet*.

DAUGHTER LIVING OF EIGHTH (AND SIXTH) BARONET

Elisabeth Anne, *b* 1931: *m* 1st, 1952 (*m diss* 1960), Richard C. Pferdner, who *d* 1989; 2ndly, 1968, Wallace G. Henry, who *d* 1972, and has issue living (by 1st *m*) Richard Charles, *b* 1959: *m* 19—, Lisa —, — Kathleen Marie, *b* 1957: *m* 19—, Robert Sacks, and has issue living, Joshua *b* 19—, Allison E. *b* 19—, — (by 2nd *m*), Eric William, *b* 1969.

HOOPER (UK) 1962, of Tenterden, co Kent (Extinct 1987)

Sir ANTHONY ROBIN MAURICE HOOPER, 2nd and last *Baronet*.

DAUGHTERS LIVING OF FIRST BARONET (*by 1st marriage*)

Bobyl Jane, *b* 1924: *m* 1945, Lt-Cdr Bernard Vann, MBE, DSC, RN, of Woodlands, Kemble Wick, Cirencester, Glos GL7 6EQ, and has issue living, Michael, *b* 1946, — James, *b* 1949.

(*by 2nd marriage*)

Emma Charlotte HOOPER, *b* 1949: *m* 1st, 1968 (*m diss* 1973), Razek Mamarbachi; 2ndly, 1979, Babar Khan Mumtaz, and has issue living (by 2nd *m*), Chungaiz, *b* 1980, — Aruna, *b* 1982.

HOPE (NS) 1628, of Craighall, co Fife

But hope is unbroken

Sir JOHN CARL ALEXANDER HOPE, 18th *Baronet*; *b* 10 June 1939; *s* his father, *Group-Capt Sir* ARCHIBALD PHILIP, OBE, DFC, AE, 1987; *ed* Eton: *m* 1968, Merle Pringle, da of late Robert Douglas, of Southside, Holbrook, Ipswich, and has issue.

Arms – Azure, a chevron or between three bezants. Crest – A broken terrestrial globe surmounted by a rainbow issuing out of a cloud at each end all proper. Supporters – Two female figures representing Hope in vestments vert, on their heads garlands of flowers, each resting her exterior hand on an anchor all proper.
Residence – 9 Westleigh Av, SW15 6RF.

SON LIVING

ALEXANDER ARCHIBALD DOUGLAS, *b* 16 March 1969; *ed* Eton.

DAUGHTER LIVING

Natasha Anne, *b* 1971.

BROTHER LIVING

Charles Archibald, *b* 1945; *ed* Eton, Balliol Coll, Oxford (BA), London Univ (MA) and — Coll Camb (MA); lecturer at Warburg Inst: *m* 1977, Jennifer Katharine, da of John Hadley, of Godmanchester, Huntingdon, and has issue living, Thomas, *b* 1978.

AUNT LIVING (*daughter of 16th Baronet*)

Katharine Anne (The Colt House, Chieveley, Newbury, Berks RG16 8XB), *b* 1916: *m* 1st, 1939, Fl-Lt Carl Raymond Davis, DFC, AAF, who was *ka* during Battle of Britain 1940; 2ndly, 1945, Maj Eric George Ewart Rayner, RA, who *d* 1978, and has issue living (by 1st *m*), Carl Michael (Marymead Cottage, Chieveley, Newbury, Berks RG16 8UX), *b* 1940: *m* 1st, 1963 (*m diss* 1987), Carolyn Rachel, da of John White, of Cushat Wood, Potten End, Berkhamsted; 2ndly, 1987, Carolyn Jane, da of late Earnest Smith Hall, of Solihull, Warwickshire, and has issue living, (by 1st *m*) Carl Robert *b* 1971, Helen Rachel *b* 1966, Julie Theresa, *b* 1968, — (by 2nd *m*) Gillian Mary, *b* 1948: *m* 1986, Peter Alan Cardiff, of 29 Stokenchurch St, Fulham, SW6 3TS.

COLLATERAL BRANCHES LIVING

Issue of late Lt-Col Hugh Alexander Hope, OBE, MC, KRRC, yst son of 16th baronet, *b* 1914, *d* 1982: *m* 1949, Cynthia Evelyn, who *d* 1997, da of late Lt-Col Algernon Corbert Turnor, MC, RHG (B Londesborough):—
Andrew Hugh, *b* 1951; *ed* Quantock Sch, Over Stowey, Somerset: *m* 1982 (*m diss* 1992), Rosanna Jane, da of Gilbert Ian Noel Johnstone, of Cross Cottage, Brixton Deverill, Warminster, Wilts, and has issue living, Oliver Hugh, *b* 1989, — Clara Harriet, *b* 1986.

Grandson of late Major Richard Berwick Hope, 3rd son of late Archibald Godfrey Hope, 2nd son of late Maj-Gen Archibald Hugh Hope, son of late Hugh Hope, 4th son of 9th baronet:—
Issue of late Alexander Erskine Hope, Lieut Bedfordshire and Herts Regt, *b* 1917, *ka* 1944: *m* 1941, Lilias Mary Phyllis (who *m* 2ndly, 1948, Lt-Col Gerard Francis Kirkpatrick Daly, RE), da of late Rev William Herbert Austwick:—
Alexander David Austwick (*posthumous*), *b* 1945; *ed* Bloxham; actor.

Granddaughter of late Major Cecil Arthur Hope, 2nd son of late James Hope, WS, *b* 1818, 4th son of late John Hope, MD, FRS, grandson of late Sir Archibald Hope (Lord Rankeillour of the Court of Session), 2nd son of 2nd baronet:—
Issue of late Lieut-Col Arthur Clement Hope, MBE, *b* 1891, *d* 1961: *m* 1933, Elizabeth Hale, da of Frederick W. Wallace, of Redjacket, Washington, USA:—
Jean Elizabeth, *b* 1937: *m* 1960, Sergio Pizzicaria.

Grandchildren of late Edward William Hope, OBE, MD, DSc (infra):—
Issue of late John Edward Bowring Hope, *b* 1901, *d* 1957: *m* 1927, Catherine, who *d* 1979, da of Robert Stephen Hubbersty, MD, of Avenue House, Sunderland:—
Michael Stephen Edward (Apt 503 Brentwood Park, Portugal Cove Rd, St Johns, Newfoundland, Canada A1B 4H9), *b* 1928; late 2nd Lieut RHG: *m* 1st, 1957, Edith Rosemary Byrne, who *d* 1962, da of late Mrs Margaret Roberts, of Bexhill-on-Sea; 2ndly, 1964, Catherine Emily, da of late Frederick Bradshaw, and widow of William Kenneth Latham, of Newfoundland, and has issue living, (by 1st *m*) Nigel John Charles *b* 1959: *m* 1983, Janet, da of Reginald Gordon Warner, of 78 Crestway, Roehampton, SW15, — Michelle Catherine Margaret, *b* 1958: *m* 1981, Nicholas Charles Devereux, of 9 Poplar Risc, Sutton Coldfield, Little Aston, W Midlands B74 4HT, and has issue living, Christopher Charles *b* 1981, Jennifer Sarah *b* 1985, — (by 2nd *m*) Catherine Charlotte, *b* 1964: *m* 1988, David John Fell, of 55 Vale Close, Harpendon, Herts, and has issue living, James Michael *b* 1990, Thomas Charles *b* 1993, — Louise Joan, *b* 1969. —— Christopher John (1 Port Hill Drive, Shrewsbury), *b* 1931; late 2nd Lt King's Shropshire LI: *m* 1956, Louise Alicia, da of late Joseph Hall, of St John's, Newfoundland, and has issue living, Peter John, *b* 1959: *m* 1989, Terry-Ann, da of Dennis Polkey, of Devon, and has issue living, Katherine Jane *b* 1990, — Susan Louise, *b* 1960. —— Catherine Eve, *b* 1941: *m* 1963, Alastair John Padraic Hardie, of Westfield House, Thropton, Northumberland NE65 7LB, and has issue living, Timothy John Alexander, *b* 1979, — Jane Catherine Sheelagh, *b* 1964: *m* 1993, Stephen Goldsmith, and has issue living, James Andrew *b* 1997, — Lucy Anne *b* 1967: *m* 1998, Matthew Thomas Meredith Broadbent, and has issue living, Tessa Catherine *b* 1998, — Catherine Mary, *b* 1980.

Granddaughters of Robert Wallis Hope, el son of late Col Robert Hope, *b* 1763, son of Capt Robert Hope, grandson of Sir Archibald Hope (ante):—
Issue of late Edward William Hope, OBE, MD, DSc, *b* 1856, *d* 1950: *m* 1899, Charlotte Rennie, who *d* 1962, da of John Bowring, of Liverpool:—
Marjory Mary, *b* 1901: *m* 1940, Francis Stephen Hubbersty, of 34 The Grove, Marton, Middlesbrough. —— Elsa Rennie (51 Caldy Rd, W Kirby, Wirral, Merseyside, L48 2HF), *b* 1905: *m* 1925, Lionel Bishop Ridley, who *d* 1965.

Granddaughter of late Col John Urmson Hope, DSO, eldest son of late Maj-Gen John Edward Hope (infra).—
Issue of late Lt-Col John Patrick Molesworth Hope, *b* 1913, *d* 1975: *m* 1938 (*m diss* 1947) (Margaret) Clare Aida, da of Lionel Julian Walford, of Middleton Stoney, Bicester, Oxon:—
Virginia Anne (4 Phillimore Gdns Close, W8), *b* 1942.

Grandchildren of late Maj-Gen John Edward Hope, el son of Col John Isaac Hope, yr son of Col Robert Hope (*b* 1763) (ante):—
Issue of late Rev George Archibald Hope, *b* 1882, *d* 1950: *m* 1929, Edith Margaret Aston, who *d* 1989, da of late Martin Aston Key, OBE, MD:—
Robert Frank Molesworth, MBE (Askenian, 7 Blvd Tanzin, 64200 Biarritz), *b* 1934; *ed* Marlborough, and New Coll, Oxford (BA 1957): *m* 1957, Jacqueline Pierrette Regine, da of Paul Marcel Albert Forer, of Marseilles, France, and has issue living, Frank George Aston, *b* 1959. — Patrick James Mailhe, *b* 1960. —— Charles Aston (16 Matford Lane, Exeter EX2 4PS), *b* 1940; *ed* Marlborough, and Emmanuel Coll, Camb (BA); Solicitor 1968: *m* 1st, 1967 (*m diss* 1992), Kathryn Elizabeth, da of Capt Wilfred Williams, Merchant Navy (ret); 2ndly, 19—, Lynda Mary Bayley, and has issue living (by 1st *m*), Philip Aston, *b* 1968, — Nicholas Astley, *b* 1970, — (by 2nd wife) Annabel May, *b* 1991. —— Elizabeth, *b* 1937: *m* 1966, Rev John Nigel Rowe, MA, BD, PhD, of 12 Begwyns Bluff, Clyro, Hereford HR3 5SR. —— Clare Urmson (18 Tonbridge House, Tonbridge St WC1H 9PA), *b* 1943.

Descendants of late Sir Charles Hope, KT (son of late John Hope, son of late Sir James Hope, KB, 6th son of 1st baronet), who was *cr Earl of Hopetoun*, 1703 (*see* M Linlithgow).

John Hope, of the High St, Edinburgh, Burgess of that City, alias Petit John, Trumpeter at the Court of King James IV, left issue three sons, the eldest of whom, Henry Hope, Burgess and Guildbrother of Edinburgh, was father of the 1st baronet, Sir Thomas, Lord Advocate of Scotland. He had fourteen children, two of whom were upon the Bench when he pleaded as Lord Advocate; from this circumstance, it is imagined, arises the privilege which that officer of the Crown enjoys of pleading with his head covered, it having been considered derogatory for a father to uncover before his sons. In 1643 he was appointed Commissioner to the General Assembly of the Church of Scotland, a dignity which was not again enjoyed by any commoner for nearly three centuries. The 11th baronet was MP for Midlothian (*C*) 1845-53. Sir John Augustus, OBE, 16th baronet, was MP for Midlothian (Edinburghshire) (*C*) Sept 1912 to Nov 1918, and for N Div of Midlothian and Peeblesshire, Dec 1918 to Oct 1922. Gp Capt Sir Archibald Hope, 17th Bt, played a distinguished role in the aviation world, served European War 1939-45 (despatches twice, DFC, OBE).

Hope-Dunbar, see Dunbar.

HORLICK (UK) 1914, of Cowley Manor, co Gloucester

By labour and knowledge

Sir JAMES CUNLIFFE WILLIAM HORLICK, 6th *Baronet*; *b* 19 Nov 1956; *s* his father, Sir JOHN JAMES MACDONALD, 1995; *ed* Eton; late Lieut Coldstream Gds 1979: *m* 1st, 1985 (*m diss* 1998), Fiona Rosalie, eldest da of Andrew Mclaren, of Alcester, Warwicks, and of Mrs Harry Digby; 2ndly, 1999, Mrs Gina Katherine K. Hudson, da of Roy Tiley, and has issue by 1st *m*.

𝔄rms – Argent, a lion rampant and on a chief gules between two bulls' heads cabossed a garb of barley or. ℭrest – In front of a garb of barley or a lion's head erased gules.
Residence – Crossways House, Hoe Benham, Newbury, Berks RG7 8LQ.

SONS LIVING (*By 1st marriage*)

ALEXANDER JAMES, *b* 8 April 1987. —— Jack Orlando, *b* 1989. —— Hugo Roland, *b* 1991.

SISTERS LIVING

Harriet Anne, *b* 1950; BA London: *m* 1970, Antony Lansdowne Granville (*see* Rose, Bt, *cr* 1872, 1995 Edn), of Tachbrook House, Stourton, nr Shipston-on-Stour, Warwicks, and has issue living, Edward James, *b* 1972; *ed* Eton, and St Catherine's Coll, Oxford, — Matilda Rose, *b* 1975. —— Araminta, *b* 1953; MCSP: *m* 1975, (Edward) Rory Carson, of Perseverance Cottage, Harpsden, Henley-on-Thames, Oxon, only son of late Hon Edward Carson (*see* Carson, By), and has issue living, Toby Edward, *b* 1977, — Jonathan Henry, *b* 1979, — Oliver James, *b* 1982, — Bartholomew John, *b* 1988.

DAUGHTERS LIVING OF THIRD BARONET

Natasha (Apt 16, Gaucin, Malaga, Spain), *b* 1935. —— Anna (17 The Little Boltons, SW10), *b* 1938: *m* 1st, 1960 (*m diss* 1971), Peter Gammon; 2ndly, 1973, Tim Fraser Wright, and has issue living (by 1st *m*), Anthony John, *b* 1965, — Tania Jane, *b* 1962.

DAUGHTERS LIVING OF SECOND BARONET

Roma Ernestine (*Roma, Countess of Dartmouth*) (15B Bedford Towers, Brighton), *b* 1903: *m* 1923, 8th Earl of Dartmouth, who *d* 1962. —— Elizabeth Ann (Betsan) (Conch, Kate St, Alexandra Headland, Sunshine Coast, Qld), *b* 1914: *m* 1933, John Balfour Symington Coats, and has issue living, Callum (Mail Service 591, Stewart's Rd, Wolvi via Gympie, Queensland 4570) *b* 1939: *m* 1st, 1967 (*m diss* 1981), Emily Jane Archer; 2ndly, 1985, Muriel Florence Wattinne, and has issue living, (by 1st *m*) Angus Orlando *b* 1968, Guy Oliver Balfour *b* 1972, — Christopher David (5156 NE 5th St, Seattle, Wa 98105, USA), *b* 1943: *m* 1966, Margaret Helen Van Etten, and has issue living, James John *b* 1978, Mercedes Jane *b* 1970, — Ian Forester Mungo (Forest Glen Sound, Forest Glen, Buderim, Queensland 4556, Australia), *b* 1953: *m* 1986, Anna Birrell, — Mary Manuela, *b* 1937: *m* 1959, Francis Skorka, of Essendon Rd, Anstead, Brisbane, Qld 4070, and has issue living, Lester Carl *b* 1963: *m* 1987, Tracey Anne Symons, of Redcliffe, Qld (and has issue living, Kelly Ann *b* 1992), Darius Brian Christopher *b* 1970, Catherine Benita *b* 1966: *m* 1984, Lennard Thomas Walbank, of Nundah, Qld (and has issue living, Thomas Shane Ronald *b* 1991, Katie Louise *b* 1993), Meri-Anne Kaye *b* 1976.

WIDOW LIVING OF FIFTH BARONET

JUNE (*June, Lady Horlick*), da of late Douglas Cory-Wright, CBE (*see* Cory-Wright, Bt): *m* 1948, Sir John James Macdonald Horlick, 5th Bt, who *d* 1995. *Residence* – Tournaig, Poolewe, Achnasheen, Ross-shire.

Sir James Horlick, 1st Bt, son of James Horlick of Ruardean, Glos was Lord of Manor of Cowley, Glos, High Sheriff of Glos 1902, and Chm and Pres of Horlicks Ltd.

HORNBY (UK) 1899, of Brookhouse, St Michael, Blackburn, County Palatine of Lancaster
(Extinct 1971)

Sir HENRY RUSSELL HORNBY, 2nd and last *Baronet.*

DAUGHTER LIVING OF SECOND BARONET

Jean Margaret (Cranford, Worlington, Mildenhall, Suffolk IP28 8RX), *b* 1915: *m* 1946, Maj-Gen Lionel Charles Manners-Smith, CBE, who *d* 1975, and has issue living, Maurice Charles Hornby, *b* 1948; Col late Royal Green Jackets: *m* 1974, Elizabeth, yst da of Maj-Gen Allan Elton Younger, DSO, OBE, of The Manor House, Twyford, Winchester, Hants SO21 1RH.

HORNE (UK) 1929, of Shackleford, Surrey

Sir (ALAN) GRAY ANTONY HORNE, 3rd *Baronet*; *b* 11 July 1948; *s* his grandfather, *Lt-Col* Sir ALAN EDGAR, MC, 1984: *m* 1980, Cecile Rose, da of Jacques Desplanche, of 5 rue de Cheverny, Romorantin, France.

𝕬rms – Gules, a fret vair between two boars passant one in chief and one in base or. 𝕮rest – A dexter arm vested gules, cuffed or, holding in the hand proper a hunting horn, and charged on the sleeve with a fret gold.
Residence – Château du Basty, Thenon, Dordogne, France.

HALF-AUNT LIVING (daughter of 2nd baronet by 1st marriage)

Edith Margery Jay, *b* 1916; European War 1939-45 as Junior Com ATS: *m* 1944, Maj Thomas Fiddian Reddaway, who *d* 1967, and has had issue, Edgar James Fiddian, *b* 1945; *ed* Oundle, and Westfield Coll, Univ of London; — William Thomas, *b* 1948; *ed* Oundle, and Bedford Coll, Univ of London: *m* 1972, Christine Mary Ann Carole, da of Consta Constantinides, of Amritsar, India, and has issue living, Chloë Rebecca *b* 1982, — Henry Sills (Bow Cottage, Lustleigh, Newton Abbot, Devon TQ13 9TS), *b* 1950; *ed* Oundle, and Bedford Coll, Univ of London: *m* 1981, Susan Elizabeth Leslie, who *d* (29 Nov) 1990, and has had issue, Alexander Thomas *b* 1984, Elizabeth Clare *b* and *d* 1988, Anne May *b* (11 July) 1990. — Richard Alan (27 Wharton St, Islington, WC1X 9PJ), *b* 1952; *ed* Oundle and Oriel Coll, Oxford: *m* 1990, Lynette Poh
Fronti Nulla Fides   Lin Eu, and has issue living, Alan Siew-Loong *b* 1995, Mary-Anne Siew-Kee *b* 1993, — (Michael) Jay, *b* 1956; *ed* Oundle, and Balliol Coll, Oxford: *m* 1989, Clare Olivia Elliott (36 Sotheby Rd, N5 2UR), and *d* (28 March) 1998, as the result of an accident on Lundy Is, leaving issue Auriol Jay *b* (25 July) 1998, — Susan Mary, *b* 1949; *ed* St Mary's, Calne, and Queen Elizabeth Coll, Univ of London: *m* 19—, —. *Residence* – Seven Edges, Brancaster, Norfolk.

The 1st baronet, Sir (William) Edgar Horne (el son of late Edgar Horne, of Witley, Surrey), was Chm of Prudential Assurance Co, and MP for Surrey, Guildford Div (U) 1910-22. Sir Alan Edgar Horne, 2nd Bt, MC, served in World War I 1914-19 in France and Balkans (despatches four times, MC and French Croix de Guerre), and in World War II in Middle East as Lt-Col Roy Pioneer Corps: *m* 1st, 1915, Florence Etty (Hetty), who *d* 1918, da of Arthur Kelly; 2ndly, 1923 (*m diss* 1931), Roslyn, who *d* 1961, da of John Bryan Robinson, and *d* 1984.

Horsbrugh-Porter, see Porter.

HORSFALL (UK) 1909, of Hayfield, Glusburn, West Riding of Yorkshire

By industry and honour

Sir JOHN MUSGRAVE HORSFALL, MC, TD, 3rd *Baronet*; *b* 26 Aug 1915; *s* his father *Sir* (JOHN) DONALD, 1975; *ed* Uppingham; late Maj Duke of Wellington's (W Riding) Regt; Underwriter at Lloyd's; formerly a Dir of Hayfield Textiles Ltd, and of Worsted Spinners Fedn, Ltd (Pres 1962-64), and of Skipton Building Soc; a JP for N Yorks County; Burma 1939-45 (MC): *m* 1940, Cassandra Nora Bernardine, da of late George Wright, of Brinkworth Hall, Elvington, York, and has issue.

𝔄rms – Gules, in chief two horses' heads couped argent bridled azure, and in base a rose of the second, barbed and seeded proper. 𝔠rest – A horse's head couped ermine, issuing from a chaplet of roses gules.
Residence – Greenfield House, Embsay, Skipton, N Yorks.

SONS LIVING

EDWARD JOHN WRIGHT (Long Thatch, Uffington, Faringdon, Oxon SN7 7RP), *b* 17 Dec 1940; *ed* Uppingham: *m* 1965, Rosemary, da of Frank N. King, of East Morton, Keighley, and has issue living, David Edward, *b* 3 Sept 1966: *m* 1996, Maria Gloria Martin Sandoval, da of late Antonio Martin, of Toro, Spain, and Señora Melanea Sandoval Rosales, and has issue living, Marie Laura *b* 1997, — Robert Ian, *b* 1968, — James Christopher, *b* 1971. —— Donald James Linton (25 Stirling Rd, Edinburgh, EH5 3JA), *b* 1942; *ed* Uppingham and Jesus Coll, Camb (MA): *m* 1965, Angela Mary, da of Henry Firth, of Ilkley, and has issue living, Peter Linton (assumed additional christian name of John by deed poll 1982), *b* 1970, — Richard Michael (assumed additional christian name of Henry by deed poll 1989), *b* 1973, — Elizabeth Jane, *b* 1968.

DAUGHTER LIVING

Henrietta Nora, *b* 1947: *m* 1987, Arthur Eubank, of Millstone Moor, Cockermouth, Cumbria.

BROTHERS LIVING AND DECEASED

†Donald Fawcett, TD, *b* (twin) 1915; *ed* Uppingham, and King's Coll, Camb (MA); formerly Capt Duke of Wellington's (W Riding) Regt; is an Underwriter at Lloyd's: *m* 1947, Jeanne Elizabeth (Fairleigh, Draughton, Skipton, N Yorks), da of Col F. Longden Smith, of Woodlands, Skipton, and *d* 1995, leaving issue, Michael Fawcett (Waulkmill, Strachan, Banchory, Kincardineshire AB3 3NS), *b* 1948: *m* 1979, Elizabeth Anne, da of Isaac Pickthall, of Barrow in Furness, and has issue living, Timothy Michael *b* 1981, Luke Benjamin *b* 1982, Donald Isaac *b* 1985, — Peter John, *b* 1953: *m* 1978, Lesley Jane, da of Robert Hardy, of Lothersdale, N Yorks, and has issue living, James Robert *b* 1983, Louise Rachael *b* 1981, — Patricia Jane, *b* 1950: *m* 1974, Thomas Andrew Hoyle, and has issue living, Katie Jane *b* 1977, Harriet Louise *b* 1979, — Susan Elizabeth, *b* 1955, — Sara Louise, *b* 1966: *m* 1996, Richard Spillett, son of Gordon Spillett, of Shrewsbury. —— Patrick David (The Nook, Arkholme, Carnforth, Lancs), *b* 1921; *ed* Uppingham; is an Underwriter at Lloyds; formerly Capt Duke of Wellington's (W Riding) Regt: *m* 1947, June, da of Capt S. H. Clough, of Bailey Cottage, Skipton-in-Craven, and has had issue, Christopher David (Overslade, Sedgwick, Kendal), *b* 1948: *m* 1st, 1970 (*m diss* 1988), Sally, da of Frank S. Greenwood, of Ingleton; 2ndly, 1995, Sylvia, da of late Sydney Sharatt, of Wigan, Lancs, and has issue living (by 1st *m*), Jonathan David *b* 1973, Philip Edward *b* 1975, Robert John *b* 1981, — Carol Anne, *b* 1951: *m* 1975, Anthony Raymond Collinson, of Lake House, Capernwray, Carnforth, Lancs LA6 1AL, and *d* 1991, leaving issue, John Horsfall *b* 1980, Poppy Henrietta *b* 1983.

The 1st baronet, Sir John Cousin, Chm of W Riding of Yorkshire County Council, was a worsted spinner and banker, and provided Glusburn Technical Institute.

HORT (GB) 1767, of Castle Strange, Middlesex

WELL·WIN·WELL·WEAR

Sir ANDREW EDWIN FENTON HORT, 9th *Baronet*; *b* 15 Nov 1954; *s* his father, *Sir* JAMES FENTON, 1995: *m* 1986, Mary, da of Jack Whibley, of Spalding, Lincs, and has issue.

𝔄rms – Azure, a cross or between in the first and fourth quarters a rose argent, barbed and seeded proper. Crest – An eagle reguardant, wings expanded, holding in the beak a chaplet of laurel all proper.

SON LIVING

JAMES, *b* ...... 1989.

DAUGHTER LIVING

Jennifer, *b* 1987.

BROTHER LIVING

Timothy George, *b* 1960.

SISTERS LIVING

Jane Antonia, *b* 1958. —— Diana Rachel, *b* 1962.

UNCLES LIVING (*sons of 7th baronet*)

Richard Patrick Arthur, *b* 1931; *ed* Harrow, and at Trin Coll, Camb (MA 1959): *m* 1956, Agnete Mannheimer, and has issue living, Nicholas Patrick Fenton, *b* 1962, — Rebecca Maria, *b* 1957, — Elsa Katinka, *b* 1960. *Address* – Kungstensg 59 4tr, S11329, Stockholm, Sweden. —— Robert William Lucas, *b* 1936; *ed* Marlborough, and at Trin Coll, Camb (MA): *m* 1973, Eleanor Mary Coburn. *Residence* – Meentashesk, Glencolumcille, co Donegal.

AUNTS LIVING (*daughters of 7th baronet*)

Elizabeth (36 Berkeley Vale Park, Berkeley, Glos GL13 9TG), *b* 1925: *m* 1951, Sqdn Ldr Eric George Holmes, MBE, RAF, who *d* 1975, and has issue living, Helen Margaret, *b* 1952, — Georgina Slaney, *b* 1954. —— Barbara Anne, *b* 1929: *m* 1961, George Bruce Sackville Berkeley, and has issue living, Martin Sackville Hamilton, *b* 1964, — Emma Louise Diana, *b* 1962, — Sara Jane Arabella, *b* 1966.

WIDOW LIVING OF EIGHTH BARONET

JOAN (*Dowager Lady Hort*), da of late Edward Peat, of Swallownest, Sheffield: *m* 1951, Sir James Fenton Hort, 8th Bt, who *d* 1995. *Residence* – Poundgate Lodge, Uckfield Rd, Crowborough, Sussex.

COLLATERAL BRANCHES LIVING

Issue of late Maj Aylmer Victor Dyson Hort, MBE, TD, yr son of 6th baronet, *b* 1897, *d* 1981: *m* 1927, Lois Mary, who *d* 1995, da of late Col Clifford Phillips, VD, TD, DL, of Coolgreany, Malpas, Newport, Monmouth:—
John Aylmer Laybourne (239 Bramcote Lane, Wollaton, Nottingham), *b* 1931; *ed* Marlborough, and Trin Coll, Camb (MA): *m* 1958, Leela, da of R. G. Senan, of 123 Anson Rd, Penang, and has issue, Peter Senan Aylmer, *b* 1958, — Michael John Laybourne, *b* 1960. — Patrick Marcus Govind, *b* 1971. —— Daphne Lois (3 Le Marchant Close, Devizes, Wilts SN10 2EZ), *b* 1930; *ed* Lady Margaret Hall, Oxford (MA). —— Frances Mary, *b* 1937: *m* 1963, John Cameron Simpson, MB, FFARCS, of 38 Kidbrooke Gdns, Blackheath, SE3, and has issue living, James Aylmer, *b* 1964, — David Cameron, *b* 1966.

Issue of late Rev Francis Fitzgerald Hort, brother of 6th baronet, *b* 1868, *d* 1942: *m* 1912, Margaret Charis, who *d* 1972, da of late Rev Joseph Henry Gray, Fellow of Queens' Coll, Camb:—
Margaret Frances, *b* 1913; *ed* Girton Coll, Camb (MA): *m* 1952, John Hunter Terry, who *d* 1976, and has issue living, Stephen John Anthony, *b* 1955, — Rosemary Frances, *b* 1953. *Residence* – 11 Bandon Rd, Girton, Cambridge.

The 1st baronet was Consul-General at Lisbon, the 2nd baronet sat as MP for Kildare 1831-2; the 3rd baronet, a Lieut-Gen in the Army, served with distinction throughout the Crimean war 1854-5, and the 6th baronet, Sir Arthur Fenton, was 33 years a Master at Harrow School.

HOSKYNS (E) 1676, of Harewood, Herefordshire

Sir BENEDICT LEIGH HOSKYNS, 16th *Baronet*; *b* 27 May 1928; *s* his brother, *Sir* JOHN CHEVALLIER, 1956; *ed* Haileybury, and at Corpus Christi Coll, Camb (MB and BChir 1952); Gen Practitioner (ret) Capt RAMC (ret): *m* 1953, Ann, da of Harry Wilkinson, and has issue.

Arms – Per pale azure and gules, a chevron between three lions rampant or.
Crest – A lion's head erased or, with flames of fire out of his mouth proper, ducally crowned of the first.
Residence – Russell House, Wherry Corner, High St, Manningtree, Essex CO11 1AJ.

VINCULA DA·LINGUÆ·VEL·TIBI·LINGUA·DABIT

Bind the tongue or the tongue will bind thee

SONS LIVING

EDWYN WREN, *b* 4 Feb 1956; Senior Chorister, King's Coll, Camb 1969; *ed* Nottingham Univ (MB, BS); MRCP (1984); Consultant Paediatrician, Leicester Gen & Leicester Royal Infirmary since 1993 *m* 1981, Jane, da of John Sellers, and has issue living Robin Chevallier, *b* 5 July 1989, — Lucy Mary, *b* 1993.
—— John Chandos, *b* 1961; *ed* Gonville and Caius Coll, Camb (BA), and Middlesex Hosp.

DAUGHTERS LIVING

Janet Mary, *b* 1954; *ed* North London Collegiate Sch, and York Univ (BA, PGCE, DPhil 1997); ARCM; Sr Academic, Music in Educn, Univ of Central England, Birmingham: *m* 1982, Christopher Harris. —— Sarah Leigh, *b* 1959; *ed* Birmingham Univ (Vice-Chancellor's Prize, BA); LGSM (MusTh), ARCM 1981; Dir Music Therapy, Guildhall Sch of Music: *m* 1989, Julian Peter C. Raphael, son of Ven Timothy John Raphael, Archdeacon of Middlesex, and has issue living, Dorothy Clare, *b* 1990.

BROTHER LIVING

Anthony Hungerford (25 Hamilton Gdns, NW8), *b* 1932; *ed* Marlborough; formerly Lt Roy Fusiliers; Korea 1952: *m* 1958, Hon Katharine Margaret Kaldor, el da of late Baron Kaldor (Life Baron), and has issue living, Nicholas Clement, *b* 1967, — Jane Frances, *b* 1962, — Teresa Mary, *b* 1963.

SISTER LIVING

Catherine Mary Trym, *b* 1935: *m* 1967, Sol Picciotto, and has issue living, Anna Rachel, *b* 1968.

COLLATERAL BRANCHES LIVING

Branch from 5th son of 9th baronet

Grandchildren of late Rear-Adm Peyton Hoskyns, CMG, MVO, 5th son of 9th baronet:—
Issue of late Major Oswald Peyton Latham Hoskyns, *b* 1883, *d* 1922: *m* 1913, Evelyn Mary, who *d* 1965, da of Joseph Herbert Blacklock, formerly of Overthorpe House, Banbury:—
Rev John Algernon Peyton (Dinham House, St Minver, Cornwall PL27 6RH) *b* 1920; *ed* Pembroke Coll, Camb (MA); formerly Maj R Signals; *m* 1st, 1944, Ann Veronica, who *d* 1968, da of C. Harrison, of King's Worthy, Winchester; 2ndly, 1970, Andrea Evelyn, who *d* 1991, da of late Adm Sir Henry Bertram Pelly, KCVO, CB (*see* Pelly, Bt, colls); 3rdly, 1995, Joanna, widow of G. Glendinning Wight, and has issue living (by 1st *m*), Oswald Christopher Peyton (Hobbit House, High St, Whitwell, Ventnor, Isle of Wight PO38 2QQ), *b* 1954; Police Inspector, Hants Constabulary: *m* 1990, Julie Anne, da of Gordon Geddes, of 22 Garden Close, Watton, Thetford, Norfolk, and has issue living, Benedict Mungo Peyton *b* 1990, Fergus Oliver McKay *b* 1991, — Rachel Susan, *b* 1946: *m* 1969, S/Ldr Robert Andrew Lund, RAF, of 16 Margerison Rd, Ben Rhydding, Ilkley, W Yorks LS29 8QU, and has issue living, Mark Edward *b* 1973, Suzanne Elizabeth *b* 1977, — Jane Elizabeth Carol, *b* 1947: *m* 1972, Rodney Alexander Sinclair, of Flat 1, 9A Buttle St, Remuera, Auckland, NZ, and has issue living, James Lawrence *b* 1980, Charlotte Ann Hoskyns *b* 1973, Amy Elizabeth *b* 1976, Sarah Jane *b* 1977, — Juliet Ann, *b* 1951: *m* 1973, Ian Richard Doswell, MRIPHH, of The Old Post Office, Shapwick, Blandford Forum, Dorset DT11 9JT, and has issue living, Ewan Rufus *b* 1978, Gwendoline Natasha *b* 1976.

Issue of late Cdr John Walter Hoskyns, RN, *b* 1892, *d* 1980: *m* 1917, Magdalen Rose Wyndham, who *d* 1991, da of late Peter Hawker, of Longparish House, Hants:—
Rosemary Eleanor Peyton (50 Greenway Lane, Bath), *b* 1919; BA (Open Univ): *m* 1949, Maj Geoffrey Nelson Stanton, KOYLI, who *d* 1978, and has issue living, David John Nelson, *b* 1958: *m* 1988, Catharine Mary Crick, and has issue living, Robert Geoffrey Mark *b* 1993, Elizabeth Ruth Eleanor *b* 1990, — Juliet Rose Brailsford, *b* 1952, — Sarah Dorothy Macduff, *b* 1955: *m* 1980, Martin Gordon Walters, of Cambridge, and has issue, three children. —— Zara Stephanie Jardine (c/o Lloyds Bank plc, Cox's & King's Branch, 6 Pall Mall, SW1), *b* 1929; F/O, WRAF (Reserve).

Branch from 6th son of 9th baronet

Grandchildren of late Ven Benedict George Hoskyns, 6th son of 9th baronet:—
Issue of late Lieut-Col Chandos Benedict Arden Hoskyns, *b* 1895, *d* of wounds received in action 1940: *m* 1920, Joyce, who *d* 1979, da of Austin Taylor, of 30 Eccleston Square, SW:—

Sir John Leigh Austin Hungerford (c/o Child & Co, 1 Fleet St, EC4Y 1BD), *b* 1927; formerly Capt Rifle Brig; Head of Prime Minister's Policy Unit 1979-82; Dir-Gen, Inst of Directors 1984-89; *cr* Kt Bach 1982: *m* 1956, Miranda, only da of Tom Mott and has issue living, Barnaby Chandos Tom, *b* 1959: *m* 1990, Victoria S., da of Conrad Sandler, and has issue living, Jake Austin Thomas *b* 1990, Fred Daniel Rufus *b* 1992, Nat Arthur Felix *b* 1996, — Benedict John Hungerford, *b* 1963: *m* 1993, Sally, yr da of C. Hodges, and has issue living, Wilf Oscar Benedict *b* 1997, Chandos Archibald John *b* (twin) 1997, — Benedicta Tamasine Maria, *b* 1961; has issue living, Alice *b* 1996. —— †David Chandos Benedict *b* 1929: *m* 1958, Sheelagh Marion (The Oast House, Wittersham, Kent), da of Hon Sir Patrick Redmond Joseph Barry, and *d* 1996, leaving two adopted children, Simon Chandos, *b* 1965, — Jessica Marion, *b* 1967: *m* 1989, Iain Macdonald Johnston, elder son of late Alan Johnston, of Wickambrook, Suffolk, and has issue living, Archie James *b* 1991, Flora Marion *b* 1992. —— Benedicta Lucia, *b* 1922: *m* 1955 (*m diss* 1989), Richard E. Vernon, actor, who *d* 1997, and has issue living, Thomas Richard Adam, *b* 1958, — Sarah Benedicta, *b* 1956.

Branch from 4th son of 6th baronet

Grandchildren of John Hoskyns (1836-1926), eldest son of Edwyn Bennet Hoskyns (1804-1848), eldest son of John Hoskyns, MD, of Dublin, 4th son of 6th baronet:—
Issue of late William John Hoskyns, *b* 1871, *d* 1948: *m* 1900, Caroline Borer:—
John D. (1804 Kenmore, Grosse Pointe Woods, MI 48236, USA), *b* 1902: *m* 1935, Therese Stascuk, and has had issue, one son (*dec*). —— Marian (3627 Millay, Troy, MI 48083, USA), *b* 1916: *m* 1935, Howard Shirkey, and has issue living, Howard, *b* 1942, — Suzanne, *b* 1936, — Joanne, *b* 1938, — Julianne, *b* 1945, — Christine, *b* 1950.

Issue of late Louis Charles Hoskyns, *b* 1878, *d* 1955: *m* 1930, Irene Beck (*neé* Pease), who *d* 1981:—
Louis C. (II) (Lan Yair Country Club, Box 18161, Spartanburg, S Carolina, USA), *b* 1930: *m* 1952 (*m diss* 1982), Joan Vandermale, and has issue living, Louis C. (III) (125 Starline Drive, Spartanburg, S Carolina 29307, USA), *b* 1964: *m* 1998, Carol Mahaffey, — Mary Jo (1415 Churchill Place, Reston, Virginia 22094, USA), *b* 1952, — Lynn Ann, *b* 1953: *m* 1st, 1973 (*m diss* 1975), Stephen Michael Sentell; 2ndly, 19—, George Chavewski, of 1 Berwick Circle, Charleston, S Carolina 29407, USA, and has issue living (by 1st *m*), Colleen Elizabeth *b* 1974, — Suzanne Arrian (103 Larkspur Lane, Spartanburg, S Carolina 29301, USA), *b* 1960: *m* 1988, Mitchell Paul Peterson. —— Gordon William (1599 14th Av, Boca Raton, Fla 33486, USA), *b* 1933: *m* 1st, 1963 (*m diss* 1974), Mary Lou Foit; 2ndly, 1976, Leah Besch Easton.

Issue of late James Patrick Hoskyns, *b* 1887, *d* 1953: *m* 1st, 1908, Lena Lusk, who *d* 1934; 2ndly, 19—, Jane Doty:—
(By 1st *m*) Alice, *b* 1909: *m* 19—, Martin Frankhouse, and has issue living, Jerrold, *b* 1931. —— Helen, *b* 1912: *m* 19—, Russell Wright, and has issue living, John, *b* 19—, — Janice, *b* 19—. —— (By 2nd *m*) James L., *b* 1935: *m* 19— (*m diss* 19—), Judith McCausland, and has issue living, James T. (11386 Farthing, Sterling Heights, MI 48078, USA), *b* 1957, — Gail E., *b* 1958.

Grandson of late Chandos Hungerford Hoskyns (1838-1929) (infra):—
Issue of late Edwin Allen Hoskyns, *b* 1871, *d* 1960: *m* 1907, Margaret Barton, who *d* 1942:—
Chandos Allen (923N 33W Av, Tulsa, Oklahoma 74127, USA), *b* 1911: *m* 1945, Mildred McPherson.

Grandchildren of late Edwyn Bennet Hoskyns (1804-1848) (ante)·—
Issue of late Chandos Hungerford Hoskyns, *b* 1838, *d* 1929: *m* 1st, 18—, Catherine, da of Ira Morris Allen, MD; 2ndly, 18—, Mary; 3rdly, ca 1901, Mary Anne, who *d* 1954, da of William Hipkiss:—
(By 3rd *m*) Wesley Lucien (19 Linwood Av, Buffalo, NY 14202, USA), *b* 1903: *m* 1st, 1930 (*m diss* 19—), Marjorie Louise, who *d* 1981, da of George Joseph Fix; 2ndly, 19— (*m diss* 19—), Alice Blythe; 3rdly, 19— (*m diss* 19—), Catherine Akester, and has issue living (by 1st *m*), Wesley Francis, *b* 1932: *m* 1958, Caroline Frances Davis, of Idaho, and has issue living, William Anthony *b* 1962: *m* 1986, Susan Patricia Bramhill (and has issue living, Spencer John Chandos *b* 1991, Alexandra Allyce Caroline *b* 1989), Robert Nicholas *b* (twin) 1962: *m* 1985, Nancy Paige Sailors (and has issue living, Wesley Sailors *b* 1987, Cooper Davis (a son) *b* 1988, Brick Carlos *b* 1993), Diane Carole *b* 1960: *m* 1982, Kevin Noble Faulkner (and has issue living, Jonathan Noble *b* 1985, Lisa Marie *b* 1983, Caroline Elizabeth *b* 1992), Nancy Renee *b* 1971: *m* 1992, Thomas Christian Nienstedt, — Joyce Louise, *b* 1933: *m* 1952, Kenneth Lawrence Cooper, and has issue living, Steven Alfonse *b* 1953, Donald Kenneth *b* 1956, Kenneth Lawrence *b* 1958, Michael Joseph *b* 1961: *m* 1991, Cheryl Ann Marquart (and has issue living, Dylan Michael *b* 1993), Thomas William *b* 1964. —— Chandos (Mike) (508 Cayuga Creek Rd, Alden, NY 14004, USA), *b* 1906: *m* 1942, Eleanor Hoskins, and has issue living, Clayton Chandos (303 Broadway, Darien Center, NY 14040, USA), *b* 1949: *m* 1974, Barbara Sobolewski, and has issue living, Sarah Ann *b* 1981, Laura Elizabeth *b* 1985, — Loren Russell (509 Cayuga Creek Rd, Alden, NY 14004, USA), *b* 1951: *m* 1983, Barbara Holtenhoff, and has issue living, Michael Chandos *b* 1983, Caitlyn Elizabeth *b* 1986, — Nancy Elizabeth, *b* 1952: *m* 1970, Michael Paul Noody, and has issue living, Brian Michael *b* 1971, Kevin Paul *b* 1973. —— Lucy Caroline, *b* 1911: *m* 1942, Willard Wakeman English.

Grandsons of late Chandos Hungerford Hoskyns (1838-1929) (ante):—
Issue of late William James Hoskyns, *b* 1908, *d* 1983: *m* 1st, 1934 (*m diss* 1953), Jean Louise McMullen, who *d* 1988; 2ndly, 1959, Margaret Norman:—
(By 1st *m*) William Roy (4819 W Desert Hills Drive, Glendale, Arizona 85304, USA), *b* 1936: *m* 1956, Marilyn Jane Miller, and has issue living, Donald James (10030 N 49th Lane, Glendale, Arizona 85302, USA), *b* 1960: *m* 1st, 1980 (*m diss* 1987), Rika Rundall; 2ndly, 1989, Tamra Garcia, and has issue living (by 1st *m*), Chelsea *b* 1982, Alyssa *b* 1984, (by 2nd *m*) Elayna *b* 1993, — Robert John (adopted son), *b* 1964, — Brenda Jeanne, *b* 1957: *m* 1st, 1975 (*m diss* 1991), Rodney Abbott; 2ndly, 1992, Wade Beauchaine, and has issue living (by 1st *m*), Justin *b* 1986, Stacie Joy *b* 1976, Tina Winifred *b* 1981. —— Leslie Laing (6119 Pine Wood Rd, Oakland, Calif 94611, USA), *b* 1941: *m* 1970 (*m diss* 1974), Stephanie Irene Muth.

Grandson of John Hoskyns (*b* 1827), 4th son of John Hoskyns, MD (ante):—
Issue of late John Hoskyns, *b* 1872, *d* 1963: *m* 1911, Florence May, who *d* 1966, da of Alfred Taylor, of Sydney, NSW:—
Chandos John (29 Woodcroft Av, St Georges, Adelaide, S Australia), *b* 1915: *m* 1938, Harriet Anderson, da of Andrew Anderson Sundquist, of NSW, and has issue living, Max (6 Cumulus Place, Willeton, W Australia 6155), *b* 1940: *m* 1964,

Lottie Jolliffe, of Manilla, NSW, and has issue living, Wayne Gregory *b* 1967, Lena Gay *b* 1965: *m* 1985, John Kraima, Mandy Jane *b* 1969, — Craig (Warners Rd, Upper Hermitage, Houghton, S Australia 5131), *b* 1944: *m* 1962, Beverley Joan Westbrook, of Loxton, S Australia, and has issue living, Joanne Kaye, *b* 1962: *m* 1982, Joseph Anthony Mamone (and has issue living, Rachel *b* 1982, Rebecca *b* 1985), Sharon Julie *b* 1965: *m* 1987, Martin Leigh Goldsworthy, of Loxton, S Australia (and has issue living, Benjamin Nathan *b* 1990), Natalie Ruth *b* 1970, — Paul (20 Morland Av, Stoneyfell, S Australia 5066), *b* 1945: *m* 1969, Deirdre Margaret Saunders, of Adelaide, and has issue living, Andrew John *b* 1970, Elizabeth Anne *b* 1972, Sarah Louise *b* 1974.

Branch from youngest son of 2nd baronet

Grandchildren of late James Hoskyns-Abrahall, 2nd son of late Rev John Charles James Hoskyns-Abrahall, el son of late Rev John Hoskyns-Abrahall (*b* 1773), el son of late Rev John Hoskyns-Abrahall, son of late Rev John Hoskyns-Abrahall (who assumed the additional surname and arms of Abrahall), yst son of 2nd baronet:—
Issue of late Major John Hoskyns Hoskyns-Abrahall, *b* 1864, *d* 1924: *m* 1900, Frances Elizabeth, who *d* 1941, da of late J. H. Vessey, of Halton Manor, Spilsby, Lincolnshire:—
Dorothea Frances, *b* 1916: *m* 1st, 1942 (*m diss* 1962), Charles Robert Gardiner; 2ndly, 1962, Lt-Cdr Alliston Temple Clough Hazledine, RNR, of 61 Regents Park, Exeter EX1 2NZ, and has issue living (by 1st *m*), Christopher Charles, *b* 1942: *m* 1st, 1967, Janet Marie Lack; 2ndly, 1986, Brenda Hebb, and has issue living, (by 1st *m*) Rebekah Jane *b* 1968: *m* 1991, Gerald Cooper (and has issue living, Joseph *b* 1993), Alice Mary *b* 1972, (by 2nd *m*) Claire Christine *b* 1986, — Peter Patrick Fairfax (177 Avenue Louise, 1050 Brussels, Belgium), *b* 1945: *m* 1974, Nicole Adrienne Marie Stalleart, and has issue living, Miles Dexter *b* 1988, — Catherine Juliet, *b* 1944: *m* 1970, Richard Stephen George Sale, Barrister, of 23 Denmark Av, Woodley, Reading, Berks RG5 4RS, and has issue living, George William Alexander *b* 1972, Mary Margaret *b* 1971: *m* 1993, Philip Richards, of Fairseat House, Fairseat, Kent, Juliet Anne *b* 1974, Jessica May Victoria *b* 1977, Fenella Grace Dorothea *b* 1983, Emily Caroline *b* 1985, — Victoria, *b* 1947: *m* 1972, Derrick William Swain, of 2 Englewood Rd, SW12 9NZ, and has issue living, Andrew Charles *b* 1972, Christy-Anne *b* 1974, Naomi Frances *b* 1980.

Issue of late Major Christopher Henry Hoskyns-Abrahall, *b* 1871, *ka* 1915: *m* 1895, Alice Maude Mary, da of — Allen:—
†James, MM, *b* 1897; European War 1914-19 with Australian Forces (wounded, MM): *m* 1923, Minnie Elizabeth Holland, who *d* 1990, of Coolup, WA, and *d* 1967, leaving issue, Christopher Leslie (27 Norman St, Innaloo, W Australia 6018), *b* 1925: *m* 1947, Phyllis Mae Sansome, of Gosnells, WA, and has issue living, Terrence Ross *b* 1954: *m* 1978, Beverley Ann Keeley, of Harvey, WA (and has issue living, Shaun Ross *b* 1981, Adam James *b* 1984), Brian Leslie *b* 1956: *m* 1984, Kerry Nelson, of Balga, WA (and has issue living, Joshua Andrew *b* 1985), Kathleen Elizabeth *b* 1950: *m* 1st, 1970, John Leslie Brewer, of Claremont, WA; 2ndly, 1978, Alan Ronald Dawson, of Carine, WA (and has issue living (by 1st *m*), Michael John *b* 1972, Shelly Anne *b* 1970, (by 2nd *m*) Philip Gregory *b* 1979), Lynette Jean *b* 1953: *m* 1973, Kevin Malcolm Langman, of Dargaville, NZ (now of Port Hedland, WA) (and has issue living, Daniel Graham *b* 1976, Sandra Alice *b* 1978), — Ernest John, *b* 1926: *m* 1948, Margaret Winscom, of Katanning, WA, and has issue living, Ian John *b* 1948, Douglas Frank *b* 1950, Gregory Alan *b* 1955, Mary Pauline *b* 1954, — Colin James, *b* 1927, — Ellen Maude, *b* 1923: *m* 1946, Leslie Charles Limbrick, of Fremantle, WA, and has issue living, Raymond George *b* 1948, Keith Leslie *b* 1950, Kevin Colin *b* 1951, Philip John *b* 1954, — Beatrice Angela, *b* 1930: *m* 1952, Hamilton McCormick, of Gingin, WA, and has issue living, Gary Thomas *b* 1953, Jeffrey David *b* 1954.

Grandchildren of late Bennet Hoskyns-Abrahall, CBE, el son of late Theophilus Bennet Hoskyns-Abrahall, 2nd son of late Rev John Hoskyns-Abrahall (*b* 1773) (ante):—
Issue of Rt Rev Anthony Leigh Egerton Hoskyns-Abrahall, Bishop Suffragan of Lancaster, *b* 1903; *d* 1982: *m* 1937, Margaret Ada, who *d* 1986, da of late F. G. Storey, Bar-at-law, of Sunderland, and sister of late Lord Buckton (ext):—
(John) Benedict Leigh (Earby Hall, Newsham, Richmond, N Yorks), *b* 1939; *ed* St John's Sch, Leatherhead, and RAC Cirencester; FRICS: *m* 1970, Mary Delamain, who *d* 1998, da of late Lt-Col Mansel Jackson, DSO and bar, MC, and has issue living, Bennet Mansel Leigh (140 Stephendale Rd, SW6), *b* 1971; *ed* Eton, and Durham Univ (BA), — (John) Harry Wren, *b* 1975; *ed* Radley, and Durham Univ (BSc), — Edward Anthony Egerton (Bertie), *b* 1977; *ed* Eton, and Newcastle Univ (BSc). —— Anthony David Wren (Lochside House, Yetholm, Kelso, Roxburghshire), *b* 1943; Lt RN (ret): *m* 1965, Phyllis Penrose, yr da of late Rear-Adm William Penrose Mark-Wardlaw, DSO, and has issue living, Mark Egerton Wren (41 West Reluges Rd, The Grange, Edinburgh), *b* 1966: *m* 1992, Fiona J., elder da of Alasdair Gordon, of Chorleywood, Herts, and has issue living, Sam *b* 1996, Elena Daisy Claire *b* 1998, — Sarah Katherine Phyllis, *b* 1971. —— Janet Elizabeth Rosemary, *b* 1938: *m* 1962, Nicholas George Hurry, of 10 Cedars Rd, SW13, and has issue living, Fiona Elizabeth, *b* 1963: *m* 1991, Jeffrey P. Cohen, of 2940 SW 155th Lane, Davie, Florida 33331, USA, and has issue living, Max Egerton *b* 1994, Victoria Rose-Mary *b* 1998, — Victoria Mary, *b* 1967: *m* 1994, Patrick Prendergast, of 1 Rotherwood Rd, Ivanhoe, Melbourne, Vic 3079, Australia, and has issue living, Harry Nicholas *b* 1997, Mollie Elizabeth *b* 1995.

Issue of late (Andrew) John Chandos Hoskyns-Abrahall, *b* 1905; *d* 1978: *m* 1935, Awdey Lorraine, BEM, who *d* 1992, da of Sir Norman Alexander Leslie, KBE:—
John Hungerford Leslie (RD3, Box 3951, Reading, Pa 19606, USA), *b* 1945: *m* 1973, Winifred Scherrer, of Calif, USA, and has issue living, Alexander Philip, *b* 1978, — Megan Selina, *b* 1976. —— Harriet HOSKYNS-ABRAHALL (1025 Lindbergh Drive, Atlanta, Georgia 30324, USA), *b* 1939; legally resumed her maiden name 1989: *m* 1965 (*m diss* 1981), Edward Brendan Lynch, WS, and has issue living, Bahama Leslie Chandos *b* 1977. —— Lucinda, *b* 1940: *m* 1972, Graham de Putron Tardif, of Cranbrook, Kent, and has issue living, Benjamin Charles de Putron, *b* 1972, — Kate Amanda de Putron, *b* 1975, — Lucy Mia de Putron, *b* 1981. —— Amanda (Cedarwood Lane, Carrboro, N Carolina 27510, USA), *b* 1940 (twin): *m* 1972 (*m diss* 1985), Burton K. Fox, and has issue living, Joshua Maxwell, *b* 1976, — Gemma Lorraine, *b* 1979.

Grandchildren of late Sir (Theo) Chandos Hoskyns-Abrahall, CMG, son of late Chandos William Hoskyns-Abrahall, MRCS, 2nd son of late Theophilus Bennet Hoskyns-Abrahall (ante):—
Issue of late Robin Chandos Hoskyns-Abrahall, *b* 1928, *d* 1998: *m* 1st, 1950 (*m diss* 1962), Petronella Elisabeth, da of John E. Cantlon, of co Carlow; 2ndly, 1962, Margaret Angela (63 Cowper Rd, Boxmoor, Hemel Hempstead, Herts HP1 1PF), da of Frank Keggins, of Knowle, Warwicks:—
(By 1st *m*), Scarlett, *b* 1952: *m* 1984 (*m diss* 1997), John Punthöller, of Amsterdam, and has issue living, Theo Alexander, *b* 1990. —— Gail, *b* 1955: *m* 1979, Stephen Brendell, of Jade House, Holme Lacy, Herefordshire HR2 6LJ,

and has issue living, Dominic, *b* 1980, — Rebecca, *b* 1984. —— (By 2nd *m*), Charles Chandos, *b* 1964; *ed* Haileybury; *m* 1997, Teresa Jordano, of Barcelona, Spain.

      Issue of late Follett Peter Hoskyns-Abrahall (actor, as Mark Follett), *b* 1934, *d* 1983: *m* 1960, Carole, da of Edwin Alexander Marks, of Chigwell, Essex:—
Edwin Follett Eden, *b* 1965; *ed* The Leys Sch. —— Emma Clare Elizabeth, *b* 1963.

    The 1st baronet, Sir Bennet, MP for Herefordshire, was son of Serjeant John Hoskyns MP, whose courageous and patriotic eloquence in the House of Commons, *temp* James I, against the encroachments of the Stuart dynasty upon the liberty of Parliament and the people, occasioned his confinement in the Tower, — hence the motto since borne by his descendants. Sir John, 2nd baronet, one of the founders of the Royal Society, succeeded his friend Sir Christopher Wren as President thereof, and received the honour of knighthood. Sir Hungerford, 4th baronet, a distinguished soldier throughout Marlborough's campaigns, was MP for Hereford. The 9th baronet, Rev Sir John Leigh, was R of Aston Tyrrold and Hon Canon of Ch Ch, Oxford. The 12th baronet, Rt Rev Sir Edwyn Hoskyns, DD, Bishop of Burnley (Suffragan for Diocese of Manchester) 1901-4, and Lord Bishop of Southwell 1904-25. The 13th baronet, Rev Sir Edwyn Clement, MC, DD, Chap to Bishop of Derby, Pres, Fellow, Dean and, Librarian of Corpus Christi Coll, Camb, and Hon Canon of Derby Cathedral. The 14th baronet, Sir Chandos Wren, F/O RAF VR, was *k* on flying operations over Norway 1945.

HOULDSWORTH (UK) 1887, of Reddish, Manchester, co Lancaster, and Coodham, Symington, Ayrshire
(Name pronounced "Hoaldsworth")

To be bent, not to be broken

Sir RICHARD THOMAS REGINALD HOULDSWORTH, 5th *Baronet*; *b* 2 Aug 1947; *s* his father, *Lt-Col Sir* REGINALD DOUGLAS HENRY, OBE, TD, 1989; *ed* Bredon Sch, Tewkesbury: *m* 1st, 1970 (*m diss* 1979), Jane, only da of Alistair Orr, of Sydehead, Beith, Ayrshire; 2ndly, 1992, Ann Catherine, eldest da of late Capt Jean Jacques Tremayne, MN, of Sway, Hants, and has issue by 1st and 2nd *m*.

𝕬rms – Ermine, the trunk of a tree in bend raguly eradicated at the base proper, between three foxes' heads erased gules. 𝕮rest – A stag's head erased gules, attired and collared or, the attires banded with a hank of cotton argent.
Residence – Kirkbride, Glenburn, Crosshill, Maybole, Ayrshire.

SONS LIVING (*By 1st marriage*)

SIMON RICHARD HENRY *b* 6 Oct 1971. —— Nicolas Peter George, *b* 1975.

(*By 2nd marriage*)

Matthew James, *b* 1992.

SISTERS LIVING

Myrtle Janet Mary, *b* 1935; *m* 1959, Philip Nicholas Charles Howard, of 47 Ladbroke Grove, W11 3AR, and has issue living, John Henry Nicholas (76 Cobbold Rd, W12), *b* 1961: *m* 1994, Judy, da of late John Heffernan, of Memphis, Tennessee, USA, — James Reginald Mark, *b* 1976, — Juliette Margaret, *b* 1960: *m* 1988, Justin Henry Francis Whiteley, yr son of Peter John Henry Whiteley (*see* E Guilford). —— Rosemary Margaret, *b* 1939: *m* 1962 (*m diss* 1990), (William) John Tevenar Usher (later Sir John Usher, 7th Bt), who *d* 1998, and has issue (*see* Usher, Bt).

UNCLE LIVING (*son of 3rd Baronet*)

Walter William Whitmore, TD, *b* 1906; Major (ret) Sherwood Foresters, served 1939-45 War (despatches): *m* 1945, Hazell Marcella, da of late J. P. Shepherd, of Barbados, and has issue living, Charles William Shepherd (Hailey House, Duntisbourne Abbots, Cirencester, Glos GL7 7JL), *b* 1946: *m* 1971, Jacqueline, only da of Paul Smith, of Biddestone, Wilts, and has issue living, Zoë Anne *b* 1974, Joanna Clare *b* 1976, — Hazell Mary Fiona, *b* 1954. *Residence* – The Fold, Sheep St, Stow-on-the-Wold, Glos GL54 7JL. *Club* – Caledonian.

    The 1st baronet, Sir William Henry Houldsworth, sat as MP for Manchester (C) 1883-5, and for N-W Div of Manchester 1885-1906. The 3rd baronet, Sir William Thomas Reginald, Houldsworth, CBE, TD, was Hon Col Ayrshire Yeo (Lieut-Col Comdg 1923).

HOULDSWORTH (UK) 1956, of Heckmondwike, West Riding of Yorkshire (Extinct 1990)

Sir (HAROLD) BASIL HOULDSWORTH, 2nd and last *Baronet*.

DAUGHTER LIVING OF SECOND AND LAST BARONET

(Sarah) Belinda Clifford, *b* 1949.

Houstoun-Boswall, see Boswall.

HOWARD (UK) 1955, of Great Rissington, co Gloucester

Sir (HAMILTON) EDWARD DE COUCEY HOWARD, GBE, 2nd *Baronet*; *b* 29 Oct 1915; *s* his father *Sir* (HAROLD WALTER) SEYMOUR 1967; *ed* Radley, and Worcester Coll, Oxford; Hon DSc, London; Lord Mayor of London 1971-72; HM Lieut for City of London; an Alderman of City of London; Chm of the firm of Charles Stanley & Co Ltd, Stockbroker; a Liveryman of Gardeners' Co (Master 1961-62); 1939-45 War as F/O RAF (despatches); GBE (Civil) 1972: *m* 1943, Elizabeth Howarth, da of late Maj Percy H. Ludlow, and has issue.

Arms – Azure, two wings conjoined in lure and in chief as many cross-crosslets fitchée or, a chief of the last thereon between two leaves of the india rubber tree proper a pale vert charged with a bezant. **Crest** – A toucan holding in the dexter claw and feeding on an apple slipped and leaved all proper.
Residence – Courtlands, Bishops Walk, Shirley Hills, Surrey CR0 5BA. *Clubs* – City Livery, City of London.

SONS LIVING

DAVID HOWARTH SEYMOUR (25 Luke St, EC2), *b* 29 Dec 1945; *ed* Radley, and Worcester Coll, Oxford (MA); an Alderman of the City of London; Man Dir Charles Stanley & Co Ltd, Stockbroker, and Liveryman of Gardeners' Co (Master 1990-91): *m* 1968, Valerie Picton, only da of late Derek Weatherly Crosse, of Chase House, Callis Court Rd, Broadstairs, and has issue living, Robert Picton Seymour, *b* 28 Jan 1971, — James Picton Seymour, *b* 1979, — Caroline Picton Seymour, *b* 1970, — Victoria Picton Seymour, *b* 1975. —— John Ludlow Seymour, *b* 1948; *ed* Grenville Coll, Devon: *m* 1983, Virginia Margaret, only da of Richard J. Purkis, of Shirley, Surrey, and has issue living, Rupert, *b* 1988, — Emily, *b* 1990, — Harriet Elizabeth, *b* 1993.

COLLATERAL BRANCH LIVING

Issue of late David Seymour de Coucey Howard, yr son of 1st baronet, *b* 1919, *d* 1954: *m* 1942 (*m diss* 1949), Jean McMurdo, da of late Thomas McMurdo Heywood:—
Jennifer Anne de Coucey, *b* 1945.

Hudson-Kinahan, see Kinahan.

HUGHES (GB) 1773, of East Bergholt, Suffolk

Sir DAVID COLLINGWOOD HUGHES, 14th *Baronet*; *b* 29 Dec 1936; *s* his father, *Sir* RICHARD EDGAR 1970; *ed* Oundle and Magdalene Coll, Camb (MA): *m* 1964, Rosemary Ann (DL Cambs 1997), only da of late Rev John Pain, and has had issue.

𝕬rms – Quarterly, 1st azure, a lion rampant or, *Hughes*; 2nd gules, a lion rampant reguardant or, *Elistan Glodrydd*; 3rd, azure, three crowns in pale or, *Beli Mawr*; 4th, per bend sinister ermine and ermines, a lion rampant or, *Tudor Trevor*; 5th, or, a lion rampant reguardant sable, *Gwaeth Voyd*; 6th, per pale azure and sable, three fleur-de-lis or, *Ynyr, King of Gwent*; 7th, sable, a chevron between three goats' heads erased or, *Ithel Velyn;* 8th, azure, a lion cowed passant guardant or, *Llewellyn Aur Dorchog.*
Residence – The Berristead, Wilburton, Ely, Cambs.

SONS LIVING AND DECEASED

THOMAS COLLINGWOOD, *b* 16 Feb 1966; MRCP, FRCS: *m* 1996, Marina Louise, DPhil, MRCP, FRACP, da of Richard Barbour, of Albany, Western Australia. —— Timothy John Pell, *b* 1968. —— Benjamin Richard, *b* 1969. —— †Anthony George David, *b* 1972; *d* in a road accident 1991.

SISTER LIVING

Elizabeth Barbara, *b* 1933: *m* 1964, Paul Ronald Scott Lever, 33 Wimpole St, W1, and has issue living, Christopher Mark, *b* 1965: *m* 1989, Susan Elizabeth Mullin, and has issue living, James Richard *b* 1993, — Alison Clare, *b* 1967, — Catherine Elizabeth, *b* 1969: *m* 1995, Andrew Bradley.

COLLATERAL BRANCHES LIVING

Issue of late Cdr Alfred Marcus Hughes, OBE, RN, brother of 13th baronet, *b* 1900, *d* 19—: *m* 1934, Hope Frances, who *d* 19—, da of late Arthur George Pritchard:—
Pamela Mary, *b* 1939: *m* 1965, Col Colin Humphrey Cowley Howgill, ret, of 1020 Bal Harbour Drive, Apollo Beach, Florida 33572, USA, and has issue living, Michael Colin, *b* 1968, — David Charles, *b* 1970, — Susan Rosemary, *b* 1967.

Issue of late Capt Charles Collingwood Hughes, brother of 13th baronet, *b* 1907, *d* 1997: *m* 1937, Sheila Dorothea, who *d* 1998, da of late Col Walter Henry Patrick Law, DSO (*see* Brooke, Bt, *cr* 1919, 1948 Edn):—
Peter Collingwood (32 Inkerman Rd, NW5 3BT), *b* 1943; *ed* Oundle, and Pomfret Sch, Conn, USA: *m* 1965 (*m diss* 1989), Susan Elizabeth Ann Cubitt, and has issue living, Natasha Sarah, *b* 1967: *m* 1989, Richard Gray, and has issue living, Louis *b* 1995, Francesca *b* 1994, — Kate, *b* 1970, — Victoria, *b* 1972.

Grandchildren of late Arthur Hughes, eldest son of late Arthur Hughes (*b* 1836), 3rd son of William Hughes, Barrister-at-law, 4th son (2nd by 2nd *m*) of 3rd baronet:—
Issue of late Richard Arthur Warren Hughes, OBE, *b* 1900, *d* 1976: *m* (Jan) 1932, Frances Catharine Ruth, who *d* 1985, da of late Gardner Sebastian Bazley (*see* Bazley, Bt):—
Rev Robert Elyston-Glodrydd (Clogwyn Melyn, Talsarnau, Gwynedd LL47 6TP), *b* 1932; *ed* Trin Coll, Oxford (MA); M Litt, Birmingham Univ: *m* 1960, Sheila Basketts, and has issue living, Claire Frances Rosemary, *b* 1961, — Rachel Catherine, *b* 1964. —— Owain Gardner Collingwood, *b* 1943. —— Penelope, *b* 1934; *ed* Somerville Coll, Oxford (MA): *m* 1958, Robin Paul Minney, and has issue living, Thomas, *b* 1960, — Hugo Benjamin Paulus, *b* 1962, — James, *b* 1963, — Richard, *b* 1967. —— Lleky Susannah, *b* 1936: *m* 19—, Stavros J. Papastavrou, MA, who *d* 19—, and has issue living, Vassili Alexander Dimitri, *b* 1960. —— Catherine Phyllida, *b* 1940: *m* 1960, Colin Michael Wells, of 39 Charles St, Ottawa, Canada, and has issue living, Christopher William Llewellyn, *b* 1961, — Dominic Richard Alexander, *b* 1963.

Grandchildren of late Arthur Hughes (*b* 1836) (ante):—
Issue of late Alfred Collingwood Hughes, *b* 1864, *d* 1915: *m* 1897, Ada Mary, who *d* 1940, da of Edmond Drage:—
Stanley Collingwood, *b* 1903. —— Jack Collingwood, *b* (twin) 1903. —— Harry Leonard Collingwood, *b* 1906: *m* 19—, Pamela Phillips, and has issue living, a son, *b* 1943.

Issue of late Robert Hughes, *b* 1870, *d* 1929: *m* 1900, Ella Fanny, who *d* 1953, da of Frederick Boldero:—
Robert Bernard (26 Calle Buen Aire, 3rd Piso B, Minorca, Spain), *b* 1906. —— Margaret Rosemary (Residencia de Ancianos, Calle J. Anselmo Clave 7, Mahon 07703, Minorca, Spain), *b* 1909: *m* 1938 (*m diss* 1976), John Hannaford; 2ndly, 1979, William Woodward, who *d* 1991.

Granddaughter of late Capt John William St John Hughes, 5th son of 8th baronet:—
Issue of late Major Frederick St John Hughes, MVO, OBE, *b* 1866, *d* 1956: *m* 1908, Mabel, who *d* 1965, da of late David Evans, of Ffrwdgrech, Breconshire:—
April Mary (Ivy Cottage, Sprayton, Crediton, Devon), *b* 1913: *m* 1939, Gp Capt Hugh Smeddle, DFC, and has had issue, Robert Adam Hughes, *b* 1948: *m* 1st, 1972 (*m diss* 1982), Sarah Anne, da of late Maj Ernest Gerald Howarth, MBE (*see* E Meath); 2ndly, 1988, Daryl Anne, da of Maj R. E. Brookes, of West Hill Farm, Okehampton, and has issue living, (by

1st *m*) William Robert *b* 1976, Vanessa Mary *b* 1974, (by 2nd *m*) Samuel Edward *b* 1988, Lucy Susan *b* 1990, — Susan Ostara Mary, *b* 1947, *d* in a motor accident 1967, while on a Durham Univ expdn to India.

This ancient family, according to the College of Arms, is descended from Elistan Glodrydh, Earl of Hereford (*b* 933). The 1st baronet, Capt Sir Richard Hughes, RN, when Commissioner of Portsmouth Dockyard (1773), entertained George III. Sir Richard, the 2nd baronet, Adm of the Red, was second in command under Lord Howe at the relief of Gibralter; he also captured the "Solitaire," and gained victory against the French off Barbados 1782. The 10th baronet Sir (Alfred) Collingwood Hughes, served during European War 1914-18, as Major 4th Vol Batn Suffolk Regt (despatches), and was High Sheriff of Suffolk 1923-4.

Hughes-Hunter, see Hunter.

HULSE (GB) 1739, of Lincoln's Inn Fields

To be rather than to seem

Sir EDWARD JEREMY WESTROW HULSE, 10th *Baronet*; *b* 22 Nov 1932; *s* his father, *Wing-Cdr Sir* (HAMILTON) WESTROW, 1996; *ed* Eton, and RMA Sandhurst; late Capt Scots Gds; High Sheriff Hants 1978, DL 1989: *m* 1957, (Sylvia) Verity Ann, only child of William Lee Pilkington, of Ivywell, Routes des Issues, St John, Jersey, and has issue.

𝕬rms – Per fesse argent and ermine, three piles, one issuing from the chief, between the others reversed, sable. 𝕮rest – A buck's head couped proper attired or, charged on the neck with a place surmounted by two bezants; between the attires a sun of the last.
Residence – Breamore House, Fordingbridge, Hants SP6 2DF. *Club* – White's.

SON LIVING

(EDWARD) MICHAEL WESTROW, *b* 10 Sept 1959; *ed* Eton, and RAC Cirencester: *m* 1986, Doone Anne, da of Iain Brotherton, of London, and has issue living, Edward Westrow William, *b* 4 March 1993, — Samuel Arthur Michael, *b* 1995, — Matthew Jack Hamilton, *b* 1998, — Venetia, *b* 1987, — Roseanne, *b* 1989, — Natasha, *b* 1990.

DAUGHTER LIVING

Camilla Ann, *b* 1962: *m* 1991, (Maurizio) Luca Corona, son of Giuseppe Corona, of 36 Via Poerio, Milan, and has issue living, Alexander Tenzin, *b* 1991. *Address* – PO Box 7003, Kathmandou, Nepal.

BROTHER LIVING

Richard Arthur Samuel, *b* 1936; *ed* Eton; late 2nd Lieut Scots Gds: *m* 1963, Caroline Susan Joan, da of Lt-Col Sir George David Elliott Tapps Gervis Meyrick, 6th Bt, MC, and has issue living, George Richard, *b* 1967; *ed* Harrow, and St Andrews Univ, — Frances Caroline Jacintha, *b* 1968: *m* 1996, Guy Martin Carne Rasch (*see* Rasch, Bt). *Residence* – The Old Chapel, Netton, Salisbury SP4 6AW.

WIDOW LIVING OF NINTH BARONET

LUCY ELIZABETH SMITHEYT (*Elizabeth, Lady Hulse*), elder da of late Col George Redesdale Brooker Spain, CMG, TD, FSA, of 7 Tankerville Place, Newcastle-upon-Tyne: *m* 1954, as his 4th wife, Wing-Cdr Sir (Hamilton) Westrow Hulse, 9th Bt, who *d* 1996. *Residence* – Cross Trees, Breamore, Fordingbridge, Hants SP6 2BU.

This family descends from the Hulses of Norbury, Cheshire, and has common origin with the Holles Earls of Clare, of whom the 4th and last Earl was *cr* Duke of Newcastle (*cr* 1694, ext 1711), when his Holles estates were devised to his nephew, Thomas Pelham who was *cr* Duke of Newcastle 1715. The 1st baronet was Physician to Queen Anne, and to Kings George I and George II.

HULTON (UK) 1905, of Hulton Park, Parish of Deane, and co Palatine of Lancaster (Extinct 1993)

Sir GEOFFREY ALAN HULTON, 4th and last *Baronet.*

SISTER LIVING OF FOURTH BARONET

Barbara Joan, *b* 1921; formerly Junior Com ATS: *m* 1945, Capt John Edward Vincent Butterfield, Duke of Wellington's Regt, only son of late Lt-Col Edward Butterfield, DSO, of Bexhill-on-Sea, Sussex, and has issue living, Hugh Alan John, *b* 1946; *ed* Wellington, — Neil Roger, *b* 1949; *ed* Wellington, — Gillian Diana, *b* 1955. *Residence* – Borden House, off West St, Alresford, Hants SO24 9AU.

Hume-Campbell, see Campbell.

Hume-Williams, see Williams.

Hunter Blair, see Blair.

Huntington-Whiteley, see Whiteley.

HUTCHISON (UK) 1923, of Hardiston, co Kinross (Extinct 1972)

Sir ERIC ALEXANDER OGILVY HUTCHISON, 2nd and last *Baronet.*

DAUGHTERS LIVING OF SECOND BARONET (*By 1st marriage*)

Morna, *b* 1925: *m* 1st, 1947, Desmond Berry, who *d* 19—; 2ndly, 19—, James Lang, and has issue living (by 1st *m*), Bruce Graham, *b* 1948, — Michael John, *b* 1950, — Patricia Fayrer, *b* 1949, — Morna Lilian, *b* 1952, — Marian Loraine, *b* (twin) 1952. —— Sheila, *b* 1926: *m* 1956 (*m diss* 1985), Eric Alexander Masterton Wood, MB, ChB, MRCP, MRCPE, DPM, who *d* 19—, and has issue living, Jonathan Paul Masterton, *b* 1958, — Christopher Malcolm Fayrer, *b* 1962, — Alastair Graham Spens, *b* 1964, — Jeremy Douglas, *b* 1966. —— Patricia, *b* 1928: *m* 1st, 1950 (*m diss* 1954), Julian St Leger (*see* B Bagot, colls, 1990 Edn); 2ndly, 1955, Michael Cain, FRIBA, and has issue living, (by 1st *m*), Harriet Claire, *b* 1951, — (by 2nd *m*) Sebastian, *b* 1957, — Marius, *b* 1958, — Benedict, *b* 1960. *Residence* – 3 Rosemont Rd, Richmond, Surrey.

Jane Moir Ogilvy, *b* 1958.

HUTCHISON (UK) 1939, of Thurle, Streatley, co Berks

Sir ROBERT HUTCHISON, 3rd *Baronet*; 25 May 1954; *s* his father, *Sir* PETER, 1998; *ed* Marlborough: *m* 1987, Anne Margaret, elder da of Sir (Godfrey) Michael David Thomas, 11th Bt (*cr* 1694), and has issue.
Residence – Hawthorn Cottage, Lower Rd, Grundisburgh, Suffolk IP13 6UQ.

SONS LIVING

HUGO THOMAS ALEXANDER, *b* 16 April 1988. —— Guy Piers Giles, *b* 1990.

BROTHER LIVING

Mark Seymour, *b* 1960: *m* 1997, Sarah E. L., el da of John Nicholson, of Waltham St Lawrence, Berks, and has issue living, Freddie Peter, *b* 1997. *Residence* – Mulberry House, East Lane, Chieveley, Berks RG20 8UZ.

SISTERS LIVING

Elspeth, *b* 1950: *m* 1975, John Richard Feneran Bryers, son of late Brig R. H. C. Bryers, of The Old Hall, Kilnwick, Driffield, Yorks, YO25 9JG, and has issue living, Henry Peter Newman, *b* 1977, — George Richard Timothy, *b* 1983, — Charlotte Emily, *b* 1979. —— Alison Margaret, *b* 1951: *m* 1990, Peter Brendon Wintgens, of 5 Beechmore Rd, SW11 4ET, elder son of late Leonard Wintgens.

UNCLE LIVING (*son of 1st baronet*)

Michael Duncan, *b* 1912; *ed* Eton, and Magdalen Coll, Oxford: *m* 1945, Margery Betty Martin, who *d* 1998, and has issue living, Paul Michael, *b* 1959, — Sara Laetitia, *b* 1949, — Margaret Ann, *b* 1953. *Residence* – 1 Brooklands Court, 35 Brooklands Av, Cambridge CB2 2BP.

WIDOW LIVING OF SECOND BARONET

MARY-GRACE (*Mary-Grace, Lady Hutchison*), MBE, da of Very Rev Algernon Giles Seymour (*see* Culme-Seymour, Bt, colls): *m* 1949, Sir Peter Hutchison, 2nd Bt, who *d* 1998. *Residence* – Melton Mead, nr Woodbridge, Suffolk IP12 1PF.

The 1st baronet, Sir Robert Hutchison, MD, CM (son of Robert Hutchison, of Carlowrie, Kirkliston) was Pres of Roy So of Med 1934-6, and of Roy Coll of Physicians 1938-41.

HUTCHISON (UK) 1956, of Rossie, co Perth

Sir PETER CRAFT HUTCHISON, CBE, 2nd *Baronet*; *b* 5 June 1935; *s* his father, *Sir* JAMES RILEY HOLT, DSO, TD, 1979; *ed* Eton, and Magdalene Coll, Camb (BA); Lt late R Scots Greys; Chm of Hutchison & Craft Ltd, insurance brokers, Glasgow, and sometime Chm Board of Trustees Royal Botanical Gardens, Edinburgh; Vice-Chm British Waterways Board, and Board Memb Scottish National Heritage; Chm Forestry Commn since 1994; CBE (Civil) 1992; FRSE 1997; *m* 1966, Virginia, da of late John Millar Colville, of Gribloch, Kippen, Stirlingshire, and has issue.

Arms – Argent, an arrow fessways vert, feathered gules and barbed or, between two lymphads vert, sails furled gules, in chief, and a parachute azure, stringed vert and ringed or, in base; in dexter chief the canton of a Baronet of the United Kingdom. Crest – A parachute as in the arms, the ring transversed of an arrow fessways also as in the arms.
Residences – Broich, Kippen, Stirlingshire FK8 3EN; 32 Moore St, SW3. *Club* – Cavalry and Guards', Western (Glasgow).

SON LIVING

JAMES COLVILLE, *b* 7 Oct 1967: *m* 1996, Jane F. E., da of Peter Laidlaw, of Edinburgh, and has issue living, Harry Leo Peter, *b* 23 Aug 1998.

Imbert-Terry, see Terry.

INGILBY (UK) 1866, of Ripley Castle, Yorkshire.

My right

Sir THOMAS COLVIN WILLIAM INGILBY, 6th *Baronet*; *b* 17 July 1955; *s* his father *Maj Sir* JOSLAN WILLIAM VIVIAN, 1974; *ed* Eton, and Royal Agric Coll, Cirencester; ARICS 1982; CAAV 1983: *m* 1984, Emma Clare Roebuck, da of Maj Richard R. Thompson, of Whinfield, Strensall, York, and has issue.

Arms – Sable, an estoile argent within a bordure engrailed gobony or and gules. Crest – A boar's head couped and erect argent, tusked or, in the mouth an estoile of the last.
Seat – Ripley Castle, Harrogate, N Yorkshire HG3 3AY.

SONS LIVING

JAMES WILLIAM FRANCIS, *b* 15 June 1985. —— Joslan Richard Ryland, *b* 1986. —— Jack Henry Thomas, *b* 1990. —— Richard Joseph Frederick, *b* 1994.

DAUGHTER LIVING

Eleanor Jane Pamela, *b* 1989.

SISTERS LIVING

Caroline Diana Colvin, *b* 1949: *m* 1986, David Francis Wakefield, eldest son of late F.H. Wakefield, of Ogston Hall, Higham, Derbyshire. —— Katherine Benita Colvin, *b* 1951: *m* 1974, Richard Denis Kingsmill Wallace, and has issue living, Sally Diana, *b* 1981.

WIDOW LIVING OF FIFTH BARONET

DIANA (*Diana, Lady Ingilby*) (Ripley Castle, Harrogate, Yorks), da of late Brig-Gen Sir George Lethbridge Colvin, CB, CMG, DSO: *m* 1948, Maj Sir Joslan William Vivian Ingilby, 5th Bt, who *d* 1974.

COLLATERAL BRANCH LIVING

Issue of late Lt-Col John Uchtred Macdowall Ingilby, OBE, brother of 4th baronet, *b* 1874, *d* 1948: *m* 1904, Marjorie Cecily, MBE, who *d* 1957, el da of late William Robert Phelips, of Montacute House, Stoke-under-Ham:—
Joan Alicia, MBE, *b* 1911; MBE (Civil) 1997. *Residence* – Coleshouse, Askrigg, Leyburn, Yorks DL8 3HH.

This family, of great antiquity, has been seated at Ripley Castle since *temp* Edward III, and has three times received the honour of a baronetcy. Sir William Ingilby, of Ripley, was created a baronet in 1642, which baronetcy became ext in 1772, on the death of his gt-grandson, Sir John Ingilby, 4th Bt. In 1781, John Ingilby, natural son of the 4th Bt, who inherited his estates was *cr* a baronet. This title became ext in 1854 on the death of his son, Sir William Amcotts-Ingilby, 2nd Bt (who also inherited, by special remainder in 1805, the baronetcy conferred in 1796 upon his maternal grandfather, Sir Wharton Amcotts). Sir Henry John Ingilby, of Ripley, 1st Bt of the third creation in 1866 was eldest son of the Rev Henry Ingilby, brother of the 1st Bt of the second creation (1781) and succeeded by devise to the family estates.

<h1 style="text-align:center">Inglefield-Watson, see Watson.</h1>

INGLIS (NS) 1703, of Glencorse, Midlothian (formerly Mackenzie of Gairloch, Ross-shire)
(Name pronounced "Ingles")

Sir RODERICK JOHN INGLIS OF GLENCORSE, 10th *Baronet*; *b* 25 Jan 1936; *s* his father, Sir MAXWELL IAN HECTOR, 1974; *ed* Winchester and Edinburgh Univ (MB, ChB): *m* 1st, 1960 (*m diss* 1975), Rachel Evelyn, da of Lt-Col N. M. Morris, of Dowdstown, Ardee, co Louth; 2ndly, 1975 (*m diss* 1977), Geraldine, yr da of R. H. Kirk, of Thaxted, Essex; 3rdly, 1986, Marilyn, da of A.L. Irwin, of Glasgow, and has issue by 1st, 2nd and 3rd *m*.

Arms – Azure, a lion rampant argent, armed and langued gules, on a chief of the second three mullets sable. **Crest** – A demi-lion as in the arms, holding in his dexter fore-paw a mullet argent.
Residence – 18 Cordwalles Rd, Pietermaritzburg, Natal, S Africa 3201. *Club* – Country, Pietermaritzburg.

SONS LIVING *(By 1st marriage)*

IAN RICHARD, *b* 1965. —— Alexander Colin, *b* (twin) 1965.

(By 3rd marriage)

Harry Mackenzie, *b* 1987.

DAUGHTERS LIVING *(By 1st marriage)*

Amanda Fiona, *b* 1963.

(By 2nd marriage)

Harriet, *b* 1977.

COLLATERAL BRANCHES LIVING

Grandchildren of late Lt-Col Harry Maxwell Mackenzie, RA, grandson of 4th baronet:—
Issue of late Engineer-Com Harry Ponsonby MACKENZIE, RN (ret), *b* 1877, *d* 1948: *m* 1915, Gladys Dalziel, who *d* 1966, yr da of late William Weatherly, of Woolongoon, Mortlake, Victoria, Australia:—
Alastair John, *b* 1922; formerly Lt Roy Austn Naval VR; 1939-45 War (despatches twice): *m* 1955, Isabel Anne, da of late Capt Andrew Kelt, RAMC, of Pickdick, Brede, Sussex, and has issue living, Roderick John Andrew, *b* 1962, — Kythé Jane, *b* 1956: *m* 1978 (*m diss* 1982), Francis Gurry, — Iona Margaret, *b* 1957, — Mairi Anne, *b* 1959, — Margaret Isabel Alexandra, *b* 1970. *Residence* – Hillside, Ararat, Vic, Aust. —— Kenneth William, *b* 1928: *m* 1962, Jennifer Margaret, only da of late Col Patrick Hyde, OBE, and has issue living, Caroline Margaret, *b* 1963, — Elizabeth Georgina, *b* 1965, — Fiona Jennifer, *b* 1970. *Residence* – Trawalla, Vic, Aust.

Issue of late Colin Rae MACKENZIE, b 1887, d 1973: m 1913, Nora Constance, da of late Herbert Guernsey, of Victoria, BC, Canada:—
Margaret Elaine (Grianach, Lettock, N Kessoch, Inverness-shire), b 1914: m 1st, 1937 (m diss 1958), Gerald Ashby Wodehouse Garland, who d 1965; 2ndly, 1958, C. R. Cuthbert (dec), and has issue living, (by 1st m) Angela Robin, b 1938, — Jennifer Sara, b 1942: m 1965, Edward John Roberts, and has issue living, Benjamin Alexander b 1966, Nicholas Justin b 1967, William Wayland b 1970. —— Nora Kythé b 1917; 1939-45 War as Section Officer WRCAF: m 1944, Capt Victor Browne, RCN, of 9 Seagate, 10110 3rd St, Sidney, BC V8L 3B3, Canada, and has issue living, Colin Victor Alleyne, b 1946, — Susan Kythé, b 1949. —— Christine Ponsonby, b 1928: m 1953 (m diss 19—), Adrian C. Boehme, and has issue living, Justin Christian, b 1959, — Nicholas Christian, b 1962, — Anna Kythé, b 1958.

Grandchildren of late Marjory Kythé (Lady Stirling of Fairburn), only da of 7th baronet:—
Issue of late Marjory Charlotte Mackenzie of Gairloch (s to the baronial estate of Gairloch on the death of her uncle, Sir Hector David Mackenzie, 8th Bt), and, with her husband, was recognized in the surname of Mackenzie of Gairloch by decree of Lyon Court 1959, b 1920, d 1988: m 1941, Brig William Alexander Mackenzie of Gairloch (formerly Stevenson), DSO, OBE, late Queen's Own Cameron Highrs, who d 1982:—
John Alexander MACKENZIE OF GAIRLOCH (Conan House, Conan Bridge, Ross-shire; c/o Glyn Mills & Co, Holt's Branch, Kirkland House, Whitehall, SW1), b 1944; late 2nd Lieut Queen's Own Highrs: m 1969, Marian, da of late Col E. Seabourne Williams. —— Andrew James, b 1949. —— James, b 1957. —— Alexandra Mary, b 1941: m 1962, Andrew Gray Muir (see Montgomery, Bt, colls, 1976 Edn), of Sundial, Gilmerton, Edinburgh 9, and has issue living, William John, b 1966, — Elizabeth Kythé, b 1963: m 1990, Archibald Stirling, yr of Garden, of Drumerchin, Kippen, nr Stirling FK8 3EZ, and has issue living James Andrew b 1999, Amy Sophia Marjory b 1993, Katrina Kythé b 1994. —— Sara Marjory, b 1945: m 1967, James MacAlpine Gregor Grant, of Roskill House, Munlochy, Ross-shire (see Arbuthnot, Bt, cr 1823, colls, 1909 Edn), and has issue living, Annabel Elizabeth, b 1968, — Clare Marjory, b 1970: m 1996, Rupert Lumsden, and has issue living, Anastasia Poppy b 1997, Georgiana Zinnia b 1998, — Lucy Sara, b 1975.

Kenneth Mackenzie, created a Baronet of Nova Scotia 1703, was son of Alexander Mackenzie, 7th of Gairloch, and sat as MP for Ross-shire 1702. Sir Kenneth John Mackenzie, 7th Bt, was King's and Lord Treasurer's Remembrancer for Scotland 1900-21, and a Scottish Ecclesiastical Commr 1925-9. On the death in 1958 of the 8th baronet, Sir Hector Mackenzie, MC, Lord-Lt of Ross-shire, the baronial estate of Gairloch, held from 1476, devolved on his niece, Marjory Charlotte Stirling, Mrs Stevenson, as Mrs Mackenzie, 15th of Gairloch, whilst the baronetcy passed to the heir male as Sir Maxwell Ian Hector Inglis of Glencorse, 9th Bt, under this name and designation, pursuant to the entail of the Rt Hon John Inglis, Lord Glencorse, Lord Justice-General of Scotland. Sir Maxwell was son of Hector Ian Maxwell Mackenzie-Inglis of Glencorse (who both assumed 1929 the additional surname of Inglis of Glencorse), son of Lt-Col Harry Maxwell Mackenzie, RA, son of John Mackenzie, 4th son of 4th Bt. In 1958 Sir Maxwell was recognized by decree of Lyon Court in the surname of Inglis of Glencorse. He was in Political Ser Gold Coast 1928-37, and Lord Lt of Midlothian 1964-72.

INGRAM (UK) 1893, of Swineshead Abbey, Lincolnshire.

In hoc signo vinces

Under this sign you
shall conquer

Sir JAMES HERBERT CHARLES INGRAM, 4th Baronet; b 6 May 1966; s his grandfather, Sir HERBERT, 1980; ed Eton, and Cardiff Univ: m 1998, Aracea Elizabeth, da of Graham Pearce, of Brampton, Cambs.

Arms – Quarterly, argent and or, gutée de poix, on a fesse invected gules four escallops of the second. Crest – On a rock proper, issuant from a wreath of cinquefoils or, a griffin's head erased quarterly gules and argent, charged on the neck with an escallop countercharged.
Residence – 8 Lochaline St, W6 9SH.

HALF-BROTHER LIVING

NICHOLAS DAVID, b 12 June 1975; ed Stowe, and RAC Cirencester.

SISTER LIVING

Frances Jane, b 1964.

HALF-SISTER LIVING

Caroline Robin, b 1979.

AUNTS LIVING (Daughters of 3rd baronet)

Marion Judith, b 1937: m 1969, Graham H. Harvey-Evers, and has issue living, Charles James Herbert, b 1970, — David Edward Herbert, b 1971. Address – PO Box 393, Britannia Place, St Helier, Jersey JE4 8US. —— Vivian Helen, b (twin) 1937: m 1963, Oliver Turnbull, of The Old Vicarage, Wickham Market, Woodbridge, Suffolk (see E Stamford, 1990 Edn), and has issue living, Harry Jonathan Peveril, b 1971: m 19—, Sarah Robbins, and has issue living, Holly Elizabeth Amy b 1995, — Jane Lucy, b 1965: m 1991, Charles Waddington, and has issue living, Toby George b 1993, Nicholas James b 1996, — Clare Catherine, b 1966: m 1990, Edward Barham, and has issue living, George Wilfrid b 1994, Emily Catherine *b* 1993, Helena Jane *b* 1997, — Sarah Mary, *b* 1968. —— Anne Carolyn, *b* 1952: *m* 1974, Alan C. Weston Peck, of Hurst Lodge, nr Twyford, Berks, and has issue living, Alexander Robin, *b* 1981, — Frances Miranda, *b* 1978.

GREAT UNCLE LIVING *(Son of 2nd baronet)*

Michael Warren, OBE, *b* 1917; *ed* Winchester, and Balliol Coll, Oxford (BA 1945); a JP and DL for Glos, Maj late Gren Gds; OBE (Civil) 1986: *m* 1944, Auriol Blanche, el da of late Lt-Gen Sir Arthur Francis Smith, KCB, KBE, DSO, MC (*see* E Kintore, colls), and has issue living, Andrew David Michael (30 King Henry's Rd, NW3 3RP), *b* 1945: *m* 1969, Carole Letitia, da of Maj John David Summers, of Marsh Cottage, Old Romney, Romney Marsh, Kent, and has issue living, Matthew William Michael *b* 1971, Toby David Warren *b* 1972, — Susan Elizabeth, *b* 1947: *m* 1969, John Humphrey Colquhoun (*see* Greenwell, Bt), of Brooke House, Frocester, Stonehouse, Glos, and has issue living, Mark Humphrey *b* 1973, James Arthur *b* 1975, Auriol Emma *b* 1982, — Nicola Mary, *b* 1951; JP Cornwall: *m* 1970, Paul Archer Tyler, CBE, MP, and has issue living, Dominick Michael Archer *b* 1975, Sophie Grace Auriol *b* 1972, — Auriol Jacqueline, *b* 1957. *Residence* – The Manor House, S Cerney, Cirencester.

WIDOW LIVING OF SON OF THIRD BARONET

Sallie Willoughby (Southridge House, nr Streatley, Reading, Berks RG8 9SJ), da of late Frank Hilary Minoprio, of Hessle Well House, Heswall, Cheshire: *m* 1973, as his 2nd wife, (Herbert) Robin Ingram (only son of 3rd baronet), who *d* 1979.

MOTHER LIVING

Shiela (8 Pitt St, W8), only da of Charles Peczenik, of 7 Grosvenor Sq, W1: *m* 1st, 1963 (*m diss* 1971), as his 1st wife, (Herbert) Robin Ingram (only son of 3rd baronet), who *d* 1979; 2ndly, 1972 (*m diss* 1985), Count Fritz Dietlof von der Schulenburg.

COLLATERAL BRANCHES LIVING

Grandchildren of late Collingwood Ingram (infra):—
Issue of late Ivor Laing Ingram, *b* 1907, *d* 1990: *m* 1936, Winifred (26 West Knowe, Bidston Rd, Birkenhead), da of late William Battle Waterhouse, of Wallasey, Cheshire:—
John Anthony (Wardle Old Hall, Wardle, Nantwich, Cheshire), *b* 1941: *m* 1963, Jacqueline Ann, da of William Alexander Lockley Cook, of Gotley, Westerham, Kent, and has issue living, Christopher William Ivor Lockley, *b* 1965, — Louis Anthony Lockley (Hospital House, Hospital St, Nantwich, Ches), *b* 1968: *m* 1998, Ruth Helen Shapland. —— Jill Susan Rosemary, *b* 1948: *m* 1969, Clyde Dennis Gordon Coltart, of Browfield, Dale End Rd, Barnston, Wirral, Cheshire, and has issue living, Rupert Gordon, *b* 1971, — Amanda Jane, *b* 1973.

Issue of late Mervyn Jeffrey Ingram, MB, BCh, MRCS, LRCP, *b* 1909, *d* 1993: *m* 1936, Joan Doreen (Westbrook Cottage, W Bradley, Glastonbury, Som), da of late Engr Capt Arthur Philip Leslie Dupen, RN:—
Collingwood William Malcolm (37 Poplar Grove, W6), *b* 1939: *m* 1976, Susan Anne, da of late Dudley Love, of Solihull, and has issue living, William Mervyn, *b* 1980, — Rosalind Annabel, *b* 1978. —— Priscilla Jane, *b* 1937: *m* 1963, Dudley Allen Doust, of Westbrook House, West Bradley, Glastonbury, Som, and has issue living, Hannah Victoria, *b* 1963: *m* 1990, Sean Michael Gresham Barrington, of The Old College Arms, Stour Row, Dorset (and has issue living, Harry Jake *b* 1997), — Elinor Jane, *b* 1966. —— Charlotte Certhia, *b* 1944: *m* 1964 (*m diss* 1993), Charles St Vigor Fox, and has issue (*see* Orr-Ewing, Bt, cr 1886, colls).

Issue of late Maj William Alastair Ingram, RA, *b* 1913, *d* 1975: *m* 1947, Daphne Anne, ARRC (8 St James Villas, Winchester), el da of late Reginald Bramley Van Wart, OBE, of Llwyngwril, Merionethshire:—
Peter William Irving (40 Landford Rd, SW15 1AG), *b* 1950; *ed* Winchester, and Univ of Kent (BA 1977): *m* 1979, Christina Mary, 2nd da of Sir James Holmes Henry, 2nd Bt, CMG, MC, TD, and has issue living, Sarah Christina, *b* 1980, — Corinna Alice, *b* 1983. —— Heather Anne, *b* 1948: *m* 1969, Michael Paget Bowyer, of Lockerley Water House, Lockerley, Romsey, Hants, and has issue living, James William Paget, *b* 1974, — Caroline Sarah, *b* 1972.

Issue of late Collingwood Ingram, yst son of 1st baronet, *b* 1880, *d* 1981: *m* 1906, Florence Maude, who *d* 1980, only child of Henry Rudolph Laing, of 5 Cadogan Gdns, SW3:—
Certhia Mary (Springhill Oast, Iden Green, Benenden, Cranbrook, Kent), *b* 1917: *m* 1940, Charles Gerald Harden, who *d* 1983, and has issue living, Alastair Geoffrey (4 Ashfield Crescent, Belfast BT15 3FR), *b* 1943: *m* 1982, Evelyn Maguire, and has issue living, Niall Charles Brendan *b* 1983, Alastair Francis *b* 1984, Marina Catherine *b* 1990, — Richard Charles (New Lindsey, Spring Lane, Burwash, Etchingham, E Sussex), *b* 1946: *m* 1976, Elizabeth Catherine Lacy, el da of Evelyn Charles Lacy Hulbert-Powell (*see* B St Levan), and has issue living, Charles John *b* 1981, Annabel Mary *b* 1977, Rosemary Juliet *b* 1979, — Veryan Penelope, *b* 1941: *m* 1964, Ernest Pollard, of Springhill Farm, Benenden, Kent, and has issue living, John Collingwood *b* 1968, Tessa Mary *b* 1966, — Frances Mary, *b* 1956: *m* 1980, Paul Stryker Meier, of Eastham Park, Eastham, Tenbury Wells, Worcs.

The 1st baronet, Sir William James Ingram, sometime Managing Director of the *Illustrated London News*, sat as MP for Boston (*L*) 1874-80, 1885-6, and 1892-5.

INNES (NS) 1628, of Balvenie, Bannffshire.
(Name pronounced "Innis")

Let it be done without blemish

SINE CRIMINE FIAT

Sir PETER ALEXANDER BEROWALD INNES OF BALVENIE, 17th *Baronet*; *b* 6 Jan 1937; *s* his father, *Lt-Col Sir* (RONALD GORDON) BEROWALD, OBE, 1988; *ed* Prince of Wales Sch, Nairobi, and Bristol Univ (BSc); FICE: *m* 1959, Julia Mary, yr da of late Alfred Stoyell Levesley, MSc, FRSC, of Burlington Rd, Bristol, and has issue.

𝔄rms – Argent, three mullets in chief azure. 𝔠rest – A dexter arm, armed and couped at the elbow, holding a broadsword in pale proper. 𝔖upporters – Two greyhounds argent.
Seat – Balvenie Castle, Banffshire. *Residence* – The Wheel House, Nation's Hill, Kings Worthy, Winchester, Hants S023 7QY.

SONS LIVING

(ALEXANDER) GUY BEROWALD (Rosebank, Church Rd, Longhope, Glos GL17 0LG), *b* 4 May 1960; *ed* Queen Mary's Coll, Basingstoke; Fellow Property Consultants Soc: *m* 1986 (*m diss* 1990), Sara-Jane, da of late Dennis Busher, of Moraira, Spain; has issue living (by Susan, da of late Peter Barwick), Laura Jane, *b* 1997. —— Alastair John Peter, *b* 1965; *ed* Newcastle Univ (BSc).

DAUGHTER LIVING

Fiona Julie, *b* 1963.

BROTHER LIVING

George Guy Alfred, *b* 1941; *ed* Massey Univ, NZ (Dip Agric). *Address* – PO Box 1069, Esperance, W Australia.

SISTER LIVING

Catherine Eythan, *b* 1940: *m* 1st, 1962 (*m diss* 1970), Mark Grant Oliver; 2ndly, 1974, Hugh Leslie Sanderson, who *d* 1985; 3rdly, 1993, Donald Campbell Dawson, and has issue living (by 1st *m*), Karen Elizabeth, *b* 1965, —— Alison Mary, *b* 1967: *m* 19—, Douglas Atkinson, of 98 Rosebery St, Bedford, W Aust 6052, and has issue living, Peggy *b* 19—. *Residence* – Lesmurdie House, Lesmurdie, W Australia 6076.

UNCLE LIVING (*brother of 16th baronet*)

William Alexander Disney, *b* 1910; *ed* Marlborough; Lt-Col (ret) Gordon Highlanders; Vice-Lieut for Banffshire 1971-87; served 1939-45 War: *m* 1939, Mary Alison, who *d* 19—, only da of late Francis Burnett-Stuart, of Howe Green, Hertford, and has issue living, Michael Alexander (St Mary's Farm, Cupar, Fife KY15 4NF), *b* 1954; *ed* Glenalmond, and Durham Univ (BA), Dip Hort Kew; and has issue living (by Carolyn Ann Scott), Rosanna Mary Scott INNES *b* 1988, —— Jonathan Berowald (33 Croft Rd, Thame, Oxon OX9 3JF), *b* 1955; *ed* Glenalmond, St Andrew's Univ (MA), and Reading Univ (MSc): *m* 1986, Jane Angela, da of Lt-Col John Dalton Stephenson, of Cefn Parc, Brecon. *Residence* – Heath Cottage, Aberlour, Banffshire AB3 9QD.

AUNT LIVING (*sister of 16th baronet*)

Elizabeth Katherine Mary, *b* 1918: *m* 1st, 1943 (*m diss* 1948), Maj James Robertson-McIsaac; 2ndly, 1948, Col Eric Dighton Mackenzie, CMG, CVO, DSO, who *d* 1972, and has issue living, (by 2nd *m*) (*see* Mackenzie, Bt, *cr* 1890).

WIDOW LIVING OF SIXTEENTH BARONET

ELIZABETH CHRISTIAN (*Christian, Lady Innes*), el da of late Lt-Col Charles Henry Watson, DSO: *m* 1961, as his 2nd wife, Lt-Col Sir (Ronald Gordon) Berowald Innes of Balvenie, 16th Bt, OBE, who *d* 1988. *Residence* – The Loom House, Aultgowrie, Muir of Ord, Ross-shire IV6 7XA.

COLLATERAL BRANCHES LIVING

Grandsons of late Col Sydney Armitage Innes, DSO (*infra*):—
Issue of late Lt-Col Berowald Alfred Innes, The Black Watch, *b* 1904, *d* 1981: *m* 1931, Betty Ida, who *d* 1997, da of late Alastair Campbell Sandeman, of Fonab, Pitlochry, Perthshire:—
Colin Berowald (Easter Dunbog, Newburgh, Cupar, Fife KY14 6JF), *b* 1936; *ed* Wellington; Maj late The Black Watch: *m* 1971, Clovannis Jane, da of late Lt-Col Charles Frederick Cathcart, DSO (*see* E Cathcart, colls), and has had issue. †Andrew Berowald, *b* 1963; *d* 1991, —— Katherine Candida, *b* 1967: *m* 1994, Giles Ernest Peppiatt, yr son of Jonathan Peppiatt, of Ford, Bucks, and has issue living, Dominic Andrew Slingsby *b* 1997, Oliver Brian Berowald *b* 1999, —— Emily Jane, *b* 1969: *m* 1997, Edward John Timothy Taylor, of Grove Place, Goudhurst, Kent. —— Malcolm Alastair (132 Wakehurst Rd, SW11 6BS; New (Edinburgh), and Caledonian Clubs, Highland Society of London [President]), *b* 1939; *ed* Wellington, and Trin Hall, Camb; late 2nd Lt Scots Gds: *m* 1976, Celia Jane Strang, LVO, el da of Jock Wykeham Strang

Steel (*see* Steel, Bt, colls), and has issue living, Robert Alexander, *b* 1980, — Fiona Bridget, *b* 1983. —— James Alexander (Newbigging Birks, Oxnam, Jedburgh TD8 6NA), *b* (twin) 1939; *ed* Gordonstoun: *m* 1969, Frances, yst da of Hugh Leggat, and has issue living, Rory Alexander, *b* 1977, — Melissa Jane, *b* 1972.

Granddaughter of late Alexander Innes, *b* 1846, son of late Alexander Innes, *b* 1812, el son of William Innes, son of Alexander Innes of Breda and Cowie, 2nd son of John Innes of Edingight, grandfather of 9th baronet:—
Issue of late Col Sydney Armitage Innes, DSO, The Black Watch, *b* 1879, *d* 1960: *m* 1903, Constance Edith, who *d* 1957, da of late Samuel Blain:—
Sylvia, *b* 1909: *m* 1944, Maj-Gen Frank McLean Richardson, CB, DSO, OBE, RAMC, who *d* 1996, and has issue living, Hugh Alexander, *b* 1946: *m* 1981, Zaleha Pawan, of Kuala Lumpur, and has issue living, Christopher Johan Roland *b* 1984, Noelle *b* 1988, — Alastair Neil, *b* 1953: *m* 1980, Mariane Angela, da of John Curry, of co Mayo, and has issue living, Simon Alexander *b* 1988, Saoirse Joanna *b* 1981, — Jennifer Jane, *b* 1944. *Residence* – 4B Barnton Av West, Edinburgh.

Grandchildren of late Lt-Col Francis Newell Innes of Learney, son of Col Thomas Innes of Learney, CVO, LLD, 2nd son of William Innes, son of Alexander Innes of Breda and Cowie, 2nd son of John Innes of Edingight, 7th in descent from Robert Innes of Innermarkie (infra):—
Issue of late Sir Thomas Innes of Learney, GCVO, LLD, FSA (Scot), Lord Lyon King of Arms 1945-69, *b* 1893, *d* 1971: *m* 1928, Lady Lucy Buchan (56 Darnell Rd, Edinburgh EH5 3PJ), da of 18th Earl of Caithness:—
Thomas Innes of Learney (West Learney, Torphins, Banchory, Kincardineshire, AB31 4LU; Roy Northern and University Club, Aberdeen); *b* 1930; *ed* Edinburgh Acad, and Edinburgh Univ (BSc Agric); late R Signals; OStJ; Pres of Deeside Field Club 1971-76: *m* 1958, Rosemary Elizabeth, yr da of late Brig Cecil Vivian Staveley Jackson, CIE, CBE, of Burnside, Aboyne, Aberdeenshire, and has issue living, Maureen Cecilia, *b* 1962: *m* 1985, Duncan John Cullen Grant, yst son of late Sir Francis Cullen Grant of Monymusk, 12th Bt, and has issue (*see* Grant, Bt, *cr* 1705). —— Berowald Fortescue, FSA (Scot) (18 Old Mill Lane, Inverness IV2 3XP), *b* 1931; *ed* Melville Coll. —— Sir Malcolm Rognvald of Edingight, KCVO, WS (35 Inverleith Row, Edinburgh; New (Edinburgh) and Puffin's Clubs), *b* 1938; *ed* Edinburgh Acad, and Edinburgh Univ (MA, LLB); CVO 1981, KCVO 1990; KStJ; Falkland Pursuivant Extraor 1957-58, Carrick Pursuivant 1958-72, Marchmont Herald 1972-81, and Lord Lyon King of Arms and Sec of the Order of the Thistle since 1981; Lyon Clerk and Keeper of the Records, Lyon Court 1966-81; a Member of Queen's Body Guard for Scotland (Royal Company of Archers): *m* 1963, Joan, only da of late Thomas D. Hay, CA, and has issue living, John Berowald of Edingight (Edingight, Keith, Banffshire), *b* 1965; *ed* Edinburgh Acad, Heriot Watt Univ (BSc), and RMA Sandhurst; Capt late The Gordon Highlanders, — Colin William of Kinnairdy (Kinnairdy Castle, Bridge of Marnoch, Banffshire), *b* 1967; *ed* Edinburgh Acad, and Aberdeen Univ (LLB, LLM): *m* 1993, Joanna, only da of David Judge, of Birchwood, Herefordshire, and has issue living, Thomas David *b* 1995, William *b* 1997, — Michael Thomas of Crommey (Crommey Castle, Aberchirder, Banffshire), *b* 1970; *ed* Edinburgh Acad, St Andrews Univ (MA), and Chester Law Sch: *m* 1998, Robyn, elder da of Stewart Milne, of Edinburgh. —— Sybil Marjorie (56 Darnell Rd, Edinburgh), *b* 1934.

Descendants of late Major James Innes of Thrumster, great-grandson of James Innes of Thursater, 5th in descent from William Innes of Thursater, yst son of Robert Innes, 2nd of Innermarkie and great-great-uncle of 1st Baronet:—

Granddaughter of late Lt-Gen James John McLeod Innes, VC, CB, only son of James Innes, 5th son of Major James Innes of Thrumster (ante):—
Issue of late Hugh McLeod Innes, *b* 1862, *d* 1944: *m* 1894, Margaret, who *d* 1948, da of James Bird:—
Christina McLeod, *b* 1902: *m* 1925, Frank Vigor Morley, PhD, who *d* 1980, and has had issue, John Donald Innes (Chalfont St Peter, Bucks), *b* 1926; *ed* New Coll, Oxford (MA): *m* 1962, Alice Millicent, da of J. T. Flook, and widow of George Boast, — Hugh Oliver, *b* 1928; FRCO, ARCM; *d* 1987, — Susanna Loveday, *b* 1932: *m* 1956, John Guthrie Smithson, of Jordans, Bucks, and has issue living, Michael John *b* 1957; BSc: *m* 1982, Emilia, da of Klimos Shaylou, of Nicosia, Cyprus (and has issue living, Sophie Marina *b* 1984), Robert Hugh *b* 1963; BSc: *m* 1996, Jacqueline Seal, Deborah Mary *b* 1959: *m* 1981, Richard Zealey, of Chalfont St Peter, Bucks (and has issue living, David John *b* 1983, Phillip James *b* 1989, Christina May *b* 1986), — Christina Margaret Peregrine, *b* 1940; *ed* The Open Univ (BA).

Grandchildren of late Arthur Donald Innes, yr son of late Lt-Gen James John McLeod Innes, VC, CB (ante):—
Issue of late Neil McLeod Innes, *b* 1903, *d* 1989: *m* 1931, Nancy Audrey, who *d* 1987, da of James Temple Stephens, of Melbourne, Australia:—
Roderick Temple McLeod (Rose Cottage, Upper Swanmore, Hants SO32 2QQ), *b* 1938: *ed* Marlborough; Lt Cdr RN (ret); FRICS: *m* 1962, Diana Selkirk, da of late Eric S. Drew, and has issue living, James McLeod, *b* 1966; *ed* Milton Abbey; ARICS, — Charles McLeod, *b* 1969; *ed* Sherborne, and Reading Univ (BSc): *m* 1994, Nathalie, da of Giles Sharp, of Tanworth-in-Arden, Warwicks. —— Catherine McLeod, *b* 1935: *m* 1954, Guy Francis Symondson, of St Anthony's, Somers Rd, Lyme Regis, Dorset DT7 3EX, and has issue living, Bevil Charles, *b* 1955: *m* 1985 (*m diss* 1999), Lucy Elizabeth, da of Douglas Hardinge Anderson, of 56036 Palaia, Prov di Pisa, Italy (*see* E Halsbury, 1995 Edn), and has issue living, Robert Michael *b* 1986, Foy Rohais *b* 1987, Minnette Elizabeth *b* 1989, — Robin Francis, *b* 1957: *m* 1986, Alison Gaddie, and has issue living, Angus John *b* 1988, Alexandra Mary Catherine *b* 1989, — Alastair James Guy, *b* 1958: *m* 1st, 1985 (*m diss* 1993), Mrs Rosemary Hardingham (*née* Cole); 2ndly, 1995, Sheila McCartney, who *d* 1997, and has issue living, (by 2nd *m*) Hamish Ronald *b* 1995. —— Fiona McLeod (Briar Cottage, Uploders, Bridport, Dorset DT6 4PG), *b* 1939: *m* 1st, 1960, Simon Noel Chick, who *d* 1982; 2ndly, 1986, Barry Gray Brookes, who *d* 1995, and has issue living (by 1st *m*), Theresa Nicola, *b* 1960: *m* 1987, Maj Jeremy Russell, RGJ, of Manor Farm, Compton Valence, Dorchester, Dorset DT2 9ES, and has issue living, Edward Simon Chick, *b* 1993, Alice Elizabeth Newton *b* 1991, Camilla Louise Newton *b* (twin) 1993, — Philippa Helen, *b* 1963: *m* 1986, Hugo James, of Pigeon House, Hampton, Dorchester, Dorset DT2 9DZ, and has issue living, Grace Daisy *b* 1992, Flora Emily *b* (twin) 1992, — Sarah Rebecca (Thrae, Compton Valence, Dorchester, Dorset DT2 9ER), *b* 1967.

Grandchildren of late Ven George Archibald Clunes Innes, Archdeacon of Hamilton, Vic, Aust, son of late Maj Archibald Clunes Innes, 3rd Buffs, 6th son of Maj James Innes of Thrumster (ante):—
Issue of late George Archibald Clunes Innes, *b* 1870, *d* 19—: *m* 1900, Agnes Mary Gowthorpe, who *d* 1937:—
Charles McLeod, *b* 1902: *m* 1931, Elspeth Anne, da of Charles Bilbe, of Dululu, N Qld, and has issue living, Lorraine, *b* 1932, — Ian, *b* 1933, — Colin, *b* 1935, — Alan, *b* 1947, — Patty, *b* 1935, — Mary, *b* 1938, — Jillian, *b* 1941. —— Enid Emily, *b* 1904: *m* 19—, Donald James Mackay, and has issue living, Shirley, *b* 1931.

Descendants of Captain Peter Innes, 79th Foot, 3rd son of William Innes in Olliclate, and younger brother of Major James Innes of Thrumster (ante):—

Granddaughter of late Peter Innes, son of late Robert Innes of Hayfield in Olrig, only son of Capt Peter Innes, 79th Foot (ante):—
Issue of late Lt-Col Robert Innes, b 1891, d 1963: m 1913, Charlotte Lloyd Heming, who d 1972:—
Margaret Joan, b 1925: m 1952, Douglas Comrie, who d 1993, and has issue living, Laurie Douglas, b 1954: m 1979, Maria Claire Allard, — Michael Raoul, b 1962, — Charlotte Ann, b 1953: m 1980, T. Jeffrey Davidson, and has issue living, John Douglas b 1983, Alexander James Charles b 1992, Jessica Jane b 1982, — Mary Jane, b 1963.

Descendants of John Innes of Coxton, grandson of Patrick Innes of the Keam of Duffus, great-great-great-uncle of 1st baronet (see that title).

The limitations of this baronetcy are to heirs male whatsoever, as contained in the "signature," or warrant for the patent and heredibus masculis quibuscunque in the latter, on record in Lyon Court, and on the death of the 8th baronet in 1817, John Innes, of Edingight (having been served heir male general to his predecessor in the title on 12 Jan 1818), assumed the baronetcy as 9th Bt, and as heir male of John Innes of Edingight, great-great-uncle of the 1st baronet. The 12th baronet was Vice-Lieut for Banffshire.

INNES (NS) 1686, of Coxton, co Moray.

Sir DAVID CHARLES KENNETH GORDON INNES OF COXTON, 12th Baronet; b 17 April 1940; s his father, Sir CHARLES KENNETH GORDON, 1990; ed Haileybury, and London Univ (BScEng); AGGI: m 1969, Marjorie Alison, da of Ernest Walter Parker, and has issue.

Arms – Argent, three mullets within a bordure embattled azure, in dexter canton argent a saltire azure surmounted of an inescutcheon or charged with a lion rampant within a double tressure flory counterflory gules (for his Baronetcy of Nova Scotia). Crest – A dexter arm in armour, the hand naked holding a skean in pale, both proper, issuing from an embattled tower argent masoned sable, port gules.
Residence – 28 Wadham Close, Shepperton, Middx TW17 9HT.

SON LIVING

ALASTAIR CHARLES DEVERELL, b 17 Sept 1970; ed Haileybury, and Southampton Univ.

DAUGHTER LIVING

Dione Elizabeth Colquhoun, b 1974.

SISTER LIVING

Daphne Margaret Colquhoun, b 1948: m 1971, Nigel Geoffrey Wolseley Haig, of Sparkfield House, High St, Newnham on Severn, Glos, and has issue living, Jonathan Peter Wolseley, b 1975, — Katharine Jane Innes, b 1976.

AUNT LIVING (Daughter of de jure 10th baronet)

Eleanor Joan, b 1913: m 1938, Trevor Walter Mimpriss, MB, MS, FRCS, and has issue living, Timothy John (27 Lon-y-Bryn, Bangor, Gwynedd), b 1940; MA, MB, BChir, Camb; FFARCS: m 1964, Wendy Anne, da of Donald Pryce, and has issue living, Robert Charles b 1971, Rosemary Jill b 1965, Hilary Anne b 1967, — John Graham (Orchard Close, The Downs, Givons Grove, Leatherhead, Surrey), b 1944: m 1966, Lorraine, da of Donald Lovell, and has issue living, Graham Donald b 1968, James Christopher b 1970, — Jill Alison, b 1942. m 1966, Lt-Cdr David Richard Monro Gregory, RN, of 32 Midmar Gdns, Edinburgh, son of Vice-Adm Sir (George) David (Archibald) Gregory, KBE, CB, DSO, and has issue living, Peter James b 1967, Caroline Joan b 1969, Nicola Helen b 1972. Residence – 4 Midmar Avenue, Edinburgh EH10 6BS.

COLLATERAL BRANCHES LIVING

Grandchildren (by 1st m) of late Edward George Innes (b 1854), son of Edward Innes (b 1827), next brother of de jure 9th baronet:—
Issue of late Edward David Ballantyne Innes, b 1884, d 1967: m 1st, 1906, Ethel Agnes Isobel, who d 1929, da of Charles Lucas; 2ndly, 1933, Viney Isobel, da of Patrick Keogh, of Gawlls, NWC, Tasmania:—
(By 1st m) John Holdsworth, b 1915: m 1960, — . —— Robert Maxwell, b 1917: m 19—, Jean Marshal, and has issue living, Barbara Ann, b 1944, — Margaret Diane, b 1946. —— Gwendolen Eleanor (6 Randall St, Sandy Bay, Hobart, Tasmania), b 1906. —— Marjory Betty, b 1913: m 1939, James Benjamin Greer. —— (By 2nd m) George Berowald, b 1938. —— Jean Elizabeth, b 1934. —— Pauline Margaret, b 1939.

Issue of Vivian Oswald Innes, b 1888, d 1971: m 1912, Teresa, da of Matthew Fitzpatrick:—
Gordon Vivian (Lymington Rd, Cygnet 7112, Tasmania), b 1922: m 1951, Rhonda Helen, da of Denis Green, of Lymington, Hants, and has issue living, David John, b 1956: m 19—, Robyn Massie, and has issue living, Adrian Ronald b 19—, Bradley John b 19—, — Helen Marie, b 1951: m 1972, Peter Michael Stevens, and has issue living, Mark Patrick b 19—, Andrew b 19—, Emma Louise b 19—, Sarah Marie b 19—, — Mary Frances b 1957: m 1982, Graham Charles Gordon, and has issue living, Kate Frances b 19—. —— Cecil Alfred, b 1923: m 19—, ……, and has issue living, Warren, b 19—, — Rodney, b 19—, — Jenny, b 19—, — Lynette, b 19—. —— Leila Anne, b 1913: m 1938, Francis Dillon, who d 1951, and d 1981, having had issue, Francis, b and d 1940, — Marie Therese, b 1942: m 19—, Richard Phab.

Issue of late Eric Edward Innes, b 1891: m 1st, 1917, Winifred Shelma, who d 1921, da of Edward Charles O'Brien; 2ndly, 1925, Doris Cecilia, da of Brian Kilmartin:—
(By 1st m) Edward George (Linga Longa, Port Cygnet, Tasmania), b 1919: m 1942, Ruth Minnie, da of Ralph Norris, and has issue living, Nigel David, b 1944: m 1st, 19—, Carmel Anne Johnstone; 2ndly, 19—, Bozena Teresa Wieclawska; 3rdly, 19—, Elizabeth Bassillio, and has issue living, (by 2nd m) Damien b 19—, Nathan b 19—, Heather b 19—, Sally b 19—, — Christopher Wayne, b 1948.

Issue of late Athol Rupert Innes, b 1893, d 1973: m 1922, Kathleen (Kia Ora Mail Box, Lymington Rd, Cygnet, 7112, Tasmania), da of Edward Crease:—
William James, b 1924: m 1st, 1950, Avis Lorraine, da of Victor Eugene Yelland; 2ndly, 1967, Claire Adelaide, da of R. A. Batty, of Adelaide, SA, and has issue living, (by 1st m) Wendy Beryl Anne, b 1951: m 19—, Peter Shoobridge, who d 1997, and has had issue, Rebecca b 1979; k 1997, Anna b 1982; k 1997, Sara b 1985; k 1997, Georgina b 1987; k 1997, — Josephine Lilian, b 1953: m 1st, 19— (m diss 19—), Anthony Friend; 2ndly, 19—, Anthony Kafer, and has issue living (by ? m), David b 1988, Guilliame b 1985, Joanne b 1984, — (by 2nd m) Bronwyn Heather, b 1971.

Grandchildren of late Edward Innes (b 1827), next brother of de jure 9th baronet:—
Issue of late Edward George Innes, b 1854, d 1904: m 1st, 1880, Jane, who d 1884, da of Philip Ballantyne; 2ndly, 1886, Marjory, who d 1946, da of Jacob Christie:—
(By 2nd m) †Adrian Arthur, b 1900: m 1927, Daisy, who d 1996, da of Francis Calvert Smith, and d 1995, leaving issue, Roy Edward (Clifton Beach Rd, Sandford, Tasmania), b (Dec) 1927: m 1963, Shirley Esther, da of Victor Richardson Clements, and has issue living, Shane Edward b 1969, Kim Nyree b 1972, — George Calvert (1 Lanena St, Bellerive, Tasmania), b 1932: m 1965, Chou Seng, da of Thar Yu Mok, and has issue living, Andrew Gary b 1969, Trevor Craig (Dept of Engineering, Univ of Tasmania, PO Box 1214, Launceston, Tasmania 7250), b 1971. —— Ismay Anne, b 1898. Residence –

Issue of late William Innes, b 1859, d 1928: m 1887, Adelina Bianca Alexandrina, who d 1946, da of William Allsopp:—
Francis Allsopp, b 1888; Lieut-Com RNR; European War 1914-18 (Croix de Guerre with palms): m 1926, Marjorie Rolleston, da of William Tucker Pyke, and has issue living, Berowald Francis, b 1928, — William, b 1935. Residence – 61 Seaview Street, Balgowlah, Sydney, NS Wales. —— William Edward Allsopp, b 1893: m 1923, Lyla Alta, da of Frederick Charles Thomson-Brown, of Launceston, Tasmania, and has issue living, Desmond Erick, b 1926, — Patricia Joan, b 1925. —— Arthur Berowald, b 1899: m 1926, Irene Eva Eastman, and has issue living, Graeme Alastair, b 1932, — Darren Arthur, b 1936, — Janet Lucille, b 1930, — Sandra Ann, b 1938. —— Gordon Tulloh, b 1904: m 1931, Brienetta Grace, da of Leonard Harold O'Brien. —— Clothilde, b 1897. Residence – Hobart, Tasmania.

Grandchildren of late George Innes, yst brother of de jure 9th Bt, and of Edward Innes (b 1827) (ante):—
Issue of late George Peacock Innes, b 1863, d 1936: m 1893, Susanna Robina, da of Robert Mills:—
George Donald (or Arnold ?), b 1905; is Municipal Engineer at Miniwa: m 1932, Florence Elizabeth Younger. —— Myrtle Robina, b 1894. —— Elizabeth Stuart, b 1898; Emergency Ambulance Corps 1939-44. Residence – 56 Shirley Rd, Wollstonecroft, Sydney, NS Wales.

Granddaughters of late Edward Henry Innes, Fleet Paymaster RN, son of Rev Dr James Innes, uncle of de jure 9th Bt:—
Issue of late Lt-Col George William Holt Innes, MBE, b 1900, d 1983: m 1931, Alexandra, who d 1977, da of Dunbar Marshall, of Natchez, Mississippi, USA, and formerly wife of Count Malagola Cappi:—
Vivien Holt, b 1932: m 1959, John Kennedy Wagstaff, of 52 Salmons Lane, Whyteleafe, Surrey CR3 0AN, and has issue living, Clarissa Christine, b 1960: m 1983, Phillip John Dann, of 1b Claremont Rd, Highgate, N6 5DR, and has issue living, Isabelle Alexandra b 1990, Eleanor Louise b 1993, — Martine Charis, b 1962: m 1st, 1986 (m diss 1990), Stephen Patrick Cotton; 2ndly, 1991, Lawrence Michael Biddle, of 33 Blenheim Rd, W4, and has issue living (by 2nd m), Thomas Lawrence b 1993, Alexandra Grace b 1991, — Vanessa Jacynth, b 1971. —— Valerie Evelyn (16 Newark Rd, S Croydon, Surrey CR2 6HQ), b 1935: m 1958 (m diss 1978), Mervyn Russell Chute, and has issue living, Nigel Anthony, b 1960, — Rosalind Alexandra, b 1962.

This baronetcy was conferred on Sir Alexander Innes, of Coxton, MP for Moray (with remainder to heirs male whatsoever). The Coxton family is a yr branch of Innes of Balvenie, cr Bt 1628, descending from Patrick, in the Keam of Duffus, 5th son of Walter Innes of Innermarkie (d ca 1499). Sir Alexander Innes' direct line became ext with his gt-grandson, Sir David, 5th Bt, who d 1803. The baronetcy descended to Sir Alexander, gt-grandson of John, 1st of Inaltrie, yr brother of 1st Bt. On the death in 1886 of Sir George, 8th Bt, succession reverted to (Sir) Charles Innes, FRIBA, de jure 9th Bt, son of Edward Innes (b 1792) and 6th in descent from John, 3rd son of John Innes, 2nd of Coxton, and gt-uncle of 1st Bt. Sir Charles Kenneth Gordon, grandson of (Sir) Charles, was placed on the Roll of Baronets in 1973, as 11th Baronet of Coxton.

ISHAM (E) 1627, of Lamport, Northamptonshire.
(Name pronounced "Eye-shum")

I show, I sham not

Sir IAN VERE GYLES ISHAM, 13th *Baronet*, el son of late Lt-Col Vere Arthur Richard Isham, MC, el son of Arthur Charles Isham, only son of Rev Arthur Isham, yr son of Rev Henry Charles Isham, 5th son of 7th baronet; *b* 17 July 1923; *s* his kinsman, *Sir* GYLES, 1976; *ed* Eton, and Worcester Coll, Oxford; NW Europe 1944, BAOR 1945-47 as Capt Co of London Yeo; patron of one living.

𝕬rms – Gules, a fesse wavy and in chief three piles also wavy, points meeting in fesse argent. 𝕮rest – A demi-swan, wings displayed argent, beaked sable. 𝕸ottoes – "Ostendo non Ostento", and "On things transitory resteth no glory."
Residence – 40 Turnpike Link, Croydon, Surrey, CR0 5NX. *Club* – Overseas.

BROTHER LIVING

NORMAN MURRAY CRAWFORD, OBE (5 Langton Way, Park Hill, Croydon, Surrey); *b* 28 Jan, 1930; *ed* Stowe, and Univ of Cape Town; BArch (Distn); RIBA; OBE (Civil) 1988: *m* 1956, Joan, da of late Leonard James Genet, of Umtali, Zimbabwe, and has issue living, Richard Leonard Vere (22 Telford Av, SW2 4XL), *b* 1958: *m* 1990, Julia Claire Mary, da of David Frost Pilkington, CBE, of 6 Cherry Green Close, Oaklands Park, Redhill, Surrey RH1 6RY, and has issue living, Angus David Vere *b* 26 Oct 1992, Charles Vere Ian *b* 1996, — Vere Murray Gyles (Hill Pasture, Broxted, Dunmow, Essex CM6 2BZ), *b* 1960: *m* 1991, Lynne Janette, da of late Howard Warren Armishaw, of Alberta, Canada, and has issue living, Maximilliano Vere *b* 1991, Oscar Howard Vere *b* 1993, — Elizabeth Angela, *b* 1957: *m* 1980, Richard Nigel Brayshaw.

The Isham family took their name from the village of Isham in Northamptonshire, where they were found holding land under William I. A cadet branch of the family was established at Pytchley in the 13th century, from whom the present family descend. Robert Isham of Pytchley was Escheator of Northamptonshire under Henry VI, and Solicitor to Elizabeth, Queen of Edward IV. Gyles Isham was MP for Peterborough twice in the reign of Queen Mary I. His younger brother, John, a prosperous Mercer, established himself at Lamport in 1560, and his grandson Sir John, High Sheriff of Northamptonshire, was created a baronet in 1627, having previously been knighted by James I. His son, Sir Justinian, a staunch Royalist, suffered severely for his loyalty, but became MP for Northamptonshire on the Restoration. Sir Justinian, the 4th baronet, MP for Northants, upon the landing of the Prince of Orange appeared in arms against James II at Nottingham. The 5th and 6th baronets were also MPs for Northamptonshire. Sir Gyles Isham, 12th Bt, FSA, was High Sheriff of Northants in 1958 and a Trustee of the National Portrait Gallery 1964-76.

ISHERWOOD (UK) 1921, of Raggleswood, Chislehurst, Kent (Extinct 1946)

Sir WILLIAM ISHERWOOD, 2nd and last *Baronet*.

DAUGHTERS LIVING OF SECOND BARONET

Annette Marie, *b* 1934: *m* 1956, J. D. Smyth, of 27 Bath Rd, Emsworth, Hants. —— Diane Joan, *b* 1936: *m* 1957, F. B. Green. *Residence* – Englefield Court, Bickley, Kent.

WIDOW LIVING OF SECOND BARONET

IRENE JEANNE, da of C. Pittolo: *m* 1932, Sir William Isherwood, 2nd Bt, who *d* 1946, when the title became ext; 2ndly, 1947, David Stevenson Watt. *Residence* – 8 Henty Gdns, Chichester, W Sussex.

JACKSON (UK) 1815, of Arlsey, Bedfordshire

Sir ROBERT JACKSON, 7th *Baronet*, only son of late Maj Francis Gorham Jackson, RE, 2nd son of 4th Baronet; *b* 16 March 1910; *s* his cousin, *Sir* JOHN MONTRESOR, 1980, but his name does not appear on the Official Roll of the Baronetage; *ed* St George's Coll: *m* 1943, Maria Esther, da of Leon P. Casamayou, of Montevideo, Uruguay, and has had issue.

ᴀrms – Argent, on a fesse between a goat's head couped in chief and a ship in full sail in base proper, a greyhound courant between two pheons or, within a bordure of the second charged with eight bezants. ᴄrest – A goat's head couped argent guttée de sang, armed and bearded or, gorged with a collar gules charged with three bezants, from the collar a line reflexed of the third, the rings gold.
Residence – Bulevard Artigas 266, Flat 601, Montevideo, Uruguay.

DAUGHTERS LIVING AND DECEASED

Victoria Maria, *b* 1945; *d* 1993. ——— Bertha Mary, *b* 1949.

DAUGHTER LIVING OF FIFTH BARONET

Bernice Evelyn Abrey, *b* 1917: *m* 1st, 1940, Wing-Com Patrick Edward Geoffrey Gunnell Connolly, RAF; 2ndly, 1954, Frederick John Ralph, and has issue living, (by 1st *m*) Richard Edward Geoffrey Gunnell, *b* 1942, — Penelope Ann, *b* 1941: *m* 1970, W. J. R. Govett, of 62 Glebe Place, SW3 5JB. *Residence* – Hawkswood, Stevens Crouch, Battle, Sussex.

COLLATERAL BRANCHES LIVING

Grandchildren of late Welby Charles Jackson, 2nd son of John Jackson, 2nd son of 1st baronet:—
Issue of late John Keith Jackson, *b* 1872, *d* 1957: *m* 1914, Anna Maria Bertha, who *d* 1953, da of —Arnold, of Freeling, South Australia:—
KEITH ARNOLD, *b* 24 April 1921: *m* 1950, Pauline Mona, da of B. P. Climo, of Wellington, New Zealand, and has issue living, Neil Keith, *b* 12 May 1952: *m* 1973, Sandra Whitehead, and has issue living, Stephen Keith *b* 27 Sept 1973, Paul Alan *b* 1976, — Colin Paul, *b* 1954: *m* 1976, Shirley Hair, — Bruce John *b* 1957, — Kenneth Grant, *b* 1961, — Claire Alison, *b* (twin) 1954: *m* 1979, Graham John Close, and has issue living, Jason John *b* 1980, Tyrell Dan *b* 1983. *Residence* – 6 Coast Rd, Wainuiomata, Lower Hutt, NZ. ——— Noela Grace, *b* 1916: *m* 1945, Arthur Lambourn, of 16 Beaumont Av, Lower Hutt, NZ, and has issue living, Graham John *b* 1946: *m* 1968, Ngaire Johnson, and has issue living, Clynton Arthur *b* 1970, Suesan Barbara *b* 1968.

Issue of late William Alfred Jackson, *b* 1878, *d* 1965: *m* 1904, Emily, who *d* 1952, da of John Hale, formerly of Westport, NZ:—
Grace Irene, *b* 1906: *m* 1937, Stephen Frederick Louis Cooper, of Gladstone, Wairarapa, NZ, and has issue living, Stephen Jackson, *b* 1952. ——— Elizabeth, *b* 1911: *m* 1937, Arthur David McKay, of 62B Essex St, Masterton, Wairarapa, NZ, and has issue living, Arthur Thomas *b* 1937: *m* 1960, Jocelyn Celia Goodwin, and has issue living, David William, *b* 1961, Iain Thomas *b* 1967, Shona Margaret *b* 1963, — Rex David, *b* 1953: *m* 1975, Beverley Ann O'Dea, and has issue living, Andrew Thomas *b* 1985, Natasha Louise *b* 1982, Kate Amanda *b* 1990, — Colleen Mary, *b* 1941: *m* 1963, Philip Cotter, and has issue living, Kathryn Mary *b* 1964, Tania Elizabeth *b* 1965, Maria Louise *b* 1967, Julia Jane *b* 1971, — Marie Elizabeth, *b* 1943: *m* 1974, Maurice Doran, and has issue living, James Gerard *b* 1976, Richard John *b* 1979.

Issue of late Sidney Leybourne Jackson, *b* 1886, *d* 1974: *m* 1915, Daphne, who *d* 1948, da of William Halse, of Wellington, NZ:—
Peggy Elinor, *b* 1917: *m* 1941, Archibald Douglas Wallace, who *d* 1986, of 80a Te Mata Rd, Havelock North, Hawkes Bay, NZ, and has issue living, James Leybourne (Sundrum Woodbury, RD 21, Geraldine, NZ); LLB; *b* 1946: *m* 1973, Evelyn Wilder, 2nd da of Sir (Hugh) John Dyke Acland, KBE, of Mount Peel, Canterbury, NZ (*see* Acland, Bt, *cr* 1678, colls), and has issue living, James Ormond, *b* 1974, Antonia Acland, *b* 1977, Henrietta Harper *b* 1979, — Simon John Lewis (87 Clyde St, Island Bay, Wellington, NZ), *b* 1949: *m* 1st, 1978 (*m diss* 19—), Anne Braithwaite; 2ndly, 19—, Susan Patterson, and has living (by 2nd *m*), George *b* 1988, Henry *b* 1992, — Judith Margaret, *b* 1943: *m* 1964, Col Thomas Arthur Aldridge, of 48 Omahu Rd, Remuera, Auckland, NZ, and has issue living, Michael Douglas Arthur, *b* 1966, Patrick Leybourne Thomas *b* 1970, Louise Elizabeth *b* 1965.

Grandchildren of late Gordon Francis Welby Jackson, 4th and yst son of late Welby Charles Jackson (ante):—
Issue of late John Richard Jackson, *b* 1924, *d* 1987: *m* 1947, Leslie Kay, da of James McKay Heise, of Raetihi, NZ:—
Peter, *b* 1951: *m* 1991, Guadalupe Rosales, and has issue living, Igor, *b* 1991. ——— John Terence (59 Glen Rd, Kelburn, Wellington 5, NZ), *b* 1956: *m* 1989, Toni, da of Ernest Cornish Cosgrove, of Wellington, NZ, and has issue living, Timothy Richard *b* 1989, — Lillian Jane, *b* 1991. ——— James, *b* 1964; has issue living (by Désirée Marie Jones), Hayden Jesse Jones JACKSON, *b* 1991, — Mitchell Lee Jones JACKSON, *b* 1993. ——— Margaret Gail, *b* 1949: *m* 1968 (*m diss* 1994), Wong Teck Sing, of Melbourne, Victoria, Australia, and has issue living, Geoffrey Peter Dow, *b* 1968, — Conrad Dow, *b* 1972, — Vera Dow, *b* 1971. ——— Kathleen, *b* 1954.

Descendants (if any) of late Hugh Whiteman Jackson (3rd son of John Jackson — ante), *b* 1842, *d* 1929: *m* 1869 Charlotte, who *d* 1929, da of A. W. Hayward, of Wellington New Zealand, and had issue, sons and das.

Grandchildren of late Murray James Hamilton Jackson, 4th son of John Jackson (ante):—
Issue of late William John Jackson, *b* 1895, *d* 1980: *m* 1924, Ella, da of Robert Guppy:—
Alan Hamilton (8 Hunter Place, New Plymouth, NZ), *b* 1924: *m* 1949, Lynn, da of late Arthur Prichard Lindsay, of 106 Spring St, Tauranga, NZ, and has issue living, William Lindsay, *b* 1956, — Murray Grant, *b* 1959, — Anne Agnes, *b* 1953. —— Robert John, *b* 1939: *m* 1962, Ruth Wynitta Lamb, and has issue living, Stephen John, *b* 1965, — Andrew Phillip, *b* 1969, — Brenden James, *b* 1970, — Pauline Ruth, *b* 1963: *m* 1989, Craig Robert Whiting. —— Esme Ruth, *b* 1925. —— Ella Marion, *b* 1927: *m* 1950, Cecil Edmund Rawhiti Smith, of 20 Bracken Av, Epsom, Auckland 3, NZ, and has issue living, Cecil David, *b* 1951, — Bruce Edmund, *b* 1953, — Peter Raymond, *b* 1954, — Paul Barry, *b* 1959, — Rodney John, *b* 1964, — Margaret Ann, *b* 1957, — Beverley Joy, *b* 1962. —— Evelyn Isabel, *b* 1931: *m* 1956, Ashley Gordon Howan, of 7 Hunter Place, New Plymouth, NZ, and has issue living, Lance, *b* 1959, — Philip, *b* 19—, — Cherry, *b* 1957.

Issue of late Murray Spearink Jackson, *b* (twin) 1895, *d* 1979: *m* 1921, Mary, who *d* 1983, da of William Robinson:—
David Murray James (3D Lovatt Crescent, Whangarei, NZ), *b* 1921; Salvation Army Offr: *m* 1950, Olive, da of Reginald Frederick Wilde, of Yeovil, Som, and has issue living, Paul Murray *b* 1951, — Verna Elizabeth, *b* 1954. —— Edmund Robinson (Apotu Rd, RD5, Hikurangi, Whangarei, NZ), *b* 1923; sheep farmer: *m* 1st, 1945, Viola Thelma, who *d* 1966, da of late Hans Ries, of Pohokura, NZ; 2ndly, 1968, Nancy Elizabeth Pyle, and has issue living, (by 1st *m*) Peter Edmund, *b* 1948; has issue living, Quentin Peter *b* 1974, Shaun Lewis *b* 1976, — Geoffrey Kendal, *b* 1952; has issue living, Dianna *b* 19—, Carolyn *b* 19—, — Raewyn Ada, *b* 1947: *m* 1968, Alan Cole, of Kaitaia, NZ, and has living, Ruth *b* 1969, — Linda Mary, *b* 1954, — Zoe, *b* 1963, — (by 2nd *m*) Russell Joseph, *b* 1970. —— Harold Stuart, *b* 1926: *m* 1961, Eleni, da of Savvas Michalis, of Dhymes, Limmasol, Cyprus, and has issue living, Andros Vassilis, *b* 1962, — Nikos Manolis, *b* 1963. —— Graham George, *b* 1935; MA, MD; lecturer in anthropology, Auckland Univ.

Grandchildren of late Mountstuart Hungerford Jackson, eldest son of late Judge Elphinstone Jackson, el son of Judge Welby Brown Jackson, 3rd son of 1st baronet:—
Issue of late Cecil Hungerford Jackson, *b* 1887, *d* 1978: *m* 1916, Marian Blanche, who *d* 1971, da of late Cdr Francis S. Wheeler, RN:—
Audrey Madeline Hungerford, *b* 1920: *m* 1944, Robert Douglas Howe, MBE, SQA, ICS, of The Manor House, Martock, Som, and has issue living, Peter Mountstuart (41 Drax Av, Wimbledon, SW19), *b* 1948: *m* 1983, Anne-Marie Boys, and has issue living, Michael Mountstuart *b* 1984, — Veronica Joan, *b* 1946: *m* 1968, James William Goodford, of The Old Rectory, Chilton Cantelo, Yeovil, Som, and has issue living, Andrew Christopher John *b* 1970, Richard Michael James *b* 1972, Simon Charles Jasper *b* 1979, Georgina Helen Jane *b* 1975.

Issue of late Col Laurence Hungerford Jackson, IA, *b* 1889, *d* 1985: *m* 1919, Freda Isabella Mary, who *d* 1978, da of Col Edmund Henry Dalgety, CB:—
Peter Hungerford (Hadstock Hall, Hadstock, Cambridge), *b* 1925; is Maj RE (ret): *m* 1953, Joyce Thomasina, da of Lt-Col V.H. Wells-Cole, late KOYLI, and has issue living, Amelia Mary Hungerford (*Hon Mrs James R. V. Brandon*), *b* 1955: *m* 1991, Hon James Roderick Vivian Brandon, eldest son of Baron Brandon of Oakbrook (Life Baron), — Catherine Ann Hungerford, *b* 1957.

Grandchildren of late Maj-Gen George D'Aguilar Jackson, 4th son of Judge Welby Brown Jackson (ante):—
Issue of late Harold Frederick D'Aguilar Jackson, *b* 1877, *d* 1942: *m* 1903, Anna Lillian, widow of Count von Stadle, of Kœnigsberg, Germany:—
William Douglas D'Aguilar, *b* 1904; *ed* California Institute of Technology, and at S California Univ; is Col US Army, and Ch of Research and Development Div, Office of QMG, US Army; has Legion of Merit with Oak Leaf Cluster: *m* 1933, Margaret Williams, and has issue living, Margaret Anne, *b* 1938, — Susan, *b* 1940. —— Hyacinthe Lilian D'Aguilar, *b* 1908; *ed* S California Univ: *m* 1933, John Machell Procter, who *d* 1941.

The 1st baronet, an East Indian Co Director, sat as MP for Dover, and the 3rd baronet was murdered at Lucknow in 1857 during the Indian Mutiny.

JACKSON (UK) 1869, of The Manor House, Birkenhead

Boldly, faithfully, successfully

Sir (WILLIAM) THOMAS JACKSON, 8th *Baronet*; *b* 12 Oct 1927; *s* his father, *Sir* WILLIAM, 1985; *ed* Mill Hill, and RAC Cirencester: *m* 1951, Gilian Malise, elder da of late Col John William Stobart, MBE, of Farlam Ghyll, Brampton, Cumbria, and has issue.

Arms – Azure, a fesse between two goat's heads couped in chief and a fleur-de-lis in base argent, two flaunches of the last. Crest – On a ragged staff fessewise sable, a goat's head couped argent, semée of trefoils vert.
Residence – Fell End, Mungrisdale, Penrith, Cumbria CA11 0XR.

SONS LIVING

(WILLIAM) ROLAND CEDRIC (Summer Hill, 14 Glebe Rd, Welwyn, Herts AL6 9PB), *b* 9 Jan 1954; *ed* Wycliffe Coll, St Peter's Coll, Oxford (MA), and Exeter Coll, Oxford (DPhil): *m* 1977, Nicola Mary, MA, DPhil, yr da of Prof Peter Reginald Davis, MB, BS, PhD, FRCS, of Polvean, St Mawes, Cornwall, and has issue living, Adam William Roland, *b* 19 May 1982, — James Anthony Foljambe, *b* 1984, — Oliver Thomas Peter, *b* 1990. —— Piers Anthony (26 Astral Av, Hipperholme, Halifax, W Yorks HX3 8NN), *b* 1955; *ed* Keswick Sch, and Derwent Coll, York (BA): *m* 1980, Anne-Marie, elder da of late Patrick Quigg, of Norfolk Dr, Belfast, and has issue living, Carl Patrick Thomas, *b* 1981, — Luke Dominic Gregory, *b* 1985, — Ben Philip Joseph, *b* 1988. —— Jolyon Thomas, *b* 1957; *ed* Keswick Sch, and RMA Sandhurst; Col RGJ: *m* 1986, Serena A., elder da of David Howell, of Monks Mead, Charlton Musgrove, Som, and has issue living, Thomas Sebastian Esme, *b* 1993, — Alicia Sophie, *b* 1989.

SISTER LIVING

Ankaret Tarn, *b* 1934: *m* 1955, Maj Timothy Richard Riley DL, The Rifle Bde, of Burbank House, Blencow, Penrith, Cumbria, and has issue living, Nicola Ankaret Katherine, *b* 1959, — Antonia Elizabeth Tarn, *b* 1962: *m* 1992, Michael Reid, of 7 New Cottages, Snailwell, Newmarket, Suffolk, and has issue living, Ben Riley, *b* 1997, Jennifer Tarn *b* 1993.

DAUGHTERS LIVING OF SIXTH BARONET

Angela Mary Mather (Sansomes Farm House, Ellen's Green, Rudgwick, Sussex), *b* 1925: *m* 1947, Francis Ambrose More O'Ferrall, who *d* 1976, and has issue living, Susan Angela (*Baroness Beaverbrook*), *b* 1948: *m* 1974, 3rd Baron Beaverbrook, — Theresa Mary (*Hon Mrs Wentworth P. I. Beaumont*), *b* 1950: *m* 1975, Hon Wentworth Peter Ismay Beaumont, el son of 3rd Viscount Allendale, — Emma Rose, *b* 1956. —— Elizabeth Georgiana Mather (*Elizabeth, Viscountess Cowdray*), *b* 1926: *m* 1953, as his 2nd wife, 3rd Viscount Cowdray, who *d* 1995. —— Sarah Gillian Mather (36 Cambridge Rd, SW11), *b* 1929: *m* 1955, Henry Lester Louis Morriss, who *d* 1963, and has had issue, James Nicholas, *b* 1958; *d* 1993, in Thailand, — Annabel Ruth (*Lady Fairfax of Cameron*), *b* 1957: *m* 1982, 14th Lord Fairfax of Cameron, — Henrietta Sarah, *b* 1961: *m* 1988, James W. Petit, and has issue living, William Francis *b* 1989, Henry James *b* 1995, Eliza Mary Lara *b* 1991.

WIDOW LIVING OF SEVENTH BARONET

INA (*Ina, Lady Jackson*), da of James Leonard Joyce, FRCS: *m* 1966, as his 2nd wife, Sir William Jackson, 7th Bt, who *d* 1985. *Residence* – 8 West View, Gelt Rd, Brampton, Cumbria, CA8 1QC.

COLLATERAL BRANCHES LIVING

Grandson of late Rt Hon Frederick Huth JACKSON (infra):—
Issue of late Frederick Huth Jackson, *b* 1896, *d* 1966: *m* 1st, 1920 (*m diss* 1929), Helen, da of late Prof Sir Paul Vinogradoff, LLD; 2ndly, 1940, Frederica Frances, who *d* 1975, da of Duncan Tucker, of Burnham-on-Sea:—
(By 1st *m*) Patrick Huth, *b* 1922.

Granddaughters of late Lt-Col Henry Humphrey Jackson, OBE, MC, TD (infra):—
Issue of late Brig Thomas Geoffrey Henry Jackson, R Green Jackets, *b* 1926, *d* 1979: *m* 1957, Judith Margaret (who *m* 2ndly, 1981, Colin MacPherson), da of Capt Henry Mangles Denham, CMG, RN:—
Catherine Margaret, *b* 1958: *m* 1983, Howard William Arthur Palmer, QC, son of William Alexander Palmer, CBE, DL, of Bussock Wood, Newbury, Berks, and has issue living, Thomas Howard, *b* 1988, — Laura Margaret, *b* 1984, — Emily Rose, *b* 1986, — Harriet Bridget *b* 1991. —— Victoria Georgina, *b* 1960: *m* 1987, David Mark Stewart, and has issue (*see* E Galloway, colls). —— Louise Sarah, *b* 1966. —— Joanna Henrietta, *b* (twin) 1966: *m* 1995, James William Jeremy Ritblat, and has issue living, Daisy Paja Silver, *b* 1998.

Issue of late John Guy Carmichael Jackson, *b* 1931, *d* 1997: *m* 1973, Flora Mary Margaret (Copse Hill, Osmaston, Ashbourne, Derbys DE6 1LU), da of late Lt-Col William Herbert Olivier, TD, DL (*see* Jones, Bt, *cr* 1919, colls):—
Georgina Mary, *b* 1974. —— (Ann) Margaret, *b* 1976.

Grandchildren of late Brig-Gen Geoffrey Meinertzhagen JACKSON, TD, 3rd son of late Thomas Hughes Jackson (*b* 1834) (infra):—

Issue of late Lt-Col Henry Humphrey Jackson, OBE, MC, TD, *b* 1895, *d* 1969: *m* 1924, Georgina, who *d* 1974, da of H. Howard Middleditch, JP, of Tamworth House, Duffield:—

Ann Georgina Laird, *b* 1928: *m* 1952, Maj Colville Graham Wemyss, Rifle Bde, of West Lodge, Upham, Southampton SO31 1JP, son of late Gen Sir Henry Colville Barclay Wemyss, KCB, KBE, DSO, MC, and has issue living, Henry Graham, *b* 1956; *ed* Wellington Coll: *m* 1984, Diana Bridget, da of R. K. Selby, of Halsemere, Surrey, and has issue living, Nicholas Henry, *b* 1988, Eleanor Rose *b* 1986, — Alice Caroline, *b* 1953: *m* 1986, Stephen Walter Hubert Lacey, son of late David Lacey, of Highgate, London, and has issue living, William David *b* 1990, Alice Megan *b* 1987.

Issue of late Capt Guy Rolf Jackson, MC, *b* 1896, *d* 1966: *m* 1937, Shelagh (St Andrews, Higham, Derby), da of late A. Ignatius Tolhurst, of Gravesend:—

Geoffrey Laird (Plas Newydd, Llanfair DC, Ruthin, Clwyd LL15 2EP), *b* 1940; *ed* Ampleforth, and RAC, Cirencester: *m* 1963, Ruth Clare, JP, da of D. F. N. Campion, of Okirai, Wanganui, NZ, and has issue living, Jonathan Guy Campion, *b* 1964: *m* 1990, Mary Rose M., only da of late Col Peter Arkwright, OBE, and has issue living, Phoebe Clare *b* 1999, — Charles Desmond Bertram, *b* 1965, — Rupert James Humphrey, *b* 1966, — William David Geoffrey, *b* 1970. —— Robert Humphrey (14 Dewhurst Rd, W14 0ET), *b* 1943; *ed* Ampleforth, and Brasenose Coll, Oxford: *m* 1971, Margaret Letitia, da of James Matthew Barrie, of Polruan, Cornwall, and has issue living, Guy Nicholas Barrie, *b* 1975, — David Geoffrey Barrie, *b* 1978. —— Jane Mary, *b* 1938.

Granddaughters of late Thomas Hughes Jackson (*b* 1834), 3rd son of 1st baronet:—
Issue of late Rt Hon Frederick Huth JACKSON, *b* 1863, *d* 1921: *m* 1895, Clara Annabel Caroline, who *d* 1944, da of late Rt Hon Sir Mountstuart Elphinstone Grant-Duff, GCSI, CIE, FRS, of 11 Chelsea Embankment, SW, and Lexden Park, Colchester:—

Anne Marie Huth (*Hon Mrs Christopher E. Fremantle*), *b* 1909; *ed* Cheltenham Ladies' Coll, and Lady Margaret Hall, Oxford (MA); *m* 1930, Hon Christopher Evelyn Fremantle (*see* B Cottesloe). *Residence* – St Wilfred's Convent, 29 Tite St, SW3.

Issue of late Thomas Hughes JACKSON, *b* 1872, *d* 1926: *m* 1910, Eileen, who *d* 1980, da of late Edward Devery, of Gisborne, New Zealand:—

Barbara Eileen Marian, *b* 1918: *m* 1947, Lt Thomas Joseph Bourke RNZNVR, who *d* 1987, and has issue living, Gerard Thomas Hughes (Ratanui, 92 Waterloo Rd, Lower Hutt, NZ), *b* 1948: *m* 1974, Joy Patricia, da of R. H. Matthews, JP, of Otoka, Waipukurau, Hawkes Bay, NZ, and has issue living, James Thomas Henry *b* 1976, Amanda Joy *b* 1978, Hannah Kathryn *b* 1980, — John Patrick, *b* 1955. *Residence* – 99 Waterloo Rd, Lower Hutt, NZ.

Sir William Jackson, 1st Bt, son of Peter Jackson of Warrington, Surg, by his wife, Sarah, only da of Henry Mather of Warrington, was MP (*L*), Newcastle-under-Lyne 1847-65 and N Derbys 1865-68. The 3rd baronet, Lord Lieut of Mon, assumed in 1886 the additional surname of Mather.

JACKSON (UK) 1902, of Stansted House, Stansted, Essex.

Sir MICHAEL ROLAND JACKSON, 5th *Baronet*; *b* 20 April 1919; *s* his father, *Sir* (WALTER DAVID) RUSSELL, 1956; *ed* Stowe, and Clare Coll, Camb (MA); formerly Fl Lt RAFVR Chartered Engineer (MIEE, FIQA) (ret): *m* 1st, 1942 (*m diss* 1969), (Hilda) Margaret, da of late Cecil George Herbert Richardson, CBE; 2ndly, 1969, Hazel Mary, da of late Ernest Harold Edwards, and has issue by 1st *m*.

Arms – Ermine, on a pile azure, between two fountains proper, a sheldrake or. Crest – On a fountain proper a sheldrake or.
Residence – Jolliffe's House, Stour Row, Shaftesbury, Dorset SP7 0QW.

Aut mors aut victoria

Either death or victory

SON LIVING (*By 1st marriage*)

THOMAS ST FELIX, *b* 27 Sept 1946, *ed* Stowe, and Southampton Univ (BA Hons); Dep Chm Billington Jackson Advertising Ltd: *m* 1980, Georgina Victoria, da of George Harold Malcolm Scatliff, of The Gate, Wineham, Sussex, and has issue, Lucy Harriet *b* 1982, — Charlotte Dare, *b* 1986. *Residence* – Springlands Farm, Wineham, Henfield, W Sussex BN5 9BP.

DAUGHTER LIVING (*By 1st marriage*)

Sally Ann, *b* 1944. *Residence* – The Folly, High St, Buxted, E Sussex TN22 4LA.

DAUGHTER LIVING OF SECOND BARONET

Nancy Amelia, *b* 1924: *m* 1948, Michael John Bowman-Vaughan, and has issue living, Michael Thomas, *b* 1959, — Annabel Leslie, *b* 1949, — Juliet Euphrosyne, *b* 1951: *m* 1995, Brian McDonald, — Venetia Mary, *b* 1954. *Residence* – 9 Cope Place, W8.

DAUGHTERS LIVING OF THIRD BARONET

Dawn Nesta (Fairview, Carter's Corner, Hilsham, Sussex BN27 4HY), *b* 1909. —— Joyce Katherine (Nyton House, Nyton Rd, Westergate, Sussex PO20 6UL), *b* 1910: *m* 1937 (*m diss* 1954), Lt-Col John Ralph Walker, and has had issue, Gay, *b* 1941; *d* 1986. —— Daphne Myddelton (Garden Hill Cottage, Steep, Petersfield, Hants), *b* 1914: *m* 1st, 1939, Sqdn Ldr Frederick U. Hollins, AFC, RAFVR, who was *ka* 1942; 2ndly, 1948, Maj Malcolm Comrie Gray, Worcestershire Regt, and has issue living, (by 1st *m*) Sarah Daphne, *b* 1941: *m* 1963 (*m diss* 19——), John Anthony Massereene-James, and has issue living, Toby Julius *b* 1969, — (by 2nd *m*) Fiona Catherine, *b* 1949: *m* 1974, Edward James Fairbairn, and has issue (*see* Fairbairn, Bt, colls).

The 1st baronet, Sir Thomas, was Chm and Director (sometime Ch Manager) of Hong Kong and Shanghai Bank, Hong Kong. The 2nd baronet, Brig-Gen Thomas Dare Jackson, DSO, MVO, late King's Own Roy Regt, was Assist Mil Sec to Gov of Gibraltar 1910-14, and served in S African War 1901-2 and European War 1914-17.

JACKSON (UK)1913, of Eagle House, Wimbledon, Surrey

Sir NICHOLAS FANE ST GEORGE JACKSON, 3rd *Baronet*; *b* 4 Sept 1934; *s* his father, *Sir* HUGH NICHOLAS, 1979; *ed* Radley, Wadham Coll, Oxford, and Royal Academy of Music; Organist, Composer and Harpsichordist; Member of Court of Drapers' Co (Junior Warden 1985, Warden 1993, Master 1994-95); Dir Concertante of London, St David's Cathedral Bach Festival, and Santes Creus Festival, Spain; Organist at St Anne's Ch, Soho 1963-71, and St James's Piccadilly 1971-74, St Lawrence Jewry-next-Guildhall 1974-77 and of St David's Cathedral 1977-84; annual tours of Spain 1979-89; Recitals and Broadcasts in Berlin 1967, Recitals in Paris 1972, and 1975, and USA 1975-88, etc: *m* 1st, 1961 (*m diss* 1968), Jennifer Ann, da of F. A. Squire, of 8 Marylebone St, W1; 2ndly, 1972, Nadia Françoise Genevieve, da of Georges Michard, Director de la Maison de la Culture, St Etienne, 42, France, and has issue by 2nd *m*.

Arms – Argent, a greyhound courant ermines, between three eagles' heads erased sable. Crest – A demi-horse argent, guttée de sang, maned and hoofed sable.
Residence – 42 Hereford Rd, W2 5AT. *Club* – Bath.

SON LIVING (*By 2nd marriage*)

THOMAS GRAHAM ST GEORGE, *b* 5 Oct 1980.

SISTER LIVING

Louise Loftus, *b* 1946.

WIDOW LIVING OF SECOND BARONET

VIOLET MARGUERITE LOFTUS (*Violet, Lady Jackson*), da of late Loftus St George (*see* St George, Bt, colls): *m* 1931, Sir Hugh Nicholas Jackson, 2nd Bt, who *d* 1979.

Sir Thomas Graham Jackson, RA, 1st Bt was an architect who designed many churches, private houses, and scholastic and public buildings in Oxford and Cambridge and elsewhere, and was author of many books on architecture.

Mather-Jackson, see Jackson, Bt, cr 1869.

JAFFRAY (UK) 1892, of Skilts, Studley, Warwickshire

Sir WILLIAM OTHO JAFFRAY, 5th *Baronet*; *b* 1 Nov 1951; *s* his father, *Col Sir* WILLIAM EDMUND, TD, 1953; *ed* Eton: *m* 1981 (*m diss* 1997), Cynthia Ross (*née* Corrington), da of Mrs William M. Geering, of Montreal, Quebec, Canada, and has issue.

Arms – Argent, three pallets sable on a fesse cotised gules, four mullets or. Crest – On a mound in front of two palm branches in orle vert, a mullet as in the arms.
Residence – Priors Dean, Petersfield, Hants GU32 1BP.

SONS LIVING

NICHOLAS GORDON ALEXANDER, *b* 18 Oct 1982. —— Jack Henry William, *b* 1987. —— William Lawrence Paget, *b* 1990.

DAUGHTER LIVING

Post nubila Phoebus
After clouds sunshine

Alexandra Marina Ross, *b* 1984.

WIDOW LIVING OF FOURTH BARONET

ANNE (*Lady Jaffray*), only da of late Capt John Otho Paget, MC, of Thorpe Satchville Hall, nr Melton Mowbray, and formerly wife of late Sir John Godfrey Worsley-Taylor, 3rd Bt, a Member of Hants Co Council 1964-80: *m* 1950, as his second wife, Col Sir William Edmund Jaffray, TD, DL, 4th Bt, who *d* 1953. *Residence* – Flat A9, Sloane Avenue Mansions, Sloane Av, SW3 3JF.

The 1st baronet, Sir John, founded the Jaffray Chronic Hospital, Birmingham, and was many years connected with the *Birmingham Daily Post*. The 3rd baronet, Sir John Jaffray (Lt Worcestershire Yeo), was *ka* 1916. The 4th baronet, Sir William Edmund Jaffray, TD, was Col (ret) late Comdg Warwickshire Yeo and a JP and DL for Warwickshire.

JAMES (UK) 1823, of Dublin (Dormant or Extinct 1979)

Sir FULLARTON JAMES, CBE, 6th and last *Baronet*.

COLLATERAL BRANCH LIVING

Granddaughters of late Charles Pierce Rowley James, 2nd son of Charles Henry James, 4th son of 1st baronet:—
Issue of late Rowley Kingston James, *b* 1901, *d* 1938: *m* 1926, Vera Léontine, who *d* 1983, da of Arnold Fatio Rideleux:—
Elizabeth Virginia, *b* 1928: *m* 1953, William John Hindmoor Youdale, of St Martin, Mougins, France, 06, and has had issue, James Robert (23 Rue Pres Kennedy, 91440 Bures/Yvette, France), *b* 1954: *m* 1982, Alicia, da of Julian Vasquez, of Glendale, California, USA, and has issue living, Laura Jane *b* 1987, — Peter William, *b* 1958: *m* 19— (*m diss* 19—), — , and has issue living, Clara *b* 1989, — Frederic Michael, *b* 1969, — Angela Jane, *b* 1956; *d* 1979. —— Sheila Margaret, *b* 1931: *m* 1955, Nigel Henry Whitfeld, and has issue living, Nicholas Rowley, *b* 1958, — Toby Martin, *b* 1959, — Lisa Gabrielle, *b* 1966. —— Patricia Mary, *b* 1933.

This family came originally from Somersetshire. Thomas, — whose father, Capt Thomas James, undertook, by the command of Charles I, a voyage to discover the north-west passage, — sold his estates in Somersetshire, went to Ireland, as an officer in Cromwell's army at the time of the Rebellion, and eventually settled in King's County. The 1st baronet, Sir John Kingston, KB, was Lord Mayor of Dublin 1821-2 and 1840-41, and the 2nd baronet, as el son of a baronet, received knighthood 1854. The 6th baronet, Sir Fullarton, CBE, Ch Constable of Radnorshire and Northumberland, *d* 1955, when the baronetcy became Dormant. The last heir Mr Gerard Bowes Kingston James *d* 1979.

Jamsetjee Jejeebhoy, see Jejeebhoy.

JARDINE (NS) 1672, of Applegirth, Dumfriesshire

Beware: I am present!

Sir ALEXANDER MAULE JARDINE OF APPLEGIRTH, 12th *Baronet; b* 24 Aug 1947; *s* his father, *Col Sir* WILLIAM EDWARD, OBE, TD, 1986; 23rd Chief of Clan Jardine; *ed* Gordonstoun; a Member of Queen's Body Guard for Scotland (Royal Company of Archers): *m* 1982, Mary Beatrice, only da of late Hon John Michael Inigo Cross (*see* V Cross), and has issue.

Arms – Argent, a saltire and chief gules, the last charged with three mullets of the field pierced of the second. Crest – A spurrowel of six points argent. Supporters – *Dexter,* a horse at liberty proper; *sinister,* a man in armour having a scimitar at his side proper.
Residence – Ash House, Thwaites, Millom, Cumbria LA18 5HY.

SONS LIVING

WILLIAM MURRAY, yr of Applegirth, *b* 4 July 1984. —— John Alexander Cross, *b* 1991. —— Douglas Edward, *b* 1994.

DAUGHTERS LIVING

Kirsty Sybil, *b* 1986. —— Jean Maule, *b* 1988.

BROTHER LIVING

William (Driftway Cottage, Dullingham Ley, Newmarket, Suffolk), *b* 1952; *ed* Sedbergh.

AUNT LIVING (*Daughter of 10th baronet*)

Christian Maule: *m* 1940, Lieut-Col Charles Patrick Anderson, Argyll and Sutherland Highlanders, and has issue living, Charles Adair (Ravensheugh, Selkirk), *b* 1946: *m* 1973, Patiénce, da of Joseph Crewdson Howard, and has issue living, Lewis Adair *b* 1978, Ralph Oliver *b* 1985, Alice Selby *b* 1976, — Roderick William (Blantyre, Lenox, Mass, USA), *b* 1950: *m* 1983, Evelyne Corbier, — Andrena Christian, *b* 1943: *m* 1st, 1969 (*m diss* 1996), Col Alastair William Scott-Elliot, Argyll & Sutherland Highrs; 2ndly, 1996, Nicholas S. R. Duffin, of Grey Point, Helen's Bay, Bangor, co Down, and has issue living (by 1st *m*), Robin James *b* 1970: *m* 1994, Emma V., da of Alan Walker, of Alne, N Yorks, Simon Charles *b* 1972, — Araminta Patricia, *b* (twin) 1950: *m* 1st, 1985, Peter John Hall, of Colorado, USA; 2ndly, 1994, Æneas Mackay, of Ardalanish Farm, Bunessan, I of Mull. *Residence* – Ulva Ferry, I of Mull, Argyllshire.

WIDOW LIVING OF ELEVENTH BARONET

ANN GRAHAM MAITLAND (*Ann, Lady Jardine of Applegirth*), da of late Lt-Col Claud Archibald Scott Maitland, Gordon Highlanders, of Dundrennan and Cumstoun, Stewartry of Kirkcudbright: *m* 1944, Sir William Edward Jardine of Applegirth, 11th Bt, OBE, TD, who *d* 1986. *Residence* – Little Dyke, Dalton, Lockerbie, Dumfriesshire.

COLLATERAL BRANCHES LIVING

Grandchildren of late Rev Charles John Jardine, 3rd son of 7th baronet:—
Issue of late Edward William Ratcliff Jardine, *b* 1872, *d* 19—: *m* 1910, May Janet, da of Capt J. Hubby, of El Toro, Calif, USA:—
Dorothea Twining, *b* 1911.

Issue of late Peter St John Jardine, *b* 1879, *b* 1957: *m* 1919, Monica Maud, who *d* 1951, da of Capt Leonard Head, MRCS, of Walthamstow:—
Piers Leonard St John, *b* 1921: *m* 1950, Jean Marjorie, da of Thomas James Vallis, of W Wickham, Kent, and has a son, Timothy Piers, *b* 1967. *Residence* – Lockerbie, 53 Barrow Green Rd, Oxted, Surrey RH8 ONJ.

Granddaughters of late Frank Lascelles Jardine (*infra*):—
Issue of late Bertie Bootle Arthur Lascelles Jardine, *b* 1884, *d* 1973: *m* 1919, Bessie Duffy, who *d* 1966:—
Marie Dempster Lascelles (Unit 2, 3 Ruth St, Como, W Australia 6152), *b* 1920: *m* 1987, Ian Campbell Shaw. —— Elizabeth Margaret Lascelles, *b* 1927: *m* 1948, Ronald Williamson, of 22 Mainsail St, Marlin Waters, Gold Coast, Qld 4223, Australia, and has issue.

Grandsons of late Alice Maule Lascelles Jardine (who *m* 1900, Capt Herbert Graham Vidgen, who *d* 1960), elder da of late Frank Lascelles Jardine, eldest son of Capt John Jardine (*infra*):—
Issue of late Maj Herbert Somerset Vidgen, Royal Australian Engrs, *b* 1901, *d* 1973: *m* 1936, Beatrice Werna Reid:—
Grahame Lascelles JARDINE-VIDGEN (Applegirth, 83 Terowi St, Sunnybank Hills, Qld 4109, Australia), *b* 1941; Capt 2/14 LH (QMI) RAAC (Armoured) Res (National Medal); JP Queensland; assumed the surname of Jardine-Vidgen by deed poll 1980, for himself and his issue: *m* 1967, Judith Elizabeth McMullan, and has issue living, Catherine Elizabeth, *b*

1968: *m* 1997, Dr Gary Ronald Hughes (grandson of Chief of Clan Chisholm), and has issue living, Lauren Amelia *b* 1994, Beth Louise *b* 1997, — Melinda Louise, *b* 1971: *m* 1999, Steven Michael Toomey, — Roslyn Annette, *b* 1973. —— John Newton VIDGEN, *b* 1944; Lt Royal Australian Commando (Res). —— Bruce Somerset VIDGEN, *b* (twin) 1944.

Grandson of late John Robert Jardine, yst son of Capt John Jardine, 4th son of 6th baronet:—
Issue of late Francis Alexander Lascelles Jardine, *b* 1893, *d* 1950: *m* 1924, Madge Dorothy Ellen Blackman, who *d* 1977, of Brisbane:—
Murray Hugh Lascelles (5 Somerset St, Toowoomba, Queensland 4350, Australia), *b* 1925: *m* 1950, Alma Glenise Byrne, and has issue living, Jan Frances Lascelles, *b* 1952, — Mary Elizabeth Lascelles, *b* 1958: *m* 1996, Gordon Dudley Bossley, of 31 Royal Terrace, Hamilton, Brisbane, Qld 4007, Australia.

Sir Alexander Jardine was *cr* a baronet of Nova Scotia with remainder to his heirs male whatsoever. This line are Chiefs of the Clan Jardine.

JARDINE (UK) 1916, of Godalming, co Surrey

Beware: I am here

Sir ANDREW COLIN DOUGLAS JARDINE, 5th *Baronet*; *b* 30 Nov 1955; *s* his father, *Brig Sir* IAN LIDDELL, OBE, MC, 1982; *ed* Charterhouse, RAC Cirencester, and Reading Univ; late RGJ; Henderson Administration Group plc 1981-92, Dir Gartmore Investment Trust Management Ltd 1992-93, Strutt & Parker since 1996; ARICS; Member Securities Inst; Member Queen's Body Guard for Scotland (Royal Company of Archers): *m* 1997, Dr Claire Vyvien, da of Dr William Griffith, of The White House, Lyth Hill, Shrewsbury, and has issue.

Arms – Gules, a saltire argent charged in the centre point with a lotus flower proper, on a chief of the second six mullets of the first. **Crest** – A mullet of six points pierced gules, between two palm branches proper.
Residence – Crabtree Barn, Duntisbourne Leek, Cirencester, Glos GL7 7AS.

DAUGHTER LIVING

Iona Claire, *b* 1999.

BROTHER LIVING

MICHAEL IAN CHRISTOPHER, *b* 4 Oct 1958; *ed* Charterhouse: *m* 1982, (Maria) Milky Pineda, and has issue living, Oliver Michael Ian, *b* 20 Feb 1983, — Adrian Douglas Francis, *b* 1986. *Residence* – 12 Graham Av, Ealing, W13 9TQ.

SISTERS LIVING

Harriet Ann, *b* 1949: *m* 1972, Maj-Gen Anthony Malcolm Douglas Palmer, late RGJ, and has issue living, Edward Anthony Douglas, *b* 1975, — Henry Arthur Douglas, *b* 1982, — Alice Georgina, *b* 1976. —— Jean Margaret, *b* 1951: *m* 1984 (*m diss* 1988), (James) Andrew Gardiner Baird (later 11th Bt), and has issue (*see* Baird, Bt, *cr* 1695).

AUNTS LIVING (*Daughters of 3rd baronet*)

Elizabeth, *b* 1921: *m* 1946, John Edward Sharpley, BM, BCh, and has had issue, Mark Alastair, *b* 1947, — Oliver John, *b* 1949, — Sarah Marily, *b* 1952; *d* 1992. *Residence* – Ravenshaw, Tanners Lane, Burford, Oxon OX18 4NA. —— Gillian Fiona, *b* 1930: *m* 1954, Ian Grant MacKenzie, MD, FRCS, who *d* 1986, and has issue living, Alistair Grant, *b* 1955, — Angus Colin, *b* 1957, — Andrew Kenneth, *b* 1958. *Residence* – Nether Kingshill, Kingswells, Aberdeenshire.

WIDOW LIVING OF FOURTH BARONET

PRISCILLA DAPHNE (*Priscilla, Lady Jardine*), da of Douglas Middleton Parnham Scott-Phillips, of Halkshill, Largs, Ayrshire: *m* 1948, Brig Sir Ian Liddell Jardine, 4th Bt, OBE, MC, who *d* 1982. *Residence* – Teal House, Cheriton, Alresford, Hants SO24 0PW.

COLLATERAL BRANCHES LIVING

Issue of late Lionel Westropp Jardine, CIE, 3rd son of 1st baronet, *b* 1895, *d* 1980: *m* 1922, Marjorie Mildred, who *d* 1994, da of Maj Richard John Woods, OBE:—
John Alexander, *b* 1939; *ed* Charterhouse: *m* 1971, Catherine Marie, da of André Trentesaux, of Lille, France, and has issue living, Emily, *b* 1979, — Alice, *b* 1980. —— Barbara Ann, *b* 1925: *m* 1964, Neville John Cooper, of 6 Victoria Rd,

W8 5RD, and has issue living, Susan Ann, b 1964, — Henrietta Jane, b 1967. ——— (Jean) Alison, b 1928: m 1949, Frederick Disney Rivers Currie, and has issue (see Currie Bt, colls).

Issue of late Rev Canon Kenneth William Seymour Jardine, 4th son of 1st baronet, b 1899, d 1960: m 1926, Katharine Frances, who d 1932, da of W. Cranswick Noad, formerly of Mount Tabor House, Perth:—
Rev David Eric Cranswick (44 Taptin Hill Rd, Crosspool, Sheffield S10 5AQ), b 1930; ed Corpus Christi Coll, Oxford (MA, Dip Th 1954); formerly R Christ Church, Smannell with St George, Enham Alamein, Andover: m 1955, Elsie Vera Susan Shanks, and has issue living, Charles Kenneth Herbert, b 1960: m 1988, Jacqueline Hannah, and has issue living, Ruari John b 1994, Catriona Louise b 1992, — Katharine Shelagh Margaret, b 1957: m 1984, Angus G. Grandfield, and has issue living, Colin Douglas Hugh b 1988, Alexander David George, b 1992, Francis Gregory Charles b 1994, Ruth Katriona b 1986, — Rachel Heather Agnes, b 1965: m 1995, David Schoon.

The 1st baronet, Sir John Jardine, KCIE, LLD, JP, was a Puisne Judge of Bombay High Court 1885-97, and sat as MP for Roxburghshire (L) 1906-18. The 3rd baronet, Maj-Gen Sir Colin Arthur Jardine, CB, DSO, MC, DL, late RA, was Dep Gov of Gibraltar, a Member of House of Laity, Church Assembly, Mil Sec to Com-in-Ch, British Expeditionary Force 1939-40, and Director of Army Welfare 1943. The 4th baronet, Brig Sir Ian Liddell Jardine, OBE, MC, Coldm Gds, was ADC to HM 1976-78.

BUCHANAN-JARDINE (UK) 1885, of Castle Milk, co Dumfries.

Beware: I am present!

The lion's anger is noble

Sir (ANDREW) RUPERT JOHN BUCHANAN-JARDINE, MC, 4th *Baronet*, b 2 Feb 1923; s his father, *Capt Sir* JOHN WILLIAM, 1969; ed Harrow, and RAC Cirencester; Maj RHG; DL of Nithsdale and Annandale and Eskdale: m 1950 (m diss 1975), Jane Fiona, da of Sir Archibald Charles Edmonstone, 6th Bt, and has issue.

𝕬rms – Quarterly 1st and 4th per pale argent and or a saltire gules, on a chief engrailed of the third three mullets of the first, *Jardine*; 2nd, or, a lion rampant gules with a double tressure flory counter-flory, sable, *Buchanan*; 3rd, sable, a chevron, between three bears' heads argent, muzzled gules, *Leny*. 𝕮rests – 1st, a spur rowel of six points gules, *Jardine*; 2nd, a sword erect in pale proper, hilted and pommelled or.
Seat – Castle Milk, Lockerbie, Dumfries-shire. *Residence* – Dixons, Lockerbie, Dumfries-shire. *Club* – MCC.

SON LIVING

JOHN CHRISTOPHER RUPERT (Castle Milk, Lockerbie, Dumfries-shire), b 20 March 1952; ed Harrow, and RAC Cirencester: m 1975, Pandora Lavinia, yr da of Peter Murray Lee, and has issue living, James Rupert, b 28 July 1994, — Tessa Mary, b 1979, — Katie Luella, b 1980, — Lorna Jane, b 1984, — Juliet Marina, b 1986, — Alice Fiona, b 1988.

DAUGHTER LIVING

Diana Gwendolyn Jean (27 Pier House, Cheyne Walk, SW3), b 1955.

HALF-BROTHER LIVING

(Charles) James (27 Queens Gate Place Mews, SW7; Turf, New (Edinburgh), White's, and R Hong Kong Jockey Clubs), b 1946; ed Stowe, and Trin Coll, Camb; ARIBA: m 1967 (m diss 1978), Lady Susan Ankaret Howard, da of 11th Earl of Carlisle; 2ndly, 1978, Irmgard Margarethe, da of Maj Rudolf Bormann, and has issue living, (by 1st m) Flora Jane, b 1971, — (by 2nd m) Claire Isabel, b 1980, — Olivia Rose, b 1982.

HALF-SISTER LIVING

Caroline Anne, b 1952.

WIDOW LIVING OF THIRD BARONET

PRUDENCE AUDREY (*Prudence, Lady Buchanan-Jardine*) (Moulin de la Mourachonne, 06370 Mouans Sartoux, France, AM), da of William Haggie, of Knayton, Thirsk, Yorks: m 1944, as his 2nd wife, Capt Sir John William Buchanan-Jardine, 3rd Bt, who d 1969.

The 1st baronet, Sir Robert Jardine, the 2nd baronet, Sir Robert William Buchanan Jardine, and the 3rd baronet, Sir John William Buchanan-Jardine, were successively head of the firm of Jardine, Matheson and Co, merchants in China. The 1st baronet also sat as MP for Ashburton (L) 1865-8, for Dumfries Burghs 1868-74, and Dumfriesshire 1880-92. The 3rd baronet assumed the additional surname of Buchanan since his grandmother, Margaret Seton, wife of the 1st baronet, was da of John Buchanan Hamilton of Leny, Perthshire, and sister and heir of John Hamilton-Buchanan, Ch of Clan Buchanan.

JARVIS (UK) 1922, of Hascombe Court, co Surrey (Extinct 1965)

Sir (ARNOLD) ADRIAN JARVIS, 2nd and last *Baronet*.

DAUGHTER LIVING OF FIRST BARONET

Brenda Beryl (*Lady Williams*), *b* 1907; a JP for Denbighshire: *m* 1932, Sir Francis John Watkin Williams, 8th Bt, QC, JP, of Llys, Middle Lane, Denbigh.

DUNNINGTON-JEFFERSON (UK) 1958, of Thorganby Hall East Riding of Yorkshire

Salvation by the Cross

Sir MERVYN STEWART DUNNINGTON-JEFFERSON, 2nd *Baronet*; *b* 5 Aug 1943; *s* his father *Lt-Col Sir* JOHN ALEXANDER, DSO, 1979; *ed* Eton: *m* 1971, Caroline Anna, only da of late John Bayley, of Hillam Hall, Monk Fryston, Yorks, and has issue.

Arms – Quarterly: 1st and 4th, gules, a griphon sejant wings addorsed argent, a bordure engrailed of the last charged with eight pellets, *Jefferson*; 2nd and 3rd, paly of six argent and azure, on a chief gules a bezant between to annulets or, *Dunnington*. Crests – 1st griphon as in the arms gorged with a collar gemel, azure in the beak a lily slipped proper, *Jefferson*; 2nd, a horse current argent gorged with a collar gules charged with a bezant between two annulets or, *Dunnington*.
Residence – 7 Bolingbroke Grove, SW11 6ES. *Clubs* – MCC, and Queen's.

SON LIVING

JOHN ALEXANDER, *b* 23 March 1980.

DAUGHTERS LIVING

Annabelle Mary, *b* 1973. —— Emma Elizabeth, *b* 1978.

SISTER LIVING

Rosemary Nicolette, *b* 1941.

WIDOW LIVING OF FIRST BARONET

(FRANCES) ISOBEL (*Isobel, Lady Dunnington-Jefferson*) (Rectory Cottage, Escrick, York Y04 6LE), da of Col Herbert Anderson Cape, DSO, of Thorganby, York: *m* 1938, Lt-Col Sir John Alexander Dunnington-Jefferson, DSO, 1st Bt, who *d* 1979.

JEHANGIR (UK) 1908, of Bombay

Sir HIRJI JEHANGIR, 3rd *Baronet*, *b* 1 Nov 1915: *s* his father, *Sir* COW-
ASJI, GBE, KCIE, 1962; *ed* St Xavier's Sch, Bombay, and Magdalene
Coll, Camb; Chm of Jehangir Art Gallery, Bombay, Pres Parsi Public
Sch Soc, Chm Cowasji Jehangir Charitable Trust: *m* 1952, Jinoo, elder
da of late Kakushroo H. Cama, and has issue.

Arms – Azure, a sun in splendour within an orle of mullets, or, on a canton argent a
rose gules slipped proper in bend surmounting a lotus flower in a bend sinister also
proper. **Crest** – Upon a mount a column, thereon flames of fire all proper.
Residences – Readymoney House, 49 Nepean Sea Rd, Bombay, 400 036; 24 Kensington
Court Gdns, Kensington Court Place, W8. *Clubs* – Royal Over-Seas League, Willingdon (Bombay).

SONS LIVING

JEHANGIR, *b* 23 Nov 1953: *m* 1988, Jasmine, da of Beji Billimoria, and has issue living,
Cowasji (a son), *b* 28 March 1990, — Simone, *b* 1994. —— Ardeshir, *b* 1956.

SISTER LIVING

Sylla, *b* 1914: *m* 1946, Richard Holmes, of 24 Kensington Court Gdns, W8.

By special Act of Legislative Council of India 1911 (dissolved 1964), all future
holders of the title were to relinquish their own names and assume those of the 1st
baronet. The 1st baronet, Sir Cowasjee Jehangir (who assumed the name of Cowasjee
Jehangir in lieu of Jehangir Cowasjee), was nephew and adopted son and heir of late Sir Cowasjee Jehangir, CSI, a
leader of the Parsee Community, a great Philanthropist, and Industrialist, and a lineal descendant of Hirji Jehangir
Readymoney, who resided in Bombay in 1717, and was the Banker to East India Company. Sir Cowasjee Jehangir, GBE,
KCIE, 2nd Bt, was Member of Bombay Corporation 1902-21, and Chm 1914-15, a MEC Bombay 1921-26, and a MLA
Delhi 1932-47.

JEJEEBHOY (UK) 1857, of Bombay

Sir JAMSETJEE JEJEEBHOY, 7th *Baronet*, el son of late Rustamjee J.
C. Jamsetjee, nephew of 4th Baronet: *b* 19 April 1913; *s* his kins-
man, *Sir* Jamsetjee, 1968, when he assumed the name of
Jamsetjee Jejeebhoy, in lieu of Maneckjee Rustamjee Jamsetjee;
ed Bombay Univ (BA): *m* 1943, Shirin, da of late Jehangir
Hormusjee Cama, and has issue.

Arms – Azure, a sun rising above a representation of "the Ghauts" (mountains
near Bombay) in base, and in chief two bees volant, all proper. **Crest** – A
mount vert, thereon a peacock (close) amidst wheat, and in the beak an ear of
wheat all proper.
Residence – Beaulieu, 95 Worli Seaface, Bombay 400 025.

SON LIVING

Rustomjee, *b* 16 Nov 1957; *ed* Bombay Univ; B Com, LLM: *m* 1984, Delara, da
of late Jal Nariman Bhaisa, and has issue living, Jehangir, *b* 20 Jan 1986.

DAUGHTER LIVING

Ayesha, *b* 1952.

DAUGHTERS LIVING OF SIXTH BARONET

Shireen (Sett Minar, Pedder Rd, Bombay 26, India) *b* 1952. —— Deanna, *b*
1953. —— Geeta, *b* 1955.

COLLATERAL BRANCH LIVING

Granddaughter of late Jamsetjee Cursetjee Jamsetjee, brother of 4th baronet, *b* 1860, *d* 1916: *m* 1882,
Awabai Sharpurjee Dhunjeebhoy, who *d* 1926:—
Issue of late Cursetjee J. C. Jamsetjee, *b* 1897, *d* 1982: *m* 1937, Mary Feroze Jehangir, who *d* 1997:—
Pirojbai, *b* 1938: *m* 1988, Burjor Sorabji Cooper, of Darbhanga Mansion, Carmichael Rd, Bombay 400026.

The 1st baronet, Sir Jamsetjee, Knt, a wealthy Parsee merchant, was renowned for his benevolence, charity, munificence, and loyalty, a reputation that was also earned by his son, the 2nd baronet. In 1860 a special Act of the Legislative Council of India was passed, with the sanction of HM Queen Victoria, by which all future holders of the title are to relinquish their own names and assume that of the 1st baronet. The 3rd baronet was MLC of Bombay. The 4th baronet was Sheriff of Bombay 1900. The 5th baronet was Dep Pres of Indian Legislative Assembly 1921-31. The 6th baronet was an Industrialist and Banker.

JENKINSON (E) 1661, of Walcot, Oxfordshire, and Hawkesbury, Gloucestershire

I obey, I do not serve

Sir JOHN BANKS JENKINSON, 14th *Baronet*; *b* 16 Feb 1945; *s* his father, *Sir* ANTHONY BANKS, 1989; *ed* Eton, and Univ of Miami: *m* 1979, Josephine Mary, da of late Samuel William Marshall-Andrew, and has issue.

𝕬rms – Azure, on a fesse wavy argent, a cross-patée gules, in chief two estoiles or. ℭrest – A sea-horse assurgent, or maned azure, supporting a cross-patée as in the arms.
Seat – Hawkesbury, Badminton, Glos. *Residence* – Hawkesbury Home Farm, Badminton, Glos.

SON LIVING

GEORGE ANTHONY SAMUEL BANKS, *b* 8 Nov 1980.

DAUGHTER LIVING

Samantha Emma, *b* 1983.

SISTERS LIVING

Jennifer Ann, *b* 1947: *m* 1976, Robert Waddington, son of late George Waddington, of Lytham, Lancs, and has issue living, Thomas Anthony, *b* 1977, — Guy George, *b* 1979. *Residence* – The Old Vicarage, Upper Minety, Malmesbury, Wilts SN16 9PY. —— Emily Frances Joan, *b* 1953: *m* 19—, Miguel Malgaret, of Fort Lauderdale, Florida, USA, and has issue living, Christopher, *b* 1977.

COLLATERAL BRANCH LIVING

Grandchildren of Lt-Col George Seymour Charles Jenkinson, DSO, son of late John Henry Jenkinson, brother of 11th baronet:—
Issue of late Capt Robert Charles Horace Jenkinson, *b* 1900, *d* 1970: *m* 1st, 1925 (*m diss* 1936), Hon Barbara Vernon Harcourt, OBE, who *d* 1961; 2ndly, 1938, Gwyneth, who *d* 1988, da of A. Llewellyn Matthews:—
(By 1st *m*) Julian Charles Lewis (Folly Faunts House, Goldhanger, Maldon, Essex), *b* 1926; *ed* Eton: *m* 1953, Diana Catherine, only da of late Maj George Henry William Baird (*see* Baird, Bt, *cr* 1809, colls), and has issue living, Dermot Julian, *b* 1954: *m* 1979, Miranda Jane, el da of John Maxwell Menzies, of Kames, Berwickshire (*see* Dawson Bt *cr* 1920), and has issue living, Oliver John Banks *b* 1984, Emily Lavinia *b* 1981, — Karen Barbara, *b* 1957: *m* 1981, Capt Robert Sturdee Mason, WG, — Laura Louise Diana, *b* 1966: *m* 1994, John Mackay. —— Clare Barbara, *b* 1933: *m* 1955 (*m diss* 1984), William McCully, of Leitrim Farm, Loughries, Newtownards, co Down, and has issue living, Patrick William, *b* 1965, — Lucinda Barbara, *b* 1962: *m* 1981, Robert Wallace McKee, of Ballydoo House, Ballyblack, Newtownards, co Down. —— (By 2nd *m*) Frances Caroline (Sycamore House, Swanton Novers, nr Melton Constable, Norfolk NR24 2RB), *b* 1942.

The 1st, 2nd, 3rd, 4th and 5th baronets were successively Members of Parliament for Oxfordshire; the 7th baronet, celebrated statesman, was created Earl of Liverpool, and his son, the 8th baronet and 2nd earl, was for many years Prime Minister of England. The peerage became extinct on the death of the 3rd earl, when the baronetcy devolved upon his cousin, Sir Charles, 10th Bt, MP for Dover, who was nephew of the 1st Earl of Liverpool. Sir George, 11th Bt, sat as MP for Wiltshire, N (*C*) 1868-80.

JENKS (UK) 1932, of Cheape, in the City of London

Sir (MAURICE ARTHUR) BRIAN JENKS, 3rd *Baronet*; *b* 28 Oct 1933; *s* his father, *Sir* RICHARD ATHERLEY, 1993; *ed* Charterhouse; CA: *m* 1962, Susan Lois, eldest da of (Frank) Leslie Allen, of Glenside, Star Lane, Hooley, Coulsdon, Surrey, and has issue.

Arms – Per fesse indented sable and argent, on a pile or a boar's head, and in base two boars' heads all couped sable; on a chief ermine a representation of the sword and mace of the City of London in saltire proper. *Crest* – A sinister arm embowed vested sable, cuffed argent, grasping in the hand a sword in bend proper, pommel and hilt or, enfiled with a ducal coronet gold.
Residence – Warren House, Savernake, Marlborough, Wilts SN8 3BQ.

ADOPTED SON LIVING

Timothy Charles, *b* 1967.

DAUGHTER LIVING

Marjorie Emma, *b* 1964: *m* 1994, William Valerian Wellesley, and has issue (*see* E Cowley, colls).

BROTHER LIVING

DECVS·RECTE·PETO

I seek honour honourably

RICHARD JOHN PETER (81 Onslow Sq, SW7), *b* 28 June 1936; *ed* Charterhouse; late 5th Royal Inniskilling Dragoon Guards; FCA: *m* 1963, Juniper Li-Yung, eldest da of late Tan Sri Y. C. Foo, of 18 Golf Club Rd, Ipoh, Malaysia, and has issue living, Richard Albert Benedict, *b* 1965; *ed* Eton, and New Coll Oxford: *m* 1998, Jo, da of Sydney Webster, of Biddulph, Staffs, and of Mrs Pauline Cree, of Shavington-cum-Gresty, Ches, — Melissa Kate Rosalind, *b* 1967, — Serena Anne Louise, *b* 1970.

WIDOW LIVING OF SECOND BARONET

MARJORIE SUZANNE ARLETTE (*Dowager Lady Jenks*), da of Sir Arthur Philip du Cros, 1st Bt: *m* 1932, Sir Richard Atherley Jenks, 2nd Bt, who *d* 1993. *Residence* – 42 Sussex Sq, W2 2SR.

COLLATERAL BRANCH LIVING

Issue of late Cdr Robert Fergus Jenks, DSC, RN, yr son of 1st baronet, *b* 1909, *d* 1982: *m* 1st, 1933 (*m diss* 1938), Joyce Wynne, only da of A. E. Booth, of Hendon; 2ndly, 1939, Molly Estelle (46 Woodgreen Rd, Harestock, nr Winchester, Hants), 3rd da of Lt Cdr Albert Edward Griffiths, RN (ret), of Parkstone, Dorset, and formerly wife of Fl Lt John F. Dales, RAF:—
(By 2nd *m*) Robert Philip (Menmar, Moll de Llevant 303, Mahon, Menorca, Spain), *b* 1948; *ed* in Rhodesia, and HMS Worcester; Yacht Broker: *m* 1st, 1968 (*m diss* 1983), Susan, only da of John B. Campbell, of Henley-on-Thames, Oxon; 2ndly, 1990, Tracy Jane, only da of Colin V. Hives, of Stone Farm, Hailey, Ipsden, Oxon. —— Sally Elizabeth, *b* 1945: *m* 1968 (*m diss* 19—), John Norman Anderson Wylie, only son of late Lieut John Norman Anderson, USN, and Mrs Joan Wylie, and adopted son of Amos K. Wylie, of New York, and has issue living, Peter, *b* 1978, — Sarah, *b* 1974.

The 1st baronet, Sir Maurice Jenks (son of Robert Isaac Jenks, of Clapham, SW), was an Alderman of City of London (Sheriff 1930-31, and Lord Mayor 1931-32).

JEPHCOTT (UK) 1962, of East Portlemouth, co Devon.

Sir (JOHN) ANTHONY JEPHCOTT, 2nd *Baronet*; *b* 21 May 1924; *s* his father, *Sir* HARRY, 1978; *ed* Aldenham, St John's Coll, Oxford, and LSE (BCom); Hon FFA, RACS 1990, Hon FANZCA 1992; 1939-45 War with REME, later RAEC; formerly Manufacturer of Anaesthesia Equipment; Man Dir Penlon Ltd 1952-73, and of Pen Medic Ltd, NZ, 1973-78: *m* 1st, 1949 (*m diss* 1978), Sylvia Mary, da of Thorsten F. Relling, of Wellington, NZ; 2ndly, 1978, Josephine Agnes, da of Philip Sheridan, of Perth, W Aust, and has issue by 1st *m*.

𝕬rms – Azure two chevronels between in chief a mortar and pestle between two escallops or and in base an open book proper edged and clasped or. 𝕮rest – A dove supporting with dexter claw a rod of Æsculapius proper the serpent vert. 𝕸otto – Scientia Salutem Feramus.
Address – 26 Sage Rd, Kohimarama, Auckland 5, NZ.

DAUGHTERS LIVING (*By 1st marriage*)

Helen Mary (13A Tullis Close, Sutton Courtenay, Abingdon, Oxon), *b* 1953: *m* 1977 (*m diss* 1989), David Asbury, and has issue living, Richard Andrew James, *b* 1982, — Alexander Philip Ralph, *b* 1984, — Anna Ruth, *b* 1980. —— Caroline Ruth, *b* 1955: *m* 1979, Nigel Clark Flower, of Hill Farm House, Brinton, Melton Constable, Norfolk, and has issue living, Hugo Gregory, *b* 1985, — Felix James, *b* 1988, — Harriet Christina, *b* 1990.

BROTHER LIVING

NEIL WELBOURN (Thalassa, E Portlemouth, Salcombe, S Devon TQ8 8PU), *b* 3 June 1929; *ed* Aldenham, and Emmanuel Coll, Camb (MA): *m* 1st, 1951, Mary Denise, who *d* 1977, da of Arthur Muddiman, of Abbots Mead, W Clandon, Surrey; 2ndly, 1978, Mary Florence, da of late James John Daly, and has issue living (by 1st *m*), David Welbourn, *b* 1952, — Mark Lanwer, *b* 1957: *m* 1983, Lysa Ann, da of Francis John Rigden, of 50 Cliff Garden, Telescombe Cliff, Sussex, and has issue living, Richard Lanwer *b* 1989, — Penelope Mary, *b* 1955.

The first baronet was Hon Pres and Chm Glaxo Group Ltd; also Pres Assocn of British Chemical Manufacturers 1952-55, Pres of Roy Institute of Chemistry 1953-55, and Chm of Council for Scientific and Industrial Research 1956-61, and of Sch of Pharmacy, Univ of London, 1948-69; also Gov LSE 1952-68, and of N London Collegiate Sch 1957-*ca* 1976.

CLARKE-JERVOISE (UK) 1813, of Idsworth Park, Hampshire (Extinct 1933)

Sir DUDLEY ALAN LESTOCK CLARKE-JERVOISE, 7th and last *Baronet*.

DAUGHTER LIVING OF SEVENTH BARONET

Gladys Agnes, *b* 1909: *m* 1936, Kenneth Southam, MRCS, LRCP, and has issue living, Gilian Margaret, *b* 1938, — Bridget Anne, *b* 1940; *m* 1966, Henry Charles Frank Wickham-Smith, RD, of 8 Wellswood Gdns, Rowlands Castle, Hants, and has issue living, Simon James Southam *b* 1968; BA. *Residence* – 78 Bowes Hill, Rowlands Castle, Hants.

JESSEL (UK) 1883, of Ladham House, Goudhurst, co Kent

Sir CHARLES JOHN JESSEL, 3rd *Baronet*; b 29 Dec 1924; s his father, Sir GEORGE, MC, 1977; ed Eton, and Balliol Coll, Oxford; 1939-45 War as Lieut 15/19th Hussars (despatches); JP (Kent) 1960-78: m 1st, 1956, Shirley Cornelia, who d 1977, da of John Waters, of Northampton; 2ndly, 1979 (m diss 1983), Gwendoline Mary, da of late Laurence Devereux, OBE, and widow of Charles Langer, and has issue by 1st m.

Arms – Azure, a fesse raguly ermine, between three eagles' heads erased argent, in the centre chief point a torch erect fired proper. Crest – A torch fessewise fired proper, surmounted by an eagle volant argent, holding in the beak a pearl of the last.
Residence – South Hill Farm, Hastingleigh, Ashford, Kent TN25 5HL. *Club* – Cavalry and Guards'.

SONS LIVING (By 1st marriage)

GEORGE ELPHINSTONE, b 15 Dec 1957; ed Milton Abbey, and RAC Cirencester: m 1st, 1988 (m diss 1993), Rose Amelia, yr da of James Coutts-Smith, of Wallington, Herts; 2ndly, 1998, Victoria, yst da of Capt Arthur John Brabant Naish, CBE, RN, of Ditteridge, Wilts, and has issue living (by 2nd m), Amelia Holly b 1999. *Residence* – Stoakes Cottage, Hastingleigh, Ashford, Kent TN25 5HG. *Clubs* – Cavalry and Guards', Farmers'. —— Alastair John (Ladham House, Goudhurst, Kent TN17 1DB), b 1959; ed Stowe: m 1988, Gail Alexandra, only da of Gordon Partridge, of Belfry Flat, Scotney Castle, Lamberhurst, Kent, and has issue living, Thomas George William, b 1990, — Camilla Alice Louise, b 1991.

DAUGHTER LIVING (By 1st marriage)

(Cornelia) Sarah, b 1963: m 1999, B. Michael Covell, son of Anthony Covell, of Morebath, Devon, and Mrs Quentin Hogg, of Kensington.

COLLATERAL BRANCH LIVING

Grandchildren of late Sir Richard Hugh Jessel (infra):—
Issue of late David Charles George Jessel, b 1924, d 1985: m 1st, 1950 (m diss 1978), Hon Amelia Grace FitzRoy, da of 2nd Viscount Daventry; 2ndly, 1980, Matilda McCormick, of Kentucky, USA (22 Cambridge Rd, SW11):—
(By 1st m) Richard James, b 1954; ed Eton: m 1982 (m diss 1998), Harriot Josephine, da of late Wilfred J. (Mike) St Pierre Bunbury, and has issue living, David Hugh Joseph, b 1986, — George FitzRoy, b 1990, — Edwina Mary Grace, b 1984. *Residence* – Wanstead House, Alchester Rd, Chesterton, Oxon OX6 8UN. —— Davina Jane, b 1952: m 1st, 1970 (m diss 1976), Hon Richard Tyrell-Kenyon, who d 1982 (see B Kenyon); 2ndly, 1977 (m diss 1984), James Remington-Hobbs; 3rdly, 1988, Charles Richard Markham Phillips, and has issue living (by 1st m: see B Kenyon), — (by 2nd m), Max Hugh, b 1979, — (by 3rd m) Richard David Markham, b 1988, — David Charles, b 1991. *Residence* – Ashland House, N Sydmonton, Newbury, Berks RG20 9JL.

Issue of late Sir Richard Hugh Jessel, yr son of 1st baronet, b 1896, d 1979: m 1st, 1923, Margaret Ella, who d 1953, 2nd da of Sir George James Graham Lewis, 2nd Bt; 2ndly, 1954, Daphne, who d 1971, da of late William Buckley Gladstone, and widow of Maj Thirlwall Philipson, MC, Life Gds; 3rdly, 1972, Diana Mary (who m 4thly, 1981, Col J. C. Cockburn, DSO, MBE, Argyll and Sutherland Highers (ret), who d 1997), da of Maj William Edward Gatacre, of de Wiersse, Vorden, Holland, widow of Col George Richard Trotter, R Scots Greys, and formerly wife of James Edward Michael Clark-Hall:—
(By 1st m) Robin Richard (12 Crooms Hill Grove, Greenwich SE10 8HB. *Club* – Garrick), b 1930; ed Eton, and at Balliol Coll, Oxford (BA); Bar Lincoln's Inn 1953: m 1957, Audrey Gertrude, el da of late Alexander Newman Howard, and has issue living, Simon Dana (36 Erlanger Rd, SE14 5TG), b 1958: m 1986, Christina Julia, yst da of Dennis Reeves, of Parkstone, Dorset, and has issue living, William George b 1995, Ella b 1988, Sarah Louise b 1990, Madeleine Tasia b 1993, — Alexander Robin, b 1961: m 1998, Nicola Ellen Thomas, da of Ellen Vera Thomas, of Dursley, Glos, — Michael Richard (38 Dunsmure Rd, N16 5PW), b 1965: m 1996, Kate Ann, only da of Gordon Wing, of Powick, Worcs, and has issue living, Matilda Rose b 1998, — Virginia Penelope, b 1967. —— Edith Marie, b 1926; ed St Hilda's Coll, Oxford (MA): m 1947, William Joseph Straker-Smith, late Capt Coldm Gds, who d 1987, of Carham, Cornhill-on-Tweed, Northumberland, and has issue living, Peter Dalrymple (Wark Common Farm, Cornhill-on-Tweed, Northumberland TD12 4RR), b 1951; ed Eton, and Pembroke Coll, Camb (BA): m 1981, Susan Steuart, and has issue living, Henry Falkland b 1982, Willa b 1984, — Richard David (3 Berkeley Gdns, W8), b 1959; ed Harrow, — Tessa Diana, b 1949: m 1969, John Robert Robson, of Melbourne Stud, Ayot Green, Welwyn, Herts, and has issue living, James b 1973, Claire b 1972.

The 1st baronet, Charles James (High Sheriff of Kent 1903), was el son of late Rt Hon Sir George Jessel, PC, Master of the Rolls and one of the most eminent Judges of his time. The 2nd son, Herbert Merton, was cr a Baronet 1917 and Baron Jessel 1924.

JOHNSON (GB) 1755, of New York, in North America

Deo Regique debeo
I owe all to God and the King

Not even difficulties frighten me

Sir PETER COLPOYS PALEY JOHNSON, 7th *Baronet*, *b* 26 March 1930; *s* his father, *Lt-Col Sir* JOHN PALEY, MBE, 1975; *ed* Wellington Coll; late Capt RA; Dir of Nautical Publishing Co Ltd 1971-81; author of *Ocean Racing and Offshore Yachts, Guinness Book of Yachting Facts and Feats*, etc: *m* 1st, 1956 (*m diss* 1972), Clare, da of late Dr Nigel Patrick Bruce, BM, BCh (*see* Bruce, Bt, *cr* 1804, colls); 2ndly, 1973, Caroline Elisabeth, twin da of late Wing-Cdr Sir (Eric) John Hodsoll, CB, and has issue by 1st and 2nd *m*.

Arms – Argent, two lions counter-rampant supporting a dexter hand gules, in chief three estoiles of the last, and in base a salmon naiant in water proper. Crest – An arm gules, encircled with a ducal coronet or, the hand grasping a sword proper, pommel and hilt gold.
Residence – Dene End, Buckland Dene, Lymington, Hants SO41 9DT. *Clubs* – Royal Ocean Racing, Royal Yacht Squadron.

SONS LIVING (By 1st marriage)

COLPOYS GUY, *b* 13 Nov 1965; *ed* Winchester, and King's Coll, London (BA); FRGS: *m* 1990, Marie Louise Carmel, da of John Holroyd, of Guildford, Surrey, and has issue living, Colpoys William, *b* 28 Dec 1993, — Rufus George, *b* 1996. *Residence* – Hollygate, Sleepers Hill, Winchester, Hants SO22 4ND. *Club* – Royal Ocean Racing

(By 2nd marriage)

Nicholas Frederick, *b* 1977.

DAUGHTERS LIVING (By 1st marriage)

Marina Grace, *b* 1960. —— Alison Fiona, *b* 1961.

SISTER LIVING

Wanda Helene Paley (1a Cobb's Well, Fowey, Cornwall PL23 1BP), *b* 1933: *m* 1955 (*m diss* 1977), Paul Weychan, and has issue living, Paul Corydon, *b* 1960, — Charlotte Sophia Carol, *b* 1956.

HALF-SISTER LIVING

Issue of late Lt-Col Sir John Paley Johnson, 6th Bt, MBE, by his 2nd wife, Jasmine Lydia, Announcer-Hostess, Directorate of Television BBC, who *d* 1991 (having *m* 2ndly, 1948 (*m diss* 1953), Frank Hugh Shirley Fox; 3rdly, 1954, Howard Marshall, who *d* 1974), da of late Lt-Col Hon Noel Gervase Bligh, DSO, yr son of 8th Earl of Darnley:—
Sarah Jack Paley (26 Abercrombie St, Battersea, SW11 2JD), *b* 1942: *m* 1st, 1963 (*m diss* 1970), Ezra Mager, of New York City; 2ndly, 1972 (*m diss* 1983), Nels Royden Johnson, and has issue living, (by 1st *m*) Dickon Porter, *b* 1969, — Emma Rachel, *b* 1964, — (by 2nd *m*) Daniel Alexander, *b* 1972.

COLLATERAL BRANCHES LIVING

Issue of late Group Capt Peter Warren Johnson, DSO, OBE, DFC, AFC, brother of 6th baronet, *b* 1980, *d* 1999: *m* 1st, 1934 (*m diss* 1961), Joan Agnes, who *d* 1972, da of late Capt Percy Richard Hare, TD (*see* E Listowel, colls); 2ndly, 1961, Margaret Anne, who *d* 1987, da of Capt Guy Wychelo Bower, DSC, RN:—
(By 1st *m*) Hugo Robert Warren (The New House, Deacon's Lane, Hermitage, Newbury, Berks RG16 5PH), *b* 1939: *m* 1st, 1963 (*m diss* 1968), Sally, da of John Allen, of Boston, Mass, USA; 2ndly, 1969 (*m diss* 1973), Rosalynd M., da of David Marrett Tims; 3rdly, 1973 (*m diss* 1981), Diana M., da of Charles Knight; 4thly, 1983 (*m diss* 1995), Wendy A. E., da of William Hodgson; 5thly, 1996, Valerie Elspeth Mary, da of David Ranald Johnston-Jones, and has issue living (by 1st *m*), Claudia Agnes, *b* 1964: *m* 1987, Philip duPont, of USA, and has issue living, Sam *b* 1993, Olivia *b* 1995, — (by 4th *m*), William Peter Warren, *b* 1985, — Edward Hugo Warren, *b* 1987. —— Virginia (1 Bachelors Row, Hempton, Deddington, Banbury, Oxon OX5 4QY), *b* 1936: *m* 1961 (*m diss* 1983), Marchese Umberto Valdambrini-Accoramboni, and has issue living, Robert, *b* 1963: *m* 1997, Sarah Virginia Holt, — Richard Warren, *b* 1965, — Julia Louise, *b* 1971.

Granddaughters of late Major Frederick Colpoys Ormsby Johnson, 2nd son of late Vice-Adm John Ormsby Johnson (infra):—
Issue of late Brigadier Guy Allen Colpoys Ormsby Johnson, CBE, MC, *b* 1886, *d* 1957: *m* 1911, Mary Isabella, who *d* 1977, da of late Col Benjamin Geale Humfrey (E Ranfurly, colls):—
Emily Mary Ormsby (Langleys, The Chalk, Iwerne Minster, Dorset), *b* 1912: *m* 1st, 1934, Group-Capt Edward Stephen Dru Drury, RAF, who *d* 1948; 2ndly, 1951, Maj Miles Garrick, who *d* 1978, and has issue living, (by 1st *m*) Stephen Guy Dru, MBE (Herons, Corfe Castle, Dorset), *b* 1939; Group-Capt RAF; MBE (Mil) 19—. — Michael Humfrey Dru, MBE (Mazowe House, Holt Wood, Wimborne, Dorset), *b* 1942; Lt-Col LI; MBE (Mil) 1977. —— Eileen Ormsby, *b* 1918: *m* 1945, Finlay George Mackintosh, MB, ChB, of 21 Wynmore Av, Bramhope, Leeds, and has issue living, Alan Finlay, *b* 1948, — Fiona Mary, *b* 1945, — Diana Barbara, *b* 1952.

Grandchildren of late Capt Alexander Adair Johnson, FRCVS (infra):—
Issue of late Ralph Harold Ormsby Johnson, *b* 1897, *d* 19—: *m* 1923, ...:—
Alexander Ormsby, *b* 1929.

Issue of late John Ormsby Johnson, *b* 1909, *d* 1990: *m* 1936, ...:—
Patricia Adair, *b* 19—: *m* 19—, G. K. Whyte, of Woodlawn, Warrington, 1 RD Waikouaiti, Otago, New Zealand.

Granddaughter of late Vice-Adm John Ormsby Johnson, son of late Col Charles Christopher Johnson, 7th son of 2nd baronet:—
Issue of late Capt Alexander Adair Johnson, FRCVS, *b* 1873, *d* 1927: *m* 1894, Emma Jane, who *d* 1940, da of —:—
Phyllis Ormsby, *b* 1917: *m* 1st, 19—, — Savage; 2ndly, 19—, — Eden. *Residence* –

Grandson of late Capt Edward Colpoys Johnson, son of late Col Charles Christopher Johnson (ante):—
Issue of late Hubert Colpoys Johnson, *b* 1878, *d* 1925: *m* 1916, Mary Anne, da of Thomas Philip Howe, formerly of Newport Pagnell, Bucks:—
Graham Christopher Colpoys, *b* 1917: *m* 1951, Joan Winifred Mary, who *d* 1958, da of John Bernard Colbeck, of Wakefield, Yorkshire, and has issue living, Anne Winifred Mary, *b* 1952.

The 1st baronet, Gen Sir William Johnson, of an ancient family in Ireland named Macshane, went in early life to America, and conducted the expedition to Crown Point, and gained the battles of Crown Point and Niagara, for which services he was created a baronet, and received £5,000 from the Government, and also large grants of land in the Province of New York, then part of the British dominions. He settled on the Mohawk river, and brought the Senecas—one of the revolted tribes, and inveterate enemies of the English—to a treaty in 1764. He was sole representative of Indian affairs for the northern parts of America for George II, and Col of the six united nations, their allies and dependants. Sir John, the 2nd baronet, was also Superintendant-Gen of Indian Affairs in North America. He remained loyal to the Crown at the outbreak of the American Revolution, and raised two battalions of King's Royal Regt of New York ("Johnson's Greens") which he commanded (now restored in Canada as a recreated unit). He was largely responsible for loyalist settlement in Canada. Sir William Johnson built Johnson Hall in 1764 three miles from Fort Johnson. This is now a fully restored NY State Historic Site, at Johnstown, NY, USA.

JOHNSON (UK) 1818, of Bath

Thou hast conquered, and we live

Never unready

Sir PATRICK ELIOT JOHNSON, 8th *Baronet*; *b* 11 June 1955; *s* his father, *Sir* ROBIN ELIOT, 1989, but no name has been entered on the Official Roll of the Baronetage since death of 6th Bt in 1986; *ed* Hilton Coll, S Africa: *m* 1980 (*m diss* 1989), Rose, da of Olav Alfhein, of Namibia, formerly of Norway, and has issue.

Arms – Per pale sable and azure, on a saltire argent between three towers or, fired proper, one in chief and two in fesse, and two tilting spears saltirewise in base of the second, five cocks of the first. Crest – A tower argent, on the battlements a cock proper. Supporters – *Dexter*, a grenadier habited and accoutred, arms ordered proper; *sinister*, a light infantry man habited and accoutred, arms trailed proper, supporting with his exterior hand a flagstaff also proper, therefrom flowing a banner gules, inscribed "New Ross" in letters of gold.
Residence – Port Macquarie, NSW 2444, Australia.

SONS LIVING

RICHARD ELIOT, *b* 8 Jan 1983. —— Peter Eliot, *b* (twin) 1983.

SISTERS LIVING

Judith Marguerite, *b* 1956: *m* 1986, Bryan Rochfort Vere Hodge, of 30 Calwalla Crescent, Port Macquarie, NSW 2444, Australia, and has issue living, Stephen William Vere, *b* 1987, — Ruth Ellen, *b* 1991. —— Heather Mary, *b* 1959: *m* 19—, Niall Haygarth, of 2a Ferndale Av, Westville, Durban, S Africa, and has issue living, Russell, *b* 19—, — Melissa, *b* 19—.

DAUGHTERS LIVING OF FIFTH BARONET

Barbara Patty, *b* 1918: *m* 1942, Charles Frederick Roetter, who *d* 1977, and has issue living, Martyn Frederick Alexander Gurney, *b* 1944; *ed* St Paul's (Foundation Scholar), and Brasenose Coll, Oxford (Scholar); Research Fellow, Univ Coll, Oxford: *m* 1976, Joyce Stevens, and has issue living, Alexander Charles *b* 1978, Nicolas Martyn *b* 1980, Natasha Chantal *b* 1983, — Christine Frances Ada, *b* 1946: *m* 1971, Stephen A. Rhodes, and has issue living, Molly Jane *b* 1975, Colette Lindsay *b* 1977. —— Monica Lena, *b* 1921: *m* 1st, 1941 (*m diss* 1952), Marshall Douglas Clare; 2ndly, 1957, Dr Florencio Enrique Escardo of Juncal 1335-1C, Buenos Aires, Argentina, and has issue living, (by 1st *m*) Michael Charles Allen, *b*

1945: *m* 1st, 1969 (*m diss* 1974), Dianae, da of Bruce Hamilton Wardrope, of 758 Waterford Av, Winnipeg, Manitoba, Canada; 2ndly, 1980, Fay Margaret Foster, and has issue living (by 2nd *m*), Brendan Marshall Foster *b* 1982, — Marcia Dorothy, *b* 1943: *m* 1965, Michael Bennie, who *d* 1974, and has issue living, Christopher Michael *b* 1966, Claire Julia *b* 1969, — (by 2nd *m*) Florencio Julian, *b* 1958: *m* 1981, Irene Matyas, — Monica Carmen, *b* 1960: *m* 1982, Fernando Garcia-Pullés, and has issue living, Josefina Maria *b* 1984, — Pilar, *b* 1963.

WIDOW LIVING OF SEVENTH BARONET

Barbara Alfreda, da of late Alfred T. Brown, of Germiston, Transvaal: *m* 1st, 1954, Sir Robin Eliot Johnson, 7th Bt, who *d* 1989; 2ndly, 19— (*m diss* 19—), Harold Bowling; has resumed surname of Johnson. *Residence* – Port Macquarie, NSW, Australia.

COLLATERAL BRANCHES LIVING

     Granddaughter of late Maj Arthur Cyril Beaumont Johnson, son of Gen Sir Charles Cooper Johnson, GCB, 6th son of 2nd baronet:—
     Issue of late Lt-Col Charles Robert Johnson, *b* 1902, *d* (of wounds received in action) 1941: *m* 1935, Mrs Eileen Agnes Johnson, who *d* 1976, da of late G. C. Mothersill, of Bedford:—
Diana Evelyn, *b* 1935.

     Granddaughter of late Maj-Gen Alured Clarke Johnson, CB, 8th son of 2nd baronet:—
     Issue of late Lt-Col Gilbert Ward Johnson, *b* 1866, *d* 1924: *m* 1923, Marion, da of C. H. Truslove, of Sale, Cheshire:—
Patricia Danino, *b* (*posthumous*) 1924.

     Grandson of late Col Archibald Acheson Johnson, 9th son of 2nd baronet:—
     Issue of late Lt-Col Allen Edwin Johnson, DSO, *b* 1878, *d* 1972: *m* 1913, Phoebe Dora Wynn, who *d* 1961, da of late Maj Alfred Elias:—
Allen Antony Wynn (Pond Cottage, Potten End, Berkhamsted, Herts), *b* 1916; *ed* Charterhouse, and St John's Coll, Oxford; formerly RA: *m* 1939, Helen Janet Margaret, only da of W. A. Annett, of Greystoke, Berkhamsted, and has issue living, Mark Allen William Wynn (12 Routh Rd, SW18), *b* 1946; *ed* Berkhamsted Sch (Foundation Scholar), and St John's Coll, Oxford: *m* 1969, Caroline Jane, only da of C. R. E. Bowles of London, and has issue living, Alexander Mark Wynn, *b* 1970, Melissa Caroline *b* 1973, Lydia Jane *b* 1980, — Christopher Wynn, *b* 1948; *ed* E Anglia Univ.

     The 1st baronet, Sir Henry, GCB, son of Allen Johnson of Kilternan, co Dublin, and yr brother of Sir John Johnson-Walsh, 1st Bt, of Ballykilcavan, (ext 1953), was Col of the 5th Regt and Governor of Ross Castle. The 2nd baronet, Sir Henry Allen, was a distinguished military officer in the Peninsular War. The 3rd baronet, Sir Henry Franks Frederic, was Col Comdg Forces in Jamaica, Windward and Leeward Islands. The 4th baronet, Sir Henry Allen William, CB, was Brig-Gen late KOYLI.

Johnson-Ferguson, see Ferguson.

Johnson-Walsh, see Walsh.

JOHNSTON (NS) 1626, of Caskieben, Aberdeenshire

Sir THOMAS ALEXANDER JOHNSTON, 14th *Baronet*; *b* 1 Feb 1956; *s* his father, Sir THOMAS ALEXANDER, 1984.

Live that you may live hereafter

Arms – Quarterly: 1st and 4th, argent, a saltire sable, on a chief gules, three cushions or, *Johnston*; 2nd and 3rd, azure, on a bend or between three harts' heads erased argent, attired of the second, as many cross-crosslets fitchée of the second, *Mar* and *Garioch* of *Caskieben*, composed together on one coat. **Crest** – A Phœnix in flames proper. **Supporters** – Two naked Indians proper, wreathed about the head and middle with laurel vert.
Residence – .

SISTERS LIVING

Helen Du Bois, *b* 1944: *m* 1969, Phillip Thomas Sargent, of 857 Rim Crest Drive, Thousand Oaks, Cal 91361-2074, USA, and has issue living, John Harrison, *b* 1972, — Bradford Gage, *b* 1976, — Lydia Gaillard, *b* 1981. —— Leslie Sheldon, *b* 1951: *m* 1972, David Charles Krempa, and has issue living, David Alexander, *b* 1984, — Mary Helen, *b* 1978, — Melissa Leslie, *b* 1980.

AUNT LIVING (*Daughter of 12th Baronet*)

Dianne, *b* 1926: *m* 1948, Samuel H. Andrews III, and has issue living, Samuel Henry, *b* 1949, — Bruce Sheldon, *b* 1950, — John Norville, *b* 1960, — Mark Alexander, *b* 1961, — Paula Burke, *b* 1952, — Lucia Dianne Andrews, *b* 1958. *Residence* – Citronelle, Alabama, USA.

WIDOW LIVING OF THIRTEENTH BARONET

HELEN TORREY, da of Benjamin Franklin Du Bois: *m* 1st, 1941, Sir Thomas Alexander Johnston, 13th Bt, who *d* 1984; 2ndly, 1989, Dr Charles Trewartha Lenton, Jr.

COLLATERAL BRANCHES LIVING

Grandchildren of late William Norville Johnston (*b* 1894) (infra):—
Issue of late William Norville Johnston, *b* 1922, *d* 1989: *m* 1952, Kathrine Pauline, da of Herbert Sigfred Solberg, of Mobile:—
WILLIAM NORVILLE, *b* 1955. —— Stephen Gregory, *b* 1958. —— Paul Brady, *b* 1959. —— Kathryn Mary, *b* 1953.

Issue of late William Norville Johnston, 2nd son of 11th baronet, *b* 1894, *d* 1959: *m* 1921, Catherine, da of Thomas Murray, of Mobile, Alabama, USA:—
Claude Edward, *b* 1930: *m* 1960, Lucy, da of Bernard Teague Mahorner, of Mobile, and has issue living, Edward Ryan *b* 1961, — Bernard Mathias, *b* 1965, — Mary Teague, *b* 1960, — Laura Jean, *b* 1964, Courtney Anne, *b* 1971, — Elizabeth Leigh, *b* (twin) 1971. —— Marion, *b* 1924: *m* 1955, Thomas Ross Johnson, of 7 Dogwood Circle, Spring Hill Station, Mobile, Alabama, USA, and has issue living, Thomas Ross III, *b* 1957. — Margaret Murray, *b* 1956: *m* 1986, Edward Luckett King, son of Dr Robert King, of Spring Hill, Alabama, — Elizabeth Barry, *b* 1961. —— Helen Jean, *b* 1926: *m* 1955, William Earle Bidez, of 14 Bienville Av, Mobile, Alabama 36606-1406, USA, and has issue living, William Earle, *b* 1957, — Jeanne Marie, *b* 1956, — Erin Anne, *b* (twin) 1957, — Catherine Leary, *b* 1961.

Issue of late Frederick Rukard Johnston, 3rd son of 11th baronet, *b* 1897, *d* 1962: *m* 1925, Grace (decd), da of John A. McRae, of Clio, Alabama, USA:—
Joyce Rukard, *b* 1926: *m* 1951, Wallace Abney Burgess, US Navy (ret), of 1007 Whitestone Lane, Houston, Texas 77073-1268, USA, and has issue living, Douglas Abney, *b* 1956, — Patricia Olivia, *b* 1952, — Suzanne McRae, *b* 1954, — Joyce Johnston, *b* 1957, — Carolyn Norville, *b* 1962.

Sir George Johnston (son of John Johnston, of Caskieben, Aberdeenshire), Sheriff of Aberdeen, was created a baronet of Nova Scotia 1626 with remainder to his heirs male whatsoever. Sir Thomas Alexander Johnston, 12th Bt, was Ch of Hydro-Power Branch, Dist Office, Mobile, Alabama.

JOHNSTONE (NS) 1700, of Westerhall, Dumfriesshire

Sir (GEORGE) RICHARD DOUGLAS JOHNSTONE, 11th *Baronet*; *b* 21 Aug 1948; *s* his father, *Sir* FREDERIC ALLAN GEORGE, 1994; *ed* Leeds Gram Sch, and Magdalen Coll, Oxford: *m* 1976, Gwyneth, da of Arthur Bailey, of Hastings, and has issue.

Arms –

SON LIVING

FREDERIC ROBERT ARTHUR, *b* 18 Nov 1981; *ed* Warwick Sch.

DAUGHTER LIVING

Caroline, *b* 1983.

BROTHER LIVING

Ian Allan, *b* 1954; *ed* Leeds Gram Sch.

WIDOW LIVING OF TENTH BARONET

DORIS (*Dowager Lady Johnstone*), da of late William Lancaster Shortridge, of Blackheath, SE: *m* 1946, as his 2nd wife, Sir Frederic Allan George Johnstone, 10th Bt, who *d* 1994.

COLLATERAL BRANCHES LIVING

Grandchildren of late Major James Henry L'Estrange Johnstone, MVO, son of James Johnstone, eldest son of James Raymond Johnstone, only son of John Johnstone, MP, 5th son of 3rd baronet:—
Issue of late Capt Henry James Johnstone, RN, *b* 1895, *d* 1947: *m* 1923, Alison, who *d* 1984, da of late T. W. McIntyre, of Sorn Castle, Ayrshire:—
Sir (John) Raymond, CBE (Wards, Gartocharn, Dunbartonshire G83 8SB), *b* 1929; *ed* Eton, and Trin Coll, Camb; Managing Dir of Murray Johnstone & Co Ltd, Glasgow; Chm Forestry Commn 1989-94; Chm Historic Buildings Council for Scotland since 1995, and Chm Nuclear Trust since 1995: *m* 1979, Susan Sara, only da of late Capt Christopher Gerald Gore (*see* E Eglinton, 1990 Edn), formerly wife of late Basil Reginald Vincent Ziani de Ferranti, and widow of Peter Quixano Henriques; *cr* CBE (Civil) 1988, and Ktd 1993. —— Christine Alison (*Lady Erskine-Hill*), *b* 1924: *m* 1942, Sir Robert Erskine-Hill, 2nd Bt, who *d* 1989. *Residence* – Harelea House, Libberton, Carnwath, Lanarkshire ML11 8LX.

Issue of late Andrew Wauchope Johnstone, *b* 1903, *d* 1980: *m* 1932, Eleanor Blanche Helen Margaretta Vere-Laurie, da of Lt-Col George Brenton Laurie, RIR (*see* V Massereene, colls):—
James Andrew Francis (35 Front St South, Unit 209, Mississauga, Ont, Canada L5H 2I6), *b* 1939; *ed* Eton, and Mil Coll, Canada: *m* 1st, 1963 (*m diss* 1978), Helen Christina, el da of late Ivan F. Wade, of 4 Pointe Claire, PQ, Canada; 2ndly, 1982, Carole, widow of Norman Burke, of Westmount, Quebec, and has issue living (by 1st *m*), Sheila Christine, *b* 1964, — Anne Laurie, *b* 1965, — Jennifer Frances, *b* 1968: *m* 1994, Donald Scott, of Port Moody, BC, Canada, — Kathleen Helen, *b* 1970. —— Gillian Margaret (Springfield House, Aldringham, Leiston, Suffolk, IP16 4PZ), *b* 1935: *m* 1957 (*m diss* 1985), Rev Edmund Selwyn Haviland, and has issue living, Andrew Mark James, *b* 1965, — Margaret Vivienne, *b* 1958, — Angela Helen, *b* 1960, — Jane Eleanor, *b* 1963. —— Jacqueline Veronica (10 O'Connor's Rd, Beacon Hill, NSW, Australia), *b* 1936: *m* 1st, 1966 (*m diss* 1975), Thomas Patrick Fitzgerald, of Sydney, NSW; 2ndly, 1977 (*m diss* 1980), Mark Anthony Salfus, and has issue living, (by 1st *m*) John Wauchope, *b* 1967, — (by 2nd *m*) Damien Anthony James, *b* 1978.

Grandchildren of late Maj FitzRoy Augustus Beauclerk Johnstone (infra):—
Issue of late FitzRoy Montague Veitch Johnstone, *b* 1922, *d* 1979: *m* 1956, Dora (Cornaa Mill, Maughold, IoM), da of late Alexander Lofthouse:—
FitzRoy Jonathan (24 Middlehead Rd, Mosman, NSW 2088, Australia), *b* 1957; *ed* Stowe: *m* 1989, Jane Alexandra, da of Peter Crothers, of Mildura, Australia, and has issue living, Alexander FitzRoy, *b* 1996, — Alice Grace, *b* (twin) 1996. —— Judith Helen, *b* 1959: *m* 1984, John Stewart Morton, of Lake View House, Guilford Rd, Lurgan, Craigavon, co Armagh, and has issue living, Alexander James, *b* 1985, — Thomas Oliver, *b* 1988, — Stewart John, *b* 1989, — William Roy, *b* 1991. —— Jennifer Alison, *b* 1962: *m* 1990, Patrick Douglas Gerard Hodson, and has issue living, James Roy Namani, *b* 1994, — Joseph Patrick Luke, *b* 1997, — Hannah Rachel, *b* 1992.

Grandson of late Lieut-Com Somerset James SOMERSET-JOHNSTONE, RN (infra):—
Issue of late Major FitzRoy Augustus Beauclerk Johnstone, *b* 1878, *d* 1931: *m* 1915, Alida Helen, who *d* 1968, da of late Andrew Veitch—
James Veitch (Glasfryn, Valley Rd, Llanfairfechan, Conwy, N Wales), *b* 1924; *ed* Lancing; Sub-Lieut RNVR 1943-45: *m* 1950, Nancy Hayes, who *d* 1998, da of late Henry Atkinson, and has issue living, Ian James FitzRoy (Glasfryn, Valley Rd, Llanfairfechan, Conwy, N Wales), *b* 1952; *ed* St Paul's, and Aston Univ; Dir Real Car Co Ltd: *m* 1989, Rosalynde Patricia, eldest da of Michael John Mills, and has issue living, Callum James *b* 1988, Noah *b* 1982 (adopted), — Peter Montague Veitch (34 Bell Rd, Bottisham, Cambs), *b* 1956; *ed* Holland Park; Conservationist: *m* 1990, Fiona Catherine, yr da of late Lt-Cmdr C. A. J. French, RN, and has issue living, Jamie Peter *b* 1994.

Grandsons of late Gen Montague Cholmeley Johnstone, 3rd son of late James Raymond Johnstone (ante):—
Issue of late Lt-Cdr Somerset James SOMERSET-JOHNSTONE, *b* 1864, *d* 1942, having assumed by deed poll 1900 the additional surname of Somerset: *m* 1st, 1877, Elizabeth Ann, who *d* 1886, da of William Jackson Johnson, of

Hootton, Cheshire; 2ndly, 1887 (*m diss* in America 1900), Isabel Ann, who *d* 1934, da of Joseph Charles Mappin, formerly of 38 Harrington Gardens, SW; 3rdly, 1900 (*m diss* 1910), Louisa Hodder, who *d* 1914:—
(By 2nd *m*) James Montague Cholmely, *b* 1889; *ed* Bedford Sch; a Master Mariner; late Lieut RNR; sometime in Australian Navy; European War 1914-17, present at surrender of German New Guinea Sept 1914, and at destruction of the *Emden* Nov 1914: *m* 1917, Alice Maud, da of Frederick Witham, and has issue living, Fitzroy Somerset, *b* 1927; European War 1943-5 as Radio Officer in Merchant Navy: *m* 1952, Francesca Hodson, da of Edward Wareing, of 20 Craven Gardens, Wimbledon, SW, and has issue living, Peter James *b* 1955, Susan Frances *b* 1953, — Mauriel Sydney, *b* 1918, — Audrey Philippa, *b* 1923, — June Octavia, *b* 1932. ——— Malcolm Bruce Somerset, *b* 1893; *ed* Sherborne; European War 1914-18 on Staff 2nd Army Head Quarters for defence of Sussex, Capt Reserve of Cav attached Army Remount Ser, and Comdg 49th Remount Squadron in Salonika (despatches); assumed by deed poll 1932, the surname of Somerset only.

Grandchildren of late Col Montague George Johnstone, DSO, 2nd son of late Gen Montague Cholmeley Johnstone (ante):—
Issue of late Major Montague Joseph Charles Somerset Johnstone, late RSG, *b* 1882, *d* 1953: *m* 1st, 1900, Victoria Louise, who *d* 1916, da of late James Stewart, of Glasgow; 2ndly, 1916 (*m diss* 1928), Mary Marion Spottiswood, who *d* 1949, da of late George Bayley, of Manuel, Stirlingshire; 3rdly, 1928, Margaret, da of late Sir John Foster Fraser:—
(By 2nd *m*) Roy Henry Montague, MBE, *b* 1919; *ed* Eton, and Magdalene Coll, Camb; 1939-45 War as Maj 60th Rifles, on Staff, War Office, and in France and Germany (despatches, MBE); MBE (Mil) 1945; a Member of London Stock Exchange 1956-74; Trustee St Clement Danes Holborn Estate Charity: *m* 1st, 1939 (*m diss* 1960), Barbara Marjorie, who *d* 1990, da of late Maj Felix Walter Warre, OBE, MC, of Wytherston, Powerstock, Dorset; 2ndly, 1961, Mme Françoise Terlinden, and has issue living, (by 1st *m*) Roland Richard Montague (Poorton Hill, Powerstock, Bridport, Dorset), *b* 1941; *ed* Eton; late Lt 60th Rifles; Solicitor 1967; Partner, Slaughter & May 1973-91: *m* 1968, Sara Outram Boileau, da of late Lt-Col John Garway Outram Whitehead, MC, of 10 Blackfriars St, Canterbury, and has issue living, Andrew Henry Montague, *b* 1969; *ed* Eton, — William Arthur Montague, *b* 1973; *ed* Clayesmore, — Mark Montague (42 Howards Wood Drive, Gerrards Cross, Bucks), *b* 1944; *ed* Eton; late Lt Queen's R Rifles (TA): *m* 1971, Rosalind Margaret, da of late Donald Macphee, DSC, FRICS, of Tylers Green, Bucks, and has issue living, Kerry Montague *b* 1972, Amanda Lee Montague *b* 1974, — Torquil James Montague, *b* 1953; *ed* Eton; CA 1977; merchant banker: *m* 1988, Irena Katharin Buller, da of Maj Ivor Roger Harding Curtis, VRD, RMR, of Wareham, Dorset, and has issue living, Joshua James *b* 1991, Alice Victoria *b* 1993, Eliza Clementine *b* 1996, — Fiona Montague, *b* 1946: *m* 1977, David Wilkins, of 75 Kenley Rd, Kingston-on-Thames, Surrey, and has issue living, Peter Jonathan *b* 1978, Helen Sarah *b* 1981, — (by 2nd *m*) Carol Peter Montague *b* 1961. *Residence* – 16 Leonard Court, Edwardes Sq, Kensington, W8. *Club* – Pratt's. ——— (By 1st *m*) Désirée Barbara Montague, *b* 1908. ——— Eileen Agnes Montague, *b* 1909: *m* 1931 (*m diss* 19—), Raymond Horwood Hazell, and has issue living, Charles Jonathan, *b* 1938, — Louise, *b* 1933, — Anastasia, *b* 1936. ——— Rosemary Maud Montague, *b* 1913: *m* 1936 (*m diss* 19—), Nicholas Desborough Burnell. ——— (By 2nd *m*) Gloria Montague (Rashwood, Droitwich, Worcs), *b* 1918. ——— (By 3rd *m*) Alastair Montague, *b* 1928.

Granddaughters of late Gen Montague Cholmeley Johnstone (ante):—
Issue of late Lieut-Col Francis Fawkes Johnstone, *b* 1849, *d* 1919: *m* 1st, 1878 (*m diss* 1886), Henrietta Jane, da of James Sullivan; 2ndly, 1887, Harriet Lavinia, who *d* 1910, da of late Richard Sargent and widow of Capt Charles Francis Gregg, of 7th Hussars and 6th Inniskilling Dragoons:—
(By 1st *m*) Mary Louisa Leonora: *m* 1897, Percy Kitchin. ——— Frances Geraldine Jane.

Granddaughters of late Lt-Col Francis Fawkes Johnstone (ante):—
Issue of late Major Charles Campbell Gosling Johnstone, *b* 1889, *d* 1942: *m* 1st, 1912 (*m diss* 1927), Laura Mary, da of late Lt-Col Willoughby B. Hemans, RA; 2ndly, 1928, Nina, da of late Col Valentine de Sventorgetsky, Russian Imperial Guard:—
(By 1st *m*) Violet Mary St Clair, *b* 1914. ——— Jean Hermione, *b* 1922.

Granddaughter of late John Heywood Johnstone, MP, son of late Rev George Dempster Johnstone, 4th son of late James Raymond Johnstone (ante):—
Issue of late George Horace Johnstone, OBE, DL, *b* 1882, *d* 1960: *m* 1910, Alison, who *d* 1978, da of the Ven Stamford Raffles Raffles-Flint (Archdeacon of Cornwall, and Canon of Truro), of Nansawsan, Ladock, Cornwall:—
Elizabeth Alison, *b* 1911.

Descendants of late Richard Johnstone (el son of late Col John Johnstone, 2nd son of 2nd baronet), who was *cr* a *Baronet* 1797 (with special remainder to the male issue of his brother, Charles John) (*see* B Derwent).

Descendants of late Charles John Johnstone (2nd son of late Col John Johnstone (ante)), (*see* B Derwent).

This family descend from Matthew Johnstone of Pettinain (later called Westraw), Lanarkshire, said to have been a yr son of Sir Adam Johnstone of that Ilk (*d* 1454), ancestor of the Marquesses of Annandale (dormant 1792). Sir John Johnstone of Westershall, 8th in descent from Matthew was *cr* a Baronet with remainder to his heirs male. He represented Dumfries in the Scottish Parliament, and voted for the Union. Sir William, 5th Bt, assumed the surname of Pulteney on marriage to Frances Pulteney, heir to her cousin the Earl of Bath, and died without male issue 1805; his only child Henrietta Laura, was created Countess of Bath, and died without issue 1808. The 6th baronet, Sir John Lowther, MP for Weymouth 1810-11, twice declined a peerage offered to him by Spencer Perceval.

JONES (UK) 1919, of Treeton, West Riding of Yorkshire

Sir SIMON WARLEY FREDERICK BENTON JONES, 4th *Baronet*; *b* 11 Sept 1941; *s* his father, *Sir* PETER FAWCETT BENTON, OBE, 1972; *ed* Eton, and Trin Coll, Camb (MA); JP for Lincs; High Sheriff of Lincs 1977-78: *m* 1966, Margaret Fiona, OBE, DL Lincs 1997, da of David Rutherford Dickson, of Barrow Lodge, Bury St Edmunds, and has issue.

𝕬rms – Per chevron argent and sable, in chief two dragons heads erased gules, and in base two crosses patée fitchée in saltire or. Crest – A demi gryphon gules, grasping a miner's pickaxe, head downwards in pale or.
Seat – Irnham Hall, nr Grantham, Lincs.

SONS LIVING

JAMES PETER MARTIN, *b* 1 Jan 1973: *m* 1997, Lucy A., only da of David Briggs, of Blackwell Farm, Latimer, Bucks. —— David William Anthony, *b* 1975. —— Alastair Frederick Malcolm *b* 1981.

DAUGHTERS LIVING

Fiona Charlotte, *b* 1967: *m* 1996, Rupert J. A. Farquharson, yst son of Rt Hon Sir Donald Henry Farquharson, of Bures, Suffolk, and has issue living, Alexander James, *b* 1998. —— Fleur Alexandra, *b* 1970: *m* 1997, Robert A. Collins, only son of Sir John Alexander Collins, of Beaulieu, Hants.

SISTER LIVING

Jill Benton (*Hon Lady McAlpine*), *b* 1937: *m* 1959, Hon Sir William Hepburn McAlpine, 6th Bt, of Fawley Hill, Fawley Green, Henley-on-Thames.

AUNT LIVING (*Daughter of 2nd baronet*)

Rachael Mary Benton, *b* 1918: *m* 1941, George Ronald Murray Kydd, and has issue living, Ian Murray, *b* 1945: *m* 1972, Elizabeth, da of Richard Blackburn, and has issue living, Benjamin Murray *b* 1972, Joel Murray *b* 1975, — Donald Hamish, *b* 1947: *m* 1970, Christine, da of Owen Gough, and has issue living, Lorraine Grace *b* 1971, Samantha Melanie Jane *b* 1973. *Residence* – 23 Chapel St, Grassington, Skipton, N Yorks BD23 5BE.

GREAT-AUNT DECEASED (*Daughter of 1st baronet*)

Katharine Mary, *b* 1904: *m* 1933, Lt-Col William Herbert Olivier, TD, JP, DL, LLD, who *d* 1992, and *d* 1998, leaving issue, Jasper William Dacres (Ashford Hall, Bakewell, Derbys DE5 1QA), *b* 1938: *m* 1973, Virginia Whitaker, and has issue living, Alice Dione Rose *b* 1976, Emma Louise *b* 1977, — James Stephen (60 Grove Lane, Camberwell, SE5 8ST), *b* 1944; Lt-Col RHG: *m* 1968, Sally Anne Simonds, and has issue living, Charles Stephen *b* 1969, Julian Henry *b* 1973, — Flora Mary Margaret, *b* 1936: *m* 1973, John Guy Carmichael Jackson, who *d* 1997, of Copse Hill, Osmaston, Ashbourne, Derbys DE61 1LU, and has issue (*see* Jackson, Bt, *cr* 1869, colls), — Julie Katharine, *b* 1941: *m* 1966, Patrick Julian Dawnay, and has issue (*see* V Downe, colls). *Residence* – Ashford Hall, Bakewell, Derbyshire, DE5 1QA.

COLLATERAL BRANCH LIVING

Issue of late Capt Charles Frederick Ward Jones, yr son of 1st baronet, *b* 1884, *d* 1971: *m* 1921, Dorothy, who *d* 1962, only da of R. H. Allen, of Hemingfield, Worksop, Notts:—
†David Robert Ward, *b* 1925; *ed* Repton; Capt RHG (Reserve): *m* 1954, Sally (23 Bettridge Rd, SW6), da of Col H. Cantan, of Bridport, Dorset, and *d* 1998, leaving issue, Emma, *b* 1956, — Kathryn, *b* 1960, — Harriet, *b* 1963. —— Anne Ward (The Old School, Ranby, nr Market Rasen, Lincs), *b* 1922: *m* 1950, Charles Douglas Pain, who *d* 1996, and has issue living, Michael Ward Eames, *b* 1957: *m* 1986, Christina Elisabeth Ljungström. —— Beth Ward, *b* 1924: *m* 1950, Michael William Ollyver Antill, of Woodhouse Hill, Holbeck, Worksop, Notts, and has issue living, Timothy William, *b* 1954: *m* 1987, Elaine Ward, and has issue living, Emily *b* 1988, Holly *b* 1989, Georgina *b* (twin) 1989, — Sarah Penelope, *b* 1952.

Sir Frederick John Jones, 1st Bt, was Pres Mining Assocn of Gt Britain, Chm, S Yorks Coal Trade Assocn, and Miners' Conciliation Board.

LAWRENCE-JONES (UK) 1831, of Cranmer Hall, Norfolk

Sir CHRISTOPHER LAWRENCE-JONES, 6th *Baronet*, 2nd son of late Cmdr Bertram Edward Jones, RN, 3rd son of 4th baronet, *b* 19 Jan 1940; *s* his uncle, *Sir* LAWRENCE EVELYN, MC, TD, 1969; *ed* Sherborne, and Gonville and Caius Coll, Camb (MA, MB, BChir); DIH, FRCP, FFOM; formerly Ch MO ICI Group, Millbank, SW1; past Chm Medichem, and past Pres section of Occ Med Royal Soc of Medicine; formerly Memb Management Cttee, British Occ Health Research Foundation, and formerly Memb of Board, Faculty of Occ Med RCP; Lord of Manor of Fakenham, Norfolk: *m* 1967, Gail, da of late Cecil Arthur Pittar, FRACS, of Auckland, NZ, and has issue.

Marte et arte

By war and art

Ꭺᵣᵐˢ – Azure, on a fesse or, three grenades fired proper; in chief a castle, and over it the word "Netherlands" in letters of gold; in base a lion couchant argent, gorged with a ribbon gules fimbriated azure, therefrom suspended a representation of the gold medal presented to the 1st baronet for his services at Badajoz. Ꮯʳᵉˢᵗ – In front of a castle a lion couchant argent gorged with a wreath of laurel, and pendent therefrom an escutcheon gules charged with a representation of the Badajoz medal as in the arms.
Club – Royal Cruising.

SONS LIVING

MARK CHRISTOPHER, *b* 28 Dec 1968. ⎯⎯ John Alexander, *b* 1971.

DAUGHTERS LIVING OF FIFTH BARONET

Vivien Lawrence, *b* 1923: *m* 1942, Simon Anthony Roland Asquith, who *d* 1973 (*see* E Oxford and Asquith, colls). *Residence* – 44 Gilpin Av, East Sheen, SW14 8QY. ⎯⎯ Lavinia Lawrence, *b* 1925: *m* 1980, Frank Monaco. *Residence* – 28 Radnor Walk, SW3.

This family was settled at Sunny Hill, Carmarthenshire for several generations. David Jones moved to Norfolk in the 17th century. Maj-Gen Sir John Jones, 1st Bt, was a distinguished officer in RE, serving in the Peninsular War. He *m* 1816, Catherine, da of Effingham Lawrence, of Long Island, NY. Sir Lawrence Jones, 2nd Bt, was murdered at Macri, in Turkey, 1845. Sir Lawrence Jones, MC, 5th Bt, was author of "Victorian Boyhood", "Edwardian Youth" and "Georgian Afternoon".

PRICHARD-JONES (UK) 1910, of Bron Menai, Dwyran, Llangeinwen, Anglesey

Sir JOHN PRICHARD-JONES, 2nd *Baronet*; *b* 20 Jan 1913; *s* his father, *Sir* JOHN, 1917; *ed* Eton, and Ch Ch, Oxford (BA honours 1934, MA); Bar Gray's Inn 1936; Capt late The Queen's Bays: *m* 1st, 1937 (*m diss* 1950), Heather Vivian Mary, da of Sir Walter Richard Nugent, 4th Bt, *cr* 1831 (of Donore); 2ndly, (Feb) 1959, Helen Marie Thérèse, da of late J. F. Liddy, Dental Surg, of 20 Lawrence St, Drogheda, and has issue by 1st and 2nd *m*.

Ꭺᵣᵐˢ – Gules, a lymphad in full sail or, on a chief of the second, two escutcheons of the first. Ꮯʳᵉˢᵗ – A demi-lion gules, resting the sinister paw on a boar's head erased or.
Residence – Allenswood House, Lucan, co Dublin.

SON LIVING (By 1st marriage)

DAVID JOHN WALTER, *b* 14 March 1943; *ed* Ampleforth, and Ch Ch, Oxford (BA Hons).

DAUGHTER LIVING (By 2nd marriage)

Susan Marie *b* (Nov) 1959.

COLLATERAL BRANCH LIVING

Issue of late Capt Richard William Prichard-Jones, yr son of 1st baronet, *b* 1914, *d* 1986: *m* 1943, Margaret Woodburn (Sally) (The Forge, Whittlesford, Cambs), da of Sqdn-Ldr Ronald Herbert Wingfield Davidson, of 605 Hood House, Dolphin Sq, SW1:—
Richard Stephen, *b* 1952; *ed* Bryanston. ⎯⎯ Marie Anne, *b* 1948: *m* 1970 (*m diss* 19—), Edward Pearce Serocold.

Sir John, JP, DL, LLD, 1st Bt, sometime head of the firm of Dickins and Jones (Limited), of 226-244 Regent Street, W, founded and endowed the Prichard-Jones Institute and Cottage Homes, Newborough, Anglesey, and donated the

Prichard-Jones Hall of Univ Coll of N Wales, of which he was Senior Vice-Pres; he assumed by deed poll (registered at the College of Arms) 1917 the surname of Prichard-Jones.

PRYCE-JONES (UK) 1918, of Dolerw, co Montgomery (Extinct 1963)

Sir PRYCE VICTOR PRYCE-JONES, 2nd and last *Baronet.*

WIDOW LIVING OF SECOND BARONET

SYRA ROANTREE (*Lady Pryce-Jones*) (The Manor Cottage, Great Ryburgh, Norfolk), only da of late Francis O'Shiel, of Omagh, co Tyrone: *m* 1938, Capt Sir Pryce Victor Pryce-Jones, 2nd Bt, who *d* 1963, when the title became ext.

JOSEPH (UK) 1942, of Stoke-on-Trent, co Stafford (Extinct 1951)

Sir FRANCIS L'ESTRANGE JOSEPH, KBE, 1st and last *Baronet.*

DAUGHTERS LIVING OF FIRST BARONET

Rosamund Mary, *b* 1919: *m* 1st, 1942 (*m diss* 1956), Maj Peter Rouse Addison Birley, 17th/21st Lancers; 2ndly, 1956, Christopher Bevis Sanford; 3rdly, 1968, Daniel Vincent O'Donovan, Barrister, who *d* 1977, and has issue living, (by 1st *m*) David Peter Francis (56 Huron Rd, SW17), *b* 1943; *ed* Harrow, and Ch Ch, Oxford: *m* 1985, (Carole) Jan, da of late Dr John Foxton, of Brigg, Lincs, and has issue living, Sam David John *b* 1986, George Charles Foxton *b* 1989, Frederick Peter Francis *b* 1989, — (by 2nd *m*), Francis L'Estrange, *b* 1957. —— Cynthia Violct Maud, *b* 1921: *m* 1946, Col Peter Stanley Walter Dean, R Anglian Regt (ret), of Foresters, Tostock, Bury St Edmunds, Suffolk, and has two adopted das, Diana L'Estrange, *b* 1956, — Rosemary Rust, *b* 1958.

JOSEPH (UK) 1943, of Portsoken, City of London

(*Hon*) (*Sir*) JAMES SAMUEL JOSEPH, 3rd *Baronet*; *b* 27 Jan 1955; *s* his father, KEITH SINJOHN, Baron Joseph, CH, PC (Life Baron), in his Baronetcy 1994, but does not use the title, or the courtesy title; *ed* Harrow: *m* 1990, Sarah Jane Thwaites, and has issue.

Arms – Per chevron gules and barry wavy of ten azure and or a fesse embattled of the last masoned sable in chief a sun in splendour gold. **Crest** – In front of an annulet azure encircling a tower gules two sprigs of honesty leaved and slipped saltire-wise proper.

SONS LIVING

SAM NATHAN, *b* 1991. —— Thomas Owain, *b* 1994.

SISTERS LIVING

Hon Emma Catherine Sarah, *b* 1956. *Residence* – ......
Hon Julia Rachel, *b* 1959: *m* 1985, Jonathan David Rolnick, only son of Jacob Rolnick, of New York, USA, and has issue living, David Sebastian, *b* 1991. *Residence* – ......
Hon Anna Jane Rebecca, *b* 1964. *Residence* – ......

MOTHER LIVING

Hellen Louise, yr da of Sigmar Guggenheimer, of New York: *m* 1951 (*m diss* 1985), as his 1st wife, Rt Hon Sir Keith Sinjohn Joseph, 2nd Bt (later Baron Joseph, CH, PC, Life Baron), who *d* 1994.

WIDOW LIVING OF LIFE BARON AND SECOND BARONET

YOLANDA VICTORIA (*Baroness Joseph*), da of Charles V. Castro, and formerly wife of Leonard S. Sheriff, of New York, USA: *m* 1990, as his 2nd wife, Baron Joseph, CH, PC (Life Baron), who *d* 1994. *Residences* – 63 Limerston St, SW10 0BL; Sunnyside Farm, Washington, Connecticut, USA.

The 1st baronet, Sir Samuel George Joseph, son of Abraham Joseph, was Co-Chm and Man Dir Bovis Ltd, Underwriter of Lloyd's, Hon Col 56th (1st London) Div RE; also Mayor of St Marylebone 1928-30, Sheriff of City of London 1933-34, Alderman thereof 1933, and Lord Mayor 1942-43; served European War 1914-19 (wounded, despatches); *d* 1944; *s* by his son, Sir Keith Sinjohn Joseph, 2nd Bt, *b* 1918; Bar Middle Temple 1946, Min of State Board of Trade 1961-62, Min of Housing and Local Govt, and Min for Welsh Affairs 1962-64, Sec of State for Social Services 1970-74, for Trade and Industry 1979-81, and for Educn and Science 1981-86; Bovis Holdings Ltd 1951-59 (Dep Chm 1964-70, Chm Bovis Ltd 1958-59); MP for NE Div of Leeds (*C*) 1956-87; *cr* PC 1962, CH 1986, and *Baron Joseph*, of Portsoken, City of London (Life Baron) 1987; *d* 1994.

KABERRY (UK) 1960, of Adel cum Eccup, City of Leeds

Hon Sir CHRISTOPHER DONALD KABERRY, 2nd *Baronet*; *b* 14 March 1943; *s* his father, DONALD, Baron Kaberry of Adel, TD (Life Baron) in his baronetcy, 1991; *ed* Repton; FCA 1967: *m* 1967, Gaenor Elizabeth Vowe, yr da of Cecil Vowe Peake, MBE, of Redbourn, Herts, and has issue.

Arms – Per fesse argent and azure and a pile reversed counterchanged three double-warded, keys wards upwards also azure each enfiled by a chaplet of holly proper and of roses argent barbed and seeded also proper. **Crest** – On a wreath of sable and azure a weeping willow tree proper pendent from the trunk thereof by a ring a fleece or.
Residence – Rock View, Chiddingstone Hoath, Kent TN8 7BT.

SONS LIVING

JAMES CHRISTOPHER, *b* 1 April 1970; *ed* Oakham: *m* 1989 (*m diss* 1996), Juliet Clare, eldest da of Sir James Frederick Hill, 4th Bt (*cr* 1916), and has issue living, Jonathan James Alexander, *b* 12 May 1989, — Oliver George Henry, *b* 1991, — Imogen Camilla, *b* 1994. —— Angus George, *b* 1972.

DAUGHTER LIVING

Claire Elizabeth, *b* 1974.

BROTHERS LIVING

Hon Andrew Murdoch Scott, *b* 1946; *ed* Repton, and E Anglia Univ (BA); FCA 1972. *Residence* – Thorpe Arch Hall, Boston Spa, W Yorks.

Hon Simon Edmund John, *b* 1948; *ed* Repton; admitted Solicitor 1974.

The 1st baronet, Donald Kaberry, TD, son of Abraham Kaberry, of Leeds, was admitted Solicitor 1930, Dep Lord Mayor of Leeds 1946-47, Parl Sec Board of Trade April to Oct 1955, Member of Mr Speaker's Panel of Chairmen 1974-83, etc; MP for NW Div of Leeds (*C*) 1950-83, DL W Yorks 1976; 1939-45 War as Col 63rd Medium Regt, Dunkirk and NW Europe RA (despatches twice); *cr Baron Kaberry of Adel*, of Adel, City of Leeds (Life Baron) 1983; *d* 1991.

KAYE (UK) 1923, of Huddersfield, co York

Spectemur agendo

Let us be judged by our actions

Maj Sir PAUL HENRY GORDON KAYE, 5th *Baronet*; *b* 19 Feb 1958; *s* his father, *Sir* DAVID ALEXANDER GORDON, 1994; Maj Australian Intelligence Corps: *m* 1984, Sally Ann Louise, da of ...... of ......

Arms – Or, a bend cotised invected between two escutcheons sable each charged with a rose argent, barbed and seeded proper. Crest – Upon a staff raguly fessewise or a goldfinch proper, holding in the beak a rose argent, barbed, seeded, leaved and slipped proper.
Residence – 15 Muston Court, Carrara, Queensland 4211, Australia.

BROTHER LIVING

JOHN EGIDIO GORDON, *b* 1967. *Address* – Hyatt Regency Guam, 1155 San Vitores Rd, Tumon, Guam 96911, USA.

SISTERS LIVING

Yvonne Marie, *b* 1956: *m* 1984, and has issue living, three children. —— Denise Anne, *b* 1960. —— Alaine Freda, *b* 1962. —— Marita Margaret, *b* 1970.

WIDOW LIVING OF FOURTH BARONET

ADELLE FRANCES (*Dowager Lady Kaye*), da of Denis Lionel Thomas, of Brisbane, Queensland, Australia: *m* 1955, as his 2nd wife, Sir David Alexander Gordon Kaye, 4th Bt, who *d* 1994. *Residence* – 594 Lower Bowen Terrace, New Farm, Brisbane, Queensland 4005, Australia.

COLLATERAL BRANCH LIVING

Issue of late Brian Joseph Gordon Kaye, yst son of 2nd baronet, *b* 1920, *d* 1986: *m* 1st, 1947 (*m diss* 1980), Anne, only da of late Frederick Henry Grisewood, OBE, of Hewshotts, Liphook, Hants; 2ndly, 1980, Ereca Mrosewski:—
(By 1st *m*) Angus Frederick Gordon, *b* 1962; WO2 (CSM) REME: *m* 1st, 1986 (*m diss* 1989), —; 2ndly, 1999, Natasha Hammond.

The 1st baronet, Sir Joseph Henry, was Senior Director of Kaye and Stewart (Limited), of Huddersfield, and a Director of London, Midland and Scottish Railway Co, and of Lloyds Bank (Limited).

LISTER-KAYE (UK) 1812, of Grange, Yorkshire

Keep your own kin kind

Sir JOHN PHILIP LISTER LISTER-KAYE, 8th *Baronet*; *b* 8 May 1946; *s* his father, *Sir* JOHN CHRISTOPHER LISTER, 1982; *ed* Allhallows Sch; Hon D Univ Stirling 1995; lecturer, writer and broadcaster on Conservation of Nature and the Environment; founder dir of Scottish Conservation Charity, The Aigas Trust, 1979; Exec Dir Aigas Field Centre Ltd since 1980; Member Internat Cttee World Wilderness Foundation since 1984, Chm Scottish Advisory Cttee RSPB 1986-92; Nature Conservancy Council 1989-91; NW Regional Chm Nature Conservancy Council for Scotland 1992; NW Regional Chm Scottish Natural Heritage 1992-97; Pres Scottish Wildlife Trust 1996; author of *The White Island* (1972), *Seal Cull* (1979), *The Seeing Eye* (1980), *One For Sorrow* (1994), and *Ill Fares the Land* (1995): *m* 1st, 1972 (*m diss* 1988), Sorrel Deirdre, el da of Count Henry Noel Bentinck (later 11th Earl of Portland); 2ndly, 1989, Lucinda Anne, JP for Ross-shire, eldest da of Robin Law, of Withersfield, Suffolk, and formerly wife of Hon Evan Michael Ronald Baillie (*see* B Burton), and has issue by 1st and 2nd *m*.

Arms – Quarterly, 1st and 4th, argent, two bendlets sable, *Kaye*; 2nd and 3rd, ermine on a fesse sable three mullets or, the whole within a bordure wavy azure, *Lister*. Crests – 1st, a goldfinch proper, charged on the breast with a rose gules; 2nd, a buck's head proper, erased wavy or, attired sable, and in the mouth a bird-bolt bendwise of the third, flighted argent.
Residence – House of Aigas, Beauly, Inverness-shire IV4 7AD. *Club* – Caledonian.

SON LIVING (By 1st marriage)

JOHN WARWICK NOEL LISTER, b 10 Dec 1974; ed Glenalmond, and RMA Sandhurst; commn'd The Highlanders (Seaforth, Camerons & Highlanders) 1996.

DAUGHTERS LIVING (By 1st marriage)

Amelia Helen, b 1976. —— Melanie Jenifer, b (twin) 1976.

(by 2nd marriage)

Hermione Anne Lucinda Lorne, b 1990.

SISTER LIVING

Mary Eugenia Helen, b 1944: m 1970 (m diss 1994), Nigel Carrel, of Biggarshiels Farm, Biggar, Lanarkshire, and has issue living, Christopher-James, b 1971, — Gareth Nigel Andrew, b 1974, — Huw Stephen, b 1981, — Lucinda Helen Jane, b 1977.

AUNT LIVING (Daughter of 6th baronet)

Rosamond Eugenia Mary, b 1912: m 1945, Maj Edward Osmond Thornhill Simpson, who d 1992, and has issue living, Mark Thornhill, b 1951, — Sarah Thornhill, b 1946, — Julia Thornhill, b 1947. Residence – 7275, Balaclava St, Vancouver V6N 1M7, BC, Canada.

COLLATERAL BRANCHES LIVING

Grandchildren of late Arthur Lister-Kaye (infra):—
Issue of late John Arthur Lister-Kaye, b 1895, d 1974: m 1923, Emily Alice, da of James Henry Cooper, of Hayling Island:—
Warwick Arthur, b 1929. —— Stella Maud, b 1924: m 1943, William John Stewart Boyd, of Vic, BC, Canada.

Issue of late Arthur Lister-Kaye, brother of 6th baronet, b 1876, d 1943: m 1st, 1895, Lottie Emmeline, da of John Woodward; 2ndly, 1900, Gertrude, who d 1945, da of J. Hall, formerly of Gore House, New Milton, Hants:—
(By 2nd m) †Arthur Lister, b 1903, d 19—.

Sir John Kaye, of Woodsome, Almondbury, Yorks, Col of Horse in the service of Charles I, was created a baronet in 1642. He later raised 700 men to fight for the King but suffered heavily at the Battle of Naseby 1645. His title and estates were forfeit as a result of his loyalty to the Crown, but he survived the Restoration in 1660, paying £50 to Parliament for the redemption of his estates. The 4th Bt, Sir John, MP for York 1734-40 and Lord Mayor of York 1737, was responsible for the restoration of Micklegate Bar, which bears his arms. He was also a known Jacobite sympathizer and harbored Jacobite rebels after the Battle of Culloden. This baronetcy became extinct on the death of the 6th Bt in 1809, but in 1812 Sir John Lister-Kaye, natural son and testamentary heir of the 5th Bt received a Baronetcy. The 3rd Bt, Sir John Pepys Lister-Kaye, was a Groom-in-Waiting to King Edward VII 1908-10.

KEANE (UK) 1801, of Cappoquin, co Waterford

The stroked cat is meek

Sir RICHARD MICHAEL KEANE, 6th *Baronet*; *b* 29 Jan 1909; *s* his father, *Lt-Col Sir* JOHN, DSO, 1956; *ed* Sherborne, and Ch Ch Oxford: *m* 1939, Olivia Dorothy, da of Oliver Hawkshaw, TD, of Chisenbury Priory, Wilts, and has issue.

Arms – Gules, three salmon naiant in pale argent. **Crest** – A cat-a-mountain sejant proper, in his dexter paw a staff displaying a banner. *Residence* – Cappoquin House, co Waterford.

SONS LIVING

JOHN CHARLES, *b* 16 Sept 1941; *ed* Eton, and Ch Ch, Oxford: *m* 1977, Corinne, da of Jean Everard de Harzir, of Waroux, Alleur, Belgium, and has issue living, Christopher, *b* 1981, — Gregory, *b* 1982, — Amelia, *b* 1987. —— David Richard, *b* 1950; *ed* Eton, and Balliol Coll, Oxford: *m* 1973, Julia, da of Henry Bowring, of The Old Orchard, Bembridge, Isle of Wight, and has issue living, Henry, *b* 1982, — Jessica, *b* 1978, — Rosanna Emily, *b* 1980, — Camilla, *b* 1985.

DAUGHTER LIVING

Vivien Eleanor, *b* 1940: *m* 1961, Simon Pleydell-Bouverie (*see* E Radnor, colls). *Residence* – The Castle House, Deddington, Oxon.

SISTERS LIVING

Sheila, *b* 1911: *m* 1935, Christopher Edward Knight, and has issue living, Michael John, *b* 1939; *ed* Eton, and New Coll, Oxford: *m* 1970, Caroline Francesca, el da of Alexander Kendal Humphrey Fletcher, and has issue living, Julian Francis *b* 1971, Cassandra Louise *b* 1972, Claudia Helen *b* 1977, — Jonathan Christopher, *b* 1943; *ed* Eton, and Architectural Association: *m* 1977, Hilary Anne Durnford, and has issue living, Oliver James *b* 1977, Imogen Laura *b* 1979, — Martin David, *b* 1946, *ed* Eton, and Trin Coll, Dublin: *m* 1971, Eleanor Clare, da of James Malcolm Harrison, and has had issue, Edward Martin *b* 1976, Tamsin Jane *b* 1974, Hermione Clare *b* 1982, *d* 1985, Sophie Clare *b* 1988, — Susan Jane, *b* 1937. *Residence* – Quarry House, East St, Turners Hill, W Sussex RH10 4PU. —— Madeline Lucy; *b* 1914: *m* 1938, Donald Godfrey Emerson, CBE, of Meads House, Leighterton, Tetbury, Glos, GL8 8UW, and has issue living, James Seymour, *b* 1941; *ed* Marlborough, and Trin Coll, Dublin: *m* 1st, 1964 (*m diss* 1971), Bridget Eileen Mary, da of Lt-Col Wyndham Marsden Knatchbull (*see* B Brabourne, colls); 2ndly, 1971, Jennifer Ruth Clement, and has issue living, (by 1st *m*) Suzanne Mary *b* 1964, Gillian Lucy *b* 1966, (by 2nd *m*) Richard Donald *b* 1971, Sarah Louise *b* 1974, — Judith Lucy, *b* 1943: *m* 1967, Michael Maurice Fletcher Watson, and has issue living, — Carol Georgena, *b* 1944: *m* 1971, Robert Lorne Hyndham, of Ottawa, Canada, and has issue living, — Mary Eleanor, *b* 1953.

COLLATERAL BRANCHES LIVING

Issue of late Capt George Michael Keane, RN, 2nd son of 4th baronet, *b* 1875, *d* 1957: *m* 1909, Violet, who *d* 1974, da of late Theodore McKenna, of 22 Portland Place, W1:— Ann Patricia, *b* 1910: *m* 1934, Christopher Leslie Thompson, Group Capt, RAF (ret), and has issue living, Christopher Mark, *b* 1935, — Jonathan Michael Adrian, *b* 1938: *m* 1970, Barbara Anne, da of F. Scrowcroft, — Andrew Theodore, *b* 1941. *Residence* – Coldenhale, Eastham, Tenbury Wells, Worcs.

Granddaughters of late Lieut-Col Richard Henry Keane, CBE (infra):— Issue of late Robert Lumley Keane, *b* 1910, *d* 1946: *m* 1938, Mary Nesta, author (as Molly Keane, and as M. J. Farrell), who *d* 1996, aged 91, da of late Walter C. Skrine, of Ballyrankin House, Ferns, co Wexford:— Adele Sara, *b* 1940: *m* 1972, George Pyne Phipps, of Kilcor Castle, Castle Lyons, co Cork —— Virginia, *b* 1945: *m* 1969, Kevin Brownlow, film historian, of 7 Manor Mansions, Belsize Park Gdns, NW3, and has issue living, Julia, *b* 1984.

The 1st baronet was successively MP for Bangor and Youghal, the 2nd baronet sat as MP for Waterford (*L*) 1832-5, and the 3rd baronet was High Sheriff for co Waterford in 1856 and the 4th baronet in 1881. Sir John Keane, 5th Bt was a Senator of Irish Free State for 26 years a Councillor of State, Republic of Ireland, Gov of Bank of Ireland, and High Sheriff of co Waterford in 1911.

KELLETT (UK) 1801, of Lota, Cork

Sir STANLEY CHARLES KELLETT, 7th *Baronet; b* 5 March 1940; *s* his father, *Sir* STANLEY EVERARD KELLETT, 1983, but no name has been entered on the Official Roll of the Baronetage since death of 4th Bt in 1966; *m* 1st, 1962 (*m diss* 1968), Lorraine May, da of F. Winspear; 2ndly, 1968 (*m diss* 1974), Margaret Ann, da of James W. Bofinger; 3rdly, 1982, Catherine Lorna, da of W. J. C. Orr, and has issue by 3rd *m*.

ℜrms – Quarterly: 1st and 4th, argent, on a mount vert a boar passant sable, armed, bristled, and chained or *Kellett*; 2nd and 3rd, argent, a cross gules, in the first quarter a fleur-de-lis of the second, *Haddock.* Crest – An armed arm proper, holding a truncheon or.
Residence – 58 Glad Gunson Drive, Eleebana, NSW 2280.

DAUGHTER LIVING (*By 3rd marriage*)

Leah Catherine Elizabeth, *b* 1983.

SISTER LIVING

Margaret Joy, *b* 1942: *m* 1963, Percival William Horton, AASA(S), of 506 Great Western Highway, Faulconbridge, NSW 2776, and has issue living, Phillip William, *b* 1967, — Colin Stanley, *b* 1969, — Deborah Jane, *b* 1964: *m* 1983, Andrew Philip Howe.

Feret ad astra virtus

Virtue will bear you to the skies

UNCLES LIVING AND DECEASED (*Brothers of 6th baronet*)

CHARLES REX (9 Ashfield Place, Glen Alpine, NSW 2560, Australia), *b* 1916: *m* 1940, Florence Helen Bellamy, who *d* 1984, and has issue living, Maxwell Rex (4 Daisy St, Roselands, NSW 2195, Australia), *b* 1947; FCPA: *m* 1968, Jennifer, da of N. Maher, and has issue living, Jane Maxine *b* 1974, — Peter Charles (9 Ashfield Place, Glen Alpine, NSW 2560, Australia), *b* 1949: *m* 1973, Jennifer, da of K. Pike, of W Aust, and has issue living, Renee Helen *b* 1977: *m* 1997, Allen Matthew Plunkett, of 51 Lysander Av, Rosemeadow, NSW 2560 (and has issue living, Ethan Jay *b* 1997, Caleb Levi *b* 1999), Lauren Ann *b* 1979, — Marilyn Helen, *b* 1942: *m* 1966 Bruce Malcolm Morgan, of 18 Grevillea Grove, Narellan, NSW 2567, Australia, and has issue living, Gavin Charles *b* 1974, Karen Lee *b* 1969: *m* 1990, Ian William Spedding, of 13A Elm Place, Narellan, NSW 2567, Australia (and has issue living, Jack William *b* 1995, Toni Lee *b* 1997), Joanne Lynne *b* 1971: *m* 1991, Jason Kenneth Watson, of 52 Castlereagh St, Tahmoor, NSW 2573, Australia (and has issue living, Matthew James *b* 1992, Ashley Lee *b* 1995). —— †Ray Weaver (10 Cutler Rd, Engadine, NSW 2233, Australia), *b* 1916: *m* 1940, Daisy Miriam Payne, and *d* 1997, leaving issue, *Rev* John Raymond (153 Brooks St, Bar Beach, Newcastle 2300, NSW), *b* 1942; *ed* Univ of NSW (BSc), and Melbourne Coll of Divinity (BD): *m* 1st, 1965 (*m diss* 1982), Sandra, da of N. Holman; 2ndly, 1982, Rita Marjorie, da of G. Wiggins, and has issue living, (by 1st *m*) David John *b* 1973, Michelle Ruth *b* 1971, — Bruce Lawrence (121 Washington Dr, Bonnet Bay, NSW 2226, Australia), *b* 1945: *m* 1969, Susan, da of J. Butler, and has issue living, Bronwyn Jane *b* 1973, Jacqueline Ruth *b* 1975, — Graham Edward (23 Taft Place, Bonnet Bay, NSW, 2226), *b* 1948; BSc: *m* 1970, Leonie, da of R. Adams, and has issue living, Joshua Morgan *b* 1977, Skye Emma *b* 1975.

WIDOW LIVING OF FIFTH BARONET

IDA MARY GRACE WEAVER (*Ida, Lady Kellett*): *m* 1952, Sir Henry de Castres Kellett, 5th Bt, who *d* 1966.

WIDOW LIVING OF SIXTH BARONET

AUDREY MARGARET PHILLIPS (*Audrey, Lady Kellett*) (33 Caroma Av, Kyeemagh, NSW): *m* 1938, Sir Stanley Everard Kellett, 6th Bt, who *d* 1983.

COLLATERAL BRANCH LIVING

Issue of late William Augustus Kellett, 3rd son of 3rd baronet, *b* 1889, *d* 1952: *m* 1919, Janet Victoria, who *d* 1936, da of Andrew Peart:—
†William Andrew Henry, *b* 1920; AASA: *m* 1945, Florence (32 Panoramic Grove, Glen Waverley, Victoria, Australia), da of late Leslie James Williamson, of Koornang Rd, Carnegie, Victoria, and *d* 1996, leaving issue, James Andrew (8 Royal Av, Sandringham, Vic 3191, Australia), *b* 1952: *m* 1st, 1974 (*m diss* 1987), Kveta, da of Karel Prochazka, of Johannesburg, S Africa; 2ndly, 1993, Dianne, da of John Goddard, of Glen Waverley, Vic, Australia, and has issue living (by 1st *m*), Tamara *b* 1977, — Anne Louise, *b* 1947: *m* 1968 (*m diss* 1994), Robert James Fitzpatrick, and has issue living, David James *b* 1972, Scott Andrew *b* 1973, Sarah Louise *b* 1978, — Christine Elizabeth, *b* 1950: *m* 1st, 1970 (*m diss* 1980), John Adrian Bailey; 2ndly, 19—, Robert A. Crewdson, and has issue living (by 1st *m*), Justin Daniel *b* 1973, Jacqueline Maree *b* 1971: *m* 1993, Russell Philip Hughes (and has issue living, Lachlan Richard *b* 1998, Olivia Maree *b* 1995).

This baronetcy was created with special remainder to the heirs male of Richard Kellett, of Lota, co Cork, the father of the 1st baronet. On the death of the 2nd baronet, Sir William, in 1886 the title passed (in accordance with the special remainder) to the descendants of the yr brother (Henry de Castres Kellett, *b* 1776) of the 1st baronet, whose third son was Henry de Castres Kellett, father of Sir Henry de Castres Kellett, 3rd Bt (for 40 years a Councillor of Kew, Melbourne). He did not assume the title until 1906. Sir Henry de Castres Kellett, 4th Bt, *d* 25 July 1966. His only son Sir Henry de Castres Kellett, 5th Bt, *d* 6 Aug 1966.

KEMP (E) 1642, of Gissing, Norfolk (Extinct 1936)

Sir KENNETH HAGAR KEMP, CBE, 12th and last *Baronet*.

COLLATERAL BRANCH LIVING

Issue of late Capt Robert Hamilton Kemp, only son of 12th baronet, *b* 1877, *d* 1933: *m* 1908, Violet Mary, da of late Capt R. C. Dalrymple Stewart-Muirhead, Roy Horse Guards:—
Margaret Violet Nancy (43 Coniston Court, Holland Rd, Hove, E Sussex), *b* 1910: *m* 1932, Henry Richard Hurrell, who *d* 1973. —— Peggy Isabelle, *b* 1914: *m* 1939, Major Richard Harold Arnaud Painter, Essex Regt, of 2 Aylesbury, York Ave, Hove, E Sussex, and has issue living, Richard Hamilton, *b* 1947: *m* 1979, Patricia Leslie Hook, and has issue living, Mark Richard *b* 1986, Kathleen Leslie *b* 1984, — Gillian Mary, *b* 1943: *m* 1972, Daniel J. De Groote, and has issue living, Neal *b* 1973, Jason *b* 1976.

KENNARD (UK) 1891, of Fernhill, co Southampton

At spes non fracta

But hope is not broken

Sir GEORGE ARNOLD FORD KENNARD, 3rd *Baronet*; *b* 27 April 1915; *s* his brother, *Sir* LAURENCE URY CHARLES, 1967; *ed* Eton; Lt-Col (ret) late Comdg 4th Queen's Own Hussars; 1939-45 War (despatches twice, prisoner): *m* 1st, 1940 (*m diss* 1958), Cecilia Violet Cokayne, only da of Maj Cecil John Cokayne Maunsell, JP (E Munster, colls); 2ndly, 1958 (*m diss* 1974), Mrs Molly Jesse Rudd Miskin, yr da of late Hugh Wyllie, of Fishbourne, Sussex; 3rdly, 1985, Nicola CAREW, only da of late Capt Peter Gawen Carew (*see* Carew, Bt, colls), and formerly wife of Charles Louis Breitmeyer; 4thly, 1992, Georgina, da of Sir Harold Augustus Wernher, 3rd Bt, GCVO, TD, and widow of Lt-Col Harold Pedro Joseph Phillips, and has issue by 1st *m*.

ᴀrms – Per chevron gules and azure, a chevron engrailed argent between in chief two keys, wards downwards, or, and in base a sword erect proper, pommel and hilt or. Ꞓrest – A dexter cubit arm erect in armour proper, charged with a buckle gules, the hand grasping a key in bend or, and a broken sword in bend sinister proper.
Residence – 13 Burton Court, Franklin's Row, SE3 4TA. *Club* – Cavalry and Guards'.

DAUGHTER LIVING (*By 1st marriage*)

Zandra, *b* 1941: *m* 1962, Maj John Middleton Neilson Powell, Queen's R Irish Hussars (Rye Hill, Thorpe Malsor, Kettering, Northants), and has issue living, Edward Coleridge Cokayne, *b* 1964, — Louise Cecilia Middleton, *b* 1966: *m* 1994, Crispin David Jermyn Holborow (*see* E Courtown), and has issue living, George *b* 1997, William *b* 1999.

Queen Victoria signified her intention of bestowing a Baronetcy upon Coleridge John Kennard but he having died before the patent was gazetted, the dignity was conferred on his grandson Coleridge Arthur FitzRoy Kennard, only child of late Hugh Coleridge Downing Kennard.

KENNAWAY (GB) 1791, of Hyderabad, East Indies

Sir JOHN LAWRENCE KENNAWAY, 5th *Baronet*; *b* 7 Sept 1933; *s* his father, *Sir* JOHN, 1956; *ed* Harrow, and Trin Coll, Camb; patron of one living: *m* 1961, Christina Veronica Urszenyi, MB, ChB, and has issue.

Arms – Argent, a fesse azure between two eagles displayed in chief gules, and in base, through an annulet of the third, a slip of olive and another of palm in saltire proper. Crest – An eagle rising proper, from the beak an escutcheon pendent azure, charged with the sun in splendour also proper. *Seat* – Escot, Ottery St Mary, Devon EX11 1LU.

SON LIVING

JOHN MICHAEL, *b* 17 Feb 1962; *ed* King Edward's Sch, Bath, and Hampshire Coll of Agric: *m* 1988, Lucy Frances, yr da of Dr Jeremy Houlton Bradshaw-Smith, of Ottery St Mary, Devon, and has issue living, Olivia Ursula, *b* 1993, — Jessica Imogen, *b* 1995.

DAUGHTERS LIVING

Julia Frances, *b* 1965. —— Irma Annabelle, *b* 1968.

I shall ascend

BROTHER LIVING

Richard Noel (19 MacMillan Av, Christchurch, NZ) *b* 1935; *ed* Eton (King's Scholar) and King's Coll, Camb (Scholar); Sen lecturer in Political Science.

SISTER LIVING

Mary Joyce, *b* 1940. *Residence* – 3 Brookside, Sidmouth, Devon EX10 9UN.

COLLATERAL BRANCHES LIVING

Granddaughters of late Rev Richard Arthur Kennaway, 4th son of 2nd baronet:—
Issue of late Mark John Kennaway, *b* 1880, *d* 1960: *m* 1920, Dorothy, who *d* 1958, da of late Edward Hick, formerly of Chartridge, Chesham:—
Anne, *b* 1922: *m* 1946, Gerald Wardlaw Scott, who *d* 1988, of Corner Cottage, Fletching, Uckfield, E Sussex, and has issue living, Philip Wardlaw, *b* 1950: *m* 1977, Julia Margaret Newnham (*née* Newbery), and has issue living, Oliver Wardlaw *b* 1978, — Deborah, *b* 1948: *m* 1973 (*m diss* 1980), Torbjorn Stene, and has issue living, Rebecca *b* 1973. —— Mary Elizabeth, *b* 1924: *m* 1948, Bernard Stratton Davis, OBE, who *d* 1983, Malayan Civil Ser, of PO Box 269, Girne, Mersin 10, Turkey, and has issue living, Mark John Stratton, *b* 1952: *m* 1980, Valerie Rainsbury, and has issue living, John Charles Stratton *b* 1981, William Adam *b* 1985, Catherine Rose *b* (twin) 1981, — Sarah Elizabeth, *b* 1951; has issue living (by John Wyllie), Jack WYLLIE-DAVIS *b* 1985, Joel WYLLIE-DAVIS *b* 1987, — Maroulla Judith, *b* 1954: *m* 1979, Jeremy Peter Haile, and has issue living, Scott Matthew *b* 1983, Peter Brendan *b* 1988, Sarah Deborah *b* 1982, Emily Rebecca *b* 1985. —— Philippa Jane, *b* 1927: *m* 1962, Alexander Keith Boyle, of 4 White Point Rd, Whitby, N Yorks YO21 3JR, and has issue living, David Kennaway, *b* 1964: *m* 1987 (*m diss* 19—), Armida Asunta Eslava, — Michael Kennaway, *b* 1967, — Kirsteen Susan, *b* 1965: *m* 1989, Herbert Van Courtlandt Bailey, and has issue (*see* B Glanusk, colls). —— Susan Helen, *b* 1928: *m* 1966, His Honour John Reginald Whitley, of Kingsrod, Kingsley Green, Haslemere, Surrey, and has issue living, Elizabeth Rose, *b* 1967.

Grandson of late Rev Charles Lewis Kennaway, grandson of 1st baronet:—
Issue of late Charles Roger Kennaway, *b* 1880, *d* 1914: *m* 1907, Margaret Evelyn, who *d* 1917, da of Rev Robert Bagot Chester Everard (B Bagot, colls):—
†Roger Charles Lewis, *b* 1910; *ed* Harrow; Capt late Oxfordshire and Bucks LI (Supplementary Reserve): *m* 1st, 1936 (*m diss* 1947), Alethea Winifrede, da of late F. N. Lloyd; 2ndly, 1947, Pamela Lavender, da of Lt-Cdr T. C. M. Bellairs, RN, and widow of Group-Capt Patrick Bruce Bine Ogilvie, DSO, DFC (Renshaw, Bt, 1956 Edn), and *d* 1995, leaving issue, (by 1st *m*) Roger Ian (32 Rylett Crescent, W12 9RL), *b* 1938; FRICS: *m* 1964, Gabrielle Mary Anna, da of late Lt-Col D. I. C. Tennant, of Bosham, Sussex, and has issue living, Charles Lewis *b* 1966, Hugh Edward *b* 1969: *m* 1997, Alyson Clare Monica Fiott, Anthony Francis *b* 1973, — (by 2nd *m*) Rose Margaret Ruth (Pengelly, Barton Breage, Helston, Cornwall), *b* 1949: *m* 1970 (*m diss* 1993), Quintin Gerald Wyvern Batt, and has issue living, Camilla Louise *b* 1973. *Residence* – Tremoor Combe, St Breward, Cornwall.

The 1st baronet, Sir John, in 1788 was appointed Resident at the Court of the Nizam, with whom, on the breaking out of the war with Tippoo Sultan, he concluded treaties of peace between the allied powers and Tippoo, who ceded half his dominions and paid £3,300,000 to the Allies. The 3rd baronet, the Rt Hon Sir John Henry, PC, CB, sat as MP for Devonshire (C) 1870-85, and for Honiton Div of Devonshire 1885-1910.

KENNEDY (UK) 1836, of Johnstown Kennedy, co Dublin

I adhere to virtue

Sir MICHAEL EDWARD KENNEDY, 8th *Baronet*; *b* 12 April 1956; *s* his father, *Lt-Col Sir* (GEORGE) RONALD DERRICK, OBE, RA, 1988; *ed* Rotherfield Hall, Sussex; *m* 1984, Helen Christine, da of Patrick Lancelot Rae, of Nine Acres, Halstead, Kent, and has issue.

𝕬rms – Sable, on a fesse between three esquires' helmets argent, a fox courant proper. 𝕮rest – A dexter arm embowed in armour, the hand grasping an oak-branch all proper.
Seat – Johnstown Kennedy, Rathcoole, Co Dublin. *Residence* – 48 Telston Lane, Otford, Kent TN14 5LA.

SON LIVING

GEORGE MATTHEW RAE, *b* 9 Dec 1993.

DAUGHTERS LIVING

Constance Andrea Rae, *b* 1984. —— Josephine Jennifer Rae, *b* 1986. —— Katherine Colleen Rae, *b* 1997.

SISTER LIVING

Carolyn Phyllis, *b* 1950: *m* 1979, Jan Gerard Willemszoon Blaauw, of Hong Kong, and has issue living, Keir Alexander Kennedy, *b* 1982, — Patrick Jan Kennedy, *b* (twin) 1982. *Residence* – 7 Beverly Court, 2D Shui Fai Terrace, Stubbs Rd, Hong Kong.

AUNT LIVING *(daughter of 6th baronet)*

Julia Maureen Patricia, *b* 1934: *m* 1961, George Hector Miller, of Middle Chantry, Carter's Lane, Wickham Bishops, Essex, and has issue living, Rupert Leslie Derrick, *b* 1965: *m* 1986, Yvette Marie Gabrielle Brewster, and has issue living, Sian Louise Georgina *b* 1988, Sophie Jane Yasmin *b* 1990, Natasha Leslie *b* 1993, — Katrina Phyllis Evelyn, *b* 1962: *m* 1993, Ian Roy Cooke, and has issue living, Frederick Roy *b* 1997, — Rachel Susan, *b* 1964: *m* 1992, Stuart Michael Banning, and has issue living, Joshua Charles *b* 1995, Sean Henry *b* 1998, — Grania Sarah, *b* 1968.

WIDOW LIVING OF SEVENTH BARONET

NOELLE MONA (*Noelle, Lady Kennedy*), da of Charles Henry Green, of Hunworth, Melton, Constable, Norfolk: *m* 1949, Lt-Col Sir (George) Ronald Derrick Kennedy, 7th Bt, OBE, RA, who *d* 1988. *Residence* – Harraton Square, Church Lane, Exning, Suffolk CB8 7HF.

COLLATERAL BRANCHES LIVING

Granddaughter of late Capt Francis Kennedy, 4th son of 1st baronet:—
Issue of late John Arthur Kennedy, *b* 1858, *d* 1913: *m* 1881, Evelyn Maude, who *d* 1921, da of late H. G. Bromilow, of Southport:—
Olive Eileen, *b* 1889.

Grandchildren of late Edward Robert Kennedy (*infra*):—
Issue of late Robert Kennedy, *b* 1911, *d* 1990: *m* 1935, Catherine Frances (Loughananna House, Kilbehenny, co Limerick), da of late Maj Robert Gregory, MC, of Coole Park, co Galway:—
Robert Edward (Creighton Park, Dandaragan, WA, Australia), *b* 1940: *m* 1969, Sandra Joan, da of S. A. Giles, of Yericoin, W Australia, and has issue living, Edward Robert, *b* 1980, — Jane Catherine, *b* 1972, — Megan Anne, *b* 1974. —— Benjamin James, *b* 1942: *m* 1980, Margaret Lorna, da of George Clark, of Portsoy, Banff, and has issue living, Graham John Clark, *b* 1982, — Heather Catherine, *b* 1983, — Julia Susan, *b* 1985. —— Susan, *b* 1936: *m* 1970 (*m diss* 19—), Wing-Cdr Ian Traill Sutherland, RAAF. —— Margaret Jane, *b* 1937: *m* 1964, Col David Andrew Robert Murray Brown, late The Queen's Royal Irish Hussars, of Warren End Cottage, Warren End, Crowborough, E Sussex, and has issue living, Robin David (150 Blythe Rd, W14), *b* 1964: *m* 1997, Rachel Margaret, only da of Ven Richard Acworth, Archdeacon of Wells, — Belinda Jane, *b* 1966: *m* 1994, Miles William Rupert Hunt, of Laburnham Cottage, Fairwarp, E Sussex, and has issue living, Thomas David *b* 1998, Susannah Jane *b* 1996.

Grandchildren of late Robert Kennedy, 5th son of 1st baronet:—
Issue of late Edward Robert Kennedy, *b* 1860, *d* 1925: *m* 1905, Beryl Doris, who *d* 1988, aged 101, da of E. Lumsdaine, of Sydney, NS Wales:—
Percy William, *b* 1914: *m* 1936, Joan, da of Sydney Cooper, and has issue living, William Roger, *b* 1940: *m* 1966, Vivienne Gloria, da of James O'Shea, and has issue living, John Edward *b* 1967, Darby James *b* 1971, *d* 1993, — Richard August, *b* 1943, — Rosemary Ann Caroline, *b* 1937: *m* 1957, Allan Ross, — Evelyn Geraldine Margaret, *b* 1942, — Judith Patricia Wilhelmena, *b* 1953. *Residence* – Weston Park, Leixlip, co Dublin. —— Maeve: *m* 1932, George John Robinson, who *d* 1958, and has issue living, John Edward Bernard, *b* 1933, — George William Richard, *b* 1934: *m* 1964, Susan, da of late Maj Cyril Hall, of Gilltown, Kilcullen, co Kildare, and has issue living, Emma Jane Anna *b* 1965, Lara Camilla Patricia *b* 1060, — Dryan Patrick Valentine, *b* 1940, — Mary Rose, *b* 1936: *m* 1961, Seamus Hayes, — Doris Teresa, *b* 1943: *m* 19—, T. O'Hanlon. *Residence* – Phepotstown, Kilcock, co Meath. —— Grania Geraldine: *m* 1947 (*m diss* 1956), Capt Edward de Lérisson Cazenove, late Coldm Gds, and has issue living, Patrick Ralph de Lérisson, *b* 1947, Nicola Louise (Cola), *b* 1949: *m* 1st, 1976 (*m diss* 1983), Sir (Brian) Charles Pennefather Warren, 9th Bt; 2ndly 1994, as his 2nd wife,

Charles St Vigor Fox (see Orr-Ewing, Bt, colls), of Langham House, Gillingham, Dorset. *Residence* – Synone Stud, Cashel, co Tipperary.

　　　　Grandchildren of Adm Francis William Kennedy, CB, son of late Robert Kennedy (ante):—
　　　　Issue of late Capt Francis Henry Kennedy, RN, *b* 1900; *d* 1981: *m* 1931, Magdalen Frances, who *d* 1976, da of late George FitzAdam-Ormiston, of Pockeridge Park, Wilts:—
Robert Francis (Melcombe House, Pen Selwood, Somerset), *b* 1935; Maj Irish Gds (ret); *ed* Stowe, and RMA Sandhurst: *m* 1976, Sally Mary, da of A. B. Antram of Keyes Wells, Petworth, and has issue living, Andrew Francis, *b* 1980. —— John Ormiston, TD (20 Greville Park Rd, Ashtead, Surrey), *b* 1938; *ed* Stowe, Queen's Coll, Camb (MA), and CEng: *m* 1969, Margaret Mary, el da of H. G. N. Lee, of Holmwood Lodge, Frome, Som, and has issue living, Christopher Patrick, *b* 1971, Annabel Margaret, *b* 1973. —— Bridget Magdalen, *b* 1942: *m* 1974, Alexander Lindsay, of Balgedie House, Easter Balgedie, by Kinross KY13 7HQ, and has issue living, Philip John, *b* 1975.

　Sir John Kennedy, 1st Bt, was great-grandson of Darby O'Kennedy, of Ballikeiroge Castle, co Waterford.

KIMBER (UK) 1904, of Lansdowne Lodge, Wandsworth, co London

You may break, but you shall not bend me

Sir CHARLES DIXON KIMBER, 3rd *Baronet*; *b* 7 Jan 1912; *s* his father, Sir HENRY DIXON, 1950; *ed* Eton, and Balliol Coll, Oxford (BA 1933); Dip Social Anthropology 1948: *m* 1st, 1933 (*m diss* 1950), Ursula, who *d* 1981, da of late Ernest Roy Bird, MP; 2ndly, 1950 (*m diss* 1965), Margaret only da of late Francis John Bonham, of 13 Dudley Rd, Wimbledon, SW, and has had issue by 1st and 2nd *m*.

𝔄rms – Argent, a torteau between three choughs proper, on a chief engrailed gules, three estoiles of the first. 𝔠rest – A bull's head cabossed sable horned argent, between the horns an estoile or.
Residence – Lower End Farm, Great Comberton, Pershore, Worcs WR10 3DU.

SONS LIVING AND DECEASED (By 1st marriage)

TIMOTHY ROY HENRY (Newton Hall, nr Carnforth, Lancs LA6 2NZ), *b* 3 June 1936; *ed* Eton; High Sheriff Lancs 1996: *m* 1st, 1960 (*m diss* 1974), Antonia Kathleen Brenda, da of Sir Francis John Watkin Williams, 8th Bt, QC, (*cr* 1798); 2ndly, 1979, Susan Hare, da of late J. K. Brooks, and widow of Richard Coulthurst North, of Newton Hall, nr Carnforth, Lancs, and has issue living (by 1st *m*), Rupert Edward Watkin, *b* 1962: *m* 1997, Lisa C. S., da of David Cave, of Alma Lodge, Terrington, Norfolk, — Hugo Charles, *b* 1964: *m* 1996, Alexandra S. J., yst da of Andrei Hoogeweegen, of Sandridge Park, Melksham, Wilts, and has issue living, Kitty Annelike India *b* 1998. —— †Nicholas John, *b* 1937; *ed* Eton; *dunm* 1996. —— Robert (New Bois, Windsor Lane, Little Kingshill, Gt Missenden, Bucks HP16 0DP), *b* 1941; *ed* Eton: *m* 1964, Carolyn Evelyn Garth, da of Frederick Griffiths-Jones, of West Barn, Little Missenden, Bucks, and has issue living, Jane Guthrie, *b* 1967: *m* 1989, Mark Charles Etheridge, and has issue living, Charles Robert Guthrie *b* 1994, Lucy Kate *b* 1996, — Amanda Ann, *b* 1970: *m* 1999, Charles Lewarne Perkin.

DAUGHTER LIVING (By 2nd marriage)

Rhys Catherine (4F Victoria Works, Graham St, Birmingham B1 3PE), *b* 1951; Dip in Landscape Architecture (Glos), ALI: *m* 1977, Michael Fox, RIBA, who *d* 1993.

COLLATERAL BRANCHES LIVING

　　　　Grandchildren of late Percy Dixon Kimber, 3rd son of 1st baronet:—
　　　　Issue of late Guy Mackenzie Kimber, *b* 1899, *d* 1985: *m* 1926, Ellen Elizabeth Margaret, who *d* 1977, da of late Rev J. Jardine-Lockhart, of Paignton, Devon:—
David Percy (Maritzdaal, Dargle, Natal), *b* 1930: *m* 1953, Elizabeth Mary Paterson, da of Tom Paterson Owens, CBE, of Weybridge, Surrey, and has issue living, Richard Guy, *b* 1956, — Christopher David, *b* 1961: *m* 1988, Shelley Bennett, and has issue living, Daniel Christopher *b* 1993, Annabel Shelley *b* 1990, — Jeannet Elizabeth, *b* 1954: *m* 1976 (*m diss* 1992), Jean-Henri Coppez, and has issue living, Henri Jean-Patric *b* 1978, Jean-Marc Guy *b* 1980, — Georgina Louise, *b* 1957: *m* 1985 (*m diss* 1992), Roland Zittera. —— Michael Jardine (Selsley, Dargle, Natal), *b* 1932: *m* 1957, Mary Elizabeth, da of late J. A. Dales, of Pietermaritzburg, Natal, and has issue living, James Michael, *b* 1958, — Guy Barrington, *b* 1962, — Kathryn Mary, *b* 1966: *m* 1992, Grantley Colin Jacques, of Durban, and has issue living, Matthew Jardine *b* 1994, Timothy Hugh *b* 1997.

　　　　Grandchildren of late Walter Dixon Kimber, 4th son of 1st baronet:—
　　　　Issue of late Eric Dixon Kimber, *b* 1898, *d* 1956: *m* 1926, Gwendolen Isa Dow, who *d* 1980, da of late Lawrence C. French, of High Trees, Godalming, Surrey:—

Anthony Dixon (Greytown, Natal), *b* 1927: *m* 1957, Joan Lilian Patterson, and has issue living, Brett Dixon, *b* 1960, — Erica-Jane, *b* 1959: *m* 1988, Paul Richard Benham, — Carolyn Suzanne, *b* 1963. —— Roger Dixon, *b* 1929: *m* 1957, Sandra, da of late Leslie Guy Gold, MC, of Sussex House, 35 Sussex Place, W2, and has issue living, Richard Orlando Dixon, *b* 1957: *m* 1984, Nicola Anne, da of Christopher Andrew Balck-Foote, of Stockcross, Berks, and has issue living, Henry Dixon Balck *b* 1988, Alexander Hudson Balck *b* 1993, Jessica Poppy Balck *b* 1985, — Eric Guy Piers, *b* 1961, — Catherine Miranda, *b* 1959: has issue living, Jaime Rose Muir *b* 1988. *Residence* – Higher Menchine Down, Black Dog, Crediton, Devon. —— Winifred Margaret (10 Nelson St, Woollahra, Sydney, NSW, Australia), *b* 1930: *m* 1959, Lawrence Kevin Tonkin, MB BS, who *d* 1993, and has issue living, Lawrence Eric, *b* 1963, — Shauna Kerry, *b* 1960: *m* 19—, Frank Curreti, and has issue living, Edwardo *b* 1989, Isobella *b* 1992.

Issue of late Allan Dixon Kimber, *b* 1903, *d* 1987: *m* 1st, 1939 (*m diss* 1959), Daphne Mary, da of Richard Guy Chaloner Ogle, of Natal; 2ndly, 1964, Sylvia Margaret, da of late Garnet Edwin Driver, solicitor, of Natal:— (By 1st *m*) Daphne Jane, *b* 1940: *m* 1st, 1964 (*m diss* 1966), John Campbell, of Natal; 2ndly, 1968 (*m diss* 1973), Peter Glen Cox, and has issue living (by 1st *m*), Paula Catherine, *b* 1965, — (by 2nd *m*) Glen Alexander Marc, *b* 1969, — Michael Piers, *b* 1970, — Joshua Richard Alan, *b* 1971. —— Susan Mary, *b* 1942: *m* 1963 (*m diss* 1974), George Desmond Fairfoot, and has issue living, Samuel Christian, *b* 1964, — Thomas Jason, *b* 1968, — Matthew Adam, *b* 1969. —— Nancy Florence, *b* 1946: *m* 1974, Henry Clive Bowring, of Park Farm House, Bodiam, Sussex, and has issue living, Guy Allan Clive, *b* 1975, — Hugh Rennie, *b* 1977.

The 1st baronet, Sir Henry, founded the legal firm of Kimber and Ellis, and sat as the first MP for Wandsworth (C) 1885-1913. The 2nd baronet, Sir Henry Dixon, was Ch Commoner, City of London 1919, and Senior Partner in the legal firm of Kimber, Williams, Sweetland & Stinson.

KING (UK) 1815, of Charlestown, Roscommon

Sir WAYNE ALEXANDER KING, 8th *Baronet*; *b* 2 Feb 1962; *s* his father, *Sir* PETER ALEXANDER, 1973; *ed* Sir Roger Mawood's Sch, Sandwich, Kent, and Algonquin Coll, Ottawa: *m* 1984, Laura Ellen, da of Donald James Lea, of Almonte, Ontario, and has issue.

𝕬rms – Sable, a lion rampant double queued or. 𝕮rest – An escallop gules.
Residence – 146 High St, Almonte, Ontario K0A 1A0, Canada.

SON LIVING

PETER RICHARD DONALD, *b* 4 May 1988.

SISTER LIVING

Spes tutissima coelis   Dorothy Jane *b* 1964.

Our safest hope is in
Heaven

WIDOW LIVING OF SEVENTH BARONET

JEAN MARGARET, da of Christopher Thomas Cavell, of Deal: *m* 1st, 1957, Sir Peter Alexander King, 7th Bt, who *d* 1973; 2ndly, 1978, Rev Richard Graham Mackenzie.

KING (UK) 1888, of Campsie, Stirlingshire

Honour is the reward of industry

Sir JOHN CHRISTOPHER KING, 4th *Baronet*; *b* 31 March 1933; *s* his father, *Sir* JAMES GRANVILLE LE NEVE, TD, 1989; *ed* Eton; Sub-Lt RNVR, 1 Lt Berks Yeo TA: *m* 1st, 1958 (*m diss* 1972), Patricia Monica, only da of late Lieut-Col Kingsley Osbern Nugent Foster, DSO, OBE; 2ndly, 1984, Mrs (Aline) Jane Holley, el da of late Col Douglas Alexander Brett, GC, OBE, MC, and has issue by 1st *m*.

Arms – Azure, on a fesse argent between a lion's head erased or in chief, and two billets of the third in base, three round-buckles of the field. **Crest** – A red-breast proper.
Residence – Stillwater, Box 218 Mathews Courthouse, Va 23109, USA.

SON LIVING (*By 1st marriage*)

JAMES HENRY RUPERT, *b* 24 May 1961; *ed* Eton: *m* 1995, Elizabeth D., yst da of Richard Ellingworth, of Budleigh Salterton, Devon.

DAUGHTER LIVING (*By 1st marriage*)

Melanie Avril, *b* 1963: *m* 1989, Jeremy Legge, and has issue living, Hamish, *b* 1991, — Charles, *b* 1992.

SISTER LIVING

Susan Penelope, *b* 1929: *m* 1957, Christopher Marsden-Smedley, yr son of late Basil Futvoye Marsden-Smedley, OBE, and has issue living, Timothy Charles, *b* 1959: *m* 1996, María Cristina, da of Don Jaime Rodríguez, of Tunja, Colombia, — Philip John, *b* 1961, — Catherine Penelope, *b* 1964: *m* 1992, Christopher D. Miller, yr son of Maj David Miller, of Pyrford, Surrey, and has issue living, George Alexander *b* 1996, Anna Penelope *b* 1999. *Residence* – Church Farm, Burrington, nr Bristol, Avon.

COLLATERAL BRANCH LIVING

Issue of late John Alastair King 2nd son of 2nd baronet, *b* 1905, *d* 1991: *m* 1st, 1929 (*m diss* 1939), Veronica Mary, who *d* 1967, only da of late Col Bertram Abel Smith, DSO, MC; 2ndly, 1939 (*m diss* 1956), Ruby Enid, who *d* 1984, yr da of late Henry George Atkinson-Clark; 3rdly, 1957, Pierina (Downs Farmhouse, Baunton, Cirencester, Glos), da of — Holt, of —:—
(By 1st *m*) Rhona Lavinia, *b* 1932. —— (By 2nd *m*), Elisabeth Jane, *b* 1941: *m* 1973, Henry William Garrood, and has issue living, Charles William *b* 1976, Caroline Anne *b* 1975. —— (By 3rd *m*) Sarah Rosemary, *b* 1959: *m* 1983, Charles Langdale Stebbing, of Mustard Field House, Burneston, Bedale, N Yorks DL8 2JD.

Sir James King, 1st Bt (son of John King, of Campsie, co Stirling, a merchant of Glasgow), was Lord Provost of Glasgow 1886-89. He received Queen Victoria on her visit to Glasgow in 1888.

King (Stafford-King-Harman), see Harman.

DUCKWORTH-KING (GB) 1792, of Bellevue, Kent (Extinct 1972)

Sir JOHN RICHARD DUCKWORTH-KING, 7th and last *Baronet*.

DAUGHTERS LIVING OF SIXTH BARONET

Anne Eva Katharine *b* 1915: *m* 1940, Christopher Willoughby Jardine, CB, who *d* 1982, and has issue living, Theresa Barbara Lettice (31 Great Tattenhams, Epsom Downs, Banstead, Surrey KT18 SRF), *b* 1942: *m* 1st, 1961 (*m diss* 1973), Anthony Harold Hazell; 2ndly, 1979, Reginald Alfred William Jones, and has issue living, (by 1st *m*), James Christopher *b* 1962, Deborah Anne *b* 1963, — Victoria Agnes, *b* 1945: *m* 1968, Peter Nicholas Christian Bordewich, of Rock Hill, Wolverley, Kidderminster, Worcs DY11 5XE, and has issue living, Luke George Batchelor *b* 1974, Magnus James Roness *b* 1975, Camilla Anne *b* (twin) 1975, — Cassandra Caroline Mary, *b* 1954: *m* 1988, William John Jeremy Chubb, of Brunswick House, 97 Knatchbull Rd, SE5 9QU, son of late John Chubb, CMG, of Beckley, E Sussex, and has issue living, Oliver Octavius *b* 1989, George Jerome Quentin *b* 1999, Elizabeth Anne *b* 1992, Dido Mary Francesca *b* 1994, Christabel Victoria *b* 1995. *Residence* – 8 St Loo Court, Flood St, SW3. —— Caroline Agnes (2 Erskine Rd, NW3 3AJ), *b* 1916.

WIDOW LIVING OF SEVENTH BARONET

ALICE PATRICIA (*Lady Duckworth-King*) (7 Mabon Place, Duns, Berwickshire; 47 Avenue de Hassan 11, Tangier, Morocco), da of Thomas Rutledge, of Fugar House, Ravensworth, co Durham; *m* 1943, as his 2nd wife, Sir John Richard Duckworth-King, 7th Bt, who *d* 1972, when the title became ext.

KINLOCH (NS) 1686, of Gilmerton, East Lothian

I aspire higher

Sir DAVID KINLOCH, 13th *Baronet*; *b* 5 Aug 1951; *s* his father, *Maj Sir* ALEXANDER DAVENPORT, 1982; *ed* Gordonstoun: *m* 1st, 1976 (*m diss* 1986), Susan, da of Arthur Middlewood, of North Side Farm, Kilham; 2ndly, 1987, Maureen, da of Robert Carswell, and has issue by 1st and 2nd *m*.

Arms – Azure, a boar's head erased between three mascles or. **Crest** – An eagle rising proper.
Seat – Gilmerton House, North Berwick, East Lothian.

SONS LIVING (By 1st marriage)

ALEXANDER, *b* 31 May 1978.

(by 2nd marriage)

Christopher Robert, *b* 1988. —— Matthew Carswell, *b* 1990.

DAUGHTER LIVING (By 1st marriage)

Alice, *b* 1976.

HALF-BROTHER LIVING (Son of 12th baronet by 3rd m)

James Alexander (23 Lauriston Gdns, Edinburgh EH3 9HH), *b* 1967: *m* 1993, Jill D., only da of Brian Bamber, of Slyne-with-Hest, Lancaster.

SISTERS LIVING (Daughters of 12th baronet by 2nd wife, Hilda Anna, who d 1986, da of Thomas Walker, of Edinburgh)

Victoria, *b* 1947: *m* 1981, Martin Teale, of 99 White Lion Rd, Amersham, Bucks. —— Harriet, *b* 1949: *m* 1st, 1967 (*m diss* 1973), Colin John Weddell; 2ndly, 1988, Ian Napier Thomson, of The Kennels, W Saltoun, by Pencaitland, E Lothian, and has issue living (by 1st *m*), Jennifer Katherine Graham, *b* 1968. —— Ann (twin with her brother David), *b* 1951: *m* 1984, George Kenneth Banks, and has issue living, Justin Christopher, *b* 1985.

HALF-SISTERS LIVING (Daughters of 12th baronet by 1st wife, Alexandra, da of Frederick Y. Dalziel, of New York, USA)

Emily Lucy (*Hon Mrs Hugh Astor*), *b* 1930: *m* 1950, Hon Hugh Waldorf Astor, who *d* 1999, and has issue (*see* B Astor of Hever, colls). *Residences* – Folly Farm, Sulhamstead, Berks; 79 Ashley Gdns, Thirleby Rd, SW1P 1HG. —— Jean Alexandra (Champions Place, Kent Hatch Rd, Limpsfield Chart, Surrey RH8 0TA), *b* 1934.

WIDOW LIVING OF TWELFTH BARONET

ANN MAUD (*Ann, Lady Kinloch*), da of late Group-Capt Frank Leslie White, of London: *m* 1965, as his 3rd wife, Maj Sir Alexander Davenport Kinloch, 12th Bt, who *d* 1982. *Residence* – Greenacre, 87 Hepburn Gdns, St Andrews, Fife KY16 9LT.

COLLATERAL BRANCHES LIVING

Issue of late Francis Kinloch, 3rd son of 10th baronet, *b* 1863, *d* 1916: *m* 1896, Marion Eva, da of late Charles Nairne Marshall, of Curriehill, New Zealand:—
Lucy Margaret, *b* 1899.

Granddaughter of late Charles Henry Alexander Frederick Camillo Everard John James Rocheid, great-grandson of Alexander Kinloch (who assumed the surname of Rocheid), 4th son of 3rd baronet:—
Issue of late Colin William Hilmar Otto Rocheid, *b* 1881, *d* 1954: *m* 1st, 1911, Elizabeth, who *d* 1935, da of late Ernst von Schröder; 2ndly, 1942, Catherine Jung, who *d* 1959:—
(By 1st *m*) Elisabeth Marie Olga Harriet Ernestine, *b* 1912: *m* 1936, Capt Joachim von Sametzki, who *d* 1946. *Residence* –

The 1st baronet, Sir Francis Kinloch (son of Andrew Kinloch, merchant of Rochelle), was Lord Provost of Edinburgh. The 10th baronet, Capt Sir Alexander Kinloch, Grenadier Guards, served in Crimea 1854-5. The 11th baronet, Brig-Gen Sir David Alexander Kinloch, CB, MVO, served with Grenadier Guards in S Africa 1899-1902, and in European War 1914-19.

KINLOCH (UK) 1873, of Kinloch, co Perth

Not degenerate

Sir DAVID OLIPHANT KINLOCH, 5th *Baronet*; *b* 15 Jan 1942; *s* his father, *Sir* JOHN, 1992; *ed* Charterhouse; CA: *m* 1st, 1968 (*m diss* 1979), Susan Minette, yst da of late Maj-Gen Robert Elliott Urquhart, CB, DSO; 2ndly, 1983, Sabine, only da of Philippe de Loes, of 5 Rampe de Cologny, 1223 Cologny, Geneva, Switzerland, and has issue by 1st and 2nd *m*.

Arms – Quarterly; 1st, grand quarter azure, a boar's head erased between three mascles or, a crescent of the second in chief for difference, *Kinloch*; 2nd, grand quarter gules, a chevron embattled between three crescents argent, *Oliphant*; 3rd, grand quarter parted per fesse argent and sable, a chevron between three cinquefoils counter-changed, *Balneavis*; 4th grand quarter counter-quartered; 1st, gules, a broken spear and a standard saltireways argent, the last charged with a cross of the field and fringed or; 2nd, azure, a cat salient argent; 3rd, argent, on a saltire sable nine mascles of the first within a bordure azure; 4th, or, three bars wavy gules, each charged with an escallop of the field, all *Smyth*. **Crest** – A young eagle perched, looking up to the sun in his splendour all proper.
Residences – House of Aldie, Fossoway, Kinross, Kinross-shire KY13 0QH; 29 Walpole St, SW3 4QS.

SON LIVING (*By 2nd marriage*)

ALEXANDER PETER, *b* 30 June 1986.

DAUGHTERS LIVING (*By 1st marriage*)

Katherine Cecilia, *b* 1972. —— Emily Nicole, *b* 1974. —— Nicola Marjorie, *b* 1976.

(*by 2nd marriage*)

Sophie, *b* 1994.

SISTER LIVING

Susan Cecilia, *b* 1935: *m* 1960, Malcolm Henry Rogers, of 11 Warrender Court, North Berwick, E Lothian EH39 4RR, and has issue living, John Andrew, *b* 1965: *m* 1997, Ann Edwards, —— Wendy Diana, *b* 1962.

AUNT LIVING (*daughter of 3rd baronet*)

Barbara Cecilia, *b* 1913: *m* 1937, Charles Gairdner Dalrymple Tennant, Maj late RASC, who *d* 1991, and has issue living, Thomas Peregrine, *b* 1939; Lt RN (ret): *m* 1972, Finella Susan, da of Geoffrey Hooper, and has issue living, Edward Charles *b* 1978, Emma Clare *b* 1975, —— Edward Kinloch, *b* 1943, —— Tanera Cecilia, *b* 1940: *m* 1962, Michael Charles Averdieck, of 5 Rock Terrace, Scotgate, Stamford, Lincs PE9 2YJ, and has issue living, William John *b* 1963: *m* 1995, Sarah Jane Crozier, Charles Edward *b* 1965, James Ulric *b* (twin) 1965: *m* 1993, Anne Geddes (and has issue living, Rory Edward *b* 19—), —— Victoria Margaret, *b* 1950: *m* 1976, Peter Mackenzie Duke, of Oldtown of Carnaveron, Muir of Foulis, Alford, Aberdeenshire, and has issue living, Robert Mackenzie *b* 1980, Kirstie Mary *b* 1982. *Residence* – Cruivie, Rosemount, Blairgowrie, Perths.

COLLATERAL BRANCH LIVING

Issue of late James Kinloch, 2nd son of 2nd baronet, *b* 1884, *d* 1950: *m* 1909, Julia Madeline, who *d* 1962, da of late George W. Boase, of Broughty Ferry:—
Colin David (26 Curtis Rd, Ashdell Park, Alton, Hants GU34 2SD), *b* 1918; a Chartered Engineer: *m* 1945, Gertrude Lilian Mary, da of E. R. Bollom, and has issue living, Nigel George, *b* 1951: *m* 1976, Elizabeth Anne, da of Geoffrey

Browning, of Winchester, and has had issue, David Geoffrey Ian *b* 1982, James Colin George *b* 1986 *d* 1987, Andrew Malcolm Robert *b* 1989, Jennifer Mary Ruth *b* 1984, Catherine Brenda Anne *b* 1988, — Bridget Eleanor Mary, *b* 1948: *m* 1974, Christopher James Biggs, of 16 Nuneham Sq, Abingdon, Oxon OX14 1EH, and has issue living, Patrick Mark James *b* 1980, Alison Samantha Mary *b* 1978, Deborah Katharine Louise *b* 1981, Sarah Elizabeth Helen *b* 1982. —— Sheila Maysie, *b* 1910: *m* 1938, Brig Arthur Catchmay Tyler, CBE, MC, DL, Mil Knt of Windsor, late Welch Regt, who *d* 1998, and has issue living, Richard Hugh (Sheldon House, Monyash, Derbys), *b* 1939; Capt late R Regt of Wales: *m* 1st, 1963 (*m diss* 1981), Suzan Gaynor, da of Lt-Col Sam Griffith, OBE; 2ndly, 1982, Beverley Gayle, da of late Arthur Rodgers, OBE, of Kuwait, and has issue living (by 1st *m*), Christopher Charles Griffith, *b* 1965, Nicholas Hugh Griffin *b* 1966, (by 2nd *m*) Caroline Mary *b* 1984, Eleanor Jane *b* 1992, — Andrew James, *b* 1950: *m* 1971, Judith Margaret, da of Alan Gale, — John Philip, *b* 1951: *m* 1973, Valerie Eileen, da of R. L. Luckin, and has issue living, Christopher Philip *b* 1978, — Mary Joyce, *b* 1941: *m* 1966, Bruce George Draper, of 25 Odenwald Rd, Eaglemont, Vic 3084, Aust, and has issue living, Jeremy Charles Bruce *b* 1971, Nicholas James *b* 1973, Catherine Louise *b* 1969. *Residence* – Kenwith Castle, Abbotsham, Bideford, Devon. —— Elspeth (Halliwell Nursing Home, Kingswood Rd, Tunbridge Wells, Kent TN2 4UN), *b* 1912: *m* 1938, Lt-Cdr Malcolm David Wanklyn, VC, DSO (two Bars), RN, who was *ka* 1942, and has issue living, Ian David Kinloch (Ashwick House, Chelmarsh, Bridgnorth, Shropshire), *b* 1939, Lt-Cdr RN: *m* 1971, Penelope, el da of Capt Charles Wickham Malins, DSO, DSC, RN, and has issue living, Alastair David *b* 1973, Oliver Charles *b* 1975, Catriona Louise *b* 1977.

 The lands of Kinloch of that Ilk were situated at Collessie, the head of Rossie Loch, Fifeshire, of which family charters date from 1210, but were sold in the 16th century. David Kinloch, physician and traveller, a descendant of this line, acquired lands in Perthshire which were erected into the Barony of Kinloch temp James VI. His grandson, Sir David Kinloch of that Ilk was created a baronet 1685, it is said to have been with remainder to his heirs male whatsoever though no record exists in the Great Seal Register, Sir James Kinloch, 3rd Bt, took part in the 1745 rising, was tried and condemned to death, and the baronetcy became forfeited, but having escaped to France he was subsequently pardoned. His son William, who dsp, sold Kinloch to his kinsman, Capt George Oliphant Kinloch (grandson of James, yr brother of 1st baronet), whose son George Kinloch of Kinloch fled to France as an outlaw 1819 for advocating reform, but in 1832 was elected the first MP for Dundee. His son, Sir George Kinloch, was the 1st Bt of the present creation.

KIRKPATRICK (NS) 1685, of Closeburn, Dumfriesshire

Sir IVONE ELLIOTT KIRKPATRICK, 11th *Baronet*; *b* 1 Oct 1942; *s* his father, *Sir* JAMES ALEXANDER, 1954; *ed* Wellington Coll, and St Mark's Coll Univ Adelaide.

Arms – Argent, a saltire and chief azure, the last charged with three cushions or. Crest – A hand holding a dagger in pale, distilling drops of blood. Supporters – Two talbot hounds argent.

BROTHER LIVING

ROBIN ALEXANDER, *b* 19 March 1944; *ed* Wellington Coll.

MOTHER LIVING

Ellen Gertrude, only da of Capt Robert Perceval Elliott, late RNR, of Ismailia: *m* 1st, 1941 (*m diss* 1953), Sir James Alexander Kirkpatrick, 10th Bt, who *d* 1954; 2ndly, 1955, John Ogilvie Corbin, MB, BS, FRCS.

COLLATERAL BRANCHES LIVING

Granddaughter of late Charles William Sharpe Kirkpatrick, 4th son of 6th baronet:—
Issue of late Thomas Stripling Kirkpatrick, *b* 1867, *d* 1937: *m* 1903, Amy Louisa, who *d* 1962, da of Walter Norris:—
Grace Amy May, *b* 1905: *m* 1926, William Henry Williams, and has issue living, Derek Henry (44 Ammersham Av, Paddonhurst, Bulawayo, Zimbabwe), *b* 1929: *m* 1953, Kathleen Elizabeth Knipe, and has issue living, Peter Duncan *b* 1956, Paul Arnold *b* 1957, Margaret Ann *b* 1959, — Olive Amy, *b* 1932: *m* 1954, John Faulding Sissison, of 16 Willow Way, Pinelands, Cape Province, S Africa, and has issue living, Michael Faulding *b* 1959, Noel Faulding *b* 1961, — Janet Ann, *b* 1943: *m* 1960, Roger Stewart Johnson, and has issue living, Susan Barbara *b* 1960, Shirley Catherine *b* 1961.

 Grandchildren of late Thomas Frederick Kirkpatrick (infra):—
Issue of late Leslie Maurice Kenneth Kirkpatrick, *b* 1925, *d* 1962: *m* 1948, Rose Lillian May, da of late Frederick George Walker:—
David Christopher (7 Fulbourne Close, Luton, Beds LU4 9PW), *b* 1950: *m* 1973, Betty Margaret, da of Leslie Augustus Radford, and has issue living, Victoria Alice, *b* 1981, — Joanna Louise, *b* 1985. —— Paul Anthony, *b* 1953. —— Stephen Robert *b* 1960: *m* 1983, Jill, da of Ernest Albert Flewin. —— Maureen Ann *b* 1952.

 Grandchildren of late Charles Bartram Kirkpatrick (*b* 1873) (infra):—
Issue of late Thomas Frederick Kirkpatrick, *b* 1094, *ku* 1940: *m* 1920, Mabel who *d* 1971, da of late John James Childs:—
Beryl, *b* 1920: *m* 1941, Stanley R Fairbrass, and has issue living, Alan, *b* 1942, — Brian Malcolm, *b* 1944, — Melvyn Denis, *b* 1948, — Geoffrey, *b* 1950, — Keith Anthony, *b* 1958.

Issue of late Charles Bartram Kirkpatrick, *b* 1899, *d* 1936: *m* 1921, Lillian (who *m* 2ndly, 1950, George Albert May, of 63 The Fairway, Bickley, Bromley Kent), da of Samuel Charles Podd:—
Charles Bartram, *b* 1922: *m* 1944, Winifred Rosa, da of George Gaffney, and has issue living, Charles Bartram (49 Norheads Lane, Biggin Hill, Kent) *b* 1945: *m* 1967, Angela Mary, da of Sidney Ernest MacClaren Dooley, and has issue living, Paul Charles *b* 1972. *Residence* – 16 Foyle Drive, South Ockendon, Essex. —— Donald (Closeburn, 4 Wilderness Rd, Hurstpierpoint, Sussex), *b* 1934: *m* 1st, 1964, Janet Olive, da of late Walter Young; 2ndly, 1990, Valerie Rose, da of James Mills, of Oldham, and has issue living, Kay, *b* 1965, — Linda, *b* 1967. —— Edna Florence, *b* 1924: *m* 1946, Henry Crook, of Flat 12, St John's House, St John's Rd, Eastbourne, E Sussex BN20 7JB, and has issue living, John David, *b* 1951, — Hilary June, *b* 1955. —— Lilian, *b* 1926: *m* 1945, Sydney Thew, and has issue living, Sydney Charles, *b* 1946, — Colin James, *b* 1947, — Robert John, *b* 1948, — Donald Patrick, *b* 1950, — Michael Allan, *b* 1952. *Residence* – 22 Terrigal Crescent, Southport, Qld 4215, Australia.

Issue of late James Arthur Kirkpatrick, *b* 1902, *d* 1935: *m* 1929, Ruby, da of Charles Heat, of Brixton, SW:—
Barbara, *b* 1931. *Residence* –

Grandson of Charles William Sharpe Kirkpatrick (ante):—
Issue of late Charles Bartram Kirkpatrick, *b* 1873, *d* 1944: *m* 1893, Helena Sarah Riches, who *d* 1936, da of William Minns, of Peckham, SE:—
Sydney Frank, *b* 1912; late Flying Officer RAF Vol Reserve; 1939-45 War as Flight-Sergeant RAF (Belgian Croix de Guerre with palm): *m* 1943, Margaret Elizabeth Cowell, and has issue living, Valerie, *b* 1946; BA, — Sandra Kirkpatrick, *b* 1953: *m* 1974, Stephen Gent, of 32 Thompson Rd, Brighton, Sussex.

Grandson of late Robert Herries Kirkpatrick, 5th son of 6th baronet:—
Issue of Wallace Herries Kirkpatrick, *b* 1886, *d* 1967: *m* 1920, Lilian Ivy, who *d* 1976, da of late Walter Oughton Hill:—
Wallace Bruce (Duke's Lodge, Alresford Rd, Winchester), *b* 1921; late Lt N Staffs Regt: *m* 1946, Irene Sylvia, who *d* 1990, da of late Harold Victor Colls, and has issue living, Scott Herries (The Arches, Broughton, Hants), *b* 1947: *m* 1970, Sandra Jean, da of Leonard Arthur Charles Hall, and has issue living, Gavin James *b* 1972, Charles Stuart *b* 1981, Victoria Jane *b* 1974, — Gavin Bruce (Croft Cottage, Lower Moors Rd, Colden Common, nr Twyford, Hants), *b* 1951: *m* 1st, 1973 (*m diss* 1987), Linda, da of William Prosser, of Llandrindod Wells; 2ndly, 1994, Susan Mary, da of Walter Marr, of Winchester, and has issue living (by 1st *m*), James William Bruce *b* 1976, Emily Elizabeth *b* 1979.

Grandchildren of late Maj-Gen Charles Kirkpatrick, CB, CBE (infra):—
Issue of late Air Vice-Marshal Herbert James Kirkpatrick, CB, CBE, DFC, *b* 1910, *d* 1977: *m* 1937, Pamela Evelyn Darvill (Gretton Court, Girton, nr Cambridge), da of late Lt-Col H. D. Watson, Indian Army:—
Roger Hugh (3 Cambridge Rd, E Twickenham, Middx), *b* 1939: *m* 1965, Julia Margaret, da of late John W. Mortimore, of Broadstone, Dorset, and has issue living, Amanda Dorothy, *b* 1974, — Christabel Pamela, *b* 1977. —— John Edward (30 Petworth St, Cambridge), *b* 1944: *m* 1964, Johanna Elizabeth, da of late Patrick Johnston, of Guildford, Surrey, and has issue living, Jeremy Mark, *b* 1964, — Julian Gwinell, *b* 1966, — Dustin John, *b* 1971. —— Christopher Charles, *b* 1948: *m* 1984, Kathleen Anne, formerly wife of John Walsh, and da of late Thomas Christopher Purcell, of co Kilkenny, and has issue living, James Charles John, *b* 1981. —— Elizabeth Susan, *b* 1942: *m* 1966, Fl-Lt Kenneth A. D. Evans, RAF, of 60 Carlyle Rd, Cambridge, and has issue living, Nicholas Christopher, *b* 1966, — Rebecca Kate, *b* 1968. —— Grizelda Jean, *b* (twin) 1948: *m* 1st, 1967, Hugh John Allen; 2ndly, 1974, Alan Graham Stuck, of 62 High St, Hampton, Middx, and has issue living (by 1st *m*), Jonathan Spencer, *b* 1968.

Granddaughters of late Dep Surg-Gen James Kirkpatrick, MC, son of late Roger Kirkpatrick (*b* 1779), 2nd son of 4th baronet:—
Issue of late Maj-Gen Charles Kirkpatrick, CB, CBE, *b* 1879, *d* 1955: *m* 1909, Elsie Isobel, who *d* 1970, da of late Herbert John Hamilton Fasson, ICS:—
Hilda May (Ashdean, Whiteparish, Salisbury), *b* 1920: *m* 1st, 1940, Maj James Michael Jourdier, E Surrey Regt; 2ndly, 1954, David Arthur Yellowlees; 3rdly, Brian Butler, and has issue living, (by 1st *m*) Anthony Maxwell Kirkpatrick (The Shrubbery House, Stanford Bridge, Worcester), *b* 1946: *m* 1974, Cecilia Maye, da of Lt-Col R. A. Conner, of Maldon, Essex, and has issue living, Peter Gilbert Kirkpatrick *b* 1983, Sophie Maye *b* 1975, Jessica Isobel *b* 1977, Louise Caroline *b* 1980, — Avril Patricia, *b* 1947: *m* 1969, John Hamish Carysfort Loch, of Monksford Cottage, St Boswells, Roxburghshire, and has issue living, Rupert John Carysfort *b* 1970, Rosalind Cecilia Carysfort *b* 1972.

Grandson of late James Ivone Kirkpatrick, son of late Dep Surg-Gen James Kirkpatrick, MC, son of late Roger Kirkpatrick (*b* 1779), 2nd son of 4th baronet:—
Issue of late Group-Capt Ivone Kirkpatrick, WS, *b* 1907, *d* 1989: *m* 1936, Ruth, da of late W...... R...... Peterson, of E London, S Africa:—
Ivone William (Swiss Lodge, Althorp, Northants NN7 4HE), *b* 1944; a Co Dir: *m* 1st, 1967 (*m diss* 1983), Velia Elizabeth Mignon, da of John Hartdegan, of Parys, Orange Free State; 2ndly, 1987, Lyn Lithgoe, and has issue living (by 1st *m*), Sean Roger, *b* 1968, — Anne Margaret, *b* 1971.

The 1st baronet, Sir Thomas Kirkpatrick was created a baronet with remainder to heirs male whatsoever. He built the mansion of Closeburn, which was burnt to the ground through the carelessness of drunken servants on 29 August 1748, and all the portraits, plate, etc, with most of the family papers, were consumed. Two boxes of papers dating back to the 16th century were deposited in Register House, Edinburgh in 1952. HIM the Empress Eugénie, wife of HIM Napoleon III, Emperor of the French, was descended from the Kirkpatricks, Barons of Closeburn. Her great-grandfather was William Kirkpatrick, of Conheath, and her lineage traces back through the Conheath and Kirkmichael branches of the family to Alexander Kirkpatrick, of Kirkmichael, who was yr brother of Sir Thomas Kirkpatrick (who *d* 1502), ancestor of the 1st baronet. Sir James Alexander Kirkpatrick, 10th Bt, was Flight-Lieut RAF Vol Reserve and Assist Game Warden, Kenya.

KLEINWORT (UK) 1909, of Bolnore, Cuckfield, Sussex

Nil sine labore

Nothing without labour

Sir RICHARD DRAKE KLEINWORT, 4th *Baronet; b* 4 Nov 1960; *s* his father *Sir* KENNETH DRAKE, 1994; *ed* Stowe, and Exeter Univ (BA): *m* 1989, Lucinda, da of William Shand Kydd, of Horton Hall, Horton, Bucks, and has issue.

Arms – Or, a lion rampant sable, on a chief of the last three oak trees eradicated proper. **Crest** – On a mount vert, three leaves of clover proper. *Residence* – Heaselands, Haywards Heath, W Sussex RH16 4SA.

SONS LIVING

RUFUS DRAKE, *b* 16 Aug 1994. —— Tristan William, *b* 1997. —— Ivo John, *b* 1999.

DAUGHTER LIVING

Héloïse, *b* 1996.

HALF-BROTHERS LIVING

Alexander Hamilton, *b* 1975. —— Michael Drake, *b* 1977.

SISTER LIVING

Marina Rose, *b* 1962.

HALF-SISTER LIVING

Selina Helen Louisa, *b* 1981.

AUNT LIVING (*sister of 3rd baronet*)

Gillian Mawdsley, *b* 1937: *m* 1957, Michael Raymond Warren, JP, and has issue living, Charles Raymond, *b* 1963: *m* 1993, Sarah Elizabeth, da of Richard Lionel Mather, and has issue living, Alexander Finlay *b* 1997, Iona Katherine *b* 1998, — Davina Mary, *b* 1958: *m* 1979, Rev Peter Elliot Irwin-Clark, of Desmond's Castle, The Hyde, Handcross, W Sussex, and has issue living, Benjamin John *b* 1983, Jessamy Claire *b* 1987, — Susanna Rachel, *b* 1975. *Residence* – Banks Farm, Barcombe, Lewes, Sussex.

WIDOW LIVING OF THIRD BARONET

MADELEINE HAMILTON (*Madeleine, Lady Kleinwort*), eldest da of Ralph Taylor, of Juncal 721, Buenos Aires, Argentina: *m* 1973, as his 2nd wife, Sir Kenneth Drake Kleinwort, 3rd Bt, who *d* 1994. *Residence* –

COLLATERAL BRANCH LIVING

Issue of late Sir Cyril Hugh Kleinwort, 5th son of 1st baronet, *b* 1905, *d* 1980: *m* 1933, Elisabeth Kathleen, who *d* 1997, da of Francis Forde, of Newbury, Berks:—
Serena Elizabeth, *b* 1936: *m* 1960, David Alfred Acland (*see* Acland, Bt, *cr* 1890, colls). —— Charlotte, *b* 1938: *m* 1st, 1965, (Richard) Lawrence Baillieu; 2ndly, 1972, (Nevile) Martin Gwynne (*see* Morrison-Bell, Bt (ext)); 3rdly, 1980, Alan Cyril Heber-Percy, who *d* 1998 (*see* D Northumberland, colls), and has issue living (by 1st *m*), Richard Alexander, *b* 1970, — Joanna Alice Serena, *b* 1966: *m* 1993, Rupert H. Prest, 2nd son of late James Prest, — (by 2nd *m*) (*see* Morrison-Bell, Bt (ext)). —— Susanna, *b* 1942: *m* 1962, David Alphy Edward Raymond Peake, son of late Sir Harald Peake (*see* V Ingleby).

Sir Alexander Drake Kleinwort, 1st Bt (son of late Alexander Frederic Henry Kleinwort), was a Banker and Partner in the firm of Kleinwort, Sons & Co, of 20 Fenchurch Street, EC3; Sir Kenneth Drake, 3rd baronet: *m* 1st, 1959, Lady Davina Rose Pepys, who *d* 1973, da of 7th Earl of Cottenham.

KNILL (UK) 1893, of The Grove, Blackheath, Kent

Sir THOMAS JOHN PUGIN BARTHOLOMEW KNILL, 5th *Baronet*; *b* 23 Aug 1952; *s* his father *Sir* JOHN KENELM STUART, 1998: *m* 1977, Kathleen Muszynski, and has issue.

Arms – Gules, semée of crosses botonnée fitchée a lion rampant, all or, on a chief of the last a fasces fessewise, head to the dexter proper. **Crest** – A demi-lion or, holding in the dexter paw a cross botonnée fitchée azure, and supporting with the sinister a fasces in bend proper.
Residence – Flat 3, 3 Widcombe Terrace, Bath, Somerset BA2 6AJ.

DAUGHTERS LIVING

Claire Rosemary, *b* 1978. —— Bryony Jane, *b* 1981. —— Lucy Jasmine, *b* 1983.

BROTHER LIVING

Nil desperandum
Never despairing

JENKYN MARTIN BENEDICT STUART, *b* 19 Jan 1954: *m* 1978, Helen Marguerite, da of late Noel Geoffrey Arthur Gulliver, of Batheaston, Bath, and has issue living, Benedict Noel Jenkyn, *b* 20 Nov 1979, — Leo Martin Barnabus, *b* 1981, — Abigail Amice Lilly, *b* 1984. *Residence* – Longhope, Packhorse Lane, Southstoke, Bath, Som.

HALF-UNCLES LIVING (*sons of 3rd baronet*)

Gyles Braoze Hamish Stanislas Stuart, *b* 1945: *m* 19—, ..., and has issue living, a da, *b* 19—, — a da, *b* 19—. *Residence* – 37 Byron Rd, Weston-super-Mare, Som. —— Rognvald Gabriel Nigel Alistair Stuart, *b* 1946: *m* 1984, Evelin Gollner, and has issue living, Julia Anne, *b* 1984; has issue (by Josephine Doherty) Rory Alec, *b* 1973, — Emma Marie, *b* (twin) 1973. *Residence* – Giore Buechner Strasse 26, 64572 Buettelborn, Germany.

HALF-AUNT LIVING (*daughter of 3rd baronet*)

Gloriana Leonora Dorothea Marie, *b* 1937: *m* 1959, CPO William Charles Morehead, RN (ret), of 33 Brompton Walk, Darlington, co Durham DL3 8RT, son of William Morehead, of Blaston, nr Market Harborough, Leics, and has issue living, Simon William (30 Ennerdale Terrace, Low Westwood, Tyne and Wear), *b* 1961: *m* 198—, Stephanie, — Sarah Maria Evelyn, *b* 1960: *m* 1983, Peter McDonnell, of 4 Coniscliffe Mews, Darlington, co Durham DL3 8UZ.

Sir Stuart Knill, 1st Bt, was head of the firm of John Knill and Co, wharfingers, and Lord Mayor of London 1892-3. Sir (John) Stuart Knill, 2nd Bt, was Lord Mayor of London 1909-10.

KNOWLES (GB) 1765, of Lovell Hill, Berkshire

Always ready

Sir CHARLES FRANCIS KNOWLES, 7th *Baronet*; *b* 20 Dec 1951; *s* his father, *Sir* FRANCIS GERALD WILLIAM, FRS, 1974; Dip Arch, RIBA, FRSA, Oxford School of Architecture, Architect: *m* 1979, Amanda Louise Margaret, da of Lance Lee Bromley, MA, M Chir, FRCS, of 26 Molyneux St, W1, and has issue.

Arms – Azure, a naval crown between four crosses crosslet in cross, all within a cross resarcelly disjoined between as many crosses crosslet all or. **Crest** – An elephant statant argent, supporting with the trunk an anchor or.
Residence – Wyndham Croft, Turners Hill, W Sussex RH10 4PS.

SONS LIVING

(CHARLES) WILLIAM FREDERICK LANCE, *b* 27 August 1985. ——— Edward Francis Annandale Bromley, *b* 1989.

SISTERS LIVING

Averina Constance Frances, *b* 1950: *m* 1969, Martin Dacre Northmore-Ball, FRCS, Orthopaedic Surg, of Higher Grange, Ellesmere, Shropshire SY12 9DH, and has issue living, Lawrence Henry Arthur Knowles, *b* 1986, — Laetitia Emily Ruth, *b* 1976. ——— Emma Irene Anne, *b* (twin) 1951: *m* 1976, Michael Henry Geddes Ablitt of 14 Westland Rd, Faringdon, Oxon, and has issue living, Zoë Christiana, *b* 1979, — Helen Angela Emma, *b* 1981, — Sophie Hannah Rachel, *b* 1985, — Tessa Catherine Ruth, *b* 1988. ——— Christiana Joan Elizabeth Ruth, *b* 1956: *m* 1979, Giles Adrian Ivo Payne, of 210 Marlborough Rd, Oxford, only son of Ivo Payne (infra), and has issue living, Charlotte Liberty Ruth, *b* 1987.

WIDOW LIVING OF SIXTH BARONET

RUTH, da of late Rev Arthur Brooke-Smith, and widow of P/O Richard Guy Hulse, RAF: *m* 2ndly, 1948, Sir Francis Gerald William Knowles, FRS, 6th Bt, who *d* 1974; 3rdly, 1979, Ivo Payne, of West Ridge, Manton Down Rd, Marlborough, Wilts (ante).

COLLATERAL BRANCH LIVING

Issue of late Robert Cosby Knowles, 5th son of 4th baronet, *b* 1888, *d* 1972: *m* 1929, Phyllis Eve, who *d* 1992, da of late Rev Canon Ward Thomas, of Lorne, Vic, Aust:—
Peter Cosby (Namarva, Winton, Qld, Aust), *b* 1930: *m* 1st, 1957 (*m diss* 1977), Gloria, da of H. Oaten; 2ndly, 1977, Jane Winifred, da of B. Cooper, of Kenmore, Brisbane, and has issue living, (by 1st *m*) Richard Cosby, *b* 1969, — Sandra, *b* 1969, — Kerry, *b* 1964, — Judith Anne, *b* 1967, — (by 2nd *m*) Imogen Winifred, *b* 1988. ——— Michael Cosby (21 Bonview Rd, Malvern, Vic, Aust), *b* 1936; M Com Qld; PhD Edinburgh; Sr lecturer, Monash Univ, Aust: *m* 1965, Ann, da of G. R. Mountain, MA, AM, of Malvern, Vic, Aust, and has issue living, Stephen Francis, *b* 1970, — Fiona Mary, *b* 1972.

This family is descended from Charles Knollys, titular 4th Earl of Banbury *temp* James II. The 1st baronet, Sir Charles, Adm of the White, and Rear-Adm of Great Britain, a distinguished naval commander, was Governor of Louisburg, Cape Breton, 1745-6, and of Jamaica 1752-6, and in 1770 was appointed, by the Empress Catherine II of Russia, Chief President of HIM's Admiralty, with a seat in the Russian Council. Adm Sir Charles Henry, GCB, 2nd Bt, distinguished himself in his profession, and commanded the "Goliath" in the memorable battle of Capt St Vincent, 14th Feb 1797, when the Spanish fleet was defeated. The 3rd baronet, Sir Francis Charles, FRS, was a mathematician who gained the Telford Prize and was elected FRS in 1830. Vice-Adm Sir Charles G. F. Knowles, 4th Bt, served in Burma War 1852-3, commanded Niger Expedition 1864, and was thanked by Admiralty for services on Coast of Cuba during insurrection of 1870-71, and for quelling in 1880 insurrection in Danish Island of Santa Cruz, and by Colonial Office for services on Newfoundland Fisheries when in command of the "Lapwing" 1872. The 5th baronet, Sir Francis Howe Seymour Knowles, was Physical Anthropologist to Geographical Survey, Canada, and a prehistorian of note. The 6th baronet, Sir Francis Gerald William, MA, DPhil, DSc, FRS, was a distinguished pioneering research biologist and author. He was Head of Biology Dept, Marlborough College, 1938-58, Reader and Prof of Comparative Endocrinology, 1967, at Birmingham Univ, and Prof of Anatomy and Head of Dept of Anatomy, Kings Coll, London Univ, 1967-74.

LACON (UK) 1818, of Great Yarmouth, Norfolk.

Probity is true honour

Sir EDMUND VERE LACON, 8th *Baronet*; *b* 3 May 1936; *s* his father *Sir* GEORGE VERE FRANCIS, 1980; *ed* Woodbridge Sch: *m* 1963, Gillian, only da of Jack Henry Middleditch, of Wrentham, and has issue.

𝕬rms – Quarterly, per fesse indented erminois and azure, in the 2nd quarter a wolf's head erased or. Crest – On a mount vert a falcon proper, belled or, collared and charged on the breast with a cross flory gules.
Residence – Milbrook, Holton St Peter, Halesworth, Suffolk IP19 8PN.

SON LIVING

EDMUND RICHARD VERE, *b* 2 Oct 1967: *m* 1997, Natalie, only da of Joginder Shinh, of High Wycombe, Bucks.

DAUGHTER LIVING

Anna Kathryn, *b* 1965.

BROTHER LIVING

George Julius (Larcombe Farmhouse, Diptford, Totnes, S Devon TQ9 7PD), *b* 1938; *ed* Duncan Hall Sch: *m* 1968, Elizabeth Rodger, only da of Archibald Kelly, of Sheffield, and has issue living, Sarah Elizabeth, *b* 1970: *m* 1998, Russell P. Hammond, yr son of George Hammond, of Edenbridge, Kent, — Emma Blanche, *b* 1973.

DAUGHTER LIVING OF FIFTH BARONET

Dorothy Beecroft, *b* (*posthumous*) 1912: *m* 1st, 1932 (*m diss* 1946), Robert Desmond Ropner (Knt 1959), who *d* 1977 (*see* Ropner, Bt, *cr* 1904, colls); 2ndly 1946, Capt D. B. M. Curtis, and has issue living, (by 1st *m*) (*see* Ropner, Bt, *cr* 1904, colls), — (by 2nd *m*) Amanda Murray, *b* 1948.

COLLATERAL BRANCHES LIVING

Grandson of late Thomas Beecroft Ussher Lacon, 2nd son of 3rd baronet:—
Issue of late Henry Reginald Dunbar Lacon, *b* 1884, *d* 1960: *m* 1912, Hilda Mary, who *d* 1965, da of late William Bruce Slayter, MD, FRCS, of Halifax, Nova Scotia:—
Reginald William Beecroft, DSC, *b* 1913; Cdr RN (ret); 1939-45 War (despatches four times, DSC, and Bar): *m* 1st, 1948 (*m diss* 1976), Joan Denyer Briscoe (DUNOLLY), da of late Albert J. George; 2ndly, 1976, Beatrice, da of late G. H. V. Burroughs, of Calgary, Alberta, and widow of Myles A. Ellissen, MC, and has had two adopted children, George Christopher Jocelyn, *b* 1955, *d* 1973, — Victoria, *b* 1952: *m* 19—, Richard H. St M. Kemmis Betty, The Queen's Own Hussars, eldest son of Lt. Col Peter Kemmis Betty, of Hampton Hill House, Swanmore, Hants.

Granddaughter of late Capt Henry Sidney Hammet Lacon, 3rd son of 3rd baronet:—
Issue of late Gordon Massy Lacon, *b* 1886, *d* 1918: *m* 1909, Phyllis, who *d* 1963 (having *m* 2ndly, 1920, John Alan Clutton-Brock, of Oakfield, Weybridge, who *d* 1925, and 3rdly, 1926, Charles Geoffrey Keith Hulbert, who *d* 1963), da of His Honour late Judge Robert Woodfall, Judge of County Court Circuit No 44, of Nutfield, Weybridge:—
Pamela Abbott, *b* 1912: *m* 1st, 1936 (*m diss* 1946), John Edward Hodgson; 2ndly, 1949, Wing-Cdr Philip S. Gage, RAF (ret), of 38 Headbourne Worthy House, Winchester, Hants SO23 7JG, and has issue living, (by 1st *m*) Robert John (2 St Hilda's Rd, SW13 9JQ), *b* 1937: *m* 1st, 1963 (*m diss* 1971), Caroline Joan Eve Kingdon; 2ndly, 1976, Hon Jean Margaret Brand, da of 5th Viscount Hampden, and has issue living, (by 1st *m*) Jonathan Charles *b* 1968, Sarah Jane *b* 1965, (by 2nd *m*) Thomas Edward *b* 1981, — Penelope Jane, *b* 1939: *m* 1st, 1964 (*m diss* 1967), John Harmon Clary; 2ndly, 1976 (*m diss* 1985), David Gavin Clark; 3rdly, 1988, William Love, of 3 Swallow St, Turners Hill, Crawley, W Sussex and has issue living, (by 1st *m*) James Alistair *b* 1965: *m* 1987, Lara Jayne Pope (and has issue living, Max McKinley *b* 1994, Alana Louise *b* 1990).

The present baronet is in direct descent from Edmund Lacon, who settled in Yorkshire early in the seventeeth century, belonging to a yr branch of the very ancient family of Lacon settled in Shropshire *temp* Edward III. Sir Edmund Lacon was created a baronet in 1818 and *d* 1839. The 2nd baronet, Sir Edmund Knowles Lacon, was High Sheriff of Norfolk. The 3rd baronet was MP for Great Yarmouth (*C*) 1852-7, and 1859-68, and for Norfolk N 1868-88. The 5th baronet was Capt 12th Lancers, and served in S African War 1899-1901 (Queen's medal with 3 clasps, King's medal with 2 clasps). The 6th baronet, Sir George Haworth Ussher Lacon, DSO served in S Africa 1901, and during European War 1914-19 as Lieut-Col Roy Warwickshire Regt (DSO).

LACY (UK) 1921, of Ampton, co Suffolk.

Sir PATRICK BRYAN FINUCANE LACY, 4th *Baronet*; *b* 18 April 1948; *s* his brother, *Sir* HUGH MAURICE PIERCE, 1998; *ed* Downside: *m* 1971, Phyllis Victoria, da of Edgar P. H. James, of 6 Berkeley Rd, Barnes, SW13, and has issue.

𝕬rms – Gyronny or and gules, on a bend sable a Lacy knot between two martlets of the first. 𝕮rest – An eagle rising or, gorged with a collar gemelle gules and resting the dexter claw on a Lacy knot sable.
Residence – 26B Wellesley Rd, W4B 4BN.

SON LIVING

FINIAN JAMES PIERCE, *b* 24 Sept 1972.

DAUGHTER LIVING

Alexandra Victoria, *b* 1997.

SISTER LIVING

Jeanne Clare, *b* 1942: *m* 1st, 1965 (*m diss* 1973), David Leslie Morgan; 2ndly, 1976, Andrew Findlay, of Trochelhill, Fochabers, nr Elgin, Morayshire IV32 7LN, and has issue living, (by 1st *m*) Dominic Maurice David, *b* 1969, — Miranda Jean, *b* 1967, — (by 2nd *m*) John Andrew Pierce, *b* 1977.

WIDOW LIVING OF THIRD BARONET

Honours are enhanced by deserts

DEANNA (*Deanna, Lady Lacy*), da of Howard Bailey, of Stourbridge: *m* 1968, Sir Hugh Maurice Pierce Lacy, 3rd Bt, who *d* 1998. *Residence* –

COLLATERAL BRANCH LIVING (*not in remainder to baronetcy*)

Issue of late Capt Anthony John Alfred Lacy, elder son of late James Stanislaus Lacy, brother of 1st baronet, *b* 1911, *d* 1975: *m* 1945, Patricia Angela Mary, who *d* 1998, yr da of late Adm of the Fleet Sir Reginald Yorke Tyrwhitt, GCB, DSO, 1st Bt (*see* Tyrwhitt, Bt (*cr* 1919), 1995 Edn):—
Rev David Anthony (41 Ickneild Close, Bidford-on-Avon Alcester, Warws B50 4BZ), *b* 1947; ordained RC Priest 1972. —— John Reginald (Llanfachreth, Gwynedd), *b* 1948: *m* 1970, Johneen Florence, da of Michael Whitfield, of Wellesbourne, Warws, and has issue living, Mark Logan Tyrwhitt *b* 1973: *m* 1998, Lois Ann, da of Alan Norman Clingo, of Downham Market, Norfolk, Michael John *b* 1981, Olivia Johneen *b* 1976. —— Richard Patrick James (The Moat Farmhouse, Mill Green, Edwardstone, Sudbury, Suffolk), *b* 1950: *m* 1973, Penelope Anne, da of Hon Simon Chelmsford Loader Maffey (*see* B Rugby), and has issue living, Timothy James *b* 1985, Laura Penelope *b* 1980, Diana Louise *b* 1984. —— Anne Mary, *b* 1953: *m* 1994, Capt Anthony Mervyn Poulter, OBE, RN, of Four Winds, Woodbine, Newton-in-Furness, Cumbria LA13 0NF, son of late Mervyn Brian Poulter.

The 1st baronet, Sir Pierce Thomas Lacy (2nd son (by 2nd *m*) of John Pierce Lacy, of Oak Mount, Edgbaston, Birmingham) was Chm of Birmingham Stock Exchange, and Founder of British Trusts Asso and of British Shareholders' Trust.

LAKE (GB) 1711, of Edmonton, Middlesex.

Sir (ATWELL) GRAHAM LAKE, 10th *Baronet*; *b* 6 Oct 1923; *s* his father, *Capt Sir* ATWELL HENRY, CB, OBE, RN, 1972; *ed* Eton; Sr Tech Adviser MOD; ret 1983; Gilbert and Ellice Mil Forces 1944-45; Colonial Admin Ser 1945-55 (Sec to Govt of Tonga 1950-53); British High Commn New Delhi 1966-68; FCO 1969-72: *m* 1983, Mrs Katharine Margaret Lister, da of late D. W. Last.

𝕬rms – Quarterly: 1st, (coat of augmentation) gules, a dexter arm embowed in armour, issuing from sinister side of the shield, holding in the hand a sword erect, all proper, thereto affixed a banner argent charged with a cross between sixteen escutcheons gules, on the centre of the cross a lion of England; 2nd, sable, a bend, between six crosslets fitchée, argent; 3rd, quarterly, argent and sable, on a bend gules, three mullets argent; 4th argent, a chevron between three boars' heads couped sable. 𝕮rest – 1st, a cavalier in a fighting posture, his scarf gules, his left arm hanging down as wounded and useless, holding the bridle in his teeth, his face, sword, armour, and horse embrued, all proper; 2nd, a horse's head argent, charged with a fesse, cottised gules.
Address – Magdalen Laver Hall, Chipping Ongar, Essex.

Un Dieu, un roy, un coeur
One God, one king,
one heart

BROTHER LIVING

EDWARD GEOFFREY (High Acre, Cowgill, Dent, Cumbria), *b* 17 July 1928; *ed* Eton: *m* 1965, Judith Ann, da of John Fox, and has issue living, Mark Winter, *b* 1968, — Sophie Louise, *b* 1971.

COLLATERAL BRANCHES LIVING

Issue of late Willoughby Alfred Lake, 2nd son of 9th baronet, *b* 1925, *d* 1986: *m* 1952, Elizabeth Elsie Faith (Horseshoe Farm, Hargham Rd, Shropham, Norfolk), da of Sir Rupert Turner Havelock Clarke, 2nd Bt:—
Susan Kathleen, *b* 1961. —— Catherine Jane, *b* 1962.

Grandsons of late Winter Atwell Edward Lake, son of late Capt Andrew Winter Lake, 5th son of 4th baronet:—
Issue of late Lieut-Col Ernest Atwell Winter Lake, CBE, Indian Army (ret), *b* 1886, *d* 1945: *m* 1924, Phyllis Marjorie, da of J. G. Silcock, formerly ICS:—
John Winter Atwell, *b* 1925: *m* 1955, Elsie, da of R. Milburn, of Long Marton, Westmorland. —— Winter Philip Edward, *b* 1930: *m* 1956, Vera, da of A. G. Liddell, of Durham.

Sir Edward Lake, Chancellor of the Diocese of Lincoln, and Advocate-General in Ireland, was, for his loyalty and services to Charles I, granted by that monarch the coat of augmentation now borne by the family, and the exceptional privilege of nominating a person to be created a baronet. He did not, however, avail himself of this privilege, and, in consequence, a baronetcy was in 1711 conferred on his great-nephew and heir, Bibye Lake, Sub-Governor of the African Co.

LAKIN (UK) 1909, of The Cliff, Borough of Warwick.

One God, one king, one heart

Sir MICHAEL LAKIN, 4th *Baronet*; *b* 28 Oct 1934; *s* his father, *Sir* HENRY, 1979; *ed* Stowe: *m* 1st, 1956 (*m diss* 1963), Margaret, da of Robert Wallace, of Mount Norris, co Armagh; 2ndly, 1965, Felicity, da of Anthony Denis Murphy, of Londiani, Kenya, and has issue by 2nd *m*.

Arms – Quarterly: indented argent and azure, in the 1st and 4th quarters a pellet charged with a lion's head erased of the first. Crest – A dexter cubit arm vested sable cuffed azure, the hand grasping a plasterer's trowel proper.
Address – Little Sherwood Hill, Tunley, nr Cirencester, Glos.

SON LIVING (*By 2nd marriage*)

RICHARD ANTHONY, *b* 26 Nov 1968: *m* 1997, Lara Maryanne, da of E. J. Rose, of Nairobi, Kenya.

DAUGHTER LIVING (*By 2nd marriage*)

Mary Jane, *b* 1966: *m* 1992, Charles Adrian Clark, of Lowesmoor Farm, Cherrington, Tetbury, Glos GL8 8SP, son of late Walter Clark, and has issue living, Timothy Anthony, *b* 1995, — Benjamin Louis, *b* 1999, — Emma Louise, *b* 1993.

COLLATERAL BRANCHES LIVING

Grandson of late Henry Gilbert Lakin, 2nd son of 1st baronet:—
Issue of late Lt-Col John Lakin, TD, *b* 1910, *d* 1989: *m* 1939, Hon (Helena) Daphne Pearson (Hammerwood House, Iping, Midhurst, Sussex GU29 0PF), da of 2nd Viscount Cowdray:—
Michael Simon, *b* 1955: *m* 1st, 1977 (*m diss* 1987), Mireille Farjon; 2ndly, 1987, Amanda Ann, only da of James Thomas Durrant Shaw, TD, of Scottow Hall, Norfolk (*see* Durrant, Bt, 1960 Edn), and has issue living (by 1st *m*), Benjamin John, *b* 1981, — (by 2nd *m*) Johnathan James, *b* 1989, — Piers Thomas, *b* 1991, — Hugo Alexander, *b* 1995, — (by 1st *m*) Laura Daphne, *b* 1984.

Issue of late Edward Lyon Lakin, 3rd son of 1st baronet, *b* 1879, *d* 1922: *m* 1912, Dorothy Barklie, who *d* 1969, da of Col Barklie Cairns McCalmont, CB (B Kingsale):—
Richard Barklie, DSO, DSC, *b* 1914; *ed* RNC Dartmouth; is Lt-Cdr RN (ret); 1939-45 War (despatches, DSO, DSC and Bar, USA Legion of Merit); DSO 1943: *m* 1st, 1936, Pamela Mary Helen, who *d* 1981, da of late Group Capt Philip Jackson-Taylor, RAF; 2ndly, 1987 (*m diss* 1998), Pansy Myra Edith, da of late Col Algernon Lothian Bonham Carter, DSO, of Buriton, Petersfield, Hants, and widow of Cdr Jo Allan Phillips, RN, and has issue living (by 1st *m*), Robin Lyon (PO Box 2625, Mill Valley, CA 94941, USA), *b* 1938; *ed* Eton: *m* 1964 (*m diss* 1997), Gillian Claire, da of Peter Baily, of South Farm, Gt Whittington, Northumberland, and has issue living, Jessica Honor Katherine *b* 1966, Nicola Anne Pamela *b* 1970 (who has issue living, Rosy Honor LAKIN *b* 1994); Robin L. Lakin has further issue (by Jo Susan, only child of late S/Ldr Roy G. Whitehead, DFC, RAF), Judy Clementine Francesca Whitehead LAKIN *b* 1974, — Mark Philip (72 Drayton Gdns, SW10 9SB), *b* 1941; *ed* Eton: *m* 1988, Christina Lisa Josephine, da of late Patrick Dolan (USA Legion of Merit), of Much Hadham, Herts, and widow of Peter Gordon Shiach, of Ardgilzean, Elgin, Morayshire, and has issue living, Patrick Barklie *b* 1989, Henry Lyon *b* 1991, Molly Kathleen *b* 1993, — Julian Barklie (Juniper Cottage, Farringdon, Hants GU34 3DT), *b* 1948; *ed* Eton: *m* 1973, Penelope Jane, da of John Almond, of Burghclere, Berks, and has issue

living, Olivia Mary b 1978, Arabella Louise b 1980, — Amanda Joy (Well House, Aldsworth, Cheltenham, Glos GL54 3QZ), b 1947: m 1981 (m diss 1990), Christopher Euan Philip Charles Courtney, — Caroline Madeline, b 1953: m 1984, Richard Frederick Wallis, of Tump Hill, Arlington, Bibury, Glos GL7 5ND, yr son of late Charles Wallis, of Bryanston Square, W1, and has issue living, Jack Charles Lyon b 1990, Daisy Pamela b 1987, — Serena Pamela, b (twin) 1953: m 1986 (m diss 1997), Giles Selwyn Robinson, of Isis Cottage, 10 Bath Rd, Cricklade, Wilts SN6 6AT, eldest son of Donald Edgar Robinson, of Perthshire, and has issue living, Harry Edgar Selwyn b 1989, Molly Pamela b 1992. Residence – Seaview House, Seaview, Isle of Wight PO34 5ET.

Grandsons of late Maj Michael Lawrence Lakin, DSO, MC, 11th Hussars, 4th son of 1st baronet:—
Issue of late Maurice Victor Lakin, MC, b 1919, d 1995: m 1st, 1951 (m diss 1956), Huguette Paule Clémence, da of Robert Cauvin, of Paris; 2ndly, 1959 (m diss 1971), Silvanni, da of Ngot-Vong, of Pnom Penh, Cambodia:—
(By 2nd m) Michael, b 1960: m 1999, Bénédicte Marie-Charlotte, da of Jacques Laurent, of Neublans 39120, France. Residence – 38 avenue Emile Zola, 75015 Paris, France. —— Richard, b 1964: m 1990, Claire, da of Roland Coutant, of Vinon sur Verdon, Var, France, and has issue living, Alexandre Gerald, b 1992, — Thibaud Victor, b 1998, — Camille Sylvie, b 1991. Residence –

Sir Michael Henry Lakin, 1st Bt (son of Henry Lakin, of Malvern), was Mayor of Warwick, Vice-Chm of County Council for Warwickshire, and High Sheriff of that County.

LAMBERT (GB) 1711, of London.

By pursuing one attains

Sir PETER JOHN BIDDULPH LAMBERT, 10th *Baronet*, only son of late John Hugh Lambert, elder son of Hugh Biddulph Lambert, only son of Rev William Henry Lambert, 6th son of 5th baronet; b 5th April 1952; s his cousin, Sir GREVILLE FOLEY 1988, but his name does not appear on the Official Roll of the Baronetage; ed Upper Canada Coll, Toronto, Trent Univ, Peterborough (BSc), and Univ of Manitoba, Winnipeg (MA): m 1989, Leslie Anne, da of Richard Welkos Lyne, and has issue.

Arms – Argent, on a mount an oak-tree vert, and a greyhound courant gules. Crest – Out of a ducal coronet or three ostrich feathers, the dexter feather gules, the centre argent, and the sinister azure.
Residence – 67 Lauder Av, Toronto, Ontario M6H 3E2, Canada.

SON LIVING

THOMAS JOHN, b 1999.

DAUGHTER LIVING

Maeve Edith Jean, b 1992.

AUNTS LIVING (*daughters of late Hugh Biddulph Lambert, ante*)

Nina Joan b 1916: m 1st, 1941 (m diss 1948), Guy Duncan Tucker; 2ndly, 1951, Eric Harold Dehn, and has issue living (by 1st m), Michael Duncan Hugh (1 Trelawncy Rd, Bristol 6), b 1942: m 1970, Stephanie West, and has issue living, Rebecca b 1971, Zoë b 1974: m 1998, Cary Colosimo, — (by 2nd m) Jacqueline Tessa, b 1952: m 1980, Robert Baxter, of 82 De Beauvoir Rd, N1 5AT, — Nicola Louisa, b 1954: m 1981, Dominique Bonnard, of 26 Rue Amiral d'Aboville, Cherbourg 50100, France, and has issue living, Camille André Jean b 1984, Thomas Michel Eric b 1987. Residence – 5 Trelawncy Rd, Bristol 6. —— Julia Margaret, b 1920; 1939-45 War in WAAF. Residence – Priory Cottage, Heythrop Rd, Chipping Norton, Oxon OX7 5TA.

DAUGHTERS LIVING OF NINTH BARONET

(Isabel) Pamela, b 1933: m 1979, Denys Leonard Taaffe, of Trevalor, 6 St Matthew's Hill, Wadebridge, Cornwall PL27 6DX. —— Carole Joy (16 High House Drive, Inkberrow, Worcs WR7 4EG), b 1940: m 1st, 1960 (m diss 1963), Raymond Bennett; 2ndly, 1968 (m diss 1987), Nicholas Jason Hill; 3rdly 1991, Colin Geoffrey Russell, and has issue living, (by 2nd m) Jason Stirling, b 1970, — Michelle Jane, b 1973.

DAUGHTER LIVING OF EIGHTH BARONET

Eileen Grey, b 1922: m 1st, 1942 (m diss 1940), 11th Earl of Harrington; 2ndly, 1947, John Phillip Bissill, MC, who d 1988, and has issue living, (by 2nd m) Alexandra Diana, b 1950: m 1979, Peter Brinton Williams, of The Home Farm, Enville, nr Stourbridge, and has issue living, Harry John b 1981, George Edward b 1985, Jane Charlotte b 1982. Residence – Enville Hall, Stourbridge, Worcs.

WIDOW LIVING OF NINTH BARONET

(EDITH) ROMA (*Roma, Lady Lambert*), da of Richard Batson: *m* 1932, Sir Greville Foley Lambert, 9th Bt, FCA, who *d* 1988. *Residence* – Flat 5, Henleydale, Stratford Rd, Shirley, Solihull, Warwicks.

COLLATERAL BRANCHES LIVING

Grandson of late Mortan Lambert, son of Alan Lambert, son of Francis John Lambert, 3rd son of 4th baronet :—
Issue of late Montague Victor Lambert, *b* 1904; *d* 1979: *m* 1st, 1931, Ena Sylvia Victoria, who *d* 1944, da of late George Grossmith; 2ndly, 1948, Janis Mary, who *d* 1984, da of late Capt Wilfrid Brittain Squirl-Dawson, of Higham, Suffolk:—
(By 2nd *m*) Charles Geoffrey Mortan, *b* 1956.

Grandson of late Jasper Lambert, son of late Alan Lambert (ante):—
Issue of late Alan Forsyth Lambert, *b* 1901, *d* 19—: *m* 1935, Olive Edith, who *d* 1990, da of late Frederick Long:—
Philip Jasper, *b* 1936.

Sir John Lambert, 1st Bt, of the Isle of Rhé, France, settled in England as a merchant, and was one of the Directors of the South Sea Co. In 1710 he supplied the Treasury with money, and for this service was created a baronet. The 7th baronet, Sir Henry Foley, assumed by Roy licence, 1905, for himself and issue, the surname of Grey in lieu of his patronymic, and the arms of Grey quarterly with those of Lambert, and was High Sheriff of Worcestershire 1901.

LANE (UK) 1913, of Cavendish Square, St Marylebone. (Extinct 1972).

Sir WILLIAM ARBUTHNOT LANE, CBE, 2nd and last *Baronet*.

DAUGHTER LIVING OF SECOND BARONET

Susan Charlotte Arbuthnot, *b* 1938: *m* 1964, John Nicolas Bowker, and has issue living, Mark James Arbuthnot Lane, *b* 1967, — Katy Louise, *b* 1968.

LANGHAM (E) 1660, of Cottesbrooke, Northampton.

Sir JAMES MICHAEL LANGHAM, TD, 15th *Baronet*; *b* 24 May 1932; *s* his father, *Sir* JOHN CHARLES PATRICK, 1972; *ed* Rossall; Capt N Irish Horse: *m* 1959, Marion Audrey Eleanor, da of Oswald Barratt, of Tanzania, and has issue.

𝔄rms – Argent, three bears' heads erased sable, muzzled or. ℭrest – A bear's head as in the arms.
Residence – Claranagh, Tempo, Enniskillen, co Fermanagh.

SONS LIVING

JOHN STEPHEN, *b* 14 Dec 1960: *m* 1991, Sarah Jane, da of late John Denis Verschoyle-Greene, of Bushfield House, Cashedermot, co Kildare, and of Mrs John Alexander, of Milford House, co Carlow, and has issue living, Tyrone Denis James, *b* 13 Aug 1994. *Residence* – Tempo Manor, Tempo, Enniskillen, co Fermanagh. —— Rupert William (27 Broadley Street, NW8 8BN), *b* 1963: *m* 1989, Karen, da of M. Soderberg, of Runcorn, Cheshire.

DAUGHTER LIVING

Lucinda Jane, *b* 1966.

Nor suffers them to be savage

The 1st baronet, Sir John, was knighted by Charles II at The Hague, being one of a deputation from the city of London to wait on HM in Holland. When Sheriff of London in 1642, he, with several other gentlemen, was imprisoned for refusing to publish "An Act for the exheridation of the Royal line, the abolishment of Monarchy in the Kingdom, and the setting up of a Commonwealth". Sir John, 6th Bt, left £6,000 to the Corporation of London to found a society for the relief of poor soldiers, sailors and their wives. Sir (Herbert) Charles Arthur, 13th Bt, was High Sheriff of co Fermanagh 1930.

LANGMAN (UK) 1906, of Eaton Square, City of Westminster (Extinct 1985).

Sir JOHN LYELL LANGMAN, 3rd and last *Baronet*.

DAUGHTERS LIVING OF THIRD BARONET

Josephine Frances, *b* 1938. —— Judith Ann Camilla, *b* 1949: *m* 1972, Ian K. Gibson.

DAUGHTERS LIVING OF SECOND BARONET

Mary Eleanor, *b* 1908. —— (Nora) Elizabeth Ferrar, *b* 1919: *m* 1955, John Archibald Montgomery, and has issue living, Archibald John, *b* 1957, — James Lyell, *b* 1961, — Katherine Elizabeth, *b* 1956. *Residence* – North Cadbury Court, Somerset.

WIDOW LIVING OF THIRD BARONET

IRIS PAMELA GASKELL (*Lady Langman*), only da of Capt Spencer Kennard, formerly of Purslow Hall, Craven Arms, Shropshire: *m* 1936, Sir John Lyell Langman, 3rd Bt, who *d* 1985. *Residence* – The Goslings, Gooseacre Lane, Cirencester, Glos.

LANGRISHE (I) 1777, of Knocktopher Abbey, Kilkenny

Sir JAMES HERCULES LANGRISHE, 8th *Baronet; b* 3 March 1957; *s* his father, *Sir* HERCULES RALPH HUME, 1998; *ed* Boveridge House Sch, Cranborne: *m* 1985, Gemma Mary Philomena, eldest da of Patrick O'Daly, of Ferndale, Kiltale, Dunsany, co Meath, and has issue.

𝔄rms – Quarterly, or and sable, four covered cups counterchanged. ℭrest – A lion rampant per fesse or and sable.
Residence – Derrypatrick, Drumree, co Meath.

SON LIVING

RICHARD JAMES HERCULES, *b* 8 April 1988.

DAUGHTER LIVING

Medio tutissimus ibis
You will walk safest in a middle path

Victoria Anna Jean, *b* 1986.

SISTERS LIVING

Miranda Grania, *b* 1959: *m* 1984, Christopher John Markes, of Old Kilcarty, Dunsany, co Meath, eldest son of late John Edward Markes, of Recess, co Galway, and has issue living, Alice Olivia, *b* 1987, — Louisa Meriel, *b* 1990, — Julia Sarah, *b* 1995. —— Georgina Emma, *b* 1961: *m* 1989, Dr S. Ross Wallace, son of Dr John Wallace, of Clare, S Australia, and has issue living, Oliver William, *b* 1993, — Sam Edward, *b* 1996. —— Atalanta Sue, *b* 1963: *m* 1992, J. Arthur R. Pollock, elder son of John David George Pollock, of Mountainstown, Navan, co Meath (*see* Barrington, Bt, 1947 Edn), and has issue living, Marina Ella, *b* 1996, — Josephine Anna, *b* 1998.

UNCLE LIVING (*son of 6th baronet*)

Patrick Nicholas, TD (The Manor House, Sellindge, Ashford, Kent), *b* 1932; *ed* Eton; late Maj Leicestershire and Derbyshire Yeo (TA) and formerly a Member of Lloyd's: *m* 1957, Penelope Jill, only child of the late Lt-Cdr Kenneth Horley, RN, and has issue living, Caroline, *b* 1958: *m* 1984, Patrick J. Drury, and has issue living, Leonie Marianne *b* 1983, Rosalind Elizabeth *b* 1985, — Marianne Stuart, *b* 1961: *m* 1988, Nicholas Di Biasio, and has issue living, Adam *b* 1987, Jamie *b* 1990, George *b* 1993.

WIDOW LIVING OF SEVENTH BARONET

Hon GRANIA SYBIL ENID WINGFIELD (*Hon Lady Langrishe*), only da of 9th Viscount Powerscourt: *m* 1955, Sir Hercules Ralph Hume Langrishe, 7th Bt, who *d* 1998. *Residence* – Arlonstown, Dunsany, co Meath.

COLLATERAL BRANCHES LIVING

Issue of late Robert Gore Langrishe, yst son of 6th baronet, *b* 1936, *d* 1982: *m* 1966, (Eleanor) Barbara Muriel (who *m* 3rdly, 1983, Hugh Curran), da of late Reginald Arthur Lygon (*see* E Beauchamp, colls), and formerly wife of William James Cavendish-Bentinck (D Portland, colls):—
Robin Stuart, *b* 1967.

Grandson of late Henry Hoadly Langrishe, eldest son of late Richard Langrishe, 5th son of 3rd baronet:—
Issue of late Lt-Col Roger Patrick Hercules Langrishe, *b* 1905, *d* 1969: *m* 1949, Doris May, who *d* 1988, da of late Thomas Sidney Bott, of 16 Beech Rd, Oxford:—
James Hoadly (55 Wych Lane, Gosport, Hants PO13 0JA), *b* 1951; *ed* King's Sch, Canterbury; Lt-Cdr RN: *m* 1979, Ann Helen, da of late Robert Arthur Jutson, of Bushey, Herts, and has issue living, Katherine Jane, *b* 1980, — Claire Jennifer, *b* 1982.

Grandchildren of late Richard Langrishe, 5th son of 3rd baronet:—
Issue of late Lieut-Col John du Plessis Langrishe, DSO, RAMC, *b* 1883, *d* 1947: *m* 1914, Helen Dorothy, who *d* 1981, da of late Philip George Collins:—
Philip John Duppa (Birches, Pembroke Rd, Woking, Surrey), *b* 1917: *ed* Cheltenham, and Pembroke Coll, Camb (BA 1938); formerly Capt RA: 1939-45 War (prisoner, escaped); solicitor: *m* 1st, 1948 (*m diss* 1963), Phyllis Edwina, da of C. V. Vanbergen, of Bassetts, Hildenborough, Kent; 2ndly, 1963, Isabel Angus, yr da of Sir (Alexander) Knox Helm, GBE, KCMG, of The Old Rectory, Tewin, Herts, and has issue living, (by 1st *m*) Charles William John (Greystones, 27 Hawkhirst Rd, Kenley, Surrey CR2 5DN), *b* 1949: *m* 1973, Philippa Anne, da of John Jenkins, and has issue living, Philip Charles Nicholas *b* 1976, Emma Charlotte *b* 1978, Nicola Anne *b* 1980, — Patrick du Plessis (Weston Manor, Weston, Honiton, Devon), *b* 1952; *ed* Exeter Univ (LLB 1973); solicitor: *m* 1972, Lynda Audrey, da of Stanley Edward Bellman, and has issue living, Thomas du Plessis *b* 1980, Catherine Mary *b* 1976, Tamsin Clare Audrey *b* 1978, Frances Anne *b* 1983, Clare Madeleine *b* 1986, Marie Anna *b* 1992. —— Hugh Richard (7 Stonehill Close, Bromyard, Herefs HR7 4XD) *b* 1923; *ed* Cheltenham; formerly Lt (A)RNVR: *m* 1955, Pamela Mary, da of late William E. Downes, of Bourton Hall, Much Wenlock, Shropshire, and has issue living, John William (4 Blenheim Gdns, Kinston-upon-Thames, Surrey KT2 7BW), *b* 1959; *ed* Wrekin Coll, and Southampton Univ (BSc), — Jane Dorothy, *b* 1956: *m* 1985, Charles John Miller, MICE, of 34 Gilmais, Bookham, Leatherhead, Surrey KT23 4RP, son of late C. H. Miller, and has issue living, Philip James *b* 1990, Hollie Claire *b* 1988. —— Dorothy Pratt (3 Palace Gate, High St, Odiham, Hook, Hants RG29 1JZ), *b* 1921: *m* 1st, 1946 (*m diss* 1972), Clifford Anthony Weston, formerly Capt RA; 2ndly, 1974, Robert Lonsdale Fell, DFC,

RAFVR, who *d* 1985, and has issue living (by 1st *m*), Richard Anthony, *b* 1947, — Christopher Nigel (Main Street, Tur Langton, nr Kibworth, Leics LE8 0PJ), *b* 1949: *m* 1977, Mary Louise, da of late George Clifford Morris, of Hall Farm, Shangton, Leics, and has issue living, Helen Louise *b* 1979, Anna Mary *b* 1981, Sally Jean *b* 1988, — *Rev* (Douglas) Neil (2 Vicarage Lane, Radcliffe on Trent, Nottingham NG12 2FB), *b* 1951; ordained priest 1977: *m* 1977, Maureen Patricia, da of late Keith Walton Dowell, and has issue living, Rosemary Jane *b* 1979, Elizabeth Anne *b* 1982.

Grandsons of late Lt-Col Richard Bellingham Langrishe, 3rd son of late Richard Langrishe (ante):—
Issue of late Lt-Col Richard Courtenay Gibson Langrishe, *b* 1912, *d* 1983: *m* 1940, Jean Gertrude Abercrombie (who *m* 2ndly, 1984, S/Ldr Michael Edward Townsend, RAF), da of late George Dingwall Thomson, MRCS:—
Richard Dingwall (The Moorings, Upper Clatford, Andover, Hants SP11 7QL), *b* 1941; *ed* Cheltenham, and RMCS Shrivenham (BSc Eng); Maj (Ret): *m* 1964, Angela Walmsley Marett, el da of David Walmsley Marett Tims, of Crookham Village, Hants, and has issue living, Belinda Jane Marett, *b* 1967: *m* 1995, Capt Richard E. van der Horst, RM, son of Brig Rupert van der Horst, of Stoke Trister, Som, and has issue living, Anna Ruth *b* 1998, — Rebecca Kate, *b* 1970. —— Nicholas du Plessis (Avery Cottage, Pinckney Green, Bradford-on-Avon, Wilts BA15 2PZ), *b* 1942; *ed* Cheltenham: *m* 1966, Anna Victoria Airy, only da of S/Ldr Michael Edward Townsend, RAF (ante), and has issue living, Oonagh Richarda du Plessis, *b* 1972.

This family is descended from Sir Nicholas Langrish, Kt, who was seized of the Manor of Langrish, Hants, AD 1273. The Irish branch is descended from Rafe, or Ralph (of Borden), 3rd son of Nicholas Langrishe, of Langrishe. Ralph Langrishe of Borden died between 1542-59; the 3rd in descent from him was Major Hercules Langrishe, Carver in Ordinary to Queen Henrietta Maria, who prevented the arrest of the "Five Members" by Charles I, and the 7th was the 1st baronet, Sir Hercules, who sat for forty years as MP for Knocktopher in the Irish Parliament. He was a Privy Councillor, and foremost in his advocacy for repealing the severe laws enacted against Roman Catholics.

LARCOM (UK) 1868.

Sir (CHARLES) CHRISTOPHER ROYDE LARCOM, 5th *Baronet*; *b* 11 Sept 1926; *s* his father, *Sir* PHILIP, 1967; *ed* Radley, and Clare Coll, Camb (MA); a FCA: *m* 1956, Barbara Elizabeth, da of Balfour Bowen, and has issue.

Arms – Argent, on a mount a hawthorn bush proper, and in chief an eagle displayed gules. **Crest** – On a cap of maintenance azure turned up ermine a martlet sable, with a fleur-de-lis in its beak or.
Residence – 4 Village Cay Marina, PO Box 145, Road Town, Tortola, British Virgin Islands.
Club – Bath.

DAUGHTERS LIVING

Le Roy, la Loy
The King, the Law

Mary Elizabeth, *b* 1957: *m* 1983, Joseph William Arnold. —— Jane Catherine, *b* 1958: *m* 1988, Andrew J. Edyvean, of Grey Cottage, 48 Far St, Wymeswold, Leics, son of L. A. Edyvean, of Urchfont, Wilts, and has issue living, Charlotte Louise, *b* 1994. —— Julia Dorothy, *b* 1961: *m* 1982, John Dyer, and has issue living, Benjamin Charles, *b* 1985, — Sophie Claire, *b* 1984. —— Anna Balfour, *b* 1962.

SISTER LIVING

Monica Rosemary Georgina, *b* 1921: *m* 1942, William Eric Walrond, of 7 Old House Close, Church Rd, Wimbledon, SW19, and has issue living, Patricia Mary, *b* 1943, — Anne Carol, *b* 1947, — Christine Diana, *b* 1953.

The 1st baronet, Maj-Gen Rt Hon Sir Thomas Aiskew Larcom, KCB, PC (son of late Capt Joseph Larcom), served in RE, and was subsequently Under-Sec of State for Ireland. The 2nd baronet, Lieut-Col Sir Charles Larcom served in NZ War 1863-4. The 3rd baronet, Major Sir Thomas Perceval Larcom, DSO, served with RA during European War 1914-18.

LATHAM (UK) 1919, of Crow Clump, Walton-upon-Thames, co Surrey.

Sir RICHARD THOMAS PAUL LATHAM, 3rd *Baronet*: *b* 15 April 1934; *s* his father, *Sir* (HERBERT) PAUL, 1955; *ed* Eton, and Trin Coll, Camb (BA 1957, MA 1962): *m* 1958, (Marie-Louise) Patricia, da of late Frederick Hooper Russell, of Vancouver, British Columbia, and has issue.

𝕬rms – Gules, an eagle displayed or, between two bezants in fesse, on a chief of the second a cross moline sable between two roses of the field. 𝕮rest – An eagle, wings elevated, inverted and addorsed or, resting the dexter claw on a torteaux and charged on the wing with a cross as in the arms.
Residence – 2125 Birnam Wood Drive, Santa Barbara, California 93108, USA.

DAUGHTERS LIVING

Nicola Patricia, *b* 1959: *m* 1986, Colin David Jones, of Vancouver, BC, Canada. —— Alison Kathleen, *b* 1965: *m* 19—, Gary W. Schilds.

By fortune and labour

The 1st baronet, Sir Thomas Paul Latham, was many years Joint Managing Director, and sometime Dep Chm of Courtaulds, Ltd, also rendered sers to Min of Pensions during European War 1914-19. The 2nd baronet, Sir (Herbert) Paul Latham was a Co Councillor for London, E Lewisham Div 1928-34, and sat as MP for Scarborough and Whitby Div of N Riding of Yorkshire (C) 1931-41.

DICK-LAUDER (NS) 1690, of Fountainhall, Haddingtonshire.

Prudence is the guardian of the tower

Sir PIERS ROBERT DICK-LAUDER, 13th *Baronet*; *b* 3 Oct 1947; *s* his father, *Maj Sir* GEORGE ANDREW, 1981.

𝕬rms – Gules, a griffin salient within a bordure argent. 𝕮rest – A tower with portcullis down, the head and shoulders of a sentinel appearing above the battlements in a watching posture proper. 𝕾upporters – Two lions rampant argent.
Residence – 91 Womerah Av, Rush Cutters Bay, Sydney, Australia.

BROTHER LIVING

MARK ANDREW, *b* 3 May 1951: *m* 1970 (*m diss* 1982), Jeanne, da of — Mullineaux, of Bolton, Lancs, and has issue living, Martin, *b* 1976. *Residence* – 3 Sunnymead Terrace, Totnes, Devon.

SISTERS LIVING

Georgina Jane, *b* 1949: *m* 1973, her cousin, Nicholas Ernest Kerr-Smiley, and has issue (*see* Smiley, Bt, colls). —— Selina Rose, *b* 1955: *m* 1978, Piers Henry Chandler, son of D. C. B. Chandler, of Sutton Coldfield, Warwicks, and has issue living, a son, *b* 1988, — a da, *b* 1995.

WIDOW LIVING OF TWELFTH BARONET

HESTER MARGUERITE (*Lady Dick-Lauder*), da of late Lt-Col George Cecil Minett Sorell-Cameron, CBE (B Tollemache): *m* 1945, Maj Sir George Andrew Dick-Lauder, 12th Bt, who *d* 1981. *Residence* – 17 Vine Court Rd, Sevenoaks, Kent TN13 3UU.

Dwell as if about to depart

This family is of Norman origin, De Lavedre being mentioned among the barons who accompanied Malcolm Canmore into Scotland. Sir Robert de Lawedre, a companion in arms of Sir William Wallace, was several times Ambassador to England from Robert I. William Lauder was Bishop of Glasgow and Chancellor of Scotland 1423, and his brother was Bishop of Dunkeld. Many of the family attained knightly honours. The 2nd baronet was a Senator of the College of Justice, with the courtesy title of Lord Fountainhall; and the 5th baronet, who assumed the additional surname of Dick, married his cousin, Isabel, heiress of William Dick, of Grange, who was in direct descent from the Royal House of Plantagenet. Sir John North Dalrymple Dick-Lauder, 11th Bt, was Lt-Col Indian Army.

LAURIE (UK) 1834, of Bedford Square, Middlesex.

Virtue is always flourishing

Sir ROBERT BAYLEY EMILIUS LAURIE, 7th *Baronet*; *b* 8 March 1931: *s* his father, *Maj-Gen Sir* JOHN EMILIUS, CBE, DSO, 1983; *ed* Eton: *m* 1968, Laurelie Meriol Winifrida, da of late Sir Reginald Lawrence William Williams, MBE, ED, 7th Bt (*cr* 1798) and has issue.

𝕬rms – Sable, a cup argent with a chaplet between two laurel branches, all issuing out of the same, vert. 𝕮rest – Two laurel branches in saltire proper. *Residence* – The Old Rectory, Little Tey, Colchester, Essex C06 1JA.

DAUGHTERS LIVING

Clare Meriol, *b* 1974. —— Serena Catherine, *b* 1976.

SISTERS LIVING

Rosemary Evelyn Anne, *b* 1924: *m* 1949, Cdr Robin Henry Ramsay Moodie, RN (ret), who *d* 1994, and has issue living, John Ramsay, *b* 1955: *m* 1989, Caroline Mary Hughes, and has issue living, Sam Ramsay *b* 1991, Iona Vive *b* 1993, —— Edward Robin, *b* 1956: *m* 1993, Patricia Fitzgerald, and has issue living, Jack Henry Fitzgerald *b* 1995. *Residence* – Red Roof, Penton Mewsey, Andover Hants SP11 0RQ. —— Marian Clare (*Baroness Laing of Dunphail*), *b* 1927: *m* 1950, Baron Laing of Dunphail (Life Baron). *Residence* – High Meadows, Windsor Rd, Gerrards Cross, Bucks SL9 8ST.

COLLATERAL BRANCHES LIVING

Issue of late Cecil Emilius Laurie, 3rd son of 3rd baronet, *b* 1862, *d* 1919: *m* 1900, Helen Janet Douglas, who *d* 1919, da of late Lieut Robert Douglas Campbell, RN (B Blythswood, colls):—
Christina Eve, *b* 1912: *m* 1938, Kenneth Murray McCall, who *d* 1987, and has issue living, David James, *b* 1941: *m* 1971, Evelyn Lucy, da of late Thomas McCosh, of Pitcon, Dalry, Ayrshire, and has issue living, Philippa *b* 1973, Sarah Christina *b* 1978, Emma Elizabeth *b* 1982, —— William Kenneth, *b* 1944: *m* 1971, Hon Gillian Patricia Denman, da of 5th Baron Denman, and has issue living, Hamish Spencer Murray *b* 1972, Robert Andrew Calum *b* 1981, Fiona Jane *b* 1975, —— Patricia Helen, *b* 1942: *m* 1970, Timothy Morgan Hughes, of Fanville Head Farm, Hook Norton, Oxon, and has issue living, Charles Edward Kenneth *b* 1971, Davina Jane *b* 1973, Iona Caroline *b* 1978, —— Joan, *b* 1948: *m* 1969, Capt John James Dean Barrow, of Camp Farm, Farmington, Northleach, Glos, and has issue living, Richard Raymond *b* 1971, Georgina Rachael *b* 1975. *Residence* – Barbuie, Moniaive, Dumfriesshire. —— Elizabeth Janet, *b* 1915: *m* 1st, 1947 (*m diss* 1960), Francis Marshall; 2ndly, 1960, Francis Dudley Rose, who *d* 1968, and has issue living, (by 1st *m*) Julian Emilius Harold, *b* 1950, —— Janet Philippa Ann, *b* 1949.

Grandchildren of late Cecil Emilius Laurie (ante):—
Issue of late Ronald Edward Laurie, *b* 1911, *d* 1952: *m* 1941, Rosemary Lilian Fullerton, who *d* 1995:—
ANDREW RONALD EMILIUS (7 St Oswalds Rd, Hexham, Northumberland), *b* 20 Oct 1944: *m* 1970, Sarah Anne, el da of C. D. Patterson, of Hexham, and has issue living, John Christopher Emilius, *b* 1971, —— Michael James Edward, *b* 1973. —— (Rosemary) Helen, *b* 1942: *m* 1966, David McMullan, of 2 Lostock Av, Poynton, Cheshire SK12 1DR, and has issue living, Andrew David Sean, *b* 1970.

Grandchildren of late Kennett BAYLEY, son of late Rev Kennett Champain Bayley, 2nd son of 1st baronet:—
Issue of late Kennett Champain BAYLEY, *b* 1873, *d* 1935: *m* 1902, Norah Kathleen, who *d* 1963, only da of late Capt Henry William Roberts, formerly 98th Regt, of Hollingside, Durham:—
¦John Maurice, DSC, *b* 1905; *ed* Rugby; Cdr (ret) RN: *m* 1935, Mary Boyd, da of F. M. Osborn, of Sheffield, and *d* 1995, leaving issue, *Rev* Michael John (27 Meadow Bank Av, Sheffield, S7 1PB), *b* 1936: *ed* Rugby, and Corpus Christi Coll, Camb (MA); PhD Sheffield: *m* 1963, Fleur, da of J. Jones, of Calverley, and has issue living, Robin Kennett *b* 1966, Andrew John *b* 1968, Jill Ruth *b* 1964: *m* 1987, Hugh Bowden, son of Rev Dr J. S. Bowden, of Highgate, Emma Susan *b* 1970, — †Kennett Ian, *b* 1941: *ed* Bradfield; Capt 1st R Green Jackets: *m* 1955, Helen Julia, who *d* 1994, da of P. D. Benjafield, of Shalford, Surrey, and *d* 1996, leaving issue, Benjamin George Robson *b* 1967: *m* 1993, Sarah, da of P. R. Dawson, of Wanaka, New Zealand (and has issue living, Hannah Julia *b* 1997), Sarah Mary Helen *b* 1969, — Peter Charles, *b* 1943: *ed* Durham: *m* 1980, Catherine Anne, da of Dr J. Dunclee, of Saskatoon, Canada, and has issue living, Johnathan Edward *b* 1986, Ellen Elizabeth *b* 1984.

Issue of late Col Arthur George BAYLEY, CBE, DSO, *b* 1878, *d* 1949: *m* 1923, Katharine Mary Frederica, who *d* 1952, da of late Brig-Gen Francis Alexander Fortescue, CB, CMG (E Fortescue, colls):—
Elizabeth Frances Mary Louise (26B Elm Park Rd, SW3), *b* 1924: *m* 1st, 1947 (*m diss* 1953), John David Nicholas Retallack, late Maj Welsh Gds; 2ndly, 1953, Francis Trelawny Williams, late Lieut KRRC, who *d* 1977 (*see* Salusbury-Trelawny, Bt, 1959 Edn); 3rdly, 1983, James Andrew Moffett, Lt-Cdr USNR (ret), and has issue living, (by 2nd *m*) Trelawny Michael, *b* 1957: *m* 1994, Olivia Rosemary, da of late Cmdr Axel Mortensen, of Oxton, Notts, and has issue living, Merlin Francis *b* 1999, Amber May *b* 1996.

The 1st baronet, Right Hon Sir John Bayley, was for many years a Judge of the Queen's Bench, and subsequently a Baron of the Exchequer. Rev Sir John Robert Laurie Emilius Bayley, 3rd Bt, assumed by Roy licence 1887 the surname and arms of Laurie of Maxwelton, in lieu of his patronymic. The 4th baronet, Col Sir Claude Villiers Emilius Laurie, CB, DSO, served in S Africa 1900-1902 (despatches, DSO).

LAWES (UK) 1882, of Rothamsted, co Hertford.

Pour la Foi
For the faith

Sir (John) Michael Bennet Lawes, 5th *Baronet; b* 24 Oct 1932; *s* his father, *Sir* John Claude Bennet, 1979; *ed* Elizabeth Coll, Guernsey.

Arms – Quarterly: 1st and 4th argent, three bendlets gules on a chief sable, a barrulet dancettée or; 2nd and 3rd or, two flaunches azure, on a chief nebuly of the second three estoiles or. **Crest** – 1st, a Saracen's head affrontée, and couped below the shoulders proper, wreathed about the temples, and tied in a bow or and gules; 2nd, on a mount vert the trunk of a tree fessewise eradicated and sprouting to the dexter, surmounted by an ermine passant proper.
Address – c/o Coutts & Co, Truchot, St Peter Port, Guernsey, CI.

HALF-SISTER LIVING

Janet Caroline, *b* 1940: *m* 1964, John Christopher Berney-Ficklin, and has issue living, Todd Alexander, *b* 1975, — Karen Lawes, *b* 1973.

The 1st baronet, Sir John Bennet Lawes, DSc, FRS, achieved considerable fame as a practical experimental agricultural chemist. He was grandson of Thomas Lawes, who inherited Rothamsted from his maternal uncle John Bennet. Rothamsted was inherited by the last named from his cousin Thomas Wittewronge in 1763, as the maternal grandson of James Wittewronge of Rothamsted, Recorder of St Albans.

LAWRENCE (UK) 1858, of Lucknow.

Never give in

Sir John Waldemar Lawrence, OBE, 6th *Baronet; b* 27 May 1907; *s* his brother, *Sir* Henry Eustace Waldemar, 1967; *ed* Eton, and New Coll, Oxford (MA); editor of *Frontier;* late Press Attaché at Moscow; Chm of GB-USSR Assoc; Pres of Keston Institute; Officer of Order of Orange Nassau of the Netherlands; OBE (Civil) 1945: *m* 1st, 1948, Mrs Mary Jacynth Donaldson-Hudson, who *d* 1987, da of late Rev Francis George Ellerton, and formerly wife of (i) Guy Douglas Hamilton Warrack, and (ii) Michael Donaldson-Hudson; 2ndly, 1988, Mrs Audrey Viola Woodiwiss, widow of John Woodiwiss.

Arms – Ermine, on a cross raguly gules an eastern crown or; on a chief azure two swords in saltire proper, pommels and hilts gold, between as many leopards' heads argent. **Crest** – Out of an eastern crown or, a cubit arm entwined by a wreath of laurel and holding a dagger all proper.
Residence – 36A Norham Rd, Oxford OX2 6SQ.

BROTHER LIVING

George Alexander Waldemar, *b* 22 Sept 1910; *ed* Eton, and Trin Coll Camb: *m* 1949, Olga, da of Peter Schilovsky, and formerly wife of Alexander Chkiantz, and has issue living, Henry Peter (The Mall House, Brockham End, Bath BA1 9BZ), *b* 2 April 1952: *m* 1979, Penelope Maureen Nunan, and has issue living, Christopher Cosmo *b* 1979, Isabelle Olga Jane *b* 1984, — Natalie Honoria, *b* 1951: *m* 1980, Mehrdad Shokoohy, — Catherine Letitia, *b* 1953: *m* 1976, Stephen James Paul Todd, of 10 Christchurch Rd, Winchester, Hants SO23 9SR, and has issue living, Peter James *b* 1982, Helen Anna *b* 1979. *Residence* – Brockham End, Bath, Som BA1 9BZ.

Sir Alexander Hutchinson Lawrence, 1st Bt, was *cr* a Baronet with remainder to his issue male, failing which to his yr brother, and was accidentally killed, 27 Aug 1864, by the falling of a bridge on the Tibet road, India. He was el son of the illustrious Sir Henry Montgomery Lawrence, KCB, who fell in defence of Lucknow in 1857.

LAWRENCE (UK) 1867, of Ealing Park, Middlesex.

Sir WILLIAM FETTIPLACE LAWRENCE, 5th *Baronet; b* 23 Aug 1954; *s* his father, *Maj Sir* WILLIAM, 1986; *ed* King Edward VI Sch, Stratford upon Avon.

𝕬rms – Ermine, a cross raguly gules, in the first and fourth quarters a serpent nowed proper. 𝕮rest – A griffin's head couped argent, in front thereof a serpent nowed proper.
Residence – The Knoll, Walcote, Alcester, Warwicks B49 6LZ.

SISTERS LIVING

Lavinia Margaret, *b* 1947: *m* 1971, Julian Conway Seymour, of Waterdale House, E Knoyle, Salisbury, Wilts, and has issue (*see* M Hertford, colls). —— Carolyn Mary, *b* 1949: *m* 1972 (*m diss* 1990), Nicholas Peter Evelyn, and has issue living, Rupert Peter, *b* 1973, — James Nicholas, *b* 1976.

WIDOW LIVING OF FOURTH BARONET

PAMELA MARY (*Lady Lawrence*), yr da of James Edgar Gordon, of Beechbank, Bromborough, Wirral, Cheshire: *m* 1945, as his 2nd wife, Maj Sir William Lawrence, 4th Bt, who *d* 1986. *Residence* – The Knoll, Walcote, nr Alcester, Warwicks B49 6LZ.

By mind and work

COLLATERAL BRANCH LIVING

Issue of late Aubrey Trevor Lawrence, MBE, KC, 2nd son of 2nd baronet, *b* 1875, *d* 1930: *m* 1901, Constance Emily Fanning, who *d* 1957, da of late Joseph McGaw, of Mickleham Downs, Dorking, and Kooba, NS Wales:—
Peter Stafford Hayden (Simeons, Little Milton, Oxford), *b* 1913; *ed* Eton, and Ch Ch, Oxford (MA); Assist Master at Eton Coll 1936-77 (House Master 1951-68); 1939-45 War as Lt-Cdr RNVR, Radar Officer (despatches): *m* 1940, Helena Frances, da of late Hon George William Lyttelton (*see* V Cobham, colls), and has issue living, Aubrey Lyttelton Simon, *b* 1942; *ed* Eton, and Ch Ch, Oxford (MA 1985): *m* 1984, Danielle de Froidmont, and has issue living, Thomas Lyttelton de Froidmont *b* 1985, — Robin Peter Charles, *b* 1950; *ed* Millfield, — Pamela Jane, *b* 1945; *ed* North Foreland Lodge, and Univ Coll, London (BA, 1970, PGCE 1978): *m* 1981, Stuart Wooler, and has issue living, Harry Peter Lawrence *b* 1988, Alice Honor Lawrence *b* 1982, — Anthea Mary, *b* 1947; *ed* North Foreland Lodge, and London Univ (BEd): *m* 1980, Clinton Cavers, — Jemima Rachel, *b* 1956; *ed* Wycombe Abbey, and Royal Northern Coll of Music (GMus): *m* 1978, Joseph Severs Taylor, and has issue living, Oscar George *b* 1987, Rowan Joseph *b* 1988, Bryn Hugh *b* 1990, Ivy Rosanna *b* 1985, — Susanna Lucy, *b* 1958; *ed* Lord Williams's Sch, Thame, and Leeds Univ (MB ChB 1981).

The 1st baronet, a distinguished surgeon, was a FRS, a Corresponding Member of Institute of France, a Member of the principal scientific socs of Europe and America, twice President of the College of Surgeons, and for many years Sergeant-Surgeon to HM Queen Victoria. The 2nd baronet, Sir Trevor, sat as MP for Mid Surrey 1875-85 and for S-E Div of Surrey 1885-92, and was 28 years Pres of Roy Horticultural So and 12 years Treasurer of St Bartholomew's Hospital.

LAWRENCE (UK) 1906, of Sloane Gardens, Chelsea.

Sir DAVID ROLAND WALTER LAWRENCE, 3rd *Baronet; b* 8 May 1929; *s* his father, *Lt-Col Sir* (PERCY) ROLAND (BRADFORD), MC, 1950; *ed* Radley, and RMC; sometime Capt Coldstream Guards: *m* 1955, Audrey, who *d* 1998, da of Brigadier Desmond Young, MC, and formerly wife of 11th Duke of Leeds.

𝕬rms – Ermine, an escarbuncle or, surmounted by a lotus flower proper, on a chief arched gules a dragon passant or. 𝕮rest – A cubit arm, vested gules, cuffed ermine, holding in the hand a plane leaf proper, and charged on the sleeve with a trefoil slipped or. 𝕾upporters – On either side a heron holding in the beak a sprig of plane fructed proper.
Residence – 28 High Town Rd, Maidenhead, Berks SL6 1PB.

BROTHER LIVING

CLIVE WYNDHAM (Woodside, Frant, nr Tunbridge Wells, Kent TN3 9HW), *b* 6 Oct 1939, *ed* Gordonstoun; late Lt Coldm Gds: *m* 1966, Sophia Annabel Stuart, da of Ian Hervey Stuart Black, of Dumbarnie Cottage, Bridge of Earn, Perthshire, and has issue living, James Wyndham Stuart, *b* 1970, — Simon Roland Stuart, *b* 1973, — Hugo Hervey Stuart, *b* 1975.

SISTERS LIVING

Jean Jacqueline, *b* 1926: *m* 1950, Harold Channing Quitman, and has issue living, Jeremy Roland Channing, *b* 1953, — Annabel Susan Maude, *b* 1951. *Residence* – Rookley Farmhouse, Upper Somborne, Stockbridge, Hants. —— Susan Louise, *b* 1944: *m* 1965, Norman Gardner, of Montreal, and has issue living, Suzanne Vanessa *b* 1965, — Amanda Sarah, *b* 1968.

COLLATERAL BRANCH LIVING

Issue of late Capt (Henry Walter) Neville Lawrence, 2nd son of 1st baronet, *b* 1891, *d* 1959: *m* 1933, Sarah, who *d* 1947, da of Nicholas Murray Butler, of New York, USA:—
Walter Nicholas Murray, *b* 1935: *m* 1961, Sally Louise, da of Lt-Col A. B. O'Dwyer, and has issue living, Sarah Louise, *b* 1962: *m* 1986, Andrew Crawley, who *d* 1988, and has issue living, Charles Murray *b* 1987, Jessica Mary *b* 1988, — Catherine Jane, *b* 1964: *m* 1992, Rupert Edmund Ivo Elliott, and has issue living, Hector Edmund Murray *b* 1996, Ivo Matthew Lawrence *b* 1998, Eliza Harriet Rosemary *b* 1994. *Residence* – Grey Walls, Hook Heath, Woking.

The 1st baronet, Sir Walter Roper Lawrence, GCIE, GCVO, CB (son of George Lawrence, JP, of Trevella, Llangwm, Monmouthshire), was Private Sec to Viceroy of India 1898-1903, Ch of Staff for visit of TRH the Prince and Princess of Wales to India 1905-6, and a member of Council of India 1907-9. The 2nd baronet, Sir (Percy) Roland (Bradford) Lawrence, MC, was Lt-Col Coldstream Guards.

Lawrence-Jones, see Jones.

LAWSON (UK) 1900, of Weetwood Grange, Headingley-cum-Burley, West Riding of Yorkshire.

Arise, and shine forth

Sir JOHN CHARLES ARTHUR DIGBY LAWSON, DSO, MC, 3rd *Baronet*; *b* 24 Oct 1912; *s* his father, *Maj Sir* DIGBY, TD, 1959; *ed* Stowe, and RMC; Chm of Fairbairn Lawson, Ltd and subsidiary cos 1968-79; a Member of Council Univ of Leeds 1972-79; 2nd Lt 11th Hus (PAO) 1933; served in Palestine 1936 (despatches); seconded Transjordan Frontier Force 1939-40; Western Desert 1940-43 (wounded, despatches thrice); T/Lt-Col 1943 as Gen Montgomery's apptd advisor on Armoured reconnaissance to Gen Patton in N Africa 1943 (wounded); US Marine Staff Course, Quantico, Virginia 1944; Personal Liaison Offr to Gen Montgomery at 21st Army GP, N France 1944; Cmdg Inns of Court Regt 1944-46; ret 1947; Col 11th Hus (PAO) 1965-69, and on their amalgamation with 10th Hus (PWO), Col R Hus 1969-72; MC 1940; DSO 1943; US Legion of Merit 1943: *m* 1st, 1945 (*m diss* 1950), Rose, who *d* 1972, da of late David Cecil Bingham, Lt Coldm Gds (E Lucan, colls), and widow of William M. L. Fiske, P/O RAF, who *d* (of wounds received in action in Battle of Britain) 1940, previously wife of 7th Earl of Warwick; 2ndly, 1954, Tresilla Anne Eleanor, who *d* 1985, da of late Maj Eric Buller Leyborne Popham, MC, and formerly wife of John Garland de Pret Roose, and has issue by 2nd *m*.

Arms – Per chevron argent and or, a chevron invected sable, plain cotised vert, between two martlets in chief of the third and a trefoil slipped in base of the fourth. **Crest** – Between two arms embowed, proper the hands holding a sun in splendour a trefoil, as in the arms the whole surmounted by a rainbow also proper.
Residence – Hillmore Cottage, Bishops Hull Rd, Taunton, Som TA1 5ER. *Club* – Cavalry and Guards'.

SON LIVING (*By 2nd marriage*)

CHARLES JOHN PATRICK, *b* 19 May 1959; *ed* Harrow, Univ of Leeds, and RAC, Cirencester (Dip Est Mng); ARICS; Dir Jackson Stops and Staff Consortium, Exeter: *m* 1987, Lady Caroline Lowther, 3rd da of 7th Earl of Lonsdale, and has issue living, Jack William Tremayne, *b* 6 Dec 1989, — Thomas Charles Lancelot, *b* 1992, — Ralph Hugh Arthur, *b* 1995, — Tess, *b* 1988. *Residence* – Heckwood, Sampford Spiney, Yelverton, Devon PL20 6L9.

BROTHER LIVING

Patrick William, *b* 1914: *m* 1939, Jean Mary, da of late Col Sydney Ernest Smith, CBE, of Stuckeridge, Oakford, Devon, and has issue living, Nicholas Patrick David (Morestead, Windlesham Rd, Chobham, Surrey); *b* 1940: *m* 1st, 1962 (*m diss* 1970), Anne Sommerville de Laval Harvie; 2ndly, 1971, Jill, da of Clifford Wendover Beeson, and formerly wife of Duncan M. Atkinson and has issue living, (by 1st *m*) Julian Alexander Nicholas *b* 1963, Rebecca de Laval *b* 1965, — (by 2nd *m*) Rupert Christopher David *b* 1972, — Timothy James (Bourn Lodge, Bourn, Cambs CB3 7SX; MCC and Farmers), *b* 1942; FRICS: *m* 1965 Elizabeth White, and has issue living, Mark James *b* 1968, Simon Alexander *b* 1970, Peter John *b* 1974, — Michael Shaun (Great House Farm, Lynwick St, Rudgwick, Sussex), *b* 1945: *m* 1970, Jane Hamilton, and has issue living, James Patrick *b* 1972 Richard Shaun, *b* 1973, Henry John, *b* 1978. *Residence* – St Mary's House, Langford, nr Bristol.

HALF-BROTHERS LIVING AND DECEASED

†Arthur Simon Albert (Tithe Barn, Crowcombe, nr Taunton, Somerset), *b* 1925; Lt-Col N Somerset Yeo; formerly Lieut 11th Hussars: *m* 1st, 1953 (*m diss* 1961), Virginia Elizabeth Grace, da of late Maj William Steel Huddleston, RHA; 2ndly, 1961 (*m diss* 1986), Alison Deirdre, el da of Lt-Col Ian Balmain; 3rdly, 1987, Magdalen Cecilia, widow of John Eric Staniland, and elder da of late Lt-Col Francis Michael Benedict Carey Boylan, MBE, of Collierstown House, Bellewstown, Drogheda, co Meath, and *d* 1995, leaving issue (by 1st *m*), Piers James, *b* 1957: late Maj Royal Hussars (PWO): *m* 1985 (*m diss* 1998), Belinda, eldest da of R. Garnham, of Bethersden, Kent, and has issue living, Bertram Digby Alexander *b* 1991, Arabella Harriet *b* 1987, Phoebe Elizabeth Grace *b* 1989, — (by 2nd *m*), Frances Lisa Victoria, *b* 1962, — Louise Christian, *b* 1963: *m* 1992, Michael Gatcombe, — Clare Alison, *b* 1968: *m* 1989, David Burnett, and has issue living, Aaron *b* 1991, Rebecca *b* 1990. —— Simon Digby (Moat Cottage, Stratton Audley, nr Bicester, Oxon OX6 9BW), *b* 1945; *ed* Sherborne, London Univ (BA), and Oxford Univ (MLitt, DPhil)· *m* 1972, Georgina Mary, da of Sqdn Ldr J. C. G. Sarll, DFC, and has issue living, Thomas Digby, *b* 1975, — Daisy Alexandra Ruth, *b* 1983.

SISTER LIVING

Daphne Olive, *b* 1910: *m* 1936, Maj Richard Edwin Fearing Cely Trevilian, TD, DL, and has issue living, John Maurice Richard, *b* 1948: *m* 1971, Penelope, yst da of Raymond Hodgson, of Craig, Balmaclellan, Kirkcudbrightshire, and has issue living, Thomas Richard John *b* 1976, Alice Mary *b* 1974, — Jane Mary, *b* 1938: *m* 1960, Adam Stanislaus Kwiatkowski, and has issue living, Damian Michael Richard *b* 1965: *m* 1994, Miranda Harriet, yr da of Andrew John Hunter Rodwell, of The Dower House, Holbrook, Ipswich, Suffolk (and his issue living, Alexander Peter *b* 1997), Sophia Helena *b* 1963: *m* 1984, Nicholas James Prestige, stepson of late Maj John Prestige, — Susanna Rose, *b* 1939: *m* 1st, 1962 (*m diss* 1970), Jeremy Gwynne Pilcher; 2ndly, 1972, Ewan Iain MacLeod Hilleary, of 197 Pottle St, Horningsham, Wilts, and has issue living (by 1st *m*), Jonathan Swaine *b* 1965, Katharine Alexandra *b* 1963: *m* 1991, Charles Rupert Hunter, son of late Brig (Henry) Michael Allan Hunter, CVO, DSO, MBE (*see* Vy Plumer, 1968 Edn) (and has issue living, Sam Alexander *b* 1992, Lily Rose *b* 1995), Charlotte Serena *b* (twin) 1963: *m* 1992, James Paul Gilfred Studholme, yr son of Sir Paul Henry William Studholme, 2nd Bt, and has issue (see that title), (by 2nd *m*) Angus Ewan MacLeod *b* 1977, — Teresa Melliscent, *b* 1946: *m* 1971, Edward Anthony Dawson, and has issue living, Edward Finch *b* 1971, Hannah Dinah *b* 1974. *Residence* – Midelney Manor, Langport, Somerset.

The influential Co of Lawson's of Leeds, textile machinery manufacturers, was founded by Samuel Lawson in 1812. His grandson, the 1st baronet, Sir Arthur Tredgold Lawson, was Chm of Fairbairn, Lawson, Combe-Barbour Ltd, a Director of Great Eastern Railway, Vice-Chm Yorkshire Conservative Newspaper Co, Dir *Yorkshire Post*, and a Chevalier of the Legion of Honour. The 2nd baronet, Major Sir Digby Lawson, TD, was Chm of Fairbairn, Lawson, Combe-Barbour, Ltd, of Leeds and Belfast, and of Urquhart Lindsay & Robertson Orchar, Ltd, of Dundee.

HOWARD-LAWSON (UK) 1841, of Brough Hall, Yorkshire

Sir JOHN PHILIP HOWARD-LAWSON, 6th *Baronet*; *b* 6 June 1934; *s* his father, *Sir* WILLIAM HOWARD LAWSON, 1990; *ed* Ampleforth; assumed by Royal Licence 1962 the surname and arms of Howard, and subsequently resumed his patronymic in addition to the surname of Howard 1992: *m* 1960, Jean Veronica, only da of late Col John Evelyn Marsh, DSO, OBE, and has issue.

Arms – Gules on a bend between six cross crosslets fitchee argent an escutcheon or charged with a demi lion rampant pierced through the mouth with an arrow within a double tressure flory counterflory of the first in chief a mullet for difference and (for distinction) a cross botonny gules. Crest – On a chapeau gules turned up ermine a lion statant guardant the tail extended or ducally gorged argent charged on the shoulder with a mullet for difference and (for distinction) on the body with a cross botonny gules.
Seat – Corby Castle, Carlisle. *Residence* – Hunter Hall, Great Salkeld, Penrith, Cumbria CA11 9NA.

SONS LIVING

PHILIP WILLIAM HOWARD, *b* 28 June 1961; *ed* Ampleforth: *m* 1st, 1988 (*m diss* 1992), Cara Margaret, only da of Hon Martin Michael Dominick Browne (*see* B Oranmore and Browne); 2ndly, 1993, Isobel Anne Oldridge, elder da of late Christopher George James Oldridge de la Hey, and of Mrs Peter Vivian Lloyd Verney, of Skiveralls House, Chalford Hill, Glos, and has issue living (by 2nd *m*), Cécile Delphine Aurore, *b* 1997. —— Thomas John HOWARD, *b* 1963; *ed* Ampleforth: *m* 1998, Megan Louise, only da of Brian John Tyquin, of Sydney, Australia, and has issue living, Charles John, *b* 1998.

DAUGHTER LIVING

Julia Frances, *b* 1964: *m* 1998, William Alexander Ratcliffe Davie, elder son of William Davie, of Glenmillan, Aberdeenshire, and of Mrs Ian Sinclair, of Hertford.

BROTHERS LIVING

Hugh William LAWSON (Croftlands, Heads Nook, Carlisle), *b* 1936; *ed* Ampleforth; High Sheriff Cumbria 1995: *m* 1961, (Margaret) Ann, elder da of late Maj Richard Gubbins Mounsey Heysham, of Castletown, Carlisle, and has issue living, Simon David, *b* 1962; *ed* Ampleforth: *m* 1989, Lucy Rose, da of James Morrish, of Ham Farm, Wellington, Somerset, and has issue living, Oliver Hugh *b* 1994, Sebastian James *b* 1997, — Philippa Joan, *b* 1963: *m* 1993, Philip A. J. Leech, elder son of Jeremy Leech, of Hovingham, York, and has issue living, William Jeremy *b* 1995, Georgina Florence *b* 1996, — Pollyanne Lucy, *b* 1970: *m* 1997, Julian Edward Roberts, yr son of David Edward Roberts, of Solihull, W Midlands. —— (Arthur) Mark LAWSON (Brough House, Alves, by Forres, Moray), *b* 1940; *ed* Ampleforth: *m* 1968, Rosemary Veronica, da of Samuel Parkington Vickery, of Ardwell, Newland, Glasgow, and has issue living, (Henry) Benedict, *b* 1970; *ed* Ampleforth: *m* 1998, Iona E., only da of Sheriff John Colin McInnes, QC, of Parkneuk, Blebocraigs, Fife, — Charlotte Niamh, *b* 1975.

SISTER LIVING

Mary Frances, *b* 1947: *m* 1969, Julian Rupert Smithers, of Haversham Grange, Haversham, nr Milton Keynes, Bucks, and has issue living, William Rupert John, *b* 1973; *ed* —, — Louisa Jane, *b* 1971.

DAUGHTERS LIVING OF FOURTH BARONET

Valerie Anne, *b* 1936: *m* 1960, Benjamin Worthington (*see* E Aylesford, 1940 Edn), who *d* 1984, and has issue living, Greville Thomas, *b* 1963; *ed* Ampleforth: *m* 1995, Hon Sophia Mary Stapleton-Cotton, yr da of 5th Viscount Combermere, — Ursula, *b* 1962: *m* 1988, Capt (Archibald) Edward (Charles) Edmonstone, eldest son of Sir Archibald Bruce Charles Edmonstone, 7th Bt, — Lucy, *b* 1967: *m* 199—, Oliver Nigel Leatham, 2nd son of John Lawson Leatham, MBE, of Athens, and has issue living, Ben *b* 1996, Lily *b* 1997. *Residence* – Wood House, Brough Park, N Yorks. —— Alethea Jill Clare, *b* 1939. *Residence* – The Stallion Box, High Green, Catterick Village, N Yorks.

Sir William, 1st Bt, was son of John Wright, of Kelvedon, by Elizabeth, yr da of Sir John Lawson, 5th Bt (*cr* 1665), of Brough Hall, whose surname he assumed. Sir Henry Joseph Lawson, 3rd Bt, *m* 1899, Ursula Mary, who *d* 1960, only child and heir of Philip John Canning Howard, of Corby Castle, Cumberland, descended from Col Sir Francis Howard, of Corby Castle, son of Lord William Howard, 3rd son of 4th Duke of Norfolk, and yr brother of Sir Philip Howard, ancestor of the Earls of Carlisle.

Lawson-Tancred, see Tancred.

LEA (UK) 1892, of The Larches, Kidderminster, Worcestershire, and Sea Grove, Dawlish, Devon

Semper fidelis
Always faithful

Sir THOMAS WILLIAM LEA, 5th *Baronet*; *b* 6 Sept 1973; *s* his father, *Sir* (THOMAS) JULIAN, 1990; *ed* Uppingham.

𝕬rms – Or, a fesse indented gules, between in chief two lions passant of the second, in base a rock, thereon a beaver proper, spotted ermine, holding in the mouth a sprig of willow slipped vert. 𝕮rest – In front of a mount vert, thereon a demi-heraldic antelope argent, supporting a bird bolt erect or, three pheons fessewise sable.

BROTHERS LIVING

ALEXANDER JULIAN, *b* 28 Oct 1978; *ed* Oakham. —— Oliver David Pell, *b* 1983.

SISTERS LIVING AND DECEASED

Rebecca Barbara, *b* 1972. —— Henrietta Katherine, *b* 1976; *d* 1989.

AUNTS LIVING (*Daughters of 3rd baronet*)

Rosemary, *b* 1927. *Residence* – 1245 Park Av, New York, NY, USA. —— Philippa Margaret, *b* 1929: *m* 1960, Orlando Michael Philip Kenyon-Slaney (*see* B Kenyon, colls). *Residence* – Bachelors Cottage, High Halden, Ashford, Kent. —— Lavinia Ann, *b* 1932: *m* 1960, Andrew Bethell Marsden-Smedley (*see* B Westbury, colls, 1985 Edn), and has issue living, Robert Andrew, *b* 1962: *m* 1996, Claudia V. M., yr da of Wyndham Holmes Austen Knight, of Wakeford Farm House, Pamber End, Basingstoke, Hants, — William Bethell (Tower Hill House, Chaddleworth, Newbury, Berks), *b* 1964: *m* 1991, Alexandra G. B., elder da of John Kirkland, of Lochbie, Duddenhoe End, Saffron Walden, Essex, and has issue living, Alfred *b* 1997, Rosie *b* 1995. *Residence* – The Glebe House, Bayton, nr Kidderminster, Worcs.

WIDOWS LIVING OF THIRD AND FOURTH BARONETS

DIANA SILVA (*Diana, Lady Lea*), only da of James Howard Thompson, MIME, of Coton Hall, Bridgnorth, Shropshire, and formerly wife of Capt Guy William Bannar-Martin, IA: *m* 1950, as his 2nd wife, Sir Thomas Claude Harris Lea, 3rd Bt, who *d* 1985. *Residence* – Harp House, Lower Broad St, Ludlow, Shropshire.

GERRY VALERIE (*Lady Lea*), only da of late Capt Gibson Clarence Fahnestock, USAF: *m* 1970, Sir (Thomas) Julian Lea, 4th Bt, who *d* 1990.

COLLATERAL BRANCHES LIVING

Issue of late Wing Cdr Robert Francis Gore Lea, OBE, 2nd son of 2nd baronet, *b* 1906, *d* 1994: *m* 1st, 1939, Valerie Josephine, who *d* 1948, da of Lieut Sir James Henry Domville, RN, 5th Bt; 2ndly, 1956, Susan (Le Clos du Chemin, St Peter, Jersey, CI), da of late John Greenwood, of The Priory of Lady St Mary, Wareham, Dorset:—
(By 2nd *m*) Francis Rupert Chad (Duxford Mill, Cambridgeshire), *b* 1957; *ed* Eton: *m* 1987, Hon Susan Kinnaird, da of 13th Lord Kinnaird. —— (By 1st *m*) Annabel Ophelia Clare, *b* 1945: *m* 1973, Simon Ricketts, of 69 Fentiman Rd, SW8 1LH, and has issue living, Theo, *b* 1975, — Catriona, *b* 1977.

Issue of late John Sydney Birch Lea, 3rd son of 2nd baronet, *b* 1911, *d* 1984: *m* 1954, Elisabeth Edith Maunsell (Kemerton House, Crowle, Worcs), da of Lt-Col Philip Victor Willingham Gell, of Hopton Hall, Wirksworth, Derbyshire:—
Richard John Philip, *b* 1957: *m* 1990, Jane Hopkins. —— Sarah Caroline Aileen, *b* 1956: *m* 1st, 1986, Robin Greenshields (later Davenport Greenshields), of Davenport House, Worfield, Shropshire; 2ndly, 1991, Peter William Richard Sankey (*see* Milburn, Bt), of Cranmere, Worfield, nr Bridgnorth, Shropshire WV15 5LP, and has issue living (by 1st *m*), William John Peter, *b* 1988, — (by 2nd *m*) (*see* Milburn, Bt).

Grandson of late Rev Percy Harris Lea, yr son of 1st baronet:—
Issue of late George Francis Percivale Lea, *b* 1901, *d* 1987: *m* 1934, Maria, who *d* 1987, da of Wilhelm Schultz, of Vienna, and of Bratislava, Czechoslovakia:—
Francis William Peter, *b* 1944; *ed* Hill Sch, Pottstown, PA, USA, and Brown Univ, RI, USA; FCA: *m* 1977, Audrey Christine, da of Maurice Davison, of Cuckfield, Sussex. *Residence* – 129 High St, Berkhamsted, Herts HP4 2DJ.

William Butcher: *m* 1792, Elizabeth, da of Francis Lea, of Kidderminster. Their son, George Butcher Lea, assumed by Roy Licence 1834, the surname of Lea. His son, Sir Thomas Lea, of the Larches, Kidderminster, MP for Kidderminster, co Donegal and S Londonderry, was *cr* a Baronet 1892.

LECHMERE (UK) 1818, of The Rhydd, Worcestershire
(Name pronounced "Letchmere")

Christ in the pelican

Sir BERWICK HUNGERFORD LECHMERE, 6th *Baronet*; *b* 21 Sept 1917; *s* his father, *Capt Sir* RONALD BERWICK HUNGERFORD, 1965; *ed* Charterhouse, and Magdalene Coll, Camb; FRICS; JP and DL; High Sheriff of Worcs 1962; Vice-Lieut for co Hereford and Worcester 1977; CStJ: *m* 1st, 1952 (*m diss* 1954), Susan Adele Mary, only child of Cdr George Henry Maunsell-Smyth, RN; 2ndly, 1954, Norah Garrett, el da of late Col Christopher Garrett Elkington, DSO, DL, of The Moat House, Cutnall Green, Worcs.

𝕬rms – Gules, a fesse, and in chief two pelicans vulning themselves or. 𝕮rest – A pelican as in the arms.
Residence – Church End House, Hanley Castle, Worcester WR8 0BL.

SISTER LIVING

Joan Penelope Alice, *b* 1919.

COLLATERAL BRANCH LIVING

Issue of late Anthony Hungerford Lechmere, 3rd son of 3rd baronet, *b* 1868, *d* 1954: *m* 1920, Cicely Mary, who *d* 1964, da of late Rev Charles Bridges, R of Bredenbury, Herefordshire, and widow of William George Lupton, of The Green, Bromyard, Herefordshire:—
REGINALD ANTHONY HUNGERFORD (Primeswell, Evendine Lane, Colwall, nr Malvern, Worcs), *b* 24 Dec 1920; *ed* Charterhouse, and Trin Hall, Camb; formerly Capt 5th Roy Inniskilling Dragoon Guards: *m* 1956, Anne Jennifer, da of late A. C. Dind, of Orbe, Switzerland, and has issue living, Nicholas Anthony Hungerford, *b* 24 April 1960: *m* 1991, Caroline Jane, yr da of Lt-Col Gerald Patrick Gahan, of Tisbury, Wilts, and has issue living, Frederick Patrick Hungerford *b* 9 Dec 1992, George Nicholas Alfred *b* 1998, Charlotte *b* 199—, — Adam Francis, *b* 1962: *m* 1993, Rosalind G., 3rd da of Rt Rev Philip Harold Ernest Goodrich, DD, Bishop of Worcester, — Mark Edmund Dind, *b* 1966, — Jennifer Sarah, *b* 1959.

This family obtained lands at Hanley, Worcestershire, in the eleventh century, which have been in the family ever since. Sir Nicholas Lechmere, of Severn End, MP for Bewdley, was a Baron of the Exchequer temp William III. His grandson, Nicholas, sometime Solicitor and Attorney-General, Chancellor of the Duchy of Lancaster, was created Baron Lechmere of Evesham 1721. The 3rd baronet sat as MP for Tewkesbury (C) 1866-68, for Worcestershire W 1876-85, for Worcestershire W, or Bewdley Div 1885-92, and for Worcestershire S or Evesham Div 1892-94.

LEEDS (UK) 1812, of Croxton Park, Cambridgeshire

Vigilate!
Watch ye!

Sir CHRISTOPHER ANTHONY LEEDS, 8th *Baronet*, only child of late Maj Geoffrey Hugh Anthony Leeds, yr brother of 6th Baronet; *b* 31 Aug 1935; *s* his cousin, *Sir* GEORGE GRAHAM MORTIMER, 1983; *ed* King's Sch, Bruton, Lond Univ (BScEcon), and Univ of S California (MA): *m* 1974 (*m diss* 1980), Elaine Joyce, da of late Sq Ldr Cornelius Harold Albert Mullins.

𝕬rms – Argent, a fesse gules between three eagles displayed sable, within a bordure wavy of the second. 𝕮rest – A staff raguly vert, thereon a cock gules wings expanded, combed, wattled, beaked, and legged or, debruised by a bendlet wavy sinister ermine.
Address – University of Nancy II, 23 Blvd Albert 1er, BP 33-97, 54015 Nancy, France.
Residence – 7 Rue de Turique, 54000 Nancy, France. *Club* – Lansdowne.

DAUGHTERS LIVING AND DECEASED OF SEVENTH BARONET

Miranda Noel Winnaretta, *b* 1956: *m* 1980, Maxim Alexander Mackay-James, of Higher Wynford House, Wynford Eagle, Dorchester, Dorset DT2 0ET, yr son of late Lt-Cdr Peter M. Mackay-James, DSC, RN, of La Rochelle, Lake Alfred, Florida, USA, and has issue living, Thomas George Peter, *b* 1984, — Archie Alexander, *b* 1986. —— Anthea Jane, *b* 1958: *d* in Indonesia 1989. —— Harriet Annabelle, *b* 1962: *m* 1983, Maj Richard John Carrow, RGJ, only son of David Carrow, of Little Hill, Hartley Wintney, Hants, and has issue living, Anthony, *b* 19—, — Hugh David, *b* 1991, — Rozel Anthea, *b* (twin) 1991, — Eloise, *b* 1995.

DAUGHTER LIVING OF SIXTH BARONET

Rhodanthe Winnaretta, *b* 1929: *m* 1st, 1952, Ronald David Hutton, MC, late Capt RE, who *d* 1984; 2ndly, 1991, Cmdr Gerald M. B. Selous, OBE, VRD, JP, and has issue living (by 1st *m*), Matthew Charles Arthur (Broom Farm, Chedgrave,

Norwich NR14 6BQ), *b* 1953; *ed* Eton, and Ch Ch, Oxford (MA); Solicitor and Tax Consultant: *m* 1984, Anne Elizabeth Caroline, elder da of Leslie Leppard, of Axminster, Devon, and has issue living, David Thomas Charles *b* 1988, Victoria Emily Louise *b* 1986, Alexandra Charlotte Kate *b* 1990, — Deborah Helen, *b* 1955; *ed* Benenden, and York Univ; journalist: *m* 1984, Charles David Sandys Stebbings, of 21 Highbury Terrace, N5 1UP, son of late David Stebbings, of Wapping Pierhead, E1, and has issue living, Archie David *b* 1987, Frederick Mortimer Lincolne *b* 1996, Romilly Paris (da) *b* 1989, Eleanor Clemency *b* 1993, — (Cecilia) Paris, *b* (twin) 1955; *ed* Bedgebury Park; schoolteacher: *m* 1982, Nigel Quarles Back, FCA, of Washingford House, Bergh Apton, Norfolk NR15 1AA, and has issue living, Charles *b* 1986, Emma *b* 1984, Katherine *b* 1988, — Louisa Winn (74 Ledbury Rd, W11), *b* 1957; *ed* Benenden, Bristol Univ and AA; architect: *m* 1991, Matthias Friedrich Sauerbruch. *Residence* – Langley Grange, Langley, Norwich, Norfolk, NR14 6BL.

COLLATERAL BRANCHES LIVING

Granddaughter of late Henry Leeds, 2nd son of 2nd baronet:—
Issue of late Edward Adderley Oglander Leeds, *b* 1869, *d* 1923: *m* 1895, a da of R. F. Vevers, of Hereford:—
Vera Mary, *b* 1898.

Grandchildren of late William Henry Montagu Leeds, eldest son of late Capt William Montagu Leeds, 3rd son of 2nd baronet:—
Issue of late Aubrey Leeds, *b* 1903, *d* 1992: *m* 1933, Barbara, who *d* 1994, only child of J. Travis, of Lightcliffe, Yorks:—
ANTONY HILDYARD *b* 15 Dec 1937: *m* 1966 (*m diss* 1973), Elizabeth Helen Cornell, of Toronto. —— Sally Gillian *b* 1936: *m* 1961, John A. Nation, BSc, PhD, and has issue living, Phllip David Oliver, *b* 1962, — Robert James Anthony, *b* 1964. —— Sharman, *b* 1953.

Grandchildren of late Charles Frederick Augustus Leeds, 3rd son of late Capt William Montagu Leeds (ante):—
Issue of late Charles Hildyard Denham Leeds, *b* 1902, *d* 1975: *m* 1940, Merran Elizabeth (Box 927, Claresholm, Alberta T0L 0T0, Canada), da of late J. H. Drew, of Kitscoty, Alberta, Canada:—
John Charles Hildyard (408 Ranch Estates Bay, NW, Calgary, Alberta, T3G 1T6 Canada), *b* 1941; BSc, Civil Eng: *m* 1965, Eileen Rose, da of late Joseph F. Shalka, of Fort Kent, Alberta, and has issue living, Michael John Hildyard, *b* 1975, — Diane Katherine, *b* 1967: *m* 1992, Rodney Orr, — Brenda Merran, *b* 1971. —— Charles Eric Montagu (Box 927, Claresholm, Alberta T0L 0T0, Canada), *b* 1945: *m* 1971, Patricia Marlene, da of Irwin E. Brown, of Stavely, Alberta, and has issue living, Montagu Charles, *b* 1975, — Shayne Irwin, *b* 1977, — Cameron Wesley, *b* 1981. —— James Douglas Logie (Box 42, Claresholm, Alberta T0L 0T0, Canada), *b* 1948: *m* 1972, Irene Mary, da of J. R. Hughes, of Longview, Alberta, and has issue living, Anthony Hildyard, *b* 1975, — Christopher James, *b* (twin) 1975, — Mark Douglas, *b* 1983, — Paula Marie, *b* 1978. —— Helen Merran, *b* 1951; BSc Pharmacy.

Issue of late Eric Edward Leeds, *b* 1907, *d* 1994: *m* 1934, Freda Foster:—
Jacqueline May, *b* 1935: *m* 1955, Robert Radleigh Hugh Tatham, and has issue living, Roderick Hugh, *b* 1958, — Catherine Ann, *b* 1956, — Carolyn Jill, *b* 1960, — Susan Margaret, *b* 1963.

Granddaughter of late Edward Montagu Leeds, 5th son of 1st baronet:—
Issue of late Lieut-Col Thomas Louis Leeds, CMG, DSO, *b* 1869, *d* 1926: *m* 1904, Clara Guion, who *d* 1940, da of Lieut-Col Henry S. Kilbourne, US Army:—
Sylvia Guion, *b* 1914: *m* 1943, Douglas Campbell Ward-Campbell, who *d* 1976, and has issue living, Iain Gordon Leeds (12 Rossett Green Lane, Harrogate, Yorks), *b* 1944; *ed* Marlborough, and Trin Coll, Camb (MA); FCA: *m* 1966, Christine Mary, da of late Dr Bernard Clive Nicholson, of Harrogate, and has issue living, Robert Iain Nicol *b* 1969: *m* 1993, Diane Jennifer Martin, Gordon James *b* 1970: *m* 1995, Catherine Clare Veltman, David Leeds *b* 1975, Andrew Douglas Clive *b* 1979, John Alexander *b* 1981, Mary Sylvia Frances *b* 1973, — Nicholas Carlton Guion (47 Brewster Place, Cambridge, Ontario, Canada), *b* 1947; *ed* Marlborough: *m* 1973, Dorothee Anastasia, who *d* 1997, only da of Wasyl Pikula, of Cambridge, Ontario, Canada, and has issue living, Belinda Maria Sylvia *b* 1977, Kimberley Meghann Leeds *b* 1979. *Residence* – 37 Church Square Mansions, Harrogate, Yorks.

Sir George William Leeds, 1st Bt, of Croxton Park, Cambs, was Equerry to the Duke of Sussex. The manor of Croxton was purchased by an ancestor of this family about 1568.

LEES (UK) 1804, of Blackrock, Dublin

I have accomplished

EXEGI

AN HONEST MAN'S THE NOBLEST WORK OF GOD

Sir THOMAS HARCOURT IVOR LEES, 8th *Baronet*; *b* 6 Nov 1941; *s* his father, *Sir* CHARLES ARCHIBALD EDWARD IVOR, 1963; no information concerning this baronet has been received since 1970.

Arms – Azure, a fesse checky argent and sable, between six cross-crosslets fitchée, three in the chief and three in the nombril points or, and three billets, two in the honour and one in the base, points of the second. Crest – A dexter hand couped above the wrist and erect proper, grasping a crescent or.

DAUGHTER LIVING OF FIFTH BARONET

Mary Helen, *b* 1928: *m* 1949, David Stuart Hahn, and has issue living, Stuart Arthur, *b* 1949, — Harold Daniel, *b* 1953. *Address* – 3 Valsayn Av, Valsayn Park, Curepe, Trinidad.

COLLATERAL BRANCHES LIVING

Issue of late Edwin Leslie Lees, 4th son of 4th baronet, *b* 1866, *d* 1937: *m* 1900, Annie, who *d* 1961, da of Jabez Charlton, of Southall, Middlesex:—
Josephine Edwina Agnes, *b* 1917: *m* 1940, Edmund Ross Spencer, who *d* 1942.

Grandchildren of late John Cathcart Lees, son of Cathcart Lees, MD, son of 2nd son of 1st baronet:—
Issue of late John Rutherfoord D'OLIER-LEES, *b* 1887, *d* 1972: *m* 1923, Margery, who *d* 1975, da of Thomas H. Scott, of Sunderland:—
JOHN CATHCART (The Cottage, Southampton Rd, Ringwood, Hants BH24 1JD), *b* 12 Nov 1927; formerly Lt 2nd Bn Border Regt and SAS Regt (Artists Rifles) TA: *m* 1957, Wendy Garrold, yr da of late Brian Garrold Groom, of Craig Elm, Eskbank, nr Edinburgh, and has issue living, Trevor John Cathcart, *b* 1961: *m* 1990, Susan Ciambriello, and has issue living, Isabella Rutherfoord *b* 1998, — James Scott Lewis, *b* 1963. —— Edmund Campbell (Lapley Farmhouse, Coaley, Dursley, Glos), *b* 1929; FCA: *m* 1960, Hilary Vernon, da of John Harbord, of Englewick, Englefield Green, Surrey, and has issue living, Robert Arthur Campbell, *b* 1963, — Caroline Margery, *b* 1961: *m* 1990, Richard James Dean, and has issue living, Edward James *b* 1992, Sophie Catherine *b* 1994, — Deborah Helen, *b* 1962. —— Elizabeth, *b* 1925: *m* 1956, Geoffrey John Martin, of Flagstones, Brattlewood, Sevenoaks, Kent TN13 1QS, and has issue living, Timothy John Hoit, *b* 1958: *m* 19—, Merryn Blacklock, and has issue living, Thomas Geoffrey Hoit *b* 1986, Lisa Adele *b* 1984, Catherine Lee *b* 1989, — Robin Geoffrey, *b* 1959. —— Helen Campbell (15c Whittingstall Rd, Parsons Green, SW6), *b* 1926.

Grandchildren of late John Rutherfoord D'OLIER-LEES (ante):—
Issue of late Thomas Rutherfoord D'OLIER-LEES, *b* 1931, *d* 1984: *m* 1960, Anne Elizabeth (Old Post Office, Oving, nr Chichester, Sussex), da of William Simpson Dalgetty, MB, ChB, of 1 Polwarth Terr, Edinburgh 11:—
Guy Rutherfoord, *b* 1962. —— Mark Angus, *b* 1964. —— Catherine Anne, *b* 1966. —— Julia Elizabeth, *b* 1968.

Grandchildren of late Edward Lees, 2nd son of William Eden Lees, 5th son of 1st baronet:—
Issue of late Harcourt Lees, *b* 1843, *d* 1939: *m* 1867, Mary Masey, who *d* 1914, da of Joseph Burke, formerly of The Lodge, Templemore:—
Harcourt Edward, *b* 1884: *m* 1961, Eileen, widow of Edward Byron de Lacy. *Residence* – Flat 25, Brunswick Manor, Bangor, co Down. —— Ethel Sophia Harriet Western.

Granddaughter of late Thomas Orde Hastings Lees, only son of late Rev John Lees, el son of late Thomas Orde Lees, 6th son of 1st baronet:—
Issue of late Lt-Col Thomas Orde Hans Lees, OBE, AFC, *b* 1877; *d* 1958: *m* 1st, 1902, Rhoda Isabel, who *d* 1930, da of late P. Musgrave, and widow of R. Lovat Fraser; 2ndly, 1932, Ellaline Hisako:—
(By 2nd *m*) Zoe Orde Eloise, *b* 1936.

Sir John Lees, 1st Bt, son of Adam Lees of Cumnock, Ayrshire, distinguished himself with the British troops in Germany under the Marquess of Granby. He was afterwards successively Usher of the Black Rod, Secretary of War, and Secretary to the Post Office in Ireland.

LEES (UK) 1897, of South Lytchett Manor, Lytchett Minster, Dorset

Sir THOMAS EDWARD LEES, 4th *Baronet*; *b* 31 Jan 1925; *s* his father, *Col Sir*
JOHN VICTOR ELLIOTT, DSO, MC, 1955; *ed* Eton, and Magdalene Coll, Camb;
is a JP for Dorset, High Sheriff 1960; European War 1943-5 as Aircraftsman
RAF (wounded): *m* 1949, Faith Justin, who *d* 1996, only da of George
Gaston Jessiman, OBE, of Swaynes Living, Great Durnford, Wilts, and has
issue.

Arms – Per chevron dovetail argent and gules, in chief two millrinds sable, and in base an
owl of the first. **Crest** – On a millrind fessewise sable an owl argent.
Residence – Post Green, Lytchett Minster, Dorset.

*Without haste, without
rest*

SON LIVING

CHRISTOPHER JAMES (Race Farm, Lytchett Minster, Poole, Dorset BH16 6BB), *b* 4 Nov 1952;
ed Eton, and Edin Univ (BSc 1976); Royal Wessex Yeo: *m* 1st, 1977 (*m diss* 1988), Jennifer,
da of John Wyllie, of Newton Stewart, Wigtownshire; 2ndly, 1989, Clare, da of Austen
Young, FRCS, of Sheffield and Ynyslas, and has issue living (by 2nd *m*), John, *b* 1992, —
Edward, *b* 1997, — Gabriel (da), *b* 1990, — Rosamund, *b* 1994.

DAUGHTERS LIVING

Sarah Margaret, *b* 1951: *m* 1979, John Marcus Omond, and has issue living, Marcus James Mucha, *b* 1979, — Andrew
Simon Mucha *b* 1981, — Tamsin, *b* 1984. —— Bridget Selina, *b* 1954: *m* 1976, Martin Christopher Green, of Kitcher-
mans, Huntick Rd, Lytchett Minster, Dorset, and has issue living, Thomas Andrew, *b* 1978, — Alice Hannah, *b* 1981.
—— Elizabeth Jane, *b* 1957.

SISTERS LIVING

Rosamund Elizabeth, *b* 1921: *m* 1943, Prof Dominick Conway, MD, FRCP, DCH, who *d* 1989, and has issue living, James
Robin, *b* 1945, — Oliver Patrick, *b* 1951, — Bryony May, *b* 1946, — Dawn Madeline, *b* 1948, — Alison Elizabeth, *b* 1949,
— Diana Rosemary, *b* 1956, — Florentia Anne, *b* 1959, — Emily Rosamund, *b* 1960. *Residence* – 1822 Elm Ridge Drive,
Gloucester, Ontario, Canada. —— (Benita) Anne, *b* 1923: *m* 1949, Lt-Col John Anthony Sandbach Barkworth, 3rd
Carabiniers, of Sackville Cottage, Sackville St, Winterborne Kingston, Dorset, and has issue living, Anthony Julian Sand-
bach, *b* 1955: *m* 1985, Catherine, da of Bruce Barnard, of New Zealand, — Primrose Madeline, *b* 1951: *m* 1974, Jonathan
Oscar Cyril Dewhurst, of Barmere, Whitchurch, Shropshire, and has issue living, Anthony John *b* 1978, Anastasia *b* 1977,
— Clare Helena (c/o World Bank Mission, PO Box 50268, Lusaka, Zambia), *b* 1953: *m* 1995, Adam Jonothon Pope.
—— Jane Madeline (Jarvis, Lytchett Minster, Dorset), *b* 1926: *m* 1st, 1946 (*m diss* 1962), Sq Ldr Simon Hugh Kevill-
Davies, RAF (*dec*); 2ndly, 1966 (*m diss* 1971), Michael Vaughan Brian, DSc (*dec*), and has issue living, (by 1st *m*) Hugh
John *b* 1948, — Sheila Anne, *b* 1950: *m* 1979 (*m diss* 1997), Patric Morrissey, of South View, Pleck, Marnhull, Dorset
DT10 1NY, and has issue living, Benita Jo *b* 1980, Jessica Gabriel *b* 1982, Annie Jane *b* 1985, — Benita Jane *b* 1954: *m*
1985, Thomas Francis Coningham Denny, and has issue (*see* Denny, Bt, *cr* 1782).

COLLATERAL BRANCH LIVING

Granddaughters of late Capt Bernard Percy Turnbull Lees, MC (infra):—
Issue of late Michael Lees, late Capt The Queen's Own Dorset Yeo and SOE, author *The Rape of Serbia* (1990),
b 1921, *d* 1992: *m* 1944, Gwendolen (Portman Place, Blandford Forum, Dorset), elder da of late (Edgar) Stanley
Johnson, of Meadowside, Twickenham:—
Christine Mary, *b* 1946; Bar Inner Temple 1967: *m* 1966, Antonio de Padua Jose Maria Bueno, QC, of 12 Canning Place
Mews, W8 5AJ, and has issue living, Nicola Anna Christina, *b* 1967: *m* 1992, Jonathon Richard Brill, and has issue living,
Jake Jonathon Antonio *b* 1998, — Julia Catherine Mary, *b* 1972, — Emily Antonia Mercedes, *b* 1988. —— Michèle Anne,
b 1954.

Issue of late Capt Bernard Percy Turnbull Lees, MC, 3rd son of 1st baronet, *b* 1891, *d* 1922: *m* 1919,
Mary, who *d* 1980, da of late Col Philip John Joseph Radcliffe, CMG (*see* Radcliffe, Bt, colls, 1980
Edn):—
Bernadette Mary, *b* (*posthumous*) 1923; formerly 3rd Officer WRNS; Master of Applied Psychology, Clinical and
Educational, Murdoch Univ, Western Australia 1981: *m* 1st, 1943, Fl-Lt Richard Osborne Curtis, RAFVR (*ka* 1944); 2ndly,
1956, Lt-Col Gordon Robin Kingston Lyon, OBE, 3rd Carabiniers, of Lot 9, Wilderness Rd, Margaret River, W Aust 6285,
and has issue living (by 2nd *m*) Kim Philip, *b* 1960.

The 1st baronet, Sir Elliott Lees, DSO, sat as MP for Oldham (C) 1886-1892, and for Birkenhead 1894-1906, and served
during S African War 1900-1901. The 2nd baronet, Sir Thomas Evans Keith Lees, Lieut Dorset Yeo, was *ka* 1915. The
3rd bronet, Sir John Victor Elliott Lees, DSO, MC, was Lt-Col KRRC and subsequently Col Comdg 5th Batn Dorset
Regt, and was twice wounded during European War 1914-18.

LEES (UK) 1937, of Longdendale, co Chester

Sir (WILLIAM) ANTONY CLARE LEES, 3rd *Baronet; b* 14 June 1935; *s* his father, *Sir* WILLIAM HEREWARD CLARE, 1976; *ed* Eton, and Magdalene Coll, Camb (MA): *m* 1986, Joanna Olive Crane.

Arms – Sable, two bars argent, on a chief of the last a garb or, between two roses gules, barbed and seeded proper. Crest – Upon a rock proper, a lion rampant gules, supporting a flagstaff, also proper, flowing therefrom a banner sable, charged with a garb or.

SISTER LIVING

Jennifer Dorothy Clare, *b* 1932: *m* 1953, John Benn Arnold Wallinger, of Beechland Farmhouse, Newick, Sussex BN8 4RX, and has issue living, John Christopher Arnold, *b* 1956, — Timothy Hereward Arnold, *b* 1960, — Vanessa Jennifer Clare, *b* 1962.

AUNT LIVING (*Daughter of 1st baronet*)

Enid Clare, *b* 1901.

The 1st baronet, Sir (William) Clare Lees, OBE, LLD (son of late William Lees, of Birkdale), was Chm of Bleachers' Asso, Ltd, Dep Chm of Martins Bank, and Chm of Martins Bank, Ltd (Manchester Board).

PERGE·SED·CAUT

Go on, but cautiously

LEESE (UK) 1908, of Send Holme, Send, Surrey (Extinct 1979)

Sir ALEXANDER WILLIAM LEESE, 4th and last *Baronet; d* 1979.

COLLATERAL BRANCH LIVING

Granddaughters of late Vernon Francis Leese, OBE, 2nd son of 1st baronet:-
Issue of late John Henry Vernon Leese (in previous editions erroneously described as having *s* his cousin, Sir Alexander William Leese, 4th Bt, who in fact outlived him), *b* 1901, *d* 1970: *m* 1939, Mrs Norah Collins Lightfoot, who *d* 1991, da of late John Joseph Carter, of The Old Bells, Hordle, Lymington, Hants, and formerly wife of Arthur Thomas Churchill Lightfoot:-
Pamela Margaret, *b* 1935: *m* 1958, Peter Edmund Pike, of 68 Parkfield Rd, Taunton, Som, and has issue living, David Steven, *b* 1960, — Heather Christine, *b* 1963: *m* 1991, Michael Patrick Mcmenamin, and has issue living, Sean James *b* 1989, Hayley Elizabeth *b* 1992, — Linda Carol, *b* 1968: *m* 1991, Leonard Mark Harris, and has issue living, Jack William *b* 1993, Joseph Peter *b* 1999, Katherine Jane *b* 1996. —— Daphne Ann, *b* 1937: *m* 1st, 1957, Arthur George Henry Taviner, who *d* 1984; 2ndly, 1988, Samuel Lionel James Godwin, of 36 Dane Rise, Winsley, Bradford-on-Avon, Wilts BA15 2ND, and has issue living (by 1st *m*), Susan Wendy, *b* 1958: *m* 1979 (*m diss* 1992), Michael Bartlett, and has issue living, Kevin Mark *b* 1981, Shaun Matthew *b* 1983, — Pauline Mary, *b* 1961: *m* 1980, Roger Edward Foote, and has issue living, Samantha Pauline *b* 1984, Penny Elizabeth *b* 1990. —— Iris Joan, *b* 1943: *m* 1st, 1963 (*m diss* 1981), John Robert Falcon; 2ndly, 1993, Richard Earl Bailey, of Old Brick Yard Farm, Penny Hill, Holbeach, Spalding, Lincs, and has issue living (by 1st husband), Michael John, *b* 1967, — Deborah Grace, *b* 1964: *m* 1989, Ian James Brindley, and has issue living, Max James *b* 1995, Joe Michael *b* 1998, Faye Elizabeth *b* (twin) 1998, — Alison Helen, *b* 1965: *m* 1990, Anthony Clive Michael, — (by 2nd husband), Laura Jessica Mary, *b* 1982.

le FLEMING (E) 1705, of Rydal, Westmorland

Sir DAVID KELLAND LE FLEMING, 13th *Baronet*; *b* 12 Jan 1976; *s* his father, *Sir* QUENTIN JOHN, 1995.

Arms – Gules, a fret argent. **Crest** – A serpent nowed holding in its mouth a garland of olive and vine all proper.
Residence – 147 Stanford St, Ashhurst, NZ.

BROTHER LIVING

ANDREW JOHN, *b* 4 Oct 1979.

SISTER LIVING

Josephine Kay, *b* 1973.

Pax, copia, sapientia

Peace, plenty, wisdom

UNCLES LIVING (*sons of 11th baronet*)

Peter Douglas (11 Lowestoft Place, Palmerston North, NZ), *b* 1958. —— Murray Kelland, *b* 1960.

AUNTS LIVING (*daughters of 11th baronet*)

Rosemary Lynette, *b* 1951: *m* 1975, Howard Asplin, of 316 Ruahine St, Palmerston North, NZ, and has issue living, Steven, *b* 1977, — Blair, *b* 1979, — Neil, *b* 1982. —— Elaine Dawn, *b* 1953: *m* 1980, John Buchanan (*see* Miller, Bt, *cr* 1705, 1980 Edn), of Mayfield, RD9, Feilding, NZ, and has issue living, Timothy, *b* 1983, — Richard, *b* 1986. —— Marie Louise, *b* 1955. —— Vicki Karin, *b* 1964: *m* 1989, Roger Whitmore, of 15 Aquarius Drive, Rotorua, NZ, and has issue living, Matthew William James, *b* 1994, — Ashleigh Simone, *b* 1998.

GREAT UNCLES LIVING (*sons of 10th baronet*)

Gordon Halsey (78 Ngatai St, RD Manaia, Taranaki, NZ), *b* 1925: *m* 1962, Lorna Margorie, da of Ronald Felthorn Trim, of Trimoana, RD Eltham NZ, and has issue living, Mark Ronald Felthorn, *b* 1965: *m* 1989, Brigitt Taisesa, da of Joseph Martin Sidler, of 121 Fairfield Rd, Hawera, S Taranaki, NZ, and has issue living, David Andra *b* 1993, Sheree Isobel *b* 1990, Renee Elizabeth *b* 1995. —— Roderick Gordon Hudleston, *b* 1970: *m* 1994, Cheran L., da of John T. Bakewell, of 36 Domett St, Chunake, Taranaki, NZ, — Ruth Maree, *b* 1963: *m* 1983, Gary Francis Brieseman, son of Ian Brieseman, of 2 Buchanan St, Hawera, S Taranaki, NZ, and has issue living, John Gordon *b* 1990, Hannah Maree *b* 1992, Sarah Jean *b* 1993, — Helen Lorna, *b* 1964: *m* 1989, Michael Patrick Kowalewski, son of Michael Patrick Kowalewski, — Alison Halsey, *b* 1967: *m* 1989, Peter John Bishop, son of Ross Bishop, of 196 Cross Rd, RD24, Midhurst, Stratford, Central Taranaki, NZ, and has issue living, Brendan John *b* 1990, Kelly May *b* 1992. —— Lindsay Craig (31 Whakapaki St, PO Box 108, Urenui, NZ), *b* 1927: *m* 1955, Jean Irene, da of Francis Gordon Campbell, of Patea, Taranaki, NZ, and has had issue, John Fraser, *b* 1958: *m* 1997, Linda, da of Barry Hoskin, of Taranaki, NZ, and has issue living, Suzy Kate *b* 1999, – Hugh Vincent, *b* 1959: *m* 1984, Darla Michelle, da of Graham Barnard, of Hawera, NZ, and has issue living, Emerald May *b* 1988, Aimee Rachael *b* 1991, Irene Jade *b* 1994, — Frances Mary, *b* 1956, — Annette Isabel, *b* 1963, *d* 1998, — Louise Joy, *b* 1969: *m* 1995, Andrew Colin Smith, son of Colin Smith, of Auckland, NZ, and has issue living, Fraser le Fleming, *b* 1999.

WIDOW LIVING OF ELEVENTH BARONET

NOVEEN AVIS (*Noveen, Lady le Fleming*), da of Clarence Charles Sharpe, of Rukuhia, Hamilton, NZ: *m* 1948, Sir William Kelland le Fleming, 11th Bt, who *d* 1988. *Residence* – c/o Palmerston North Retirement Village, Box 624, RD6, Palmerston North, NZ.

WIDOW LIVING OF TWELFTH BARONET

JUDITH ANN (*Lady le Fleming*), da of C. J. Peck, JP, of Ashhurst, Manawatu, NZ: *m* 1971, Sir Quentin John le Fleming, 12th Bt, who *d* 1995. *Residence* – 147 Stanford St, Ashhurst, NZ.

COLLATERAL BRANCH LIVING

Grandchildren of late Richard Thomas le Fleming, son of late William le Fleming, 2nd son of 6th baronet:—
Issue of late Richard Henry Edward le Fleming, *b* 1892, *d* 1960: *m* 1918, Mabel Gladys (of 151, Seaview Rd, Westown, New Plymouth, New Zealand), da of Henry Parslow:—
Albert Edward (3 Kauri St, Inglewood, NZ), *b* 1923; European War 1939-45 with Roy New Zealand Air Force: *m* 1946, Eileen Ellen, da of John Moffet, and has issue living, Richard John (289 Old Te-kuiti Rd, Otorohanga, NZ), *b* 1953: *m* 1976, Yvonne Leanne, da of Owen Bulter, and has issue living, Nathan John *b* 1978, Jared Paul *b* 1980, Daniel Richard *b* 1985, — Judith Merle, *b* 1949: *m* 19—, Paul Eric Scown, of 380 Upper Durham Rd, Inglewood, NZ, and has issue living, Darren Matthew *b* 1967, Kylie Jane *b* 1971: *m* 1997, Murray Owen Cameron, son of Owen Bruce Cameron, of 110 Pembroke St, New Plymouth, NZ (and has issue living, Kristian Cole *b* 1998). —— Noala Doris, *b* 1920: *m* 1942, Raymond Peterson, and has issue living, Janice Margaret, *b* 1945, — Fay Maralyn, *b* 1948. *Residence* - Manutake, Hawera, New Zealand.

This family claims to be descended from Sir Michael le Fleming, of Furness living in 1127. The Visitation of Westmorland 1665 carried the pedigree down to Sir Daniel Fleming of Rydal Hall, Cumberland, father of 1st baronet. The 1st baronet sat as MP for Westmorland 1696-1707, and the 2nd baronet was Bishop of Carlisle 1734-47.

LEGARD (E) 1660, of Ganton, Yorkshire

By the cross to heaven

Sir CHARLES THOMAS LEGARD, 15th *Baronet*; *b* 26 Oct 1938; *s* his father, *Sir* THOMAS DIGBY, 1984; *ed* Eton: *m* 1st, 1962, Elizabeth, da of late John M. Guthrie, of Church Meadows, Hutton Buscel, Scarborough; 2ndly, 1987, Caroline Sarah, da of late Maj Arthur Ralph Kingsley Weston, of Howlet Hall, Sleights, Whitby, Yorks, and has issue by 1st *m*.

𝕬rms – Argent, on a bend between six mullets pierced of the field gules, a cross-patée or. Crest – A greyhound passant or, collared sable, studded argent. *Seat* – Scampston Hall, Malton, N Yorks.

SONS LIVING (*By 1st marriage*)

CHRISTOPHER JOHN CHARLES, *b* 19 April 1964; *ed* Eton: *m* 1986, Miranda M., da of Maj Edward Fane Travers Gaffney, of Crossbank Hill, Hurworth, co Durham (*see* Feilden, Bt, colls), and has issue living, Benjamin Fane John, *b* 12 May 1995. *Residence* – Grizzlefield House, Felixkirk Rd, Thirsk, N Yorks YO7 2ED. —— Edward Thomas, *b* 1966; Capt The Light Dragoons: *m* 1993, Lucy F., eldest da of Ivone Peter Kirkpatrick, of Donhead St Andrew, Dorset, and has issue living, Oliver Robert, *b* 1995, — Alexander Thomas, *b* 1999, — Celia Mary, *b* 1996. *Residence* – The Manor House, Whitwell-on-the-Hill, York YO6 7JJ.

DAUGHTER LIVING (*By 1st marriage*)

Louise Elizabeth, *b* 1969.

BROTHERS LIVING

William Robert (Lowthorpe Lodge, Lowthorpe, Driffield, Yorks), *b* 1943; *ed* Eton, and Roy Agric Coll, Cirencester: *m* 1st, 1967, Sally Ann, da of late W. H. Craig; 2ndly, 1978, Helen, only da of late R. Geoffrey Le-Pine, of Little Driffield, Yorks, and has issue living, (by 2nd *m*) Arabella Mary Elaine, *b* 1978, — Victoria Helen, *b* 1980. —— James Digby (The Mill Farmhouse, Wintringham, Malton, N Yorks YO17 8HW), *b* 1946; *ed* Eton: *m* 1969, Daphne Jane, el da of Denis West, of Belgrave Lodge, Chester, and has issue living, Thomas James St Quintin, *b* 1971; *ed* St Edward's Oxford, and RAC Cirencester, — Sophie Jane, *b* 1973.

COLLATERAL BRANCHES LIVING

Issue of late William Ernest Legard, F/O RAF, yst son of 13th baronet, *b* 1911, *ka* 1940: *m* 1939, Alice (Appleton House, Appleton-le-Street, Malton, Yorks, who *m* 2ndly, 1943, Col Basil Perry Beale, OBE, MC, DL, who *d* 1967), da of Hon George Ellis Vestey (*see* B Vestey, colls):—
Anne, *b* 1940: *m* 1st, 19—, Frank Curtis Luckow; 2ndly, 1965, Harry O'theil Seymour, and has issue living, (by 1st *m*) William Frank, *b* 1962, — Laura *b* 1963, — (by 2nd *m*) Donna Anne, *b* 1966: *m* 1992, Michael Whiteside, and has issue living, Siena Katherine Seymour *b* 1993.

Granddaughter of late Col Sir James Digby Legard, KCB, el son of late Capt James Anlaby Legard, RN, el son of late Rev William Legard, 4th son of 5th baronet:—
Issue of late Col Alfred Digby Legard, CBE, *b* 1878, *d* 1939: *m* 1902, Winifred (who *d* 1962, having *m* 2ndly, 1947, as his second wife, Maj-Gen George Henry Addison, CB, CMG, DSO, who *d* 1964), only da of late Col Sir William George Morris, KCMG, CB:—
Diana, *b* 1918: *m* 1950, John Percival Wheeler, and has issue living, Michael John, *b* 1952, — Bridget Diana, *b* 1954: *m* 1983, Michael Wood, son of Brig R. B. P. Wood, of Leverstock Green, Herts, and has issue living, Patrick Michael Olive *b* 1991, Rebecca Diana *b* 1989. *Residence* – Bockingfold, near Marden, Kent.

Granddaughters of late Lieut George Percy Legard, RN, 2nd son of late Col Sir James Digby Legard, KCB (ante):—
Issue of late Lt-Col Charles Percy Digby Legard, *b* 1906, *d* 1980: *m* 1934, Gertrude Kate, who *d* 1969, da of Arthur Thomson, late of Heathside, Wimbledon Common, SW, and Java:—
Sarah Anthea, *b* 1939: *m* 1966, Capt Malcolm James Sherwin, Queen's Own Hussars, and has issue living, Simon Patrick, *b* 1967, — Amanda Kate, *b* 1969. —— Dinah Annabel (Stearsby Hagg Farm, Stearsby, York), *b* 1941: *m* 1964 (*m diss* 1984), James Harrison Holt (*see* Reckitt, Bt, ext), and has issue living, Philip James Harrison, *b* 1965: *m* 1990, M. Jane

R., eldest da of Ewan Harper, of Titchmarsh, Northampton, — Michael Vernon Charles, *b* 1966, — Elizabeth Rebecca, *b* 1969. —— Lavinia Anlaby, *b* 1944: *m* 1982, Robin George Newman (*see* E Clarendon, 1971 Edn).

Grandson of late Col Sir James Digby Legard, KCB (ante):—
Issue of late Richard Anlaby Legard, *b* 1880, *d* 1973: *m* 1929, Dorice, who *d* 1976, da of late Harold Ostler, of Hull:—
Richard Digby (Apartado 110, Garrucha, Almeria, Spain), *b* 1930: *m* 1st, 1966 (*m diss* 1975), Mrs Jean H. Dodd, of York; 2ndly, 1985, Joan Frances Hall, da of late Francis Johnson Flynn, and has issue living (by 1st *m*), James Richard Anlaby, *b* 1967; *ed* Worksop, and RMA Sandhurst.

Grandsons of late Rev Francis Digby Legard, son of late George Legard, el son of late Digby Legard, 5th son of 5th baronet :—
Issue of late Brig-Gen D'Arcy Legard, CMG, DSO, *b* 1873, *d* 1953: *m* 1908, Lady Edith Margaret Emily Mary Foljambe, who *d* 1962, da of 1st Earl of Liverpool (*cr* 1905):—
Antony Ronald, MBE, *b* 1912; *ed* Winchester, and Trin Coll, Oxford; formerly Maj RE (TA); 1939-45 War (MBE); MBE (Mil) 1940: *m* 1946, Maud, da of Clifford Schwabe, of Cuddington Grange, Northwich, Ches, and has issue living, Simon Littledale (Codd Hall, Common Lane, South Cave, Brough, N Humberside), *b* 1947: *m* 1971, Heather Temperton, and has issue living, Richard Simon *b* 1976, Helen Louise *b* 1974, — David Antony, *b* 1953, — Diana May, *b* 1950. *Residence* – Fairway, Delamere, Northwich, Ches. —— Peter Herbert, *b* 1917; *ed* Shrewsbury, and Edinburgh Univ; late Lt Lanarkshire Yeo: *m* 1959, Brenda Valerie, only da of late Lt-Col Stanley Kidd, TD, DL, of Harcsgill, Penrith, Cumbria, and has issue living, Jonathan Antony (9 Bridgman Rd, W4 5BA), *b* 1961; *ed* Shrewsbury, Leeds Univ (BA), and Peterhouse, Camb; BBC Sports Commentator: *m* 1996, Katharine Sally Wenlock, only da of Wing Cdr Christopher Clive Chacksfield, of Windwhistle, Bourne End, Bucks, and has issue living, Piers Benjamin Antony *b* 1999, — Edith Veronica Jane *b* 1964. *Residence* – 11 Glan Aber Park, Chester, CH4 8LE.

Grandchildren of late Rev Charles Legard, MC (infra):—
Issue of late Lt-Cdr George Hugo Digby Legard, MBE, RN, *b* 1920, *d* 1966: *m* 1944, Eve Lilian (who *m* 2ndly, 1973, Guy Alexander Hughes, of Winchelsea Cottage, 7 Bells Lane, Tenterden, Kent TN30 6ES), da of late Capt Francis Howard, DSC, RN:—
Robin Hugo Charles (53 Harwood Rd, SW6), *b* 1945; *ed* Milton Abbey, and Selwyn Coll, Camb (MA). —— Joanna Frances (19 Rankeillor St, Edinburgh), *b* 1948. —— Hilary Jane (18 Leighton Gdns, NW10), *b* 1951.

Grandson of late Digby Charles Legard, only son of late Rev Digby Charles Legard, yr son of late Digby Legard (ante):—
Issue of late Rev Charles Legard, MC, *b* 1887, *d* 1976: *m* 1918, Ethel Gertrude, who *d* 1973, da of late Rev George Strickland Marriott, R of Sigglesthorne:—
John Bruce (75 Holland Park, W11 3SL), *b* 1924; *ed* Cheltenham Coll.

This family is of great antiquity in Yorkshire, and possessed the manor of Anlaby as early as the 12th century. The 1st baronet, Sir John, was MP for Scarborough, and an eminent royalist. Sir Charles, 11th Bt, was Chm of E Riding of Yorkshire County Council, and MP for Scarborough (C) 1874-80.

LEICESTER (I) 1671, of Timogue, Queen's co (Extinct 1968)

Sir CHARLES BYRNE WARREN LEICESTER, 9th and last *Baronet*.

DAUGHTER LIVING OF EIGHTH BARONET

(By 2nd *m*) Meriel Jeanne, *b* 1931: *m* 1956, Sidney John Winder, and has issue living, Michelle Ann, *b* 1958: *m* 1978, Patrick Oliver Da Costa, and has issue living, Tanya Michelle *b* 1984, — Nicola Jane, *b* 1960: *m* 1997, David Lyle McConnell, — Robyn Marte, *b* 1968: *m* 1990, Jeffrey Lynn Rowe. *Residence* – 1595 Amberlea Drive South, Dunedin, Florida 34698, USA.

COLLATERAL BRANCH LIVING

Granddaughter of late Maj William Frederick Leicester, father of 9th baronet:—
Issue of late Lieut-Col George William Frederic Leicester, *b* 1895, *d* 1944: *m* 1932, Katherine Anne (who *m* 2ndly, 1945, Lt-Col A. Frankland, of The Gables, Hopton Cangeford, Ludlow), da of late Col Lawrence Chenevix Trench, CMG, DSO (*see* B Ashtown, colls):—
Elizabeth Meriel Anne, *b* 1935.

LEIGH (UK) 1918, of Altrincham, Cheshire

Sir RICHARD HENRY LEIGH, 3rd *Baronet*, *b* 11 Nov 1936; *s* his uncle, Sir JOHN, 1992; *ed* Aiglon Coll, Switzerland: *m* 1st, 1962 (*m diss* 1977), Barbro Anna Elizabeth, el da of late Stig Carl Sebastian Tham, of Sweden; 2ndly, 1977, Cherie Rosalind, el da of late Douglas Donald Dale, of La Blanchie, Cherval, France, and widow of Alan Reece, RMS.

Arms – Argent, on a cross engrailed quadrant gules, a garb or between in chief two roses of the second, barbed and seeded proper. Crest – A cubit arm vested gules, cuffed argent, grasping a staff in bend sinister proper, pendant therefrom a banner of the second, charged with a cross-couped of the first.
Residence – Trythall Vean, Madron, Penzance, Cornwall TR20 8SY.

HALF-BROTHER LIVING

CHRISTOPHER JOHN (The Spinney, Wendens Ambo, Saffron Walden, Essex), *b* 6 April 1941; *ed* Radley: *m* 1963, Gillian Ismay, only da of late William King Lowe, of The Bell House, Guiting Power, Glos, and has issue living, Edward John, *b* 1 April 1970; *ed* Bishop's Stortford Coll: *m* 1999, Rebecca Mary Streeter, — Caroline Nicola, *b* 1967.

HALF-SISTER LIVING

Victoria Anne, *b* 1945; *ed* St James's, Malvern: *m* 1967, Jasper Rodney Archer, of The Malt House, Stapleford, nr Salisbury, Wilts, son of late Lt-Col Rodney Archer, MC, 4th Hussars, of Millfield, Haslemere, Surrey, and has issue living, Nicholas Jasper, *b* 1971, — Sophie Louise, *b* 1973.

UNCLE LIVING (*son of 1st baronet*)

David, BM, BCh, *b* 1921; *ed* Eton, and New Coll, Oxford (MA); CStJ: *m* 1945, Rosemary Eleanor, da of late William Henry Wyburn-Mason, of Rosemont, Clytha Park, Newport, Mon, and has issue living, Peregrine William Roger Wyburn, *b* 1955; *ed* Eton, Exeter Univ (BA), and RAC, Cirencester (DipSurv): *m* 1992, Laura Dawn, da of Col Vincent Warwick Calmady-Hamlyn, of Leawood, Bridestowe, Devon, and has issue living, Ranald Geoffrey Merlin *b* 1992, — Corinna Eleanor Elizabeth Wyburn, *b* 1951; *ed* Westonbirt: *m* 1992, Col Keith George Turner, MBE, son of late Maj Herbert George Turner. *Residence* – High Coombe, Coombe Hill, Bruton, Somerset BA10 0QA.

The 1st baronet, Sir John Leigh (son of John Leigh, JP, of Brooklands, Cheshire), was proprietor of *The Pall Mall Gazette* (before amalgamation with *Evening Standard*). In European War 1914-18 he equipped a hospital for wounded officers at Altrincham, and founded, maintained, and was Chm of Canadian Officers' Club. He sat as MP for Clapham Div of Wandsworth (*C*) 1922-45.

LEIGHTON (E) 1693, of Wattlesborough, Shropshire

Sir MICHAEL JOHN BRYAN LEIGHTON, 11th *Baronet*; *b* 8 March 1935; *s* his father, *Col Sir* RICHARD TIHEL, TD, 1957; *ed* Stowe, and RAC Cirencester; is patron of one living: *m* 1st, 1974 (*m diss* 1980), Mrs Amber Mary Ritchie; 2ndly, 1991, Mrs Diana Mary Gamble, and has issue by 2nd *m*.

Arms – Quarterly, per fesse indented or and gules. Crest – A wyvern with wings expanded sable.
Seat – Loton Park, Shrewsbury. *Club* – MCC.

DAUGHTER LIVING (*By 2nd marriage*)

Eleanor Angharad Diana, *b* 1992.

SISTERS LIVING

Dread shame

Lavinia Ann, *b* 1932: *m* 1958, Major Edward Arthur Trevor Bonnor-Maurice, Coldstream Guards, and has issue living, Emma Mary, *b* 1959: *m* 1986, Mark William Fane, and has issue living, Harry Lachlan *b* 1992, Alice Daisy (twin) *b* 1992, — Frances Flavia, *b* 1962. —— Judy Johanna Kathleen, *b* 1937. —— Elizabeth Linda Mary *b* 1938: *m* 1st, 1977 (*m diss* 1984), David James Treasure, Monmouthshire Regt; 2ndly, 1988, Vyvyan Clover, Parachute Regt.
Residence – Bodynfoel Hall, Llanfechain, Montgomeryshire.

The Leightons derive their name from Leighton in Shropshire, where they were seated in the 12th century. They inherited, *temp* Edward IV, the estates of Wattlesborough and Loton, through the Mawddwys and the Burghs by the marriage of John Leighton with a coheiress of the last-named family. The county of Shropshire was represented in Parliament by Richard de Leighton, AD 1312-18, and has since often been represented by members of this family. Sir Edward Leighton, 2nd Bt changed the residence from the ancient castle of Wattlesborough to the house at Loton, which he greatly enlarged in 1712. Sir Baldwyn Leighton, 8th Bt, sat as MP for Shropshire S (C) 1877-85. Col Sir Richard Tihel Leighton, 10th Bt, Shropshire Yeo, was High Sheriff of Salop 1956.

FORBES-LEITH OF FYVIE (UK) 1923, of Jessfield, co Midlothian

I wait in hope
God assisting

Sir ANDREW GEORGE FORBES-LEITH OF FYVIE, 3rd *Baronet*; *b* 20 Oct 1929; *s* his father, *Sir* (ROBERT) IAN (ALGERNON), KT, MBE, 1973; *ed* Eton: *m* 1962, Jane Kate, who *d* 1969, only da of late David McCall-McCowan, of Dalwhat, Moniaive, Dumfries, and has issue.

Arms – Quarterly, 1st grand quarter or, a cross-crosslet fitchée sable between three crescents in chief and as many fusils in base gules, *Leith*; 2nd grand quarter quarterly, 1st and 4th azure, on a chevron between three bears' heads couped argent, muzzled gules, a man's heart proper, between two skenes of the first, pommelled or, *Forbes of Balfing*; 2nd azure, a fesse chequy argent and of the first between three boars' heads erased or, within a bordure indented of the second, *Gordon of Badenscoth*; 3rd argent, a fir-tree growing out of a mount in base vert, surmounted of a sword in bend, supporting on its point an Imperial head erased azure, armed and langued gules, *Gregory*; crown proper, in sinister chief and dexter base a lion's 3rd grand quarter, parted per fesse azure and argent, in chief three bears' heads couped of the second, muzzled gules, and in base as many unicorns' heads erased sable, *Forbes of Ballogie*; 4th grand quarter argent, on a bend gules between two mullets in chief, and in base a hunting horn, sable, stringed of the second, three buckles or, *Burn*. **Crest** – 1st, a cross-crosslet fitchee sable *Leith*; 2nd, a bear's head and neck couped argent, muzzled azure, *Forbes*; 3rd a dexter cubit arm in armour bendways, the hand naked proper holding a cross-crosslet fitchée erect in pale gules, *Burn*.
Residence – Dunachton, Kingussie, Inverness-shire. *Clubs* – Royal Northern (Aberdeen), Highland (Inverness).

SONS LIVING

GEORGE IAN DAVID, *b* 26 May 1967: *m* 1995, Camilla Frances, eldest da of Philip Ely, of Crawley, Hants, and has issue living, Alexander Philip George, *b* 4 Feb 1999, — India Rose, *b* 1997. —— John Charles, *b* 1969: *m* 1999, Marina, da of Christopher Burges-Lumsden, of Pitcaple, Aberdeenshire.

DAUGHTERS LIVING

Miranda Jane, *b* 1963: *m* 1990, Julian N. W. McHardy, son of Col W. G. McHardy, CVO, MBE, MC, of Woodend House, Banchory, Kincardineshire, and has issue living, Andrew William Jock, *b* 1992, — Iona Jane, *b* 1994, — Clodagh June, *b* 1996. —— Louisa Mary, *b* 1965: *m* 1991, Thomas William Leader, yr son of Henry William Leader, of 41 Warwick Gdns, W14, and of Mrs G. H. Maingot, of Sugar House, Tobago, and has issue living, Frederick Henry, *b* 1996, — Ruaraidh William Percy, *b* 1998, Josephine Kate, *b* 1994.

SISTERS LIVING

Anne Rosdew, *b* 1932: *m* 1959, Angus Maitland Pelham Burn, of Kennels Cottage, Dess, Aboyne, Aberdeenshire, and has issue living, Amanda Mary, *b* 1961: *m* 1995, Michael Green, son of William Green and has issue living, Sam William Curtis *b* 1996, — Lucy Rosdew, *b* 1963, — Emily Louise, *b* 1964, — Kate Ruth, *b* 1966. —— Mary Elizabeth, *b* 1934: *m* 1961, Maj James Gresley McGowan, 15th/19th King's Roy Hussars, of Benridge Hall, Ponteland, Northumberland (*see* Gresley, Bt, colls, 1973-74 Edn), and has issue living, Charles Gresley (Southlands Farm, Gunnerton, Hexham, Northumberland NE48 4EA), *b* 1962: *m* 1989, Deborah Ann, da of Dr Joseph Edward Gordon, of The Villa, Seaton Burn, Newcastle upon Tyne, and has issue living, Hector Joseph Gresley *b* 1991, Rosanna Mary *b* 1994, — Hugo John, *b* 1964, — Lorna, *b* 1967

Sir Charles Rosdew Forbes-Leith of Fyvie, OBE, 1st Bt, yst son of Gen Robert Burn, Col Comdt RA: *m* 1891, Hon Ethel Louise Forbes-Leith, OBE, only da of and heir of 1st Baron Leith of Fyvie (*ext*), and by edict of Lord Court 1925, assumed the surname and arms of Forbes-Leith of Fyvie, for himself, his wife and son, under terms of the will of his father-in-law; MP for Torquay (*U*) 1910-23, Col TA and Lt-Col R Dragoons; served in Hazara Expedition 1888, S African War 1900 and 1914-18 War. His el son Arthur Herbert Rosdew was *ka* Ypres 1914; the yr son, Sir (Robert) Ian (Algernon) Forbes-Leith of Fyvie, KT, MBE, was Lord Lt of Aberdeenshire 1959-73.

Alexander Burn bought Kingston, East Lothian 1765, which was sold in 1813 by his son, John Burn, grandfather of 1st Bt. Baron Leith of Fyvie was el son of Rear-Adm John James Leith (descended from the Leiths, successively of Barnis, co Aberdeen, Edingarioc, New Leslie in the Garioch, and Leith Hall) by his wife Margaret, da and heir of Alexander Forbes of Blackford, Aberdeenshire, descended from Duncan Forbes of Corsindae, 2nd son of 2nd Lord Forbes.

Leith-Buchanan, see Buchanan.

LE MARCHANT (UK) 1841, of Chobham Place, Surrey

Sir FRANCIS ARTHUR LE MARCHANT, 6th *Baronet*; *b* 6 Oct 1939; *s* his father, Sir DENIS, 1987, *ed* Gordonstoun, and RA Schools.

Arms – Azure, a chevron or between three owls argent. **Crest** – Out of a ducal coronet an owl's leg erect or.
Seat – Hungerton Hall, Grantham, Lincolnshire. *Address* – c/o Midland Bank plc, 88 Westgate, Grantham, Lincs NG31 6LF.

SISTER LIVING

(Penelope) Clare (Colston Bassett House, Colston Bassett, Notts), *b* 1944: *m* 1st, 1964 (*m diss* 1990), Capt John Henry Warrand Hanmer; 2ndly, 1995, Frederick Connell, son of late Rev Richard Connell, and has issue (by 1st *m*) (*see* Hanmer, Bt, colls).

Me Minerva lucet

Minerva is my light

WIDOW LIVING OF FIFTH BARONET

ELIZABETH ROWENA (*Lady Le Marchant*), da of Arthur Hovenden Worth, of Hovenden House, Fleet, Lincs: *m* 1933, Sir Denis Le Marchant, 5th Bt, who *d* 1987. *Residence* – Hungerton Hall, Grantham, Lincs.

COLLATERAL BRANCHES LIVING

Granddaughters of late Alfred Gaspard Le Marchant (infra):—
Issue of late Sir Spencer Le Marchant, *b* 1931, *d* (7 Sept) 1986: *m* 1955, Lucinda Gaye (*Lady Le Marchant*) (The Saltings, Yarmouth, Isle of Wight), da of Brig Hugh Nugent Leveson-Gower, late RA (*see* D Sutherland, colls):—
Perronelle Jane, *b* 1956: *m* 1979, James Wallace Hudleston, yr son of Wilfrid Andrew Hudleston, and has issue living, Hugh Edward, *b* 1983, — Tamara Avril, *b* 1980. —— Geva Ann, *b* 1958: *m* 1991, Dr Michael McCaldin, elder son of Dr John McCaldin, of Down House, Anerley, Natal, and has issue living, Elvira Joy, *b* 1994, — Leonora Xa, *b* 1997.

Issue of late Alfred Gaspard Le Marchant, yr son of 4th baronet, *b* (twin) 1906, *d* (3 March) 1986: *m* 1929, Turdis, who *d* (11 March) 1986, da of late Einar Mortensen, of Holte, Denmark:—
MICHAEL, *b* 28 July 1937; *ed* Eton: *m* 1st, 1963 (*m diss* 19—), Philippa, eldest da of late Ralph Batchelor Denby, of Tanyard, Sharpthorne, Sussex; 2ndly, 1981, Sandra Elisabeth Champion, da of — Kirby, and has issue living (by 1st *m*), Piers Alfred, *b* 1964: *m* 1995, Hon Silvia Maria Francesca Pearson, eldest da of Baron Pearson of Rannoch (Life Baron), and has issue living, Edward Charles Carey *b* 1998, Olivia Francesca *b* 1996, — Dickon John, *b* 1968, — Melissa Winifred, *b* 1965, — Antonia Ruth, *b* 1970. *Residence* – White Lodge, 15 Bathwick Hill, Bath, Avon BA2 6EW. —— Pamela, *b* 1933: *m* 1st, 1957, Henry Douglas-Pennant, who *d* 1986 (*see* B Penrhyn, colls); 2ndly, 1988, Very Rev Patrick Reynolds Mitchell, Dean of Windsor. *Residence* – The Deanery, Windsor Castle, Berks SL4 1NJ.

The father of Sir Denis Le Marchant, 1st Bt, Maj-Gen John Gaspard Le Marchant (a lineal descendant of Peter Le Marchant, President of the States, and Lieut-Governor of Guernsey in the 13th century), was killed at the battle of Salamanca, while leading the heavy brigade of cavalry. Brig-Gen Sir Edward Thomas Le Marchant, KCB, CBE, 4th Bt, was High Sheriff of Nottinghamshire 1930, Chm of Nottinghamshire TA Asso 1931-45, and Dep Chm of Quarter Sessions, Nottinghamshire 1933-45. Sir Denis Le Marchant, 5th Bt, was Capt Cheshire Yeo (Res), and Lieut Nottingham (Sherwood Rangers) Yeo, and High Sheriff of Lincolnshire 1958-59; his elder son, Peter Edward, *b* 1934, *ed* Eton, and Lincoln Coll, Oxford, *dvp*.

BARRETT-LENNARD (UK) 1801, of Belhus, Essex

Rev Sir HUGH DACRE BARRETT-LENNARD, 6th *Baronet*; only son of late Sir Fiennes Cecil Arthur Barrett-Lennard, el son of Capt Thomas George Barrett-Lennard, grandson of John Barrett-Lennard, 2nd son of 1st baronet; *b* 27 June 1917; *s* his kinsman, *Sir* (THOMAS) RICHARD FIENNES, OBE, 1977; *ed* Radley; formerly Capt Essex Regt; 1939-45 War (despatches); a Priest of London Oratory.

Arms – Quarterly: 1st and 4th, or, on a fesse gules three fleurs-de-lis or, within a bordure wavy, *Lennard*; 2nd and 3rd, party per pale barry of four counterchanged argent and gules, *Barrett*; all within a bordure wavy sable. **Crest** – Out of a ducal coronet or an Irish wolf dog's head per fesse argent and ermine, charged with an escallop per fesse nebuly, gules and sable. (The 1st baronet also obtained from the Lyon office in Edinburgh a grant of supporters, viz.—two lions rampant or, each charged with a collar quarterly argent and gules; but the grantee's domicile being in England this grant was illegal.)
Address – The Oratory, SW7 2RP.

To wish well

Pour bien désirer

DAUGHTER LIVING OF FIFTH BARONET

Anne, *b* 1923: *m* 1949, Rev John Charles Pollock (*see* Pollock, Bt, *cr* 1866, colls). *Residence* – Rose Ash House, South Molton, Devon EX36 4RB.

COLLATERAL BRANCHES LIVING

Branch from brother of 2nd baronet

Granddaughter of late Rev Dacre Barrett-Lennard, brother of 2nd baronet:—
Issue of late Dacre Barrett-Lennard, *b* 1884, *d* 1948: *m* 1915, Mabel Ella, da of James Sage, of The Yew Tree Farm, Aldham, Suffolk:—
Viva Dacre, *b* 1923. *Residence* –

Branch from 2nd son of 1st baronet

Grandchildren of late Trenchard Goodenough Barrett-Lennard, yst son of late George Barrett-Lennard, 2nd son of John Barrett Lennard, 2nd son of 1st baronet:—
Issue of late Sqdn-Ldr Dacre Barrett-Lennard, RAF *b* 1906, *ka* 1944: *m* 1938, Una (37 The Cliff, Wellington Rd, Wallasey, Merseyside L45 2NL), da of Leo Burn, of Wallasey, Cheshire:—
Paula, *b* 1943: *m* 1969, David Ambrose Staines, of 1 Old Orchard, Hawthorne Lane, Wilmslow, Cheshire SK9 5DH, and has issue living, Dacre Ambrose, *b* 1977, — Rachel, *b* 1975.

Issue of late Roy Barrett-Lennard, *b* 1909, *d* 1979: *m* 1939, Joyce Christine Elizabeth, who *d* 1985, da of Stuart Robert Drinkwater, of Coventry:—
RICHARD FYNES, *b* 6 April 1941. —— Peter John (2 Farmhouse Cottage, Leatherhead Rd, Oxshott, Surrey KT22 0EZ), *b* 1942: *m* 1979, Sonja, da of Vladimir Belacic, of 23 Autuna Branka Simica, 41000 Zagreb, Yugoslavia, and has issue living, Simon James, *b* 1980. —— Penelope Anne, *b* 1948.

Branch from 3rd son of 1st baronet

Grandchildren of late Edmund Thomas Dacre Barrett-Lennard (infra):—
Issue of late Geoffrey Barrett-Lennard, *b* 1908, *d* 1988: *m* 1933, Lorna Margaret, da of A. B. Lodge, of York:—
John (Annandale, Beverley, W Aust), *b* 1949: *m* 1976, Leita Catherine, da of R. A. McLean, of Beverley, W Aust, and has issue living, James Dacre, *b* 1981, — Claire, *b* 1979, — Marie, *b* 1984. —— Sarah Margaret, *b* 1936: *m* 1963, Archibald Stewart Fraser, of 17 Euston Av, Highgate, S Aust, and has issue living, John Buchanan, *b* 1966, — Geoffrey Lodge, *b* 1968, — Catherine Margaret, *b* 1971. —— Judith (17 Forrest St, Beverley 6304, W Aust), *b* 1938: *m* 1969, Robert Henry Magill, who *d* 1974, and has issue living, Peter John, *b* 1972, — David James Henry, *b* 1974, — Catherine Elizabeth, *b* 1970: *m* 1996, David Alexander Edgar, of Yaraandoo, Boddington, W Aust.

Issue of late Edmund Thomas Keith Barrett-Lennard, *b* 1911, *d* 19·: *m* 1938, Margaret (Woonderlin, Beverley, W Aust), da of A. V. Clarke, of Beverley, W Aust:—
Edmund Timothy Dacre, *b* 1941. —— Douglas John (Woonderlin, Beverley, W Aust), *b* 1944: *m* 1974, Dorothy Marianne, el da of Gordon Derwent Crosthwaite, of Glenroa, Margaret River, W Aust, and has issue living, Derwent Thomas Keith, *b* 1976. —— Richard (Milepool, Beverley, Western Australia), *b* 1950; AMF Vietnam: *m* 1975, Lorna Jean, da of Donald A. Sprigg, of Strathallen, Wagin, W Aust, and has issue living, Michael James, *b* 1978, — Jeremy, *b* 1980. —— Helen Mary (Forrest St, Beverley, Western Australia), *b* 1939: *m* 1959, Michael Seed, and has issue living, Christopher James Blake, *b* 1960, — Thomas William Timothy, *b* 1966, — Catherine Jane Blake, *b* 1962: *m* 1999, — .

Grandchildren of late Edmund George Barrett-Lennard, son of late Edmund Thomas Henry Barrett-Lennard, son of George Barrett-Lennard, 3rd son of 1st baronet:—

Issue of late Edmund Thomas Dacre Barrett-Lennard, b 1881, d 1945: m 1907, Kathleen Rosina who d 1939, da of Thomas D. Pettigrew:—
Anthony Leslie (84/31 Williams Rd, Nedlands, W Aust 6009), b 1913: m 1943, Ethel Barbara, da of R. F. Adams, of Sydney, NSW, and has issue living, Antony John William, b 1953: m 1981, Alison, da of P. R. Bremner, of Beverley, WA, and has issue living, Benjamin James b 1987, Jodie Louise b 1985, — Carmen Lesley, b 1944, — Jill Kathleen, b 1946: m 1974, Allan Wall, of 63 Webster St, Nedlands, W Aust, and has issue living, Timother Lawler b 1976, Carmen Belinda b 1978, — Sally Anne, b 1951: m 1979, George Jenkin Ellis Smith, and has issue living, Thomas William b 1983, Hilary Rebecca b 1981.

Issue of late Francis Barrett-Lennard, b 1882, d 1960: m 1910, Elsie Selina, who d 1950, da of Thomas George Walker, of Beverley, W Australia:—
Thomas Edmund (Drumclyer, Beverley, W Australia), b 1916; is a Farmer: m 1948, Lesley Vernon, da of Vernon Bland Gibson, of Perth, W Australia, and has issue living, Graham Francis, b 1953: m 1984, Dina Campbell, da of John Pike Campbell Curlewis, of Toronto, NSW, Australia, and has issue living, Edmund George b 1986, Marika Joan b 1984, — Felicity Anne, b 1949; BEd, Dip PE: m 1977, Russell John Perry, PhD, BSc, son of Alfred Trevor Perry, of Perth, Western Australia, and has issue living, Philippa Louise b 1982, Elizabeth Emma b 1985, — Jennifer Jane, b 1950; WATC: m 1975, Vernon Ashley, son of Julius Vernon Brockman, of Beach Grove, Busselton, Western Australia, and has issue living, James Julius b 1977, Ashley Edmund Vernon b 1980, — Dinah Louise, b 1955; WATC, BHSAI: m 1987, Ronald John Fleming, of Glenesk, Muchea, Western Australia. —— Launa, b 1911: m 1940, Horace Arnold Butler, of Beverley, W Australia, and has issue living, Lennard Wilfred, b 1944, — Frances Merrilyn, b 1943.

Issue of late Henry Barrett-Lennard, b 1884, d 1960: m 1912, Muriel Ellen, da of John Trevelyan:—
Trevor Henry (Camblebren, Gairdner River, W Australia), b 1922, is a Farmer; European War 1939-45, with Australian Imperial Force: m 1951, Audrey, yr da of Albert E. Wilhelm, of Beverley, W Australia, and has issue living, Cameron (Beaming Hill, Gairdner River, W Australia), b 1952: m 1979, Kathryn Faye, da of Colin V. Ellis, of Violet Town, Victoria, and has issue living, Dale Cameron b 1982, Deanna Jane b 1981, Krystelle Amy b 1985, — Brent, b 1957: m 1984, Jillian Elizabeth, da of William E. Meier, of Toocelup, Bremer Bay, W Australia, and has issue living, Clay b 1988, Holly Elizabeth b 1985, — Leonie Gaye, b 1954: m 1977, Raymond John Ward, of Bridgetown, W Australia, and has issue living, Benjamin Trevor b 1978, — Belinda Anne, b 1963: m 1987, Graham John Yuill (PO Box 8, Esperance, W Australia), and has issue living, Rhys Raymond b 1989, Kyra Corrine b 1990.

Issue of late Alexander Forrest Barrett-Lennard, b 1895, d 1941: m 1917, Eva May, who d 1973, da of Edward Berry:—
Alexander Dacre (Belhus, Box 58, Beverley, W Aust), b 1921; F/Sgt RAAF: m 1949, Dorothea Ann, da of James Davidson Weaver, of Beverley, W Aust, and has issue living, Gregory Dacre, b 1958: m 1985, Margaret Louise, da of Alan J. Croft, of City Beach, W Aust, and has issue living, Jackson Dacre b 1988, Alix Louise b 1990, Rebecca Ann b 1992, Kym Elizabeth b 1998, — Susan, b 1950: m 1st, 1971, Kenneth Charles Baston; 2ndly, 1981, Phillip James Hill, of PO Box 225, Beverley, Western Australia 6304, and has issue living, (by 1st m) George Derek b 1974, Richard Charles b 1976, (by 2nd m) Guy Phillip b 1982, — Meredith, b 1953: m 1973, Philip Anthony Cockerill, of Geraldton, W Aust, and has issue living, Benjamin Dacre b 1976, Joseph Anthony b 1978, Samuel Charles b 1980, Zachary Philip b 1984, — Vicki, b 1955: m 1997, Simon Lewis Potter, of Perth, W Aust, and has an adopted da, Frehiwot Gabriella b 1995. —— Peggy Amy, b 1918: m 1946, Durward Toleman, who d 1981, and has issue living, David Forrest, b 1952; ed Univ of Melbourne (BSc (Hons), BCom), — Michael Fiennes, b 1955: m 1985, Suzanne Joy, da of Bruce Herbert Whitaker, of Donvale, Victoria, and has issue living, Kate Suzanne b 1986, Penny Nicole b 1988. *Residence* – 208 Mahoney's Rd, Burwood East, 3151, Victoria, Aust.

Branch from 5th son of 1st baronet

Grandchildren of George Hardey Barrett-Lennard, eldest son of late Edward Graham Barrett-Lennard, eldest son of late Edward Pomeroy, 5th son of 1st baronet:—
Issue of late George Graham Barrett-Lennard, b 1887, d 1968: m 1911, Maud Gladys Hastings, da of G. W. Hester, of Dalgarup Park, Bridgetown, W Aust:—
Fynes (St Leonards, Kondut, W Aust), b 1915: m 1949, Florence Ray, da of W. C. Williams, of Nedlands, W Aust, and has issue living, Kingsley Ian Michael, b 1954, — William Ashley Dacre, b 1957, — Wendy Roslyn, b 1950: m 1972, Ralph Dunstan Pomery, of, and has issue living, Sharon Anne b 1974, Michelle Louise b 1977, — Helen Elizabeth, b 1951: m 1974, Kimberley John Clifton. —— Douglas Graham (The Crescent, Gingin, W Aust), b 1916: m 1943, Olive Davidson, and has issue living, David Thomas, b 1945 (Belhus, Upper Swan, W Aust), — Joan, b 1946: m 1970, Keith McMullan, of Caprice Rd, Geraldton, W Aust, — Kaye Julie, b 1959. —— Lancelot (Averley Downs, Kondut, W Aust), b 1918; MB and BS Adelaide: m 1945, Patricia Ida, da of J. Porter, of Northam, W Aust, and has issue living, Michael Scott, b 1949, — Rev Richard John Stirling (16 Bellairs Road, Kardinya, W Aust) b 1951; BA (Hons), MA (Oxon), PhD: m 1st 1973 (m diss 1990), Rosalind, da of late Robert Willis; 2ndly, 1990, Julie Louise, da of Leslie Gibson, and has issue living (by 1st m), David John b 1978, Jeremy Robert b 1981, — Simon Hugh b 1957, — Patricia Ruth, b 1947: m 1972, Richard Stevenson, — Kathleen Ann, b 1954. —— Godfrey Trevor, b 1926; ed Perth Univ, W Aust (BSc, BA and at Chicago Univ) (Dr in Psychology 1959); Prof in Psychology, Univ of Waterloo, Ont: m 1948, Helen, da of William Love, of 40 Harvey St, Mosman Park, W Aust, and has issue living, John Graham, b 1953, — Lance Godfrey, b 1955, — Sirri Anne, b 1960, — Katherine Gail, b (twin) 1960, — Judith Helen, b 1966. —— Irwin Prescott (St Leonards, Kondut, W Australia), b 1929; ed W Australia Univ (BSc Agriculture, MSc): m 1953, Berwine Ruth, da of Dr Leigh Cook, of Stirling Highway Claremont, W Australia, and has issue living, Edward Graham, b 1953, — Hugh Anthony, b 1955, — James Irwin, b 1961, — Ann Mary, b 1958. —— Hester, b 1913: m (Feb) 1937, Hubert Leake Shields, of Glenvar, Wongan Hills, W Aust 6603, and has issue living, Graham Michael, b 1946: m 1969, Lynette, da of John Gale, of Yelbeni, W Aust, and has issue living, Michael Graham b 1973, Marnie Jane b 1974, Kellie Anne b 1977, — Peter William Hubert, b 1950: m 1980, Mary Charm, da of Frederick Hamilton, of Moora, W Aust, and has issue living, William Hubert b 1984, Stuart Frederick b 1986, Philippa Robin b 1981, — Anthony Hubert, b 1955, — Robin Wendy, b (Dec) 1937: m 1961, Dr Roy Montague Green MSc (17 Piridari Rd, City Beach, W Aust) and has issue living, Julie Anne b 1964, Cathy Susan b 1965, — Waverley Hester, b 1939: m 1970, Robin Ladyman, of Katanning, W Aust, and has issue living, Lara b 1972, Tanya b 1974, — Christine Mary, b 1944: m 1967, Robert Weise, of Highbury 6313, W Aust, and has issue living, Michael William b 1969, Timothy b 1971, Anthony b 1973, — Elizabeth Ann, b 1953: m 1980, John Casey, of Auckland, NZ, and has issue living, Nicola Simone b 1985, Asha b 1987.

Issue of late Trevor St Aubyn Barrett-Lennard, *b* 1889, *d* 1970: *m* 1st, 1912, Susan Mary, who *d* 1939, da of C. W. Ferguson, of Houghton, Swan, W Aust; 2ndly, 1942, Edith Mary, who *d* 1968, da of John Edward Wedge:—— (By 1st *m*) Ferguson (W Swan Rd, W Swan 6056, W Aust) *b* 1913. —— Donald (Houghton, Middle Swan, W Aust), *b* 1916: *m* 1940, his cousin, Dorothy, da of C. O. Ferguson (*see* Barrett-Lennard, Bt, colls, 1985 Edn), and has had issue, Bruce, *b* 1944, *d* 1950, — Brian, *b* 1952, — Flora, *b* 1947: *m* 1972, Lawrence Alec Smith, and has issue living, Kathryn Rachel *b* 1980. —— (By 2nd *m*) Barbara, *b* 1948: *m* 1968, Stuart William Green, of 25 Gloucester St, Victoria Park 6100, W Aust, and has issue living, Philip Edward Spencer, *b* 1968, — Julian St Aubyn, *b* 1973, — Rosemarie Catherine, *b* 1970. —— Elizabeth, *b* 1949; *m* 1968, Gregory Allan Harris, of 7 Rubida Court, Boronia 3155, Victoria, Australia, and has issue living, Trevor Allan, *b* 1968, — Daniel Raymond, *b* 1974.

Issue of late St Aubyn Edward Barrett-Lennard, *b* 1899, *d* 1956: *m* 1933, Betty Corona, who *d* 1981, da of Edward Sidney Simpson, DSc, of Millpoint, South Perth, W Australia:—
Richard St Aubyn (Belhus Farm, Upper Swan, W Aust), *b* 1938: *m* 1965, Sandra, el da of Keith Irwin Bedford Smith, of Alfred Cove, W Aust, and has issue living, Nigel Dacre, *b* 1968, — Philip St Aubyn, *b* 1972, — Amy Wilson *b* 1966. —— John Dacre, *b* 1940: *m* 1970, Lynette Marie, el da of Robert Atkinson of W Perth, W Aust, and has issue living, Mark Robert, *b* 1970, — Timothy Stewart, *b* 1972: *m* 1997, Siobhan Alice, yst da of Peter Ackland Waring, of Mt Lawley, W Aust, — Daniel Thomas John, *b* 1977, — Bethwyn Ruth, *b* 1975.

Grandchildren of late St Aubyn Edward Barrett-Lennard (ante):—
Issue of late George Simpson Barrett-Lennard, *b* 1934, *d* 1972: *m* 1961, Angela Clare (who *m* 2ndly, 1978, Rev Frank Bazely, of The Rectory, Yule Av, Middle Swan, W Aust 6056), da of Alfred Raymond Stevens, of W Swan, W Aust:—
David Anthony, *b* 1966: *m* 1993, Julieanne, da of Theodore Charles Fisher, of Lockridge, W Aust. —— Michael John, *b* 1972. —— Susan Fairlie, *b* 1963: *m* 1990, Phillip Stephen Hall, son of Ronald Alan Hall, of Red Hill, W Aust, and has issue living, Teresa Elisabeth, *b* 1992, — Kate Louise, *b* 1993.

Granddaughter of late Edward Graham Barrett-Lennard (ante):—
Issue of late Victor Dacre Barrett-Lennard, *b* 1874, *d* 1930: *m* 1906, Blanche Isabel, who *d* 1958, da of Robert Allen:—
Lucille (57 Watkins Rd, Dalkeith, W Aust), *b* 1915: *m* 1940, John Hill Chellew, who *d* 1981, and has issue living, John Alexander, *b* 1949: *m* 1974, Penny, da of Malcolm Devine, of Melrose Station, Leonora, W Aust, and has issue living, Cameron John *b* 1977, Amanda Jane *b* 1981, — William Lennard, *b* 1951: *m* 1976, Billie Keiller, and has issue living, Duncan *b* 1985, Jacqui (twin) *b* 1985, — Mary Diane, *b* 1941: *m* 1965, John Kingsley Baldock, of Wattle Grove, W Aust, and has issue living, Jeremy John *b* 1971, Catherine Jane *b* 1968, Judith Mary *h* (twin) 1971, — Margaret Anne, *b* 1947: *m* 1969, Andrew Henry Skreiner, and has issue living, Hugh Michael *b* 1976, Anna Nadine *b* 1973, — Elizabeth Jill, *b* 1953: *m* 1st, 1977, David Arthur Cannon; 2ndly, 1982, Dr Henly Harrison, and has issue living, (by 2nd *m*) Amy Elizabeth *b* 1982.

Grandchildren of late Victor Dacre Barrett-Lennard (ante):—
Issue of late Dacre Barrett-Lennard, *b* 1906, *d* 1961: *m* 1943, Maisie, da of J. Vile, of Aubury, NSW:—
John Dacre (Mobedine, York, W Aust), *b* 1944: *m* 1972, Margaret, da of Peter Lee, of Cottesloe, W Aust, and has issue living, Dacre, *b* 1974, — Peter John, *b* 1977, — Elizabeth May, *b* 1982.

Issue of late Ernest Stuart Barrett-Lennard, *b* 1910, *d* 1980: *m* 1939, Lorraine, da of Allen Mair, of Swanbourne, W Aust:—
Robert Allen, *b* 1941: *m* 1965, Judith Anne, da of Horace Joseph Stone, of Merredin, W Aust, and has issue living, Clare Lois, *b* 1967, — Melissa, *b* 1969. —— Sandra Lorraine, *b* 1942: *m* 1966, Geoffrey Wackett, of Quairading, W Aust, and has issue living, Andrew, *b* 1968. —— Jennifer Jill, *b* 1947.

Granddaughter of late Arthur St Aubyn Barrett-Lennard (infra):—
Issue of late Arthur Viveash Barrett-Lennard, *b* 1910, *d* 1983: *m* 1952, Joan, da of Frederick Short, of Claremont, W Aust:—
Jane Margaret, *b* 1953: *m* 1973, Bernard Drag, of Cirencester, Glos, and has issue living, Timothy Viveash, *b* 1979, — Heather Rosalie, *b* 1976. *Residence* – 100 O'Connor Rd, Mahogany Creek, W Aust 6072.

Grandchildren of late Edward Graham Barrett-Lennard (ante):—
Issue of late Arthur St Aubyn Barrett-Lennard, *b* 1876, *d* 1953: *m* 1906, Fanny Susan, who *d* 1949, da of Samuel Henry Viveash:—
Frank St Aubyn (17 Martock Way, Karrinyup, W Aust 6018), *b* 1912: *m* 1942, Constance Rosalie, da of the Ven Archdeacon L. W. Parry, of Perth, W Aust, and has issue living, Rosalie Susan (22 Ken St, Wembley Downs 6019, W Aust), *b* 1945: *m* 1st, 1966, Ian Maxwell Greenham, who *d* 1988; 2ndly, 1991, Kim Sears, and has issue living (by 1st *m*), Anthony Ian St Aubyn *b* 1970, Deborah Susan *b* 1968: *m* 1994, Geoffrey Michael Reilly, of Perth, W Aust (and has issue living, Eliza Susan *b* 1998), — Marian Ruth, *b* 1947: *m* 1977, S/Ldr Roger Ashton Clark, RAAF, and has issue living, Paul Robert *b* 1980, Nicholas James *b* 1982, — Constance Anne, *b* 1951: *m* 1st, 1972 (*m diss* 19—), Neil Bates; 2ndly, 1995, Michael John O'Donoghue, of Port Hedland, W Aust, — Jennifer Robyn, *b* 1954: *m* 1978, Bryce Edward Hayes-Thompson, of Doodlakine, W Australia, and has issue living, Owen Bryce *b* 1980, David Frank *b* 1983, Ruth Verna *b* 1985. —— Edward Guy (Nundah, Northam, W Aust; 7 Albert St, S Perth, W Aust), *b* 1919: *m* 1960, Dymity Ann, da of V. W. Shotter, of Perth, W Aust, and has issue living, Edward William, *b* 1967, — Guy St Aubyn, *b* 1969, — Lindal Dymity, *b* 1963: *m* 1988, Herbert Dennis Wessels, of Bannister Springs, Boddington, W Aust.

Issue of late John Evelyn Barrett-Lennard, *b* 1881, *d* 1967: *m* 1911, Frances Amy, who *d* 1954, da of Edward Kay Courthope, of Perth, W Australia:—
Frances Josephine (9 Alexander Rd, Dalkeith, W Australia 6009), *b* 1913: *m* 1940, Geoffrey Howard Gwynne, who *d* 1984, and has issue living, John Howard, *b* 1946, el W Aust Univ (BSc): *m* 1969, Deborah Judith, da of A. B. Walton, of Perth, W Aust, and has issue living, Christopher *b* 1976, Belinda Judith *b* 1972, Katherine Anne *b* (twin) 1972, — Geraldine Frances, *b* 1941: *m* 1967, Jens Dalhoff Jorgensen, of Aalborg, Denmark, and has issue living, Michael Dalhoff *b* 1971, Frances Dalhoff *b* 1968: *m* 1990, Scott Leary (and has issue living, Daniel Scott *b* 1996), Pia Dalhoff *b* 1982, — Angela

Madeline, *b* 1953. —— Judith, *b* 1914: *m* 1941, Ashburton Hall Clark, who *d* 1975, and *d* 1998, leaving issue, John Jeremy, *b* 1941: *m* 1969, Geraldine Lesley, da of L. J. Locke, of Perth, W Aust, and has issue living, Anthony Phillip *b* 1974, Catherine Rosanne, *b* 1971, — Frances Louise, *b* 1946: *m* 1974, Trevor William Tyson, of 101 Townshend Rd, Subiaco, W Aust, and has issue living, Dale Lee *b* 1982. —— Anne (37 Fifth Av, Mt Lawley 6050, W Aust), *b* 1916: *m* 1946, Edward Alexander Glyn Watkins, who *d* 1985, and has issue living, Jonathon George Glyn, *b* 1948: *m* 1986, Rhonda Evelyn, da of Thomas Benton, and has issue living, Isaac Thomas Edward *b* 1987, — Daniel Glyn, *b* 1955: *m* 1986, Frances Anne, da of Eugene Patrick O'Callaghan, of Perth, W Aust, and has issue living, Chauncy Patrick *b* 1990, Hamish Eugene *b* 1993, Connor Edward *b* 1996, Bridget Glyn *b* 1987, — Miranda Glyn, *b* 1952: *m* 1977, Andrew Forte, and has issue living, Woodrow Andrew *b* 1983, Georgina Amy *b* 1979. —— Prudence, *b* 1918: *m* 1946, Frank Ernest Heymanson, who *d* 1989, and *d* 1995, leaving issue, John Simon, *b* 1953: *m* 1st, 1975, Jane Carruthers; 2ndly, 1990, Concetta Caratazzolo, and has issue living (by 1st *m*), Jonathon Simon *b* 1980, Kate Louise *b* 1977 (by 2nd *m*) Antonina *b* 1994, Rebecca *b* 1996, — Janet Louise, *b* 1947: *m* 1976, Patrick John Nodwell, and has issue living, Joanne Helen *b* 1977, Emma Louise *b* 1979, Shelly Prudence *b* 1983, — Elizabeth Jane, *b* 1948, — Deborah Dacre, *b* 1950: *m* 1976, Jack McAdam, and has issue living, Samson Roscoe *b* 1976: *m* 1997, Alina Price, Luke *b* 1986. —— Charlotte Virginia, *b* 1920: *m* 1945, Alleyne Bruce Giles, and *d* 1977, leaving issue, John Nicolas, *b* 1946: *m* 1974, Christine Linfoot, and has issue living, Natalie Simone, *b* 1976, Kelly Vanessa *b* 1978, — Richard Courthope, *b* 1953: *m* 1974, Barbara Flower, and has issue living, Daniel Peter *b* 1978, Kristen Jasmine *b* 1980, — Susanne Virginia, *b* 1949: *m* 1971, Jack Herbert Dowling, and has issue living, Paul Brian *b* 1978, Karen Mena *b* 1976.

Branch from 8th son of 1st baronet

Grandchildren of late William Barrett-Lennard, eldest son of late Walter James Barrett-Lennard, 8th son of 1st baronet:—
Issue of late Walter James Barrett-Lennard, *b* 1883, *d* 1954: *m* 1904, Mary, who *d* 1967, da of late James Lawther, of Russell, Manitoba:—
Walter James (4023 Vine St, Vancouver, BC, Canada V6L 3C1), *b* 1914; served 1939-45 War as Lieut RCNVR: *m* 1947, Beatrice Elizabeth, da of late Dr C. T. Crowdy, of Montreal W, Quebec, and has issue living, James Thomas (39-8868 16th Av, Burnaby, BC V3N 5A6, Canada), *b* 1956: *m* 1983, Gabrielle Ann, da of late Volker H. Evers, of Vancouver, and has issue living, Brenna Darby *b* 1994, — Elizabeth Jane, *b* 1948, — Deborah Dacre (7329 Old Redmond Rd, Redmond, WA 98052, USA), *b* 1949: *m* 1972 (*m diss* 1982; re-*m* 1984 and *m diss* 1993), James M. Cleland, jr, — Naomi Barbara (10 Patience Lane, Ajax, Ontario, Canada L1S 3B4), *b* 1952: *m* 1981, Craig Kempton Hutcheon. —— Margaret Kinnaird, *b* 1911: *m* 1936, Col Donald Spankie, OBE, CM, ED, Canadian Inf, of 3869 W 12th Av, Vancouver, BC, Canada V6R 2N9, and has issue living, James Robert, *b* 1955, — Caroline Margaret Dacre, *b* 1943: *m* 1971, Roy Finklea Knight, and has issue living, James Andrew Drogo *b* 1976, Dacre Roy Thomas *b* 1983, Rollo William Gilbert *b* 1985, Alexandra Margaret Julia *b* 1973, — Mary Isobel Priscilla, *b* 1945: *m* 1981, Christopher Stanbury, and has issue living, Roland Donald Norman *b* 1982.

Issue of late Hardinge Barrett-Lennard, *b* 1890, *d* 1959: *m* 1st, 1922, Annie, da of Harry Wyles, of Victoria, BC; 2ndly, 1930, Leontine Leffler, who *d* 1975, of New York City, NY:—
(By 2nd *m*) Joan, *b* 1933: *m* 1955, Roy Hubbard, of 1740 Aladdin Av, New Hyde Park, NY 11040, USA, and has issue living, Catherine Julia, *b* 1957: *m* 19— (*m diss* 19—), Edward Figueroa, and has issue living, Edward *b* 1978, Eric *b* 1988, — Annabel Joan, *b* 1962: *m* 1991, Alberto Bazante, and has issue living, Maxwell Arthur *b* 1992, — Dorothy Jean, *b* 1963.

Issue of late William Louis Barrett-Lennard, MC, Canadian Inf, *b* 1893, *d* 1970: *m* 1920, Agnes Mildred, who *d* 1982, da of late Nathaniel Dowsett, of Lethbridge, Alberta, Canada:—
Beverley Agnes, *b* 1921: *m* 1st, 1951, William James Fieldhouse, who *d* 1967; 2ndly, 1974, Capt Charles Hardwick Jancowski, who *d* 1992, and has issue living (by 1st *m*), Carol Jacqueline, *b* 19—: *m* 1974, Robert Joseph Lasota, of Winnipeg, Manitoba, and has issue living, Eleanor Rachel *b* 1976, Michelle Rose *b* 1977. *Residence* – 942 Highview Terrace, Nanaimo, BC, Canada V9R 6K5.

Grandchildren of late Lt-Col John Barrett-Lennard, CBE, 3rd son of Walter James Barrett-Lennard, 8th son of 1st baronet:—
Issue of late Rev Dacre Fiennes Barrett-Lennard, *b* 1888, *d* 1975: *m* 1st, 1910, Charlotte Dorothy Evelyn, who *d* 1937, da of late Rev Henry Chichele Hart Bampton (E Albemarle, colls); 2ndly, 1940, Irene Phyllis, who *d* 1986, da of Mark Moss, of Rook Hall, Cressing:—
(By 1st *m*) Richard Dacre (Flat 8, 42 Nevern Square, SW5 9PG), *b* 1921. —— Michael Henry (12 Chisholm Court, St Peters Rd, W6), *b* 1923. —— John Fiennes (Glendale, Cranleigh Rd, Ewhurst, Surrey GU6 7RJ), *b* 1926: *m* 1984, Monica Anne, da of late Henry John Wood. —— Rachel Margaret (26 Grange Av, New Duston, Northampton NN5 6SR), *b* 1928: *m* 1950, Maurice Harry Dickenson, who *d* 1993, and has issue living, Trevor David, *b* 1955. —— (By 2nd *m*) Philip Francis Dacre (Six Mile House, Acle Rd, Great Yarmouth, Norfolk NR30 1TH), *b* 1947: *m* 1986, Josephine Albertina Elizabeth, da of late Joseph Albert Colchester.

Grandchildren of late Villiers Barrett-Lennard, 4th son of late Walter James Barrett-Lennard (ante):—
Issue of late Richard Barrett-Lennard, *b* 1892, *d* 1967: *m* 1917, Kathleen, who *d* 1988, da of Alfred Blake, of Duxmere, Ross-on-Wye:—
Robert Villiers, *b* 1924. —— June Rosemary (85 Compton Place, Carpenders Park, Herts), *b* 1922.

The 1st baronet, Sir Thomas, of Belhus, Essex (natural son and testamentary heir of Thomas Barrett-Lennard, 17th Lord Dacre), was MP for S Essex, and the 2nd, Sir Thomas, was High Sheriff of co Monaghan 1868.

LEON (UK) 1911, of Bletchley Park, Bletchley, Buckinghamshire

SEEK THE TRUTH

Sir JOHN RONALD LEON, 4th *Baronet*; *b* 16 Aug 1934; *s* his father, *Sir* RONALD GEORGE, 1964; *ed* Eton, Millfield, and Byam Shaw Sch of Art; late 2nd Lt King's Roy Rifle Corps; actor (as John Standing) *m* 1st, 1961 (*m diss* 1972), Jill, da of Jack Melford, actor; 2ndly, 1984, Sarah Kate, da of Bryan John Forbes, the film dir, and has issue by 1st and 2nd *m*.

Arms – Gules: two sunflowers erect, slipped, leaved, and eradicated or, seeded sable. **Crest** – Issuant out of a mural crown or, a demi-lion gules supporting between the paws a sunflower erect, slipped and leaved gold, seeded sable.

SON LIVING (*By 1st marriage*)

ALEXANDER JOHN, *b* 3 May 1965; *ed* Bryanston: *m* 1996, Susan Janice, da of late Derek Francis Paul, of 44 Granville Park, Blackheath, SE3, and has issue living, Thomas Alexander Melford, *b* 16 April 1998.

(By 2nd marriage)

Archie, *b* 1986.

DAUGHTERS LIVING (*By 2nd marriage*)

India, *b* 1985. —— Octavia, *b* 1989.

BROTHER LIVING

Timothy Michael George (26 Benbow Rd, W6; Fermor House, Somerton, Oxon), *b* 1938; *ed* Stowe; late Sub-Lt RNVR: *m* 1969, Suzanne, da of Col H. Kinnear, JP, late KOYLI.

COLLATERAL BRANCH LIVING

Grandson of late Reginald Herbert Leon, 2nd son of 1st baronet:—
Issue of late Richard Neville Leon, *b* 1909, *d* 1981: *m* 1941, Margery Frances, who *d* 1991, only da of Sir William Henry Robinson, KCMG, CBE:—
David Richard, *b* 1946: *m* 1970, Maria Amelia da Conceicao, only da of Domingos Jacinto, of Lisbon, and has issue living, Daniel James, *b* 1976, —— Jennifer Rachel, *b* 1972. *Residence* – Benton Cottage, Peters Green, Bodiam, E Sussex TN32 5UN.

The 1st baronet, Sir Herbert Samuel Leon (High Sheriff of Bucks 1909), sat as MP for Bucks N, or Buckingham, Div (L) 1891-5. Sir Ronald George Leon, 3rd Bt, *b* 1902, Memb London Stock Exchange: *m* 1st, 1924, Rosemary Armstrong; 2ndly, 1932 (*m diss* 1945), Dorothy Katherine (Kay Hammond, the actress, who *d* 1980, having *m* 2ndly, 1946, Sir John Selby Clements, CBE, actor and dir, who *d* 1988), da of Sir Guy Standing, KBE; 3rdly, 1947, Alice Mary Holt.

LESLIE (NS) 1625, of Wardis and Findrassie, Morayshire (Dormant 1967)

Sir (HENRY JOHN) LINDORES LESLIE, 9th *Baronet*, *d* 1967, and at the time of going to press no name appears on the Official Roll of Baronets in respect of this title.

DAUGHTER LIVING OF NINTH BARONET

Elizabeth Jean (*Lady Hyde Parker*) *b* 1952: *m* 1972, Sir Richard William Hyde Parker, 12th Bt, of Melford Hall, Long Melford, Suffolk, and has issue (*see* Parker, Bt, cr 1681).

DAUGHTER LIVING OF EIGHTH BARONET

Nancy Jean, *b* 1923: *m* 1946, Col (William Henry) Gerard Leigh, CVO, CBE, Life Gds, and has issue living, John Norman Gerard (The Old Rectory, Doynton, Bristol), *b* 1949; *ed* Eton: *m* 1977, Lavinia Sheila, da of Leopold (Leo) Richard Seymour (*see* M Hertford, colls) and has issue living, Louisa Helen *b* 1980, Emily Rose *b* 1982, Laura Katherine *b* 1984,

— David William Philip (16 Ormeley Rd, SW12 9QE), *b* 1958: *m* 1990, Julie S., eldest da of H. A. Rall, of Forrest Town, Johannesburg, S Africa, and has issue living, James Henry *b* 1991, Jessica Rose *b* 1993, — Carolyn Jane Gerard, *b* 1947: *m* 1977, as his 2nd wife, Charles Edward Riou Benson, of 7 Trevor Sq, SW7, and has issue living, Honor May *b* 1980, — Camilla Madeleine Gerard *b* 1952: *m* 1979 (*m diss* 1998), as his 2nd wife, Hugh Leopold Seymour, elder son of Leopold (Leo) Richard Seymour, and has issue (*see* M Hertford, colls). *Residences* – 15 Eaton Mansions, Cliveden Place, SW1; Hayes, East Woodhay, Newbury, Berks RG15 0AN.

WIDOW LIVING OF NINTH BARONET

COLETTE KATHLEEN (RUSSEL-WALLING), (*Lady Leslie*) (The Garden House, Melford Hall, Long Melford, Suffolk), da of late Dr George Theodore Cregan, MC, Croix de Guerre, of 57 Sloane St, SW1: *m* 1950, Capt Sir (Henry John) Lindores Leslie, 9th Bt, who *d* 1967.

COLLATERAL BRANCHES LIVING

Grandson of late John Leslie, el son of late Thomas Leslie, 3rd son of 4th baronet:—
Issue of late Frank Harvey Leslie, *b* 1874, *d* 1965: *m* 1st, 1915, Amelia Caroline, who *d* 1918, da of Alexander Russon; 2ndly, 1918, Agnes Maude, who *d* 1948, da of Frank Spooner:—
(By 1st *m*) (PERCY) THEODORE, *b* 19 Nov 1915; presumed heir to Baronetcy.

(In remainder)

Descendants of George Leslie of Crichie, uncle of 1st baronet (*see* Leslie, Bt, *cr* 1876).

This family is descended from the ancient family of Leslie of Balquhain, who are also ancestors of the Counts Leslie of the Holy Roman Empire. The lands of Balquhain in 1340 were erected into a barony by Charter from David II. Sir Andrew Leslie, 3rd Baron of Balquhain, was Master of the Horse in the Royal Army at Harlaw, 1411. Sir John Leslie, 1st Bt of Wardis was created a Baronet in 1625 with remainder to his heirs male whatsoever. On the death of the 2nd baronet the baronetcy reverted to his uncle, William, 2nd son of John Leslie, of Wardis, father of the 1st baronet, but he declined to assume the title as the Wardis estates did not accompany it. His four sons, all died without issue. The baronetcy remained dormant for many years, until it was assumed (without service of heirship) by John Leslie, who was 4th in descent from Norman, next brother of 3rd Bt. The Baronets of Glaslough, co Monaghan *cr* (UK) 1876, are therefore in remainder.

LESLIE (UK) 1876, of Glaslough, co Monaghan

GRIP FAST!

Sir JOHN NORMAN IDE LESLIE, 4th *Baronet*; *b* 6 Dec 1916; *s* his father, Sir (JOHN RANDOLPH) SHANE, 1971; *ed* Downside, and Magdalene Coll, Camb (BA); Capt Irish Gds, Knt of Honour and Devotion Sovereign Mil order of Malta, and Knt Cdr Order of St Gregory the Great; 1939-45 War (prisoner).

Arms – Quarterly, 1st and 4th argent, on a bend azure between two holly leaves vert, three buckles or; 2nd and 3rd or, a lion rampant gules, debruised by a ribbon sable. Crest – A griffin's head erased gules.
Residence – Glaslough, co Monaghan. *Clubs* – Travellers', Circolo della Caccia (Rome).

BROTHER LIVING

DESMOND PETER ARTHUR (Castle Leslie, Glaslough, co Monaghan), *b* 29 June 1921; *ed* Ampleforth, and Trin Coll, Dublin; Composer, Author, Film Producer, and Discologist; late Fl Sgt Pilot RAF: *m* 1st, 1945, Agnes, only da of Rudolph Bernauer, of Budapest, Hungary; 2ndly, 1970, Helen Jennifer, da of late Lt-Col E. I. E. Strong, of Tor House, Wiveliscombe, Som, and has issue living (by 1st *m*), Shaun Rudolph Christopher, *b* 1947, — Christopher Mark, *b* 1952: *m* 1982, Cliona Manahan, and has issue living, Luke Daniel *b* 1987, Leah *b* 1992, — Antonia Kelvey, *b* 1963: *m* 1995, Colm Nolan, and has issue living, Lola Sasfi Gwen *b* 1998, — (by 2nd *m*) Samantha Helen, *b* 1966, — Camilla Patricia, *b* 1968: *m* 1994 (*m diss* 1998), Craig Woodgate, son of Barry Woodgate.

COLLATERAL BRANCHES LIVING

Issue of late William Seymour Leslie, 3rd son of 2nd baronet, *b* 1889, *d* 1979: *m* 1929, Gwenyth Rawdon (Castle Leslie (West), Glaslough, co Monaghan), da of Rawdon Roden:—
Jennifer Constance, *b* 1930. *Residence* – Castle Leslie (West), Glaslough, co Monaghan.

Issue of late Capt Lionel Alister David Leslie, sculptor, author and explorer, 4th and yst son of 2nd baronet, *b* 1900, *d* 1987: *m* 1942, Barbara Yvonne, da of Edwin Alexander Enever:—
Leonie Deirdrie Elise, *b* 1944: *ed* Trin Coll, Dublin (BA 1967): *m* 1975, Luiz Monteiro de Barros, of Rio de Janeiro, and has issue living, Leo Alexander, *b* 1976, — Jaime Norman Jerome, *b* 1977. *Residence* – 38 Bloemfontein Av, W12 7BL.

John Leslie, DD, Bishop of the Isles, Scotland, translated to Raphoe, Ireland 1633, and Clogher 1661, was the first of this family to possess Castle Leslie or Glaslough. He was son of George Leslie of Crichie, 2nd son of Walter Leslie of Wardis (*see* E Rothes) and uncle of 1st Bt (*cr* NS 1625), to which baronetcy his line is in remainder. Sir John Leslie, 1st baronet, sometime Capt 1st Life Guards, was MP for co Monaghan and a noted painter. The 2nd baronet, Sir John, CBE, was Lt Grenadier Guards and Lt-Col Roy Irish Fusiliers, and served in Egypt 1882, in S Africa 1900, and in 1914-18 War (CBE). Sir John, who was the last Lord Lieut and Custos Rotulorum co Monaghan, *m* 1884, Leonie Blanche, da of Leonard Jerome, of New York (grandfather of Sir Winston Churchill). The 3rd baronet was the writer Sir (John Randolph) Shane Leslie, and his da, Anita Leslie, was also a distinguished writer.

LETHBRIDGE (UK) 1804, of Westaway House, and Winkley Court, Somerset

My hope is in God

Sir Thomas Periam Hector Noel Lethbridge, 7th *Baronet*; *b* 17 July 1950; *s* his father, *Sir* Hector Wroth, 1978; *ed* Milton Abbey, and RAC Cirencester: *m* 1976 (*m diss* 1998), Susan Elizabeth, el da of Lyle Rocke, of Maryland, USA, and has issue.

𝔄rms – Argent, over water proper, a bridge of five arches embattled gules, and over the centre arch a turret, in chief an eagle displayed sable charged on the breast with a bezant. ℭrest – From a bridge embattled of one arch gules a demi-eagle displayed sable, wings erminois charged on the breast with a leopard's face or. 𝔐otto over ℭrest – "*Truth*".
Clubs – Farmers', Voles.

SONS LIVING

John Francis Buckler Noel, *b* 10 March 1977. —— Edward Christopher Wroth, *b* 1978. —— Alexander Ralph Periam, *b* 1982. —— Henry Charles Hesketh, *b* 1984.

DAUGHTERS LIVING

Georgina Rose Alianore, *b* 1980. —— Rachel Elizabeth Mary, *b* 1986.

SISTER LIVING

Mary Jacintha, *b* 1948: *m* 1974, Brig Richard J. Heywood, OBE, Coldm Gds, of Manor Farm Stables, Ingoldisthorpe, King's Lynn, Norfolk, and has issue living, Richard Anthony, *b* 1977, — Anna Rose, *b* 1975.

COLLATERAL BRANCHES LIVING

Issue of late Hugh Francis Hesketh Lethbridge, 4th son of 4th baronet, *b* 1867, *d* 1935: *m* 1912, Edith Maude, da of Thomas Mellor Robinson, of Metford, Natal:—
Hugh Mytton Fitzwarine, *b* 1913: *m* 1945, Elsie Murray, da of late Very Rev Dean Bartlet, of Aberdeen, and has issue living, Hugh George, *b* 1948, — Jennifer Murray, *b* 1946. —— Wroth Thomas Hesketh Bourchier, *b* 1914. —— Delphine Edith Conyers Bourchier, *b* 1922.

Grandchildren of late John Acland Musgrave Lethbridge (infra):—
Issue of late Duncan John Leghe Lethbridge, *b* 1898, *d* 1962; *m* 1922, Phyllis Muriel (Anderson), who *d* 1971, da of T. Stanley Chappell, of Chadshunt, Warwicks:—
June Florence, *b* 1926: *m* 1944, Mario A. Fog, of 217A Lucy Creek Drive, Beaufort, S Carolina 29902, USA, and has issue living, Duncan Lethbridge, *b* 1948: *m* 1989, Sarah McLane, — Stephen Chase, *b* 1952: *m* 1979, Wendy Merritt Dixon, and has issue living, Merritt Lawrence *b* 1981, Courtnay Andrews *b* 1984. —— Ann, *b* 1930: *m* 1951, Graham Lusk Platt, of 40 Walnut Tree Lane, Cold Spring Harbor, Long Island, New York 11724, USA, and has issue living, Graham Leghe, *b* 1959: *m* 1995, Laura Ann Allen, and has issue living, Dillon Weil *b* 1997; also has issue, Jeremy Redding Knox *b* 1983, — Gordon Lethbridge, *b* 1962: *m* 1993, Mary M. Walsh, — Christina May, *b* 1956: *m* 1980, Michael J. Nelson, and has issue living, Adrien Leghe *b* 1979, Lindsay Ann *b* 1981, Louisa May *b* 1985, Sandi Grey *b* 1989.

Issue of late Harold Reginald Lethbridge, *b* 1901, *d* 1972: *m* 1942, Shirley Ivy Grace (Lidstone), da of William Mascall, of Cambridgeshire:—
Duncan Stuart (St Francis Bay, S Africa), *b* 1943: *m* 1969, Catherine Jean Beveridge, da of late John Sneddon, of Kinross, Scotland, and has issue living, Duncan Reginald John, *b* 1973, — Claire Cecilia, *b* 1975. —— Reginald Martin Peter, *b* 1946. —— Richard Christopher Noel, *b* 1949; *d* 1968.

Issue of late John Acland Musgrave Lethbridge, 5th son of 4th baronet, *b* 1869, *d* 1934: *m* 1894, Florence Martin, who *d* 1931, da of Sidney Wood Cooper, of New York, USA:—
Annie Gwendoline, *b* 1896: *m* 1st, 1916, Capt Guy Clavering Wetherall, formerly RASC; 2ndly, 1945, Capt Thorold Murray Smith, MC, and has issue living, (by 1st *m*) Robert Guy, *b* 1917, — Peter Martin, *b* 1919.

Grandchildren (by 3rd *m*) of late Capt Walter Miguel Lethbridge, MC (infra):—
Issue of late Walter Miguel Lethbridge, *b* 1923, *d* 1991: *m* 1st, 1949 (*m diss* 1956), Nora, da of Eduardo Barrios; 2ndly, 1957 (*m diss* 1982), Jill Margaret, da of late Robert Gibson Nethery, MRCS, LRCP, of 5 St Patrick's Court, Bath; 3rdly, 1982, Silvely (Calle Pedroza, Residencias Miami, Piso 6 Apt 20, La Florida, Caracas 1030, Venezuela), da of late Viktor Kalve Grandin, of Riga, Latvia:—
(By 1st *m*) Walter Alexander, *b* 1950: *m* 1st, 1971 (*m diss* 1988), Elsie, da of Guy Derozieres-Le comte, of Lille, France; 2ndly, 1988, Patricia Douglas, and has issue living, (by 1st *m*) Alexis Guillaume, *b* 1971, — Chloé, *b* 1980. —— (By 2nd *m*) Arabella Margaret, *b* 1962: *m* 1986, Charles Edward Budgett, son of Rev Preb Anthony Thomas Budgett, of Wellington, Som, and has issue living, Holly Katharine, *b* 1989, — Vanessa Margaret, *b* 1992.

Issue of late Rodney Thomas Lethbridge, *b* 1925, *d* 1978: *m* 1st, 1942 (*m diss* 1944), Sara, da of R. Miranda; 2ndly, 1949 (*m diss* 1955), Fedora, da of Ernesto Moya; 3rdly, 1956, Marcelle Goulet:—
(By 2nd *m*) Doris Elizabeth, *b* 1950. —— (By 3rd *m*) Rodney Thomas, *b* 1957. —— Michael Walter, *b* 1964. —— Suzanne Carmen, *b* 1962.

Grandchildren of late Capt Walter Alexander Charles Lethbridge (infra):—
Issue of late Capt Walter Miguel Lethbridge, MC, *b* 1886, *d* 1964: *m* 1st (Jan) 1907 (*m diss* 19—), Anna Agnes, da of V. Gunter; 2ndly, 1913 (*m* annulled 19—), Catherine Matilda, da of F. M. Marsh; 3rdly, 1919, Carmela, who *d* 1980, da of Miguel I. Aguilera:—
(By 1st *m*) Frances Rose, *b* (Nov) 1907. —— (By 3rd *m*) Douglas Nelson, *b* 1933: *m* 1st, 1954 (*m diss* 196-), Margaret, da of George Isnor; 2ndly, —; 3rdly, —; 4thly, —; 5thly, —; 6thly, 19— (*m diss* 19—), Maria Cecilia Urrutia, of Columbia; 7thly, — ; 8thly, — and has issue living, (by 1st *m*) Michael, *b* 1955, — Maureen, *b* 1956, — (by later *m*) 2 children. —— Carmen Rosa, *b* 1927: *m* 1st, 1950 (*m diss* 19—), Luis F. Pineiro; 2ndly, 19—, — Menendes, of Lodlam Point, 6880 SW 44th St, Apt 204, Fla 33155, USA, and has issue living (by 1st *m*) Luis Felipe, *b* 1952, — Rose Marie, *b* 1959, — Katherine, *b* 1968.

Grandsons of late Capt Walter Alexander Charles Lethbridge, only son of late Walter Buckler Lethbridge, 6th and yst son of 3rd baronet:—
Issue of late John George Jules Lethbridge, late RAF and US Navy, *b* 1888, *d* 1968 (Washington, DC): *m* 1917, Dorothy Josephine, da of late Le Roy M. Taylor, of Washington, DC:—
John George, *b* 1917. —— Robert Mortimer, *b* 1921.

Sir John Lethbridge, 1st Bt, was the only son of John Lethbridge, of Westaway House, Pilton, and *m* Dorothea, el da and co-heir of William Buckler, of Boreham, Wilts. The 2nd baronet, Sir Thomas Buckler, Lethbridge, sat as MP for Somersetshire 1806-12 and 1820-30.

LETT (UK) 1941, of Walmer, co Kent (Extinct 1964)

Sir HUGH LETT, KCVO, CBE, DCL, ScD, MB, FRCS, 1st and last *Baronet*.

DAUGHTERS LIVING OF FIRST BARONET

Sheila Buckston, *b* 1910: *m* 1946, Maj Gordon Appleford Lett, DSO, who *d* 1989, and has issue living, Hugh Brian Gordon, *b* 1949; Bar Inner Temple 1972: *m* 1979, Angela Susan Jaques, and has issue living, Julian Peter Hugh *b* 1984, Robin Jonathan Hugh *b* 1986, Toby Alexander Hugh *b* 1992, Stephanie Rachel Buckston *b* 1988, — Valerie Buckston, *b* 1947; LRAM. ——Joan Buckston, *b* 1918: *m* 1941, Hugh William Cochrane Bailie, MB, FRCS (Edin), late Capt RAMC, who *d* 1980, and has issue living, Hugh Richard Molyneux (Honeymead, 64 Raglan Rd, Reigate, Surrey RH2 0HP), *b* 1950; FRICS, FRVA: *m* 1975, Susan Jane Rees, and has issue living, Hugh Alistair Cochrane *b* 1981, Catherine Anne *b* 1978, — Lyndon Lett, *b* 1942; MB, BCh, DO: *m* 1974, Richard Austen Bloxham, MB, BS, MRCP, of 7 Langston Av, Palmerston North, North Island, NZ, and has issue living, David Andrew *b* 1975, Helen Jane *b* 1977, Megan Louise *b* 1979, — Fiona Buckston, *b* 1944; MB BCh, FRCS (Edinburgh): *m* 1990, Michael Taylor, of 12 Chartwell Grove, Mapperley Plains, Nottingham NG3 5RD. *Residence* – 2A Orchard Drive, Tonbridge, Kent.

LEVER (UK) 1911, of Hans Crescent, Chelsea

Sir (Tresham) Christopher Arthur Lindsay Lever, 3rd *Baronet, b* 9 Jan 1932; *s* his father, *Sir* Tresham Joseph Philip, FRSL, 1975; *ed* Eton, and Trin Coll, Camb (MA); commn'd 17th/21st Lancers 1950; naturalist and author; FLS: *m* 1st, 1970 (*m diss* 1974), Susan Mary, da of late John Armytage Nicholson, of Enniscoe, Crossmolina, co Mayo, and Milestown, Dunboyne, co Meath; 2ndly, 1975, Linda Weightman McDowell, da of late James Jepson Goulden, of Tennessee, USA.

𝔄rms – Quarterly 1st and 4th, tierce in pairle sable, gules and azure, three bear's heads one and two erased, muzzled or; 2nd and 3rd argent, a chevron invected ermines between two keys erect the wards to the dexter in chief sable, and an Esquire's helmet in base proper. 𝔠rest – 1st, in front of a rising moon proper, a cormorant sable; 2nd, a dexter arm embowed in armour, the hand proper holding a key in bend sinister, the wards upwards sable, and encircled above the elbow with a chaplet or roses argent, leaved vert.
Residence – Newell House, Winkfield, Berks SL4 4SE. *Club* – Boodle's.

WIDOW LIVING OF SECOND BARONET

(Clodagh) Pamela (*Pamela, Lady Lever*) (Lessudden, St Boswells, Roxburghshire), only child of late Lt-Col Hon Malcolm Bowes-Lyon, CBE (*see* E Strathmore, colls), and formerly wife of the late Lord Malcolm Avondale Douglas-Hamilton, OBE, DFC (D Hamilton): *m* 1962, as his 2nd wife, Sir Tresham Joseph Philip Lever, FRSL, 2nd Bt, who *d* 1975.

By courage and faith

Sir Arthur, 1st Bt, a JP for Essex, was a yr brother of Sir Maurice Levy, 1st Bt (*cr* 1913), of Great Glen House, co Leicester, and son of late Joseph Levy, of Leicester; he was a member of Roy Commn on Coast Erosion, and sat as MP for Harwich (*L*) 1906-10, and Hackney, Central (NL) 1922-23; assumed by deed poll 1896 and by Roy licence 1911 the additional surname of Lever; Sir Tresham Joseph Philip, 2nd Bt, was author of various historical works including *The Life and Times of Sir Robert Peel, The House of Pitt,* and *The Herberts of Wilton.*

LEVINGE (I) 1704, of High Park, Westmeath

Sir Richard George Robin Levinge, 12th *Baronet; b* 18 Dec 1946; *s* his father, Major *Sir* Richard Vere Henry, MBE, TD, 1984; *m* 1st, 1969 (*m diss* 1978), Hilary Jane, da of Dr Derek Mark, of Wingfield, Bray, co Wicklow; 2ndly, 1978, Donna Maria Isabella d'Ardia Caracciolo, yr da of Don Ferdinando d'Ardia Caracciolo dei Principi di Cursi, of Haddington Rd, Dublin 4, and has issue by 1st and 2nd *m.*

𝔄rms – Vert, a chevron or, three escallops argent in chief. 𝔠rest – An escallop argent, within a garland proper.
Residences – Clohamon House, Bunclody, co Wexford, Republic of Ireland.

SONS LIVING (*By 1st marriage*)

Richard Mark, *b* 1970.

(*By 2nd marriage*)

Robin Edward, *b* 1978.

DAUGHTER LIVING (*By 2nd marriage*)

Melissa Louise, *b* 1980.

BROTHER LIVING

No footsteps backwards

Michael James, *b* 1948. *Residence* – 2 Vicarage Crescent, Hatfield Peverel, Chelmsford, Essex.

SISTERS LIVING

Elizabeth Anne (104 Beechwood Lawn, Killiney, Co Dublin), *b* 1937: *m* 1957, Walter Wright Lee, Jr, only son of Walter Wright Lee, of 145 East 35th St, New York. —— Susan Maureen (Bulland Cottage, Wiveliscombe, nr Taunton, Somerset), *b* 1944: *m* 1965 (*m diss* 19—), Douglas P.W. Wright, yr son of late Rev E.H. Wright, and has issue living, Slaney, *b* 1976. — Clody, *b* 1979. —— Mary Irene, *b* 1952: *m* 1976, Charles Philip Cooper, of Markree Castle,

Collooney, co Sligo, yst son of late Lt-Cmdr Edward Francis Patrick Cooper, of Markree Castle, co Sligo, and has issue living, Patricia, *b* 1982, — Siobhan, *b* 1984.

WIDOW LIVING OF ELEVENTH BARONET

JANE ROSEMARY (*Jane, Lady Levinge*), da of John Thomas Stacey, of East Dereham, Norfolk, and formerly wife of Dennis Millward: *m* 1976, as his 2nd wife, Sir Richard Vere Henry Levinge, 11th Bt, MBE, TD, who *d* 1984. *Residence* – Abbey Lodge, Rectory Lane, Itchen Abbas, Hants.

COLLATERAL BRANCHES LIVING

Grandchildren of late Maj Thomas Vere Levinge (infra):—
Issue of late William James Levinge, *b* 1929, *d* 1987: *m* 1954, Heather Mary Johnson (41 Bridge Rd, Welwyn Garden City, Herts), of Brackley, Northants:—
Nicholas Vere, *b* 1955: *m* 1983, Kathryn Bampton, and has issue living, Thomas John, *b* 1986. —— Edward James, *b* 1957: *m* 1984, Sandra Ann Dunne, and has issue living, Andrew William, *b* 1992, — Joanna Louise, *b* 1990. —— Sarah Jennifer Louise, *b* 1961.

Issue of late Major Thomas Vere Levinge, 2nd son of 9th baronet, *b* 1880, *d* 1949: *m* 1928, Dorothy, who *d* 1977, da of J. Ingman, of Northampton:—
Thomas Gerald, *b* 1934: *m* 19—, Stella Field, and has issue living, a son, *b* 1964.

Issue of late Bernard George Levinge, 5th son of 9th baronet, *b* 1887, *d* 1953: *m* 1912, Stella Parsons:—
Reginald Noel (9 Dent St, Penrith, NSW), *b* 1927: *m* 1950, Pearl Kathleen, da of late Walter Wright Armstrong, and has issue living, Geoffrey Paul, *b* 1952: *m* 1970, Sandra, da of A. Kiggins, and has issue living, Mark Andrew *b* 1974, Kerry Ann *b* 1971, Tracy Maree *b* 1980, — Maureen Ann, *b* 1956: *m* 1978, Christopher Fehon, of 1B Minna St, Burwood, NSW 2134, and has issue living, Luke *b* 1985, Rebecca *b* 1982, Emma *b* (twin) 1985, — Sharon Maree, *b* 1963: *m* 1983, Christopher Carl, and has issue living, Michael James *b* 1985, Adrian Noel *b* 1986, Amanda Lee *b* 1984.

Issue of late Major George Edward Levinge, brother of 9th baronet, *b* 1862, *d* 1926: *m* 1895, Elizabeth Louisa, da of John Wiley, of Brisbane, Queensland:—
George Onslow, *b* 1896. —— William John, *b* 1903.

Granddaughter of late Harry Corbyn Levinge, eldest son of 6th baronet:—
Issue of late Sir Edward Vere Levinge, KCIE, CSI, *b* 1867, *d* 1954: *m* 1900, Alys Adèle, who *d* 1952, da of Maj-Gen Charles Frederic Thomas:—
Vera Alys, *b* 1911: *m* 1938, Count (Michael) Karl von Althann, who *d* 1978, and has issue living, *Count* (Michael) Robert, *b* 1939, — *Count* (Michael) Alexander, *b* 1940: *m* 1978, Maria Kammerlander, and has issue living, *Count* Wenzel *b* 1979, *Count* Quintin *b* 1982, *Countess* Clementine *b* 1980, — *Count* (Michael) Victor, *b* 1944: *m* 1972, Maria de la Natividad del Valle, of Haverford, Pa, USA, and has issue living, *Count* Charles *b* 1982, *Countess* Caroline *b* 1980, — *Countess* Maria Olga, *b* 1941: *m* 1975, Count Ferdinand von Coreth zu Coredo, and has issue living, *Countess* Julie *b* 1976, *Countess* Isabelle *b* 1978, — *Countess* Maria Christina *b* 1942: *m* 1966, Don José Manuel de Ruiz Gonzalez, who *d* 1980, and has issue living, José Carlos *b* 1967, Alejandro Miguel *b* 1970, Veronica *b* 1974, — *Countess* Maria Therese Margarethe, *b* 1949: *m* 1983, François-Charles Pictet, Swiss Amb to the Court of St James's (Swiss Embassy, 21 Bryanston Sq, W1). *Residence* – A3435, Zwentendorf a d Donau, Lower Austria.

Grandson of late Capt Richard Hugh Levinge, 2nd son of late Richard William Chaworth Levinge (infra):—
Issue of late Rev (Evelyn) Hugh Jenoyr Levinge, RN, *b* 1915, *d* 1981: *m* 1955, Sheila Joy, who *d* 1992, da of S. L. R. Etherton, LLB, BSc, of Detroit, USA:—
Richard St John (Broadway, 8 Hall Rd, Leckhampton, Cheltenham, Glos GL53 0HE), *b* 1956: *m* 1979, Mary Juliet, da of Radnor Outhwaite, of Cale Green, Stockport, and has issue living, Daniel Richard, *b* 1983, — Victoria Louise, *b* 1984.

Grandson of late Richard William Chaworth Levinge, eldest son of Charles William Levinge (infra):—
Issue of late Frederick Rufane Levinge, *b* 1890, *d* 1981: *m* 1929, Rona Elizabeth, who *d* 1971, da of late Richard M. Hawker, of Bungaree, Clare, S Aust:—
Frederick Charles Richard (13 McIntyre St, Robe, S Aust 5276), *b* 1939: *m* 1969, Tessa Mary, only da of R. W. Barton, of Gisborne, NZ, and has issue living, Charles Richard Wynne, *b* 1973, — Georgina Rona, *b* 1971: *m* 1996, Richard Allan Oates, of Elouera, Purlewaugh, NSW 2357, Aust.

Grandchildren of late Surg-Maj Edward Levinge, 2nd son of late Charles William Levinge, only son of late Richard Hugh Levinge, 4th son of 4th baronet:—
Issue of late Edward Vere Bryce Levinge, *b* 1889, *d* 1922: *m* 1916, his cousin, Ethel Violet, who *d* 1924, da of late George Cardwell Porter, MD, of Castleacre, Norfolk (*see* Levinge, Bt, 1924 Edn):—
Bryce Leonard, *b* 1922; is a Farmer. —— Avice Ethel Mary: *m* 1st, 1944, Ward Shepard, who *d* 1953; 2ndly, 1953, George Alfred Robinson, and has issue living, (by 1st *m*) Carol Jean, *b* 1946, — (by 2nd *m*) Bryce Levinge, *b* 1954, — Guy Herrick, *b* 1957. *Address* – PO Box 275, Falls Church, Virginia, USA.

Granddaughters of late Robert Degennes Levinge, 4th son of late Marcus Anthony Levinge, only son of late Mark Anthony Levinge, 5th son of 4th baronet:—
Issue of late Walter Hodson Levinge, *b* 1894, *d* 1982: *m* 1945, Marion Blanche, who *d* 1974, da of Rev Francis Cockle, Rector of Aasleagh, Leenane, co Galway:—

Hester Sylvia, *b* 1947: *m* 1970, Trevor David Scott, of Mount Venus House, Woodtown Rd, Rathfarnham, co Dublin. —— Daphne Elaine Sybil, *b* 1950; PhD: *m* 1979, Jonathan Joseph Shackleton, and has issue living, David Levinge, *b* 1981, — Jane Hester, *b* 1984, — Hannah Lydia, *b* 1987. —— Marion Alison Patricia, *b* 1951: *m* 1981, Charles Gillard Couper, of Creaghduff, Athlone, co Westmeath, and has had issue, Alister Milne, *b* 1984, *d* 1987, — Tristan Richard, *b* 1988, — Sally Marion, *b* 1981, — Elaine Judith, *b* 1989.

The 1st baronet, Right Hon Sir Richard Levinge, was Lord Chief Justice of the Common Pleas in Ireland and the 7th baronet, Sir Richard George Augustus, sat as MP for co Westmeath (*L*) 1857-65. The 10th baronet, Sir Richard William, Lieut 1st Life Guards, was *ka* Oct 1914.

LEVY (UK) 1913, of Humberstone Hall, co Leicester (Extinct 1996)

Sir EWART JOSEPH MAURICE LEVY, 2nd and last *Baronet*.

DAUGHTER LIVING OF SECOND BARONET

Caroline Anne Patricia, *b* 1933: *m* 1st, 1965 (*m diss* 1971), George Robert Paterson Coles; 2ndly, 1971, Terence John McInnes Skinner, of John O'Gaunt House, Melton Mowbray, Leics.

ORR-LEWIS (UK) 1920, of Whitewebbs Park, Enfield, co Middlesex (Extinct 1980)

Sir (JOHN) DUNCAN ORR LEWIS, 2nd and last *Baronet*; *d* 1980.

DAUGHTER LIVING OF SECOND BARONET

Marie Ardyn, *b* 1922: *m* 1942, Affleck Macpherson and has issue living, Alastair Duncan, *b* 1960, — Marjorie Gay, *b* 1946. *Residence* –

LEWTHWAITE (UK) 1927, of Broadgate, Parish of Thwaites, co Cumberland

Sir RAINALD GILFRID LEWTHWAITE, 4th *Baronet*, CVO, OBE, MC; *b* 21 July 1913; *s* his brother, *Sir* WILLIAM ANTHONY, 1993; *ed* Rugby, and Trin Coll Camb (BA 1934); Brig late Scots Gds; Mil Attche 1964, and Defence Attache at British Embassy, Paris, 1965-68; 1939-45 War in Middle East (MC), France, Holland, Germany and Italy; OBE (Civil) 1974, CVO 1975: *m* 1936, Margaret Elizabeth, MBE, who *d* 1990, da of Harry Edmonds, of New York, USA, and has had issue.

Arms – Ermine, a cross flory azure, fretty or. **Crest** – A garb or, bound by a serpent nowed proper, holding in the mouth a cross-crosslet fitchée gules. *Residence* – Broadgate, Millom, Cumbria LA18 5JZ.

Virtus·ad·æthera·tendens

Virtue reaching towards heaven

SONS LIVING AND DECEASED

DAVID RAINALD (49 Ranelagh Grove, SW1W 8PB), *b* 26 March 1940; *ed* Rugby, and Trin Coll Camb (BA 1960): *m* 1969, Diana Helena, twin da of late William Robert Tomkinson, TD (*see* Blane, Bt (ext)), and has issue living, Emma Victoria, *b* 1971: *m* 1997, Andrew A. Pitt, son of late David Pitt, of Macclesfield, Cheshire, — Mary-Claire, *b* 1972. —— †John Valentine, *b* 1944; *ed* Eton, and Harvard: *m* 1967, Elizabeth Georgiana (Combe Farm, Battisborough Cross, Plymouth, Devon PL8 1JQ), da of Richard John Bramble Mildmay-White (*see* By Mildmay of Flete, 1990 Edn), and *d* 1990, leaving issue, Alice Georgiana, *b* 1969: *m* 1997, Andrew G. Page, elder son of Michael Page, of Piltdown, Sussex, — Martha Grace, *b* 1970: *m* 1994, Brendan T. Desmond, yst son of late George Desmond, of Fulham, SW, and has issue living, Fred Valentine *b* 1996, Elsa Georgina *b* 1997.

DAUGHTERS DECEASED

Margaret Sylvia, *b* 1937; *dunm* 1994. —— Mary Rose, *b* 1946; *d* 1949.

DAUGHTER LIVING OF THIRD BARONET

Catherine Jane, *b* 1954: *m* 1986, William Tobias Hall, 2nd son of late S. J. Hall, of Stratfield Turgis, Hants, and has issue living, Francesca, *b* 1990, — Sophie, *b* (twin)1990.

WIDOW LIVING OF THIRD BARONET

LOIS MAIRI (*Lady Lewthwaite*), only child of late Capt Struan Robertson Kerr-Clark (*see* E Drogheda, 1966 Edn): *m* 1936, Sir William Anthony Lewthwaite, 3rd Bt, who *d* 1993. *Address* – c/o 73 Dovehouse Street, SW3 6JZ.

Sir William Lewthwaite, 1st Bt (Vice-Lieut of Cumberland 1921-2 and 1923-4, and Dep Chm of Quarter Sessions) was Chm Conservative Asso of Egremont Div of Cumberland 1904-24 (many years Treasurer).

LEY (UK) 1905, of Epperstone Manor, Epperstone, co Nottingham
(Name pronounced "Lee")

Sir IAN FRANCIS LEY, 5th *Baronet*; *b* 12 June 1934; *s* his father, *Major Sir* FRANCIS DOUGLAS, MBE, TD, 1995; *ed* Eton; late 2nd Lieut 10th Royal Hussars; High Sheriff Derbys 1985: *m* 1957, Caroline Margaret, elder da of late Maj George Henry Errington, MC, of Zimbabwe, and has issue.

Arms – Argent, six lozenges conjoined in bend between two broken tilting spears gules. **Crest** – In front of a cubit arm in armour a hand grasping a broken tilting spear, four lozenges conjoined fesseways gules.
Residence – Fauld Hall, Tutbury, Staffs. *Club* – White's.

SON LIVING

CHRISTOPHER IAN, *b* 2 Dec 1962; *ed* Eton: *m* 1999, Henrietta M., yr da of David Nicholls, of Manningtree, Essex. *Residence* – 74 Coniger Rd, SW6 3TA.

DAUGHTER LIVING

Virginia Mary, *b* 1960: *m* 1988, Samuel C. Thomasson, eldest son of Christopher Thomasson, of Boothby Graffoe, Lincs, and has issue living, Jack James, *b* 1990, — Laurie Francis, *b* 1992, — Cicely, *b* 1996. *Residence* – Spring Garden, Horse Croft, Stanford in the Vale, Oxon.

SISTER LIVING

After death I hope for life

POST·MORTEM·SPERO·VITAM

Susan Alison, *b* 1937: *m* 1960, Charles Edward Weatherby, of Mixbury Lodge Farm, Brackley, Northants, and has issue living, Camilla Jane, *b* 1963: *m* 1993, William John Haviland Hiley (*see* M Linlithgow, colls), and has issue (see that title), — Fiona Mary, *b* 1965: *m* 1990, Paul Richard Webber, of Cropredy Lawn, Banbury, Oxon, son of late John Huyshe Webber, of Cropredy, Oxon, and has issue living, Sophie Rose *b* 1998.

AUNT LIVING (*daughter of 2nd baronet*)

Mary Rhoda (Ilsom House, Tetbury, Glos), *b* 1906: *m* 1944, Maj Geoffrey Charles Bishop, 9th Lancers, who *d* 1970.

DAUGHTERS LIVING OF THIRD BARONET (*By 1st marriage*)

(Elizabeth) Bridget Rhoda, *b* 1937: *m* 1965, Roger Humphrey Boissier, CBE, High Sheriff Derbys 1988-89, of Easton House, The Pastures, Repton, Derby DE65 6GG, and has issue living, Rupert John *b* 1967: *m* 1996, Isabel Mary, da of Spencer Rodney Osborne Barratt, and has issue living, Thomas Samuel *b* 1998, — Clare Louise, *b* 1968. ———— Annabel Alison (Townhead of Glencairn, by Moniaive, Dumfriesshire DG3 4HD), *b* 1939: *m* 1960 (*m diss* 1999), David Eric Cramer Stapleton, and has issue living, Serena Jane Clare, *b* 1961: *m* 1990, David Hugo Martyn Williams-Ellis, of Lazonby Manor, Lazonby, Penrith, Cumbria CA10 1BA, son of late John Williams-Ellis, of Carregfelen, Porthmadog, N Wales, and has had issue, Hugo John George *b* 1992, Jack David Clough *b* 1997, Emily Rose *b* and *d* 1991, Phoebe Constance Mary *b* 1994, — Charlotte Jessica Louise, *b* 1963: *m* 1987, Bertrand Maurice Van Houtte de la Chaise, of 30 rue Montmartre, 75001 Paris, France, son of Jacques Van Houtte de la Chaise, of Deauville, France, and has issue living, Edward Henri Cramer *b* 1991, Pierre Maxim Charles *b* 1994, Alexandra Constance Marie *b* 1989, — Victoria Lucy Annabel, *b* 1967: *m* 1999, Jonathan Mark Pilkington, of 30 Lots Rd, SW10 0QF, yr son of Ronald Charles Leslie Pilkington, and has issue living, Jesse Honor *b* 1997, — Lara Alexandra Mary-Rose, *b* 1974. ———— Caroline Sheila (*Countess of Lonsdale*), *b* 1943: *m* 1975, as his 4th wife, 7th Earl of Lonsdale, and has issue (see that title).

Sir Francis Ley, 1st Bt, Gov, Director, and Founder of Ley's Works in Derby, later Leys Foundries and Engineering plc, was High Sheriff of Notts 1905.

NAYLOR-LEYLAND (UK) 1895, of Hyde Park House, Albert Gate, co London

Sir PHILIP VYVIAN NAYLOR-LEYLAND, 4th *Baronet*; *b* 9 Aug 1953; *s* his father, *Sir* VIVYAN EDWARD, 1987; *ed* Eton, RMA Sandhurst, NY Univ Business Sch, and RAC Cirencester; Lieut LG; MFH: *m* 1980, Lady Isabella Lambton, yst da of Antony Claud Frederick Lambton (6th Earl of Durham until he disclaimed his title 1970), and has issue.

𝕬rms – Quarterly, 1st and 4th, ermine, on a fesse engrailed sable, between nine ears of barley, three, three, and three vert, banded or in chief, and three like ears in base, a lion passant of the last between two escallops argent and for distinction a canton gules, *Leyland*; 2nd and 3rd, per pale or and argent, a pale sable fretty of the first between two lions rampant of the third, and for distinction a canton gules, *Naylor*. 𝕮rest – 1st, A mount vert, thereon an escallop argent, surmounted by a demi-eagle erminois, wings endorsed azure, bezantée, in the mouth three ears of barley vert, and charged for distinction with a cross-crosslet gules, *Leyland*; 2nd, a lion passant sable, charged on the body with two saltires or, resting the dexter forepaw upon a shield, charged with the arms of Naylor, and charged further for distinction with a cross-crosslet also or, *Naylor*.
Residences – Milton, Peterborough, Cambs PE6 7AA; Nantclwyd Hall, Ruthin, Denbighshire LL15 2PR.

Faithful and bold

SONS LIVING

THOMAS PHILIP, *b* 22 Jan 1982. —— George Antony, *b* 1989. —— Edward Claud, *b* 1993.

DAUGHTERS LIVING

Violet Mary, *b* 1983. —— Beatrix Rose Elizabeth, *b* 1998.

HALF-SISTERS LIVING (*Daughter of 3rd baronet by 2nd wife*)

Cleone Mary Veronica, *b* 1968.

(*Daughter of 3rd baronet by 3rd wife*)

Virginia, *b* 1983. —— Jessica Pamela, *b* 1987.

UNCLE LIVING (*Son of 2nd Baronet*)

Michael Montagu George, MC, *b* 1926; formerly Capt The Life Guards: *m* 1953, Jacqueline Marie Françoise, yr da of Maj Ides Floor, DSO, MBE, of Lullenden, East Grinstead, Sussex, and has issue living, David George Edward, *b* 1955; Lt LG: *m* 1978, Jane Lucinda, el da of Lt-Col John Monsell Christian, MC, KRRC, of Clifferdine House, Rencomb, Glos, and has issue living, John *b* 1984, Frederick George *b* 1987, Victoria *b* 1982, — Joanna Rosemary Jane, *b* 1961: *m* 1st, 1985 (*m diss* 1989), Nigel James Norman, elder son of Sir Mark Annesley Norman, 3rd Bt; 2ndly, 1989, Philip S. O. Lambert, of 8 Soudan Rd, SW11, yr son of Capt Richard Lambert, RN, CBE, DL, of Garthgwynion, Machynlleth, Wales, and has issue living (by 2nd *m*), Jack *b* 1990, Tom *b* 1994, Laura *b* 1992. *Residence* – The Red House, Lacock, Chippenham, Wiltshire SN15 2LB.

AUNT LIVING (*Daughter of 2nd baronet*)

Veronica Rosemary, *b* 1932: *m* 1955 (*m diss* 1975), Peter Cyril Alexander Munster (*see* E Dudley, colls, 1980 Edn), and has issue living, Alexander Paul, *b* 1961, — Sarah Hélène, *b* 1957, — Marina Claire, *b* 1960. *Residence* – 3 Queens Gate Place Mews, SW7 5BG.

WIDOW LIVING OF THIRD BARONET

JAMEINA FLORA (*Jameina, Lady Naylor-Leyland*), da of James Freeman Reid: *m* 1980, as his 3rd wife, Sir Vivyan Edward Naylor-Leyland, 3rd Bt, who *d* 1987. *Residence* – Le Neuf Chemin, St Saviours, Guernsey, CI.

COLLATERAL BRANCH LIVING

Issue of late (Alick) David Yorke Naylor-Leyland, LVO, late Lieut Gren Guards, yst son of 2nd baronet, *b* 1929, *d* 1991: *m* 1st, 1953 (*m diss* 1962), Diana Elizabeth Lea (who *m* 2ndly, 1962, 7th Earl of Wilton), da of Roy Galway, of St Ronans, Winkfield Row, Berks; 2ndly, 1962 (*m diss* 1969), Dita Douglas (AMORY), da of J. Gordon Douglas, Jr, of Prince's Neck, Newport, Rhode Island, USA; 3rdly, 1973, Carolyn S. Neilson, who *d* 1989:—

(By 1st *m*) Michael Alexander Robert, *b* 1956: *m* 1st, 1984 (*m diss* 19—), Lucy Clare, da of Henry Potts, of Eglingham Hall, Alnwick, Northumberland; 2ndly, 1990, HRH Princess Tania Saskia Viktoria-Luise of Hanover, only child of HRH late Prince Welf Ernst August Andreas Philipp Georg Wilhelm Ludwig Berthold of Hanover (*see* ROYAL FAMILY), and has issue living, (by 2nd *m*) Jake John, *b* 1993. —— Amanda Jane, *b* 1954: *m* 1st, 1977 (*m diss* 1982), Thomas Skiffington; 2ndly, 1996, as his 2nd wife, Thomas Mervyn Brudenell (*see* M Ailesbury, colls). *Residence* – Lark Hall, Fordham, Ely, Cambs. —— (By 2nd *m*) Nicholas Edward, *b* 1962. —— (By 3rd *m*) Edward Frederick, *b* 1975.

The 1st baronet, Sir Herbert Scarisbrick, was MP for Colchester (*C*) 1892-95, and for Lancashire (S-W), Southport Div (*L*) 1898-9. The 2nd baronet, Sir Albert Edward Herbert, was Sheriff of Denbighshire 1921, and was sometime an Hon Attaché, British Legation, Berne, and British Embassy, Paris. The 3rd baronet, Sir Vivyan Edward, *b* 1924, late Lieut Gren Gds: *m* 1st, 1952 (*m diss* 1960), Hon Elizabeth Anne Marie Gabrielle Fitzalan-Howard, who *d* 1997, yr da of 2nd Viscount FitzAlan of Derwent (*see* B Mowbray, colls); 2ndly, 1967 (*m diss* 1975), Noreen Starr, da of late W/Cdr Peter Anker-Simmons, DFC, RAF (*see* Bailey, Bt); 3rdly, 1980, Jameina Flora, da of James Freeman Reid; *d* 1987.

LIGHTON (I) 1791, of Merville, Dublin

Sir THOMAS HAMILTON LIGHTON, 9th *Baronet*; *b* 4 Nov 1954; *s* his father, *Sir* CHRISTOPHER ROBERT, MBE, 1993; *ed* Eton: *m* 1990, Belinda Jean, elder da of John Fergusson, of Barnhillies, Castle Douglas, Kirkcudbrightshire, and has had issue.

𝕬rms – Barry of eight argent and vert, over all a lion rampant crowned with an eastern crown or, armed and langued azure, a canton of Ireland. 𝕮rest – A lion's head erased crowned with an eastern crown or, langued azure.

SONS LIVING AND DECEASED

JAMES CHRISTOPHER HAMILTON, *b* 20 Oct 1992. —— Harry John Hamilton, *b* (twin) 1992. —— †Christopher, *b* and *d* 1994.

Fortitudine et prudentia

By fortitude and prudence

DAUGHTER LIVING

Celina Hamilton, *b* 1991.

HALF-SISTERS LIVING

Bridget Mary, *b* 1927: *m* 1949, Brig Anthony Onslow Lawrence Lithgow, MC, late Black Watch (RHR) (E Onslow, colls), who *d* 1988, and has issue living, Nigel Christopher Douglas, *b* 1950, — Sarah Vivienne Hamilton, *b* 1952, — Grania Claire Bridget, *b* 1953. —— Virginia Hamilton, *b* 1929.

WIDOW LIVING OF EIGHT BARONET

EVE (*Eve, Lady Lighton*), only da of Rear Adm Alexander Livingston Penrose Mark-Wardlaw, of Loseberry, Claygate, Surrey, and widow of Maj Henry Stopford Chetwode Ram, RE: *m* 1985, as his 3rd wife, Sir Christopher Robert Lighton, 8th Bt, MBE, who *d* 1993.

Sir Thomas Lighton, 1st Bt, son of John Lighton of Raspberry Hill, co Derry, was a Dublin banker, High Sheriff of Co Dublin 1790 and co Tyrone 1801, and MP for Tuam 1790-97, and Carlingford 1798-1800. At the time of his death his firm was known as Lighton, Needham & Shaw. The last named partner, Robert Shaw, was also created a baronet.

LINDSAY (UK) 1962, of Dowhill, co Kinross

Sir RONALD ALEXANDER LINDSAY OF DOWHILL, 2nd *Baronet*; *b* 6 Dec 1933; *s* his father, *Sir* MARTIN ALEXANDER, CBE, DSO, 1981; is 23rd representer of baronial house of Dowhill; *ed* Eton, and Worcester Coll, Oxford (MA); Lieut Gren Gds 1952-54; FCII (1964); insurance broker and Lloyd's members' agent 1958-1993; an underwriting member of Lloyd's 1962-98; Member of Queen's Body Guard for Scotland (Royal Company of Archers); a Vice-pres Anglo-Spanish Soc since 1993 (Vice-chm 1985-93); Encomienda de la Orden de Isabel la Católica 1988; Member (Chm 1987-89) Standing Council of the Baronetage; a Vice-pres Clan Lindsay Soc since 1999: *m* 1968, Nicoletta, yr da of late Capt Edgar Storich, Royal Italian Navy (ret), and has issue.

Arms – Gules, a fess chequy argent and azure, between a mullet of the second in chief and the base barry undy or and of the third; in a dexter canton argent a sinister hand couped apaume erect of the first. **Crest** – A castle triple-towered proper, port gules, tower-caps argent. **Supporters** – Two doves proper, gorged of collars chequy argent and azure.
Residence – 104 Edith Rd, W14 9AP.

SONS LIVING

JAMES MARTIN EVELYN, *b* 11 Oct 1968; *ed* Shiplake Coll, and RMA Sandhurst; Lieut Gren Gds 1988-93. *Club* – Cavalry and Guards. —— Hugo Edgar, *b* 1970. —— Robin Ronald Edward, *b* 1972.

DAUGHTER LIVING

Lucia Linda, *b* 1974.

BROTHER LIVING

Oliver John Martin, CBE (c/o Child and Co, 1 Fleet St, EC4Y 1BD), *b* 1938; Col Gren Gds (ret); a Member of Queen's Body Guard for Scotland (Royal Company of Archers); FRHistS, MICFM; author of *The Lasting Honour - The Fall of Hong Kong 1941* (1978) and *At The Going Down of the Sun - Hong Kong and South East Asia 1941-45* (1981), editor of *A Guards General: The Memoirs of Sir Allan Adair* (1986); CBE (Mil) 1993: *m* 1964, Lady Clare Rohais Antonia Elizabeth Giffard, yr da of 3rd Earl of Halsbury, and has issue living, Mark Oliver GIFFARD-LINDSAY, *b* 1968, — Victoria Louise Elizabeth Clare, *b* 1967: *m* 1988, Gregory F. M. T. Wheatley, 2nd son of Anthony Wheatley, — Fiona Emily Margaret, *b* 1972.

SISTER LIVING

Jacynth Rosemary (*Lady Mark Fitzalan Howard*), *b* 1934: *m* 1961, Lord Mark Fitzalan Howard, and has issue (*see* D Norfolk). *Residence* – 13 Campden Hill Sq, W8 7LB.

Sir Martin Alexander Lindsay, the 1st baronet, was 22nd in descent from Sir William Lindsay of Rossie, 1st of Dowhill, half-brother of 1st Earl of Crawford. The estate was sold by James, 13th Laird, and his son Martin in the 18th century. The coat of arms of Adam, 5th of Dowhill (*d* 1544) is shown in the armorial of Sir David Lindsay of the Mount, Lyon King of Arms. Adam had a crown charter of confirmation of "his barony of Crambeth called Dowhill" in 1541. Earlier such charters are in 1353 by David II, in 1397 by Robert III and in 1447 by James II. The 1st baronet, Sir Martin, explorer, soldier and author, was Solihull's first MP from 1945 to 1964.

Lindsay-Hogg, see Hogg.

Lister-Kaye, see Kaye.

Liston Foulis, see Foulis.

LITHGOW (UK) 1925, of Ormsary, co Argyll

By sea and land

PER·MARE·PER·TERRAS

Sir WILLIAM JAMES LITHGOW, 2nd *Baronet*; *b* 10 May 1934; *s* his father, *Sir* JAMES LITHGOW, GBE, CB, MC, TD, 1952; *ed* Winchester; Hon LLD Strathclyde 1979; CEng, FRINA, CBIM, FRSA, Fellow Scottish Council, Member of Queen's Body Guard for Scotland (Royal Company of Archers) 1964; DL Renfrewshire 1970; Chm of Lithgows Ltd 1959-1984 and since 1988, Dir since 1956; Chm Scott Lithgow Drydocks Ltd 1967-78; Vice-Chm Scott Lithgow Ltd 1968-78; Chmn Western Ferries (Argyll) Ltd 1972-85; Chmn Hunterston Development Co Ltd since 1987, Dir since 1981; Chm Campbeltown Shipyard Ltd 1970-85, Dir since 1985; Chm Landcatch 1981-85, Dir since 1985; Shipbuilding Employer's Federation 1961-62; Dir Bank of Scotland 1962-86; Dir Lithgows Pty Ltd since 1972; Member, British Committee Det Norske Veritas 1966-92; Exec Cttee Scottish Council for Development and Industry 1969-85; Greenock Dist Hosp Bd 1961-66; Gen Bd Nat Physical Lab 1963-66; Hon Pres Students Assoc and Member Court of Univ of Strathclyde 1964-69; Clyde Port Authority 1969-71; Scottish Regional Council of CBI 1969-76; W. Central Scotland Plan Steering Cttee 1970-74; National Ports Council 1971-78; Scottish Milk Marketing Board 1979-83; Chm Iona Cathedral Management Bd 1979-83; Winston Churchill Memorial Trust Council 1979-83: *m* 1st, 1964, Valerie Helen, who *d* 1964, da of late Denis Herbert Scott, CBE, of Farley Grange, Westerham, Kent; 2ndly, 1967, Mary Claire, DL Argyll and Bute 1998, da of Col Frank Moutray Hill, CBE, of East Knoyle, Salisbury, Wilts, and has issue by 2nd *m*.

Arms – Per chevron sable and argent three estoiles in chief of the second, and in base in a seaundy azure and of the second a galley, sails furled of the first, flagged gules. Crest – An otter on a rock proper.
Seat – Ormsary, by Lochgilphead, Argyllshire.

SONS LIVING *(By 2nd marriage)*

JAMES FRANK (Drums, Langbank, Renfrewshire), *b* 13 June 1970: *m* 1997, Claire Felicity, yr da of Nicholas du Cane Wilkinson, of Croy, Inverness, and has issue living, Henry James, *b* 23 Oct 1998. —— John Alexander, *b* 1974.

DAUGHTER LIVING *(By 2nd marriage)*

Katrina Margaret, *b* 1968.

SISTERS LIVING

Margaret Helen, *b* 1928: *m* 1951, Geoffrey Robert Rickman, and has issue living, Stephen Lithgow, *b* 1952, — Robert James, *b* 1957, — Andrew George, *b* 1960, — Catherine Margaret, *b* 1953. *Residence* – Sullington Old Rectory, Storrington, Pulborough, W Sussex. —— Ann Barlow, MBE, *b* 1931: *m* 1952, William Simon Wilson, and has issue living, Mark Lithgow, *b* 1960, — Sarah Rosalind, *b* 1953, — Judith Clare, *b* 1957. *Residence* – Ballochmorrie House, Barrhill, by Girvan, Ayrshire.

The 1st baronet, Sir James Lithgow, GBE, CB, MC, TD, DL, JP, LLD (son of late W. T. Lithgow, of Drums, Renfrewshire), was a Shipbuilder of Port Glasgow, a Member of Board of Admiralty 1940-46, Vice-Lieut for Renfrewshire, Hon Col TA, and first Freeman of Burgh of Port Glasgow.

LLEWELLYN (UK) 1922, of Bwllfa, Aberdare, co Glamorgan

Character is destiny

Sir HENRY (HARRY) MORTON LLEWELLYN, CBE, 3rd *Baronet*; *b* 18 July 1911; *s* his brother, *Sir* RHYS, 1978; *ed* Oundle, and Trin Coll, Camb (MA); DL for Mon, and a JP 1953-67; High Sheriff of Mon 1966; Chm C. L. Clay and Co (coal importers) 1936-46, Chm Whitbread Wales Ltd 1958-72, Member Wales Tourist Board 1968-74, Chm Sports Council for Wales 1971-81; Dir Chepstow Racecourse; Vice-Chm of Civic Trust for Wales, Chm Wales Bd Nat Building Soc, and formerly Chm Eagle Star Assurance Co (Wales Board); a Member of Nat Hunt Cttee 1946, Jockey Club since 1969, and Council of World Wildlife Fund since 1986; Chm of British Show Jumping Assoc 1972-76; Pres British Equestrian Fedn 1976-80 and of the Roy Welsh Agricultural Soc 1984; joined Warwicks Yeo 1939 and Staff Coll Haifa 1942, GSO II OPS 8th Army Oct 1942, GSOI (Operational Liaison) 21st Army Group 1944; 1939-45 War in Iraq, Syria, Western Desert, N Africa, Sicily, Italy, and NW Europe (despatches twice, OBE, US Legion of Merit); has Roy Humane Soc's Medal: show jumping Olympic Gold Medallist, Helsinki 1952, and Olympic Bronze Medallist, London 1948; OBE (Mil) 1945, CBE (Civil) 1953, Knt 1977: *m* 1944, Hon Christine Saumarez, who *d* 1998, da of 5th Baron de Saumarez, and has issue.

Arms – Per chevron or and gules, in chief a lion passant and in base three chevronels all counterchanged. Crest – A demi-dragon holding in the mouth a dexter hand couped proper.
Residence – Ty'r Nant, Llanarth, Raglan, Gwent. *Clubs* – Cavalry and Guards', Jockey, Shikar.

SONS LIVING

DAVID ST VINCENT, *b* 2 April 1946; *ed* Eton: *m* 1980 (*m diss* 1987), Vanessa Mary Theresa, yr da of Lt-Cdr Theodore Bernard Peregrine Hubbard, RN (*see* D Norfolk), and has issue living, Olivia Anna Christina, *b* 1980, — Arabella Dominica, *b* 1983. —— Roderic (Roddy) Victor (Old George House, Leafield, nr Whitney, Oxon OX8 5NP), *b* 1947; *ed* Shrewsbury; landscape gardener, journalist, broadcaster, and author: *m* 1981, Tatiana Manora Caroline, da of late Paul Soskin, film producer, and has issue living, Alexandra Manora Tatiana, *b* 1982, — Natasha Anna Christina, *b* 1984, — Rose-Anna Alice, *b* 1987.

DAUGHTER LIVING

Anna Christina, *b* 1956: *m* 1987, Christopher Charles Elletson, of 5A Egerton Terrace, SW3 2BX, son of late C. E. Elletson, of Douglas, IoM.

BROTHER LIVING

(William Herbert) Rhidian, MC, *b* 1919; *ed* Eton; Maj late Welsh Gds; DL of Cardiganshire, High Sheriff 1967-68; Member Cardiganshire Co Council 1961-70, Member of Cardiganshire Agric Exec Cttee, and Traffic Commr, S Wales; and a Member of Court of Govs, Nat Library of Wales 1967-68, and Univ of Wales 1968-70; 1939-45 War in France, N Africa, Italy and Greece (despatches, MC): *m* 1943, Lady Honor Morvyth Malet Vaughan, da of 7th Earl of Lisburne, and has issue living, Trefor Wilmot (Hill Farm House, Ipsden, Oxon), *b* 1947: *m* 1973, Heather Mary, da of Richard Lucas, of The Lydiate, Heswall, and has issue living, Catrin Sarah Malet *b* 1981, Elinor Victoria Sian *b* 1985, — Cordelia, *b* 1949: *m* 1969, Angus Lamont, of Beech House, Chiddingfold, Surrey, and has issue living, Douglas Ross *b* 1973, Camilla Rose *b* 1971, — Gaynor Malet, *b* 1952: *m* 1977, Edward James Sutcliffe Garrett, of 146 New Kings Rd, SW6, and has issue living, Nicholas Edward Sutcliffe *b* 1982, Lucinda Felicity *b* 1979, Melissa Kinvara *b* 1987. *Residence* – 4 St Omer Rd, Guildford, Surrey GU1 2DB.

SISTERS LIVING

Margaret Elaine (*Lady Anderson*), *b* 1913: *m* 1935, Sir Donald Forsyth Anderson, who *d* 1973, son of late Sir Alan Garrett Anderson, GBE, and has issue living, Gillian Elizabeth (21 Carlotta Rd, Sydney, NSW), *b* 1936; MB BS, MRCS, LRCP 1961: *m* 1966 (*m diss* 19—), William Peter Grant Davies, — Jennifer Forsyth, *b* 1937: *m* 1965, Anthony David Loehnis, CMG, of Haughton House, Churchill, Oxon (*see* E Harrowby, colls), — Lindsay Garrett, *b* 1942; JP for Droxford, Hants: *m* 1962, Robert Trench Fox, CBE (*see* B Ashtown, colls), of Cheriton House, Alresford, Hants, — Susan Elaine (*Countess of Darnley*), *b* 1945; JP for Severnminster, Worcs: *m* 1965, 11th Earl of Darnley, of Netherwood Manor, Tenbury Wells, Worcs. *Residence* – 9 Hamilton House, Vicarage Gate, W8 4HL. —— Elizabeth Aileen Maud, *b* 1914; formerly Wing Officer WAAF; 1939-45 War: *m* 1946, Lt-Col David Mathew Caradoc Prichard, Roy Welch Fusiliers, who *d* 1986, and has had issue, Robert David Caradoc, *b* 1947; *d* 1995, — Colin Hubert Llewellyn (Lodge Farm, Barcombe, Lewes, E Sussex), *b*

1949: *m* 1977, Jane Helen, da of Paul Chamberlain, of Groombridge, E Sussex, and has issue living, Claire Helen *b* 1982, Eleanor Jane *b* 1984, Lydia Diana *b* 1988, — William de Burgh (Gobion Manor, Abergavenny, Gwent), *b* 1953; Capt Welsh Guards: *m* 1983, Judith Elizabeth Thorneycroft, da of late Richard Thorneycroft Salt, of The Old Farm, Over Whitacre, Warwicks, and has issue living, Thomas David Caradoc *b* 1990, Georgina Lydia *b* 1986, Olivia Charlotte *b* 1988. *Residence* – Gobion Manor, Abergavenny, Gwent.

COLLATERAL BRANCH LIVING

Issue of late Sir David Treharne Llewellyn, 3rd son of 1st baronet, *b* 1916, *d* 1992: *m* 1950, Joan Anne, OBE, formerly Squadron Officer WAAF, Head of War Cabinet Cipher Office (The Well House, Yattendon, Berks), da of late Robert Henry Williams, of Bonvilston House, Bonvilston, nr Cardiff:— Robert Crofts Williams (The Old Rectory, Hopton, Suffolk IP22 2QX), *b* 1952; *ed* Eton; ACII; Dir Bain Clarkson Ltd 1986-87; Dir Jardine Insurance Brokers International Ltd 1987-93, Johnson and Higgins Ltd 1994-97: *m* 1st, 1975, Susan Constance, who *d* 1980, el da of late Hubert Miller-Stirling, of Cape Town, S Africa; 2ndly, 1981 (*m diss* 1989), Lucinda Roberte, only da of Alexander Clement Gilmour (*see* B Gilmour of Craigmillar); 3rdly, 1989, Sarah Dominica, da of Maj Gavin Anderson, of Swallow Cottage, Little Cressingham, Norfolk, and of late Mrs Michael Giles (*see* B Kilmaine, 1990 Edn), and has issue living (by 2nd *m*), Dominic Robin Crofts, *b* 1984, — Zara Marie-Louise, *b* 1986. —— David Rhidian, *b* 1957: *m* 1984, Mrs Susan Edwards, elder da of late Edward Edmiston, Headmaster Papplewick Sch Ascot. —— Emma Victoria, *b* 1951: *m* 1974, Bruce H. Dinwiddy, c/o Foreign and Commonwealth Office (Dar es Salaam), SW1A 2AH, and has issue living, Thomas Rhidian, *b* 1979. —— Celia Rose, *b* 1976.

LLEWELLYN (UK) 1959, of Baglan, co Glamorgan (Extinct 1994)

Sir MICHAEL ROWLAND GODFREY LLEWELLYN, 2nd and last *Baronet*.

DAUGHTERS LIVING OF SECOND BARONET (By 2nd marriage)

Sarah Janet, *b* 1958. —— Carolyn Frances, *b* 1959. —— Lucy Mary, *b* 1963.

DAUGHTER LIVING OF FIRST BARONET

Wenllian Kennard, *b* 1923: *m* 1949, Maj Wyndham Jermyn Hacket Pain, JP, DL, late Gren Gds, High Sheriff of Surrey 1988-89, who *d* 1998, of Dixton Lodge, Hadnock, Monmouth, Mon NP5 3NQ, elder son of late Col Michell Hacket Pain, of Upper Lostiford, Wonersh, nr Guildford, Surrey, and has issue living, Nicholas Wyndham Llewellyn (Tredunno, Cwmyoy, Abergavenny, Mon NP7 7NG), *b* 1953; *ed* Harrow, and RMA; served Gren Gds 1972-76 (despatches, Ulster 1974): *m* 1994, Elizabeth Jean, only da of late Kenneth Lewis Richard Greves, and has issue living, Wyndham Richard Llewellyn *b* 1994, Emma Edith Wenllian *b* 1997, — Simon Michell (15 Tainui Rd, Titirangi, Auckland, NZ), *b* 1956; *ed* Harrow: *m* 1993, Vicky Robyn, elder da of N. C. Myers, of Cambridge, NZ.

WIDOW LIVING OF SECOND BARONET

JANET PRUDENCE (*Lady Llewellyn*), yst da of Lt-Col Charles Thomas Edmondes, JP, DL, of Ewenny Priory, Bridgend, Glamorgan: *m* 1956, as his 2nd wife, Capt Sir Michael Rowland Godfrey Llewellyn, 2nd Bt, who *d* 1994. *Residence* – Glebe House, Penmaen, nr Swansea, W Glamorgan SA3 2HH.

DILLWYN-VENABLES-LLEWELYN (UK) 1890, of Penllergaer, Llangyfelach and Ynis-y-gerwn, Cadoxton juxta Neath, Glamorganshire

(Name pronounced "Dilwin-Venables-Hlooellin")

Dread shame

Sir JOHN MICHAEL DILLWYN-VENABLES-LLEWELYN, 4th *Baronet*; *b* 12 Aug 1938; *s* his father, *Brig Sir* (CHARLES) MICHAEL, MVO, 1976; *ed* Eton, and Magdalene Coll, Camb: *m* 1963 (*m diss* 1972), Nina, da of late Lt J. S. Hallam, KRRC; 2ndly, 1975, Nina Gay Richardson Oliver, who *d* 1995, and has issue by 1st *m*.

Arms – Quarterly: 1st and 4th, argent, gutée de poix, three chevronels gules, in base a lamb passant proper, *Llewelyn*; 2nd, azure, two bars each cotised between five mullets, three in chief and two in base all argent, and for difference a cross-crosslet or, *Venables*; 3rd gules, on a chevron nebulée argent, five trefoils slipped of the first, *Dillwyn*; on an escutcheon of pretence the Arms of *Venables* without distinctions. Crests – 1st, on a trunk of a tree fessewise eradicated and sprouting to the dexter, a lamb passant proper, bearing a banner gules charged with three chevronels argent, *Llewelyn*; 2nd, a wyvern wings expanded gules, each wing charged with a fesse argent, issuant from a weir basket proper, the dexter claw resting on a mullet azure, charged for difference as in the arms, *Venables*; 3rd, in front of a stag's head couped proper three trefoils slipped vert, *Dillwyn*.
Residence – Llysdinam, Newbridge-on-Wye, Llandrindod Wells, Powys LD1 6NB.

DAUGHTERS LIVING (*By 1st marriage*)

Georgina Katherine, *b* 1964: *m* 1989, Antony H. Mead, 2nd son of Humphrey Mead, of Moyaux, Normandy. —— Emma Susan, *b* 1967.

SISTER LIVING

Mary Julia, *b* 1936: *m* 1971, Michael B. Elster, of Gwarcae, Llanddew, Brecon, Powys, and has issue living, Jake, *b* 1972, — Caitlin, *b* 1974.

WIDOW LIVING OF THIRD BARONET

Lady DELIA MARY (*Lady Delia Dillwyn-Venables-Llewelyn*), (Llysdinam, Newbridge-on-Wye, Llandrindod Wells, Powys LD1 6NB), da of late Capt Michael Hugh Hicks-Beach, MP, Viscount Quenington (*see* E St Aldwyn); raised to the rank of an Earl's da 1920: *m* 1934, Brig Sir (Charles) Michael Dillwyn-Venables-Llewelyn, MVO, 3rd Bt, who *d* 1976.

The 1st baronet, Sir John Talbot Dillwyn-Llewelyn (son of late John Dillwyn-Llewelyn, FRS, of Penllergaer, co Glamorgan), was Mayor of Swansea 1890, and sat as MP there (C) July 1895 to Oct 1900. The 2nd baronet, Col Sir Charles Leyshon Dillwyn-Venables-Llewelyn, CB, was High Sheriff of Radnorshire 1924, and Lord Lieut 1929-49, and sat as MP for Radnorshire (C) Jan to Nov 1910. The 3rd baronet, Sir (Charles) Michael Dillwyn-Venables Llewelyn, MVO, was Lord Lieut of Radnorshire 1949-74, and Vice-Lieut of Powys 1974-76.

LLOYD (UK) 1960, of Rhu, co Dunbarton

Sir RICHARD ERNEST BUTLER LLOYD, 2nd *Baronet*; *b* 6 Dec 1928; *s* his father, *Maj Sir* (ERNEST) GUY RICHARD, DSO, 1987; *ed* Wellington, and Hertford Coll, Oxford (MA); commn'd The Black Watch 1948; ADC to GOC Malaya 1948-49; banker, Dir Glyn Mills and Co 1964-70, Chief Executive Williams and Glyn's Bank 1970-78, successively Dep Chm, Chief Executive and Chm Hill Samuel Bank Ltd 1978-91, Chm Vickers 1992-97, and dir of other public companies; Chm Business Industry Advisory Cttee to the OECD Paris since 1998; Gov Ditchley Foundation, Pres British Heart Foundation; Member Ind Dev Advisory Board 1972-76, NEDC 1973-77, Overseas Projects Board 1981-85, and Advisory Board Royal Coll of Defence Studies 1987-95. *m* 1955, Jennifer Susan Margaret, elder da of late Brig Ereld Boteler Wingfield Cardiff, CB, CBE, of Easton Court, nr Ludlow, Shropshire, and has issue.

Arms – Per bend, sable and gules, a lion rampant regardant argent, goutté of the second, surmounted of a fess or, charged with a barrulet dancette azure, a bordure invected of the fourth. Crest – A demi-lion argent goutté and langued gules, holding in bend forward two spears sable points upwards or.
Residence – Sundridge Place, Sundridge, Sevenoaks, Kent TN14 6DD.

SONS LIVING

(RICHARD) TIMOTHY BUTLER (Howe Combe Farm House, Watlington, Oxon), *b* 12 April 1956; *ed* Wellington, and RAC Cirencester: *m* 1989, Wilhelmina S. M., yr da of G. H. A. Schut, of Amstelveen, The Netherlands, and has issue living, Sebastian George Butler, *b* 11 Nov 1996, — Daphne Florence Wilhelmina, *b* 1993. —— Simon Wingfield Butler, *b* 1958; *ed* Eton, and Hertford Coll, Oxford (BA): *m* 1984, Catherine Rosemary Chanter, and has issue living, Christopher Timothy Butler, *b* 1986, — Jeremy Richard Butler, *b* 1988, — Jessica Chanter, *b* 1991. —— Henry Butler, *b* 1965; *ed* Eton, and Bristol Univ (BSc): *m* 1992, Joanna M., elder da of James Gourlay Freeland, of Staplewood, Nether Wallop, Stockbridge, Hants, and has issue living, Edward James Butler, *b* 1994, — Thomas Butler, *b* 1996, — Alice Elizabeth, *b* 1997.

SISTERS LIVING

Margaret Kynaston, *b* 1920: *m* 1948, Percy Bruce Southmayd Fowler, DM, FRCP, late Maj RAMC, and has issue living, Michael Bruce, *b* 1951; *ed* Harrow; MB, FRCP, FACC: *m* 1st, 1978, Dr Linda Jane Fenney; 2ndly, 1992, Sherry Farr, and has issue living (by 1st *m*), Jack *b* 1981, Katherine Jane *b* 1980, Emily Louise *b* (twin) 1981, (by 2nd *m*) Jenna Morgan *b* 1994, — Guy Richard John, *b* 1961; *ed* Harrow; MB, BS: *m* 1994, Vanessa Stuttaford, and has issue living, Angus *b* 1998, Holly Victoria *b* 1997, — Susanne Jane, FRCGP, *b* 1949: *m* 1970, Richard Antony Savage, FRCGP, and has issue living, Thomas Michael *b* 1978, Samuel Richard *b* 1984, Emma Louise *b* 1981, — Amanda Jill, *b* 1952; MRCP, MRCGP: *m* 1979, Andrew Duncan Platts, FRCS (Edin), FRCS (Lond), FRCR, and has issue living, Nicholas James *b* 1982, Helen Jane *b* 1981, Catherine Frances *b* 1987. *Residence* – Shirley Holms, Gerrards Cross, Bucks SL9 8JH. —— Elizabeth Hunt (*Dowager Lady Denny*), *b* 1924: *m* 1949, Sir Alistair Maurice Archibald Denny, 3rd Bt (*cr* 1913), who *d* 1995, and has issue. *Residence* – Crombie Cottage, Abercrombie, Anstruther, Fife KY10 2DE.

The 1st baronet, Maj Sir (Ernest) Guy Richard Lloyd, of Rhu Cottage, Carrick Castle, Lochgoilhead, Argyll (*see* Green-Price, Bt, 1961 Edn), served in European War 1914-18 (despatches, DSO), and European War 1939-40 with Royal Warwickshire Regt in France; sat as MP for Renfrewshire, E Div (*U*) 1940-59; ktd 1953; DL Dunbartonshire 1953-87.

SINCLAIR-LOCKHART (NS) 1636, of Murkle, co Caithness, and Stevenson, co Haddington

Corda serrata fero
I bear a locked heart

Sir SIMON JOHN EDWARD FRANCIS SINCLAIR-LOCKHART, 15th *Baronet*; *b* 22 July 1941; *s* his father, *Sir* MUIR EDWARD, 1985: *m* 1973, Felicity Edith, only da of late Ivan Lachlan Campbell Stewart, of Havelock North, New Zealand, and has issue.

Arms – Quarterly: 1st and 4th, argent, a man's heart proper within a fetter-lock sable, on a chief azure three boar's heads erased argent all within a bordure, ermine, charged with three crosses patee gules; 2nd and 3rd, argent, on a saltire engrailed gules, four bezants. **Crest** – A boar's head erased argent.
Address – 62 Muritai Crescent, Havelock North, Hawkes Bay, New Zealand.

SONS LIVING

ROBERT MUIR, *b* 12 Sept 1973. —— James Lachlan, *b* (twin) 1973.

DAUGHTER LIVING

Fiona Mary, *b* 1979.

SISTER LIVING

Sara Ann May (Camnethan, RD7, McKay's Rd, Feilding, New Zealand), *b* 1942; has resumed the surname of Sinclair-Lockhart: *m* 1968 (*m diss* 1980), Nicholas Welcome Willcock.

WIDOW LIVING OF FOURTEENTH BARONET

(OLGA) ANN (*Ann, Lady Sinclair-Lockhart*), da of late Claude Victor White Parsons, of Hawkes Bay, New Zealand: *m* 1940, Sir Muir Edward Sinclair-Lockhart, 14th Bt, who *d* 1985. *Residence* – Camnethan, RD7, McKay's Rd, Feilding, New Zealand.

COLLATERAL BRANCH LIVING

Issue of late Bruce Sinclair-Lockhart, LLM, yst son of 11th baronet, *b* 1910, *d* 1965: *m* 1940 (*m diss* 1949), Joan Marian Belle Quilliam, of New Plymouth, NZ:—
Sally Elisabeth, *b* 1942: *m* 1964, Stuart William Veitch, c/o Private Bag, Waimata, Gisborne, NZ, and has issue living, Guy Bruce, *b* 1966, — William Ronald *b* 1968, — Michael Richard, *b* 1970, — Katie Jane, *b* 1973.

Sir John Sinclair (son of George Sinclair of Edinburgh) was created a baronet of Nova Scotia with remainder to heirs male whatsoever. Sir Robert, 3rd Bt was a Privy Councillor and a Baron of the Exchequer. Sir John Sinclair, 4th Bt: *m* 1698, Martha, da and eventually heir of Sir John Lockhart of Castlehill, a Lord of Session (Lord Castlehill). Sir John Gordon Sinclair, 8th Bt, a distinguished Admiral, served sixty-three years in the Royal Navy. On the death of his son Sir Robert Charles Sinclair, 9th Bt in 1899 the baronetcy passed to a descendant of James Sinclair, yr son of the 5th baronet, who on inheriting Castlehill 1764, assumed the surname of Lockhart. The 10th baronet Maj-Gen Sir Græme A. Lockhart, CB (who served during Persian and Indian Mutiny Campaigns) assumed the additional surname of Sinclair. Sir Robert Duncan Sinclair-Lockhart, 11th Bt, was son of late George Duncan Lockhart (whose grandfather assumed the surname of Lockhart in lieu of his patronymic), a descendant of late James Lockhart Sinclair, 2nd son of 5th baronet. The 12th baronet, Sir Graeme Sinclair-Lockhart, sometime 2nd Lieut Scottish Horse (Scouts), served 1914-18 and 1939-45 Wars, and in the Russo-Finnish War. He was *s* by his brother, Sir John, 13th Bt, Maj RA, District Commr Kenya, Colonial Serv.

LOCOCK (UK) 1857, of Speldhurst, Kent (Extinct 1965)

Sir CHARLES BIRD LOCOCK, 3rd and last *Baronet*.

DAUGHTER LIVING OF THIRD BARONET

Vera Frances, *b* 1920: *m* 1st, 1939, Capt Philip McDonald Bottome, RASC; 2ndly, 1946, Cyril Stevens: *m* 3rdly, 1972 (*m diss* 1978), Malcolm Paul Holman, and has issue living, (by 2nd *m*) Anthony Charles, *b* 1948: *m* 1st, 1972 (*m diss* 1979), Sally Jean Boyns; 2ndly, 1979, Carolyn Ann Mason, and has issue living, (by 2nd *m*) Robin William *b* 1979, — Nigel Derek, *b* 1951: *m* 1972 (*m diss* 1975), Susan Hilary Saunders, and has issue living, Michelle Jane, *b* 1972 — (by 1st *m*) Patricia Anne, *b* 1941: *m* 1st, 1960 (*m diss* 1966), Raymond Bey-Leveld; 2ndly, 1987, Roger Alan Geddes, and has issue living, (by 1st *m*) Kevin Wayne, *b* 1961: *m* 1987, Sharon Amoedo, Barry Gordon, *b* 1963, — (by 2nd *m*) Anita Janet Christine, *b* 1956: *m* 1980, Michael Vaughan Johnson, and has issue living, James Michael *b* 1989, Kate Louise *b* 1987.

COLLATERAL BRANCHES LIVING

Issue of late Charles Bardolf Locock, son of 3rd baronet, *b* 1905, *d* 1961: *m* 1950, Frances Daphne, who *d* 1974, eldest da of late Cdr Ralph Hicks, RN, of Pyrford, Surrey:—
Frances Anne, *b* 1951: *m* 1986, Quentin Turton Cross, and has issue living, Alexander Orlando, *b* 1989. *Residence* – Two Ways, Madeira Rd, W Byfleet, Surrey.

Granddaughter of late Rev Alfred Henry Locock, 2nd son of 1st baronet:—
Issue of late Charles Dealtry Locock, *b* 1862, *d* 1946: *m* 1889, Ida Gertrude, who *d* 1962, da of late Col Herbert Locock, 5th son of 1st baronet:—
Elsa, *b* 1891. *Residence* –

LODER (UK) 1887, of Whittlebury, Northamptonshire, and of High Beeches, Slaugham, Sussex

Sir EDMUND JEUNE LODER, 4th *Baronet; b* 26 June 1941; *s* his father, *Sir* GILES ROLLS, 1999; *ed* Eton; FCA: *m* 1st, 1966 (*m diss* 1971), Penelope Jane, da of Ivo Forde; 2ndly, 1992, Susan Warren, da of V. W. Warren Pearl, of Lindfield, Sussex, and has issue.

Arms – Azure, on a fesse between two escallops or, three bucks' heads cabossed proper. **Crest** – Between two escallops or, a bucks head cabossed and pierced with an arrow bendwise point to the sinister proper. *Residence* – Eyrefield Lodge, The Curragh, co Kildare.

A sound conscience is a wall of brass

DAUGHTER LIVING (*By 1st marriage*)

Gillian Marie, *b* 1968: *m* 1992, James D. P. Morgan, son of David Morgan, of Northchapel, Sussex, and has issue living, Mathew James David, *b* 1995, — Olivia, *b* 1996.

BROTHER LIVING

ROBERT REGINALD (ROBIN) (Leonardslee Gardens, Horsham, W Sussex), *b* 12 Nov 1943; *ed* Eton, and Trin Coll, Camb (MA): *m* 1967, Quenelda Jane, da of Sir John Ledward Royden, 4th Bt, and has issue living, Christopher Giles, *b* 1968: *m* 1997, Antonia Lucy, yr da of Michael Holland, of Broad Oak, Sussex, — Peter Thomas, *b* 1972, — Catherine Marie Violet, *b* 1970, — Mary Charlotte, *b* (twin) 1972: *m* 1996, Stephen John Davies, son of T. Davies, of Llanelli, Dyfed.

WIDOW LIVING OF THIRD BARONET

MARIE VIOLET PAMELA (*Dowager Lady Loder*), OStJ, only da of late Bertram Hanmer Bunbury Symons-Jeune, of Runnymede House, Old Windsor: *m* 1939, Sir Giles Rolls Loder, 3rd Bt, who *d* 1999. *Residence* – Ockenden House, Cuckfield, Sussex RH17 5LD.

COLLATERAL BRANCHES LIVING

Grandchildren of late Wilfred Hans Loder, 2nd son of 1st baronet:—
Issue of late Hubert Sydney Loder, *b* 1888, *d* 1982: *m* 1918 (*m diss* 1944), Brenda, who *d* 1981, da of Charles McNeill:—
Simon John (Manor Farmhouse, Cruxton, Dorchester, Dorset DT2 0DZ), *b* 1932; *ed* Eton; late Capt Gren Gds: *m* 1st, 1962 (*m diss* 1978), Kathleen Alexandra, el da of Richard Evelyn Fleming, MC, TD (*see* B Wyfold); 2ndly, 1979, Penelope Anne Mary, da of Sir Charles Marcus Mander, 3rd Bt, and formerly wife of Michael Rollo Hoare, and has issue living, (by 1st *m*) David Richard, *b* 1964: *m* 1990, Cressida, da of Ian Landless, of Duns Tew, Oxon, and has issue living, Katherine Rose *b* 1996, Flora *b* 1998, — Alexander Hugh, *b* 1965: *m* 1996, Anna L., da of Michael Green, of Bucks, and has issue living, Robert Hamish *b* 1997, Edward Alastair, *b* 1999, — John Alistair, *b* 1968, — (by 2nd *m*) James Robert, *b* 1981, — Jean Mary (Dam Farm House, Brailsford, Derby), *b* 1919: *m* 1939, Stephen Dane Player, who *d* 1979, and has issue living, Peter Dane (Whatton Manor, Whatton in the Vale, Notts), *b* 1941: *m* 1970, Catherine Esther, eldest da of Col Gerald Vigors de Courcy O'Grady (The O'Grady), MC, of Kilballyowen, Bruff, co Limerick, and formerly wife of Rupert Hugh Stobart, and has issue living, Edward Dane *b* 1973, Alice Mary *b* 1971, — James Stephen (Bradley Park South, Brailsford, Derby), *b* 1945: *m* 1968, Philippa Headley, da of Frank Headley Richardson, and has issue living, Andrew Headley *b* 1970, Duncan James *b* 1972, — Nicholas Charles William, *b* 1948, *d* 1909, — Karen Jean, *b* 1940: *m* 1963, Dermot Kelly, of The Coach House, Dowdeswell, Cheltenham, Glos GL5 J44, and has issue living, Patrick Dermot Stephen *b* 1968, Doone *b* 1963, Anna *b* 1966. — Gillian, *b* 1925: *m* 1952, John Johnston Kirkpatrick, FLAS, FRICS, of Horn Park, Beaminster, Dorset, and Church Hill, Newcastle, co Down, N Ireland, and has issue living, Christopher James (Sydenham Farm, Broadwell, Moreton-in-Marsh, Glos), *b* 1953: *m* 1978, Annabel Susan, da of Frederick McLean Hayward, of Gosebury Hall Farm, Nonnington, Kent, and has issue living Lucy Diana *b* 1984, Sophie Clare *b* 1986, Chloe Laura *b* 1991, — Nicholas Yvone John (Ownham Old Farm, Boxford, Newbury, Berks RG16 8RJ), *b* 1959: *m* 1990, Hon Joanna Norrie FitzRoy Newdegate, only da of 3rd Viscount Daventry, and has issue living, William John Francis *b* 1992, Rosanagh Charlotte *b* 1994, — Francis Hugh (Hunters Hill, Hartley Wintney, Hants RG27 8JG), *b* 1962: *m* 1990, Miranda J., eldest da of David Fitzwilliam-Lay, of Bloxham, Savernake Forest, Wilts, and has issue living, George Hugh *b* 1992, Henry James *b* 1993, Augustus John *b* 1996, Laura Rose *b* 1998, — Robin Kenneth Anthony, *b* 1969, — Rose Cecilia, *b* 1955: *m* 1977 (*m diss* 1991), James Adair Wigan, and has issue (*see* Wigan, Bt, colls), — Sara Gillian, *b* 1956: *m* 1983,

Preston Martin Charles Rabl, of Winterbourne Manor, Newbury, Berks RG16 8AU, and has issue living, Francesca Sara *b* 1984, Sophia Rose *b* 1986, Georgina Moira *b* 1988.

Issue of late Gerald Walter Erskine Loder, 5th son of 1st baronet, who was *cr Baron Wakehurst* 1934 (see that title).

The 3rd baronet, Sir Giles Rolls Loder, was a noted horticulturist. The family's garden at Leonardslee is renowned for its rhododendrons and camellias, and was the location for the 1947 Powell and Pressburger film of Rumer Godden's novel *Black Narcissus*.

MORRISON-LOW (UK) 1908, of Kilmaron, co Fife

Perils delight me. Prudence excels

Sir JAMES RICHARD MORRISON-LOW, 3rd *Baronet*: *b* 3 Aug 1925; *s* his father, *Sir* WALTER JOHN, 1955; DL of Fife: *m* 1953, Anne Rawson, da of late Air Commodore Robert Gordon, CB, CBE, DSO, and has issue.

Arms – Quarterly, 1st and 4th argent, two wolves counterpassant sable, armed and langued gules, on a chief of the last three fleurs-de-lis of the first, *Low*; 2nd and 3rd per chevron or and ermine three saracens' heads couped at the neck proper, turbaned vert, *Morrison*. Crest – 1st, and eagle's head between two thistles slipped proper, *Low*; 2nd, a saracen's head proper, turbaned vert, *Morrison*.
Seat – Kilmaron, near Cupar, Fife KY15 4NE.

SON LIVING

RICHARD WALTER, *b* 4 Aug 1959: *m* 1994, Sandra, da of late Syndey Scott Newman, of Edinburgh, and has issue living, Victoria Ann-Louise, *b* 1996. *Residence* – Kilmaron Farm, Cupar, Fife KY15 4NE.

DAUGHTERS LIVING

Alison Dorothy, *b* 1955. —— Jean Elspeth, *b* 1957: *m* 19—, Larry Keim. —— Susan Elizabeth, *b* 1963: *m* 1989, Graham William Latham, of No 1 Meadow Cottages, Church St, Sturminster Marshall, Dorset BH21 4BU, eldest son of K. O. E. Latham, of Poole, Dorset.

BROTHER LIVING

(Colin) John (Route 1, Box 302, Easton, Maryland 21601, USA), *b* 1928: *m* 1st, 1953, Susan Désirée MacDougal, who *d* 1977, da of P. C. M. Watson, of George, S Africa; 2ndly, 1980, Mrs Anne de Clerk, and has issue living, (by 1st *m*) Katherine Dorothy, *b* 1955: *m* 1978, Peter Jarman, of Stirling, Australia, — Corinna Helen, *b* 1959: *m* 1984 (*m diss* 1989), Mark Brettel, son of Ray Brettel, of Teulada, Alicante, Spain.

WIDOW LIVING OF SECOND BARONET

(HENRIETTA) WILHELMINA MARY (*Dowager Lady Morrison-Low*), da of late Maj Robert Walter Purvis, of Gilmerton, Fife (Gilmour, Bt, cr 1897): *m* 1948, as his second wife, Sir Walter John Morrison-Low, 2nd baronet, who *d* 1955. *Residence* – Kingsbarns House, 6 The Square, Kingsbarn, nr Andrews, Fife.

Sir James Low, Knt, 1st Bt, el son of William Low, of Kirriemuir, by Janet, his wife, da of Alexander Morrison, of Kirriemuir, was Lord Provost of Dundee 1893-6. Sir Walter John Morrison-Low, 2nd Bt, assumed by deed poll (enrolled at College of Arms) 1924, the additional surname of Morrison.

LOWE (UK) 1918, of Edgbaston, City of Birmingham

I hope for better things

Sir THOMAS WILLIAM GORDON LOWE, 4th *Baronet*; *b* 14 August 1963; *s* his father, *Sir* FRANCIS REGINALD GORDON, 1986; Bar-at-law; *ed* Stowe, LSE London Univ (LLB), and Jesus Coll, Camb (LLM): *m* 19—, Mozhgan, da of H. Asilzaden.

Arms – Erminois, on a bend engrailed cottised plain azure between two Stafford knots sable, three wolves' heads erased or. **Crest** – A demi-gryphon erminois, resting the sinister paw on a Stafford knot sable.
Residence – 8 Seymour Walk, SW10.

BROTHER LIVING

CHRISTOPHER FRANCIS, *b* 25 Dec 1964. *Residence* – Lake Constance, W Germany.

MOTHER LIVING

Francesca Cornelia, da of Siegfried Steinkopf, of Berlin: *m* 1961 (*m diss* 1971), as his 1st wife, Sir Francis Reginald Gordon Lowe, 3rd Bt, who *d* 1986. *Residence* –

ADOPTED SON LIVING OF THIRD BARONET

William John, *b* 1972; *ed* Ryde Sch, IOW, and Middlesex Univ. *Residence* – Pelham House, 9 Bath Rd, Cowes, IOW PO31 7QN.

WIDOW LIVING OF THIRD BARONET

HELEN SUZANNE (*Helen, Lady Lowe*), da of late Sandys Stuart Macaskie, solicitor: *m* 1971, as his 2nd wife, Sir Francis Reginald Gordon Lowe, 3rd Bt, who *d* 1986. *Residence* – Pelham House, 9 Bath Rd, Cowes, Isle of Wight PO31 7QN.

COLLATERAL BRANCHES LIVING

Issue of late Arthur Holden Lowe, 2nd son of 1st baronet, *b* 1886, *d* 1958: *m* 1924, Evelyn, who *d* 1949, da of Alfred Philpot, of Bexhill-on-Sea:—
John Evelyn, *b* 1928; MA, FSA; author: *m* 1st, 1956 (*m diss* 1981), Susan Helen Sanderson; 2ndly, 1989, Yukiko Nomura, and has issue living (by 1st *m*), Mark John, *b* 1957, — Dominic Simon, *b* 1961, — Judith Anne, *b* 1962, — (by 2nd *m*), Miki (a da), *b* 1991. *Residence* – Paillole-Basse, Cours, 47360 Praysass, France. ⸺ Jill Rosemary (170 Cambridge St, SW1), *b* 1937: *m* 1957 (*m diss* 1980), (Ronald) Peter Gibbons, who *d* 1999; 2ndly, 1994, Lal Singh Yadav, and has issue living, (by 1st *m*) Nicholas Arthur, *b* 1960, — Caroline Evelyn, *b* 1958, — Lucinda Mary, *b* 1961, — Julia Anne, *b* 1963, — Mary Jane, *b* 1967: *m* 1997, Jamie John Lillingston-Paterson (*see* McLintock, Bt).

Issue of late Wing Cdr John Claude Malcolm Lowe, yst son of 1st baronet, *b* 1888, *d* 1970: *m* 1912, Winifred Olsson, who *d* 1968:—
†Anthony John, *b* 1913: *m* 1948, Mrs Rosemary Beatrice Richards, elder da of late Capt A.H. Hollins, and *d* 1992, leaving issue, Charles *b* 1949, — Nicholas (twin), *b* 1949: *m* 1974, Rosemary Jane, da of Maurice Henry Frank Charman, and has issue living, Christopher Peter *b* 1986, Elizabeth Jane *b* 1980, Katherine Louisa *b* 1981, — Timothy, *b* 1953, — Joanna, *b* 1958. ⸺ Elizabeth Sydney, *b* 1928: *m* 1957, Edward C. Richardson, of 66 Godstow Rd, Oxford OX2 8NY, and has issue living, Henry Edward Carleton, *b* 1961, — Conan Sacheverell Carleton, *b* 1963, — Emma, *b* 1958, — Sophie, *b* 1959.

The 1st baronet, Rt Hon Sir Francis William Lowe, DL, was sometime a partner in the legal firm of Lowe and Jolly, and sat as MP for Birmingham, Edgbaston Div (C) 1898 to 1929.

LOWSON (UK) 1951, of Westlaws, co Perth

Sir IAN PATRICK LOWSON, 2nd *Baronet*; *b* 4 Sept 1944; *s* his father, *Sir* DENYS COLQUHOUN FLOWERDEW, 1975; *ed* Eton, and Duke Univ, USA; an OStJ: *m* 1979, Mrs Tanya Theresa H. Du Boulay, only da of Raymond F. A. Judge.

Arms – Quarterly; 1st and 4th per saltire argent and azure, in chief a sealion sejant and in base a fleur-de-lys sable, in each flank a garb or, *Lowson*; 2nd per chevron argent and pean a chevronel invected on the upper side between two sealions segant sable in chief and another in base of the first, *Flowerdew*; 3rd erminois, three catherine-wheels two and one sable within a bordure engrailed azure, over all a chief gules thereon a hill with lines of defence all proper, in dexer chief a mullet argent, *Scott*. **Crest** – 1st a garb or; 2nd a demi-man habited azure, garnished gules wreathed about the temples argent and sable holding in the right hand a sprig of two roses, one of the second, the other of the third, stalked and leaved proper.
Residence – 23 Flood Street, SW3 5ST. *Clubs* – Boodle's, Pilgrims, Brook (NY).

SON LIVING

HENRY WILLIAM, *b* 10 Nov 1980.

DAUGHTER LIVING

Katherine Louisa Patricia, *b* 1983.

SISTERS LIVING

Gay Ann (*Countess of Kinnoull*), *b* 1938: *m* 1961, 15th Earl of Kinnoull (15 Carlyle Sq, SW3 6EX; Pier Hse, Seaview, I of Wight). —— Melanie Fiona Louisa, *b* 1940: *m* 1964, Charles Archibald Adam Black, of 1 Astell St, SW3 3RT (*see* D Roxburghe, 1970 Edn), and has issue living, Adam Sebastian, *b* 1965, — Holly Patricia Louisa, *b* 1968.

WIDOW LIVING OF FIRST BARONET

Hon ANN PATRICIA MACPHERSON (*Hon Lady Lowson*) (Oratory Cottage, 33 Ennismore Gdns Mews, SW7 1HZ), da of 1st Baron Strathcarron; an OStJ: *m* 1936, Sir Denys Colquhoun Flowerdew Lowson, 1st Bt, who *d* 1975.

Sir Denys Colquhoun Flowerdew Lowson, 1st Bt, son of James Gray Flowerdew Lowson JP, PhD, of Balthayock, Perthshire, was Lord Mayor of London 1950-51 (Festival of Britain year).

LOWTHER (UK) 1824, of Swillington, Yorkshire

Sir CHARLES DOUGLAS LOWTHER, 6th *Baronet*, *b* 22 Jan 1946; *s* his father, *Lt-Col Sir* WILLIAM GUY, OBE, 1982; *ed* Winchester; Col, commanded Queen's R Irish Hus 1986-89; Memb HM Body Guard of Hon Corps of Gentlemen at Arms since 1997; High Sheriff Clwyd 1997: *m* 1st, 1969 (*m diss* 1975), Melanie Pensée FitzHerbert, da of late Roderick Christopher Musgrave; 2ndly, 1975, Florence Rose, yst da of late Col Alexander James Henry Cramsie, OBE, of O'Harabrook, Ballymoney, co Antrim, and has issue by 2nd *m*.

Arms – Or, six annulets sable, a crescent for difference. **Crest** – A dragon passant argent.
Seat – Erbistock Hall, nr Wrexham, Clwyd LL13 0DE.

SON LIVING (*By 2nd marriage*)

PATRICK WILLIAM, *b* 15 July, 1977.

DAUGHTER LIVING (*By 2nd marriage*)

The magistrate shows the man   Alice Rose, *b* 1979.

SISTER LIVING

Grizelda Leonora, *b* 1948: *m* 1968, Capt Timothy Michael Bell, Scots Gds, and has issue living, Matthew Guy, *b* 1974, — Katherine Leonora, *b* 1971.

WIDOW LIVING OF FIFTH BARONET

GRANIA SUZANNE (*Grania, Lady Lowther*), yst da of late Maj Archibald James Hamilton Douglas-Campbell, OBE, of Blythswood House, Renfrew (By Clarina, ext); OStJ: *m* 1939, Lt-Col Sir William Guy Lowther, OBE, 5th Bt, who *d* 1982. *Residence* – Cefyndd Farm, Erbistock, Wrexham.

COLLATERAL BRANCHES LIVING

Grandchildren of late Col John George Lowther, CBE, DSO, MC, TD (infra):—
Issue of late Capt George Hugh Lowther, *b* 1912, *d* 1976: *m* 1938, Sheila Rachel Isabel, who *d* 1980, da of late Maj Phipps Foster:—
James, *b* 1947; *ed* Eton: *m* 1987, Karen H., da of James Wallace, of Boston, Mass, USA, and has issue living, James William Dolfin, *b* 1991, — Natasha Jane, *b* 1988, — Mamie Grace, *b* 1994. *Residence* – Holdenby House, Northampton.
—— Sheila Ann, *b* 1943: *m* 1964 (*m diss* 19—), John Byng Oswald Carleton Paget, and has issue living, James Nicholas, *b* 1966: *m* 1995, Lauren E., da of Mrs Taryn Baldwin Edwards, of Chicago, Illinois, USA, and has issue living, Emily Josephine *b* 1997, — William Byng, *b* 1968: *m* 1996, Fiona V. M., eldest da of late Adrian Maynard, of Wolverton, Hants, — Rory Edward, *b* 1971.

Issue of late Col John George Lowther, CBE, DSO, MC, TD, brother of 4th baronet, *b* 1885, *d* 1977: *m* 1911, Hon Lilah Charlotte Sarah White, who *d* 1976, da of 3rd Baron Annaly:—
Sir John Luke, KCVO, CBE (Nortoft Grange, Guilsborough, Northants NN6 8QB), *b* 1923; Capt late KRRC; Lord Lieut Northants 1984-98; CBE (Civil) 1983; KCVO 1997: *m* 1952, Jennifer Jane, el da of late John Henry Bevan, CB, MC (E Lucan), and has issue living, Hugh William (Guilsborough Court, Northants NN6 8QW), *b* 1956: *m* 1985, Hon Amanda Ursula Georgina Vivian, elder da of 4th Baron Swansea, and has had issue, †Bertie *b* and *d* 1989, Flora Miriam *b* 1988, Georgia *b* 1991, Lucia *b* 1994, — Sarah Charlotte Margaret, *b* 1954: *m* 1977, Henry Merton Henderson, 2nd son of John Ronald Henderson, CVO, OBE, of West Woodhay House, Newbury, and has issue living, Harry Oliver *b* 1979, Katie Sarah *b* 1981, — Lavinia Mary, *b* 1958: *m* 1983, Julian Edward Tomkins, of South Lodge Farm, Holdenby, Northants NN6 8DL, son of Sir Edward Emile Tomkins, GCMG, CVO, of Winslow Hall, Winslow, Bucks, and has issue living, Benjamin Henry *b* 1988, Geordie Edward *b* 1991. —— Bridget Elizabeth, *b* 1921: *m* 1947, Robert Alister Henderson (*see* Clerke, Bt, 1980 Edn), of North Ecchinswell Farm, Ecchinswell, nr Newbury, Berks, and has had issue, Robert David Charles (Battle House, Goring-on-Thames, Oxon), *b* 1948: *m* 1975, Odette Anne, da of late Lloyd Llewellyn Andersson, of Parktown, Johannesburg, and has issue living, Camilla Elizabeth *b* 1977, Laura Catherine *b* 1979, Celia Anne *b* 1982, — James, *b* 1955: *m* 1978, Susan Clare Evelyn (who *m* 2ndly, 19—, Charles Dingwall), da of David Cuthbert Tudway Quilter (*see* Quilter, Bt, colls), and *d* 1991, leaving issue, Sophie Elizabeth *b* 1979, Emily Anne *b* 1981, Alice Beatrice *b* 1985, — Emma Mary, *b* 1950: *m* 1st, 1971 (*m diss* 1978), Hugh Leopold Seymour (*see* M Hertford, colls); 2ndly, 1979, J. L. David Aschan; 3rdly, 1982, Paul Anthony Irby, of Garth House, Highclere, nr Newbury, Berks RG20 9RE, and has issue living, (by 2nd *m*), Clare Louise *b* 1979, Eliza Beatrice *b* 1981, (by 3rd *m*) (*see* B Boston).

The 1st baronet, many years, MP for Cumberland, was brother to William, 1st Earl of Lonsdale, and the 2nd baronet was successively MP for Cockermouth, Wigton, and York. The 4th baronet, Lieut-Col Sir Charles Bingham, CB, DSO, was Lieut-Col Northants Yeo and High Sheriff of Northants 1926.

LUCAS (UK) 1887, of Ashtead Park, Surrey, and of Lowestoft, co Suffolk

Hope and faith

Sir THOMAS EDWARD LUCAS, 5th *Baronet*, son of late Ralph John Scott Lucas, 2nd son of Maj Ernest Murray Lucas, 3rd son of 1st baronet; *b* 16 Sept 1930; *s* his cousin, Maj Sir JOSCELYN MORTON, KBE, MC 1980, but his name does not appear on the Official Roll of the Baronetage; *ed* Wellington Coll, and Trin Hall, Camb (MA): *m* 1st, 1958, Charmian Margaret, who *d* 1970, only da of late Col James Stanley Powell, of Drayton Court, SW10; 2ndly, 1980, Mrs Ann J. Graham Moore, and has issue by 1st *m*.

𝕬rms – Per bend argent and gules, a bend dovetailed between six annulets, all counterchanged. Crest – Issuant from a wreath of oak or a dragons head, wings addorsed gules, semée of annulets argent.
Address – Shermans Hall, Dedham, Essex CO7 6DE.

SON LIVING (By 1st marriage)

STEPHEN RALPH JAMES, *b* 11 Dec 1963; *ed* Wellington Coll, and Edinburgh Univ (BCom): *m* 1993, Charlotte A., yst da of late J. E. B. Johnson, of Lockerbie, Dumfries, and has issue living, Olivia May, *b* 1997.

BROTHER LIVING

Patrick Timson, VRD and bar (The Hollies, Court Green Heights, Hook Heath, Woking, Surrey; Royal Naval Club), *b* 1933; *ed* Wellington Coll; Maj (RMR): *m* 1958, Anne, da of Jack Westcott, of Yeovil, Som, and has issue living, Simon James Timson, *b* 1960; *ed* Wellington Coll, and City Univ, London (BSc), — Julian Patrick, *b* 1962; *ed* Wellington Coll, and Univ Coll, Cardiff (BSc).

COLLATERAL BRANCHES LIVING

Grandchildren of late Rev Francis Granville Lewis Lucas, 4th son of 1st baronet:—
Issue of late Maj Arthur John Lucas, *b* 1903, *d* 1986: *m* 1930, Margaret Ruth, who *d* 1989, da of late Col Joseph Francis Noel Baxendale, CB, TD (Heathcoat, Bt):—
James Granville (Yew Tree Cottage, Port Navas, Falmouth, Cornwall), *b* 1932; *ed* Harrow; Lt Cdr RN (ret): *m* 1st, 1957 (*m diss* 1973), Suzanne Molly, da of late Edward FitzRoy Talbot-Ponsonby (*see* E Shrewsbury, colls); 2ndly, 1973, Ann Marie Mason, and has issue living (by 1st *m*), Jonathan Delight, *b* 1964, — Charles Granville *b* (twin) 1964, — (by 2nd *m*) Serena Kate, *b* 1977. —— Jennifer, *b* 1936: *m* 1972, Hugh Cecil Toomer, of 5 Eccleston Sq, SW1.

Grandchildren of late Maj Evelyn Penn Lucas, MC, yst son of 1st baronet:—
Issue of late Capt Timothy Stovin Lucas, MC, TD, *b* 1916; *d* 1981: *m* 1942, Joanna Repington (Sharow Hall, Ripon, N Yorks), only child of Charles Bernard Mathews, of Lob's Wood, Ilkley, Yorks:—
Charles Evelyn Penn (Sharow Hall, Ripon, N Yorks), *b* 1943; *ed* Eton: *m* 1967 (*m diss* 1989), Antoinette Maria, only da of late Baron Henri von Westenholz, of Blakesware, Much Hadham, Herts, and has issue living, Piers Timothy Everard, *b* 1970, — Harry Rudolph Penn, *b* 1976, — Nina Antoinette, *b* 1971. —— Charlotte Theresa Stovin (Weavers, Fewcott, nr Bicester, Oxon), *b* 1945: *m* 1966 (*m diss* 1971), Christopher Frank Stuart Irwin, and has issue living, Alexander Christian Stovin, *b* 1970, — Sophia Georgette Kate, *b* 1968.

Lucas (Munro-Lucas-Tooth), see Tooth.

RAMSAY-FAIRFAX-LUCY (UK) 1836, of The Holmes, Roxburghshire

Sir EDMUND JOHN WILLIAM HUGH RAMSAY-FAIRFAX-LUCY, 6th *Baronet*; *b* 4 May 1945; *s* his father, *Maj Sir* BRIAN FULKE, 1974; *ed* Eton; Dip RA Schs: *m* 1st, 1974 (*m diss* 19—), Sylvia, da of Graeme Ogden, of The Old Manor, Rudge, Somerset; 2ndly, 1986 (*m diss* 1989), Lady Lucinda Lambton, eldest da of Antony Claud Lambton (6th Earl of Durham until he disclaimed his title 1970); 3rdly, 1994, Erica Everina Penelope, only da of Simon Folliott Warren Thomas Barton Loane, of Crocknacrieve, co Fermanagh, and has issue by 3rd *m*.

Arms – 1st and 4th grand-quarters, gules, 1st semée of cross crosslets, three lucies haurient argent, a canton of the last, *Lucy;* 2nd and 3rd grand quarters, quarterly 1st and 4th argent, three bars gemel sable surmounted by a lion rampant gules, armed and langued azure, *Fairfax;* 2nd, per pale argent and or, an eagle displayed sable, armed, beaked and membered gules, *Ramsay;* 3rd counter-quartered, 1st and 4th azure, a branch of palm between three fleurs-de-lis or, 2nd and 3rd gules, three annulets or, stoned azure, in the centre of three counter-quarters a crescent or for difference, *Montgomerie.* Crests – 1st, out of a ducal coronet gules a boar's head argent guttée de poix, between two wings sable: billettée or charged on the neck, with a cross-crosslet sable, *Lucy;* 2nd, a lion passant guardant proper, *Fairfax.* Mottoes – *Dexter,* By truthe and diligence, *Lucy; sinister,* Fare fac, *Fairfax.*
Seat – Charlecote Park, Warwick.

SONS LIVING *(by 3rd marriage)*

PATRICK SAMUEL THOMAS FULKE, *b* 3 April 1995. —— John Frederick Hugh, *b* 1998.

SISTER LIVING

(Mary Caroline Alys) Emma, *b* 1946: *m* 1st, 1967, James Empson Scott, MA, MB, BCh, FRCS; 2ndly, 1982, as his 2nd wife, James Louis Lambe (*see* Corbet, Bt, 1990 Edn), and has issue living, (by 1st *m*) Sophie Katherina Rosie, *b* 1970, — Charlotte Christina Bianca, *b* 1974. *Residence* – The Castle, Upton Bishop, Ross-on-Wye, Herefords HR9 7UW.

COLLATERAL BRANCHES LIVING

Issue of late Capt Ewen Aymer Robert Ramsay-Fairfax-Lucy, yst son of 3rd baronet, *b* 1899, *d* 1969: *m* 1930, Margaret Westall, who *d* 1994, da of Sir John Westall King, 2nd Bt (*cr* 1888):—
Duncan Cameron (The Malt House, Charlecote, Warwick CV35 9EW), *b* 1932; *ed* Eton; FCA: *m* 1964, Janet Barclay, da of P. A. B. Niven, of Malt Cottage, Charlecote, Warwick, and has issue living, (Spencer) Angus, *b* 1966: *m* 1995, Daoruang, da of Mrs Kumpaa Duanjangram, of Buriram, Thailand, — Anna Margaret Barclay, *b* 1969. —— Robin Spencer, *b* 1937. —— Jennifer Frances, *b* 1935: *m* 1st, 1962, Dr (Ronald) Ian Talbot Cromartie, CMG, who *d* 1987; 2ndly, 1995, James Stuart Lechmere Macaskie, and has issue living, (by 1st *m*) Alan Duncan Talbot, *b* 1964, — David Francis Ian, *b* 1970, — Selina Margaret Lucy, *b* 1967. —— Christina Alison, *b* 1943: *m* 1964, John Anthony Chandley Pugh, FCA, and has issue living, Jonathan Chandley, *b* 1966: *m* 1994, Jennifer Ruth, yst da of G/Capt John Horrell,

OBE, — Rosanna Lucy, *b* 1968: *m* 1996, Andrew Jonathan Bentley, 3rd son of Michael John Bentley, — Martha Elizabeth, *b* 1971.

Issue of late Com William George Astell RAMSAY-FAIRFAX, CMG, DSO, RN, 3rd son of 2nd baronet, *b* 1876, *d* 1946: *m* 1909, Lilian Kate, who *d* 1957, da of late Henry Rich, of Abbey Lodge, Malmesbury:—
Victor George Hargrave, DSC, *b* 1912; Lt-Cdr (ret) RN; 1939-45 War (despatches, DSC): *m* 1939, Christian Geraldine Mary, who *d* 1967, only child of late Lt-Col Frederick Arthur Irby (B Boston, colls), and has issue living, Victor Ferdinand Desmond, *b* 1944, — Pepita Christian, *b* 1942. *Residence* – 73 High St, Lavenham, Suffolk, CO10 9PT. *Club* – Army and Navy.

This family claims descent from the same stock as Lord Fairfax of Cameron. Vice-Adm Sir William George Fairfax, a distinguished naval officer, was made a Knight Banneret for bravery displayed by him at the battle of Camperdown, and in consideration of his services a baronetcy was conferred upon his only surviving son, Col Sir Henry Fairfax, who *m* 1830 (as his 1st wife) Archibald Montgomerie, da and eventually heir of Thomas Williamson (afterwards Williamson-Ramsay), by Elizabeth, da and co-heir of Robert Ramsay of Camno and Arthurstown, Forfar. The 2nd baronet, Col Sir William George Herbert Taylor, assumed the additional surname and arms of Ramsay 1876, and the 3rd baronet, Sir Henry William, CB, assumed by Royal Licence the additional surname of Lucy 1892, and Cameron 1921, having *m* 1892, Ada Christina, da and heir of Henry Spencer Lucy, of Charlecote, Warwickshire.

LUSHINGTON (GB) 1791, of South Hill Park, Berkshire

Fides nudaque veritas

Faith and naked truth

Sir JOHN RICHARD CASTLEMAN LUSHINGTON, 8th *Baronet*; *b* 28 Aug 1938; *s* his father, *Sir* HENRY EDMUND CASTLEMAN, 1988; *ed* Oundle; Partner MaST (Management and Skills Training): *m* 1966, Bridget Gillian Margaret, only da of late Col John Foster Longfield, of Knockbeg, Saunton, N. Devon, and has issue.

Arms – Or, on a fesse wavy between three lions' heads erased vert, as many ermine spots or. **Crest** – A lion's head erased vert, charged on the erasure with three ermine spots or, ducally gorged argent.
Residence – The Glebe House, Henham, Bishops Stortford, Herts.

SONS LIVING

RICHARD DOUGLAS LONGFIELD, *b* 29 March 1968; BA; Fl Lt RAF. —— Greville Edmund Longfield, *b* 1969; BA: *m* 1998, Tracey Nicola, only da of Leslie B. Binns, of Scissett, Yorks. —— Thomas Robert Longfield, *b* 1975.

SISTERS LIVING AND DECEASED

Caroline Elizabeth, *b* 1942: *m* 1964, Patrick Donald Bloss, FCA, of Dene House, The Green, Shamley Green, Guildford, Surrey GU5 0UA, and *d* 1995, leaving issue, James Patrick, *b* 1972, — Diana Elizabeth, *b* 1967, — Victoria Caroline *b* 1970. —— Penelope Daphne, *b* 1945: *m* 1967, Ronald Gulliver, LLB, FCA, of The Old Chapel, New Mill, Eversley, Hants, and has issue living, Christopher Ronald, *b* 1974, — Patricia Jean, *b* 1976.

HALF-UNCLE LIVING (*son of 6th baronet by 2nd marriage*)

Patrick Hay Castleman (56 Suzanne Av, Morphett Vale, S Aust 5162) *b* 1931; late RAF: *m* 1957, Ann Marie, el da of Ferdinand Mohr, of 37 Neutorstrasse, Mainz, Germany, and has issue living, Kurt, *b* 1958: *m* 1985, Susane Annette, da of Lionel Burton, of 14 Lochness Av, Adelaide, and has issue living, Joshua Hay Castleman *b* 1991, Caleb James *b* 1997, Grace Alexandra *b* 1992, Hanna Victoria *b* 1995, — Werner, *b* 1960: *m* 1985, Sylvia Angelika, da of Sigismund Krause, of 81 O'Sullivan Beach Rd, Morphett-Vale, and has issue living, Sean Matthew *b* 1987, Alexander James *b* 1992 Tarryn Rebecca *b* 1985, — Horst, *b* 1966: *m* 1995, Faerlie Eveline Powell, da of Colin Ross Gordon, of Kangarilla, S Australia, and has issue living, Finneas Colin Ross Gordon *b* 1997, Millicent Anita Hay Castleman *b* 1999, — Elke Christine, *b* 1964: *m* 1992, Robert Melten, yst son of Nicholas Melton, and has issue living, Kathleen Gabrielle *b* 1995, Genevieve Ingrid *b* 1998.

HALF-AUNT LIVING (*daughter of 6th baronet by 2nd marriage*)

Pamela Anne, *b* 1929: *m* 1952, Peter Lindsay Jones, of 19 Aberdare Av, Drayton, Cosham, Portsmouth PO6 2AT, and has issue living, Alistair, *b* 1953: *m* 1st, 1975 (*m diss* 1986), Heather McKennes; 2ndly, 1993, Shaari Horowitz, — Laurence, *b* 1959, — Martin Edward, *b* 1964, — Margaret Amanda, *b* 1955: *m* 1976, Michael Joseph Reilly, of Denver, USA, and has issue living, Patrick Joseph *b* 1977, Dennis John *b* 1979, — Rosemary Anne, *b* 1957: *m* 1989, Nicholas John Pullen, and has issue living, Adam James *b* 1990, Rebecca Louise *b* 1992, — Sarah Louise, *b* 1966.

WIDOW LIVING OF SEVENTH BARONET

PAMELA ELIZABETH DAPHNE (*Pamela, Lady Lushington*), elder da of late Maj Archer Richard Hunter, of The White Cottage,

Rectory Rd, Wokingham, Berks: *m* 1937, Sir Henry Edmund Castleman Lushington, 7th Bt, who *d* 1988. *Residence* – Gramerci, Eversley Centre, Hants RG27 0NB.

COLLATERAL BRANCH LIVING

Grandson of late Sydney George Lushington, 2nd son of late Edward Harbord Lushington, eldest son of late Rt Hon Stephen Lushington, MP, 2nd son of 1st baronet:—
Issue of late Lt-Col Franklin Lushington, *b* 1892, *d* 1964: *m* 1st, 1916 (*m diss* 1948), (Mary Marjorie) Bridget, who *d* 1977, da of Ernest Howard; 2ndly, 1949, Eleanora, who *d* 1964, da of Niels Illeris, of Bagsvaerd, Denmark:—
(By 1st *m*) Stephen (9 High Wickham, Hastings, E Sussex TN35 5PB), *b* 1917; *ed* Eton, and New Coll, Oxford; late RA: *m* 1st, 1941 (*m diss* 1951), Maureen, da of Maj John Pook; 2ndly, 1951 (*m diss* 1972), Sonia, da of Harry Ratoff; 3rdly, 1972, Beatrice, da of Irvan O'Connell, of Winchester, Va, USA, and widow of Theodore Roethke, and has issue living, (by 1st *m*) Mark (72 Dynevor Rd, N16), *b* 1942: *m* 1966, Cora, da of Sidney Kaplan, of Northampton, Mass, USA, and has issue living, Jacob *b* 1968, — (by 2nd *m*) Catherine Rachel, *b* 1953: *m* 1975, Richard Marc Greenblatt, of 22 Palmerston Gdns, Toronto, Ontario M6G 1V9, Canada, and has issue living, William *b* 1987, Luke *b* 1990, Natasha Grace *b* 1984.

This family was settled in E Kent from the 14th century. Sir Stephen Lushington, 1st Bt, of South Hill Park, Berks (grandson of Stephen Lushington of Sittingbourne, who purchased the Manor of Rodmersham) was Chm of Hon East India Co 1790.

LYLE (UK) 1929, of Glendelvine, co Perth

Sir GAVIN ARCHIBALD LYLE, 3rd *Baronet*, son of late Capt Ian Archibald de Hoghton Lyle, Black Watch, el son of 2nd baronet; *b* 14 Oct 1941; *s* his grandfather, *Col Sir* ARCHIBALD MOIR PARK, MC, 1946; *ed* Eton: *m* 1967 (*m diss* 1985), Susan, only da of John Vaughan Cooper, and has issue.

Arms – Gules, fretty or surmounted of a gallery, oars in saltire, sails furled sable, flagged gules, the sails charged with a crescent of the second for difference. **Crest** – A cock or crested gules.
Residence – Glendelvine, Caputh, Perthshire, PH1 4JN.

SONS LIVING

IAN ABRAM, *b* 25 Sept 1968. —— Jake Archibald, *b* 1969. —— Matthew Alexander, *b* 1974. —— Joshua, *b* 1979. —— Samuel, *b* 1981.

DAUGHTER LIVING

Rachel, *b* 1971.

SISTER LIVING

Lorna, *b* 1939: *m* 1st, 1959, Timothy Cyprian George Thomas Elwes (*see* B Rennell, 1973-74 Edn); 2ndly, 1979, (Walter) Ronald Alexander, of Moonzie Mill, Balmallow, Fife KY16 OAH, and has issue living, (by 1st *m*) Ian Anthony Archibald de Hoghton Cary (34 Lanarch Rd, W6 9NX), *b* 1961: *m* 1990, Deborah J., elder da of David Winckles, of Bovey Tracey, Devon, — Gavin Esmond Cary, *b* 1962, — Amanda Dorothy Cary, *b* 1964: *m* 1992, Matthew D. Austin, of 53 Heathfield Rd, SW18 2PH, only son of John Austin, of Arden House, Warwicks, — Lydia Elinor Cary *b* (twin), 1964.

UNCLE LIVING (*Son of 2nd baronet*)

Archibald Michael, OBE, *b* 1919; *ed* Eton, and Trin Coll, Oxford; Lt-Col (ret) Scottish Horse, and late Maj Black Watch; Vice Lord Lieut, DL and JP for Perthshire, and a Member Queen's Body Guard for Scotland (Royal Company of Archers); OBE (Civil) 1995; *m* 1942, Hon Elizabeth Sinclair, who *d* 1994, yr da of 1st Viscount Thurso, and has three das, Veronica (*Baroness Linklater of Butterstone*), *b* 1943; *cr* Baroness Linklater of Butterstone (Life Baroness) 1997: *m* 1967, Magnus Duncan Linklater, of 5 Drummond Place, Edinburgh EH3 6PH, and has issue (see that title), — Janet, *b* 1944: *m* 1975, Richard Cooper, and has issue living, Daisy *b* 1983, Hester *b* 1985, Matilda *b* 1988, — Sarah Caroline, *b* 1963: *m* 1996, Dr Owen John Day, son of Prof Nicholas Edward Day, of Haddenham, Cambs, and has issue living, Alastair Nicholas Michael *b* 1997, James Archibald John *b* 1999. *Residence* – Riemore Lodge, Dunkeld, Perths.

AUNT LIVING (*Daughter of 2nd baronet*)

Dorothea, *b* 1914, *m* 1937 (*m diss* 1962), Rear-Adm Viscount Kelburn, CB, DSC (subsequently 9th Earl of Glasgow), who *d* 1984. *Residences* – Marwell House, Owlesbury, nr Winchester, and Albany, Piccadilly, W1.

MOTHER LIVING

Hon Lydia Yarde-Buller, da of 3rd Baron Churston: *m* 1st, 1938, Capt Ian Archibald de Hoghton Lyle, Black Watch (ante), who was *ka* 1942; 2ndly, 1947 (*m diss* 1960), 13th Duke of Bedford. *Residence* – Little Ribsden, Windlesham, Bagshot, Surrey.

Sir Alexander Park Lyle, 1st Bt, was a shipowner, and gt-grandson of Abram Lyle, of Greenock, who founded the firm of Abram Lyle & Sons in 1796 (previously MacDonald & Lyle). The 1st Lord Lyle of Westbourne was a nephew of the 1st Bt.

Lynch-Blosse, see Blosse.

Lynch-Robinson, see Robinson.

McALPINE (UK) 1918, of Knott Park, co Surrey

Hon Sir WILLIAM HEPBURN MCALPINE, 6th *Baronet*; *b* 12 Jan 1936; *s* his father, (ROBERT) EDWIN, Baron McAlpine of Moffat (Life Baron) in his Baronetcy 1990; *ed* Charterhouse; a Dir Sir Robert McAlpine Ltd: *m* 1959, Jill Benton, only da of late Lt-Col Sir Peter Fawcett Benton Jones, 3rd Bt, OBE, and has issue.

𝕬rms – Per chevron vert and or, two chevronels one in chief argent the other in base azure. 𝕮rest – A cubit arm grasping a chaplet of pine fructed all proper.
Residence – Fawley Hill, Fawley Green, Henley-on-Thames, Oxon RG9 6JA.

SON LIVING

ANDREW WILLIAM, *b* 22 Nov 1960; *ed* Stowe: *m* 1991, (Caroline) Claire, yr da of Frederick A. Hodgson, of Sheffield, Yorks, and has issue living, Frederick William Edwin, *b* 25 Aug 1993, — Fergus Andrew Algernon, *b* 1994, — Henry Arthur, *b* 1998, — Archie Robert, *b* (twin) 1998.

DAUGHTER LIVING

Lucinda Mary Jane, *b* 1964.

BROTHERS LIVING

Hon Robert Alistair (*Baron McAlpine of West Green*), *b* 1942; *cr* Baron McAlpine of West Green (Life Baron) 1984 (see that title).
Hon David Malcolm, *b* 1946; *ed* Stowe; Dir Sir Robert McAlpine Ltd: *m* 1971 (*m diss* 1993), Jennifer Anne, da of Eric Hodges, and has issue living, Robert Edward Thomas William, *b* 1978, — Katherine Alexandra Donnison, *b* 1972, — Elizabeth Louise, *b* 1973.

SISTER LIVING

Hon Patricia Garnett, *b* 1932: *m* 1950, Hon Robin Sandbach Borwick, Lieut The Life Guards (ret), of Neptune House, Newells Lane, Bosham, Sussex PO18 8PS, son of 3rd Baron Borwick.

DAUGHTER LIVING OF SECOND BARONET

Zelie Agnes Elise Conde (Woodgates Cottage, Ford Manor, Dormansland, Lingfield, Surrey), *b* 1910: *m* 1934, Surg-Cdr Wilfred Treize Rougier Chapman, VD, RNVR, MRCS, LRCP, who *d* 1981, and has issue living, Zeralda Lillias, *b* 1939: *m* 1st, 1962 (*m diss* 1970), Trevor Adrian Soutry; 2ndly, 1977, Alphonse Michaele Micallef, MD, of Lower Stonehurst Farm, E Grinstead, Sussex, and has issue living (by 1st *m*), Giles Robert Adrian *b* 1964: *m* 1994, Mrs Anne Yolande Tranter Broadbent, da of Peter Cartwright, Lucinda Caroline *b* 1969, — Nonie Elizabeth, *b* 1942, — Penelope Margaret, *b* 1944: *m* 1966, David Ronald Adam, of Lower Sandhill House, Halland, nr Uckfield, Sussex, and has issue living, Angus Ronald *b* 1969: *m* 1996, Yasemin Sina Osman, Gavin David *b* 1976, Annabelle Jane *b* 1968: *m* 1993 (*m diss* 1998), Maj Charles Andrew Stuart (and has issue living, William James *b* 1996), Katherine Lucy *b* 1972: *m* 1997, Michael Greville Tufnell (*see* B Chesham).

COLLATERAL BRANCHES LIVING

Grandchildren of late William McAlpine, 2nd son of 1st baronet:—
Issue of late Malcolm Donnison McAlpine, *b* 1909; *d* 1982: *m* 1939, Diana Mary (Little Burton, Burton Lazars, Melton Mowbray, Leics), da of Sidney Bruce Askew, of Nutfield, Surrey:—
Ian Malcolm, OBE, *b* 1942; *ed* Oundle, and Clare Coll, Camb (MA); High Sheriff Leics 1998; OBE (Civil) 1995: *m* 1967, Caroline Mary, da of late William Henry Ward, of Wisbech, Cambs, and has two adopted children, Julian Angus Ian, *b* 1970, — Susannah Melanie, *b* 1972: *m* 1998, Edward Aston Wass, 2nd son of Nigel Samuel Wass, of Highgate. *Residence* – Peatling Hall, Peatling Parva, Leics. —— Bruce Andrew, *b* 1947; *ed* Oundle, and Clare Coll, Camb: *m* 1st, 1974 (*m diss* 1992), Ingrid Christliebe, da of Alfred Reynolds Schlosshauer, of Neckarhausen, Germany; 2ndly, 1993, Marina Ernestine Hirschberg, da of late Hubert, Baron von Breisky, of Salzburg, Austria. —— Susan Mary, *b* 1945: *m* 1968, Leonard Maxwell Harvey, of Lyneham House, Yealmpton, nr Plymouth, Devon, and has issue living, Damon Maxwell, *b* 1970.

Granddaughter of late Sir (Thomas) Malcolm McAlpine, KBE (infra):—
Adopted da of late Sir Robin McAlpine, CBE, *b* 1906; assumed by deed poll 1939 the christian name of Robin in lieu of Robert; *d* 1993: *m* 1st, 1939, Nora Constance, who *d* 1966, yr da of F. H. Perse, formerly of Rochester, Kent; 2ndly, 1970, Mrs Philippa Janet Nicolson, who *d* 1987, da of Sir (Eustace) Gervais Tennyson d'Eyncourt, 2nd Bt, and formerly wife of Nigel Nicolson, MBE (*see* B Carnock, colls):—
Carolyn Peta, *b* 1944: *m* 1965, Nigel Robert Elwes, and has issue living, Andrew Julian Robert, *b* 1969; *ed* Eton, and Edinburgh Univ, — Serena Clare, *b* 1967: *m* 1996, Jeremy J. C. Bradbeer, only son of Sir Derek Bradbeer, of Shilvington, Northumberland, and has issue living, Charles Julian Chantler *b* 1997, Eliza Jennifer *b* 1999, — Melisa, *b* 1973. *Residence* – Aylesfield, Alton, Hants GU34 4BY.

Issue of late Sir (Thomas) Malcolm McAlpine, KBE, 3rd son of 1st baronet, *b* 1877, *d* 1967: *m* 1903, Maud, who *d* 1969, da of James Gibson Dees:—
Malcolm Hugh Dees (Highfields, Withyham, Hartfield, E Sussex TN7 4DB), *b* 1917; late Lt-Col RE; a Dir of Sir Robert McAlpine Ltd: *m* 1944, Sheila Margaret, el da of late Maj F. Raeburn Price, of Fordyce, N Foreland, Thanet, and has issue living, Adrian Neil Raeburn, *b* 1944; Dir Sir Robert McAlpine Ltd; a Gov Milton Abbey Sch since 1987: *m* 1983, Angela Mary, yr da of Dr George Hickie, of Mill House, Ashton Keynes, Wilts, and has issue living, Angus Neil Adrian *b* 1993, Antonia Louise Philippa *b* 1984, Olivia Alice Gemma *b* 1986, — Cullum (Cold Ashton Manor, Chippenham, Wilts SN14 8JU), *b* 1947; assumed the forename of Cullum in lieu of Malcolm Robert by deed poll 1963; Dir Sir Robert McAlpine Ltd: *m* 1973, Amanda, yr da of Robert Lamdin, of Horsted Keynes, Sussex, and has issue living, Robert Harry *b* 1975, Gavin Malcolm *b* 1976, Hector George *b* 1980, Douglas James *b* 1983, — Hamish (79 Wardour St, W1V 3TH), *b* 1954: *m* 1997, Karen J., eldest da of Trevor Nicholls, of St Albans, Herts. —— Kenneth, OBE (The Priory, Lamberhurst, Kent), *b* 1920; late F/O RAFVR; High Sheriff of Kent 1973-74, DL Kent 1976; Gov St Bartholomew's Hosp 1972-74, Gov and Dep-Chm Eastbourne Coll 1968-84; OBE (Civil) 1997; FRAeS: *m* 1955, Patricia Mary, da of late Capt Francis William Hugh Jeans, CVO, RN, and has issue living, Richard Hugh, *b* 1958; Dir Sir Robert McAlpine Ltd: *m* 1991, Linda Elizabeth, only da of late William Leighton Wee, of San Francisco, USA, and has issue living, Thomas Leighton *b* 1992, — James Thomas Hemery, *b* 1960; Dir McAlpine Helicopters Ltd: *m* 1995, Heather Alison, only da of Andrew Baillie, of Edinburgh, and has issue living, Melissa Abigail Nicola *b* 1998.

Grandchildren of late Sir Alfred (David) McAlpine, 4th son of 1st baronet:—
Issue of late Alfred James McAlpine, *b* 1908, *d* 1991: *m* 1st, 1931 (*m diss* 1940), Peggy Barbara, eldest da of late John Ernest Sanders, of Gresford, Denbighshire; 2ndly, 1940 (*m diss* 1951), Mary Kinder, da of Frank Musgrave Read; 3rdly, 1951 (*m diss* 1959), Mrs Rosemary Lavery, who *d* 1983, da of late Maj Charles Hugh Gregory-Hood (*see* V Hood, colls, 1980 edn); 4thly, 1959 (*m diss* 1979), Eleanor Margaret Rangel, da of late John Nicholson Wallace, of Lisbon; 5thly, 1979, Cynthia Greenaway (Gerwyn Hall, Marchwiel, nr Wrexham, Denbighshire), da of Harry Whitney:—
(By 1st *m*) Robert James (Tilstone Lodge, Tilstone Fearnall, Tarporley, Cheshire CW6 9HS), *b* 1932; *ed* Harrow; a Dir Sir Alfred McAlpine & Son Ltd: *m* 1st, 1956 (*m diss* 19—), Jane, who *d* 1992, eldest da of James Anton, of Tudor House, Rumsley, nr Bridgnorth, Shropshire; 2ndly, 1981, Mrs Angela J. Bell, only da of late Maj E. W. Langford-Brooke, of Cheshire, and formerly wife of Christopher Bell, and has issue living (by 1st *m*), Euan James, *b* 1958: *m* 1983, Fiona Elizabeth, eldest da of Charles Aylmer Eade, of Uppington House, Telford, Shropshire, and has issue living, Tom *b* 1991, Flora *b* 1989, Rosie *b* 1993, — Christopher William, *b* 1965: *m* 1991, Sarah Louise, da of Anthony Rundell, of Clapham, SW, — Sara Jane, *b* 1961: *m* 1982 (*m diss* 1994), Hon (Herbert) Robin Cayzer (later 3rd Baron Rotherwick), — (by 2nd *m*) Emma Antonia, *b* 1982. —— †Alfred William, *b* 1935; *ed* Harrow; *d* as the result of a road accident 1962, *unm*. —— (By 2nd *m*) Valerie Ann, *b* 1942: *m* 1st, 1962 (*m diss* 1966), Julian Noyes; 2ndly, 1967, Peter Shaw, and has issue living (by 1st *m*), William, *b* 1963, — (by 2nd *m*) Samantha Margaret, *b* 1969, — Joanna Mary, *b* 1972. —— (By 3rd *m*) Sally Dorothy (49 Campden Hill Rd, W8 7DY), *b* 1952: *m* 1975 (*m diss* 1990), as his 3rd wife, (Bernard) Godfrey Argent, and has issue living, Jenna Charlotte, *b* 1980.

Issue of late Granville Ramage McAlpine, 5th son of 1st baronet, *b* 1883; *d* 1928: *m* 1922, Beatrice Mary Donald, who *d* 1936:—
Maureen Agnes, *b* 1925: *m* 1949, Frederick Stanley Thornton, MBE, who *d* 1994, and has issue living, David Malcolm, *b* 1950: *m* 1973, Stephanie Patricia Mills, and has issue living, Simon Edward *b* 1983, — Andrew William (Willow Orchard, Frating Rd, Gt Bromley, Colchester, Essex C07 7JW), *b* 1953: *m* 1981, Jacqueline Mary Deane, and has issue living, James Ashley *b* 1984, Tobias William *b* 1987. *Residence* – 12 Mossfield Close, Colchester, Essex C03 3RG.

Issue of late (Archibald) Douglas McAlpine, MD, FRCP, 6th son of 1st baronet, *b* 1890, *d* 1981: *m* 1st, 1917, Elizabeth Meg Sidebottom, who *d* 1941; 2ndly, 1945, Diana Christina Dunscombe, who *d* 1981, da of late Bertram Plummer:—
(By 1st *m*) (Robert Douglas) Christopher, CMG (Longtree House, Cutwell, Tetbury, Glos GL8 8EB), *b* 1919; *ed* Winchester, and New Coll, Oxford (MA); Foreign Office 1946-47, Assist Private Sec to Sec of State 1947-49, Control Commn for Germany as 2nd and later 1st Sec 1949-52; Foreign Office 1952-54, British Embassy, Lima 1954-56, and Moscow 1956-59, Foreign Office 1959-62, Dep Consul-Gen, New York 1962-65, and Counsellor, British Embassy, Mexico City 1965-68; a Dir of Baring Bros & Co Ltd 1969-79, Dir Clarkson (Holdings) plc 1980-87; 1939-45 War as Lt-Cdr RNVR (Fleet Air Arm) CMG 1967): *m* 1943, Helen Margery Frances, da of late Capt Astley Cannan, and has issue living, David Douglas Christopher (64 Gloucester Rd, Kew, Richmond, Surrey), *b* 1949; *ed* Winchester, and E Anglia Univ: *m* 1973, Susan Mary, da of Richard John Boileau Walker, and has issue living, Thomas David *b* 1977, Laura Esme *b* 1980, Martha Rose *b* 1983, Jessica Mary Sucharita *b* 1986, — Robert John (5935 Coach Hill Rd, SW, Calgary, Alberta, Canada

T3H 1E3), *b* 1953: *m* 1987, Sheila Maureen, da of E. J. Arseneault, of Winnipeg, Manitoba, Canada, and has issue living, Sophia Madeleine *b* 1993, — Sarah Margaret, *b* 1946: *m* 1971, Timothy George Holloway, of Glebe House, Lamer Lane, Wheathampstead, St Albans, Herts AL4 8RH, and has issue living, Benjamin Richard *b* 1973, Katharine Helen *b* 1975. —— Florence Mary, *b* 1922; formerly 3rd Officer WRNS: *m* 1952, Peter Alexander MacDonell, who *d* 1986, of Rose Court, Fortrose, Ross-shire, and has issue living, Charlotte Anne, *b* 1954: *m* 1979, Peter Maltin, and has issue living, Charles Alexander *b* 1992, Zoe Alexandra *b* 1987, — Maria Christian, *b* 1959; has issue living, Calanach Jack *b* 1994, Molly Isolde *b* 1992, Georgina Primrose *b* 1996, Juno Isabella *b* 1999. —— (By 2nd *m*) Alastair Bertram, *b* 1945: *m* 1968 (*m diss* 1973), Ann, da of Maj Bernard Winchester.

The 1st baronet Sir Robert McAlpine, JP (son of Robert McAlpine of Newarthill, Lanarks), founded the firm of Sir Robert McAlpine & Sons, civil engineering and building contractors, and *d* 3 Nov 1934. He was *cr* a *Baronet* (UK) of Knott Park, co Surrey 1918. The 5th baronet, Sir (Robert) Edwin McAlpine, ptnr Sir Robert McAlpine & Sons Ltd, was *cr* Knt 1963, *s* his brother in his baronetcy 1983, and was *cr Baron McAlpine of Moffat*, of Medmenham, co Bucks (Life Baron) 1980.

MACARA (UK) 1911, of Ardmore, St Anne-on-the-Sea, co Lancaster

By wisdom not by might

Sir HUGH KENNETH MACARA, 4th *Baronet*; *b* 17 Jan 1913; *s* his brother, *Sir* (CHARLES) DOUGLAS, 1982.

Arms – Ermine, an oak tree eradicated in bend dexter, surmounted by a sword proper, hilted and pommelled or, in bend sinister, supporting on its point an Imperial Crown of the second, on a chief of the third, a spider sable between two thistles also proper. **Crest** – A stag reguardant lodged in front of an oak tree proper.
Residence –

SISTER LIVING

Aileen Lillah, *b* 1908.

DAUGHTERS LIVING OF THIRD BARONET

Pamela Alison, *b* 1927: *m* 1954, John Gordon Raymond Romer, and has issue living, Charles John, *b* 1958, — Gordon Clive, *b* 1960, — Gillian Avril, *b* 1955, — Susan Claire, *b* 1970. *Residence* – 22 Cranston Grove, Gatley, Ches. —— Quenilda Jennifer, *b* 1929: *m* 1954, Peter Graham Dobson, and has had issue, Trevor William, *b* 1957, — John Keith, *b* 1963, *d* 1982, — Susan Jane, *b* 1954, — Valerie, *b* 1956, — Kay Elizabeth, *b* 1960. *Residence* – 7 Clyst Valley Rd, Clyst, St Mary, Exeter.

The 1st baronet, Sir Charles Wright Macara (son of Rev William Macara, Min of Free Church, Strathmiglo, Fife), was Chm of Henry Bannerman & Sons, Ltd.

MACARTNEY (I) 1799, of Lish, Armagh

It stimulates, but it adorns

Sir JOHN BARRINGTON MACARTNEY, 6th *Baronet*, el son of late John Barrington Macartney, 3rd son of 3rd baronet; *b* 1917; *s* his uncle, *Sir* ALEXANDER MILLER, 1960; is a retired Dairy Farmer: *m* 1944, Amy Isobel Reinke, who *d* 1978, and has issue.

Arms – Or, a stag trippant, within a bordure gules. **Crest** – A hand holding a slip of a rose tree with three roses thereon all proper.
Residence – 37 Meadow St, N Mackay, Queensland 4740.

SON LIVING

JOHN RALPH (1 Kookaburra St, Slade Point, Queensland 4740), *b* 1945; Petty Officer RAN (ret); served in Malaya 1964-65 and Vietnam 1968-69; Teacher at Bruce Coll of Technical and F Education 1979-82; Facilities Manager Mackay TAFE, Qld; Communications Offr Oaky North Underground Mine, Qld: *m* 1966, Suzanne Marie Fowler, of Nowra, NSW, and has issue living, Donna Maree, *b* 1968 (has issue living, Peter John *b* 1990, Cody Alexander *b* 1993, Lisa Maree *b* 1986): *m* 1999, James William Lakin, — Karina Lee, *b* 1971: *m* 1997, Stephen Mark Anthony Power, and has issue living, Samuel Isaac *b* 1998, Grace Zara *b* 1997, — Katherine Anne, *b* 1974, — Anita Louise, *b* 1979.

SISTERS LIVING

Evelyn Catherine, *b* 1911: *m* 1931, Albert Edward Ellwood, of 23 Milne Lane, W Mackay, Qld 4740, and has issue living, Alan John (4740 Gargett via Mackay, Qld), *b* 1935: *m* 1963, Hester da of H. Lewis, of Mackay, Qld, and has issue living, Derek John *b* 1968, Charmaine Mary *b* 1964, Dianne Lucy *b* 1966, — Edward Graham (5 Piccadilly St, Geebung 4734, Aust 2611), *b* 1945: *m* 19—, Helen Mary, da of Thomas Chadwick of Dalby, Qld, and has issue living Damian Ralf *b* 1974, — Audrey Philomene, *b* 1932: *m* 1952, Noel Nathaniel Perry, of Matcham, Gracemere, via Rockhampton, Qld 4702, and has issue living, Gregory John *b* 1957, Shane Nathaniel *b* 1971, Christine Anne *b* 1953, Janette Patricia *b* 1955, Judith Marie *b* 1956, Kathleen Ellen *b* 1959, — Marie Claire, *b* 1934: *m* 1956, Franciscao Antonius Brieffres, of 4740 Kuhabul, via Mackay, Qld, and has issue living, Frank John *b* 1957, Peter Eugene *b* 1961, Anthony John *b* 1964, Lynette *b* 1958, Trudy Bernadette *b* 1959, Melita Maree *b* 1963, Yvonne *b* 1966. —— Constance (Mail Service 656, Mackay, Queensland 4740, Australia), *b* 1912: *m* 1939, Stanley Dan Desbois, who *d* 1983, and has issue living, Kevin, *b* 1941: *m* 1966, Janet Elizabeth Gordon, of Mackay, Qld, and has issue living, Sean Kevin *b* 1975, Michelle Maree *b* 1968, Andrea Jane *b* 1969, — Clive John, *b* 1948: *m* 1973, Bernadette Mary Murphy, and has issue living, Timothy John *b* 1976, Graham Stanley *b* 1983, Sharon Ann *b* 1978, Jennifer Mary *b* 1981.

COLLATERAL BRANCHES LIVING

Issue of late Herbert Charles Macartney, 4th son of 3rd baronet, *b* 1876, *d* 1953: *m* 1913, Frances, da of Mountiford Tooker, of Yeppoon, Queensland:—
Patricia Catherine, *b* 1917: *m* 1941, Leslie John Campbell, of Inverness, Calliope, Gladstone, Qld, and has issue living, Alan Leslie John Macartney, *b* 1952, — Diana Ruby, *b* 1942, — Rosemary Frances, *b* 1945, — Ailsa Catherine, *b* 1947. —— Frances Evelyn, *b* 1924: *m* 1953, John Smith. *Residence* – Brisbane, Qld.

Issue of late David Edwin Macartney, 6th son of 3rd baronet, *b* 1880, *d* 1957: *m* 1st, 1912, Flora Gordon, who *d* 1914, da of E. K. Ogg, of Rockhampton, Queensland; 2ndly, 1920, Ella Margaret McCulloch, who *d* 1978, da of Daniel Craig, of Longreach, Qld:—
(By 2nd *m*) †Alexander Macdonald, *b* 1921; formerly Flight-Lt RAAF: *m* 1959, Penelope Ann (11 Chermside Drive, Warwick, Qld 4370, Australia), da of C. B. Freeman, of Brisbane, Qld, and *d* 1996, leaving issue, John Alexander OAM (154 Millpoint Rd, South Perth, WA), *b* 1961; Fl Lieut RAAF; with Ansett, Australia: *m* 1986, Robyn Mary, da of E.M. Norling, of Wellington, NZ, — Deborah Ann, *b* 1962: *m* 1985 (*m diss* 1994), — , and has issue living, Arianna Ella *b* 1990, — David Edwin, *b* 1924; formerly in R Austn Navy: *m* 1948, Elizabeth Lillias, da of L. Ewert, of Rotorua, NZ, and has issue living, David Edwin, *b* 1951, — Anthony Craig, *b* 1956, — Diane Ewert, *b* 1952: *m* 1977, David John McBryde, and has issue, James David *b* 1983, Fiona Diane *b* 1981. —— John Craig (PO Box 1, Mount Nebo, Qld 4520) *b* 1927; formerly in AIF: *m* 1951, Betty Katrine, da of Dr Leckie, of Ingham, Qld, and has issue living, — Belinda Lee, *b* 1952. —— Wallace Herbert (49 Nevin St, Aspley, Brisbane, Qld 4034), *b* 1929: *m* 1973, Judith Anne, da of A. K. Addison, of Brisbane, and has issue living, Robyn Judith, *b* 1976. —— Margaret Miller, *b* 1923: *m* 1949, Capt David Henry Hopton, formerly Ansett Airlines, of PO Box 242, Edge Hill, N Qld 4870, and has issue living, John Macartney, *b* 1950: *m* 1980, Diane Rita Cavanagh, — Peter Coulter, *b* 1955: *m* 1980, Christine Ann Cosgriffe, and has issue living, James Duncan *b* 1988, Stephanie Lee *b* 1984, Angela Margaret *b* 1986, — Jason Craig, *b* 1956: *m* 1983, Julie Ann McLaren, and has issue living, Toby John *b* 1985, Fraser McLaren *b* 1987, Joshua Craig *b* 1989 . —— Catherine Ella, *b* 1926: *m* 1962, Donald Grayling, RN, of 13 Cliff Av, Winston Hills, Sydney, NSW 1253, and has issue living, Donald David, *b* 1968, — Fiona Ella, *b* 1964.

Issue of late Victor Alan Macartney, yst son of 3rd baronet, *b* 1887, *d* 1969: *m* 1915, Elsie Maria, da of late Robert McKie, of Brisbane:—
Harold Kenneth, *b* 1919; Singapore 1941 with AIF (prisoner): *m* 1951, Beatrice, da of Henry Apsley Carlyle Lowe, of Burling, Terrigall, NSW, and has issue living, William John, *b* 1959, — Diana Eileen, *b* 1955. —— Elinor Macartney, *b* 1917; late Sister Austn Army Nursing Ser; Middle East 1940-41: *m* 1942, Maj Francis Stephen Small, AIF, of Royston Park, Ourimbah, NSW, and has issue living, Roderick Cameron Macartney, *b* 1943, — Robert Francis, *b* 1949, — Rosemary Elinor, *b* 1945, — Margaret Anne (twin), *b* 1949.

Issue of late William George Macartney, 2nd son of 2nd baronet, *b* 1835, *d* 188-: *m* 1872, Bessie, da of late Robert Bayley Tyser, of Wellington, New Zealand:—
Ernest George, *b* 1880. —— Eileen Agnes. *Residence* –

Grandsons of late Edward Hussey Burgh Macartney (infra):—
Issue of late James Edward Macartney, *b* 1911, *d* 1977: *m* 1946, Margaret Casson, da of late Herbert Ernest Bennett:—
John Alexander, *b* 1947: *m* 1977, Lynette Kathleen, da of Gordon Vaughan, and has issue living, Edward John *b* 1978. —— William James, *b* 1948: *m* 1970, Sherryl, da of Wallace George Humfry, and has issue living, Benjamin Wallace, *b* 1972, — Christopher John, *b* 1973, — Jack Hussey Burgh, *b* 1981.

Grandchildren of late Edward Hardman Macartney, son of the Very Rev Hussey Burgh Macartney (first Dean of Melbourne), yr son of 1st baronet:—
Issue of late Edward Hussey Burgh Macartney, *b* 1867, *d* 1930: *m* 1st, 1904, Jane Alexandra, who *d* 1909, da of Alexander Richardson McNab; 2ndly, 1910, Constance May, who *d* 1960, da of Edward Griffith:—
(By 2nd *m*) John Hussey Burgh (7 Tutus St, Balgowlah, NSW 2093), *b* 1915; Lt-Cdr RAN (ret): *m* 1945, Geraldine, da of Eli Leach, of Darwen, Lancs, England, and has issue living, Francesca May, *b* 1948; BA, LLB, Sydney: *m* 1972, Christopher William Beale, BA, LLB Sydney, MBA Harvard, and has issue living, Julian Macartney *b* 1986, Andrew Macartney *b* 1988. —— (By 1st *m*) Jean Marion Isobel, *b* 1908: *m* 1954, William Balston, who *d* 1960. —— (By 2nd *m*) Catherine Frances, *b* 1913: *m* 1933, A. N. Magnus. —— Constance Eleanor, *b* 1922, *m* 1950, David Howley.

Issue of late Charles Perry Macartney, *b* 1880, *d* 1947: *m* 1912, Daphne Violet, who *d* 1976, da of Henry King:—
Violet Moore, *b* 1914. *Residence* – 33 Proctors Rd, Dynnyrne, Hobart, Tasmania. —— Nancy Gower (43 Tramway Parade, Beaumaris, Melbourne, Vic 3193) *b* 1920: *m* 1958, Leonard J. Basterfield, who *d* 1988, and has issue living, Josephine Nancy, *b* 1960.

The 1st baronet, Sir John, MP (yr son of William Macartney of Lish, co Armagh, MP for Belfast), prior to his being created a baronet, received knighthood for his services in promoting inland navigation in Ireland.

McCONNELL (UK) 1900, of The Moat, Strandtown, Belfast

(*Sir*) ROBERT SHEAN MCCONNELL, 4th *Baronet*; *b* 23 Nov 1930; *s* his father, *Sir* ROBERT MELVILLE TERENCE, VRD, 1987, but does not use the title; *ed* Stowe, Queens' Coll, Camb (MA), and Univ of British Columbia (MSc); ARICS, FRTPI.

A conquerer amidst difficulties

Arms – Per pale azure and gules, to the dexter a ship in full sail proper, to the sinister an arm embowed and couped at the shoulder argent, the hand grasping a trefoil slipped or, on a chief of the fourth, three stags' heads cabossed sable. Crest – A stag's head erased azure attired and charged on the neck with a bee volant or.

BROTHERS LIVING

JAMES ANGUS (Rory's Glen, 219 Old Holywood Rd, Holywood, co Down), *b* 18 Dec 1933; *ed* Stowe; FSVA; JP; Capt RARO: *m* 1957, Elizabeth Jillian, da of late Derek Edmund Harris, of Sydenham, Belfast, and has issue living, Terence Reade, *b* 16 Nov 1959; Maj Royal Irish Regt (ret): *m* 1987, Lorel Natalie Willetts, and has issue living, James Alexander *b* 1989, Kitty Sarah *b* 1991, — Edmund Fraser, *b* 1961: *m* 1998, Heidi Portig, — Joanne Christina, *b* 1958: *m* 1979, Richard Sholdis, and has issue living, Robert James *b* 1984, Christopher John *b* 1989; Jennifer Elizabeth (twin) *b* 1984, Rachel Rosemary *b* 1987, — Victoria Wylie, *b* 1965, — Emma-Jane Wylie, *b* (twin) 1965: *m* 1995, David Michael Allen, and has issue living, Sophie Emma *b* 1998, — Alison Clare, *b* 1967: *m* 1998, Andrew Lester Ruddy. —— William Donn (Laurelbrae, Saintfield Rd, Lisburn, co Antirm), *b* 1938; *ed* Stowe: *m* 1963, Daphne Elisabeth, only da of late Robert Simms, of Bangor, co Down, and has had issue, Robert Randal, *b* 1966: *m* 1993, Sarah Annaliese Kirk, and has issue living, Jacob (Jake) *b* 1997, Ellie Alicia *b* 1999, — Stewart Neale, *b* 1972, — Penelope Elisabeth, *b* 1964, *d* 1970.

SISTER LIVING

Elisabeth Moyne, *b* 1935: *m* 1958, Robert Henry Cooke Ramsay (Ardreagh, Marino, Holywood, co Down), and has issue living, Richard Patrick James, *b* 1960: *m* 1995, Carey Duffin, and has issue living, Mary-Rose Elizabeth *b* 1997, — Magnus Robert Neale, *b* 1967, — Roslyn Moyne Elisabeth, *b* 1962.

WIDOW LIVING OF THIRD BARONET

ALICE ANN MARY (*Alice, Lady McConnell*), da of late Robert Graham Glendinning, of Lennoxvale, Belfast, and formerly wife of James Hillis, of Newgrove, Ballylesson: *m* 1967, as his 2nd wife, Sir Robert Melville Terence McConnell, 3rd Bt, VRD, who *d* 1987. *Residence* – Pigeon Hill, Island Rd, Killyleagh, co Down.

COLLATERAL BRANCH LIVING

Issue of late (Jackson) Desmond McConnell, yr son of 2nd baronet, *b* 1912, *d* 1986: *m* 1948, Honor Muriel (Little Galleons, 52 Craigdarragh Rd, Helen's Bay, Bangor, co Down BT19 1UB), da of late Robert Henry Cooke Ramsay, of Fairholme, Craigdarragh Rd, Helen's Bay, co Down, and widow of Sqdn Ldr Richard Ashton Shuttleworth, RAF:—
Rory Desmond Ramsay (Ardville, 19 Ballyalgan Rd, Crossgar, co Down BT30 9DR), *b* 1957; *ed* Marlborough: *m* 1982, Karen, da of late James McClean, of Bangor, co Down, and has issue living, Jamie Desmond, *b* 1984, — Hayley Elizabeth, *b* 1987, — Alexandra Jane, *b* 1991. —— Kathryn Fiona, *b* 1948: *m* 1970, Maj Anthony Randel, of Langdon, Langdon Cross, Launceston, Cornwall, and has issue living, Sophia Honor, *b* 1971: *m* 1996, Matthew David Murr.

Issue of late Alfred Edward McConnell, 2nd son of 1st baronet, *b* 1880, *d* 1963: *m* 1919, Emma (Yvonne) Dougal, who *d* 1957:—
Robert William Brian, PC, *b* 1922; *cr Baron McConnell* (Life Baron) 1995 (see that title).

The first baronet, Sir Robert John McConnell (son of Joseph McConnell, of Clougher, co Antrim), was Lord Mayor of Belfast 1900, and the 2nd baronet, Sir Joseph, was MP for co Antrim at Westminster (*U*) May 1929 to Aug 1942.

McCOWAN (UK) 1934, of Dalwhat, co Dumfries

We press forward to heaven

Sir DAVID CARGILL McCOWAN, 4th *Baronet*; *b* 28 Feb 1934; *s* his brother, Sir HEW CARGILL, 1998: *m* 1995, Jean, da of Arthur Roland McGhee, and has issue.

Arms – Argent, a saltire between four anchors sable roped or. **Crest** – An eagle rising proper.
Residence – Auchendennan Farm, Alexandria, Dunbartonshire.

SON LIVING

DAVID JAMES CARGILL, *b* 2 June 1975.

DAUGHTER LIVING

Caroline Elizabeth, *b* 1966.

The 1st Baronet, Sir David McCowan (son of Hew McCowan, of Ayr), was a Senior Partner in the firm of William Euing & Co, marine insurance brokers, of 8 Royal Exchange Buildings, Glasgow, and Hon Pres of Scottish Unionist Assocn.

McCULLAGH (UK) 1955, of Lismara, Parish of Carnmoney, co Antrim (Extinct 1974)

Sir JOSEPH CRAWFORD McCULLAGH, 2nd and last *Baronet*.

WIDOW LIVING OF SECOND BARONET

ELIZABETH (*Lady McCullagh*), da of James Copeland: *m* 1937, Sir Joseph Crawford McCullagh, 2nd Bt, who *d* 1974, when the title became ext.

BOSVILLE MACDONALD (NS) 1625, of Sleat, Isle of Skye

By sea and land. Virtue for its own sake

Sir IAN GODFREY BOSVILLE MACDONALD OF SLEAT, 17th *Baronet* and 25th *Chief of Sleat*; *b* 18 July 1947; *s* his father, Sir (ALEXANDER) SOMERLED ANGUS, MC, 1958; High Sheriff Humberside 1988, DL E Riding Yorks 1998: *m* 1970, Juliet Fleury, only da of late Maj-Gen John Ward-Harrison, of Hazel Bush House, Malton Rd, York, and has issue.

Arms – (as recorded at Lyon Office)—Quarterly, 1st and 4th grand quarters counter-quartered, 1st argent, a lion rampant gules, armed and langued azure, 2nd or, a hand in armour fessewise proper, holding a cross-crosslet fitchée gules, 3rd argent a lymphad, sails furled and oars in action sable, flagged gules, and 4th vert a salmon naiant in fesse proper, *Macdonald*; 2nd and 3rd grand quarters, argent, five lozenges conjoined in fesse gules and in chief three bears' heads erased at the neck sable, muzzled or, a canton, ermine, *Bosville*. **Crest** – 1st, a hand in armour fessewise, holding a cross-crosslet fitchée gules *Macdonald*; 2nd, a bull passant argent, armed or, issuing from a hurst of oaks, charged on the shoulder with a rose proper, *Bosville*. **Supporters** – Two leopards proper, collared or.
Seats – Thorpe Hall, Rudston, Driffield, E Yorks YO25 0JE; Osmigarry Lodge, Isle of Skye.

SON LIVING

SOMERLED ALEXANDER, *b* 30 Jan 1976.

DAUGHTERS LIVING

Deborah Fleury, *b* 1973. —— Isabel Mary, *b* 1983.

BROTHER LIVING

James Alexander (12 Poplar Grove, W6), b 1949; ed Ardingly: m 1995, Mary Lucinda, da of Lt-Col L. C. Connolly, of Nortoft House, Guilsborough, Northants.

SISTERS LIVING

Janet Elizabeth, b 1950: m 1980, John Joseph Trapp, of Swann House, Swaffham Bulbeck, Cambs CB5 0NE, elder son of late R. E. Trapp and Mrs L. Reynolds, and has issue living, Alexander John Nicolai, b 1984. —— Annabel Celia Dorothy, b 1953: m 1987, Clive Duncan Evans, of West Croft Farm, Rudston, Driffield, E Yorks, son of late M. R. Evans, of Swansea, and has issue living, Benedict Ian, b 1989, — Caitlin Mary, b 1993.

UNCLE LIVING (Son of 15th baronet)

Nigel Donald Peter CHAMBERLAYNE-MACDONALD, CVO, OBE, b 1927; Maj (ret) late Scots Guards; a Member of the Queen's Body Guard for Scotland (Royal Company of Archers); Equerry to HRH the Duke of Gloucester 1954-55, and again 1958-60, and Assist Private Sec to HRH the Duke of Gloucester 1958-60; Extra Equerry to HRH the Duke of Gloucester 1964-74; a Gentleman Usher to HM The Queen 1979-97, since when an Extra Gentleman Usher; High Sheriff of Hants 1974, and DL 1975; OStJ; assumed by deed poll 1958 the surname of Chamberlayne before his patronymic; Chm of Hants and I of Wight Assocn of Boys' Clubs 1967-83, a Vice-Pres 1983, and a Vice-Chm of Nat Assocn of Boys' Clubs 1969-90, Pres Coaching Club 1982-90; LVO 1960, OBE (Civil) 1981, CVO 1997: m 1958, Penelope Mary Alexandra, only child of late Tankerville Chamberlayne, of Cranbury Park, Hants, and has had issue, Alexander Nigel Bosville, b 1959· m 1991, Shirley Irene, da of late George Cecil Pridmore, of Swayfield, Lincs, — Thomas Somerled, b 1969, — Diana Mary (Countess of Lindsay) b 1961: m 1982, 16th Earl of Lindsay, — Frances Penelope, b 1965; d 1985. Residences – Cranbury Park, Winchester SO21 2HL; 17 William Mews, Lowndes Sq, SW1; Glaschoille House, Knoydart, Mallaig, Inverness-shire.

AUNTS LIVING (Daughters of 15th baronet)

Jean Alice, b 1919: m 1952, Lieut-Col Basil John Ringrose, DSO, TD, who d 1995, of Royal Oak, Morby, nr Boston, Lincs. ——Angela Daphne Rachel, b 1923: m 1957, James Michael Gardner Fell, and has issue living, Peter James, b 1960, — Rachel Mary, b 1959. Address – University of Pennsylvania, Philadelphia, USA.

WIDOW LIVING OF SIXTEENTH BARONET

MARY ELIZABETH (Mary, Lady Bosville Macdonald of Sleat), da of late Lt-Col Ralph Crawley-Boevey Gibbs: m 1946, Sir (Alexander) Somerled Angus Bosville Macdonald of Sleat, 16th baronet, MC, who d 1958. Residence – West Croft Farm, Rudston, Driffield, E Yorkshire.

COLLATERAL BRANCHES LIVING

Descendants of Godfrey William Wentworth Macdonald, 4th Baron Macdonald, 3rd (but el born after the English m of his parents) son of late Godfrey Macdonald, 3rd Baron Macdonald and 11th baronet (see B Macdonald).

Descendants of late Donald Macdonald 1st of Castleton, 2nd son of 1st baronet:—

Grandchildren of late Rev James Alexander Donald John Macdonald, 10th of Castleton, son of James Alexander Macdonald, 9th of Castleton, eldest son of James Macdonald, 8th of Castleton, 6th in descent from Donald Macdonald (ante):—
Issue of late Donald John Macdonald, 12th of Castleton, b 1897, d 1984: m 1932, Cecilie Frances Jess, who d 1987, da of Ernest George Evan-Williams, of Johannesburg, S Africa, and adopted da of Maj James Alexander Macdonald, DSO, MC:—
Ranald Alasdair, 13th of Castleton (12 Wren St, WC1), b 1937; late Cameron Highlanders: m 1st, 1964, Eleanor Russell; 2ndly, 1988, Lee Honeyman, and has issue living (by 1st m), Shona, b 1965, — (by 2nd m) Callum, b 1995, — Catriona Michelle, b 1990. —— Cecilie Ruth Faith, b 1933: m 1974, Andrew Barclay, of 109 Hyndland Rd, Glasgow, and has issue living, Carol Hope, b 1975. —— Catherine Stella, b 1941: m 1962, Graham Robertson Harvey, of Ferndale, Forres, Morayshire IV36 0PH, and has issue living, David Ranald Macdonald, b 1965: m 1995, Lucy Marie Pease, — Dawn Caroline, b 1968: m 1991, William Andrew Hawking, of Oldfield Farm, Wilts, and has issue living, Angus William Macdonald b 1995, Flora Louise b 1994, — Louise Robertson, b 1969: m 1994, Gavin John Logan Willins, of Edinburgh. —— Frances Ruth (Achnandarrach, Plockton, Ross-shire), h 1944: m 1968, Austin Bankhead, who d 1990, and has issue living, Jamie Macdonald, b 1969, — Patrick Augustine, b 1971, — Robin Francis, b 1978.

Grandson of late Edward William Johnstone Macdonald, yr son of late James Alexander Macdonald, 9th of Castleton (ante):—
Issue of late Roderick Norman Douglas Macdonald, b 1886, d 1971: m 1912, Eleanor Davison, of Toronto, who d 1969:—
Alexander Douglas, b 1923: m 1941, Gertrude Noreen Davis, of Toronto, and has issue living, Geoffrey Alex, b 1952, — Pamela, b 1948.

Grandsons of late Inspector-Gen Sir John Denis Macdonald, KCB, MD, FRS, 3rd son of late James Macdonald, 8th of Castleton (ante):—
Issue of late Capt John Denis Macdonald, Roy Canadian Veterinary Corps, b 1873, d 1940: m 1908, Minnie Gunter:—
Geoffrey John Gunter, b 1910: m 1930, Muriel Eleanor Tingle, and has issue living, Michael Douglas, b 1940, — Heather Margaret, b 1942, — Janet Elizabeth, b 1947. ——James Edward Somerled, b 1912. —— Ewen Reginald, b 1915; European War 1939-45 with Gordon Highlanders: m 19—, Elsie Glanville, and has issue living, Angus John, b 1943, — Alison Celia, b 1947.

Issue of late William Richard Macdonald, b 1876, d 1950: m 1st, Olive—; 2ndly, 19—, Erina Archer:—
(By 2nd m) Richard John, b 1940.

This Baronetcy was created with remainder to heirs male whatsoever and a special clause of precedency provided that it should have precedency of all former baronets (Sir Robert Gordon only excepted) "tho' their patents were of a prior date", whereby, if that clause is in force, it is now second in the order of Nova Scotia baronets. In 1776, Sir Alexander Macdonald, 9th Bt, was created *Baron Macdonald*, of Slate, co Antrim (peerage of Ireland). Godfrey Macdonald (afterwards 3rd Baron and 11th Baronet) assumed by Roy licence 1814, on inheriting the estates of Bosville of Thorpe and Gunthwaite, the surname of Bosville in lieu of his patronymic. On succession to the titles in 1824 he resumed the surname of Macdonald after that of Bosville. He died in 1832, having m (in an English Church) 15 Dec, 1803, Louisa Maria La Coast, da of HRH Prince William Frederick, Duke of Gloucester by Lady Almeria Carpenter, and ward of Farley Edsir. The validity of a Scottish m said to have taken place with the same lady in 1799 having been disputed, he was s in the Irish peerage by his son Godfrey William Wentworth, born after the date of the English m, but according to a decree of the Court of Session in June 1910, the father being domiciled in Scotland, that m legitimated according to the law of Scotland, Alexander William Robert Macdonald, b 12 Sept 1800, prior to the date of the English m, who had s to the Thorpe and Gunthwaite estates, and to whom therefore the Nova Scotia baronetcy of 1625 passed de jure. On entering into possession of the Bosville estates in 1832 he assumed by Roy licence the surname of Bosville in lieu of Macdonald. His grandson, Alexander Wentworth Macdonald Bosville, thus became 14th Baronet in 1910, and resumed the family surname of Macdonald after that of Bosville (recognised by Court of Lord Lyon 1910). The present baronet is heir-male and representative of Sir Donald Macdonald, 1st Bt (descended from Hugh Macdonald, first of Sleat, a son of Alexander, Lord of the Isles, Earl of Ross, by a da of Gillepatrick Roy), and representative of the family of Macdonald of Sleat, in the Island of Skye.

McEWEN (UK) 1953, of Marchmont, co Berwick, and Bardrochat, co Ayr

Dieu Premier Servi

Sir JOHN RODERICK HUGH McEWEN, 5th *Baronet*; b 4 Nov 1965; s his brother, Sir JAMES FRANCIS LINDLEY, 1983; ed Ampleforth, Univ Coll, London, and Glasgow Univ.

Arms – Quarterly: 1st and 4th, or, a lion rampant azure, gorged with a ducal crown proper, on a chief of the second three garbs of the field, *McEwen*; 2nd and 3rd, gules, three headless cranes argent, *Finnie*. **Crest** – The trunk of an oak tree sprouting proper.
Residence – Polwarth Crofts, Greenlaw, Duns, Berwickshire TD10 6YR.

SISTERS LIVING AND DECEASED

Mary Christian, b 1956. —— Catherine Veronica, b 1958; d 1983. —— Helena Mary Elizabeth, b 1961. —— Isabella Gabriel Anne, b 1968.

DAUGHTERS LIVING OF SECOND BARONET

Margaret, b 1959: m 1980, Edward John Ivo Stourton (see B Mowbray, colls). —— Mary Gabriel, b 1963: m 1989, (Vincent) Patrick Byrne (see B Lawrence). —— Christina, b 1964: m 1992, Anthony D. L. Norton, son of David Norton, of Buckland St Mary, Somerset, and has issue living, Hector Benedict, b 1995, — Madeleine Hope, b 1997.

UNCLES LIVING (Sons of 1st baronet)

Alexander Dundas, b 1935; ed Eton; late Queen's Own Cameron Highlanders: m 1960, (Princess) Cecilia, da of HSH late Franz, 2nd Prince Weikersheim, and has issue living, Alexander Francis, b 1962: m 1988, Natasha Durac, elder da of Peter H. D. Marr, and has issue living, Thomas Peter Dundas b 1989, Archie James b 1992, Maximilian Francis b 1996, — Hugo Gabriel, b 1965: m 1996, Monica, yst da of Lennart Blom, of Stockholm, — Sophia Christina, b 1961. *Residence* – Bardrochat, Colmonell, Ayrshire. —— John Sebastian, b 1942; ed Eton, and Trin Coll, Camb: m 1975, Gillian, da of D. M. Heeley, and has issue living, David, b 1977, — Duncan Dundas, b 1979. *Residence* – 74 St Augustine's Rd, NW1 9RP.

AUNT LIVING *(Daughter of 1st baronet)*

Christian Mary, OBE *(Dowager Baroness Hesketh)*, *b* 1929; High Sheriff of Northants 1981; a DL of Northants; Hon LLD (Univ of Leicester) 1982, Hon PhD (London) 1999; OBE (Civil) 1983: *m* 1949, 2nd Baron Hesketh, who *d* 1955. *Residences* – Pomfret Lodge, Hulcote, Towcester, Northants; 20a Tregunter Rd, SW10.

WIDOW LIVING OF SECOND BARONET

CLARE ROSEMARY, only child of Col John William Eric Graves Sandars, OBE, TD, of Gate Burton Hall, Gainsborough, Lincs *(see* B Graves, 1959 Edn): *m* 1st, 1958, Sir James Napier Finnie McEwen, 2nd Bt, who *d* 1971; 2ndly, 1973, Kenneth Wagg.

WIDOW LIVING OF THIRD BARONET

BRIGID CECILIA *(Lady McEwen)*, only da of late James Laver, CBE: *m* 1954, Sir Robert Lindley McEwen, 3rd Bt, who *d* 1980. *Residence* – Polwarth Crofts, Duns, Berwickshire TD10 6YR.

COLLATERAL BRANCH LIVING

Issue of late Roderick (Rory) McEwen, 3rd son of 1st Baronet, *b* 1932, *d* 1982: *m* 1958, Romana, da of late Raimund von Hofmannsthal:—
ADAM HUGO, *b* 9 Feb 1965. —— Flora Mary Alice, *b* 1959: *m* 1988, Anthony David Willard Mason, son of late John Harradine Mason, of Haddenham, Bucks, and has issue living, Nathaniel Home, *b* 1994, — Brooke Emmeline Harradine, *b* 1997. —— Samantha Mary, *b* 1960. —— Christabel Mary, *b* 1962: *m* 1983 *(m diss* 1995), Hon Edward Richard Lambton (styled Lord Durham since 1970), only son of Antony Claud Frederick Lambton (6th Earl of Durham until he disclaimed his title 1970), and has issue *(see* E Durham), — and further issue (by Julian Miles Holland), Mabel Ray Britannia, *b* 1990.

Sir John (Helias Finnie) McEwen, 1st Bt, was MP for Berwick and Haddington (C) 1931-45, Parliamentary Under-Sec of State for Scotland 1939-40, and a Lord Commr of the Treasury 1942-44: *m* 1923, Bridget Mary, who *d* 1971, eldest da of Rt Hon Sir Francis Oswald Lindley *(see* B Lovat, 1949 Edn); *d* 1962; *s* by his eldest son, Sir James Napier Finnie McEwen, 2nd Bt; served 1939-45 War (wounded): *m* 1958, Clare Rosemary, only child of Col John William Eric Graves Sandars, OBE, TD *(see* B Graves, 1959 Edn), *d* 1971; *s* by his brother, Sir Robert Lindley McEwen, 3rd Bt; barrister-at-law: *m* 1954, Brigid Cecilia, only da of late James Laver, CBE; *d* 1980; *s* by his elder son, Sir James Francis Lindley McEwen, 4th Bt; *dunm* 1983; *s* by his brother, Sir John Roderick Hugh McEwen, 5th Bt.

McFARLAND (UK) 1914, of Aberfoyle, co Londonderry

This I'll defend

Sir JOHN TALBOT McFARLAND, 3rd *Baronet*, TD; *b* 3 Oct 1927; *s* his father, Sir BASIL ALEXANDER TALBOT, CBE, ERD, 1986; *ed* Marlborough, and Trin Coll, Oxford; Capt RA ret; a DL of City of co of Londonderry 1956-82; Councillor, Londonderry Corp 1955-69; High Sheriff of co Londonderry 1958, and of City of co of Londonderry 1965 and 1966; mem Londonderry Port Harbour Commrs 1965-73, NW Hosp Management Cttee 1960-73; Chm Lanes Gp of Cos, Dir Londonderry Gaslight Co Ltd 1960, and Donegal Holdings Ltd 1966; Chm Londonderry & Lough Swilly Rlwy Co 1978-81, McFarland Farms Ltd, and J.T. McFarland Holdings 1984: *m* 1957, Mary Scott, el da of late Dr William Scott Watson, of Dunmore House, Carrigans, co Donegal, and has issue.

Arms – Argent, a saltire engrailed gules, between two roses in pale and a thistle and shamrock in fesse all proper. Crest – A demi savage holding in the dexter hand an antique crown all proper.
Residence – Dunmore House, Carrigans, Co Donegal. *Clubs* – Kildare and University (Dublin), Northern Counties (Londonderry).

SONS LIVING

ANTHONY BASIL SCOTT, *b* 29 Nov 1959; *ed* Marlborough, and Trin Coll, Dublin (BA); ACA: *m* 1988, Anne Margaret, 3rd da of Thomas Kennedy Laidlaw, of Gernonstown, Slane, co Meath, and has issue living, Max Anthony, *b* 1993, — Rory John, *b* 199—, — Amelia Elizabeth, *b* 1990. —— Stephen Andrew John, *b* 1968; *ed* Glenalmond, and RAC Cirencester.

DAUGHTERS LIVING

Shauna Jane, *b* 1957: *m* 1982, Andrew Louis Hamilton Gailey, MA, PhD, and has issue living, Emily Mary Lara, *b* 1988. *Residence* – The Manor House, Eton, Berks. —— Fiona Kathleen, *b* 1963: *m* 1993, William Edward Orme, and has issue living, Shane (a son), *b* 1994. *Residence* – The Orchard, Fen Ditton, Cambs.

The 1st baronet, Sir John, was a partner in the firm of McCrea and McFarland, engineering contractors, of Belfast and Londonderry, Chm of Mulhollands (Limited), drapers and of Brewsters (Limited), bakers, of Londonderry, Proprietor of Lough Swilly Steamship Co, and Chm of Lough Swilly Railway Co. The 2nd baronet, Sir Basil Alexander Talbot, CBE, ERD, was a Senator of N Ireland and HM Lt for the City of Londonderry.

MACGREGOR (UK) 1828, of Savile Row, Middlesex

Sir EDWIN ROBERT MACGREGOR, 7th *Baronet*; *b* 4 Dec 1931; *s* his father, *Sir* ROBERT JAMES McCONNELL, MM, 1963; *ed* Univ of British Columbia (BA Sc 1955, MA Sc 1957): *m* 1st, 1952 (*m diss* 1981), Margaret Alice Jean, da of Arthur Peake, of Haney, British Columbia; 2ndly, 1982, Helen Linda Herriott, and has issue by 1st *m*.

Arms – Argent, from a mount base an oak-tree surmounted by a sword in bend proper, and in chief two eastern crowns gules, all within a bordure engrailed of the last. Crest – A human hand couped at the wrist and holding a dagger erect proper, pommel and hilt gold.
Address – Scarlet Oak, 6136 Kirby Rd, Sooke, BC VOS INO, Canada.

SON LIVING (*By 1st marriage*)

Ian Grant, *b* 22 Feb 1959. *Residence* – 3886 Kings Rd, East Bay, Nova Scotia, Canada B0A 1H0.

DAUGHTERS LIVING (*By 1st marriage*)

Valerie Jean, *b* 1956. —— Jessie Elizabeth Marlene, *b* 1963.

BROTHER LIVING

Arthur Joseph, *b* 1933; *ed* Univ of British Columbia (MD 1958): *m* 1st, 1957, Carole Isabel, who *d* 1984, da of W. L. Valens, MD, of Victoria, British Columbia; 2ndly, 1985, Brenda Margaret Hanson, and has issue living (by 1st *m*), Ann Lorraine, *b* 1960, — Jean Louise, *b* 1962. *Residence* – 2597 Vista Bay Rd, Victoria, British Columbia.

SISTERS LIVING

Margaret Gertrude, *b* 1937: *m* 1963, Cyril George White, of 6172 Pepperell St, Halifax, Nova Scotia. —— Patricia Elizabeth (981 Gloria Place, Victoria, BC, Canada), *b* 1939: *m* 1966 (*m diss* 1983), John Peramaki. —— Nancy Lane, *b* 1942: *m* 1972, Hubert Foulds, who *d* 1991. *Residence* – 3871 High St, Victoria, British Columbia.

COLLATERAL BRANCH LIVING

Issue of late Brig-Gen Charles Reginald Macgregor, CB, DSO, 2nd son of 3rd baronet, *b* 1847, *d* 1902: *m* 1893, Maud (who *m* 2ndly, 1903, Addison Yalden Thomson), da of A. dés Moustiers Campbell, formerly of Oakley House, Abingdon, Berks:—
Helen Maud, *b* 1894. *Address* – c/o Westminster Bank, Terminus Road, Eastbourne, Sussex.

Sir Patrick Macgregor, 1st Bt, son of James Macgregor of Bellimore, Inverness-shire, was Serjeant-Surgeon to King George IV.

MAC GREGOR OF MAC GREGOR (GB) 1795, of Lanrick, co Perth

Srioghal mo dhream
Royal is my race

E'en do and spair nocht

Sir GREGOR MAC GREGOR OF MAC GREGOR, 6th *Baronet*; *b* 22 Dec 1925; *s* his father, *Capt Sir* MALCOLM, CB, CMG, RN, 1958; *ed* Eton; Brig late Scots Guards; ret 1980; a Member of Queen's Body Guard for Scotland (Roy Co of Archers), and 23rd Chief of Clan Gregor; Grand Master Mason of Scotland 1988: *m* 1958, Fanny, only da of Charles Hubert Archibald Butler, of Le Pavillon, Newport, Essex, and has issue.

ᴀrms – Argent, an oak-tree eradicated and fructed in bend sinister proper, surmounted of a sword in bend azure, carrying on its point in the dexter canton an antique crown gules. ᴄrest – A lion's head proper crowned with an antique crown or. ᴚupporters – Dexter, a unicorn argent, crowned and horned or; sinister, a stag proper, tyned azure.
Residence – Bannatyne, Newtyle, Angus PH12 8TR. *Clubs* – Pratt's, and New (Edinburgh).

SONS LIVING

MALCOLM GREGOR CHARLES (43 Kinnoul Rd, W6 8NG) *b* 23 March 1959, *ed* Eton, and Cranfield Univ (MBA); Maj Scots Guards (ret), a Member of Queen's Body Guard for Scotland (Royal Company of Archers); FRGS: *m* 1988, Cecilia Margaret Lucy, elder da of Sir Ilay Mark Campbell, 7th Bt (*cr* 1808). —— Ninian Hubert Alexander *b* 1961: *m* 1999, Fiona M. N., da of David Graham, of Chute, Wilts.

COLLATERAL BRANCHES LIVING

Grandchildren of late Alexander Ronald Mac Gregor of Cardney, yr son of 4th baronet:—
Issue of late Lt-Cdr Malcolm Findanus Mac Gregor of Cardney, *b* 1908, *d* 1990: *m* 1st, 1930 (*m diss* 1940), Rachel Katharine, who *d* 1996, da of Hon Eustace Scott Hamilton-Russell, OBE (*see* V Boyne); 2ndly, 1941, Mariquita Gwen Alison (Cardney, Dunkeld, Perthshire PH8 0EY), da of A.J. Webbe:—
(By 2nd *m*) Alpin Findanus (79 Stockwell Park Rd, SW9 0DB), *b* 1941: *m* 1965, Maria Christina Elisabeth, da of Dage Collin Brunow, OBE, of Kotka, Finland, and has issue living, Euan Alexander, *b* 1972, — Callum Randal, *b* 1977, — Alasdair Duncan, *b* 1979.

Issue of late Maj Donnchadh Tearlach Mac Gregor, ERD, R Scots Greys, *b* 1914, *d* 1974: *m* 1st, 1944 (*m diss* 1949), Nighean, da of Col Alastair Norman Fraser, DSO, MB; 2ndly, 1954, Roxana Mary Jocelyn, who *d* 1989, da of Jocelyn Walker, of Oaklands, Isfield, Sussex:—
(By 1st *m*) Randal Alasdair (Came, Dorchester, Dorset DT2 8NU), *b* 1945, Capt R Scots Dragoon Gds: *m* 1st, 1973 (*m diss* 1977), Lynn Vanessa, da of Maj Tommy Vale, MBE, of Farthings, Kingston Broadway, Shoreham by Sea, Sussex; 2ndly, 1978, Sarah, da of Maj Nigel Martin, of Came House, Dorchester, and has issue living (by 2nd *m*) Morag Nicotina, *b* 1978, — Malvina Iona, *b* 1982. —— (By 2nd *m*) Isabel Maryel, *b* 1956. —— Catriona Gabrielle, *b* 1968.

The royal descent of this ancient clan can be traced to remote antiquity, Gregor Garubh, or "The Stout", having fought under King Duncan I. In the early part of the 17th century there were feuds between numerous clans, the Mac Gregors being persecuted with such fury that any person might mutilate or slay them with impunity. In this situation they continued till they were courted to join the Solemn League and Covenant, upon promises of future friendship; but they declared, "That as they *bore the crown on the point of their swords*, they would not fail to use the latter in support of the former". They are the only instance of a race being forbidden to bear their family name, which was first proscribed by James VI, owing to treachery and misrepresentation. They were restored by Charles II, 1661, to their estates, and permitted to bear their own name. In the reign of William and Mary the law of proscription was again revived, and continued in force until its repeal in 1774. The name was not, however, restored until a Royal Licence to resume it was obtained by Sir John Murray (properly Mac Gregor) 1822. Sir Malcolm, CB, CMG, 5th Bt was Capt RN and served in European War 1914-18.

McGRIGOR (UK) 1831, of Campden Hill, Middlesex

Royal is my tribe

S'rioghal mo dhream

Sir CHARLES EDWARD McGRIGOR, 5th *Baronet*; *b* 5 Oct 1922; *s* his father, *Lieut-Col Sir* CHARLES COLQUHOUN, OBE, 1946; *ed* Eton; formerly Capt Rifle Bde; Exon of Queen's Body Guard, Yeoman of the Guard 1970-85, and Member of Queen's Body Guard for Scotland (Roy Co of Archers); DL Argyll and Bute 1980; 1939-45 War in N Africa and Italy (despatches): *m* 1948, Mary Bettine, da of Sir Archibald Charles Edmonstone, 6th Bt, and has issue.

𝕬rms – Argent, a fir-tree growing out of a mount in base vert surmounted by a sword point upwards in bend proper, pommel and hilt gold, in the dexter chief an eastern crown gules, on a chief azure a tower or, between the badge of the Order of the Tower and Sword on the dexter, and that of the Crescent on the sinister. 𝕮rest – A lion's head erased gules, crowned with an eastern coronet or.
Residences – Upper Sonachan, by Dalmally, Argyll PA33 1BJ.

SONS LIVING

JAMES ANGUS RHODERICK NEIL (Ardchonnel House, by Dalmally, Argyll PA33 1BW), *b* 19 Oct 1949; *ed* Eton: *m* 1st, 1987 (*m diss* 1994), Caroline F., da of late Jacques Roboh, of Paris; 2ndly, 1997, Emma Mary Louise, da of David Lyon Fellowes, of Inistrynich, by Dalmally, Argyll, and has issue living (by 1st *m*), Sibylla, *b* 1988, — Sarah, *b* 1989, — (by 2nd *m*), Alexander James Edward Lyon, *b* 5 Aug 1998. —— Charles Edward, *b* 1959: *m* 1996, Melissa Susan, eldest da of Thomas R. Merryweather, of 465 Bastogne Drive, Akron, Ohio.

DAUGHTERS LIVING

Lorna Gwendolyn, *b* 1951. —— Kirsty Rowena Amabel, *b* 1953; resumed her maiden name 1991 until remarriage: *m* 1st, 1979, David Norman G. Barraclough, eldest son of Geoffrey Barraclough, of Madrid; 2ndly, 1993, as his 2nd wife, Roderick John Maclaren (*see* Cs Loudoun) and has issue living (by 1st *m*), Hector, *b* 1979, — Amabel, *b* 1983, — (by 2nd *m*) (*see* Cs Loudoun).

The 1st baronet, Sir James, KCB, FRS, was for thirty-six years Director-General of the Army Medical Department, and three times Lord Rector of Marischal College, Aberdeen. A statue of him erected outside the Barracks at Chelsea was subsequently removed and re-erected at the RAMC buildings at Millbank, while there is a bust of him in Wellington College, and a stall dedicated to his memory in the Garrison Church at Portsmouth. The 3rd baronet, Sir James Roderick Duff, Capt late Rifle Brig, was many years senior partner in the late firm of Sir Charles R. McGrigor, Bart, and Co, army agents and bankers. The 4th baronet, Sir Charles Colquhoun, OBE, was Lieut-Col Rifle Brig.

MACKENZIE (NS) 1673, of Coul, Ross-shire

Purified by adversity

Sir PETER DOUGLAS MACKENZIE, 13th *Baronet*, only son of late Henry Douglas Mackenzie, elder son of Keith Douglas Mackenzie, yr son of Col Henry Douglas Mackenzie, eldest son of Rev Charles Mackenzie, 3rd son of John Mackenzie of Torridon (*d* 1820), 4th in descent from Simon Mackenzie, 2nd son of 1st baronet; *b* 23 April 1949; *s* his kinsman, *Sir* ROBERT EVELYN, 1990; *ed* —: *m* 1982, Jennifer, da of Ridley Boyce, and has issue.

𝕬rms – Quarterly: 1st and 4th azure, a deer's head cabossed or, *Mackenzie*; 2nd and 3rd gules, a boar's head couped argent, *Chisholm*. 𝕮rest – A boar's head erect or between the attires of a stag fixed to a scalp sable. 𝕾upporters – *Dexter*, an armed Highlander in full custume proper; *sinister*, a roebuck proper.
Residence –

DAUGHTERS LIVING

Alison Douglas, *b* 1985. —— Sarah Douglas, *b* 1988.

SISTER LIVING

Ann Douglas, *b* 1943: *m* 1975, Michael Wallace Mayne, and has issue living, Douglas Wallace, *b* 1976, — Rory Douglas, *b* 1979. *Address* – PO Box 10036, Rivonia 2128, S Africa.

AUNT LIVING (*daughter of late Keith Douglas Mackenzie, ante*)

Joan Douglas (Nashleigh Cottage, Chesham, Bucks), *b* 1909: *m* 1943, Maj Kenneth David Harris, King's Dragoon Gds, who *d* 1967, and has issue living, Peter David (Ring Cottage, Wissenden Green, Bethersden, Kent), *b* 1949: *ed* —: *m* 1981, Anne Elizabeth, da of — Anwyl-Davies, — Gillian Diana, *b* 1947: *m* 1981, Raymond Wright, of 13 Bardwell Rd, Oxford, and has issue living, David William Benedict *b* 1988, Eleanor Faith Rosina *b* 1986.

COLLATERAL BRANCHES LIVING

Granddaughters of late Keith Douglas Mackenzie, yr son of Col Henry Douglas Mackenzie (ante):—
　　Issue of late Keith Douglas Mackenzie, *b* 1912, *b* 1984: *m* 1937, Thelma, da of — Reeders:—
Judy Douglas, *b* 1940: *m* 1962 Lt Graham Douglas Ferguson, SAAF, of 294 Albert St, 0181 Waterkloof, Pretoria, Transvaal, S Africa, and has issue living, Ian Douglas, *b* 1964, — Kim Douglas, *b* 1962: *m* 1984, David James Sharp, — Lynn Douglas, *b* 1968, — Lee-Ann Douglas, *b* 1971. —— Jenifer Mary Douglas, *b* 1994: *m* 1965, Jeremy David Garrett, of 7 Dromedaris Rd, Somerset West 7130, Cape Province, S Africa, and has issue living, Craig Douglas, *b* 1968: *m* 1998, Karen van den Velden, of Rotterdam, Netherlands, — Geoffrey Keith, *b* 1972, — Nikki Jane, *b* 1970.

Granddaughters of late Henry Augustin Ornano Mackenzie, 8th son (only son by 2nd *m*) of 7th baronet:—
　　Issue of late George Henry Louis Mackenzie, *b* 1872, *d* 1960: *m* 1907, Lilian Mary, who *d* 1958, el da of Richard Rodney Pope, formerly ICS:—
Mary Zeta Bingham, *b* 1909: *m* 1931, Philip Henry Burch, who *d* 1932, Lieut Indian Army, and has issue living, Deirdre Raine Mary, *b* 1932, — Phillida Mary, *b* (*posthumous*) 1933: *m* 1965, Aloysius John Zadnik (Box 33, Taber, Alberta, Canada), and has issue living, Philip John *b* 1967, Michael Peter *b* 1968, Elizabeth Anne *b* 1970. *Address* – c/o National & Grindlays Bank, 13 St James's Sq, SW1. —— Eira Margaret Antonia, *b* 1913: *m* 1938, Owen James Esmonde, who *d* 1993, of Cloneen, Glendalough, co Wicklow (*see* Esmonde, Bt).

Grandchildren (by 1st *m*) of late Capt Roderick Henry Turing Mackenzie (infra):—
　　Issue of late Maj Keith Roderick Turing Mackenzie, OBE, MC, *b* 1921, *d* 1990: *m* 1949, Barbara Kershaw (Garden Cottage, Thistle Lane, South St, St Andrews, Fife), da of late W. H. Miles, of Deal, Kent:—
MILES RODERICK TURING, *b* 18 April 1952; *ed* Essex Univ (MA): *m* 1983, Hiroko Sato, of Tokyo, Japan. —— Angus Keith Turing, *b* 1965: *m* 1995, Funda Perciner, of Istanbul. —— Sarah Jane Kershaw, *b* 1950: *m* 1975, Alan Forrest Franchi, of 9 Osborne Pl, Aberdeen. —— Susannah Mary, *b* 1957: *m* 1979, Seumas McKinnon Lorimer, of Spott Mill, Spott, E Lothian.

Grandsons of late Henry Turing Mackenzie, son of late Rt Rev Henry Mackenzie, DD (infra):—
　　Issue of late Capt Roderick Henry Turing Mackenzie, *b* 1891, *d* 1963: *m* 1st, 1920 (*m diss* 1932), Helen Margaret, da of late J. P. Dalzell; 2ndly, 1934, Helen Monica Bradley (14 Gybbons Rd, Rolvenden), da of late Lt-Col William Bradley Roberts, DSO:—
(By 2nd *m*) Bruce Sydenham, *b* 1935; Maj late Queen's Lancashire Regt: *m* 1963, Sheila Hope Evan, da of late Rev Aubrey Lionel Evan Hopkins, late V of Holy Trin, Folkestone, and has issue living, Kevin Roderick, *b* 1964; *ed* Lancaster Univ (BA), and Hong Kong Univ (MA): *m* 1992, Alexandra Jane Morton, and has issue living, Joseph Michael *b* 1994, Esme Elizabeth *b* 1996, — Neil Kenneth, *b* 1966; *ed* Nene Coll, Northampton (BA), and Lancaster Univ (MA): *m* 1996, Teresa Mary Brayshaw, — Tessa Claire, *b* 1970; *ed* Leeds Univ (BA), — Kirsty Celia, *b* 1971; *ed* Leeds Univ (BA). —— Michael Sydenham *b* 1940; *ed* Trin Coll, Dublin (BA).

Grandson of late Stanley John Mackenzie (by 1st *m*) (infra):—
　　Issue of late Stanley Charles William WYNN-MACKENZIE, *b* 1870, *d* 19—: *m* 1900, G Whitehouse:—
Douglas Stanley, *b* 1903.

Issue, if any, of late Kenneth Maurice WYNN-MACKENZIE, *b* 1880, *d* 19—: *m* 1917.

Grandchildren (by 2nd *m*) of late Stanley John Mackenzie, son of Rt Rev Henry Mackenzie, DD (Bishop Suffragan of Nottingham), yst son of late John Mackenzie of Torridon (*d* 1820) (ante):—
　　Issue of late Noel Donald George Mackenzie, *b* 1899, *d* 1981: *m* 1931, Elsie Kate (Sunnydene, 27 Greensleeves Av, Broadstone, Dorset, BH18 8BJ), da of William Henry Mitchell:—
Donald William John (41 Lertpanya Building, Room 905, Soi Lertpanya, Sri Ayuthaya Rd, Khet Rajathewee, Bangkok 10400, Thailand), *b* 1935: *m* 1969, Cheryl Patricia Elizabeth, da of Cyril Leslie Charles Allen, of Cheriton, Llyswen, Breconshire, and has issue living, Nicholas Richard John, *b* 1974, — Christopher Stuart, *b* 1977. —— Marian Audrey, *b* 1944: *m* 1966 (*m diss* 1975), Kaddour Amari, and has issue living, Nadia, *b* 1966, — Samira, *b* 1970.

Grandchildren of late Capt Kenneth Mackenzie, only son of late John Ord Mackenzie, WS son of late Richard Mackenzie, son of late John Mackenzie of Dolphinton, son of late Kenneth Mackenzie, 2nd son of late John Mackenzie of Delvine, 3rd son of 1st baronet:—
　　Issue of late John Moncreiff Ord Mackenzie, WS, *b* 1911, *d* 1986: *m* 1936, Delia Alice, da of Lt-Col Wyndham Damer Clark, JP, DL (E Mayo, colls):—
Richard Wyndham John (Dunclotha, Ayton, Eyemouth, Berwicks), *b* 1939: *m* 1969, Diane Gracie Petters, and has issue living, Douglas John, *b* 1972, — Delia Joan, *b* 1970. —— Elizabeth Anne, *b* 1937. —— Diana Ord, *b* 1944. —— Cynthia Rose, *b* 1946: *m* 1969, Capt Colin Grant Ogilvie Hogg, KOSB, of Mounthooly, Jedburgh TD8 6TJ, and has had issue, Vanessa Charlotte Ogilvie, *b* 1972, — Nicola Joanna Ogilvie, *b* and *d* 1974, — Sarah Jane Ogilvie, *b* 1976. —— Angela Viviane, *b* 1949.

Issue of late Kenneth Ord Mackenzie, *b* 1912, *d* 1994: *m* 1955, Penelope June (Springfield Cottage, Sherborne St John, Basingstoke), da of Neville Brace Colt (Rawlinson, Bt, colls):—
Virginia Anne, *b* 1958: *m* 1988, Hans H. von Celsing, of Pyt House, Ashampstead, Reading, Berks RG8 8RA, yr son of Capt Folke von Celsing, of Stockholm, Sweden, and has issue living, Henrik Alexander Folke, *b* 1990, — Christian Frederick, *b* 1992, — Isabel Alexandra, *b* 1995. ——— Caroline Jane, *b* 1960: *m* 1987, Hector W. H. Sants, of Court Farm, Worminghall, Bucks HP18 4LD, son of John Sants, of Oxford, and has issue living, Hector Alexander, *b* 1989, — Edward Kenneth Richard, *b* 1990, — Arthur Frederick Joseph, *b* 1994.

Issue of late Col Alastair Douglas Mackenzie, CBE, *b* 1917, *d* 1989: *m* 1945, Diane, da of late Col Arthur John Henry Sloggett, CBE, DSO:—
Mark Tresloggett, *b* 1950.

Alexander Mackenzie of Coul, father of Sir Kenneth Mackenzie, 1st baronet, was a natural son of Colin Cam (one-eyed) Mackenzie, 11th of Kintail (*d* 1594) and half-brother of 1st Lord Mackenzie of Kintail (ancestor of the Earls of Seaforth) and of Sir Roderick Mackenzie of Tarbat (ancester of the Earls of Cromartie). Sir John Mackenzie, 3rd baronet, participating in the Jacobite rising 1715, was included in the act of attainder passed against the Earl of Mar and his adherents. He died without male issue, and despite the forfeiture, the Baronetcy has been assumed since 1702, it being claimed that the attainder did not extend to collateral branches, and that the *title* as well as the estates devolved upon his brother.

Mackenzie (NS) 1703, of Gairloch, Ross-shire, see Inglis.

MACKENZIE (NS) 1703, of Scatwell, Ross-shire

I shine but do not burn

Without stain

Sir RODERICK MCQUHAE MACKENZIE, 12th *Baronet*; *b* 17 April 1942; *s* his father, *Capt Sir* RODERICK EDWARD FRANÇOIS MCQUHAE, CBE, DSC, 1986, but no name has been entered on the Official Roll of the Baronetage since death of 9th Bt in 1972; *ed* Sedbergh, King's Coll, Univ of London, and St George's Hosp; MB, BS, MRCP (UK), FRCP (C), DCH: *m* 1970, Nadezhda (Nadine), da of Georges Frederic Leon Schlatter, Baron von Rorbas of Buchs-K-Zurich, Switzerland, and has issue.

Arms – Quarterly, 1st, azure, a deer's head cabossed or, *Mackenzie of Scatwell*; 2nd, or, a mountain azure, inflamed gules; 3rd, gules, three legs of a man in armour proper flexed in triangle, garnished and spurred or, *Macleod of Lewis*, 4th, azure, a deer's head cabossed or within a bordure of the last charged with eight crescents of the first, *Mackenzie of Findon*. Crest – The sun in his splendour or. Supporters – *Dexter*, a savage wreathed about the head and middle with laurel and carrying with his dexter hand a club over his shoulder, all proper; *sinister*, a deer proper.

SON LIVING

GREGORY RODERICK MCQUHAE, *b* 8 May 1971.

DAUGHTER LIVING

Nina Adelaïda, *b* 1973.

SISTERS LIVING

Marie Isobel Campbell, *b* 1939: *m* 1964, Air Vice-Marshal Richard C. Allerton, CB (DL Cornwall 1995), of Bicton Mill, Bicton, Liskeard, Cornwall, and has issue living, James Roderick Orde (Rooksmoor, Buckland Monochorum, Devon), *b* 1967: *m* 1995, Marion E. C., da of Guy Hayward, of Harleston, Norfolk , — Christopher Edward Orde, *b* 1970; Capt Life Gds. ——— Fiona Louise, *b* 1943: *m* 1969, Lt-Cdr Timothy Patrick Havers, RN, of Corner House, 153 Dalling Rd, Ravenscourt Park, W6 0ER, and has issue living, (James) Angus, *b* 1978, — Louisanna Marie, *b* 1973, — Laetitia Anastasia Sophie, *b* 1982.

MOTHER LIVING OF TENTH BARONET

Elizabeth Carrington, da of late William Barbee Settle, Counsellor-at-law, of S Boston, Va, USA: *m* 1954, Kenneth Roderick Mackenzie, who *d* 1960.

The 1st baronet sat as MP for Ross-shire 1702-07, and the 5th baronet was Lord-Lieutenant of that county, and MP thereof 1822-31. This family is a collateral branch of the Mackenzies, Earls of Cromarty (title attainted 1746), and the present baronet claims he is representative, as heir male collateral, of Sir John Mackenzie of Tarbat (created a baronet of Nova Scotia by Charles I, 21 May 1628, with remainder to heirs male whatsoever, — "haeredibus masculis et talliae"). This same Sir John Mackenzie of Tarbat was the father of George, 1st Earl of Cromarty. The great-grandfather eight times removed of the present baronet was Sir Roderick Mackenzie of Tarbat and Coigeach, who was knighted in 1609 by James I of England and VI of Scotland.

MACKENZIE (UK) 1890, of Glen Muick, Aberdeenshire

SIC

ITUR AD ASTRA

This is the way to the stars

Sir (ALEXANDER GEORGE ANTHONY) ALLAN MACKENZIE, CD, 4th *Baronet*, *d* 5 Jan 1993, since when the succession to the baronetcy has not been established.

Arms – Per pale indented azure and or, a stag's head cabossed counter-changed. Crest – A dexter hand grasping a sword bendwise proper.

DAUGHTERS LIVING AND DECEASED OF FOURTH BARONET

Margaret Ann, *b* 1939: *m* 1974, Richard L. Mullin, and *dsp* 1989. —— Kathryn Heather, *b* 1946. —— Linda Alexandra MACKENZIE, *b* 1949; has resumed her maiden name: *m* 1970, Brock J. Eayrs, BA, LLB, and has issue living Jennifer Alexandra MACKENZIE, *b* 1973, — Alison Marjorie Ellen MACKENZIE, *b* 1977, — Elizabeth Brooke Jane MACKENZIE, *b* 1989. —— Allain Fenton, *b* 1953: *m* 1974, J. F. M. Beltgens, and has issue living, Christopher John Mackenzie, *b* 1978, — Jessica Kathryn Ann, *b* 1982.

WIDOW LIVING OF FOURTH BARONET

MARJORIE (*Lady Mackenzie*), da of A. F. McGuire, of Vancouver, BC, Canada: *m* 1937, Sir (Alexander George Anthony) Allan Mackenzie, 4th Bt, CD, who *d* 1993.

COLLATERAL BRANCH LIVING

Issue of the late Col Eric Dighton Mackenzie, CMG, CVO, DSO, yst son of 2nd Bt, *b* 1891, *d* 1972: *m* 1948, Elizabeth Kathrine Mary, da of late Capt James William Guy Innes, CBE, JP, RN, (*see* Innes, Bt, *cr* 1628), and formerly wife of Maj James Robertson-McIsaac:—
(James William) Guy (Tresowes Hill Farm, Ashton, nr Helston, Cornwall), *b* 1946; *ed* Stowe: *m* 1972 (*m diss* 1980), Paulene Patricia Simpson, and has issue living, Amanda Louise, *b* 1972, — Iona Elizabeth Rose, *b* 1978. —— Allan Walter, *b* 1952. —— Lucy Elizabeth Victoria, *b* 1949.

The 1st baronet, Sir James Thompson Mackenzie (son of George Mackenzie, of Aberdeen), was a DL for Ross-shire and Middlesex. The 3rd baronet, Sir Victor Audley Falconer, DSO, MVO, was Col Scots Guards, a Groom-in-Waiting to King George V, and an Extra Groom-in-Waiting to King Edward VIII and King George VI. He served during European War 1914-18 (DSO). The descendants of Sir Allan Mackenzie, 4th Bt, CD, are also in remainder to the barony of Berners.

MUIR MACKENZIE (UK) 1805, of Delvine, Perthshire

Straight at difficulties

Sir ALEXANDER ALWYNE BRINTON MUIR MACKENZIE, 7th *Baronet*; *b* 8 Dec 1955; *s* his father, *Capt Sir* ROBERT HENRY, 1970; *ed* Eton and Trin Coll, Camb: *m* 1984, Susan Carolyn, yst da of John David Henzell Hayter, of Dollivers, Holwell, Sherborne, Dorset, and has issue.

Arms – Quarterly: 1st and 4th, argent, on a fesse azure, three estoiles or, *Muir*; 2nd and 3rd, azure, a buck's head cabossed or, *Mackenzie*, all within a bordure nebuly quarterly gules and argent, the badge of a British baronet being placed in surtout. **Crest** – 1st, a sword and olive-branch in saltire proper; 2nd, a dexter hand grasping a dart in bend sinister proper. **First Motto** – "In utrumque paratus" (*In everything prepared*). **Second Motto** – "Recte ad ardua" (*Straight at difficulties*).

SON LIVING

ARCHIE ROBERT DAVID, *b* 17 Feb 1989.

DAUGHTER LIVING

Georgina Mary, *b* 1987.

SISTER LIVING

Prepared for either fortune

(Charmian) Miranda, *b* 1948: *m* 1968, Robert Dennis Smyly (*see* By of Buckland, 1980 Edn), of Sunderland Hall, Galashiels, Selkirkshire, TD1 3PG, and has issue living, Richard, *b* 1972, — Henrietta, *b* 1970: *m* 1997, Edward T. Gimlette, yst son of Dr T. M. D. Gimlette, of Teffont Magna, Wilts, and has issue living, Alistair *b* 1999.

WIDOW LIVING OF SIXTH BARONET

MARY TERESA (*Mary, Lady Muir Mackenzie*) (51 Elizabeth Court, Milman St, SW10 0DA), da of late Dr James Mathews, and widow of John Geoffrey Turner, of Lower Old Park, Farnham, Surrey: *m* 1963, as his 2nd wife, Capt Sir Robert Henry Muir Mackenzie, 6th Bt, who *d* 1970.

The 1st baronet, Sir Alexander Muir, descended from the Muirs of Cassencarrie (a very ancient family), assumed the additional surname of Mackenzie upon succeeding to the estates of his great-uncle John Mackenzie, of Delvine, Perthshire, 3rd son of Sir Kenneth Mackenzie, 1st baronet of Coul. The 4th baronet *d* 1918, and the 5th baronet, Sir Robert Cecil, MC, Lieut Durham LI, was *ka* 1918.

MACKESON (UK) 1954, of Hythe, co Kent

Sir RUPERT HENRY MACKESON, 2nd *Baronet*, *b* 16 Nov 1941; *ed* Harrow, and Trin Coll, Dublin (MA); late Capt RHG, and Lt Buffs Regt (TA); *s* his father, *Brig Sir* HARRY RIPLEY, 1964: *m* 1968 (*m diss* 1972), Hon Camilla Margaret, da of Baron Keith of Castleacre (Life Baron) (*see* E Kintore).
Residence –

Arms – Vair four roses three and one or. **Crest** – A lion's gamb erased or supporting an escutcheon gules charged with a rose or.

SISTER LIVING

Fiona Mariella, *b* 1946: *m* 1965, Capt Hamish Leslie Gray-Cheape, late Gren Gds, JP, High Sheriff Warwicks 1984, and DL 1990, of Hill House, Walcot, Alcester, Warwicks, and has issue living, Hugo James, *b* 1968, — George Hamish, *b* 1971.

Sir Harry Ripley Mackeson, 1st baronet, son of Henry Mackeson of Littlebourne House, Littlebourne, Kent, was MP for Hythe (*C*) 1945-50, and for Folkstone 1950-59. He was Dep Ch Conservative Whip 1950-52, Senior Lord Commr of the Treasury 1951-52, and Sec for Overseas Trade 1952-53.

MACKWORTH (GB) 1776 of The Gnoll, Glamorganshire

Rather death than shame

Sir DIGBY JOHN MACKWORTH, 10th *Baronet*; *b* 2 Nov 1945; *s* his father *Sir* DAVID ARTHUR GEOFFREY, 1998; *ed* Wellington; late Lt Aust Army Air Corps in Malaysia and Vietnam; Pilot Bristow Helicopters, British Airways: *m* 1971, Antoinette Francesca, da of Henry James McKenna, of Ilford, Essex, and has issue.

𝕬rms – Per pale indented sable and ermine, on a chevron gules, five crosses-patée or. Crest – A cock proper.
Residence – Blagrove Cottage, Fox Lane, Boars Hill, Oxford OX1 5DS.

DAUGHTER LIVING

Octavia, *b* 1977.

AUNTS LIVING (*daughters of 5th son of 6th baronet*)

Betty Mabel (23 Shipley Close, S Brent, Devon TQ10 9PS), *b* 1911.
—— Lorna Alice (known as Mrs Lorna Alice ELDRED) (RR1, Smith Rd, Falkland, BC V0E 1W0, Canada), *b* 1918.

WIDOW LIVING OF NINTH BARONET

BERYL JOAN (*Beryl, Lady Mackworth*), 3rd da of late Pembroke Henry Cockayn Cross, and formerly wife of late Ernest Henry Sparkes: *m* 1973, as his 2nd wife, Sir David Arthur Geoffrey Mackworth, 9th Bt, who *d* 1998. *Residence* – 36 Wittering Rd, Hayling Island, Hants PO11 9SP.

COLLATERAL BRANCHES LIVING

Issue of late Capt Francis Julian Audley Mackworth, 2nd son of 6th baronet, *b* 1876, *ka* 1914: *m* 1910, Dorothy Conran, who *m* 2ndly, 1922, Charles Edward Gatehouse, and *d* 1976, da of late Arthur Hastings Lascelles, of Belmore, Narbeth, Pembroke:—
Cecily Joan (6 Rue des Coutures-St Gervais, Paris 75003), *b* 1911: *m* 1st, 1935, Leon Donckier de Donceel, who *d* 1938; 2ndly, 1956, Marquis de Chabannes la Palice, of Château du Brèvedent, Calvados, France, who *d* 1980, and has issue living, (by 1st *m*) Pascale, *b* 1936.

Issue of late Col John Dolben Mackworth, CBE, 7th son of 6th baronet, *b* 1887, *d* 1939: *m* 1913, Marianne Annette, who *d* 1968, da of H. W. Sillem, of The Pines, Horsell, Surrey:—
Josephine Ann, *b* 1914: *m* 1st, 1937, Major Patrick Owen Lyons, who *d* 1941, Indian Army Ordnance Corps; 2ndly, 1942, Lt-Col Noel James, MBE, RAOC, of Tower House, 4 Bath Rd, Cowes, I of Wight, and has issue living, (by 2nd *m*) Christopher Noel Mackworth, *b* 1946. — John Gwyn Mackworth, *b* 1951. — (by 1st *m*) Mary Annette, *b* 1939, — Bridget Carol Dolben, *b* 1940.

Grandson of late Horace Euguene Mackworth, 2nd son of 4th baronet:—
Issue of late Lt-Col Norman Walter Mackworth, MB, ChB, FRCS, IMS, *b* 1878, *d* 1950: *m* 1908, Isabel Largie, MA, who *d* 1967, da of late William Anderson:—
NORMAN HUMPHREY, PhD, MB, ChB (16232 Camellia Terr, Los Gatos, Cal 95030, USA), *b* 1917; *ed* Aberdeen Univ (MB and ChB); PhD Camb; *m* 1941, Jane Felicity, MB, BChir, PhD, yr da of late Capt Walter Hugh Charles Samuel Thring, CBE, RN, and has issue living, Alan Keith (4433 West 9th Av, Vancouver, BC, Canada V6R 2C9), *b* 1945: *m* 1969, Marian Elizabeth, da of J. V. Fry, and has issue living, Bryn Sarah *b* 1972, — Hugh Francis, *b* 1958, — Jean Clare, *b* 1942: *m* 1964, David Surry, and has issue living, Patrick David *b* 1969, Susan Alicia Mackworth *b* 1971, Kathleen Jane Mackworth *b* 1973.

Grandchildren of late Audley Mackworth, 2nd son of late Herbert Francis Mackworth, el son of late Lieut Herbert Mackworth, RN, 2nd son of 3rd baronet:—
Issue of late Air Vice-Marshal Philip Herbert Mackworth, CB, CBE, DFC, *b* 1897, *d* 1958: *m* 1921, Winifred Kathleen June, who *d* 1967, da of William Moss:—
Richard Charles Audley (27 Wellington Sq, SW3), *b* 1924; *ed* Camb Univ (MA); MSc Eng London; MIMcchE; MIWE; DIC; formerly Fl-Lt RAF; *m* 1960, Rosalind Jean, da of Rev A. Walters, V of Wychbold, Worcs, and has issue living, Julia Kathleen, *b* 1968, — Victoria Alma Louise, *b* 1971. —— James Digby (The Old School House, Littleworth, Faringdon, Oxon SN7 8ED), *b* 1927; *ed* Camb Univ (MA); Maj (ret) REME; CEng, FIMechE: *m* 1st, 1952 (*m diss* 1968) Marjorie Wilding; 2ndly, 1968, Anna Marjorie Wilson Melling, who *d* 1983; 3rdly, 1984, Elizabeth Marianne Parsons, and has issue living, (by 1st *m*) Charles Digby *b* 1958, Amanda Jane *b* 1956.

This family is of considerable antiquity in Shropshire and Derbyshire, and a member of it fought at Poitiers in 1356. Sir Francis Mackworth, a distinguished royalist, fought on the side of Charles I. Col Humphrey Mackworth, a man of considerable note *temp* Commonwealth, was MP for Salop, was Governor for Shrewsbury, and one of Cromwell's Council. The 1st baronet sat as MP for Cardiff, and the 2nd baronet bequeathed the Gnoll Castle estate to his widow. The 8th baronet, Col Sir Harry Llewellyn Mackworth, CMG, DSO, Roy Corps of Signals, was Ch Signal Officer, Egypt 1924-27.

MACLEAN (NS) 1631, of Dowart and Morvaren, Argyllshire

Hon Sir LACHLAN HECTOR CHARLES MACLEAN, 12th *Baronet*; *b* 25 Aug 1942; *s* his father, CHARLES HECTOR FITZROY, Baron Maclean, KT, GCVO, KBE, PC (Life Baron) in his baronetcy 1990; *ed* Eton; 28th Chief of Clan Maclean; Maj Scots Guards (ret); DL Argyll and Bute 1993: *m* 1966, Mary Helen, eldest da of William Gordon Gordon, of Lude, Blair Atholl, Perthshire, and has had issue.

Arms – Quarterly: 1st, argent, a rock gules; 2nd argent, a dexter hand fessewise couped gules holding a cross-crosslet fitchée in pale azure; 3rd, or, a lymphad, oars in saltire, sails furled, sable, flagged gules; 4th, argent, a salmon naiant proper, in chief two eagles' heads erased respectant gules. **Crest** – A tower embattled argent. **Supporters** – *Dexter*, a seal proper; *sinister*, an ostrich with a horseshoe in its beak proper.
Seat – Duart Castle, Isle of Mull. *Residence* – Arngask, Glenfarg, Perthshire PH2 9QA.

SONS LIVING

MALCOLM LACHLAN CHARLES, *b* 20 Oct 1972; *ed* Eton, and Manchester Univ: *m* 1998, Anna-Michelle, eldest da of Giles Sturdy, of Trigon, Wareham, Dorset. —— Andrew Lachlan William, *b* 1979.

DAUGHTERS LIVING AND DECEASED

Emma Mary, *b* 1967: *m* 1996, Giovanni U. Amati, son of late Dr Luigi Amati, and of Signora Carla Ponziani Amati, of Lecco, Italy. —— Sarah Elizabeth Helen, *b* 1969, *d* 1971. —— Alexandra Caroline, *b* 1975.

SISTER LIVING

Hon Janet Elizabeth, *b* 1944: *m* 1974, Maj Nicholas Michael Lancelot Barne, Scots Guards (ret) (*see* Orr Ewing, Bt, *cr* 1886, colls, 1969 Edn), and has issue living, Alasdair Michael Fitzroy, *b* 1979, — Hamish Nicholas Charles, *b* 1981. *Residence* – Blofield House, Blofield, Norwich, Norfolk.

WIDOW LIVING OF LIFE BARON AND ELEVENTH BARONET

JOAN ELIZABETH (*Elizabeth, Baroness Maclean*), da of late Capt Francis Thomas Mann (*see* Mann, Bt): *m* 1941, Baron Maclean, KT, GCVO, KBE, PC (Life Baron), who *d* 1990. *Residence* – Wilderness House, Hampton Court Palace, Surrey KT8 9AR.

(1) *Sir* LACHLAN Maclean of Morvern, son and heir of Hector Og Maclean of Duart; a zealous supporter of Charles I; *cr* a Bt 1631, with remainder to his heirs male whatsoever: *m* Mary, da of Roderick Macleod of Macleod; *d* 1649; *s* by his el son (2) *Sir* HECTOR, 2nd Bt; *b* about 1625; *d* unm, *k* fighting for Royal cause at Innerkeithing 1651; *s* by his brother (3) *Sir* ALLAN, 3rd Bt; *b* about 1637: *m* Giles, da of John Macleod of Macleod; *d* 1674; *s* by his only son (4) *Sir* JOHN, 4th Bt; present with his clan at Killiecrankie 1689 and Sheriffmuir 1715; *m* about 1704 Mary, da of Sir Aeneas Macpherson of Invereshie; *d* about 1719; *s* by his son (5) *Sir* HECTOR, 5th Bt; *b* about 1704; imprisoned in Tower of London 1745-47 as a Jacobite; *d* unm 1751; *s* by his kinsman (6) *Sir* ALLAN, 6th Bt, (gt-grandson of Donald Maclean of Brolas, half-brother of 1st Bt): *m* Una, da of Hector Maclean of Coll; *d* 1783; *s* by his kinsman (7) *Sir* HECTOR, 7th Bt (grandson of Hector Og, gt-uncle of 6th Bt); *d* unm 1818; *s* by his half-brother (8) *Sir* FITZROY JEFFREYS GRAFTON, Lt-Gen; present at capture of Martinique and Guadaloupe: *m* 1st, 1794, Elizabeth, who *d* 1832, da of Charles Kidd, and widow of John Bishop of Barbados; 2ndly, 1838, Frances, who *d* 1843, da of Rev Henry Watkins, and widow of Henry Campion; *d* 1847; *s* by his el son (9) *Sir* CHARLES FITZROY, 9th Bt; *b* 1798; Col: *m* 1831, Emily Eleanor, who *d* 1838, da of Rev Canon Hon Jacob Marsham, DD (E Romney); *d* 1883; *s* by his son (10) *Sir* FITZROY DONALD, KCB, 10th Bt, *b* 1835; Ch of Clan Maclean; recovered Duart Castle 1910; Comdg 13 H; Crimean War; *m* 1872, Constance Marianne, who *d* 1920, da of George Holland Ackers, of Moreton Hall, Ches; *d* 1936; *s* by his grandson, (11) *Sir* CHARLES HECTOR FITZROY, 11th Bt, KT, GCVO, KBE, PC, *b* 1916; Lord Lieut Argyll and Bute, Chief Scout of the Commonwealth, Lord Chamberlain of the Household, Lord High Commr to Gen Assembly of Church of Scotland, a Permanent Lord in Waiting and Chief Steward of Hampton Court Palace, Chllr Royal Victorian Order (Royal Victorian Chain), author of children's books; *cr Baron Maclean*, of Duart and Morvern, co Argyll (Life Baron) 1971: *m* 1941, Joan Elizabeth, da of late Capt Francis Thomas Mann (*see* Mann, Bt); *d* 1990; *s* by his son (12) *Sir* LACHLAN HECTOR CHARLES, 12th Bt.

MACLEAN OF DUNCONNEL (UK) 1957, of Strachur and Glensluain, co Argyll

Sir CHARLES EDWARD MACLEAN OF DUNCONNEL, 2nd *Baronet*; *b* 31 Oct 1946; *s* his father, *Sir* FITZROY HEW, KT, CBE, 1996; 16th Hereditary Keeper and Captain of Dunconnel in the Isles of the Sea; *ed* Eton, and New Coll, Oxford; Writer: *m* 1986, Deborah, da of Lawrence Young, of Chicago, USA, and has issue.

Arms – Quarterly, 1st, argent, a lion rampant gules, armed and langued azure; 2nd, azure, a castle triple towered argent, masoned sable, windows, portcullis and flags gules; 3rd, or, a dexter hand couped fessways gules, holding a cross crosslet fitchée azure; 4th, or, a galley, sails furled, oars in saltire sable, flagged gules, in a sea in base vert a salmon argent; at the centre point a portcullis sable for difference. Above the shield, from which is pendent from its proper riband the Badge of a Baronet of the United Kingdom, and behind which are placed in saltire a key wards outwards or and a rod gules garnished or, being insignia for his office of Hereditary Keeper and Captain of Dunconnel Castle, is placed his chapeau gules furred ermine (as feudal baron of Strachur). Crest – A lochaber axe in pale between a branch of laurel and a branch of cypress in open chaplet all proper.
Residence – Strachur House, Strachur, Argyll.

DAUGHTERS LIVING

Margaret Augusta, *b* 1986. —— Katharine Alexandra, *b* 1988. —— Charlotte Olivia, *b* 1991. —— Diana Mary Elektra, *b* 1997.

BROTHER LIVING

(ALEXANDER) JAMES, *b* 9 June 1949; *ed* Eton: *m* 1st, 1983 (*m diss* 1989), Sarah, eldest da of Hugh Janson, of Barn House, Aldbourne, Wilts; 2ndly, 1993, Sarah Carolyn, da of Nicolas de la Mare Thompson, of 8 Ennismore Gdns, SW7, and has issue living (by 2nd *m*), Alexander Fitzroy Nicolas, *b* 19 Sept 1996. *Residence* – Flat 4, 49 Drayton Gdns, SW10 9RX.

WIDOW LIVING OF FIRST BARONET

Hon VERONICA NELL FRASER (*Hon Lady Maclean of Dunconnel*), da of 14th Lord Lovat, KT, GCVO, and widow of Lt Alan Phipps, RN (*see* M Normanby, colls): *m* 1946, Sir Fitzroy Hew Maclean of Dunconnel, 1st Bt, KT, CBE, who *d* 1996. *Residence* – Strachur House, Argyll.

Maj Charles Wilberforce Maclean, DSO, OBE, father of the 1st baronet, was 4th son of Lt-Col Allan Henry Maclean, RHA, grandson of Lt-Col Alexander Maclean, 13th Chief of Ardgour, Argyll. His ancestor, Donald, yr son of Lachlan Bronnach, 7th of Duart (*see* Maclean Bt, *cr* 1631) slew MacMaster of Ardgour and appropriated his lands, about 1432, obtaining a grant thereof from Alexander, 3rd Lord of the Isles. This was confirmed by James IV in 1494. Sir Fitzroy Hew Maclean, 1st baronet, KT, CBE, entered Diplomatic Ser 1933, served Paris and Moscow, Under-Sec of State for War and Financial Sec to War Office 1954-57; 1939-45 War with Queen's Own Cameron Highlanders and 1st SAS Regt, Brig Comdg British Mission to Yugoslav Partisans 1943-45; French Croix de Guerre, Order of Kutusov of Russia, and Yugoslav Partisan Star; MP (C) for Lancaster Oct 1941 to Oct 1959, and for Bute and N Ayrshire Oct 1959 to Feb 1974; recognised by Lord Lyon as 15th Hereditary Keeper and Captain of Dunconnel in the Isles of the Sea 1981; author of *Eastern Approaches* and other works.

MacLEOD (UK) 1924, of Fuinary, Morven, co Argyll

Hon Sir JOHN MAXWELL NORMAN MacLEOD, 5th *Baronet*; *b* 23 Feb 1952; *s* his father, Very Rev GEORGE FIELDEN, Baron MacLeod of Fuinary, MC, DD (Life Baron), in his baronetcy 1991; *ed* Gordonstoun.

Arms – Azure, a castle triple-towered argent, masoned sable, windows and protcullis gules, on a chief of the second an open book proper, leaved of the fourth. **Crest** – A bull's head cabossed sable, horned or, between two keys wards uppermost of the last.
Residence – Fuinary Manse, Loch Aline, Morven, Argyll.

BROTHER LIVING

Hon NEIL DAVID, *b* 25 Dec 1959; *ed* —. *Residence* – —.

SISTER LIVING

Hon Eva Mary Ellen, *b* 1950. *Residence* – .

The 1st baronet, Sir John Mackintosh MacLeod (son of Very Rev Norman MacLeod, DD, of Barony Church, Glasgow, and Dean of the Order of the Thistle), sat as MP for Central Div of Glasgow (*Co U*) 1915-18, and for Kelvingrove 1918-22. The 2nd baronet, Sir John Mackintosh Norman, was Unicorn Pursuivant of Arms 1925-29, and Rothesay Herald 1929-39. The 3rd baronet, Capt Sir Ian Francis Norman, Intelligence Corps, *d* on active ser during European War 1944. The 4th baronet, Very Rev Sir George Fielden, MC, DD, was Leader of Iona Community 1938-67, Moderator of Gen Assembly of Church of Scotland 1956-57, and Chaplain to HM in Scotland 1956-65; *cr Baron MacLeod of Fuinary*, of Fuinary in Morven, co Argyll (Life Baron) 1967: *m* 1948, Lorna Helen Janet, who *d* 1984, da of Rev Donald MacLeod of Balvonie, of Inshes, Inverness, and *d* 1991.

McLEOD (UK) 1925, of The Fairfields, Cobham, Surrey
(Name pronounced "McLoud")

Be thou a brazen wall

Sir CHARLES HENRY MCLEOD*, 3rd *Baronet*; *b* 7 Nov 1924; *s* his father, *Sir* MURDOCH CAMPBELL, 1950; *ed* Winchester: *m* 1957, (Anne) Gillian, who *d* 1978, yr da of Henry Russell Bowlby (V Combermere, colls), and has issue.

Arms – Ermine, on a pile azure between two lotus flowers in base or a castle triple-towered argent, masoned sable, windows and porch gules. **Crest** – In front of two flags in saltire gules, staves proper, a bull's head caboshed also gules.
Residence – Coombe Green Cottage, Lea, Malmesbury, Wilts SN16 9PF.

SON LIVING

JAMES RODERICK CHARLES, *b* 26 Sept 1960: *m* 1990, Helen M., elder da of Capt George T. Cooper, OBE, RN, of Lilliput, Poole, Dorset, and has issue living, Rory, *b* 7 July 1994, — Alexandra, *b* 1992.

DAUGHTERS LIVING

Belinda Ann McLEOD, *b* 1957; has resumed her maiden name: *m* 1990 (*m diss* 1999), Khaled Shaker, and has issue living, Zachariah, *b* 1990. —— Nicola, *b* 1958: *m* 1st, 1981 (*m diss* 1985), Nigel Iorwerth Stodart Parry, elder son of John Stanley Hammond Parry, of Staplegordon, Seale, Surrey; 2ndly, 1985, Stewart A. Duffain; 3rdly, 1990, John Spencer Warwick Bampfylde, of 120 Old Ayer Rd, Groton, MA 01450, USA (*see* B Poltimore).

The 1st baronet, Sir Charles Campbell McLeod (son of the Rev Norman McLeod, of N Uist), was Chm of National Bank of India, Ltd, and of Imperial Tea Co, Ltd.
*His el brother Roderick Campbell McLeod, *b* 1921; Lieut Scots Guards; *ka* at Salerno 1943.

McLINTOCK (UK) 1934, of Sanquhar, co Dumfries

By virtue and labour

Sir MICHAEL WILLIAM McLINTOCK, 4th *Baronet*; *b* 13 Aug 1958; *s* his father, *Sir* WILLIAM TRAVEN, 1987.

𝕬rms – Azure, a book expanded or, leaved gules, over all a writing pen palewise proper. 𝕮rest – A lion passant or, holding in his dexter paw a thistle slipped proper. *Residence* – The Cottage, Lower Woodside, Herts AL9 6DJ.

BROTHERS LIVING

ANDREW THOMSON (95 Heathcote Av, Hatfield, Herts AL10 0RL), *b* 2 Dec 1960. —— Kevin Robert (50 Chester Rd, Macclesfield, Ches FK1 8DT), *b* 1963.

UNCLE LIVING *(son of 2nd baronet)*

Peter Thomson, *b* 1933; *ed* Harrow: *m* 1st, 1954 (*m diss* 1977), Fiona, yst da of Gen Sir Philip Christian, 4th Bt, GBE, CB, DSO, MC; 2ndly, 1986, Patricia-Anne, da of —, and has issue living (by 1st *m*), Traven Thomson Christison (7 Manor Rd, Jordanhill, Glasgow G14 9LG), *b* 1957; *ed* Edinburgh Acad; MB ChB: *m* 1984, —, and has issue living, Sarah *b* 1987, — Morar, *b* 1955: *m* 1986, David Honeyman, and has issue living, Ailsa *b* 1986.

GREAT-AUNT LIVING *(daughter of 1st baronet)*

Mary Lyons, *b* 1912: *m* 1st, 1937, Capt Malcolm George Lillingston, King's Drag Gds, who was *ka* 1941; 2ndly, 1947, Maj Robert Bradford Myles, MC, late Royal Inniskilling Fus, who *d* 1981, and has issue living (by 1st *m*), Mark Campbell, *b* 1938; *ed* Eton, and Magdalene Coll, Camb, — Diane Margaret, *b* 1941: *m* 1963, Robin Andrew Paterson, CA, of Lees Court, Matfield, Tonbridge, Kent, and has issue living, Jamie John Lillingston LILLINGSTON-PATERSON *b* 1967; *ed* Eton; assumed addl surname of Lillingston 1987: *m* 1997, Mary-Jane, yst da of (Ronald) Peter Gibbons (*see* Lowe, Bt, colls), Joanna Mary Lillingston *b* 1965: *m* 1990, Michael Richard John Bell, yst son of Lt-Cdr Peter Bell, of Yeabridge Close, S Petherton, Som, and has issue living, Hollie Mary Ann *b* 1993, Camilla Margaret Lucy *b* (twin) 1993, Tara Poppy Francesca *b* 1997, — (by 2nd *m*) Nicholas Robert William Bradford, *b* 1954; *ed* Eton, — Sarah Louise Bradford, *b* 1950: *m* 1982, Michael James Corbett Robinson, of 8 Gorst Rd, SW11 6JE, and has issue living, Jonathon Myles *b* 1986, Cara Myles *b* 1984, — Penelope Jean Bradford, *b* 1952: *m* 1979, Dr Anthony Pitt Lipscomb. *Residence* – Coach House, Lees Court, Matfield, Tonbridge, Kent.

WIDOW LIVING OF THIRD BARONET

Mrs (MURIEL) HEATHER HOMFRAY NEWMAN (*Lady McLintock*), da of late Philip Dennis Homfray-Davies: *m* 1974, as his 2nd wife, Sir William Traven McLintock, 3rd Bt, who *d* 1987. *Residence* –

MOTHER LIVING

Andrée, da of Richard Lonsdale-Hands, of 6 Av Edouard Dapples, Lausanne: *m* 1952 (*m diss* 19—), as his 1st wife, Sir William Traven McLintock, 3rd Bt, who *d* 1987. *Residence* –

The 1st baronet, Sir William McLintock, GBE, CVO (son of Thomson McLintock), was senior partner in the firm of Thomson McLintock & Co, chartered accountants, of 33 King William Street, EC4, and Glasgow.

MACLURE (UK) 1898, of The Home, Whalley Range, near Manchester, co Palatine of Lancaster

Sir JOHN ROBERT SPENCER MACLURE, 4th *Baronet*; *b* 25 March 1934; *s* his father, *Lt-Col Sir* JOHN WILLIAM SPENCER, OBE, 1980; *ed* Winchester; Headmaster of Croftinloan Sch, Pitlochry 1978-92 and 1997-98: *m* 1964, Jane Monica, da of late Rt Rev Thomas Joseph Savage, Bishop of Zululand and Swaziland, and has issue.

𝕬rms – Argent, on a chevron engrailed azure between in chief two roses and in base a quatrefoil gules, a martlet between two escallops of the field. 𝕮rest – An eagle's head erased argent between four roses gules, stalked and leaved on each side proper. *Residence* – Trerice, Chevithorne, Tiverton, Devon EX16 7PY. *Club* – Royal and Ancient Golf; MCC; Royal Greenjackets.

SONS LIVING

Paratus sum
I am ready

(JOHN) MARK, *b* 27 Aug 1965; *ed* Winchester: *m* 1996, Emily Jane, yr da of Capt Peter Frean, of Connel Ha', Cothal, Aberdeen, and of Mrs Elisabeth Austing, of Brixham, and has issue living, John James, *b* 4 Sept 1997. *Residence* – Forge Cottage, Axford, Hants RG25 2EA. —— Thomas Stephen, *b* 1967. —— Graham Spencer, *b* 1970. —— Stephen Patrick Ian, *b* 1974.

BROTHER LIVING

Patrick Stanley Winton King (Flat 2, 25 Christchurch Rd, Winchester, Hants SO23 9SU; *Clubs* – Oriental, Royal Green-jackets, MCC), *b* 1939; *ed* Winchester; company secretary.

SISTER LIVING

Elspeth Rosemary, *b* 1930; SRN: *m* 1955, Maj-Gen Michael Matthews, CB, DL, who *d* 1993, and has issue living, Graeme Michael Ian (Pentwyn Farmhouse, Gwehelog, nr Usk, S Wales NP5 1RE), *b* 1959: *m* 1987, Sophie L. K., yr da of Ralph Denne, of Henley-on-Thames, and of Lady Hodson, of Romsey, and has issue living, Benjamin Michael David *b* 1989, Oscar William *b* 1991, Mungo George *b* 1993, Hamish Max *b* 1995, — James Binding, *b* 1966: *m* 1990, Jennifer J. Harper-Hill, — Nichola Jane, *b* 1957, — Elspeth Julie, *b* 1963. *Residence* – Selhurst, Bartons Lane, Old Basing, Hants RG24 8AN.

UNCLE LIVING (*Son of 2nd baronet*)

Edward Stanley Winton, *b* 1909; Lt-Com (ret) RN: *m* 1938, Jeanette Kathleen, who *d* 1969, da of late Anton Bakker, of Sydney, Aust, and has issue living, Caroline Eleanor Kathleen (Abeelstraat 154, 3329 A H Dordrecht, Netherlands), *b* 1939; *ed* London Univ (BA): *m diss* 1989, Gerard Jozef van Tienen, and has issue living, Robbert Rudolf *b* 1967, Richard Mark *b* 1970, — Margaret Elizabeth Anne, *b* 1941: *m* 1969, Raymond D. Hibberd, of 24 Warfield Av, Water-looville, Hants, and 4 rue de la Liberation, Plerguer, Brittany, France, and has issue living, Simon Philip *b* 1972, Nicholas Adam *b* 1975, — Yvonne Irene Valerie, *b* 1943: *m* 1st, 1964 (*m diss* 1972), Albert Brian Challinor; 2ndly, 1972, Brian Henry Thompson, RN, of 35 George V Av, Westbrook, Margate, Kent, and has issue living (by 1st *m*), Ian Grant *b* 1965, Susan Jane *b* 1967 (by 2nd *m*) Fiona Kate *b* 1973, Alexandra Louise *b* 1975, Caroline Elizabeth *b* 1978. *Residence* – Flat No 1, Hinton House, Jubilee Rd, Waterlooville, Hants PO7 7QX.

AUNT LIVING (*Daughter of 2nd baronet*)

Edith Mary Ursula, *b* 1916: *m* 1939, Louis Gordon Oliphant Hutchison, sometime F/O RAFVR, who *d* 1959, and has issue living, Alexander Gordon Oliphant (Batworthy Mill, Batworthy, nr Chagford, Devon), *b* 1943: *m* 1967, Jennifer Marilyn, da of Alun Blackwell, and has issue living, Alexander Valentine Oliphant *b* 1968, William Lawrence Oliphant *b* 1969, James Hardy Oliphant *b* 1973, — Susan Ruth Oliphant (Les Bourges, Salles 47150, Monflanquin, France), *b* 1940: *m* 1st, 1959, John Chislett, who *d* 1962: 2ndly, 1962 (*m diss* 1975), Jonathan Frederick Macnaught Ruddick; 3rdly, 1976, Colin Costello-Jones, and has issue living, (by 1st *m*) Miles Gordon *b* 1960: *m* 1986, Elizabeth Robinson (and has issue living, Hannah Georgina *b* 1986), (by 2nd *m*) Francis Louis *b* 1962, Simon William *b* 1964, Charlotte Nina *b* 1966, Romany Lara *b* 1974, (by 3rd *m*) Benjamin Llewelyn *b* 1981, Harriet *b* 1984, — Philippa Anne Oliphant *b* 1946: *m* 1st, 1963 (*m diss* 1970), Donald Stuart Oldham; 2ndly, 1972, Patrick John Bugg, and has issue living, (by 1st *m*) Tamsin *b* 1963: *m* 1985, Jonathan Seymour (and has issue living, Alice *b* 1986), Jessica *b* 1966: *m* 1988, James Eager (and has issue living, Amy *b* 1989), (by 2nd *m*) Fletcher Charlie *b* 1973. *Residence* – Ramon, Salles 47150, Monflanquin, France.

The 1st baronet was Hon Sec to Cotton Famine Relief Fund 1862-65, and MP for Stretford 1886-1901.

McMAHON (UK) 1817
(Name pronounced "McMahn")

Thus we defend ourselves and our sacred rights

SIC NOS, SIC SACRA TUEMUR

Sir BRIAN PATRICK McMAHON, 8th *Baronet*; *b* 9th June 1942; *s* his father, Sir (WILLIAM) PATRICK 1977; *ed* Wellington Coll, Wednes-bury Tech Coll (BSc 1964) AIM (1965): *m* 1981 (*m diss* 1991), Kathleen Joan, da of late William Hopwood.

𝔄rms – Per saltire or and ermine, a lion passant azure between two lions passant-reguardant gules. 𝔠rest – An arm embowed in armour, holding a sword wavy, all proper, surmounted of a portcullis gules, chained or. 𝔖upporters – On either side a private of the 10th Foot habited and accoutred, and holding in the exterior hand a musket proper.
Residence – Oak Ridge, School Rd, Thorney Hill, Bransgore, Christchurch, Dorset BH23 8DS.

BROTHER LIVING

SHAUN DESMOND (Dendron, 21 Old Vineyard Rd, Constantia, Cape, S Africa), *b* 29 Oct 1945; *ed* Wellington Coll: *m* 1st, 1971, Antonia Noel, da of Antony James Adie, of Rowington, Warwicks; 2ndly, 1985, Jill Rosamund, yr da of Dr Jack Cherry, of 44 Park Rd, Abingdon, Oxon, and has issue living, (by 2nd *m*) Patrick John Westropp, *b* 7 Feb 1988, — Charles Beresford, *b* 1989.

The 1st baronet, Right Hon Sir John McMahon, was a Privy Councillor for Ireland and Private Secretary and Keeper of the Privy Purse to George IV. His next brother was also created a baronet (*cr* 1815, ext 1926). The 1st baronet of this creation was succeeded under a limitation in the patent by his second brother, Gen Sir Thomas, GCB, Col of 10th Foot, and Com-in-Chief of the Forces at Bombay.

MACNAGHTEN (UK) 1836, of Bushmills House, co Antrim

Sir PATRICK ALEXANDER MACNAGHTEN, 11th *Baronet, b* 24 Jan 1927; *s* his father *Sir* ANTONY, 1972; *ed* Eton and Trin Coll, Camb: *m* 1955, Marianne, da of Dr Erich Schaefer, of Cambridge, and has issue.

Arms – Quarterly: 1st and 4th argent a dexter hand fessways proper holding a cross-crosslet fitchée azure; 2nd and 3rd argent, a tower gules. **Crest** – A tower embattled gules. **Supporters** – Two roebucks proper.
Residence – Dundarave, Bushmills, co Antrim BT57 8ST.

SONS LIVING

MALCOLM FRANCIS, *b* 21 Sept 1956. —— Edward Alexander, *b* 1958. —— David Charles, *b* 1962.

BROTHERS LIVING

Antony Martin (Ballyvester House, Donaghadee, co Down), *b* 1930; *ed* Eton, and Trin Coll, Camb: *m* 1959, Catherine Frances, da of Rev Charles ffolliott Young, and has issue living, Philip Martin, *b* 1965, — Antony Charles, *b* 1971, — Ruth Helen, *b* 1964: *m* 1992, Dr Jonathan Holbrook, — Imogen Alice, *b* 1970. —— Charles Edmund (The Croft, Church St, Seal, nr Sevenoaks, Kent), *b* 1937; *ed* Eton, and Trin Coll, Camb: *m* 1976, Mary Jane, da of John W. Saunders, of West Hartford, Connecticut, USA, and has issue living, Alexander, *b* 1977, — Mary Joanna, *b* 1979.

SISTER LIVING

Diana Mary, *b* 1929: *m* 1951, Myles Richard Eckersley, and has issue living, Alison, *b* 1954, — Fiona Jane, *b* 1955. *Residence* – Elm View, Lockerley, nr Romsey, Hants.

AUNT LIVING

Anne Catherine (23 Wymondley Rd, Hitchen, Herts), *b* 1908: *m* 1st, 1936, James Ernest Skilbeck, who *d* 1947; 2ndly, 1947, Arnold Richardson Ashby, who *d* 1994, and has issue living, (by 1st *m*) John, *b* 1942, — Catherine, *b* 1947.

WIDOW LIVING OF TENTH BARONET

MADGALENE (*Magdalene, Lady Macnaghten*) (Dundarave, Bushmills, co Antrim), el da of late Edmund Fisher: *m* 1926, Sir Antony Macnaghten, 10th Bt, who *d* 1972.

COLLATERAL BRANCHES LIVING

Granddaughter of late Alfred Hill Macnaghten, 6th son of Francis Macnaghten, 3rd son of 1st baronet:—
Issue of late Lieut-Col Balfour Macnaghten, DSO, 12th Roy Lancers, *b* 1875, *d* 1945: *m* 1902, Hilda, who *d* 1958, da of W. G. Lardner, of 11 Fourth Avenue, Hove, Sussex:—
Daphne, *b* 1914: *m* 1940, Lieut-Col Richard Percival Hawksley Burbury, Duke of Cornwall, LI, who *d* of wounds received in action in Normandy.

Granddaughter of late Elliot Macnaghten (*b* 1837), eldest son of late Elliot Macnaghten (*b* 1807), 4th son of 1st baronet:—
Issue of late Russell Elliot Macnaghten, *b* 1860, *d* 1918: *m* 1891, Mary, da of late Frederick Berry, of Church-down, Gloucestershire:—
Kathleen Edith, *b* 1903: *m* 1934, Edward C. R. Cardinall, and has issue living, Edward Russell, *b* 1936, — Sandra Margaret, *b* 1934, — Chloe Joan (twin), *b* 1936.

Grandchildren of late Col William Hay Macnaghten, CB, son of late Elliot Macnaghten (*b* 1807) (ante):—
Issue of late Brig-Gen Ernest Brander Macnaghten, CMG, DSO, *b* 1872, *d* 1948: *m* 1906, Yvonne Marie, who *d* 1950, da of late Surg-Lieut-Col J. S. Forrester, Roy Horse Guards:—
Renée Gavrelle, *b* 1918: *m* 1st, 1938, Lt-Cdr Alexander Arthur Wyndham Baker, RN, who *d* 1969; 2ndly, 1971, William Henry Guilland Stenson, and has issue living (by 1st *m*), Mark Alexander (The Old School, Fyfield, Abingdon, Oxon), *b* 1940; *ed* Ch Ch, Oxford (MA): *m* 1964, Meriel, da of Capt Edward Hugh Frederick Chetwynd-Talbot, MBE (*see* E Shrewsbury, colls), and has issue living, Alexander Duncan *b* 1968, Miranda Gavrelle *b* 1970, — Gavin Jeremy, *b* 1944: *m* 1971, Joanna Gwendoline, da of Gp Capt G. B. Bell, RAF.

Issue of late Leslie Hay Macnaghten, *b* 1875, *d* 1950: *m* 1906, Hilda Mary Ethelind who *d* 1973, da of late Rev Jocelyn Barnes, V of St Breage, Cornwall:—
Geoffrey Leslie (31 Chelsea Court, 95 Elm Park Gdns, SW10 9QW), *b* 1909; *ed* Malvern Coll; 1939-45 War as Fl-Lt RAFVR; late Imp Cancer Research Fund: *m* 1937, Hilary Marriott, who *d* 1989, da of late T. A. Marriott Castle, and has issue living, Jennifer Rosemary, *b* 1939: *m* 1968, David Guthrie Mattinson, and has issue living, John *b* 1974, Michelle *b* 1966, — Sarah Lynne, *b* 1954. ——— Douglas Melville (Hill Brow, Beacon Hill Rd, Ewshot, Farnham, Surrey GU10 5DB), *b* 1911; *ed* Wellington Coll; late Spicers Internat Ltd, of Reed House, 82 Piccadilly, W1; 1939-45 War in N Africa and Italy as Maj RASC (Africa star, Italy star, 1939-45 star): *m* 1946, Thecla Isabel, who *d* 1987, twin da of late John Mundell Reid, of Greenock, and has issue living, Lorraine Thecla Ethelind, *b* 1947: *m* 1982, Alastair Ford-Young, and has issue living, Jeremy David *b* 1984, Nicholas James *b* 1985, — Camilla Dawn (The Cottage, Holmwood Place, Ide Hill Rd, Four Elms, Edenbridge, Kent TN8 6NT), *b* 1950: *m* 1971 (*m diss* 1979), Timothy William Whittle; has issue living, Anastasia Isabella *b* 1993.

Grandchildren of late Leslie Hay Macnaghten (ante):—
Issue of late Lieut Cyril Jocelyn Gillichrist Macnaghten, RNVR, *b* 1907, *ka* 1943: *m* 1932, Mary Evelyne, who *d* 1954, da of late G. E. Mullens, of Teddington, Australia:—
Alexander Michael Gillichrist (Jabiru Jetty, 12 Kiap Rd, Yunderup Canals, W Australia 6208), *b* 1940; *ed* Wellington Coll, and at Roy Agricultural Coll, Cirencester; a Member of Commonwealth Inst of Valuers: *m* 1st, 1971 (*m diss* 1975), Vanessa, da of Duncan Charles Beresford-Ord, of Beverley Lodge, Mill Point Rd, S Perth, Aust; 2ndly, 1983, Vanessa Keran, 2nd da of late David Pay, of Palma, 1 Brock Terr, Grange, St Peter Port, Guernsey, CI. ——— Angela Kay, *b* 1935: *m* 1960, John Woodward, of High House, Scopwick, Lincs LN4 3PA, and has issue living, Andrew St John, *b* 1965, — Sarah Mary, *b* 1963.

Grandchildren of late Sir Henry Pelham Wentworth Macnaghten, elder son of late Rev Henry Alexander Macnaghten, 5th son of late Elliot Macnaghten (*b* 1807) (ante):—
Issue of late Capt Angus David Henry Macnaghten, *b* 1923, *d* 1988: *m* 1952, Sally, who *d* 1991, only child of late Edmund Hannay Watts, of Ashfields, Great Canfield, Essex:—
David Edmund, *b* 1954; *ed* Stowe. ——— Stuart Ben (Ashfields, Hole Lane, Bentley, Farnham, Surrey GU10 5LT), *b* 1957: *m* 1st, 1988, Joanna Crittall; 2ndly, 1993, Mrs Emma Monaghan (*née* Majdalany), and has issue living (by 1st *m*), Ben Henry, *b* 1989. ——— Patrick Henry (Sodston House Farm, Narberth, Dyfed SA67 8HB), *b* 1959: *m* 1986, Pamela Jane, yr da of late S/Ldr K. J. White, of Skellingthorpe, Lincs, and has issue living, Sam Anthony Angus *b* 1988, Jack Donnelly *b* 1990, Francesca Alice *b* 1987.

Adopted children of late Robin Donnelly Macnaghten, *b* 1927, *b* 1999: *m* 1961, Petronella Anne (Prospect House, Tisbury, Wilts SP3 6QQ), da of Lt-Col A. T. T. Card, of The Old Vicarage, Holt, Wimborne, Dorset:—
Alexander Hugh, *b* 1965: *m* 1994, Gillian, da of Ronald Law, of Dundee. ——— James Donnelly, *b* 1969. ——— Frances Bridget, *b* 1967: *m* 1990, Trevor William Jolley, yr son of Rev Arthur Jolley, of Boston, Lincs, and has issue living, Hannah, *b* 1992, — Laura, *b* 1994.

Adoptive granddaughter of late Capt Angus Charles Rowley Steuart Macnaghten, Lieut Black Watch (Royal Highlanders), only son of late Sir Steuart Macnaghten, 6th son of 1st baronet:—
Adopted da of late Maj Angus Derek Iain Jacques Macnaghten, *b* 1914, *d* 1992: *m* 1957, Daphne, who *d* 1984, only da of late Horace Nettleship Soper, of 15 Stanley Crescent, W11:—
Fiona, *b* 1962: *m* 1990, Martin K. Asquith, only son of late E. Asquith, of Blewbury, Oxon, and has issue living, Eleanor Daphne, *b* 1993, — Imogen Muriel, *b* 1997.

The family of Macnaghten is of great antiquity in the Western Highlands. In 1267, Alexander III granted to Gillichrist Macnaghten and his heirs the custody of the castle and island of Fraocheilean, on condition that he should rebuild it, and keep it fit for the reception of the king whenever he should visit it. His great-grandson Duncan, was one of the band that accompanied James Douglas in his attempt to deposit the heart of Robert Bruce at Jerusalem. The 1st baronet, Sir Francis, a Judge of the Supreme Court of Madras 1809-15, and of Calcutta 1815-25, assumed the additional surname and arms of Workman by Roy licence 1809. The 4th baronet, Rt Hon Sir Edward, GCB, GCMG, was MP for co Antrim (*C*) 1880-85, and for Antrim co, N Div 1885-87 when he became a Lord of Appeal in Ordinary, with title of *Baron Macnaghten* (Life Peerage). The 6th baronet, Sir Edward Henry Macnaghten, Lieut Black Watch (Royal Highlanders), was *ka* July 1916, and his yr brother, Sir Arthur Douglas Macnaghten, 7th baronet, Lieut Rifle Brig, was also *ka* Sept 1916.

Macpherson-Grant, see Grant.

MACREADY (UK) 1923, of Cheltenham, co Gloucester

Sir NEVIL JOHN WILFRID MACREADY, CBE, 3rd *Baronet*; *b* 7 Sept 1921; *s* his father, *Lieut-Gen Sir* GORDON NEVIL, KBE, CB, CMG, DSO, MC, 1956; *ed* Cheltenham and St John's Coll, Oxford (MA); Man Dir of Mobil Oil Co, Ltd 1975-85; Chm Crafts Council 1984-91; Chm Horseracing Advisory Council 1986-93; Dep Chm British Horseracing Bd 1993-95; 1939-45 War as Capt RA (despatches); CBE (Civil) 1982: *m* 1949, Mary, only da of late Sir (John) Donald Balfour Fergusson, GCB, and has issue.

Arms – Argent, on a chevron azure between three leopard's faces gules, two swords, the points in saltire proper, pommels and hilts or. **Crest** – On a wreath of the colours, in front of two swords points upwards in saltire proper, pommels and hilts or, a cubit arm also proper, grasping a snake vert.
Residence – The White House, Odiham, Hants RG29 1LG. *Clubs* – Boodles, Jockey (Paris).

SON LIVING

CHARLES NEVIL, *b* 19 May 1955: *m* 1981 (*m diss* 1994), Lorraine, da of Brian McAdam, of Connah's Quay, Deeside, Clwyd, and has issue living, James Nevil *b* 26 Nov 1982, — Laura Mary, *b* 1984.

DAUGHTERS LIVING

Caroline Elisabeth, *b* 1950: *m* 1978, Clive F Tucker, of Whitewold House, Woldingham, Surrey, and has issue living, two das. —— Sarah Diana Mary, *b* 1953. —— Anna Louise, *b* 1963.

The 1st baronet, Gen Rt Hon Sir (Cecil Frederick) Nevil Macready, GCMG, KCB (son of William Charles Macready, actor), served in Egyptian Expedition 1882, S Africa 1899-1902, and European War 1914-18 as AG (KCMG, GCMG), and was Commr of Metropolitan Police 1918-20, and Com-in-Ch of Troops, Ireland 1920-22. The 2nd baronet, Lieut-Gen Sir Gordon Nevil Macready, KBE, CB, CMG, DSO, MC, was Col Comdt RE Assist Ch of Imperial Gen Staff, War Office 1940-2, Ch of British Army Staff, Washington, USA 1942-6, Regional Commr, Hanover 1946-7, British Chm of Bipartite Economic Control Office in Germany 1947-8, Regional Commr, N Rhine-Westphalia 1948-9, and Economic Advisor to United Kingdom High Commr 1949-51.

MACTAGGART (UK) 1938, of King's Park, City of Glasgow

Sir JOHN AULD MACTAGGART, 4th *Baronet*; *b* 21 Jan 1951; *s* his father, *Sir* IAN AULD, 1987; *ed* Shrewsbury, and Trin Coll, Camb (MA): *m* 1st, 1977 (*m diss* 1990), Patricia, yst da of late Maj Harry Alastair Gordon, MC (*see* E Wavell); 2ndly, 1991, Caroline, yst da of Eric Charles Williams, of Fair Acre, 20 Meadway, Esher, Surrey, and has issue by 2nd *m*.

𝕬rms – Argent, on a bend sable between two owls proper, three escallop shells or. 𝕮rest – A tower proper masoned sable, windows and port gules.

SONS LIVING (*By 2nd marriage*)

JACK AULD, *b* 11 Sept 1993. —— Sholto Auld, *b* 1996.

DAUGHTER LIVING (*By 2nd marriage*)

Kinvara May, *b* 1992.

BROTHER LIVING

Philip Auld, *b* 1956: *m* 1978, Frances, only da of late Christy George Peters, of New York, USA.

SISTERS LIVING

Jane Lindsay MACTAGGART, *b* 1949; has resumed the surname of Mactaggart: *m* 1974 (*m diss* 1978), Keith Douglas Henry Baines. *Residence* – Ardilistry, Southdown, Wanborough, nr Swindon, Wilts SN4 0DB. —— Fiona Margaret, MP, *b* 1953; MP (*Lab*) Slough since 1997; PPS to Rt Hon Chris Smith. *Residence* – 61 Taybridge Rd, SW11 5PX.

UNCLE LIVING (*son of 2nd Baronet*)

Alastair Auld (Sandy), *b* 1928; *ed* Harvard Univ (BA, MBA); late Lieut (P) RCNR: *m* 1959, Cecile Macy, da of Josiah M. Erickson, of Greenwich, Conn, USA, and has issue living, Alastair Auld, *b* 1966; *ed* Harvard Univ (BA, MBA), — Mara Macy, *b* 1963, — Fiona Osborn, *b* 1964. *Address* – PO Box 3160, Edmonton, Alberta, Canada.

COLLATERAL BRANCH LIVING

Issue of late Neil Auld Mctaggart, late Capt RE, 2nd son of 2nd baronet, *b* 1925, *d* 1999: *m* 1st, 1953, Sheila, who *d* 1990, da of Hon Herbert A. McKinney, of Nassau, Bahamas; 2ndly, 1994, Betty Jane (PO Box EE16979, Nassau, Bahamas), only da of late Lucius E. Peterson, of NJ, USA:—
(By 1st *m*) Neil Auld, *b* 1959. —— Andrew Auld, *b* 1962: *m* 1989, Barbara ......, and has issue living, Molly Mae, *b* 199—, — Emma McKinney, *b* 199—. —— Ann Elizabeth, *b* 1955: *m* 1995, James Pleydell-Bouverie, and has issue (*see* E Radnor, colls). —— Robin, *b* 1957: *m* 1981, Theodore Brent Symonette, and has issue living, Andrew Brent, *b* 1990, — Islay Robin, *b* 1985, — Julia Elizabeth, *b* 1987. —— Tara, *b* 1960.

The 1st baronet, Sir John Auld Mactaggart (son of late Neil Mactaggart of Glasgow), was a Housing Expert, and Chm of Western Heritable Investment Co, Ltd, of Glasgow, London, and Canada. He presented King's Park to City of Glasgow. The 2nd baronet, Sir John (Jack Auld) Mactaggart was for many years Managing Dir of Mactaggart & Mickel Ltd, builders and estate developers, of Glasgow and Edinburgh. Sir Ian Mactaggart, 3rd Bt, was chm Soc for Individual Freedom and chm of Western Heritable Investment Co Ltd.

MacTaggart-Stewart, see Stewart.

MADDEN (UK) 1919, of Kells, co Kilkenny

Sir CHARLES EDWARD MADDEN, GCB, 2nd *Baronet*: *b* 15 June 1906; *s* his father, *Adm of the Fleet, Sir* CHARLES EDWARD, GCB, OM, GCVO, KCMG, DCL, LLD, 1935; Adm (ret): Ch of Naval Staff, New Zealand 1953-5, Dep Ch of Naval Personnel 1955-7, Flag Officer, Malta 1957-9, Flag Officer, Flotillas, Home Fleet 1959-60, C-in-C Plymouth 1960-63, and C-in-C Home Fleet, and C-in-C E Atlantic Command (NATO) 1963-65; Chm Roy Nat Mission to Deep Sea Fishermen 1971-81, Trustee National Maritime Museum 1968 (Chm 1972-77), and Vice-Chm Sail Training Assocn 1968-70; Vice-Lieut of Greater London 1969-81; 1939-45 War (despatches twice); *cr* CB (Mil) 1955, KCB (Mil) 1961, GCB (Mil) 1965: *m* 1942, Olive, who *d* 1989, da of late George Winchester Robins, of Caldy, Cheshire and has issue.

Arms – Sable, a falcon with his wings expanded, preying on a mallard all argent, on a chief ermine out of a naval crown between two cross-crosslets gules, from a staff in bend a flag of St George, all proper. **Crest** – On a ducal coronet or a falcon rising argent, holding in his beak a cross-crosslet fitchée gules.
Residence – 21 Eldon Rd, W8 5PT.

He is stronger who conquers himself

DAUGHTER LIVING

Roseann, *b* 1945: *m* 1972, John Richard Beddington, 3 Pine Forest Rd, Toronto, Ontario M4N 3E6, Canada, and has issue living, James Edward, *b* 1973. — David Paul Madden, *b* 1975.

SISTERS LIVING

Joan, *b* 1912: *m* 1939, Lt-Col Henry Morison Vere Nicoll, DSO, OBE, late RA, of North Field, Manton, Oakham, Rutland, and has issue living, Graham Morison (The Cottage, Church Lane, Somerby, nr Melton Mowbray, Leics), *b* 1940; *ed* Eastbourne Coll; Capt Welsh Gds: *m* 1st, 1965 (*m diss* 1972), Lucinda Marjorie, yr da of Capt Timothy John Gurney, of The White House, nr Buntingford, Herts (*see* de Bathe, Bt, ext); 2ndly, 1972, Jane, da of late Maj Thomas Edward Dealtry Kidd, MBE, RCA (*see* B Beaverbrook, 1985 Edn); 3rdly, 1980, Mrs Jacquelyn Alexander (*née* Bray); 4thly, 1994, Sally Anderton, and has issue living (by 1st *m*), Simon Morison *b* 1968, (by 3rd *m*) Harry Michael *b* 1983, (by 4th *m*) Poppy *b* 1995, Rose *b* 1997, — Kenneth Charles (28 Wallingford Av, W10), *b* 1942; *ed* Marlborough: *m* 1968, Veronica Gillian, da of C. P. Payne, of Cape Town, and has issue living, Alastair Charles *b* 1973, Sara Jane *b* 1971, Georgina Clare *b* 1981, — Adrian Michael (Freynestown Stud, Dunlavin, co Wicklow), *b* 1949; *ed* Marlborough: *m* 1976, Meriel Jane, da of late Capt James McCarthy, of Navan, co Meath, and has issue living, James Henry *b* 1981, Annabel Jane *b* 1979, — Neville Henry (6119 Andrus Rd, Boulder, Colorado 80301, USA), *b* 1954; *ed* Marlborough: *m* 1984, Carrie Virginia, only da of Dr W. Robert Wentz, of 4301 David St, Durham, N Carolina, and has issue living, Alexander Robert *b* 1986, John Morison *b* 1988, Sabrina Fiennes *b* 1993. —— Hope (120 Northumberland Court, Northumberland Rd, Leamington Spa, Warwickshire CV2 6HN), *b* 1914: *m* 1939 (*m diss* 1947), Maj John Henry Beardmore Batten, Royal Fus, and has issue living, Patrick John Beardmore, *b* 1941; *ed* Ampleforth: *m* 1965 (*m diss* 1978), Diana Lyn, da of H. L. Brooke, and has issue living, Annabell Jane Beardmore *b* 1965, Katherine Nicola Beardmore *b* 1968, Sally Elizabeth Beardmore *b* 1970. —— Mary Elizabeth (25 Eldon Rd, W8), *b* 1920: *m* 1st, 1939 (*m diss* 1952), Raymond Guy Vere Nicoll, MC, who *d* 1981; 2ndly, 1952 (*m diss* 1956), Maj Desmond Richard FitzGerald, late Irish Gds; 3rdly, 1969, Cdr Charles Raymond Barrett, RN, who *d* 1970, and has issue living (by 1st *m*) Mark Raymond (24 Eldon Rd, W8), *b* 1942; *ed* Eton: *m* 1968, Virginia Anne, da of late Maj J Christopher Vernon Miller, of Blackwell Grange, Shipton-on-Stour, and has issue living James *b* 1971, Edward *b* (twin) 1971, Claire *b* 1970, Tamara Ann, *b* 1978, — Nigel Edward (The Chantry, Upper Chute, Wilts), *b* 1947; *ed* Eton: *m* 1st, 1969 (*m diss* 1989), (Corinna) Jane, da of late John Goring, CBE, TD (*see* Goring, Bt); 2ndly, 1991, Catharine Euphan, formerly wife of Hon John Edward Malet Vaughan (*see* E Lisburne), and only da of J. P. Waterer, of Coombe Bissett, Salisbury, and has issue living, (by 1st *m*) Adam Nigel *b* 1972, Rory Raymond *b* 1978, Zoe Gabrielle *b* 1971, Corinna Mary *b* 1980, (by 2nd *m*) Frederick John *b* 1993, Siana Irene *b* 1995.

COLLATERAL BRANCH LIVING

Issue of late Lt-Col John Wilmot Madden, MC, RA, yr son of 1st baronet, *b* 1916, *d* 1990: *m* 1941, Beatrice Catherine, JP, who *d* 1989, only da of William Arthur Sievwright, WS, of Moncrieff House, St Andrews, Fife:—
PETER JOHN (Kaymito Cottage, San Carlos Heights, Quiot Pardo, Cebu City, Cebu, Philippines 6000), *b* 10 Sept 1942; *ed* Blundell's, and RMA Sandhurst; late Capt RA: *m* 1993, Mrs Vellie Laput Co, da of Cirilo Laput, and widow of Roberto Co, and has adopted his step-das, Vellie Beth Laput, *b* 1974, — Vellie Michelle Laput, *b* 1976, — Vellie Flor, *b* 1981. —— Charles Jonathan (Katherine Bank, Chapel Green, Earlsferry, Elie, Fife KY9 1AD), *b* 1949; BSc, MTech, MBA: *m* 1980, Kirsteen Victoria Ronald, da of John Ronald Noble, of Wayside, St Andrews, Fife, and has issue living, Samuel Charles John, *b* 1984, — Sophie Emma, *b* 1981. —— Susan Kate, *b* 1946: *m* 1970, Richard Leoline Jenkins, LVO, TD, late Capt 1st The Queen's Dragoon Gds, Lt-Col Royal Wessex Yeomanry (TA) of Delbridge House, Wendy, Royston, Herts SG8 0HT, and has issue living, Sarah Alexandra, *b* 1972, — Caroline Louise Gore, *b* 1973.

The 1st baronet, Adm of the Fleet Sir Charles Edward Madden, GCB, OM, GCVO, KCMG, DCL, LLD (son of Capt J. W. Madden, 4th Regt), served in Egyptian War 1882, and in European War 1914-19 as Ch of Staff and 2nd in Command of Grand Fleet (thanked by Parliament, *cr* a Baronet, granted £10,000), and was Com-in-Ch of Home and Atlantic Fleets 1919-22 and First Sea Lord of the Admiralty and Ch of Naval Staff 1927-30.

MADGE (UK) 1919, of St Margaret's Bay, co Kent (Extinct 1962)

Sir FRANK WILLIAM MADGE, 2nd and last *Baronet.*

DAUGHTERS LIVING OF SECOND BARONET

Pauline, *b* 1928: *m* 1951, Capt Peter Jack Shaw, CBE, RN, and has had issue, Christopher John, *b* 1957, *d* 1992: *m* 1983, Olive Victoria Whales, — Carol Anne, *b* 1952: *m* 1975, Michael William Livett, and has issue living, Ian Michael *b* 1979, Peta-Jane *b* 1977: *m* 1999, Philip Skedgell. *Residence* – Woodside, Rogate, Petersfield, Hants GU31 5DJ. —— Doreen (West Wold House, Prestbury, Cheltenham), *b* 1931: *m* 1954 (*m diss* 1970), Hubert Mark Thursfield, and has had three adopted children, Dominic Simon, *b* 1960: *m* 1985 (*m diss* 1988), Briony Daniell, — Susanna Katherine, *b* 1960, *d* 1989: *m* 1988, André Jacques Ernest Simon, — Sophia Belinda Rachael, *b* 1964. —— June *b* (twin) 1931: *m* 1963, Peter John Ball, MB, BChir, of 11 Nevill Park, Tunbridge Wells TN4 8NN, and has issue living, Martin Hugh, *b* 1964, — Angela Wendy, *b* 1965: *m* 19—, Lawrence Barolsky, and has issue living, Jenna *b* 1993, Nikki *b* 1995, — Louise Clare, *b* 1968: *m* 19—, Ewout Van Manen, and has issue living, Saskia Lucia *b* 1997, Evangeline May *b* 1999, — Juliet Amanda, *b* 1970. —— Gillian, *b* 1937: *m* 1972, Richard William Honner, and has issue living, Emma Sophie *b* 1973; has issue living (by Paul Caples), Sophie Katherine Honner *b* 1992, Josephine Kate *b* 1974.

MAGNUS (UK) 1917, of Tangley Hill, Wonersh, co Surrey.

By faith and work

Sir LAURENCE HENRY PHILIP MAGNUS, 3rd *Baronet*, *b* 24 Sept 1955; *s* his uncle, *Sir* PHILIP MONTEFIORE MAGNUS-ALLCROFT, CBE, 1988; *ed* Eton, and Ch Ch Oxford (MA); Exec Dir Samuel Montagu & Co Ltd 1988-95; Man Dir Investment Banking, Donaldson Lufkin & Jenrette Inc since 1995; Non-Exec Dir FIM Services Ltd since 1997; Memb Finance Cttee, National Trust since 1997: *m* 1983, Jocelyn Mary, eldest da of Robert Henry Foster Stanton, and has issue.

𝔄rms – Bendy of six gules and vert, on a fesse or an open book proper between two martlets sable. 𝔈rest – A magnolia tree flowered proper. *Residence* – Flat 8, 44 Lower Sloane St, SW1W 8BP. *Club* – Brooks's

SONS LIVING

THOMAS HENRY PHILIP, *b* 30 Sept 1985. —— Edmund Robert Hilary, *b* 1991.

DAUGHTER LIVING

Iona Alexandra, *b* 1988.

SISTER LIVING

Caroline Anne (Stokesay Court, Onibury, Shropshire SY7 9BD), *b* 1951; *ed* Benenden.

AUNTS LIVING (*sisters of 2nd baronet*)

Jessie Dora (44 Burton Court, Chelsea, SW3): *m* 1935, David Hugh Sandell, MD, FRCS, who *d* 19—, and has issue living, Robert Laurie (56 Dale St, Chiswick, W4 2BZ) *b* 1938; *ed* Eton, and Ch Ch, Oxford: *m* 1969 (*m diss* 1991), Stephanie Getz, and has issue living, Adam Jonathan William *b* 1972, Alexandra Jessica Laurie *b* 1975, — Jenifer Celia Emily (Fornham Court, Fornham St Martin, Bury St Edmunds, Suffolk), *b* 1936; Bar Lincoln's Inn 1958; LSE: *m* 1962, Nicholas Bridges-Adams, Recorder of Crown Court, who *d* 1998. —— Ruth Emily (129 Rivermead Court, Ranelagh Gdns, SW6 3SD): *m* 1946, as his 2nd wife, Denzil Charles Sebag-Montefiore, who *d* 1996, and has issue living, Charles Adam Laurie (21 Hazlewell Rd, SW15 6LT; *Clubs* – Brooks's, Beefsteak) *b* 1949: *ed* Eton, and St Andrews Univ; FSA 1995: *m* 1979, Pamela Mary Diana, yr da of late Archibald Tennant (*see* Glenconner, B, colls), and has issue living, Archibald Edward Charles *b* 1987, Elizabeth Anne *b* 1982, Laura Rose *b* 1984, — Mary Pamela, *b* 1951; Bar Middle Temple 1974: *m* 1973, David Murray Davidson, son of Col Robert St Clair Davidson, of The Manor House, Upham, Hants, and has issue living, Denzil Jonathan Robert *b* 1975, Susanna Mary *b* 1978, Felicity Dora *b* 1982.

MOTHER LIVING

Rosemary Vera Anne, eldest da of late George Henry Masefield, of 88 Chelsea Park Gdns, SW3, and widow of Quentin Berkeley Hurst: *m* 1950, Lt-Col Hilary Barrow Magnus, TD, QC, who *d* 1987, yr son of Laurie Magnus, elder son of Sir Philip Magnus, 1st Bt. *Residence* – Cragmore House, Wye, Kent TN25 5BJ.

The 1st baronet, Sir Philip Magnus, a pioneer of technical education, sat as MP for London Univ (*U*) 1906-22; *s* by his grandson, Sir Philip Montefiore Magnus-Allcroft, CBE, FRSL, FRHistS, biographer and historian, author of *Kitchener* (1950), *Gladstone* (1954), *King Edward The Seventh* (1964), etc; assumed by deed poll 1951 the additional surname of Allcroft.

MAHON (UK) 1819, of Castlegar, co Galway
(Name pronounced "Mahn")

Sir WILLIAM WALTER MAHON, 7th *Baronet*; *b* 4 Dec 1940; *s* his father, *Sir* GEORGE EDWARD JOHN, 1987; *ed* Eton; a member of HM Bodyguard of The Honourable Corps of Gentleman at Arms 1993: *m* 1968, Rosemary Jane, yr da of late Lt-Col Michael Ernest Melvill, OBE, of The Long House, W Linton, Peeblesshire, and has issue.

Arms – Per fesse sable and argent, an ostrich countercharged, in the beak a horseshoe or. Crest – A dexter arm embowed in armour in the hand grasping a sword wavy all proper. *Address* – c/o Guinness Mahon and Co Ltd Private Bank, 2 Gresham St, EC2V 5QP.

SON LIVING

JAMES WILLIAM, *b* 29 Oct 1976.

Moniti meliora sequamur

Having been warned let us follow better things

DAUGHTERS LIVING

Annabel Jane, *b* 1970: *m* 1995, Richard J. Amphlett, son of Philip Amphlett, of Ombersley, Worcs, and has issue living, George Richard Melvill, *b* 1999. —— Lucy Caroline, *b* 1972: *m* 1997, Alexander G. H. Stroud, son of Geoffrey Stroud, of Kensington, and of Mrs Shiona Johnstone, of Holland Park.

BROTHER LIVING

Timothy Gilbert, *b* 1947; *ed* Crookham Court, Newbury: *m* 1971, Penelope Telfer, elder da of Maj Thomas B McDowell, of St Thomas, Rathfarnham, co Dublin, and has issue living, Rupert Thomas George, *b* 1974, — Myles Francis James, *b* 1980, — Antonia Margaret Evelyn, *b* 1976.

SISTER LIVING

Jane Evelyn, *b* 1944: *m* 1967 (*m diss* 1978), Peter Alec Charles Moore, and has issue living, Alannah Katharine, *b* 1969. *Residence* – 12 Althorp Rd, SW17.

HALF-SISTER LIVING

Sarah Caroline, *b* 1959: *m* 1997, Charles David Montgomery Loane, only son of Simon Folliott Warren Thomas Barton Loane, of Crocknacrieve, co Fermanagh. *Residence* – 133 Westbridge Rd, SW11.

WIDOW LIVING OF SIXTH BARONET

SUZANNE (*Suzanne, Lady Mahon*), da of late Thomas Donnellan, of Pirbright, Surrey: *m* 1958, as his 2nd wife, Sir George Edward John Mahon, 6th Bt, who *d* 1987. *Residence* – 16 St James's Terr, Winchester, Hants SO22 4PP.

COLLATERAL BRANCHES LIVING

Issue of late Luke Bryan Arthur DILLON-MAHON (assumed by deed poll 1966 the surname of Dillon-Mahon), yst son of 5th baronet, *b* 1917, *d* 1997: *m* 1949, Audrey Doreen (Cooleen, Moycullen, co Galway), only da of late Ernest John Vipond, MBE, MC:—
Robert John George DILLON-MAHON (Chez Madame Deltrull, 17 rue du Ribas, 06620 Bar-sur-Loup, France), *b* 1954: *m* 1983 (*m diss* 1999), Caroline Mary, yst da of late Hon John Forbes (*see* E Granard), and formerly wife of Dominick Charles Hamilton, and has issue living, Luke John, *b* 1984. —— Susan, *b* 1950: *m* 1978, George Wilmer Hatfeild Gossip, of Tullanisk, Birr, co Offaly, and has issue living, William Luke George Hatfeild, *b* 1983.

Issue of late John FitzGerald Mahon, 4th son of 4th baronet, *b* 1858, *d* 1942: *m* 1898, Lady Alice Evelyn Browne, who *d* 1970, da of 5th Marquess of Sligo:—
Sir (John) Denis, CBE, *b* 1910; *ed* Eton, and Ch Ch, Oxford (MA); Hon DLitt Newcastle 1969, Oxford 1994; Art Historian and FBA, a Trustee of National Gallery 1957-64, and 1966-73, medal for Benemeriti della Cultura, Italy 1957, and Accademico d'Onore, Clementine Acad of Bologna 1964, and Serena Medal for Italian Studies, British Academy 1073; CBE (Civil) 1967. Knt 1986. *Residence* – 33 Cadogan Sq, SW1X 0HU.

Issue of late Edward Mahon, 6th son of 4th baronet, *b* 1862, *d* 1937: *m* 1911, Lilette Caroline Julia, da of late James K. Rebbeck, of Victoria, British Columbia:—
Bryan Edward (2003, 82nd Av SE, Mercer Island, Washington 98040, USA), *b* 1913: *m* 1960, Marolyn Miriam, da of late C. Laverne Smith, MD, of Seattle, Wash, USA, and has issue living, Ross Mackenzie, *b* 1961, — Lilette Elizabeth, *b* 1963.

Sir Ross Mahon 1st Bt, MP for Granard and Ennis, was el son of Ross Mahon of Castlegar (*d* 1788), whose grandfather Capt Bryan Mahon of Castlegar, served in Earl of Clanricarde's Regt of Inf, James II's Army at Battle of the Boyne 1690.

MAINWARING (UK) 1804, of Over Peover, Cheshire (Extinct 1934)
(Name pronounced "Mannaring")

Sir HARRY STAPLETON MAINWARING, 5th and last *Baronet*.

DAUGHTER LIVING OF FIFTH BARONET

Zara Sophie Kathleen Mary, *b* 1917: *m* 1st, 1940 (*m diss* 1949), Capt Hon (Alexander) Ronald George Strutt, Coldm Gds, afterwards 4th Baron Belper; 2ndly, 1949, Peter Victor Ferdinand Cazalet, JP, DL, Welsh Gds (Heron-Maxwell, Bt), who *d* 1973, and has issue living (by 1st *m*) (*see* B Belper), — (by 2nd *m*) Victor Anthony (13 Vicarage Gdns, W8 4AH), *b* 1951: *m* 1976, (Mary) Isabel Dorothy, da of late Hon George William ffolkes Dawnay (*see* V Downe, colls), and has issue living, Edward Peter *b* 1981, Catherine Rosemary *b* 1979, Clare Elizabeth *b* 1983, — Anthony Peter, *b* 1953. *Residence* – 26 Wilton Row, SW1.

MAITLAND (UK) 1818, of Clifton, Midlothian

By counsel and courage

Sir CHARLES ALEXANDER MAITLAND, 10th *Baronet*; *b* 3 June 1986; *s* his father, *Sir* RICHARD JOHN, 1994, but his name does not appear on the Official Roll of the Baronetage.

𝕬rms – Or, a lion rampant couped at all joints of the field gules, within a double tressure flory counterflory azure. 𝕮rest – A lion sejant, affrontée gules, ducally crowned or, and holding in his dexter paw a drawn sword proper, pommelled and hilted gold, and in the sinister a fleur-de-lis azure.

SISTER LIVING

Alice Emma, *b* 1983.

UNCLE LIVING (*Son of 8th baronet*)

ROBERT RAMSAY, *b* 14 July 1956: *m* 1984, (Georgina) Claire, yst da of John Drysdale, of Kilrie, Kirkcaldy, Fife, and has issue living, Harry Robert, *b* 1986, — John Richard, *b* 1992, — Cara Claire, *b* 1989, — Anna Victoria, *b* 1991. *Residence* – Dowalty, Crathes, Banchory, Kincardineshire.

AUNT LIVING (*Daughter of 8th baronet*)

Jane Fiona, *b* 1963: *m* 1988, Hugo Peter Haig, son of Anthony Haig, of Laggan, Scaniport, Inverness, and has issue living, Christopher Edward (Kit), *b* 1993, — Archianne Rose, *b* 1992.

GREAT UNCLES LIVING (*Sons of 7th baronet*)

John Ramsay, *b* 1924; formerly Sqdn-Ldr RAF: *m* 1st, 1952 (*m diss* 19—), Nan Margaret, da of late Brig Charles Bannatyne Findlay, CBE, MC; 2ndly, 1968, Kathleen Mary, da of late Vivian Charles Desmond, and has issue living (by 1st *m*), David Ramsay, *b* 1954, — James, *b* 1957: *m* 1987, Sarah Elizabeth, only da of Malcolm Selwyn Shaw, — Jean Findlay, *b* 1959, — (by 2nd *m*), Keith John, *b* 1969. *Residence* – Holly Cottage, Harmony St, Tunbridge Wells, Kent. —— James, *b* 1927: *m* 1959, Mavis Ann, el da of H. J. Kennaway, of Keithock, Brechin, Angus, and has issue living, Alexander Henry, *b* 1964, — Amanda Helen, *b* 1960: *m* 1994, Lt-Col David Limb, yst son of Roy Limb, of Hadley Wood, Herts, — Fiona Ann, *b* (twin) 1960. *Residence* – Clathic, Crieff, Perthshire.

GREAT AUNT LIVING (*Daughter of 7th baronet*)

Helen Florence, *b* 1923: *m* 1952, Col Thomas David Lloyd-Jones, OBE (Reswallie, Forfar, Angus), and has issue living, John Ramsay, *b* 1954: *m* 1982, Henrietta Cicely, only da of Henry Gabriel Richards Pickthorn (*see* Pickthorn, Bt), and has issue living, Alexander Richard Juxon *b* 1986, Lucy Mary Helen *b* 1989, Celia Miranda Charlotte *b* 1992, — Peter Neil, *b* 1956: *m* 1989, Victoria Rees, and has issue living, Frederick *b* 1990, George *b* 1991, — Caroline Margaret, *b* 1961: *m* 1987, Marc Villiers Townsend, son of Reginald Townsend, of Rugby, and has issue living, Emily *b* 1992, Anna *b* 1994.

DAUGHTER LIVING OF SIXTH BARONET

Petronilla Kathleen Florence, *b* 1916: *m* 1951, Malcolm Park, OBE, who *d* 1963, and has issue living, Malcolm John Maitland, *b* 1955: *m* 1982, Nicola Anne Jackson, and has issue living, David Malcolm *b* (twin) 1986, Emma Caroline *b* 1984, Marianne Beatrice *b* 1986. *Residence* – Stour Hill, Sturminster Newton, Dorset DT10 1ED.

WIDOWS LIVING OF EIGHTH AND NINTH BARONETS

LAVENDER MARY JEX (*Lavender, Lady Maitland*) (Mid Dod, Forfar, Angus), yst da of late Francis William Jex Jackson, of Kirkbuddo, Forfar: *m* 1951, Maj Sir Alexander Keith Maitland, 8th Bt, who *d* 1963.

CARINE CELIA ANN, elder da of J. St G. Coldwell, of Somerton, Oxford, and of Mrs B. P. M. Rooney, of Llandovery, Dyfed: *m* 1st, 1981, Sir Richard John Maitland, 9th Bt, who *d* 1994; 2ndly, 1995, John Christopher William Kidd (*see* E Shrewsbury, colls).

COLLATERAL BRANCHES LIVING

Grandchildren of late George Keith Maitland, yr son of George Ramsay Maitland, WS, 2nd son of Alexander Maitland, advocate at Scottish bar, eldest son of 2nd baronet:
Issue of late Angus Charles Marjoribanks Maitland, *b* 1887, *d* 1986: *m* 1923, Mary Brigid, who *d* 1946, da of Thomas O'Callaghan, of Claremorris, co Mayo:—
Rev Keith Marjoribanks, *b* 1925; a priest at Downside Abbey. —— Natalie Mary (15 Bellevue, Clifton, Bristol BS8 1DB), *b* 1924: *m* 1980, Joseph Bibbing, who *d* 1989. —— Joan Mary, *b* 1928: *m* 1952, Noel Martin Fisher, DSC, of 37A Lyncombe Hill, Bath BAZ 4PQ, and has issue living, Dominic Mayne, *b* 1953, — Andrew Martin, *b* 1954, — Aidan Hugh, *b* 1959, — Paul Gregory, *b* 1960, — Mary Brigid, *b* 1956, — Catharine Mary, *b* 1957, — Lucy Elizabeth, *b* 1963, — Anna Claire, *b* 1964, — Jane Frances, *b* 1965. —— Angela Helena Mary, *b* 1933: *m* 1959, Raymond Geoffrey Daniel, of the Willow, Willows Vale, Frome, Somerset, and has issue living, Charles Martin, *b* 1961, — Francis Keith, *b* 1965, — Brigid Mary, *b* 1959, — Helen Margaret, *b* 1963.

Grandchildren of late Lieut-Col Reginald Charles Frederick Maitland, DSO, only son of late Maj Reginald Paynter Maitland, grandson of Gen Frederick Maitland, 4th son of 1st baronet:—
Issue of late Alastair Reginald Maitland, *b* 1915, *d* 1990: *m* 1947, Mary (Gables, Linden Chase, Uckfield, Sussex), da of late Campbell Mansbridge:—
Iain David Paynter, *b* 1954: *m* 1981, Robyn-Jane Nicholl, and has issue living, James Alastair Patrick, *b* 1985, — Fiona Jane, *b* 1982. —— Andrew Reginald Campbell, *b* 1963: *m* 1994, Vivien Pemberton. —— Penelope Mary, *b* 1948: *m* 1972, Peter Bayes, who *d* 1987, and has issue living, Claire, *b* 1975. —— Carolyn Judith, *b* 1951: *m* 1976, John McArthur, and has issue living, Stephen, *b* 1977, — Christopher, *b* 1979, — David *b* 1983.

Issue of late Maj Geoffrey Ernald Maitland, *b* 1918, *d* 1992: *m* 1st, 1945 (*m diss* 1967), Diana Joy, da of Maj James Pridham, RA; 2ndly, 1971 (*m diss* 1980), Mrs Eleanor Williamson, da of James Salter:—
(By 1st *m*) Alastair Charles Frederick, *b* 1958. —— Diana Jane, *b* 1945: *m* 1967, Michael J. Brooke, of Woods Farm, Burrow Hill, Chobham, Surrey GU24 8BY, and has issue living, Mark, *b* 1969, — James, *b* 1971, — Christopher, *b* 1983, — Katie, *b* 1976. —— Patricia Anne, *b* 1947: *m* 1st, 1977 (*m diss* ca 1981-82), Robert Campbell; 2ndly 1991, Richard Law, and has issue living (by 1st *m*) Julian, *b* 1980, — (by 2nd *m*) David, *b* 1992. —— Susan Mary, *b* 1952: *m* 1991, Patrick Blackwell, of PO Box 438, Woollahra, NSW 2025, Aust. —— (Sarah Gillian) Gabrielle, *b* 1954: *m* 1987, David Hylton Briggs, of 34 Cadogan Place, SW1X 9RX, eldest son of W/Cdr G. H. Briggs, of The Farmhouse, Strettington, Sussex, and has issue living, Thomas, *b* 1990, — Lucy *b* 1992. —— (By 2nd *m*) Alexander James, *b* 1971.

The 1st baronet, Gen Hon Sir Alexander Maitland, Col of the 49th Foot, was 5th son of the 6th Earl of Lauderdale; the 2nd baronet assumed the additional surname of Gibson, and the 3rd baronet, Sir Alexander Charles Maitland, assumed the additional surname of Ramsay before those of Gibson and Maitland. The 7th baronet, Sir George Ramsay Maitland, DSO, was Lt-Col 14th Jat Lancers and a Member of Queen's Body Guard for Scotland (Roy Co of Archers).

RAMSAY-STEEL-MAITLAND (UK) 1917, of Sauchie, co Stirling (Extinct 1965)

Sir KEITH RICHARD FELIX RAMSAY-STEEL-MAITLAND, 3rd and last *Baronet*.

DAUGHTER LIVING OF SECOND BARONET

Gay, *b* 1929: *m* 1949, Lt-Com Roger Martin Stafford, RN (ret), who *d* 1990. *Residence* – Sauchiburn House, Stirling.

WIDOW LIVING OF SECOND BARONET

MATILDA BRENDA (*Lady Ramsay-Steel-Maitland*), da of late Thomas Doughty, of Coalbrookdale: *m* 1942, as his 2nd wife, Sir (Arthur) James (Drummond) Ramsay-Steel-Maitland, 2nd baronet, who *d* 1960. *Residence* – Castle Gogar, Edinburgh 12.

MAKINS (UK) 1903, of Rotherfield Court, Henley-on-Thames, co Oxford

Sir PAUL VIVIAN MAKINS, 4th *Baronet*; *b* 12 Nov 1913; *s* his brother, *Lt-Col Sir* WILLIAM VIVIAN, 1969; *ed* Eton, and Trin Coll, Camb (MA); Maj (ret) Welsh Guards; Knt of Magistral Grace of Order of Malta; 1939-45 War: *m* 1945, Maisie, who *d* 1986, da of Maj Oswald Henry Pedley, of Gibraltar, and widow of Maj Cecil Leander John Bowen.

Arms – Argent, on a fesse embattled counter embattled gules, between in chief two falcons proper belled or, and in base a lion's face of the second, an annulet or between two bezants. Crest – A dexter arm embowed in armour proper encircled by an annulet or and holding a flag staff, therefrom flowing a banner argent charged with a lion's face gules.
Address – Casas Cortijo 135, Sotogrande, Provincia de Cadiz, Spain.

DAUGHTER LIVING OF THIRD BARONET

Carolyn Diana Mary, *b* 1933: *m* 1956, LeRoy Tuttle Morgan, and has issue living, Diana Vivian, *b* 1958, — Teresa Adelaide, *b* 1959, — Eleanora Carroll, *b* 1961, — Cecilia Hay, *b* 1964, — Maria Abell (twin) *b* 1964, — Olivia Dudley, *b* 1972. *Residence* – 25214 Peachtree Rd, Clarksburg, Md 20871-9101, USA.

In lumine luce
Shine thou in the light

The 1st baronet, Sir William Thomas, sat as MP for S Essex 1874-85, SE Essex 1885-86, and Walthamstow, 1886-92. 1st Baron Sherfield (*cr* 1964) is a grandson of Henry Thomas Makins, Bar-at-law, yr brother of 1st baronet.

MALCOLM (NS) 1665, of Balbedie and Innertiel, co Fife

Ardua tendo
Attempt difficult things

Sir JAMES WILLIAM THOMAS ALEXANDER MALCOLM, 12th *Baronet*; elder son of late Lt-Col Arthur William Alexander Malcolm, CVO, only surv son of late Maj Charles Edward Malcolm, brother of 9th baronet; *b* 15 May 1930; *s* his kinsman, *Maj Sir* DAVID PETER MICHAEL, 1995; *ed* Eton, and RMA Sandhurst; late Col Welsh Guards; Appeals Dir British Heart Foundation 1976-89; High Sheriff Surrey 1991-92: *m* 1955, Gillian Heather, only child of Elton Henry Humpherus, of Kennards, Leigh, Kent, and has issue.

Arms – Or a saltire azure between four stags' heads couped gules, a bordure indented of the third. Crest – A pyramid encircled by a laurel wreath proper.
Residence – Thatchers Barn, Worplesdon, Guildford, Surrey GU3 3RD. *Clubs* – MCC, Royal St George's, Berkshire Golf.

Dei dono sum quod sum
By the grace of God I am what I am

SONS LIVING

ALEXANDER JAMES ELTON, *b* 30 Aug 1956; *ed* Eton, and RMA Sandhurst; Lt-Col Welsh Guards: *m* 1982, Virginia Elizabeth, da of late Capt Alfred Coxon, RN, and has issue living, Edward Alexander Humpherus, *b* 28 Sept 1984, — Thomas William, *b* 1990, — Camilla Petronell, *b* 1987. *Address* – c/o RHQ Welsh Guards, Wellington Barracks, Birdcage Walk, SW1E 6HQ. *Clubs* – Cavalry and Guards', MCC. —— Robin William, *b* 1958; *ed* Eton, and RMA Sandhurst; late Capt Welsh Guards.

DAUGHTERS LIVING

Julia Mary, *b* 1960: *m* 1984, Julian Neville Guy Spurling, son of Jeremy Michael Lovett Spurling, and has issue living, Jonathan Henry William, *b* 1987, — Frederic James Lovett, *b* 1989, — Harry Alexander, *b* 1992. *Residence* – Brow Cottage, Furneux Pelham, nr Buntingford, Herts SG9 0JY. —— Annabel Heather, *b* 1967: *m* 1993, Capt Patrick Cameron Doiran Toyne Sewell, son of Maj-Gen Timothy Patrick Toyne Sewell, and has issue living, Charles Alexander, *b* 1997.

BROTHER LIVING

Ian William Ruthven, *b* 1933; *ed* Eton, and Magdalene Coll, Camb (BA 1957, MA 1960): *m* 1963, Mrs Christie Moss, only da of late John Bramley, of Bloemfontein, S Africa, and has issue living, Robert van Riet, *b* 1965; *ed* Cranbrook Sch, and St Paul's Coll, Sydney Univ (BEcon 1986): *m* 1993, Susan, da of late Thomas Henry Cass, of Ruislip, Middx, — William David, *b* 1967; *ed* Cranbrook Sch, and St Paul's Coll, Sydney Univ (BA 1988), — John Alexander, *b* 1968; *ed* Cranbrook Sch, and St Paul's Coll, Sydney Univ (BEcon 1989). *Residence* – 76 Adelaide St, Woollahra, Sydney, NSW 2025, Australia.

DAUGHTER LIVING OF ELEVENTH BARONET

Fiona Alice Jane, *b* 1962: *m* 1992, Oliver George Stephenson, and has issue (*see* Stephenson, Bt, colls). *Residence* – Lomberdale Hall, Middleton by Youlgreave, Bakewell, Derbyshire DE45 1LU.

DAUGHTERS LIVING OF TENTH BARONET

(Margaret) Jane Venetia, *b* 1923; formerly 3rd Officer WRNS, served in 1939-45 War: *m* 1945, Lt-Cmdr Christopher Robert Vesey Holt, CVO, VRD, late RNVR, who *d* 1997, and has issue living, Nicholas James Vesey (84 Manor Fields, Horsham, W Sussex RH13 6SB), *b* 1947; *ed* Eton, — Ianthe Evelyn Vesey, *b* 1950: *m* 1975, Rodney Charles Hudson, of 49 Eastwood Rd, Dunkeld, Johannesburg 2196, S Africa, and has issue living, Julian Charles *b* 1979; *ed* Hilton Coll, Natal, Felicity Jane *b* 1983. *Residence* – Westbury Manor, W Meon, Petersfield, Hants. ——— Morar Catherine Beryl, *b* 1929: *m* 1959, as his 2nd wife, Oswald Whitwell Ainscough, late Maj King's (Liverpool) Regt, who *d* 1995. *Residence* – Abbots Brow, Kirkby Lonsdale, Lancs.

WIDOW LIVING OF TENTH BARONET

KATHLEEN (*Kathleen, Lady Malcolm*), da of late Cmdr George Jonathan Gawthorne, RN, and formerly wife of James Melvin: *m* 1947, as his 2nd wife, Maj Sir Michael Albert James Malcolm, 10th Bt, who *d* 1976. *Residence* – Flat 1, 11 Onslow Sq, SW7.

WIDOW LIVING OF ELEVENTH BARONET

HERMIONE (*Hermione, Lady Malcolm*), elder da of Sir David George Home, 13th Bt: *m* 1959, Maj Sir David Peter Michael Malcolm, 11th Bt, who *d* 1995. *Residence* – Whiteholm, Whim Rd, Gullane, E Lothian EH31 2BD.

COLLATERAL BRANCH LIVING

Issue of late Maj Alexander Ernest William Malcolm, TD, RA (TA), yr son of 9th baronet, *b* 1900, *d* 1958: *m* 1st, 1925, Olive Leah, yst da of Walter Scott, of Sydney, NSW; 2ndly, 1941, Mrs Sybil Mary Grenfell (who *m* 3rdly, 1963, Aubrey Vernon), da of late Hugh Peacock, of Greatford Hall, Stamford:— (By 2nd *m*) Alexandra Mary, *b* 1943: *m* (Jan) 1964, Simon Ward, actor, and has issue living, Sophie Anna, *b* (Dec) 1964; actress: *m* 1988, Paul Hobson, son of late George Hobson, and has issue living, Nathaniel *b* 1989, Joshua *b* 1992, — Claudia Thomasina, *b* 1969: *m* 1995, Benedick Devlin, son of Hon Gilpatrick Devlin (*see* B Devlin, ext), — Kitty Teresa Juniper, *b* 1976. *Residence* – 13a Lawn Rd, NW3 2XS.

John Malcolm, of Balbedie, Lochore, and Innertiel, *b* 1611, was appointed Chamberlain of Fife 1641, and Member of Scottish Parliament 1650; he *d* 1692, having *m* Margaret, who *d* 1698, aged 72, da of Sir Michael Arnot, of that Ilk, and had six sons, of whom John, the el, was created a Baronet of Nova Scotia 1665, while the third son, Alexander, became a Senator of the College of Justice with the title of Lord Lochore 1687, and Lord Justice-Clerk and a Privy Councillor 1688; James fourth son, fought at Killicrankie and was attainted. The 1st baronet was succeeded by his el son John, 2nd baronet, who was followed in the Baronetcy by his third son, Michael, served heir as 3rd baronet in 1784. The 4th baronet was James (Lieut-Gov of Sheerness), who had been served heir-general to his father, Robert Malcolm, of Grange, 2nd son of 1st baronet, in 1795. At the death of Sir James, Lieut-Gov of Sheerness, in 1805, the dignity passed to John, 8th child of Michael Malcolm, 3rd son of 1st baronet, at whose decease, in 1816, his el son, Michael, was served heir to his father, and in 1828 his son, John, as 7th baronet. In 1886 Sir James, son of James Malcolm, 2nd son of 5th baronet, was served heir to his cousin, as 8th baronet. At his death in 1901 the Baronetcy passed to his kinsman, Sir James William Malcolm, 9th Bt, who in 1897 had recorded the pedigree in the Lyon Office. The 10th baronet, Maj Sir Michael Albert James Malcolm, Scots Gds was a Member of Standing Council of The Baronetage 1954-76. The 11th baronet, Maj Sir David Peter Michael Malcolm, Scots Gds, was a Member of Royal Company of Archers (Queen's Body Guard for Scotland), and a Council Member of London Stock Exchange.

MALET (GB) 1791, of Wilbury, Wiltshire
(Name pronounced "Mallet")

My strength is from on high

Sir HARRY DOUGLAS ST LO MALET, 9th *Baronet*; *b* 26 Oct 1936; *s* his father, *Col Sir* EDWARD WILLIAM ST LO, OBE, 1990; *ed* Downside, and Trin Coll, Oxford (BA); late Lt Queen's Royal Irish Hussars; JP: *m* 1967, Julia Gresley, da of Charles Harper, of 54 Irvine St, Peppermint Grove, Perth W Australia, and has issue.

Arms – Azure, three escallops or. **Crest** – Out of a ducal coronet or, an heraldic tiger's head issuant ermine.
Address – Wrestwood, RMB 184, Boyup Brook, WA 6244, Australia.

SON LIVING

CHARLES EDWARD ST LO, *b* 30 Aug 1970; *ed* Blundell's; commd'd Queen's Royal Irish Hussars 1990: *m* 1997, Rachel L., da of Timothy P. S. Cane, of Kirby Bedon, Norfolk, and has issue living, Tabitha Louise, *b* 1999.

SISTERS LIVING

Mary Jane St Lo, *b* 1938; has Nat Diploma of Design, and Oxford Univ Certificate of Fine Art; *m* 1970, Robert Pickering, of 101 North Rd, Bassendean, Perth, W Aust, and has issue living, Samuel Thomas Carrigton St Lo, *b* 1970, — William Benedict St Lo, *b* 1972. —— Micaela Elizabeth Benedicta *b* 1939; has Oxford Univ Certificate of Fine Art; High Sheriff of Somerset 1998-99: *m* 1963, Maj-Gen Edwin Beckett, CB, MBE, Prince of Wales' Own Regt, and has issue living, Simon Turlo, *b* 1965, — Alexander Crispin, *b* 1979, — Thomas James, *b* 1980, — Diana Vola, *b* 1964.

AUNT LIVING (*Daughter of 7th baronet*)

Helen Agnes St Lo, *b* 1911: *m* 1934, Alan Douglas Stoddart, and has issue living, Alan Malet, *b* 1936: *m* 1961, Sally Noryl Harknes, and has issue living, Mark Alan *b* 1962, Benjamin Noryl *b* 1966, Emma Jane *b* 1964, Charlotte Helen *b* 1967, — Robert Douglas, *b* 1939: *m* 1967, Barbara Palmer, and has issue living, Timothy Robin *b* 1972, Rachel Louise *b* 1970, — Murray Laurence, *b* 1942: *m* 1970, Caroline Anne Windham, and has issue living, Craig Bowring *b* 1972, Duncan Laurence *b* 1974, — Gareth Bowring (Leadburn House, Leadburn, West Linton, Peeblesshire EH46 7BE), *b* 1947: *m* 1975, Lorna Christine Allan, yst da of Richard Oliver MacMahon Williams, MBE, MC, WS (*see* Rose, Bt, *cr* 1874, colls), and has had issue, Douglas Oliver Bowring *b* 1988, Sophie Helen *b* 1978, Katherine Anne *b* 1980, Camilla May *b* 1982, Alice *b* and *d* 1986, Clementine Rose *b* 1990, — Mary Lynette St Lo, *b* 1946: *m* 1968, Magnus Charles Mowat, of New Park House, Whitegate, nr Northwich, Cheshire, and has issue living, Charles Patrick Magnus *b* 1969, Alexander John *b* 1970, Hugh Laurence *b* 1973. *Residence* – Middle Halsway, Crowcombe, Taunton, Som. TA4 4BA.

COLLATERAL BRANCHES LIVING

Grandchildren of late Major Guilbert Edward Wyndham Malet, el son of Rev William Wyndham Malet, 3rd son of 1st baronet:—
Issue of late Lieut-Col Alexander Wyndham Malet, Indian Army, MVO, *b* 1886, *d* 1956: *m* 1921, Kathleen Betty, who *d* 1993, da of Brig-Gen Alexander Cadell, Indian Army:—
Richard Wyndham, *b* 1923; late Capt Indian Army; Far East 1941-47; MBIM; in management of tea estates, India and Africa 1947-60; Management Advisory Officer, Rural Development Commission: *m* 1956, Judith Winifred Ferguson, yst da of D. McEwen, of Kirkby Lonsdale, and has had issue, Claire Alexandra, *b* 1965: *m* 1993, Simon Hale, — Sarah Agnes, *b* 1969; *d* 1985 (Sarah Malet Trust Regd Charity No 299769R established in her memory). —— Sylvia Mary Fanshaw, ARCM, LRAM, *b* 1925: *m* 1948, John William Theodore Tapp, and has issue living, Nicholas Charles Theodore, *b* 1952, — Caroline Linda, *b* 1956. *Residence* – Southborough House, Ashcombe Av, Surbiton, Surrey. —— Kathleen Mary, ARCM, LRAM, *b* 1934.

Issue of late Edward Barnabas Wyndham Malet, *b* 1894, *d* 1961: *m* 1st, 1921 (*m diss* 1950), Esther Grace Macdonald, who *d* 1969, da of Rev Gilbert Lyon (formerly V of Cloford, Frome), of Wican Croft, Bishopsteignton, Teignmouth, Devon; 2ndly, 1950, Aileen Nina Mary, who *d* 1981, el da of F. W. Cumming, of Parklands, Bradninch, Devon:—
(By 1st *m*) Michael Edward Guilbert (Knockwood House, Nether Wallop, Stockbridge, Hants), *b* 1922; Maj RA (ret): *m* 1953, Judith Rowley, who *d* 1996, el da of E. Rowley Lewis, of Battledown, Cheltenham, and has issue living, Mark Wyndham (25c Route de la Chapelle, 1212 Grand Lancy, Switzerland), *b* 1956: *m* 1984, Lilyan, da of Capt M. N. Herrera, of Caracas, Venezuela, and has issue living, Barnabas Wyndham *b* 1986, Alexandra Sophie *b* 1988, — James Edward Barnabas, *b* 1964, — (Mary) Pepita, *b* 1954: *m* 1977, Michael O'Kelly Webber, and has issue living, Thomas Edward O'Kelly *b* 1984, Jessica Grace *b* 1982. —— Wendy (4 Church View, Bourton, Gillingham, Dorset), *b* 1926.

Grandchildren of late Major Harold Wyndham Malet, son of late Col Harold Esdaile Malet, son of late Rev William Wyndham Malet (ante):—
Issue of late Capt John Wyndham, *b* 1910, *ka* 1940: *m* 1937, June Rosalind (who *d* 1991, having *m* 2ndly, 1943, Capt Wladyslaw Galica, who *d* 1951), da of late Capt John Broadley Harrison Broadley, of Welton House, Brough, E Yorkshire:—

Greville John Wyndham, OBE (The Walled House, Hatherop, Cirencester, Glos), *b* 1939; *ed* Harrow; Lt-Col R Hussars: *m* 1972 (*m diss* 1993), Hon Margaret Cherry Wigram, el da of 2nd Baron Wigram, and has issue living, Charles Neville Wyndham, *b* 1976, — Henrietta Margaret June, *b* 1978. —— (Leola) Dawn Wyndham, *b* 1938: *m* 1961, Capt John David Graham Nicholson, RHA, son of Gen Sir Cameron Gordon Graham Nicholson, GCB, KBE, DSO, MC, and has issue living, John Andrew Graham, *b* 1964, — Edward Wyndham Graham, *b* 1966, — Davina June, *b* 1962.

    Grandchildren of late Allan Arthur Grenville Malet, son of late Lieut-Col George Grenville Malet, 4th son of 1st baronet:—
Issue of late Col George Edward Grenville Malet, OBE, late RAOC, *b* 1898, *d* 1952: *m* 1st, 1922 (*m diss* 1938), Gwendolen Iliffe (who *m* 2ndly, 1938, Rear-Adm Ernest William Leir, DSO, and *d* 1980), da of Brig-Gen James Aubrey Gibbon, CMG; 2ndly, 1939, Margaret Bell Wright, resumed her former married name of Malet by deed poll, who *m* 2ndly, 1967, Patrick Walsh, JP, who *d* 1980:—
(By 1st *m*) (Baldwin) Hugh Grenville (The Vyne, Blue Anchor, nr Minehead, Som TA24 6JX), *b* 1928; *ed* Wellington Coll, and King's Coll, Camb (MA); PhD (Salford); 8th Army, Italy 1946; Palestine 1947-48 (service medal); Sudan Political Ser 1950-56; author; Pres W S Village History Soc; Lecturer in Local History, Salford Univ since 1973: *m* 1959, Kathleen Patricia, who *d* 1983, da of Arthur Morris, of Whitby, Cheshire, and has issue living, Durand David Grenville, *b* 1965; *ed* St Chad's Coll, Durham; Barrister-at-law, — Jane Phoebe Grenville, *b* 1962. —— Barbara Madeline Anne, *b* 1924; JP for Somerset: *m* 1947, Edward Hugh Michael Counsell, CBE, HM Diplomatic Service (ret), and has issue living, John Aubrey Malet, *b* 1949, — Christopher Anthony Malet, *b* 1952, — Hugh Michael Malet, *b* 1962. —— (By 2nd *m*) Michael Ian Grenville, *b* 1939; *ed* Berkhamsted, and St Andrews Univ (MA); PhD (LSE London): *m* 1st, 1964 (*m diss* 1980), Alison Little; 2ndly, 1980, Jennifer Jones, and has issue living, (by 1st *m*) Iain Martin, *b* 1964, — Saffron Margaret, *b* 1968, — Jonquil May, *b* 1970, — (by 2nd *m*) Emily Helen, *b* 1980. —— Zenobia Margaret Grenville, *b* 1942; *ed* St Anne's Coll, Oxford: *m* 1967, Michael Venner, of Libra, Loders, nr Bridport, Dorset, and has issue living, Miriam Anna, *b* 1969, — Catriona Jeanne, *b* 1979.

    Grandchildren of late Cdr Herbert Rivers Malet, late RNVR, yr son of late Arthur Malet, 5th son of 1st baronet:—
Henry Guy Rivers Malet, *b* 1894, *d* 19—: *m* 1st, 1917, (*m diss* 19—), Olga Muriel, da of James Balfour, of Paignton, Devon; 2ndly, 19—, Tessa West:—
Vyvyan Arthur Rivers, *b* 1927. —— Olga Diana Valentine Rivers, *b* 1925: *m* 1951, F. A. Heilingbrunner. —— Patience Violet Rivers, *b* 1930: *m* 1954 (*m diss* 19—), Leslie G. Walton.

William Malet, founder of this family in England, was a companion of William the Conqueror at Hastings, and probably (according to Sir Anthony Wagner) the only one from whom a male line descent to the present day can be traced. His son, Robert Malet, of Eye, was the first Lord Chamberlain of England, and William Malet, of Curry Mallet, was a Magna Carta Baron. A branch was settled at Enmore, Somerset from the twelfth century to 1681. Sir Baldwin Malet, of St Audries and Poyntington, Somerset, ancestor of this branch, descended from Sir Baldwin Malet, Solicitor Gen to Henry VIII, yr son of Thomas Malet, of Enmore (*d* 1502). A Baronetcy for services during the civil war was conferred by Charles II, on Sir Thomas Malet, of Poyntington, who *d* before the patent passed under the great seal. He was one of the Judges sent to the Tower by Cromwell, from the Court at Maidstone, for refusing to grant a summons against a clergyman who would not give up using the Book of Common Prayer. Sir Charles Warre Malet, was *cr* a Bt, for diplomatic services in India. The 2nd Bt, Sir Alexander, KCB, was Min to the German Confederation 1852-66. The 4th Bt, Rt Hon Sir Edward, GCB, GCMG, PC, was Min to Belgium 1883-84, and Ambassador to Germany 1884-95. The 7th Bt, Lt-Col Sir Harry Charles Malet, DSO, OBE, served in S Africa 1899-1902, and 1914-18 War.

Mallaby-Deeley, see Deeley.

MALLINSON (UK) 1935, of Walthamstow, co Essex

Sir (WILLIAM) JAMES MALLINSON, 5th *Baronet*; *b* 22 April 1970; *s* his father, *Sir* WILLIAM JOHN, 1995; *ed* Eton (King's Scholar), St Peter's Coll, Oxford (BA), School of Oriental and African Studies (MA), and Balliol Coll, Oxford.

Arms – Ermine, three pallets gules, in chief two crescents or, and in base an acorn leaved and slipped proper. Crest – A cubit arm, the hand grasping a stock of a tree, snagged and eradicated proper.
Residence – Rawlings Farm, Cocklebury Lane, Chippenham, Wilts SN15 1RU.

SISTER LIVING

Kate Sophia, *b* 1972; *ed* Edinburgh Univ (BA). *Residence* – 13 Kilmarsh Rd, W6.

AUNT LIVING (*daughter of 3rd baronet by 1st marriage*)

Angela Mary, *b* 1941; MRCS (Eng); LRCP (London); DPM: *m* 1964, Edward Tuppin Scrase, BA, MB, BChir, FFA, RCS, of Prospect Farm, Llanidloes, Powys, and has issue living, Ivan, *b* 1968; *ed* Ch Ch, Oxford (BA), — Aeron Michael, *b* 1980, — Hannah, *b* 1967.

Thence the oak

INDE · QUERCUS

MOTHER LIVING

Rosalind Angela, only da of late Rollo Hoare, TD, of The Dower House, Dogmersfield, Hants (*see* M Bristol, 1955 Edn): *m* 1st, 1968 (*m diss* 1978), William John Mallinson (later Sir William Mallinson, 4th Bt), who *d* 1995; 2ndly, 1996, Dale C. Fishburn. *Residence* – 46 Ravenscourt Rd, W6 OUG.

WIDOW LIVING OF THIRD BARONET

MARGARET (*Lady Mallinson*), BA, MB BS 1953, only da of late Samuel Abraham Bowden, of Torquay, Devon, and formerly wife of Surg-Lieut Ronald Henry Gorrill, RNVR; Foreign Office linguist (GC and CS) 1942-45, Admiralty 1946: *m* 1968, as his 2nd wife, Sir (William) Paul Mallinson, 3rd Bt, who *d* 1989. *Residence* – 25 Wimpole St, W1M 7AD.

COLLATERAL BRANCHES LIVING

Issue of late Stanley Tucker Mallinson, 2nd son of 1st baronet, *b* 1884, *d* 1955: *m* 1919, Dora Selina, who *d* 1960, da of late William B. Burridge, of Boscombe, Hants:—
Anthony William, *b* 1923; *ed* Marlborough, and at Gonville and Caius Coll, Camb (BA and Exhibitioner 1948, LLM 1949); admitted a Solicitor (honours) 1951; formerly Major RA: *m* 1955, Heather Mary, da of late Thomas Arthur Mansfield Gardiner. *Residence* – 21 Cottesmore Court, Stanford Rd, W8 5QN.

Issue of late Col Sir Stuart Sydney Mallinson, CBE, DSO, MC, JP, DL, 3rd son of 1st baronet, *b* 1888; *d* 1981: *m* 1916, Marjorie Gray, CBE, who *d* 1969, da of late Rev Alfred Soothill, Headmaster of Ashville Coll, Harrogate:—
Justin Stuart (Bredy Farm, Burton Bradstock, Bridport, Dorset DT6 4ND), *b* 1923; *ed* Marlborough, and Jesus Coll, Camb; Paul Harris Fell 1987; sometime Capt Gren Gds: *m* 1944, Juliana Beatrice, only da of late Samuel Martin, of St Helens, I of Wight, and has issue living, John Michael Stuart (Lower Millhayes, Hemyock, Cullompton, Devon EX15 3RJ), *b* 1945; *ed* Marlborough Coll, and Reading Univ (BSc Agric): *m* 1968, Elizabeth May, da of John Cloke, MRCVS, of Walsall, Staffs, and has issue living, Jonathan Justin Stuart *b* 1971: *m* 1998, Leann Alyson Llewellyn, Elspeth May Stuart *b* 1974, Jane Marjorie *b* 1979, — Jennifer Jane Stuart, *b* 1949: *m* 1971, Lt-Cdr Nicholas Graham Talbot Harris, RN (ret), and has issue living, Charles Justin Talbot *b* 1983, Antonia Diana Stuart *b* 1975, Francesca Louise Talbot *b* 1979. —— Terence Stuart, CBE (28 Albion St, W2 2AX), *b* 1929; *ed* Marlborough, and Jesus Coll, Camb (MA); DL; CBE (Civil) 1995: *m* 1955, Anne Mary Butler, JP, Lord Mayor of Westminster 1986-87, da of late David Butler Wilson, MC, of Burlington Lodge Alderley Edge, Cheshire, and has issue living, Lawrence Stuart (65 St Michael's St, W2 1QR), *b* 1957, *ed* Marlborough, and Jesus Coll, Camb (MA): *m* 1990, Angela Marie Christine, da of Henry Sulivan, of Weybridge, Surrey and has issue living, Barnaby Henry Stuart *b* 1993, Mathilda Anne Kate *b* 1995, Phoebe Agnes Henrietta *b* 1997, — Michael David Stuart (16 Elvaston Pl, SW7 5QF), *b* 1959; *ed* Marlborough, and Fitzwilliam Coll, Camb (MA), Dip Arch, RIBA: *m* 1987, Helen P. M. (head of Coll of Architecture & Design, Univ of N London), eldest da of Alan Powell, of Cheltenham, Glos, and has issue living, Saul Antony Terence *b* 1996, Rosanna Marjorie Bernice *b* 1989, — Roland Arthur Stuart, *b* 1966; BSc: *m* 1995, Fiona M., twin da of Ian Hunter-Craig, of Reigate, Surrey, — Sheila Mary Anne, *b* 1961; BA: *m* 1988, Nicholas Spencer Charrington, eldest son of Maj Gerald Anthony Charrington, of Layer Marney Tower, Colchester, Essex CO5 9US, and has issue living, John Spencer *b* 1995, Alice Calmeyer *b* 1990, Hannah Mary *b* 1991, Grace Elizabeth *b* 1993.

Grandchildren (by 2nd *m*) of late Maj Lancelot Victor Mallinson, MC, yst son of 1st baronet:—
Issue of late Alastair Mallinson, *b* 1932, *d* 1986: *m* 1955, Rosemary (Rue des Saulniers, 44420 Mesquer, France), da of late Charles Cecil Harvey:—
Guy (23 Avenue Georges Pompidou, 92150 Suresnes, France), *b* 1958. —— Alexandre, *b* 1964. —— Florence, *b* 1962.

The 1st baronet, Sir William Mallinson (son of late John Mallinson, of Forest Gate, E7) was a JP for Essex (Chm of Beacontree Bench). The 2nd baronet, Sir William James, was High Sheriff of Surrey 1933, a DL for the County of Surrey, and JP (Croydon Bench). The 3rd baronet, Sir (William) Paul, was a medical practitioner, Surg Lt Cmdr RNVR, and held the Family Order of Brunei.

MANDER (UK) 1911, of The Mount, Tettenhall, co Stafford

Live well

VIVE · BENE

Sir CHARLES MARCUS MANDER, 3rd *Baronet*; *b* 22 Sept 1921; *s* his father, *Sir* CHARLES ARTHUR, 1951; *ed* Eton, and Trin Coll, Camb; late Capt Coldstream Guards; formerly Dir Mander Bros Ltd, Chm Arlington Securities Ltd, of St James's 1983, and London & Cambridge Investments Ltd; High Sheriff of Staffs 1962-3; European War 1939-45 a Capt Coldstream Guards in Egypt, Italy, and N-W Europe: *m* 1945, Maria Dolores Beatrice, yr da of late Alfred Edmund Brödermann, of Gross Fontenay, Hamburg, Germany, and has issue.

𝔄rms – Gules, on a pile invected erminois, three annulets interlaced, two and one of the field. 𝔄rest – A demi-lion couped ermine holding in the paws two annulets interlaced fessewise gules, between two buffalo horns of the last. *Residence* – Little Barrow, Moreton-in-Marsh, Glos GL56 9DW.

SONS LIVING

(CHARLES) NICHOLAS (Owlpen Manor, Uley, Glos GL11 5BZ) *b* 23 March 1950; *ed* Downside, and Trin Coll, Camb (MA); co-founder of Mander Portman Woodward (private tutors) of Kensington, 1973; dir of publishing and land companies in UK and Spain; Farmer; Member of Lloyd's: *m* 1972, Karin Margareta, yr da of late Gustav Arne Norin, of Stockholm, Sweden, and has issue living, (Charles) Marcus Septimus Gustav, *b* 26 July 1975; *ed* Eton, and Peterhouse, Camb, — Benedict Edward Arthur, *b* 1977; *ed* Eton, and St John's Coll, Camb, — Hugo Richard Theodore, *b* 1981; *ed* Eton, — Fabian Edmund Quintin, *b* 1987, — Sarra Mary, *b* 1973; *ed* St Mary's, Ascot, and Edinburgh Univ. —— Francis Peter Edward (Heath Barn, Donnington, nr Moreton-in-Marsh, Glos GL56 OXU; 140 Park Lane, W1Y 3AA), *b* 1952; *ed* Downside, Grenoble Univ, and RAC Cirencester; Commercial pilot, founded Mandair Promotions 1983, and Francis Mander Photography 1990; Member of Lloyds: *m* 1990, Georgina Jane, elder da of Cmdr Edward Theodore Thring, RN, of Alford House, Castle Cary, Som, and has issue living, Luke Edward Charles, *b* 1994, — Frederick George Arthur, *b* 1996.

DAUGHTER LIVING

Penelope Anne Mary, *b* 1946: *m* 1st, 1965 (*m diss* 1978), Michael Rollo Hoare; 2ndly, 1979, Simon John Loder, late Capt Gren Gds, and has issue living, (by 1st *m*) Venetia Elizabeth, *b* 1965; *ed* Trin Coll, Camb: *m* 19—, Hamish J. P. Leng, eldest son of Gen Sir Peter John Hall Leng, KCB, MBE, MC, and has issue living, Harry *b* 1997, Rosanna Elizabeth *b* 1999, — Fiona Mary, *b* 1969: *m* 1997, Charles R. Crole, yst son of Gerard Crole, of Auch Iunkart House, Banffshire, — (by 2nd *m*) (*see* Loder, Bt, colls).

SISTERS LIVING

Ann Marietta Patience, *b* 1914; JP for Glos, and Fellow King's Coll, London: *m* 1939, Hugh Patrick Stirling, who *d* 1991, of Witney House, Leafield, Oxford, and has two adopted children, Nicholas Charles (Dipton Cottage, Corbridge, Northumberland), *b* 1947; *ed* Eton; 16th/5th Queen's Royal Lancers; FRCA; MFH: *m* 1975, Elizabeth Emma, da of Brig V. W. Barlow, DSO, OBE, and has issue living, William Nelson *b* 1979; *ed* Eton, Frances *b* 1980, Patience *b* 1983, Alexandra Emma *b* 1989, — Charlotte Amelia, *b* 1950; *ed* Cranborne Chase, and Bristol Univ (BA): *m* 1973, Paul Francis Sandilands, of Falcutt House, Helmdon, Northants, and has issue living, Frederick James *b* 1982, Marietta Minette *b* 1980. —— Carinthia Jill, *b* 1920; formerly in WRNS: *m* 1st, 1944, James Ramsden, who *d* 1956; 2ndly, 1964, Lt-Cdr James de Votier Grosvenor Wallis, RN (ret), of Le Friquet, Bailiff's Cross Rd, St Andrews, Guernsey, and has issue living (by 1st *m*), James Tobit (Edmonton, Canada), *b* 1948; *ed* Radley, and Sheffield Univ (BA): *m* 1st, 1973 (*m diss* 1983), Linda, da of Walter Critchlow, of St Bruno, PQ, Canada; 2ndly, 1985, Ann Miller-Williams, and has issue living, (by 1st *m*) Sarah Jill *b* 1977, (by 2nd *m*) Edward Henry James *b* 1988, Sian Amelia *b* 1986, Daisy Katherine *b* 1990, — Charles Riordan, *b* 1949; *ed* Radley: *m* 1974, Elizabeth Mary, only da of Stewart Kilpatrick, of Fogdens Barn, Bury, Sussex.

COLLATERAL BRANCHES LIVING

Granddaughter of late Gerald Poynton Mander, FSA (infra):—
Issue of late Philip FitzGerald Mander, *b* 1915, *d* 1972: *m* 1942, Priscilla Patricia, BA (The Folley, Stableford, Bridgnorth, Shropshire), da of late Lt-Col Edmund de Warrenne Waller, MC, Indian Army:—
Rev Philippa Hazel Jeanetta (The Vicarage, 11 Brookhouse Lane, Featherstone, Wolverhampton WV10 7AW), *b* 1944; *ed* Cheltenham Ladies' Coll, Exeter Univ (BA), and Queen's Theological Coll; ordained deacon 1988, priest 1994: *m* 1965, John Patrick Thorneycroft, MA, and has issue living, Hugh Martin Sumner, *b* 1967; *ed* Wellington Coll, and Durham Univ: *m* 1995, Caroline Alison, da of George Riddington, of Crowland, Lincs, and has issue living, Harry George Sumner *b* 1998, Olivia Sophie *b* 1996, — Martin Philip, *b* 1977; *ed* Winchester, and Oxford Univ, Voryan Ruth, *b* 1971; *ed* Cheltenham Ladies' Coll, Exeter Univ (BA), and Reading Univ (MA): *m* 1997, Paul David Evans, son of John Evans, of Emmer Green, Reading, — Naomi Priscilla, *b* 1975; *ed* Oakham Sch, and Oxford Brookes Univ.

Granddaughter of late Philip FitzGerald Mander (ante):—
Issue of late (Patrick) Oliver Mander, *b* 1951, *d* 1982: *m* 1978, Gabrielle Patricia (St Andrew's East, Bedchester, Fontmell Magna, nr Shaftesbury, Dorset SP7 0JU), only da of late Geoffrey Terence Weaver:—
Hannah Rachel, *b* 1982; *ed* Bryanston Sch.

Issue of late Gerald Poynton Mander, FSA, yr son of 1st baronet, *b* 1885, *d* 1951: *m* 1913, Nancy Steward, who *d* 1960, da of late Lieut-Col R. H. Hargreaves, JP, DL, of Knightley Grange, Staffordshire:—
(Catherine) Daphne (7 Firsway, Wightwick, Wolverhampton WV6 8BJ), *b* 1914. —— Hilary Nancy, *b* 1924: *m* 1st, 1946 (*m diss* 1981), William Reginald Purslow, who *d* 1991; 2ndly, 1985, Anthony Michél Jarrey, and has issue living (by 1st *m*), Ian Gerald Steward (Auch, France), *b* 1949: *m* 1st, 1971 (*m diss* 1982), Sally Anne, only da of Gordon Matthews, of Milton House, Shipton-under-Wychwood, Oxon; 2ndly, 1988, Susan Kathryn, da of Capt Colin McKeand Little, RN (ret), of Queen Camel, Som, and has issue living (by 2nd *m*), Margaux Rose *b* 1991, Flora Louise *b* 1994. *Residence* – Casa Pepita, Partida Vinent 23, Lista de Correos, 03720 Benissa, Alicante, Spain.

The 1st baronet, Sir Charles Tertius Mander (Chm of Mander Bros Limited, of Wolverhampton), was High Sheriff of Staffordshire 1903, and Mayor of Wolverhampton 1892-6 (Hon Freeman 1897). The 2nd baronet, Sir Charles Arthur Mander, was High Sheriff for Staffordshire 1926, and Mayor of Wolverhampton, 1932 and 1936 (Hon Freeman 1946).

MANN (UK) 1905, of Thelveton Hall, Thelveton, Norfolk

Statesman

HOMME · D'ETAT

Sir RUPERT EDWARD MANN, DSO, MC, 3rd *Baronet*, el son of Edward Charles Mann, DSO, MC, only son of Maj William Edgar Mann, DSO, 2nd son of 1st Bt; *b* 11 Nov 1946; *s* his great uncle, *Sir* (EDWARD) JOHN, 1971; *ed* Malvern: *m* 1974, Mary Rose, da of Geoffrey Butler, of Cheveley Cottage, Stetchworth, Newmarket, Suffolk, and has issue.

Arms – Argent, a chevron sable, between in chief two crosses moline, and in base an annulet gules. **Crest** – A demi-man in armour proper, the helmet adorned with four feathers argent, holding in his dexter hand a cross moline as in the arms. *Seat* – Billingford Hall, Diss, Norfolk.

SONS LIVING

ALEXANDER RUPERT, *b* 6 April 1978. —— William Edward, *b* 1980.

BROTHER LIVING

Andrew William, *b* 1947, *ed* Malvern: *m* 1985, Ann Christina, da of late Michael Wyvil Lesley, of St Peter Port, Guernsey, CI, and has issue living, Jack Malcolm Wyvil, *b* 1993, — Lucy Clare, *b* 1987, — Daisy Sarah, *b* 1989, — Camilla Mary, *b* (twin)1993. *Residence* – 27 Limerick Rd, Redland, Bristol BS6 7DY.

AUNTS LIVING

Ann Sara (Westcott Barton Lodge, Middle Barton, Chipping Norton, Oxon OX7 7AA), *b* 1916; 1939-45 as Junior Cdr ATS (despatches): *m* 1950, Charles John Cunningham, MA, FRIBA, who *d* 1994, and has issue living, Alexander Kenneth, *b* 1956: *m* 1980, Frances, da of His Honour Judge John da Cunha, of Churchill, Som, and has issue living, Maximilian Edward *b* 1986, Ivo Alexander James *b* 1991, Camilla Lucy *b* 1988, — Edward James, *b* 1962: *m* 1990, Melissa Ann, da of Daryl H. Foster, of Perth, W Aust, and has issue living, James Alexander *b* 1992, Thomas Henry *b* 1995, Simon Nicholas *b* 1998, — Sara Mary, *b* 1952, — Clare Margaret, *b* 1953: *m* 1983, Edward Gold, son of Dr S. C. Gold, MD, FRCP, and has issue living, Christopher Charles *b* 1984, Simon Piers *b* 1988. —— Penelope Jane (Hoe Hall, Dereham, Norfolk), *b* 1924; a JP of Norfolk: *m* 1950, Michael Telfair Keith, who *d* 1966, and has issue living, James Edward, *b* 1960: *m* 1987, Victoria Rosemary, da of Roy E. Cook, of Cawood, N Yorks, and has issue living, Edward Michael *b* 1991, Henry Theodore Keith *b* 1998, Roseanna Victoria *b* 1989, Alicia Rose Juliet *b* 1993, — Rosemary Ann, *b* 1951: *m* 1983, Michael Charles Fetherston-Dilke, of Maxstoke Castle, Warwicks, son of Capt Charles Beaumont Fetherston-Dilke, RN, and has issue living, George Michael *b* 1985, Edward Charles *b* 1986, Sarah *b* 1989, — Priscilla Mary, *b* 1953: *m* 1979, Fergus Hew Grant Laing, of Craggan, Grantown-on-Spey, Moray, and has issue (*see* E Stair, colls).

MOTHER LIVING

Pamela Margaret, only da of late Maj Frank Haultain Hornsby, RFA (B Belper): *m* 1945, Edward Charles Mann, DSO, MC, who *d* 1959 (ante).

COLLATERAL BRANCH LIVING

Issue of late Capt Francis Thomas Mann, 3rd son of 1st Bt, *b* 1888, *d* 1964: *m* 1916, Enid Agnes, who *d* 1976, da of late George A. Tilney:—
(Francis) George, CBE, DSO, MC (Great Farm House, West Woodhay, Newbury, Berks RG15 0BL), *b* 1917; *ed* Eton, and Pembroke Coll, Camb; formerly Maj Scots Guards (Supplementary Reserve); 1939-45 War in N Africa and Italy (wounded, MC, DSO); DSO 1945, CBE (Civil) 1983: *m* 1949, Margaret Hildegarde, who *d* 1995, el da of late W. Marshall Clark, of Johannesburg, S Africa, and has issue living, Simon Francis, *b* 1952; *ed* Eton, and RMA Sandhurst; Capt Scots Guards 1971-81 and 1991-92: *m* 1977 (*m diss* 1986), Jennifer, da of David Barham, of Hole Park, Rolvenden, and has issue living, Peter George *b* 1980, Jack *b* 1982, Sophie *b* 1985, — Richard William (Goosedown Farm, Dolton, Winkleigh, Devon), *b* 1953: *m* 1983, Selina Rose Thoroton, only da of late Maj Robert Christopher Thoroton Hildyard, MC, RA, of Plaister Pitts, Scrayingham, Yorks, and has issue living, Edgar *b* 1985, Perdita *b* 1986, — Edward John, *b* 1961: *m* 1986, D. Clare de C., da of Archie A. de C. Hunter, of Southcombe Farm House, Thorncombe, Chard, Dorset, and has issue living, a son *b* 1989, Alexander Edward *b* 1995, Georgia *b* 1991, — Sarah Margaret, *b* 1960: *m* 1989, Hugh Grootenhuis, son of Peter Grootenhuis. —— John Pelham, MC (290 Weed St, New Canaan, Conn 06840, USA), *b* 1919;

ed Eton, and Pembroke Coll, Camb; formerly Maj Scots Guards; 1939-45 War (MC): *m* 1st, 1942 (*m diss* 1975), Ann Marguerite, only da of late Col John Grahame Brockbank, CMG, DSO, of The Manor House, Steeple Langford, Salisbury; 2ndly, 1976, Isabel, da of Dr Alton Ochsner, of New Orleans, USA, and has issue living, (by 1st *m*) James John Francis (Bricklayers Farm, West Woodhay, Newbury, Berks RG15 OBP), *b* 1946: *m* 1976 (*m diss* 1994), Effie Sarah Anne, da of late Norman Hepple, RA, of 10 Sheen Common, Richmond, Surrey, and has issue living, Thomas James *b* 1979, Frederick John *b* 1986, Rachel Poppy Jillian *b* 1977, — Charles Edward Lionel, *b* 1948: *m* 1980, Jane, da of Thomas Elliott, of Sale, Cheshire, and has issue living, Charlotte Joanna *b* 1981, — Celia Marguerite, *b* 1943: *m* 1964 (*m diss* 1996), 2nd Baron Norrie. —— Joan Elizabeth (*Elizabeth, Baroness Maclean*), *b* 1923: *m* 1941, Baron Maclean (Life Baron), who *d* 1990. —— Margaret Enid, *b* 1924; formerly in WRNS: *m* 1951, Maj Seaton Patrick Hayes Simonds, MC, RHA (ret), of Manor Farm, Syde, Cheltenham GL53 9PN, and has issue living, Peter Hayes, *b* 1966: *m* 1990, Karen, da of Daniel Smith, of Wellesly, Barnstaple, and has issue living, George *b* 1995, Matthew *b* 1999, Alexandra *b* 1997, Hannah *b* 1997, — Susan Enid, *b* 1954: *m* 1978 (*m diss* 1983), Timothy D. E. Rees, — Anne Margaret, *b* 1958: *m* 1989, John Treadwell, of 66 Howards Lane, SW15 6QD, son of late Lt-Col G. W. Treadwell, OBE, and has issue living, Edward *b* 1991, William *b* 1994, Louisa *b* 1993, — Nicola Mary, *b* 1968: *m* 1999, Driss Anabi, — Catherine Elizabeth, *b* 1970.

The 1st baronet, Sir Edward Mann (son of Thomas Mann, of Thelveton Hall, Scole, and Roseneath House, Winchmore Hill, N), was Chm of Mann, Crossman & Paulin, Ltd, of Brandon's Putney Brewery, Ltd.

MANSEL (E) 1622, of Muddlescombe, Carmarthenshire

What he wishes,
he wishes fervently

Sir PHILIP MANSEL, 15th *Baronet*; *b* 3 March 1943; *s* his father, *Sir* JOHN PHILIP FERDINAND, 1947; *ed* Grosvenor Coll, Carlisle, and Carlisle Gram Sch: *m* 1968, Margaret, only da of Arthur Docker, of Hainings Gate, Moorhouse, Carlisle.

Arms – Argent, a chevron between three maunches sable. **Crest** – A cap of maintenance gules, turned up ermine, enflamed on the top proper. *Seat* – Maesycrugiau Manor, Maesycrugiau, Carmarthenshire.

SONS LIVING

JOHN PHILIP, *b* 19 April 1982. —— Richard James, *b* 1990.

DAUGHTER LIVING

Nicol, *b* 1978.

AUNTS LIVING (*Daughters of 13th baronet*)

Margaretta Cecil, *b* 1913: *m* 1940, Lt-Cdr Ralph Leonard West, RN (ret), and has issue living, Richard Mansel, *b* 1946, — Christopher Leonard, *b* 1951, — Aileen Margaretta, *b* 1941. —— Juliet, *b* 1917: *m* 1939, Group Capt Richard Eric Burns, CBE, DFC, and has issue living, Richard Harcourt, *b* 1943, — Christine Georgina, *b* 1941, — Gillian, *b* 1948. *Residence* – Corner Cottage, Ashby Lane, Bitteswell, Lutterworth, Leics.

WIDOW LIVING OF FOURTEENTH BARONET

HANNAH, da of Ben Rees, of Cwmhuplyn, Pencader: *m* 1st, 1940, Sir John Philip Ferdinand Mansel, 14th baronet, who *d* 1947; 2ndly, 1949, — Harrison.

COLLATERAL BRANCHES LIVING

Issue of late Regnier Ranulf Dabridgecourt Mansel (son of 13th baronet), *b* 1919, *d* 1984: *m* 1941, Mary Germaine (Taliaris, Maesycrugiau, Carmarthenshire), da of W/Cdr W. St J. Littlewood, OBE, of Braemar, Stanmore, Middlesex:—
Anthony Ranulf, *b* 1946: AInstBM: *m* 19 , Joan Evans, of Neath, and has issue living, Richard Mark, *b* 1973, — Robert Courtney, *b* 1976. —— Robert Edward, *b* 1948; Capt RAMC (V); MB, BS Lond; FRCS Eng, LRCP Lond: *m* 1st, 19—, Ingrid Powell; 2ndly, 1987, Elizabeth C. Skone, niece of the Bishop of Tonbridge, and has issue living (by 1st *m*), Joanna Margaret, *b* 1971, — Juliet Claire, *b* 1977, — (by 2nd *m*), Rhys Edward Regnier, *b* 1989, — Courtenay Robert John, *b* 1994, — Charlotte Elizabeth, *b* 1988. —— Roderick Rhys, *b* 1959. —— Isabel Theresa, *b* 1949. —— Frances, *b* 1952.

Grandson of late Rev Canon John Colvile Morton Mansel-Pleydell, 2nd son of late John Clavell Mansel Pleydell, eldest son of Col John Mansel, CB, 3rd son of the 8th baronet:—
Issue of late Ralph Morton Mansel-Pleydell, *b* 1895, *d* 1932: *m* 1920, Countess Margurite Marie, who *d* 1968, da of Count Aymard d'Ursel:—
Philip Morton (2 Lower Clenston, Blandford, Dorset DT11 0NY), *b* 1922; *ed* Ampleforth Coll; Lt-Cdr RN (ret); 1939-45 War: *m* 1961, Dagmar Rosalie, da of late Theodore Louis Bowring, CMG, OBE, and has issue living, John Bowring Morton (6534 Flickinger Rd, Ney, OH, USA), *b* 1963: *m* 1995, Rebecca Frances, da of Robert Joseph Shininger, of Defiance, Ohio, USA, and has issue living, Joshua Francis *b* 1998, Rose Magdalene *b* 1996, — Rosanna Vivien, *b* 1965: *m* 1990, Werner van Zuylen, of Le Pavillon, Chateau de et à, 4601 Argenteau, Belgium, eldest son of Baron Edouard van Zuylen, of Argenteau, Belgium, and has issue living, Edmond Marc Dominic *b* 1992, Charles *b* 1994.

Grandsons of late Ralph Morton Mansel-Pleydell (ante):—
Issue of late David Gabriel Morton Mansel-Pleydell, DFC, *b* 1923, *d* 1973: *m* 1963, Elisabeth Susan (42 Bloomfield Terr, SW1; Barneston Manor, Steeple, Dorset), da of late John McVean Luard, of Court St, Nayland, Suffolk:—
Toby Edmond Luard Morton, *b* 1964. —— Harry Rupert Delalynde Morton, *b* 1966. —— Thomas Oliver Clavell Morton, *b* 1969. —— Charles David Luttrell Morton (*posthumous*), *b* 1973.

Grandchildren of late Col John Delalynde Mansel, eldest son of George Pleydell Mansel, 2nd son of Col John Mansel, CB, 3rd son of 9th baronet:—
Issue of late Maj Rhys Clavell Mansel, *b* 1891, *d* 1969: *m* 1st, 1916, Sylvia Nina, who *d* 1944, da of Sir Guy Theophilus Campbell, 3rd Bt; 2ndly, 1944 (*m* annulled 1946), Mrs Margaret Georgina Walker, da of late Dr H. F. G. Noyes; 3rdly, 1947, Archie Anne, who *d* 1986, da of Hugh Montgomery Cairnes, of Fox Hall, Raheny, co Dublin:—
(By 1st *m*) John Clavell (The Old Parsonage, Kimmeridge, Wareham, Dorset BH20 5PE), *b* 1917; *ed* Eton, and Ch Ch, Oxford (MA); Maj (ret) Rifle Bde; JP and DL for Dorset; High Sheriff of Dorset 1968; 1939-45 War: *m* 1945, Damaris Joan, da of late Hyde Hyde-Thomson, of 36 Victoria Rd, W8, and has had issue, †Richard John Clavell, *b* 1949; *d* 1993, — Philip Robert Rhys, *b* 1951; writer; — Lavinia Sylvia MANSEL, *b* 1946; resumed her maiden name 1991: *m* 1968 (*m diss* 1991), Alexander Quentin Jones, and has issue living, Alexander Daniel Mansel *b* 1978, Benjamin Robin Clavell *b* 1980, Owen Toby Rhys *b* 1984. —— Elizabeth Madeline Nina (Flat 11, St Martin's House, North St, Wareham, Dorset), *b* 1919: *m* 1961 (*m diss* 1966), Sir Malby Sturges Crofton, 5th Bt (*cr* 1838). —— Felicité Mary Adeline (29 Ruttan Bay, Winnipeg, Manitoba, Canada R3T 0H5), *b* 1924: *m* 1952 (*m diss* 1978), Peter Warner, and has issue living, William Francis, *b* 1957, — Susanna Elizabeth Juliet, *b* 1953: *m* 19—, Harold Polsky, and has issue living, Elizabeth *b* 19— (and has issue living, Alura Rachelle Poschner BOLDUC POLSKY *b* 19—), — Ianthe Sylvia, *b* 1954, — Sarah Adeline WARNER, *b* 1959; continues to use her maiden name: *m* 1993, Thomas Peter Kobar, of 274 1st St East (Box 4194), The Pas, Manitoba R9A 1R2, Canada, — Charlotte Anne, *b* 1965, — Oenone Jane, *b* 1966. —— Pamela Sylvia, *b* 1926: *m* 1953, Nicholas Cole McClintock, CBE, KStJ, late Snr Resident, Northern Nigeria, of Lower Westport, Wareham, Dorset BH20 4PR, and has issue living, Alexander Edward Franklin (Frank) (Barranco da Estrada, 7665 Santa Clara a Velha, Baixo Alentejo, Portugal), *b* 1959; *ed* Eton: *m* 1986, Julia (Lulu) Adeline, yr da of Thomas Henry Luckock, of Flint House, Barkway, Royston, Herts, and has issue living, Archie James Jo *b* 1988, Araby Tessa *b* 1989, Alexandra Adeline *b* 1992, — Michael Leopold Elphinstone (6 Westport Rd, Wareham, Dorset BH20 4PR), *b* 1960; *ed* Milton Abbey: *m* 1991 (*m diss* 1997), Mrs Anne K. Lee, da of R. T. Greenwood, of Shipley, W Yorks, and has issue living, Jonathan Michael *b* 1994, Thomas Alexander *b* 1997, Edward George *b* 1998, — Sylvia Araby Jane, *b* 1954: *m* 1979, Malcolm Wright, of Cricket Green Cottage, Ewhurst Green, Cranleigh, Surrey GU6 7RR, and has issue living, Pamela Melesina Marion *b* 1981, Katherine Elizabeth Jane *b* 1984, — Elizabeth Melesina, *b* 1962: *m* 1992, Anthony F. Loring, of 2 Wingate Rd, W6 0UR, son of late Brig Walter Loring, CBE, of Slingsby, Yorks, and has issue living, Joshua Nigel McClintock *b* 1995, Frances Claudia *b* 1993. —— (By 3rd *m*) Hugh Clavell (Thornmoor House, South Middlebere, nr Wareham, Dorset BH20 5DY), *b* 1948; *ed* Eton: *m* 1st, 1973, Jennifer Ann, yr da of Brian Ashford-Russell, of 1 Cheyne Walk, SW3, and The Lindens, Alresford, Hants; 2ndly, 1984, Diana Theresa Violet, yst da of late Lt-Col Conyers Stephen Scrope, MC (*see* D Sutherland, 1980 Edn), and has issue living (by 2nd *m*), Rhys Clavell, *b* 1987, — Isabella Maria, *b* 1985.

Grandchildren of late Algernon Lascelles Mansel, elder son of late Capt Arthur Edmund Mansel, yst son of Col John Mansel, CB, 3rd son of 9th baronet:—
Issue of late John William Morton Mansel, TD, *b* 1909, *d* 1974: *m* 1952, Gillian Valerie (1 Lower Barns, Salford, Chipping Norton, Oxon OX7 5YP) (who *m* 2ndly, 1977, John M. S. Barnard, who *d* 1979), el da of late Douglas Harold Whinney, of South Moreton Manor, Didcot, Berks:—
Isita Susan, *b* 1954: *m* 1st, 1978 (*m diss* 198-), J. Peter Raffe; 2ndly, 1988, Roy Thomas Pickering, of Nailsworth, Netting Close, Hook Norton, Oxon, and has issue living (by 1st *m*), Jonathan Luke, *b* 1980, — Sally Jane Isita, *b* 1979. —— Philippa Clare, *b* 1955.

Issue of late Lt-Col Edmund Clavell Mansel, OBE, MC, RA, *b* 1915, *d* 1997: *m* 1954, Ann (Rosslyn, Hindon, Salisbury, Wilts SP3 6DP), only da of late Capt Claud Anthony Merriman, RN, of Newton House, Longparish, Hants:—
Timothy Mervyn Charles, *b* 1961; *ed* Winchester, and Bristol Univ (BSc). —— Catherine Gillian, *b* 1956: *m* 1979, Rupert Michael Walter James Dilnott-Cooper, of 23 Glenmore Rd, NW3 4BY, and has issue living, Edward Kenneth Timothy, *b* 1989, — William Rupert Mansel, *b* 1993. —— Elizabeth Jane, *b* 1963; *d* 1971.

Sir Francis Mansel, 1st Bt (*cr* 1622) was a yr brother of Sir Thomas Mansel, of Margam Abbey, Glam, who was *cr* a baronet 1611. The latter's gt-grandson, Sir Thomas, 5th Bt, was *cr* Lord Mansel of Margam, in 1712, *ext* 1750. On the death of Sir John William Bell Mansel, 11th Bt (*cr* 1622), in 1883, his kinsman Richard, *b* 1850 (son of Maj Courtenay Mansel, formerly Phillips) son of Richard Phillips, formerly Mansel, yr son of 9th Bt, who *m* in Scotland, in or about 1838, Eliza, da of Rev John Sidney (a decree in Court of Session, Edinburgh, pronounced validity of this *m* in Scotland 1906). He *m* the same lady in St Paul's, Liverpool 1847, assumed the baronetcy as 12th Bt; he *d* 1892, having *m* 1st, 1878, Maud Margaretta Bowen, who *d* 1885, da of John Jones, of Maes-y-Crugiau Hall, co Carmarthen, and 2ndly, 1891, Ada Alice Lea, who *d* 1916. He was followed by his son (by 1st *m*), Courtenay Cecil Mansel (de facto 13th Bt), who in 1903, discontinued using the title, when, with his assent, it was taken up as 12th baronet, by his uncle (Sir) Edward Berkeley Mansel, *b* 1839 el son of Maj Courtenay Mansel (ante). He *dsp* 1908, when the title was resumed by his nephew Sir Courtenay Cecil Mansel (ante), as 13th Bt.

MAPPIN (UK) 1886, of Thornbury, co York (Extinct 1975)

Sir FRANK CROSSLEY MAPPIN, 6th and last *Baronet*.

DAUGHTERS LIVING OF SIXTH BARONET

Ivy Marjorie, *b* 1914: *m* 1941, Air Commodore Theodore Jasper MacLean de Lange, CBE, DFC; RNZAF (ret) of Kohanga, Otaramarae, RD4, Rotorua, NZ. —— Ethel Thorpe, *b* 1917: *m* 1944, George Fenwick, MD. *Residence* – 157 Arney Rd, Auckland 5, NZ.

SISTER LIVING OF FOURTH BARONET

Molly Violet, *b* 1907: *m* 1st, 1928 (*m diss* 1930), Francis Ferdinand Maurice Cook (afterwards 4th Bt), who *d* 1978; 2ndly 1930 (*m diss* 19—), Maj W. St. J. Macarthey; 3rdly, 19—, N. Walker.

MARKHAM (UK) 1911, of Beachborough Park, Newington, Kent

Tenax propositi

Tenacious of purpose

Sir CHARLES JOHN MARKHAM, 3rd *Baronet*; *b* 2 July 1924; *s* his father, *Sir* CHARLES, 1952; *ed* Eton; is Lieut 11th Hussars; was Vice-Chm, Nairobi Co Council 1953-55, and a MLC, Kenya 1955-60; appointed Pres, Roy Agricultural Soc of Kenya 1958; European War 1943-45 (despatches); KStJ 1973: *m* 1949, Valerie, who *d* 1998, only da of Lt-Col Evelyn Barry-Johnston, of Kenya, and has issue.

Arms – Azure, on a pale argent, three lozenges, palewise sable, issuant from a chief engrailed or, a demi-lion gules. **Crest** – A winged lion guardant or, the head surrounded by a halo gules and resting the dexter forepaw on a lozenge sable.
Address – PO Box 42263, Nairobi, Kenya. *Clubs* – MCC, and Muthaiga (Kenya).

SONS LIVING

(ARTHUR) DAVID (PO Box 42263, Nairobi, Kenya), *b* 6 Dec 1950; *ed* Milton Abbey: *m* 1977, Carolyn L., yr da of Capt Mungo Park, of Carraig, Breac, Baily, co Dublin, and has issue living, Tanya Valerie Helen, *b* 1979, — Joanna Mary Hilda, *b* 1981. —— Richard Barry, *b* 1954: *m* 1985, Ann C., yst da of late Ian Malcolm-Smith, of Mombasa, and Mrs Yvonne Malcolm-Smith, of Canterbury, Kent, and has issue living, Nicholas Charles, *b* 1987, — Matthew James, *b* 1990.

DAUGHTER LIVING

Elizabeth-Anne, *b* 1958: *m* 1983, Peter J. Bateman, elder son of Col A. J. Bateman, of Baulking, Oxon, and has issue living, Jessica Elizabeth, *b* 1987.

HALF-BROTHER LIVING

John (c/o Williams & Glyn's Bank, 9 Pall Mall, SW1), *b* 1933; *ed* Gordonstoun; is Maj RA: *m* 1st, 1961 (*m diss* 1987), Yvonne, da of Neil-Buchanan; 2ndly, 1987, Elizabeth, da of late Von Langnau, and has issue living (by 1st *m*), Toby John, *b* 1966: *m* 1994, Natasha, da of Walter Brunn, — Annalise Elizabeth, *b* 1963: *m* 1986, Anthony Cowley.

SISTER LIVING

Mary, *b* 1921: *m* 1st, 1946 (*m diss* 19—) Senator Joseph Dana Roberts; 2ndly, 1977, James Austin Hughes, who *d* 1982, and has issue living (by 1st *m*), Henry Michael, *b* 1952. *Residence* – 315 East 65th St, New York, NY 10021, USA.

COLLATERAL BRANCHES LIVING

Granddaughters (by 1st *m*) of late Mansfield Markham, 2nd son of 1st baronet, *b* 1905, *d* 1971: *m* 1st, 1927 (*m diss* 1942), Mrs Beryl Purves (the aviatrix, Beryl Markham), who *d* 1987, da of Charles B. Clutterbuck, of Kenya; 2ndly, 1944, Mary Ellen, who *d* 1987, da of late Capt A. Adley, of Calcutta:—
Issue of late Gervase Markham, *b* 1929, *d* in a motor accident 1971: *m* 1952, Viviane, who *d* 1987, da of Joseph Bruiltet, of Les Hesperides, St Germain en Laye 78100, France:—
Fleur, *b* 1953. —— Valerie-Carol, *b* 1955: *m* 1982, Daniel Rollet, of Lyon, France, son of Georges Rollet, of Lyons, and *d* 1988.

Issue of late Arthur Markham, 3rd son of 1st baronet, *b* 1911, *d* 1943: *m* 1936, Althea (who *d* 1996, having *m* 2ndly, 1946, William John Martin Begg, who *d* 1986), da of late Warren David Heinly, of Los Angeles, USA:—
Michael Arthur (Southerly, Smith's Parish, Bermuda), *b* (*posthumous*) 1944; *ed* Trin Coll Sch, Canada, Menlo Coll, CA (BS, BA), and Florida Atlantic Univ; Chm of the Pedry Mine: *m* 1976, Geke, da of D. De Jager, of Holland, and has issue living, Moshe Arthur, *b* 1977, — John Lloyd, *b* 1979, — Hanna Althea Marion, *b* 1981, — Julia Grace, *b* 1990, — Joy Elizabeth, *b* 1992, — Christy Victoria, *b* 1996.

The 1st baronet, Sir Arthur Basil Markham (son of Charles Markham, JP, of Tapton House, Derbyshire), was a Director of the Tredegar Iron and Coal Co, and Founder of Doncaster Amalgamated Collieries; and sat as MP for Mansfield Div of Notts (*L*) 1900-1916.

MARLING (UK) 1882, of Stanley Park and Sedbury Park, co Gloucester

Sir CHARLES WILLIAM SOMERSET MARLING, 5th *Baronet*; *b* 2 June 1951; *s* his father, *Lt-Col Sir* JOHN STANLEY VINCENT, OBE, 1977; *ed* Harrow: *m* 1979, Judi P., adopted da of Thomas W. Futrille, of Sunningdale, Berks, and has issue.

𝕬rms – Argent, three bars gules each charged with five bezants; in chief a lion passant gules. 𝕮rest – In front of a tower argent three bezants; the tower capped with a cupola, thereon a flag-staff proper from which flows a pennant gules.
Residence – The Barn, The Street, Eversley, Hants RG27 0PJ. *Clubs* – White's, Chelsea Arts.

DAUGHTERS LIVING

Georgina Katharine *b* 1982. —— Aimy Frances, *b* 1984. —— Laura Beatrice, *b* 1990.

SISTERS LIVING

Miranda Mary, *b* 1941: *m* 1966, Anthony John Cordle, late Capt Coldm Gds, of 23 Durand Gdns, SW9, and has issue living, Lucia Georgina Diana, *b* 1968, — Jessica Grace Rosanne, *b* 1972. —— Harriet Anne, *b* 1944. —— Virginia Frances, *b* 1946; *m* 1978, Colin Bowie, of Dragon's Lair, Moor Lane, Wincanton, Som BA9 9EJ, and has issue living, John Adrian Charles *b* 1977, — Geoffrey David *b* 1979.

We are a prey to none

The 1st baronet sat as MP for Gloucestershire West (*L*) 1868-74 and for Stroud 1875-80. The 2nd baronet was High Sheriff of Gloucestershire 1888. The 3rd baronet, Col Sir Percival Scrope Marling, VC, CB, served in S Africa 1881, in Egypt 1882, with Suakim Expedition 1884 (VC), with Nile Expedition 1884-5, in S Africa 1899-1902 (CB) and during European War 1914-15.

MARR (UK) 1918, of Sunderland, co Palatine of Durham

(*Sir*) LESLIE LYNN MARR, 2nd *Baronet*, son of late John Lynn Marr, OBE, el son of 1st Baronet; *b* 14 Aug 1922; *s* his grandfather, *Sir* JAMES, CBE, 1932, but does not use title; *ed* Shrewsbury, and Pembroke Coll, Camb (MA); late Fl Lt RAF: *m* 1st, 1948 (*m diss* 1956), Dinora Delores Mendelson; 2ndly, 1962, Lynn Heneage, and has issue by 2nd *m*.

𝕬rms – Azure, the mast and sail of a ship, pennon flying, within eight estoiles in orle or. 𝕮rest – A bell charged with a fouled anchor proper.

DAUGHTERS LIVING (*By 2nd marriage*)

Joanne Lesley, *b* 1963. —— Rebecca Lynn, *b* 1966.

COLLATERAL BRANCHES LIVING

Grandchildren of late William Bell Marr, yr son of 1st baronet:—
Issue of late Allan James Marr, CBE, *b* 1907, *d* 1989: *m* 1936, Joan de Wolf, who *d* 1990, da of John Ranken, of Sunderland:—
JAMES ALLAN (2 Peppermines, Brancepeth, Durham DH7 8ED), *b* 17 May 1939; *ed* Oundle, and Newcastle Univ: *m* 1964, Jennifer, yr da of late John William Edmund Gill,

Labour conquers all things

Issue of late Norman Carse Marr, *b* 1910, *d* 1980: *m* 1935, Flora McDonald, who *d* 1985, da of Kenneth McDonald Cameron, of West Hartlepool:—
Jeremy Norman (4430 Piccadilly, W Vancouver, BC, Canada), *b* 1940: *m* 1968, Gillian Yvonne, only da of late P. J. Hugo, of Johannesburg, S Africa, and has issue living, Kyle Jeremy, *b* 1974, — Jordan Hugo, *b* 1977. —— Dair Norman, *b* 1941: *m* 1964, Douglas Ian Henry Henderson, and has issue living, Stuart Philip, *b* 1968, — Karen Frances, *b* 1966, — Avril Louise, *b* 1971. —— Alexandra Norman, *b* 1944: *m* 1975, Ian Nicol.

Issue of late Arthur Lynn Marr, *b* 1914, *d* 1991: *m* 1941, May Victoria (12 King John's Court, Ponteland, Newcastle-upon-Tyne NE20 9AR), da of Harry Bernard Bradshaw, of St Ouen, Jersey:—
Bernard Lynn (Deneholme, Acomb Drive, Wylam, Northumberland), *b* 1943; *ed* Oundle: *m* 1968, Judith, da of late Ronald Henry Richards, of Burcroft, Wood Lane, Astwood Bank, Worcs, and has issue living, Katherine Lynn, *b* 1972, — Jane Victoria, *b* 1974, — Helen Judith, *b* 1979. —— Mary Singleton, *b* 1946: *m* 1972, Christopher Broom-Smith, of Auchenskeoch Lodge, Dalbeattie, Kirkcudbrightshire DG5 4PG. —— Victoria Lynn, *b* 1951: *m* 1976 (*m diss* 19—), Henry Jeremy Meadows, and has issue living, Carl Jeremy, *b* 1980, — James Arthur Henry, *b* 1983, — Joanna Lynn, *b* 1977.

The 1st baronet, Sir James Marr, CBE, was a shipbuilder, Chm of Sir James Laing & Sons, Ltd, of Sunderland, of Sunderland Forge & Engineering Co, Ltd, of T. W. Greenwell & Co, Ltd, of Sunderland and of Joseph I. Thompson & Sons Ltd, of Sunderland and a Member of Lloyd's Registry of Shipping.

SMITH-MARRIOTT (GB) 1774, of Sydling St Nicholas, Dorset

Sir HUGH CAVENDISH SMITH-MARRIOTT, 11th *Baronet*, *b* 22 March 1925; *s* his father, *Sir* RALPH GEORGE CAVENDISH, 1987; *ed* Bristol Cathedral Sch: *m* 1953, Pauline Anne, who *d* 1985, only da of Frank Fawcett Holt, of Abbotsway, Bristol, and has issue.

Arms – Quarterly: 1st and 4th, barry of six, or and sable, in chief two escallops gules, *Marriott*; 2nd and 3rd, sable, a fesse erminois cotised or, between three martlets of the last , each charged with an ermine spot, *Smith*. Crest – 1st, a mount vert, thereon a talbot passant sable, guttée de larmes, collared and line reflexed over the back or; 2nd, a greyhound sejant gules, collared and a line reflexed over the back or, charged on the shoulder with a mascle argent.
Residence – 26 Shipley Rd, Westbury-on-Trym, Bristol BS9 3HS.

DAUGHTER LIVING

Semper fidelis
Always faithful

Julie Anne, *b* 1958: *m* 1978, David Anthony Graveney, and has issue living, Adam Hugh Francis, *b* 1982, — Charlotte Pauline, *b* 1986. *Residence* – 6 Southover Close, Westbury-on-Trym, Bristol.

BROTHER LIVING

PETER FRANCIS, *b* 14 Feb 1927; *ed* Bristol Cathedral Sch: *m* 1961, Jean Graham Martin, only da of James Sorley Ritchie, of Harare, Zimbabwe, and has issue living, Martin Ralph, *b* 1962, — Neil Hugh, *b* 1964, — Ian Peter, *b* 1967, — Mark Nicholas, *b* 1974, — Paul Graham, *b* (twin) 1974. *Residence* – 88 Maidenhall, Highnam, nr Gloucester.

SISTER LIVING

Doris Mary, *b* 1929: *m* 1957, Alexander Stewart MacCaig, 11 Shipley Rd, Westbury-on-Trym, Bristol, and has had issue, Helen Mary, *b* 1958: *m* 1985, John Michael Burton, and has issue living, Thomas Michael *b* 1989, Andrew Jack *b* 1992, Kathryn Anne *b* 1986, — Susan Jane, *b* 1961: *m* 1988, Dr David Richardson, and *d* 1996, leaving issue, Polly Francesca *b* 1991, Maisie Jane *b* 1994, — Anne Elizabeth, *b* 1964.

WIDOW LIVING OF TENTH BARONET

BARBARA MARI (*Dowager Lady Smith Marriott*), da of G. C. Brown, ACA, and widow of Lt J. A. Cantlay, DLI: *m* 1966, as his 3rd wife, Sir Ralph George Cavendish Smith-Marriott, 10th Bt, who *d* 1987. *Residence* – 28A Westover Rd, Westbury-on-Trym, Bristol.

COLLATERAL BRANCHES LIVING

Grandchildren of late Reginald Bosworth Smith, 2nd son of Reginald Southwell Smith, 5th son of 2nd baronet:—
Issue of late Gerard Hugh Bosworth Smith, *b* 1868, *d* 1940: *m* 1893, Olive Yates:—

Reginald Claude, *b* 1899: *m* 1929, Evelyn Whittington, of Panama City, Florida, USA, and has issue living, Reginald Claude, *b* 1930, — Wayne Edward, *b* 1932, — Evelyn Joan, *b* 1935, — Geraldine, *b* 1942. —— Ellinor Joan, *b* 1896. —— Bertha Bosworth, *b* 1908: *m* 1926, Roy Bronson.

Issue of late Reginald Montagu Bosworth Smith, CBE, *b* 1872, *d* 1944: *m* 1st, 1905 Agnes Val, who *d* 1915, da of G. Val Davies; 2ndly, 1916, Kate Evelyn, who *d* 1975, da of late Frederick Charles Pardoe Radclyffe, of Birmingham:—
(By 2nd *m*) †Reginald Bosworth, LLB, *b* 1917; *d* 1996: *m* 1965, Helen Margaret, da of late Ernest R. Stidworthy, of East London, S Africa. *Address* – PO Box 577, East London, S Africa. —— †Alan Bosworth, *b* 1919: *m* 1949, Helen, da of John Mackenzie, of Johannesburg, and *d* 1996, leaving issue, Michael John Bosworth (30 Esmeralda Rd, St Francis Bay 6312, S Africa), *m* 1st, 1982 (*m diss* 1985), Colleen May Hauptfleisch; 2ndly, 1985 (*m diss* 1991), Elizabeth Ann Ringstead; 3rdly, 1999, Gaynor, da of Alf Birch, and has issue (by 2nd *m*), Matthew Edward *b* 1988, — Pamela Anne, *b* 1953: BA: *m* 1973, Keith Oliver Butler-Wheelhouse, of The Orchard, Sudbury Hill, Harrow-on-the-Hill, Middx HA1 3NA, and has issue living, Duncan *b* 1981, Andrew *b* 1985. *Address* – 4 Christopherson Rd, Dunkeld, Johannesburg 2196, S Africa.

Issue of late Bertrand Nigel Bosworth Smith, *b* 1873, *d* 1947: *m* 1912 (*m diss* 1932), Mary Constance, who *d* 1961, da of late David Inche-Bett, of New Hall, Forfarshire:—
Mary Nigella, *b* 1913: *m* 1946 (*m diss* 1960), Peter de Lande Long, FRICS, FLAS, who *d* 1981, and *d* 1995, leaving issue, Ian Bartholomew (Im Weingarten 13, D-64342, Seeheim, Germany), *b* 1949; *ed* Winchester and York Univ (MA): *m* 1971, Marjorie, da of Dr Hamilton, of Dublin, — Jonathan (425 East 58th St, Suite 48c, New York, NY 10022-2300, USA), *b* 1951; *ed* Winchester and City of London Coll; FCA: *m* 1995, Rabia, da of Jalil Rahman, of Virginia, USA, and has issue living, Peter Roderick Bartholomew *b* 1998; — Peter Graeme (Bracken Cottage, Church Rd, Scaynes Hill, W Sussex RH17 7NY), *b* 1952; *ed* Winchester and Trin Coll, Camb (BA); MICE: *m* 1986, Lucilla Eve, da of Capt Lennox William Napier, DSO, DSC, RN, of Donhead St Andrew, Dorset, and has issue living, Genevieve Anne *b* 1987, Vanessa Charlotte *b* 1989. —— Janet Wickham, *b* 1918: *m* 1939, Claude Scott Nicol, CBE, TD, MD, FRCP, late Col RAMC (V), and has issue living, Alasdair Gordon *b* 1944: *m* 1st, 1974 (*m diss* 1987), Julie Mayston Collings; 2ndly, 1987, Robyn Adair Witters, and has issue living, (by 1st *m*) Stuart *b* 1977, James *b* 1979, (by 2nd *m*) Phoebe Caroline *b* 1990, — Judy, *b* 1943: *m* 1966, John Diggory de Bourbel Rochfort, of 2 Parkside Cottages, West Bagborough, Taunton, Som, and has issue living, Christopher Michael *b* 1969: *m* 1995, Sarah, da of Gordon Andrews (and has issue living, Henry James *b* 1996), Jeremy *b* 1971, James *b* 1974, — Melany (Amberwood, The Avenue, Sherborne, Dorset DT9 3AJ), *b* 1946: *m* 1973, Piers Hayward Hughes, who *d* 1996, and has issue living, Robert *b* 1976, Katherine Melany *b* 1974, Anna Caroline Wickham *b* 1979.

Issue of late Mervyn Henry Bosworth Smith, *b* 1878, *d* 1950: *m* 1st, 1914 (*m diss* 1919), Sophie, da of John Warmington, of Ninnes, Lelant, Cornwall; 2ndly, 1920 (*m diss* 1926), Mary Annette Morcum, of Johannesburg, S Africa; 3rdly, 1927, Sarah Aletta, da of H. W. Fourie, of Johannesburg, S Africa:—
(By 2nd *m*) †Anthony Mervyn Bosworth, *b* 1925: *m* 1951, Jean Rosemary, el da of A. Peerman, of Erin Stables, Sandown, Johannesburg, S Africa, and *d* 1992, leaving issue, Mervyn Nigel Bosworth, *b* 1957; *ed* Univ of Natal (BSc) (Civil Engineering) 1981: *m* 1984, Maryna Elizabeth van Niekerk, and has issue living, Sadie Elizabeth *b* 1987, Jessica Danielle *b* 1989, — Gwen Bridget, *b* 1953: *m* 1981, Ian Watson, of Tarry-a-While, 33 Buckingham Rd, Kloof, Natal, and has issue living, Cameron Nicholas *b* 1983, Oliver Hylton *b* 1986. *Residence* – Blesbok Ridge, PO Box 132, Nottingham Rd, Natal 3280, S Africa.

Issue of late Nevil Digby Bosworth Smith, CB, *b* 1886, *d* 1964: *m* 1913, Gladys, who *d* 1965, da of late John Francis Wood, of Uffculme, Devon:—
Richard Nevil BOSWORTH-SMITH (7 Hillside Rd, Northwood, Middlesex HA6 1PY), *b* 1926; *ed* Harrow, and Balliol Coll, Oxford (MA); assumed the additional surname of Bosworth 1969: *m* 1960, Anne, el da of late John Ree, of Pinner, Middx, and has issue living, Nevil John Bosworth, *b* 1961, — Mary Margaret Bosworth *b* 1964.

Grandchildren of late Capt Hugh Francis Wyldbore WYLDBORE-SMITH, RN, eldest son of late Rev Francis Alfred Smith, eldest son of late Rev Francis Smith, 6th son of 2nd baronet—
Issue of late Lt-Cdr Hugh Deane WYLDBORE-SMITH, RN, *b* 1907, who was *ka* 1941: *m* 1937, Rachel Caroline Lucy (The White House, Husborne Crawley, Beds), el da of late Rev Edward Yarde Orlebar, of Crawley Park, Beds:—
Nicolas Hugh WYLDBORE-SMITH (The Courtiers, Clifton Hampden, Abingdon, Oxon), *b* 1938; *ed* Wellington, and St James, Maryland, USA: *m* 1964, Gillian Mary, da of late Leslie Carman, of Fareham, Hants, and has issue living, Alexander Hugh Nicolas, *b* 1969, — James William, *b* 1971.

Issue of late John Henry Wyldbore-Smith, *b* 1916; *d* 1982: *m* 1939, Robina, who *d* 1993, da of late Capt Francis Welsford Ward, of Bosloe, Cornwall:—
William Francis WYLDBORE-SMITH (Bremhill Manor, Calne, Wilts; Brooks's Club), *b* 1948; *ed* Marlborough; Solicitor; Under Sheriff Wilts 1987: *m* 1974, Mrs Prisca Faith Jenney, yr da of Rev Peter Nourse, of Leominster, Herefordshire, and has issue living, Philippa, *b* 1977. —— Robina Ann, *b* 1943: *m* 1977, (Richard Robert) Bindon Plowman, and has had issue, Andrew John Napier, *b* 1979, *d* 1989, — Felicity Frances Robina, *b* 1980. —— Susan Elizabeth, *b* 1950.

Grandsons of late Rev Francis Alfred Smith, eldest son of late Rev Francis Smith, 6th son of 2nd baronet:—
Issue of late Rev William Reginald Wyldbore Smith, *b* 1874, *d* 1943: *m* 1905, Dorothy, who *d* 1969, da of late George Green, of Watford Field House, Watford:—
†(Reginald) Anthony Wyldbore, *b* 1909: *m* 1933, Honor Christine Dyott, who *d* 1984, da of late George Wilmot, of Coleshill, Warwicks, and *d* 1987, leaving issue, Michael Anthony Wyldbore WYLDBORE-SMITH (Moat Cottage, Berkswell, W Midlands CV7 7BX), *b* 1944; *ed* Cheltenham; assumed by deed poll 1969 the additional surname of Wyldbore: *m* 1967, Sheila Margaret, da of E.C.H. Organ, of Kenilworth, and has issue living, Sarah *b* 1969: *m* 1997, Capt Stuart D. Guest, The Parachute Regt, yr son of Kenneth Guest, of Bagshot, Surrey, Nicola *b* 1971: *m* 1995, Capt Christopher M. Pullen, Coldstream Gds, yr son of James Pullen, of Marlborough, Wilts (and has issue living, Thomas Charles Wyldbore *b* 1998), Claire *b* 1977. —— *Sir* (Francis) Brian Wyldbore WYLDBORE-SMITH, CB, DSO, OBE (Grantham House, Grantham, Lincs; Naval and Military and Buck's Clubs), *b* 1913; *ed* Wellington, and RMA, Woolwich; assumed by deed poll 1966,

the additional surname of Wyldbore; Maj-Gen, late RHA and 15th/19th KR Hussars (Comdg 1953-56, Col 1970-77); Ch of Staff to C-in-C, Far East 1963-65; GOC 44th Inf Div and Home Cos Dist, and Dep Constable of Dover Castle 1965-68; ret 1968; 1939-45 War in Middle East, Italy and NW Europe (MBE, DSO, OBE); MBE (Mil) 1943, DSO 1944, OBE (Mil) 1945, CB (Mil) 1965; *cr* Knt 1980: *m* 1944, Hon Molly Angela Cayzer, da of 1st Baron Rotherwick, and has had issue, Brian Robin, *b* 1957, — Carolyn Molly, *b* 1944: *m* 1968, Harry O. Ditson, and has issue living, Sam Lennie *b* 1984, Lucy Rebecca *b* 1975, Melissa Martha *b* 1978, — Angela Maureen, *b* 1947: *m* 1975, Barrie Giffard-Taylor, of Barnbridge Farm, East Tytherton, Chippenham, Wilts, and has issue living, James William *b* 1982, Jemima Alice *b* 1977, Emily Victoria *b* 1979, — Penelope Ann, *b* 1948: *m* 1973, James E. Herdman, only son of late John Patrick Herdman, of Carricklee House, co Tyrone, and has issue living, Emerson John *b* 1979, Katherine Louise *b* 1977, — Nicola Jane, *b* 1952; *d* 1996.

Grandchildren of late Rev Heathcote Smith, son of Maj Edward Heathcote Smith, 7th son of 2nd baronet:—
    Issue of late Sir Clifford Edward Heathcote-Smith, KBE, CMG, *b* 1883, *d* 1963: *m* 1909, Elaine, who *d* 1967, da of late John J. Spiegethal de Fonton, of Cannes:—
Clifford Bertram Bruce HEATHCOTE-SMITH, CBE (4 Britts Farm Rd, Buxted, E Sussex), *b* 1912; *ed* Malvern, and at Pembroke Coll, Camb; late HM Diplo Ser; acting Senior Clerk, House of Commons; CBE (Civil) 1963: *m* 1940, Thelma Joyce Engström, and has issue living, Charles Clifford Ralph, *b* 1949: *m* 1986, Josette Lchmeisc, and has issue living, Julie *b* 1991, — Max Christopher (Jasmine Bank, 30 Ellesborough Rd, Wendover, Bucks HP22 6EL), *b* 1950: *m* 1982, Drusllla Mary Der rick, and has a da, Laura *b* 1986. ——— Elaine Mary Elizabeth, *b* 1914: *m* 1936, Rear Adm Roger Stanley Wellby, CB, DSO, DL, of 17 Honeybanks, Wendover, Bucks HP22 6NA, and has issue living, Michael Anthony (2 Kingsmere Rd, Wimbledon Common, SW19 6PX), *b* 1939: *m* 1966, Kate Frances, da of William Ram, of Berkhamsted, and has issue living, Anthony William *b* 1969, Kate d'Esterre *b* 1968, — Christopher Mark (50 Hurlingham Rd, SW6 3RQ), *b* 1943; *ed* Ch Ch, Oxford: *m* 1982, Barbara, da of Frank Elston, of Liverpool, and has issue living, Peter Nicholas Elston *b* 1985, Jack William Heathcote *b* 1987, Louise Rachel *b* 1990, — Peter Martin Heathcote (Hodgsons, Acreman St, Sherborne, Dorset DT9 3NX), *b* 1946; *ed* Ch Ch, Oxford: *m* 1988, Judith Helen Matson, and has issue living, George Francis Roger *b* 1990.

    The 1st baronet, Sir John Smith (son of late Henry Smith, of New Windsor, Berks), was High Sheriff of Dorset 1772. The 4th baronet, Sir William Marriott, assumed, by sign manual 1811, the additional surname and arms of Marriott, and the 5th was High Sheriff of Dorset 1873.

MARSDEN (UK) 1924, of Grimsby, co Lincoln

Thanks to God

Sir SIMON NEVILLE LLEWELYN MARSDEN, 4th *Baronet*; *b* 1 Dec 1948; *s* his brother, *Sir* NIGEL JOHN DENTON, 1997; *ed* Ampleforth, and Sorbonne, Paris: *m* 1st, 1970 (*m diss* 1978), Catherine Thérèsa, yr da of late Brig James Charles Windsor-Lewis, DSO, MC (*see* B Burnham, 1969 Edn); 2ndly, 1984, Caroline, yst da of John Stanton, of Houghton St Giles, Walsingham, Norfolk, and has issue by 2nd *m*.

Arms – Sable, a fesse dancettée ermine, in chief two fleur-de-lis argent and in base a ship sailing to the sinister proper. **Crest** – In front of a unicorn's head erased sable charged with two barrulets gules as many roses argent, barbed and seeded proper.
Residence – The Presbytery, Hainton, Market Rasen, Lincs LN8 6LR.

SON LIVING (*By 2nd marriage*)

TADGH ORLANDO DENTON, *b* 25 Dec 1990.

DAUGHTER LIVING (*By 2nd marriage*)

Skye Atalanta, *b* 1988.

SISTERS LIVING

Vanessa Ann, *b* 1941: *m* 1968 (*m diss* 1981), Francis John Whitehead, son of Maj Thomas B. Whitehead, of Chisbury Farm, nr Marlborough, Wilts, and has issue living, Mark John Bovil, *b* 1975. ——— Caroline Jane, *b* 1946: *m* 1970, Richard Thomas Widdowson Noton, of Bockingham Hall, Copford, Colchester, Essex CO6 1DR, and has issue living, Charles Richard Marsden, *b* 1975, — Henrietta Caroline Marsden, *b* 1979.

DAUGHTERS LIVING OF THIRD BARONET

Lucinda Ann, *b* 1962. ——— Rosa Amanda, *b* 1964 ——— Annabel Juliet, *b* 1968.

AUNT LIVING (*Daughter of 1st baronet*)

Agnes Isabelle, *b* 1920: *m* 1941, Capt Frederick William Tackaberry Storey, RASC, only son of Rev John William Storey, of Staplegrove Rectory, Taunton, and has issue living, Michael William Tackaberry, *b* 1942; *ed* Sherborne, — Jonathan William Tackaberry *b* 1948; *ed* Sherborne, — Alastair William Tackaberry, *b* 1949, — Jane Patricia, *b* 1951, — Penelope Caroline, *b* 1953, — Sally Anne, *b* 1957. *Residence* - Baymead Cottage, 2 Baymead Lane, North Pemberton, nr Bridgwater, Somerset.

WIDOWS LIVING OF SECOND AND THIRD BARONETS

HOPE (*Hope, Lady Marsden*), yr da of late G. E. Llewelyn, of Bryngawr, Aberkenfig, Glamorgan: *m* 1939, Sir John Denton Marsden, 2nd Bt, who *d* 1985. *Residence* – Holly Tree Cottage, Hainton, Market Rasen, Lincs LN8 6LR.

DIANA JEAN (*Diana, Lady Marsden*), elder da of Air Marshal Sir Patrick Hunter Dunn, KBE, CB, DFC: *m* 1961, Sir Nigel John Denton Marsden, 3rd Bt, who *d* 1997. *Residence* – 1 Grimsby Rd, Waltham, Grimsby, E Lincs DN37 0PS.

The 1st baronet, Sir John Denton Marsden (son of William Dent Marsden, of Aldmondbury, Huddersfield), was Principal of Consolidated Fisheries Ltd, of Grimsby, Swansea and Lowestoft.

Mather-Jackson, see Jackson.

MATHESON (UK) 1882, of Lochalsh, co Ross

Do and hope

Sir FERGUS JOHN MATHESON OF MATHESON, 7th *Baronet*; Ch of Clan Matheson; *b* 22 Feb 1927; *s* his brother, *Maj Sir* TORQUHIL ALEXANDER, 1993; *ed* Eton; Maj Coldm Gds 1945-64; a Member of HM's Body Guard of the Hon Corps of Gentlemen at Arms 1979-97, Standard Bearer 1993-97: *m* 1952, Hon Jean Elizabeth Mary Willoughby, JP, yr da of 11th Baron Middleton, KG, MC, and has issue.

ⓐrms – Gyronny of eight sable and gules, a lion rampant or, armed and langued azure, overall on a canton argent a dexter hand appaumée gules. Crest – Issuant from an antique crown or a hand brandishing a scimitar fessways all proper. Supporters – Two brown bears proper, each gorged with an antique crown or.
Residence – The Old Rectory, Hedenham, Norfolk NR35 2LD.
 Club – Army and Navy.

SON LIVING

ALEXANDER FERGUS, YR OF MATHESON, *b* 26 Aug 1954; *ed* Eton, and Durham Univ; Lt-Col Coldm Gds; temporary Equerry to HM The Queen 1982-84; Chief of Staff British Forces Belize 1992-94; Adjt RMA Sandhurst 1994-96; Bde Maj Household Div 1996-98; Comd Offr Oxford Univ OTC since 1998: *m* 1983, Katharine Davina Mary, only da of Sir (William Richard) Michael Oswald, KCVO (*see* M Exeter), and has issue living, Andrew William Fergus, *b* 12 March 1985; *ed* Eton, — Archie James Torquhil, *b* 1987, — Louisa Alexandra Matilda, *b* 1989.

DAUGHTERS LIVING

Elizabeth Angela Matilda, *b* 1953: *m* 1978, Martin Claude Thompson, of The Old Rectory, Little Bytham, Lincs, elder son of late Maj E. C. O. Thompson, and has issue living, Charles Guy Martin, *b* 1981, — Mara Angela Matilda, *b* 1979, — Siana Camilla Elizabeth, *b* 1989. —— Fiona Jean Lucia, *b* 1962: *m* 1986, Andrew Thomas Kendall, of The Old Rectory, Henstead, Beccles, Suffolk NR34 7LA, elder son of John Kendall, of Danybryn, Vaynor, Merthyr Tydfil, Glam, and has issue living, Edmund Andrew Fergus, *b* 1991, — Lucia Amelia Fiona, *b* 1988.

DAUGHTERS LIVING OF SIXTH BARONET

Eleanor Mary Francesca, *b* 1955. —— Isobel Sophia, *b* 1957: *m* 1986, William George Craven, of 16 Allotment Lane, Castor, Peterborough, Cambs PE5 7AS, 2nd son of John Craven, MRCVS, and has issue living, Frances Elizabeth, *b* 1987, — Emily Flora, *b* 1989.

WIDOW LIVING OF SIXTH BARONET

SERENA MARY FRANCESCA (*Serena, Lady Matheson of Matheson*), only child of late Lt-Col Sir (James) Michael Peto, 2nd Bt (*cr* 1927): *m* 1954, Sir Torquhil Alexander Matheson of Matheson, 6th Bt, DL, who *d* 1993. *Residences* – Trees Farm, Standerwick, Frome, Somerset BA11 2PT; Dalmhor, North Side, Duirinish, Kyle of Lochalsh IV40 8BE.

Mathesons occupied the lands of Lochalsh from the 13th century. Their chief being one of those arrested and executed at Inverness in 1427, the estates were granted to Celestine of The Isles, whose granddaughter, Margaret, conveyed the half to her husband Macdonell of Glengarry. John Matheson, who in 1728 married, as his second wife, Margaret Mackenzie, a descendant of this marriage, acquired Attadale in 1730. Their great-grandson and heir male, Alexander Matheson, a partner in Jardine Matheson, and Matheson & Co, having in 1851, purchased Lochalsh, was created a baronet under that designation in 1882. He sat as MP for Inverness District (*L*) 1847-68, and for Ross and Cromarty 1868-84. Sir Alexander Perceval Matheson, 3rd Bt, was a Senator of Commonwealth of Australia. Gen Sir Torquhil George Matheson, KCB, CMG, 5th Bt, commanded 3rd Coldstream Guards, 46th Inf Bde, 20th Light, 4th and Guards Divs, 1914-18, Waziristan Field Force 1920-24, and was GOC in C W Command, India, 1931-35. He also commanded a company of the 2nd Batn Ross-shire HG 1940-42, covering S W Ross-shire. Maj Sir Torquhil Alexander Matheson of Matheson, 6th Bt, s his kinsman, Col Bertram Matheson of Matheson, MC, as Ch of Clan Matheson by tanistry 1975; Member HM's Body Guard of Hon Corps of Gentlemen-at-Arms, Clerk ot the Cheque and Adjutant.

MATHIAS (UK) 1917, of Vaendre Hall, St Mellons, co Monmouth (Extinct 1991)

Sir RICHARD HUGHES MATHIAS, 2nd *Baronet*; *d* 4 Jan 1991.

DAUGHTERS LIVING OF SECOND BARONET

Anna Patricia (35 Ifield Rd, SW10), *b* 1938: *m* 1962 (*m diss* 1971), Lt-Cdr Eric Clive Hastings, RN, and has issue living, Nichola Jane, *b* 1964: *m* 1990, Peter Thomas Alistair Jessop Davis, and has issue living, William Oliver, *b* 1994, — Frederick Valentine, *b* 1996. —— Virginia Turton, *b* 1942.

MAXWELL (NS) 1681, of Monreith, Wigtownshire

I renew my strength

Sir MICHAEL EUSTACE GEORGE MAXWELL, 9th *Baronet*; *b* 28 Aug 1943; *s* his uncle, *Capt Sir* AYMER, 1987; *ed* Eton, and London Univ; ARICS.

Arms – Argent, an eagle with two heads displayed sable, beaked and membered gules; on the breast an escutcheon of the first, charged with a saltire of the second, surcharged in the centre with a hurcheon (hedgehog), or, all within a bordure gules. **Crest** – An eagle rising proper.
Seat – Monreith House, Port William, Newton Stewart DG8 9LB, Wigtownshire. *Residences* – Laundry House, Farming Woods, Brigstock, Northants NN14 3JA; 56 Queensmill Rd, SW6 6JS.

SISTER LIVING

Diana Mary, *b* 1942; has issue living (by Patrick Helmore), Katharine Diana, *b* 1984, — Charlotte Jessica, *b* (twin) 1984. *Residence* – 15 Cupar Rd, SW11.

MOTHER LIVING

Dorothy Vivien, elder da of late Capt George Ernest Bellville, JP, of Fermyn Woods Hall, Northants: *m* 1940 (*m diss* 1949), Maj Eustace Maxwell, Argyll & Sutherland Highrs, yr brother of 8th Bt, who *d* 1971. *Residence* – Fermyn Woods Hall, Brigstock, Northants.

COLLATERAL BRANCH LIVING

Descendants, if any, of Alexander Charles Maxwell, yr son of Maj Hamilton Maxwell, BSc (*d* 1829), 3rd son of 4th baronet, who left issue four sons.

The Maxwells of Monreith derive from Sir Edward Maxwell of Tinwald, co Dumfries, yr son of 1st Lord Maxwell (*cr* 1440) ancestor of the Earls of Nithsdale (*see* L Herries). The Maxwells of Tinwald became ext in early 18th century. Herbert Maxwell, yr brother of Edward Maxwell of Tinwald, *m* 1541, Margaret Maxwell, heir of Monreith. Fourth in descent from whom was the 1st baronet, Sir William. The 7th baronet, Rt Hon Sir Herbert, KT, PC, LLD, DCL, FRS, was Lord-Lieut of Wigtownshire 1903-35, MP for Wigtownshire (C) 1880-1906, and a Lord of the Treasury 1886-92.

Maxwell (Constable-Maxwell-Scott), see Scott.

HERON-MAXWELL, (NS) 1683, of Springkell, Dumfriesshire

May it flourish again

Sir NIGEL MELLOR HERON-MAXWELL, 10th *Baronet*; *b* 30 Jan 1944; *s* his father, *Sir* PATRICK IVOR, 1982; *ed* Milton Abbey: *m* 1972, Mary Elizabeth Angela, only da of William Ewing, of co Donegal, and has issue.

𝕬rms – Quarterly: 1st and 4th, argent, on a saltire sable, an annulet or, stoned azure; in base, a crescent of the second; all within a bordure gules charged with eight bezants, *Maxwell*, 2nd and 3rd, gules, on a bend argent a rose between two lions passant gules, *Heron*. 𝕮rest – A dexter hand proper holding an eagle's neck erased with two heads sable. 𝕾upporters – Two eagles close-reguardant sable.
Residence – 50 Watlington Rd, Old Harlow, Essex CM17 0DY.

SON LIVING

DAVID MELLOR, *b* 22 May 1975.

DAUGHTER LIVING

Claire Louise, *b* 1977.

BROTHERS LIVING

Colin Mellor, *b* 1952; *ed* Down House: *m* 1976, Angela, only da of Sabin Nistor, of Petrosani, Rumania, and has issue living, Kirsten Diana, *b* 1982, — Hayley Claudia, *b* 1983. —— Paul Mellor, *b* 1957; *ed* Knights Templar.

AUNT LIVING (*Daughter of 8th baronet*)

Rachel Mary, *b* 1922: *m* 1947, Roy Martin Macnab, D Litt et Phil, FRSA, and has issue living, Simon Martin, *b* 1955, — Celia Mary, *b* 1949: *m* 1988 (*m diss* 1993), Brian John Weller. *Address* – 9/86 Elm Park Gdns, SW10 9PD.

WIDOW LIVING OF NINTH BARONET

DOROTHY GERALDINE EMMA (*Geraldine, Lady Heron-Maxwell*) (9 Cowslip Hill, Letchworth, Herts), yr da of late Claud Paget Mellor: *m* 1942, Sir Patrick Ivor Heron-Maxwell, 9th Bt, who *d* 1982.

COLLATERAL BRANCH LIVING

Granddaughter of late Capt John Heron Maxwell-Heron, el son of late Rev Michael Heron Maxwell-Heron, 4th son of 4th baronet:—
Issue of late Capt Basil Charles Montagu Maxwell-Heron, *b* 1878, *ka* 1916: *m* 1905, Mary, who *d* 1957, da of late Garrett O'Byrne:—
Rita Steuart Mary *b* 1905: *m* 1927, Antony William Hamilton Nelson, Pilot-Officer RAF and has issue living, John Edward Arthur Hamilton, *b* 1935, — Patricia Anne, *b* 1930: *m* 19—, P. L. Braine, — Sheila Steuart Mary, *b* 1932: *m* 19—, J. C. Horrocks.

This baronet is head in the male line of Maxwells of Pollock, and Chief of the Clydesdale Maxwells. The 4th baronet, Sir John, assumed the additional surname and arms of Heron, having *m* 1802, Mary, da and heir of Patrick Heron of

Heron in Kirouchtree. Sir John 7th baronet, was Capt 15th Hussars, and a Member of HM's Body Guard for Scotland (Roy Co of Archers).

STIRLING-MAXWELL (NS) 1682 and (NS) 1707, of Pollock, Renfrewshire (Dormant 1956)

Sir JOHN MAXWELL STIRLING-MAXWELL, KT, 10th *Baronet, d* 30 May 1956.

DAUGHTER LIVING OF TENTH BARONET

Anne, *b* 1906: *m* 1930, John Moreton-Macdonald (later Maxwell Macdonald), who *d* 1995 (*see* E Ducie, colls), and has issue living, JOHN RONALD (Gortinanane House, Tayinloan, Argyll PA29 6XG) *b* 22 May 1936; eventual heir to the baronetcy under the terms of the 1707 remainder; *ed* Winchester: *m* 1964, Eleanor Ruth, da of T. B. Laird, and has issue living, John Ranald *b* 1965: *m* 1998, Emma, eldest da of Simon Logie, of Winson, Glos, and of Mrs Jeremy John Heming Gilkes, of Wandsworth, Angus *b* 1967, Victoria Anne *b* 1971, — Donald, *b* 1938 (*see* E Ducie, colls). *Residence* – Gortinanane House, Tayinloan, Argyll PA29 6XG.

COLLATERAL BRANCH LIVING (*Males and Females in remainder*)

Grandchildren of late Brig-Gen Archibald Stirling of Keir, 2nd son of 9th baronet:—
Issue of late Lt-Col William Joseph Stirling of Keir, *b* 1911; *d* 1983: *m* 1940, Susan Rachael, who *d* 1983, da of Lt-Col Hon Noel Gervase Bligh, DSO (E Darnley):—
Archibald Hugh STIRLING OF KEIR (Ochtertyre, Stirling FK9 4UN), *b* 1941; *ed* Ampleforth: *m* 1st, 1964 (*m diss* 1977), Charmian Rachel, yr da of Lord George Francis John Montagu-Douglas-Scott (*see* D Buccleuch); 2ndly, 1982 (*m diss* 1993), Enid Diana Elizabeth (later Dame Diana Rigg, DBE), da of late Louis Rigg, and formerly wife of Menachem Gueffen, and has issue living (by 1st *m*), William Rory Alexander, *b* 1965, — Ludovic David, *b* 1967, — (by 2nd *m*) Rachael Atlanta, *b* 1977. —— John Alexander, *b* 1948: *m* 1st, 1971, Mrs Susan Burton, only da of Edmund Black, of Johannesburg; 2ndly, 1985, Olivia Louise, da of Maj Patrick Waller, and has issue living (by 2nd *m*), Joseph Patrick William, *b* 1985, — Hugh David Archibald, *b* 1993, — Christabel Georgia, *b* 1987. —— Hannah Ann (*Viscountess Cranborne*), *b* 1944: *m* 1970, Robert Michael James, Viscount Cranborne, PC, el son of 6th Marquess of Salisbury, and has issue (*see* M Salisbury). —— Magdalen, *b* 1945: *m* 1969, Patrick Petit, and has issue living, Benjamin, *b* 1972, — Jonathan, *b* 1973.

Issue of late Margaret Elizabeth Mary, *b* 1914, *d* 1997: *m* 1940, 16th Earl of Dalhousie, KT, GCVO, GBE, MC:— *See* F. Dalhousie.

This family is of the oldest branch of the Maxwells, Earls of Nithsdale. Sir John Maxwell of Pollok distinguished himself at an early age in chivalry, especially at the celebrated battle of Otterburn, or Chevy Chase (1388), where he captured Sir Ralph Percy, son of the Earl of Northumberland, and brother of the renowned "Hotspur". The Baronetcy was first conferred in 1682 upon John Maxwell of Pollok (son of Sir George Maxwell), with remainder to heirs of the body, but a further patent was issued in 1707 extending remainder to heirs of entail in his lands and estates. The 9th baronet, Sir William Stirling-Maxwell, who as heir of entail succeeded under the special limitation, was MP for Perthshire (*C*) 1852-68 and 1874-8, and received as a Commoner the exceptional honour of being created a KT. Sir John Maxwell Stirling-Maxwell was MP for Coll Div of Glasgow (*C*) 1895-1906 and was also created a KT.

MEDLYCOTT (UK) 1808, of Ven House, Somerset

Sir MERVYN TREGONWELL MEDLYCOTT, 9th *Baronet*, son of late Thomas Anthony Hutchings Medlycott, 2nd son of 7th baronet; *b* 20 Feb 1947; *s* his uncle, *Sir* (JAMES) CHRISTOPHER, 1986; Fellow Soc of Genealogists; Memb AGRA; Pres (formerly Founder and Hon Sec 1975-77, Chm 1977-84, and Vice-Pres 1984-86), Somerset & Dorset Family History Soc.

𝕬rms – Quarterly, per fesse indented gules and azure, three lions rampant, two and one, argent. 𝕮rest – Out of a mural crown gules a demi-eagle with wings elevated or. *Residence* – The Manor House, Sandford Orcas, Sherborne, Dorset DT9 4SB.

SISTERS LIVING

Julia Elizabeth, *b* 1939: *m* 1965 (*m diss* 1986), Michael John Bazeley Smith, and has issue living, Timothy John Medlycott, *b* 1966, — Philip Anthony Medlycott, *b* 1971: *m* 1997, Georgina Abbott, and has issue living, Eleanor Mary Medlycott *b* 1998, — Catherine Frances Sarah, *b* 1968. *Residence* – Edmondsham House, Edmondsham, Cranborne, Wimborne, Dorset BH21 5RE. ——— Philadelphia Jane, *b* 1941: *m* 1967, Rupert Oliver, and has issue living, Kim, *b* 1970. — Philadelphia Jo, *b* 1972. *Residence* – The Residence, Kenchester, Hereford HR4 7QJ. ——— Sarah Nell, *b* 1944: *m* 1971, Kenneth Dale Ritchey, and has issue living, Jonathan Dale, *b* 1975, — Emily Jane, *b* 1977. *Address* – 112 Wright Rd, Beckley, W Virginia 25801, USA.

He that sows in tears shall reap in joy

MOTHER LIVING

Cecilia Mary, da of late Maj Cecil Harold Eden, of Tregonwell Lodge, Cranborne, Dorset: *m* 1938, Thomas Anthony Hutchings Medlycott, who *d* 1970, 2nd son of 7th baronet. *Residence* – Cowleaze, Edmondsham, Wimborne, Dorset BH21 5RE.

This family descends from James Medlycott, of Ven House, Milborne Port, Som, Master in Chancery, and MP for Milborne Port 1710-22. His son Thomas, of Ven House, *d* 1763 without surviving issue, and settled his estates on his maternal nephew, Thomas Hutchings, who accordingly adopted the name and arms of Medlycott. His son, Sir William Coles Medlycott, 1st Bt, was MP for Milborne Port 1790-91.

STUART-MENTETH (UK) 1838, of Closeburn, Dumfriesshire, and Mansfield, Ayrshire

Whilst I live I hope

Sir JAMES WALLACE STUART-MENTETH, 6th *Baronet*; *b* 13 Nov 1922; *s* his father, *Sir* WILLIAM FREDERICK, 1952; *ed* Fettes Coll, St Andrews Univ, and Trin Coll, Oxford (MA); sometime Lieut Scots Guards; European War 1939-44 in N Africa and Italy (wounded): *m* 1949, (Dorothy) Patricia, da of late Frank Greaves Warburton, of Thorrington, Stirling, and has issue.

𝕬rms – Quarterly: 1st and 4th, or, a bend chequy argent and sables 2nd and 3rd, azure, three buckles or; the whole within a bordure gules. 𝕮rest – A lymphad sable. *Residence* – Nutwood, Auchencairn, Castle Douglas, Kirkcudbrightshire DG7 1QZ.

SONS LIVING

CHARLES GREAVES (Monkcastle House, Kilwinning, Ayrshire KA13 6PN), *b* 25 Nov 1950; *ed* Trin Coll, Oxford: *m* 1976, Nicola Mary Jane, da of Vincent Charles Raleigh St Lawrence, of 102 Exeter St, Salisbury, and has issue living Alice Clare, *b* 1977, — Celia Jane, *b* 1978, — Sarah Harriet, *b* 1982, — Sophie Emily Flora, *b* 1995. ——— (William) Jeremy, *b* 1953: *m* 19——, Rosalind, eldest da of J. Lane, of Ruislip, Middlesex, and has issue living, James William, *b* 1987, — Lucy Ann, *b* 1985.

Sub sole nihil

Nothing under the sun

BROTHER LIVING

Charles Granville (Woodchester House, Woodchester, Glos, RAC), *b* 1928; *ed* Oxford Univ (BA); late 2nd Lt Scots Guards; Underwriting Member of Lloyd's: *m* 1963, Priscilla Helen, el da of late Thomas Newman, of Widdicombe House, Kingsbridge, Devon (*see* Newman, Bt, *cr* 1836), and has issue living, James William Francis, *b* 1965, — Alexander Granville, *b* 1971, — Alice Caroline, *b* 1969.

SISTER LIVING

Ludivina Frances (Arkaig, Tibbermallo Rd, Methven, Perthshire PH1 3QL), *b* 1927: *m* 1947, Capt William Sawbridge How, Hon Artillery Co, who *d* 1990, and has issue living, Stuart Sawbridge, *b* 1950: *m* 1974, Barbara Joan, eldest da of Charles Statters, of Newcastle, and has issue living, Michael Sawbridge *b* 1978, Andrew Charles *b* 1981, Christopher James *b* 1991, Lisa Joan *b* 1983, — Anthony Edward, *b* 1951: *m* 1997, Christine Stewart, yr da of Alexander MacLeod, of Glasgow, — Helen Frances, *b* 1955: *m* 1984, Michael Peter Stoneham, WS, and has issue living, Nicholas Alexander *b* 1986, Richard William *b* 1990, Sophie-Louisa Ludivina *b* 1994.

COLLATERAL BRANCHES LIVING

Grandchildren of late Walter Erskine Stuart-Menteth (infra):—
Issue of late Maj Walter Granville Stuart-Menteth, *b* 1906, *d* 1970: *m* 1st, 1937 (*m diss* 1950), Marianne Marguerite, who *d* 1975, da of Jules Cuenod, of La Tour de Peilz, Switzerland; 2ndly, 1957, Edith Pauline, da of James Harold Wadsworth:—
(By 1st *m*) Charles Henry, *b* 1938; *ed* Rugby. —— James Sleigh, *b* 1940: *m* 1968, Barbara Richardson. —— Marie Octavia, *b* 1939.

Issue of late Walter Erskine Stuart-Menteth, 4th son of 4th baronet, *b* 1877, *d* 1956: *m* 1905, Violet Grace, who *d* 1970, yst da Henry Lafone, formerly of 59 Onslow Sq, SW:—
Henry Alexander, DSC (16 Inverleith Terr, Edinburgh 3), *b* 1912; Cdr RN; 1939-45 War despatches, DSC: *m* 1952, Penelope, only da of Digby Giles, of Toorak, Melbourne, Aust, and has issue living, Andrew Alexander (18 Marion St, Brighton, Melbourne, Vic 3186, Australia), *b* 1954: *m* 1988, Pamela, da of Capt J. C. Chapman, of Melbourne, Australia, and has issue living, James Alexander *b* 1989, Lucy Linda *b* 1990, — Walter Henry, *b* 1957, — Harriet Lucy, *b* 1959: *m* 1991, James H. Brennan, 2nd son of Lt-Col M. W. Brennan, of Painswick, Glos, and has issue living, Thomas Michael *b* 1992, Kate Florence *b* 1994, Zoë Alice *b* 1997. —— Lucy Violet, *b* 1911: *m* 1942, Maj Donald Brain, Princess Patricia's Canadian LI, who was *ka* 1943, and has issue living, Donald Rowan, *b* 1943; *ed* Fettes. *Residence* – Crossways, Godstone, Surrey.

This family is lineally descended in the male line from Walter (third son of Walter, Lord High Steward of Scotland), who *m* 1258 the Countess of Menteth, and thus acquired that earldom. He left two sons, who both assumed the surname of Menteth, viz, Alexander, 6th Earl of Menteth, and Sir John Menteth, Lord of Arran, etc, who *m* Elyne, daughter of Gratney, Earl of Mar, and whose granddaughter, Janet Keith, *m* Robert, 1st Lord Erskine, and thus the Erskines acquired the earldom of Mar. Sir John Menteth of Ruskie (who *d* before 1333), from whom the Stuart-Menteths trace their descent, was a yr brother of Alexander, 6th Earl of Menteth. This Earldom was forfeited on the execution of Murdoch Stewart, Duke of Albany in 1425. The father of the 1st baronet, Rev James Stuart-Menteath, assumed by sign-manual, in 1770 the additional surname of Stuart "for himself and his posterity." The 2nd baronet resumed the ancient name of Menteth, but his two yst brothers retained the name of Mcnteath. Sir James, 3rd baronet, became a naturalized American.

METCALFE (UK) 1802, of Chilton, Berkshire (Extinct 1979)

Sir THEOPHILUS JOHN METCALFE, 8th and last *Baronet.*

SISTER LIVING OF EIGHTH BARONET

Peggy Theophila, LVO, OBE, *b* 1920; FCO 1947-80; 1939-45 War as Senior Com ATS (MBE); MBE (Mil) 1945, OBE (Civ) 1974, LVO 1980. *Residence* – Scribbins, Benenden, Kent.

MEYER (UK) 1910, of Shortgrove, Newport, Essex

RAST · ICH · ROST · ICH

Rest not rust not

Sir ANTHONY JOHN CHARLES MEYER, MP, 3rd *Baronet*; *b* 27 Oct 1920; *s* his father, *Sir* FRANK CECIL, 1935; *ed* Eton, and New Coll, Oxford; is a Trustee of Shakespeare National Memorial Theatre; European War 1941-45 as Lieut Scots Guards (wounded); entered HM's Foreign Ser 1947; 1st Sec Paris 1956, Moscow 1957, and at Foreign Office 1958-62; PPS to Ch Sec of the Treasury (Mr Maurice Macmillan, MP) 1970-72, and to Sec of State for Employment (Rt Hon Maurice Macmillan, MP) 1972-74; Chm, Franco-British Parl Relations Cttee; MP for Eton and Slough (*C*) 1964-66, for W Flintshire 1970-83, and for Clwyd N W 1983-92; Policy Dir European Movement since 1992; Memb Franco-British Council since 1979 (Dep Chm UK Section); Publications, "A European Technological Community 1966", "Stand Up and Be Counted" 1990, "A Federal Europe: Why Not" 1992, Founder and Dir of "Solon" 1969; Offr of Légion d'honneur 1983: *m* 1941, Barbadee Violet, only child of late A. Charles Knight, JP, FSA, of Lincoln's Inn, WC, and Herne Place, Sunningdale, Berks, and has issue.

Arms – Sable, a key wards downwards or between four bezants. Crest – A cock sable, armed, combed, and wattled or, holding in the dexter claw a key as in the arms.
Residence – 9 Cottage Place, Brompton Sq, SW3 2BE. *Club* – Beefsteak.

SON LIVING

(ANTHONY) ASHLEY FRANK, *b* 23 Aug 1944; *ed* Eton: *m* 1966 (*m diss* 1979), Susan Mathilda, da of Charles Freestone, and has issue living, Sophie Mathilda Barbadee, *b* 1972.

DAUGHTERS LIVING

Carolyn-Clare Barbadee (7 Cottage Place, Brompton Sq, SW3), *b* 1943: *m* 1965 (*m diss* 1988), Charles Francis Sands, and has issue living, Robert Charles, *b* 1970, — David Francis, *b* 1974. —— Tessa Violet, *b* 1955: *m* 1977, David Peter Murdoch, of 3 Luxemburg Gdns, W6, and has issue living, Iona Dorothy, *b* 1984, — Frances Evelyn *b* 1986, — Sienna Rose Adèle, *b* 1992. —— Sally Minette, *b* 1961: *m* 1989, Marcus John Vergette, of Coombe Farm, Highampton, Beaworthy, Devon, only son of Nicholas Vergette.

The 1st baronet, Sir Carl Ferdinand Meyer, was a Director of National Bank of Egypt, and the 2nd baronet, Sir Frank Cecil, sat as MP for Great Yarmouth (*C*) 1924-9.

MEYRICK (UK) 1880, of Bush, Pembrokeshire
(Name pronounced "Merrick")

Without God, without anything;
God and enough

Sir DAVID JOHN CHARLTON MEYRICK, 4th *Baronet*; *b* 2 Dec 1926; *s* his father, *Col Sir* THOMAS FREDERICK, TD, DL, JP, 1983; *ed* Eton, and Trin Hall Camb (MA); formerly a Chartered Surveyor and a Land Agent: *m* 1962, Penelope Anne, el da of late Cdr John Bertram Aubrey Marsden-Smedley, RN (*see* B Westbury, colls, 1985 Edn), and has issue.

Arms – Quarterly; 1st and 4th, sable, on a chevron argent between three staves raguly or, inflamed proper, a fleur-de-lys gules between two Cornish choughs respectant also proper, *Meyrick*; 2nd and 3rd, or, a lion rampant gules, a sinister quarter quarterly 1st and 4th, gules, ten besants, three, two, and one, 2nd and 3rd argent on a mount vert, a lion passant guardant or, *Charlton*. Crests – 1st, a tower argent, having on its top a mount vert, and thereon a Cornish chough proper, and holding in the dexter claw a fleur-de-lys gules, *Meyrick*; 2nd, out of an eastern coronet or, a leopard's head, issuant gules, *Charlton*.
Seat – Gumfreston, Tenby, Dyfed, Wales. *Residence* – Bush House, Gumfreston, Tenby, Pembrokeshire SA70 8RA

SONS LIVING

TIMOTHY THOMAS CHARLTON, *b* 5 Nov 1963; *ed* Eton, and Bristol Univ. —— Simon Edward, *b* 1965; *ed* Shrewsbury, and RAC Cirencester: *m* 1989, Jennifer Amanda, yr da of J. B. Irvine, of Thornton, Fife. —— Christopher John, *b* 1967; *ed* Eton, and Trin Hall Camb.

BROTHERS LIVING

Frederick Rowland, *b* 1928; *ed* Eton, and RMA Sandhurst; Maj (ret) 15th/19th King's Roy Hussars: *m* 1985 (*m diss* 1993), Patricia Anne Busswell-Dewitte, eldest da of late Dennis William Busswell, KRRC, of Lisbon. *Residence* – 27 Tudor Court, Narberth, Pembs. —— Richard Eric, *b* 1936; *ed* Monkton Combe, and RAC Cirencester; a Chartered Surveyor: *m* 1962, Catherine Ann, el da of late Col Vivian Joseph French Popham, S Wales Borderers, of Begelly, Kilgetty, Pembs. *Residence* – Lower Helland, Bodmin, Cornwall.

HALF-BROTHER LIVING

John Herbert, *b* 1952; *ed* Abbotsholme: *m* 1982, Sandra Dawn, only da of L. V. Blackman, of Lewes, E Sussex, and has issue living, Matthew Thomas, *b* 1986, — Alistair Charles, *b* 1988. *Residence* – 63 Dawson Drive, Trimley St Mary, Ipswich.

SISTERS LIVING

Susan Ethel, *b* 1932: *m* 1954, Roland Owen-George, of Hillside, Garway, Herefs HR2 8RL. —— Penelope Ann, *b* 1939: *m* 1966, Michael McGarvie, of 19 Styles Hill, Frome, Som, and has issue living, Emma Louise, *b* 1969, — Victoria Grace, *b* 1971, — Alice Katherine *b* 1974.

AUNT LIVING (*Daughter of 2nd Baronet*)

Violet (*Baroness Merthyr*), *b* 1908; is a Serving Sister of Order of St John of Jerusalem: *m* 1932, 3rd Baron Merthyr, who *d* 1977. *Residence* – Churchton, Saundersfoot, Pembrokeshire.

COLLATERAL BRANCH LIVING

Issue of late Walter Thomas Meyrick, 5th son of 1st baronet, *b* 1882, *d* 1953: *m* 1st, 1914 (*m diss* 1935), Mabel Violet Blanche, da of late Col Arthur Hill Sandys Montgomery, Rifle Brig, and widow of Percy Downes; 2ndly, 1935, Mary Jocelyn (Sawmill Close, Sharperton, Morpeth), da of Sir James Ernest Thorold, 14th Bt—
(By 2nd *m*) Walter James Charlton (Quinta Ladeira da Nora, Alvor, Portimão, Portugal), *b* 1936; *ed* Eton: *m* 1965, Gillian, yr da of late W. Macduff Urquhart, of Edinburgh, and has issue living, St John James Charlton, *b* 1969, — William Andrew Charlton, *b* 1976, — Louisa Mary Charlton, *b* 1966: *m* 1995, Count Ian Alexander Dembinski, of 204 Camberwell Grove, SE5 8RJ, yr son of Count Julius Dembinski, of Hindhead, Surrey, and has issue living, Alexander *b* 1998, Mariella *b* 1997, — Sophia Rachel Charlton, *b* (twin) 1966: *m* 1994, Aidan J. M. Jackson, of 14 South Green, Staindrop, Barnard Castle, co Durham, yr son of late J. T. Milburn Jackson, of Embleton, Northumberland, and has issue living, Maximilian James Milburn *b* 1997, Amelia Louisa Milburn *b* 1999. —— Michael Alan Charlton, *b* 1937. —— Christopher Thomas Charlton, *b* 1946: *m* 1975, Caroline Mary (who *m* 2ndly, 1985, Julian Richard Freeland, of Green Close, Combe, Oxon OX7 2N5, yst son of Maj P. K. Freeland, of Ipplepen, Devon), elder da of Iain Hugh Webster, of Forest Row, Sussex, and *d* 1979. —— Mary Rhoda Charlton, *b* 1944: *m* 1971, Colin A. Matheson, and has issue living, Nicholas Simon, *b* 1973, — Patrick William Christopher, *b* 1979, — Camilla Karen, *b* 1976.

The 1st baronet, Col Sir Thomas Charlton Meyrick, KCB, DL, JP (son of St John Chivarton Charlton, DL, JP, of Apley Castle, Salop), was MP for Pembroke Dist (C) 1868-74, and assumed 1858, by Roy licence the surname of Meyrick, his maternal grandfather being Thomas Meyrick of Bush, Pembrokeshire, descended from the Meyricks of Bodorgan, Anglesey.

TAPPS GERVIS MEYRICK (GB) 1791, of Hinton Admiral, Hampshire
(Name pronounced "Tapps Gervis Merrick")

Heb dhu, heb dhim, dhu
a digon

Without God, without anything;
God and enough

Sir GEORGE CHRISTOPHER CADAFAEL TAPPS GERVIS MEYRICK, 7th *Baronet*; *b* 10 March 1941; *s* his father *Lt-Col Sir* GEORGE DAVID ELIOTT, MC, 1988: *ed* Eton, and Trin Coll, Camb; patron of two livings; *m* 1968, Jean Louise, yst da of late Lord William Walter Montagu Douglas Scott, MC (*see* D Buccleuch, colls), and has issue.

Arms – Quarterly: 1st and 4th, sable, on a chevron argent between three bands erect raguly or, inflamed proper, a fleur-de-lis gules between two Cornish choughs respecting each other proper, *Meyrick*; 2nd, argent, six ostrich feathers, three, two, and one, sable in the centre point a pellet, *Gervis*; 2nd and 3rd, azure, on a fesse or, between three rhinoceroses argent, as many escallops gules, *Tapps*. **Crest** – 1st, a tower argent, thereon upon a mount vert a Cornish chough holding in the dexter claw a fleur-de-lis; 2nd, a mount vert, thereon three ostrich feathers, one in pale and two in saltire sable, banded by a wreath of oak or; 3rd, a greyhound couchant per pale argent and sable charged on the body with two escallops fessewise counter-charged.
Seats – Hinton Admiral, nr Christchurch, Dorset; Bodorgan, Anglesey.

SONS LIVING

GEORGE WILLIAM OWEN, *b* 3 April 1970. —— Charles Valentine Llewelyn, *b* 1972.

DAUGHTER LIVING

Suzannah Daisy, *b* 1978.

SISTER LIVING

Caroline Susan Joan, *b* 1942: *m* 1963, Richard Arthur Samuel Hulse, of The Old Chapel, Netton, Salisbury SP4 6AW, yr son of Wing-Cdr Sir (Hamilton) Westrow Hulse, 9th Bt.

AUNT LIVING (*daughter of 5th baronet*)

Susan Hermione, *b* 1919: *m* 1945, Peter John Green, MC, and has issue living, Christopher, *b* 1946. *Residence* – Minstead Manor, Minstead, Lyndhurst, Hants.

WIDOW LIVING OF SIXTH BARONET

ANN (*Dowager Lady Tapps Gervis Meyrick*), da of late Clive Miller, of Melbourne, Australia: *m* 1940, Lt-Col Sir George David Eliott Tapps Gervis Meyrick, 6th Bt, MC, who *d* 1988. *Residence* – Waterditch House, Bransgore, Christchurch, Dorset.

COLLATERAL BRANCH LIVING

Grandchildren of late Capt Richard Owen Tapps Gervis Meyrick, yr son of 4th baronet:—
Issue of late Capt Richard Anthony Tapps Gervis Meyrick, *b* 1920, *d* 1964: *m* 1949, Alexandra Adèle (Zandra) (Sheafhayne Manor, Yarcombe, Honiton, Devon) (who *m* 2ndly, 1967, Antony Rising Baxter), da of Brig Rupert John Brett, DSO, of Langsmeade House, Milton Common, Oxon:—
James David, *b* 1950: *m* 1988, Nicola Jane, da of H. M. Williams, of White House, Llantilio Crossenny, Abergavenny, Gwent. —— Sarah Jacintha Barbara, *b* 1952: *m* 1989, Walter John Dowe Taylor.

The 2nd baronet, Sir George William Tapps, MP for Christchurch 1832-6, assumed in 1835 the additional surname of Gervis, while the 3rd baronet assumed in 1876 by Roy licence the further additional surname of Meyrick. The 4th baronet, Sir George Augustus Eliott Tapps Gervis Meyrick, was High Sheriff of Hants 1900. The 5th baronet, Sir George Llewelyn Tapps Gervis Meyrick, Major (ret) 7th Hussars, was High Sheriff of Anglesey 1939.

Meysey-Thompson, see Thompson.

MIDDLETON (E) 1662, of Belsay Castle, Northumberland (Extinct 1999)

Sir LAWRENCE MONCK MIDDLETON, 10th and last *Baronet*; *d* 1999.

WIDOW LIVING OF TENTH BARONET

PRIMROSE (*Lady Middleton*), da of Lawrence Haynes Adams, of Shrubland House, Soham, Cambs, and previously wife of ...... Westcombe: *m* 1984, Sir Lawrence Monck Middleton, 10th Bt, who *d* 1999.

COLLATERAL BRANCHES LIVING

Granddaughter of late Lambert William Middleton (infra):—
Issue of late Henry Lambert Middleton, *b* 1923, *d* (17 Jan) 1998: *m* 1964 (*m diss* 1978), Susan Jenifer, who *d* (7 Nov) 1998, da of late William Arthur Fearnley-Whittingstall, TD, QC, of The Old Manor House, Melbourn, Cambs, and widow of Hon Rodney Mathias Berry, TD (*see* V Camrose):—
Laura Sybil Rose, *b* 1969: *m* 1997, Peter R. de Wesselow, yst son of Ian de Wesselow, of Shurlock Row, Berks, and has issue living, Delilah Jacaranda Jane, *b* 1999.

Granddaughter of late Henry Nicholas Middleton, brother of 7th baronet:—
Issue of late Lambert William Middleton, *b* 1877, *d* 1941: *m* 1922, Lady Sybil Grey, OBE, who *d* 1966, da of 4th Earl Grey:—
Mary Sybil, *b* 1925: *m* 1948, Capt John Brooke Boyd, KOSB, of Whiterigg, Melrose, Roxburghshire TD6 9HE, and has issue living, Simon John (34 Kimberley Rd, Cambridge), *b* 1949; *ed* Eton, and New Coll Oxford: *m* 1979, Julia Mary Seiber, — James Lambert (Rue Rotselaerlaan 13, 3180 Tervuren, Belgium), *b* 1952; *ed* Eton, — Caroline Elizabeth *b* (twin), 1952, — Diana Mary, *b* 1955: *m* 1990, Neil Braithwaite, of Aydon Grange, Corbridge, Northumberland.

MILBANK (UK) 1882, of Well, co York, and of Hart, co Durham

Sir ANTHONY FREDERICK MILBANK, 5th *Baronet*, *b* 16 Aug 1939; *s* his father, *Maj Sir* MARK VANE, KCVO, MC, 1984; *ed* Eton; Chm Moorland Assocn; DL N Yorkshire: *m* 1970, Belinda Beatrice, yr da of Brig Adrian Clements Gore, DSO (*see* Gore, Bt, colls), and has issue.

Arms – Gules, a saltire argent, gutte de poix between two lions heads couped in pale, and as many roses in fesse of the second. Crest – A lion's head couped argent, gutte de poix, charged with a pale gules, thereon three roses, also argent.
Seat – Barningham Park, Richmond, N Yorks DL11 7DW.

SONS LIVING

EDWARD MARK SOMERSET, *b* 9 April 1973. —— Toby Adrian Jameson, *b* 1977.

DAUGHTER LIVING

Alexina Victoria, *b* 1971.

BROTHER LIVING

(Arthur) John (The Old Laundry House, Smeeth, Ashford, Kent, TN25 6ST), *b* 1940; *ed* Gordonstoun: *m* 1969, Rosalind Eleanor Lucy, da of G. E. L. Townshend, of Pretoria, S Africa, and has issue living, Robert Andrew, *b* 1972, — Lucy Verena, *b* 1970.

UNCLE LIVING (*son of 3rd baronet*)

Denis William Powlett, TD, *b* 1912; *ed* Radley; is Maj RA (TA): *m* 1934, Doreen Frances, who *d* 1991, da of Sir Richard Pierce Butler, OBE, 11th Bt (*cr* 1628), and has issue living, Mark Richard (Chirume Ranch (Box 767), Marondera, Zimbabwe), *b* 1937: *m* 1st, 1966 (*m diss* 1989), Frances Elizabeth, da of Richard V. Holme; 2ndly, 1993, Mrs Nicola Mary Sclater, da of late Antony Cropper, of Tolson Hall, Kendal, Cumbria, and has issue living (by 1st *m*), Robert Frederick *b* 1968: *m* 19—, Amanda Claire, only da of Robin von der Heyde, of Vigila, Mvurwi, Zimbabwe (*see* Wake, Bt, 1980 Edn) (and has issue living, Sabrina, *b* 1997), Henry Mark Thomas *b* 1970: *m* 1999, Philippa Shaxson, Jack Patrick *b* 1979, — Penelope Ann (Box 628, Umtentweni 4235, S Africa), *b* 1935: *m* 1st, 1955, Capt John Frederick de Vere Shaw, Kenya Regt, who *d* 1960 (*see* Shaw, Bt, *cr* 1821, colls); 2ndly, 1970, Hougham Robert Mills, and has issue living (by 1st *m*) (*see* Shaw, Bt, *cr* 1821), — Susan Fiona, *b* 1942: *m* 1963, Antony Roger Pelly, and has issue (*see* Pelly, Bt). *Residence* – Southbrook, Galphay, Ripon, N Yorks.

COLLATERAL BRANCH LIVING

Issue of late Maj John Gerald Frederick Milbank, 2nd son of 3rd Bt, *b* 1909, *d* 1991: *m* 1938, Louisa Harriet, who *d* 1974, only da of late Edward Beaumont Cotton Curtis, of Caynham Cottage, Ludlow, Shropshire (Curtis, Bt):—
David John (Gayles Fields, Dalton, Richmond, Yorks), *b* 1940; *ed* Gordonstoun: *m* 1971, Clarissa Mary, da of Capt S. L. Bigge, of Langdale, Melsonby, Yorks, and has issue living, James John, *b* 1974, — Nicholas Charles, *b* 1975. —— Charles Gerald, *b* 1942; *ed* Eton; a racehorse trainer: *m* 1973 (*m diss* 1981), Mrs Wendy Wright, da of late E. N. Johnson, of Newton Firs, Newton, by Frodsham, Cheshire, and has issue living, Philip Augustus, *b* 1974, — Camilla, *b* 1975, — Sophie Kathleen, *b* 1977.

The 1st baronet, Sir Frederick Acclom Milbank, 2nd son of late Mark Milbank of Thorpe-Perrow, was MP for N Riding of York 1865-85, and for York, N Riding, Richmond Div 1885-6. The 2nd baronet, Sir Powlett Charles John, sat as MP for Radnorshire (C) 1895-1900. The 4th baronet, Sir Mark Vane, KCVO, MC, was Master of HM Household and Extra Equerry to HM 1954-67.

Milborne-Swinnerton-Pilkington, see Pilkington.

MILBURN (UK) 1905, of Guyzance, Parish of Shilbottle, Northumberland

Sir ANTHONY RUPERT MILBURN, 5th *Baronet*; *b* 17 April 1947, elder son of late Maj Rupert Leonard Eversley Milburn, yr son of 3rd baronet; *s* his uncle, *Sir* JOHN NIGEL, 1985; *ed* Eton, and RAC, Cirencester; ARICS, MRAC: *m* 1977, Olivia Shirley, yst da of Capt Thomas Noel Catlow, CBE, RN, of Rose Cottage, Tunstall, by Carnforth, Lancs, and has issue.

Arms – Per fesse or and gules, a pale counterchanged between two bears' heads erased in chief sable, muzzled of the first, and as many bear's heads also erased and muzzled in base or. **Crest** – In front of a bear's head erased sable, muzzled or, four mascles interlaced fesseways of the last. **Badge** – On a mill-rind sable, an escallop shell argent.
Seat – Guyzance Hall, Acklington, Northumberland.

SONS LIVING

PATRICK THOMAS, *b* 4 Dec 1980. —— (Edward) Jake, *b* 1987.

DAUGHTER LIVING

Lucy Camilla Anne, *b* 1982.

BROTHER LIVING

While I breathe I hope

Michael Richard, *b* 1950; *ed* Eton: *m* 1982, Carola Anneliese, da of Kurt Walter Bedau, of Schulstrasse 9, Schonebeck/Elbe, Germany, and has issue living, Mark Phillip, *b* 1987. *Address* – c/o Perlas Travel & Tours Ltd, 101, 1000 8th Ave SW, Calgary, Alberta, Canada T2P 3M7.

SISTERS LIVING

Caroline Anne (*Lady Renwick*), *b* 1945: *m* 1966, Sir Richard Eustace Renwick, 4th Bt, of Whalton House, Whalton, Morpeth, Northumberland, and has issue (see that title). —— Diana Rosemary (34 Salcott Rd, SW11), *b* 1949: *m* 1970 (*m diss* 1980), Richard Murrough Wilson, and has issue living, Nicholas Rupert Gerald, *b* 1974.

AUNTS LIVING (*Daughters of 3rd baronet*)

Darea Joan, *b* 1923: *m* 1950, Maj George Harold Michael Sankey, late Staffs Yeo, of Shackerley Hall, Albrighton, Wolverhampton, Staffs, eldest son of late Col Harold Bantock Sankey, CBE, MC, TD, DL, of Whiston Hall, Albrighton, and has issue living, Christopher Michael David (Rosedale, Church Lane, Pitton, Salisbury SP5 1DJ), *b* 1952; *ed* Shrewsbury: *m* 1995, Sarah Elizabeth, da of late Ronald Gilbert Frost, of Ham Farm, Brent Knoll, Highbridge, Som, and has issue living, Hannah *b* 1996, Catherine *b* 1998, — Peter William Richard (Cranmere Worfield, Bridgnorth, Shropshire WV15 5LP), *b* 1953; *ed* Shrewsbury: *m* 1991, Mrs Sarah Caroline Aileen Davenport Greenshields, only da of late John Sydney Birch Lea (*see* Lea, Bt, colls), and has issue living, Edward Philip George *b* 1994, Georgina Elisabeth Joan *b* 1992, — Nicola Mary Joan, *b* 1955, — Virginia Karen Margaret, *b* 1957. —— Susan Anne (*Lady Farr*), *b* 1937: *m* 1960, Sir John Arnold Farr, who *d* 1997, of 11 Vincent Sq, SW1, and Shortwood House, Lamport, Northants, elder surv son of late Capt John Farr, JP, of Worksop Manor, Notts, and has issue living, Jonathan, *b* 1962: *m* 1998, Caroline, eldest da of David Barton, of Calderstones, Liverpool, — George Nelson, *b* 1967: *m* 1992, Jane F., da of C. R. Lachlan, of Melbourne, and of Mrs David Gape, of Caxton, Cambs, and has issue living, Oliver George Tebbitt *b* 1997, James Casper *b* 1999, Harriet Philippa Joan *b* 1994, Katherine Elizabeth *b* 1996.

WIDOW LIVING OF FOURTH BARONET

DOROTHY JOAN (*Dorothy, Lady Milburn*), eldest da of Leslie Butcher, of Dunholme, Lincs: *m* 1940, Sir John Nigel Milburn, 4th Bt, who *d* 1985. *Residence* – Brainshaugh, Acklington, Morpeth, Northumberland.

COLLATERAL BRANCHES LIVING

Issue of late John Davison Milburn, 3rd son of 1st baronet, *b* 1886, *d* 1972: *m* 1922, Grace Emily, who *d* 1934, only da of late Stuart MacRae, of Conchra, Ross-shire:—
Angela Mary (Highcliff, Little Switzerland, Douglas, Isle of Man IM2 6AE), *b* 1925. —— Sybil Pauline (Highcliff, Little Switzerland, Douglas, Isle of Man IM2 6AE), *b* 1926.

Issue of late Capt Archibald William Milburn, 4th son of 1st baronet, *b* 1887, *d* 1965: *m* 1931, Eleanor Lilias (Victora), who *d* 1983, da of Maj Nevill Arthur Charles de Hirzel Tufnell, of Langleys, Chelmsford:—
Mark Anthony William (Apart 164, Arrecife de Lanzarote, Canary Islands), *b* 1932; *ed* Eton, le Rosey, and RMA; PhD, FLS, FSA; late Maj Special Air Ser (TA) and late Lt R Scots Greys: *m* 1968 (*m diss* 1976), Angela Margaret Cromwell, da of late Lt Col Geoffrey Stephen Carmac Weigall, and formerly wife of David Francis Brougham Maitland Edye, and has issue living, Francis Shahid, *b* 1969; *ed* Millfield; BSc. —— Sarah Caroline Georgiana (Langleys, Gt Waltham, Chelmsford, Essex CM3 1AH), *b* 1935: *m* 1956, David Robert Micklem, son of late Cdr Sir (Edward) Robert Micklem, CBE, RN, and has issue living, Alexander David Robert, *b* 1965: *m* 1990, Jennifer Jane, elder da of Dr Maurice Healy, and has issue living, Oliver David *b* 1991, Henry James *b* 1993, Charles Nicholas *b* 1995, — Lucy Victoria Cornelia, *b* 1958: *m* 1984, Peter John Bradford Gibson, and has issue living, Archibald John Peter *b* 1991, Olivia Emily Victoria *b* 1987, Alice Emma Louise *b* 1989, — Anna Caroline, *b* 1960: *m* 1987, Jonathan James Grew, and has issue living, James Edward *b* 1988, Jeremy Charles *b* 1993, Richard David *b* 1995, Louisa Sarah *b* 1990.

This family is descended from Thomas Milburn, of Broomhope in Birtley, North Tynedale (*d* 1705). The 1st baronet, Sir John Davison Milburn, was High Sheriff for Northumberland 1905. The 3rd baronet, Sir Leonard John Milburn, was High Sheriff of that co 1928. The mother of Sir Anthony Rupert Milburn, 5th Bt, was Anne Mary (*d* 1991), da of late Maj Austin Scott Murray, MC, of Heckfield Place, Basingstoke (*see* B Mowbray, colls). This lady, being with her cousin Mary sole co-heir to the family of Scott Murray of Danesfield and Hambledon, co Bucks, was granted by Lord Lyon the arms of *Murray of Philiphaugh* with a difference 14 Dec 1955, and of *Scott of Trabourn* with a difference 29 Aug 1966.

ST JOHN-MILDMAY (GB) 1772, of Farley, co Southampton
(Name pronounced "Sinjun-Mildmay")

Sir WALTER JOHN HUGH ST JOHN-MILDMAY, 11th *Baronet*, son of late Michael Paulet St John-Mildmay, great-grandson of Edward St John-Mildmay, 8th son of 3rd baronet; *b* 3 Sept 1935; *s* his kinsman, *Rev Sir* (AUBREY) NEVILLE, who *d* 1955, after which the baronetcy was dormant until 1998; *ed* Wycliffe Coll, Emmanuel Coll, Camb (BA), Hammersmith Coll of Art and Building, and RAC Cirencester; later Royal Engineers.

Arms – Argent, three lions rampant azure, armed and langued gules. Crest – A lion rampant guardant azure.
Residence – 9 Lansdowne Crescent, Bath BA1 5EX.

BROTHER LIVING

MICHAEL HUGH PAULET, *b* 28 Sept 1937; *ed* Wycliffe Coll, and Emmanuel Coll, Camb (MA): *m* 1965, Mrs Crystal Margaret Ludlow, and has issue living, Henry Walter, *b* 1971, — Oliver James, *b* 1973, — Emilia Alice Joan, *b* 1977, — and has adopted his step-daughter Eroica Greer, *b* 1960. *Residence* – Drakestone House, Stinchcombe, Dursley, Glos GL11 6AS.

Alla ta Hara

The 1st baronet, Sir Paulet St John (son by the 2nd wife of Ellis Mews, or Mewys, who assumed by Act of Parliament the surname of St John on his marriage in 1699 to his first cousin, Frances, da and eventual heiress of Oliver St John, MP, of Farley), was MP for Winchester 1734-41 and 1751-4, and for Hants 1741-7. The 2nd baronet, Sir Henry Paulet St

John (knighted 1760), was MP for Hants 1772-80. Sir Henry Paulet St John, 3rd Bt, MP for Westbury, Winchester, and Hants (1796-1808), *m* Jane, el da and coheir of Carew Mildmay, of Shawford House, Hampshire, and Mildmay Park, Stoke Newington; she was also heiress of her uncle, Sir William Mildmay, Bt, of Moulsham Hall, Essex, and of her great-uncle, Carew Hervey Mildmay, MP for Harwich, of Marks, Essex, and Hazlegrove, Somerset. In 1790 Sir Henry, 3rd baronet, obtained Royal permission to use the additional surname of Mildmay, and to bear the arms of Mildmay only. The 4th baronet, Sir Henry St John Carew St John-Mildmay, was MP for Winchester. The 5th baronet was Major 2nd Dragoon Guards subsequently Comdg. Hampshire Yeo., and the 6th baronet was Major Grenadier Guards. The 7th baronet assumed by Roy. licence 1900 the additional surnames and arms of Shaw-Lefevre under the will of his grand-father, Charles, Visount Eversley, G.C.B. (ext. 1888). The 8th baronet assumed by deed poll 1922, for himself and issue the surnames of St John-Mildmay only in lieu of those of Shaw-Lefever-St John-Mildmay. The 10th baronet, Rev Sir (Aubrey) Neville St John-Mildmay, *d* in 1955. His only surviving son, Verus Arundell St John-Mildmay, *dsp* in 1965, without having claimed the baronetcy. The baronetcy was revived in 1998, having been dormant since 1955, in favour of Sir Walter John Hugh St John-Mildmay, 11th Bt, son of the presumed heir to the baronetcy, Michael Paulet St John-Mildmay, who *d* 1993, without his name having been entered in the Official Roll of the Baronetage.

MILES (UK) 1859, of Leigh Court, Somersetshire

Labora sicut bonus miles

Work like a good soldier

Sir WILLIAM NAPIER MAURICE MILES, 6th *Baronet*; *b* 19 Oct 1913; *s* his father *Lt-Col Sir* CHARLES WILLIAM, OBE, 1966; *ed* Stowe, and Jesus Coll, Camb: *m* 1946, Pamela, da of late Capt Michael Dillon, and has issue.

Arms – Azure, a chevron paly of six ermine and or between three lozenges argent, each charged with a fleur-de-lis sable. Crest – Upon a rock a dexter arm embowed in armour the hand grasping an anchor entwined by a cable proper.
Residence – Old Rectory House, Walton-in-Gordano, Clevedon, Som BS21 7AW.

SON LIVING

PHILIP JOHN, *b* 10 Aug 1953.

DAUGHTERS LIVING

Catherine Anne Elizabeth, *b* 1947: *m* 1974, Peter Charles Beloe, of Madam's End Farm, Hardwicke, Gloucester and has issue living, William Alexander Peter, *b* 1977, — Phoebe Caroline, *b* 1983. —— Lorraine, *b* 1950: *m* 1972, Martin Hugh Sessions-Hodge, and has issue living, James Anthony, *b* 1975, — Henry George Patrick, *b* 1977, — Abigail Theodora, *b* 1980.

BROTHER LIVING

Charles William Noel, *b* 1915; *ed* Stowe, and Jesus Coll, Camb: *m* 1940, Jacqueline (Dickie), who *d* 1998, da of late Robert Singlehurst Cross, and has had issue, †Anthony William, *b* 1946; *ed* Stowe; *dunm* 1969, — Phinola Jane, *b* 1943: *m* 1st, 1967 (*m diss* 1991), Anthony McCandlish Smith; 2ndly, 1995, Ian Gerald Brown, of Maesachddu, Porthyrhyd, Carmarthen SA32 8PX, and has issue living (by 1st *m*), Fraser William *b* 1975, Robert Gavin *b* 1977. *Residence* – Wheelers, Hound Green, Mattingley, Basingstoke, Hants.

COLLATERAL BRANCH LIVING

Issue of late Capt William Henry Miles, yr son of 4th baronet, *b* 1888; *d* 1975: *m* 1912, Lilian, who *d* 1972, da of Hon Sir Hartley Williams, of 93 Cadogan Gdns, SW:—
Lilian Mary, *b* 1914: *m* 1939, Alan Grant Maby, who *d* 1965, and *d* 1995, leaving issue, Michael Robin Patrick (50 Stamford Court, Goldhawk Rd, W6), *b* 1944: *ed* Wellington Coll: *m* 1969, Miranda Jane, 2nd da of Edward Charles Gough Marrow, of Kingsdon, Somerton, Som, and has issue living, Alexander Miles *b* 1974, Dominic Henry *b* 1977, — Keith Alan (Old Chapel House, Long Compton, Warwicks CV36 5JS), *b* 1946: *ed* Wellington Coll, and Ch Ch, Oxford: *m* 1977, Elizabeth Symes, da of late Dr John Symes Prior, of The Old Forge, Hayden, Cheltenham, and has issue living, Thomas Edward, *b* 1979, — William Jonathan, *b* 1982. —— Pamela (Ossington House, Newark, Notts), *b* 1916: *m* 1st, 1947, Lt-Col William Maxwell Evelyn Denison, who *d* 1972; 2ndly, 1974, Prof Daniel Goedhuis, late Netherlands Embassy, who *d* 1995, and has issue living (by 1st *m*), Georgina Jane, *b* 1948: *m* 1978, George Michael Gill, of 27 Campden Hill Rd, W8, and has issue living, Chloe Francesca *b* 1981.

This family, from Ledbury, Herefordshire, became merchants of Bristol in the 18th century. Philip John Miles of Leigh Court, Som, was Mayor of Bristol 1780, and MP for Westbury, Corfe Castle and Bristol. His son, Sir William, 1st Bt, was MP for Chippenham, Romney, and E Somerset (*C*). Sir Philip John William, 2nd Bt, was MP for E Somerset (*C*) 1878-85.

MILLAIS (UK) 1885, of Palace Gate, Kensington, co Middlesex, and of St Ouen, Jersey
(Name pronounced "Millay")

Ars longa, vita brevis

Art endureth, life is short

Sir GEOFFROY RICHARD EVERETT MILLAIS, 6th *Baronet*; *b* 27 Dec 1941; *s* his father, *Sir* RALPH REGNAULT, 1992.

Arms – Per bend sinister or and azure, an estoile of eight points between three fleurs-de-lys, two in fesse and one in base, all counter-changed. **Crest** – In front of a dexter hand gauntleted and couped gules an estoile of eight points or.

SISTER LIVING

Caroline Mary Felicity, *b* 1940: *m* 1963, David Anthony Campbell-Jones, only son of late Mervyn Campbell-Jones, and has issue living, Henry David Mervyn, *b* 1972; *ed* Radley, — Serena Caroline Mary, *b* 1969; *ed* Royal Naval Sch, Haslemere.

UNCLE LIVING (*son of 4th baronet*)

EDWARD GRAY ST HELIER, *b* 15 March 1918; *ed* Radley; late Capt Anti-Aircraft Regt RA: *m* 1947, Rosemary Barbara, yr da of late Brig-Gen Frederick George Lucas, CB, CSI, CIE, DSO, 5th Royal Gurkha Rifles, and has issue living, Andrew Michael, *b* 13 April 1948; *ed* Clayesmore, — John Frederick, *b* 1949; *ed* Radley, — Peter William, *b* 1951; *ed* Radley, — David Gray, *b* 1959; *ed* Monkton Combe: *m* 1993, Susanna M., da of late Dr Patrick Maybin and of Dr Maureen Maybin, of Ballylesson, co Down, and has issue living, Patrick David *b* 1995, Niamh Esmé *b* 1997, — Fiona, *b* 1960. *Residence* – Crosswater Farm, Churt, Surrey.

WIDOW LIVING OF FIFTH BARONET

BABETTE IRENE (*Lady Millais*), yr da of late Maj-Gen Harold Francis Salt, CB, CMG, DSO (*see* Salt, Bt, *cr* 1899, colls), widow of Maj John de Grey Tatham Warter, MC, and formerly wife of Victor William Henry Sefton-Smith: *m* 3rdly, 1975, as his 3rd wife, Sir Ralph Regnault Millais, 5th Bt, who *d* 1992. *Residence* – Elizabeth Court, 47 Milmans St, SW10 0DA.

COLLATERAL BRANCH LIVING

Issue of late John Guille Millais, 4th son of 1st baronet, *b* 1865, *d* 1931: *m* 1894, Fanny Margaret, who *d* 1960, da of late Philip George Skipwith, of Hundleby, Lincolnshire:—
(Hesketh) Raoul le Jarderay, *b* 1901; Capt (ret) late Scots Guards: *m* 1st, 1926, Elinor Clare, who *d* 1953, da of late Allan Ronald Macdonell, of Montreal; 2ndly, 1949, Mrs Katharine Edith Prior-Palmer, who *d* 1985, da of late Frank Bibby, CBE, of Hardwick Grange, Shrewsbury, and has issue living, (by 1st *m*) John Ronald Raoul LEES-MILLAIS (Rockley Manor, Marlborough), *b* 1927; assumed the additional surname of Lees: *m* 1952, Lavinia Charlotte, da of late Capt Geoffrey William Martin Lees, of Falcutt House, Brackley, Northants, and has issue living, David John Geoffroy *b* 1953: *m* 1980, Jane V. H., el da of Kenneth J. Forder, of Steeple Close, Church Gate, SW6 (and has issue living, a son *b* 1982, a da *b* 1987, Catherine Dimity L. *b* 1991), Colin Everett (Whittlebury Park, nr Towcester, Northants) *b* 1957: *m* 1991, Frances Maria Loftus, only da of Humphry Stuart Loftus Tottenham, of Minchens, Bramley, Hants (*see* Archdale, Bt, 1972-73 Edn) (and has issue living, Sophie Frances Margery *b* 1994, Emily Grace *b* 1997), Patrick James *b* 1958: *m* 1987, Fiona Astrid, yst da of late Maj John Edward Joicey, MC (and has issue, Marcus John *b* 1989, Rory *b* 1990), Joanna Clare *b* 1954: *m* 1981, Thomas Hornby Graham Cooper, son of late Brig Thomas Cooper, of Bottom Farm, Eaton, Grantham, Lincs (and has issue living, Alexander Thomas *b* 1986, Louisa Clare *b* 1983, Emma Lavinia *b* 1985), Fiona Katherine *b* 1964: *m* 1996, Richard H. C. Nourse, eldest son of Dr C. H. Nourse, of Ipswich (and has issue living, Arabella Mary *b* 1999), — Hugh Geoffroy (The Stables, Kirtlington Park, Oxon OX5 3JN), *b* 1929: *m* 1st, 1957 (*m diss* 1978), Suzy Falconnet; 2ndly, 1989, Anne Mary, da of late Adin Harry Sheffield, of Galliats, Lilliput, Dorset, and has issue living (by 1st *m*), Ian *b* 1958, Joshua *b* 1961: *m* 1996, Letitia, 2nd da of Sir Thomas Raymond Dunne, KCVO (HM's Lord Lieut of Herefordshire and Worcestershire), of Gatley Park, Herefords, Tara Romaney *b* 1967, — (by 2nd *m*), Hesketh Merlin, *b* 1950; *ed* Milton Abbey; Capt R Hussars (PWO): *m* 1981, Amanda W., da of James Fletcher, of 8 Avonmore Mansions, Avonmore Rd, W14 (and has issue living, Raoul Edward *b* 1981, Iona Effie *b* 1983, Katherine Alice *b* 1986). *Residence* – Dippers Moor Manor, Wormbridge, Herefordshire.

The 1st baronet, Sir John Everett Millais (son of John William Millais, of Jersey), was an eminent painter and Pres of Roy Acad. The 5th baronet, Sir Ralph Regnault Millais, *m* 1st, Felicity Caroline Mary, who *d* 1994, da of Brig-Gen William Ward Warner, CMG. She was mother of the 6th and present baronet.

MILLER (E) 1705, of Chichester, Sussex

Sir HARRY MILLER, 12th *Baronet, b* 15 Jan 1927; *s* his brother, *Sir* JOHN HOLMES, 1995: *m* 1954, Gwynedd Margaret, da of R. P. Sherriff, of St Anthony, Paraparaumu, NZ, and has issue.

𝔄rms – Argent, a fesse wavy azure, between three wolve's heads erased gules. 𝔄rest – A wolf's head erased gules charged on the neck with a fesse azure.
Residence – 53 Koha Rd, Taupo, NZ.

SON LIVING

ANTHONY THOMAS, *b* 4 May 1955: *m* 1990, Barbara Ann, da of Herbert Kensington, formerly wife of ...... Battersby, and has issue living, Thomas Kensington, *b* 26 Feb 1994, — Richard Harry, *b* 1997. *Residence* – 86 Godden Crescent, Mission Bay, Auckland, NZ.

DAUGHTERS LIVING

Sara Margaret, *b* 1957: *m* 1986, Garth David Laing, and has issue living, Jack McIntyre, *b* 1994, — Maggie Eleanor, *b* 1992. —— Judith Christine, *b* 1960.

SISTERS LIVING

Hilary, *b* 1921: *m* 1945, John Alexander Nisbet, of 10 Weka Rd, Taupo, NZ, and has issue living Philip John, *b* 1946, — Jan, *b* 1948. —— Norah Jessie, *b* 1923: *m* 1949, Roy Galloway Gardiner, of 68A Wakeman St, Pahiatua, NZ, and has issue living John, *b* 1950, — Hugh, *b* 1956, — Margaret, *b* 1951.

DAUGHTERS LIVING OF ELEVENTH BARONET

Roslyn Mary, *b* 1955: *m* 1995, Rick McCay. —— Diana Jocelyn, *b* 1958: *m* 1991, Murray John Telford, of Paraparaumu, NZ.

COLLATERAL BRANCHES LIVING

Issue of late Charles Holmes Miller, yr son of 9th baronet, *b* 1905, *d* 1984: *m* 1st, 1936, Hester Amelia, who *d* 1974, da of E. J. Wilde; 2ndly, 1975, Pauline Rochfort (2/26 Clyde Rd, Napier, NZ):—
(By 1st *m*) Patrick Holmes, *b* 1941. —— Paul Greville, *b* 1943. —— Monica Jane, *b* 1938. —— Elizabeth Hope, *b* 1940.

Grandchildren of late Hon Sir Henry John Miller (first elected Speaker of NZ Legislative Council), 2nd son of 6th baronet:—
Issue of late William Nicholson Miller, *b* 1868, *d* 1950: *m* 1906, Edith Mary, da of J. C. Forsyth:—
William Maxwell (Chesterville Retirement Village, Unit 10/14-18, Chesterville Rd,. Cheltenham, Victoria 3192, Australia), *b* 1913; MICE Aust, Chartered Civil Engr (ret): *m* 1938, Marjory, who *d* 1996, da of late L. M. Bell, MICE, and has issue living, Leonard Maxwell (Level 11/34 Queens St, Melbourne, Victoria 3000, Australia), *b* 1948; BCEng, MICE Aust, Chartered Civil Engr; Dir LMA Partnership Pty Ltd: *m* 1975, Ruth Annette Vile, and has issue living, Daniel James *b* 1976, Katherine Rachel *b* (twin) 1976, Rebecca Sarah *b* 1977, — Diana Marjory, *b* 1940; BA, Dip Arch: *m* 1963, Jeremy David Pope (c/o Transparencey International, Otto-Suhr-Allee 97-99, D-10585, Berlin, Germany) and has issue living, Adam Quentin *b* 1969; LLB: *m* 1998, Karin A. W. Jakobsson, Samuel William *b* 1974, Jemima Mary *b* 1971; BEd, — Mary Nicholson, *b* 1947; MBA, BA, Dip Soc Studies: *m* 1st, 1976 (*m diss* 1986), Yoram Zamir, of New York; 2ndly, 1988, Faizal Khan, of 43-31 223rd St, Bayside, NY 11361, USA, and has issue living (by 1st *m*), Talor Miller *b* 1981, — Robyn Elizabeth, *b* 1951; BA, Dip Ed: *m* 1973, Geoffrey Collis, of 4 Sherwood Court, Lindisfarne, Tasmania 7015, and has issue living, Matthew William *b* 1980, Jacqueline Louise *b* 1983. —— Margaret May (Waiapu House, Havelock North, Hawkes Bay, NZ), *b* 1907: *m* 1937, Edward Ernest Zohrab, who *d* 1970, and has issue living, Margaret Ann, *b* 1938: *m* 1964, Jerome Glazebrook Whyte, of Clive, Hawkes Bay, NZ, and has issue living, — Jenny Elizabeth, *b* 1940: *m* 1964, John Mundell Ewart, of 14 Wheretia St, Taupo, NZ, and has issue living, — Patricia Joan, *b* 1947: *m* 1970, Bryan Gifford Moore, of Wharemoa, Otoroa, Kaeo, Northland, NZ, and has issue living.

Issue of late Lieut-Col George Ralph Miller, DSO, *b* 1874, *d* 1948: *m* 1916, Violet Mary, who *d* 1981, da of late W. H. Teschemaker, of Kauro Hill, Otago, New Zealand:—
Cecil Ralph, TD (70 Ballabrooie Way, Douglas, Isle of Man), *b* 1917; Maj Parachute Regt ret: *m* 1981, Marie, da of Stephen Sumner, and widow of Maj Robert Thomas Williamson, The Cameronaians (ret), of Edinburgh. —— Anthony John (142 Bothams Bend Rd, Blenheim, RD3, NZ), *b* 1920: *m* 1952, Sheila Doreen, da of Lt-Col L. Harvey, of Clare Glen, High Hurstwood, Sussex, and widow of Sqdn-Ldr M. Savage, and has issue living, Richard Charles Cecil, *b* 1956: *m* 1984, Eileen Joy, da of E. R. Odey, of Norfolk, and has issue living, Mark George Ralph *b* 1987, Matthew Anthony Edward *b* 1989, Rosemary Jane Violet *b* 1993, — Timothy John, *b* 1957: *m* 1996, Carolyn Reece-Jones, and has issue living, Holly Olivia *b* 1998, — Jennifer Anne, *b* 1952: *m* 1st, 1976, Peter Antony Twist, who *d* 1979; 2ndly, 1988, Warren Sullivan, of Sydney, NSW, Australia, and has issue living, (by 2nd *m*) Luke Anthony *b* 1989, Françoise Alice *b* (twin) 1989.

Sir Thomas Miller, 1st Bt, was son of Mark Miller, Alderman of Chichester, and was several times Mayor of that city. The 1st, 2nd, and 3rd baronets each represented Chichester in Parliament, and the 5th baronet sat as MP for Portsmouth.

MILLER (GB) 1788, of Glenlee, Kirkcudbrightshire

Sir STEPHEN WILLIAM MACDONALD MILLER OF GLENLEE, 8th *Baronet*, MB, BS, FRCS, FRCGP; *b* 20 June 1953; *s* his father, *Sir* (FREDERICK WILLIAM) MACDONALD, 1991; *ed* Rugby, and St Bart's Hosp: *m* 1st, 1978, Mary Carolyn, who *d* 1989, only da of Gwynedd Bulkeley Owens, of 2 Westfield Av, Oakes, Huddersfield; 2ndly, 1990, Caroline Mary Clark, da of Leslie A— E— Chasemore, of Shebbear, Devon, and widow of Harold Frederick Clark, and has issue by 1st *m*.

𝕬rms – Argent, a cross moline azure, in chief a lozenge between two mullets of the second and in base a bar wavy vert. 𝕮rest – Λ human hand couped at the wrist; the third and fourth fingers folded in the hand proper. 𝕾upporters – Two roebucks proper.
Residence – The Lawn, Shebbear, Beaworthy, Devon EX21 5RU.

SON LIVING (By 1st marriage)

JAMES STEPHEN MACDONALD, *b* 25 July 1981.

DAUGHTER LIVING (By 1st marriage)

Katherine Helen, *b* 1983.

SISTER LIVING

Alison Hilary, *b* 1951: *m* 1976, John Glover Freeman, of Holly Farm, Bergh Apton, Norwich, and has issue living, William Griffin Henry, *b* 1981, — Thomas Michael Percy, *b* 1984.

HALF-UNCLES LIVING (Sons of 6th baronet by his 3rd wife, Cynthia Rosemary, who d 1991, da of Frederick Edward Huish)

Graham Frederick Alastair (Coral Gables, Florida, USA), *b* (Sept) 1938; *ed* Pangbourne: *m* 1968, Gaynor, who *d* 1988, da of Tudor Whitcombe, of Cardiff, S Wales, and has issue living, Alastair, *b* 1971; B Eng, — Penelope, *b* 1969; *ed* Univ of Wales, Cardiff (BSc). —— George Edward John, *b* 1946: *m* 1970, Merrill, da of T. G. Morris, and has issue living, Christopher Carl Edward, *b* 1980, — Stephanie Claire, *b* 1971; *ed* Univ of Wales, Swansea (BSc).

HALF-AUNTS LIVING

(Daughter of 6th baronet by his 2nd wife, Margaret May, da of Frederick Shotter)

Pamela Ann Mary, *b* 1928: *m* 1950, John Ward Randolph Nicholson, of Crag View Farm, North Rigton, nr Huby, Yorks, and has issue living, Mark John Anthony, *b* 1952, — Martin Euan Thomas, *b* 1955, — Moray John Fergus, *b* 1962, — Myles Ian Vaughan, *b* 1964, — Magnus Francis Benedict, *b* 1966, — Mungo Patrick Lee, *b* 1969, — Annette Mary Ward, *b* 1951, — Philippa Mary Randolph, *b* 1954, — Iona Frances Marianne, *b* 1957, — Alexandra Mary Elizabeth, *b* 1959.

(Daughter of 6th baronet by his 3rd wife)

Teresa Rosemary Ann, *b* 1939: *m* 1961 (*m diss* 1976), Grenfell King, and has issue living, Julian Grenfell, *b* 1972.

WIDOW LIVING OF SEVENTH BARONET

(MARION JANE) AUDREY (*Audrey, Lady Miller of Glenlee*), only da of late Richard Spencer Pettit: *m* 1947, Sir (Frederick William) Macdonald Miller of Glenlee, 7th Bt, who *d* 1991. *Residence* – Ivy Grange Farm, Westhall, Halesworth, Suffolk IP19 8RN.

The 1st baronet, Sir Thomas (*d* 1789), son of William Miller, WS, and grandson of Matthew Miller of Glenlee, Kirkcudbright, was Lord President of the Court of Session in Scotland, with the title of Lord Barskimming. Sir William, the 2nd baronet (*d* 1846), was a Lord of Session with the title of Lord Glenlee.

MILLS (UK) 1921, of Ebbw Vale, co Monmouth

Sir PETER FREDERICK LEIGHTON MILLS, 3rd *Baronet*; *b* 9 July 1924; *s* his father, *Sir* (FREDERICK LEIGHTON) VICTOR, MC, 1955; *ed* Eastbourne Coll, and Natal Univ (BSc Agriculture 1952); formerly in Rhodesia Civil Ser; late Lieut Roy Gurkha Rifles; European War 1943-5: *m* 1954, Pauline Mary, da of L. R. Allen, of Calverton, Nottinghamshire, and has issue.

Arms – Sable, three millrinds in pale or between two swords erect proper, pommels and hilts of the second. **Crest** – A peewit's head, the neck encircled by a serpent nowed, both proper.
Address – PO Box A474, Avondale, Harare, Zimbabwe.

SON LIVING

MICHAEL VICTOR LEIGHTON, *b* 30 Aug 1957: *m* 1981, Susan, da of J. Doig, of Harare.

The first baronet, Sir Frederick Mills (son of late Leighton Mills, of Sunderland) was Chm of Ebbw Vale Steel and Iron Co, Ltd, Sheriff for Monmouthshire 1912, and MP for E Div of Leyton (C) 1931-45. The second baronet, Major Sir (Frederick Leighton) Victor Mills, MC, RA (Reserve) was Director of Public Works, Sierra Leone 1939-42 and of Uganda 1942-7, and served during European War 1914-18 (MC).

MILMAN (GB) 1800, of Levaton-in-Woodland, Devonshire

DEUS NOBISCUM QUIS CONTRA

God with us, who against us?

Sir DAVID PATRICK MILMAN, 10th *Baronet*; *b* 24 Aug 1945; *s* his father, *Lt-Col Sir* DEREK, MC, 1999; *ed* ......, and London Univ (BEd 1969, MA 19—): *m* 1969, Christina, da of John William Hunt, of Leigh on Sea, Essex, and has issue.

Arms – Azure, a serpent nowed or, between three sinister gauntlets open, two in chief and one in base argent. **Crest** – A hart lodged, per pale ermine and erminois attired and unguled or, charged on the body with two hurts fesseways.
Residence – 71 Camden Rd, Sevenoaks, Kent.

SON LIVING

THOMAS HART, *b* ...... 1976.

DAUGHTER LIVING

Katharine Jane, *b* 1976.

BROTHER LIVING

Terence Martin (98 New Dover Rd, Canterbury, Kent), *b* 1947; *ed* Bedford School, and London Univ: *m* 1976, Sandra Wendy Elizabeth, da of Frederick Garrett, of Canterbury, Kent, and has issue living, William Frederick, *b* 1984, — Alexandra Elizabeth, *b* 1979.

DAUGHTER LIVING OF EIGHTH BARONET

Celina Anne MILMAN (4018 Bay Ridge Crescent, W Vancouver V7V 3K4, Canada), *b* 1945: *m* 1968 (*m diss* 1980), John Springett Appleby; 2ndly, 1995, Paul Leslie Hammond, and has issue living (by 1st *m*), Tristan Dermot Springett, *b* 1968, — Tremayne Robert, *b* 1974.

WIDOWS LIVING OF EIGHTH AND NINTH BARONETS

MURIEL (*Dowager Lady Milman*), only da of John Edward Scott Taylor, of King's Lynn, Norfolk: *m* 1941, Maj Sir Dermot Lionel Kennedy Milman, 8th Bt, who *d* 1990. *Residence* – 7 Old Westhall Close, Warlingham, Surrey CR6 9HR.

MARGARET CHRISTINE (*Christine, Lady Milman*), da of Alfred Whitehouse, of Sutton Coldfield: *m* 1942, Lt-Col Sir Derek Milman, 9th Bt, MC, who *d* 1999. *Residence* – Forge Cottage, Wilby Rd, Stradbroke, Suffolk IP21 5JN.

COLLATERAL BRANCHES LIVING

Issue of late Lt-Col Malcolm Douglas Milman, RA, 2nd son of 7th baronet, *b* 1915, *d* 1987: *m* 1940 (*m diss* 1949), Sheila Maud, da of Albert Maurice Dudeney:—
Felicity Ann, *b* 1941: *m* 1965, Peter Robin Flockton, of RR#1 Apple Hill, Ontario KOC 1BO, Canada, and has issue living, Phyllida Fiona, *b* 1969: *m* 1994, Michael Gerald Gillissie, of Ottawa, Canada, — Vanessa, *b* 1971: *m* 1995, Michael John Low. —— Penelope Fiona, *b* 1943: *m* 1964, Anthony Stuart Darroch, and has issue living, Ian George, *b* 1965: *m*

1989, Victoria Jillian Elizabeth Watt —, and has issue living, Oliver William *b* 1994, George Alexander *b* 1997, — James Anthony, *b* 1967: *m* 1997, Sally-Ann Toft, and has issue living, Abigail Sophie *b* 1999.

Grandchildren of late Stephen Walter Milman, 4th son of 4th baronet:—
Issue of late Gerald Stephen Milman, *b* 1908, *d* 1987: *m* 1944, Noreen (El Venado, Casilla de Correo 27, La Cumbre, Sierras de Cordoba, Argentina), da of Thomas Johnston Elliot:—
Ian Stephen, *b* 1946: *m* 1978, Gloria Wassermann. ——Stephanie Rosalind, *b* 1949: *m* 1975, Robert Albert Christopher Lovell, and has issue living, Andrew Christopher, *b* 1979, — Mark Stephen, *b* 1982. ——Angela Caroline, *b* 1952: *m* 1974, Peter Scott Kirkwood, and *d* 1991, in an aeroplane accident, leaving issue, Catriona Alexandra, *b* 1979, — Melanie Jane, *b* 1980, — Caroline Louise, *b* 1989. ——Geraldine Stella, *b* 1956: *m* 1988, Marcelo di Tomasi, and has issue living, Stephen George, *b* 1992, — Patrick Gerald, *b* 1993.

Issue of late Com Henry Augustus Milman, OBE, RN, 5th son of 4th baronet, *b* 1882, *d* 1952: *m* 1912, Genevieve IRVING MILMAN, who *d* 1984, da of John Irving, of Victoria, BC:—
John Alexander Ralph, OBE (The Granary, Heath Rd, Petersfield, Hants GU31 4JF), *b* (Nov) 1912; *ed* Haileybury; Major (ret) Highland L I and Mil Attaché, Budapest; Mohamand Campaign 1934; Mil Attaché, Budapest, 1953-55; 1939-45 War as acting Lt-Col in Middle East, Burma, and Italy (wounded, despatches, OBE); OBE (Mil) 1943: *m* 1943, Daphne Mary, who *d* 1995, da of Alexander Andrew Bisset, and formerly wife of G. E. E. Webster, and has issue living, John Andrew Francis Pretyman (Flat C, Cossington House, Weston Rd, Petersfield, Hants GU31 4JF), *b* 1945: *m* 1st, 1977 (*m diss* 1986), Sarah Margaret, da of late William Robertson Wade-Gery, JP, of Bushmead Priory, nr Bedford; 2ndly, 1987, Lynne Duerden (*née* Sanders), and has issue living, (by 1st *m*) Oliver James Francis *b* 1980, Edward John William *b* 1982, (by 2nd *m*) Alice Sophie Mary *b* 1989, — Anne Isabel Jane, *b* 1943: *m* 1965, William Frederick Hempsall, and has issue living, Ashley *b* 1964, Miles *b* 1966.

Issue of late Major Hugh Milman, OBE, yst son of 4th baronet, *b* 1884, *d* 1959: *m* 1914, Marjorie, only da of late Malcolm McCullock Paterson, MICE, formerly of the Croft, Pannal, Harrogate:—
Stephanie Grace, *b* 1915, *d* 1994. ——Diana Constance, *b* 1920: *m* 1942, Capt John Michael Merry, RA, and has issue living, Bruce, *b* 1944: *m* 1st, 1965 (*m diss* 1980), Serenella Papi, 2ndly, 19—, Jean Marquard, who *d* 1984; 3rdly, 19—, Gina ......, and has issue living, (by 1st *m*) Ludovica *b* 1965, (by 2nd *m*) Octavius *b* 1980, — David, *b* 1945: *m* 1976 (*m diss* 19—), Anna Mai Gill, and has issue living, Louise *b* 1985, — Tessa, *b* 1947: *m* 1st, 1971 (*m diss* 1983), John Hopwood; 2ndly, 1993, Jack Hassan, and has issue living (by 1st *m*), Alastair *b* 1973, Kairst *b* 1976, — Miranda, *b* 1950; has issue living (by Eric Bowles), Felix *b* 1979, Lyndall *b* 1984, — Dilys, *b* 1956: *m* 1984, Richard John Smith, and has issue living, Louie *b* 1985, Asa *b* 1987, Alex *b* 1989. *Residence* – Tunnel Cottage, Knapp Lane, Ledbury, Herefordshire HR8 1JD.

Granddaughters of late Humphrey Radcliffe Milman, son of late Walter Charles Gordon Milman (infra):—
Issue of late John Walter Francis Milman, *b* 1928, *d* 1984: *m* 1955, Jean Margaret, who *d* 1984, da of G. C. Till, of Gunard, I of Wight:
Pamela Rosemary, *b* 1961. ——Laura Frances, *b* 1965.

Issue of late Walter Charles Gordon Milman, 3rd son of 3rd baronet, *b* 1853, *d* 1907: *m* 1886, Edie Helen Blythe, who *d* 1955, da of John Alexander Radcliffe, formerly of Ordsal, Cobham, Surrey:—
Isabel Joan, *b* 1898: *m* 1922, Maj William M. Martineau, MC, RASC, who *d* 1983, and has issue living, Josephine Helen, *b* 1923: *m* 1959, John Van Valkenburg.

Granddaughters of late Lt-Col Everard Stepney Milman, 6th son of Lt-Gen Francis Miles Milman, 2nd son of 1st baronet:—
Issue of late Lt-Col Octavius Rodney Everard Milman, DSO, *b* 1882, *d* 1971: *m* 1911, Mary Freya, who *d* 1979, el da of late Rev William Edward Haigh, Hon Canon of Bristol:—
Joanna Woolstone (Little Orchard, Bracken Rd, Seaford, Sussex), *b* 1912: *m* 1939, Maj Denys Paul Bulkeley, RA, who *d* 1981, and has issue living, Richard Milman (Lane End, 9 St Botolph's Lane, Orton Longueville, Peterborough), *b* 1940: *m* 1967, Elizabeth Mahoney, and has issue living, Thomas William *b* 1971, Joanna Louise (twin) *b* 1971. ——Patricia Freya, *b* 1920: *m* 1942, Lionel Noel Woolf, of 7B Bedford Towers, Cavendish Place, King's Rd, Brighton BN1 2JG, and has issue living, Inigo Rodney Milman, *b* 1946: *m* 1970, Susan Rebecca Davis, and has issue living, Bethia Fearne Milman *b* 1974, — Christopher Patrick Milman, *b* 1947: *m* 1969, Linda Johnston, and has issue living, Simon Justin *b* 1970, Jonathan Marcus *b* 1973: *m* 1997, Soumhya Venkatesan, — Nicholas David Milman *b* 1953: *m* 1973 (*m diss* 1996), Ann Elizabeth March, and has issue living, Benjamin Douglas *b* 1978.

Sir Francis Milman, 1st Bt of Levaton in Woodland, Devon, was Pres of Roy Coll of Physicians 1811-13, and Physician to King George III. Sir William Ernest Milman, MM, 6th Bt *d* (Aug), 1962, and his brother and successor, Brig-Gen Sir Lionel Charles Patrick Milman, CMG, 7th Bt *d* (Nov) 1962. The 9th Bt, Lt-Col Sir Derek Milman, MC, 3rd East Anglian Regt, served in 1939-45 War with 5th Indian Div in Middle East.

Milne-Watson, see Watson.

MILNER (GB) 1717, of Nun Appleton Hall, Yorkshire

Sir TIMOTHY WILLIAM LYCETT MILNER, 10th *Baronet*; *b* 11 Oct 1936; *s* his father, *Capt Sir* (GEORGE EDWARD) MORDAUNT, 1995; *ed* Michaelhouse, Natal.

Arms – Per pale or and sable, a chevron between three horses' bits counterchanged. **Crest** – A horse's head couped sable, maned and bridled or between a pair of wings gold.
Address – c/o Natte Valleij, Box 4, Klapmuts 7625, Cape Province, S Africa.

BROTHER LIVING

CHARLES MORDAUNT (Natte Valleij, Box 4, Klapmuts 7625, Cape, S Africa), *b* 18 May 1944; *ed* St Andrew's Coll, Grahamstown: *m* 1965, Lady Charlene Mary Olivia French, eldest da of 3rd Earl of Ypres, and has issue living, Marcus Charles Mordaunt, *b* 6 Jan 1968: *m* 1998, Catherine Anne, eldest da of Bruce Lane, of Kenilworth, Cape, — Patrick Edward French Mordaunt, *b* 1969: *m* 1996, Andrea, yr da of Rudolf Buys, of Stanford, Cape, — Alexander George French Mordaunt, *b* 1981.

SISTER LIVING

Addit frena feris

He puts bridles on the brutal

Georgina Madeleine Mary, *b* 1939: *m* 1961, (Arthur Henry) Bertram Grattan-Bellew, and has issue (*see* Grattan-Bellew, Bt, colls). *Residence* – Hole Farm, Gt Waldingfield, Sudbury, Suffolk.

The 1st baronet, MP for York City, was Grand Master of the Freemasons in England. The 2nd baronet was Receiver-General of Excise, the 3rd baronet sat as MP for York City 1790-1811, the 5th baronet sat as MP thereof 1848-57, and the 7th baronet, Rt Hon Sir Frederick George Milner, GCVO, PC, sat as MP thereof 1883-5 and for Nottinghamshire, Bassetlaw Div 1890-1906. The 9th baronet, Capt Sir (George Edward) Mordaunt Milner, was Steward of Cape Turf Club 1960-76, and Jockey Club of S Africa 1977-80, and was an authority on thoroughbred breeding.

Milnes-Coates, see Coates.

MOIR (UK) 1916, of Whitehanger, Fernhurst, co Sussex

Sir CHRISTOPHER ERNEST MOIR, 4th *Baronet*; *b* 22 May 1955; *s* his father, *Sir* ERNEST IAN ROYDS, 1998; *ed* King's Coll Sch, Wimbledon: *m* 1983, Vanessa, yr da of Victor Alfred Crosby, of Merton Park, SW19, and formerly wife of Joseph William Kirtikar, and has issue.

Arms – Argent, a span of a bridge enarched, embattled, and in perspective, checky or and azure, between three Moors' heads coupled sable, each banded of the second and third, and distilling three drops of blood proper. **Crest** – Upon a span of a bridge as in the arms a Moor's head affrontée couped at the shoulders sable, banded or and azure, collared checky of the same.
Residence – 77 Dora Rd, Wimbledon, SW19 7JT.

SONS LIVING

OLIVER ROYDS *b* 9 Oct 1984. —— Alexander Victor, *b* (twin) 1984.

BROTHERS LIVING

Timothy James (Crossways Cottage, Roke Lane, Witley, Surrey), *b* 1959. —— Rev Nicholas Ian (The Vicarage, 8 Chapel Street, Waterbeach, Cambs CB5 9HR), *b* 1961: *m* 1998, Rosaline, elder da of John Love, OBE, of Llangybi, Monmouthshire.

WIDOW LIVING OF THIRD BARONET

By virtue, not otherwise

MARGARET HANHAM (*Margaret, Lady Moir*), da of George Eric Carter, of Cranbrook, Netheroyd Hill, Huddersfield, *m* 1954, Sir Ernest Ian Royds Moir, 3rd Bt, who *d* 1998. *Residence* – Three Gates, 174 Coombe Lane West, Kingston-upon-Thames, Surrey KT2 7DE.

The 1st baronet, Sir Ernest William Moir, was head of the firm of Ernest William Moir & Co Ltd, engineers, which he founded, and a Director of S Pearson & Son Ltd, contracting engineers. The 2nd baronet, Sir Arrol Moir, was Vice-Pres of Institute of Patentees.

Molesworth-St Aubyn, see St Aubyn.

MOLONY (UK) 1925, of the City of Dublin

In God and not in my bow will I hope

(*Sir*) (THOMAS) DESMOND MOLONY, 3rd *Baronet*, does not appear on the Official Roll of the Baronetage, *b* 13 March 1937; *s* his father, *Sir* HUGH FRANCIS, 1976, but does not use title; *ed* Ampleforth, and Trin Coll, Dublin; late P/O RAF: *m* 1962, Doris, da of late E. W. Foley, of Cork, and has issue.

𝕬rms – Gules, six arrows in saltire between two bows erect to dexter and sinister or, a chief ermine. 𝕮rest – A dexter arm embowed in armour proper charged with a fleur-de-lys gules, the hand in a gauntlet holding a sword of the first.
Residence – 33 Ernest St, Leichhardt, Queensland 4305, Australia.

DAUGHTERS LIVING

Jennifer Mary, *b* 1963. —— Grace Ann, *b* 1964. —— Daphne Julia Rose, *b* 1965. —— Lynda Jacqueline Clare, *b* 1967.

COLLATERAL BRANCH LIVING

Grandchildren of Rt Hon Sir Thomas Francis Molony, 2nd son of 1st baronet:—
Issue of late Sir Joseph Molony, KCVO, QC, Judge of Courts of Appeal of Jersey and Guernsey, *b* 1907, *d* 1978: *m* 1936, Carmen Mary (who *m* 2ndly, 1989, Reginald A. Slay, who *d* 1994, of 45 Emmbrook Court, Woolacombe Drive, Reading, Berks RG6 5TZ), only da of late Frankland Dent, PhD, MSc:—
PETER JOHN (Rock House, Great Elm, Frome, Som BA11 3NY), *b* 17 Aug 1937; *ed* Downside, and Trin Coll, Camb (MA); FCA: *m* 1964, Elizabeth Mary, cl da of late Henry Clervaux Chaytor, of Cambridge, and has issue living, (James) Sebastian, *b* 1965, — (John) Benjamin, *b* 1966, — (Simon) Benedict, *b* 1972, — (Thomas) Francis, *b* 1975, — (Carmen) Jane, *b* 1967. —— John Fernando (30 St Ann's Lane, Godmanchester, Cambs PE18 8JE), *b* 1949; *ed* Downside and Trin Coll Camb: *m* 1985, Caroline Christine, yst da of late Brig Wilfred Montague Ponsonby, OBE, of West Burton, N Yorkshire, and has issue living, Nicola Carmen, *b* 1986, — Catherine Elizabeth, *b* 1988. —— Mary Carmen, *b* 1939: *m* 1963, Martin Noble Wells, of 34 Beeleigh Rd, Maldon, Essex CM9 7QH, and has issue living, Nicholas Thomas Clinton, *b* 1964, — Adrian Francis, *b* 1966, — Jonathan Patrick, *b* 1968, — Joanna Kate, *b* 1971. —— Angela Carmen, *b* 1942: *m* 1967, Philip Vincent, of Taverners, Woodeaton, Oxford OX3 9TH, and has issue living, Patrick Henry Morse, *b* 1970, — Bruno Charles, *b* 1979, — Antonia Louise, *b* 1968, — Katherine Eleanor, *b* 1974.

The 1st Baronet, Rt Hon Sir Thomas Francis Molony (son of James Molony, of Harcourt Street, Dublin), was appointed HM's 2nd Serjeant-at-Law, Ireland 1911, Solicitor-Gen for Ireland 1912, and Attorney-Gen for Ireland 1913, and was Judge of High Court of Justice in Ireland (King's Bench Div) 1913-15, a Lord Justice of Appeal 1915-18, and Lord Ch Justice of Ireland 1918-24.

MONCREIFFE OF THAT ILK (NS) 1685, of Moncreiffe, Perthshire.

Sir (RUPERT) IAIN KAY MONCREIFFE OF THAT ILK, 11th *Baronet*, CVO, QC, 24th Chief of the Name and Arms of Moncreiffe, *d* 1985 and was *s* by his elder son, the 24th Earl of Erroll (*see that title*).

WIDOW LIVING OF ELEVENTH BARONET

HERMIONE PATRICIA (*Lady Moncreiffe of that Ilk*), da of late Lt-Col Walter Douglas Faulkner, MC, Irish Gds (*see* D Buccleuch, colls): *m* 1966, as his 2nd wife, Sir (Rupert) Iain Kay Moncreiffe of that Ilk, 11th Bt, CVO, QC, who *d* 1985.
Residence – 24 Gordon Place, W8 4JE.

This family derives its surname from the hill of Moncreiffe, which has been in their possession since before surnames were first adopted in Scotland. "Moncreiffe" is the Old Gaelic place-name *Monadh Craoibhe* (the Hill of the Sacred Bough), and on its summit stood the dry-stone stronghold of the Pictish Kings; while the Moncreiffe arms indicate them to have probably been cadets of the same branch of the ancient royal stock as the lairds of Dundas (*see* M Zetland). Sir Mathew of Moncreiffe was confirmed in the lands by royal charter in 1248; and Malcolm Moncreiffe, 6th of that Ilk, had a new charter of the free Barony of Moncreiffe in 1455. Sir Thomas Moncreiffe, 14th of that Ilk, who was *cr* a Baronet with remainder to heirs male whatsoever in 1685, was 4th in descent from Hew Moncreiffe, 2nd son of John Moncreiffe, 8th of that Ilk (*d* 1496). The el son, Sir John Moncreiffe, 9th of that Ilk (*k* at Flodden 1513) was great-grandfather of Sir John Moncreiffe, 12th of that Ilk, who was *cr* a Baronet 1626. His son Sir John Moncreiffe of that Ilk, 2nd Bt, being childless, the Baronetcy (*cr* 1626) passed eventually to the line of his uncle Archibald Moncreiff, Heritable Prior of Elcho (*see* B Moncreiff); but in 1667 the Crown confirmed a family arrangement whereby Sir John made over the feudal Barony of Moncreiffe to his kinsman Thomas Moncreiffe, who thus succeeded him as Chief and became 14th of that Ilk and was later *cr* 1st Bt (1685). The 11th baronet, Sir (Rupert) Iain Kay Moncreiffe of that Ilk, CVO, QC, a distinguished genealogist and writer on heraldic and genealogical subjects, was successively Kintyre Pursuivant and Albany Herald.

Montagu-Pollock, see Pollock.

Montague-Barlow, see Barlow.

MONTGOMERY (UK) 1801, of Stanhope, Peeblesshire

Sir (BASIL HENRY) DAVID MONTGOMERY, 9th *Baronet*, only son of late Lt-Col Henry Keith Purvis-Russell Montgomery, OBE; *b* 20 March 1931; *s* his uncle, *Sir* BASIL RUSSELL PURVIS-RUSSELL-HAMILTON-MONTGOMERY, 1964; *ed* Eton; a JP and Lord Lieut of Perth and Kinross since 1996: *m* 1956, Delia, da of late Adm Sir (John) Peter Lorne Reid, GCB, CVO (*see* Reid, Bt, *cr* 1897, colls), and has issue.

Arms – Quarterly, 1st and 4th azure, three fleurs-de-lis or; 2nd and 3rd gules, three annulets or, stones azure, over all, dividing the quarters, a cross wavy of the second, charged with three cinquefoils, in fesse ermine. **Crest** – A Dexter Hand holding a sword indented on the back like a saw proper.
Residence – Home Farm, Kinross KY13 8EU.

SON LIVING

JAMES DAVID KEITH, *b* 13 June 1957; *ed* Eton, and Univ of Exeter; late Capt The Black Watch: *m* 1983, Elizabeth Lynette, eldest da of Lyndon Evans, of Tyla Morris Farm, Pentyrch, Mid-Glamorgan, and has issue living, Edward Henry James, *b* 1986, — Iona Rosanna, *b* 1988. *Residence* – Kinross House, Kinross KY13 8EU.

DAUGHTERS LIVING

Caroline Jean, *b* 1959: *m* 1983, Nicholas J. K. Liddle, eldest son of Alan Liddle, of Knockanboy House, Deryok, co Antrim, and has issue living, Alexander Allan Kessel, *b* 1988, — Lucy Delia, *b* 1986, — Harriet Susan, *b* 1991. —— Davina Lucy, *b* 1961: *m* 198-, Humphrey Martin Butler, eldest son of Geoffrey Butler, of Cheveney Cottage, Stetchworth, Newmarket, and has issue living, Bertie James, *b* 1991, — Hector Charles, *b* 1993. —— Iona Margaret, *b* 1972: *m* 1998, Benjamin K. Romer-Lee, elder son of Robin Romer-Lee, of Groton, Suffolk, and has issue living, Arthur Knyvett, *b* 1999. —— Laura Elizabeth, *b* 1974: *m* 1998, David Redvers, son of John Redvers, of Hartpury, Glos.

SISTER LIVING

Veronica Mary Anthea, *b* 1935.

DAUGHTER LIVING OF EIGHTH BARONET

Sheila, *b* 1923; 1941-45 War with New Zealand WAAF (Radar): *m* 1st, 1945 (*m diss* 1959), John Martin Griffith; 2ndly, 1967, Desmond Edward Widgery, who *d* 1989, and has issue living (by 1st *m*), Andrea Suzanne, *b* 1946: *m* 1975, Alexander Palmarczuk, — Gael Virginia, *b* 1949: *m* 1982, Sqdn Ldr Gordon Graham, RAF, who *d* 1990 (*k* on mil ser). *Residence* – Warroch, Newstead, RD, Hamilton, NZ.

COLLATERAL BRANCHES LIVING

Grandchildren of late Herbert Elphinstone Montgomery, yr son of Capt Thomas Henry Montgomery, yst son of 2nd baronet:—
Issue of late Brig Arthur Herbert Montgomery, OBE, TD, *b* 1902, *d* 1978: *m* 1939, Féodora Kathleen Alice, the film and stage actress (as Jane Baxter), who *d* 1996, da of late Henry Bligh Forde:—
James Henry Anson (5 Trafalgar Way, Stockbridge, Hants SO20 6ET), *b* 1945: *m* 1st, 1972 (*m diss* 1977), Carolyn Winifred Finlay; 2ndly, 1984 (*m diss* 1998), Julia Rosamund (actress Fiona Richmond), da of late Rev John Harrison, of Cornwall; 3rdly, 1999, Emma Elizabeth Sophy Pole Welman, and has issue living (by 2nd *m*), Tara Féodora, *b* 1984. —— Rachel Janet, *b* 1940: *m* 1972, Max Monsarrat, of Le Tournier, Latouille-Lentillac, St Céré, Lot 46.400, France, and has issue living, Samuel Nicholas, *b* 1972, — Thomas Anson Gordon, *b* 1976, — Marc Turney, *b* 1978. —— Sylvia Mary (*Baroness Crathorne*), *b* 1942: *m* 1970, 2nd Baron Crathorne.

Granddaughter of late William Montgomery, son of late Robert Montgomery, 4th son of 1st baronet:—
Issue of late Robert Hamilton Montgomery, *b* 1863, *d* 1943: *m* 1898, Evelyn Mary, who *d* 1951, da of late Rev Frederick Vernon, V of Shawbury, near Shrewsbury:—
Dorothy Vernon, *b* 1909: *m* 1952, William Smoot Rust, and has issue living, William Montgomery, *b* 1952.

Grandchildren of late Robert Hamilton Montgomery (ante):—
Issue of late Ian Stuart Montgomery, *b* 1900, *d* 1984: *m* 1942, Neva, da of late Ogden Minton, of Greenwich, Connecticut, USA:—
Brian Stuart, *b* 1952: *m* 1976, Patty —, of Warrenton, Va, USA. —— Ann Vernon, *b* 1945: *m* 1967, James R. Egan, and has issue living, Cheryl Ann, *b* 1970, — Mischell, *b* 1974. —— Sheila Minton, *b* 1949: *m* 1972, Mervin J. Marles, of New York, USA, and has issue living, Merv John, *b* 1978, — Ian Stuart, *b* (twin) 1978.

Issue of late Adm Alan Robert Montgomery, US Navy, *b* 1905, *d* 1964: *m* 1st, 1928 (*m diss* 1940), Josephine Marie, da of late Edward J. Straine, of Philadelphia; 2ndly, 1941, Mary Helen, da of George E. Kohlhaas, of San Bernadino, California, USA:—
(By 1st *m*) Robert Edward, *b* 1932. —— Doris Marie, *b* 1929.

Grandson of late Rev Colin Francis Montgomery, 2nd son of late William Montgomery (ante):—
Issue of late Squadron Leader Robert Maxwell Montgomery, RAF, *b* 1897, *d* 1977: *m* 1st, 1924 (*m diss* 1936), Eleanor Pierce Adams, who *d* 1957; 2ndly, 1936, Audrey Winifred, who *d* 1980, only da of C. Field, of The Hazels, Worplesdon, Surrey:—
Andrew John (Farthingham House, Farthingham Lane, Ewhurst, Surrey), *b* 1937: *m* 1965, Maureen Patricia, da of M. J. Roberts, of Morden, Surrey, and has issue living, Robert Maxwell, *b* 1968: *m* 1998, Heather, yr da of Geoffrey Yates, of Grange-over-Sands, Cumbria, — Michael Andrew, *b* 1971.

This is a younger branch of the Montgomeries, Earls of Eglinton, descended from Robert Montgomerie of Giffen, yr brother of the 1st Lord Montgomerie. William, 5th in line from Robert, acquired the lordship of Magbiehill, Ayrshire. The 1st baronet, Sir James Montgomery, MP for Peebles 1768-76, was Chief Baron of the Exchequer in Scotland 1775-81. His elder brother, William of Magbiehill, was also created a baronet, but his title became extinct 1831. Sir James, the 2nd baronet, was Lord Advocate of Scotland 1804-06, and represented Peebles for nearly thirty years. The 3rd baronet, Sir Graham (Lord-Lt of Kinross-shire), sat as MP for Peeblesshire 1852-68, and for Selkirkshire and Peeblesshire (C) 1868-80, and was a Junior Lord of the Treasury 1866-68. The 7th baronet, Sir Henry James, was Lord-Lt for Kinross-shire, and assumed 1907 for himself and issue the additional surname of Purvis-Russell (having *m* 1882 Mary Maud, MBE, da of T. Purvis-Russell of Warroch, Kinross-shire), and in 1933 the further surname of Hamilton for himself only. His son, Sir Basil Russell Purvis-Russell-Hamilton-Montgomery, 8th baronet, was recognized in that name by decree of Lord Lyon 1948.

Montgomery Cuninghame, see Cuninghame.

MOON (UK) 1855, of Portman Square, Middlesex

Keep an even mind

Sir PETER WILFRED GILES GRAHAM MOON, 5th *Baronet*; *b* 24 Oct 1942; *s* his father, *Sir* (ARTHUR) WILFRED GRAHAM, 1954; *ed* Lancing *m* 1st, 1967 (*m diss* 1992), Mrs Sarah Gillian Chater, da of late Lt-Col Michael Carson Lyndon Smith, MC, MB, BS (*see* Smith, Bt, colls, *cr* 1897); 2ndly, 1993, Mrs Terry Lynn de Vries, da of W. Coetzee, of Brackenfell, Cape Town, S Africa, and has issue by 1st *m*.

Arms – Argent, an eagle displayed gules, charged on the breast with two swords in saltire proper; on a chief nebuly azure, a fasces erect or, between two crescents argent. *Crest* – A crescent argent, in front of a fasces in bend or, surmounting a sword in bend sinister proper.
Residence – *Clubs* – Royal Cork Yacht, Master Mariners (Cape Town).

SONS LIVING (*By 1st marriage*)

RUPERT FRANCIS WILFRED GRAHAM (Cotmandene, Escot Park, Ottery St Mary, Devon EX11 1LU), *b* 29 April 1968; *ed* Marlborough, and Exeter Univ; has issue living (by Denise ......), Arthur Sidney, *b* 1992, — Tansy, *b* 19—. —— Thomas Edward Bradshaw Graham, *b* 1972; *ed* Dean Close, Cheltenham.

COLLATERAL BRANCHES LIVING

Grandchildren of late Rev Cecil Graham Moon (infra):—
Issue of late Lt-Col Edward Horace Graham Moon, 15th/19th Hussars, *b* 1904, *d* 1990: *m* 1931, Cynthia Rosamond, who *d* 1989, da of L. Avery:—
(John) Jeremy Edward Graham, MBE (Thrintoft House, Thrintoft, Northallerton, N Yorks), *b* 1932; *ed* Sherborne; Maj 15th/19th Hussars (ret); Lt-Col Army Legal Corps; MBE 1985: *m* 1st, 1958 (*m diss* 1964), Jane Mary, da of T. J. Cundy, of Brant Broughton, Lincs; 2ndly, 1966, Dorrit, el da of Gert Andersson, of Gongehusevej 174, Copenhagen, Denmark, and has issue living (by 1st *m*), Francis Edward Graham, *b* 1962: *m* 1986, Lorraine, eldest da of Michael Willoughby, of Hinton Waldrist, Oxon, and has issue living, Camilla Sarah Jane *b* 1992, — Caroline Rachel Graham, *b* 1960: *m* 1987, Charles Nicholas Frank, son of Charles Frank, of Standlake, Oxon, and has issue living, Georgina Rachel *b* 1990, Elizabeth Jane *b* 1992, — (by 2nd *m*), Christian Graham, *b* 1967, — Thomas Edward Graham, *b* 1969. —— Camilla Mary Graham, *b* 1939: *m* 1972, Clinton Bourdon, and has issue living, Jeremy Edward Currier, *b* 1979, — Timothy Francis Avery, *b* 1981.

Issue of late Rev Cecil Graham Moon, yst son of 2nd baronet, *b* 1867, *d* 1948: *m* 1898, Mary Andalusia, who *d* 1970, da of John Barnard Hankey:—
John Cecil Graham, *b* 1919; *ed* Eton; Maj (ret) 15th/19th Hussars: *m* 1952, Susan Mary Milburn, yr da of late Edward Reed, of Ghyllheugh, Longhorsley, Northumberland, and has issue living, Belinda Mary Graham, *b* 1954: *m* 1977, Marek William Kwiatkowski (*see* E Dartmouth), — Amanda Jane Graham, *b* 1958: *m* 1985, Thomas G. Bowring, eldest son of Geoffrey Bowring, of Halton Park, Lancaster, and has issue living, Cynthia *b* 1991, Flora *b* 1994, — Philippa Ann Graham, *b* 1959. *Residence* – Springfield Mews, Corbridge, Northumberland.

The 1st baronet, Sir Francis Graham Moon, an eminent fine-art publisher, and Lord Mayor of London 1854-5, was created a baronet during his Mayoralty in recognition of the visit of the Emperor Napoleon III and the Empress of the French to the Guildhall, April 1855. Sir (Arthur) Wilfred Graham Moon, the 4th baronet, was ADC to Gov of Fiji 1929-31.

MOON (UK) 1887, of Copsewood, Stoke, co Warwick

Vincit omnia veritas
Truth conquers all things

Sir ROGER MOON, 6th *Baronet*, *b* 17 Nov 1914; *s* his brother *Sir* EDWARD, MC, 1988; *ed* Sedbergh; served with Johore Volunteer Engineers in Malaya and Singapore; prisoner-of-war in Thailand 1942-45: *m* 1950, Meg, yr da of late Arthur Mainwaring Maxwell, DSO, MC, of Moss Vale, NSW, Australia, and grand-da of Maj-Gen Sir William Throsby Bridges, KCB, CMG, founder of the Australian Imperial Forces, and has issue.

Arms – Argent, an eagle displayed gules; two flaunches of the last, each charged with a fleur-de-lis of the field, on a chief of the second three crescents of the first. *Crest* – A fleur-de-lis argent in front of a demi-eagle displayed gules, charged on the breast with an escutcheon of the first bearing a crescent also gules.
Address – c/o Willis Maktoum plc, PO Box 152, City Centre, Dubai, UAE.

DAUGHTERS LIVING

Sarah Corinna, *b* 1951. —— Gillian Adèle, *b* 1954: *m* 1986, William Andrew Johnston, yr son of late Brian Johnston, CBE, and has issue living, Harry Edward Duff, *b* 1987, — Emily Rose, *b* 1988, — Georgia Grace, *b* 1990. —— Patricia Isolda, *b* 1955: *m* 1982, Peter W. A. Hogg, of House 6, Pacific View, 22 Cape Rd, Hong Hom Kok, Hong Kong, only son of late Lt-Col Anthony George Hogg, OBE, of Ibthorpe House, Hurstbourne Tarrant, Hants, and has issue living, Anthony Oliver Richard, *b* 1985, — Camilla Adèle, *b* 1983, — Arabella Louisa Daphne, *b* 1987.

BROTHER LIVING

HUMPHREY (White Rock, Llanymynech, Powys), b 9 Oct 1919: m 1st, 1955 (m diss 1964), Diana Marion, da of late F. Basil Hobson, of The Homestead, Freshwater Bay, Isle of Wight; 2ndly, 1964, Elizabeth Anne Drummond, who d 1994, da of late George Archibald Drummond Angus, and widow of Henry James Butler, of Lusaka, and has issue living (by 1st m), Susan Caroline, b 1957, — Vicki Georgina, b 1960, — (by 2nd m) Jennifer Claire, b 1966.

SISTERS LIVING

Ursula, b 1912: m 1945, Peter Henry Joscelyne, who d 1958, and has had issue, Hugh Anthony, b 1947; d 1990, — Nigel Townshend, b 1949. —— Mary, b 1913. —— Gwynneth Elinor, b 1916.

DAUGHTER LIVING OF THIRD BARONET

Lila Colleen, b 1931: m 1953, George Garroway Little, who d 1992, and has issue living, Gregory Robert, b 1959, — Sharon Colleen, b 1961. Residence – 4132 Balkan St, Vancouver 10, BC.

WIDOW LIVING OF FIFTH BARONET

MARY (Mary, Lady Moon), only child of late Capt Benjamin Conolly: m 1947, Sir Edward Moon, 5th Bt, MC, who d 1988. Residence – Heath House, Crickheath, Oswestry, Shropshire SY10 8BN.

COLLATERAL BRANCHES LIVING

Granddaughters of late Sir Ernest Moon, KCB, KC yst son of 1st baronet:—
Issue of late Arthur Moon, MC, QC, b 1882, d 1961: m 1912, Marjorie Isabel, who d 1966, da of Charles Lancelot Andrewes Skinner, formerly 4th Hussars (E Bessborough):—
Penelope Kathleen, b 1924: m 1950, (Count) Thomas Andreas Constantine Lubienski, of 60 Thorpe Lea Rd, Peterborough, and has issue living, Andrew, b 1952: m 1990, Louise King, — Henry Roger, b 1960: m 1991, Petra Limberg, and has issue living, Jonathon b 1991, Helen b 1993, — Michael Arthur, b 1962, — Clare Barbara, b 1955: m 1988, Christopher Hamilton, and has issue living, Patrick Thomas b 1989, Alex b 1992, — and also has an adopted da, Mary Elizabeth, b 1954; m 1994, Christopher Kearton, and has issue living, Harry b 1990, Louis b 1992. —— Christine Marjorie, b 1925: m 1962, Lt-Cdr John Bertram Watson, RN (ret), of The Red House, Hambledon, Hants, and has issue living, Robin Bertram Stephen, b 1967, — Rupert Phillp, b 1971, — Rosamund Isobel, b 1965.

Granddaughters of late Arthur Moon, MC, QC (ante):—
Issue of late John Richard Philip Moon, OBE, b 1915, d 1978: m 1945, Ann, (who m 2ndly, 1980, W. A. Beare, of Ledgeland, St Margaret's Bay), da of R. P. Melhuish:—
Susan, b 1947: m 1st, 1969 (m diss 1980), Cameron Murray; 2ndly, 1980, Lt-Col George Douglas Birdwood Keelan, of The Stables, Cargill, Perth, and has issue living, (by 1st m) Jamie, b 1972, — Pollyanna, b 1973. —— Elizabeth Ann, b 1949: m 1971, Matthew Gloag, of Arnaud Lanne, 32500 Urdens, Gers, France, and has issue living, Emma, b 1972; has issue living, Inde Ann b 1997, — Sorcha Ann, b 1974. —— Sarah, b 1956: m 1989, Peter Cutts, of 36 Calbourne Rd, SW12, and has issue living, Richard Adam Moon, b 1991, — Alexander Charles Famin, b 1992.

Sir Richard Moon, 1st baronet (son of Richard Moon, a Liverpool merchant) was Chm of London of London and North-Western Railway Co 1861-91.

MOORE (UK) 1919, of Hancox, Whatlington, Sussex

I strive against adversity

(*Sir*) NORMAN WINFRID MOORE, 3rd *Baronet* (has established his claim but does not use the title); *b* 24 Feb 1923; *s* his father, *Sir* ALAN HILARY 1959; *ed* Eton, and Trin Coll, Camb (BA 1943); PhD Bristol 1954; sometime Lieut RA; Senior Prin Scientific Officer, Nature Conservancy 1965-83, and Visiting Prof, Wye Coll, Univ of Lond 1979-83; sometime Chm Farming and Wildlife Advisory Group; European War 1942-45 (wounded, prisoner): *m* 1950, Janet, PhD, only da of Paul Singer, and has issue.

𝔄rms – Argent on a fesse between two garbs azure, three mullets or (also on an inescutcheon the arms of *Burrows*; azure between three fleurs de lys erminois a sword in pale point upwards proper, pommel and hilt or). 𝔠rest – In front of a Moor's head proper, a garb, barwise or.
Residence – The Farm House, 117 Boxworth End, Swavesey, Cambridge.

SON LIVING

PETER ALAN CUTLACK (23 Mount Pleasant Rd, NW10 3EG), *b* 21 Sept 1951; *ed* Eton, and Trin Coll, Camb BA (1973), DPhil (Oxon) 1980: *m* 1989, Pamela Edwardes, and has issue living, Paul Edwardes, *b* 1990, — Esther Edwardes, *b* 1993.

DAUGHTERS LIVING

Caroline Mary Phyllis MOORE, *b* 1953; Barrister-at-Law; has retained her maiden name: *m* 1982 (*m diss* 1998), Richard Anthony Cohen, of 20 Wandsworth Common West Side, SW18 2EH, and has issue living, Toby Benedict, *b* 1983, — Guy Peter Gillachrist, *b* 1988, — Mary Beatrix, *b* 1986. —— Helena Meriel MOORE, *b* 1957; has retained her maiden name: *m* 1986, David Alexander of 14 South Parade, York YO2 1BF, and has issue living, Rose Maribel, *b* 1990, — Catherine Janet, *b* (twin) 1990, — Harriet Alannah, *b* 1994.

BROTHER LIVING

Richard Gillachrist, *b* 1931; *ed* Trin Coll, Camb (BA); Pres of Union Soc, Camb 1955; formerly on editorial staff of *News Chronicle*, Sec Gen of Liberal International, and Private Sec to Leader of Liberal Party and Political Sec to Federation of Liberal and Democratic Parties of the European Community: *m* 1955, Ann Hilary, only da of late Wing-Cdr Charles Cleaver Miles, MC, RAF, and has issue living, Charles Hilary, *b* 1956; Ed *The Sunday Telegraph* 1992-95, since when Ed *The Daily Telegraph*: *m* 1981, Caroline Mary, elder da of Ralph Lambert Baxter, and has issue living, William *b* 1990, Katharine *b* (twin) 1990, — Rowan William Gillachrist, *b* 1961: *m* 1991, Elizabeth Treip, and has issue living, Helena *b* 1994, Stella *b* 1997, — Charlotte Sydney, *b* 1959: *m* 1987, Mark V. E. Smith, of Hancox, Whatlington, Battle, Sussex, and has issue living, George *b* 1990, Samuel *b* 1991, Jacob *b* 1998. *Residence* – 16 Thornhill Square, N1 1BQ.

SISTERS LIVING AND DECEASED

Hilary Mary, *b* 1927, *d* 1996. —— Meriel Edith Milicent, *b* 1936: *m* 1961, Rt Rev John Keith Oliver, Bishop of Hereford, of the Palace, Hereford, and has issue living, Thomas Hilary, *b* 1964, — Henry Caspar William, *b* 1968, — Mary Philomena, *b* 1971.

Sir Norman Moore, MD, LLD, FRCP, 1st Bt (only son of Robert Ross Rowan Moore, Bar-at-law, of Broughton, Lancashire), was Emeritus Lecturer on Principles and Practice of Med at St Bartholomew's Hospital, and Pres of Roy Coll of Physicians 1918-21.

MOORE (UK) 1923, of Colchester, Essex (Extinct 1992)

Sir EDWARD STANTON MOORE, OBE, 2nd and last *Baronet*.

SISTER LIVING OF SECOND BARONET

Doris Vera, *b* 1907: *m* 1939, Patrick Seeton of 31 York Av, Scottsville, Pietermaritzburg, Natal, and has issue living, John, *b* 1940, — David, *b* 1943: *m* 1964, Jeann Griffioen, and has issue living, Jacqueline Doris, *b* 1965.

COLLATERAL BRANCHES LIVING

Issue of late Brig Eric Edward James Moore, DSO, Col R Inniskilling Fus, 3rd son of 1st baronet, *b* 1894, *d* 1979: *m* 1928 (*m diss* 1948), Gertrude, who *d* 1972, da of Frank Fellows Vanderhoef, of New York:—

Mary Elizabeth Deirdre, *b* 1937: *m* 1965, David Tudor Evans, of Homeland, Bunbury Heath, Tarporley, Cheshire, and has issue living, Peter Edward Gwilym, *b* 1967, — Juliet Mary Enid, *b* 1969.

Issue of late Wing-Cdr Ronald George Moore, 4th son of 1st baronet, *b* 1903, *d* 1981: *m* 1st, 1928 (*m diss* 1942), Barbara Kathleen, da of Charles Richard Crampton Elwes; 2ndly, 1942, Angela Mary, da of Paul Cammiade:—

(By 1st *m*) Anne Cecilia, *b* 1929: *m* 1954, John Hetherington, and has issue living, Christopher, *b* 1955, — Cary, *b* 1957, — Philip, *b* 1958, — Simon Charles, *b* 1965.

MOORE (UK) 1932, of Moore Lodge, co Antrim

Sir WILLIAM ROGER CLOTWORTHY MOORE, TD, 3rd *Baronet*; *b* 17 May 1927; *s* his father, *Sir* WILLIAM SAMSON, DL, JP, 1978; *ed* Marlborough, and RMC; Lt R Inniskilling Fus 1945; 1950-63 Maj N Irish Horse; High Sheriff co Antrim 1964, DL 1990; Chm of board of Visitors HM Prisons in N Ireland 1971; BBC Broadcaster 1963-66; UK Gov Internat Platform Assoc, USA 1980; TD 1963: *m* 1954, Gillian, da of John Brown, of co Antrim, and has issue.

ᴀrms – Azure, on a chief indented or, a spur sable between two mullets pierced gules. Crest – Out of a ducal crest coronet or, a blackamoor's head, face to dexter proper, wreathed about the temples argent and sable.
Residence – Moore Lodge, Ballymoney, co Antrim. *Club* – Kildare and University (Dublin).

The brave may falter but never yield

SON LIVING

RICHARD WILLIAM, *b* 8 May 1955; *ed* Portora, and RMA; Lieut R Scots 1974: *m* 1985, Karyn Furness, and has issue living, Charlotte, *b* 1989, — Sophie, *b* 1991, — Fenella, *b* 1993.

DAUGHTER LIVING

Belinda Jane, *b* 1956: *m* 1978, Timothy James Bryce Duncan, yst son of late Sir Arthur Bryce Duncan, and has issue living, Sally, *b* 1980, — Gemma, *b* 1981, — Harriet, *b* 1983.

COLLATERAL BRANCH LIVING

Issue of late Capt Joseph Roger Moore, KPM, RUC, 2nd son of 1st baronet, *b* 1895, *d* 1951: *m* 1920, Florence Amy, who *d* 1948, da of Lt-Col John Patrick, of Dunminning, co Antrim:—

Jean Florence Helen, *b* 1923: *m* 1949, Robert Andrew Young, and has issue living, Timothy David (Westcote, Green Rd, Rickling Green, Saffron Walden, Essex), *b* 1950: *m* 1st, 1979 (*m diss* 1992), Sarah Elizabeth Armorel Leng; 2ndly, 1992, Moira Moon, and has issue living (by 2nd *m*), Tom Alastair *b* 1990, Lily Maeve *b* 1998, — Alexandra Louise, *b* 1952: *m* 1984, John Crawford Cone, of Holt Cottages, Kimpton, Hitchin, Herts, and has issue living, Sam Andrew Robson *b* 1987. *Residence* – School Court, Westmill, Buntingford, Herts.

The 1st baronet, the Rt Hon Sir William Moore, PC (el son of late William Moore, MD, JP, of Moore Lodge, Ballymoney, co Antrim), was Parliamentary Private Sec to Ce Sec for Ireland (Rt Hon G. Wyndham, MP) 1902-4, Senior Crown Prosecutor, Belfast 1915-17, and Treasurer, King's Inns, Dublin 1918-20; became a Judge of High Court of Justice (King's Bench Div) 1917, a Lord Justice of Appeal for N Ireland 1921, and Lord Ch Justice of N Ireland 1925; retired 1937; sat as MP for N Antrim Div of Antrim co (C) 1899-1906, and for N Armagh Div Armagh co Nov 1906-17.

MORDAUNT (E) 1611, of Massingham Parva, Norfolk
(Name pronounced "Mordant")

Ferro comite

The sword my companion

Sir RICHARD NIGEL CHARLES MORDAUNT, 14th *Baronet*; *b* 12 May 1940; *s* his father, *Sir* NIGEL JOHN, MBE, 1979; *ed* Wellington Coll: *m* 1964, Myriam, da of — Atchia, of — and has issue.

Arms – Argent, a chevron between three estoiles sable. *Crest* – A Saracen's head full faced proper, wreathed round the temples argent and sable.
Residence – ......

SON LIVING

KIM JOHN, *b* 1966.

DAUGHTER LIVING

Michele, *b* 1965.

BROTHERS LIVING

David Arthur John, *b* 1942: *m* 1969, Elizabeth Aske, da of William Edgel Luke, and has issue living, Katherine Elizabeth Aske, *b* 1970, — Alexandra Caroline Aske, *b* 1972. —— Peter Anthony Charles (The Old Farmhouse, Sulgrave, Banbury, Oxon), *b* 1946: *m* 1st, 1972 (*m diss* 1997), Angela Mary, da of Ralph Arthur Hubbard (*see* B Addington, colls), and formerly wife of (Luke Edward) Timothy Hue Williams; 2ndly, 1999, Mrs Amanda Bridget Wootton, da of Kenneth Bailey, and has issue living (by 1st *m*), Alastair Nigel Charles, *b* 1974, — Anna Rose, *b* 1981.

SISTER LIVING

Tessa Anne, *b* 1947: *m* 1974, David Anthony Nutting, DL, and has issue (*see* Nutting, Bt).

AUNT LIVING (*Sister of 13th baronet*)

Cynthia Violet, *b* 1918.

COLLATERAL BRANCHES LIVING

Grandchildren of late Gerald John Mordaunt, brother of 12th baronet:—
Issue of late Eustace John Mordaunt, *b* 1901, *d* 1988: *m* 1934, Anne Frances, who *d* 1976, only da of late Alastair Gilmour:—
David John, *b* 1937; *ed* Wellington Coll; Royal Northumberland Fus 1955-57; Assist Master Wellington Coll 1963-86, and Housemaster 1968-79: *m* 1990, Catharine Hilary, da of John Mayne, CB, of Westminster, SW1. *Residence* – Mondhuie, Nethy Bridge, Inverness-shire PH25 3DF. —— Gerald Charles *b* 1939; *ed* Wellington Coll: *m* 1965 (*m diss* 1981), Carol Elspeth, da of late Brig Richard Montagu Villiers, DSO (*see* E Clarendon, colls), and has issue living, James Richard John, *b* 1967, — Christopher Charles (59a Wix's Lane, SW4), *b* 1969: *m* 1995, Katja, da of Kim Leschly, of USA, and has issue living, Milo John Gilbert *b* 1996, — Tanya Alexandra, *b* 1974, — Harriet Georgia, *b* 1980. *Residence* – 55 Melody Rd, SW18. —— Angela Mary, *b* 1934: *m* 1955, David Neil Carr, of Riley Hill Farm House, Riley Hill, Lichfield, Staffs WS13 8HW, and has issue living, Philip Donald Mordaunt (Lambrook Haileybury School, Winkfield Row, Bracknell, Berks RG42 6LU), *b* 1959: *m* 1989, Katherine Jane, da of Richard David Cairns Hubbard, OBE, of Meadowcroft, Windlesham, Surrey, and has issue living, Charles David *b* 1994, Susannah Claire *b* 1992, — Sally Jane, *b* 1956: *m* 1st, 1977 (*m diss* 1987), Anthony Mitchell; 2ndly, 1989, Andrew Simms, of Yew Tree Cottage, Weston Bank, Weston, nr Stafford, Staffs ST18 0BA, and has issue living, (by 1st *m*) Andrew David *b* 1982, — Judith Anne, *b* 1961: *m* 1st, 1983, Patrick Dickinson; 2ndly, 1989, Geoffrey Teather, of Riley Hill Farm House, Riley Hill, Lichfield, Staffs WS13 8HW.

Issue of late Robin Charles Mordaunt, *b* 1909, *d* 1998: *m* 1940, Brita (89B Winchester St, Christchurch, NZ), da of C. Thoren, of Stockholm, Sweden:—
Timothy John (60 Karina Terrace, Palmerston North, NZ), *b* 1949: *m* 1976, Heather Gowing, and has issue living, Guy John, *b* 1977, — Anthony Charles, *b* 1979, — Samuel John, *b* 1986, — Rebecca Jean, *b* 1982. —— Kristina Birgitta (17 Repton St, Christchurch, NZ), *b* 1946: *m* 1967 (*m diss* 1986), Christopher McVeigh, and has issue living, Brita, *b* 1970, — Carlotta, *b* 1971, — Anna, *b* 1974, — Juliet, *b* 1978.

Grandchildren of late Christopher John Mordaunt (infra):—
Issue of late Lt-Cmdr Richard John Mordaunt, *b* 1908, *d* 1998: *m* 1st, 1930, Nancy, who *d* 1986, da of late Major T. C. Toler, DL, of Swettenham Hall, nr Congleton, Ches; 2ndly, 1988, Sarah Anne (Dodington Manor, Chipping Sodbury, Glos), da of late W/Cdr E. Seymour Williams:—
(By 1st *m*) (Thomas) Christopher John (Brawby Lodge, Brawby, Malton, N Yorks), *b* 1934; is a Capt 9th Queen's Roy Lancers: *m* 1959, Belinda Madeline, da of Thomas Cecil Gouldsmith (*see* Laurie Bt, colls, 1961 Edn), of Coneysthorpe, Malton, Yorks, and has issue living, (Sarah) Camilla, *b* 1961: *m* 1985, William Richard Ashton Shuttleworth, of Brook House, Stanton Lacy, Ludlow, Shropshire (*see* V Cross, 1990 Edn), and has issue living, Tom William Ashton *b* 1990, Alexandra Sophie Ashton *b* 1987, a da *b* 1994, — Sophie Jane, *b* 1967. —— Rosemary Jane, *b* 1931: *m* 1957, Lyndon Bolton, of Arrat's Mill, by Brechin, Angus, and has issue living, Lyndon, *b* 1958, — Timothy William, *b* 1963. —— Nicola Anna Mary, *b* 1944.

Issue of late Capt Stephen Clare Mordaunt, *b* 1925, *d* 1998: *m* 1950, Joan (Horseshoe House, 51 Sydney Blds, Bath BA2 6DB), da of late Louis Henry Poppleton, of Nightingale Villa, Batheaston:—
Guy Roger, *b* 1952; *ed* Grenville Coll, Bideford: *m* 1980, Deborah Anne, yst da of B. A. G. Norton, and has issue living, Simon Richard Stephen, *b* 1988, — Sally Jane, *b* 1985, — Elizabeth Muriel, *b* 1990. ——Ann Patricia, *b* 1956: *m* 1978, John Quartly, and has issue living, Amy, *b* 1979, — Ruth, *b* 1981, — Emma, *b* 1982.

Granddaughter of late Harry Mordaunt, 4th son of late John Mordaunt, 17th Lancers, son of Rev Charles Mordaunt, 2nd son of 6th baronet:—
Issue of late Christopher John Mordaunt, *b* 1879, *d* 1954: *m* 1st, 1907, Helena Charlotte, da of Capt R. N. Young, RHA; 2ndly, 1916, Mary Patricia, who *d* 1975, da of Lt-Col J. C. Cautley, Roy W Kent Regt:—
(By 2nd *m*) Katherine Patricia (Wyke Croft, 36 Brandy Hole Lane, Chichester, Sussex), *b* 1918: *m* 1950, David Isard, who *d* 1980, and has issue living, John David, *b* 1951; *ed* Cranleigh, and Leicester Univ.

Osbert le Mordaunt, a Norman knight, was possessed of Radwell, in Bedfordshire, by the gift of his brother, who had it of William I for his services, and for the services of his father, in the conquest of England. The 1st baronet, Sir l'Estrange Mordaunt, distinguished himself in the wars of the Low Countries, *temp* Elizabeth I. Sir Charles, the 3rd baronet, has his estates sequested for his loyalty to Charles I. The 5th, 6th, 7th, 9th, and 10th baronets each represented Warwickshire in Parliament, while the 7th baronet was also a Groom of the Bedchamber.

HUGHES-MORGAN (UK) 1925, of Penally, co Pembroke

His Honour Sir DAVID JOHN HUGHES-MORGAN, CB, CBE, 3rd *Baronet*; *b* 11 Oct 1925; *s* his father, *Sir* JOHN VERNON, 1969; *ed* RN Coll, Dartmouth; Sub-Lt RN (ret); Maj-Gen Army Legal Corps (ret 1984); 1939-45 War; a Recorder (1983); a Circuit Judge on South-eastern Circuit 1986-98; MBE (Mil) 1959, CBE (Mil) 1973, CB (Mil) 1983: *m* 1959, Isabel Jean Blacklock Gellatly Milne, who *d* 1994, da of John Milne Lindsay, of Annan, Dumfriesshire, and has issue.

Arms – Quarterly, 1st and 4th, a griffin segreant sable, over all a chevron of the second charged with a mullet between two fleur-de-lis of the first, *Morgan*; 2nd and 3rd, sable, a lion rampant guardant between two fleur-de-lis in fesse or; on a chief engrailed of the second, two Cornish choughs proper, *Hughes*, **Crest** – 1st, in front of a reindeer's head erased or, collared and chained sable, a fleur-de-lis between two mullets also sable, *Morgan*; 2nd, in front of a demi-lion rampant guardant argent, charged on the shoulder with a fleur-de-lis sable, two swords saltireways proper, pommels and hilts or, *Hughes*.
Residence – Chorleywood Lodge, Chorleywood, Herts WD3 5BY.

SONS LIVING

(IAN) PARRY DAVID (10 Southside, W6 0XY), *b* 22 Feb 1960: *m* 1992, Julia Katrin, elder da of R. J. S. Ward, of Amersham, Bucks, and has issue living, Isabel, *b* 1995, — Rachel, *b* 1996, — Alexandra, *b* 1999. ——Jonathan Michael Vernon (Woodthorpe, 61 Leigh Hill Rd, Cobham, Surrey KT11 2HY), *b* 1962: *m* 1996, Gail Christine, yr da of I. W. Melling, of Winnipeg, Canada, and has issue living, Charlotte, *b* 1996. —— Mark Richard Milne, *b* 1964: *m* 1988, Sophia Frances, yst da of Graham Rogers, of Hungerford House, Fordingbridge, Hants, and has issue living, Daniel, *b* 1988, — Theo, *b* 1990, — Felix, *b* 1992, — Beatrice, *b* 1995.

Without God, without anything

COLLATERAL BRANCHES LIVING

Issue of late Capt (Thomas Parry) Michael JONES-PARRY, S Wales Borderers, 2nd son of 2nd Bt, *b* 1928; *d* 1982; assumed by deed poll 1961 the surname of Jones-Parry in lieu of his patronymic: *m* 1952, Gillian (White Hart Cottage, Westbrook, Boxford, Newbury, Berks), yr da of Reginald Carter Stern, of Arden, Weybridge, Surrey:—
David Anthony, *b* 1954; *ed* Wellington Coll: *m* 1983, Jacqueline Rowland-Rouse, and has issue living, Thomas Edward, *b* 1986, — Matthew Nicholas, *b* 1991, — Gemma, *b* 1987. ——Caroline Anne, *b* 1953: *m* 1975, Baron Hugues M. F. d'Achon, of Paris, 3rd son of Baron Antoine d'Achon. —— Sarah Margaret, *b* 1961.

Issue of late Sq-Ldr David James Hughes-Morgan, RAF, yr son of 1st baronet, *b* 1903, *d* 1967: *m* 1935, Evelyn, who *d* 1965, da of John Windsor-Richards, of Plas, Caerleon, Mon:—
Elizabeth Dolores, *b* 1936: *m* 1960, John Brill, MA, of Rookhurst, Coast Hill Lane, Westcott, nr Dorking, Surrey, and has issue living, Timothy John, *b* 1965, — Jonathon Richard, *b* 1966, — Edward James, *b* 1969.

The 1st baronet, Sir David Hughes-Morgan (son of late David Morgan, of Henllys, Llandovery), was Chm of *Western Mail*, and High Sheriff of Breconshire 1898-9. He assumed by deed poll (enrolled in College of Arms) 1925 the additional surname of Hughes.

MORRIS (UK) 1806, of Clasemont, Glamorganshire

Sir ALLAN LINDSAY MORRIS, 11th *Baronet*; *b* 27 Nov 1961; *s* his father, *Sir* ROBERT BYNG, 1999, but no name has appeared on the Official Roll of the Baronetage since the death of Sir Cedric Lockwood, 9th Bt in 1982: *m* 1986, Cheronne Denise, eldest da of Dale Whitford, of Goonhavern, Cornwall, and has issue.

Arms – Sable, on a saltire engrailed ermine a bezant, charged with a cross couped gules. **Crest** – A lion rampant or, charged on the shoulder with a cross couped gules, within a chain in the form of an arch or.
Residence – 10885 15th Sideroad, RR3 Georgetown, Halton Hills, Ontario L7G 4S6, Canada.

SONS LIVING

SENNEN THOMAS, *b* 5 June 1995. —— Chance James, *b* 18 Sept 1997.

DAUGHTER LIVING

Chelsea Alana, *b* 1992.

SISTERS LIVING

By the shield of faith

Geraldine Ann, *b* 1948: *m* 1st, 1969 (*m diss* 1981), Gilbert Baxter, Jr; 2ndly, 1984, Thomas Millard of Vancouver, BC, and has issue living, (by 1st *m*) Jennifer Carly, *b* 1975. —— Gillian, *b* 1950: *m* 1st, 1972 (*m diss* 19—), Andrew Jamieson; 2ndly, 1995, Clifford Morrison. —— Roberta Crystal, *b* 1965; Jr Dressage Canadian Champion 1983: *m* 1991 (*m diss* 1998) Donald Lebrun.

WIDOWS LIVING OF SEVENTH AND TENTH BARONETS

OLIVE IRENE (*Olive, Lady Morris*), da of William Davies, of Swansea: *m* 1938, Sir Herbert Edward Morris, 7th baronet, who *d* Aug 1947.

CHRISTINE KATHLEEN (*Christine, Lady Morris*), da of Archibald Field, of Toddington, Glos: *m* 1947, Sir Robert Byng Morris, 10th Bt, who *d* 1999. *Residence* – Norton Creek Stables, RR5 Norton Creek Rd, St Chrysostome, Quebec, Canada.

COLLATERAL BRANCHES LIVING

Issue of late Frank Hall BYNG-MORRIS, brother of 8th baronet, *b* 1869, *d* 1954 (having assumed by deed poll 1927 the additional surname of Byng): *m* 1913, Irene Catherine, who *d* 1968, da of Lt-Col Rogers-Harrison, of Kenilworth, Pittville Lawn, Cheltenham:—
Daphne Veronica, *b* 1914: *m* 1942, Norman Halfhead, who *d* 1988, and has issue living, Christopher Norman, *b* 1946: *m* 1984, Francesca Waterhouse, and has issue living, Michael Christopher *b* 1986, Lucy Christina *b* 1985.

Issue of late Col John Morris, 2nd son of 3rd baronet, *b* 1850, *d* 1916: *m* 1881, Jessie who *d* 1941, da of William Fowler:—
Jessie Harriet Amy Blanche: *m* 1923, Capt Bertram Wellington Parker, late Queen's Own Roy W Kent Regt. He *d* 1966. *Residence* – The Firs, Chelston, Torquay.

This family descends from Robert Morris of Bishops Castle and Cleobury, Salop, whose grandson, Sir John Morris of Claremont, was created a baronet in 1806. The 9th Baronet, Sir Cedric, was a noted painter and horticulturalist.

Morrison-Bell, see Bell.

Morrison-Low, see Low.

Mosley (GB) 1781, of Ancoats, Lancashire, and of Rolleston, Staffordshire (see B Ravensdale).

EDWARDS-MOSS (UK) 1868, of Roby Hall, Lancashire

(*Sir*) DAVID JOHN EDWARDS-MOSS, 5th *Baronet, b* 2 Feb 1955; *s* his father, *Sir* JOHN HERBERT THEODORE, 1988, but at the time of going to press, his name does not appear on the Roll of the Baronetage, nor does he use the title; *ed* Cranleigh.

𝕬rms – 1st and 4th, quarterly, ermine and erminois a cross-patée azure between six billets, three in chief and three in base gules, *Moss*; 2nd and 3rd, argent a lion rampant-guardant sable on a chief dancetté of the last two eagles displayed of the first, a canton or, *Edwards*. 𝕮rest – 1st, issuant from the battlements of a tower or, charged with a rose gules slipped vert, a griffin's head ermine, charged on the neck with a cross-pattée azure; 2nd, a rock proper, therefrom rising a dove argent (charged on the breast, for distinction, with a cross-crosslet gules), holding in the beak an olive branch and surmounted by a rainbow also proper.
Residence –

En la rose je fleurie

I flourish in the rose

BROTHERS LIVING

PETER MICHAEL, *b* 26 Sept 1957: *m* 1988, Jenifer Cadisch, and has issue living, John Herbert Theodore, *b* 1992, — Charles Anthony, *b* 1994. —— Paul Richard, *b* 1960. —— Christopher James, *b* 1963. —— Jonathan Francis William, *b* 1967.

SISTER LIVING

Penelope Anne, *b* 1956: *m* 1988, Michael Geoffrey Jennings, and has issue living, Johnnie Sam, *b* 1991, — Kathrine Sarah, *b* 1989, — Lucie Charlotte, *b* 1995.

WIDOW LIVING OF FOURTH BARONET

JANE REBIE (*Lady Edwards-Moss*), da of Carteret John Kempson: *m* 1951, Sir John Herbert Theodore Edwards-Moss, 4th Bt, who *d* 1988. *Residence* – Ruffold Farm, Cranleigh, Surrey.

COLLATERAL BRANCH LIVING

Grandchildren of late Maj John Edwards-Moss, RGA, 2nd son of 2nd baronet:—
Issue of Capt Thomas Richard Edwards-Moss, *b* 1921, *d* 1974: *m* 1st, 1943 (*m diss* 1952), Bridget Doreen, da of late Maj Hon Richard Coke (*see* E Leicester, colls); 2ndly, 1953, Monica Hughes (3 West Court, The Hill, Langport, Som TA10 9QF), da of late Maj H. G. Wilkinson, BSc, Burma Ser (ret).—
(By 1st *m*) John Richard, *b* 1947; *ed* Eton: *m* 1976, Penelope, only da of Michael Horne, of Bath Villas, Mill Hill, Newmarket, Suffolk, and has issue living, Thomas Michael, *b* 1980, — Rose Bridget, *b* 1981, — Letitia Patience, *b* 1983. *Residence* – Glebe Farm House, E Leake, Loughborough, Leics LE12 6LE. —— (By 2nd *m*) Stella Lucy, *b* 1958.

Sir Thomas Edwards-Moss, 1st baronet, assumed, by Roy licence, 1851, the additional surname and arms of Edwards, having *m* 1847, Amy Charlotte, da and heir of Richard Edwards of Roby Hall, Lancs.

MOSTYN (E) 1670, of Talacre, Flintshire
(Name pronounced "Mostin")

Life by the death of the lion

My help is from the Lord

Sir WILLIAM BASIL JOHN MOSTYN, 15th *Baronet*; *b* 15 Oct 1975; *s* his father, *Sir* JEREMY JOHN ANTHONY, 1988.

Arms – Per bend sinister ermine, and ermines, a lion rampant or. Crest – On a mount vert a lion as in the arms.
Residence – The Coach House, Church Lane, Lower Heyford, Oxon.

SISTERS LIVING

Casimira Anita Maria, *b* 1964. —— Rachel Johanna Maria, *b* 1967.

UNCLE LIVING (*son of 13th baronet*)

TREVOR ALEXANDER RICHARD (39B Elgin Crescent, W11 2JD), *b* 23 May 1946: *m* 1986 (*m diss* 1988), Elizabeth, da of Peter Dax.

AUNTS LIVING (*daughters of 13th baronet*)

Sara Ann, *b* 1932: *m* 1957, Ranjit Banerji, of 7 London Place, Oxford OX4 1BD, and has issue living, Bijoya (10 Molescroft Park, Beverley, Humberside HU17 7EA), *b* 1957: *m* 1983, Ian Chisholm, who *d* 1998, and has issue living, Rory *b* 1989, Anna *b* 1987, — Sabita BANERJI (87 Lytton Rd, Oxford OX4 3NY), *b* 1961: *m* 1989 (*m diss* 1997), Arild Bergh, and has issue living, Maia *b* 1994, — Juthika, *b* 1963: *m* 1987, David Nicholas Slaughter, of Penny Cottage, London Rd, Henfield, W Sussex BN5 9JJ. — Joanna Mary Patricia, *b* 1939: *m* 1960, Hugh Edward Sarne Griffith, of La Mariscala 315, San Isidro, Lima 27, Peru, and has issue living, Hugh Pyers Sarne, — Isolde Gemma Sarne, *b* 1961: *m* 1988, Ian Aitken Georgeson, — Bronwen Anita, *b* 1963, — Samantha Joanna, *b* 1967, — Phoebe Abigail, *b* 1976.

GREAT AUNT LIVING (*sister of 13th baronet*)

Hermione Mary Josephine, *b* 1906: *m* 1942, Joseph Mostyn, Col Polish Army, who *d* 1969 (naturalized a British subject 1949, when he abandoned by deed poll his surname of Tuzinkiewicz), and has issue living, Richard Jan Joseph (Old Manor Farm, Broughton, Aylesbury, Bucks), *b* 1942: *m* 1966, Annette Christian Garrick, and has issue living, Suki Hermione *b* 1968, Melissa Bernadette *b* 1970, Chloe Mary *b* 1975, — Paul (Mill Hook Farm, Granborough, Buckingham), *b* 1945: *m* 1971, Elizabeth Catherine Bernadette, da of Peter Northcote Lunn, CMG, OBE (V Gormanston), and has issue living, Toby Joseph *b* 1975, Theresa Antoinette *b* 1973, Olivia Mary *b* 1977, — Simon Edward Basil (Kings Court, Talley, Carmarthenshire), *b* 1947: *m* 1973, Alison Mary Bridget, da of Capt J. Thomas, RN, and has issue living, Samuel John Savage *b* 1975, Freddy Joseph George *b* 1980, Harry Edward Llewelyn *b* 1987, Polly Elizabeth Hermione *b* 1973, Megan Myfanwy Joan *b* 1983, — Wanda Hermione Krystyna, *b* (twin) 1942: *m* 1964, Capt Terence Percyvall Hart Dyke (*see* Dyke, Bt, colls).

WIDOW LIVING OF FOURTEENTH BARONET

CRISTINA BEATRICE MARIA (*Lady Mostyn*), da of Marchese Pier Paolo Vladimiro Orengo, of Turin, Italy: *m* 1963, Sir Jeremy John Anthony Mostyn, 14th Bt, who *d* 1988. *Residence* – The Coach House, Church Lane, Lower Heyford, Oxon.

COLLATERAL BRANCHES LIVING

Grandchildren of late Lieut-Col Edward Henry Joseph Mostyn, only son of late Capt Edward Henry Mostyn, 2nd son of 7th baronet:—
Issue of late Capt Joseph Edward Hubert Mostyn, TD, *b* 1888, *d* 1960: *m* 1920, Gertrude Clare, who *d* 1974, da of late John Hutchinson:—
Edward John, TD, *b* 1922; *ed* Ampleforth; is Capt RA (TA), and a Qualified Asso of Land Agents' So; Hon Research Fellow Reading Univ; formerly Flight-Lieut RAF; European War 1941-45 (despatches): *m* 1945, Dorothy Brady, and has had issue, Francis Edward Terence (84 Ledborough Lane, Beaconsfield, Bucks HP9 2DG), *b* 1946: *m* 1981, Kathryn Jane, da of Eric William Hope Spillett, of Victoria, Australia, and has issue living, Francis Christopher Pyers *b* 1988, Isabel Sara Lisette *b* 1983, — Stephen John (Cherrywood, 1053 Oxford Rd, Tilehurst, Reading, Berks), *b* 1949, — Sara Juliet, *b* 1955; *d* 1964.

Issue of late Maj Joseph Cecil Mary Mostyn, MC, *b* 1891, *d* 1971: *m* 1924, Joan Wake, who *d* 1975, da of Guy Shorrock:—
Jerome John Joseph (c/o Lloyds Bank plc, 4 Dean Stanley St, SW1P 3HU), *b* 1933; *ed* Downside: *m* 1st, 1956 (*m diss* 1971), Mary Anna Bridget Ghislaine, da of Ronald F. Medicott; 2ndly, 1972, Ana Julia Novoa, who *d* 1980; 3rdly, 1988, Rosemary Joy Hamilton, widow of (Alan) Ross McWhirter, and da of Leslie C. H. Grice, and has issue living (by 1st *m*), Nicholas Anthony Joseph Ghislain (Danes, Little Berkhamsted, Herts SG13 8LU), *b* 1957; QC 1997, Assist Recorder of the Crown Court 1997: *m* 1981, Lucy Joanna, da of John Hodgson Willis, of Wressle House, nr Brigg, S Humberside, and has issue living, Henry Francis Joseph Ghislain *b* 1987, Gregory Thomas Joseph Ghislain *b* 1995, Charlie Otto Joseph Ghislain *b* 1998, Daisy Catherine Mary Ghislaine *b* 1989, — Mark Francis Joseph Ghislain (Walnut Cottage, Asthall, Burford, Oxon OX18 4HW), *b* 1959: *m* 1996, Gabrielle (Didi), da of P.S. de la Pena, of Elmley Castle, Worcs, and has issue living, Harry Paul *b* 1997, — Giles Patrick Joseph Ghislain, *b* 1967, — Joanna Charlotte Mary Ghislaine, *b* 1963: *m* 1992, George Thomas Treves, of Burcombe Farm, North Poorton, Bridport, Dorset DT6 3TH, and has issue living, Constance *b* 1993, Martha *b* 1996. — (by 2nd *m*) Philip Anthony Julio Jerome, *b* 1978, — Anna Teresa Joan, *b* 1973. —— Philomena Cecilia Mary (9 Abbefield, 40 Vyrnwy Place, Oswestry, Shropshire SY11 1PA), *b* 1926: *m* 1949, Hugh Dudley Symon, MA, MRCS, FRCP, who *d* 1980, and has issue living, Andrew Nicholas Dudley, *b* 1950, — Neil

Antony, *b* 1953: *m* 1981, Victoria Allison Edwards, — Pyers Hugh, *b* 1957; BSc Univ of Wales: *m* 1986, Patricia Mary Roberts. —— Charmian Mary, *b* 1938: *m* 1966, Guy Hipsley Cooper, who *d* as the result of an accident 1986, and has issue living, Tarquin Rupert Christopher Mostyn, *b* 1975, — Sophy Maria, *b* 1968, — Jonquil Kate, *b* 1971, — Alice Teresa Mostyn, *b* 1972.

Issue of late Joseph Philip David Mostyn, *b* 1894, *d* 1929: *m* (Jan) 1928, Mary Catherine (who *d* 1995, having *m* 2ndly, 1931, Brigadier Desmond Seymour Keenan, who *d* 1997), da of Richard Cecil Moss:—
Sir (Joseph) David (Frederick), KCB, CBE (c/o Lloyds Bank, Broad St, Lyme Regis, Dorset), *b* (Nov) 1928; Gen late R Green Jackets; GOC Berlin 1980-83, Military Sec 1983-86, Adjt Gen, Min of Defence 1986-88, Col Cmdt Light division 1983-86, Army Legal Corps 1983-88; MBE (Mil) 1962, Despatches Brunei 1963, CBE (Mil) 1974, KCB (Mil) 1983; Kt of the sovereign Mil Order of Malta (1974): *m* 1952, Diana Patricia, da of late Col Bertrand Cecil Owens Sheridan, MC, and has issue living, Philip Joseph, *b* 1955; Col—: *m* 1985, Helen Catharine Stewart, da of late Maj George Stewart Nickerson, of Cour, by Campbeltown, Argyll, and has issue living, Isobel Mary *b* 1987, Alice Mary *b* 1989, Rosanna Mary *b* 1990, Clare Mary *b* 1993, Lucy Mary *b* 1998, — (David) Mark (Joseph), *b* 1960: *m* 1989, Jane Carolyn, da of J. W. Rhodes, of Melbourne, Australia, and has issue living, Joshua Marcus Joseph *b* 1991, William David Joseph *b* 1992, Georgia Emma Mary *b* 1995, — Rupert Joseph Sheridan, *b* 1961, — Matthew Anthony Joseph, *b* 1971, — Celia Mary, *b* 1953, — Katherine Mary, *b* 1973.

Descendants of late George Charles Browne-Mostyn, eldest son of late Charles Browne-Mostyn (*b* 1753) (infra), who became 6th *Baron Vaux of Harrowden* on termination of the abeyance in his favour 1838 (see that title).

Granchildren of late Francis Llewellyn Mostyn, 4th son of late Charles Browne-Mostyn (*b* 1840), only son of late Henry Browne-Mostyn, 2nd son of late Charles Browne-Mostyn (*b* 1753), 2nd son of 5th baronet:—
Issue of late Charles Francis Llewellyn Mostyn, *b* 1904, *d* 1992. *m* 1933, Marion Ethel McKay, who *d* 1993:—
Francis Llewellyn (81 La Rose Drive, St Albert, Alberta, Canada T8N 2V7), *b* 1935: *m* 1958, Yvonne Brown, and has issue living, Douglas William Francis, *b* 1959: *m* 19—, Tammy Wilson, — Donald Wayne, *b* 1960, — Patricia Dawn, *b* 1964. —— Trevor Angus (RR 1, Box 4, Elko, BC, Canada V0B 1J0), *b* 1946: *m* 1966, Doris de Rosier, and has issue living, Trevor William Charles, *b* 1971, — Vincent Norman Alan, *b* 1973; has issue living (by Roxanne Baurassa), Melissa Ashley Rose *b* 1991, (by Holly Lynn Walker) Jessie Alan PIERCE MOSTYN *b* 1998, — Laurie Irene Grace, *b* 1966: *m* 1st, 19—, Ian Alexander Sheperd; 2ndly, 19—, Colin James Breakwell, and has issue living (by 1st *m*), Ian Charles Alan *b* 1986, (by 2nd *m*) James Andrew *b* 1996, — Diana Lynn Carolyn, *b* 1967: *m* 19—, Wade Richard Lightburn, and has issue living, Natasha Lynn Rose *b* 1986. —— Robert Norman, *b* 1957: *m* 1995, Twyla Dawn Sorenson, and has issue living, Zachary Peter Charles, *b* 1999. —— Gwendolyn Grace, *b* 1937: *m* 1958, Leonard Alexander Gyulai, of 40 Covington Mews NE, Calgary, Alberta, Canada T3K 4E8, and has issue living, Edward Llewellyn Alexander (215 Coachwood Crescent SW, Calgary, Alberta, Canada T3H 1E7), *b* 1959: *m* 1981, Rosemary Fiona Neumann, and has issue living, Alexander Donald James *b* 1991, Amanda Rose *b* 1989, — Donald Leonard Trevor, *b* 1966: *m* 1991, Lorraine Myrna Eriksen, and has issue living, Evan Donald Francis *b* 1996, Rebecca Gwendolyn *b* 1993, — James Robert Charles, *b* 1969: *m* 1995, Keri Lynn Babuik, and has issue living, Taylor Dawn *b* 1997, — Francis Charles Frederick, *b* 1979, — Sara Theresa Marion, *b* 1960: *m* 1980, Donald Duane Hollyoake, and has issue living, Stuart Donald Llewellyn *b* 1989, Adam Edward William *b* 1991, — Sandra Agnes Grace, *b* 1961; has issue living (by Marty Walter Gordon Anderson), Shawn Leonard James ANDERSON *b* 1986, Kelly Maybell Grace ANDERSON *b* 1989, — Susan Julianne Gladys, *b* 1964: *m* 1987, Terry Lee Swalm, and has issue living, Scott Alexander Lee *b* 1989, Jonathan David Charles *b* 1992, — Sinda Margaret Lenora, *b* 1967.

Grandchildren of late Charles Browne-Mostyn (*b* 1840) (ante):—
Issue of late Capt George William Mostyn, *b* 1874, *d* 1939: *m* 1897, Isabel Almond:—
Vaux Almond, *b* 1906; late Maj Australian Imperial Forces: *m* 1st, 1934, Mavis Jean Marshall, who *d* 1958; 2ndly, 1964, Monica Lewsey Jackson, who *d* 1985. *Residence* – 17 Frederick St, Glengowrie, S Australia.

Issue of late Iltyd Edward Mostyn, *b* 1881, *d* 1958: *m* 1901, Lily Humphry, who *d* 1984:—
†Iltyd Humphry, *b* 1907: *m* 1934, Joan Athol, who *d* 1989, da of Charles J. Radwell, and *d* 1982, leaving issue, (David) Pyers, *b* 1938: *m* 1963, Susan Wallace Johnson, and has issue living, Richard Pyers *b* 1963: *m* 1990, Shona Sugrue (and has issue living, Richard Thomas *b* 1994), David Wallace *b* 1967, Peter Llewellyn *b* 1968, — Richard Clive (1979 W 36th Av, Vancouver, BC, Canada V6M 1K7), *b* 1945: *m* 1986, Ursula Anna Schmiing. —— Charles Gerard (305-8840 No 1 Rd, Richmond, BC, Canada V7C 4C1), *b* 1910: *m* 1936, Ruth Winona, who *d* 1988, da of William Brown, and has issue living, Trevor Iltyd (380 Hidhurst Place, W Vancouver, BC, Canada V7S 1K1), *b* 1940: *m* 1979, Sarah Katherine Ford. —— Gwendolyn Mary, *b* 1905: *m* 1939, Charles Allen Higginson, and has issue living, Brenda Lynne, *b* 1940: *m* 1963, Kirby Michael O'Donaughy, DDS, of Box 276, Rossland, BC, Canada, and has issue living, Denise Margaret *b* 1964, Theresa Lynne *b* 1967, Kelly Corinne *b* 1969, — Kathleen Mary, *b* 1942: *m* 1962, Lorne Richard Simpson, of 5900 Unsworth Rd, Sardis, BC, Canada, and has issue living, Thomas Allen *b* 1967, Barbara Kathleen *b* 1964. *Residence* – 45687 Spadina Av, Chilliwack, BC, Canada V2P 1T8.

This is one of the numerous Welsh families who trace their descent in the male line from Tudor Trevor, who was the ruler of Hereford early in the tenth century. Richard ap Howell, a lineal descent from the above, was seated at Mostyn, *temp* Henry VII, and his son Thomas, who assumed the name of Mostyn, is an ancestor in female line of Baron Mostyn. Thomas Mostyn's yr brother, Pyers Mostyn, of Talacrc, was gt grandfather of Sir Edward, 1st baronet.

MOTT (UK) 1930, of Ditchling, co Sussex

Bold in dangers

Sir JOHN HARMAR MOTT, 3rd *Baronet*, *b* 21 July 1922; *s* his father, *Sir* ADRIAN SPEAR, 1964; *ed* Radley, and New Coll, Oxford (MA, BM, BCh); and Middx Hospital; MRCGP; 1939-45 War as F/O RAF: *m* 1950, Elizabeth, da of late Hugh Carson, FRCS, of Selly Oak, Birmingham, and has issue.

Arms – Sable, four crescents in cross the horns turned inwards, argent. **Crest** – An estoile of eight points argent encircled by an annulet or.
Residence – Staniford, Brookside, Kingsley, Cheshire WA6 8BG.

SON LIVING

DAVID HUGH, *b* 1 May 1952; *ed* Shrewsbury, Sussex Univ (BSC), Birkbeck Coll Lond Univ (MSc), and Queen Mary Coll, Lond Univ (PhD): *m* 1980, Amanda Jane, only da of Lt-Cdr D. W. P. Fryer, RN (ret), of 20 Westover Rd, Fleet, Hants, and has issue living, Matthew David, *b* 1982, — Jonathan William, *b* 1984.

DAUGHTERS LIVING

Jennifer, *b* 1954: *m* 1977, Robert Alexander Buckey, and has issue living, Mark Robert, *b* 1981, — James John *b* 1983. ——— Alison Mary, *b* 1958; *ed* Southampton Univ (BM); MRCP; has issue living, Jack Lewis Mott Kinnersley, *b* 1993, — Anna Morag Mott Kinnersley, *b* 1997.

SISTER LIVING

Anne Lawrence (Kerensa, 3 Chute Lane, Gorran Haven, St Austell, Cornwall), *b* 1915; *ed* St Anne's Coll, Oxford (MA): *m* 1st, 1939, Anthony Dockray Phillips, DSO, DFC, RAF, who was *ka* 1944; 2ndly, 1946 (*m diss* 1961), Wilfred Robert Peasley, DFC, RAF; 3rdly, 1983, David John Hodges, and has issue living, (by 1st *m*) Anthony Adrian (Teddington House, Warminister, Wilts), *b* 1942; *ed* Shrewsbury, and Merton Coll, Oxford: *m* 1970, Lucinda Aris, and has two adopted children, Anthony Julian *b* 1980, Katherine Mary *b* 1979, — (by 2nd *m*) Patricia Mary Anne, *b* 1947: *m* 1968, Peter James Crowe, of Tregarth, 28 Chute Lane, Gorran Haven, St Austell, Cornwall PL26 6NU, and has issue living, Tasman Peter *b* 1968, James Aylwyn *b* 1971, Matthew Tristan George *b* 1973, Elena Catherine *b* 1977, — Julia Jane (Lowenek, Tregony, Truro, Cornwall), *b* 1950: *m* 1969 (*m diss* 1988), Alan Nigel Clark, and has issue living, Alexander Edward *b* 1977, Dominic *b* 1979, Justin *b* 1982, — Lydia Elizabeth, *b* 1953: *m* 1973 (*m diss* 1988), David Charles Whetter, and has issue living, Timothy Andrew *b* 1978, Thomas Charles *b* 1985, Donna Marie *b* 1980.

COLLATERAL BRANCH LIVING

Issue of late Mark Dobell Mott, yr son of 1st baronet, *b* 1892, *d* 1975: *m* 1st, 1916 (*m diss* 1936), Mary Coryndon, da of late James Henry Greathead; 2ndly, 1936, Martha Lewis, da of Arthur Willis, of Witton Gilbert, co Durham:—
(By 2nd *m*) Peter Lewis, *b* 1944; *ed* Manchester Univ (BA) and Calif Univ (MA). ——— Diana Dobell, *b* 1947.

The 1st baronet, Sir Basil Mott, CB, FRS (son of Frederick Thompson Mott of Birstall Hill, near Leicester), was a Consulting Civil Engineer and a Past Pres of Institution of Civil Engineers.

MOUNT (UK) 1921, of Wasing Place, Reading, Berks

Prudently and constantly

(*Sir*) (WILLIAM ROBERT) FERDINAND MOUNT, 3rd *Baronet*; *b* 2 July 1939; *s* his uncle, *Sir* William Malcolm, 1993, but does not use the title: *ed* Eton, Vienna Univ, and Ch Ch Oxford (MA); Editor Times Literary Supplement since 1990: *m* 1968, Julia Margaret, twin da of Archibald Julian Lucas (*see* B Grenfell, 1980 Edn), and has issue.

Arms – Or, on a mount vert a lion rampant azure, ducally crowned or, between in chief two roses gules, barbed and seeded proper. **Crest** – Upon a mount vert a fox salient proper, supporting a ragged staff erect sable.
Residence – 17 Ripplevale Grove, N1 1HS.

SONS LIVING

WILLIAM ROBERT HORATIO, *b* 12 May 1969; *ed* Westminster, and Magdalen Coll Oxford: *m* 1997, Deborah J. K., elder da of Colin Grey, of Oxshott, Surrey.
—— Henry Francis, *b* 1971; *ed* Westminster, and Magdalen Coll Oxford.

DAUGHTER LIVING

Mary Julia, *b* 1972; *ed* Westminster, and Worcester Coll, Oxford.

SISTER LIVING

Frances Leone, *b* 1941. *Residence* – 1 Steps Farm, Polstead, Colchester, Essex.

DAUGHTERS LIVING OF SECOND BARONET

Cecilia Mary (*Lady Dugdale*), *b* 1931: *m* 1967, Sir William Stratford Dugdale, CBE, MC, 2nd Bt, of Merevale Hall, Atherstone, Warwickshire, and Blyth Hall, Coleshill, Birmingham. —— Mary Fleur, *b* 1934: *m* 1962, Ian Donald Cameron, of The Old Rectory, Peasemore, Newbury, and has issue living, (Allan) Alexander, *b* 1963: *m* 1990, Sarah Louise, 2nd da of (William) George Fearnley-Whittingstall, of Springhill, Eastington, Glos, and of Mrs Douglas Montagu Douglas Scott, of Halford, Warwicks, and has issue living, Angus *b* 1994, Imogen Clare *b* 1992, — David William Donald, *b* 1966, — Tania Rachel, *b* 1965, — Clare Louise, *b* 1971. —— Viola Clare, *b* 1938: *m* 1960, Dr John Robert Blyth Currie, and has issue living, Thomas Mark, *b* 1966, — Mary Teresa, *b* 1962, — Anna Magdalen, *b* 1964.

COLLATERAL BRANCH LIVING

Issue of late George Richard Mount, 3rd and yst son of 1st baronet, *b* 1911, *d* 1991: *m* 1936, (Patricia) Elizabeth, who *d* 19—, da of late John Anthony Baring, of New York:—
(Serena) Georganne, *b* 1941: *m* 1969, Claude Royston Johnson, of 26 Devonshire Place, W1, son of Capt (S) Royston Henry Johnson, CBE, RN, of Old Barn House, Wootton, Boars Hill, Oxford.

The 1st baronet, Sir William Arthur Mount, CBE (son of late William George Mount of Wasing Place, Berks), was MP for S, or Newbury, Div of Berkshire (C) Oct 1900 to Jan 1906, and Jan 1910 to March 1918, and for Berks, Newbury Div, Dec 1918 to May 1922. Parliamentary Private Sec to successive Chancellors of the Exchequer (Rt Hon Sir Michael Hicks-Beach, Bt, MP, and Rt Hon C. T. Ritchie, MP) 1900-1902, and Civil Member of British Claims Commn in France 1916-17.

MOUNTAIN (UK) 1922, of Oare Manor, co Somerset, and Brendon, co Devon

Safety with the Cross

Sir DENIS MORTIMER MOUNTAIN, 3rd *Baronet*; *b* 2 June 1929; *s* his father, *Sir* BRIAN EDWARD STANLEY, 1977; *ed* Eton; late Lt Royal Horse Gds; Pres Eagle Star Holdings 1958-93, Chm and Man Dir of Eagle Star Insurance Co Ltd 1974-85; Dir Rank Organisation plc 1968-94, Bank of Nova Scotia since 1978, Allied London Properties since 1986: *m* 1958, (Hélène) Fleur Mary Kirwan, da of late John William Kirwan-Taylor, of Chemin de Carvalho 3, 1009 Pully, Switzerland, and has issue.

Arms – Ermine, on a fesse azure between three lions rampant guardant sable, each holding between the forepaws an escallop gules, three cross-crosslets argent. *Crest* – Issuant from the battlements of a tower proper, a demi-lion guardant argent, holding between the paws an escallop gules.
Residences – The Manor, Morestead, Winchester, Hants S021 1LZ; 12 Queens Elm Sq, Old Church St, SW3 6ED. *Clubs* – Nat Sporting, Blues and Royals.

SONS LIVING

EDWARD BRIAN STANFORD, *b* 19 March 1961; late Maj The Blues and Royals: *m* 1987, Charlotte Sarah Jesson, da of His Honour Judge (Henry) Pownall, and has issue living, Thomas Denis Edward, *b* 14 Aug 1989, — Harry Brian Pownall, *b* 1991, — Camilla, *b* 1993. —— William Denis Charles, *b* 1966: *m* 1994, Emma V. G., da of Cmdr Patrick Mitchell, of Chorleywood, Herts, and has issue living, Rory Patrick William, *b* 1998.

DAUGHTER LIVING

Georgina Lily Fleur, *b* 1959: *m* 1986, Nigel Charles Blake Macpherson, only son of Ian Macpherson, of The Old Hall, Blofield, Norwich, Norfolk, and has issue living, Charles Edward Ian, *b* 1989, — Lara Alexandra Fleur, *b* 1991, — Katie Victoria Lily, *b* 1994.

BROTHER LIVING

Nicholas Brian Edward (17 Hollywood Rd, SW10; Lower Lanham Farm, Alresford, Hants), *b* 1936; *ed* Eton, and St Catherine's Coll, Camb; formerly Lt Royal Horse Gds: *m* 1965, Penelope, yr da of late M. H. Shearme, of 15 Astell St, SW3, and has issue living, Henry Nicholas *b* 1967: *m* 1998, Hon Camilla Sarah Cecil, yr da of 3rd Baron Rockley, — Nathalie Frances, *b* 1970.

SISTER LIVING

Fleur Caroline, *b* 1933: *m* 1955, Dane Peter Douetil, of Busbridge Lakes House, Godalming, Surrey, and has had issue, Dane Jonathan, *b* 1960, — Guy William, *b* 1963, — William Walton, *b* 1966, — Nicola Fleur, *b* 1957; *d* 1993.

WIDOW LIVING OF SECOND BARONET

DORIS ELSIE (*Doris, Lady Mountain*) (75 Eaton Sq, SW1), el da of late Eric Charles Edward Lamb, of 2 Queen St, Mayfair, W1: *m* 1926, Sir Brian Edward Stanley Mountain, 2nd Bt, who *d* 1977.

The 1st baronet, Sir Edward Mortimer Mountain (son of late Henry Stanford Mortimer Mountain), was Chm of Eagle Star Insurance Co, Ltd. The 2nd baronet, Sir Brian Edward Stanley Mountain was Pres of Eagle Star Insurance 1974-77, and Chm 1948-73.

MOWAT (UK) 1932, of Cleckheaton, West Riding of Yorkshire (Extinct 1968)

Sir ALFRED LAW MOWAT, DSO, OBE, MC, JP, DL, 2nd and last *Baronet*.

DAUGHTER LIVING OF SECOND BARONET

Joan Mary Louise (*Baroness Shaw of Northstead*), *b* 1923: *m* 1951, Baron Shaw of Northstead (Life Baron), and has issue. *Residence* – Duxbury Hall, Liversedge, Yorkshire.

MOWBRAY (UK) 1880, of Warennes Wood, Berkshire

Sir JOHN ROBERT MOWBRAY, 6th *Baronet; b* 1 March 1932; *s* his father, *Sir* GEORGE ROBERT, KBE, 1969; *ed* Eton, and New Coll, Oxford; DL Suffolk 1993: *m* 1957, Lavinia Mary, da of Lt-Col Francis Edgar Hugonin, OBE, JP, RA (Walker, Bt, *cr* 1868), and has issue.

𝕬rms – Quarterly, 1st and 4th gules, a lion rampant ermine; two flaunches or, each charged with three billets in pale azure, *Mowbray;* 2nd and 3rd per pale azure and sable a chevron embattled, between in chief two roses, and in base a cross pattée or, *Cornish.* 𝕮rests – 1st, an oak tree or, pendent from the tree an escutcheon gules charged with a lion's head erased argent; 2nd, a Cornish chough between two branches of laurel proper. 𝕾econd 𝕸otto – "Deus pascit corvos" (*God feedeth the ravens*), *Cornish.*
Residence – The Hill House, Duffs Hill, Glemsford, Suffolk CO10 7PP.

Suo stat robore virtus

Virtue stands in its own strength

William, *b* 1996.

DAUGHTERS LIVING

Mary Clare, *b* 1959: *m* 1984, James Duncan Delevingne, son of late E. N. Delevingne, and has issue living, Benjamin James, *b* 1984, — Oliver Guy, *b* 1988. —— Teresa Jane, *b* 1961. —— Katherine Diana, *b* 1965: *m* 1993, David Norman Chastel de Boinville, son of late Gerard Nicolas Pyemont Chastel de Boinville, MC, TD, of Walkern Hall, Herts, and has issue living,

SISTERS LIVING

Carolyn Mary, *b* 1930: *m* 1952, Stamford Robert Francis Vanderstegen-Drake, and has issue living, John Peter, *b* 1955: *m* 1986, Charlotte Susannah, da of Brian Gunn, of Quarry Close, Winscombe, Avon, and has issue living, John William *b* 1988, — Mark Stamford, *b* 1959: *m* 1986, Susan, da of Cmdr Alan Dickie, of Bowdown House, Rodborough Common, Stroud, — Clare Rosdew, *b* 1953: *m* 1st, 1978 (*m diss* 1984), (William) Gerald Cheyne (*see* Cheyne, Bt, colls); 2ndly, 1984, Christopher J. B. Bromfield, of The Old Coaching House, Lacock, Chippenham, Wilts, eldest son of late Dr F. B. Bromfield, of The Blue House, Rodborough Common, Stroud, Glos, and has issue living (by 1st *m*) (*see* Cheyne, Bt, colls), (by 2nd *m*), George Frank *b* 1985, Alice Mary *b* 1987. *Residence* – The Old Tannery, Ecchinswell, Newbury. —— Elizabeth Rose, *b* 1936: *m* 1964, Capt Patrick Hector Raymond Glennie, RN (The Old Mill House, Clanfield, Portsmouth, Hants), and has issue living, Christopher Arthur John, *b* 1966: *m* 1991, Christina Marie, da of Cyril Steiner, of Stevensville, Michigan, USA, — Alexander Patrick, *b* 1970, — Sarah Frances, *b* 1965.

The Rt Hon Sir John Robert Mowbray, 1st baronet, el son of Robert Stirling Cornish, of Exeter, assumed by Roy licence 1847 the surname of Mowbray in lieu of his patronymic, his wife, Elizabeth Gray, being da and heir of George Isaac Mowbray of Bishopswearmouth, co Durham, and Mortimer, Berks. He sat as MP for Durham City (*C*) 1853-68 and for Oxford Univ 1868-99, and was Judge Advocate-Gen and Judge Marshal 1858-59 and 1866-68, and "Father of the House of Commons" 1898-99. The 2nd baronet, Sir Robert Gray Cornish, sat as MP for Lancashire, SE, Preswich Div (*C*) 1886-95, and for Brixton Div of Lambeth 1900-06.

MUIR (UK) 1892, of Deanston, Perthshire

I am not broken by hardships

DURIS NON FRANGOR

(*Sir*) RICHARD JAMES KAY MUIR, 4th *Baronet; b* 25 May 1939; *s* his father *Sir* JOHN (HARLING) MUIR, 1994, but his name does not appear on the Official Roll of the Baronetage, nor does he use the title; *ed* Trin Coll, Glenalmond: *m* 1st, 1965 (*m diss* 1974), Susan Elizabeth, da of George Albert Gardener, of Calcutta and Leamington Spa; 2ndly, 1975, Lady Linda Mary Cole, da of 6th Earl of Enniskillen, and has issue by 1st and 2nd *m*.

𝕬rms – Per chevron argent and or, on a chevron cotised azure, a redbreast proper between two mullets of the first, in chief as many fleurs de lis on the third. 𝕮rest – A Saracen's head couped, wreathed with laurel proper, charged on the neck with a mullet azure.
Residence – Park House, Blair Drummond, Perthshire.

DAUGHTERS LIVING (*By 1st marriage*)

Louisa Jane, *b* 1967. —— Catherine Elizabeth, *b* 1968.

(*by 2nd marriage*)

Daisy Mary, *b* 1977. —— Anna Charlotte, *b* 1979.

BROTHERS LIVING

IAN CHARLES (Well Cottage, Poulner, Ringwood, Hants), *b* 16 Sept 1940; *ed* Gordonstoun: *m* 1967, Fiona Barbara Elspeth, da of Maj Stuart Mackenzie, of Rose Cottage, Charlton All Saints, Salisbury, and has issue living, Sophie Amanda Noël, *b* 1969, — Lisa Jane Fiona, *b* 1973, — Juliet Sara Kirstie, *b* 1978. —— Andrew Hugh John (Itchen Lodge, Itchen Abbas, Winchester, Hants), *b* 1943; *ed* Gordonstoun: *m* 1st, 1969 (*m diss* 1993), Primrose Jean Onslow, da of Robert B. How of St Andrews, Fife (*see* E Onslow, colls, 1995 Edn); 2ndly,

1993, Ann Mary, da of — Corbally, and formerly wife of Timothy Jenkins, and has issue living (by 1st *m*), Philip John Frederick, *b* 1974, — Alexandra Juliet, *b* 1971. —— James Francis (Underhill, Muthill Perthshire), *b* 1948; *ed* Gordonstoun: *m* 1975, Griselda C, da of Sir Anthony Nathaniel Stainton, KCB, QC, and has issue living, John Alexander Hector, *b* 1976, — William Anthony Nathaniel, *b* 1979. —— Robert William, *b* 1950; *ed* Tabley House.

SISTERS LIVING

Fiona Mary, *b* 1938: *m* 1968, Walter Goetz, who *d* 1995, of 19 Alexander Place, SW7, and has issue living, Sebastian, *b* 1970, — Dominic, *b* 1971. —— Margaret Elizabeth (*Lady Aird*), *b* 1946: *m* 1968, Sir (George) John Aird, 4th Bt, of Grange Farm, Evenlode, Moreton-in-Marsh, Glos, and has issue (*see* Aird, Bt).

AUNT LIVING (*Sister of 3rd baronet*)

Margaret Vivian, *b* 1912: *m* 1938, Eric Gerald Hayes, who *d* 1959, and has issue living, David Richard MUIR OF KNOCK (Pityoulish, Aviemore, Inverness-shire), *b* 1939: *m* 1968, Hon Sarah Maclay, da of 2nd Baron Maclay, — Helen Jane (*Hon Mrs Robert Younger*), *b* 1941: *m* 1971, Hon Robert Edward Gilmour Younger (*see* V Younger of Leckie). *Residence* – Tremelethen, St Mary's, Isles of Scilly.

WIDOW LIVING OF THIRD BARONET

ELIZABETH MARY (*Lady Muir*), el da of late Frederick James Dundas (*see* M Zetland, colls): *m* 1936, Sir John (Harling) Muir, 3rd Bt, who *d* 1994. *Residence* – Bankhead, Blair Drummond, Perthshire.

COLLATERAL BRANCHES LIVING

          Grandchildren of late James Finlay Muir, 2nd son of 1st baronet:—
     Issue of late Lt-Cdr Gerald Robin Muir, OBE, RN *b* 1917, *d* 1991: *m* 1st, 1940, Doreen Margaret, who *d* 1982, yr da of late Col Charles Wanford Watney, of Quay Cottage, Weare Giffard, Devon; 2ndly, 1983, Margaret Claire, da of late Llewellyn Arthur Hugh-Jones, OBE (*see* B Auckland, colls, 1980 Edn), and widow of (i) Philip Dalton Worthington, MBE, and (ii) Lt-Cdr Thomas Mervyn Smith Dorrien Smith, of Tresco Abbey, Isles of Scilly:—
(By 1st *m*) †Hugh James Robin, *b* 1944: *m* 1969, Maureen Yearsley (PO Box 521, Malanda, N Queensland 4885, Australia), and *d* 1995, leaving issue, Andrew James, *b* 1970, — Jeremy Kim, *b* 1973. —— Nicholas John (Dunduff, Braco Castle Farm, by Dunblane, Perthshire), *b* 1953: *m* 1st, 1975, Janet Mary Bain, who *d* 1978, da of Sir Colin Moffat Bain Campbell, MC, 8th Bt; 2ndly, 1980, Angela Cramp, and has issue living (by 2nd *m*), David Stuart, *b* 1981. —— Sarah Nadéjda WILLIAMS (Blaenau Dwr Farm, Froncysyllte, Llangollen, Clwyd), *b* 1940: has assumed the surname of Williams: *m* 1965 (*m diss* 1982), Alexos Katsikides, of Athens, and has had issue, Simion, *b* 1966; *d* 1987, — Maria, *b* 1967; *d* 1976. —— Anne Catriona, *b* 1943: *m* 1970, Maj John Philip Ogilvy Gibb, of Glenisla House, by Blairgowrie, Perthshire PH11 8QL, and has issue living, Alastair John Richard, *b* 1972, — Nicholas James Harry, *b* 1975, — Catriona Mary, *b* 1971. —— Jean Charlotte, *b* 1946: *m* 1970, Lieut Alexander Michael Gregory, RN, of Duncryne House, Gartocharn, by Alexandria, Dumbartonshire, and has issue living, Charlotte Clare, *b* 1971, — Katherine Jane, *b* 1973, — Helen Veronica, *b* 1979, — Sarah Rachel, *b* 1982. —— Diana Rachel, *b* 1949: *m* 1985, James Lonergan, of Graigue Little, New Inn, Cashel, co Tipperary, and has issue living, James Robin, *b* 1986, — Rosanna Rachel, *b* 1988, — Clare Charlotte, *b* 1989.

          Issue of late John Buchanan Muir, 3rd son of 1st baronet, *b* 1876, *d* 1956: *m* 1911, Agnes Heather Gardiner, who *d* 1961, da of late John Gardiner Muir, of 2 Grosvenor Cres, SW:—
Diana Heather, *b* 1915: *m* 1950, John Anthony Francis Binny, who *d* 1996, and has issue living, Anne Heather, *b* 1951: *m* 1st, 1979 (*m diss* 1982), David Child, 2ndly, 1983, Jonathan Guy Chambers, of Kiftsgate Court, Campden, Glos, and has issue living, (by 2nd *m*), Robert Edward *b* 1983, Patrick William Jack *b* 1987, Clare Heather *b* 1983, — (Katherine) Emma, *b* 1953: *m* 1976, Philip Austin George Mackenzie, and has issue (*see* D Grafton). *Residence* – Kiftsgate Court, Campden, Gloucestershire. —— Bettine Clara (Hidcote Vale, Campden, Glos), *b* 1917.

  The 1st baronet, Sir John Muir was Lord Provost of Glasgow 1889-92. The 2nd baronet, Sir (Alexander) Kay Muir, was High Sheriff of co Waterford 1929.

Muir Mackenzie, see Mackenzie.

MUNRO (NS) 1634, of Foulis-Obsdale, Ross-shire

Sir KENNETH ARNOLD WILLIAM MUNRO, 16th *Baronet*, elder son of late Arnold Harry Munro, 6th son of late Harry Munro, yr son of 9th baronet; *b* 26 June 1910; *s* his first cousin once removed, *Sir* IAN TALBOT, 1996, but his name does not appear on the Official Roll of the Baronetage: *m* 1935, Olive Freda, da of Francis Broome, of Nunhead, SE15, and has issue.

𝕬rms – Or, an eagle's head erased gules, langued azure, a label of three points of the second charged with three lions' heads erased argent, and in dexter chief a canton of a Baronet of Nova Scotia. 𝕮rest – An eagle displayed proper, charged across his breast and wings with a label of three points gules charged with three lion's heads erased argent.
Residence – 3 Courtrai Rd, Honor Oak Park, SE23.

SON LIVING

IAN KENNETH, *b* 5 April 1940. *Residence* – Foulis, Gold Cup Lane, Ascot, Berks SL5 8NP.

DAUGHTER LIVING

Christine Freda, *b* 1944: *m* 1971, Capt Kim Bridle, and has issue living, Christopher, *b* 1972, — Andrew, *b* 1975. *Residence* – Timbers, Barclay Park, Aboyne AB3 5JP.

BROTHER LIVING

Roland Alec Wilfred (Maycroft, 223 Crookston Rd, Eltham Park, SE9 1YE), *b* 1911: *m* 1937, Queenie May, da of Ernest Rose Johnson, of Nunhead, SE15, and has issue living, Godfrey Roland (184 Greenvale Rd, Eltham Park, SE9 1PQ), *b* 1938: *m* 1985, Julie Pamela, da of Reginald Gosling, of N Cheam, Surrey, and has issue living, Rupert Roland *b* 1987, Lawrence Godfrey *b* 1990, Victoria Ella May *b* 1993, — Yvonne May, *b* 1943: *m* 1967, Kenneth A. Parkes, and has issue living, Alexander James *b* 1976.

DAUGHTERS LIVING OF FOURTEENTH BARONET

Audrey Muriel, *b* 1924: *m* 1946, Donald Ernest Fifield, of 1A Rhoose Rd, Rhoose, Vale of Glamorgan, Wales CF62 3EQ, and has issue living, Richard Donald *b* 1947. —— Betty Millicent (34 Falstaff Av, Earley, Reading, Berks RG6 5TQ), *b* 1926: *m* 1950 (*m diss* 1982), Brian Leslie Wright, and has issue living, Gail Louise, *b* 1951: *m* 1973, Richard Sharp, — Linda Ann, *b* 1953: *m* 1986, Raymond Vass, and has issue living, Rosalind Natasha *b* 1987.

DAUGHTERS LIVING OF THIRTEENTH BARONET

Grace, *b* 1908: *m* 1931, William Price, who *d* 1992, of 119 Crystal Palace Rd, E Dulwich, SE22, and has issue living, Jean, *b* 1932, — Sylvia, *b* 1933, — Barbara, *b* 1939. —— Minnie Isabel, *b* 1914: *m* 1935, Ernest Price, who *d* 1981, brother of late William Price (ante), and has issue living, Ernest Talbot (11 Kinver Rd, Sydenham, SE26), *b* 1939: *m* 1977, Valarie Weatherall, who *d* 1996, and has issue living, Stuart *b* 1970: *m* 1994, Margaret Davis, Robert Ernest *b* 1981, Lisa Jane *b* 1977, — Jacqueline, *b* 1935: *m* 1958, George James Fox, of 3 Chichester Rd, Greenhithe, Dartford, Kent DA9 9JS, and has issue living, Dawn Lesley *b* 1959: *m* 1983 Anthony Jaglo (and has issue living, Stacey *b* 1986, Shelley *b* 1990).

STEPMOTHER LIVING OF FIFTEENTH BARONET

Simone (24 Bramcote, York Rd, Weybridge, Surrey), da of late Louis Jean Bareau, and widow of Rudolph Lancester Fisk: *m* 1950, as his 2nd wife, Robert Hector Munro, who *d* 1965.

COLLATERAL BRANCHES LIVING

Granddaughter of late Charles Munro, brother of 12th and 13th baronets, sons of late Harry Munro, yr son of 9th baronet:-
Issue of late Malcolm Munro, *b* 1901, *d* 1994: *m* 1931, Constance (Whitegates, Rock, Wadebridge, Cornwall PL27 6JZ), da of William Carter:-
Mary Lee, *b* 1935: *m* 1955, David Rex Denny, of Shalmar Hollow, Rock, Wadebridge, N Cornwall, and has issue living, Sally Louise, *b* 1961: *m* 1st, 1989 (*m diss* 1996), Robert Gerald Leeds Scovell; 2ndly, 1996, Stephen Bennett Mably, of Dinham Farm, St Minver, Wadebridge, Cornwall, — Felicia Mary, *b* 1965: *m* 1987, Richard Michael Latham Jones, of Merryfield Cottage, Rock, Cornwall, and has issue living, William David Studley *b* 1994, Lucy Mary Studley *b* 1992, Amy Louise Studley *b* 1996.

Granddaughter of late Harry Munro, yr son of 9th baronet:-
Issue of late Percy Munro, *b* 1870, *d* 1953: *m* 1909, Annie Louisa, who *d* 1963, da of William Henderson Pearson, of Kennington, SE:-

Irene Louisa, *b* 1915: *m* 1940, William Archer Lawrence, and has issue living, Michael, *b* 1943, — Iain, *b* 1944.

Grandchildren of late Mrs Cecil Claud Hugh Orby Gascoigne (infra):-
Issue of late Capt Patrick Munro of Foulis, TD, *b* 1912; assumed by decree of Lyon Court 1937 the surname and arms of Munro of Foulis and recognised as Chief of Clan Munro; *d* 1995: *m* 1946, Eleanor Mary (Foulis Castle, Evanton, Ross-shire IV16 9UX), da of late Capt Hon William Joseph French (*see* B de Freyne):-
Hector William MUNRO OF FOULIS, Chief of Clan Munro, *b* 1950: *m* 1974, Sarah Margaret Katharine, da of late Henry George Austen de l'Etang Herbert Duckworth (*see* B Chatfield), and has issue living, Finnian George, *b* 1975, — Isabella Katharine, *b* 1978, — Aline Angela, *b* 1981. ——— Harry Robert Gascoigne MUNRO, OC (Ardullie, Kingshead, RR1 New Glasgow, Nova Scotia B2H 5C4, Canada), *b* 1954: *m* 1976, Lynda Marion, da of Cecil Cranton, of Nova Scotia, Canada, and has issue living, Eva Marion, *b* 1983, — Fiona Louise, *b* 1986, — Monica Bernice, *b* 1988. ——— John Alexander Seymour MUNRO, *b* 1959: *m* 1979, Silvia Charlotte Maria, 4th da of Knud Johan Ludvig, Count Holstein-Ledreborg, of Ledreborg, Denmark, by his wife, HRH Princess Marie Gabrielle of Luxembourg, and has issue living, Alexander, *b* 1985, — Tatiana Angela Marie, *b* 1983, — Charlotte Tatiana Marie, *b* 1990, — Angela Charlotte Marie, *b* 1992. ——— Charlotte Eva (Keirhill, Balfron, by Glasgow G63 0LG), *b* 1947: *m* 1st, 1975, John William Betts Donaldson, who *d* 1985, son of late Norman Fraser Graham Donaldson, of Ballindalloch, Balfron, Stirlingshire; 2ndly, 1992, Col Robin Chester Vaughan Hunt, son of late Gen Sir Peter Mervyn Hunt, GCB, DSO, OBE, and has issue living (by 1st *m*), William Betts, *b* 1980, — Robert John, *b* 1983, — Joanna Eva, *b* 1977.

Issue of late Maj Robert Clifton Gascoigne, *b* 1915, *d* 1994: *m* 1st, 1940 (*m diss* 1954), Sylvia Rapozo; 2ndly, 1954, Margaret (2 Hampton Place, Edinburgh EH12 5JA), da of late N. E. Douglas-Menzies, of Newtonairds, Dumfries:-
(By 1st *m*) Robert Hugh GASCOIGNE, *b* 1941. ——— Caroline Orby, *b* 1946: *m* 1st, 1968, Michael Robarts; 2ndly, 1973, Andrew Gordon-Duff, and has issue (by 2nd *m*) (*see* Baird, Bt, *cr* 1809). ——— (By 2nd *m*) Matilda Anne, *b* 1955: *m* 1979, Michael Charles Bevan, of Sothenbury Farm, Scaynes Hill, Haywards Heath, W Sussex RH17 7PE, only son of late Maj T. H. Bevan, of Miltown Grange, co Louth, and has issue living, Conor Thomas Hector, *b* 1983, — Georgina Kathleen, *b* 1991.

Issue of later Cecil Alastair Hector Gascoigne, *b* 1916, *d* 1993: *m* 1947, Jean Muller, who *d* 1959:-
Michael Neil Clifton GASCOIGNE (Grove Cottage, Aberlady, E Lothian EH32 0RB), *b* 1949: *m* 1975, Anna Jennifer, el da of John Milne, of Nether Clifton, Southwick, Dumfries, and has issue living, James Neil Crispin, *b* 1979, — Peter John Hector, *b* 1987, — Gemma Eva Pamela, *b* 1981. ——— Patrick Edward Cecil GASCOIGNE, MBE, *b* 1950: Lt-Col Scots Gds: *m* 1979, Penny Jane, el da of late Maj Alastair Ker MacGeorge, MC, of The Glebe House, Cockpen, Bonnyrigg, Midlothian, and has issue living, Cecily Jean, *b* 1991.

Issue of late Eva Marion Munro, da of 11th baronet, *b* 1881, *d* 1976: *m* 1904, Lt-Col Cecil Claud Hugh Orby Gascoigne, DSO, who *d* 1929:—
Marion Erica, *b* 1906: *m* 1934, Brig George Des Champs Chamier, OBE, KOYLI, who *d* 1987, son of late Sir Edward Maynard Des Champs Chamier, KCSI, KCIE, and has issue living, Anthony Edward Des Champs (Achandunie House, Ardross, Ross and Cromarty), *b* 1935: *m* 1962, Anne-Carole, da of William Dalling, of Transvaal, S. Africa, and has issue living, Daniel William Des Champs *b* 1964, Amy Louise Des Champs *b* 1962, — George Washington Des Champs, *b* 1947: *m* 1974, Janet Michele St Clair, — Antoinette Des Champs, *b* 1938: *m* 1973, Angus Buchan Gordon, FRCS, and has issue living, James Buchan *b* 1974, Madeleine Claire *b* 1976, — Georgiana Des Champs, *b* 1949: *m* 1979, Adrian Gruzman, and has issue living, Angus Michael *b* 1982, Alice Freyer *b* 1980, Amelia Anastasia *b* 1989. ——— Joan Orby, *b* 1910: *m* 1st, 1937, Alastair Gordon-Ingram, Colonial Police; 2ndly, 1947, His Honour Harold William Paton, DSC, who *d* 1986, and has issue living, (by 1st *m*) Donald Alexander, *b* 1938, — (by 2nd *m*) Mary Joanne Letitia, *b* 1948.

The 1st baronet, Col Hector Munro of Foulis, Ross-shire, was created a baronet of Nova Scotia with remainder to heirs male whatsoever. On the death of his son, Sir Hector Munro in 1651, the title reverted to Sir Robert Munro, 3rd baronet (grandson of George, uncle of 1st baronet). The 6th baronet, Sir Robert Munro MP, fought at Fontenoy, and was killed at the battle of Falkirk 1746. Sir Charles Munro, 9th baronet (4th cousin of his predecessor) was distinguished in the Peninsular War, and commanded a Div of Colombian Army under Bolivar.

MUNRO (UK) 1825, of Lindertis, Forfarshire

Sir ALASDAIR THOMAS IAN MUNRO OF LINDERTIS, 6th *Baronet*; *b* 6 July 1927; *s* his father, *Sir* (THOMAS) TORQUIL ALPHONSO, 1985; *ed* Landon Sch, USA, Georgetown Univ, Washington, DC, Pennsylvania Univ, and IMEDE, Lausanne, Switzerland: *m* 1954, Marguerite Lillian, da of late Franklin R. Loy, of Dayton, Ohio, USA, and has issue.

Arms – Or, and eagle's head erased gules, encircled by a branch of laurel on the dexter and of oak on the sinister side both proper; on a chief argent the representation of an Indian hill-fort, and beneath in letters of gold the word "Badamy"; on a canton gules, a representation of a gold medal presented by the East India Co the the 1st baronet for his services in Seringapatam in 1790. Crest – An eagle close proper, having a representation of the medal above mentioned pendent from its neck by a ribbon, the dexter claw resting upon an escutcheon gules, charged with a representation of an Indian hill-fort, and beneath in letters or gold, the world "Badamy" as in the arms, and in the beak a sprig of club moss.
Residence – River Ridge, Box 940, Waitsfield, Vermont 05673, USA.

SON LIVING

KEITH GORDON, *b* 3 May 1959; *ed* Cardigan Mount Sch, Kimball Union Acad, and Univ of New Hampshire: *m* 1989, Jada Louise, da of Adrian Elwell, of Waitsfield, Vermont, and has issue living, Zachary Adrian, *b* 1992, — Mackenzie Carmen, *b* 1996.

DAUGHTER LIVING

Karen Fiona, *b* 1956: *m* 1980 (*m diss* 1988), Robert David Macmichael, Jr, who *d* 1994, of New London, New Hampshire, son of Robert David Macmichael, of New London, New Hampshire, and has issue living, Josh Munro, *b* 1981, — Blake Thomas Ian, *b* 1984.

HALF-BROTHER LIVING

James Kenneth Torquil, *b* 1941; *ed* Bradfield: *m* 1970 (*m diss* 19—), Camilla Ann, yr da of late Cdr J. Nigel Ball, DSC, RN, and has issue living, Iona Katharine, *b* 1973, — Flavia Isla, *b* 1975, — Camilla Morna, *b* 1977.

COLLATERAL BRANCHES LIVING

Grandchildren of late Ian Charles Ronald Walker-Munro (*infra*):—
Issue of late Thomas Ian Michael Walker-Munro, *b* 1922, *d* 1965: *m* 1947, Hon Marjorie Amy Biddulph, da of 3rd Baron Biddulph:—
Thomas Malcolm, *b* 1948. —— Sarah Amy, *b* 1950: *m* 1973, Brig Melville Stewart Jameson, CBE, R Scots Dragoon Gds, and has issue living, Melville Harry Stewart, *b* 1977, — Michael Andrew Stewart, *b* 1980.

Issue of late Patrick Angus Walker-Munro, *b* 1924, *d* 1993: *m* 1950, Mary Barnett, who *d* 1980, da of late R. Y. Phillips:—
Ian David Torquil (404 Galston Rd, Galston 2159, NSW, Australia), *b* 1951: *m* 1982, Mrs Suellan Lough, of Sydney, Australia, and has issue living, Brenton Neil Patrick, *b* 1985, — Alaisdair John Torquil, *b* 1988, — Catherine, *b* 1983. —— (Charles Michael) Angus (34 Forest End, Fleet, Hants GU13 9XE), *b* 1953: *m* 1981 (*m diss* 19—), Christine Margaret, da of Albert Arthur Humphrey, of 29 Marley Av, Bexleyheath, Kent, and has issue living, Peter Michael Angus, *b* 1985.

Grandchildren of late Lieut-Com Edward Lionel Walker-Munro, RN, 2nd son of 3rd baronet:—
Issue of late Ian Charles Ronald Walker-Munro *b* 1889, *d* 1952: *m* 1919, Morna Violet, who *d* 1988, da of Sir Hugh Thomas Munro, 4th Bt:—
Lionel Malcolm (64 Bourne St, SW1), *b* 1929: *m* 1998, Mrs Joan Mary Matilda (Sally) Bowler, of W Chiltington, W Sussex. —— (Roderick) Hugh (Kinnettles House, Forfar, Angus), *b* (twin) 1929: *m* 1st, 1964, Irene, who *d* 1976, da of late Roderick Watt Edgar; 2ndly, 1993, Brenda, da of late Donald Wheelton, and has issue living (by 1st *m*), Euan Torquil Drummond, *b* 1965: *m* 1993, Susan, da of Keith Howman, of Ashmere, Shepperton, Middx, — Geordie Roderick Hamish, *b* 1968: *m* 1993, Lorraine Rose, only da of Patrick Orchard, of Carandain, Perthshire, and has issue living, Rory James Christian *b* 1997, Amelia Charlotte Rose *b* (twin) 1997.

This family descends from John Munro, 1st of Miltown, yr son of Hugh Munro, 9th of Foulis. The 1st baronet, Maj-Gen Sir Thomas, KCB, was Governor of Madras 1820-27.

Munro-Lucas-Tooth, see Tooth.

MUNTZ (UK) 1902, of Clifton-on-Dunsmore, Warwickshire (Extinct 1940)

Sir GERARD PHILIP GRAVES MUNTZ, RN, 3rd and last *Baronet; ka* 1940.

DAUGHTER LIVING OF SECOND BARONET (*By 2nd marriage*)

Désirée Violet, TD, *b* 1916: *m* 1940, Capt Alfred John Spencer Hancock, King's Roy Rifle Corps, and has issue living, Gerard Spencer MOLYNEUX (Bodcott Farm, Moccas, Hereford), *b* 1948, assumed the surname of Molyneux by deed poll 1968, — Antonia *b* 1946: *m* 1st, 1977 (*m diss* 1984), Martin Whitfield; 2ndly, 1985 (*m diss* 1991), Philip Holbourn, and has issue living (by 1st *m*), John Robert *b* 1978, Simon Peter *b* 1981. *Residence* – Broad Close, Coates, Cirencester.

MURRAY (NS) 1628, of Blackbarony, Peeblesshire

Fear God

Sir NIGEL ANDREW DIGBY MURRAY OF BLACKBARONY, 15th *Baronet, b* 15 Aug 1944; *s* his father *Sir* ALAN JOHN DIGBY, 1978; *ed* St Paul's Sch, Argentina, Salesian Agric Tech Sch, Argentina, and Roy Agric Coll, Cirencester: *m* 1980, Diana Margaret, yr da of Robert Campbell Bray, of Sarmiento 1443, (2624) Arias, Prov de Córdoba, Argentina, and has issue.

Arms – Or, a fetterlock azure, on a chief of the last three mullets argent. Crest – A dexter hand holding a scroll proper.
Residence – Establecimiento Tinamú, CC 115, 2624 Arias (Prov de Córdoba), Argentina.

SON LIVING

ALEXANDER NIGEL ROBERT, *b* 1 July 1981.

DAUGHTERS LIVING

Rachel Elisabeth Vanda Digby, *b* 1982. —— Evelyn Caroline Digby, *b* 1987.

BROTHERS LIVING

Kenelm Gerald Digby (Crofts, Woodside Rd, Chiddingfold, Surrey), *b* 1946; *ed* St Paul's Sch, Argentina, and Birmingham Univ (BSc): *m* 1973, Jolandë St Clare Byrne, only child of Mrs Francis Mellor, of Nottingham, and has issue living, Alan James Digby, *b* 1980, — Olivia Lucile Caroline Digby, *b* 1977. —— Peter Francis Digby, *b* 1947; *ed* St Paul's Sch Argentina, Shuttleworth, Agric Coll (NDA), and Bangor Univ (BSc); a Missionary: *m* 1995, Rev Susan Gould. —— Denis Jermyn Digby (The Farmyard, Upper Llandwrog, Fron, Gwynedd), *b* 1949; *ed* St Paul's Sch, Argentina, and Bangor Univ (BSc): *m* 1980, Christiane Baars, who *d* 1993, and has issue living, David Christopher, *b* 1981, — Lawrence Stephan, *b* 1986, — Teresa Mabel, *b* 1983.

AUNT LIVING

Eileen Charmion Digby, *b* 1910: *m* 1930, David Hinchcliff-Mathew, who *d* 1974, and has issue living, Murray Alan, *b* 1933: *m* 1958, Marilyn Nazabal Chapman, da of Don Evaristo Nazabal, of Rufino, Argentina, and has issue living, David *b* 19—, Andrew *b* 19—, Marjory Charlotte *b* 1959, Carol *b* 1961, Rose Ann *b* 19—, Alexandra *b* 19—, — John Gervase, *b* 1947: *m* 1984, Susan Penelope, da of Donald Maxwell Jack, and has issue living, Daniel *b* 1985, Vanessa *b* 1987. *Residence* – Estancia Los Flamencos, Sancti Spiritu, Prov Sta Fé, Argentina.

WIDOW LIVING FOURTEENTH BARONET

MABEL ELISABETH (*Mabel, Lady Murray of Blackbarony*), 2nd da of late Arthur Bernard Schiele, of Arias, Argentina: *m* 1943, Sir Alan John Digby Murray of Blackbarony, 14th baronet, who *d* 1978.

COLLATERAL BRANCHES LIVING

Grandchildren of late Lt-Col Archibald Digby Murray, DSO, RA, elder son of late Col Kenelm Digby
    Murray, DSO, 4th son of 10th baronet:-
Issue of late Lt-Col Archibald John Murray, Black Watch, *b* 1907, *d* 1995: *m* 1st, 1935, Nancy, who *d* 1974, da of
late Philip George, of Barrow Gurney, Som; 2ndly, 1977, Phyllis Walker (Woodford, Dartmouth, Devon TQ6
9PA), da of late Surg Rear-Adm David Walker Hewitt, CB, CMG, MD, BCh, FRCS, and widow of Surg Capt P.
G. Burgess, MVO, RN:—
(By 1st *m*) John Archibald Digby (Churchill Court, Churchill, Somerset BS25 5QW), *b* 1941; *ed* Harrow; JP Avon 1976:
m 1975, Janet, da of Adam Johnstone, OBE, of Temple Wood, Caple, Surrey, and has issue living, Angus John Digby, *b*
1976, — Nicola Rosamund, *b* 1979, — Alice, *b* 1982. ——— Gillian Claire, *b* 1946: *m* 1978, Roger Philip Latham.

Issue of late Maj Ian Digby Murray, *b* 1912, *d* 1974: *m* 1944, Pamela, who *d* 1988, only da of Claud Parbury, of
    Dewhurst, Wadhurst, Sussex:—
Julian Charles Digby (Kelowna, BC, Canada), *b* 1949: *m* 1973, Jill Fraser, of Saskatoon, Saskatchewan, and has issue
living, Ian Thomas, *b* 1987, — Tessa Jane, *b* 1985. ——— Petrina Rosamund, *b* 1947: *m* 1970, Manuel Moran, of Madrid,
and has issue living, Mark, *b* 1977, — Sophia, *b* 1976, — Ania, *b* (twin) 1977. ——— Charlotte Davey, *b* 1954: *m* 1977,
Grahame Royds Gordon Nicholson, and has issue living, Ian Royds Gordon, *b* 1981, — Rupert Grahame Murray, *b* 1983,
— Sabrina Pamela, *b* 1989.

Grandson of late Col Kenelm Digby Murray, DSO (ante):—
Issue of late Col Kenelm Digby Bold Murray, CB, DSO, *b* 1879, *d* 1947: *m* 1911, Gwendolen, who *d* 1979, da of
    late Thomas Andrew de Wolf, of Sydney, NS Wales:—
Andrew Digby, *b* 1916; Lieut-Col (retired) RA: *m* 1947 (*m diss* 19—), Joan (ROBERTS), da of Major A. Nelson Allen, of
Leigh, Surrey, and has issue living, Anna Teresa, *b* 1947.

Grandchildren of late Lieut-Gen Sir James Wolfe Murray, KCB, son of late James Wolfe Murray (*b*
    1814), son of late James Wolfe Murray (Hon Lord Cringletie), great-grandson of late Alexander Murray,
    4th son of 2nd baronet:—
Issue of late Capt George Wolfe Murray, *b* 1876, *d* 1955: *m* 1910, Katherine, who *d* 1955, da of late Rev Thomas
    Jones, R of Llanbedr, Crickhowell:—
Thomas Wolfe, *b* 1913; *ed* St Bees, and Faraday Hse (Diploma): *m* 1946, Violet May, da of late Alexander Scott, of
Vancouver, British Columbia, and has issue living, Alexander James Wolfe, *b* 1949; *ed* Perth High Sch, and Univ of
British Columbia (BA), — Robin Wolfe, *b* 1951; *ed* Perth Academy, and St Andrews Univ (BSc (Hons), PhD), — Patricia
Ann Wolfe, *b* 1947, — Susan May Wolfe, *b* 1958. *Residence* – Hycroft, Hatton Rd, Kinnoull, Perth. ——— Katherine Jean
Wolfe, *b* 1911: *m* 1958, James Gordon Fyfe, TD, WS, DL. ——— Miriam Arabella Elizabeth Wolfe, *b* 1916: *m* 1950, Albert
Victor Baker, and has issue living, Victor George, *b* 1954: *m* 1975, Christine Mary Hollis, — Katherine, *b* 1951. *Residence*
– Inglenook, Winsor Lane, Winsor, Southampton.

Grandchildren of late Cdr Philip Charles Knightly Wolfe Murray (infra):—
Issue of late Lt-Col Robert Alexander Wolfe Murray, DSO, MC, *b* 1889, *d* 1973: *m* 1923, Isobel Mary, who *d*
    1970, da of late Edward Armistead Baxter, of Kincaldum, Forfarshire:—
James Wolfe (House of Daviot, Daviot, Inverness-shire), *b* 1931; *ed* Harrow; Capt (ret) Queen's Own Highlanders; a
Member of Queen's Body Guard for Scotland (Royal Company of Archers): *m* 1st, 1961 (*m diss* 1969), Baroness
Catherina Ingrid Madelaine, da of late Baron Eugene Fredrik Christer Con Stedingk, of Ullaberg, Stjärnhov, Sweden,
2ndly, 1976, Sally Ann, only da of Eric Gordon Bean, of Burnside, Struy, Inverness-shire, and has issue living (by 1st *m*),
Chanette Pauline Catharina, *b* 1964, — Tatjana Thesy Isma, *b* 1965, — (by 2nd *m*), James Wolfe, *b* 1978. ——— Sibil Pau-
line Wolfe, *b* 1924: *m* 1951, Lt-Col Frank Derck Carson, OBE, Queen's Own Highlanders, of 8 Kingsburgh Rd,
Murrayfield, Edinburgh, and has issue living, Philip Derek Murray, *b* 1955: *m* 1993, Alison Marguerite, da of Cdr
Graham Creedy, LVO, RN, and has issue living, Marguerite Anne Murray *b* 1998, — Rachel Isma Ann, *b* 1957: *m* 1st,
1979 (*m diss* 1984), Capt Christopher Glyn-Jones; 2ndly, 1987, Timothy Horrox, and has issue living, (by 1st *m*) Caroline
Mary *b* 1980, Alexandra Pauline *b* 1982, (by 2nd *m*) Charlotte Julia *b* 1988, Olivia Julia *b* 1990, — Iona Fairlie Edith, *b*
1959: *m* 1995, Richard Jones.

Grandchildren of late Cdr Philip Charles Knightly Wolfe Murray, son of James Wolfe Murray (*b* 1814)
    (ante):—
Issue of late Lt-Col David Knightley Wolfe Murray, *b* 1897, *d* 1970: *m* 1920, Ivry Cordelia, who *d* 1984, da of
    Montagu Townsend, of 8 North Pallant, Chichester:—
Christopher Michael Wolfe (Easter Slap, Dirleton, E Lothian), *b* 1929; *ed* Oundle; Capt Gordon Highlanders (ret): *m* 1st,
1955 (*m diss* 1980), Jacqueline, da of Col Sir John Turnbull Usher 4th Bt, OBE; 2ndly, 1980, Alison Isabel Rowe, da of
late James Boyd, TD, DL, of Carradale, Helensburgh, and has issue living, (by 1st *m*) Dorinda Mary MURRAY (Rose
Cottage, Whitsbury, nr Fordingbridge, Hants), *b* 1957; resumed her maiden name: *m* 1984 (*m diss* 1997), Murray Ross
Maclean Hancock, and has issue living, Sam Fergus *b* 1991, Benjamin Rory *b* 1993, — Erica Jacqueline, *b* 1959: *m* 1986,
Malcolm Allen Brinkworth, of The Malt House, Donhead St Mary, Shaftesbury, Dorset, and has issue living, Alexander
Charles *b* 1989, Christopher Rory *b* 1993, Robin David *b* 1995, Faye Tamsin *b* 1988, — Serena Jean, *b* 1964; resumed her
maiden name until remarriage: *m* 1st, 1989, Justin J. B. Varcoe elder son of Beaumont Varcoe, of Nanscawen, Par, Corn-
wall; 2ndly, 1998, Edward C. M. Humphrey, of Ferrar, Aboyne, Aberdeen, elder son of Marcus Humphrey, of Dinnet,
Aberdeenshire. ——— Ivri Patricia, *b* 1922: *m* 1951, Charles Mailert Wormser, of 65 East 96th St, New York 10028, USA,
and has issue living, Andrew Charles, *b* 1953, — Nina Carolyn, *b* 1955.

Grandchildren of late Brig-Gen Arthur Wolfe Murray, CB, son of James Wolfe Murray (*b* 1814)
    (ante):—
Issue of late Lt-Col Malcolm Victor Alexander Wolfe Murray, The Black Watch, *b* 1908, *d* 1985: *m* 1st, 1935,
    Lady Grizel Mary Boyle, who *d* (at sea as result of enemy action) 1942, eldest da of 8th Earl of Glasgow; 2ndly,
    1947, Zofia, who *d* 1968, da of M. Jaxa Chamiec, of Warsaw, Poland:—
(By 1st *m*) James Archibald Wolfe (Chesterhall, Melrose, TD6 9HE), *b* 1936; *ed* Eton, and Worcester Coll, Oxford;
Group Regional Dir S America of United Distillers: *m* 1st, 1963 (*m diss* 1976), Hon Diana Lucy Douglas-Home, da of
Baron Home of the Hirsel, KT, PC (Life Baron) (ext); 2ndly, 1978, Amanda Felicity, elder da of late Anthony Street, and

has issue living, (by 1st *m*) Rory James Wolfe, *b* 1965: *m* 1987, Marion J., da of late Dr Phillip Arthur Zorab, of Golden Hill, Chepstow, and has issue living, Harry *b* 1990, Flora Jessica *b* 1992, — Fiona Grizel Wolfe, *b* 1964: *m* 1991, Andrew M. Shufflebotham, son of David Shufflebotham, of Mijas, Spain, and has issue living, Molly Rita *b* 1994, Rosie Beth *b* 1995, — Clare Elizabeth Wolfe, *b* 1969: *m* 1994, John W. Flett, son of George Flett, of W Norwood, and has issue living, Cameron James *b* 1998, Zoë Elizabeth Alexandra *b* 1995, — (by 2nd *m*) Andrew Alexander Wolfe, *b* 1978. —— Angus Malcolm Wolfe, *b* 1937: *m* 1961, Stephanie Vivian, da of late Maj Hadden Royden Todd, and has issue living, Kim Alexander Wolfe, *b* 1962, — Rupert Hamish Wolfe, *b* 1963, — Gavin Scott Wolfe, *b* 1966, — Magnus Wolfe, *b* 1968. —— (By 2nd *m*) Teresa Mary Wolfe, *b* 1950.

Descendants of late Sir Gideon Murray, 3rd son of late Andrew Murray, uncle of 1st baronet, of who the el son was *cr* Lord Elibank (*see* L Elibank).

Descendants of late William Murray, yst son of late Andrew Murray, uncle of 1st baronet, whose son, late William Murray was created a baronet in 1630 (*see* Murray, Bt, *cr* 1630).

Sir Archibald Murray, 1st baronet, a first cousin of 1st Lord Elibank, was created a baronet with remainder to his heirs male whatsoever.

MURRAY (NS) 1630, of Dunerne, Fifeshire

Sir ROWLAND WILLIAM MURRAY, 15th *Baronet*, *b* 22 Sept 1947; *s* his father, Sir ROWLAND WILLIAM PATRICK MURRAY, 1994, but no name has been entered on the Official Roll of the Baronetage since death of 13th Bt in 1958; *ed* Georgia State Univ; Pres Southern Furniture Galleries; Vice-Pres Ball-Stalker Inc: *m* 1970, Nancy Diane, da of George C. Newberry, of Orlando, Florida, and has issue.

Arms – Not matriculated at Lyon Office.
Residence – 4364 E Brookhaven Drive, Atlanta, Georgia 30319, USA.

SON LIVING

ROWLAND WILLIAM (IV), *b* 31 July 1979.

DAUGHTER LIVING

Ryan McCabe, *b* 1974.

BROTHERS LIVING

Edward George (635 Creekwood Crossing, East Rowswell, Georgia 30076, USA), *b* 1951; marketing and merchandising consultant, D.C. & Co: *m* 1975, Glenda Sharon, da of John Foutes, and has issue living, Michael Betton, *b* 1971. —— Robert Michael (6819 Brewster Court, Columbus, Georgia 31904, USA), *b* 1953; *ed* Young Harris Coll, Georgia, Columbus Coll, Georgia (BS), and Troy State Univ (MBA); Lt-Col US Army: *m* 1981, Vickie, da of Helen Kent, of Augusta, Georgia, and has issue living, Robert Michael, *b* 1985, — Ashley Kathren, *b* 1989. —— Christopher Joseph, *b* 1957: *m* 1984, Kimberly Ann, da of James Johnson, and has issue living, Nicholas Christopher, *b* 1986, — Jessica Kirsten, *b* 1988.

SISTERS LIVING

Helen Brooke, *b* 1945: *m* 1st, 19—, Clinton S. Ferguson; 2ndly, 1980, Capt Ronald Grant Reppert, US Army, and has issue living, (by 1st *m*) Clinton S., *b* 1970, — Julia H., *b* 1971, — (by 2nd *m*) Stephen Harris, *b* 1984. —— Patricia Marie, *b* 1949: *m* 1977, Edward Scoloro, of 3303 Decatur Av, Tampa, Florida, USA, and has issue living, Anthony Edward *b* 1985, — Nina Murray, *b* 1988.

GREAT AUNT LIVING (*Daughter of 12th baronet*)

Laura Magdalen Irving, *b* 1887: *m* 1907, Gerald Alexander Marlowe-King, and has issue living, Alexander William (83 Hillcrest Rd, Mt Vernon, NY 19552, USA), *b* 1910; Assist Treas of Dry Dock Savings Bank, New York: *m* 1935, Helen Laurette McMahon, and has issue living, William Alexander *b* 1937; *ed* Iona Coll, New Rochelle, NY; (BA): *m* 1967, Geraldine Tierney, Junellen Mary, *b* 1940: *m* 1960, Denis Robert Sullivan (and has issue living, Steven Alexander *b* 1961, Dennis Robert *b* 1962, Kevin William *b* 1964), — George Robert (2800, N Holliston, Ataldena, Cal 91001, USA), *b* 1911: *m* 1937, Ruth Sheets, and has issue living, Gerald John *b* 1937: *m* 1967, Roxanne Pettigrew, Georgette Alexandria *b* 1939:

m 1956, Louis Griffiths (and has issue living, Stephen John *b* 1959, John Wayne *b* 1960), — Kenneth Gandy (187 Fern St, Fairfield, Conn, USA), *b* 1912: *m* 1937, Blanche Connelly, and has issue living, Kenneth Gary *b* 1939: *m* 1959, Sherrin O'Toole (and has issue living, Kenneth Michael *b* 1960), John William *b* 1942; *ed* Conn Univ; (BA); late Capt USAF: *m* 1965, Patricia Ann O'Connell (and has issue living, John Patrick *b* 1965, Kenneth Scott *b* 1968), — Donald Murray *b* 1915.

WIDOW LIVING OF THIRTEENTH BARONET

RUBY (*Ruby, Lady Murray*) da of S Hearn, of Helmdon, Northants: *m* 1938, as his second wife, Lieut-Col Sir Edward Robert Murray, 13th Bt, DSO, who *d* 1958.

WIDOW LIVING OF FOURTEENTH BARONET

SARAH JAYNE WIKLE (*Sarah, Lady Murray*), da of Walter W. LaFevre: *m* 1991, as his second wife, Sir Rowland William Patrick Murray, 14th Bt, who *d* 1994. *Residence* – 2820 Peachtree Rd NE, Apt No 1312, Atlanta, Georgia 30305, USA.

COLLATERAL BRANCHES LIVING

Issue of late Robert Lithgow Murray, 3rd son of 12th baronet, *b* 1881, *d* 1942: *m* 1908, Harriet Pope:—
Vernon Robert William (314 S Circle Dr, Boynton Beach, Florida, USA), *b* 1909: *m* 1934, Elizabeth Camberne Kirkwood, and has issue living, Vernon Kirkwood, *b* 1945: *m* 1966, Linda Tischler, and has issue living, Christine Lynn *b* 1966, — Harriet Elizabeth, *b* 1937; *ed* State Univ, New York (MS): *m* 1958, Dale Aldrich Edwards of 2 Plane Tree Lane, Dix Hills, NY, USA, and has issue living, Daniel Vernon *b* 1962, Susan Dale *b* 1959, Carolyn Kirkwood *b* 1968, — Phyllis Vernon, *b* 1939: *m* 1st, 1957 (*m diss* 1978), Adrian Cecil Stanley; 2ndly, 1981, Roy Awbrey, of 704 Abbey Arch, Virginia Beach, Va, USA, and has issue living (by 1st *m*), Kenneth William *b* 1960, Edward Murray *b* 1966, Janet Elizabeth *b* 1958, Alice Camberne Stanley *b* 1970. —— Robert Atholl, *b* 1914: *m* 1935, Mary Ellen Guinan, and has issue living, Robert Atholl, *b* 1937, — James Ivor, *b* 1947, — Diane, *b* 1942.

Grandchildren of late Robert Lithgow Murray (ante):—
Issue of late James Edward Murray, *b* 1911, *d* 1963: *m* 1934, Dorothy Elizabeth Holley (38-38, 217th St, Bayside, NY, USA):—
Donald MacLean, *b* 1945; *ed* Mass Inst of Technology. —— Elizabeth Anne, *b* 1938: *m* 1957, Louis H. Cabrol, of Route de Maraussan, Beziers, Herault, France, and has issue living, Jean Louis, *b* 1964, — Jacques, *b* 1970, — Marie Thérèse, *b* 1958, — Danielle, *b* 1960, — Alice, *b* 1961: *m* 1981, Lotfi Ech-Chaaier, of 24 Boulevard Gambetta, 13150 Tarascon, France, and has issue living, Jérémy *b* 1986, Kévin *b* 1994, — Helene, *b* 1963. —— Susan Eleanora, *b* 1939: *m* 1st, 1958 (*m diss* 1982), James A. Kowalski; 2ndly, 1984, Francis Roland, of 726 Dartmouth Av, Silver Spring, Md, USA, and has issue living, (by 1st *m*) Glenn R, *b* 1960, — Gary W, *b* 1962, — James Edward, *b* 1964, — Melissa Jill, *b* 1969.

Issue of late William Gerard Pulteney Murray, 4th son of 12th baronet, *b* 1891, *d* 1953: *m* 1919, Frances Swarts:—
Allan Gerald, *b* 1928: *m* 19—, Penny Phillips, and has issue living, William *b* 19—, — June Ann, *b* 19—, — Gail, *b* 19—.

The 7th baronet, a distinguished military officer during the first American war, was subsequently Secretary at War. He married in 1794 Right Hon Henrietta (in her own right) Countess of Bath, and assumed the surname of Pulteney but died without issue.

MURRAY (NS) 1673, of Ochtertyre, Perthshire

Sir PATRICK IAN KEITH MURRAY OF OCHTERTYRE, 12th *Baronet*; *b* 22 March 1965; *s* his father, *Sir* WILLIAM PATRICK KEITH, 1977; *ed* Christ Coll, Brecon, and London Academy of Music and Dramatic Art.

Arms – Azure, three mullets argent, in the centre a cross of the second surmounted on a saltire gules both couped, **Crest** – olive-branch proper. *Residence* – 12 Burgos Grove, Greenwich, SE10 8LL.

MOTHER LIVING

Susan Elizabeth, da of Stacey Jones, of Sheephouse, Hay-on-Wye, Powys: *m* 1st, 1963 (*m diss* 1973), as his 1st wife, Sir William Patrick Keith Murray, 11th Bt; 2ndly, 1976, James Carr Hudson, PhD, of Flat 6, 16 Harcourt Terr, SW10, and Old Ffordfawr, Hay-on-Wye, Herefordshire.

WIDOW LIVING OF ELEVENTH BARONET

Deirdra (folk singer, as Dee Dee Woods), da of Norman Wood, of Crail, Fife: *m* 1975, Sir William Patrick Keith Murray of Ochtertyre, 11th Bt, who *d* 1977.

COLLATERAL BRANCHES LIVING

Grandchildren of late Archibald Lamont Keith-Murray, 10th son of 7th baronet:—
Issue of late David KEITH-MURRAY, *b* 1900, *d* 1968: *m* 1932, Nancy May (126 Mount Baker Cres, Salt Spring Island, BC V8K 2J7), da of late Henri Gautschi, of Vancouver, BC:—
PETER (895 Brentwood Heights, Brentwood Bay, BC, Canada V8M 1A8), *b* 12 July 1935; Maj Canadian Forces (ret): *m* 1960, Judith Anne, da of late William Andrew Tinsley, of Sarnia, Ont, and has issue living, (David) Andrew, *b* 7 Dec 1965, — Leslie Anne, *b* 1961: *m* 1989, Paul Joseph Lascelle. —— (David) Mark (525 Baylis Rd, Qualicum Beach, BC V9K 2G2, Canada), *b* 1939: *m* 1960 (*m diss* 1984), Hazel, da of late Amos Pineau, of Prince Edward Is, and has issue living, David Wayne, *b* 1961, — Christopher Mark, *b* 1964. —— Marnie KEITH-MURRAY, *b* 1937; resumed her maiden name 1978: *m* 1958 (*m diss* 1979), Douglas Tufts, of Madoc, Ont, and has issue living, Paul Anthony *b* 1960, — Colin Douglas, *b* 1964, — Andrea Dee, *b* 1959.

Grandchildren of late Henry Dundas Murray, 5th son of 6th baronet:—
Issue of late William Tullibardine Murray, *b* 1863, *d* 1923: *m* 1886, May Elisabeth Margaret, da of late James Bell, MD, of Kaipara, New Zealand:—
Henry Lamont, *b* 1891. —— Yolande, *b* 1887. *Residence* – New Zealand.

Grandson of late George Joseph Murray, grandson of late Alexander Murray, son of Patrick Murray, 2nd son of 2nd baronet:—
Issue of late Capt Alexander Penrose Murray, *b* 1863, *d* 1926: *m* 1st, 1891, Nina, who *d* 1894, da of Col Alexander Solovtsoff; 2ndly, 1895, Ethel Chorley, da of late Maj-Gen Arthur Hill:—
(By 2nd *m*) Charles, *b* 1895. *Residence* –

Granddaughters of late Mackenzie Murray, son of late John Murray, great-grandson of late Mungo Murray, yst son of 1st baronet:—
Issue of late Edward Mackenzie MURRAY-BUCHANAN, *b* 1874, *d* 1956 (having assumed the additional surname of Buchanan on succeeding to the estate of Leny 1919): *m* 1913, Jean Isabella Shaw, who *d* 1952, da of James Carmichael, of Arthurstone, Meigle, Perthshire:—
Euphemia Cecilia, *b* 1915: *m* 1st, 1940, Maj Francis William Clark, of Ulva, who was *ka* 1944; 2ndly, 1956, Lieut-Col John Hay Young, DSO, MC, who *d* 1979, and has issue living (by 1st *m*) Francis Malcolm, *b* 1942: *m* 1971, Georgina Jane, da of late Maj S. J. Swinton Lee, Seaforth Higlanders, and has issue living, John Francis *b* 1971, Michael James *b* 1972, Fiona Janet *b* 1980. *Residence* – West Lodge, 3a Glen Rd, Bridge of Allan, Stirlingshire. —— Phoebe Aeonie, *b* 1922: *m* 1952, John Craufuird Roger Inglis, and has issue living, Richard David (5 Hamilton Rd, North Berwick, E Lothian), *b* 1953: *m* 1980, Pauline Goldie, and has issue living, Crawford *b* 1986, Zoe *b* 1982, Charlotte *b* 1984, — John Edward (25 Halsey St, SW3 2PT), *b* 1961: *m* 1st, 1991 (*m diss* 1993), Marina B., da of Roger Hall Lloyd, of Kensington, W8; 2ndly, 1996, Victoria H. R. Mellstrom, and has issue living (by 2nd *m*), Luella Phoebe Victoria *b* 1998, — Jean Helen, *b* 1955: *m* 1980, Christopher Smith, of 1 Wester Coates Terr, Edinburgh, and has issue living, Jeremy Gordon *b* 1983, Camilla Helen *b* 1985, — Fiona Ann, *b* 1957: *m* 1993, Mark A. Ramsay, and has issue living, James *b* 1996, — Sheena Mary, *b* 1960: *m* 1986, Michael Crerar, of The Courtyard, Kilconquhar, Fife, and has issue living, Gordon *b* 1993, Katherine *b* 1991, — Susan Patricia, *b* 1964. *Residence* – Inglisfield, Gifford, E Lothian.

The 1st baronet, Sir William Murray, a cadet of Tullibardine (*see* D Atholl), was created a baronet with remainder to his heirs male whatsoever. The 6th baronet, *Sir* Patrick Murray, sat as MP for Edinburgh (City) 1806-12, and was afterwards Baron of Court of Exchequer in Scotland. The 7th Baronet, Sir William Murray, on his marriage in 1833, to Helen Margaret Oliphant, only child of Sir Alexander Keith of Dunnottar, Knt Marischal of Scotland, assumed the name of Keith before that of Murray, which name was used by all his descendants, until the succession of the 10th Baronet, who reverted to Murray.

MUSGRAVE (E) 1611, of Hartley Castle, Westmorland

Sir CHRISTOPHER PATRICK CHARLES MUSGRAVE, 15th *Baronet*; *b* 14 April 1949; *s* his father, *Sir* CHARLES, 1970; patron of one living: *m* 1st, 1978 (*m diss* 1992), Megan, da of Walter Inman, of Hull; 2ndly, 1995, Carol, da of Geoffrey Lawson, of Chandlers Ford, Hants, and has issue by 1st *m*.

⟨rms – Azure, six annulets or, three, two, and one. ⟨rest – Two arms embowed in armour proper, the hands grasping an annulet or.
Address – c/o National Westminster Bank, West St, Fareham, Hants.

DAUGHTERS LIVING (*by 1st marriage*)

Helena, *b* 1981. —— Antonia, *b* 1987.

BROTHER LIVING

JULIAN NIGEL CHARDIN, *b* 8 Dec 1951; *ed* S Wymondham Coll, and Queen Mary Coll London (BSc): *m* 1975 (*m diss* 1999), Gulshanbanu Buddrudin, and has issue living, Anar (a da), *b* 1980, — Ruth, *b* 1983.

MOTHER LIVING

Olive Louise Avril, only da of Patrick Cringle, of Holme-on-Sea, Hunstanton: *m* 1st, 1948 (*m diss* 1961), Sir Charles Musgrave, 14th Bt, who *d* 1970; 2ndly, 1961, Peter Charles Nelson, of Tans End, Wells-on-Sea, Norfolk.

Without changing

This family was originally settled at Musgrave in Westmorland. Thomas Musgrave, *temp* Edward III, was summoned by writ and sat as peer of the realm for twenty-three years. Sir Philip, 2nd baronet, a distinguished Royalist, sat as MP for Westmorland 1640-42: after the battle of Worcester, he attended King Charles II of France, in Holland and Scotland, whence he retired to the Isle of Man, which he bravely defended under the Countess of Derby. For his great Services a Warrant creating him Baron Musgrave of Hartley Castle was issued, but he did not take out the patent. The 5th baronet, MP for Carlisle, was Clerk to the Privy Council, and the 6th baronet sat as MP for co Westmorland. Sir Philip, 8th baronet, was MP for Carlisle, and Sir Richard, 11th baronet, sat as MP for E Cumberland and was Lord-Lieut of Westmorland.

MUSGRAVE (I) 1782, of Tourin, Waterford

Sir RICHARD JAMES MUSGRAVE, 7th *Baronet*; *b* 10 Feb 1922; *s* his father, *Sir* CHRISTOPHR NORMAN, OBE, 1956; *ed* Stowe; Capt late Indian Army: *m* 1958, Maria, da of late Col Mario Cambanis, of Athens, Greece, and has issue.

⟨rms – Azure, six annulets, or, three, two, and one. ⟨rest – Two arms in proper, gauntleted and supporting an annulet or.
Residences – Knightsbrook, Trim, co Meath; Komito, Syros, Greece.

SONS LIVING

CHRISTOPHER JOHN SHANE, *b* 23 Oct 1959; *ed* Cheltenham. —— Michael Shane, *b* 1968; *ed* Cheltenham.

DAUGHTERS LIVING

Olivia Mirabel, *b* 1958. —— Anastasia Maria, *b* 1961: *m* 1980, Robert Michael Wilson-Wright (*see* Yate, By, ext), and has issue living, Michael Almroth, *b* 1983, — Sophie Margaret, *b* 1980. —— Charlotte Elizabeth, *b* 1963: *m* 1989, James Hanly, and has issue living, Jack Alexander, *b* 1991. —— Alexandra Victoria, *b* 1965.

SISTER LIVING

Elizabeth Anne, *b* 1931: *m* 1955 (*m diss* 1980), Thomas Aydon Bates, and has issue living, Giles Langley, *b* 1963; *ed* Ampleforth: *m* 1994, Emily Nott, and has issue living, Hester Isabella *b* 1993, Dominica Ruby *b* 1996, — Benedict Loftus, *b* 1964; *ed* Ampleforth: *m* 1993, Alison Kilner, and has issue living, Dominic Michael *b* 1990, William Thomas *b* 1992, Edward James *b* 1994, — Annabelle Carol Elizabeth, *b* 1955: *m* 1980 (*m diss* 1991), Samuel Rodd Morshead, yr son of late Maj Christopher Morshead, of Bellewstown House, co Meath, and has issue living, Charles Christopher Thomas *b* 1981, Samuel Harry *b* 1983, —

Without changing

Belinda Ann, *b* 1957: *m* 1st, 1981, David W. Pulford, yr son of late Rev Walter William Pulford; 2ndly, 1985 (*m diss* 1997), Robin David Erskine, and has issue (by 2nd *m*) (*see* E Mar and Kellie, colls), — Corrinne Lucy, *b* 1958: *m* 1st, 1976 (*m diss* 1982), Athanasios Komninos; 2ndly, 1982, Fawzard Saffari Shooshtari, and has issue living, (by 2nd *m*) Sebastian Thomas Dariush *b* 1985, Felix Ferrydon Benjamin *b* 1995, Francesca Elizabeth *b* 1988, — Teresa Astrid, *b* 1959: *m* 1981, Nicholas C. H. Somerville, only son of late Maj A. J. Somerville, of Bury St Edmunds, Suffolk, and has issue living, Fedora Isabella Charlotte *b* 1989. *Residence* – Pagos 85, Syros, Greece.

COLLATERAL BRANCHES LIVING

Issue of late Maj Francis Edward Musgrave, brother of 6th baronet, *b* 1894, *d* 1975: *m* 1919, Kathleen
Ethel, who *d* 1966, da of late Lt-Col Charles William Grey, Durham LI:—
Patricia Kathleen, *b* 1921: *m* 1946, David Michael Bay, of 11 E Common, Harpenden, Herts and has issue living,
Nicholas Michael (1 New Cottages, Bendish, Hitchin, Herts), *b* 1948: *m* 1st, 1975, Jane Lilly; 2ndly, 1989, Jill Walton, —
Anthony David, *b* 1951: *m* 1998, Amanda Gordard. —— Shelagh Monica, *b* 1927: *m* 1956, Michael R. P. Boyd-Moss, and
has issue living, Robin James, *b* 1959, — Nicola Margaret, *b* 1958.

Issue of late Robert Musgrave, uncle of 6th baronet, *b* 1870, *d* 1940: *m* 1905, Amy Lindsay, who *d* 1939,
da of Brig-Surg F. Lindsay Dickson, of Vancouver, British Columbia:—
Robert John, *b* 1905: *m* 1934, Marjorie Winnifred Chinneck, who *d* 1973, and has issue living, Jean Marjorie Frances, *b*
1935, — Daphne Edith Amy, *b* 1936.

Grandchildren of late Robert Musgrave (ante):—
Issue of late Edward Lindsay Musgrave, *b* 1907, *d* 1985: *m* 1949 Judith Bradfield Stevens:—
Anthony Richard, *b* 1955: *m* 1984, Celia Lydia Mary Lane, and has issue living, Alexander Anthony John, *b* 1991.
—— Robert Lindsay, *b* 1958; has issue living (by Theresa Mary Killoran), Patrick James MUSGRAVE, *b* 1994. —— Susan
Patricia, *b* 1951: *m* 1st, 19—, — Nelson; 2ndly, 1986, Stephen Douglas Reid, of PO Box 2421, Sidney, BC, Canada V8L
3Y3, and has issue living (by 1st *m*), Charlotte Amelia Musgrave, *b* 19—, — (by 2nd *m*) Sophie Alexandra Musgrave, *b*
1989. —— Mary Kathleen, *b* 1961: *m* 1982, William Arthur Broughton, and has issue living, Christopher William, *b* 1984,
— Marcus Edward, *b* 1990, — Jennifer Kathleen, *b* 1987.

This Baronetcy was conferred on Richard Musgrave, MP, el son of Christopher Musgrave, of Tourin, co Waterford,
with special remainder to his yr brothers, under which remainder the 2nd baronet, Sir Christopher, succeeded. The 3rd
baronet sat as MP for co Waterford, and the 4th baronet was Lord-Lieut and Custos Rotulorum of co Waterford.

MUSPRATT (UK) 1922, of Merseyside, City of Liverpool (Extinct 1934)

Sir MAX MUSPRATT, 1st and last *Baronet*.

DAUGHTERS LIVING OF FIRST BARONET

Frances Kate; *b* 1898: *m* 1923, Howard Raymond John Feeney, who *d* 1977, and has issue living, Max Howard, *b* 1928;
ed Stonyhurst, — Patrick Dalrymple, *b* 1931, — June Mary, *b* 1925, — Jasmine Ann, *b* 1936. —— Vanda May, *b* 1901: *m*
1926, George Frederick Killwick, and has issue living, Georgette, *b* 1926. *Residence* – Whispers, 12 Hill Brow, Hove,
Sussex.

MYNORS (UK) 1964, of Treago, co Hereford

Sir RICHARD BASKERVILLE MYNORS, 2nd *Baronet*, *b* 5 May 1947; *s* his
father, *Sir* HUMPHREY CHARLES BASKERVILLE, 1989; *ed* Marlborough,
and Corpus Christi Coll, Camb; musician; Assistant Dir of Music,
King's Sch, Macclesfield 1970-73; Dir of Music, Wolverhampton Gram
Sch 1973-81, Merchant Taylors' Sch 1981-88, Belmont Abbey Sch,
Hereford 1988-89: *m* 1970, Fiona Bridget, da of late Rt Rev George
Edmund Reindorp, DD, sometime Bishop of Salisbury, and has issue.

Arms – Sable, an eagle displayed or, beaked and membered gules, on a chief azure,
bordured argent, a chevron between two crescents in chief and rose in base of the
last.
Residence – Treago, St Weonards, Hereford HR2 8QB.

DAUGHTERS LIVING

Alexandra Fiona, *b* 1975. —— Frances Veronica, *b* 1978. —— Victoria Jane, *b* 1983.

SISTERS LIVING

Elizabeth Baskerville, *b* 1940: *m* 1962, Jeremy Longmore Russell, of Batch Cottage, Almeley, Hereford HR3 6PT, and has issue living, Thomas Lancelot, *b* 1965, — Jennifer Frances, *b* 1969. —— Catherine Baskerville, *b* 1944: *m* 1966, Christopher Mordaunt Richards, 4 St Ronan's Av, Redland, Bristol BS6 6EP, and has issue living, Benedict William Mordaunt, *b* 1972, — Sophia Janet, *b* 1969, — Clare Eleanor, *b* 1974. —— Philippa Baskerville, *b* 1950: *m* 1977, Rev Alan Duce, of 2 Temple Gdns, Lincoln, and has issue living, Patrick Richard, *b* 1984, — Eleanor Rachel, *b* 1979, — Catherine Veronica, *b* 1981. —— Jane Margery Baskerville, *b* 1952: *m* 1974, Nicholas Kersteman King, of 12 Whiteford Rd, Mannamead, Plymouth PL3 5LX, and has issue living, Hugh Samuel, *b* 1982, — Theresa Jane, *b* 1977, — Jennifer Vivien, *b* 1980.

The first baronet, Sir Humphrey Charles Baskerville Mynors, was a Dir of the Bank of England 1949-54, and Dep Gov 1954-64.

NAIRN (UK) 1904, of Rankeilour, Collessie, and Dysart House, Dysart, Fifeshire

Sir MICHAEL NAIRN, 4th *Baronet*; *b* 1 July 1938; *s* his father, *Sir* (MICHAEL) GEORGE, TD, 1984; *ed* Eton, and INSEAD; DL Perth and Kinross 1996: *m* 1st, 1972, Diana Gordon, who *d* 1982, eldest da of F. Leonard Bligh, of Pejar Park, Woodhouselee, NSW, Australia; 2ndly, 1986, Mrs Sally Jane Straker, yr da of Maj William P. S. Hastings, of Brandy Well, Eglingham, Alnwick, Northumberland, and has issue by 1st *m*.

Arms – Per fesse argent and sable, on a chaplet four escallops, all counterchanged. Crest – Three thistles conjoined in stalk entwined with two roses all slipped proper.
Address – PO Box 55, Dundee DD1 9JJ. *Club* – Caledonian.

SONS LIVING (*By 1st marriage*)

MICHAEL ANDREW, *b* 2 Nov 1973. —— Alexander Gordon, *b* 1975.

DAUGHTER LIVING (*By 1st marriage*)

Emma Helen Beatrice, *b* 1980.

BROTHER LIVING

Charles Bruce, *b* 1942; *ed* Eton, and McGill Univ, Montreal (BA): *m* 1973, Carol Ann, da of late Lt-Col Sidney Clive Blaber (*see* Hartwell, Bt, colls), and has issue living, Amy, *b* 1985.

WIDOW LIVING OF THIRD BARONET

HELEN LOUISE (*Helen, Lady Nairn*), yr da of late Maj Ernest James Webster Bruce, MC, RFA, of Melbourne, Australia: *m* 1936, Sir (Michael) George Nairn, 3rd Bt, TD, who *d* 1984.

COLLATERAL BRANCH LIVING

Issue of late Sir Robert SPENCER-NAIRN, Bt, TD (2nd son of 1st baronet), who was *cr* a *Baronet* 1933. *See* Spencer-Nairn, Bt.

The 1st baronet, Sir Michael Barker, was Chairman of Michael Nairn and Co (Limited), linoleum manufacturers, of Kirkcaldy, and of Nairn Linoleum Co, of Kearny, USA.

SPENCER-NAIRN (UK) 1933, of Monimail, co Fife

Sir ROBERT ARNOLD SPENCER-NAIRN, 3rd *Baronet*; *b* 11 Oct 1933; *s* his father, Lt-Col *Sir* DOUGLAS LESLIE SPENCER, TD, 1970; *ed* Eton, and Trin Hall, Camb; late Lt SG; DL Fife 1995, Vice Lord Lieut since 1996: *m* 1963, Joanna Elizabeth, da of late Lt-Cdr George Stevenson Salt, RN (*see* Salt, Bt, *cr* 1899, colls), and has issue.

ᴬrms – Per fesse argent and sable, on a chaplet four escallops, all counter-changed; in the chief point a crescent of the second for difference. Crest – A terrestrial sphere with semi-meridian and stand proper.
Residence – Barham, Cupar, Fife KY15 5RG.

SONS LIVING

JAMES ROBERT, *b* 7 Dec 1966; *ed* Glenalmond, and RAC Cirencester: *m* 1994, Dominique Jane, only da of Michael Williamson, of London, and of Mrs Charles Newman, of Sherborne, and has issue living, Alastair Charles, *b* 10 April 1999. —— Andrew George, *b* 1969.

DAUGHTER LIVING

Katharine Elizabeth, *b* 1964.

BROTHER LIVING

John Chaloner (2046 West 13th Av, Vancouver BC, Canada V6J 2HJ), *b* 1938; *ed* Eton; late 2nd Lt R Dragoons: *m* 1st, 1966 (*m diss* 1970), Barbara Lynn, da of Murray Kamichik, of Montreal, Canada; 2ndly, 1971, Lucie, da of late Pierre Belanger, Canada, and has issue living (by 2nd *m*), John Henderson, *b* 1973, —— Kim Sheilagh, *b* 1975, —— Tara Lucie, *b* 1977.

HALF-BROTHER LIVING

(Christopher) Frank (Culligran, Struy, Beauly, Inverness-shire), *b* 1949; *ed* Eton, and Magdalene Coll, Camb; FCA; MBA Cape Town: *m* 1975, Juliet Constance, da of Oswald Frank Baker Baker of Eskhill, Forfar, Angus (E Perth, colls), and has issue living, Douglas Frederick, *b* 1986, —— Philippa Lucy, *b* 1980, —— Jenny Anne Helen, *b* 1983.

SISTERS LIVING

Mary Elizabeth, *b* 1931: *m* 1953, Maj Andrew Beatty Houstoun, OBE, MC, DL, late R Dragoons, and has issue living, William Robert (Cairnhall, Lintrathen, Kirriemuir, Angus), *b* 1954; *ed* Harrow, and Edinburgh Univ: *m* 1981, Sarah Molly, da of Col Charles Sivewright, CB, MC, DL, of Talland House, South Cerney, Cirencester, Glos, and has issue living, Camilla Mary *b* 1983, Rosemary Sarah *b* 1984, —— David Waldron (Glenkilrie, Blacklunans, Blairgowrie, Perthshire), *b* 1957; *ed* Harrow: *m* 1989, Morag Lynne, da of John Davidson, of Forter, Glenisla, Perthshire, and has issue living, Andrew James *b* 1990, Claire Kathryn *b* 1992, Rachel Elizabeth *b* 1995, —— Alexander Michael (Kerbet House, Kinnettles, by Forfar, Angus DD8 1TQ), *b* 1958; *ed* Harrow: *m* 1988, Margaret Susan, da of Duncan Kerr, of Kingennie, Angus, and has issue living, Michael Paterson *b* 1990, Robert Duncan *b* 1992, —— Andrew Neil (Little Fithie, Farnell, Brechin, Angus DD9 6UF), *b* 1961; *ed* Harrow, and RAC Cirencester: *m* 1995, Victoria Margaret, da of David Laird, of West Memus, Forfar, Angus. *Residence* – Kirkhill, Lintrathen, Kirriemuir, Angus DD8 5JH.

HALF-SISTER LIVING

Teresa Leslie, *b* 1952: *m* 1975, John Mungo Ingleby, of Malling Farm, Port of Menteith, Stirling, and has issue living, Mungo Henry *b* 1981, —— (John) Frederick, *b* 1988, —— Kim Louise, *b* 1978, —— Rosie, *b* 1990.

UNCLES LIVING AND DECEASED (*Sons of 1st baronet*)

Michael Alastair Spencer, TD, *b* 1909; *ed* Trin Hall, Camb (MA); JP; formerly Major Fife and Forfar Yeo (TA): *m* 1935, Ursula Helen, da of late Howson Foulger Devitt (*see* Devitt, Bt, *cr* 1916, colls), and has issue living, Angus (La Fontaine, Rue du Pont, St John, Jersey), *b* 1947: *m* 1968, Christina Janet, da of late Col Hugh Gillies, and has issue living, Michael Angus *b* 1975, Fiona Louise *b* 1974, —— Sarah Ursula, *b* 1937: *m* 1967, John Scoular, of Tonderghie, Whithorn, Wigtownshire, and has issue living, Alastair John Greenshields *b* 1972, Anys Helen *b* 1978, —— Catriona Jane, *b* 1945: *m* 1st, 1969 (*m diss* 1980), Paul Hosegood Kirton, elder son of late Robert James Kirton, CBE; 2ndly, 1986, George Edward Derrington Tremlett, of River House, The Green, Elstead, Godalming, Surrey GU8 6DA, son of late Laurence Edward Paul Tremlett, and has issue living (by 1st *m*), Ian Nigel *b* 1970: *m* 1999, Tara Louise Owen, da of Robert Glen, of Forest Hill House, Forest Hill, Oxford, Clare Helen *b* 1972, Lena Harriett *b* 1974, Mary Rose *b* (twin) 1974. *Residence* – Baltilly House, Ceres, Fife KY15 5QG. —— †Robert Frank, *b* 1912; *ed* Trin Hall, Camb (BA 1932, MA 1936); sometime Capt The Black Watch (TA): *m* 1st, 1936 (*m diss* 1949), Caroline Isabel, da of H. A. Chadwick, of Calgary, Canada; 2ndly, 1954, Mary Anna, da of Walter E. Hettman, of San Francisco, California, and *d* 1995, leaving issue, (by 1st *m*) Isabel Susan *b* 1937: *m* 1966, Brig Nicholas John Ridley, OBE, Queen's Own Highlanders (Christison, Bt), and has had issue, Nicholas Charles Philip Christison *b* 1973, Alexia Kathleen *b* 1967, *d* 1992, Susanna Mary *b* 1969, —— (by 2nd *m*) Martha Ann (13 Redcliffe Place, SW10), *b* 1955: *m* 1984 (*m diss* 19—), Seth M. Milliken II, and has issue living, Eliza Clark *b* 1987, —— Charlotte Emily, *b* 1957: *m* 1989, Duncan MacGuigan, of 5 East 75th St, New York, NY 10021, —— Elspeth Margaret NAIRN (5320 Brookview Av, Edina, Mass 55424, USA), *b* 1958; has resumed her maiden name: *m* 1981 (*m diss* 1988), Edgar W. Swift, and has issue living, Clinton Spencer *b* 19—, —— Margaret Cynthia, *b* 1965. *Residence* – Castle Carey, St Peter Port, Guernsey.

AUNTS LIVING (*Daughters of 1st baronet*)

Kathleen Matilda, MBE, *b* 1913: *m* 1st, 1938 (*m diss* 1948), Maj Ronald Richards, TA; 2ndly, 1948, William Webb, who *d* 1991, and has issue living, (by 2nd *m*) William Spencer, *b* 1948, — Alan Gordon, *b* 1951, — Michael Charles, *b* 1952. *Residence* – Mendlesham Manor, Stowmarket, Suffolk. ——Helen Clare, *b* 1917: *m* 1st, 1939, Maj John Henry Courthope Powell, Fife and Forfar Yeo (TA), who was *ka* 1944; 2ndly, 1945, John William Gardner Hume, who *d* 1976, and has issue living, (by 1st *m*) Elizabeth Clare, *b* 1942: *m* 1965, Rev Canon Colin T. Scott Dempster, of Old Faskally House, Killiecrankie, Pitlochry, Perthshire, and has issue living, Robert Andrew (6 Dean Terrace, Edinburgh) *b* 1967; late Capt The Black Watch (Royal Highland Regt): *m* 1995, Camilla Helen, elder da of P. M. Lockhart Smith, of Manor House Farm, W Drayton, Notts (and has issue living, Lorne Robert *b* 1998), Harry Colin *b* 1985, Clare Ann *b* 1969, — Margaret Ann, *b* 1944: *m* 1966, Lt-Col Stephen James Lindsay, and has issue (*see* E Crawford, colls), — (by 2nd *m*) Mary *b* 1947: *m* 1972, John FitzGerald, of The Old Rectory, Rodmarton, Cirencester, Glos, and has issue living, John William Broun *b* 1973, Edward James Broun *b* 1975, Katherine Mary *b* 1979, Louisa Clare *b* 1984. *Residence* – Damside, Auchterarder, Perthshire. ——Adela Margaret (*Baroness Colnbrook*), *b* 1924: *m* 1944, Baron Colnbrook, KCMG, PC (Life Baron), who *d* 1996.

The 1st baronet, Maj Sir Robert Spencer-Nairn, TD (2nd son of Sir Michael Barker Nairn 1st Bt, of Rankeilour, Springfield, Fife), by Emily Frances, da of Alfred Rimington Spencer, was Major Fife and Forfar Yeo. In 1928 he adopted the surname of Spencer-Nairn.

NALL (UK) 1954, of Hoveringham, co Nottingham

Sir MICHAEL JOSEPH NALL, 2nd *Baronet*; *b* 6 Oct 1921; *s* his father *Col* Sir JOSEPH, DSO, TD, 1958; *ed* Wellington Coll; Lt-Cdr RN (ret); DL Notts 1970, High Sheriff 1971-72, and Vice Lord-Lieut 1989-91; Pres of Nottingham Chamber of Commerce and Industry 1972-74; 1939-45 War: *m* 1951, Angela Loveday Hanbury, da of Air Ch Marshal Sir (William) Alec Coryton, KCB, KBE, MVO, DFC, and has issue.

𝔄rms – Per chevron barry of six gules and or and of the first, in chief two stag's heads caboshed proper and in base a lion rampant guardant of the second. ℭrest – Within a leathern garter buckled gules, a bee or.
Residence – Hoveringham Hall, Nottingham, NG14 7JR.

SONS LIVING

EDWARD WILLIAM JOSEPH, *b* 24 Oct 1952; *ed* Eton; late Maj 13th/18th Royal Hussars (QMO) Light Dragoons. ——Alexander Michael (Lodgefield Farm, Hoveringham, Notts NG14 7JQ), *b* 1956; *ed* Eton; late Capt 2nd RGJ; High Sheriff Notts 1999; Man Dir Louis Latour Ltd since 1992: *m* 1982, Caroline Jane (JP Notts 1996), yr da of Anthony L. à'C. Robinson (*see* B Heytesbury, 1990 Edn), and has issue living, William Alexander Coryton, *b* 1985, Katharine Caroline, *b* 1986.

BROTHER LIVING

William George Joseph, *b* 1926; *ed* Wellington Coll; European War 1944-45 as Lieut 13th/18th Royal Hussars (QMO): *m* 1961, Jennifer Jane, el da of L. Aylwin Richardson, FRCS, of Minstead, Hants, and has issue living, Charles William Joseph, *b* 1965; *ed* Rugby; BA, ACA, MBA, — Richard George Aylwin, *b* 1966; *ed* Rugby; BA, DipM: *m* 1993, Sarah Helen, el da of B. J. Wood, of Ablington, Glos, and has issue living, Edward James Richard *b* 1996, Sophia Rosemary Eleanor *b* 1999, — Olivia Jane Caroline, *b* 1970: *m* 1997, Neil Milburn Reynolds, of Farm House, Wellow, Newark-on-Trent, Notts NG22 0EA, yr son of Ian W. Reynolds, OBE, TD, of Corwen, N Wales. *Residence* – Farm House, Wellow, Newark-on-Trent, Notts NG22 0EA.

SISTERS LIVING

Elizabeth Josephine, TD, *b* 1920; a JP of Notts (Supplementary List); 1939-45 War with ATS. *Residence* – Hall Close, Hoveringham, Notts NG14 7JR. ——Rosemary Alice Anne, *b* 1923; 1939-45 War, Army Remount Depot, Melton Mowbray 1939-41, Admiralty Ops Sigs 1942-45: *m* 1947, Peter Bingham Inchbald, Capt RA (*see* Bingham, Bt, ext, 1985 Edn), and has issue living, Peter Joseph Nicholas, *b* 1951, — Guy William Benjamin, *b* 1952: *m* 1981, Hazel Brenda, yst da of E. Trant, of Esk Bank, Dalkeith, Midlothian, and has issue living, Robin Peter Guy *b* 1991, Joanne Elizabeth *b* 1982, Jenny Anne *b* 1984. *Residence* – Holdfast Manor, Upton-on-Severn, Worcs. ——Diana Christian Isabella, *b* 1924; 1939-45 War with Mobile Red Cross attached RN: *m* 1950, Col Sidney John Watson, MBE, late RE (B Dulverton), of Ballingarrane, Clonmel, co Tipperary, and has issue living, John Wilfred, *b* 1952; *ed* Eton and RAC Cirencester; ARICS; 1978 World three-day-event Championship (Silver Medal): *m* 1977, Julia Morrish, and has issue living, Samuel James *b* 1985, Suzannah Irene *b* 1980, Rosalind Sara *b* 1982, — Elizabeth Sandra, *b* 1953; SRN: *m* 1975, Richard Vincent Craik-White, and has issue living, James Richard *b* 1977, Henry William *b* 1979.

The 1st baronet, Col Sir Joseph Nall, DSO, TD (el son of Joseph Nall, of Hoveringham and Broom Cottage, High Legh, Cheshire) was a Director of several Transport and Industrial undertakings; ktd 1924, a DL for Lancashire and Notts

(High Sheriff 1952-3), Pres of Institute of Transport 1925-26, and MP for Hulme Div of Manchester (*U*) 1918-29, and 1931-45. He served in European War 1914-18 (wounded, despatches, DSO).

NAPIER (NS) 1627, of Merchistoun

Faith preserved renders prosperous;
Look well; Without stain

Sir JOHN ARCHIBALD LENNOX NAPIER OF MERCHISTOUN, 14th *Baronet*; *b* 6 Dec 1946; *s* his father, Sir WILLIAM ARCHIBALD, 1990; *ed* St Stithians, and Witwatersrand Univ, Johannesburg; MSc (Eng), PhD: *m* 1969, Erica, da of late Kurt Kingsfield, of Johannesburg, and has issue.

𝕬rms – Quarterly, 1st and 4th argent, on a saltire engrailed between four roses gules, the roses barbed vert, five mullets of the field, *Napier of Merchistoun*; 2nd, azure, a lion rampant argent, crowned or, *MacDowall of Garthland*; 3rd argent, a fess azure voided of the field, between three demi-lions crowned gules, *Milliken of that Ilk.* 𝕮rests – *Dexter*, on a chapeau gules furred ermine, *for the feudal Barony of Merchistoun*; an arm grasping an eagle's leg proper, talons expanded gules, *Napier of Merchistoun; Sinister*, A demi-lion rampant gules, holding in his dexter forepaw a dagger or, *Milliken of Culcreuch.* 𝕾upporters – Two eagles with their wings closed proper.
Residence – Merchiston Croft, PO Box 65177, Benmore, 2010, S Africa.

SON LIVING

HUGH ROBERT LENNOX, *b* 1 Aug 1977.

DAUGHTER LIVING

Natalie Ann, *b* 1973.

WIDOW LIVING OF THIRTEENTH BARONET

KATHLEEN MABEL (*Dowager Lady Napier of Merchistoun*), da of late Reginald Greaves, of Tafelberg, Cape Province: *m* 1942, Sir William Archibald Napier of Merchistoun, 13th Bt, who *d* 1990. *Residence* – Merchistoun Croft, P.O. Box 65177, Benmore 2010, S Africa.

COLLATERAL BRANCHES LIVING

Grandchildren of late William Edward Stirling Napier (*b* 1858), 3rd son of 9th baronet:—
Issue of late Lt-Col William Edward Stirling Napier, MC, TD, *b* 1893, *d* 1983: *m* 1919, Audrey, who *d* 1986, da of late William Houlding, of Liverpool, and Arcachon, France:—
Elizabeth June Houlding (Culcreuch Cottage, 6 Milton St, Bowral, NSW 2576, Australia), *b* 1920: *m* 1947, Lt-Col Gerald Patrick Gardner-Brown, RA (ret), who *d* 1994, and has had issue, Elspeth Susan, *b* 1948, — Vivien Patricia, *b* 1951, *d* 1987: *m* 1974, John Grant Pagan, only son of late Brig Sir John Ernest Pagan, CMG, MBE, TD, FRGS, and has issue living, Jonathan Edward *b* 1981, Peter Napier *b* 1983. —— Lavinia NAPIER (30 Beatrice Terrace, Ascot, Queensland 4007, Australia), *b* 1924; has resumed her maiden name: *m* 1947, Capt C. Czarkowski-Golijeivski, 14th Polish Lancers. —— Elspeth Mary, *b* 1933: *m* 1957, Denbigh Hamilton-Harding, of 7 Lodersfield, Lechlade, Glos GL7 3DJ and has issue living, Caroline, *b* 1958, — Fiona, *b* 1960, — Unity, *b* 1962.

Issue of late Aleck Douglas Napier, *b* 1894, *d* 1965: *m* 1927, Dorris Mary Clara, da of late Victor Hide Hill:—
Alexander Colin, *b* 1930. —— John Stirling, *b* 1935.

This family is a branch of the Earls of Levenax or Lennox (title extinct), and is said to have taken its name from a saying by Alexander III (of Scotland), after battle, that Lennox had *na peer* (no equal). Sir William, the 8th baronet, was served heir male general to Archibald, 3rd Baron Napier, 1817, and afterwards assumed the baronetcy—one of the oldest in Scotland—which had remained dormant for 134 years. Sir Alexander Lennox Milliken Napier, 11th Bt, Capt Grenadier Guards, was ADC to Gov-Gen and Com-in-Ch of Australia (Earl of Dudley) 1910-12; he served in S Africa 1902, and in European War 1914-17 (twice wounded).

NAPIER (UK) 1867, of Merrion Square, Dublin

Sir CHARLES JOSEPH NAPIER, 6th *Baronet; b* 15 April 1973; *s* his father, *Sir* ROBERT (ROBIN) SURTEES, 1994; *ed* Eton, and Edinburgh Univ.

Arms – Argent, on a saltire engrailed between four roses gules, five escallops or. **Crest** – A dexter cubit arm erect proper, charged with a rose gules, the hand grasping a crescent argent.
Residence – Woodlands, Martyr Worthy, Winchester, Hants SO21 1AT.

UNCLE LIVING (*son of 4th baronet*)

JOHN LENNOX (86 Ennerdale Rd, Kew, Richmond, Surrey; MCC), *b* 25 Jan 1934; *ed* Eton: *m* 1967, Cecily, da of late Arthur Mortimer, of Malta, and has issue living, James Alexander, *b* 1969; *ed* Oundle, — Jessica, *b* 1971.

WIDOW LIVING OF FOURTH BARONET

ISABEL MURIEL (*Isabel, Lady Napier*), 2nd da of late Maj Henry Siward Balliol Surtees, JP, DL, of Redworth Hall, co Durham: *m* 1931, Sir Joseph William Lennox Napier, 4th Bt, OBE, who *d* 1986. *Residence* – 17 Cheyne Gdns, SW3 5QT

WIDOW LIVING OF FIFTH BARONET

JENNIFER BERYL (*Lady Napier*), da of late Herbert Warwick Daw, of Flint Walls, Henley-on-Thames, and formerly wife of Mark R. Palmer, of Houston, Texas: *m* 1971, Sir Robert (Robin) Surtees Napier, 5th Bt, who *d* 1994. *Residence* – Woodlands, Martyr Worthy, Winchester, Hants SO21 1AT.

Without blemish

COLLATERAL BRANCH LIVING

Issue of late Maj Charles MacNaughten Napier, 2nd son of 3rd baronet, *b* 1896, *d* 1967: *m* 1923 (*m diss* 1939), Dorothy Constance, who *d* 1960, da of late Col Reginald Hawkins Hall Dempster, DSO, of Dunnichen and Auchterforfar:—
Lennox Alexander Hawkins, CB, OBE, MC (Osbaston Farm, Monmouth, Mon), *b* 1928; Maj-Gen late RRW (ret); DL Gwent 1984, High Sheriff 1988, Vice Lord Lieut 1995; formerly Chm Central Transport Consultative Cttee, and Inspector Public Inquiries, and Memb British Transport Police Cttee; OStJ; MBE (Mil) 1965, OBE (Mil) 1970, CB (Mil) 1983: *m* 1959, Jennifer Dawn, da of B Wilson, and has issue living, Philip Martin Lennox, *b* 1964; Maj RRW: *m* 1990, Philippa N., elder da of James Rawson, of Shire Lane House, Hurst Green, Lancs, and has issue living, Harry James Lennox *b* 1996, Phoebe Henrietta *b* 1992, Isabel Louisa Rodier *b* 1994, — Joanna Dawn, *b* 1962: *m* 1987, Col Robert Hanbury Tenison Aitken, Royal Regt of Wales, ot Wallnut Tree Farm, Croesyceiliog, Mon, only son of Capt Harry Kerr Aitken, MC, Argyll and Sutherland Highrs, and has issue living, Robert Frederick *b* 1994, James Lennox Oliver *b* 1996, — Sally Vanessa, *b* 1967. —— Audrey Lennox, *b* 1926: *m* 1958, Lt Col Henry Christian Ewart Harding, MC, of Furzey Lodge, Beaulieu, Hants, and has issue living, William George Charles, *b* 1964, — Sarah Constance Hope, *b* 1961: *m* 1992, Oliver Dacres Wise, el son of R. Derek Wise, of Barcombe, Sussex, and has issue living, Henry Gerard Dacres *b* 1993, Eleanor Lucy Constance *b* 1995, — Susan Jane Napier, *b* 1966.

This family claim descent from a branch of the family of Sir Robert Napier, Bt, of Luton Hoo (*cr* 1611) which established itself in Ireland about 1700 and from which the 1st baronet, Sir Joseph Napier, of Merrion Square, descended.

The 1st baronet, Sir Joseph, PC, DCL, LLD, sat as MP for Dublin University (*C*) 1848-57 and was Lord Chancellor of Ireland 1858-9, a member of the Judicial Committee of the Privy Council 1868-81, First Lord Commissioner for Custody of Great Seal in Ireland 1874, and Vice-Chancellor of Dublin University 1867-80. The 3rd baronet, Lieut-Col Sir William Lennox, was *ka* in the Dardanelles 1915, when serving as Major with 4th Batn S Wales Borderers. The 5th baronet, Sir Robert (Robin) Surtees, assumed the forename of Surtees in lieu of those of Aubone Siward.

Naylor-Leyland, see Leyland.

NEAVE (GB) 1795, of Dagnam Park, Essex

Sir PAUL ARUNDELL NEAVE, 7th *Baronet*; *b* 13 Dec 1948; *s* his father, *Sir* ARUNDELL THOMAS CLIFTON, 1992; *ed* Eton; stockbroker: *m* 1976, Coralie Jane Louise, eld da of Sir Robert George Caldwell Kinahan, ERD, of Castle Upton, Templepatrick, co Antrim, and has issue.

Arms – Argent, on a cross sable five fleurs-de-lis or. Crest – Out of a ducal coronet gold a lily, stalked and leaved vert, flowered and seeded or.
Residence – Queen's House, Monk Sherborne, Hants RG26 5HH. *Club* – Boodle's.

SONS LIVING

FREDERICK PAUL KINAHAN, *b* 25 Jan 1981. —— Julian Robin Kinahan, *b* 1983.

BROTHER LIVING

Robert Joshua (Greatham Moor, Liss, Hants), *b* 1951; *ed* Eton.

SISTERS LIVING

Dilys Richenda, *b* 1947: *m* 1968, Timothy Hayward Hobson, of Harvard Farm, Halstock, Yeovil, Som BA22 9SZ, and has issue living, Jake Timothy, *b* 1971, — Barnaby John, *b* 1974, — Samuel Jeffrey, *b* 1979, — Richenda Eveline, *b* 1969. —— Serena Mary, *b* 1955.

Those things only are becoming which are honourable

UNCLE LIVING (*son of 5th baronet*)

Kenelm Digby (Saunders Farm, Camden Hill, Sissinghurst, Kent TN17 2AR), *b* 1921; *ed* Harrow; Capt (ret) Welsh Gds; N-W Europe 1944-45 (wounded): *m* 1st, 1949, Venetia, only child of late Harold Digby Neave (gt-grandson of William Augustus Neave, 4th son of 2nd Bt), and late Mrs Johnson; 2ndly, 1970, Marian Rosamond, da of late Gerald Hartley Lees, and has issue living (by 1st *m*), Nicola Venetia, *b* 1956: *m* 1976, Robert Reagan, of 19 Ullswater Rd, Hatherley, Cheltenham, Glos, and has issue living, Paul *b* 1979, Jonathan *b* 1984, Louise *b* 1982, — Dorinda Mary, *b* 1958: *m* 1985, Barry Shell, of 4692 Quebec St, Vancouver, BC, Canada, and has issue living, Samuel *b* 1987, Davina *b* 1991.

COLLATERAL BRANCHES LIVING

Grandchildren of late Sheffield Airey Neave, CMG, OBE (infra):—
Issue of late Lt-Col Airey Middleton Sheffield Neave, DSO, OBE, MC, TD, MP, *b* 1916, assassinated 1979: *m* 1942, Diana Josceline Barbara (*cr Baroness Airey of Abingdon*, 1979), who *d* 1992, da of Thomas Arthur Walter Giffard, MBE, of Chillington Hall, Wolverhampton (Trollope Bt):—
Hon (Richard) Patrick Sheffield (16 Maze Rd, Kew, Richmond, Surrey), *b* 1947; *ed* Eton, and City of London Poly: *m* 1980, Elizabeth Mary Catherine, yr da of late Cuthbert Edward Alphonso Riddell, of Hermeston Hall, Worksop, Notts, and has issue living, James Riddell Airey, *b* 1983, — Thomas Edward Riddell Airey, *b* 1985, — Matthew Robert Riddell Airey, *b* 1993. —— *Hon* William Robert Sheffield (20 Kirkstall Rd, SW2), *b* 1953; *ed* Eton: *m* 1986, Joanna Mary Stuart, 2nd da of James Stuart Paton, of The Old Vicarage, Gt Hockham, Norfolk, and has issue living, Richard Digby Stuart, *b* 1987, — Sebastian Airey Stuart, *b* 1989. —— *Hon* Marigold Elizabeth Cassandra, *b* 1944: *m* 1968, William Richard Broughton Webb, DL, of Barbers, Martley, Worcs, and has issue living, Edward Alexander Broughton, *b* 1974, — Katherine Angela Mary, *b* 1970: *m* 1995, Christian R. Holland, son of Rodney Holland, of Holland Park W11, and has issue living, a son *b* 1997.

Grandchildren of late Sheffield Henry Morier Neave, el son of Sheffield Neave, 3rd son of 2nd baronet:—
Issue of late Sheffield Airey Neave, CMG, OBE, *b* 1879, *d* 1961: *m* 1st, 1915, Dorothy, who *d* 1943, da of late Lt-Col Arthur Thomson Middleton, JP, 13th Hussars, of Ayshe Court, Horsham, Sussex; 2ndly, 1946, Mary Irene, who *d* 1993, da of Henry Hodges, of Broadway Hall, Churchstoke, Montgomery:—
(By 1st *m*) Digby John Sheffield (1 Rue Champflour, 78160 Marly-le-Roi, France), *b* 1928; *ed* Eton, and at Merton Coll, Oxford: *m* 1st, 1958, Ulla, who *d* 1963, da of A. B. Schmidt, of Gilleleje, Denmark; 2ndly, 1966, Christiane, da of E. J. Corty, of L'Etang-la-Ville, France, and has issue living, (by 1st *m*) Victoria Janet (*Hon Mrs Hugh N. T. Fairfax*), *b* 1959: *m* 1984, Hon Hugh Nigel Thomas Fairfax, 2nd son of 13th Lord Fairfax of Cameron, — Philippa *b* 1960, — (by 2nd *m*), Lionel Digby Sheffield (10 Bolingbroke Grove, SW11 6ER), *b* 1966: *m* 1992, Hon Victoria Alice, 2nd da of Baron McAlpine of West Green (Life Baron), and has issue living, Digby Julius Sheffield *b* 1996, Alice Artemis *b* 1994. —— Rosamund Malua, *b* 1921: *m* 1939, Capt Edward Noble Sheppard, Essex Yeo.

Issue of late Lt-Col Richard Neave, *b* 1881, *d* 1962: *m* 1912, Helen Elizabeth Mary, who *d* 1976, da of late Robert Miller:—
†Robert Morier Sheffield, MC, MRCVS, *b* 1917, *ed* London Univ; Major 13th/18th Hussars (Supplementary Reserve); European War 1939-44 (wounded, MC): *m* 1952, Philippa Elizabeth (Mallards, Bear St, Nayland, Suffolk CO6 4HY), only da of late Lt-Col (Vincent) Basil Ramsden, DSO, MC (*see* V St Davids, colls, 1977 Edn), and *d* 1995, leaving issue, Julia Helen, *b* 1953: *m* 1976, Jonathan Bennett Walker, of 12 Japonica Drive, Lititz, Pennsylvania 17543, USA, and has issue living, Bennett Neave *b* 1984, Megan Philippa *b* 1980, Lydia Joy *b* 1982, — Lucinda (Lucy) Philippa, *b* 1954: *m* 1983, Michael Philip Muller, of Tithe Farmhouse, Hitcham Lane, Burnham, Bucks SL1 7DP, elder son of Dr Walter Muller, of Cheltenham, and has issue living, Thomas Robert *b* 1992, Katharine Elise *b* 1985, Jessica Philippa *b* 1986, Rebecca Madeleine *b* 1989, — Harriet Elise Bunty, *b* 1957: *m* 1998, Michael Charles Justin Ellis, of The Paddocks, Tidney, Haselbury Bryan, Sturminster Newton, Dorset DT10 2EB, 2nd son of Lt-Col John Ellis, of Fifehead St Quintin, Sturminster Newton, Dorset. —— Julius Arthur Sheffield, CBE (Mill Green Park, Ingatestone, Essex), *b* 1919; *ed* Sherborne; Maj (ret), 13th/18th Hussars (Reserve); JP and DL for Essex; OStJ 1988; 1939-45 War (despatches, MBE); MBE (Mil) 1945,

CBE (Civil) 1978: *m* 1951, Helen Margery, da of late Lt-Col Percy Morland Acton-Adams, DSO, of Clarence Reserve, Kaikoura, NZ, and has issue living, (Helen) Penelope, *b* 1952: *m* 1981, Michael Wilson, and has issue living, Esme Beatrice *b* 1983, Julia Rose *b* 1985, — (Joan) Miranda Mary, *b* 1954: *m* 1979, (George) Anthony John Bowles, of Holmhead, Corsock, Castle Douglas, Kirkcudbrightshire DG7 3DT, and has issue (*see* Barwick, Bt, colls), — Venetia Beatrice, *b* 1958: *m* 1982, William Lebus, yr son of Oliver Lebus, of 25 Victoria Rd, W8, and has issue living, Frederick Oliver *b* 1985, Henry William *b* 1991, Tomasina Olivia *b* 1987. —— Beatrice Honoria Sheffield, *b* 1916: *m* 1952, Eustace Blewitt Robinson, who *d* 1992, and has had issue, Eleanor Mary, *b* 1953: *m* 1977, Julian Richard Edwards, and *d* 1992, leaving issue, Alexander Julian *b* 1981, James Blewitt *b* 1984.

Grandchildren of late Edward Strangways Neave, 2nd son of late Sheffield Neave, 3rd son of 2nd baronet (ante):—
Issue of late Edward Arthur Neave, *b* 1883, *d* 1960: *m* 1916, Evelyn Margaret, who *d* 1966, da of George Augustus Lamb (British Guiana Police), of Rye, Sussex:—
Digby Seymour, *b* 1921; is a FRICS; Senior Partner Messrs Neave, Tinworth and Nuan, Chartered Quantity Surveyors; 1939-45 War as Lieut RA in N-W Europe: *m* 1948, Chrystel, authoress, only da of Prof Poul P. Outzen-Boisen, Knt of Dannebrog, OBE, of Rungsted Kyst, Denmark.

Issue of late Guy Morier Neave, *b* 1886, *d* 1950: *m* 1925, Dorothy, who *d* 1961, da of late J. E. Ponsonby-Steel:—
June Violet, *b* 1928: *m* 1956 Bryan Francis Blake, of 115 Meadvale Rd, Ealing, W5, and has issue living, Stephen Guy, *b* 1958, — Judith Clare, *b* 1960: *m* 1987, Bernard Carl Greatbatch, of Holly House, Tower Rd, St Helier, Jersey, CI, and has issue living, Toby William *b* 1990, Robin Stephen *b* 1991, Chloë Ruth *b* 1988. —— Rose Ann, *b* 1930: *m* 1955, Robert Arthur Jackman, of 6 Overwood Drive, King's Park, Glasgow, S4, and has issue living, Scott Robert, *b* 1963: *m* 1991, Eileen Jane, da of Robert Trail, of Paisley, Renfrewshire, — Lindsey Ann *b* 1961: *m* 1984, Stuart Allan Horton, Fl Sgt RAF, and has issue living, Sarah Ann *b* 1985, Michelle Ashley *b* 1989, Philippa Abigail *b* 1990.

Grandchildren of late Rev William Alexander Neave, el son of late William Augustus Neave, 4th son of 2nd baronet:—
Issue of late Lionel Digby Neave, MRCS, LRCP, *b* 1873, *d* 1951: *m* 1909, Winifred, who *d* 1956, da of Michael Burke:—
Nelson Digby (Kiah, 1300 Glenhuntly Rd, Carnegie, Victoria 3163, Australia), *b* 1914; 1939-45 War as F/Lt RAFVR: *m* 1936, Betty Ross, who *d* 1998, of Liverpool, and has issue living, Marilyn Kathryn (Unit 2, 59 Foam St, Elwood, Vic 3184, Australia), *b* 1938: *m* 1st, 1958 (*m diss* 1974), Samuel Shub, MRACP, of Victoria, Australia; 2ndly, 1983, Dr Anthony Challinor, BSc, PhD (Camb), FGS, who *d* 1996, and has issue living (by 1st *m*), Martin David Neave (29 Lancelot St, Five Dock, Sydney, NSW 2046, Australia) *b* 1959: *m* 1991, Helen Bongiorno (and has issue living, Joshua Lorenzo *b* 1994, Nicholas Digby *b* 1996), Caroline Leanne (13 Mountain St, S Melbourne, Vic 3205, Australia) *b* 1960: *m* 1987 (*m diss* 19—), James Ford (and has issue living, Charles James *b* 1988, Oliver *b* 1990), Melissa Louise *b* 1965: *m* 1996, Grant Rutherford, of 1/12 Wimbledon Av, Elwood, Vic 3184, Australia (and has issue living, Lily Annabel *b* 1997). —— John Alexander (17 Netheredge Drive, Knaresborough, N Yorks, HG5 9DA), *b* 1919: *m* 1946, Jacqueline, only child of F. Ranger, of Holyhead, Anglesey, and has issue living, David John *b* 1954: *m* 1976, Jacqueline Irene, da of Peter Flack, of Haughley, Suffolk, and has issue living, Danielle 1980, Kimberley 1982, — Judith Marlon, *b* 1948: *m* 1969, James Brame, of Highwood, Topcliffe, N Yorks, and has issue living, James Kenneth *b* 1969, — Margaret Alison, *b* 1950: *m* 1st, 1969, (*m diss* 1981), Jean-Claude Estripeau; 2ndly, 1983, Alan Parnham, and has issue living by 1st *m*, Natalie Isabelle *b* 1970, Tamsin Jane *b* 1976, — Catherine Mary, *b* 1951: *m* 1971, Hartwig Waldemar Nicolaus, and has issue living, Heidi Marie *b* 1971. —— Geoffrey Lionel (Flat 1, 1 Marmara Dr, Elsternwick, Vic 3185, Australia), *b* 1920; *ed* Ascham Coll, and County High Sch, Clacton-on-Sea; 1939-45 War with Roy Hampshire Regt in Italy and Greece: *m* 1964, Freda Mary Walmsley, da of late G. H. Hobson, of Lincoln. —— Mary Winifred, *b* 1913: *m* 1933, Rev Dennis Victor Wright, AKC, who *d* 1982, and has issue living, Stephen John Neave, *b* 1934; *ed* Brentwood Sch, and at Co High Sch, Buckhurst Hill, Essex: *m* 1960, Jennifer Anne, SRN, da of Arthur John Carter, of Chingford, Essex, and has issue living, Christopher Jonathan Neave *b* 1961, Nigel Robin Neave *b* 1962, Samantha Jane *b* 1966, — Rev Martin Neave, *b* 1937; *ed* King's Coll, London (AKC); Bishop of Coventry's Officer for Social Responsibility, — Ruth Mary, *b* 1943; SRN. *Residence* – 6 Willoughby Rd, Banbury, Oxon.

Grandchildren of late Francis Digby Spencer Neave, 2nd son of late William Augustus Neave (ante):—
Issue of late Francis Digby Neave, *b* 1874, *d* 1943: *m* 1910, Ethelberta, who *d* 1970, da of late Edward Washbourn, of St Albans, Christchurch, New Zealand:—
†John Digby, *b* 1916; formerly Ch Instructor at Canterbury Aero Club: *m* 1939, Martha Dorothy, who *d* 1985, da of late R. F. Francis, of St Albans, Christchurch, NZ, and *d* 1994, leaving issue, Richard Francis, *b* 1941: *m* 1962, Patricia Lorraine McGuire, and has issue living, Roger John Francis *b* 1962, Deborah Michelle *b* 1965, Amanda Gaye *b* 1969, — Barbara Alice, *b* 1940: *m* 1962, Ramon Juan Saunders, of 54 Holland Av, Hillcrest, Auckland 10, NZ, and has issue living, David John *b* 1968, James Richard Neave *b* 1972, Rachael Louise *b* 1974, — Eleanor Elizabeth, *b* 1943: *m* 1964, Bruce Peter Anderson, and has issue living, Thomas Digby *b* 1970, Philip Richard *b* 1972. —— Henry Washbourn, *b* 1918: *m* 1st, 1945 (*m diss* 1949), Doreen Melba, da of late J. W. Wright Spreydon; 2ndly, 1953, Sheila Duncan, da of R. H. Bennetts, of Christchurch, NZ, and has issue living, (by 2nd *m*) Alistair Dudley Digby (1351, Whangaparaoa Rd, Hibiscus Coast, NZ), *b* 1956: *m* 1978, Lorraine Mary, da of J. Irvine, of Auckland, NZ, and has issue living, Hamish Irvine Digby *b* 1990, Michelle Mary Ellen *b* 1993, — Richard Henry Digby (4 Denley Gdns, Avonhead, Christchurch 5, NZ), *b* 1960, — Diana Sheila, *b* 1954: *m* 1979, Brett Michael Russell, of Christchurch, NZ. *Residence* - 8 Moor Park Place, Ilam, Christchurch, NZ. —— Arthur Kenelm, *b* 1924: *m* 1st, 1951, Elizabeth Marie (DOYLE), who *d* 1983, da of late George Brady; 2ndly, 1984 (*m diss* 1993), Winifred Emma Bates, da of Roy Stiggants. *Residence* - Ceduna, S Aust. —— Elizabeth Marjorie, *b* 1911: *m* 1941, Grgo Franicevic, who *d* 1981, of 5 Tui St, Fendalton, Christchurch, NZ, and has had issue, Vincent Peter Ivan, *b* 1942: *m* 1st, 1963 (*m diss* 1972), Maritza Ann Frances Glucina; 2ndly, 1979, Maria Bartolovic, and *d* 1994, leaving issue (by 2nd *m*), Dean Peter *b* 1980, — Edward John Grgo, *b* 1946: *m* 1967 (*m diss* 1986), Margaret Anne Blay, and has issue living, Lisa Marie *b* 1967, Anita Margaret *b* 1969: *m* 19—, Alan Bigwood (and has issue living, Kelsi *b* 1996), Terry *b* 1974: *m* 1999, Karin Tonkin, Paul Francis Anton, *b* 1949: *m* 1983, Shona Lorna Mitchell, and has issue living, Scott Anton *b* 1989, Kim Marie *b* 1991, — Lois Ethel Yurka (74 Point Rd, Monaco, Nelson), *b* 1944: *m* 1st, 1966 (*m diss* 1988), Geoffrey Herbert Heath; 2ndly, 1990, Robert Basil Thombs Colley, and has issue living (by 1st *m*), Michael Geoffrey *b* 1969: *m* 1995, Sarah Melina Jolliffe, Thomas James *b* 1970: *m* 1999, Samantha Julie Cummings, Katrina Louise *b* 1973, — Mara Elizabeth, *b* 1948: *m* 1978, Peter Charles Abrams, and has issue living, Anna Mara *b* 1979, Sarah Katherine Louise, *b* 1981.

Granddaughters of late Lt-Col Everard Strangways Neave, 3rd son of late William Augustus Neave (ante):—

Issue of late Everard Reginald Neave, *b* 1877, *d* 1951 (having assumed in 1910 the additional surname of Hay before his patronymic): *m* 1910, Amy Charlotte Paterson Balfour Hay of Leys and Randerston, who *d* 1971, da of late Peter Hay-Paterson:—
Beatrice Rosemary, *b* 1911; is a SRN: *m* 1939, Capt Colin Napier Christie, Black Watch, and has issue living, Mary Helen, *b* 1941: *m* 1970, James Beaton Marshall, of Ormlie, Bankend Rd, Bridge of Weir, Renfrewshire, — Anna Margaret, *b* 1943: *m* 1970, Derek O'Shea, of 49 Woodfield Cres, Ealing, W5, and has issue living, Catherine Janet *b* 1972, Linda Margaret *b* 1975. —— Diana Hope, *b* 1918 late WRNS: *m* 1st, 1940, David James Reoch Ritchie, P/O RAFVR, who was *ka* 1943; 2ndly, 1950, Ryszard Habdank-Kolaczkowski, late Lt RA and Polish AF, of 280 Easy St, 515 Mountain View, Cal 94043, USA, and has issue living, (by 2nd *m*) Anita Marya Star *b* 1951: *m* 1976, Piotr Daniel Moncarz, of 3255, Emerson St, Palo Alto, Cal 94306, USA and has issue living, Sylvana Marya, *b* 1981. —— Griselda Nancy, *b* 1920; formerly Subaltern ATS: *m* 1943, Henry Feliks Jascoll (formerly Jaszczolt), late Polish Army, of 28 Ravensbourne Gdns, Ealing, W13, and has issue living, Dominic Peter HAY OF LEYS (21 Warrenside Close, Blackburn, Lancs, BB1 9PE), *b* 1945; recognised in the surname of Hay of Leys by decree of Lord Lyon 1986, — John Henry David (2633 Hazelwood Rd, Lancaster, PA 17601, USA), *b* 1949; *ed* London Sch of Econs, London Univ (MScEcon): *m* 1974, Dorothy (Dorie) Ann, da of Homer K. Luttringer, and has issue living, Jennifer Elizabeth *b* 1983.

Grandchildren of late Arundell Francis Robert Irvine Neave (infra):—
Issue of late Lt-Cdr Arundell Richard Yorke Irvine Neave, DSC, RN, *b* 1915, *d* 1977: *m* 1941, Barbara Marie, only da of late Frederick Charles Evelyn Liardet, of Beech Park, Newton Abbot:—
Guy Richard Irvine, *b* (Dec) 1941; *ed* King's Sch, Worcester, and Queen Mary's Coll, London (PhD); research member of Inst D'Education, Fondation Européenne de la Culture, Université Dauphine, Paris. —— Penelope Gay, *b* 1945: *m* 1966 (*m diss* 1977), Duncan Edward McBarnet, and has issue living, Justin Guy, *b* 1970, — Alasdair Mathew, *b* 1972.

Granddaughter of late Richard Irvine Neave, el son of late George Peters Neave, son of late Richard Neave, 3rd son of 1st baronet:—
Issue of late Arundell Francis Robert Irvine Neave, *b* 1874, *d* 1918: *m* 1902, Mona Lewis, who *d* 1958:—
Muriel Catherine, *b* 1907: *m* 1928, Graham Thorpe, of Westfield, Calpe Av, Lyndhurst, Hants.

Granddaughter of late Cecil Howard Neave; elder son of George Howard Neave, yr son of George Peters Neave (ante):—
Issue of late Geoffrey Howard Neave, *b* 1917, *d* 1983: *m* 1946, (Mary) Therese Jeanette (21 Cornell Av, Rumford, Rhode Is, USA), da of late Joseph Adelard Voyer:—
Bernadette Blanche Dolores, *b* 1947: *m* 1968, Arvid Charles Nelson, late US Marines, and has issue living, Michael Shawn, *b* 1969, — Robert David, *b* 1973.

The Neave family lived at Tivetshall, Norfolk, temp Henry IV. Sir William Le Neve, Clarenceux King of Arms 1660, belonged to a younger branch. Sir Richard Neave, of Dagnam Park, Essex, 1st Bt, was Governor of the Bank of England 1780.

NELSON (UK) 1912, of Acton Park, Acton, of Denbigh

Sir JAMIE CHARLES VERNON HOPE NELSON, 4th *Baronet*; *b* 23 Oct 1949; *s* his father, *Sir* WILLIAM VERNON HOPE, OBE, 1991; *ed* Redrice: *m* 1983, Maralynn Pyatt, da of late Albert Pyatt Hedge, of Audenshaw, Lincs, and has issue.

𝕬rms – Quarterly, 1st and 4th gules, on a fesse between three daggers points downwards or, two sinister hands couped of the field; 2nd and 3rd argent, a pile engrailed ermines between two lions' heads erased in base gules, langued azure, a chief vair all within a bordure vert. 𝕮rests – 1st, in front of a sun rising or, a sinister arm embowed in armour proper, the hand grasping a dagger point downwards as in the arms; 2nd, issuant from clouds proper charged with three mullets azure, a globe fracted at the top under a rainbow with clouds at each end proper.
Residence – 39 Montacute Rd, Tintinhull, Yeovil, Somerset BA22 8QD.

SON LIVING

Liam Chester, *b* 1982.

BROTHERS LIVING

Per se confidens
Confident in oneself

DOMINIC WILLIAM MICHAEL (Barratts Mill, Corton Denham, Sherborne, Dorset), *b* 13 March 1957; *ed* St Edward's, Malta: *m* 1981, Sarah, el da of late John Neil Hylton Jolliffe (*see* B Hylton, colls), and has issue living, Barnaby John, *b* 1982, — Thomas Dudley, *b* 1984, — George Marcus, *b* 1987, — Henrietta Penelope, *b* 1994. —— Declan Hugh Plantagenet, *b* 1968.

SISTERS LIVING

Deirdre Elizabeth Ann (Bently Cottage, Cuckfield, Sussex), *b* 1947: *m* 1st, 1980 (*m* annulled 1985), Martin Thomas; 2ndly, Dr John Dillow Macguire, of Bently Cottage, 12 The Highlands, Cuckfield, W Sussex RH17 5HL, and has issue living (by 1st *m*), Peter, *b* 1981. —— Cary Georgina (2 Court Barton, Crewkerne, Somerset), *b* 1952. —— Sophie Lucia, *b* 1971.

WIDOW LIVING OF THIRD BARONET

Hon ELIZABETH ANN BEVIL CARY (*Hon Lady Nelson*), da of 14th Viscount Falkland: *m* 1945, Sir William Vernon Hope Nelson, 3rd Bt, OBE, who *d* 1991. *Residence* – The Old Post House, Chiselborough, Somerset.

Sir William, 1st Bt (son of James Nelson, of Cooldrinagh, Ireland), was Chm of the Nelson Line (Liverpool) (Limited), and of the Nelson Steam Navigation Co.

NEPEAN (UK) 1802, of Bothenhampton, Dorsetshire
(Name pronounced "Nepeen")

Sir EVAN YORKE NEPEAN, 6th *Baronet*; *b* 23 Nov 1909; *s* his father, *Major Sir* CHARLES EVAN MOLYNEUX YORKE, 1953; *ed* Winchester, and Downing Coll Cambridge (BA 1931, MA 1947); Lt-Col (ret) R Corps of Signals; Mohmand Operations 1936 (medal with clasp); 1939-45 War in Middle East and Western Desert (Africa Star with clasp): *m* 1940, (Georgiana) Cicely, da of late Maj N. E. G. Willoughby, Middlesex Regt, and has issue.

Arms – Gules, a fesse wavy erminois between three mullets argent. **Crest** – On a mount vert a goat passant sable, charged on the side with two ermine spots in fesse or, collared and horned gold.
Residence – Elm View, 31 High St, W Lavington, Devizes, Wilts SN10 4HQ.

DAUGHTERS LIVING

Respice
Look back

Susan Cicely, *b* 1941: *m* 1961, James Martin Norman Aylmer Hall, of 1 Partridge Down, Olivers Battery, Winchester, and has issue living, Richard John Nepean Aylmer, *b* 1964: *m* 1988, Tracy-Jane Boal, — Patrick Robert Aylmer, *b* 1966: *m* 1995, Elizabeth Wood, and has issue living, Kieran James *b* 1998, — Katherine Mary Aylmer, *b* 1963: *m* 1986, Russell Wheeldon, and has issue living, Christopher Andrew *b* 1989, Helen Rebecca *b* 1995, — Carole Margaret Aylmer, *b* 1967: *m* 1997, Robert Robotham. —— Judith Sarah, *b* 1946: *m* 1993, Edgar Noel Goldthorp, of Black Sheep House, Healey, nr Masham, Ripon, N Yorks HG4 4LH. —— Gillian Helen, *b* 1950: *m* 1982, Paul Stevens, and has issue living, David Yorke, *b* 1986, — Jonathan Edward, *b* 1988.

COLLATERAL BRANCH LIVING

Granddaughter of late Cdr St Vincent Nepean, MVO, RN, 4th son of Col Herbert Augustus Tierney Nepean, 3rd son of late Rev Evan Nepean, 4th son of 1st baronet:—
Issue of late Leonard Percyval St Vincent Nepean, *b* 1879, *d* 1932: *m* 1909, Ellen Mary, who *d* 1957, da of late Matthew Edwards, of St Petersburg:—
Anne Camilla Catharine, *b* 1910: *m* 1st, 1932 (*m diss* 1947), Alfred Lingley Bennett; 2ndly, 1948, John Herbert McQuade, who *d* 1980, and has issue living, (by 1st *m*) Gordon Lingley Nepean (Portree, 109 Guildford Rd, Bagshot, Surrey), *b* 1936: *m* 1st, 1958 (*m diss* 1972), Faith Merritt, who *d* 1988; 2ndly, 1979, Christine Stephanie Barbara Maria Whipps, and has issue living, (by 1st *m*) Lingley Graham Nepean *b* 1959: *m* 1989, Fiona, da of — Eccleston (and has issue living, Harry Lingley Nepean *h* 1992), Robert *b* 1966: *m* 1993, Valerie Anderson (and has issue living, Ashleigh *b* 1995, Melissa *b* 1998), Sally Jacqueline *b* 1957: *m* 1980 (*m diss* 1991), Duncan Edward Sibbald (and has issue living, Kieran *b* 1982, Kimberley *b* 1981), Angela *b* 1961: *m* 1984, Ian Bowerman (and has issue living, Andrew *b* 1991, Amy Samantha *b* 1989, Faith *b* 1994), (by 2nd *m*) Christian *b* 1980, — Roger Lingley Nepean, *b* 1937: *m* 1966, Diana Jacqueline Westcob, and has issue living, Nicola *b* 1967: *m* 1991, Simon Bush (and has issue living, Ryan Michael *b* 1994), Tamsin *b* 1970, Justine *b* 1978: *m* 1994, Richard Letcher (and has issue living, Nicholas *b* 1999). *Residence* – Moorlands Nursing Home, Macdonald Rd, Lightwater, Surrey.

This family came from St Just, Cornwall. Right Hon Sir Evan Nepean, 1st Bt, was MP for Queensborough and Bridport, Sec of the Admiralty, Chief Sec for Ireland, and Gov of Bombay.

NEVILLE (UK) 1927, of Sloley, co Norfolk (Extinct 1994)

Capt Sir RICHARD LIONEL JOHN BAINES NEVILLE, 3rd and last *Baronet*; *d* 1994.

DAUGHTERS LIVING OF SECOND BARONET

Rosalind Angela Mary, *b* 1933: *m* 1954, Philip Murray Gorton, of The Emplins, Gamlingay, Sandy, Beds, yr son of late Rev John Percival Page Gorton, and has issue living, Simon Neville (The Hall, Sloley, Norwich), *b* 1957: *m* 1985, Ann, da of Peter Donald Hull and has issue living, Peter Neville *b* 1986, Emma Jane *b* 1987, — Mark Philip (The House, Brooms Green, Dymock, Glos), *b* 1960: *m* 1st, 1982 (*m diss* 1990), Elizabeth Jane, da of Brian David Carter; 2ndly, 1990, Deborah, da of Harry Cook, and has issue living (by 2nd *m*), Alice Muriel *b* 1990, — David Colin (C Cortes Catalones, Bayo 2A, 08140 Caldes de Montbui, Barcelona, Spain), *b* 1962: *m* 1998, Mercédes, da of Emilio Bonilla, — Elizabeth Clare, *b* 1958: *m* 1983, Quenton Hayton Hill, of Golder Cottage, Sloley, Norwich, and has issue living, James David *b* 1988, Hannah Christine *b* 1986. —— Jane Shirley (Cubitt Cottage, Sloley, Norfolk), *b* 1934: *m* 1st, 1963 (*m diss* 1977), Vivian Vincent Esch, yr son of late Vincent Jerome Esch, CVO, FRIBA; 2ndly, 1977 (*m diss* 1985), Patrick Thomas Foulkes, and has issue living (by 1st *m*), Nicholas Charles (7a Bassein Park Rd, W12 9RN), *b* 1966; *ed* Eton, — Rupert Vivian Neville (Lot 450, Simes Rd, Grady's Creek, via Kyogle, NSW 2474, Australia), *b* 1967; *ed* Stowe.

WIDOW LIVING OF SECOND BARONET

BETTY (*Lady Neville*) (61 Yarmouth Rd, N Walsham, Norfolk), da of George Legerton Cowell, and formerly wife of Peter Thornton Cowell: *m* 1981, as his 2nd wife, Lt-Col Sir James Edmund Henderson Neville, 2nd Bt, who *d* 1982.

NEWMAN (UK) 1836, of Mamhead, Devonshire

Sir GEOFFREY ROBERT NEWMAN, 6th *Baronet*; *b* 2 June 1947; *s* his father, *Sir* RALPH ALURED, 1968; *ed* Kelly Coll; late Lieut Gren Gds: *m* 1980, Mary Elizabeth, yr da of late Col Sir Martin St John Valentine Gibbs, KCVO, CB, DSO, TD (*see* Fowler, Bt ext, 1966 Edn), and has issue.

𝕬rms – Azure, three demi-lions rampant argent, semée of cross-crosslets, langued gules. 𝕮rest – A lion rampant per chevron azure gutté-de-l'eau and argent gutté-de-sang.
Residence – Blackpool House, Dartmouth, S Devon TQ6 0RG.

SON LIVING

ROBERT MELVIL, *b* 4 Oct 1985.

DAUGHTERS LIVING

Frances Joyce, *b* 1983. —— Elsie Laura, *b* 1987. —— Louisa Bridget, *b* 1990.

BROTHER LIVING

Richard Claude, *b* 1951: *m* 1992, Louise Dorothy Catherine, only child of late Gordon Alexander Egerton Ruck (*see* B Braybrooke), and has issue living, Henry Ralph Gordon, *b* 1997, — Georgina Dorothy Catherine, *b* 1995.

SISTERS LIVING

Zabian Carlotta Annette Alfreda, *b* 1948. —— Louisa Ann (Melverley, Ravensbourne Lane, Stoke Fleming, Dartmouth, S Devon TQ6 0QZ), *b* 1955: *m* 1st, 1977 (*m diss* 1992), Andrew William Kingsley Thomas; 2ndly, 1997, Michael Clive Bowker Smith, yr son of John Smith, of Dartmouth, Devon, and has issue living (by 1st *m*), William Lydston, *b* 1983, — Rachael Elizabeth Ann, *b* 1987.

WIDOW LIVING OF FIFTH BARONET

Hon ANN ROSEMARY HOPE (*Hon Lady Newman*), (Blackpool House, Dartmouth, S Devon), da of late Capt the Hon Claude Hope-Morley (*see* B Hollenden, colls): *m* 1946, Sir Ralph Alured Newman, 5th Bt, who *d* 1968.

COLLATERAL BRANCHES LIVING

Grandchildren of late Robert Lydston Newman, el son of Thomas Holdsworth Newman, 3rd son of 1st baronet:—
Issue of late Capt Thomas Newman, *b* 1906, *d* 1980: *m* 1938, Helen, who *d* 1972, da of Sir (Charles) Alban Young, KCMG, MVO, 9th Bt (*cr* 1769):—
Peter Thomas Lydston (The Manor House, Coryton, Okehampton, Devon), *b* 1944; *ed* Eton, and Ch Ch, Oxford (MA); FCA: *m* 1981, Catherine Jane, da of Alistair James Lilburn, of Coull, Aboyne, Aberdeenshire (*see* Reid, Bt, *cr* 1922, 1980 Edn), and has issue living, Rupert Thomas Lydston, *b* 1984, — William Alistair, *b* 1988, — Harriet Joan, *b* 1986. —— Priscilla Helen, *b* 1939: *m* 1963, Charles Granville Stuart-Menteth, of Woodchester House, Woodchester, Glos, and has issue (*see* Stuart-Menteth, Bt). —— Elizabeth Clare, *b* 1941: *m* 1964, (Robert Myles) Randal MacDonnell, of 17 Malbrook Rd, SW15, and has issue living, Julian Sorley Randal, *b* 1967: *m* 1992, Sophia Helen, da of David Reed, of Bath, and has issue living, Amity Catherine *b* 1993, — Natasha Clare, *b* 1965, — Louisa Helen, *b* 1971.

Grandchildren of late Alured Newman, 4th son of 1st baronet:—
Issue of late Maj Edward Devon Newman, *b* 1885, *d* 1977: *m* 1st, 1909 (*m diss* 1926), Violet Ethel, da of late Rev Morgan Kirby; 2ndly, 1926, Hilda, who *d* 1970, da of Leonard Norman Barrow, JP, of Normanton Hall, Southwell, Notts:—
(By 1st *m*) Edward John Alured (PO Box 1216, Pinetown, Natal 3600, S Africa), *b* 1915; *ed* Radley: *m* 1st, 1947 (*m diss* 1958), Katherine Dolores, formerly wife of Stephen Townsend, and da of Frank Bazette, of Newbury, Berks; 2ndly, 1964, Winifred Betty, formerly wife of Eric Paull, and da of Charles Rowe, of Wellington, NZ, and has issue living, (by 1st *m*) Priscilla Elizabeth (Bori 1 Fontesta 39, 1A, 08021 Barcelona, Spain), *b* 1949: *m* 1969 (*m diss* 1989), Eugene de Pau, and has issue living, Gregory, *b* 1972: *m* 1999, Monica Soler Vidal, of Matadepera, Spain. —— Myra Beatrice, *b* 1914: *m* 1946, Lt-Col William Bagnall, OBE, who *d* 1984, of Upper Brook House, Marchington, Uttoxeter, Staffs, and has issue living, William Edward Hampshire (2 Brook House, New Pond Rd, Compton, nr Guildford, Surrey), *b* 1947: *m* 1969, Bridget, da of Kenneth Charles Pearce, and has issue living, William Richard *b* 1978, Jessica Jane *b* 1976, — Felicity Jane, *b* 1951: *m* 1977, Nicholas John Sutton Mills, of Bank House Farm, Hyde Lea, Stafford.

The 1st baronet, Sir Robert William Newman (son of Thomas Newman, of Dartmouth) sat as MP for Exeter, and was High Sheriff of Devon 1827. The 2nd baronet, Capt Sir Robert Lydston, Grenadier Guards, was *ka* 1854. The 3rd baronet, Sir Lydston, was High Sheriff of Devon, 1871. The 4th baronet, Sir Robert Hunt Stapylton Dudley Lydston, sat as MP for Exeter (*U* latterly *Ind*) 1918-31 and was *cr Baron Mamhead*, of Exeter, co Devon 1931.

NEWMAN (UK) 1912, of Cecil Lodge, Newmarket, co Cambridge

By hard work and with honour

Sir FRANCIS HUGH CECIL NEWMAN, 4th *Baronet*; *b* 12 June 1963; *s* his father, Sir GERARD ROBERT HENRY SIGISMUND, 1987; *ed* Eton, and Univ of Pennsylvania, USA: *m* 1990, Katharine M., yr da of late (Cecil Ralph) Timothy Edwards, of Grendon Court, Upton Bishop, Herefords, and has issue.

Arms – Argent, an ostrich proper, on a chief azure, a lozenge of the field between two bezants. Crest – Out of an antique coronet or, a springbok's head proper.
Residence – Burloes Hall, Royston, Herts SG8 9NE.

SONS LIVING

THOMAS RALPH GERARD, *b* 7 Jan 1993. —— Arthur Guy Hugh, *b* 1996.

DAUGHTER LIVING

Lily May Violet, *b* 1994.

BROTHERS LIVING

Geoffrey John, *b* 1966; *ed* Eton, and Bristol Univ. —— Christopher George *b* 1969; *ed* Eton, and Napier Univ, Edinburgh.

SISTER LIVING

Susanna Philippa Helen, *b* 1962: *m* 1985, Julian Eldon Gorst, eldest son of Sir John Michael Gorst, and has issue living, Henry Eldon Geoffrey, *b* 1991, — Edward John, *b* 1997, — Rose Philippa Tatiana, *b* 1990, — Alice Caroline Natasha, *b* 1999. *Residence* – Oxcombe Manor, Horncastle, Lincs.

UNCLE LIVING (*son of 2nd baronet*)

John Francis (Compton Park, Compton Chamberlayne, Salisbury, Wilts SP3 5DE), *b* 1930; *ed* Eton; late Lt Roy Horse Gds; Dir Blick plc, Avocet Mining plc, and other Cos: *m* 1963, Caroline Henrietta, yr da of Lt-Col Angus John Campbell Rose, of Dunira Garden House, Comrie, Perthshire, and has issue living, Anthony John Cecil, *b* 1966; *ed* Harrow, and RAC Cirencester, — Henrietta Mary Alison (*Countess of Caledon*), *b* 1964: *m* 1989, as his 2nd wife, 7th Earl of Caledon, — Sarahjane Caroline, *b* 1968; *ed* Bristol Univ.

AUNTS LIVING (daughters of 2nd baronet)

Annabel Cecilia Mary, *b* 1922: *m* 1947, Maj Peter Merton Beckwith-Smith, who *d* 1984, and has issue living, James Merton, *b* 1948; *ed* Tabley House, Knutsford, — Anne Honor Mary, LVO, *b* 1951; appointed Lady in Waiting to HRH The Princess of Wales 1981; LVO 1990. *Residence* – Bishopstone House, Salisbury, Wilts SP5 4AS. —— Lynette Johanna Violet (1 Sloane Court East, SW3), *b* (twin) 1927. —— Rosalind Cynthia (Chestnut Brow, Church Rd, Bramshott, Liphook, Hants), *b* 1936: *m* 1969, Francis Albert John Watson, who *d* 1973, and has issue living, Jeremy John Albert, *b* 1970, — Joanna Clare Elizabeth, *b* 1972.

WIDOW LIVING OF THIRD BARONET

CAROLINE PHILIPPA, da of late Brig Alfred Geoffrey Neville, CBE, MC (*see* B Braybrooke, colls): *m* 1st, 1960, Sir Gerard Robert Henry Sigismund Newman, 3rd Bt, who *d* 1987; 2ndly, 1996, Andrew F. B. Crawshaw. *Residence* – The Manor House, Fowlmere, Royston, Herts SG8 7SJ.

COLLATERAL BRANCH LIVING

        Issue of late Guy Arthur Newman, son of 1st baronet, *b* 1904, *d* 1982: *m* 1930, Hon Jean Sybil Loch,
        who *d* 1994, da of 2nd Baron Loch:—
Mary Ella, *b* 1931: *m* 1954, Lt Col William Richard Edgedale, The Life Guards, who *d* 1996, of 34 Edna St, SW11, and has issue living, James William, *b* 1963: *m* 1993, Sarah Louise Jenkinson, and has issue living, Rupert Guy *b* 1997, Alice Lucy *b* 1995, — Mirabel Jean Elaine, *b* 1955, — Emma Margaret, *b* 1956: *m* 1983, Orlando dos Santos, of 55 Rowena Crescent, SW11, and has issue living, Frederick Andrew William *b* 1986, Ella Clementine *b* 1989, Charlotte Maria Elizabeth *b* 1993, — Sarah Jane, *b* 1965: *m* 1996, Robert P. P. Donlan, and has issue living, Imogen Emily Zöe *b* 1998. —— Diana Margaret Anna (23 Glebe Place, SW3), *b* 1934. —— Ann Elizabeth, *b* 1937: *m* 1965, Richard James Randal MacDonnell, of Ivy Lodge, Churchill, N Som, and has issue living, Simon Guy Randal, *b* 1968: *m* 1996, Sara Catrin Evans, — Crispin Paul Geoffrey Randal, *b* 1974, — Tania Alice, *b* 1966.

  Sir Sigmund NEUMANN, 1st Bt (son of Gustav Neumann, of Fuerth, Bavaria), was partner in the firms of S Neumann and Co, merchants, of Salisbury House, EC, and Neumann, Luebeck and Co, bankers. Sir Cecil Gustavus Jacques Newman, 2nd Bt, who was High Sheriff of Herts 1939, and Pres of National Asso Fishery Board 1946-51, assumed by Roy licence 1936 the surname of Newman in lieu of Neumann. Sir Gerard Robert Henry Sigismund Newman, 3rd Bt, was High Sheriff Herts 1981, Chm Galloway Group Ltd 1974-87, and Chm Rom River Co 1954-69.

NEWSON (UK) 1921, of Framlingham, co Suffolk (Extinct 1950)

Sir PERCY WILSON NEWSON, 1st and last *Baronet*.

DAUGHTER LIVING OF FIRST BARONET

Audrey Joan (*Audrey, Lady Twisleton-Wykeham-Fiennes*), *b* 1912: *m* 1931, Lieut-Col Sir Ranulph Twisleton-Wykeham-Fiennes, 2nd Bt, DSO, R Scots Greys, who *d* of wounds received in action 1943. *Residence* – Robins, Church Lane, Lodsworth, Petworth, Sussex.

Newson-Smith, see Smith.

NEWTON (UK) 1900, of The Wood, Sydenham Hill, Lewisham, Kent, and Kottingham House, Burton-on-Trent, co Stafford

Sir (HARRY) MICHAEL REX NEWTON, 3rd *Baronet; b* 7 Feb 1923; *s* his father, *Sir* HARRY KOTTINGHAM, OBE, 1951; *ed* Eastbourne Coll; late Lieut King's Roy Rifle Corps; Past Master The Girdlers' Co; 1939-45 War in N Africa and Middle East (wounded): *m* 1958, Pauline Jane, only da of Richard John Frederick Howgill, CBE, of Branscombe, Sullington Warren, Storrington, Sussex and has issue.

Arms – Azure, two bones in saltire between as many roses argent, on a chief or, a lotus flower slipped proper. Crest – Out of the battlements of a tower an arm erect, the hand grasping a sword in bend sinister proper suspended therefrom a flag argent charged with a sword erect between two branches of oak proper.
Residence – Cliff House, Old Lyme Rd, Charmouth, Dorset DT6 6BW. *Club* – R Ocean Racing.

Faveat fortuna
May fortune favour

SON LIVING

Rev GEORGE PETER HOWGILL, *b* 26 March 1962; *ed* Sherborne, and Pembroke Coll, Camb (MA); Priest-in-charge Holy Trinity, Aldershot, since 1999: *m* 1988, Jane L., twin da of John Rymer, and has issue living, Sarah Rebecca, *b* 1991, — Kate Evangeline, *b* 1992. *Residence* – 2 Cranmore Lane, Aldershot, Hants GU11 3AS.

ADOPTED DAUGHTERS LIVING

Lucinda Jane, *b* 1964. —— Julia Kate, *b* 1967: *m* 1994 (*m diss* 19—), Daryn K. Hufton-Rees, only son of Kenneth Rees, of Manchester. —— Jennifer Anne, *b* (twin) 1967.

BROTHER LIVING

Rev Canon Christopher Wynne, *b* 1925; *ed* Eastbourne Coll, and Trin Hall, Camb (MA); formerly Urban Dean of Milton Keynes: *m* 1950, Margaret, da of John Ormerod, of Accrington, and has issue living, Jeremy John, *b* 1952, — Peter Michael, *b* 1953. *Residence* – 24 Slade Court, Watling St, Radlett, Herts.

The 1st baronet, Sir Alfred James Newton, Chm of Harrods (Limited), was Lord Mayor of London 1899-1900, when he founded City of London Imperial Vol during S African War (Baronetcy conferred); also an Hon Freeman of Scarborough and Londonderry, and sixteen years Gov of the Hon the Irish So. The 2nd baronet, Sir Harry Kottingham Newton, OBE, was Vice-Chm of Harrods (Limited), and was MP for N-E Div of Essex (*U*) 1910-18, and for Harwich Div thereof 1918-22.

NEWTON (UK) 1924, of Beckenham, co Kent

Sir KENNETH GARNAR NEWTON, OBE, TD, 3rd *Baronet, b* 4 June 1918; *s* his father, *Sir* EDGAR HENRY, 1971; *ed* Wellington; Master of Leathersellers' Co 1977-78, Master of Feltmakers' Co 1983-84; Gen Commr for Income Tax 1961; Pres British Leather Fedn 1968-69; Pres Internat Council of Tanners 1972-78; Chm Garnar Booth plc 1972-87; chm Govs Colfe's Sch 1982-93; Lt-Col RASC (TA); 1939-45 War; MBE (Mil) 1944, OBE (Civil) 1969: *m* 1st, 1944, Margaret Isabel, who *d* 1979, da of Rev Dr George Blair, of Dundee; 2ndly, 1980, Pamela Sidney, widow of F. T. K. Wilson, and has issue by 1st *m*.

Arms – Argent, on a chevron between three eagles displayed azure, as many garbs or. Crest – A bear's head couped argent, muzzled gules, charged on the neck with three crescents interlaced azure.
Residence – Oaklands, Harborough Gorse, W Chiltington, W Sussex RH20 2RU.

SONS LIVING (*By 1st marriage*)

JOHN GARNAR (North House, Wyboston, Beds), *b* 10 July 1945; *ed* Reed's Sch, Cobham: *m* 1972, Jacynth Anne Kay Miller, and has issue living, Timothy Garnar, *b* 4 Sept 1973, — Alistair Blair, *b* (twin) 1973, — Andrew Robert, *b* 1975. —— Peter Blair (Park House, Souldern, nr Bicester, Oxon), *b* 1950; *ed* Wellington: *m* 1983, Fiona S., only da of W.Q. FitzGerald, of Penny Broom, Burnham Market, Norfolk, and has issue living, Alex Blair, *b* 1988, — Rory James, *b* 1990.

Faveat fortuna
May fortune favour

WIDOW LIVING OF SECOND BARONET

ALICE MARY (*Alice, Lady Newton*) (14 Castle Hill View, Sidford, Sidmouth, Devon), da of late Henry Barber, of Surbiton, and widow of Glyn Rosser: *m* 1968, as his 2nd wife, Sir Edgar Henry Newton, 2nd Bt, who *d* 1971.

COLLATERAL BRANCH LIVING

Issue of late Sidney Arthur Newton, 2nd son of 1st baronet, *b* 1901, *d* 1978: *m* 1933, Oonagh, who *d* 1990, da of late John Fleming, of Dublin:—
Hedley John (Moat Farm House, Kettle Green, Much Hadham, Herts), *b* 1936; *ed* Charterhouse, and Trinity Hall, Camb (MA, LLB); solicitor 1960; a Liveryman of Vintners' Co: *m* 1964, Virginia, da of James Archibald Baiss, and has issue living, Marcus James, *b* 1966, — Charles Benedict, *b* 1968, — Caspar John, *b* 1971. —— Shane (*Baroness Gisborough*), *b* 1934: *m* 1960, 3rd Baron Gisborough, of Gisborough House, Guisborough, Cleveland. —— Gaidagh, *b* 1947: *m* 1968, James Martin Strong, of West Bradley, Templeton, Tiverton, Devon.

The 1st baronet, Sir Louis Arthur Newton (son of late Reuben Newton, of Macclesfield), was a Surveyor, and an Alderman and Lieut of City of London (Senior Sheriff 1916-17, Lord Mayor 1923-4), a County Councillor for London 1931-4, High Sheriff of Kent 1940-41, and sometime Hon Col 56th (1st London) Div Train RASC.

NICHOLSON (UK) 1912, of Harrington Gardens, Royal Borough of Kensington

Sir CHARLES CHRISTIAN NICHOLSON, 3rd *Baronet*; *b* 15 Dec 1941; *s* his father, Sir JOHN NORRIS, KBE, CIE, 1993; *ed* Ampleforth, and Magdalen Coll, Oxford: *m* 1975, Martha Rodman, da of Col Stuart Warren Don, and widow of Niall Hamilton Anstruther-Gough-Calthorpe (*see* Anstruther-Gough-Calthorpe, Bt).

Arms – Per pale nebuly azure and gules two bars argent guttée de poix, in chief two suns in splendour proper. **Crest** – A lion's head couped sable guttée d'eau before a sun in splendour proper.
Residence – Turners Green Farm, Elvetham, Hartley Wintney, Hants RG27 8BE. *Clubs* – Brooks's, Pratt's, Royal Yacht Squadron.

BROTHER LIVING

JAMES RICHARD LOTHIAN, *b* 24 Oct 1947; *ed* Ampleforth, and Churchill Coll, Camb: *m* 1st, 1974 (*m diss* 1980), Charmian Joy, da of Maj Harcourt Michael Scudamore Gold, MC (*see* By of Trent); 2ndly, 1980, Sarah Hazel, da of Richard Alan Budgett, of Kirtlington, Oxford, and has issue living (by 2nd *m*), Edward, *b* 1983, — Lara, *b* 1986. *Residence* – The Stableyard, Kirtlington Park, Oxford.

SISTERS LIVING

Quietate et Confidentia

Tessa Mary, *b* 1944: *m* 1967, Piers Anthony Constantine Howard Phipps, of Trerose Manor, Mawnan, Falmouth, Cornwall, only son of late Sqdn Ldr Francis Constantine Phipps. —— Mary Louise Petronella, *b* 1950: *m* 1973, Adam Trevor Kelly Smail, of Spring Hill, Compton Abdale, Glos, son of Lt-Col Adam Trevor Smail, DSO, of Edgeworth Manor, Stroud, Glos.

The 1st baronet, Sir Charles Norris Nicholson, sat as MP for Doncaster Div of S Part of W Riding of Yorkshire (*L*) 1906-18. The 2nd baronet, Sir John Norris Nicholson, KBE, CIE, was Chm Ocean Steamship Co 1957-71 and of Martin's Bank 1962-64, Vice Lord-Lieut of Isle of Wight 1974-80 and Lord-Lieut 1980-86.

NICHOLSON (UK) 1958, of Winterbourne, Royal co of Berks (Extinct 1991)

Sir GODFREY NICHOLSON, 1st and last *Baronet*, *d* 14 July 1991.

DAUGHTERS LIVING OF FIRST BARONET

Rose Helen (*Lady Luce*), *b* 1937: *m* 1961, Rt Hon Sir Richard Napier Luce, of Dragons Farmhouse, Cowfold, Horsham, Sussex, son of late Sir William Henry Tucker Luce, GBE, KCMG, and has issue living, Alexander Richard, *b* 1964, — Edward Godfrey, *b* 1968. —— Laura Violet (*Lady Montgomery Cuninghame*), *b* 1939: *m* 1964, Sir John Christopher Foggo Montgomery Cuninghame, 12th Bt, of The Old Rectory, Brightwalton, Newbury, Berks and has issue (*see* Cuninghame, Bt). —— Emma Harriet (*Baroness Nicholson of Winterbourne*), *b* 1941: MP for Devon West and Torridge 1987-97 (*C* 1987-Dec 1995, *Lib Dem* 1995-97); *cr* Baroness Nicholson of Winterbourne (Life Baroness) 1998: *m* 1987, Sir Michael Harris Caine, who *d* 1999, son of late Sir Sydney Caine, KCMG. —— Harriet Mary, *b* 1946: *m* 1969, Charles Hamilton Flower (D Abercorn, colls, 1976 Edn), and has issue living, Katharine Mary, *b* 1972, — Sarah Constance, *b* 1976.

NICOLSON (NS) 1629, of that Ilk, and of Lasswade, Midlothian (Dormant 1961)

Sir HAROLD STANLEY NICOLSON, 14th *Baronet*, *d* 1961, and at the time of going to press no name appears on the official Roll of Baronets in respect of this title.

COLLATERAL BRANCH LIVING

Issue of late Lionel Rutherford Nicolson, WS, 3rd son of 12th baronet, *b* 1887, *d* 1957: *m* 1932, Kathleen Mary, who *d* 1995, da of late Henry Gane Moon:—
Anne, *b* 1939: *m* 1963, Miles Hansen, of Bletchinglye Farm, Bletchinglye Lane, Rotherfield, Sussex, and has issue living, Piers James, *b* 1966, — Clare Louise, *b* 1969: *m* 1995, Timothy J. Bennett, son of Rev Arnold Bennett.

John Nicolson of that Ilk and Lasswade, Midlothian, was *cr* a baronet 1629 with remainder to his heirs male whatsoever, with a grant of land in Nova Scotia. On the death of Sir James, 7th Bt, 1713, the baronetcy became dormant. Arthur, *de jure* 8th Bt (*d* 1793) was a great-grandson of James, Bishop of Dunkeld, next brother of 1st Bt. In 1826, Sir Arthur, *de jure* 10th Bt, grandson of Arthur, was served heir male of 7th Bt. The Baronetcy again became dormant on the death of the 14th Bt in 1961.

NIGHTINGALE (E) 1628, of Newport Pond, Essex

Sir CHARLES MANNERS GAMALIEL NIGHTINGALE, 17th *Baronet*; *b* 21 Feb 1947; *s* his father, *Sir* CHARLES ATHELSTAN, 1977; *ed* St Paul's Sch; BA (Open Univ) 1990; Grade 7, Dept of Health.

Arms – Per pale ermine and gules, a rose counterchanged. *Crest* – An ibex sejant argent, tufted, armed, and maned or.
Residence – 16 Unity Grove, Harrogate, N Yorks HG1 2AQ.

SISTERS LIVING

Nadine Mary Rosalie (54 Willow Close, Quintrell Downs, Newquay, Cornwall TR8 4NQ), *b* 1938: *m* 1st, 1959 (*m diss* 1972), Peter Maurice Edmunds; 2ndly, 1972 (*m diss* 1989), Derek Frederick Curtis, and has issue living, (by 1st *m*) Thomas Charles, *b* 1961, — David Michael, *b* 1963, — Jeremy John, *b* 1964, — Jane Elizabeth, *b* 1965, — (by 2nd *m*) James *b* 1972. —— Clothilde Muriel Frances, *b* 1939: *m* 1964, Derek Edward Glenister, of 2 Albany Close, Ickenham, Middx, and has issue living, Frances Mary, *b* 1966, — Clare Julia, *b* 1968.

COLLATERAL BRANCHES LIVING

Grandchildren of late Lacy Gamaliel Nightingale, KC, son of late Percy Nightingale, el son of late Thomas Henry Nightingale, RN, 2nd son of 11th baronet:—
Issue of late Manners Percy Nightingale, MRCS, LRCP, *b* 1908, *d* 1974: *m* 1936, Mary Ursula, who *d* 1983, da of late Rev George Saunders Gilbert, of Groombridge, Sussex:—
EDWARD LACY GEORGE (Kneesworth, Lynton, N Devon), *b* 11 May 1938; *ed* Exeter Sch; Master Mariner. —— Jane Elizabeth, *b* 1940.

For king and country

Issue of late Neville Gascoyne Nightingale, *b* 1911, *d* 1989: *m* 1946, Nancy Esther (6 Long Lane, Southrepps, Norfolk), da of late Godfrey James Whistler, of Ross-on-Wye, Hereford:—

Thomas Lacy Manners, *b* 1947: *m* 1993, Lois Allison, only da of late Rev Thomas Oswald Welch Glass, of Roydon, Norfolk. *Residence* – Wellsprings Farmhouse, Wellsprings Rd, Southrepps, Norfolk NR11 8XA.

Grandsons of late Maj-Gen Manners Ralph Wilmott Nightingale, CB, CMG, CIE, DSO, 4th son of late Percy Nightingale, eldest son of late Thomas Henry Nightingale, RN (ante):—
Issue of late Lt-Col George Manners Nightingale, MC, *b* 1913, *d* 1992: *m* 1946, Mrs Alison Cornwallis Sutton, who *d* 1996, da of late Col James Cameron, RE, and formerly wife of Stanley William Vernon Sutton:—
Christopher George Manners, *b* 1949; *ed* Kelly Coll, and RMA Sandhurst; Capt Staffordshire Regt: *m* 1st, 1971, Marie-Claudette, da of Marc Roger Tenermont; 2ndly, 1978, Anna Sorina, da of Christian Niels Fischer, and has issue living (by 2nd *m*), Edward George Manners, *b* 1985. —— Jeremy John Charles, *b* 1952; *ed* Wellington Coll.

Granddaughters of late James Edward Nightingale, 2nd son of Thomas Henry Nightingale, RN (ante):—
Issue of late Ernest Albert Nightingale, *b* 1867, *d* 1945: *m* 1893, Sarah Annette Thorntone, who *d* 1947, da of late John Austen:—
Irene Mary (Imperani Park, Ficksburg, S Africa), *b* 1899: *m* 1926, Norman Owen Halse, who *d* 1966, and has issue living, Norma Rene, *b* 1927, — Varney Marren, *b* 1934, — Rosemary Joy, *b* 1943.

Issue of late Thomas Cecil Parry Nightingale, *b* 1885; *d* 1950: *m* 1911, Anita Adendorff:—
Joy Thelma, *b* 1913: *m* 1936, Cornie Hugo Liesching, and has issue living, Frederick Jabris, *b* 1937, — Cornie, *b* 1940, — Anita Lorraine, *b* 1945, — Margaret, *b* 1947.

Grandchildren of late Claud Robert Nightingale, MC, son of late Frederick Charles Nightingale, son of late Geoffrey Nightingale, 7th son of 10th baronet:—
Issue of late Christopher Carnac Nightingale, *b* 1913, *d* 1970: *m* 1941, Muriel de Lissa (39 Gander Hill, Haywards Heath, Sussex), da of late F. D. Philips, of Leatherhead:—
Nicholas John, *b* 1942: *m* 1968, Susan Kay, da of Philip Lyth, of Park Hill, Southwell, Notts and has issue living, Thomas James, *b* 1977, — Rebecca Jane, *b* 1972, — Elizabeth Jane, *b* 1976. —— Anne Christine, *b* 1944: *m* 1972, Kenneth Ian Murchison, of 21 Calvert Av, Killara, NSW 2071, Aust, and has issue living, Scott Timothy, *b* 1973, — Hamish Charles, *b* 1977, — Emma Georgina, *b* 1974. —— Patricia Ruth, *b* 1950: *m* 1979, Ian Christie of 131 Mount View Rd, N4, and has issue living, Edward Nightingale, *b* 1987, — Beatrice Nightingale, *b* 1980, — Laura Nightingale, *b* 1982, — Isabel Nightingale, *b* 1985.

Issue of late Robert Forbes Nightingale, *b* 1917, *d* 1993: *m* 1st, 1940 (*m diss* 1956), Lesley Phyllis, da of late S. Kenneth West; 2ndly, 1956, Dora, who *d* 1992, da of George Henry Kirkpatrick:—
(By 1st *m*) Peter Robert (Meadowbank, The Avenue, Godalming, Surrey), *b* 1947: *m* 1968, Joan Anne, da of late J. A. Kerr, and has issue living, James Peter, *b* 1974, — Andrea Jane, *b* 1969: *m* 1995, Andrew John Hurley, and has issue living, Megan Anne *b* 1997, — Helen Mary, *b* 1971. —— Richard John (Blackdown Cottage, Denbigh Rd, Haslemere, Surrey), *b* 1948: *m* 1971, Frances Catherine, da of late C. B. Green, and has issue living Catherine, *b* 1972.

Sir Thomas Nightingale, 1st Bt, of Newport Pond, Essex, was High Sheriff of Essex 1627. On the death in 1722 of Sir Robert, 4th Bt, a Dir of Hon East India Co, his estates devolved on his cousin, Robert Gascoyne. The baronetcy should have passed to Edward Nightingale, of Kneesworth, Cambs, son of Geoffrey, yr son of 1st Bt, but succession was not established until Sir Edward Nightingale recorded his pedigree and established his right to the title as 10th baronet in 1797. Sir Charles Athelstan Nightingale, 16th Bt, *b* 1902: *m* 1932, Nadine, who *d* 1995, da of late Arthur Diggens, and *d* 1990.

NIXON (UK) 1906, of Roebuck Grove, Milltown, co Dublin, and Merrion Square, City of Dublin

Sir SIMON MICHAEL CHRISTOPHER NIXON, 5th *Baronet*, eldest son of late Maj Cecil Dominic Henry Joseph Nixon, MC, 3rd son of 2nd baronet; *b* 20 June 1954; *s* his uncle, *Rev Fr Sir* KENNETH MICHAEL JOHN BASIL, SJ, 1997; *ed* ......

Arms – Azure, on a chevron engrailed between three frets couped or, as many trefoils vert, on a chief indented of the second, a cat passant between two fleams of the field. **Crest** – A leopard rampant azure bezantee, holding in the dexter paw a fleam or. *Address* – Salt Winds, Torridge Rd, Appledore, N Devon.

BROTHERS LIVING

MICHAEL DAVID HUGH, *b* 19 May 1957; *ed* .... —— Kenneth Philip Guy, *b* 1959; *ed* ......

SISTER LIVING

Susan Penelope, *b* 1955.

Always ready

DAUGHTERS LIVING OF THIRD BARONET

Anne Louise Catherine, *b* 1954; MB, BSc, FRCP, FRC (Path): *m* 1980, Jonathan Anthony Miller, MB, BCh, FRCP, and has issue living, David Christopher, *b* 1987, — Nicholas Jonathan, *b* 1989. —— Mary Joan Teresa, *b* 1957; MCSP, SRP: *m* 1988, Eric Olivier Léchaire, and has issue living, Jeremy, *b* 1989, — Samuel, *b* 1992. —— Sally Veronica Rose, *b* 1961; BDS, MSc, FDS (RCS): *m* 1989, Andrew Kenneth Robson, MB, BSc, FRCS, and has issue living, Toby Christopher Kenneth, *b* 1996, — Lucy Dorothy Julia, *b* 1990, — Rosie Esme Dorothy, *b* 1992.

MOTHER LIVING

Brenda, only da of late Samuel Lycett Lewis, and widow of Maj M. F. McWhor: *m* 1953, Maj Cecil Dominic Henry Joseph Nixon, MC, who *d* 1994. *Residence* – Salt Winds, Torridge Rd, Appledore, N Devon.

WIDOW LIVING OF THIRD BARONET

JOAN LUCILLE MARY (*Lady Nixon*) (c/o Lloyds Bank, St George's Rd, Wimbledon, SW19), only da of Robert Felix Mervyn Brown, of Rangoon, Burma: *m* 1949, Maj Sir Christopher John Louis Joseph Nixon, MC, 3rd Bt, who *d* 1978.

The Rt Hon Sir Christopher John Nixon, PC, MD, LLD, 1st Bt, was an eminent physician, Vice-Chancellor of National Univ of Ireland, and Pres of Veterinary Coll of Ireland. The 2nd Bt, Major Sir Christopher William Nixon, DSO, RA (ret), served during European War 1914-18 (DSO). The 3rd baronet was a Maj in R Ulster Rifles and served in Burma (MC) and Palestine in WW II, and in Korea 1950-51 (wounded, despatches). The Rev Father Sir Kenneth Michael John Basil Nixon, SJ, 4th Bt, was a Roman Catholic Priest and Member of the Society of Jesus; *d* in Harare, 1997.

NOBLE (UK) 1902, of Ardmore and Ardardan Noble, Cardross, co Dumbarton

By virtue and valour

Sir DAVID BRUNEL NOBLE, 6th *Baronet*; *b* 25 Dec 1961; *s* his father, *Sir* MARC BRUNEL, CBE, 1991; *ed* Eton: *m* 1st, 1987 (*m diss* 1993), Virginia Ann, yr da of late Roderick Lancaster Wetherall, MBE, of Platt Oast, St Mary's Platt, Kent; 2ndly, 1993, Stephanie, da of Daniel Digby, of Rainham, Kent, and has had issue by 1st and 2nd wives.

Arms – Argent, three bay leaves slipped proper. **Crest** – A dexter hand couped, holding a dagger all proper. **Supporters** – Two wild men, wreathed and cinctured with bay leaves, each supporting with the exterior hand a holly tree eradicated, and resting the exterior foot on the roots thereof, all proper (These were granted to descend hereditarily.)
Residence – Deerleap House, Knockholt, Sevenoaks, Kent, TN14 7NP.

SONS LIVING AND DECEASED (*By 1st wife*)

RODERICK LANCASTER BRUNEL, *b* 8 Dec 1988. —— Alexander David, *b* 1990.

(By 2nd wife)

Connor Daniel, *b* 1993. —— †Drew Marc (twin), *b* and *d* 1993.

DAUGHTER LIVING (*By 2nd wife*)

Megan Lorna Annette, *b* 1995.

BROTHER LIVING

Charles Richard Austin, *b* 1963; *ed* Harrow. *Residence* – Deerleap House, Knockholt, Sevenoaks, Kent TN14 7NP.

SISTER LIVING

Anna Margaret, *b* 1957: *m* 1984, John Edward Llewellyn Porter, who *d* 1987, son of late Stephen Porter, and has issue living, George Edward, *b* 1986. *Residence* – Deerleap House, Knockholt, Sevenoaks, Kent TN14 7NP.

AUNT LIVING (*daughter of 4th baronet*)

Lilias Mulgrave, *b* 1931: *m* 1951, Capt Robin John Sheepshanks, CBE, DL, late King's Dragoon Guards (V Chelmsford), and has issue living, David Richard, *b* 1952, — Richard John, *b* 1955, — Andrew Charles, *b* 1960, — Christopher James, *b* 1964. *Residence* – The Rookery, Eyke, Woodbridge, Suffolk.

WIDOW LIVING OF FIFTH BARONET

JENNIFER LORNA (JANE) (*Dowager Lady Noble*), da of late John Mein Austin, of Flinthill, W Haddon, Northants: *m* 1956, Sir Marc Brunel Noble, 5th Bt, CBE, who *d* 1991. *Residence* – Deerleap House, Knockholt, Sevenoaks, Kent TN14 7NP.

COLLATERAL BRANCHES LIVING

Issue of late Peter Saxton Fitzjames Noble, CBE, 2nd son of 4th baronet, *b* 1929, *d* 1998: *m* 1st 1954 (*m diss* 1966), Elizabeth Emmeline, da of late Launcelot William Gregory Eccles, CMG, MC; 2ndly, 1966 (*m diss* 1980), Helena Margaret, da of late Thomas Essery Rose-Richards, and previously wife of David Anthony Harries; 3rdly, 1980, Penelope Margaret (Flax Cottage, Ham Common, Richmond, Surrey TW10 7JB), da of late Leslie Landau:—
(By 1st *m*) Simon Peter Saxton Fanshaw, *b* 1958. —— (By 2nd *m*) James Essery Brunel, *b* 1968.

Issue of late Sir John Henry Brunel Noble (3rd son of 1st baronet), who was *cr* a *Baronet* 1923:—
See Noble, Bt, *cr* 1923.

Grandson of late Philip Ernest Noble, 4th son of 1st baronet:—
Issue of late Maj Horace Westmacott Noble, *b* 1899, *d* 1980: *m* 1st, 1929 (*m diss* 1934), Joan Marion, only child of H. R. Miller, of New York, USA; 2ndly, 1946, Mrs Edna Louise Malone, da of late Charles Johnson, of Chicago, USA:—
(By 1st *m*) Philip Ralph, *b* 1930; *ed* Eton, and Sir George Williams Univ, Montreal: *m* 1955, Joane McNamara, da of late John Hawkins, of Bathurst, Cape Province, S Africa, and has issue living, Robin Louise, *b* 1960, — Simone Alexandra, *b* 1962. Resides in Canada.

The 1st baronet, Sir Andrew Noble, the well-known expert on explosives, joined the firm of Sir W. G. Armstrong & Co in 1860, and eventually became Chm; he was a Member of the first Committee of Explosives until dissolved in 1880, and High Sheriff of Northumberland 1896. The 4th baronet, Sir Humphrey Brunel Noble, MBE, MC, was High Sheriff of Northumberland 1956. Sir Marc Brunel Noble, 5th Bt, was High Sheriff of Kent 1985-86.

NOBLE (UK) 1923, of Ardkinglas, co Argyll

Sir IAIN ANDREW NOBLE, OBE, 3rd *Baronet*: *b* 8 Sept 1935; *s* his father, *Sir* ANDREW NAPIER, KCMG, 1987; *ed* Eton, and Univ Coll, Oxford (MA); Scottish Council (Development and Industry) Edinburgh 1964-69; Joint Founder and Man Dir Noble Grossart Ltd 1969-72; Joint Founder and Chm Seaforth Maritime Ltd 1972-77; Chm Noble Group Ltd, Merchant Bankers, of Edinburgh, since 1980; Dir Adam & Co plc, Bankers, of Edinburgh, 1983-93; Dir New Scotland Insurance Gp plc, of Glasgow, since 1986; Dir Premium Investment Trust plc since 1993; Proprietor Fearann Eilean Iarmain and Barony of MacDonald, Isle of Skye since 1972, Chm Pràban Ltd (whisky proprietors) of Eilean Iarmain since 1977; a founding trustee Coll of Sabhal Mor Ostaig 1974-84; Memb Edinburgh Univ Court 1970-73; Dep Chm Traverse Theatre Club, Edinburgh 1966-69; Trustee Nat Museums of Scotland 1987-91; Chm Scots Australian Council; Pres Saltire Soc: *m* 1990, Lucilla Charlotte James, da of late Col Hector Andrew Courtney Mackenzie of Dalmore, OBE, MC, TD, JP, DL.

Arms – Per pale Argent and Vert three bay leaves counterchanged, and on a canton Argent a sinister hand couped apaumé Gules for his Baronetcy. Above the Shield from which is pendent the proper badge of a Baronet of the United Kingdom is placed an Helm befitting his degree with a Mantling Vert doubled Argent, and on a Wreath of the Liveries is set for. **Crest** – A bay tree Vert, trunk Sable, ensigned with an estoile Argent and in an Escrol over the same this Motto "Mairidh an Duilleag".
Residence – An Lamraig, Eilean Iarmain, Isle of Skye IV43 8QR. *Club* – New (Edinburgh).

BROTHER LIVING

TIMOTHY PETER *b* 21 Dec 1943; *ed* Eton, and Univ Coll, Oxford (MA); Bar Gray's Inn 1969; INSEAD, Fontainebleau (MBA) 1970; Exec Dir Lyle Shipping plc, Glasgow, 1976-1984, Ch Exec Noble Group Ltd, Merchant Bankers, of Edinburgh, since 1984; Dir Waverley Mining Finance plc since 1987, Medway Insurance Group plc since 1996, Darnaway Venture Capital plc since 1995, and The British Snowsport Federation Ltd 1993-98; Chm Business Archives Council of Scotland 1986-95; Chm RSNO Endowment Trust since 1994, and Chm British Ski Academy since 1997: *m* 1976, Elizabeth Mary, da of late Alexander Wallace Aitken, and has issue living, Lorne Andrew Wallace, *b* 1980, — Andrew Iain Brunel, *b* 1984, — Sasha Heidi Elizabeth, *b* 1978. *Residence* – Ardnahane, Barnton Avenue, Edinburgh EH4 6JJ. *Club* – New (Edinburgh).

SISTER LIVING

Laila Ilona, *b* 1937: *m* 1958, Kenneth Magnus Spence, who *d* 1989, son of late Col Patrick Magnus Spence, MC, and has issue living, Magnus Andrew, *b* 1959: *m* 1994, Sarah yr da of FM Sir Nigel Thomas Bagnall, GCB, CVO, MC, — Patrick Matthew, *b* 1967, — Melanie Jane, *b* 1961: *m* 1995, George Robert Embelton, of Melbourne, Australia. *Residences* – 15 Millicent Av, Toorak, Vic 3142, Australia; Flat 7, 53 Kensington Court, W8 5DE.

AUNT LIVING *(daughter of 1st baronet)*

Anastasia Mary Elizabeth (The Square, Ardkinglas, Cairndow, Argyll), *b* 1911.

WIDOW LIVING OF SECOND BARONET

SIGRID (*Sigrid, Lady Noble*), 2nd da of Johan Michelet, Norwegian Diplo Ser: *m* 1934, Sir Andrew Napier Noble, 2nd Bt, KCMG, who *d* 1987. *Residence* – Galsworthy House, 177 Kingston Hill, Kingston upon Thames, Surrey KT2 7LX.

COLLATERAL BRANCHES LIVING

Issue of late John Samuel Brunel Noble, 2nd son of 1st baronet; *b* 1909, *d* 1972: *m* 1934, Elizabeth Virginia, who *d* 1983, da of late William Louis Lucas (Goldsmid, Bt, ext):—
Simon John (Ardkinglas, Cairndow, Argyll; Boodle's, New Club (Edinburgh)) *b* 1936; *ed* Eton, and Oxford Univ; Chm Wine Imports Edinburgh Ltd and Loch Fyne Oysters Ltd; Dir of Noble Group Ltd, and Edinburgh Tapestry Co Ltd. —— Sarah, *b* 1935: *m* 1957, Peter Whitton Sumsion, of Bachie Barn House, Cairndow, Argyll, and 42 Dudley Dr, Glasgow, and has issue living, David, *b* 1958, — Daniel, *b* 1967, — Virginia, *b* 1960, — Lucy, *b* 1963. —— Christina Campbell, *b* 1942: *m* 1980, Kranti Singh, who *d* 1992, of 66 Hungerford Rd, N7 9LP, and has issue living, Rahul John, *b* 1976, — Tara Anastasia, *b* 1977.

Issue of late Rt Hon Michael Antony Cristobal Noble (Baron Glenkinglas), yst son of 1st baronet, *b* 1913, *d* 1984: *m* 1940, Anne (*Baroness Glenkinglas*) (Strone, Cairndow, Argyll), da of late Sir Neville Arthur Pearson, 2nd Bt, of Dunstan's (ext):—
See Glenkinglas, By.

The 1st baronet, Sir John Henry Brunel Noble (3rd son of Sir Andrew Noble, CB, 1st Bt, of Ardmore (*cr* 1902)), awarded the Order of the Sacred Treasure of Japan, was a Director of London and N-E Railway and many other Cos. Sir Andrew Napier Noble, 2nd Bt, was HM Min to Helsinki and HM Amb to Warsaw, Mexico and The Hague.

Norie-Miller, see Miller.

NORMAN (UK) 1915, of Honeyhanger, Parish of Shottermill, co Surrey

Live but do not forget

Sir MARK ANNESLEY NORMAN, 3rd *Baronet*, DL; *b* 8 Feb 1927; *s* his father, *Air-Commodore Sir* (HENRY) NIGEL ST VALERY, CBE, 1943: *ed* Winchester, and RMA; Lieut Coldstream Guards 1945-47 and Flying Officer, No 601 Squadron, R Aux AF (GD Pilot 1953-56); High Sheriff of Oxfordshire 1983-84; DL Oxfordshire (1985); Gazetted Air Commodore, R Aux AF, and appointed Hon Air Commodore No 4624 (County of Oxford) Movements Sqdn, R Aux AF 1983: *m* 1953, Joanna Camilla, da of Lt-Col Ian James Kilgour (*see* Forestier-Walker, Bt, colls, 1985 Edn), and has issue.

Arms – Sable, a thunderbolt, and in chief two crosses patée pierced with the eight symbols of Fhohe or the Pa-qua and charged with a rounder containing the eastern symbol known as Tae Keigh' all or. **Crest** – Upon mount vert a spear erect, transfixing a Saracen's head, all proper. **Supporters** – On either side a Norseman proper.
Residence – Wilcote Manor, Wilcote, Chipping Norton, Oxon, OX7 3EB. *Clubs* – White's, MCC, Pratt's, Royal Air Force, Royal Southern Yacht, SWSYC.

SONS LIVING

NIGEL JAMES, *b* 5 Feb 1956; late Maj 13th/18th Royal Hussars (QMO) (despatches 1989), Sultan of Oman's Armoured Regt; Dir Morgan Grenfell International Funds Management Ltd: *m* 1st, 1985 (*m diss* 1989), Joanna Rosemary Jane, da of Michael Montagu George Naylor-Leyland, MC, of Church Farm, Coates, Cirencester, Glos (*see* Naylor-Leyland, Bt); 2ndly, 1994, Mrs Juliet Clare Louise Marriott, da of Richard Lloyd Baxendale, of Aston Park House, Aston Rowant, Oxon, and has issue living (by 2nd *m*), Antony Richard St Valery, *b* 10 March 1995, — Mark Henry Kilgour, *b* 1996, — Sophie Patricia Clare, *b* 1997. *Clubs* – White's, Annabels. —— (Antony) Rory, *b* 1963: *m* 1998, Camilla, A. C., yr da of Kenneth Baker, of Taunton, Som.

DAUGHTER LIVING

Lucinda Fay, *b* 1965: *m* 1988, Stanislas Richard Marie Aubertin, son of Christian Aubertin, of Neuilly-sur-Seine, France, and has issue living, Nicholas Helli, *b* 1991, — Ludovic Matthieu, *b* 1994.

BROTHERS LIVING

(Nigel) Desmond, CBE, *b* 1929; CBE (Civil) 1971: *m* 1st, 1956 (*m diss* 1965), Barbara Anne, only da of late Capt Mark Fogg Elliot, DSO, RN; 2ndly, 1965, Mrs Boel Elisabeth Holmsen, only da of late Gösta Suenson, of Malmo, Sweden, and has issue living, (by 1st *m*) Henry Mark Desmond, *b* 1957, — Alexander Robert, *b* 1959, — (by 2nd *m*) Roderick Peregrine, *b* 1966, — Roland, *b* 1971, — Lisa Jemima, *b* 1969. —— Torquil Patrick Alexander (62 Gloucester Crescent, NW1 7EG), *b* 1933: *m* 1961, Elizabeth Anne, da of Alexander Victor Edward Paulet Montagu (10th Earl of Sandwich until he disclaimed his title 1964), and has issue living, Alexander Jesse, *b* 1962, — Casey William, *b* 1963, — Caspar Joe, *b* 1966, — Lucy Patricia, *b* 1964, — Amy Jean Mary, *b* 1969.

COLLATERAL BRANCH LIVING

Issue of late Major Willoughby Rollo Norman, 2nd son of 1st baronet, *b* 1909, *d* 1997: *m* 1st, 1934 (*m diss* 1973), Hon Barbara Jacqueline Boot, da of 2nd Baron Trent; 2ndly, 1973, Anna Caroline (The Grange, South Harting, Petersfield, Hants), da of late William Greville Worthington (E Aylesford), and formerly wife of Oliver Patrick Miller Haskard:—
(By 1st *m*) Jeremy Nicholas, *b* 1935: *m* 1980, Mrs Danuska Maria Weeks, da of late Mr Grajewski, of Wroclaw, Poland. —— Sarah Jessica, *b* 1940: *m* 1st, 1960 (*m diss* 1967), Peter Egerton-Warburton (*see* Grey-Egerton, Bt, colls); 2ndly, 1967, Peter David Rickett, and has issue living, (by 1st *m*) (*see* Grey-Egerton Bt, colls), — (by 2nd *m*) Nicola Barbara, *b* 1970, — Lucinda Frances, *b* 1971. —— Tessa Roselle, *b* 1944: *m* 1968, George Maurice Pope, late Capt Coldm Gds, and has issue living, Edward, *b* 1970, — Emily, *b* 1972, — Arabella, *b* 1975.

The 1st baronet, Rt Hon Sir Henry Norman, PC (son of late Henry Norman), was MP for S Div of Wolverhampton (*L*) 1900-1910, and for Blackburn 1910-23. The 2nd baronet, Air Commodore Sir (Henry) Nigel St Valery, CBE, Auxiliary Air Force (Reserve), was *ka* 1943.

NORTH (UK) 1920, of Southwell, co Nottingham

Sir (WILLIAM) JONATHAN FREDERICK NORTH, 2nd *Baronet*, son of late Hon John Montagu William North (*see* E Guilford); *b* 6 Feb 1931; *s* his maternal grandfather, *Sir* WILLIAM NORTON HICKING, 1947; *ed* Marlborough Coll: *m* 1956, Sara Virginia, da of late Air Ch Marshal Sir (James) Donald Innes Hardman, GBE, KCB, DFC, and has issue.

𝕬rms – Quarterly, 1st and 4th azure, a lion passant or, three fleurs-de-lis argent, *North*; 2nd and 3rd, argent, semée of lozenges vert, a bordure, gules, *Hicking.* 𝕮rest – A dragon's head erased sable, ducally gorged and chained or.
Residence – Frogmore, Weston-under-Penyard, Herefordshire HR9 5TQ.

SON LIVING

JEREMY WILLIAM FRANCIS, *b* 5 May 1960; *ed* Marlborough: *m* 1986, Lucy A., da of G. A. van der Meulen, of Tunbridge Wells, Kent, and has issue living, Jocelyn Montagu Dudley, *b* 23 March 1989, — Francis Augustus Roderick, *b* 1990, — Polly Antonia, *b* 1992, — Lydia Calypso Helena, *b* 1995. *Residence* – Standerwick Court, Frome, Som BA11 2PP.

DAUGHTERS LIVING

With courage and fidelity

Charlotte Amelia, *b* 1958: *m* 1989, Matthew Dufton Tester, yst son of late Maurice Tester, of Long Barn House, Cowfold, Sussex. *Residence* – 12 Crowood Lane, Ramsbury, nr Marlborough, Wilts SN8 2PT. —— Harriet Cordelia Henrietta, *b* 1963: *m* 1984, (Seymour) Thomas Thistlethwayte, son of Seymour Thistlethwayte, of Sheet Mill House, Petersfield, Hants, and has issue living, Oliver Seymour, *b* 1990, — Edmund Thomas, *b* 1996, — Daisy Alexandra, *b* 1988, — Cecily Alice, *b* 1992. *Residence* – South Collingham House, Newark, Notts NG24 7LQ.

SISTER LIVING

Georgiana Mary, *b* 1928: *m* 1960, Esmond Unwin Butler, CM, CVO, Sec to Gov-Gen of Canada, who *d* 1989, and has issue living, Mark William, *b* 1961, — Clare Martine, *b* 1963. *Residence* – 149 Rideau Terrace, Ottawa, Ontario, Canada.

The 1st baronet, Sir William Norton Hicking (son of late George Hicking, of Nottingham), sometime Chm of Nottingham and Notts Banking Co, and High Sheriff of Notts 1913-14, was *cr* a Baronet in 1917 with the usual limitation to heirs male of the body, but in 1920 a further creation was granted failing heirs male of the body of the grantee, with special remainder to the first and every other son of Mabel Doris Willoughby (el da of 1st Bt), and the heirs of their bodies and with like remainder to the male issue of any yr das of the 1st Bt. On the death of the 1st Bt in 1947 the Baronetcy of 1917 became ext and that of 1920 passed to the son of his yr da, Muriel Norton, formerly wife of the Hon John Montagu William North, 2nd son of 8th Earl of Guilford.

Norton-Griffiths, see Griffiths.

NUGENT (I) 1795, of Ballinlough, co Westmeath

Sir JOHN EDWIN LAVALLIN NUGENT, 7th *Baronet*, and 4th Count of the Austrian Empire; *b* 16 March 1933; *s* his father, *Sir* HUGH CHARLES, 1983; *ed* Eton; late Lieut Irish Gds; High Sheriff of Berks 1981; JP Berks: *m* 1959, Penelope Anne, elder da of late Brig Richard Nigel Hanbury, CBE, TD, and has issue.

𝔄rms – Ermine, two bars gules. ℭrest – A cockatrice vert. *Seat* – Ballinlough Castle, Clonmellon, co Westmeath.

Decrevi

I have decreed

SON LIVING

NICHOLAS MYLES JOHN, *b* 17 Feb 1967; *ed* Eton.

DAUGHTER LIVING

Grania Clare, *b* 1969.

BROTHER LIVING

David Hugh Lavallin (Clobemon Hall, Ferns, Enniscorthy, co Wexford. *Club* – Cavalry and Guards'), *b* 1935; *ed* Eton; late Lt Irish Gds; Kt Cmdr of Order of Holy Sepulchre of Jerusalem with Star Grand Officer, Lord of Castletown Delvin, co Westmeath, and Baron of Fore, co Westmeath: *m* 1st, 1960 (*m diss* 1990), Lady Elizabeth Maria Guinness, da of late Maj Arthur Onslow Edward, Viscount Elveden, el son of 2nd Earl of Iveagh; 2ndly, 1991 (*m diss* 1996), Djong-Zha, only da of In-Suk Hyun, of Seoul, Korea, and formerly wife of Sir Richard Heygate, 6th Bt, and has had issue (by 1st *m*), Charles Rupert, *b* 1962: *m* 1989, Louise V., yr da of Timothy Nixon, of The Old Vicarage, Pampisford, Cambridge, and has issue living, Hugh Frederick *b* 1995, James Timothy *b* 1996, — Hugo John, *b* 1963: *m* 1989, Louise, yr da of Thomas Elliot Rutherford, of Parkdaill, Hawick, Scotland, and has issue living, Isaac Séan Rutherford *b* 1992, Finn Ruaridh Rutherford *b* 1995, — Rory David Neeld Lavallin, *b* 1971, — (Sheelin) Rose, *b* 1967: *m* 1996 (*m diss* 1998), Dominic Scriven, son of Timothy Scriven, of London, and *d* after an accident 1998.

WIDOW LIVING OF SIXTH BARONET

MARGARET MARY LAVALLIN (*Margaret, Lady Nugent*), da of late Rev Herbert Lavallin Puxley, of The White House, Chaddleworth, Newbury, Berks (Neeld, Bt): *m* 1931, Sir Hugh Charles Nugent, 6th Bt, who *d* 1983. *Residence* – Cronk Ghennie House, Bowring Rd, Ramsey, IoM.

COLLATERAL BRANCH LIVING

Grandchildren of late Charles James Nugent (*b* 1881) (infra):—
Issue of James Andrew William Nugent, *b* 1909, *d* 1965: *m* 1936, Dardanella, who *d* 1983, da of David Webber, of Wairoa, NZ:—
Trevor Charles, *b* 1940. —— Brian David, *b* 1942. —— Rayna Joy, *b* 1941.

Issue of Frederick Nugent, *b* 1914, *d* 1983: *m* 1939, Rita Kara (Mahia, Hawke's Bay, NZ), da of T. Carrol of Wairoa, NZ:—
Mark, *b* 1950. —— Valentine, *b* 1952. —— Pearl, *b* 1940. —— Brenda, *b* 1941. —— Diana, *b* 1954. —— Dixie, *b* 1957.

Issue of Charles Joseph Nugent, *b* 1918, *d* 1980: *m* 19—, Kathleen, da of Edgar Jenkinson of Gisborne, NZ:—
Peter James, *b* 1947. —— Graham, *b* 1953. —— Kenneth John, *b* 1955. —— Margaret Anne, *b* 1950. —— Raewyn Gay, *b* 1961.

Grandchildren of late James O'Reilly Nugent, 4th son of 3rd baronet:—
Issue of late Charles James Nugent, *b* 1881, *d* 1961: *m* 1907, Anne, who *d* 1961, da of William King, formerly of Napier, New Zealand:—
Patrick Hulme, *b* 1912: *m* 1940, Mary McFalls Quin, of Glasgow, who *d* 198—, and has issue living, Barry Hulme Joseph, *b* 1946, — Darryl Charles, *b* 1952, — Lynette Ann, *b* 1940, — Janice Patricia, *b* 1944. ——†Richard King, *b* 1923: *m* 1947, Doreen Mabel, da of Townsend May, of New Plymouth, New Zealand, and *d* 1992, leaving issue, Sandra May, *b* 1947, — Karen Louise, *b* 1952, — Anne Marie Eva, *b* 1954. —— Hubert Thomas Michael, *b* 1925: *m* 19—, Ngaire, da of George Able, of Wairoa, New Zealand, and has issue living, Alan Grant, *b* 1949, — Glenis Joy, *b* 1950. —— Florence Maud, *b* 1916: *m* 19—, Norman Jones, and has issue living, Howard Gilbert, *b* 1939: *m* 1963, Kathleen Elizabeth Sherridan, — Warren Charles, *b* 1942, — Michael O'Reilly, *b* 1947. *Residence* – Frasertown Rd, Wairoa, Hawke's Bay, New Zealand. —— Marie Tepaea Diana (3/10 Geddis Av, Maraenui, Napier, NZ), *b* 1921: *m* 1938, Moat Mervyn Hoggard, who *d* 1982, and has issue living, Shona Faye, *b* 1939: *m* 1960 (*m diss* 197—), Colin Thomas William Bailey, and has issue living, Andrea Jane *b* 1960: *m* 1991, David Paul Burton (and has issue living, Rea Louise *b* 1993), Grant Colin *b* 1962: *m* 1991, Lynda Gwenith O'Brien (and has issue living, Laura Jayne *b* 1993, Lisa Marie *b* 1969). —— (Anne) Barbara, *b* 1927: *m* 1st, 1951, Roy Alexander Andrew Ross; 2ndly, 19—, — Todd, of 14A Laurent Place, Greenmeadows, Napier, NZ, and has issue living (by 1st *m*), Judith Ann, *b* 1953: *m* 1976, Robert Chadwick Smith (c/o Lakeland Marine Ltd, Rauhato, Taupo, PO Box 827, NZ), and has issue living, Haylee Ann *b* 1980, Renee Adrienne *b* 1982, — Deborah Irene, *b* 1956: *m* 19— and has issue, — Sharon Barbara, *b* 1959: *m* 19—, and has issue, — Angela Leslie, *b* 1961: *m* 19—, and has issue.

Issue of late Walter Lonergan O'Reilly Nugent, *b* 1884, *d* 1949: *m* 1911, Amelia Bateup, who *d* 1966:—

Joan Florence, *b* 1917: *m* 1940, Donald Evelyn Fenner, and has issue living, Janet Nugent, *b* 1946: *m* 1971, Michael Cansdale, of 84 Capelands, New Ash Green, Kent DA3 8LQ, and has issue living, Andrew Richard *b* 1976, Penelope Alice *b* 1972: *m* 1998, Lee Gardham. *Residence* – 24 The Boulevard, Pevensey Bay, E Sussex BN24 6SB. —— Gwennyth Eileen Mary, *b* 1928: *m* 1949, Alfred Stokes, of 25 Victoria Rd, Mayfield, Sussex, and has issue living, Patrick John, *b* 1954: *m* 1979, Jenny Garsad, and has issue living, William Conrad *b* 1980, — Sally Ann, *b* 1950: *m* 1970, Graham White, and has issue living, Sarah Jayne *b* 1974, — Jennifer Mary, *b* 1952: *m* 1972, Malcolm Palmer, and has issue living, Aaron James *b* 1975, Paul Malcolm *b* 1978, Michelle Louise *b* 1982, — Teresa Jill, *b* 1962.

Issue of late Wilfrid Basil Nugent, *b* 1885, *d* 1976: *m* 1916, Alice Isobel, da of late Theodore Manson West:— Diana Mary Hampshire, *b* 1918.

The original surname of this Family was O'Reilly (a very ancient Irish sept). Sir Hugh O'Reilly, 1st Bt, assumed by Royal Licence 1812 the surname of Nugent on the death without issue of his maternal uncle, John Nugent of Tulloughan, Gov of Tortola and the Virgin Islands, el son of Andrew Nugent, of Dysart, co Westmeath, and Lady Catherine Nugent, yr da of Thomas, 4th Earl of Westmeath. His brother was the Austrian Field Marshal Count Andrew O'Reilly (*cr* Count of the Holy Roman Empire 1797), and their sister was created Baroness Talbot of Malahide. The 3rd baronet, Sir John Nugent, was Chamberlain to the Emperor of Austria and was created a Count of the Austrian Empire.

NUGENT (UK) 1806, of Waddesdon, Berkshire

I have decreed

Sir ROBIN GEORGE COLBORNE NUGENT, 5th *Baronet, b* 11 July 1925; *s* his father, *Capt Sir* (GEORGE) GUY BULWER, 1970; *ed* Eton; ARIBA; Lt Gren Gds 1943-48; Italy 1944-45: *m* 1st, 1947 (*m diss* 1967), Ursula Mary, da of late Lt-Gen Sir Herbert Fothergill Cooke, KCB, KBE, CSI, DSO; 2ndly, 1967, Victoria Anna Irmgard, da of late Dr Peter Cartellieri, and has issue by 1st *m*.

Arms – Ermine, two bars within a bordure engrailed gules, on a canton of the last a dagger erect proper, pommel and hilt or. Crest – A cockatrice vert, gorged with a plain collar or, pendent therefrom an escutcheon gules, charged with a dagger erect as in the arms. Supporters – Two cockatrices vert, wings endorsed, collared or, pendent therefrom a shield gules, charged with a dagger as in the arms.

SONS LIVING (*By 1st marriage*)

CHRISTOPHER GEORGE RIDLEY, *b* 5 Oct 1949; *ed* Eton and East Anglia Univ; *m* 1985, Jacqueline Vagba, and has issue living, Terence, *b* 1 March 1986, — Rufus, *b* 1987, — Benjamin, *b* 1991. —— Patrick Guy, *b* 1959.

DAUGHTER LIVING (*By 1st marriage*)

Philippa Mary, *b* 1951.

BROTHER LIVING

Jeremy Charles Clare, *b* 1936: *m* 1960, Joy, da of A. H. Waterson, and has issue living, Nigel Howard Clare, *b* 1963, — Julian Guy Bulwer, *b* 1965, — Fiona Clare, *b* 1967.

SISTER LIVING

Dinah, *b* 1922; 1942-45 War in WRNS: *m* 1950, Capt John William Huyshe Bennett, DSC, RN, of Farleigh Plain, Hinton Charterhouse, Bath, and has issue living, Timothy Nugent Huyshe, *b* 1951, — Nicholas John William, *b* 1957.

The 1st baronet, Sir George Nugent GCB, DCL, was a Field Marshal in the Army.

NUGENT (UK) 1831, of Donore, Westmeath

I have decreed

Sir PETER WALTER JAMES NUGENT, 5th *Baronet*; *b* 26 Jan 1920; *s* his father, *Sir* WALTER RICHARD, 1955; *ed* Downside; European War 1940-45 as Major Hampshire Regt: *m* 1947, Anne Judith, only da of Major Robert Smyth, of Gaybrook, Mullingar, co Westmeath, and has issue.

Arms – Ermine, two bars gules; in dexter chief a martlet azure for difference. **Crest** – A wyvern vert on the breast a martlet or.
Residence – Baybush, Straffan, co Kildare.

SONS LIVING

(WALTER) RICHARD MIDDLETON, *b* 15 Nov 1947; *ed* Downside; FCA: *m* 1985, Okabe Kayoko. —— Andrew Robert (7 Liffey Court, Clane, co Kildare), *b* 1951.

DAUGHTERS LIVING

Fiona Aileen, *b* 1949: *m* 1989, John Stuart Bellingham (*see* Bellingham, Bt colls). —— Laura Anne (46 Sister's Av, SW11 5SN), *b* 1954.

SISTERS LIVING

Heather Vivian Mary, *b* 1917: *m* 1937 (*m diss* 1950), Sir John Prichard-Jones, 2nd Bt. *Residence* – 30 Claylands Rd, SW8 1NZ. —— Gloria Aileen, *b* 1925: *m* 1946, Michael Meade Carvill, Capt Irish Guard's Reserve.

James Nugent, of Donore, was created a baronet 1768, but on the death of his brother, who succeeded by special remainder, the title became extinct. The Donore estate passed to their nephew, Thomas Fitzgerald, RN, who assumed, without Roy licence, the name of Nugent, and his son was created a baronet. Sir Walter Richard Nugent, 4th Bt, was High Sheriff of co Westmeath 1922-3, a Director and Dep Gov of Bank of Ireland, and Chm of Great Southern Railways of Ireland. He sat as MP for S Westmeath Div of co Westmeath (*N*) 1907-18, and was a Senator of Irish Free State 1928-39.

NUTTALL (UK) 1922, of Chasefield, Parish of Bowdon, co Chester

Either do not attempt, or complete

Sir NICHOLAS KEITH LILLINGTON NUTTALL, 3rd *Baronet*; *b* 21 Sept 1933; *s* his father, Lieut-Col *Sir* (EDMUND) KEITH, 1941; *ed* Eton and RMA; Maj (ret) R Horse Gds: *m* 1st, 1960 (*m diss* 1971), Rosemary Caroline, el da of late Christopher York, DL, of Long Marston Manor, York (Milner Bt); 2ndly, 1971 (*m diss* 1975), Julia Jill Beresford, da of late Col Thomas Cromwell Williamson, DSO, of Beaumont Hall, Thorpe-le-Soken, Essex, and formerly wife of Darel Sausmarez Carey; 3rdly, 1975 (*m diss* 1983), Miranda Elizabeth Louise, da of Richard St John Quarry, and formerly wife of late Peter Richard Henry Sellers, CBE, the actor; 4thly, 1983, Eugenie Marie Alicia, eldest da of William Thomas McWeeney, and has had issue by 1st, 3rd and 4th *m*.

Arms – Or, on a pile sable between in base two roses gules barbed and seeded proper, a shacklebolt of the field. **Crest** – A Dalmatian hound sejant proper, collared and chained and resting the forefoot on a shacklebolt sejant.
Address – PO Box N7776, Nassau, Bahamas. *Club* – White's.

SONS LIVING (By 1st marriage)

HARRY, *b* 2 Jan 1963: *m* 1996, Kelly Marie, only da of Anthony E. Allen, of Raleigh, N Carolina, USA. *Residence* – Flat 1, 15 Sloane Court West, SW3.

(By 4th marriage)

Nicholas Alexander David, *b* 1985.

DAUGHTERS LIVING AND DECEASED (By 1st marriage)

Tamara, *b* 1967: *m* 199—, Lorenzo Cardi, yst son of Francesco Cardi, of Rome, and *d* 1997, leaving issue, Tommaso, *b* 19—.

(By 3rd marriage)

Gytha Miranda, *b* 1975. ── Amber Louise, *b* 1976. ── Olympia Jubilee, *b* 1977.

COLLATERAL BRANCH LIVING

Issue of late Clive Nuttall, 3rd son of 1st baronet, *b* 1906, *d* 1936: *m* 1931, Eileen Daphne Elizabeth, da of late Lt-Col Horatio Douglas Russell, DSO:—
Clive Patrick, *b* 1933.

The 1st baronet, Sir Edmund, was head of the firm of Nuttall and Co, civil engineering contractors, of Trafford Park, Manchester. The 2nd baronet, Lieut-Col Sir (Edmund) Keith, was *ka* 1941.

NUTTING (UK) 1902, of St Helens, Booterstown, co Dublin

Death rather than disgrace

Sir JOHN GRENFELL NUTTING, QC, 4th *Baronet*; *b* 28 Aug 1942; *s* his father, *Rt Hon Sir* (HAROLD) ANTHONY, 1999; *ed* Eton, and McGill Univ, Canada (BA); Bar Middle Temple 1968; Bencher 1991; Recorder of the Crown Court 1988; QC 1995; Judge of the Courts of Appeal of Jersey and Guernsey 1995; Dep High Court Judge 1998; elected to Senate of Inns of Court and Bar 1978-80, 1986-87 and 1995-97; Chm of the Young Bar 1980; Junior Treasury Counsel 1981-88 (First Junior Treasury Counsel 1987-88); Senior Treasury Counsel 1988-95 (First Senior Treasury Counsel 1993-95); Memb Lord Chancellor's Advisory Cttee on Legal Educn and Conduct 1997-99: *m* 1973, Diane Patricia, OBE, da of John Rutherford Blundell, of Havant, Hants, adopted da of Capt Duncan Kirk, and widow of 2nd Earl Beatty.

Arms – Chevrony of six gules and vert three gryphons segreant or, on a chief of the last as many nut branches slipped proper. Crest – A demi gryphon segreant enclosed between two nut branches proper.
Seat – Achentoul, Kinbrace, Sutherland. *Residences* – Chicheley Hall, Newport Pagnall, Bucks MK16 9JJ; K3 Albany, Piccadilly, W1.

SON LIVING

JAMES EDWARD SEBASTIAN, *b* 12 Jan 1977.

DAUGHTER LIVING

Victoria Emily, *b* 1975.

BROTHER LIVING

David Anthony (New House, Terling, Chelmsford, Essex CM3 2JF), *b* 1944; *ed* Eton, and Trin Coll, Camb (BA); DL Essex 1988: *m* 1974, Tessa Anne, da of Lt-Col Sir Nigel John Mordaunt, 13th Bt, MBE, and has issue living, Belinda, *b* 1975, — Serena, *b* 1977, — Alexandra, *b* 1978.

SISTER LIVING

Zara Nina, *b* 1947: *m* 1966 (*m diss* 1970), Martin Guy Stephenson (V Hawarden, colls), and has issue living, Katya, *b* 1967.

MOTHER LIVING

Gillian Leonora, da of late Capt Edward Jolliffe Strutt (*see* B Rayleigh, colls): *m* 1st, 1941 (*m diss* 1959), as his 1st wife, Rt Hon (Harold) Anthony Nutting (later 3rd Baronet), who *d* 1999; 2ndly, 1961, Brig Oliver George Brooke, CBE, DSO (*see* V Brookeborough, colls, 1985 Edn), who *d* 1987. *Residence* – The Manor House, Gt Cheverell, Devizes, Wilts.

WIDOW LIVING OF THIRD BARONET

MARGARITA (*Dowager Lady Nutting*), da of late Carlos Sanchez, of Havana, Cuba: *m* 1991, as his 3rd wife, Rt Hon Sir (Harold) Anthony Nutting, 3rd Bt, who *d* 1999. *Residence* – 7 Ashchurch Park Villas, W12.

COLLATERAL BRANCH LIVING

Issue of late Capt Arthur Ronald Stansmore Nutting, OBE, MC, 3rd son of 1st baronet, *b* 1888, *d* 1964: *m* 1st, 1912 (*m diss* 1932), Edith Allen, who *d* 1953, da of Walter Brooks; 2ndly, 1932, Patricia Elizabeth (Stable Cottage, North Breache, Ewhurst, Surrey), da of Henry R. Jameson, of Drumleck, Howth, co Dublin:—

(By 2nd *m*) Peter Robert (North Breache Manor, Ewhurst, Surrey; 610 Nelson House, Dolphin Sq, SW1), *b* 1935; *ed* Eton; Late Irish Guards; past Chairman of Edward & John Burke, Ltd; J P (Inner Lond); High Sheriff Surrey 1999-2000; Financial Consultant and Dir of Companies: *m* 1965, Cecilia Hester Louise Constance, el da of Cosmo Rex Ivor Russell (*see* B Ampthill, colls), and has issue living, William Frederick, *b* 1968, — Rupert Edward, *b* 1971, — Amanda Charlotte, *b* 1966: *m* 1991, James Edward Thornton, eldest son of Michael Thornton, of Ringwood, Hants, and has issue living, Max *b* 1995, Emma *b* (triplet) 1995, Lucy *b* (triplet) 1995. —— Nicholas Ronald (Yard Farm, Ewhurst, Surrey), *b* 1937; *ed* Eton: *m* 1st, 1962, Caroline Elise Houghton, da of Brig F. W. Houghton Beckford, RA, of Vancouver, BC; 2ndly, 1977, Annette Moira, da of Percy Charles Briscoe, and has issue living (by 1st *m*), (Ann) Olivia, *b* 1963: *m* 1991, Rupert Hew Williams Barrington, and has issue (*see* Barrington, Bt, colls), — Sarah Caroline, *b* 1965: *m* 1991, Sean Eugene John Martin McDonald, elder son of John McDonald, of Ballyholland, Newry, co Down.

The 1st baronet, Sir John Gardiner Nutting, DL, was Chm of E and J Burke, Ltd, a JP and DL, and High Sheriff of co Dublin 1895-6.

OAKELEY (GB) 1790, of Shrewsbury

I fear not, but am cautious

Sir JOHN DIGBY ATHOLL OAKELEY, 8th *Baronet*; *b* 27 Nov 1932; *s* his father, *Sir* (EDWARD) ATHOLL, 1987; *ed* privately; holder of 24 World, European and National sailing titles, author of several books on sailing; Man Dir Miller and Whitworth, Freedom Yachts, Dehler Yachts UK: *m* 1958, Maureen Frances, da of late John Cox, of Hamble, Hants, and has issue.

Arms – Argent, on a fesse between three crescents gules as many fleurs-de-lis or. **Crest** – A dexter arm, embowed in armour proper charged with two fleurs-de-lis or, each in a crescent gules, in the hand a scimitar proper hilt or.
Residence – 10 Bursledon Heights, Long Lane, Bursledon, Hants.

SON LIVING

ROBERT JOHN ATHOLL, *b* 13 Aug 1963, Man Dir Rowles-Picador plc: *m* 1989, Catherine Amanda, da of late William Knowles, FRCS, and has issue living, William Robert Atholl, *b* 13 Oct 1995, — Olivia Kate, *b* 1993.

DAUGHTER LIVING

Marina Anne, *b* 1961; *ed* Southampton Univ (LLM, BA): *m* 19—, Capt Robert E. Gordon (LLM, LLB), son of late Frank Gordon, and of Mrs Pamela Davies, of Vancouver, BC, and has issue living, Conrad James, *b* 1991, — Fraser, *b* 1998, — Rebecca Elise, *b* 1993.

HALF-SISTER LIVING (*daughter of 7th baronet by 4th marriage*)

Lorna Olivia Athole, *b* 1961; RGN: *m* 1987 (*m diss* 1998), Julian Roe, and has issue living, Oliver, *b* 1993, — Claudia, *b* 1990. *Residence* – 6 Birbeck Way, Frettenham, Norwich NR12 7LG.

UNCLE LIVING (*brother of 7th baronet*)

Rowland Henry, *b* 1909; *ed* Clifton Coll, and at New Coll, Oxford (BA 1930); in Malayan Civil Ser 1931-58, Commonwealth Relations Office 1959-65, and Diplo Ser 1966-69: *m* 1940, Diana Margaret, da of late John Arthur Hayward, MD, FRCS, and has issue living, Christopher Rowland (295 Short St, Mt Helena, W Aust 6082), *b* 1941; *ed* Winchester, Trin Coll, Dublin (BA), and Univ of W Aust (MBA): *m* 1973, Margaret, da of late Gilbert Carson, of Merredin, W Aust, and has issue living, Andrew Gilbert *b* 1974, Timothy Christopher *b* 1976, Paul David *b* 1978, Caroline Rachel *b* 1981, — Henry Francis (77 Copers Cope Rd, Beckenham, Kent BR3 1NR), *b* (twin) 1941; *ed* Clifton, and St Thomas's Hosp (MB BS); FRCP (London), MRCPsych, FLS; formerly Consultant Psychiatrist St Thomas's Hosp, SE1: *m* 1968 (*m diss* 1988), Penelope Susan, LRCP, MRCS, da of Wilfred Barlow, BM, BCh, of 3 Albert Court, Kensington Gore, SW7, and has issue living, Matthew Thomas *b* 1968, Edward James *b* 1970, Rachel Mary *b* 1973, — Rosamond Margaret, *b* 1946; *ed* Walthamstow Hall, and Sheffield Univ: *m* 1969, Henry David Warriner (Broadmoor Farm, Little Wolford, Shipston-on-Stour, Warwicks), and has issue living, Michael Francis *b* 1970, Timothy David *b* 1974, Sarah Caroline *b* 1971, — Auriol Mary, *b* 1947; *ed* Walthamstow Hall, Roy Ballet Sch, and Bishop Otter Coll: *m* 1977, Peter Nicolas Chisholm, of Headmaster's House, Yehudi Menuhin School, Cobham, Surrey KT11 3QQ. *Residence* – Gowerbank, Littleworth, Chipping Campden, Glos GL55 6BB.

AUNT LIVING (*sister of 7th baronet*)

Rosemary, *b* 1903; *ed* Headington Sch, Oxford, and Evendine Court, Colwall: *m* 1940, Mervyn Cecil ffranck Sheppard, CMG, MBE, Malayan Civil Ser, who *d* 1994, and has issue living, Lavender Frances, *b* 1941: *m* 1st, 1962 (*m diss* 1981), Richard Giles Saker, Lt RN (ret); 2ndly, 1987, Francis John Buckland, of Tandlaw Steading, Hawick, Roxburghshire TD9

7NY (see E Lichfield, colls, 1990 Edn), and has issue living (by 1st m), Iain Richard Mark b 1962; ed Radley; 1st The Queen's Dragoon Gds: m 1992, Kate, da of Ian Macdonald, of Higher Hill Farm, Butleigh, Som, Robin David Mervyn b 1963; ed Radley, Emma-Rose Everilde b 1968; ed Wychwood Sch, Oxford, and Eastbourne Coll: m 1st, 1988 (m diss 1994), Joseph Jasiewicz; 2ndly 19—, Edward Ralston Johnstone (and has issue living (by 1st m), Charles Alexander Francis Beaumont b 1992, (by 2nd m), Eva Rose Elizabeth b 1997, Lorna Rosemary b 1998), Zoë Arabella Helena b 1970; ed Oxford High Sch, and Durham Univ (BA). Residence – Linden House, West Wittering, nr Chichester, Sussex PO20 8QF.

WIDOW LIVING OF SEVENTH BARONET

SHIRLEY (Shirley, Lady Oakeley) (Nomad, Lynton, Devon), da of Herbert W. Church, of 2 Northwood Rd, Tonbridge, Kent: m 1960, as his 4th wife, Sir (Edward) Atholl Oakeley, 7th Bt, who d 1987.

This family was long settled at Oakeley, Bishop's Castle, Shropshire, and Sir Charles Oakeley, 1st Bt, was Governor of Madras 1790-94. Sir Charles Richard Andrew Oakeley, 6th Bt, was Joint Managing Director of the firm of Oakeley Vaughan & Co Ltd, insurance brokers. Sir (Edward) Atholl Oakeley, 7th Bt, was European Heavy-weight Wrestling Champion 1932.

OAKES (UK) 1939, of Nassau, Bahama Islands

Through difficulties

Sir CHRISTOPHER OAKES, 3rd *Baronet*; b 10 July 1949; s his father, Sir SYDNEY, 1966: m 1978, Julie Dawn, da of Donovan Cowan, of Canada, and has issue.

𝕬rms – Or on a fesse sable between in chief an acorn slipped and leaved and in base a maple leaf proper, three maple leaves of the field. 𝕮rest – Issuant from a chaplet of roses gules a demi-lion rampant or, grasping in the dexter paw an acorn slipped and leaved proper.
Address – 4215-20 St, Vernon, BC, Canada V1T 4E2.

SON LIVING

VICTOR, b 6 March 1983.

DAUGHTER LIVING

Greta Anna Eunice, b 1979

SISTERS LIVING

Felicity, b 1952: m 1987, Steven Stuart Simpson. —— Virginia Viveca, b 1954: m 1982, Gavin Andrew McKinney, son of J. Andrew McKinney, and has issue living, Morgan Gavin, b 1983, — Sydney Analia (a da), b 1987. *Address* – PO Box 556330, Nassau, Bahamas.

UNCLE LIVING (Son of 1st baronet)

Harry Philip (PO Box N222, Nassau, Bahamas), b 1932: m 1958, Christiane, only da of Rudolf Botsch, of Hamburg, Germany, and has issue living, Harry Newell, b 1958, — Philip Gale, b 1961, — Michael Lewis, b 1966, — Bianca Eunice, b 1963.

AUNT LIVING (Daughter of 1st baronet)

Nancy VON HOYNINGEN-HUENE (PO Box N3229, 28 Queen St, Nassau, Bahamas, and Marsella 44, Mexico 6, DF Mexico), b 1925; resumed by deed poll in the Bahamas 1975 the surname of von Hoyningen-Huene: m 1st, 1942 (m annulled 1949), Alfred de Marigny; 2ndly, 1952 (m diss 1956), Baron Ernst-Lyssardt von Hoyningen-Huene; 3rdly, 1962 (m diss 1973), Patrick Claude Henry Tritton, who d 1998, and has issue living, (by 2nd m) Baron Alexander George Lyssardt, b 1955.

The 1st baronet, Sir Harry Oakes (son of William Pitt Oakes, of Sangerville, Maine, USA), was a Member of Legislative Council of Bahamas.

OAKSHOTT (UK) 1959, of Bebington, co Palatine of Chester

Hon Sir ANTHONY HENDRIE OAKSHOTT, 2nd *Baronet; b* 10 Oct 1929; *s* his father, HENDRIE DUDLEY, *Baron Oakshott* (Life Baron) and 1st Baronet, 1975; *ed* Rugby: *m* 1965 (*m diss* 1981), Valerie Anne Doreen, who *d* 1988, da of Jack Vlasto, of 2 Denbigh House, Hans Place, SW1, and formerly wife of (i) Donald John Ross, and (ii) Michael de Pret-Roose.

𝕬rms – Per chevron azure and gules in chief two arrows in saltire between as many branches of oak slipped and fructed or an in base a bear passant argent. 𝕮rest – In front of a mount vert thereon an oak tree proper fructed gold the main-stem transfixed by two arrows in fesse points to the dexter also proper a bow fessewise or.
Residence – Beckley House, Bledington, Oxfordshire OX7 6UX. *Club* – White's.

BROTHER LIVING

Hon MICHAEL ARTHUR JOHN (16 Dee Walk, Kircudbright DG6 4DR), *b* 12 April 1932; *ed* Rugby: *m* 1st, 1957, Christina Rose Methuen, who *d* 1985, da of late Thomas Banks, of Solai, Kenya; 2ndly, 1988, Mrs Helen Clare JONES, da of late Edward Ravell, of Woodhall Spa, Lincs, and has issue living (by 1st *m*), Thomas Hendrie, *b* 1959, — Charles Michael (Fares Stables Ltd, Newsells Park, Barkway, Royston, Herts), *b* 1961: *m* 1989, Anne C., da of William Stapleton, of Newry, co Down, and has issue living, Patrick Charles *b* 1996, Roseanne *b* 1990, Alice *b* 1993, — Angus Withington, *b* 1965: *m* 1998, Sarah J., da of late George McElwee, of Hamilton, NZ.

Sir Hendrie Dudley Oakshott, MBE, 2nd son of Arthur John Oakshott of Merle Dene, Bidsdon, Cheshire, was a Lord Commr of HM Treasury 1952-55, Comptroller of HM Household 1955-57, Treasurer 1957-59, and PPS to Sec of State for Foreign Affairs 1959-60, and to Chancellor of Exchequer 1961-62; MP for Bebington (*C*) 1950-64; *cr* a Baronet 1959, and Baron Oakshott, of Bebington, co Palatine of Chester (Life Baron) 1964.

O'BRIEN (UK) 1849, of Merrion Square, Dublin, and Boris-in-Ossory, Queen's County

The strong hand uppermost

Sir TIMOTHY JOHN O'BRIEN, 7th *Baronet; b* 6 July 1958; *s* his grandfather, *Sir* DAVID EDMOND, 1982; *ed* Millfield, and Univ of Hartford, Connecticut, USA.

𝕬rms – Argent, three lions passant-guardant per pale gules and azure, armed or, all within a bordure vert. 𝕮rest – From a castle argent in flames, a naked arm embowed, the hand grasping a sword, all proper.
Residence – Stable Flat, The Old Vicarage, Bishopstone, Swindon, Wilts.

BROTHER LIVING

JAMES PATRICK ARLAND, *b* 22 Dec 1964; *ed* Millfield: *m* 1992, Lianna, da of Alan Mace, and has issue living, Silas Benjamin Arland, *b* 26 Nov 1993, — Jesse John, *b* 1997. *Residence* – Bury Town Farm, Blunsdon, Swindon, Wilts SNZ 4DR.

SISTERS LIVING

Doone Victoria, *b* 1959: *m* 19—, Lincoln McMullan, and has issue living, two das. —— Melanie Frances Ann, *b* 1961: *m* 19—, Michael Hugh Duff, and has issue living, two sons.

AUNT LIVING (*Daughter of 6th baronet*)

Audrey Mary, *b* 1935: *m* 1963, Conrad Andrew Roman Dobrzynski, and has issue living, Sophia Catherine, *b* 1966: *m* 1997, Allan Hepworth, — Emma Natasha, *b* 1972. *Residence* – Ballacleator, St Judes, I of Man.

DAUGHTER LIVING OF FIFTH BARONET

Mary Clare (43 Finstock Rd, W10), *b* 1943: *m* 1st, 1961 (*m diss* 1976), John Peter James Hare; 2ndly, 1990, Frederick Edward Pearson, and has issue living (by 1st *m*), David John Brent (Iskeroon, Caherdaniel, co Kerry), *b* 1963: *m* 1995, Geraldine Burkitt, — Kerry-Jane, *b* 1966: *m* 1989, Stephen Henry Martin, son of René Martin, and has issue living, Guy Henry *b* 1997, Venetia Rose *b* 1995.

DAUGHTERS LIVING OF FOURTH BARONET

Patricia Mary Gabrielle (45 Burntwood Grange Rd, Wandsworth Common, SW18 3JY): *m* 1955 (*m diss* 1961), Walter William Burgoyne Chalwin, and has issue living, Simon William Burgoyne (77 Hendham Rd, Wandsworth, SW17 7DH), *b* 1956: *m* 1983, Teresa Mary Young, — Nicola Clare, *b* 1957: *m* 1st, 1978 (*m diss* 1981), Nicholas George Mark Seymour (*see* M Hertford colls); 2ndly, 1981, Richard Eric Champion Jones, of 37 Lower Camden, Chislehurst, Kent. —— Sheelagh Tessa Ursula: *m* 1954, Caird Wentworth Gordon Wilson, son of late Lt-Gen Sir Gordon Wilson, KCSI, CB, CBE, MC, and has issue living, Robert Caird, *b* 1955: *m* 1993, Diana Rosemary, da of David Lethbridge, of Hawkes Bay, NZ, and has issue living, Rebecca Frances *b* 1994, — Alexander Hugh Gordon, *b* 1957: *m* 1982, Susan Katharine, da of Capt H. R. C. Young, RN (ret), and has issue living, Philip Hugh Caird *b* 1984, Angus Robert Gordon *b* 1992, Miranda Frances Katharine *b* 1986. *Residence* – Ramsden Farm, Bethersden, Kent TN26 3JR. —— Shaunagh Gundrede: *m* 1972, John Nares Addinsell, who *d* 1991.

MOTHER LIVING

Sheila Winifred, only da of Sir Charles Arland Maitland Freake, 4th Bt (ext): *m* 1957, John David O'Brien, el son of 6th Bt, who *d* 1980. *Residence* – Eastrop Grange, Highworth, nr Swindon, Wilts.

COLLATERAL BRANCH LIVING

Issue of late Gerald Patrick O'Brien, yr son of 6th Bt, *b* 1930, *d* 1979: *m* 1960, Frances Huband de Savoie (30 Applegarth Rd, W14), yst da of Col William Thornton Huband Gregg, DSO, OBE, of Ballyknockane House, Clonmel, co Tipperary:—

Lyndall Jane, *b* 1961; has issue living, Daniel O'BRIEN, *b* 1986, — Jack O'BRIEN, *b* 1996. —— Lucy Frances, *b* 1964: *m* 19—, Dr Mark Sacks, and has issue living, Ben, *b* 1994, — Maya, *b* 1997. —— Rachel Shirin, *b* 1965; has issue living, Laura O'BRIEN, *b* 1986. —— Deborah Susan, *b* 1969.

This family claims to represent the powerful house of O'Brien Ara, of the line of Thomond. Sir Timothy O'Brien, son of Timothy O'Brien of co Tipperary, 1st Bt, MP for Cashel (*L*) 1846-59, was a merchant of Dublin who took a leading part in the reform of its Corporation and contributed largely to the redemption of the Municipal property. He was Lord Mayor of Dublin 1844 and again 1849, being specially elected to receive Her Majesty on her first visiting Ireland, on which occasion he was created a baronet. Sir Patrick, 2nd Bt, sat as MP for King's co (*L*) 1852-85. Sir Timothy Carew, 3rd Bt, was a DL and JP of co Cork, and served in 1914-18 War as Capt R Irish Fusiliers, and as Maj Remount Ser (despatches).

O'CONNELL (UK) 1869, of Lakeview, Killarney, co Kerry, and of Ballybeggan, Tralee, co Kerry

Reason and strength

Sir MAURICE JAMES DONAGH MacCARTHY O'CONNELL, 7th *Baronet*; *b* 10 June 1958; *s* his father, *Sir* MORGAN DONAL CONAIL, 1989; *ed* Ampleforth: *m* 1993, Francesca Susan, only da of Clive Raleigh, of Hong Kong.

𝔄rms – Per fesse argent and vert, a stag trippant proper between three trefoils slipped counterchanged. 𝔠rest - A stag's head erased argent, charged with trefoil slipped vert (Ulster Office 1667).
Residence - Lakeview House, Killarney, Co Kerry.

BROTHER LIVING

JOHN MORGAN ROSS MacCARTHY, *b* 17 April 1960; *ed* Ampleforth, Regents Park Coll, Oxford (MA), and Guildhall Sch of Music (AGSM).

SISTERS LIVING

Frances Mary Margaret MacCarthy, *b* 1954: *m* 1986, Roy W. Telling, of The Old Forge, Upton, nr Didcot, Oxon, only son of late W. Telling, of Wolverhampton, and has issue living, Ross Morgan William, *b* 1989. —— Susan Jane Anne, *b* 1956: *m* 1993, Julian R. Glasgow, yr son of Dr James Glasgow, of Rockland St Mary, Norwich. —— Katherine Lucila Jean, *b* 1964. —— Claire Helen Pauline, *b* 1969.

AUNT LIVING (*Daughter of 5th baronet*)

Joan Mary Lucilla Margaret, *b* 1926; formerly 3rd Officer WRNS: *m* 1953, Lieut-Com John Allen Victor Hickley, RN (ret), of Birchdale, RD10, Waimate, S Canterbury, NZ, and has issue living, Martin Maurice Victor, *b* 1957: *m* 1984, Robyn Myrie, eldest da of Douglas Williams Jenkins, of Mosgiel, NZ, and has issue living, Cameron Douglas Victor *b* 1988, Patrick Joseph Victor *b* 1991, Joanna Louise *b* 1985, — Grania Margaret Leslie, *b* 1959.

WIDOW LIVING OF SIXTH BARONET

ELIZABETH (*Elizabeth, Lady O'Connell*), only child of late Maj John MacCarthy-O'Leary, of Lavenders, West Malling, Kent: *m* 1953, Sir Morgan Donal Conail O'Connel, 6th Bt, who *d* 1989. *Residence* - Lakeview House, Killarney, co Kerry.

COLLATERAL BRANCH LIVING

Issue of late Basil Morgan O'Connell, KPM, yst son of 4th baronet, *b* 1900, *d* 1971: *m* 1st, 1935, Lucila, who *d* 1953, da of Maj Henry Hugh Peter Deasy, of Cnoc Na Faire, Carrigahorig, Eire; 2ndly, 1962, Georgia Bard Shearer (Box 131, Solebury, Pa 18963, USA), widow of Mortimer Haldeman O'Connor:—
(By 1st *m*) Maurice Hugh Ricardo Ross (12 Rostrevor Rd, Dublin 6), *b* 1936; *ed* Ampleforth, Peterhouse, Camb (MA) and Trin Coll, Dublin (MEd, HDip Ed); NUI (Dip Cat) a Member of Dublin City Council 1967-74; Seanad Eireann 1981-83, Nat Exec, Fine Gael Party; Replacement Candidate, European Parl Elections, Dublin 1984: *m* 1961, Ann, el da of Hugh Gillespie, of the Old Rectory, Kiltegan, Baltinglass, co Wicklow, and has issue living, Carlos Donal John, *b* 1963; Irish Junior Decathlon Champion, — Morgan Basil Peter, *b* 1965, — Maurice William Hugh Rickard, *b* 1966, — Ross Paul Francis, *b* 1968, — Lucila Marie Valdemara Georgia, *b* 1962, — Sarah Emily, *b* 1973. —— Seamus Morgan Basil Ross, *b* 1941; *ed* Ampleforth, and Trin Coll, Dublin (BA).

The 1st baronet was the yst and last surviving brother of Daniel O'Connell, QC, MP, of Darrinane Abbey, Senior Representative of the ancient Irish sept of O'Connell, and nephew of Lieut-Gen Count Daniel O'Connell of the French Service by whose efforts the officers of the disbanded French Irish Brig enrolled in the Service of King George III in 1794.

OGILVY (NS) 1626, of Inverquharity, Forfarshire

I despise earthly dangers

Sir FRANCIS GILBERT ARTHUR OGILVY, 14th *Baronet*; *b* 22 April 1969; *s* his father, *Sir* DAVID JOHN WILFRID, 1992; *ed* Glenalmond, and RAC Cirencester (BSc): *m* 1996, Dorothy Margaret, eldest da of Rev Jock Stein, of Carberry Tower, Midlothian, and has issue.

𝕬rms – Quarterly: 1st and 4th, argent, a lion passant-guardant gules, gorged with an open crown, and crowned with a close imperial one or, *Ogilvy*; 2nd and 3rd, argent, an eagle displayed sable, beaked and membered gules, *Ramsay of Auchterhouse*. 𝕮rest – A demi-lion gules. 𝕾upporters – Two wild men wreathed about the head and temples with leaves, trampling upon serpents, and holding branches in their exterior hands all proper.
Seat – Winton House, Pencaitland, East Lothian. *Residence* – Winton House, Pencaitland, East Lothian EH34 5AT.

SON LIVING

ROBERT DAVID, *b* 8 July 1999.

AUNTS LIVING (*Sisters of 13th baronet*)

Katharine Olivia Mary, *b* 1916: *m* 1947, William Packe, of Low Wood, Winthorpe, Newark, Notts, son of Charles James Melville Packe, of Rothley, Leics, and has issue living, Thomas Gilbert (East Philipstoun Farmhouse, Linlithgow, W Lothian EH49 7RY), *b* 1948; *ed* Gordonstoun, and RAC Cirencester: *m* 1994, Sally Margaret, yr da of late Maj John Basil Ready, — Andrew James (The Steward's House, Bledington, Oxford OX7 6UZ), *b* 1951; *ed* Radley, and RAC Cirencester: *m* 1981, Aloÿse Anne, only da of Christopher James Morrell Blackie, and has issue living, Frederick Christopher William *b* 1987, James Anthony Charles *b* 1999, Olivia Aloÿse Hester *b* 1984, Katherine Amelia Caroline *b* (twin) 1999. —— Hester Mary, *b* 1921; *ed* Edinburgh Univ (MA), and Oxford Univ (BA): *m* 1951, David Scott of Glenaros, who *d* 1996, of Glenaros, Aros, Isle of Mull, elder son of late Sir Basil Scott, former Chief Justice of Bombay, and has issue living, Colum Basil, *b* 1954; *ed* Stowe, and RAC Cirencester: *m* 1992, Sarah Louise, yr da of Michael Charles Watson Credland, and has issue living, Angus Michael David *b* 1993, Robin Francis William *b* 1994, Emily Louise *b* 1996, — Margaret Isobel, *b* 1952: *m* 1991, Brian Simons, and has issue living, Jamie Mark *b* 1987, Samuel Isaac Michael *b* 1992, — Christian Mary Gertrude, *b* 1955: *m* 1984, Anthony Latham, son of Leslie Latham, and has issue living, Andrew David *b* 1987, Brendan Michael *b* 1994, Helen *b* 1986, Mairi Isobel *b* 1992, — Helen Olivia Katharine, *b* 1958: *m* 19—, Alistair Danter, son of John Danter, and has issue living, Fiona Marie Josée Scott *b* 1993, Molly Katherine Scott *b* 1996, Tara Jeannine Scott *b* 1998.

WIDOW LIVING OF THIRTEENTH BARONET

PENELOPE MARY URSULA (*Penelope, Lady Ogilvy*), only da of late Capt Arthur Lafone Frank Hills, OBE, of White Court, Penshurst Station, Kent: *m* 1966, Sir David John Wilfrid Ogilvy, 13th Bt, who *d* 1992. *Residence* – Winton Cottage, Pencaitland, East Lothian EH34 5AT.

COLLATERAL BRANCHES LIVING

Issue of late Lt Cmdr John Augustine Ogilvy, RN, brother of 13th baronet and yr son of late Gilbert Francis Molyneux Ogilvy, JP, yst son of 10th baronet, *b* 1915, *d* 1993: *m* 1942, Margaret Vivienne

Lyndall (Old North Manse, E Linton, E Lothian), eldest da of late Col William Thornton Huband Gregg, DSO, OBE, late Royal Irish Fus, of Ballynockane House, co Tipperary:—
†Angus William, *b* 1945; *ed* Eton, and Stirling Univ (BA Hons): *m* 1st, 1968 (*m diss* 1980), Sally, da of Michael Long; 2ndly, 1980, Helen (6 Queen's Rd, King Park, Stirling FK8 2QY), da of John Dudley Massingham, CMG, of Pershore, Worcs, and *d* 1989, leaving issue, (by 1st *m*) Andrew John, *b* 1972, — Robert Iain Michael, *b* 1974, — (by 2nd *m*) James Angus John, *b* 1982, — Thomas Alasdair William, *b* 1984. —— Diana Lyndall, *b* 1946.

Grandchildren of late Walter Tulliedeph Ogilvy (*b* 1852) (infra):—
Issue of late Angus Edward Ogilvy, *b* 1880, *d* 1928; *m* 1910, Margaret, who *d* 1956, da of Lieut-Col Sir James Frederick Stuart-Menteth, 4th Bt, of Rownhams Mount, near Southampton:—
†Walter Tulliedeph, *b* 1911: *m* 1st, 1947, Christina Alexandra Sutherland, who *d* 1949, da of A. Polson, of Spinningdale, Sutherland; 2ndly, 1950, Audrey Kingsley, da of A. G. Weeks, of Limpsfield, Surrey, and *d* 1987, leaving issue, (by 2nd *m*) Fiona Audrey, *b* 1952: *m* 1974 (*m diss* 1980), Christopher Cook, and has issue living, Nicola Jane *b* 1975, Claire Annabel *b* 1977, — Susan Margaret, *b* 1955: *m* 1974 (*m diss* 1978), John Pelly. *Residence* – Rosemary Cottage, Buxted, Sussex.

Issue of late Brigadier David Ogilvy, CIE, DSO, OBE, *b* 1881, *d* 1949: *m* 1906, Vere Grace, da of late Sir Henry Fawcett, KCMG, Ch Justice of the Levant.—
Vere Edith OGILVY, *b* 1912; resumed by deed poll 1955 the surname of Ogilvy: *m* 1932, Lt-Col Charles Herbert Harberton Eales, MC, Indian Cav, who *d* 1941, and has issue living, John David OGILVY, *b* 1934; assumed by deed poll 1955 the surname of Ogilvy in lieu of his patronymic; *ed* Wellington Coll; Lt-Cdr RN (ret): *m* 1958, Felicity Neilson, da of late Maj Hugh Jack Melville, of Wendover, Bucks, and has issue living, David Guy Francis Melville *b* 1960, Alasdair James Eales (Battlehurst, Kirdford, W Sussex) *b* 1961: *m* 1989, Fleur S. C., da of Ian Vergin Brooke, of The Quell, Blackdown, W Sussex (and has issue living, Flora Alexandra Claire *b* 1992, Tara Clementine Alice *b* 1994), — Mary Ann Vere, *b* 1935: *m* 1st, 1957 (*m diss* 1973), Maj Charles Pepler Norton, who *d* 1994; 2ndly, 1980, Capt James Quintin Penn Curzon (*see* E Howe, colls), who *d* 1985; 3rdly, 1987, as his 2nd wife, Maj John David Makgill-Crichton-Maitland (*see* E Lauderdale, colls), and has issue living, (by 1st *m*) Anthony Charles Pepler *b* 1958: *m* 19—, S. C. Jane, only da of Dr Keith Haward Bywater, of Haward House, Old Rd, Ruddington, Notts (and has issue living, Edward James Pepler *b* 1987), Julian Alexander Pepler *b* 1959, Marina Caroline Vere *b* 1961: *m* 1985, Capt James Farquhar Robin Campbell, late The Queen's Own Highlanders (*see* E Cawdor, colls), Josephine Sarah Vere *b* 1964.

Issue of late Lieut-Col Gilbert Mark Haworth Ogilvy, King's Own Scottish Borderers, *b* 1887, *d* on active ser 1945: *m* 1915, Mildred Scott, who *d* 1925:—
Mildred Cecil, *b* 1916: *m* 1944, Lieut Thomas Duerdin-Dutton, RNVR.

Granddaughter of late David Ogilvy, son of late Alexander Ogilvy, 6th son of 5th baronet:—
Issue of late Walter Tulliedeph Ogilvy, *b* 1852, *d* 1927: *m* 1st, 1878, Eleanor May Edith Lumley, who *d* 1902, da of late Edward Lumley Haworth, 28th Regt; 2ndly, 1903, Winifred, who *d* 1909, da of Rev Henry Edward Maskew; 3rdly, 1910, Christina, who *d* 1956, da of Col Bannatyne Macleod, formerly Bombay Artillery:—
(By 2nd *m*) Earna, *b* (twin) 1909: *m* 1931, W. J. Forrester, who *d* 1975, and has issue living, David Alton (18 Shasta Rd, Lesmurdie, W Aust), *b* 1932; *ed* Camb Univ (MA, LLM, ACIS); Barrister: *m* 1959, Fay Garner, who *d* 1979, and has issue living, Richard Alton *b* 1961, Susan May *b* 1965, — Thelma *b* 1934: *m* 1960, Neil Pearson, of Box BE46, Belvedere, Harare, Zimbabwe, and has issue living, Lesley Dawn *b* 1961, Janette Nancy *b* 1962. *Residence* – c/o 18 Shasta Rd, Lesmurdie, W Aust.

Sir John Ogilvy was created a Baronet with remainder to heirs male whatsoever. The 2nd baronet was MP for Angus 1665-78. The 5th baronet sold the estate of Inverquharity, which had been in the family for fourteen generations. Sir John, 9th Bt, sat as MP for Dundee (*L*) 1857-74. The 11th baronet Sir Gilchrist Nevill, Lieut Scots Guards, was killed in action during European War Oct 1914.

Ogilvy-Wedderburn, see Wedderburn.

OHLSON (UK) 1920, of Scarborough, North Riding of co of Yorkshire

Alteri · Si · tibi

Do to others as thyself

Sir BRIAN ERIC CHRISTOPHER OHLSON, 3rd *Baronet*; *b* 27 July 1936; *s* his father, Sir ERIC JAMES, 1983; *ed* Harrow, and RMA; late Lieut Coldstream Gds; money broker (ret).

Arms – Argent, in waves of the sea a steamer proper, on a chief azure three fir trees eradicated also proper. **Crest** – In front of a sun in splendour proper, a motor wheel sable.
Residence – 1 Courtfield Gdns, SW5 0PA. *Clubs* – Hurlingham, MCC, and Cavalry and Guards'.

BROTHER LIVING

PETER MICHAEL, *b* 18 May 1939; *ed* Harrow, and Trin Coll, Camb (BA): *m* 1968, Sarah, only da of Maj-Gen Thomas Brodie, CB, CBE, DSO. *Residence* – 33 The Avenue, Kew, Surrey TW9 2AL.

SISTER LIVING

Christine Rose, *b* 1950.

WIDOW LIVING OF SECOND BARONET

MARJORIE JOAN (*Lady Ohlson*), 2nd da of late Charles Henry Roosmale-Cocq, of Dorking, Surrey: *m* 1935, Sir Eric James Ohlson, 2nd Bt, who *d* 1983. *Residence* – 15 Kathleen Godfree Court, Queens Rd, Wimbledon, SW19 8LB.

COLLATERAL BRANCH LIVING

Issue of late Gerald Thomas Ohlson, 2nd son of 1st baronet, *b* 1917, *d* 1971: *m* 1943, Marjorie Beryl, da of Trevor Davies:—
Christopher Mark, *b* 1944.

The first baronet, Sir Erik Olof Ohlson (who had been knighted in 1915), son of Anders Ohlson, of Fellingsbro, Sweden, was a shipowner, a coal and coke exporter, and a timber importer, of Hull.

WALKER-OKEOVER (UK) 1886, of Gateacre Grange, co Lancaster, and Osmaston Manor, co Derby

ESTO · VIGILANS

Sir PETER RALPH LEOPOLD WALKER-OKEOVER, 4th *Baronet*; *b* 22 July 1947; *s* his father, *Lt-Col Sir* IAN PETER ANDREW MONRO, DSO, TD, 1982; *ed* Eton, and RMA Sandhurst; Capt Blues and Royals; DL Staffs 1992; patron of one living: *m* 1st, 1972 (*m diss* 1991), Catherine Mary Maule, el da of Col George Patrick Maule Ramsay (*see* Dalhousie, colls); 2ndly, 1993, Patricia Margaret, eldest da of Laurence Berry Sanderson, and has issue by 1st *m*.

Arms – Quarterly, 1st and 4th, ermine, on a chief gules three bezants, *Okeover*; 2nd and 3rd or, three pallets gules surmounted of a saltire argent charged with a stag's head erased proper on a chief azure a garb between two stars of six points of the first, *Walker*. **Crests** – 1st, an oak tree eradicated proper fructed or mantled gules doubled argent; 2nd, out of a ducal coronet or a dragon ermine armed azure langued gules, mantled gules doubled argent, both *Okeover*; 3rd, a cornucopia proper, *Walker*.
Seats – Okeover Hall, Ashbourne, Derbyshire; House of Glenmuick, Ballater, Aberdeenshire.

SONS LIVING (By 1st marriage)

ANDREW PETER MONRO, *b* 22 May 1978. —— (Patrick) Ralph, *b* 1982.

DAUGHTER LIVING (By 1st marriage)

Georgina Elizabeth, *b* 1976.

SISTERS LIVING

Elizabeth Anne, *b* 1940: *m* 1969, Lt-Cdr Timothy William Clowes, RN (ret), and has issue living, Catriona Helen, *b* 1971, — Sophie Fiona, *b* 1974. —— Jane Katharine, *b* 1942; Extra Woman of the Bedchamber to HM Queen Elizabeth the Queen Mother since 19—.

WIDOW LIVING OF THIRD BARONET

DOROTHY ELIZABETH (*Elizabeth, Lady Walker-Okeover*) (Park Cottage, Osmaston, Ashbourne, Derbyshire DE6 1LT), da of late Josceline Reginald Heber Percy (*see* D Northumberland, colls): *m* 1938, Lt-Col Sir Ian Peter Andrew Monro Walker-Okeover, 3rd Bt, DSO, TD, who *d* 1982.

COLLATERAL BRANCHES LIVING

Granddaughter of late Col John Reid WALKER, TD, 2nd son of 1st baronet:—
Issue of late Capt Codrington Gwynne Reid Walker, *b* 1895, *d* 1963: *m* 1921, Gwendoline Phyllis, who *d* 1974, da of late James Munro Walker (infra):—
Jean, *b* 1922; WRNS 1942-45: *m* 1949, Nicholas Knoop, BSc(Eng), FICE, of Ville ès Normans, Trinity, Jersey, CI, and has issue living, Alexander Jonathan, *b* 1951: *m* 1988, Cheryl Magundi (*née* George) (medaille d'or, piano), da of Achilles George, of Long Island, NY, — Sandra, *b* 1950: *m* 1973, Jean-Paul Vonrospach, of 11 Rue des Etats, 54000 Nancy, France, and has issue living, Alexander Kerry *b* 1982, Melany Claire *b* 1980.

Granddaughter of Capt Codrington Gwynne Reid WALKER (ante):—
Issue of late Giles Reid Walker, *b* 1925, *d* 1951: *m* 1949, Catherine Elaine (who *m* 2ndly, 1955, Patrick Campbell Hall, of Cae Grugog, Trearddur Bay, Holyhead, Anglesey), da of late Maj Charles Edward Hickman (*see* Hickman, Bt, colls):—
Gilean Phyllis (*posthumous*), *b* 1951.

The 1st baronet, Sir Andrew Barclay Walker (son of Peter Walker, of Auchinflower, near Ballantrae, co Ayr, and Warrington, co Lancaster), was Mayor of Liverpool 1873-4, and 1876-7 and High Sheriff of Lancashire 1886, and made many munificent gifts to the City of Liverpool. The 2nd baronet, Lt-Col Sir Peter Carlaw Walker, TD: *m* 1899, Ethel Blanche, sister and co-heir of Haughton Ealdred Okeover, MVO, of Okeover, Staffs, descended from Orme de Okeover living 1138. The 3rd baronet, Sir Ian Peter Andrew Monro Walker-Okeover, assumed by Roy Licence 1956 the additional surname of Okeover after his patronymic, and the Arms of Okeover quarterly with those of Walker.

O'LOGHLEN (UK) 1838, of Drumconora, Ennis
(Name pronounced "O'lochlen")

The anchor of safety

Sir COLMAN MICHAEL O'LOGHLEN, LLB, 6th *Baronet*, son of late Henry Ross O'Loghlen, 6th son of 3rd baronet; *b* 6 April 1916; *s* his uncle, *Sir* CHARLES HUGH ROSS, 1951; *ed* Xavier Coll, Melbourne, and Melbourne Univ; is a Stipendiary Magistrate, Lae, Territory of New Guinea, and late Capt Australian Imperial Force; was Acting Judge of Supreme Court of Territory of Papua and New Guinea May to Aug 1957: *m* 1939, Margaret, da of Francis O'Halloran, of Melbourne, Australia, and has issue.

ᴀrms – Gules, a man in armour in the act of shooting an arrow from a longbow towards the sinister, all proper. Crest – On a ducal coronet or, an anchor erect entwined with a cable, all proper.
Residence – Ellengrove, Queensland 4077, Australia.

SONS LIVING

MICHAEL, *b* 21 May 1945. —— Bryan, *b* 1946. —— Ross, *b* 1948. —— Hugh, *b* 1952.

DAUGHTERS LIVING

Margaret, *b* 1940. —— Janet, *b* 1942.

SISTERS LIVING

Ella Allison: *m* 1944, John Cardiff O'Connell, Flying Officer Roy Australian Air Force, and has issue living, Ross John *b* 1945. —— Doreen Sinclair.

AUNTS LIVING (*Daughters of 3rd baronet*)

Ella Maude: *m* 1922, George Herbert Williams, who *d* 1957, son of late Hon Sir Hartley Williams. —— Frances Mary; a nun. —— Clare Mary.

MOTHER LIVING

Doris Irene, da of late Percival Horne, RA: *m* 1912, Henry Ross O'Loghlen (ante), who *d* 1944. *Residence* – Melbourne, Australia.

COLLATERAL BRANCHES LIVING

Issue of late Bryan James O'Loghlen, 4th son of 3rd baronet, *b* 1875, *d* 1920: *m* 1909, Violet Elizabeth Amelia, who *d* 1951, da of late Daniel Grant, of Bendigo, Australia:—
Elizabeth: *m* 1944, Fl-Lt Ian Cutler, RAAF, and has issue living, Elizabeth Ann, *b* 1945, — Felicity Margaret, *b* 1948.

Granddaughter of late Henry Ross O'Loghlen, 6th son of 3rd baronet:—
Issue of late Ross Bryan O'Loghlen, Flying Officer Roy Australian Air Force, *b* 1914, presumed *d* (as a prisoner in Japanese hands) 1944: *m* 1941, Phyllis, da of George Nason, of Horsham, Victoria, Australia:—
Susan Anne, *b* 1943.

The 1st baronet, Right Hon Sir Michael, a distinguished lawyer, was MP for Dungarvan (*L*) 1835-6, a Baron of the Exchequer in Ireland 1836-7, and Master of the Rolls there 1837-42. He was the first Roman Catholic who, since the Revolution of 1688, was raised to a judicial office either in England or Ireland. The 2nd baronet was a Privy Councillor, and MP for co Clare (*L*) 1863-77. The 3rd baronet was Attorney-Gen of Victoria (Australia) 1878-81, Premier thereof 1881-3, and again Attorney-Gen 1893-4, and sat as MP for co Clare (HR) 1877-9. The 4th baronet was HM's Lieut for co Clare.

ONSLOW (GB) 1797, of Althain, Lancashire

Forward with caution

Sir JOHN ROGER WILMOT ONSLOW, 8th *Baronet*; *b* 21 July 1932; *s* his father, *Sir* RICHARD WILMOT, TD, 1963; *ed* Cheltenham: *m* 1st, 1955 (*m diss* 1973), Catherine Zoia, da of Henry Atherton Greenway, of The Manor, Compton Abdale, nr Cheltenham; 2ndly, 1976, Susan Fay, who *d* 1998, 2nd da of E. M. Hughes, of Frankston, Vic, Aust, and has issue by 1st *m*.

𝕬rms – Argent, a fesse gules between six Cornish choughs proper. 𝕮rest – An eagle sable preying upon a partridge or. 𝕾econd 𝕸otto – 'Semper fidelis' (*Always faithful*).
Residence – 85 Leila Rd, Ormond, Vic 3163, Australia. *Club* – Nautico (Majorca).

SON LIVING (*By 1st marriage*)

RICHARD PAUL ATHERTON, *b* 16 Sept 1958.

DAUGHTER LIVING (*By 1st marriage*)

Joanna Elizabeth, *b* 1956.

SISTERS LIVING

Tessa Elizabeth, *b* 1930: *m* 1st, 1953 (*m diss* 1964), John Leonard Hargrave; 2ndly, 1969, John Vernon Mossman, and has issue living (by 1st *m*), Belinda Anne Constance, *b* 1955, — Jane, *b* 1956. ——— Jill Angela, *b* 1941: *m* 1962, Patrick E. Lavin, of Casilla 14220, Santiago 15, Chile, and has issue living, Sean Paul, *b* 1967, — Christopher Patrick, *b* 1970, — Cecily Ann, *b* 1965. ——— Sally Constance, *b* 1946.

AUNT LIVING (*Daughter of 6th baronet*)

Ursula Joan, *b* 1916: *m* 1948, John Archibald Harris and has issue living, Robert James Onslow, *b* 1952, — Geoffrey Archibald Onslow, *b* 1954, — Richard Charles Onslow, *b* 1958. *Residence* –

COLLATERAL BRANCHES LIVING

Issue of late John Vernon Onslow, yr son of 6th baronet, *b* 1919, *d* 1985; *m* 1946, Anne Broun (Luckington Manor Stables, Luckington, Chippenham, Wilt), da of Gavin Hutchison:—
Charlotte Anne Mildred, *b* 1947: *m* 1974, Charles E. Wilkinson, of The Coach House, Sutton Benger, Chippenham, Wilts, and has issue living, James Maurice, *b* 1975, — John Charles, *b* 1977, — Anne Nora, *b* 1980. ——— Victoria Joy Nora, *b* 1950: *m* 1972, (Lionel) Jeffrey Lippiatt, of Manor Farm, Alderton, Chippenham, Wilts, and has issue living, Miranda Kate, *b* 1978, — Emma Suzanna, *b* 1982.

Grandchildren of late Rev Matthew Richard Septimus Onslow, 4th son of 4th baronet:—

Issue of late Capt Richard Francis John Onslow, MVO, DSC, RN, *b* 1896, *ka* 1942: *m* 1st, 1920, Sylvia Rachel, who *d* 1933, da of Rev Alfred Edward Green-Price, V of Norton, Radnorshire (Green-Price, Bt); 2ndly, 1939, Jessie Violet Betty (CStJ) (who *d* 1993, having *m* 2ndly, 1951 (*m diss* 1956), Major Arthur Christopher John Congreve, who *d* 1992), da of late Brig-Gen Reynold Alexander Gillam, CMG, DSO:—
(By 1st *m*) Anthea Mary, *b* 1925; formerly in WRNS: *m* 1947, Lt-Col Edward Courtenay Phillips, MC, JP, DL, 60th Rifles, of Chase House, Monnington-on-Wye, Herefordshire, and has issue living, Sarah Angela Josephine, *b* 1948: *m* 1968, Robert Anthony Corbett, of Newchurch Farm, Kinnersley, Hereford, and has issue living, Benjamin *b* 1969, Thomas R. *b* 1971: *m* 1996, Sarah F., yr da of John Moore, of Sawbridgeworth, Herts, Hannah *b* 1977, — Harriet Anne Jennifer, *b* 1953: *m* 1977, Maj Peter Edward Cheney, MBE, WG (ret), and has issue living, Joss Edward *b* 1990, Melita Clare *b* 1982, Theodora May *b* 1983, Lettice Rose *b* 1986.

Issue of late Herbert Frank Onslow, *b* 1899, *d* 1970: *m* 1934, Hon Lena Barbara Joan Ogilvie-Grant, who *d* 1981, da of 4th Baron Strathspey:—
Roger Cranley Seafield (7 Links View, Baunton Lane, Cirencester, Glos), *b* 1934; *ed* Christ's Hosp: *m* 1959, Eileen Margaret, da of late J. A. J. Barnard, of The Borough, Crondall, Hants, and has issue living, Susan Helen, *b* 1965: *m* 1990, Philip Tattersall, — Clare Louise, *b* 1967: *m* 1988, Alan Robert Smith, and has issue living, Holly Iris *b* 1988.

Granddaughters of late Capt Richard Francis John Onslow, MVO, DSC, RN (ante):—
Issue of late Capt Richard Thomas Onslow, RM, *b* 1922; *d* 1983: *m* 1947, Gillian Doriel (Westend House, Hambledon, Hants P07 6TB), el da of Edward Clemson, of Gaston House, E Bergholt, Suffolk:—
(Sylvia) Jane, *b* 1951. —— Geraldine Victoria, *b* 1954: *m* 1987, Nicholas Mark Keith, of 16 St John's Hill Grove, SW11 2RG, son of late J. R. Keith, and has issue living, William Richard, *b* 1977, — Hebe, *b* 1990.

Granddaughter of late Brig-Gen Cranley Charlton Onslow, CB, CMG, CBE, DSO (infra):—
Issue of late Lt-Cdr Denzil Richard Cranley Onslow, RNR, *b* 1909, *d* 1973: *m* 1940, Bernadine, who *d* 1976, da of David Blackburn:—
Judith Marylyn, *b* 1946: *m* 1970, George Sheffield Kinnear, of 3 Abbots Way, Hartford, Northwich, Ches, and has issue living, James Onslow Glyn, *b* 1986, — Amanda Jane, *b* 1971, — Felicity Esther Helen, *b* 1975.

Granddaughters of late Hamilton Cranley Onslow, el son of late Thomas Onslow, 3rd son of 2nd baronet:—
Issue of late Brig-Gen Cranley Charlton Onslow, CB, CMG, CBE, DSO, *b* 1869, *d* 1940: *m* 1904, Sydney Alice Hastings, who *d* 1962, da of late Surg-Gen Sir Benjamin Franklin, KCIE:—
Margaret Vivien, *b* 1918: *m* 1943, Johnston McDowell, of The Old Quaker House, Milverton, Som, and has issue living, Hugh Geoffrey, *b* 1947; *ed* Swansea Univ: *m* 1976, Merle Argosino, and has issue living, Peter Johnston *b* 1980, — Brian Johnston (Barnsfield, Blundell Rd, Tiverton, Devon EX16 4NB), *b* 1954: *ed* Haberdashers' Aske's: *m* 1980, Diana Stella Carr, and has issue living, Harry Cranley Onslow *b* 1989, Hugh Donald Johnston *b* 1992, Sarah Frances *b* 1981, Emily Jane *b* 1983, — Jane Maureen, *b* 1944: *m* 1966, Norman Roberts, of 169 Belswaine Lane, Hemel Hempstead, Herts HP3 9XF, and has issue living, John Michael *b* 1971: *m* 1997, Mandy Haydon (and has issue living, Hannah Jane *b* 1999, Kira Louise *b* (twin) 1999), Andrew David *b* 1972, — Fiona Margaret, *b* 1961. —— Jocelyn Anne Sydney (4 Chapel Close, Castle Cary, Som BA7 7AX), *b* 1922: *m* 1953, Cdr Leonard Charles Sutton Sheppard, OBE, RN (rct), who *d* 1992.

Granddaughter of late Lt-Col Arthur Walton Onslow, 4th son of 2nd baronet:—
Issue of late Lieut-Col Richard Cranley Onslow, Indian Army, *b* 1857, *d* 1934: *m* 1883, Edith Margaretta, who *d* 1934, da of Francis Beer:—
Alice Mary (Fairfield Hotel, Aliwal Rd, Wynberg, Cape Town, S Africa): *m* 1914, Capt Francis Richard Savage, formerly Cheshire Regt, who *d* 1960, and has issue living, Gerald Onslow, *b* 1916; Maj late Queen's Roy Regt.

This family is descended from Lieut Gen Richard Onslow, nephew of 1st Baron Onslow, and uncle of the 1st Earl of Onslow, and is in special remainder to the Barony of Onslow (*see* E Onslow, colls). The 1st baronet, Admiral Sir Richard Onslow, GCB, and General of Marines, was second in command at Camperdown, and was created a baronet for distinguished services at that battle.

OPPENHEIMER (UK) 1921, of Stoke Poges, co Bucks

Sir MICHAEL BERNARD GRENVILLE OPPENHEIMER, 3rd *Baronet*; *b* 27 May 1924; *s* his father, *Sir* MICHAEL, 1933; *ed* Charterhouse, and Ch Ch, Oxford (MA 1952, B Litt 1955); late Lieut S African Artillery: *m* 1947, (Laetitia) Helen, BPhil, MA, DD, da of Lieut-Col Sir Hugh Vere Huntley Duff Munro-Lucas-Tooth, 1st Bt (*cr* 1920), and has issue.

Arms – Azure, two swords in saltire proper, pommeled and hilted or, between two lions passant of the last. **Crest** – A demi-koodoo proper, resting the sinister hoof on a rose gules, barbed and seeded proper.
Residence – L'Aiguillon, Rue des Cotils, Grouville, Jersey JE3 9AP. *Clubs* – Kimberley (S Africa), Victoria (Jersey).

DAUGHTERS LIVING

Henrietta Laetitia Grenville, *b* 1954: *m* 1978, Adam Lawrence Scott, and has issue living, Patrick Aaron, *b* 1986, — Eleanor Rose, *b* 1989. —— Matilda Magdalen Grenville, *b* 1956: *m* 1978, Neil G. A. King, and has issue living, Dorothy Xanthe, *b* 1987, — Hannah Magdalen, *b* 1988, — Elsa Mary, *b* 1990, — Lily Alexandra, *b* 1993. ——Xanthe Jennifer Grenville (*Hon Mrs Ivo A. R. Mosley*), *b* 1958: *m* 1977, Hon Ivo Adam Rex Mosley, and has issue (*see* B Ravensdale).

AUNT LIVING (*Daughter of 1st baronet*)

Madeleine Hilda (*Baroness Devlin*), *b* 1909; formerly a JP for Wilts: *m* 1932, Baron Devlin, a Lord of Appeal in Ordinary (Life Baron), who *d* 1992. *Residence* – West Wick House, Pewsey, Wilts.

In adversity undismayed

Sir Bernard Oppenheimer, 1st Bt (son of Edward Oppenheimer), was Chm of S African Diamond Corporation, Ltd, and the New Vaal River Diamond and Exploration Co. In 1917 he inaugurated diamond-cutting factories for Discharged and Disabled Soldiers.

CAMPBELL-ORDE (GB) 1790, of Morpeth, Northumberland

Gentle and Strong

Sir JOHN ALEXANDER CAMPBELL-ORDE, 6th *Baronet*; *b* 11 May 1943; *s* his father, *Maj Sir* SIMON ARTHUR, TD, 1969; *ed* Gordonstoun: *m* 1973 (*m diss* 1988), Lacy Rals, only da of T. Grady Gallant, of Nashville, Tennessee, USA, and has issue.

Arms – 1st and 4th sable, three salmon hauriant per pale argent and or, *Orde*; 2nd and 3rd, gyronny of eight or and sable within a bordure componée ermine and vert, in the centre a crescent of the last for difference, *Campbell*. **Crests** – 1st, an elk's head erased or, gorged with a collar invected sable; 2nd, a dexter hand proper, holding a spur or, strap also proper.
Address – PO Box 22974, Nashville, Tennessee 37202, USA.

SON LIVING

JOHN SIMON ARTHUR, *b* 15 Aug 1981.

DAUGHTERS LIVING

Alexandra Louise, *b* 1974. —— Alice Theodora, *b* 1976. —— Octavia Maie, *b* 1978.

BROTHER LIVING

Peter Humphrey, *b* 1946; *ed* Gordonstoun: *m* 1st, 1976 (*m diss* 1992), Mrs Perdita Bennett, da of Alexander Peter Fordham Watt, and formerly wife of Richard Bennett, 2ndly, 1992, Penelope Jane Armstrong, da of late Mark Alexander Wynter-Blyth, MA, FRES, Prin The Rajkumar Coll, Rajkot, India. *Residence* – 53 Bell St, Shaftesbury, Dorset SP7 8AE.

SISTER LIVING

Caroline Jane, *b* 1940; *ed* N Foreland Lodge, and the Sorbonne: *m* 1967, Christopher John Davies, MA, of Westgate House, Dedham, Colchester, Essex CO7 6HJ, and has issue living, John Humphrey Stewart, *b* 1969, — Simon William Gardner, *b* 1970; MA, PhD (Cantab), — Caroline Celia Hyde, *b* 1973; BA.

Granddaughter of late Colin Ridley Campbell-Orde, 2nd son of 3rd baronet:—
Issue of late Bernard Arthur Campbell-Orde, *b* 1901, *d* 1974: *m* 1st, 1939 (*m diss* 1955), Pamela, who *d* 1979, da of late Brig-Gen John Cecil Wray, CB, CMG, CVO, TD, and formerly wife of Col Robert Hugh Arthur Lucas; 2ndly, 1955, Nancy Mabyn Bradley (Old Farm, Trebetherick, Wadebridge, Cornwall), da of Maj Thomas Langdon Trethewy, DCLI:—
Jennifer Mary, *b* 1940: *m* 1st, 1959 (*m diss* 1971), Robin Alfred Clive Salmon, Merchant Navy; 2ndly, 1977, Reuben Harry Gunn, of 39 Whitworth Close, Gosport, Hants, and has issue living (by 1st *m*) Timothy John, *b* 1960, — Robert Bernard, *b* 1961, — Belinda Jane, *b* 1964, — (by 2nd *m*) Sarah Louise, *b* 1978.

Issue of late Henry Campbell Campbell-Orde, yst son of 3rd baronet, *b* 1877, *d* 1954: *m* 1st, 1901, Marie Elizabeth, who *d* 1913, da of John S. Barr, of Newcastle-on-Tyne; 2ndly, 1927, Ruth, who *d* 1985, da of late Robert Thomas, of Penarth, S Wales:—
(By 2nd *m*) Alexander Powlett (Willow Cottage, Newbridge Green, Upton-on-Severn, Worcs), *b* 1928; Petty Officer (Radar Electrical Artificer) RN (ret). —— Colin Robert (Cruachan, Kingweston Rd, Charlton Mackrell, Somerton, Som TA11 6AH), *b* 1935; CEng, MIMechE, MRAeS: *m* 1959, Audrey Isobel, da of Raymond S. Griffiths, of Brentford, Middx, and has issue living, Andrew Colin (48 Oak Terrace, Board Walk, Shepton Mallet, Som BA4 5DY), *b* 1969; *ed* Millfield; ACCA: *m* 1991, Susan, da of Brian Parsons, and formerly wife of Peter Hill, and has issue living, Joseph Harry *b* 1993, Annie Grace *b* 1995, — Tamzin Ruth, *b* 1960: *m* 1985, Dennis David James Elliott, of 60 Grove Av, Yeovil, Som, and has issue living, Adam David Stewart *b* 1986, Christopher James Robert *b* 1988, Daniel David James *b* 1991, — Sarah Elizabeth, *b* 1965: *m* 1993, David Montagu Read, of RR1, Rapid City, Manitoba, Canada R0K 1W0, and has issue living, Callum Stuart Montagu *b* 1995, Benjamin Robert William *b* 1997. —— Morwenna (4 Heol-y-Delyn, Lisvane, Cardiff CF4 5SQ), *b* 1929; SRN: *m* 1951 (*m diss* 19—), George Ernest Turner, and has issue living, Ian George, *b* 1965, — Tracey Christine, *b* 1958, — Alison Meryl, *b* 1961: *m* 1984, Stephen Kingdon.

The 1st baronet, Adm Sir John Orde, Adm of the White, and, finally, Vice-Adm of the Red, Governor of Dominica 1783-93, was yr brother of the 1st Baron Bolton. The 3rd baronet assumed by Roy licence 1880 the additional surname of Campbell, his mother having been Eliza, el da and co-heir of Peter Campbell of Kilmory, Argyll, descended from Campbell of Auchinbreck (*see* Campbell Bt, *cr* 1668).

Orr Ewing, see Ewing.

Orr-Lewis, see Lewis.

OSBORN (E) 1662, of Chicksands, Bedfordshire

Sir RICHARD HENRY DANVERS OSBORN, 9th *Baronet*; *b* 12 Aug 1958; *s* his father, *Sir* DANVERS LIONEL ROUSE, 1983; *ed* Eton; Christie's 1979-83, Colnaghi 1984-86, Fine Art Consultant; Assoc Dir Paul Mitchell Ltd.

Arms – Argent, a bend between two lions rampant sable. Crest – A lion's head argent ducally crowned or.
Residence – 25 Queen's Gdns, W2 3BD.

Quantum in rebus inane

How much vanity there is in human affairs

SISTER LIVING

Sarah, *b* 1950: *m* 1989, Christopher Gwyn Saunders-Davies, of The Mill House, Greatbridge, Romsey, Hants S051 0HP, son of late A. O. Saunders-Davies, of The Island, Romsey, Hants.

COLLATERAL BRANCH LIVING

Grandson of late Lieut-Col Danvers Henry Osborn, 5th son of 5th baronet:—
Issue of late Danvers Osborn, *b* 1864, *d* 1929: *m* 1906, Inez, who *d* 1953, 2nd da of Henry Smith, of Victoria, British Columbia:—
WILLIAM DANVERS, *b* 4 June 1909; assumed the names of William Danvers in lieu of his Christian names of George Schomberg by deed poll (registered in Supreme Court of British Columbia) 1936: *m* 1939, Jean Burns, da of R. B. Hutchinson, of Vancouver, British Columbia, and has issue living, Cheryl Elizabeth, *b* 1945. *Residence* – 2676 Seaview Rd, Victoria, British Columbia.

The 1st baronet, Sir John Osborne, was son of Sir Peter Osborne, Governor of Guernsey, grandson of Peter Osborne, who purchased Chicksands Priory in 1576, and was Treasurer's Remembrancer to Henry VIII, Keeper of the Privy Purse to Edward VI and Commr of Ecclesiastical Affairs to Queen Elizabeth I. He was Treasurer's Remembrancer 1674-98 and received his Baronetcy in recognition of all the family had suffered in the cause of Charles I. Sir Danvers, 3rd baronet, was son of John Osborne (el son of 2nd baronet), who altered the spelling of his name to Osborn to avoid confusion with the family of the Duke of Leeds. He was Governor of New York before the War of Independence. Sir George, 4th Bt, commanded Scots Gds 1779 and was a Gen in the Army, MP for Bedford, and Groom of the Bedchamber to George III. Sir John, 5th Bt, was for many years an MP, and was a Lord Commr of the Admiralty. Sir Peter Osborne's da Dorothy *m* Sir William Temple, to whom she wrote the famous love letters.

OSBORNE (I) 1629, of Ballintaylor, co Tipperary

Sir PETER GEORGE OSBORNE, 17th *Baronet*; *b* 29 June 1943; *s* his father, Lieut-Col Sir GEORGE FRANCIS, MC, 1960; *ed* Wellington Coll, and Ch Ch, Oxford: *m* 1968, Felicity, da of late Grantley Loxton-Peacock, of 13 Eaton Place, SW1, and has issue.

Arms – Gules, on a fesse cotised or two fountains, over all a bend argent. Crest – A sea-lion holding a trident.
Residence – 67 Lansdowne Rd, W11 2EG.

SONS LIVING

GEORGE GIDEON OLIVER, *b* 23 May 1971; assumed the additional forename of George by deed poll 1988: *m* 1998, Hon Frances Victoria Howell, elder da of Baron Howell of Guildford, PC (Life Baron). —— Benedict George, *b* 1973. —— Adam Peter, *b* 1976. —— Theo Grantley, *b* 1985.

Pax in bello
Peace in war

BROTHER LIVING

James Francis (Elbridge House, Sturry, Kent CT3 4AU), *b* 1946: *m* 1971, Felicity Jane, only da of Peter Boutwood, of Holmes Farm, W Wittering, Sussex, and has three sons, Toby James Robert, *b* 1977 (adopted), — George Dominic Peter, *b* (twin) 1977 (adopted), — Harry Lucas, *b* 1988.

SISTERS LIVING

Jennifer Jane, *b* 1939: *m* 1966, Antony Rufus Little, of Flat 3, 55 Drayton Gdns, SW10 9RU. —— Caroline Mary, *b* 1941: *m* 19—, Michael Dodd, who *d* 1987, and has issue living, Andrew, *b* 19—, — Simon, *b* 19—, — Sara, *b* 19—: *m* ...... *Residence* – 32 Farley Av, Gorton, Manchester.

COLLATERAL BRANCH LIVING

Grandsons of late Edward Osborne, only brother of 15th baronet:—
Issue of late Stanley Patrick Osborne, *b* 1904, *d* 1989: *m* 1st, 1931, Muriel Harvey, who *d* 1967, da of Llewellyn Harvey Matthews, of Shrewsbury; 2ndly, 1969, Mary Enid Lyon:—
(By 1st *m*), Anthony Trevor (22 St Peter's Way, Edgmond, Shropshire), *b* 1934; *ed* Felsted, and Emmanuel Coll, Camb (MA); MICE: *m* 1958, Beryl Anne Shadbolt, of Cambridge, and has issue living, Marcus Duncan Fitzwilliam, *b* 1967, — Catherine Frances, *b* 1961, — Nicola Clare, *b* 1963. —— Edward Peter (Fairview Cottage, West Down, Ilfracombe, Devon), *b* 1938; *ed* Felsted, and Peterhouse, Camb (BA): *m* 1961, Marjorie, da of William Newton, of Fleetwood, Lancs, and has issue living, John Philip, *b* 1963, — Judith Carol, *b* 1962, — Janet Elizabeth, *b* 1964.

The 2nd and 7th baronets each represented the co of Waterford in Parliament. The 8th baronet was a Privy Councillor in Ireland, and sat as MP for Carysfort. The 9th baronet was MP for Carysfort and Sheriff of Waterford 1795. The 11th baronet was MP for Carysfort and subsequently for Enniskillen. Sir George Francis Osborne, MC, 16th baronet was Lieut-Col Roy Sussex Regt.

Osborne-Gibbes, see Gibbes.

OUTRAM (UK) 1858
(Name pronounced "Ootram")

I know not how to change my faith

Sir ALAN JAMES OUTRAM, 5th *Baronet*, son of late James Ian Outram, son of late Rev Arthur Outram, 3rd son of 2nd baronet; *b* 15 May 1937; *s* his great-uncle, *Sir* FRANCIS DAVIDSON, OBE, 1945; *ed* Marlborough, and St Edmund Hall, Oxford (MA); Lt-Col TAVR: *m* 1976, Victoria Jean, da of late George Dickson Paton, of Bexhill-on-Sea, E Sussex, and has issue.

🛡️rms – Or, on a chevron embattled, between three crosses flory gules, five escallops of the first. Crest – Out of an eastern crown a demi-lion or, gorged with a wreath of laurel proper, holding between the paws a cross-flory gules. Supporters – On either side a royal Bengal tiger guardant proper, gorged with a wreath of laurel vert and on the hand an eastern crown or.
Residence – Chase House, Moorside, Sturminster Newton, Dorset DT10 1HQ.

SON LIVING

DOUGLAS BENJAMIN JAMES, *b* 15 March 1979.

DAUGHTER LIVING

Alison Catharine, *b* 1977.

SISTER LIVING

Margaret Evelyn, *b* 1935: *m* 1st, 1956, Richard Coverley Champion; 2ndly, 1985, Peter Denby Gilbert, of 47 Hollis Way, Southwick, Trowbridge, Wilts BA14 9PH, and has had issue (by 1st *m*), Anthony Richard Coverley, *b* 1964, — Jean Margaret, *b* 1958: *m* 1989, Martin Galloway Booth, and has issue living, Christopher Albert Galloway *b* 1990, Edward Martin Galloway *b* 1992, — Jennifer Fleur, *b* 1960: *m* 1983, David Reginald Higgins, and has issue living, Stephen Richard *b* 1988, Katherine Joanna *b* 1990, Rebecca Fleur *b* 1994, — Joanna Esmé, *b* 1963: *m* 1984, Michael William Gooden, and *d* 1986.

COLLATERAL BRANCHES LIVING

Grandchildren of late Rev William Outram, yst son of 2nd baronet:—
Issue of late Rev Francis Henry Outram, *b* 1907, *d* 1972: *m* 1946, Eileen Grace, who *d* 1995, da of late Rev L. A. McClintock Newbery:—
John Douglas (Haining House, Taylor's Lane, Bosham, Chichester), *b* 1947; *ed* Marlborough, Liverpool Univ (BEng), and Birmingham Univ (MSc); Man Dir Outram Research Ltd: *m* 1970, Valerie Ann, da of Geoffrey Wilson, of Whitley Bay, and has issue living, Nicholas Francis, *b* 1973, — Philip Maxwell, *b* 1976, — Rachel Helen, *b* 1978, — Katy Ann, *b* 1981. —— Margaret Eleanor, *b* 1949: *m* 1975, Peter Francis Charters, of Red Gables, 9 Pagnell Lane, Littleton Panell, nr Devizes, Wilts SN10 4EW, and has issue living, Richard Francis, *b* 1977, — Simon James, *b* 1979, — Robin Andrew, *b* 1982.

Issue of late James Richard Outram, *b* 1911, *d* 1986: *m* 1939, Lucy Dora (Richardson House, Englefield Green, Surrey TW20 OJY), yst da of late Jacob Andreas Frerichs, of Johannesburg, S Africa:—
Francis William, *b* 1946; *ed* Scarborough Coll: *m* 1996, Joanna Catherine Royle, and has issue living, Henry Sebastian *b* 1998. *Residence* – 70 Wroughton Rd, SW11 6BG. —— Richard Graham (43 Richmond Place, Bath BA1 4QA), *b* (twin) 1946; *ed* Marlborough. —— Keith Alastair, *b* 1947; *ed* Scarborough Coll. —— Nicola Elspeth (Greenhayes, West Hill, Ottery St Mary, Devon EX11 1UY), *b* 1940: *m* 1962, David Alistair Kingsley Cooper, who *d* 1988, son of late Thomas Esmond Kingsley Cooper, MA, and has issue living, James Alexander (181 Leathwaite Rd, SW11 6RW), *b* 1969; *ed* King's Sch, Worcs, and Exeter Univ, — Jennifer Mary, *b* 1967: *m* 1994, Malcolm Bernard Yallop, of Russetts, Weston, Honiton, Devon EX14 0PQ, and has issue living, Alexander Malcolm *b* 1996, Nicholas David *b* 1998.

OWEN (UK) 1813, of Orielton, Pembrokeshire

Sir HUGH BERNARD PILKINGTON OWEN, 5th *Baronet*; *b* 28 March 1915; *s* his father, *Capt Sir* JOHN ARTHUR, 1973; *ed* Chillon Coll, Switzerland.

Arms – Gules, a chevron or, between three lions rampant or.
Residence – 63 Dudsbury Rd, Ferndown, Dorset.

John Lord, MP for the Pembroke Burghs, and Lord-Lieut of Pembrokeshire, assumed the name of Owen on inheriting the estates of Sir Hugh Owen, 6th Bt (*cr* 1641). Sir Arthur Owen, MP, 3rd Bt of the first creation, is stated to have given the deciding vote for a Bill containing provisions for ensuring the Protestant succession to the British Throne, after riding in unprecedented haste from Wales for that purpose. Sir Arthur Owen's grandda, Corbetta, was mother of the Sir John Owen, *cr* a baronet 1813. The 2nd baronet sat as MP for Pembroke

Honesty is the best policy

Dist (*L*) 1826-38 and 1861-68: he *m* 1st, 1825, Angelina, who *d* 1844, sister of 1st Lord Tredegar; 2ndly, 1845, Henrietta, who *d* 1894, da of Hon Edward Rodney, RN, son of the famous Adm, 1st Lord Rodney. The baronetcy of the first creation (1641) became ext at the death in 1851 of Sir William Owen-Barlow, 8th baronet. The 3rd baronet of this creation, Sir Hugh Charles, served at siege of Montevideo 1845-46, and in Kaffir War 1846-47 (medal).

CUNLIFFE-OWEN (UK) 1920, of Bray, co Berks

Sir HUGO DUDLEY CUNLIFFE-OWEN, 3rd *Baronet*; *b* 16 May 1966; *s* his father, *Sir* DUDLEY HERBERT, RN, 1983; *ed* King William's Coll, Isle of Man.

Arms – Quarterly, 1st and 4th, sable, a lion rampant between three crosses couped within a bordure, all or, *Owen*; 2nd and 3rd, sable, three conies courant in pale with two flaunches argent, *Cunliffe*. **Crests** – 1st, a lion rampant sable charged with three crosses couped in pale or, *Owen*; 2nd, a greyhound sejant argent, collared sable, in front of a flag-staff proper, flowing therefrom a banner also charged with a cross gules.
Residence –

SISTER LIVING (*Daughter of 2nd baronet by 3rd marriage*)

Sophia Jean, *b* 1965.

HALF-SISTER LIVING (*Daughter of 2nd baronet by 2nd marriage*)

Juliana Diana, *b* 1957: *m* 1980, Stephen Markeson, and has issue living, Oliver James, *b* 1984, — Lucy Juliana, *b* 1982.

AUNTS LIVING (*Daughters of 1st baronet*)

Honesty is the best policy

Philippa Helen (Felstead House, 11 Cannock Close, Maidenhead, Berks SL6 1XB), *b* 1926: *m* 1st, 1945 (*m diss* 1952), Denis Macduff Burke, who *d* 1999; 2ndly, 1952 (*m diss* 1963), Archie Alistair Baring; 3rdly, 1966, Peter William Thorn Warren, who *d* 1973; 4thly, 1979, Gilbert Hugh Sandbach Toller, and has issue living (by 1st *m*), David Macduff, *b* 1948; *ed* Uppingham: *m* 1976, Sally Anne Elizabeth, 3rd da of late William Antony Hamer, of Thorndon Green, Lyndon, Rutland, and has issue living, William Macduff *b* 1978, Harriet Victoria *b* 1980, — Alexandra Yvette, *b* 1946: *m* 1968, Edward Maurice Pierce Butler, and has issue living, Simon Maximillian *b* 1984, Michael Edward *b* 1986, Katie Serena *b* 1973, Emma Siobhan *b* 1975, — (by 2nd *m*), Adrian Allistair (47 Blackburn Way, Godalming, Surrey GU7 1JY), *b* 1957: *m* 1993, Sally Anne Harrison, da of Norman Nash, and has issue living, Lucy Harrison *b* 1994, Scarlett Harrison *b* 1996, — Sarah Elizabeth (Flat 3, 24 Carlton Way, Southampton SO15 2HE), *b* 1954: *m* 1st, 19—, ... Gosden; 2ndly, 1982 (*m diss* 1987), William Knight, and has issue living (by 1st *m*), Ronald Lance *b* 1976, (by 2nd *m*), Peter Edward *b* 1980.
—— Diana Elizabeth (Queens Lodge, Beldam Bridge Rd, Chobham, Surrey), *b* 1928: *m* 1st, 1947 (*m diss* 1955), William Gavin Buchanan; 2ndly, 1964 (*m diss* 1967), Cdr Richard O'Brien, RN; 3rdly, 1967 (*m diss* 1991), Antony Hanbury, and has issue living, (by 1st *m*) Gray Hugo (194 Clive Rd, Dulwich, SE21 8BS), *b* 1948, — Diana Victoria, *b* 1951: *m* (March) 1989, Andrew Scott Thorburn, of 20 Lennox St Mews, Edinburgh EH4 1PZ, and has issue living, Clare Elizabeth Scott *b* (Dec) 1989.

WIDOW LIVING OF SECOND BARONET

JEAN (*Lady Cunliffe-Owen*), only da of late Surg-Cdr A. N. Forsyth, RN: *m* 1964, as his 3rd wife, Sir Dudley Herbert Cunliffe-Owen, 2nd Bt, RN, who *d* 1983.

This family descends from Joseph Owen of Crookes Moor, Shelfield, who *m* 1746, Sarah, da and co-heir of Samuel Skargell, by Elizabeth da of John Cunliffe. The 1st baronet, Sir Hugo Cunliffe-Owen (son of Sir (Francis) Philip Cunliffe-Owen, KCB, KCMG, CIE, great-grandson of Joseph Owen), was Pres of British-American Tobacco Co.

Page-Wood, see Wood.

PAGET (UK) 1871, of Harewood Place, Middlesex

Sir JULIAN TOLVER PAGET, CVO, 4th *Baronet*, son of late Gen Sir Bernard Charles Tolver Paget, GCB, DSO, MC, 3rd son of Rt Rev Francis Paget, DD, 2nd son of 1st baronet; *b* 11 July 1921; *s* his 1st cousin once removed, *Sir* JAMES FRANCIS, 1972; *ed* Radley, and Ch Ch, Oxford (MA); Lt-Col Coldm Gds; 1939-45 War; a Gentleman Usher to HM 1971-91; CVO 1984: *m* 1954, Diana Frances, da of late Frederick Spencer Herbert Farmer, of Vicars Hill Lodge, Lymington, Hants, and has issue.

𝕬rms – Sable; on a cross engrailed, between in the 1st and 4th quarters an eagle displayed and in the 2nd and 3rd a heraldic tiger passant argent, an escallop of the first. Crest – A heraldic tiger passant argent, gorged with a collar and charged with two escallops sable. *Residence* – 4 Trevor St, SW7 1DU. *Clubs* – Cavalry and Guards', Flyfishers'.

SON LIVING

Labor ipse voluptas
Work itself is pleasure

HENRY JAMES (Summerfield, Little London, Heathfield, Sussex TN21 0NU), *b* 2 Feb 1959; *ed* Radley: *m* 1993, Mrs Margarete E. Varvill, da of late Halfdan Lynner, and has issue living, Bernard Halfdan, *b* 4 July 1994, — Daphne Ampuria, *b* 1996.

DAUGHTER LIVING

Olivia Jane, *b* 1957: *m* 1992, Nigel J. Cox, son of Basil Cox.

COLLATERAL BRANCH LIVING

Granddaughters of late Rt Rev Francis Paget, DD, Lord Bishop of Oxford, 2nd son of 1st baronet:—
Issue of late Lt-Col Humphrey Paget, MC, *b* 1891, *d* 1985: *m* 1918, Elizabeth Caroline, who *d* 1970, da of Sir Lewis Tonna Dibdin:—
Elizabeth Frideswide, *b* 1921; 1939-45 War in ATS: *m* 1950, Lt-Col John Darwin Maling, DSO, MC, RA, of 10 Warbler Grove, Waikanae, NZ, and has issue living, Thomas Anthony Darwin, *b* 1951, — Sarah Geraldine, *b* 1952, — Elizabeth Anne, *b* (twin) 1952, — Joanna Katherine, *b* 1956. —— Jean Marianne, *b* 1924; 1939-45 War in WAAF: *m* 1966, Robert Ian Cheyne Macpherson, of 16 Williams Av, New Pakuranga, Auckland, NZ. ——Helen Rosemary, *b* 1929: *m* 1966, George Albert Longman, of 2 Doatshayne Close, Musbury, Axminster, Devon EX13 6BQ.

Sir James Paget, 1st Bt, son of Samuel Paget of Great Yarmouth, was Sergeant-Surg to Queen Victoria and Surg to King Edward VII when Prince of Wales. Sir John Rahere, 2nd Bt, was a KC.

PAGET (UK) 1886, of Cranmore Hall, co Somerset

Sir RICHARD HERBERT PAGET, 4th *Baronet*; *b* 17 Feb 1957; *s* his father, *Sir* JOHN STARR, 1992; *ed* Eton: *m* 1985, Richenda Rachel, da of Rev Preb John Theodore Cameron Bucke Collins (*see* B Hazlerigg, 1990 Edn), and has issue.

𝔄rms – Sable, on a cross invected argent, between four eagles displayed ermine, an eagle displayed between four lions passant of the first. Crest – A demi-heraldic tiger sable, maned, tufted, and gorged with a collar vallary argent, and holding in its mouth an eagle's leg erased at the thigh or.
Residence – Burridge Heath Farm, Little Bedwyn, Marlborough, Wilts SN8 3JR.

DAUGHTERS LIVING

Emma Rachel, *b* 1986. —— (Richenda) Elizabeth, *b* 1988. —— Camilla Mary, *b* 1991.

BROTHER LIVING

DAVID VERNON JOHN, *b* 26 March 1959; *ed* Eton, and Trinity Coll, Cambridge: *m* 1990, Cluny Patricia Maxine, da of late Cmdr Duncan Macpherson, of Gaskmore, Laggan, Scotland, and Radbroke Hall, Shrewsbury, and has issue living, Alexander Lachlan John, *b* 14 June 1994, — Antonia, *b* 1992, — Catriona Isabel, *b* 1997. *Residence* – Chenies, Liphook Rd, Headley, Bordon, Hants GU35 8NF.

Saying and doing

SISTERS LIVING

Patricia Mary, *b* 1945: *m* 1975, Philip John Anthony Hawkes, of 60 rue de Varenne, 75007 Paris, and Château de Missery, 21210 Saulieu, France, and has issue living, Lucy Mary, *b* 1980. —— Rosemary Muriel, *b* 1948: *m* 1971, Christopher Ralph William Richard Inge, of Westmead, Bleadney, nr Wells, Som BA5 1PF, and has issue living, Alexia Diana Nancy, *b* 1977, — Olivia Dorothy Jane, *b* 1980. —— Elizabeth Frances, LVO, *b* 1950, Lady-in-Waiting to HRH The Princess Margaret, Countess of Snowdon since 1979; LVO 1998: *m* 1st, 1981 (*m diss* 1985), Dr Angus A. D. Blair; 2ndly, 1989, Maj-Gen Charles Gerard Courtenay Vyvyan, CB, CBE, RGJ (*see* Vyvyan, Bt, colls). —— Davina Jane, *b* 1951: *m* 1972, Rev (James) Adrian Hunter Pollard, and has issue living, (Etienne) James Hunter, *b* 1979, — Benjamin David Hunter, *b* 1979. —— Susan Glynne, *b* 1960: *m* 1988, Maj Simon Thornhill, late SG, of Troubadour, 265 Old Brompton Rd, SW5 9JA, yr son of late Thomas Thornhill, of Buzzards Bay, Mass, USA, and has issue living, Thomas, *b* 1999, — Catherine Starr, *b* 1991, — Fiona Surtees, *b* 1993.

WIDOW LIVING OF THIRD BARONET

NANCY MARY (*Dowager Lady Paget*), da of late Lt-Col Francis Woodbine Parish, DSO, MC: *m* 1944, Sir John Starr Paget, 3rd Bt, who *d* 1992. *Residence* – Haygrass House, Taunton, Somerset TA3 7BS.

Rev John Paget, R of Pointington, Somerset, for 54 years until his death 1745, purchased that manor and sold his lands at Daventry. His son, Rev Thomas Paget, held the same living 1745 until his death 1783. By the marriage of his son Richard to Mary, el da and eventually heir of James Moore, Cranmore Hall, Somerset, passed to this family. Their great grandson, Rt Hon Sir Richard Horner Paget, 1st baronet was many years Chm of Somerset Quarter Sessions and County Council, and sat as MP for E Somerset (*C*) 1865-68, for Mid Somerset 1868-85, and for Wells Div of Somersetshire 1885-95.

PALMER (E) 1660, of Carlton, Northamptonshire

May the success be equal to the labour

Sir GEOFFREY CHRISTOPHER JOHN PALMER, 12th *Baronet*; *b* 30 June 1936; *s* his father *Lieut-Col Sir* GEOFFREY FREDERICK NEILL, 1951; *ed* Eton; is patron of two livings: *m* 1957, Clarissa Mary, DL Leics 1994, el da of Stephen Francis Villiers-Smith (*see* B Northbourne, colls, 1980 Edn), and has issue.

Arms – Sable, a chevron or, between three crescents argent. Crest – A wyvern, wings addorsed or, armed and langued gules.
Seat – Carlton Curlieu Hall, Leicestershire.

DAUGHTERS LIVING

Sophia Mary, *b* 1959: *m* 1987, Michael H. W. Neal, of Legsheath Farm, nr E Grinstead, Sussex, only son of (Harry) Morton Neal, CBE, of Great Sarratt Hall, Sarratt, Herts, and has issue living, Harry Morton Geoffrey, *b* 1988. — Jemima Mary, *b* 1991. —— Celina Lucinda, *b* 1961. *m* 1986, William Alexander Mavourn Francklin, of Clavering Hall, Clavering, Essex, yr son of Cmdr (Mavourn Baldwin) Philip Francklin, DSC, of Gonalston Hall, Notts, and has issue living, Henry Alexander John, *b* 1988, — Clementine, *b* 1990, — Daisy, *b* 1993. —— Isabella Anne, *b* 1962: *m* 1993, David W. R. Harrington, son of Ronald Harrington, of Shatwell Cottage, Yarlington, Som, and has issue living, Edward David Francis, *b* 1995, — Nicholas Richard John, *b* 1997, — Lavinia Juliet, *b* 1994. —— Rosanna Jane, *b* 1967: *m* 1993, Edward J. G. Peel, son of John Peel, of Dudgrove, Fairford, Glos, and has issue living, Zachary Geoffrey Gretton, *b* 1997, — Jacob John Gretton, *b* 1998.

BROTHER LIVING

JEREMY CHARLES (Westwater House, Axminster, Devon), *b* 16 May 1939; *ed* Eton, and Univ of Tours: *m* 1968, Antonia, yr da of late Astley Dutton, and has issue living, Drew Herrick, *b* 1974, — Tom Jeremy, *b* 1977.

COLLATERAL BRANCHES LIVING

Grandchildren of late Major Herrick Augustus Palmer, son of late Rev Henry Palmer, 3rd son of 5th baronet:—
Issue of late Frederick Charles Palmer, *b* 1866, *d* 1930: *m* 1897, Eleanor Annie, who *d* 1942, da of late Henry Wilson Sharpin, FRCS, of 34 Sillwood Rd, Brighton:—
Dorothy Esther, *b* 1898.

Issue of late Lieut-Col Robert Henry Palmer, DSO, *b* 1868, *d* 1947: *m* 1909, Margaret Finch, who *d* 1955, el da of late Gerard Finch Dawson:—
Robert Henry Charles, *b* 1916; *ed* Clifton, and Wadham Coll, Oxford (Organ Scholar, MA, BMus); Organist, St Mary's, Oak Bay, Victoria, BC 1961-83; Conductor of Choir, Univ of Victoria 1965-69; formerly Music Master, Westminster Abbey Choir Sch, and an ARCM; 1939-45 War with RAF. —— Mary Margaret Elizabeth, *b* 1914: *m* 1944, Genille Hilton Jordayne Cave Browne-Cave, PhD (*see* Cave Browne-Cave, Bt, colls).

The 1st baronet, Sir Geoffrey, sat as MP for Stamford in the Long Parliament, and was subsequently one of the Commissioners at the Treaty of Uxbridge, Attorney-General to Charles II, and Chief Justice of Chester. The 3rd, 4th, and 5th baronets successively represented Leicestershire in Parliament.

PALMER (GB) 1791, of Wanlip Hall, Leicestershire

Sir JOHN EDWARD SOMERSET PALMER, 8th *Baronet*; *b* 27 Oct 1926; *s* his father, *Sir* JOHN ARCHDALE, 1963; *ed* Canford, Pembroke Coll, Camb (BA 1951, MA 1957), and Durham Univ (MSc Agric Eng 1953); late Lt, RA; Colonial Agricultural Ser, N Nigeria 1953-62, R. A. Lister & Co, Dursley 1962-63, and at Overseas Liaison Unit, National Institute of Agricultural Engineering, Silsoe, Beds 1964-68; a consultant, Dir W. S. Atkins Agriculture 1979-87: *m* 1956, Dione Catharine, da of late Charles Duncan Skinner, and has issue.

Arms – Argent, on two bars sable three trefoils slipped of the first, in chief a greyhound courant of the second, collared or. Crest – On a mount vert a greyhound sejant sable, gorged with a collar or, rimmed gules, and charged on the shoulder with a trefoil slipped argent. *Seat* – Newland, nr Coleford, Glos. *Residence* – Court Barton, Feniton, Honiton, Devon EX14 0BD.

SON LIVING

ROBERT JOHN HUDSON (31 Wandle Rd, SW17 7DL; Royal Ocean Racing Club), *b* 20 Dec 1960; *ed* St Edward's Sch, Oxford, Grey Coll, Univ of Durham (BA), and Cambridge Univ (BA): *m* 1990, Lucinda Margaret, da of late Michael Barker, of 14 Harley Gdns, SW10, and has issue living, Charles Henry Somerset, *b* 12 Oct 1992, — Alice Harriet, *b* 1994.

DAUGHTER LIVING

Harriet Alyson Ducarel, *b* 1959: *m* 1987, Andrew Lorne Campbell Byatt, son of Sir Hugh Campbell Byatt, KCVO, CMG, of Leargnahension, by Tarbert, Argyll, and has issue living, Douglas Edward Campbell, *b* 1989, — Emma Harriet Campbell, *b* 1992.

BROTHER LIVING

Robert Archdale (Dorhall Farm, Chaddesley Corbett, nr Kidderminster, Worcs DY10 4QQ), *b* 1930; *ed* Canford, and St Andrews Univ (MA 1951); late 2nd Lt RA; HM Overseas Civil Ser, Uganda 1955-62; Sr Assist Sec Univ of Birmingham 1962-89: *m* 1963, Rosalie Margaret, da of late Keith Newell, of Wentworth, Neston, Ches, and has issue living, Philip David Archdale, *b* 1969: *m* 1997, Alison, da of Howard Murray, of Stockton-on-Tees, Cleveland, — Jeremy Frederick Mathews, *b* 1972, — Catherine Ducarel, *b* 1963: *m* 1991, Stephen William Milgrew Piggin, son of Desmond Piggin, of Auckland, NZ, and has issue living, Hannah Ducarel *b* 1995, Louise Frances Sturtevant *b* 1998, — Sarah Rosalie, *b* 1965: *m* 1992, Peter Mark Creber, son of David Creber, of Saltash, Cornwall, and has issue living, Thomas Jack *b* 1994, David Alexander *b* 1996.

The 1st baronet, Sir Charles Grave Hudson, was a Director of the South Sea Co, and High Sheriff of Leicestershire 1780. Sir Charles Thomas, 2nd baronet, assumed the surname of Palmer, by Royal sign-manual, 1813, on succeeding to the estates of his maternal grandfather, Henry Palmer, of Wanlip.

PALMER (UK) 1886, of Grinkle Park, co York, and of Newcastle-upon-Tyne

May the success be equal to the labour

Sir (CHARLES) MARK PALMER, 5th *Baronet, b (posthumous)* 21 Nov 1941; *s* his father, *Major Sir* ANTHONY FREDERICK MARK, 1941; *ed* Eton; was a Page of Honour to HM 1956-59: *m* 1976, Hon Catherine Elizabeth Tennant, yr da of 2nd Baron Glenconner, and has issue.

ᴀrms – Sable, on a chevron between three crescents in chief and a lion passant in base argent, two tilting spears chevronwise proper. Crest – In front of a tilting spear erect proper a wyvern or, resting the dexter foot on a crescent argent. *Residences* – Mill Hill Farm, Sherborne, Glos; 15 Bramerton St, SW3.

SON LIVING

ARTHUR MORRIS, *b* 9 March 1981.

DAUGHTER LIVING

Iris Henriette, *b* 1977.

SISTER LIVING

Antonia Mary (*Lady Christopher J. Thynne*), *b* 1940: *m* 1968, Lord Christopher John Thynne, of Britmore House, Donhead St Andrew, nr Shaftesbury, Dorset SP7 9EB (*see* M Bath).

AUNTS LIVING

Diana Mabel, *b* 1917: *m* 1939, Squadron-Leader Vivian William Huntington, JP, who *d* 1989, and has had issue, Nicholas Charles, *b* 1940; *ed* Eton, — Anthony Patrick, *b* 1942; *ed* Eton: *m* 1982, Ann Jehle, da of Edward Hance Letchworth, of Buffalo, NY, USA, — Peter William, *b* 1945; *ed* Tabley House: *m* 1983 (*m diss* 1994), Philippa Carolyn, elder da of Sir Archibald Bruce Charles Edmonstone, 7th Bt, and *d* 1998, leaving issue, Thomas William *b* 1988, Louise Mary *b* 1986, — Richard Ian, *b* 1946; *ed* Gordonstoun: *m* 1983, Polly Ann Thelma, da of late William Thomas Smith, and has issue living, James William *b* 1986, Robin Anthony, *b* 1988. *Residence* – Bonawe House, Taynuilt, Argyll. —— Angela, *b* 1921; sometime in WRNS: *m* 1948, Lt-Col John Turnbull, MC, 11th Hussars, who *d* 1986, and has issue living, Richard (Cabrachan, Sir William Hill Rd, Grindleford, Sheffield S30 1HS), *b* 1951; *ed* Eton: *m* 1978, Sally, da of Donald Gordon Mackean, of Fern Grove, Welwyn Garden City, Herts, and has issue living, Robert *b* 1980, James *b* 1982, — Michael (8 Mackay Rd, SW4 0ND), *b* 1953; *ed* Eton: *m* 1990, Christine, da of late Reginald Charles Peter, of Marlborough, Wilts, — Anna (Jasmin Cottage, Pound Lane, Presteigne, Powys), *b* 1950. *Residence* – Well Cottage, Lingen, Bucknall, Shropshire.

WIDOW LIVING OF FOURTH BARONET

Henriette Alice, DCVO (*Lady Abel Smith*), da of late Cdr Francis Charles Cadogan, RN (*see* E Cadogan, colls); a JP; appointed a Lady-in-Waiting to HM the Queen when HRH Princess Elizabeth 1949, a Woman of the Bedchamber to HM the Queen 1952-53, an Extra Woman of the Bedchamber 1953-73, since when again a Woman of the Bedchamber to HM the Queen; CVO 1964, DCVO 1977: *m* 1st, 1939, Maj Sir Antony Frederick Mark Palmer, 4th baronet, who was *ka* 1941; 2ndly, 1953, Brig Sir Alexander Abel Smith, KCVO, TD, JP (D Somerset, colls), who *d* 1980. *Residence* – The Garden House, Quenington, Cirencester, Glos.

COLLATERAL BRANCHES LIVING

Grandaughters of Capt Lionel Hugo Palmer, 6th son of 1st baronet:—
Issue of late Charles Lionel Palmer, *b* 1909, *d* 1987: *m* 1937, Karoline (LRAM), who *d* 1995, da of late Maj Carl Gach, of Vienna:—
Diana Lillian (7811 Yonge St, Apt 1110, Thornhill, Ontario L3T 4S3, Canada), *b* 1939. —— Marjorie Tessa, *b* 1950: *m* 1978, Dennis Tallevi, of 3430 Halstead Rd, Mississauga, Ontario L5L 4H2, Canada.

Grandchildren of late Godfrey Mark Palmer (infra):—
Issue of late Maj Mark Palmer, TD, *b* 1917, *d* 1995: *m* 1939, Rosemary Aileen, elder da of late Edward Welton, of 31 Knightsbridge Court, SW:—
†Adrian Mark, *b* 1944; *k* in a motor accident 1967, *unm.* —— Ferelith Alison (*Hon Mrs James Drummond*), *b* 1946: *m* 1st, 1971 (*m diss* 1984), Ashley Gordon Down; 2ndly, 1988, Hon James Reginald Drummond (*see* E Perth), and has issue living (by 1st *m*), John Mark Palmer, *b* 1979, — Selina Eleanor, *b* 1975.

Issue of late Godfrey Mark Palmer, 7th son of 1st baronet, *b* 1878, *d* 1933: *m* 1906, Eleonora Mary, who *d* 1965, da of late Alexander Geddes, of Blairmore, Aberdeenshire:—
Myrtle Frances (East Cottage, Oswaldkirk, York YO6 5XZ), *b* 1912: resumed the surname of Palmer in lieu of Robinson by deed poll 1944: *m* 1st, 1940 (*m diss* 1944), Fl-Lt Guy Robinson, RAF; 2ndly, 1948 (*m diss* 1962), Horace Barker; 3rdly, 1967, Edward Walsh Tetley, and has issue living (by 2nd *m*), Rachel Kay, *b* 1950: *m* 1974, Christopher Rodney Wilson, of 8 Foskett Rd, SW6, and has issue living, Mark Christopher *b* 1984, Serena Annabel *b* 1980.

The 1st baronet, Sir Charles Mark, was a coal-owner and founder of the town of Jarrow, of which he was the first Mayor 1875, and was MP for N Durham (*L*) 1874, and from 1874 to 1885, and for Jarrow Div of co Durham 1885 to 1907. The 4th baronet, Major Sir Anthony Frederick Mark, RA, was *ka* 1941.

Palmer (Fuller-Palmer-Acland), see Acland.

PARKER (E) 1681, of Melford Hall, Suffolk

Sir RICHARD WILLIAM HYDE PARKER, 12th *Baronet*; *b* 5 April 1937; *s* his father, *Sir* WILLIAM STEPHEN HYDE, 1951; *ed* Millfield, and RAC, Cirencester; High Sheriff, and DL Suffolk 1995: *m* 1972 (Elizabeth) Jean, da of late Sir (Henry John) Lindores Leslie, 9th Bt (*cr* 1625), and has issue.

Arms – Quarterly: 1st and 4th, sable, a buck's head cabossed, between two flaunches argent, *Parker*; 2nd and 3rd azure, a chevron between three lozenges or, *Hyde*. **Crest** – A dexter arm erect, vested azure, slashed and cuffed argent, holding in the hand proper an attire of a stag gules.
Seat – Melford Hall, Long Melford, Suffolk.

SON LIVING

WILLIAM JOHN HYDE, *b* 10 June 1983.

DAUGHTERS LIVING

Beata Hyde, *b* 1973. —— Margaret Hyde *b* (twin), 1973. —— Lucy Hyde, *b* 1975.

SISTER LIVING

Elisabeth Mary Hyde (*Baroness Camoys*), *b* 1939: *m* 1966, 7th Baron Camoys, of Stonor Park, Henley on Thames, Oxon, and has issue (see that title).

COLLATERAL BRANCHES LIVING

Grandchildren of late Laurence Hyde Parker, 5th son of 9th baronet:—
Issue of late Laurence Edmond Hyde Parker, *b* 1912, *d* 1994: *m* 1953, Margarethe Van Thörne (Smeetham Hall, Bulmer, Sudbury, Suffolk), da of Mrs Ditlef Nielsen, of Gothenburg, Sweden:—
Anthony Laurence Hyde, *b* 1958: *m* 1986, Bridget Charlotte, yst da of late Arthur Stearns, of Ranworth House, Harleston, Norfolk, and has issue living, Thomas Frederick Laurence Hyde, *b* 1989, — Sophie Antonia Hyde, *b* 1992. —— Michael Edmond Hyde, *b* 1961. —— Jane Katarina Hyde, *b* 1954: *m* 1977, J. Skybak.

Granddaughters of Capt John Barnardiston Hyde Parker, 7th son of 9th baronet:—
Issue of late Edmond Francis Hyde Parker, *b* 1912, *d* 1966: *m* 1946, Naomi (Huish Farm, Huish Episcopi, Langport, Somerset), da of late Dr. D. Carmichael Thomas, of Langport, Som:—
Auriol Katharine Hyde, *b* 1950: *m* 1974, Maj Meyrick David Griffith-Jones, 13th/18th R Hussars (Queen Mary's Own) (ret), of King's Stag House, King's Stag, Sturminster Newton, Dorset, and has had issue, Edmond Laugharne Hyde, *b* 1979, — Jocelyn Hyde Laugharne *b* 1980, *d* 1988, — Piers Laugharne Hyde, *b* 1989, — Eluned Hyde Laugharne (twin), *b* 1989. —— Sophia Naomi Lucy Hyde, *b* 1952: *m* 1970, Glynn Mark Alexander Gray-Read, of 3 The Manor, Halse, Taunton, Somerset, and has issue living, Oliver Mark Forrester, *b* 1980, — Julian Frederick Thomas, *b* 1982. —— Harriet Ann Hyde, *b* 1953: *m* 1953, Alexander John Maxwell Findlater, of The Grammar House, Langport, Som, only son of Herbert Maxwell Findlater, of The Glebe Cottage, Bucklebury, Reading, Berks, and has issue living, Frederica Harriet Maxwell, *b* 1986, — Leonora Frances Maxwell, *b* 1988.

Grandchildren of late Harry Richard Hyde Parker, yst son of Maj-Gen John Boteler Parker, son of Adm Sir Hyde Parker, 2nd son of 5th baronet:—
Issue of late Reginald John Hyde Parker, *b* 1894, *d* 1957: *m* 1927, Violet Jackson:—
(Reginald Harry) Richard Hyde, *b* 1931: *m* 1st, 1957 (*m diss* 1961), Dorothy Margaret Stanley; 2ndly, 1962, Anne Bulmer, and has had issue (by 2nd *m*), †Simon Richard Hyde, *b* 1966, *d* 1985, — Emma Jayne Hyde, *b* 1962. —— Eve Frances Hyde, *b* 1932; is a SRN: *m* 1968, William Leavey.

Issue of late Edward Hyde Parker, *b* 1899, *d* 19—: *m* 1928, Ethel, who *d* 19—, da of Henry Mortimore:—
Alan Hyde, *b* 1933; *ed* Hertford, and Birmingham Univ (BSc). —— David Hugh Hyde, *b* 1934: *m* 1959, Brenda, da of Henry McIntosh, BEM, and has issue living, Rosemary Hyde, *b* 1960, — Anne Hyde, *b* 1962, — and an adopted son, Michael Hyde, *b* 1964.

The 1st baronet, Sir Hugh, was an Alderman of London. The 2nd baronet, Sir Henry, *m* Margaret, da and heir of Alexander Hyde, Bishop of Salisbury, 1st cousin of 1st Earl of Clarendon, Lord Chancellor. The 5th baronet, Adm Sir Hyde, commanded in the action of St Lucia 1780, and in the memorable action with the Dutch on the Dogger Bank 1781. In 1782 he was nominated to the chief command of the British Fleet in the East Indies. He sailed from England in the 'Cato,' which vessel never having been heard of after leaving Rio de Janeiro, is supposed to have been lost with all hands. Other members of this family have also been distinguished both in the Navy and the Army.

PARKER (UK) 1844, of Shenstone Lodge, Staffordshire

Sir (WILLIAM) PETER BRIAN PARKER, 5th *Baronet*; *b* 30 Nov 1950; *s* his father, Sir (WILLIAM) ALAN, 1990; *ed* Eton; FCA; ptnr Stephenson Nuttall & Co, Newark: *m* 1976, Patricia Ann, da of R. and Dorothy Evelyn Filtness, of Lea Cottage, Beckingham, Lincoln, and has issue.

Arms – Gules, a chevron or between three leopoards' faces or. **Crest** – A leopard's head erased, affrontée, ducally gorged or.
Residence – Apricot Hall, Sutton-cum-Beckingham, Lincoln, LN5 0RE.

SON LIVING

JOHN MALCOLM, *b* 14 May 1980.

DAUGHTER LIVING

Sub libertate qui etem
Under liberty rest

Lucy Emma, *b* 1977.

SISTER LIVING

Lindy Ruth, *b* 1947; *ed* Durham Univ (BA): *m* 1969, Prof Robert Samuel Moore, PhD, of Bennachie, Carmel Rd, Holywell, Clwyd CH8 6DD, and has issue living, David Kenneth, *b* 1974, — Heloise Catherine, *b* 1976.

AUNT LIVING (*Daughter of 3rd baronet*)

(Ruth Kathleen) Betty, *b* 1920; 1939-45 War with First Aid Nursing Yeo: *m* 1947, Richard Arthur Cole-Hamilton (*see* E Enniskillen, colls), who *d* 1992. *Residence* – Hawthorn Villa, 386 Ferry Rd, Edinburgh EH5 3QG.

WIDOW LIVING OF FOURTH BARONET

SHEELAGH MARY (*Sheelagh, Lady Parker*), only da of late Dr Sinclair Stevenson, of Beech Lawn, Fareham, Hants: *m* 1946, Sir (William) Alan Parker, 4th Bt, who *d* 1990. *Residence* – Apricot Hall, Sutton-cum-Beckingham, Lincoln LN5 0RE.

COLLATERAL BRANCHES LIVING

Issue of late John Douglas Parker, 2nd son of 3rd baronet, *b* 1924, *d* 1980: *m* 1958, Iris Anne, who *d* 1959, yst da of late Cdr G. A. Titterton, RN, of 4 Clarence House, Granville Rd, Eastbourne:—
Timothy John, *b* 1959. *Residences* – 266 Latymer Court, Hammersmith, W6; King's Sch, Canterbury.

Grandchildren of late Col William Frederick Parker, elder son of Adm George Parker, 2nd son of 1st baronet:—
Issue of late Capt William Mackworth Parker, Rifle Brig (Prince Consort's Own), *b* 1886, *ka* 1915: *m* 1912, Lillian Ursula, an OStJ, who *d* 1966 (having *m* 2ndly, 1921, Vice-Adm Everard John Hardman-Jones, CB, OBE, who *d* 1962), da of late Col Sir Arthur Pendarves Vivian, KCB (B Swansea, colls):—
Letitia Margaret (Delamore, Cornwood, Ivybridge, Devon), *b* 1914: *m* 1942, Dennis Seaver Dollard, who *d* 1983, and has issue living, Anthony Brian Christopher (Bridge House, Gilling East, York YO6 4JN), *b* 1949; *ed* Downside: *m* 1979, Caroline Lucy, da of John Martin Baskerville Edwards, of 91 Binfield Rd, Bracknell, Berks, and has issue living, Thomas Vivian Alexander *b* 1981, William Michael Frederick *b* 1985, Benedict Richard Seaver *b* (twin) 1985, Lucy Letitia *b* 1983, Mary-Clare Elizabeth *b* 1990, — Gavin James Dominic (East Rooke, Delamore Estate, Cornwood, Ivybridge, Devon PL21 9RF), *b* 1950; *ed* Downside: *m* 1st, 1979 (*m diss* 1983), Colleen Catherine, da of late G. M. O. Robinson, of Lansdowne, Bath; 2ndly, 1995, Nicola Jayne, elder da of late George Edward Sealy Woodhouse, of West Lodge, Blandford, Dorset, and has issue living (by 2nd *m*), Dominic Sebastian George *b* 1996.

Issue of late Cyril George Parker, *b* 1890; *d* 1968: *m* 1st, 1921, Beatrice, who *d* 1928, da of W. Harris; 2ndly, 1934, Margaret May, da of John Holmes Graham, and widow of Wallace Bruce MagDougall:—
(By 1st *m*) Laurence Frederick Cyril, *b* 1922: *m* 1951, Dorothy May, da of R. S. Kent, and has issue living, Allen Kent, *b* 1954, — Beatrice Anne, *b* 1952, — Donna Gail, *b* 1956, — Nancy Kay, *b* 1958.

Grandchildren of late Mackworth Praed Parker, yr son of Adm George Parker (ante):—
Issue of late Capt Gerard Parker, b 1896, d 1976: m 1st, 1921, Dorothy, who d 1954, da of late Lt-Col Francis Marwood Hext, of Redhayes, nr Exeter; 2ndly, 1958, Jill Lettice Mary (who m 2ndly, 1982, David Joseph Scott Roberts, of Slade, Timberscombe, Som), elder da of Richard William Kandahar Nott, of Penkenna, Westward Ho!, N Devon:—
(By 2nd m) Gerard Mackworth, b 1958: m 1987, Michaela Louise, elder da of John Frank William Burton, of Hockley, Essex, and has issue living, Christopher Mackworth John, b 1994, — Alexandra Nichola Mary, b 1990. ——— Julius Praed (97 Chilcombe Way, Lower Earley, Berks), b 1959: m 1992, Doreen, da of Finbar Murphy, and has issue living, Laura Katie Christina, b 1992, — Clare Phyllis Jill, b 1995. ——— Susan Mary, b 1961: m 1987, David Carroll, of The Manor, Weston Rd, Lewknor, Oxon, and has issue living, William Gerard John, b 1993, — Sophie Letitia, b 1990, — Isabella Jessica, b 1996.

The 1st baronet, grandson of the Right Hon Sir Thomas Parker (of Park Hall, Staffordshire, Lord Chief Baron of the Exchequer), commanded in the Tagus during the war between Dom Pedro and Dom Miguel; he was a Lord of the Admiralty in 1834 and 1835-41, principal naval ADC to HM Queen Victoria. Commander-in-Chief during Chinese war 1841-2, in Mediterranean 1845-52, and at Devonport 1854-57, and sometime Senior Admiral of the Fleet. Thomas Parker, father of 1st Earl of Macclesfield, was a yr son of George Parker, of Park Hall (d 1675).

PARKYNS (E) 1681, of Bunney Park, Nottinghamshire (Dormant 1926)

(Although the existence of an heir is probable, since the death of the 6th Baronet in 1926 a right to the Baronetcy has not yet been officially established).

DAUGHTER LIVING OF SIXTH BARONET

Sylvia Dorothy, b 1887: m 1912 (m diss 1931), Allan Gilbert Cram, and has issue living, Thomas, b 191—, — a da, b 19—.

COLLATERAL BRANCHES LIVING

Grandchildren of late Edwin Garling Territt Parkyns (infra):—
Issue of late Garling Alfred Parkyns, b 1913, d 1984: m 1935, Lucy Frances Laycock (Lot 3, 50 Bent St, Tuncurry, NSW, Australia):—
Garling Alfred (Lot 72, Sprimont St, Canterbury Estate, Bald Hills, Queensland 4036, Australia), b 1936: m 19—, and has issue living, Alan, b 19—, — Geoffrey, b 19—. ——— Frances Ann, b 1938. ——— Yvonne, b 1943. ——— Janette, b 1945. ——— Marie, b 1948.

Grandchildren of late Francis Charles Parkyns, son of Edward Territt Parkyns, son of Capt Levett Broadley Parkyns (b 1779), grandson of George Parkyns, brother of 3rd baronet:—
Issue of late Edwin Garling Territt Parkyns, b 1890, d 1975: m 1912, Emily Alice, who d 1974, da of late George Walter Wood, JP, of Mill Rd, Liverpool, NSW:—
Kenneth George (2 Rose St, Liverpool, NSW 2170), b 1917: m 1945, Patricia May Robins, and has issue living, Robert Carswell, b 1946, — Lindsay Hampton, b 1948. ——— Clifford Edwin Frederick (26 Rose St, Liverpool, NSW 2170, Australia), b 1926: m 1950, Shirley Dawn Hornby, and has issue living, Gregory Edwin, b 1952: m 1979, Mary Richards, and has issue living, Ryan b 1979, Guy b 1991, Clayton b 1984, — Vicki Anne, b 1962: m 1985, Christopher Andrew Livingstone, and has issue living, Jayde b 1987, Emily b 1991, Kyrstal b 1992. ——— Gladys Lorraine (4 Rose St, Liverpool, NSW 2170), b 1915: m 1936 (m diss 19—), Kenneth Leonard Weston-Brown, and has issue living, Brian, b 1936: m 1956, Margaret Calpin, and has issue living, Deborah b 1958: m 1987, Dennis Low, and has issue living, Briana b 1989, Lian 1991, Megan b 1965: m 1984, David Spencer, and has issue living, Joshua b 1985, Elizabeth b 1990, — Kenneth Weston, b 1938: m 1959, Hazel Cheesman, and has issue living, Andrew b 1964: m 1991, Rosemary Christopher, Craig b 1973, Murray b 1975, Justine b 1968: m 1990, Jason Thelander, and has issue living, Georgia b 1991, — Peter Weston (Lot 1, Lake Rd, Elrington, NSW 2325, Australia), b 1946: m 1966, Joy Clark, and has issue living, Ian b 1974, Glen b 1976, Ryan b 1984, Emily b 1979, Sara b 1981, — Wendy Lorraine, b 1940: m 1960, Bruce McGowan, and has issue living, Robert b 1962: m 19—, Dianne Allison, and has issue living, Christopher b 1993, Sharon b 1960: m 19—, Peter Hellyer, and has issue living, Mark b 1990, Nicole b 1988. ——— Enid Dorothy, b 1922: m 1947, Donald Douglas Floyd, of 14 Rose St, Liverpool, NSW, Australia, and d 1991, leaving issue, Douglas Stewart, b 1948: m 1970, Christine Holland, and has issue living, Bradley b 1981, Michele b 1972, Kylie b 1974, Renee b 1979, — Robyn Lorraine, b 1950: m 1972, Robert Perrim, of 18 Gardenia Av, Emu Plains, NSW, and has issue living, Brett b 1974, Stuart b 1980, Amanda b 1976, Narelle b 1978.

Grandsons of late Edward Territt Parkyns (ante):—
Issue of late Edwin Downing Parkyns b 1865, d 19—: m 1896, Cassilla Cole, who d 1955:—
Henry Jones, b 1896. ——— Edwin Arnold Allan, b 1898.

Issue of late Henry Garling Parkyns, b 1867, d 1938: m 1907, Mary McClifty, who d 1944:—
Daniel George, b 1916: m 1942, Evelyn Mary Cook.

PASLEY (GB) 1794, of Craig, Dumfriesshire
(Name pronounced "Paisley")

*Fighting for my king
and country*

Sir (JOHN) MALCOLM SABINE PASLEY, 5th *Baronet*; *b* 5 April 1926; *s* his father, *Sir* RODNEY MARSHALL SABINE, 1982; *ed* Sherborne, and Trin Coll, Oxford (MA); Emeritus Fellow of Magdalen Coll, Oxford, FBA: *m* 1965, Virginia Killigrew, da of Peter Lothian Killigrew Wait, of Kew, Surrey, and has issue.

Arms – Azure, on a chevron argent between two roses in chief of the last, and an anchor in base or, three thistles slipped proper. Crest – Out of a naval coronet gold, a sinister arm in armour proper, grasping in the hand a staff thereon a flag argent, charged with a cross couped gules, and on a canton azure a human leg erect, couped above the knee or.

SONS LIVING

ROBERT KILLIGREW SABINE, *b* 23 Oct 1965. —— Humphrey Sabine, *b* 1967.

COLLATERAL BRANCHES LIVING

Grandsons of late William Sabine Pasley (infra):—
Issue of late Eric Kinnersley Sabine Pasley, *b* 1900, *d* 1975: *m* 1st, 1928, Thelma, who *d* 1948, da of late John Power, of Auckland, NZ; 2ndly, 1949, his cousin, Rona Norma Sabine, who *d* 1978, da of late Russell Sabine Pasley (infra):—
(By 1st *m*) Thomas Sabine (141 Moana Av, Nelson, NZ), *b* 1929; a Member of Real Estate Inst NZ: *m* 1958, Helen Aroha, da of Justin Beauchamp Foster-Barham, of Nelson, NZ, and has had issue, Malcolm Sabine, *b* 1960, — Alastair Sabine, *b* 1963: *m* 1993, Elizabeth, da of William Rackley, of Nelson, — Hamish Sabine *b* 1964; *h* in an accident 1982. —— Warren Sabine (3 Butler St, Opawa, Christchurch, NZ), *b* 1931: *m* 1955 (*m diss* 1980), Margaret Mae, el da of John Douglas McIntosh, of Dunedin, NZ, and has issue living, Jonathan Douglas Sabine, *b* 1961, — Joanne Tui Sabine, *b* 1959. —— John Clinton Sabine (116 Queen St, Northcote, Auckland, NZ), *b* 1936: *m* 1960, Monica Therese, da of Patrick Reilly, of Christchurch, NZ, and has issue living, Matthew Patrick (106 Queen St, Northcote Pt, Auckland, NZ), *b* 1961: *m* 1984, Julie, da of Roderick Langridge, of Auckland, and has issue living, Thomas Michael *b* 1988, James Matthew *b* 1992, — Paul Joseph Eric, *b* 1962: *m* 1991, Amanda, da of John Fear, of Auckland, and has issue living, Emma Rose *b* 1994, — John Nicholas, *b* 1963, — Thomas Anthony, *b* 1966: *m* 1988, Jane, da of Sean Walsh, of Auckland, and has issue living, Andrew Sean Sabine *b* 1990, Alexandra Hannah Sabine *b* 1992, Francesa Kate Sabine *b* 1996, Isabella Paris Sabine *b* 1998, — Clare Monica, *b* 1968.

Granddaughters of late Rodney Stewart Lyons Sabine Pasley, 2nd son of 2nd baronet:—
Issue of late Montagu Thomas Sabine Pasley, *b* 1869, *d* 1947: *m* 1900, Agnes Jane, who *d* 1965, da of late John Innes, of Invercargill, NZ:—
Nancy Sabine, *b* 1907: *m* 1932, Robert Paterson Barr.

Issue of late William Sabine Pasley, *b* 1870, *d* 1938: *m* 1900, Florence Annie Heloise, who *d* 1959, da of late W. H. Kinnersley:—
Dorothy Madelene Sabine, *b* 1906: *m* 1939, Victor Patrick Coghlan, who *d* 1986. *Residence* – 8 Victoria Rd, Nelson, NZ.

Grandchildren of late Russell Sabine Pasley, yst son of late Rodney Stewart Lyons Sabine Pasley (ante):—
Issue of late Maitland Sabine Pasley, *b* 1914, *d* 1972: *m* 1943, Nancy Molyneux (56 Severn St, Islands Bay, Wellington, NZ), da of John Phillips, of Te Puke, NZ:—
Philip Sabine (Bamfords Rd, R.D.1 Lyttelton, Christchurch, NZ), *b* 1945: *m* 1969, Colleen Monica, el da of Daniel Doyle, of Ch Ch, NZ, and has issue living, Stuart Sabine, *b* 1974, — Andrea Sabine, *b* 1972, — Vanessa Sabine, *b* 1977. —— Russell Sabine, *b* 1947. —— Christine Sabine, *b* 1950: *m* 1972, Robert John Lang, of 36 Raymond Terrace, Birkenhead, Auckland, NZ, and has issue living, John Maitland, *b* 1980, — Deborah Maree, *b* 1975, — Karen Ellen, *b* 1977.

Grandchildren of late Capt Montagu Wynyard Sabine Pasley, RA, 3rd son of late Maj Maitland Warren Bouverie Sabine Pasley, 3rd son of 2nd baronet:—
Issue of late Maj-Gen Joseph Montagu Sabine Pasley, CB, CBE, MVO, *b* 1898, *d* 1978: *m* 1st, 1926 (*m diss* 1948), Christina Joan, da of John Darby, of Hillmorton House, nr Rugby; 2ndly, 1950, Dorothy Beatrice, da of W. J. Fance, of Parkstone, Dorset, and widow of F/Lt C. W. Parsons:—
(By 1st *m*) Anne Sabine, *b* 1929: *m* 1st, 1951 (*m diss* 1977), Maj John G. Melsom; 2ndly, 1978, Brig Guy Reginald Rowbotham, CBE, of Nobles House, 18 Station Rd, Petersfield, Hants GU32 3ES, and has issue living (by 1st *m*) Andrew John (South House, Ham, nr Marlborough, Wilts), *b* 1953; *ed* Uppingham: *m* 1980, Melanie Claire, da of Maj James Derek Kenyon-Hague, MC, of South House, Ham, Marlborough, Wilts (*see* Thompson, Bt, cr 1806), and has had issue, Harry George *b* 1984, Andrew Jack *b* 1987 *d* 1988, Edwina Lily *b* 1989, Cecily Kate *b* 1992. —— (By 2nd *m*) Malcolm Peter Sabine, *b* 1956; *ed* Marlborough.

Grandchildren of late Capt Hamilton Sabine Pasley, 5th son of 2nd baronet:
Issue of late Richard Sydney Sabine Pasley, *b* 1862, *d* 1911: *m* 1897, Mary Victoria, who *d* 1942, da of Sir Henry Dalrymple Des Vœux, 5th Bt:—
Audrey Christina Sabine, *b* 1905. *Residence* – Wistaria Cottage, Maresfield, Sussex.

Issue of late Charles Malcolm Sabine Pasley, *b* 1864, *d* 1907: *m* 1903, Berthe, who *d* 1964, da of late Comte de Rilly:—
Charles Hamilton Sabine (55 Ewan St, Margate 4019, Qld, Aust), *b* 1906; Roy Australian Air Force (ret); 1939-45 War (despatches): *m* 1933, Marjorie May Heales, and has issue living, Helen Sabine, *b* 1934.

Granddaughter of late Richard Sydney Sabine Pasley (ante):—
Issue of late Arthur Dalrymple Sabine Pasley, *b* 1903, *d* 1980: *m* 1st, 1943, Doris, who *d* 1950, da of Herbert Rastell; 2ndly, 1950, Hilda Mary, da of William H. Gardner:—
(By 2nd *m*) Victoria Mary Sabine, *b* 1952: *m* 1975, Fernando Antonio Palacios, of Santiago, Chile.

The 1st baronet, Adm Sir Thomas Pasley, was created a baronet, with remainder to the issue male of his daughters successively, and in 1808 was succeeded by his grandson, Thomas Sabine, who assumed by Roy licence the surname of Pasley, 1809.

Paston-Bedingfeld, see Bedingfeld.

Pauncefort-Duncombe, see Duncombe.

PEARSON (UK) 1916, of St Dunstan's, co London (Extinct 1982)

Sir NEVILLE ARTHUR PEARSON, 2nd and last *Baronet*.

DAUGHTERS LIVING OF SECOND BARONET (*By 1st marriage*)

Anne (*Baroness Glenkinglas*), *b* 1923: *m* 1940, Baron Glenkinglas (Life Baron), of Strone, Cairndow, Argyll, who *d* 1984. *Residence* – 7 Egerton Gdns, SW3 2BP.

(*By 2nd marriage*)

Sally, *b* 1929: *m* 1961 (*m diss* 1986), (Timothy Sydney) Robert Hardy, CBE, actor, and writer, and has issue living, Emma Jocelyn Cressida Myfanwy, *b* 1963: *m* 1989, Hamish A. Bullough, son of Alaisdhair Bullough, and has issue living, Robert Gabriel *b* 1994, Alice Miranda *b* 1991, Cressida Hope *b* 1997, — Justine Elinor Eldrydd, *b* 1966.

PEARSON (UK) 1964, of Gressingham, co Palatine of Lancaster

Sir (FRANCIS) NICHOLAS FRASER PEARSON, 2nd *Baronet*; *b* 28 Aug 1943; *s* his father, *Sir* FRANCIS FENWICK, MBE, 1991; *ed* Radley; Capt 3rd Bn Rifle bde 1961-60; ADC to C-in-C Far East 1969; company dir: *m* 1978, Henrietta, da of Cdr Henry Pasley-Tyler, of Coton Manor, Guilsborough, Northants.
Address – c/o Natwest Bank, Kirkby Lonsdale, Cumbria. *Club* – Carlton.

SISTER LIVING

Susan Alison Mary, *b* 1941: *m* 1961, Peter Sharp, of Linden Hall, Borwick, Carnforth, Lancs, and has had issue, James Edward, *b* 1967, — Harriet Nicola, *b* 1962, — Joanna Katharine Rose, *b* 1963, *d* 1989.

WIDOW LIVING OF FIRST BARONET

KATHARINE MARY (*Katharine, Lady Pearson*), da of Rev David Denholm Fraser, of Sprouston, Kelso, Roxburghshire: *m* 1938, Sir Francis Fenwick Pearson, 1st Bt, MBE, who *d* 1991. *Residence* – The Old Vicarage, Burton in Lonsdale, Carnforth, Lancs.

The 1st baronet, Sir Francis Fenwick Pearson, MBE, son of Frank Pearson, of Kirkby Lonsdale, Westmorland, was ADC to Viceroy of India 1934-36, Under Sec Indian Political Dept 1942-45, and Ch Min Maipur State 1945-47, MP (C) for Clitheroe Div of Lancs 1959-70, PPS to Rt Hon Alec Douglas-Home 1963-64, and Chm Central Lancs New Town Development Corpn 1971.

PEASE (UK) 1882, of Hutton Lowcross and Pinchinthorpe, co York

Sir (ALFRED) VINCENT PEASE, 4th *Baronet*; *b* 2 April 1926; *s* his half-brother, *Sir* EDWARD, 1963, *ed* Bootham Sch, York.

Peace and hope

Arms – Per fesse azure and gules, a fesse nebuly ermine between two lambs passant in chief argent, and in base upon a mount proper a dove rising argent, holding in the beak a pea stalk, the blossom and pods proper. **Crest** – Upon the capital of an Ionic column a dove rising, holding in the beak a pea stalk as in the arms.
Residence – 149 Aldenham Rd, Guisborough, Cleveland TS14 8LB.

BROTHER LIVING

JOSEPH GURNEY, *b* 16 Nov 1927; *ed* Bootham Sch, York; was a Member of Guisborough Urban District Council 1950-53; Pres NW Regional Liberal Party 1970 and 1971: *m* 1953, Shelagh Munro, da of Cyril G. Bulman, of Great Langdale, Ambleside, Westmorland, and has issue living, Charles Edward Gurney, *b* 1955, — Jane Elizabeth Gurney, *b* 1957: *m* 1990, Colin Charles Bright, elder son of William C. J. Bright, of Southsea, Hants, and has issue living, Thomas *b* 199—, Olivia Lucy Kate *b* 1995.

SISTER LIVING

Anne Phillida, *b* 1923; formerly in WRNS: *m* 1946, Major Edward Mark Chetwynd-Stapylton, King's Roy Rifle Corps (*see* V Chetwynd, colls), who *d* 1995. *Residence* – 110 Western Rd, Lewes, E Sussex BN7 1RR.

COLLATERAL BRANCHES LIVING

Issue of late Capt Christopher York Pease, Yeo, younger son of 2nd baronet, *b* 1886; *ka* 1918: *m* 1910, Margaret Philippa, who *d* 1959, da of late Walter Johnson, JP (Bell, Bt, *cr* 1885):—
Rachel Hebe Philippa, *b* 1911: *m* 1940, Richard Selby Smith, Lieut-Com, RNVR, and Prof Emeritus of Educ Tasmania Univ, and has issue living, Christopher Selby (50 Rotherwood St, Richmond, Victoria 3121), *b* 1942; DPhil Oxon; Visiting Prof, Monash Univ: *m* 1967, Joy Miriam, da of Thomas McGeehan, of Myrtleford, Vic, Aust, and has issue living, David Selby *b* 1969, Hugh Thomas *b* 1975, — Peter Selby (1 Hill St, Blackburn, Vic 3101, Aust), *b* 1948; BCE: *m* 1971, da of John Holroyd, of Rosanna, Vic, Aust, and has issue living, Andrew Selby *b* 1976, Anne Jane *b* 1974, Robyn Clare *b* 1980. *Residence* – Derwent Waters Residential Club, Cadbury Rd, Claremont, Tasmania 7011.

Issue of late Rt Hon Joseph Albert Pease (2nd son of 1st baronet), who was *cr Baron Gainford* 1916 (see that title).

PEASE (UK) 1920, of Hummersknott, Borough of Darlington, co Durham

Peace and hope

Sir RICHARD THORN PEASE, 3rd *Baronet*, *b* 20 May 1922; *s* his father, *Sir* RICHARD ARTHUR, 1969; *ed* Eton; late Capt 60th Rifles: *m* 1956, Anne, da of late Lt-Col Reginald Francis Heyworth, 1st R Dragoons (*see* By Tweedmouth, 1995 Edn), and formerly wife of Fl Lt David Henry Lewis Wigan, RAFVR, and has issue.

𝕬rms – Per fesse azure and gules, a fesse nebuly ermine between two lambs passant in chief argent, and in base upon a mount proper a dove rising argent, holding in the beak a pea stalk, the blossom and pods proper. 𝕮rest – Upon the capital of an Ionic column a dove rising, holding in the beak a pea stalk as in the arms.
Residence – Hindley House, Stocksfield-on-Tyne, Northumberland.

SON LIVING

RICHARD PETER, *b* 4 Sept 1958: *m* 1995, T.C.C. (Cecilie), da of P. H. Tholstrup, of Copenhagen, Denmark. *Residence* – 6 Eversley Park, SW19 4UU.

DAUGHTERS LIVING

Carolyn Thorn, *b* 1957: *m* 1981, John Silvester Varley, only son of Philip Varley, of Garden House, Barford Hill, Warwicks, and has issue living, George, *b* 1994, — Emma Thorn Anne, *b* 1989. —— Nichola, *b* 1961: *m* 1991, R. Crispin Odey, only son of Richard Odey, of The Kennels, Hotham, York, and has issue living, Felix, *b* 1994, — Maximillian Alexander Tom, *b* 1998, — Sophia, *b* 1997.

SISTER LIVING

Aline Thorn, *b* 1919: *m* 1st, 1940, Patrick Claude Hannay, Flying Officer Aux Air Force, who was *ka* 1940; 2ndly, 1941 (*m diss* 1954), 3rd Earl of Inchcape; 3rdly, 1955 (*m diss* 1968), Thomas Chambers Windsor Roe, who *d* 1988, and has issue living (by 2nd *m*) (*see* E Inchcape), — (by 3rd *m*) Patrick Rupert Windsor (73 Chemin des Osches, CH-1009 Pully, Switzerland), *b* 1960: *m* 1993, Maria João Lopes, da of João Carlos Lourenço da Purificação, of Queluz, Portugal, and has issue living, Simon Daniel *b* 1996, — Oriel Melanie Thorn (Rue Caroline 10, 1003 Lausanne, Vaud, Switzerland), *b* 1956. *Residence* – 63 Chemin des Osches, CH-1009 Pully, Switzerland.

COLLATERAL BRANCH LIVING

Issue of late Derrick Allix Pease, yr surviving son of 2nd baronet, *b* 1927, *d* 1998: *m* 1951, Hon Rosemary Portman (Folly Farm, Ashill, Ilminster, Som), da of 5th Viscount Portman:—
Jonathan Edward, *b* 1952: *m* 1979, Mary, da of Francis Moore Dutton, of Tushingham Hall, Whitchurch, Shropshire, and has issue living, Catherine Annie, *b* 1982, — Victoria Margaret, *b* 1983, — Alice Rosie, *b* 1991, — Christopher Berkeley, *b* 1958: *m* 1989, Mariana, elder da of Robert Scrymsoure Steuart Fothringham, of Pourie-Fothringham and Murthly (*see* E Gainsborough, colls, 1985 Edn), and has issue living, Edward Robert, *b* 1991, — Dorothea Elizabeth, *b* 1992, — Sybilla Mary, *b* 1994, — Carola Rosemary, *b* 1996, — Arthur David, *b* 1961: *m* 1994, Lucilla K. H., da of late T. H. Regis, of Wheathampstead, Herts, and has issue living, Thomas, *b* 1995, — George David, *b* 1998. —— Rosalind Jeanette, *b* 1954: *m* 1st, 1974, Evan Robert (Joss) Hanbury; 2ndly, 1997, Rodney John Berkeley Portman (*see* V Portman, colls), and has issue living, (by 1st *m*) James Robert, *b* 1979, — William Edward, *b* 1983, — Susanna Rosemary, *b* 1977.

The 1st baronet, Sir Arthur Francis Pease, son of late Arthur Pease, MP, brother of 1st Bt (*cr* 1882 ante), was 2nd Civil Lord of the Admiralty, Jan 1918 to March 1919, and High Sheriff for co Durham 1920.

PECHELL (GB) 1797, of Paglesham, Essex (Extinct 1984)
(Name pronounced "Peechell")

Sir RONALD HORACE PECHELL, 9th and last *Baronet*.

SISTER LIVING OF NINTH BARONET

Pauline Ruth Margaret, *b* 1923: *m* 1941, Rear-Adm Edmund Nicholas Poland (ret), CB, CBE, of 39 Limmer Lane, Felpham, Bognor Regis, W Suss PO22 7HD, and has issue living, Raymond Anthony, *b* 1942; *ed* King's Coll, Taunton, and Imp Coll, London Univ (MSc): *m* 1974, Lucy Sayers, — Roger Hugh, *b* 1949; *ed* King's Coll, Taunton, and Leeds Univ (BSc): *m* 1973, Elisabeth Gutleiben, of Bad Aibling, Bavaria, and has issue living, Eva Ruth Elisabeth *b* 1978, —

Andrew Quentin, *b* 1960, — Celia Frances, *b* 1947: *m* 1st, 1969 (*m diss* 1974), John Neil Gardener Govan; 2ndly, 1975 (*m diss* 1977), Richard Rohan-Irwin; 3rdly, 1978, Alfred Wolff, and has issue living (by 2nd *m*), Tracey Elizabeth *b* 1975.

PEEK (UK) 1874, of Rousdon, Devon

Sir WILLIAM GRENVILLE PEEK, 5th *Baronet*; *b* 15 Dec 1919; *s* his cousin, *Sir* FRANCIS HENRY GRENVILLE, 1996; *ed* Eton; Capt late 9th Lancers; 1939-45 War (despatches): *m* 1950, Lucy Jane, yst da of late Maj Edward Dorrien-Smith, of Weir Point, Restronguet, Falmouth, and has issue.

𝔞rms – Azure, an estoile argent; in chief three crescents of the last. ℭrest – Two hazel nuts, slipped proper. *Residence* – Weekemoor, Loddiswell, Kingsbridge, Devon TQ7 4DY. *Club* – Royal Western Yacht.

SON LIVING

RICHARD GRENVILLE, *b* 3 Feb 1955; *ed* Eton: *m* 1983, Melanie Jane, da of late George Waterson, of Broad Close, N Molton, N Devon, and has issue living, Timothy Grenville, *b* 1989, — Matthew William, *b* 1991, — Michael George, *b* 1994. *Residence* – Wallover Barton, Bratton Fleming, Barnstaple, N Devon EX31 4TP.

DAUGHTERS LIVING

Jane Elizabeth, *b* 1952: *m* 1974, James McIntyre Robertson, elder son of Prof Noel Farnie Robertson, of Woodend, Walkerburn, Peebles, and has issue living, Andrew Roger, *b* 1978, — Joanna Frances, *b* 1980. *Residence* – 9 Dagden Rd, Shalford, Guildford, Surrey GU4 8DD. —— Mary Susannah, *b* 1957: *m* 1990, Malcolm Hugh Campbell Robertson, 3rd son of Alistair Campbell Robertson, and has issue living, Thomas Grant Campbell, *b* 1992, — Eleanor Ruth Campbell, *b* 1994. *Residence* – Newhall, Drumoak, Banchory, Kincardineshire. —— Katherine Julia, *b* 1960: *m* 1982, James Edward David Hughes, 2nd son of late Trevor George Edward Hughes, of Downderry, nr Torpoint, Cornwall, and has issue living, Simon Timothy Edward, *b* 1987, — David William George, *b* 1990. *Residence* – The Round House, 53 Astrop Rd, Kings Sutton, Banbury, Oxon OX17 3PS.

The Master comes

WIDOW LIVING OF FOURTH BARONET

CAROLINE ANNE (*Caroline, Lady Peek*), elder da of late Sir Robert Lucien Morrison Kirkwood, KCMG, of Three Kings, Sandwich, Kent, and formerly wife of John Wolfgang von Kotze: *m* 1967, as his 3rd wife, Sir Francis Henry Grenville Peek, 4th Bt, who *d* 1996. *Residence* – Villa du Parc, 8 Avenue Jean de Noailles, Cannes 06400, France.

Sir Henry William Peek, 1st baronet, sat as MP for Mid Surrey (C) 1868-84. The 3rd baronet, Sir Wilfrid, was High Sheriff of Devon 1912, and served in Mesopotamia 1916-19 on Staff, despatches, DSO. Sir Francis Henry Grenville Peek, 4th baronet, was ADC to Gov of Bahama Islands 1938-39.

BERESFORD-PEIRSE (UK) 1814, of Bagnall, Waterford

Sir HENRY GRANT DE LA POER BERESFORD-PEIRSE, 6th *Baronet*; *b* 7 Feb 1933; *s* his father, *Sir* HENRY CAMPBELL DE LA POER, CB, 1972; *ed* Eton and Ontario Agric Coll; formerly Lt Scots Gds: *m* 1966, Jadranka, da of Ivan Njerš, of Zagreb, Croatia, and has issue.

Arms – Quarterly, 1sts and 4th, azure, a ducal coronet between three cross-crosslets fitchée or, *Peirse*; 2nd and 3rd, argent, semée of cross-crosslets fitchée, three fleur-de-lis sable, within a bordure wavy ermines, *Beresford*. **Crest** – 1st, a cross-crosslet fitchée or, ensigned by a mural crown gules, *Peirse*, 2nd, out of a naval crown or, a dragon's head per fesse wavy azure and gules, the lower part of the neck transfixed by a broken tilting spear in bend sinister, in the mouth the remaining part of spear in the bend, the point upwards or, *Beresford*. **Mottoes** – Nil Nisi Cruce (*Beresford*); Non Sine Pulvere Palma (*Peirse*).
Seat – Bedale Manor, Bedale, Yorks. *Residence* – 34 Cadogan Sq, SW1.

SONS LIVING

HENRY NJERŠ DE LA POER, *b* 25 March 1969. —— John de la Poer, *b* 1973.

Nil nisi cruce
Depend only on the cross

ADOPTED DAUGHTER OF FIFTH BARONET

Mary Spiers, *b* 1947; is a SSStJ: *m* 1971, Andrew Frank Gilmour, of Pratis House, Leven, Fife KY8 5NX, yr son of Col Sir John Edward Gilmour, 3rd Bt, DSO, TD, and has issue (*see* Gilmour, Bt, *cr* 1897).

COLLATERAL BRANCHES LIVING

Issue of late Rev Peter de la Poer Beresford-Peirse, yr son of 4th baronet, *b* 1907, *d* 1984: *m* 1940, Muriel, who *d* 1996, da of late Joseph Griffiths, of Barry, S Wales:—
Hugh de la Poer, *b* 1941: *m* 1963, Carolyn Ann Elizabeth, elder da of late Hubert George Frederick Barker, and has issue living, Julian de la Poer, *b* 1966: *m* 1994, Tracy Dawn, da of Robin Adrian Gates, of Clenchwarton, Norfolk, and has issue living, Thomas de la Poer *b* 1996, — Claire Elizabeth, *b* 1969: *m* 1994, Iain Wilson, son of Geoffrey Wilson, of Gayton, Wirral. —— Rev Mark de la Poer (21 Crimple Meadows, Pannal, Harrogate, N Yorks), *b* 1945; *ed* Richmond Sch, Magdalen Coll, Oxford, and Coll of St Mark and St John, Chelsea: *m* 1976, Margaret Joan, da of Prof David W. Arnott, and has had issue, †Duncan de la Poer, *b* and *d* 1980, — Rachel Helen, *b* 1977, — Sophia Rosemary, *b* 1981. —— Mary, *b* 1948. —— Ruth, *b* (twin) 1948: *m* 1976, Hugh Charles Wrigley, of Danby Hall, Danby Wiske, Northallerton, N Yorks, and has issue living, Elspeth Rosemary, *b* 1977, — Camilla Mary, *b* 1980.

Granddaughters of late Rev Richard Windham de la Poer Beresford-Peirse (infra):—
Issue of late Group Capt Francis Campbell de la Poer Beresford-Peirse, RAF, *b* 1911, *d* 1986: *m* 1st, 1936 (*m diss* 1957), Lady Katharine Lillian Edgcumbe, da of 6th Earl of Mount Edgcumbe; 2ndly, 1958, Kathleen Graham, da of late Charles Machattie:—
(By 1st *m*) Susan Katherine, *b* 1940: *m* 1972, John Miles Bird, and has issue living, Tiffany, *b* 1973. —— Philippa Jane, *b* 1944: *m* 1970, Nigel Hope.

Issue of late Rev Richard Windham de la Poer Beresford-Peirse, 2nd son of 3rd baronet, *b* 1876, *d* 1952: *m* 1st, 1910, Lady Lilian Katharine Campbell, who *d* 1918, da of 3rd Earl Cawdor; 2ndly, 1924, Katherine Mabel Helen, who *d* 1974, da of William James Yorke-Scarlett, of Fyfield House, Andover (V Valentia, colls):—
(By 1st *m*) Sybil Adelaide, OBE (6 Queensdale Walk, W11 4QQ), *b* 1912; OBE (Civil) 1990; LRAM. —— Barbara, *b* 1915: *m* 1942, Barry Martin Baker, of 6 Gloucester Mews, W2, and has issue living, Janet Bridget, *b* 1943, — Katherine Elizabeth, *b* 1946. —— Lilian Bridget, *b* 1918: *m* 1945, Godfrey John Mapplebeck, OBE, who *d* 1991, and has issue living, Anthony Peirse, *b* 1946, — Althea Rosamund Louise, *b* 1951, — Selina Bridget Lucy, *b* 1960.

Grandchildren of late Rev Windham de la Poer Beresford-Peirse, Hon Canon of Ripon, 6th and yst son of Henry William de la Poer Beresford-Peirse, 2nd son of 1st baronet:—
Issue of late Capt Arthur Cecil Proctor de la Poer Beresford-Peirse, MBE, *b* 1890, *d* 1970: *m* 1916, Gertrude Anne Ormonde, who *d* 1974, da of late Maj Henry Wallis Prior-Wandesforde, BA, of Kirklington Hall, Yorks:—
Michael Wandesforde de la Poer (Padgepool House, Wooler, Northumberland NE71 6BD), *b* 1917; *ed* Lancing Coll; a farmer (ret): *m* 1944, Joyce Franklin, who *d* 1997, da of Phillip Hope Percival, of Potha Machakos, Kenya, and has issue living, Judith Anne Vivian, *b* 1948: *m* 1980, James Stephen Bingham Kennedy, of Dunlossit Estate, Ballygrant, Isle of Islay, Argyll PA45 7QL, and has issue living, Thomas James Peirse *b* 1984, Clare Louise *b* 1982, — Susan Alice Prior, *b* 1950: *m* 1st, 1975 (*m diss* 1982), Phillip Hamilton Newman; 2ndly, 1983, Richard William Margesson, of 27 Bridge Rd, Welwyn Garden City, Herts AL8 6UG (*see* Hagart-Alexander, Bt, 1985 Edn), and has issue living (by 2nd *m*), Lucy Emma Alexander *b* 1986. —— Rev Robert Henry Windham de la Poer, OBE (30 Burt St, Albany 6330, W Aust), *b* 1922; *ed* Eton; late Flt LtRAF; Dist Officer, British N Borneo, ret 1964; OBE (Civil) 1963: *m* 1st, 1943, Margaret, who *d* 1972, da of late Edward Giles, of 72 Rue Kitchener, Alexandria, Egypt; 2ndly, 1974, Dorothy Maud, da of Percy Donald Beard, of Mel, Vic, and has issue living (by 1st *m*), Ian Arthur de la Poer (1/16 Quinton Rd, Manly, NSW 2095, Aust), *b* 1944; *ed* Tabley House: *m* 1968, Janice Patricia, SRN, el da of Lt-Cdr Lawrence Edward Murphy, RANR, of Perth, W Aust, and has issue living, Giles Windham de la Poer *b* 1969, Angus Arthur de la Poer *b* 1971, Digby John de la Poer *b* 1975, — Patricia Margaret, *b* 1950: *m* 1972, Richard Stuart Callander, of Adelaide, S Aust, and has issue living, Ian Stuart *b* 1974, Fiona Margaret *b* 1978. —— Anne Ethel Mary, *b* 1919: late Junior Cdr ATS: *m* 1942, Col Peter Anthony Lowe, late RA, of Tamerton, Upton Lovell, Warminster, Wilts, and has issue living, David Michael Peirse, *b* 1944; *ed* Sherborne, and RMA Sandhurst; Col late RA: *m* 1968, Catherine, widow of Capt J. A. Fleming, RA, and has issue living, Peter David *b* 1969, — Michael Peter, *b* 1949; *ed* Sherborne and Pa Univ, USA: *m* 1st, 1971 (*m diss* 1984), Rorie, da of G. K. Waters, of Waymart, Pa, USA; 2ndly, 1984, Sheilah Zaha, of Bensalem, Pa, USA, and has issue living, Matthew Peter *b* 1985, Jeremy David *b* 1988, Victoria (adopted da) *b* 1977, — Elizabeth Anne, *b* 1948: *m* 1970, Richard George Goodman, and has issue living, Thomas Richard *b* 1978, James Anthony *b* (twin) 1978.

Grandchildren of late John Peirse de la Poer Beresford, el son of Rev John George Beresford, 3rd son of 1st baronet:—
Issue of late Capt George Wilfred Bruce de la Poer Beresford, b 1888, d 1931: m 1920, Louise Barbara (who m 2ndly, 19—, Ralph Jones Coles, who d 1969), da of Jacob Frederick Beck:—
John George, b 1923: m 1947, Edith Joan, da of Henry Thomas John Mellaby, and has issue living, John Henry, b 1948: m 1971, Meredith Jean, da of Murray Victor Jones, — Peter Bruce, b 1950: m 1972, Julianne La Far, da of Julian La Far Smith, — Diane Louise, b 1949: m 1972, Glen Churchill. — Cynthia Joan, b 1952. —— James Francis (London, Ontario), b 1925: m 19—. —— Mary Isabel, b 1921, Robert Campbell Moreland, and has issue living, George Alexander, b 1947: m 1969, Marilyn Christine, da of William Reginald Lower, — David Beresford, b 1951: m 1973, Leslie Michelle, da of George Franklin Bowles.

Grandchildren of late Rev Walter Vevers de la Poer Beresford, yst son of Rev John George Beresford, 3rd son of 1st baronet:—
Issue of late Charles Denman de la Poer Beresford, b 1906, d 1990: m 1950, Pamela Croot (50 Ryan Court, Whitecliffe Mill St, Blandford Forum, Dorset DT11 7DQ), da of late Rev Frank Stone, MC:—
Marcus John de la Poer, b 1954; ed Clifton, and Balliol Coll, Oxford (BA). —— Julia Caroline, b 1951: m 1979, Simon Mark Amos, who d 1987, son of late E. Amos, of Blunham, Beds, and has issue living, Rosemary Cecilia, b 1984.

Issue of late Marcus Walter de la Poer Beresford, b (posthumous) 1909, d 1995: m 1942, Patricia Muriel, who d 1992, da of late C. Reginald Fox, of Plymouth:—
Charles Richard de la Poer (Barn Hall, The Rideaway, Hemingford Abbots, Cambs PE18 9AG), b 1943; ed Clifton, Gonville and Caius Coll, Camb (MA), and London Univ (PhD): m 1967, Tessa, da of late H. William Dean, of Cambridge, and has issue living, John Charles de la Poer, b 1973, — Fiona Carolyn, b 1969: m 1995, Lt-Cmdr Michael John Doodson Beardall, RN, son of Kenneth Beardall, of Gerrards Cross, Bucks, and has issue living, Molly Rose Beresford b 1999. —— Rev Peter Marcus de la Poer (The Rectory, 2 Rectory Lane, Barby, nr Rugby, Warwicks CV23 8TZ), b 1949; ed Cranmer Hall, Durham Univ: m 1979, Charlotte Frances Hester, elder da of late Rev John Grenfell McClintock, MC, and has issue living, Helen Caroline, b 1981, — Elizabeth Joy, b 1985.

The 1st baronet, Adm Sir John Poo Beresford, KCB, GCH, MP (Knight of the Tower and Sword), natural son of 1st Marquess of Waterford, and brother of Viscount Beresford (ext), sat as MP for Coleraine 1809-12 and 1814-23, for Berwick-on-Tweed 1823-26, for Northallerton 1826-32, again for Coleraine 1832-33, and for Chatham 1835-37. The 3rd Bt, Sir Henry, was Chm of N Riding of Yorkshire County Council. The 4th baronet, Major Sir Henry Bernard de la Poer, DSO, was Under-Treasurer, Middle Temple for 17 years, and served in S Africa 1900-01 as Major Imperial Yeo (DSO). The 5th Bt, Sir Henry Campbell de la Poer, CB, was Dir-Gen Forestry Commn 1962-68: m 1932, Margaret, who d 1995, da of Frank Morison Seafield Grant, of Knockie, Whitebridge, Invernesshire.

PELLY (UK) 1840, of Upton, Essex

God guiding, nothing hurts

Sir RICHARD JOHN PELLY, 7th *Baronet*; b 10 April 1951; s his uncle, Sir JOHN ALWYNE, 1993; ed Wellington Coll, and Wadham Coll, Oxford (BA); Farmer: m 1983, Clare Gemma, da of late Harry Wilfred Dove, of Winchester, Hants, and has issue.

Arms – Or, on a bend engrailed azure, between two trefoils slipped vert, three martlets argent. Crest – Issuant from a crown vallery or, charged on the rim with three hurts, an elephant's head argent.
Residence – The Manor House, Preshaw, Upham, Southampton, Hants SO32 1HP.

SONS LIVING

ANTHONY ALWYNE, b 30 Oct 1984. —— James Richard, b 1986. —— Harry Philip, b 1988.

SISTER LIVING

Jane Carol, b 1949; BA: m 1974, Charles Scott Bowring, PhD, son of late Frederick Bowring, of Tunbridge Wells, and has issue living, Thomas Scott, b 1975, — Rosemary Carol, b 1977.

DAUGHTER LIVING OF SIXTH BARONET (by 2nd m to Elsie May (Hazel), who d 1987, da of late Louis Thomas Dechow)

Margaret Elizabeth Rosanne, b 1952.

UNCLE LIVING (son of 5th baronet)

Frederick Michael (West Lodge, Preshaw, Upham, Hants), b 1926: m 1952, Jill Elizabeth, el da of late Col William Patrick Stewart Curtis, OBE (see Curtis, Bt, colls), and has had issue, Patrick Michael (Wormit House, Wormit, Fife), b 1954: m 1980, June, da of late W. G. Edgar, and has issue living, Louise Mary b 1986, Charlotte Elizabeth b 1991, — †Alwyne Nicholas, b 1955; BSA Police; d 1987, in Harare, Zimbabwe, — Frederick Peter Douglas (La Boine, St Jean de Côle, France), b 1959: m 1987, Evelyne, yst da of Maurice Souilhe, of Paris, and has issue living, Curtis Vincent b 1987, Alwyne Nicolas b 1988, Adderley Charlotte b 1991.

AUNT LIVING (*daughter of 5th baronet*)

Carol Patricia Benita, *b* 1928: *m* 1947, Lieut Cmdr Thomas Michael Blake, RN, who *d* 1984, and has issue living, Caroline Patricia (Pink's Hill, Warnford, Hants), *b* 1949: *m* 1976, John Henry Edmund Lushington, who *d* in a motor accident 1998 (*see* B Kensington, 1962 Edn), and has issue living, Katherine Elizabeth *b* 1979, Phillipa Alice *b* 1981, — Juliet, *b* 1950: *m* 1972, Howard Neil Fairman, and has issue living, Lutia Charlotte *b* 1974, Georgina *b* 1976, — Annabel, *b* 1953: *m* 1974, Richard Huxley Cowen, and has issue living, Emma *b* 1976, Victoria *b* 1977, Charlotte Annabel *b* 1982. *Residence* – Lippen Wood Farm, West Meon, Hampshire.

MOTHER LIVING

Mary Elizabeth, da of late John Luscome, of N Huish, Devon: *m* 1948, Richard Heywood Pelly, 2nd son of 5th baronet, who *d* 1988. *Residence* – Loup House, Lyme Rd, Axminster, Devon.

WIDOW LIVING OF SIXTH BARONET

(AVA) BARBARA ANN (*Barbara, Lady Pelly*), only da of late Brig Keith Frederick William Dunn, CBE: *m* 1st, 1945 (*m diss* 1950), as his 1st wife, Sir John Alwyne Pelly, 6th Bt; 2ndly, 1951 (*m diss* 1964), Maj David Michael de Lérisson Cazenove; 3rdly, 1990, as his 3rd wife, her 1st husband, Sir John Alwyne Pelly, 6th Bt, who *d* 1993. *Residence* – 9 Brook St, Bishop's Waltham, Hants SO3 1AX.

COLLATERAL BRANCHES LIVING

Branch from 4th Baronet

Issue of late Philip Vincent Pelly, yr son of 4th baronet, *b* 1898, *d* 1991: *m* 1932, Pamela Mary, who *d* 1970, only child of Sir Frederick Henry Arthur Des Voeux, 7th Bt (ext 1944):—
Brian Raymond (1253 Via Landeta, Palos Verdes Est, Calif 90274, USA), *b* 1935; *ed* Lancing: *m* 1962, Dinah, er da of late Rev Gerald Alfred Hutchison, of Littleton Drew Rectory, Chippenham, Wilts, and has issue living, Ivan Raymond, *b* 1963, — Oliver Harding, *b* 1966, — Annabel Marguerite Pamela, *b* 1970. ——— Antony Roger (Commongate, Holnest, Sherborne, Dorset DT9 6HY), *b* 1937; *ed* Lancing; BSc, FRICS, late RHA: *m* 1963, Susan Fiona, yr da of Maj Denis William Powlett Milbank, TD (*see* Milbank, Bt), and has issue living, (Helen) Fiona, *b* 1964: *m* 1989, Nicholas J. Chapman, of 16 Lessar Av, SW4, only son of J. A. Chapman, of Little Blair, Hill Head, Hants, and has issue living, Fredrick Nicholas Anthony *b* 1992, Katie Calypso Fiona *b* 1995, Tatiana Poppy Ruth *b* 1996, — Anna Maria Alice, *b* 1967: *m* 1988, Nicholas Mark Ryman Richards, of Hill View, Wheatley Rd, Forest Hill, Oxon OX33 1EW, er son of Nigel Richards, of 37 Evelyn Rd, Richmond, Surrey, and has issue living, Benita Frances *b* 1994, Lottie Mariah *b* 1997. ——— Roland Des Voeux (Limes Court, Stanstead, Essex), *b* 1943; *ed* Cheltenham; solicitor 1967: *m* 1968, Diana, da of Capt James FitzGibbon, RN (ret), of Thames, NZ, and has issue living, Richard Philip, *b* 1971, — Claire Mary, *b* 1982. ——— Philip Harold (Purples Farm, Bardfield Saling, nr Braintree, Essex CM7 5EJ), *b* 1948; BSc; DipEd; admitted a solicitor 1977; District Judge 1997: *m* 1970, (Margaret) Helen, da of late Canon Daniel Ernest John Anthony, of Sherston, Wilts, and has issue living, Thomas Philip Anthony, *b* 1980, — Katherine Louisa, *b* 1977. ——— Pamela Margaret Evelyn, *b* 1933: *m* 1957, Maurice John Greening, of Ladyfield, Acton Turville, Badminton, Glos, only child of John Greening, of Purton, Wilts, and has issue living, Harold John, *b* 1958, — James Timothy, *b* 1960, — Maurice Vincent, *b* 1964, — Mary Jacqueline, *b* 1962. ——— Clare Richenda, *b* 1940: *m* 1963, Henry Hartley, and *d* 1987, leaving issue, Mark William, *b* 1964, — Madeline Mary, *b* 1967.

Branch from 2nd son of 1st Baronet

Grandchildren of late Rev Douglas Raymond Pelly, DSO (infra):—
Issue of late Air Ch Marshal Sir Claude Bernard Raymond Pelly, GBE, KCB, MC, *b* 1902, *d* 1972: *m* 1930, Margaret Ogilvie, who *d* 1990, da of late E. J. Spencer, of Hove:—
Rev Raymond Blake (12 Kio Crescent, Hataitai, Wellington, NZ), *b* 1938; *ed* Rugby, and Worcester Coll, Oxford: *m* 1st, 1964, Joanna Bickmore, yr da of John Anthony Clarke, of Home Orchard, Street, Som; 2ndly, 1990, Barbara Helen, elder da of Alan Craig, and has had issue (by 1st *m*), Aidan John Raymond, *b* 1970, — Gail, *b* and *d* 1965, — Monica, *b* 1966, — Catherine Hilda, *b* 1967; *ed* Dartington; *d* 1984, — (by 2nd *m*), Thomas Douglas Raymond Craig, *b* 1993. ——— David Claude Raymond (Dairy Farmhouse, Coltishall, Norwich, Norfolk NR12 7AH), *b* 1941; *ed* Rugby: *m* 1974, Philippa Margaret, only da of Anthony Peter Bowman, of Hitchin, Herts, and has issue living, Tessa Patricia *b* 1977, — Lorna Jane, *b* 1979. ——— Jane Elizabeth, *b* 1931: *m* 1960, John I. Guest, of 760 Eden Pl, W Vancouver, BC, Canada, and has issue living, John William *b* 1961, — Margaret Elizabeth *b* 1960, — Maire Frances, *b* 1963.

Issue of late Rear-Adm Peter Douglas Herbert Raymond Pelly, CB, DSO, *b* 1904, *d* 1980: *m* 1932, Gwenllian Violet, who *d* 1987, da of late Capt Hon George Henry Edwardes, MC (*see* B Kensington, colls):—
Sara Ann, *b* 1937: *m* 1968, Peter Low, who *d* 1997, of Darsham House, nr Saxmundham, Suffolk, and has issue living, Tobias Blake, *b* 1969, — Nathaniel Peter, *b* 1971. ——— Richenda, *b* 1939: *m* 1959, Col Douglas Alexander Nigel Capel Miers, Queen's Own Highlanders (East Farmhouse, Wylye, Warminster, Wilts), and has issue living, Lucian Douglas Ronald Capel, *b* 1962, — Mary Ann Capel, *b* 1961, — Victoria Jane Capel, *b* 1964, — Henrietta Alice Capel, *b* 1966. ——— (Margaret) Clare, *b* 1942: *m* 1963, Timothy Lawrence Ireland, of Eatons Farm, Ashurst, nr Steyning, W, Sussex, and has issue living, Mark Peter Lawrence, *b* 1965, — Blake Timothy Lawrence, *b* 1972, — Nicola Gwenllian, *b* 1966: *m* 1995, Doron Rigel, of Tel Aviv, Israel, and has issue living, Itamar Blake *b* 1995, Guy Liam *b* 1998, — Gemma Mary Clare, *b* 1974.

Issue of late Blake Raymond Pelly, OBE, *b* 1907, *d* 1990: *m* 1938, Mary Pamela Laidley (3 Vaucluse Rd, Sydney, NSW 2030), da of Vincent Laidley Dowling:—
Andrew Douglas Blake (8 Johnston Crescent, Lane Cove, Sydney, NSW), *b* 1939; *ed* Tudor House, and The King's Sch, Sydney; Television Producer and Dir 1964-87: *m* 1st, 1961 (*m diss* 1978), Gaye Delyss, da of Gordon Clempson Evans, of Chatswood, NSW; 2ndly 1983, Maria Rita, da of Frank Van Ierland, of The Netherlands, and has issue living, (by 1st *m*) Fiona Elizabeth, *b* 1964, — Vanessa Pamela, *b* 1967, — (by 2nd *m*) Richard Francis Blake, *b* 1984. —— Michael Francis Blake (56 Crescent Rd, Hamilton, Brisbane, Qld), *b* 1947: *m* 1983, Nora Danaher, and has issue living, Martine Pamela, *b* 1984, — Simone Veronica, *b* 1986. —— Angela Mary Blake, *b* 1942: *m* 1965, Cdr John Spencer Compton, RAN (ret) (248 La Perouse St, Red Hill, ACT) and has issue living, James Gregory Spencer *b* 1967, — Blake John Raynor *b* 1970, — Henry Charles Grenville *b* 1977.

Granddaughter of late Rev Canon Raymond Percy Pelly, yr son of late Raymond Pelly, 2nd son of 1st baronet:—
Issue of late Rev Douglas Raymond Pelly, DSO, *b* 1865, *d* 1943: *m* 1898, Verena Noélie, who *d* 1952, da of late Rev George W. Herbert, V of St Peter's, Vauxhall, SE:—
Stella Elizabeth Mary (15 The Mint, Wallingford, Oxon), *b* 1908: *m* 1934, William Richard Gowers, CBE, DCL, who *d* 19—, only son of late Sir Ernest Arthur Gowers, GCB, GBE, and has issue living, William Patrick, *b* 1936; PhD; *m* 1961, Caroline Molesworth, yr da of Dr Timothy Maurice, OBE, of 10 Kingsbury St, Marlborough, and has issue living, William Timothy *b* 1963, Rebecca *b* 1965, Katherine *b* 1970, — Ann Elizabeth Mary, *b* 1938; BEd, PhD: *m* 1963, Prof Roger Dennis Scott, DPhil, of 417 Swann Rd, St Lucia, Brisbane, Aust, and has issue living, Richard Andrew *b* 1964; Midshipman RAN, Alexander Patrick *b* 1967.

Granddaughters of late Rev Canon Raymond Percy Pelly, yr son of late Raymond Pelly, 2nd son of 1st baronet:—
Issue of late Brig-Gen Raymond Theodore Pelly, CB, CMG, DSO, late Loyal Regt, and a Mil Knight of Windsor, *b* 1881, *d* 1952: *m* 1910, Moriet Elsie Maxwell, who *d* 1965, da of late Maj-Gen Arthur Gethin Creagh, CB (Wolseley, Bt, *cr* 1744, colls):—
Pamela Moriet, *b* 1911: *m* 1st, 1935, Frank Rough, who *d* 1966; 2ndly, 1968, John Moore Lorimer, who *d* 1982; 3rdly, 1993, Donald Pearson Paton, DFC, MA, who *d* 1998, of 22 North Mill Place, Halstead, Essex CO9 2FA, and has issue living, (by 1st *m*) Caroline, *b* 1940: *m* 1963, John Ralph Lawrenson, of The Old Rectory, Great Waldingfield, Sudbury, Suffolk CO10 0TL, and has issue living, Frank Ralph *b* 1967, Sophie Patricia *b* 1968. —— Patricia Carlota, *b* 1915: *m* 1948, Alan H. Maccoy, DSC, RNVR, of The Coach House, Church Rd, Shillingstone, Blandford Forum, Dorset DT11 0SL, and has an adopted son and da, Paul John Raymond, *b* 1958: *m* 1st, 1986 (*m diss* 1993), Leigh Thelma Sessions; 2ndly, 1995, Miriam Constance Dudden, — Catherine Richenda, *b* 1959: *m* 1981, David Peter Pickering of Bermuda, and has issue living, Samantha Clare *b* 1990.

Branch from 3rd son of 1st Baronet

Grandchildren of late Charles Brent Neville Pelly, el son of Rev Charles Henry Pelly, el son of Charles Pelly, MCS, 3rd son of 1st baronet:—
Issue of late Cdr Charles Sinclair Pelly, RN, *b* 1902, *d* 1967: *m* 1928, Caroline Mary, who *d* 1992, da of Charles Samuel Facey, MB, of Chickerell, Weymouth:—
Charles Patrick (St Mary's Lodge, Chitterne, Wilts), *b* 1935: *m* 1966, Avis Olga, da of W. H. T. Woon, and has issue living, Nigel William Sinclair, *b* 1968, — Stephen Grenville, *b* 1970, — Simon Charles Tregoning, *b* 1973. —— William Rupert Brent (Bell Cliff House, 7 Broad St, Lyme Regis, Dorset DT7 3QD), *b* 1943: *m* 1st, 1967 (*m diss* 19—), Judith Rowena, da of Prof Norman Henry Gibbs, DPh (*see* E Leven and Melville, colls); 2ndly, 1994, Louisa Maria Trufelli, and has issue living (by 1st *m*), Benjamin Rupert William, *b* 1972, — Joel Peter Sinclair, *b* 1980, — Zinnia Joanne, *b* 1970: *m* 1995, Christopher (Kester) S. J. Wilkinson, yst son of late Surg Cmdr (D) Kit Wilkinson, and of Mrs William Minchin, of Midhurst, Sussex, and has issue living, India Jane *b* 1998, — Tabitha Louise, *b* 1978. —— Jane *b* 1931: *m* 1957, Capt Kenneth Mills, RN, The Elms, Chickerell, Weymouth, Dorset, and has issue living, Charles Richard, *b* 1958, — Patrick George, *b* 1963, — Cecilia Jane, *b* 1959.

Issue of late Major Henry Patrick Neville Pelly, *b* 1912, *ka* in Assam 1945: *m* 1939, Marion Veronica, who *d* 1992, el da of Maj Harry Sanderson of Galashiels, Roxburghshire:—
George Michael Harvey (Arosa, Hawksdown, Walmer, Deal, Kent CT14 6PN), *b* 1944; Maj RA: *m* 1979, Diana, el da of Maj D. Montgomery, of Wotton, Surrey, and has issue living, Henry David Patrick, *b* 1983, — Grace Catherine, *b* 1981, — Rachel Caroline, *b* (twin) 1983. —— Sarah Rutherford, *b* 1941: *m* 1966, Jonathan Coldstream Lawley, of 56 Nightingale Lane, SW12, and has issue living, Thomas Henry, *b* 1973, — Juliet Rosemary, *b* 1969: *m* 1998, Koert Otto Erhardt, and has issue living, Matthew Otto Robert *b* 1999, — Katherine Jane, *b* 1970.

Grandchildren of late Maj William Francis Henry Pelly, 2nd son of Rev Charles Henry Pelly (ante):—
Issue of late Capt Charles Nigel Pelly, OBE, *b* 1908, *d* 1966: *m* 1934, Betty Joan, who *d* 1995, da of Lt-Col Leo Webster Cole, OBE, of Cairo:—
Christopher Patrick Cavendish (57 Corbière Av, Parkstone, Poole, Dorset), *b* 1939; MA: *m* 1969, Brenda Amy Grosvenor, da of Alfred Mutlow Grosvenor Herd (M Bute, colls), and has issue living, Nigel Christopher Grosvenor, *b* 1973, — Amanda Rachel, *b* 1970. —— †Marcus Nigel, *b* 1941; R Hong Kong Police: *m* 1st, 1971, Peggy Jane, da of Robert A. Wright, of Vic, BC, Canada; 2ndly, 1978, Barbara (22 Nicholli St, S Duncraig, W Australia 6023), da of S. Mason, of Harare, Zimbabwe, and *d* 1996, leaving issue (by 2nd *m*), Nicholas Julian, *b* 1982, — Andrew Jonathan, *b* 1984. —— Sally Joan, *b* 1944: *m* 1967, Paul Edmond de Rham, of The Lawns, 17 Moorlands Rd, West Moors, Wimborne, Dorset, and has issue living, Marc Edmond, *b* 1970, — Joanna Claire, *b* 1968, — Lucy Caroline, *b* 1976, — Sophie Charlotte, *b* 1979.

Grandchildren of late Richard Stewart Pelly, 2nd son of Charles Pelly, MCS (ante):—
Issue of late Henry Conway Dobbs Pelly, *b* 1878, *d* 1908: *m* 1903, Brenda, who *d* 1935, da of W. D. Horsley, MCS:—
Stuart Horsley, *b* 19—. —— Ralph Horsley, *b* 1907; BC Civil Ser: *m* 1928, Jacobina Benson, da of G. N. Landscrown, of Aberdeen, and has issue living, Bruce Conway, *b* 1933; RCN 1950-55, served Korean War: *m* 1962, Lucille Odette, da of Rev Ernest Amex, of Grande Ligne Mission, Quebec City, and has issue, Scott *b* 1965, Susanne Lucille *b* 1963, — Brian

George, b 1938: m 1958, Bernice Lorraine, da of E. E. Cave, Sgt RCMP, of Vancouver, BC, and has issue living, Michael George, b 1961, Steven Todd, b 1963, Lisa Lorraine, b 1964, Michele Kim, b 1966, — Patricia Landscrown, b 1929: m 19—, George E. Belsham, and has issue. ——— Conway Horsley, b 19—.

　　　　　　Grandchildren of late Edward Pelly, 3rd son of Charles Pelly, MCS (ante):—
　　　Issue of late Edward Raymond Pelly, b 1890, d 1963: m 1st, 1918, Frances Muriel, who d 1943, da of late Rev Alfred Shidrick, V of Milton-under-Wychwood, Oxon; 2ndly, 1944, Dorothy Jean Edna (8 Carlton House, 1251 Lawrence Av, Kelowna, British Columbia V17 6M5), el da of late J. M. Dadson, of Winnipeg, Canada:—
(By 2nd m) †John Edward, b 1947: m 1975, Patricia (2576 Bendale Rd, N Vancouver, BC, Canada), 2nd da of Jack F. Cogger, of Surrey, and d 1995, leaving issue, Tod Cogger, b 1978, — Edward Reid, b 1979. ——— Mary Ann, b 1945: m 1967, Douglas Alva Snowsell, of Casilla 312V, Correro 21, Santiago, Chile, and has issue living, Brandon James b 1969, — Colin David, b 1970.

　　　　　　Granddaughter of late Rear-Adm Francis Raymond Pelly, 4th son of Charles Pelly, MCS (ante):—
　　　Issue of late Lt-Col Hutcheson Raymond Pelly, IA, b 1887, d 1979: m 1913, Kathleen Mary, who d 1984, da of Edward Clifford-Walsh, of St Aidens, Arklow, co Wicklow:—
Dorothy Mary Fleurette (77 Archway St, Barnes, SW13 0AN), b 1921; 1939-45 War (despatches).

Branch from 4th son of 1st Baronet

　　　　　　Grandchildren of late Albert Edgar Champion Pelly, el son of late Albert Champion Pelly, el son of Albert Pelly (b 1813), 4th son of 1st baronet:—
　　　Issue of late John Pelly, b 1905, d 1981: m 1st, 1931, Bertha, who d 1935, da of John William Selwin Taylor, of Alfreton, Derby; 2ndly, 1942, Hilda May, who d 1977, elder da of Thomas Brewer Barrow, of Bedminster, Bristol:—
(By 2nd m) Derek John (Jakob-Schmid-Str 19, 85221 Dachau, Germany), b 1946: m 1985, (m diss 1993), Elvira Maria Lute.

　　　Issue of late Noel Henry Pelly, b 1906, d 1974: m 1932, Marjorie, who d 1992, da of late Frank Harold Hinton, of Forest Hill, SE:—
Raymond Frank (27 Harrington Villas, Brighton BN1 6RG), b 1940: m 1st, 1964, Janet, da of late Alexander Head, of 6 Long Lodge Drive, Walton-on-Thames; 2ndly, 1994, Pauline Ruth Rowlands, da of late William Dey, of Ripon, N Yorks, and has issue living, Nicole Louise, b 1966; has issue living, Grace b 1991, — Lisette Suzanne, b 1969.

　　　Issue of late Edgar Frank Pelly, b 1919, d 1954: m 1941, Dulcie Vera Manning, who m 2ndly, 1959, Dennis Smith, and d 1997:—
Dorinda May, b 1945: m 1st, 1965 (m diss 1985), John Scoltock; 2ndly, 1992, Roger James Channon, of 7 Oakdale Rd, Downend, Bristol, and has issue living (by 1st m), Simon John, b 1969. — Amanda Louise, b 1968. ——— Julia Ruth, b 1947: m 1966, Terry Gilborson, of 1 College Court, Glaisdale Rd, Fishponds, Bristol, and has issue living, Mark Julian, b 1966, — Sarah Louise, b 1969.

　　　　　　Granddaughters of late Russell George Pelly, son of late William Henry Pelly, 2nd son of Albert Pelly (b 1813) (ante):—
　　　Issue of late Russell Steele Pelly, b 1910, d 1993: m 1945, Agnes Mysie (32 Verena Terr, Perth PH2 0BZ), da of late F. H. Macpherson, solicitor of Ayr:—
Frances Elsie, ARSA, b 1947. ——— Lindsay Grace, b 1950: m 1976, John Warrender Gow, and has issue living, David Russell, b 1979, — Hazel Joan, b 1977, — Morven Elizabeth, b 1983. ——— Mysie Ann, b 1953: m 1981, Robert Ferguson, and has issue living, Ruaraidh, b 1989, — Shuna Margaret, b 1985.

　　　Issue of late Anthony Roger Pelly, b 1915, d 1972: m 1st, 1947, (m diss 1965), Joan, da of late Gp Capt Martin William Flack, CBE, MB; 2ndly, 1968, Mrs Eileen Cleveland (73 Warrington Cres, Maida Vale, W9), da of late Joseph Prior:—
(By 1st m) Sarah Jane, b 1949.

　　　　　　Granddaughter of late Capt John Henry Pelly, RN, 3rd son of late Albert Pelly (b 1813) (ante):—
　　　Issue of late Charles Thorne Pelly, b 1890, d 1966: m 1922, Lilian May, who d 1976, da of late Rear-Adm John William Ham, CB:—
Pauline Elizabeth, b 1927: m 1st, 1948, Peter Anthony Welsford; 2ndly, 1961, Aveling Jocelyn Pickard, of 17 The Leys, Esher Rd, Walton-on-Thames, Surrey KT12 4LP, and has issue living (by 1st m) Paul Simon, b 1953: m 1998, Artemis Tsimrikidou, — Penelope Ann, b 1949: m 1975, Stuart Hall, and has issue living, Simon Leslie b 1983, Oliver Charles b 1986.

Branch from 5th son of 1st Baronet

　　　　　　Grandson of late John Gurney Richard Pelly, eldest son of late Capt Richard Wilson Pelly, RN, 5th son of 1st baronet:—
　　　Issue of late Vivian Gurney Pelly, b 1881, d 1949: m 1st, 1907, Dorothy Penrose, who d 1972, el da of William Henry Sewell, formerly of Epping Place, Epping; 2ndly, 1946, Hilda Victoria Cole:—
(By 1st m) Douglas Gurney, b 1910; formerly Lt Maritime RA; High Sheriff of Essex 1962: m 1935, Monica, da of late Lt-Col Arthur Wignall Tate, DSO (see Tate, Bt, colls), and has issue living, John Gurney (Spring Hill, E Malling, Kent), b 1938: m 1973, Vanda Joan, da of Col Hubert Mortimer Allfrey, MC, TD (E Romney, colls), and has issue living, Sam Gurney b 1974, James Rupert b 1976, Guy Wignall b 1982, — William Henry (The Old Rectory, Sherrington, Warminster,

Wilts), *b* 1946: *m* 1975, Anne, yr da of Francis Byrne, and has issue living, Henry Francis *b* 1978, Rupert Alexander *b* 1980, — Claire Rose *b* 1943: *m* 1st, 1966 (*m diss* 1981), 17th Earl of Pembroke and Montgomery; 2ndly, 1984, Stuart Wyndham Murray Threipland, of Dunbeath Castle, Dunbeath, Caithness. *Residence* – Swaynes Hall, Widdington, nr Newport, Essex.

Grandchildren of late Rev Canon Richard Arnold Pelly, 2nd son of late Capt Richard Wilson Pelly (ante):—
Issue of the Rev Canon Richard Lawrence Pelly, *b* 1886, *d* 1976: *m* 1927, Rosa Salome, MB, who *d* 1995, da of late Rt Rev John Wordsworth, DD, 93rd Lord Bishop of Salisbury (Williams, Bt, *cr* 1915):—
Richard Christopher Wordsworth (Stonyroad, Audishaw Lane, Boylestone, Derbys DE6 5AE), *b* 1938; *ed* Marlborough, and Clare Coll, Camb (BA): *m* 1962, Ruth Elinor, da of Philip Askey, of Weaverham, Ches, and has issue living, Richard Hugh, *b* 1964, — David John, *b* 1972: *m* 1996, Paula Weston, and has issue living, Jordan *b* 19—, Chad *b* 19—, — Katherine Jane, *b* 1966: *m* 1991, Jasper John Pleydell-Bouverie, yr son of Hon Reuben Pleydell-Bouverie, and has issue (*see* E Radnor). —— Hugh John Wordsworth (Wake House, Ebbesbourne Wake, Salisbury, Wilts SP5 5JL), *b* 1945; *ed* Marlborough; MB, BS, DCH: *m* 1972, Jane Mary Fergusson, and has issue living, Tom Fergus, *b* 1975, — Matthew David, *b* 1977, — Adam, *b* 1979, — Christopher Hugh, *b* 1982, — Claire Alexandra, *b* 1990. —— Elizabeth Mary, *b* 1929: *m* 1952, Wyndham M. Jordan, MA, BM, BCh, DRCOG, who *d* 1996, of 81A Beccles Rd, Bungay, Suffolk NR35 1IIU, and has issue living, Christopher Wyndham (Highbury, Love Lane, Shaw, Newbury, Berks RG13 2DY), *b* 1956; BSc: *m* 1979, Gillian Smith, and has issue living, Anthony *b* 1989, Zhala *b* 1987, — Rosalind Cicely, *b* 1955; MA: *m* 1986, Robert Tatam, of 21 Sheredan Rd, Highams Park, E4 9RW, and has issue living, Luke Wyndham Charles *b* 1989, — Diana Salome, *b* 1959; BA: *m* 1983, Timothy Benge-Abbott, of 7 Southland Close, Colchester, Essex CO4 4QH, and has issue living, Daniel *b* 1986, Joel *b* 1989, — Alison Faith, *b* 1961; MB, BS, DRCOG, DCH, MRCGP: *m* 1983, Timothy Clarke, BSc, PhD, of Norfolk House, 1 Grange Rd, Bishop's Stortford, Herts, and has issue living, Alexander *b* 1998, Fiona *b* 1994. —— Rosa Jane, *b* 1931. —— Juliet Rachel, *b* 1933: *m* 1964, William Gibbins Webb, of 44 Mill Rd, Salisbury, Wilts SP2 7RZ, and has issue living, Rachel Sally, *b* 1965, — Rhoda Jane, *b* 1966: *m* 1989, Andrew Thomas Agerbak, of 32 Butler Rd, Harrow, Middx HA1 4DR, and has issue living, Elinor *b* 1995, Isabel *b* 1997. —— Robina Catherine, *b* 1935: *m* 1958 (*m diss* 1986), Timothy Sherwood Hattersley, MB, BChir, of 3 Mill Race, Salisbury, and has issue living, Andrew Tym, *b* 1958; MB, BChir, MRCP: *m* 1986, Katharine Dick, and has issue living, Mark *b* 1995, Ruth *b* 1991, Rosie *b* 1993, — William John, *b* 1960; BSc, — Richard Wordsworth, *b* 1964; MB, BS: *m* 1991, Susan Herbert, and has issue living, Emma Rachel *b* 1998.

Issue of late Francis Brian Pelly, AFC, *b* 1889, *d* 1984: *m* 1913, (Edith) Beatrice, who *d* 1984, da of late Rev William James Packe, V of Feering, Kelvedon:—
†Michael Brian, *b* 1915; *ed* Bryanston; CEng: *m* 1946, Mary Margaret (Fairview, 71 High St, Rode, Bath BA3 6PB), da of late Herbert Southerden Burn, CBE, and *d* 1994, leaving issue, Roger Brian, *b* 1950; *ed* Bryanston, Southampton Univ and Birmingham Univ (MSc), MIOSH: *m* 1st, 1980 (*m diss* 1986), Monica Giovanna Deorsola; 2ndly, 1987, Christine Joyce McFarlane, — David Arnold (29 Leaside Av, N10), *b* 1954; *ed* Bryanston, York Univ and Bradford Univ (BTech): *m* 1989, Deborah Susan Mattinson, and has issue living, Henry Theodore Mattinson *b* 1992, Francis Michael Mattinson *b* 1994, Clara May Mattinson *b* 1990, — Nicola Susan (3255 Cedar Av, Westmount, Montreal, Quebec, Canada), *b* 1948; *ed* Sherborne Sch for Girls and Sidcot Sch: *m* 1st, 1972 (*m diss* 1977), Peter Charles Jeffery; 2ndly, 19—, Harry Parnass, and has issue living (by 2nd husband), Arik Shaan Mika-El *b* 1992, Talia Shane *b* 1984. —— Peter Richard (Green Farm, Bovingdon Green, Bovingdon, Herts HP3 0LF), *b* 1916; *ed* Bryanston; CEng; *m* 1945, Kathleen Irene, da of late S. W. Moorhouse, of Guildford, and has issue living, Lynda Ann, *b* 1947: *m* 1980, Edward Macalister-Smith, of 9 Whittox Lane, Frome, Somerset BA11 3BY, and has issue living, Sam Henry *b* 1982, Mathilda Rose *b* 1983, — Kathleen Georgina, *b* 1951: *m* 1975, E. V. Caldwell, of Moses Plat Farm, Speen, Aylesbury, Bucks. —— Margaret Beatrice (Rosebay Cottage, 15 Langham Place, Rode, Bath, Avon BA3 6PL), *b* 1921: *m* 1st, 1943 (*m diss* 1959), Theodore Sanger; 2ndly, 1969, Jovan Ulic, of Belgrade, and has issue living (by 1st *m*), Melody, *b* 1947: *m* 1970, Peter Wright, and has issue living, Megan Jenett *b* 1973, Alice Rosamund *b* 1979, Madelene Rose *b* 1980, — Katrina Scarlett, *b* 1952: *m* 1977, Michael Power, and has issue living, Katherine *b* 1978, Molly *b* 1980, Ellen *b* 1983.

Issue of late Capt Arthur Roland Pelly, *b* 1895, *d* 1966: *m* 1920, Phyllis Elsie, who *d* 1974, da of late Alexander Duff Henderson, of Hampstead, NW:—
John Gordon (Aniceford House, Stockton-on-Teme, Worcs WR6 6UX), *b* 1923; *ed* Marlborough; Lt RNVR; 1939-45 War (despatches): *m* 1947, Patricia Maureen, da of late Maj Hugh Clarence Fuller, of Arran Lodge, Crossabeg, co Wexford, and has issue living, John Henry Patrick Fuller (Cleave House, Fordcombe, Kent TN3 0RJ), *b* 1953; *ed* Marlborough: *m* 1980, Susan Elizabeth, da of Michael A. Briggs, of Harts, Penshurst, Kent, and has issue living, Freddie John Fuller *b* 1986, Clare Elizabeth *b* 1984, Serena Rose *b* 1989, — Priscilla Jane, *b* 1949: *m* 1972, David Dalziel Mundell, of Nelgai, Condamine, Qld, and has issue living, John Dalziel *b* 1977, Andrew Hugh Dalziel *b* 1979, Sarah Richenda *b* 1973, Lucinda Clare *b* 1975, — Caroline Anne, *b* 1950: *m* 1973, Michael Eliot Howard, of Green Farm, Sankyns Green, Worcester, and has issue living, Nicholas Henry *b* 1979, Harry Eliot *b* 1982, Joanna Clare *b* 1977. —— Derek Roland (Kenbank, St John's Town of Dalry, Kirkcudbrightshire DG7 3TX), *b* 1929; *ed* Marlborough and Trin Coll, Camb (MA): *m* 1953, Susan, da of John Malcolm Roberts, of 4 Macartney House, Chesterfield Walk, Greenwich, SE10, and has issue living, Samuel Roland, *b* 1960, — Rosemary Jane *b* 1955: *m* 1988, Mark C. Campbell, son of D. M. Campbell, of Colesbourne, Glos, and has issue living, Alexander Leo *b* 1990, Euan Henderson *b* 1992, — Catherine Susan, *b* 1958: *m* 1982, Simon A. W. Osborn, only son of Col M. A. C. Osborn, of Shaftesbury, Dorset, and has issue living, George Ashby Arthur *b* 1990, Cicely Mai Elsie *b* 1986, Anna Catherine Pelly *b* 1988. —— Mary Duff, *b* 1921: *m* 1945, George T. B. Stevens, solicitor, of Barn Corner, All Cannings, Devizes, Wilts, and has issue living, Charles Bridges, *b* 1946; *ed* Cheltenham Coll; ACIB, FAAI, MSI: *m* 1972, Jeanette MacDonald, da of late Walter Moore, of Barbados, and has issue living, Edward George Bridges *b* 1976, — David George, *b* 1951; *ed* Cheltenham Coll, and St Bartholomew's Hosp (BSc, MB, BS, MRCGP, MRCPsych): *m* 1976, Philippa Mary, da of Charles Richard Pemberton Steer, of Llandevaud, Gwent, and has issue living, Hugh Richard *b* 1979, Alec Charles *b* 1982, — Lucia Mary, *b* 1956: *m* 1981, Philip Charles Dinkel, RIBA, son of Prof Michael Dinkel, of Bussage, Glos, and has issue living, Henry Michael George *b* 1988, William Theodore John *b* 1990, Charlotte Mary *b* 1986. —— Janet Elizabeth (83 Bainton Rd, Oxford OX2 7AG), *b* 1926: *m* 1953 (*m diss* 1981), Michael L. Fenwick, PhD, and has issue living, Allison Jane, *b* 1955, Anne Richenda, *b* 1957. — Juliet Nicola, *b* 1959: *m* 1992, Derwin Nazarino, of 4305 SW 100th St, Seattle, USA.

Grandsons of late Capt Richard Wilson Pelly, RN (ante):—
Issue of late Adm Sir Henry Bertram Pelly, KCVO, CB, *b* 1867, *d* 1942: *m* 1904, Lilian Katharine Hawkshaw, who *d* 1966, da of Sir William Vincent, 12th Bt (*cr* 1620, ext):—
Douglas Charles Vincent (4 Shapley Hill, Winchfield, Hants, RG27 8BU), *b* 1908; Com RN (ret); 1939-45 War (despatches): *m* 1938, Catherine Loraine, da of Edwyn Conran, of Hurlingham, Buenos Aires, and has issue living, Douglas Edwyn Vincent (10 Freelands Rd, Cobham, Surrey KT11 2ND), *b* 1951: *m* 1974, Susan Margaret, da of George Hards, of Cobham, Surrey, and has issue living, Matthew James *b* 1984, Jessica *b* 1975, Samantha *b* 1976, — Anne

Loraine, *b* 1939: *m* 1966, Lachlan Nicholas Ferrar Forbes, of St Andrew's School, Private Bag, Molo, Kenya, and has issue living, Lachlan Pelly Ferrar *b* 1970: *m* 1999, Melanie, da of Jonathan Knights, of Bletsoe, Beds, Angus Maxwell Pelly *b* 1971: *m* 1998, Anne-Kathrin, da of Jochen Neumann, of Berlin, Germany, — Gillian Esmé, *b* 1942: *m* 1983, Timothy C. Caffell, of 7 Waverley Rd, Stoke d'Abernon, Surrey, 2nd son of E. W. Caffell, of Cobham, Surrey, and has issue living, Anna Margaret Juliet *b* 1985, — Catherine Elizabeth, *b* 1948: *m* 1973, Simon Maxwell, and has issue living, Daniel *b* 1976, Oliver *b* 1977, Dominic *b* 1981. —— Adrian Vincent, LVO (Coombeside, E Meon, Petersfield, Hants GU32 1PB), *b* 1919; late Lt RNVR; HM's Land Steward at Windsor 1951-71; a JP; *cr* MVO 1962, LVO 1971: *m* 1975, Margaret Esterel, who *d* 1997, el da of late Lt-Col Roger Uvedale Lambert, MBE, of Cuckseys Farm, Bletchingley, Surrey.

Grandchildren of late Edmund Nevill Richard Pelly, 3rd son of late Capt Richard Wilson Pelly, RN (ante):—
Issue of late Capt John Noel Pelly, CBE, RN, *b* 1888, *d* on active ser 1945: *m* 1924, Rosalind, who *d* 1957, da of late R. G. Gatehouse, of Abbot's Grange, Bebington, Cheshire:—
John Stewart Gatehouse, *b* 1930: *m* 1960, Helen Josephine, da of Denys Heaton Hirst, of 46 Lightridge Rd, Fixby, Huddersfield, and has issue living, Jennifer Œnone, *b* 1965, — Catherine Allison, *b* 1967, — Helen Rosalind, *b* 1969, — Isobel Serena, *b* 1973. *Residence* – Great Wilsey Farm, Haverhill, Suffolk. —— Rosemary Œnone, *b* 1927: *m* 1956, Gordon Nelmes, who *d* 1992, and has issue living, John Pelly, *b* 1957: *m* 1988, Fiona Jane, da of Robert Nalder, of Underriver, Kent, and has issue living, Flora Mary *b* 1991, Emma Rosemary *b* 1993, Elizabeth Margaret *b* 1996, — Godfrey Edward, *b* 1959: *m* 1998, Judith Ann, da of Norman Oliver, of Newmarket, and has issue living, Oliver Ernest Noel *b* 19—, — Edmund Gordon, *b* 1965, — Rosalind Jane, *b* 1962: *m* 1986, Charles Richard Maurice Bishop, and has issue living, Thomas Richard Chilton *b* 1993, Rosanna Emily Margaret *b* 1990, Victoria Œnone Jane *b* 1994. *Residence* – Gardeners, Hatfield Peverel, nr Chelmsford, Essex CM3 2NS.

Issue of late Lt-Col (Edmund) Godfrey Pelly, DSO, MC, *b* 1889, *d* on active ser 1939: *m* 1919, Isabel Amy, who *d* 1988, da of late Robert Henry Fowler, of 5 Park Square West, NW:—
Robert Hubert (Victoria House, Pierce Lane, Fulbourn, Cambridge CB1 5DL), *b* 1923; *ed* Shrewsbury, and Trin Coll, Camb (BA 1950); 1939-45 War as Capt Lothians and Border Yeo (despatches): *m* 1951, Eirolys Elizabeth, da of late Maj le Gendre George William Horton-Fawkes, OBE, of Farnley Hall, Otley, Yorks, and has issue living, Richard Fowler, *b* 1955: *m* 1983, Michelle Colette, yr da of Dr Henri Bouteille, of St Etienne, France, and has issue living, Isabelle *b* 1986, Victoria Sarah *b* 1988, Mathilde *b* 1990, — Robert Simon Horton (47 Isis St, SW18 3QL), *b* 1960: *m* 1989, Rachel M., yst da of Peter Hamilton-Ely, of Fovant, Wilts, and has issue living, Hugh *b* 1995, Rupert *b* 1997, Camilla *b* 1993, — Serena Louise, *b* 1953: *m* 1974, Stephen John Richards, and has issue living, Thomas Linton *b* 1980, Clare Lucy *b* 1979.

Grandchildren of late Herbert Cecil Pelly, 4th son of late Capt Richard Wilson Pelly, RN (ante):—
Issue of late Humphrey Richard Pelly, *b* 1886, *d* 1955: *m* 1916, Barbara Vidal, who *d* 1965, da of Frederick Scrutton, of Woolpits, Nutfield, Surrey:—
Juliet (Cobblers Cottage, Bishop Monkton, Harrogate, N Yorks), *b* 1920: *m* 1946, George Ian Bray, MBE, who *d* 1985, and has issue living, Rose Elizabeth, *b* 1950, — Annabel Lucy, *b* (twin) 1950.

Issue of late Capt Gilbert Cecil Pelly, RN, *b* 1892, *d* 1961: *m* 1921, Constance Margery, who *d* 1952, da of late F. E. Tweenbrook Glazebrook, of Manila:—
David Cecil, *b* 1922; Lt-Cdr RN (ret); 1939-45 War (despatches, French Croix de Guerre); yr brother of Trinity House: *m* 1950, Angela Mary, da of late Capt Wilfrid Pearse Gandell, CBE, RN (ret), and has issue living, Richard Cecil, *b* 1951; *ed* Marlborough, and Selwyn Coll, Camb (MA, MSc, CEng, MI MechE); Capt RN; yr brother of Trinity House: *m* 1974, Fleur Veronica, only da of late John Desmond Proctor, of North View, High Trees Rd, Reigate, Surrey, and has issue living, Jonathan Henry *b* 1988, Cécile *b* 1977, Victoria Clare *b* 1982, — Nicholas John, *b* 1953; *ed* Marlborough, Birmingham Univ (BSc), and London Business Sch (MSc): *m* 1st, 1977 (*m diss* 1987), Elaine Margaret, el da of George G. Illingworth, of Dalmore, West Park Rd, Cupar, Fife; 2ndly, 1990, Sally, da of late Jack Odell, of Topeka, Kansas, USA, and has issue living (by 1st *m*), Alistair George *b* 1981, Catriona Marie *b* 1983, (by 2nd *m*) James David *b* 1992, — Patrick David (18 Badshot Park, Badshot Lea, Farnham, Surrey GU9 9JZ), *b* 1955; *ed* Marlborough, and Manchester Univ (BSc): *m* 1985, Margaret Julie, da of Scott Gray, of Coal Aston, Sheffield, and has issue living, Ralph Jonathan *b* 1986, Christopher Scott *b* 1988, — Gilbert Ralph, *b* 1966; *ed* Marlborough; Maj RM: *m* 1995, Jane A., da of J. A. Bagley, of Godalming, — Alexandra Helen, *b* 1961; *ed* Midhurst Gram Sch, and Birmingham Univ (BSocSc): *m* 1988, Ian Mark McLaren Pearson, eldest son of Malcolm J. S. Pearson, of Kingsgate, Chapel Sq, E Hendred, Oxon, and has issue living, Hamish James McLaren *b* 1993, Catherine Rose McLaren *b* 1995. *Residence* – Westerly, 5 The Marches, Fernhurst, Haslemere, Surrey GU27 3DT. —— John Kenneth (Cedar Croft, Rural Route 5, Bolton, Ont, Canada, L7E 5S1), *b* 1923; Lt (ret) RN: *m* 1946, Joan Campbell, only da of late J. C. Fraser, of Cedar Ridge, Scarborough, Ont, Canada, and has issue living, David Fraser (908-475 Laurier Av W, Ottawa, Ont, Canada K1R 7X1), *b* 1948; BSc (RMC), Lt-Cdr (ret); FRGS, FRCGS: *m* 1st, 1970 (*m diss* 1974), Sara Lynn, da of late Alan Nicholson, of Charlottetown, Prince Edward Island, Canada, 2ndly, 1991, Laurie, da of Joseph McGinnis, of New Jersey, USA, — Brian Gordon (41 Underhill Crescent, Aurora, Ontario, Canada L4G 5S3), *b* 1954; BMath (Univ of Waterloo); ASA, FCAS, FCIA: *m* 1978, Lynn Dorothy, el da of late Russell Henry Pearson, of Manitoulin Island, Ontario, and has issue living, Kyle Russell John *b* 1984, Heather Kathryn *b* 1981, Colleen Leslie *b* 1986, — Elizabeth Gail, *b* 1951: *m* 1975, John David Henry, of 127 Parkview Av, Willowdale, Ontario, Canada M2N 3Y4, and has issue living, Kimberly Beth *b* 1981, Robyn Lynn *b* 1984, Laura Louise *b* 1986. —— Peter Jeremy (Under Westwood, Upper Swainswick, Bath BA1 8BZ), *b* 1930: *m* 1953, Dorothy Joan (Joanna), da of Capt Thomas William Robert Hill, RA (*see* Dick-Cunyngham, Bt (ext), 1980 Edn), and adopted da of late Christopher Ransom, of Monk's Wall, Otterton, Budleigh Salterton, and has issue living, Anthony John, *b* 1956: *m* 1983, Jane Chisholm, only da of Noel Hair, of Wylam, Northumberland, and has issue living, Stephen Nicholas James *b* 1985, David Samuel Henry *b* 1988, Joanna Elizabeth Chisholm *b* (twin) 1988, — Lyndsay Madeleine, *b* 1954: *m* 1980, Peter St L. Kyrke-Smith, son of late B. H. S. Kyrke-Smith, of Penbedw, Nannerch, Clwyd, and has issue living, George Henry *b* 1991, Laura Elizabeth *b* 1983, Hannah Sarah *b* 1985, Rebecca Lucy *b* 1987, — Elizabeth Joanna Clare (Ovington House, Ovington, Northumberland), *b* 1958: *m* 1990 (*m diss* 19—), Anthony John Fielding, and has issue living, Leo Anthony *b* 1993, Molly Alexandra *b* 1992, — Nicolette Jane, *b* 1960, — Ann Catherine, *b* 1964.

Issue of late Sir Kenneth Raymond Pelly, MC, *b* 1893, *d* 1973: *m* 1919, Elspeth Norna, who *d* 1978, da of late Robert Campbell Grant, of Hale Edge, S Nuffield:—
Andrew Desmond, DFC (Halings, Balcombe, Haywards Heath, Sussex), *b* 1923; formerly F/Lt RAF: *m* 1945, Nancye Jean, da of Lt-Col Eric Tillyer Tatham (*see* B Digby, colls), and has issue living, Ian Raymond, *b* 1949: *m* 1974 (*m diss* 1993), Alana Murray, of Brisbane, Aust, — Angela Pauline (133 Georgia, Pointe Claire, Quebec, Canada), *b* 1947: *m* 1970 (*m diss* 1987), Douglas Frederick Wentzel, and has issue living, Kristian Douglas Andrew *b* 1979, Karla Juli-Anne *b* 1973,

Alexandra Korin *b* 1975, — Christine Mary, *b* 1952: *m* 1972, Timothy Cross, Col RAOC, and has issue living, Alexander Leigh *b* 1974, Stephen David *b* 1990, Gemma Charlotte *b* 1977, — Fiona Elizabeth, *b* 1955. —— Ursula Elspeth (New Barn, Colgate, Sussex), *b* 1921; formerly WRNS: *m* 1945, Lt Robert George Malloch Brown, SANF(V), who *d* 1967, and has issue living, George Mark, *b* 1953: *m* 1989, Patricia Anne Cronam, and has issue living, Maddison Jane *b* 1991, Isabel Anne *b* 1994.

Grandson of late Capt Richard Wilson Pelly, RN (ante):—
Issue of late Alfred Digby Pelly, *b* 1862, *d* 1940: *m* 1899, Evelyn Sophia, who *d* 1970, da of late Rev Edward John Harford (Bridges, Bt):—
Richard Edward, *b* 1905: *m* 1941, Diana Marthe Desgrand Mitchell, who *d* 1991, and has issue living, Louise Sophia PELLY (500 Avenue Rd, Apt 1407, Toronto, Ont, Canada M4V 2J6), *b* 1943; *ed* Concordia Univ, Montreal (BA 1973), McGill Univ, Montreal (LLB 1976, BCL 1977), and Harvard Univ (LLM 1978); Bar Quebec 1979, and Onnt 1990; QC 1991; joined Stikeman, Elliott 1980, ptnr since 1985; joined Gowing, Strathy & Henderson 1994; Commemorative Medal for 125th Confedn of Anniversary of Canada 1992; has resumed the surname of Pelly: *m* 1967 (*m diss* 1971), Donald MacTaggart; has issue living, Alexandra Caroline Diana PELLY *b* 1985, — Harriet Elizabeth Annabel (70 Third Av, Ottawa, Ont, Canada K1S 2J8), *b* 1948; *ed* McGill Univ, Montreal (BAPsych 1977, MSW 1985); resumed the surname of Pelly until re-marriage: *m* 1st, 1984 (*m diss* 1988), Francis Rohland Stark; 2ndly, 1991, Gerald Graham. *Residence* – West End, Coggeshall, Essex.

Branch from 8th son of 1st Baronet

Granddaughter of late Leonard Pelly, yr son of late Percy Leonard Pelly, 8th son of 1st baronet:—
Issue of late Eric Percy Leonard Pelly, *b* 1894, *d* 1978: *m* 1924, Helen Marjorie, who *d* 1968, da of late Edmund Richmond Wade, of Boston, USA:—
Rosamund Ann, *b* 1927: *m* 1950, Elliott Merriam Viney, DSO, MBE, TD, FSA, of Cross Farmhouse, Quainton, Aylesbury, Bucks HP22 4AR, and has issue living, Diana Susan, *b* 1952: *m* 1979, Hugh Scrimgeour, of 1 Teignmouth Rd, NW2 4HR, son of late Robin Scrimgeour, of Lockeridge, Marlborough, and has issue living, Daniel Viney Carron *b* 1981, Alexander Tom Viney *b* 1984, Sophie Rebekah Viney *b* 1988, — Amanda Louise, *b* 1954: *m* 1983, Tom Deakin, of 9 Hazlebury Rd, SW6, and has issue living, Jack Elliott *b* 1987, Charley *b* 1989.

The Pellys were settled in Dorset from the early 14th century, continuing with John Pelly of the co of Dorset, living 1419, William Pelly, gentleman, of Sturminster Marshall, living 1431/32, John Pelly, Kt (*ca* 1430-1510), William, of Sturminster Newton, living 1539, and John of Okeford Fitzpaine living 1539/69. In 1581 Thomas Pelly *m* Mary, da of Robert Nicles, Mayor of Poole, the family continuing in that town, as merchants, and ship owners with William (1593-1659) Overseer of the Poor 1622, William (1620-91) and John (1644-1720) Younger Brother of Trinity House. His son, Capt John Pelly (1683-1762) Elder Brother of Trinity House married, 2ndly, Grisella, da of Capt Thomas Collet, HEICS, of Barking, Essex. His son (by his 1st wife, Martha Lapthorne), was Capt John Pelly, HEICS, of Upton and Aveley (1711-1762), Younger Brother of Trinity House, who *m* Elizabeth, da of Henry Hinde, of Upton. Their son, Henry Hinde Pelly (1744-1818) inherited the Upton and Aveley estates. He was Capt HEICS, Elder Brother of Trinity House and High Sheriff of Essex in 1780; *m* Sally, da of Capt John Blake, HEICS, of Watcombe, Hants. Their eldest son, John Henry Pelly (1777-1852), of Upton, was created 1st baronet in 1840. He was Gov of Bank of England, Gov of Hudson's Bay Co and Deputy Master of Trinity House. He was *s* by his eldest son, Sir John Henry (1809-64), 2nd Bt, who was *s* by his eldest son, Sir Henry Carstairs (1844-77), 3rd Bt, who was *s* by his half-brother, Sir Harold (1863-1950), 4th Bt, who was *s* by his eldest son, Sir Harold Alwyne (1893-1981), 5th Bt, who was *s* by his eldest son, Sir John Alwyne (1918-1993), 6th Bt.

Pennington-Ramsden, see Ramsden.

PERKS (UK) 1908, of Wykham Park, Neithrop, co Oxford (Extinct 1979)

Sir (ROBERT) MALCOLM MEWBURN PERKS, 2nd and last *Baronet*.

DAUGHTERS LIVING OF SECOND BARONET

Rosemary (Oak Hall, Bartholomew St, Hythe, Kent CT21 5BT), *b* 1919; sometime Section Officer WAAF: *m* 1st, 1942, Lieut-Col Frederick Onslow Alexander Godwyn Bennett, who *d* 1993; 2ndly, 1995, A/Cdre Richard Julian Paget Prichard, CB, CBE, DFC, AFC, and has had issue (by 1st *m*), James Malcolm Alexander (68 Webcowet Rd, Arlington, Mass 02474, USA), *b* 1949: *m* 1984, Judith Krieger, and has issue living, Rachel Jennifer *b* 1992, — Elaine Roselle (29 East London St, Edinburgh EH7 4BN), *b* 1945: *m* 1976 (*m diss* 1996), Grant Bannatyne Fraser-Tytler, and has issue living, Alexander Hugh Bannatyne *b* 1978, — Louise Rosemary, *b* 1946: *m* 1968 (*m diss* 1986), Leonard Russell Hone, and *d* 1998, leaving issue, Andrew Nicholas Withers *b* 1972: *m* 1998, Jemma Curry (and has issue living, Laura *b* 1998), Jasper

George Edward Russell *b* 1976, Alexandra Belinda Louise *b* 1974: *m* 1999, Matthew Thomas Chivers, — Claire Rosamund, *b* 1951: *m* 1981, Oliver Riviere, of 34 St Giles Rd, Swanton Novers, Melton Constable, Norfolk NR24 2RB, and has issue living, Samuel James *b* 1981, Matthew David *b* 1985, Hannah Rose *b* 1983, — Francesca Rosalind, *b* 1959. —— Felicia Dorothy (The Barn, King Steps, Brecon, Powys), *b* 1921: *m* 1st, 1940 (*m diss* 1958), Robert Lyle; 2ndly, 1959 (*m diss* 1986), Ruggero Galletta, and has issue living, (by 1st *m*) Hugh Robert (now known as Ralph) (Glynderi, Senny-bridge, Brecon, Powys), *b* 1941: *m* 1968, Catherine (now known as Ruth) Steadman, da of Rupert Hector Greig, of Abbeyfield House, Camden Rd, Brecon, and has issue living, Robin *b* 1969, Leonard *b* 1972, Ellen *b* 1970, — Philip Dominic (Brussels, Belgium), *b* 1949, — Felix Gregory, *b* 1953: *m* 19—, Yolanda, da of ......, and has issue living, Benedict *b* 19—, — Thelma Cristina Elizabeth (now known as Virginia), *b* 1944: *m* 19—, Richard Swan, and has issue living, Reynold *b* 19—, Richard *b* 19—, Ralph *b* 19—, — Miranda Maria (now known as Agnes) (Paris, France), *b* 1946, — (by 2nd *m*) Flavio Raul Turiddù, *b* 1960; has issue living, Massimo *b* 19—, — Giuseppina Graziana Eva Francesca (8 The Wotton, Brecon, Powys), *b* 1959; has issue living, Oliver Benjamin Turiddù GALLETTA *b* 1981, Henry Arthur Rhys GALLETTA-WILLIAMS *b* 1993, Jessica Rhiana Elizabeth GALLETTA-WILLIAMS *b* 1991.

PERRING (UK) 1963, of Frensham Manor, Surrey

Sir JOHN RAYMOND PERRING, TD, 2nd *Baronet; b* 7 July 1931; *s* his father, *Sir* RALPH EDGAR, 1998; *ed* Stowe; Master Merchant Taylors' Co 1988 and 1994; Sheriff of City of London 1991: *m* 1961, Ella Christine, da of late Maj Anthony George Pelham (*see* E Chichester, colls), and has issue.

𝔄rms – Argent, on a pile barry wavy of eight azure and of the field, between two walnut trees eradicated proper, a lion rampant gules. 𝔠rest – Upon the trunk of a walnut tree, fessewise with two branches sprouting therefrom proper a sword erect or.
Residence – 21 Somerset Rd, Wimbledon, SW19 5JZ.

SONS LIVING

JOHN SIMON PELHAM, *b* 20 July 1962. —— Mark Ralph Pelham, *b* 1965: *m* 1999, Sophie, da of Anthony McPherson.

DAUGHTERS LIVING

Emma Mary, *b* 1963: *m* 1994, Christian Philip Heyman, son of Hans Heyman, of Dorking, Surrey, and has issue living, Benjamin Edward, *b* 1997, — Kate Isabelle, *b* 1999. —— Anna Margaret, *b* 1968: *m* 1992, Edward Pery Standish (*see* B Byron).

BROTHER LIVING

Michael Arthur (114 Harley St, W1N 1AG), *b* 1937; *ed* Stowe, and Trin Coll, Camb (MA, MB, BChir): *m* 1961 (*m diss* 1988), Elizabeth, da of late Air Commodore Eric Delano Barnes, CB, AFC, and has issue living, Nicholas David Delano, *b* 1963, — Michael Charles Delano, *b* 1965, — Thomas Edward Delano, *b* 1971, — Ralph Andrew Delano, *b* 1973.

COLLATERAL BRANCH LIVING

Issue of late Richard Eric Perring, 2nd son of 1st baronet, *b* 1933, *d* 1971: *m* 1964, Faith (17 Red House Close, Beaconsfield, Bucks HP9 1XU) (who *m* 2ndly, 1974 (*m diss* 1982), William John Stainton Clutterbuck, and resumed her former surname of Perring by deed poll, 1983), da of late Sir Peter (Arthur Percival Hay) Aitken:—
Christopher James, *b* 1965. —— Antony William, *b* 1967: *m* 1995, Victoria, C., only da of Michael Barham, of Quenington, Glos, and has issue living, Thomas Richard, *b* 1998. —— Graham Michael, *b* 1970.

The 1st baronet, Sir Ralph Edgar Perring, son of Col Sir John Ernest Perring, was Chm of Perring Furnishings Ltd 1948-81, and John Perring Ltd, and Lord Mayor of London 1962-63.

PERROTT (UK) 1911, with precedence from 1 July, 1716 (Extinct 1922)

Sir HERBERT CHARLES PERROTT, CH, CB (6th of GB 1716 creation according to Roll of Baronets), 1st (of UK 1911 creation), and last *Baronet*.

DAUGHTER LIVING OF SIXTH (GB) AND FIRST (UK) BARONET

Helena Ruth (*Helena, Viscountess Maitland*), *b* 1912; is an OStJ: *m* 1936, Viscount Maitland, who was *ka* 1943, only son of 15th Earl of Lauderdale. *Residences* – Park House, Makerston, Kelso, Roxburghshire TD5 7PA; Flat E, 34 Cadogan Sq, SW1X 0JL.

PETIT (UK) 1890, of Petit Hall, Island of Bombay

Sir DINSHAW MANOCKJEE PETIT, 5th *Baronet; b* 21 Jan 1965; *s* his father, *Sir* DINSHAW MANOCKJEE, 1998, and changed his name from Jehangir Petit to Dinshaw Manockjee Petit; *ed* Pierrepont Sch, New Hampshire Coll: *m* 1994, Laila, da of Homi F. Commissariat, and has issue.

Arms – Azure, on a chevron argent, between three urns of the last, therefrom issuant flames proper, as many bees volant, also proper. **Crest** – A ship under sail at sea, in front thereof an anchor fessewise, all proper.
Seat – Petit Hall, Nepean Sea Rd, Bombay 400 006, India.

Consequitur quodcunque petit

He obtains whatever he seeks

SON LIVING

REHAN, *b* 4 May 1995.

DAUGHTER LIVING

Aisha, *b* 1998.

BROTHER LIVING

Framjee, *b* 1968.

AUNT LIVING (*daughter of 3rd baronet*)

Dina, *b* 1931: *m* 1961, Yves Jean Robert Louis Morange, who *d* 1992, and has issue living, Shireen Isabelle, *b* 1962, — Anne Dina, *b* 1965.

MOTHER LIVING

Nirmala, da of Maj Gen Nanavati, of Bombay; assumed by deed poll 1964 her stepfather's surname of MODY in lieu of her patronymic: *m* 1st, 1964 (*m diss* 1985), as his 1st wife, Sir Dinshaw Manockjee Petit, 4th Bt; 2ndly, 1996, John Michael Henry Anderson, of Garden Flat, 225 Elgin Av, W9 1NH.

WIDOW LIVING OF FOURTH BARONET

ELIZABETH MARIA (*Lady Petit*), da of Hendrik Tinkelenberg: *m* 1986, as his 2nd wife, Sir Dinshaw Manockjee Petit, 4th Bt, who *d* 1998. *Residence* – Ruimzicht 281, Amsterdam 1068 CX, Netherlands.

COLLATERAL BRANCHES LIVING

Grandchildren of late Cowasjee Dinshaw Petit, el son of 1st baronet:—
Issue of late Pestonjee Cowasjee Petit, *b* 1866, *d* 1932: *m* 1894, Perzojbai Cowasjee Parukh:—
Hirabai (Hill Side, Nepean Sea Rd, Bombay), *b* 1898.

Issue of late Hormusjee Cowasjee Petit, *b* 1868, *d* 1939: *m* 1891, Perojbai Sorabjee Patuck, who *d* 1945:—
Cowasjee (Petit House, 25 Pali Mala Rd, Bandra, Bombay, 400050), *b* 1893: *m* 1919, Nawajbai (Nancy) Pherozeshaw Dadyburjor, and has issue living, Sorabjee (Solie) (Petit House, 25 Palimala Rd, opp. Hill Queen, Bandra (West), Bombay 400 050), *b* 1921: *m* 1946, Cleta Mathias, and has had issue, Marius *b* 1948: *m* 19—, Phil Brown (and has issue living, Marius Junius *b* 1971, Vanessa *b* 1974, Shareen *b* 1979), Stephen *b* 1950: *m* 1971 (*m diss* 19—), Marilyn Pereira (and has issue living, Stephanie *b* 1971), Sean *b* 1953: *m* 1990, Deborah Pavey (and has issue living, Nathan *b* 1991), Gavin *b* 1960, *d* 1985, Cory Ann *b* 1951: *m* 19—, Sharad Shelar (and has issue living, Sonia *b* 1981, Anisa *b* 1982), Jenny Lou *b* 1955: *m* 19—, Dosu Bhiwandiwalla (and has issue living, Neville *b* 1977, Zarir (a son) *b* 1980, Vera *b* 1976). — †Dinshawjee, *b* 1903: *m* 1940, Mithibai D. Poocha, and *d* 19—, leaving issue, Homa (Ram Mansion, Nepean Sea Rd, Bombay 400 006), *b* 1945, — Freny, *b* 1941. — Mithibai, *b* 1892. *Residence* – Ram Mansion, Nepean Sea Rd, Bombay, India.

Grandchildren of late Bomanjee Dinshaw Petit, 3rd son of 1st baronet:—
Issue of late Dhunjibhoy Bomanji Petit, *b* 1881, *d* 1957: *m* 1900, Humabai, who *d* 1949, el da of Jalbhoy Ardeshir Sett:—
†Maneckji, *b* 1900: *m* 1927, Perin Maneckji Vacha, and *d* 1082, without leaving issue. *Residence* – Sett Minar, Peddar Road, Bombay. — Ratanbai, *b* 1906: *m* 1st, 1934 (*m diss* 19—), Karl J. Khandalawalla; 2ndly, 1947, Lama Anagarika Govinda, and *d* 1986 (having changed her name to Li Gotami), without issue. — Kuverbai (Coomie), *b* 1908; BA 19—, LLB 19—: *m* 1939, Rustom F. Vakharia, of Silvan Roche, 21 Carmichael Rd, Mumbai, India, and has issue living, Sylla, *b* 1940: *m* 1964, Girish Malvi, of Anand, 8th Rd, Khar, Bombay 400 052, India (and has issue living, Shona *b* 1969, Rahul *b* 1970), — Roshan, *b* 1943: *m* 1969, Darayus Cooper (and has issue living, Lara *b* 1974, Rishad *b* 1976).

This baronetcy was granted with remainder to (i) Framjee Dinshaw Petit, 2nd son of the 1st baronet (Sir Dinshaw Manockjee Petit, a merchant and millowner of Bombay, who had served as Sheriff of Bombay and been Knighted 1887), and the heirs male of his body lawfully begotten, and (ii) the heirs male of the body of the 1st baronet. By special Act of the Legislative Council of India, all holders of the title relinquish their own name on succession and assume those of the 1st baronet. The 2nd baronet's daughter Ruttenbai, who *d* 1929, was the wife of Mohamed Ali Jinnah, later Governor-General and President of Pakistan.

PETO (UK) 1855, of Somerleyton Hall, Suffolk

Sir HENRY GEORGE MORTON PETO, 4th *Baronet*, *b* 29 April 1920; *s* his father, *Sir* (HENRY) FRANCIS MORTON, 1978; *ed* Sherborne, and Corpus Christi Coll, Camb: *m* 1947, Frances Jacqueline, JP, da of late Ralph Haldane Evers, of Milan, and has issue.

𝕬rms – Per pale indented or and gules barry of six, two annulets in fesse, all counterchanged. 𝕮rest – On a rock proper a sinister wing or, thereon three annulets gules.
Residence – Stream House, Selborne, Alton, Hants GU34 3LE.

SONS LIVING

FRANCIS MICHAEL MORTON (Cowdenknowes Mains, Earlston, Berwickshire TD4 6AA), *b* 1949: *m* 1974, Felicity Margaret, da of late Lt-Col John Alan Burns, of Fairfield, Cole Rd, Bruton, Som (*see* Hope-Dunbar, Bt, colls), and has issue living, David James Morton, *b* 25 Aug 1978, — George Francis John, *b* 1980. —— Robert Henry Haldane (117 East Sheen Av, SW14 8AX), *b* 1950: *m* 1975, Susan, only da of William Judge, of 25 Model Cottages, East Sheen, SW14, and has issue living, Thomas William Morton, *b* 1977, — Edward Henry Haldane, *b* 1979.

Ad finem fidelis
Faithful to the end

BROTHER LIVING

William Neill (Lapfordwood House, Lapford, Crediton, Devon EX17 6QU), *b* 1922; *ed* Sherborne: *m* 1st, 1943 (*m diss* 1962), Jacqueline Mary Valentine, who *d* 1971, da of late Gurth Edelsten, of Eastmore, PO Flora, Marquard, OFR; 2ndly, 1962, Ann Bernal, who *d* 1996, only da of late Lt-Col Theodore Thompson Laville, of Little Garth, Sampford Peverell, nr Tiverton, Devon; 3rdly, 1997, Mrs Rowan Margaret Crichton (*née* Cunningham), widow of Lt-Cmdr David Dewar Crichton, RN, and has issue living (by 1st *m*), James Francis Morton (Glan Cerrig, Llanfaglan, Caernarfon, Gwynedd LL54 5RS), *b* 1944: *m* 1st, 1969, Daphne, who *d* 1981, yr da of Thomas Henry Kennedy, of Blackwood, Auldgirth, Dumfries; 2ndly, 1987, Dorothy, yr da of Maurice Wilson, of Cooper House, Selside, Kendal, and has issue living, (by 1st *m*) Mark Edward *b* 1971, Alexander George *b* 1979, Rebecca Jane *b* 1975, — William Gurth (Anwoth House, Gatehouse-of-Fleet, Castle Douglas, Kirkcudbrightshire DG7 2EF), *b* 1949; *ed* Wellington, and RMA Sandhurst; late Maj 13th/18th R Hussars: *m* 1976, Alice Caroline, da of late Dermot Holdsworth Harling Turner, of Kildalloig, Campbeltown, Argyll, and has issue living, Roland Harry Morton *b* 1982, Alice Jane *b* 1979.

HALF-BROTHER LIVING

Raymond John (Westfield House, Puncknowle, Dorset DT2 9BP), *b* 1950; *ed* Ampleforth, and Brunel Univ: *m* 1986, Monica Marie, da of Thomas Barlow, of Chapeltown, Yorks.

COLLATERAL BRANCHES LIVING

Granddaughter of late Sir Geoffrey Kelsall Peto, KBE, 2nd son of late William Herbert Peto, 3rd son of 1st baronet:—
Issue of late Anthony Peto, *b* 1907, *d* 1994: *m* 1936, Baroness Barbara Wrangel, who *d* 1987, da of Baron Hermann Wrangel, of Genarp, Sweden:—
Ursula, *b* 1938: *m* 1960, Richard Alan Opperman, and has issue living, Mark Richard Charles, *b* 1963, — Nicholas Richard James, *b* 1965.

Issue living of late Basil Edward Peto (7th son of 1st baronet), who was *cr* a *Baronet* 1927:—
See Peto, Bt, *cr* 1927.

Sir Samuel Morton Peto, 1st Bt, MP for Norwich (*L*) 1847-55, and subsequently for Finsbury and Bristol, was the el son of William Peto, of Cookham, Berks.

PETO (UK) 1927, of Barnstaple, co Devon

Sir MICHAEL HENRY BASIL PETO, 4th *Baronet*; *b* 6 April 1938; *s* his father, *Brig Sir* CHRISTOPHER HENRY MAXWELL, DSO, 1980; *ed* Eton, and Ch Ch, Oxford (MA); Bar Inner Temple 1960; Member of Stock Exchange 1963: *m* 1st, 1963 (*m diss* 1970), Sarah Susan, yst da of Maj Sir Dennis Frederick Bankes Stucley, 5th Bt; 2ndly, 1971, Mrs Lucinda Mary Hilleary, da of Sir Charles Douglas Blackett, 9th Bt, and has issue by 1st and 2nd *m*.

Arms – Barry or and gules per pale indented counterchanged in chief a boar's head erased proper and in base two annulets counterchanged. **Crest** – On a rock proper a sinister wing or, thereon three annulets gules.
Residence – Lucker Southside Farmhouse, Belford, Northumberland NE75 7JW. *Clubs* – Pratt's, Northern Counties.

Faithful to the end

SONS LIVING (*By 1st marriage*)

HENRY CHRISTOPHER MORTON BAMPFYLDE, *b* 8 April 1967; *ed* Eton, and Oxford Brookes Univ (BSc): *m* 1998, Louise Imogen, yst da of Christopher Balck-Foote, of Stockcross, Berks. *Residence* – Court Hall, North Molton, Devon EX36 3HP.

(*By 2nd marriage*)

Hugh David, *b* 1974. —— Charles Michael, *b* 1977.

DAUGHTERS LIVING (*By 1st marriage*)

Emma Rose, *b* 1965: *m* 1994, Harry N. Matovu, yr son of late Leonard Matovu, of Vienna, and has issue living, Joseph Nathaniel Bukenya, *b* 1997. —— Marina Sarah, *b* 1968.

BROTHER LIVING

Nicholas John (Grey Walls, Chadlington, Oxon; Turf and Pratt's Clubs), *b* 1939; *ed* Eton, and RMA Sandhurst; Capt 9th/12th Lancers, ADC (to Gen Norman Wheeler) BAOR 1964: *m* 1st, 1969 (*m diss* 1978), Anne Colquhoun, el da of late John Tysen, New York; 2ndly, 1979 (*m diss* 1989), Lucinda Hilary, da of late Owen George Endicott Roberts, and formerly wife of Demetri P. Marchessini; 3rdly, 1991, Mrs Zoë Westropp, da of Charles Douglas Neville Walker, of 58 rue Singer, Paris, and formerly wife of Anthony Henry (Harry) Westropp, and has issue living (by 1st *m*), Alexander Tysen, *b* 1973.

SISTER LIVING

Elizabeth Mary, *b* 1936: *m* 1958, Ronald Philip Murphy, of Shippool House, Innishannon, co Cork, and has issue living, Charles Christopher Ronald, *b* 1959, — Richard Norbert, *b* 1961.

DAUGHTER LIVING OF SECOND BARONET

Serena Mary Francesa (*Serena, Lady Matheson of Matheson*), *b* 1928: *m* 1954, Maj Sir Torquhil Alexander Matheson of Matheson, 6th Bt, who *d* 1993. *Residences* – Trees Farm, Standerwick, Frome, Somerset BA11 2PP; Dalmhor, Duirinish, Kyle of Lochalsh, Ross-shire IV4 8BE.

COLLATERAL BRANCH LIVING

Issue of late Major (Basil Arthur) John Peto, King's Dragoon Guards, 3rd son of 1st baronet, *b* 1900, *d* 1954: *m* 1934, Patricia Geraldine (66 Whitelands House, Cheltenham Terr, SW3) (who *m* 2ndly, 1955, Lt-Col Hugh Granville Leveson Dudley Ryder, TD (*see* E Harrowby, colls)), da of late Gerald Macleay Browne, OBE:—
Jonathan Basil Morton (Bealings House, Woodbridge, Suffolk; Pratt's Club), *b* 1942; *ed* Eton; Coldm Gds 1962-66; ADC to Gov of Qld 1963-66: *m* 1969, Hon Selina Lilian Hughes-Young, da of 1st Baron St Helens, and has issue living, Amyas John, *b* 1969. — Harold Patrick Basil, *b* 1974, — Daisy Elizabeth, *b* 1971, — Augusta Mary, *b* 1977, — Violet Selina, *b* 1984. —— Virginia Anne (Raswell Cottage, Loxhill, Godalming, Surrey), *b* 1935: *m* 1st 1955 (*m diss* 1981), Gerard Wyndham Morgan-Grenville (*see* Ly Kinloss, colls); 2ndly, 1998, George A. Cox, and has issue (by 1st *m*) (*see* Ly Kinloss, colls). —— Joanna Dava, *b* 1938: *m* 1957, Capt Charles St John Graham Moncrieff, Scots Gds (*see* V Bolingbroke, colls, 1985 Edn), and has issue living, Alexander Charles Graham, *b* 1967, — Charlotte Henrietta, *b* 1959: *m* 1987, Benjamin Heath, yr son of William Heath, of Guildford, Surrey, and has issue living, Rory William *b* 1988, Pollyanna Rose *b* 1992, — Miranda Caroline (*Hon Mrs Mark F. R. Baring*), *b* 1961: *m* 1983, Hon Mark Francis Robert Baring, el son of 7th Baron Ashburton, and has issue (*see* B Ashburton), — Rosanna Claire, *b* 1965: *m* 1995, David Charles McCraith, elder son of Anthony McCraith, and has issue living, Natasha Phyllis *b* 1998. *Residence* - Easter Elcho, Rhynd, Perthshire. —— Sarah Christian Pandora (*Lady Bathurst*), *b* 1940: *m* 1959, Adm of the Fleet Sir David Benjamin Bathurst, GCB (*see* E Bathurst, colls).

The 1st baronet, Sir Basil Edward Peto (7th son of Sir Samuel Morton Peto, 1st Bt (*cr* 1855)), was MP for E or Devizes Div of Wilts (*C*) 1910-18 and for Barnstaple Div of Devon 1922-3, and 1924-35. Lt-Col Sir J. Michael Peto, 2nd Bt, Coldm Gds, served in World War I 1915-18 (despatches), and in World War II 1939-45.

PETRIE (UK) 1918, of Carrowcarden, Castleconnor, Barony of Tireragh, co Sligo

Trust, but observe

Sir PETER CHARLES PETRIE, CMG, 5th *Baronet*; *b* 7 March 1932; *s* his half-brother, *Lt-Col Sir* (CHARLES) RICHARD BORTHWICK, 1988; *ed* Westminster, and Ch Ch Oxford (MA); HM Diplomatic Service, 2nd Sec UK Del NATO Paris 1958, 1st Sec New Delhi 1961, Chargé d'Affaires Kathmandu 1963, 1st Sec UK Mission to UN, New York 1969, Counsellor Bonn 1973; Head of European Integration Dept, FCO 1976, Minister Paris 1979-85, HM Amb to Belgium 1985-89, since when Adviser to Governor of Bank of England; Memb Franco-British Council since 1994 (Chm British Section since 1997); Council Memb City Univ since 1997; late 2nd Lieut Gren Gds; CMG (1980): *m* 1958, Countess Lydwine Maria Fortunata, da of Count Charles Alphonse v Oberndorff, of The Hague and Paris, and has issue.

𝔄rms – Azure, on a bend between a stag's head couped and three cross crosslets fitchée argent, as many escallops gules. 𝔄rest – A demi-eagle displayed proper gazing at a sun or.
Residences – 16A Cambridge St, SW1V 4QH; 40 rue Lauriston, Paris 16e; Hameau du Jardin, Lestre, 50310 Montebourg, Normandy.

SONS LIVING

CHARLES JAMES, *b* 16 Sept 1959; *ed* American Coll, Paris (BA), INSEAD, Fontainebleau; 2nd Lieut 67th French Inf Regt; chief senior consultant Coopers and Lybrand 1987-90, UN Emergency Unit Sudan 1990-92, UN Operation Somalia 1992-94: *m* 1981, France, da of Comte Bernard de Hauteclocque, of Chateau d'Etrejust, Picardie, and has had issue, Arthur Cecil, *b* 15 Feb 1987, — Oliver Bernard, *b* 1989, — Victor François, *b* 1992, — Cecilia Marie Bernard, *b* and *d* 1985. ——— Wilfrid John, *b* 1965; *ed* Ecole St Jean de Passy, Lycée Louis Le Grand, and Ecole Polytechnique: *m* 1989, Fabienne, da of Louis Lacaille, of 3 Blvd Flandrin, 75116 Paris.

DAUGHTER LIVING

Leticia Jacqueline Fortunata Cecilia, *b* 1961: *m* 1989, Pierre-André de Chalendar, and has issue living, François, *b* 1990, — Jacques, *b* 1992, — Antoine, *b* 1997, — Laure, *b* 1994.

DAUGHTER LIVING OF SECOND BARONET

Violet Haddon, *b* 1913: *m* 1st, (Jan) 1937, Charles Edward Wilson Sleigh; 2ndly, 1950, William Dalziel Mungall Allison, who *d* 1957, and has issue living (by 1st *m*) Thomas Edward (The Gardens Cottage, E Saltoun, nr Pencaitland, E Lothian EH34 5DS), *b* 1939: *m* 1965, Daphne Mary Walker, da of Dr Charles Boness-Jones, of Bengal, India, and has issue living, David Edward *b* 1969, Charles Timothy Fisher *b* 1971, Patricia Mary *b* 1967, — Rosemary Anne ALEXANDER (Stoneacre, Otham, Maidstone, Kent), *b* (Dec) 1937; has resumed surname of Alexander: *m* 1st, 1956 (*m diss* 1975), (Walter) Ronald Alexander; 2ndly, 1982, His Honour Judge (George Leon Severyn) Dobry, CBE, and has issue living (by 1st *m*), Walter *b* 1957, Charles Edward *b* 1963, Rosalind *b* 1959, Caroline *b* 1961, — (by 2nd *m*) Robert William Mungall (6 Camus Park, Edinburgh EH10 6RY), *b* 1951: *m* 1st, 1982 (*m diss* 1991), Pamela Louise, da of William Dougal Taylor; 2ndly, 1996, Pauline Janice Anne, da of Samuel McCartney. *Residence* – 6 Camus Park, Edinburgh EH10 6RY.

Sir Charles Petrie, 1st baronet (son of Alexander Petrie, of Carrowcarden, Enniscrone, co Sligo, grandson of Peter Petrie, of Newburgh, Fife, and great grandson of George Petrie, of Port Leithen, Aberdeen), was Lord Mayor of Liverpool 1901-2, and Leader of Conservative Party. His son, Sir Charles Petrie, 3rd baronet, CBE, the eminent historian and author, was Knt Order of Civil Merit (Spain), Com of Orders of Crown of Italy, of George I of Greece, and of Isabella the Catholic of Spain, and Pres of Mil History Soc of Ireland.

PEYTON (GB) 1776, of Doddington, Cambridgeshire (Extinct 1962)

Sir ALGERNON THOMAS PEYTON, 7th and last *Baronet*.

DAUGHTERS LIVING OF SEVENTH BARONET

Delia, *b* 1916: *m* 1943, Major Benjamin George Barnett, MBE, TD, Oxfordshire Yeo; High Sheriff of Oxon 1969, who *d* 1998; and has issue living, David John Wheate, *b* 1946: *m* 1971, Annabel Mary, da of Peter Owen of Mixbury, Northants, and has issue living, James Peter Wheate *b* 1973, Toby Luke *b* 1981, Hermione, *b* 1975, — Charles Henry, *b* 1948: *m* 1978, Georgina Ross, da of David Coventry Greig, of Muirhead of Balgray, Irving, Ayrshire, and has issue living, John Robert *b* 1983, Flora Anne *b* 1979, — Rosemary Dorothea, *b* 1953. *Residence* – The Stud House, Great Purston, Brackley, Northants NN13 5PL. —— Elisabeth Rosamund, *b* 1919: *m* 1943, Capt John Nigel Bingham, Coldstream Guards (*see* E Lucan, colls). *Residence* – Stone House, Brimpton, Reading.

Philipson-Stow, see Stow.

FOLEY-PHILIPPS (UK) 1887, of Picton Castle, co Pembroke (Extinct 1962)

Sir RICHARD FOLEY FOLEY-PHILIPPS, 4th and last *Baronet*.

DAUGHTER LIVING OF SECOND BARONET

Sheila Victoria Katrin (*Dowager Lady Dunsany*), *b* 1912; is DStJ: *m* 1st, 1932, Major John Frederick Foley, Baron de Rutzen, Welsh Guards, who was *ka* in Italy 1944, having in 1918 received Roy licence (for himself and the heirs male of his body on succession) to use the title within the British Dominions; 2ndly, 1947, as his 2nd wife, the 19th Baron of Dunsany, who *d* 1999, and has issue living (by 2nd *m*) (*see* B Dunsany). *Residence* – Dunsany Castle, co Meath.

PHILLIPS (UK) 1912, of Tylney Hall, Rotherwick, co Southampton

Truth conquers

Sir ROBIN FRANCIS PHILLIPS, 3rd *Baronet*; *b* 29 July 1940; *s* his father, *Capt Sir* LIONEL FRANCIS, 1944; *ed* Aiglon Coll, Switzerland.

Arms – Or, on a pile azure, between two greyhounds courant in base sable, a lion rampant of the first, guttée-des poix. **Crest** – A demi-lion azure, charged on the shoulder with two annulets interlaced paleways or, between as many nuggets of gold.
Residence – 12 Manson Mews, SW7.

AUNT LIVING

Mary Pamela, *b* 1919: *m* 1943, Arthur Owen Hunt, who *d* 1988, and has issue living, Clive Anthony, *b* 1944: *m* 1980, Philippa Jane Samuel, and has issue living, William Edward *b* 1987, Annabel Carolyn Philippa *b* 1984, — David Charles, *b* 1947: *m* 1974, Julia Vivian Bennett, and has issue living, Peter Lionel *b* 1981, Gemma Helen *b* 1976, Vanessa Caroline *b* 1979, — Paula Caroline, *b* 1950. *Residence* – 4 Leicester Close, Henley-on-Thames, Oxon RG69 2LD.

WIDOW LIVING OF SECOND BARONET

CAMILLA MARY, da of late Capt Hugh Algernon Parker (*see* E Macclesfield, colls): *m* 1st, 1939, Capt Sir Lionel Francis Phillips, 2nd Bt, who was *ka* in Italy 1944; 2ndly, 1950, John George Pisani, who *d* 1982, of 21 Chancellor House, 17 Hyde Park Gate, SW7 5DQ.

The 1st baronet, Sir Lionel Phillips (son of late Philip Saunders Phillips, merchant of London), was a partner in the late firm of Wernher, Beit & Co, of 1 London Wall Buildings, EC; sometime Chm Central Mining & Investment Corporation Ltd, and Rand Mines Ltd; Hon Col 10th S African Inf and 1st S African Field Ambulance; one of the leaders of the Transvaal Reform Movement 1896, resulting in Jameson Raid (sentenced to death by Judge Gregorovski, sentence commuted to fine of £25,000); a MLA, S Africa 1910-15; prominently associated with Transvaal gold-mining industry, and five times Pres of Transvaal Chamber of Mines. The 2nd baronet, Capt Sir Lionel Francis, RA (TA), was *ka* in Italy 1944.

FAUDEL-PHILLIPS (UK) 1897, of Grosvenor Gardens, St George, Hanover Square, co London, and Queen's Gardens, West Brighton, co Sussex (Extinct 1941)

Sir LIONEL LAWSON FAUDEL FAUDEL-PHILLIPS, 3rd and last *Baronet*.

DAUGHTER LIVING OF THIRD BARONET

Helen Bridget (*Countess of Kilmorey*), *b* 1918; resumed her former style 1990: *m* 1st, 1941, 5th Earl of Kilmorey, who *d* 1977; 2ndly, 1978 (*m diss* 1990), Harold William Elliott. *Residence* – 8 The Dormers, Highworth, Swindon, Wilts.

PICKTHORN (UK) 1959, of Orford, co Suffolk

Sir JAMES FRANCIS PICKTHORN, 3rd *Baronet*; *b* 18 Feb 1955; *s* his father, *Sir* CHARLES WILLIAM RICHARDS, 1995; *ed* Eton: *m* 1997, Clare, yr da of Brian Craig-McFeely, of Sevenoaks, Kent, and has issue.
Residence – 45 Ringmer Av, SW6 5LP.

SON LIVING

WILLIAM EDWARD CRAIG, *b* 2 Dec 1998.

SISTERS LIVING

Caroline, *b* 1958. —— Frances, *b* 1960: *m* 1982, Crispin Bernard Noël Kelly, and has issue (*see* D Norfolk). *Residence* – Wrights Farm, Combe, Hungerford, Berks RG17 9EL.

UNCLE LIVING (*son of 1st baronet*)

Henry Gabriel Richards, *b* 1928; *ed* Eton, and Trin Coll, Camb: *m* 1955, Mary, da of Cecil James Juxon Talbot Barton, CMG, OBE, and has issue living, John, *b* 1957, — Andrew, *b* 1961: *m* 1995, Katherine S., elder da of Anthony Garnett, of Gastard, Wilts, and of Mrs William Dudgeon, of Stainforth, N Yorks, and has issue living, Arthur William Garnett *b* 1996, Edward James Henry *b* 1998, — Thomas David Alexander, *b* 1967: *m* 1993, Nicola, da of His Honour Judge (John Declan) Sheerin, of Rougham, Suffolk, and has issue living, Alice Mary Ella *b* 1996, Emma Frances Suzanne *b* 1997, — Henrietta Cicely, *b* 1959: *m* 1982, John Ramsay Lloyd-Jones, and has issue (*see* Maitland, Bt). *Residence* – 54 Chelsea Park Gdns, SW3.

AUNT LIVING (*daughter of 1st baronet*)

Catherine Ann Monica, *b* 1925: *m* 1950, Neil Atkinson Iliff, CBE, who *d* 1973, and has issue living, Charles, *b* 1952; *ed* Eton and Trin Coll, Camb: *m* 1989, Monica, da of Jerome Dessain, and has issue living, Jonathan, *b* 1993, Lucy *b* 1991, — Catherine, *b* 1955: *m* 1989, Andrew Saul, and has issue living, Edmund *b* 1990, Nancy *b* 1994, — Elizabeth Ann Julia, *b* 1957, — Mary, *b* 1958, — Georgina Margaret Pickthorn, *b* 1963: *m* 1994, Tobias Farrell, and has issue living, Gabriel *b* 1995. *Residences* – 32 Chipstead St, SW6 3SS; Rosehill, Orford, Woodbridge, Suffolk.

WIDOW LIVING OF SECOND BARONET

HELEN ANTONIA (*Dowager Lady Pickthorn*), only da of late Sir James Gow Mann, KCVO: *m* 1951, Sir Charles William Richards Pickthorn, 2nd Bt, who *d* 1995. *Residence* – 3 Hobury St, SW10.

Rt Hon Sir Kenneth William Murray Pickthorn, 1st Bt, was MP for Camb Univ (*C*) 1935-50, and Carlton, Notts 1950-66. He was Parl Sec, Min of Education 1951-54.

PIERS (I) 1661, of Tristernagh Abbey, Westmeath

Noble is the lion's anger

Sir JAMES DESMOND PIERS, 11th *Baronet*; *b* 24 July 1947; *s* his father, Sir CHARLES ROBERT FITZMAURICE, 1996; partner in law firm Russell & DuMoulin: *m* 1975, Sandra Mae Dixon, and has issue.

𝕬rms – Azure, three lions passant-guardant in fesse, between two double cotises argent. 𝕮rest – An arm embowed vested azure, charged with three plates and cuffed argent the hand holding a broken flagstaff, the flat azure, on a chief argent three torteaux.
Address – 3635 Bluebonnet Rd, N Vancouver, BC, Canada V7R 4C9.

SON LIVING

STEPHEN JAMES, *b* 14 Sept 1979.

DAUGHTER LIVING

Christine Sarah, *b* 1976.

COLLATERAL BRANCHES LIVING

Grandsons of late Lt-Col William Barrington Piers, el son of late Col Thomas Tristram Piers, 5th son of late Rev Octavius Piers, 5th son of 5th baronet:—
Issue of late William Price Barrington Piers, *b* 1905, *d* 1974: *m* 1935, Ursula Mary Bence, who *d* 1993, da of Rev George Alfred Charles Smith-Cranmoor, R of Baldock, Herts:—
Anthony Tristram Barrington (Withy Cottage, Wrantage, Taunton, Som TA3 6DJ), *b* 1939; Maj 1st Devonshire and Dorset Regt (ret): *m* 1st, 1964 (*m diss* 1981), Susan Jacqueline Dawn, only da of Lt-Col H. T. Bayldon, MC, of Las Palmas, Canary Islands; 2ndly, 1981, Mrs Mary Gertrude Eveleen Croft, da of D.H. Baker, of Farnham, Surrey, and has issue living (by 1st *m*), Christopher William Barrington, *b* 1973, — Ann-Marie Barrington, *b* 1965: *m* 1988, Kevin Crampton, and has issue living, Connor Sebastian *b* 1990, Rory Leto *b* 1992, Bran Zak *b* 1995, — Bridget Dawn Barrington, *b* 1967: *m* 1993, Anton Matthews, and has issue living, Isaac William *b* 1998, Lucy Ruby *b* 1995. —— Brian William Barrington (7 Ross St, Toowoomba, Queensland 4350, Australia), *b* 1941: *m* 1970, Stephanie Ellen Elizabeth, da of late Capt Attoe, of London, and has issue living, Robert Courtney Barrington, *b* 1973, — Samantha Barrington, *b* 1971. —— Charles Barrington (95 Belladona Rd, Roodekranz Ext 7, Roodepoort 1725, Transvaal, S Africa), *b* 1943; Lt-Col (ret) Rhodesian African Rifles: *m* 1980, Judy Melanie Pamela, da of P. D. Fuller, of Shurugwi, Zimbabwe, and has issue living, Niall Barrington, *b* 1984.

Granddaughters of late Col Thomas Tristram Piers (ante):—
Issue of late Rev Samuel Octavius Piers, *b* 1869, *d* 1940: *m* 1901, Mabel Marion, who *d* 1951, da of G. Smith, of Ipswich:—
†Charles Stuart Tristram, *b* 1920; Sub-Lt, RN; served 1939-45 War; *d* as a result of enemy action 1941. —— Violet Marion, *b* 1905: *m* 1st, 1931, Louis Brown, who *d* 1934; 2ndly, 1939, George Paul, and has issue living, (by 2nd *m*) Jacqueline Evelyn, *b* 1940: *m* 1961, Henry Charles Pope, of RR4, Paisley, Ontario, Canada N0G 2N0, and has issue living, David Henry (377 Russell St, Kincardine, Ontario, Canada N2Z 2A9) *b* 1964: *m* 1988, Heather Ann Sale (and has issue living, Jacob Davis *b* 1993, Chelsea Anne *b* 1995), Christopher Charles (1179 Colville Rd, Victoria, BC, Canada V9A 4R1) *b* 1969; PO 2nd class RCN: *m* 1993, Tracey Jean Stonehouse (and has issue living, Courtney Amanda *b* 1995), Jonathan George (931 Bewdley St, Esquimalt, BC, Canada V9A 5M4) *b* 1971: PO 2nd class RCN: *m* 1993, Jennifer Lynn Thede (and has issue living, Dylan Michael *b* 1994, Hayden Jonathan *b* 1996), James Stuart (1363 Ewert St, Prince George, BC, Canada V2N 5H2) *b* 1975, Brenda Kathleen *b* 1961: BA: *m* 1st, 1983, Dr Kenneth Lee Bridge; 2ndly, 1997, Gregory Neil McKeachnie, of 415 Durham St, Kincardine, Ontario, Canada N2Z 2B5 (and has issue living (by 1st *m*), Gordon Alexander Henry (Sandy) *b* 1985, Brian William Harrison *b* 1986, Robyn Lee *b* 1984, Rebecca Lynne *b* 1990), Deborah Lynne *b* 1963; BSW: *m* 1987, Kenneth Robert McCulloch, of 690 Albert St, Port Elgin, Ontario, Canada N0H 2C1 (and has issue living, Curtis Matthew *b* 1989, Jared Michael *b* 1991, Brett Fraser *b* 1994, Bethany Dawn *b* 1992). *Residence* – 510 Wellington St, Apt 102, Port Elgin, Ontario, Canada. —— Evelyn Helena, *b* 1909: *m* 1st, 1938, George Damer, Lt RCA, who was *ka* in Italy 1944; 2ndly, 1972, Robert Owen Fowler, AMIEE, of Liverpool, Nova Scotia, and has issue living (by 1st *m*), George Terence Stuart (Hazelbank, 14 Beech Rd, Reigate, Surrey), *b* 1940; BSc: *m* 1964, Michèle Mary Godwin Prouten, and has issue living, Justin Dawson *b* 1967, Miranda Jane *b* 1968, Annabel Katie Louise *b* 1974. *Residence* – 1 Brooklands Court, Wray Park Rd, Reigate, Surrey RH2 0EE. —— Ruth Pauline, *b* 1925: *m* 1946, Thomas Eric Hazeldine, AMICE, and has issue living, Keith Trevor, *b* 1947; BEng, MBA: *m* 1970, Ethel Mae Fraser, and has issue living, Julia Lee *b* 1975, Amy Katherine *b* 1977, Laura Mae *b* 1979, — Piers Martyn, *b* 1957: *m* 1st, 1984, Iva MacKenzie, who *d* 1992; 2ndly, 1994, Wendy Wyer, and has issue living (by 1st *m*), Tia Lee-Anne *b* 1984, Dana Christine *b* 1986, (by 2nd *m*) Heidi Lee Grace *b* 1994, — Carol Anne, *b* 1948: *m* 1970, James E. Dewar, and has issue living, Brydone Michael *b* 1980, Jennifer Laura *b* 1975, Kimberly Margaret *b* 1978, — Sally Jane, *b* 1949: *m* 1971, Dr Arnie Chestnut, and has issue living, Matthew Robert *b* 1979, Heidi Anne *b* 1974, Shannon Gail *b* 1977, — Gail Melissa, *b* 1955: *m* 1980, William Moffatt, of 6620 Jubilee Rd, Halifax, Nova Scotia B3H 2H4, Canada, and has issue living, Jonathan

Eric Douglas *b* 1991, Luke Stuart *b* 1994, Rachel Alexandra Hazeldine *b* 1990. *Residence* – Blueberry Shores, RR1, Liverpool, Nova Scotia BOT 1KO, Canada.

      Grandchildren of late Walter Barrington Piers (infra):—
      Issue of late Grahame Barrington Piers, *b* 1913, *d* 1980: *m* 1950, Shirley O'Brien (Suite 310, 404, E 80th Av, Vancouver, BC, Canada):—
Richard Barrington, *b* 1953.

      Issue of late Cecil Edwin Piers, *b* 1914, *d* 1987: *m* 1941, Ethel Sheppard (PO Box 301, Montrose, BC, Canada V0G 1P0):—
Kenneth Barrington (Schelf Straat No 1, 3295 TK S'Gravendeel, Holland), *b* 1943: *m* 1966, Maartje Wolf. —— Penelope Ann, *b* 1946: *m* 1972, Brian Denton, of 2134 Graham Av, Prince Rupert, BC V8J 1C8, Canada, and has issue living, Trevor Piers, *b* 1975, — Laura Lynn, *b* 1973.

      Grandchildren of late Shute Barrington Piers (infra):—
      Issue of late Walter Barrington Piers, *b* 1890, *d* 1964: *m* 1913, Mary Cecilia Onn, who *d* 1983:—
Harry Gordon, *b* 1920; formerly Warrant Officer, RCAF; Inspector of Customs and Immigration (ret): *m* 1st, 1946, Sally Chisholm; 2ndly, 1970, Helen Street, and has issue living (by 1st *m*), James Walker, *b* 1947.

      Issue of late Grahame Sedway Piers, *b* 1892, *d* 1970: *m* 1917, Dorothy Mary, who *d* 1971, da of G. D. Heather:—
Heather, *b* 1918: *m* 1945, Anthony Freeman, FCA, and has issue living, Michael Edmund Piers, *b* 1946, — Anthony Piers, *b* 1956, — Chloe Anne, *b* 1949, — Amanda Jane, *b* 1953.

      Granddaughters of late Capt Shute Barrington Piers, RN, 6th son of late Rev Octavius Piers (ante):—
      Issue of late Shute Barrington Piers, *b* 1864, *d* 1947: *m* 1888, Gertrude, who *d* 1938, da of Charles Henry Nottingham:—
Gladys Nottingham, *b* 1893: *m* 1920, W. Serle, who *d* 1940, and has issue living, Patrick Philip Oswald, *b* 1921; Sqdn Ldr RAF (ret): *m* 1st, 1940, Sheila Foster, of Bexhill-on-Sea; 2ndly, 1965, Nicole Lecoq, and has issue living (by 1st *m*) Roy Anthony Michael *b* 1941; Inspector, Metropolitan Police: *m* 1964, Elizabeth Mary, da of —, (and has issue living, Paul *b* 1966, Keith *b* 1968, Fiona *b* 1965), John Patrick David *b* 1944; Capt RAOC, Peter Norman James, *b* 1949; RAF (by 2nd *m*) Robert Barrington *b* 1966.

      Issue of late Henry Handyside Bruce Piers, *b* 1865, *d* 1935: *m* 1902, Eva Gertrude, who *d* 1962, da of G. B. Pennell:—
Helen Alice, *b* 1914: *m* 1944, Rev John Lionel Mortimer, who *d* 1983, and has issue living, *Rev* Lawrence George, *b* 1945; Communications Officer, Diocese of Coventry: *m* 1st, 1973, Catriona Lane, who *d* 1982; 2ndly, 1992, Rosemary Bartlett, and has issue living (by 1st *m*), John Lawrence *b* 1978, Rebecca Magdalena Helen *b* 1974, Rosamund Clare *b* 1976, — Michael Piers, *b* 1946: *m* 1985, Ann, da of James Jenkinson, of Aldershot, and has issue living, Benjamin *b* 1987, Emily *b* 1985, — Christopher Hugh, *b* 1949. *Residence* – The Old Rectory, High Street, Nunney, nr Frome, Somerset BA11 4LZ.

      Grandchildren of late Henry Handyside Bruce Piers (ante):—
      Issue of late Maj Eustace Pennell Piers, *b* 1910; *d* 1979: *m* 1941, Jean Mavis (1 Mitre Place, The Park, Castle Cary, Somerset BA7 7EP), da of John Edward Ralph, of Streatham Hill, SW:—
William James Shute Barrington, *b* 1948; *ed* Millfield, and Brunel Univ; BTech, MIMech E: *m* 1978, Janet Anne, da of late Kenneth Arthur Fream, of Bristol, and has had issue, Adam Ralph Barrington *b* 1980, — Oliver Henry, *b* 1982, *d* 1984, — Thomas Michael, *b* 1985, — Sarah Elizabeth, *b* 1987. *Residence* – 48 Stokes End, Haddenham, Bucks HP17 8DX. —— Angela Mary, *b* 1942: *m* 1965, Peter Kiero Watson, of 49 Brookway, Lindfield, W Sussex RH16 2BP, and has had issue, James Kiero, *b* 1966, — Thomas Piers Kiero, *b* 1969, *d* 1970, — Edward Piers Kiero, *b* 1970. —— Clare Rosamund Pennell (twin), *b* 1948: *m* 1984, Peter William Dodd, of 4 Russell Rd, W14 8JA.

  This baronet is descended from William Piers, son of Henry Piers, of Piers Hall, Yorks, who is said at one time to have saved the Princess Elizabeth from the fury of her sister, Queen Mary, by conveying her privately away. After that princess ascended the throne, he was sent by Her Majesty to Ireland, and received a grant of the abbey of Tristernagh, in Westmeath. He was afterward appointed Governor of Carrickfergus and Seneschal of the county of Antrim, and in 1565 obtained the reward of 1,000 marks for bringing in the head of the rebel Shane O'Neil. The 9th baronet, Sir Charles Pigott, was Major (ret) Canadian Mil and served in S Africa 1900-1901, and in European War 1914-19.

PIGOT (GB) 1764, of Patshull, Staffordshire

Sir GEORGE HUGH PIGOT, 8th *Baronet, b* 28 Nov 1946; *s* his father *Maj-Gen Sir* ROBERT ANTHONY, CB, OBE, 1986; *ed* Stowe: *m* 1st, 1967 (*m diss* 1973), Judith Sandeman, elder da of late Maj John Hele Sandeman-Allen, RA (*see* E Woolton, 1985 Edn); 2ndly, 1980 (*m diss* 1993), Lucinda Jane, yr da of Donald Charles Spandler, of Chiddingfold, Surrey, and has issue by 1st and 2nd *m.*

𝔄rms – Ermine, three lozenges conjoined in fesse sable. ℭrest – A Wolf's head erased argent.
Residence – Mill House, Mill Lane, Padworth, Berks RG7 4JX.

SON LIVING (*By 2nd marriage*)

GEORGE DOUGLAS HUGH, *b* 17 Sept 1982. —— Robert Edward Richard, *b* 1984.

DAUGHTER LIVING (*By 1st marriage*)

Melanie Barbara, *b* 1969.

HALF-BROTHER LIVING

Robert James, *b* 1971; *ed* Eton.

Always ready

SISTER LIVING

Louise, *b* 1943: *m* 1966, Peter Mellor, of Brinksway House, Shottermill, nr Haslemere, Surrey son of A. R. Mellor, of Lamb Cottage, Newtown, IoW, and has issue living, Nicola, *b* 1970, — Suzanna, *b* 1975, — Katherine, *b* 1979.

HALF-SISTER LIVING

Sarah Sophia, *b* 1975.

DAUGHTERS LIVING OF SIXTH BARONET

Margaret, *b* 1914: *m* 1st, 1940, Maj Donald Ian Molteno, Black Watch, who was *ka* 1944; 2ndly, 1949, (Edward) John Macdonald Dent, of Manor Farm, Broughton, Stockbridge, Hants, and has issue living, (by 1st *m*) Susan Ferelith, *b* 1941: *m* 1961, Timothy Robert Malden Ashfield, and has issue living, a son *b* 1970, Gillian, *b* 1942: *m* 1969, Jeremy James. —— Jean (twin), *b* 1914: *m* 1944, Capt Atholl Murray Robertson, Black Watch, of The Lowes, Dunkeld, Perths, and has issue living, Alastair John, *b* 1946; *ed* Trinity Coll Glenalmond. —— Diana Gillian, *b* 1918.

WIDOW LIVING OF SEVENTH BARONET

SARAH ANNE (*Sarah, Lady Pigot*), eldest da of late David Richard Colville (*see* V Colville, colls): *m* 1968, as his 2nd wife, Sir Robert Anthony Pigot, CB, OBE, RM, who *d* 1986. *Residence* – Garden House, St Luke's Drive, Bembridge, IoW PO35 5XA.

The 1st baronet, Sir George Pigot (Governor of Madras 1755-63 and 1775-7, and MP for Wallingford 1765-8 and subsequently for Bridgnorth), was created a Baronet with special remainder to his brothers Robert and Hugh; in 1765 he became Baron Pigot, which title expired on his death 1777. He bequeathed the celebrated Pigot diamond, valued by skilful lapidaries at £30,000, to his brothers, Gen Sir Robert, the 2nd baronet, and Adm Hugh Pigot, and his sister, Margaret Fisher; it was subsequently disposed of under an Act of Parliament 1800, by way of lottery, for £23,998 16s. The 4th baronet sat as MP for Bridgnorth (*C*) 1832-53. The 7th baronet, Sir Robert Pigot, CB, OBE, was Maj-Gen RM, Dep Standing Group NATO, Rep with N Atlantic Council, Paris, and Ch of Staff RM.

PIGOTT (UK) 1808, of Knapton, Queen's County

Here and elsewhere

Sir (BERKELEY) HENRY SEBASTIAN PIGOTT, 5th Baronet; *b* 24 June 1925; *s* his father, *Maj Sir* BERKELEY, 1982; *ed* Ampleforth; European War 1944-45 with RM: *m* 1954, Jean Olive, only da of late John Williams Balls, of Holly Lodge, Surlingham, Norfolk, and has issue.

Arms – Ermine, three lozenges in fesse sable, a crescent for difference. Crest – A wolf's head erased proper, collared or.
Residence – Brook Farm, Shobley, Ringwood, Hants.

SONS LIVING

DAVID JOHN BERKELEY (91 Bellemoor Rd, Upper Shirley, Southampton S015 7QW), *b* 16 Aug 1955; *ed* Moor Park, Ludlow, and Hurn Court, Bournemouth: *m* 1st, 1981 (*m diss* 1984), Alison Fletcher; 2ndly, 1986, Julie, da of Eric Gordon Wiffen, of 28 Fitzroy Close, Bassett, Southampton, and has issue living (by 2nd *m*), Christabel Maria, *b* 1989. —— Antony Charles Philip, *b* 1960.

DAUGHTER LIVING

Sarah Jane Mary, *b* 1964.

SISTERS LIVING

Mary Stephanie, *b* 1920: *m* 1st, 1951, Peter Friedrich Sika; 2ndly, 1959, Com Walter Higham, RN, who *d* 1990, and has issue living, (by 2nd *m*), Stephen Walter, *b* 1960: *m* 19—, Janet Hazel, da of Geoffrey Lamb, of Fletcham. *Residence* – 12 King George Av, Petersfield, Hants. —— Mary Veronica, *b* 1922: *m* 1944, Stefan Wysogota-Kwasniewski, and has issue living, Casimir Stefan, *b* 1946: *m* 1973, Laura Clements, and has issue living, Alexandra Christabel *b* 1980, — Sabina Orietta, *b* 1945: *m* 1st, 1964, Derek Johnstone Brooke; 2ndly, 1968, Andrew Holt, and has issue living, (by 1st *m*) Gregory Damien Amadeus *b* 1965, (by 2nd *m*) Trystan *b* 1969, Thor *b* 1973, Luke *b* 1977. *Residence* – Martyr's Way, Walsingham, Norfolk.

The 1st baronet, Sir George, was son of Major-Gen Thomas Pigott, MP, of Knapton, Queen's Co, and Sir Charles, 3rd Bt, served in the Crimea.

PILDITCH (UK) 1929, of Bartropps, Weybridge, co Surrey

He conquers who conquers himself

Sir RICHARD EDWARD PILDITCH, 4th *Baronet*; *b* 8 Sept 1926; *s* his brother, *Sir* PHILIP JOHN FREDERICK, 1954: *ed* Charterhouse: European War 1944-45 with RN, in India and Ceylon: *m* 1950, Pauline Elizabeth Smith, and has issue.

Arms – Per chevron invected sable and or, two ancient galleys in chief, and in base an eagle displayed all counter changed. Crest – A bear sejant proper, muzzled and gorged with a chain or, pendent therefrom an escutcheon sable charged with an eagle displayed gold.

SON LIVING

JOHN RICHARD, *b* 24 Sept 1955.

DAUGHTER LIVING

Fiona, *b* 1951: *m* 1982, Patrick John Payne, son of Austin Ralph Payne.

DAUGHTERS LIVING OF THIRD BARONET

Frances Jean, *b* 1952: *m* 1978, George Phillips Yeats, son of George Yeats, and has issue living, Frederick Xavier, *b* 1983. —— Felicity Mary, *b* (*posthumous*) 1954: *m* 1975, Richard Austin, of Buttergate Barn, Sykes' Fold, Leeming, Oxenhope, nr Keighley, W Yorks BD22 9SH, son of Herbert Wilfred Charles Austin, and has issue living, Nicholas Charles, *b* 1982, — Charlotte Susannah Frances, *b* 1985.

HALF-SISTER LIVING

Rosalind Phyllis Muriel, *b* 1946: *m* 1969, Allan Owen-Taylor.

WIDOW LIVING OF THIRD BARONET

PHYLLIS JEAN, el da of Maj Dudley Cautley Stewart Smith, MBE, of Weybridge, Surrey: *m* 1st, 1948, Sir (Philip John) Frederick Pilditch, 3rd Bt, who *d* 1954; 2ndly, 1977, David Smith. *Residence* – 2 St Mary's Mews, Ludlow, Shropshire SY8 1DZ.

COLLATERAL BRANCH LIVING

Issue of late Maj Edgar Lewis Pilditch, TD, yr son of 1st baronet, *b* 1901, *d* 1986: *m* 1936, Anne (4 St James Close, Ruscombe, Twyford, Reading, Berks), da of Richard Llewellyn Weeks, of Broomhaugh House, Riding Mill, Northumberland, and formerly wife of — Goodchild:—

Simon Andrew Llewellyn, MRAC, *b* 1938; *ed* Eton, McGill Univ, Montreal (BA), and RAC Cirencester; Company Dir: *m* 1969 (*m diss* 19—), Ute, da of late Siegfried Johannes Mayr, of Kitzbühel, Tyrol, and has issue living, Olivia Margaret, *b* 1970.

The 1st baronet, Sir Philip Edward Pilditch (son of late Philip John Pilditch, of Plymouth), sat as MP for Spelthorne Div of Middlesex (*U*) 1918-31.

PILE (UK) 1900, of Kenilworth House, Rathgar, co Dublin

Sir FREDERICK DEVEREUX PILE, MC, 3rd *Baronet*; *b* 10 Dec 1915; *s* his father, *Gen Sir* FREDERICK ALFRED, GCB, DSO, MC, 1976; *ed* Weymouth Coll, and RMC Sandhurst; Col late R Tank Regt; British Joint Sers Mission Washington, DC 1957-60; Comdt RAC Driving and Maintenance Sch 1960-62; 1939-45 War (MC): *m* 1st, 1940, Pamela, who *d* 1983, el da of late Philip Henstock, of Newbury, Berks; 2ndly, 1984, Mrs V. Josephine A. Culverwell, previously wife of late Gerald D. Culverwell, and has issue by 1st *m*.

Arms – Azure, three piles argent, on a chief ermine, a castle with two towers proper between two harps or, stringed of the second. Crest – on a ducal coronet or, charged with a cross-botonée azure, a pelican with wings addorsed and inverted proper. *Residence* – Beadles, Cowbeech, E Sussex. *Club* – MCC.

Sine labe nota

Known without dishonour

DAUGHTERS LIVING (*By 1st marriage*)

Fiona Devereux, *b* 1941: *m* 1976, Mark William Towse. —— Vanessa Anne, *b* 1951: *m* 1972, Rory Gilchrist Graham Mackean, of 4 Colyton Rd, SE22, and has issue living, Thomas, *b* 1985, — Charlotte, *b* 1979, — Virginia, *b* 1980.

COLLATERAL BRANCHES LIVING

Issue of late Major Walter Devereux Pile, yr son of 1st baronet, *b* 1887, *d* 1959: *m* 1921, Margaret Lucy, MBE, who *d* 1989, el da of Thomas Irvine Bonner, MA, MB, CM, formerly of 22 Ivy Rd, Shipley, Yorkshire:—

Anne Devereux, *b* 1932: *m* 1961, David Evan Daniel, of The White House, 56 Lark Lane, Liverpool L16 8YA.

Issue of late Sir John Devereux Pile, yr son of 2nd baronet, *b* 1918; *d* 1982: *m* 1946, Katharine Mary (Munstead, Godalming, Surrey GU8 4AR), da of late Austin George Shafe:—

ANTHONY JOHN DEVEREUX (The Manor House, Pitsford, Northampton NN6 9AZ), *b* 7 June 1947; *ed* Durham Sch; Maj LI (ret): *m* 1977, Jenny Clare, da of late Peter H. Youngman, of Fenn St, Westleton, Suffolk, and has issue living, Thomas Charles Devereux, *b* 6 April 1978, — Hugh James Devereux, *b* 1980, — Harriet Rose Devereux, *b* 1983. —— Timothy Simon Devereux (1 Beech Park Drive, Barnt Green, Birmingham B45 8LZ), *b* 1953; *ed* Haileybury, and Durham Univ (BA): *m* 1977, Jean Patricia Lynne Thomas, and has issue living, Jonathan Matthew Devereux, *b* 1981, — Christopher James Devereux, *b* 1984, — Victoria Jane Devereux, *b* 1987, — Rebecca Claire Devereux, *b* 1991. —— Jennifer Jane Devereux, *b* 1950: *m* 1973, Huw J. Alban Davies, DM, FRCP, of Troutbeck, Otford, Sevenoaks, Kent TN14 5PH, and has issue living, Henry Christopher, *b* 1975, — Hester Margaret, *b* 1977, — Katharine Clare, *b* (twin) 1977. —— Sarah Katharine Devereux, *b* 1960; BA: *m* 1st, 1987, C. Richard J. Bate; 2ndly, 1994, David Alan Jones, of Clumber, Linkside East, Hindhead, Surrey GU26 6NY, and has issue living (by 2nd *m*), Oliver David *b* 1994, Emma Elizabeth *b* 1998.

The 1st baronet, Sir Thomas Devereux Pile, was High Sheriff of Dublin 1898, and Lord Mayor 1900.

MILBORNE-SWINNERTON-PILKINGTON (NS) 1635, of Stanley, Yorkshire

Now thus, now thus

Sir THOMAS HENRY MILBORNE-SWINNERTON-PILKINGTON, 14th *Baronet; b* 10 March 1934; *s* his father, *Sir* ARTHUR WILLIAM, MC, 1952; *ed* Eton; formerly in Roy Scots Greys; Chm of Thomas and James Harrison Ltd 1980-99, Dep Chm Cluff Mining Ltd since 1997, and Chm Charente Steamship Co Ltd 1977: *m* 1961, Susan, da of Norman Stewart Rushton Adamson, of Durban, S Africa, and has issue.

Arms – Quarterly: 1st and 4th, argent, a cross flory, voided gules, *Pilkington*; 2nd, argent, a cross formé fleuretté sable, surmounted by a bend engrailed gules, *Swinnerton*; 3rd, per pale, argent and gules, a cross patonce between, in the sinister chief and dexter base two leopards' faces counter-changed, *Milborne*. Crests – 1st, on a mount vert a boar passant argent, charged with a cross formé fleuretté sable; 2nd, a mower with his scythe proper, habited per pale argent, and sable; 3rd, a demi-lion per fesse argent and gules, holding between the paws a leopard's face of the first.
Residence – King's Walden Bury, Hitchin, Herts. *Club* – White's.

SON LIVING

RICHARD ARTHUR, *b* 4 Sept 1964; *ed* Eton, and RAC Cirencester: *m* 1994, Katya T., da of Terence J. Clemence, of Wilton Crescent, SW1, and has issue living, Elizabeth Rose, *b* 1994.

DAUGHTERS LIVING

Sarah Elizabeth, *b* 1962: *m* 1993, James Burnes Anderson, son of Ian Robert Anderson, of Les Frêtes, Vaulion, Switzerland, and has issue living, Alexander Burnes, *b* 1997. —— Joanna, *b* 1967.

SISTERS LIVING

Sonia Margery, *b* 1937: *m* 1st, 1965, Anthony Dominic Dyke Rogers, who *d* 1984; 2ndly, 1990, Ib Jorgensen, of Airlie Stud, Grangewilliam, Maynooth, co Kildare, and has issue living (by 1st *m*), John Dyke Darby, *b* 1968, — Anthony Patrick, *b* 1971. —— Carole Mary (Brainge, Putley, Ledbury, Herefordshire), *b* 1942: *m* 1962, James Bowes Daly, who *d* 1989 (B McGowan), and has issue living, Dermot Christopher, *b* 1964: *m* 1998, Louise, elder da of Simon Harrap, of Bentley (*see* Darell, Bt), — Henry Duncan James (Birches House, Downton Hall, Ludlow, Shropshire SY8 3DX), *b* 1966: *m* 1994, Clarissa Ferelith, da of Simon Thomas Clarke, of Kingsettle Farmhouse, Semley, Shaftesbury, and has issue living, Davina Clare *b* 1997. —— Moira Elizabeth, *b* 1943: *m* 1969, Benjamin Hanbury, of Green Man House, Cowlinge, Newmarket, and has issue living, Emma Jane, *b* 1970, — Amanda Aline, *b* 1973.

COLLATERAL BRANCH LIVING

Issue of late Ulick O'Connor Milborne-Swinnerton-Pilkington, 2nd son of 12th baronet, *b* 1903; *d* 1979: *m* 1951, Angela Mary Purcell (who *m* 2ndly, 1981, Cdr Edward Alfred Eborall, RNVR, FIEE, who *d* 1992, of Tally Ho House, Castletownshend, co Cork), da of late Gerald de Purcell Cotter (*see* Cotter, Bt, colls):—
Lionel Ulick (62 Manor Court, Knocknacarra, Salthill, Galway), *b* 1956; *ed* Univ Coll, Cork (MA), and Toronto Univ (PhD): *m* 1990, Elizabeth Susan, PhD, da of Col Hugh Tilley, of Ottawa, Canada, and has issue living, Colin Patrick, *b* 1993. —— Michael Gerald, *b* 1959; *ed* Trin Coll, Dublin (BSc).

This family descends from Robert Pilkington, of Sowerby, Yorks, 3rd son of Sir John Pilkington, of Pilkington, Lancs (*d* 1421). Sir Arthur Pilkington, of Stanley, nr Wakefield, received a Baronetcy of Nova Scotia, probably with remainder to heirs male whatsoever (the patent was not entered in the Geat Seal Register of Scotland), and a grant of 6,000 acres in Nova Scotia. Sir William Pilkington, 8th Bt (*d* 1850): *m* Mary, da and co-heir of Thomas Swinnerton, of Butterton Hall, Staffs, by Mary, da and heir of Charles Milborne, of Wonastow, Monmouth. His yst son, Sir Lionel Pilkington, 11th Bt, took by Roy Licence 1856 the surnames of Milborne-Swinnerton but subsequently resumed the final name of Pilkington. The 13th baronet, Sir Arthur William Milborne-Swinnerton Pilkington, MC, was Major 16th/5th Lancers.

PINSENT (UK) 1938, of Selly Hill, City of Birmingham

Sir CHRISTOPHER ROY PINSENT, 3rd Baronet; *b* 2 Aug 1922; *s* his father *Sir* ROY, 1978; *ed* Winchester; taught at Camberwell Sch of Art 1962-86; 1939-45 War as Leading Aircraftman RAF: *m* 1951, Susan Mary, da of John Norton Scorer, of Fotheringhay, and has issue.

𝕬rms – Argent a saltire flory vert, between four chaffinches proper. 𝕮rest – Upon a fleur-de-lis couped vert, two chaffinches addorsed proper.
Residence – Ramblers, The Cricket Green, Woodside Rd, Chiddingfold, Surrey GU8 4UG.

SON LIVING

THOMAS BENJAMIN ROY, *b* 21 July 1967.

DAUGHTERS LIVING

Laura Candace, *b* 1954: *m* 1978, Timothy Bartel Smit, son of Jan Adrianus Bartel Smit, of Arnhem, Holland, and has issue living, Jeremy Alexander Bartel, *b* 1980, — Samuel Christopher, *b* 1984, — Laura Marian, *b* 1982. —— Joanna Mary, *b* 1957: *m* 1991, James David Simpson, son of John Leonard Simpson, of Wetherby, Yorks, and has issue living, Ella Bennett, *b* 1993, — Alice Mary Ann, *b* 1996.

BROTHER LIVING

Michael Roy (61 Wellington Rd, Birmingham), *b* 1927; *ed* Marlborough; admitted a solicitor 1952; 1939-45 War as Lt R Signals: *m* 1952 (*m diss* 19—), Stella Marie, da of late Basil Priestman, of Birmingham, and has issue living, William Ross, *b* 1955, — Nicola Jane, *b* 1957, — Tonya Mary, *b* 1959: *m* 1986, William James Wood, yr son of late Sir Frank Wood, KBE, CB, and has issue living, Richard Foucard *b* 1989.

SISTER LIVING

Rosemary, *b* 1930; *ed* Edgbaston High Sch: *m* 1960, Keiden John Knapp Barrow, of Hazelhope, Stalisfield, Faversham, Kent ME13 0HY, and has issue living, Clive Andrew Knapp, *b* 1962: *m* 1991, Lynne Catherine, da of Roy Thornton Marsden, of Taupo, NZ, and has issue living, Daniel James Knapp *b* 1994, Alexandra Catherine *b* 1991, Georgia Nicol *b* 1997, — Clare, *b* 1964: *m* 1987, Alastair Michael Gordon, son of late Alexander Nigel Gordon, and has issue living, Tom Alex *b* 1995, Katie *b* 1999.

COLLATERAL BRANCHES LIVING

Grandchildren of late Com Clive Pinsent, RN (infra):—
Issue of late Lt-Cdr Andrew Clive Macpherson Pinsent, RN, *b* 1922, *d* 1982: *m* 1945, Gloria Poppy Marie, who *d* 1979, da of late Capt (Cecil) Herbert Tollemache:—
Anthony Andrew Macpherson (4 North Pallant, Chichester, W Sussex), *b* 1946; *ed* Radley: *m* 1969, Clare Natalie, da of Victor Reynolds, of Estremoz, Portugal, and has issue living, Charles Victor R., *b* 1973, — Amelia Clare, *b* 1976. —— David Tollemache, *b* 1948; *ed* Radley: *m* 1976, Susie, da of Mrs J. Chandler, of Mosman, NSW, and has issue living, Rollo Tollemache, *b* 1978, — Hugo G., *b* 1980. —— Susan Catherine, *b* 1953: *m* 1976, Kerry John Pfeiffer, and has issue living, Olivia K., *b* 19—.

Issue of late Lt-Cdr James Macpherson Pinsent, RN, *b* 1925, *d* 1983: *m* 1st, 1956 (*m diss* 1972), Daphne Miranda, who *d* 1991, da of Capt Kenneth Lanyon Harkness, CBE, DSC, RN (ret); 2ndly, 1976, Eleanor Mary Penrose (Audrey) (13 Felden St, SW6), da of late Dr Victor Penrose Robinson, MA, BM, BCL:—
(By 1st *m*) Oliver Clive (Cheddington, Quarry Close, Limpley Stoke, Bath BA3 6HN), *b* 1964: *m* 1989, Catherine C., da of R. C. Bennett, of Bath, and has issue living, Benjamin James Oliver, *b* 1992, — Hannah Miranda Crawford, *b* 1994. —— Camilla Louise (Ariel Cottage, Graffham, nr Petworth, W Sussex), *b* 1962: *m* 1983 (*m diss* 1996), Capt Mark P. Colacicchi, 13th/18th R Hus (QMO), eldest son of late Count Paul Colacicchi, of 9 St Dionis Rd, SW6, and has issue living, James Paul, *b* 1985, — Rory Adam, *b* 1986, — Sophie Antonia, *b* 1989.

Issue of late Com Clive Pinsent, RN, 2nd son of 1st baronet, *b* 1886, *d* 1948: *m* 1921, Kathleen Jane, who *d* 1974, da of late George Macpherson, DL, JP, of The Lloyd House, Wolverhampton:—
Rev Ewen Macpherson, *b* 1930: formerly Lt RN: *m* 1962, Jean Grizel, da of late Maj-Gen Neil McMicking, CB, CBE, DSO, MC, and has issue living, Matthew Clive, MBE, *b* 1970; *ed* Eton, and St Catherine's Coll, Oxford; MBE (Civil) 1993, — Katherine Jane *b* 1963: *m* 1991, Thomas W. Tyson, twin son of D. Tyson, of Dorf House, Widdington, Essex, — Emma Charlotte, *b* 1964: *m* 1992, Erik Thomson, son of Andrew Thomson, of 4 New Mills Crescent, Balerno, Midlothian, and has issue living, Magnus Thomas *b* 1995, Findlay David *b* 1998, Catriona Rose *b* 1994. *Residence* – The Cross House, Child Okeford, Blandford, Dorset.

Issue of late Col John Ryland Pinsent, CBE, DSO, 3rd son of 1st baronet, *b* 1888, *d* 1957: *m* 1915, Kathleen May, who *d* 1969, da of late Col E. G. Boyce:—
John Laurance, *b* 1916; admitted a solicitor 1946; is a farmer; European War 1939-45 as Major RA: *m* 1940, Margaret Molyneux, el da of late R. Yernon Favell, and has issue living, John Edward, *b* 1950: *m* 1985, Susan Elizabeth Mallett, da of late John Mallett Hughes, and has issue living, Harry Edward *b* 1991, Joss Richard *b* (twin) 1991, Laura Elizabeth *b* 1989, — Margaret Anne, *b* 1941: *m* 1968, Rev Canon John Lawrence Simpson, of Yardes Cottage, Ashill, Ilminster, Som TA19 9NT, and has issue living, Benjamin John Lawrence *b* 1970, Joanna Mary *b* 1965: *m* 1996, Daniel Quentin Salmons, Jessamie Anne *b* 1968: *m* 1999, Simon Jonathan Thomas, — Mary, *b* 1943: *m* 1964, Denis Theodore Archdale, of

Roseworthy Barton, Camborne, Cornwall, and has issue living, Nicholas Henry *b* 1966 (has issue living, William Laurence *b* 1998), Audley Mervyn *b* 1969: *m* 1998, Kerry, da of Alec Robinson, of Southfleet, Kent (and has issue living, Thomas Audley *b* 1998), Rachael Mary *b* 1968: *m* 1991, Michael David Norman (and has issue living, Joshua Kyle *b* 1991, Josceline Leanne *b* 1993), — Jennifer, *b* 1944: *m* 1969, Capt Christopher Louis Wreford-Brown, DSO, RN, and has issue living, Paul Christopher *b* 1972, Julia Anne *b* 1970: *m* 1994, William Gifford Scott (and has issue living, George William Gifford *b* 1997), Amanda Jane *b* 1976, — Elizabeth Jane *b* 1948. *Residence* – Higher Ludbrook, Ermington, S Devon. —— Richard Alan, *b* 1931: *m* 1954, Mary Matruh, da of Group-Capt John Benjamin Graham, OBE, MC, AFC, and has issue living, Dinah, *b* 1955, — Susan Melanie *b* 1964.

The 1st baronet, Sir Richard Alfred Pinsent (son of late Richard Steele Pinsent), was Pres of Law So 1918-19.

PLATT (UK) 1958, of Rusholme, City of Manchester (Extinct 1998)

Sir (FRANK) LINDSEY PLATT, 2nd and last *Baronet*.

SISTERS LIVING OF SECOND BARONET

Rosemary Elizabeth (76 Peppercombe Rd, Eastbourne, E Sussex BN20 8JN), *b* 1921: *m* 1948, Trevor Lewis Midgley, who *d* 1978, and has issue living, Jonathan David, *b* 1950: *m* 1983, Julia Margaret Chinnery, and has issue living, James Alexander Lewis *b* 1986, — Amanda Jane Elizabeth, *b* 1953: *m* 1979, Jerome Peter Duncanson, and has issue living, Peter Robin *b* 1994, Sophie Elizabeth *b* 1984. —— Sara Margaret Helen (*Lady Williams*), *b* 1927: *m* 1952, Capt Sir Lawrence Hugh Williams, 9th Bt, RM, and has issue (*see* Williams, Bt, *cr* 1798). *Residence* – Old Parciau, Marianglas, Anglesey. —— Diana Primrose Rowley, *b* 1932: *m* 1955, Robin Gwynne Jennings, of 134 Rosendale Rd, Dulwich, SE21 8LG (Wake, Bt, *cr* 1621, colls), and has issue living, Nicholas David de Burgh, *b* 1959, — Robin Hereward, *b* 1963: *m* 1997, Emma Burch, and has issue living, Rachel *b* 1999, — Charles Rupert, *b* 1968, — Sarah Primrose, *b* 1961: *m* 1990, Anthony Hook, and has issue living, Megan Elizabeth April *b* 1993, Katharine Rachel *b* 1994.

PLATT (UK) 1959, of Grindleford, co Derby

Hon Sir PETER PLATT, AM, 2nd *Baronet*; *b* 6 July 1924; *s* his father ROBERT Baron Platt (Life Baron) in his Baronetcy, 1978, *ed* Abbotsholme Sch, The Royal Sch of Music, and Magdalen Coll, Oxford (BMus, BLitt, MA, FGSM); Prof of Music, Sydney Univ, Aust; 1939-45 War with RNVR (despatches); AM 1999: *m* 1948, Jean Halliday, da of Dr Charles Philip Brentnall, and has issue.

Arms – Or fretty sable plate on a pale gules a rod of aesculapius gold. **Crest** – In front of a demi plate a nightingale in full song proper.
Residence – 1 Ellison Pl, Pymble, NSW 2073, Australia.

SON LIVING

MARTIN PHILIP (Wyllies Crossing, RD1, Dunedin, NZ), *b* 9 March 1952: *m* 1971, Frances Corinne Moanna, da of Trevor Samuel Conley, and has issue living, Philip Stephen, *b* 17 Oct 1972, — Timothy Martin, *b* 1980, — Suzanne, *b* 1971, — Rachael, *b* 1976.

DAUGHTERS LIVING

Margaret, *b* 1949: *m* 1969 (*m diss* 1978), Anthony Pratt Kaye. —— Katherine, *b* 1956: *m* 1988, Alexander Hendrik Vincent Beasley, son of Robert Beasley, of Auckland, NZ.

SISTERS LIVING

Hon Joan Elizabeth, *b* 1927: *m* 1952, John Bunting Allen, of 10 Buckwood Close, Hazel Grove, Stockport, Cheshire SK7 4NG, and has issue living, Jonathan Robert, *b* 1953, — Paul Bunting, *b* 1956, — Mark Benedict, *b* 1965. —— *Hon* Helen Margaret, *b* 1933: *m* 1954, Cecil Henry Stowasser, of 10 Lantana Lane, PO Box 256, Mapleton, Queensland 4560, Australia, and has issue living, Peter, *b* 1955, — Robert, *b* 1956, — Michael, *b* 1960.

WIDOW LIVING OF LIFE BARON AND FIRST BARONET

SYLVIA JEAN, ARCM (*Sylvia, Lady Platt*) (40 Arthurs Bridge Rd, Horsell, Woking, Surrey GU21 4NT), da of late Sidney Charles Caveley, and formerly wife of John Alfred Haggard: *m* 1974, as his 2nd wife, Baron Platt (Life Baron), 1st Bt, who *d* 1978, when the peerage became ext.

Robert Platt, MSc, MD, FRCP, son of William Platt, schoolmaster, of London and Grindleford, Derbys; was Editor of *Quarterly Journal of Medicine* 1948-55, Pres of Roy Coll of Physicians, London 1957-62, and Chm of Clinical Research Board, Med Research Council 1964-67; 1939-45 War as Brig RAMC; was *cr* a baronet 1959 and *Baron Platt*, of Grindleford, co Derby (Life Baron) 1967.

POLE (E) 1628, of Shute House, Devonshire

Pollet virtus
Virtue is powerful

Sir (JOHN) RICHARD WALTER REGINALD CAREW POLE, 13th *Baronet*; *b* 2 Dec 1938; *s* his father, *Sir* JOHN GAWEN CAREW, DSO, TD, 1993; *ed* Eton, and Royal Agric Coll, Cirencester; late Lt Coldm Gds; a Liveryman of Fishmongers' Co, elected to Court 1993; a Co Councillor for Cornwall 1973-93, High Sheriff 1980, and DL 1988; Devon and Cornwall Cttee, Nat Trust 1978-83; Min of Agriculture's Regional Advisory Cttee 1970-80; Gov Seale Hayne Agric Coll 1979-89, and Plymouth Coll 1985-95; part-time Dir SW Electricity Bd 1981-90; Devon and Cornwall Police Authority 1973-89 (Chm 1985-87); Pres R Cornwall Show 1981; Member SW Regional Cttee W of England Building Soc 1989-91; Dir Theatre Royal Plymouth 1985-97; Pres Surf Life Saving Assocn of Great Britain 1975-86; Countryside Commissioner 1991-96; Trustee of National Heritage Memorial Fund since 1991, and Tate Gallery since 1993: *m* 1st, 1966 (*m diss* 1973), Hon Victoria Marion Ann Lever, da of 3rd Viscount Leverhulme, KG, TD; 2ndly, 1974, Mary, LVO, da of late Lt-Col Ronald Dawnay (*see* V Downe, colls), and has issue living by 2nd *m*.

Arms – Azure, semée of fleurs-de-lis or, a lion rampant argent.
Seat – Antony House, Torpoint, Cornwall PL11 2QA. *Clubs* – Pratt's.

SONS LIVING (*By 2nd marriage*)

TREMAYNE JOHN CAREW, *b* 22 Feb 1974, *ed* Eton, and Manchester Univ. —— John Alexander George Carew, *b* 1975; *ed* Eton, and Brasenose Coll, Oxford; a Page of Honour to HM Queen Elizabeth The Queen Mother 1990-92.

SISTERS LIVING

Elizabeth Mary, *b* 1929: *m* 1953, David Cuthbert Tudway Quilter, DL (*see* Quilter, Bt). *Residence* – Milton Lodge, Wells, Somerset. —— Caroline Anne (*Hon Mrs Paul Asquith*), *b* 1933: *m* 1963, as his 2nd wife, Hon Paul Asquith, who *d* 1984 (*see* E Oxford and Asquith, colls). *Residence* – 41 Quarrendon St, SW6.

WIDOW LIVING OF TWELFTH BARONET

JOAN SHIRLEY (*Joan, Lady Carew Pole*), da of late Rear Adm Charles Maurice Blackman, DSO, and widow of (i) Maj Jocelyn Arthur Persse, Rifle Bde, and (ii) Lt-Col Francis Edgar Fulford, of Great Fulford, Dunsford, Exeter: *m* 1979, as his 2nd wife, Sir John Gawen Carew Pole, 12th Bt, DSO, TD, who *d* 1993. *Residence* – Horson House, Torpoint, Cornwall.

COLLATERAL BRANCHES LIVING

Issue of late Maj Patrick William Butler POLE-CAREW, brother of 12th baronet, *b* 1913, *d* 1971: *m* 1st, 1939 (*m diss* 1950), Sonia, who *d* 1976, da of Sir (William Eley) Cuthbert Quilter, 2nd Bt; 2ndly, 1950, Mary Patience (Clashaphouca, Clogheen, co Tipperary) da of late Maj Richard Ernest Gilchrist Phillips, and formerly wife of Ronald Ewan Cameron:—
(By 1st *m*) Rosemary, *b* 1940.

Grandchildren of late Charles Edward Pole-Carew, uncle of 12th baronet:—

Issue of late Maj Gerald Ayshford Pole-Carew, *b* 1887, *d* 1969: *m* 1915, Eileen Flora Lismore, who *d* 1989, da of late Surg-Maj George Henry Kenneth MacDonald O'Callaghan, CMG:—
Charles Oliver (Flat B, 1 Royal Cres, W11 4SL), *b* 1923; *ed* Claysmore. ——— Christopher Gerald (Shute Barton, Shute, Devon), *b* 1931; *ed* RNC Dartmouth; formerly Lt RN; High Sheriff of Notts 1979-80: *m* 1954, Gillian, only da of Clive Burton, of Addo, Cape Province, S Africa, and has issue living, (Gerald Anthony) Peregrine (Higher Waterston Farm, nr Dorchester, Dorset DT2 7SW), *b* 1957; *ed* Radley, and RMA Sandhurst; late Lt Coldstream Gds: *m* 1st, 1984, Claudia A., only da of David Wolfers, of Barnes, London; 2ndly, 1991, Georgina E. M., da of Charles Harris, of Longonot Farm, Naivasha, Kenya (*see* V Hill, colls), and has issue living (by 2nd *m*), Tatiana Cecily Alice *b* 1993, Alexandra Cornelia Rose *b* 1996, — Delia Elizabeth, *b* 1955: *m* 1981, Charles Benedict de Broca Madden, yst son of Dr James George Madden, of the Glebe House, Tollesbury, Essex, and has issue living, James Antony Grellan *b* 1982, Edward Christopher Otha *b* 1984, Thomas Mark Ambrose *b* 1988, — Camilla Janet, *b* 1962: *m* 1982, Dominic John Earle Welby, yr son of Sir (Richard) Bruno Gregory Welby, 7th Bt, and has issue (*see* Welby, Bt). ——— Geraldine Frances Flora, *b* 1917. ——— Eileen Loveday (83 Gowan Av, SW6 6RQ), *b* 1930: *m* 1955 (*m diss* 1964), Brian Arnold Miller.

Grandchildren of late Reginald Charles Somers Pole, eldest son of late Reginald Carolus Pole (infra):—
Issue of late Reginald Edward Morice de la Pole, *b* 1893, *d* 1948: *m* 1924, Dorothy Ethel Christine, who *d* 1998, aged 102, da of late Charles William Searle, JP, of Larchwood, Sunninghill, Ascot, Berks:—
Pauline Marjorie Doreen, *b* 1925: *m* 1951, Squadron-Leader Frederick John Crewe, RAF (ret), of 2A Birchwood Rd, Maidstone, Kent, and has issue living, Roderic Guy Pole, *b* 1952: *m* 1987, Tina Norris, and has issue living, Daniel Roderic *b* 1990, Eleanor Marie *b* 1992, — Alastair Frederick, *b* 1954: *m* 1978 (*m diss* 19—), Elaine Ruth Blackburn, and has issue living, Sam Richard *b* 1978, Joseph Paul *b* 1982, — Felicity Jane, *b* 1953: *m* 1978 (*m diss* 1983), Paul Antoni Coleburt, — Virginia Rosemarie Pauline, *b* 1955: *m* 1984 (*m diss* 1999), Derek Alan Lawrence. ——— Rosemary Ethel Greason, *b* 1927: *m* 1957 (*m diss* 1996), Patrick Eric Edward Walsh, and has issue living, Guy Patrick, *b* 1957: *m* 1982 (*m diss* 1989), Rachel Gough, and has issue living, Martin Alexander *b* 1987, — Penelope Jane, *b* 1958: *m* 1990, Roy Whiteman, and has issue living, Daisy Caroline *b* 1986, — Jill Christine, *b* 1960, — Kim Elizabeth, *b* 1962. ——— Lucille Dorothy Carew, *b* 1938: *m* 1969, Stuart Malcolm Forbes Keir, of Brook Cottage, Tanhouse Rd, Oxted, Surrey, and has issue living, James Alexander, *b* 1976.

Issue of late Lionel Robert Glanville Pole, *b* 1902, *d* 1965: *m* 1924 (*m diss* 19—), Gertrude Gregory:—
Reginald Robert, *b* 1925: *m* 1953, Sylvia Patricia Sullivan, and has issue living, a son, *b* 19—, — Susan Carole, *b* 1954, — a da, *b* 19—. Resides in USA.

Issue of late Percival Arthur Carew Pole, *b* 1904, *d* 1965: *m* 1934, Irene Clare French, who *d* 1975:—
Geoffrey Arthur (3 Mill Pond Rd, Windlesham, Surrey), *b* 1935: *m* 1961, Patricia, da of W. Sweetman, of Birmingham, and has issue living, Julia, *b* 1963, — Diana (twin), *b* 1963, — Susan Caroline, *b* 1964. ——— Roger Charles, *b* 1939: *m* 1959, Joyce, only da of W Powell, of Worcester Park, Surrey, and has issue living, Mark Nicholas Charles, *b* 1961, — John Damian, *b* 1967, — Carey Thérèse, *b* 1959, — Joanne Sarah, *b* 1963. ——— Jennifer Clare, *b* 1937: *m* 1961, Dudley Hasting Wheeler, of Friars Pardon, Hurworth-on-Tess, co Durham, and has issue living, Clare Frances, *b* 1963, — Alison Mary, *b* 1966.

Grandchildren of late Reginald Carolus Pole, 2nd son of Rev Edward Pole (*b* 1805), 2nd son of Rev Edward Pole, DD, 3rd son of Reginald Pole, son of Rev Carolus Pole, 3rd son of 3rd baronet:—
Issue of late Clarence Dyke Pole, Major 2nd Bn Royal Warwickshire Regt, *b* 1871, *d* 1940: *m* 1893, Alice Mary, da of William Davies, of 1 St Paul's St, Warwick:—
†Hubert, *b* 1895; *d* 1907. ——— †Alfred Eden, *b* 1897: *m*, and *dsp* 1963. ——— †Francis John, *b* 1899: *m*, and *dsp* 1971. ——— †Reginald Edward, *b* 1902; *dunm* 1975. ——— Robert Stuart (2 William Bristow Rd, Cheylesmore, Coventry CV3 5LQ), *b* 1913: *m* 1939, Stella Kathleen, da of Henry Clarke, of 2 Highbury Place, Abbots Lane, Coventry, and has issue living, Graham Robert, *b* 1948: *m* 19—, Mrs ......, and has issue living, Emma *b* 19—, — Julia, *b* 1940: *m* 19—, ... Galbraith, who *d* 19—, and has issue living. ——— Winifred Alice, *b* 1900; *dunm* 1925.

Issue of late Albert Edward Pole, *b* 1875, *d* 1940: *m* 1907, Sophia Buckingham, who *d* 1955, el da of late Edward Alexander Buckingham Hay, of Alaington, Dalkeith Avenue, Dumbreck, Glasgow:—
Reginald Carew, *b* 1914: *m* 1939, Mary MacKinnon, da of R. P. Don, of 46 Walnut Crescent, Possilpark, Glasgow, and has issue living, Reginald Carew, *b* 1942, — Isobel Buchannan Colquhoun, *b* 1947. ——— Annie Laing Hay, *b* 1908.

Issue of late Courtenay Alexander Pole, *b* 1888, *d* 1967: *m* 1917, Janet Watson, who *d* 1955, da of late James Deans, of Highbury Park, Mount Florida, Glasgow:—
Reginald Alexander Carolus (Ardfern, 126 Cawdor St, Nairn), *b* 1920; Lt (Ex Sp) RNVR 1939-45, Clyde Div RNR 1946-65, late Lt-Cdr VRD, RNR; founder Member RNVR Club Scotland (S V Carrick), Glasgow: *m* 1959, Dorothy Betty Wallace, da of late David Green Roddick, of 47 Moraine Dr, Glasgow.

Grandson of late Courtenay Alexander Pole (ante):—
Issue of late Courtenay Deans Carew Pole, *b* 1925, *d* 1984: *m* 1951, Aileen Munro, da of John M. Crawford:—
Alan John Carew (37 Lechford Rd, Horley, Surrey RH6 7AB), *b* 1958: *m* 1980, Susan Lindsay, yst da of Frederick Holroyd, of 31 Woodvale Av, Giffnock, Renfrewshire, and has issue living, Stuart Alan, *b* 1988, — Caroline Susan, *b* 1986.

Granddaughter of late John Pole, 5th son of Rev Edward Pole (ante):—
Issue of late Herbert Edward Pole, *b* 1882, *d* 1965: *m* 1930, Ena Marsh (Glenloch, Rowley Drive, nr Cranleigh, Surrey):—
Millicent Rosemary, *b* 1933: *m* 1958, Peter Cox, of Petamille, 3 Park Way, Gt Bookham, Surrey, and has issue living, Gawen Peter, *b* 1967, — Emma Louise, *b* 1964.

The 1st baronet was MP for Devonshire, the 2nd Baronet represented Honiton in Parliament, and the 3rd and 5th baronets each sat as MP for co Devon. The 6th baronet assumed in 1790 the surname of De-la-Pole, which his successor discontinued, and the 8th baronet assumed in 1838 the surname of Reeve-de-la-Pole, and afterwards discontinued it. The 10th Baronet resumed the surname of de la Pole 1895. Sir Frederick Arundell de la Pole, 11th baronet, was High Sheriff of Devon 1917.

POLE (GB) 1791, of Wolverton, Hampshire

Sir PETER VAN NOTTEN POLE, 5th *Baronet,* son of late Arthur Chandos Pole, grandson of late Gen Edward Pole, 4th son of 2nd Baronet; *b* 6 Nov 1921; *s* his kinsman, *Sir* CECIL PERY VAN-NOTTEN-POLE, 1948; FASA; ACIS; accountant; 1939-45 War as Flight-Sgt R Aust AF: *m* 1949, Jean Emily, da of late C. D. Stone, of Borden, W Aust, and has issue.

Arms – Argent, a chevron between three crescents gules, a mullet for difference. **Crest** – A falcon rising proper, a mullet for difference. **Supporters** – On either side a lion reguardant proper (the Supporters of HSH William, Landgrave of Hesse-Cassel), debruised by a pale of three tinctures, the first half per pale gules and argent, the second half azure (originally conferred on the 1st Baronet by the Landgrave and confirmed by Roy Warrant of 1794 to the Baronet and his successors).
Residence – 130/60 Kalinda Drive, City Beach, W Australia 6015.

SON LIVING

PETER JOHN CHANDOS (41 Webster St, Nedlands 6009, W Australia), *b* 27 April 1952: *m* 1973, Suzanne Norah, da of Harold Raymond Hughes, of 214/60 Kalinda Drive, City Beach, W Aust 6015, and has issue living, Michael Van Notten, *b* 12 May 1980, — Andrew Van Notten, *b* 1986, — Naomi Suzanne, *b* 1983.

DAUGHTER LIVING

Anne, *b* 1957: *m* 1982, Martin Paul Carr, of Bridgetown, W Australia 6025.

SISTER LIVING

Marjorie van Notten, *b* 1923. *Residence* – 83/60 Kalinda Drive, City Beach, W Australia 6015.

This is a branch of the ancient Derbyshire family of Pole, many members of which have distinguished themselves in the field, notably German Pole, who commanded in Ireland, and served against the Armada. They were also descended in the female line from a sister of Sir John Chandos, KG, chief commander at Crecy and Poitiers. Millicent, daughter of Charles Pole, of Holcroft, married Charles Van-Notten, a London merchant, son of Charles Van-Notten (a descendant of Henry Van-Notten, ennobled 1499 by the Emperor Maximilian I, and whose only son Charles received from Charles V the titles of Lord of Ath and Vander-Notten, and Chatelaine of Alost), a merchant of Amsterdam and London. He assumed the surname of Pole, and was created a baronet with remainder to the heirs male of his body, failing which to those of his daughter Susannah. Susannah *m* 1802 Isaac Minet, but her male line is understood to have become ext with the death of her son without male issue. The 3rd baronet assumed in 1853, by Roy licence, the additional and original paternal name of Van-Notten. On his death in 1948, the baronetcy reverted to the line of Gen Edward Pole, Col 12th Lancers, 4th son of 2nd Bt.

POLLEN (GB) 1795, of Redenham, Hampshire

Sir JOHN MICHAEL HUNGERFORD POLLEN, 7th *Baronet*, only son of late Lieut-Com John Francis Hungerford Pollen, RN, el son of late Capt Francis Gabriel Hungerford Pollen, CBE, RN, 4th son of late John Hungerford Pollen, yr brother of 3rd baronet; *b* 6 April 1919; *s* his kinsman, *Sir* JOHN LANCELOT HUNGERFORD, 1959; *ed* Downside, and Merton Coll, Oxford; is Capt RA: *m* 1st, 1941 (*m diss* 1956), Angela Mary Oriana, who *d* 1990, da of late Maj Felix John Russi, MC, 5th Roy Inniskilling Dragoon Guards; 2ndly, 1957, Mrs Diana Alice Jubb, who *d* 1995, da of late A. E. Timbrell, and has issue by 1st *m*.

Arms – Azure, on a bend cotissed or, five escallops vert between six lozenges argent, each charged with an escallop sable. Crest – A pelican per pale or and azure, vulning herself, and feeding her young proper, charged on the wings elevated with a lozenge, as in the arms. *Residence* – Rodbourne, Malmesbury, Wilts.

SON LIVING (*By 1st marriage*)

RICHARD JOHN HUNGERFORD, *b* 3 Nov 1946; *ed* Worth: *m* 1971, Christianne Mary, da of late Sir (William) Godfrey Agnew, KCVO, CB, and has had issue, William Richard Hungerford, *b* 28 June 1976, — Jonathan Charles, *b* 1979, — Andrew Francis, *b* 1982, — Alexander Christian, *b* 1986, — Joseph Anthony, *b* and *d* 1991, — Isabel Mary Ruth, *b* 1975, — Alice Charlotte Mary, *b* 1984, — Beatrice Veronica Mary, *b* 1992. *Residence* – Three Firs House, Bramshott Chase, Hants GU26 6DG

DAUGHTER LIVING (*By 1st marriage*)

Jane Oriana Mary, *b* 1942: *m* 1962, Roger Tilney Grafftey-Smith, of Monks Farmhouse, Sherborne, Cheltenham, Glos GL54 3DR, son of late Sir Laurence Barton Grafftey-Smith, KCMG, KBE, and has issue living, Simon Laurence (29E Warwick Sq, SW1V 2AD), *b* 1968; *ed* Winchester, and Exeter Univ; Guinness Mahon & Co Ltd since 1989: *m* 1999, Miranda Elizabeth E., only da of Timothy Parson, of Hunstrete, Bristol, — Max Anthony, *b* 1974, — Selina Dora, *b* 1971: *m* 1996, Charles Edward Hooton Faircloth, of 208 Stanley Hill, Amersham, Bucks HP7 9ET, son of John Faircloth, of Chesham Bois, Bucks, and has issue living, Felix Hooton *b* 1996, Mia Amy *b* 1998.

SISTER LIVING

Susan Mary, *b* 1917. *Residence* – By Scarlett's Wood, Hare Hatch, Twyford, Berks.

COLLATERAL BRANCHES LIVING

Issue of late Sir Walter Michael Hungerford Pollen, MC, uncle of 7th baronet, *b* 1894, *d* 1968: *m* 1925, Rosalind Frances, who *d* 1983, da of late Robert Benson, of Buckhurst, Withyham, Sussex, and 16 South St, Park Lane, W1:—
Peregrine Michael Hungerford (The Farmhouse, Norton Hall, Mickleton, Glos; Balranald House, N Uist), *b* 1931; *ed* Eton, and Ch Ch Oxford: *m* 1958, Patricia Helen, da of late Lt-Col Gerald Barry, MC (*see* Barry, Bt, colls), and has issue living, (Peregrine) Marcus Hungerford, *b* 1964; *ed* Eton, — Susannah Hungerford, *b* 1959, — Arabella Rosalind Hungerford (*Hon Mrs David Macmillan*), *b* 1961; *ed* St Swithun's, Winchester, and Queen's Coll London; designer: *m* 1st, 1985, Giacomo Dante Algranti; 2ndly, 1995, Hon David Maurice Benjamin Macmillan (*see* E Stockton), and has issue living (by 1st *m*), Jesse Gilberto *b* 1986, Samuel Peregrine *b* 1989, (by 2nd *m*) (*see* E Stockton). —— Pandora Mary Hungerford (Argyll House, Cirencester, Glos), *b* 1928; LRCP & S Ireland; formerly Prin, Hatherop Castle Sch, Coln-St-Aldwyn, Glos: *m* 1949, Charles Edward Moorhead, who *d* 1953, and has issue living, Rosalind Catherine, *b* 1950: *m* 19—, Dermot Gleeson, and has issue living, Patrick Charles Thomas *b* 1984, Catherine Mary *b* 1981, — Annabel Mai, *b* 1951: *m* 19—, Hjalmar Schiøtz, of Norway, and has issue living, Tanja Katrine *b* 1976, Marianne *b* 1981, Nina *b* 1985.

Grandchildren of late Arthur Joseph Lawrence Pollen (*infra*):—
Issue of late Francis Anthony Baring Pollen, *b* 1926, *d* 1987: *m* 1950, Marie Thérèse (*Viscountess Sidmouth*) (who *m* 2ndly, 1993, as his 2nd wife, 7th Viscount Sidmouth), da of His Honour late Sir Joseph (Alfred) Sheridan:—
John Stephen Hungerford, *b* 1959: *m* 1988, Jacqueline Ann, yr da of Brian H. Caro, of Applehayes, Curry Rivel, Som, and has issue living, Francis Arthur Hungerford, *b* 1989, — Anthony Oswald Lawrence, *b* 1992. —— Clare (*Viscountess Asquith*), *b* 1951: *m* 1978, Raymond Benedict Bartholomew Michael, Viscount Asquith, elder son of 2nd Earl of Oxford and Asquith, KCMG, and has issue (see that title). *Residence* – Branch Farm, Mells, Frome, Somerset. —— Katharine, *b* 1954: *m* 1979, Richard Pflaum, and has issue living, Dominic Richard, *b* 1985, — Julia, *b* 1982, — Thea Mary, *b* 1990. —— Roseanna, *b* 1956: *m* 1984, Ferdinand Carabott-Tortell, and has issue living, Arthur John Rupert *b* 1986, — Juno Clare Emily, *b* 1989. —— (Mary) Louise, *b* 1969.

Grandchildren of late Arthur Joseph Hungerford Pollen, son of John Hungerford Pollen, next brother of 3rd baronet:—
Issue of late Arthur Joseph Lawrence Pollen, *b* 1899, *d* 1968: *m* 1926, Hon Daphne Baring, who *d* 1986, da of 3rd Baron Revelstoke:—
Patrick Laprimaudaye (USA), *b* 1928: *m* 1963, Nell, yst da of late John Murphy, of Sweetmount House, New Ross, co Wexford, and has issue living, Patrick Benedict Peter, *b* 1965, — Laurence Joseph, *b* 1968, — Ciaran, *b* 1966, — Christopher, *b* 1972, — Patricia, *b* 1970. —— Cecilia Mary, *b* 1930: *m* 1952, Christopher Robert Hull, and has issue living,

Rupert Teilo David, *b* 1959, — Caspar William, *b* 1960, — Thomas Richard, *b* 1964, — Simon Paul Timothy, *b* 1966, — Lucy Bridget, *b* 1955, — Barbara Margaret, *b* 1957. —— Lucy Margaret, *b* 1932: *m* 1955, Philip Vincent Belloc Jebb, who *d* 1995, of Beenham Hatch, Bucklebury, Berks RG7 6NR, and has issue living, Matthew Hilary, *b* 1958: *m* 1987, Serena Emma Rose, elder da of Hon Richard Morgan Oliver Stanley, and has issue (*see* B Stanley of Alderley), — Louis Bernard, *b* 1959, — Magdalen Marianne Francesca, *b* 1956, — Christian Agnes Valentine, *b* 1961: *m* 1993, Nigel A. Spence, yr son of Julian Spence, of Burnham Thorpe, Norfolk, and has issue living, George Julian *b* 1995, Isabel *b* 1994, Charlotte *b* 1998. —— Mary Rose Catherine, *b* 1940: *m* 1967, Hugo Laurence Joseph Brunner, of 26 Norham Rd, Oxford (*see* Brunner, Bt). —— Margaret Mary Clare, *b* 1943: *m* 1966, Patrick Hyde Kelly, of 23 Charleville Rd, Rathmines, Dublin, and has issue living, Arthur Edmund Campion, *b* 1971, — James Patrick Simeon, *b* 1980, — Beatrice Maeve, *b* 1968.

Issue of late John Anthony Lawrence Pollen, *b* 1900, *d* 1998: *m* 1931, Bridget Gertrude, who *d* 1956, da of late Maj Cuthbert Leigh Blundell-Hollinshead-Blundell (*see* Astley, Bt, 1954 Edn):—
Anne Bridget, *b* 1934.

Granddaughters of late Lt-Col Stephen Hungerford Pollen, CMG son of late John Hungerford Pollen (ante):—
Issue of late Lt-Col Stephen Derek Hungerford Pollen, MBE, *b* 1908; *d* 1969: *m* 1944, Marion Leigh Howard, who *d* 1990, da of late Capt Thomas Storie Dixson:—
Helen Leigh, *b* 1948. —— Margaret Anne, *b* 1952.

Grandchildren of late John Hungerford Pollen (ante):—
Issue of late Lieut-Col Clement Hungerford Pollen, *b* 1869, *d* 1934: *m* 1912, Mabel Brenda who *d* 1964, da of late Alan Southey Dumbleton of Victoria, British Columbia:—
Hubert Clement Hungerford (3 Dinorben Av, Fleet, Hants GU13 9SG), *b* 1913; *ed* Downside; late Maj Indian Army: *m* 1954, Quita, da of late A. Edward Baker, of Salop, and Fiji. —— Cynthia Brenda, *b* 1914: *m* 1943, Lt Ronald Malcolm Marshall, RN (ret), who *d* 1981, and has issue living, Robin Michael Hungerford, *b* 1943, — Bernard Mark Sebastian, *b* 1945, — John Henry Hubert, *b* 1948, — Clement Wilfrid Ronald Pollen, *b* 1951, — Rosemary Winetride Brenda, *b* 1950. *Residence* – 7 Mount Terrace, Taunton.

This family came originally from Lincs. Edward Pollen became London Merchant temp James I and *d* 1636. His son, grandson and great-grandson, all named John, were MPs for Andover. The last named, father of Sir John, 1st baronet, was one of the Judges of Wales and *d* 1776.

POLLOCK (UK) 1866, of Hatton, Middlesex

Boldly and strenuously

Sir GEORGE FREDERICK POLLOCK, 5th *Baronet*; *b* 13 Aug 1928; *s* his father, Sir (FREDERICK) JOHN 1963; *ed* Eton, and Trin Coll, Camb (MA); solicitor 1956; late 2nd Lt 17th/21st Lancers; Hon Fellow of Roy Photographic Soc, Pres (1978); FBIPP; FRSA; former Chm of London Salon of Photography, and of Photeurop (UK) Cttee: *m* 1951, Doreen Mumford, da of late Norman Ernest Keown Nash, CMG, and has issue.

Arms – Quarterly, 1st and 4th azure, three fleurs-de-lis within a bordure engrailed or, in dexter chief point on a canton ermine a portcullis of the second, *Pollock of Balgray*; 2nd and 3rd vert, a saltire or, between three bugles in fess and in base argent, garnished gules, within a bordure engrailed, dexter chequy of the second and first, sinister of the second, the whole within a bordure ermine for difference, *Pollock of that Ilk.* **Crest** – A boar passant, quartered or and vert, pierced through the sinister shoulder with an arrow proper. **Supporters** – Two talbots sable, each gorged with a collar or and pendent therefrom a portcullis of the last.
Residence – 83 Minster Way, Bathwick, Bath, Avon BA2 6RL. 3QH. *Club* – Downhill Only.

SON LIVING

DAVID FREDERICK, *b* 13 April 1959: *m* 1985, Helena R, only da of late L.J. Tompsett, OBE, of Tadworth, Surrey, and has issue living, Anna-Lisa Frances, *b* 1989.

DAUGHTERS LIVING

Charlotte Anne, *b* 1952: *m* 1976, David D. Swift. —— Catherine Frances Jill, *b* 1955: *m* 1976, Robert A. Hiron.

COLLATERAL BRANCHES LIVING

Grandchildren of late Archibald Gordon Pollock, yr son of Robert John Pollock, 3rd son of 1st baronet:—
Issue of late Hamilton Rivers Pollock, *b* 1884, *d* 1940: *m* 1912, Eveline Morton, who *d* 1940, da of Thomas Bell, of Newcastle-on-Tyne:—

Martin Rivers (Marsh Farm House, Margaret Marsh, Shaftesbury, Dorset SP7 0AZ), *b* 1914; *ed* Winchester, and Trin Coll, Camb (BA and Senior Scholar 1936, MB, ChB 1940, MA 1951): Prof of Biology Edinburgh Univ 1965-76, since when Emeritus; FRS 1962: *m* 1st, 1941 (*m diss* 19—), Jean Ilsley, who *d* 1997, elder da of Frank Ilsley Paradise; 2ndly, 1979, Janet Frances Machen, and has issue living (by 1st *m*), Julian Rivers (13 Guilford Rd, Leicester), *b* 1942; *ed* William Ellis Sch, and Edinburgh Univ (MA 1967): *m* 1969, Patricia Diana, yr da of AV-M John Chegwyn Thomas Downey, CB, DFC, AFC, and has issue living, Benjamin James *b* 1973, Joanna Ruth *b* 1982, — Jonathan Ilsley (25 Florence Park, Westbury Park, Bristol BS6 7LS), *b* 1948; *ed* William Ellis Sch, and Edinburgh Univ: *m* 1980, Susan, da of Dr Tom Pollock, and has issue living Jennifer Claire *b* 1983, Eleanor Daisy *b* 1987, — Jessamy, *b* 1941, — Lisa Jane, *b* 1944: *m* 1968, Richard Robinson, of 27 de Freville Av, Cambridge CB4 1HW, and has issue living, Sam Jonathan *b* 1972, Sara Miranda *b* 1969; (who has issue living, by Grahame Alexander, Rosa ROBINSON ALEXANDER *b* 1994), Katie Alice *b* 1978. —— Marian Eveline, *b* 1918: *m* 1956, Thomas Edgar Foulkes, of 10 Singleton Rd, N Balwyn, Melbourne, Vic 3104, Australia, and has issue living, Paul Vincent (64 Northcote Rd, Armadale, Vic 3143, Australia), *b* 1958; MB BS, FRANZCP Melbourne Univ: *m* 1986, Debra, da of Clive Anthony Levy, and has issue living, Callum James Rivers *b* 1998. —— Margaret Gordon, *b* 1921: *m* 1st, 1943 (*m diss* 1961), Boris Kidel, who *d* 1991; 2ndly, 1962, Paul Lendvai, of Gonzagagasse 15/10, 1010 Vienna, Austria, and has issue living (by 1st *m*), Andrey (40 Park Drive, NW11 7SP), *b* 1943; *ed* French Lycee, Vienna, Oxford Univ (BA 1964), and LSE (MSc 1966): *m* 1969, Sara Jacinta Nadal, and has issue living, Alexei *b* 1972, Carlos *b* 1974, Rafael Ivan *b* 1978, Nicholas *b* 1985, — Mark Rivers, *b* 1947.

Granddaughter of late Col Ralph Charles Geoffrey Pollock, el son of Harry Frederick Pollock, el son of George Frederick Pollock (infra):—
Issue of late Maj (Ralph) John Hamilton Pollock, RA, *b* 1921, *d* 1980: *m* 1st, 1948 (*m diss* 1955), Patricia Clarice Marion, who *d* 1999, da of Capt Arthur Thompson, late Northants Regt; 2ndly, 1957 (*m diss* 1968), Elizabeth Ormond, da of late Charles Mills Maclean, of Savannah, Georgia, USA, and formerly wife of Robert Martin; 3rdly, 1968, Lady Zinnia Rosemary Cantlie (who *d* 1997, having *m* 5thly, 1982, Jamie H. Judd, of Stewkley Grange, Leighton Buzzard, Beds), da of 4th Earl of Londesborough:—
(By 1st *m*) Sally Anne St George, *b* 1952: *m* 1975, Ian Kenneth Francis Robertson, of Coolnaskeagh Lodge, Templecarig, Greystones, co Wicklow, and has issue living, Rebecca Alexandra, *b* 1977, — Holly Anne, *b* 1986.

Granddaughters of late William Rivers Pollock, MD, MRCS, FRCP, 4th son of late George Frederick Pollock (infra):—
Issue of late Humphrey Rivers Pollock, MRCS, LRCP, *b* 1889, *d* 1964: *m* 1920, Eleanor Violet, who *d* 1973, da of late Willoughby Aston Littledale (Thursby, Bt):—
Mary Rivers, *b* 1921; MCSP: *m* 1st, 1960, Charles Tristan D'Oyly, MBE, who *d* 1981; 2ndly, 1990, Philip R. R. Coad, MC, who *d* 1993. *Residence* – 129 Swan Court, SW3. —— Joan Littledale, *b* 1924; *ed* Otago Univ (MA): *m* 1948, Francis Alexander de Hamel, MD, of 25 Howard St, Macandrew Bay, Dunedin, NZ, and has issue living, Michael Alexander, *b* 1949; *ed* Otago Univ (MA); MRSP: *m* 1982, Alison Patricia Holcroft, of Nelson, NZ, and has an adopted son, Stephen Wai Lam *b* 1984, — Christopher Francis Rivers, *b* 1950; *ed* Otago Univ (BA), and New Coll, Oxford (D Phil); FSA; Dir Sotheby's: *m* 1st, 1978 (*m diss* 1989): Christine Leslie Carmody, of Nelson, NZ; 2ndly, 1993, Mette Tang, da of Axel Tang Svendsen, of Copenhagen, and formerly wife of David Melville Bromby Simpson, and has issue living (by 1st *m*), Alexander John Pudsay *b* 1981, Edwin Willoughby Rivers *b* 1984, — Geoffrey William, *b* 1953: *m* 1981, Philippa Sarah, da of Dr Max Nash, of Remuera, NZ, and has issue living, Adam Culyer Nash *b* 1983, Jane Sarah Nash *b* 1985, — Richard John Bruno, *b* 1960: *m* 1987, Philippa Lynne White, MD, of Blenheim, NZ, and has issue living, Roy William *b* 1991, James Michael *b* 1993, Thomas Richard *b* 1997, — Quentin David Humphrey, *b* 1963: *ed* Otago Univ (LLB): *m* 1991, Judith Anne Clark, of Christchurch, NZ, and has issue living, Stephanie Jane Littledale *b* 1992, Kathryn Anne Taylor *b* 1995.

Issue of late Rt Hon Sir Ernest Murray Pollock, KBE (5th son of late George Frederick Pollock (infra)), who was *cr Viscount Hanworth* 1936 (see that title).

Granddaughter of late George Frederick Pollock, 4th son of 1st baronet:—
Issue of late Rt Rev Bertram Pollock, KCVO, DD, Lord Bishop of Norwich 1910-42, *b* 1863; *d* 1943: *m* 1928, Joan Florence Helena, who *d* 1986, da of late Rev Algernon Charles Dudley Ryder (*see* E Harrowby, colls):—
Mary Rosalind Frances Felicia, *b* 1931.

Grandchildren of late Hon Sir Charles Edward Pollock, 5th son of 1st baronet:—
Issue of late George Hume Pollock, *b* 1870, *d* 1924: *m* 1900, Margaret Agnata, who *d* 1954, da of Sir Richard Harington, 11th Bt:—
Agnata Cecilia, *b* 1907. *Residence* – Quendon Cottage, Quendon, nr Saffron Walden, Essex. —— Margaret Georgina, *b* 1913; *m* 1948, Richard Tresillian Gabb, MB, BCh, who *d* 1986. *Residence* – Beverley House, Stansted Mountfitchet, Essex CM24 8AE.

Issue of late Robert Pollock, *b* 1874, *d* 1957: *m* (Jan) 1914, Ethel Mary Purefoy, who *d* 1970, da of James Crofts Powell, of 13 Chester St, Grosvenor Pl, SW:—
Martin James, *b* (Dec) 1914; *ed* Charterhouse, and Trin Coll, Camb (BA 1936); admitted a solicitor 1946; is Lieut RNVR: *m* 1942, (Pamela) Valentine, who *d* 1997, da of late Valentine Leslie Douglas Uzielli, and has issue living, Robert Valentine, *b* 1957, — Carolyn Alice, *b* 1944: *m* 1st 1967 (*m diss* 1971), Michael Bernard Thorold, Scots Gds (*see* Thorold, Bt, colls); 2ndly, 1976, Anthony Edward Henson, of Elm Tree House, Tillers Green, Dymock, Glos, and has issue (by 1st *m*) (*see* Thorold, Bt, colls), — Rosalind Janet, *b* 1948; SEN: *m* 1975, John Edward Fawkes, of Kenyons, W Horsley, Surrey, and has issue living, Mark Alexander *b* 1977, Juliette Elizabeth *b* 1982. *Residence* – West Crosside, Knowstone, S Molton, N Devon. —— *Rev* John Charles, *b* 1923; *ed* Charterhouse, and Trin Coll, Camb (BA 1946, MA 1948); formerly Capt Coldm Gds: *m* 1949, Anne, da of Sir Thomas Richard Fiennes Barrett-Lennard, 5th Bt, OBE. *Residence* – Rose Ash House, S Molton, Devon EX36 4RB. —— Honor Purefoy, *b* 1916: *m* 1939, James Frederick Priestley, MC, and has issue

living, Hugh Michael (52 Stanford Rd, W8), *b* 1942; *ed* Winchester and Worcester Coll, Oxford: *m* 1968, Caroline Clarissa Duncan, only da of Brig John Hume Prendergast, DSO, MC, and has issue living, Alexandra Mary Duncan *b* 1971, Susannah Caroline Louise *b* 1974, — Richard James (The Old Rectory, Houghton, nr Stockbridge, Hants SO20 6LJ), *b* 1947: *m* 1980, Iona Rosalind, da of Maj Ion Melville Calvocoressi, MBE, MC, of Court Lodge, Westerham, Kent (*see* M Ailsa, colls), and has issue living, Laura Katherine *b* 1982, Rosanna Victoria *b* 1985, Isabel Louise *b* 1988, — Sarah Veronica (Ovington House, Alresford, Hants SO24 0RB), *b* 1944: *m* 1st, 1967, Brian David Bond, who *d* 1981; 2ndly, 1990, Robert George Thorne, and has issue living (by 1st *m*), Michael Alan Shaw *b* 1968; *ed* Eton, and Durham Univ (BSc), Edward Brian Shaw *b* 1970; *ed* Eton, and Newcastle Univ (BA): *m* 1999, Virginia, da of Michael Melville, of Deep Well House, Gt Chishill, Herts, Annabel Clare *b* 1971; *ed* Durham Univ (BA): *m* 1997, Michael Alexander Smyth-Osbourne (*see* Ramsden, Bt), Marina Alice *b* 1976. *Residence* – Headbourne Worthy House, Winchester, Hants SO23 7JG.

Granddaughter of late George Hume Pollock (ante):—
Issue of late Com Charles Harington Pollock, DSC, RN, *b* 1906; *d* 1983: *m* 1938, Patricia Aileen Domville, who *d* 1957, da of late Herbert Payne Heming, of Victoria, BC, Canada, and widow of Capt H. Leicester Leverin, RCE:—
Ann Patricia, *b* 1939: *m* 1961, Maj Richard Cecil Wallace, RCT, of Kemps, Hill Green, Clavering, Saffron Walden, Essex, and has had issue, Charles Pollock, *b* 1963, — Oliver James Shannon, *b* 1970, *d* 1976.

Grandchildren of late Maj-Gen Sir (Frederick) Richard Pollock, KCSI, 7th son of 1st baronet:—
Issue of late Dighton Nicolas Pollock, *b* 1864, *d* 1927: *m* 1921, Hon Margaret Anna Buckmaster, who *d* 1929, da of 1st Viscount Buckmaster:—
Richard Stanley, *b* 1922. *Residence* – 20 Porchester Terrace, W2. —— John Dighton, *b* 1924.

Grandchildren of late Douglas Warren Pollock, MBE, yst son of late Sir Edward James Pollock, 9th son of 1st baronet:—
Issue of late Maj Jack Warren Pollock, RA, *b* 1913; *d* 1981: *m* 1949, Hazel (The Bridge House, Shoreham, Kent TN14 7SJ), da of late Henry Arthur Hinton, of Shrewsbury, and widow of Maj Howard Bourne, Hon Artillery Co:—
Nicholas Charles Valentine (22 Oaklands Grove, W12), *b* 1950; *ed* Winchester, New Coll, Oxford (MA), and Southampton Univ (MSc). —— Christopher James Douglas (30 London St, Whitchurch, Hants), *b* 1956; *ed* Winchester, and Worcester Coll, Oxford: *m* 1984, Sarah, da of David Geddes Mitchell, of Iffley, Oxford, and has issue living, Felix Alexander, *b* 1989, — Tobias Frederick, *b* 1992, — Eliza Madeline *b* 1995. —— Miranda Penelope Gillian, *b* 1952: *m* 1992, (Brian Edward) Nicholas O'Brien (*see* B Inchiquin, colls), of Hawthorn Cottage, Milford, Surrey GU8 5BH.

The Right Hon Sir Frederick, 1st baronet, was Lord Chief Baron of the Court of Exchequer, 1844-68. He was a son of David Pollock, saddler, of Charing Cross, a descendant of David Pollock, of Balgray, Renfrewshire, *b* about 1631, great-grandson of Charles Pollock of Greenhill, yr son of David Pollock of that Ilk. David Pollock, the saddler, also had two other sons who attained great eminence, viz, Sir David Pollock, Chief Justice of Bombay, and Field Marshal Sir George Pollock, Baronet, GCB, GCSI, Constable of the Tower of London. The senior line Pollock of Pollock became ext in the 19th century. The 2nd baronet was for many years Senior Master of the Supreme Court of Judicature and Queen's Remembrancer. The 3rd baronet was a Privy Councillor, KC and Admiralty Judge of the Cinque Ports 1914-36. The 4th baronet was an Officer Legion of Honour.

MONTAGU-POLLOCK (UK) 1872, of the Khyber Pass

Boldly and strenuously

Let us be examined by our conduct

Sir GILES HAMPDEN MONTAGU-POLLOCK, 5th *Baronet*; *b* 19 Oct 1928; *s* his father, *Sir* GEORGE SEYMOUR, 1985; *ed* Eton, and de Havilland Aeronautical Tech Sch; De Havilland Enterprise 1949-56, Bristol Aeroplane Co Ltd 1956-59, Bristol Siddeley Engines Ltd 1959-61, J. Walter Thompson Co Ltd 1961-69, C. Vernon and Sons Ltd 1969-71, Acumen Marketing Group Ltd 1971-74, 119 Pall Mall Ltd 1972-78, John Stork and Partners Ltd 1980-89, Management Consultant since 1974, Associate Korn/Ferry International since 1989: *m* 1963, Caroline Veronica, yr da of late Richard Francis Russell, of 18 The Grange, Wimbledon, SW19, and has issue.

Arms – Quarterly, 1st and 4th, azure, three fleurs-de-lis within a bordure embattled or for his distinguished services in the Afghan war on a chief of the second an eastern crown gules, superinscribed "Khyber," and on a canton ermine three cannons fessways in pale sable *Pollock*; 2nd and 3rd, parti per pale argent and gules, a fesse lozengy counterchanged *Montagu*; in the middle chief point a cross moline, also counterchanged. **Crests** – 1st, a lion rampant guardant argent adorned with an eastern crown or, holding in his dexter paw in bend sinister an Afghan banner displayed gules, bordered or and vert, the staff broken in two, in his sinister paw a part of the broken staff in an escrol over the motto, "Affghanistan" *Pollock*; 2nd, a boar passant quarterly embattled or and vert, pierced through the sinister shoulder with an arrow proper *Pollock*; 3rd, a griffin's head couped, wings expanded

or, gorged with a collar lozengy *Montagu*. ≋upporters – *Dexter*, an heraldic tiger sable, maned, tufted, and gorged with an eastern crown, and chained, chain being reflexed over the back or, and pendent from the collar an escutcheon or, charged with a bomb fired proper; *sinister*, a talbot gorged, chained, and charged as the dexter.
Residence – The White House, 7 Washington Rd, Barnes, SW13 9BG. *Club* – Inst of Directors.

SON LIVING

GUY MAXIMILIAN, *b* 27 Aug 1966; *ed* Eton, and Hatfield Poly.

DAUGHTER LIVING

Sophie Amelia, *b* 1969; *ed* Godolphin and Latymer.

SISTER LIVING

Karen Aagot Georgina, *b* 1931: *m* 1952, Richard Eliot Hodgkin, yr son of late Brig Adrian Eliot Hodgkin, OBE, MC, and has issue living, Harry John, *b* 1961; *ed* Radley and Ealing College (LLB); Bar: *m* 1990, Karen Lesley Pearce, and has issue living, Polly Grace *b* 1992, — Edward Eliot, *b* 1963; *ed* Radley, and Jesus Coll, Oxford (BA, DPhil): *m* 1993, Karen Lesley Jones, — Georgina Elizabeth, *b* 1954: *m* 1975 (*m diss* 1979), Nicholas David Douro Hoare, and has issue living, Caspar Michael Douro *b* 1977. *Address* – c/o Drummonds Branch, The Royal Bank of Scotland, 49 Charing Cross, SW1A 2DX.

COLLATERAL BRANCHES LIVING

Issue of late Hubert Vernon Montagu-Pollock, 2nd son of 3rd baronet, *b* 1902; *d* 1970: *m* 1945, Delia Florence Alice, who *d* 1977, da of late Herbert Snowden, and widow of Harold Edward Pearce:—
Jonathan David (Bridge Cottage, Winterbourne Stoke, Salisbury, Wilts SP3 4SW; Army and Navy and RGJ (London) Clubs), *b* 1947; *ed* Charterhouse; late 2nd Lt R Green Jackets: *m* 1979, Deirdre Clare, yr da of John Edward Binding, of Rock, N Cornwall, and has issue living, Thomas George, *b* 1983, — Archer William, *b* 1986.

Issue of late Sir William Horace Montagu-Pollock, KCMG, 3rd son of 3rd baronet, *b* 1903, *d* 1993: *m* 1st, 1933 (*m diss* 1945), (Frances Elisabeth) Prudence, who *d* 1985, da of late Sir John Fischer Williams, CBE, KC, of Lamledra, Gorran Haven, Cornwall (D Atholl, colls); 2ndly, 1948, Barbara, who *d* 1998, da of late Percy Hague Jowett, CBE, of 28 Drayton Gds, SW10, and formerly wife of Thomas Josceline Gaskell (*see* B Bagot, colls):—
(By 1st *m*) Hubert George Murray (Low Beckfoot, Barbon, Carnforth, Cumbria LA6 2LE), *b* 1935; *ed* Winchester; MA; PhD; Past Fellow of Trin Coll, Camb; Reader in Surface Physics, Lancaster Univ: *m* 1960, Emmerentia Johanna, yr da of J.B. de Jong Cleyndert, of Palegates Farm, Henham, Essex, and has issue living, Harriet Marthe, *b* 1961, — Catherine Juliet, *b* 1963, — Annabel Frances, *b* 1966: *m* 1997, Stewart McWilliam, and has issue living, Rachel *b* 1998. —— Fidelity Juliet, *b* 1940: *m* 1962, Alan Charles Barclay Dean, MB, FRCS, of Balgone House, N Berwick, E Lothian EH39 5PB, and has issue living, Marcus William Fischer, *b* 1963; RIBA, RIAS, — Juliet Augusta Carolyn, *b* 1965, — Corinna Lucy Henrietta, *b* 1967. —— (By 2nd *m*) Matthew John (7 Yap Compound, Bauhinia Drive, Banilad, Cebu City, Philippines), *b* 1951; *ed* Westminster, and Ch Ch, Oxford: *m* 1984, Aliaa, da of late Abdel Rahman Zayed, and has issue living, Gabriel (a son), *b* 1994, — Sasha (a da), *b* 1991.

Issue of late John Gathorne Montagu-Pollock, 4th and yst son of 3rd baronet, *b* 1911, *d* 1995: *m* 1943, Elizabeth Metcalf, who *d* 1989, da of late Carl Herbert Coston, of South Hadley Falls, Mass, USA:—
Stephen Hull (850 Berkshire Drive, Westbury, Long Island, NY 11590, USA), *b* 1945: *m* 1979, Barbara Ann, da of Ralph J. Betschart. —— Christopher James (2604 W County Rd 8, Berthoud, Colorado 80513, USA), *b* 1952: *m* 1980, Dianne Kristen, da of Eugene M. Spear, and has issue living, Toby William, *b* 1986, — Jennifer Ann, *b* 1982. —— Margaret Bell (2340 Abingdon Way, Long Lake, MN 55356, USA), *b* 1948: *m* 1972, Robert Lewis Merkow, who *d* 1989, of Hartland, Wisconsin, USA, and has issue living, Sarah Ellen, *b* 1981, — Carla Lauren, *b* 1984.

Granddaughters of late Hugh Pollock, 2nd son of late George David Pollock, FRCS (infra):—
Issue of late Hugh Wykeham David Pollock, *b* 1900, *d* 1972: *m* 1934, Barbara, who *d* 1993, da of Sir Philip Bealby Reckitt, OBE, 3rd Bt (ext):—
Bridget Wykeham (Lowlands Farm, Shrewley, Warwicks), *b* 1935: *m* 1960 (*m diss* 1977), Michael John Marshall, son of Sir Arthur Gregory George Marshall, OBE, DL, and has issue living, Robert David, *b* 1962: *m* 1992, Julia Kathleen, yr da of Timothy Patrick Hamilton-Russell (*see* B Ashbourne), and has issue living, Bethany Finn *b* 1996, — James Gregory, *b* 1964, — Belinda Louise, *b* 1960: *m* 1988, Adrian Richard Hill, — Cressida Micael, *b* 1967. —— Ann Catherine (Coshandrochaid, Tayvallich, Argyll), *b* 1938. —— Jane (Winderwath, Penrith, Cumbria), *b* 1945.

Granddaughter of late George David Pollock, FRCS, 2nd son of 1st baronet:—
Issue of late Col Evelyn Pollock, CBE, RA, *b* 1861, *d* 1951: *m* 1890, Mary, who *d* 1936, da of late Henry Jefferd Tarrant, Bar-at-law:—
Jean, *b* 1914: *m* 1st, 1940, Maj Gerard Joseph McCann, RM, who was *ka* 1943; 2ndly, 1951, Group Capt Slocombe Gomez, CBE, RAF, who *d* 1972, and has had issue, (by 1st *m*) Peta Jean Madeleine, *b* 1941; *d* 1996, — (by 2nd *m*) Nicholas David (Carretera de Boadilla del Monte, 52-7°B, Madrid 28024, Spain), *b* 1952; *ed* Sherborne: *m* 1976, Felicidad Mediavilla, and has issue living, Karen Alexandra *b* 1978, Gillian *b* 1982. *Residence* – Carretera de Boadilla del Monte, 52-7°B, Madrid 28024, Spain.

Granddaughter of late Col Evelyn Pollock, CBE, RA (ante):—
Issue of late Sir Ronald Evelyn Pollock, *b* 1891, *d* 1974: *m* 1st, 1921, Margery, who *d* 1959, da of late Samuel Fitze; 2ndly, 1963, Pamela, who *d* 1989, only da of late Francis Winckworth Anstice Prideaux, OBE, and widow of Percy John Hodsoll Stent, CIE, ICS:—
(By 1st *m*) Anne Margery, *b* 1924; formerly in WRNS: *m* 1st, 1958 (*m diss* 1979), Clive Robert Basche; 2ndly, 1981, Richard Holman Parsons, Lt-Cdr RN, of Fiddlers Green, 9 Grenehurst Way, Petersfield, Hants, and has issue living (by 1st *m*), Timothy James, *b* 1961: *m* 1988 (*m diss* 1997), Melanie Jane Lawson, and has issue living, Charlotte Louise *b* 1990, Sophie *b* 1993, — Clare Nicola, *b* 1959: *m* 1983, Jonathan Gordon Drew, and has issue living, James Newcombe *b* 1983, Robert Edmund *b* 1986, Christopher Gordon *b* 1987.

Grandchildren of late Lt-Col Frederick George Pollock, el son of late Archibald Reid Swiney Pollock, 4th son of 1st baronet:—
Issue of late Lt-Col Harry Clement Pollock, MBE, *b* 1883, *d* 1971: *m* 1st, 1914 (*m diss* 1928), Dorothy Beatrice, da of late Sir Theodore Caro Piggott; 2ndly, 1929, Constance Ferne, who *d* 1943, da of late Alfred Russell, of Rushall, Staffs; 3rdly, 1944, Winifred Eileen (14A Queens Rd, Royston, Herts), da of late W. T. C. Macgregor, of Wick, Caithness:—
(By 1st *m*) John Basil (224A Connaught Rd, Brookwood, Woking, Surrey, GU24 0AH), *b* 1920; BSc London Eng (Metallurgy); ARSM: *m* 1949, Betty Angela, da of H. A. Lusher, of Sevenoaks, Kent, and has issue living, Christopher Robert, *b* 1954, — Anne Patricia, *b* 1951, — Sarah Gillian, *b* 1957. ▬▬ (By 3rd *m*) Martin Donald, *b* 1948; *ed* Churchill Coll, Camb (MA); PhD (Cosmology).

Issue of late Archibald Frederick Pollock, *b* 1885, *d* 1941: *m* 1922, Ada Gertrude, who *d* 1979, da of late Albert Imossi, of Gibraltar:—
David Francis, *b* 1928; *ed* RMA Sandhurst; late Major RA: *m* 1959, Diana Mary, da of late Maj F. J. Andrews, of Hemingford Lodge, London Rd, Cheam, Surrey, and has issue living, James Robert, *b* 1962; *ed* King's Coll, Taunton, and Univ of W Aust (BCom): *m* 1994, Lucy, da of late Simon Chapman, of Mudgee, NSW, and has issue living, Harry Francis *b* 1998, Eleanor Sophie *b* 1996, — Gillian Mary, *b* 1960; *ed* Royal Sch, Bath: *m* 1983, David Ian Hill, son of Ian Hill, of Auckland, NZ, and has issue living, Marcus David *b* 1991, Stephanie Jane *b* 1995. ▬▬ Mary, *b* 1924: *m* 1946, Bryan L. Epsom, late Capt Queen's Own Roy W Kent Regt, and has issue living, Hugh David, *b* 1949, — Guy Bryan, *b* 1954, — Paul Robert, *b* 1956. *Address* – c/o PO Box 40026, Nairobi, Kenya.

Issue of late William Hamilton Pollock, *b* 1887, *d* 1976: *m* 1915, Sara Amanda, who *d* 1981, da of late Jose Santos Tello, of Chile:—
†Richard Douglas, *b* 1924; a Chemical Engineer, Federico Santa Maria Univ, Chile: *m* 1956, María Helia, da of late Ceferino Veloso, of Santiago, Chile, and *d* 1990, leaving issue, William Douglas, *b* 1957; Industrial Engr, Chile Univ: *m* 1990, Agnes Joyce, da of Richard Sharman Claude, of Viña del Mar, Chile, and has issue living, Michael Douglas *b* 1993, Agnes Marianne *b* 1990, — James Edward, *b* 1959; Electrical Engr, Chile Univ: *m* 1986 (*m diss* 1992), Macarena, da of Claudio Mas Ferret, of Santiago, Chile, and has issue living, Benjamin Edward *b* 1988, Vincent *b* 1991, Macarena Sofía *b* 1987, — Philip Andrew, *b* 1962; Industrial Engr, Chile Univ: *m* 1988, María Gabriela, da of Juan Lasnibat Aninat, of Santiago, Chile, and has issue living, Philip Anthony *b* 1990, Anne Mary *b* 1991, — Maureen Elizabeth, *b* 1960: *m* 1986, Pablo Emanuel Quiñones de León, of Santiago, Chile, and has issue living, Luis Felipe *b* 1987, Juan Pablo *b* 1989, José Antonio *b* 1992.

Granddaughter of late Archibald Reid Swiney Pollock (ante):—
Issue of late Maj-Gen John Archibald Henry Pollock, CB, *b* 1856, *d* 1949: *m* 1898, Lillian Forrester, who *d* 1954, da of J. Fortune:—
Justina Lillian (Pansy), *b* 1902: *m* 1926, Frederic Whigham McConnel, of Blair House, 8 High St, Kirkcudbright, and has issue living, James Frederic Whigham (Whitehouse, Newcastle, Monmouth, Gwent), *b* 1929: *m* 19—, Judith Marian Culpin, — John William (Lettrick, Dunscore, Dumfries-shire DG2 0UX), *b* 1931: *m* 19—, Lois Christine Lyon, and has issue living, James Archibald Robert *b* 1958: *m* 19—, Sarah Helen Walker (and has issue living, James Archibald Frederic Whigham *b* 1994), John Andrew Douglas *b* 1961, William Kennedy *b* 1962. *m* 19—, Susan Mary, da of Edward Alfred Heycock (*see* Halsey, Bt, colls) (and has issue living, Jennifer Kathryn Halsey *b* 1993), Fiona Mary *b* 1957: *m* 19—, Ian Macpherson (and has issue living, Morag Fiona *b* 1988, Katherine Anne *b* 1989).

Sir George Pollock, 1st baronet, yr brother of Rt Hon Sir Frederick Pollock, 1st baronet of Hatton (*cr* 1866) commanded the army with great distinction in the first Afghan war. He attained the rank of Field-Marshal, and was sometime Constable of the Tower. Sir Frederick, 2nd baronet, assumed by Roy licence in 1873 the additional surname of Montagu, having *m* 1861, Laura Caroline, da of Henry Seymour Montagu of Westleton Grange, Suffolk.

PONSONBY (UK) 1956, of Wootton, co Oxford

Sir ASHLEY CHARLES GIBBS PONSONBY, KCVO, MC, 2nd *Baronet*; *b* 21 Feb 1921; *s* his father, *Col Sir* CHARLES EDWARD, TD (*see* B de Mauley, colls) 1976; *ed* Eton, and Balliol Coll, Oxford; late Capt Coldm Gds 1939-45 War (wounded, MC, 1945); Lord Lieut of Oxfordshire 1980-96; *cr* KCVO 1993; KStJ 1989: *m* 1950, Lady Martha Butler, yr da of 6th Marquess of Ormonde, and has issue.

Arms – Gules, a chevron between three combs argent. Crest – Out of a ducal coronet or three arrows, points downwards, one in pale and two in saltire, entwined at the intersection by a snake proper.
Residence – Woodleys, Woodstock, Oxford OX20 1HJ.

SONS LIVING

CHARLES ASHLEY (Grim's Dyke Farm, Woodstock, Oxford OX20 1HJ), *b* 10 June 1951; *ed* Eton, and Ch Ch, Oxford (MA): *m* 1983, Mary Priscilla, yr da of late Maj Arthur Richard Bromley Davenport, of Knutsford, Cheshire, and has issue living, Arthur Ashley, *b* 15 Sept 1984, — Frederick Edward, *b* 1986, — Alice Elizabeth, *b* 1988. —— Rupert Spencer, *b* 1953; *ed* Eton, and Reading Univ: *m* 1985, Amanda, MBE, elder da of Michael Keith Beale Colvin, MP, of Tangley House, Andover, Hants (*see* Barony of Cayzer), and has issue living, George Edward Michael, *b* 1996, — Emily Mary, *b* 1990, — Eleanor Rose, *b* 1993. —— Luke Arthur *b* 1957; *ed* Eton: *m* 1985, Nicola J., yr da of Gen Sir Roland Kelvin Guy, KCB, CBE, DSO, of Stourpaine, Dorset, and has issue living, Edmund (Ned) Brabazon, *b* 1989, — William Roland Ashley, *b* 1995, — Lucy India Clare, *b* 1991. —— John Piers, *b* 1962; *ed* Eton, and Gonville and Caius Coll, Camb: *m* 1994, Serena N., da of Robert Marshall, of Nairobi, Kenya, and has issue living, James Robert Edwin, *b* 1997, — Henry Alexander, *b* 1998.

SISTERS LIVING

Priscilla Dora (*Priscilla, Lady Bacon*), *b* 1913; a DL of Norfolk: *m* 1936, Lt-Col Sir Edmund Castell Bacon, KG, CBE, TD, 14th Bt, who *d* 1982. *Residence* – Orchards, Raveningham, Norwich NR14 6NS. —— Diana Mary, *b* 1916: *m* 1940, Rev Canon Mark Meynell (*see* E Halifax, colls). *Residence* – 2 Double St, Framlingham, Suffolk. —— Lavinia Rosalind (*Lady Hamilton*), *b* 1919: *m* 1947, Sir Michael Aubrey Hamilton, of Lordington House, Chichester, W Sussex PO18 9DX and has issue living, John Ashley, *b* 1948: *m* 1975, Audrey Carola, only da of Capt Nigel William Ivo Naper, of Loughcrew, Oldcastle, co Meath (V Valentia), and has issue living, Mark Emmanuel Naper *b* 1979, Robin Michael Elijah *b* 1982, Oliver *b* 1985, Meg Rosaleen Gabriel, *b* 1977, — Caroline Mary, *b* 1950: *m* 1980, Stephen M. Codner, son of John Codner, of Breadstone House, Glos, and has issue living, Jesse Anne *b* 1981, Rose Elizabeth *b* 1983, Alice *b* 1990, — Susanna, *b* 1954: *m* 1982, Rufus Anthony Reade, and has issue living, Benedict *b* 1984, Hannah *b* 1988, — Jane Lavinia, *b* 1958, *m* 1984, Garth K. P. Watkins, and has issue living, Jonathan Michael *b* 1986, Simon Alexander *b* 1988. —— Juliet Barbara Anna, *b* 1923: *m* 1949, Rt Hon James Edward Ramsden, and has had issue, Thomas James Ponsonby, *b* 1950: *m* 1983, Jane Ann, yr da of late John Eustice, of Omaha, Nebraska, USA, and has issue living, James Thomas Eustice *b* 1985, Matthew John *b* 1987, William Joseph *b* 1990, Mary Juliet Eustice *b* 1984, — George Edward (The Old Rectory, Settrington, Malton, Yorks), *b* 1953: *m* 1986, Jane Slane Sloan, formerly wife of Anthony Charles Vaughan Wynn (*see* B Newborough), and elder da of Rev William Thompson, of Oxnam Manse, Jedburgh, Roxburghshire, and has issue living, Edward William *b* 1989, Laura Vida *b* 1988, Juliet Charlotte Rose *b* 1992, — Richard Ashley (10 Michael Fields, Forest Row, E Sussex RH18 5BH), *b* 1954: *m* 1978, Kristin Maria, only da of John Waldroup, of Carmel, Calif, USA, and has issue living, Thalia *b* 1985, Marika *b* 1986, Kaelyn *b* 1988, — Emma Juliet Geraldine, *b* 1957: *m* 1981, Rev John G. W. Oliver, only son of G. F. Oliver, MBE, of Mistley, Van Dieman's Lane, Bath, and has issue living, Joseph Mark Ashley *b* 1994, Sarah Charlotte Coolwe *b* 1992, — Charlotte Mary Rose, *b* 1960: *m* 1982, Mark Lawrence Cheverton, yr son of Rev David Cheverton, of Cruachan Cottage, Preston-under-Scar, Leyburn, Yorks, and was *k* with her husband in a motor accident 1991. *Residences* – Old Sleningford Hall, Ripon, Yorks; 10 Cleaver Sq, Kennington, SE11.

Sir Charles Edward Ponsonby, TD, DL, 1st Bt, grandson of 2nd Baron de Mauley, was MP for Sevenoaks (*C*) 1935-50, PPS to Sec of State for War 1940, and to Sec of State for Foreign Affairs 1941-45.

POORE (GB) 1795, of Rushall, Wiltshire

Sir HERBERT EDWARD POORE, 6th *Baronet*; *b* April 1930; *s* his father, *Sir* EDWARD, 1938.

Arms – Argent, a fesse azure between three mullets gules. **Crest** – A cubit arm erect vested sable, slashed argent, cuffed ermine, charged with two mullets in fesse or, grasping in the hand an arrow proper.
Residence – Argentina.

SISTERS LIVING

Elsie Nelly, *b* 1923: *m* 1947, Jorge Ball, and has issue living, Jorge Eduard, *b* 1948, — Alberto Carlos, *b* 1949, — Roberto, *b* 1954, — Susana Beatriz, *b* 1952. —— Betty Gladys, *b* 1926.

UNCLE LIVING

Pauper, non in spe

Poor, but not in spirit

NASIONCENO, *b* 1900: *m* 19—, Juana Borda, who *d* 1943, and has issue living, Roger Ricardo, *b* 1930, — Roberto, *b* 1932: *m* 1964, Norma Onhaso, — Percy Nasionceno, *b* 1933, — Argentina *b* 1927, — Gloria *b* 1928, — Tady Esterlina, *b* 1938.

AUNTS LIVING

Francesca, *b* 1898. —— Rosalie, *b* 1905: *m* 1930, Juan F. Garmedia. *Residence* – Belgrano, 912 Curuzu Cuatia, Argentina.

WIDOW LIVING OF FIFTH BARONET

AMELIA (*Lady Poore*), da of Senor Santiago Guliemone, of Estancia La Blanca, Estacion Acuna, Corrientes, Argentine Republic: *m* 1922, Sir Edward Poore, 5th baronet, who *d* 1938.

COLLATERAL BRANCHES LIVING

(In special remainder)

Grandsons of late Capt Mark Saurin Poore, 2nd son of late Maj Robert Poore (infra):—
Issue of late Robert Poore (who assumed by Roy Licence 1932 the surname of Poore-Saurin-Watts), *b* 1904, *d* 1973: *m* 1945, Rosemary Philippa (Brown Edge, W Malvern, Worcs WR14 4BJ) (who *m* 2ndly, 1974, James Richardson, MRCS, LRCP, who *d* 1986), da of Maj Richard Norman Winstanley, of Rownhams House, nr Southampton:—
†(Robert) Mark, *b* 1946; *d* 1953. —— †Edward Richard POORE, *b* 1948; *ed* Harrow, and Lausanne Univ; relinquished the additional surnames of Saurin-Watts 1983; *d* 1991, in Haifa, Israel. —— Andrew Philip POORE-SAURIN-WATTS (22 Vanneck Sq, Roehampton, SW15 5DY), *b* 1951; *ed* Milton Abbey, and Lausanne Univ.

Granddaughter of late Maj Roger Alvin Poore, DSO, RWF, 3rd son of late Maj Robert Poore (infra):—
Issue of late W/Cdr Roger Dennistoun Poore, RAF, *b* 1916, *d* 1987: *m* 1949, Peta, widow of W/Cdr Walter Ronald Farley, DFC, and da of late William George Coast, of Finchley:—
Victoria Lorne Peta, *b* 1956: *m* 1981, (Geoffrey Robert) James Borwick, elder son of Hon Robin Sandbach Borwick, and has issue (*see* B Borwick).

Grandchildren of late Major Robert Poore, son of late Robert Montagu Poore, son of late John Montagu Poore, 2nd son of late Edward Poore, brother of 1st baronet:—
Issue of late Capt Mark Saurin Poore, *b* 1869, *d* 1931: *m* 1900, Irene, who *d* 1943 (having *m* 2ndly, 1933, Major Harry Grant Thorold, of Cranford Hall, Northants), da of late Edward Hanslope Watts, of Hanslope Park, Bucks:—
(Louisa) Florentia, *b* 1905: *m* 1932, Leslie Woods Haslett, who *d* 1992, of Apart 404, 1460 Docteur Penfield, Montreal, Canada, and has issue living, (Leslie) Mark, *b* 1933: *m* 1959, Jane Aikins, da of Robert David Mulholland, of Montreal, and has issue living, Andrew Mark *b* 1961, Thomas Leslie *b* 1962, Peter Aikins *b* 1964, Jennifer Anne *b* 1968, — Robert David, *b* 1937: *m* 1963, Lucy, da of Christopher Eberts, of Ottawa, and has issue living, Elizabeth *b* 1964, Mary Martha *b* 1966, — Richard Stuart, *b* 1940: *m* 1965, Katharine, da of Ernest Boyne, of St John, New Brunswick, and has issue living, Christopher Leslie *b* 1967, Michael *b* 1970, Robert *b* 1974, — Christian Florentia, *b* 1935: *m* 1956, David Gladwin Turnbull, of Rothesay, New Brunswick, and has issue living, Douglas Alasdair Stuart *b* 1958, Charles Laughlin *b* 1960, Douglas David *b* 1963, Christian Benita *b* 1957, — Benita Jane, *b* 1938.

Issue of late Philip Poore, *b* 1874, *d* 1937: *m* 1918, Cicely Eleanor who *d* 1978, da of Sir Edward Arthur Barry, 2nd Bt:—
Philip Barry, MC, *b* 1919; formerly Capt and temporary Major Wilts Regt; Burma 1944-5 with Gold Coast Regt (MC): *m* 1954, Jennifer Mary, da of Lieut-Col S. C. H. Worseldine, IMS (ret), of Nelson, New Zealand, and has issue living, Philip William, *b* 1956, — Anna Cicely, *b* 1954, — Sara Eleanor, *b* 1958, — Helen Jennifer, *b* 1960. *Residence* – Pakaraka, RD2 Kaikohe, Bay of Islands, New Zealand. —— Robert Roger, *b* 1924; BSc Engineering 1949: *m* 1952, Diana Marion, who *d* 1996, da of John Davis Canning, of Oakbourne, Waipukurua, New Zealand, and has issue living, Marion Rosalind, *b* 1953, — Caroline Louise, *b* 1955, — Elizabeth Julia, *b* 1957, — Judith Rosamund, *b* 1958. *Residence* – 21B Kelvin Rd, Remuera, Auckland, NZ. —— Anne Benita (PO Box 164, Kerikeri, Bay of Islands, NZ), *b* 1922: *m* 1946, Thomas Camp-

bell Lindesay, who *d* 1989, and has issue living, Philip Edward (9 St Benedict St, Auckland, NZ), *b* 1947: *m* 1971, Barbara Lesley Hargrave, — Thomas Reginald, *b* 1953, — Clare (Inlet Rd, Kerikeri, NZ), *b* 1950: *m* 1st, 1972 (*m diss* 19—), Rodney Burke; 2ndly, 19— (*m diss* 19—), Michael Gadsby, — Erica Anne, *b* 1955: *m* 19—, Scott Sinel.

The family descends from Philip Poore of Amesbury, Wilts (will proved 15 July 1585), whose son Philip was settled at Durrington, nearby. Though earlier genealogical proof has not been established, it is likely that this family has common ancestry with the brothers Herbert le Poer or Poore, last Bishop of Old Sarum, who *d* 1217, and Richard who succeeded him as Bishop of Salisbury, and built the Cathedral at New Sarum, which was consecrated in 1225.

PORRITT (UK) 1963, of Hampstead, co London

Hon Sir JONATHON ESPIE PORRITT, 2nd *Baronet*; *b* 6 July 1950; *s* his father, ARTHUR ESPIE, Baron Porritt, GCMG, GCVO, CBE (Life Baron) in his Baronetcy 1994; *ed* Eton, and Magdalen Coll, Oxford; Dir Friends of the Earth 1984-90: *m* 1986, Sarah, da of Malcolm Staniforth, of Malvern, Worcs, and has issue.

𝕬rms – Or, a serpent in bend vert between two lions heads erased gules, on a chief of the last two swords points upwards in saltire of the first, between as many roses argent both surmounted by another gules barbed and seeded proper. 𝕮rest – On a wreath or and gules, a demi heraldic antelope gules armed azure collared or; holding a torch of the last enflamed proper between two fern fronts vert.
Residence – 9 Lypiatt Terrace, Cheltenham, Glos GL50 2SX.

DAUGHTERS LIVING

Eleanor Mary, *b* 1988. ——— Rebecca Elizabeth, *b* 1991.

BROTHER LIVING

Hon JEREMY CHARLES, *b* 19 Jan 1953; *ed* Eton: *m* 1980, Penny, da of J. H. Moore, of London, Ontario, Canada, and has issue living, Andrew Sebastian Alexander, *b* 1982, — Hugo James, *b* 1986. *Residence* – ....

SISTER LIVING

Hon Joanna Mary, *b* 1948: *m* 1969, Simon Patrick Meredith Hardy, and has issue living, Henry Patrick, *b* 1975, — George Peter, *b* 1978. *Residence* – 23 Baronsmead Rd, SW13.

The 1st baronet, Brig Sir Arthur Espie Porritt, GCMG, GCVO, CBE, *b* 1900, was Surg to HM King George VI 1946-52, Sjt-Surg to HM The Queen 1952-67, and Gov-Gen of NZ 1967-72; Pres BMA 1960-61, Royal Coll of Surgs 1960-63, and Royal Soc of Medicine 1966-67; also Memb Internat Olympic Cttee (Bronze Medallist 100 metres Paris Olympics 1924); *cr Baron Porritt*, of Wanganui, NZ, and of Hampstead, Greater London (Life Baron) 1973; *d* 1994.

PORTAL (UK) 1901, of Malshanger, Church Oakley, co Southampton

Sir JONATHAN FRANCIS PORTAL, 6th *Baronet; b* 13 Jan 1953; *s* his father, *Sir* FRANCIS SPENCER, 1984; *ed* Marlborough, and Edin Univ: *m* 1982, Louisa Caroline eldest da of Sir (Frederick) John Charles Gordon Hervey-Bathurst, 7th Bt, and has issue.

𝕬rms – Per Saltire azure and gules, a portal flanked by two towers argent; on a chief ermine a crescent of the first betwen two mullets of the second. 𝕮rest – A portal flanked by two towers argent, each charged with a fleur-de-lis azure, and a wreath of laurel in base vert.
Residence – Burley Wood, Ashe, Basingstoke, Hants RG25 3AG.

SONS LIVING

WILLIAM JONATHAN FRANCIS, *b* 1 Jan 1987. —— Robert Jonathan, *b* 1989, —— John Arthur Jonathan, *b* 1993.

BROTHER LIVING

Philip Francis, *b* 1957; *ed* Radley, and Durham Univ: *m* 1989, Catherine Helen Monica Deckers, and has issue living, Simon Joe Philip, *b* 1988, — Louis Raymond Philip, *b* 1991, — Daniel Sandy Philip, *b* 1995. *Residence* – Urbanização Areia Mar-Lote 2, Rue de São José-Areia, 2750 Cascais, Portugal.

SISTER LIVING

Mary Jane, *b* 1955.

HALF-SISTER LIVING (*Daughter of 5th baronet by 1st wife, Rowena, who d 1948, da of Paul Selby, of San Francisco, California, and Johannesburg*)

(Rowena) Jeanne, *b* 1931: *m* 1957, Richard James Livingstone Altham, of Crunnells Green House, Preston, Hitchin, Herts, and has issue living, David Richard Spencer, *b* 1959; *m* 1993, Sandra Louise Bunn, — Robert Patrick James, *b* 1960: *m* 1998, Caroline Louise Margaret England, — Alastair John Livingstone, *b* 1963: *m* 1994, Caroline Wilhelmina Koopmanns, and has issue living, Harry Willem Livingstone *b* 1995, Angus John Learmonth *b* 1997.

WIDOW LIVING OF FIFTH BARONET

JANE MARY (*Jane, Lady Portal*), DL (Hants 1991), da of late Albert Henry Williams, OBE (mil), of The Flint House, Langstone, Havant, Hants: *m* 1950, as his 2nd wife, Sir Francis Spencer Portal, 5th Bt, who *d* 1984. *Residence* – Priors Barton Cottage, Kingsgate Rd, Winchester, Hants SO23 9QF.

COLLATERAL BRANCHES LIVING

Grandson of late Brig-Gen Sir Bertram Percy Portal, KCB, DSO (infra):—
Issue of late Maj Melville Edward Bertram Portal, MBE, *b* 1900, *d* 1971: *m* 1926, Hon Cicely Winifred Goschen, who *d* 1980, da of 2nd Viscount Goschen:—
Simon George Melville (9 Kelso Place, W8; Cavalry Club), *b* 1927; late Capt 17th/21st Lancers, Palestine 1948, Korea 1950-51 (attached 8th Hussars), attached Trucial Oman Levies 1955-56; ADC to C-in-C Far East Land Forces 1958-59; a Member of London Stock Exchange 1960-65: *m* 1962 (*m diss* 1971), Gillian, yst da of late Maj James Cyril Aubrey George Dance, MP, of Moreton House, Moreton Morrell, Warwicks, and has issue living, Robert Melville, *b* 1967; actor.

Issue of late Brig-Gen Sir Bertram Percy Portal, KCB, DSO, 3rd son of 1st baronet, *b* 1866, *d* 1949: *m* 1899, Hon Margaret Louisa Littleton, who *d* 1945, da of 3rd Baron Hatherton:—
Charlotte Mary, *b* 1903: *m* 1929, Col Richard James Longfield, late RA, who *d* 1987, and has issue living, *Brig* Desmond Richard Henry (Paccombe Farm House, Downton, Salisbury, Wilts SP5 3PP; *Club* – Army and Navy), *b* 1931; *ed* Wellington Coll; late RA: *m* 1959, Jennifer, yr da of Clement William Robert Spencer Thomas, of Upper Honeydon, Bedford, and has issue living, James Desmond Spencer *b* 1964: *m* 1993, Rosalind S. G., 2nd da of Michael Pulvertaft, of Sunshine Beach, Qld, Australia (and has issue living, Matilda Sarah Graham *b* 1996, Rosanna Harriet Graham *b* 1998), Melanie Louisa *b* 1961: *m* 1986, Simon Jonathan Hoare (and has issue living, Oliver George David *b* 1990, Robert Patrick James *b* 1992, Sophie Charlotte *b* 1995), Harriet Sarah *b* 1965: *m* 1996, Jeremy Richard Skeet (and has issue living, Eloise Kate *b* 1996), Charlotte Jane *b* 1970. *Residence* – Lower Silton, Gillingham, Dorset. —— Hyacinthe Eveline, *b* 1904: *m* 1929, Malcolm Arthur Æneas Mackintosh, who *d* 1966, and has issue living, Angus Malcolm (St Algar's Farm, W Woodlands, Frome, Somerset), *b* 1930: *m* 1958, Brenda Joyce, el da of Clement William Robert Spencer Thomas (ante), and has had issue, Ewan Angus *b* 1960 *d* 1977, Robert Malcolm *b* 1962, Alexander William *b* 1963, William Aeneas *b* 1973, — Anne Evelyn, *b* 1936: *m* 1986, John Harrison, of Ashford House, Madley, Hereford. *Residence* – Orchard Plot, E Chaldon, Dorset. —— Margaret Cecilia, *b* 1908: *m* 1939, Capt John Shirley Sandys Litchfield-Speer, OBE, RN, who *d* 1993 (having subsequently relinquished the surname of Speer, and used that of Litchfield only), and has issue living, Mark Shirley Portal (The Hermitage, Boxley, Maidstone, Kent) *b* 1940; Lt RN (ret): *m* 1974 (*m diss* 1978), Marcia Osorio, and has issue living, Vasco *b* 1974, Larissa *b* 1975, — Sophie Mary Cecilia, *b* 1942: *m* 1970, John Irvin, of 6 Lower Common South, SW15, and *d* 1992, leaving issue, Luke Litchfield *b* 1973, Emilie Jane *b* 1970, Amy Hyacinthe *b* 1978, — Virginia Margaret, *b* 1945. *Residence* – Snowfield, Bearsted, Kent. —— Sophie, MBE, *b* 1910; sometime Junior Com ATS; MBE (Mil) 1947. —— Cecilia Violet, *b* 1911: *m* 1937, Lt-Col Nigel Walter Hoare, OBE, TD, who *d* 1988, and has issue living,

Hyacinthe Cecilia (Spring Cottage, Winford, Bristol), *b* 1938: *m* 1961 (*m diss* 1972), Piers Scandrett Harford, son of Sir George Arthur Harford, 2nd Bt, and has issue (see that title), — Joanna Bridget, *b* 1940: *m* 1961, Jeremy Francis Patrick Durham-Matthews, late Capt Irish Gds, of Southington House, Overton, Basingstoke, Hants, and has issue living, John Patrick Nigel *b* 1967: *m* 1995, Helen J., eldest da of Peter Smith, of Taverham, Norwich (and has issue living, Cecilia Emily *b* 1998), Miranda Elizabeth *b* 1962: *m* 1988, Simon John Hitchman Collins, of The Elms, Tilshead, Salisbury, Wilts (and has issue living, Timothy Walter Hitchman *b* 1988, Isabel Cecilia *b* 1990, Frances Joanna *b* 1994), Lucy Mary *b* 1965: *m* 1989, Richard John Bamford, of 26 Strutton Ground, SW1P 2HR (and has issue living, Constance Amelia *b* 1991, Elizabeth Maria *b* 1993, Henrietta Mary *b* 1996), Catherine Ann *b* 1972. — Louisa Margaret, *b* 1945: *m* 1968, Trevor John Bissett Newman, of The Holt, Ashford Hill, Newbury, Berks, and has issue living, Zachary John Bissett *b* 1972: *m* 1996, Rachel Maria, da of Michael Carter, of Chorley, Lancs (and has issue living, Gabriel Bissett *b* 1998), Henrietta Louisa *b* 1975, Veronica Margaret *b* 1977. *Residence* – Southington House, Overton, Basingstoke, Hants.

The 1st baronet, Sir Wyndham Spencer Portal (7th son of late John Portal, JP, DL, of Laverstoke, Hants), was Chm of London and S-W Railway Co, and *d* 1905. The 2nd baronet, Sir William Wyndham, was Chm of Portals, Ltd and Dep Chm of London and S-W Railways. The 3rd baronet, Sir Wyndham Raymond, GCMG, DSO, MVO, was Managing Director of Portals Ltd, a Director of Great Railway Co, and Min of Works and Buildings and First Commr of Works 1942-4, and was created *Baron Portal*, of Laverstoke, co Southampton (peerage of United Kingdom) 1935, and *Viscount Portal*, of Laverstoke, co Southampton (peerage of United Kingdom) 1945. He *d* 1949, when the Barony and Viscountcy became ext and the Baronetcy devolved upon his uncle, Sir Spencer John, 4th baronet, who was Pres of Trustee Savings Bank Asso, and a Dir of Portals. His only surv son, Sir Francis Spencer, 5th Bt, DL Hants 1967, and High Sheriff 1963, was Chm and later Dir of Portals Ltd 1949-68, Dir of Wiggins Teape, and Royal Exchange Assurance Co, Pres and Chm Southern Region YMCA, etc.

HORSBRUGH-PORTER (UK) 1902, of Merrion Square, City and Co of Dublin

Sir JOHN SIMON HORSBRUGH-PORTER, 4th *Baronet*; *b* 18 Dec 1938; *s* his father, *Sir* ANDREW MARSHALL, DSO, 1986; *ed* Winchester, and Trin Coll, Camb: *m* 1964, Lavinia Rose, 2nd da of Ralph Meredyth Turton, of Kildale Hall, Whitby (*see* V Chetwynd, colls), and has issue.

Arms – Argent, on a bend azure between in chief a portcullis, and in base two keys saltirewise sable, three bells of the field. Crest – On a fasces fessewise a cherub, all proper. *Residence* – Bowers Croft, Coleshill, Amersham, Bucks HP7 0LS.

SON LIVING

ANDREW ALEXANDER MARSHALL, *b* 19 Jan 1971; *ed* Winchester.

DAUGHTERS LIVING

Anna Josephine, *b* 1965: *m* 1993, Nicholas J.F. McNulty, son of John McNulty, of Liverpool, and has issue living, Hal Alexander John, *b* 1997, — Ella Hero, *b* 1995. —— Zoë Mary, *b* 1967: *m* 1994, Nicholas S. Curtis, only son of Andrew Curtis, of Knutsford, Cheshire, and has issue living, Harry Theodore, *b* 1999, — Natasha Alexandra, *b* (twin) 1999.

SISTERS LIVING (*Daughters of 3rd baronet*)

Susan (*Lady Barlow*), *b* 1936: *m* 1962, Sir John Kemp Barlow, 3rd Bt, of Brindley, Nantwich, Cheshire, and has issue (*see* Barlow, Bt, *cr* 1907). —— Caroline Elaine, *b* 1940: *m* 1986, Col J. B. Henderson, of Cottage-on-the-Green, Barton-on-the-Heath, Moreton-in-Marsh, Glos GL56 0PJ.

COLLATERAL BRANCH LIVING

Granddaughters of late Alexander Horsbrugh Porter, 2nd son of 1st baronet:—
Issue of late William Eric Horsbrugh Porter, *b* 1905, *d* 1985: *m* 1929, Monica Ruth Lisalie, who *d* 1986, da of late Capt Anthony Fitz Maude (*see* V Hawarden, colls):—
Dympna Monica, *b* 1931: *m* 1st, 1950, Patrick St John Brawn, who *d* 19—; 2ndly, 1975, Richard Jones, and has issue living, (by 1st *m*) Daniel, *b* 1954, — Michael Patrick, *b* 1958, — Anna Livia, *b* 1955, — Isabel Frances, *b* 1965. —— Phyllida, *b* 1934: *m* 1956, Donald Kenneth McAlpine, of 12 Martindale Rd, SW12, and has issue living, Louisa Ngaire, *b* 1958, — Fiona Caroline, *b* 1961.

The 1st baronet, Rt Hon Sir Andrew Marshall Porter (son of late Rev John Scott Porter), was Master of the Rolls in Ireland 1883-1906 and sat as MP for co Londonderry (*L*) Dec 1881 to Dec 1883. The 2nd baronet, Sir John Scott Porter, assumed the additional surname of Horsbrugh 1911.

POUND (UK) 1905, of Stanmore, co Middlesex

By good faith and vigilance

Quay St, Orford, Suffolk IP12 2NU.

FIDE·ET·VIGILANTIA

Sir JOHN DAVID POUND, 5th *Baronet*; *b* 1 Nov 1946; *s* his father, *Sir* DEREK ALLEN, 1980; *ed* Burebank Sch, Aylsham, Norfolk: *m* 1st, 1968 (*m diss* 1978), Heather Frances O'Brien, only da of Harry Jackson Dean; 2ndly, 1978, Penelope Ann, el da of Grahame Rayden, and has issue by 1st and 2nd *m*.

Arms – Argent a sword erect proper surmounted of a fesse gules, thereon three mullets argent, in chief two boars' heads erased sable. **Crest** – A castle proper, charged with a shield argent, thereon a sword erect proper.
Residence – Coppice Lodge, Lythe Hill, Shrewsbury, Shropshire SY3 0BS.

SONS LIVING (*By 1st marriage*)

ROBERT JOHN, *b* 12 Feb 1973; *ed* St Edmund's Coll, Ware, Herts, and Southampton Univ (BSc); CA. *Residence* – 26 West Hill Way, Totteridge, N20 8QP.

(*By 2nd marriage*)

Christopher James, *b* 1982. —— Nicholas Edward, *b* 1986.

SISTER LIVING

Diana Marilyn, *b* 1944: *m* 1966, Keble Stuart Paterson, and has issue living, Timothy Keble, *b* 1968, — Caroline Elizabeth, *b* 1971. *Residence* – Black Cottage,

WIDOW LIVING OF FOURTH BARONET

JOAN AMY (*Joan, Lady Pound*) (Hill Farm Bungalow, Fern Hill, Dersingham, Norfolk PE31 6HT), da of James Woodthorpe, of Boston, Lincs: *m* 1942, Sir Derek Allen Pound, 4th Bt, who *d* 1980.

The 1st baronet, Sir John Pound, head of the firm of John Pound and Co, portmanteau manufacturers, of 81-4, Leadenhall Street, EC, was Sheriff of London 1895-6, and Lord Mayor of London 1904-5, and the 2nd baronet, Sir (John) Lulham, was an Alderman of City of London (Aldgate Ward) 1915-21. The 3rd baronet, Sir Allen Leslie, was a Solicitor and sole member of the firm of Pound & Pound, of Egham and Bracknell.

POWELL (UK) 1897, of Wimpole Street, St Marylebone, co London
(Name pronounced "Poel")

Anima in amicis una
One mind amongst friends

Sir NICHOLAS FOLLIOTT DOUGLAS POWELL, 4th *Baronet*; *b* 17 July 1935; *s* his father *Sir* RICHARD GEORGE DOUGLAS, MC, 1980; *ed* Gordonstoun; late Lt Welsh Gds: *m* 1st, 1960 (*m diss* 1987), Daphne Jean, yr da of Maj George Henry Errington, MC, of Chadwell Hall, Essex, and Chadwell, Ruwa, Zimbabwe; 2ndly, 1987, Davina Hyacinth Berners, elder twin da of Michael Edward Ranulph Allsopp (*see* B Hindlip, colls), and has issue by 1st and 2nd *m*.

Arms – Gules, a lion rampant within a bordure engrailed or, in the dexter chief point a mullet argent within an annulet of the second. **Crest** – A lion's head erased argent, charged with a collar flory counter flory gules.
Residence – Hillside Estate, Bromley, Zimbabwe.

SONS LIVING (*By 1st marriage*)

JAMES RICHARD DOUGLAS (Westhide Cottage, PO Box 1269, Marondera, Zimbabwe), *b* 17 Oct 1962: *ed* Peterhouse, Zimbabwe, and RAC Cirencester: *m* 1991, Susanna Frances, eldest da of David Murray Threipland, and has issue living, Douglas James Folliott, *b* 22 Oct 1992, — Hamish William David, *b* 1998, — Cordelia Catherine, *b* 1995.

(*By 2nd marriage*)

Benjamin Ranulph Berners, *b* 1989. —— Oliver Michael Folliott, *b* 1990.

DAUGHTER LIVING (*By 1st marriage*)

Catherine Mary, *b* 1961: *m* 1991, Walter Ruprecht, eldest son of Joseph Ruprecht, and has issue living, Nicholas Joseph Lawrence, *b* 1995, — Alexander Dominic, *b* 1998, — Anastasia Laura, *b* 1993. *Address* – Gum Gully, PO Box GD 1005, Greendale, Harare, Zimbabwe.

(*By 2nd marriage*)

Maimie Josephine Berners, *b* 1992.

SISTERS LIVING

Bryony Josephine Anne (19 Ackmar Rd, SW6 4UP), *b* 1933: *m* 1955 (*m diss* 1968), Christopher Lucas Thomasson, and has issue living, Samuel Charles, *b* 1956, — Mary Elizabeth, *b* 1958. —— Julia Mary, *b* 1943: *m* 1973, Jeremy John Twynam, of Kitemore House, Faringdon, Oxon SN7 8HR, and has issue living, Henry Thomas Alexander, *b* 1977, — Leonora Mary Alexandra, *b* 1975.

WIDOW LIVING OF THIRD BARONET

Alice Maria, el da of Wilhelmus den Bode, of Utrecht: *m* 1st, 1980, as his second wife, Sir Richard George Douglas Powell, 3rd Bt, MC, who *d* 1980; 2ndly, 1982, Lt-Col Donald John Arthur Grant.

The 1st baronet, Sir Richard Douglas Powell, KCVO, MD, FRCP, was Physician Extraor to Queen Victoria 1887-99, and Physician-in-Ord 1899-1901, Physician Extraor to King Edward VII 1901-7, and Physician-in-Ord 1907-10, and to King George V 1910-25; also Pres of Roy Coll of Physicians 1905-10. The 3rd baronet, Sir Richard George Douglas Powell, MC, was Dir-Gen of Inst of Directors 1954-74: *m* 1st, 1933, Elizabeth Josephine, who *d* 1979, only da of late Lt-Col Osmond Robert McMullen, CMG, of Presdales Hall, Ware, Herts; 2ndly, 1980, Alice Maria, el da of Wilhelmus den Bode, of Utrecht.

POWER (UK) 1836, of Kilfane, Kilkenny (Dormant 1928)

Sir GEORGE POWER, 7th *Baronet*, *d* 1928, and the next heir, his cousin, GERVASE PARKER POWER, is believed to have died in America some years ago. At the time of going to press no name appears on the Official Roll of Baronets in respect of this title.

COLLATERAL BRANCH LIVING

Granddaughers of late Maj Ambrose Grattan Power (infra):—
Issue of late Maj Anthony Ambrose Grattan Power, *b* 1917, *d* 1994: *m* 1961, Sarah Judith, only da of late Joseph Halford Gough, of Cookham, Berks:—
Lavinia Frances, *b* 1964: *m* 1995, W/Cmdr M. Paul Colley, elder son of late Thomas Colley, of Clifford, W Yorks. —— Georgina Rachel, *b* 1966: *m* 1992, Adrian Hall, son of late James Hall, of Kingston-upon-Thames, Surrey, and has issue living, Charles Anthony James, *b* 1998. —— Amy Katherine, *b* 1968: *m* 1997, John Keir Kimmance, elder son of Dr Keir Kimmance, of Whiteparish, Wilts.

Granddaughter of late Ambrose William Bushe Power, eldest son of Ven Ambrose Power, Archdeacon of Lismore, 4th son of 1st baronet:—
Issue of late Maj Ambrose Grattan Power, *b* 1887, *d* 1926: *m* 1908, Ada Mary, who *d* 1968, yst da of late Richard Austin Cooper Chadwick, of Ballinard, co Tipperary:—
Iris Frances Mary, *b* 1914: *m* 1943, as his 2nd wife, Capt Thomas Abdy Combe, Gren Gds, who *d* 1983. *Residence* – Oaks Corner, Hemingford Abbots, Huntingdon, Cambs PE18 9AP.

Sir John Power, 4th baronet, died of wounds received at Lindley during S African War 1900, and Sir Derrick, 5th baronet, died in S Africa during the same war 1902.

POWER (UK) 1924, of Newlands Manor, Milford, Southampton

Sir ALASTAIR JOHN CECIL POWER, 4th *Baronet*; *b* 15 Aug 1958; *s* his father, *Sir* JOHN PATRICK McLANNAHAN, 1984: *m* 1981, Virginia, da of Gordon Edward Lawrence Newton, and has issue.

Arms – Or, on a bend gules between two foxes' heads erased proper three crescents of the first; on a chief of the second as many escallops argent. Crest – A stag's head erased proper, gorged with an antique crown and between the attires a cross patée or.

SON LIVING

MARK ALASTAIR JOHN, *b* 15 Oct 1989.

DAUGHTERS LIVING

Melanie-Anne Louise, *b* 1984. —— Amanda Jane, *b* 1986.

BROTHER LIVING

Adam Patrick Cecil, *b* 1963.

For my country always

SISTER LIVING

Belinda Jane, *b* 1960.

AUNT LIVING (*Daughter of 2nd baronet*)

Hilary Diana Cecil (*Countess of Buchan*), *b* 1930: *m* 1957, 17th Earl of Buchan, of Newnham House, Basingstoke, Hants.

MOTHER LIVING

Melanie, adopted da of Hon Richard Alastair Erskine (*see* E Buchan): *m* 1957 (*m diss* 1967), as his 1st wife, Sir John Patrick McLannahan Power, 3rd Bt, who *d* 1984; 2ndly, 1968, William Barnsley Allen, who *d* 1974; 3rdly, 1974, Douglas Reginald Joseph Patrick Ward. *Residence* – 19 St Keyna Av, Hove, E Sussex BN3 4PN.

GREAT UNCLE LIVING (*son of 1st baronet*)

George Frederick Cecil McLannahan, *b* 1919; *ed* Eton and in Switzerland; formerly acting Maj Welch Regt; Liaison Officer to RAF 1940; Capt late War Dept Fleet (salvage explosives); Councillor of Lymington Borough 1948-65, and a Member of Co Council Adoption Cttee 1950-65, and HM Harbour Commr 1960-65; Founder of Sea Rescue Ser, now Inshore Rescue RNLI, and a Gov of RNLI; Admiralty Ferry Crew 1941 (now known as Admiralty Ferry Crew Assocn); a Gov of Wessex Hosp Group, a Member of Territorial Cttee (Army South), and a Gov of County Council Schs in Hants; Ch Eng RNXS 1965, AFCA; Dir Arthur Beale 1950-68; assumed the additional name of McLannahan 1954: *m* 1st, 1940 (*m diss* 1947), Joy Mervyn, da of late Dr Geoffrey Noott, of Fern Down Hill, Ferndown, Dorset; 2ndly, 1948, (Monica) Angela Mary, who *d* 1990, da of late Lt-Com Henry Guy Stanton, RN (ret) (B Castlemaine, colls); 3rdly, 1995, Elizabeth (LLOYD-ROBERTS), da of Dr George Anthony Rawlins, of Garn Dolbenmaen, Gwynedd, and has issue living, (by 1st *m*) David George Cecil (Islands, Acedia, Casares, Malaga, Costa del Sol, Spain), *b* 1941; *ed* Repton: *m* 1968, Jennifer Anne, da of late Cdr Thompson, of

Arms of Capt George F. C. McL. Power

Jersey, and has issue living, January Georgina *b* 1979, —— Mervyn Peter, *b* 1944; *ed* Repton: *m* 1976, Diana Louise, da of late Graham Alexander Michael, of Wigston, Leicester, and has issue living, Henry George Alexander *b* 1978, Camilla Joy Cynthia *b* 1976 (has issue living, Joseph Dallas Dorrington *b* 1999), —— (by 2nd *m*) Bridie Maureen McLannahan, *b* 1951: *m* 1972, Joseph Gavin Bonello, of The Cottage, Stuckton, Fordingbridge, Hants SP6 2HG, and has two adopted children, Michael Gavin James Stuart *b* 1976, George Gavin Richard Matthew *b* 1977, —— Sheena Patricia McLannahan, *b* 1954: *m* 1975, Capt Peter Jeremy Walton Ledger, RM (ret) of Old Well House, 1 Cobbs Rd, Wimborne, Dorset BH21 2RL, and has issue living, Araminta Elizabeth Walton *b* 1984, —— Louisa Roxane McLannahan (Le Poher Cottage, Verwood Rd, Ringwood, Hants BH24 2DD), *b* 1957: *m* 1st, 1976, Robert Derek Philp (Metropolitan Police), who was *k* 1983; 2ndly, 1987 (*m diss* 1991), Jeremy David Barrell, BSc; 3rdly, 1997, Ivan David Halford, and has issue living, (by 1st *m*) Neisha Roxane McLannahan *b* 1983, (by 2nd *m*) Susannah Louise Roxane *b* 1988, (by 3rd *m*) Rowan Ashley Anastasia *b* 1998. *Residence* – Le Poher Cottage, Verwood Rd, Ringwood, Hants BH24 2DD. *Clubs* – Royal Yachting Assocn (Life Memb), RN Sailing Assocn, Keyhaven Yacht Club (Life Memb), Inland Waterways Assocn (Life Memb).

GREAT AUNT LIVING (*daughter of 1st baronet*)

Lilian Hartley Cecil: *m* 1930, Paul Van Kleeck Kingston, MD, who *d* 1988, and has issue living, Peter Charles (688 Hillsdale Av, Toronto, Canada), *b* 1945: *m* 1983, Nancy Allison, da of Oscar Clark, and has issue living, Alexander *b* (twin) 1984, Christopher *b* (twin) 1984, Philip *b* 1988, —— Timothy Paul, *b* 1949: *m* 1st, 1983 (*m diss* 1987), Kathleen Procopio; 2ndly, 1992, Tani Bowman, —— Katharine Martha, *b* 1943: *m* 1968 (*m diss* 1993), Jack Calvin Hartje, PhD, of 6120 San

José Blvd W, Jacksonville, Florida, USA, and has issue living, Neil *b* 1978, Naomi *b* 1974. *Residence* – 400 N Flagler Drive, Apt 1105, W Palm Beach, Florida 33401, USA.

The 1st baronet, Sir John Cecil Power (son of William Taylor Power, of Belfast, co Down, and Sheen, Surrey) sat as MP for Wimbledon (*U*) 1924-45, and was Founder of Roy Institute of International Affairs. Sir Ivan McLannahan Cecil Power, 2nd Bt, was Chm of various industrial Cos in Union of S Africa and a Co Councillor for London. Sir John Patrick McLannahan Power, 3rd Bt, was a Dir of Arthur Beale, Ltd.

PRESCOTT (UK) 1938, of Godmanchester, co Huntingdon

Sir MARK PRESCOTT, 3rd *Baronet*, son of late Maj (William Robert) Stanley Prescott, MP, yr son of 1st baronet; *b* 3 March 1948; *s* his uncle, *Sir* RICHARD STANLEY, 1965; *ed* Harrow.

𝕬rms – Per chevron pean and erminois, on a chief or, a rose gules, barbed and seeded proper, between two leopards' faces sable. 𝕮rest – Upon the battlements of a tower proper, a leopard statant sable.
Residence – Heath House, Moulton Rd, Newmarket CB8 8DU.

AUNT LIVING (*daughter of 1st baronet*)

Louise Bernice, MBE, *b* 1903; MBE (1978): *m* 1928, Reginald Gray, and has issue living, David Stanley, *b* 1931.

The 1st baronet, Col Sir William (Henry) Prescott, CBE, DL (son of John Prescott, of Blackburn), was an Alderman and Chm of Middlesex County Council, Chm of Metropolitan Water Board, and of Lee Conservancy Board, High Sheriff for Middlesex 1929, and for Cambs and Hunts 1938, and MP for N Div of Tottenham (*Co U*) 1918-22.

He conquers who endures

Prescott-Westcar, see Westcar.

PRESTON (UK) 1815, of Beeston St Lawrence, Norfolk

Sir PHILIP CHARLES HENRY HULTON PRESTON, 8th *Baronet*; son of late Lt-Col Philip Henry Herbert Hulton Preston, OBE, MC, son of late Col Philip Henry Hulton Preston, son of late Lt-Col Henry Edward Preston, son of late Thomas Edward Preston, 2nd son of 1st baronet; *b* 31 Aug 1946; *s* his kinsman, *Sir* RONALD DOUGLAS HILDEBRAND, 1999; *ed* Nautical Coll, Pangbourne; architect: *m* 1980, Kirsi Sylvi Annikki, da of late Eino Yrjö Pullinen, of Mukkulankaju 29, F46 Lahti, Finland, and has issue.

𝕬rms – Ermine, on a chief sable three crescents or. 𝕮rest – A crescent or.
Residence –

SON LIVING

PHILIP THOMAS HENRY HULTON, *b* 1990.

DAUGHTERS LIVING

Katherine Louise Tuula, *b* 1982. —— Emily Jean Charlotte, *b* 1985.

SISTER LIVING

Caroline Elizabeth, *b* 1943: *m* 1974, Paul Louis Edelin de la Praudiere, of 128 Palewell Park, SW14 8JH, and has issue living, Philip Louis, *b* 1975, — William Francis Paul, *b* 1977.

I hope for a brighter light

AUNT LIVING (*daughter of late Col Philip Henry Hulton Preston*)

Marjorie, *b* 1917: *m* 1939, Miles Pacey Cheales, of Clovers, Knowle Lane, Cranleigh, Surrey, and has issue living, Justina Victoria, *b* 1945, — Briony Margaret, *b* 1948, — Mary Henrietta Miles, *b* 1951: *m* 1971, Philip Alistair Barter, and has issue living, Oliver Philip Tom *b* 1975, Alexander John *b* 1975, — Alexandra Marjorie, *b* 1952: *m* 1976, Charles Thornton Hardy.

DAUGHTER LIVING OF SIXTH BARONET

Stella Tatiana Gertrude, *b* 1920; former opera singer and UN civil servant: *m* 1962, Eugene Hartzell, Mus Bach and Mus M (Yale Univ), of Pfarrhofgasse 13/21, Vienna III, and has issue living, Eugenie Belinda Tamara, *b* 1963, — Melanie Anne Sonia, *b* 1964.

DAUGHTERS LIVING OF FIFTH BARONET

Juliet Mary (*Hon Mrs Richard N. Manners*), *b* 1921: *m* 1945, Hon Richard Neville Manners, of Cromer Hall, Norfolk (*see* B Manners). —— Patricia Evelyn (Home Farm House, Cromer, Norfolk NR27 9JG), *b* 1923: *m* 1962, John Louis Benedict Todhunter, OBE, who *d* 1980 (B Kenyon, colls).

WIDOW LIVING OF SEVENTH BARONET

PAULEEN JANE (*Dowager Lady Preston*), da of late Paul Lurcott, of Albany Cottage, Fairwarp, Sussex: *m* 1972, as his 2nd wife, (her 2nd cousin) Sir Ronald Douglas Hildebrand Preston, 7th Bt, who *d* 1999.

The 1st baronet, Sir Thomas, was a son of Henry Hulton, of Andover, by Elizabeth, eldest daughter of Isaac Preston of Beeston St Lawrence, whose estates he inherited, and in 1804 assumed the name and arms of Preston. The Prestons have held Beeston since 1640. According to family tradition, Jacob Preston was one of four confidants who attended Charles I during his imprisonment, and who was presented by that monarch, as a last mark of attachment, with an emerald ring still preserved in the family. The 6th Baronet, Sir Thomas Hildebrand, was British Consul at Ekaterinburg in 1918 at the time of the murder of the Tsar and his family.

PREVOST (UK) 1805, of Belmont, Hampshire
(Name pronounced "Prev-o")

Servatum cineri
Kept for the dead

Sir CHRISTOPHER GERALD PREVOST, 6th *Baronet*; *b* 25 July 1935; *s* his father, *Sir* GEORGE JAMES AUGUSTINE, 1985; *ed* Cranleigh; late 60th Regt: *m* 1964, Dolores Nelly, only da of late Dezo Hoffmann, of 1 Crispian Close, Neasden Lane, NW10 1PW, and has issue.

Arms – Azure, a dexter arm in fesse issuing from a cloud in the sinister fesse point, the hand grasping a sword erect proper, pommel and hilt or, in chief two mullets argent. **Crest** – A demi-lion rampant azure, charged on the shoulder with a mural crown or, the sinister paw grasping a sword erect as in the arms. **Supporters** – Two grenadiers of the 16th Foot, each supporting with exterior hand a flag flying, that on the dexter flying to the sinister and inscribed "West Indies," and that on the sinister gules, to the dexter, and inscribed "Canada."
Residence – Box 3072, Vale da Rabelho, 8200 Albufeira, Portugal.

SON LIVING

NICHOLAS MARC, *b* 13 March 1971.

DAUGHTER LIVING

Ruth Annette, *b* 1964: *m* 1986, Steven Walter Wrench, of 18 Swallowdale, Great Clacton, Essex CO15 4HA, and has issue living, Laura Annette, *b* 1988.

HALF BROTHERS LIVING (Sons of 5th baronet by 3rd marriage)

James William, b 1952, ed Aldenham. —— Edward Charles, b 1953; ed Aldenham.

SISTER LIVING

Felicity Jane, b 1936: m 1970, Hisham Pilus, of 192 Jalan Terasek, Bangsar, Kuala Lumpur 59100, Malaysia, and has issue living, Muhammad Yusuf, b 1977, — Sofia Jane, b 1972, — Sarah Louise, b 1974.

WIDOW LIVING OF FIFTH BARONET

PATRICIA BETTY (Patricia, Lady Prevost), da of late William Porter, of Kilburn, NW: m 1952, as his 3rd wife, Sir George James Augustine Prevost, 5th Bt, who d 1985. Residence – 45 Carneton Close, Quantock, Newquay, Cornwall.

The 1st baronet, Lt-Gen Sir George Prevost (el son of Gen Augustine Prevost, of Geneva, who settled in England), was Col of the 60th Regt, Gov of Canada and Commander of the Forces in British North America. The Supporters were granted in 1816 by King George III to the widow of the 1st baronet in lieu of a Peerage, as Lady Prevost felt she did not have sufficient means to support the dignity.

PRICE (UK) 1815, of Trengwainton, Cornwall

All depends on God

Sir FRANCIS CARADOC ROSE PRICE, 7th Baronet, b 9 Sept 1950; s his father, Sir ROSE FRANCIS, 1979; ed Eton, Melbourne Univ (LLB), and Alberta Univ (LLM); QC 1992: m 1975, (Hon Madam Justice) Marguerite Jean, da of Roy Samuel Trussler, of Victoria, BC, and has issue.

Arms – Sable, a chevron erminois between three spear-heads argent, embrued at the points proper. Crest – A dragon's head vert, erased gules, holding in the mouth a sinister hand erect couped at the wrist and dropping blood all proper.
Residence – 9626-95 Avenue, Edmonton, Alberta, Canada, T6C 2A4. Clubs – Centre Club and Faculty Club (Edmonton)

DAUGHTERS LIVING

Adrienne Calantha Rose, b 1976. —— Megan Kathleen Rose, b 1977. —— Glynis Nicola Rose, b 1982.

BROTHER LIVING

NORMAN WILLIAM ROSE (73 Fawnbrake Av, SE24 0BE), b 17 March 1953; ed Eton, and Gordonstoun: m 1987, Charlotte Louise, da of Randolph Rex Bivar Baker, of Yelverton, Devon, and has issue living, Benjamin William Rose, b 16 Sept 1989, — Timothy Charles Rose, b 1991.

AUNT LIVING (Daughter of 5th baronet)

Helen Jocelyn, b 1920: m 1950, Maj-Gen Logan Scott-Bowden, CBE, DSO, MC, of Prospect Farm, Cottesmore Lane, Ewelme, Oxon, and has issue living, Robert Logan (Graden, 14 High St, Tisbury, Wilts), MBE, b 1955; Col late Royal Scots; served NI (MBE 1992): m 1980, Nicola Frances, yr da of Maj H. T. K. Phillips, of The Clock House, Uffington, Oxon, and has issue living, Christopher William b 1987, Camilla Frances b 1984, — James Russell, b 1958; Maj WG: m 1988, Nicola Jane, yr da of Anthony J.V. Shepherd, of Park Farm, Alderley, Glos, and has issue living, Harry Russell b 1989, Edward Jonathan b 1991, Arthur James b 1993, Matilda b 1997, — Peter William, b 1962: m 1993, Caroline A., only da of D. J. Mangham, of Wethersfield, Essex, and has issue living, Angus Logan b 1995, Jack David b (twin) 1995, William b 1997, Henry Philip b 1998, — Claire Anne, b 1951, — Fiona Susan, b 1952: m 1978, Charles John Maitland Wilmoth, of 2 Bould Farm Cottages, Bould, Chipping Norton, Oxon OX7 6RT, and has issue living, George James b 1980, Harriette Jocelyn b 1984, — Alexandra Marjorie, b 1960: m 1990, Andrew H. C. Ballingall, of Flat 3, 5 Sinclair Gdns, Shepherds Bush, W14 0AU, only son of of late H. Campbell Ballingall, of Simonstown, Cape Province, S Africa, and has issue living, Archibald Andrew b 1990.

WIDOW LIVING OF SIXTH BARONET

KATHLEEN JUNE (June, Lady Price) (Dormer Cottage, Park Rd, Stoke Poges, Bucks), da of late Norman William Hutchinson, of Toorak, Melbourne, Australia: m 1949, Sir Rose Francis Price, 6th baronet, who d 1979.

COLLATERAL BRANCHES LIVING

Issue of late Maj William Russell Rose Price, yr son of 5th baronet, *b* 1916, *d* 1985: *m* 1st, 1945 (*m diss* 1953), Joan Ross-Hurst, of Calcutta; 2ndly, 1954, Aline Flora (9 Cowbar Bank, Staithes, Saltburn by Sea, Cleveland TS13 5BZ), da of David Silverman:—
(By 2nd *m*) Gillian Isobel, *b* 1959: *m* 1984, David William Frith, of Grove End, 14 Newlay Grove, Horsforth, Leeds LS18 4LH, and has issue living, Mark William, *b* 1989, — Jessica Sarah, *b* 1986. —— Julia Jane, *b* 1962: *m* 1984, Dennis Alfred Underwood, of Woodlands, 8 Aintree Av, Hunters Croft, Eckington, Derbyshire S21 4JA, and has issue living, David William, *b* 1989.

Grandchildren of late Capt Francis Henry Talbot Price (infra):—
Issue of late Leslie Frederick TALBOT PRICE, *b* 1904, *d* 1972: *m* 1924 (*m diss* 1953), Hon Diana Frederica, who *d* 1979, da of late Hon Maurice Raymond Gifford, CMG (*see* B Gifford):—
Maurice Rose (32 Clearview St, Bowral, NSW 2576, Australia), *b* 1929: *m* 1959, Elaine, only da of C. J. Burford, of Kuala Lumpur, Malaya, and Sydney, Australia, and has issue living, Martin Paul, *b* 1961: *m* 1996, Alana Jane, eldcr da of Harold Alan Fairclough, of Witchampton, Dorset, — Michael John, *b* 1964. —— Michael Henry Charles (558 Greenhill Rd, Burnside, Adelaide, S Australia 5066), *b* 1932: *m* 1962, Lyndsay June, da of late Cedric L. Messner, of Harpenden, Herts, and has issue living, Nicholas Frederick, *b* 1964: *m* 1992, Caroline Anne, elder da of Keith Platts, of Harpenden, Herts, and has issue living, Charlotte Anne *b* 1994, Isabelle Caroline *b* 1997, — David Aldrich, *b* 1966. —— Pamela, *b* 1925: *m* 1944, F/Lt John William Reid, DFC, RNZAF, and has issue living, Martin James, *b* 1946: *m* 1970, Elizabeth, da of H. H. Harvey Renwick, of Marlborough, NZ, and has issue living, Timothy Edward *b* 1974, David Charles *b* 1976, Nicholas Martin *b* 1977, — William John, *b* 1952: *m* 1980, Robyn, da of L. McNeill, of Nelson, NZ, and has issue living, Toby John *b* 1984, Amelia Jane *b* 1986, — Julia, *b* 1948: *m* 1978, Philip de Weck, — Diana, *b* 1949: *m* 1972, Peter Vernon Arnott Anderson, and has issue living, George Peter *b* 1979, Caroline *b* 1977, — Isabella Patricia, *b* 1957: *m* 1983 (*m diss* 1996), Gerrit Vlaming.

Granddaughter of late Capt Henry Talbot Price, RN, brother of 3rd baronet:—
Issue of late Capt Francis Henry Talbot Price, *b* 1872, *d* 1930: *m* 1899, Florence, only da of Frederick Hurdle:—
Olive May Talbot, *b* 1900: *m* 1924, Count St John Vivian Beaumont de Beaufort Molyneux (*cr* Holy Roman Empire 1710), who *d* 1962, and *d* 1999.

Granddaughters of late Col Thomas Caradoc Rose Price, CB, 3rd son of John Price, 4th son of 1st baronet:—
Issue of late Brig-Gen Thomas Rose Caradoc Price, CMG, DSO, *b* 1875, *d* 1949: *m* 1911, Dorothy Patience, who *d* 1969, only da of late Sir Henry William Verey:—
Mary Dorothy Rose, *b* 1918: *m* 1948, John Dugdale Holt Wiseman, MA, PhD, formerly Dep Keeper of Mineralogy, British Museum of Natural History, and has issue living, John Paul Holt (Coarsewell Farm, Ugborough, Ivybridge, Devon), *b* 1949; *ed* Shrewsbury: *m* 1989, Jane Trant, and has issue living, Catherine Jane *b* 1990, Alice Mary *b* 1995. *Residence* – Hornbeam House, Waltham St Lawrence, Berks.

Issue of late Lieut-Com Vivian Franklin Lyon Rose Price, RN, *b* 1881; *d* on active ser 1915: *m* 1912, Jean Purvis Mills, who *d* 1939:—
Vivian Judith Elizabeth Rose, *b* 1915: *m* 1937, Col George Francis Taylor, CBE, who *d* 1979, and has issue living, Jeremy Vivian George, *b* 1940: *m* 1967, Sally, da of John Parnell, and has issue living, Gemma Vivian *b* 1971, — Sarah Jane Elizabeth, *b* 1943: *m* 1968, Thomas Peart, and has issue living, Rachel *b* 1969, Scarlett *b* 1971, — Anna-Lisa, *b* 1949.

Grandchildren of late Brig-Gen Thomas Rose Caradoc Price, CMG, DSO (ante):—
Issue of late Lt-Col Robert ROSE PRICE, DSO, OBE, Welsh Gds, *b* 1912, *d* 1988: *m* 1946, Hon Maureen Maude Tower Butler (98 Old Church St, SW3), 2nd da of 27th Baron Dunboyne:—
(Thomas Geoffrey) Timothy Rose (The Wadfield, Winchcombe, Cheltenham, Glos), *b* 1948; *ed* Eton: *m* 1975, Leila Anne Katherine, da of Sir Richard Guy Carne Rasch, 3rd Bt, and has issue living, Dominic Charles Rose, *b* 1978, — Patrick David Caradoc, *b* 1980, — Katherine Leila Sarah, *b* 1985. —— Sarah Maureen Rose, *b* 1947: *m* 1968, Michael John Burrell, barrister, of 6 St Peter's Sq, W6, and has issue living, James Michael, *b* 1976, — Amanda Caroline, *b* 1971, — Nicola Sarah, *b* 1973.

Issue of late Dennistoun John Franklyn Rose Price (actor Dennis Price), *b* 1915, *d* 1973: *m* 1939 (*m diss* 1950), Joan Schofield:—
Susan Joan Rose, *b* 1940: *m* 1967, Thomas H. Mapp, of 85 Langham Rd, Teddington, Middx, and has issue living, Joel Dennis, *b* 1979, — Kate Miranda, *b* 1972. —— Tessa Alexandra Rose, *b* 1943: *m* 1965, Hugh Thomas Burnett, FCA, of 36 Wilbury Villas, Hove, E Sussex BN3 6GD, and has issue living, Rupert Thomas, *b* 1971, — Lucy Eleanor, *b* 1966: *m* 1990, Roger Bracken, and has issue living, Sophie Madeleine *b* 1992, Lily Matilda *b* 1997, Phoebe Rose *b* 1998, — Emily Tamelayne, *b* 1968: *m* 1994, Gavin McWhirter, and has issue living, Felix George *b* 1997.

Grandson of late George Price, 5th son of 1st baronet:—
Issue of late Cyril Oliver Rose Price, MBE, *b* 1880, *d* 1961: *m* 1910, Edith Muriel, who *d* 1956, da of late Donald Campbell Ridout, of Toronto:
George Donald Rose (26 Utkinton Rd, Tarporley, Ches), *b* 1911; *ed* Haileybury, and Emmanuel Coll, Camb (MA): *m* 1947, Dorothy Christine, da of late Major Eric Fairclough, DSO.

Granddaughters of late Arthur Henry Price (infra):—
Issue of late Arthur Douglas Price, *b* 1873, *d* 1951: *m* 1st, 1901 (*m diss* 1922), Wilhelmine Marion, who *d* 1955, da of late Robert Adolphe Claude, of Valparaiso; 2ndly, 1922, Augustine Laetitia, da of Jacques Benoit:—
(By 1st *m*) Violet Marion Rose, *b* 1902: *m* 1926, Joaquín Santiago Andrés Muñoz Arlegui, who *d* 1939, and *d* 1969, leaving issue, Joaquin Santiago Federico (Los Radales 789, Pinares de Montemar, Con-Con, Chile), *b* 1930: *m* 1964, Maria Eugenia Bravo, and has issue living, Joaquin Santiago Caradoc Price *b* 1970, Carolina Vivian Rose *b* 1967: *m* 1987,

Diego Alonso Montero (and has issue living, Daniel Andres *b* 1989, Joaquin Alonso *b* (twin) 1989, Diego Ismael *b* 1996, Valentina Victoria Rose *b* 1992), Moira Violet Rose *b* 1976, — Veronica Marion, *b* 1927: *m* 1st, 1951, Alexander Edmund Gough Gubbins Browne, who *d* 1952; 2ndly, 1960, Alfonso Necocha Beauchemin, and has issue living (by both *m*). —— Beatrice Mary Rose, *b* 1904, *d* 1987: *m* 19—, —, who *d* 19—. —— Olivia Margaret Rose, *b* 1910: *m* 1932, José-Maria Souviron, and has issue living, Alvaro Souviron Price, *b* 1933: *m* 1958, Ximena Grebe, and has issue living, Pilar Souviron *b* 1959, Beatrice Souviron *b* 1960, — Jacqueline Souviron Price, *b* 1936: *m* 1958, Luis Urrejola Dittborn, of Santiago, Chile, and has issue living, Daniel Urrejola *b* 1959, Sebastian Urrejola *b* 1961, Caroline Urrejola *b* 1962. —— Eveleen Mina Rose, *b* 1913, *d* 1978: *m* 19—, (*m diss* 19—).

Grandchildren of late Rev Thomas Rose Price (infra):—
Issue of late Rev Thomas Neville Vreichvras Churchill Rose Price, MA, *b* 1911, *d* 1970: *m* 1939, Edna Mary, who *d* 1979, da of late Howard Edge, of Wolverhampton:—
Robin Francis Neville Rose (Startlea House, Torcross, nr Kingsbridge, Devon TQ7 2TQ), *b* 1945: *m* 1970, Alison Margaret, da of Denis Rogers, of Torcross, Devon, and has issue living, Andrew Rose, *b* 1975, — Sarah Rose, *b* 1973. —— Heather Mary Rose, *b* 1942: *m* 1st, 1965 (*m diss* 1976), Richard James Biddle; 2ndly, 1978, Harry Denys Barron, of Denysholme, Chilworth, Old Village, Southampton, and has issue living (by 1st *m*), Marc Jonathan Seymour (Long Bangan, Sarawak, Malaysia), *b* 1967: *m* 1993, Payang Tingan, — Roy Lindley Stirling, *b* 1969, — Paul Ashley Sheridan, *b* 1974, — Tiffany Lynn, *b* 1970.

Grandchildren of late Arthur Henry Price, yr son of Thomas Price, 6th son of 1st baronet:—
Issue of late Rev Thomas Rose Price, *b* 1874, *d* 1940: *m* 1901, Frances Louisa Salisbury, who *d* 1943, da of Frederick Churchill, MD, FRCS:—
Joy Gerrardine Salisbury Rose, *b* 1918: *m* 1939, Rupert George Pearce, and has issue living, Peter Wayne, *b* 1947: *m* 1969, Kay Teresa Harris, and has issue living, Jeremy Robert *b* 1974, Lisa Kelly *b* 1972, Anna *b* 1977, — Wendy Lynne, *b* 1941: *m* 1964, William Harper Ritchie, and has issue living, Peter Graham *b* 1966, Grant Phillip *b* 1970, Kathryn Margaret *b* 1968, — Pauline Frances, *b* 1944: *m* 1968, Donald George Foster, and has issue living, Daniel Richard *b* 1970, Emily Victoria *b* 1971, Faye Louise *b* 1974, — Faye Fiona, *b* 1949: *m* 1970, Wayne Allan Parkhill, and has issue living, Jesse Andrew *b* 1981, Charlotte Faye *b* 1979, — Estelle Suzanne, *b* 1951: *m* 1972, Christopher John Alleyne, and has issue living, Timothy Francis *b* 1984, Melissa Gerrardine *b* 1975, Holly Felicity *b* 1979. *Residence* – Hoon Hay Valley, Christchurch 3, NZ.

Issue of late Samuel Percy Price, *b* 1878, *d* 19—: *m* 1st, 1906, Margaret Elinor, who *d* 1906, da of late James Grant, of Dunheanish, Oban; 2ndly, 1912, Anita, da of T.A. Mackay, of Concepcion, Chile:—
(By 2nd *m*) John Samuel (PO Box 916, Concepcion, Chile), *b* 1921: *m* 1943, Joan Margaret, who *d* 1954, da of Frank Williams, of Cochabamba, Bolivia, and has issue living, Samuel John Rose, *b* 1950, — Peter Rose, *b* 1954, — Anita Margaret Rose, *b* 1944, — Sandra Joan *b* 1947, — Jennifer Rose, *b* 1953. —— Michael Patrick (PO Box 492, Concepcion, Chile), *b* 1922: *m* 1945, Evelyn Mabel, da of late Eric Saffery, of Talcahuano, Chile, and has issue living, Anthony Samuel Patrick Rose, *b* 1953, — Thomas Eric Rose, *b* 1956, — Heather Evelyn Rose, *b* 1946, — Marilyn Rose, *b* 1949, — Gillian Rose, *b* 1951. —— Carmen (Almirante Latorre 399, Ancud, Chile), *b* 1915: *m* 1st, 1935, Lt Oswald Marcus Cheke, DSC, RN, who was *ka* 1941; 2ndly 1942 (*m diss* 1951), James Byrne; 3rdly, 1953, Manuel Hidalgo, and has issue living, (by 1st *m*) Marcus Oswald, *b* 1936, — Francis Patrick, *b* 1940, — (by 2nd *m*) Jacqueline, *b* 1945, — Rosanna Amber, *b* 1949, — (by 3rd *m*) Ana Manuela, *b* 19—, — Maria Victoria, *b* (twin) 19—. —— Pearl Rose (General Ludwig 4747, Las Condes, Santiago, Chile), *b* 1917: *m* 1st, Rudolph Seyler; 2ndly, 1947, Edward George Yriberry, and has issue living, (by 1st *m*) Christopher Louis, *b* 1939, — (by 2nd *m*) Pearl Anita, *b* 1954.

Francis Price, *b* about 1635, believed to be descended from Caradoc Vreichvras, Prince between the Wye and Severn, settled in Jamaica soon after its conquest in 1655. He acquired Worthy Park in St Johns 1670, and was a Member of House of Assembly and Maj of Militia. He married Elizabeth Booth, widow of Col William Rose, of Rose Hall, Jamaica. His son, Col Charles Price, was testamentary heir of his uterine brother, Thomas Rose, and inherited his Jamaica estates. His el son Charles, Speaker of House of Assembly, was *cr* a Bt 1768, which title became ext on the death of the 2nd Bt 1788 (also Speaker of House of Assembly). John Price, 2nd son of Col Charles Price, was grandfather of Sir Rose Price, 1st Bt of the 2nd and present creation. Sir Rose Price, 4th Bt, was *k* during S African War 1901.

GREEN-PRICE (UK) 1874, of Norton Manor, Radnorshire

Live to-day

Sir ROBERT JOHN GREEN-PRICE, 5th *Baronet*; *b* 22 Oct 1940; *s* his father, Capt *Sir* JOHN, 1964; *ed* Shrewsbury; Capt (ret) RCT; ADC to Gov of Bermuda 1969-72; Instructor Concord Sch of English, Tokyo 1973-76; Lecturer in English, Teikyo Univ 1976-82, and Chiba Univ of Commerce 1982-1997.

𝕬rms – Sable, a chevron invected argent betwen three escutcheons of the last, each charged with a spear-head of the first embrued proper. 𝕮rest – In front of a dragon's head erased vert, holding in the mouth a dexter hand, couped at the wrist gules, three escallops argent.

SISTER LIVING

Roseanne, *b* 1943: *m* 1st, 1963, Richard Lowe, Maj Queen Elizabeth's Own Gurkha Rifles; 2ndly, 1984, Michael Hender, and has issue living, (by 1st *m*) Timothy, *b* 1963, — Deborah, *b* 1965, — Sophie Louise, *b* 1969. *Residence* – Dukes, Bradninch, nr Exeter, Devon EX5 4QN.

COLLATERAL BRANCHES LIVING

Issue of late John Powell Green-Price, 5th son of 2nd baronet, *b* 1878, *d* 1927: *m* 1907, Julia Helen Ouchterlony Norman, who *d ca* 1959, da of Harold Manners-Norman:—
(POWELL) NORMAN DANSEY, *b* 22 July 1926; adopted by his uncle Sir Robert Green-Price, 3rd Bt, 1944; *ed* Shrewsbury; late Lieut WG; High Sheriff Radnorshire 1969; MFH· *m* 1963, Ann Stella, da of late Brig Harold George Howson, CBE, MC, TD, of North House, Carlton-in-Lindrick, Worksop, Notts, and has issue living, Simon Richard, *b* 10 May 1964, — Stella Rachel, *b* 1965. *Residence* – Hivron, Bleddfa, Knighton, Radnorshire LD7 1NY.

Issue of late Llewellyn James Green-Price, yst son of 2nd baronet, *b* 1881, *d* 1962: *m* 1919, Ethel Lilian, da of S. Faram, of Kepax, Worcester:—
Olive Maude, *b* 1922.

Grandchildren of late Rev Herbert Chase Green-Price, 2nd son of 1st baronet:—
Issue of late Lt-Col Francis Chase Green-Price, *b* 1896, *d* 1975: *m* 1934, Joan Atcherley, who *d* 1991, da of late Guy Dobell, of Crickhowell:—
John Chase, *b* 1947: *m* 1986 (*m diss* 1989), Susan Elizabeth, da of Kenneth Woodyatt. *Residence* – Wendover, Moor Lane, Croyde Bay, N Devon EX33 1NP. —— Susan Marion, *b* 1939. *Residence* – Breezelands, Moor Lane, Croyde Bay, N Devon EX33 1NU.

Issue of late Richard Henry Green-Price, *b* 1905, *d* 1998: *m* 1931, Ruby Beatrix, who *d* 19—, da of late Robert Thomas Rowan, of Shanghai:—
†Anthony Chase, *b* 1933: *m* 1980, Joyce Betty Schrieber. —— Susan Anne, *b* 1943: *m* 1967, Alfred Ian Ryder.

Issue of late Rev Alfred Edward Green-Price, 4th son of 1st baronet, *b* 1860, *d* 1940: *m* 1893, Mary Louisa, who *d* 1922, da of late Very Rev H. Edwards, Dean of Bangor:—
Alice Monica (Nash Cottage, Fownhope, Hereford), *b* 1907: *m* 1969, Richard Vivian Glynne Williams.

The 1st baronet, Sir Richard, son of late George Green, of Knighton, assumed, by Roy licence 1874, the additional surname of Price, being heir to his maternal uncle, Richard Price, of Norton Manor, Radnorshire. He sat as MP for Radnor Boroughs (*L*) 1862-9, and for Radnorshire 1880-85. Sir Robert Henry, 3rd Bt was High Sheriff of Radnorshire 1930.

RUGGE-PRICE (UK) 1804, of Spring Grove, Richmond, Surrey

Live (here) so that you may live
(thereafter)

Sir (CHARLES) KEITH NAPIER RUGGE-PRICE, 9th *Baronet*; *b* 7 Aug 1936; *s* his father, *Lt-Col Sir* CHARLES JAMES NAPIER, 1966; *ed* Middleton Coll, Ireland: *m* 1965, Jacqueline Mary, yr da of Maj Pierre Paul Loranger, MC, CD, and has issue.

𝕬rms – Quarterly, 1st and 4th, gules, a lion rampant argent, *Price*; 2nd and 3rd, sable, on a chevron invected argent, between three mullets or pierced of the field, an unicorn's head erased of the first, *Rugge*. 𝕮rests – 1st, a lion rampant argent, holding in the dexter paw a rose slipped proper; 2nd, a talbot passant argent, gored with a collar and pendent therefrom an escutcheon sable, thereon the head of an ibex couped, also argent.
Residence – 2 Lorne Cres, St Albert, Alberta, Canada T8N 3R2.

SONS LIVING

JAMES KEITH PETER, *b* 8 April 1967. —— Andrew Philip Richard, *b* 1970.

SISTERS LIVING

Angela Muriel Frances, *b* 1938: *m* 1970, Martyn Samuel, of 3 Hillside Av, Exeter EX4 4NW, and has issue living, Bernard Charles, *b* 1971, — Edward Hugh, *b* 1974. —— Jane Marjorie Agnes, *b* 1943: *m* 1965 (*m diss* 19—), Leslie C. Tankard, and has issue living, Nigel Peter Stewart, *b* 1970, — Wendy Julie Angela, *b* 1967. —— Catharine Sarah Christina, *b* 1948.

COLLATERAL BRANCHES LIVING

Issue of late Col Anthony Arthur Keith Rugge-Price, CBE, yr son of 7th baronet, *b* 1914, *d* 1997: *m* 1st, 1939 (*m diss* 1948), Joan Lisette Douglas, yst da of Alan Douglas Pilkington, of Dean Wood, Newbury, Berks; 2ndly, 1952, Mrs Mary Joy Campbell (47 Draycott Place, SW3), da of late John Eric Horniman, and formerly wife of Nigel Keith Graham Campbell:—
(By 1st *m*) (Anthony) Jeremy (132 Oak Hill Rd, Hudson, NY 12534, USA), *b* 1940; *ed* Harrow; late Capt 13/18th Royal Hussars (Queen Mary's Own): *m* 1st, 1963 (*m diss* 19—), Sarah Olivia Valentine, only da of Maj Thomas Adam, of Denmore, Bridge of Don, Aberdeenshire; 2ndly, 1972, Beverly Ann Davidson, of Lt-Col Lance Granville Davidson Brett, of Corfe, Som; 3rdly, 1981, Mrs Carolyn Anne Hicks Beach, only da of Sir Richard Ashton Beaumont, KCMG, OBE, and formerly wife of Michael Brodrick Hick Beach (*see* E St Aldwyn, colls), and has issue living (by 1st *m*), (Andrew) Christian (26 Sutton Court Rd, W4), *b* 1964: *m* 1991 (*m diss* 1994), Sophie A., yr da of A. J. Hind, and of Mrs W. Hipwell, of Norwich, — Barnaby Douglas, *b* 1969, — Matilda Candida, *b* 1970, — (by 2nd *m*), Edward Jason Napier, *b* 1973, — (by 3rd *m*), Robert Jake, *b* 1982, — †Andrew Douglas Napier, *b* 1943; *d* 1957. —— James Keith Alan (Stainswick Manor, Shrivenham, Swindon, Wilts) *b* 1944; *ed* Harrow; *m* 1st, 1967 (*m diss* 1972), Elizabeth Mary, only da of Lt-Col James Innes, of Larkenshaw, Chobham, Surrey (*see* B Westbury); 2ndly, 1976, (Mary) Alexa, da of late Arthur Patrick Usher Crookshank, and has issue living (by 1st *m*), Lucy Caroline, *b* 1969, — (by 2nd *m*), Samantha, *b* 1979, — Kinvara, *b* (twin) 1979, — Alice, *b* 1985. —— (By 2nd *m*) Juliet, *b* 1954: *m* 1979, Thomas M. S. Hughes Hallett, of 20 Stanley Gdns, W11, and has issue living, Archie James Arthur, *b* 1983, — Arthur Thomas M......, *b* 1989, — Grace Marjorie, *b* 1986.

Grandchildren of Alfred Adams Price, grandson of Ralph Price, 3rd son of 1st baronet:—
Issue of late Kenneth Alexander Price, *b* 1869, *d* 19—: *m* 1904, Helen Mary, who *d* 1942, 2nd da of William Baldwin George:—
Arthur Basil, *b* 1916: *m* 1939, Ethel Frances Brindle. —— Douglas Leonard, *b* 1922: late Fl Lt RAF: *m* 1943, Hazel Irene Boyles. —— Ethel Marian, *b* 1905: *m* 1930, Kenneth Couch. —— Phyllis, *b* 1908: *m* 1941, Leslie Henry, late Canadian Army.

Grandchildren of late Petley Lloyd Augustus Price (infra):—
Issue of late Capt Augustus Robert Petley Price, *b* 1885, *d* 1945: *m* 1922, Augusta Elsy Maud, who *d* 1980, da of Gilbert Wilkes, of Ganges, British Columbia:—
Augustus Robert Kenrick, *b* 1927. —— Elsy Mary, *b* 1923: *m* 1963, Raymond Perks, and has issue living, John Robert Raymond, *b* 1965, — David Raymond, *b* 1966.

Granddaughter of late Lieut-Col Augustus Price, el son of late Richard Price, 4th son of 1st baronet:—
Issue of late Petley Lloyd Augustus Price, *b* 1856, *d* 1910: *m* 1884, Mary Cotton, who *d* 1946, da of late Com Frederick Arthur Egerton, RN (Grey-Egerton, Bt, colls):—
Elizabeth Rosina May, *b* 1886: *m* 1915, Alexander Thomas Benthall Charlesworth Lt RFC, who was *ka* 1917.

Grandchildren of late Petley Lloyd Augustus Price (ante):—
Issue of late Harold Tudor Egerton Price, *b* 1888, *d* 1965: *m* 1927, Margaret Frances, da of Edward Fotheringham Layard, of Southsea, Hants:—
John Harold Petley, *b* 1928: *m* 1953, Edith, da of late J. Lee, of Victoria, BC. —— Ruth Gladys, *b* 1930.

Granddaughter of late Major Edward Augustus Uvedale Price (infra):—
Issue of late Lt-Cdr Geoffrey Uvedale Price, RNVR, *b* 1885, *d* 1960: *m* 1908, Winifred Ethel, who *d* 1963, only da of late Edgar L. Price, of The Bays, Oakhill Rd, East Putney, SW:—

Vivienne Betty Henrietta, *b* 1910: *m* 1934, Brigadier Maurice Rapinet Mackenzie, DSO, RA, and has issue living, Michael Philip Uvedale Rapinet, *b* 1937; *ed* Downside, and Oxford Univ.

Grandchildren of late Gen George Uvedale Price, 4th son of late Richard Price, 4th son of 1st baronet:—
Issue of late Major Edward Augustus Uvedale Price, *b* 1854, *d* 1905: *m* 1881, Elizabeth Henrietta, who *d* 1905, da of Henry J. P. Dumas, JP for Surrey:—
Kathleen Janette: *m* 1912, Capt Leslie Granville Waller, late Intelligence Corps, and has issue living, Margaret Evelyn Henrietta, *b* 1913: *m* 1939, Jacques Lioni, of Mr Sixlaan 3, Amstelveen, Holland, and has issue living, David Alexander *b* 1941, John Christopher Granville *b* 1945, Helen Mary *b* 1947. *Residence* – 62 Melbury Gardens, Wimbledon, SW20.

Issue of late Col Cyril Uvedale Price, CMG, *b* 1868, *d* 1956: *m* 1st, 1902, Ethel Maude, who *d* 1916, da of late Capt William Henry Ashe; 2ndly, 1919, May Edith, who *d* 1967, da of late Robert Lewis, of Damaraland:—
(By 2nd *m*) Roger Uvedale, *b* 1921; Burma 1942-45 as Capt Indian Army: *m* 1946, Angela Marcella Exton, da of Brig Wallis, Indian Army and has issue living, Myfanwy Uvedale, *b* 1948: *m* 1st, 1968 (*m diss* 1989), Peter John Penney; 2ndly, 1992, Michael John Payne, of South Lodge, 22 Lansdowne Rd, Angmering, W Sussex BN16 4JX, and has issue living (by 1st *m*), Ian Richard *b* 1970, Samantha Helen *b* 1973.

Grandson of late Ralph Mountague Rokeby Price, 4th son of the Rev Thomas Charles Price, el son of Thomas Price, 5th son of 1st baronet:—
Issue of late Arthur Mountague Rokeby Price, *b* 1892, *d* 1941: *m* 1916, Eliza, who *d* 1983, da of Victor Kuylen, of Stann Creek, British Honduras:—
Ralph Mountague Rokeby, CPM (4244 Kawanee Av, Metairie, La 70002, USA), *b* 1917; formerly Principal Assist Sec, British Honduras, CPM for Meritorious Ser; 1939-45 War Capt Caribbean Regt: *m* 1942, Margarita Matilda Ernestina, da of Nazario Cervantes, of Belize, British Honduras, and has had issue, Ralph Mountague Rokeby, *b* 1946: *m* 1976, Kim, da of Harold Maranto, Jr, of Louisiana, USA, and has issue living, Jared *b* 1978, Joshua *b* 1980, Andrew *b* 1982, Adam *b* 1984, Jennifer Leigh *b* 1977, — Arthur Richard Rokeby (41228 Eldorado Dr, Hammond, LA 70403, USA), *b* 1949: *m* 1972, Elaine Sand, and has issue living, Jason Richard *b* 1974, Scott Richard *b* 1979, — †David Francis Rokeby, *b* 1956, *d* 1986, — †Michael John Rokeby, *b* 1958, *d* 1987, — Patricia Elizabeth Rokeby, *b* 1943: *m* 1963, Marvin Robert Sabido, of 1905 Kent Av, Metairie, La 70001, USA, and has issue living, Marvin Robert *b* 1964, David Andrew *b* 1967: *m* 1991, Laura Michele, da of Michael Williams, of Louisiana, USA (and has issue living, Brandon Michael *b* 1995, Ashley Nichole *b* 1992), Christopher Ian *b* 1967, Steven Scott *b* 1975: *m* 1997, Denise Ann, da of Dennis Couret, of Louisiana, USA, — Alice Mae Rokeby, *b* 1948: *m* 1972, Lloyd Perrien, of 2604 N Sibley St, Metairie, La 70003, USA, and has issue living, Todd Andrew *b* 1973, Derek Lloyd *b* 1976, — Margaret Joan Rokeby, *b* 1952, — Carolyn Mary Rokeby, *b* 1962.

Grandchildren of late Arthur Mountague Rokeby Price (ante):—
Issue of late Arthur Victor Rokeby Price, *b* 1921, *d* 1964: *m* 1955, Bridget Ellen, da of Micheal Austin Flynn, of Canada:—
Michael Craig, *b* 1959. —— Richard Arthur (twin), *b* 1959. —— Bridget Ellen, *b* 1956. —— Judith *b* 1958. —— Jennifer, *b* (twin) 1958. —— Margaret Mary, *b* 1961. —— Sheila Rose, *b* 1962. —— Elizabeth Anne, *b* 1964.

Grandchildren of late Thomas Plumer Price, 5th son of late Rev Thomas Charles Price, el son of late Thomas Price, 5th son of 1st baronet:—
Issue of late Capt Thomas Ralph Plumer Price, *b* 1885, *d* 1967: *m* 1916, Ruth Beatrice, who *d* 1978, da of late Sydney Harris, of The Gables, Hagley Rd, Edgbaston:—
Richard Ralph Plumer (1-1019 Pemberton Rd, Victoria BC, Canada, V8S 3R5), *b* 1926: *m* 1954, Audrey Chrystal, da of late James Anderson Gray, of London, Ont, and has issue living, James Plumer, *b* 1957, — Norman Plumer (2236 Florence St, Victoria, BC V8R 5E8), *b* 1959: *m* 1979, Bronwyn Anne, da of Robert Fox, of Victoria, BC, and has issue living, Tristian Christina *b* 1980. —— Ruth Rosemary Plumer (10 Garden Mews, Warsash, Southampton SO31 9GW), *b* 1920: *m* 1946 (*m diss* 1953), Robert Alfred John Sindall, FO, RAF, and has issue living, David Robert Plumer *b* 1947: *m* 1978 Susan Jane Humby, and has issue living, Thomas David Plumer *b* 1982, Emily Jane *b* 1980, — Sally Ann, *b* 1949: *m* 1st, 1969 (*m diss* 1975) Stephen Philip Clarke; 2ndly, 1977 (*m diss* 19—), Roger David Hogben, and has issue living (by 1st *m*), Rachel Melanie *b* 1970, Sarah Elizabeth *b* 1972, — (by 2nd *m*) Helen Abigail *b* 1977.

Grandchildren of late Capt Spencer Cosby Price, 3rd son of late Thomas Price (ante)—
Issue of late Spencer Edward Cosby Price, *b* 1873, *d* 19—: *m* 1894, his cousin, Eleanor Ann, of Mark Whatmore:—
Spencer Kendrick Sydney, *b* 1902. —— Nesta Joan Cosby, *b* 1900.

The 1st baronet, Alderman Sir Charles Price, was MP for the City of London 1802-12, and Lord Mayor thereof 1802-3. Sir Arthur James, 5th baronet, assumed in 1874, by Roy licence, the additional surname of Rugge. Lieut-Col Sir Charles Frederick Rugge-Price, 7th baronet RFA, served in S Africa 1900-1901, and in European War 1914-18.

Prichard-Jones, see Jones.

PRIMROSE (UK) 1903, of Redholme, Dumbreck, Govan, co of City of Glasgow

Fidelity and confidence

Sir JOHN URE PRIMROSE, 5th *Baronet*; *b* 28 May 1960; *s* his father, *Sir* ALASDAIR NEIL, 1986; *ed* Buenos Aires: *m* 1983 (*m diss* 1987), Marion Cecilia, da of Hans Otto Altgelt, of Buenos Aires, Argentina, and has issue.

Arms – Per fesse argent and ermines, on a fesse vert between in chief a mill rind between two cross-crosslets fitchée gules, and in base a salmon on its back argent, holding a signet ring in its mouth, three primroses slipped proper. **Crest** – A hand couped at the wrist grasping a primrose slipped proper.
Residence – Puerto Victoria, Alto Parana Misiones, Argentina.

DAUGHTERS LIVING

Christine Anne, *b* 1984. —— Jennifer Diana, *b* 1986.

BROTHER LIVING

ANDREW RICHARD, *b* 19 Jan 1966.

SISTERS LIVING

Doris Sofia, *b* 1962. —— Deborah Marina, *b* 1964.

WIDOW LIVING OF FOURTH BARONET

(ELAINE) NOREEN (*Lady Primrose*), only da of Edmund Cecil Lowndes, of Buenos Aires, Argentina: *m* 1958, Sir Alasdair Neil Primrose, 4th Bt, who *d* 1986. *Residence* – Ada Elflein 3155, 1642 San Isidro, Provincia de Buenos Aires, Argentina.

COLLATERAL BRANCH LIVING

Issue of late Hugh Dunsmuir Primrose, yr son of 2nd baronet, *b* 1909, *d* 1979: *m* 1935, Kathleen, da of late Samuel Tyler, of Long Sutton, Lincs:—
Iain Dunsmuir (Lymburghs Farm, Marnhull, Sturminster Newton, Dorset DT10 1HN), *b* 1941; *ed* King's Coll, Taunton: *m* 1971, Roberta Jeanette, da of Frederick Clapp, of Bristol, and has issue living, James Robert, *b* 1973, — Fiona Joanne, *b* 1971, — Nicola Kathryn, *b* 1976.

The 1st baronet, Sir John Ure Primrose (senior partner in the firm of William Primrose and Sons, flour millers, of Centre Street, Glasgow), was Chm of Clyde Navigation Trustee 1907-9, Lord Provost of Glasgow 1903-5, and Lord-Lieut of co of the City of Glasgow.

Prince-Smith, see Smith.

PRINGLE (NS) 1683, of Stichill, Roxburghshire

Faith crowns

Lt-Gen Sir STEUART ROBERT PRINGLE, KCB, 10th *Baronet*; *b* 21 July 1928; *s* his father, *Squadron Leader Sir* NORMAN HAMILTON, 1961; *ed* Sherborne; Hon DSc City Univ (1982), Hon LLD Exeter Univ (1994); formerly Commandant Gen RM; formerly Chm and Ch Exec Chatham Historic Dockyard Trust; Pres St Loye's Coll Foundation, Exeter; KCB (Mil) 1982: *m* 1953, Jacqueline Marie, only da of Wilfrid Hubert Gladwell, of La Rocque, Jersey, and has issue.

ⁿⁿ**Arms** – Azure, three escallops or. **Crest** – A saltire azure within a garland of bay-leaves proper. *Residence* – 76 S Croxted Rd, Dulwich, SE21 8BD.

SONS LIVING

SIMON ROBERT (5 Hyde Vale, Greenwich, SE10 8QQ), *b* 6 Jan 1959; *ed* Worth Abbey, and Trinity Coll Oxford (BA): *m* 1992, Pamela Margaret, da of George Hunter, of Belfast, and has issue living, Siena Evangeline, *b* 1994. —— Julian Andrew James, *b* 1961.

DAUGHTERS LIVING

Shelagh Mary Frances, *b* 1954: *m* 1st, 1975, Jasper J. H. Dale; 2ndly, 19—, Gary Nicholas Newton, and has issue living, Jessica Anne, *b* 1978, — Katherine Frances, *b* 1980, — Alexa Mary Elizabeth, *b* 1983. —— Nicola Ann, *b* 1956: *m* 1981, Clive Gordon Harris, and has issue living, Robert Keith, *b* 1985, — Callum Charles, *b* 1993, — Geraldine Marie, *b* 1982.

Friendship reflects honours

COLLATERAL BRANCHES LIVING

Issue of late Ronald Steuart Pringle, 2nd son of 8th baronet, *b* 1905; *d* 1968: *m* 1938, Janet Patricia Todd, who *d* 1983, da of late Capt George Todd Pickford, RNR, of Wallasey, Ches:—
Norman Murray, *b* 1941; BA, FCIS, FCMA: *m* 1st, 1966, Lysbet Watkins-Pitchford; 2ndly, 1992, Patricia Nadine Millem, and has issue living (by 1st *m*), Alastair Steuart Ronald, *b* 1972, — Sian Amanda, *b* 1972. Resides in Maadi, Cairo. —— James Bruce (5 St Mary's Pl, Newbury, Berks), *b* 1943: *m* 1965, Rosemary Jean Collis, and has issue living, Andrew James Edward, *b* 1975, — Jean Frances, *b* 1967: *m* 1996, David Antony Paddick, and has issue living, Alexander James *b* 1998, — Marion Clare, *b* 1970, — Angela Mary, *b* 1971. —— Priscilla Frances, *b* 1944: *m* 1st, 1964 (*m diss* 1972), Anthony Mark Dorman; 2ndly, 1976 (*m diss* 1991), Derek John McIntosh, and has issue living (by 1st *m*), Louise Margaret, *b* 1965: *m* 198-, Paul John Preston, and has issue living, Leigh Mark *b* 1985, Christopher James *b* 1988, Robert Steven *b* 1990, Steven Jonathan *b* 1992, Lisa Clare *b* 1987.

Issue of late James Drummond Pringle, yst son of 8th baronet, *b* 1906, *d* 1960: *m* 1st, 1932 (*m diss* 1946), Nina Beryl, who *d* 1988, el da of P. W. Trutwein, formerly Sessions Judge, Burma; 2ndly, 1947, Mrs Pauline Cunliffe:—
(By 1st *m*) Norman Alastair (27 Lynton Green, Maidenhead), *b* 1933; *ed* Stonyhurst: *m* 1956 (*m diss* 1979), Diana Joan, da of Victor Clarke, and has issue living, Robin Alastair, *b* 1962: *m* 1984 (*m diss* 1996), Anne Samuel, — Susan Jane, *b* 1960: *m* 1st, 1977 (*m diss* 1980) Alan Watkins; 2ndly, 1980 (*m diss* 1994), Tony Bennett; 3rdly, 1995, Alan Singleton, and has issue living (by 2nd *m*), Nadia *b* 1980, (by 3rd *m*), Alex *b* 1995, — Dawn Anne, *b* 1965: *m* 1982, Terry Spracklen, and has issue living, Kayleigh Louise *b* 1985, — Beth Kelcei, *b* 1991, — Lydia Kimberley, *b* 1993. —— (By 2nd *m*) John, *b* 1948. —— Melanie, *b* 1955.

The Pringles of Stichill are heirs male and representatives of the Hop-Pringles of Craglatch and Newhall, co Selkirk. Sir Robert Pringle of Stichill, 1st baronet, *s* to Newhall 1667 on the extinction of the elder branch of the family.

PROBY (UK) 1952, of Elton Hall, co Huntingdon

Sir PETER PROBY, 2nd *Baronet, b* 4 Dec 1911; *s* his father, Maj *Sir* RICHARD GEORGE, MC, JP, 1979; *ed* Eton, and Trin Coll, Oxford (BA); Capt Irish Gds; Bursar of Eton 1953-71; a DL for Cambs, and Lord Lieut 1981-85; FRICS: *m* 1944, Blanche Harrison, only da of Col Henry Harrison Cripps, DSO, R Fus, and has issue.

Arms – Quarterly: 1st and 4th, ermine on a fesse gules a lion passant or, *Proby,* 2nd and 3rd, argent, two bars wavy azure, on a chief of the last an estoile between two escallops or, *Allen;* Crest – An ostrich's head erased proper, ducally gorged and holding in the beak a key or.
Residence – No 2 St Botolph's Green, Elton, Peterborough PE8 6SG. *Club* – Travellers'.

Manus haec inimica Tyrannis

This hand is unfriendly to tyrants

SON LIVING

WILLIAM HENRY, *b* 13 June 1949; *ed* Eton, Lincoln Coll, Oxford (MA), and Brooksby Coll of Agric; DL Cambs 1995; FCA; Chm HHA Taxation Comm 1986-94; Pres Historic Houses Assocn 1993-98; farmer; financial adviser: *m* 1974, Meredyth Anne, da of Dr Timothy David Brentnall, of Corner Cottage, Preston, nr Uppingham, Leics, and has issue living, Alexandra Meredyth Anne, *b* 1980, — Alice Katherine, *b* 1982, — Frances Rose Gwyneth, *b* 1986, — Isabella Victoria Hamilton, *b* 1991. *Residence* – Elton Hall, Elton, Peterborough PE8 6SH.

DAUGHTERS LIVING

Sarah Blanche, *b* 1945; *ed* Lady Margaret Hall, Oxford (MA, BM, BCh): *m* 1968, Peter George Mills, MA, BCh, FRCP, of 158 Tachbrook St, SW1, son of Dr George William Mills, MBE, and has issue living, James Douglas George, *b* 1972, — Robert Peter, *b* 1975, — Elizabeth Sarah Jane, *b* 1980. — Charlotte Mary, *b* 1957; *ed* Lady Margaret Hall, Oxford (MA, MB, BS), MRCP: *m* 1984, Stephen John Hay, son of Maj John Hay, of Cheltenham, and has issue living, Matthew John Claud, *b* 1990, — Francis Michael Bruce, *b* 1999, — Matilda Blanche, *b* 1989, — Flora Millie Rose, *b* 1994. — Christine Elisabeth, *b* (twin) 1957; *ed* New Hall, Camb (MA, VetMB, MRCVS): *m* 1983, Christopher T. C. Dobbs, yst son of J. A. Dobbs, CMG, OBE, TD, of Charlton Musgrave, Som, and has issue living, Rachel Alice, *b* 1992, — Lucy Harriet, *b* 1995.

SISTERS LIVING

Margaret *b* 1920; a JP for Dorset: *m* 1948, Jack Harry Harrison Cripps, of Bramble Cottage, 10 French Mill Lane, Shaftesbury, Dorset, and has issue living, Harry Richard, *b* 1949: *m* 1974, Vivien Barbara, da of Roy North, and has issue living, Elizabeth Blanche *b* 1977, Sarah Margaret *b* 1979, — Peter John, *b* 1954: *m* 1983, Hazel Anne, da of Jack Fox, — Thomas Philip (twin), *b* 1954: *m* 1979, Elizabeth Margaret, da of Oliver Sugden, and has issue living, Margaret Jane *b* 1981, — Barbara Mary, *b* 1952: *m* 1973, Giles T. R. Droop, and has issue living, Alastair Philip *b* 1980, Alison Jane *b* 1978. — Patience (*Lady Moberly*) (twin), *b* 1923; *ed* Lady Margaret Hall, Oxford (BA, BM and BCh); MRCP: *m* 1959, Sir John Campbell Moberly, KBE, CMG, HM Diplo Ser, of The Cedars, Temple Sowerby, Penrith, and 35 Pymers' Mead, Croxted Rd, SE21 8NH, son of Sir Walter Hamilton Moberly, GBE, KCB, DSO, and has issue living, Richard John, *b* 1962: *m* 1992, Catharine J. F., da of Noel Baker, and has issue living, Joanna Clare *b* 1996, — Nicholas Hamilton, *b* 1963: *m* 1991, Margaret Fiona Clare, da of J. H. Callan, of Horley, Surrey, and has issue living, James Hamilton *b* 1994, Emma Lucy Victoria *b* 1993, — Clare Elizabeth, *b* 1967.

WIDOW LIVING OF FIRST BARONET

EILEEN YVONNE (Abbey Lodge, Beverley, Harrogate, N Yorks GH3 5AX), da of Walter Edwin Ambrose Helps, of Trevarth Manor, Gwennap, Cornwall, and widow of F/Lieut Reginald Kenneth Harris, RAF: *m* 2ndly, 1972, as his 2nd wife, Maj Sir Richard George Proby, 1st Bt, MC, JP, who *d* 1979; 3rdly, 1991, Eric Holman Stirk, of Abbey Lodge, Bewerley, Harrogate, Yorks.

COLLATERAL BRANCH LIVING

Issue of late Capt Claud Proby, IG, 2nd son of 1st baronet, *b* 1917, *d* 1987: *m* 1942, Patricia Amelia (1 Chestnut Close, Gt Waldingfield, Sudbury, Suffolk), da of Lt-Cmdr Vyvyan Whitmore Pearce, RN:—
Patrick James (21 Greenacres, Gt Waldingfield, Sudbury, Suffolk), *b* 1944; *ed* Eton. — Caroline Fiona, *b* 1943: *m* 1st, 1969 (*m diss* 1988), 6th Viscount Hampden; 2ndly, 1990, Christopher Kanthack St John Bird. — Joanna Margaret, *b* 1946: *m* 1970, Edward Richard Woods, NZ Ambassador to Russia, son of Archdeacon Samuel Woods, and has issue living, James Christopher, *b* 1972, — Samuel Richard, *b* 1973. *Address* – NZ Foreign Ministry, Parliament Bldgs, Wellington, NZ. — Jocelyn Elizabeth, *b* 1950; *m* 1993, Donald Retson, of Edmonton, Alberta, Canada, and has issue living, Serena Christine, *b* 1992.

This family is descended in the female line from William Proby, first cousin of Sir Thomas Proby, Bt, upon whose death in 1689 the baronetcy became extinct, and from the Earls of Carysfort, whose Irish Earldom and Barony, and English Barony became extinct on the death of the 5th Earl in 1909. Lady Elizabeth Emma Proby, a sister of the last Earl of Carysfort, married Rt Hon Lord Claud Hamilton, MP, brother of 1st Duke of Abercorn, and their son, Col Douglas James Hamilton, assumed by Roy licence 1904 the surname of Proby. The 1st baronet, Maj Sir Richard Proby, was Pres of Country Landowners' Assocn 1947-51.

Probyn-Jones, see Jones.

Proctor-Beauchamp, see Beauchamp.

Pryce-Jones, see Jones.

PRYKE (UK) 1926, of Wanstead, co Essex

Sir CHRISTOPHER DUDLEY PRYKE, 4th *Baronet*; *b* 17 April 1946; *s* his uncle, *Sir* DAVID DUDLEY, 1998, *ed* Hurstpierpoint; chartered surveyor: *m* 1973 (*m diss* 1986), Angela Gay, who *d* 1995, da of late Harold Noel Meek, of Holly Cottage, Crowell, nr Kingston Blount, Oxon, and has issue.

Arms – Per pale or and argent, on a cross invected azure two fasces erect in pale and as many mascals in fesse all of the first. Crest – Two arms embowed, the hands proper supporting a fasces erect or, each arm charged with a mascal of the last.
Residence – 23 Wavendon Av, Chiswick, W4 4NP.

SON LIVING

JAMES DUDLEY, *b* 29 Dec 1977.

SISTER LIVING

Rosemary Susan, *b* 1949. *Residence* – 26 St Augustine's Rd, NW1 9RN.

DAUGHTERS LIVING OF THIRD BARONET

Madge, *b* 1946: *m* 1971, Keith Robert Pettit, of 21 Wards Rd, Newbury Park, Ilford 1G2 7BA, son of Harry Pettit, of Brightlingsea, and has issue living, Stephen Robert, *b* 1975, — Christine Yvonne, *b* 1978. ——— Anita, *b* 1949: *m* 1969, Edwin Mark Lightstone, of 4 Fairlight Court, Welland Rd, Tonbridge TN10 3TR, and has issue living, Alexander James Mark, *b* 1976, — Peter David Edward, *b* 1982, — Tamsin Anna Frances, *b* 1980.

The 1st baronet, Sir William Robert Pryke (son of Richard Reeve Pryke), of Bury St Edmunds, was Chm of Pryke & Palmer, Ltd, iron and hardware merchants of 40 and 41 Upper Thames Street, EC, and Lord Mayor of London 1925-6. The 2nd baronet, Sir (William Robert) Dudley Pryke, was Chm of Pryke & Palmer, Ltd, iron and hardware merchants, of 40 and 41 Upper Thames Street, EC.

SAUNDERS-PRYSE (UK) 1866, of Gogerddan (Extinct 1962)

Sir PRYSE LOVEDEN SAUNDERS-PRYSE, 5th and last *Baronet*.

DAUGHTER LIVING OF FOURTH BARONET

Margaret Angharad Elinor, *b* 1903: *m* 1930, Godfrey S. Briggs, who *d* 1941.

Purves (Home-Purves-Hume-Campbell), see Campbell.

QUILTER (UK) 1897, of Bawdsey Manor, Bawdsey, Suffolk

Sir ANTHONY RAYMOND LEOPOLD CUTHBERT QUILTER, 4th *Baronet*; *b* 25 March 1937; *s* his father, *Sir* (JOHN) RAYMOND CUTHBERT, 1959; *ed* Harrow: *m* 1964, (Mary) Elise, el da of Col Brian Sherlock Gooch, DSO, TD, of Tannington Hall, Woodbridge (*see* Gooch, Bt, *cr* 1746, colls), and has issue.

𝕬rms – Argent, on a bend invected gules, between three Cornish choughs proper, two cross crosslets of the first. 𝕮rest – In front of an arm vambraced proper, the hand grasping a battle-axe in bend sinister sable, head argent, the wrist entwined by a wreath of the third and second, a Cornish chough proper.
Seat – Sutton Hall, Woodbridge, Suffolk.

SON LIVING

GUY RAYMOND CUTHBERT, *b* 13 April 1967: *m* 1992, Jenifer J., only da of John Redvers-Cox, of Melton, Suffolk, and has issue living, William Raymond Cuthbert, *b* 29 Nov 1995, — Henry Guy Cuthbert, *b* 1997.

Plutôt mourir que
changer

Rather die than change

DAUGHTER LIVING

Juliet Elise, *b* 1965.

WIDOW LIVING OF THIRD BARONET

MARGERY MARIANNE (*Margery, Lady Quilter*) (Pettistree Hall, Sutton, Woodbridge, Suffolk), da of late Sir (James) Douglas Cooke, of Kingston House, Princes' Gate, SW7: *m* 1935, Sir (John) Raymond Cuthbert Quilter, 3rd Bt, who *d* 1959.

COLLATERAL BRANCHES LIVING

Issue of late Percy Cuthbert Quilter, 4th son of 1st baronet, *b* 1879 *d* 1947: *m* 1909, Gladys Clare Alice, who *d* 1973, da of late Charles Clement Tudway (Hervey-Bathurst, Bt):—
David Cuthbert TUDWAY QUILTER, *b* 1921; *ed* Eton; assumed by deed poll 1962 the additional surname of Tudway before his patronymic; DL Somerset (Vice Lord-Lieut since 1978): *m* 1953, Elizabeth Mary, da of Sir John Gawen Carew Pole, 12th Bt, DSO, TD, and has issue living, Simon John Cuthbert, *b* 1955, — Susan Clare Evelyn, *b* 1957: *m* 1st, 1978, James Henderson, who *d* 1991; 2ndly, 19—, Charles Dingwall, of The Manor House, W Hendred, nr Wantage, Oxon OX12 8RP, and has issue living, (by 1st *m*) (*see* Lowther, Bt, *cr* 1824, colls), (by 2nd *m*) John Patrick D...... J......*b* 1993, — Lucy Anne, *b* 1961: *m* 1984, Dr Christopher D. B. Daniel, yr son of Ian Daniel, of Oaklands, Fressingfield, Eye, Suffolk, and has issue living, Jonathan David *b* 1985, Katie *b* 1987. *Residence* – Milton Lodge, Wells, Som. —— Diana Primrose, *b* 1916: *m* 1st, 1942 (*m diss* 1945), as his 2nd wife, Brig Lancelot Merivale Gibbs, CVO, DSO, MC, who *d* 1966; 2ndly, 1947, Archibald Tennant, who *d* 1955 (*see* B Glenconner, colls). *Residence* – 12 Victoria Sq, SW1.

Grandchildren of late Ronald Eustace Cuthbert Quilter, elder son of late Maj Eustace Cuthbert Quilter, OBE, 5th son of 1st baronet:—
Issue of late William Ronald Cuthbert Quilter, *b* 1937; *d* 1981: *m* 1962, Jennifer Ann (who *m* 2ndly, 1985, Reginald J.T. Hill, of Holfield Grange, Coggeshall, Essex CO6 1NU), da of Cdr Evelyn John Tamlyn, RD, RNR (ret), of Yew Tree Farm, Pleshey, Chelmsford, Essex:—

Benjamin William Cuthbert, b 1963: m 1992, Helen Lidwina, da of Hendrik Akerboom, of Henderson, Auckland, NZ, and has issue living, Samuel William John, b 1993, — Laurence Benjamin John, b 1995. Residence - 61 Konini Rd, Titirangi, Auckland, NZ. — Melissa Jane, b 1966: m 1992, Dennis Embleton, son of late Dr Philip Embleton, of Aldeburgh, Suffolk, and has issue living (Dennis) Harry Faraday, b 1993, — Freddie Philip, b 1995. Residence - Lime Tree Farm, Badingham, Woodbridge, Suffolk.

The 1st baronet, Sir Cuthbert, was one of the Founders of the National Telephone Co (Limited), and sat as MP for S, or Sudbury, Div of Suffolk (LU) 1885-1906. The 2nd baronet, Sir (William Eley) Cuthbert, sat as MP for Suffolk, S or Sudbury Div (C) 1910-18.

RADCLIFFE (UK) 1813, of Milnesbridge House, Yorkshire

Virtue for its own sake

Sir SEBASTIAN EVERARD RADCLIFFE, 7th *Baronet*; b 8 June 1972; s his father, *Capt Sir* (JOSEPH BENEDICT) EVERARD HENRY, MC, 1975.

Arms – Argent, a bend engrailed sable charged with a crescent of the field for difference. **Crest** – A bull's head erased sable, horns argent, tipped or, gorged with a ducal coronet of the second.

HALF-SISTER LIVING

Susan Elizabeth Mary, b 1940.

WIDOW LIVING OF SIXTH BARONET

MARCIA HELEN (Château de Cheseaux, 1033 Vaud, Switzerland), da of Maj David Turville-Constable-Maxwell (see L Herries of Terregles): m 1st, 1968, as his 2nd wife, Sir (Joseph Benedict) Everard Henry Radcliffe, MC, 6th Bt, who d 1975; 2ndly, 1988, Howard Montagu Stuart Tanner.

COLLATERAL BRANCHES LIVING

Issue of late Hugh John Reginald Joseph Radcliffe, MBE, 2nd son of 5th baronet, b 1911, d 1993: m 1937, Marie-Therese (Mariquita) (The White House, Stoke, Andover, Hants SP11 0LU), yst da of Maj-Gen Sir Cecil Edward Pereira, KCB, CMG:—
MARK HUGH JOSEPH (The Malt House, Upton, Andover, Hants SP11 0JS; Cavalry and Guards' Club), b 22 April 1938; ed Downside; High Sheriff Hants 1996, DL 1997: m 1963, Anne, da of Maj-Gen Arthur Evers Brocklehurst, CB, DSO, and has issue living, Lucinda Mary, b 1964, — Emily Marie Louise, b 1968: m 1996, Alex J. S. Rogers, eldest son of B. Rogers, of Dyfed, — Camilla Mary, b 1971. ——Anthony Joseph (The Vicarage, Langford, Glos), b 1942; ed Downside: m 1964, Rachel Mary, eldest da of Joseph Russell Goddard, of Harmony Hall, Barbados, and has issue living, James Russell Joseph, b 1965: m 1992, Anne Louisa, yst da of Mrs Elizabeth Poyser, of South Place, Moor Park, Middlesex, and has issue living, Polly Anna b 19—, Helena b 1994, — Julian Everard Joseph, b 1967: m 1991, Deborah, el da of T. Key, of Compton, Berks, and has issue living, Matthew Joseph b 1998, — Philippa, b 1975. ——Most Rev Fr Timothy Peter Joseph, OP (Convento S. Sabino, Piazza P. d'Illiria 1, Aventino, 00153 Rome, Italy), b 1945; ed Downside, and St John's Coll, Oxford (MA, Hon Fellow 1993); Prior Provincial of the English Province of the Order of Preachers (The Dominicans), 1988-92, since when Master of the Order of Preachers. ——Paul John Joseph (Rudges Hill, Ramsden, Oxon OX7 3AT), b 1949; ed Downside: m 1978, Nora H., yr da of late Sigmund Hjornevik, and has issue living, Alexander Hugh Joseph, b 1982, — Emma Marie Clare, b 1980. ——Richard Joseph (14 Langham Place, W4 2QL), b 1954; ed Downside: m 1981, Gillian, da of Maj D.W. Mart, of Felixstowe, Suffolk, and has issue living, Harry Hugh Joseph, b 1985, — Lucy Elizabeth, b 1983. ——(Teresa) Jane (97 Altenburg Gdns, SW11 1JQ), b 1939.

Issue of late Joseph Francis Edward Radcliffe, 2nd son of 4th baronet, b 1891, d 1940: m 1922, Marjorie Sophia, who d 1973, da of Sir Francis Charles Edward Denys-Burton, 3rd Bt (Denys, Bt):—
Elizabeth Denyse Mary, b 1923; 1941-45 War with WAAF: m 1952, Ives Bonapace, and has issue living, Charles, b 1953, — Mark, b 1955, — William, b 1958, — Caroline, b 1954, — Jane Mary, b 1961, — Isabelle, b 1964. —— Louise Marie Antoinette, b 1928: m 1956, Alec Pearson Carn, of Highbury, Thornford, Sherborne, Dorset, and has issue living, Nicholas Denys Pearson (4 Park Village E, NW1 7PX; The Old Manse, Stansfield, Suffolk), b 1957; ed Bradfield; MA Oxon 1987: m 1987, Eveline Cécile Barbara, da of late Louis Ochtman, of Brussels, and has issue living, Alexander Nicholas Radcliffe b 1993, Gabrielle Emily Johanna b 1996, — Jonathan, b 1960; ed Bradfield, and Reading Univ (BSc), — Vanessa Mary, b 1963; MRCVS Bristol 1987; PhD 1994, — Francesca Georgina, b 1969; ed Exeter Univ (BSc), — Alexandra Sophia, b 1972; BA London Univ 1993.

Issue of late Robert John Peter Joseph Radcliffe, 4th son of 4th baronet, b 1898, d 1974: m 1929, Ursula Evelyn Mary, who d in a house fire 1977, da of late Lt-Col Miles John Stapylton, OBE, of Myton Hall, York:—
Peter Martin Joseph, b 1941: m 1963, Pamela Ann, 2nd da of George C. Johnson, of 2 Castle Terr, Husthwaite, York. —— Thomas Joseph Henry, b 1943. —— Rosemary Anne Ursula Katherine, b 1930: m 1950, Louis Bertram Hawkswell, who d 1987, and has issue living, Frederick Andrew Joseph, b 1951; ed Belmont Abbey, Hereford: m 1974, Linda Anne Todd, and has issue living, Michael Andrew William b 1976, Benjamin James b 1977, — Martin Louis, b 1955; ed Belmont Abbey, Hereford: m 1976, Elsa Catherine Hall, and has issue living, Oliver Alan Louis b 1979, Nicholas Martin b 1983, — Anthony Robert, b 1956; ed Belmont Abbey, Hereford: m 1979, Linda Middleton, — Philip William, b 1958; ed Belmont Abbey, Hereford: m 1981, Jill Patricia Dorrington, and has issue living, Jon William Robert b 1984, Rebecca Eleanor Ann b 1981, — Simon, b 1968, — Elizabeth Ann, b 1960: m 1980, Anthony George Dorrington, and has issue, Daniel George Louis b 1980, Bronwen Ann b 1982. —— Mary Elizabeth Jane (The Colt House, Easingwold, York), b 1939: m 1st, 1957, John William Courtney, who d 1969; 2ndly, 1985, Philip Leslie Abbott, who d 1991, and has issue

living (by 1st *m*), Miles Stewart John, *b* 1965: *m* 1989, Tracy Anne Clarke, — Rosemary Elizabeth, *b* 1967: *m* 1995, David Patrick Kuba, and has issue living, Claire Laura *b* 1996, Lauren *b* 1998.

Issue of late (Charles Joseph) Basil Radcliffe, 5th and yst son of 4th baronet, *b* 1900, *d* 1983: *m* 1939, (Kathleen) Norah Anne, who *d* 1994, only da of late Norman Percy, of Maloya, Colombo, Sri Lanka:— Francis Charles Joseph (78 Millfield Rd, York), *b* 1939; *ed* Ampleforth, and Gonville and Caius Coll, Camb; Bar Gray's Inn 1962; a Recorder 1979-83: *m* 1969 (*m diss* 1982), Nicolette Hélène, el da of Eugene Randag, of Lodge Hill Farm, Butler's Cross, Aylesbury, Bucks, and has issue living, Edward Eugene Joseph, *b* 1969, — Colette Anne, *b* 1971, — Alexandra Mary, *b* 1972. —— (Bryan) Anthony Joseph (24 Abbotsbury Close, W14), *b* 1941; *ed* Ampleforth; Solicitor 1963: *m* 1965, Pisana, yr da of late Conte Giuseppe Petrobelli, of Prato della Valle, Padua, Italy, and has issue living, Mark Anthony Joseph, *b* 1967, — Harry Joseph, *b* 1972, — Isabella Carolina, *b* 1974. —— Kathryn Anne (Cockenskell, Blawith, Ulverston, Cumbria), *b* 1943: *m* 1965, Anthony John Tulk-Hart Bigland, of Bigland Hall, Ulverston, Cumbria, and has issue living, Benedict James, *b* 1972, — Emma Lucy, *b* 1967, — Sophie Kathryn, *b* 1970.

Issue of late Capt Henry Joseph Francis Radcliffe, 2nd son of 3rd baronet, *b* 1862, *d* 1928: *m* 1896, Gertrude Mary Philomena, who *d* 1955, da of late Rev John Coventry (E Coventry, colls):— Henry Edward Joseph (Manor Cottage, Lympsham, Weston-Super-Mare), *b* 1904: *m* 1939, Ursula Mary Skeet, who *d* 1996, yr da of F. D. Workman, and has issue living, Sally Anne Ursula, *b* 1940: *m* 1966, Geoffrey P. M. Taylor, of Willow Cottage, Dundry, Bristol, and has issue living, Justin Peter *b* 1968, Juliet Clare *b* 1970, Lucinda Jane *b* 1971, Kirsty Anna *b* 1974. —— Gertrude Mary Katherine, *b* 1903: *m* 1925, Philip George Bower, who *d* 1939.

This family took its name from the village of Radcliffe in Lancashire. Richard de Radclyffe, Seneschal and Minister of the Forests in Blackburnshire, accompanied Edward I in his wars in Scotland, and received from that monarch a grant of a charter of freewarren and chase in all his demesne lands of Radcliffe. Mary, da of William Radcliffe of Milnsbridge, Yorks (a descendant of William 2nd son of Richard), and sister and heir of William Radcliffe of Milnsbridge (*d* 1795): *m* Joseph Pickford of Ashton-under-Lyne, Lancs. Their son Joseph Pickford, who assumed the surname of Radcliffe in 1795, was created a baronet for distinguished public services.

RAEBURN (UK) 1923, of Helensburgh, co Dunbarton

Safe if strong

(*Sir*) MICHAEL EDWARD NORMAN RAEBURN, 4th *Baronet*; *b* 12 Nov 1954; *s* his father, *Sir* EDWARD ALFRED, 1977, but does not use title: *m* 1979, Penelope Henrietta Theodora, da of late Alfred Louis Penn, of London, and has issue.

Arms – Or, on a piece of ground in base vert a roebuck statant proper, drinking out of a burn or brook undy argent and azure running bendways, in chief an anchor sable between two roses gules, barbed and seeded of the second. **Crest** – A stag's head proper.
Residence – Fourways, Turners Green, Wadhurst, E Sussex TN5 6TU.

SONS LIVING

CHRISTOPHER EDWARD ALFRED, *b* 4 Dec 1981. —— Martin Phillip, *b* 13 Jan 1989.

DAUGHTERS LIVING

Gwendoline Mary Joan, *b* 1983. —— Janet Maria, *b* 1986. —— Victoria Beatrix Sarah Gabrielle, *b* 1992.

AUNTS LIVING (*Daughters of 2nd baronet*)

Sheila Saisie (Denecourt, Cuckmere Rd, Seaford, E Sussex), *b* 1913. —— Irene Muriel (Denecourt, Cuckmere Rd, Seaford, E Sussex), *b* 1914.

WIDOW LIVING OF THIRD BARONET

JOAN (*Lady Raeburn*) (Fourways, Turners Green, Wadhurst, E Sussex), da of late Frederick Hill, of Dartford, Kent, and Boston, Mass, USA: *m* 1950, Sir Edward Alfred Raeburn, 3rd Bt, who *d* 1977.

COLLATERAL BRANCH LIVING

Issue of late Sir Ernest Manifold Raeburn, KBE, 2nd son of 1st baronet, *b* 1878, *d* 1922: *m* 1910, Greta Mary Alison, who *d* 1975, da of late Engineer-Capt James Herbert Watson, RN:— Sir (William) Digby Manifold, KCVO, CB, DSO, MBE (25 St Ann's Terrace, NW8 6PH; *Clubs* – Pratt's, Cavalry and Guards', Royal Yacht Squadron), *b* 1915; *ed* Winchester and Magdalene Coll, Camb (MA); Maj-Gen (ret) late Scots Gds; Comdg 2nd Bn Scots Gds 1953-55; Lt-Col Comdg Scots Gds 1958-59, Comd 1st Gds Bde Group 1960-61, Dir of Combat Development (Army) 1963-65, Ch of Staff Allied Forces N Europe 1965-68, and Ch, Army Instructor Imperial Defence Coll 1968-70; Resident Gov and Keeper of Jewel House of HM Tower of London 1971-79; 1939-45 War in Middle East, Italy and NW Europe (despatches, MBE, DSO); MBE (Mil) 1941, DSO 1945, CB (Mil) 1966, KCVO 1979: *m* 1960, Adeline Margaret, yst da of late Thomas Selwyn Pryor, MC (*see* Halsey, Bt).

The 1st baronet, Sir William Hannay Raeburn (son of late William Raeburn, of Glasgow), was head of firm of Raeburn & Verel, Ltd, and sat a MP for Dunbartonshire (*U*) 1918-23. The 2nd baronet, Sir William Norman Raeburn, CBE, was a KC.

RALLI (UK) 1912, of Park Street, City of Westminster

Keep to the straight path

Sir GODFREY VICTOR RALLI, TD, 3rd *Baronet*; *b* 9 Sept 1915; *s* his father, Sir STRATI, MC, 1964; *ed* Eton; 1939-45 War, as Capt Berks Yeo RA (despatches): *m* 1st, 1937 (*m diss* 1947), Nora Margaret, only child of late Charles Forman, of Lodden Court, Spencers Wood, nr Reading; 2ndly, 1949, Jean, who *d* 1998, da of late Keith Barlow, of 3 Vicarage Gate, W8, and has issue living by 1st *m*.

𝕬rms – Azure, a lion rampant argent semée ot lozenges of the first in chief a crescent between two crosses couped of the second. 𝕮rest – A lion as in the arms holding between the paws a cross couped argent.
Residence – Piers House, 52 New St, Sandwich, Kent CT13 9BB. *Club* – Naval and Military.

SON LIVING (*By 1st marriage*)

DAVID CHARLES (The Old Hall, Hardingham, Norfolk NR9 4EW), *b* 5 April 1946; *ed* Eton, and Harper Adams Agric Coll: *m* 1975, Jacqueline Cecilia, da of David Smith, and has issue living, Philip Neil David, *b* 31 March 1983, — Marina Louise, *b* 1980. *Clubs* – White's, Farmers'.

DAUGHTERS LIVING (*By 1st marriage*)

Louise, *b* 1942: *m* 1964, Ewen James Fassiefern Cameron, of The Old Vicarage, Harringworth, Corby, Northants NN17 3AF, and has issue living, James Allan Godfrey, *b* 1965, — Alistair Ewen David, *b* 1968: *m* 1998, Lucy, yr da of Michael Sutton-Scott-Tucker, of Riversbridge, Dartmouth, Devon. —— Tessa TITTERTON, *b* 1945; adopted by her mother and her stepfather, Philip Arthur Titterton, MB, ChB, whose surname she assumed in 1952.

BROTHER LIVING

Lucas John, *b* 1920; *ed* Eton; 1939-45 War as Maj Roy Signals (despatches): *m* 1st, 1950 (*m diss* 1989), Katia, da of Constantine Droulia, of Athens, Greece; 2ndly, 1989, Mrs Jean Patricia Barrett, da of Capt Edward Morden Bennett, RN, of Wolfcton Manor, Charminster, Dorchester, and has issue living (by 1st *m*), John Strati (97 Bryanston Court, George St, W1H 7HE), *b* 1956: *m* 1986, Kathryn Martin, and has issue living, Helen Elizabeth *b* 1987, Stephanie Catherine *b* 1990, — Dora Louise, *b* 1953: *m* 1984, Nicolas Rakić, of 18 Bury Walk, SW3 6QB, and has issue living, Peter Lucas Gradimir *b* 1988, Alexander Minas Cedomir *b* (twin) 1988, Anna Katharina Lila *b* 1985. *Residence* – 14 Oxford Sq, W2 2PB.

SISTERS LIVING

Diana Myrtle (Arlington Lodge, Bibury, Glos), *b* 1918: *m* 1939, Lt-Col John Herbert (Jack) Walford, DSO, Seaforth Highlanders, who *d* 1976, and has issue living, Michael Carr (The Old House, Wolverton, Basingstoke, Hants RG26 5RS), *b* 1943; *ed* Harrow and Royal Agric Coll, Cirencester, — (Ewan) John (203 West Prairie, Wheaton, Illinois 60187, USA), *b* 1945; *ed* Harrow, Law School (London and Guildford), and Free Univ, Amsterdam; Speelman Fellow, Wolfson Coll, Camb, 1976; PhD; Prof of Art History, Wheaton Coll, Illinois since 1981: *m* 1972, Maria, only da of late Pietro Angelo Eligio Dellù, of Milan, and has issue living Samuel Michael *b* 1973; *ed* Wheaton Coll, and Western Carolina Univ (BA, MA): *m* 1998, Ginger Elizabeth, da of Dr John Bewick Gouch, of Charlotte, N Carolina, USA, David John *b* 1980, Deborah Maria *b* 1978, — Delinda Mary (8 St Mary Abbot's Terrace, W14), *h* 1941: *m* 1st, 1961 (*m diss* 1968) John William Hayter; 2ndly, 1986, Colin Norman McCorquodale, only son of late Maj Angus McCorquodale, and has issue living (by 1st *m*), Sarah Miranda *b* 1964: *m* 1989, Angus Sladen, of The Old House, Wolverton, Basingstoke, Hants RG26 5RS, son of late Toby Sladen, of Baughurst, Hants (and has issue living, Archie Jack Murray *b* 1996, Olivia Henrietta Malvina *b* 1992, Georgina Ann Diana *b* 1994). —— Patience Louise, *b* 1922: *m* 1944, Lt-Cdr William Edward Michael de Sivrac Dunn, RNVR (despatches), of Awliscombe House, Honiton, Devon EX14 0NP, and has issue living, Mark de Sivrac, *b* 1947, — Karen Louise, *b* 1945: *m* 1971, Alan Grieve, of Stoke Lodge, Clee Downton, Ludlow, Salop SY8 3EG, and has issue living, Thomas de Sivrac *b* 1973, Lara Louise *b* 1974.

The 1st baronet was head of the firm of Ralli Bros, East India merchants, of 25, Finsbury Circus, EC.

RAMSAY (NS) 1666, of Bamff, Perthshire (Extinct 1986)

Sir NEIS ALEXANDER RAMSAY, 12th and last *Baronet*; *d* 1986.

COLLATERAL BRANCH LIVING

Grandchildren of late William Alexander Ramsay, el son of George Gilbert Ramsay, 3rd son of 9th baronet:—
Issue of late Lt-Col George William Neil Ramsay, RA, *b* 1907, *d* 1976: *m* 1st, 1932, Maryel Hope, who *d* 1935, 2nd da of late Col Robert William Pigott Clarke-Campbell-Preston, of Ardchattan Priory, Connel, Argyllshire; 2ndly, 1937 (*m diss* 1947), Catherine Trewyn, only da of Charles Bernard Dougherty, of Ottawa, Canada; 3rdly, 1948, Muriel (80 Comares Ave, St Augustine, Florida 32084, USA), only da of late Sydney Haslett, of St Leonards-on-Sea, Sussex:—
(By 1st *m*) Maryel Susan, *b* 1935: *m* 1965, Peter Callanan Battin, of Albany, NY, USA, and has issue living, Peter Ramsay, *b* 1970, — Maia Hope, *b* 1967. —— (By 2nd *m*) Catherine Ann, *b* 1938: *m* 1st, 1959 (*m diss* 1969), Russell Payson, of Cambridge, Mass, USA; 2ndly, 1970 (*m diss* 1973), Peter Alexander Altman, of Washington, DC, USA, and has issue living (by 1st *m*), Gilbert Russell, *b* 1962, — Katherine Ann, *b* 1964. —— Priscilla Maud, *b* 1940: *m* 1968, Robert Taylor Adams, of Richmond, Virginia, USA, and has issue living, Priscilla Susan, *b* 1972.

RAMSAY (UK) 1806, of Balmain, Kincardineshire

Sir ALEXANDER WILLIAM BURNETT RAMSAY, 7th *Baronet*; *b* 4 Aug 1938; *s* his father, *Sir* ALEXANDER BURNETT, 1965; the presumed heir to the Baronetcy of Burnett of Leys (*cr* 1626): *m* 1963, Neryl Eileen, da of J. C. Smith Thornton of Trangie, NSW, and has issue.

Arms – Argent, an eagle displayed sable, beaked and membered gules, charged on the breast with a rose of the field. **Crest** – A demi-eagle displayed sable.
Residence – Banchory, PO Box 274, Warren, NSW 2824, Australia.

Aspiro

I aspire

SONS LIVING

ALEXANDER DAVID, *b* 20 Aug 1966: *m* 1990, Annette Yvonne, da of M. Plummer, of Trigoona, Tottenham, NSW, and has issue living, Kate Victoria, *b* 1995, — Saye, *b* 1997. —— Ian John, *b* 1968: *m* 1993, Kerry Louise, da of L. Calvert, of Warren, NSW. —— David Burnett, *b* 1971: *m* 1998, Alexandra Richmond.

SISTERS LIVING

Enid Ellice, *b* 1937: *m* 1961, Reginald Geoffrey Capel, who *d* 1999, of Calool, Manilla, NSW, and has issue living, Peter Geoffrey, *b* 1963: *m* 1992, Louise Johnston, and has issue living, Jock Ian Geoffrey *b* 1997, — Dianna Enid, *b* 1965: *m* 1994, Alexander William Campbell Martin, of Jamestown, SA, and has issue living, Isabel Dianna *b* 19—, Rachel Ellice *b* 1998. —— Patricia Thirza, *b* 1940: *m* 1965, Anthony Osborne McAlary, of Milawa, Warren, NSW, and has issue living, Anthony Alexander, *b* 1970, — Anna, *b* 1968.

AUNT LIVING (*Daughter of 5th baronet*)

Constance Agnes, *b* 1912: *m* 1938, Arthur Thomas Baldwin (Bundilla, Young, NSW, Australia), who *d* 1977, and has issue living, Ross Ramsay, *b* 1943: *m* 1971, Susan Joan, da of S. R. Oldham, of Matta Mia, Wagga Wagga, NSW, and has issue living, Angus Oldham *b* 1972, Richard Arthur *b* 1973, — Malcolm Ramsay (Brisendon Av, Collaroy, NSW, Australia), *b* 1946, Janet Mabel, *b* 1941: *m* 1962, John Lyle Francis, of Tara, Mumbril, NSW, Australia, son of G. H. Francis, and has issue living, Hubert Thomas Lyle *b* 1967, Regina Constance *b* 1965: *m* 1999, Andrew Parkes (and has issue living, Lucy *b* 1999).

COLLATERAL BRANCHES LIVING

Issue of late Herbert William Alexander Ramsay, yr son of 5th baronet, *b* 1907, *d* 1987: *m* 1936, Bessie Billingsley, who *d* 1997, yst da of Dr Wilfred Billingsley Dight, of Sydney, NSW, Australia:—
William Macalister (Girraween, Bonshaw, NSW, Australia), *b* 1939: *m* 1967, Susan Thornton, da of R T Parkinson, of Camla, Wellington, and has issue living, Timothy William, *b* 1969. — William Ross, *b* 1971, — Jennifer Susan, *b* 1972. —— Elizabeth Barton, *b* 1945: *m* 1966, Peter Angus Gough, of 8 Crane Place, Moree, NSW, Australia, and has issue living, Simon John, *b* 1972, — Phillipa Anne, *b* 1968: *m* 1st, 1989, Stephen John Smith; 2ndly, 19—, Andrew Paul Maguire, of 7 Myall Place, Moree, NSW, Australia, and has issue living, (by 1st *m*) Nicola Elizabeth Winter *b* 1994, — Sandra Elizabeth, *b* 1969: *m* 1995, Kevin Law, and has issue living, Kate Elizabeth *b* 19—. —— Roslyn Barton, *b* 1946: *m* 1st, 1967, Geoffrey Robert Burcham, who *d* 1998; 2ndly, 1987, Keith Donald Glasson, of Kingaroy, Queensland,

Australia, and has issue living, (by 1st *m*) David William, *b* 1969, — Jacqueline Judith, *b* 1971, — Georgina Elizabeth, *b* 1979.

Granddaughter of late Hugh Francis Ramsay, 2nd son of 3rd baronet:—
Issue of late Hugh Entwistle Ramsay, *b* 1871, *d* 1960: *m* 1901, Elsie Lavater, who *d* 1960, da of William Cox:—
Irene Beatrice, *b* 1902: *m* 1929, Ivor George Sullivan, who *d* 1955, and has issue living, Ramsay Wakeford (4460 Cottonwood Drive, Burlington, Ontario, Canada), *b* 1933: *m* 1957, Eleanor Mary Thorpe, and has issue living, Richard Andrew Ramsay *b* 1960, Fiona Clare *b* 1962, Jennifer Mary *b* 1965, — Patricia Berenice, *b* 1934; ARCA: *m* 1961, Professor Michael Edward Mallett, DPhil, of 2 Lansdowne Circus, Leamington Spa, and has issue living, Lucien Christian Ramsay *b* 1976, Cyprian Casper Alexander *b* 1978.

Grandchildren of late Hugh Entwistle Ramsay (ante):—
Issue of late Alexander Hugh Ramsay, *b* 1905, *d* 1962: *m* 1937, Ethel Charlotte, who *d* 1993, da of late Albert Upton, of Waimai, NZ:—
Patricia Marion, *b* 1945: *m* 1976, Carl Donald Tyndale Watson-Gandy, PhD, of 3 South Lodge, Stanton Fitzwarren, Swindon, Wilts SN6 7SF, and has issue living, Hugh James Ramsay, *b* 1981, — (Jane) Vere, *b* 1979. —— Eleanor Margaret, *b* 1949: *m* 1991, Serge Artemiev, of 12 Stansell St, Shannon, Levin, NZ.

Issue of late John Entwisle Ramsay, *b* 1908, *ka* 1942: *m* 1937, Elizabeth Frances, da of A. H. Crichton, of Kelowna, British Columbia:—
Ian Alexander (62 Lemington Rd, Westmere, Auckland, NZ), *b* 1939: *m* 1st, 1963 (*m diss* 1988), Rosalind Sheila Tolliss, of Hildenborough, Kent; 2ndly, 1988, Lorraine Gillian Kelly, and has two sons (by 1st *m*) Norman Francis, *b* 1967, — Nicholas John, *b* 1968, — (by 2nd *m*) Alexandra Grace, *b* 1988.

Grandson of late Noel Bannerman Ramsay (infra):—
Issue of late Lieut Noel Entwistle Burnett Ramsay, RNVR, *b* 1907, *ka* 1942: *m* 1932, Phyllis Agnes, who *d* 1999 (having *m* 2ndly, 1949, Lt-Col Eric T. Cuthbert, who *d* 1974, and 3rdly, 1982, Ronald George Fielder, FICS, who *d* 1996) da of Arthur H. Kilner:—
Rev Canon Alan Burnett (St Marks Vicarage, Locks Lane, Mitcham, Surrey CR4 2JX), *b* 1934; AKC: *m* 1967, Elisabeth, da of Norman Marsh, and has issue living, Christopher, *b* 1968, — Matthew John, *b* 1971, — Francis, *b* 1973, — Rachel, *b* 1969.

Grandchildren of late Lieut Noel Entwistle Burnett Ramsay, RNVR (ante):—
Issue of late Duncan Soutter Burnett Ramsay, *b* 1937, *d* 1988: *m* 1967, Carole Anne (17 Lambourn Gdns, Harpenden, Herts), da of late D. H. Briars:—
Benjamin Noel, *b* 1969. —— Daniel Bruce, *b* 1971. —— Helen Jayne, *b* 1973.

Granddaughter of late Hugh Francis Ramsay (ante):—
Issue of late Noel Bannerman Ramsay, *b* 1875, *d* 1958: *m* 1905, Edith Katharine, who *d* 1962, da of Francis Johnson, MD:—
Edith Rosemary Patricia, *b* 1915: *m* 1st, 1937, Thomas Martin Homfray Pardoe, Capt 2nd Batn Worcestershire Regt, who was *ka* Hong Kong 1941; 2ndly, 1943, Col Thomas Brian Carey, RA, who *d* 1970; 3rdly, 1975, Prof James Carl Gilbert, Univ of Hawaii, and has issue living, (by 1st *m*) Hermione Ann Felicity, — (by 2nd *m*) Shane Peter, *b* 1944, — Peter Brian Ramsay, *b* 1948. *Residences* – Rigden's Farm, Leigh, nr Reigate, Surrey; 2969 Kalakaua Av, Honolulu, Hawaii 96815, USA.

Issue of late Capt John Ramsay, 3rd son of 3rd baronet, *b* 1843, *d* 1913: *m* 1876, Florence Mary, who *d* 1936, only child of late Richard J. Hilton, of Preston House, Faversham:—
Ethel, MBE, *b* 1882; MBE (Civil) 1918: *m* 1906, Major William Thompson Armitage, formerly RA. —— Hilda, *b* 1885: *m* (Jan) 1912, Eugene Spinney, and has issue living, David John, *b* Oct 1912, — Martin Giles, *b* 1916, — Juliet Ethel, *b* 1914. —— Evelyn, *b* 1887: *m* 1909, Cuthbert Radcliffe, who *d* 1924, and has issue living, Richard, *b* 1912, — Norman, *b* 1914, — Michael, *b* 1918.

Grandsons of late Brig-Gen William Alexander Ramsay, el son of Capt Francis Ramsay, 3rd son of 2nd baronet:—
Issue of late Adm Sir Bertram Home Ramsay, KCB, KBE, MVO, *b* 1883, *ka* 1945: *m* 1929, Helen Margaret, who *d* 1993, da of Col Charles Thomson Menzies, of Kames, Greenlaw, Berwickshire:—
David Francis (74857 South Cove Drive, Indian Wells, Calif 92210, USA). *Club* – New (Edinburgh), *b* 1933; *ed* Eton, and Camb Univ (BA): *m* 1st, 1963 (*m diss* 1973), Stacey Rogers; 2ndly, 1988, Pamela —, of Calif, USA, and has issue living (by 1st *m*), Michael Stuart, *b* 1964; *ed* Stanbridge Earls: *m* 1993, Beatriz, da of Jesus Paris Gonzales Trapiello, of Aviles, Spain, and has issue living, William Bertram Alexander *b* 1997, — James Alexander, *b* 1967; *ed* Eton, and Bristol Univ. —— Charles Alexander (Bughtrig, Coldstream, Berwicks TD12 4JP; Chesthill, Glenlyon, Perthshire; *Clubs* – Boodle's, Cavalry and Guards', and New (Edinburgh)), *b* 1936; *ed* Eton, and RMC; served R Scots Greys; Maj-Gen 1984 a Member of Queen's Body Guard for Scotland (Royal Company of Archers): *m* 1967, Hon Mary Margaret Hastings MacAndrew, da of 1st Baron MacAndrew, PC, TD, and has issue living, William Bertram, *b* 1969; *ed* Eton, Newcastle Univ (BA), and RMA Sandhurst; commn'd Royal Scots Dragoon Gds 1992: *m* 1997, Natasha Alexandra, da of Lt-Col Dudley Gordon de Chair, of Tulloch, Inverness-shire (*see* D Fife, colls), — Charles Burnett, *b* 1981; *ed* Eton, — Rowena Cecilia, *b* 1973; *ed* Edinburgh Univ, — Camilla Georgina, *b* 1976; *ed* Northumbria Univ.

Grandchildren of late Marmaduke Francis Ramsay, eldest son of late Robert Ramsay (infra):—
Issue of late Robert Ottiwell Ramsay, *b* 1900, *d* 1996: *m* 1937, Constance Aileen (Kinblethmont, Arbroath, Angus), only da of late Maj Hugh Bernard German, MC, RAMC:—
Robert David (Kinblethmont, by Arbroath, Angus DD11 4RW), *b* 1942; *ed* Harrow, and Glasgow Univ (BSc 1965): *m* 1966, Penelope Anne, only da of Michael Gladstone, of Gt Shelford, Cambridge, and has issue living, Robert Nicholas, *b* 1968; *ed* Harrow, and Reading Univ: *m* 1993, Jessica, da of Sir Robin John Taylor McLaren, KCMG, of Wimbledon

SW19, and has issue living, Thomas *b* 1996, Nicholas *b* 1998, — Alexander John, *b* 1969; *ed* Harrow, and Brasenose Coll, Oxford: *m* 1999, Elizabeth Anne, only da of Colin Archer, of Richmond, Yorks, — Jonathan Charles, *b* 1973; *ed* Harrow, Edinburgh Univ, and Leeds Coll of Music. —— John Lauderdale, *b* 1945; *ed* Harrow. —— Sarah Margaret (*Dowager Madam Campbell of Dunstaffnage*), *b* 1937: *m* 1st, 1962 (*m diss* 1973), Capt David John Walter Anstice, 10th Royal Hussars, son of Vice Adm Sir Edmund Walter Anstice, KCB; 2ndly, 1976, as his 2nd wife, Michael John Eadon Campbell of Dunstaffnage, 21st Hereditary Capt of Dunstaffnage, who *d* 1981, of Dunstaffnage Castle, Connel, Argyllshire, and has issue living (by 1st *m*), Christian Edmund, *b* 1963, — David Henry, *b* 1964, — James Richard, *b* 1965. —— Lavinia Jane (Nerja, Spain), *b* 1938: *m* 1959, Patrick Robert Chalmers, who *d* 1982, and has had issue, Patrick Robert Graham, *b* 1960: *m* 1990, Josien Posthumus, and has issue living, Jonathon Patrick Hendrik *b* 1995, Lydia Lara *b* 1992, — Virginia Jane, *b* 1961: *m* 1993, Timothy Paul Staples, and has issue living, James Marshal *b* 19—, — Lindsay, *b* 1962, *d* 1998, leaving issue, Daisy Olivia *b* 1996, — Nicola Catherine, *b* 1964. —— Aileen Susanna, *b* 1941: *m* 1964, Colin Gibb, of Inshewan, Forfar, and has issue living, John Alexander, *b* 1968, — Shanestra Margaret, *b* 1966.

      Grandchildren of late Robert Ramsay, son of late Capt Robert Ramsay, 3rd son of 1st baronet:—
      Issue of late Robert Christian Ramsay, *b* 1861, *d* 1957: *m* 1907, Olive Zillah, who *d* 1957, da of W. W. Voss, of Penrice, Queensland:—
Alexander Robert (44/10 Lower River Terrace, S Brisbane, Qld 4101, Australia), *b* 1910; Cdr RNVR; 1939-45 War (DSC and Bar): *m* 1944, Helen MacGregor, da of J. M. Shaw, of Lisburn, co Antrim, and has issue living, Colin Robert (87 Gurney Crescent, Seaforth, Sydney, Australia), *b* 1945: *m* 1968, Lyndall Clare Sundstrom, of Gatton, Qld, and has issue living, Robert Andrew *b* 1974, Susan Belinda *b* 1976, Sandra Leigh *b* 1977, — Celia Grace, *b* 1947: *m* 1st, 1966 (*m diss* 1974 in Zimbabwe), 10th Viscount Chetwynd; 2ndly, 1974, Geoffrey Burnett-Smith, of 13 Gloucester Av, Belair, S Australia, and has issue living, (by 1st *m*) (*see* V Chetwynd), (by 2nd *m*) Angus *b* 1977, — Alexandra Helen Fleur, *b* 1955: *m* 1st, 1977, Iain Lovat Fraser, who was *ka* 1978; 2ndly, 1986, Terrence John Tarlinton, of 40/10 Lower River Terrace, S Brisbane, Qld 4101, Aust. —— †David Malcolm (The Woodlands, Navenby, Lincoln), *b* 1924: *m* 1948, Joan Esme, da of C. J. Murphy, and *d* 1995, leaving issue, Alan David (PO Box 408, Unley, Adelaide, S Aust 5061), *b* 1951: *m* 19—, Janice Boardman, and has issue living, Miranda Christine *b* 1980, — *Rev* James Anthony, *b* 1952: *m* 1st, 19— (*m diss* 19—), Anne Depaulis; 2ndly, 19—, Celia Wood, — Oliver Dermot (McBride, BC, Canada), *b* 1954: *m* 1st, 19— (*m diss* 19—), Susan Eriksen; 2ndly, 19—, Maureen Knowles, and has issue living, Jesse *b* 1980, Kevin *b* 1982, Nikolas *b* 1989, — Malcolm Robert, *b* 1956. —— Olive Joan, *b* 1916: *m* 1948, Wing-Cdr Eric Comyn Boucher, RAF, who *d* 1981, and has issue living, Angus Comyn, *b* 1949, — Esther Dawn, *b* 1951, — Vanessa Jayne, *b* 1954. *Residence* – The Hollies, Bredgar, Kent.

      Issue of late Arthur Douglas Ramsay, OBE, *b* 1868, *d* 1952: *m* 1914, Winifred who *d* 1979, da of W. H. Turner, of Geraldton, W Aust:—
Susan Patricia (18 Cristowe Rd, SW6), *b* 1926: *m* 1st 1950 (*m diss* 1965), Maj Sir Francis David Somerville Head, 5th Bt; 2ndly, 1967 (*m diss* 1988), Henry Jagoe Shaw, FRCS, and has issue (by 1st *m*) (*see* Head, Bt).

      Grandson of late Arthur Douglas Ramsay (ante):—
      Issue of late Capt Michael Douglas Ramsay, Seaforth Highlanders, *b* 1918, *d* 1983: *m* 1949, Eleanor Kinsell (Lyford Cay, PO Box N7776, Nassau, Bahamas), of Florida, USA:—
Jonathan Chandler Burnett, *b* 1950: *m* 1979, Keren Jane Livingstone-Leonard, and has issue living, Alexander Douglas Burnett, *b* 1984, — Kia Nikisha Burnett, *b* 1982. *Residence* – Aerie, PO Box N52, Nassau, Bahamas.

  Sir Alexander, 1st Bt (2nd son of Sir Thomas Burnett of Leys, 6th (*see* Burnett, Bt)), by his wife Catherine, sister of Sir Alexander Ramsay of Balmain, 6th and last Bt, succeeded his uncle in the Ramsay estates 1806, and assumed, by Roy licence, the surname and arms of Ramsay. Sir John Ramsay, *cr* Lord Bothwell 1485 and killed at Flodden 1513, was ancestor of Sir Gilbert Ramsay of Balmain, 1st Bt (*cr* 1625).

Ramsay-Fairfax-Lucy (Cameron-Ramsay-Fairfax-Lucy), see Lucy.

Ramsay-Steel-Maitland, see Maitland.

RAMSDEN (E) 1689, of Byram, Yorkshire

Sir JOHN CHARLES JOSSLYN RAMSDEN, 9th *Baronet*; *b* 19 Aug 1950; *s* his father, *Maj Sir* CARYL OLIVER IMBERT, CMG, CVO, 1987; *ed* Eton, and Trin Coll, Camb (MA); HM Foreign Ser: *m* 1985, (Jennifer) Jane, yr da of Rear Adm Christopher Martin Bevan, CB, of Cranborne, Dorset, and has issue.

𝔄rms – Argent on a chevron between three fleurs-de-lis sable, as many ram's heads couped at the neck argent. 𝔠rest – A cubit arm in armour proper, the gauntlet holding a fleur-de-lis sable.
Address – c/o Foreign and Commonwealth Office, King Charles St, SW1.

DAUGHTERS LIVING

Isobel Lucy, *b* 1987. —— Stella Evelyn, *b* 1989.

DAUGHTERS LIVING OF SEVENTH BARONET

Phyllida Rosemary, *b* 1929: *m* 1955, Patrick Thomas Gordon-Duff-Pennington, OBE, DL (who assumed by deed poll 1955, the final surname of Pennington), and has issue living, Prunella Melissa Phyllida, *b* 1956: *m* 1980, Donald Gordon, of 9 East Rd, N Berwick, E Lothian, — Anthea, *b* 1958: *m* 1982, Timothy Charles Osborn-Jones, of 3 Norman Av, Henley-on-Thames, Oxon, son of Rev Arthur Osborn-Jones, of 24 Ainsworth Av, Ovingdean, Brighton, and has issue living, Rupert Alexander *b* 1987, Katharine Louisa *b* 1986, — Iona Arabel, *b* 1961: *m* 1988, Peter Edward Frost (who assumed the surname of Frost Pennington 1988), son of Robert C. Frost, of Balloch, Inverness-shire, and has issue living, Ewan Patrick *b* 1990, Fraser Robert *b* 1991, Isla Rose *b* 1993, — Rowena, *b* 1963: *m* 1987, (Martin) Robert Morris-Eyton, of Hallbeck, Whicham, Millom, Cumbria LA18 5LU, only son of John Reginald Morris-Eyton, of Beckside, Whicham, Millom, Cumbria, and has issue living, Patrick Geordie *b* 1993, Isobel Rosemary *b* 1989, Rebecca Melissa *b* 1991. *Residence* – Muncaster Castle, Ravenglass, Cumbria CA18 1RQ. —— Penelope Lucinda, *b* 1930: *m* 1958, Peter Anthony Neville Pennethorne Laing, of Turweston Manor, Turweston, Brackley, Northants, and has issue living, Arabella Charlotte Lucinda, *b* 1960: *m* 1988, Toby James Foster, elder son of David Foster, of Lea Farm, Stopham, Sussex, and has issue living, Alexandra Constance Harriet *b* 1990, Prudence Charlotte Victoria *b* 1993, Hermione Lydia Grace *b* 1998, — Venetia Alexandra Veronica Cayetana, *b* 1961: *m* 1987, James Anthony Findlay, eldest son of John Findlay, of Carnell, Kilmarnock, and has issue living, Christopher Anthony Genghus *b* 1991, Oliver Angus Ruaridh *b* 1995. —— Annabel (Versions Farm, Brackley, Northants), *b* 1931: *m* 1958, Col (Edward) Timothy Smyth-Osbourne, Coldm Gds, who *d* 1987, and has issue living, Charles William (Rectory Farm, Sulgrave, Banbury, Oxon OX17 2SG), *b* 1959: *m* 1986, Joanna Mary, elder da of Sir Hugh Guy Cubitt, CBE (*see* B Ashcombe), and has issue living, Edward John *b* 1988, William Hugh *b* 1991, Archie Alexander *b* 1994, — Julian George (Highfields Stables, Adstone, Towcester, Northants), *b* 1964: *m* 1990, Claudia A., yr da of late C. N. R. Procter, of Ripon, N Yorks, and has issue living, Luke *b* 1996, Timothy *b* 1998, Sophie Charlotte *b* 1997, — Michael Alexander, *b* 1967: *m* 1997, Annabel Claire, elder da of late Brian David Bond, and of Mrs Robin Thorne, of Ovington House, nr Alresford, Hants (*see* Pollock, Bt, colls), — Rachel Rosa, *b* 1961: *m* 1989 (*m diss* 1994), Robert Drysdale, yst son of late W. A. Drysdale, and has issue living, Francis William *b* 1992, Veronica Mary *b* 1991.

SISTER LIVING OF SEVENTH BARONET

Mary Joyce (*Lady Feilden*), *b* 1907: *m* 1929, Maj-Gen Sir Randle Guy Feilden, KCVO, CB, CBE, Coldstream Guards, who *d* 1981 (*see* V Hampden, colls). *Residences* – Cot Farm, Minster Lovell, Oxford OX8 5RS; Aberardur Lodge, nr Newtonmore, Inverness-shire PH20 1BX.

WIDOW LIVING OF EIGHTH BARONET

ANNE (*Anne, Lady Ramsden*), elder da of Lt-Col Sir Charles George Wickham, KCMG, KBE, DSO, of Ashdene, Comber, co Down: *m* 1945, Maj Sir Caryl Oliver Imbert Ramsden, 8th Bt, CMG, CVO, who *d* 1987. *Residence* – Vallance Cottage, Upper Chute, nr Andover, Hants SP11 9EH.

COLLATERAL BRANCHES LIVING

Issue of late John St Maur Ramsden, el son of 6th Baronet, *b* 1902, *d* 1948: *m* 1935 (*m diss* 1948), Lady Catherine Mary Clementine Heathcote-Drummond-Willoughby, who *d* 1990, da of 2nd Earl of Ancaster (*see* Bs Willoughby de Eresby):—
(Eloise) Carola, *b* 1938: *m* 1st, 1961, George Fillmore Miller III; 2ndly, 1974, Robert E. J. Philippi, and has issue living, (by 1st *m*) Sebastian St Maur, *b* 1965; Capt The Blues and Royals: *m* 1991, Emma Caroline, da of John Harries, of Esher, Surrey, — (by 2nd *m*) James Jeremy George, *b* 1975. *Residence* – Kinlochlaggan, Inverness-shire

Granddaughter of late Capt John Charles Francis Ramsden, son of late Capt Henry James Ramsden, 3rd son of 4th baronet:—
Issue of late Lieut-Col Henry RAMSDEN-JODRELL, CMG, *b* 1871, *d* 1950 (having assumed by Roy Licence 1920 the

additional surname of Jodrell): *m* 1902, Dorothy Lynch, CBE, JP, who *d* 1958, el da of late Col Sir Edward Thomas Davenant Cotton-Jodrell, KCB (V Combermere, colls):—
Mary Angela (*Lady Fielden*), *b* 1916: *m* 1940, Air Vice-Marshal Sir Edward Hedley Fielden, GCVO, CB, DFC, AFC, RAF, who *d* 1976, and has issue living, Fiona, *b* 1944: *m* 1966, Christopher Norman Hart, of Eastcourt Farm, Crudwell, Malmesbury, Wilts. *Residence* – Park Thatch, Sutton Manor, Sutton Scotney, Winchester, Hants SO21 3JX.

Granddaughter of late Robert Henry Ramsden, son of late Robert John Ramsden, son of Robert Ramsden (*b* 1784), of Carlton Hall, Notts, son of Robert Ramsden (*b* 1753), of Carlton Hall, Notts, son of Robert Ramsden, of Osberton, Notts, 4th son of 2nd baronet:—
Issue of late Robert Charles Plumptre Ramsden, *b* 1874, *d* 1964: *m* 1934, Mary Isiline (who *m* 2ndly, 1964, David William Smith, of Wigthorpe Hill, Wigthorpe, Worksop), only da of Lt-Col W. Wetwan, of Ashley Grove, Worksop:—
Mary, *b* 1938: *m* 1960, William Arthur Butroid, of Wigthorpe Farm, Wigthorpe, Worksop, Notts S81 8BT, son of Herbert Butroid, and has had issue, Christine Joanna, *b* 1961: *m* 1994, Andrew Jonathan Walker, son of George Geoffrey Walker, of Whitwell, and has issue living, William George Butroid *b* 1996, — Sarah Isiline, *b* 1963, *d* 1984, — Janet Elizabeth, *b* 1965: *m* 1995, Iain Turley, son of late William Turley, of Lesmahagow, and has issue living, Lisa Mary *b* 1999.

Grandchildren of late Edward Plumptre Ramsden (infra):—
Issue of late (John Edward) Cecil Ramsden, *b* 1881, *d* 1933: *m* 1907, Mabel, who *d* 1950, da of Rev Samuel Hewlett:—
†Robin John Edward, *b* 2 Sept 1917: *m* 1942, Mary Veronica, da of John Francis Kenny, and *d* 3 Oct 1967, leaving issue, COLIN JOHN (Tasmania), *b* 22 Jan 1949: *m* 1st, 1976 (*m diss* 19—), Kim O'Halloran; 2ndly, 1994, Sandra Robinson, and has issue living, (by 1st *m*) Richard *b* 1979, Angela Lee *b* 1981, (by 2nd *m*) Rachael Mary *b* 1996, — Robyn Anne, *b* 1953: *m* 19—, Ross Anderson, and has issue living, Steele *b* 1985, Storm *b* 1983. —— Louisa Margaret, *b* 1909: *m* 1940, Herbert Gibbons Hooper, who *d* 1987, and *d* 1995, having had issue. —— Annie Elizabeth, *b* 1911, *m* 1933, Trevor Maxwell Cooper, who *d* 1978, and *d* 1956, leaving issue. —— Charlotte Mabel, *b* 1913: *m* 1933, Lindsey Llewelyn Bramwell Dew, who *d* 1990, and has issue living. —— Edith Catherine, *b* 1920: *m* 19—, W. Elliott, and *d* 1966, leaving issue. —— Ruth May, *b* 19—: *m* 19—, Owen Etherton, and has issue living.

Issue of late William Eustace Ramsden, *b* 1882, *d* 1967: *m* 1909, Camelia Jane, who *d* 1971, da of Henry Mutlow Biddle:—
†Charles Arthur, *b* 1911: *m* 1938, Irene, who *d* 1996, da of John James Day, of Birregurra, Victoria, Aust, and *d* 1991, leaving issue, William Arthur (PO Box 405, Currie, King Island, Tasmania 7256, Aust), *b* 1938: *m* 1st, 1963 (*m diss* 1992), Pamela Jean, da of Roy Manning Richards; 2ndly, 1993, Barbara Cazaly, and has issue living, (by 1st *m*) William John *b* 1978, Sandra Jean *b* 1966: *m* 1993, Michael Shane East (and has issue living, Nathan William *b* 1996, Aaron Michael *b* 1998), Cherie Lynn *b* 1969: *m* 1989, Peter William Caddy (and has issue living, Brett William *b* 1990, Dale Peter *b* 1992, Kaine Winton *b* 1994), — Raymond Noel (37 Brookman St, Esperance 6450, W Aust), *b* 1940: *m* 1960, Janice Martha Maguire, and has issue living, Jennifer Anne *b* 1960, Denise Irene *b* 1963: *m* 1995, Desmond Hazel (and has issue living, Bredon James *b* 1996, Serena Ann *b* 1998), Anne-Maree *b* 1969 (and has issue living, by John Thomas O'Dea, Sean Patrick *b* 1994, Ryan Jessie *b* 1996), — (Marlene) Joyce, *b* 1939: *m* 1960, Ian James Valentine, and has issue living, Peter James *b* 1960: *m* 1986, Sandra Janet Mogridge (and has issue living, Timothy James *b* 1987, Jeffrey Arthur *b* 1988, Michael Shane *b* 1990, Ciara May *b* 1993), Gregory Paul *b* 1966: *m* 1991, Rachel Clare Matthews (and has issue living, Astrid Ruby *b* 1998), Julie Gaye *b* 1962: *m* 1985, Neal Vivian (and has issue living, Matthew Paul *b* 1987, Robert Neal *b* 1988, Brendan James *b* 1992, Stephen Thomas *b* 1998), — Aileen Patricia, *b* 1942: *m* 1961, Raymond Edward Fearnley, and has issue living, Mark Raymond *b* 1962 (and has issue living, by Rosalind Gail Turner, Aaron Raymond *b* and *d* 1989, Nicholas Charles *b* (twin) and *d* 1989, Damien Mark *b* 1990, Kayla Jean *b* 1988, Bianca Aileen *b* 1997, Cassandra Irene *b* (twin) 1997), Paul Robert *b* 1964: *m* 1st, 1985 (*m diss* 1991), Donna Marita Lade; 2ndly, 1997, Kerry Leanne Powney (and has issue living, by 1st *m*, Courtney Lee *b* 1987, by 2nd wife, Jake Raymond *b* 1994, Clancee Shaye *b* 1995), Rayleen *b* 1968: *m* 1989, Bruce David Glover (and has issue living, Ryan Bruce *b* 1991, Joshua Aaron *b* 1993, Taylor Aileen Bernice *b* 1998), — (Judith) Gaye (Port Welshpool, Victoria 3965, Aust), *b* 1948: *m* 1964, Philip Allan Stephens, and has issue living, Craig Allan *b* 1964: *m* 1992, Jennifer Lee Scales (and has issue living, Samuel Allan *b* 1993, Curtis Lee *b* 1999, Anna Rose Celeste *b* 1995), Vicki Marie *b* 1966: *m* 1986, Terence Athanas Stoitse (and has had issue, Shane Athanus *b* 1987, *d* 1992, Wade Athanus *b* 1994, Vanessa Gaye *b* 1989, Kristina Shauna *b* 1997), Kim Joy *b* 1969 (and has had issue, by Anthony James LeBlanc, Phillip John *b* 1995, James Arthur *b* and *d* 1998, Rebecca Storm *b* 1993). —— †William Pemberton (Noel), *b* 1912, *d* 1919. —— Frances Elizabeth, *b* 1910: *m* 1938, Rev Harold Percival Keith Gordon, who *d* 1992, and *d* 1964, leaving issue, David Leander, *b* 1943: *m* 1965, Faye D'Esterre Wray, and has issue living, Rodney D'Esterre *b* 1972, Jeffery Mark *b* 1974: *m* 1996, Jennifer Lexley Buxton (and has issue living, Mitchell Thomas *b* 1997), — Karl Soren, *b* 1946: *m* 1969, Kay Robertson, and has issue living, Rohan Leslie *b* 1973, Cameron James *b* 1974, Shannon Stuart *b* 1979, — Beryl, *b* 1939: *m* 1966, Alexander Hamilton Hill, and has issue living, Malcolm Alexander *b* 1967, Stuart Gordon *b* 1968: *m* 1997, Susan Nicole Ferris (and has issue living, Jarrod Samuel *b* 1998), Andrew Keith *b* 1970: *m* 1992, Carolyn Francis Scammell (and has issue living, Lachlan Joe *b* 1996, Austin Tyler *b* 1997), — Yvonne (10 Shoubra Drive, Highton, Victoria 3216, Aust), *b* 1940: *m* 1962, Charles John Fox, and has had issue, Darren John *b* 1967: *m* 1992, Joanne Maree Clissold, Joanne Tricia *b* and *d* 1963, Deanne Tricia *b* 1969: *m* 1993, Anthony Paul Kluytmans (and has issue living, Jarrod Michael *b* 1998), — Karmen, *b* 1944: *m* 1967, Eric Allan Pollock, and has issue living, Jonathan David *b* 1968: *m* 1991, Catherine Lee Dowse (and has issue living, Morgan David *b* 1996, Emily Beth *b* 1998), Andrew James *b* 1969: *m* 1993, Wendy Gaye McConville (and has issue living, Timothy Jordan *b* 1995, Joshua Lucas *b* 1997, Caroline Joy *b* 1998), — Glenda, *b* 1948: *m* 1968, Leslie William Leach, and has issue living, Damien Leslie *b* 1975, Michelle Elizabeth *b* 1971: *m* 1994, Scott Richard Quaill (and has issue living, Cory William *b* 1998), Rebecca Jane *b* 1973: *m* 1998, Scott Alpert Iseppi. —— Muriel Camella, *b* 1914: *m* 1st, 1934, Gordon Thomson, who *d* 1976; 2ndly, 1978, John Robert Sexton, who *d* 1991, and has issue living, (by 1st *m*) Kevin William John (98 Brisbane St, Berwick, Vic 3806 Aust), *b* 1936: *m* 1965, Alison Edith Dennis, and has issue living, Blair Gordon *b* 1974, Shelley Annette *b* 1967: *m* 1999, Dale Edward Burnside, Kathryn Jane *b* 1968, Dana Louise *b* 1972, Jillian Elizabeth *b* 1978, — Ailsa Muriel, *b* 1941; has resumed her maiden name of THOMSON: *m* 1963 (*m diss* 1980), Colin Stanley Lucas, and has issue living, Brett Anthony *b* 1967: *m* 1998, Nerissa Phipps, Karen Elizabeth *b* 1964: *m* 1986, Thomas Gregory Blakey (and has issue living, Daniel Gregory *b* 1990, Kahlia Elisa *b* 1992). —— Ila May (687 The Esplanade, Mornington, Vic 3931, Aust), *b* 1919: *m* 1940, Maurice Archibald Rhodes, and has issue living, Noel Maurice, *b* 1943: *m* 1968, Judith Alexandra Shardey, and has issue living, Alexander Noel *b* 1976, Colette Jane *b* 1971, Nicole Regina *b* 1973, — Carolyn May, *b* 1941: *m* 1962, Eldric William Marshall McKinley, and has issue living, Gavin Marshall *b* 1964: *m* 1991, Connie Leah Anne Cernec (and has issue living, Balin Thomas *b* 1997), Jason Rhodes *b* 1967: *m* 1992, Donna Catrine Wheeler (and has issue living, Rhodes Leighton *b* 1995, Tyla Sheridan *b* 1994), Edan Shane, *b* 1972: *m* 1st, 1992 (*m diss* 1995), Leca Landon; 2ndly, 1999, Donna Loone (and has issue living, (by 1st *m*) Jesse Edan *b* 1991, (by 2nd wife) Jordyn Lee *b* 1996), Callen Marcus *b* 1974, Hayden Maurice *b* 1979, Ilana Jane *b* 1976, Cara Lynne *b* 1984, — Meryl Patricia, *b* 1946: *m* 1970, Peter William James Ashworth, and has issue living, Travis Benjamin *b* 1971, Yolande Louise *b* 1972. —— Edna Beryl (11 Kenneth St, Belmont, Vic 3216, Aust), *b* 1924: *m* 1950, Edgar Robert Hoe, and has had issue, Roger Hadley, *b* 1955: *m* 1st, 1981 (*m diss* 1991), Debra Patricia Sherwood; 2ndly, 1996, Robyn Ann

Chamberlain, and has issue living, (by 1st *m*) Ashley James *b* 1984, — Lois Muriel, *b* 1952, *d* 1971, — Alison Jane, *b* 1959: *m* 1982, Gary Ian Stevenson, and has had issue, Krystle Jane *b* 1986, Beth Alison *b* 1988, *d* 1996. —— Eleanor Patricia (312 Jetty Rd, Drysdale, Vic 3222, Aust), *b* 1926: *m* 1951, Maxwell George Brown, and has had issue, Philip Maxwell, *b* 1952: *m* 1972, Lorraine Marjory McFarlane, and has issue living, Gavin Paul *b* 1972, Shane Andrew *b* 1975, Travis James *b* 1977, — Vaughan Robert, *b* 1955: *m* 1977, Nancy Elizabeth Buckenara, and has issue living, Matthew Leigh *b* 1982, Megan Elizabeth *b* 1980, Ellen May *b* 1988, — Owen Leigh, *b* 1956: *m* 1980, Heather Ann McPadden, and has issue living, Joel Michael *b* 1986, Kylie Jade *b* 1984, — Andrew William George, *b* (March) 1959, *d* (Sept) 1959, — Glenn Paul, *b* 1963, — Patricia Anne, *b* 1954: *m* 1974, Roger James Grant, and has issue living, Lachlan Craig *b* 1988, Michelle Lee *b* 1981, Andrea Jane *b* 1983, — Lynne Marijane, *b* 1962. —— Hazel Aileen Margaret (312 Jetty Rd, Drysdale, Vic 3222, Aust), *b* 1933: *m* 1957 (*m diss* 1968) Ian Macdonald Tonkin; 2ndly, 1968, Rex Archibald Smith, who *d* 1984, and has issue living (by 1st *m*) Alister William John, *b* 1958: *m* 1976 (*m diss* 1980) Jan Bennet; 2ndly, 1984, Jan Stuart, and has issue living (by 1st *m*) Travis John *b* 1978; has issue living (by Chantelle Knight), Troy John *b* 1996, — Malcolm Ian David TONKIN-SMITH (12 Holyman St, Scullin, ACT 2614, Aust), *b* 1962; adopted additional surname of SMITH by Deed Poll 1987: *m* 1987, Bernadette Maree Clouton, and has issue living, Steven James *b* 1984, Matthew Scott *b* 1988, Benjamin James *b* 1992, Samantha-Lee *b* 1986, Courtney Maree *b* 1994, — Susanne Margaret, *b* 1959: *m* 1981 (*m diss* 1982), Andrew Valintine Fairall, and has issue living, Kirsty Maree *b* 1980; has issue (by Mark Nells), Melonie Jayne SMITH *b* 1978, (by Joe Urosevic), Kassie Jillian SMITH-FAIRALL *b* 1986, — Fiona Christina Jane, *b* 1964: *m* 1987 (*m diss* 1992), John Ken Banks, and has issue living, Jay Dyllon *b* 1986, Bobbi Jayne *b* 1989; has issue (by Kevin Carter), Krystle Aileen CARTER *b* 1983.

Granddaughters of late Robert John Ramsden, son of late Robert Ramsden (*b* 1784) (ante):—
Issue of late Edward Plumptre Ramsden, *b* 1848, *d* 1916: *m* 1875, Frances Elizabeth, who *d* 1941, da of William Kelly, of Blackheath, SW:—
Mary Louise, *b ca* 1877: *m* 1897, Frank Cavanagh Grace, and died leaving issue. —— Frances Eleanor, *b ca* 1878: *m* 1910, George Herbert McKay, and died leaving issue. —— Elizabeth Amy, *b* 1885: *m ca* 1959, ..., and died without issue. —— Charlotte Emma, *b* 1889: *m* 19—, Alec White, and died without issue. —— Leila Margaret, *b* 1891: *m* 19—, Ernest Marsh, and died without issue. —— A son and two daughters died in infancy.

Grandchildren of late Algernon Feilden Ramsden, 4th son of late Robert John Ramsden (ante):—
Issue of late Edward Feilden Ramsden, *b* 1893, *d* 1973: *m* 1928, Rhoda Helen, who *d* 1971, da of late Ashmore Mitchell, of Edinburgh:—
Geoffrey Ashmore, *b* 1930. —— Marjorie Neish, *b* 1929: *m* 1954, Paul Hastings Tennent, of 104 Lynton Rd, Acton, W3, and has issue living, Timothy Feilden, *b* 1955, — Stephen John, *b* 1958, — Adrian Paul, *b* 1961, — Mary Frances, *b* 1963.

Granddaughter of late Robert John Ramsden (ante):—
Issue of late John Pemberton Ramsden, *b* 1854, *d* 1911: *m* 1883, Alice Louisa, who *d* 1924, da of late Arthur Malet (Malet, Bt, colls):—
Frances Teresa: *m* 1928, James Tisdall Davidson.

Grandchildren of late Charles Harold Lowther Ramsden (infra):—
Issue of late Charles Dean Ramsden, BSc, *b* 1915, *d* 1981: *m* 1940, Katherine, who *d* 1979, da of Homer F. Lightfoot:—
Charles Anthony (178 Patricia Dr, Atherton, California, USA), *b* 1943; *ed* Stanford Univ (BSc, MBA); late Lieut USNR: *m* 1969, Naomi, da of Robert F. Robinson, MD, and has issue living, Abigail Leah, *b* 1976. —— Katherine Cecile, *b* 1945: *m* 1st, 1967 (*m diss* 1971), Grant A. Mitchell, late 2nd Lieut, US Army Res; 2ndly, 1972, Michael James Gannon, of 859 Acalanes Rd, Lafayette, California 94549, USA, and has issue living, (by 2nd *m*) Geoffrey Michael, *b* 1974, — Victoria Cecile, *b* 1976.

Grandchildren of late Charles Hamilton Ramsden, son of late Rev Charles Henry Ramsden, son of late Robert Ramsden (*b* 1784), grandson of late Robert Ramsden (*b* 1708), 4th son of 2nd baronet:—
Issue of late Charles Harold Lowther Ramsden, BSc, *b* 1883, *d* 1965: *m* 1st, 1912, Cecile W., who *d* 1933, da of W. S. Childs; 2ndly, 1936, Alice Voice, who *d* 1963, widow of William R. Henderson:—
(By 1st *m*) Scott Carlton (226 Hall Drive, Orinda, Cal, USA), *b* 1923; *ed* Cal Univ (BSc); late Lt, USN Reserve: *m* 1952, Mary Alice, da of Walter Garms, and has issue living, *Rev* Linda Alice (456 S 12th St, San Jose, Cal 95112, USA), *b* 1954; has an adopted son, Benjamin RAMSDEN-STEIN *b* 1984. —— Dorothy Childs (4720 W Continental Drive, Glendale, AZ 85308, USA), *b* 1913: *m* 1947, Paul R. Coombs, who *d* 1992, and has issue living, Walter Ramsden (3916 W Yucca Dr, Phoenix, Ariz, USA 85029), *b* 1950: *m* 1972, Joan Vivian, da of Robert Grant Comstock, and has issue living, Paul Charles *b* 1986, Michele Ramsden *b* 1979, — David Paul (3529 Newland Rd, Baltimore, Md, USA), *b* 1952: *m* 1974, Vivien Gale, da of Karnig Paternayan, and has issue living, Christopher Paternayan *b* 1983, Carolyn Paternayan *b* 1985, — Marjorie Cecile (2711 Ordway St NW, Washington, DC 20008, USA) *b* 1954. —— Helen Caroline, (twin) 1923: *m* 1946, Fred Albert Wagner, of 2405 Wedgewood Way, Livermore, Cal 94550, USA, and has issue living, Fred Albert, *b* 1950: *m* 1997, Mrs Dale Halton, widow of Phillip Halton, — Jay Thomas (1485 W Greenfield, Ann Arbor, MI 48108, USA), *b* 1952: *m* 1989, Debra Garcia Tearney, — Caroline Cecile, *b* 1948: *m* 1974, William Wesley Constable, of 8 Memory Lane, Clearlake Highlands, Calif 95422, USA, and has issue living, Remington Peter *b* 1983, Wendy Erin *b* 1979, — June Marseillette, *b* 1955: *m* 1978, David Robert Bedford, of 368 Beaten Path, Mooresville, NC 28115, USA, and has issue living, Ryan David *b* 1981, Lauren Anne *b* 1982.

Issue of late Percival Scott Webber Ramsden, *b* 1886, *d* 1968: *m* 1910, Abigail E., who *d* 1979, da of F. F. Philbrick:—
Shirley Carolyn (3721 Albion Little River Rd, Box 515, Albion, CA 95410, USA), *b* 1916: *m* 1942 (*m diss* 1948), Leslie A. Peek, and has had issue, Lynne, *b* 1943; *d* 1993. —— Marjorie (San Ramon, CA, USA), *b* 1917.

Grandchildren of late Cmdr Francis Edward Ramsden, RN, 3rd son of late Rev Charles Henry Ramsden (ante):—
Issue of late Francis Charles Home Ramsden, *b* 1880, *d* 1955: *m* 1927, Lilla Marguerite, da of Charles Mackenzie:—

Francis Birch (Box 670, Wembley, Alberta, Canada T0H 3S0), *b* 1928. ——— June Elizabeth (1430 72nd Av, Box 413, Grand Forks, BC, Canada V0H 1H0), *b* 1929: *m* 1952, Gordon Floyd Brox, and has issue living, Gary Allan, *b* 1954, — Wayne Dale, *b* 1959, — Dean Ross, *b* 1962.

Grandchildren of late Major Arthur Geoffrey Francis Ramsden, DSO, RA (infra):—
Issue of late Peter Derek Frecheville Ramsden, *b* 1922, *d* 1993: *m* 1958, Barbara, who *d* 1992, da of W. S. Alexander:—
Gordon Benjamin Frecheville, *b* 1961. ——— Elizabeth Lee, *b* 1959: *m* 19—, Hans-Peter Lehmann, of 2311 Birdie Lane, Duluth, Georgia 30136, USA, and has issue living, Kim Alexandra, *b* 1988. ——— Beverley Anne, *b* 1962: *m* 19—, Carl Harth, of PO Box 905, Jukskei Park, Randburg 2153, S Africa.

Grandchildren of late Arthur John Ramsden, el son of Col Arthur Charles, 3rd son of Rev William Ramsden, son of Capt George Ramsden, only son of Lt-Col Frecheville Ramsden, 6th son of 2nd baronet:—
Issue of late Major Arthur Geoffrey Francis Ramsden, DSO, RA, *b* 1887, *d* on active ser 1945: *m* 1918, Winifred, who *d* 1958, da of late S. B. Cowan, LLD:—
Justin John Frecheville (8 St Margaret's Rd, Hillcrest 3610, S Africa), *b* 1927; Group Accountant-Sec of Tozer, Kemsley & Millbourn (S Africa) (Pty), Ltd, Johannesburg: *m* 1960, Brigit Joy Barry, da of Barry Smith, of Hill Crest, Natal, and has had issue, John Henry Frecheville *b* 1963, *d* 1997, — Timothy Geoffrey Frecheville, *b* 1965, — Paula Frances Barry, *b* 1967. ——— David Bruce Frecheville (PO Box 140, Magaleissig 2067, S Africa), *b* 1929; late Capt RA: *m* 1958, Deirdre Mary Bouchier, and has issue living, Bruce Charles Frecheville (1144 Montrose Abbey Drive, Oakville, Ontario, Canada), *b* 1959: *m* 1989, Sarah, el da of R. Garnett, and has issue living, Nicola Jane *b* 1991, Laura *b* 1994, — Paul David Frecheville (13 Morrell Rd, Blairgowrie, Randburg, S Africa), *b* 1961; has issue living, James *b* 1996, — Debra Gail, *b* 1960: *m* 1st, 1982 (*m diss* 19—), Bruce Franklin, son of R. Franklin; 2ndly, 19—, Graham Jeffery, of 3 Beech Av, Robin Acres, Randburg, S Africa, el son of S. Jeffery, of Springs, S Africa, and has issue living, (by 1st *m*) Brendan *b* 1985, Sean *b* 1987, — Penelope Ray, *b* 1963: *m* 19—, Ian Rickleton, of 28 Glen Rd, Bramley, Johannesburg, S Africa, son of Cliff Rickleton, and has issue living, Dean *b* 1994, Ryan *b* 1996. ——— Myra Patricia (The Cottage, Carlton Scroop, Kesteven, Lincs), *b* 1921: *m* 1953, Alan Rowland Lingard Escombe. ——— Arminel Jill, *b* 1925: *m* 1952, Lt-Cdr Richard Thomas Leggott, MBE, RN, and has issue living, Arminel Ruth, *b* 1953: *m* 1984, Jonathan Levi, of PO Box 27143, Hout Bay, Cape Town 7872, S Africa, and has issue living, Richard Ernst *b* 1988, Arminel Jenna *b* 1985, — Susan Elizabeth, *b* 1955: *m* 19—, Anthony G. Pick, of North Leas, Church Lane, Londonthorpe, Lincs, — Jenifer Leigh (50 Fairfield St, S Wigston, Lincs LE18 4SL), *b* 1958. *Residence* – 56 Edwin St, Boston, Lincs.

Issue of late John Hope Frecheville Ramsden, *b* 1896, *d* 1955: *m* 1930, Hilda Marguerite Lonnen, who *d* 1979, da of late E. J. Simmons:—
Margaret Elizabeth Anne (Cherry Garth, East Stoke, Stoke-sub-Hamdon, Somerset), *b* 1932: *m* 1966, Major T. L. Browne, MBE, Int Corps, who *d* 1995, and has issue living, Richard Kimberley John (The Colonnade, 347 West 57th St, Apt 27F, New York, NY 10019, USA), *b* 1968: *m* 1999, Jane Sarah Thatcher.

Robert Ramsden was seated at Longley Hall, *temp* Henry VIII. The 1st baronet received his baronetcy for his essential services and the distinguished zeal exhibited by him at the Revolution. The 5th baronet, Sir John William, sat as MP for Taunton (*L*) 1853-7, for Hythe 1857-9, for W Riding of York 1880-85, for Osgoldcross Div of E Part of W Riding of York 1885-6, and was Under-Sec of State for War 1857-8. Sir John Frecheville Ramsden, 6th Bt was High Sheriff of Bucks 1920. Maj Sir (Geoffrey) William Pennington-Ramsden, 7th Bt, assumed by deed poll 1925 the surname of Pennington in lieu of his patronymic, and the arms of Pennington (differenced with a canton sable) quartered with those of Ramsden, in accordance with the will of the late Lord Muncaster, and by deed poll 1958 resumed the surname of Ramsden after that of Pennington; was patron of four livings, and High Sheriff of Cumberland 1962.

RANKIN (UK) 1898, of Bryngwyn, Much Dewchurch, co Hereford

Sir IAN NIALL RANKIN, 4th *Baronet*; *b* 19 Dec 1932; *s* his uncle, *Sir* HUGH CHARLES RHYS, 1988; *ed* Eton, and Ch Ch, Oxford (MA), FRGS, Lieut Scots Gds (Reserve): *m* 1st, 1959 (*m diss* 1967), Alexandra, only da of late Adm Sir Laurence George Durlacher, KCB, OBE, DSC (*see* Hanson, Bt, *cr* 1887, 1968 Edn); 2ndly, 1980, June, elder da of late Capt Thomas Marsham-Townshend (*see* E Romney, colls), and formerly wife of Bryan Montagu Norman, and has issue by 1st and 2nd *m*.

𝕬rms – Or, a cinquefoil gules, in chief a battle-axe erect between two boars' heads couped, and in base a boar's head between two battle-axes erect sable. 𝕮rest – In front of a cubit arm holding a battle-axe proper, three cinquefoils gules.
Residence – 97 Elgin Av, W9 2DA.

SONS LIVING (*By 1st marriage*)

GAVIN NIALL, *b* 19 May 1962; a Page of Honour to HM The Queen 1977-79; *ed* Eton, and Buckingham Univ: *m* 19—, Alexandra, da of Dr Jürgen von Knieriem, and of Mrs Monica von Pott, of Heidelberg and Vienna, and has issue living, Tassilo Laurence, *b* 1998, — Xenia Sophia, *b* 1996. *Residence* – 13 Addison Rd, W14 8DJ.

(By 2nd marriage)

Lachlan John, *b* 1980.

DAUGHTER LIVING *(By 1st marriage)*

Zara Sophia (*Hon Mrs Humphrey Drummond*), *b* 1960: *m* 1997, Dr the Hon Humphrey John Jardin Drummond, 2nd son of Baroness Strange. *Residence* – 64 Comeragh Rd, W14.

BROTHER LIVING

Sir Alick Michael, *b* 1935; *ed* Eton, Lieut Scots Gds (Reserve); Kt Bach 1992: *m* 1st, 1958 (*m diss* 1976), Susan Margaret, elder da of Lt-Col Hugh Littleton Dewhurst (*see* B Forteviot, 1985 Edn); 2ndly, 1976, Suzetta, da of Patrick Nelson, of Seafield, IoM, and has issue (by 1st *m*), Rupert Mark, *b* 1962, — Clare Joanna, *b* 1961, — Annabel Louise, *b* 1964, — Juliet Rachel, *b* 1970. *Residence* – Tullimoy House, Glenalmond, Perths PH1 3SL.

MOTHER LIVING

Lady Jean Margaret Dalrymple, DCVO, da of 12th Earl of Stair: *m* 1931, Lt-Col (Arthur) Niall Talbot Rankin, yr son of 2nd baronet, who *d* 1965. *Residences* – House of Treshnish, Calgary, I of Mull; 97 Elgin Av, W9 2DA.

WIDOW LIVING OF THIRD BARONET

Robina (*Robina, Lady Rankin*), FSA Scot, SRN, da of Steurt Finlay, of Comrie, Perthshire: *m* 1946, as his 2nd wife, Sir Hugh Charles Rhys Rankin, 3rd Bt, who *d* 1988. *Residence* – ......

COLLATERAL BRANCH LIVING

Grandchildren of late Charles Herbert Rankin, CB, CMG, DSO, 2nd son of 1st baronet:—
    Issue of late Brig William Rankin, OBE, *b* 1909, *d* 1968: *m* 1939, Pauline Sinclair (Dowdeswell Hall, Dowdeswell, Glos), da of late Oswald Sinclair Haggie:—
Mark (5 Albany Mews, Albany Rd, SE5 0DQ), *b* 1941, late Capt 15th/19th King's R Hussars. —— Christopher John (535 E 86th St, Apt 19A, New York, NY 10028, USA), *b* 1946: *m* 1st, 1968 (*m diss* 1974), Lucinda Jane, el da of Lt-Cdr Christopher Godfrey de Lisle Bush, RN; 2ndly, 1975 (*m diss* 1989), Penelope Jane, da of Nicholas Robin Benson, of Aycote House, Rendcombe, Cirencester (D Rutland); 3rdly, 1999, Ingrid, da of Ottokar Schroeder, of Koenigsberg, Germany, and has issue living (by 1st *m*), Peter William, *b* 1969, — James Christopher, *b* 1972, — (by 2nd *m*), Clare Louise, *b* 1978, — Katherine Emily, *b* 1981. —— Carolyn, *b* 1943: *m* 1967, Edmund Brooke Alexander, of 465 W 23rd St, Apt 9A, New York, NY 10011, USA, and has issue living, Emily Sinclair, *b* 1971, — Jessica Brooke, *b* 1973. —— Jean Mary, *b* 1952: *m* 1977, Charles Anthony Letts, of The Hendom Barn, Llowes, Herefordshire HR3 5JK, and 9 Stanley Gdns, W11 2ND, and has had issue, Charles Alexander Frazer, *b* 1980, — Benjamin James Mark, *b* and *d* 1982, — Jeremy Finan, *b* 1984.

The 1st baronet, Sir James (Ch Steward of the City of Hereford), was High Sheriff of Hereford 1873, and sat as MP for Herefordshire, N, or Leominster, Div (*C*) 1880-85, 1886-1906, and 1910-12. The 2nd baronet, Lieut-Col Sir Reginald, FRHS, FRGS, Bar-at-law, was Private Sec to Sec of State for the Colonies (Rt Hon A. Lyttleton, KC, MP) 1903-4, and *Times* War Correspondent in Morocco 1908, and with Bulgarian Forces 1912; he was Lieut-Col Comdg Herefordshire Regt (TD), and second in command of W Kent Yeo; served in S Africa 1900 as trooper and Lieut Rimington's Guides (medal with three clasps); author of *A Subaltern's Letters to His Wife*, *With General d'Amade in Morocco* (translated into Spanish and French), *The Inner History of the Balkan War*, *The Royal Ordering of Gardens*, etc. Sir Hugh Rankin, 3rd Bt (*d* 1988), was a noted eccentric whose interests embraced golf (held amateur record of GB for having played on 382 courses in UK and Eire), mountain cycling (Pres Rough Stuff Cycling Accocn 1956) and comparative religion; became a Moslem (British Rep all European Moslem Congress in Geneva), and later a non-Theistic Theravda Buddhist; campaigner for 'an independent Red Republic of all Scotland, excluding Orkneys and Shetland'; Trooper 1st Royal Drag Gds 1920-22 (invalided out), 1939-45 War in India; assumed by deed poll 1932 the addl surname of Stewart, discontinued same by deed poll 1946, and assumed the forename of Hugh in lieu of his patronymic Hubert.

RASCH (UK) 1903, of Woodhill, Danbury, Essex

Sir SIMON ANTHONY CARNE RASCH, 4th *Baronet*; *b* 26 Feb 1948; *s* his father, *Maj Sir* RICHARD GUY CARNE, 1996; *ed* Eton, and RAC Cirencester; Page of Honour to HM 1962-64: *m* 1987, Julia, elder da of Maj Michael Godwin Plantagenet Stourton (*see* B Mowbray, colls), and has issue.

Arms – Quarterly; azure and gules, a cross parted and fretted or, between in the first quarter a lion rampant per bend sinister ermine and erminois; in 2nd quarter a pelican in her piety, argent; in 3rd quarter a griffin segreant of the third; and in the 4th quarter a lion rampant of the last. **Crest** – Upon a rock proper a gryphon's head azure, collared gemel or, in front thereof a leopard's face between two fleurs-de-lis of the last.
Residence – The White House, Manningford Bruce, nr Pewsey, Wilts. *Club* – Pratt's.

SON LIVING

TOBY RICHARD CARNE, *b* 28 Sept 1994.

DAUGHTER LIVING

Molly Clare Anne, *b* 1990.

SISTER LIVING

Leila Anne Katherine, *b* 1952: *m* 1975, Thomas Geoffrey Timothy Rose Price, and has issue (*see* Price, Bt, *cr* 1815, colls). *Residence* – The Wadfield, Winchcombe, Cheltenham, Glos.

UNCLE LIVING (*brother of 3rd baronet*)

David Alwyne Carne, *b* 1922; *ed* Eton; Maj late Grenadier Gds: *m* 1953, Lady (Elizabeth) Anne Somerset, who *d* 1995, sister of 11th Duke of Beaufort, and has issue living, Guy Martin Carne (Heale House, Woodford, Salisbury SP4 6NT), *b* 1959; *ed* Millfield: *m* 1996, Frances Caroline, only da of Richard Arthur Samuel Hulse (*see* Hulse, Bt), — Jane Catherine RASCH (The Round House, Netton, Salisbury), *b* 1955; has resumed her maiden name: *m* 1976 (*m diss* 1980), Michael Smedley, — Emma Caroline (The Mill House, Middle Woodford, Salisbury), *b* 1962: *m* 1996, Robert James Jackson, son of late Harry Wallace Jackson, of Chorleywood, Herts. *Residence* – Heale Stables, Woodford, Salisbury, Wilts SP4 6NT.

WIDOW LIVING OF THIRD BARONET

FIONA MARY (*Fiona, Lady Rasch*), eldest da of Robert Douglas Shaw, of St Leonards-on-Sea, Sussex, and formerly wife of Humphrey John Rodham Balliol Salmon: *m* 1961, as his 2nd wife, Maj Sir Richard Guy Carne Rasch, 3rd Bt, who *d* 1996. *Residences* – The Manor House, Lower Woodford, Salisbury, Wilts; 30 Ovington Sq, SW3.

The 1st baronet, Sir Frederic Carne Rasch, sat as MP for S-E Div of Essex (C) 1886-1900 and for Chelmsford Div of Essex 1900-1908. The 3rd baronet, Maj Sir Richard Guy Carne Rasch, was a Member HM Body Guard of Hon Corps of Gentlemen-at-Arms 1968-88: *m* 1st, 1947 (*m diss* 1959), Anne Mary (who *d* 1989, having *m* 2ndly, 1959, Marchese Paolo Sersale, who *d* 1991), eldest da of late Maj John Henry Dent-Brocklehurst, OBE, of Sudeley Castle, Glos (*see* B Trevor, 1962 Edn); 2ndly, 1961, Fiona Mary, eldest da of Robert Douglas Shaw, of St Leonard's-on-Sea, Sussex, and formerly wife of Humphrey John Rodham Balliol Salmon.

RASHLEIGH (UK) 1831, of Prideaux, Cornwall

Sir RICHARD HARRY RASHLEIGH, 6th *Baronet*; *b* 8 July 1958; *s* his father, *Sir* HARRY EVELYN BATTIE, 1984; *ed* All Hallows' Sch, Dorset: *m* 1996, Emma F. C., eldest da of John McGougan, of London, and of Lady Acland, of Provost's Lodge, Eton Coll, and has issue.

Arms – Sable, a cross or, between in the 1st quarter, a Cornish chough argent; in the 2nd quarter a text T, and in the 3rd and 4th a crescent all argent.
Residence – Menabilly, Par, Cornwall PL24 2TN. *Club* – Royal Fowey Yacht.

SON LIVING

DAVID WILLIAM AUGUSTINE, *b* 1 April 1997.

DAUGHTER LIVING

Ruth Honora, *b* 1999.

SISTERS LIVING

Susanna Jane, *b* 1955: *m* 1984, Timothy John Peter Emerson, of Coleraine, Yelverton, Devon PL20 6BN, son of Col John Emerson, OBE, TD, DL, of Yelverton, Devon, and has issue living, Thomas Alexander, *b* 1987, — Charlotte Jane, *b* 1985. —— Frances Elisabeth (Bess), *b* 1956: *m* 1982, Jonathan Ayton Haward, of 5 Stratton Terr, Truro, Cornwall TR1 3EW, son of Dr Michael Haward, of Quethiock, Liskeard, Cornwall, and has issue living, Harry Thomas, *b* 1986, — Emma Elisabeth, *b* 1988. —— Anne Henrietta, *b* 1959: *m* 1989, Peter B. R. Argles, of Green Lane Gardens, Buckland Monachorum, Yelverton, Devon PL20 7NP, son of late Guy Kingston Argles, of Sutton Valence, Kent, and has issue living, Edward Hugh Rashleigh, *b* 1992, — Arthur Peter Kingston *b* 1994, — Christopher Jonathan Sneyd, *b* 1995, — Isobel Lydia Anne, *b* 1997.

AUNTS LIVING (*Sisters of 5th baronet*)

Elizabeth, *b* 1915. —— (Mary) Vivien (Lawhyre Cottage, Fowey, Cornwall), *b* 1917: *m* 1941, Cdr Philip Kidd, RN, and has had issue, Christopher Hugh Rashleigh *b* 1949: *m* 1975, (Anne) Louise Houblon (Lower Trengale, Doublebois, nr Liskeard, Cornwall), only da of Maj Richard de Warrenne Waller, RA, of Evergreens, The Avenue, Ascot, Berks, and *d* 1994, leaving issue, George Philip Houblon *b* 1977, Toby Richard Rashleigh *b* 1979, Emily Louisa Vivien *b* 1980, — Judith Anne, *b* 1941: *m* 1966, Robin Alec Stables, of 26 Daglands Rd, Fowey, Cornwall, and has issue living, Timothy Hugh *b* 1969, Susanna Vivien *b* 1967, — Sarah Vivien, *b* 1943: *m* 1st, 1967 (*m diss* 1981), Angus Dormer Crichton; 2ndly, 1982, Desmond George Uniacke Bain, of Lawhyre Cottage, Fowey, Cornwall, and has issue living (by 1st *m*), Thomas *b* 1975, Camilla *b* 1969, Anne *b* 1970, — Elizabeth, *b* 1946: *m* 1st, 1967 (*m diss* 1970), John Ronald Hoskins; 2ndly, 1979 (*m diss* 1987), Robin Kemp; 3rdly, 1988, Christopher Stuart Conwy Morgan, of 68 Esplanade, Fowey, Cornwall PL23 1JA, and has issue living (by 2nd *m*), Charles Frederick *b* 1972, Henry Selby *b* 1977.

COLLATERAL BRANCH LIVING

Issue of late Peter Rashleigh, yr brother of 5th baronet, *b* 1924, *d* 1990: *m* 1949, Lola, who *d* 1998, da of Thomas Edmonds, of NSW:—
†Edward Harry, *b* and *d* 1952. —— Margaret Anne, *b* 1950: *m* 1970, Geoffrey Carruthers, of 43 Archdall St, McGregor, Canberra 2615, ACT, Australia, and has issue living, Richard, *b* 1976, — Keryn, *b* 1973. —— Bettine Jane, *b* 1954. —— Jill Vivien, *b* 1956: *m* 1982, Max Steiger, of 171 Carrington Av, Hurstville, Sydney, NSW 2220, Australia, and has issue living, Ben, *b* 1988, — Todd, *b* 1989.

The family of Rashleigh has been seated in Cornwall since the early part of the 16th century. The 2nd baronet was MP for Cornwall E (*L*) 1874-80.

RAWLINSON (UK) 1891

Sir ANTHONY HENRY JOHN RAWLINSON, 5th *Baronet*; *b* 1 May 1936; *s* his father, *Sir* (ALFRED) FREDERICK, 1969; *ed* Millfield: *m* 1st, 1960 (*m diss* 1967), Penelope Byng, da of late Rear-Adm Gambier John Byng Noel, CB (*see* E Gainsborough, colls); 2ndly, 1967 (*m diss* 1976), Pauline Strickland, da of John Holt Hardy, of Sydney, NSW; 3rdly, 1977 (*m diss* 1997), Helen Leone, da of Thomas Miller Kennedy, of Glasgow, and has issue by 1st, 2nd, and 3rd *m*.

Arms – Sable, three swords in pale proper, pommels and hilts or, two erect points upwards and between them the other, point downwards; on a chief embattled of the third an antique crown gules. **Crest** – Out of an antique crown or, a cubic arm erect in armour, the hand grasping a sword in bend sinister, and the wrist encircled by a laurel wreath proper. *Residence* – Heath Farm, Guist, Norfolk NR20 5PG.

SONS LIVING (*By 1st marriage*)

ALEXANDER NOEL, *b* 15 July 1964.

(*By 2nd marriage*)

Rupert Seymour, *b* 1970.

(*By 3rd marriage*)

Christopher Thomas Seymour, *b* 1981.

DAUGHTER LIVING (*By 1st marriage*)

Caroline Louise Byng, *b* 1962.

BROTHER LIVING

(Marcus) Andrew Frederick (Stody Hall, Melton Constable, Norfolk), *b* 1940; *ed* Canford: *m* 1964, Miriam Diana, el da of Richard Joice, of Mill Farm, Newton by Castle Acre, Kings Lynn, Norfolk, and has issue living, Joanna Jane, *b* 1965: *m* 1992, Patrick Andrew Tristram (Todd) Watt, of Little Monks Farm, Wickhambrook, Suffolk, son of Capt Harry Watt, of Carrablagh, co Donegal, and has issue living, Patrick Andrew Harry *b* 1997, Tara Rosanna *b* 1994, — Nicola Abigail, *b* 1967: *m* 1995, as his 2nd wife, Evan Robert (Joss) Hanbury (*see* Birkin, Bt, 1976 Edn), of Burley-on-the-Hill, Oakham, Rutland, and has issue living, Sophie Rose *b* 1996, — Candida Louise, *b* 1974.

SISTER LIVING

Sarah Jane, *b* 1939: *m* 1962, Capt William Hanslip Bulwer Bulwer Long, 9th/12th Roy Lancers, DL Norfolk 1992 (who *d* 1996, having assumed by deed poll 1963 the additional surname of Bulwer), of Heydon Hall, Heydon, Norwich, and has issue living, Edward Hanslip, *b* 1966, — Benjamin Earle, *b* 1970: *m* 1997, Rhona J. K., da of Timothy Brindley, of Patchetts Green, Herts, and has issue living, Letitia *b* 1999, — Daisy Lydia, *b* 1975.

Henry Creswicke Rawlinson, GCB (son of Abraham Tyzack Rawlinson, of Chadlington, Oxford), a distinguished Orientalist, and the first decipherer of cuneiform inscriptions; MP for Reigate 1858, and for Frome (*L*) 1865-8; re-organized Shah's Army 1833-9, Political Agent at Candahar 1840-43, and a Member of Council of Sec of State for India 1858-9 and 1868-95; *cr* a *Baronet* 1891. His son, Gen Sir Henry Seymour, GCB, GCSI, GCVO, KCMG, 2nd Bt; served with Burma Expedition 1886-87, with Nile Expeditions 1897 and 1898, at battles of Atbara and Khartoum, in S Africa 1899-1902, 1914, GOC 4th Div 4th Army Corps, and 4th Army 1915-18, and as GOC in C, N Russia 1919; C in C Aldershot 1919-10, and India 1920-25; *cr Baron Rawlinson*, of Trent, co Dorset (peerage of UK) 1919; *d* 1925, when the Barony became ext, and the Baronetcy devolved upon his brother, Lt-Col Sir Alfred, CMG, CBE, DSO, 3rd Bt.

READE (E) 1661, of Barton, Berkshire

Sir KENNETH RAY READE, 13th *Baronet*; *b* 23 March 1926; yr son of LaVerne Elton Reade, 5th son of 9th baronet; *s* his cousin, *Sir* CLYDE NIXON, 1982: *m* 1944, Doreen, da of Edward Vinsant, of Ann Arbor, Michigan, USA, and has issue.

𝔄rms – Gules, a saltire between four garbs or. ℭrest – On the stump of a tree vert, a falcon rising proper, belled and jessed or.
Residence – 1102 Lariot Loop, Apt 201, Ann Arbor, MI 48108-2493, USA.

DAUGHTERS LIVING

Sandra, *b* 1945: *m* 1966, Douglas Crawford, of 3479 Central St, Dexter, Michigan 48130, USA, and has issue living, Michael, *b* 1966, — John, *b* 1970, — Beth, *b* 1975. —— Karen, *b* 1948: *m* 1968, James Lamb, of 8531 Jackson Rd, Dexter, Michigan 48130, USA, and has issue living, Tammy, *b* 1970, — Jennifer, *b* 1973, — Angie, *b* 1974, — Bonnie, *b* 1975, — Jackie, *b* 1978, — Karen Ann, *b* 1980. —— Norma (425 East Av A, Newberry, Michigan 49868, USA), *b* 1953; has issue living, Richard, *b* 1972, — William, *b* 1988, — Sara, *b* 1984.

SISTER LIVING OF TWELFTH BARONET

Hazel, *b* 1899: *m* 1919, John Neil, and has issue living, Donald George (6051 Daft St, Lansing, Ingham Co, Michigan, USA), *b* 1921. *Residence* –

COLLATERAL BRANCHES LIVING

Issue of late Elmer Compton Reade, 2nd son of 9th baronet, *b* 1877, *d* 1918: *m* 1902, Leticia Wylie:—

Laura Leticia, *b* 1908: *m* 1930, Gordon Heston. *Residence* –

Issue of late Emory Isaac Reade, 4th son of 9th baronet, *b* 1887, *d* 1939: *m* 1908, Millicent da of G. Fisk:—

Irene Norah, *b* 1911: *m* 1931, Hugh Peebles, and has issue living, Robert Bradley, *b* 1932, — David, *b* 1943, — Gloria Ann, *b* 1935. —— Eileen, *b* 1913: *m* 1935, Ronald Durrett. —— Esther, *b* 1918: *m* 1934, Lawrence Durrett. *Residence* –

The 1st baronet's paternal grandfather was knighted by Queen Elizabeth I, and a baronetcy conferred upon his uncle, John, in 1641, became extinct 1712. The 3rd baronet of the present creation sat as MP for Cricklade. Sir George Compton Reade, 9th Bt, son of John Stanhope Reade (*d* 1883) (who emigrated to Dexter Township, Washtenaw Co, Michigan, *ca* 1835, with his first cousin, Edwyn Bennet Hoskyns), was a great-grandson of the 6th Bt, *d* in April 1908.

READHEAD (UK) 1922, of Westoe, Borough of South Shields, co Palatine of Durham (Extinct 1988)

(*Sir*) JAMES TEMPLEMAN READHEAD, 3rd and last *Baronet* (but did not use the title).

DAUGHTER LIVING OF THIRD BARONET

Charlotte Susan Carolynn, *b* 1947. *Residence* – Flat 18, Ladbroke Square House, 2/3 Ladbroke Sq, W11 3LX.

DAUGHTER LIVING OF SECOND BARONET

Doreen Evelyn, *b* 1916: *m* 1946, John P. Glaisyer. *Residence* – Gallowhill, Whalton, Morpeth, Northumberland.

WIDOW LIVING OF THIRD BARONET

HILDA ROSEMARY, da of G. H. Hudson, of The Manor, Hatfield, Doncaster: *m* 1946, (Sir) James Templeman Readhead, 3rd Bt (who did not use the title), who *d* 1988. *Residence* – Marlish Cottage, High St, Woodgreen, nr Fordingbridge, Hants SP6 2AU.

Reardon-Smith, see Smith.

REDMAYNE (UK) 1964, of Rushcliffe, co Nottingham

Hon Sir NICHOLAS JOHN REDMAYNE, 2nd *Baronet*; *b* 1 Feb 1938; *s* his father, MARTIN, Baron Redmayne, DSO, TD, PC (Life Baron), in his Baronetcy, 1983; *ed* Radley, and RMA Sandhurst; late Lt Gren Guards; Dept Chm Kleinwort Benson Grp 1996-97; Chm ENBA plc since 1999: *m* 1st, 1963 (*m diss* 1976), Ann, who *d* 1985, da of Frank Birch Saunders, of The Mews, Kineton, Warwicks; 2ndly, 1978, Mrs Christine Diane Wood Hewitt, da of late Thomas Wood Fazakerley, and has issue by 1st *m*.

Arms – Gules two chevronels, between three cushions ermine tasselled or, a bordure engrailed argent. Crest – In front of a cushion as in the arms fessewise, a horse's head argent mane gules.
Residence – Walcote Lodge, Walcote, Lutterworth, Leics.

SON LIVING (*By 1st marriage*)

GILES MARTIN, *b* 1 Dec 1968; *ed* Radley: *m* 1994, Claire Ann, da of Sean O'Halloran.

DAUGHTER LIVING (*By 1st marriage*)

Camilla Jane, *b* 1966: *m* 1st, 1989 (*m diss* 1992), Julian Howard Trevor Beach; 2ndly, 1996, Kevin Peacock, and has issue living, (by 2nd *m*) Olivia, *b* 1996.

Martin Redmayne, DSO, TD, PC, son of Leonard Redmayne, was Ch Govt Whip 1959-1964, MP for Rushcliffe Div of Notts (*C*) 1950-66, and was *cr* a baronet 1964, and *Baron Redmayne*, of Rushcliffe, co Notts (Life Baron) 1966.

REDWOOD (UK) 1911, of Avenue Rd, St Marylebone

We have disseminated knowledge from of old

Sir PETER BOVERTON REDWOOD, 3rd *Baronet*; *b* 1 Dec 1937; *s* his father, *Sir* THOMAS BOVERTON, 1974; *ed* Gordonstoun; late Col KOSB: *m* 1964, Gilian Waddington, only da of John Lee Waddington Wood, of Limuru, Kenya, and has issue.

𝕬rms – Paly of six or and ermine, a lion rampant sable, on a chief azure an embattled gateway proper between two mullets of six points of the first. 𝕮rest – A rock, therefrom an eagle rising proper, charged on each wing with a mullet of six points, in the beak a staff raguly or.
Address – c/o National Westminster Bank, Warminster Branch, 80 Market Place, Warminster, Wilts BA12 9AW.

DAUGHTERS LIVING

Anna Kathryn, *b* 1967: *m* 1993, Capt Patrick M. Thomson, eldest son of Brig Michael Thomson, of Trouville, France, and has issue living, Archibald William Boverton, *b* 1995, — Finlay Thomas Macdonald, *b* 1998, — Octavia Flora, *b* 1997. —— Colina Margaret Charlotte, *b* 1969. —— Gaynor Elizabeth, *b* 1972.

HALF-BROTHERS LIVING

ROBERT BOVERTON, *b* 24 June 1953; *ed* Truro Cathedral Sch: *m* 1978, Mary Elizabeth Wright, and has issue living, James Boverton, *b* 2 Oct 1985, — Morwenna Anne Carlile, *b* 1982. —— Charles Boverton, *b* 1956.

HALF-SISTER LIVING

Anne Boverton, *b* 1947: *m* 1968, James Embury, and has issue living, Tristan James, *b* 1971, — Bartholomew Boverton, *b* 1972.

AUNT LIVING

Patricia Boverton, *b* 1910: *m* 1965, Harold Box, of Spring Ducks, Horton Rd, Ashley Heath, Ringwood, Hants.

WIDOW LIVING OF SECOND BARONET

URSULA (*Ursula, Lady Redwood*), da of late Rev Herbert Percy Hale: *m* 1944, as his 2nd wife, Sir Thomas Boverton Redwood, 2nd Bt, who *d* 1974.

The 1st baronet, Sir Boverton, was a well-known authority on Petroleum, and was Adviser on Petroleum to Admiralty, India Office, and Home Office.

REID (UK) 1897, of Ellon, Aberdeenshire

Nothing is hard for one who loves

Sir ALEXANDER JAMES REID, 3rd *Baronet*; *b* 6 Dec 1932; *s* his father, *Sir* EDWARD JAMES, KBE, 1972; *ed* Eton, and Magdalene Coll, Camb; Capt (ret) 3rd Bn Gordon Highlanders; Malaya 1951-53; JP Cambridgeshire and Isle of Ely 1971, DL 1973; High Sheriff Cambridgeshire 1987-88; a Dir of Cristina Securities Ltd since 1970, Ellon Castle Estates Co Ltd 1965-96; Chm Clan Donnachaidh Soc since 1994; Gov (Chm 1976-92) Heath Mount Sch, Hertford since 1970: *m* 1955, Michaela Ann, da of late Olaf Kier, CBE, of Cokenach, Barkway, Royston, Herts, and has issue.

𝕬rms – Azure, a stag's head erased or, between two torches fired proper; (as an honourable augmentation) on a chief gules a lion passant guardant or, armed and langued azure (being one of the lions from the Royal arms). 𝕮rest – A pelican in its piety proper. 𝕾upporters – On either side a Royal stag or, round the neck a chain proper suspended therefrom an escutcheon azure, charged with a representation of the Imperial Crown proper.
Residence – Lanton Tower, Jedburgh, Roxburghshire TD8 6SU. *Clubs* – Caledonian, and New (Edinburgh).

SON LIVING

CHARLES EDWARD JAMES, *b* 24 June 1956; *ed* Rannoch, and RAC Cirencester.

DAUGHTERS LIVING

Christina, *b* 1958. —— Jennifer, *b* 1959: *m* 1st, 1986 (*m diss* 1991), Stephen J. Marsh-Smith; 2ndly, 1991, Rory Collins, only son of Bernard Collins, of Bisley, Glos, and has issue living, (by 1st *m*) Edward Leo, *b* 1988, — Henrietta, *b* 1987, — (by 2nd *m*) Alexander James Rhuaraidh, *b* 1993. —— Alexandra Catherine, *b* 1965: *m* 1992, Charles A. Lloyd, only son of John Lloyd, of Tiverton, Devon, and has issue living, Thomas Alexander, *b* 1998, — Eleanor Mary, *b* 1996, — Serena Caroline, *b* (twin) 1998.

COLLATERAL BRANCH LIVING

Issue of late Adm Sir John Peter Lorne Reid, GCB, CVO, yr son of 1st baronet, *b* 1903; *d* 1973: *m* 1933, Jean, who *d* 1971, da of Sir Henry Herbert Philip Dundas, MVO, 3rd Bt (*cr* 1898):—
David Lorne Dundas (Quinta das Murtas, Rua Eduardo Van-Zeller, 2710 Sintra, Portugal), *b* 1938; late Lt 15th/19th King's R Hussars: *m* 1st, 1968 (*m diss* 1979), Mrs Elizabeth Wilkinson, da of late Adam Natt; 2ndly, 1979, Tedda Ann, da of Albert Charles Webber, of Litton Cheney, Dorchester, Dorset, and formerly wife of James Sholto Arthur Douglas (*see* E Morton, colls), and has two adopted das (with 1st wife), Jacqueline Dundas (*Countess of Northesk*), *b* 1956: *m* 1979, 14th Earl of Northesk, and has issue (*see* E Northesk), — Lorna Victoria, *b* 1972, — and issue living (by 2nd wife) Benjamin James Dundas, *b* 1983, — Leonora Emily Louise, *b* 1981. —— Delia (*Lady Montgomery*), *b* 1935: *m* 1956, Sir (Basil Henry) David Montgomery, 9th Bt, of Kinross House, Kinross.

This Baronetcy was created on the occasion of HM Queen Victoria's Diamond Jubilee in recognition of the 1st baronet's personal services to HM, Sir James, GCVO, KCB, MD, LLD, 1st Bt, being successively Physician to Queen Victoria, to King Edward VII, and to King George V.

REID (UK) 1922, of Springburn, Co of City of Glasgow, and of Kilmaurs, co Ayr

Sir HUGH REID, 3rd *Baronet*; *b* 27 Nov 1933; *s* his father, *Sir* DOUGLAS NEILSON, 1971; *ed* Loretto.

By fortitude and labour

Arms – (as recorded at Lyon Office) Argent, a demi-eagle, wings expanded, in chief an ancient handbell between a mullet in the dexter and a cross moline in the sinister, all sable. **Crest** – A demi-eagle, wings expanded sable.
Seat – Caheronaun Park, Loughrea, co Galway.

SISTER LIVING

Joan Murray, *b* 1929: *m* 1953, John Francis Quinn, and has issue living, John Douglas, *b* 1954, — Peter Francis, *b* 1956, — James Hugh, *b* 1959, — Michael Joseph, *b* 1967, — David Paul, *b* 1969, — Kevin, *b* 1974, — Mary Teresa, *b* 1955, — Margaret Joan, *b* 1960, — Anne Bernadette, *b* 1962, — Pauline, *b* 1965. *Residence* – Caheronaun, Loughrea, co Galway.

The 1st baronet, Sir Hugh Reid, CBE, VD, LLD, MICE, DL, JP (son of James Reid of Auchterarder, JP, MICE), was Chm and Managing Director of N British Locomotive Co, Ltd.

RENALS (UK) 1895

Sir STANLEY RENALS, 4th *Baronet*; *b* 20 May 1923; *s* his brother, *Sir* HERBERT, 1961; *ed* City of London Freemen's Sch; late Merchant Navy: *m* 1957, Maria Dolores Rodriguez Pinto, da of late José Rodriguez Ruiz, and has issue.

Arms – Per pale gules and sable, on a fesse nebuly argent between in chief two lozenges, and in base as many fleurs-de-lis or, a fasces fessewise proper. Crest – On a rock a fox reguardant supporting with its dexter foot a fasces erect proper, and charged on the shoulder with a lozenge or.
Residence – 52 North Lane, Portslade, E Sussex BN4 2HG.

Cavendo tutus
Safe by being cautious

SON LIVING

STANLEY MICHAEL, *b* 14 Jan 1958; *ed* Falmer High Sch, and Brighton Polytechnic (BSc, CEng, MIMechE, MIEE, MInstD); Eur Ing; Man Dir Crossflow International: *m* 1982, Jacqueline Ann, da of Roy Dennis Riley, of 26 Uplands Rd, Hollingdean, Brighton, Sussex, and has issue living, Lloyd James, *b* 17 May 1985, — Frances Emma, *b* 1986. *Residence* – 72 Parsonage Rd, Henfield, W Sussex BN5 9HZ.

The 1st baronet, Sir Joseph Renals (son of late William Renals, of Nottingham), was a Partner in the firm of Renals & Co, merchants, and was Lord Mayor of London 1894-5.

RENSHAW (UK) 1903, of Coldharbour, Wivelsfield, Sussex

Sir (CHARLES) MAURICE BINE RENSHAW, 3rd *Baronet*; *b* 7 Oct 1912; *s* his father, *Capt Sir* (CHARLES) STEPHEN BINE, 1976; *ed* Eton; late F/O RAF: *m* 1st, 1942 (*m diss* 1947), Isabel Bassett, da of late Rev John L. T. Popkin; 2ndly, 19—, Winifred May, da of H. F. Gliddon, of Ashwater, Devon, and formerly wife of James H. T. Sheldon, and has had issue by 1st and 2nd wives.

Arms – Per pale and per chevron or and azure, in chief two martlets, and in base a bull's head couped all counterchanged. Crest – In front of a griffin's head erased sable a decrescent and an increscent argent.
Residences – Tom-na-Margaidh, Balquhidder, Perthshire FK19 8PB; Linwood, Instow, N Devon EX39 4HX.

Esse quam videri
To be rather than to seem

SONS LIVING AND DECEASED (*by 1st wife*)

†Charles Edward Bine, *b* 1944; *d* 1954. —— JOHN DAVID (8 Graham House, Birdcage Walk, Newmarket, Suffolk), *b* 9 Oct 1945; *ed* Army Catering Corps, Aldershot; Furniture Maker: *m* 1970 (*m diss* 1988), Jennifer, da of late Group Capt Frederick Murray, RAF, and has issue living, Thomas Charles Bine, *b* 3 March 1976, — Joanna Caroline Graham, *b* 1973, — Catherine Elisabeth Graham, *b* 1978.

(*by 2nd wife*)

Andrew (UK MOD SAP, Khamis Mushayt, BFPO 633), *b* 1947; *ed* McLaren High Sch, Callander; Wing Cdr RAF: *m* 1977, Cherry Rose, da of Cdr John Blakeley Russell, DSC, RN, of 37 Horne Rd, Ilfracombe, N Devon (*see* Chichester, Bt), and has issue living, Edward Chichester, *b* 1979, — Rory Andrew, *b* 1980, — Harry John, *b* 1983, — Eloise Rose, *b* 1986. —— Quintus (Pentwater Inn, 180 E Lowell St, Pentwater, Michigan 49449, USA), *b* 1952; *ed* McLaren High Sch, Callander, and Dundee Univ: *m* 1st, 1976 (*m diss* 1979), Heather, da of ...... MacGillivray, of Sydney, NSW; 2ndly, 1986, Donna Lee Helmkamp, da of late Stephen Chutorash, of Grosse Point, Michigan, USA. —— Edward (9 Bevan Rd, Barnstaple, N Devon EX32 8LJ), *b* 1965; *ed* ......

DAUGHTERS LIVING (*By 1st wife*)

Margaret, *b* 1943: *m* 1st, 1967 (*m diss* 1988), Dr Lee Coulter Chumbley, of Nashville, Tennessee, USA; 2ndly, 1990, Dr John Bellamy, of 8 Graham House, Birdcage Walk, Newmarket, Suffolk, and has issue living (by 1st *m*), Roger Renshaw, *b* 1973, — Justin Renshaw, *b* 1977, — Lucy, *b* 1970.

(by 2nd wife)

Caroline, *b* 1948: *m* 1987, Richard Dumbrill, of 52 Elsham Rd, W14 8HD. —— Janet RENSHAW (8 Kennet Mews, Marlborough, Wilts SN8 1NU), *b* 1950; has resumed her maiden name by deed poll 1994: *m* 1970 (*m diss* 1989), Dr Colin Dodd, PhD, and has issue living, Benjamin, *b* 1976, — Jennifer, *b* 1971. —— Helen, *b* 1951: *m* 1st, 1976 (*m diss* 19—), Douglas Arthur Coutts, of Lerwick; 2ndly, 19—, Ian Macdonald, of 9 Fraser Crescent, Portree, Isle of Skye, and has issue living (by 1st *m*), Andrew, *b* 1977, — (by 2nd *m*), Calum Ian Berge, *b* 1982, — Findlay Charles, *b* 1986, — Eilidh, *b* 1981, — Fiona Mary, *b* 1984.

SISTERS LIVING

Julia Noble Bine, *b* 1914: *m* 1940, Capt Edward William Whitfield, Indian Army, and has issue living, Michael Stephen (Plymtree, PO Box 721, Marondera, Zimbabwe), *b* 1941; late Maj R Scots Dragoon Gds: *m* 1969, Lady Fiona Catharine Sinclair, da of late 19th Earl of Caithness, and has issue living, Edward James *b* 1971, Christine Louise *b* 1973, — Christopher George, *b* 1945: *m* 1976, Moira Everitt, and has issue living, Ivan Edward, *b* 1978, Delia Joy *b* 1980, — Wendy Martina, *b* 1942: *m* 1963, Arthur Guiffré, of Portsmouth, Rhode Island, USA, and has issue living, Christopher Paul *b* 1965, Stephen *b* 1966, Karen Elizabeth *b* 1963, — Diana Mary *b* 1952: *m* 1975, David Bridge, and has issue living, Justyn *b* 1977, Martin *b* 1979. *Address* – PO Box 3721, Marondera, Zimbabwe. —— (Catherina) Margot, *b* 1917: *m* 1945, William Robert Percy Wall, Lt S African Air Force, who *d* 1988, and has issue living, Mary Jane, *b* 1948: *m* 1969, Louis George von Bratt Reynolds, MB, ChB, of Capetown, — Jessica, *b* 1950. *Residence* – Oakleigh, Greytown, Natal.

The 1st baronet, Sir Charles Bine Renshaw (son of late Thomas Charles Renshaw, QC, of Sandrocks, Sussex), sat as MP for W Div of Renfrewshire (*C*) July 1892 to Jan 1906.

RENWICK (UK) 1921, of Newminster Abbey, Morpeth, Northumberland

FOR TRUE LIVERTY

Sir RICHARD EUSTACE RENWICK, 4th *Baronet*; *b* 13 Jan 1938; *s* his father, *Sir* EUSTACE DEUCHAR, 1973; *ed* Eton: *m* 1966, Caroline Anne, da of late Maj Rupert Leonard Eversley Milburn, of Ghyllheugh, Longhorsley, Morpeth (*see* Milburn, Bt), and has issue.

𝔄rms – Per chevron sable and argent, in chief two lymphads of the second and in base on a mount vert a horse courant of the first. 𝔠rest – In front of a lion's head erased proper, a bugle horn stringed gules.
Residence – Whalton House, Whalton, Morpeth, Northumberland NE61 3UZ.

SONS LIVING

CHARLES RICHARD, *b* 10 April 1967; Capt The Light Dragoons: *m* 1993, Mrs Jane Ann Lyles, only da of Stuart Bush, of Holly Farm, Wendling, Norfolk, and has issue living, George Charles Eustace, *b* 8 Jan 1995, — Frederick Richard, *b* 1996. —— Harry Timothy, *b* 1968. —— Rory Eustace Deuchar *b* 1975.

BROTHER LIVING

George Eustace, *b* 1947; *ed* Eton.

SISTER LIVING

Julia Diana, *b* 1935: *m* 1957 (*m diss* 1979), Jervis Joscelyn Percy, and has issue living, Corinna Josceline, *b* 1964: *m* 1992, Maj A. O. McC. Waddell, RHA, and has issue living, Kitty Diana Osborne *b* 1997, — Jane Diana, *b* 1966, — Charlotte Elizabeth, *b* 1967: *m* 1994, Charles Edward Bennett. *Residence* – Greenfield, Wall, Hexham, Northumberland.

WIDOW LIVING OF THIRD BARONET

DIANA MARY (*Diana, Lady Renwick*) (Whalton, Morpeth, Northumberland), da of Col Bernard Cruddas, DSO, of Middleton Hall, Morpeth: *m* 1934, Sir Eustace Deuchar Renwick, 3rd Bt, who *d* 1973.

COLLATERAL BRANCHES LIVING

　　　　　Issue of late Dudley Cyril Deuchar Renwick, yr son of 2nd baronet, *b* 1907, *d* 1984: *m* several times:—
Three daughters.

Issue of late William Henry Renwick, 2nd son of 1st baronet, *b* 1880, *d* 1961: *m* 1899, Ethel Maud, who *d* 1944, da of William Ratcliffe:—

†Eric Montagu, *b* 1904: *m* 1956 (*m diss* 1960), Marie Sandra, who *d* 19—, da of ......, and *d* 19—, without issue. —— †Aubrey Forster, *b* 1912: *m ca* 1940, Elizabeth, who *d* 199—, da of ......, and *d* 19—, leaving issue, Timothy, *b* 19—, — Penelope, *b* 19—: *m* 19—, Philip Armitage, of Mount Farm, Whenby, Brandsby, Yorks. —— Alexandra Constance, *b* 1902: *m* 19—, Dr John Williams, of Richmond, Yorks, and *d* 19—, leaving issue, Sheila, *b* 19—. —— Dorothy Forster, *b* 1905: *m* 19— (*m diss* 19—), Edward Leatham Whitwell, and *d* 1994, without issue. —— Pamela Mary (40 Harlow Terrace, Harrogate, N Yorks HG2 0PN), *b* 1920.

Issue of late George Renwick, 3rd son of 1st baronet; *b* 1881, *d* 1937: *m* 1906, Nina, da of John Best Ferrier:—

Peter, *b* 1913: *m*, and has issue. —— Peggy, *b* 1907: *m* 1931, Claude Chessher Darling, and has issue living, David, *b* 1932, — Timothy, *b* 1944, — Diana Jane, *b* 1938: *m* 1968, Peter George Cary Summers, and has issue living, Jonathan Peter *b* 1969, Caroline Cary *b* 1971.

Grandson of late Gustav Adolph Renwick, 4th son of 1st baronet:—

Issue of late Denis Adolph Renwick, *b* 1907; *d* 1983: *m* 1934, Phyllis, who *d* 1983, only da of A. B. Atkinson:—

Guy Philip (Holystone Grange, Sharperton, Morpeth, Northumberland), *b* 1936; *ed* Stowe, and Christ's Coll, Camb; late 2nd Lt R Scots: *m* 1966, (Janet) Melanie, only da of late H. James Franklin, FRIBA, of West Hepple Farmhouse, Hepple, Morpeth, Northumberland, and has issue living, Shaun Maurice, *b* 1970, — Maxwell Mark, *b* 1972.

Issue of late Septimus Renwick, MC, Scots Guards, 5th son of 1st baronet, *b* 1886, *d* 1966: *m* 1916, Margaret, who *d* 1983, da of James Turnbull:—

(George) Lionel (Upend, Newmarket, Suffolk CB8 9PH), *b* 1917. —— Barbara (Upend, Newmarket, Suffolk CB8 9PH), *b* 1922.

The 1st baronet, Sir George Renwick (son of John Nixon Renwick, of Newcastle-upon-Tyne) was a member of the firm of Fisher Renwick & Co, shipowners and brokers of Newcastle, and Managing Director of Fisher Renwick Manchester-London Steamers, Ltd; he sat as MP for Newcastle-on-Tyne (C) Oct 1900 to Jan 1906 and Sept 1908 to Jan 1910, and for Central Division thereof Dec 1918 to Oct 1922.

REYNOLDS (UK) 1923, of Woolton, Co Lancaster

Sir DAVID JAMES REYNOLDS, 3rd *Baronet*; *b* 26 Jan 1924; *s* his father, *Lieut-Col Sir* JOHN FRANCIS ROSKELL, MBE, 1956; *ed* Downside; active service 1942-47, Capt 15th/19th Hussars: *m* 1966, Charlotte Baumgartner, and has issue.

Arms – Per chevron ermine and or, in chief two lions passant gules, and in base three leopards' faces sable. **Crest** – A demi moorcock displayed proper, charged on each wing with a leopard's face or.
Residence – Blanchepierre House, Rue de la Blanchepierre, St Lawrence, Jersey.

SON LIVING

JAMES FRANCIS, *b* 10 July 1971.

DAUGHTERS LIVING

Lara Mary, *b* 1967. —— Sophie Josephine, *b* 1968.

SISTER LIVING

Hermione Mary Elizabeth, *b* 1922: *m* 1948, Edward Raymond Courage, CBE, who *d* 1982, and has issue living, Christopher John, *b* 1962: *m* 1991, Alexandra Louise, elder da of John Charles Haynes (*see* B Vaux of Harrowden), and has issue living, Edward Francis *b* 1992, Beatrice Millicent *b* 1995. *Residences* – Edgcote, Banbury, Oxon, and 31 Abbotsbury House, Abbotsbury Rd, W8.

By persevering

HALF-SISTER LIVING

Mary Merilyn, *b* 1935: *m* 1954 (*m diss* 1963), Peter Guy Henry Thorold, and has issue (*see* Thorold, Bt, colls). *Residence* Dutch Barge Wiljan, St Mary's Church, Battersea Church Rd, SW11 3NA.

COLLATERAL BRANCH LIVING

Issue of late James Roskill Reynolds, 2nd son of 1st baronet, *b* 1904, *d* 1982: *m* 1931, Helen Mary, who *d* 1977, el da of late Charles Richard Gillow, of Leighton Hall, co Lancaster:—

Richard James Gillow (Leighton Hall, Carnforth, Lancs), *b* 1933; *ed* Ampleforth; late 2nd Lieut IG: *m* 1968, Caroline Susan, da of late Terence Kenyon, and has issue living, Katherine Elizabeth Gillow, *b* 1971, — Lucy Helen Gillow, *b* 1975. —— Simon Anthony (64 Lonsdale Rd, SW13 9JS), *b* 1939; *ed* Ampleforth: *m* 1970, Beata, el da of late Baron Siegfried von Heyl zu Herrnsheim, and has issue living, Stefan Damian, *b* 1970, — Rupert Christian, *b* 1979, — Olivia Helen, *b* 1972, — Leila Barbro, *b* 1976.

Issue of late William Francis Roskell Reynolds, 3rd son of 1st baronet, *b* 1911, *d* 1978: *m* 1934, Nancy Planche, who *d* 19—, da of Rupert Bendall:—
Nicholas Francis (Thornley House, Nether Wallop, Stockbridge, Hants SO20 8HA), *b* 1938; *ed* Downside, and Ch Ch, Oxford (MA); late 2nd Lt IG; FCA: *m* 1964, Wendy Helen Broke, twin da of late Lt Nigel Vere Broke Thurston, RN, and has issue living, Alexander, *b* 1971, — Lucy Claire Thurston, *b* 1966, — Charlotte Louise, *b* 1967. —— Juliet Mary, *b* 1936: *m* 1962, Neville Anthony Leonard Whitbread, ACA, of Lower Huxley Hall, Chester, and has issue living, James Rupert Sinanian, *b* 1970, — Victoria Mary, *b* 1963, — Alice Mary, *b* 1964, — Emilia Ann, *b* 1967.

The 1st baronet, Sir James Philip Reynolds, DSO, MP (son of Francis William Reynolds, of Hillside, Woolton, Liverpool), was senior partner of Reynolds & Gibson, cotton brokers of Liverpool, a Director of Martins Bank, Ltd, of The Royal Insurance Co (Limited), Liverpool, London and Globe Insurance Co (Limited), and Thames and Mersey Marine Insurance Co (Limited), a JP and DL, and MP for Exchange Div of Liverpool (*U*) 1929-32. The 2nd baronet, Sir John Francis Roskell Reynolds, MBE, was a partner of Reynolds & Gibson, Chm of Combined English Mills (Spinners) Ltd, and Lieut-Col Irish Guards.

RHODES (UK) 1919, of Hollingworth, co Palatine of Chester

By good ways

Sir JOHN CHRISTOPHER DOUGLAS RHODES, 4th *Baronet*; *b* 24 May 1946; *s* his father, *Lt-Col Sir* CHRISTOPHER GEORGE, 1964.

Arms – Azure, on a bend between two lozenges or a leopard's face gules between two holly leaves vert. **Crest** – Two lions' gambs erased gules supporting a lozenge charged with a holly leaf, both as in the arms. *Residence* –

BROTHER LIVING

MICHAEL PHILIP JAMES, *b* 3 April 1948: *m* 1973, Susan Elizabeth, 2nd da of Richard Patrick Roney-Dougal, of South Lodge, Norton, Shifnal, Shropshire, and has issue living, Louise, *b* 1974. *Residence* – Southdown, Blakeney, Holt, Norfolk.

SISTER LIVING

Ursula Catherine, *b* 1944: *m* 1967, Capt Peter Herbert Roberts, RA, only son of Maj Herbert Thomas Roberts, of Bexhill-on-Sea, Sussex. *Residence* – 8 Letheringsett Hill, Holt, Norfolk.

WIDOW LIVING OF THIRD BARONET

MARY FLORENCE (*Lady Rhodes*) (Purvis Lodge, Cley-next-the-Sea, Holt, Norfolk), da of late Dr Douglas Wardleworth: *m* 1943, as his 2nd wife, Lt-Col Sir Christopher George Rhodes, 3rd Bt, who *d* 1964.

COLLATERAL BRANCH LIVING

Issue of late Com Philip Wood Rhodes, RN (ret), 2nd son of 1st baronet, *b* 1894, *d* 1956: *m* 1st, 1919, Judith Beresford, who *d* 1942, da of Trevelyan Martin; 2ndly, 1944, Elspeth (181 Cranmer Court, Sloane Av, SW3), da of T. Tod, of Durban:—
(By 1st *m*) Pamela Beresford, *b* 1920: *m* 1944, Peter Coleclough, of Longlands Hall, Stonham Aspal, Stowmarket, and has had issue, Jeremy Nigel (Butterfield House, W Pinchbeck, Spalding, Lincs), *b* 1945: *m* 1979, Clare, da of Dr Wilfred O. Nowlan, and has issue living, Jonathan Peter *b* 1982, Catherine Helen *b* 1985, Elisabeth Rachel *b* 1988, — Martin Timothy, *b* 1947: *m* 1969, Carolyn Morva, da of John E. Stark, of Vancouver, and *d* 1985, leaving issue, Nigel Martin *b* 1974, Jennifer Nerissa *b* 1971.

Sir George Rhodes, 1st Bt, was a JP for Cheshire. Lt-Col Sir John Phillips Rhodes, DSO, late RE, 2nd Bt, was Chm of Thomas Rhodes (Limited), cotton spinners and manufacturers, of Hollingworth, Cheshire, and sat as MP for Cheshire, Stalybridge and Hyde Div (*C*) 1922-23.

Rhys-Williams, see Williams.

RICH (GB) 1791, of Shirley House, Hants (Dormant 1983)

Sir ALMERIC FREDERIC CONNESS RICH, 6th *Baronet*; *d* 1983, and at the time of going to press no name appears on the Official Roll of Baronets in respect of this title.

COLLATERAL BRANCHES LIVING

Grandchildren of late Harold A. S. P. Rich (*b* 1865), 3rd son of Henry Osborne Ludlow Rich (*b* 1822), only son of William Osborne Ludlow Rich, 3rd son of 1st baronet:—
Issue of late Leonard H. Rich, *b* 1898, *d* 1969: *m* 19—, —:—
Gordon Leonard (*presumed heir*) (Sydney, NSW, Australia), *b* 1921: *m* 1942, Olive Gilks, and has issue living, Gregory, *b* 1947, — Stephen Gordon, *b* 1949: *m*, and has issue. —— Joyce, *b* ca 1923. —— Shirley Osborne, *b* 1926.

Grandchildren of late Lt-Col Charles Edwin Frederick Rich, DSO, only son of late Rev John Rich, el son of late Rev John Rich (*b* 1789), 4th son of 1st baronet:—
Issue of late Cdr Charles Rodney St John Rich, RN, *b* 1900, *d* 1970: *m* 1st, 1928 (*m diss* 1936), Felicity Chesterton, da of late Sir George Thompson Hutchinson; 2ndly, 1937, Georgina Blanche, only da of late Donald Francis Napier Dalrymple, of 48 Hans Place, SW1:—
(By 1st *m*) Miles Rodney (Winkton Acre, Winkton, Dorset), *b* 1931; *ed* Bradfield; MBIM; Maj RE (ret): *m* 1959, Patricia Mary, only da of late George Stuart Castle, of Stone House Farm, Frindsbury, Rochester, and has issue living, Geoffrey Stuart, *b* 1969; *ed* Canford; BA, — Alexandra Mary, *b* 1960; BSc: *m* 1988, Nicholas David Mills, — Frances Catherine St John, *b* 1962; MEng: *m* 1984, Stephen Craig Anderson, — Philippa Clare St John, *b* 1965: *m* 1999, Dirk Stibbe. —— Deirdre Frances, *b* 1934: *m* 1958, Maj James Sidney Nobbs, MBE, RE (ret), of 9 Green Lane, Ford, Salisbury, Wilts, and has issue living, Nicolas Finch, *b* 1959; late Maj RTR: *m* 1985 (*m diss* 19—), Sara Jane Dolding, — Anthony James, *b* 1961; BSc: *m* 1st, 1992, Natalie Diane Magnaldi; 2ndly, 1998, Kate Louise Humphries, — Alison Frances, *b* 1963.

Grandsons of late Edwin William Gordon Rich, el son of late William Gordon Rich, 3rd son of late Rev John Rich (*b* 1789), 4th son of 1st baronet:—
Issue of late William Gordon Rich, *b* 1897, *d* 19—: *m* 1st, 1931, Henrietta Dorothy, who *d* 1955, da of Henry Donate Tyacke, of Westmeath, Ireland; 2ndly, 1958, Rhona Elizabeth, second da of late Thomas Lyons, of Hobart, Tasmania, and widow of John Matthew Clarke:—
(By 1st *m*) Urquhart David Gordon, *b* 1934; B Agriculture; is a Solicitor. —— John Patrick Gordon, *b* 1936: *m* 19-, Jillian, da of Helyar Bishop, of Papanui, Christchurch, New Zealand, and has issue living, Nicola, *b* 1960, — Joanna, *b* 1963.

Granddaughters of late Maitland Gordon Rich, yr son of late William Gordon Rich, 3rd son of late Rev John Rich (*b* 1789), 4th son of 1st baronet:—
Issue of late Geoffrey Gordon Rich, MC *b* 1889, *d* 1975: *m* 1924, Sybil Catherine Dorothy (14 Lysaght St, Timaru, NZ), da of Maj P. H. Johnson, of Mount Torlesse Station, Springfield, Canterbury, NZ:—
Dorothy Georgiana Gordon, *b* 1927: *m* 1951, Anthony Derek Morley Pinfold, of 187 Sawyers Arms Rd, Papanui, Christchurch, NZ, and has issue living, Giles Derek, *b* 1953, — Hamish Gordon Pinfold, *b* 1972, — Mary Kathryn, *b* 1954, — Judy Cassandra, *b* 1956. —— Penelope Rosamund, *b* 1929: *m* 1953, Frederick Gerard Ulrich, of The Rock, Cave, S Canterbury, NZ, and has issue living, Peter Herstall, *b* 1954, — Sally Rosamund, *b* 1956, — Robyn Penelope, *b* 1957, — Jan Belinda, *b* 1959. —— Angela Maitland, *b* 1932; *m* 1957, Lennox Mounsey, Master Mariner, of 77 Bann St, Bluff, NZ, and has issue living, Gordon Lennox, *b* 1958, — Timothy John, *b* 1965, — Prudence Jane, *b* 1960, — Annabel Kay, *b* 1963.

Grandsons of late Edwin Francis Rich, son of Vice-Adm Edwin Ludlow Rich, 5th son of 1st baronet:—
Issue of late Francis Arthur Rich, *b* 1859, *d* 1938: *m* 1st, 1890, Mary Catherine, who *d* 1899, da of Gerard Spooner, formerly of Elmdon, Warwickshire; 2ndly, 1899, Henrietta, da of Gerard Spooner (ante):—
(By 2nd *m*) Ronald Philip, *b* 1900. —— Edwin Francis, *b* 1903.

RICHARDSON (UK) 1924, of Yellow Woods, Province of Cape of Good Hope, South Africa

By courage, faith and honour

Sir ANTHONY LEWIS RICHARDSON, 3rd *Baronet*; *b* 5 Aug 1950; *s* his father, *Sir* LESLIE LEWIS, 1985; *ed* Diocesan Coll, Cape Town; Dir, Barclays Private Bank: *m* 1985, Honor Gillian, da of Robert Anthony Dauney, of Darling Point, Sydney, Australia, and has issue.

𝕬rms – Argent, an ostrich proper, on a chief sable three lions' heads erased of the field. 𝕮rest – Upon a rock a lion rampant guardant proper resting the sinister paw on a mullet, gold.
Residence – Triggs, Crondall Rd, Crondall, Hampshire GU10 5RU.

SON LIVING

WILLIAM LEWIS, *b* 15 Oct 1992.

DAUGHTER LIVING

Honor Olivia Phoebe, *b* 1990.

BROTHER LIVING

Charles John (7 Franconia Rd, SW4 9NB); *b* 1955; *ed* Diocesan Coll, Cape Town: *m* 1987, Gigi D. M., da of late Lt-Col R. R. Morris, of Huish Farm, Sydling St Nicholas, Dorset, and has issue living, George Leslie, *b* 1991, — Jessica Kate, *b* 1988.

SISTER LIVING

Jennifer, *b* 1947: *m* 1984, Richard Michael Fearon Gold, of Windrush Farm, Stowell, Dorset, eldest son of Rev Guy Alastair Whitmore Gold, of Bridge House, Great Bealings, Woodbridge, Suffolk, and has issue living, Alexander Leslie Fearon, *b* 1985, — Edward Guy Fearon, *b* 1986.

AUNT LIVING *(Daughter of 1st baronet)*

Audrey Anne, *b* 1909: *m* 1st, 1939, John Henry Muers-Raby, who *d* 1973; 2ndly, 1983, Maj-Gen Raymond Cyril Alexander Edge, CB, MBE, and has issue living, (by 1st *m*) Nicholas Jonathan (Townhead House, Stainforth, Settle, N Yorks), *b* 1941: *m* 1973, Victoria, da of Lt-Col Henry Christopher White Bowring, MA, FLAS, of Whelprigg, Casterton, Carnforth, Cumbria, and has issue living, Rosanna Louise *b* 1975, — Nigel Andrew (Higher Vexford House, Higher Vexford, Lydeard St Lawrence, Taunton, Som), *b* 1949: *m* 1986, Fiona Jane, da of Maj Geoffrey Lloyd, and has issue living, Thomas Sebastian *b* 1987, Oliver Henry *b* 1991. *Residence* – Amesbury Abbey, Amesbury, Wilts.

WIDOW LIVING OF SECOND BARONET

JOY PATRICIA (*Joy, Lady Richardson*), da of John Percival Rillstone, of Johannesburg, S Africa: *m* 1946, Sir Leslie Lewis Richardson, 2nd Bt, who *d* 1985. *Residence* – Constantia Village, Cape Town, S Africa.

The 1st baronet, Sir Lewis Richardson, CBE (son of Kaufmann Richardson), was head of the firm of L. Richardson & Co, of Port Elizabeth, London, New York, and Boston.

RICHARDSON (UK) 1929, of Weybridge, co Surrey (Extinct 1981)

Sir GEORGE WIGHAM RICHARDSON, 3rd and last *Baronet*.

DAUGHTERS LIVING OF THIRD BARONET *(By 2nd m)*

Jenifer Winifred Wigham, *b* 1945: *m* 1973, David M. Drayson, of Studmore, Brenchley, Kent, and has issue living, Timothy James, *b* 1975, — Jonathan Charles, *b* 1980, — Melanie Sarah, *b* 1976. —— Caroline Rosa Wigham, *b* 1950. —— Patricia Barbara Wigham, *b* 1953: *m* 1982, Alastair Currie Begg, who *d* 1994, of Monks Manor, Fir Toll Lane, Mayfield, E Sussex, and has issue living, Andrew Henry Wigham, *b* 1985, — Camilla Rosemary Wigham, *b* 1984.

STEWART-RICHARDSON (NS) 1630, of Pencaitland, Haddingtonshire

Honour is gained by valour

Sir SIMON ALAISDAIR (IAN NEILE) STEWART-RICHARDSON, 17th *Baronet*; *b* 10 June 1947; *s* his father, *Sir* IAN RORIE HAY, 1969; *ed* Trin Coll, Glenalmond.

Arms – Quarterly of six: 1st and 6th, argent, on a fesse azure between a bull's head or in chief and in base a lymphad sable, a saltire of the field *Richardson*; 2nd, argent, a lion rampant azure within a bordure gules *Stewart*; 3rd, azure, three garbs or *Comyn*; 4th, argent on a bend azure three buckles or *Leslie*; 5th, gyronny of eight or and sable *Campbell*. **Crest** – A cubit arm in armour grasping a sword all proper. **Supporters** – *Dexter*, a wyvern and *sinister*, an eagle wings erect, both proper.
Residence – Lynedale, Longcross, Chertsey, Surrey, KT16 0DP.

BROTHER LIVING

NINIAN RORIE (Rua Irlanda, Jardim Europa, CEP 01450-050, São Paulo, Brazil), *b* 20 Jan 1949; *ed* Rannoch Sch, Perthshire; industrialist, late Commercial Air Pilot: *m* 1983, Joan Kristina, da of Howard Smee, of Rio de Janeiro, Brazil, and has issue living, Edward Rorie, *b* 22 July 1988, — William Howard, *b* 1990, — Olivia Joan, *b* 1987.

SISTERS LIVING

Claudia Mavis, *b* 1946: *m* 1970, R. Anthony Wainwright, of 29 Stratford Rd, W8, and has a son and da, Guiam Edward, *b* 1985, — Sarah, *b* 1987. —— (Roslyn) Alison, *b* 1952: *m* 1984, Peter Glennerster Wear, of 33 Findon Rd, W12 9PP, and has issue living, Christopher Algernon, *b* 1988, — Jessica, *b* 1986.

WIDOW LIVING OF SIXTEENTH BARONET

AUDREY MERYL (Lynedale, Longcross, Chertsey, Surrey KT16 0DP), da of Claude Odlum, of Leinster Grove, Naas, co Kildare: *m* 1st, 1944, as his 2nd wife, Sir Ian Rorie Hay-Stewart-Richardson, 16th Bt, who *d* 1969; 2ndly, 1975, Patrick Allan Pearson Robertson, CMG.

COLLATERAL BRANCHES LIVING

Issue of late Lieut-Col Neil Graham Stewart-Richardson, DSO, 3rd son of 14th baronet; *b* 1881, *d* 1934: *m* 1924, Alexandra, who *d* 1972, da of late Peter Ralli, of 11 Hyde Park Gardens, W2:—
Peter Neil Ralli, MBE, *b* 1926; *ed* Eton; High Sheriff Norfolk 1989; Maj Coldstream Gds; Brig late Parachute Regt, Croix de Guerre 1950, MBE (Mil) 1964: *m* 1954, Patricia Ann, da of late Maj John Michael Evans Lombe, MC, RA, and has had issue, †Neil Graham John, *b* 1955; *ed* Eton; *d* 1978, — Michael Peter Alastair, *b* 1957: *m* 1982, Amanda L., only da of John Baker, of Higher Shortwood Farm, Litton, Bath, and has issue living, Rory Neil John *b* 1989, Lucy Alexandra *b* 1987, — Mary-Ann, *b* 1961: *m* 1st, 1981 (*m diss* 19—), (George) Dominic Mackintosh Warre, yst son of Maj John Antony Warre, MC, of Barrowden, Oakham, Leics (*see* D Devonshire, 1973-74 Edn); 2ndly, 1987, David Stewart Gemmell, of Delvine, Murthly, Perthshire PH1 4LD, son of Lt-Col Arthur Stewart Gemmell, of Ingarsby Old Hall, Leics, and has issue living, (by 2nd *m*) George Neil *b* 1988, Mary Rose *b* 1990, — Katharine Jane, *b* 1966. *Residence* – Creake Abbey, Fakenham, Norfolk NR21 9LF. —— Alastair Lucas Graham (120 Woodsford Sq, W14 8DT; 7 Kings Bench Walk, Temple, EC4) *b* 1927; *ed* Eton, and Magdalene Coll, Camb (MA); Bar Inner Temple 1952: *m* 1969, (Diana) Claire, yr da of late Brig George Streynsham Rawstorne, CBE, MC, and has issue living, James George, *b* 1971, — Hugh Neil, *b* 1977, — Sarah Alexandra, *b* 1974.

Grandchildren of late Henry Gresham Stewart-Richardson, 2nd son of 13th baronet:—
Issue of late Charles Robert Stewart-Richardson, *b* 1877, *d* 1954: *m* 1905, Edith, who *d* 1950, 2nd da of Albert Berryman, formerly of Bath:—
†Alistair De Vere (Australian, Union and Pioneers Clubs), *b* 1906; Dep Gen Manager of Bank of NSW, Sydney: *m* 1944, Joan Wilson, da of late Edward Wilson Hunt, of Lane Cove, NSW, and *d* 1983, leaving issue, Donald Bruce, *b* 1946: *m* 19—, —, and has issue living, a son *b* 19—, a da *b* 19—. —— Dudley Austin (322 Hector St, Tuart Hill, W Aust), *b* 1924: *m* 1948, Barbara Jean Clark, and has issue living Kenneth John, *b* 1950, — Peter Dudley, *b* 1953. —— Beatrice Edith, *b* 1909: *m* 1948, Clive Edwards. —— Constance, *b* 1918: *m* 1941, Harry Hatch, and has issue living, Geoffrey Neil, *b* 1943, — Brian Richard, *b* 1946 — Lorraine Elizabeth, *b* 1950. —— Sadie Mary, *b* 1921: *m* 1963, Frank Chinnock, of Mt Barker, W Aust.

Issue of late John Henry Stewart-Richardson, *b* 1879, *d* 1952: *m* 1924, Anne, who *d* 1980, da of late Thomas Jackson, of Carnforth, Lancashire:—
Ian Douglas, *b* 1925. *Residence* –

Grandchildren of late John Ramsay Stewart-Richardson, 3rd son of 13th baronet:—
Issue of late Arthur James Stewart-Richardson, *b* 1884, *d* 1950: *m* 1913, Kathleen Mary, who *d* 1964, da of late Charles Hunter, of Cambridge, New Zealand:—

Edward James (PO Box 10038, Arataki, Mt Maunganui 3030, NZ), *b* 1915; 1939-45 War with RNZAF: *m* 1948, Heather Gladys, who *d* 1985, da of Charles Scott, of Auckland, and has issue living, John Scott (11c Birdwood Crescent, Parnell, Auckland, NZ), *b* 1950; *ed* King's Coll, Auckland, and Auckland Univ; stockbroker, — Julia, *b* 1954; *ed* St Cuthberts Sch for Girls, Auckland, and Otago Univ: *m* 1990, Christopher William Cornthwaite, of 41 Dudley Rd, Mission Bay, Auckland, NZ, and has issue living, Guy Edward *b* 1991, James William *b* 1994. —— John Charles (1 Haworth Av, Cambridge, NZ) *b* 1925; 1939-45 War with RNZAF: *m* 1950, Edith Margaret, da of Percival McIver, of Wellington, NZ and has issue living, Ian, *b* 1954: *m* 1984, Patricia, da of Robert Searle, of Cambridge, NZ, and has issue living, Kurt Jon *b* 1984, — June, *b* 1950: *m* 1970, Allan Ross Browne, son of Ivan Browne, of Cambridge, NZ, and has issue living, Scott Michael *b* 1973, Glen Andrew *b* 1977, Aaron Paul *b* 1978. —— Kathleen Sheila, *b* 1921: *m* 1946, Derek Pocknall, of 4A Oxford St, Masterton, NZ, and has issue living, Robert, *b* 1949, — Graeme (twin), *b* 1949, — David Thomas, *b* 1953, — Susan Mary, *b* 1948, — Helen Jean, *b* 1958. —— Barbara Mary, *b* 1930: *m* 1st, 1950, Harold Vosper, who *d* 1960; 2ndly, 1962, Peter G. Wilson, of 4 Oleander Lane, Mt Maunganui, NZ, and has issue living, (by 1st *m*), Frank Stewart, *b* 1951; *ed* Wanganui Collegiate: *m* 1979, Claire Jeannette, da of Lionel Montague, of Matamata, NZ, and has issue living, Kirk James *b* 1981, Lauren Jane *b* 1980, Brook Jade *b* 1986, — Richard Arthur, *b* 1953; *ed* Wanganui Collegiate, and Matamata Coll: *m* 1st, 1979, —; 2ndly, 1984, —, da of Noutsos, of Athens, Greece; 3rdly, 1997, Dione Haswell, and has issue living (by 2nd *m*), Nikolas *b* 1984, Sarah Elizabeth *b* 1987, — Jennifer Kaye, *b* 1955: *m* 1980, Neil Brooks, son of Keith Brooks, and has issue living, Mitchell Peter *b* 1987, Jackson Stewart *b* 1998, — (by 2nd *m*), Stewart James, *b* 1968: *m* 1999, Angela McAleese, — Robyn Jane, *b* 1963: *m* 1997, Paul Kenna.

Sir Robert Richardson of Pencaitland, Haddingtonshire, was created a baronet with remainder to heirs male whatsoever. On the death of the 2nd baronet 1640, the title passed to Sir James Richardson of Smeaton, grandson of Sir James, el brother of 1st baronet. This baronetcy was dormant 1821-37, when John Stewart-Richardson assumed the title on being served heir of the 12th baronet. The mother of the 13th baronet was Elizabeth, el da and co-heir of James Stewart of Urrard, Perths. The 15th baronet, Sir Edward Austin, Capt Black Watch, was *ka* 1914.

Richardson-Bunbury, see Bunbury.

RICHMOND (UK) 1929, of Hollington, co Sussex

Sir JOHN FREDERICK RICHMOND, 2nd *Baronet*; *b* 12 Aug 1924; *s* his father, Sir FREDERICK HENRY, 1953; *ed* Eton, and at Jesus Coll, Camb; formerly Lieut 10th Hussars (seconded Provost branch): *m* 1965, Mrs Anne Moreen Bentley, who *d* 1997, da of late Dr Robert William Paylor Hall, MC, and has issue.

Labour conquers

Arms – Gules, on a fesse cotissed or, between two roses argent, barbed and seeded proper, a lion passant of the field. Crest – A demi-stag proper, charged on the shoulder with a rose as in the arms, and holding between the forelegs a rose argent, barbed, seeded, leaved, and slipped, also proper.
Residence – Shimpling Park Farm, Bury St Edmunds, Suffolk. *Club* – MCC.

DAUGHTER LIVING

Caroline Sarah, *b* 1966.

SISTER LIVING

Anne Elizabeth, *b* 1926: *m* 1958, Dudley William Reeves, and has issue living, Nicholas Mark Renny, *b* 1964, — Heather Jennifer, *b* 1962: has issue living, Myles Edward REEVES *b* 1987. *Residence* – Filgrave House, Newport Pagnell, Bucks.

The 1st baronet, Sir Frederick Henry Richmond (son of late Henry Richmond, of Marnham), was Chm of Debenhams Ltd, of 91 Wimpole Street, W1, and of Harvey Nichols and Co, Ltd.

RICKETTS (UK) 1828, of The Elms, Gloucestershire, and Beaumont Leys, Leicestershire

Prend moi tel que je suis

Take me as I am

Sir ROBERT CORNWALLIS GERALD ST LEGER RICKETTS, 7th *Baronet*; *b* 8 Nov 1917; *s* his father, *Sir* CLAUDE ALBERT FREDERICK, 1937; *ed* Haileybury, and Magdalene Coll, Camb (MA); admitted a Solicitor 1949; FRSA; formerly Partner in Wellington and Clifford; 1939-45 War as Capt Devonshire Regt; Personal Assist to Ch of Staff, Gibraltar, 1942-45 and ADC to Lt-Gov of Jersey 1945-46; Hon Citizen of Mobile, Alabama, USA: *m* 1945, (Anne) Theresa, CBE, who *d* 1998, da of late Rt Hon Sir (Richard) Stafford Cripps, CH, QC (*see* B Parmoor, colls), and has issue.

Arms – On a chevron azure between three roses gules, barbed and seeded proper, two swords in chevron also proper, pommels and hilts or, their points crossing each other in saltire (that on the dexter surmounted by that of the sinister) and passing through a wreath of laurel or; on a chief of the second a naval crown between two anchors erect or. **Crest** – Out of a naval crown or, a dexter arm embowed, habited azure and charged on the sleeve with two roses argent, the hand grasping a scimitar, the arm in front of an anchor in bend sinister sable.
Residence – Forwood House, Minchinhampton, Stroud, Gloucestershire GL6 9AB.

SONS LIVING

(ROBERT) TRISTRAM (47 Lancaster Av, SE27 9EL), *b* 17 April 1946; *ed* Winchester, and Magdalene Coll, Camb (MA): *m* 1969, Ann, yr da of late Eric William Charles Lewie, CB, of 31 Deena Close, Queen's Drive, W3, and has issue living, Stephen Tristram, *b* 1974, — Clare Jessica *b* 1977. —— John Stafford (92 Thompson Av, Richmond, Surrey), *b* 1956; *ed* Winchester, and King's Coll, London: *m* 1986, Jacqueline Zifteh, and has issue living, Joseph Robert *b* 1988.

DAUGHTERS LIVING

Sarah Lilian, *b* 1947: *m* 1981, His Honour (George Frederick) Peter Mason, QC, of Lane Cottage, Amberley, Glos GL5 5AB. —— (Isobel) Theresa, *b* 1952: *m* 1973, John Anthony Bird, MBE, and has issue living, Patrick Jack, *b* 1975, — Eileen Diana, *b* 1977.

COLLATERAL BRANCHES LIVING

Grandchildren of late Rev Richard Ernest Ricketts, son of late Com Simpson Hicks Ricketts, RN, 3rd son of 1st Baronet:—
Issue of late Rt Rev Clement Mallory Ricketts, formerly Suffragan Bishop of Dunwich, *b* 1885, *d* 1961: *m* 1920, Dorothy Frances, who *d* 1984, da of late Rt Rev George Rodney Eden, DD (*see* Eden of Winton, B, colls, 1985 Edn):—
Michael Rodney, *b* 1923 (Breakers, Atlantic Terrace, New Polzeath, N Cornwall PL27 6UG); *ed* Sherborne and Trin Coll, Oxford (MA); formerly Maj KRRC; a House Master, Bradfield Coll 1950-67, Headmaster of Sutton Valence Sch 1967-80, 1939-45 War (wounded): *m* 1958, Judith Anne Caroline, el da of late Col Thomas Stanley Courtenay-Clack, TD, RA, and widow of H. J. Corry, and has issue living, Charles Michael Thomas, *b* 1960: *m* 1990, Jill Elizabeth Davies, and has issue living, Joseph Charles *b* 1992, Thomas Benjamin *b* 1993, Luke William *b* 1997, — James Rodney Eden, *b* 1964, — Rosemary Courtenay, *b* 1958, — Katharine Elizabeth, *b* 1962. —— John Eden (World's End, Reepham, Norwich), *b* 1926; *ed* Sherborne, and Trin Coll, Oxford (MA); formerly in RM; Housemaster of School House, Worksop Coll 1959-74: *m* 1970, Isobel Claridge, da of late Charles Claridge Druce, of Flishinghurst, Cranbrook, Kent, and has issue living, Michael Tristram *b* 1971, Christopher Eden *b* 1973: *m* 1994, Loretta Wendy, el da of Anthony Wood, of Dartmouth. —— Rosemary Ellison, *b* 1928; *ed* Cheltenham Ladies' Coll: *m* 1949, Rev Frank Richard Knight Hare, of 14 Lee Rd, Aldeburgh, Suffolk IP15 5HG, and has issue living, Roger John, *b* 1957; assumed the additional surname of Shelmerdine by deed poll 1989, but subsequently discontinued; Maj Anglian Regt: *m* 1981, Caroline Philippa Shelmerdine, and has issue living, Thomas Shelmerdine *b* 1985, Rayner Harry *b* 1990, Alicia Caroline *b* 1983, Brioni Alexandra *b* 1988, — Elizabeth, *b* 1952: *m* 1972, Richard Cane, and has issue living, Rachel Simone *b* 1974, Annabel Louise *b* 1977.

The 1st baronet, Sir Robert Tristram Ricketts, DCL, was a Vice-Admiral, and the 2nd baronet was an Admiral. The 3rd baronet in 1884 succeeded to the estates of his maternal uncle (Col Thomas R. Plumbe-Tempest), and assumed by Roy licence in that year the surname of Tempest in lieu of his patronymic.

RIDDELL (NS) 1628, of Riddell, Roxburghshire

Sir JOHN CHARLES BUCHANAN RIDDELL, CVO, 13th *Baronet; b* 3 Jan 1934; *s* his father, *Sir* WALTER ROBERT BUCHANAN, 1934; *ed* Eton, and Ch Ch, Oxford (BA, MA); Dep Chm IBA 1981-85; Private Sec to TRH the Prince and Princess of Wales 1985-90, a Member of the Prince's Council 1985-90; CVO 1990; DL Northumberland 1990: *m* 1969, Hon Sarah Richardson, LVO, da of Baron Richardson of Duntisbourne, KG, MBE, PC (Life Baron), of Chelsea, SW3, and has issue.

Arms – Argent, a chevron gules between three ears of rye slipped and bladed vert. Crest – A demi-greyhound argent. Supporters – Two grey-hounds argent.
Residences – Hepple, Morpeth, Northumberland; 49 Campden Hill Sq, W8.

SONS LIVING

WALTER JOHN, *b* 10 June 1974. —— Hugh Gordon, *b* 1976. —— Robert Henry, *b* 1982.

SISTERS LIVING

Jean (*Lady Pumphrey*), *b* 1920: *m* 1945, Sir John Laurence Pumphrey, KCMG, of Caistron, Thropton, Morpeth, Northumberland NE65 7LG, and has issue living, Matthew James, *b* 1946: *m* 1976, Pamela Mary Clare, da of James Wyllie Irving, and has issue living, John Wyllie Francis *b* 1979, Maximilian Oscar Edward *b* 1982, India Victoria *b* 1988, — Charles Walter Bartholomew, *b* 1948: *m* 1981, (Cynthia) Penelope Helen, only child of late David Bruce (*see* E Elgin, colls), and has issue living, Oliver James *b* 1986, David Laurence *b* 1989, Katharine Elizabeth *b* 1983, — Jonathan Henry, *b* 1954: *m* 1982, Nicola, only da of late J. A. R. N. White, of Ladbroke Rd, W8, and has issue living, Jonathan Vivian *b* 1985, Rebecca Elisabeth *b* 1986, Olivia Rachel *b* 1989, — James Laurence, *b* 1964: *m* 1991, Katherine Lucy, yr da of David Sanders, of Winchester, and has issue living, Oliver Thomas *b* 1996, Camilla Louise *b* 1993, — Laura Mary Beatrice, *b* 1951: *m* 1983, Robert James Longair, son of Arthur Longair, of Calgary, Alberta, Canada, and has issue living, Samuel Christopher *b* 1985, Alexander Hugh *b* 1988, a da *b* 1990. —— Mary, *b* 1922: *m* 1954, Richard Laurence Ollard, of Norchard Farmhouse, Morecombelake, Bridport, Dorset DT6 6EP, and has issue living, William Richard, *b* 1957, — Edward Christopher, *b* 1959, — Elizabeth Rachel, *b* 1961. —— Anne, *b* 1924. —— Hester, *b* 1927: *m* 1956, Christopher Henry Pemberton, of Place Farmhouse, Bardwell, Bury St Edmunds, Suffolk, and has issue living, Jethro Francis *b* 1987, Sophia Rosamund *b* 1991, — (Richard) Mark (The Old Diary, Stoughton, W Sussex PO18 9JQ), *b* 1961: *m* 1993, Mrs Olivia Mary Rokeby Nicolson, da of Antony Charles Reynardson Fane (*see* E Westmorland, colls), and formerly wife of Adam Nicolson (*see* B Carnock), and has issue living, Joseph Oliver *b* 1995, Oscar Hugh *b* 1998, — Daniel Hugh Vincent, *b* 1962, — Thomas William, *b* 1964, — Isobel Beatrice *b* 1959: *m* 1994, David Goldblatt, 2nd son of Samuel Goldblatt, of Ra'anana, Israel, and has issue living, Oliver Solomon *b* 1999, Rachel Mathilda *b* 1994, Lily Judith *b* 1997.

COLLATERAL BRANCHES LIVING

Grandsons of late Major Ralph Gervase Riddell-Carre, son of late Thomas Alexander Riddell-Carre, son of late Walter Riddell-Carre, 2nd son of Thomas Riddell (*b* 1777) (infra):—
Issue of late Sqdn Ldr Gervase Robert Riddell-Carre, RAFVR, *b* 1906, *d* 1989: *m* 1940, Eileen Inez, who *d* 1993, only da of late John Tweedie, of Edradour, North Berwick:—
Ralph John (31 Hillway, N6 6QB), *b* 1941: *ed* Harrow: *m* 1972, Valerie Caroline Wells, only da of late W. T. W. Tickler, of White-ladies, Frinton-on-Sea, Essex, and has issue living, John Timothy, *b* 1976, — Peter Thomas, *b* 1979, — David Alexander, *b* 1983. —— Walter Gervase (Cavers Carre, Melrose, Roxburghshire TD6 9EJ), *b* 1944; *ed* Harrow; CA: *m* 1975, Carolyn Anne, eldest da of Maj A. P. P. Ricketts, of The Old Manse, Nigg, Ross-shire, and has issue living, Andrew Gervase, *b* 1979, — James Walter, *b* 1981.

Grandson of late Col Thomas William Carre Riddell, VD, son of John Carre Riddell, 3rd son of late Thomas Riddell (*b* 1777), el son of William Riddell, son of Thomas Riddell (*b* 1696), 2nd son of 4th baronet:—
Issue of late Col Consett Carre Riddell, DSO, VD, BSc, BME, MIE (Aust), *b* 1887, *d* 1953: *m* 1923, Thora, who *d* 1963, da of J. L. Menzies:—
John Walter Carre, MB, BS, *b* 1925: *ed* Melbourne Univ; *m* 1957, Margaret Louise, who *d* 1986, only da of R. W. Krohn, and has issue living, Malcolm John Carre, *b* 1960, — David Ronald Carre, *b* 1966: *m* 19—, Jaki, 2nd da of John Lagos, of The Entrance N, NSW, and has issue living, Taylor Lagos Carre *b* 1997, — Fiona Carre, *b* 1958: *m* 1989, James Posillico, of Bayville, New York, — Susan Patricia Carre, *b* 1962: *m* 1989, Michael Underwood Felton. *Residence* – 2/547 Whitehorse Rd, Surrey Hills, Vic 3127, Aust.

Grandson of late Col Edward Vansittart Dick Riddell, 2nd son of late Col Robert Vansittart Riddell, eldest son of late Robert Riddell (*b* 1804), great-grandson of late Walter Riddell, son of late William Riddell, 2nd son of 2nd baronet:—
Issue of late Major Edward Alexander Buchanan Riddell, *b* 1903, *d* 1986; *m* 1st, 1928, Mary, eldest da of Stuart Cameron, of Caulfields, Vancouver, BC, Canada: 2ndly, 1939, Mrs Irene Julia Ballance, who *d* 1961, da of late A.W.E. Bullmore, of Letchworth, Herts: 3rdly, 1962, Mrs Mary Kingzett, da of late Lt-Col John Kennington, DSO, MC, JP, DL, of Riby, Lincs:—
(By 1st m) Stuart Edward, *b* 1929: *m* 1960, Emily Spitzer, da of late Whiting N. Shepard, of Montclair, New Jersey, USA, and has issue living, Cameron Alexander, *b* 1962, — Romayne Bouvée, *b* 1964.

Grandsons of late Brig John Balfour Riddell, DSO, 3rd son of late Col Robert Vansittart Riddell (ante):—
Issue of late Lt-Col John L'Estrange Riddell, TD, *b* 1910, *d* 1984: *m* 1939, Barbara Agnes, da of late M. McC. Fairgrieve, of Edinburgh:—
Robert Balfour (c/o AIICO Insurance (Nigeria) plc, PO Box 2577, Lagos, Nigeria), *b* 1940; *ed* Edinburgh Acad; ACII: *m* 1966 (*m diss* 1984), Jean, da of late M. Allen, of London. —— John Gifford (61 Belle Vue Rd, Salisbury, Wilts SP1 3YE), *b* 1942; *ed* Edinburgh Acad: *m* 1966, Belinda Irene, da of late E. C. Hensler, of 20 Fisherton St, Salisbury, and has issue living, Benedict Charles John, *b* 1969: *m* 1991, Karen Anne, da of Christopher Jones, of Swanfield by Dunnet, Thurso, and has issue living, Christopher John *b* 1994, Anna Louise *b* 1996, — Jonathan David, *b* 1973. —— Archibald George Vansittart (31 Marlston Av, off Lache Lane, Chester), *b* 1954; *ed* Oundle: *m* 1982, Patricia Maria, 2nd da of late John B. Axon, of 18 Panton Rd, Chester, and has issue living, Andrew John, *b* 1986, — Alexander George, *b* (twin) 1986, and an adopted da, Kelly Jayne, *b* 1979.

Granddaughters of late William Riddell, 2nd son of late Rev Henry Riddell, 2nd son of Henry Riddell (*b* 1745), grandson of John Riddell, 2nd son of the Rev Archibald Riddell, 3rd son of 2nd baronet:—
Issue of late John Riddell, *b* 1895, *d* 1959: *m* 1st, 1918 (*m diss* 1923), Doris Alice Victoria Jones; 2ndly, 1925, Alys, who *d* 1982, da of John R. Savage, of Edinburgh:—
(By 1st *m*) Irene Yvonne, *b* 1919: *m* 1943, Richard Adamson Crow, TD, who *d* 1998, of 24 Abbey Walk, Gt Missenden, Bucks HP16 0AY, and has issue living, Richard Michael, *b* 1944: *m* 1st, 1964 (*m diss* 1974), Alexandra Drysdale Love; 2ndly, 1980, Jean Marie Westbeach, and has issue living (by 1st *m*), Simon Richard *b* 1969, Victoria Caroline *b* 1965: *m* 1991, Jason Bacon (and has issue living, Emily Alexandra Mathewson *b* 1994, Georgia Victoria *b* 1998) (by 2nd *m*) Richard James *b* 1981, William Thomas Adamson *b* 1984, Caroline Rose *b* 1987, — Michael Anthony, *b* 1948: *m* 1st, 1972 (*m diss* 1984), Penelope Laura Carter; 2ndly, 1987, Jill MacKay Ballantyne, and has issue living (by 1st *m*), Benjamin James *b* 1976, Rebecca Jane *b* 1974, and has two adopted das, Tracey Michele, *b* 1960: *m* 1982 (*m diss* 1992), Andrew Robert Banks, and has issue living, Harrison Andrew *b* 1986, Hetty Mae *b* 1984, — Katherine Margaret Lindsay, *b* 1962: *m* 1997, Adam Glyn Gillespie Jones, and has issue living, Cameron Peter Adamson *b* 1998. —— (By 2nd *m*), Audrian, *b* 1926: *m* 1950, William Burns Hutchinson, and has issue living, Michael William (53 Heathfield Crescent, Waterdown, Ont L0R 2H5), *b* 1961: *m* 1991, Patricia Eileen Tendam, and has issue living, Matthew Benjamin *b* 1992, Nicholas William *b* 1996, — Gregory John (28 Pearl St, Leamington, Ont N8H 1J6), *b* 1962: *m* 1987, Rebecca Ann Clark, and has issue living, Andrew John *b* 1991, Ryan William *b* 1993, — Janet Louise, *b* 1954. *Residence* – 9 Lorne Av, Leamington, Ont, Canada N8H 2H6.

Grandchildren of James Riddell, yst son of Rev Henry Riddell (ante):—
Issue of late Walter Riddell, *b* 1874, *d* 1951: *m* 1917, Mary Ellinor, who *d* 1958, da of late Dr John Garbutt Hutchinson, of North Lodge, Kineton:—
John Walter Rowland, *b* 1919.

Issue of late Lt-Col Archibald Riddell, DSO, *b* 1882, *d* 1970: *m* 1907, Edith Mary, who *d* 1947, da of late William Lawrie, of Seleng, Assam:—
William James, MBE (Foresters, Hightown Hill, Ringwood, Hants), *b* 1909; late Maj Gen List; served in World War II; *ed* Harrow, and Clare Coll, Camb; MBE (Mil) 1944: *m* 1st, 1959, Jeannette Anne, who *d* 1972, da of late Edward Kessler, and widow of Ripley Oddie; 2ndly, 1973, Alison Frances, da of late Arthur Newton Jackson, of Wilmslow, Cheshire, and has issue living (by 2nd *m*), Jemma Jeannette, *b* 1976.

Grandchildren of late Lt-Col Archibald Riddell, DSO (ante):—
Issue of late Group-Capt Peter John Archibald Riddell, CBE, *b* 1914, *d* 1985: *m* 1940 (*m diss* 1968), Cynthia Mary, who *d* 1993, da of late Brooks Crompton Wood, of Bruern Abbey, Churchill, Oxford:—
Nicholas Peter (18 Myddelton Sq, EC1), *b* 1941; *ed* Harrow, and Magdalene Coll, Camb (BA); Bar Inner Temple 1964: *m* 1st, 1967 (*m diss* 1976), Felicity Jane, eldest da of D.G. Rolfe, of Kensington; 2ndly, 1976, Barbara Helen, eldest da of Peter Glucksmann, of 53 Hendon Lane, N3, and has issue living, (by 1st *m*) Eleanor Mary, *b* 1972, — (by 2nd *m*) Juliet Clare, *b* 1979, — Laura Virginia, *b* 1982. —— Catherine Mary, *b* 1944: *m* 1976, Timothy Clare O'Rorke, FRICS, of 1 St James's Gdns, W11, and has issue living, Mark Henry, *b* 1978, — David Anthony, *b* 1981.

Grandchildren of late William Law Riddell, son of Robert Riddell (*b* 1797), yst son of Henry Riddell (*b* 1745) (ante):—
Issue of late Robert Riddell, *b* 1879, *d* 1958: *m* 1908, Flora McDonald, who *d* 1961, da of Charles Samuel George Nicholson, of Duntulm, Isle of Skye:—
William Law, *b* 1909: *m* 1941, Jean, da of late Edwin Charles Hocking, of Dunedin, NZ, and has issue living, Robert James (40 Oriel Av, Tawa, Wellington, NZ), *b* 1942; BAgricSc NZ: *m* 1965, Marion Gwynneth, da of K. McIntosh, of Rangiora, N Canterbury, NZ, and has issue living, William Grant *b* 1973, Anna Ruth *b* 1969, Lynette Judith *b* 1970, — Eleanor Mary, *b* 1943; BA (NZ): *m* 1st, 1964 (*m diss* 1978), David John Sutherland; 2ndly, 19—, Bruce Charles Smart, of 7 Kirkdale Place, Ilam, Christchurch, New Zealand, and has issue living (by 1st *m*), Elliot David Law *b* 1969, Meredith Lawrie *b* 1970, Fiona Jean *b* 1967, — Helen Annette *b* 1946; MA (NZ): *m* 1967, Roger Beach Balfour Mee, MB, ChB, FRACS(NZ), and has issue living, Jared James Balfour *b* 1968, Nicholas Roger Alexander *b* 1970, Michaela-Jean Coates *b* 1975, Josephine Bridie Mary *b* 1982. —— Flora McDonald (39 Chapter St, Christchurch, NZ), *b* 1910: *m* 1944, John Campbell Wilson, who *d* 1964, and has issue living, Elizabeth, *b* 1946; MA (NZ). —— Charlotte Isabel, *b* 1913: *m* 1938, Ralph Alan Gibson, of Wellington, NZ, and has issue living, John Hastings, *b* 1938; BEng (NZ): *m* 1964, Barbara Dawn Shepherd, of Timara, S Canterbury, NZ, and has issue, — Margaret Flora, *b* 1940: *m* 1961, Murray Bennett, and has issue. —— Margaret Carlina, *b* 1914: *m* 1939, William Kemp Paterson, of 2 Kirrimuir St, Dunedin, NZ, and has issue living, Gaynor Margaret, *b* 1941: *m* 1969, John Lyall, of Dunedin, NZ, — Roberta Joy, *b* 1946; BSc (NZ): *m* 1968, Ian Leslie Stephenson, BSc, of Hamilton, NZ, — Isabel Janice, *b* 1950: *m* 1970, Bruce Ronald Cowan, of Dunedin, NZ. —— Joan Doreen, *b* 1927: *m* 1948, Herbert Rance Brenton, and has issue living, Mervyn Robert, *b* 1940, Lyal James, *b* 1953, — Robyn Joan, *b* 1951. *Residence* – Geraldine, Canterbury, NZ. —— Mary Frazer (165 Weston Rd, Christchurch, NZ), *b* 1922.

Grandchildren of late Robert Riddell (*b* 1879) (ante):—
Issue of late James Riddell, *b* 1920, *d* 1972: *m* 1950, Annette Lucy (The Downs, Geraldine, S Canterbury, NZ), da of P. Forde, of 62 Darby St, Christchurch, NZ:—
Peter James, *b* 1958. —— Judith Mary, *b* 1952. —— Sally Anne, *b* 1954. —— Annette Joan, *b* 1956.

Issue of late John Buchanan Riddell, *b* 1924, *d* 1969: *m* 1948, Barbara Frances, da of F. H. Ruddenklau, of Rangatata Island, Temuka, NZ:—
Frank Buchanan, *b* 1951. —— David John, *b* 1953. —— Graham Samuel, *b* 1961. —— Gail, *b* 1949. —— Sandra Ngaire, *b* 1958.

This family is of Norman descent, and was early settled in Roxburghshire, Gervase de Ridle, or Ridel, being High Sheriff of that county in 1116. The 9th baronet was successively MP for Selkirkshire and Lanarkshire, and the 10th baronet was Recorder of Maidstone and Tenterden 1846-63, and Judge of County Courts for N Staffordshire 1859-63, and for Whitechapel 1863-79. Sir John Walter, 11th Bt, was High Sheriff of Northumberland 1897. Sir Walter Robert, 12th Bt, was Principal of Hertford College, Oxford 1922-28 and Chm U.G.C. 1930-34.

RIGBY (UK) 1929, of Long Durford, Rogate, co Sussex

I would rather die than be dishonoured

Sir ANTHONY JOHN RIGBY, 3rd *Baronet*; *b* 3 Oct 1946; *s* his father, *Sir* (HUGH) JOHN MACBETH, ERD, 1999: *m* 1978, Mary, eld da of late R. G. Oliver, of Hope Green, Adlington, Macclesfield, and has issue.

Arms – Argent, on a cross flory sable a rod of Æsculapius or. Crest – In front of an antelope's head erased proper gorged with an antique crown or, two ostrich feathers saltirewise argent.

SONS LIVING

OLIVER HUGH, *b* 20 Aug 1979. —— Rollo Macbeth, *b* 1981. —— Tom Gladwin, *b* 1985.

DAUGHTER LIVING

Flora Charlotte Leacock, *b* 1989.

BROTHERS LIVING

Hugh Macbeth, *b* 1948: *m* 1970, Kathleen Mary, da of Conrad Salber, of Rochester, NY, USA, and has issue living, Zachary John, *b* 1974, — Rachel Mary, *b* 1971. —— James Erskine, *b* 1949: *m* 1979, Victoria Mary, da of late Charles Noel Edmeston, of Rush Cottage, Gore Lane, Alderley Edge, Cheshire, and has issue living, Simon Henry Erskine, *b* 1984. —— Stephen Leacock, *b* 1952: *m* 1st, 1979 (*m diss* 19—) Sally Anne, da of H. E. W. (Peter) Kirby, of 20 Admiralty Rd, Felpham, W Sussex; 2ndly, 1998, Frances Christine, da of late J. Lill, of Almodington, Chichester, W Sussex, and has issue living, (by 1st *m*) William Peter, *b* 1986, — Emily Flora, *b* 1983, — Alice Olivia, *b* 1988, — Melissa Mary, *b* 1989.

UNCLE LIVING (*son of 1st baronet*)

Roger Macbeth, *b* 1922; *ed* Winchester, and Magdalene Coll, Camb; is Hon Capt Roy Armoured Corps: *m* 1957, Patricia Ann, who *d* 1996, yr da of late Capt Desmond Nevill Cooper Tufnell, DSC, RN, and has issue living, Melissa Terwick, *b* 1959: *m* 1989, Christopher Wills, and has issue living, India Macbeth *b* 1991, Iona Christie *b* 1993, — Tanya Macbeth, *b* 1961: *m* 1993, Mark Anthony Lole, and has issue living, William Thomas *b* 1996, Amber Macbeth *b* 1994. *Residence* – Ansty Plum, Ansty, Salisbury, Wilts SP3 5QD.

AUNT LIVING (*daughter of 1st baronet*)

Margaret Hamilton, *b* 1919: *m* 1951, Richard Kynaston Briscoe (*see* Briscoe, Bt). *Residence* – 12 Rosemary Court, Church Rd, Haslemere, Surrey GU27 1BH.

The 1st baronet, Sir Hugh Mallinson Rigby, KCVO, FRCS (son of late John Rigby), was for several years Surg to HM Queen Alexandra, Serjeant-Surg to HM King George V, and Surg-in-Ord to HM King Edward VIII when Prince of Wales.

RIPLEY (UK) 1880, of Rawdon, Yorkshire

While I breathe I hope

Sir HUGH RIPLEY, 4th *Baronet*; *b* 26 May 1916; *s* his father, *Sir* HENRY WILLIAM ALFRED, 1956; *ed* Eton; late Dir of John Walker and Sons; Major (ret) King's Shropshire LI; European War 1942-5 in Tunisia and Italy (wounded, despatches twice, American Silver Star); author of *Whisky for Tea* (1991): *m* 1st, 1946 (*m diss* 1971), Dorothy Mary Dunlop, da of J. C. Bruce Jones (Dunlop Bt); 2ndly, 1972, Susan, da of W. Parker, of Keythorpe Grange, E Norton, Leicester, and has issue by 1st and 2nd *m*.

𝕬rms – Per chevron nebuly or and vert, three lions rampant counterchanged between three cross crosslets, two in base or, and one in chief vert. 𝕮rest – A demi-lion reguardant vert, collared or, charged on the shoulder with a cross crosslet of the second, and holding between the paws an escutcheon argent charged with a cockerel proper.
Seat – Bedstone, Bucknell, Shropshire. *Residences* – 20 Abingdon Villas, W8 6BX; The Oak, Bedstone, Shropshire. *Club* – Boodle's.

SON LIVING (*By 1st marriage*)

WILLIAM HUGH (Dove Cottage, Bedstone, Bucknell, Shropshire), *b* 13 April 1950; *ed* Eton, and McGill Univ (BA); bookseller.

DAUGHTERS LIVING (*By 1st marriage*)

(Dorothy) Caroline, *b* 1947: *m* 1983, as his 2nd wife, Hugh John Montgomery-Massingberd, the writer, of 101 Hereford Rd, W2 5BB, only son of John Michael Montgomery-Massingberd, of Gunby, Lincs (*see* V Hawarden, colls, 1928 Edn).

(*By 2nd marriage*)

Katherine, *b* 1974.

SISTER LIVING

Suzan, *b* 1919; European War 1939-45 with ATS: *m* 1951 Robert de la Garde Savery, and has issue living, Christopher Robert de la Garde, *b* 1954: *m* 1980, Margaret, yst da of Ian Archibald Slater, of Wellside, Livesey Rd, Ludlow, Shropshire, and has issue living, Alice Eugénie de la Garde *b* 1983, — Chloë Abigail de la Garde, *b* 1955: *m* 1979, Andrew John Scott Calder. *Residence* – Orchard House, Bedstone, Bucknell, Shropshire.

COLLATERAL BRANCH LIVING

Issue of late Lieut-Col Edward Robert Guy Ripley, King's Shropshire LI, el son of 3rd baronet, *b* 1911, *ka* in Normandy June 1944; *m* 1944, Sarah Stella (Cripplegate, Llanidloes, Powys SY18 6AP), elder da of late Col Arthur George Pardoe, RE (TF), of Gravel Hill, Kington, Herefords (*see* Every, Bt, colls):—
Patience Anna, *b* (*posthumous*) (Dec) 1944: *m* 1963, Richard Michael Tudor Morgan, of Llwyn, Llanidloes, Powys, and has issue living, David Paul Edward (Swyn-y-Lli, Llanidloes, Powys SY18 6IIG), *b* 1964: *m* 1991, Anna Maureen, da of Vincent Samuel Hodgson, and has issue living, Jessica Chelsea *b* 1993, Imogen Rose *b* 1995, — Timothy Michael Julian, *b* 1969, — Charlotte Sarah, *b* 1965: *m* 1985, Kevin Thomas Ingram, of Llawryllan, St Harmon, Rhayader, Powys LD6 5LU, and has issue living, Rebecca Sarah *b* 1988, Rachel Elizabeth *b* 1990, Abigail Jane *b* 1993.

Sir Henry William Ripley, 1st Bt, son of Edward Ripley of Bowling, near Bradford, was MP for Bradford (*L*) 1868-9 and 1874-80. Sir Frederick Ripley of Acacia, Rawdon, 3rd son of 1st Bt, was *cr* a baronet 1897, which became ext on death of 3rd Bt in 1954.

RITCHIE (UK) 1918, of Highlands (Extinct 1991)

Sir JAMES EDWARD THOMSON RITCHIE, TD, 2nd and last *Baronet*.

HALF-SISTER LIVING OF SECOND BARONET

Barbara Anne Lydia Janet, *b* 1916; European War 1940-43 with ATS attached RA. *Residence* – Crackshill Cottage, Yelvertoft, near Rugby.

Rivett-Carnac, see Carnac.

ROBERTS (UK) 1809, of Glassenbury, Kent, of Brightfieldstown, co Cork and of the City of Cork

Sir GILBERT HOWLAND ROOKEHURST ROBERTS, 7th *Baronet*; *b* 31 May 1934; *s* his father, Col *Sir* THOMAS LANGDON HOWLAND, CBE, 1979; *ed* Rugby, and Gonville and Caius Coll, Camb (BA; CEng, MIMechE); served in Kenya with RE (East African GS Medal): *m* 1958, Ines Eleonore, only da of late Alfons Leo Labunski, of Danzig, and has issue.

Arms – Azure, on a chevron argent cotised or, three mullets of six points sable, pierced of the field. Crest – On a mount vert an eagle displayed ermine, wings argent, gorged with a chaplet of ivy proper.
Residence – 3340 Cliff Drive, Santa Barbara, Calif 93109-1079, USA.

SON LIVING

HOWLAND LANGDON, *b* 19 Aug 1961.

DAUGHTER LIVING

Solveig Margaret, *b* 1959.

BROTHER LIVING

Walter Rookehurst (72 Eccleston Square, SW1V 1PJ), *b* 1951; *ed* King's Sch, Canterbury, and Gonville and Caius Coll, Camb (MA); admitted a Solicitor England and Wales 1978, Hong Kong 1985; Capt 4th RTR (TA): *m* 1988, Caroline Heather, da of Hugh Cocks, of Woodside Green, Essex.

ADOPTIVE SISTER LIVING

Virtue survives death

Rosamund Margaret (Kings Farm, Noar Hill, Selborne, nr Alton, Hants GU34 3LW), *b* 1951: *m* 1988, Steven R. Noel-Hill.

COLLATERAL BRANCH LIVING

Issue of late Capt Gilbert Howland Roberts, CBE, RD, RN, yr son of 5th baronet, *b* 1900, *d* 1986: *m* 1st, 1930 (*m diss* 1947), Marjorie, da of John Boultbee Brooks, of Blackwell Court, nr Bromsgrove, Worcs; 2ndly, 1947, Jean, da of Edward Warren, of Yelverton, Devon:—
(By 1st *m*) Michael Gilbert, *b* 1932, formerly Lieut RM: *m* 1960 (*m diss* 1970), Felicity Roberts, da of Gordon Charles Sheppard, of Cape Town, South Africa, and has issue living, Mark Howland, *b* 1961, — John Langdon, *b* 1964, — Jennifer Leigh, *b* 1962. ⸺ Jill Morna Boultbee, *b* 1933.

The former baronetcy of 1620 (claimed by the present holder of the 1809 creation as 14th Bt, which claim, however, has not been officially established at the Heralds' College), belonged to the old Kentish family, originally called Rookehurst and later Roobertes, and apparently became extinct on the demise in 1745 of Sir Walter, 6th Bt, who left an only daughter, Jane, who married 3rd Duke of St Albans. About 1775 the Duchess believed she had discovered the descendants of Thomas, second son of the 1st baronet, seated at Brightfieldstown, Roberts' Cove, co Cork; and the title was assumed by the then head of that family, Randal, and subsequently by his eldest son Thomas, to whom, however, a new patent of Baronetcy was passed in 1809. The ancient property of Glassenbury, Cranbrook, Kent, which had then been in the direct line for nearly seven centuries, was left by the Duchess of St Albans to the second son of this Sir Thomas, viz, Col Thomas Walton Roberts, JP (High Sheriff of Kent 1879), who *d* 1882, and devised the said property by will to his nephew, the late Major John Atkin-Roberts, JP.

ROBERTS (UK) 1909, of Milner Field, Bingley, West Riding of Yorkshire

Justly and firmly

Sir WILLIAM JAMES DENBY ROBERTS, 3rd *Baronet*; *b* 10 Aug 1936; *s* his father, *Sir* JAMES DENBY, OBE, 1973; *ed* Rugby, and Roy Agric Coll, Cirencester.

Arms – Vert, on a pile or, between two saltires in base of the last an Angora goat statant proper. **Crest** – Upon two millrinds fesseways or, an Angora goat as in the arms.
Seat – Strathallan Castle, Auchterarder, Perthshire PH3 1JZ. *Residence* – Combwell Priory, Flimwell, Wadhurst, Sussex.

SISTER LIVING

Susan Elisabeth, *b* 1934; MA Oxford: *m* 1st, 1956, Roger John Edward Liddiard, BA; 2ndly, 1974, Douglas Hills, and has issue living (by 1st *m*), Nicholas Anthony, *b* 1958, — Timothy Mark, *b* 1960, — Jonathan Miles, *b* 1962, — Rupert Alexander, *b* 1966.

AUNT LIVING

Catherine Elizabeth, *b* 1907: *m* 1928, Robert Hope Donaldson, who *d* 1964, and has issue living, Robert Bertram, *b* 1929, — William James, *b* 1934. *Residence* – 17 East Rd, W Mersea, Colchester, Essex.

COLLATERAL BRANCHES LIVING

Issue of late David Gordon Denby Roberts, yst son of 2nd baronet, *b* 1940, *d* 1971. *m* 1962, Diana Frances, (Lawhill House, Auchterarder, Perths (who *m* 2ndly), 1973, Cameron Roy Marchand Buchanan), only da of Hugh Wilson-Jones, of The White Hose, N Lopham, Diss, Norfolk:—
JAMES ELTON DENBY ROBERTS-BUCHANAN, *b* 12 July 1966. ── Gail Antoinette ROBERTS-BUCHANAN, *b* 1964.

Issue of late William Denby Roberts, 2nd son of Bertram Foster Roberts, el surv son of 1st baronet, *b* 1909, *d* 1966: *m* 1935, Helen Fyans, who *d* 1963, yr da of late Herbert Shakespeare Fenwick, of Dunedin, NZ:—
Anthony Fenwick Denby (Mossdale, Conistone-with-Kilnsey, nr Skipton, Yorks), *b* 1938; *ed* Rugby, and Univ Coll, Oxford (BA): *m* 1964, Vanessa Jean Wishart, da of Sir (James) Douglas Wishart Thomson, 2nd Bt (*cr* 1929), and has issue living, Jonathan William Denby, *b* 1966, — Nicholas David Denby, *b* 1967, — James Anthony Denby, *b* 1974. ── Peter William Denby *b* 1945; *ed* Rugby, and Roy Agric Coll, Cirencester: *m* 1st, 1970 (*m diss* 1977), Christine Margaret Hermione, da of late Capt Hon Anthony Gerard Hugh Bampfylde (*see* B Poltimore, colls); 2ndly, 1977 (*m diss* 1988), Grizel Elizabeth-Anne (Lulla), only da of Col Anthony Gerald Way, MC, of Kincairney, Dunkeld, Perthshire, and formerly wife of (Patrick) Joseph Scott-Plummer (*see* B Kinross), and has issue living (by 1st *m*), Emma Louise, *b* 1972, — Lucinda Ann, *b* 1973, — (by 2nd *m*), William Gerald Denby, *b* 1980. ── Ann, *b* 1936.

Issue of late Joseph Henry Nicholson Roberts, 2nd surv son of 1st baronet, *b* 1887, *d* 1946: *m* 1920, Frances Eleanor, who *d* 1983, da of G. Partington, of The Laurels, Tilehurst, Reading:—
John, *b* 1921: *m* 1st, 1949 (*m diss* 1961), Diana Emily, da of late Lawrence Norris Evans; 2ndly, 1962 (*m diss* 1972), Hon Juliana Eveline (CUNLIFFE-OWEN), da of 2nd Viscount Scarsdale; 3rdly, 1974, Maryan Gwyneth, da of Patrick Edward Aston Talbot (*see* E Shrewsbury, colls), and has had issue (by 1st *m*), Jane, *b* 1953: *m* 1st, 1972 (*m diss* 1977), Robin John Kershaw Roberts; 2ndly, 1978 (*m diss* 1988), Nicholas John Foster Robinson; 3rdly 1989, Robert Walter Armstrong, and has issue living, (by 2nd *m*) Max Nicholas John *b* 1984, — Sally (*Hon Mrs James Bethell*), *b* 1955: *m* 1st, 1979 (*m diss* 1986), Nicholas Albert Le Gallais; 2ndly, 1987, Hon James David William Bethell, 2nd son of 5th Baron Westbury, and has issue (by 2nd *m*) (*see* B Westbury), — (by 2nd *m*) †John James, *b* 1964, *d* 1986. — Lucinda Elizabeth, *b* 1963: *m* 1989, Pearse Bergin, and has issue living, James Michael *b* 1993, Laura Alice *b* 1991. *Residence* – L'Etoquet House, St Ouen, Jersey. ── Henry, *b* 1923: *m* 1955, Anne Dorothy, da of late John Huelin, of Cape Town, S Africa, and has issue living, Lesley Ann, *b* 1957, — Frances Mary, *b* 1963. *Residence* – La Fontaine, Trinity, Jersey.

The 1st baronet, Sir James Roberts (son of James Roberts, of Haworth, Yorkshire), was former owner of the town of Saltaire, and Chm of Sir Titus Salt, Bt, Sons & Co, Ltd, of Saltaire.

ROBERTS (UK) 1919 of Ecclesall and Queen's Tower, City of Sheffield, and West Riding of Yorkshire

Sir SAMUEL ROBERTS, 4th *Baronet*; *b* 16 April 1948; *s* his father, *Sir* PETER GEOFFREY, 1985; *ed* Harrow, and Sheffield Univ (BA); Bar Inner Temple 1972: *m* 1977, Georgina Ann, yr da of David Cory, of Bluetts, Peterston-super-Ely, S Glam, and has issue.

ᴀrms – Sable, on a chevron couped argent, three mullets of the field, a chief dancettée or. Crest – Issuant out of a circlet or, a demi-lion rampant gules holding in the paws a mullet gold.
Residences – Cockley Cley Hall, Swaffham, Norfolk PE37 8AG; 6 Caversham St, SW3.

SON LIVING

SAMUEL, *b* 12 Aug 1989.

DAUGHTERS LIVING

Eleanor Judith, *b* 1979. —— Olivia, *b* 1982. —— Amelia, *b* 1985.

SISTERS LIVING

Jane, *b* 1940: *m* 1962, Claude Henri Jean-Jacques Maurin, of La Tour Villedon, 18260 Subligny, and 65 rue de Cévennes, Paris 75015, France, and has issue living, Sébastien Alexandre, *b* 1965: *m* 1994, Alison, da of Jonathan Durr, of Cape Town, SA, — Edmond Peter, *b* 1974, — Alicia, *b* 1967: *m* 1997, Matthew Suminski, of Milwaukee, USA, and has issue living, Crispin Randell *b* 1998, — Constance, *b* (twin) 1974. —— Catherine, *b* 1943: *m* 1965, John Andrew Longworth, of 34 Westmoreland Terrace, SW1V 4AL, and has issue living, Stephanie Lydia, *b* 1968, — Charlotte Gay, *b* 1970: *m* 1998, Adam P. Spiegel, only son of late Sam Spiegel, — Joanna Catherine, *b* 1973. —— Deborah, *b* 1946: *m* 1967, Peter Constantin Brun, of 60 Captain Pipers Rd, Vaucluse, Sydney, NSW 2030, Australia, and has issue living, Henry Constantin, *b* 1971, — Peter Maximilian, *b* 1974, — Julian Constantin, *b* 1981, — Rachel, *b* 1970: *m* 1997, David Scanlon. —— Rebecca, *b* 1955: *m* 1978, Guy Mark Vernon Whitcombe, and has issue living, Claudia Elizabeth, *b* 1984, — Madeleine Rebecca, *b* 1989.

The 1st baronet, Rt Hon Sir Samuel Roberts, was Lord Mayor of Sheffield 1899-1900, and sat as MP for Ecclesall Div of Sheffield (C) 1901-23. The 2nd baronet, Sir Samuel Roberts, was Lord Mayor of Sheffield 1919-20, MP for Hereford Div of Herefordshire (C) 1921-9, and for Ecclesall Div of Sheffield 1929-35, and Master Cutler of Sheffield 1935-6. The 3rd baronet, Sir Peter Geoffrey Roberts, was MP for Ecclesall Div of Sheffield (C) 1945-50, and for Heeley Div of Sheffield 1950-66, Master Cutler of Sheffield 1956-57, and High Sheriff of Hallamshire 1970.

ROBINSON (E) 1660, of London

Sir JOHN JAMES MICHAEL LAUD ROBINSON, 11th *Baronet*; *b* 19 Jan 1943; *s* his grandfather, *Maj Sir* FREDERICK VILLIERS LAUD, MC, Croix de Guerre 1975; *ed* Eton, and Trin Coll, Dublin (MA); a Chartered Financial Analyst; DL of Northants since 1984; Pres British Red Cross (Northants Branch) 1982-90; Chm St Andrews Hospital Northampton 1984-94, Northampton General Hospital NHS Trust 1994-98: *m* 1968, (Kathryn) Gayle Elizabeth, only child of Stuart Nelson Keyes, of Orillia, Ont, Canada, and has issue.

ᴀrms – Quarterly: 1st and 4th, quarterly crenellée gules and or in the first quarter a lion passant-guardant or standing on a tower argent; 2nd and 3rd, vert, a buck trippant within an orle of trefoil slipped or. Crest – A buck trippant or, collared and lined vert, the collar charged with three trefoils slipped or.
Residence – Cranford Hall, Cranford, Kettering NN14 4AD.

SONS LIVING

MARK CHRISTOPHER MICHAEL VILLIERS, *b* 23 April 1972. —— Alexander Frederick Stuart Laud, *b* 1973.

DAUGHTER LIVING

Kathryn Anne Elizabeth, *b* 1985.

SISTER LIVING

Anne Elizabeth Villiers, *b* 1950: *m* 1975, Derek Alan Buckley, and has issue living, Samuel Michael, *b* 1978.

The 1st baronet, Sir John Robinson, nephew of Archbishop Laud, and Lord Mayor of London, was Lieut of the Tower, and did great service in promoting the coronation of Charles II. The 5th and the 6th baronets each sat as MP for Northampton.

ROBINSON (UK) 1854, of Toronto, Canada

Quickly and cautiously

Sir CHRISTOPHER PHILIPSE ROBINSON, 8th *Baronet*; son of late Christopher Robinson, QC, son of late Christopher Charles Robinson, KC, eldest son of late Christopher Robinson, KC, 3rd son of 1st baronet; *b* 10 Nov 1938; *s* his kinsman, *Sir* JOHN BEVERLEY, 1988: *m* 1962, Barbara Judith, da of Richard Duncan, of Ottawa, Canada, and has issue.

Arms – Or, on a chevron between three stags trippant vert, as many cinquefoils of the field. Crest – A stag trippant vert bezantée.
Residence – 460 RR1, Chelsea, PQ, Canada J0X 1N0.

SONS LIVING

PETER DUNCAN, *b* 31 July 1967. —— Jonathan Richard, *b* 1969.

BROTHERS LIVING

Walter Gherardi (69 Douglas Crescent, Toronto, Ont M4W 2E6), *b* 1940; QC; *m* 1963, Alison Jean, da of Robert Stewart Fraser, of Toronto, Canada, and has issue living, Hilary Elizabeth, *b* 1967, — Alicia Isabel, *b* 1970. —— John Mowat (117 Pineridge Rd, Carp, Ontario, Canada K0A 1L0), *b* 1942: *m* 1st, 1969 (*m diss* 1982), Joyce, da of Roy Harrod, of Orsett, Essex; 2ndly, 1988, Jane Stewart, da of Duncan K. MacTavish, QC, OBE, of Ottawa, and has issue living (by 1st *m*), Graeme Harrod, *b* 1970, — Christopher Mowat, *b* 1972.

SISTER LIVING

Neville Gherardi (31 Acacia Av, Ottawa, Ontario, Canada), *b* 1935: *m* 1956 (*m diss* 1967), Georges-Henri Carasso, of Paris, who *d* 1974, and has issue living, John Christopher, *b* 1959, — Robin, *b* 1979.

UNCLE LIVING

Hugh Lukin, *b* 1916: *m* 1st, 1941 (*m diss* 1972), Ruth Elizabeth, da of John Cotter, of Ottawa, Ont; 2ndly, 1973, Lillian Ruth, da of Jacob Milton, of Toronto, and has issue living (by 1st *m*), John Michael (Thunder Bay, Ont, Canada), *b* 1946, — David Lukin (Los Angeles, Calif, USA), *b* 1952, — Elizabeth, *b* 1955: *m* 1976, Kenneth Quinlan, of Saskatoon, Saskatchewan, Canada, and has issue living, Andrea *b* 1984. *Residence* – 401 Woburn Av, Toronto, Canada.

AUNTS LIVING

Laura Beverley, *b* 1913: *m* 1st, 1937 (*m diss* 1956), Andrew Kalitinsky; 2ndly, 1957, Adolf Kurt Placzek, and has issue living, (by 1st *m*) Sylvia (1724 Kellogg Dr, Anaheim, California 92807, USA), *b* 1945: *m* 1966 (*m diss* 1979), Roger Alan Barkley, and has issue living, Ian Andrew *b* 1970. *Residence* – . —— Wendela Isabel, *b* 1918: *m* 1957, Andrew Kalitinsky (ante), of La Jolla, California, USA.

SISTER LIVING OF SEVENTH BARONET

Constance Suzette Beverley, *b* 1914: *m* 1939 (*m diss* 1969), Edward William Sutherland, and has issue living, John Warren, *b* 1942: *m* 1962, Kathleen Croft, of Hamilton, Ontario, and has issue living, David *b* 1963, Beth *b* 1964, — Harley Peter, *b* 1948: *m* 1966, Patricia Carter, of Guelph, Ont, and has issue living, Kimberley Deanne *b* 1967, Joy Patrick *b* 1969, — David Victor, *b* 1948: *m* 1971, Jacquie Smith, of Hamilton, Ont, and has issue living, Tracey, *b* 1973, — Wendy Gayle, *b* 1940: *m* 1961, Anthony Ian Roberts, of London, Ont, and has issue living, Paul Douglas *b* 1968, Nancy Marie *b* 1962, Patricia *b* 1964, — Suzette Marion, *b* 1944: *m* 1964 (*m diss* 1969), David Teft, of Grimsby, Ontario.

COLLATERAL BRANCHES LIVING

Grandchildren of late Christopher Charles Robinson, KC (ante):—
Issue of late Peter Beverley Robinson, *b* 1915, *d* 1992: *m* 1st, 1938, Elizabeth, who *d* 1965, da of Halsey Frederick, of Mountain Lakes, New Jersey, USA; 2ndly, 1966, Nancy Carol, who *d* 1994, da of Norris Konheim, of Woodmere, NY:—
(By 1st *m*) Wendy Bouquet, *b* 1944: *m* 1965 (*m diss* 1975), Martin V. Boelitz, and has issue living, Jessica Elizabeth, *b* 1968. —— Susan Celina, *b* 1946: *m* 1st, 1966 (*m diss* 1967), Ira James Sandperl; 2ndly, 1969 (*m diss* 1981), Pierre Bain, of Comps-sur-Artuby, Var, France; 3rdly, 19—, David Peterson. —— (By 2nd *m*) Kenneth Beverley, *b* 1967. —— Alice Natalie, *b* 1969.

Issue of late (John) Beverley Robinson, *b* 1884, *d* 1954: *m* 1920, Marion (28 Foxbar Rd, Toronto, 7 Canada), da of Weymouth de Lisle Schreiber, of Toronto Canada.
John Beverley, *b* 1922: *m* 1948, Constance Anne, da of James Bruce Mackinnon, of Toronto, and has issue living, Bruce Beverley, *b* 1952, — Christopher Charles, *b* 1957, — Linda de Lisle, *b* 1949, — Hilary Anne, *b* 1953. *Residence* – 194 Inglewood Drive, Toronto, Canada. —— Weymouth Hugh Beverley, *b* 1927: *m* 1956, Patricia Elizabeth, el da of Robert James Glendenning Innes, of Toronto, Canada, and has issue living, Judith Suzanne, *b* 1957, — Jennifer Leslie, *b* 1960. —— Elizabeth de Lisle, *b* 1924: *m* 1st, 1946, John Kingsford Herbert Mason, who *d* 1952; 2ndly, 1959, Capt John Littler, RCN, and has issue living, (by 1st *m*) David *b* 1950, Marion Thonia *b* 1948, Philippa *b* 1952.

Issue of late Duncan Strachan Robinson, *b* 1886, *d* 1956: *m* 1916, Emily, el da of Gordon Watson, formerly of Brandon, Manitoba:—
Duncan Gordon Strachan, *b* 1917. —— John Attrachay, *b* 1920. *Residence* – Toronto, Canada. —— Mary Emily, *b* 1917. *Residence* – Guelph, Ontario, Canada. —— Anne, *b* 1922. *Residence* – Phoenix, Arizona, USA. —— Daphne, *b* 1928. *Residence* – Toronto, Canada.

Issue of late Maj-Gen Sir Charles Walker Robinson, KCB, 4th son of 1st baronet, *b* 1836, *d* 1924: *m* 1884, Margaret Frances, who *d* 1940, da of Gen Sir Archibald Alison, GCB, 2nd Bt:—
Joan Emma Beverley, *b* 1892. —— Dorothy Margaret, *b* 1895. *Residence* – Bideford, Devon.

This family is descended from Christopher Robinson, or Cleasby, Yorkshire, who emigrated to Virginia about 1670, and was elder brother of the Rt Rev John Robinson, Ambassador to Sweden 1683-1708, Bishop of Bristol and London 1710-23, and First Plenipotentiary at the Congress of Utrecht 1713. The 1st baronet, Sir John Beverley, CB, DSL, of Oxford, having served as a Volunteer in the war of 1812 with America, was admitted to the Bar in Canada and at Lincoln's Inn, and was subsequently (1829-62) Chief Justice of Upper Canada, and for many years member for the town of York and Speaker of the Legislative Council in the Old Province of Upper Canada. Sir John Beverley Robinson, 4th Bt, was el son of late Hon John Beverley Robinson, Lieut-Gov of Ontario 1880-87.

ROBINSON (UK) 1908, of Hawthornden, Wynberg, Cape Province, S Africa and Dudley House, City of Westminster

I have found

Sir WILFRED HENRY FREDERICK ROBINSON, 3rd *Baronet*, son of late Wilfred Henry Robinson, 3rd son of 1st baronet; *b* 24 Dec 1917; *s* his uncle, *Sir* JOSEPH BENJAMIN, 1954; *ed* Diocesan Coll, Rondebosch, and St John's Coll, Camb (BA 1939, MA 1944); Vice-Prin of Diocesan Coll Sch, Rondebosch; late Major Parachute Regt; Finance Offr, Soc of Genealogists 1980-92: *m* 1946, Margaret Alison Kathleen, da of late Frank Mellish, MC, of Cape Town, S Africa, and has issue.

Arms – Vert, three bezants chevronwise between two chevronels, the whole between three demi-stags couped or. Crest – A demi-stag or, charged with two chevronels vert, supporting with the dexter leg a flagstaff in bend sinister proper, pendant therefrom a banner bert charged with a bezant. *Residence* – 24 Ennismore Gdns, SW7 1AB.

SON LIVING

PETER FRANK (14 Wellgarth Rd, NW11 7HS), *b* 23 June 1949: *m* 1988, Alison Jane, eldest da of D. Bradley, of Rochester, Kent.

DAUGHTERS LIVING

Suzanne Moira, *b* 1947: *m* 1969, J. Steen Flamand, of Copenhagen, Denmark. —— Clementine Anne Eileen, *b* 1957: *m* 1981, Jeffrey Foulser.

Sir Joseph Benjamin Robinson, 1st Bt (sometime a MLA, Mayor of Kimberley 1880, and Chm of Robinson's South Africa Banking Co, Ltd, and of many gold mines in Transvaal Colony), was yst son of late Robert John Robinson, and was nominated to a peerage in June 1922, but declined the honour. Sir Joseph Benjamin Robinson, 2nd Bt, sat in Union Parliament of S Africa 1915-19, and 1932-34.

LYNCH-ROBINSON (UK) 1920, of Foxrock, co Dublin

Sir DOMINICK CHRISTOPHER LYNCH-ROBINSON, 4th *Baronet*; *b* 30 July 1948; *s* his father, *Sir* NIALL BRYAN, DSC, 1996; *m* 1973, Victoria, da of Kenneth Weir, of 37 Stokesay Rd, Sale, Manchester, and has issue.

Arms – Quarterly: 1st and 4th, vert, a chevron engrailed between three stags at gaze or, each charged with a fleur-de-lis azure, *Robinson*; 2nd and 3rd, azure a chevron between three trefoils and two voiders or, *Lynch*. Crests – 1st, Out of a crown vallery or a mount vert, thereon a stag as in the arms; 2nd, a lynx passant argent gorged with a collar gules with chain reflexed over the back or.
Residence – Flat 3, 34 Montagu Square, W1H 1TL.

SON LIVING

CHRISTOPHER HENRY JAKE, *b* 1 Oct 1977.

DAUGHTER LIVING

Anne Elizabeth Seaton, *b* 1973.

WIDOW LIVING OF THIRD BARONET

Faithful to the law and the king

ROSEMARY SEATON (*Rosemary, Lady Lynch-Robinson*), elder da of late Capt Harold John Eller: *m* 1940, Sir Niall Bryan Lynch-Robinson, 3rd Bt, DSC, who *d* 1996. *Residence* – The Dower House, Headbourne Worthy House, Winchester, Hants S023 7JG.

The 1st baronet, Rt Hon Sir Henry Augustus Robinson, KCB, was Vice-Pres of Local Govt Board for Ireland 1898-1920. The 2nd baronet, Sir Christopher Henry Robinson, assumed by deed poll 1947 (registered in College of Arms) the additional surname and arms of Lynch before his patronymic. The 3rd baronet, Sir Niall Bryan, served 1939-45 War with RNVR (DSC, Croix de Guerre), and was Chm Leo-Burnett Ltd 1970-78.

ROCHE (UK) 1838, of Carass, Limerick

Sir DAVID O'GRADY ROCHE, 5th *Baronet*; *b* 21 Sept 1947; *s* his father, *Lt-Cdr Sir* STANDISH O'GRADY, DSO, RN, 1977; *ed* Wellington Coll, and Trin Coll, Dublin; FCA; Chm Baltic Forest Lines Ltd; Cllr Lond Borough of Hammersmith & Fulham 1978-82; Worshipful Co of Saddlers: *m* 1971, Hon (Helen) Alexandra Briscoe Gully, da of 3rd Viscount Selby, and formerly wife of late Roger Moreton Frewen, and has issue.

Arms – Gules, three roaches naiant within a bordure engrailed argent. Crest – A rock, thereon a stork close, charged on the breast with a torteau, and holding in his dexter claw a roach all proper.
Residence – Norris Castle Farm, I of Wight P032 6AZ; Bridge House, Starbotton, Skipton, N Yorks. *Clubs* – Buck's, Kildare Street, University (Dublin), Royal Yacht Squadron.

SON LIVING

DAVID ALEXANDER O'GRADY, *b* 28 Jan 1976.

DAUGHTER LIVING

Cecilia Evelyn Jonnë, *b* 1979.

BROTHER LIVING

God is my rock

Timothy O'Grady *b* 1948; *ed* St Columba's Coll, Dublin; Lt (ret) 1st Bn IG; a Freeman of City of London: *m* 1975, Lorna, da of A. T. R. Nicholson, of Ashcombe, Merstham, Surrey, and has issue living, Patrick Timothy O'Grady, *b* 1978, — Simon James O'Grady, *b* 1980. *Residence* – 40 Redstone Park, Redhill, Surrey.

WIDOW LIVING OF FOURTH BARONET

EVELYN LAURA (*Evelyn, Lady Roche*) (Monte de Cerro, Corotelo, São Bras d'Alportel, Algarve, Portugal), da of Maj William Andon, W Yorks Regt, of Jersey: *m* 1946, Lt-Cdr Sir Standish O'Grady Roche, DSO, RN, 4th Bt, who *d* 1977.

The 1st baronet, Sir David Roche, was MP for Limerick City 1832-44. Sir David Vandeleur, 2nd Bt, was Vice-Lieut of co Limerick (High Sheriff 1865), and Master of Limerick Hunt. Sir Standish Roche, 3rd Bt, was DL Carlow.

RODGERS (UK) 1964, of Groombridge, Kent

Sir (ANDREW) PIERS (WINGATE) RODGERS, 3rd *Baronet*; *b* 24 Oct 1944; *s* his brother, *Sir* (JOHN FAIRLIE) TOBIAS, 1997; *ed* Eton, and Merton Coll, Oxford (BA); Sec to Royal Academy of Arts (also Sec of Chantrey Bequest and British Inst Fund) 1981-96; Member Board Warburg Inst, London Univ since 1993; Freeman City of London; Member Co of Merchant Adventurers City of York, Hon Court Member Masons' Co; FRSA; Chevalier de l'Ordre des Arts et des Lettres (France) 1987, Ordre National de Merite (France) 1991, Cavaliere Ufficiale Ordine al Merito della Repubblica Italiana 1992: *m* 1979, Marie-Agathe, da of late Charles-Albert Houette, Croix de Guerre, of Bléneau, France, and has issue.

Arms – Azure two bars gemel dancetty argent, over all two palm branches in saltire enfiled through an ancient crown or. **Crest** – Two ravens' heads addorsed sable and gules both within a collar or pendant therefrom a rose argent barbed and seeded proper. *Residence* – Peverell House, Bradford Peverell, Dorset. *Clubs* – Brook's, Pratt's, MCC.

SONS LIVING

Experience is knowledge　　　THOMAS, *b* 18 Dec 1979; *ed* Eton. —— Augustus, *b* 1983; *ed* Marlborough.

The first baronet, Sir John Charles Rodgers, son of Charles Rodgers, of York, was MP (C) for Sevenoaks Div of Kent 1950-79, held several ministerial posts, and was a DL of Kent. The second baronet, Sir (John Fairlie) Tobias Rodgers, was an antiquarian bookseller.

ROLL (UK) 1921, of The Chestnuts, Wanstead, Essex (Extinct 1998)

Rev Sir JAMES WILLIAM CECIL ROLL, 4th and last *Baronet*.

DAUGHTER LIVING OF SECOND BARONET

Betty Catherine, *b* 1910: *m* 1932, Charles Algernon Sharman, who *d* 1988, and has issue living, Charles James Roll, *b* 1934, — John Frederick (180 Thorpe Rd, Peterborough PE3 6JJ), *b* 1936, — Patrick George, *b* 1939, — Nicholas Algernon, *b* 1945, — Briony Anna, *b* 1942. *Residence* – Front Park, 110 Thorpe Rd, Peterborough PE3 6AP.

The 1st baronet, Sir James Roll, was Chm of Pearl Assurance Co Ltd, and Lord Mayor of London 1920-21.

ROPNER (UK) 1904, of Preston Hall, Stockton-on-Tees, Co Palatine of Durham, and Skutterskelfe Hall, Hutton Rudby, North Riding of Yorkshire

Sir ROBERT DOUGLAS ROPNER, 4th *Baronet*, *b* 1 Dec 1921; *s* his father, *Sir* (EMIL HUGO OSCAR) ROBERT, 1962; *ed* Harrow; formerly Capt RA: *m* 1943, Patricia Kathleen, da of W. E. Scofield, of West Malling, Kent, and has issue.

Arms – Per fesse indented sable and or, a pale, with three mullets pierced two and one, and as many roebucks' heads erased one and two, all counterchanged. Crest – In front of three tilting spears, one erect, and two in saltire, or, as many mascles interlaced fesswise of the last, thereon, a roebuck's head erased sable.
Residence – Rose Cottage, Swaffham Prior, Norfolk CB5 0LD.

SON LIVING

ROBERT CLINTON, *b* 6 Feb 1949; *ed* Harrow; FCA: *m* 1978, Diana Felicia, 2nd da of late W/Cmdr Arthur Henri Abbott, of Henville House, Hamble, Hants, and has issue living, Christopher Guy, *b* 18 Jan 1979, — Katherine Anne, *b* (twin) 1979.

DAUGHTER LIVING

Serena Gay, *b* 1953.

SISTERS LIVING AND DECEASED

Diana Joan, *b* 1919: *m* 1941, John Randal Elliot. —— Patricia Elizabeth, *b* 1923: *m* 1944, Lt-Col Claude MacDonald Hull, MC, who *d* 1979, and *d* 1983, leaving issue, Susan Patricia Macdonald, *b* 1948, — Fiona Elizabeth Macdonald, *b* 1950.

COLLATERAL BRANCHES LIVING

Grandchildren of Emil Hugo Oscar Robert Ropner, 2nd son of 1st baronet:—
Issue of late Lt-Col Richard Ropner, TD, *b* 1898, *d* 1975: *m* 1928, Margaret Forbes, who *d* 1976, da of John Gilfillan Ronald, MD, of Torwood Hall, Larbert, Stirlingshire:—
Richard John Ronald (Rossett, Balcarras Rd, Charlton Kings, Glos GL53 8QG), *b* 1941; *ed* Harrow, and Edinburgh Univ (MB, ChB); D(Obst) RCOG; DPM; MRC Psych: *m* 1974, Janet Elizabeth, FRCP, FRCPath, el da of Joseph William Fox, PhD, of Marlow House, 3 Camden Park Rd, Chislehurst, Kent, and has issue living, James Richard Alexander, *b* 1977; *ed* Harrow, and Univ Coll London Med Sch (BSc 1998), — Victoria Elizabeth Louise, *b* 1979; *ed* Cheltenham Ladies Coll, and Leeds Univ. —— Alison Margaret, *b* 1930: *m* 1957, Gerald Robert Savage, who *d* 19—, of 21B Calle Donana, 11310 Sotogrande, Cadiz, Spain, and of 2 Rose Cottage, Hascombe, Surrey GU8 4JG, and has issue living, Nichola Mary, *b* 1958. —— Pamela Christine, *b* 1931; *ed* Edinburgh Univ (MA): *m* 1957 (Irving) Thomas Stuttaford, OBE, MRCS, LRCP, of Houghton St Giles, Walsingham, Norfolk NR22 6AQ, and has issue living, Andrew Irving Ropner, *b* 1958, — Thomas Richard Ropner, *b* 1961, — Hugo John Ropner *b* 1964: *m* 19—, Joanna M., only da of late Keith Davenport, and has issue living, Oliver George Watkin *b* 1994, Alice Catherine Royden *b* 1997.

Issue of late Capt (Cuthbert) Maurice Ropner, King's Own Scottish Borderers, *b* 1905, *ka* 1945: *m* 1929, Dorothea Seymour, who *d* 1994, da of Rev Robert William Bell, V of Stamfordham:—
George Maurice, *b* 1934; Maj (ret) Northumberland Hussars (TA). *Residence* – Gallowshaw, Netherwitton, Morpeth, Northumberland. —— (Vivien) Anne (Tethermill House, 2A Mill Field Rd, Whickham, Newcastle on Tyne NE16 4QA), *b* 1930; *ed* Durham Univ (MB BS 1955). —— (Caroline) Jane, *b* 1945; *d* 19—.

Grandchildren of late William Ropner, 3rd son of 1st baronet:—
See Ropner Bt, *cr* 1952.

Issue of late Sir (William) Guy Ropner, *b* 1896, *d* 1971: *m* 1921, Margarita, who *d* 1973, da of Sir William Cresswell Gray, 1st Bt:—
(William Guy) David (1 Sunningdale Gdns, Stratford Rd, W8 6PX; The Lodge, Accommodation Rd, Longcross, Surrey), *b* 1924; *ed* Harrow; late Capt RHA: *m* 1st, 1955, (Mildred) Malise Hare, da of late Col George Armitage, MC, TD, of Newburgh House, Coxwold, Yorks; 2ndly, 1985, Hon Charlotte Mary, da of 2nd Baron Piercy, and formerly wife of Paolo Emilio Taddei, and has issue living (by 1st *m*), Guy David Armitage (N Stanmore Farm, Stanmore, Newbury, Berks RG20 8SR), *b* 1959: *m* 1991, Annabel Frances, elder da of Michael Odiarne Coates, of Great Shoesmiths Farm, Wadhurst, E Sussex, and has issue living, Amy Grace Coates *b* 1992, Molly *b* 1996, Flora *b* (twin) 1996, — Roderick John, *b* 1962, — Peter Gavin Malise, *b* 1964, — Lucy Armitage, *b* 1957: *m* 1985, Christopher Goelet, of 15115 Wheeler Lane, Sparks, Maryland 21152, USA, yst son of John Goelet, of New York, and has issue living, Eloise Ropner *b* 1987, Isabelle Guestier *b* 1989, Henrietta Zoe *b* 1992, — (by 2nd *m*) Nicholas David Piercy *b* 1986. ——Jonathan Gray (Dalesend, Patrick Brompton, Bedale, N Yorks, DL8 1JL), *b* 1931; late Lt IG: *m* 1953, Edith Avril, da of Charles Urie Peat, MC, of Wychffe Hall, Barnard Castle, co Durham, and has issue living, (Jonathan) Mark, *b* 1954: *m* 1985, Madelyn K., only da of W. Stefanech, of San Luis Obispo, California, USA, and has issue living, James *b* 1986, Jasmine *b* 1989, Charles Guy Corban, *b* 1959: *m* 1989, Emma J. F. E., yr da of Richard Andrews, of Courtyard House, Westow, N Yorks, and has issue living, Richard Jonathan Charles *b* 1995, Mary Rose Avril *b* 1991, Eugenie Annabel Pearl *b* 1993, — Paul Benedict Peat, *b* 1965: *m* 1992, Peggy A., da of Willard A. Ison, Warrant Officer USN (ret), of Salt Lake City, Utah, USA, and has issue living, Luke Asa Gray *b* 1996, Chloe *b* 1993, — Dominic Adam, *b* 1968: *m* 1991, Abigail, da of Peter de Barros Clay, of The Old Court House, The Green, Richmond-upon-Thames, Surrey, and has issue living, Inigo Thomas Robert *b* 1993, Daisy Manina Debarros *b* 1992, — Margarita Carey, *b* 1956: *m* 1979, John Dickson, and has issue living, Tobyn Benedict *b* 1981, Amelia Sophie *b* 1983, Leila Florence *b* 1989. —— Rita Gray (13 Old Palace Lane, Richmond, Surrey), *b* 1922: *m* 1947 (*m diss* 1967), Alan Maskew Hodson, and has issue living, Alexandra Mary, *b* 1958.

Issue of late John Raymond Ropner, *b* 1903, *d* 1996: *m* 1928, Joan, who *d* 1993, da of late William Redhead:— William David Jock, *b* 1929; *ed* Harrow: *m* 1961 (*m diss* 1962), Elizabeth Anne, eldest da of Elmer Ellsworth Jones, of 23 Lowndes Sq, SW1. ——— Jeremy Vyvyan (Firby Hall, Bedale, N Yorks; Brooks's Club), *b* 1932; *ed* Harrow, and RNC Dartmouth: *m* 1955, his cousin, Sally Talbot, da of late Maj George Talbot Willcox, MC (*see* Ropner, Bt, *cr* 1904, colls, 1985 Edn), and has issue living, †Clive Vyvyan Peter, *b* 1957; *d* 1979, — Simon Jock Wilks (4 Bettridge Rd, SW6), *b* 1962: *m* 1993, Suzanne L., da of Ivor Roberts, of Bradford-on-Tone, Som, and has issue living, Harry Jeremy Ivor *b* 1996, James Clive Leopold *b* 1998, — Sophia Sally, *b* 1959: *m* 1991, Christopher John Mansfield, of 53 Campana Rd, SW6 4AT, son of Kenneth Mansfield, of Quarry House, Malton, N Yorks, and has issue living, William Vyvyan Haldane *b* 1994, Isabella Mary *b* (twin) 1994, — Lisa Cleone Vivian, *b* 1964: *m* 1985, Capt (Timothy) Mark Nicole, 4/7th Royal Dragoon Gds, son of Tom Nicole, of Slape Manor, Netherbury, Bridport, Dorset, and has issue living, Edward Tom George *b* 1990, George Charles Jeremy *b* 1993, Lucy Sophia Katherine *b* 1987. ——— Susan Carole, *b* 1936: *m* 1957, Maj Charles Peter Martel, of The Manor House, Gayles, Richmond, Yorks, only son of late Lt-Gen Sir Giffard le Quesne Martel, KCB, KBE, DSO, MC, and has issue living, Nicholas Charles Giffard, *b* 1960: *m* 1987 (*m diss* 1997), Sarah Jane Maxwell, only da of J. S. M. Barlow, of Minshull Hall, Nantwich, Cheshire, and has issue living, Charles *b* 1988, Hugo *b* 1993, — Carole Valerie, *b* 1958, — Virginia Jill, *b* 1964, *d* 1971, — Sarah Charlotte, *b* 1973.

Issue of late Sir Robert Desmond Ropner, *b* 1908, *d* 1977: *m* 1st, 1932 (*m diss* 1946), Dorothy Beecroft, da of Sir Edmund Lacon, 5th Bt; 2ndly, 1947, Sibyl, who *d* 1969, da of late Thomas O. Carter:— (By 1st *m*) (Robert) Bruce Beecroft (Camp Hill, Kirklington, Bedale, Yorks) *b* 1933; Lt Welsh Gds: *m* 1960, Willow, da of James Hare, of Fieldhead, Thorner, Leeds, and has issue living, Robert James Bruce, *b* 1962: *m* 1986, Johanna Louise, yr da of Colin Strathearn Ropner Stroyan, of Teith, Doune, Perthshire (*see* Ropner, Bt, *cr* 1904, 1985 Edn), and has issue living, (Robert) Angus *b* 1988, Max *b* 1990, Poppy *b* 1993, — Nicola Molly, *b* 1965. ——— Garry Lacon Jock (Rookery House, Crayke, York YO61 4TN), *b* 1937; late 2nd Lt, Welsh Gds: *m* 1st, 1962 (*m diss* 1973), Antonia, yr da of Maj-Gen Edward Charles Colville, CB, DSO (*see* V Colville of Culross, Colls); 2ndly, 1974, Mrs Julie Marie Swanwick, da of O. B. Aarvold; 3rdly, 1987, Mrs Marie-Louise (Sally) Raynar, da of Arthur Southcombe Brook, of Mount Dart, Totnes, Devon, previously wife of (i) late Antony Stuart Trotter, and (ii) late Geoffrey Kenneth Sefton Raynar, and has issue living (by 1st *m*), Emma Louise, *b* 1963.

Issue of late Leonard Ropner, 5th son of 1st baronet, *b* 1873, *d* 1937: *m* 1904, Georgina, who *d* 1930, da of late Murdock Mackay:— Leonard Robert, *b* 1910: *m* 1934, Agnes Deans Bennett.

The 1st baronet, Sir (Emil Hugo Oscar) Robert Ropner (a steamship owner of West Hartlepool and a steamship builder of Stockton-on-Tees), son of Henry Ropner, of Magdeburg, sat as MP for Stockton-on-Tees (C) 1900-10.

ROPNER (UK) 1952, of Thorp Perrow, N Riding of Yorkshire

Faith and Fortitude

Sir JOHN BRUCE WOOLLACOTT ROPNER, 2nd *Baronet*; *s* his father *Sir* LEONARD, MC, TD, 1977; *b* 16 April, 1937; *ed* Eton, and St Paul's Sch, USA; High Sheriff N Yorks 1991-92: *m* 1st, 1961 (*m diss* 1970), Anne Melicent, da of late Sir Ralph Hubert Joan Delmé-Radcliffe; 2ndly, 1970 (*m diss* 1994), Auriol Veronica, yr da of late Capt Graham Lawrie Mackeson-Sandbach, of Caerllo, Llangernyw, Abergele, Denbighshire; 3rdly, 1996, Mrs Diana Nicola (Niki) Tippett, yr da of Wing-Cmdr Peter Graeme Agnew, MBE, RAF (*see* Agnew, Bt, *cr* 1895, colls) and has issue by 1st and 2nd *m*.

𝕬rms – Per fesse indented sable and or, a pale, with three mullets pierced two and one, and as many roebucks' heads erased one and two, all counterchanged; a crescent or for difference. €rest – In front of three tilting spears, one erect and two in saltire or, as many mascles interlaced fessewise of the last, thereon a roebuck's head erased sable.
Residence – Thorp Perrow, Bedale, N Yorks.

SON LIVING (*By 2nd marriage*)

HENRY JOHN WILLIAM, *b* 24 Oct 1981.

DAUGHTERS LIVING (*By 1st marriage*)

Jenny, *b* 1963; resumed her maiden name 1988 until remarriage: *m* 1st, 1985, William H. Bullard, son of late Gerald Bullard, of Hill Farm, Gressenhall, Norfolk; 2ndly, 1990, Graham G. D. Simpson, of Hungry Lodge, Maple Durwell, Basingstoke, Hants RG25 2LQ, son of Brig John Simpson, of Hants and Sydney, and has issue living, Alexander John Drysdale, *b* 1992, — Miranda Lucy Araminta, *b* 1994. ——— Katherine (*Hon Mrs Henry Holland-Hibbert*), *b* 1964: *m* 1988, Hon Henry Thurstan Holland-Hibbert, elder son of 6th Viscount Knutsford, and has issue (*see* V Knutsford).

(*By 2nd marriage*)

Carolyn Esme, *b* 1971: *m* 1999, Christopher James, son of Capt Jeremy James, of Julians Park, Herts. ——— Annabel Mariella, *b* 1974.

SISTERS LIVING

Merle Aurelia, *b* 1939: *m* 1st, 1960 (*m diss* 1968), Christopher John Spence; 2ndly, 1968, Maj Laurence Hew Williams Barrington, who *d* 1998, of Church End House, Great Rollright, Oxon (*see* Barrington, Bt colls), and has had issue, (by 1st *m*) Jeremy Mark, *b* 1964; *d* 1982, — Miranda Jane, *b* 1963: *m* 1989, Patrick Robin Barran (*see* Barran, Bt, colls), — (by 2nd *m*) (*see* Barrington Bt, colls). ⸺ Virginia June, *b* 1941: *m* 1st, 1962 (*m diss* 1973), Anthony David Arnold William Forbes (*see* B Faringdon, colls, 1980 Edn); 2ndly, 1974, Capt John Alexander Henderson, late 14th/20th Hus, of Holly Hill, Well, Bedale, Yorks, and has issue living (by 1st *m*), Jonathan David, *b* 1964: *m* 1993, Sacha Louisa, da of Hon Robin Charles Denison-Pender (*see* B Pender), and has issue living, Jack Alexander David *b* 1996, — Susanna Jane, *b* 1966: *m* 1993, William M. Amberg, yr son of Michael Amberg, of Ravenstone, Bucks, and has issue living, Daisy Silvi *b* 1998.

Sir Leonard Ropner, MC, TD, 1st Bt, son of William Ropner, (*see* Ropner Bt, *cr* 1904), was MP (*C*) for Sedgfield Div of co Durham, and for Barkston Ash Div of W Riding of Yorks. 1931-64, Senior partner Sir R. Ropner & Co Ltd, Ship-owners, Chm of Conservative Shipping and Shipbuilding Cttee 1946-64, PPS to Sec of State for War 1924-28, and temp Chm of Cttees, House of Commons 1945-58.

ROSE (UK) 1872, of Montreal, Dominion of Canada; and 1909, of Hardwick House, Whitchurch, Oxfordshire

I dare

Sir JULIAN DAY ROSE, 5th *Baronet* of 1st, and 4th of 2nd, creation; *b* 3 March 1947; *s* his father, Sir CHARLES HENRY, 1966, in the Baronetcy of Rose of Hardwick House, and *s* his kinsman, Sir FRANCIS CYRIL, 1979, in the Baronetcy of Rose of Montreal; *ed* Stan-bridge Earls Sch, Romsey, and RADA; Actor and Assist Dir; co-founder of Inst for Creative Development, Antwerp; organic farmer, writer and broadcaster: *m* 1976, Elizabeth Good, da of Derrol Johnston, of Columbus, Ohio, USA, and has issue.

Arms – Or, a boar's head couped gules between three water bougets sable; on a chief of the second three maple leaves of the first. **Crest** – A harp or, stringed azure.
Residence – Hardwick House, Whitchurch, nr Reading, Oxon RG8 7RB.

SON LIVING

LAWRENCE MICHAEL, *b* 6 Oct 1986.

DAUGHTER LIVING

Miriam Margaret, *b* 1984.

SISTERS LIVING

Margaret Minna, *b* 1938: *m* 1966, John Alexander Cochrane, of Fairspear House, Leafield, Oxford, OX8 5NT, and has issue (*see* B Cochrane of Cults). ⸺ Penelope Clare, *b* 1945: *m* 1975, Francis Anthony Armstrong Carnwath, CBE, el son of late Sir Andrew Hunter Carnwath, KCVO, and has had issue, Alexander Patrick, *b* 1980, — Flora Helen, *b* 1976, — Catriona Rose, *b* 1978; *d* 1985.

WIDOW LIVING OF THIRD BARONET

Hon PHOEBE MARGARET DOROTHY PHILLIMORE (*Hon Lady Rose*) (Hardwick House, Whitchurch-on-Thames, Oxon RG8 7RB), da of 2nd Baron Phillimore: *m* 1937, Sir Charles Henry Rose, 3rd Bt, (Rose Bt, *cr* 1909), who *d* 1966.

Rt Hon Sir John Rose, GCMG, 1st baronet (of Montreal), was Min of Finance, Canada 1868-69, and Receiver-Gen for Duchy of Cornwall 1883-88. He was son of William Rose of Huntingdon, Canada, who was *b* at Turiff, Aberdeenshire, of a family originally from co Nairn.

The 1st baronet (of Hardwick House), Sir Charles Day Rose, 2nd son of late Rt Hon Sir John Rose, GCMG, 1st Bt (of Montreal, ante), sometime a partner in the American Banking firm of Morton Rose and Co, of Bartholomew Lane, EC, sat as MP for Newmarket, (*L*) 1903-10 and 1910-13. The 2nd baronet, Capt Sir Frank Stanley, 10th R Hussars, was *ka* 1914.

ROSE (UK) 1874, of Rayners, Buckinghamshire

Sir DAVID LANCASTER ROSE, 4th *Baronet*, son of late Ronald Paul Lancaster Rose, only son of Bateman Lancaster Rose, 5th son of 1st Baronet; *b* 17 Feb 1934; *s* his cousin, *Sir* PHILIP HUMPHRY VIVIAN, 1982: *m* 1965, Dorothy, da of Albert Edward Whitehead, and has issue.

𝕬rms – Azure, a chevron invected erminois, between three water bougets in chief and one in base argent. 𝕮rest – A stag argent, collared, and resting the dexter fore-leg on a water bouget azure.
Residence – 20 Kingston Close, Seaford, Sussex.

SONS LIVING

PHILIP JOHN LANCASTER, *b* 1966. —— Christopher David, *b* 1968.

DAUGHTER LIVING

Probitate ac virtute

By probity and valour   Angela Mary, *b* 1967.

DAUGHTERS LIVING OF THIRD BARONET

Petica Mary, *b* 1929: *m* 1955, Judge Andrew Felix Waley, VRD, QC, and has issue living, Simon Felix, *b* 1964, — Sarah Elizabeth, *b* 1958, — Jane Felicity, *b* 1959, — Juliet Anne, *b* 1960. *Residence* – Pleasure House, East Sutton, Kent ME17 3NW. —— Susan Elizabeth Ann, *b* 1932.

SISTER LIVING OF THIRD BARONET

June Dorothy (House of Rothschild, 675 S University Blvd, Denver, Colorado 80209, USA), *b* 1913: *m* 1938 (*m diss* 19—), Marcel Brennan, and has issue living, Christopher (3356 Bird Av, Apt 16, Coral Gables, Florida 33133, USA), *b* 1939: *m* 1963, his cousin, Elisa Virginia Mary, da of Wilfred Eyre, of Denver, Colorado (*see* Rose, Bt, *cr* 1874, 1995 Edn), and formerly wife of Charles Bennet Cobb, and has issue living, Christopher Thomas *b* 1972.

MOTHER LIVING

Shelagh Grant Lindsay, da of Maj Joseph Lindsey Curtis: *m* 1933 (*m diss* 1937), Ronald Paul Lancaster Rose, who *d* 1977.

COLLATERAL BRANCHES LIVING

Grandchildren of late George Alfred Sainte Croix Rose, 6th son of 1st baronet:—
Issue of late Major Ivor Sainte Croix Rose, OBE, *b* 1881, *d* 1961: *m* 1st 1907, Etta Mabel, who *d* 1918, yst da of late Com Sebastian Gassiot, RN; 2ndly, 1918 (*m diss* 1935), Nancy who *d* 1968, da of Arthur Conran Blomfield; 3rdly, 1936 (*m diss* 1951), Ruth Elldale, who *d* 1952, da of Richard White, of Nain, Labrador:—
(By 3rd *m*) George Vivian Sainte Croix (45 Woodfield Lane, Ashtead, Surrey), *b* 1939: *m* 1960, Audrey Rosamond, da of Lawrence Frederick Barrow, and has issue living, Philip Vivian Sainte Croix, *b* 1961, — Alison Charlotte, *b* 1960: *m* 1979, Adrian Christopher Rowe, of 191 Downs Barn Blvd, Milton Keynes, Bucks, and has issue living, Katherine Nancy Charlotte *b* 1991. —— (By 2nd *m*) Camilla Mary Sainte Croix (Moss Bank, Howgate, Penicuik, Midlothian EH26 8QB), *b* 1919; 2nd Offr WRNS 1939-45 War: *m* 1945, Richard Oliver MacMahon Williams, OBE, MC, WS, who *d* 1981, and has issue living, Caroline Jane Sainte Croix, *b* 1947: *m* 1983, Jeremy Peter Marriage, and has issue living, Frederick Peter Oliver *b* 1986, Clare Felicity *b* 1984, Lucy Diana *b* 1989, — Nicola Valentine Blomfield, *b* 1948: *m* 1972, Maj-Gen Alistair Stuart Hastings Irwin, OBE, The Black Watch (R Highland Regt), and has issue living, George Ronald Valentine Hastings *b* 1983, Mary Rose Elizabeth *b* 1975, Laura Bridget *b* 1978, — Rosemary Anne MacMahon (38 Elsynge Rd, SW18 2HN), *b* 1952: *m* 1973 (*m diss* 1989), Adrian Gerald Burns, and has issue living, Thomas Michael Macmahon *b* 1979, Emily Caroline *b* 1981, — Lorna Christine Allan, *b* 1954: *m* 1975, Gareth Bowring Stoddart, and has issue (*see* Malet Bt).

Issue of late Harcourt George Sainte Croix Rose, *b* 1883, *d* 1955: *m* 1st, 1908 (*m diss* 1920), Florence Norah, who *d* 1970, da of Arthur Elliot Deane, of Littleton House, Winchester (Hughes, Bt, *cr* 1773); 2ndly, 1920 (*m diss* 1930), Freda Victoria, who *d* 1972, da of late C. A. Keyser; 3rdly 1930, Estelle Marie, da of late Marquis of Sarzano, 8th Hussars:—
(By 1st *m*) Jean *b* 1915; European War 1939-45 with WAAF: *m* 1953, Lieut-Com Henry Francis Ormsby Hale, RN, of High View House, Langtree, Torrington, Devon, who *d* 1984.

Sir Philip Rose, 1st Bt, was Founder of the Brompton Hospital for Consumption (Hon-Sec 1841-83), and High Sheriff of Bucks 1878.

ROSE (UK) 1935, of Leith, Co of City of Edinburgh (Extinct 1976)

Sir HUGH ROSE, TD, 2nd and last *Baronet.*

DAUGHTER LIVING OF SECOND BARONET

Alison Mary (Whitfield Farm, Hawick, Roxburghshire), *b* 1936: *m* 1st, 1964 (*m diss* 1972), Ian Napier; 2ndly, 1985, John Risk Buchanan.

ROSS (UK) 1960, of Whetstone, Middlesex

Sir (JAMES) KEITH ROSS, RD, MS, FRCS, 2nd *Baronet*; *b* 9 May, 1927; *s* his father, *Sir* JAMES PATERSON, KCVO, 1980; *ed* St Paul's, and Middx Hosp; MB and MS London; FRCS 1956; Surg Lt-Cdr RNR; Consultant cardiac surgeon Wessex Region 1972-90: *m* 1956, Jacqueline Annella, da of late Francis William Clarke, of Banstead, Surrey, and has issue.

Arms – Per pale argent and sable a chevron between in chief lion passant and in base an anchor all counterchanged. **Crest** – A hawk rising sable between two branches of juniper leaved and fructed proper.
Residence – Moonhills Gate, Hilltop, Beaulieu, Hants SO42 7YS.

SON LIVING

ANDREW CHARLES PATERSON, *b* 18 June 1966; Maj RM: *m* 1997, Surg Cmdr Sarah J., yr da of J. Dennis Murray, of Curbar, Derbys.

DAUGHTERS LIVING

Susan Wendy, *b* 1958: *m* 1983, Nigel Timothy Wolstenholme, of The Oast House, Hoplands Farm, Kings Somborne, Stockbridge, Hants SO20 6QH, son of late J. M. Wolstenholme. —— Janet Mary, *b* 1960: *m* 1990, Timothy N. Morgan, of Moonhills Gate Cottage, Beaulieu, Hants, son of late N. V. Morgan, of Dibden Purlieu, Hants. —— Anne Townsend, *b* 1962: *m* 1993, Murray J. S. Anderson-Wallace, of 20 Heathfield Terrace, Far Headingley, Leeds LS6 4DE, yr son of J. Wallace, of York.

BROTHER LIVING

Harvey Burton, RD, MS, FRCS (Springvale, Brewery Common, Mortimer, Reading, RG7 3JE, Berks), *b* 1928; FRCS 1957: *m* 1st, 1962, Nancy Joan, da of B. C. Hilliam, of Bank Lyndhurst; 2ndly, 1988, Susan Christine, da of P. M. Blandy, of Reading, Berks, and has issue living (by 1st *m*), Edward Paterson, *b* 1963, — James Hilliam, *b* 1972, — Imogen, *b* 1970.

The first baronet, Sir James Paterson Ross, was Surg to HM 1952-64; Pres Royal College of Surgeons 1957-59; *cr KCVO* 1949.

ROTHBAND (UK) 1923, of Higher Broughton, Salford, co Palatine, of Lancaster (Extinct 1940)

Sir HENRY LESSER ROTHBAND, 1st and last *Baronet.*

GRANDDAUGHTER LIVING OF FIRST BARONET

Issue of late Percy Lionel Rothband, only son of 1st baronet, *b* 1884, *d* 1926: *m* 1918, Ellen Elizabeth Marjorie (who *d* 1956, having *m* 2ndly, 1935, Capt Wilfred Henry Furlonger, who *d* 1945), el da of William Francis Fisher, of Altrincham:—
Joan Olga Eleanor, *b* 1920: *m* 1942, Dennis Arthur Treves Atkins, who *d* 1993, and has issue living, Timothy Simon Treves, *b* 1951, — Penelope Jane, *b* 1943: *m* 1969, Peter Nicholas Geer, of 537 Eastcot Rd, W Vancouver, BC V7S 1E5, Canada, and has issue living, Noel *b* 1976, Samantha *b* 1970, Jill *b* 1973, — Marilyn Jill ATKINS, *b* 1947; has resumed her

maiden name: *m* 1974 (*m diss* 1985), Johann Klein, — Priscilla Dawn, *b* 1948: *m* 1973 (*m diss* 1984), Bruce Higham, and has issue living, Alice *b* 1973. *Residence* – 21 Courtyards, Little Shelford, Cambridge CB2 5ER.

Rouse-Boughton, see Boughton.

ROWLAND (UK) 1950, of Taunton, co Somerset (Extinct 1970)

Sir WENTWORTH LOWE ROWLAND, 2nd and last *Baronet*.

DAUGHTER LIVING OF SECOND BARONET

Georgina Elizabeth Mary, *b* 1952: *m* 1977, John George Stewart Scott, of Lower Street Farmhouse, Hildenborough, Tonbridge, Kent, and has issue living, Victoria Katharine, *b* 1979, — Charlotte Elizabeth, *b* 1982.

WIDOW LIVING OF SECOND BARONET

(VIOLET MARY) ELIZABETH MACBETH (*Lady Rowland*) (4 Stonewall Park Rd, Langton Green, Tunbridge Wells, Kent), da of late A. C. Macbeth Robertson, of Dumfries: *m* 1947, Sir Wentworth Lowe Rowland, 2nd Bt, who *d* 1970.

ROWLEY (GB) 1786, of Tendring Hall, Suffolk (Dormant 1997)

Sir JOSHUA FRANCIS ROWLEY, 7th *Baronet*; *d* 1997.

DAUGHTER LIVING OF SEVENTH BARONET

Susan Emily Frances, *b* 1965: *m* 1988, Robert David Holden (*see* E Powis, 1995 Edn), and has issue living, Hubert Joshua Robert, *b* 1997, — Lucia Hermione Sophia, *b* (twin) 1997. *Residence* – Sibdon Castle, Craven Arms, Shropshire SY7 9AQ.

DAUGHTER LIVING OF SIXTH BARONET

Alethea Susan, *b* 1922: *m* 1949, Henry Reginald Townshend, MBE, of Brook Hall, Bramfield, Suffolk IP19 9HN, and has issue living, James Reginald (Melbury House, Dorchester, Dorset DT2 0LF), *b* 1954; *ed* Eton, and RAC Cirencester: *m* 1st, 1980 (*m diss* 1995), Olivia Mora, da of Peter Matthey, of Snowshill House, Fifield, Oxon; 2ndly, 1995, Hon Mrs Charlotte Anne Morrison, da of 9th Viscount Galway, and has issue living (by 1st *m*), Henry Roscoe *b* 1984, Georgina Hermione *b* 1982, (by 2nd *m*), Melissa Susan Charlotte *b* 1996, — Robert Charles (Holbecks, Hadleigh, Suffolk IP7 5PF), *b* 1956; *ed* Eton: *m* 1983, Fiona Elizabeth Mary, da of late John Hugh McLeod Fraser, and has issue living, Hugh Charles *b* 1984, Alexander George Rupert *b* 1991, Arabella Charlotte *b* 1987, — Albinia Jane, *b* 1952: *m* 1977, James Anthony Stoddart Murray, of Alde House, The Street, Bruisyard, Saxmundham, Suffolk IP17 2DT, and has issue living, Susannah Albinia Frances *b* 1979, Annabel Katharine Law *b* 1981.

COLLATERAL BRANCHES LIVING

Descendants, if any, of late Rev Joshua Rowley, Rector of Bergholt, Suffolk, 3rd son of 1st baronet.

Descendants of late Adm Sir Charles Rowley, GCB, GCH, 4th son of 1st baronet, who was *cr a Baronet* 1836:—
See Rowley, Bt, *cr* 1836.

ROWLEY (UK) 1836, of Hill House, Berkshire

With favouring winds

Sir CHARLES ROBERT ROWLEY, 7th *Baronet*; *b* 15 March 1926; *s* his father, *Lt-Col Sir* WILLIAM JOSHUA, 1971; *ed* Wellington; Senior known heir to baronetcy of Rowley of Tendring Hall, Suffolk (dormant 1997): *m* 1952, Astrid, da of late Sir Arthur Massey, CBE, MD, of 93 Bedford Gdns, W8, and has issue.

Arms – Argent, on bend engrailed between two Cornish choughs sable, three escallops of the field. **Crest** – A Mullet pierced or. **Supporters** – Two Cornish choughs proper, navally crowned or, gorged with the riband and therefrom pendent a representation of the badge of the Imperial Austrian Order of Maria Theresa also proper.
Residences – Naseby Hall, Northants NN6 6DP; 21 Tedworth Sq, SW3 4DR.

SON LIVING

RICHARD CHARLES, *b* 14 Aug 1959; *ed* Eton, and Exeter Coll, Oxford (BA): *m* 1989, (Elizabeth) Alison, da of late (Arthur) Henry Bellingham (*see* Bellingham, Bt, colls), and has issue living, Joshua Andrew, *b* 1989, — William Henry Stuart, *b* 1992. *Residence* – 15 Worfield St, SW11 4RB.

DAUGHTER LIVING

Caroline Astrid, *b* 1955: *m* 1979, Edwin Rudolph Joseph March Phillipps de Lisle, and has issue living, Alexander Edwin, *b* 1983, — Nicholas Charles, *b* 1991.

BROTHER LIVING

(Joshua) Christopher, *b* 1928.

SISTER LIVING

Avice Gwendoline, *b* 1920: *m* 1953, John Arderne Mere Latham, and has issue living, Mark Joshua Arderne, *b* 1955, — Robert William Mere, *b* 1956. *Residence* – The Forge, Cawston, Norfolk.

HALF-SISTERS LIVING

Felicity Margaret, *b* 1945: *m* 1967, (Alexander) Michael Foulds Slinger, of River Green House, Great Chesterford, Saffron Walden, Essex, CB10 1NP, and 34 Hornton St, W8, and has issue living, Arabella Claire Felicity, *b* 1972, — Katharine Merianna Sarah, *b* 1977. —— Prudence Elizabeth, *b* 1951: *m* 1972 (*m diss* 1998), Simon Geoffrey Hull, and has issue living, Thomas Gresham, *b* 1975, — Louisa Claire, *b* 1977.

COLLATERAL BRANCHES LIVING

Grandchildren of late Capt Charles Donovan Rowley, MBE (infra):—
Issue of late John Howard Rowley, *b* 1931, *d* 1997: *m* 1963, Aileen Margery (Monks' Orchard, Blakeney, Holt, Norfolk), da of late R. Clifford Freeman:—
Charles John Freeman, *b* 1969. —— Irene Frances Elizabeth, *b* 1965.

Granddaughters of late Julius Richard Capel Molyneux Rowley, el son of late Rev Julius Henry Rowley, son of late Capt Richard Freeman Rowley, RN, 4th son of 1st baronet:—
Issue of late Capt Charles Donovan Rowley, MBE, *b* 1889, *d* 1935: *m* 1917, Hon Irene Evelyn Beatrice (who *d* 1949, having *m* 2ndly, 1941, Frank Ash, who *d* 1974, of Narborough Hall, King's Lynn, Norfolk), da of 9th Viscount Molesworth:—
Nina Irene (PO Box 1451, Dassenberg 7350 S Africa), *b* 1922. —— June Rose (PO Box 1012, Darwin, NT 0801, Australia), *b* 1924: *m* 1963, Thomas Opitz, who *d* 1982. —— Julia May, *b* 1934: *m* 1955, Anthony Frederick Twist, and has issue living, Andrew Charles, *b* 1958: *m* 1st, 1977, Bronwen Anne Bowden; 2ndly, 1987, Sally Michael Mangos, and has issue living (by 1st *m*), Rebecca Catherine *b* 1985, (by 2nd *m*) Samuel Wilfrid *b* 1993, Sara Lucy *b* 1995, — Julian Richard, *b* 1960: *m* 1981, Gillian Sandra Hooper, and has issue living, Jennifer Megan *b* 1987, Helen Victoria *b* 1989, Sarah Catherine *b* 1991, Catherine Olivia *b* 1994, Martha Alice *b* 1998, — Philip Michael, *b* 1962: *m* 1983, Elspeth Jane Barr, and has issue living, Lucy Alice *b* 1987, Emily Charlotte *b* 1989, Rosie Francesca *b* 1993, — Catherine Julia, *b* 1956; has issue living, Jessica May *b* 1995, — Mai Alison (adopted da), *b* 1970. *Residence* – Clements End, Conduit Head Rd, Cambridge CB3 0EY.

Grandchildren of late Julius Leigh Rowley (infra):—
Issue of late Robin Julius Leigh Rowley, *b* 1892, *d* 1974: *m* 1920, Edith May, who *d* 1984, da of Sidney Hugo Mumford, of Eton, Bucks:—
Thelma Jeanne, *b* 1923: *m* 1946, René Georges Lucien Paul Lefevre, of Ivydene, East Drive, Bracklesham Bay, W Sussex PO20 8JH, and has issue living, Julian Howard Georges Alphonse (United Nations WFP, PO Box 25, Hanoi, Vietnam), *b* 1949; *ed* Leeds Univ (BA), — Michelle Edith Germaine, *b* 1946, — Christine Rene Jeanne, *b* 1948, — Jacqueline Marguerite Frederica, *b* 1951. —— Audrey Frederica, *b* 1928: *m* 1949, Thomas Arthur Smith, of Walnut Trees, Cemetery Lane, Woodmancote, Emsworth, Hants, and has issue living, Ivan Howard Lee (Lordington Park, Lordington, Chichester, W Sussex), *b* 1952: *m* 1st, 1978, Pamela Joan, da of late Ronald Janman; 2ndly, 19—, Jessica Jane, da of David Rutland, and has issue living (by 1st *m*), James Leigh Thomas *b* 1983, Luke Robin Anthony *b* 1984, (by 2nd *m*) Harriet Jane *b* 1993, — Stephen Frederick John (Downs View, East Marden, Chichester, W Sussex), *b* 1955: *m* 1983, Shona Joyce, da of Peter McCall, and has issue living, Nicholas Edward Peter *b* 1984, Charlotte Louise *b* 1986.

Issue, if any, of late Julius Henry Rowley, *b* 1905, *d* 1982.
Issue, if any, of late Douglas Lionel Rowley, *b* 1911, *d* 1991.

Grandchildren of late Rev Julius Henry Rowley (ante):—
Issue of late Julius Leigh Rowley, *b* 1863; *d* 1943: *m* 1st, 1890, Florence, who *d* 1895, da of Harry Coe; 2ndly, 1899, Alma, da of Harry Welch:—
(By 2nd *m*) Violet Frances, *b* 1903: *m* 19—, — Fenwick, formerly of 2159, Mission St, San Francisco, Calif, USA. —— Geraldine Winifred, *b* 1909: *m* 1932, Clarence Arthur Allendin, of Geyserville, Sonoma Co, Cal, USA. —— Hildred Vivian, *b* 1912: *m* 19—, — Wycoft. —— Alma Julia, *b* 1915.

Granddaughters of late Richard Julius Molyneux Rowley (infra):—
Issue of late Frederick Duncan Lorin Rowley, *b* 1912, *d* 1968: *m* 1941, Dale (2388 East Racquet Club Rd, Palm Springs, Cal, USA), da of Joseph Antellin:—
Pamela Dale, *b* 1942. —— Loryn Lee, *b* 1946.

Granddaughter of Rev Julius Henry Rowley (ante):—
Issue of late Richard Julius Molyneux Rowley, *b* 1865, *d* 1948: *m* 1900, Idabe Sophia, who *d* 1951, da of Oscar T. Nelson, of Gothenburg, Sweden:—
Constance Frederica Julia Christina, *b* 1901: *m* 1922, Burnell Hamilton De Vos, and has issue living, Burnell Hamilton, *b* 1927, — Richard Glenn, *b* 1932.

Descendants, if any, of late Com Robert Hibbert Bartholomew Rowley, RN, 5th son of 1st baronet, *b* 1817, *d* 1860: *m* 1845, Donna Juanita di Latzona, who left issue, two sons and two das, concerning whom no details are available.

The 1st baronet, Adm Sir Charles, GCB, GCH (also Knight of Order of Maria Theresia of Austria), was 4th son of Sir Joshua Rowley, 1st Bt (creation 1786), of Tendring Hall.

ROYDEN (UK) 1905, of Frankby Hall, co Palatine, of Chester

Sir CHRISTOPHER JOHN ROYDEN, 5th *Baronet*; *b* 26 Feb 1937; *s* his father, *Sir* JOHN LEDWARD, 1976; *ed* Winchester, and Ch Ch, Oxford (MA): *m* 1961, Diana Bridget, only da of Lt-Col Joseph Henry Goodhart, MC, of Keldholme Priory, Kirkbymoorside, Yorks, and has issue.

Arms – Vert, three stags' heads erased in pale between two hunting horns in fesse or.
Crest – A stag's head erased or, collared gemel vert, holding in the mouth a riband also vert, suspended therefrom a shield of the Royden arms.
Residence – Bridge House, Ablington, Bibury, nr Cirencester, Glos.

SONS LIVING

JOHN MICHAEL JOSEPH, *b* 17 March 1965; *ed* Stowe, and Reading Univ (LLB): *m* 1989, Lucilla Mary, da of John Ralph Stourton (*see* B Mowbray), and has issue living, Charlotte Alice Maude, *b* 1992, — Lucinda Catherine Quenelda, *b* 1995. —— Richard Thomas Bland (25 Porten Rd, W14 0LQ), *b* 1967; *ed* Stowe, New York Inst of Finance, and London Business Sch: *m* 1994, Annabel Julia, yr da of David Darling, of Leeson House, Abthorpe, Northants, and has issue living, Minnie, *b* 1999.

DAUGHTER LIVING

Emma Mary Bridget, *b* 1971.

BROTHER LIVING

Thomas Cecil (Netherfield Place Farm, Battle, Sussex), *b* 1938; *ed* Winchester, Ch Ch Oxford, Univ of Maryland, LSE, Utah State Univ (MSc), and Calif State Poly Univ Pomona; Master of USA Agric; Settlement Manager, Kitale, Tanzania; Consultant Utah State Univ.

SISTERS LIVING

Catherine Anne, *b* 1945: *m* 1965 (*m diss* 1979), Christopher Synge Barton (*see* Synge, Bt, colls, 1985 Edn), and has issue living, James Edward Synge, *b* 1974, — Sarah Melissa Synge, *b* 1970. —— Quenelda Jane, *b* 1947: *m* 1967, Robert Reginald (Robin) Loder, of Leonardslee Gardens, Lower Beeding, Horsham (*see* Loder, Bt).

COLLATERAL BRANCH LIVING

Issue of late Thomas Jerome Royden, yr son of 3rd Bt, *b* 1913, *d* 1991: *m* 1st, 1937, Catherine Mary Denton, who *d* 1970, da of late Charles Denton Toosey, of Oxton, Birkenhead; 2ndly, 1970, Lynn (201 Sweetwater Creek Drive E., Longewood, Fla 32779, USA), da of late Lloyd Aspinwall, Jr, of Mountain Lake, Lake Wales, Fla, USA:—
(By 1st *m*) Ernest Jerome, *b* 1944: *m* 1974, Suzanne Adams, and has issue living, Catherine Helene, *b* 1982. —— Anne Elizabeth Mary, *b* 1945: *m* 1967, Barry Lewis Gerken, of 37 Woodside Dr, Bolton, Mass 01740, USA, and has issue living, Heather Kristin, *b* 1969, — Stefanie Rebecca, *b* 1971. —— (By 2nd *m*) Thomas, *b* 1976. —— Alexa, *b* 1972.

The 1st baronet, Sir Thomas Bland Royden, was Mayor of Liverpool 1878-9, and MP for W Toxteth Div of Liverpool (C) 1885-92. The 2nd baronet, Sir Thomas Royden, CH, was Chm of Cunard Steamship Co, Ltd, and a Director of Phoenix Assurance Co, Ltd, and other Cos, and sat as MP for Bootle (*Co U*) 1918-22. He was *cr Baron Royden*, of Frankby, co Chester (peerage of United Kingdom) 1944 and *d* 1950, when the Barony became ext, and the Baronetcy devolved upon his brother, Sir Ernest Bland Royden. Sir Ernest Bland Royden, 3rd Bt, was High Sheriff of Anglesey 1920.

Rugge-Price, see Price.

Ruggles-Brise, see Brise.

RUMBOLD (GB) 1779, of Wood Hall, Watton, Herts

Praise is the excitement
of virtue

Sir HENRY JOHN SEBASTIAN RUMBOLD, 11th *Baronet*; *b* 24 Dec 1947; *s* his father, *Sir* (HORACE) ANTHONY CLAUDE, KCMG, KCVO, CB, 1983; *ed* Eton, and William and Mary Coll, Va, USA: *m* 1978, Frances Ann, da of late Dr Albert Whitfield Hawkes, of New York City, NY, USA, and formerly wife of Julian Berry.

ârms – Or, on a chevron gules three cinquefoils of the field; a canton of the second charged with a leopard's face erminois. Crest – A demi-lion rampant erminois.
Residences – 19 Hollywood Rd, SW10 9HT; Hatch House, Tisbury, Wilts.

SISTERS LIVING

Serena Caroline, *b* 1939: *m* 1959, Jeremy Lancaster, of The Gables, Broadwell, Moreton-in-Marsh, Glos, and has issue living, Nicholas Horace John, *b* 1966, — Emma Charlotte, *b* 1961, — Joanna Elizabeth, *b* 1963, — Frances Mary, *b* 1968. —— Venetia Mary *b* 1941. —— Camilla Charlotte, *b* 1943: *m* 1st, 1962 (*m diss* 1970), Hon Christopher Lionel Baliol Brett (*see* V Esher); 2ndly, 1972 (*m diss* 1983), Giles Oliver Cairnes Swayne, only son of late Sir Ronald Oliver Carless Swayne, MC, and has issue living (by 1st *m*) (*see* V Esher), — (by 2nd *m*) Orlando Benedict Carlos, *b* 1974.

AUNT LIVING (*Daughter of 9th baronet*)

Constantia Dorothy, *b* 1906: *m* 1944, Hugh William Farmar, MVO, LLD, who *d* 1987, and has issue living, (Hugh Alexander) Peregrine (Saltway House, Bibury, nr Cirencester, Glos), *b* 1945; *ed* Eton, and Keble Coll, Oxford: *m* 1973, Carole Mary Phillips, and has issue, Samuel Hugh Gregory *b* 1977, Rebecca Lucy *b* 1975, Georgina Frances *b* 1980, Charlotte Felicity *b* 1985, — Francis Edmund (1 Rectory Cottages, Sedgehill, Shaftesbury, Dorset), *b* 1948; *ed* Eton, St Martin's Coll of Art, and West of England Coll of Art: *m* 1982 (*m diss* 1997), Judith Madeline Povoas. *Residence* – Wasing Old Rectory, Aldermaston, Berks.

WIDOW LIVING OF TENTH BARONET

PAULINE LAETITIA (*Pauline, Lady Rumbold*), da of late Hon David Francis Tennant (*see* B Glenconner, colls), and formerly wife of (1) Capt Julian Alfred Lane-Fox-Pitt-Rivers (*see* By Forster, 1980 Edn), and (2) Euan Douglas Graham (*see* D Montrose, colls): *m* 3rd, 1974, as his 2nd wife, Sir (Horace) Anthony Claude Rumbold, 10th Bt, KCMG, KCVO, CB, who *d* 1983. *Residence* – Hatch Cottage, Coker's Frome, Dorchester, Dorset.

COLLATERAL BRANCHES LIVING

Issue of late Col William Edwin Rumbold, CMG, 2nd son of 8th baronet, *b* 1870, *d* 1947: *m* 1903, Elizabeth Gordon, who *d* 1948, da of late Rev J. Cameron, of Burntisland:—
Violet Elizabeth, *b* 1907: *m* 1934, Andrew Atha, who *d* 1967, and has issue living, Charles Antony (Wandle Villa, 98 Phipps Bridge Rd, SW19 2ST), *b* 1937: *m* 1st, 1971 (*m diss* 1989), Bridget Amanda Macgregor, da of late Robert Snaith, of Clifton, Bristol; 2ndly, 1990, Anthea Helen Skilbeck, da of late Cmdr Malcolm Stuart Leslie Burnett, OBE, RN, of Williamston House, by Insch, Aberdeenshire, and has issue living (by 1st *m*), Antonia Susan *b* 1975, Annabella Faith Marie *b* 1977, Araminta Tamsin Lucy *b* 1980, — Elizabeth Amanda, *b* 1940: *m* 1967, Michael David Abrahams, CBE, DL, of Newfield, Mickley, Ripon, Yorks HG4 3JH, and has issue living, Rupert Edward Charles, *b* 1972, Emily Anne *b* 1968, Victoria Ruth *b* 1970.

Grandchildren of late Col William Edwin Rumbold, CMG (ante):—
Issue of late Sir (Horace) Algernon Fraser Rumbold, KCMG, CIE, *b* 1906, *d* 1993: *m* 1946, Margaret Adel (Shortwoods, West Clandon, Surrey GU4 7UB), da of late Arthur Joseph Hughes, OBE, of Pages, Chigwell Row, Essex:—
Sara Josephine, *b* 1948: *m* 1969, Robert Michael Owen, QC, of Shortwoods, Oak Grange Rd, W Clandon, Guildford, Surrey GU4 7UB, and has issue living, Thomas Llewellyn, *b* 1973, — Huw Algernon, *b* 1976. —— Caroline Elizabeth, *b* 1950: *m* 1981, Richard James Keevil, of Clevancy, Calne, Wilts, and has issue living, Katharine Elizabeth Adele, *b* 1982, — Cordelia Jane, *b* 1988.

Issue of late William Robert Rumbold, *b* 1912, *d* 1983: *m* 1st, 1942 (*m diss* 1952), Pamela Mary Dewe; 2ndly, 1957, Sylvia Violet, only da of Lawrence John Smith:—
(By 1st *m*) Cheryl Anne, *b* 1944: *m* 1968 (*m diss* 1979), Luca C. Dotti. *Residence* – 5 Av Calas, Geneva, Switzerland. —— (By 2nd *m*) CHARLES ANTON (Flat 1, 239 Earls Court Rd, SW5), *b* 7 Feb 1959: *m* 1987, Susan, elder da of J. M. Tucker, of Melbourne, Aust. —— Alexander Robert, *b* 1971.

Issue of late Lt-Col Alastair Gordon Rumbold, OBE, MC, *b* 1914, *d* 1992: *m* 1st, 1941 (*m diss* 1952), Tania, da of late Michael Borzakovsky; 2ndly, 1958, Auriol Cressida (4 North St, Castle Cary, Som), da of Col William Rixon Bucknall:—
(By 1st *m*) Michael Alastair, *b* 1943; *ed* Wellington: *m* 1976, Katherine Mary, da of Donal John Cagney, of Broadstairs, Kent, and has issue living, Angus Michael, *b* 1982, — Victoria Catherine, *b* 1977, — Lucinda, *b* 1979. —— (By 2nd *m*) Belinda Cressida, *b* 1962.

Granddaughter of late Thomas Henry Rumbold, 2nd son of Charles Edmund Rumbold, 5th son of 1st baronet:—

Issue of late Thomas Arthur Rumbold, *b* 1882, *d* 1972: *m* 1st, 1911, Evelyn Mary, who *d* 1954, only da of late Walter Comyn Jackson, JP; 2ndly, 1959, Elizabeth, who *d* 1973, da of late Rev T. M. B. Paterson, of Laighstone Hall, Hamilton:—

(By 1st *m*) Elizabeth Anne, MBE (*Baroness Hayter*) (Ashtead House, Ashtead, Surrey), *b* 1919; MBE (Civil) 1975: *m* 1940, 3rd Baron Hayter.

The 1st baronet, Sir Thomas, sometime MP for Melcombe Regis Dorset, and New Shoreham, Sussex, served as Aide-de-Camp to Lord Clive at Plassey (1757), was severely wounded, and was afterwards Governor of Madras. The 2nd baronet was HM's Minister at Hamburg. The 5th baronet, a Capt in the Army, was President of Nevis 1857-63, and Virgin Islands 1865-9; he was also a Col in the Ottoman Army, served with the Turkish Contingent during the Crimean war. The Rt Hon Sir Horace Rumbold, GCB, GCMG, PC, 8th Bt, was Sec of Legation at Athens 1862-4 and at Berne 1864-8, Sec of Embassy at St Petersburg 1868-71 and at Constantinople 1871-72, Min Resident and Consul-Gen in Chile 1872-78 and to Swiss Confederaton 1878-9, Envoy Extraor and Min Plen to Argentine Republic 1879-81, to Stockholm 1881-5, to Athens 1885-8, and to The Hague 1888-96, and Ambassador Extraor and Plen at Vienna 1896-1900. The 9th baronet, Rt Hon Sir Horace George Montagu, GCB, GCMG, MVO, PC, was Envoy Extraor and Min Plen to Switzerland 1916-19, and to Poland 1919-20, High Commr at Constantinople 1920-23, and Ambassador Extraor and Plen to Spain 1923-8, and Berlin 1928-33. The 10th baronet, Sir (Horace) Anthony Claude, KCMG, KCVO, CB, was Min in Paris 1960-63, Ambassador to Thailand 1964-67, and to Austria 1967-70.

Runchorelal (UK) 1913, of Shahpur, Ahmedabad, India (see Chinubhai)

RUSSELL (UK) 1812, of Swallowfield, Berkshire

Sir (ARTHUR) MERVYN RUSSELL, 8th *Baronet*, 2nd son of *Sir* ARTHUR EDWARD IAN MONTAGU RUSSELL, 6th Bt; *b* 7 Feb 1923; *s* his half-brother, *Sir* GEORGE MICHAEL, 1993; late RN: *m* 1st, 1945 (*m diss* 19—), Ruth, da of Charles George Holloway, of Wandsworth; 2ndly, 1956 Kathleen Joyce Searle, and has issue by 1st and 2nd *m*.

Arms – Argent, a chevron sable between three cross-crosslets fitchée azure within a bordure engrailed gules, bearing alternate bezants and escallops or. **Crest** – A demi-lion rampant ermine, charged with a fasces proper, and bearing in his dexter paw a cross-crosslet fitchée sable.

SONS LIVING (*By 1st marriage*)

STEPHEN CHARLES, *b* 12 Jan 1949; artist. *m* 1974, Dale Frances, da of late George Gustav Markstein, novelist and scriptwriter, and has issue living, Lucy Scarlett, *b* 1974.

(*By 2nd marriage*)

Ian Mervyn, *b* 1956.

HALF-BROTHER LIVING

Christopher, *b* 1937; *ed* Charterhouse: *m* 1st, 1962 (*m diss* 1983), Ann, da of late Lt-Col (Clifford) Donald Battersby Campling, of Syngate House, Stelling Minnis, Canterbury, Kent; 2ndly, 1983, Loveday Mary, widow of Cdr P. D. Davey, RN.

Learn justice being admonished

DISCITE · JUSTITIAM · MONITI

DAUGHTERS LIVING OF SEVENTH BARONET

Marie Clotilde, *b* 1939: *m* 1965 (*m diss* 1984), Nelson Grant Mews, son of late P. Mews, of Perth, W Australia, and has issue living, Josephine Lucy, *b* 1974. —— Mary Christina, *b* 1944.

WIDOWS LIVING OF SIXTH AND SEVENTH BARONETS

MARJORIE ELISABETH JOSEPHINE (*Dowager Lady Russell*) (Little Struan, Pangbourne, Berks), da of Ernest Rudman, of Foxhangers, Earley, Berks: *m* 1933, as his 3rd wife, Sir Arthur Edward Montagu Russell, 6th Bt, who *d* 1964.

JOY FRANCES BEDFORD (*Joy, Lady Russell*), da of late W. Mitchell, of Irwin, W Australia: *m* 1936, Sir George Michael Russell, 7th Bt, who *d* 1993.

COLLATERAL BRANCHES LIVING

Grandchildren of late Major Francis Whitworth Russell, son of late Francis Whitworth Russell, 3rd son of 1st baronet:—
Issue of late Francis Whitworth Russell, b 1854, d 19—: m 1886, Maude Agnes, da of late Denis O'Brien, of Knockroe, Fermoy, co Cork:—
Francis Whitworth, b 1888. Residence –

Issue of late Edward Stuart Marjoribanks Harley Russell, b 1857, d 1926: m 1882, Mary, who d 1938, da of late Capt W. Phipps:—
Alice. —— Rachel. —— Kate. Residence –

Grandchildren of late Whitworth Russell, son of late Henry Russell, son of late Rev Whitworth Russell, 4th son of 1st baronet:—
Issue of late John Whitworth Russell, b 1891, d 1982: m 1915, Mary Alice, who d 1985, da of J. R. Anderson:—
Whitworth Athol (23 Ingleton Terr, Hamilton, NZ), b 1918; MB, ChB, DCP; assumed 2nd christian name of Athol by deed poll in lieu of Athelstan: m 1946, Marjory Ellen Ross, and has issue living, Anthony Whitworth (15 Insoll Av, Hamilton, NZ), b 1951; ACA, ACIS: m 1st, 1971 (m diss 1986), Catherine Sylvia Bradley; 2ndly, 1993, Catherine Patricia Felicity Orange, and has issue living (by 1st m), James Whitworth b 1979, Joanna Alice b 1976, Claire Jennifer b 1980, — Michael David, b 1959, — Juliet Ethne, b 1962: m 1983 (m diss 1990), Shaughan Bruce, and has issue living, Alexandra Ellen b 1987. —— Richard Hudson, b 1928. —— Elizabeth Alison, b 1934; BA: m 1956, David Ernest Poswillo, CBE, DDS, MD, DSc, Emeritus Prof UMDS, Guy's Hosp, Univ of London, of Ferndale, 7 Oldfield Rd, Bickley, Kent BR1 2LE, and has issue living, Stephen David, b 1962: m 1988, Michelle Lynn Narcisse, and has issue living, Maxwell Stephen b 1994, Chloe Dale b 1999, — Mark Geoffrey, b 1964, — Deborah Jane, b 1958: m 1989, Robert William Caton, and has issue living, Harry James b 1997, Lucy Harriett b 1994, — Mary Jill, b 1961: m 1987, Robert William Gerald Battye, and has issue living, Alexander Robert b 1989, Emma Alice b 1991.

Grandchildren of late George Cecil Russell, eldest son of late Cecil Henry Russell, son of late George Lake Russell, 5th son of 1st baronet (infra):—
Issue of late Evelyn Aylmer Cecil Russell, b 1891, d 1963: m 1st, 1916 (m diss 1923), Alice Edith, da of W. H. Wallis, of California Gully, Bendigo, Victoria 3806, Australia; 2ndly, 1924, Irene, da of John Brodrick, JP, of Nangana, Victoria:—
(By 2nd m) William Henry Cecil (Strensham, Beaumont Rd, Berwick, Victoria 3806, Australia), b 1927: m 1953, Margaret Winifred, da of Gordon Newton, of Mornington, Victoria, Australia, and has issue living, William James Cecil b 1994, Mark Newton Cecil (Russmoore, Norbury Rd, Upper Beaconsfield, Victoria, Australia), b 1959: m 1987, Rosemary Anne, da of Alan Moore, of E Bentleigh, Victoria, Australia, and has issue living, William James Cecil b 1994, Briony Jane b 1990, — Jane Elizabeth, b 1956: m 1976, Timothy Leslie Moore, 2nd son of Lt-Col Colin Moore, of East Brighton, Victoria, Australia, and has issue living, Jayce William b 1980, Ebby Margaret b 1983, — Kim Margaret, b 1964: m 1989, Mark Raymond Bloodworth, son of Raymond Bloodworth, of Rosanna, Victoria, Australia. —— Harry Arthur Cecil (Quarry Hill, 19 Belmont Av, Upwey, Victoria 3158, Australia), b 1931; JP: m 1959, Marjorie Ailsa, da of Alfred Sutton, of Hawthorn, Victoria, Australia, and has issue living, Ewen James Cecil, b 1967, — Sarah Anne Cecil b 1962, — Virginia Kate Cecil (twin), b 1962: m 1992, David Robert Edwards, son of Philip Edwards, of Hawthorn, Victoria, Australia, and has issue living, Stephanie Kate b 1996. —— (By 1st m) Sadie Evelyn, b 1917; ed Melbourne Univ (BA): m 1940, Harold William Halls, and has issue living, Peter John, b 1944: m 1969, Marjorie, da of Rev Maurice Padman, of Snowtown, S Australia, and has issue living, Evelyn Marie b 1972, Joanne Michele b 1973, — Robin, b 1958; BCom LLB.

Issue of late John Hardress Cecil Russell, b 1896, d 1979: m 1927, Doris Marion, da of Ernest Reginald Green, of Colac, Victoria, Australia:—
John Alan Cecil (Protea Bowl, Gembrook 3782, Victoria, Australia), b 1928: m 1955, Patricia Mary Gordon, da of late Roddam Morris Douglas, of Emerald, Victoria, Australia, and has issue living, Susan Patricia, b 1956, — Penelope Ann, b 1959, — Lynette Margaret, b 1963, — Diane Marion, b 1964.

Sir Henry, 1st Bt, son of Michael Russell of Dover, was Chief Justice of Bengal. Sir Henry, 2nd Bt, was for many years Resident at the Court of Hyderabad, Sir Charles, VC, 3rd Bt, received Victoria Cross in Crimea 1854, and was MP (C) for Berks and Warminster. Sir George, 4th Bt, was a Judge of County Courts, Recorder of Wokingham and MP for Berks E Div (C).

RUSSELL (UK) 1916, of Littleworth Corner, Burnham, co Buckingham

Sir CHARLES DOMINIC RUSSELL, 4th *Baronet*; *b* 28 May 1956; *s* his father *Sir* CHARLES IAN, 1997; *ed* Worth Abbey: *m* 1986 (*m diss* 1995), Sarah Jane Murray, only da of Anthony Chandor, of Brock St, Bath, Avon, and has issue.

What will be, will be

Arms – Argent, a lion rampant gules, on a chief sable three escallops of the first, the whole a bordure engrailed vert. **Crest** – A goat passant argent, armed or, charged on the body fessewise with three trefoils slipped or.
Residence – Flat 12, 39 Egerton Gdns, SW3 2DD.

SON LIVING

CHARLES WILLIAM, *b* 8 Sept 1988.

SISTER LIVING

Clare Harriet Faviell, *b* 1949: *m* 1974, Richard James Shepherd, of Stratton End, Cirencester, Glos, and has issue living, Edward James, *b* 1977, — Andrew Charles, *b* 1979, — Thomas Richard, *b* 1982.

COLLATERAL BRANCHES LIVING

(In special remainder)

Issue of late Gerald Cyril Russell, MC, brother of 2nd baronet, *b* 1896, *d* 1962: *m* 1923, Barbara, who *d* 1985, da of Lieut-Col Sir James Philip Reynolds, 1st Bt, DSO:—
Cyril (The Covert, Aldeburgh, Suffolk), *b* 1924: *m* 1949, (Eileen Mary) Elizabeth, da of late Major W. D. G. Batten, 3rd Gurkha Rifles, and has issue living, Gerald William, *b* 1950: *m* 1976, Tessa, da of Richard Rumsey, and has issue living, James Alexander *b* 1978, Sophie Annabel *b* 1980, Lucy Victoria *b* 1983, Kate Elizabeth *b* 1985, Emma Rose *b* 1989, — Patrick James, *b* 1952: *m* 1977, Pamela Jill, da of Phillip Chesterman, and has issue living, Oliver William Grant *b* 1981, Charles *b* 1990, Jessica Helen *b* 1984, Camilla Ellinora *b* 1987, — Nicholas Alastair (151 Lower Rd, Gt Bookham, Surrey), *b* 1958: *m* 1986, Heather B. L., da of Col John Burrell, MBE, of 4 Lee Rd, Aldeburgh, Suffolk, and has issue living, Alastair Hamish *b* 1987, Philippa Barbara *b* 1990. —— †Rev John Alastair, *b* 1928, *d* 1997; was in Holy Orders of Church of Rome. —— Colin Patrick (Long Ford, Duntisbourne Leer, Cirencester Glos), *b* 1944: *m* 1978, Jessica Margaret, only da of Ramsay William Rainsford-Hannay, of Kirkdale, Kirkcudbright (see Wiseman, Bt). —— Moira, *b* 1927, *d* 1992. —— Clodagh Mary, *b* 1933: *m* 1971, Brig David William Reid, MBE, of The Studio, Priors Hill Rd, Aldeburgh, Suffolk, son of late Sir Robert Neil Reid, KCSI, KCIE.

Grandchildren of late Maj Denis Leslie Russell, MBE, TD (infra):—
Issue of late (Denis) Anthony Russell, *b* 1934, *d* 1966: *m* 1961, Charlotte Mary (who *m* 2ndly, 1970, John Watcyn Lewis, of 66 Clifton Hill, NW8), yr da of late Lt-Col Sir Ian Frank Bowater, GBE, DSO, TD (see Bowater, Bt, cr 1939):—
William Anthony Bowater, *b* 1965: *m* 1989, Hilary Ann, only da of John Chaplin, of Cambridge, and has issue living, Edward John Bowater, *b* 1992, — Nicholas William Albert, *b* 1995, Alistair, *b* 1997. —— Amanda Charlotte, *b* 1963: *m* 1987, Charles Nicholas Yaxley, only son of John Yaxley, of Hong Kong, and has issue living, Thomas, *b* 1989, — Joshua Robert, *b* 1995.

Issue of late Maj Denis Leslie Russell, MBE, TD, yr brother of late Gerald Cyril Russell, MC (ante), *b* 1909, *d* 1986: *m* 1932: Verena, who *d* 1995, yr da of late George Henderson, of 55 Cadogen Pl, SW1, and Orchard House, Crastock, Surrey:—
David Ian (4 Westover Rd, SW18), *b* 1943; *ed* Ampleforth: *m* 1976, Hon Frances Marian Chant-Sempill, da of Lady Sempill, and has a da, Katherine Ann, *b* 1980. —— Sally Verena, *b* 1937: *m* 1956, William Bertram Weatherall, of Shorn-down, Mursley, Bucks, son of late Lt-Col Nigel Edward Weatherall, of Caldwell House, Gilling W, Richmond, Yorks, and has issue living, Michael William (4 Hosack Rd, SW17 7QP), *b* 1958: *m* 1987, Penelope Ann, da of late Frederick Wharton Askew, of Caroline House, Redhill, Surrey, and has issue living, Edward Frederick *b* 1991, Toby William *b* 1993, — Annabel Jane, *b* 1960: *m* 1985, William George Briscoe Bevan, and has issue (see Brocklebank, Bt, colls), — Clare Victoria, *b* (twin) 1960: *m* 1987, James Bunten de Sales La Terrière, eldest son of Capt Ian Cameron de Sales La Terrière, of Dunalastair, Perthshire, and has issue living, Archie *b* 1990, Dominic John *b* 1993, Emma *b* 1988.

Issue of late Lt-Col Cyril Alan Russell, yst brother of late Gerald Cyril Russell (ante), *b* 1910, *d* 1986: *m* 1st, 1937, Grace Evelyn, who *d* 1943, eldest da of William Thomas Moore, of New York, USA; 2ndly, 1944, Jean Patricia (23 Park Lane, Aldburgh, Suffolk), da of Stafford Croom Johnson, of Greenacre, Stoke Bishop, Bristol, and widow of Wing-Cdr John Ryan Cridland, AAF:—
(By 2nd *m*) Michael Alan, *b* 1947; *ed* Beaumont: *m* 1972, Penelope, yr da of Lt-Col A. R. Dawe, OBE, of Wyke Lodge, Normandy, and has issue living, Toby Alan, *b* 1974, — Michaella Katherine, *b* 1976, — Hannah, *b* 1982.

Grandchildren of late Rt Hon Francis Xavier Russell, brother of 1st Bt, *cr Baron Russell of Killowen* (Life Baron) 1929, son of Charles Russell, *cr Baron Russell of Killowen* (Life Baron) 1894:—
Issue of late Rt Hon Charles Ritchie Russell, *cr Baron Russell of Killowen* (Life Baron) 1975, *b* 1908, *d* 1986: *m* 1st, 1933, Joan Elizabeth, who *d* 1976, only child of late James Aubrey Torrens, MD, FRCP, of 46 Wimpole St, W1; 2ndly, 1979, Elizabeth Cecilia (*Baroness Russell of Killowen*), da of AV-M William Foster Macneece Foster, CB, CBE, DSO, DFC, and widow of Judge Edward Hey Laughton-Scott, QC:—

(By 1st *m*) *Hon* Valentine Francis Xavier Michael (CP51, 1631 Moléson, Fribourg, Switzerland), *b* 1938; *ed* Beaumont, and Oriel Coll, Oxford. —— *Hon* (Francis) Damian (17 Lurline Gdns, SW11), *b* 1947; *ed* Beaumont, and Trin Coll Dublin: *m* 1994, Carole Myers, BSc, DPhil, of Hillsborough, S Yorks. —— *Hon* Julian Mary, *b* 1935; *m* 1st, 1955 (*m diss* 1974), Anthony Rodney Allfrey; 2ndly, 1975, Dr Harlan Ullman, of 1245 29th St NW, Washington DC, USA, and has issue (by 1st *m*) (*see* Fox, Bt, ext).

Grandchildren of late Charles Russell, *cr Baron Russell of Killowen* (Life Baron) 1894 (ante):—

Issue of late Lieut-Col Hon Bertrand Joseph Russell, DSO, *b* 1876, *d* 1960: *m* 1st, 1902, Dorothy, who *d* 1921, da of late John George Leeming; 2ndly, 1922 (*m diss* 1936), Mavis Winifred, da of late Frederick Hazell, of Frinton-on-Sea:—

(By 2nd *m*) †Michael Dudley, *b* 1923: *m* 1st, 1949 (*m diss* 1959), Jeanette Meryen, da of Major Arthur Sinclair Cannon, of Rangoon, Burma; 2ndly, 1960, Judy, yr da of Dr M. A. W. Roberts, of Dublin, and *d* 1993, leaving issue (by 1st *m*), Christopher John (19 Charles St, W1), *b* 1951; *ed* Worth: *m* 1976 (*m diss* 1981), Nicola, only da of James de Courcy Hughes, and has issue living, Dominic John *b* 1979, Lucienne Eva *b* 1977; has further issue, (by Alexandra Bex) William *b* 1987, — Julia Meryen, *b* 1954: *m* 1986, Timothy Ashworth, of Old Marsham Farm, Pett, Hastings, Sussex, and has issue living, Daniel James Michael *b* 1996, Camilla Eileen *b* 1989, Elizabeth Annabelle *b* 1990, — (by 2nd *m*) Anna Katherine, *b* 1961, — Verena Grace, *b* 1962: *m* 1989, Andrew Bruce Weir, of 52 Kings Rd, SW19 8QU, and has issue living, Oliver Michael *b* 1994, Isobelle Katherine *b* 1991, a da *b* 1998. *Residence* – Meadow Court, Coombe Hill Rd, E Grinstead, W Sussex. —— (By 1st *m*) Joan, *b* 1908: *m* 1933, Charles Gordon Brand, CBE, who *d* 1966, and *d* 1997, leaving issue, Andrew Charles, *b* 1938, — Duncan Valentine, *b* 1941, — Felicity *b* 1945. —— Clodagh, *b* 1912: *m* 1939, Brigadier Thomas Haddon, CBE, late Border Regt, who *d* 1993, and has issue living, Paul Antony, *b* 1940; *ed* Beaumont, and Campion Hall, Oxford, — Martin Thomas, *b* 1944; *ed* Beaumont, and Worcester Coll, Oxford, — John Richard, *b* 1947; *ed* Beaumont, and Worcester Coll, Oxford. *Residence* – Mole End, Churt, Farnham, Surrey.

This Baronetcy was conferred with a special remainder (in default of heir male of the body of the grantee) to the heirs male of the body of Charles, Baron Russell of Killowen (Life Baron, *cr* 1894), father of the 1st baronet. The 1st baronet, Hon Sir Charles Russell (senior partner in the firm of Charles Russell and Co solicitors, of 37 Norfolk Street, Strand, WC), was 2nd son of late Charles, Baron Russell of Killowen (Life Baron *cr* 1894), Lord Ch Justice of England. The 2nd baronet, Sir Alec Charles Russell, MC, was Capt (retired) RA. The 3rd baronet, Sir Charles Ian Russell, was a partner in the family firm of solicitors for over thirty years.

RUTHERFORD (UK) 1923, of Liverpool, co Palatine of Lancaster (Extinct 1942)

Sir (JOHN) HUGO RUTHERFORD, 2nd and last *Baronet*.

DAUGHTERS LIVING OF SECOND BARONET

Elspeth, *b* 1914: *m* 1939, Lieut-Col Francis William Bartlett, REME (ret), and has had issue, William John, *b* 1940, *d* 1997, — Charles Hugo, *b* 1943, — Francis Murray, *b* 1945, — James Peter, *b* 1947, — Isabel, *b* 1951. *Residence* – 36 Laurel Drive, Willaston, Neston, Ches CH64 1TW. —— Isabel Lavender, *b* 1925: *m* 1948, Peter Thomas Crook, and has had issue, Jeremy Peter, *b* 1954; *d* 1993, — Matthew Lancelot, *b* 1969, — Jean Isabel, *b* 1951. *Residence* – 28 Beacon Dr, W Kirby, Wirral, Merseyside L48 7ED.

RYAN (UK) 1919, of Hintlesham, Suffolk

Nothing without labour

Sir DEREK GERALD RYAN, 4th *Baronet*; *b* 25 March 1954; *s* his father, *Sir* DEREK GERALD, 1990; *ed* Univ of California at Berkeley (BA (Environmental Design) 1977): *m* 1986 (*m diss* 1990), Maria Teresa, da of Juan G. Rodriguez, of Lexington, Kentucky, USA.

Arms – Gules, in chief two griffins sejant respectant and combatant or, and in base a garb of rye proper. Crest – Upon a mount vert a griffin sejant sable, holding in the dexter claw a sword erect, and resting the sinister on a sickle or.
Address – 4618 South Austin, St, Seattle, WA 98118, USA.

SISTERS LIVING

Anne Katherine, *b* 1951: *m* 1st, 1977 (*m diss* 1989), Edgard Puente; 2ndly, 1989, Steven Casciola. *Residence* – Villa Marjorie Apartments no 411, 1711 East Olive Way, Seattle, WA 98102, USA. —— Jenifer Hylda, *b* 1955: *m* 1985, Christopher Stirling Newall, son of Peter Newall, of Crookham Westfield Farmhouse, Cornhill on Tweed, Northumb, and has issue living, Alfred Stirling, *b* 1987, — George Stirling, *b* 1990. *Residence* – 17 Lonsdale Sq, N1 1EN. —— Caroline Sarah, *b* 1956: *m* 1990, Jeff Chase, and has issue living, Perry *b* 1994, Monica Kristi, *b* 1991, Liza (twin) *b* 1994. *Residence* – 15 Brook Rd, Topsfield, MA 01983, USA.

MOTHER LIVING

Penelope Anne, da of late Rex Hawkings, of 139 East 94th St, New York: *m* 1947 (*m diss* 1971), as his 1st wife, Sir Derek Gerald Ryan, 3rd Bt, who *d* 1990. *Residence* – 14 Longbrook Rd, Byfield, MA 01922, USA.

WIDOW LIVING OF THIRD BARONET

KATJA (*Dowager Lady Ryan*), da of late Ernest Best, of 35 Kassel, Fuhrmannsbreite 11, Germany: *m* 1972, as his 2nd wife, Sir Derek Gerald Ryan, 3rd Bt, who *d* 1990. *Residence* – Scharfensteinstrasse 36, 6228 Eltville a Rh1, Germany.

COLLATERAL BRANCH LIVING

Issue of late Vivian Desmond Ryan, yr son of 1st baronet, *b* 1893, *d* 1950: *m* 1st, 1917, Kathleen Frances, who *d* 1945, da of late James William Helps, MICE, of Berisal, Normanton Rd, S Croydon; 2ndly, 1946, Nanny, who *d* 1988, da of late Dixon Slater, of 24 Belleview, Skipton, Yorks:—
(By 1st wife) DESMOND MAURICE (S15 C8 RR4 Gower Point, Gibsons, BC, Canada V0N 1V0), *b* 1918: *m* 1942, Margaret Catherine, da of A. H. Brereton, and has issue living, Barry Desmond, *b* 1943: *m*, and has issue living, Andrew *b* 19—, — Kevin Vivian, *b* 1951: *m*, and has issue living, Martin *b* 19—, — Michael Brereton, *b* 1954: *m*, and has issue living, Aaron *b* 19—. —— †Adrian James, *b* 1920: *m* 1st, 1941 (*m diss* 1950), Peggy Rose; 2ndly, 1952, Barbara Pitt; 3rdly, 1977, Susan Curnow (8 Camden Studios, Camden St, NW1), and *d* 1998, leaving issue, (by 1st *m*) Geraldine Daphne, *b* 1943, — (by 2nd *m*) Kathleen Scarlett, *b* 1954, — Vivien Frances, *b* 1957. —— Jeanette Daphne, *b* 1929. —— (By 2nd wife) John Desmond, *b* 1945: *m* 1969, Tina, da of late Arthur Percy Gregory, and has issue living, Nicola Jane, *b* 1972, — Rosalind Anne, *b* 1975. *Residence* – 11 Compton Rise, Pinner, Middx HA5 5IIS.

The 1st baronet, Sir Gerald Hemmington Ryan (son of Michael Desmond Ryan, of Kildare Terr, W) was later Gen Manager and Chm of Phoenix Assurance Co.

RYCROFT (GB) 1784, of Calton, Yorkshire

Sir RICHARD JOHN RYCROFT, 8th *Baronet*; son of late Cdr Henry Richard Rycroft, OBE, DSC, RN, 4th son of 5th baronet; *b* 15 June 1946; *s* his cousin, *Sir* (RICHARD) NEWTON, 1999; *ed* Sherborne; marine environmental scientist with MAFF; Burnham-on-Crouch RNLI Lifeboat crew 1987-96, Deputy Launching Authority since 1996.

౼rms – Quarterly: 1st and 4th, per bend or and azure, three griffins, heads erased counterchanged; on a chief ermine, a fleur-de-lis between two roses gules, *Rycroft*; 2nd and 3rd, party per pale or and sable, a chevron between three fleurs-de-lis all counterchanged, *Nelson*. ౼rest – A griffin's head erased per bend or and azure, charged with two fleurs-de-lis counter- changed.
Residence – Mariners, Ship Rd, Burnham-on-Crouch, Essex CMO 8JX. *Club* – Royal Corinthian Yacht Club.

SISTERS LIVING

Caroline Mary, *b* 1944: *m* 1966, Nicholas Wolryche Meyrick, of Church Farm House, Empingham, Rutland, and has issue living, Julian Timothy, *b* 1968, — Oliver Michael, *b* 1978, — Hilary Jocelyn, *b* 1970. ⸺ Philippa Eve, *b* 1949: *m* 1981, Peter Edward Jenkinson, of Fringford Cottage, Fringford, Oxon, and has issue living, Susanna Emily, *b* 1982, — Olivia Mary, *b* 1984, — Harriet Anne, *b* 1989. ⸺ Jocelyn Penelope, *b* 1955: *m* 1984, Michael Piers Lawton, of The Lodge, Bryngarw Country Park, Bryncethin, Mid Glamorgan, and has issue living, Piers Simon George, *b* 1990, — Sarah Louise, *b* 1988.

AUNTS LIVING (*Daughters of 5th baronet*)

Alice Juliana Rosamond (The Paddock, 4 South Place, Lee on the Solent, Hants), *b* 1915: *m* 1st, 1938, Neil Malise Graham, who *d* 1939; 2ndly, 1943, Rev Patrick Roger Harvey, who *d* 1986, and has issue living, (by 1st *m*) Charles Edward Malise (Riccards Down House, Abbotsham, Bideford, Devon EX39 5BG), *b* 1939; *ed* Exeter Univ (LLB); Master Marine, Younger Brother of Hull Trinity House: *m* 1976, Lynn Marie, da of Stanley Carter, — Bruce Torquil Irving (twin) (Penhoat Luon, Guimiliau, Landivisiau, France), *b* 1939, — (by 2nd *m*) Michael Timothy John, *b* 1944; *ed* Keble Coll, Oxford (MA), and Lyons Univ, France, — Diana Lavender Mary, *b* 1946: *m* 1970, Robert Ian Fellows, and has issue living, Gregory Chad *b* 1974, Charlotte Claire *b* 1976, — Primrose Miranda Margaret, *b* 1953: *m* 1989, Michael Robert Line, and has issue living, Harriet Clare *b* 1992. ⸺ Eleanor Mary (Resthaven, Pitchcombe, Stroud, Glos GL6 6LS), *b* 1918; 1942-45 War in WRNS.

DAUGHTERS LIVING OF SEVENTH BARONET

Susan Marilda, *b* 1948; *ed* Trin Coll Dublin (MA): *m* 1974, Ian Martell, of Wood House, Shotley Bridge, co Durham, and has issue living, Jonathan Newton, *b* 1978, — Alice, *b* 1976. ⸺ Sally Ann (*Viscountess FitzHarris*), *b* 1950; *ed* Magdalen Coll, Oxford (MA): *m* 1969, James Carleton Harris, Viscount FitzHarris, of Greywell Hill, Greywell, Hook, Hants RG29 1DG, el son of 6th Earl of Malmesbury, and has issue (see that title).

MOTHER LIVING

Penelope Gwendoline, da of late Lt-Col Charles Spenser Browne Evans-Lombe: *m* 1941, Cdr Henry Richard Rycroft, OBE, DSC, RN, who *d* 1985. *Residence* – 19 Marcuse Fields, Bosham, Chichester, Sussex.

WIDOW LIVING OF SEVENTH BARONET

ANN (*Lady Rycroft*), da of the late Hugh Bellingham Smith: *m* 1947, Sir (Richard) Newton Rycroft, 7th Bt, who *d* 1999. *Residence* – Winalls Wood House, Stuckton, Fordingbridge, Hants SP6 2HG.

COLLATERAL BRANCHES LIVING

Issue of late Rev Richard Michael Rycroft, 3rd son of 5th baronet, *b* 1897, *d* 1968: *m* 1924, Evelyn Maud, who *d* 1969, da of late Francis James Driscoll, of Jersey:—
Jean Dorothea, *b* 1925; 1943-45 in WRNS: *m* 1945, Charles Spencer Goldring, of Yarmouth, Nova Scotia, and has issue living, Paul Michael (4085 Rue Berri, Montreal, Quebec, Canada), *b* 1947; *ed* St Mary's Univ (BA): *m* 1983, Ryoko Mine, and has issue living, Matthew John Wallace Yotaru Mine *b* 1985, Nathan Charles Toshiharu Mine *b* 1987, — James Philip (53 Pooler Av, Ottawa, Ontario, Canada), *b* 1948; *ed* Lond Univ (PhD): *m* 1969, Marianne Louise McLean, and has issue living, Andrew Michael Dmitri *b* 1970, Hugh Douglas Arthur *b* 1986, — Nicholas John, *b* 1954, — Hilary Adrian Jerome, *b* 1959; *ed* W Ontario Univ (Bus Ad), — Stephen Gerard, *b* 1961, — Christopher Septimus Denison (twin), *b* 1961, — Felicity Jocelyn, *b* 1965; *ed* Dalhousie Univ, Halifax (BSc). ⸺ (Mary) Elizabeth (8 Southcote Rd, N19), *b* 1935; *ed* Royal Coll of Art (MA).

Issue of late Charles Frederick Rycroft, MB, BS, 5th son of 5th baronet, *b* 1914, *d* 1998: *m* 1st, 1947 (*m diss* 1963), Chloe, da of late Edouard Majolier; 2ndly, 1977, Jenny (2 Modbury Gdns, NW5 3QE), da of William Pearson:—
(By 1st *m*) FRANCIS EDWARD (School Farm Barn, Denton Rd, Aldeburgh, Suffolk IP20 0BY) *b* 1950; *ed* Gresham's Sch, Holt: *m* 1975, Cherry, da of Kenneth Willmott, and has issue living, Michael Kenneth Edward, *b* 1979, — Kelly Jane *b* 1977. —— Alice Julia, *b* 1947; *ed* Univ of Kent (BA): *m* 1978, Ibrahim Jama, of 3 Woodside Rd, Manchester 16, and has issue, Adan, *b* 1981, — Malik, *b* 1986, — Miriam, *b* 1979. —— Catherine Ann, *b* 1949: *ed* Univ of Kent (BA): *m* 1970, Christopher Piers Merriman, of Tankers' Row, S Clydach, Abergavenny, Gwent, and has issue living, Roger Christopher, *b* 1975, — Chloe Catherine, *b* 1977.

Granddaughters of late Maj-Gen Sir William Henry Rycroft, KCB, KCMG, 2nd son of 4th baronet:—
Issue of late Major Julian Neil Oscar Rycroft, DSO, MC, *b* 1892, *d* 1928: *m* 1920, Elizabeth Mildred Louisa, who *d* 1932, da of Sir Ralph William Anstruther, 6th Bt:—
Cynthia Margaret, *b* 1922: *m* 1949, Col Philip Dives Stenning, late RE, and has issue living, Christopher John William (15 Peterborough Rd, SW6 3BT), *b* 1950; *ed* Marlborough: *m* 1981, Ruth, da of George T. C. Draper, of Swaffham, Norfolk, and has issue living, Jonathan *b* 1985, Rachel *b* 1983, — Nicholas Julian Seymour (Medstead House, Medstead, nr Alton, Hants GU34 5LY), *b* 1952; *ed* Marlborough, and Pembroke Coll, Oxford: *m* 1976, Caroline, da of late Michael Livingstone-Learmonth, MC, of Minchinhampton, Glos, and has issue living, Alexander *b* 1985, Clare *b* 1979, Emily *b* 1981, — Richard Neil (Meadcrott, Sidmouth Rd, Colyton, Devon EX13 6NP), *b* 1955; *ed* Marlborough, and Nottingham Univ: *m* 1988, Alison, da of Mrs A. E. Hooper, and has issue living, Aisha *b* 1989, Eliana Grace *b* 1990. *Address* – Sunnyside, Elie, Fife KY9 1DN. —— Evelyn Joanna Christian, *b* 1925: *m* 1953, Martin Claridge, MCh, FRCS, and has issue living, Simon Julian, *b* 1954: *m* 19—, Marit McKerchar, and has issue living, Rebecca Tatsachen *b* 1987, Jessica *b* 1989, — Tobias James, *b* 1963: *m* 19—, Victoria Hartnell, and has issue living, Fergus *b* 1994, Hester *b* 1996, — Anna Louise, *b* 1958, — Katharine Georgina, *b* 1960: *m* 19—, Richard Fuller, and has issue living, Caspar Furneaux *b* 1995, Marlda Grace *b* 1997. *Residence* – St Martin's House, St Martin's Av, Canterbury.

Issue of late Rev Edmund Hugh Rycroft, 3rd son of 4th baronet, *b* 1862, *d* 1932: *m* 1902, Winifred Edith, who *d* 1968, el da of late Adm of the Fleet Sir Arthur Dalrymple Fanshawe, GCB, GCVO:—
Arthur John, *b* 1905; *ed* Radley, and Corpus Christi Coll, Oxford (BA 1927). *Residence* – The Old Vicarage, Wilsford, Pewsey, Wilts.

Grandson of late Rev Edmund Hugh Rycroft (ante):—
Issue of late Col David Hugh Rycroft OBE, *b* 1907 *ka* 1944: *m* 1st, 1930 (*m diss* 1934), Elizabeth Edith Dilys, da of late Capt Miles Bertie Cunningham Carbery, Roy Irish Fusiliers; 2ndly, 1939, Cicely Phoebe Susanna, who *d* 1980, da of late Lt-Col Robert Bruère Otter-Barry, OBE, of Glazeley Hall, near Bridgnorth (Cs Dysart, colls, 1968 Edn):—
(By 2nd *m*) Henry David (58 Garscube Terr, Ravelston, Edinburgh EH12 6BN), *b* 1943; *ed* Radley, and St Andrews Univ (BSc); MB BS: *m* 1st, 1972 (*m diss* 1983), Nicole Elizabeth, MB, BS, da of Maurice Kenig, MD; 2ndly, 1983, Mrs Dorothea Ann Joan HEANEY, yr da of late Robert William Nicholson Evans (*see* Lees, Bt, *cr* 1804, colls, 1990 Edn), and has issue living (by 1st *m*), Alexander Theophilus, *b* 1975.

The 1st baronet, Rev Sir Richard Rycroft, DD, only surviving son of John Nelson, assumed the surname of Rycroft by royal sign-manual 1758. Sir Richard Nelson Rycroft, 5th Bt, and Sir Nelson Edward Oliver Rycroft, 6th Bt, were High Sheriffs of Hants 1899, and 1938, respectively.

MOLESWORTH-ST AUBYN (E) 1689, of Pencarrow, Cornwall

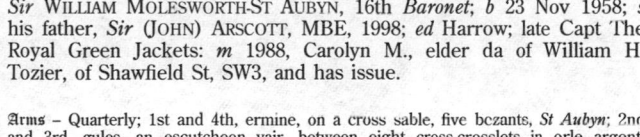

In se teres
Complete in itself

Sic fidem teneo
Thus I hold the faith

Sir WILLIAM MOLESWORTH-ST AUBYN, 16th *Baronet*; *b* 23 Nov 1958; *s* his father, *Sir* (JOHN) ARSCOTT, MBE, 1998; *ed* Harrow; late Capt The Royal Green Jackets: *m* 1988, Carolyn M., elder da of William H. Tozier, of Shawfield St, SW3, and has issue.

Arms – Quarterly; 1st and 4th, ermine, on a cross sable, five bezants, *St Aubyn*; 2nd and 3rd, gules, an escutcheon vair, between eight cross-crosslets in orle argent, *Molesworth*. Crest – A rock, thereon a Cornish chough rising, all proper.
Residence – Pencarrow, Bodmin, Cornwall PL30 3AG.

SON LIVING

ARCHIE HENDER, *b* 27 March 1997.

DAUGHTER LIVING

Jemima, *b* 1995.

BROTHER LIVING

James Francis, *b* 1960; *ed* Harrow.

SISTER LIVING

Emma Jane, *b* 1971: *m* 1996, Maj Simon David Oliver, The Royal Scots Dragoon Gds (Carabiniers and Greys), yr son of Lt-Col M. D. Oliver, of Pimperne, Dorset.

AUNTS LIVING (*Daugthers of 14th baronet*)

Johanna Katherine (*Countess of Morley*) (Pound House, Yelverton, Devon PL20 7LJ), *b* 1929: *m* 1955, Lt-Col 6th Earl of Morley, KCVO. —— Prudence Aline, *b* 1937: *m* 1969, Joseph Robertson Cooke-Hurle, of Long Ash, Buckland Monachorum, nr Yelverton, Devon, and has issue living, Celia Hermione, *b* 1970, — Penelope Joy, *b* 1971: *m* 1998, Edward James Douglas Miller, yst son of Robert Douglas Miller, of Barelaw Castle, Midlothian.

WIDOW LIVING OF FIFTEENTH BARON

IONA AUDREY ARMATRUDE (*Iona, Lady Molesworth-St Aubyn*), da of late Adm Sir Francis Loftus Tottenham, KCB, CBE: *m* 1957, Sir (John) Arscott Molesworth-St Aubyn, 15th Bt, who *d* 1998. *Residence* – Pencarrow, Bodmin, Cornwall PL30 3AE.

COLLATERAL BRANCHES LIVING

Issue of late Maj Hender Charles Molesworth-St Aubyn, 2nd son of 13th baronet, *b* 1901, *d* 1986: *m* 1935 (*m diss* 1946), Dulciebella Joy, da of Lt-Col John Cayzer Medlicott-Vereker (*see* V Gort, colls):— Caroline Gay, *b* 1940: *m* 1963, Edward Simon Foord, of Hill Farm House, Bures, Suffolk CO8 5EW, only son of late Brig Edward John Foord, CBE, and has issue living, Edward Richard, *b* 1965, — Nicola Samantha, *b* 1967: *m* 1995, Paul Richard Sercombe, of Costers Mill Cottage, W Lavington, Midhurst, W Sussex GU29 0EN, and has issue living, Oliver James *b* 1999, Alice Olivia *b* 1996, — Annabel Jane, *b* 1971.

Issue of late Guy Kemyel Molesworth-St Aubyn, yst son of 13th baronet, *b* 1904, *d* 1981: *m* 1931, Catherine, JP, who *d* 1979, yst da of late Richard Tattersall Hargreaves, of Benington Park, Herts:— Anthony William (Cobbs, Howe Street, nr Chelmsford, Essex), *b* 1936; *ed* Eton: *m* 1964, Mary Evelyn, only da of late Kenneth Meiklejohn, and has issue living, Charles Hugh, *b* 1966; *ed* Eton; late Capt RGJ: *m* 1992, Zoë, da of J. J. Prow, and of Mrs F. M. Gibson, of Notts, and has issue living, Samuel Guy *b* 1994, Alexandra Frances *b* 1992, — Anna Victoria, *b* 1970: *m* 1997, Count Peter Z. M. Krasiński, son of Count Stanislaw Krasiński, of Cuckfield, Sussex, and has issue living, Adam Tadeusz Anthony *b* 1999. —— †Simon Guy, *b* 1944; *ed* Eton; Maj late 60th Rifles: *m* 1977, Amanda Jane, el da of George Walker, of Knutsford, Cheshire, and *d* 1995, leaving issue, Thomas Kemyel, *b* 1981, — Cressida Juliet, *b* 1988. —— Felicity Sybil (*Hon Lady Butler*), *b* 1932: *m* 1955, Rt Hon Sir Adam Courtauld Butler, of The Old Rectory, Lighthorne, Warwick, 2nd son of late Baron Butler of Saffron Walden (Life Baron), and has issue living (*see that title*).

Grandson of late Col St Aubyn Molesworth, RA, son of late Col St Aubyn Molesworth, RE, son of late Rev John Molesworth, 2nd son of 5th baronet:— Issue of late Major Edward Algernon Molesworth, DSO, *b* 1875, *d* 1939: *m* 1916, Ruth, da of Leslie Creery, of Lisnalurg, Shankill, co Dublin:— St Aubyn, *b* 1917; sometime Engineer in Merchant Navy.

This family descends from Sir Walter de Molesworth, who in 1270 accompanied Edward I, when Prince Edward, to the Holy Land. The 1st baronet, Sir Hender, was Lieut-Gov of Jamaica. The 2nd baronet, MP for Bossiney, was knighted by Charles II. The 4th baronet sat as MP for Newport, Cornwall, 1734, and for Cornwall 1744-61. The 5th and 6th baronets respectively represented Cornwall 1765-75, and 1784-90. The 8th baronet, MP for East Cornwall 1832-7, for Leeds 1837-41, and for Southwark 1841-55, was Privy Councillor, and successively First Commissioner of Works, and Secretary of State for the Colonies. The 11th baronet sat as MP for Cornwall S-E, or Bodmin Div (LU) 1900-6. The 12th baronet, Rev Sir Hender, was son of late Rev Hender Molesworth (great-grandson of 5th baronet), who assumed by Roy licence 1844, the additional surname and arms of St Aubyn, his mother Catherine being da and co-heir of Sir John St Aubyn, baronet.

ST GEORGE (I) 1766, of Athlone, co Westmeath

Sir JOHN AVENEL BLIGH ST GEORGE, 10th *Baronet*; *b* 18 March 1940; *s* his father, *Sir* GEORGE BLIGH 1995; *ed* Christian Brothers' Coll, Kimberley: *m* 1st, 1962 (*m diss* 1979), Margaret, da of John Leonard Carter, MBE, of Mayes Park House, Warnham, Sussex; 2ndly, 1981, Linda, da of Robert Perry, of 10 Dubton St, Bishoploch, Glasgow, and has issue by 1st and 2nd *m*.

𝕬rms – Argent: a chief azure, over all a lion rampant gules, ducally crowned or, armed and langued of the second, a crescent for difference. Crest – A demi lion rampant gules, ducally crowned or, armed and langued azure.
Residence – 2 Curzon St, Ibstock, Leics LE67 6LA.

Firmitas in coelo

Stability in heaven

SONS LIVING (By 2nd marriage)

ROBERT ALEXANDER BLIGH, *b* 17 Aug 1983. —— Benjamin Bligh, *b* 1986.

DAUGHTERS LIVING (By 1st marriage)

Elinor Jane Bligh, *b* 1963: *m* 1990, Richard Newbold, of Birchwood House, 32 Blackhills, Esher, Surrey, and has issue living, Cameron, *b* 1991, — Georgia, *b* 1992. —— Catherine Bligh, *b* 1966.

BROTHER LIVING

Peter Bligh, *b* 1946; MBA (Cape Town), CA (SA); formerly Dir County Natwest, Investment Bankers, Australia: *m* 1974, Elizabeth Meyrick, eldest da of late Alan Meyrick Williams, of Newport, Gwent, and has issue living, William Bligh, *b* 1984, — Caroline Bligh, *b* 1976, — Alice Mary Bligh, *b* 1981. *Residence* – 130 Wolseley Rd, Point Piper, Sydney, NSW 2027, Australia.

SISTERS LIVING

Elizabeth Margaret Bligh, *b* 1936: *m* 1962, Peter Ivor Baikie, CA (SA), FSAA, of 21 Garrard Rd, Banstead, Surrey, and has issue living, David Peter, *b* 1963, — Derek John, *b* 1973: *ed* Dundee Univ (BSc), — Fiona Margaret, *b* 1965, — Linda Jeanne, *b* 1969. —— Catherine Mary, *b* 1937: *m* 1964, John Douglas Walker, MB, ChB, FRCOG, of 33 Fourth Av, Houghton, Johannesburg 2198, S Africa, and has issue living, John Paul Douglas, *b* 1968: *ed* St John's Coll, Johannesburg, — Jane Philippa Douglas, *b* 1966, — Felicity Mary Douglas, *b* 1974. —— Angela Bligh, *b* 1952; *ed* Natal Univ (BEd).

WIDOW LIVING OF NINTH BARONET

MARY SOMERVILLE (*Mary, Lady St George*), da of Francis John Sutcliffe, of Durban, Natal: *m* 1935, Sir George Bligh St George, 9th Bt, who *d* 1995. *Residence* – 4 Lucas Gdns, 541 Ridge Rd, Durban 4001, S Africa.

COLLATERAL BRANCHES LIVING

Granddaughter of Robert James Ker St George, 2nd son of Robert St George, 3rd son of 2nd baronet:—
Issue of late Richard Christopher Bligh St George, *b* 1875, *d* 1945: *m* 1916, Alice Rosabel, who *d* 1964, el da of Lt-Col Hugh L. Donovan, of Oakhurst, S Yardley, Worcs:—
Catherine Harriet Mary Bligh (1346 Coventry Rd, Yardley, Birmingham, B25 8AN), *b* 1917.

Granddaughters of late Howard Bligh St George, 3rd son of Robert St George (ante) :—
Issue of late George Baker Bligh St George, *b* 1892, *d* 1957: *m* 1917, Katharine (a Member of House of Representatives, USA Congress), who *d* 19—, da of Price Collier, of Tuxedo Park, New York, USA:—
Priscilla Avenel, *b* 1919: *m* 1st, 1936 (*m diss* 1939), Angier Biddle Duke; 2ndly, 1941 (*m diss* 1950), Allan A. Ryan, Jr, and *d* 1995, leaving issue (by 1st *m*), St George Biddle (PO Box 610, Absarokee, Montana 59001, USA), *b* 1938: *m* 1st, 1959, Jeanne S. Farmer; 2ndly, 1973, Mary Ellen, da of late Ora Cecil Haga, and has issue living (by 1st *m*), George St George *b* 1960, Benjamin Buchanan *b* 1963, — (by 2nd *m*) Katharine Delano (Good Hap, Barrytown, NY 12507, USA), *b* 1942: *m* 1st, 1963 (*m diss* 1972), Keith Torrey Middleton, Jr; 2ndly, 1973, John Winthrop Aldrich, and has issue living (by 1st *m*), Daniel Torrey Tack *b* 1965, Laura Delano Ryan *b* 1964, (by 2nd *m*) Margaret Livingston *b* 1974, Katharine Delano *b* 1976.

Issue of late Col Frederick Ferris Bligh St George, CVO, *b* 1908, *d* 1970: *m* 1932, Meriel Margaret, JP, who *d* 1966, da of late Lt-Col William Scott Warley Radcliffe (E Macclesfield, colls):—
Meriel Jane Bligh ST GEORGE (424 E 52 St, Apt 2A, New York, NY 10022), *b* 1933; has resumed her maiden name: *m* 1966 (*m diss* 1971), Benjamin Brandreth McAlpin. —— Elizabeth Sally Bligh, *b* 1936: *m* 1965, John Richard Alford, of Hammatethy House, St Breward, Bodmin, Cornwall, and has issue living, Charles William Bligh, *b* 1971, — Julia Meriel Bligh, *b* 1967, — Nicola Jane Bligh, *b* 1969. —— Diana Gillian Bligh (*Lady Earle*), *b* 1939: *m* 1967, Sir Hardman George Algernon Earle, 6th Bt, of Abington, Murroe, co Limerick, and has issue (see that title).

Grandchildren of late George Edward St George, 3rd son of late William Oliver St George (infra):—

Issue of late Leslie George St George, *b* 1896, *d* 1968: *m* 1918, Gladys, who *d* 1941, da of Alfred McGillivray, of Ottawa:—
Leslie Richard (3 Goodwin Av, Nepean, Ont, K2E 5C4), *b* 1924: *m* 1946, Muriel Winnifred, da of John Edwards, and has issue living, Barry Edward, *b* 1949: *m* 1978, Catherine Jean, da of George P. Campbell, of Ottawa, and has issue living, Joshua Adam *b* 1980, Lauren Ashley *b* 1982, — Leslie Timothy, *b* 1961: *m* 1986, Janet Lee, da of Robert Ross Wilson, of Nepean, Ont, and has issue living, Lindsay Blair *b* 1989, Laura Leigh *b* 1991, — Gayle Mary, *b* 1953, — Beverly Ann, *b* 1954: *m* 1979, Kerry Patrick Scullion, of Ottawa, and has issue living, Timothy Patrick Pearse *b* 1983, Rory Joseph Anthony 1987. —— Robert John, *b* 1941: *m* 1968 (*m diss* 1984), Vivien Jill, da of David G. Walters, of London, England, and has issue living, Christian Robert David, *b* 1974, — Catherine Lesley, *b* 1970. —— Mary Audrey (1308-1701 Kilborn Av, Ottawa, Ont K1H 6M8), *b* 1927: *m* 1949, John Scarcella, who *d* 1989, and has issue living, Byron Michael, *b* 1949: *m* 1973, Annette, da of Lionel Aucoin, of Ottawa, and has issue living, Lisa Marie *b* 1977, — David Louis Anthony, *b* 1955, — Gordon Kenneth John *b* 1960.

Grandchildren of late George Edgar St George (I) (infra):—
Issue of late George Edgar St George (II), *b* 1929, *d* 1992: *m* 1954, Lise Lamothe, of Hull, Quebec (80 Nevers St, Gatineau Pte, Quebec, Canada J8T 4R5):—
George Edgar (III) (Eddie), *b* 1957: *m* 1984, Linda Ruth Redmond, and has issue living, James Ryan, *b* 1992, — Danielle Lise, *b* 1990. —— Richard, *b* 1962; has issue living (by Debbie Yuill), Christopher YUILL, *b* 19—. —— Suzanne, *b* 1955: *m* 1978 (*m diss* 1984), Michael Grégoire, and has issue living, Eric, *b* 1982, — and further issue (by Richard Poirier), Carl, *b* 1990, — Lianne, *b* 1993. —— Julie, *b* 1959; has issue living (by Pierre Gagné), Jacob, *b* 1997, — Nellie Kim, *b* 1984.

Grandchildren of late Robert St George (1856-1939), 4th son of late William Oliver St George (infra):—
Issue of late George Edgar St George (I), *b* 1882, *d* 1965: *m* 1929, Ruth Mary, da of Harold Richardson, of Ottawa, Ont:—
(Richard Bligh) Harold (3199 Riverside Drive, Ottawa, Ont, Canada K1V 8H8), *b* 1935: *m* 19—, Gail Conway, and has had issue, Anthony, *b* 1967, — †Jonathan, *b* 1965; *d* 1996, — Robin (a da), *b* 1975. —— Michael Patrick (274 N Gorsuch Rd, Westminster, MD 21157, USA), *b* 1940: *m* 1st, 1968 (*m diss* 1975), Yvonne M., da of William Palmer, of Baltimore, Maryland; 2ndly, 1977, Carol, da of Rev Dr James Gaiser, of Scranton, Penn, and has issue living (by 2nd *m*), James Gavin, *b* 1989, — Tara Elizabeth Victoria, *b* 1983. —— (Ruth Mary) Madora (2197 Fife Crescent, Ottawa, Ont, Canada K1V 2Z3), *b* 1931: *m* 1955, John L. Bove, who *d* 1997, and has issue living, Tony, *b* 1968. —— Tovey Elizabeth (1590 Baseline Rd, Ottawa, Ont, Canada K2C 0B5), *b* 1947: *m* 1970 (*m diss* 1985), William Charles O'Halloran, and has issue living, Tara Elizabeth, *b* 1970, — Virginia Anne, *b* 1974: *m* 1996, Wayne Ladouceur.

Grandchildren of late William Oliver St George, 4th son of 2nd baronet:—
Issue of late Hercules Frank St George, *b* 1867, *d* 1938: *m* 1895, Rosaline, who *d* 1901, da of John Dunn, of Gaspé, Quebec, Canada:—
Hercules Frank, *b* 1896: *m* 1939, Marie Adeline Juliette, da of Eugene Larocque, of Ottawa.

Issue of late John Arthur St George (twin), *b* 1867, *d* 1912: *m* 1900, Lily Belle, da of John Magladry:—
William John, *b* 1907. —— Gladys Ellen, *b* 1901. —— Marjorie Ellen, *b* 1903: *m* 19—, Lawrence J. Desjardins. —— Fanny Evelyn, *b* 1905. —— Sarah Alice, *b* 1909.

Grandson of late Loftus St George (infra):—
Issue of late Clifford Fortescue Loftus St George, CBE, *b* 1894, *d* 1966: *m* 1931, Gwen Marjorie Chisholm, who *d* 1982, da of Rev William Dalton, V of Glynde, Sussex:—
John (Warren Farm, Wilmington, E Polegate, Sussex BN26 6RL), *b* 1942: *m* 1st, 1965 (*m diss* 1975), — da of —; 2ndly, 1975, Elizabeth Jane, el da of Herbert Westgate, of Shabbards, Berwick, Sussex, and has issue living (by 1st *m*), William, *b* 1967, — Lucy, *b* 1969, — Marina, *b* 1970.

Granddaughter of late James Cuffe St George, 5th son of 2nd baronet:—
Issue of late Loftus St George, *b* 1858, *d* 1952: *m* 1893, Marguerite Isabel Clifford, who *d* 1956, da of late Clifford Fortescue Borrer, of Pickwell, Cuckfield, Sussex:—
Violet Marguerite Loftus (*Violet, Lady Jackson*), *b* 1904: *m* 1931, Sir Hugh Nicholas Jackson, 2nd Bt (*cr* 1913), who *d* 1979.

The 1st baronet, Sir Richard St George (second son of George St George, of Woodsgift, co Kilkenny), was MP for Athlone 1763-89. The 2nd baronet, Sir Richard Bligh, was Sec of Order of St Patrick. The 6th baronet, Sir Theophilus John, was sometime Assist Master of Supreme Court, Natal.

SALT (UK) 1869, of Saltaire, Yorkshire

What not with God helping?

Sir PATRICK MACDONNELL SALT, 7th *Baronet*; *b* 25 sept 1932; *s* his brother, *Sir* ANTHONY HOULTON, 1991; *ed* Stowe: *m* 1976, Ann Elizabeth Mary, da of late Dr Thomas Kay Maclachlan, and widow of Denys Kilham Roberts, OBE.

Arms – Azure, a chevron indented between two mullets in chief, and a demi-ostrich displayed, holding in the beak a horse-shoe in base or. Crest – Upon a rock, an alpaca statant, proper. *Residence* – Hillwatering Farmhouse, Langham, Bury St Edmunds, Suffolk IP31 3ED.

DAUGHTERS LIVING OF SIXTH BARONET

Fenella Mary Houlton, *b* 1959: *m* 1995, Nicholas Cosmo de Satgé, yr son of late Rev Canon John de Satgé, and has issue living, Davina Mary Valentine, *b* 1996, — Laura Frances Houlton, *b* 1998. —— Rebecca Madeleine Harris, *b* 1961: *m* 1993, Alexander I.M. Kennedy, 2nd son of John Kennedy, of Kensington, and has issue living, Edward Anthony Maxwell, *b* 1996, — James Titus Maxwell, *b* 1998. —— Lucinda Mary Harriet, *b* 1964: *m* 1996, Stuart Leslie Feast, yr son of Donald Feast, of Lower Skerrisdale, Kirk Michael, I of Man, and has issue living, Louisa Emily Frances, *b* 1998. —— Charlotte Lavinia Francis, *b* 1967: *m* 1993, Christopher James Walter Trower, 3rd son of Anthony Gosselin Trower, of Stansteadbury, Ware, Herts, and has issue living, Arabella Olivia Francis, *b* 1995, — Zara Rose Catherine, *b* 1998.

WIDOW LIVING OF SIXTH BARONET

PRUDENCE MARY DOROTHEA FRANCIS (*Prudence, Lady Salt*), yst da of late Francis Meath Baker, of Hasfield Court, Glos: *m* 1957, Sir Anthony Houlton Salt, 6th Bt, who *d* 1991. *Residence* – Dellow House, Ugley Green, Bishop's Stortford, Herts.

COLLATERAL BRANCHES LIVING

Grandchildren of late Gordon Locksley Salt; eldest son of late Titus Salt, 5th son of 1st baronet:—
Issue of late John Scarlett Alexander Salt, *b* 1905, *d* 1947: *m* 1939, Olive Mary (who *d* 1999, having *m* 2ndly, 1952, Christopher Gorton), da of William Gilbert Shapley:—
DANIEL ALEXANDER (14531 South East 196 Place, Renton, WA 98058, USA), *b* 1943: *m* 1968, Mehrchide, da of Dr A. Emami, of Teheran, and has issue living, Firoozeh Katherine, *b* 1971, — Maryam Rachel, *b* 1974. —— Nicholas John (Tyllottyn, Llawryglyn, Caersws, Powys SY17 5RJ), *b* 1945: *m* 1971, Catherine Kimerling, da of Charles Grun, of New York, and has issue living, Aaron, *b* 1972. —— Christina Mary, *b* 1947: *m* 1976, Anthony Hart, of 106A Raglan Rd, Mosman, NSW 2088, Australia, son of Benjamin Hart, and has issue living, Adam John, *b* 1981.

Grandsons of late Titus Salt (ante):—
Issue of late Harold Crossley Salt, *b* 1868, *d* 1943: *m* 1906, Grace Ethel Muriel, da of late Rev Henry Madan Pratt, R of Cottesbrooke, Northamptonshire (Wilson, Bt, *cr* 1874):—
Denys Geoffrey Crossley (38 Holland Park, W11), *b* 1918; *ed* Marlborough, and St Edmund Hall, Oxford (MA): *m* 1st, 1956 (*m diss* 1963), Patricia Lee, da of late Lt-Col D. C. Pope, MC, of Red House, Sutton Montis, Somerset; 2ndly, 1989, Eva Klesling, of Graz, Austria. —— Peter Hubert Wharton, *b* 1920; *ed* Cheltenham, and St Edmund Hall, Oxford (MA); India 1944-46 with Intelligence Corps: *m* 1951, Gillian Caryl, who *d* 1983, da of late John Hill, of Westhill, Ledbury, and has issue living, Jonathan Wharton, *b* 1953: *m* 1981 (*m diss* 1996), Susan Lee Jeanette, da of William McGann, of 39 Broomfield Av, Telscombe Cliffs, Brighton, and has issue living, Benjamin Wharton *b* 1982, Kate Alicia Gillian Samantha *b* 1986, — Miranda Elisabeth Caryl, *b* 1955: *m* 1980, Carteret Hunter Maunsell, of 19 Velmore Rd, Chandlers Ford, Hants, and has issue living, Mark Hugo *b* 1986, Hannah Caryl *b* 1982, Cara Alison *b* 1984. *Residence* – 6 Romanby Court, Mill St, Redhill, Surrey.

Sir Titus, 1st baronet, son of Daniel Salt of Bradford, sat as MP for Bradford (*L*) 1859-61.

SALT (UK) 1899, of Standon, and of Weeping Cross, co Stafford

Sir (THOMAS) MICHAEL JOHN SALT, 4th *Baronet; b* 7 Nov 1946; *s* his father, Lt-Col *Sir* THOMAS HENRY, 1965; *ed* Eton: *m* 1971, Caroline, el da of late Henry Robert John Hildyard (*see* B Kindersley, 1980 Edn).

Arms – Argent, a chevron rompu between three mullets in chief and a lion rampant in base sable. Crest – Three annulets interlaced sable, thereon a dove holding an olive branch proper, charged on the neck with a chevron also sable.
Residence – Shillingstone House, Shillingstone, Dorset DT11 0QR. *Club* – Boodle's.

In sale salus

DAUGHTERS LIVING

Henrietta Sophia Meriel, *b* 1978. —— Alexandra Georgia May, *b* 1982.

BROTHER LIVING

ANTHONY WILLIAM DAVID, *b* 5 Feb 1950; *ed* Milton Abbey: *m* 1978, Olivia Anne, yr da of Martin Morgan Hudson, and has issue living, Edward James Stevenson, *b* 11 June 1981, — Henry Martin Morgan, *b* 1983. *Residence* – Fryern Court Farm, Burgate, Fordingbridge, Hants.

SISTERS LIVING

Sarah Meriel, *b* 1944: *m* 1977, Malcolm David Coombs, of 10 The Close, Rickmansworth, Herts, and has issue living, Dominic Nathaniel Thomas, *b* 1986, — Augusta Elinor Lettice, *b* 1979, — Octavia Alexandra Elizabeth, *b* 1981. —— Jennifer Mary, *b* 1951: *m* 1977, John Joseph William Clark, of Moyston, Victoria, and has issue living, Thomas William, *b* 1979, — Anthea Mary, *b* 1981.

WIDOW LIVING OF THIRD BARONET

MERIEL SOPHIA WILMOT (*Meriel, Lady Salt*) (Shillingstone House, Shillingstone, Dorset), da of late Capt Berkeley Cole Wilmot Williams (B Addington): *m* 1943, Sir Thomas Henry Salt, 3rd Bt, who *d* 1965.

COLLATERAL BRANCHES LIVING

Issue of late Lt-Cdr George Stevenson Salt, RN, 2nd son of 2nd baronet, *b* 1908, *d* on active service 1940: *m* 1935, Lilian Bridget (who *m* 2ndly, 1948, Capt William John Lamb, CVO, OBE, RN (ret), who *d* 1993, of Brookway, Rhinefield Rd, Brockenhurst, Hants), da of late F. S. Francis, of Champion's Farm, Pulborough, Sussex:—
James Frederick Thomas George, CB (Salterns, Lock Lane, Birdham, Chichester, W Sussex), *b* 1940; Rear Adm; cmd'd HMS *Sheffield* (sunk S Atlantic Campaign 1982); sr Naval Directing Staff at Royal Coll of Defence Studies 1988-90; ACNS (Gulf War) 1990-91; Mil Dep Defence Export Services 1992-97; Marketing Dir Colebrand Ltd since 1998; CB (Mil) 1991: *m* 1975, Penelope, only da of Anthony Walker, of 47 Warkton, nr Kettering, Northants, and has issue living, George William, *b* 1977, — Charles James *b* 1979, — Thomas Edward *b* 1983, — John Philip, *b* 1986. —— Joanna Elizabeth (*Lady Spencer-Nairn*), *b* 1937: *m* 1963, Sir Robert Arnold Spencer-Nairn, 3rd Bt, of Barham, Cupar, Fife.

Issue of late Herbert Edward ANDERDON, 2nd son of 1st baronet, *b* 1870, *d* 1938 (having assumed by deed poll 1923, the surname of Anderdon in lieu of his patronymic): *m* 1899, Ethel Menie, who *d* 1966, da of late Henry Manisty of 169 Queen's Gate, SW7:—
Henry Manisty ANDERDON, *b* 1900; *ed* Haileybury: *m* 1929, Sybilla Marjorie, da of Lt-Col Reginald Holden Steward, OBE, and has issue living, (John) Nigel Steward (Nursling House, Nursling, Soton, Southampton), *b* 1931; Cdr RN (ret): *m* 1961, Mavis Marjorie, who *d* 1999, da of Lester Gibson, of Bristol, and has issue living, Alexander Philip *b* 1963, and an adopted son, James *b* 1954, — Ian George Carlyle (Henlade, Taunton, Som), *b* 1936. *Residence* – Henlade, Taunton, Som.

Issue of late Rev William Manning Salt, 5th son of 1st baronet, *b* 1876, *d* 1947: *m* 1907, Mildred Nairne, who *d* 1926, da of late Col C. H. E. Graeme:—
Joan Mildred, *b* 1908; JP of Monmouth: *m* 1938, Frederick Newman Tanner. *Residence* – The Vaga, Monmouth. —— Elisabeth, *b* 1915.

Issue of late Maj-Gen Harold Francis Salt, CB, CMG, DSO, yst son of 1st baronet, *b* 1879, *d* 1971: *m* 1914, Phyllis Dulce, who *d* 1965, da of late Maj E. D. Cameron, RFA:—
Primrose Phyllis, *b* 1915: *m* 1st, 1935, Maj Anthony Hope Osborne, The Queen's Bays, who was *ka* 1943; 2ndly, 1944 (*m diss* 1948), Capt Philip Quellyn Roberts, RN; 3rdly, 1962, James Mansfield Niall, of 99 Empire Circuit, Deakin, Canberra, Aust, and has issue living, (by 1st *m*) Duncan Norton Hope, *b* 1936, — (by 2nd *m*) Paul Quellyn, *b* 1945. —— Babette Irene (*Lady Millais*), *b* 1922: *m* 1st, 1941, Maj John De Grey Tatham Warter, MC, 2nd Dragoon Gds (The Queen's Bays), who was *ka* 1942; 2ndly, 1948 (*m diss* 1972), Victor William Henry Sefton-Smith; 3rdly, 1975, as his 3rd wife, Sir Ralph Regnault Millais, 5th Bt, of Elizabeth Court, 47 Milmans St, SW10 0DA, and has issue living (by 2nd *m*) Ewan Victor William, *b* 1950, — Susan Jane, *b* 1948: *m* 1st, 1971 (*m diss* 1976), John Henry Deen; 2ndly, 1976 (*m diss* 1987), John Leslie McClue; 3rdly, 1987, David Hyman, of 101 Flood St, SW3 5TD, and has issue (by 2nd *m*), Linsey Jane *b* 1976, Laura Leslie *b* 1977, — Lucy Annabelle, *b* 1952: *m* 1977, Richard Hobart John de Courcy Moore, of 11 Chelsea Park Gdns, SW3 6AF, and has issue living, Francis Richard Hobart de Courcy *b* 1985, Natalie Elizabeth Victoria de Courcy *b* 1993.

The 1st baronet, Sir Thomas, a partner in the private banking firms of Stevenson, Salt and Co (Stafford Old Bank), and Bosanquet, Salt and Co (London), and Chm of Lloyds Bank, sat as MP for Stafford (C) 1859, 1869-80, 1881-5, and 1886-92. He was son of Thomas Salt of Standon and Weeping Cross, Staffs, whose family was settled at Rugeley in the seventeeth century. Sir Thomas Salt, 1st baronet, *m* 1861, Emma Helen Mary, da of John Lavicount Anderdon of Chislehurst, Kent, niece of Cardinal Manning.

Salusbury-Trelawny, see Trelawny.

SAMUEL (UK) 1898, of Nevern Square, St Mary Abbots, Kensington, co London

A pledge of better times

Sir JON MICHAEL GLEN SAMUEL, 5th *Baronet*; *b* 25 Jan 1944; *s* his father, *Sir* JOHN OLIVER CECIL, 1962; *ed* Radley, and Univ Coll, London (BSc): *m* 1st, 1966, Antoinette Sandra, da of late Capt Anthony Hewitt, RE; 2ndly, 1982, Mrs Elizabeth Ann Molinari, yst da of late Maj R. G. Curry, of Bournemouth, Dorset, and has issue by 1st *m*.

Arms – Party per chevron argent and gules, two wolves' heads erased in chief sable, and in base as many squirrels sejant addorsed, each cracking a nut of the first. **Crest** – On a rock in front of three spears, one in pale and two in saltire proper, a wolf courant sable, pierced in the breast by an arrow argent, flighted or.
Residence – Dean House, Vernham Dean, Hants SP11 0LA.

SONS LIVING (By 1st marriage)

ANTHONY JOHN FULTON, *b* 13 Oct 1972. —— Rupert Casper James, *b* 1974.

SISTER LIVING

Jane Lesley, *b* 1947: *m* 1966, John Henry Newman, of Gilson Court, Old Windsor, Berks SL4 2JL, and has issue living, James Michael, *b* 1969, — Timothy John Hoyt, *b* 1972.

AUNT LIVING

Eva Elizabeth, *b* 1905: *m* 1934, George Brian Stafford Cothay, who *d* 1983, and has issue living, Charlotte Ann Stafford, *b* 1936: *m* 1962, Cdr John May, LVO, RN, of Woodside, Eastergate, Chichester, and has issue living, Alexandra Louise Stafford *b* 1965. *Residence* – 29 Windmill Court, East Wittering, Chichester, W Sussex.

WIDOW LIVING OF FOURTH BARONET

CHARLOTTE MARY (The Old School House, W Horsley, Surrey), da of late R. H. Hoyt, of Calgary, Alberta, Canada: *m* 1st, 1942, Sir John Oliver Cecil Samuel, 4th Bt, who *d* 1962; 2ndly, 1966, Heremon James Patrick Desmond, who *d* 1971.

The 1st baronet, Hon Sir Saul, KCMG, CB, was Agent-Gen in England for NSW 1880-98.

SAMUELSON (UK) 1884, of Bodicote, Banbury, Oxfordshire

Light after darkness

Sir (BERNARD) MICHAEL FRANCIS SAMUELSON, 5th *Baronet*; *b* 17 Jan 1917; *s* his father, *Capt Sir* FRANCIS HENRY BERNHARD, 1981; *ed* Eton; late Lt RA; Burma 1939-45 War (despatches): *m* 1952, Janet Amy, yr da of Lt-Cdr Lawrence Garrett Elkington, of Chelsea, SW3, and has issue.

𝕬rms – Sable, three piles wavy two issuant from the chief and one from the base or, each charged with a phoenix proper. 𝕮rest – A phoenix holding in its beak a torch, and charged on each wing with a scroll.
Residence – Hollingwood, Stunts Green, Herstmonceux, E Sussex BN27 4QG.

SONS LIVING

JAMES FRANCIS (3 Manor Cottages, Buckhorn Weston, Gillingham, Dorset SP8 5HH), *b* 20 Dec 1956; *ed* Hailsham: *m* 1987, Caroline Anne Woodley, and has issue living, Miranda Alice, *b* 1990, — Naomi Harriet, *b* 1992. —— Edward Bernard, *b* 1967; *ed* Hailsham.

DAUGHTERS LIVING

Nancy Amy, *b* 1953. —— Angela Margaret, *b* 1962.

BROTHERS LIVING

Christopher Blundell, *b* 1920; *ed* Eton, and Trin Coll, Camb; 1940-45 War with Staffordshire Yeo. —— Richard (11 Heath Rd, Petersfield, Hants), *b* 1925; *ed* Eton; 1943-45 War as Lt Fleet Air Arm.

SISTER LIVING

Diana Frances (Little Lodge, Jarvis Lane, Steyning, Sussex), *b* 1922: *m* 1943, William Ord Blacklock, who *d* 1958, and has issue living, Catherine Margaret, *b* 1945: *m* 1970, Alistair Donald Mant, of Sydney, NSW, and has issue living, Eleanor Frances *b* 1972, Isabel Catherine *b* 1973, — Frances Elizabeth, *b* 1946: *m* 1st, 1970 (*m diss* 1981), Dennis Thomas Conroy; 2ndly, 1990, Allan Jarvis, of Perth, W Australia, and has issue living, (by 1st *m*), Thomas Liam *b* 1974, Joanna Mary *b* 1971, Alice Frances *b* 1973, Kate Diana May *b* 1980, — Stephanie, *b* 1952: *m* 1972, Barrie Weir, and has issue living, Adam James *b* 1976, Gemma Fay *b* 1974, Natasha Hope *b* 1977.

COLLATERAL BRANCHES LIVING

Grandchildren of late Capt Bernard Godfrey Samuelson, 3rd son of late Godfrey Blundell Samuelson (infra):-
Issue of late Peter Bernard Samuelson, painter, *b* 1912, *d* 1996: *m* 1935 (*m diss* 1949), Wilhelmina Van Blaaderen, who *d* 1997:-
Jean Paul (1 High Rd, Roleystone, W Australia 6111), *b* 1939: *m* 1962, Annette Louise, who *d* 1998, da of Hubertus Johannes Richardus Ponjee, and has issue living, Dennis John, *b* 1963, — Nicolas Andrew, *b* 1966, — Quentin Jeremy, *b* 1969, — Natasha Nicole, *b* 1972. —— Bridget (The Green, Shenington, Oxon OX15 6NQ), *b* 1935: *m* 1986, William Allan Dickie, who *d* 1993. —— Zandra Serafina, *b* 1937: *m* 1962, Paul de Maar, of 7 Regentesselaan, Amersfoort, The Netherlands, and has issue living, Onno, *b* 1969, — Annekatrien, *b* 1967.

Granddaughter of late Godfrey Blundell Samuelson, 3rd son of 1st baronet:——
Issue of late Carol Hubert Francis Samuelson, *b* 1899, *d* 1984: *m* 1st, 1920, Doris, who *d* 1959, da of Capt John George Edmund Templer, formerly of Lindridge, Bishop's Teignton, Devon; 2ndly, 1961, Marjorie Hilda Donisthorpe (Strand House, Ringmore, Shaldon, Teignmouth, Devon):——
(By 1st *m*) Eleanor Caroline, *b* 1921: *m* 1946, Capt Marc Anderson Kerr, MBE, IA (ret), of Windrush, Poltimore, Exeter, Devon, and has issue living, Vyvian Frances, *b* 1947: *m* 1972, John Charles Gundry, and has issue living, Mark Alexander *b* 1983, — Fiona Charlotte Eleanor, *b* 1953: *m* 1978, Anthony Garne Fraser Peal, and has issue living, Alastair Mark Fraser *b* 1980, Nicholas Hugh Anderson *b* 1983.

Grandchildren of late Capt Guy Weston Samuelson, 2nd son of late Godfrey Blundell Samuelson (ante):——
Issue of late Lt-Col John Peel Weston Samuelson, MC, *b* 1917, *d* 1988: *m* 1st, 1943 (*m diss* 1951), Pamela, who *d* 1989, eldest da of late Cecil E. Winter, of Surrenden Dering, Pluckley, Kent; 2ndly, 1952, Grace Eleanor, who *d* 1998, da of late R. C. Dawson, of Ball Hill, Newbury, Berks:——
(By 1st *m*) Nigel John Esdaile (Fronwen, Alexandra Rd, Brecon, Powys), *b* 1944; Solicitor: *m* 1971, Angela Margaret, who *d* 1999, da of late Bruce Samways, of Bleadon, Weston-super-Mare, Avon, and has issue living, Alistair Paul, *b* 1976, — Robert Ernest, *b* 1979, — Diana Helen Esdaile, *b* 1973. —— Christopher Richard Leney (PO Box 472, Gibraltar), *b* 1946: *m* 1st, 1968 (*m diss* 1980), Catherine Elizabeth, da of late George M. Cooper, of Charnwood, Idutywa, S Africa; 2ndly, 1980, Diana Margaret, da of Richard Lewis, of Lahore, and has issue living (by 1st *m*), John Michael Winter, *b* 1974, — (by 2nd *m*) Nichola Robyn, *b* 1981, — Lucy Anne, *b* 1986. —— (By 2nd *m*) Robin Dawson, *b* 1953, *d* 1978. —— Eleanor Clare, *b* 1958.

Issue of late Henry Bernard Samuelson, *b* 1919, *d* 1988: *m* 1st, 1947 (*m diss* 1949), Evelyn Patience, da of John Nairn Burt, of Ashwell House, Knaresborough, N Yorks; 2ndly, 19— (*m diss* 1961), Barbara Crossley, of Sydenham; 3rdly, 1961, Anita Jill Waring, yst da of Frederick William Guard, of Barnstaple, Devon:——

(By 3rd *m*) Francis Peel Waring (8 Burrows Close, Braunton, Devon), *b* 1961. —— Godfrey Weston Rhodes, *b* 1962. —— Kevin Guard Leney, *b* 1965. —— Clife Bernard Waring, *b* 1967. —— Henry Rhodes Hulke, *b* 1970.

Granddaughters of late Sir Herbert Walter Samuelson, KBE, 4th son of 1st baronet:—
Issue of late Maj Rupert Eric Herbert Samuelson, *b* 1899, *d* 1993: *m* 1930, Eileena Jane, who *d* 1998, da of Arthur Reece-Jones, of Cefn-y-Parc, Barry:—
Doriel Sybil (1 Beacon Hill Park, Hindhead, Surrey GU26 6HU), *b* 1931: *m* 1st, 1955 (*m diss* 1972), Andrew Ridgway; 2ndly, 1972 (*m diss* 1981), Aldwin David James Hall, and has had issue (by 1st *m*), Peter Eric, *b* 1958: *m* 1st, 19— (*m diss* 19—), Maria Anderton; 2ndly, 1996, Maxine Taylor, and has issue living (by 2nd *m*), one child, — Amanda Jane, *b* 1956: *m* 1st, 19— (*m diss* 1991), Neil Palmer; 2ndly, 1992, Toby Heppel, and has issue living, (by 1st *m*) two children, (by 2nd *m*) two children, — Joanna Kate, *b* 1962, *d* 1995, — Charlotte Rose, *b* 1965: *m* 1995, Adrian Wainwright, and has issue living, two children. —— Philippa Margaret, *b* 1934.

The 1st baronet, Rt Hon Sir Bernhard Samuelson, FRS, founder and Chm of Sir B. Samuelson and Co (Limited) of Middlesbrough, and of Samuelson and Co (Limited) of Banbury, was Chm of Roy Commn on Technical Instruction 1881, and sat as MP for Banbury (*L*) Feb to April 1859 (when he was defeated) and 1865-85, and for N, or Banbury, Div of Oxfordshire 1885-95. He was the Pioneer of Technical Education, and sat on several Roy Commns, his baronetcy being conferred for his services in the cause of education. Sir Henry Bernard Samuelson, 2nd Bt, sat as MP for Cheltenham (*L*) 1868-74, and for Frome 1876-85.

SANDERSON (UK) 1920, of Malling Deanery, South Malling, co Sussex

Without God nothing

Sir FRANK LINTON SANDERSON, 3rd *Baronet*; *b* 21 Nov 1933; *s* his father, *Sir* (FRANK PHILIP) BRYAN, 1992; *ed* Stowe, and Salamanca Univ; RNVR 1950-65: *m* 1961, Margaret Ann (Margot), da of late John Cleveland Maxwell, of New York, USA, and has issue.

Arms – Azure, a maunch between three annulets or. **Crest** – Between two wings or a sinister arm embowed in chain-mail grasping a scimitar proper, pommelled and hilted or.
Residence – Grandturzel Farm, Burwash, E Sussex TN19 7DE.

SONS LIVING

DAVID FRANK, *b* 26 Feb 1962; *ed* Stowe, and Univ of Sussex (BA); Bar Inner Temple 1985: *m* 1990, Fiona Jane, da of Robert Bruce Ure and Mrs Barbara Michael, of Bristol, and has issue living, Hannah Clare, *b* 1997. —— Michael John, *b* 1965; *ed* Stowe.

DAUGHTERS LIVING

Caroline Anne, *b* 1966: *m* 1996, Simon John Kennedy, and has issue living, Amy Elizabeth, *b* 1998. —— Nina Margaret, *b* 1968. —— Katherine Claire, *b* (twin) 1968: *m* 1996, James Michael Douglas Thomson, son of late Paul Thomson, and of Mrs Michael Cuddigan, of Sandhill, Aldeburgh, Suffolk, and has issue living, Bronwen Olivia Africa, *b* 1998.

BROTHER LIVING

Peter Bryan (Hole Farm, North Chailey, E Sussex BN8 4EJ), *b* 1946; *ed* Stowe, and Salamanca Univ: *m* 1970, Elizabeth Magdalena, da of late John Grün, of Hove, Sussex, and has issue living, Roberta Caroline, *b* 1974.

SISTER LIVING

Merry Claire, *b* 1936: *m* 1959, David Lyle, late Capt 16th/5th R Lancers, of Yew Tree Cottage, Scaynes Hill, Sussex, and has issue living, James Robert Bryan, *b* 1961; *ed* Charterhouse, and St Edmund Hall, Oxford (BA), — Robert Giles, *b* 1964; *ed* Charterhouse, and London Sch of Economics (BA), — Edward Hugh, *b* 1970; *ed* Hurtwood House, Univ of London (BA).

AUNT LIVING (*daughter of 1st baronet*)

Pearl, *b* 1906: *m* 1st, 1928, Gerald Melville Donner (Macnaghten, Bt, colls); 2ndly, 1947, Maj Alan Sherman James, who *d* 1963, and has issue living (by 1st *m*), John Melville (Heddon Oak House, Crowcombe, Somerset), *b* 1930; *ed* Stowe, and RMA; Coldm Gds 1948-53 and 1956 (Suez); Underwriting Member of Lloyd's 1964-94; Man Dir Fenchurch Insurance Holdings plc 1969-74; Chm DUA Ltd 1974-90; Queen's Award for Export 1983, 1988: *m* 1952, Patricia Mary, da of late Barnet Thomas Jenkins, of Bickleigh, S Devon, and has issue living, Rupert Melville *b* 1955; *ed* Stowe, and Exeter Univ (BA); Solicitor, Annabel Elizabeth *b* 1958; *ed* Benenden, and Exeter Univ (BA): *m* 1995, Michael Vernon, — Gillian Pearl (Clayton, Sussex), *b* (twin) 1930: *m* 1963, Cdr Kenneth Coburn, USN, who *d* 1971, and has issue living, John Bruce *b* 1967; *ed* Tonbridge, Kimberly Gillian *b* 1965: *m* 1992, John Garth Kirkland, of Sydney, Australia, — Rosita Ann, *b* 1933: *m* 1954, Michael Beresford Burtenshaw, who *d* 1994.

COLLATERAL BRANCH LIVING

Issue of late Derek Maxwell Sanderson, yr son of 1st baronet, *b* 1914, *d* 1983: *m* 1936, Daphne (34 Delves House, The Green, Ringmer, Lewes, E Sussex BN8 5QG), elder da of late Frederick Ernest Bayard Elton (*see* Elton, Bt, colls):—
John Maxwell (Brook House, Tinkers Lane, Blackboys, Uckfield, East Sussex TN22 4EU), *b* 1938; *ed* Pangbourne: *m* 1962, Susan Elizabeth, WVSM, elder da of Brig Randall Thomas Kellow Pye, DSO, OBE, of Horsted Keynes, West Sussex, and has issue living, Christian Maxwell, *b* 1966; *ed* Wellington, and Univ of the West of England (BA Hons), Charlotte Jane, *b* 1964; *ed* Downe House. —— Richard Bryan (Finca Argaga, Valle Gran Rey, La Gomera, Canary Islands), *b* 1942; *ed* Harrow; Coldm Guards 1960-63: *m* 1964, Narima, yr da of late Louis Jonquier of Lausanne, Switzerland, and has issue living, Mark Bryan, *b* 1967, — Caspar Jason Manfred Henrique, *b* 1969. —— Christopher Derek (37 Glendavis Crescent, Toronto, Ontario ME4 16X, Canada), *b* 1948; *ed* Milton Abbey, and Dalhousie Univ (BA). —— Sally Greet, *b* 1939; *m* 1st, 1966, Lother John; 2ndly, 1988, Rev Anthony Talbot Hindley, of The Rectory, School Rd, Ringsfield, Beccles, Suffolk NR34 8NZ, and has issue living (by 1st *m*), Rolf Peter, *b* 1967, — Dominique (da), *b* 1969.

Sir Frank Sanderson, 1st Bt, 7th son of John Sanderson of Hull, was founder of Wray, Sanderson & Co, Ltd, Controller (unpaid) Trench Warfare National Filling Factories, Ministry of Munitions 1915-19, sat as MP for Darwen Div of Lancs (*U*) 1922-23, and 1924-29, for Ealing 1931-45, and for E Ealing 1945-50, Public Accounts Cttee, House of Commons 1942-50.

Saunders-Pryse, see Pryse.

SAVORY (UK) 1890, of Brook Street, St George, Hanover Square, co London (Extinct 1961)

Sir WILLIAM BORRADAILE SAVORY, 3rd and last *Baronet.*

DAUGHTERS LIVING OF THIRD BARONET

Diana Victor, *b* 1913: *m* 1934, James Nigel Jackaman, and has issue living, Nigel Victor Charles, *b* 1939, — Elizabeth Mary, *b* 1936. *Residence* – Glebe House, Stoke Poges, Bucks SL2 4PE. —— Pamela Frances, *b* 1916: *m* 1939, Douglas Burbridge, and has issue living, Howard Harry Borradaile, *b* 1941, — Robert Anthony Carruthers, *b* 1952. *Residence* – 2 Selsey Rd, Donnington, Chichester, W Sussex PO19 2SN.

SCHUSTER (UK) 1906, of Collingham Rd, Royal Borough of Kensington (Extinct 1996)

Sir (FELIX) JAMES MONCRIEFF SCHUSTER, OBE, TD, 3rd and last *Baronet.*

DAUGHTERS LIVING OF THIRD BARONET

Sarah Lavinia, *b* 1941: *m* 1st, 1962 (*m diss* 1966), Theodore Phillips Burgess; 2ndly, 1972, Patrick O'Neill, and has issue living, (by 2nd husband) Sam Edward, *b* 1971, — Felix Jake, *b* 1972, — Ben Darcy, *b* 1974. —— Inger Marion Averil, *b* 1944: *m* 1967, Hugh Reginald Newcomb, of Black Swan Hall, Goudhurst, Kent, and has issue living, Toby James Moncrieff, *b* 1969, — Rupert, *b* 1971.

SISTER LIVING OF THIRD BARONET

Dorothy Ann Violet, *b* 1921: *m* 1st, 1940, Brig Arthur Frederick Crane Nicholls, GC, Coldstream Guards, who was *ka* 1944; 2ndly, 1944, Sqdn-Ldr Archibald George Dunlop Mackenzie, RAF, and has issue living, (by 2nd *m*) Andrew Robert Archibald Dunlop, *b* 1945; *ed* Stowe: *m* 1st, 1968, Herdis Pelle; 2ndly, 19—, Sarah Anne Orme, and has issue living (by 1st *m*), Louisa *b* 1970, Sonja *b* 1972, (by 2nd *m*) Alexander Dunlop *b* 1983, Isla Clare *b* 1985, — (by 1st *m*) Jennifer Ann Crane, *b* 1943, — (by 2nd *m*) Catriona, *b* 1947: *m* 1969, Michael Dollin, and has issue living, Laura *b* 1971.

SCOTT (UK) 1806, of Great Barr, Staffordshire

Sir DOUGLAS FRANCIS SCOTT, 9th *Baronet*; *b* 26 Aug 1908; *s* his brother, *Sir* EDWARD ARTHUR DOLMAN, 1980.

Arms – Argent, on a fesse gules, cotissed azure, between three catherine-wheels sable, as many lambs passant argent. **Crest** – On a mount vert a beacon fired proper, ladder argent.

Faithful to king and country

SISTERS LIVING

Florence Susan Helen, *b* 1901. —— Frances Lucy Mary, *b* 1904.

WIDOW LIVING OF EIGHTH BARONET

DOROTHY ELSIE (*Lady Scott*), da of W. H. Winchcombe, of Yorktown, S Australia: *m* 1943, Sir Edward Arthur Dolman Scott, 8th Bt, who *d* 1980.

The 1st baronet (of Great Barr, creation April 1806) was MP for Worcester 1802-6, and his son the 2nd baronet, sat as MP for Lichfield 1831-7. The 3rd baronet of 1st, and 2nd baronet of 2nd creation, inherited at his birth the baronetcy of his maternal grandfather, Sir Hugh Bateman, of Hartington, who had, in Dec 1806, been created a baronet, with remainder (primogeniturely) to the male descendants of his daughters, Catherine Juliana (afterwards wife of Sir Edward Dolman Scott, 2nd baronet) and Amelia Anne (afterwards wife of Sir Alexander Hood, 2nd Bt of St Audries); the latter Baronetcy passed on the death of Sir Edward Dolman Scott, 6th Bt of 1st and 5th of 2nd creation in 1905 to Rt Hon Sir Alexander Fuller-Acland-Hood, PC, MP, 4th Bt of St Audries (afterwards Baron St Audries). The 7th baronet was sometime R of Teffont Ewyas.

SCOTT (UK) 1821, of Lytchett Minster, Dorsetshire (Extinct 1961)

Sir ROBERT CLAUDE SCOTT, 7th and last *Baronet*.

DAUGHTER LIVING OF SEVENTH BARONET

Hope Berthe Turner, MB, ChB, DPH, *b* 1925: *m* 1960, William Alexander Hogg, who *d* 1989, and has issue living, William Scott (2 The Paddocks, Waverton, Chester CH3 7RB), *b* 1963: *m* 1994, Hilary Alison, da of Norman Jones, of High Kinnerton, Cheshire, and has issue living, Cameron William Scott *b* 1995, Catriona Beatrix *b* 1998. *Residence* – 7 Westside Gdns, Partickhill, Glasgow, G12 9DW.

SCOTT (UK) 1907, of Beauclerc, Bywell St Andrews, co Northumberland

Sir (WALTER) JOHN SCOTT, 5th *Baronet*; *b* 24 Feb 1948; *s* his father, *Sir* WALTER, 1992; *ed* privately; farmer: *m* 1st, 1969 (*m diss* 1971), Lowell Patria, da of late S/Ldr Pat Vaughan Goddard, of Auckland, NZ; 2ndly, 1977, Mary Gavin, only da of Alexander Fairly Anderson, of Gartocharn, Dunbartonshire, and has issue by 1st and 2nd *m*.

𝔄rms – Per chevron azure and or, in chief two bees volant, and in base a crescent all counterchanged. 𝔠rest – Between the hornes of a crescent sable a bee volant proper. *Residence* – Priestlaw, Cranshaws, Duns, Berwickshire TD11 35N.

SON LIVING (By 2nd marriage)

WALTER SAMUEL, *b* 6 Dec 1984.

DAUGHTERS LIVING (By 1st marriage)

Rebecca, *b* 1970: *m* 1999, Andrew James Leslie Beatson, son of His Honour Judge Beatson, of Taupo, NZ.

(by 2nd marriage)

Honour follows though unsought for

Diana Helen Rose *b* 1977.

WIDOW LIVING OF FOURTH BARONET

ANNA-LOUISE (*Dowager Lady Scott*), da of late Aubrey Derwent Healing, of Lewes, Sussex: *m* 1991, as his 2nd wife, Sir Walter Scott, 4th Bt, who *d* 1992. *Residence* – New House West, Church Lane, Ripe, Lewes, East Sussex BN8 6AS.

COLLATERAL BRANCHES LIVING

Grandchildren of late Mason Thompson Scott, 4th son of 1st baronet:—
Issue of late William Walter Brough Scott, *b* 1902, *d* 1980: *m* 1st, 1925 (*m diss* 1937), Bridget Margaret, da of late Charles Leigh Clay, of Wyndcliffe Court, Chepstow; 2ndly, 1937, Pamela, who *d* 1992, da of late Sir Charles William Fielding, KBE (*see* E Denbigh, colls, 1990 Edn):—
(By 2nd *m*) Charles Martin Fielding (Mawley Farm House, Quenington, Cirencester, Glos GL7 5BW), *b* 1945; late Lt, 1st R Dragoons: *m* 1970, Jill, da of late Wing-Cdr Marcus Mowbray Hutchinson, AFC, AAF, and has issue living, Camilla Jane, *b* 1971. —— Maxine Ling Elizabeth, *b* 1939: *m* 1st, 1966 (*m diss* 1975), Manuel Diaz Camacho; 2ndly, 1975, Edward Martin Anthony Northey, of Kingston Common Farm, Kingston Lisle, Wantage, Oxon, and has issue living, (by 1st *m*) Roderigo Manuel, *b* 1967, — Carolina del Roccio, *b* 1969, — (by 2nd *m*) Andrew Edward William, *b* 1978, — Lucinda Elizabeth, *b* 1976.

Grandchildren of late Charles Thomas Scott, 5th son of 1st baronet:—
Issue of late Capt Mason Hogarth Scott, RN, *b* 1900, *d* 1971: *m* 1924, Hon Irene Florence Seely, who *d* 1976, da of 1st Baron Mottistone:—
Mason Charles, *b* 1930; late Capt Scots Gds: *m* 1953, Judith Allison Dalgleish, and has issue living, Mason Stapleton, *b* 1955, — Adam, *b* 1963: *m* 1991, Louise Sinclair Maddocks, and has issue living, Rory Sinclair *b* 1992, Laura Sinclair *b* 1993, — Emma, *b* 1957. —— John Brough, *b* 1942: *m* 1973, Susan, da of R. G. MacInnes, of Meadow House, Ewhurst, Surrey, and has issue living, Charles Ronald Brough, *b* 1976, — James Seely, *b* 1979, — Sophie Diana, *b* 1974, — Tessa Irene, *b* 1984. —— Jane Emily (*Lady Gow*), *b* 1925: *m* 1946, Gen Sir James Michael Gow, GCB, late Scots Gds, of 18 Ann St, Edinburgh, and has issue living, Roderick Charles (49 Grahampton Lane, Greenwich, CT 06830, USA), *b* 1947; late Capt Scots Gds: *m* 1977, Anne Bayart, and has issue living, Andrew Jonathan *b* 1978, Neil James *b* 1981, — Susan Jane, *b* 1949: *m* 1969, Lt-Col Malcolm Ross, CVO, OBE, late Scots Gds, of Netherhall, Bridge of Dee, Castle Douglas, Kirkcudbrightshire, and has issue living, Hector Walter James *b* 1983, Tabitha Alice *b* 1970, Flora Jane Josephine *b* 1974, — Anna Katharine, *b* 1952: *m* 1977 (*m diss* 1991), Charles Hunter, and has issue living, Timothy Michael *b* 1981, Patrick James Simon *b* 1984, Sophie Irene *b* 1977, — Belinda Catriona, *b* 1958: *m* 1987, Julius M. Drake, of 21 Creighton Rd, NW6 6EE, eldest son of Michael Drake, of 37 Rundall Cres, NW3, and has issue living, Katherine Molly Myrtle *b* 1992, — Clunie Fiona Mary, *b* 1964: *m* 1990, Samuel Cornelius Dominic Phipps and has issue (*see* M Normanby, colls). —— (Irene) Jill, *b* 1928: *m* 1951, John Gore Phillimore, CMG, of Brooklyn House, Kingsclere, Newbury, Berks, and has issue living, John Francis, *b* 1952, — Hugh Richards, *b* 1959, — Louisa Mary, *b* 1954: *m* 1975, John C. R. Paravicini, — Penelope Jane (Polly), *b* 1956: *m* 1987 (*m diss* 1996), John Vidal, elder son of late Roland Espeut Vidal, of Oswestry, Shropshire. —— Janet Sylvia, *b* 1941: *m* 1963, Simon John Chamberlayne, of Oakham, Little Compton, Glos, and has issue living, Edward Charles, *b* 1966: *m* 1990, Zoë E., da of John Cursham, of Nottingham, and has issue living, Henry John Tankerville *b* 1995, Charles Simon Tankerville *b* 1997, — Thomas Simon, *b* 1979, — Sarah Caroline, *b* 1964: *m* 1993, G. William Allardice, son of His Honour Judge Allardice, of Stafford, and has issue living, Madeleine Jane *b* 1995, Clara Daphne *b* 1997, — Laura Katherine Jane, *b* 1972. —— Jennifer Teresa, *b* 1945: *m* 1967, Alexander Patrick Scott, of 20 Bloomfield Terrace, SW1W 8PQ and has issue living, Emily Mary, *b* 1968: *m* 1997, Robert David Huxley Turner, and has issue living, David Patrick Apollo *b* 1998, — Catherine Charlotte, *b* 1970: *m* 1994, Henry Fiddian Birtles, and has issue living, Jack Victor Patrick *b* 1998, — Claire Penelope Rose, *b* 1975, — Jill Henrietta Caroline, *b* 1980.

The 1st baronet, Sir Walter Scott, JP, son of late Samuel Scott, of Holm Cultram, Cumberland; was Chm of Walter Scott (Limited), of Walter Scott and Middleton (Limited), and of Walter Scott Publishing Co (Limited).

SCOTT (UK) 1909, of Yews, Undermilbeck, Westmorland

Sir OLIVER CHRISTOPHER ANDERSON SCOTT, MD, 3rd *Baronet*; *b* 6 Nov 1922; *s* his father, *Sir* SAMUEL HASLAM, 1960; *ed* Charterhouse, and King's Coll, Camb (MA); FRCR 1998, Memb British Inst of Radiology 1999; Dir of Research Unit in Radiobiology, British Empire Cancer Campaign; Mount Vernon Hosp 1966-69; Consultant, Inst of Cancer Research 1974-82; Radiobiologist, St Thomas's Hosp London 1982-88; High Sheriff of Westmorland 1966: *m* 1951, Phoebe Anne, elder da of late Desmond O'Neill Tolhurst, of The Gateways, Chelsea, SW, and has issue.

Arms – (as granted 1570 to Jean Schotte, infra)—Azure a greyhound courant argent, collared gules, and attached by a line of the second to a sphere in chief or. **Crest** – A sphere or, encircled by four feathers erect, severally argent, azure, gold, and gules.
Seat – Yews, Undermilbeck, Windermere, Westmorland. *Residence* – 31 Kensington Square, W8 5HH. *Club* – Brooks's.

SON LIVING

CHRISTOPHER JAMES ANDERSON, *b* 16 Jan 1955; *ed* Bryanston, Trinity Coll, Camb, and INSEAD: *m* 1988, Emma Jane, only da of Michael John Boxhall, of Chichester, Sussex, and has issue living, Edward James Saim, *b* 25 Oct 1990, — Charles James Michael, *b* 1994, — Oenone Jennifer Katharine, *b* 1992, — Cressida Jane Phoebe, *b* 1997.

DAUGHTERS LIVING

Hermione Mary, *b* 1952: *m* 1978, Dr Miles Richard Stanford, yr son of K.J. Stanford, of Langton Matravers, Dorset, and has issue living, Emma, *b* 1984, — Harriet, *b* 1986, — Olivia, *b* 1989. —— Camilla Nancy, *b* 1956: *m* 1990, David Bruce Withington, yr son of James Withington, of Competa, nr Malaga, Spain, and has issue living, Oliver, *b* 1991, — Samuel Peter, *b* 1993.

HALF-SISTER LIVING

Anne Katharine Sibella, RIBA, *b* 1912: *m* 1944, Jocelyn Wiseman Fagan Morton, who *d* 1987, son of late Sir James Morton, LLD, and has issue living, Eleanor Katharine Mary, *b* 1948: *m* 1977, Ali Resa Afsari, and has issue living, Anna Rose *b* 1979, — Frances Anne Marylee, *b* 1950: *m* 1972, Benjamin Charles Ruck Keene, and has issue living, Alexander Charles Edward *b* 1976, Dominic Nicholas John *b* 1982, Hermione Katharine Mary *b* 1978, — Beatrice Emily Margareta, *b* 1952: *m* 1980, Reginald Henry L. R. Norton, and has issue living, Thomas Henry Jocelyn *b* 1981, Natalia Beatrice Adelaide *b* 1985, — Lucia Katharine Fagan, *b* 1954: *m* 1975, Andrew Francis King, and has issue living, Robert Jocelyn Morton *b* 1985, Rosalind Frances *b* 1981, Carmel Katharine *b* 1983, Frances Sibella *b* 1987. *Residence* – 13 Acacia Gdns, NW8 6AH.

COLLATERAL BRANCH LIVING

Issue of late Francis Clayton Scott, yr son of 1st baronet, *b* 1881, *d* 1980: *m* 1911, Gwendolen Frieda Martha, who *d* 1973, da of George Jäger, of Lingdale, Birkenhead, Cheshire:—
Peter Francis, CBE (58 Cumberland St, SW1), *b* 1917; *ed* Oriel Coll, Oxford (BA 1939); formerly Capt KRRC (Supplementary Reserve); CBE 1982: *m* 1953, Prudence Mary, da of Capt Grenville Milligan, RN, and has issue living, Francis Alexander, *b* 1959, — Charlotte Rose, *b* 1954, — Madeleine Mary, *b* 1957, — Rebecca Anne, *b* 1960. —— Joan Frieda, BM, BCh (21B Inverleith Place, Edinburgh EH3 5QD), *b* 1912: *m* 1949 (*m diss* 1959), John Trevelyan, CBE (*see* Trevelyan, Bt, *cr* 1662, colls).

Sir James William Scott, 1st Bt (head of several manufacturing and mercantile firms in Lancashire, founded by John Haslam of Larkhill 1771-1820), was 12th in descent (as registered at the Heralds' Coll) from Emricus Scotus, Seneschal of the co of Solms 1484, grandfather of Jean Schotte, historian of the family, ennobled by Charles III of Lorraine. The name is now spelt Scott in accordance with its original signification, the family being descended from Scottish settlers in Franconia, a branch of whom became settled in England early in the 19th century. Sir Samuel Haslam Scott, 2nd Bt, was High Sheriff of Westmorland 1926.

SCOTT (UK) 1913, of Witley, Surrey.

Sir ANTHONY PERCY SCOTT, 3rd *Baronet*; *b* 1 May 1937; *s* his father, *Col Sir* DOUGLAS WINCHESTER, 1984; *ed* Harrow, and Ch Ch, Oxford; Bar Inner Temple 1960: *m* 1962, Caroline Teresa Anne, elder da of (William Charles) Edward Bacon, of Hill House, Mobberley, Cheshire, and has issue.

ᴀrms – Argent, pelletty, in base a lymphad sable, pennons flying to the dexter gules, in chief two crescents azure. ᴄrest – An ancient cannon, firing to the dexter proper.
Residence – Long Barrow, Goodworth Clatford, Andover, Hants SP11 7SE.

SONS LIVING

HENRY DOUGLAS EDWARD, *b* 26 March 1964; *ed* Harrow: *m* 1993, Carole Ruth, elder da of Derek Maddick, and of Mrs E. Roberts, of Auckland, NZ. *Residence* – 46 Ashburnham Mansions, Ashburnham Rd, SW10 0PB. —— *Rev* Simon James, *b* 1965; *ed* Harrow, Ch Ch, Oxford, and Wycliffe Hall, Oxford; ordained 1991.

DAUGHTER LIVING

Miranda Claire, *b* 1967.

BROTHER LIVING

Alastair John Douglas *b* 1940; *ed* Harrow, and McGill Univ, Canada: *m* 1965, Virginia Mary, da of late John Gaynor, of Fairfield, Pyrford Wood, Surrey, and has issue living, William Douglas, *b* 1966, — Sarah Victoria, *b* 1969, — Penelope Mary, *b* 1974.

SISTER LIVING

Diana Jean, *b* 1934: *m* 1956, John Peter Fraser-Mackenzie, and has issue living, Robert Douglas, *b* 1959: *m* 1992, Philippa Mary, da of Harold Jones, of Harare, Zimbabwe, — Elizabeth Henrietta, *b* 1958: *m* 1988, Count Thomas Ahlefeldt-Laurvig-Lehn, of Nielstrup Hovedgaard, 5762 Vester-Skerninge, Denmark, — Georgina Ann, *b* 1963: *m* 1989, Maj Charles P. H. Knaggs, son of George H. Knaggs, — Catherine Beatrice (*Lady Calum Graham*), *b* 1966: *m* 1991, Lord Calum Ian Graham, yst son of 7th Duke of Montrose. *Residence* – Lone Cow Estate, PO Box 22, Mutorashanga, Zimbabwe.

The 1st baronet, Adm Sir Percy Moreton Scott, KCB, KCVO, LLD, served during Ashantee War 1873-4, in Expedition up the Congo against pirates 1875, in Egyptian War 1882, in S Africa 1899-1900 as Comdt of Durban, when he devised special mounting for the Naval Gun used for defence and relief of Ladysmith, and in China 1900; invented night signalling apparatus used in RN; in command of Gunnery Sch, and a Naval ADC to HM 1903-5, Inspector of Naval Target Practice 1905-7, and in command of First Cruiser Squadron 1907-8, and of Second Cruiser Squadron 1908-9 (Comdg in S African Federation Convention); appointed or Special Ser at the Admiralty 1914; took charge of Gunnery Defences of London 1915-16.

SCOTT (UK) 1962, of Rotherfield Park, Alton, Hants

Sir JAMES JERVOISE SCOTT, 3rd *Baronet*; *b* 12 Oct 1952; *s* his father, Sir JAMES WALTER, 1993; *ed* Eton, and Trin Coll, Camb; Editor of *Big Farm Weekly* 1984-88: *m* 1982, Judy Evelyn, da of Brian Sadler Leigh Trafford (*see* B Taylor of Hadfield), of Tismans, Rudgwick, W Sussex, and has issue.

Arms – Per pale indented argent and sable a saltire counterchanged. Crest – Out of a circlet of pales or, a cubit arm erect habited gules cuffed ermine, the hand proper holding a paper scroll argent.
Residence – Rotherfield Park, Alton, Hants GU34 3QL.

SON LIVING

ARTHUR JERVOISE TRAFFORD, *b* 2 Feb 1984; *ed* Eton.

DAUGHTER LIVING

Alexandra Lilian, *b* 1986; *ed* Wycombe Abbey.

BROTHERS LIVING AND DECEASED

Charles Clive, *b* 1954; *ed* Eton, and Trin Coll, Camb: *m* 1979, Caroline Frances, da of Hugh Grahame Jago, of Old Cottage, Campfield Pl, Leith Hill, Dorking, Surrey, and has issue living, Eleanor Gabriel, *b* 1981, — Rose Loveday, *b* 1983, — Alice Olivia, *b* 1987. *Residence* – Manor Farm, Colemore, Alton, Hants GU34 3RX.
—— †Alexander Archibald, *b* 1960; *ed* Eton, and Queen's Coll, Cambridge: *m* 1986, Julia Mary Mackenzie, eldest da of Patrick William Mackenzie Dean, of E Mere, Lincs (*see* B Raglan, colls), and *d* 1994, leaving issue, Daniel Fitzroy, *b* 1987, — Rupert Patrick, *b* 1992, — Emily Rosanna, *b* 1990. *Residence* – Glebe House, Cheveley, Newmarket, Suffolk CB8 9DG.

SISTER LIVING

Susannah Maria, *b* 1963: *m* 1990, Major James Richard Kelly, Scots Guards, only son of John Kelly, of Barnes, SW, and has issue living, Archibald Clive, *b* 1992, — George Claude, *b* 1993, — James Charles, *b* 1995. *Residence* – Ardovie House, by Brechin, Angus DD9 6ST.

UNCLE LIVING (*Son of 1st baronet*)

Samuel Arthur (Thatched Cottage, East Tisted, Alton, Hants), *b* 1926; *ed* Eton, and RMC Sandhurst; Lt 7th Queen's Own Hussars, late Capt 4th Royal Hampshire Regt (TA); Korea with 8th Hussars 1950-51: *m* 1952, Juliet Modwena, elder da of Samuel Ranulph Allsopp, CBE (*see* B Hindlip, colls), and has issue living, Henry Samuel Jervoise, *b* 1955; *ed* Eton, and RMAS; Lt-Col The Life Guards: *m* 1979, Joanna Sarah, da of James Brownlow, of The Old Rectory, Kelling, Holt, Norfolk, and has issue living, Geoffrey James Ranulph *b* 1980, Rory Samuel Jervoise *b* 1982.

WIDOW LIVING OF SECOND BARONET

ANNE CONSTANTIA (*Dowager Lady Scott*), eldest da of Late Lt-Col Clive Grantham Austin, DL, of Roundwood, Micheldever, Hants (*see* E Scarbrough, 1980 Edn): *m* 1951, Sir James Walter Scott, 2nd Bt, who *d* 1993. *Residence* – The Knapp, Colemore, Alton, Hants GU34 3RX.

COLLATERAL BRANCH LIVING

Issue of late Maj Richard Jervoise Scott, TD, yst son of 1st baronet, *b* 1929, *d* 1974: *m* 1955 (*m diss* 1972), Julia Maud, who *d* 1974, yr da of Sir Henry Robert Kincaid Floyd, 5th Bt, CB, CBE:—
Victoria Kathleen, *b* 1956: *m* 1977, Charles Herbert Parker, and has issue living, Thomas Richard, *b* 1982, Samuel George, *b* 1984, — Emma Louise, *b* 1987. —— Camilla Julia (*Lady Michael Cecil*), *b* 1986: *m* 1986, Lord Michael Hugh Cecil, yst son of 6th Marquess of Salisbury, and has issue (*see* M Salisbury). *Address* – PO Box 49428, Nairobi, Kenya.

This family descends from John Scott of Hatfield Regis, Essex, 4th son of William Scott, lord of the manor of Stapleford Tawney, Essex, who *d* 1491. Rotherfield Park, Hants, was purchased in 1808 from the 14th Marquess of Winchester by James Scott of Hammersmith, 8th in descent from John. His grandson, Archibald Edward Scott, of Rotherfield Park was father of Sir Jervoise Bolitho Scott, 1st Bt, High Sheriff of Hants 1936, and a Co Councillor 1932-65, and Official Verderer of New Forest 1950-64. Sir James Walter Scott, 2nd baronet, was Lord Lieut Hants 1982-93.

MAXWELL SCOTT (E) 1642, of Haggerston, Northumberland

Sir DOMINIC JAMES MAXWELL SCOTT, 14th *Baronet*; *b* 22 July 1968; *s* his father, Sir MICHAEL FERGUS CONSTABLE, 1989; *ed* Eton, and Sussex Univ.

Arms – Quarterly, grand-quartered; 1st grand-quarter; or, two mullets in chief and a crescent in base azure, within an orle or the second and charged at the middle chief point with a crescent sable (*Scott*); 2nd grand-quarter; azure on a bend cotised argent three billets sable (*Haggerston of Haggerston*); 3rd grand-quarter; quarterly; 1st and 4th quarters argent an eagle displayed with two heads sable, beaked and membered gules, surmounted on an escutcheon of the first charged with a saltire of the second and surcharged in the centre with an hurcheon or (*Maxwell, E of Nithsdale*); 2nd quarter counter quartered (i) and (iv) argent a saltire sable, in chief a label of three points gules (*Maxwell*); (ii) and (iii) argent three hurcheons sable (*Herries of Terregles*) 3rd quarter, quarterly, gules vair a bend or (*Constable of Everingham*); 4th grand-quarter, or on a bend azure three mascles of the first in the sinister chief point a buckle of the second (*Haliburton*). Crest – 1st, a nymph richly attired holding in her dexter hand the sun and in her sinister the moon all proper (*Scott*); 2nd a lion passant argent (*Haggerston of Haggerston*).
Residence – 130 Ritherdon Rd, SW17.

BROTHER LIVING

MATTHEW JOSEPH, *b* 27 Aug 1976.

SISTER LIVING

Annabel Jane, *b* 1973.

DAUGHTERS LIVING OF ELEVENTH BARONET

Belinda Ann de Marie (*Lady Haggerston Gadsden*), *b* 1933: *m* 1955, Sir Peter Drury HAGGERSTON GADSDEN, GBE, AC, FREng (who assumed by Royal Licence 1973 the additional surname of Haggerston), of Harelaw House, Chathill, Northumberland NE67 5HE, and has issue living, Juliet Mary Haggerston, *b* 1956: *m* 1978, Nigel John Cartwright, of Cherry Tree House, Ramsden, Chipping Norton, Oxon OX7 3AR, and has issue living, Nicholas John Haggerston Gadsden *b* 1980, James Alexander Haggerston Gadsden *b* 1982, Charles Peter Haggerston Gadsden *b* 1989, Georgina Mary Haggerston Gadsden *b* 1984, — Caroline Mabel, *b* 1957: *m* 1983, Capt Graham C. Simpson, RA, of The Home Farm, Ellingham, Chathill, Northumberland NE67 5HG, and has issue living, Matthew Caveen Drury *b* 1985, Oliver Peter Carnaby *b* 1989, Amelia Ann de Marie *b* 1987, Belinda Rose de Marie *b* 1991, — Clare Louise, *b* 1960: *m* 1985, Iain C. H. McWhirter, elder son of late A. Ross McWhirter, of The Old Rectory, Little Blakenham, Ipswich, Suffolk, and has issue living, (Alexander) Ross *b* 1988, Annabelle Louise *b* 1986, Lucy Belinda *b* 1990, Camilla Rosemary *b* 1991, Charlotte Elizabeth *b* 1993, Christabel Katharine de Marie *b* 1996, Flora Clare de Marie *b* 1999, — Elizabeth Ann, *b* 1962: *m* 1999, Claude Edward Partridge, yr son of John Arthur Partridge, of Empingham, Rutland (*see* B Brownlow). —— Jennifer Veronica Louise de Marie (4 Guion Rd, SW6 4UE), *b* 1938: *m* 1959 (*m diss* 1987), Anthony Lambert Forward, and has issue living, Hugh Carnaby, *b* 1959: *m* 1st, 1988 (*m diss* 1989), Veronique Cavallier; 2ndly, 1997, Fiona Mary Joiner, — Andrew Lambert, *b* 1964: *m* 1996, Lisa Anna Ciolli, and has issue living, Gabriella Louise *b* 1999. —— Phyllida Angela de Marie, *b* 1945: *m* 1967, Antony Roland Richard Woosnam Mills, of Mother Ivey Cottage, Trevose Head, Padstow, Cornwall PL28 8SL, and has an adopted son and da, Alexander Ross, *b* 1984, — Victoria Anne, *b* 1977; has issue, Holly Anne *b* 1999.

WIDOWS LIVING OF TWELFTH AND THIRTEENTH BARONETS

JOAN ADELENE (*Lady Haggerston*), da of late William Blythe-Perrett, of Ludgershall, Wilts: *m* 1956, Sir Ralph (Raphael) Stanley de Marie Haggerston, 12th Bt, who *d* 1972. *Residence* – 62 Longston Park, Beadnell, Chathill, Northumberland NE67 5BP.

DEIRDRE MOIRA (*Lady Maxwell Scott*), da of late Alexander McKechnie: *m* 1963, Sir Michael Fergus Constable Maxwell Scott, 13th Bt, who *d* 1989. *Residence* – 130 Ritherdon Rd, SW17 8QQ.

COLLATERAL BRANCHES LIVING (*see also* L Herries of Terregles, colls)

Issue of late Ian Malcolm Maxwell Scott, brother of 13th baronet, *b* 1927, *d* 1993: *m* 1958, Susan Mary (12 Kelmscott Rd, SW11 6QY), yr da of Sir Andrew Edmund James Clark, 3rd Bt, MBE, MC, QC (*cr* 1883):—
Malcolm Fergus, *b* 1960: *m* 1990 (*m diss* 1993), Tanya, yr da of William Church. —— Simon Magnus, *b* 1962: *m* 1986 (*m diss* 1994), Gaynor, yst da of Daniel Jones, and has issue living, Hector George, *b* 1986, — Amelia Elizabeth, *b* 1989. —— Andrew Nicholas Hugh, *b* 1966. —— Lucy Ann, *b* 1958. —— Sarah Secunda, *b* 1959. —— Catherine Monica Jane, *b* (twin) 1966.

Sir Thomas Haggerston, who commanded a regt in Charles I's army, was *cr* a Bt in 1642. On the death in 1972 of Sir Ralph (Raphael) Stanley de Marie Haggerston, who had *s* as 12th Bt in 1971, the line from Sir Thomas, 4th Bt became ext, and the title reverted to that of the 2nd son of the 3rd Bt, William Haggerston-Constable (who in 1746 inherited Everingham Park, Yorks, from his great uncle, Sir Marmaduke Francis Constable, 4th Bt, and thereupon assumed the additional name of Constable). He *m* 1758 (Lady) Winifred, da of Robert Maxwell, titular 6th Earl of Nithsdale, when he assumed by Roy Licence the surname of Constable-Maxwell. Their grandson William *s* as 10th Lord Herries of Terregles. This peer's el son Marmaduke, 11th Lord Herries, *d* 1908 without male issue (*see* L Herries), and his 3rd son Joseph assumed by Roy Licence the surname of Constable-Maxwell-Scott, on *m* 1874 to Monica, da of J. Robert Hope Scott, of Abbotsford (by his wife Charlotte Lockhart, grandda and heiress of Sir Walter Scott, 1st Bt, the eminent writer). Joseph's el son, Sir Walter Joseph was *cr* a Bt in 1932 (which became ext on his death without male issue 1954), and his 3rd son Adm Malcolm Joseph Raphael, DSO, was father of the 13th Bt.

CONSTABLE-MAXWELL-SCOTT (UK) 1932, of Abbotsford, Melrose, co Roxburgh (Extinct 1954)

Maj-Gen Sir WALTER JOSEPH CONSTABLE-MAXWELL-SCOTT, CB, DSO, 1st and last *Baronet*.

DAUGHTER LIVING OF FIRST BARONET (*By 1st marriage*)

Dame Jean Mary Monica, DCVO, *b* 1923; *ed* Convent des Oiseaux, Westgate-on-Sea; a Lady-in-Waiting to HRH Princess Alice, Duchess of Gloucester since 1959; 1939-45 War as VAD; CVO 1969, DCVO 1984. *Residence* – Abbotsford, Melrose, Scotland; New Cavendish Club.

SEALE (UK) 1838, of Mount Boone, Devonshire

In heaven salvation

Sir JOHN HENRY SEALE, 5th *Baronet*; *b* 3 March 1921; *s* his father, *Sir* JOHN CARTERET HYDE, 1964; *ed* Eton, and Ch Ch, Oxford; Capt late RA; patron of one living; RIBA: *m* 1953, Ray Josephine, da of late Robert Gordon Charters, MC, of Christchurch, New Zealand, and has issue.

Arms – Or, two barrulets azure between three wolves heads erased sable, in the fesse point a mural crown gules. Crest – Out of a crown vallery or a wolf's head argent, the neck encircled with a wreath of oak vert.
Residence Slade, near Kingsbridge, Devon TQ7 4BL.

SON LIVING

(JOHN) ROBERT CHARTERS, *b* 17 Aug 1954; *ed* Eton, and Univ Coll of N Wales, Bangor: *m* 1996, Michelle Judith, da of Kevin William Taylor, of Mattishall, Norfolk.

DAUGHTER LIVING

Elizabeth Margaret Anne, *b* 1956.

BROTHER LIVING

Richard Styleman (Conduit Rise, Conduit Head Rd, Cambridge), *b* 1924; *ed* Eton, and Pembroke Coll, Camb: *m* 1963, Elizabeth Vazeille, da of late T. B. Bright, of Silverdale, Lancs, and has issue living, William Thomas Carteret, *b* 1964, — Margaret Rachel Vazeille, *b* 1966: *m* 1991, Paul Atputhakumar Jebarajasingam Supramaniam, of London and Singapore, and has issue living, James Timothy Bright Aiyathuraisingam *b* 1993, — Matthew Edward Herring Jeyathuraisingam, *b* 1998.

SISTER LIVING

Mary Paulina, *b* 1920: *m* 1945, Col George Robert Melville Harvey More, MC, RE, who *d* 1991, and has issue living, Robert Harvey, *b* 1946: *m* 1989, Claire, da of Cdr H. Harwood, RN, of Rowde, Wilts, and has issue living, Caspar George Harvey *b* 1992, Harriet Caroline Eaton *b* 1990, Marina Elizabeth Eaton *b* 1994, — Henry Sanctuary (1436 Miramonte Av, Los Altos, Calif 94022, USA), *b* 1948: *m* 1977, Adelle Anne, da of late Harold Mackenzie Smith, of Sacramento, Calif, and has issue living, Paul Henry *b* 1979, Stephen Henry *b* 1981, Susannah Mary *b* 1993, — John William, *b* 1953: *m* 1987, Martine, da of Jacques Wolf, of Paris, and has issue living, Ludéric Norman James *b* 1994, Noëlie Joanna *b* 1991, — Sarah Frances, *b* 1952. *Residence* – Bazzleways, Milborne Port, Sherborne, Dorset DT9 5EH.

COLLATERAL BRANCHES LIVING

Issue of late Maj Henry Dendy Seale, yr son of 3rd baronet, b 1882, d 1974: m 1914, Lora May, who d 1974, da of late Cecil Hurst Bisshopp, of Fernlea, Oban, Argyllshire:—
Mary Désirée, b 1915: m 1st, 1946, Stanley James Meyers, who d 1974; 2ndly, 1978, Charles Eastman Adams, who d 198-; 3rdly, 198-, George Hutchison, of 601 Monkland Av, Montreal, Prov Quebec, Canada H4B 1J2, and has issue living (by 1st m), Linda May, b 1948: m 1973 (m diss 1981), Robert Donald Giroux, and has issue living, Sean Robert b 1975, Scot Donald b 1977.

Grandchildren of Frederick Hayne Seale (infra), 2nd son of late George Thomas Seale, yr son of late Rev Edward Taylor Seale, 3rd son of 1st baronet:—
Issue of late Richard Wentworth Seale, b 1904, d 1972: m 1927, Edith Hazel, who d 1990, da of William Brown Birch:—
Richard Laurie (32 Kincardine Crescent, Floreat Park, W Australia 6014), b 1930: m 1956, Paula Cathleen, da of late Hans Carl Bruechle, and has issue living, Richard Beaumont, b 1966, — Stacey Jennifer, b 1958, — Leanda Jane, b 1960, — Petrina Louise, b 1962.

Issue of late Gordon Frederick Seale, b 1906, d 1985: m 1936, Eva Vera (37 Marlow St, Wembley, W Australia), da of Charles Adams:—
Elizabeth Lenore, b 1939: m 1961, Horace Charles Kennedy, and has issue living, Shane Brett, b 1967, — Natalie Lisa, b 1965. —— Carolyn Margaret, b 1943.

Issue of late Walter Douglas Seale, b 1907, d 1989: m 1st, 1935 (m diss 1967), Mons Carruthers, da of Sidney Herbert Reidy-Crofts; 2ndly, 1974, Barbara Topping, who d 1993:—
(By 1st m) John Digby, b 1937: m 1st, 1960 (m diss 1973), Roslyn Edith, da of David Englander; 2ndly, 1980, Ann, da of James Thomas Collingwood Mullner. —— Felicity Jane, b 1939: m 1st, 1961, Evan Owen; 2ndly, 1987, Sidney Donald Bradshaw, of 156 Hensman Rd, Subiaco 6008, W Aust, and has issue living (by 1st m), Simon Llewellyn, b 1963, — Sarah Alexander, b 1967, — Sophia Jane, b 1971.

Issue of late Allan Dudley Seale, b 1911, d 1989: m 1947, Ilma Ruth (25 Fortune St, S Perth, W Australia 6151), da of Edward John Barrett:—
Phillip Gregory (27 Deakin St, Forestville, NSW 2087, Australia), b 1948: m 1st, 1978 (m diss 1981), Cheryl Davis; 2ndly, 1991, Adele Sharam. —— Brian Wentworth (11 Annetts Rd, Dalwallinu, WA 6609, Australia), b 1950: m 1st, 1970 (m diss 1997), Cheryl Lynne, da of Stanley Raey Gibb; 2ndly, 1998, Debra Rose, da of John William Elliott Baldrey, of 52 Manning Rd, Wilson, WA, and has issue living (by 1st m), Paul Langdon Wentworth, b 1973, — Belynda Ruth, b 1971, — Rebekah Michaela Alyse, b 1976, — (by 2nd m) Allana Emily Rose, b 1999. —— Marlene Ruth, b 1952: m 1974, Lance Rattigan, of 13 Roseberry Av, S Perth, W Australia, and has issue living, Jeremy Lance, b 1977, — Timothy Neal, b 1979, — Andrew Stephen, b 1982.

Issue of late Frederick Hayne Seale (ante), b 1878, d 1931: m 1903, Ethel Lenore, who d 1959, da of Joseph Nathan:—
Grace Mildred, b 1909: m 1946, Vice Adm Brian Betham Schofield, CB, CBE, who d 1984, and has issue living, Elizabeth Virginia, b 1948, — Rosemary Victoria, b 1950: m 1982, Stephen Mark Willis, of 48 Westbourne Park Rd, W2 5PH, and has issue living, Anthony Brian b 1987, Alexandra Rose b 1985, Olivia Grace b 1990. Residence – Holme, Lower Shiplake, Henley-on-Thames, Oxon RG9 3JS.

This family can trace its descent from John Seale of St Brelade, Jersey, who was b about 1512. According to Payne's Armorial of Jersey, the earliest reference is to Robert Seale, or Scelle, a "gens de bien" of St Brelade 1292, and other Scelles of St Brelade are mentioned in the Rolls of the Assizes 1309. John Seale Constable of St Brelade 1644-51, a yr son of John Seale Constable 1615-21 was great-grandfather of John who purchased Mount Boone, Dartmouth, about 1720. His grandson, the 1st baronet, Sir John Henry Seale, sat as MP for Dartmouth (L) 1832-44. The 2nd baronet, Sir Henry Paul Seale, was sixteen times Mayor of Dartmouth.

SEBRIGHT (E) 1626, of Besford, Worcestershire

Sir PETER GILES VIVIAN SEBRIGHT, 15th *Baronet*; *b* 2 Aug 1953; *s* his father, *Sir* HUGO GILES EDMUND, 1985, but his name does not appear on the Official Roll of the Baronetage; is patron of one living: *m* 1st, 1977 (*m diss* 19—), Regina Maria, da of Francis Steven Clarebrough, of Melbourne, Australia; 2ndly, 1987, Madeleine, and has issue by 1st and 2nd *m*.

Arms – Argent, three cinquefoils sable. Crest – A tiger sejant argent, maned and crowned or. Badges – A garb of oats or band azure inscribed with the motto "Pro Rege".
Address – PO Box 15527, Lynne East, Pretoria 0039, S Africa.

SONS LIVING (*By 1st marriage*)

RUFUS HUGO GILES, *b* 31 July 1978.

(*By 2nd marriage*)

Dashiell, *b* 1987.

DAUGHTER LIVING (*By 2nd marriage*)

Klara, *b* 1993.

MOTHER LIVING

To preserve equanimity

Deirdre Ann, da of late Maj Vivian Lionel Slingsby Bethell (*see* B Westbury, colls): *m* 1st, 1952 (*m diss* 1964), Sir Hugo Giles Edmund Sebright, 14th Bt, who *d* 1985; 2ndly, 1965, Anthony Melbourne-Hart, who *d* 1988.

WIDOW LIVING OF FOURTEENTH BARONET

VICTORIA ROSAMOND (*Dowager Lady Sebright*), da of late Capt Richard Taylor White, DSO, RN (ret) (*see* White, Bt, *cr* 1802), and formerly wife of David Ashton Ashton-Bostock: *m* 1984, as his 3rd wife, Sir Hugo Giles Edmund Sebright, 14th Bt, who *d* 1985. *Residence* – BP3, Clarensac 30870, France.

The 1st baronet, Sir Edward Sebright, was High Sheriff of Worcestershire *temp* Charles I. He was a warm royalist, and paid £1,109 composition for his estate to the sequestrators. Sir Thomas Saunders, the 4th baronet, was MP for Hertford 1715-36. The 7th baronet also sat as MP for Hertford, Lt-Col Sir Edgar Sebright, 11th Bt, was Equerry to HRH Princess Mary Adelaide (Duchess of Teck) 1882-92 and Extra Equerry 1892. Sir Giles Sebright, CBE, 13th Bt, was Lt-Col late Comdg Herts Regt (TA), and temporary Equerry to HM King George VI when Duke of York 1922-23.

SEELY (UK) 1896, of Sherwood Lodge, Arnold, Notts, and Brook House, Brook, Isle of Wight

NIGEL EDWARD SEELY, 5th *Baronet*, *b* 28 July 1923; *s* his father, *Maj Sir* VICTOR BASIL JOHN, 1980; *ed* Stowe: *m* 1st, 1949, Loraine, only da of late Wilfred W. Lindley-Travis, of Gatehead, Fulstone, Yorks; 2ndly, 1984, Trudi, da of Sydney Pacter, of Tunbridge Wells, and has issue by 1st *m*.

Arms – Azure, three ears of wheat banded or between two marlets in pale, and as many wreaths of roses in fesse argent. Crest – In front of three ears of wheat banded or, the trunk of a tree fessewise eradicated and sprouting to the dexter proper.
Residence – 3 Craven Hill Mews, W2. *Clubs* – Buck's, Royal Solent.

DAUGHTERS LIVING (*By 1st marriage*)

Charlotte Alexandra Mary, *b* 1954: *m* 1st, 1980 (*m diss* 19—), Paul Arthur Schwartz, of New York, USA; 2ndly, 1988, Allen Lawrence Levy, and has issue living (by 2nd *m*), Emily Rose, *b* 1989. —— Catherine Lucy Emily, *b* 1957: *m* 1994, William Gatacre (*see* Paget, Bt, *cr* 1886, 1995 Edn), and has issue living, Amelia Lettice, *b* 1997. —— Henrietta Louise, *b* 1962.

HALF-BROTHER LIVING (*Son of 4th baronet by his 3rd wife, Mary Frances Margaret, da of late William Ronald Collins*)

VICTOR RONALD (Newlands Farm, Farfield Cam, Dursley, Glos GL11 5HE; *Club* – Army & Navy), *b* 1 Aug 1941; *ed* Eton, RMA Sandhurst and the Army Staff Coll, Camberley; Maj R Hus (PWO), served on secondment to the Sultan of Oman's Armed Forces 1970-71: *m* 1972, Annette Bruce, da of late Lt-Col J. A. D. McEwen, of Salperton House, Salperton, Cheltenham, and has issue living, William Victor Conway, *b* 16 Sept 1983, — Natasha Wilhelmina Annette, *b* 1979.

HALF-SISTERS LIVING (*Daughter of 4th baronet by his 2nd wife, Hon Patience Kemp, da of 1st Baron Rochdale*)

Victoria (Bridgewater, Spy Lane, Loxwood, W Sussex RH14 0SS), *b* 1933: *m* 1954 (*m diss* 1975), (Francis Arthur) Michael Bray, DSC, and has issue living, Charles Michael Francis (61 Fentiman Rd, SW8 1LH), *b* 1957: *m* 1992, Elspeth J., yr da of Alastair Moncrieff, of Old Bosham, Sussex, and has issue living, Alastair Charles Michael *b* 1993, Oliver Valentine Chancourt *b* 1995, Floriana (Flora) Victoria *b* 1997, — Mariana Victoria Magdalen, *b* 1956: *m* 1985, Maj Richard C.B. Sampson, The Life Guards, of Manor House, Calton, Stoke on Trent, Staffs ST10 3JX, son of Maj Richard C. Sampson, of Norwich, Norfolk, and has issue living, George Edward Richard *b* 1986, Charles Michael Henry *b* 1988, Hugo Miles Evelyn *b* 1991, — Amelia Mary, *b* 1962: *m* 1985, Andrew James Randolph Macpherson, elder son of Colin Macpherson, of Martyr Worthy, Hants, and has issue living, Matilda Mary *b* 1987, Cluny Amelia *b* 1991, Ottilie Elizabeth *b* 1993.

(*Daughter of 4th baronet by his 3rd wife, Mary Frances Margaret, da of late William Ronald Collins*)

Alexandra Mary Hilda, *b* 1938: *m* 1st, 1966 (*m diss* 19—), Henry Charles Seymour, yr son of late Lt-Col Sir Reginald Henry Seymour, KCVO (*see* M Hertford, colls); 2ndly, 1995, Capt Michael Patrick Radcliffe Boyle (*see* E Shannon, colls).

COLLATERAL BRANCHES LIVING

Issue of late Sqdn-Ldr Nigel Richard William Seely, AuxAF (Reserve), 4th son of 2nd baronet, *b* 1902; *d* on active ser 1943: *m* 1937, Isabella Elinor Margarete (who *d* 1957, having *m* 2ndly, 1949, Edward Bromley-Davenport, who *d* 1990), da of Eugen Bernhard Adolf Erdmann von Rieben:—
Charles John Howell (La Bosnière, Cussay, France), *b* 1937; *ed* Eton. —— Hilton Nigel Matthew (45 Sterndale Rd, Brook Green, W14 0HT), *b* 1940; *ed* Eton: *m* 1st, 1971, Leonie Mary, da of late Brig George Taylor, CBE, DSO and Bar, of North Manor, Strathwell Park, I of Wight; 2ndly, 1993, Denise M., da of Thomas Muckle, of Rothbury, Northumberland, and has issue living (by 1st *m*), Charles Hilton, *b* 1972; *ed* Eton, — Dominic Edward *b* 1975; *ed* Eton, — (by 2nd *m*) Max Anthony Philip, *b* 1993. —— Elinor Ivy, *b* 1941: *m* 1st, 1968, Maj Martin Vyvyan Carleton-Smith, Irish Gds; 2ndly, 1990, Ian V. Fletcher, of Johannesburg, and has issue living (by 1st *m*), Robin Francis Popham *b* 1972, — Camilla Alison, *b* 1969. —— Isabella Frances, *b* (twin) 1941: *m* 1st, 1961 (*m diss* 1966), Simon James Scrimgeour; 2ndly, 1966, Anthony Piers Covill, of 97 Arthur Rd, SW19, and has issue living, (by 1st *m*) Lucilla Jane, *b* 1963: *m* 1996, Jeremy P. Lavender, yr son of Laurence Lavender, of Cheam, Surrey, — (by 2nd *m*) Piers Anthony Charles, *b* 1967: *m* 1995, Kate Henrietta, only da of David Covell, of Chelsea, SW3, — Joseph William Edward, *b* 1969.

Grandsons of late Lt-Col Frank Evelyn Seely, 3rd son of 1st baronet:—
Issue of late Lt-Col (Frank) James (Wriothesley) Seely, MFH, *b* 1901, *d* 1956: *m* 1925, Vera Lilian, who *d* 1970, da of late Col Charles Wilfrid Birkin, CMG (*see* Birkin, Bt):—
†Michael James, *b* 1926: *m* 1st, 1952 (*m diss* 1966), Barbara Patricia Callaghan; 2ndly, 1966, Patricia Ann Auchterlonie, who *d* 1990; 3rdly, 1993, Irene Heath, and *d* 1993, leaving issue, (by 2nd *m*) Rachel (Rosie), *b* 1967. —— Timothy Ward (Ramsdale Farm, Oxton Lane, Arnold, Notts NG5 8PU), *b* 1935; *ed* Eton; an actor: *m* 1960 (*m diss* 19—), Anne Henrietta Maria St Paul, who *d* 1996, formerly wife of James Dugdale Burridge, and only da of Horace George St Paul Butler, of High Humbledon, Wooler, Northumberland, and has issue living, Hugo Michael David St Paul (Bickerton Grange, Tom Cat Lane, Wetherby, Yorks LS22 5ES), *b* 1961: *m* 1991, J. Caroline, elder da of Dr. A. Milner, of Islip, Oxon, and has issue living, Toby Hugo St Paul *b* 1996, India Grace St Paul *b* 1992. —— James Richard Francis, *b* 1940: *m* (Jan) 1960, Wendy Mary Hutchinson, and has issue living, Christian James Russell, *b* (Dec) 1960, — Jonathan Sebastian, *b* 1962.

Issue of late Lt-Col William Evelyn Seely, *b* 1902, *ka* 1942: *m* 1927, Irene Lavender (who *d* 1977, having *m* 2ndly, 1943, as his 2nd wife, Maj-Gen Sir Miles William Arthur Peel Graham, KBE, CB, MC, who *d* 1976 (E Peel, colls)), da of Richard Francklin (V St Vincent):—
Richard Evelyn (33 Upper Park Rd, NW3), *b* 1928; *ed* Eton; Bar Gray's Inn, 1961; JP: *m* 1960, Helga, da of Wilhelm Schnarr, of Mainz, Germany, and has issue living, Philip Frank Evelyn, *b* 1963; *ed* Harrow, — Robert William Henry, *b* 1966; *ed* Harrow: *m* 1995, Nata, da of Algirdas Rashimas, of Vilnius, Lithuania. —— Charles William (Rendham Barnes, Saxmundham, Suffolk), *b* 1935; *ed* Eton: *m* 1958, Morvyth, da of late George Arthur St George, of 4 Dyke Rd Pl, Brighton, 5, and has issue living, Amy Jane Lavender *b* 1969, — Camilla Rose, *b* 1972, — Joanna Matilda, *b* 1974.

Issue of late Maj-Gen Rt Hon John Edward Bernard Seely, CB, CMG, DSO (4th son of 1st baronet), who was *cr* Baron Mottistone 1933 (*see* that title).

Charles Seely, father of the 1st Bt, was MP for Lincoln 1847-48 and 1861-85 and High Sheriff of Hants 1860. The 1st Bt, Col Sir Charles, of Brook House, I of Wight, and of Sherwood Lodge, Arnold, Notts, DL, JP Notts, and High Sheriff 1890, sat as MP for Nottingham (*L*) 1869-74, and 1880-85, and for W Nottingham 1885-86, and again for Nottingham (LU) 1892-95; founder and benefactor Nottingham Gen Hosp. The 2nd Bt, Sir Charles Hilton, High Sheriff Notts 1912, JP Notts and Hants, DL Notts, was MP for Lincoln (LU) 1895-1906, and for Mansfield (*Co L*) 1916-18. The 3rd Bt, Sir Hugh Michael, JP Notts, High Sheriff 1925, MP E Div Norfolk (*L*) 1923-24, and for Berwick-upon-Tweed 1935-41, PPS to Sec of State for Air 1940, Joint Under-Sec of State for Air 1941-45, was *cr* Baron Sherwood 1941; he *d* 1970, when the peerage became ext. His brother, Sir Victor Basil John, 4th Bt, was Master Gunmakers' Co 1957 and 1964, and Chm Purdey's 1970.

Selby-Bigge, see Bigge.

SETON (NS) 1663, of Abercorn, Linlithgowshire

Sir IAIN BRUCE SETON, 13th *Baronet, b* 27 Aug 1942; *s* his father, *Sir* CHRISTOPHER BRUCE, 1988, *ed* Colchester, and Chadacre Agric Inst: *m* 1963, Margaret Ann, only da of Walter Charles Faulkner, of Barlee Rd, W Australia, and has issue.

Arms – Quarterly: 1st and 4th, or, three crescents within a double tressure flory, counterflory gules, *Seton*; 2nd and 3rd, argent, three in escutcheons gules, *Hay*. Crest – A boar's head couped or, armed and langued azure. Supporters – Two greyhounds proper.
Address – Bella Vista, PO Box 253, Bridgetown 6255, W Australia.

SON LIVING

LAURENCE BRUCE, *b* 1 July 1968: *m* 1990, Rachel, da of Jeffery Woods, of Bridgetown, W Australia, and has issue living, Rowan Ann, *b* 1996, — Sarah Jane, *b* 1998.

DAUGHTER LIVING

Amanda Jane, *b* 1971; *m* 1999, Brent Joseph Pritchard, of Katanning, W Australia.

BROTHER LIVING

Michael Charles, *b* 1944; *ed* Colchester Tech Coll: *m* 1973, Vida Millicent, da of late Sidney Clarence Smith, of Boxted, Essex, and has issue living, Philip Charles, *b* 1975, — Helen Mary, *b* 1978.

Residence – Fingringhoe, Colchester, Essex.

SISTERS LIVING

Sarah Ann, *b* (twin) 1944: *m* 1st, 1968 (*m diss* 1970), Thomas Charles Usher; 2ndly, 1974 (*m diss* 1988), Ferdinand Winston Good. *Address* – Box 443, Belton, Missouri 64012, USA. ——Joanna Mary, *b* 1946: *m* 1983, Peter Gillespie, and has issue living, Giles Peter Seton, *b* 1986. *Residence* – Vicarage Farm, Halliford Rd, Sunbury on Thames, Middx.

DAUGHTER LIVING OF TENTH BARONET

Egidia Hay, *b* 1928: *m* 1st, 1948 (*m diss* 1949), her cousin, Andrew George Seton Arnot, who *d* 1988 (*see* Seton, Bt, *cr* 1663, 1980 Edn); 2ndly, 1953, Norman Haynes, and has issue living (by 2nd *m*), Hamish (40 Jessica Rd, SW18), *b* 1956: *m* 1982, Carmella Milne-Buckley, — Alasdair, *b* 1960: *m* 1993, Jane Elizabeth Bridgman. *Residence* – 2 Old Palace Terrace, Richmond, Surrey.

DAUGHTER LIVING OF ELEVENTH BARONET (*By 2nd marriage*)

Lydia Antoinette Gordon, *b* 1941: *m* 1st, 1966 (*m diss* 1981), Peter Stanley Spratt; 2ndly, 1982, Norman Victor Vine, of The Old Rectory, Church Rd, Tharston, Norfolk NR15 2YG, and has issue living (by 2nd *m*), Antony Patrick Seton, *b* 1982.

WIDOW LIVING OF TENTH BARONET

JULIA, OBE, VMH (*Julia, Lady Seton*) (122 Swan Court, Chelsea Manor St, SW3), da of late Frank Clements, OBE (Civil) 1989: *m* 1962, as his 3rd wife, Sir Alexander Hay Seton, 10th baronet, who *d* 1963.

WIDOW LIVING OF TWELFTH BARONET

JOYCE VIVIEN (*Dowager Lady Seton*), eldest da of late Oliver George Barnard, of Lockington House, Stowmarket, Suffolk: *m* 1939, Sir Christopher Bruce Seton, 12th Bt, who *d* 1988. *Residence* – Flat 1B, Papillon House, Balkerne Gdns, Colchester, Essex CO1 1PR.

COLLATERAL BRANCH LIVING

        Issue (by 2nd *m*) of late Major Henry James Seton, *b* 1854, *d* 1920: *m* 1st, 1888, Elizabeth, who *d* 1897, da of late Henry James Byron (B Byron, colls); 2ndly, 1899, Marie Bowles (who *d* 1928, having *m* 2ndly, 1922, Sir Charles George Walpole, who *d* 1926 (E Orford, colls)), da of late Percy Hale Wallace:—

Marie, *b* 1910; author of *Sergei M Eisenstein, A Biography, Portrait of a Director: Satyajit Ray,* and *Paul Robeson: m* 1942 (*m diss* 1958), Donald Louis Hesson.

  Sir Walter Seton of Abercorn, 1st Bt, was *cr* a Bt with remainder to heirs male whatsoever. The present baronet is the direct male representative of Sir Alexander Seton, who *m* Elizabeth, sister and heir of John Gordon of Gordon. She in 1408 (in conjunction with her husband) received a charter of the land of Gordon. Sir Alexander was held to have been *cr* a Lord of Parliament as Lord Gordon in or before 1429. Their son Alexander, 1st Earl of Huntly, was father (by his 1st wife, Egidia Hay) of Sir Alexander Seton, ancestor of this family, and (by his 2nd wife Elizabeth Crichton) of George Seton, late Gordon, on whom he obtained a charter to settle the Earldom. In 1923 Sir Bruce Gordon Seton, 9th Bt, CB, petitioned the Crown to admit his succession and declare his right to the title of Lord Gordon in the peerage of Scotland (*cr* in or before 1429). After a lengthy hearing the Committee for Privileges of the House of Lords, while admitting that he was heir male to Sir Alexander Seton, Dominus de Gordon (subsequently created Earl of Huntly)—eldest son of Sir Alexander—could not recognize that the evidence submitted by the petitioner established the creation and existence of the dignity. Col Sir Bruce Gordon Seton, 9th Bt, CB, in 1929 unsuccessfully claimed this Lordship before the Committee for Privileges of the House of Lords. Sir Alexander Hay Seton, 10th Bt, was Carrick Pursuivant of Arms 1935-9.

SETON (NS) 1683, of Pitmedden, Aberdeenshire

I sustain the standard with my blood

Sir CHARLES WALLACE SETON, 13th Baronet; *b* 25 Aug 1948; *s* his uncle, *Sir* JAMES CHRISTALL, 1998: *m* 1974 (*m diss* 1994), Rebecca, da of Robert Lowery.

Arms – Quarterly: 1st and 4th, or, three crescents, and in the centre a man's heart distilling blood, the whole within a double tressure flory counter-flory gules, *Seton*; 2nd and 3rd, argent, a demi-otter sable, crowned or issuing out of a bar wavy of the second, *Meldrum*. **Crest** – A demi-man in military habit holding the banner of Scotland. **Supporters** – *Dexter*, a greyhound proper, collared gules; *sinister*, an otter sable. *Residence* – 2332 15th Street, Vero Beach, Florida 32960, USA.

DAUGHTER LIVING

Jennifer, *b* 1985.

This is the sure reward of labor

BROTHER LIVING

BRUCE ANTHONY, *b* 29 April 1957: *m* 1991, Paula, da of Emmett Harper, and has issue living, Dylan Harper, *b* 1998, — Olivia, *b* 1994. *Residence* – Indianapolis, Indiana, USA.

SISTERS LIVING

      Judith Allen, *b* 1944. —— Marsha Ann, *b* 1947: *m* 1981 (*m diss* 1984), Glen Duffy, and has issue living, Steven Seton, *b* 1968. —— Terri Michele, *b* 1958: *m* 1984, William Dick, of 7418 Zimmerman Av, Apt 2, Delair, NJ 08110, USA, son of William Dick Sr, and has issue living, David, *b* 1985, — Thomas, *b* 1987, — Desire Michelle, *b* 1983.

WIDOW LIVING OF TWELFTH BARONET

EVELYN (*Evelyn, Lady Seton*), da of Ray Hafer: *m* 1939, Sir James Christall Seton, 12th Bt, who *d* 1998. *Residence* – Otterbein-Lebanon, 585 North State, Route 741, Lebanon, Ohio 45036-9551, USA.

COLLATERAL BRANCHES LIVING

      Issue of late Robert Benjamin Seton, brother of 12th baronet, *b* 1917, *d* 1993: *m* 1940, Martha Mae, who *d* 1984, da of Fred Minich:—

Karen Louise, *b* 1941: *m* 1963, Michael Conrad, of 878 Viewland, Rochester Hills, Michigan 48309, USA, and has issue living, Dennis Michael, *b* 1964: *m* 1993, Bridgett, da of John George Heal III. —— Dorothy Jean, *b* 1947: *m* 1975, Jerry L. Hill, of Johnstown, Ohio, USA.

  James Seton 1st of Pitmedden (gt grandfather of the 1st baronet) was 5th son of William Seton of Meldrum who descended from William Seton, 2nd son of Sir Alexander Seton of that ilk who *m* Elizabeth, heir of the Gordons. The

1st baronet, Sir Alexander, sat as MP for Aberdeenshire, and was subsequently a Lord of Justiciary, with the title of Lord Pitmedden. The 2nd baronet was MP for Aberdeenshire, and one of the Commissioners appointed to treat about the union of England and Scotland. Sir James Lumsden Seton, 8th Bt, was Capt 102nd Regt, and received 2nd class of Order of Iron Cross of Germany for saving life in the field during Franco-Prussian War 1870.

CULME-SEYMOUR (UK) 1809, of Highmount,co Limerick, and Friery Park, Devonshire
(Name pronounced "Cowlme-Seamer")

Faith for duty

Sir MICHAEL CULME-SEYMOUR, 5th *Baronet; h* 26 April 1909; *s* his father, *Vice-Adm Sir* MICHAEL, KCB, MVO, 1925; Cdr RN (ret 1947); *s* to the Rockingham estate upon the death of his great-uncle, Rev Wentworth Watson (*see* E Sondes, 1925 Edn), 1925, which he subsequently devised upon his nephew, Cdr L. M. M. Saunders Watson 1967 (infra); RN 1926, ADC to Gov-Gen of Canada 1934-36, served 1939-45 War, Atlantic, N Africa, Normandy, and Far East (despatches); served Imperial Defence Coll 1946-47 (ret); CC Northants 1948-55, JP 1949, DL 1958-71, High Sheriff 1966; Farmer and Landowner (Bledisloe Gold Medal 1972); active Member Contemporary Art Soc: *m* 1948, Lady (Mary) Faith (NESBITT), who *d* 1983, elder da of 9th Earl of Sandwich, and formerly wife of late Philip Booth Nesbitt, and has had issue (two sons who *d* in infancy), and has adopted his stepda.

Arms – Azure, a pair of wings conjoined in pale and surmounted of a naval crown or; on a canton argent an anchor sable. Crest – On a naval crown or, two brands in saltire inflamed at the ends proper, thereon an eagle rising, also proper, looking at the sun or. Supporters – *Dexter,* A sailor in the Royal Navy; *sinister,* a soldier of the Royal Marines holding in his exterior hand a rifle, the butt resting upon the ground, all proper. Motto – Foy pour devoir. *Residence* – Wytherston, Powerstock, Bridport, Dorset DT6 3TQ. *Club* – Brooks's.

ADOPTED STEPDAUGHTER LIVING

(Caroline) Gemma, *b* 1939: *m* 1964 (*m diss* 1976), Andrew H. Best, and has issue living, Matthew Thomas, *b* 1966, — Anna Josephine, *b* 1965. *Residence* – Sort, Wytherston, Powerstock, Dorset DT6 3TQ.

COLLATERAL BRANCHES LIVING

Issue of late Elizabeth Culme-Seymour, only da of 4th Bt, *b* 1904, *d* 1963: *m* 1933, Capt Leslie Swain Saunders, DSO, RN (ret), who *d* 1988, of South Lodge, Rockingham Castle, Market Harborough, Leics:—
Leslie Michael MacDonald SAUNDERS WATSON, CBE (Rockingham Castle, Market Harborough, Leics; Brooks's Club), *b* 1934; assumed by deed poll 1971 the surname of Saunders Watson; *ed* Eton; Chm The British Library 1990-93; Cdr RN (ret); High Sheriff of Northants 1978; CBE (Civil) 1993; DL Northants 1979; Hon DLitt, Warwick Univ: *m* 1958, Georgina Elizabeth Laetitia, da of Adm Sir William Wellclose Davis, GCB, DSO (*see* M Normanby, 1985 Edn), and has issue living, James Michael Ross, *b* 1961: *m* 1990, Elizabeth, da of Dr Christopher Brown, and has issue living, Eleanor *b* 19—, Beatrice Elizabeth Rose *b* 1997, — David William Wentworth, *b* 1968, — Fiona Jane Liebe, *b* 1965. —— Alasdair James Hew (17 The Little Boltons, SW10), *b* 1938; *ed* Eton: *m* 1974, Joanna Christina, da of Col John Offley Crewe-Read, OBE (*see* By Robins), and formerly wife of Capt John Anthony Frank Morton, late RHA, and has issue living, Thomas Alasdair, *b* 1978, — Alice Elizabeth, *b* 1975. —— Iain Ogilvy Swain, *b* 1947; *ed* Radley: *m* 1976, Roberta Ann Phoenix, of Laguna Beach, California, USA, and has issue living, Christina Ann Swain, *b* 1983. —— Elizabeth Christina, *b* 1941: *m* 1963, William Lawrence Banks, CBE, of Ridgebourne, Kington, Herefordshire, HR5 3EG, and has issue living, Richard Michael, *b* 1965: *m* 1992, Chloë Berenice Josephine Macaskie, and has issue living, William Ferdinand *b* 1995, Rose Esther Doune *b* 1998, — Edward Joseph, *b* 1967: *m* 1998, Julia Ruth Sutherland, and has issue living, Frederick Michael *b* 1999.

Granddaughter of late John Wentworth Culme-Seymour, (infra):—
Issue of late John Dennis Culme-Seymour, *b* 1923, *d* 1982: *m* 1957, (Elizabeth) Jane, who *d* 1989, da of Lt-Col Kenneth Mackessack, of Ardgye, Elgin (Craik, Bt ext):—
Caroline, *b* 1959.

Issue of late John Wentworth Culme-Seymour, 2nd son of 3rd baronet, *b* 1876, *d* 1962: *m* 1918, Evelyn Mary, who *d* 1977, da of late C. A. Smith-Ryland, of Barford, Warwick:—
Jane, *b* 1925: *m* 1959, Com John Hocken Joughin, DSC, RN, who *d* 1986. *Residence* - Flat 2, 11 St Fimbarrus Rd, Fowey, Cornwall, PL23 1JJ.

Grandchildren of late Capt George Culme-Seymour (infra):—
Issue of late Maj Mark Charles Culme-Seymour, *b* 1910, *d* 1990: *m* 1st, 1935 (*m diss* 1938), Babette, only child of late David Llewelyn Patric-Jones; 2ndly, 1941 (*m diss* 1949), Princesse Hélène Marie de la Trémoïlle, 3rd da of Prince Louis Charles Marie, 12th Duc de Thouars, Prince and 11th Duc de la Trémoïlle, Premier Duc de France, 12th Prince de Tarente, and 15th Prince de Talmond, and formerly wife of Sir (William) Campbell Mitchell-Cotts, 2nd Bt; 3rdly, 1956 (*m diss* 1967), Patricia June, da of late Charles Reid-Graham, and widow of Geoffrey Edward Ansell; 4thly, 1973, Mary Darrall, only da of late Leander Armistead Riely, of Oklahoma City, USA, and widow of Philip Kidd:—
(By 3rd *m*) MICHAEL PATRICK (Swissair, 435 Orchard Rd No18-04, Wisma Atria, Singapore), *b* 28 April 1962; Regional Vice-Pres Swissair, Asia, Pacific and India: *m* 1986, Karin Fleig, and has issue living, Michael, *b* 1986, — Julian, *b* 1988. —— Miranda CULME-SEYMOUR (7311 Waring Av, Los Angeles, CA 90046, USA), *b* 1959; has retained her maiden name: *m* 1990, Jonathan Fuller. —— Sarah Louise, *b* 1961: *m* 1990, Laurence Stewart Treloar, of 30 Canoon Rd, S Turramurra, NSW 2074, Australia, and has issue living, Hugh Michael James, *b* 1995, — Alice Patricia, *b* 1991.

Issue of late Capt George Culme-Seymour, 3rd son of 3rd baronet, *b* 1878, who was *ka* 1915: *m* 1909, Janet Beatrix (who *d* 1943, having *m* 2ndly, 1918, Rev Geoffrey Harold Woolley, VC, MC, Chap to Forces, Chap at Harrow Sch, formerly Capt London Regt (TA)), da of late Charles Lindsay Orr Ewing, MP (Ewing, Bt colls):—
Angela Mary, *b* 1912: *m* 1st, 1934 (*m diss* 1938) John George Spencer Churchill, who *d* 1992 (*see* D Marlborough, colls); 2ndly, 1938 (*m diss* 1942), 3rd Baron Kinross, who *d* 1976; 3rdly, 1948 (*m diss* 19-), Count René de Chatellus; 4thly, 1977, Mehmet Ali Bulent Rauf, who *d* 1987. *Residence* – 90 Vicarage Court, Vicarage Gate, W8 4HQ.

Issue of late Major Henry Hobart Culme-Seymour, 3rd son of 2nd baronet, *b* 1847, *d* 1920: *m* 1878, Kate, who *d* 1931, da of William Charles Lucy:—
Violet Katharine Maria, *b* 1891: *m* 1926, Charles de la Cour Le Maistre, CBE, who *d* 1953.

Granddaughters of late Cdr Evelyn Culme-Seymour, RN (infra):—
Issue of late Lt-Cdr Gerald Henry Hobart Culme-Seymour, RN, *b* 1914, *d* 1973: *m* 1st, 1939, Constance Helen, who *d* 1959, da of late Alfred Rendell Street (Dashwood, Bt, *cr* 1684); 2ndly, 1960, Patricia Mary (Well Cottage, Cartmel, Cumbria LA11 6PP), eldest da of late Edward Pearson Hewetson, JP, of 15 Glebelands, Brampton, Oxon, and formerly wife of 3rd Viscount Cross:—
(By 1st *m*) Victoria, *b* 1940: *m* 1963, Manouchehr Haeri, of 625 Main St, #1130, New York, NY 10044, USA, and has issue living, David, *b* 1967, — Mina (41 Gowrie Rd, SW11 5NN) *b* 1964, — Sophia Helen, *b* 1978. —— Anne Evelyn, *b* 1941: *m* 1st, 1961 (*m diss* 1970) John Lang Mangles Denham; 2ndly, 1972, (David) Michael (Richard Cecil) Allen, of Kidmore House, Kidmore End, Oxon, and has issue living (by 1st *m*), James Henry Seymour, *b* 1964: *m* 1996, Katharine Dunning, — Alexandra Sophia, *b* 1966 — (by 2nd *m*), Louisa Chelsea, *b* 1975. —— Catherine, *b* 1945: *m* 1972, Christopher James Munro Hartley, of Lavethan, Blisland, Bodmin, Cornwall, and has issue living, Melissa Charlotte Victoria, *b* 1974, — Victoria Elizabeth Anne, *b* 1978. —— Alexandra, *b* 1953: *m* 1975, Simon Webb, of 7 Burlington Rd, Redland, Bristol BS6 6TJ, and has issue living, Rowland Henry, *b* 1978, — Clementine Laura, *b* 1982. —— (By 2nd *m*) Caroline Eve, *b* 1961: *m* 1996, Rupert Spira, of Church Farm, More, Bishops Castle, Shropshire SY9 5HH.

Granddaughter of late Maj Henry Hobart Culme-Seymour (ante):—
Issue of late Cdr Evelyn Culme-Seymour, RN, *b* 1881, *d* 1970: *m* 1908, Laura Maude Amy, who *d* 1958, da of late Sir Steuart Macnaghten (Macnaghten, Bt colls):—
Patience Ann (17 Child's St, SW5 9RY), *b* 1912: *m* 1939 (*m diss* 1951), Lt-Cdr David Robert Fremantle, RNVR, who *d* 1989, and has issue (*see* B Cottesloe, colls).

Grandchildren of late Rev Richard Seymour (*b* 1877) (infra):—
Issue of late Com John Richard Arthur Seymour, OBE, DSC, RN, *b* 1905, *d* 1957: *m* 1941, Helen Augusta (who *d* 1988, having *m* 2ndly, 1973, John Edward Francis Rawlins, who *d* 1991), da of late Lt-Col Richard Edmund Corydon Luxmoore-Ball, DSO, DCM, Welsh Guards:—
Richard Paul (Sunnybrook Cottage, Lyatts Hill, Hardington Mandeville, Yeovil, Som BA22 9NR), *b* 1943; Cdr RN; AFC: *m* 1971, Valerie Ann, da of P. L. Foulsham, and has issue living, Alexander John, *b* 1974, — Mark Richard, *b* 1980. —— Anthony John, *b* 1946.

Issue of late Michael Ernest Seymour, *b* 1906, *d* 1973: *m* 1931, Gwendoline Arran, who *d* 1993, da of William Stuart Gore (*see* E Arran, colls):—
Eleanor, *b* 1932: *m* 1953, John Ferrari, of 57 McArthur St, Guildford 2161, NSW, Australia, and has issue living, Timothy John (45 Tenth Av, Oyster, Bay 2225, NSW, Australia) *b* 1954: *m* 1980, Christine Elizabeth Hanson, and has issue living, Jillian Elizabeth *b* 1984, Emma Elise *b* 1988, — Michele Jane, *b* 1958: *m* 1979, Ronald Arthur Adam, of 6 Arthur Street, Blacktown 2148, NSW, Australia, and has issue living, Mathew James *b* 1985.

Granddaughter of late Ven Albert Eden Seymour, son of late Rev Richard Seymour, 5th son of 1st baronet:—
Issue of late Rev Richard Seymour, *b* 1877, *d* 1958: *m* 1903, Annie Louisa Mary, who *d* 1909, da of late W. E. Arthur, JP, formerly of Marwood Hill, Barnstaple, Devon:—
Ruth Mary (18 Wilder Park, Horne Rd, Ilfracombe, Devon EX34 8HH), *b* 1909: *m* 1939 (*m diss* 1949), Wilfrid Harold Gillard, and has issue living, John Michael Patrick, *b* 1940.

Grandsons of late Edward Albert Seymour, MB (infra):—
Issue of late Edward Richard Fortescue Seymour, *b* 1915; *d* 1981: *m* 1943, Margaret Eileen (48 Military Rd, Rye, Sussex TN31 7NY), da of late Maj Grantham Dodd, TD, RAMC:—
Edward Grantham (4 Rue du Pont, L-5355 Oetrange, Luxembourg GD), *b* 1945: *m* 1969, Philippa Rosalie Jane, da of Geoffrey Mollet, of Henley-on-Thames, and has issue living, Edward Hugo, *b* 1979, — Guinevere Jane, *b* 1974: *m* 1998, Philip Webster, of 6 Charles St, Oxford OX4 3AS, — Susanna Rosalie, *b* 1977, — Augustina Maria, *b* 1981. —— Charles Adrian (3 Stocklands Close, Cuckfield, Sussex), *b* 1947: *m* 1970, Sylvia Ellen, da of late A. Kimber, of Hurstpierpoint, Sussex, and has issue living, Brendan Charles, *b* 1980, — Richard Edward, *b* 1982. —— (Michael) Shaughan (4

Chelsham Rd, Clapham, SW4 6NP), *b* 1949: *m* 1975, Jane Constance Madeleine, da of late James Lytton, and has issue living, Toby James Edward, *b* 1982, — Zoë Jane, *b* 1978, — Lucy Margaret, *b* 1980. —— Gervais Richard Hugh (179 Oundle Rd, Woodston, Peterborough PE2 9QZ), *b* 1952: *m* 1st, 1973 (*m diss* 1984), Ann Shirley Trowbridge; 2ndly, 1984, Victoria Louise, da of Robert Brewer, of Newborough, Cambs, and has issue living (by 1st *m*), Rebecca Ann, *b* 1980, — (by 2nd *m*) Thomas Christopher Gervais, *b* 1984, — Ellena Victoria, *b* 1986, — and two adopted das, Joanna Claire Marie, *b* 1978, — Michaella Jayne, *b* 1980. —— James Quentin (1 Shepherd's Way, Cirencester, Glos GL7 2EY), *b* 1953: *m* 1979, Rosemary Yvonne, da of Lt-Cdr Peter Hampson Wailes, RN (ret), of Thetford, Norfolk, and has issue living, Michael James, *b* 1980, — Alice Victoria, *b* 1982.

Granddaughters of late Ven Albert Eden Seymour (ante):—
Issue of late Edward Albert Seymour, MB, *b* 1884, *d* 1946: *m* 1914, Gwendolen Emily, who *d* 1980, da of late Rev William Birch Gascoigne, formerly R of Wood Eaton, Oxfordshire:—
Hester Mary, *b* 1917, *d* 1995. —— Joyce Eleanor, *b* 1918. *Residence* – 52 Lombard Court, Old Portsmouth, Hants PO1 2HU.

Issue of late Very Rev Algernon Giles Seymour, *b* 1886, *d* 1933: *m* 1921, Ida Grace, who *d* 1971, da of late Vice-Adm Robert Frederick Hammick (*see* Hammick, Bt):—
Mary-Grace (*Mary-Grace, Lady Hutchison*), MBE, *b* 1924; MBE (Civil) 1999: *m* 1949, Sir Peter Hutchison, 2nd Bt, who *d* 1998. *Residence* – Melton Mead, nr Woodbridge, Suffolk.

Grandsons of late Very Rev Algernon Giles Seymour (ante):—
Issue of late Cdr Timothy Maurice Barnabas Seymour, RN, *b* 1932, *d* 1975: *m* 1954, Monica (5 Tarleton Gardens, SE23), da of late Rt Rev Wilfred Arthur Westall, Bishop of Crediton:—
Michael Nicholas, *b* 1960. —— Charles Richard, *b* 1963: *m* 1992, Deborah Miller.

The 1st baronet, Adm Sir Michael Seymour, KCB, when in command of the "Amethyst" frigate on the night of 10 Nov 1808, fell in with the French frigate "La Thetis" off L'Orient, which, after a gallant resistance, was captured. This action, for gallantry, skill, and courage, has scarcely been equalled. George III signified his approbation by presenting him with a gold medal, and Lloyd's Patriotic Fund voted him 100 guineas. The 2nd baronet assumed by Roy licence in 1842 the additional surname of Culme to perpetuate the name of his first wife, which would otherwise have become extinct. The 3rd baronet, Adm Sir Michael, GCB, GCVO, served during Crimean War 1854-55, and commanded Pacific Station 1885-7, the Channel Squadron 1890-92, and the Mediterranean Fleet 1893-6, and was Com-in-Ch at Portsmouth 1897-1900, Principal Naval ADC* to HM Queen Victoria 1899-1901, and to HM King Edward VII: Vice-Adm of Great Britain and Ireland, and Lieut of Admiralty thereof 1901-20. He married Mary Georgiana, da of Hon Richard Watson of Rockingham Castle (son of 2nd Baron Sondes). This estate was inherited by the 5th Bt in 1925. The 4th baronet, Vice-Adm Sir Michael Culme-Seymour, KCB, MVO, who commanded HMS *Centurion* at battle of Jutland 1916, was Director of Mobilizations 1916-18, Comdg British Ægean Squadron 1918-19, British Naval Forces in Black Sea, Sea of Marmara, and Caspian Sea 1919-20, 2nd in command Mediterranean 1920-23, Com-in-Ch N America and W Indies 1923-4, and Second Sea Lord of the Admiralty and Ch of Naval Personnel 1924-5.

*In which capacity Adm Sir Michael was in charge of the transportation of the Queen's body from Osbourne to Windsor Castle. When the procession reached the steep hill within the castle walls, the horses pulling the gun-carriage slipped on the icy ground, and bolted, breaking the traces, whereupon the gun carriage bearing the Queen's coffin threatened to run back into the procession. The Admiral ordered the naval contingent to take up the traces by hand, which was done with great efficiency, and a serious disaster was averted. In recognition of this, the Admiral was granted supporters to his arms by Royal Licence 1913, in perpetuity.

SHAKERLEY (UK) 1838, of Somerford Park, Cheshire

Sir GEOFFREY ADAM SHAKERLEY, 6th *Baronet*; *b* 9 Dec 1932; *s* his father, *Maj Sir* CYRIL HOLLAND, 1970; *ed* Harrow and Trin Coll, Oxford; late 2nd Lt KRRC dir of Photographic Records Ltd since 1970; *m* 1st, 1962, Virginia Elizabeth, who *d* 1968, el da of W. E. Maskell, of Little Down, Bury, Sussex; 2ndly, 1972, Lady Elizabeth Georgiana Anson, da of late Thomas William Arnold, Viscount Anson (*see* E Lichfield), and has issue by 1st and 2nd *m*.

Arms – Argent, a chevron between three hillocks vert. Crest – A hare rampant sable supporting a garb or.
Residence – Brent House, N Warnborough, Hants RG29 1BE.

SONS LIVING (*By 1st marriage*)

NICHOLAS SIMON ADAM, *b* 20 Dec 1963. —— Peter Jonathan, *b* 1966.

DAUGHTER LIVING (*By 2nd marriage*)

Fiona Elizabeth Fenella, *b* 1973.

BROTHER LIVING

Charles Frederick Eardley (Cudworth Manor, Newdigate, Surrey RH5 5BH), *b* 1934; *ed* Harrow, and Ch Ch, Oxford: *m* 1962, Lucy Carolyn, el da of Francis St G. Fisher, of Cragg, Cockermouth, Cumbria, and has issue living, Eleanor Jane, *b* 1963, — Victoria Lee, *b* 1965: *m* 1990, Maj Charles William Nepean Crewdson, 9th/12th Royal Lancers (Prince of Wales's), son of John Crewdson, of Winster House, Winster, Windermere, Westmorland, — Philippa Patricia Alice, *b* 1970: *m* 1997, Maj William A. Grace, yr son of Antony Grace, of Frampton, Dorset, and has issue living, Matilda Imogen *b* 1998.

SISTER LIVING

Jane Eve, *b* 1930: *m* 1963, David William Phillips, of The Old Rectory, Stedham, Midhurst, Sussex, and has issue living, Katherine Elizabeth, *b* 1966: *m* 1992, Leonard J. Wadstein, of Cannes, France, and has issue living, Alexander James *b* 1996, Georgina *b* 19—.

COLLATERAL BRANCH LIVING

Grandchildren of late Major Ernest Alfred SHAKERLEY-HOWELL, 3rd son of 2nd baronet:—
Issue of late Col Peter Francis Shakerley, OBE, *b* 1906, *d* 1994: *m* 1934, Alison May, who *d* 1992, da of late Alexander Sands, of Aberdeen:—
(Geoffrey) Clive Howell (Tredudwell Manor, Lanteglos by Fowey, Cornwall) *b* 1935; *ed* Radley, and St Edmund Hall, Oxford (BA): *m* 1965, Rosanna Ruth, da of late Thomas P. Barneby, of The Hill, Duloe, Cornwall, and has issue living, Alastair Justin Charles, *b* 1972, — Alison Clare, *b* 1970. —— (Peter) Gavin David (Pont House, Lanteglos-by-Fowey, Cornwall), *b* 1950; *ed* Radley, and Durham Univ (BA); Maj IG: *m* 1976, Margaret Ann, da of Bernard Hammond, of Chichester, and has issue living, Charles Alaister, *b* 1981, — Antonia Elizabeth, *b* 1983. —— Angela Madeleine (1 Arthur St, Seacliff Park, S Australia 5049), *b* 1938: *m* 1st, 1958 (*m diss* 1978), William Trevor Stephens; 2ndly, 1978, Harry Dudley Phillips, who *d* 1982; 3rdly, 1987, Valentino Greck, and has issue living (by 1st *m*) Richard Gwyn, *b* 1961: *m* 1995, Leanne, da of Peter Woods, — John Angelo, *b* 1963: *m* 1984, Elizabeth Louise, da of late Peter V. Walter, and has issue living, Matthew John *b* 1987, Sean Adam *b* 1989, Catherine Louise *b* 1993, — David Paul, *b* 1965: *m* 1983, Michelle Anne, da of Jack Bunfield, and has issue living, Rebecca Jane *b* 1984, Jessica Louise *b* 1987, — Teresa Madeleine, *b* 1959: *m* 1996, Kurt Fitzpatrick, son of John Fitzpatrick, — and an adopted son and da, Patrick Joseph, *b* 1962: *m* 1995, Kerrie Louise, da of Gary Douglas, and has issue living, Caitlin Jayne *b* 1998, — Sandie Patricia, *b* 1966; has issue living (by Neil Barham), Bianca Lee *b* 1984, Melissa Jayne *b* 1986, (by Shane Tugwell) Rhianna Sue *b* 1989, — (by 2nd *m*) Harry Sydney, *b* 1977. —— Dawn Michelle Alison, *b* 1942: *m* 1965 (legally separated 1984), Peter Joseph Knight, of 21D Russell Crescent, Rotorua, NZ, and has issue living, Timothy William Francis, *b* 1968, — Karen Francesca, *b* 1966: *m* 1986, Richard Mallinson, and has issue living, James Sean *b* 1992, Kate Judith *b* 1994, — Sarah Melody Foye, *b* 1969: *m* 1991, Christopher Bramwell Jans, and has issue living, Danielle Frances *b* 1989, Zoe-Rose *b* 1995.

SHAKESPEARE (UK) 1942, of Lakenham, City of Norwich

(*Sir*) THOMAS WILLIAM SHAKESPEARE, 3rd *Baronet*; *b* 11 May 1966; *s* his father, *Sir* WILLIAM GEOFFREY, 1996, but does not use the title; *ed* Radley, Pembroke Coll, Camb (BA 1987, MA 1990), and King's Coll, Camb (MPhil 1990, PhD 1995); Research Fellow in Sociology, Leeds Univ since 1996; Member Northern Arts Board 1995-99; co-author *Sexual Politics of Disability: Untold Desires* (1996), and *Exploring Disability* (1999); editor *The Disability Reader* (1998); has issue.

Arms – Or, on a bend between in chief a portcullis and in base an anchor sable, a spear of the field. Crest – In front of a portcullis sable an eagle rising, grasping with the dexter claw a spear or, barbed argent.
Residence – 13 Wood Terrace, Bill Quay, Gateshead, Tyne and Wear NE10 0UD.

SON LIVING (*by Judy Brown*)

Robert Samuel BROWN, *b* (Nov) 1988.

DAUGHTER LIVING (*by Lucy Anne Broadhead*)

Ivy Connor BROADHEAD, *b* (June) 1988.

BROTHER LIVING

Rev JAMES DOUGLAS GEOFFREY, *b* 12 Feb 1971; *ed* Radley, Fitzwilliam Coll, Camb (BA 1993, MA 1997), and Manchester Univ (MA 1996); Curate, St John the Evangelist Church, Cambridge: *m* 1996, Alison Jean, da of Martin Lusby, of Manchester. *Residence* – 46 Holbrook Rd, Cambridge CB1 7ST.

WIDOW LIVING OF FIRST BARONET

ELIZABETH (*Elizabeth, Lady Shakespeare*) (36 Clare Park, Crondall, nr Farnham, Surrey GU10 5DT), da of late Brig-Gen Robert William Hare, CMG, DSO, DL (*see* E Listowel, colls); Section Offr WAAF 1940-45 (despatches, Bronze Star of USA); Freeman of City of London 1974: *m* 1952, as his 2nd wife, Rt Hon Sir Geoffrey Hithersay Shakespeare, 1st Bt, who *d* 1980.

WIDOW LIVING OF SECOND BARONET

SUSAN MARY (*Lady Shakespeare*), da of late A. Douglas Raffel, of Colombo, Ceylon: *m* 1964, Sir William Geoffrey Shakespeare, 2nd Bt, who *d* 1996. *Residence* – Manor Cottage, Stoke Mandeville, Aylesbury, Bucks HP22 5XA.

The 1st baronet, Rt Hon Sir Geoffrey Hithersay Shakespeare, sat as MP for Wellingborough (*L*) 1922-23, and Norwich 1929-45; also Parliamentary and Financial Sec to Admiralty 1937-40, Parliamentary Sec to Dept of Overseas Trade April-May 1940, and Under-Sec of State for Dominion Affairs and Chm of Children's Overseas Reception Board May 1940 - March 1942. The second baronet, Sir William Geoffrey Shakespeare, was a GP Aylesbury 1968-86, Hospital Practitioner, Manor House Hosp, Aylesbury 1972-96, and was previously Registrar St George's Hosp and Stoke Mandeville Hosp, Member Snowdon Working Party into Integration of Handicapped 1974-76, Vice-Pres Nat PHAB 1977-96, and Vice-Pres Restricted Growth Assocn 1982-96. Trustee Shakespeare's Globe Theatre 1990-96.

SHARP (UK) 1920, of Heckmondwike, West Riding, co York

I strive till I overcome

(*Sir*) SHERIDAN CHRISTOPHER ROBIN SHARP, 4th *Baronet*, only son of late Reginald Sharp, 3rd son of 1st baronet; *b* 25 April 1936; assumed the forenames of Sheridan Christopher Robin in lieu of Samuel Christopher Reginald by deed poll 1971; *s* his cousin, *Maj Sir* MILTON REGINALD, 1996 (although his name does not appear on the Official Roll of the Baronetage, nor does he use the title); *ed* Rugby: *m* 1st 1958 (*m diss* 1967, and annulled 1971), Sheila Aileen, da of J. Denzil Moodie, of Campbell's Bay, Quebec; 2ndly, 1969, Anna Maria, da of NH Saverio Rossi, of Rome, and has issue by 2nd *m*.

ᴀrms – Azure, on a fesse engrailed argent between two plates, a torteaux between two pheons gules. Crest – In front of a pheon sable, an eagle's head erased azure, charged with a cross-crosslet or.
Residences – The Old Pavilion, Whiteway, nr Stroud, Glos GL6 7ER; 5 Harrowby Court, Harrowby St, W1H 5FA.

SON LIVING (*By 2nd marriage*)

FABIAN ALEXANDER SEBASTIAN, *b* 5 Nov 1973; *ed* City of London Sch, and Univ Coll, London (BA 1997).

DAUGHTER LIVING (*By 2nd marriage*)

Leonora Nicola, *b* 1970.

SISTERS LIVING

Caroline Eve, *b* 1944: *m* 1970 (*m diss* 1981), Richard Anthony Sheldon, and has issue living, Saul Christopher Alaric, *b* 1970, — Nicholas Hugh Alexander, *b* 1972. *Residence* – May Cottage, Wells Rd, Eastcombe, nr Stroud, Glos GL6 7EE. —— Rosemary Anne, *b* 1946. *Residence* – 55 Richmond Rd, Twickenham, Middx TW1 3AW.

MOTHER DECEASED

Doris Eve (known latterly as Mrs Eve Langtry), da of Henry Saville Faulder: *m* 1933 (*m diss* 1958), as his 2nd wife, Reginald Sharp, who *d* 1969, and *d* 1985.

COLLATERAL BRANCHES LIVING

Grandson of late Herbert Sharp, 4th son of 1st baronet:—
Issue of late John Herbert Sharp, *b* 1920, *d* 1992: *m* 1st, 19—, ...; 2ndly, 19—, ...; 3rdly, 1953, Lily, da of Edward Hassam:—
(By 3rd *m*) John Henry-Edward, *b* 1965.

Issue of late Harold (Jack) Sharp, 6th son of 1st baronet, *b* 1895, *d* 1965: *m* 19—, —, da of —Lister:—
Jack (3 Newstead Av, Bushby, Leics LE7 9QE), *b* 1932. —— Barbara Elizabeth, *b* 1931.

Sir Milton Sheridan Sharp, 1st Bt, was Chm Bradford Dyers Asso Ltd.

SHARP (UK) 1922, of Warden Court, Maidstone, Kent

Sir ADRIAN SHARP, 4th *Baronet*; *b* 17 Sept 1951; *s* his father, *Sir* EDWARD HERBERT, 1985; *ed* Boxhill Sch, and Nat Business Coll, Cape Town; Exec Mgr Toyota Motor Co: *m* 1st, 1976 (*m diss* 1986), Hazel Patricia, only da of James Trevor Wallace, of Box 2574, Pietersburg, S Africa, and formerly wife of William Ian Barrett Bothwell; 2ndly, 1994, Denise, only da of Percy Edward Roberts, of Ironbridge, Shropshire, and has issue by 2nd *m*.

Arms – Argent, on a fesse indented between two falcons' heads erased sable, three pheons or. Crest – Upon a mount vert a falcon rising proper, belled and resting the dexter claw upon a pheon or.
Residence – 91 Pentz Drive, Flamingovlei, Table View, Cape Town, S Africa.

SON LIVING (*By 2nd marriage*)

HAYDEN SEAN, *b* 27 Aug 1994.

BROTHER LIVING

Owen, *b* 1956; *ed* Waterford, Swaziland, and Durham Univ: *m* 1980, Caroline, da of late Jerrard Collings Van Beuge, of Durban, Natal, S Africa, and has issue living, Declan, *b* 1980, — Lyndall, *b* 1983. *Residence* – Ballito, Natal, S Africa.

Victory in truth

SISTER LIVING

Terry, *b* 1950: *m* 1969, Ian Wilson, of La Lucia, Durban, Natal, S Africa, son of Ennis Wilson, of Ashtead, Surrey, and has issue living, Karen, *b* 1969, — Tracey, *b* 1971, — Lee, *b* 1972.

COLLATERAL BRANCH LIVING

Issue of late Wilfred James Sharp, 2nd son of 1st baronet, *b* 1880, *d* 1945: *m* 1909, Ada Frances, who *d* 1936, da of George Meek, of Beckenham:—
Edward Harold Wilfred, *b* 1910; Past Chm of Edward Sharp & Sons Ltd, Manufacturing Confectioners. *Residence* – Brymere, Norton Rd, Chart Sutton, Maidstone, Kent.

The 1st baronet, Sir Edward, was Founder and Chm of Edward Sharp & Sons Ltd, manufacturing confectioners of Maidstone.

SHAW (UK) 1821, of Bushy Park, Dublin

Sir ROBERT SHAW, 7th *Baronet*; *b* 31 Jan 1925; *s* his father, *Lt-Col Sir* ROBERT DE VERE, MC, 1969; *ed* Harrow, and Oklahoma (BS) and Missouri (MS) Univs; Professional Engineer (Alberta); Lt RN (ret); 1939-45 War in NW Europe, and W Pacific: *m* 1954, Jocelyn Mary, da of late Andrew McGuffie, of Mbabane, Swaziland, and has issue.

Arms – Or, on a chevron engrailed sable, between three eagles displayed of the second, as many trefoils slipped of the first. Crest – A hart's head couped sable, transfixed through the neck with an arrow or, feathered argent.
Residence – 234 40th Av, Calgary, Alberta, Canada. *Club* – Alberta United Services Institute (Calgary).

DAUGHTERS LIVING

Grania, *b* 1955. —— Reinet, *b* 1960.

COLLATERAL BRANCHES LIVING

Issue of late Capt John Frederick de Vere Shaw, Kenya Regt, yr son of 6th baronet, *b* 1930, *d* 1960: *m* 1955, Penelope Ann, who *m* 2ndly, 1970, Hougham Robert Mills (PO Box 628, Umtentweni, 4235 Natal, S Africa), da of Maj Denis William Powlett Milbank (*see* Milbank, Bt):—
CHARLES DE VERE (Pigeon Farmhouse, Greenham, Newbury, Berks RG19 8SP), *b* 1 March 1957; *ed* Michaelhouse, S Africa; Maj 5th R Inniskilling Drag Gds 1975-87; businessman: *m* 1985, Sonia, elder da of Thomas Geoffrey Eden, of Dean Cottage, 23 The Street, Wrecclesham, nr Farnham, Surrey, and has issue living, Robert Jonathan de Vere, *b* 7 Aug 1988, — Alexandra Frances, *b* 1986. —— Jane Frances, *b* 1958. —— Ann Vivian, *b* 1960.

Te ipsum nosce
Know thyself

Issue of late Lieut-Col Frederick Charleton Shaw, OBE, 2nd son of 5th baronet, *b* 1895, *d* (on active service in Germany) 1945: *m* 1922, Angela (SEWALL), who *d* 1978, da of late Ricardo de Acosta:—
Mercedes Eile, *b* 1926: *m* 1956, Capt Miles Matthew Lee Hudson, 12th R Lancers, of The Priors Farm, Mattingly Green, Basingstoke, and has issue living, Mark John Frederick, *b* 1957, — Peter Charles, *b* 1960, — Richard Miles, *b* 1966, — Veronica Mary, *b* 1958.

Granddaughter of late Maj-Gen George Shaw, CB, 2nd son of 3rd baronet:—
Issue of late Frederick Shaw, *b* 1850, *d* 1928: *m* 1873, Ella Jane, da of William Willis, of USA:—
Cora Desfontaines: *m* 1909, Charles Abner Howard, LLD. *Residence* –

Grandson of late Lt-Col Wilkinson Jocelyn Shaw, 5th son of 3rd baronet:—
Issue of late Major Jocelyn Frederick de Fonblanque Shaw, *b* 1874, *d* 1936: *m* 1921, May Alberta, who *d* 1930, da of late Robert Cecil Kenward:—
Jocelyn Frederick Basil, *b* 1923; *ed* Wellington, King's Coll, London, and Miami Univ (PhD); Consulting Engineer: *m* 1964 (*m diss* 1971), Carolyn Ann, da of late Samuel Bexton Guynes, of Waco, Texas, and has issue living, Jocelyn Robert Guynes, *b* 1965, — John Frederick Darin, *b* 1967, — Edward Henry David, *b* 1969.

Granddaughter of late Charles Shaw, QC, 5th son of 1st baronet:—
Issue of late William Shaw, *b* 1857, *d* 1939: *m* 1889, Roxanna Massie, da of James Henry Bowles:—
Emily Newell, *b* 1902: *m* 1921, Charles Franklin Jenness, and has issue living, Charles Franklin, *b* 1924, — Stuart Barton, *b* 1928, — Barbara Claire, *b* 1932. *Residence* – 5621 Randall Avenue, Richmond, Virginia, USA.

The 1st baronet, Sir Robert, sat in the Irish Parliament for New Ross, and for Dublin in the Imperial Parliament 1804-26; the 3rd baronet, who was Recorder of Dublin 1828-76, and a PC of Ireland, sat as MP for Dublin (*C*) 1830-32, and for University of Dublin 1832-48.

SHAW (UK) 1908, of Wolverhampton, co Stafford (Extinct 1942)

Sir (THEODORE FREDERICK) CHARLES EDWARD SHAW, 1st and last *Baronet*.

DAUGHTER LIVING OF FIRST BARONET

Vera Stafford, *b* 1901: *m* 1922, Charles Bradshaw Shard, formerly Lieut 14th Hussars, and has issue living, Charles William George, *b* 1927, — Johane Dawson, *b* 1925.

BEST-SHAW (E) 1665, of Eltham, Kent

Sir JOHN MICHAEL ROBERT BEST-SHAW, 10th *Baronet, b* 28 Sept 1924; *s* his father, *Com Sir* JOHN JAMES KENWARD, RN, 1984; *ed* Lancing, Hertford Coll, Oxford (BA 1950, MA 1954), and Lond Univ (Cert of Ed); formerly Capt Queen's Own R West Kent Regt; R Federation of Malaya Police Force 1950-58; WW II 1942-45 (three medals); Church work 1959-71, teacher 1972-82: *m* 1960, Jane Gordon, 2nd da of Alexander Gordon Guthrie, of Hampton Court House, Farningham, Kent, and has issue.

Arms – Quarterly, 1st and 4th argent, a chevron between three fusils ermines, *Shaw;* 2nd and 3rd sable, a cinquefoil pierced, and in chief two cross-crosslets fitchée or, *Best.* **Crests** – 1st, six arrows interlaced, saltirewise or, tied together with belt gules, the buckle and pendant or; 2nd, issuing out of a mural crown or, a demi-ostrich argent holding in the beak a cross-crosslet fitchée or.
Residence – Belmont, 104 High St, W Malling, Maidstone, Kent ME19 6NE. *Club* – R Commonwealth Soc.

SONS LIVING

THOMAS JOSHUA, *b* 7 March 1965; *ed* Maidstone Gram Sch, and Reading Univ (BSc 1987); Surveyor: *m* 1992, Emily Susan, da of Vivian Rubin, of Wateringbury, Kent, and has issue living, Joshua John Kirkland, *b* 17 Jan 1995, — William Vivian Guthrie, *b* 1997. —— Samuel Stevenson, *b* 1971; *ed* Maidstone Gram Sch, and Exeter Coll, Oxford (BA 1992, MA 1997); Financial Analyst; *m* 1997, Elena, da of late Michail Arch, of St Petersburg, Russia.

DAUGHTER LIVING

Lucy Ann (73 Otley Old Rd, Lawnswood, Leeds, W Yorks LS16 6HG), *b* 1961; *ed* Bedgebury Park, and Maidstone Sch for Girls; RNMH 1986: *m* 1985 (*m diss* 1989), Terence Wentworth-Wood, and has issue living, Alexander, *b* 1985, — Christina Lily, *b* 1987.

BROTHERS LIVING

Charles John Hughes (Cornerfield House, The Hill, Charing, Ashford, Kent TN27 0LU), *b* 1928: *m* 1971, Carol Mary, 2nd da of late Joseph Martin Drew, and has issue living, Helen Mary Elizabeth, *b* 1972; *ed* Ashford Sch, and St Chad's Coll, Durham Univ (BSc 1994, MA 1996). —— Stephen Bosanquet (Boxley Abbey, Maidstone, Kent), *b* 1935: *m* 1964, Elizabeth Annette Freda, yst da of late Gerald Baldwin Hayward, MBE, of Athens, and has issue living, James Robert Hawley, *b* 1965: *m* 1992, Charlotte Louise, 2nd da of Nigel Ashley, of Mijas, Spain, and has issue living, Harry *b* 1996, — Hugh Edward Gerald, *b* 1975, — Louisa Margaret Aylmer *b* 1967: *m* 1988 (*m diss* 1998), Andrew Charles Robert Beale, son of Robert Beale, of Wellington Sq, SW3, and has issue living, Freddie James Robert *b* 1993, Roseanna Mary Elizabeth *b* 1991, Polly Theodora *b* 1997.

SISTERS LIVING

Mary Elisabeth Helen (Jonstone West, Egerton, Ashford, Kent TN27 9DR), *b* 1922; a JP of Kent: *m* 1st, 1943, Patrick Henry Coates, late Capt RA, who *d* 1949; 2ndly, 1968, John Melliar Adams-Beck, who *d* 1979, and has issue living, (by 1st *m*) David Carlyon (Mark's Farmhouse, Bramshaw, Lyndhurst, Hants), *b* 1944; FRICS: *m* 1970, Lavinia Jane, da of Alan O'Connor-Fenton, and has issue living, Emma Mary *b* 1973, Alice Julia *b* 1975, Georgina Ruth *b* 1980, — Simon Patrick (Rectory Farm, Raddington, Taunton, Som), *b* 1948; JP Som: *m* 1979, Katherine Jane, 2nd da of late Maj Richard Hodgkinson Jessop, IA (ret), and has issue living, Thomas George Carlyon *b* 1981, Nicholas Henry Jessop *b* 1983. —— Julia Aylmer (Boxley Abbey, Maidstone, Kent), *b* 1923; 1939-45 War in WRNS. —— Hermione Theodora (Boxley Abbey, Maidstone, Kent), *b* 1926. —— Martha Mary (Boxley Abbey, Maidstone, Kent), *b* 1934.

COLLATERAL BRANCHES LIVING

Grandchildren of late Rev Robert John Shaw, son of late Rev Robert William Shaw, 5th son of 5th baronet:—
Issue of late Lewis Hugh de Visme Shaw, *b* 1865, *d* 1931: *m* 1901, Edith Mary, who *d* 1929, da of late Capt John Smyth Nelson, S Staffordshire Regt:—
Horatia Edith de Visme (Nazareth House, Queen Wilhelmina AV, Waterkloof, Pretoria 0002, S Africa), *b* 1902.

Issue of late Henry Augustus Gregory Shaw, *b* 1875, *d* 1954: *m* 1925, Eileen, who *d* 1973, el da of Charles William Howard:—
John Gregory Monson de Visme (22 Brunswick Terrace, Hove, Sussex), *b* 1930: *m* 1st, 1959 (*m diss* 1972), Helene Maud, da of Cyril Ernest Kerslake Baker, of co Down; 2ndly, 1976, Joan Phyllis, elder da of late Alfred Frank Elphick. —— Robert Henry Barnardiston de Visme (9 Cranswick Rd, Willowild, Sandton, Transvaal, S Africa), *b* 1932: *m* 1961, Valerie Ann, only da of B. R. Lobb, of Johannesburg and London, and has issue living, Philip Gregory de Visme, *b* 1970, — Christine Ann de Visme, *b* 1965: *m* 1991, Mark John Fraser-Valentine, and has issue living, Katelyn Ann *b* 1991, Emily Jo *b* 1993. —— Eileen Ann de Visme, *b* 1928: *m* 1952, Alan Baker, and has issue living, Robert Alan, *b* 1960, — James Paul, *b* 1963, — Catherine Ann, *b* 1953.

Sir John, the 1st baronet, having rendered great service to Charles I during the Rebellion, and having advanced several sums of money to Charles II during that King's exile was after the Restoration appointed one of the Farmers of the Customs; Com Sir John James Kenward Best-Shaw, RN, High Sheriff of Kent, assumed by R Licence (1956) the additional surname of Best before that of Shaw and the Arms of Best quarterly with those of Shaw.

Shaw-Stewart, see Stewart.

SHEFFIELD (GB) 1755, of Normanby, Lincolnshire

Blandly, but determinedly

Sir REGINALD ADRIAN BERKELEY SHEFFIELD, 8th *Baronet*, son of late Maj Edmund Charles Reginald Sheffield, 2nd son of 6th Bt; *s* his uncle, *Sir* ROBERT ARTHUR, 1977; *b* 9 May 1946; *ed* Eton; DL Lincs 1985; *m* 1st, 1969 (*m diss* 1975), Annabel Lucy Veronica, da of Timothy Angus Jones (*see* B Clifford of Chudleigh, colls, 1985, Edn); 2ndly, 1977, Victoria Penelope, da of late Ronald Clive Walker, DFC, and has issue living by 1st and 2nd *m*.

Arms – Argent, a chevron engrailed between two garbs in chief gules, and in base a sheaf of arrows proper, banded also gules. **Crest** – A boar's head erased at the neck or between two arrows points downwards proper. *Seat* – Normanby Park, Normanby, Scunthorpe, N Lincs.

SON LIVING (*By 2nd marriage*)

ROBERT CHARLES BERKELEY, *b* 1 Sept 1984.

DAUGHTERS LIVING (*By 1st marriage*)

Samantha Gwendoline, *b* 1971: *m* 1996, David W. D. Cameron, yr son of Ian Cameron. —— Emily Julia, *b* 1973.

(*By 2nd marriage*)

Alice Daisy Victoria, *b* 1980. —— Lucy Mary, *b* 1981.

SISTER LIVING

Fiona Mary (*Baroness Inchyra*), *b* 1939: *m* 1961, 2nd Baron Inchyra.

UNCLE LIVING (*son of 6th Baronet*)

John Vincent, CBE, *b* 1913; *ed* Eton, and Magdalene Coll, Camb (MA); is an OStJ; High Sheriff of Lincs 1944-45; CBE (civil) 1984: *m* 1st, 1936, Anne Margaret, who *d* 1969, da of Sir Lionel Lawson Faudel-Faudel-Phillips, 3rd Bt; 2ndly, 1971, France Mary Agnes, da of late Brig-Gen Goland Clarke, CMG, DSO and formerly wife of Major Ivor Crosthwaite, DSO, and has issue living (by 1st *m*), (John) Julian Lionel George (Spring Pond, Laverstoke, Whitchurch, Hants), *b* 1938; *ed* Eton, and Camb Univ; High Sheriff Hants 1998: *m* 1961, Carolyn Alexandra, da of late Brig Sir Alexander Abel Smith, of Quenington Rectory, Cirencester, Glos (D Somerset, colls), and has issue living, John David *b* 1963, Simon Robert Alexander *b* 1964: *m* 1996, (Clare Elizabeth) Dido, yst da of Sir John Lindsay Eric Smith, CH, CBE, FRIBA (*see* E Northesk, colls) (and has issue living, Helen Christina Anne *b* 1998), Lionel Julian *b* 1969: *m* 1997, Nathalie Emma Jane, eldest da of Maurice Norton, of Saffron Walden, Essex, Nicola Elizabeth Anne *b* 1973, — Jane Armyne, LVO (The Mill House, Sutton Courtenay, Abingdon, Oxford) *b* 1937; LVO 1993: *m* 1956 (*m diss* 1979), Jocelyn Edward Greville Stevens (later Sir Jocelyn Stevens), CVO, and has had issue, Charles Greville Vincent (643 Evergreen Point Rd, Medina, WA 98039, USA) *b* 1957: *m* 1980, Delphine Suzanne, da of late John Dove, of Douglas, IoM (and has issue living, Nicholas Jocelyn Edmund *b* 1988, Leonora Mary *b* 1985, Amanda Julia *b* 1992), Rupert Jocelyn Sebastian *b* 1964 *d* 1989, Pandora Anne *b* 1959: *m* 1983, Charles Hamar Delevingne, of Paddock House, 9 Spencer Park, SW18, and has issue (*see* V Greenwood), Melinda Armyne *b* 1972, — Diana Anne, *b* 1942: *m* 1966, David Mark Norman, of Burkham House, Alton, Hants GU34 5RS, and has issue living, Jonathan Mark Ronald *b* 1972, Anna Helen *b* 1967, Isabella Julia (*Hon Mrs Timothy Knatchbull*) *b* 1971: *m* 1998, Hon Timothy Nicholas Sean Knatchbull, yst twin son of 7th Baron Brabourne, CBE, by his wife Countess Mountbatten of Burma, CBE, Davina Penelope *b* 1981, — Angela Margaret, *b* 1947: *m* 1966, (Anthony) Richard Brocas Burrows, of The Hall, Barham, Ipswich, and has issue living, (Edward) Brocas *b* 1975, Carey Jane *b* 1968: *m* 1995, Rupert L. A. English, son of Peter English, of Argyll Rd, W8 (and has issue living, Brett Brocas Alexander *b* 1999, Grace Angela Amba *b* 1997), Joanna Molly Anne *b* 1969: *m* 1997, Charles Ashley Cunningham-Reid (*see* By Mount Temple, 1985 Edn) (and has issue living, Louis Noel Richard, *b* 1998), (Angela) Petra *b* 1972. *Residence* – New Barn House, Laverstoke, Whitchurch, Hants.

COLLATERAL BRANCHES LIVING

Issue of late Maj George Berkeley Sheffield, 3rd son of 6th baronet, *b* 1910, *d* 1968: *m* 1st, 1935, Psyche Isabel Joan, who *d* 1945, da of late Capt Edward Altham, CB, RN; 2ndly, 1949, Hon Agnes Wilson McGowan, who *d* 1976, da of 1st Baron McGowan, and formerly wife of Maj Dermot Ralph Daly:—
(By 2nd *m*) Laura Diana, *b* 1949: *m* 1st, 1969 (*m diss* 1984), George William Pilkington; 2ndly, 1990, Paul Sednaoui, and has issue living (by 1st *m*), Harry George, *b* 1971, — Martha Mary, *b* 1972. *Residence* – Ramsden House, Ramsden, Oxon. —— Davina Mary, *b* 1951: *m* 1981, Jonathan Derek Morley, yr son of late Brig Michael Frederick Morley, MBE, of Marlborough, Wilts, and has issue living, Thomas George Jonathan, *b* 1983, — William Frederick Duncan, *b* 1984, — Henry Quintus, *b* 1987. *Residence* – Westerdale, nr Whitby, N Yorks.

Grandsons of late Robert Stoney OLIPHANT-SHEFFIELD (who assumed the additional surname of OLIPHANT 1901), son of Capt John Charles Sheffield, 3rd son of 4th baronet:—
Issue of late Edmund George Sheffield, *b* 1913; discontinued use of additional surname of Oliphant; *d* 1976: *m* 1939, Eva May, who *d* 1988, eldest da of Charles Blood Mulville, of Hampstead, NW3:—
John Robert (Broadfield, Southwaite, Carlisle, Cumbria CA4 0LR), *b* 1941; *ed* Harrow: *m* 1st, 1967 (*m diss* 1971), Valerie Jean, da of Capt George Ernest Towill, of St Aidans Rd, Carlisle; 2ndly, 1978, Elizabeth Helen, who *d* 1991, da of late James Turner, 3rdly, 1994, Jean Ann, da of late Charles Edward Lomas, and has issue living, (by 1st *m*) Edward John, *b* 1968, — Andrew George, *b* 1970. —— Richard Charles, *b* 1944; *ed* Harrow: *m* 1st, 1966 (*m diss* 1972), Cheryl Mary Eleanor, only da of David Lloyd McNeil Williams, of Haling Park Rd, S Croydon, Surrey; 2ndly, 1972 (*m diss* 1982), Caroline Alison, da of Everett Ryshworth Unwin, of The Court House, Lelant, Cornwall; 3rdly, 1986, Mary Morrice, da of Charles Maclay Scott, of Ornum, 3 Camstradden Dr, Bearsden, Glasgow. —— George Henry Oliphant, *b* 1948; *ed* Rannoch: *m* 1974, Christine Holdsworth.

Grandson of late Rev Frank Sheffield, 5th son of 4th baronet:—
Issue of late Rev Arthur Digby Sheffield, *b* 1897, *d* 1975: *m* 1932, Alice Katharine, who *d* 1982, da of late Donald Malcolm Scott, of 8 Chandos St, W1:—
Nigel Digby (Rookery Farm, Earl Soham, Woodbridge, Suffolk), *b* 1933; *ed* Eton and Ch Ch, Oxford (MA): *m* 1960, Helen Jane Ann Russell, el da of Lt Col Bernard Russell French, DSO, of Edgeworth, Glos, and has issue living, Timothy John Digby *b* 1966: *m* 1994, Alexandra C., da of Nicholas Butterworth, of St Leonards, Herts, and has issue living, Frederick Arthur Digby *b* 1997, — Ann Margot, *b* 1963: *m* 1997, Jonathan T. Underwood, only son of Raymond Underwood, of Wells-next-the-Sea, Norfolk, and has issue living, Oscar Ernest Digby *b* 1998, — Susan Margaret, *b* 1965: *m* 1992, Michael Lock, son of Peter Lock, of Shape, Suffolk, and has issue living, Thomas Hugo *b* 1996, Alice Jane *b* 1996.

The 1st baronet, Sir Charles Sheffield (originally Herbert), was an illegitimate son of John Sheffield 1st Duke of Normanby and Buckingham; he inherited the estates of his legitimate brother Edmond last Duke of Buckingham. The 6th baronet, Sir Berkeley Digby George, sat as MP for N Lindsey, or Brigg, Div of Lincolnshire (C) 1907-10 and 1922-9, and was High Sheriff of Lincolnshire 1905.

SHELLEY (E) 1611, of Michelgrove Sussex

As I find

(*Sir*) JOHN RICHARD SHELLEY, 11th *Baronet* (has established his claim but does not use the title), *b* 18 Jan 1943; *s* his grandfather, *Maj Sir* JOHN FREDERICK, 1976; *ed* King's Sch, Bruton, Trin Coll, Camb (MA), (MB, BChir) and St Mary's Hosp, London Univ, DObstRCOG, MRCGP; Partner in Drs, Shelley, Doddington and Gibb, Medical Practitioners; Member Exeter Diocesan Synod 1976-79: *m* 1965, Clare, da of Claud Bicknell, OBE, ret law Commr, of Newcastle upon Tyne, and has issue.

Arms – Sable a fesse, engrailed, between three whelks or. Crest – A griffin's head erased, beaked argent, and ducally gorged or.
Residence – Shobrooke Park, Crediton, Devon EX17 1DG.

DAUGHTERS LIVING

Diana Elizabeth, *b* 1970: *m* 1993, John S. Moule, son of B. J. Moule, of Wellington, Shropshire, and has issue living, Benjamin John Enoch, *b* 1998, — Emily Rebekah, *b* 1996. —— Helen Ruth, *b* 1972: *m* 1994, Amos James Storkey, son of Alan Storkey, of Southgate, N.

BROTHER LIVING

THOMAS HENRY, *b* 3 Feb 1945; *ed* King's Sch, Bruton, and Trin Coll, Camb (BA): *m* 1970 (*m diss* 1992), Katharine Mary Holton, and has issue living, Kirsten Rachel Irvine, *b* 1973, — Victoria Juliet, *b* 1974, — Benita Mary, *b* 1978.

UNCLE LIVING (*Son of 10th baronet*)

Philip Spencer, *b* 1921; late FO RAF: *m* 1st, 1947 (*m diss* 1963), Pamela Grace, da of late Lt-Col Henry Nigel Kermack, RE; 2ndly, 1968 (*m diss* 1978), Elizabeth Philippa, da of Leonard George Edward Llewellyn, of Nairobi, and has issue living (by 1st *m*), Nigel Antony (82 Selborne Drive, Boyatt Wood, Eastleigh, Hants SO50 4PH), *b* 1948: *m* 1st, 1972 (*m diss* 1984), Pamela Mary Inder; 2ndly, 1987, Amanda Jayne, da of Pat Alan Fletcher, and has issue living, (by 1st *m*) Alexandra Margaret *b* 1975, (by 2nd *m*) Samuel Nicholas *b* 1992, — Malcolm Frederick (33 St Piran Rd, Perranporth, Cornwall TR6 0EY), *b* 1953: *m* 1974, Lynne Sharon, da of late Richard Alfred Buckingham, and has two adopted sons, Glenn James Thomas *b* 1984, Joshua Luke *b* 1989. —— Marian Pamela, *b* 1950: *m* 1991, David Edward Unwin, of 183 John Ruskin St, SE5 0PT, son of late Rear Adm John Harold Unwin, CB, DSC, — (by 2nd *m*) Nora Elizabeth, *b* 1969: *m* 1st, 1992 (*m diss* 1996), Anthony Edward Irwin; 2ndly, 1996, Sgt Stephen Johnstone, and has issue living (by 2nd *m*), Benjamin Stephen *b* 1996, — Sebastian Philip, *b* 1997, — Gillian Philippa, *b* 1971: *m* 1993 (*m diss* 1996), Mark McKinetry.

AUNTS LIVING (*Daughters of 10th baronet*)

Mary Nora (67 Birch Av, Sheffield S30 4RQ), *b* 1913: *m* 1940, Maj Robin Paige, MC, TD, who *d* 1969, and has issue living, Michael Robert (Rose Cottage, Low Hameringham, Horncastle, Lincs LN9 6PG), *b* 1941: *m* 1966, Patricia Margaret Appleby, and has issue living, Nicholas Robert *b* 1972, Catherine Mary *b* 1968: *m* 1994, Alexander Stuart Gray (and has issue living, Rebecca Elizabeth *b* 1998), Sarah Jane *b* 1970: *m* 1998, Max William Frick, — Timothy John (twin), *b* 1941, — Christopher David, TD (2 Mallard Close, Thorpe Hesley, Rotherham, S Yorks S61 2TW), *b* 1945; Maj RE (*V*): *m* 1970, Cynthia Ann Ison, and has issue living, David Hugh *b* 1976, Joanne Lesley *b* 1983. —— Frances Elizabeth, *b* 1914: *m* 1938, Rev Henry John Allen Rusbridger, who *d* 1985, and has issue living, Peter Henry James, *b* 1941: *m* 1969, Geraldine Johnston, and has issue living, Charles Peter James *b* 1971, Lucy Victoria *b* 1973, — Elizabeth Jean, *b* 1939: *m* 1963, Rev Preb Michael Bowles, of Stanmore Rectory, Middx, and has issue living, Jeremy Michael *b* 1966, Catherine Elizabeth *b* 1964, Jennifer Susan *b* 1974, — Margaret Anne, *b* (twin) 1941: *m* 1st, 1965 (*m diss* 1976), Arthur William Frederick Sacheverel Pulford; 2ndly, 1979, Kenneth E. R. Hawkins, and has issue living (by 1st *m*), Claire *b* 1966. —— Gillian Hester (Southern Wood, Peter Tavy, Devon), *b* 1918: *m* 1949, Capt Michael William Howard, MC, Devonshire Regt, who *d* 1994 (*see* E Carlisle, colls).

MOTHER LIVING

Dorothy Irvine (Westacott, Shobrooke, Crediton, Devon), el da of late Arthur Irvine Ingram, MA, solicitor, of Bath: *m* 1940, John Shelley, who *d* 1974, el son of 10th baronet.

COLLATERAL BRANCHES LIVING

Issue of late Vice-Adm Richard BENYON, CB, CBE (assumed by deed poll 1964, and by Roy Licence 1967 (for himself and el son) the surname of Benyon in lieu of Shelley), yr son of 9th baronet; *b* 1892; *d* 1968: *m* 1929, Eve Alice, who *d* 1995, da of late Rt Rev Lord *Sir* William Rupert Ernest Cecil, DD, 65th Lord Bishop of Exeter (*see* M Salisbury, colls):—
Sir William Richard BENYON (Englefield House, Reading), *b* 1930; Lt RN (Reg Reserve); High Sheriff Berks 1995; MP for Buckingham (*C*) 1970-83, and Milton Keynes (*C*) 1983-92; *cr* Kt Bach 1994: *m* 1957, Elizabeth Ann, yr da of late Vice-Adm Ronald Hamilton Curzon Hallifax, CB, CBE (*see* Hughes, Bt, *cr* 1773, 1972-73 Edn), and has issue living, Richard Henry Ronald (The Lambdens, Beenham, Reading, Berks RG7 5LD), *b* 1960: *m* 1988, Emma Helen, yr da of Capt Anthony Henry Heber Villiers (*see* E Clarendon, colls), and has issue living, Harry Charles William *b* 1990, Thomas Anthony Edward *b* 1992, Frederick Richard *b* 1994, — Edward William, *b* 1962: *m* 1989, Katy E. M., yr da of Robin Crofts, of Nethercote House, Flecknoe, Warwicks, and has issue living, Charles *b* 1991, Victoria *b* 1993, — Catherine Rose Ingrid, *b* 1958: *m* 1984, Peter David Ian Haig, son of Maj Andrew Haig, of Norfolk, and has issue living, William Robin *b* 1988, Georgiana Elizabeth *b* 1989, Rachel Louisa *b* 1992, — Mary Elizabeth, *b* 1965: *m* 1990, Capt Thomas R. P. Riall, 15th/19th The King's Royal Hussars, son of Maj Patrick Riall, of Knockbawn, Kilmacanogue, co Wicklow, and has issue living, Phineas Patrick *b* 1993, Matthew *b* 1996, Rosanna Eleanor *b* 1992, — Susannah Eve, *b* 1969: *m* 1996, G. Neville McBain, elder son of George McBain, of Lower Woodshaw Farm, Wootton Bassett, Wilts, and has issue living, Joseph George *b* 1999, Samuel William *b* (twin) 1999. —— James Edward SHELLEY, CBE (Mays Farm House, Ramsdell, Tadley, Hants RG26 5RE), *b* 1932: *m* 1956, Judith, da of George Grubb, and has issue living, Timothy James, *b* 1966: *m* 1993, Emma Jane, eldest da of David Dinkeldein, of Whiteway Farmhouse, nr Newbury, and has issue living, Jemima Louise *b* 1996, Lucy Rose *b* 1998, — Philip John, *b* (twin) 1966: *m* 1994, Joanne Marie, da of Stewart England, of Ravenshead, Nottingham, and has issue living, Jack Alexander Stewart *b* 1996, Genevieve Mary *b* 1997, — Alison Jane, *b* 1959: *m* 1990 Anthony Clavane, son of Emile Clavane, of Leeds, and has issue living, Rosa *b* 1992, Miriam *b* 1996, — Penelope Sarah, *b* 1960. —— Andrew Thomas Rupert SHELLEY (Oakfield, Cox Green, Rudgwick, Horsham, W Sussex RH12 3DD), *b* 1933; late Maj R Green Jackets: *m* 1971, Joanna M., only da of Adm Sir (Randolph Stewart) Gresham Nicholson, KBE, CB, DSO, DSC, and has issue living, Nicholas Charles, *b* 1978, — Sarah Lucy, *b* 1974. —— David Robert SHELLEY (Church End Cottage, Kensworth, Dunstable, Beds LU6 3RA), *b* 1937: *m* 1971, Elisabeth Rhoda, yr da of late Gilbert Graham Balfour (*see* Halsey, Bt, 1990 Edn), and has issue living, Peter David, *b* 1972, — Jonathan Rupert, *b* 1974.

Grandchildren of late Spencer Shelley (*b* 1843), elder son of late Spencer Shelley (*b* 1813), 4th son of 6th baronet:—
Issue of late Spencer Shelley, *b* 1878, *d* 1941: *m* 1917, Gladys, who *d* 1947, da of E. Mulligan, of Sydney, NS Wales:—
Spencer, *b* 1920; sometime Lieut RNVR; a JP for Glos: *m* 1946, Maureen, da of Commodore Trevor Lewis Owen, OBE, RD, and has issue living, Elizabeth Grey, *b* 1948: *m* 1976, Michael D. R. Oakley, of Wyngates Farm, Mayhill, Longhope, Glos GL17 0RF, and has had issue, James Spencer *b* 1981, *d* 1998, Laura Elizabeth *b* 1978, — (Anna) Frances, *b* 1950: *m* 1983, Edward Osborne Cavendish, and has issue (*see* D Devonshire, colls), — Katherine Jane, *b* 1954: *m* 1981, Roger David Keyworth, of Tuatea wa, Kennedy Bay Rd, Coromandel, NZ, and has issue living, Billy Finn Shelley *b* 1988, Moana Grace Shelley *b* 1986. *Residence* – Tigh-na-Sithe, Comrie, Perthshire. —— Charles Francis, *b* 1925, sometime Sub-Lt RNVR: *m* 1st, 1951, Elizabeth Jane, who *d* 1992, only child of late Brig Sir Francis Smith Reid, CBE; 2ndly, 1995, Mrs Mary Anne Gough, da of Ronald Arthur Savidge, and formerly wife of Keith Locke Gough, and has issue living (by 1st *m*), Sarah Jane, *b* 1952, — Julia Frances, *b* 1954: *m* 1980, Charles Brereton Frater, and has issue living, George Kenneth Charles *b* 1987, Rebecca Jane *b* 1984, — Caroline Ruth, *b* 1957. *Residence* – Little Conigree, Mitcheldean, Glos. —— Frederick Norman (2 Ferguson Street, Alfred Cove, 6154, Perth, Western Australia), *b* (twin) 1925; CEng; MIMechE; *m* 1958, Ruth Mary, only da of late Rowland Colley Skitt, of Barakat, Sudan, and has issue living, Stephen Spencer (11 Peacock St, Burwood, Vic, Australia), *b* 1959: *m* 1990, Heidi Kaupert, and has issue living, James Spencer *b* 1991, Thomas Joseph *b* 1993, Guy William *b* 1997, — Philip Norman, *b* 1960: *m* 1992, Anna Uszko, of Kew, Melbourne, Vic, — William Rowland, *b* 1964, — Anne Lucy, *b* 1963: *m* 1988, Peter James Franklin, of Perth, W Australia, and has

issue living, Matilda Ruth *b* 1995, Lucy Cynthia Shelley *b* 1997. ⸺ Cynthia Kathleen, *b* 1921, sometime in WRNS: *m* 1943, Michael Richard Lloyd Hayes, DL, KStJ, CEng, FIMechE, FRINA, FIMarE, High Sheriff, Pembs, and has issue living, Sylvia Josephine Ruth (*Hon Mrs G. Andrew Lawson Johnston*), *b* 1945: *m* 1968, Hon George Andrew Lawson Johnston, of Invernan House, Strathdon, Aberdeenshire AB3 87A (*see* B Luke), ⸺ Frances Patricia Jane, *b* 1948: *m* 1971, Julian Dyson Seddon, of The Old Vicarage, 26 Wandle Rd, Wandsworth, SW17 7DW, and has issue living, Alexander James Dyson *b* 1973, Zoe Louisa *b* 1974, ⸺ Ann Wendy Felicity, *b* 1950: *m* 1972, Peter A. Cartwright, of Marren, Holworth, Dorchester, Dorset DT2 8NJ, and has issue living, Thomas Aubrey *b* 1975, William Cloudesley *b* 1989, Emma Juliet *b* 1973. *Residence* – Four Ashes, Cosheston, Pembroke Dock, Pembs, SA72 4TX.

Thomas Shelley was Lord of the Manor of Shelley, Kent, *temp* Edward I. This family can prove seven royal descents in unbroken legitimate lines from Henry III and Edward I. Michelgrove, the seat of the Shelley family for more than 300 years, was sold at the end of the 18th century, to the Duke of Norfolk, whose family later demolished it. Sir John Shelley, 9th Bt, was High Sheriff of Devon 1895. Maj Sir John Frederick Shelley, 10th Bt, was High Sheriff of Devon 1938.

SHEPPERSON (UK) 1945, of Upwood, Co Huntingdon (Extinct 1949)

Sir ERNEST WHITTOME SHEPPERSON, 1st and last *Baronet*.

DAUGHTERS LIVING OF FIRST BARONET

Rosemary Jane, *b* 1921; *ed* Newnham Coll, Camb (BA 1943): *m* 1947, Eric Arthur North Whitehead, and has issue living, Simon Ambrose North, *b* 1952, ⸺ Margaret Loveday, *b* 1948. ⸺ Mary Elizabeth, *b* 1927: *m* 1st, 1945, Ian Loudon Spofforth (MA Oxon), late Fl Lt RAF, who *d* 1964; 2ndly, 1968, Brig Henry Ralph Orton, of Ashbourne, Thornton Av, Warsash, Southampton, SO3 9FJ, and has issue living (by 1st *m*), Timothy Markham Shepperson, *b* 1947, ⸺ Sally Jane, *b* 1950, ⸺ Belinda Anne, *b* 1952, ⸺ Virginia Elizabeth, *b* 1956.

Sherston-Baker, see Baker.

SHIFFNER (UK) 1818, of Coombe, Sussex

Sir HENRY DAVID SHIFFNER, 8th *Baronet*; *b* 2 Feb 1930; *s* his father, *Major Sir* HENRY BURROWS, OBE, 1941; *ed* Rugby, and Trin Hall, Camb: *m* 1st, 1951 (*m diss* 1956), Dorothy, da of W. G. Jackson, of Coventry; 2ndly, 1957 (*m diss* 1970), Beryl, da of George Milburn, of Saltdean, Sussex; 3rdly, 1971, Joaquina Ramos Lopez, of Madrid, Spain, and has issue by 1st and 2nd *m*.

Arms – Azure, a bend sinister, in chief two estoiles in like bend or; in base, the end and stock of an anchor gold, issuing from waves of the sea proper. **Crest** – An estoile or, between the rays six annulets azure.

DAUGHTERS LIVING (*By 1st marriage*)

Elizabeth Marilyn, *b* 1953. ⸺ (*By 2nd marriage*) Linda Mary, *b* 1957: *m* 1994, Maj Roger B. C. Holden, elder son of D. J. Holden, of Ditchling, Sussex.

COLLATERAL BRANCHES LIVING

Grandchildren of late George Bridger Shiffner, 2nd son of 4th baronet:—
Issue of late Capt George Edward Shiffner, *b* 1901, *d* 1956: *m* 1935, Kathleen Patricia, who *d* 1978, da of Lt-Col Sir Edward Boscawen Frederick, CVO, 9th Bt:—

GEORGE FREDERICK (14 Coggeshall Rd, Braintree, Essex CM7 6BY; Searles, Alderford St, Sible Hedingham, Essex), *b* 3 Aug 1936; *ed* Wellington: *m* 1961, Dorothea Helena Cynthia, da of late T. H. McLean, and has issue living, Michael George Edward, *b* 1963: *m* 1996, Suzanne E., da of late Dennis Buss, of Clifton, Beds, and has issue living, Scarlett Vegas Rosie *b* 1998, — Penelope Ann Dorothy, *b* 1962. —— Susan Georgiana, *b* 1938: *m* 1st, 1963, Henry Pickup, who *d* 1975; 2ndly, 1975, Michael Scales, of Culverdown, Great Henny, Sudbury, Suffolk, and has issue living (by 2nd *m*), Timothy Michael Edward, *b* 1977.

Issue of late Capt John Scarlett Shiffner, RN, *b* 1910, *d* 1980: *m* 1940, Margaret Harriet (10 Malvern Court, Onslow Sq, SW7), da of George Tullis, of Strathenry, Leslie, Fife:—
John Robert, CB (c/o Royal Bank of Scotland, Leslie, Fife), *b* 1941; BSc Lond CEng, FIMarE; Rear Adm RN; CB (Mil) 1995: *m* 1969, Rosemary Anne Creyghton, da of Brig Alfred Tilly, CBE, DL, and has issue living, John Edward, *b* 1971, — Henry Charles Alexander, *b* 1975, — Caroline Mary Tilly, *b* 1973. —— Charles Tullis, *b* 1944; *ed* St Andrews Univ (MA): *m* 1978, Rosamund Mary, da of James London, of Woods Hill, W Chiltington, W Sussex, and has issue living, Robin John Landon, *b* 1982, — Katherine Landon, *b* 1979, — Elizabeth Margaret Mary, *b* 1981. —— Priscilla Mary Scarlett (37 Lexham Gdns, W8 5JR), *b* 1949.

The 6th baronet, Sir John Bridger Shiffner, Lieut Roy Sussex Regt, was *ka* 1918. The 7th baronet, Major Sir Henry Burrows Shiffner, OBE, RA, was *ka* 1941.

SHUCKBURGH (E) 1660, of Shuckburgh, Warwickshire

Sir RUPERT CHARLES GERALD SHUCKBURGH, 13th *Baronet*; *b* 12 Feb 1949; *s* his father, *Maj Sir* CHARLES GERALD STEWKLEY, JP, TD, 1988: *ed* Worksop Coll: *m* 1st, 1976 (*m diss* 1987), Judith, da of late William Gordon Mackaness, of Paddock Lodge, Everdon, Daventry; 2ndly, 1987, Margaret Ida, da of late William Evans, of Middleton, Derbys, and has issue by 1st *m*.

𝕬rms – Sable, a chevron between three mullets argent. 𝕮rest – A blackamoor couped at the waist proper, with a dart in his hand or.
Seat – Shuckburgh Hall, near Daventry NN11 6DT.

SONS LIVING (*By 1st marriage*)

JAMES RUPERT CHARLES, *b* 4 Jan 1978. —— Peter Gerald William, *b* 1982.

Haec manus ob patriam

This hand for my country

SISTERS LIVING

Remony Charmian, *b* 1938: *m* 1st, 1963 (*m diss* 1978), Hugo Macdonald Price; 2ndly, 1983, Michael Taylor-Downes, and has issue living (by 1st *m*), Robin Macdonald, *b* 1970, — Justin Bryan, *b* 1973; has issue living, Amber Remony *b* 1995. *Residence* – 60 Shingham, Beachamwell, Swaffham, Norfolk PE37 8AY. —— Amanda Maria, *b* 1946. *Residence* – The Gate House, White Colne, Colchester, Essex C06 2PW.

This family takes its name from Shuckburgh in Warwickshire. Richard Shuckburgh, Esq, MP for the county in 1641, and father of the 1st baronet, armed all his tenants, and joined King Charles I at Edgehill, where he was knighted. After the battle of Edge Hill he retired and fortified himself on Shuckburgh Hill, where most of his tenantry were slain, and he himself was taken prisoner. After being confined in Kenilworth Castle for a considerable time, he purchased his liberty at a dear rate. His eldest son, John, was created a baronet by Charles II.

SIMEON (UK) 1815, of Grazeley, Berkshire

Neither rashly nor timidly

Sir JOHN EDMUND BARRINGTON SIMEON, 7th *Baronet*; *b* 1 March 1911; *s* his father, Sir JOHN WALTER BARRINGTON, 1957; *ed* Eton, and Ch Ch, Oxford; Flight-Lieut (ret) RAF: *m* 1937, Anne Robina Mary, elder da of Hamilton Dean, and has issue.

Arms – Per fesse sable and or a pale counter-changed three trefoils slipped, two and one of the second, and three ermine spots one and two of the first. **Crest** – A fox passant-regardant proper, in the mouth a trefoil slipped vert. **Supporters** – *Dexter*, a fox reguardant proper, in the mouth a trefoil slipped vert; *sinister*, a lion gules, ducally crowned or.
Address – Jerome & Co, Solicitors, Newport, Isle of Wight.

SON LIVING

RICHARD EDMUND BARRINGTON (20 Biggar Av, Toronto, Ontario, Canada), *b* 2 March 1943; *ed* St George's Sch, Vancouver, Univ of British Columbia (BA) and Yale (MA, PhD) Univ; Prof of Political Science and Law, Toronto Univ, subsequently Dir of Inst of Intergovernmental Relations 1976-83 and Dir of Sch of Public Admin since 1986-90; Vice-Chm Ontario Law Reform Commn since 1989: *m* 1st, 1966 (*m diss* 1989), Agnes Joan, only da of George Frederick Weld; 2ndly, 1993, Maryetta Cheney, and has issue living (by 1st *m*), Stephen George Barrington, *b* 29 Oct 1970: *m* 1996, Michelle Owens, and has issue living, Ewan Barrington Harold *b* 1998, — Rachel Elizabeth, *b* 1973.

DAUGHTERS LIVING

Anne Emily Philippa, *b* 1938: *m* 1962, Nigel Leonard Harper Gow, of 6129 Highbury, Vancouver, BC, Canada, and has issue living, Ian Harper, *b* 1968: *m* 1995, Holly Lear, — Lisa Harper, *b* 1965: *m* 1996, Jeff Burke, and has issue living, Ariane *b* 1999. —— Sara Alexandra, *b* 1946: *m* 1st, 1967 (*m diss* 1994), Anthony John Williams; 2ndly, 1996, Christopher Foster, of 134 Caprice Heights, Saltspring Island, BC, Canada, and has issue living (by 1st *m*), Derek John, *b* 1973, — Trevor Michael, *b* 1975, — Adria Elizabeth, *b* 1971.

COLLATERAL BRANCHES LIVING

Grandchildren of late Stephen Louis Simeon, 4th son of 3rd baronet:—
Issue of late Leonard Stephen Barrington Simeon, MC, *b* 1891, *d* 1978: *m* 1924, Ella Hazel Powys, who *d* 1980, da of late Col Powys Lane, IA, of Upper Ward, Bonchurch, I of Wight:—
Miles Powys Barrington (Suffolk House, St Osyth, Clacton, Essex), *b* 1927: *m* 1956, Joan Mary, da of Laurence Frederick Underhay, of Clacton, Essex, and has issue living, Michael John Barrington, *b* 1957, — Robert Miles (Daltes Farm, St Osyth, Clacton, Essex), *b* 1959: *m* 1988, Carol Ann Newcombe, and has had issue, John Robert *b* 1992, James Kenneth Barrington *b* 1995, Laura Ann *b* and *d* 1988, Samantha Ann *b* 1989. —— Anne Primrose Louise (Home Field, Broke Rd, Wollombi, NSW 2325, Australia), *b* 1925: *m* 1st, 1944 (*m diss* 1959), Louis Gustave Julian Strauss; 2ndly, 1959, Leonard Townsend, who *d* 1971; 3rdly, 1973, Gp Capt John Michael Skelton Adams, RAF (ret), CEng, FIEE, FIMechE, who *d* 1993, and has issue living (by 1st *m*), Linda Evelyn *b* 1947: *m* 1974, Thomas Kennedy Nelson, of Killiecrankie Farm, Wollombi, NSW 2325, Australia, and has issue living, Hamish Kennedy Strauss *b* 1975, Robin Simeon *b* 1977, — Caroline Louise (6/30 Park Avenue, Mosman, Sydney, NSW 2088, Australia), *b* 1948: *m* 1974 (*m diss* 1981), Nicholas John de Jongh, — Diana Margaret (5 Box House, Luddenden, nr Halifax, W Yorks), *b* 1955: *m* 1978 (*m diss* 1984), Peter Gilbert Marsland, and has issue living, Christopher Barrington *b* 1981.

Grandson of late Rev Geoffrey Barrington Simeon, 3rd son of Capt Charles Simeon, 75th Regt, 2nd son of 2nd baronet:—
Issue of late Geoffrey Nelthorpe Simeon, *b* 1888, *d* 1923: *m* 1919, Henrietta Mary Collingwood, who *d* 1989, da of late Rev W. Collingwood Carter, formerly V. of Shipton-under-Wychwood:—
Geoffrey John Barrington, *b* 1923; Lt-Cdr RN (ret); FRICS: *m* 1954, Elizabeth Frances Richenda, da of late Rev R. C. Rham, of Feock, Cornwall, and has issue living, Charles Richard Barrington (8 Arle Close, Alresford, Hants SO24 9BG), *b* 1958; *ed* Sherborne: *m* 1999, Caroline Sarah, da of late Keith J. Salter, of Ascot, Berks, — Sarah Richenda Barrington, *b* 1956, — Elizabeth Anne Barrington, *b* 1960: *m* 1987, Anthony George Harrison (11 Chilton Candover, Alresford, Hants SO24 9TX), son of late G. G. Harrison, of St Ives, Cornwall, and has issue living, George Geoffrey *b* 1988, Robert William *b* 1990. *Residence* – Maple House, Chilbolton, Stockbridge, Hants SO20 6BQ.

Grandson of late Perceval Barrington Simeon, el son of Cornwall Simeon, 3rd son of 2nd baronet:—
Issue of late Cornwall Barrington Simeon, *b* 1889, *d* 1957: *m* 1st, 1928 (*m diss* 1947), Ellaline Margery Mary, who *d* 1966, da of late Arnold le Poer Power, of Clonmel, co Tipperary; 2ndly, 1947, Violet, MBE, who *d* 1979, only da of late Algernon Hodson, and widow of Lt-Col Neal William Douglas-Matheson, DSO, MC:—
(By 1st *m*) John Power Barrington, OBE (4 Cliff Rd, Dovercourt, Harwich, Essex CO12 3PP), *b* 1929; *ed* Beaumont Coll, and RMA Sandhurst; entered HM Dip Serv 1965, First Sec (Commercial) Colombo 1967, Bonn 1968-70, Port of Spain 1970-73 (sometime Acting High Commr), FCO 1973-75, Dep High Cmmr and Head of Post, Ibadan, Nigeria 1975-79, HM Consul Gen Berlin 1979-81 and Hamburg 1981-84 (ret); OBE (Civil) 1978: *m* 1st, 1951 (*m diss* 1955), Margareta Valborg Johanna, only da of late Erik Ahlstrom, of Norrmark, Finland; 2ndly, 1966, Norma, who *d* 1969, da of late Capt Norman Herbert Dopson; 3rdly, 1970, Carina Renate Elisabeth, da of late Michael Schüller, of Bonn, W Germany, and has issue living (by 2nd *m*), Charles John Barrington (15 Varna Rd, Fulham SW6 7LB), *b* 1967; *ed* King's Sch, Canterbury: *m* 1997, Sarah Catherine, yr da of David Keith Youngman, of Chipstead, Surrey, and has issue living, Ella Sarah Barrington *b* 1999.

Granddaughter of late Cornwall Simeon, 3rd son of 2nd baronet:—
Issue of late Rev John Pole Simeon, *b* 1872, *d* 1951: *m* 1908, Dorothy, who *d* 1955, da of late Rev Sydney
Benjamin Field, formerly V of Patcham:—
Joan Edith Barrington, *b* 1909: *m* 1st, 1938 (*m diss* 1945), Richard William Barnes Clarke; 2ndly, 1945, Wenzel Jaksch,
who *d* 1966, and has issue living, (by 2nd *m*) George Barrington, *b* 1945: *m* 1974, Carmen Julia, da of Don Constantino
Torres, of Colombia, and has issue living, David Wenzel *b* 1977, Sandra Mary *b* 1978, — Mary Dorothy Plantagenet, *b*
1947: *m* 1981, Uwe Grodd, son of Reinhold Grodd, of Stuttgart, and has issue living, Sebastian Wenzel *b* 1981. *Residence*
– 62 Wiesbaden, Kohlheck, Wenzel-Jaksch St 32, Germany.

Grandchildren of late Edward Archibald Simeon, MRCS, LRCP, el son of Lt-Col Edward Simeon, 3rd
son of Rear-Adm Charles Simeon, 3rd son of 1st baronet:—
Issue of late Vice-Adm Sir Charles Edward Barrington Simeon, KBE, CB, *b* 1889, *d* 1955: *m* 1918, Gladys, who *d*
1983, da of Benjamin Arkle, formerly of Spital, Cheshire:—
Hugh Michael (3 Westview Lane, S Norwark, Conn 06854, USA), *b* 1926; Cdr RN (ret): *m* 1966, Ilona Maria, da of Prof
Dr Med Gustav Christian Schimert, of Munich, and has issue living, George Edward, *b* 1969, — John David, *b* 1971, —
Diana Maria, *b* 1967: *m* 1995, Robert John Spadoni, and has issue living, Nora Maria *b* 1998. —— William Martin (Lot
49, Condor Drive, Nikenbah, 4655 Qld, Australia), *b* 1936; late Rifle Brig: *m* 1st, 1959 (*m diss* 1964), Doreen Mary Wren;
2ndly, 1971, Jane Naik, who *d* 1996, and has issue living (by 2nd *m*), Kathryn Mary Anne *b* 1972, Samantha Mervena *b*
1974. —— Marguerite Gladys (3 Farmhill Rd, Waltham Abbey, Essex EN9 1NE), *b* 1922; sometime in WRNS: *m* 1946,
Maj Peter Rainier Adams (ret), late RA, and Indian Army, who *d* 1993, and has issue living, John Rainier, *b* 1947, —
Hugh Robert, *b* 1949, — Charles David, *b* 1951. —— Josephine Osyth, *b* 1932: *m* 1956, Lt-Cdr Thomas David Alexander
Kennedy, RN (ret), MIMechE; CEng, and has issue living, Martin Charles, *b* 1958: *m* 1985, Suzanne Jayne, elder da of
Ronald Charles Brown, of Ayr, Scotland, and has issue living, Peter Charles *b* 1997, Lucy Joanne *b* 1994, — Ian David, *b*
1965, — Fiona Osyth, *b* 1960: *m* 1st, 1984 (*m diss* 1988), Dominic James Shaw; 2ndly, 1989 (*m diss* 1997), Hugh
Anstruther Rance, and has issue living (by 1st *m*), Katurah Osyth *b* 1987, (by 2nd *m*), Eleanor Yaiah Tara *b* 1990, Saskia
Leah Channah *b* 1992, Demelza Chloe Mae *b* 1995. *Residence* – Hill House, Berecourt Rd, Pangbourne, Berks.

Grandson of late Lt-Col Edward Simeon, son of late Rear-Adm Charles Simeon (ante):—
Issue of late Herbert Richard Simeon, *b* 1865, *d* 1926: *m* 1892, Effie Dean Florence, who *d* 1938, da of Walter
Moss, of Ashburton, New Zealand:—
Percival Edward Ralph (c/o Memorial Home, Gisborne, NZ), *b* 1898.

Descendants of John, Lt 54th Regt (*b* 1841) and Albert (*b* 1841), sons of Rear-Adm Charles Simeon
(ante), who both left numerous issue.

Sir John Simeon, 1st baronet, MP for Reading, was senior Master of the Court of Chancery, Sir Richard Godin Simeon,
2nd baronet: *m* 1813, Louisa Edith, da and heir of Sir Fitzwilliam Barrington, 10th Bt of Barrington Hall, Essex (*cr* 1611,
ext 1833).

Sinclair-Lockhart (cr 1636), see Lockhart.

SINCLAIR (NS) 1704, of Dunbeath, Caithness-shire

Fidelity

Sir PATRICK ROBERT RICHARD SINCLAIR, 10th *Baronet*; *b* 21 May 1936, son of late Alexander Robert Sinclair, brother of 8th Bt; *s* his cousin, *Sir* JOHN ROLLO NORMAN BLAIR, 1990; *ed* Winchester, and Oriel Coll, Oxford (MA); Bar Lincoln's Inn 1961, Bencher 1994; Sub Lt RNVR: *m* 1974, Susan Catherine Beresford, eldest da of Geoffrey Clive Davies, OBE, of Greenshaw, Holbrook, Ipswich, Suffolk (*see* Knowles, Bt), and has issue.

Arms – Quarterly: 1st azure, a ship at anchor, oars in saltire or, flagged gules, within a double tressure counterflory of the second; 2nd and 3rd, or, a lion rampant gules, armed and langued azure; 4th, azure, a ship under sail or, sails argent and flags gules; over all, dividing the four quarters, a cross engrailed, sable, *Sinclair;* the whole within a bordure parted per pale, the dexter side indented gules, the sinister ermine. Crest – A cock proper.
Address 5 New Sq, Lincoln's Inn, WC2A 3SA.

SON LIVING

WILLIAM ROBERT FRANCIS, *b* 27 March 1979.

DAUGHTER LIVING

Helen Margaret Gwendolen, *b* 1984.

DAUGHTERS LIVING OF EIGHTH BARONET

Georgina Margaret Snowdrop SINCLAIR, *b* 1932: *m* 1955 (*m diss* 1968), John Leonard Maddocks, and has issue living, John Alexander SINCLAIR-MADDOCKS (202 Battersea Bridge Rd, SW11), *b* 1960: *m* 1995, Sara Sonia Browne, and has issue living, Angus Henry Sinclair *b* 1997. — Margaret Louise Sinclair, *b* 1962: *m* 1991, Adam Piers Scott, of Barrock House, Lyth, Caithness, KW1 4UD and has issue living, Rory Alexander Sinclair *b* 1991, Oliver Roderick Archibald Sinclair *b* 1995, Timothy Charles Sinclair *b* 1997, Laura Rose Sinclair *b* 1993. *Residence* – The Mount, Brewood, Staffs. —— Susan Lilian Primrose (*Countess of Swinton*), *b* 1935 (*cr* a Life Baroness, with the title of Baroness Masham of Ilton, 1970): *m* 1959, 2nd Earl of Swinton. *Residences* – Dykes Hill House, Masham, Ripon, Yorks; 46 Westminster Gdns, Marsham St, SW1P 4JG.

COLLATERAL BRANCH LIVING

Granddaughter of late Rt Hon John Sinclair, GCSI, GCIE (*cr* Baron Pentland 1909), el son of Capt George Sinclair, Bengal Army, yst son of 6th baronet:—
Issue of late Henry John, 2nd Baron Pentland, *b* 1907, *d* 1984: *m* 1941, Lucy Elisabeth Babington (*Baroness Pentland*) (4670 Independence Av, New York City, NY 10471, USA), da of late Sir Henry Babington Smith (*see* E Elgin 1944 Edn):—
Hon Mary, *b* 1942; BA Mount Holyoke, USA (1964): *m* 1976, Jon Anderson Rothenberg, of 131 East 66 St, New York, NY 10021, USA, and has issue living, Laura, *b* 19—.

This family is a younger branch of the Earls of Caithness, Sir James Sinclair of Dunbeath, 1st baronet, being a descendant of the 4th Earl. The baronetcy was *cr* with remainder to heirs male whatsoever, and on the death of the 5th baronet in 1842, it was assumed by his cousin, John Sinclair, of Barrock, as great-great-grandson of George Sinclair of Barrock, brother of William Sinclair of Dunbeath, uncle of 1st baronet, the propinquity being proved by a retour of general service 23 Dec 1842. The 7th baronet, Sir John Rose George Sinclair, DSO, was Vice-Lt for co Caithness, and served in S Africa 1900-01, and during European War 1914-18, Sir Ronald Norman John Charles Udny Sinclair, TD, DL, JP, 8th Bt, was Maj Seaforth Highlanders and Dist Resident Officer, Norderdithmarschen 1947, and British Resident Heide/Holstein 1949.

SITWELL (UK) 1808, of Renishaw, Derbyshire

Sir (SACHEVERELL) RERESBY SITWELL, 7th *Baronet*; *b* 15 April 1927; *s* his father, *Sir* SACHEVERELL, CH, 1988; *ed* Eton, and King's Coll, Camb; formerly Lieut Gren Gds, BAOR 1946-48; Advertising and PR exec 1948-60, vending machine operator 1960-70, wine merchant 1960-75; High Sheriff of Derbys 1983, Freeman of City of London 1984; a DL for Derbys since 1984, Lord of Manors of Eckington and Barlborough, Derbys, and of Whiston and Brampton-en-le-Morthen, Yorks: *m* 1952, Penelope, yr da of late Col Hon Donald Alexander Forbes, DSO, MVO (*see* E Granard, colls), and has issue.

𝔄rms – Barry of eight or and vert, three lions rampant sable. 𝔠rest – A demi-lion rampant, erased sable, holding between the paws an escutcheon per pale or and vert.
Seat – Renishaw Hall, Derbys; *Town Residence* – 4 Southwick Place, W2 2TN.

Yield not to misfortune

DAUGHTER LIVING

Alexandra Isobel Susanna Edith, *b* 1958: *m* 1991, Richard A. Hayward, elder son of Sir Jack Hayward, OBE, and has issue living, Jack Osbert Reresby Sitwell, *b* 1994, — Rosaleen Catriona Sitwell, *b* 1993.

BROTHER LIVING

FRANCIS TRAJAN SACHEVERELL, *b* 17 Sept 1935; *ed* Eton; Sub-Lieut RNVR 1954-56; Royal Dutch/Shell Group 1956-66; Advertising, Public Affairs and Public Relations Consultant; Memb of Council, Lond Philharmonic Orchestra 1965-84 (Vice-Chm 1983-84), and of Byam Shaw Sch of Art 1975-91; Chm Park Lane Group 1978-91; Memb of UK Council, World Wild Fund for Nature since 1985; Chm City Liaison Group since 1988: *m* 1966, Susanna Carolyn, da of late Rt Hon Sir Ronald Hibbert Cross, KCMG, KCVO, 1st Bt, and has issue living, George Reresby Sacheverell, *b* 1967, — William Ronald Sacheverell, *b* 1969, — Henrietta Louise Vereker, *b* 1973. *Residence* – Weston Hall, Towcester, Northants NN12 8PU.

COLLATERAL BRANCH LIVING

      Granddaughter of Capt Herbert Cecil FitzRoy Sitwell, son of Herbert Wellington Sitwell, son of Capt George Frederick Sitwell, 2nd son of 2nd baronet:—
   Issue of late Lt-Col George FitzRoy Sitwell, US Army, *b* 1923, *d* 198-: *m* 1945 (*m diss* 1971); Elizabeth, da of Paul Freed, of Waynesboro, Virginia, USA:—
Elizabeth, *b* 1951: *m* 1969, Alfred Townsend Truitt, of Bradenton, Florida, USA, and has issue living, Anne, *b* 1972.

  The Sitwells appeared early in Eckington, Derbyshire; William Cytewell, *temp* Edward III, and Roger Cytewell, *temp* Edward IV, both being holders of land there. The eventual heiress of the family, Katherine Sitwell, *m* 1727, Jonathan Hurt, and her son Francis succeeded to the Renishaw estates and assumed the name of Sitwell. The Sitwells are the only remaining representatives of the family of Reresby of Thribergh, through Mary Reresby, who in 1693 *m* William Sitwell. Sir George Reresby, 4th Bt, sat as MP for Scarborough (C) 1885-86 and 1892-95. His only da Dame Edith Louisa Sitwell, DBE, *b* 1887, *d* 1964, author, poet and critic, was Vice-Pres of R Soc of Literature 1958. His el son Sir (Francis) Osbert Sacheverell Sitwell, CH, CBE, CLitt, 5th Bt, was the poet and author; *d* 1969; his brother, Sir Sacheverell Sitwell, CH, 6th Bt, was also a noted poet and author; *d* 1988.

SKINNER (UK) 1912, of Pont Street, Borough of Chelsea

I neither fear nor despise

Sir (THOMAS) KEITH HEWITT SKINNER, 4th *Baronet; b* 6 Dec 1927; *s* his father *Sir* (THOMAS) GORDON, 1972; *ed* Charterhouse; Chm and Ch Exec of Reed Publishing Ltd, and a Dir of other cos: *m* 1959, Jill, da of late Cedric Ivor Tuckett, of Yardley Gables, Tonbridge, and has issue.

Arms – Ermine, on a bend or, between in chief a port between two towers, flying therefrom two pennons gules to the sinister, and in base an ancient ship of the second, three maple leaves slipped vert. **Crest** – A griffin's head couped at the neck or, between two dragons' wings gules.
Residence – Wood Farm, Reydon, nr Southwold, Suffolk IP18 6SL.

SONS LIVING

(THOMAS) JAMES HEWITT, *b* 11 Sept 1962. —— Ian Ivor Hewitt, *b* 1964.

BROTHERS LIVING

(Gordon) Michael Hewitt (Juani Farm, PO Box 1375, Nakuru, Kenya), *b* 1930: *m* 1st, 1955 (*m diss* 1960), Josephine Dawn, da of D. S. Redman, of Bleak Hall, Biggleswade; 2ndly, 1961, Eve, da of late Vernon John Fullforth, of Whitehall Court, Whitehall, SW1; 3rdly, 1968, Jean Margaret, who *d* 1995, da of late Donald Sharp, and widow of Robin Vetch, and has issue living, (by 1st *m*) Dudley Mark Hewitt, *b* 1956, — (by 2nd *m*) Sarah Patricia, *b* 1963. —— Peter Girling Hewitt (Highway Model Farm, Downside, Cobham, Surrey), *b* 1938: *m* 1966, Jennifer, da of J. Corbett, of Perrymill, Bradley Green, nr Redditch, Worcs, and has issue living, Justin Mark Thomas, *b* 1968, — (Peter) Dominic Thomas, *b* 1970, — Gemma Sophia Nicola, *b* 1977.

AUNT LIVING (*Daughter of 2nd baronet*)

Constance Irene, *b* 1901: *m* 1936, Claude Harry Mills, who *d* 1971. *Residence* – Pett Place, Charing, Kent.

COLLATERAL BRANCHES LIVING

Issue of late Ernest Skinner, 2nd son of 1st baronet, *b* 1880, *d* 1919: *m* 1903, Leonie Mercedes, who *d* 1964, da of late Henry William Doll, of Lancing, Sussex:—
Eva Jacqueline Leonia, *b* 1914. *Residence* – 8 Tarring Gate, St Lawrence Av, Worthing.

Issue of late John Skinner, 3rd son of 1st baronet, *b* 1882, *d* 1939: *m* 1904, Angela, da of William Dunn:—
John Reginald, *b* 1909: *m* 1949, Shirley Evelyn, da of late James Roddick, of Melbourne, Aust, and has issue living, Dawn Rosalyn, *b* 1952.

Grandchildren of late Charles Henry Skinner, yst son of 1st baronet:—
Issue of late Charles David Evelyn Skinner, *b* 1916, *d* 1987: *m* 1940, Pamela (The Pound, Yarmouth, I of Wight), da of Dr S. B. Couper, of Blaby, Leicester:—
Peter David (Elm Tree House, Kemble, Cirencester), *b* 1941; Fl Lt RAF (ret): *m* 1964, Susan Mary, da of Keith Francis Thompson, of Worcester, and has issue living, Mark David Francis, *b* 1966: *m* 1998, Francesca Kirsten, da of Anthony Hay, of Chobham, Surrey, — James Nicholas Peter, *b* 1982, — Sarah Lucinda, *b* 1968. —— Carol, *b* 1944: *m* 1st, 1967 (*m diss* 1993), Peter De Villiers; 2ndly, 1993, Alwyn Landman, of Elgin Villa, Marlborough Lane, Bath, Som, and has issue living (by 1st *m*), Nicholas James, *b* 1971, — Brigitte Pamela, *b* 1973. —— Susan Pamela, *b* 1945: *m* 1965, Robert Webb, and has issue living, Georgie Suzanne, *b* 1971, — Polly Louisa, *b* 1973.

The 1st baronet, Sir Thomas, was a Director of Canadian Pacific Railway, of Hudson's Bay Co, and of Bank of Montreal, founder and editor of Thomas Skinner & Co (Publishers) Ltd, and founder and editor of "Stock Exchange Official Year Book" and "The Directory of Directors". Sir (Thomas) Hewitt, 2nd baronet, was Pres of Thomas Skinner & Co (Publishers) Ltd.

SKIPWITH (E) 1622, of Prestwould, Leicestershire

Without God I cannot

Sir PATRICK ALEXANDER D'ESTOTEVILLE SKIPWITH, 12th *Baronet*, son of late Grey d'Estoteville Townsend Skipwith, Flying Officer RAF Vol Reserve, el son of 11th baronet; *b* 1 Sep 1938; *s* his grandfather, *Sir* GREY HUMBERSTON D'ESTOTEVILLE, 1950; *ed* Harrow, Dublin Univ (MA), and Imperial Coll, London Univ (PhD); marine geologist in Tasmania 1966-67, Malaysia 1967-69, W Africa 1969-70, then at the Directorate Gen of Mineral Resources, Jeddah, Saudi Arabia 1970-71 and 1972-73, geological editor, Bureau de Recherches Géologiques et Minières, Jeddah, Saudi Arabia, 1973-86; Dir Immel Publishing Ltd, London 1987-96 (Man Dir 1988-89), and Dir GeoEdit, London 1987-96; Head of Translation, BRGM, Orléans, since 1996: *m* 1st, 1964 (*m diss* 1970), Gillian Patricia, adopted da of late Charles Frederick Harwood; 2ndly, 1972 (*m diss* 1997), Ashkhain, da of late Bedros Atikian, of Calgary, Alberta, Canada; 3rdly, 1997, Martine Sophie Yvonne, only da of Joseph de Wilde, of 2 Allée des Bouleaux, Theillay, Loir-et-Cher, France, and has issue by 1st and 3rd *m*.

Arms – Argent, three bars gules, in chief a greyhound courant sable, collared or. Crest – A turnstile or.
Residence – 76 rue de Pont-aux-Moines, 45450 Donnery, France. *Club* – Chelsea Arts.

SONS LIVING (*By 1st marriage*)

ALEXANDER SEBASTIAN GREY D'ESTOTEVILLE, *b* 9 April 1969; *ed* Harrow, and Kingston Univ (BA); Man Dir Pepperhead (Original Designs) Ltd, London.

(*By 3rd marriage*)

Grey Camille d'Estoteville, *b* 1997. —— Louis Peyton d'Estoteville, *b* (twin)1997.

DAUGHTER LIVING (*By 1st marriage*)

Zara Alexandra Jane d'Estoteville, *b* 1967: *m* 1998, Nigel Francis Moran, of Port Douglas, Queensland, Australia, yst son of Edward Moran.

UNCLES LIVING (*Sons of 11th baronet*)

Egerton Grey d'Estoteville (Langton Old Rectory, Blandford Forum, Dorset DT11 9HS), *b* 1935; *ed* Canford; late National Service 13th/18th Roy Hussars and Royal Ulster Rifles: *m* 1997, Deirdre Veronica, yst da of late Richard Smythe Guinness, of Lodge Park, Straffan, co Kildare, and formerly wife of Alberto Neyra, of Lima, Peru. —— Peyton Stephen (c/o The Fine Art Society, plc, 148 New Bond St, W1), *b* 1939; *ed* Canford: *m* 1971, Anne, da of Capt C. E. Barren, of Seasalter, Kent, and has issue living, Grey Egerton d'Estoteville, *b* 1981, — Selina, *b* 1972, — Amber Louise, *b* 1974.

AUNT LIVING (*Daughter of 11th baronet*)

Audrey Elsie Townsend, *b* 1911: *m* 1943, Paul Antony Negretti, formerly Maj The Black Watch, and has issue living, (Antony) Simon Timothy, *b* 1945: *m* 1981, Lucinda G., yst da of late Guy Lawrence, and has issue living, Guy *b* 1983, Gipsy *b* 1989, — Annelise Audrey, *b* 1948: *m* 1975, Alexander G. M. Kemp, of Homewood Farm, Mulgowie, Qld 4341, Australia, son of J. E. Kemp, of Queensland, Australia, and has issue living, Simon James *b* 1977, Emma Bay *b* 1979. *Residence* – Thornborough Thatch, Sutton Manor, Sutton Scotney, Hants SO21 3JX.

COLLATERAL BRANCHES LIVING

Grandson of late Col Grey Townsend Skipwith, only son of Fulwar Skipwith, 3rd son of 8th Bt:—
Issue of late Lt-Col James Wemyss Skipwith, RE, *b* 1875, *d* 1950: *m* 1911, Estelle, who *d* 1961, da of late Robert Henderson, of The Wylds, Liss, Hants:—
Patrick James Townsend, *b* 1915; Lt-Col (ret) RA; Hong Kong 1941 (prisoner): *m* 1941, Beryl Daisy, who *d* 1999, da of late Arthur A. Fair, of Montree, Athlone, co Westmeath, and has issue living, Michael James Grey (Swyncombe Old School, Cookley Green, nr Nettlebed, Oxon), *b* 1951: *m* 1988, Jacqueline, da of J. Ould, of Coventry, Warwicks, — Susan Virginia, *b* 1947: *m* 1988, Christopher James Frederick Blumer (*see* E Lauderdale), — Bridget Ann, *b* 1948: *m* 1981, John Macaskill, of 12 Sheep Lane, LI, New York, NY 11560, son of late Dr John Macaskill, of Moray Place, Edinburgh, and has issue, John *b* 1984, Ben *b* 1986. *Residence* – North End, Chiddingfold, Surrey.

Grandsons of late Lt-Col James Wemyss Skipwith, RE (ante):—
Issue of late Maj John Granville Wemyss Skipwith, RA, b 1921, d 1991: m 1st, 1947, Margaret Lettice Mary, who d 1968, only da of late Col William Paget-Tomlinson, DSO, of Biggins House, Kirkby Lonsdale, Carnforth, Lancs; 2ndly, 1977, Eva Agnes, who d 1997, da of George Cooper Ingall, of Croft End, Kendal, and widow of Maj James Cameron Campbell, RE (ret):—
(By 1st m) Guy Paget Grey (107 Cheshire St, Market Drayton, Shropshire), b 1951; ed Shrewsbury, and Nottingham Univ: m 1972, Pamela, da of late Thomas N. Foster, of Edgmond, Shropshire, and has living, Thomas Grey, b 1979, — Robert John, b 1985, — Judith Lakshmi, b 1988. ——Philip James Henderson (Biggins Grange, Kirkby Lonsdale, Carnforth, Lancs), b 1957; ed Shrewsbury.

Grandchildren of late Col Grey Townsend Skipwith (ante):—
Issue of late Lt-Col Frederick Skipwith, b 1877, d 1964: m 1916, Lily Spence, who d 1979, da of late Lt-Col John Garvie, MD, IMS:—
Wendy Elisabeth, b 1927: m 1955, Capt Thomas Peter Robin Crane, CBE, late RSNC, of Bridge Cottage, Well Lane, Midhurst, Sussex, and has issue living, Jennifer Anne, b 1958: m 1988, David Michael Corner, of 105 Listria Park, N16, son of late Freddie Corner, of Dorking, Surrey, and has issue living, Kai Louis Thomas Freddie b 1997, Caroline Virginia b 1968, — Caroline Virginia, b 1969.

Issue of late Charles Grey Yule Skipwith, b 1890, d 1967: m 1926, Althea Kathleen Joyce, who d 1973, da of late Charles Hunting, of Slaley Hall, Northumberland:—
Michael Charles (The Lotus Pottery, Stoke Gabriel, S Devon), b 1928: m 1957, Mary Elizabeth, da of R Barthram Wood, of Croft House, Kirkbymoorside, Yorks, and has issue living, Jonathan Charles d'Estoteville (The Palms, Venn Grove, Plymouth, Devon), b 1962; BSc: m 1993, Gina, da of M. P. Ferrigno, of Dournazac, France, — Joanna Lisette, b 1960.

Grandchildren of late Lionel Skipwith, 7th son of 8th baronet:—
Issue of late Frederick Charles Skipwith, b 1857, d 1940: m 1893, Mary Annie, da of G. F. Cremer, formerly of Wanganui, New Zealand:—
Gore Peyton Lewis, b 1894. ——Lionel Ernest, b 1896: m 1929, Eva May, da of J. Hopkins, of Auckland, New Zealand, and has issue living, Ronald Hugh, b 1930. Residence – Auckland, New Zealand.

Grandchildren of late Francis Skipwith, 4th son of late Lionel Skipwith (ante):—
Issue of late Robert Grey Skipwith, b 1900, d 1989: m 1937, Annemarie (7 Trust Cottages, 15 Murambi Drive, Mutare, Zimbabwe), da of late Hans Evers, of Ratzeburg, German:—
Francis Grey (Crosfields School, Shinfield, Reading, Berks), b 1940: m 1968, Jacqueline Ann, da of Charles Albert Frederick Kettley, and has issue living, Andrew William Grey, b 1969: ed Charterhouse, and Trin Coll, Camb, — Timothy Edward, b 1972; ed Charterhouse, — Barnaby James, b 1974; ed St Edward's Sch, Oxford. ——Robert Frederick (PO Box 327, Kwe Kwe, Zimbabwe), b 1941: m 1st, 1965 (m diss 1971), Patricia Ann Saville; 2ndly, 1971, Judith Ann, da of late Thomas Stephen Johnson, of Que Que, Zimbabwe, and has issue living (by 1st m), Charles Robert, b 1969: m 1998, Deborah, da of Thomas Edwin Cox, of Goromonzi, Zimbabwe, — (by 2nd m) Thomas Stephen, b 1975, — James Grey b 1976.

Issue of late Capt Lionel Peyton Skipwith, RN, b 1902; d 1978: m 1926, Thelma Westwood, who d 1988, only child of late Surg Cdr Andrian A. Forrester, of Weymouth:—
Venetia Forrester (11 Castle St, Totnes, Devon TQ9 5NU), b 1932: m 1951 (m diss 1991), Cdr James Michael Burnard Walkey, RN, and has issue living, Anthony Charles d'Estouteville, b 1955, — Justin Robert Chichester (42 Orpington Rd, Winchmore Hill N21 3PG), b 1957.

Grandchildren of late Rev Granville Gore Skipwith (infra):—
Issue of late Philip Lionel d'Estouteville SKIPWITH-TYSER, b 1904, d 1991; assumed by Royal Licence 1958 the additional surname and arms of Tyser: m 1932, Elsie Barbara, who d 1999, da of late Col Arthur Edward Phillips, DSO, of Elm House, Winterbourne Dauntsey, nr Salisbury:—
Richard Peyton SKIPWITH (Wisteria House, Wickham, Hants PO17 5JG), b 1937; ed Eton: m 1965, Annie Carmen Angele Marie, eldest da of André Bonnor, of Château Leyran, Villenave d'Ornon, Bordeaux, and has issue living, Julian Alexandre d'Estoteville (203B Camberwell Grove, SE5 8JU), b 1972: m 1997, Caroline M. C. BIRCH, da of R. and F. Birch, of London, — Anouk Barbara Hélène, b 1974. ——Charles Fulwar SKIPWITH (Le Cros, Salle Bruneau, 33760 Frontenac, France), b 1946, ed Wellington: m 1969, Lucie, da of late Maurice Othon, and has issue living, Naomi Barbara Marie-Françoise, b 1972, — Alissa Caroline Marie-Thérèse, b 1975, — Georgina Marie-Louise Selina, b 1979. ——Noel Camilla, b 1934: m 1959, Capt Anthony Charles Alston Benda, 1st The Queen's Dragoon Gds (The Old Vicarage, Crondall, Hants GU10 5QQ), son of Charles Kenneth Benda, and has issue living, Nicholas James Alston, b 1960, — Jonathan Charles Alston, b 1962, — William Philip Alston, b 1966.

Grandchildren of late Lionel Skipwith (ante):—
Issue of late Rev Granville Gore Skipwith, b 1865, d 1955: m 1899, Violet Mary, who d 1957, da of late George Walter Tyser, JP (Parkyne, Bt):—
Rev Osmund Humberston (23 Heathdene Manor, Grandfield Av, Watford, Herts), b 1906; ed Harrow, and New Coll, Oxford (MA); sometime a Chap to Forces; formerly a Missionary; Africa and SE Asia 1941-54: m 1946, Philippa Katharine Jane, da of late Richard Edward Skipwith, MBE, of Ruddington, Notts, and has issue living, Peter Michael (25 The Ridgeway, Watford, Herts), b 1947; BSc: m 1970, Patricia Mary, BA, ARICS, da of David Allan, of Penrith, and has issue living, Susan Katharine, b 1972; MA: m 1998, Charles Joseph Andrew Tugendhat, elder son of Michael George Tugendhat, QC, Rebecca Vivienne b 1974; MA, MPhil. ——Barbara Nannette, b 1902: m 1928, Gerald William Kenyon-Slaney, OBE, who d 1953 (see B Kenyon, colls). Residence – 16 Smith Terrace, SW3, and Six Mount Pleasant, Tenterden, Kent.

Granddaughters of late Ernest d'Estoteville Skipwith, son of late Rev Randolph Skipwith, 10th son of 8th baronet:—
Issue of late Randolph Bruce d'Estoteville Skipwith, b 1880, d 1939: m 1906, Adelia L. Warnken, who d 1938:—

Margery Louise, *b* 1908: *m* 1936, Earle Sydney Chard, and has issue living, Carole Elizabeth: *m* 1958, Gordon Lorne Down. —— Lorraine Gladys, *b* 1909: *m* 1936, Herbert Roberts Adams, who *d* 1983, and has issue living, Donald Bruce, *b* 1942.

Grandchildren of late Reginald Skipwith, elder son of late Cmdr Sidmouth Stowell Skipwith, RN, 12th and yst son of 8th baronet:—
Issue of late Cmdr Arthur Grey Skipwith, RN, *b* 1902, *d* 1997: *m* 1933, Sarah Hope, who *d* 1994, yst da of late Maj Alfred James Fraser, DSO, of Woodside, Hardingstone, Northampton:—
(William) Grey, *b* 1938. —— Sarah Jane, *b* 1943: *m* 1967, John William Finlay Robins. *Residence* – Manor Farm, Longbridge Deverill, Wilts. —— (Rosemary) Ann (*Baroness Iliffe*), *b* (twin) 1943: *m* 1966, 3rd Baron Iliffe, and has issue. *Residence* – Yattendon Park, Yattendon, Berks RG16 0UT.

This baronet claims descent from Robert d'Estoteville, Baron of Cottingham, *temp* William the Conqueror. Many of his descendants were of knightly rank, and distinguished both in war and in law, a Sir William Skipwith having been a Justice of the Queen's Bench *temp* Edward III and Richard II, and a Sir Thomas having achieved honour in the French wars was knighted by Henry V. The 1st baronet, who achieved reputation as a poet, sold the Prestwold estates in 1653. The 3rd baronet emigrated to Virginia, USA, in the middle of the 17th century. Sir Peyton Skipwith, who died in Virginia in 1805, was domiciled in England, as were his successors.

SLADE (UK) 1831, of Maunsel House, Somersetshire

Faithful and bold

Sir (JULIAN) BENJAMIN ALFRED SLADE, 7th *Baronet*; *b* 22 May 1946; *s* his father, *Capt Sir* MICHAEL NIAL 1962; *ed* Millfield; Dir of Shirlstar Container Transport Ltd, etc; Mem Worshipful Co of Ironmongers and Freeman of City of Lond (1979): *m* 1977 (*m diss* 1991), Pauline Carol, el da of Maj Claude Myburgh, of Inholmes Court, Hartley Wintney, Hants.

ᴬrms – Per fesse argent and sable, a pale countercharged and three horses' heads erased two and one of the second; on a chief ermine, two bombs fired proper. ᶜrest – On a mount vert, a horse's head erased sable, encircled by a chain in the form of an arch gold.
Residence – Maunsel, North Newton, Bridgwater, Somerset. *Club* – Turf.

COLLATERAL BRANCHES LIVING

Issue of late Basil Alfred Slade, 2nd son of 3rd baronet, *b* 1865, *d* 1930: *m* 1st, 1891 (*m diss* 1925), Louisa Mary, who *d* 19—, da of William Clements, of Kingsclere, Hants; 2ndly, 1925, Grace Joanna, who *d* 1975, da of Edward Harrison Tame, of Whitecote, nr Halstead, Essex:-
(By 2nd wife) Barbara Agnes, *b* 1916: *m* 1949, as his 2nd wife, A/Cdre Allen Henry Wheeler, CBE, RAF, who *d* 1984, of Whistley Bridge Field, Whistley Green, Hurst, Reading, Berks RG10 0RA (*see* Bs Berners, colls).

Granddaughter of late Marcus Warre Slade, KC, 2nd son of late Rev George Fitz Slade, 11th son of 1st baronet:—
Issue of late Marcus George Savill Slade, *b* 1906, *d* 1972: *m* 1944 (*m diss* 1953), Rita Annie, da of William James Motton, of Plymouth:—
Susan Rebecca (2 Walton House, Walton St, SW3), *b* 1945; painter.

Granddaughter of late Henry Adolphus Warre Slade, 3rd and yst son of Rev George FitzClarence Slade (ante):—
Issue of late Maurice Gordon Slade, *b* 1902, *d* 1971: *m* 1934, Margaret, who *d* 1980, da of Hew Congreve Kennedy:—
Primrose, *b* 1934: *m* 1957, John Patrick Roger Heather Hayes, Lt-Col RE, of Tivoli Farms, Tivoli, NY 12583, USA, and has issue living, Phoebe, *b* 1960.

The 1st baronet, Gen Sir John, GCH, served with great distinction in the Peninsular War. The 2nd baronet was an eminent QC. Sir Alfred, 3rd baronet, who served during the Crimean War, was Receiver-Gen of Inland Revenue 1875-90.

SLEIGHT (UK) 1920, of Weelsby Hall, Clee, co Lincoln

Sir RICHARD SLEIGHT, 4th *Baronet*; *b* 27 May 1946; *s* his father, *Sir* JOHN FREDERICK, 1990: *m* 1978, Marie-Thérèse, only da of O. M. Stepan, of London W3, and has issue.

Arms – Per chevron or and sable, in chief two cross-crosslets and in base a lymphad with sail hoisted countercharged. Crest – A mast with sail hoisted argent charged with three cross-crosslets sable.
Address – c/o National Westminster Bank, 6 High St, Teddington, Middx TW11 8EP.

SONS LIVING

JAMES ALEXANDER, *b* 5 Jan 1981. ———— Nicholas Edward *b* 1985.

WIDOW LIVING OF THIRD BARONET

JACQUELINE MARGARET (*Jacqueline, Ludy Sleight*), eldest da of Maj H. R. Carter, of Brisbane, Queensland, and widow of Ronald Mundell: *m* 1942, Sir John Frederick Sleight, 3rd Bt, who *d* 1990. *Residence* – ......

COLLATERAL BRANCHES LIVING

Serve all, slight none

Granddaughter of late Maj Rowland Sleight, 2nd son of 1st baronet:—
Issue of late Rowland Derek Lambert Sleight, *b* 1908, *d* 1994: *m* 1939, Winifred (The White House, Quidenham, Norfolk NR16 2PB), da of late Calvert Hunt, of London:-
Lesley, *b* 1943: *m* 1978, Crispin de Boos. *Residence* – The Old Bakery, Banham, Norfolk NR16 2HW.

Grandchildren of late Nelson Sleight (infra):—
Issue of late Sqdn-Ldr Peter Sleight, DFM, AE, *b* 1920, *d* 1995: *m* 1947, Joyce Elizabeth (Herons Flight, 11 Manor Park, Legbourne, Louth, Lincs), eldest da of J. H. Dale, of The Langmore, Wold Newton, Lincs:-
(John) Nelson (51 Park Drive, Grimsby, NE Lincs), *b* 1947: *m* 1974, Susan Jennifer, da of J. C. Hewson, of Tetney, Lincs, and has issue living, Lucy Margaret, *b* 1979, — Sophie Elizabeth, *b* 1982. ———— Diana Margaret, *b* 1950: *m* 1974, (James) Stewart Atkinson, of Chartwell House, Messingham Lane, Scawby, Brigg, N Lincs, and has issue living, Charles William James, *b* 1977, — Charlotte Diana, *b* 1980, — Louise Joanna, *b* (twin) 1980.

Issue of late Nelson Sleight, 3rd son of 1st baronet, *b* 1883, *d* 1939: *m* 1915, Edith Mary, who *d* 1966, da of late Christopher Dewick Charles Hunt, of Gainsborough:—
Violet Mary, *b* 1917: *m* 1938, Frederick Ousey Redshaw, late Lieut RNVR, who *d* 1980, and has issue living, Pamela Mary, *b* 1942: *m* 1968, George Bryan O'Toole, of Field House, Duton Hill, Great Dunmow, Essex, and has issue living, Laurence James *b* 1969: *m* 1996, Anna Hadland, and has issue living, Eleanor Grace, Howard Charles *b* 1975, Stella Elizabeth *b* 1971: *m* 1999, Adrian Stuart Westbrook Douglas, Lucy Alicia *b* 1978. *Residence* – 9 Croft Court, Braintree Rd, Gt Dunmow, Essex CM6 1HR.

Issue of late George Frederick Sleight, yst son of 1st baronet, *b* 1890, *d* 1954: *m* 1915, Edith Mary, who *d* 1963, da of late Edwin James Brockway, JP, of Oakham, Rutland:—
Michael Marcus, *b* 1924; *ed* privately, and Camb Univ. *Residence* – Binbrook Hall, Binbrook, Lincs LN3 6BW. ———— Edith Mary, *b* 1918: *m* 1947, James Davey, and has issue living, Veronica Mary, *b* 1950, — Caroline Frances, *b* 1954. *Residence* – Kelstern Hall, Louth, Lincs.

Sir George, 1st Bt, was Lord of the Manor of Kelstern, Lincolnshire. Sir Ernest, OBE, TD, 2nd Bt, was High Sheriff, DL, and JP of Lincolnshire 1946.

SMILEY (UK) 1903, of Drumalis, Larne, co Antrim, and Gallowhill, Paisley, co Renfrew

By industry, valour, and
fortitude

Lt-Col Sir JOHN PHILIP SMILEY, 4th *Baronet*; *b* 24 Feb 1934; *s* his father, *Sir* HUGH HOUSTON, 1990; *ed* Eton, and RMA Sandhurst; Lt-Col late Gren Guards; Cyprus 1958; ADC to Gov of Bermuda 1961-62; Master Grocers' Co 1992-93: *m* 1963, Davina Elizabeth, el da of late Denis Charles Griffiths, of Orlingbury Hall, nr Kettering, Northants, and has issue.

Arms – 1st and 4th, per bend azure and or, a lion rampant ermine between three pheons counterchanged, *Smiley*; 2nd and 3rd gules, on a chevron argent two mullets azure, in base a fusil of the second, *Kerr*. Crest – A lion's jamb erased, and holding in bend sinister a pheon shafted proper, head or.
Residence – Cornerway House, Chobham, Surrey GU24 8SW. *Club* – Army and Navy.

SONS LIVING

CHRISTOPHER HUGH CHARLES, *b* 7 Feb 1968; *ed* Eton, and Edinburgh Univ (MA): *m* 1998, Clare Annabel Barr Smith, yr da of Maj Henry Charles Blosse-Lynch, Irish Gds, of Longcross House, Headley, Berks (*see* Yate, Bt (ext), 1990 Edn). *Residence* – 81 Montholme Rd, SW11 6HX. —— William Timothy John, *b* 1972; *ed* Eton, and Bristol Univ (BSc); Capt Gren Gds.

DAUGHTER LIVING

Melinda Elizabeth Eirène, *b* 1965: *m* 1991, Jonathon Mark Midelton Baker, son of John Baker, of Charlton, Horethorne, Dorset, and has issue living, Archie John Midelton, *b* 1993, — Herbert Douglas Midelton, *b* 1995. *Residence* – Lovel House, Upton Noble, Som.

UNCLE LIVING (*son of 2nd baronet*)

David de Crespigny, LVO, OBE, MC (30 Kensington Mansions, Trebovir Rd, SW5 9TQ. *Clubs* – White's, MCC, Special Forces), *b* 1916; *ed* Nautical Coll, Pangbourne, and RMC Sandhurst; Col late Royal Horse Gds, commanded Royal Horse Gds 1952-54, Mil Attaché Stockholm 1955-58 (Knight Cdr of Order of the Sword of Sweden), and Cdr of Armed Forces of Sultan of Muscat and Oman 1958-61, and Mil Adviser to Imam of Yemen 1963-68; a Member of HM Body Guard of Corps of Gentlemen-at-Arms 1966-68; 1939-45 War with 1st Household Cav Regt in Middle East (despatches) and with Special Forces in the Balkans (MC and Bar), Far East 1945 (OBE); OBE (Mil) 1946, LVO 1952; Grand Cordon of the Order of Skanderbeg of Albania, Albanian Order of Liberty, 1st class, 1994: *m* 1947, Moyra Eileen, da of late Lt-Col Lord Francis George Montagu Douglas Scott, KCMG, DSO (*see* D Buccleuch, colls), and widow of Maj Hugo Douglas Tweedie, Scots Gds, and has issue living, Xan de Crespigny (68 Lonsdale Rd, Oxford OX2 7EP; White's, Beefsteak, and Polish Hearth Clubs), *b* 1949; *ed* Eton and New Coll, Oxford (MA); Editor of *Africa Confidential* 1977-81; Leader writer, *The Times* 1982-83; Foreign Specialist, *The Economist* 1983-86; Moscow Correspondent, *The Daily Telegraph* 1986-89, and Washington Correspondent *The Sunday Telegraph* 1990-92, since when Political Editor *The Economist*: *m* 1983, Hon Jane Lyon-Dalberg-Acton, yst da of 3rd Baron Acton, and formerly wife of late Charles Thomas Pugh, and has issue living, Ben Richard Philip de Crespigny *b* 1983, Adam David Emerich *b* 1988, — Philip David (157 Mount Pleasant Rd, Singapore), *b* 1951; *ed* Eton, and St Andrews Univ (MA); Solomon Islands Govt 1974-80, Hong Kong Govt 1980-85; W. I. Carr (Far East) 1985-90, since when Man Dir Jardine Fleming Securities: *m* 19—, So-Hyung, yr da of Gen Young-Woo Kim, of Seoul, Korea, and has issue living, Francis Hugh Kim *b* 1996, Dominic David *b* 1998.

AUNT LIVING (*Daughter of 2nd baronet*)

Patricia Margaret (3 The Lilypool, Melbourne, Derbys), *b* 1907: *m* 1st, 1931, Rupert Douglas Tollemache, who *d* 1933 (B Tollemache, colls); 2ndly, 1941, Col Charles Dalby, CBE, KRRC, who *d* 1981, and has issue living (by 2nd *m*), Charles Gerald (Castle Donington, Leics) *b* 1942; *ed* Eton; Arch Assocn Dip; ARIBA: *m* 1980, Kathleen Margaret, el da of late Stanley Hodson, of Luska, Puckane, Nenagh, co Tipperary (*see* Hodson, Bt, colls), and has issue living, Edward Charles Gerald *b* 1982, Lucy Margaretta Hyacinthe *b* 1981, — Patrick Claude John (40 Chester Row, SW1W 8JP; White's Club), *b* 1948; *ed* Rugby; late Royal Green Jackets.

COLLATERAL BRANCHES LIVING

Issue of late John Claude Smiley, 2nd son of 2nd baronet, *b* 1910, *d* 1995: *m* 1st, 1936 (*m diss* 1942), Lady Cecilia Katherine Wellesley, who *d* 1952, yr da of 3rd Earl Cowley; 2ndly, 1947, Mrs Sheila Joyce Otter-Barry, who *d* 1978, da of late Hon Stanhope Alfred Tollemache (B Tollemache):-
(By 1st *m*) David Valerian, *b* 1938; *ed* Wellington Coll; Maj late Royal Horse Gds: *m* 1st, 1962 (*m diss* 1987), Rose-Ann, el da of Col David Greig; 2ndly, 1988, Jill Velia, da of late Cdr John Kershaw, DSO, and widow of Lionel William (Robin) Huntington, MC, and has had issue (by 1st *m*), Patrick Valerian, *b* 1965; *ed* Glenalmond, and Durham Univ (BA): *m* 1998, Arabella Faith, da of late Brian J. Chapman, of Leics, and of Mrs David Jinks, of Gaddesby Hall, Leics, — †Thomas Edward de Crespigny, *b* 1967; *ed* Kiel Sch; *d* 1989, — (Katherine) Cecilia, *b* 1963: *m* 1990, Tom Julian Beaumont Varcoe, of 77 Winchester St, Overton, Hants, yr son of late Beaumont Varcoe, of Nanscawen, Par, Cornwall, and has issue living, Thomas Anthony Beaumont *b* 1991, Xan John Felix *b* 1992.

Issue of late Major Peter Kerr KERR-SMILEY, 2nd son of 1st baronet, *b* 1879, *d* 1943 (having assumed in 1905 the additional surname of Kerr): *m* 1905, Maud, who *d* 1962, da of Ernest L. Simpson, of New York:—

Elizabeth Maud, *b* 1907: *m* 1936, Christopher Edward Clive Hussey, CBE, who *d* 1970 (E Powis, colls). *Residence* – Scotney Castle, Lamberhurst, Kent.

Grandsons of late Maj Peter Kerr-Smiley (ante):—
Issue of late Lt-Col Cyril Hugh Kerr-Smiley, TD, *b* 1906, *d* 1980: *m* 1933, Agnes, who *d* 1986, el da of late Lt-Col George Cecil Minett Sorel Cameron, CBE (*see* B Tollemache, colls):—
Peter Simon (Towranna Farm, Huntingfield, Suffolk; Naval and Military Club), *b* 1934; *ed* Ampleforth, and RMA Sandhurst; Lt-Col Queen's Own Cameron Highlanders, Arabian Peninsula 1956-57, ADC to Gov of Malta 1959-61, Queen's Messenger 1984-96: *m* 1960 (*m diss* 1981), Jennifer Guise, only da of late Lt-Col Thomas Guise Tucker, MC, and has issue living, Mark Alexander (15 Granard Rd, SW12), *b* 1961; *ed* Ampleforth: *m* 1988, Manuela Marie, da of S. M. Raquez, of 205 Av Brugmann, Brussels, and has issue living, Frederick Hugh *b* 1992, Isabella Louise *b* 1990, Eloise Olivia *b* 1995, — Justin Robert, *b* 1965; *ed* Ampleforth, and Newcastle Univ (BA), — Emma Caroline Hyde, *b* 1963: *m* 1994, Euan D. Nicolson, yr son of late Timothy Nicolson, of Kintbury, Berks, and of Mrs Nicholas Embiricos, of Kirdford, Sussex. —— Hector Robert (Elms Hall, Colne Engaine, Essex; Boodle's Club), *b* 1937; *ed* Ampleforth; Lt Queen's Own Cameron Highlanders (TA Reserve): *m* 1962, Eleanor Jill, da of Cdr Peter Wadlow, RN (ret), and has issue living, Simon Alastair Hugh, *b* 1964; *ed* Gordonstoun: *m* 1992, Nony Mary Louise, da of Sir Richard John Uniacke Barrow, 6th Bt, and has issue living, Eleanor Sophie Frances *b* 1994, (Fiona) Emma Victoria *b* 1996, — Christopher Peter Nicholas, *b* 1967; *ed* Eton, — Charlotte Elizabeth, *b* 1963: *m* 1990, Christopher Hugh Courtney Smith, son of Sir Robert Courtney Smith, CBE, and has issue living, George Hector Courtney *b* 1993, Harriet Rose Constance *b* 1995. —— Nicholas Ernest, *b* 1940; *ed* Ampleforth, and Kalgoorlie Sch of Mines (MAusIMM): *m* 1973, Georgina Jane, el da of late Maj Sir George Andrew Dick-Lauder, 12th Bt, and has issue living, Samantha Fiona Marguerite, *b* 1976.

Grandchildren of late Hubert Stewart Smiley, 3rd son of 1st baronet:—
Issue of late Maj (Charles) Michael Smiley, CVO, JP, *b* 1910, *d* 1991: *m* 1939, Lavinia, who *d* 1991, da of late Capt Hon (Bernard) Clive Pearson (*see* V Cowdray, colls):—
James Robin Clive (50 Martin Rd, Centennial Park, Sydney 2021, NSW, Aust), *b* 1947; *ed* Gordonstoun: *m* 1981, Jane Suzanne, da of late James Gorrie, of 24 Lynwood Av, Killara, NSW, and has issue living, Alexander Orlando Charles, *b* 1981, — Thomas Robin James, *b* 1983. —— Andrew Michael, *b* 1952; *ed* Eton; Gren Gds: *m* 1975, (Sarah) Caroline, da of late Lt-Col C. C. Coade, and has issue living, Charlotte Sarah, *b* 1983, — Sarah Miranda, *b* 1986. —— Miranda Daphne Jane (*Countess of Iveagh*) (Wilbury Park, Newton Toney, Wilts SP4 0HS), *b* 1940: *m* 1963 (*m diss* 1984), 3rd Earl of Iveagh, and has issue (*see* E Iveagh).

The 1st baronet, Sir Hugh Houston Smiley (1841-1909), was Principal Proprietor of the *Northern Whig*. The 2nd baronet, Major Sir John Smiley (1876-1930), 6th Dragoon Guards, served during S African War 1900-1902, and European War 1914-18. The 3rd baronet, Sir Hugh Smiley (1905-90), Gren Guards, served in European War 1939-45, and was High Sheriff for Hants (1959), and Vice Ld-Lieut (1973-82). He *m* 1933, Nancy Elizabeth Louise Hardy, who *d* 1999, aged 89, da of late Ernest Walter Hardy Beaton (and sister of late Sir Cecil Beaton, CBE, the photographer and designer).

SMITH (UK) 1809, of Eardiston, Worcestershire

Sir CHRISTOPHER SYDNEY WINWOOD SMITH, 5th *Baronet*; *b* 20 Sept 1906; *s* his father, *Sir* WILLIAM SYDNEY WINWOOD, 1953: *m* 1932, Phyllis Berenice, yst da of late Thomas Robert O'Grady, of Waterford, Ireland, and Grafton, NSW, and has issue.

Arms – Sable, a cross flory or, on a chief engrailed ermine, a demi-lion issuant between two cross-crosslets gules. **Crest** – A greyhound couchant, sable, collared and line reflexed over the back or, the body charged with a cross-crosslet of the last, the dexter paw resting upon a cross flory as in the arms.
Residence – 349 Fry St, Grafton, NSW 2460, Australia.

SONS LIVING

ROBERT CHRISTOPHER SYDNEY WINWOOD, *b* 1939: *m* 1972, Roselyn Nellie, eldest da of late James Keith McKensie, of Sydney, NSW 2444, and has issue living, Craig Robert Winwood *b* 1974, — Robyn Louise Winwood, *b* 1978. *Residence* – 13 Siren St, Port Maquarie, NSW. —— Hugh William Standish Winwood, *b* 1942: *m* 1966, Clare Philomena, eldest da of late Leslie Arthur Stinson, of Sydney, NSW, and has issue living, Christopher Hugh Winwood, *b* 1966, — Gregory Robert Winwood, *b* 1971, — Catherine Anne Winwood, *b* 1969, — Julie Stella Winwood, *b* 1973. —— Terence John Winwood, *b* 1945: *m* 1967, Helen June, da of late Donald W. McLeod, of Cootamunda, NSW, and has issue living, Ian James Winwood, *b* 1969, — Richard Charles Winwood, *b* 1972, — Jaqueline Nicole Winwood, *b* 1975. —— Matthew Roy Winwood, *b* 1947: *m* 1975, Janette Leferve, eldest da of late John Truman, of Sydney, NSW, and has issue living, Michael Winwood, *b* 1977. —— David Anthony Winwood, *b* 1949: *m* 1976, Judith Chaffey, of Grafton, NSW, and has issue living, Simon Winwood, *b* 1976, — Steven Winwood, *b* 1977. —— Ronald James Thomas Winwood, *b* 1951: *m* 1976, Rhonda Jean, eldest da of late Ronald Raine, of Sydney, NSW, and has issue living, Gary Winwood, *b* 1978, — Benjamin Winwood, *b* 1981, — Megan Winwood, *b* 1984.

Residence – 15 Jordan St, Fairfield, NSW 2169.

DAUGHTERS LIVING

Villette Mary Winwood, *b* 1935: *m* 1961, Roger Hore, and has issue living, Andrew, *b* 1962. —— Helen Eve Winwood, *b* 1936: *m* 1958, Arthur Sydney Macalpine, and has issue living, Arthur David, *b* 1959. — Ian Christopher, *b* 1961, — Alison Helen, *b* 1966, — Jillian Elizabeth, *b* 1970. —— Frances Caroline Winwood, *b* 1941: *m* 1973, Kenneth James Hebblewhite, and has issue living, Mark Kenneth, *b* 1976, — Simon James, *b* 1978, — Rebecca Frances, *b* 1978.

BROTHER LIVING

Rupert William Winwood (42 Campbell St, Toowoomba, Queensland), *b* 1908: *m* 1940, Nancia Jean Margaret, da of John Bailey Cave, of Grafton, NS Wales, and has issue living, Geoffrey Stirling Winwood, *b* 1945: *m* 1972, Stephanie Sue, el da of W. Kelly, of Tallowoods, Cabarlah, Queensland, and has issue living, Nicholas William Winwood *b* 1977, Hugh Stirling Winwood *b* 1981, — Adrian John Winwood, *b* 1955: *m* 1984, Luciana Tranquilla, da of A. Gastaldo, of Adelaide, S Australia, — Merran Joy Winwood, *b* 1942: *m* 1977, Virgil Joseph Hull, PhD, of Keyser, W Virginia, USA, and has issue living, Meredith Fleur Winwood *b* 1980.

COLLATERAL BRANCH LIVING

Granddaughter of late William Arthur Winwood Smith, yst son of 3rd baronet:—
Issue of late Instr-Cdr Christopher William Winwood Smith, RN (ret), *b* 1893, *d* 1969: *m* 1916, Alice Muriel, who *d* 1969, da of Capt W. F. Garside, of Morden, Seaford:—
Pauline Muriel Winwood, *b* 1918: *m* 1st, 1949, James Mayhew; 2ndly, 1977, Richard Tudor Archer, of 7 Laurel Drive, Southmoor, Abingdon, Oxon.

SMITH (UK) 1897, Stratford Place, St Marylebone, co London

Dabit qui dedit
He will give who hath given

Sir (THOMAS) GILBERT SMITH, 4th *Baronet*; *b* 2 July 1937: *s* his father, *Sir* THOMAS TURNER, 1961; *ed* Huntley Sch, and Nelson Coll; Exec: *m* 1962, Patricia Christine, da of David Cooper, of Paraparaumu, NZ, and has issue.

Arms – Quarterly, or and gules, a fret between three fleurs-de-lis all counterchanged. **Crest** – A fret gules, issuant therefrom a fleur-de-lis or.
Address – PO Box 654, Masterton, New Zealand.

SONS LIVING

ANDREW THOMAS, *b* 17 Oct 1965. —— Alistair Blair, *b* 1969.

DAUGHTER LIVING

Janne Fiona, *b* 1963: *m* 1988, David Carl Finlayson, of Levin, NZ, and has issue living, Nicholas David Thomas, *b* 1993, — Hamish Patrick George, *b* 1996.

BROTHER LIVING

Denis Michael, *b* 1945: *m* 1967, Janet, da of L. Eckhoff, of Ambarwood, RD3, Drury, NZ, and has issue living, Richard Michael, *b* 1968, — Joanna Marie, *b* 1969.

SISTERS LIVING

Barbara Elizabeth, *b* 1939: *m* 1967, Selwyn Lloyd Harris, of Sanson, NZ, and has issue living, Boyd John, *b* 1968, — Peter Thomas, *b* 1970, — Quentin Patrick, *b* 1972, — Zane Gilbert, *b* 1974. —— Gillian Madelaine, *b* 1941: *m* 1978, Michael Nicholas McCarthy, JP, of Wanganui, NZ, and has issue living, Samuel Thomas O'Meara, *b* 1980, — Trinity Madeleine, *b* 1979.

COLLATERAL BRANCH LIVING

Issue of the Lieut-Col Michael Carson Lyndon Smith, MC, MB, BS, MRCS, LRCP, IMS, brother of 3rd baronet, *b* 1908, *d* 1961: *m* 1936, Pauline, who *d* 1988, da of Charles Rowlatt:—
Sarah Gillian, *b* 1937: *m* 1st, 1958 (*m diss* 1966), Maj Anthony Gibbon Chater; 2ndly, 1967 (*m diss* 1992), Sir Peter Wilfred Giles Graham Moon, 5th Bt, and has issue living, (by 1st *m*) James Michael Douglas, *b* 1959, — Giles Addison, *b* 1961, — Piers Antony Rowlatt, *b* 1963, — (by 2nd *m*) (*see* Moon, Bt, *cr* 1855). —— Elizabeth Caroline, *b* 1940: *m* 1987, Christopher Ravenscroft, and has issue living, Michael Jack, *b* 1973. —— Alexa Pauline Lovedy, *b* 1945: *m* 19—, John Davenport. —— Joanna Esmée, *b* 1948: *m* 1969, John Alexander Broom, and has issue living, Alexander Rui Tomas, *b* 1972, — Daniel John, *b* 1978, — Orlanda Maria, *b* 1974. *Residence* – Headley Grange, Bordon, Hants.

Sir Thomas Smith, KCVO, FRCS, 1st baronet was so created on the occasion of HM Queen Victoria's Diamond Jubilee in recognition of his eminence as a Surgeon; he was Surg Extraor to Queen Victoria, Hon Sergeant-Surg to King Edward VII, and a Vice-Pres of Roy Coll of Surgeons. Sir (Thomas) Rudolph Hampden Smith, CBE, FRCS, 2nd baronet, was Hon Surg Comdg Torquay Hospital for Wounded Soldiers 1914-18.

SMITH (UK) 1920, of Kidderminster, co Worcester (Extinct 1961)

Sir HERBERT SMITH, 2nd and last *Baronet.*

DAUGHTERS LIVING OF SECOND BARONET

Emily Lindsay Cherrington, *b* 1930: *m* 1958, Joseph Thwaites. —— Martha Theresa Belinda, *b* 1933: *m* 1956, Robin Houghton Stretton, and has issue living, Martin John, *b* 1959, — Bridget Claire, *b* 1957.

DAUGHTERS LIVING OF FIRST BARONET

Mabel Merci, *b* 1899. —— Dora, *b* 1901: *m* 1922 (*m diss* 1929), George Edgar Ingman.

WIDOW LIVING OF SECOND BARONET

E. M. (GRIFFIN) (*Lady Smith*): *m* 1948, as his 2nd wife, Sir Herbert Smith, 2nd Bt, who *d* 1961, when the title became ext.

SMITH (UK) 1945, of Crowmallie, co Aberdeen

Sir ROBERT HILL SMITH, MP, 3rd *Baronet; b* 15 April 1958; *s* his father, *Lt-Cdr Sir* (WILLIAM) GORDON, VRD, RN, 1983; *ed* Merchant Taylors', and Aberdeen Univ; MP (*Lib Dem*) Aberdeenshire W and Kincardine since 1997: *m* 1993, Fiona Anne, da of Col J. D. Cormack, and has issue.

Arms – Or, on the waves of the sea, a three masted ship in full sail proper flagged gules on a chief engrailed, vert, a flame of fire between two horse-shoes of the first. **Crest** – A sea-horse argent.
Seat – Crowmallie, Pitcaple, Aberdeenshire.

DAUGHTERS LIVING

Helen Rosemary, *b* 1994. —— Kirsty Diana, *b* 1997.

BROTHER LIVING

CHARLES GORDON, *b* 21 April 1959; *ed* Merchant Taylors', St Andrews Univ, Univ of Oregon, and Trin Hall, Camb (PhD): *m* 1990, Dr Ann Maria Kennedy, da of Joseph Kennedy, of Ballycastle, co Antrim, and has issue living, Samuel Gordon, *b* 11 Nov 1993, — Rory Donal, *b* 1996. *Residence* – 21 Kimberley Rd, Cambridge CB4 1HG.

UNCLE DECEASED (*Son of 1st Baronet*)

Robert Alexander, *b* 1920; *ed* Stowe, and Trin Coll, Camb; European War 1940-45 as Lieut RNVR: *m* 1945, Marianne, da of Serge Denissieff, and widow of George Plaoutine, of Philippeville, Algeria, and *d* 19—, leaving issue, Andrew Alexander, *b* 1946; *ed* Gordonstoun, — Robert Serge, *b* 1948; *ed* Gordonstoun. *Residence* – East Crowmallie, Pitcaple, Aberdeenshire.

WIDOW LIVING OF SECOND BARONET

DIANA MAY VIOLET PEEL (*Diana, Lady Smith*), da of Warwick Goodchild, and formerly wife of George Ian Young: *m* 1958, as his 2nd wife, Lt-Cdr Sir (William) Gordon Smith, 2nd Bt, VRD, RN, who *d* 1983. *Residence* – East Crowmallie, Pitcaple, Aberdeenshire.

The 1st baronet, Sir Robert (Workman) Smith, yr son of late George Smith (Chm of "City Line", Glasgow), of Glenmorag, Argyllshire, was MP for Central Div of Aberdeenshire and Kincardineshire (C) 1924-1945.

SMITH (UK) 1947, of Keighley, co York

Sir CHARLES BRACEWELL SMITH, 4th *Baronet*; *b* 13 Oct 1955; *s* his brother, *Sir* GUY BRACEWELL, 1983; *ed* Harrow; Author (as Francis O'Donovan) *The Song of the Saints*: *m* 1st, 1977, Carol Vivien, who *d* 1994, da of Norman Hough, of Cookham, Berks; 2ndly, 1996, Nina, da of Kuldip Kakkar, of New Delhi, India.

Arms – Tierce in pairle reversed argent, gules and azure; in chief, two roses counterchanged barbed and seede proper, and in base a London pride plant flowered and eradicated also proper. **Crest** – Upon a rock a moorcock rising, resting the dexter foot on a double convex lens, all proper. *Residence* – 7 Clarence Gate Gdns, Glentworth St, NW1 6AY.

Sir Bracewell Smith, KCVO, 1st Bt, son of Samuel Smith of Keighley, Yorks, was MP for Dulwich (C) 1932-45, and Lord Mayor of London 1946-47.

CUSACK-SMITH (I) 1799, of Newtown, King's County (Extinct 1970)

Sir (WILLIAM ROBERT) DERMOT JOSHUA CUSACK-SMITH, 6th and last *Baronet*.

DAUGHTERS LIVING OF SIXTH BARONET

(By 1st *m*) Berry, *b* 1937: *m* 1960, (Hugh) Jon Foulds, and has issue living, William Mark Aubrey (109 Cathles Rd, SW12), *b* 1963. — Hugo Charles Berry, *b* 1967. —— (By 2nd *m*) Oonagh Mary, *b* 1948: *m* 1972, John Michael Hyland, of Bermingham House, Tuam, co Galway, and has issue living, Charles Stuart, *b* 1976, — Joanna Mary, *b* 1972, — Sarita Catherine, *b* 1979.

Hamilton Spencer-Smith, see Spencer-Smith.

NEWSON-SMITH (UK) 1944, of Totteridge, co Hertford

Sir Peter Frank Graham Newson-Smith, 3rd *Baronet*; *b* 8 May 1947; *s* his father, *Sir* John Kenneth, 1997; *ed* Dover Coll, and Trin Coll of Music: *m* 1974, Mary Anne, da of Cyril C. Collins, of Sturminster Newton, Dorset, and formerly wife of Anthony Owens, and has issue.

Arms – Gules, on a chevron or, between in chief two bezants, and in base a cross pattée fitchée of the second, a pellet between two crosses patteé fitchée sable. Crest – Issuant from a mural crown or, a goat's head argent, armed and bearded or, eared sable and charged with a sword erect gules.
Residence – Lovells Court, Burton St, Marnhull, Sturminster Newton, Dorset DT10 1JJ.

SON LIVING

Oliver Nicholas Peter, *b* 12 Nov 1975.

DAUGHTER LIVING

Emma, *b* 1977.

SISTERS LIVING

Susan Rosemary, *b* 1946: *m* 1978, Charles Reiss, of 91 Belsize Lane, NW3, eldest son of late Dr J. C. Reiss, and has issue living, Rowan Susannah Charlotte, *b* 1978, — Holly Clare, *b* 1980, — (Catherine) Bryony Aspen, *b* 1986. —— (Elizabeth) Jane, *b* 1953: *m* 1978, Kenneth Hall, of Lynwood, 21 Midhurst Rd, Fernhurst, Haslemere, Surrey GU27 3EJ, and has issue living, Katherine Louise, *b* 1979, — Rachel Helen, *b* 1980.

WIDOW LIVING OF SECOND BARONET

Sarah Lucretia Wimberly (*Sarah, Lady Newson-Smith*), da of Robert Bicknell, and formerly wife of M. G. Ramsay: *m* 1988, as his 3rd wife, Sir John Kenneth Newson-Smith, 2nd Bt, who *d* 1997. *Residence* – 67 East St, Warminster, Wilts BA12 9BZ.

MOTHER LIVING

Vera Margaret, da of late Dr Wilfrid Greenhouse Allt, CBE, CVO: *m* 1945 (*m diss* 1971), as his 1st wife, Sir John Kenneth Newson-Smith, 2nd Bt, who *d* 1997. *Residence* – Lynwood, 21 Midhurst Rd, Fernhurst, nr Haslemere, Surrey GU27 3EJ.

COLLATERAL BRANCH LIVING

Issue of late Capt Peter Henry Newson-Smith, RA, yr son of 1st baronet, *b* 1914, *ka* in Italy 1944: *m* 1939, Gertrude Irene (who *m* 2ndly, 1948, Bertrand Milton Walker, of 1200 Cherokee Drive, Waycross, Georgia, USA), da of Frederick Lester Walker, of Georgia, USA:—
Carole Irene, *b* 1943.

Sir Frank (Edwin) Newson-Smith, 1st Bt, son of Henry Newson-Smith, DL, CA, of London, was Lord Mayor of London 1943-44.

PRINCE-SMITH (UK) 1911, of Hillbrook, Keighley, W Riding of Yorkshire

The more prepared, the more powerful

Sir (WILLIAM) RICHARD PRINCE-SMITH, 4th *Baronet; b* 27 Dec 1928; *s* his father, *Sir* WILLIAM, OBE, MC, 1964; *ed* Charterhouse, and Clare Coll, Camb (MA): *m* 1st, 1955, Margaret Ann, only da of late Dr John Carter, of Goldings, Loughton, Essex; 2ndly, 1975, Ann Christina, da of Andrew Faulds, OBE, of Lee Wick Farm, St Osyth, Clacton-on-Sea, Essex, and has issue by 1st *m.*

Arms – Per chevron nebuly or guttée de sang and gules, two stags' heads cabossed in chief of the last and a rose in base argent, barbed and seeded proper. Crest – A dragon's head erased gules, charged with a rose as in the arms, between a stag's attired or.
Residence – 40735 Paxton Drive, Rancho Mirage, California 92270-3519, USA.

SON LIVING (*By 1st marriage*)

JAMES WILLIAM (Morton Hall, Norwich, Norfolk NR9 5JS), *b* 2 July 1959; *ed* Gresham's, and Buckingham Univ; Capt 13th/18th Royal Hussars (Queen Mary's Own) 1979-87, Yorks Sqdn Q0Y.

DAUGHTER LIVING (*By 1st marriage*)

Elizabeth Ann, *b* 1957: *m* 1987, Colin Earl, of Heath Green Farmhouse, Hattingley, Medstead, Alton, Hants GU34 5NG, and has issue living, Katie Louise, *b* 1994.

SISTER LIVING

Eileen Marjorie Clare, *b* 1932: *m* 1959, Stephen Hattersley Smith, and has issue living, Christopher Stephen Hattersley (Yew Tree Farm, Yew Tree Lane, Burn Bridge, Harrogate HG3 1NR), *b* 1963: *m* 1988, Tanya Gwynne Hutchinson, and has issue living, William Richard Hattersley *b* 1993, Lucy Georgina Hattersley *b* 1991, Katie India Hattersley *b* 1995, — Jane Clare Hattersley, *b* 1961: *m* 1985, Michael John Clark, of 89 Pool Rd, Otley, W Yorks LS21 1HL, and has issue living, Emma Jane *b* 1987, Georgina Marie *b* 1990, — Vanessa Jill Hattersley, *b* 1965: *m* 1990, Daniel James Martin, of Old Smithy Cottage, Kirby Lane, Kearby, Wetherby, Yorks LS22 4BR, and has issue living, Victoria Kate *b* 1993, Sophie Elizabeth *b* 1995. *Residence –* Eastlands, 91 Pool Rd, Otley, W Yorks LS21 1DY.

The 1st baronet, Sir Prince Smith (son of late Prince Smith, of Holly House, Keighley), was a JP for W and E Ridings of Yorkshire. The 2nd baronet, Sir Prince, assumed by deed poll 1922, the additional surname of Prince.

REARDON SMITH (UK) 1920, of Appledore, co Devon

What I do I do earnestly

Sir WILLIAM ANTONY JOHN REARDON SMITH, 4th *Baronet; b* 20 June 1937; *s* his father, *Sir* WILLIAM REARDON 1995; *ed* Wycliffe Coll, Gloucester: *m* 1962, Susan Wight, da of Henry Wight Gibson, of Cardiff, and has issue.

Arms – Argent, upon a mount vert in front of an oak tree fructed proper a lion passant gules, in chief three estoiles sable. Crest – In front of a mast and sail of a ship proper charged with a sphinx couchant sans wings argent, an anchor fessewise sable, entwined with a scroll silver, inscribed "HMS Romulus", in letters also sable.
Residence – 26 Merrick Sq, SE1 4JB.

SONS LIVING

WILLIAM NICOLAS HENRY, *b* 10 June 1963; *ed* Milton Abbey. —— Giles Antony James, *b* 1968; *ed* St Edward's Sch, Oxford: *m* 1998, A. Janie, 2nd da of Charles Rowe, of Little Thurlow, Suffolk, and has issue living, Sophie Megan Susan, *b* 1998. —— Harry Alexander, *b* 1979; *ed* Bearwood Coll.

DAUGHTER LIVING

Henrietta Nesta, *b* 1965; *ed* North Foreland Lodge.

BROTHERS LIVING

Barrie Alan, *b* 1942; *ed* Wycliffe Coll, Gloucester: *m* 1965, Wendy Elizabeth, da of George William Bigglestone, of Coventry, and has issue living, Samantha Elizabeth, *b* 1966: *m* 1991, Adam Whittaker, — Louise Suzanne, *b* 1968: *m* 1991, Sylvain Bouteiller, and has issue living, Alexander *b* 1995. *Residence –* Mill House, Ogbourne St George, Marlborough, Wilts. —— Timothy Henry Neale, *b* 1944; *ed* Wycliffe Coll, Gloucester: *m* 1966, Lynda Madeleine, da of Francis Wallace Preston, of Redditch, Worcs, and has issue living, Philip Timothy Edward, *b* 1969; *ed* Monmouth Haberdashers, — James Henry Charles, *b* 1971; *ed* Crickhowell, — Edward William Neale, *b* 1977; *ed* Crickhowell. *Residence –* Pentre House, Llanwenarth, Abergavenny, Gwent.

HALF-BROTHER LIVING

David Joseph William, *b* 1960: *ed* .... *Residence* – ......

SISTER LIVING

(Nesta) Suzanne, *b* 1939: *m* 1958, Francis Edward Sutherland Hayes, DL, and has issue living, Patrick Neil Sutherland, *b* 1961; *ed* Marlborough, and Birmingham Univ: *m* 1988, Jacqueline, da of late John Ford, and has issue living, Samuel *b* 1993, Aimée *b* 1990, — Thira Nesta, *b* 1960: *m* 1991, John Rudd, — Elizabeth Ann, *b* 1964: *m* 1990, Ian Mellett, and has issue living, Caroline Elizabeth *b* 1994, — Philippa Vera, *b* 1966: *m* 1994, Vincent Brigode. *Residence* – Llansannor House, Cowbridge, Glam.

HALF-SISTERS LIVING

Deirdre Ellen, *b* 1955. ——— Amanda Mary, *b* 1958. ——— Penelope Ann, *b* 1962.

UNCLE LIVING (*yst son of 2nd baronet*)

Douglas Hamlyn (West Ash Hill, Forches Cross, Newton Abbot, Devon), *b* 1928; *ed* Marlborough, and Roy Agric Coll, Cirencester: *m* 1949, Minnie Wanna, da of John Dawson, and has had two adopted sons and an adopted da, Hugh David, *b* 1957; *ed* Marlborough, — Jonathan Owen, *b* 1961; *ed* Marlborough: *m* 19—, Diane H., only da of Douglas Webb, of Blakeney, Glos, and has issue living, Oliver *b* 1993, — Jane Elizabeth, *b* 1959; *d* 1977.

AUNT LIVING (*only daughter of 2nd baronet*)

Mary Ellen, *b* 1922: *m* 1947, Dr David Kenneth Lewis Davies, OBE, and has issue living, David Christopher (57 Cheriton Drive, Thornhill, Cardiff CF4 9DF), *b* 1948; *ed* Bromsgrove Sch: *m* 1st, 1974 (*m diss* 1978), Elizabeth, da of Dr Anthony Thomas, of Cardiff; 2ndly, 1981, Terry Anne, da of Colin Smale, CBE, of Cardiff, and has issue living (by 1st *m*), Lucy Alexandra *b* 1974, (by 2nd *m*), Timothy John *b* 1984, James Frederick *b* 1987, — Simon James (34 Bron Haul, Pentyrch, Cardiff CF4 8TA), *b* 1952; *ed* Bromsgrove Sch: *m* 1974, Carolyn Margaret, da of William Sutton, of St Fagans, Cardiff, and has issue living, Katie Elizabeth *b* 1976, Karen Ann *b* 1979, — William Peter (19 Cory Crescent, Peterston-super-Ely, Cardiff CF5 6LS), *b* 1953; *ed* Bromsgrove Sch: *m* 1985, Heather Roslyn, da of John Patterson, of Radyr, Cardiff, and has issue living, Phillip John *b* 1989, Robert William *b* 1992, — Mark Hamlyn (98 Foxbourne Rd, Balham, SW17 8EN), *b* 1961; *ed* Clifton: *m* 1998, Sarah, da of Leonard Condi, of Banstead, Surrey, — Siân Elizabeth (Brooklyn, Cardiff Rd, Creigiau, Cardiff CF4 8NL), *b* 1956: *m* 1979, Prof R. K. Lewis, and has issue living, Matthew Owain *b* 1985, Huw Rhodri *b* 1993, Catrin Angharad *b* 1987, Ceri Elin *b* 1990. *Residence* – 54 Palace Rd, Llandaff, Cardiff.

WIDOW LIVING OF THIRD BARONET

BERYL FRANCES (*Dowager Lady Reardon Smith*), da of William Henry Powell, of Cardiff: *m* 1954, as his 2nd wife, Sir William Reardon Reardon Smith, 3rd Bt, who *d* 1995. *Residence* – Rhode Farm, Romansleigh, S Molton, N Devon EX36 4JW.

COLLATERAL BRANCH LIVING

Issue of late Alan John Reardon Smith, 2nd son of 2nd baronet, *b* 1914, *d* 1970: *m* 1937, Winifred Maud, who *d* 1975, da of Frederick C. Williams:—
John Philip (Greenleaves, 301 Marshfield Rd, Castleton, nr Cardiff CF3 8UU), *b* 1941: *m* 1st, 1964 (*m diss* 1996), Josephine Mireille, da of Frederick Wilding, of Barry, Glam; 2ndly, 1997, Deborah Margaret, da of Russell Hibbs, of 106 Spring Hill, Weston-super-Mare, and has issue living (by 1st *m*), Charles Alan, *b* 1965: *m* 1997, Elizabeth Hobbs, of Stroud, — Simon John, *b* 1966: *m* 1998, Lauren Sylvester, of Belize, and has issue living, Tara Bella *b* 1998, — Katharine Lisa, *b* 1971: *m* 1995, Christopher Lloyd Williams, son of D. I. Williams, of Peterston-super-Ely, S Glamorgan, and has issue living, Morgan Lloyd *b* 1997. ——— Richard William Alan, *b* 1946: *m* 1st, 1970 (*m diss* 1990), Suzanne Ward, da of Jonathan Preece Jones, of Coychurch, Glam; 2ndly, 1990, Nicola Jane, eldest da of Christopher Denis Yapp, of Plough House, Druidstone Rd, St Mellons, S Glamorgan, and has issue living (by 1st *m*), Dylan Alan John, *b* 1972, — Zahra Elizabeth, *b* 1973, — (by 2nd *m*) Samuel William, *b* 1990.

The 1st baronet, Sir William Reardon Smith (son of Capt Thomas Reardon Smith, of Appledore, N Devon), was a Ship-owner, a Coal Exporter, an an Insurance Broker. Sir Willie, 2nd baronet, assumed by deed-poll 1929 the surname of Reardon-Smith in lieu of his patronymic.

SPENCER-SMITH (UK) 1804, of Tring Park, Hertfordshire

Sir JOHN HAMILTON SPENCER-SMITH, 7th *Baronet*; *b* 18 March 1947; *s* his father, *Sir* THOMAS COSPATRIC, 1959; *ed* Milton Abbey, and Lackham Coll of Agric: *m* 1980 (*m diss* 1992), Mrs Christine Sandra Parris, da of late John Theodore Charles Osborne, of Durrington, Worthing, Sussex, and has issue.

Arms – Sable, on a fesse cottised between three martlets or, as many crescents azure, **Crest** – A sword proper, pommel and hilt or, and a pen argent in saltire.
Residence – Hazel House Quarantine Kennels, Elsted, Midhurst, W Sussex GU29 0JT.

DAUGHTER LIVING

Jessica Kirsten, *b* 1985.

WIDOW LIVING OF SIXTH BARONET

LUCY ASHTON (*Lady Spencer-Smith*), only da of late Thomas Ashton Ingram: *m* 1944, Sir Thomas Cospatric Hamilton Spencer-Smith, 6th Bt, who *d* 1959.

COLLATERAL BRANCHES LIVING

By war and wit

Grandchildren of late Lt-Col Michael Seymour Spencer-Smith, DSO, MC, son of late Rev Spencer Compton Spencer-Smith, 3rd son of late Spencer Smith, yr brother of 2nd baronet:—
Issue of late Maj Peter Compton Spencer-Smith, *b* 1912, *d* 1993: *m* 1950, Philippa Mary (Tingley House, Hexton Rd, nr Hitchin, Herts SG5 3BJ), yr da of late Capt Richard Ford, Rifle Brig:—
MICHAEL PHILIP (7 Redcliffe Sq, SW10 9LA), *b* 2 April 1952; *ed* Eton. —— Gerald Peter Harry (36A Walham Grove, SW6 1QR), *b* 1954.

Grandchildren of late Rev Orlando Spencer SMITH, 4th son of late Spencer Smith (ante):—
Issue of late Col Richard Osbaldeston SPENCER-SMITH, *b* 1885, *d* 1962: *m* 1st, 1912, Murielle Alethe Victoria, who *d* 1931, da of Leonard Guise John Wingfield-Stratford (V Powerscourt, colls); 2ndly, 1932, Christian Louisa, who *d* 1962, da of late Lt-Col H. E. Passy:—
(By 1st *m*) Drummond Mervyn (Jade Cottage, Bidford-on-Avon, Alcester, Warwicks B50 4NL), *b* 1920, *ed* Wellington; Capt (ret) R Tank Regt: *m* 1960, June Patrysha, da of Bertram George Finn, and has issue living, Christopher Rex, *b* 1962: *m* 1986, Serena Richwood, and has issue living, Naomi Kate *b* 1987, Danielle Eve *b* 1990. — Rosalind Muriel, *b* 1960: *m* 1988, Colin George Woodnutt, and has issue living, Simon Edward *b* 1989. —— (By 2nd *m*) Rosan Winifred, *b* 1934.

Grandchildren of late Col Richard Osbaldeston SPENCER-SMITH (ante):—
Issue of late Maj Roland Wingfield SPENCER-SMITH, Royal Hampshire Regt, *b* 1916, *d* 1988: *m* 1948, Helen Rosamund, who *d* 1999, da of Lt-Col James Percy Earp, OBE, MC:—
Richard Mervyn (124 Hampstead Way, NW11 7XY), *b* 1954: *m* 1989, Sotiria Dracopoulou, and has issue living, Roland Mikhail Alexander, *b* 1990. —— Jennifer Murielle, *b* 1952: *m* 1st, 1973 (*m diss* 1984), Peter Leslie Riley; 2ndly, 1990, Simon Andrew Cyprian Dunstan, and has issue living (by 2nd *m*), Ysobel Sophie Helen, *b* 1991.

The 1st baronet, Sir Drummond Smith, not having issue, the patent of baronetcy was conferred with remainder to the issue male of his niece, Augusta (daughter of his el brother, Joshua Smith), who *m* 1798 Charles Smith, MP, of Suttons, Essex, descended from Robert Smith of Ilminster, ancestor of Smith-Marriott, Bt. Sir Drummond Cospatric Hamilton-Spencer-Smith, 5th Bt, OBE, (whose father the Rev Spencer Compton Hamilton-Spencer-Smith assumed the additional names of Hamilton and Spencer 1872, having *m* Mary, da of Adm Cospatric Baillie-Hamilton, descended from 6th Earl of Haddington), was Mil Sec to Comdt of New Zealand Forces 1910-13, and a Member of Mil Inter-Allied Commn of Control 1920-24. The 7th Bt discontinued the use of the surname of Hamilton.

VASSAR-SMITH (UK) 1917, of Charlton Park, Charlton Kings, co Gloucester

Sir JOHN RATHBORNE VASSAR-SMITH, 4th *Baronet*; *b* 23 July 1936; *s* his father, *Sir* RICHARD RATHBORNE, 1995; *ed* Eton; formerly Headmaster of St Ronans Prep Sch, Hawkhurst, Kent (ret 1997): *m* 1971, Roberta Elaine, da of W/Cdr Norman Williamson, and has issue.

Arms – Quarterly, 1st and 4th per bend embattled azure and or, in sinister chief point a cuirass with tasces attached and in the dexter base point a well-head all counterchanged, *Smith*; 2nd and 3rd, argent, an Etruscan vase gules, in chief two fusils azure, each charged with a fleur-de-lis or, *Vassar*. **Crests** – 1st, a dexter arm embowed in armour proper, bound above the elbow with a scarf gules and holding in the hand an arrow in bend point downwards or and a pair of pincers in fesse sable, *Smith*; 2nd, an Etruscan vase gules between two branches of oak fructed proper, *Vassar*.
Residence – 24 Haywards Close, Wantage, Oxon OX12 7AT.

SONS LIVING

RICHARD RATHBORNE, *b* 29 Dec 1975. —— David Rathborne, *b* 1978.

SISTER LIVING

Juliet Rathborne, *b* 1941.

Labour and truth

WIDOW LIVING OF THIRD BARONET

DAWN MARY (*Dowager Lady Vassar-Smith*), da of late Sir Raymond Wybrow Woods, CBE: *m* 1932, Sir Richard Rathborne Vassar-Smith, 3rd Bt, TD, who *d* 1995. *Residence* – Chestnut, Rye Rd, Hawkhurst, Kent TN18 4HD.

The 1st baronet, Sir Richard (son of late Richard Tew Smith), assumed by Roy licence 1904, the additional surname of Vassar, and was Chm of Lloyds Bank (Limited). Sir Richard, 3rd Bt, was Headmaster St Ronan's Preparatory Sch 1957-7—.

WALKER-SMITH (UK) 1960 of Broxbourne, co Herts.

Hon Sir (JOHN) JONAH WALKER-SMITH, 2nd *Baronet*; *b* 6 Sept 1939; *s* his father, DEREK COLCLOUGH, Baron Broxbourne, TD, QC, PC (Life Baron) in his baronetcy 1992; *ed* Westminster, and Ch Ch Oxford: *m* 1974, Aileen Marie, only da of late Joseph Smith, and has issue.

Arms – Quarterly: 1st and 4th, per fesse or and argent a portcullis sable throughout raised to the nombril point within a bordure per fesse gules and or, charged with ten acorns counter coloured, *Smith*; 2nd and 3rd, per pale azure and gules a horse passant argent hooved and crined or, between three caltrops gold, *Walker*. **Crests** – 1st, out of a mural crown gules masoned or a mount vert thereon a lion statant argent holding in the dexter forepaw a sword proper pommel hilt and quillons also or, the blade environed by an oak branch fructed gold, *Smith*; 2ndly, between two ostrich feathers gules quilled or a leg in armour azure garnished gold, *Walker*.
Address – 11 Doughty St, WC1.

SON LIVING

DANIEL DEREK, *b* 26 March 1980.

DAUGHTER LIVING

Charmian Lucinda, *b* 1977.

SISTERS LIVING

Hon Deborah Susan, *b* 1941: *m* 1965, Christopher Terence Sinclair-Stevenson, publisher, of 3 South Terrace, SW7 2TB. —— *Hon* Berenice Mary, *b* 1946: *m* 1967, William Andrew Weston, of 7 Royal Arcade, Albemarle St, W1X 3HD.

Smith-Dodsworth, see Dodsworth.

Smith-Gordon, see Gordon.

Smith-Marriott, see Marriott.

SMYTH, (UK) 1956, of Teignmouth, co Devon

NEC·TIMEO·NEC·SPERNO

*I neither fear mine enemy
nor do I despise him*

Sir TIMOTHY JOHN SMYTH, 2nd *Baronet*; *b* 16 April 1953; *s* his grandfather, *Brig Rt Hon Sir* JOHN GEORGE, VC, MC, 1983; *ed* Univ of NSW, MB BS (NSW); MBA (AGSM), LLB (NSW), FRACMA: *m* 1981, Bernadette Mary, da of Leo Askew, and has issue.

Arms – Ermine, on a bend beneath two unicorns' heads erased azure, three lozenges or. Crest – A demi bull rampant argent, issuing from a ducal coronet or, armed and horned of the same, and gorged with a collar azure, charged with three lozenges and rimmed or.
Address – PO Box 421, New Lambton, NSW 2305, Australia.

SONS LIVING

BRENDAN JULIAN, *b* 4 Oct 1981. —— Gerard Timothy, *b* 1988.

DAUGHTERS LIVING

Kathryn Mary, *b* 1983. —— Emma Louise, *b* 1985.

BROTHERS LIVING

Christopher Charles, *b* 1954. —— John George, *b* 1957. —— Simon Gerard, *b* 1961. —— Andrew, *b* 1964.

SISTERS LIVING

Margaret Mary, *b* 1955. —— Clare Marie, *b* 1960.

AUNT LIVING *(Daughter of 1st baronet)*

Jillian Margaret, *b* 1929: *m* 1968, David George Firth, of 98 Sussex Way, N7.

MOTHER LIVING

Philomena Mary, da of John Francis Cannon: *m* 1952, Julian Smyth, who *d* 1974, el son of 1st Bt. *Residence* – 22 Ina Gregory Court, Conder, ACT 2906, Australia.

COLLATERAL BRANCH LIVING

> Issue of late Robin Smyth, yst son of 1st baronet, *b* 1926, *d* 1992: *m* 1961, Joan Harrison, da of late W. J. Williams, of Worthing, Sussex:—
John Julian, *b* 1961.

The 1st Bt, Rt Hon Sir John George Smyth, VC, MC, served with distinction in both World Wars and was MP for Norwood Div of Lambeth 1950-66, being *cr* PC 1962.

BOWYER-SMYTH (E) 1661, of Hill Hall, Essex

Sir THOMAS WEYLAND BOWYER-SMYTH, 15th *Baronet*; *b* 25 June 1960; *s* his father *Capt Sir* PHILIP WEYLAND, RN, 1978: *m* 1992 (*m diss* 1996), Sara Louise Breinlinger.

Arms – Quarterly: 1st and 4th sable, a fesse, dancettée argent, billettée sable between three lioncels reguardant of the second, each supporting an altar or, flaming proper, *Smyth*; 2nd and 3rd, or, a bend vair, cotised gules, *Bowyer*. **Crests** 1st, a salamander in flames proper, *Smyth*; 2nd, on a ducal coronet or, an heraldic tiger sejant argent, *Bowyer*.
Address – c/o Stour House, Fordwich, Canterbury, Kent CT2 0DA.

SISTER LIVING

Amelia, *b* 1958: *m* 1982, James Duncan Johnstone Gracie, son of Rev Anthony Johnstone Gracie, of 53 Ashford Rd, Swindon, Wilts, and has issue living, Luke, *b* 1986, — Leah, *b* 1989. *Residence* – Le Moulin de Gillebert, Montjean, 16240 Villefagnan, France.

Qua pote lucet

AUNT LIVING (*Daughter of 13th baronet*)

Lily Marcia BOWYER-SMYTH, *b* 1905.

WIDOW LIVING OF FOURTEENTH BARONET

VERONICA MARY (*Lady Bowyer-Smyth*), da of Capt C. W. Bower, DSC, RN (ret), of Fordwich, Kent: *m* 1951, as his 2nd wife, Capt Sir Philip Weyland Bowyer-Smyth, RN, who *d* 1978.

COLLATERAL BRANCHES LIVING

> Grandchildren of late William Baird BOWYER-SMYTH (declaration of legitimacy granted in Scotland 1918, but not in succession to the baronctcy), son of 11th baronet, *b* 1859, *d* 1940: *m* 18—, C. V. Sweeney, who *d* 1892:—
Issue of late William Bowyer-Smijth, *b* 1889, *d* 1937: *m* 1913, Janie Isabel Norman, who *d* 1972, of Monaro Vale, Berringan, NSW:—
†William, *b* 1915: *m* 1941, Eileen May Peterson, (9/601 Wyse St, Albury, NSW 2640, Australia), and *d* 1989, leaving issue, Ian William (16 Yattenden Crescent, Baulkham Hills, NSW 2153), *b* 1942; Inspector, NSW Police Service, JP; A Dip JA, BA: *m* 1964, Jennifer Shepherd, and has issue living, Stuart *b* 1965: *m* 1st, 1985 (*m diss* 1998), Liana Cooper; 2ndly, 1998, Kerrie-Ann Cocker (and has issue living, (by 1st *m*) Fiona *b* 1987, (by 2nd *m*), Natasha *b* 1998), Mark *b* 1968: *m* 1999, Joanne Littler, — Keith Raymond (Burrows St, Albury, NSW 2640), *b* 1945: *m* 1973, Lorraine Campbell, and has issue living, Bruce *b* 1977, Louise *b* 1975. *Residence* – 619 Wyse St, Albury, NSW. —— Henry, *b* 1916. —— Edward, *b* 1930. —— Betty, *b* 1921.

> Issue of David Malcolm BOWYER-SMYTH (declaration of legitimacy granted in Scotland 1918, but not in the succession to the baronetcy), 5th son of 11th baronet, *b* 1869, *d* 1930: *m* 1900 (*m diss* 1910), Miriam McCheyne, da of Maj Legh Richmond Battye:—
Basil Malcolm, *b* 1901: *m* 1924, Mabel Henrietta, da of late James Samuel Tetlock, and has issue living, Barrie Malcolm (1090 Keith Rd, W Vancouver, BC), *b* 1925: *m* 1959, Margaret, da of George Kilpatrick Morrison, and has issue living, John Barrie *b* 1962, Jane Catherine *b* 1965, Elizabeth Margaret *b* 1968, — James Brian (8300 Victoria Dr, Vancouver, BC), *b* 1929: *m* 1965, Marianne, da of Max Bruno Schwaerzler, and has issue living, Marc *b* 1967, Simone *b* 1969, — David Anthony, *b* 1931: *m* 1953 (*m diss* 1972), Lee Smith, and has issue living, David *b* 1954, Michael *b* 1956, Kathie *b* 1955, Lisa *b* 1958. —— Evangeline Battye, *b* 1904: *m* 1928, Reginald John Veale, who *d* 1986, and has had issue, Robert Brian, *b* 1929: *m* 1960 (*m diss* 1965), Del Elizabeth Demack, of Brisbane, Australia, and *d* 1989, leaving issue, Jill Wilde *b* 1961: *m* 1982, Graham New, of Brisbane, Australia (and has issue living, Jacob Allan *b* 1983, Thomas Graham *b* 1985, Gemma Elizabeth *b* 1991), — John Douglas de Coverley (2025 Beach Drive, Comox, BC, Canada V9M 1T7), *b* 1933: *m* 1960, Shauna Arlene Allen, of Red Deer, Alberta, Canada, and has issue living, Jonathan Peter de Coverley *b* 1968: *m* 1999, Marlies Tinkler, Jenifer Leslie *b* 1964: *m* 1988, David Bradley Boylan, of Glencoe, Ontario (and has issue living Angus Allen Nathaniel *b* 1996, Cecilie Evangeline *b* 1997), — Joan Kathleen Battye, *b* 1931: *m* 1954 (*m diss* then re-*m*), Stuart Henry Orge, and has issue living, Bradford William *b* 1954, Mark Phillip *b* 1961, Hilory Anne Theresa *b* 1964, —

Nellie Alice Miriam, *b* 1934: *m* 1969, Graham Wilkie; has issue, Timothy Joseph Reginald Malcolm VEALE *b* 1974, Melody Suzanne VEALE *b* 1963, — Daphne Beverly Diane, *b* 1936.

Grandchildren of late Maj Ashe WINDHAM (*b* 1863), el son of Ashe WINDHAM (*b* 1830) (who assumed the surname of Windham in lieu of Smijth-Windham by Roy Licence 1888), 2nd son of late Capt Joseph SMIJTH-WINDHAM, of Waghen Hall, Yorks (who assumed the additional surname and arms of Windham by Roy Licence 1823), yst son of 7th baronet:—

Issue of late Sir Ralph Windham, *b* 1905, *d* 1980; Ch Justice of Tanganyika: *m* 1946, Kathleen Mary (Hook's Cottage, Kingscote, Tetbury, Glos), da of Capt Cecil Henry Fitzherbert, of Millbrook, Abbeyleix, co Leix, Eire:—
JOHN JEREMY (The Hyde, Woolhope, Herefords HR1 4RE), *b* 22 Nov 1948; *ed* Wellington Coll; Capt (ret) Irish Gds and 22 SAS Regt: *m* 1976, (Rachel) Mary, 2nd da of late Lt-Col (Walter) George Finney, TD, RA (TA) (*see* E Perth, colls, 1995 Edn), and has issue living, (Thomas) Ralph, *b* 5 Aug 1985, — Katharine Anne, *b* 1981, — Emma Georgina, *b* 1983. —— Andrew Guy (Shobdon Farm, Newton St Margaret's, Vowchurch, Herefordshire HR2 0QW), *b* 1949; *ed* Wellington Coll, and Trin Coll Camb (MA); solicitor: *m* 1976, Diana Susan, yr da of Hon Norman Dunlop Galloway Galbraith (*see* B Strathclyde), and has issue living, Rory Michael, *b* 1978, — Ruth Emily, *b* 1980, — Lydia Mary, *b* 1982, — Harriet Rachel, *b* 1984. —— Penelope Susan, *b* 1952. —— Belinda Mary Victoria, *b* 1955: *m* 1989, Mark Baxter, 2nd son of David Baxter, and has issue living, Thomas Mark, *b* 1990, — Luke Jacob, *b* 1993.

Grandchildren of late Ashe Windham (*b* 1830) (ante):—
Issue of late Major Ashe WINDHAM, *b* 1863, *d* 1937: *m* 1903, Cora Ellen Sowerby, who *d* 1948, 2nd da of late Capt Henry Sowerby Middleton, Oxfordshire LI:—
Ashe, MBE *b* 1916; *ed* Radley; Maj (ret) E Yorks Regt & ADC to Gov of Assam 1938-40: *m* 1940, Iris Daphne, da of Col Edward Selby Phipson, CIE, DSO, MD, IMS (ret), and has issue living, Ashe Adrian (Rectory Lodge, The Fairland, Hingham, Norfolk), *b* 1941; late Capt RA; Diplomatic Ser (ret): *m* 1969, Daphne Anne, da of late Maj A. A. P. C. Thomas, TD (ret), and has issue living, Philippa Mary *b* 1977, — Daniel Harry (Willow Cottage, Hackford, Wymondham, Norfolk), *b* 1948; *ed* Radley, and Magdalene Coll, Camb; late R Irish, and Muscat Regt SAF: *m* 1975, Caroline Mary, da of late Richard Pelham Warren, FRCS, of Epping, Essex, and has issue living, William *b* 1978; *ed* Norwich Sch, and Magdalene Coll, Camb, Alexa *b* 1980. —— Ruth (Little Beechwood, Child Okeford, Dorset), *b* 1912: *m* 1st, 1938 (*m diss* 1962), Robert Bellord, Maj IG, who *d* 1970; 2ndly, 1972, Brig John Henry Patrick Woodroffe, DSO, who *d* 1996, and has had issue (by 1st *m*), Robert WINDHAM-BELLORD, *b* 1943: *m* 1st, 1968, Jane Elinor, 2nd da of Carleton John Richard Tufnell; 2ndly, 1978, Marika, da of Tore Sellberg, of Stockholm, and *d* 1987, having had issue, (by 1st *m*) Charles Robert Carleton *b* 1971; *ed* Downside, and King's Coll, London, Henry Jake Ashe *b* 1972; *ed* Downside: *m* 1995, Sarah Kate, da of David F. Wade, of New Hampshire, USA (and has issue living, Amaris *b* 1996), Thomas Daniel Tufnell *b* 1975; *ed* Downside, and Oxford Brookes Univ, (by 2nd *m*) Marisa *b* 1984, *d* 1985, Hanna Sofia Irma *b* 1986, — Edward James WINDHAM-BELLORD (The Cottage, Cucklington, Som), *b* 1947; *ed* Downside, and Wadham Coll, Oxford; assumed the surname of Windham-Bellord 1965: *m* 1972 (*m diss* 1976), Caroline Irene, who *d* 1979, only da of Robert Grenville Plantagenet Morgan-Grenville (*see* L Kinloss), and has issue living, James Robert Grenville, *b* 1973; *ed* Downside, and King's Coll, London, — Richard Valentine, *b* 1949: *m* 1st, 1974 (*m diss* 1982), Cheung Wai Lan; 2ndly, 1982, Julieta Espiña Bisco, and has issue living, (by 1st *m*) Richard Valentine (Siddha) *b* 1975, Satya *b* 1976, Subhadra *b* 1977, (by 2nd *m*) Rupa (son) *b* 1985, Jamuna *b* 1983, — Ellen Mary, *b* 1938, — Alice Mary, *b* 1939.

Granddaughters of late Sir William Windham, CBE, 2nd son of late Ashe Windham (*b* 1830) (ante):—
Issue of late William Evan Windham, *b* 1904, *d* 1977: *m* 1st, 1932, Constance Lloyd, who *d* 1939, da of James Hope Loudon, of Olantigh, Wye, Kent; 2ndly, 1962, Dorothy Muir, who *d* 1996, da of Robert Deans Johnston, of Lenzie, Lanarkshire, and widow of Carl Raymond Davis:—
(By 1st *m*) Elizabeth Aylva, *b* 1935: *m* 1955 (*m diss* 1974), George Alfred Bakewell, and has issue living, Constance Louise *b* 1957, — Charlotte Alice, *b* 1959. —— Juliet Alexa WINDHAM HACKETT, *b* 1938; assumed the additional surname of WINDHAM 1978: *m* 1962 (*m diss* 1971), Raymond Bingham Hackett.

Grandchildren of late Lt-Col Henry Steuart WINDHAM (infra):—
Issue of late Maj James Steuart WINDHAM, *b* 1917, *d* 1989: *m* 1957, Annette de Mestre (May Hill House, Longhope, Glos), da of William John Wilkin, FRCS:—
Mark Hastings Wriothesley, *b* 1959. —— Tobias Cosmo Russell, *b* 1962. —— Sophia Louise de Mestre *b* 1958: *m* 1982, Bruce Robinson, film writer and dir, and has issue living, Willoughby, *b* 1993, — Lily India, *b* 1986.

Grandchildren of late Major George Smijth-Windham, 4th son of late Capt Joseph SMIJTH-WINDHAM (ante):—
Issue of late Lt-Col Henry Steuart WINDHAM (twin), *b* 1873, *d* 1958: *m* 1915, Marjory Russell, who *d* 1971, da of late Henry McLean Dymock:—
William Ashe Dymoke (Parc Gwynne, Glasbury-on-Wye, via Hereford, Radnorshire), *b* 1926; *ed* Bedford Sch (Scholar), and Christ's Coll, Camb (Scholar) (MA); High Sheriff Powys 1996; Chm, Skelmersdale Development Corpn 1979-85: *m* 1956, Alison Audrey Primrose, da of late Maj Philip Pinckney Curtis, MC (*see* Curtis, Bt, colls), and has issue living, Ashe George Russell, LVO, *b* 1957; *ed* Eton, and RMA Sandhurst; Capt IG; Temp Equerry to HM Queen Elizabeth, The Queen Mother 1980-82, and an Extra Equerry since 1993; LVO 1982: *m* 1997, Arabella Peggy Marian, only da of Francis Hoare (*see* King, Bt, *cr* 1888, 1995 Edn), — (Charles) William Fitz-Roy, *b* 1960, — Emma Rose Dymock *b* 1959: *m* 1991, Simon Vivian Surtees Phillpotts of The White House, White St, Market Lavington, Devizes, Wilts, son of late Christopher Phillpotts, CMG, of 27 Merrick Sq, SE1, and has issue living, Archie Christopher Louis *b* 1992, Lara Georgina Windham *b* 1995. —— Rachel Russell, *b* 1916: *m* 1963, Lt-Col George Kinloch Sheppard, who *d* 1963, el son of late Sir William Didsbury Sheppard, KCIE.

Issue of late Arthur Russell Smijth-Windham, *b* 1874, who *d* 1915: *m* 1901, Brenda Helen, who *d* 1947, da of late Gerald Hall:—
†William Russell, CBE, DSO, *b* 1907; *ed* Wellington Coll; Brigadier late Royal Signals, a FIEE; appointed an ADC to HM 1957; Mount Everest Expeditions 1933 and 1936; 1939-45 War in Middle East and NW Europe (despatches, DSO, CBE); DSO 1942, CBE (Mil) 1946: *m* 1934, Helen Teresa Clementi, da of late Brig Hubert Clementi Smith, DSO (Clarke-Jervoise, Bt, ext), and *d* 1994, leaving issue, Simon William (Middle Lodge, Hughenden Estate, High Wycombe, Bucks MP14 4LA), *b* 1937: *m* 1960, Wendy Myra, da of Edgar William John Albrow, and has issue living, Alistair William *b* 1966, Tanya Myra *b* 1961, — Joanna Felicity (Fairseat Farm, Chew Stoke, nr Bristol), *b* 1938: *m* 1st, 1963, Peter Anthony Lazarus, who *d* 1980; 2ndly, 1984, Alan Robert Brown, and has issue living (by 1st *m*), George William, *b* 1969, Mary Helen *b* 1966, — Prudence Helen, *b* 1945; *ed* St Hugh's Coll, Oxford (MA); Solicitor: *m* 1967 (*m diss* 1985), John Derek

Walter Murdoch, and has issue living, Thomas Duncan *b* 1970, Clarissa Helen *b* 1972, Rosamond Elsie *b* 1977, — Rachel Beatrice, *b* 1946: *m* 1970, John Santer, of 78 Enborne Rd, Newbury, Berks, and has issue living, William Robert Clive *b* 1976, Harry Joseph *b* 1978, Evelyn Margaret *b* 1973, Anne Dorothy Sarah *b* 1981. *Residence* – Estate Corner, Pitney, Langport, Som.

Sir Thomas Smith, 1st Bt of Hill Hall, Essex, High Sheriff 1663, was grandson of George, brother of Sir Thomas Smith, of Hill Hall, Sec of State to Edward VI and Elizabeth I. His son, Sir Edward 2nd Bt, adopted the spelling of Smyth, and Sir William, 7th Bt about 1796, that of Smijth. He *m* 1779, Anne, da of John Windham-Bowyer, of Woodmansterne, Surrey, and sister and heir of Joseph Windham. Her mother, Mary, was da and heir of Joseph Windham, of Twickenham, Middlesex (afterwards Ashe), by Catherine, da and co-heir of Sir Edmund Bowyer, of Camberwell. Sir Edward, 10th Bt, assumed by Roy Licence 1839 the name and arms of Bowyer-Smijth. Sir Alfred John, 13th Bt, reverted to former spelling of surname from Bowyer-Smijth to Bowyer-Smyth.

SNADDEN (UK) 1955, of Coldoch, co Perth (Extinct 1959)

Sir WILLIAM MCNAIR SNADDEN, 1st and last *Baronet*.

DAUGHTER LIVING OF FIRST BARONET

Rosemary Adele McNair, *b* 1926: *m* 1st, 1944, Capt Charles Napier Frederick Webb, S Wales Borderers, who *d* 1945 while on active ser abroad; 2ndly, 1947, Patrick Heatley Dickson, and has had issue (by 1st *m*) James Charles Napier, *b* 1946: *m* 1974, Mary Thomas, of The Old Mill, Easingwold, Yorks, and *d* 1980, — (by 2nd *m*) Elizabeth Jane, *b* 1948: *m* 1st, 1969, Michael Alexander Ligertwood, who *d* 1982; 2ndly, 1984, John Alexander Fell, of Levenside, Haverthwaite, Cumbria, and has issue living, (by 1st *m*) Mark Murray *b* 1972, Guy Alexander *b* 1975, Andrew Patrick *b* 1979, — Deborah Rose, *b* 1953: *m* 1982 (*m diss* 1989), Nigel Everard Barnes, of Johannesburg, S Africa, and has issue living, Tugela Jane *b* 1985. *Residences* – Langthorne St, SW6; Craighead House, Blair Drummond, by Stirling.

BUCKWORTH-HERNE-SOAME (E) 1697, of Sheen, Surrey

Sir CHARLES JOHN BUCKWORTH-HERNE-SOAME, 12th *Baronet*; *b* 28 May 1932; *s* his father *Sir* CHARLES BURNETT, 1977: *m* 1958, Eileen Margaret Mary, da of Leonard Minton, of Caughley, Shropshire, and has issue.

𝕬rms – Quarterly: 1st and 4th, gules, a chevron between three mallets or, a canton argent for difference, *Soame*; 2nd and 3rd, sable, on a chevron between three cross-crosslets fitchée argent, an ermine spot, *Buckworth*. 𝕮rests – 1st, a lure gules, garnished and stringed argent, thereon a falcon or, beaked and legged of the second; 2nd a man's head in profile armed with a helmet, the beaver up all proper. *Residence* – Sheen Cottage, Coalbrookdale, Shropshire.

SON LIVING

RICHARD JOHN, *b* 17 Aug 1970.

SISTER LIVING

Mary, *b* 1936: *m* 1958, Keith Howard Edwards, of 27 Woodside, Coalbrookdale, Shropshire, and has issue living, Robert John Edwards, *b* 1971, — Carol Jane, *b* 1964.

Sir John Buckworth, 1st baronet, was High Sheriff of London 1704. Sir Everard, the 3rd baronet, was Assist Gentleman Usher to King George II. Sir Everard, the 5th baronet, Gentleman-Pensioner and Exon of the Guard, *temp* George III, assumed the additional surname of Herne, having *m* Anne Herne, of Haviland Hall, Norfolk. Sir Buckworth Buckworth-Herne, the 6th baronet, assumed, in 1806, the additional surname of Soame by Roy licence, in compliance with the will of Sir Peter Soame, 4th baronet (title now extinct).

SOMERVILLE (I) 1748, of Dublin (Dormant 1929)

Since the death of the 2nd Baron Athlumney (who was also 6th Baronet of this creation) in 1929, the Baronetcy has remained dormant, and at time of going to press no name appears in respect of it on the Official Roll of Baronets.

COLLATERAL BRANCHES LIVING

Descendants, if any, of late Archibald James Somerville (son of late Capt William Somerville, only son of late Major William Somerville, 2nd son of 1st baronet), *b* 1803, *d* 1871: *m* 1836, Elizabeth, da of Jason Crawford, of Ballyholly, co Cavan; he left issue, Archibald James, William, Jason, Bellingham Brookes.

Grandchildren of late Capt Bellingham Arthur Somerville, 2nd son of Tenison Alan Somerville, 5th son of Capt William Somerville (ante):—
Issue of late Lt-Col Gualter Hugh Rodger Bellingham Somerville, MC, *b* 1894, *d* 1947: *m* 1925, Heather Edith, who *d* 1994, da of late Col Cecil Norris Baker, CIE:—
Patricia May Naomi (20 Carlton Rd, Oxford OX2 7SA), *b* 1929: *m* 1st, 1951 (*m diss* 1973), Lt Michael William Richmond Nicholas, RN; 2ndly, 1974, Robert James Henderson, who *d* 1977; 3rdly, 1978, Prof Thomas David Duncan Williams, who *d* 1985, and has issue living (by 1st *m*), Patrick Richmond, *b* 1952, — Elizabeth Richmond, *b* 1954: *m* 1st, 1978 (*m diss* 1984), Capt Andrew Malcolm Wright, RE; 2ndly, 1991, Robert James Turner, who *d* 1995 (*m diss* 1998), Richard Perceval Graves, and has issue living (by 2nd *m*), Samuel David Richmond *b* 1993, Zoë Elizabeth Richmond *b* 1992. —— Julia Heather Margaret, *b* 1931: *m* 1958, as his 2nd wife, William Bristow Stevenson, DL, MA, High Sheriff co Londonderry 1971, Chancellor Diocese of Derry and Raphoe, and has issue living, James Roger, *b* 1963; MRAC, — Henry Bristow, *b* 1970; *ed* Bristol Univ (LLB Hons), — Diana Margaret Julia, *b* 1961; BMus, ARCM, LGSM: has issue living (by Dr Kevin Richardson), Joseph Michael RICHARDSON *b* 1992, Anna Heather Margaret RICHARDSON *b* 1995. *Residence* – Knockan, Feeny, co Londonderry.

Issue of late Reginald Malcolm John Bellingham Somerville, *b* 1897, *d* 1971: *m* 1st, 1928, Maude Gwendoline Constance Violet, who *d* 1935, da of late Capt A. E. H. Moore, R Dublin Fus; 2ndly, 1936, Honor Lucretia Philippa, who *d* 1985, da of late Rev Canon Philip B. Johnson, of the Rectory, Wicklow:—
(By 1st *m*) Juanita Elizabeth Maude, *b* 1932; *ed* Hillcourt Sch, and The Ling Physical Training Coll, Dublin: *m* 1964, Peter Brumby, late Chief Pilot, E African Airways. *Residence* – The Lodge, Dargle Hill, Enniskerry, co Wicklow. —— (By 2nd *m*) William Barnard Reginald Bellingham, *b* 1937; *ed* Trin Coll, Dublin (BA); Solicitor 1967; late Admin Officer, HM Colonial Ser, Tanganyika: *m* 1968, Margery Manon, el da of George Clemenger Vincent Brittain, of Craigfoodie House, Dairsie, Fife, and has issue living, James William Reginald Bellingham, *b* 1969; *ed* Radley, and Trin Coll, Dublin (LLB), — Charles John George Bellingham, *b* 1971: *ed* Kelly Coll, — Edward Henry Tenison Bellingham, *b* 1972; *ed* Radley. *Residence* – Dargle Hill, Enniskerry, co Wicklow.

The 1st baronet, Sir James Somerville, KB, was MP for Dublin City 1729, and Lord Mayor of Dublin 1737, the 4th, Sir Marcus, was MP for co Meath 1801-3, and the 5th, Rt Hon Sir William Meredyth, PC, MP for Drogheda (*L*) 1837-52, and for Canterbury 1854-65, Under-Sec for Home Depart 1846-7, and Ch Sec for Ireland 1847-52, was *cr Baron Athlumney* (peerage of Ireland) 1863, and *Baron Meredyth* (peerage of United Kingdom) 1886, in which Baronies the Baronetcy remained merged until the death of the 2nd Baron Athlumney in 1929, when both Peerages became extinct, and the Baronetcy became dormant.

AGNEW-SOMERVILLE (UK) 1957, of Clendry, co Wigtown.

Sir QUENTIN CHARLES SOMERVILLE AGNEW-SOMERVILLE, 2nd *Baronet*; *b* 8 March 1929; *s* his father, *Cdr Sir* PETER GARNETT AGNEW, RN, 1990; assumed by Royal Licence 1950 the additional surname of Somerville after that of Agnew, and the arms of Somerville quarterly with those of Agnew, in compliance with the will of his uncle (by marriage), 2nd and last Baron Athlumney; *ed* RNC Dartmouth: *m* 1963, Hon (Margaret Irene) April Drummond, yst da and co-heiress of 15th Baron Strange, and has issue.

Arms – Quarterly, 1st and 4th, azure three mullets or, two and one, between seven cross-crosslets fitchée, three, one, two and one argent, a canton voided of the last charged with four mullets gules and as many cross-crosslets fitchée sable (*Somerville*); 2nd and 3rd, parted per saltire argent and gules, two cinquefoils in pale and as many saltires couped in fess, all counterchanged, a bordure azure (*Agnew*). **Crests** – *Dexter*, a demi-lion rampant sable, charged on the shoulder with a cross-crosslet fitchée between two mullets argent; *sinister*, an eagle rising reguardant proper, holding in the dexter claw a sword proper hilted and pommelled or.
Residence – Mount Auldyn House, Ramsey, I of Man IM8 3PF.

SON LIVING

JAMES LOCKETT CHARLES, *b* 26 May 1970; *ed* Milton Abbey.

DAUGHTERS LIVING

Amelia Rachel, *b* 1965: *m* 1992, Nicholas C. Hannaford, only son of I. G. Hannaford, of Adelaide, S Australia. *Residence* – The Stone House, Whyanbeel Valley, PO Box 460, Mossman, Queensland 4873, Australia. —— Geraldine Margaret, *b* 1967: *m* 1998, William G. Osborne-Young, yst son of late Kenneth Osborne-Young, of Pensax, Worcs.

Cdr Sir Peter Garnett Agnew, 1st Bt, RN, was MP for Cambourne Div of Cornwall (C) 1931-50, and for S Div of Worcs 1955-66; also a Trustee of Historic Churches Preservation Trust.

SOUTHBY (UK) 1937, of Burford, co Oxford

Sir JOHN RICHARD BILBE SOUTHBY, 3rd *Baronet*; *b* 2 April 1948; *s* his father, *Lt-Col Sir* (ARCHIBALD) RICHARD CHARLES, OBE, 1988; *ed* Peterhouse, Zimbabwe, and Loughborough Univ (BSc): *m* 1971, Victoria Jane, eldest da of John Wilfred Sturrock, of 88 Wrottesley Rd, Tettenhall, Wolverhampton, and has issue.

Arms – Or, a chevron between three apples gules. **Crest** – A demi lion or holding in the dexter paw an apple gules.
Residence – Lomagundi, High St, Nash, Bucks MK17 0EP.

SONS LIVING

PETER JOHN, *b* 20 Aug 1973; *ed* Oundle, and Magdalen Coll, Oxford (MA); ACA: *m* 1995, Katherine M., da of Dr Neal Priestland, of Radcliffe-on-Trent, Notts. *Residence* – 315 High Rd, Chilwell, Beeston, Notts NG9 5DL. —— James William, *b* 1984.

DAUGHTER LIVING

Sarah Jane, *b* 1975.

UNCLE LIVING (son of 1st baronet)

Patrick Henry James, *b* 1913; Lt-Cdr RN (ret): *m* 1939, Lady Anne Adeline Hope, da of 2nd Marquess of Linlithgow, and has issue living, Richard Henry Alexander (The Red House, Overbury, Tewkesbury, Glos GL20 7PB), *b* 1941; *ed* Eton, and Worcester Coll, Oxford (MA): *m* 1985, Nicola Claire Wallop, eldest da of Jonathan Janson (*see* E Portsmouth, colls), and has issue living, Alexander Richard Janson *b* 1987, Henrietta Elizabeth *b* 1989, —— Mary Anne, *b* 1946; *ed* Benenden, and Courtauld Inst, London Univ: *m* 1975, Martin Robert Kenyon, of 70 Stockwell Park Rd, SW9, and has issue (*see* B Kenyon, colls). *Residence* – Robins Mill, Overbury, Tewkesbury, Glos GL20 7NT.

WIDOW LIVING OF FIRST BARONET

NOREEN VERA (*Noreen, Lady Southby*) (18 Harbour View Rd, Parkstone, Poole, Dorset BH14 0PE), da of late Bernard Compton Simm, of Ashbourne, Derbys: *m* 1962, as his 2nd wife, Cdr Sir Archibald Richard James Southby, RN, 1st Bt, who *d* 1969.

WIDOW LIVING OF SECOND BARONET

IRIS MACKAY (*Iris, Lady Southby*), da of late Lt-Col Granville Mackay Heriot, DSO, RM, and widow of Brig Ian Charles Alexander Robertson: *m* 1979, as his 4th wife, Lt-Col Sir (Archibald) Richard Charles Southby, 2nd Bt, OBE, who *d* 1988. *Residences* – Greystone House, Stone, Tenterden, Kent.

 Cdr Sir Archibald Richard James Southby, RN, 1st Bt, 2nd son of Richard Southby of Hodcott and Chieveley, Berks, was MP for Epsom 1928-47, Assist Govt Whip 1931-35, and a Jnr Lord of the Treasury 1935-37; Lt-Col Sir Richard Southby, 2nd Bt, OBE, was awarded American Medal of Freedom.

SPEARMAN (UK) 1840, of Hanwell, Middlesex

While I breathe I hope

Sir ALEXANDER YOUNG RICHARD MAINWARING SPEARMAN, 5th *Baronet*; *b* 3 Feb 1969; *s* his father *Sir* ALEXANDER BOWYER, 1977: *m* 1st, 1994 (*m diss* 1997), Anne Stine, da of Kaj Munch, of Hyllinge, Denmark; 2ndly, 1997, Theresa Jean, da of Dr Thomas Sutcliffe, of Cape Town, and has issue by 2nd *m*.

𝕬rms – Azure, on a chevron ermine between three tilting spears, argent, headed or, a red deer's head erased proper. 𝕮rest – A lion rampant proper, gorged with a collar gemelle or, supporting a tilting spear also proper, enfiled with a mural crown or.
Address – PO Box 10004, Vredekloof 7560, Cape, S Africa.

SON LIVING (*By 2nd marriage*)

ALEXANDER AXEL, *b* 9 March 1999.

SISTERS LIVING

Catherine Wendy Nest, *b* 1959: *m* 1979, Jonathan Mort, and has issue living, Rebecca Claire Spearman, *b* 1994. —— Lynne Dorothy Ann, *b* 1962: *m* 1982, Gregory Lloyd, and has issue living, Nicola, *b* 1988, — Chelsea Anne, *b* 1991. —— Daphne Joan Constance Eileen, *b* 1965.

UNCLE LIVING (*Son of 3rd baronet*)

Richard Ian Campbell, *b* 1926; *ed* Clayesmore Sch, and Birkbeck Coll, London (BSc special honours in Zoology, PhD, DSc); Hon Sr Lecturer Univ Coll London, FLS, FZS, Fellow of Inst of Biology, Member of Soc of Experimental Biology, and of British Ecological Soc. *Residence* – 70 Hatherley Rd, Winchester, Hants S022 6RR.

COLLATERAL BRANCHES LIVING

 Issue of late Joseph William Spearman, eldest son of 2nd baronet, *b* 1879, *dvp* 1917: *m* 1900, Evelyn Daisy Oram:—
Gwendoline Daisy Elizabeth, *b* 1911: *m* 19—, — , and *d* 1994, leaving issue, Valerie, *b* 19—: *m* 19—, Guy Godefroy, of SC1 Les Vigneaux, 41130 Chatillon sur Cher, France, and has issue.

 Grandchildren of late Com Alexander Young Crawshay Mainwaring Spearman, RN, half-brother of 2nd baronet:—
Issue of late Sir Alexander Cadwallader Mainwaring Spearman, *b* 1901; *d* 1982: *m* 1st, 1928 (*m diss* 1951), Diana Violet Edith Constance, who *d* 1991, da of Col Sir Arthur Havelock James Doyle, 4th Bt; 2ndly, 1951, Diana Josephine (The Old Rectory, Sarratt, Herts; Fealar, Enochdhu, Blairgowrie, Perthshire; 32 Queen Anne's Gate, SW1), only child of Col Sir (Albert) Lambert Ward, 1st Bt, CVO, DSO, TD:—
(By 2nd *m*) Lochain Alexander, *b* 9 April 1952: *m* 1977, Pilin, da of Senor de Garrigues, and has issue living, Alexander James, *b* 27 March 1984, — Jack, *b* 1986, — a da, *b* 1980. —— John Dominic, *b* 1954: *m* 1976 (*m diss* 1978), Rebecca, da of Sir Alan Lewis Wigan, 8th Bt. —— Andrew Mark, *b* 1960: *m* 1994, Elisa, da of Rt Hon Thomas Jeremy King, CH, MP, and has issue living, a son, *b* 1994, — a da, *b* 1997, — a da, *b* 1999. —— James, *b* 1964. —— Zara Ann Louise, *b* 1956: *m* 1979, Iain A. Milligan.

 Granddaughters of late Alexander Young Spearman, el son of 1st baronet:—
Issue of late Charles Edward Spearman, *b* 1863, *d* 1945: *m* 1901, Frances Henrietta Priaulx, who *d* 1955, da of John Aikman, MD, of Birnam, Guernsey:—

Alice Louisa Jean *b* 1903: *m* 1928, Martin William Strong, who *d* 1978, and has issue living, Richard Martin (25 Newstead Way, Wimbledon, SW19), *b* 1929: *m* 1st, 1956 (*m diss* 1969), Ann Georgina, da of late Richard P. Sargent; 2ndly, 1971, Venetia Mary, da of late Ian T. Henderson, of Crawley, Hants, and has issue living (by 1st *m*), Simon Alexander *b* 1959: *m* 1997, Vilma Lucia, da of Humberto Tarazona, — Christopher John, *b* 1932; Sqdn-Ldr RAF: *m* 1956, Brenda Mary, da of late A. Willbery, and has issue living, Michael Alexander *b* 1957, Penelope Ann *b* 1959, Helen Jean *b* 1960, — Michael Charles (2727 Windover Drive, Corona del Mar, Calif 92625, USA), *b* 1935: *m* 1st, 1963 (*m diss* 1968), Lysbeth Joanna, who *d* 1970, el da of Dr C Lanyon, of Falmouth; 2ndly, 1968, Margaret Christine, da of late Edwin V. Price, of Chester, and has issue living, (by 2nd *m*), Edward Charles *b* 1970, James Alexander *b* 1972, Christopher Edwin *b* 1977, — Patricia Anne (The Gables, 17 Brightmans Drive, Maulden, Bedford), *b* 1931: *m* 1957, John Barrett, who *d* 19—, and has issue living, Hazel Jean *b* 1963. *Residence* – 35 Arterberry Rd, SW20. —— Ivy Joy, *b* 1912: *m* 1939, Lt-Col Thomas Harold Barnes, TD, who *d* 1971, and has issue living, Belinda Marion, *b* 1941: *m* 1963 (*m diss* 1997), John Part, and has issue living, Emma Josephine *b* 1967: *m* 1993, Benjamin Oliver Hugh Robson, of The Little House, Biddestone, Wilts (and has issue living, Polly Anna Kate *b* 1995, Rosie *b* 1998), Tracy Belinda *b* 1970, Joanna Frances *b* 1974, — Susannah Mainwaring, *b* 1944: *m* 1966, Andrew Wilson Thomson, of Ashgate Old Forge, Fivehead, Curry Rivel, Taunton, Som.

Grandchildren of late Col Horace Ralph Spearman, 3rd son of 1st baronet.
Issue of late Horace Ralph Spearman, *b* 1868, *d* 19—: *m* 1890, Louisa, da of James Parker:—
Horace Layton, *b* 1896. —— Lily Alexandrina Campbell, *b* 1892. —— Isabella Lucy, *b* 1893.

Issue of late Major Alexander Young Spearman, *b* 1872, *d* 1911: *m* 1898, Mary Cramond, da of late Edward Etches, of Litchurch Grange, Derby:—
Horace Edward James, *b* 1899; *ed* Trin Coll, Glenalmond, and Uppingham; Major late RA: *m* 1934, Mary, da of late Jon Constantinescu, of Braila, Roumania.

The family of Spearman is of considerable antiquity in Durham. John Spearman, a lawyer and antiquary, was many years Under-Sheriff of Durham, and in 1678 he purchased the manor of Thornley in that county. The 1st baronet, Right Hon Sir Alexander Young, was for a long period Comptroller-General and Secretary to the Commissioners for the Reduction of the National Debt.

SPEELMAN (E) 1686

Jonkheer Sir CORNELIS JACOB SPEELMAN, 8th *Baronet*; *b* 17 March 1917; *s* his father, *Jonkheer Sir* Cornelis Jacob, 1949; *ed* Perth Univ, W Australia (BA 1958); formerly in Education Depart of Roy Dutch Army, and a Master at Geelong Gram Sch, and Clifton Coll; Tutor, Exeter Tutorial Coll; is a British subject: *m* 1972, Julia Mona Le Besque, who *d* 1978.

John Cornelis Speelman, of Batavia, *b* 1659, *d* June 1686 before the Royal Warrant directing his creation as a *Baronet* had passed the Great Seal. By Letters Patent of 9 Sept 1686, his widow, Debora, da of John Nicolaes Kievit (Attorney Fiscal to the Admiralty of the Maes), of Rotterdam, was raised to the rank of a Baronet's widow, the same Letters Patent also creating their only son and heir Cornelis, a *Baronet*. The 6th Baronet was in Royal Dutch Navy 1870-83, and sometime Burgomaster of Harlingen. The holders of this title remained resident in the Netherlands until the 8th Baronet.

Spencer-Nairn, see Nairn.

Spencer-Smith, see Smith.

SPEYER (UK) 1906, of Grosvenor Street, St George, Hanover Square, co London (Extinct 1932)

Sir EDGAR SPEYER, 1st and last *Baronet*.

DAUGHTERS LIVING OF FIRST BARONET

Pamela, *b* 1903: *m* 1926, Count Hugo Carl Maria Moÿ de Sons, who *d* 1938. *Residence* – Bell Cottage, Bury Gate, near Pulborough, Sussex. —— Vivien Clare, *b* 1907. *Residence* – 22 Irving Pl, New York City, NY 1003, USA.

SPICER (UK) 1906, of Lancaster Gate, Borough of Paddington

In God alone my hope

Sir NICHOLAS ADRIAN ALBERT SPICER, 5th *Baronet*; *b* 28 Oct 1953; *s* his father, (*Sir*) PETER JAMES (who did not use the title), 1993; *ed* Eton, and Birmingham Univ (MB, ChB 1977); medical practitioner: *m* 1992, Patricia Carol, 2nd da of Warwick Dye, of Auckland, NZ, and has issue.

ᴀrms – Per chevron or and sable, in chief two cinquefoils and in base a tower, all counterchanged. ℭrest – Out of the battlements of a tower a cubit arm erect in armour proper, holding in the gauntlet an annulet or.
Residence – The Old Rectory, Malvern Rd, Stanford Bishop, Bringsty, Worcs WR6 5TT.

SONS LIVING

JAMES PETER WARWICK, *b* 12 June 1993. —— Andrew Nicholas Kingsley, *b* 1 Aug 1995.

SISTERS LIVING

Phyllida Margaret, *b* 1950: *m* 1979, David John Worcester, of Gillham's Croft, Highleigh Rd, Sidlesham, Chichester, W Sussex PO20 7NR. —— Alison Celia, *b* 1955: *m* 1980, Giles Marshall Hallam Mills, of Brixey's Farmhouse, Sandford, Ringwood, Hants BH24 3BU. —— Susanna Juliet (Flat 3, 12 Palace Rd, SW2 3NG), *b* 1963.

AUNTS LIVING (*Daughter of 3rd baronet*)

Janet Dykes, *b* 1931. —— Margaret Grace Gillespie, *b* 1933: *m* 1960, John Arnfield Heap, CMG, PhD, of The Old House, Harston, Cambridge and has issue living, Thomas John Gillespie, *b* 1966: *m* 1992, Tammany Robin Stone, —— Sarah James, *b* 1961: *m* 1991, Leonard Joseph Byatt, — Alice Margaret, *b* 1964: *m* 1st, 1988 (*m diss* 1994), Andrew Richard Ginger; 2ndly, 1994, Neil Michael Preston Gough.

DAUGHTERS LIVING OF SECOND BARONET

Pamela Rosamond, *b* 1914: *m* 1936, John Stuart Johnstone, of Mole Hall, Widdington, nr Saffron Walden, Essex, and has issue living, Douglas Stuart, *b* 1953; *ed* Harrow, — Caroline Rosamond, *b* 1938: *m* 1963, Paul-Louis Mascaux, and has issue living, Pascal René Stuart *b* 1965. —— Althea Dykes, *b* 1918: *m* 1st, 1939, Joseph Alwyn Francis Baxendale, Lieut Surrey and Sussex Yeo, who *d* of wounds received in action 1940; 2ndly, 1945, Capt John Wynne Bankes, 14th/20th King's Hussars, of Mynachlog, Northop, Mold, Clwyd CH7 6AF, and has had issue, (by 2nd *m*) Nigel John Eldon, *b* 1946; *ed* Eton, — Andrew Dykes Scott, *b* 1955; *ed* Eton: *m* 1984, Ariane, da of late Arthur John Goodman (*see* M Anglesey, colls), and *d* 1987, — Althea Lavinia, *b* 1949: *m* 1972, Capt Andrew Duncan Gordon, Army Air Corps, of The Steading, Blair Atholl, Perthshire. *Residence* – Mynachlog, Northop, Flints.

WIDOW LIVING OF FOURTH BARONET

MARGARET, da of late Sir (James) Steuart Wilson, of Fenn's, Petersfield, Hants: *m* 1949, (Sir) Peter James Spicer, 4th Bt (who did not use the title), who *d* 1993. *Residence* – 15 Washington St, Chichester, W Sussex PO19 3BN.

The Rt Hon Sir Albert Spicer, PC, 1st baronet, was Chm of James Spicer & Sons, Ltd (later Spicers, Ltd), paper makers, wholesale stationers, and manufacturers, of 19 New Bridge Street, EC4, and sat as MP for Monmouth Dist (*L*) 1892-1900, and for Central Div of Hackney 1906-18. He was First Lay Chm of Congregational Union of England and Wales 1893, Treasurer of London Missionary So 1885-1910, and of Mansfield Coll, Oxford 1888-1921, Chm of Govs Mill Hill Sch, and Pres of London Chamber of Commerce 1907-10.

Stafford-King-Harman, see Harman.

STAMER (UK) 1809, of Beauchamp, Dublin

By valor and strength

Sir (LOVELACE) ANTHONY STAMER, 5th *Baronet*; *b* 28 Feb 1917; *s* his father, *Lt-Col Sir* LOVELACE, 1941; *ed* Harrow, Trin Coll, Camb (MA) and Roy Agric Coll, Cirencester; an AMIMI 1963; PO RAF 1939-41, and 1st Officer Air Transport Aux 1941-45; Exec Dir of Bentley Drivers Club Ltd, 1969-73, and of Bugatti and Ferrari Owners Clubs 1973-75; Hon Treas, Ferrari Owners Club 1975-81: *m* 1st, 1948 (*m diss* 1953), Stella Huguette, da of late Paul Burnell Binnie, of Brussels; 2ndly, 1955 (*m diss* 1959), Margaret Lucy, da of late Maj T. A. Belben, Indian Army; 3rdly, 1960 (*m diss* 1968), Marjorie June, da of T. C. Noakes, of St James, Cape Province, S Africa; 4thly, 1983, Elizabeth Graham, who *d* 1992, widow of G. P. H. Smith, and da of late C. J. R. Magrath; 5thly, 1997, Pamela Grace (*née* Hawkins), widow of P. B. Cheston, of Moreton-in-Marsh, Glos, and has issue by 1st *m*.

𝕬rms – Quarterly: 1st and 4th gules on a fesse indented argent, a lion passant azure armed and langued gules, 2nd and 3rd azure the civic cap between three castles inflamed proper. Over all a cross ermine charged with the sword of state of the City of Dublin in pale proper. 𝕮rest – A stag's head erased proper, gorged with a mural crown or.
Residence – 5 Windrush Court, 175 The Hill, Burford, Oxon OX18 4RE.

SON LIVING (By 1st marriage)

PETER TOMLINSON, *b* 19 Nov 1951; *ed* Malvern, and Southampton Univ; late Sqdn-Ldr RAF: *m* 1st, 1979 (*m diss* 1989), Dinah Louise, da of late Thomas Selwyn Berry; 2ndly, 1999, Věra Řeháková, of Prague, Czech Republic, and has issue living (by 1st *m*), William Peter Alexander, *b* 20 Sept 1983, — Antonia Louise, *b* 1981.

DAUGHTER LIVING (By 1st marriage)

Lucinda Jane, *b* 1949.

COLLATERAL BRANCHES LIVING

Grandchildren of late Rev Frederick Charles Stamer, 2nd son of 3rd baronet:—
Issue of late Hugo Frederick Barnabas Stamer, *b* 1900, *d* 1980: *m* 1925, Kathleen Florence Louise, da of J. Whittome, of Vancouver:—
James Alexander Donovan, *b* 1928: *m* 1951, Patricia Louise, da of A. J. McNeil, of Duncan, BA, and has issue living, Gregory McNeil, *b* 1956. —— Marion Joan, *b* 1926: *m* 1947, John Ernest Fox, of 1147 Williams Rd, Richmond, Vancouver, BC, and has issue living, John Patrick, *b* 1950, — Geoffrey Ernest, *b* 1951, — Kathleen Jennifer, *b* 1948, — Diane Joan, *b* (twin) 1950.

Grandchildren of late William Edward Stamer, 3rd son of 3rd baronet:—
Issue of late William Arthur John Stamer, *b* 1899, *d* 1991: *m* 1935, Helen, da of Dr Wilfred Anthony Legh Jackson, of Lavington, BC:—
William John Derek (PO Box 247, Barrière, BC, Canada, VOE IEO), *b* 1940: *m* 1st, 1961 (*m diss* 1964), Marcelle Blanche, da of David Howrie, of Vernon, BC; 2ndly, 1967, Valerie Margaret, da of Roy MacQuarrie, of Revelstoke, and has had issue (by 1st *m*), Rodney William, *b* 1961, — (by 2nd *m*) John Edward, *b* 1962: *m* 1990, Carleen Gail, da of Gordon Zerr, of Barrière, BC, and has issue living, Brittany Marie *b* 1993, Nicole Alexandra *b* 1994, — Cory Wayne, *b* 1963: *m* 1994, Barbara Lynn, da of Barry Ross, of Barriere, BC, and has issue living, Tiana Leah *b* 1995, Trista Lynn *b* 1998, — William John David, *b* 1970; *d* 1989, — Patricia Leah, *b* (twin) 1970. —— Judith Cicely, *b* 1939: *m* 1st, 1957 (*m diss* 1961), Glen Fletcher, of Lavington, BC, Canada; 2ndly, 1964, Arthur G. Jaik, of 6909 Palfrey Drive, Vernon, BC, Canada V1B 1A7, and has issue living, (by 1st *m*), Rhondda Jane, *b* 1957: *m* 1981, Christopher Oostlander, and has issue living, Adam Nickolas *b* 1983, Ryan Jeffrey *b* 1985, — (by 2nd *m*), Catherine Louise, *b* 1965: *m* 1994, Paul Chabot, and has issue living, Jennifer Rose *b* 1989, Saleena Irene, *b* 1993, Caitlyn Christine *b* 1995, — Susan Christine, *b* 1968. —— Rosemary Shane, *b* 1943: *m* 1964, Ronald Edwin Haywood, of 1191 Crestwood Drive, Kamloops, BC, Canada V2C 5G8, and has issue living, John Christopher (321 Stevens Drive, Kamloops, BC, Canada V2H 1L5), *b* 1968: *m* 1997, Elaine Starlene Klein, da of Doug Chambers, of Kamloops, BC, Canada, and has issue living, Julia Crystal Gail *b* 1988, Jillene Ann *b* 1998, — Alison Jane, *b* 1966: *m* 1st, 1989 (*m diss* 1994), Clayton Jay Paull; 2ndly, 1995, Brent Ernest Miller, of 1953 Gardiner Rd, Kamloops, BC, Canada V2C 6V8, and has issue living (by 2nd *m*), Lauren Elizabeth *b* 1995, Sarah Kathleen *b* 1997.

The 1st baronet, Sir William Stamer, was Lord Mayor of Dublin 1809 and 1819, and commanded a regiment of the Dublin Yeomanry during the Irish rebellion. The Rt Rev Sir Lovelace Tomlinson Stamer, DD, 3rd Bt, was Suffragan Bishop of Shrewsbury 1888-1905.

STANIER (UK) 1917, of Peplow Hall, Hodnet, co Shropshire

Sir BEVILLE DOUGLAS STANIER, 3rd *Baronet; b* 20 April 1934; *s* his father, *Brig Sir* ALEXANDER BEVILLE GIBBONS, 1995; *ed* Eton; late Capt Welsh Guards; ADC to Gov-Gen of Australia 1959-60; Stock Exchange 1960-76, Partner Messrs Kitcat and Aitken 1969-74; Farmer since 1976: *m* 1963, (Violet) Shelagh, eldest da of late Maj James Stockley Sinnott, of Tetbury, Glos, and has issue.

𝔄rms – Or, on a pile azure ten escallops, four, three, two and one of the first. 𝔄rest – In front of a griffin's head, erased proper three escallops or. *Residence* – Kings Close House, Whaddon, Bucks MK17 0NG. *Club* – MCC.

SON LIVING

ALEXANDER JAMES SINNOTT, *b* 10 April 1970; *ed* Eton.

DAUGHTERS LIVING

Henrietta Claire, *b* 1965. —— Lucinda Katherine, *b* 1967: *m* 1996, James R. Martin, yr son of late John Martin, and of Mrs John Simpson, of Exeter.

SISTER LIVING

Stronger by piety

Sylvia Mary Finola, LVO, *b* 1928; LVO 1981. *Residence* – Manor Farm, Maidwell, Northampton NN6 9JB.

This family, originally spelt Stonhewer, was settled at Biddulph, Staffs, from the 16th century. Sir Beville Stanier, 1st Bt, MP for Newport, Salop (*C*) 1908-18, and Ludlow 1918-21 and Lord of the Manors of Peplow and High Hatton, was 2nd son of Francis Stanier of The Moor House, Biddulph, Staffs, and Peplow Hall, Salop, High Sheriff of Salop, 1894. Brig Sir Alexander Beville Gibbons Stanier, 2nd Bt, was JP, DL and High Sheriff Shropshire; Brig Welsh Guards (comdg 1945-48); patron of two livings.

STAPLES (I) 1628, of Lissan, co Tyrone

Sir GERALD JAMES ARLAND STAPLES, 16th *Baronet, b* 2 Dec 1909; *s* his brother, *Sir* THOMAS, 1997, but his name does not appear on the Official Roll of the Baronetage: *m* 1951, Henrietta, da of late Arland Ussher, of Blackrock Dublin, and has issue.

𝔄rms – Quarterly, 1st and 4th, argent, on a fesse engrailed sable between three hurts, as many ermine spots between two dragons' heads erased or, *Staples*; 2nd and 3rd, argent, a cross ragulé gules, on a chief sable two pheons or, *Jones.* 𝔄rest – A demi-savage azure, girt with a belt with two rings, charged with four torteaux, and holding in his hands a large staple or. *Residence* – 5 Little Stodham House, Liss, Hants GU33 6LJ.

DAUGHTERS LIVING

Emily Ann, *b* 1952: *m* 1st, 1974 (*m diss* 1984), Howard George Smith; 2ndly, 1988, Kerry William John McDonald, of 11 Rhoscolyn Drive, Tattenhoe, Milton Keynes, Bucks MK4 3AE, and has issue living (by 1st *m*), Juliet Clare, *b* 1980. —— Jacqueline Mary, *b* 1954: *m* 1985, Timothy Pullen, of 19 Willowdale Close, Petersfield, Hants.

BROTHER LIVING

RICHARD MOLESWORTH (22 New St, Lismore, co Waterford, Republic of Ireland), *b* 11 June 1914: *m* 1954, Marjorie Charlotte Thomas, who *d* 1998, of Christchurch, NZ.

SISTERS LIVING

Elizabeth Lindsay, *b* 1911: *m* 1st, 1933, Henry Eric St George Harper, who *d* 1947; 2ndly, 1961, John Frank Harris, who *d* 1971; 3rdly, 1972, James Victor Thomas Rawlence, MBE, RN, who *d* 1993, of 42 Ridgeway, Sherborne, Dorset, and has issue living (by 1st *m*), Elizabeth Lindsay St George, *b* 1937: *m* 1961, Trevor Arthur Lant, and has issue living, Myles Arthur *b* 1963, Philippa Lindsay *b* 1969. —— June Pamela (22 New St, Lismore, co Waterford), *b* 1923.

DAUGHTERS LIVING OF FOURTEENTH BARONET

Eileen Sybell, *b* 1939: *m* 1968, Timothy Geary Edward Kilpatrick, of Hale House, Churt, Surrey, and has issue living, Amanda Charlotte, *b* 1971, — Sarah Patricia, *b* 1974. —— Barbara Helen, *b* 1941: *m* 1st, 1970, Alistair John Hutchinson-

Russell, who *d* 1973; 2ndly, 1974, Anthony Warren England; 3rdly, 1988, Keith James Burton, of 55 Harbord St, SW6 6PL, and has a son, Mark James, *b* 1990.

DAUGHTER LIVING OF THIRTEENTH BARONET

Hazel Marion, *b* 1923: *m* 1970, Harry Holbeche Radclyffe Dolling, who *d* 1986. *Residence* – Lissan House, Cookstown, co Tyrone BT80 98W.

SISTER LIVING OF FOURTEENTH BARONET

Eileen Patience, *b* 1917. *Residence* – St John's, 202 Merrion Rd, Dublin 4.

COLLATERAL BRANCHES LIVING

Granddaughters of late Maj-Gen Thomas Staples, BSC, 3rd son of Rev John Molesworth Staples, and next brother of 10th baronet:—
Issue of late Noel Richard Ponsonby Staples, *b* 1879, *d* 1958: *m* 1905, Kathleen, who *d* 1966, da of late Alexander Ross Hamilton, of Glensavage, Blackrock, co Dublin:—
Anne Veronica (RR1 Maple Bay, Duncan, BC, Canada), *b* 1910: *m* 1936, Lt-Col Richard MacNaughton Lendrum, DSO, who *d* 1976, and has issue living, Richard Brian, *b* 1949: *m* 1970, Gail Jeanette Robinson, — Jillian Anne, *b* 1944: *m* 1965 Raymond Thomas Benwell. —— Flora Hamilton, *b* 1912. —— Kathleen (twin), *b* 1920: *m* 19— (*m diss* 1972), Alexander Clarke Wilson, of 305-1676 West 11th St, Vancouver 9, BC, Canada.

Granddaughters of late Noel Richard Ponsonby Staples (ante):—
Issue of late Richard Nathaniel Staples, *b* 1908, *d* 1975: *m* 1939, Isabel MacMillan:—
Heather Anne, *b* 1941. —— Sheila Isabel, *b* 1944.

Issue of late Anthony Staples, *b* 1920, *d* 1975: *m* 1950, Margaret Eva Duffield, who *d* 1970:—
Noel Leslie, *b* 1954: *m* 1972, Dwaine Grant Van Eeuwen.

Descendants, if any, of Thomas Staples (*b* 1823), Samuel Montgomery Staples (*b* 1830), and Robert Staples (*b* 1832), 3rd, 4th and 5th sons of Rev Alexander Staples, Rector of Gowran, 2nd son of Rev Alexander Staples, 2nd son of Rev Thomas Staples, 3rd son of 4th baronet.

The 1st baronet, Sir Thomas Staples of Lissan, co Tyrone and Faghanvale, co Derry, High Sheriff of co Tyrone 1640, was 5th son of Alexander Staples, of Yate Court, Glos. The 9th baronet, Sir Thomas, QC, Queen's Advocate in Ireland, who *d* 1865, was a distinguished lawyer.

STAPLETON (E) 1679, of The Leeward Islands (Extinct 1995)

DAUGHTER LIVING OF NINTH BARONET (*By 2nd marriage*)

Susan Penelope, *b* 1937: *m* 1964, Roger Fulford-Dobson, who *d* 1986, of Shepherds, Rotherfield Greys, Henley-on-Thames, Oxon, and has issue living, Giles Roger, *b* 1965, — Jasper William, *b* 1970, — Emma Susan, *b* 1967.

STARKEY (UK) 1935, of Norwood Park, Parish of Southwell, and co of Nottingham

Man proposes, God disposes

Sir JOHN PHILIP STARKEY, 3rd Baronet; *b* 8 May 1938; *s* his father, *Lt-Col Sir* WILLIAM RANDLE, 1977; *ed* Eton, and Ch Ch Oxford (MA), Sloan Fellow London Business Sch; DL (Notts) 1981; High Sheriff 1987-88: *m* 1966, Victoria Henrietta Fleetwood, da of late Lt Col Christopher Herbert Fleetwood Fuller, TD (*see* Fuller Bt, colls) and has issue.

Arms – Argent, a bend engrailed vair between six storks sable. *Residence* – A stork argent, semée of estoiles azure.
Residence – Norwood Park, Southwell, Notts NG25 0PF.

SONS LIVING

HENRY JOHN, *b* 13 Oct 1973.

DAUGHTERS LIVING

Suzannah Clare, *b* 1966: *m* 1989, Jonathan Beatson-Hird, yr son of Dr John Beatson-Hird, of Oldwell, Ashton-under-Hill, nr Evesham, Worcs, and has issue living, Hubert John, *b* 1992, — Digby George, *b* 1994. —— Elizabeth Victoria, *b* 1975. —— Katherine Alexandra, *b* 1977.

BROTHER LIVING

Michael William, *b* 1946; *ed* Eton, Newcastle Univ, Trent Business Sch, and Nottingham Univ; BSc, MBA, MCIM: *m* 1974, Gillian Mary, da of late E. Treflyn Roberts, of Shotton, Deeside, Clwyd, and has issue living, Edward Thomas William, *b* 1978, — Isabella Irené Marianne, *b* 1983. *Residence* – Cutlersforth Farm, Halam, nr Newark, Notts NG22 8AP.

SISTER LIVING

Caroline Myrtle (*Lady Hervey-Bathurst*), *b* 1936: *m* 1957, Sir (Frederick) John Charles Gordon Hervey-Bathurst, 7th Bt. *Residence* – Somborne Park, King's Somborne, Hants.

The 1st baronet, Sir John Ralph (el son of late Lewis Randle Starkey, DL, JP, of Norwood Park, Notts), sat as MP for Newark (*C*) 1906-22, Lt-Col Sir William Randle, 2nd Bt, was High Sheriff of Notts 1954-55.

STEEL (UK) 1938, of Philiphaugh, co Selkirk

Sir (FIENNES) MICHAEL STRANG STEEL, CBE, 3rd *Baronet*; *b* 22 Feb 1943; *s* his father, Sir (FIENNES) WILLIAM STRANG, 1992; *ed* Eton; Maj (ret) 17th/21st Lancers; DL Borders Region 1990; Forestry Commr since 1988; Member Queen's Body Guard for Scotland (Royal Company of Archers); CBE (Civil) 1999: *m* 1977, Sarah Jane, el da of late J. A. S. Russell, of Mayfield, Lochmaben, Dumfriesshire, and has issue.

Arms – Argent, a bend chequy sable and ermine, between two lions' heads erased gules, on a chief azure, two billets or, a crescent of the first for difference. Crest – A lion's head erased gules.
Residence – Philiphaugh, Selkirk TD7 5LX.

SONS LIVING

FIENNES EDWARD, *b* 8 Nov 1978; *ed* Glenalmond. —— Sam Arthur, *b* 1983.

DAUGHTER LIVING

Tara Diana, *b* 1980.

BROTHER LIVING

Colin Brodie Strang (Threepwood, Blainslie, Galashiels, Selkirkshire TD1 2PY), *b* 1945; *ed* Eton, and RAC Cirencester; chartered surveyor; FRICS: *m* 1970, April Eileen, da of Aubrey Fairfax Studd, of Cahoo House, Regaby West, Ramsey, IoM, and has issue living, James William, *b* 1973, — Alistair Fairfax, *b* 1975, — Peter Brodie, *b* 1977.

UNCLE LIVING (*son of 1st baronet*)

Robert Stanley Strang, *b* 1934; *ed* Eton, and RAC Cirencester: *m* 1958, Caroline Angela Elaine, only da of late Lt-Col William Hugh Carter, of Rosslyn, Tain, Ross-shire, and has issue living, David William Strang, *b* 1961; *ed* Glenalmond, and RAC Cirencester; Chartered Surveyor: *m* 1991, Fiona Louise, yr da of Dr Richard Legge, of Edinburgh, and has issue living, Charles William Brooke Strang *b* 1995, Alice Charlotte Strang *b* 1993, Olivia Rose *b* 1997, — Richard James Strang, *b* 1963; *ed* Eton: *m* 1996, Sophia Juliet, da of Rodney Shirley of Buckingham. *Residence* – Sluie, Banchory, Kincardineshire AB31 4BA.

AUNT LIVING (*daughter of 1st baronet*)

Grizel Mabel Strang, *b* 1921. *Residence* – Beechwood, Selkirk TD7 5LU.

COLLATERAL BRANCH LIVING

Issue of late Jock Wykeham Strang Steel, 2nd son of 1st Bt, *b* 1914, *d* 1991: *m* 1945, Lesley (Haydean, Haddington, E Lothian EH41 4HN), da of late Lt-Col Sir (John) Reginald Noble Graham, 3rd Bt, VC, OBE:—
Malcolm Graham Strang, WS (Barrowmore, Milnathort, Kinross KY13 9SL), *b* 1946; *ed* Eton, Trin Coll, Camb (BA), and Univ of Edinburgh (LLB); solicitor; sec Standing Council of Scottish Chiefs 1973-83; memb Queen's Body Guard for Scotland (Royal Company of Archers); FRSA: *m* 1972, Margaret Philippa, da of late William Patrick Scott, OBE, TD, DL, of Kierfiold, Stromness, Orkney, and has issue living, Patrick Reginald Strang, *b* 1975; *ed* Eton, and Manchester Univ, — Laura Strang, *b* 1977. —— Celia Jane Strang, LVO, *b* 1948; Lady in Waiting to HRH The Princess Royal since 1977; LVO (1989): *m* 1976, Malcolm Alastair Innes (*see* Innes Bt (*cr* 1628), colls). —— Susan Rachel Strang (*Lady Agnew of Lochnaw*), *b* 1952: *m* 1980, Sir Crispin Hamlyn Agnew of Lochnaw, 11th Bt.

The 1st baronet, Sir Samuel Strang Steel (son of late William Strang Steel, JP, DL, of Philiphaugh, Selkirk), was Major Lothians and Border Horse, MP for Ashford Div of Kent 1918-29, Pres Scottish Unionist Assoc 1937-38 and 1942-43, Lord Lieut of Selkirkshire 1948-58, Forestry Commr, a Dir of LNER and a Dir of Bank of Scotland.

Steel (Ramsay-Steel-Maitland), see Maitland.

STEPHENSON (UK) 1936, of Hassop Hall, co Derby

Sir HENRY UPTON STEPHENSON, TD, 3rd *Baronet*; *b* 26 Nov 1926; *s* his father, *Col Sir* HENRY FRANCIS BLAKE, OBE, TD, 1982; *ed* Eton; late Capt Yorkshire Yeo; TD 19—: *m* 1962, Susan, da of late Maj John Ernest Clowes, of Clifton, Ashbourne, Derbys, and has issue.

Arms – Vair, on a pale between two pallets gules, three leopard's faces or, two flaunches of the second. **Crest** – A rock, thereon a falcon's head erased proper, gorged with a collar vair, pendent therefrom an escutcheon vert, charged with two arrows, saltirewise, points downwards or.
Residence – Tissington Cottage, Rowland, Bakewell, Derby DE4 1NR.

DAUGHTERS LIVING

Fiona Kathleen, *b* 1964. —— Annabel Mary, *b* 1965. —— Emma Frances, *b* 1968. —— Lucy Clare, *b* 1970.

Medio tutissimus ibis

Thou will go safest in the middle course

AUNTS LIVING (*Daughters of 1st baronet*)

Cynthia Margaret, MBE, *b* 1910; MBE (Civil) 1948. —— Emma Letitia Gertrude, *b* 1914: *m* 1941, Philip Charles Fenner Lawton, CBE, DFC, who *d* 1993, of Fenner House, Glebe Way, Wisborough Green, W Sussex, and has had issue, Charles Henry Huntly, *b* 1946: *m* 1979, Sarah Margaret, da of Rev Christopher Hugo Lambert, of 26 Abingdon Villas, W8, and has issue living, Timothy Philip Hugo *b* 1982, Hermione Margaret Clare *b* 1984, — Philippa Rosemary, *b* 1943: *m* 1974, Lt-Cdr Michael Henry White, RN, and *d* 1999, leaving issue, Richard *b* 1978, Serena *b* 1976, Lucinda *b* 1983.

WIDOW LIVING OF SECOND BARONET

JOAN (*Joan, Lady Stephenson*) (Hassop Green, Bakewell, Derbyshire), el da of late Maj John Herbert Upton, JP, of Ingmire Hall, Sedbergh: *m* 1925, Col Sir Henry Francis Blake Stephenson, OBE, TD, 2nd Bt, who *d* 1982.

COLLATERAL BRANCHES LIVING

Issue of late William Raymond Shirecliffe Stephenson, 2nd son of 1st baronet, *b* 1898, *d* 1977: *m* 1923, Madeleine Rose, who *d* 1990, da of George Montagu Butterworth, of Westward Ho!, Devon:—
TIMOTHY HUGH, TD (Lomberdale Cottage, Bakewell, Derby DE45 1LU), *b* 5 Jan 1930; *ed* Eton, and Magdalene Coll, Camb; JP for Sheffield: *m* 1959, Susan Lesley, yr da of late George Arthur Harris, of Sheffield, and has issue living, Matthew Francis Timothy (3 Stoke Park Rd, Stoke Bishop, Bristol BS9 1LE), *b* 1960: *m* 1984, Philippa Delphine, da of John Lincoln, of Aldersley House, Chester, and has issue living, John Lewis *b* 1986, Jessica Frances *b* 1985, Madeleine Claire *b* 1990, — Oliver George (Lomberdale Hall, Middleton by Youlgreave, Bakewell, Derby DE45 1LU), *b* 1962: *m* 1992, Fiona Alice Jane, da of Maj Sir David Peter Michael Malcolm, 11th Bt, and has issue living, Augustus William Malcolm *b* 1994, Alfred Hugh Malcolm *b* 1996, Arabella Constance Hermione *b* 1998. —— Susan Madeleine, MBE, *b* 1924; MBE 1995: *m* 1949, Charles Graham Murray, MBE, JP, DL, of 3 Belgrave Drive, Sheffield S10 3LQ, and has issue living, Elizabeth Susan, *b* 1951, — Jane Madeleine, *b* 1953: *m* 1983, John Ferretti, of 10 Chorley Drive, Sheffield S10 3RR, and has issue living, Matthew Robert *b* 1987, James Alexander *b* 1990, — Anne Catriona, *b* 1955: *m* 1982, Frank W. Womack, of 68 Banner Cross Rd, Sheffield S11 9HR, and has issue living, Alastair Edward *b* 1984, Thomas Martin *b* 1986. —— Jocelyn Frances, *b* 1926: *m* 1948, David Clement Wilson, of 363 Fulwood Rd, Sheffield, and has issue living, Christopher Michael Rockley, *b* 1957, — Olivia Frances (38 Stumperlowe Crescent Rd, Sheffield 10), *b* 1952: *m* 1976 (*m diss* 1989), Christopher A. Cooke, — Sarah Margaret, *b* 1954: *m* 1982, Jaime Acosta (AA 85101, Bogotá, Colombia), and has issue living, Simon *b* 1985, Nicolas *b* 1988.

Issue of late Percival John Parker Stephenson, 3rd son of 1st baronet, *b* 1900, *d* 1973: *m* 1930 (*m diss* 1948) Pamela Benton (*dec*), da of Sir Walter Benton Jones 2nd Bt:—
Jennifer Barbara, *b* 1931: *m* 1958, John Henry Thornton, DL, of Alburgh House, Alburgh, Harleston, Norfolk, and has issue living, Edward John (29 Broxash Rd, Clapham, SW11), *b* 1963: *m* 1994, Fiona Ward, and has issue living, Thomas Henry *b* 1996, Charlotte Elizabeth *b* 1998, — Robert Walter (24 Mattock Lane, Ealing, W5), *b* 1968: *m* 1996, Keara Veronica Grace, and has issue living, George William *b* 1997, — Katherine Louise, *b* 1961: *m* 1986, Timothy James Stapleton Harris, of 7 Selwyn Av, Richmond, Surrey, and has issue living, Georgina Rose *b* 1991, Annabel Louise *b* 1994.

Issue of late Lt-Col Charles Eustace Kenyon Stephenson, yst son of 1st baronet, *b* 1903, *d* 1971: *m* 1930, Nancy Barbara (The Outrake, Bakewell, Derbys), da of Harry Limnell Lyon, JP, of Hillam Hall, Monk Fryston, Yorks:—
Charles Lyon, TD (The Cottage, Gt Longstone, Derbys DE45 1UA), *b* 1935; *ed* Eton; Maj Royal Yeo; Man Dir Stephenson Blake (Holdings) Ltd: *m* 1st, 1960 (*m diss* 1972), Margot Jane, da of late Tony Malcolm Tinker; 2ndly, 1974, Hon Sarah Merryweather Norrie, da of 1st Baron Norrie, and has issue living (by 1st *m*), George Lyon (Hurdcott, Barford St Martin, nr Salisbury SP3 4BA), *b* 1962: *m* 1990, Lucilla, da of Jeremy Peter Foster Clay, of Fawley Court, nr Hereford, and has issue living, Alexander *b* 1995, Tarquin *b* 1996, — Rupert Nicholas, *b* 1964, — Belinda Jane, *b* 1963. —— Harriet Ann, *b* 1931: *m* 1951 (*m diss* 1973 and re-married 1976), John Bulkley Herbert Francis of The Well House, Cowley, nr Cheltenham, Glos GL53 9NJ, and has issue living, Charles Mark (Southmoor, Brampford Speke, Exeter EX5 5DY), *b* 1952: *m* 1978, Pamela, da of Ronald George Frankland, of 67 Garden House Estate, Crawcrook, Tyne and Wear, and has issue living, Anna Louise *b* 1987, — Timothy, *b* 1960: *m* 19—, Louise Halstead, and has issue living, William *b* 1992, Oliver *b* 1994, Sophie Louise *b* 1998, — Clare Victoria, *b* 1955: *m* 1984, Mark Millington Synge, and has issue (*see* Synge, Bt, colls), — Charlotte Ann (82 Islip Rd, Oxford OX2 7SW), *b* 1963.

The 1st baronet, Sir Henry Kenyon Stephenson, DSO, VD (son of late Sir Henry Stephenson, of the Glen, Endcliffe, Sheffield), was Pro-Chancellor of Sheffield Univ, Chm of Stephenson, Blake & Co, typefounders, Lord Mayor of Sheffield 1908-09 and 1910-11, Master Cutler of Sheffield 1919-20, and High Sheriff of Derbyshire 1932. He sat as MP for Park Div of Sheffield (*L*) 1918-23, and served during European War 1914-18 (DSO).

STEWART (I) 1623, of Ramelton, co Donegal

Nothing is to be despaired of

NIL DESPERANDVM

Sir ALAN D'ARCY STEWART, 13th *Baronet; b* 29 Nov 1932; *s* his father, Sir JOCELYN HARRY, 1982; *ed* All Saints', Bathurst, NSW: *m* 1952, Patricia, da of Lawrence Turner, of Ramelton, co Donegal, and has issue.

Arms – (recorded at Lyon Office)—Or, a fesse chequy azure and argent surmounted of a bend engrailed and in chief a rose gules, all within a bordure of the third charged with three lions rampant of the fourth. **Crest** - A dexter arm erect couped at the elbow, the hand holding a heart all proper.
Residence – One Acre House, Church St, Ramelton, co Donegal.

SONS LIVING

NICHOLAS COURTNEY d'ARCY, *b* 4 Aug 1953; *ed* New Univ of Ulster (BSc, Dip Ed). —— Lindsay Stephen d'Arcy, *b* 1956: *m* 1983, Jane Maria d'Arcy, da of Albert Rossley, of The Haw House, Ray, co Donegal, and has issue living, Emma Naomi d'Arcy *b* 1983.

DAUGHTERS LIVING

Constance Patricia, *b* 1954: *m* 1978, Malcolm McMillan, and has issue living, James, *b* 1980, — Peter, *b* 1981. —— Siobhan d'Arcy, *b* 1960.

HALF-BROTHERS LIVING

Brian Jocelyn, *b* 1948. —— Terence Annesley, *b* 1949.

HALF-SISTERS LIVING

Marie Jeanette, *b* 1947: *m* 19—, Harry Scott, of Greenhill, Convoy, co Donegall, and has issue living, a son, *b* 19—. —— Katherine Benedicta, *b* 1951.

COLLATERAL BRANCHES LIVING

Issue of late Malcolm Geoffrey Stewart, 4th son of 11th baronet; *b* 1908, *d* 1974: *m* 1946, Joan Cox, who *d* 1968:—
Robin Gordon Alan (50 Parkholme Rd, E8) *b* 1948: *m* 1973, Barbara Anne, da of Wilfred Miller, of Grasscroft, Yorks, and has issue living, James Malcolm, *b* 1978, — Thomas Annesley, *b* 1979, — William Francis, *b* 1984. —— Jonathan Malcolm (South View, Rectory Rd, Great Haseley, Oxford), *b* 1951; has issue living, Sorrel STEWART, *b* 1984.

Granddaughter of late Col Harry Hutchinson Augustus Stewart, brother of 9th baronet:—
Issue of late Walter Annesley Stewart, *b* 1883, *d* 1937: *m* 1920, Phyllis Lucie (who *d* 1981, having *m* 2ndly, 1938, Benjamin Worthy Horne, of Norfolk Cottage, Waldron, Heathfield, Sussex), da of late Edmund Larkin Horne, of 34 Bolton Gdns, SW5:—
Rosemary, *b* 1928: *m* 1950, Col John Arthur Haire, late RA, of Somerville, Woodlands Rd, Bromley, Kent, and has issue living, John Stewart (33 Radnor Walk, SW3), *b* 1957; BA, — Susan Mary, *b* 1952; BA, RAS Cert (PG): *m* 1982, Frank Peter Hinks, of The Old Vicarage, Shoreham, Sevenoaks, Kent, and has issue living, Julius James *b* 1984, Alexander John *b* 1985, Benjamin Stewart *b* 1987, — Anne Rosemary, *b* 1954; MRCGP, DRCOG, DCH, MFFP: *m* 1981, Alan Frederick Graeme Groom, FRCS, of 65 Lee Rd, Blackheath, SE3 9EN, and has issue living, William Douglas Ian *b* 1985, Frederick Thomas *b* 1990, Alice Suzanne *b* 1987.

Granddaughter of late Lorenzo Moore Stewart (infra):—
Issue of late Trevor Eugene St Quinton Stewart, *b* 1907, *d* 1980: *m* 1932, Edna Maude (Unit 4/5 Woodrow Place, Dianella, Perth, WA), da of late Richard Sherman Wood:—
Pamela Jean, *b* 1934: *m* 1962, Leon Allan Kings. *Residence* - 18 Norton Drive, Dianella, Perth, W Australia.

Grandson of late Richard Quinton Stewart, yr son of late Lorenzo Moore Stewart, uncle of 9th baronet:—
Issue of late Lorenzo Moore Stewart, *b* 1882, *d* 1926: *m* 1906, Ivy Mercilla, who *d* 1967, da of late Walter Edmund Pachaud Wordsworth, of Rampur Haut, India:—
Harold Vivian Moore, *b* 1908; CEng, MIMechE; *m* 1st, 1932 (*m diss*), Ella Marie, who *d* 1986, da of late John Tracey Falconer; 2ndly, 1956, Helen Elizabeth, da of late Archibald Ronald Robb, and has issue living (by 1st *m*), Olga Deidre Moore (52 Victoria Rd, Cowes, Isle of Wight PO31 7JJ), *b* 1936: *m* 1964 (*m diss* 1991), Gordon Edward Malone, and has issue living, Amanda Jane *b* 1966; BA London, Catherine Ellen *b* 1968; BA, PhD Oxon, — Roslyn Anne Moore, *b* 1944: *m* 1966, Alan Gray Rutherford, OBE, BSc, PhD, CChem, CEng, FRSC, FInstE, FRSA, Hon Col The Parachute Regt, of 18 Murrayfield Gdns, Edinburgh EH12 6DF, and has issue living, Simon Gray *b* 1967, Sarah Caroline *b* 1971; *ed* Merton Coll, Oxford (MA), and Edinburgh Univ (PhD); FRSA: *m* 1999, Danny Morrison, MD, BMedSc, FRCOphth, FRSA, — (by 2nd *m*) Michael Ian Moore (118 Bagnall Beach Rd, Corlette, NSW 2515, Australia), *b* 1958; *ed* WA Univ (BCom); Master Management Studies, Univ SW; Maj RACT: *m* 1988, Janelle Skehan, BPharm (Sydney), Dip Hospital Pharmacy, and has issue living, Callam Michael *b* 1994, Ellenore Anne *b* 1991, — Richard Quinton Moore, *b* 1964; *ed* Curtain Univ, WA (B(app)Sc). *Residence* - 18 Nangkita Rd, Kalamunda, Perth, W Australia 6076.

This family is of common ancestry with the Earls of Galloway and Barons Blantyre (ext 1900). The 1st baronet greatly distinguished himself as a Mil Comd in the troubles of Ireland, and was created a Privy Councillor. The 3rd baronet, Master-General of the Ordnance in Ireland, was in 1682 created Lord Stewart of Ramelton and Viscount Mountjoy. The 2nd Viscount and 4th Baronet was also Master-General of the Ordnance; and the 3rd Viscount and 5th Baronet was created Earl of Blessington, but his peerages became extinct at his death in 1769. The 6th baronet sat as MP for Charlemont 1763-97, and the 7th baronet represented in Parliament Enniskillen 1783-90 and Donegal co 1802-18.

STEWART (UK) 1803, of Athenree, Tyrone

Sir DAVID JOHN CHRISTOPHER STEWART, 7th *Baronet; b* 19 June 1935; *s* his father, *Maj Sir* HUGH CHARLIE GODFRAY, 1994; *ed* Bradfield, and RMC Sandhurst; late Capt Royal Inniskilling Fus, and Trucial Oman Scouts: *m* 1959, Bridget Anne, eldest da of late Patrick Wood Sim, and has issue.

𝕬rms – Quarterly, 1st, or, a lion rampant within a double tressure flory counter-flory gules; 2nd, or, a fess chequy azure and argent, in chief a portcullis sable, *Stewart*; 3rd, argent, a saltire between four roses gules, barbed vert, *Fife*; 4th, or, a lion rampant gules, *Lennox*; the whole within a bordure compony argent and azure charged with three thistles proper. 𝕮rest – A unicorn's head coupled argent, armed and crined or, between two olive branches proper.
Residence – Tower View, 8 Silver St, Wiveliscombe, Taunton, Som TA4 2PA.
Club – MCC.

DAUGHTERS LIVING

Siobhan Amanda, *b* 1961: *m* 1986, Toby Mark Andrew Holland, of 21 Rockwell Green, Wellington, Som TA21 9BT, son of Bryant Holland, of London, and has issue living, George David Bryant, *b* 1988, — Aimée Grace, *b* 1990. —— Selina Godfray (49 Allfarthing Lane, SW18), *b* 1964. —— Sophie Caroline, *b* 1966: *m* 1990, Jonathan à Court-Wills, of 2 Upper Holway Rd, Taunton, Som TA1 2HD, son of Anthony Wills, of Wellington, Som, and has issue living, Patrick David Anthony, *b* 1992, — Alice Victoria Ann, *b* 1996.

HALF-BROTHER LIVING

HUGH NICHOLAS, *b* 20 April 1955; *ed* Portora Royal Sch: *m* 1976, Anna, da of Frank Llewellyn Leeke, of Kingsbury, Middx, and has issue living, Kieran Andrew Liam, *b* 22 Jan 1979, — Cherisma, *b* 1974, — Tamesin Kerry, *b* 1977, — Lauren, *b* 1987. *Residence* – Lowlands, Tibberton, Glos.

SISTER LIVING

Elinor Godfray, *b* 1930: *m* 1953, John Michael Macdonell, of 3 Blackhouse Rise, Hythe, Kent CT21 5UX, and has issue living, Michael John Alistair (The Park, Weston Underwood, Bucks MK46 5JZ), *b* 1960; *ed* Winchester: *m* 1988, Sara Belinda Bleakly, of Rochdale, and has issue living, Charlie Michael *b* 1995, Lydia Rose *b* 1997, — Sarah Jane Elinor, *b* 1959: *m* 1st, 1981 (*m diss* 1985), Brian Cadogan; 2ndly, 1988, Graham Shewell, of Plaxtol, Tonbridge, Kent, and has issue living (by 1st *m*), Jonathan Joseph *b* 1981, Patrick Michael *b* 1983, (by 2nd *m*) Hugh Timothy *b* 1989, Teresa Elinor *b* 1992.

HALF-SISTER LIVING

Jane Diana, *b* 1949: *m* 1973, John Thomas Costelloe, of Bartlow, Leckhampton, Cheltenham, Glos, and has issue living, Hugh John, *b* 1974, — Nicola, *b* 1977, — Jessica, *b* 1981.

WIDOW LIVING OF SIXTH BARONET

DIANA MARGARET (*Dowager Lady Stewart*), da of late Capt James Edmond Hibbert, MC, DFC: *m* 1948, as his 2nd wife, Maj Sir Hugh Charlie Godfray Stewart, 6th Bt, who *d* 1994. *Residence* – Cottesbrook, Sandy Pluck Lane, Bentham, Cheltenham, Glos GL51 5UB.

COLLATERAL BRANCHES LIVING

Granddaughter of late Capt Hugh Stewart, 2nd son of 2nd baronet:—
Issue of late Lieut-Col Hugh Stewart, DSO, MC, MB, *b* 1881, *ka* 1918: *m* 1907, Muriel Dalzell, da of Hugh McKean, of 19 Zion Rd, Rathgar, Dublin:—
Muriel Denise Evelyn, *b* 1913: *m* 1942, John Gunn Murray-Matheson, MB, ChB, and has issue living, Desmond John, *b* 1950, — Nigel Hugh, *b* 1951, — Ann Christine, *b* 1943: *m* 1966, Dr Richard John Purvis, of 2 Queen's Av, Dorchester, Dorset, — Rosemary Jean Denise, *b* 1947. *Residence* – 32 Elmfield Rd, Gosforth, Newcastle-upon-Tyne.

Grandchildren of late George Vesey Stewart, MBE, 3rd son of Mervyn Stewart, 2nd son of 1st baronet:—
Issue of late Mervyn Archdale Stewart, *b* 1859, *d* 1951: *m* 1881, Phœbe, who *d* 1951, da of late Robert Hornidge-Gledstanes:—
Mary Sophia Ethel: *m* 1918, Robert Rutland Turner, who *d* 1927, formerly of Tauranga, New Zealand, and has issue living, Stewart Rutland, *b* 1919: *m* 1942, Kathleen, da of W. O'Connor, of Ashburton, New Zealand, and has issue living, a son *b* 1943, — Phœbe Ethne, *b* 1923: *m* 1944, Clifford Cedric Mountier.

Issue of late George Vesey Stewart, *b* 1861, *d* 1892: *m* 1890, Cecilia Isabella, who *d* 1947, da of Thomas Anderson, formerly of Jesmond, Newcastle-upon-Tyne:—
Georgina Frances (*posthumous*): *m* 1925, Norman Lawrence Wilson, and has issue living, Lawrence Stewart, *b* 1928, — George Archdale, *b* 1930, — Kerry Robin (5 Maungarei Rd, Remuera, Auckland 5, New Zealand), *b* 1933, — Patricia Cecilia, *b* 1934.

Grandsons of late John Rowley Miller Stewart (infra):—
Issue of late Mervyn Oswald Stewart, *b* 1888, *d* 1946: *m* 1915, Ivy Mona, who *d* 19-, da of Robert Ernest Lester, of Kohukohu, Auckland, NZ:—
Mervyn Leslie Lester, *b* 1916: *m* 19-, and has issue living, Trevor Rex (Takanini, Auckland, NZ), *b* 1940. —— Donald Walton (1 Mainston Rd, Remuera, Auckland, NZ), *b* 1919: *m* 1941, Joan Eunice, yst da of late Harry John Brunsdon, of Christchurch, NZ, and has issue living, Roger Alan (78 Morey Rd, Beaumaris, Melbourne, Aust), *b* 19—: *m* 19—, Linda Denise Marsden, and has issue living, Hamish *b* 19—, Stephanie Gina *b* 19—: *m* 19—, Alistair Woodhead, Alexia *b* 19—, Sarra-Jane *b* 19—, — Ian Murray (33 Hopkins Crescent, Kohimaramara, Auckland, NZ), *b* 19—: *m* 19—, Jo-Anne Mills, and has issue living, Barnaby *b* 19—, Felicity *b* 19—, — Evan Alistair (29 Tandanya St, Mansfield, Brisbane 4122, Aust), *b* 19—: *m* 19—, Avril Burberry, and has issue living, Troy Anthony *b* 19—, Andrew *b* 19—, Lucinda *b* 19—, — Peter Mark (22a, Manawa Rd, Remuera, Auckland, NZ), *b* 19—: *m* 1987, Jennifer Dowling, — Juliet Cynthia, *b* 1942: *m* 1969, Donald Rex Worrall, of 16 Awatea Rd, Parnell, Auckland, NZ, and has issue living, Allister Stewart *b* 1971, Marcus James *b* 1973, Elliot John *b* 1974, Jonathan Charles *b* 1978. —— Kenneth Archdale (70 Ray Small Drive, Papakura, NZ), *b* 1922; Sr Clerk of Works, Min of Works, Auckland: *m* 1951, Elma Pearl, da of Harold Kirtlan, of Kaitai, NZ, and has issue living, Murray Kenneth, *b* 1952: *m* 19—, Barbara Lynn, da of Hugh Douglas, of Wellington, NZ, and has issue living, Daniel Craig *b* 1978, Kristy Nicole *b* 1981, — Gael, *b* 1953: *m* 19—, David Alexander Splek, of Fielding Rd, Drury, Auckland, NZ, and has issue living, Mathew David *b* 1975, Allister Lee *b* 1978, — Jennifer Anne, *b* 1958: *m* 1983, Peter George Neate, and has issue living, Sam George *b* 1988, Anna-Marie *b* 1985.

Issue of late George Leslie Stewart, *b* 1893, *d* 1938: *m* 1927, Lillian Alice Ridsdale:—
Ross Ridsdale (c/o PO Box 407, Gisborne, NZ), *b* 1934: *m* 1966, Jillian Michelle, da of Robert Hamilton Bartie, of Gisborne, NZ, and has issue living, Jonathan Bruce, *b* 1969.

Grandchildren of Trevor Rowley Stewart (infra):—
Issue of late Colin Trevor Stewart, *b* 1925, *d* 1968: *m* 1948, Bessie Rebie, da of Frederick Clarke Shroff, of Tauranga, NZ:—
Gary Colin, *b* 1953. —— Peter Gregory, *b* 1958. —— Colette Marie, *b* 1950.

Grandchildren of George Vesey Stewart, MBE (ante):—
Issue of late John Rowley Miller Stewart, *b* 1862, *d* 1945: *m* 1st, 1886, Ellen Louisa, who *d* 1912, da of late Henry Furness, of Kyber Pass, Auckland, New Zealand; 2ndly, 1913, Louisa Beatrice, da of Thomas Gorst Travis, of Dunedin, NZ:—
(By 1st *m*) Trevor Rowley (149 Edgecumbe Rd, Tauranga, NZ), *b* 1896: *m* 1920, Dora, da of late Edwin Hall, of Waihi, NZ, and has issue living, Shirley Rita, *b* 1921: *m* 1st, 1945 (*m diss* 1950), William Lloyd Stevens; 2ndly, 1969, Francis Victor Parker, who *d* 1973, and has issue living (by 1st *m*), Kay Stewart, *b* 1947. —— (By 2nd *m*) Lorraine Travis, *b* 1917: *m* 1937, Alfred Shepherd Willan, of Hastings Rd, Stratford, Taranaki, NZ, and has issue living, Michael Frederick Stewart, *b* 1941, — Jock Stewart, *b* 1944, — Bruce Stewart, *b* 1946, — Pamela Stewart, *b* 1939.

Issue of late Hugh Alexander Montgomery Moore Stewart, *b* 1868, *d* 1954: *m* 1st, 1891, Susan, who *d* 1926, da of late William Tasman Clark, CE, of Hobart, Tasmania; 2ndly, 1932, Edith, el da of Joseph Cantwell, of Hawke's Bay, New Zealand:—
(By 1st *m*) James Edward Frederick Vesey Tasman, *b* 18-: *m* 19-, and has issue living, Noel Montgomery, *b* 19-. —— Gilbert Harry Ranfurly, *b* 18-. —— Christina Martina Alice, *b* 19-. —— Myrtle, *b* 19-. —— (By 2nd *m*) Coral Elizabeth, *b* 19-.

Grandchildren of late Hugh Alexander Murray Stewart, 2nd son of Hugh Alexander Montgomery Moore Stewart (ante):—
Issue of Ranfurly Henry Stewart, *b* 1899, *d* 1972: *m* 19-, Emma Frances Newman, who *d* 1967:—
William Henry Albert Harvey (Ohauiti Rd, RD3, Tauranga, NZ), *b* 1929: *m* 1951, Joan Alison, da of David Prestney, and has issue living, Brian William (209 James St, Whakatare, NZ), *b* 1966, — Julie Frances, *b* 1953: *m* 19—, Peter Robert Gray, of 11 Heritage Av, Hamilton, NZ, son of Jack Gray, of Te Puke, and has issue living, Richard Bruce *b* 1977, Jennifer Louise *b* 1975, Alison Julie *b* 1980, — Colleen Margaret, *b* 1955: *m* 19—, Philip Edward Watts, of Esdailes Rd, RD8, Tauranga, NZ, son of Thomas Watts, of Tauranga, and has issue living, Andrew Thomas *b* 1980, Ryan Philip *b* 1983, Anna Liese *b* 1987, — Janelle Beverley, *b* 1957: *m* 19—, John Anthony Arts, son of Bernhard J. Arts, of Tauranga, and has issue living, Anthony James *b* 1989, Renée Marise *b* 1982, Sarah Rochelle *b* 1900, Katie Monique *b* 1986, Debora Joy STEWART (has kept her maiden name), *b* 1959: *m* 1st, 19—, Paul Anthony Hogg; 2ndly, 19—, Tom Smith, and has issue living (by 1st *m*), Adam Stewart *b* 1984. —— Trevor Ernest (PO Box Ormand, Gisborne, NZ), *b* 1931: *m* 1955, Joan Alice, da of Andrew Stanley Fisher, and has issue living, Kevin Mark, *b* 1959; has issue living, Dion Mark *b* 1984, — Steven Wayne, *b* 1962; has issue living, Matthew Allan *b* 1986, Stacey Janna *b* 1992, — David Ernest, *b* 1968, — Philip Trevor, *b* 1972, — Maureen Anne, *b* 1957; has issue living, Philippa Joan *b* 1988, — Shona Joy, *b* 1961; has issue living, Rory Shane *b* 1988, Hayley Maree *b* 1991, — Sarah Lisa-Maree, *b* 1970. —— Valerie Elizabeth Grace, *b* 1933: *m* 19—, Patrick John Donovan, and has issue living, Bruce Charles, *b* 1955; has issue living, Gene *b* 1987, — Raymond John, *b* 1957, — Suzanne Jean, *b* 1959. —— Dawn Frances, *b* 193-: *m* 19—, Ronald Leslie Nicholson, and has issue living, Linda Dawn, *b* 19—, — Christine, *b* 19—, — Ronda, *b* 19—.

Grandchildren of late Hugh Stewart, yst son of late Mervyn Stewart, 2nd son of 1st baronet:—
Issue of late Rev Mervyn James Stewart, *b* 1871, *d* 1961: *m* 1910, Margaret Emma, who *d* 1968, da of late Frederick Jeffray Steuart, formerly of Carfin, Melbourne, Victoria, Australia:—

Hugh St Clair, MBE (Oak Cottage, Cheapside Lane, Denham, Bucks UB9 5AD; Savile Club), *b* 1910; *ed* St John's Coll, Camb (MA); 1939-45 War as Lt-Col Comdg an Army Film and Photographic Unit; MBE (Mil) 1945: *m* 1934, Frances Henley, BA, who *d* 1982, only child of late Dr Henley Frank Curl, of Wokingham, and has issue living, Andrew Mervyn (37 Park Rd, Rickmansworth, Herts WD3 1HU), *b* 1943; *ed* Rugby: *m* 1st, 1966 (*m diss* 1991), Carol-Anne, da of Stanley Burritt Featherstone, of Uitenhage, S Africa; 2ndly, 1991, Maaike, da of Dr Ir Johan Joseph Breen, of Gorinchem, Holland, and has issue living (by 1st *m*), Zoë Abbygail *b* 1971, — Michael Henley (Heathlands, Keepers Lane, Hyde Heath, Bucks HP6 5RJ), *b* 1949; *ed* Rugby, and Southampton Univ: *m* 1st, 1971, Jillian Maureen, who *d* 1980, da of Stanley Gold, of Reigate; 2ndly, 1985, Ann Frances, da of Frank Harris, of Feltham, and has issue living (by 1st *m*), Simon Mark Hugh *b* 1977, Paul Daniel *b* 1978, (by 2nd *m*) Sally Ann *b* 1985, Clare Henley June *b* 1987, Hannah Daisy *b* 1989, — Penelope Agnes, *b* 1939; *ed* Somerville Coll, Oxford (MA): *m* 1962, Hugh Macdonald Eales Forsyth, of Linden Lodge, Austen Way, Chalfont St Peter, Bucks, and has issue living, Kevin Hugh *b* 1969, Angus Edward Eales *b* 1975, — Sophie Frances *b* 1971, — Trottie (twin), *b* 1949; legally assumed the forename of Trottie in lieu of Margaret; *ed* Queenswood Sch, and Girton Coll, Camb; MD: *m* 1971, Anthony Kirwan, and has issue living, Jonathan Anthony *b* 1987, Eleanor Catherine *b* 1979, Frances Marguerite *b* 1982. —— David (2425 153rd Av SE, Bellevue, Washington 98007, USA), *b* 1912; is an Assocn-Fellow of R Aeronautical Soc: *m* 1st, 1942, Marjorie Susan Carroll, who *d* 1961, yr da of the Rev Frederick Charles Costeloe, formerly V of Staveley, Carlisle; 2ndly, 1963, Grace Edman Cunningham, of Madison, Connecticut, USA, and has had issue (by 1st *m*), Gordon Archdale (9760 Barnett Valley Rd, Sebastopol, CA 95472, USA), *b* 1944; *ed* St Columba's, and Pacific Lutheran Univ (BA): *m* 1982, Cora Docken, of St Paul, Minnesota, — †Simon Jeffray, *b* 1945: *ed* St Columba's, and Washington Univ (MBA): *m* 1968, Carolyn Sroufe, who *d* 1992, and *d* 1993, leaving issue, Patrick Jeffray *b* 1979, Rachel Elizabeth *b* 1976: *m* 1999, Jason Mark, of Bellevue, Washington, — David James (7338 47th Av N.E., Seattle, Washington 98115, USA), *b* 1952; *ed* Washington Univ (MBA): *m* 1st, 1979 (*m diss* 1994), Carole Cummins; 2ndly, 1997, Vickie Davie, of Seattle, Washington, and has issue living (by 1st *m*), Michael Cameron *b* 1985, Susan Blake *b* 1989. —— Mary Jeffray (Estone, Steeple Aston, Oxon), *b* 1913; formerly Section Officer, WAAF: *m* 1944, Dr John Edgar Furness, formerly Wing-Cdr RAF, who *d* 1974, and has issue living, Diana Ruth, *b* 1944: *m* 1973, Ronald Gardner, of Spring Vale, Steeple Aston, Oxon, and has issue living, Samantha Kim *b* 1975, Karen Louise *b* 1978, Sally Marie *b* 1984.

This family descends from Capt Andrew Stewart who accompanied Lord Ochiltree from Scotland, and settled at Gortigal, co Tyrone, about 1620. The 1st baronet, the Right Hon Sir John, Attorney-General for Ireland in 1799, drafted the Act of Union, and was successively MP for cos Down and Tyrone.

STEWART (UK) 1920 of Fingask, co Perth (Extinct 1979)

Sir BRUCE FRASER STEWART, 2nd and last *Baronet*.

DAUGHTER LIVING OF SECOND BARONET

Joy Elizabeth, *b* 1932: *m* 1955, Anthony Maxwell Deans, of 14 Petworth Place, Westmorland, Christchurch 8003, NZ, and has issue living, Robert Maxwell, *b* 1959: *m* 1986, Penelope Jane Russell, and has issue living, Samuel John Maxwell *b* 1989, Annabel Jane *b* 1991, Sophie Ellen *b* 1996, — Ian Bruce, *b* 1960. — Joanne Stewart, *b* 1956: *m* 1986, Stephen McAtamney, of Oregon, Ruapuna RD5, Ashburton, NZ, and has issue living, Daniel *b* 1987, Anthony Joshua *b* 1988, Matthew *b* 1990, — Nicola Anne, *b* 1957: *m* 1983, Michael James Bowie Hobbs, of 19 Seaview Terrace, Northlands, Wellington, NZ, and has issue living, Michael *b* 1987, Emily *b* 1985, Penny *b* 1990, Isabelle *b* 1994, — Sarah, *b* 1962.

STEWART (UK) 1920, of Balgownie, Bearsden, co Dumbarton

Sir (JOHN) SIMON WATSON STEWART, 6th *Baronet*; *b* 5 July 1955; *s* his father, *Sir* JOHN KEITH WATSON, 1990; *ed* Uppingham, and Charing Cross Medical Sch; MD, FRCP, FRCR: *m* 1978, Dr Catherine Stewart, da of Henry Gordon Bond, of Heyeswood House, Shiplake, Oxon, and has issue.

𝔄rms – (as recorded at Lyon Office)—Or, a fesse checky azure and argent between in chief a Roman Charioteer driving a chariot with two horses, and in base a demi-figure of St Kentigern habited, bearing a crozier in his left hand, his right hand raised in benediction, all proper. 𝔠rest – A dexter hand couped at the wrist holding a sword erect in pale proper hilted and pommelled or. *Residence* – 38 Duke's Av, W4 2AE. *Club* – Oriental.

SON LIVING

JOHN HAMISH WATSON, *b* 12 Dec 1983.

DAUGHTER LIVING

Anna Rebecca Watson, *b* 1987.

BROTHER LIVING

James Watson, *b* 1960; *ed* Winchester, Durham Univ, and RMA Sandhurst: *m* 1987, Judy Anne, da of late John George Bamford, of Uttoxeter, Staffs, and has issue living, Thomas Murdoch Watson, *b* 1992, — Emma Victoria Watson, *b* 1990, — Alice Georgina Watson, *b* 1993. *Residence* – The Old Vicarage, Melchbourne, Beds MK44 1BQ.

SISTER LIVING

Caroline Felicity Watson STEWART, *b* 1958; *ed* Lycée Française de Londres; has resumed her maiden name: *m* 1982, Neil Barry Solomons, FRCS (Ed), son of Dr Arthur Solomons, of Port Elizabeth, S Africa, and has issue living, Lucy, *b* 1983, — Kate, *b* 1985.

WIDOW LIVING OF FOURTH BARONET

AVRIL VERONICA, DStJ, FRSA, Hon FBID, Hon MASC (*Avril, Lady Watson Stewart*), only da of late Andrew Adamson Gibb, of Glasgow; artist, calligrapher and lecturer: *m* 1980, as his 2nd wife, Sir James Watson Stewart, 4th Bt, who *d* 1988. *Residence* – Undercliff Court, Wemyss Bay, Renfrewshire PA18 6AL. *Club* – Royal Scottish Automobile.

WIDOW LIVING OF FIFTH BARONET

MARY ELIZABETH (*Mary, Lady Stewart*), elder da of late John Francis Moxon, of Horton Hall, Leek, Staffs: *m* 1954, Sir John Keith Watson Stewart, 5th Bt, who *d* 1990. *Residence* – Flat 55, Hans Rd, SW3 1RN.

COLLATERAL BRANCH LIVING

Issue of late Fl Lt Malcolm Gilbert Watson Stewart, DFC, yst son of 1st baronet, *b* 1898, *d* 1971: *m* 1923, Evelyn Maud, da of late John A. Stewart, of Glasgow:—
John Allan (Tepic 80 Col Roma, Mexico DF, Mexico), *b* 1928: *m* 1959, Maria del Rufugio Vargas, of Mexico City, and has issue living, John Eric, *b* 1960. —— Edith Mary Hedley, *b* 1924: *m* 1948, Francis Lockhart McCall, of 5 Clyde Park Redland, Bristol, and has issue living, Peter Lockhart, *b* 1949, — Charles Michael Lockhart, *b* 1956, — Aline Mary, *b* 1950, — Sara Elizabeth, *b* 1954, — Louise Evelyn, *b* 1963.

Sir James Watson Stewart, 1st Bt (a Chartered Accountant), was a Member of Glasgow Corporation 1904-20, and Lord Provost of Glasgow and Lord-Lieut of Co of City of Glasgow 1917-20.

STEWART (UK) 1937, of Stewartby, co Bedford (Extinct 1999)

Sir RONALD COMPTON STEWART, 2nd and last *Baronet*; *d* 1999.

HALF-SISTER LIVING OF SECOND BARONET

Yvonne Elizabeth Diana, *b* 1915; *ed* Somerville Coll, Oxford (BA 1937, MA 1950): *m* 1948, Thomas Doggett Savory, who *d* 1988, and has issue living, Thomas Stewart, *b* 1949: *m* 1975, Susan Elizabeth Allen, and has issue living, Elizabeth Susan *b* 1986, — Malcolm Doggett, *b* 1950: *m* 1975, Julia Mary Dring, and has issue living, Edward James Doggett *b* 1980, Hannah Caroline *b* 1977, Jessica Mary Alice *b* 1987.

STEWART (UK) 1960, of Strathgarry, co Perth

Sir ALASTAIR ROBIN STEWART, 3rd *Baronet*; *b* 26 Sept 1925; *s* his brother, *Sir* DAVID BRODRIBB, TD, 1992; *ed* Marlborough; Man Dir (ret) of Stewart and Harvey Ltd; Lieut Royal Glos Hussars: *m* 1953, Patricia Helen, MBE, BA, ARIBA, da of late John Alfred Merrett, of Pondhead Farm, Forest Green, Surrey, and has issue.

Arms – Quarterly, 1st and 4th; of, a fess chequy azure and argent, *Stewart*; 2nd and 3rd; argent, a galley sable, sails furled, oars in action proper, flagged gules, *Lorne*; the whole within a bordure per pale dexter vert, sinister argent, charged with three roses gules barbed and seeded vert. **Crest** – A unicorn's head couped argent and armed and crined or. **Badges** – On escutcheon at centre of quarters.
Residence – Walter's Cottage, Little Baddow, Chelmsford, Essex CM3 4TQ.

SON LIVING

JOHN KENNETH ALEXANDER, *b* 15 Dec 1961; *ed* Marlborough, and Pembroke Coll, Camb (BA).

DAUGHTERS LIVING

Judith Patricia, *b* 1954; *ed* St Felix, Chelmsford County High Sch, and Bristol Polytechnic: *m* 1993, David Harley Usill, eldest son of late Harley Usill, of London. —— Lucy Janetta, *b* 1956; *ed* St Felix, Chelmsford County High Sch, and Newcastle Polytechnic (BA). —— Catherine Helen, *b* 1958; *ed* St Felix, Marlborough Coll, and Trin Hall, Camb (BA).

SISTERS LIVING

Janetta Kenric (1 The Ridings, Links Rd, Ashtead, Surrey), *b* 1918; *ed* Lady Margaret Hall, Oxford (BA 1942). —— Leslie Mary (No 3 Collingham-Blue Water Rd, Beacon Way, East London, S Africa), *b* 1921; *ed* Malvern Girls' Coll: *m* 1942, John Berger, MRCVS, who *d* 1982, son of Harry August Emil Berger, of Bickley, Kent, and has issue living, David Kenneth, *b* 1964; *ed* Univ of Cape Town (PhD): *m* 19—, Eldje Strijdom, and has issue living, Kenneth *b* 1995, Heidi *b* 1996, — Jennifer, *b* 1944; *ed* Aberdeen Univ (BSc), and Berkeley Univ, Cal, USA (PhD), — Vere, *b* 1946; *ed* Aberdeen Univ (BA), and Sussex Univ (MA), — Elizabeth, *b* 1948; *ed* Nottingham Univ (BSc); MSc Nairobi: *m* 1972 Peter Moore, and has issue living, Kathleen Lesley *b* 1980, Carissa *b* 1981.

WIDOW LIVING OF SECOND BARONET

BARBARA DYKES (*Dowager Lady Stewart*), da of late Harry Dykes Lloyd, of Hull, and widow of Donald Ian Stewart, MC: *m* 1963, Sir David Brodribb Stewart, 2nd Bt, TD, who *d* 1992. *Residence* – Sasella, 5 Niklausen, Horw, Switzerland.

This family descends from the Rev Duncan Stewart, 1st of Strathgarry, son of Donald, 4th son of Alan Stewart, 3rd of Appin. Sir Kenneth Dugald Stewart, 1st Bt, yst son of Hinton Daniell Stewart, 6th of Strathgarry, was Chm of Lancs Cotton Corporation 1928-32, and of Trustee Savings Banks Assocn, 1946-65.

HENDERSON-STEWART (UK) 1957, of Callumshill, co Perth

Sir DAVID JAMES HENDERSON-STEWART OF CALLUMSHILL, 2nd *Baronet*; *b* 3rd July 1941; *s* his father, *Sir* JAMES, MP, 1961; *ed* Eton, and Trin Coll, Oxford: *m* 1972, Anne, da of Count Serge de Pahlen, and has issue.
Residence – 90 Oxford Gdns, W10.

SONS LIVING

DAVID, *b* 2 Feb 1973. —— Nicolas, *b* 1974. —— André, *b* 1976.

DAUGHTER LIVING

Nathalie, *b* 1981.

SISTER LIVING

Annabel HENDERSON-STEWART, *b* 1943; has resumed surname of Henderson-Stewart: *m* 1966, Andrew Alastair Borthwick, and has issue living, Selena Margaret, *b* 1967, — Emilie Anna, *b* 1970.

WIDOW LIVING OF FIRST BARONET

ANNA MARGARET, da of Sir Bernard Eyre Greenwell, MBE, 2nd Bt: *m* 1st, 1940, Sir James Henderson-Stewart, MP, 1st baronet, who *d* 1961; 2ndly, 1965, Geoffrey Walford Wilks, CBE, TD, of 64 Cadogan Sq, SW1, who *d* 1987.

Sir James Henderson-Stewart, MP, 1st Bt (son of late Matthew Deas Stewart), sat as MP for E Div of Fife (LU) 1933-61, and was Joint Parliamentary Under-Sec of State for Scotland 1952-57. He was officially recognised in the surname of Henderson-Stewart and the designation of Callumshill by warrant of Lord Lyon 1957.

SHAW-STEWART (NS) 1667, of Greenock and Blackhall, Renfrewshire

I hope for better things

Maj Sir HOUSTON MARK SHAW-STEWART, MC, 11th *Baronet*, *b* 24 April 1931; *s* his brother, *Sir* EUAN GUY, 1980; *ed* Eton; Maj Ayrshire Yeo; late 2nd Lt R Ulster Rifles, Korea 1950-51 (MC 1950): *m* 1982, Lucinda Victoria, yr da of Alexander K. H. Fletcher, of the Old Vicarage, Wighill, Tadcaster, N Yorks, and has issue.

𝔄rms – Quarterly: 1st and 4th, or, a fesse chequy azure, over all a lion rampant gules, *Stewart of Blackhall*; 2nd and 3rd, azure, three covered cups or *Shaw of Greenock*. ℭrests – 1st, a lion's head erased gules, armed and langued azure, *Stewart of Blackhall*; 2nd, holding a club over his shoulder proper, a demi-savage wreathed about the head and middle with a laurel vert, *Shaw of Greenock*. 𝔖upporters – *Dexter*, a lion rampant gules, armed and langued azure, gorged with a collar checky argent and azure; *sinister*, a savage, holding a club over his shoulder all proper, wreathed round the middle with laurel leaves vert.
Seat – Ardgowan, Inverkip, Renfrewshire

SON LIVING

LUDOVIC HOUSTON, *b* 12 Nov 1986.

DAUGHTERS LIVING OF TENTH BARONET (*By 1st marriage*)

Fiona Mary Onyx, *b* 1954: *m* 1981, Guy Nicholas John Jewers, son of Maj J.S. Jewers, RM (ret), and has issue living, a son, *b* 1995.

(By 2nd marriage)

Claudia Mary, *b* 1963.

COLLATERAL BRANCHES LIVING

Issue of late Rev Charles Robert Shaw-Stewart, 2nd son of 7th baronet, *b* 1856, *d* 1932: *m* 1890, Ida Fannie Caroline, who *d* 1940, da of H. W. Alfken:—
Una Mary, *b* 1890: *m* 1916, Walter Rupert Reynell, MD, FRCP, who *d* 1948, and has issue living, Peter Carew, *b* 1917, — Anthony Charles, *b* 1930, — Joan Katharine, *b* 1918, — Anne Lenore, *b* 1923.

Grandchildren of late Michael Patrick Stewart, son of late John Erskine Douglas Stewart, son of late Adm of the Fleet Sir Houston Stewart, GCB, 2nd son of 5th baronet:—
Issue of late George Archdale Stewart, *b* 1893, *d* 1959: *m* 1921, Myrtle, who *d* 1971, da of John Wheeler, of Auckland, NZ:—
Lois Frances, *b* 1925. *Residence* – Unit 4, No 8 Bowling Av, Epsom, Auckland, NZ.

Issue of late Donald Erskine Stewart, *b* 1905, *d* 1985: *m* 1936, Ailsa Violet Annie, who *d* 1970, da of John Forbes, of Auckland, NZ:—
Donald Michael (699 Mt Eden Rd, Mt Eden, Auckland, NZ), *b* 1944: *m* 1970 (*m diss* 1979), Jill Mary Smith, and has issue living, Bradley James, *b* 1970, — Jonathan Paul, *b* 1973, — Joanne Clare, *b* 1975.

Grandsons of late Maj-Gen John Heron Maxwell Shaw-Stewart, son of late John Shaw-Stewart, 3rd son of 5th baronet:—
Issue of late Col Basil Heron Shaw-Stewart, CMG, DSO, *b* 1877, *d* 1939: *m* 1916, Vera, who *d* 1993, da of W. H. Caldwell, of Morar, Inverness-shire:—
Michael (Linthill, Melrose, Roxburghshire TD6 9HU), *b* 1925: *m* 1951, Grizel Margaret Lighton, da of late Maj Alexander Caldwells Stewart, MC (Lighton, Bt), and has issue living, Archibald John (Drummore, Doune, Perthshire), *b* 1953: *m* 1983, Judy Ann, el da of Maj Robert Courage, CVO, MBE, of Greenlanes, Windlesham, Surrey, and has issue living, James Robert Houston *b* 1986, Mary Ann *b* 1987, Phoebe Kate *b* 1990, — Robert Hugh, *b* 1960, — Helen Katharine, *b* 1959: *m* 1994, Alastair George Bradstock, of 14 Dawson Place, W2 4TJ, and has issue (*see* V Hawarden, colls). —— John William Archibald, *b* 1929: *m* 1955, Vora June Douglas, who *d* 1998, da of Charles Whistler Mackintosh (*see* D Hamilton and Brandon, 1985 Edn), and has issue living, David Hugh (Hailes, Haddington, E Lothian), *b* 1956: *m* 1984, Linda Mary Catherine, elder da of late Terence Malin Dare Sorby, CBE, of the Old Vicarage, Markbeech, Edinbridge, Kent, and has issue living, Lachlan Hugo Terence *b* 1988, Guy Philip *b* 1990, Alexandra Linda Vora *b* 1986, — Patrick Douglas, *b* 1958: *m* 1995, Minnie J., da of John Stephens, of Otham, Kent, and has issue living, Thomas Dougal *b* 1996, — Alexander Malcolm, *b* 1960, — Mairi Hermione Margaret, *b* 1962: *m* 199—, Barry K. Hextall, son of Kenneth Hextall, of Guiseley, Leeds, and has issue living, Lily Vora *b* 1999. *Residence* – Traigh House, Arisaig, Inverness-shire.

Granddaughter of late George Steuart, son of Lt-Gen George Mackenzie Steuart, great-grandson of Walter Steuart, 3rd son of 1st baronet:—
Issue of late Capt James McAlpine Steuart, *b* 1868, *d* 1946: *m* 1921, Mary, who *d* 1981, da of late John Edward Compton-Bracebridge, of Atherstone Hall, Warwickshire:—
Mary Veronica GOLDBERG-STEUART, *b* 1926; assumed the addl surname of Steuart by deed 1981: *m* 1950, Donald Arthur Goldberg, who *d* 1988, of Street Ashton House, Stretton under Foss, Rugby.

The present baronet is in direct male descent from Sir John Stewart, natural son of Robert III, King of Scotland, to whom was granted the family seat of Ardgowan. Sir Michael Stewart, 3rd Bt, *m* 1738, Helen, sister and co-heir of Sir John Houston of that Ilk, 4th Bt. Her mother, Margaret, was da of Sir John Shaw, of Greenock, 2nd Bt. Sir John Shaw-Stewart, 4th Bt in 1752, on the death of his great-uncle, Sir John Shaw of Greenock, 3rd and last Bt, inherited the entailed estate of Greenock and assumed the additional surname of Shaw. Sir Euan Guy Shaw-Stewart, 10th Bt, *b* 1928: *m* 1st, 1953 (*m diss* 1956), Mary Louise, da of late Lt-Col Geoffrey Reginald Devereux Shaw (*see* Durrant, Bt, 1960 Edn) (she *m* 2ndly, 1957, Patrick James Lysaght (*see* B Lisle), and 3rdly, 1987, David Blackwell); Sir Euan *m* 2ndly, 1962 (*m diss* 1969), Victoria Anne, yr da of W. Fryer, of 8 Springfield Av, SW10, and *d* 1980.

Stewart-Clark, see Clark.

Stewart-Rankin, see Rankin.

Stewart-Richardson, see Richardson.

STIRLING (NS) 1666, of Glorat, Stirlingshire (Dormant 1949)

Sir GEORGE MURRAY HOME STIRLING OF GLORAT, CBE, DSO, 9th *Baronet*, *d* 1949, and at time of going to press no name appears on the Official Roll of the Baronetage in respect of this title.

DAUGHTERS LIVING OF NINTH BARONET

Jean Margaret, *b* 1908: *m* 1939, Maj Frederick Graham Sheppard Graham, Argyll and Sutherland Highlanders, who *d* 1990. *Residence* – Rednock House, Port of Menteith, Perths. ———— Marjorie Marigold Anne, *b* 1920: *m* 1943, Edward Alan Langley, Lt RAMC, who *d* 1982, and has issue living, David Stirling (Glorat, Milton of Campsie, Stirlingshire), *b* 1945, — George Arthur Stirling (Little Baldoran, Milton of Campsie, Stirlingshire), *b* 1948, — John Charles Mark (5 Fettes Row, Edinburgh), *b* 1950: *m* 1st, 1981 (*m diss* 1993), Christina Maria Cavedon; 2ndly, 1995, Philippa Jayne White, and has issue living (by 2nd *m*), Max Edward Stirling *b* 1995, Raife Murray Stirling *b* 1997. *Residence* – Little Baldoran, Milton of Campsie, Stirlingshire.

COLLATERAL BRANCH LIVING

Grandson of late Charles Stirling, son of late Robert Dundas Stirling, 5th son of 5th Bt:—
Issue of late Robert Wilson Stirling, *b* 1890, *d* 1970: *m* 1920, Hazel, da of John Heidenreich:—
†John Charles, *b* 1922: *m* 1944, Evelyn Essig, and *d* 1998, leaving issue, John Charles (10838, Wonderland Drive, Indianapolis, Indiana, 46239, USA), *b* 1948; probable heir to Baronetcy: *m* 1966, Valborg-Nelson, and has issue living, Jeffery Dundas *b* 1969, April Cheryl *b* 1967, — Sherry Lynn (2405, Greentree, Indianapolis, Indiana 46227, USA), *b* 1951.

Stirling-Hamilton, see Hamilton.

Stirling-Maxwell, see Maxwell.

STOCKDALE (UK) 1960, of Hoddington, co Southampton

Sir THOMAS MINSHULL STOCKDALE, 2nd *Baronet*; *b* 7 Jan 1940; *s* his father, *Sir* EDMUND VILLIERS MINSHULL, 1989; *ed* Eton, and Worcester Coll, Oxford (MA): *m* 1965, Jacqueline, da of Ha-Van-Vuong, of 293 Phan, Thanh-Gian, Saigon, and has issue.

𝔄rms – Ermine on a bend sable between two escallops gules three pheons argent. ℭrest – Issuant from a crown or a griffin's head gules.
Residence – Manor Farm, Weston Patrick, Basingstoke, Hants RG25 2NT. *Club* – Turf.

SON LIVING

JOHN MINSHULL, *b* 13 Dec 1967.

DAUGHTER LIVING

Charlotte Fermor, *b* 1970.

BROTHER LIVING

Frederick Minshull (Thorpe Tilney Hall, Lincoln; Eastwood Farm, Herstmonceux, Sussex), *b* 1947; *ed* Eton, and Jesus Coll, Camb (MA): *m* 1st, 1970 (*m diss* 1989), Joanna Lennox, yr da of Capt Roger Edward Harvey, JP, DL, Scots Gds, of Parliament Piece, Ramsbury, Wilts (*see* Mainwaring, Bt, ext, 1990 Edn); 2ndly, 1992, Adele Elizabeth Lavinia, da of Lincoln Mason, of Swinton, Manchester, and has issue living (by 1st *m*), Harry Tevis Minshull (47 Basuto Rd, SW6 4BL), *b* 1973; *ed* Eton, and UEA (MA), — Alexander Breckenridge Minshull (3 Snowbury Rd, SW6), *b* 1975; *ed* Eton, and Nottingham Trent Univ (MA), — Valentine Frederick Minshull, *b* 1981; *ed* Eton, — (by 2nd *m*) Charles Lincoln Minshull, *b* 1994.

Sir Edmund Stockdale, 1st Bt, son of late Maj Henry Minshull Stockdale, JP, of Mears Hall, Northants, was Dep Prin Bank of England 1941-45, Alderman 1948-63, Lord Mayor of London 1959-60, and one of HM Lieuts of City of London.

STOCKENSTRÖM (UK) 1840, of Maasström, Cape of Good Hoope (Extinct 1957)

Sir ANDERS JOHAN STOCKENSTRÖM, 4th and last *Baronet*.

DAUGHTER LIVING OF FOURTH BARONET

Andrée Mabel, *b* 1939: *m* 1960, James Norman Pringle Gardiner. *Residence* – 22 Fraser St, Hunters Home, Knysna, S Africa.

STOKES (UK) 1889, of Lensfield Cottage, St Paul, Cambridge (Extinct 1916)

Sir ARTHUR ROMNEY STOKES, 2nd and last *Baronet*.

DAUGHTER LIVING OF SECOND BARONET

Mary Muriel, *b* 1899. *Address* – c/o Barclays Bank, White River 1240, Transvaal, South Africa.

STONHOUSE First Creation (E) 1628; Second Creation (E) 1670, of Radley, Berkshire.

Rev Sir MICHAEL PHILIP STONHOUSE, 19th *Baronet*; *b* 4 Sept 1948; *s* his father, *Sir* PHILIP ALLAN, 1993; *ed* Medicine Hat Coll, Univ of Alberta (BA), Wycliffe Coll (MDiv); deacon 1977, priest 1978 (Diocese of Calgary, Alberta, Canada); assist Curate, St Peter's Calgary 1977-80; Rector and Incumbent, Parkland Parish, Alberta 1980-87, St Mark's, Innisfail and St Matthew's, Bowden, Alberta 1987-92, since when of St James, Saskatoon, Saskatchewan: *m* 1977, Colleen Eleanor, da of late James Albert Councill, of Toronto, Ontario, Canada, and has issue.

𝖠rms – Argent, on a fesse sable between three hawks volant azure, a leopard's face between two mullets or. 𝖢rest – A talbot's head couped argent, collared sable, lined and catching a dove volant of the first.
Residence – 3413 Balfour St, Saskatoon, Saskatchewan, Canada S7H 3Z3.

SONS LIVING

ALLAN JAMES, *b* 20 March 1981. —— David Michael, *b* 1983. —— Philip Radley, *b* 1987.

BROTHER LIVING

Let us seek sublimer objects

Timothy Allan, *b* 1950; BA, Dip Ed, LLB: *m* 1976, Marija, da of George Baros, of Edmonton, Alberta, and has issue living, Matthew Paul, *b* 1980, — Benjamin Judah, *b* 1983, — Danica, *b* 1987. *Residence* – 6 Glacier Place, St Albert, Alberta, Canada T8N 1H6

AUNT LIVING (*Daughter of 17th baronet*)

Margaret Eleanor, *b* 1924: *m* 1953, Lt Cdr William Mansfield La Nauze, CD, RCN, of #47 120 Finholm St, Parksville, BC, Canada V9P 1J5, and has issue living, Patricia Joan, *b* 1954: *m* 1980, Paul Williams.

Sir George, the 3rd baronet, was fined £1,460 for his loyalty to Charles 1. In 1670 he obtained a new patent granted to himself, with the old precedency and with a special remainder to his second son, John, and his heirs male, intending thereby to exclude his first son. The el son, however, on his father's decease, claimed and enjoyed the baronetcy created by the original patent, so that there were two baronetcies in the family till, on the death (without issue) of Sir John, 6th baronet under the old creation, they became united in Sir John, 3rd baronet of the new. The 11th baronet, having been for twenty years Physician to the Northampton Infirmary, took Holy Orders, and subsequently became an eminent preacher.

STOREY (UK) 1960, of Settrington, co York

Hon Sir RICHARD STOREY, 2nd *Baronet*, CBE; *b* 23 Jan 1937; *s* his father, SAMUEL, Baron Buckton (Life Baron) in his Baronetcy, 1978; *ed* Winchester, and Trin Coll, Camb (BA LLB); High Sheriff N Yorks 1992; Bar Inner Temple 1962; Chm Portsmouth & Sunderland Newspapers plc 1973-98 (Dir 1962-99); Pres Newspaper Soc 1990-91 (Member of Council 1980-98), Press Council 1980-86; Member of Nat Council and Executive of the County of Landowners Assoc 1980-84 (Chm of Yorks Executive 1974-76); Member CBI Employment Policy Cttee 1984-88; Council Member of INCA-FIEJ Research Assoc 1983-88; Chm Hillier Arboretum Mgmt Cttee since 1989, Dir The Fleming Enterprise Investment Trust plc since 1989 (Chm since 1990), Reuters Holdings plc 1986-92, The Press Assocn Ltd 1986-95 (Chm 1991-95); served on Yorkshire and Humberside CBI Regional Council 1974-76; CBE (Civil) 1996: *m* 1961, Virginia Anne, da of late Sir Kenelm Henry Ernest Cayley, 10th Bt, and has issue.

𝖠rms – Per fesse argent and sable a pale counter charged three storks also sable. 𝖢rest – In front of an escallop or a stork's head erased sable gorged with a mural crown gold.
Residences – Settrington House, Malton, Yorks YO17 8NP; 11 Zetland House, Marloes Rd, W8 5LB.

SON LIVING

KENELM, *b* 4 Jan 1963; *ed* Winchester, and George Washington Univ, Washington DC (BBA).

DAUGHTERS LIVING

Elisabeth, *b* 1964: *m* 1988, Rowland Bruce Ranald Critchley, of Crawhill Manor, Westfield, Bathgate, W. Lothian EH48 4NH, elder son of Col I. R. Critchley, of Altina, by Crieff, Perthshire, and has issue living, Fergus Ranald, *b* 1990, — Douglas Bruce, *b* 1994, — Lucilla, *b* (twin) 1990. —— Melissa, *b* 1968: *m* 1992, Christophe Nigel Paul Stourton, of 37 Patience Rd, SW11, and has issue living (*see* B Mowbray, colls).

SISTER LIVING

Hon Jacquetta, *b* 1930: *m* 1956, Francis Cator, of The Old House, Ranworth, Norfolk, and 12 Warwick Sq Mews, SW1, and has issue living, Charles Francis, *b* 1959: *m* 1987, Jane, widow of William J. Russell, and da of Robert Culverwell, of Luckington, Wilts, and has issue living, Samuel Charles *b* 1992, Rosanna *b* 1988, Jessica Clare *b* 1989, Eleanor Camilla *b* 1995, — Mark, *b* 1960: *m* 1991, Hon Isabel Alicia Claire Crossley, eldest da of 3rd Baron Somerleyton, and has issue living, Benjamin Hugo *b* 1988, Oscar William *b* 1996, Lara Louise *b* 1992, — Harry, *b* 1964: *m* 1992, Kathleen Jean, da of Capt Alan Mackay, of Port Macquarrie, Australia, and has issue living, Frederick Francis *b* 1993, Jeremy Alan *b* 1995, Annabel Sophia *b* 1997, — Elisabeth Anne, *b* 1957: *m* 1982, Rupert Thomas Newton Thistlethwayte, and has issue (*see* E Portsmouth, colls).

Samuel Storey, Life Baron and 1st Baronet, el son of late Frederick George Storey, JP, was Chm, of Ways and Means 1965-66, Pres of Portsmouth and Sunderland Newspapers, and MP for Sunderland (*C*) 1931-45, and for Stretford 1950-66; *cr* a Baronet (UK) 1960, and *Baron Buckton*, of Settrington, in E Riding, Co York (Life Baron) 1966.

STOTT (UK) 1920, of Stanton, co Gloucester

He aims at high things

Sir ADRIAN GEORGE ELLINGHAM STOTT, 4th *Baronet*, *b* 7 Oct 1948; *s* his father, *Sir* PHILIP SIDNEY, 1979; *ed* Univ of British Columbia (BSc, MSc) and Univ of Waterloo, Ontario (MMaths); Dir of Planning rural region of BC 1974-77; Town planning consultant 1977-80; Real estate portfolio manager 1980-86, Man Dir Marketing Co 1987-91, since when management consultant; MCIP.

𝖆rms – Gules, three pallets or, each charged with as many pellets, on a chief of the second a heart between two battle-axes of the first. 𝕮rest – Upon a chaplet of roses fessewise gules a martlet sable.
Residence – The Downs, Little Amwell, Herts SG13 7SA.

BROTHER LIVING

VYVYAN PHILIP (Box 1150, Atherton, Queensland 4883, Australia), *b* 5 Aug 1952.

UNCLES LIVING (*Sons of 2nd baronet*)

Christopher George Swailes, *b* 1924; *ed* Malvern; MRAC; European War 1939-45 in RAF Vol Reserve: *m* 1st, 1953 (*m diss* 19—), Winifred Marshall (MOSSFORD), da of William Don; 2ndly, 19—, Anne, da of — McMahon, of Lisdoonvarna, co Clare, and has issue living, (by 1st *m*) Sarah Caroline, *b* 1956, — (by 2nd *m*) Christopher John McMahon, *b* 19—. —— Derek Nicholson (29 Birngana Av, Sandy Bay, Tas, 7005 Aust), *b* 1928; *ed* Malvern; is a MIEE: *m* 1993, Eileen Bridget, da of Dr D. G. Wilde, of Epsom, Surrey.

The 1st baronet, Sir Philip Sidney Stott (son of late Abraham Henthorne Stott, of Oldham), was an architect, JP for Gloucestershire, and High Sheriff of Gloucestershire 1925. The 2nd baronet, Sir George Edward Stott, was a registered Architect, and High Sheriff of Gloucestershire 1947. The 3rd baronet, Sir Philip Sidney Stott, was a registered architect and a composer.

PHILIPSON-STOW (UK) 1907, of Cape Town, Colony of Cape of Good Hope, and Blackdown House, Lodsworth, co Sussex

Sir CHRISTOPHER PHILIPSON-STOW, 5th *Baronet*; *b* 13 Sept 1920; *s* his cousin, *Maj Sir* EDMOND CECIL, 1982; *ed* Winchester; late Fl Lt RAFVR: *m* 1952, Elizabeth Nairn, da of late James Dixon Trees, of Toronto, and widow of Maj Frederick George McLaren, 48th Highrs, of Canada, and has issue living.

𝔄rms – Quarterly, 1st and 4th vert, on a cross nebulée between four leopards' faces or, a rose gules, *Stow*; 2nd and 3rd gules two chevronelles between three boars' heads couped ermine, *Philipson*. 𝔄rest – 1st issuant from an antique crown or, charged with a rose gules, a leopard's face gold between two wings vert, *Stow*; 2nd, issuant from a mural crown or, charged with a rose gules, a plume of five ostrich feathers alternately argent and gules, *Philipson*.
Residence – 26 Cambridge St, Penetanguishene, Ont, Canada L9M 1E6.

SONS LIVING

ROBERT MATTHEW (32 John St, Thornhill, Ontario, Canada L3T 1X8), *b* 29 Aug 1953; *ed* Thornhill Secondary Sch, and Univ of Waterloo, Ont (BASc, PEng). —— Rowland Frederic (23 Robinson Rd, PO Box 1260, Nobleton, Ontario, Canada L0G 1N0), *b* 1954; *ed* Thornhill Secondary Sch, and Univ of Waterloo (BASc, PEng): *m* 1979, Mary Susan, da of William J. N. Stroud, of Thornhill, Ont, and has issue living, Christopher William, *b* 1983, — Kimberly Susan, *b* 1981.

Fide non fraude

By faith, not by fraud

COLLATERAL BRANCH LIVING

Issue of late Maj Guyon Philipson Philipson-Stow, 6th and yst son of 1st baronet, *b* 1898, *d* 1983: *m* 1925, Alice Mary, who *d* 1989 only da of R. Hilton Fagge:—
Robert Nicholas (Priors Court, Long Green, Glos; White's Club), *b* 1937; *ed* Winchester; late Lt RHG: *m* 1963, Nicolette Leila, el da of late Hon Philip Leyland Kindersley (*see* B Kindersley, colls), and has issue living, Robert Rowland, *b* 1970; *ed* Malvern; Capt Blues and Royals (White's Club), — Edward Miles, *b* 1972; *ed* Malvern, and RAC Cirencester, — Georgina Mary, *b* 1976; *ed* Malvern Girls' Coll. —— Helen Rosemary, *b* 1934.

Sir Frederick Samuel Philipson Stow, 1st baronet, assumed by Roy licence 1891, the additional surname and arms of Philipson, being 4th in descent from George Stow of Sutton in Ashfield, Notts, who *m* 1767, Elizabeth, da and eventual heir of John Wilberfoss, by Elizabeth, el da and eventual heir of Richard Philipson, of Beverley.

STRACEY (UK) 1818, of Rackheath, Norfolk

Sir JOHN SIMON STRACEY, 9th *Baronet*, only son of late Capt Algernon Augustus Henry Stracey, 2nd son of 6th Bt; *b* 30 Nov 1938; *s* his cousin, *Sir* MICHAEL GEORGE MOTLEY, 1971; *ed* Wellington Coll, and McGill Univ: *m* 1968, Martha Maria, da of late Johann Egger, of Innsbrück, and has issue.

𝔄rms – Ermine, on a cross engrailed between four eagles displayed gules five cinquefoils or. 𝔄rest – A lion rampant erminois, ducally crowned gules supporting a cross patée-fitchée of the last.
Residence – Holbeam Wood Cottage, Wallcrouch, Wadhurst, E. Sussex TN5 7JT.

DAUGHTERS LIVING

Daniela, *b* 1968. —— Nadja, *b* 1973.

SISTER LIVING

Ramona Beryl, *b* 1930: *m* 1959, Theodore Frederic Darvas, Flat 1, 5 St George's Terrace, NW1 8XH, and has issue living, Jane Caroline, *b* 1963, — Anna Judith, *b* 1966.

SISTER LIVING OF EIGHTH BARONET

Margaret Rosalind Linley, *b* 1907: *m* 1959, Peter Edward Clement Harris, who *d* 1976, son of late Sir Austin Edward Harris, KBE. *Residence* – 189 Cranmer Court, Sloane Av, SW3.

HALF-SISTER LIVING OF EIGHTH BARONET

Dereen Elizabeth Paulette, *b* 1937: *m* 1965, James Douglas Bartlett, of Paddocks Farm, Cranbrook, Kent, and has issue living, Christopher James Edward Douglas, *b* 1966, — Peter Sean Charles, *b* 1969, — Richard Gerald Patrick, *b* 1971.

COLLATERAL BRANCHES LIVING

Grandchildren of late Gilbert Hardinge Stracey, 5th son of 5th baronet:—
Issue of late Lt-Col Ernest Henry Denne Stracey, *b* 1871, *d* 1948: *m* 1907, Faith Dorothy Beatrice Mounteney, who *d* 1965, da of late Henry Downes Popham:—
HENRY MOUNTENEY, *b* 24 April 1920: *m* 1st, 1943, Susanna, da of Adair Tracey; 2ndly, 1950, Lysbeth, da of Charles Ashford; 3rdly, 1961, Jeltje, yst da of Scholte de Boer, of Oppenhuizen, Friesland, Holland, and has issue living, (by 1st *m*) Amarilla, *b* 1943, — (by 2nd *m*), Rupert, *b* 1951, — Miranda Hinemoa, *b* 1955. *Residence* – White Barn, Walberswick, Suffolk. —— Noel Margaret Jephson (Durham House, Balsham, Cambs), *b* 1908: *m* 1933, Maj Charles Robert Purdon Coote, who *d* 1954 (*see* Coote, Bt, *cr* 1621, colls).

Granddaughters of late Hardinge Robert Stracey, 3rd son of 4th baronet:—
Issue of late Lt-Col Hardinge Richard Stracey, *b* 1840, *d* 1924: *m* 1883, Mary Henrietta Rennel, who *d* 1944, da of late Adm Frederick Byng Montresor:—
Constance Mary, *b* 18—. —— Elizabeth Julia, *b* 18—: *m* 1909, Charles Henry Garner Richardson and has issue living, Richard Hearle, *b* 1914, — Peter Tremayne, *b* 1916, — Elizabeth Barbara, *b* 1911, — José Antonia Doreen, *b* 1921. —— Ruth: *m* 1930, J. Wilfred Wickes, consulting engineer, of Durban, Natal, and has issue living, a da, *b* 1931. —— Margaret Diana, *b* 1896.

Grandson of late Lt-Cdr Eustace William Clitherow STRACEY-CLITHEROW (infra):—
Issue of late Cdr Christopher Bryan STRACEY CLITHEROW, DSC, RN, *b* 1903, *d* 1977: *m* 1928, Maida Daughne Laurel, da of late Capt Hon Francis Almeric Butler (*see* E Lanesborough, colls):—
Dominic Peter (3 St Aubyn St, Devonport, Auckland 9, NZ), *b* 1939; *ed* Harrow and London Univ (BSc); C Eng; Lt Cdr RN (ret); employed by NZ navy: *m* 1971, Penelope Bronwen, da of L. Griffiths, of Henley-in-Arden, and has issue living, Henry Dominic, *b* 1979, — Simon Andrew, *b* (twin) 1979, — Charlotte Emma, *b* 1972, — Virginia Louise, *b* (twin) 1972.

Granddaughter of late Rev William James STRACEY-CLITHEROW (who assumed by Roy licence 1900, the additional surname and arms of Clitherow), son of late John Stracey, 5th son of 1st baronet:—
Issue of late Lieut-Com Eustace William Clitherow STRACEY- CLITHEROW, *b* 1864, *d* 1930: *m* 1900, Frances Evelyn Veronica, who *d* 1962, da of late John Birkbeck Evelyn Stansfeld, sometime Capt 3rd Btn Duke of Wellington's (W Riding Regt):—
Mary Barbara (2 Sheldon Av, Broadway, Worcs), *b* 1909: *m* 1938, Francis Stanton Blake, who *d* 1947.

Sir Edward Stracey, 1st baronet, was the el surviving son of Sir John Stracey, Knt, Chief Judge of the Sheriffs' Court, and Recorder of London in 1746. The 5th baronet sat as MP for Norfolk East (C) 1855-7, for Yarmouth 1859-65, and for Norwich 1868-9. Sir Edward Paulet Stracey, 7th baronet, was appointed High Sheriff of Norfolk 1928.

STRACHEY (UK) 1801, of Sutton Court, Somerset

(*Sir*) CHARLES STRACHEY, 6th *Baronet*, son of late Rt Hon Evelyn John St Loe Strachey, MP; *b* 20 June 1934; *s* his 1st cousin once removed EDWARD, 2nd Baron Strachie, 1973, but his name does not appear on the Official Roll of the Baronetage, nor does he use the title; *ed* Westminster Sch, and Magdalen Coll, Oxford: *m* 1973, Janet Megan, da of Alexander Miller, of Earls Barton, Northants, and has issue.

𝕬rms – Quarterly: 1st and 4th argent, a cross between four eagles displayed gules, *Strachey*; 2nd and 3rd or, three crescents, two and one, sable; on a canton of the last a ducal crown, or, *Hodges*. 𝕮rest – An eagle displayed gules, charged on the breast with a cross-crosslet fitchée argent. *Address* – 30 Gibson Sq, N1.

The circumstances may Change, but not the mind

DAUGHTER LIVING

Jane Alice, *b* 1975.

SISTER LIVING

Elizabeth, *b* 1936: *m* 1958, Hamid al Qadhi, who *d* 1986, and has issue living, Mohammed Jemil, *b* 1959, — Samia, *b* 1964, — and an adopted da, Hannah, *b* 1962.

COLLATERAL BRANCHES LIVING

Grandchildren of late Ralph Strachey, 2nd son of late Lt-Gen Sir Richard Strachey, GCSI, FRS, LLD
(infra):—
Issue of late Richard Philip Farquhar Strachey, *b* 1902, *d* 1976: *m* 1st, 1927 (*m diss* 1940), Frances Esme, da of
Charles John Rudd; 2ndly, 1943, Mrs Simonette Mary Reynolds Woods (25 Park Town, Oxford), da of Charles
Foster Atchison, of Cliff Cottage, Bonchurch, Isle of Wight, and formerly wife of S. John Woods:—
(By 1st *m*) Philippa HAWTIN (La Casita Vieja, Pt da El Collado, 03729 Lliber, Alicante, Spain), *b* 1927; assumed the
surname of Hawtin by deed poll 1961. —— Victoria (9 Dolforgan Court, Louisa Terrace, Exmouth, Devon EX8 2AQ), *b*
1929; assumed the surname of Hunter by deed poll 1951 (and has issue, Matthew HUNTER, *b* 1951): *m* 1952, Mark
Graham Holloway, and has further issue, Sam HOLLOWAY, *b* 1953: *m* 1983, Elizabeth Anne Cotterill, and has issue living,
Laura Esme *b* 1985, Rachael Emma *b* 1987, — Sophy, *b* 1955; has issue living (by John David Weaver), Frederick Mark
Richard WEAVER *b* 1987, Victoria Lilian WEAVER *b* 1985, — Sarah Louise, *b* 1957; has issue living (by Jonathan Peter
White), Matthew William WHITE *b* 1993, Katie May WHITE *b* 1992.

Issue of late John Ralph Severs Strachey, *b* 1905, *d* 1983: *m* 1st, 1933 (*m diss* 1942), Isobel Bertha, who *d* 1987,
da of Ronald Leslie; 2ndly, 1944, Rosemary, da of Douglas Mavor:—
(By 2nd *m*) HENRY LEOFRIC BENVENUTO, *b* 17 April 1947: *m* 1st, 1971 (*m diss* 1982), Julie Margaret Hutchens; 2ndly, 1983,
Susan Christine, da of John Ernest Skinner, of Manor Cottage, 41 Court Lane, Cosham, Hants. *Address* – c/o Middleton
& Upsall, Solicitors, 39 Silver St, Warminster, Wilts BA12 8PP.

Granddaughter of late Lt-Gen Sir Richard Strachey, GCSI, FRS, LLD, 3rd son of Edward Strachey
(infra):—
Issue of late Oliver Strachey, CBE, *b* 1874; *d* 1960: *m* 1st, 1901 (*m diss* 1908), Ruby Julia, da of late Julius
Mayer; 2ndly, 1911, Rachel Conn, who *d* 1940, da of late Benjamin Francis Costelloe:—
(By 2nd *m*) Barbara, *b* 1912: *m* 1st, 1934 (*m diss* 1937), Olav Hultin; 2ndly, 1937, Wolf Halpern, Leading Aircraftman,
RAFVR, who *d* on active ser 1943, and has issue living (by 1st *m*), Roger Olavson, *b* 1934. *Residence* – 3 Woodlands
Walk, Boars Hill, Oxford.

Grandchildren (if any) of late William Strachey, son of late George Strachey, 6th son of late Edward
Strachey, 2nd son of 1st baronet:—
Issue (if any) of late Reginald Strachey, *b* 1905, *d* 1973 (NY, USA).

The Strachie family was settled at Saffron Walden, Essex, until the 16th century. John Strachey, *b* 1634, inherited
Sutton Court, Som, from his mother Elizabeth Cross: *m* 1662, Jane, da and co-heir of George Hodges, of Wedmore,
Somerset, Their great-grandson, Sir Henry Strachey, of Sutton Court, MP 1770-1810, was Sec to Lord Clive 1764, and
Commn for Restoring Peace to America 1774, an Under Sec of State 1782, and Master of the Household 1794. He was *cr*
a *Baronet* 1801. His great-grandson, Sir Edward, PC, 4th Bt, Treasurer of the Household 1905-10, Paymaster-Gen. 1912-
15, and MP for S Som (*L*) 1892-1911, was *cr Baron Strachie*, of Sutton Court, Somerset, 1911. This Barony became ext
on the death of his son Edward, 2nd Baron and 5th Bt in 1973, when the baronetcy reverted to Sir Charles, 6th Bt,
grandson of John St Loe Strachey, yr brother of 1st baron.

Strickland-Constable, see Constable

Strang Steel, see Steel

STRONGE (UK) 1803, of Tynan, co Armagh

Sir JAMES ANSELAN MAXWELL STRONGE, 10th *Baronet*; son of late Maxwell Du Pre James Stronge; *b* 17 July 1946; *s* his 2nd cousin, *Capt Sir* JAMES MATTHEW*, 1981; *ed* Privately.

Arms – Argent, a chevron wavy sable between three lozenges azure, in the centre chief point an estoile gules. Crests – 1st an eagle with two heads displayed sable, beaked and legged azure, langued gules; 2ndly, a cluster of wine grapes proper. Second Motto – Dulce quod utile (*That is sweet which is useful*).
Residence – Shannagh Camp Hill Community, Kilkeel, co Down.

SISTER LIVING

Helen Mary, *b* 1948: *m* 1971, Philip Rodney Allen-Morgan, of Manor South, Bishopstone, E Sussex BN25 2VD, and has issue living, William Frederick Stronge, *b* 1975, — Allanah Mary, *b* 1974, — Laura Myfanwy, *b* 1978.

DAUGHTERS LIVING OF EIGHTH BARONET

A way is to be attempted

Daphne Marian, *b* 1922; late WRNS: *m* 1954, Thomas John Anthony Kingan, late Irish Guards, and has issue living, James Anthony John, *b* 1957. *Residence* – Glenganagh, Bangor, co Down. —— Evelyn Elizabeth, *b* 1925; late WRNS: *m* 1960, Brig Charles Harold Arthur Olivier, CBE, who *d* 1992. *Residence* – Rosemary Cottage, Amport, Andover.

ſENTANDA·VIA·EST

*By decision of House of Lords 10 Sept 1941, approved by HM King George VI, which provides that where two persons have died in circumstances rendering it uncertain as to which of them survived the other, such deaths should be presumed to have occurred in order of seniority.
Sir James Matthew, DCL, 2nd baronet, was a Gentleman of the Privy Chamber, and Sir James Matthew, 3rd baronet, sat as MP for Armagh (*C*) 1864-74. The 7th baronet, Sir Charles, Sir Charles Edmond Sinclair, was HM Lieut for co Londonderry. The 8th baronet, Rt Hon Sir (Charles) Norman Lockhart, MC, was Lord Lieut for co Armagh 1939-81, Member of House of Commons, N Ireland (*U*) 1938-69 (Speaker 1945-69), and was murdered by terrorists at his residence, Tynan Abbey, co Armagh, 1981. His son, the 9th baronet, Capt Sir James Matthew MP Mid-Armagh (*U*), NI Parl 1969-72, MP for NI Assembly (Armagh) 1973-74, was murdered with his father.*

STUART (E) 1660, of Hartley Mauduit, Hampshire.

Sir PHILLIP LUTTRELL STUART, 9th *Baronet* (but his name does not, at time of going to press, appear on the official Roll of Baronets), son of late Luttrell Hamilton Stuart, brother of 8th baronet; *b* 7 Sept 1937; *s* his uncle, *Sir* HOULTON JOHN, 1959; late F/O RCAF: *m* 1st, 1962 (*m diss* 1968), Marlene Rose, da of Otto Muth, of 1172, Pembina Highway, Winnipeg, Manitoba, Canada; 2ndly, 1969, Beverley Claire Pieri, and has issue by 1st and 2nd *m*.

Arms – Or, a fesse checky azure and argent, an inescutcheon argent charged with the lion of Scotland debruised with a bendlet raguly or. Crest – A roebuck statant argent, ducally gorged gules.
Residence – 10980 Westdowne Rd, #50, RR2, Ladysmith, BC, Canada V0R 2E0.

Avito viret honore

He flourishes by ancestral honors

SON LIVING (*By 2nd marriage*)

GEOFFREY PHILLIP, *b* 5 July 1973. *Residence* – 3 Windermere Bay, Winnipeg, Manitoba, Canada R3T 1B1.

DAUGHTERS LIVING (*By 1st marriage*)

Cynthia Louise, *b* 1963. *Residence* – 42 Arthur St N, Guelph, Ontario, Canada N1E 4T8.

(*By 2nd marriage*)

Brenda Claire, *b* 1969. *Residence* – 3 Windermere Bay, Winnipeg, Manitoba, Canada R3T 1B1.

COLLATERAL BRANCH LIVING

Grandchildren of late Major Arthur John Stuart, RM, 3rd son of 5th baronet:—
Issue of late Arthur Kennedy Stuart, *b* 1859, *d* 19—: *m* 1892, Luise Franziska, da of Carl Joseph Pfeifer, of
Freiburg-in-Baden, Germany:—
Arthur Ernest, *b* 1896. —— Charles Edwin, *b* 1897.

The 1st baronet, Sir Nicholas Stuart (son of Simeon Stuart, of Hartley Mauduit), and the 2nd baronet, Sir Simeon, each held the office of a Chamberlain of the Exchequer. The 2nd and 3rd baronets successively sat as MP for Hampshire. In 1829, on the death of his grandfather, the last Earl of Carhampton, the 5th baronet was offered a fresh patent by George IV, which however, he did not accept. The 7th Baronet, Sir Simeon Henry Lechmere, was City Marshal of London 1893-9. The present baronet is representative of the Earldom of Carhampton (*ext*) and the Barony of Waltham (*ext*).

Stuart-Menteth, see Menteth.

Stuart Taylor, see Taylor (cr 1917).

STUCLEY (UK) 1859, of Affeton Castle, Devonshire
(Name pronounced "Stukeley")

Softly but boldly

Sir HUGH GEORGE COPLESTONE BAMPFYLDE STUCLEY, 6th *Baronet*; *b* 8 Jan 1945; *s* his father, *Maj Sir* DENNIS FREDERIC BANKES, 1983; *ed* Milton Abbey, and RAC Cirencester; late Lieut RHG; Chm Devon CLA 1995-97; Pres The Devonshire Assoc 1997; DL Devon 1997: *m* 1969, Angela Caroline, el da of Richard Toller, of Orchard House, Kingston Lisle, Wantage, Berks, and has issue.

Arms – Quarterly: 1st and 4th, azure, three pears or, *Stucley*; 2nd and 3rd, per fesse embattled argent and sable, three bucks attires, each fixed to the scalp, counterchanged, *Buck*. **Crest** – Between a buck's attires as in the arms sable, a lion rampant or, the sinister paw holding a battleaxe resting on the shoulder proper.
Residence – Affeton Castle, Worlington Crediton, Devon.

SONS LIVING

GEORGE DENNIS, *b* 26 Dec 1970: *m* 1997, Amber Camilla, yr da of Thomas Ælla Godfrey Gage (*see* V Gage, colls). —— Peter Richard, *b* 1972; *ed* Harrow, and RMA Sandhurst; commn'd RHG/D 1995.

DAUGHTERS LIVING

Charlotte Catherine, *b* 1975. —— Lucinda Sarah, *b* 1977.

SISTERS LIVING

Margaret Cynthia, *b* 1934: *m* 1953, Gerald Arthur Hohler (V Gort), and has issue living, (Thomas) Edward, *b* 1958: *m* 1998, Georgina Caroline, elder da of John Ralph Stourton (*see* B Mowbray, colls). —— Henrietta Margaret Cynthia, *b* 1955: *m* 1994, Charles Richard Seymour (*see* M Hertford, colls), — Lucinda Jane Astell, *b* 1960: *m* 1982, Richard Clephane Compton (*see* M Northampton, colls). *Residence* – Trent Manor, Sherborne, Dorset. —— Rosemary Anne (*Rosemary, Viscountess Boyne*), *b* 1936: *m* 1956, 10th Viscount Boyne, KCVO, who *d* 1995. *Residence* – The Old Dairy, Burwarton, Bridgnorth, Shropshire WV16 6QH. —— Christine Elizabeth (*Baroness Cobbold*), *b* 1940: *m* 1961, 2nd Baron Cobbold. *Residences* – Knebworth House, Knebworth, Herts; 2d Park Place Villas, W2. —— Sarah Susan, *b* 1942: *m* 1st, 1963 (*m* diss 1970), Michael Henry Basil Peto (later Sir Michael Peto, 4th Bt); 2ndly, 1971, Charles Worthington, and has issue living (by 1st m) (see Peto, Bt, cr 1927), — (by 2nd m) Anna, b 1972. *Residence* – Court Hall, N Molton, N Devon.

AUNT LIVING (*Daughter of 4th baronet*)

Priscilla (90 Fentiman Rd, SW8 1LA), b 1911: m 1936 (m diss 1956), Count Andrzej Zygmunt Zamoyski, who d 1964, and has issue living, *Count* Zygmunt Ignacy Stukeley, b 1937, ed Stowe, and Ch Ch, Oxford, — *Countess* Betka Marya, b 1948; ed Cranborne Chase, and Lady Margaret Hall, Oxford; journalist: m 1988 (m diss 1993), Benjamin Hargreaves.

The Stucley family (which has possessed Affeton Castle for over 600 years) came from Stukeley, Huntingdonshire, and were Sheriffs of that county, *temp* John. Sir George, 1st baronet, assumed by Roy licence, 1858, the surname of Stucley in lieu of his patronymic of Buck as lineal representative of that ancient family, and was MP for Barnstaple (C) 1855-9 and 1865-8. Maj Dennis F. B. Stucley, 5th Bt, was a DL and High Sheriff of Devon; Chm Regional Advisory Cttee, Forestry Comm SW 1958-75, of Timber Growers' Organisation 1966-69, and of Exmoor Nat Park (Devon) Cttee 1968-74; Master Hartland Harriers 1932-35, N Eggesford Foxhounds 1936-38, and jt Master Dulverton West Foxhounds 1952-54.

STUDD (UK) 1929, of Netheravon, Wilts

Sir EDWARD FAIRFAX STUDD, 4th *Baronet*; b 3 May 1929; s his brother, *Sir* (ROBERT) KYNASTON, 1977; ed Winchester; formerly Dir of Inchcape plc, and Member of Court of Assistants of Merchant Taylors' Co (Master 1987-88 and 1993-94); late Lt Coldm Gds; Malaya: m 1960, Prudence Janet, da of late Alastair Douglas Fyfe, OBE, of Grey Court, Riding Mill, Northumberland, and has issue.

Arms – Gules, lion rampant between three crescents argent, on a chief masoned two tilting spears in saltire, all proper. Crest – Out of a mural crown two arms embowed in armour, the hands in gauntlets holding two tilting spears saltirewise, all proper.
Residence – Kingsbury House, Kingsbury Episcopi, Martock, Som TA12 6AU.
Clubs – Boodle's, and Pratt's.

Nous tenons le droit

SONS LIVING

PHILIP ALASTAIR FAIRFAX, b 27 Oct 1961: m 1987 (m diss 199—), Georgina A. G., da of Sir Roger Albert Gartside Neville, VRD, of Possingworth Manor, Blackboys, nr Uckfield, E Sussex, and has issue living, Kynaston Roger Fairfax, b 31 Dec 1993, — Imogen Mary Henrietta, b 1991. —— Christopher Andrew Eric, b 1968.

DAUGHTER LIVING

Alexandra Mary, b 1965.

BROTHER LIVING

Rev John Eric (Albion Lodge, Halterworth Lane, Romsey, Hants), b 1934; ed Winchester, and Clare Coll, Camb (MA): m 1969, Nea Mildred, yr da of late Gordon Penn Kennett, of 35 Kireep Rd, Balwyn, Vic, Aust.

SISTER LIVING

Elizabeth Stephana, b 1924: m 1954, Victor Erwin Spindel, who d 1996, and has issue living, Daniel Jonas Arthur, b 1962; has issue living (by Emma Caroline Adams), Jonah Adam SPINDEL b 1998, Julia Mereden Stephana SPINDEL b 1993, Eliza Katharine SPINDEL b 1996. *Residence* – Court Barn, Pond Meadow, West Wickham, Cambs CB1 6RY.

DAUGHTERS LIVING OF THIRD BARONET

Sara Alexandra, b 1959. —— Jane Anastasia, b 1961: m 1988, Christopher John Hall, elder son of Sir Peter Hall, KBE, of Chelsea, and of Leslie Caron, actress, of Rue de Bellechasse, Paris, and has issue living, Frederick Amery Kynaston, b 1989, — Benjamin Charles Edward, b 1992. —— Anne Elizabeth, b 1964.

WIDOW LIVING OF THIRD BARONET

ANASTASIA (*Anastasia, Lady Studd*) (Manor Farm, Rockbourne, Fordingbridge, Hants), da of late Lt-Col Harold Boscawen Leveson-Gower (see D Sutherland, colls): m 1958, *Sir* (Robert) Kynaston Studd, 3rd Bt, who d 1977.

COLLATERAL BRANCH LIVING

Issue of late Bernard Cyril Studd, yst son of 1st baronet, *b* 1892, *d* 1962: *m* 1925, Caryl Theodora, who *d* 1977, el da of Brig-Gen Charles de Winton, CMG:—
Diana Caryl, *b* 1928: *m* 1st, 1954 (*m diss* 1976), Anthony Ross Pope; 2ndly, 1976, Anthony Carroll Cavalier, who *d* 1986, of 1213 Shady Av, Pittsburgh, Pa, USA, and has issue living (by 1st *m*), David Bernard Anthony Edward Beauchamp, *b* 1961: *m* 1991, Janice Ann Woolheater, and has issue living, Nicholas Anthony *b* 1993, Jonathan Robert *b* 1996, — Simon Charles Kynaston Beauchamp, *b* 1964: *m* 1989, Felicia Anna Maria Campano, and has issue living, Desirae Jeanene *b* 1993, — Sara Caryl Beauchamp, *b* 1955: *m* 1978, Colin Weston Patrick Chase, of Meadow Cottage, Wineham, nr Henfield, Sussex, and has issue living, David Weston *b* 1982, Kathryn Diana *b* 1986, — Caroline Diana Beauchamp, *b* 1957: *m* 1988, Michael Joseph Mackenzie Thorne, of Cranes Farm, Epwell, nr Banbury, Oxon OX15 6LH, and has issue living, Joseph William Ross *b* 1992, Pia Sophie Elizabeth *b* 1991. —— Joanell Vera, *b* 1933: *m* 1959, Lt-Col Robert Henville Chappell, OBE, late Queen's Regt, of Arndown, 7 Elm Hill, Warminster, Wilts BA12 0AV, and has issue living, Gavin Bernard (Southdown House, Westbury Rd, Warminster, Wilts BA12 0AP), *b* 1963: *m* 1988, Dr Jessica Lynn Holm, da of Sir Ian Holm, CBE, and has issue living, Tierney Brook *b* 1997, — Kathryn Joanell, *b* 1966: *m* 1992, Capt Simon William David Butt, Capt RRW, son of Lt-Col William Butt, of Cirencester, Glos, and has issue living, Tobias, Simon Benjamin *b* 1997, Imogen Hannah Joanell *b* 1995.

The 1st baronet, Sir (John Edward) Kynaston Studd (son of Edward Studd, of Tidworth House, Wilts, and 2 Hyde Park Gardens, W), was Pres and Chm of Polytechnic, and an Alderman of City of London (Sheriff 1922-3, and Lord Mayor 1928-9).

STUDHOLME (UK) 1956, of Perridge, co Devon

Sir HENRY WILLIAM STUDHOLME, 3rd *Baronet*; *b* 31 Jan 1958; *s* his father, Sir PAUL HENRY WILLIAM, 1990; *ed* Eton, and Trin Hall, Camb (MA); ACA, ATII: *m* 1988, (Sarah) Lucy Rosita Deans-Chrystall, only da of Richard S. Deans, of Christchurch, NZ, and has issue.

𝔄rms – Vert, a horse statant argent, caparisoned or, on a chief of the second three mullets of six points pierced gules. ℭrest – A horse's head argent, bridled, and charged on the neck with a spur or.
Residence – Halscombe Farm, Ide, nr Exeter, Devon EX2 9TQ. *Clubs* – Brooks's, MCC.

SONS LIVING

JOSHUA HENRY PAUL, *b* 2 Feb 1992.
Jacob William Richard, *b* 1993.

DAUGHTER LIVING

Lorna Jane, *b* 1990.

BROTHER LIVING

James Paul Gilfred, *b* 1960; *ed* Eton, and Reading Univ (BSc): *m* 1992, Charlotte Serena, twin da of Jeremy Gwynne Pilcher, of Seymour Walk, SW10 (*see* Lawson, Bt, *cr* 1900), and has issue living, Arthur James Gilfred, *b* 1996, — Rafe Henry Wyndham, *b* 1998.

SISTER LIVING

Anna Katherine, *b* 1965; *ed* St Mary's, Calne, and York Univ (BSc): *m* 1992, Duncan M. Watts, yr son of T. C. Watts, of Rottingdean, E Sussex, and has issue living, Isabella Virginia Charlotte, *b* 1994.

UNCLE LIVING (*son of 1st baronet*)

Joseph Gilfred, *b* 1936; *ed* Eton, and Magdalen Coll, Oxford (MA); late 2nd Lt 60th Rifles; Chm and MD Editions Alecto Group since 1963: *m* 1959, Rachel, yr da of late Capt Sir William Albemarle Fellowes, KCVO (*see* V Hampden, colls), and has issue living, Andrew Gilfred, *b* 1962; *ed* Univ of E Anglia (BA): *m* 1988, Joanna, yr da of Eric D Thompson, of Shamley Green, Surrey, and has had issue, †Edward William Gilfred *b* and *d* 1992, Cosmo Edward Gilfred *b* 1993, Nancy Elisabeth Rachel *b* 1998, — Henry Alexander, *b* 1967; *ed* Magdalen Coll, Oxford (DA), — Hugo William Robert, *b* 1968; *ed* Bristol Univ (BSc): *m* 1996, Charlotte L., yst da of J. V. Hagestadt, of Westminster. *Residence* – The Court House, Lower Woodford, Salisbury, Wilts SP4 6NQ.

AUNT LIVING (*Daughter of 1st baronet*)

Henrietta Mary, *b* 1931: *m* 1953, Major Thomas Edward St Aubyn, 60th Rifles, CVO (*see* B St Levan colls). *Residence* – Dairy House Farm, Ashford Hill, Thatcham, Berks RG19 8BL.

WIDOW LIVING OF FIRST BARONET

JUDITH JOAN MARY (*Judith, Lady Studholme*), da of late Henry William Whitbread, of Norton Bavant Manor, Wilts: *m* 1929, Maj Sir Henry Gray Studholme, 1st Bt, CVO, who *d* 1987. *Residence* – Amesbury Abbey, Amesbury, Wilts SP4 7EX.

Maj Sir Henry Studholme, 1st Bt, CVO, was DL for Devon 1969, MP (*C*) for Tavistock 1942-66, Conservative Whip 1945-56, Joint Hon Treas of Conservative Party 1956-62 and Vice-Chamberlain to HM Household 1951-56.

STURDEE (UK) 1916, of the Falkland Islands (Extinct 1970)

Rear-Adm Sir LIONEL ARTHUR DOVETON STURDEE, CBE, 2nd and last *Baronet*.

DAUGHTER LIVING OF SECOND BARONET

Elizabeth Mary Doveton (*Lady Ashmore*), *b* 1919; 1939-45 War as 2nd Officer WRNS: *m* 1942, Adm of the Fleet Sir Edward Beckwith Ashmore, GCB, DSC, and has issue living, Thomas Sturdee, *b* 1955, — Susan Alexandra (*Lady Sykes*), *b* 1943: *m* 1966, Sir (Francis) John Badcock Sykes, 10th Bt (*cr* 1781), of Kingsbury Croft, Kingsbury St, Marlborough, Wilts, and has issue.

STYLE (E) 1627, of Wateringbury, Kent

Sir WILLIAM FREDERICK STYLE, 13th *Baronet*; *b* 13 May 1945; *s* his father, *Sir* WILLIAM MONTAGUE, 1981, but his name does not appear on the Official Roll of the Baronetage: *m* 1st, 1968 (*m diss* 1971), Wendy Gay, da of Gene Wittenberger, of Hartford, Wisconsin 53066, USA; 2ndly, 1986, Linnea Lorna, da of Donn Erickson, of Sussex, Wisconsin 53089, USA, and has issue by 1st and 2nd *m*.

ᴁrms – Sable, a fesse or fretty of the field between three fleurs-de-lis gold, all within a bordure of the second. ᴀrest – A wolf's head couped sable, collared or, the lower part of the neck fretty of the last.
Residence – ......

SON LIVING (*By 2nd marriage*)

WILLIAM COLIN, *b* ...... 1995.

DAUGHTERS LIVING (*By 1st marriage*)

Shannon Gay, *b* 1969. —— Erin Kay, *b* 1972.

(by 2nd marriage)

McKenna Ashleigh, *b* 1987. —— McKayla, *b* 1990.

BROTHER LIVING

Frederick Montague (N5866 Rockland Beach, Hilbert, WI 54129, USA), *b* 1947: *m* 1971 (*m diss* 1988), Sharon, da of William H. Kurz, of Menomonee Falls, Wisconsin, USA, and has issue living, Jennifer K., *b* 1977, — Christina S., *b* 1979.

AUNT LIVING (*Daughter of 11th baronet by 1st marriage*)

Helen, *b* 1913: *m* 19—, Gilbert L. Schiltz, and has issue living, Susan, *b* 19—: *m* 19—, Dennis Grosse, — Mary Lou, *b* 19—: *m* 19—, Michael Duell.

WIDOW LIVING OF TWELFTH BARONET

LA VERNE (*La Verne, Lady Style*), da of late Theron M. Comstock, of Palm Springs, California, USA: *m* 1941, Sir William Montague Style, 12th baronet, who *d* 1981. *Residence* – 334B Riverview Drive, Delafield, Wisconsin 53018, USA.

COLLATERAL BRANCHES LIVING

Branch from 3rd son of 9th baronet

Grandchildren of late Glenmore Rodney Style (infra):—
Issue of late Rodney Henry Style, *b* 1914, *d* 1975: *m* 1st, 1941, Kathleen, who *d* 1952, da of Jack Quillan; 2ndly, 1959, Loretta Goodyear; 3rdly, 19—, Lois Franke:—
(By 1st *m*) Mary Kathryn, *b* 1947: *m* 1st 19— (*m diss* 19—), James Zarling; 2ndly, 19—, Michael Murphy, and has issue living (by 1st *m*), Heather Marie, *b* 1971: *m* 19—, Steve Scheer, and has issue living, Ireland Kathryn *b* 1999, — Erin Kathleen, *b* 1975: *m* 19—, Joe Maidl.

Issue of late Gerald Eugene Style, *b* 1922, *d* 1966: *m* 1945, Marguerite, da of Edward Keogan:—
James Robert, *b* 1948. —— Ann Marie, *b* 1951.

Grandchildren of late Henry Albert Glenmore Style (infra):—
Issue of late Glenmore Rodney Style, *b* 1887, *d* 1971: *m* 1913, Mary Margaret, who *d* 1979, da of John M. Tobin:—
†James Glenmore, *b* 1919: *m* 1943, LeEtta Smith, and was *ka* 1944. —— †Robert George, *b* 1920, and was *ka* 1944. —— William Hugh (426 Saratoga Drive, Green Bay, WI 54303, USA), *b* 1924: *m* 1956, Mary Ann, da of Patrick Farrell, and has issue living, Robert George, *b* 1959: *m* 19—, Laura Bair, and has issue living, Keenan McKenna *b* 1994, Etta McKibben *b* 1995, — William Edward, *b* 1961: *m* 19—, Cynthia, da of James Wills, and has issue living, William Eric *b* 1993, Austin Wills *b* 1996, — John Paul, *b* 1970, — Susan Marie, *b* 1957, — Margaret Mary, *b* 1965: *m* 19—, Curt Yakel, and has issue living, Connor James *b* 1996. —— Charles Albert (1001 S Orient St, Fairmont, MN 56031-4347, USA), *b* 1926: *m* 1950, Delores, da of Frank Jaqua, and has issue living, Gregory Charles, *b* 1951: *m* 19— (*m diss* 19—), Deb Scheef, and has issue living, Natasha Marie *b* 1982, — Gary Kevin, *b* 1952: *m* 19—, Michelle, da of Lloyd Morin, and has issue living, Alyssa Michelle *b* 1984, Lynnea Charlene *b* 1987. —— Jerome Everett (106 14th St W, Glencoe, MN 55336-1116, USA), *b* 1932: *m* 1955, Margaret, da of Dorrance Ryan, and has issue living, David Ryan, *b* 1964: *m* 19—, Lisa, da of Gilbert Hasse Jr, and has issue living, Ryan David *b* 1991, Casey Matthew *b* 1993, — Kathleen Michelle, *b* 1956: *m* 19—, Bruce Homa, and has issue living, Patrick Thomas *b* 1984, Beth Kathryn *b* 1985, — Maureen Anne, *b* 1954: *m* 1st, 19—, Kevin Boesche; 2ndly, 19—, David Drew, and has issue living, (by 1st *m*) Jackson Ryan *b* 1978, Maria Lynn *b* 1975, Courtney Elizabeth *b* 1982, (by 2nd *m*) Jonathan David *b* 19—, Hailey Rose *b* 1995, — Barbara Jo, *b* 1959, — Sara Therese, *b* 1970: *m* 19—, Mark Uecker. —— Vincent Joseph (900 10th St S, St James, MN 56081, USA), *b* 1934: *m* 1956, Jane, da of George Sizer, and has had issue, †Matthew Vincent, *b* 1958, *d* 1961, Steven Joseph, *b* 1959: *m* Deb, da of Duane Nessler, and has issue living, Tucker Steven *b* 1992, Alyssa Lynn *b* 1990, — Chad Patrick, *b* 1963: *m* 19— (*m diss* 19—), Denise Pryer, and has issue living, Zachary Levi *b* 1988, — Nona Marie, *b* 1962: *m* 19—, Keith Runge, and has issue living, Matthew Keith *b* 1984, Adam Vincent *b* 1987, William Walter *b* 1996, Jaime Rae *b* 1985, Jena Marie *b* 1988, Julie Jane *b* 1993. —— Margaret Clare (Assisi Heights, 1001 14th St NW, Rochester, MN 55901-2511, USA), *b* 1918; is a Franciscan Nun. —— Mary Crescent (1400 17th Av N, Minneapolis, MN 55411-3123, USA), *b* 1923: *m* 1944 (*m diss* 19—), Maurice Finney. —— Elizabeth Ann (1400 17th Av N, Minneapolis, MN 55411-3123, USA), *b* 1928: *m* 1955 (*m diss* 19—), Eugene Sullivan, and has issue living, Joseph Donald, *b* 1956: *m* 19—, Judy, da of Gustave Hieke, and has issue living, Conor Joseph *b* 1991, — Thomas Michael, *b* 1958. —— Catherine Therese (502 N 7th St, Brainerd, MN 56401-3020, USA), *b* 1929: *m* 1951, Robert E. Olson, and has issue living, Mark Joseph, *b* 1952, — Stephen George, *b* 1953: *m* 19—, Cherie, da of Robert Barsness, and has issue living, Carston Robert *b* 1986, Blake Steven *b* 1990, — Jonathan Robert, *b* 1954, — Eric James, *b* 1961: *m* 19—, Juliana, da of L. Birkes, and has issue living, Evan Thomas *b* 1996, Gabriel James *b* 1998, — Christopher Style, *b* 1966: *m* 19—, Laurie Vidmar, and has issue living, Nathaniel Style *b* 1997, — Julie Ann, *b* 1951: *m* 19—, James Kaul, and has issue living, Andrew James *b* 1977, William Estvand *b* 1978, Patrick Dillon *b* 1982, Elizabeth Ann *b* 1975, — Jennifer Catherine, *b* (twin) 1954: *m* 19—, Kevin Hoffman, and has issue living, Anthony Hugh *b* 1982, Ahnna Marie *b* 1978, — Mary Beth, *b* 1957: *m* 19—, Thomas Luckemeyer, and has issue living, Catherine Tobin *b* 1989, Bethany Ann *b* 1991, — Lisa Marie, *b* 1959: *m* 19—, Michael Morgan, and has issue living, Joseph Patrick *b* 1982, Thomas Lee *b* 1985, — Ellen Christine, *b* 1962: *m* 19—, John Fussy, and has issue living, Mason Thomas *b* 1992, Reno Thomas *b* 1994, Rylie Christine *b* 1991, — Therese Lynn, *b* 1963: *m* 19—, Steven Johnson, and has issue living, Eric Edward *b* 1991, Luke Steven *b* 1994.

Daughters of late Henry Albert Glenmore Style, 3rd son of 9th baronet, *b* 1862, *d* 1916: *m* 1886, Anna Lydia, who *d* 1951, dau of Samuel Fletcher Goldsmith:—
Rosamond Lydia, *b* 1891: *m* 1st, 19—, Jack Dagnon; 2ndly, 19—, ... Smith, and *d* 1976, leaving issue, (by 1st *m*) Raymond Style, *b* 1910: *m* 19—, Adeline Wannarka, and *d* 1999, leaving issue, Candace Lee *b* 1950, — (by 2nd *m*) Rodney Style, *b* 1918: *m* 19—, Evelyn Beaton, and *d* 1996, leaving issue, Michael Banco, Beach Rex (has issue, Barry, Kevin), Janet Rainwater, Terri McKnight. —— Brenda Helen, *b* 1897: *m* 19—, Oscar Tonnesson, and *d* 1996. —— Viola, *b* (twin) 1897: *m* 19—, Merton Crandall, and *d* 1989, leaving issue, Dayton, *b* 19—.

Branch from 4th son of 9th baronet

Issue of late Brig-Gen Rodney Charles Style, 4th son of 9th baronet, *b* 1863, *d* 1957: *m* 1911, Hélène Pauline, who *d* 1975, da of late Herman Greverus Kleinwort, of 45 Belgrave Square, SW1, and Wierton Pl, Maidstone:—
Sir Godfrey William, CBE, DSC, *b* 1915; *ed* Eton; Lt-Cdr RN; an Underwriting Member of Lloyd's; served in HM Yacht "Victoria and Albert" 1938; Flag Lt to Com-in-Ch Home Fleet 1939-41; a Member of the Nat Advisory Council on Employment of Disabled People 1944-74 (Chm of Council 1964-74), of Advisory Panel to Disabled Living Foundation since 1965, and of Nat Star Centre for Youth, Cheltenham, Advisory Panel since 1966, and Council since 1970; a Gov Sir

Oswald Stoll Foundation 1975-84, and of Queen Elizabeth's Foundation for the Disabled since 1975; a Member of Disablement Advisory Cttee, Maidstone, 1945-64 and Chm of Sheltered Employment Cttee of Nat Advisory Council 1954-64; 1939-45 War (despatches twice, DSC, invalided); CBE (Civil) 1960, Knt 1973: *m* 1st, 1942 (*m diss* 1951), Jill Elizabeth, da of late George Bellis Caruth, of Drumard Cottage, Ballymena, co Antrim; 2ndly, 1951, Sigrid Elisabeth, who *d* 1985, da of late Per Stellan Carlberg, of Jönköping, Sweden; 3rdly, 1986, Valerie Beauclerk, widow of Duncan McClure, and da of late Lt-Com Cecil Hulton-Sams, RN (*see* V Hawarden, colls, 1976 Edn), and has issue living (by 1st *m*) Montague William (27 rue des Romains, 68480 Bettlach, France), *b* 1943; *ed* Eton; Diplome de l'Académie des Hautes Etudes Commerciales, Paris; MBA, INSEAD: *m* 1970, Susan Jennifer, yr da of Peter Wrightson, OBE (*see* Wrightson, Bt), and has issue living, Oliver Rodney *b* 1976, Sophie Elizabeth *b* 1974, — Helen Anne, *b* 1946: *m* 1971, Lt-Col Charles Frederick Byng Stephens, Welsh Gds, of Brook House, Amport, Andover, Hants, and has issue living, Alexandra Claire *b* 1973, Georgina Kate *b* 1976, — Marieka Louise, *b* 1947: *m* 1969, Charles John Hamilton Fisher, of 15 Foskett Rd, SW6 3LY, and has issue living, Hugo Hamilton *b* 1970, Louise Hamilton *b* 1973, — (by 2nd *m*) Charles Rodney (Wood Cottage, Cornwood, Ivybridge, Devon), *b* 1954; *ed* Eton, and Camb Univ; Cdre RN: *m* 1981, Charlotte Amanda, el da of late Lt Timothy Martin Woodford, RN (*see* Stirling-Hamilton, Bt), and has issue living, Amanda Clare *b* 1981, Annabel Daisy *b* 1983, Elizabeth Sigrid *b* 1990. *Residence* – 30 Carlyle Court, Chelsea Harbour, SW10 0UQ. *Club* – Naval and Military. —— Rodney Gerald, *b* 1920; *ed* Eton; Col RRF (OC 1st Bn RNF 1962-65); Comdt RMSM, Kneller Hall 1973-75; 1939-45 War with Coldm Gds; Licentiate of Brit Inst of Professional Photography: *m* 1st, 1944 (*m diss* 1952), Melloney, da of late Maj-Gen Sir (Sandford) John Palairet Scobell, KBE, CB, CMG, DSO; 2ndly, 1952, Barbara, da of late John A. Hill, of 102 Pond St, Natick, Massachusetts, USA, and has issue living (by 2nd *m*), William Bryant (c/o RHQ Coldstream Gds, Wellington Barracks, Birdcage Walk, SW1), *b* 1954; Maj Coldm Gds: *m* 1977, Celia Maria, yr da of Hon Robert Latham Baillieu, MBE, TD (*see* B Baillieu), and has issue living, Edward Rodney *b* 1980, Robert William *b* 1982, Jennifer Hélène *b* 1988, — Rodney Hill (Knowle Farmhouse, North Newington, Oxon OX15 6AN), *b* 1956; ACA, ATII: *m* 1982, Georgina Eve, yr da of John Kinloch Kerr of Abbotrule (*see* M Lothian, colls), and has issue living, George Oliver *b* 1985, Hugo Gerald *b* (twin) 1985, Elizabeth Daisy *b* 1989, — John Glenmore (Calle Rafel Ripolles 13, La Selva del Camp, Tarragona, Spain), *b* 1957: *m* 1988, Concepción, only da of José Muñoz Sainz, of Corral de Calatrava, Ciudad Real, Spain, and has issue living, Helena Barbara *b* 1995, — Caroline Mary, *b* 1964: *m* 1988, Adam Francis Southwell, of Prince Hall Hotel, Two Bridges, Yelverton, Devon PL20 6SA. *Residence* – Fairmont, Sands Rd, Seale, Farnham, Surrey GU10 1LW. —— Rosamond Marguerite, *b* 1912: *m* 1st, 1934, Rear-Adm John Harvey Forbes Crombie, CB, DSO, who *d* 1972; 2ndly, 1980, Antony William Allen, and has issue living, (by 1st *m*) James Rodney Forbes, *b* 1935; Capt late Queen's Own Highlanders: *m* 1961 (*m diss* 1977), Lee Adrienne Chavet, — Rosanna Mary, *b* 1937: *m* 1964, Maj Malcolm Kenneth Shennan, late R Scots Greys, and has issue living, Mark Douglas *b* 1970: *m* 1998, Victoria Ann Litherland, Melissa *b* 1967: *m* 1996, Hugh Alexander Stewart (and has issue living, Alice Flora Rosamond *b* 1998), — Annabel Jean, *b* 1944: *m* 1964, Simon Gerard Younger, of Baro House, Haddington, East Lothian EH41 4PF, and has issue living, James Henry *b* 1965, Jonathan Simon *b* 1979, Mary-Claire *b* 1967, Eugenie *b* 1968, Sophie Rosamond *b* 1973, — Julia Rosamond, *b* 1947: *m* 1974, John Henry Trotter, of Mordington House, Berwick-upon-Tweed, TD15 1XA, and has issue living, Thomas Henry *b* 1978, Alexander Harry *b* 1981, Victoria Rosamond *b* 1980. *Residence* – The Garden House, Mordington, Berwick-on-Tweed, Northumberland TD15 1XA. —— Mary Dorothy, *b* 1918: *m* 1939, Neil Arthur Campbell, TD, of Chennell Park, Tenterden, Kent, and has issue living, Alistair Neil, *b* 1941: *m* 1970 (*m diss* 1975), Jane, da of Michael Gatehouse, — Jeremy George, *b* 1948: *m* 1973, Penelope Hudson, and has issue living, Toby George Mungo *b* 1975, Angus Neil Morgan *b* 1977, Camilla Mary *b* 1981, — Gerald Angus (Keeper's Cottage, Chennell Park, Tenterden, Kent TN30 6XA), *b* 1951: *m* 1976 (*m diss* 1998), Dorian Isobel, da of late Maj Anthony Peter Howorth Greenly (*see* Gibson, Bt, *cr* 1926, 1995 Edn), and has issue living, George Richard Angus *b* 1979, Henry Neil Edward *b* 1980, — Joanna Mary, *b* 1946: *m* 1972, Philip Thompson, and has issue living, James Courtney *b* 1974, Charles Neil *b* 1976.

Branch from brother of 9th baronet

Grandchildren of late Maj George Montague Style, eldest son of late Albert Frederick Style (infra):—
Issue of late Oliver George Style, *b* 1897, *d* 1973: *m* 1923, Guinevere, who *d* 1975, da of late Rev Walter Matthew Parker (Molesworth St Aubyn, Bt, colls):—
George Michael Oliver, *b* 1927: *m* 1951, Mary Jeans, and has issue living, Elizabeth Mary, *b* 1952, — Sarah Jane, *b* 1955, — Caroline Ann, *b* 1956. —— Patricia Nora, *b* 1924: *m* 1946 (*m diss* 1970), Gp Capt Deryck Hugo Cross, RAF (ret), and has issue living, Robert Humphrey Hugo *b* 1951, — Alison Guinevere Hugo, *b* 1947: *m* 1972, Gerald Bunyan, and has issue living, Kathleen Jill *b* 1973, — Frances Jane Hugo, *b* 1949: *m* 1969, Richard Charles Mortimore.

Grandson of late Albert Frederick Style, brother of 9th baronet:—
Issue of late Charles Humphrey Style, *b* 1877, *d* 1936: *m* 1899, Anne Maud Harriet, who *d* 1942, da of late Gen Sir Hugh Henry Gough, VC, GCB:—
Humphrey Bloomfield, *b* 1902; *ed* Marlborough, and Pembroke Coll, Camb: *m* 1935, Anita Dolores, who *d* 19—, da of Charles Brunson, of Antofagasta, Chile, and has issue living, Charles Humphrey, *b* 1945: *m* 1971, Elizabeth Ann Hoskin, of London, Ont, Canada, — Ursula Anne, *b* 1936: *m* 1959, William Swaisland Carter, of Toronto, Canada, and has issue living, William Alarik, *b* 1963, Roberta Jean *b* 1960, Jacqueline Anne *b* 1966, Adrienne Julia *b* 1971, — Ingrid Priscilla, *b* 1939: *m* 1960, Henry Evan Cockshutt Schulman, and has issue living, Charles Eric *b* 1965, Frances Yvonne *b* 1961, Audrey Alexis *b* 1963, — Diana Maria, *b* 1941: *m* 1965, Robert Tweedy, of 7 Royal Oak, Don Mills, Toronto, Canada, and has issue living, Laura Anne *b* 1968, Lisa Diana *b* 1973.

Grandsons of late Charles Humphrey Style (ante):—
Issue of late Hubert Anthony Style, *b* 1910, *d* 1992: *m* 1942, Enid Margaret (Broomscroft Cottage, 144 Canon Lane, Wateringbury, nr Maidstone, Kent ME18 5PQ), only da of Leonard Frederick Leonard, of Reigate, Surrey:—
John Richard (c/o Jardine Fleming Investment Management Ltd, 47th Floor Jardine House, Hong Kong), *b* 1943; *ed* Marlborough, and Coll of Law; Solicitor 1970: *m* 1990, Caroline A.M., only da of Anthony Sparrow, of Abinger Hammer, Surrey, and has issue living, Alexander Nicholas Hubert, *b* 1991, — Toby James Anthony, *b* 1994. —— (Robert) Nicholas Humphrey (11th 16th Av, Rivonia, Sandton, Transvaal, S Africa), *b* 1949; *ed* Marlborough: *m* 1982, Mrs Diana Schoeller, da of J. Leal, of Johannesburg, and has issue living, Jonathan Rupert Anthony, *b* 1982, — Freddy, *b* 1984, — Sophy, *b* (twin) 1984.

Issue of late Capt Robert Henry Style, Yeo, *b* 1881, *d* 1945: *m* 1905, Grace Winnifred, who *d* 1977, da of John Bazley-White (E Rothes):—
David Leslie, *b* 1913; *ed* Radley; European War 1939-45 as Able Seaman RN. *Residence* – Hampton Court, Isle of Man.

This family, originally seated in Suffolk, is descended from William Style, of Ipswich, father of Sir John Style Alderman of London, grandfather of Sir Humphrey Style Knt, one of the Esquires to the Body of Henry VIII, and grandfather of Sir Thomas, 1st baronet.

SULLIVAN (UK) 1804, of Thames Ditton, Surrey

What we gain by conquest we secure by clemency

(*Sir*) RICHARD ARTHUR SULLIVAN, 9th *Baronet*; *b* 9 Aug, 1931; *s* his father, *Sir* RICHARD BENJAMIN MAGNIAC, 1977, but does not use his title; *ed* Univ Cape Town (BSc), and at Massachusetts Inst of Technology (SM); MICE, PE, MASCE; Man of operations, Woodward Clyde Oceaneering: *m* 1962, Elenor Mary, el da of Kenneth Merson Thorpe, of 7 Jacqueshill Crescent, Somerset West, Cape Prov, S Africa, and has issue.

Arms – Per fesse, the base per pale; in the chief or, a dexter hand couped at the wrist grasping a sword erect gules, the blade entwined by a serpent proper, between two lions rampant respecting each other of the second; the dexter base vert, charged with a buck trippant or, on the sinister base per pale argent and sable, a boar passant counterchanged. Crest – On a ducal coronet or, a robin holding in the beak a sprig of laurel proper.
Residence –

SON LIVING

CHARLES MERSON, *b* 15 Dec 1962; *ed* — Coll, Camb (BA).

DAUGHTERS LIVING

Katherine Ann, *b* 1963. —— Sarah Elizabeth, *b* 1965. —— Margaret Mary, *b* 1969.

BROTHER LIVING

Michael Francis (12 Gloucester Crescent, NW1 7DS), *b* 1936; *ed* Camb Univ (MA, MB, BCh), FRCS (Eng): *m* 1st, 1957 (*m diss* 1978), Inger, only da of Arne Mathieson, of Oslo, Norway; 2ndly, Caroline Mary, el da of Maj Christopher John Griffin, of Hall Farmhouse, Oxborough, Norfolk, and has issue living, (by 1st *m*) Richard Alexander Dermot, *b* 1961; *ed* Reading Univ (BA): *m* 1993, Julia Elizabeth, eldest da of Peter Graham Macdonald-Smith, of Bloxworth, Dorset, —— Vivienne Nicola, *b* 1965. —— (by 2nd *m*) Emma Lucy Mary, *b* 1980.

COLLATERAL BRANCH LIVING

Issue of late Valentine Arthur Sullivan, 2nd son of Capt Richard Sullivan, RN, 2nd son of 7th baronet, *b* 1907, *d* 1965: *m* 1937, Mollie Maureen Madge, who *d* 1985, da of late W. N. Craig, of Sale, Cheshire:—
Peter Craig Valentine (Mercury House, Riebeek St, Wynberg 7800, Cape), *b* 1941; *ed* Univ of Cape Town.

The 6th baronet, Adm Sir Francis William Sullivan, KCB, CMG, was an ADC to Queen Victoria 1877-8. The 7th baronet, Rev Sir Frederick, was 20 years R of Southrepps.

SULLIVAN (UK) 1881, of Garryduff, co Cork (Extinct 1937)

Sir WILLIAM SULLIVAN, 3rd and last *Baronet*.

DAUGHTER LIVING OF THIRD BARONET (*By 1st marriage*)

Kathleen Mary: *m* 1914, Wilmot Humphrey Clifford Lloyd, who *d* 1948, and has issue living, Desmond Humphrey Clifford, *b* 1917; *ed* Trin Coll, Dublin (BA 19-); European War 1942-5 with London Irish Rifles, —— Wilmot Anthony Clifford, *b* 1928; is Fl-Lt RAF, —— Nedda Cecil Clifford: *m* 19-, James Davis.

SUMMERS (UK) 1952, of Shotton, co Flint (Extinct 1993)

(*Sir*) FELIX ROLAND BRATTAN SUMMERS, 2nd and last *Baronet*.

DAUGHTER LIVING OF SECOND BARONET

Micheline, *b* 1947: *m* 1970, Mark Dudley Langridge, of Shepherds Down, 3 The Ridgeway, Friston, Eastbourne, E Sussex BN20 0EZ.

DAUGHTERS LIVING OF FIRST BARONET (*by 1st marriage*)

Anne Griselda (Plas-yn-Gerddi, Lloc, Holywell, Flintshire), *b* 1916: *m* 1953, Maj Alan Edward Curtis Lake, TD, who *d* 1980.

(*by 2nd marriage*)

Judith Margaret, *b* 1932: *m* 1958, Gordon Elliott, of Low Abbey, Bay Horse, Lancaster, and has issue living, Geoffrey Ian, *b* 1960, — Martin Anthony, *b* 1963, — Catherine Elizabeth, *b* 1961, — Lucy Helen, *b* 1966. —— Carolyn Elizabeth, *b* 1936: *m* 1958, Robin Hilary Beaumont Malim, of Croose Farm, Woolhope, Hereford, and has issue living, Peter Beaumont, *b* 1963, — Karen Elizabeth, *b* 1960, — Sophie Hilary, *b* 1968.

WIDOW LIVING OF SECOND BARONET

ANNA MARIE LOUISE (Shepherds Down, 3 The Ridgeway, Friston, Eastbourne, E Sussex BN20 0EZ), da of late Gustave Demaegd, of Brussels: *m* 1945, (Sir) Felix Roland Brattan Summers, 2nd Bt (who did not use the title), who *d* 1993.

SUTHERLAND (UK) 1921, of Dunstanburgh Castle, Embleton, co Northumberland

Without fear

(*Sir*) JOHN BREWER SUTHERLAND, 3rd *Baronet b* 19 Oct 1931; *s* his father, *Sir* (BENJAMIN) IVAN, 1980, but does not use title; *ed* Sedbergh, and St Catharine's Coll, Camb: *m* 1st, 1958, Alice Muireall, JP, who *d* 1984, da of late William Stamford Henderson, of Usan, Makerstoun, Kelso, Roxburghshire; 2ndly, 1988, (Ailsa) Heather, da of late David Alexander Gray, of Langley Mill, Lanchester, co Durham, and has issue by 1st *m*.

𝕬rms – Gules, a chevron flory-counterflory between in chief three mullets and in base a lymphad all or. 𝕮rest – Upon the trunk of a tree a cat salient proper.
Residence – Ross, Belford, Northumberland.

SONS LIVING (*By 1st marriage*)

PETER WILLIAM, *b* 18 May 1963: *m* 1988, Suzanna Mary, da of R. Michael Gledson, of Newlands Mill Lane, Little Shrewley, Warwick, and has issue living, Kate Alice, *b* 1993, — Lucy Suzanna, *b* 1995. *Residence* – Swarland East House Farm, Swarland, Felton, Morpeth, Northumberland. —— Christopher John, *b* 1965. —— Robert Brewer, *b* 1970: *m* 1998, Rebecca, da of Michael Trickey, of Sannacott, North Molton, Devon.

DAUGHTER LIVING

Susan Muireall, *b* 1960: *m* 1992, Alastair Peter Jollans, of Southfield House, Painswick, Glos, and has issue living, Daniel John Peter, *b* 1994, — William *b* 1998, — Alice Jane, *b* 1995.

BROTHER LIVING

(David) Michael (Northfield, Lowick, Northumberland), *b* 1940; *ed* Sedbergh, and St Catharine's Coll, Camb: *m* 1966, Caroline Mary, da of late Robert Simon Hogan, of Blackrock, co Dublin, and has issue living, Julia Ruth, *b* 1967: *m* 1998, Edward J. Banks, yr son of (William) Lawrence Banks, CBE, of Ridgebourne, Kington, Herefordshire, — Serena Louise, *b* 1971, — Polly Anne, *b* 1975.

HALF-BROTHERS LIVING

William, *b* 1945; *ed* Leys Sch, Cambridge, and St Catharine's Coll, Camb: *m* 1966, Sarah Lucy, da of Dr Cecil Gilbert, of Benton, Newcastle upon Tyne, and has issue living, Mark Rupert, *b* 1967, — Dylan Paul, *b* 1970, — Hal, *b* 1988, — Ceri

Jane, *b* 1968, — Amy Gael, *b* 1969. —— Owen, *b* 1947; *ed* The Leys Sch, Cambridge, and St Catharine's Coll, Camb: *m* 1971, Margaret Ann, da of Daniel Herbert Williams, of Rainhill, Liverpool, and has issue living, Jonathan Ben, *b* 1976, — Victoria Jane, *b* 1974. —— Ben (USA), *b* 1949; *ed* The Leys Sch, Cambridge, and Essex Univ: *m* 1986, Bonna Howell, and has issue living, Lesley Ann, *b* 1986.

UNCLE LIVING (Son of 1st baronet)

Robert Gordon (Piper's Hill, Castle Terrace, Berwick-upon-Tweed), *b* 1908: *m* 1st, 1934 (*m diss* 1958), Helen Wallace, da of late Edward Farish, of Wigton, Cumberland; 2ndly, 1958 Emily, da of late Lavinia Hayes, of Hanwell, Middlesex, and has issue living, (by 1st *m*) Arthur Ian *b* 1936, — David Wallace, *b* 1938.

WIDOW LIVING OF SECOND BARONET

MARGARET, JP (*Margaret, Lady Sutherland*) (The Smithy, Embleton, Northumberland), da of Albert Owen, of Fairways, Chalfont St Giles, Bucks: *m* 1944, as his 2nd wife, Sir (Benjamin) Ivan Sutherland, 2nd Bt, who *d* 1980.

COLLATERAL BRANCH LIVING

Issue of late Arthur Munro Sutherland, el son of 1st baronet, *b* 1894, *d* 1941: *m* 1921, Nina Marguerite Crawshay, da of late Arthur Skelton Wimble, of Whitley Bay, Northumberland, and St Helier, Jersey:—
Nina Marguerite Munro, *b* 1923: *m* 1949, James Keith W. Slater, who *d* 1968, and has issue living, Gail Munro, *b* 1950, — Kim Munro, *b* 1952, — Bill Munro, *b* 1953, — Peter Munro, *b* 1956. *Residence* – The Mill Cottage, Eglingham, Alnwick, Northumberland. —— Ann Munro, *b* 1928.

The 1st baronet, Sir Arthur Munro Sutherland, KBE (son of B. J. Sutherland of Newcastle-on-Tyne), Chm of Newcastle Commercial Exchange; was Lord Mayor of Newcastle-on-Tyne 1918-19, Pres of Chamber of Shipping of the United Kingdom 1930, and High Sheriff of Northumberland 1943.

Sutherland-Dunbar (Duff-Sutherland-Dunbar), see Dunbar.

GRANT-SUTTIE (NS) 1702, of Balgone, Haddingtonshire

Nothing hazard, nothing have

Sir JAMES EDWARD GRANT-SUTTIE, 9th *Baronet*; *b* 29 May 1965; *s* his father, *Sir* (GEORGE) PHILIP, 1997: *m* 1st, 1989 (*m diss* 1992), Emma Jane, yr da of Peter Craig, of Innerwick, East Lothian; 2ndly, 1997, Sarah Jane, da of Alan Smale, and has issue by 1st and 2nd *m*.

Arms – Quarterly: 1st and 4th, barry wavy of six azure and or; on a chief of the last, a lion rampant naissant with two tails vert, armed and langued gules, *Suttie*; 2nd and 3rd, or a chevron checky gules and of the first, between three hunting-horns sable, garnished of the second, all within a bordure of the same, *Semple*. **Crest** – A ship under full sail proper.
Residence – Sheriff Hall Farm, Balgone, N Berwick, E Lothian.

SONS LIVING (By 1st marriage)

GREGOR CRAIG, *b* 29 Oct 1991.

(by 2nd marriage)

Andrew James, *b* 1997. —— David Philip, *b* 1999.

AUNT LIVING

Ann, *b* 1940: *m* 1st, 1958, —; 2ndly, 1967, Marinus Jan Luitwieler, of Calgary, Alberta, Canada, and has issue living (by 1st *m*), Susan Ann McGEE GRANT-SUTTIE (63121 2604 Kensington Rd NW, Calgary AB, Canada T2N 4S5), *b* 1960: *m* 1st 19— (*m diss* 19—), — Olson; 2ndly, 1994, Barclay Todd Redman, and has issue living (by 1st *m*), Nicole Noël Ann OLSON *b* 1984, — (by 2nd *m*) Rinus Jon, *b* 1968, — Melissa Ann, *b* 1970.

MOTHER LIVING

ELSPETH MARY, el da of late Maj-Gen Robert Elliott Urquhart, CB, DSO: *m* 1st, 1962 (*m diss* 1969), Sir (George) Philip Grant-Suttie, 8th Bt, who *d* 1997; 2ndly, 1970, Rt Hon (Walter) Menzies Campbell, CBE, QC, MP.

COLLATERAL BRANCH LIVING

Grandson of late Robert Grant-Suttie, 4th son of 5th baronet:—
Issue of late Col Hubert Francis Grant-Suttie, CBE, DSO, MC, *b* 1884, *d* 1973: *m* 1920, Torfrida Alianore, who *d* 1971, da of Sir Wroth Periam Christopher Lethbridge, 5th Bt:—
(Robert) Ian (17 Mountain Av, Woodstock, Vermont 05091, USA), *b* 1926; *ed* Wellington Coll, Sorbonne, and New Coll, Oxford; late Lt Black Watch: *m* 1951, Juliet Carmen, yr da of late Lt-Col Nigel Eustace Philip Sutton (*see* Sutton, Bt, colls), and has issue living, Francis Æneas, *b* 1957: *m* 1983, Carolyn Forrest, da of Maj-Gen Robert Ginsburgh, of Chevy Chase, Maryland, USA, and has issue living, Ian Hamilton *b* 1991, Katherine Myers *b* 1988, — James Archibald, *b* 1964, — Atalanta Theresa, *b* 1955, — Roxana Idonea, *b* 1961: *m* 1986, Ogden Mills Reid, of Ophir West, 09 Evergreen Drive, Placitas, New Mexico 87043, USA, son of Ogden Rogers Reid, of Purchase, New York, and has issue living, Lindsay Sutton *b* 1990, Ashley Louise *b* 1993, Natalie Mills *b* 1995.

The 2nd and 4th baronets successively represented Haddingtonshire in Parliament, and the 4th baronet assumed the additional surname of Grant on succeeding to the estates of his aunt, Janet Grant, Countess of Hyndford.

SUTTON (GB) 1772, of Norwood Park, Nottinghamshire

Sir RICHARD LEXINGTON SUTTON, 9th *Baronet*; *b* 27 April 1937; *s* his father, Sir ROBERT LEXINGTON, 1981; *ed* Stowe: *m* 1959, Fiamma, only da of Giuseppe Marzio Ferrari, of Via S Giacomo 28, Rome, and has issue.

𝕬rms – Quarterly: 1st and 4th argent, a canton sable, *Sutton*; 2nd and 3rd, argent, a cross flory azure, *Lexington*. 𝕮rest – A wolf's head erased gules.
Residence – Moor Hill, Langham, Gillingham, Dorset.

SON LIVING

DAVID ROBERT, *b* 26 Feb 1960; *ed* Milton Abbey: *m* 1992, Annette, only da of B. David, of Aller, Langport, Somerset, and has issue living, Charlotte Emily, *b* 1994, — Harriet Eugenie, *b* 1995.

Always ready

DAUGHTER LIVING

Caroline Victoria, *b* 1965: *m* 1989, Alexander C. Gibbs, son of C. E. Gibbs, of Bourton, Dorset, and has issue living, Charles Toby, *b* 1991, — Robert Alexander, *b* 1993.

BROTHER LIVING

James Anthony (Marsh Cottage, Penselwood, nr Wincanton, Som), *b* 1940; *ed* Stowe: *m* 1964, Dale, only da of Capt Cecil William Stevens, of Windrush Mill, Windrush, Burford, Oxford, and has issue living, Tristan Antony, *b* 1966: *m* 1995, Catherine Louise, da of David Masters, and has issue living, William Oliver *b* 1998, — Chloe Emma, *b* 1968.

WIDOW LIVING OF EIGHTH BARONET

DAPHNE GWLADYS (*Daphne, Lady Sutton*) (Clinger Farm, Wincanton, Som), only da of Maj Arnold Charles Gover, MC, of Pilton: *m* 1936, Sir Robert Lexington Sutton, 8th Bt, who *d* 1981.

COLLATERAL BRANCHES LIVING

Grandchildren of late Thomas Alexander Sutton (infra):—
Issue of late John Alexander Sutton, *b* 1915, *d* 1981: *m* 1950, (Violet) Deirdre (Badbury Wick House, Chiseldon, Wilts), el da of late James Sheringham Shepherd, of Kilbrack, Doneraile, co Cork:—
Charles Alexander, *b* 1950; *ed* Millfield: *m* 1979, Susan Nita, yr da of Brian Richard Notton, of The Old Malthouse, Wanborough, Wilts. ——— Grania Jane, *b* 1952: *m* 1985, (Robert) Nicholas Bovill Whitehead, of Badbury Wick Farm-house, Chiseldon, nr Swindon, Wilts, eldest son of T. B. Whitehead, of Chisbury, nr Marlborough, Wilts, and has issue living, Hugh Alexander Bovill, *b* 1989, — Thomas James Bovill, *b* 1989 (twin), — Eleanor Amanda Deirdre, *b* 1987.

Granddaughter of late Alexander George Sutton, 3rd son of 4th baronet:—
Issue of late Thomas Alexander Sutton, *b* 1888, *d* 1945: *m* 1913, Gwendoline, da of Thomas Forsyth-Forrest, formerly of The Querns, Cirencester:—

Margaret Pamela (*Pamela, Lady Bunbury*), *b* 1919: *m* 1940, Sir (John) William Napier Bunbury, 12th Bt, who *d* 1985. *Residence* – 9 Lee Rd, Aldeburgh, Suffolk.

Granddaughter of late Lt-Col Francis Henry Sutton, MC, 11th Hussars (PAO), only son of late Maj Francis Richard Hugh Seymour Sutton, only surv son of late Capt Francis Sutton, RHG, 3rd son of 2nd baronet:—
Issue of late Lt-Col Richard David Sutton, 11th Hussars (PAO), *b* 1923, *d* 1965: *m* 1965, Sally Christine (Evergreen Cottage, Cherington, Tetbury, Glos GL8 8SH), da of late J. D. Graeme Reid, of Gruivie, Wormit, Fife:——
Frances Elizabeth (*posthumous*) *b* 1966.

Grandchildren of late Gilbert William Sutton, 3rd son of late Rev Augustus Sutton, 5th son of 2nd baronet:—
Issue of late Cdr John Gilbert Sutton, DSC, *b* 1892, *d* 1982: *m* 1st, 1918, Eva Maud, who *d* 1919, only child of Thomas Cook, of Hobland, Bradwell, Great Yarmouth; 2ndly, 1920 (*m diss* 1940), Ida Margaret, who *d* 1984, da of Charles Halls; 3rdly, 1940 (*m diss* 1950), Katherine, who *d* 1977, da of Charles Balfour-Kinnear, WS (Montgomery, Bt); 4thly 1950, Violet (Manor House, Portesham, nr Weymouth, Dorset), da of late Herbert James Godwin, OBE, of Greatham, Petersfield, Hants:—
(By 2nd *m*) Richard John Beverley (Foxfield, Ansty, Dorchester, Dorset DT2 7PJ), *b* 1922; Lt-Cdr RN; *ed* Imp Service Coll, Windsor: *m* 1949, Ann Stella, da of late Brig Charles Hall Woodhouse, OBE, MC, and has issue living, Richard Charles, *b* 1955; Maj 4th/7th R Drag Gds: *m* 1985, Jane Elizabeth, only da of Lt-Cdr John Alan Bird, RN, of The Cottage, Nottington Lane, Nottington, Weymouth, Dorset, and has issue living, Hugo George Richard *b* 1990, Sophie Georgina Elizabeth *b* 1988, — Amanda Clare, *b* 1952: *m* 1973, Robert Stephen MacKenzie, Queens R Irish Hussars, and has issue living, Rupert Charles Robert *b* 1982, Emily Amanda *b* 1977. —— Felicity Ruth (Home Cottage, Puddletown, Dorchester, Dorset DT2 8TL), *b* 1926: *m* 1951, Maj Denis Cary Atkinson, 4th/7th Royal Dragoon Gds, who *d* 1985, and has issue living, Timothy Charles Garnet (2 Clyffe Stables, Tincleton, Dorchester, Dorset DT2 8QR), *b* 1960, — Tessa Margaret (Yew Tree Cottage, Barton Stacey, nr Winchester, Hants SO21 3RT), *b* 1952: *m* 1977 (*m diss* 1999), Maj Michael John Herbert Malyon, Roy Hus, and has issue living, Giles William Herbert *b* 1989, Mary Louise *b* 1980, Isobel Alice *b* 1982. —— (By 3rd *m*) Henry Richard (c/o Sun House, Lower Burton, Dorchester, Dorset), *b* 1945. —— Judith (14B Nevoria Place, Padbury, W Australia 6025), *b* 1942: *m* 1st, 1961 (*m diss* 1971), Michael William Cox; 2ndly, 1971 (*m diss* 1982), Peter Victor Langley, and has issue living (by 1st *m*), Anthony William, *b* 1961, — Nicholas Michael, *b* 1963: *m* 1987, Lisa Shilling, and has issue living, Christopher *b* 1989, — (by 2nd *m*), Scott Victor, *b* 1973, — Samantha Kate, *b* 1971: *m* 1996, Antonio Sepulcri, RAN.

Granddaughters of late Rowland Sutton, 4th son of late Rev Augustus Sutton, 5th son of 2nd baronet:—
Issue of late Lawrence Seymour Sutton, *b* 1905, *d* 1967: *m* 1st, 1936, Muriel Geraldine, who *d* 1940, da of Maj L. A. Sherrard; 2ndly, 1942, Martha Joyce, da of W. L. Williams, of Cefn-y-dre, Pembrokeshire:—
(By 1st *m*) Rosemary Margaret (29 Darwin House, Australia Close, Landport, Portsmouth PO1 1JW), *b* 1937: *m* 1962 (*m diss* 1974), Jack Anthony Eden, MBE, who *d* 1990, and has issue living, Sally Jane, *b* 1963: *m* 1986, Stephen Butcher, and has issue living, Matthew William *b* 1998, — Susan Rosemary EDEN-BROWNE (52 Arminers Close, Alverstoke, Gosport, Hants PO12 2HB), *b* 1964: *m* 1st, 1981 (*m diss* 1988), John Patrick Vickery; 2ndly, 1998, Mark Anthony Eden-Browne, and has issue living (by 1st *m*), Anthony John *b* 1983, Laura Jane *b* 1981. —— Molly, *b* 1940: *m* 1966, Graham J. Waterman, of Springate Farm, Henham, Bishops Stortford, Herts CM22 6BQ, and has issue living, Matthew Charles, *b* 1967, — Julian Rupert, *b* 1969, — Charlotte Lucy, *b* 1973.

Grandchildren of late Maj-Gen Hugh Clement Sutton, CB, CMG (infra):—
Issue of late Lt-Col Nigel Eustace Philip Sutton, *b* 1896, *d* 1956: *m* 1st 1921, Stella Clementina, who *d* 1945, da of late Montague Whittingham Price, of 67 Eaton Place, SW (E Clarendon, colls); 2ndly, 1951, Elisabeth Clothilde Hedwige (Mrs Zita Gielgud), da of late Zoltan Gruszer, of Budapest, Hungary:—
(By 1st *m*) John Hugh Torquil, *b* 1923; *ed* Eton, and Ch Ch, Oxford; Major (retired) Coldstream Guards: *m* 1952, Carola Mariette, da of late Ulick Otway Vortigern Lloyd-Verney, OBE (*see* Verney, Bt, *cr* 1818, colls), and has issue living, Hugh Nigel John (Old Rectory, Pimperne, Blandford, Dorset), *b* 1954: *m* 1987, Miranda F., only da of John Goldsmid, of Copyhold Farm, Goring Heath, Oxfordshire, and has issue living, Emma Frances Juliet *b* 1989, Olivia Henrietta Jonquille *b* 1991, Rebecca Virginia Jonquille *b* 1991, — Mark Richard (42 Clarendon Drive, Putney, SW15), *b* 1956: *m* 1985, Rose, yst da of Samuel Carr, of Paultons Square, Chelsea, and has issue living, Thomas Samuel *b* 1991, Phoebe Esmé *b* 1988, Chloe Patricia *b* 1995, Eloise Rose *b* (twin) 1995, — Catherine Stella Louise, *b* 1959. *Residence* – Bayfield Brecks, Holt, Norfolk. —— Juliet Carmen, *b* 1930: *m* 1951, Robert Ian Grant-Suttie, of 17 Mountain Av, Woodstock, Vermont 05091, USA (*see* Grant-Suttie, Bt, colls).

Granddaughter of late Henry George Sutton, 6th son of 2nd baronet:—
Issue of late Maj-Gen Hugh Clement Sutton, CB, CMG, *b* 1867, *d* 1928 : *m* 1st, 1891, Mabel Ida, who *d* 1896, da of Sir Campbell Munro, 3rd Bt (*cr* 1825); 2ndly, 1898, Hon Alexandra Mary Elizabeth Wood, who *d* 1965, el da of 2nd Viscount Halifax (E Halifax):—
(By 2nd *m*) Elizabeth Mary, *b* 1910: *m* 1st, 1931 (*m diss* 1936), (Ronald) Mark Cunliffe Turner (knighted 1946, and *d* 1980); 2ndly, 1936 (*m diss* 1976), John Tindall-Lister, son of Col late Sir William Tindall Lister, KCMG, KCVO, MD, FRCS, and has had issue (by 1st *m*), Elizabeth Undine, *b* 1931: *m* 1953, Christopher Palgrave Barker, — (by 2nd *m*) Francis Hugh William Bernard, *b* 1937, — Charles John Alexander, *b* 1945, Mary Nerissa Anna, *b* 1941, — Sarah Janet Consuelo, *b* 1947. *Residence* – Luccas Farm, Powerstock, Bridport, Dorset.

Grandchildren of late Major Robert Nassau Sutton Nelthorpe, OBE, el son of late Rev Robert Sutton, el son of late Capt Robert Nassau Sutton, 3rd son of 1st baronet:—
Issue of late Col Oliver Sutton Nelthorpe, CBE, DSO, MC, *b* 1888, *d* 1963: *m* 1914, Marjorie Elspeth Constable, who *d* 1976, da of Charles Constable Curtis (E Onslow, colls):—
Roger SUTTON NELTHORPE, MBE, TD (Scawby Hall, Brigg, Lincs), *b* 1918; *ed* Eton; late Lt-Col Nottinghamshire (Sherwood Rangers) Yeo, and a JP and DL (High Sheriff of Lincs 1970); Palestine and Middle East 1939-44, NW Europe 1944-45 (MBE); MBE (Mil) 1945. —— †John Richard SUTTON NELTHORPE, *b* 1923; *ed* Eton; was Lt RNVR: *m* 1946, Mary Elizabeth, who *d* 1992, only da of T. C. Brown, of The Cottage, Scawby, Lincs, and *d* 1994, leaving issue, Anthony Julian (Orchard House, Carters Lane, Henham, Bishops Stortford, Herts CM22 6AQ), *b* 1948; *ed* Charterhouse: *m* 1973, Margaret, yst da of R. F. Schumacher, of Upton, Didcot, Oxon, and has issue living, Thomas Max *b* 1977; *ed* Uppingham, and Univ Coll, Oxford, Clare Lydia *b* 1979. —— Ann, *b* 1919.

Grandson of late Richard Coningsby Sutton, elder son of late Francis Richard Sutton, 3rd son of late Rev Robert Sutton (ante):—
Issue of late Col Francis Richard Heywood Sutton, MC, TD, *b* 1905, *d* 1970: *m* 1st, 1929 (*m diss* 1937), Barbara Jean, da of A. D. Tait; 2ndly, 1939 (*m diss* 1958), Vera Kathleen, da of W. J. Waldock; 3rdly, 1960, Mrs Audrey Theodosia Madeleine Davies, who *d* 1974, da of Lancelot Squarey (E Gosford):—
(By 2nd *m*) Richard Oliver (1 Route de Duillin, 1261 Trelex, Switzerland), AFC; late Lieut RN; *b* 1940; *ed* Eton: *m* 1967, Helene, da of Ministro Carlo de Franchis, of Rome, and has issue living, Francesco Charles, *b* 1967.

Granddaughter of late Herbert Arthur Sutton, 5th son of late Capt Frederick Sutton (infra):—
Issue of late Roland Manners Verney Sutton, *b* 1895, *d* 1957: *m* 1927, Dora, who *d* 1984, da of Elijah White-hurst, formerly of Overdale, Brinnington, Stockport:—
Ursula Constance, *b* 1929: *m* 1963, Norman Yearsley, of Windbrow, 307 Cromwell Lane, Burton Green, Kenilworth, and has issue living, Jonathan Manners, *b* 1968.

Grandchildren of late Maj Charles Lexington Manners Sutton, MBE (infra):—
Issue of late John Charles Ludlow Manners Sutton, *b* 1921, *d* 1992: *m* 1st, 1946, Daphne Agnes, who *d* 1961, only da of William Francis Wormald, JP; 2ndly, 1962, Gillian, da of Edwin Stanley Harris, of Newcastle-upon-Tyne:—
(By 1st *m*) Richard Manners, *b* 1947: *m* 1st, 1972 (*m diss* 1979), Mary de Witt, da of Charles Diebold, of Buffalo, New York; 2ndly, 1979, Penelope Jane, da of Anthony Gray Quinlan, of Scarborough, N Yorks, and has issue living (by 2nd *m*), William Lexington Manners, *b* 1980, — Thomas Anthony Manners, *b* 1982. ⸺ William Reginald Manners, *b* 1949: *m* 1982, Janet Risa, da of Benjamin Chubac, of New Jersey, USA, and has issue living, Emily Anne, *b* 1983, — Lydia Beth, *b* 1985. ⸺ Oliver Ludlow Manners, *b* 1950: *m* 1980, Virginia Sarah, da of Paul Lipscombe Marriott, of Welshpool, and has issue living, Philip Ludlow Manners, *b* 1984, — Anna Lucy, *b* 1983. ⸺ (By 2nd *m*) Virginia Anne, *b* 1964: *m* 1st, 1989 (*m diss* 1995), Sebastian J. T. Foster, of Harrogate, son of Lt Cdr J. R. Foster, RN (ret), of Godalming, Surrey, and Mrs N. Ward, of Cleckheaton, W Yorks; 2ndly 1998, Jeremy H. Thomas, son of Reginald S. Thomas, of Chester.

Granddaughter of late Rev Charles Nassau Sutton, yst son of late Capt Frederick Sutton, 3rd son of late Capt Robert Nassau Sutton (ante):—
Issue of late Maj Charles Lexington Manners Sutton, MBE, *b* 1891, *d* 1962: *m* 1st, 1917 (*m diss* 1932), Amabel Anne, da of Major Ludlow Coape Ludlow, of Beech Green, Withyham, Sussex; 2ndly, 1932, Gladys Louise (RICHARDSON), who *d* 19—, da of Percy Gubb:—
(By 2nd *m*) Philippa Mary, *b* 1936: *m* 1st, 1956, Derek Walter Pryke; 2ndly, 1982, John Selby-Green of Pashley Farm, Ticehurst, Wadhurst, Sussex, and has issue living, (by 1st *m*) Kelham Charles Manners, *b* 1959, — Timothy John Manners, *b* 1961, — Flavia Anne, *b* 1957: *m* 1986, (Leslie) Andrew Jackson, of 26 Bassingham Rd, SW18 3AG, eldest son of late Ralph Jackson, of Hopehay, Cartmel, Cumbria.

Roland de Sutton, of Sutton upon Trent, Notts: *m* Alice, da of Richard de Lexington (now spelt Laxton), and sister and co-heir of Robert de Lexington, of Averham, Notts, which manor was inherited by their son Robert de Sutton, who *d* 1281. William Sutton of Averham (or Aram), Notts was father of Robert, who was *cr Baron Lexinton*, of Aram 1645 (which peerage became ext in 1723, and whose da and heiress *m* the 3rd Duke of Rutland), and Henry, grandfather of the Rt Hon Sir Robert Sutton. The 1st baronet, Sir Richard Sutton (son of late Rt Hon Sir Robert Sutton, KB, a distinguished diplomat) sat as MP for St Albans 1768-80, for Sandwich 1780-84, and for Boroughbridge 1784-96, and was an Under-Secretary of State 1766-72. Capt Sir Richard Vincent Sutton, MC, 1st Life Gds and Capt and Adj, Machine Gun Regt, who *s* as 6th Bt at his birth, in April 1891, was *ka* 1918.

SWANN (UK) 1906, of Prince's Gardens, Royal Borough of Kensington

Sir MICHAEL CHRISTOPHER SWANN, TD, 4th *Baronet*; *b* 23 Sept 1941; *s* his father, *Sir* ANTHONY CHARLES CHRISTOPHER, CMG, OBE, 1991; *ed* Eton; late 60th Rifles; TD: *m* 1st, 1965 (*m diss* 1985), Hon Lydia Mary Hewitt, da of 8th Viscount Lifford; 2ndly, 1988, Mrs Marilyn Ann Morse, da of Leslie Charles Tobitt, of Montevideo, Uruguay, and previously wife of late Michael Haig Morse, and has issue by 1st *m*.

𝕬rms – Azure, a swan rousant proper within an orle of lymphads, sails furled, flags flying to the dexter, or. 𝕮rest – Between two buffalo's horns a demi-swan wings expanded, all proper.
Residence – 38 Hurlingham Rd, SW6 3RQ.

SONS LIVING (*By 1st marriage*)

JONATHAN CHRISTOPHER, *b* 17 Nov 1966; *ed* Eton: *m* 1994, Polly M., da of Cmdr David Baston, of Compton Dundon, Som. ⸺ Toby Charles, *b* 1971; *ed* Stowe: *m* 1997, Tanna, da of Keith Bradley, of Salem, Oregon, USA.

DAUGHTER LIVING (*By 1st marriage*)

Tessa Margaret, *b* 1969; *ed* Sacred Heart, Tunbridge Wells.

WIDOW LIVING OF THIRD BARONET

JEAN MARGARET (*Dowager Lady Swann*), da of late John Herbert Niblock-Stuart, of Nairobi, Kenya: *m* 1940, Sir Anthony Charles Christopher Swann, 3rd Bt, CMG, OBE, who *d* 1991. *Residence* – 25 Hurlingham Sq, Peterborough Rd, SW6 3DZ.

COLLATERAL BRANCHES LIVING

Granddaughters of late Harold Swann, 2nd son of 1st baronet, *b* 1880, *d* 1953: *m* 1907, Dorothea Alma, who *d* 1969, da of late Henry De Courcy Agnew (Agnew, Bt, *cr* 1629, colls):—
Issue of late Charles Brian Swann, *b* 1913, *d* 1966: *m* 1st, 1939 (*m diss* 1955), Vanessa, da of Ernest William Dalrymple Tennant; 2ndly, 1955, Ann Corben, da of Cyril Alwyn Harrison:—
(By 1st *m*) Julia Vanessa, *b* 1940: *m* 1960, Blyth Metcalf Thompson, of Applecross, 150 Empire Pl, Sandhurst, Johannesburg, S Africa, and has issue living, William Rowland Blyth, *b* 1962, — Dendy Martin Blyth, *b* 1972, — Vanessa Eirene, *b* 1961, — Moya Ann, *b* 1965, — Hannah Yvonne, *b* 1967, — Sonia Suzanne, *b* 1969. —— Karin Clarissa, *b* 1942. —— Virginia Caroline, *b* 1948: *m* 1971, David Winkfield Hughes, of Mid Lambrook Manor, S Petherton, Yeovil, and has issue living, Thomas Percy Winkfield, *b* 1974, — Harriet Elfreda, *b* 1972.

Grandchildren of late Geoffrey Swann (infra):—
Issue of late Major Kenneth Geoffrey Swann, MC, RA, *b* 1915, *ka* 1944: *m* 1942, Delmira Marion (who *d* 1947, having *m* 2ndly, 1947, Peter Richard Hampton), da of Sir (Ferdinand) Michael Kroyer-Kielberg, KBE:—
Christopher Kenneth (Santa Barbara, Calif, USA), *b* 1942; *ed* Eton, and Internat Sch of Geneva: *m* 1968, Kathleen Harriet Brodarick. —— Penelope Ann, *b* 1944.

Issue of late Geoffrey Swann, 4th son of 1st baronet; *b* 1883; *d* 1965: *m* 1911, Florence Mildred, who *d* 1964, da of John Brodie:—
Janet Elizabeth, *b* 1913; a JP for Herts: *m* 1939, Charles Gifford Bardswell, AE, late RAFVR, Kt of the Order of Dannebrog of Denmark, of The Grange, Walkern, nr Stevenage, Herts, and has issue living, Charles Nicholas, *b* 1941: *m* 1969, Sarah Josephine, el da of Sir (Thomas) Leslie Rowan, KCB, CVO, and has issue living, Charles Leslie Geoffrey *b* 1981, Catherine Jane Elizabeth *b* 1971, Alice Victoria Josephine *b* 1974, Isabella Louise Clementine *b* 1979, — Philip Geoffrey, *b* 1948: *m* 1973, Alexandra Augusta, only child of Iver Lunn, of Towersley, Oxon, and has issue living, Josephine Elizabeth *b* 1977, Sonya Caroline *b* 1979, — Veronica Elizabeth, *b* 1945: *m* 1974, Roger Gaymer Broadie (formerly Broadie-Griffith), and has issue living, Helen Elizabeth *b* 1978, Charlotte Anne *b* 1981. —— Phyllis Mildred, *b* 1919: *m* 1946, John Charles Fegen, DSC, late RNVR, of Porta-beg, Ballykeeran, co Westmeath, and has issue living, Richard Kenneth, *b* 1947: *m* 1982, Charmian Sadgrove, and has issue living, Robin *b* 1985, Polly Lucinda *b* 1983, — Frances Lynette, *b* 1950, — Lucy Mildred, *b* 1953: *m* 1976, Simon Burdett, and has issue living, Jonathan *b* 1983, Chloe *b* 1979, Katherine Mildred *b* 1988. —— Kathleen Prudence, *b* 1921: *m* 1945, Allan Priestley Thomson, QSO, late Capt NZ Engineers, former Dir Gen of NZ Forest Ser, of 8 Nicholson Rd, Wellington 6004, NZ, and has issue living, Michael Kenneth, *b* 1951, — Peter Geoffrey, *b* 1955: *m* 1990, Anne Wittholz, and has issue living, Daniel Allan *b* 1993, Chamolie Rose *b* 1992, — Andrew Brodie, *b* 1958: *m* 1987, Razimah Ishmail, and has issue living, Amir Geoffrey *b* 1996, — Celia Margaret, *b* 1946: *m* 1970, Brian Herbert Bockett, and has issue living, David Arthur *b* 1972, Nicholas Andrew *b* 1977, Kirsten Margaret *b* 1974.

The Rt Hon Sir Charles Ernest Swann, 1st Bt (son of late Frederick Schwann, of 23 Gloucester Square, W), sat as MP for N Div of Manchester (*L*) 1886-1918, and assumed by Roy licence, 1913, for himself and his issue, the surname of Swann in lieu of his patronymic.

SWINBURNE, (E) 1660, of Capheaton, Northumberland (Extinct 1967)

Sir SPEARMAN CHARLES SWINBURNE, MRCS, LRCP, 10th and last *Baronet*.

DAUGHTER LIVING OF EIGHTH BARONET

Joan Mary, *b* 1906: *m* 1937, Richard Granville Browne, who assumed by deed poll 1937 the additional surname of Swinburne, and has issue living, John *b* 1937; High Sheriff of Northumberland 1978: *m* 1966, Susan, da of Anthony Comar Wilson, and has issue living, William *b* 1967, Alice *b* 1968, — Rosalind Mary, *b* 1939: *m* 1966, Francesco Parlade, of Marbella, Spain, and has issue living, Jaimie *b* 1967, Marie Anna *b* 1971, Teresa *b* 1974. *Residence* – Capheaton Hall, Newcastle upon Tyne.

Swinnerton (Milborne-Swinnerton-Pilkington), see Pilkington.

SYKES (GB) 1781, of Basildon, Berkshire

Sir (FRANCIS) JOHN BADCOCK SYKES, 10th *Baronet*; *b* 7 June 1942; *s* his father, *Sir* FRANCIS GODFREY, 1990; *ed* Shrewsbury, and Worcester Coll, Oxford (MA); Solicitor 1968; partner in legal firm of Townsends, Swindon & Newbury: *m* 1966, Susan Alexandra, art history lecturer, da of Adm of the Fleet Sir Edward Beckwith Ashmore, GCB, DSC, of South Cottage, Headley Down, Hants (*see* Sturdee, Bt (ext)), and has issue.

Arms – Argent, an eagle rising between three sykes or fountains proper; on a canton gules, a caduceus of the first. Crest – A demi-lady of Bengal in the complete dress of that country, holding in the dexter hand a rose gules.
Residence – Kingsbury Croft, Kingsbury St, Marlborough, Wilts SN8 1HU.

SONS LIVING

FRANCIS CHARLES, *b* 18 June 1968; *ed* Malvern, and Worcester Coll, Oxford (BA). —— Edward William, *b* 1970; *ed* Winchester, and Manchester Univ (BA). —— Alexander Henry Ashmore, *b* 1974; *ed* Marlborough, and Newcastle Univ.

SISTER LIVING

Elizabeth Ann Bowen (19 Torriano Cottages, off Leighton Rd, NW5), *b* 1936; *ed* Howells, Denbigh, Bedford Coll, London (BSc, MSc), and Edinburgh Univ (PhD); AFBPsS, CPsychol, ScFZS; Prof and Head of Sch of Psychology, Middx Univ, and Hon Research Fell, Univ Coll, London.

He is wise who is assiduous

UNCLES LIVING (*Brothers of 9th baronet*)

John Patrick (Craig View, 41/143 Stock Rd, Bicton, WA 6157, Australia), *b* 1909: *m* 1955, Patricia Cecily, who *d* 1979, da of E. P. Graham Little. —— Paul Lionel (Unit 53, Retirement Village, Charlotte St, Burradoo, NSW 2576, Australia), *b* 1915: *m* 1946, Mrs Ann Stewart, of Sydney, Australia.

AUNTS LIVING (*Sisters of 9th baronet*)

Beatrice Honora (17 Holloway Drive, Pershore, Worcs), *b* 1910: *m* 1949, Cdr Frederick D'Oyly Nind, RN, who *d* 1962, son of late Frederick William Nind. —— Mary Agatha (Flat 14, St Nicholas Hospital, Salisbury, Wilts), *b* 1913: *m* 1944, William Thomas Moran Gilbert, LRCPI, LRCSI, Colonial Medical Service, who *d* 1970, son of William Reilley Starkie Gilbert. —— Janet Edith (Flat 18, St Nicholas Hospital, Salisbury, Wilts), *b* 1916.

WIDOW LIVING OF NINTH BARONET

ETHEL FLORENCE (*Ethel, Lady Sykes*), da of Lt-Col John Sinclair Liddell, and widow of (i) Brian G. Macartney-Filgate, and (ii) Cdr W. Graeme Ogden, DSC, RNVR (ret): *m* 1985, as his 3rd wife, Sir Francis Godfrey Sykes, 9th Bt, who *d* 1990. *Residence* – ......

COLLATERAL BRANCHES LIVING

Grandchildren of late Lt-Col William Sykes, 3rd son of Rev John Heath Sykes (infra):—
Issue of late Brig John Henry Sykes, *b* 1896, *d* 1975: *m* 1st, 1919, Leila, who *d* 1970, da of late D. S. Macphee; 2ndly, 1971, Florence Cathleen, who *d* 1983, da of William Turner, and widow of (1) James Mackay, and (2) Sir (Stanley) Herbert Howard:—
Margery Hope, *b* 1921: *m* 19—, — ...... Eliot-Sutton. *Residence* – Brookfield, Silkmill Lane, Winchcombe, Glos GL54 5HZ.

Issue of late Richard Alexander Sykes, *b* 1912, *d* 1981: *m* 1942, Freda Serita (20 Ashdale Av, Pershore, Worcs), da of Lewis Field:—
William David (18 Markby Close, Duxford, Cambs), *b* 1946; *ed* St Edward's Sch, Oxford: *m* 1978, Josephine Helen White, and has issue living, Archie Frederick William *b* 1984, — Chloë Alexandra, *b* 1981. —— Anthony Richard John (Willoughby House, High St, Dorchester-on-Thames, Oxon), *b* 1950; *ed* St Edward's Sch, Oxford: *m* 1982, Tessa Cox, and has issue living, Thomas Neill Alexander, *b* 1984, — Amanda Marie, *b* 1986.

Grandson of late Frederick Sykes, 4th son of Rev John Heath Sykes, yst son of Rev William Sykes, 2nd son of 2nd baronet:—
   Issue of late Frederick Heath Cyril Sykes, b 1897, d 1959: m 1934, Judith Helen, who d 1982, da of Wyndham Henry Stubbs, of The Leasowes, Cressage, Salop:—
Harry Wyndham, b 1936: m 1956, Magdalena (Lena) Amelia, da of Edward Julius Schulze, of Grande Prairie, Alberta, and has issue living, Ronald Frederick, b 1963, — Dianne Lea, b 1957: m 1978 (m diss 1986), Martin Lavoie, and has issue living, Harvest Serena b 1979, Yarrow Lee (a da) b 1983, — Patricia Lynn, b 1960.

Granddaughter of late Rev John Heath Sykes (ante):—
   Issue of late Alfred Sykes, b 1872, d 1954: m 1902, Scènie Marguerite Genelle, who d 19—:—
Marcedèsse Doyley, b 1904: m 1st, 1932, R. Alston Jones; 2ndly, 1947, Brock R. Darling, and has issue living, (by 1st m) George Sykes, b 1935.

Grandchildren of late Edward Ernest Sykes, 7th son of late Rev John Heath Sykes (ante):—
   Issue of late Clement Edward Heath Sykes, b 1911, d 1987: m 1951, Isabel L., da of Robert Parry, of N Wales:—
Sean Edward Heath, b 1952. —— David Robert Heath, b 1954. —— Sheila Anne Heath, b 1952.

This family have held lands in England since before 1220, in which year they were described as being in possession of land previously held by them. The 1st baronet, Sir Francis, of Ackworth Park, Yorkshire, and subsequently of Basildon Park, Berks, Chief Governor of Cossimbazar, Bengal, and Resident at the Court of the Nawab of Bengal, was successively MP for Shaftesbury and Wallingford. The 2nd baronet also sat as MP for Wallingford. The 8th baronet, the Rev Sir Frederick John was V of Stoke Canon, Exeter 1936-46. The 9th baronet, Sir Francis Godfrey, was Regional Sec (Shropshire, Cheshire, Staffs) of the Country Landowners' Assocn 1956-71.

SYKES (GB) 1783, of Sledmere, Yorkshire

Sir TATTON CHRISTOPHER MARK SYKES, 8th Baronet; b 24 Dec 1943; s his father, Lt-Col Sir (MARK TATTON) RICHARD TATTON-SYKES 1978; ed Eton, and Univ d'Aix-Marseilles, and Royal Agric Coll, Cirencester.

Arms – Argent, a chevron sable between three sykes or fountains proper. Crest – A demi-triton issuant from flags or reeds, blowing a shell, and wreathed about the temples with like flags or reeds, all proper.
Seat – Sledmere, Driffield, E Yorkshire.

BROTHERS LIVING

JEREMY JOHN (The Villa, Sledmere, Driffield, E Yorks), b 8 March 1946; ed Ampleforth: m 1982, Pamela June, only da of late Thomas Wood. —— Christopher Simon (96 Brondesbury Villas, NW6 6AD), b 1948; ed Eton: m 1st, 1982 (m diss 1997), Belinda Susan Mary, yr da of Frank Thomas Robertson Giles (see E De La Warr); 2ndly, 1997, Mrs Isabella Bywater, 3rd da of Thomas Charles Gerard Stacey of 128 Kensington Church St, W8, and has issue living (by 1st m), Joseph Francis Richard, b 1990, — Lily, b 1984. —— (Richard) Nicholas Bernard (17 Thames Walk, Hester Rd, SW11 4AN), b 1953; ed Ampleforth.

SISTERS LIVING

Arabella Lilian Virginia, b 1950: m 1975, Kevin Delahunty, of Scotts Farm, Stockley, Calne, Wilts, and has issue living, Damian John Richard, b 1976. —— Henrietta Caroline Rose, b 1957: m 1986, Nigel Kenneth Cayzer of Thriepley House, Lundie, Dundee, 2nd son of Anthony Malcolm Galliers-Pratt, CBE, and has issue (see Cayzer, Bt).

COLLATERAL BRANCH LIVING

Issue of late Christopher Hugh Sykes, FRSL, author, 2nd son of 6th baronet, b 1907, d 1986: m 1936, Camilla Georgiana, who d 1983, da of late Maj-Gen Sir Thomas Wentworth Russell, KBE, CMG (see D Bedford, colls).—
Mark Richard, b 1937; ed Eton, and Ch Ch, Oxford: m 1st, 1962 (m diss 1965), Helen, only da of late Dr Arthur Norman Homewood, of Melbourne, Aust; 2ndly, 1968, Valerie, da of Robert Goad, and has issue living (by 2nd m), Thomas, b 1974, — Frederick, b 1983, — Joshua, b 1988, — Lucy, b 1969, — Victoria, b (twin) 1969; journalist for American Vogue, — Alice, b 1972.

The 1st baronet, the Rev Sir Mark, was son of Richard Sykes, an eminent merchant in Hull; the 2nd baronet, Sir Christopher, sat as MP for Beverley; the third baronet, Sir Mark, was High Sheriff and MP for York 1807-20; and the 4th baronet was the well-known sportsman, Sir Tatton Sykes. Sir Tatton, 5th baronet, was High Sheriff of Yorkshire

1869. The 6th baronet, Sir Mark, was Private Sec to Ch Sec for Ireland 1904-05, MP for Central Div of Hull (C) 1911-18, and for Kingston-upon-Hull, Central Div Dec 1918-19, and served during 1914-18 War as Col 5th Batn Yorkshire Regt, and as Assist Sec to War Cabinet; Signatory to the Sykes-Picot Agreement 1917. The 7th baronet, Lt-Col Sir (Mark Tatton) Richard was High Sheriff of Yorks 1948, and Pres of E Riding Georgian Soc and Northern Counties Concert Soc. He adopted the surname of Tatton-Sykes by deed poll 1977.

SYKES (UK) 1921, of Kingsknowes, Galashiels, co Selkirk

Sir JOHN (CHARLES ANTHONY LE GALLAIS) SYKES, 3rd *Baronet*, el son of late Capt Stanley Edgar Sykes, Duke of Wellington's Regt, yr son of 1st baronet; *b* 19 April 1928; *s* his uncle, *Sir* (BENJAMIN) HUGH, 1974; *ed* Churchers Coll; export merchant (ret): *m* 1954 (*m diss* 1970), Aitha Isobel, yr da of Lionel Dean, of New Mill, Huddersfield.

Arms – Per chevron gules and sable, in chief two sykes (fountains) proper, and in base a fleece or. **Crest** – A cubit arm, habited in a khaki sleeve and holding in the hand a teazle slipped and leaved proper.

WIDOW LIVING OF SECOND BARONET

AUDREY WINIFRED (*Audrey, Lady Sykes*) (Kestrel Grove, Hive Rd, Bushey Heath, Herts WD2 1JQ), da of Frederick Charles Thompson, of Cricklewood, NW2: *m* 1935, Sir (Benjamin) Hugh Sykes, 2nd Bt, who *d* 1974.

COLLATERAL BRANCH LIVING

Issue of late Michael le Gallais Sykes, yr son of late Capt Stanley Edgar Sykes (ante), *b* 1932, *d* 1981: *m* 1st, 1953, Joan, only da of Cecil Groome, of 14 Highfield Rd, Nuthall, Notts; 2ndly, 1976, Jacqueline Susan, only da of Capt C. Melia:—
(By 1st *m*) DAVID MICHAEL (The Chestnuts, Middle Lane, Nether Broughton, Leics), *b* 10 June 1954: *m* 1st, 1974 (*m diss* 1987), Susan Elizabeth, 3rd da of G. W. Hall; 2ndly, 1987, Margaret Lynne, only da of John Thomas McGreavy, and has issue living (by 1st *m*), Stephen David *b* 14 Dec 1978, — (by 2nd *m*) Joanna Lauren, *b* 1986. —— Christopher Cary, *b* 1959: *m* 1st, 1978 (*m diss* 1984), Tina, da of —; 2ndly, 1989, Anne Marie, da of —, and has issue living (by 1st *m*), Lisa Tina, *b* 1979, — Kelly, *b* 1981.

The 1st baronet, Sir Charles Sykes, KBE (son of Benjamin Sykes), was a woollen manufacturer, MP for Huddersfield (*Co L*) 1918-22, and Govt Dir of Textile Prodcn 1914-18, for which he was ktd.

SYNGE (UK) 1801, of Kiltrough
(Name pronounced "Sing")

We sing of heavenly things

Sir ROBERT CARSON SYNGE, 8th *Baronet*, son of late Neale Hutchinson Synge, 2nd son of 6th baronet; *b* 4 May 1922; *s* his uncle, *Sir* ROBERT MILLINGTON, 1942: *m* 1944, Dorothy Jean, da of Theodore Johnson, of Cloverdale, British Columbia, and has issue.

Arms – Quarterly: 1st and 4th, azure, three millstones proper; 2nd and 3rd, argent, an eagle displayed with two heads sable, beaked and legged gules. **Crest** – Out of a ducal coronet or, an eagle's claw proper.
Residence – 19364, Fraser Valley Highway, RR4, Langley, BC, Canada.

DAUGHTERS LIVING

Donna Joan, *b* 1946: *m* 1967, Richard David Harvey. ——— Wendy Marleen, *b* 1949.

SISTER LIVING

Patricia Neale, *b* 1924: *m* 1948, Emerson Edgar Barden. *Residence* – 14227, 110th Avenue, North Surrey, British Columbia.

AUNT LIVING (*Daughter of 6th baronet*)

Jessica Helen (c/o Lloyds Bank, High St, Berkhamsted, Herts), *b* 1914: *m* 1940 (*m diss* 1949), Fl-Lt Alfred Davidson Colin Cleugh Fair, RAF.

COLLATERAL BRANCHES LIVING

Issue of late Edward Synge, yst son of 6th baronet, *b* 1882, *d* 1966: *m* 1901, Agnes Emily, da of James Jelley:—
NEALE FRANCIS, *b* 28 Feb 1917: *m* 1939, Katherine Caroline Bowes, and has issue living, Allen James Edward, *b* 1942, — Sharon Eileen, *b* 1943. ——— Molly Eileen, *b* 1908: *m* 1929, Raymond Augustus McCarthy, and has issue living, Raymond Edward, *b* 1930: *m* 1950, Helen, da of Roy Dagg, of Prince George, BC, and has issue living, Sharon Patricia *b* 1951: *m* 1973, Gerhard Mueller (and has issue living, Marcus Raymond George *b* 1978, Christa, *b* 1974), — Stanley Norman (1075 Lamar Place, Kamloops, BC, Canada), *b* 1941: *m* 1961, Karen Maureen, da of Maurice Gregoire, of Penticton, BC, and has issue living, Gregory Douglas *b* 1967, Edward Morris *b* 1970, Judith Maureen *b* 1962.

Granddaughter of late Edward Synge (ante):—
Issue of late Edward Synge, *b* 1902, *d* 1928: *m* 1925, Alma (Apt 206, 1050, W 10th Av, Vancouver, BC), da of Martin Hansen:—
Marjorie Irene, *b* 1926: *m* 1946, William Thomas Kidner, of 1005, Beaumont St, N, Vancouver, BC, Canada, and has issue living, Jacquelyn Ann, *b* 1951, — Patricia Lynn, *b* 1952.

Grandson of late Major Robert Follett Synge, el son of late Rev Robert Synge, 3rd son of 1st baronet:—
Issue of late Lieut-Col Robert Follett Muter Foster Millington Synge, *b* 1857, *d* 1941: *m* 1884 (*m diss* 1900), Charlotte Granville, who *d* 1942, da of Maj-Gen William James Stuart, formerly RE:—
Alan Hamilton Stuart, *b* 1886: *ed* Wellington Coll; European War 1914-19 with RFC: *m* 1920, Alice May Bradley, of Washington, USA.

Grandchildren of late Francis Julian Synge, 2nd son of William Webb Follett Synge (infra):—
Issue of late Capt Robert Millington Synge, *b* 1894, *d* 1964: *m* 1922, Cristabel Etrenne, who *d* 1988, da of late Charles Lyon Liddell, of The Place House, Peasmarsh, Sussex (*see* B Ravensworth, colls):—
Allen John Millington (2 Diamond Terrace, Greenwich SE10 8QN), *b* 1930; *ed* Trin Coll, Dublin: *m* 1955, Olive Rachel, da of Thomas Weir, of Ballymena, co Antrim, and has issue living, Daniel Thomas Millington, *b* 1963, — Timothy Auchmuty, *b* 1968, — Frances Clare, *b* 1959: *m* 1986, Bernard Fitzgerald Clark, of Goose Cottage, 14 Fearon St, Greenwich SE10 0RS, yr son of late Richard Clark, of Dibden Purlieu, Southampton. ——— Gillian Frances, *b* 1933: *m* 1952, Col George Stanley Ames, US Marine Corps, of 305 Old Pickard Rd, Concord, Mass, USA, and has issue living, Richard Millington, *b* 1955, *ed* Gordonstoun, Duke Univ, and Georgia Univ: *m* 1982, Laura Mahone, da of Thomas Mahone Tolleson, of Atlanta, Georgia, USA, and has issue living, Alexander Millington *b* 1985, Ian Mahone *b* 1988, Hannah Suzanne *b* 1987, — John Bruton, *b* 1960: *m* 1989, Donna Jean, da of Mario Chiaravelotti, of N Conway, NH, and has issue living, Evan George *b* 1991, Shanna Mae *b* 1993, — Robert Oakes *b* 1969: *ed* Gordonstoun, and Rice Univ, — Elizabeth Whiting, *b* 1953, *ed* Concord Academy, and Duke Univ: *m* 1984, Alan Thomas Macdonald, son of Thomas Hugh Macdonald, of Canton, Mass, USA, and has issue living, Hugh Oakes Ames *b* 1986, Adrian Synge *b* 1988.

Grandsons of late William Makepeace Thackeray Synge, yst son of William Webb Follett Synge, 4th son of late Rev Robert Synge (ante):—
Issue of late Capt William Alfred Thackeray Synge, *b* 1893, *d* 1968: *m* 1920, Hilda Marjorie, who *d* 1967, da of Ebenezer Pike, formerly of Kilcrenagh, co Cork:—
Brian Thackeray (4 Pembroke Close, Grosvenor Cres, SW1), *b* 1920; formerly Hon Maj Irish Gds; a Serving Brother of Order of St John of Jerusalem: *m* 1st, 1945 (*m diss* 1970), Alison Patricia, da of Brig Victor Francis Staples Hawkins, DSO, MC, late Lancashire Fusiliers; 2ndly, 1970, Mrs Pamela Columbine de Meo, and has issue living, (by 1st *m*) Barry Edward Thackeray (c/o 4 Pembroke Close, Grosvenor Cres, SW1), *b* 1949: *m* 1986 (*m diss* 1990), Moira French, da of Thomas Macdonald, of Ancrum, Roxburghshire, — Mark Millington, *b* 1953: *m* 1984, Clare Victoria, elder da of John Bulkley Herbert Francis (*see* Stephenson, Bt, colls), of Cowley, nr Cheltenham, Glos, and has issue living, Annabel *b* 1987, Georgina Rose *b* 1989, — (Norah) Melanie, *b* 1947: *m* 1st, 1969 (*m diss* 1976) Anthony Elliott; 2ndly, 1984, Charles Ross Birkett, of 29 Rozel Rd, Clapham Old Town, SW4 0EY, and has issue living, (by 1st *m*) Rupert Francis William *b*

1970, Francesca Elisabeth *b* 1972, (by 2nd *m*) (Charles) John Ross *b* 1987, Alice Emily Rose *b* 1984. —— †John Millington, *b* 1923, *d* 1999.

The family of Synge was seated at Bridgnorth early in the 16th century, the original name of Millington having been changed to Synge. The Rt Rev Dr Samuel Hutchinson, Lord Bishop of Kilala, was father of Sir James Hutchinson, 1st Bt (*cr* 1782, ext, 1906) who sat as MP for Jamestown in Irish Parliament. The Rev Sir Samuel Synge, 3rd Bt, grand-nephew of the 1st and 2nd baronets, *s* under special remainder, and assumed the additional surname and arms of Hutchinson; his 2nd brother, Robert, was *cr* a baronet as above. Sir Edward Synge, 3rd Bt (*cr* 1801), was High Sheriff of co Cork 1844.

LAWSON-TANCRED (E) 1662, of Boroughbridge, Yorkshire

Aimez Dieu
Love God

Sir HENRY LAWSON-TANCRED, 10th *Baronet*; *b* 12 Feb 1924; *s* his father, *Major Sir* THOMAS SELBY, 1945; *ed* Stowe, and Jesus Coll, Camb; a JP of W Riding of Yorks; 1939-45 War as Flying Officer, RAFVR: *m* 1st, 1950, Jean Veronica, who *d* 1970, yst da of late Gerald Robert Foster, of Stockeld Park, Wetherby, Yorks (*see* Ogilvy, Bt, 1955 Edn); 2ndly, 1978, Susan Dorothy Marie-Gabrielle, 2nd da of late Sir Kenelm Henry Ernest Cayley, 10th Bt, and formerly wife of Maldwin Andrew Cyril Drummond (*see* E Perth, colls), and has issue by 1st *m*.

𝕬rms – Argent, a chevron between three escallops gules. 𝕮rest – An olive tree fructed proper.
Residence – Aldborough Manor, Boroughbridge, Yorkshire YO5 9EP.

SONS LIVING (*By 1st marriage*)

ANDREW PETER, *b* 18 Feb 1952; *ed* Eton, and Leeds Univ; Bar Middle Temple 1977. *Residence* – 13 Musgrave Crescent, SW6 4PT. —— Rupert Thomas, *b* 1953; *ed* Gordonstoun. —— James Gilchrist Henry, *b* 1956; *ed* Trin Coll, Glenalmond. —— Gerald Nicholas, *b* 1961; *ed* Trin Coll, Glenalmond. —— Alastair David Piers, *b* 1964; *ed* Bootham Sch, York: *m* 1993, Virginia C., only da of Col Joseph Hordern, OBE, of Radwinter, Essex, and has issue living, Robert Henry Montague, *b* 1999, — Georgina Mary Christina, *b* 1997.

DAUGHTER LIVING (*By 1st marriage*)

Finella Mary, *b* 1959: *m* 1991, Nicholas S. Orr, yr son of late George Alistair Orr, of Montgreenan, Ayrshire, and has issue living, James Charles Tancred, *b* 1995, — Rosamond Anne Jane, *b* 1993.

SISTER LIVING

Pauline, *b* 1916: *m* 1937, (Frank) Douglas Nicholson, TD, who *d* 1984, and has issue living, *Sir* Paul Douglas (Quarry Hill, Brancepeth, co Durham), *b* 1938; *ed* Harrow, and Clare Coll, Camb; late Lieut Coldm Gds; Chm Vaux Group plc 1976-99; High Sheriff co Durham 1980, DL 1980, and Lord Lieut since 1997; Ktd 1993: *m* 1970, Sarah, yst da of Sir Edmund Castell Bacon, KG, KBE, TD, 13th Bt, and has issue living, Lucy *b* 1972, — Nigel Frank, *b* 1940: *m* 1982, Mrs S.A. Barnes, of Durban, S Africa, — Andrew, *b* 1945: *m* 1972, Angela, da of Vice-Adm Denis Bryan Harvey Wildish, CB, and has issue living, Rosemary *b* 1975, Caroline *b* 1976, — Mark Thomas, *b* 1950: *m* 1996, Lucille Diana Butler, — Frank, *b* 1954: *m* 1986, Lavinia Margaret Grace, da of Nigel John Ivo Stourton, OBE (*see* B Mowbray, colls), and has issue living, Simon Douglas *b* 1989, Hugo Frank *b* 1991, Edward Ivo *b* 1994. *Residence* – Harbour House, Plawsworth, nr Chester-le-Street, co Durham.

COLLATERAL BRANCHES LIVING

Issue of late *Rev* Christopher Lawson-Tancred, yst son of 9th baronet, *b* (twin) 1924, *d* 1998: *m* 1951, Cerise Eyre Campbell (3 Minterne House, Minterne Magna, Cerne Abbas, Dorset DT2 7AX), el da of late Sir Hugh Eyre Campbell Beaver:—
Hugh Christopher (97 Third Av, W10), *b* 1955: *m* 1993, Emily C.A.R., da of James Macaskie, of Yarlington, Som, and has issue living, Josephine Rose, *b* 1993. —— Cerise Elinor, *b* 1952: *m* 1988, David Holmes, MRCVS, son of Dudley Holmes, and has issue living, Finella Harriet Rachel, *b* 1991. —— Olivia Eyre, *b* 1957: *m* 1986, Richard L. Bourne, Cdr RN, of Petvins Cottage, Haselbury Plucknet, Som, son of Leonard Richard Thomas Bourne, and has issue living, Simon Richard, *b* 1989, — Nicholas Hugh, *b* 1992.

Grandson of late Clement William Tancred, 4th son of 7th baronet:—
Issue of late Christopher Humphrey Tancred, OBE, *b* 1888, *d* 1971: *m* 1st, 1915 (*m diss* 1923), Gladys Winifred, da of late Walter Chandler; 2ndly, 1927 (*m diss* 1938), Margery Agnes, da of late Samuel Henry Slater, CMG, CIE; 3rdly, 1938 (*m diss* 1943), Priscilla Nöel Cecilia, da of John A. Barclay, of New York; 4thly, 1944, Sadika (21 Lexham Gdns, W8 5JJ), da of R. Miligui, of Cairo, Egypt:—
(By 2nd *m*) Anthony Christopher, *b* 1930; *ed* Eton.

Grandchildren of Harry George Tancred (infra):—
Issue of late Bertram Selby Tancred, *b* 1895, *d* 1965: *m* 1924, Elsa (83 Young St, New Plymouth, NZ), da of A. V. Sims:—
Rex Selby Assheton (12B Oleander Pl, Bell Block, New Plymouth, NZ), *b* 1925: *m* 1948, Shirley Edith, da of H. Box, and has issue living, Philip Rex, *b* 1952, — Linda Joanne, *b* 1954: *m* 1972, Allan John Brooking, son of Frederick John Brooking, of New Plymouth, and has issue living, Daniel John *b* 1976, Jemma Claire *b* 1977, Talia Louise, *b* 1979, — Susan Shirley, *b* 1955: *m* 1975, Stephan Thomas Kerr (King Rd, RD6 Inglewood, NZ), son of Kelvyn Thomas Kerr, of New Plymouth, and has issue living, Alisha Maree *b* 1981, Rachel Lee, *b* 1983. —— Lyle Ashley (205 Frankley Rd, New Plymouth, NZ), *b* 1933: *m* 1959, Beverley Ethel, da of Nelson Howard Bishop, of New Plymouth, NZ, and has issue living, Stephen Ashley (4 Barry Lane, New Plymouth, NZ), *b* 1962: *m* 1994, Stacey Joan, da of Ivan John Woodward, of New Plymouth, NZ, and has issue living, Brock Ashley *b* 1998, Samantha Joan *b* 1993, Aleisha Jade *b* 1995. —— Elwyn Elsa, *b* 1927: *m* 1954, Archibald James Gamble, of 20 Cousins Av East, Foxton Beach, Wellington, NZ, and has an adopted son, Craig Anthony, *b* 1965.

Issue of late Cecil Mount-Stewart-Tancred, *b* 1884, *d* 19—: *m* 1907:—
Emmie, *b* 1908.

Issue of late Harry George Tancred, 6th and yst son of 7th baronet, *b* 1858, *d* 1945: *m* 1st, 1881, Emily Alicia de Courcy, who *d* 1907, elder da of late Major Slingsby Bell, of Purneah, India, and the Bungalow, Napier, New Zealand; 2ndly, 1908, Rosie Elphinstone, da of late Major Slingsby Bell, and widow of Henry Warren, of New Zealand:—
(By 1st *m*) Zillah Selby, *b* 1893: *m* 1915, Raymond F. M. Atkinson, and has issue living, Veronica Selby *b* 1915: *m* 1943, Gary Elmer Gorsline, of 4304 Jeffries Av, Burbank, Cal, 91505 USA, and has issue living, Victoria Elizabeth Selby *b* 1945: *m* 1963, David Wayne Maske, of 7550 Coldwater Canyon, N Hollywood, California 91605, USA, and has issue living, Michael Andrew (6489 Hope St, Simi Valley, California 93063, USA) *b* 1964, Douglas Adam (2374 Timber Lane Circle, Simi Valley, California 93063, USA) *b* 1965: *m* 1988, Jennifer Ellen Weyand (and has issue living, Kirstie Adrianna *b* 1991), Julie Michelle *b* 1970: *m* 1992, Andi Costin Gorgescu, of 12203 Magnolia Blvd, Apt 106, Valley Village, California 91607, USA (and has issue living, Christopher David *b* 1992). *Residence* – 4304 Jeffries Av, Burbank, California 91505, USA.

This family is descended from Richard Tankard, who soon after the Conquest was possessed of lands at Borough-bridge, where still remains the ancient family house. A Christopher Tancred founded a retreat for poor gentlemen at Whixley, and also scholarships at Oxford, Cambridge, and Lincoln's Inn. The 9th baronet, Major Sir Thomas Selby, Indian Army, assumed by deed poll the additional surname of Lawson 1914, having *m* 1912 Margery Elinor, el da and co-heir of Andrew Sherlock Lawson, of Aldborough Manor, Yorks. Sir John Grant Lawson, 1st Bt (*cr* 1905), was his yr brother.

TANGYE (UK) 1912, of Glendorgal, St Columb Minor, Cornwall (Extinct 1969)

Sir BASIL RICHARD GILZEAN TANGYE, 2nd and last *Baronet*.

DAUGHTER LIVING OF SECOND BARONET

Gitta Clarisse Gilzean, *b* 1928. *Residence* – 4 Farquhar Rd, Edgbaston, Birmingham.

Tapps-Gervis-Meyrick, see Meyrick.

TATE (UK) 1898, of Park Hill, Streatham, co London

Sir (HENRY) SAXON TATE, CBE, 5th *Baronet*; *b* 28 Nov 1931; *s* his father, *Sir* HENRY, TD, DL, 1994; *ed* Eton, and Ch Ch, Oxford; Lt Life Gds (Army Emergency Reserve); Dir Tate & Lyle plc 1956-99, Chm Exec Cttee 1973-78, Man Dir 1978-80, Vice-Chm 1980-82; Chief Exec Offr Redpath Industries Ltd Canada 1965-73; Dir Tate Appointments Ltd since 1982, Chm 1991-96; Dir other Cos; FIMgt 1975; CBE 1991: *m* 1st, 1953 (*m diss* 1975), Sheila Ann, who *d* 1987, eldest da of late Duncan Robertson, of Llantysilio, Llangollen (*see* Williams-Wynn, Bt, 1985 Edn); 2ndly, 1975, Virginia Joan Sturm, and has issue by 1st *m*.

𝕬rms – Ermine, on a pale invected azure between four Cornish choughs proper two roses argent. 𝕮rest – A dexter arm embowed and vested azure, cuffed or, the arm charged with two roses argent, the hand grasping a pineapple erect slipped proper between two ears of wheat saltirewise all proper. *Residence* – 26 Cleaver Square, SE11 4EA. *Club* – Buck's.

Thincke and thancke

SONS LIVING (*By 1st marriage*)

EDWARD NICOLAS, *b* 2 July 1966. —— Duncan Saxon, *b* 1968. —— John William, *b* 1969. —— Paul Henry, *b* (twin) 1969.

BROTHER LIVING

(William) Nicolas, *b* 1934; *ed* Eton, and Ch Ch, Oxford; Lt Gren Gds (Emergency Reserve): *m* 1960, Sarah Rose, eldest da of Lt-Col Angus John Campbell Rose, of Dunira Garden House, Comrie, Perthshire, and has had issue, Rupert Sebastian, *b* 1962, — a son, *b* and *d* 1966, — Melissa Nairne, *b* 1964, *d* 1969, — Georgina Nairne, *b* 1969. *Residence* – 69 Claylands Rd, SW8 1PJ.

WIDOW LIVING OF FOURTH BARONET

EDNA STOKES (*Dowager Lady Tate*): *m* 1988, as his 2nd wife, Sir Henry Tate, 4th Bt, TD, DL, who *d* 1994. *Residence* – The Cottage, Galltfaenan, Trefnant, Clwyd.

COLLATERAL BRANCHES LIVING

Grandchildren of late Alfred Herbert Tate, 3rd son of 2nd baronet:—
Issue of late Louis William Tate, *b* 1911, *d* 1986: *m* 1934, Mary Christine (Little Sadlers, Grayswood Rd, Haslemere, Surrey), da of late R. C. Bolton, of Anstey Lane, Alton, Hants:—
Jeremy Louis (Old Quarry Rise, Hargate Hill, Glossop, Derbys), *b* 1937: *m* 1961, Rosemary Helen, da of D. Collins, of East Drive, Sawbridgeworth, Herts, and has issue living, William James Louis, *b* 1965, — Julia Rosemary, *b* 1963, — Emma Margaret Rebecca, *b* 1976.

Issue of late Francis Herbert Tate, *b* 1913, *d* 1998: *m* 1937, Esther Frances (Little Wissett, Hook Heath Gdns, Woking, Surrey GU22 0QG), da of late Sir (John) Bromhead Matthews, KC:—
David Anthony (Stone Cross House, Crowborough, E Sussex TN6 3SH), *b* 1941: *m* 1969, Jennifer, da of Mrs Evelyn MacAndrews, of Littlestone, Kent, and has issue living, Rupert David, *b* 1974, — Matthew Francis, *b* 1976. —— Caroline Frances TATE (14 Balaclava Rd, Surbiton, Surrey KT6 5PN), *b* 1946; has resumed her maiden surname: *m* 1st, 1973 (*m diss* 1984), Bruce Jerrit; 2ndly, 1984 (*m diss* 1991), Guy William Brisbane, and has issue living, (by 1st *m*) Benedict Sinclair, *b* 1976, — Giles Zachary, *b* 1978, — (by 2nd *m*) Tessa Jennifer, *b* 1986. —— Marianne Esther, *b* 1949.

Issue of late John Frederick Peter Tate, *b* 1923, *d* 1989: *m* 1949, Celia Judith (7 Fisherton Island, Salisbury, Wilts SP2 7TG), da of late Sir Adrian Corbett:—
Christopher John (The Coach House, Langton Hall, W Langton, Leics LE16 7TY), *b* 1953: *m* 1978 (*m diss* 1991), Jane, eldest da of Capt A. Bicket, of Derwas, Dolwen, Abergele, Clwyd, and has issue living, Alexander John, *b* 1984, — Daisy Virginia, *b* 1981. —— Anne Teresa, *b* 1951; FRCR: *m* 1982, Prof Rodney H. Reznek, FRCR, FRCP, of 15 Park Avenue North, N8 7RU. —— Nicola Helen, *b* 1955: *m* 1976, Michael Van der Gucht, of Plume House, Up Nately, Basingstoke, Hants RG27 9PR, and has issue living, Charles Graham, *b* 1980, — Benjamin Michael, *b* 1985, — Sarah Celia, *b* 1982, — Victoria Anthea, *b* 1992. —— Sophia Louise, *b* 1958: *m* 1986, Capt Thomas Wright, RGJ (c/o John Swire & Sons (HK) Ltd, PO Box 1, 9P0 Hong Kong), and has issue living, Matthew Adam Christopher, *b* 1989, — Katharine Elizabeth, *b* 1992.

Granddaughters of late Henry Tate, 6th son of 1st baronet:—
Issue of late Capt Henry Burton Tate, *b* 1883, *d* 1962: *m* 1st, 1909 (*m diss* 1925), Ida Guendolen, who *d* 1969, da of Robin H. Legge; 2ndly, 1925 (*m diss* 1944), Mavis Constance, who *d* 1947, da of Guy Weir Hogg (B Magheramorne, colls); 3rdly, 1944, Gwen, who *d* 1957, da of late Herbert Edwards, of The Old Hall, Findern, Derbys:—
(By 1st *m*) Julia Elizabeth Mary, *b* 1919: *m* 1959, Paul Georges Bernard, of 22 Rue des Réservoirs, Versailles, France.

Issue of late Lt-Col Arthur Wignall Tate, DSO, *b* 1888, *d* 1939: *m* 1910, Violet Elaine, da of F. W. Few:—

Monica, *b* 1912: *m* 1935, Douglas Gurney Pelly (*see* Pelly, Bt, colls). *Residence* – Swaynes Hall, Widdington, near Newport, Essex.

Issue of late George Booth Tate, 7th son of 1st baronet, *b* 1857, *d* 1936: *m* 1884, Edith Katherine, who *d* 1937, da of James Walker Yates, formerly of Ashton-on-Mersey, Cheshire:—
Jane Marjorie, *b* 1895: *m* 1920, Redvers Arthur Oldham, who *d* 1960, and has issue living. *Residence* – Birchwood, Sunningdale, Berks.

Granddaughter of late George Booth Tate (ante):—
Issue of late George Vernon Tate, MC, *b* 1890, *d* 1955: *m* 1922, Evelyn Victoria Anne, who *d* 1979, da of Walter Robert Chandler, and widow (1) of 25th Baron de Clifford, and (2) of Capt Arthur Boy Stock:—
Pamela Aloysia, *b* 1923: *m* 1946, Henry Forbes, son of Adm of the Fleet Sir Charles Morton Forbes, GCB, DSO, and has issue living, Timothy John (Seend Head House, Seend, Devizes, Wilts SN12 6PP), *b* 1947; *ed* Stowe: *m* 1973, Rosemary Elisabeth Balliol, da of Humphrey John Rodham Balliol Salmon, and has issue living, Charles Morton *b* 1975, Edward (Ned) Alexander *b* 1983, — Amanda Aloysia, *b* 1950: *m* 1973, Peter Mackelean Woodroffe, of 13 Cadogan St, SW3 2PP, and has issue living, Justin Mackelean *b* 1977, Clifford Derry *b* 1979, — Vanessa Christina, *b* 1955: *m* 19—, John Kelly, of Glenwood, 5 King Edward Rise, Ascot, Berks SL5 8JZ. *Residence* – 5 Lyne Place Manor, Bridge Lane, Virginia Water, Surrey GU25 4ED.

Sir Henry Tate, 1st Bt, the sugar magnate, gave the Tate Gallery to the nation. Sir William Henry Tate, 2nd Bt, was High Sheriff of Lancashire 1907. Sir Henry Tate, 4th Bt, TD, was Co Councillor for Rutland 1958-74, a DL 1964, and High Sheriff of Rutland 1949-50.

TAYLOR (UK) 1963, of Cawthorne in the West Riding, co York (Extinct 1972)

Sir WILLIAM JOHNSON TAYLOR, CBE, 1st and last *Baronet*.

DAUGHTERS LIVING OF FIRST BARONET

Pauline Mary, *b* 1932: *m* 1963, Dr Brian Kenneth Schlotel, of 35 The Grove, Woking, Surrey GU21 4AF, and has issue living, Mary Julia Taylor, *b* 1964. — Helen Rosalind Taylor, *b* 1967. — Carol Margaret, *b* 1937: *m* 1959, Robert Nigel David Bruce, of 20 Jackson's Edge Rd, Disley, Stockport, Cheshire SK12 2JL, and has issue living, Robert Torfine William, *b* 1962, — Robert Thurstan Taylor, *b* 1965, — Robert Andrew Johnson, *b* 1967, — Katherine Isabelle Zoe, *b* (twin) 1967.

STUART TAYLOR (UK) 1917, of Kennington, co London

Sir NICHOLAS RICHARD STUART TAYLOR, 4th *Baronet*; *b* 14 Jan 1952; *s* his father *Sir* RICHARD LAURENCE, 1978; *ed* Bradfield; Solicitor 1977: *m* 1984 (*m diss* 1999), Malvena Elizabeth, BSc, MB, BS, FRCA, only da of Daniel David Charles Sullivan, of E Finchley, London, and has issue.

Arms – Per pale gules and azure a fox's brush erect or between two bezants in fesse. Crest – A demi-fox gules tailed or, supporting a banner also gules, charged with a seax or.
Address – White Lodge, Hambrook, Chichester, W Sussex PO18 8RG.

DAUGHTERS LIVING

Virginia Caterina, *b* 1989. —— Olivia Malvena, *b* 1991.

SISTER LIVING

(Anne) Caroline, *b* 1955; *ed* St Michael's Sch, Petworth, and Grenoble Univ; Chief Exec Ski Club of Great Britain since 1997.

WIDOW LIVING OF THIRD BARONET

IRIS MARY (*Iris, Lady Stuart Taylor*) (White Lodge, Hambrook, Chichester, Sussex PO18 8RG), da of the Rev Edwin John Gargery: *m* 1950, Sir Richard Laurence Stuart Taylor, 3rd Bt, who *d* 1978.

Sir Frederick Taylor, 1st Bt, MD, FRCP, was an eminent Consulting Physician, and Pres of R Coll of Physicians. He was *s* in 1920 by his son Sir Eric Stuart Taylor, OBE, MD, MRCP, who *d* 20 Oct 1977, having assumed the addl surname of Stuart. His son, Sir Richard Laurence Stuart Taylor, who served in World War II with RAC and R Glos Hussars, was Man Dir of Powell Duffryn Fuels Ltd. He *d* 10 Sept 1978.

WORSLEY-TAYLOR (UK) 1917, of Moreton Hall, Parish of Whalley, Co Palatine of Lancaster (Extinct 1958)

Sir FRANCIS EDWARD WORSLEY-TAYLOR, 4th and last *Baronet*.

DAUGHTER LIVING OF SECOND BARONET

Dorothea Margaret, *b* 1920. *Residence* – The Old Forge, Bashall Eaves, Clitheroe, Lancs.

DAUGHTER LIVING OF THIRD BARONET

Annette Pamela, *b* 1944: *m* 1997, Anthony Sheil. *Residence* – 57 Drayton Gdns, SW10 9RU.

TEMPLE (UK) 1876, of The Nash, Kempsey, co Worcester

Templa quam dilecta

How beloved are thy temples

Sir RICHARD ANTONY PURBECK TEMPLE, MC, 4th *Baronet*; *b* 19 Jan 1913; *s* his father, *Sir* RICHARD DURAND, DSO, 1962; *ed* Stowe, and Trin Hall, Camb; sometime Maj King's Roy Rifle Corps; European War 1939-45 (wounded, MC): *m* 1st, 1936 (*m diss* 1946), Lucy Geils, 2nd da of late Alain Joly de Lotbiniere of Montreal; 2ndly, 1950, Jean, da of late James T. Finnie, and widow of Oliver P. Croom-Johnson, and has issue by 1st and 2nd *m*.

Arms – Quarterly: 1st and 4th, or, an eagle displayed sable; 2nd and 3rd, argent, two bars sable each charged with three martlets or. **Crest** – On a ducal coronet or, a martlet of the last.
Address – c/o The National Westminster Bank Ltd, 94 Kensington High St, W8.

SONS LIVING (*By 1st marriage*)

RICHARD (6 Clarendon Cross, W11 4AP), *b* 17 Aug 1937: *m* 1964, Emma Rose, da of late Maj-Gen Sir Robert Edward Laycock, KCMG, CB, DSO (*see* E Dudley, colls), and has issue living, Lucy Martha, *b* 1965: *m* 1993, Julian G. Brookhouse, son of Ralph Brookhouse, of Putney, SW, — Alice Frances, *b* 1967, — Daisy Louise, *b* 1971. —— Anthony St George (31 Gascony Av, NW6), *b* 1941: *m* 1986, Angelika Reda, and has issue living, Nicholas Christopher, *b* 1986.

DAUGHTER LIVING (*By 2nd marriage*)

Anne Sophia, *b* 1951: *m* 1974, Jeremy Christopher Peter Amos, of 24 Holland Park Av, W11, and has issue living, Alexander Rudolph, *b* 1978, — Benjamin Christopher, *b* 1980.

HALF-BROTHERS LIVING

Peter Paul Grenville (resides in Florida, USA), b 1941: m 1st, 1975 (m diss 1980), Heather Joy, da of Duncan Alistair McKellar (see Cayzer, Bt), and formerly wife of Kenneth Leonard Hyman; 2ndly, 1983 (m diss 1987), Veronica Margaret, 2nd da of Geoffrey Trigg, of Norfolk, and has issue living (by 2nd m), Richard John Geoffrey, b 1984. —— John Anthony (25 Square du Val de la Cambre, 1050 Brussels, Belgium), b 1942: m 1967, Dominique Francine Paule Ghislaine Maire, da of Jean-Maurice Vaes, of Antwerp, and has issue living, Jean-Marc Peter Grenville (20 rue Ernest Laude, 1030 Brussels), b 1968: m 1995, Odile Arlette Joséphine, da of Jean-Jacques Matthieu de Wynendaele and Mme née Baronne Marie-Claire van der Elst, of Château de Wynendaele, Belgium, and has issue living, Basile Jérôme Grenville b 1999, — Sophie Anne Jacqueline, b 1970, — Vanessa Chantal Marie, b 1973.

This family descends from William Dicken, of Shenton, Salop, who m 1740, Henrietta, da and co-heir of Sir William Temple, 5th Bt of Stowe, Bucks. Their son John (grandfather of 1st baronet) assumed by Royal Licence 1796 the surname of Temple. The 1st baronet, Rt Hon Sir Richard Temple, GCSI, CIE, was Financial Member of Govt of India 1868-74, Lieut-Gov of Bengal 1874-7, Gov of Bombay 1877-80, and MP for Worcestershire S, or Evesham, Div 1885-92, and for Surrey, Kingston Div 1892-6. The 2nd baronet, Lieut-Col Sir Richard Carnac Temple, CB, CIE (Indian Army, and sometime Ch Commr Andaman and Nicobar Islands), raised and commanded Upper Burmah Vol Rifles 1887-90, raised Rangoon Naval Vol 1892, and Rangoon Vol Engineers (Submarine Miners) 1893, and was Editor and Proprietor of the Indian Antiquary 1884-1931. The 3rd baronet, Lt-Col Sir Richard Durand Temple served in the S African War and World War I (DSO, Croix de Guerre with palm) and was later Col cmdg 1st Army BEF, Col cmdg 27th Bn Northumberland Fus, and Col cmdg 5th Bn Worcester Regt.

Tennyson-d'Eyncourt, see d'Eyncourt.

IMBERT-TERRY (UK) 1917, of Strete Ralegh, Whimple, co Devon

Sir MICHAEL EDWARD STANLEY IMBERT-TERRY, 5th Baronet; b 18 April 1950; s his brother, Sir ANDREW HENRY BOUHIER, 1985; ed Cranleigh: m 1975, Frances Dorothy, da of late Peter Scott, of 25 Corfton Rd, Ealing, W5, and has issue.

Arms – Azure, guttée d'or three, four, three and four, on a chief of the last a bull's head caboshed between two mullets of the first. Crest – Issuant from the coronet of a French Seigneur an eagle rising proper, crowned with an Eastern crown or.
Address – c/o Lady Sackville, Knole, Sevenoaks, Kent.

SONS LIVING

BRYCHAN EDWARD, b 1975. —— Jack b 1985.

DAUGHTERS LIVING

Song, b 1973. —— Bryony Jean, b 1980.

SISTERS LIVING

Carolyn Rose (Hollymead, Bagshot Rd, West End, Chobham, Woking, Surrey), b 1947: m 1st, 1973 (m diss 1981), Peter Lauderdale Mackintosh; 2ndly, 1984, Christopher Goode, son of Brig Ernest Reginald Goode, CBE, of Milford, Surrey, and has issue living (by 1st m), Rory Edward Christopher, b 1976, — Catherine Rose, b 1977. —— Alison Jean, b 1952: m 1981, Julian Lorimer Sanger of The Vale House, Frostenden, Beccles, Suffolk, and has issue living, Jonathan Edward, b 1983, — Rachel Mary, b 1981.

AUNTS LIVING (Daughters living of 2nd baronet)

Rosanne Mildred Clothilde, b 1913. —— Marie Jacqueline, b 1923: m 1st, 1947 (m diss 1954), McRae Wyndham Green hill; 2ndly, 1972, William Maurice Williams.

WIDOW LIVING OF THIRD BARONET

JEAN (Baroness Sackville), da of late Arthur Stanley Garton, of Danesfield, Marlow, Bucks; JP 1973: m 1st, 1944, Maj Sir Edward Henry Bouhier Imbert-Terry, MC, 3rd Bt, who d 1978; 2ndly, 1983, as his 3rd wife, 6th Baron Sackville. Residence – Knole, Sevenoaks, Kent.

The 1st baronet, Sir Henry Machu Imbert-Terry (2nd son of Henry Imbert-Terry), was Chm of Central Organization Committee of Unionist Party 1907-17. Lt-Col Sir Henry Bouhier Imbert-Terry, DSO, MC, 2nd Bt, late RA, was High Sheriff of Devon 1948.

THATCHER (UK) 1991, of Scotney, co Kent

Sir DENIS THATCHER, MBE, TD, 1st *Baronet*, son of Thomas Herbert Thatcher, of Uffington, Oxon; *b* 10 May 1915; *ed* Mill Hill; served European War 1939-45 as Maj RA (TD 1940); Dir Burmah Castrol 1970-75, Vice-Chm Attwoods plc 1983-93, Dir Quinton Hazell plc since 1968, Consultant Amec plc and CSX Corpn (US) since 1988; MBE (Mil) 1945: *m* 1st, 1942 (*m diss* 1946), Margaret Doris, only da of Leonard Kempson, of Potters Bar, Middx; 2ndly, 1951, Margaret Hilda, LG, OM, PC (*Baroness Thatcher*) (see that title), da of late Alfred Roberts, of Grantham, Lincs, and has issue by 2nd *m*.

𝕬rms – Gules, two chevrons or between three crosses moline argent, on a chief azure, between two fleurs-de-lys also argent, a mural crown or masoned gules. 𝕮rest – A demi-lion rampant or within a circlet of New Zealand ferns argent, holding between the fore-paws a pair of shears proper.
Residence – 73 Chester Sq, SW1. *Clubs* – Carlton, Buck's, E India, Pratt's.

SON LIVING (*By 2nd marriage*)

Hon MARK, *b* 15 Aug 1953; *ed* Harrow: *m* 1987, Diane, only da of T. C. Burgdorf, of Dallas, Texas, USA, and has issue living, Michael, *b* 1 Feb 1988, — Amanda Margaret, *b* 1993.

DAUGHTER LIVING (*By 2nd marriage*)

Hon Carol, *b* (twin) 1953; journalist and broadcaster.

THOMAS (E) 1694, of Wenvoe, Glamorganshire

Sir (GODFREY) MICHAEL DAVID THOMAS, 11th *Baronet*; *b* 10 Oct 1925; *s* his father, *Rt Hon Sir* GODFREY JOHN VIGNOLES, GCVO, KCB, CSI, 1968; *ed* Harrow; late Capt Rifle Bde; late Member of London Stock Exchange: *m* 1956, Margaret Greta, yr da of John Cleland, of Stormont Court, Godden Green, Sevenoaks, and has issue.

𝕬rms – Sable, a chevron and a canton ermine. 𝕮rest – A demi-unicorn ermine, armed, crined, and unguled or, supporting a shield sable.
Residence – 81 Rivermead Court, Ranelagh Gdns, SW6 3SA. *Clubs* – MCC; Hurlingham.

SON LIVING

DAVID JOHN GODFREY, *b* 11 June 1961.

DAUGHTERS LIVING

Anne Margaret, *b* 1957: *m* 1987, Sir Robert Hutchison, 3rd Bt (*cr* 1939). —— Diana Elizabeth, *b* (twin) 1961: *m* 1985, Richard Allan Halford Brooks (*see* B Crawshaw, colls).

Invincible virtue is glorious

Sir John Thomas, 1st Bt, of Wenvoe, Glam (grandson of James, yr son of Edmond Thomas, of Wenvoe temp James I and Charles I) *m* 1694, Elizabeth, sister of Edmond Thomas, of Wenvoe (*d* 1677), and widow of Gen Edmund Ludlow. The baronetcy was *cr* 1694 with remainder to his brothers Edmond (who *s* 1703 as 2nd Bt) and William. Brig Sir Godfrey Vignoles Thomas, CB, CBE, DSO, 9th Bt, commanded 24th Div RA and 2nd Reserve Bde RA during 1914-18 War, was *ka* 1919. His son Rt Hon Sir Godfrey John Vignoles Thomas, GCVO, KCB, CSI, 10th Bt, was Private Sec to the Prince of Wales 1919-36, and Assist Sec when King Edward VIII, and Private Sec to the Duke of Gloucester 1937-57; PC 1958.

THOMAS (UK) 1918, of Garreglwyd, Anglesey

Sir (WILLIAM) MICHAEL MARSH THOMAS, 3rd *Baronet, b* 4 Dec 1930; *s* his father, *Major Sir* WILLIAM EUSTACE RHYDDLAD, MBE, 1958, *ed* Oundle: *m* 1957, Geraldine, da of Robert Drysdale, of Trearddur Bay, Anglesey, and has issue.

𝕬rms – Per pale gules and azure, on a chevron argent between in chief a sower in the attitude of scattering seed and an eagle displayed both or, and in base a garb of the last, three fleurs-de-lis sable. 𝕮rest – On waves of the sea proper between two anchors sable, a ship in full sail proper.
Residence – Belan Fawr, Rhosneigr, Anglesey, Gwynedd LL64 5JE.

DAUGHTERS LIVING

Geraldine Dawn, *b* 1958. —— Elizabeth Penelope Kim, *b* 1959. —— Pippa-Jane, *b* 1963.

WIDOW LIVING OF SECOND BARONET

PATRICIA (LARKINS) (*Patricia, Lady Thomas*): *m* 1957, as his 3rd wife, Major Sir William Eustace Rhyddlad Thomas, MBE, 2nd Bt, who *d* 1958.

COLLATERAL BRANCH LIVING

Do right and fear nothing

Issue of late Col Robert FREEMAN THOMAS, yr son of 1st baronet, *b* 1911, *d* 1972: *m* 1947, Marcia (who *d* 1992, having *m* 2ndly, 1955, Anthony Melville-Ross, of Lewes, Sussex, who *d* 1993), da of Maurice Sandberg:—
Sarah Anne, *b* 1948: *m* 1981, Alexander James Smith, of 3 Wallands Crescent, Lewes, E Sussex BN7 2QT, and has issue living, Luke Alastair Robert, *b* 1982.

The 1st baronet, Sir Robert John Thomas (son of late William Thomas, of Liverpool), was a Ship and Insurance Broker, and was High Sheriff of Anglesey 1912. He founded and contributed £20,000 to Welch Heroes Memorial Fund and sat as MP for Wrexham Div of Denbighshire (*Co L*) 1918-22, and for Anglesey Co (*L*) 1923-29.

THOMAS (UK) 1919, of Ynyshir, co Glamorgan

Sir WILLIAM JAMES COOPER THOMAS, TD, 2nd *Baronet*; *b* 7 May 1919; *s* his father, *Sir* (WILLIAM) JAMES, 1945; *ed* Harrow, and Downing Coll, Camb; Bar Inner Temple 1948; is a JP and a DL for Gwent (High Sheriff of co Monmouth 1973-74); 1939-45 War with RA: *m* 1947, Freida Dunbar, who *d* 1990, da of late F. A. Whyte, of Montcoffer, Banff, and has issue.

𝕬rms – Argent, a bend gules, between in chief a pick sable and in base a rose of the second, barbed and seeded proper, all within a bordure also of the second. 𝕮rest – Upon a branch of olive fessewise an owl affrontée proper.
Seat – Tump House, Llanrothal, Monmouth, Gwent NP5 3QL.

SONS LIVING

WILLIAM MICHAEL, *b* 5 Dec 1948; *ed* Harrow, and Ch Ch, Oxford. —— Stephen Francis (Flat 6, 31 Dorset Square, London NW1), *b* 1951; *ed* Harrow, and Oriel Coll, Oxford: *m* 1986, Hon Jane Ridley, eldest da of late Baron Ridley of Liddesdale, PC (Life Baron), and has issue living, Toby James, *b* 1988, — Humphrey William, *b* 1991.

DAUGHTER LIVING

Sara Roberta Mary *b* 1954: *m* 1988, Ian W. Jones, yr son of late G. V. Jones, of Walton-on-the-Hill, Surrey, and has issue living, Nicholas David Richard, *b* 1991, — Katherine Louise, *b* 1989.

The 1st baronet, Sir (William) James Thomas (son of Thomas James Thomas), built Welsh National Med Sch at Cardiff, and was High Sheriff of Glamorganshire 1936.

THOMPSON (UK) 1806, of Hartsbourne Manor, Hertfordshire

Sir (THOMAS) LIONEL TENNYSON THOMPSON, 5th *Baronet*; *b* 19 June 1921; *s* his father, *Lt-Col Sir* THOMAS RAIKES LOVETT, MC, 1964; *ed* Eton; Bar Lincoln's Inn 1952; 1939-45 War as Flying Officer RAFVR (invalided), and subsequently as Able Seaman Roy Fleet Auxiliary (1939-45, and Aircrew (Europe) stars, Defence and Victory Medals): *m* 1955 (*m diss* 1962), Mrs Margaret van Beers, da of late Walter Herbert Browne, and has issue.

𝔄rms – Per fesse argent and sable, a fesse counter-embattled between three falcons belled and jessed or, all within a bordure engrailed, and all counter-changed; in the chief point, also within the bordure, an anchor erect azure, cable proper. 𝔠rest – Out of a naval crown or, an arm in armour embowed proper, garnished gold, the hand supporting a lance erect also proper. *Address* – 16 Old Buildings, Lincoln's Inn, WC2A 3UP.

SON LIVING

THOMAS D'EYNCOURT JOHN (c/o King Sturge & Co, 7 Stratford Place, W1N 9AE), *b* 22 Dec 1956; *ed* Eton; BA, MSc; ARICS.

DAUGHTER LIVING

Sarah Catherine Elizabeth (2330 Larkin St, 5, San Francisco, CA 94109, USA), *b* 1955.

SISTER LIVING

Not by whom but in what manner

Jane Olivia Marion, *b* 1918: *m* 1st, 1938 (*m diss* 1947), David Owen Nares; 2ndly, 1948, Maj James Derek Kenyon Hague, MC, Bar-at-law, who *d* 1966, and has issue living (by 1st *m*), Caroline Harriette, *b* 1940: *m* 1961, Robert Belmont, — (by 2nd *m*) Melanie Clare, *b* 1957: *m* 1980, Andrew John Melsom (*see* Pasley, Bt, colls). *Residence* – Stud House, Chilton Foliat, Hungerford, Berks.

The 1st baronet, Vice-Adm Sir Thomas Boulden Thompson, GCB (MP for Rochester 1807-16), greatly distinguished himself, as Captain of the *Leander*, at the battle of the Nile, and afterwards in the action between *Leander* (50) and *Le Genereux* (74), and on his return to England he was knighted 1799; subsequently engaged at the battle of Copenhagen 1801, where he lost a leg; and was appointed Comptroller of the Navy 1806, being created a baronet in the last-mentioned year. Subsequently he was appointed Treasurer of Greenwich Hospital.

THOMPSON (UK) 1890, of Park Gate, Guiseley, Yorkshire

Lt-Col Sir CHRISTOPHER PEILE THOMPSON, 6th *Baronet*; *b* 21 Dec 1944; *s* his father, *Lt-Col Sir* PEILE, OBE, 1985; *ed* Marlborough; Lt-Col (ret) R Hussars (PWO); Equerry to HRH Prince Michael of Kent: *m* 1969 (*m diss* 1997), Anna Elizabeth, da of Maj Arthur George Callander, of Silbury House, Avebury, Marlborough, Wilts, and has issue.

𝔄rms – Azure, a bridge of three arches embattled proper, in chief the sun in his glory between two mullets of six points pierced or in base an eagle displayed with two heads argent. 𝔠rest – In front of embattlements proper, a cubit arm erect, habited azure, cuffed argent, and charged with a mullet as in the arms, the hand grasping five ears of wheat or. *Clubs* – Cavalry and Guards', Woodroffes, St Moritz Tobogganing, Mill Reef (Antigua).

SON LIVING

PEILE RICHARD, *b* 3 March 1975; *ed* Harrow, and Bristol Univ.

Wheare vertue lys love nevr dys

DAUGHTER LIVING

Alexandra Lucy (*Hon Mrs Piers Portman*), *b* 1973: *m* 1995, Hon Piers Richard Berkeley Portman, 4th son of 9th Viscount Portman.

SISTER LIVING

Ann Mary, *b* 1939: *m* 1st, 1965 (*m diss* 1973), Arturo Cesare Pilato, son of late Gino Pilato, of Naples; 2ndly, 1973, Raymond Benjamin Cheetham, late R Hong Kong Police Force, of Hillbrook House, Dipford, Trull, Somerset, son of late

Benjamin Cheetham, of Lismore, Feniton, Devon, and has issue living (by 1st *m*), Roberto Arturo Kenneth, *b* 1966; *ed* King's Coll, Taunton, and Cardiff Univ, — Leonardo Cesare, *b* 1970; *ed* King's Coll Taunton, and De Montfort Univ.

AUNT LIVING (*Daughter of 4th baronet*)

Mary Winifred, *b* 1909: *m* 1941, Hugh Kenyon, of 9 Frobisher Gdns, Boxgrove, Guildford, Surrey, son of Rev Thomas Kenyon, of Malham, Skipton, Yorks, and has issue living, Hugh Matthew, *b* 1944; *ed* Rugby, — Elizabeth Katharine, *b* 1942: *m* 1977, Francis Pasco Grenfell (*see* B Grenfell, colls).

COLLATERAL BRANCHES LIVING

Grandchildren of late Capt Gilbert Thompson, Connaught Rangers (infra):—
Issue of late Maj Christopher Smith Byrom THOMPSON ROYDS, *b* 1907; assumed by Roy licence 1936, the additional surname and arms of Royds; *d* 1967: *m* 1936, Yolande Anne (Walton House, Boston Spa, Yorks), yr da of late A. T. Hodgson, of Tatchbury Manor House, New Forest, Hants:—
Gilbert (Seymour House, Market St, Charlbury, Oxon), *b* 1939; *ed* Eton: *m* 1976, Vanessa Maxine, da of Mark Leslie Brandon (*see* V Selby). — Matthew, *b* 1942; *ed* Eton: *m* 1969, Susan (Damaris), el da of Arthur Robert Jarrett, of Chedgrove Manor, Loddon, Norfolk. — Timothy Christopher, *b* 1950; *ed* Stowe: *m* 1983, Anne Penelope, yr da of Gordon Shafto Hedley (*see* E Waldegrave, 1995 Edn), and has issue living, Mark Christopher, *b* 1989, — Kate, *b* 1985. — Laura Yolanda, *b* 1947.

Grandchildren of late Reginald Thompson, 2nd son of 1st baronet:—
Issue of late Capt Gilbert Thompson, Connaught Rangers, *b* 1877, *ka* 1915: *m* 1906, Ethel Isabella, who *d* 1959, da of late Marmaduke D'Arcy Wyvill (B Rookwood):—
Laura Barbara Frances (*Lady Inglefield*), *b* 1908: *m* 1933, Sir Gilbert Samuel Inglefield, GBE, TD, who *d* 1991, and has issue living, David Gilbert Charles (The Old Rectory, Staunton-in-the-Vale, Orston, Notts), *b* 1934: *m* 1970, Jean Mary, only da of late Col Sir Alan Gomme-Duncan, MC, and has issue living, Charles Nicholas David *b* 1977, Mary Victoria *b* 1974, — (Christopher) Samuel (Bryngwyn Manor, Raglan, Gwent), *b* 1936: *m* 1971, Susan Lilias, da of Henry Turcan, of Lindores House, Newburgh, Fife, and has issue living, Edward Henry Samuel *b* 1973, Frederick Thomas Christopher, *b* 1982, Olivia Barbara Jane *b* 1972, Katherine Lilias Cecilia *b* 1977, — Elizabeth Isabel Albinia (Orchard Grange, Old Warden, Biggleswade, Beds SG18 9HB), *b* 1942: *m* 1962, Maj Christopher Wyndham Diggle, who *d* 1986, and has issue living, Robert Dominic Charles *b* 1969, Jonathan Benjamin Christopher *b* 1973, Albinia Julia *b* 1964: *m* 1988, Richard Malcolm Jannion Trustram Eve, and has issue (*see* B Silsoe), Louise Georgina *b* 1966. *Residence* – 6 Rutland House, Marloes Rd, W8 5LE. — Naomi Isabella, *b* 1912: *m* 1935, Maj D'Arcy Armitage Dawes, late 15/19th King's R Hussars, who *d* 1967 (Armytage, Bt, colls), and has issue living, Charles Lancelot (Leacon Hall, Warehorne, Ashford, Kent), *b* 1938, Capt (ret) late 15th/19th King's R Hussars: *m* 1964, Valerie Ann, el da of Col Edward Townsend, of Fencote Hall, Northallerton, Yorks, and has issue living, Nicholas Halford *b* 1967: *m* 1994, Katharine Lucy, da of Derrick Penrose, of Park House, Baslow, Derbys (and has issue living, Thomas Charles D'Arcy *b* 1998), James Christopher *b* 1968: *m* 1996, Victoria Mary, da of late Morris Clough, of 8 Stockers Green, Knebworth, Herts (and has issue living, Freya *b* 1998), Isla Caroline *b* 1971, — Hermione Ann, *b* 1941: *m* 1964, John Oliver Birkbeck, of Litcham Hall, King's Lynn (*see* E Munster, 1990 Edn), and has issue living, Oliver Benjamin *b* 1973, Lucy Claire *b* 1966: *m* 1995, Robert M. Leitão, only son of Eduardo Francisco Felipe Read Leitão, of Estoril, Portugal (and has issue living, Felix Edward Oliver *b* 1998), Roseanna Mary *b* 1974. *Residence* – Forge Cottage, Warehorne, Ashford, Kent.

Issue of late Col Reginald Thompson, DSO, *b* 1884, *d* 1965: *m* 1st, 1922, Marjorie Olive, who *d* 1929, da of late James Arthur, of Montgomerie, Tarbolton (B Glenarthur); 2ndly, 1932, Ruth Eleanor, who *d* 1986, da of the Rev J. H. Hodgson, and widow of John C. Bradley Firth, of Blyth, Notts.
(By 1st *m*) Elizabeth Olive (Failford House, Mauchline, Ayrshire), *b* 1923: *m* 1948, Maj George Malcolm Graham, KRRC, who *d* 1980, and has issue living, James Anthony (La Hille, Fanjeaux 11270, France), *b* 1953; *ed* Sorbonne: *m* 1978 (*m* diss 1993), Hayat Lebbar, — Alexandra Mary, *b* 1949: *m* 1974, Adrian John Speir, of The Old Rectory, Melsonby, nr Richmond, N Yorks, son of late Michael Adrian Speir, of Foresters Hall, Middleton Tyas, N Yorks, and has issue living, Edward Francis *b* 1976, Harry James *b* 1979. — Judith Mary (Day Ash, Darley, Yorkshire) *b* 1927.

The 1st baronet sat as MP for Bradford (*L*) 1867-8, and was Chm of the Forth Bridge and the Midland Railway Cos.

THOMPSON (UK) 1963, of Reculver, co Kent

†*Sir* RICHARD HILTON MARLER THOMPSON, 1st *Baronet*, son of late Richard Smith Thompson; *b* 5 Oct 1912; *ed* Malvern Coll; a Co Dir; Assist Govt Whip 1952-54, Lord Commr of Treasury 1954-56, Vice Chamberlain, HM Household 1956-57, Parl Sec, Min of Health 1957-59, Parl Under-Sec of State, Commonwealth Relations Office, 1959-60, and Parl Sec, Min of Works 1960-62; a Trustee of British Museum, 1951-84; Dir of Rediffusion TV Ltd and Rediffusion Holdings 1966-83; Chm of Capital & Counties Property Co Ltd 1971-76 and Pres of British Property Federation 1976-77; Chm of British Museum Soc 1970-74 and a Member of Council, Nat Trust 1978-84; 1939-45 War as Lt-Cdr RNVR (despatches); MP Croydon W (*C*) 1950-55, and of Croydon S 1955-66 and 1970-74: *m* 1939, Anne Christabel de Vere, only da of late Philip de Vere Annesley (*see* V Valentia, colls), and has issue. Sir Richard H. M. Thompson, 1st Bt, *d* 15 July 1999.

𝖆rms – Azure a bend argent between two ship's wheels or. 𝕮rest – A demi figure representing a Moorish Prince proper, wreathed about the temples with a torse argent and azure, vested of a tunic paly argent and azure fringed and garnished or, at his back supported by a guige gules baldrickwise across the right dexter shoulder, a quiver azure replenished with arrows argent flighted or, from the dexter hand a martlet rising azure and in the other a bow palewise stringed gules. Inescutcheon of pretence, paly of six argent and azure, over all a hand gules, *Annesley.*
Residence – Rhodes House, Sellindge, Ashford, Kent TN25 6JA. *Clubs* – Carlton, Army and Navy.

SON LIVING

NICHOLAS ANNESLEY MARLER (Maxgate, George Rd, Kingston-upon-Thames, Surrey KT2 7NR; Carlton Club), *b* 19 March 1947; *ed* King's Sch, Canterbury, and Univ of Kent at Canterbury (BA); admitted a solicitor 1973; Mem Westminster City Council 1978-86; Dep Lord Mayor of Westminster 1983-84: *m* 1982, Venetia Catherine, yr da of John Horace Broke Heathcote, of Conington House, Peterborough, Cambs (*see* Heathcote, Bt, of London), and has issue living, Simon William, *b* 10 June 1985, — Charles Frederick, *b* 1986, — David Jonathan, *b* 1990, — Emma Louise, *b* 1991.

THOMPSON (UK) 1963, of Walton-on-the-Hill, City of Liverpool

Sir PAUL ANTHONY THOMPSON, 2nd *Baronet*; *b* 6 Oct 1939; *s* his father, *Sir* KENNETH PUGH, 1984; *ed* Aldenham: *m* 1971, Pauline Dorothy, da of late Robert Orrell Spencer, of Tippett House, Smithills, Bolton, Lancs, and has issue.

𝖆rms – Per fess dancetty argent and sable of two upward and one downward points, each ending in a cross potent, three swans one in chief and two in base counterchanged. 𝕮rest – A demi figure affronty representing Neptune wreathed about the middle with laver proper, the mantle gules clasped and crowned with an antique crown or, supporting in the dexter hand a trident sable and in the sinister a spear proper.
Residence – Woodlands Farmhouse, 56 Ruff Lane, Ormskirk, Lancs L39 4UL.

SONS LIVING

RICHARD KENNETH SPENCER, *b* 27 Jan 1976. —— David Paul Charles, *b* 1978.

DAUGHTERS LIVING

Karena Melanie, *b* 1973. —— Nicola Robyn, *b* 1974.

SISTER LIVING

(Nanne) Patricia, *b* 1942: *m* 1st, 1966, Tredinnick Michael Johns; 2ndly, 1989, Neil Charles Bedford, and has issue living (by 1st *m*), Anna Melinda, *b* 1969, — Charlotte, *b* 19—, — Polly, *b* 19—.

MEYSEY-THOMPSON (UK) 1874, of Kirby Hall, Yorkshire

Sir (HUMPHREY) SIMON MEYSEY-THOMPSON, 4th *Baronet*, son of late Guy Herbert Meysey-Thompson, grandson of 1st Baronet; *b* 31 March 1935; *s* his kinsman, *Sir* ALGAR DE CLIFFORD CHARLES, 1967.

Arms – Quarterly: 1st and 4th, per fesse argent and sable, a fesse counterembattled between three falcons counterchanged, belled and jessed or; 2nd and 3rd, argent, a fesse between three cinquefoils sable. **Crests** – 1st, an arm embossed quarterly or and azure, gauntleted proper, grasping a broken tilting spear in bend sinister or; 2nd, a dragon's head quarterly or and azure, eared gules.
Residence – 10 Church St, Woodbridge, Suffolk.

SISTER LIVING

Sarah Horatia, *b* 1944: *m* 1969, Charles William Spencer Paterson, of 31 Ranelagh Grove, SW1, and has issue living, Charles Joseph Alexander, *b* 1983.

DAUGHTER LIVING OF SECOND BARONET

See Barony of Knaresborough.

I wish for fair fight

The 1st baronet, Sir Harry Stephen Meysey-Thompson, sat as MP for Whitby (*L*) 1859-65. The 2nd baronet, Sir Henry Meysey-Thompson, sat as MP for Knaresborough (*L*) April to July 1880, for N Lindsey, or Brigg, Div of Lincolnshire 1885-6, and for Handsworth Div of Staffordshire (LU) 1892-1905, and was *cr Baron Knaresborough*, of Kirby Hall, co York (peerage of United Kingdom) 1905 (ext 1929).

THOMSON (UK) 1925, of Old Nunthorpe, co York

Sir MARK WILFRID HOME THOMSON, 3rd *Baronet*; *b* 29 Dec 1939; *s* his father, *Sir* IVO WILFRID HOME, 1991; *ed* —; Lieut RN (Fleet Air Arm) 1957-65: *m* 1976 (*m diss* 1996), Lady Jacqueline Rosemary Margot Rufus Isaacs, only da of 3rd Marquess of Reading, and has issue.

Arms – Ermine, a lion passant guardant or, on a chief azure two keys, wards inwards of the second. **Crest** – A lion rampant or, gorged with an antique crown gules, between two roses argent barbed, seeded, leaved and slipped proper.
Residence – 53 Drayton Gdns, SW10 9RX.

SONS LIVING

ALBERT MARK HOME, *b* 3 Aug 1979. —— Jake Michael Alfred, *b* 1983. —— Luke Ivo Charles, *b* (twin) 1983.

DAUGHTER LIVING

Daisy Jacqueline Carol, *b* 1977.

WIDOW LIVING OF SECOND BARONET

VIOLA MABEL (*Lady Thomson*), da of Roland Dudley, of Linkenholt Manor, Andover, Hants, and formerly wife of Keith Home Thomson, MBE: *m* 1954, as his 2nd wife, Sir Ivo Wilfrid Home Thomson, 2nd Bt, who *d* 1991.

Always faithful

The 1st baronet, Sir Wilfrid Forbes Home Thomson (el son of Most Rev and Rt Hon William Thomson, DD, PC, Archbishop of York), was a partner in the firm of Beckett & Co, bankers, of York.

THOMSON (UK) 1929, of Glendarroch, co Midlothian

God will provide

providebit

Deus

Sir (FREDERICK DOUGLAS) DAVID THOMSON, 3rd *Baronet; b* 14 Feb 1940; *s* his father, *Sir* (JAMES) DOUGLAS WISHART, 1972; *ed* Eton, and Univ Coll, Oxford (BA); Dir Britannia Steam Ship Insurance Assocn since 1965 and Chm since 1986; Dir Cairn Energy plc since 1971; Dir Danae Investment Trust plc since 1979; Chm Jove Investment Trust since 1983; Dir Kynoch Group plc since 1990; Dir Martin Currie Pacific Trust plc since 1985; Chm Ptarmigan International Capital Trust plc since 1990; Dir Through Transport Mutual Insurance Association Ltd since 1973, Chm since 1983; Dir Bolero International Ltd since 1998; Chm Laurence J. Smith Ltd since 1993; Mem of the Queen's Body Guard for Scotland (Royal Company of Archers): *m* 1967 (*m diss* 1994), Caroline Anne, da of Maj Timothy Stuart Lewis, R Scots Greys (*see* V Daventry, 1995 Edn), and has issue.

Arms – Argent, a stag's head cabossed gules between the attires a shakefork sable, on a chief engrailed of the second, a galley, sail furled, oars in saltire between two towers triple towered of the field. **Crest** – A dexter hand couped proper holding a cross crosslet fitchée azure.
Residence – Holylee, Walkerburn, Peeblesshire EH43 6BD.

SONS LIVING

SIMON DOUGLAS CHARLES, *b* 16 June 1969. —— Christopher Michael David, *b* 1970.

DAUGHTER LIVING

Sarah Anne Vanessa, *b* 1974.

BROTHER LIVING

William Andrew Charles (24 Hermitage Drive, Edinburgh), *b* 1948; *ed* Gordonstoun: *m* 1976, Cecilia Bernadette Gill, and has issue living, Douglas Charles, *b* 1978, — William Frederick *b* 1981, — Charles David, *b* 1988, — Julia Margaret Clare, *b* 1983.

SISTERS LIVING

Susan Evelyn Margaret, *b* 1936: *m* 1961, Capt John Michael Cavenagh, GM, and has issue living, Thomas Douglas, *b* 1966, — Sarah Louise, *b* 1964, — Bettina Susan Margaret, *b* 1971. *Residence* – Withcote Hall, Oakham, Rutland. —— Vanessa Jean Wishart, *b* 1942: *m* 1964, Anthony Fenwick Denby Roberts, of Mossdale, Conistone with Kilnsey, Skipton, Yorks (*see* Roberts, Bt, *cr* 1909 colls), and has issue (see that title). —— Jennifer Constance Anne, *b* 1945: *m* 1989, Howard Pighills, of Conistone Fold, Conistone with Kilnsey, Skipton, N Yorks.

WIDOW LIVING OF SECOND BARONET

BETTINA (*Bettina, Lady Thomson*) (Old Caberston, Walkerburn, Peebles-shire), da of late Lt-Cdr David William Shafto Douglas, RN: *m* 1935, Sir (James) Douglas Wishart Thomson, 2nd Bt, who *d* 1972.

Sir Frederick Charles Thomson, KC, 1st Bt (son of late James Wishart Thomson, shipowner, of Glenpark, Balerno, Midlothian), sat as MP for S Div of Aberdeen (*U*) 1918-35, and was a Junior Lord of the Treasury Feb to April 1923, Solicitor-Gen for Scotland April 1923 to Jan 1924, again a Junior Lord of the Treasury Nov 1924 to Jan 1928, Vice-Chamberlain of HM's Household Jan 1928 to June 1929, and Sept to Nov 1931, and Treasurer of HM's Household Nov 1931 to April 1935. The 2nd Bt, Sir (James) Douglas Wishart Thomson sat as MP for S Aberdeen (U) 1935-46, was PPS to Minister of Shipping 1940, and Chm Ben Line Steamers Ltd 1964-70.

THOROLD (E) 1642, of Marston, Lincolnshire

The stag is not a slave

Sir (ANTHONY) OLIVER THOROLD, 16th *Baronet; b* 15 April 1945; *s* his father, *Captain Sir* ANTHONY HENRY, OBE, DSC, RN, 1999; *ed* Winchester, and Lincoln Coll, Oxford; Bar Inner Temple 1971: *m* 1977, Genevra, yst da of John L. Richardson, of Broadshaw, West Calder, Midlothian, and has issue.

𝔄rms – Sable: three goats salient argent. 𝔠re𝔰t – A roebuck passant argent, attired or.
Seat – Syston Old Hall, Grantham, Lincs. *Residence* – 8 Richmond Crescent, N1 0LZ.

SON LIVING

HENRY LOWRY, *b* 6 Aug 1981.

DAUGHTER LIVING

Lydia Josephine, *b* 1985.

SISTERS LIVING

Celia, *b* 1940: *m* 1962, Capt Bryan David Salwey, RN, of 5 West Hill Rd, Wandsworth, SW18 1LH, and has issue living, Roger Penruddocke (30 Sarsfeld Rd, SW12 8HN), *b* 1964: *m* 1996, Julie Erica, da of Neville Bennett Randall, of Tower Cottage, The High St, Bletchingley, Surrey RH1 4PB, and has issue living, Saskia Alice Bauwina *b* 19—, Claudia Celia Clementine *b* 1999, — David Guy, *b* 1966, — Nicholas Anthony, *b* 1969. —— Diana Jocelyn (21 Gerrard Rd, N1 8AY), *b* 1942; MA, Edinburgh, and London; Senior Lecturer, Univ of Westminster.

AUNTS LIVING (*Daughters of 14th baronet*)

Dorothy Aline, *b* 1908. *Residence* – 24 Bowling Green Court, Hospital Rd, Moreton-in-Marsh, Glos GL56 0BX. —— Mary Jocelyn (Sawmill Close, Sharperton, Morpeth, Northumberland), *b* 1914: *m* 1935, as his 2nd wife, Walter Thomas Meyrick, who *d* 1953 (*see* Meyrick, Bt, colls).

COLLATERAL BRANCHES LIVING

Issue of late Lt-Col Montague Thorold, yr son of 14th baronet, *b* 1906, *d* 1974: *m* 1946, Helen Moye (The Old Rectory, Stainby, Grantham, Lincs NG33 5QX), da of late Capt Barnard Stone:—
John Richard (52 Danemere St, SW15), *b* 1947; *ed* Kelly Coll, Tavistock; 2nd Lt 9/12th R Lancers; ARICS, land agent: *m* 1991, Elizabeth A., da of Lt-Col A. J. E. Cruickshank, of Coxbridge, Som, and has issue living, Guy, *b* 1992, — Alexandra, *b* (twin) 1992. —— (Rosemary) Julia (203A Castelnau, Barnes, SW13), *b* 1950.

Grandchildren of late Reginald Henry Thorold, 2nd son of late Rev Henry Baugh Thorold, el son of late Rev George Thorold, 2nd son of 9th baronet:—
Issue of late Reginald Charles Thorold, *b* 1871, *d* 1956: *m* 1906, Elizabeth McMaster, who *d* 1965, da of Nicolas Moncrieff Howitt, of Gawonga, Victoria:—
Reginald Moncrieff (21 River Rd, Camden, NSW 2570), *b* 1914: *m* 1942, Sheila Frances, who *d* 1968, da of Hugh Sinclair Mackay, of Tasmania, and has issue living, Reginald David, *b* 1945. — Elizabeth Helen, *b* 1948. —— Katharine Florence, *b* 1907. —— Elizabeth, *b* 1909. —— Bertha Edith, *b* 1911: *m* 1941, Christo Albertyn Smith, of Falmouth, Tasmania, and has issue living, Christopher John, *b* 1945. — Lillemor Elizabeth, *b* 1942. —— Margaret, *b* 1918. *Residence* – Falmouth, Tasmania.

Grandsons of late Reginald Charles Thorold (ante):—
Issue of late John Charles Nicolas Thorold, *b* 1916, *d* 1961: *m* 1948, Barbara Nicolson Arthur (Brambletye, Conara 7211, Tasmania), da of late John Nicolson Archer, of Conara, Tasmania:—
Barry John Archer, *b* 1949: *m* 1975, Joanna, only da of Keith Ian Benson, of Launceston, Tasmania, and has issue living, John Charles Nicholas, *b* 1988, — Lydia Jane, *b* 1979, — Sabina Lucy, *b* 1980, — Emma Elizabeth, *b* 1985. —— †David Nicholas, *b* 1951, *d* 1952. —— †Simon Charles, *b* 1953, *d* 1970. —— Marcus Jonathan, *b* 1958.

Grandchildren of late Rev Algernon Herbert Thorold, eldest son of late Rev Algernon Charles Edward Thorold (infra):—
Issue of late Rev Michael Herbert Thorold, *b* 1904, *d* 1956: *m* 1931, Dorothy (180a Gloucester Pl, NW1), da of late George Patrick Henfrey, of The Dower House, Beckenham, Kent:—
Anthony Patrick de Buckenhold (c/o Barclays Bank, Marble Arch, W1; *Club* – Junior Army and Navy), *b* 1938; *ed* Brighton Coll, and at Sidney Sussex Coll, Camb; Maj RCT: *m* 1962, Jane Antoinette, only da of William Francis Paul Corbould of Purley, Surrey, and has issue living, Emma Jane, *b* 1963: *m* 1988, Andrew Michael Tomalin, of 7 Vale Rd North, Surbiton, Surrey, elder son of David A. Tomalin, of Crowborough, Sussex, and has issue living, Victoria Alice *b* 1989, — Antonia Cecilia, *b* 1966: *m* 1993, Robert B. C. Goodman, eldest son of N. J. Goodman, and of Mrs J. Campbell-Davys. —— Ia Cecilia, *b* 1935; BA: *m* 1966, John Hamish St John McIlwaine, of 10 Cromwell Close, E Finchley, N2, and has issue living, Katherine Anne, *b* 1969.

Grandsons of late Rev Michael Herbert Thorold (ante):—

Issue of late Michael Bernard Thorold, *b* 1942, *d* 1979: *m* 1st, 1967 (*m diss* 1971), Carolyn Alice, da of Martin James Pollock (*see* Pollock, Bt, colls); 2ndly, 1971, Mary Nihan (20 Silsoe House, Park Village East, NW1 4AS), da of James Mackenzie-Mair, of Beachborough Park East, Folkestone:—
(By 1st *m*) Rupert Michael James de Buckenhold, *b* 1969. —— (By 2nd *m*) Crispin Crispian James Leofric, *b* 1973.

Grandsons of late Rev Algernon Charles Edward Thorold, el son of Charles Thorold, 3rd son of Rev George Thorold, 2nd son of 9th baronet:—
Issue of late Arthur Charles Campbell Thorold, *b* 1873, *d* 1939: *m* 1st, 1913, Kathleen May, who *d* 1922, only da of late Frederick Jeffery; 2ndly, 1925, Jessie Isobel Marjory, who *d* 1954, da of late Francis Wellington Were, of Heidelberg, Melbourne, Australia:—
(By 1st *m*) Patrick Hayford (7 Broadbeach Blvd, Broadbeach 4218, Qld), *b* 1916: *m* 1st, 1940 (*m diss* 1949), Dorrit Wilhelmina, da of J. H. Charles, of 270 Burke Rd, Glen Iris, Melbourne, Australia; 2ndly, 1949, Naureen Margaret, only da of late William George Mason, of Armadale, Melbourne, and has issue living, (by 1st *m*) Ruth Patricia, *b* 1942: *m* 1966, Roger MacLeod Dunn, of 109 Wellington St, Kew, Melbourne, Vic, Aust, and has issue living, Lachlan Thorold MacLeod *b* 1968, Tarquin Charles MacLeod *b* 1972, Phoebe Rebecca *b* 1969, — (by 2nd *m*) Joan Michele, *b* 1952: *m* 1974, Andrew Howard Knox Wilson, of 12 Seymour Av, Armadale 3143, Vic, Aust, and has issue living, Benjamin Thorold Knox *b* 1983, Nicholas Andrew Jeffery *b* 1985, Patrick Howard Knox *b* 1989.

Issue of late Rev Ernest Hayford Thorold, CB, CBE, DD (Chap-Gen to Forces 1931-9, and Chap to HM 1935-40), *b* 1879, *d* 1940: *m* 1913, Dorothy Frances, who *d* 1969, da of Edward Herbert, of Ludford House, Duppas Hill, Croydon:—
Rev John Robert Hayford, *b* 1916; *ed* Westminster, and at King's Coll, Camb (BA 1943, MA 1945); sometime Sub-Lieut (Sp) RNVR, and an Assist Master at Eton; is Priest of the Oratory of the Good Shepherd, and co-patron of five livings. *Residence* – St Deiniol's Library, Hawarden, Chester CH5 3DF. —— *Rev* Henry Croyland, *b* 1921; *ed* Eton, and at Ch Ch, Oxford; FSA; sometime Chap RN, and Chap to Bishop of Brechin; House Master and Chap at Lancing Coll 1949-68 and co-patron of five livings; author of *Shell Guide to Derbyshire, Shell Guide to Staffordshire, Shell Guide to County Durham, Shell Guide to Nottinghamshire* and joint-author of *Shell Guide to Lincolnshire*, also author of *Collins Guide to Cathedrals, Abbeys and Priories of England and Wales, Lincolnshire Churches Revisited* (with foreword by HRH The Prince of Wales), *Lincolnshire (Pimlico County History Guide)*, and *Collins Guide to the Ruined Abbeys of England, Wales and Scotland. Residence* – Marston Hall, Grantham.

Grandsons of late Cdr Hubert Gould William Thorold, RN, 2nd son of late Rev William Thorold, 6th son of Rev George Thorold, 2nd son of 9th baronet:—
Issue of late Sir Guy Frederick Thorold, KCMG, *b* 1898, *d* 1970: *m* 1928, Mary Wilder, who *d* 1963, da of late Henry Mildmay Husey:—
Peter Guy Henry (25 Stanley Crescent, W11 2NA), *b* 1930; *ed* Eton, and New Coll, Oxford: *m* 1st, 1954 (*m diss* 1963), Merilyn Mary, who *d* 1999, da of Lt-Col Sir John Francis Roskell Reynolds, MBE, 2nd Bt; 2ndly, 1964, Anne, yr da of Robert Evelyn Herbert Fender, AFC, of The Manor House, Withington, Glos, and has issue living, (by 1st *m*) Marcus Guy Francis, *b* 1955: *m* 1992, Georgina C., elder da of Peter Armitage, of Tarporley, Cheshire, and has issue living, Jack Guy Peter *b* 1995, Iona Sophie *b* 1997, — Daniel Edward, *b* 1960, — Caroline Emelia, *b* 1956, — (by 2nd *m*) Nicola Anne, *b* 1965. —— Julian Hubert, *b* 1933; *ed* Eton, and New Coll, Oxford.

Granddaughters of late Rev John Leofric de Buckenhold Thorold, 3rd son of late Rev William Thorold (ante):—
Issue of late George Preston Thorold, *b* 1896, *d* 1964: *m* 1940, Madeleine Beatrice, who *d* 1988, da of Aubrey Carteret de Carteret:—
Laelia Karslake, *b* 1942: *m* 1964, Julian Rodney Hartnoll, of 8 Etherden Rd, W12, and has issue living, Emma de Carteret, *b* 1965, — Jenny Moulton, *b* 1967.

Issue of late Edward Leofric Thorold, *b* 1898, *d* 1965: *m* 1st, 1928 (*m diss* 1942), Phyllis Frances, da of A. C. Hills; 2ndly, 1942, Agnes Phyllis, who *d* 1996, da of late Albert Humphrey Johnson:—
(By 1st *m*) Brenda Frances, *b* 1929: *m* 1947, R. Hillier, of Flat 10, 19 Holland Park, W11, and has issue living, Anthony Edward, *b* 1949, — Nicholas Leofric, *b* 1952. —— (By 2nd *m*) Judith Rose, *b* 1947: *m* 1969, Michael Thorold-Palmer (surname assumed by deed poll), of Walkleigh House, South Holmwood, Dorking, Surrey, and has issue living, Edward James, *b* 1972, — Alexandra Louise, *b* 1974.

Issue of late Charles Aubrey Thorold, *b* 1906, *d* 1998: *m* 1949, Katharine Mary (11 Tower Rd, Twickenham, Middx), da of late Rt Rev Algernon Augustus Markham, Bishop of Grantham:—
Philippa Markham, *b* 1951: *m* 1981, Nicolas Killin, MBA, of 50 Samdon St, Hamilton, NSW 2303, Australia, and has issue living, Thomas William, *b* 1983, — Samuel Charles, *b* 1989, — Emily Katharine, *b* 1991. —— Joanna Mary, *b* 1955; MA (Oxon), MA (Lond): *m* 1977, Paul Clifford, MA, of 14 Lakeside, Oxford, and has issue living, Sarah Katharine, *b* 1981, — Elizabeth Rose, *b* 1984.

Grandchildren of late Algar Labouchere Thorold, son of Rt Rev Anthony Wilson Thorold DD, son of Rev Edward Thorold, 4th son of 9th baronet:—
Issue of late Francis John Anselm Thorold, *b* 1901, *d* 1958: *m* 1932, Ann Amelia, who *d* 1979, da of late William Somers, of Wick, Somerset:—
John Christopher, *b* 1940: *m* 1966, Elizabeth Ann, da of Noe John Colborne, of Chippenham, and has issue living, Justin Algar *b* 1967. —— Catherine Ann, *b* 1933: *m* 1960 (*m diss* 1965), John Blaker (now 3rd Bt). *Residence* – Woodcote Farm, Nutley, nr Uckfield, Sussex.

Grandson of late Michael Richard Thorold, son of late Michael Wynne Thorold, son of late Rev Michael Thorold, son of late Samuel Thorold (*b* 1748), 2nd son of 8th baronet:—
Issue of late Richard Gillbee Thorold, *b* 1859, *d* 1940: *m* 1900, Ellen Irene, who *d* 1958, da of late Edward Hogg, of The Lodge, Pinner:—
(Edward) Lionel, *b* 1905. *Residence* – Potterspury Lodge School, Towcester, Northants NN12 7LL.

The first proved ancestor of this family, Sir Richard Thorold of Selby, co York, acquired the Manor of Marston, co Lincoln by *m* (temp Edward III) to Joan, da and heir of Robert de Hough by his wife Maud da and heir of Michael de Marston. William Thorold (*d* 1569), 5th in descent from Sir Richard, purchased Cranwell, co Lincoln (demolished 1815, estates, requisitioned 1915, and sold to RAF 1920) and his son, Sir Anthony (*d* 1594) purchased Syston, Lincs. His grandson, Sir William, 1st Bt, was knighted by James I when aged 16 years. He was a Royalist and paid £4,460 to the sequestrators of his estate. Sir John Thorold, 9th Bt, built the new house of Syston 1766/75 which was enlarged by his son Sir John Hayford Thorold, 10th Bt, the book collector (*d* 1815). This house was demolished 1934 when Syston Old Hall became the seat of the Baronets. Marston Hall, the principal seat of Baronets until the 18th century, is still in the possession of this family. Three other Baronetcies of Hough-on-the-Hill (*cr* 1644), of Harmston (*cr* 1709), and of Harmston (*cr* 1740), have been conferred on this family, all of which have become extinct.

THROCKMORTON (E) 1642, of Coughton, Warwickshire (extinct 1994)

Sir ANTHONY JOHN BENEDICT THROCKMORTON, 12th and last *Baronet.*

SISTER LIVING OF ELEVENTH BARONET

Ann Barbara (Spiney House, Coughton, Alcester, Warwicks), *b* 1911: *m* 1939, Ludwig Freiherr von Twickel, who *d* 1945, and has issue living, *Freiherr* Johann (John) Robert (Bethmannstrasse 7, Frankfurt/M, Germany), *b* 1940: *m* 1st, 1968 (*m diss* 1993), HSH Princess Victoria Benigna Ina Marie Cecile Friederike Luise Helene, da of HSH Prince Karl Peter Franz Andreas Biron von Curland (*see* ROYAL FAMILY); 2ndly, 1993, HSH Princess Charlotte Alexandra Marie Clothilde, da of HSH Prince Alexander Georg Maria Josef Ignatius of Croy, and formerly wife of HSH Kraft Alexander Ernst Ludwig Georg Emich, 9th Prince of Hohenlohe-Langenburg (*see* ROYAL FAMILY), and has issue living (by 1st *m*), *Freiherr* Nikolaus Maximilian *b* 1969, *Freiherr* Tassilo *b* 1976, — *Freiherr* Alexander Rudolf Ferdinand Nikolaus Zdenko (123 Warwick Way, SW1V 4HS; Tidmington Corner, Shipston-on-Stour, Warwicks CV36 5LR) *b* 1941; Lt-Col 9th/12th R Lancers (Prince of Wales's): *m* 1973, Neville Christine, da of Garth Priestman, and has issue living, *Freiin* Angela Margaret Walburga Faith Zdenka *b* 1975; *ed* Heathfield, and Edinburgh Univ, *Freiin* Matilda Victoria Louise Ann Zdenka *b* 1976; *ed* North Foreland Lodge, and Newcastle Univ.

WIDOW LIVING OF ELEVENTH BARONET

Lady ISABEL VIOLET KATHLEEN MANNERS (*Lady Isabel Throckmorton*), da of 9th Duke of Rutland, and formerly wife of late Gp Capt Thomas Loel Evelyn Bulkeley Guinness, OBE: *m* 1953, as his 2nd wife, Sir Robert George Maxwell Throckmorton, 11th Bt, who *d* 1989. *Residence* – Coughton Court, Alcester, Warwickshire B49 5JA.

WIDOW LIVING OF TWELFTH BARONET

VIOLET VIRGINIA (*Lady Throckmorton*), da of late Anders William Anderson: *m* 1972, Sir Anthony John Benedict Throckmorton, 12th Bt, who *d* 1994. *Residence* – 2006 Oakes, Everett, Washington 98201, USA.

COLLATERAL BRANCH LIVING

Issue of late Elizabeth Ursula Arienwen Throckmorton, sister of 11th baronet, *b* 1906, *d* 1970: *m* 1935, Prof Alphonsus Ligouri d'Abreu, CBE, FRCS, who *d* 1976:—
(Elizabeth) Clare McLAREN-THROCKMORTON, *b* 1935; *ed* Mayfield, and Birmingham Univ (BA 19—); Bar Inner Temple 1968, QC 1988; assumed addl surname of Throckmorton by deed poll 1991 upon *s* her uncle in the Throckmorton estates: *m* 1st, 1958 (*m diss* 1971), Alan George Tritton; 2ndly, 1973, Andrew McLaren, and has issue living (by 1st *m*), (Robert) Guy Henton, *b* 1963: *m* 1995, Jane Pycraft and has issue living, Luke Charles Henton *b* 1998, Lara Ursula *b* 1996, — Charles Courtenay, *b* 1965: *m* 1993, Anneli Clare Pougatch, and has issue living, Felix Michael Courtenay *b* 1996, Theodore *b* 1998, — Christina Margaret, *b* 1960: *m* 1st, 1984 (*m diss* 1990), Rupert Birch; 2ndly, 1993, (Adam) Benedict N. Williams, son of late Sir Anthony Williams, KCMG, of Salehurst, E Sussex (*see* B Wrenbury, 1976 Edn), and has issue living (by 1st *m*), Magnus Courtenay, (by 2nd *m*), Merlin Anthony Baillie *b* 1994, Jasper Ambrose George *b* 1997, Flavia Elizabeth Ruth *b* 1995. *Seats* – Coughton Court, Alcester, Warwicks B49 5JA; Manor House, Molland, S Molton, N Devon EX36 3ND. —— Felicity Ann, *b* 1938: *m* 1st, 1959 (*m diss* 19—), Charles Reginald Hugh Crosland; 2ndly, 1983, as his 2nd wife, Roald Dahl, the writer, who *d* 1990, and has issue living (by 1st *m*), Camilla Emma, *b* 1960, — Charlotte Ann, *b* 1961, — Lucy Lorina, *b* 1963. *Residence* – Gipsy House, Gt Missenden, Bucks HP16 0PB. —— Veronica Tessa, *b* 1948; *ed* Somerville Coll, Oxford (BA 1970), and Newnham Coll, Camb: *m* 1972, Marius Peregrine Lechmere Barran, and has issue (*see* Barran, Bt) *Residences* – The Poplars, 64 St Marks Rd, W10 0NN; Lower Hill, Molland, S Molton, N Devon E36 3NE.

DOUGHTY-TICHBORNE (E) 1621, of Tichborne, Hampshire (Extinct 1968)

Sir ANTHONY JOSEPH HENRY DOUGHTY DOUGHTY-TICHBORNE, 14th and last *Baronet*.

DAUGHTERS LIVING OF FOURTEENTH BARONET

Miranda Frances, *b* 1941: *m* 1961, Christopher Stephen Motley, of Sonas, Ardentallen, By Oban, Argyll PA34 4SF (*see* E Ranfurly, colls, 1980 Edn), and has issue living, William Michael, *b* 1962, — Mark Charles, *b* 1966, — Samantha Antonia Clare *b* 1964, — Abigail Anne Louise, *b* 1970, — Pandora Mary Denise, *b* 1971. —— Denise Mary Magdalene, *b* 1949: *m* 1986, Michael Hendrie, of Down Farmhouse, Kilmeston, Hants, only son of John Hendrie, of Harewood End, Herefs, and has issue living, Harry John, *b* 1988.

EVANS-TIPPING (UK) 1913, of Oaklands Park, Awre, co Gloucester

Sir DAVID GWYNNE EVANS-TIPPING, 5th *Baronet*; *b* 25 Nov 1943; *s* his father, *Sir* FRANCIS LORING GWYNNE-EVANS, 1993; *ed* Trin Coll, Dublin (B Agric Sci).
Residence – 11 rue Angelique-Verien, Neuilly-sur-Seine, France.

BROTHER LIVING

CHRISTOPHER EVAN EVANS-TIPPING (Symonds Farmhouse, Childrey, Wantage, Oxon OX12 9UA), *b* 1946: *m* 1974, Fenella Catherine, 2nd da of Cdr Edwin Allen Morrison, OBE, DL, of The Bury House, Odiham, Hants, and has issue living, Guy Edward Francis, *b* 1978, — Amy Clare, *b* 1976.

HALF-BROTHER AND ADOPTIVE HALF-BROTHER LIVING

Francis Tristan GWYNNE-EVANS, *b* 1960. —— Teo Leslie GWYNNE-EVANS (adopted), *b* 1962.

SISTER LIVING

Carolyn Eve, *b* 1947: *m* 1984, Eamon Peter Toner, and has issue living, Edward Evan, *b* 1987, — Evelyn Frances, *b* 1985.

HALF-SISTERS LIVING

Melody Louise Bernadette GWYNNE-EVANS, *b* 1958. —— Clelia Marie GWYNNE-EVANS, *b* 1965. —— Soraya Charlotte GWYNNE-EVANS, *b* 1967.

DAUGHTERS LIVING OF THIRD BARONET (*By 1st marriage to Elspeth, da of Rt Hon Sir Godfrey Patison Collins KBE, CMG, MP*)

Sylvia Ada, *b* 1938: *m* 1967, Duncan Godfrey Stableford Smith, of 1 Almond Way, Annaty Bank, Tokai, Cape Town, S Africa, yst son of Clifford Edgar Smith, of Lynedoch, Cape Province, S Africa, and has issue living, Andrew Duncan, *b* 1973, — Philippa Silvia, *b* 1976. —— Gwenllian Mary Hope, *b* 1939: *m* 1963, Robert Chumley Bryce Neill, of 10 Cecil Av, Melrose, Johannesburg, S Africa, elder son of R. C. Neill, of 19 Adlam Rd, Durban, S Africa, and has issue living, Robert Ian Grant, *b* 1965, — Angela Elspeth, *b* 1970, — Belinda Gwen, *b* 1973.

HALF-GREAT UNCLE LIVING (*Son of 1st baronet*)

John (c/o Barclays Bank DCO, PO Box 1004, Johannesburg, S Africa), *b* 1910.

WIDOWS LIVING OF THIRD AND FOURTH BARONETS

MONICA (*Monica, Lady Gwynne-Evans*), da of Douglas Clinch, of Durban, S Africa, and formerly wife of William Dalrymple: *m* 1946, as his 2nd wife, Sir Ian William Gwynne-Evans, 3rd Bt, who *d* 1985. *Residence* – 57 Eastwood Rd, Dunkeld, Johannesburg, S Africa.

GLORIA MARIE (*Lady Gwynne-Evans*), da of Thomas Reynolds: *m* 1958, as his 2nd wife, Sir Francis Loring Gwynne-Evans, 4th Bt, who *d* 1993. *Residence* – Casa Rosada, C/Los Jazmines 329, Urb El Rosario, 29600 Marbella, Spain.

The 1st baronet, Sir William Gwynne-Evans (only son of Evan Evans, of Wain, Cardiganshire, by Mary Gwynne, widow of Charles Gwynne Pryse, of Gogerddan, Cardiganshire), received Royal Licence 1913 to continue to use the additional surname of Gwynne. Sir Evan Gwynne Gwynne-Evans, 2nd baronet, was High Sheriff of Gloucestershire 1943. Sir Francis Loring Gwynne-Evans, 4th baronet, assumed by deed poll 1943 the names of Francis Loring Gwynne Evans-Tipping in lieu of those of Francis Loring Gwynne-Evans and reverted to his patronymic by deed poll 1958. He was a professional singer under the name of Francis Loring.

TOLLEMACHE (GB) 1793, of Hanby Hall, co Lincoln

CONFIDO · CONQVIESCO

I trust and am content

Sir LYONEL HUMPHRY JOHN TOLLEMACHE, 7th *Baronet*; *b* 10 July 1931; *s* his father, Maj-Gen *Sir* HUMPHRY THOMAS, CB, CBE, DL, 1990; *ed* Uppingham, and RAC Cirencester; Maj (ret) Coldm Gds; FRICS; JP and DL of Leics, High Sheriff 1978-79, and CC 1985-97: *m* 1960, Mary Joscelyne, el da of late Col William Henry Whitbread, TD, of Warren Mere, Godalming, and has had issue.

Arms – Argent, a fret sable (a label of three points for difference). Crest – A horse's head erased gules, between two wings or pelletée (differenced as the arms).
Residence – Buckminster Park, Grantham NG33 5RU.

SONS LIVING AND DECEASED

†Lyonel Thomas, *b* 23 Jan 1963; *ed* Stanbridge Earls; *d* 22 Aug 1996. —— RICHARD JOHN, *b* 4 May 1966; *ed* Uppingham: *m* 1992, Amanda Louise, elder da of Gordon Phillips, of Brickhill Pastures, Maulden, Bedford, and has issue living, Alice Mary, *b* 1997. *Residence* – Wymondham Manor, Wymondham, Melton Mowbray, Leics LE14 2AJ.

DAUGHTERS LIVING

Katheryne Mary, *b* 1960. —— Henrietta Joscelyne, *b* 1970: *m* 1993, Capt David J. Chubb, late The Light Dragoons, son of Cmdr Edwin Chubb, of Pennaton, S Brent, Devon. *Residence* – Mill Farm, Coston, Melton Mowbray, Leics LR14 2RP.

BROTHER LIVING

Robert Hugh Thomas, *b* 1937; *ed* Uppingham, and Magdalene Coll, Camb (BA): *m* 1962, Lorraine Frances Lougheed, el da of Brig Frederick Joshua Allen, OBE, of Hambledon Cottage, Lower Bourne, Surrey, and has issue living, William Benjamin (32 Spring St #2, New York, NY 10012, USA), *b* 1966; *ed* City of London Sch, and Univ Coll, London: *m* 1995, Minna Sarah, da of late Gerald Ian Lacey, of 56 Hamilton Park West, N5, — Rosa Frances Laila, *b* 1970. *Residence* – 27 Aubert Park, N5 1TP.

SISTERS LIVING AND DECEASED

Priscilla Joan, *b* 1927: *m* 1952, John Chetwynd Gillett, of Gulworthy Farm, Tavistock, Devon, son of Col Sir (William) Alan Gillett, TD, DL (V Chetwynd, colls), and has issue living, Robert John Chetwynd (Rock Park, Gulworthy Farm, Tavistock, Devon), *b* 1954: *m* 1977, Clara Elizabeth, da of Gordon William Heath, PhD, of Paignton, Devon, and has issue living, Ella Clare *b* 1980, Sophie Louise *b* 1982, — Andrew William Tollemache (72 Heavitree Rd, Exeter, Devon), *b* 1958: *m* 1979, Rosemary McMahon, and has issue living, David *b* 1983, Edward *b* 1989, Esther *b* 1980, — (Diana) Mary, *b* 1953: *m* 1983, Hugh Davies, of Cherry Brook House, Tavistock, Devon, and has issue living, Peter *b* 1987, Thomas *b* (twin)1987, — Sara Jane, *b* 1962: *m* 1989, Michael Woolley, and has issue living, Daniel *b* 1991, Alice *b* 1990. —— †Diana Margaret, *b* 1929: *m* 1953, Daniel Johannes Haak, of Uplands Stud, Scotland Farm, Hawkley, Liss, Hants GU33 6NH, and *d* 1996, leaving issue, Jonathan Daniel, *b* 1955: *m* 1978, Annabella Edith, da of John Wickins, of Eastergate, Chichester, and has issue living, Jochen Daniel *b* 1981, Anoushka Lara *b* 1979, Naomi Tara *b* 1985, — Roderick Johannes, *b* 1957: *m* 1980, Nicola Jane, da of Michael Cameron, MD, FRCS, FRCOG, and has issue living Sam Michael *b* 1984, Toby Daniel *b* (twin) 1984, Charlie *b* 1985, Poppy Anna *b* 1990, — Venetia Priscilla, *b* 1959: *m* 1988, Phillip Robinson, of Southampton, and has issue living, Tristan Joshua *b* 1994, — Felicity Nora, *b* 1961: *m* 1987, Colin Rodger, of Petersfield, and has issue living, Megan Diana *b* 1988, Hannah Margaret *b* 1990, Tamsin Janna *b* 1994.

COLLATERAL BRANCHES LIVING

(*See* Cs Dysart, colls).

This baronetcy was granted to William Manners, subsequently Lord Huntingtower, el son of Louisa, Countess of Dysart, who assumed by Roy Licence the surname and arms of Talmash 1821. On his death in 1833, he was succeeded by his el son, Lionel William John Tollemache, Lord Huntingtower, who succeeded his grandmother as 8th Earl of Dysart in 1840, the baronetcy thus becoming merged in the Earldom. In 1935, on the death of the 9th Earl of Dysart, the baronetcy was released and passed to his kinsman, Sir Lyonel Felix Carteret Eugene Tollemache, who succeeded as 4th baronet.

LUCAS-TOOTH (UK) 1920, of Bught, Inverness

Perseverantia palmam obtinebit

Perseverance will obtain the palm

Sir (HUGH) JOHN LUCAS-TOOTH, 2nd *Baronet*; *b* 20 Aug 1932; *s* his father, *Sir* HUGH VERE HUNTLY DUFF MUNRO-LUCAS-TOOTH, 1985; *ed* Eton, and Balliol Coll, Oxford; late Lt Scots Guards: *m* 1955, Hon Caroline Poole, eldest da of 1st Baron Poole, CBE, TD, PC, and has issue.

𝕬rms – Quarterly, 1st and 4th gules, a demi-gryphon segreant between three feathers argent; 2nd and 3rd azure, on a bend between in chief two crescents and in base an estoile argent, three vine leaves proper. 𝕮rests – 1st, a gryphon segreant gules, semée of mullets, and holding in the sinister claw a feather argent; 2nd, a demi-dragon azure, holding in the paws a vine branch fructed and leaved proper.
Residences – Parsonage Farm, East Hagbourne, Didcot, Oxon OX11 9LN; 41 Lancaster Rd, W14 1QJ.

DAUGHTERS LIVING

(Caroline) Maria, *b* 1956: *m* 1980, William John Hibbert, of 41 Lancaster Rd, W11, yr son of Sir Reginald Alfred Hibbert, GCMG, and has issue living, Cosima Mary, *b* 1984, — Clover Frances, *b* 1988. ——— (Lucinda) Kate, *b* 1958: *m* 1980, David Mark Ackroyd, son of L. M. Ackroyd, and has issue living, Frederick William, *b* 1981, — Nancy Caroline *b* 1983, — Beatrice Alice Violet, *b* 1988. ——— (Belinda) Alice, *b* 1966: *m* 1990, Aubrey Duarte Simpson-Orlebar, elder son of Michael Keith Orlebar Simpson-Orlebar, CMG, of The British Embassy, Mexico.

SISTERS LIVING

Laetitia Helen (*Lady Oppenheimer*), *b* 1926; BPhil, MA, DD: *m* 1947, Sir Michael Bernard Grenville Oppenheimer, 3rd Bt, of L'Aiguillon, Rue des Cotils, Grouville, Jersey, CI. ——— Jennifer Mary, *b* 1929: *m* 1949, Maj John Desmond Henderson, Scots Guards, who *d* 1990, and has issue living, Richard, *b* 1951, — Alexander, *b* 1971, — Patricia, *b* 1950: *m* 19—, Charles Brims, of Brimpton Lodge, Brimpton, Reading, Berks RG7 4TG. *Residence* – Hatch Gate, Hatch Lane, Bucklebury, Berks RG7 6NX.

COLLATERAL BRANCH LIVING (*In special remainder*)

Issue of late Com Selwyn John Power WARRAND, RN, brother of 1st baronet, *b* 1904, *ka* 1941: *m* 1933, Frena Lingen (who *m* 2ndly, 1947, Henry Richard Charles Humphries), da of late Everard Crace, of Canberra, Aust:—
JAMES LINGEN, *b* 6 Oct 1936: *m* 1960, Juliet Rose, yr da of late T.A. Pearn, of Plymouth, Devon, and has issue living, Patrick Duncan, *b* 18 March 1962: *m* 1989, Elizabeth Margaret, yst da of Bernard Bowen, of Perth, Western Australia, — Edward Jonathon, *b* 1968: *m* 1993, Lisa Ann, eldest da of Graham Wagg, of Kentlyn, NSW, Australia, — Anna-Claire, *b* 1964: *m* 1991, Christopher George Coore, yst son of George Coore, of Canberra, ACT, and has issue living, George Thomas *b* 1993. *Residence* – Ryefields, Cobbity, NSW 2570. ——— Joanna Christine, *b* 1938.

Sir Hugh Vere Huntly Duff Lucas-Tooth, 1st Bt, was the grandson of Sir Robert Lucas Lucas-Tooth, 1st Bt (*cr* 1906, ext), whose surname and arms he assumed by Roy licence 1920, and whose three sons had been killed during 1914-18 War, leaving no male issue. In default of heirs male of the body of the grantee this Baronetcy has special remainder to the other heirs male of the body of his mother, Beatrice Maude, da of 1st baronet (*cr* 1906). In 1965 Sir Hugh assumed for himself only the additional surname of Munro.

TOUCHE (UK) 1920, of Westcott, co Surrey

Be Watchful

Sir ANTHONY GEORGE TOUCHE, FCA, 3rd *Baronet*; *b* 31 Jan 1927; *s* his uncle, *Sir* NORMAN GEORGE, 1977; *ed* Eton; Chm Touche, Remnant and Co 1971-81; Dep Chm Nat Westminster Bank plc 1977-87 and a Dir of other financial cos: *m* 1961, Hester Christina, el da of Dr August Friedrich Werner Pleuger, of Linden Lodge, Green Rd, Birchington, Kent, and has issue.

Arms – Argent, a lion salient between a fleur-de-lis in the sinister chief and a like fleur-de-lis in the dexter base vert. Crest – Two fleur-de-lis gules, resting thereon a mullet of six points or.
Residence – Stane House, Ockley, Dorking, Surrey, RH5 5TQ.

SONS LIVING

WILLIAM GEORGE, *b* 26 June 1962: *m* 1987, Elizabeth Louise, yst da of Allen Bridges, of Lyford Cay, Nassau, Bahamas, and has issue living, Harry George, *b* 3 June 1992, — James Alexander, *b* 1994, — Edward William, *b* 1999, — Lucy Madeleine, *b* 1996. —— Peter Francis, *b* 1968: *m* 1996, Laura Jefferson, who *d* (15 Feb) 1999, elder da of Thomas Richards Coolidge, of Red Fox Farm, Falls Village, Connecticut, USA, and has issue living, Alexander Thomas Coolidge, *b* (6 Feb) 1999, — Charles Randolph Jefferson, *b* (twin) 1999.

DAUGHTER LIVING

Helen Mary, *b* 1966.

SISTER LIVING

Isabel Amy, *b* 1930: *m* 1962, David Murray Arthur Reid, of The Folly, Tetbury, Glos GL8 8XN.

DAUGHTERS LIVING OF SECOND BARONET

Penelope Maitland, *b* 1930; BSc Edinburgh 1952: *m* 1954, Joseph Edwin Mason, PhD, of Crabtree Meadow, Hope, Sheffield, and has issue living, Donald George, *b* 1955, — Brian Richard, *b* 1960, — Barbara Jane, *b* 1956. —— Brenda Margaret, *b* 1932; *ed* Newnham Coll, Camb (BA): *m* 1956 (*m diss* 1987), Ronald Edward Artus, MA, and has issue living, Colin Edward, *b* 1957, — Alan Norman, *b* 1959, — Philip Matthew, *b* 1964, — Lucy Katharine, *b* 1961.

COLLATERAL BRANCH LIVING

Issue of late Rt Hon Sir Gordon Cosmo Touche, 3rd son of 1st baronet (*b* 1895, *d* 1972), who was *cr* a *baronet* 1962 (see that title).

The 1st baronet, Sir George Alexander Touche (son of Anthony Murray Touche, banker, of Inverleithfield, Edinburgh), was Senior Partner in the firm of George A. Touche & Co, chartered accountants, and a Lieut for City of London (Sheriff 1915-16, and an Alderman 1915-21), and sat as MP for N Div of Islington (*C*) 1910-18.

TOUCHE (UK) 1962, of Dorking, co Surrey

Be Watchful

Sir RODNEY GORDON TOUCHE, 2nd *Baronet*; *b* 5 Dec 1928; *s* his father, *Rt Hon Sir* GORDON COSMO, 1972; *ed* Marlborough, and Univ Coll Oxford: *m* 1955, Ouida Ann, el da of late Frederick Gerald MacLellan, of Moncton, New Brunswick, Canada, and has issue.

Arms – Vert, a lion rampant argent holding between the forepaws a portcullis chained or, between two fleurs-de-lis, one in sinister chief, the other in dexter base argent. Crest – Between two fleurs-de-lis or, a Dorking cock proper.
Residence – 2403 Westmount Pl, 1100 8th Av SW, Calgary, Alberta, T2P 3T9, Canada.

SON LIVING

ERIC MacLELLAN (PO Box 72, Cochrane, Alberta T0L 0W0, Canada), *b* 22 Feb 1960: *m* 1990 (*m diss* 1998), Leanne Marie, da of Arthur Stringer, of Pontiex, Saskatchewan, Canada, and has issue living, Braden Stringer, *b* 1990, — Danielle Erica, *b* 1992.

DAUGHTERS LIVING

Amanda Ann *b* 1956: *m* 1978, Peter M. Bowler, of 4557 Bordeaux Av, Dallas, Texas 75205-3608, USA, and has issue living, Samuel McNamara, *b* 1987, — Sarah Jane, *b* 1983, — Anne MacLellan, *b* 1985. —— Susan Ruth, *b* 1957: *m* 1st, 1983 (*m diss* 1986), Pasquale Tartaglia; 2ndly, 1992, Trevor B. Arends, of Newport, Rhode Island, USA, son of Kaj Arends, of USA, and has issue living, (by 1st *m*) Cosmo Alexander Touche, *b* 1990, — (by 2nd *m*), Sebastian Valdimar Touche, *b* 1992, — Finnley Angus Yuri Touche, *b* 1999, — Islah Valerie Touche, *b* 1993, — Siri Ouida Elizabeth Touche, *b* 1995. —— Karen Marie, *b* 1961: *m* 1986, Michael Lightstone, of 6369 Seaforth St, Halifax, Nova Scotia B3L 1R2, Canada, and has issue living, Jesse Lyon, *b* 1990, — Samantha Touche, *b* 1988, — Kate Annie, *b* 1992.

SISTER LIVING

Daphne Margaret, *b* 1927: *m* 1952, Patrick Wilfred Wells, of Snells, Great Henny, Sudbury, Suffolk, and has issue living, Derrick Gordon, *b* 1956: *m* 1st, 1984 (*m diss* 1991), Katherine Ann, yr da of Guy Simpson, of Earl Soham, Suffolk; 2ndly, 1997, Diana, da of Robert Long, of Bishops Waltham, Hants, and has issue living, (by 1st *m*) George Patrick Charles *b* 1985, Elizabeth Florence *b* 1987, (by 2nd *m*) James Rodney Mitchell *b* 1997, Charles Gordon Alexander *b* 1999, — William Patrick, *b* 1960: *m* 1985 (*m diss* 1995), Jane Elizabeth, da of John Alexander, of Ufford, Suffolk, and has issue living, Thomas Alexander *b* 1987, Robert William *b* 1990, — Jennifer Margaret, *b* 1953.

The 1st Bt, Rt Hon Sir Gordon Cosmo Touche (3rd son of 1st Bt 1920 creation), MP for Reigate (*C*) 1931-50, and Dorking 1950-64, was Chm of Ways and Means, House of Commons 1960-62.

SALUSBURY-TRELAWNY (E) 1628, of Trelawny, Cornwall
(Name pronounced "Saulsbury-Trelawny")

Deeds consonant with words

Virtue is more noble than patrimony

Sir JOHN BARRY SALUSBURY-TRELAWNY, 13th *Baronet; b* 4 Sept 1934; *s* his father, *Sir* JOHN WILLIAM ROBIN MAURICE, 1956; *ed* HMS Worcester; Sub Lt RNVR; Dir of the Martin Walter Group Ltd 1971-74, of the Korn Ferry International Inc 1977-83, and of Goddard Kay Rogers Assoc 1984-95 (Chm 1993-95); F Inst M 1974; JP (Kent) 1973-78: *m* 1958, Carol Knox, yr da of late C. F. K. Watson, of Saltwood, Kent, and has issue.

Arms – Quarterly: 1st and 4th, argent, a chevron sable, *Trelawny;* 2nd and 3rd, gules, a lion rampant per bend sinister argent and erminois ducally crowned between three crescents or, *Salusbury,* on a canton of the last (for *Brereton*) a bear's head erased sable, muzzled argent. Crests – 1st, a wolf passant proper; 2nd, a demi-lion rampant per bend sinister, as in the arms, holding in the paws a shield or charged with a bear's head sable, muzzled argent.
Residence – Beavers Hill, Rectory Lane, Saltwood, Hythe, Kent CT21 4QA.
Clubs – Army and Navy.

SON LIVING

JOHN WILLIAM RICHARD (278 Seabrook Rd, Hythe, Kent) *b* 30 March 1960: *m* 1st, 1980 (*m diss* 1986), Anita, yr da of Kenneth Snelgrove; 2ndly, 1987 (*m diss* 1993), Sandra Patricia, da of Joseph Thompson, of Seabrook, Hythe, Kent, and has issue living (by 1st *m*), Harry John, *b* 10 Dec 1982, — Victoria Hayley, *b* 1981, — (by 2nd *m*) Thomas Jonathon, *b* 1989.

DAUGHTERS LIVING

Jane Louise, *b* 1958: *m* 1977, Maj John R. Martin, Parachute Regt, and has issue living, James Jonathan, *b* 1982, — Emma Jane, *b* 1980. —— Amanda Sarah, *b* 1961: *m* 1980, Capt Alan M. Startin, Devonshire and Dorset Regt, and has issue living, Matthew Guy, *b* 1982, — Benjamin Marcus, *b* 1984, — Hamish William, *b* 1988, — Pollyanna Knox, *b* 1992. —— Emma Mary, *b* 1966: *m* 1988, William Ernle Hardy Vernon (*see* E Harrowby, colls), and has issue (see that title).

HALF-BROTHER LIVING

William Hamelin (Southtown House, W Pennard, Glastonbury, Som), *b* 1942: *m* 1967, Meline Martha Katharina, who *d* 1969, da of late Dr Ir Cornelius P. A. Zeijlmans van Emmichoven, of The Hague.

WIDOW LIVING OF TWELFTH BARONET

ROSAMUND HELEN, da of late Arthur Reed Ropes (Adrian Ross, author and playwright): *m* 1st, 1937, as his second wife, Sir John William Robin Maurice Salusbury-Trelawny, 12th Bt, who *d* 1956, 2ndly, 1990, Christopher R. V. Bell, OBE. *Residence* – 32 Harvest Vale, Lindfield, Haywards Heath, W Sussex.

COLLATERAL BRANCHES LIVING

Grandchildren of late Lt-Col James Edward Salusbury-Trelawny, OBE, 2nd son of 10th Baronet:—
Issue of late James Reginald Dorrington Salusbury-Trelawny, *b* 1908, *d* 1980; *m* 1st, 1932, Muriel Mary, who *d* 1970, da of Sir Eustace William Windham Wrixon-Becher, 4th Bt; 2ndly, 1971, Vieno Helinä, yr da of late Väinö Junno, of Keni, Finland:—
(By 1st *m*), Jonathan William, OBE, *b* 1934; *ed* Charterhouse; Col Coldm Gds, OBE (Mil) 1976; *m* 1st, 1959 (*m diss* 1969), Jill Rosamonde, da of Maj-Gen Cecil Benfield Fairbanks, CB, CBE; 2ndly, 1970 (*m diss* 197—), Gillian, only child of R. J. Ratcliff, of Fossebridge House, nr Cheltenham, and has issue living (by 2nd *m*), Katherine Sophie, *b* 1972. —— Mary Letitia, *b* 1937; *m* 1966, Procter Naylor, OBE, of 17 Chapel St, Bildeston, Ipswich, and has issue living, Edward Trelawny Procter, *b* 1969: *m* 1996, Barbara, da of Bernard Thole, of Holland, and has issue living, James Alexander *b* 1998, — William James, *b* 1977, — Harriet Mary, *b* 1967: *m* 1999, Josef Antoni Lampart, son of Antoni Lampart, of Bury St Edmunds, Suffolk, and has issue living, Florence Harriet *b* 1998.

Grandchildren of late John Salusbury-Trelawny, son of late Col Harry Reginald Salusbury-Trelawny, 4th son of 8th baronet:—
Issue of late Major John Maitland Salusbury-Trelawny, MC, *b* 1892, *d* 1954: *m* 1919, Louisa Frederica, who *d* 1985, da of late Capt Guy Mainwaring, RN:—
John Guy, *b* 1919; *ed* Bradfield Coll; Capt (ret) Duke of Cornwall's LI; European War 1939-45 (wounded, prisoner): *m* 1948, Ruth Gertrude, da of late Edward Richard Marker (B Bagot, colls), and has issue living, Richard John MARKER (Combe, Honiton, Devon), *b* 1953; assumed the surname of Marker in lieu of his patronymic 1974: *m* 1978, Petronela Johana van der Mortel, of Victoria, BC, Canada, and has issue living, Karissa Ann *b* 1980, Stephanie Michelle *b* 1984, Angela Nicole *b* 1986, Joanna Petronela *b* 1988, — Peter Michael, *b* 1956, — Patrick Charles, *b* 1958, — Daphne Anne, *b* 1950, — Jill Margaret, *b* 1951. —— †Philip Michael, MC, *b* 1921; *ed* Winchester; Lt-Col The LI; N Africa and Italy 1942-45 (MC); DL Cornwall 1982: *m* 1946, Jean Mary (Flt Officer WAAF), who *d* 1988, only da of late Col Herbert Cecil Fraser, DSO, OBE, TD, and *d* 1998, leaving issue, Simon Jonathan (120 Earlsfield Rd, SW18. *Club* – Army and Navy), *b* 1948; *ed* Nautical Sch, Pangbourne: *m* 1st, 1974 (*m diss* 1978), Caroline Margaret, only da of Sir Nigel John Douglas

Vernon, 4th Bt; 2ndly, 1978, Marian Janet, da of John MacAulay, of Poplar Hall, Ramsey, nr Harwich, Essex, and has issue living (by 2nd *m*) Edward John *b* 1979, Harry Philip *b* 1980, — Diana Jane, *b* 1947: *m* 1970, Robert Jessop Blake, of Harrington House Farm, Spilsby, Lincs, and has issue living, James Trelawny *b* 1971, Jonathan Jessop *b* 1973. —— Ann Laetitia, *b* 1924: *m* 1953, David Neil Courtenay MacWatters, and has issue living, Jonathan Courtenay, *b* 1954, — Victoria Courtenay, *b* 1956, — Jennifer Laetitia, *b* 1962.

This family takes its name from Trelawn or Treloen, in Cornwall. The Right Rev Sir Jonathan Trelawny, 3rd Bt, a man of great learning, was consecrated Bishop of Bristol 1685, and was one of the seven Bishops committed to the Tower by James II, which act caused a great rising among the people of Cornwall. After the Revolution, he was successively Bishop of Exeter and Winchester. Capt Sir William, RN, 6th Bt, was Governor of Jamaica. Sir William Lewis, 8th Bt, MP for East Cornwall, and Lord-Lieutenant of the county, assumed, in 1802, the additional surname of Salusbury.

TREVELYAN (E) 1662, of Nettlecombe, Somerset (Dormant 1976)
(Name pronounced "Trevillian")

Sir Willoughby John Trevelyan, 9th Bt, of Nettlecombe, died unmarried in 1976, since when no name has been entered on the Official Roll of the Baronetage. Succession to the Baronetcy is held to have passed to *Sir* George Lowthian Trevelyan, 4th Bt, of Wallington, who *d* 1996, and subsequently to his brother *Sir* Geoffrey Washington Trevelyan, 5th Bt, of Wallington (and *de jure* 11th Bt, of Nettlecombe).

COLLATERAL BRANCH LIVING *(not in remainder to Baronetcy)*

Grandchildren of late Edward Walter Trevelyan, yr son of late George Edward Trevelyan (whose issue was legitimated by his subsequent *m*, but not for succession to Baronetcy), 2nd son of late Rev George Trevelyan, 3rd son of late Rev Walter Trevelyan, 2nd son of 4th baronet:—
Issue of late Norman Irving Trevelyan, *b* 1915, *d* 1996: *m* 1951, Jennifer Mary (1041 Adella Av, Coronado, CA 92118, USA), only da of late Arthur Elliott Riddett, of Burgh Heath, Surrey:—
Edward Norman (3180 Via Real, Carpinteria, CA 93013, USA), *b* 1955: *m* 1993, Debbie J., da of Robert A. Mullin, of Corpus Christi, Texas, and has issue living, Reed Edward, *b* 1996. —— George Arthur (Cayucos, CA 93430, USA), *b* 1958; has issue living, Charles, *b* 1985, — Luke, *b* 1991, — Miles, *b* 1996, — Mia, *b* 1987. —— Jane, *b* 1953: *m* 1978, David Floyd Lewis, of Fairfield, Iowa, USA, and has issue living, Katie, *b* 1993.

(Male line in remainder to baronetcy)

Descendants of late Sir Charles Edward Trevelyan, KCB, son of late Ven George Trevelyan, Archdeacon of Taunton, 3rd son of 4th baronet, who was *cr* a *baronet* 1874:—
See Trevelyan, Bt, *cr* 1874.

Grandchildren of late Rev Preb Charles William Trevelyan, MC (infra):—
Issue of late John Francis Trevelyan, *b* 1934, *d* 1996: *m* 1958, Elizabeth Mary (RD2, Te Puke, NZ), da of Harvey Brockenshaw:—
Andrew John (6 Watea Rd, Mount Albert, Auckland, NZ), *b* 1961: *m* 1991, Jenny Elizabeth, da of Michael James Grainger, of Bramhall, Cheshire, and has issue living, Matthew Grainger, *b* 1994, — Thomas Michael, *b* 1998, — Sarah Jane, *b* 1996. —— James Edward, *b* 1962; BE: *m* 1994, Vicki Kathryn, da of Anthony Wilfred Long, of Rotorua, NZ. —— Fiona Catherine, *b* 1965. —— Katrin Elizabeth, *b* 1966.

Grandchildren of late Rev John Charles Trevelyan, 2nd son of Rev William Pitt Trevelyan (infra):—
Issue of late Rev Prebendary Charles William Trevelyan, MC, *b* 1887, *d* 1974: *m* 1930 Maud Dorothe, who *d* 1986, da of late Frederick Augustus Dixey, MD, FRS:—
Rev Preb James William Irvine (The Rectory, Rookwood Close, Honiton, EX14 8BH), *b* 1937; *ed* Wellington Coll, and Selwyn Coll, Camb (MA); V of Lenham with Boughton Malherbe, Kent, 1972-78, since when R of Honiton: *m* 1969, Felicity Jane, da of Joseph Gibson and has issue living, Robert William Dixey, *b* 1970, — Lucy Catherine, *b* 1974. —— Janet Isabel, *b* 1932. —— Elizabeth Margaret, *b* 1939: *m* 1964, Robert Adrian Franklin, MA, MB (Cantab), FRCPsych, of Verno House South, Lyndhurst Rd, Christchurch, Dorset BH23 4SG, and has issue living, Nicholas Robert, *b* 1969, — Clare Elizabeth, *b* 1965, — Susan Dorothe, *b* 1967.

Granddaughter of late Rev William Pitt Trevelyan, 6th son of late Ven George Trevelyan, Archdeacon of Taunton, 3rd son of 4th baronet:—
Issue of late Rev George Philip Trevelyan, *b* 1858, *d* 1937: *m* 1896, Monica Evelyn Juliet, who *d* 1962, da of late Rev Sidney Philips, Hon Canon of Worcester (sometime V of Kidderminster), of The Blanquettes, Worcester:—
Urith Monica *b* 1909; *ed* Somerville Coll, Oxford (BA 1937, MA 1941): *m* 1940, Rt Rev Harry James Carpenter, 37th Bishop of Oxford, who *d* 1993, of St John's Home, St Mary's Rd, Oxford OX4 1QE, and has issue living, Humphrey

William Bouverie (6 Farndon Rd, Oxford OX2 6RS) *b* 1946; *ed* Marlborough, and Keble Coll, Oxford (MA, DipEd); author, broadcaster and musician; FRSL 1983: *m* 1973, Mari Christina, da of late Caradog Prichard, and has issue living, Clare Nia *b* 1978, Katherine Sioned *b* 1981.

Grandchildren of late Rev George Philip Trevelyan (ante):—
Issue of late John Trevelyan, CBE, *b* 1903, *d* 1986: *m* 1st, 1928 (*m diss* 1949), Kathleen Margaret, da of late Charles Pass; 2ndly, 1949 (*m diss* 1959), Joan Frieda, BM, BCh, da of Francis Clayton Scott (*see* Scott, Bt, *cr* 1909, colls); 3rdly, 1959, Jean, who *d* 1972, da of Robert Mutch; 4thly, 1974, Rosalie Evelyn, who *d* 1979, da of Joseph Lopez-Salzedo:—
(By 2nd wife) James Philip (33 Brockman Av, Dalkeith, W Aust 6009), *b* 1948; *ed* Univ of W Aust (BEng, MEngSc); ASME, MIEAust: *m* 1st, 1971 (*m diss* 1994), Jolin, da of late Frank Edmondson, of Floreat Park, W Aust; 2ndly, 1994, Dr Samina Yasmeen, da of Malik Mohammad Iqbal, of Islamabad, Pakistan, and has issue living (by 1st *m*), Charles Francis, *b* 1974, — Nicholas James, *b* 1976, — Clare Rose, *b* 1983. —— Sarah Juliet, *b* 1950: *m* 1980, James (Jimmy) Boyle, writer and sculptor, of 21a Inverleith Place, Edinburgh EH3 5QD, and has issue living, Suzannah Angela, *b* 1984, — Kydd, *b* 1987. —— (By 3rd wife) Jonathan (33 Archery Rise, Durham DH1 4LA), *b* 1959; *ed* Bristol Univ (BSc, PhD): *m* 1980, Karen Elizabeth, da of late Kenneth Frank Ireland, and has issue living, David John, *b* 1988, — Sally, *b* 1991. —— Simon (66 Manor Rise, Lichfield, Staffs WS14 9RF), *b* (twin) 1959; *ed* Birmingham Univ (BSc): *m* 1982, Isobel Catherine, da of Dr Oliver Watt, OBE, of Glasgow, and has issue living, James Oliver, *b* 1988, — Anna Joëlle, *b* 1985.

Issue of late Humphrey, Baron Trevelyan, KG, GCMG, CIE, OBE, *b* 1905, *d* 1985 (see that title).

Grandchildren of late John Spencer Trevelyan, eldest son of late Thornton Roger Trevelyan, only son of late Raleigh Trevelyan, 2nd son of Walter Trevelyan (infra):—
Issue of late John Thornton Trevelyan, *b* 1898, *d* 1970: *m* 1928, Anne Georgina, who *d* 1989, da of Prof John Dobson, Wardale, of Newcastle upon Tyne:—
John Cecil Raleigh (Netherwitton Hall, Morpeth, Northumberland NE61 4NW), *b* 1933; *ed* Marlborough: *m* 1962, Jane, yr da of late Brig Roger Peake, DSO, OBE, and has issue living, John Henry Thornton, *b* 1968; *ed* Radley: *m* 1998, Anne-Marie, only da of late Leonard Beaton, and has issue living, James Francis Thornton *b* 1999, — Caroline Georgina, *b* 1962, — Tessa Margaret Thornton, *b* 1966: *m* 1995, Jonathan L. H. Goodhart, of Woodyard House, Potcote, Towcester, Northants NN12 8EH, son of Lt-Col Mark H. Goodhart, of Fighledean, Wilts, and has issue living, Serena Caroline Margot *b* 1998. —— Edward Calverley Thornton (Dalton House, Dalton, Northumberland), *b* 1935; *ed* Marlborough: *m* 1962, Elizabeth Anne, el da of late Geoffrey Blayney, of High Shield, Hexham, and has issue living, Julian Blackett Thornton, *b* 1963: *m* 1995, Helen, yr da of Thomas Bevan, of Bellawongarah, NSW, Australia, — Hugh Robert Thornton, *b* 1973, — Rosemary Joy, *b* 1965, — Amanda Fay, *b* 1967. —— Anne Margaret Thornton, *b* 1930: *m* 1953, John Humphrey Usborne, of Glan-Nant, Crickhowell, Breconshire, and has issue living, Richard Thomas, *b* 1954: *m* 198-, Henrietta E. M., 6th da of B. C. White-Spunner, of Brookes Hall, Horsington, Somerset, and has issue living, Thomas Masters *b* 1983, Alice *b* 1985, — John Edward, *b* (twin) 1954: *m* 1980, Diana, da of late A. Glynne-Percy, of Tomatin, Inverness-shire, and has issue living, Joanna Susan *b* 1983, Sarah Margaret *b* 1985, — Andrew Thornton (George House, 21 High St, Colsterworth, Lincs NG33 5NE), *b* 1956; CEng, MICE: *m* 1983, Lamorna, yr da of K. J. Hammond Forder, of Napier Cottage, Napier Av, SW6, and has issue living, Harriet Georgina *b* 1991, a da *b* 1995. —— Joan Mary Thornton, *b* 1932: *m* 1963, George Campbell Wilkinson, TD, of Upper End Lodge, Eckington, Pershore, Worcs WR10 3DQ, and has issue living, Anne Margaret, *b* 1965: *m* 1995, Gary Clarke, of 3 Copes Lane, Bramshill, Hook, Hants, and has issue living, Jacqueline Mary *b* 1997.

Grandsons of late Capt Walter Raleigh Trevelyan, son of late Walter Raleigh Trevelyan (infra):—
Issue of late Col Walter Raleigh Fetherstonhaugh Trevelyan, Indian Army, *b* 1893, *d* 1953: *m* 1921, Olive Beatrice, who *d* 1976, (having *m* 2ndly, 1953, Col William Henry Ralston, DSO, OBE, MC, who *d* 1962), da of late Thomas Gibbons Frost, of Mollington Hall, Chester:—
Walter Raleigh, *b* 1923; *ed* Winchester; 1942-45 War as Capt Rifle Bde. *Residences* – 18 Hertford St, W1Y 7DB; St Cadix, St Veep, Cornwall PL22 0PB. —— John Amyas (1 Roscacre, Tye Green, Alpheton, Suffolk CO10 9BW), *b* 1928; *ed* Winchester; sometime 2nd Lt Rifle Bde. *m* 1954, Patricia Mary, da of late Stuart Moore, and has issue living, Amyas John Stuart, *b* 1957: *m* 1988, Claire Diane, da of Harry Whittle, and has issue living, Philip John Amyas *b* 1991, Alice Margaret *b* 1989, — Oliver Willoughby, *b* 1961: *m* 1990, Louise Elizabeth, da of Alan Thompson, and has issue living, Mary Elizabeth *b* 1991, Katherine Louise *b* 1993, Esme Olivia *b* 1996, — Rupert Patrick, *b* 1963: *m* 1987, Sara Jane, da of Richard Glanville, and has issue living, Grace Kathryn *b* 1989, Olivia Jane *b* 1991, Anna Florence *b* 1993, — Elizabeth Virginia, *b* 1955: *m* 1984, Anthony Terrell Webb-Martin, of Bishopslea School, PO Belvedere, Harare, Zimbabwe, eldest son of late J. J. Webb-Martin, of Marondera, Zimbabwe, and has issue living, Stuart John *b* 1987, Matthew Trevelyan *b* 1990.

Grandsons of late Charles Leslie Calverley Trevelyan, yr son of Walter Raleigh Trevelyan, only son of Walter Calverley Trevelyan, 3rd and yst son of Walter Trevelyan, yr son of 3rd baronet:—
Issue of late Leslie Calverley Trevelyan, *b* 1912; *d* 1982: *m* 1939, Prudence Mary, who *d* 1986, da of late Alfred S. Fawcett, of Standhills, Dore Moor, Derbyshire:—
Anthony Leslie Calverley (Three Gables, Kemerton, Glos GL20 7HR), *b* 1941; *ed* Seaford Coll: *m* 1972, Victoria, da of late Lt-Col Gordon Kenward Barker, DSO, of Bourton-on-the-Water, and has issue living, Charlotte Louise, *b* 1973, — Esmé Gwendolen, *b* 1975, — Alexandra Mary *b* 1979. —— (Amyas) Charles (Wood Stanway, nr Cheltenham, Glos GL54 5PG; Cavalry and Guards' Club), *b* 1946; *ed* Harrow, and RMA; Maj R Scots Dragoon Gds (Carabiniers and Greys): *m* 1989, Angela Joan, SRN, RSCN, da of Cecil Pike, of The Wagon House, Higher Langham, Nimmer, Chard, Som, and has had issue, Piers Calverley Charles, *b* 1990, — Prudence, *b* and *d* 1993, — Henrietta Prudence Angela, *b* 1994.

The family of Trevelyan takes its name from Trevelyan in the parish of St Veep, Cornwall. The 1st baronet, Sir George, was son of George Trevelyan, who suffered greatly for his fidelity to the royal cause during the civil war. The 2nd and 4th baronets each represented Somersetshire in Parliament. Sir Walter Calverley Trevelyan, 6th Bt, was a noted geologist, whose wife Pauline was a confidant of Ruskin and Swinburne, and a patron of the Pre-Raphaelites.

TREVELYAN (UK) 1874, of Wallington, Northumberland
(Name pronounced "Trevillian")

Sir GEOFFREY WASHINGTON TREVELYAN, 5th *Baronet*; *b* 4 July 1920; *s* his brother, *Sir* GEORGE LOWTHIAN, 1996; his claim to the Trevelyan of Nettlecombe Baronetcy has been accepted by the College of Arms, although no name has been entered on the Official Roll of the Baronetage; *ed* Oundle, and Trin Coll, Camb (MA); Dir Chatto and Windus Ltd, Hogarth Press Ltd 1962-78, Chatto, Bodley Head and Jonathan Cape Ltd 1970-78; Chm Thames North Region of Abbeyfield Soc 1985-94: *m* 1947, Gillian Isabel, MBE, eldest da of late Alexander Louis Sandison Wood, OBE, of Spencer's Farm, Whelpley Hill, Chesham, and has issue.

Arms – Gules, a demi-horse argent, hoofed and maned or, issuing out of water in base proper. Crest – Two arms counter-embowed proper, habited azure, holding in the hands a bezant.
Seat – Wallington, Cambo, Morpeth, Northumberland. *Residence* – Lower Silkstead, 3 Abbey Mill End, St Albans, Herts AL3 4HN.

SON LIVING

PETER JOHN, *b* 11 Sept 1948; *ed* Oundle, and Trinity Coll, Camb (MA): *m* 1996, Diane Christine Terry, and has issue living, Julian Miles, *b* 29 Oct 1998. *Residence* – Lower Silkstead, 3 Abbey Mill End, St Albans, Herts AL3 4HN.

DAUGHTER LIVING

Sandra Mary, *b* 1951: *m* 1974, David Bradley, and has issue living, Robert David, *b* 1980, — James Thomas, *b* 1982. *Residence* – Northrigg Hill, Brampton, Cumbria CA8 2BX.

SISTERS LIVING

Marjorie (*Lady Weaver*), *b* 1913: *m* 1941, Sir Tobias Rushton Weaver, CB, son of late Sir Lawrence Weaver, KBE, and has issue living, Lawrence Trevelyan (4 Huntley Gdns, Dowanhill, Glasgow G12 9AS), *b* 1948: *m* 1991, Camilla Rohini Simmons, and has issue living, Robin Lintorn *b* 1993, Marion Sophia *b* 1995. — Kathleen, *b* 1943; JP Dunmow, Saffron Walden and Harlow: *m* 1966, Nicholas John Milford Abbott, of Crouches, Church End, Great Dunmow, Essex CM6 3BQ, and has issue living, Simon Milford *b* 1971, Benjamin Tobias *b* 1973, Rachel Mary *b* 1967 (has issue living, Stan Jean *b* 1995, Louis Pascal *b* (twin) 1995), Judith Caroline *b* 1969, — Caroline, *b* 1945: *m* 1986, Michael Herbert Baker, of 26 Wellington Park, Clifton, Bristol BS8 2UT, eldest son of Henry Baker, — Rachel, *b* 1950: *m* 1974, Charles David Munn, of Hodore, Hartfield, Sussex, and has issue living, George Patrick *b* 1976, Toby Charles *b* 1984, Louise Caroline *b* 1978, Emily Claire *b* 1980. *Residence* – 14 Marston Close, NW6 4EU. —— Florence Patricia, *b* (twin) 1915: *m* 1st, 1942, Lt Frederick Philip Cheswright, RNVR, who *d* 1946; 2ndly, 1950 (*m diss* 1975), Sqdn-Ldr Reginald Joseph Jennings, MC, RAFVR, and has issue living (by 1st *m*), Hugh Weeden Nicholas (The 2 Queens, Cambo, Morpeth, Northumberland NE61 4AR), *b* 1942: *m* 1st, 1968 (*m diss* 1979), Rosemary Frances, da of late Norman Walduck, of Hatfield, Herts; 2ndly, 1980, Jean Moya, da of David William Barratt, and has issue living, (by 1st *m*) Sebastian Charles Philip *b* 1971, Rupert James Macaulay *b* 1972, — Janet Vanessa, *b* 1943: *m* 1st, 1964 (*m diss* 1985), Geoffrey Brian Parker; 2ndly, 1988, David G. Hall, MBE, of Longfield House, Fairview Rd, Dartmouth, Devon TQ6 9EN, and has issue living, (by 1st *m*) Philip Christopher Liam *b* 1967, Jonathan Hugh *b* 1968. *Residence* – Wallington, Cambo, Morpeth, Northumberland NE61 4AR.

COLLATERAL BRANCHES LIVING

Grandson of late Robert Calverley Trevelyan, poet and dramatist, 2nd son of 2nd baronet:—
Issue of late Julian Otto Trevelyan, *b* 1910, *d* 1988; painter: *m* 1st, 1934 (*m diss* 1950), Ursula Frances Elinor, elder da of late Bernard Richard Meirion Darwin, CBE; 2ndly, 1951, Mary (Durham Wharf, Hammersmith Terr, W6 9TS), da of late Vincent Fedden:—
(By 1st *m*) Philip Erasmus, *b* 1943; *ed* Bryanston, Dept. of Fine Art, King's Coll, Newcastle-upon-Tyne, and Royal Coll of Art: *m* 1975, Eleanor, da of late Matthew Prior, of Cambridge, and has issue living, Jack Elisha, *b* 1977, — Matthew Robert, *b* 1978, — Susannah, *b* 1987. *Residence* – Hilltop Farm, Appleton-le-Moors, Kirkbymoorside, N Yorks.

Grandchildren of late George Macaulay Trevelyan, OM, CBE, FRS, the famous historian, 3rd son of 2nd baronet:—
Issue of late Charles Humphry Trevelyan, *b* 1909, *d* 1964: *m* 1936, Mary Trumbull (6 Walton Av, Henley-on-Thames, Oxon RG9 1LA), yst da of Winchester Bennett, of Everitt St, New Haven, Conn, USA:—
Thomas Arnold (31 Orbel St, SW11 3NX), *b* 1942; *ed* Bryanston, and King's Coll, Camb (MA); MB BChir, MRCGP: *m* 1st, 1965 (*m diss* 1974), Ann, da of James Jones; 2ndly, 1974, Anita, da of Reginald Martyn Smith, of Chaddesley Corbett, Worcs, and has had issue (by 1st *m*), Harry, *b* 1968, — Emma, *b* 1966, — Selina Rose, *b* 1969, — (by 2nd *m*) Jack Humphry, *b* and *d* 1984, — Clare, *b* 1981, — Victoria Rossanna, *b* 1986. —— George Macaulay (6 Walton Av, Henley-on-Thames, Oxon RG9 1LA), *b* 1944; *ed* Bryanston, Queen's Coll, Oxford, and London Sch of Econ: *m* 1st, 1967, Susan, da of Mark Pearson, of Burton Joyce, Notts; 2ndly, 19—, Valerie Elizabeth, da of Tom Preston, of School Lane, Dewsbury, W Yorks, and has issue living (by 1st *m*), Will Mark, *b* 1971, — Sasha France, *b* 1969, — Laura Kate, *b* 1968, — (by 2nd *m*) Thomas Trumbull, *b* 1988. —— Humphry Bennett (Diamond Cottage, Keyhaven, Hants SO41 0TP), *b* (twin) 1944; *ed* Bryanston, and Trin Coll, Camb: *m* 1st, 1972, (*m diss* 1978), Jane Bannatyne COTTER, da of Peggy Cotter, of Guildford; 2ndly, 1981 (*m diss* 1992), Valerie May, da of Reginald Phillips, of Saltdean, Sussex; 3rdly, 1994, Patricia Ramos, da of José Costa, of Rio de Janeiro, Brazil, and has issue living (by 2nd wife), Stephanie Leah, *b* 1979. —— Jane

Winchester (188 Peckham Rye, SE22), *b* 1938: *m* 1960 (*m diss* 1984), David Armstrong, and has issue living, Richard Michael Boris, *b* 1961, — Sarah Jane, *b* 1965, — Rachel Elizabeth, *b* 1966. —— Mary Harriet, *b* 1939; MB, BS: *m* 1971, James Barton.

This family is a younger branch of the Trevelyans, baronets of Nettlecombe (see colls, thereof). The 1st baronet was Gov of Madras 1859-60, and Financial member of Gov-Gen's Council at Calcutta 1862-5. The 2nd baronet, Rt Hon Sir George Otto Trevelyan, OM, DCL, LLD (a historian, and author of *The Life and Letters of Lord Macaulay*, and other works), was a Lord of the Admiralty 1869-70, Parliamentary Sec to Admiralty 1880-82, Ch Sec for Ireland 1882-4, Chancellor of Duchy of Lancaster 1884-5, and Sec for Scotland and ex-officio Keeper of the Great Seal of Scotland 1886 and 1892-5, and MP for Tynemouth (*L*) 1865-8, for the Border Burghs 1868-86 (when he was defeated), and for Bridgeton Div of Glasgow (*L*) 1887-97. The 3rd baronet, Rt Hon Sir Charles Philips Trevelyan, was Parliamentary Sec to Board of Education 1908-14, and Pres of Board of Education Jan to Nov 1924 and 1929-31, and sat as MP Elland Div of N Part of W Riding of Yorkshire (*L*) 1899-1918, and for Newcastle-upon-Tyne (*Lab*) 1922-31. The 4th baronet, Sir George Trevelyan, was Warden Attingham Park, Shropshire (adult education centre) 1947-71, and Founder (1971) Wrekin Trust (Pres 1971-86).

On the death of Sir Willoughby John Trevelyan, 9th Bt, of Nettlecombe, who died unmarried in 1976, succession to the Baronetcy of Nettlecombe is held to have passed to Sir George Trevelyan, 4th Bt, of Wallington, who *d* 1996, and subsequently to his brother Sir Geoffrey Trevelyan, 5th Bt, of Wallington (and *de jure* 11th Bt, of Nettlecombe).

TRITTON (UK) 1905, of Bloomfield, Borough of Lambeth, co London

Forward

Sir ANTHONY JOHN ERNEST TRITTON, 4th *Baronet*; *b* 4 March 1927; *s* his father, *Maj Sir* GEOFFREY ERNEST, CBE, 1976; *ed* Eton; Maj (ret) The Queen's Own Hussars: *m* 1957, Diana, da of late Rear-Adm St John Aldrich Micklethwait, CB, DSO (*see* Welby, Bt, colls, 1990 Edn), and has issue.

Arms – Argent, on a bend cotised gules a besant between two esquires' helmets or. **Crest** – A horse statant argent, resting the dexter forefoot upon a besant proper.
Residence – River House, Heytesbury, Warminster, Wilts BA12 0EE. *Club* – Cavalry and Guards'.

SON LIVING

JEREMY ERNEST (6 St Stephen's Terrace, SW8 1DH), *b* 6 Oct 1961.

DAUGHTER LIVING

Clarissa Mary Penelope, *b* 1959: *m* 1988, John Charles Joseph Delamere, yr son of late F. A. Delamere, of Rathgowan, Mullinger, co Westmeath, and has issue living, Hugo Fitzherbert, *b* 1989, — Camilla Sophia, *b* 1991. *Residence* – The Old Rectory, Avening, Glos GL8 8NF.

SISTER LIVING

Julia Mary, *b* 1930. *m* 1952, Richard Norman Kingzett (*see* Agnew, Bt, *cr* 1895, 1985 Edn), and has issue living, Jan Antony, *b* 1955, — Christopher Richard Colin (68 Camberwell Grove, SE5), *b* 1958: *m* 1989, Madeleine Anne, da of Theodore Peter Donahue, of North St, Litchfield, Conn, USA, and has issue living, Emily Rose Julia *b* 1990, Catherine Augusta Mary *b* 1992. *Residence* – 18 Sloane Avenue, Chelsea, SW3.

The 1st baronet, Sir (Charles) Ernest Tritton, sat as MP for Norwood Div of Lambeth (*C*) July 1892 to Jan 1906.

TROLLOPE (E) 1642, of Casewick, Lincolnshire

I hear, but am Silent

Sir ANTHONY SIMON TROLLOPE, 17th *Baronet*; *b* 31 Aug 1945; *s* his father, *Sir* ANTHONY OWEN CLAVERING, 1987; *ed* Sydney Univ (BA), and New England Univ (MBA); breeder of Rhodesian Ridgebacks and Anglo-Arab horses: *m* 1969, Denise, da of Trevern Thompson, of N Sydney, NSW, and has issue.

𝕬rms – Vert, three stags courant argent, attired or, within a bordure of the second. 𝕮rest – On a mount vert, a stag courant as in the arms, holding an oak-leaf in his mouth proper.
Residence – Churinga Lodge, 28 Midson Rd, Oakville, NSW 2765, Australia.

DAUGHTERS LIVING

Kellie Yvette, *b* 1970. —— Analese Christine, *b* 1972.

BROTHER LIVING

HUGH IRWIN (Casewick Cottage, 26 Bayswater Rd, Lindfield, NSW 2070, Australia), *b* 31 March 1947: *m* 1971, Barbara Anne, da of William Ian Jamieson, of Lawley Crescent, Pymble, NSW, and has issue living, Andrew Ian, *b* 1978, — Edwina Anne, *b* 1976, — Jennifer Kate, *b* 1980.

UNCLE LIVING (*son of 15th Baronet*)

Gordon Paul Clavering (Dougherty Apartments, 1 Victor St, Chatswood, NSW 2067, Australia), *b* 1918.

WIDOW LIVING OF SIXTEENTH BARONET

JOAN MARY ALEXIS (*Dowager Lady Trollope*), da of Alexis Robert Gibbes, of Balgowlah, NSW: *m* 1942, Sir Anthony Owen Clavering Trollope, 16th Bt, who *d* 1987. *Residence* – 31 Pacific Highway, Wahroonga, NSW 2076, Australia.

COLLATERAL BRANCHES LIVING

Granddaughters of late Herbert Edward Trollope, only son of late Edward Hazel Trollope, 2nd son of late Rev John Trollope, son of late Rev Thomas Daniel Trollope, grandson of late Henry Trollope, 3rd son of 3rd baronet:—
Issue of late John Herbert Hazel Trollope, *b* 1908, *d* 1991: *m* 1939, Ruth, who *d* 1987, da of Frederick Warry, of Freshford, Somerset:—
Beatrice Mary, *b* 1942: *m* 1963, Peter Old, of Featherlands, Honeycroft, Chilsworthy, Holsworthy, Devon EX22 7JJ, and has issue living, Andrew (Silworthy Farm, Bradworthy, Holsworthy, Devon), *b* 1967: *m* 1997, Diane Mary Wickett, — Rachel, *b* 1964: *m* 1986, Mervyn William Bate, of Splatt Farm, Tresmeer, Launceston, Cornwall, and has issue living, Verity Ruth *b* 1989, Hannah Rachel *b* 1992, — Sarah, *b* 1971: *m* 1993, Wagner Rangel, Jr, of 127 Ringway, Southall, Middx UB2 5ST. —— Maureen Hazel, *b* 1945: *m* 1973, Ian Joseph Kampel, CEng, MIEE, MBIM, of 101 Broadway, Southbourne, Bournemouth, and has issue living, Timothy Ian, *b* 1978, — Alison Jane, *b* 1975: *m* 1999, Shaun Cole, of 206 Runnymede Av, Bearwood, Bournemouth. —— Susan Bridget, *b* 1947: *m* 1969, Elemér Fejér, and has issue living, Karen Lisa, *b* 1974, — Trudy Lynne, *b* 1977.

Grandsons of late Henry Trollope, 3rd son of late Rev John Trollope (ante):—
Issue of late John Trollope, *b* 1880, *d* 1927: *m* 1911, Florence Evelyn, who *d* 1977, da of James Grose, of Oshawa, Ont, Canada:—
John Henry James (Canada), *b* 1916: *m* 1940, Elizabeth, da of Archibald Eugene McKinnon, of Canada, and has issue living, John Brian (2146 Bickerton Av, Gloucester, Ont, Canada K1J 6Y3), *b* 1941: *m* 1965, Carol Ann, da of Blake Weir, of Canada, and has issue living, Teresa Dione Weir *b* 1972: *m* 1993, Jasvinderpal Singh Brar, of England, — Robert Donald, *b* 1945: *m* 1969, Bonnie Laurene, da of Willis David Murray, of Canada, and has issue living, Heather Anne *b* 1970: *m* 1995, Miles Edward Nellis, of Canada, — Susan Diane Elizabeth, *b* 1943. —— Donald Herbert (Stonehouse, Glos), *b* 1925: *m* 1955, Doris, da of Arthur James Eborall, and has issue living, Anthony John Christopher James (109 Charleswood Drive, Downsview, Ont, Canada M3H 1X5), *b* 1959: *m* 1990, Linda, da of Russell Saunders, of Canada, and has issue living, Anthony Michael Jeffrey *b* 1992, Jillian Victoria *b* 1995, — Kathleen Elizabeth Victoria Beaumont, *b* 1964.

The Rt Hon Sir John Trollope, PC, 7th Bt, MP for Lincolnshire (*C*) 1861-68, was *cr* Baron Kesteven (peerage of United Kingdom) 1868, when the Baronetcy remained merged in the Barony until the death of the 3rd Baron (*ka* 1915), when it devolved upon his cousin, Sir William Henry Trollope, 10th Bt. Sir Gordon Clavering Trollope, 15th Bt *s* Nov 1957 and *d* Oct 1958, when he was *s* by his son, Sir Anthony Owen Clavering Trollope, 16th Bt.

TROUBRIDGE (GB) 1799, of Plymouth
(Name pronounced "Troobridge")

Sir THOMAS RICHARD TROUBRIDGE, 7th *Baronet*; *b* 23 Jan 1955; *s* his father, *Lieut-Cdr Sir* PETER, RN, 1988; *ed* Eton, and Univ Coll, Durham: *m* 1984, Hon Rosemary Douglas-Pennant, yr da of 6th Baron Penrhyn, and has issue.

ᴀrms – Or, on a bridge embattled of three arches, through which water is flowing towards the base proper, a tower of the second, thereon hoisted a broad pennant flying towards the sinister; on a canton azure, two keys in saltire, the wards upwards or. ᴄrest – A dexter arm-embowed, habited azure, holding a flagstaff, thereon a flag azure charger with two keys in saltire or.
Residences – 96 Napier Court, Ranelagh Gardens, SW6 3XA; The Manor House, Elsted, Midhurst, W Sussex GU29 0JY. *Clubs* – Hurlingham, Itchenor Sailing.

SONS LIVING

EDWARD PETER, *b* 10 Aug 1989. —— Nicholas Douglas St Vincent, *b* 1993.

DAUGHTER LIVING

Emily Rose, *b* 1987.

SISTERS LIVING

Amanda Marguerite, *b* 1957: *m* 1991, Timothy M. H. Payne, yst son of Anthony D. Payne, of Marnhull, Dorset, and has issue living, Daisy, *b* 1997. —— Camilla June, *b* 1961.

UNCLE LIVING (*brother of 6th baronet*)

Thomas (1B Gertrude St, SW10), *b* 1939: *m* 1st, 1971 (*m diss* 1977, annulment by Roman Catholic Church 1978), Baroness Marie Christine Hedwig Agnes Ida, da of late Baron Günther Hubertus von Reibnitz (*see* Royal Family, D Kent); 2ndly, 1981, Mrs Petronella Forgan (*née* von Woyrsch), formerly wife of James Russell Forgan.

AUNT LIVING (*sister of 6th baronet*)

(Elizabeth) June, *b* 1933: *m* 1956, Alan G. L. Baxter, who *d* 1988, and has issue living, Edward Thomas, *b* 1960, —— Elizabeth Anne, *b* 1958, —— Sarah Evelyn, *b* 1962, —— Mary Emma, *b* 1965, —— Louisa Jane, *b* 1969. *Residence* – 46 South St, St Andrews, Fife KY16 9JT.

WIDOW LIVING OF SIXTH BARONET

Hon VENETIA DAPHNE WEEKS, da of 1st Baron Weeks: *m* 1st, 1954, Lieut-Cdr Sir Peter Troubridge, 6th Bt, RN, who *d* 1988; 2ndly, 1995, as his 2nd wife, William Frederick Eustace (Derick) Forbes (*see* V De Vesci, colls, 1990 Edn). *Residence* – Earlstoun Lodge, Dalry, Castle Douglas, Kircudbrightshire DG7 3TY.

COLLATERAL BRANCH LIVING

Issue of late Maj Edward St Vincent Troubridge, RM, brother of 6th baronet, *b* 1930, *d* 1992: *m* 1st, 1955 (*m diss* 1974), Jennifer Anne, da of late Edward Billing-Lewis, of Maidstone, Kent; 2ndly, 1974, Patricia Barbara (7 Liskeard Gdns, SE3), da of Maj Chevalier Hannibal Alexander Scicluna, OBE, of 29 Milner St, Sliema, Malta, and formerly wife of Cmdr P. G. Nelson, of Oslo, Norway:—
(By 1st *m*) Rodney St Vincent, *b* 1957. —— Charlotte Louise, *b* 1960. —— Emma Marguerite, *b* 1963. —— (By 2nd *m*) Amelia Clare, *b* 1974.

The 1st baronet, Adm Sir Thomas (son of late Richard Troubridge, of London), was a distinguished naval commander, and sat as MP for Yarmouth 1802-6. The 2nd baronet, Adm Sir Edward Thomas, CB, sat as MP for Sandwich 1831-47, and Col Sir Thomas, CB, 3rd Bt, greatly distinguished himself in the Crimea, where he was severely wounded. Sir Peter Troubridge, 6th Bt, was Chm of the Standing Council of the Baronetage 1981-84.

TRUSCOTT (UK) 1909, of Oakleigh, East Grinstead, Sussex

Sir GEORGE JAMES IRVING TRUSCOTT, 3rd *Baronet*; *b* 24 Oct 1929; *s* his father, *Sir* ERIC HOMEWOOD STANHAM, 1973; *ed* Sherborne: *m* 1st, 1954 (*m* annulled on his petition 1958), Irene Marion Craig Barr Brown; 2ndly, 1962, Yvonne Dora, yr da of late Frank Edward Nicholson, of Carshalton, Surrey, and has issue by 2nd *m*.

Prepared for either

Truth against all the world

Arms – Argent, three chevronels gules, between two mullets in chief of the last, pierced of the field, and a knight's helmet in base proper; a chief checky of the second and first. **Crest** – A fasces erect, surmounted by a palm branch slipped and an arrow saltireways, all proper.
Address – BM Quill, London WC1N 3XX.

SON LIVING

RALPH ERIC NICHOLSON, *b* 21 Feb 1966.

DAUGHTER LIVING

Ruth Emma, *b* 1967.

SISTER LIVING

Jennifer Margaret Anne, *b* 1932: *m* 1958, Lt-Cdr Edward Martyn Theodore Segar, RN (ret), of Stanton Hill, Priorsfield Rd, Godalming, Surrey GU7 2RQ, and has issue living, John Edward, *b* 1965, — Jane Margaret, *b* 1959, — Anne Mary, *b* 1962.

The 1st baronet, Sir George Wyatt Truscott (son of Sir Francis Wyatt Truscott, Lord Mayor of London 1879-80), was Chm of Brown, Knight & Truscott, Ltd, printers and stationers, of Suffolk Lane, EC, and an Alderman of City of London (Sheriff 1902-3, Lord Mayor 1908-9, Hon Freeman 1937).

TUCK (UK) 1910, of Park Crescent, St Marylebone

Sir BRUCE ADOLPH REGINALD TUCK, 3rd *Baronet*, *b* 29 June 1926; *s* his father, *Major Sir* (WILLIAM) REGINALD, 1954; *ed* Canford Sch; sometime Lieut Scots Guards: *m* 1st, 1949 (*m diss* 1964), Luise, da of John C. Renfro, of Sán Angelo, Texas, USA; 2ndly, 1968, Pamela Dorothy, da of Alfred Michael Nicholson, of London, and has issue by 1st and 2nd *m*.

With God

Arms – Or, an antique lamp flaming azure, in base a hurt charged with four F's in cross of the field, on a chief of the same two hands in the act of blessing of the first. **Crest** – A lion sejant sable supporting with the paws an artist's palette proper, inscribed thereon the word "Thorough" sable.
Residences – Newmarket, Suffolk; Montego Bay, PO Box 274, Jamaica. *Club* – Lansdowne.

SONS LIVING (*By 1st marriage*)

RICHARD BRUCE, *b* 7 Oct 1952; *ed* Millfield. —— Christopher John, *b* 1954.

DAUGHTER LIVING (*By 2nd marriage*)

Charlotte Emily Pamela, *b* 1974.

SISTER LIVING

Moyra Grace, *b* 1920: *m* 1st, 1947, Lee David Greif, who *d* 1950; 2ndly, 1951, Major Alvin Greif, US Army Air Force, who *d* 1958; 3rdly, 1959, Nigel Digby Pemberton. *Residence* – Montego Bay, Jamaica.

Sir Adolph Tuck, 1st Bt, son of late Raphael Tuck, fine art publisher, was Chm and Managing Director of Raphael Tuck and Sons (Limited), of Raphael House, Moorfields, EC.

TUITE (I) 1622, of Sonnagh, Westmeath
(Name pronounced "Tute")

Sir CHRISTOPHER HUGH TUITE, 14th *Baronet; b* 3 Nov 1949; *s* his father, *Maj Sir* DENNIS GEORGE HARMSWORTH, 1981; *ed* Wellington Coll, and Liverpool Univ (BSc); PhD Bristol: *m* 1976, Deborah Anne, da of A. E. Martz, of Pittsburgh, USA, and has issue.

𝕬rms – Quarterly, argent and gules. 𝕮rest – An angel vested argent, holding in the dexter hand a flaming sword proper, the sinister resting on a shield of the arms.
Residence – 120 Main St, Yarmouth, MA 02675, USA.

SONS LIVING

THOMAS LIVINGSTONE, *b* 24 July 1977. —— Jonathan Christopher Hannington, *b* 1981.

BROTHERS LIVING

Jeremy Dennis (4 Culvert Close, Coggeshall, Essex CO6 1PB), *b* 1951; *ed* Wellington Coll, and Leeds Univ (MB, FRCS): *m* 1st, 1978 (*m diss* 1997), Anne, da of J. Ebdon-Robinson; 2ndly, 1999, Mrs Rosemary Wardle, da of J. P. Meighan, of Glasgow, and has issue living (by 1st *m*), Anthony Dennis, *b* 1982, — Edward Jeremy, *b* 1984, — James Carey John, *b* 1987, — Sally Anne, *b* 1990. —— Patrick Leslie, *b* 1954; *ed* Wellington Coll, and Leeds Univ (BSc): *m* 1992, Gillie M., da of Dr K. Martin McNicol, of Grayshott, Surrey.

WIDOW LIVING OF THIRTEENTH BARONET

MARGARET ESSIE (*Margaret, Lady Tuite*) (7 Vicarage Gdns, Grayshott, Hindhead, Surrey GU26 6NH), only da of late Col Walter Leslie Dundas, DSO: *m* 1947, Maj Sir Dennis George Harmsworth Tuite, MBE, 13th Bt, who *d* 1981.

This family, which has been settled in Ireland since 1172, is descended from Sir Richard de Tuitt who that year accompanied the Earl of Pembroke to that country. The 7th baronet was murdered at Sonnagh in 1783.

TUPPER (UK) 1888, of Armdale, Halifax, Nova Scotia

Sir CHARLES HIBBERT TUPPER, 5th *Baronet; b* 4 July 1930; *s* his father, *Sir* JAMES MACDONALD, 1967: *m* 1959 (*m diss* 1975), Bernice Yvonne Quinn, and has issue.

𝕬rms – Per fesse azure and or, on a fesse ermine between two boars passant in chief or, and a sprig of may flower slipped and leaved in base proper, three escallops gules. 𝕮rest – On a mount vert, a greyhound statant sable, charged on the body with two escallops or, and holding in the mouth a sprig of mayflower as in the arms.
Residence – Suite 1101, 955 Marine Drive, W Vancouver, BC, V7T 1A9.

SON LIVING

CHARLES HIBBERT, *b* 10 July 1964: *m* 1987, (Elizabeth) Ann Heaslip, and has issue living, Cara-Lyn Ann, *b* 1991. *Address* – 5164 Sam's Way, Nanaimo, British Columbia, Canada V9T 6C4.

SISTER LIVING

Janet Mary, *b* 1929: *m* 1951, William John Couldwell, MD, CM, of #50-5880 Hampton Place, Vancouver, British Columbia V6T 2E9, and has issue living, William Tupper (16 Tarry a Bit Drive, Waccabuc, NY 10597, USA), *b* 1955; MD, PhD: *m* 1990, Marie Francoise Simard, and has issue living, Mitchell William Galen *b* 1991, Sandrine Marie Camille *b* 1991, Genevieve Christine *b* 1993, — Susan Janice, *b* 1953; BA, BArch: *m* 1977, John Joseph McCormack, Dip Arch, MRAIC, of 4666 West 3rd Av, Vancouver, BC, Canada V6R 1N4, and has issue living, John Paget *b* 1981, Brendan William *b* 1984, Liam James Couldwell *b* 1988, — Sandra Lee (Apt 204, 3641 West 28th Av, Vancouver, BC, Canada V6S 1S3), *b* 1954; BA: *m* 1982 (*m diss* 1987), Gabor Hegedus, who *d* 1990, and has issue living, Andras Zoltan Couldwell *b* 1983.

Hope is my strength

DAUGHTER LIVING OF SECOND BARONET

Margot Stewart, *b* 1928. *Residence* – Portage Sch, Portage La Prairie, Manitoba, Canada.

DAUGHTERS LIVING OF THIRD BARONET

Janet Macdonald, *b* 1920: *m* 1944, Philip Lionel Underwood, late Capt Roy Canadian Artillery, PO Box 117, Grafton, Ont, Canada, and has issue living, Harry Charles Gordon, *b* 1951: *m* 1984, Denise Ireland, — Mary Fielding, *b* 1946: *m* 1969, Claude-Frédéric Roger Marie Ingell de Kerckhove Varent, and has issue living, Charles André Philippe *b* 1976, Derrick Tupper Daniel *b* 1978. — Nora Frances, *b* 1958: *m* 1984, Gary Jay Tenenbaum. —— Dorothy Joyce, *b* 1922: *m* 1944, Maj Edward Arunah Dunlop, OBE, GM, Queen's Own Rifles of Canada, and has issue living, Edward Arunah, *b* 1946: *m* 1976, Valerine Glen Hardacre, — Charlotte Mary Ferguson, *b* 1949. *Residence* – 6 Meredith Cres, Toronto, Canada, M4W 3B6.

COLLATERAL BRANCHES LIVING

Grandchildren of late Maj Reginald Hibbert Tupper, QC, LLD, brother of 3rd and 4th baronets:—
Issue of late Charles Gordon Hibbert (Victor) Tupper, *b* 1918, *d* 1996: *m* 1946, Margaret Ada, da of James Albert Campbell, QC, of Vancouver:—
Charles Reginald Hibbert (121-6450 East Blvd, Vancouver, BC, Canada V6M 3V9), *b* 1947.

Issue of late David Wilson Hibbert Tupper, LLB, *b* 1921, *d* 1999: *m* 1st, 1947, Joan Margot, who *d* 1985, da of late Col Austin Gillies, VD, of Ottawa; 2ndly, 1986, Jacqueline Caroline (5615 Hampton Place, Apt 105, Vancouver, BC, Canada V6T 2H1), da of ...... Haddock:—
(By 1st *m*) Sidney Victor Hibbert (7611 Moffat Rd, Apt 32, Richmond, BC, Canada V6H 1X9), *b* 1948: *m* 1974, Josephina Rosa Vassallo, of Peru, and has issue living, Jesse Derek, *b* 1980, — Cecilia Alexandra, *b* 1976. —— Charles Austin Hibbert (510 W 13th Av, Vancouver, BC, Canada V5Z 1N1), *b* 1951. —— Julia Isabel (1304 SE Reynolds St, Portland, Oregon 97202, USA), *b* 1953.

Grandchildren of late William Johnson Tupper, KC (Lt-Gov of Manitoba), 3rd son of 1st baronet:—
Issue of late Charles William Tupper, QC, *b* 1898, *d* 1960: *m* 1st, 1929, Ray Macdonald; 2ndly, 1941, Winifred Lillian Craske, who *d* 1956:—
(By 2nd *m*) Charles James (1428-75 Bamburgh Crescent, Scarborough, Ontario, Canada M1W 3W1) *b* 1942; BScE. —— (By 1st *m*) Margaret Ray, *b* 1931; BA, BLS: *m* 1956, William Macdonald Price, of 700 Cardinal, St Laurent, Quebec, Canada H4L 3C7, and has issue living, Charles Macdonald (1354 Gatehouse Drive, Mississauga, Ontario, Canada L5H 1A5), *b* 1958; MD, CM: *m* 1983, Mary Shanahan, B Eng, and has issue living, Rae Frances *b* 1989, Thomas McMurray *b* 1990, Joseph Charles *b* 1992, — Scott William (117 Laurier, Dollard des Ormeaux, PQ, Canada H9B 3B1), *b* 1960; ARCT: *m* 1988, Martine Chevrier, and has issue living, Jennifer Martine *b* 1994, Audrey Margaret *b* 1995.

The name of Tupper can be traced at Bury and vicinity, W Sussex, from the 13th century. Thomas Tupper emigrated from Kent to Massachusetts in 1635. Charles Tupper, 4th in descent from him, moved to Cornwallis, Nova Scotia 1760. His grandson, Rt Hon Sir Charles Tupper, GCMG, CB, LLD, MD, 1st Bt, was fourteen consecutive times returned as MP for his native co (Cumberland, NS), and represented it for thirty-three years in the Canadian House of Commons, was Prime Min of Nova Scotia 1864-67, and was High Commr in Great Britain for Dominion of Canada 1883-87, and 1888-96, and Premier of Canada 1896.

TURING (NS) 1638, of Foveran, Aberdeenshire

Fortune aids the daring

Sir JOHN DERMOT TURING, 12th *Baronet*; son of late John Ferrier Turing, gt grandson of John Robert Turing, brother of 7th baronet; *b* 26 Feb 1961; *s* his kinsman, Sir JOHN LESLIE, MC, 1987; *ed* Sherborne, King's Coll, Camb, and New Coll, Oxford: *m* 1986, Nicola Jane, da of Malcolm Douglas Simmonds, of Wimborne, Dorset, and has issue.

𝕬rms – Argent, on a bend sable, three boars' heads or. 𝕮rest – A hand holding a helmet proper. 𝕾upporters – Two stags proper. *Residence* – ......

SONS LIVING

JOHN MALCOLM FERRIER, *b* 5 Sept 1988. —— James Robert Edward, *b* 1991.

HALF-SISTERS LIVING

Inagh Jean, *b* 1936: *m* 1st, 1960 (*m diss* 1980), Warren Gray, solicitor; 2ndly, 1980, Herbert Aspinall, who *d* 1997, 3rdly, 1998, John Alexander Payne, and has issue living (by 1st *m*), Mark Warren, *b* 1961: *m* 1994, Rita Keller, and has issue living, Natalie Lisa *b* 1995. — Stephen Paul, *b* 1969, — Rachel Mary, *b* 1963: *m* 1990, Mark Richard Barnes, and has issue living, Thomas David *b* 1993, George Christopher *b* 1997, Anna Clare *b* (twin) 1997, — Deborah Jean, *b* 1964: *m* 1995, Jason Wright, and has issue living, Zachary Jared *b* 1998, Kiah Callula *b* 1996. *Residence* – 105 Wades Hill, Winchmore Hill, N21 1AP. —— Shuna, *b* 1940: *m* 19— (*m diss* 1983), Albert Hunt, and has issue living, Nevil, *b* 1970. *Residence* – 3 The High St, Small Dole, Henfield, Sussex. —— Janet Ferrier, *b* 1947: *m* 1981, Alan John Robinson, ARICS, and has issue living, Lisa Ferrier, *b* 1982, — Clare Elizabeth, *b* 1985. *Residence* – 137 Westfields, St Albans, Herts AL3 4JR.

MOTHER LIVING

Beryl Mary Ada, da of Herbert Vaughan Hann: *m* 1960, as his 2nd wife, John Ferrier Turing, who *d* 1983. *Residence* – 72 Chirgwin Rd, Truro, Cornwall TR1 1TT.

COLLATERAL BRANCH LIVING

Granddaughter of late Rev John Robert Turing, brother of 7th baronet:—
Issue of late Harvey Doria Turing, *b* 1877, *d* 1950: *m* 1918, Violet, who *d* 1961, da of late Rev Harry Alsager Sheringham:—
Penelope Anne Tryon, *b* 1925. *Residence* – 411 Beatty House, Dolphin Sq, SW1 3PL.

Sir William Turyn attached himself to the fortunes of King David II, and shared that monarch's exile; his loyalty was however subsequently rewarded by a grant of the barony of Foveran, in Aberdeenshire, which his descendants held more than 300 years. Sir John Turing of Foveran, 1st Bt, espoused the cause of Charles I. He was taken prisoner by the Covenanters 1639 who later sacked Foveran. He fought at Battle of Worcester 1651. The right to this baronetcy was sustained by the Lyon Office in 1882 to Sir Robert Fraser Turing, 8th Bt, by a Committee of the Privy Council in 1912, and by Interlocutor of the Lord Lyon 1.

Twisleton (Twisleton-Wykeham-Fiennes), see Fiennes.

TWYSDEN (E) 1611, of East Peckham, Kent (Extinct 1970)

Sir WILLIAM ADAM DUNCAN TWYSDEN, 12th and last *Baronet*.

WIDOW LIVING OF ELEVENTH BARONET

MARY, da of late Rear Adm H. E. C. Blagrove: *m* 1st, 1945, Sir Anthony Roger Duncan Twysden, 11th Bt, who *d* 1946; 2ndly, 1949, Capt Peter Gerald Charles Dickens, DSO, MBE, DSC, RN, of Lye Green Forge, Crowborough, Sussex, who *d* 1987, el son of late Adm Sir Gerald Charles Dickens, KCVO, CB, CMG.

TYRWHITT (UK) 1919, of Terschelling, and of Oxford
(Name pronounced "Tirrit")

Sir REGINALD THOMAS NEWMAN TYRWHITT, 3rd *Baronet*, *b* 21 Feb 1947; *s* his father, *Adm Sir* ST JOHN REGINALD JOSEPH, KCB, DSO, DSC and bar, 1961; *ed* Downside; 2nd Lieut RA 1966, Lieut 1969, RARO 1969: *m* 1st, 1972 (*m diss* 1980 and annulled 1984), Sheila Gail, da of William Alistair Crawford Nicoll, MA, LLB, of Kingsham Old Farm, Milland, Hants; 2ndly, 1984, Charlotte, only da of late Capt Angus Jeremy Christopher Hildyard, DL, RA (*see* B Morris, 1995 Edn), and has issue by 2nd *m*.

Arms – Gules, three tyrwhitts (lapwings) or. Crest – A woodman wreathed with oak and holding a club, all proper. Supporters – *Dexter*, a savage wreathed about the loins and head with oak proper, and holding over the shoulder in the exterior hand a club or; *sinister*, a sailor of the Royal Navy holding in the exterior hand a coil of rope proper.
Residence – 51 Whitecross St, Barton-on-Humber, S Humberside.

SON LIVING (*By 2nd marriage*)

ROBERT ST JOHN HILDYARD, *b* 15 Feb 1987.

DAUGHTER LIVING (*By 2nd marriage*)

Letitia Mary Hildyard, *b* 1988.

BROTHER LIVING

John Edward Charles, *b* 1953; MA Cantab 1975; ACA 1979: *m* 1978, Melinda Ngaire, only da of Capt Anthony Philip Towell, MC, of Long Island, New York, USA, and has issue living, St John Thomas Anthony, *b* 1980, — Oliver Edward John, *b* 1982, — Alexander William James, *b* 1984.

SISTER LIVING

Veronica Mary, *b* 1944: *m* 1979, Christopher Miles Boast, of 15 Ilfracombe Drive, Wattle Park, SA 5066, Australia, and has issue living, Charles St John, *b* 1980, — Timothy William, *b* 1982.

WIDOW LIVING OF SECOND BARONET

NANCY VERONICA (*Lady Agnew*), only child of late Capt Charles Newman Gilbey, of Folkestone, Kent: *m* 1st, 1944, Adm Sir St John Reginald Joseph Tyrwhitt, KCB, DSO, DSC, 2nd Bt, who *d* 1961; 2ndly, 1965, Sir (William) Godfrey Agnew, KCVO, CB, who *d* 1995. *Residence* – 25 Huntsman's Meadow, Ascot, Berks SL5 7PF.

This family descends from Sir Robert Tyrwhitt, of Kettleby, Lincs, living 1322, whose ancestor was Sir Hercules Tyrwhitt, of High Trewhitt, Northumberland, 1097. This family was also seated at Cammeringham and Scotter, co Lincs. Sixteenth in descent from Sir Robert was Richard Tyrwhitt of Nantyr Hall, Denbighshire, Recorder of Chester (*d* 1836), 3rd son of John Tyrwhitt of Netherclay House, Som, and brother of Sir Thomas Tyrwhitt (later Jones), who was *cr* a Bt 1808, ancestor of Barons Berners. The 1st baronet, Adm of the Fleet Sir Reginald Yorke Tyrwhitt, GCB, DSO (son of Rev Richard St John Tyrwhitt, Rector of St Mary Magdalen, Oxford), *m* Angela Mary, da of Mathew Corbally, JP, DL, of Rathbeale Hall, co Dublin, cmd'd 1st and 3rd Flotilla and the Harwich Force 1914-18, and was Com-in-Ch China Station 1927-29, and Com-in-Ch at the Nore 1930-33. The 2nd baronet, Adm Sir St John Reginald Joseph Tyrwhitt, KCB, DSO, DSC and bar, was Ch of Staff to Com-in-Ch Allied Forces Mediterranean 1958-9, and a Lord Commr of Admiralty, Second Sea Lord and Ch of Naval Personnel 1959-61.

USHER (UK) 1899, of Norton, Ratho, Midlothian, and of Wells, Hobkirk, Roxburghshire

With nothing base

Sir ANDREW JOHN USHER, 8th *Baronet*, *b* 8 Feb 1963; *s* his father, *Sir* (WILLIAM) JOHN TEVENAR, 1998; *ed* Hilton Coll, S Africa: *m* 1987, Charlotte Louise Alexandra, only da of Robert Barry Eldridge, of SW10, and has issue.

Arms – Gules, a saltire between four barons argent, garnished sable. Crest – A dexter arm couped below the elbow, vested azure, cuffed argent, holding in the hand a baton proper. *Seat* – Hallrule, Hawick, Roxburghshire. *Residence* – 61 Waldron Rd, SW18 3TA.

SONS LIVING

RORY JAMES ANDREW, *b* 11 June 1991. —— Callum William Edward, *b* 1994.

BROTHER LIVING

Michael William Reginald, *b* 1967; *ed* Maritzburg Coll, S Africa; *m* 1993, Belinda Anne, da of Franklin Neil Keevy Webber, of Grahamstown, S Africa, and has issue living, Angus, *b* 1995. *Residence* – 1 Radcliffe Crescent, Cherry Hills, Mount Edgecombe Country Club, Durban, Natal, S Africa.

SISTER LIVING

Caroline Rosemary, *b* 1966: *m* 1st, 1987 (*m diss* 1991), Ian Britz, who was *k* in a motor accident 1993, son of Carl Britz; 2ndly, 1998, Digby Coulson Guy, and has issue living (by 1st *m*), Julie Caroline, *b* 1988. *Residence* – Deargacha, Glen Masson, Dunoon, Argyllshire.

UNCLE LIVING (*son of 5th son of 2nd baronet*)

Stuart Alexander, *b* 1941; *ed* Uppingham: *m* 1981, Gillian Anne, da of late Dr Herbert Creeke, of Pietermaritzburg, and has issue living, Richard William, *b* 1986, — Katherine Anne, *b* 1983. *Residence* – Under Langlee, Jedburgh, Roxburghshire TD8 6PB.

DAUGHTER LIVING OF THIRD BARONET

Jacqueline, *b* 1931: *m* 1st, 1955 (*m diss* 1980), Capt Christopher Michael Wolfe Murray, Gordon Highlanders (ret); 2ndly, 1998, Cmdr William John Macnamara Faulkner, RN (ret), and has issue (by 1st *m*) (*see* Murray, Bt, *cr* 1628, colls). *Residence* – Stoner End, Froxfield, Petersfield, Hants GU32 1DX.

MOTHER LIVING

Rosemary Margaret, da of Col Sir Reginald Douglas Henry Houldsworth, OBE, TD, 4th Bt (*cr* 1887): *m* 1962 (*m diss* 1990), as his 1st wife, (William) John Tevenar Usher (later Sir John Usher, 7th Bt), who *d* 1998. *Residence* – Glenburn, Crosshill, Maybole, Ayrshire.

WIDOW LIVING OF SEVENTH BARONET

GEORGINA ELIZABETH (*Dowager Lady Usher*), da of Charles Manclark: *m* 1992, as his 2nd wife, Sir (William) John Tevenar Usher, 7th Bt, who *d* 1998. *Residence* – 7 Thorngate Rd, Hayfields, Pietermaritzburg 3201, S Africa.

COLLATERAL BRANCHES LIVING

Granddaughter of late Lieut Ronald James Usher, DSC, RN, 2nd son of 2nd baronet:—
Issue of late Lieut Robert Ronald Harry Usher, RN, *b* 1924, *d* 1947: *m* 1945, Jane Hall, who *d* 1989, having *m* 2ndly, 1954, James Murray Gregory-Jones:—
Elizabeth Margaret (Wild Thyme Cottage, The Square, Dinas Powis, Vale of Glamorgan), *b* 1946: *m* 1969 (*m diss* 1982), David Patrick Richards, and has issue living, Peter James, *b* 1970, — Owain David *b* 1973.

Issue of late Brig Thomas Clive Usher, CBE, DSO, 6th and yst son of 2nd Bt, *b* 1907; *d* 1982: *m* 1939, Valentine (Wells Stables, Hawick, Roxburghshire), da of Brig C. V. Stockwell, of Victoria, BC:—
Margaret Anne, *b* 1941: *m* 1964, Alan Harry Mactaggart, of Hallrule Farm, Bonchester Bridge, Hawick, Roxburghshire and has issue living, David Clive, *b* 1966, — William Jeremy, *b* 1970.

Issue of late Frederick Usher, 4th son of 1st baronet, *b* 1862, *d* 1909: *m* 1901, Rosie Emil (who *d* 1958, having *m* 2ndly, 1911, Colin Mackenzie Black, CVO, WS, who *d* 1943), el da of late Rev William John Knox Little, formerly V of Hoar Cross, Burton-on-Trent, and Canon and Sub-Dean, of Worcester:—

Neil John William Heriot (Culachy, Fort Augustus, Inverness-shire. *Club* – New), *b* 1903; *ed* Eton, and Trin Coll, Oxford; is Lieut 7th Batn King's Own Scottish Borderers; assumed on his marriage the additional surname of Murray, but has discontinued its use: *m* 1st, 1929 (*m diss* 1937), Elizabeth Evelyn, who *d* 1990, da of late Lieut-Col Frederick David Murray Baillie (4th Hussars), of Broughton and Cally, and of Ilston Grange, Leicester; 2ndly, 1938, Dorothy Margaret, da of Rev Colin William Scott-Moncrieff, and has issue living, (by 1st *m*) James Neil (Murrayton, Gatehouse of Fleet, Kirkcudbrightshire), *b* 1931; *ed* King's Sch, Canterbury: *m* 1957 (*m diss* 1977), Sara Winefred, da of late Lt-Col Laurence Richardson Younger, and has issue living, Peter James *b* 1961, Rozanne Helen *b* 1960, Diana Katherine *b* 1968.

Grandson of late Francis James Usher, 5th son of 1st baronet:—
   Issue of late Francis Simeon Caverhill Usher *b* 1902, *d* 1954: *m* 1935, Jean Lindsay, who *d* 1954, da of W. E. Kitson, of Blanerne, Berwickshire:—
Francis John (Dunglass, Cockburnspath, Berwickshire TD13 5XF), *b* 1937: *m* 1967, Merilyn Haswell, only da of late William Lyle Brown, DSO, TD, MD, of White Ridge, Bamburgh, Northumberland, and has two adopted children, Simon Francis, *b* 1975, — Katharine Caverhill, *b* 1972.

Sir John Usher, 1st Bt, yst son of Andrew Usher, of Edinburgh, assisted in founding a chair of public health, Edinburgh Univ 1898, and built a public health institute 1902.

Vassar-Smith, see Smith.

VAVASOUR (UK) 1828, of Haslewood, Yorkshire

Sir ERIC MICHEL JOSEPH MARMADUKE, VAVASOUR, 6th *Baronet*, only son of late Hugh Bernard Moore Vavasour, only surv son of late Oswald Joseph Stanislaus Vavasour, eldest son of late Oswald Hugh Stanislaus Vavasour, uncle of 4th baronet; *b* 3 Jan 1953; *s* his 2nd cousin once removed, *Cmdr Sir* GEOFFREY WILLIAM, DSC, RN, 1997; *ed* St Joseph's Coll, Stoke on Trent, and University of Manchester (BSc 1974); AMIEE: *m* 1976, Isabelle Baudouin Françoise Alain Cécile Cornelie Ghislaine, da of André van Hille, of 102 Hoften Berg, Brussels 1200, and has issue.

Arms – Quarterly: 1st and 4th, or a fesse dancettée sable, in the dexter chief a cross-crosslet for difference of the second, *Vavasour*; 2nd and 3rd, sable, a bend or, between six fountains, *Stourton*. **Crests** – 1st, a cock gules charged with a fountain, *Vavasour*; 2nd, a demi-monk habited in russet, his girdle or, and wielding in his dexter hand a scourge or, thereon five knotted lashes, and in his sinister an open book or, *Stourton*.
Residence – 15 Mill Lane, Earl Shilton, Leics LE9 7AW.

SONS LIVING

JOSEPH IAN HUGH ANDRÉ, *b* 22 Jan 1978; *ed* English Martyrs RC School, Leicester. —— Thomas Bernard André Hugh, *b* 1984.

DAUGHTER LIVING

Emilie Isabelle Marguerite Monique, *b* 1980.

SISTER LIVING

Anne Pauline Mary Draycot, *b* 1969. *Residence* – 17 Oakhill Close, Tean, Stoke on Trent ST10 4JP.

DAUGHTERS LIVING OF FIFTH BARONET (*By 1st marriage*)

Jacqueline Mary, *b* 1941: *m* 1966, Capt Peter John Whittington (ret) 14/20th King's Hussars, of Townhouse, 99 Upper Grosvenor Rd, Tunbridge Wells, Kent TN1 1EA, and has issue living, Edward James, *b* 1977, — Anna Catherine, *b* 1974. —— Elizabeth Anne, *b* 1943: *m* 1st, 1965 (*m diss* 1968), Terence Hickman; 2ndly, 1968 (*m diss* 1988), James Monroe Woodman; 3rdly, 1989, Calvin Palme Winn, of PO Box 4577, 460 Hammerstone Lane, Frisco, Colorado 80443, USA, and has issue living (by 2nd *m*), Elizabeth Anne, *b* 1969: *m* 1994, John William Fefley, Jr, and has issue living, Aubin (a da) *b* 1996, Olivia *b* 1999, — Lara, *b* 1970.

DAUGHTERS LIVING OF FOURTH BARONET

Elizabeth Mary, *b* 1917: *m* 1st, 1940, Lieut Michael John Priaulx Walters, RN, who *d* on active ser 1941; 2ndly, 1942, Brigadier Garth Raymond Godfrey Bird, of The Oast House, Gt Broadhurst Farm, Broad Oak, Heathfield, Sussex, and has issue living, (by 1st *m*) Simon de Lancey (Tundry House, Dogmersfield, Hants), *b* (*posthumous*) 1941: *m* 1966, Sarah, da of late Brig Thomas Gwythr Charles, and has issue living, Mark *b* 1967: *m* 1996, Victoria Helmore Elizabeth, da of Simon Anthony Aldridge, of Little Walden, Essex (and has issue living, Luke Michael *b* 1999), Barnaby *b* 1974, Gemma *b* 1969: *m* 1997, Benedict J. Scott Knight son of Adrian Scott Knight (and has issue living, Madeline Elizabeth *b* 1999), Abigail *b* 1976, — (by 2nd *m*) Christopher John Godfrey (40 London Rd, Garsington, Oxon), *b* 1946: *m* 1972 (*m diss* 1989), Hon Catherine Mary Dormer, yr da of 15th Baron Dormer, — Anthony Nigel Godfrey (47 Buckingham Place, Brighton, Sussex), *b* 1953, — Fiona Mary, *b* 1943: *m* 1969, Robin Alaster Nicholson, of 7 Highbury Place, N5 1QZ (*see* E Waldegrave, 1959 Edn), and has issue living, Zachary Luke *b* 1971, Solomon Rufus *b* 1974, Caspian Ned *b* 1978. —— Josephine Mary, *b* 1921; formerly 3rd Officer WRNS: *m* 1942, Rear Adm Derick Henry Fellowes Hetherington, CB, DSC, who *d* 1992, and has issue living, Mark, *b* 1950, — Virginia Mary, *b* 1947, — Teresa, *b* 1951, — Dinah Mary, *b* 1957.

COLLATERAL BRANCHES LIVING

Grandchildren of late Oswald Hugh Stanislaus Vavasour, uncle of 4th baronet:—
Issue of late Oswald Joseph Stanislaus Vavasour, *b* 1883, *d* 1973: *m* 1915, Mary Dorothy, who *d* 1952, da of late Bernard Moore, of The Grange, Draycott, Stoke-on-Trent:—
Dorothy Constance (Provincial House, The Broadway, Mill Hill, NW7 1EH), *b* 1916; a Sister of Charity of St Vincent de Paul.

Issue of late John Wilfred Leonard Vavasour, *b* 1891, *d* 1955: *m* 1940, Joyce, who *m* 2ndly, 1961, Robert William Ellett Ware, da of late George Frederick Mayer, of Ardleigh, Keddington Rd, Louth, Lincolnshire:—
Margaret Ann *b* 1940. —— Angela Mary VAVASOUR (Southampton), *b* 1943; has resumed her maiden surname: *m* 1963 (*m diss* 19—), Ronald James Edgington, and has had issue, Alexander James *b* 1968, — Fiona Anne, *b* 1966, *d* 1981. —— Frances Joyce Sarah, *b* 1949.

Grandchildren of late Henry Dunstan Vavasour (infra):—
Issue of late Edward Joseph Henry Vavasour, *b* 1898, *d* 1978: *m* 1927, Mary, who *d* 1975, da of late Duncan Leslie, of Perth:—
Paul (41 Serpentine Rd, Sevenoaks, Kent TN13 3XS), *b* 1929; *ed* Stonyhurst; BSc, (Lond) FICE, FIHT: *m* 1952, Pauline Mary, da of late Charles John Cable, of Sevenoaks, Kent, and has issue living, Dunstan Edward, *b* 1963; *ed* Stonyhurst; MA (Oxon); MIEE: *m* 1988, Jill, da of John Edward Fellows, of Stonebroom, Derbys, and has issue living, Oliver James *b* 1991, William Alistair John *b* 1995, — Catriona Mary *b* 1955: BSc (Dunelm): *m* 1992, Maj Nigel D. Wylie Carrick, 2nd King Edward VII's Own Goorkhas (The Sirmoor Rifles), elder son of Maj N. Wylie Carrick, of Duntisbourne Abbots, Cirencester, and has issue living, Harry Norbert Paul *b* 1994, Lucy Elizabeth Mary *b* 1993, — Elspeth Anne, *b* 1956: *m* 1979, Paul Julian Fox, of Yeoman Oast, Manor Farm, Laddingford, Kent, and has issue living, Miles Edward *b* 1983, Oriana Mary *b* 1980, Miranda Jane *b* 1985, — Matilda Alice, *b* 1961: MA (Oxon): *m* 1987, Lt-Col Nicholas Keith Cooper, RAMC, elder son of Basil Keith Cooper, of Croyde, Devon, and has issue living, Hugh Edward Keith *b* 1990. —— Christopher Edward (187 Glenmore Rd, Paddington, NSW 2021, Australia), *b* 1938; *ed* King's Sch, Canterbury, and Roy Agric Coll, Cirencester: *m* 1st, 1963 (*m diss* 19—), Cecilie May, da of late Cecil Dudley Morris, of Maidlands Farm, Brede, Sussex; 2ndly, 1987, Penelope Joanne, da of H. David S. Luetchford, of Noosa, Queensland, Australia, and has issue living, (by 1st *m*) Philip James Edward (282 Beaver Rd, Ashford, Kent), *b* 1964; *ed* Kelly Coll: *m* 1990, Joanna Marjorie, da of Alan George Smith, of Burwash, Sussex, and has issue living, Fenella Molly May *b* 1993, — Simon Mark Andrew (9 Wood St, Norwich, Norfolk), *b* 1966; *ed* King's Sch, Canterbury, and London Univ (MB, BS): *m* 1992, Sarah Lucy, elder da of Geoffrey Jacques, of SW7, and has issue living, Harry Geoffrey George *b* 1997, Rosie Charlotte May *b* 1993, Kate Victoria Alice *b* 1995, — Charles William Alexander (Magpie House, Stubbs Cross, Ashford, Kent), *b* 1971; *ed* King's Sch, Canterbury, and Oxford Brookes Univ (BA), — (by 2nd *m*) Susannah Mary-Jane, *b* 1989.

Issue of late Harold Hugh Vavasour, *b* 1902, *d* 1989: *m* 1939, Margery Constance (12 Munro St, Blenheim, NZ), da of Harold Oakley Goulter, of Blairich Station, Blenheim, NZ:—
Hugh Gerald (Hazlewood, 34 Brook St, Blenheim, NZ), *b* 1940: *m* 1966, Belinda Mary, da of Leonard Clarke, of Wellington, NZ, and has issue living, Andrew Philip Henry, *b* 1968; B Ag (Massey), — Sarah Mary Constance *b* 1967: *m* 1988, James Hadden Barr, son of Henry John Haddon Barr, of Invercargill, NZ, and has issue living, Angus Haddon Dunstan *b* 1991, Jock Henry Hugh *b* 1993, — Rachel Isolda Mary, *b* 1972, — Alice Francesca Mary *b* 1977. —— Philip Joseph (112 Karori Rd, Wellington, NZ), *b* 1943: *m* 1973, Elizabeth Robyn, da of Robert Barnett, of Bronte St, Nelson, NZ, and has issue living, Jonathan Charles, *b* 1982, — Carolyn Elizabeth, *b* 1980. —— Nicola Mary Clare, *b* 1947: *m* 1972, Kerry Gould Louis Nolan, of Coops Rd, Kaiapoi RD, NZ, and has issue living, David, *b* 1976, — Rosamond Mary Hope, *b* 1974, — Abigail *b* 1978.

Issue of late Gerard Aloysius Vavasour, *b* 1904, *d* 1983: *m* 1930, Lilian Frances, who *d* 1997, da of late Francis Campbell, of Blenheim, NZ:—
Michael Philip (Titania, Oberon, NSW 2787, Aust), *b* 1932: *m* 1st, 1955, Margaret Anne, who *d* 1963, da of Frederick H. B. Redward, of New Plymouth, NZ; 2ndly, 1965, Pamela Anne, da of Reginald B. Marston, of Sydney, and has issue living, (by 1st *m*) Gerard Joseph (19 Powell Drive, Queanbeyan, NSW, Australia), *b* 1956: *m* 1st, 1978 (*m diss* 1983), Colleen Bishop, of Sydney, Aust; 2ndly, 1984, Sonja Westerburg, of Queanbeyan, NSW, and has issue living, (by 1st *m*) Daniel *b* 1980, (by 2nd *m*) Alexander *b* 1990, Tamara *b* 1987, — Phillip Charles Dunstan (21 Alice Jackson Crescent, Gilmore, ACT, Aust), *b* 1960: *m* 1987, Katherine Lions, of Sydney, Aust, and has issue living, Nicola Frances *b* 1993, — Angela Margaret, *b* 1959: *m* 1979, Gary Smith, of Terrigal, NSW, and has issue living, Scott Aaron *b* 1983, Shaun Thomas *b* 1986, Jessica Leanne *b* 1989, — Rose Lillian Mary, *b* 1962, — (by 2nd *m*) Christopher Paul (4 Dart St, Oberon, NSW 2787, Aust), *b* 1966. —— Bernard John (Toi Downs, RD4, Blenheim, NZ), *b* 1933; Dip CAC: *m* 1964, Susan Ferrier, da of Bruce Colville Morton, of Wai Whiro, Takapau, and has issue living, Thomas William, *b* 1964: *m* 1992, Kris Mills, and has issue living, Kelsey May *b* 1993, Dayle Marshall *b* 1996, — Joseph Murray, *b* 1970, — Matthew Colville, *b* 1971, — Dominic Gerard, *b* 1977: *m* 1998, Robyn Galbraith, — Maria, *b* 1966, — Katherine Mary, *b* 1968: *m* 1987, Andrew Keith Boniface, and has issue living, Karl Andrew *b* 1989, Christopher Ryan *b* 1994, Stacey Marie *b* 1986. —— Priscilla, *b* 1936: *m* 1959, Marian Josef Adamski (Kahui Rd, RD 34, Rahotu Taranaki,

NZ), and has issue living, Peter Bernard, *b* 1961, — Anthony John, *b* 1968: *m* 1988, Leanne, da of Peter Tanner, and has issue living, Haiden James *b* 1989, — Damian Joseph, *b* 1969, — Maria Ann, *b* 1963, — Frances Mary, *b* 1964, — Theresa, *b* 1966. —— Bertha Eleanor Mary, *b* 1942: *m* 1st, 1967 (*m diss* 1987), Michael John Baldwin; 2ndly, 19—, Michael Newman, of Cowslip Valley, Marlborough, NZ, and has issue living (by 1st *m*), Bruce Phillip, *b* 1970, — Anita Jane, *b* 1968, — Penelope Debra, *b* 1975: *m* 1995, Stephen Baker, of Hawkes Bay, NZ, and has issue living, Ashley Debra *b* 1996, Tiffany Ann *b* 1997. —— Colleen Mary, *b* 1943: *m* 1973, Don Alan Robertson, of 133 Ranzau Rd, Hope, Nelson, NZ, and has issue living, Gilbert Alan, *b* 1974, — James Wallace, *b* 1977, — Phillip Duncan, *b* 1981, — Colette Marie, *b* 1976, — Sophie Anne, *b* 1979.

Issue of late John Louis Vavasour, *b* 1905, *d* 1987: *m* 1937, Madeleine Hope (who *m* 2ndly, 1988, her late husband's younger brother, Henry Philip Bede Vavasour) (infra), da of Ernest John Brammall, of Blenheim, NZ:— Jeremy Dunstan Trevor (Koitaki Plantation, PO Box 133, Port Moresby, Papua New Guinea), *b* 1942: *m* 1966, Joan Reilly, da of late George Robert Moss, of Melbourne, Aust, and has issue living, Simon John, *b* 1974, — Peta, *b* 1967, — Kimble, *b* 1971. —— Anne, *b* 1938: *m* 1963, David Eric Stewart Adams, of 23 Mulara St, Alice Springs 0870, NT, Aust, and has issue living, Jacqueline Anne, *b* 1968, — Gillian Merle, *b* 1970, — Sandra Claire, *b* 1972. —— Teresa Virginia, *b* 1939: *m* 1962, Brian John Cowan, of 15 Harrier Crescent, Umhlanga Rocks 4320, Natal, S Africa, and has issue living, John Michael, *b* 1964, — Anne Juliet, *b* 1967, — Sara Jill, *b* 1971. —— Marcia Jane, *b* 1952: *m* 1979, Owen William Finger, of Debesa Station, PO Box 356, Broome 6725, W Aust, and has issue living, Kurt John, *b* 1980, — Graeme William *b* 1982.

Issue of late Henry Dunstan Vavasour, uncle of 4th baronet, *b* 1850, *d* 1927: *m* 1887, Bertha Eleanor Mary, who *d* 1959, da of Thomas Peter Redwood, of Burleigh, Blenheim, New Zealand:— Henry Philip Bede, *b* 1907: *m* 1st, 1949, Rosamond Mary, who *d* 1973, da of Daniel Riddiford, of Featherston, NZ; 2ndly, 1988, Madeleine Hope, widow of his brother John Louis Vavasour (ante), and has issue living (by 1st *m*), Peter Dunstan (The Favourite, Blenheim, NZ), *b* 1950: *m* 1978, Anna Caroline, who *d* 1985, da of David Churchill Gould, of Sunsfield, Christchurch, NZ, and has issue living, Louis Dunstan *b* 1980, Felix William *b* 1982, Claudia Annabelle *b* 1984, — Francis William Joseph, *b* 1958, — Rollo Charles Joseph (twin), *b* 1951, — Charles Edward, *b* 1954, — Mary Rosamond (twin) *b* 1954, — Aletha Thérèse, *b* 1955. *Residence* – Harford, 72 Murphy's Rd, Blenheim, NZ. —— Pearl Constantia, *b* 1895: *m* 1924, Francis Felix Reid, CBE, who *d* 1966, and has issue living, Christopher Robin (Redwood, Blenheim, NZ), *b* 1925: *m* 1958, Clare, widow of Peter Goulter, — Angela *b* 1929: *m* 1956, Richard Fawcett, and has issue living, Thomas Francis *b* 1957; *ed* Ampleforth and RAC, Cirencester, Anthony James *b* 1961; *ed* Ampleforth, Peter Edward *b* 1963; *ed* Ampleforth, Teresa Mary *b* 1958, Sarah Jane *b* 1959.

Sir Thomas Vavasour, Knt, of Hazlewood, co York, was created a baronet 1628. The title became extinct on the death of the 7th baronet 1826. The estates devolved upon his maternal cousin, the 3rd son of the 17th Baron Stourton, Hon Edward Marmaduke Joseph Stourton, who assumed the name of Vavasour, and was created a baronet (*see* B Mowbray, colls) in 1828.

Venables (Dillwyn-Venables-Llewelyn), see Llewelyn.

VERNEY (UK) 1818, of Claydon House, Buckinghamshire

*One faith,
one sun*

*The promise made
to my ancestor has
been kept*

Sir RALPH BRUCE VERNEY, KBE, 5th *Baronet; b* 18 Jan 1915; *s* his father, Sir HARRY CALVERT WILLIAMS, DSO, 1974; *ed* Canford, and Balliol Coll, Oxford (BA); Java 1945 as Maj RA; Vice-Lt for Bucks 1965-86; High Sheriff 1957; Co Councillor of Bucks 1952-73, and Co Alderman 1961-73; Chm, Nat Cttee for England of Forestry Commn 1968-80 (Produced plan for the Chiltern Hills in 1971); Pres Country Landowners' Assocn 1961-63; Chm Nature Conservancy Council 1980-83; Member of Royal Commn on Environmental Pollution 1973-79; former Trustee of Radcliffe, Ernest Cook and Chequers Trusts; KBE (Civil) 1974: *m* 1948, Mary (LRAM), da of late Percy Charles Vestey (*see* Vestey, Bt, colls), and has issue.

𝔄rms – Quarterly: 1st and 4th, azure, on a cross argent, fimbriated or, five mullets gules, *Verney;* 2nd and 3rd, paly of six erminois and pean, a bend engrailed counterchanged, *Calvert.* ℭrests – 1st, a demi-phœnix in flames proper, charged with five mullets in cross or and looking at the rays of the sun, *Verney;* 2nd out of a mural crown argent two spears erect therefrom two pennons flowing towards the dexter, one erminois, the other pean, *Calvert.*
Seat – Claydon House, Buckingham, MK18 2EX. *Residence* – Ballams, Middle Claydon, Buckingham MK18 2ET. *Club* – Cavalry and Guards'.

SON LIVING

EDMUND RALPH (Claydon House, Buckingham, MK18 2EX) (Brooks's Club), *b* 28 June 1950; *ed* Harrow, and York Univ; High Sheriff Bucks 1998; FRICS: *m* 1982, Daphne Primrose, da of late Col Andrew Hamilton Farquhar Fausset-Farquhar, DSO, TD, JP (*see* Macpherson-Grant, Bt, ext, 1995 Edn) and has issue living, Andrew Nicholas, *b* 9 July 1983, — Ella, *b* 1985.

DAUGHTERS LIVING

Sarah Dorothy, *b* 1953: *m* 1974, George Caird, of 15 Chad Rd, Birmingham B15 3ER, and has issue living, Adam Benjamin, *b* 1977, — Oliver Ralph, *b* 1978, — Edmund George, *b* 1989, — Iona Katharine Mary, *b* 1991. — Mary Jane, *b* 1957. —— Francesca Marjorie VERNEY, *b* 1963; has retained her maiden surname: *m* 1997, Peter Kershaw, of The Old Cottage, London Rd, Bourne End, Hemel Hempstead, Herts HP1 2RJ.

BROTHERS LIVING

Rt Rev Stephen Edmund, MBE (Charity School House, Church Rd, Blewbury, Didcot, Oxon OX11 9PY), *b* 1919; *ed* Harrow, and Balliol College, Oxford (MA); late Lt and temp Capt Intelligence Corps; Canon of St George's Chapel, Windsor 1970-77; consecrated Bishop of Repton (Suffragan for Diocese of Derby) 1977; 1939-45 War in Greece and Central Mediterranean (MBE); MBE (Mil) 1945: *m* 1st, 1947, Priscilla Avice Sophie, who *d* 1974, only da of George Schwerdt, of Alresford, Hants; 2ndly, 1981, Mrs Sandra Bailey, and has issue living (by 1st *m*), Robert Francis (Lower Camelot, S Cadbury, Yeovil, Som BA22 7HA), *b* 1949; *ed* Harrow: *m* 1974, Marianne Juliet, da of Francis Henry Haine, of Box Cottage, Blockley, Glos, and has issue living, Alistair Francis *b* 1976, Nicholas Stephen *b* 1978, Christopher Felix *b* 1982, — Rachel Penelope, *b* 1952: *m* 1982, Nicholas Wheeler-Robinson, of Pigotts, North Dean, High Wycombe, Bucks HP14 4NF, and has issue living, Charles Ralph *b* 1988, Caleb John *b* 1992, Olivia Alice *b* 1989, — Helen Mary, *b* 1955: *m* 1986, Jonathan Impett, and has issue living, Thomas Gabriel *b* 1986, Lara Priscilla *b* 1989, — Katharine Priscilla, *b* 1958: *m* 1985, Michael Berman, of 19 Moreton Pl, SW1, and has issue living, Jonathan Stephen *b* 1986, Adam Michael *b* 1993, Imogen Emily *b* 1989. —— Hugh Alexander, *b* 1920; *ed* Harrow, and Oriel Coll, Oxford (BA 1946, MA 1958); sometime Lt Gren Gds; 1939-45 War (wounded): *m* 1950, Ann Mary, da of late S. E. Chesterman, of Wing, Rutland, and has had issue, †Thomas Harry, *b* 1958; *ed* Harrow; *d* 1988, as the result of a road accident, — Mark, *b* 1962; *ed* Harrow, — Jonathan *b* (twin), 1962; *ed* Harrow, — Fiona Ann, *b* 1952: *m* 1975, Mark Hope, of Sunninghill, Banchory, Kincardineshire AB31 3TR, and has issue living, Harry Alexander *b* 1988, Jonathan Mark *b* 1990, — Teresa Joan, *b* 1954: *m* 1975 (*m diss* 1980), Robin Hales, — Julia Mary, *b* 1956: *m* 1992, Iain Smith. *Residence* – The Mill, Snowshill Rd, Broadway, Worcs. —— Andrew Felix (White House, Pewsey, Wilts SN9 5DW), *b* 1921; *ed* Harrow, and Balliol Coll, Oxford; MRCS and LRCP 1948: *m* 1955, Mrs Theodosia Olive Craig, da of James W. Cropper, of Ellergreen, Kendal, and has issue living, Caspar Charles Andrew (Ashfield House, 56 Kirk Lane, Yeadon, Leeds LS19 7ET), *b* 1961: *m* 1986, Wilma Birnie Thomson, and has issue living, Joseph Alexander *b* 1984, George Andrew *b* 1987, Edward Jonathan *b* 1991, — Caroline Rachel, *b* 1956: *m* 1985, Guy Robert Dagul, of Britwell Lodge, Benson, Oxon OX9 6SD, son of Harvey Dagul, of St Albans, Herts, and has issue living, Samuel Matthew *b* 1990, William Arthur *b* 1993, Rose Elizabeth *b* 1988. —— Sir Lawrence John, TD (Windmill House, Church Lane, Oving, Aylesbury, Bucks HP22 4HL), *b* 1924; *ed* Harrow, and Oriel Coll, Oxford (MA); Bar Inner Temple 1952; Hon LLD London Guildhall Univ 1998; late Lt-Col RA (TA) (R Bucks Yeo); a DL of Bucks; Dep Chm Bucks Quarter Sessions 1962-71; Dep Chm Middx Sessions 1971; a Circuit Judge 1972-90, Recorder of London 1990-98 (ret); 1939-45 War as Capt Gren Gds and Lt Col in Roy Bucks Yeo TA 1947-68; Hon Col of Bucks Army Cadet Force 1075 80, Roy Bucks Yeo Signal Sqdn 1997-99; OStJ 1992; ktd 1993: *m* 1972, Zoë Auriel, yr da of Lt-Col Peter Goodeve Goodeve-Docker, of Kealkil, Bantry, co Cork.

SISTERS LIVING

Mary Rachel, *b* 1916: *m* 1947, Rev Geoffrey Thomas Roberts, who *d* 1999, of West Flat Riding School, Grimsthorpe, Bourne, Lincs PE10 0LY, and has issue living, Gillian Marjorie, *b* 1950. — Susan Jane, *b* 1953: *m* 1982, Paul Morgan, and has issue living, Benjamin Andrew *b* 1992, Claire Susan *b* 1983, Anna Mary (twin) *b* 1983, Lucy Rachel *b* 1987. —— Catherine, *b* 1925: *m* 1947, Richard Mervyn Hare, FBA, White's Prof Emeritus of Moral Philosophy, Oxford, and has issue living, John Edmund (144 Benjamin St SE, Grand Rapids, Michigan 49506, USA), *b* 1949; *ed* Rugby, and Balliol

Coll, Oxford; Prof: *m* 1976, Teresa, da of William Forsyth, of Princeton, New Jersey, USA, and has issue living, Andrew Forsyth *b* 1983, Catherine Elizabeth *b* 1980, — Bridget Rachel, *b* 1950: *m* 1976, William Toy George, Jr, of Little Pond, 5 Penn Dixie Rd, Nazareth, PA, 18064, USA, and has issue living, Samuel Benton *b* 1980, Anisa Louise *b* 1982, — Amy Louise, *b* 1953: *m* 1984, Philip Gerald Knight, of 92 Hamilton Rd, Reading RG1 5RD, and has issue living, Hannah Ellin *b* 1987, — Ellin Catherine, *b* 1955; has issue living, Matt Martin *b* 1992. *Residence* – Bywater, The Street, Ewelme, Oxon OX10 6HQ.

COLLATERAL BRANCHES LIVING

Grandchildren of late Sir Harry Lloyd-Verney, GCVO, 2nd son of Col George Hope Lloyd-Verney (who assumed the additional surname of LLOYD by Roy Licence 1888), 3rd son of 2nd baronet:—
Issue of late Maj-Gen Gerald Lloyd Verney, DSO, MVO, late Irish Guards, *b* 1900, *d* 1957, having discontinued the use of the Christian names of Harry George by deed poll 1941: *m* 1926, Hon Joyce Sybil Vivian, who *d* 1983, da of 1st Baron Bicester:—
Peter Vivian, *b* 1930; *ed* Eton, and Trin Coll, Dublin (MA); late Maj Irish Gds; an author: *m* 1st, 1959 (*m diss* 1982), Caroline Evelyn, el da of late George Anthony Harford, of Widden Hill House, Horton, Chipping Sodbury, Glos; 2ndly, 1983, Elizabeth Anne, da of Wing Cdr Harry St George Burke, RAF, of Auberies, Bulmer, Essex, and widow of Christopher George James Oldridge de la Hey, and has issue living (by 1st *m*), Harry George Vivian (The Old Forge, Ewen, Cirencester, Glos), *b* 1960: *m* 1st, 1985 (*m diss* 1989), Sarah Mary Cotterill, da of Richard P. Voelcker, of Stanton St Quintin, Wilts; 2ndly, 1992, Mrs Lavinia Mary Delves Dawes, yst da of Sir Evelyn Delves Broughton, 12th Bt, and widow of Douglas D. Dawes, and has issue living (by 2nd *m*), Harriet Charity *b* 1992, — Louisa Margaret, *b* 1962: *m* 1993, Matthew Jeremy Higgs, and has issue living, Florence Nettle *b* 1994, — Henrietta Nell, *b* 1965: *m* 1987, Thomas Richard William Lapage-Norris, eldest son of Capt T. E. Lapage-Norris, of Worton, Wilts.

Issue of late Lt-Col Ulick Otway Vortigern Lloyd-Verney, OBE, *b* 1902, *d* 1979: *m* 1929, Esmé Louise, who *d* 1978, da of Charles Alston Smith-Ryland, of Barford Hill, Warwick:—
Harry Ulick Dennis (The Garden House, Cheriton, Alresford, Hants), *b* 1940; *ed* Eton; FCA: *m* 1976, Sarah Fane, yr da of Maj A. P. P. Ricketts, of The Old Manse, Nigg, Ross and Cromarty, and has issue living, Louisa Florence, *b* 1977, — Alice Sarah, *b* 1979, — Camilla Anne, *b* 1981. —— Anne Margaret, *b* 1930; JP Shrewsbury; DL Shropshire 1986: *m* 1951, Col John Montagu Flint, MBE, late RE, of The Dower House, Great Ness, Shrewsbury, and has issue living, Charles John Raffles QC (Blackstone Chambers, EC4Y 9BW), *b* 1952; Barrister-at-law: *m* 1978, Diana Rosemary, el da of late Maj Robert Topham, of Plas-yn-Grove, Ellesmere, Shrops, and has issue living, William Charles Raffles *b* 1982, Julia *b* 1984, — Michael Edward Stamford, *b* 1956: *m* 1981, Fiona, 2nd da of Prof Alasdair Steele-Bodger, of The Old Rectory, Hale, Fordingbridge, Hants, and has issue living, Alasdair Stamford *b* 1987, Oliver John Montagu *b* 1989, — Sarah Esmé, *b* 1955: *m* 1976, Maj Christopher Thomas Stanton Prestwich, 15th/19th King's R Hussars, and has issue living, Edward Joseph Stanton *b* 1985, Emma Charlotte Esmé *b* 1983, — Elizabeth Anne, *b* 1958: *m* 1983, Colin Michael Wood, and has issue living, Christopher James *b* 1987, Helen Sarah *b* 1990. —— Carola Mariette, *b* 1932: *m* 1952, Maj John Hugh Torquil Sutton, late Coldm Gds, of Bayfield Brecks, Holt, Norfolk (*see* Sutton, Bt, colls), and has issue (see that title).

Grandchildren of late Frederick William Verney, 4th son of 2nd baronet:—
Issue of late Sir Ralph Verney, CB, CIE, CVO, who was *cr* a *Baronet* 1946:—
See Verney, Bt, *cr* 1946.

The 1st Bt, Gen Sir Harry CALVERT, GCB, GCH, was Adjt-Gen of the Forces for 21 years. The Rt Hon Sir Harry, 2nd Bt, in 1827 assumed the surname of Verney by Roy licence (his father having discontinued the name of Calvert, having *s* to the Verney estates (his cousin Richard Calvert *m* the widow of Hon John Verney, el son of 1st Earl Verney). He sat as MP for Buckingham (*L*) and Bedford. The 3rd baronet, Sir Edmund Hope, Capt RN, served in Crimean War 1854-55, and Indian Mutiny 1857-58, and sat as MP for Buckingham (*L*). The 4th Bt, Sir Harry Calvert Williams Verney, DSO, was PPS to Ch Sec for Ireland 1911-14, and Parl Sec to Board of Agric 1914; MP for Bucks (*L*) 1910-18; author of *The Verneys of Claydon* and *Florence Nightingale at Harley Street*.

VERNEY (UK) 1946, of Eaton Square, City of Westminster

One faith,
one sun

The promise made
to my ancestor has
been kept

(*Sir*) (JOHN) SEBASTIAN VERNEY, 3rd *Baronet*; *b* 30 Aug 1945; *s* his father, *Sir* JOHN, MC, 1993, but his name does not appear on the Official Roll of the Baronetage, nor does he use the title.

Arms – Quarterly: 1st and 4th, azure, on a cross argent, fimbriated or, five mullets gules, *Verney*; 2nd and 3rd, paly of six erminois and pean, a bend engrailed counterchanged, *Calvert*. Crests – 1st, a demi-phœnix in flames proper, charged with five mullets in cross or, and looking at the rays of the sun, *Verney*; 2nd, out of a mural crown argent two spears erect, therefrom two pennons flowing towards the dexter, one erminois, the other pean, *Calvert*.

SISTERS LIVING

Sabrina Anne, *b* 1947: *m* 19—, — Reid Mar (PO Box 203, Idyllwild, California 92549, USA). —— Juliet Rose, *b* 1949: *m* 1st, 1970 (*m diss* 19—), Michael Benjamin; 2ndly, 1979, Simon Hugh Arden Acworth, of Flat 1A, 58 Chilbolton Av, Winchester, Hants, only son of Maj G. W. Acworth, MVO, of Woodeaton, Oxford, and has issue living (by 1st *m*) Thomas Michael, *b* 1971, — Julian, *b* 1973, — (by 2nd *m*) Robin, *b* 1983, — Florence Mary, *b* 1980. —— Rose Lucinda, *b* 1950: *m* 1978, Peter Zinovieff, of 16 Hardwick St, Cambridge CB3 9JA, elder son of late Maj Leo Zinovieff, and has issue living, Olga, *b* 1978, — Katarina, *b* 1981, — Iliena, *b* 1983. —— Candida Harriet, *b* 1953: *m* 1980, Timothy C. Molloy, of Peartree Cottage, 29 Ashley Rd, Bradford-on-Avon, Wilts BA15 IRU, son of Maj T. R. Molloy, MC, of Wincanton, Somerset, and has issue living, Henry, *b* 1981, — Ned, *b* 1984, — Theo, *b* 1986. —— (Alice) Angelica, *b* 1956: *m* 1984, David James Risk Kennard, of Merriott House, Powerstock, Bridport, Dorset DT6 3SZ, yr son of late Maj Robert William Kennard, MC, TD, of Barton Farm, Guiting Power, Glos, and has issue living, Paris Timothy, *b* 1986, — Hector James, *b* 1988, — Edgar Robert, *b* 1991.

AUNT LIVING (*daughter of 1st baronet*)

Joscelyne, *b* 1915: *m* 1941, Capt Andrew Thorne, late Gren Gds (B Penrhyn), who *d* 1991, and has had issue, Nicholas Andrew, *b* 1942; Capt Gren Gds: *m* 1969, Diana Lesley Kathryn (who *m* 2ndly, 1977 (*m diss* 1998), Ian Mitchell Thomas), da of late Donald Leslie, of Horley Place, Horley, Surrey, and *d* 1976, leaving issue, Alexander Francis Andrew Nicholas *b* 1972, Camilla Claire Louise *b* 1976, — Joanna Mary, *b* 1945: *m* 1966, Maj-Gen John Peter William Friedberger, CB, CBE, of North Woolding Cottage, The Harrow Way, Whitchurch, Hants RG28 7QT, and has issue living, Richard Mark *b* 1973, William John *b* 1995, Oliver James *b* 1997, Rosanna Catharine *b* 1967: *m* 1991, James Robert Perceval Armitage, son of Jeremy Armitage (and has issue living, Luke Robert *b* 1993), Lucinda Jane *b* 1970: *m* 1999, Andrew Pietro Fitch Pincott, son of Gerald Pincott, — Carola Joscelyne, *b* 1948: *m* 1978, Nigel Howard Symington (Parsonage Farm House, Fletching, Uckfield, E Sussex), and has issue living, Lucy Elizabeth Joscelyne *b* 1980, Fiona Juliet *b* 1982, Victoria Carola *b* 1984. *Residence* – Cottage 32, Headbourne Worthy House, Winchester SO23 7JG.

WIDOW LIVING OF SECOND BARONET

(JEANIE) LUCINDA (*Lady Verney*), da of late Maj Herbert Musgrave, DSO, RE: *m* 1939, Sir John Verney, 2nd Bt, MC, who *d* 1993. *Residence* – The White House, Clare, Suffolk.

COLLATERAL BRANCH LIVING

Issue of late Lt Cdr David Verney, RN, yr son of 1st Bt, *b* 1918, *d* 1992: *m* 1948, Hon Mary Kathleen Boscawen (Trevella, St Erne, nr Truro, Cornwall), only da of 8th Viscount Falmouth:—
CHRISTOPHER RALPH EVELYN (50 Abbotsbury Close, W14 8EQ), *b* 4 Oct 1948; *ed* Eton: *m* 1976, Madeliene, da of — Lindberg, of — . —— Margaret Mary (Coco's Box, Dauntsey, Chippenham, Wilts), *b* 1950: *m* 1071 (*m diss* 1995), Peter Michael Bickford-Smith, and has issue living, Michael Rupert David, *b* 1984, — Sacha Ann Mary, *b* 1975, — Charlotte Ann Bertha, *b* 1977, — Stephanie May, *b* 1989. —— Rosemary Janette, *b* 1958: *m* 1982 (*m diss* 1991), John Kenna, yst son of Raymond Kenna, of The Pines, Foxrock, co Dublin, and has issue living, Justin, *b* 1987, — Nicholas Harry, *b* 1990, — Lamorna Daisy, *b* 1985.

The 1st baronet, Lt-Col Sir Ralph Verney, CB, CIE, CVO, Rifle Brig, son of late Frederick William Verney (yst son of Sir Harry Verney, 2nd Bt, *cr* 1818), was appointed Mil Sec to Viceroy of India, 1916-21, Sec to Speaker of House of Commons 1921-55, and an Examiner for Private Bills and Taxing Master House of Commons 1927-45: *m* 1909, Janette Cheverié Hamilton, da of Senator Hon James Thomas Walker of Sydney, Aust.

VERNON (UK) 1914, of Shotwick Park, co Chester

Spring does not always flourish

Sir NIGEL JOHN DOUGLAS VERNON, 4th *Baronet*; *b* 2 May 1924; *s* his father *Sir* (WILLIAM) NORMAN, 1967; *ed* Charterhouse; late Lt RNVR and RNR; Dir Hogg Insurance Brokers: *m* 1947, Margaret Ellen, da of late Robert Lyle Dobell, of The Mount, Waverton, Chester, and has had issue.

𝔄rms – Or, on a fesse azure between two cross molines in pale gules three garbs of the field. Crest – In front of a demi-female figure affrontée proper vested azure, around the temples an oak wreath vert, holding in the dexter hand a sickle and in the sinister two ears of wheat slipped also proper, a garb fessewise or.
Residence – Top-y-Fron Hall, Kelsterton, nr Flint, Flints CH6 5TF. *Clubs* – Naval, Army and Navy.

SONS LIVING AND DECEASED

JAMES WILLIAM, *b* 2 April 1949; FCA; *ed* Shrewsbury: *m* 1981, Davinia Elizabeth, elder da of late Christopher David Howard (*see* V Portman, colls), and has issue living, George William Howard, *b* 25 July 1987, — Guy Alexander Howard, *b* 1993, — Harriet Lucy Howard, *b* 1985. *Residence* – The Hall, Lygan-y-Wern, Pentre Halkyn, Flints. ——†John Alan, *b* 1956; *ed* Shrewsbury; *d* 1987.

DAUGHTER LIVING

Caroline Margaret, *b* 1953: *m* 1974 (*m diss* 1978), Simon Jonathan Salusbury-Trelawny (*see* Salusbury-Trelawny, Bt, colls).

SISTER LIVING

Diana Elizabeth, *b* 1922; formerly Section Officer WAAF: *m* 1st, 1943 (*m diss* 1949) (annulment Roman Catholic Church 1951), Bohuslav F. Kovarik, DFM, Czechoslovak Air Force, who *d* 1969; 2ndly, 1951, Joseph Olivier Hamelin de Grondines de Landry, who *d* 1995. *Residence* – Flat 9, Batworth Park House, Crossbush, Arundel, W Sussex BN18 9PG.

COLLATERAL BRANCHES LIVING

Issue of late Humphrey Bagnall Vernon, MC, 3rd son of 2nd baronet, *b* 1895, *d* 1979: *m* 1938, Sibyl (Beechdale House, Stonecross, Exford, Somerset), yst da of late Samuel Mason Hutchinson, of The Marfords, Bromborough, Cheshire:—
John Humphrey (26 Pembroke Place, Bampton, Oxon), *b* 1940: *m* 1st, 1973 (*m diss* 1996), Alison Margaret, only da of William Warnock Watt, of Sheriffhales, Shrops; 2ndly, 1997, Tina Jeanette, eldest da of James Carlson, of Sandbourne, New York, USA, and has issue living, (by 1st *m*) Andrew William, *b* 1981, — Nicola Jane, *b* 1978. —— Richard Bagnall (Little Tranby, Seven Corners Lane, Beverley, E Yorks), *b* 1944: *m* 1969, Deborah Florence, el da of Geoffrey Oswald Atyeo Briggs, MB, BCh, of The Kennels, Thoresby Park, Notts, and has issue living, Toby Richard, *b* 1971.

Grandchildren of late William Allen Vernon, 2nd son of 1st baronet:—
Issue of late Herbert Wallace Vernon, *b* 1890, *d* 1974: *m* 1924, Gertrude, who *d* 1959, el da of Tom Jackson, JP, of Waterfoot, Heaton, Bolton:—
Bryan Tom Jackson (The Deacons, High St, Yarmouth, I of Wight), *b* 1925; *ed* Loretto; late Sub-Lt RNVR: *m* 1955, Anne Cecilia, da of late Harry S. Burgess, of Beck Hall, Thornton Dale, Yorks, and has issue living, Andrew Bryan, (The Old Vicarage, Tideswell, nr Buxton, Derbys SK17 8LD), *b* 1955: *m* 1982, Patricia May Gorecki, and has issue living, Thomas Andrew *b* 1983, Alexandra Mary *b* 1985, — Charles Harry (16 Dexter Way, Kinderton Manor, Middlewich, Ches CW10 9UJ), *b* 1960, — Timothy William (The Old Vicarage, W Peckham, Kent ME18 5JH), *b* 1962: *m* 1988, Tessa Hodgson, — Belinda Anne (49 The Mall, Newport, I of Wight), *b* 1957: *m* 1980 (*m diss* 1987), Timothy John Hughes-Williams, of Valbonne, Provence, France, and has issue living, Mark Alan *b* 1983, Victoria Anne *b* 1981. —— Richard Wallace (Park Lodge, 46 Park Rd, Aldeburgh, Suffolk IP15 5EU), *b* 1927; *ed* Camb Univ (MA); late 2nd Lt RA: *m* 1955, Pamela Violet, da of late Lt-Col Alexander George William Grierson, RM (ret) (*see* Grierson, Bt, colls), and has issue living, David Grierson (Adam House, Mark Way, Godalming, Surrey GU7 2BN), *b* 1956: *m* 1988, Rosemary Nicola Myer, and has issue living, William Grierson *b* 1990, Hannah Emily *b* 1992, Lucy Nicola *b* 1994, — Simon Richard (Upcote, Drove Rd, Chilbolton, Stockbridge, Hants SO20 6BA), *b* 1958: *m* 1985, Vanessa Ann Hudson, and has issue living, James Richard Alexander *b* 1988, Tobias Edward *b* 1990, Melissa Anne *b* 1992, — Sally Pamela Clare, *b* 1960: *m* 1986, Robert William Blackburn Daniell, of 8 Arminger Rd, W12 7BB, and has issue living, Thomas Christopher Hebden *b* 1988, Patrick Richard *b* 1990, Natasha Annette *b* 1993, — Joanna Caroline, *b* 1963: *m* 1986, Charles Albury George Bennett, of The Old Forge, Elmdon, nr Saffron Walden, Essex CB11 4NL, and has issue living, George Albury Richard *b* 1992, Edward Charles *b* 1994.

Issue of late Reginald Thornycroft Vernon, *b* 1892, *d* 1977: *m* 1920, Margarita Grace, who *d* 1989, yr da of Joseph Constantine, of Harlsey Hall, Northallerton, Yorks:—
George Thornycroft (2539 Benvenue Av, Berkeley, Calif 94704, USA), *b* 1935, *ed* Eton, and Trin Coll, Camb. —— James Loudon (310 Fulham Rd, SW10 9UG), *b* 1940; *ed* Eton, and Trin Coll, Dublin (BA): *m* 1971, Elspeth Mary Stewart, da of late Rev Cyril Raby Thomson, of Holy Trinity Vicarage, Southwell, Notts, and has issue living, Alexander James Constantine, *b* 1971, — Eliot Antony Stewart, *b* 1975, — Rossanna Mary Anderson, *b* 1976, — Tara Katharine Loudon, *b* 1979. — Pamela Margaret, *b* 1924. —— Jean Winifred, *b* 1926: *m* 1954, John Stewart Prescot, of Fairlight House, E Grinstead, Sussex, and has issue living, Charles Stewart, *b* 1957, — Alastair John Vernon, *b* 1960, — Nigel Kenrick Grosvenor, *b* 1962, — Margaret Louise, *b* 1955. —— Margaret Elizabeth, *b* 1933; *ed* Lady Margaret Hall, Oxford (BA): *m* 1972, Ven Jeremy Peake, Archdeacon of the Aegean and the Danube (c/o British Embassy, Vienna), son of late Sir Charles Brinsley Pemberton Peake.

Issue of late Sir Wilfred Douglas Vernon, *b* 1897, *d* 1973: *m* 1923, Nancy Elizabeth, who *d* 1999, aged 100, yr da of Tom Jackson, JP, of Waterfoot, Heaton, Bolton:—
Sir (William) Michael (Fyfield Manor, Fyfield, Hants), *b* 1926; *ed* Trin Coll, Camb (MA); late Lt RM; Chm of Spillers Ltd 1968-80, and Chm RNLI 1989-96 (Dep Chm 1981-89); Ktd 1995: *m* 1st, 1952 (*m diss* 1977), Rosheen Elizabeth Mary, da of late George O'Meara, of Johannesburg, S Africa; 2ndly, 1977, Mrs Jane Olivia Colston, who *d* 1998, da of late Denys Kilham-Roberts, and formerly wife of Michael Colston, and has issue living (by 1st *m*), Mark Thornycroft, *b* 1958: *m* 1986, Harriet Laura, eldest da of John Bertrand Worsley (*see* Clark, Bt, ext 1979), and has issue living, Wilfred Alec *b* 1996, Jessica Rosheen *b* 1988, Phoebe Rose *b* 1991.

Sir William Vernon, 1st Baronet, was head of the firm of W Vernon and Sons, millers, of London and Liverpool. The 2nd baronet, Sir (John) Herbert Vernon, was High Sheriff of Cheshire 1926.

VESTEY (UK) 1921, of Shirley, Surrey

Sir (JOHN) DEREK VESTEY, 2nd *Baronet*, son of late John Joseph Vestey (*b* 1888, *d* 1932: *m* 1913, Dorothy Mary, who *d* 1918, only da of John Henry Beaver, of Gawthorpe Hall, Bingley, Yorks), el son of 1st baronet; *b* 4 June 1914; *s* his grandfather, *Sir* EDMUND HOYLE, 1953; *ed* The Leys Sch, Camb; European War 1940-45 as Flight-Lieut RAF Vol Reserve: *m* 1938, Phyllis Irene, da of H. Brewer, of Banstead, and has issue.

From work stability

Arms – Argent, on a fesse between two flaunches gules each charged with a cross throughout of the field, three roses also of the field. Crest – In front of a springbok's head proper three mullets argent.
Residence – Park Penthouse, 355 King's Rd, Chelsea, SW3 5ES. *Club* – MCC.

SON LIVING

PAUL EDMUND (53 Cheval Place, SW7; Manor House Farm, Bishops Sutton, Hants; *Club* – British Racing Drivers), *b* 15 Feb 1944; *ed* Radley: *m* 1971, Victoria Anne Scudamore, da of John Salter, of Old Ford House, Tiverton, Devon, and has issue living, Joanna Clare, *b* 1972, — Caroline Louise *b* 1975, — Georgina Jane, *b* 1977.

DAUGHTER LIVING

Rosamund Hope, *b* 1940: *m* 1st, 1961 (*m diss* 1980), Anthony Charles Brown; 2ndly, 1982, Karl Ove Arvidsson, and has issue living (by 1st *m*), Mark Nigel Alastair, *b* 1964: *m* 1993, Elizabeth Ann Julien, and has issue living, Vita Rosamund *b* 1993, — Julia Caroline, *b* 1962. *Residence* – Longdown Cottage, Longdown, Guildford, Surrey.

COLLATERAL BRANCHES LIVING

Issue of late Charles Gordon Vestey, brother of 2nd baronet, *b* 1916, *d* 1986: *m* 1946, Monica Hope (Little Haley, Oxenhope, Keighley, Yorkshire), yr da of Arthur John Parker Heaton, of Manorlands, Oxenhope, Keighley:—
Diana Mary, *b* 1947: *m* 1st, 1968, Kenneth Cameron Simm, who *d* 1977; 2ndly, 1987, Thomas Mark Blackburn, of Prospect House, Bradley, Skipton, N Yorks, and has issue living, (by 1st *m*) Gordon Christopher Cameron, *b* 1970, — Holly Ann Cameron, *b* 1971. ——Rachel Margaret, *b* 1949: LRAM: *m* 1970, Philip Anthony Hills, BA, PhD, of The Mill House, Gt Horkesley, Colchester, Essex, and has issue living, Thomas Edmund, *b* 1977, — Matthew William, *b* 1979.

Issue of late Percy Charles Vestey, 3rd son of 1st baronet, *b* 1893, *d* 1939: *m* 1916, Dorothy Emmeline, who *d* 1976, da of late Charles David Johnson:—
Roger Edmund (11 Hyde Park Gardens, W2. *Club* – Cavalry), *b* 1921; *ed* Harrow, and Clare Coll, Camb (BA 1946, MA 1951); late Capt Berks Yeo; European War 1940-45: *m* 1950, Penelope Jane, only da of late Lieut-Col Robert Arthur Little, DSO, late Australian Forces, of Melbourne, Australia, and has had issue, †Charles Julian, *b* 1952; *ed* Harrow, Munich Univ and Sorbonne, Paris; *d* 1993, — James Patrick, *b* 1954: *ed* Harrow, and Southampton Univ; DM, FRCP (Edin): *m* 1981, Nicola Jane, da of late Harold Vernon Knight. ——Patricia (34 Bryanston Square, W1), *b* 1922: *m* 1945, Lt William Reginald Servaes, RN, who *d* 1999, and has had issue, Michael Maxwell, *b* 1947, *d* 1986, — James William (Carlton House Farm, Mettingham, Bungay, Suffolk NR35 1TF; *Club* – Cavalry and Guards'), *b* 1948; *ed* Harrow, and RMA: *m* 1st, 1972 (*m diss* 1975), Phoebe, da of Keith Pither Cox, of Sydney; 2ndly, 1978, Harriet, yr da of Maj Richard Neville Barclay, of Pond House, Boxted, Colchester, and has issue living (by 2nd *m*), Rebecca Mansel *b* 1981, Alice Harriet *b* 1984, — Andrew Mark (South Green House, Southwold, Suffolk), *b* 1900: *m* 1995, Samantha, da of William Sajjan, of Glasgow, and has issue living, Luke Jo *b* 1996, India Kate *b* 1999, — Diana Patricia (2 Chalfont Rd, Oxford OX2 6TH), *b* 1951; BA (Mus): *m* 1978 (*m diss* 1994), James Norman Hiddleston, and has issue living, Thomas William *b* 1981, Sarah Alexandra *b* 1979, Emma Elizabeth *b* 1986, — Elizabeth Mary, *b* 1953: *m* 1978, Timothy John Russell Fargher, of The Old Rectory, Orford, Woodbridge, Suffolk IP12 2NN, and has issue living, Matthew Philip Michael *b* 1981, Edmund James Timothy *b* 1986, Zoe Clare *b* 1979, Anna Patricia *b* 1984. ——Mary (*Lady Verney*), *b* 1925; LRAM: *m* 1948, Sir Ralph Bruce Verney, KBE, 5th Bt (*cr* 1818), and has issue (see that title).

Issue of late Ronald Arthur Vestey, 4th son of 1st baronet, *b* 1898, *d* 1987: *m* 1923, Florence Ellen McLean, who *d* 1966, da of late Col Theodore George Luis, VD, of Broughty Ferry, Angus:—

Edmund Hoyle (Little Thurlow Hall, Haverhill, Suffolk; Iolaire Lodge, Lochinver, Sutherland. *Clubs* – Cavalry and Guards', Carlton), *b* 1932; *ed* Eton, High Sheriff Essex 1977, DL 1980, DL Suffolk 1991; late Lieut City of London Yeo; patron of five livings: *m* 1960, Anne Moubray, yr da of Gen Sir Geoffry Allen Percival Scoones, KCB, KBE, CSI, DSO, MC, and has issue living, Timothy Ronald Geoffry (Waltons, Ashdon, nr Saffron Walden, Essex), *b* 1961: *m* 1995, Mrs Tessa M. Shepherd-Barron, and has issue living, Jack Arthur *b* 1996, — James Edmund McLean, *b* 1962, — George Moubray William (Great Thrulow Hall, Haverhill, Suffolk), *b* 1964: *m* 1989, Rachel, yr da of Patrick Osborne, of Currandooley, NSW, and has issue living, Thomas Hector Moubray *b* 1993, Edmund Arthur Valentine *b* 1995, Richard George Archibald *b* 1997, Ruby Constance *b* 1991, — Robin John Henry, *b* 1968: *m* 1993, Victoria Eileen Herbert, yst da of Robin Waddell, of Edinburgh, and has issue living, Henry Robin Edmund *b* 1997, Georgina *b* 1994. Rose Elizabeth Jean *b* 1996. —— Florence Elizabeth Lindsay, *b* 1926: *m* 1952, Robert Lawrence Clifton-Brown (*see* Brown, Bt, colls). —— Jane McLean, *b* 1928: *m* 1956, John Richard Baddeley, of Great Butts, Cousley Wood, Wadhurst, Sussex, and has had issue, Mark Christian Jon, *b* 1960: *m* 1987, Brigette Susan Alfille, and has issue living, Matthew *b* 1989, Charles David James *b* 1991, Lucy Elizabeth Jane *b* 1995, — Gary Christopher, *b* 1965; assumed the names of Gary Christopher in lieu of Edward Christopher Francis by deed poll: *m* 1989, Cecilia Barker, — Melissa Jane Elizabeth, *b* 1963, *d* 1980. —— Margaret, *b* 1929: *m* 1954, James Gladstone Payne, of Ardvar, Drumbeg, via Lairg, Sutherland, and has issue living, Michael Edmund (Severals Farm, Arkesden, Saffron Walden, Essex), *b* 1959: *m* 1986, Sophie Corinne Banks, da of Jeremy John Banks Skinner, of Stocking Farm, Stocking Pelham, Buntingford, Herts, and has issue living, Fergus Edmund *b* 1990, Hector Cameron *b* 1992, Caspar James *b* 1994, Lochlan Troy *b* 1998, — Nichola Rosemary, *b* 1955: *m* 1981, Alastair Ian McArthur, and has had issue, Matthew James *b* 1984, Harry Simon *b* 1987, Samuel George *b* 1988, Emily Clare *b* and *d* 1983, — Philippa Margaret, *b* 1963: *m* 1982, Simon Hamilton Shirley-Beavan, and has issue living, Charles Michael *b* 1984, George Ronald Benjamin *b* 1987.

Issue of late William Vestey, yst son of 1st baronet, *b* 1902, *d* 1971: *m* 1928, Ursula Frances Bowring, who *d* 1993, da of Edward H. Bowring Skimming, of Taplow House, Taplow:—
John (Orbetello, Italy; Bath and Boodles Clubs), *b* 1929: *ed* Eton: *m* 1958 (*m diss* 1977), Felicity Gay, da of Kenneth H. Crawford, of Holbrook, NSW, and has issue living, Victoria Gay, *b* 1960: *m* 1986, David Michael Russell-Hills, and has issue living, Mark William *b* 1988, Lucy Scarlett *b* 1986, — Angela Caroline, *b* 1962: *m* 1987, Paul Coleman, and has issue living, Luca John *b* 1988, — Georgina Ann, *b* 1964, — Sara Frances, *b* 1966: *m* 1991, Santiago Gaztambide, — Christina Mary, *b* 1969.

The 1st baronet, Sir Edmund Hoyle Vestey (third son of Samuel Vestey, of Liverpool), was Chm of Union International Co, and Joint Head of Blue Star Line, Ltd with his elder brother 1st Baron Vestey.

VINCENT (E) 1620, of Stoke d'Abernon, Surrey (Extinct 1941)

Rt Hon Sir EDGAR VINCENT, GCB, GCMG, FRS, 16th and last Baronet (who was *cr Baron D'Abernon* 1914, and *Viscount D'Abernon* 1926).

DAUGHTERS LIVING OF FOURTEENTH BARONET

Una Claire Margaret (Lyells, Hollam Drive, Dulverton, Somerset), *b* 1926: *m* 1950, Air Commodore Nicholas Roger Lyell Bristow, RAF, who *d* 1996, and has issue living, Robert Nicholas, *b* 1954: *m* 1982 (*m diss* 1997), Linda Mary Dickinson, and has issue living, Thomas Francis Edward *b* 1990, Rosemary Clare Margaret *b* 1986, — Edward Anthony (twin), *b* 1954: *m* 1983, Susan Sadaukas, — Clare Margaret, *b* 1951: *m* 1972, Colin Ian Liddell, and has issue living, Victoria Clare Margaret *b* 1981, — Jane Elizabeth, *b* 1953: *m* 1st, 1974 (*m diss* 1987), Michael Balfour Hutchings; 2ndly, 1990, William Richard Oake Holmes, and has issue living, (by 1st *m*) William Benjamin Balfour *b* 1981, Anna Clare *b* 1978, (by 2nd *m*) Katharine Alexandra *b* 1991. —— Pamela Helen Frances (Combe House, Titcomb Way, Kintbury, Berks), *b* 1928: *m* 1951, Douglas R. Whittaker, who *d* 1974, and has issue living, Suzanne, *b* 1951: *m* 1973, Spencer Charles Hilton Barrett, and has issue living, Rowan Douglas Hilton *b* 1980, Seth Arthur Vincent *b* 1983, — Helen Gay, *b* 1953: *m* 1973, Timothy Philip Lyth Badgett, and has issue living, Henry Vincent *b* 1979, Katherine Joanna *b* 1981, — Judith Frances, *b* 1959: *m* 1985, Ashley Dominic Griffith, and has issue living, Rebecca Jane *b* 1989, Hannah Lucinda *b* 1991.

VINCENT (UK) 1936, of Watton, co Norfolk

Sir WILLIAM PERCY MAXWELL VINCENT, 3rd *Baronet*; *b* 1 Feb 1945; *s* his father, *Sir* LACEY ERIC, 1963; 2nd Lt Irish Gds: *m* 1976, Christine Margaret, da of Rev Edward Gibson Walton, and has issue.

Arms – Azure, a chevron between two garbs in chief and in base a castle all or. **Crest** – In front of two bird bolts points downwards saltirewise or a Labrador retriever dog, statant sable.
Residence – Whistlers, Buriton, Petersfield, Hants.

SONS LIVING

EDWARD MARK WILLIAM, *b* 6 March 1978. —— Charles Michael Lacey, *b* 1979. —— John James Robertson, *b* 1981.

SISTER LIVING

Amanda Mildred, *b* 1942: *m* 1st, 1961, John Barry Henry Dinan, late Capt Irish Guards; 2ndly, 1984, as his 2nd wife, Gerald John Ward, of Chilton Park Farm, Hungerford, Berks (*see* E Dudley, colls), and has issue living (by 1st *m*), Mark Henry *b* 1963, — Dominic John, *b* 1966.

By Fortitude and Endeavour

WIDOW LIVING OF SECOND BARONET

HELEN MILICENT (*Helen, Lady Vincent*) (179 Cranmer Court, Sloane Av, SW3 3HN), yr da of late Field-Marshal Sir William Robert Robertson, 1st Bt, GCB, GCMG, GCVO, DSO (*see* B Robertson of Oakridge): *m* 1938, Sir Lacey Eric Vincent, 2nd baronet, who *d* 1963.

The 1st baronet, Sir Percy Vincent (son of Lacey Andrews Vincent, of Watton, Norfolk), was an Alderman City of London 1929-42 (Sheriff 1926-27, and Lord Mayor 1935-36).

Vœux, see Des Vœux.

VYVYAN (E) 1645, of Trelowarren, Cornwall

Sir (RALPH) FERRERS ALEXANDER VYVYAN, 13th *Baronet*; *b* 21 Aug 1960; *s* his father, *Major Sir* JOHN STANLEY, 1995; *ed* Charterhouse, RMA Sandhurst, and The Architectural Assocn: *m* 1986, Victoria Arabella, yst da of M. B. Ogle, of Skerraton, Buckfastleigh, Devon, and has issue.

Arms – Argent, on a mount vert a lion rampant gules, armed sable. **Crest** – A horse passant furnished proper.
Residence – Trelowarren, Mawgan, Helston, Cornwall TR12 6AF.

SONS LIVING

JOSHUA DRUMMOND, *b* 10 Oct 1986. —— Frederick George, *b* 1987, —— Rowan Arthur, *b* 1989. —— Inigo Valentine, *b* 1994. —— Gabriel Francis, *b* 1999.

SISTER LIVING

Amanda Clare, *b* 1959: *m* 1st, 1984 (*m diss* 1988), Mark Ian Richard, Baron von Brockdorff; 2ndly, 1991, David John Judson, and has issue living (by 1st *m*), Alexander Mark Edward John Vyvyan, *b* 1984, — (by 2nd *m*), Josiah Barclay, *b* 1992, — Mariana Grace, *b* 1995. *Residence* - 16 Kenwyn Rd, Truro, Cornwall.

While we live, let us live

HALF-SISTER DECEASED (*daughter of 12th baronet by 1st marriage*)

Lorraine, *b* 1942; *d* 1983.

HALF-AUNT LIVING (*half-sister of 12th baronet*)

(Mary) Virginia, *b* 1934; JP Berks 1973: *m* 1st, 1956 (*m diss* 1963), Harold Markham Mills, who *d* 1995; 2ndly, 1975 (*m diss* 1978), William Archibald Wilson, who *d* 1995; 3rdly, 1979, Douglas Frederick Redrup, and has issue living (by 1st *m*), Julian Maximilian Vyvyan (72 Lyford Rd, SW18 3JW), *b* 1957; *ed* Charterhouse: *m* 1987, Isla Fiona Gail Johnston, and has issue living, Alexander Frederick Johnston *b* 1988, Edward Charles Harold Johnston *b* 1990, Olivia Joan Johnston *b* 1995, — Antonia Helen (4 Porter Av, Newport, Rhode Is 02840, USA), *b* 1958, — Charlotte Elisabeth (Chyrune, Bonallack Lane, Gweek, Cornwall TR12 6UJ), *b* 1960: *m* 1986 (*m diss* 1998), Paul Robert Frewin Howse, and has issue living, Sholto Douglas Frewin *b* 1987, Antonia Vyvyan *b* 1992. *Residence* – Little Compton, Samarkand Close, Camberley, Surrey GU15 1DG.

WIDOW LIVING OF TWELFTH BARONET

JONET NOÉL (*Dowager Lady Vyvyan*), eldest da of Lt-Col Alexander Hubert Barlcay, DSO, MC, Queen's Bays (*see* Mitchelson, Bt (ext 1945), 1965 Edn): *m* 1959, as his 3rd wife, Major Sir John Stanley Vyvyan, 12th Bt, who *d* 1995. *Residence* – Trelowarren Mill, Mawgan, Helston, Cornwall TR12 6AF.

COLLATERAL BRANCHES LIVING

Branch from brother of 9th baronet

Grandson of late Stanhope Trefusis Vyvyan, 4th son of late Rev Herbert Francis Vyvyan, brother of 9th baronet:—
Issue of late Lester Trefusis Vyvyan, *b* 1905, *d* 1952: *m* 1934, Mary Clare Frances (2 Trenoweth, Carwinion Rd, Mawnan Smith, Falmouth, Cornwall), da of John Leeming, of Chalfont St Peter, Bucks:—
Anthony Beville (Merthen, Constantine, Falmouth, Cornwall TR11 5RU), *b* 1935; *ed* Downside: *m* 1960, Mary Winifred da of Arthur Joseph Quin-Harkin, OBE, and has issue living, Richard Trefusis, *b* 1961: *m* 1993, Claire Susan, yr da of David Williets, of Fairfield Cottage, Middleton, Warwicks, and has issue living, Max Anthony *b* 1998. — Jonathan Vyell, *b* 1962, — Simon Courtenay, *b* 1964: *m* 1992, Jane E., elder da of Michael Lodge, of Lighthorne Rough, Lighthorne, Warwicks, and has issue living, Edward Michael Trevidren *b* 1995, Alexandra *b* 1993, Georgia *b* 1997, — Charles Bevil (Riverbank House, Wharfeside Av, Threshfield, N Yorks), *b* 1965: *m* 1990, Amelia Jane, only da of G. A. Boyd, of Threshfield, N Yorks, and has issue living, George Anthony Bevil *b* 1993, Isabella Mary *b* 1991, — Paul Grenville, *b* 1969, — James Hannibal, *b* 1972, — Hugh Donnithorne, *b* 1976, — Katharine Anne, *b* 1967: *m* 1996, Robert Wall, only son of Brian Wall, of Perth, W Aust, and has issue living, Demelza Jane *b* 1998.

Grandchildren of late Rev Herbert Francis Vyvyan (ante):—
Issue of late Capt William Geoffrey Vyvyan, Roy Welch Fusiliers, *b* 1876, *ka* 1914: *m* 1904, Frances Mary, who *d* 1964, da of the late Edmund Salwey Ford, of Pengreep, Perranwell, Cornwall, and 17 Hyde Park Sq, W:—
James Graham (Weston House, Gresford, Wrexham, Clwyd LL12 8EN), *b* 1905; *ed* Wellington Coll and RMC; Hon Lt-Col late R Welch Fus, and DL of Denbighshire: *m* 1934, Guenilda Mary, da of late Rev Preb Arthur Harvey Thursby-Pelham, R of Upton Magna, Shrewsbury, and has issue living, Anthony Geoffrey (Villa Marguerite, 3 Avenue Fabre, 06270 Villeneuve-Loubet, France), *b* 1940; *ed* Wellington Coll, RMA, and Magdalen Coll, Oxford (MA); late Capt R Welch Fus: *m* 1970, Miranda Violet Marguerite, yr da of late Rev Robnett Walters, BD, of North Tamerton, Cornwall, and has issue living, Philip James *b* 1975, David Robnett *b* 1977, Nicholas George *b* 1980, — Cicely Mary, *b* 1936: *m* 1961, Maj Peter Leslie Rawll, late RM, of The Gables, 39 Cotswold Green, Stonehouse, Glos, and has issue living, Andrew Charles Vyvyan *b* 1963, Katherine Frances *b* 1965, — Daphne Elizabeth, *b* 1937: *m* 1965, Edward Christopher Mumford, and has issue living, Robert Vyvyan *b* 1970, Alison Clare Mary *b* 1966: *m* 1991, Timothy Robert Hazlitt Love, son of Col Stephen Love, Jane Myfanwy *b* 1968: *m* 1997, Ian Thomson. —— Opre (*Lady Maclean*), *b* 1910: *m* 1933, Vice-Adm Sir Hector Charles Donald Maclean, KBE, CB, DSC, DL (M Linlithgow, colls), of Deepdale Old Rectory, Brancaster Staithe, King's Lynn, Norfolk, and has issue living, Charles David Hector (8 Eardley Cres, SW5), *b* 1936; *ed* Wellington Coll; Capt R Scots (Lothian) Regt: *m* 1966, Judith, el da of late Donald MacLehose, of Glengair, Clynder, Dunbartonshire, and has issue living, Charles Hector *b* 1968, James Lachlan *b* 1970, — Sara, *b* 1934: *m* 1955, Maj Anthony Michael Everett, Wiltshire Regt (ret), of Enford Grange, Pewsey, Wilts, and has issue living, Simon Anthony Cunningham *b* 1956; *ed* Ampleforth, Rupert James Hector *b* 1959; *ed* Ampleforth, — Katherine Mary, *b* 1937. —— Joan Mary (*Lady Ford*) (twin), *b* 1910: *m* 1937, Sir (Richard) Brinsley Ford, CBE, FSA, who *d* 1999, and has issue living, Francis Vyvyan, *b* 1941; *ed* Eton, and Ch Ch Oxford: *m* 1979, Katherine Elizabeth, da of John Owen, of Playden, Rye, Sussex, and has issue living, Arthur Richard *b* 1988, Lily Rosamund Elizabeth *b* 1980, Gloria Frances Mary *b* 1983, Sylvia Agnes Helen *b* 1985, — (Richard) Augustine, *b* 1943; *ed* Ampleforth: *m* 1978, Elizabeth, da of late Edward Frost, and has issue living, Thomas Augustine *b* 1978, Edward Brinsley *b* 1980, (Richard) Sebastian *b* 1983, Susanna Clare *b* 1986, — Marianne Adele Hermione, *b* 1937: *m* 1966 (*m diss* 1973), Patrick Martin Laver, and has issue living, Harriet Joanna Veronica *b* 1967. *Residence* – 14 Wyndham Pl, W1.

Grandchildren of late Capt William Geoffrey Vyvyan (ante):—
Issue of late (Frederick) Richard Vyvyan, *b* 1913, *d* 1991: *m* 1937 (*m diss* 1957), Barbara, da of late Montague Jones, of Hartpury, Glos:—
(Charles) Richard (82 rue de Graman, Puplinge, CH 1241 Geneva, Switzerland), *b* 1938; *ed* Clifton, and Trin Coll, Camb (MA). —— Priscilla Mary, *b* 1941: *m* 1972, John Loraine Cherry (*see* Rankin, Bt (ext 1960), 1967 Edn), of Mill House, Iping, Midhurst, Sussex GU29 0PF, and has issue living, Tarquin Loraine, *b* 1974, — Amanda Clare, *b* 1978. — Clare, *b* 1944: *m* 1st, 1966 (*m diss* 1978), Martin Austrey Kendall; 2ndly, 1984, Richard Clarke-Hall, of Greenway Manor, Luppitt, Devon, and has issue living (by 1st *m*), Jonathan Austrey, *b* 1966, — Charles Vyvyan, *b* 1971, — Robert Bradley, *b* 1973, — (by 2nd *m*) Henrietta Vyvyan, *b* 1986.

Branch from 3rd son of 7th baronet

Grandchildren of late Capt Richard Norman Vyvyan, eldest son of late Rev Thomas Grenfell Vyvyan, eldest son of late Rev Thomas Hutton Vyvyan, 3rd son of 7th baronet:—
Issue of late Capt (John) Michal Kenneth Vyvyan, *b* 1907, *d* 1991: *m* 1941 (*m diss* 1971), Elizabeth Mary, da of Hugh Gordon Lowder:—
Charles Gerard Courtenay, CB, CBE, *b* 1944; *ed* Winchester, and Balliol Coll, Oxford (BA); Maj-Gen, Defence Attaché, and Head of British Defence Staff (Washington) 1997, Col Comdt R Green Jackets; MBE (Mil) 1974, CBE (Mil) 1990, CB 1998: *m* 1989, Mrs Elizabeth Frances Blair, da of Sir John Starr Paget, 3rd Bt. —— George James Tawney, TD (46 Claylands Rd, SW8), *b* 1951; *ed* Eton; Barrister-at-law; late Capt R Green Jackets; Maj TA: *m* 1st, 1980 (*m diss* 1991), Diana Elizabeth Mary, da of Richard Desmond Hill, OBE, of Kingston Bagpuize, Oxon; 2ndly, 1993, Venetia Ruth Caroline, elder da of John Philip Turner, of Cheyne Walk, SW10, and has issue living (by 2nd *m*), Charlotte Elisabeth Constance *b* 1996. —— Caroline Mary Louise, *b* 1942: *m* 1963, Stephen Charles Archibald Pryor, of Brackengarth, Keasden, Clapham via Lancaster, and has issue living, Henry Charles Lister, *b* 1965, — Charles James Archibald, *b* 1971, — William Tawney Charles, *b* 1973, — Richard Charles Stephen, *b* 1976, — James Charles Edward, *b* 1979, — Rachel Elizabeth (*Hon Mrs Montagu J. Erskine*), *b* 1966: *m* 1997, Hon Montagu John Erskine, yr son of 17th Earl of Buchan.

Branch from 2nd son of 2nd son of 3rd baronet

Grandchildren of late Philip Augustus Vyvyan-Robinson, el son of Rev Philip Vyvyan-Robinson (*b* 1820), el son of Philip Vyvyan-Robinson (*b* 1777), 2nd son of Rev Richard Vyvyan, 2nd son of Richard Vyvyan, 2nd son of 3rd baronet:—
Issue of late Arthur Claude Vyvyan-Robinson, *b* 1880, *d* 1960: *m* 1923, Patricia, who *d* 1982, only child of late F. T. MacDonnell:—
†Arthur Frederick, RD, *b* 1925; *ed* Nautical Coll, Pangbourne, and Pembroke Coll, Camb (MA); Lt-Cdr RNR (ret); 1939-45 War; formerly Headmaster of Royal Masonic Sch, Bushey, and Woodbridge Sch, Suffolk: *m* 1951, Patricia Jill, who *d* 1997, el da of I. W. G. Freeman, of Woking, Surrey, and *d* 1999, leaving issue, Patrick John, *b* 1955; formerly Maj R Regt Fus: *m* 1978, Rosamund Mary, el da of Maj Acton Henry Gordon Gibbon, GM, of Errington, Trillick, co Tyrone, and has issue living, Rachel Louise *b* 1981, Joanna Elizabeth *b* 1983, Tamsin Sarah *b* 1987, Henrietta Frances *b* 1989, — James Courtenay, MBE, *b* 1958; formerly Maj R Green Jackets; MBE (Mil) 1988: *m* 1988, Nicola S., da of N. Poston, of Waltham St Lawrence, Berks, and has issue living, Christopher Courtenay *b* 1994, Jessica Josselyn *b* 1990, — David Augustus, *b* 1960: *m* 1988, Charlotte, da of Oscar Husum, of Cascais, Portugal, and London, — Amanda, *b* 1953: *m* 1974, Charles Philip Metcalfe Yeoman, ARICS, el son of late P. M. Yeoman, FRCS, of Monkton Combe, Bath, and has issue living, Charles William Metcalfe *b* 1978, Thomas Frederick Metcalfe *b* 1980, Harriet Vyvyan *b* 1983. —— Cecil Courtenay, *b* 1928; *ed* Charterhouse, and Jesus Coll, Camb (MA): *m* 1955, Ann Leonora Dirom, el da of V. Berwyn Jones, MRCVS, of Frocester, Glos, and has issue living, Peter Dirom Courtenay, TD (85 Finlay St, SW6 6HF; *Club* – Cavalry and Guards), *b* 1958; Maj HAC; TD: *m* 1994, Elizabeth A. M., da of Derek Guy, of Blackwell, Bristol, — Frances Jane, *b* 1957; AGSM· *m* 1981, Michael Vincent Berrett, of 49 Charlton Village Rd, Wantage, Oxon OX12 7HQ, only son of I.V. Berrett, of Woodford Green, Essex, and has issue living, Peter Michael Vyvyan *b* 1990, Joseph Benedict Vyvyan *b* 1994, Elizabeth Tamsin Mary *b* 1985, Anna Rosamunde Dirom *b* 1987, — Katherine Armorel, *b* 1959: *m* 1986, Mark Peter Stanford, of 12b Arterberry Rd, Wimbledon SW20 8AJ, eldest son of P. J. Stanford, of Dartford, Kent, and has issue living, Charlotte June *b* 1987, Sarah Vyvyan *b* 1989, — Diane Elizabeth, *b* 1963; BA: *m* 1990, Ian Charles Cornock, ARICS, of The Tile House, Hadley, Droitwich, Worcs WR9 0AU, elder son of Maj-Gen Charles Gordon Cornock, CB, MBE, of Cranleigh, Surrey, and has issue living, Harriet Lucy *b* 1993, Pippa Ann *b* 1995, Camilla Fran *b* 1997. *Residence* – The Old House, Horsham, Martley, Worcs WR6 6PN. —— Richard, MBE, *b* 1937; *ed* Bradfield; Maj late LI; MBE (Mil) 1968: *m* 1968, Virginia Ann, da of late Lt-Col William Maitland Brewster Dunn, and has had issue, †Charles Arthur, *b* 1970, *d* 1989, — Mark William, *b* 1972; *ed* Blundell's, and Sidney Sussex Coll, Camb (BA). *Residence* – Mellingey Mill House, St Issey, Wadebridge, Cornwall PL27 7QU. —— Susan Philippa, *b* 1924; 1939-45 War in WRNS: *m* 1954, John Dugmore, of 816 Ely Blvd South, Petaluma, Cal 94952, USA and has issue living, Neil Vyvyan, *b* 1957, — Geoffrey Roland, *b* 1959, — Christopher John, *b* 1965. —— Jane Theodora, *b* 1930: *m* 1955, David Kenneth Wilton Cox, and has issue living, Timothy Michael Wilton, *b* 1959, — Richard Wilton, *b* 1962, — Sarah Lamorna, *b* 1957, — Victoria Tamsin, *b* 1964. *Residence* – Preston Farm, Drewsteignton, Devon. —— Claudia Franeca, *b* 1932: *m* 1957, Henry Graham Tom, and has issue living, Elizabeth Vyvyan (Tregeare, Pendoggett, St Kew, Bodmin, Cornwall PL30 3LW), *b* 1959; has issue living, (by Alastair James MacDonald Baird) Hedrek Henry Vyvyan TOM-BAIRD *b* 1991, Trystan Courtenay Avalon TOM-BAIRD *b* 1998, Damaris Ygerna MacDonald TOM-BAIRD *b* 1989, Ezeld Lalage McDonnell TOM-BAIRD *b* 1997, — Juliet Vyvyan, *b* 1965. *Residence* – Lower Trewiggett, St Teath, Bodmin, Cornwall.

Issue of late Lt Col Francis Vyvyan-Robinson, MC, 1897, *d* 1975: *m* 1926, Aileen, da of late Dr R. H. Powers, of Southend:—
Henry Francis, *b* 1928; *ed* King's Coll, Taunton; late F/O RAAF; Civil Air Pilot: *m* 1957, Susan Rosamond, da of P. A. H. Pettman, of Bournemouth, and has issue living, Hugh, *b* 1958, — Peter Francis (rue des Paquis 5, CH-1201 Geneva, Switzerland), *b* 1963: *m* 1996, Catherine, da of Philippe Emile Robert Böhler, of Montey, Switzerland, and has issue living, Tristan Francis Ulysses *b* 1997, — Sally, *b* 1960: *m* 1986, Walter Albrecht, of Ob der Mur 18, 8173 Riedt, Switzerland, and has issue living, Yannik Vyvyan *b* 1991, Michael *b* 1993, Stefanie *b* 1987, Jennifer *b* 1989, Melanie *b* (twin) 1993. —— Loveday, *b* 1930: *m* 1951, Dr Keith Maxwell Fergusson, of Cranmere, South Rd, Newton Abbot, Devon, and has issue living, Neil Vyvyan, *b* 1952, — Graham Moore, *b* 1955, — Fiona Margaret, *b* 1959, — Elizabeth Loveday, *b* 1963. —— Caroline, *b* 1934: *m* 1957, James Caruth Moore Pryde, of Arden Cottage, 19 Harefield Av, Cheam, Surrey, and has issue living, Catherine Ann, *b* 1960, — Juliet Clare, *b* 1968; has issue living, (by Andrew Holdford) James Andrew *b* 1998.

Grandchildren of late Hugh Norris Vyvyan, 2nd son of Rev Philip Vyvyan-Robinson (*b* 1820) (ante):
Issue of late Capt Hugh Wren Vyvyan, MC, *b* 1890, *d* 1966: *m* 1st, 1917, Mary, who *d* 1930, da of Patrick Lowe, of Bridge of Allan; 2ndly, 1945, Nellie Ryan Sibson:—
(By 1st *m*) Patrick Hugh (71 Mary St, Barrie, Ontario, Canada), *b* 1918; late Sergt Royal Signals; served in World War II 1939-45 (wounded, despatches), formerly Assist Supt of Police, Federation of Malaya: *m* 1959 (*m diss* 19—), Angela, da of Viggo Christensen, of London, and has issue living, Patrick Hugh Beresford, *b* 1959. —— Beresford Haughton, *b* 1929: *m* 19—, Enid Baker, and has issue living, Geoffrey, *b* 19—, — Maryann, *b* 19—, — Wendy, *b* 19—, — Laura, *b* 19—. —— Rosemary Constance, *b* 1929 (twin): *m* 1959, Richard David Messano.

Grandchildren of late Capt Hugh Wren Vyvyan, MC (ante):—

Issue of late Capt Peter Gerald Vyvyan, RCEME, b 1921, d 1962: m 19—, Marjorie Thurman:—
Peter Hugh, b 19—. —— Rosemary Ann, b 19—.

Granddaugher of late Rev Henry Vyvyan, 3rd son of Rev Philip Vyvyan-Robinson (b 1820) (ante):—
Issue of late Lt-Col Philip Henry Nugent Norris Vyvyan, OBE, MC; b 1881; d 1967: m 1917, Mary Caroline, who
d 1982, da of late Rev John Stephen Flynn:—
Lalage Nugent (Well Cottage, White Chimney Row, Westbourne, Emsworth, Hants), b 1921: m 1943, John Derek
Atheling Boustead, Lt R Ulster Rifles, who was ka in Normandy 1944, and has issue living, Lalage Tamsin Vyvyan, b
1943: m 1964, Richard Hugh Lee, Lt RE, and has issue living, James Nugent b 1968, Nicholas Harry Atheling b 1984,
Angela Caroline b 1967.

Granddaughters of late Capt Albert O'Donnel Colley Vyvyan, yr son of late Rev Henry Vyvyan (ante):—
Issue of late Henry O'Donnel Vyvyan, OBE, b 1910, d 1998: m 1936, June (Try-le-Bois, Greencliffe, St Martin,
Jersey), da of John Humphries, of Napier, NZ:—
Wendy (c/o Try-le-Bois, Greencliff, St Martin, Jersey), b 1937: m 1957, Lt Graham George Bell, RASC, and has issue
living, Christopher Graham Vyvyan, b 1960, — Simon Bruce O'Donnel, b 1961, — Robin Benjamin, b 1963, — Bruce St
John, b 1966. —— Valerie Cecilia, b 1941: m 1st, 1966 (m diss 1975), David Henry La Cagnina; 2ndly, 1979, Henry
Fielding Thoresby, of 12 Wexford Rd, SW12 8NH, and has issue living (by 1st m), Adam Vyvyan, b 1970, — Dominic
Vyvyan, b 1973.

Grandson of late Rev Charles Shimmin Vyvyan, 4th son of Rev Philip Vyvyan-Robinson (b 1820)
(ante):—
Issue of late Norris Vyvyan, b 1900, d 1963: m 1925, Florence Elizabeth (Betty), who d 1967, da of the Rev W.
J. Tristram, of Oldham:—
Bertram Charles Boucher, b 1930: m 1965, Jean Margaret Taylor, and has issue living, Catherine Margaret, b 1967.

Grandchildren of late Frederick Albert VYVYAN (who discontinued the surname of Robinson 1879), 5th
son of Rev Philip Vyvyan-Robinson (b 1820) (ante):—
Issue of late Philip Vyvyan, b 1892, d 1985: m 1926, Mary Jacqueline, who d 1970, da of late John Milberne Leacock (Erskine, Bt, cr 1821, colls):—
Rev John Philip (Club — Royal Commonwealth Society), b 1928; ed Charterhouse, and New Coll, Oxford (MA 1959); a
priest in the Anglican Church, Borneo 1961-64, since when Vicar of Adderbury with Milton, Oxon; late DCLI (Regular
Army Reserve); Malaya 1947-48; in Overseas Service, N Borneo 1952-57: m 1957, Monica Yin Tsu, da of Fu Yun Fatt, of
Sandakan, N Borneo, and has issue living, Richard Mark Augustine, b 1960: m 1988, Nada, da of ......, and has issue
living, Oliver Luke b 1995, Ella May Kerie b 1998, — Henry Arthur Luke (4 Philip St, Bondi, NSW 2026, Australia), b
1961: m 19—, Jenette Wylie, — Francis Michael Hannibal, b 1971, — (Honor Mary) Anastasia, b 1968: m 19—, Andrew
W. Panoho, yst son of Charles Panoho, of Auckland, NZ, and has issue living, Charlotte Aroha Gabriella b 1998.
—— Bernard Jeremy (37 West Hill Av, Epsom, Surrey), b 1930; ed Charterhouse, and London Univ (BScEng), FICE; late
REME: m 1964, Constance Joan Steel, da of late Ronald Ismay Pattinson, of Stanwix, Carlisle, and has issue living, David
Jeremy, b 1972, — Mary Louise, b 1965: m 1996, Iain Edward Gibb, elder son of Edward Gibb, of 24 Aberdour Rd,
Dunfermline, and has issue living, Samuel Callum b 1997, — Juliet Penelope, b 1967.

Grandchildren of late Edwin Vyvyan, 6th son (but only son by 2nd m) of late Rev Philip Vyvyan-
Robinson (b 1820) (ante):—
Issue of late Henry Edwin Vyvyan, b 1896, d 1978: m 19—, Grace, who d 19—, da of ......
Malcolm, b 19—: m 19—, and has issue. —— Mamie, b 19—: m 19—, and has issue, one da. —— Betty, b 19—: m
19—, N...... Brook, of 14 Doonside Rd, Doonside, NSW 2767, Australia, and has issue, five children.

The 1st baronet, Sir Richard Vyvyan, MP, was Master of the Mint during the reign of Charles I, and followed the King
to Oxford. He was one of the last six baronets created by that monarch. The 2nd and 3rd baronets each sat as MP for
Cornwall, and the 8th baronet sat as MP for Cornwall (C) 1825-31 for Bristol 1832-7, and for Helston 1841-57. The 10th
baronet, Col Sir Courtenay Bouchier Vyvyan, CB, CMG, served in S African War 1879, Matabeleland Campaign 1896, S
African War 1900-1902, and European War 1914-18 (CMG).

WAECHTER (UK) 1911 of Ramsnest, Chiddingfold, Surrey (Extinct 1985)
(Title pronounced "Vechter")

Sir (HARRY LEONARD) D'ARCY WAECHTER, 2nd and last Baronet.

COLLATERAL BRANCH LIVING

Issue of late John d'Arcy Waechter, PhD, yr son of 1st Bt, b 1915, d 1978: m 1952, Caroline Dymond
(46 Thames St, Sunbury-on-Thames, Middlesex), yr da of the Ven Edgar Francis Hall, Archdeacon of
Totnes:—

Andrea Caroline, *b* 1953. —— Suzanne Anstice Eveline, *b* 1957.

WAKE (E) 1621, of Clevedon, Somerset

Watch and pray

Sir HEREWARD WAKE, MC, 14th *Baronet*; *b* 7 Oct 1916; *s* his father, *Maj-Gen Sir* HEREWARD, CB, CMG, DSO, 1963; *ed* Eton; Maj (ret) KRRC; Vice Lord-Lieut of Northants 1984-91; High Sheriff 1955; 1939-45 War (MC, wounded); *m* 1952, Julia Rosemary, JP, DL, yr da of Capt Geoffrey William Martin Lees, of Falcutt House, nr Brackley, Northants, and has issue.

𝔄rms – Or, two bars gules, in chief three torteaux. Crest – The Wake knot.
Residence – The Old School House, Courteenhall, Northampton NN7 2QD.
Club – Brooks's.

SON LIVING

HEREWARD CHARLES, *b* 22 November 1952: *m* 1st, 1977 (*m diss* 1995), Lady Doune Mabell Ogilvy, el da of 13th Earl of Airlie, KT, GCVO, PC; 2ndly, 1998, Mrs Joan Elizabeth Barrow, da of late Kenneth Murray McCall and has had issue (by 1st *m*), John Hereward, *b* 6 Oct 1978, — Henry, *b* 1980, — †Tom, *b* 1984; *d* 1985, — Laura Katherine, *b* 1986.

DAUGHTERS LIVING

Diana Julia, *b* 1955: *m* 1979, Roderick John Fleming, and has issue (*see* B Wyfold). *Residence* – The Dower House, Sarsgrove, Churchill, Oxon. —— Caroline Jane, *b* 1957: *m* 1979, Adam Richard Fleming, and has issue (*see* B Wyfold). *Address* – Curdle Hill Farm, Chadlington, Chipping Norton, Oxon OX7 3NS. —— Sarah Jennifer, *b* 1960: *m* 1985, Rodney C.H. Morgan-Giles, son of Rear Adm Sir Morgan Charles Morgan-Giles, DSO, OBE, GM, of Upton Park, Alresford, Hants, and has issue living, August George H., *b* 1988, — Julius, *b* 1995, — Max, *b* 1998, — George, *b* (twin) 1998, — Tilia Julia C., *b* 1990.

SISTER LIVING

Mary, *b* 1927: *m* 1947, Capt James Howard Weatherby, late 10th Hussars, and has had issue, Jeremy James, *b* 1949; *ed* Eton; *d* 1998, — Susan (*Viscountess Ullswater*) *b* 1947: *m* 1967, 2nd Viscount Ullswater, of The Old Rectory, Docking, Kings Lynn, Norfolk. *Residence* – Cleeve House, East Knoyle, Salisbury, Wilts.

COLLATERAL BRANCHES LIVING

Issue of late Roger Wake, 2nd son of 13th baronet, *b* 1918, *d* 1988: *m* 1st, 1944 (*m diss* 1969), Olwyn Mary, da of late Col John Charles Wynne-Finch, CBE, MC (*see* E Aylesford, colls); 2ndly, 1984, Belinda Joan, da of Charles Patrick Crossley, and formerly wife of Timothy Michael Nicholl:—
(By 1st *m*) John, *b* 1945; *ed* Eton: *m* 1969, Isabelle, 2nd da of Comte Charles-Evrard de Dreux-Brézé, of Paris, and has issue living, Christopher, *b* 1969, — Jeremy Alistair, *b* 1974, — Charlotte, *b* 1971, — Annabelle, *b* 1986. *Residence* – L'Aumonerie, 49124 St Barthelemy d'Anjou, France. —— Charles Julian, *b* 1947; *ed* Eton, and Univ of BC, Canada: *m* 1977, Josie Abata, of Canada, and has issue living, Callum, *b* 1983, — Rowena, *b* 1978. *Residence* – PO Box 1003, Queen Charlotte City, BC V0T 1S0, Canada. —— William, *b* 1949; *ed* Eton: *m* 1986, Jehanne Deirdre Alexandra, biographer, only da of late James Hamilton Williams, of Anderidan House, Curtisden Green, Kent, and has issue living, David, *b* 1991, — Catherine Mary, *b* 1986. *Residence* – 57 Macfarlane Rd, W12. —— Jane, *b* 1950: *m* 1977, (Simon) Hugh Arnold Potter, and has issue living, Simon, *b* 1982, — Emma, *b* 1979. *Residence* – Cuckoo Bush Farmhouse, Reybridge, nr Lacock, Wilts.

Issue of late Peter Wake, yst son of 13th baronet, *b* 1921, *d* 1993: *m* 1960, Marion Margaret, DL (Fairfield House, Hambledon, Hants PO7 4RY), yr da of late John Henry Bevan, CB, MC, TD, and of Lady Barbara Violet Bingham, elder da of 5th Earl of Lucan:—
Edward, *b* 1965; *ed* Eton: *m* 1991, Katherine Yvonne, only da of John Alfred Leavett-Shenley (*see* B Amherst of Hackney, colls, 1990 Edn), and has issue living, George *b* 1999, — Eliza, *b* 1994, — Mary, *b* 1997. —— Philip Hereward, *b* 1967; *ed* Eton. —— Susan *b* 1963: *m* 1994, John Mervyn Edward Pugh, son of John Mervyn Cullwick Pugh, of Fernhill Heath, Worcs, and has issue living, Lucy, *b* 1996, — Flora, *b* 1997.

Grandchildren of late Col Edward St Aubyn Wake, CMG, son of late Adm Charles Wake (infra):—
Issue of late Rev Hugh Wake, *b* 1916, *d* 1993: *m* 1944, (Catherine) Marigold, who *d* 1999, da of late Adm Sir (William) Frederic Wake-Walker, KCB, CBE (*see* Walker Bt, *cr* 1856, colls, 1995 Edn):—
Vincent Hugh (800 Crow Rd, Glasgow), *b* 1947, SRN, RSCN: *m* 1977, Ruth Mary Petersen, da of William McAulay, of Glasgow, and has issue living, Christine Grace, *b* 1978, — Rebekah Sarah, *b* 1980. —— (Cedric) Philip (22 Lytton Grove, SW15), *b* 1950; MSc; FNI, Master Mariner, Lt Cdr RD RNR (ret): *m* 1978, Claire Susan Woodburn, da of William Vinten, OBE, of Suffolk, and has issue living, Marcus Philip Vinten, *b* 1990, — Charlotte Elizabeth Vinten, *b* 1982, — Suzannah Catherine Vinten, *b* 1985, — Henrietta Claire Vinten, *b* 1992. —— Thomas Baldwin (30 Moss Gdns, Leeds), *b* 1960: *m* 1986, Valerie, da of Harry Green, of Aston, Sheffield, and has issue living, Alexander Harry, *b* 1996, — Christopher Edward, *b* 1998. —— Catherine Frances, *b* 1945: *m* 1st, 1966, Michael Edward Turpin, who *d* 1972; 2ndly, 1973, Vernon Charles Nott, BSc, MIAgrE, of Pelham Hall, Twinstead, Essex, and has issue living, (by 1st *m*) Edward, *b* 1969, — Sarah Jane, *b* 1967, — Rosanna Elspeth, *b* 1972, — (by 2nd *m*) Benjamin Porter, *b* 1976.

Grandson of late Maj Hugh St Aubyn Wake, MVO (infra):—
Issue of late Hugh Edward William Wake, b 1900, d 1967: m 1928, June Brotherton:—
Charles Hugh Edward, b 1930; d 1976, USA.

Grandchildren of late Adm Charles Wake, 2nd son of 10th baronet:—
Issue of late Major Hugh St Aubyn Wake, MVO, b 1870, ka 1914; m 1899, Kathleen Mary, who d 1938, da of Lieut-Col Edward Evans Grigg, Indian Army (formerly Commr of Kamoun):—
Kathleen Josephine (Little Garth, Forest Rd, Hale, Fordingbridge, Hants), b 1909: m 1934, Lt-Col George Douglas James McMurtrie, Somerset LI, and has issue living, Hugh Wake, b 1936, — Michael St Aubyn (twin), b 1936; Maj, 3rd Bn, Princess Patricia's Canadian LI; OMM: m 1958, Bridget Constantia Rubery, and has issue living, Nigel Andrew James b 1959, Paul Marcel b 1971, Marcia Kathleen b 1961, — Jonathan Philip James, b 1941: m 1975, Anne Kelly, and has issue living, Andrew b 1975, Jane b 1977.

Issue of late (Arthur) Leofric St Aubyn Wake, b 1879, d 1957: m 1911, Elma, who d 1971, only da of late William Edward Highett, of Melbourne, Victoria:—
Geoffrey St Aubyn, b 1914; is Capt Australian Imperial Force: m 1943, Lois Ivan-Smith, and has issue living, Carolyn Fearnley St Aubyn, b 1945, — Cheryl Anne, b 1949. Residence – 43 Kooyong Rd, Armadale, SE3, Victoria, Australia. —— Elma Thurfrida, b 1912. —— Diana, b 1913: m 1940, Desmond George Grace, and has issue living, Simon George, b 1948, — Diana Gillian, b 1941, — Susan Elizabeth, b 1943. ——Audrey, b 1916: m 1946, Angus Manning Watson. Residence – 43 Kooyong Rd, Armadale, SE3, Melbourne, Aust.

Grandsons of late Rev Hereward Eyre Wake, only son of late Rev Baldwin Eyre Wake, eldest son of late Rev James Hare Wake, eldest son of late Baldwin Wake, MD, elder son of late Drury Wake, 3rd son of 7th baronet:—
Issue of late Lt-Col Hereward Baldwin Lawrence Wake, b 1900, d 1983: m 1926, Sheila, who d 1991, da of late Capt Henry William Fraser Harris:—
Hereward Michael Wilfred (High Ridge, Knoll Wood, Godalming, Surrey), b 1927. —— Robin Eyre (Polgreen Farm, St Mawgan-in-Pydar, Cornwall TR8 4AG), b 1933; international ornithologist: m 1962, Judith Ann (Judith Wake, NDD, artist), da of Eric Hayden Barry, of West Chiltington, Sussex.

This ancient family is descended from Hugh Wac or Wake (baron by tenure of Bourne and Deeping) (temp King Stephen), from whom the 1st baronet was 15th in male descent. The 2nd baronet assumed the additional surname of Jones, but d without issue. Sir Herewald, 12th baronet, was High Sheriff of Northants 1879. Maj-Gen Sir Hereward Wake, CB, CMG, DSO, 13th baronet, was Dep Constable of Dover Castle 1929-32, and Col Comdt 1st Bn, KRRC 1938-46, and High Sheriff of Northants 1945.

WAKEFIELD (UK) 1962, of Kendal, co Westmorland

Sir (Edward) Humphry Tyrrell Wakefield, 2nd Baronet, b 11 July 1936; s his father, Sir Edward Birkbeck, CIE, 1969; ed Gordonstoun, and Trin Coll, Camb (MA); Fellow of Pierrepont Morgan Library, USA; founder of Stately Homes Collection of Antique Furniture and Objects of Art; Exec Vice Pres of Mallett America Ltd 1970-75; Dir of Mallett and Son Antiques 1970-78, the Spoleto Festival, and the Tree of Life Foundation; Chm of Tyrell Moore Ltd, Sir Humphry Wakefield and Partners Ltd; joined NZ Everest Team on their first ascent of Mount Wakefield 1991, attempted Everest 1992, member Norman Vaughan Antarctic Expedition 1993; President The Northumberland National Park Search and Rescue Team, and The Avison Trust; Patron Actors North East, Medicine for Chernobyl; member of Standing Council of Baronetage, and Lord of the Manor of Chillingham, Northumb, and of Sedgwick, Cumbria; late Capt 10th R Hussars, Freeman of Kansas City, and Hon Citizen of Houston and New Orleans in USA; Hon Col in State of Louisiana; Fell of Pierrepont Morgan Library, USA: m 1st, 1960 (m diss 1964), Priscilla, el da of Oliver Robin Bagot (B Bagot, colls); 2ndly, 1966 (m diss 1971), Hon Elizabeth Sophia Sydney, el da of 1st Viscount De L'Isle, VC, KG, GCMG, GCVO, PC, and formerly wife of George Silver Oliver Annesley Colthurst (see Colthurst, Bt); 3rdly, 1974, Hon Katherine Mary Alice Baring, da of 1st Baron Howick of Glendale, KG, GCMG, and has issue by 2nd and 3rd m.

Arms – Argent two barrulets sable between three owls proper. Crest – A bat displayed proper, charged on each wing with a crescent argent.
Seat – Chillingham Castle, Chillingham, Northumberland NE66 5NJ. Clubs – Turf, Cavalry and Guards', Harlequin Rugby Football, Scott Polar Inst.

SONS LIVING (By 2nd marriage)

MAXIMILIAN EDWARD VEREKER, b 22 Feb 1967; ed Milton Abbey, and RMA Sandhurst; Capt Royal Hussars (PWO): m 1994, Lucinda Katharine Elizabeth, da of Lt-Col David Pipe, of Windlesham, Surrey, and has issue living, William, b 1998.

(By 3rd marriage)

John Humphry Baring, b 1977; ed Eton, and New Coll, Oxford.

DAUGHTER LIVING (by 3rd marriage)

Mary Elizabeth Lalage, b 1975; ed Wycombe Abbey, and Edinburgh Univ.

BROTHER LIVING

Gerald Hugo Cropper (Bramdean House, Alresford, Hants. Club – White's, and The Brook [NY]), b 1938; ed Eton, and Trin Coll, Camb (MA) Chm CT Bowring & Co Ltd, and Guy Carpenter & Co Inc, New York 1996-99: m 1971, Victoria Rose, el da of late Maj Cecil Henry Feilden, of Bramdean House, Alresford, Hants (see V Hampden colls), and has issue living, Edward Cecil, b 1973; ed Eton, and Durham Univ.

WIDOW LIVING OF FIRST BARONET

CONSTANCE LALAGE (Dowager Lady Wakefield) (13 St Mary Abbots Terr, W14), da of late Sir John Perronet Thompson, KCSI, KCIE: m 1929, Sir Edward Birkbeck Wakefield, CIE, 1st Bt, who d 1969.

This family can trace its lineage to Roger Wakefield, of Challon Hall, Westmorland, temp Elizabeth I. Sir Edward Birkbeck Wakefield, CIE, 1st baronet (whose el brother was cr Baron Wakefield of Kendal 1963) was a great-grandson of Edward William Wakefield, of Birklands, Kendal, 3rd son of John Wakefield of Stricklandgate, Kendal (d 1829), 6th in descent from Roger; was Comptroller, HM Household 1958-60 and Treasurer, HM Household 1960-62, 1st UK Commr in Malta 1962-64 and 1st High Commr to Malta 1964-65.

WAKELEY (UK) 1952, of Liss, co Southampton

Sir JOHN CECIL NICHOLSON WAKELEY, 2nd Baronet, b 27 Aug 1926; s his father, Sir CECIL PEMBREY GREY, KBE, CB, 1979; ed Canford, and London Univ (MB BS); LRCP; FRCS; FACS; formerly Ch Inspector, City of London Special Constabulary; former senior Consulting Surg, W Cheshire Group of Hosps, a CStJ, and a former Member of Council RCS England; former Member of Liverpool Regional Hosp Board, and of Mersey Regional Health Authority; Civil Consultant Adviser in Surgery to RAF: m 1954, June, da of Donald Frank Leney, of Shottermill, Haslemere, Surrey, and has issue.

Arms – Argent on a chevron sable between in chief two eagles displayed azure and in base a Rod of Aesculapius proper three crescents of the field. Crest – A demi horse argent supporting between the legs a Rod of Aesculapius proper.
Residence – Mickle Lodge, Mickle Trafford, Chester CH2 4EB.

SONS LIVING

NICHOLAS JEREMY, b 17 Oct 1957: m 1991, Sarah Ann, da of AV-M Brian Lewis Robinson, of Cheldon House, Cheldon, Devon, and has issue living, Joshua Jeremy, b 27 Sept 1993. —— Charles John (Old Bittern Barn, W Harptree, Bristol BS40 6HQ), b 1959; BSc, MB BS, FRCS, FRCSEd, FRCR: m 1984, Rachel Morag Louise, yr da of George Penrose, of Elk House, N Elkington, Lincs, and has issue living, Rupert William, b 1990, — Arthur Charles, b 1993.

DAUGHTER LIVING

Amanda Jane, b 1962; fashion designer: m 1st, 1985 (m diss 1987), Alan Louis Bresler, elder son of late Judge Max Bresler, of Memphis, Tennessee; 2ndly, 1992, Neil David Gillon, son of Norman Keith Gillon, of Perth, Western Australia. Residence – ......

BROTHERS LIVING

Richard Michael (Coves Cottage, High St, St Peters, Broadstairs, Kent CT10 2TH), *b* 1933; *ed* Winchester; MB and BS 1957. —— William Jeremy (Pope's Hall, Hartlip, Sittingbourne, Kent), *b* 1935; *ed* Radley; former JP for Kent: *m* 1959, Veronica, 3rd da of John Dunning Aysh, of Hardham Priory, Pulborough, Sussex, and has issue living, James Richard William, *b* 1963: *m* 19—, Gaynor Rowena, da of David Morgan, of The Hollow, Caistor Lane, Tealby, Market Rasen, Lincs, and has issue living, Alice Angharad *b* 1991, Imogen Cross *b* 1993, — Adam John Paul, *b* 1965: *m* 1991, Melanie Henrietta, da of Michael David Brash Dingley, of Foxcote Hill, Ilmington, Warwicks, and has issue living, Lily Evelyn *b* 1993, — Miranda Elizabeth, *b* 1967: *m* 1992, John Edward Segar, son of Martin Segar, of Stanhill, Godalming, Surrey, and has issue living, Amelia *b* 19—, Arabella Katherine *b* 1998.

WAKEMAN (UK) 1828, of Perdiswell Hall, Worcestershire

Nec temere, nec timide

Neither rashly nor timidly

Sir EDWARD OFFLEY BERTRAM WAKEMAN, 6th *Baronet*; *b* 31 July 1934; *s* his half-brother, *Sir* (OFFLEY) DAVID, 1991.

Arms – Paly wavy of six vert and argent, a saltire engrailed ermine. **Crest** – Between two palm-branches proper, a lion's head erased argent, vomiting flames, gorged with a collar engrailed and cotised vert, and charged with three ermine spots. or.

WIDOW LIVING OF FIFTH BARONET

PAMELA ROSE ARABELLA (*Lady Wakeman*), da of late Lt-Col Cecil Hunter Little, DSO, MBE: *m* 1946, Sir (Offley) David Wakeman, 5th Bt, who *d* 1991. *Residence* – Peverey House, Bomere Heath, Shrewsbury, Shropshire.

Sir Henry Wakeman, 1st Bt, of Perdiswell, Worcs, and Hinton Hall, Salop. Was a Member of HEICS. He was 2nd son of Thomas Wakeman, of Worcester, and *m* 2ndly, 1797, Sarah, da of heir of Richard Ward Offley of Hinton, Salop, Sir Offley, 3rd Bt, was Chm Salop Quarter Sessions 1889-1914, and Capt Sir Offley, CBE, 4th Bt, was Chm, Salop Co Council 1943-63, and a Member of LCC 1922-25.

Waley-Cohen, see Cohen.

WALKER (UK) 1856, of Oakley House, Suffolk

Sir (BALDWIN) PATRICK WALKER, 4th *Baronet*, el son of late Com Baldwin Charles Walker, only son of 3rd baronet; *b* 10 Sept 1924; *s* his grandfather, *Sir* FRANCIS ELLIOT, 1928; *ed* Gordonstoun; Lieut RN (ret); is an hereditary Pasha of Ottoman Empire: *m* 1st, 1948 (*m diss* 1954), Joy Yvonne, da of Sir Arrol Moir, 2nd Bt; 2ndly, 1954, Sandra, da of Henry Stewart; 3rdly, 1966, Rosemary Ann, da of late Henry Hollingdrake; 4thly, 1980, Vanessa Hilton, and has issue by 3rd *m*.

𝕬rms – Gules, on a chevron between three cross-crosslets argent, an anchor sable; on a chief of the second, three stags, heads cabossed proper, a canton azure, thereon a representation of the diamond decoration of a Pasha of the Ottoman Empire, conferred on late Sir Baldwin by the Sultan for his services in Syria. 𝕮rest – Out of a naval crown azure, a stag's head proper, gorged with an eastern crown or.
Address – 5 Voortrekker Rd, Blanco 6531, S Africa.

SON LIVING (*By 3rd marriage*)

CHRISTOPHER ROBERT BALDWIN, *b* 25 Oct 1969.

DAUGHTER LIVING (*By 3rd marriage*)

Amanda Jane *b* 1967: *m* 1993, Michael Grant Fenner-Solomon.

COLLATERAL BRANCHES LIVING

Issue of late Francis Donald Baldwin Walker, yr brother of 4th baronet, *b* (*posthumous*) 1927, *d* 1994; *m* 1st, 1955, Joanna, only da of late Sir John Weir Russell; 2ndly, 1965, Jennifer Mary (Robin Hill, Josephine Rd, Claremont, Cape Town, Cape Province, S Africa), only da of late Lt-Cdr Eric Stokoe, RN (ret):—
(By 1st *m*) Caroline Lucy Marjorie, *b* 1958. —— (By 2nd *m*) Anthony Eric Charles, *b* 1966.

Grandchildren of late Frederic George Arthur WAKE-WALKER, yst son of 1st baronet:—
Issue of late Adm Sir (William) Frederic WAKE-WALKER, KCB, CBE, *b* 1888, *d* 1945: *m* 1916, Muriel Elsie, who *d* 1963, only da of Sir Collingwood Hughes 10th Bt (*cr* 1773):—
†Christopher Baldwin HUGHES-WAKE-WALKER, *b* 1920; Capt RN (ret), assumed the additional surname of Hughes; *ed* RNC Dartmouth; Commander RN Coll Greenwich 1959-61; Naval Attaché in Paris 1962-64; Capt Dartmouth Training Squadron 1964-66; Dir of Naval Signals 1966-68; DL Suffolk 1983, High Sheriff 1985: *m* 1944, Lady Anne Spencer (sometime 3rd Officer WRNS), only da of 7th Earl Spencer, and *d* 1998, leaving issue, David Christopher (82 Royal Hill, SE10 8RT), *b* 1947; *ed* St Andrews Univ (MA); Page of Honour to HM The Queen 1960-62; Dir Kleinwort Benson Group 1990-95: *m* 1979, Jenni Rosemary, only da of late Capt Patrick Vaulkhard, of Stone Cottage, Snape, Saxmundham, Suffolk, and has issue living, Frederic David *b* 1981, Nicholas John *b* 1985, — Richard Anthony, *b* 1951; *ed* St Andrews Univ (MA); Co Dir, and diamond valuer to Federal Canadian Govt: *m* 1980, Sharon Pamela, yr da of late Gordon Stuart Little, of Crowborough, Sussex, and has issue living, Robert Michael *b* 1990, Kate Louise *b* 1982, Olivia Rose *b* 1984, — Michael John (East Bergholt Lodge, East Bergholt, Suffolk), *b* 1958; *ed* RMA Sandhurst; Capt Coldstream Guards: *m* 1992 (*m diss* 1999), Catherine Patricia, eldest da of B. R. Hazlitt, of Billingshurst, Sussex, and has issue living, George *b* 1995, — Elizabeth Sarah, *b* 1944: *m* 1970, Anthony Nicholas George Duckworth-Chad, DL (High Sheriff Norfolk 1992), of Pynkney Hall, King's Lynn, Norfolk, and has issue living, James Anthony de l'Etang *b* 1972, William George Christopher *b* 1975, Davina Alice *b* 1978, — Diana Mary, *b* (twin) 1958: *m* 1980, Maj Charles Keble Macfarlane, Coldstream Guards, and has issue living, Thomas Christopher Keble *b* 1983, Georgina Cynthia *b* 1986. *Residence* – East Bergholt Lodge, Colchester, Suffolk. —— Cedric Collingwood, *b* 1923; Lt-Cdr RN (ret): *m* 1949, Margaret Iona Letitia, MBE, JP, DL, da of Capt J. C. Maclean, RN, and has issue living, Edward Collingwood (5 West St, Kingston, Wareham, Dorset), *b* 1952: *m* 1982, Fiona Margaret, da of Cdr Michael J. Hodgson, DSC, RN (ret), of Westwood, Bradford-on-Avon, Wilts, and has issue living, Thomas Collingwood *b* 1987, Eleanor May *b* 1989, — Susanna, *b* 1950: *m* 1974, Christopher Mark Dancy, MA, BM, BCh, FRCP, of 41 Berwyn Rd, Richmond, Surrey, and has issue living, Luke Henry *b* 1983, Arabella Clare *b* 1977, Martha Caroline *b* 1979, — Corinna Elizabeth, *b* 1957: *m* 1983, Francis Christopher (Fred) Carr, of 49 Moore Park Rd, Fulham, SW6 2HP, son of A. E. J. Carr, of San Francisco, California, USA, and has issue living, Polly Catherine Alice *b* 1985, Matilda Rose *b* 1987. *Residence* – Terwick Wood, Rogate, Petersfield, Hants. —— Penelope Hughes (*Lady Eley*), *b* 1917: *m* 1937, Sir Geoffrey Cecil Ryves Eley, CBE, who *d* 1990, and has issue living, Piers David Christopher (35 Montague Rd, Richmond, Surrey), *b* 1941; MA, MSc: *m* 1967, Sarah Cloudesley, da of late Lt-Col David Edward Long-Price, OBE, and has issue living, Damian Edward Piers *b* 1970: *m* 1997, Alison J., eldest da of Michael Somers, of Churt, Surrey, Thalia Catherine *b* 1971, — Gavin Michael Geoffrey (40 Woolmead Av, NW9), *b* 1945: *m* 1st, 1974 (*m diss* 1984), Mary Belinda (Holly), el da of Maj Bruce Edward Arthur Urquhart of Craigston, Craigston Castle, Aberdeenshire, and formerly wife of Fabrizio Pratesi; 2ndly, 1994, Virginia Jo, da of Peter Williams, of 31 Parliament Hill Mansions, Lissenden Gdns, NW5, — (Susan) Ianthe, *b* 1938: *m* 1st, 1963 (*m diss* 1985), Paul Edward Cornwall Jones; 2ndly, 1985, Peter R. del Tufo, eldest son of late Sir Vincent del Tufo, KBE, and has issue living (by 1st *m*), Imogen Annabel *b* 1967; *ed* Edinburgh Univ (MA), Theresa Hermione Chloë *b* 1971, — Chloë Sarabella, *b* 1950: *m* 1st, 1971 (*m diss* 1984), Richard Christian Wynne Fremantle (*see* B Cottesloe); 2ndly, 1986, Peter Blegvad, of 22 Anley Rd, W14, son of Erik Blegvad, of Wardsboro, Vermont, USA, and has issue living (by 2nd *m*), Kaye Eley *b* 1987, Alec Viggo Eley *b* 1990. *Residence* – The Change House, Gt Yeldham, Essex.

The 1st baronet, Adm Sir Baldwin Wake Walker, KCB (only surviving son of late John Walker, of Whitehaven), was Comptroller of the Navy 1847-60. He served many years in the Turkish service, and was made a Pasha for his services on the coast of Syria. The 2nd baronet, Sir Baldwin Wake Walker, CMG, CVO, was a Vice-Adm.

WALKER (UK) 1868, of Sand Hutton, co York, and of Beachampton, Bucks

How great is honesty

Sir JAMES HERON WALKER, 5th *Baronet*; *b* 7 April 1914; *s* his father, *Sir* ROBERT JAMES MILO, 1930; *ed* Eton, and Magdalene Coll, Camb: *m* 1st, 1939 (*m diss* 1972), Angela Margaret, who *d* 1993, only da of late Victor Alexandre Beaufort, OBE, MC, of Steephill, Jersey; 2ndly, 1972, Sharrone Babette, el da of David Philip Read, of Clanfield, Oxon, and has issue by 1st and 2nd marriages.

Arms – Argent, on a chevron gules, between three crescents azure, as many annulets or. Crest – Out of a battlement argent, a dexter arm embowed in armour azure, in the hand proper a lizard vert.
Residence – Oakhill, Braddan, IoM.

SONS LIVING (*By 1st marriage*)

VICTOR STEWART HERON (Old Cadet House, Gorey, Jersey JE3 6DS, CI), *b* 8 Oct 1942; *ed* Eton; 2nd Lt Gren Gds 1962-65, and Lt R Wilts Yeo and R Yeo 1965-73: *m* 1st, 1969 (*m diss* 1982), Caroline Louisa, yst da of late Lt-Col Frederick Edwin Barton Wignall (*see* Acland, Bt, *cr* 1678, colls, 1980 Edn); 2ndly, 1982, Svea, only da of late Capt (Ernst) Hugo Gothard Knutson Borg, and has issue living (by 1st *m*), James Frederick Heron, *b* 1970, — Andrew Robert Heron, *b* 1973, — Rosanna Celia Louisa, *b* 1979.

(*By 2nd marriage*)

Simon Peter, *b* 1974.

COLLATERAL BRANCHES LIVING

Branches from younger sons of 3rd baronet

Issue of late Capt Ronald Heron Walker, 3rd son of 3rd baronet, *b* 1896, *d* 1964: *m* 1921, Noel, who *d* 1972, da of Maj Guy Edward Wentworth, of Woolley Park, Wakefield:—
Michael Anthony (Pantyffynnon, Salem, Llandeilo, Dyfed), *b* 1924: *m* 1st, 1948, Ann, who *d* 1978, da of John E. Ferguson, of Busbridge Wood, Godalming; 2ndly, 1978, Anne Lavinia, el da of Capt John Henderson, and has issue living (by 1st *m*), Caroline Margaret, *b* 1950: *m* 1969, Ian D. Doulton (Beechcroft, Tunworth, Basingstoke, Hants), and has issue living, David Peter Michael *b* 1974: *m* 1998, Laura Caldwell (and has issue living, Jack Peter *b* 1998), Jonathan Duke *b* 1980, Lucy Catherine *b* 1971: *m* 1995, Gavin Alan Tyte (and has issue living, Gemma Louise *b* 1999), — Rosemary Ann, *b* 1954: *m* 1981, Capt Robert Lincoln Guy, LVO, RN, of 11 Dornton Rd, SW12 9NB, and has two adopted das, Laura Susan *b* 1992, Anna Caroline *b* 1996. — Frances Mary, *b* 1965: *m* 1999, Maarten Christopher Westerduin, — (by 2nd *m*), John Michael, *b* 1979, — Andrew James, *b* (twin) 1979, — James, *b* 1984, — Ruth, *b* 1982. ⸻ Diana Mary, *b* 1923: *m* 1969, Simon Neville Turner, who *d* 1990, of Achnashellach, by Strathcarron, Ross-shire.

Issue of late Patrick Bruce Walker, MBE, 4th and yst son of 3rd baronet, *b* 1898, *d* 1988: *m* 1928, Sybil, who *d* 1986, da of Charles Byron Turner, MRCS, of Ashby-cum-Fenby, Lincs:—
Susan Anne Maud (*Hon Lady Butler*), *b* 1930: *m* 1952, Hon Sir Richard Clive Butler, of Gladfen Hall, Halstead, Essex, son of Baron Butler of Saffron Walden, KG, CH, PC (Life Baron), and has issue (see that title).

Branches from younger sons of 2nd baronet

Grandsons of late Rev Reginald Edmund Walker (infra):—
Issue of late Rupert Alexander Seymour Walker, *b* 1910, *d* 1973: *m* 1942, Edith Mary Sutherland:—
Jack Mervyn, CD (Suite 802, 829 Norwest Rd, Kingston, Ont, Canada K7P 2N3), *b* 1946; CD 19—: *m* 1968, Marjorie Aline, da of Herbert Buske, of Pembroke, Ont, and has issue living, Victoria Edith *b* 1974. ⸻ Raymond Earle, *b* 1950.

Issue of late Rev Reginald Edmund Walker, 2nd son of 2nd baronet, *b* 1866, *d* 1945: *m* 1895, Lady Emily Mary Seymour, who *d* 1948, da of 6th Marquess of Hertford:—
Margaret Edith Mary, *b* 1901: *m* 1st, 1920, Frank Caffery; 2ndly, 1941, William Derbyshire, and has issue living, (by 1st *m*) Kathleen Ethel Mary, *b* 1934: *m* 1st, 19—, Robert Coates; 2ndly, 19—, John Jeffrey, of Burnaby 1, BC, Canada, and has issue living (by 1st *m*), Edward Francis *b* 19—: *m* 1970, Jo-Ann Shepherd (and has issue living, Jolene Mary *b* 1974), Douglas Colin Paul *b* 1953, Robert James *b* 1958, Kathleen Wendy Maki *b* 19—: *m* 1972, Matthew Mackie (and has issue living, Matthew Maki *b* 1974), Anita Marie *b* 1955: *m* 1973, George Polburn (and has issue living Shayne Gregory *b* 1974), Sharon Leigh *b* 1957, Phyllis Margaret *b* 1959, Debra Joan *b* 1960.

Issue of late Ernest Robert Walker, 5th son of 2nd baronet, *b* 1872, *d* 1942: *m* 1901, Beatrice Mary, who *d* 1938, da of Rt Hon Sir Herbert Eustace Maxwell, 7th Bt, MP (*cr* 1681):—
Kathleen Elizabeth Jean (Cannons, Tibberton, Glos), *b* 1908.

Branches from younger sons of 1st baronet

Grandchildren of late Frederick James Walker, MVO, 2nd son of 1st baronet:—

Issue of late Capt Hugh Edward Walker, b 1865, d 1935: m 1913, Hon Marjory Winifred, who d 1945, da of 21st Baron Forbes:—
Rosemary Alice Champney b 1917: m 1948, Capt Hugh Shelley Le Messurier, Duke of Wellington's Regt, of 48 E Witton, nr Leyburn, N Yorks DL8 4SL, and has issue living, Jacquine Shelley, b 1949: m 1960, Lt Jeremy John Gaskell, The Kings' Regt, and has issue living, Victoria Jacquine b 1971: m 1999, Matthew Power, Joanna Louise b 1973, — Susan Rosemary, b 1950: m 1977, John McDonald Green-Armytage (The Cedars, Barnes Common, SW13), and has issue living, Matthew Whitla b 1978, Anna Claire b 1981, Camilla Rose b 1983, Elizabeth Caroline b 1985. —— Marguerite Helena Mary, b 1919: m 1942, Capt Giles Grierson Tweedie, of Glencairn, Church Crescent, Dunscore, Dumfriesshire DG2 0TA, late Argyll and Sutherland Highlanders, and has issue living, Marion Veronica, b 1943: m 1978, Michael Frank Walter, and has issue living, Patrick Douglas b 1980, — Jacqueline Alice, b 1944, — Rosalind Mary, b 1947: m 1979, Derek Gwynn Evans, who d 1994, and has issue living, Mark Edward b 1982, Eifion Charles b 1983, Alison Margaret b 1985, Pamela Sian b 1988. —— Daphne Elizabeth (3 Barford St, N1 0QB), b 1926.

Grandsons of late Rear-Adm Charles Francis Walker, 3rd son of 1st baronet:—
Issue of late Capt Edgar Wilmer Walker, E Yorkshire Regt, b 1875, ka 1914: m 1906, Charlotte Rankin, who d 1954, having m 2ndly, 1919, (7th Viscount Lifford), da of Sir Robert Maule:—
Francis Robert, b 1910.

Issue of late Rev Philip Charles Walker, b 1878, d 1933: m 1916, Dorothy Ann, who d 1936, da of late Col Frederick Compton Howard, Rifle Brig (E Carlisle, colls):—
Anthony Charles Howard, b 1917; ed Wellington Coll: m 1st, 1939, Lorna (m diss 1946), da of H. Crabtree; 2ndly, 1952, Peggy Foster, da of John T. Hewes, of Cambridge, and has issue living, (by 2nd m) Timothy Heron, b 1954, — Elizabeth Cavendish, b 1956, — Ann Cavendish, b 1958. Residence – 58 Balfour Rd, Blackbird Leys, Oxford. —— Philip James, b 1920; ed Uppingham Sch; formerly in RAF; European War 1939-45 in India: m 1951, Helen Gibson, da of Dr Milligan, late of Hessle, E Yorkshire. Residence – Halse Springs, Macheke, Zimbabwe.

Granddaughter of late Capt Edwyn Walker, 4th son of 1st baronet:—
Issue of late Capt Oswald Bethell Walker, 15th Hussars, b 1875, ka 1914: m 1910, Marcia Eugenia (who d 1973, having m 2ndly, 1920, Francois de Juge Montespieu), da of late Col John Delalynde Mansel (Mansel, Bt, colls):—
Lois Adeline, b 1912: m 1932, George Nickerson, late Coldstream Guards, who d 1976, and has had issue, David George Francois, b 1933: m 1957, Sara Elizabeth (who m 2ndly, 1997, Maj Charles Christopher Sebastian Fenwick (see B Lilford, colls), of Barhams Manor, Higham, Suffolk), da of late Col John Howlett Jewson, MC, of Mergate Hall, Norwich, and d 1995, leaving issue, William John George b 1958: m 1989, Jayne, eldest da of Roland Pickering (and has issue living, Joshua b 1992, Alfred William Sparrow b 1995, Ella b 1997), James David Rivers b 1960: m 1993, Ann D. L., da of Horace Reynolds, of Inkberrow, Worcs (and has issue living, Daisy b 1996, Florence b 1998), Camilla b 1965: m 1995, Neville H. F. Wakefield, son of Humfrey Wakefield, of Tresco, Isles of Scilly (and has issue living, Atticus b 1998), — Mark Oswald Julian (Boxted Lodge, Colchester), b 1935: m 1974, Elizabeth, da of F. P. Birch, and has issue living, Emma b 1975, Caroline b 1978. Residence – Burnt Fen, Horning, Norfolk.

Grandson of late Capt Gerald Walker, 5th son of 1st baronet:—
Issue of late Lieut-Col Bertram James Walker, CMG, DSO, b 1880, d 1947: m 1st, 1909 (m diss 1926), Josepha Margaret, who d 1972, da of late Sir George Donaldson, of 1 Grand Av, Hove, Sussex; 2ndly, 1940, Countess Lucie Marie Reventlow, who d 1984, aged 99, of Brahe Trolleborg, Denmark:—
(By 1st m) †Anthony Gerald Bartholomew, b 1912; ed Harrow and RMC Sandhurst; Lieut-Col (ret) Somerset LI: m 1939, Margaret Cumberland, who d 1987, only da of late Col C. P. Templeton, CB, DSO, of Victoria, British Columbia, and d 1999, leaving issue, Rev Christopher James Anthony (Horseshoe Meadow Farm, Cholderton, Salisbury, Wilts SP4 0ED), b 1943; ed Harrow, and RMA Sandhurst; Lt-Col (ret) 17th/21st Lancers; Chaplain to the Forces 1987: m 1971, Ronwen Melody, eldest da of late Lt-Col E. C. Barton, MC, and has issue living, Rupert Anthony Edward b 1972, Alice Melody Margaret b 1974, Lavinia Verity Rose b 1977, Cicily Primrose Amy b 1979, — Robin Charles Andrew (The Garden Flat, 30 Maida Av, W2 1ST), b 1944, ed Harrow, and McGill Univ, Montreal. m 1975, Selina Margaret, el da of Maj Patrick Dudley Erskine Riall, of Ballyorney House, Enniskerry, co Wicklow, and has issue living, Lucinda Margaret Riall b 1983, Sophie Claire b 1985, — Peter Gerald Edward (Binghams Farmhouse, Bower Chalke, Salisbury SP5 5BN), b 1948; ed Harrow: m 1980, Anne Susan Lyon, only da of late Capt N. Fellowes, and has issue living, Harry Bertram Templeton b 1984, Charles Peter Templeton b 1987, Emily Rose Cumberland b 1983, Amelia Anne Cumberland b 1989, — John Perry Donaldson (44 Cornwall Gdns, SW7 4AA), b 1951: ed Harrow; Capt 17th/21st Lancers, — Morella Cumberland, b 1942: m 1967, Robert Gwynne Cottam, of 7 Stanford Rd, W8 5PP, and has issue living, Charles Robert Edward b 1969, Henry Gerald Alexander b 1973, Rosemary Margaret Cumberland b 1971: m 1999, Kevin Thomas Maher.

Grandchildren of late Arthur Walker, 8th son of 1st baronet:—
Issue of late Edward Arthur Walker, b 1883, d 1950: m 1911, Frances Beatrice, who d 1961, da of James Davis:—
Harold Edward Palmes, TD (Springwood Tower Rd North, Heswall, Ches), b 1917; 1939-45 War as Maj Indian Army in Burma: m 1951, Phyllis Nora Green, and has issue living, Michael Anthony, b 1951; ed St David's Coll, Llandudno: m 1983, Frances Helen Price, of Mount Isa, Qld, Aust, and has issue living, James Heron Palmes b 1986, Ross Francis b 1988, — Joan Olive Beatrix, b 1912: m 1940, Geoffrey Norman Booth, solicitor, of 77 Palm Grove, Oxton, Birkenhead, and has issue living, David Parkin, b 1943. —— Stella Rowena Palmes (3 Halifax Close, Wellesbourne, Warwicks), b 1920: m 1944, Cdr Harold Jack Edmund Dugdale, RNR, who d 1975, and has issue living, Janet Beatrice, b 1947: m 1972, Robert Lewes Sinkinson, and has issue living, Mark Luis b 1985, James Alexander b 1991, — Diana Elizabeth, b 1952: m 1989, Jan Ryszard Kacperek, and has issue living, Paul Anthony b 1993.

Grandchildren of late Henry Walker (infra):—
Issue of late Maj Henry Arthur Walker, b 1913, d 1994: m 1st, 1935 (m diss 1947), Rose Vivien, who d 1993, da of Raymond Robert Ulyate, of Arusha, Tanzania; 2ndly, 1948, Christine Mabel, who d 1973, da of Ollive Edward Hollingworth, of Step Cottage, Witchampton, Dorset; 3rdly, 1980, Patricia Blanche Neville (The Bridge House, Spetisbury, Blandford Forum, Dorset DT11 9EB), da of Ralph Neville Neville-Jones, of Broadstone Dorset, and widow of Capt C. H. Hammer, MBE, RN:—
(By 1st m) Robert Christopher Arthur (PO Box 835, Robertson 6705, Western Cape, S Africa), b 1938; ed King's Sch, Bruton: m 1964, Melody Glorianna Mignonette, yst da of late Gustavus Adolfus Carl de Friedland, of Cape Town, S Africa, and has issue living, Grant Robert James (Sunninghill, Johannesburg, SA), b 1968; ed St Martin's, Johannesburg:

m 1999, Janine, yst da of Vic Worthmann, of Sunninghill, Johannesburg, — Juanita Marguerite Vivien *b* (Jan) 1965: *m* 1983, Ferdinando Ganchinho Carlos, of N Budrim, Maroochydore, Brisbane, Qld, Australia, and has issue living, Sheyne Robert Martins *b* 1984, Ivan Anibal Christopher *b* 1986, Ricardo Fernando *b* 1987, — Karine Madelaine Mignonette Tanya (Kenridge, Durbanville, Cape Town, SA), *b* (Nov) 1965; has issue living, Devon Christopher *b* 1994. —— (By 2nd *m*) Mary Woodroffe Margaret, *b* 1957: *m* 1980, John Stephen Lucas, of Wychwood, 4 Field Way, Corfe Mullen, Wimborne, Dorset BH21 3XH, and has issue living, Emma Annabel Mary, *b* 1983, — Sophie Elizabeth, *b* 1985.

Grandchildren of late Arthur Walker (ante):—
Issue of late Henry Walker, *b* 1885, *d* 1965: *m* 1913, Margaret, who *d* 1974, da of Robert Rowlands:—
Monica Diana (5 Bon Accord, Victoria Av, Swanage, Dorset), *b* 1915: *m* 1939, Archibald Robert Octavius McMillan, OBE, who *d* 1988. —— Margaret Patricia (1 Richmond Lodge, Victoria Av, Swanage, Dorset), *b* 1919: *m* 1944 (*m diss* 1966), Eugene Larner, who *d* 1989, and has issue living, Felicity Gay (15 Gayford Rd, W12 9BJ), *b* 1945: *m* 1980 (*m diss* 1985), William McKinney, and has issue living, Clinton William Eugene *b* 1981.

Issue of late Maj Ernest Walker *b* 1887, *d* 1970: *m* 1st, 1921, Mildred Katherine Grace, who *d* 1952, da of late Lt-Col Sir Charles Henry Brabazon Heaton-Ellis, CBE; 2ndly, 1953, Dorothy Hyacinthe, who *d* 1993, only child of late Maj Cecil William Bunbury Eames, JP, RE:—
(By 1st *m*) Peter Martin Brabazon, CBE (Drumlaggan, The Ross, Comrie, Perthshire), *b* 1922; *ed* Haileybury, and Trin Coll, Camb; Prof of Natural Hist, Edinburgh Univ; FRSE: *m* 1st, 1943, Violet Wright; 2ndly, 1986, Joan Patricia Taylor, and has issue living, (by 1st *m*) Robin John, *b* 1947: *m* 19—, Barbara Ovens, and has issue living, Sam Brabazon *b* 1972, — Marian Elizabeth, *b* 1943: *m* 1st, 19— (*m diss* 19—), David Malcolm; 2ndly, 1985, Dr Maurice Shepherd, and has issue living, (by 1st *m*) James Murdo Walker *b* 1967, Tobias Peter Walker *b* 1972, — Sonia Elidh, *b* 1954: *m* 19—, Stephen Turley, and has issue living, Jonathan William Peter *b* 1984, Frederick James Robin *b* 1990, Nicholas Liam Sydney *b* 1993, Rosemary Anna Violet *b* 1987, — Caroline Jane Palmes, *b* 1960, — (by 2nd *m*) Hannah Virginia, *b* 1987. —— Jonathan Mungo Palmes (Lythanger, Empshott, Hants), *b* 1929; Maj (ret) The Black Watch: *m* 1955, Diana Mary, el da of late Brig Otho William Nicholson, TD, DL (*see* E St Aldwyn 1939 Edn), and has issue living, Timothy William Mungo, *b* 1956; *ed* Millfield: *m* 1989, Julia Suzanne, eldest da of John Clifford Groves, of Lundie Castle, Edzell, Angus, and has issue living, Max John Mungo *b* 1990, — Jonathan Alexander James, *b* 1961; *ed* Millfield, — Juliette Elisabeth Charmian (*Hon Mrs William Wilson*), *b* 1958; *ed* St Mary's, Calne and Homerton Coll, Camb: *m* 1989, Hon William Edward Alexander Wilson, yr son of 2nd Baron Moran, KCMG.

Granddaughter of late Maj Ernest Walker (ante):—
Issue of late Lt Cdr Timothy Robin Charles Walker, RN, *b* 1925, *d* 1964: *m* 1958, Dilys, who *d* 1964, da of late Brig John Victor Dykes Radford, OBE, MC, of Clayhanger, Purse Caundle, Sherborne, Dorset:—
Sabrina Louise, *b* 1962: *m* 1983 (*m diss* 1986), Maj Roderick Alexander Ingleby-Mackenzie, Scots Gds.

Sir James Walker, 1st Bt, of Sand Hutton, Yorks, only son of James Walker of Springhead, Hull, was High Sheriff of York 1846. Sir James Robert Walker, 2nd Bt, was MP for Beverley (*C*), 1859-65.

WALKER (UK) 1906, of Pembroke House, City of Dublin

Sir HUGH RONALD WALKER, 4th *Baronet*; *b* 13 Dec 1925; *s* his father, *Maj Sir* CECIL EDWAR , DSO, MC, 1964; *ed* Wellington Coll; Member of Assoc of Supervisory and Exec Engineers; Maj (ret) RA: *m* 1971, Norna, el da of Lt-Cdr R.D. Baird, RNR (ret), of Yarford Orchards, Kingston St Mary, nr Taunton, and has issue.

𝕬rms – Ermine, on a chevron engrailed plain cotised azure, between three hurts, each charged with a portcullis or, as many trefoils slipped of the last. 𝕮rest – On a Roman fasces or, banded azure, a dove of the last, holding in its beak a trefoil slipped of the first.
Address – Ballinamona Hospital, Kilmallock, co Limerick.

SONS LIVING

ROBERT CECIL, *b* 26 Sept 1974. —— Roy Edward, *b* 1977.

SISTER LIVING

Sheilagh Rosemary, *b* 1928.

The 1st baronet, Rt Hon Sir Samuel, PC, was Solicitor-Gen for Ireland 1883-5, Attorney-Gen of Ireland 1885 and 1886, Lord Chancellor of Ireland 1892-5, a Lord Justice of Appeal 1895-1905, and again Lord Chancellor 1905-11.

Walker-Okeover, see Okeover.

Walker-Smith, see Smith.

FORESTIER-WALKER (UK) 1835
(Name pronounced "Forest-tier-Walker")

Sir MICHAEL LEOLIN FORESTIER-WALKER, 6th *Baronet*; only son of Lt-Col Alan Ivor Forestier-Walker, MBE, elder son of Ivor Augustus Forestier-Walker, 5th son of 2nd Bt; *b* 24 April 1949; *s* his kinsman, *Sir* CLIVE RADZIVILL, 1983; *ed* Wellington Coll, and R Holloway Coll, London Univ (BA Hons, Cert Ed); Schoolmaster at Feltonfleet School, Cobham: *m* 1988, Elizabeth, da of Joseph Hedley, of Bellingham, Northumberland, and has issue.

Arms – Erminois, on a pile embattled azure, a mural crown charged with the word "Badajos" between two galtraps in pale or. **Crest** – On a mural crown or, encircled by a wreath of laurel vert, an ostrich proper, resting the dexter foot on a shell exploding proper. **Supporters** – *Dexter*, a lion reguardant proper, gorged with a riband gules, fimbriated azure, therefrom pendent a representation of the medal and claps presented to the 1st baronet for his services in the Peninsula; in the mouth a broken flagstaff reversed, with the eagle and French tricolored flag also proper, the latter inscribed with the word "Orthes"; *sinister*, an ostrich supporting the colours of the 50th Regt, thereon an escroll gules inscribed with the word "Vimiera" in letters of gold.
Residence – Bibury, 116 Hogshill Lane, Cobham, Surrey.

SON LIVING

JOSEPH ALAN, *b* 2 May 1992.

DAUGHTER LIVING

Chloë, *b* 1990.

SISTER LIVING

Michelle, *b* 1946: *m* 1970, Christopher K. C. Metz, of North Brook End House, Steeple Morden, Royston, Herts, and has issue living, Camilla, *b* 1977, — Rosamond, *b* 1979, — Marguerite, *b* 1984.

DAUGHTERS LIVING OF FIFTH BARONET

Lesley Jane, *b* 1951: *m* 1968, John Wheaton, of 23 Grove Rd, Rayleigh, Essex SS6 8PU, and has issue living, Joanna Lesley, *b* 1970, — Jacqueline, *b* 1971. —— Heather, *b* 1954. *m* 1972, John Gray of 20 Grove Rd, Rayleigh, Essex SS6 8PU, and has issue living, Steven John, *b* 1977, — Adam James, *b* 1981. —— Elizabeth, *b* 1958: *m* 1974, David King, of 21 Juniper Rd, Leigh-on-Sea SS9 4BQ, and has issue living, Daniel David, *b* 1975, — Kerryann, *b* 1976.

COLLATERAL BRANCHES LIVING

Granddaughter of late Radzivill Frederick Forestier-Walker, 2nd son of 2nd Baronet:—
Issue of late Radzivill Clive Forestier-Walker, *b* 1895; *d* 1973: *m* 1921, Kathleen Rose, who *d* 1975, da of late William George Tinkler, of King's Lynn, Norfolk:—

June Vivienne, *b* 1923: *m* 1954, Leonard Raymond Hayes, of Chinook, Castle Rising Rd, S Wootton, King's Lynn, Norfolk.

Grandson of late Ivor Augustus Forestier-Walker, 5th son of 2nd baronet:—
Issue of late Urbain Evelyn Forestier-Walker, *b* 1915, *d* 1974: *m* 1941, Aileen, who *d* 1976, da of Thomas Morrissey:—
Alan David, *b* 1944; *ed* Prior Park Coll, Bath; Lt-Col 7th Duke of Edinburgh's Own Gurkha Rifles: *m* 1969, Adela, da of Simon Phillip Davis, and has issue living, Robin Peter, *b* 1978, — Clare Elaine, *b* 1971, — Louise Anne *b* 1972. —— Anne Patricia, *b* 1942.

Issue of late Capt Devereux Philip Forestier-Walker, 6th son of 2nd baronet, *b* 1864, *d* 1936: *m* 1896, Isabella Constance, who *d* 1949, da of late F. G. Dalgety, of Lockerley Hall, Hants, and widow of Capt C. W. Selwyn:—
Freda Gladys (17, 31313 Livingstone Av, Cleasbrook, BC, V2S 5W6), *b* 1897: *m* 1921, William Henry Cartwright, who *d* 1962, and has issue living, Julian William Devereux, *b* 1923: *m* 1949, Margaret Elaine, da of E. Ewing, and has issue living, Elena Marr *b* 1950: *m* 1976, Donald John Rouse, Lorena Joanne *b* 1951: *m* 1972, Jacobus Antonius Ferdinand Remak (and has issue living, Jason William Johannes *b* 1976) Shelley Rae *b* 1953: *m* 1973, Terrance Glenn Pruden, Tracy Dell *b* 1961, — Barbara Mary, *b* 1922: *m* 1954, John Bannatyne McLeod, of 920 Smith Av, Coquitlam, BC. —— Honor Dorothy, *b* 1899: *m* 1934, Capt Thomas Willington Lane, late RA; MA Camb and ADC to Gov of Mauritius, who *d* 1977, and has issue living, Patrick Anthony Willington (28 High St, Manton, Marlborough, Wilts SN8 4HH), *b* 1938: *m* 1978, Dinah, da of late B. W. Righton, of Town Farm, Ebrington, Glos, and has issue living, Martin Nicholas *b* 1980, Sarah Ann *b* 1979, — Gillian, *b* 1935. *Residence* – Longdon, Bath Rd, Marlborough, Wilts.

Grandchildren of late Charles Evelyn Forestier-Walker, 9th son of 2nd baronet:—
Issue of late Charles Jocelyn Forestier-Walker, *b* 1912, *d* 1992: *m* 1942, Joy (19 High St, Hanslope, Bucks MK19 7LQ), da of late Lt-Cdr John Robert Gill, RNR, of Christchurch, Newport, Mon:—
Charles Robert Piers (385 Rt 217, Claverack, Hudson, NY 12534, USA), *b* 1950; *ed* Wellington College: *m* 1st, 1974 (*m diss* 1979), Philippa Jean White, step-da of Dr C. Bondy; 2ndly, 1996, Carla Jo, da of James Cashen, and has issue living, (by 1st *m*) Rowan, *b* 1977. —— Elenith Camilla, *b* 1947: *m* 1st, 1968 (*m diss* 1982), Malcolm Anthony Luker; 2ndly, 1983, James Stephen Allen, of 46 Hertford St, Cambridge CB4 3AG, and has issue living, (by 1st *m*) James Robert, *b* 1971, — Benjamin Gavin, *b* 1975, — (by 2nd *m*) Richard Arthur Llewellyn, *b* 1983, — Charles Alexander Titus, *b* 1988, — Camilla Imogen Maud, *b* 1984.

Issue of late (Robert Jestyn) Gwent Forestier-Walker, *b* 1919, *d* 1994: *m* 1956, Elizabeth Ann (Barberry House, Clifford, Herefords HR3 5HF), da of late Brig J. H. Willans, of Newton House, Sneaton, Yorks:-
(Charles) Aidan Gwent, *b* 1966: *m* 19—, Nicola, da of Gerald Anthony Fulton Tinto, of Mallorca, Balearics. —— (Evelyn) Rosamond, *b* 1961: *m* 1987 (*m diss* 1990), Hon Hugh Francis Kindersley, who *d* 1991, 2nd son of 3rd Baron Kindersley. —— Vivien Serena Charlotte, *b* 1963: *m* 19—, G. Nicholas Tucker, son of late Maj K. O. Tucker, and has issue living, Harry Albert, *b* 1994, — George, *b* 1997. —— (Daphne) Miranda Clare, *b* 1964: *m* 1998, Nicholas de Bellaigue, son of Eric de Bellaigue (*see* B Rodney, 1985 Edn), and has issue living, Otto, *b* 1997.

Grandchildren of late Lieut-Col Edmond Somerville Forestier Walker, el son of Maj-Gen George Edmond Lushington Walker, 4th son of 1st baronet:—
Issue of late Col Edmond Alec FORESTIER-WALKER, *b* 1888, *d* 1952 (having assumed by deed poll 1909, the additional surname of Forestier): *m* 1921, Eileen de Renzy, who *d* 1977, da of late Col O. H. Channer, of Brookheath, Fordingbridge, Hants:—
Edmond Annesley (Broombank, Aldeburgh, Suffolk IP15 5PQ), *b* 1922; *ed* Felsted Sch, Maj (ret) RA; 1939-45 War in N Africa and Italy (despatches); Administration Manager, Touche Ross 1969-83: *m* 1st, 1944, Bridget, who *d* 1961, da of Cdr Sir Geoffrey Henry Hughes-Onslow, KBE, DSC, RN (ret) (E Onslow, colls), 2ndly, 1968, Dreenagh Denise, da of Kenneth G. Chavasse, MVO, of London, and has issue living, (by 1st *m*) George Clive (Plum Tree Cottage, North Heath, Chieveley, Newbury, Berks RG20 8UD), *b* 1946; Maj Coldm Gds (ret): *m* 1970, Ruth Christian, yst da of John Gurney, of Walsingham Abbey, Norfolk (*see* Ogilvy Bt, colls, 1995 Edn), and has issue living, Camilla Christian *b* 1973: *m* 1994, Robert A. Byk, yst son of Peter H. J. Byk, of Bickley, Kent, Susanna Charlotte *b* 1976, Liza Bridget *b* 1980, Mary Sarah *b* 1983, — Sally Eileen, *b* 1948: *m* 1972, Mark Andrew Muspratt-Williams, of Springfields, 94 The High St, Sutton Veny, Warminster, Wilts BA12 7AW, and has issue living, Alexander Mark *b* 1977, Catriona Louise *b* 1975, — (by 2nd *m*) David Anthony, *b* 1972, — Annabel Dreenagh, *b* 1974; MSc. —— Claude Osborne (Babbacombe, Snape Bridge, Saxmundham, Suffolk IP17 1ST), *b* 1924; *ed* Felsted Sch; is a Co Dir: *m* 1950, Gillian Mary, da of Maj Guy Pedder, of Park House, Hoxne, nr Diss, Norfolk, and has issue living, Hugh Anthony Claude (Kencot Hill Farmhouse, Filkins, Lechlade, Glos GL7 3QY), *b* 1954; *ed* Abbotsholme; Co Dir: *m* 1976, (Elizabeth) Jane, da of Rev Christopher Birdwood, and has issue living, Edward *b* 1982, Caroline Louise *b* 1978, Rebecca Jane *b* 1980, — Melanie Diana, *b* 1956, — Katherine Susan, *b* 1960; MA (Cantab); journalist (as Katherine Forestier): *m* 1988, Zhang Zeming, of 58 Po Wah Yuen, Yung Shue Wan, Lamma Island, Hong Kong, and has issue living, Lydia Yishi *b* 1990, Laura Yiya *b* 1992.

The 1st baronet, Gen Sir George Townshend, GCB, KCTS, was a distinguished Peninsular officer, C-in-C at Fort St George, India, and Lt-Gov of Chelsea Hospital. The 2nd baronet assumed by deed poll 1893, the additional surname of Forestier.

WALLER (I) 1780, of Newport, Tipperary

Honour and truth

Sir ROBERT WILLIAM WALLER, 9th *Baronet*; *b* 16 June 1934; *s* his father, *Sir* ROLAND EDGAR, 1958; *ed* Newark Coll of Engineering, and Fairleigh Dickinson Univ; formerly Business Manager with General Electric Co (ret 1991); a citizen of USA: *m* 1960 (*m diss* 1975; re-*m* 1997), Carol Anne, da of John E. Hines, of 45 Bellevue Rd, Lynn, Mass, USA, and has issue.

Arms – Checky or and azure, on a canton gules, a lion rampant double queued of the first. Crest – Out of a ducal coronet a plume of five ostrich feathers, 2nd and 4th azure, 1st, 3rd and 5th argent, surmounted by an eagle's claw gules. *Residence* – 5 Lookout Terr, Lynnfield, Mass 01940, USA.

SONS LIVING

JOHN MICHAEL, *b* 14 May 1962: *m* 1986, Maria Renee Gonzalez, and has issue living, John Michael, *b* 1990, — Patrick Joseph de Warren, *b* 1992, — Victor Robert, *b* 1995, — William Thomas *b* 1998, — Jocelyn Anne, *b* 1988, — Mary Katherine, *b* 1994. *Residence* – USA. ———— David Peter *b* 1963: *m* 1990, Lynn Riddle, and has issue living, Wyatt Owen, *b* 1998, — Isabel Jeannette, *b* 1996. *Residence* – 22 Mountain Av, Malden, Mass 02148, USA.

DAUGHTERS LIVING

Susan Carol, *b* 1968. ———— Kathleen Anne, *b* 1970. *m* 1998, William D. Grant, V.

SISTERS LIVING

Helen Mary, *b* 1924: *m* 1945, Arthur Paul Warshauer, who *d* 1990, and has issue living, Shawn Matthew, *b* 1962, — Sandra Ann, *b* 1945, — Mary Susan, *b* 1950. *Residence* – 144 W Webster St, Apt 4F, Manchester, NH 03104-2939, USA. ———— Patricia Ann, *b* 1930: *m* 1st, 1949 (*m diss* 1974), Howard George Schier; 2ndly, 19—, Leonard Monroe, of 3321 19th St CT East, Bradenton, Fla 34208, USA, and has issue living (by 1st *m*), Virginia Gail, *b* 1949, — Nancy Lee, *b* 1954, — Linda Jean, *b* 1957.

COLLATERAL BRANCHES LIVING

Branch from brother of 7th baronet

Grandson of late Elwood Eccleston Waller, brother of 7th baronet, *b* 1876, *d* 1944: *m* 1895, Francina Claire Shaunesy, who *d* 1958:—
Issue of late Elwood Eccleston Waller, *b* 1896, *d* 1976: *m* 1921, Jane Eden, who *d* 1977:—
Elwood Eccleston (3511 Hargill Drive, Orlando, Florida 32806, USA), *b* 1922; formerly Lieut USA Air Force: *m* 1st, 1946, Marie Maupin; 2ndly, 1956, Marie Benton, and has issue living (by 1st *m*), Patrick, *b* 1949, — Susan (3019 Emerson St, Tampa, Florida 33629, USA), *b* 1947.

Branch (if any) from 3rd brother of 6th baronet

Descendants (if any) of Edmund Waller, 3rd brother of 6th baronet, *b* 1844, *m* 1861 and *d* 1899, leaving issue.

Branch from 3rd brother of 4th baronet

Descendants (if any) of Augustus Edmund Waller, *b* 1871, and Philip Percy Waller, *b* 1877, sons of Jocelyn Waller, el son of Samuel Waller, MD, 3rd brother of 4th baronet.

Grandchildren of late John Stanton Waller (infra):—
Issue of late John Clifton Waller, *b* 1903, *d* 1985: *m* 1st, 1939 (*m diss* 19—), Priscilla Frost, of Marblehead, MD, USA; 2ndly, 1953 (*m diss* 19—), Christine E. Todtschinder, of Manchester Centre, VT, USA:—
(By 1st *m*) John Clifton, Jr, *b* 1940: *m* 1st, 1964 (*m diss*), Donna Lee Smethurst, of Marblehead, MA, USA; 2ndly, 1977, Diana Casey, of Salem, MA, USA, and has issue living, (by 1st *m*) John Clifton III, *b* 1965, — Michael, *b* 1973. *m* 19—, — , and has issue living, Timothy Michael French *b* 1991, — Donna Leann, *b* 1969: *m* 19—, — , and has issue living, Shawn William Somers *b* 1989, Jeremy Michael Somers *b* 1991, — (by 2nd *m*) Darrell Hawkes, *b* 1977, — Annette Michelle, *b* 1984, — Alan Peyton Hawkes, *b* 1946: *m* 1st, 19— (*m diss*), Susan Jan Halloran, of Marblehead, MA, USA; 2ndly, 1980, Christine Renée Whalen, of Princeton, NJ, USA, and has issue living, (by 1st *m*) Todd Alan Hawkes, *b* 1968, — (by 2nd *m*) Benjamin Edward Austin Hawkes, *b* 1990. ———— (by 2nd *m*) Sandra Gail, *b* 1957.

Granddaughter of late Samuel William Waller (*b* 1844), yr son of Samuel Waller, MD (ante):—
Issue of late John Stanton Waller, *b* 1868, *d* 1921: *m* 1888, Ida Anna Finley, who *d* 1950, da of James Peyton, of Montreal, Canada:—

Margaret Patricia Eunice, *b* 1907: *m* 1928, Walter Brown Power, Jr, and has issue living, Walter Brown III, *b* 1930: *m* 1955, Sandra Sherman, and has issue living, Walter Brown IV *b* 1958, Sherman Douglas *b* 1961: *m* 1989, Christine Landry, Matthew Eli *b* 1963, Elizabeth Atwood *b* 1970, — James Peyton, *b* 1933: *m* 1965, Virginia O'Meara, and has issue living, Peyton Jay *b* 1975, Tara O'Meara *b* 1966: *m* 1991, Bradley James Gilbert, Laurel Peyton *b* 1969: *m* 1990, Michael Perry.

Grandchildren of late Edmund Henry Colclough Waller (infra):—
Issue of late Herbert Montague Waller, *b* 1907, *d* 1971: *m* 1942, Vera Germain (245 Denis St, Thunder Bay, Ont, Canada):—
Edgar Herbert (239 Bluejay Crescent, Oshawa, Ont, Canada L1G 6X4), *b* 1942; *ed* Lake Head Univ, Thunder Bay, Ont: *m* 1966, Sandra Yvonne Egan, and has issue living, Scott Edward (104 Covington Bend, Whitehouse, Tenn, USA), *b* 1967: *m* 1995, Carolyn Mitchell, and has issue living, Carly Nicole *b* 1998. —— Brian Robert (1 Mango Lane, Blenheim, Ont, Canada), *b* 1944; *m* 1965 (*m diss* 1982), Joan Gloria Woodgate, and has issue living, Faye Kathleen, *b* 1969: *m* 1993, Tim Fox, of 213 Tenth Av, Crambrook, BC, Canada, and has issue living, Adam Timothy *b* 1997, Kathleen Gloria Maria *b* 1995, — Karen Louise, *b* 1972: *m* 1999, James Coffey, of 123 Eric Clarke Drive, Whitby, Ont, Canada, and has issue living, Devon McKenzie *b* 1994, China Rose *b* 1998. —— Sharon Claire, *b* 1946: *m* 1965, Robert Bruce Nicholl, of RR 2, Devlin, Ont, and has issue living, Laura Cecile, *b* 1966, — Rhonda Jean, *b* 1968: has issue living, Robert Herbert James *b* 1989, Shaleigh *b* 1995. —— Jean Patricia, *b* 1952: *m* 1972, John Charles Mayo, of RR1, Thunder Bay, Ont, and has issue living, Jennifer Ann, *b* 1975.

Grandchildren of late Samuel William Waller (*b* 1844) (ante):—
Issue of late Edmund Henry Colclough Waller, *b* 1879, *d* 1970: *m* 1906, Caroline Agnes, who *d* 1967, da of late John Mann, of Grand Valley Ont:—
†Arthur Edmund (6711 Dover Rd, Nanaimo, BC, Canada V9T 2L9), *b* 1909: *m* 1st, 1941 (*m diss* 1967), Frances, da of John Martin, of Vancouver BC; 2ndly, 1968, Mrs Alma Rickerby, da of — Taylor, and *d* 1999, leaving issue (by 1st *m*), Lynne Diane, *b* 1944: *m* 1996, Fred Penland, of Richmond, BC. —— William Hugh, *b* 1912: *m* 1944, Alvina Koch. —— Cedric Henry, *b* 1914: *m* 1939, Flora Margaret da of John George Campbell, of MacDowell, Sask, Canada, and has issue living, Cedric Lorne, *b* 1940; *ed* BC Univ (BEd) and W Washington Univ, USA (MEd); Sch Administrator: *m* 1st, 1964 (*m diss* 1977), Doris Lorraine, da of Edward Sweetman, of Trail, BC; 2ndly, 1977, Julia Carolyn, da of George Dennison Glanville, of W Vancouver, BC, and has issue living, (by 1st *m*) Stephen Lorne *b* 1966, Richard Lawrence *b* 1968, Daniel Leonard *b* 1970 (by 2nd *m*) Jennifer Louise *b* 1980, Allison Patricia *b* 1982, — Ronald Henry (1940 Treetop Rd, Kelowna, BC, Canada V1P 1C5) *b* 1943; *ed* BC; Univ (BSP, MSc): *m* 1965, Gwendolyn Anne, da of William Wright, of Nelson, BC, and has issue living Michael Ronald *b* 1966, Donald William Henry *b* 1969, Christopher Bradley *b* 1970, Darren Lorne *b* 1971, Heather Diane Habiza *b* 1972. —— †Thomas Geoffrey, *b* 1916; Forestry Dept Supervisor, BC Govt (ret): *m* 1st, 1947 (*m diss* 1975), Elizabeth Margaret Esther, da of William J. Brodie, of Nelson, BC; 2ndly, 1994, Evelyn Cogill, and *d* 1997, leaving issue, (by 1st *m*), and has issue living, Donna Elaine, *b* 1949: *m* 1971, Edward Charles Anderson, and has issue living, Nicole Dawn *b* 1974, Tara Leigh *b* 1979, — Glowena Margaret, *b* 1950: *m* 1st, 1969, Allen Lee Hutchinson; 2ndly, 1986, Leslie Alexander Cook, and has issue living (by 1st *m*), Celeste Marie *b* 1969, Michelle Jeanette *b* 1972, — Judith Darlene, *b* 1953: *m* 1st, 1973 (*m diss* 1977), Joseph Martin Walker; 2ndly, 1983, Frederick Louis Tuttosi, and has issue living (by 1st *m*), Cassandra Lee *b* 1981, (by 2nd *m*) Michael Ryne *b* 1984. —— Arnold Blair (401-154 Promenade Drive, Nanaimo, BC, Canada V9R 6Y3), *b* 1924: *ed* BC Univ (BASc): *m* 1951, Janet Louise, who *d* 1994, da of William Paton Montgomery, of Montreal, and has an adopted son, Jonathan Blair, *b* 1962, — Laurie Jane, *b* 1953: *m* 1984, Christopher Benson, of 63 Anne St, Cannington, Ont L0E 1E0, and has issue living, Robin Patrick Waller *b* 1989, Mairen Rose Montgomery *b* 1992, — Elizabeth Sue, *b* 1958: *m* 1989 (*m diss* 1993), Christopher Thor Asp, of Neustadt, Ont N0G 2MO, Canada. —— Evelyn Agnes *b* 1918: *m* 1st 1937 (*m diss* 1954), James Donald Ross; 2ndly, 1961, William Wilson, and has issue living, (by 1st *m*) Shirley Norma, *b* 1938: *m* 1st, 1955 (*m diss* 1969), Allen William Wilson; 2ndly, 1980 (*m diss* 1989), Póvl Frederich Holm, and has issue living (by 1st *m*), Michael Allen (26136 Camelot Av, Loma Linda, Calif 92354, USA) *b* 1963; *ed* Loma Linda Univ, Calif; MD, Shelley Norma *b* 1957: *m* 1983, Michael Collins. —— Beatrice Alice (Nanaimo, BC, Canada), *b* 1922: *m* 1949, Ernest John Moretti, who *d* 1971, and has issue living, Ernest James, *b* 1950.

Grandchildren of late Hugh Jocelyn Waller (infra):—
Issue of late Hector Hugh Waller, *b* 1910, *d* 1986: *m* 1945, Mary Patricia (N Vancouver, BC, Canada), da of Ivor John Everson, of Gravesend, Kent:—
Thomas Hector (1935 West View Drive, N Vancouver, BC, Canada V7M 3B1), *b* 1947: *m* 1969, Margaret Quilliam, and has had issue, Michael Hugh, *b* 1974, — †Ian Denny, *b* 1976; *d* 1994. —— Sean Ivor, *b* 1957. —— Mary Kathleen, *b* 1950: *m* 1972, Gerald St Laurent, of N Vancouver, BC, and has issue living, Jocelyn Kathleen, *b* 1974, — Tannis Patricia Marie, *b* 1977. —— Valerie Jane, *b* 1954: *m* 19—, William Truttman; 2ndly, 1988, Pal Levitt.

Issue of late Gordon Jocelyn Waller, *b* 1912, *d* 1992: *m* 1937, Pearl Solie:—
Dennis Raymond, *b* 1938. —— Gordon Edmund (6370 Old W Saanich Rd, Victoria, BC, Canada V8M 1W8), *b* 1948: *m* 1985, Diane Victoria Chestnut, and has issue living, Mark Allan, *b* 1986, — Erin Victoria, *b* 1990.

Grandchildren of late Samuel William Waller (*b* 1844) (ante):—
Issue of late Hugh Jocelyn Waller, *b* 1887, *d* 1981: *m* 1909, Olive Maria, who *d* 1959, da of John Mann:—
Hugh Macartney (119 Heritage Cres, Nanaimo, BC, Canada), *b* 1922: *m* 1st, 1943, Betty Hallat; 2ndly, 1951, Florence —, and has issue living (by 2nd *m*), Kenneth Hugh, *b* 1953: *m* 1975, Anne Beswetherwick, of New Haven, Sussex, and has an adopted son, Liam Kenan Hugh *b* 1987, — Gregory Allen, *b* 1955: *m* 1980, Judith Anne Yule, and has issue living, Sean Steven *b* 1987, — Douglas William, *b* 1959: *m* 1983, Kathleen Freeman, and has issue living, Nicholas Hugh *b* 1986, Jessica Rachelle *b* 1988, — Denise Jean, *b* 1951: *m* 1973, Arthur Stanley Webb, and has issue living, Ryan Gregory *b* 1980, Jaye Scott *b* 1981, Lauren Ashley *b* 1987, — Kathleen Marie, *b* (twin) 1953: *m* 1983, Johannes Verhagen, and has issue living, Gregory William *b* 1986, Caitlin Johanna *b* 1989. —— Lilian Gladys, *b* 1911: *m* 1935, Clinton Geddes, and has issue living, Gordon, *b* 1936: *m* 1958, Judith Anne Hall, and has issue living, Clinton Douglas *b* 1965, Michael *b* 1970, Cinda Marie *b* 1959, Dayna *b* 1960. —— Muriel Eleanor, *b* 1919: *m* 1941, Charles Guiguet, who *d* 1999, Curator of Birds and Mammals, Provincial Museum, Victoria, BC, of 2399 Dalhousie St, Victoria, BC, and has issue living, Mark Laurence, *b* 1950: *m* 19—, Victoria —, and has issue living, Colin *b* 19—, Michelle *b* 19—, — Joan Muriel, *b* 1942, — Patricia Lynda, *b* 1947: *m* 1969, John —, and has issue living, Matthew Guiguet *b* 1969, — Suzanne Maria, *b* 1955: *m* 198-, Bryce —, and has issue living, Tyson Bancroft *b* 1987. —— Jean Pearl, *b* 1923: *m* 1946, Laurence Cutler, and has issue living, Jerry, *b* 1947, — Ross, *b* 1952, — Gregory, *b* 1955: *m* 19—, Sherry —, and has issue living, Ryan *b* 19—, — Janet, *b* 1949: *m* 1968, Len Thony, and has issue living, Paul John *b* 1970, Corry Lynne *b* 1969, Dana Marie *b* 1973, — Debra, *b* 1957.

Branch from youngest brother of 4th baronet

Grandchildren of late Robert William Waller, el son of late Robert Waller, yst brother of 4th baronet:—
Issue of late Frank Hastings Waller, *b* 1871, *d* 1953: *m* 1914, Elvie Grace, *d* as a result of enemy action 1940, da of late William Bedford, of Landour, India:—
Marjorie, *b* 1919.

Issue of late Charles Robert Waller, *b* 1877, *d* 1933: *m* 1905, Agnes Helen, da of late Francis Thorne, of Launceston, Cornwall:—
†Robert William, *b* 1910: *m* 1936, Daphne Mabel, who *d* (Oct) 1992, el da of Herbert Clifton Morton, of Pretoria, S Africa, and *d* (Aug) 1992, leaving issue, Robert David (Morville Farm, Le Hurel, St Ouen, Jersey) *b* 1939: *m* 1961, Rosalie Beryl, da of late Wilfred Easter, of Southampton, and has issue living, Hugh *b* 1965, Vanessa *b* 1963, Ursula (twin) *b* 1963: *m* 19—, Douglas A. Richardson, of Morville Farm, Le Hurel, St Ouen, Jersey, CI, — Leonard Harold (1 Ivy Place, Vincent Heights, E London 5247, S Africa), *b* 1953: *m* 1st, 1976, Moira, who *d* 1981, da of Frank Ferreira, of Queenstown; 2ndly, 1982, Helen Louise, da of Raymond George Hewson, of East London, and has issue living (by 1st *m*), Stephen *b* 1976, Marc *b* 1977, (by 2nd *m*), Peter *b* 1984, — Delene Ruth, *b* 1937: *m* 1961, Edgar E. Esselen, of 132 Golf Av, Club View West, Pretoria, S Africa, and has issue living, Deborah *b* 1962: *m* 1980, Gary Alan Gordon (and has issue living, Justin *b* 1984, Megan *b* 1986), Ingrid *b* 1965, — Thalia Lynnette, *b* 1943: *m* 1965, Allan Harry Griffin, of 14 Hill Cres, Amanzimtoti, Natal, and has issue living, Helen Eileen *b* 1969; *m* 1998, Richard Zulch, Louise Daphne *b* 1971: *m* 1995, John Dennison, — Daphne Jess, *b* 1945: *m* 1985, Peter Alan Anscombe, of Johannesburg, S Africa, — Heather Lynn, *b* 1949. —— Edmund John (31 Kingston Drive, Umhlanga Rocks, Natal), *b* 1919; 1939-45 War as Warrant Officer SAAF, in Middle East, Malta, Sicily, and Italy: *m* 1944, Alma, yst da of Edwyn Treffry-Goatley, of Durban, Natal, and has issue living, Virginia Helen, *b* 1945, — Hazel Louise, *b* 1948: *m* 1968, John Robert Lockwood, of E Yorks, England, and has issue living, Edmund Sean *b* 1973, Amanda Jane *b* 1969.

Grandchildren of late Jocelyn Waller, 2nd son of late Robert Waller (ante):—
Issue of late Robert Martin Jocelyn Waller, *b* 1862, *d* 1936: *m* 1896, his cousin, Emily Mary, who *d* 1951, da of late Robert William Waller:—
Frank Martin Roden, *b* 1909: *m* 1948, Nora Dale, who *d* 1965, da of late Rev Cyril Edgington, of Bath, and has issue living, Robert Cyril Hardress Jocelyn, *b* 1949. —— Dorothy Minnie, *b* 1898: *m* 1919, Reginald Carp, of 12 Grange Av, Highbridge, Som, and has issue living, Thomas Walter Waller, *b* 1924, — Pamela Mary, *b* 1923.

Grandchildren of late Rev William Dillon Waller, 3rd son of late Jocelyn Waller (ante):—
Issue of late Hans Jocelyn, *b* 1897, *d* 1978: *m* 1922, Mildred, da of Dr Vivian Pennock, MD, of Longmont, Colorado:—
Edmund Hugh (8656 W Progress Place, Littleton, Colorado 80123, USA), *b* 1929: *m* 1951, Barbara Yetter, and has issue living, Kenneth Scott, *b* 1959: *m* 1982, Karen Staley, and has issue living, Tyler Paul *b* 1989, Danielle Renée *b* 1986, — Wendy Ann, *b* 1957: *m* 1st, 1983 (*m diss* 1985), Randall J. Brunko; 2ndly, 1987, Timothy Todd, and has issue living (by 2nd *m*), Joseph Lee *b* 1988. —— Patricia Gene, *b* 1925: *m* 1948, Rev Dr Vern L. Klingman, of 1020 14th St W, Billings, Montana 59102, USA, and has issue living, Stephen Wesley (1910 3rd Av N, Seattle, Washington 98109, USA), *b* 1957: *m* 19—, Janel Erickson, and has issue living, Peter Craig *b* 1990, August Hans *b* 1993, — Nancy Rose, *b* 1955, — Candace Martha, *b* 1961, — and has an adopted son, Paul Bryan, *b* 1953: *m* 19—, Peecheng Chen, and has issue living, Bryan Waller *b* 1986, Rei Lin *b* 1988.

Grandson of late Rev Alfred Jocelyn Waller (infra):—
Issue of late Hardress Jocelyn Waller, *b* 1905, *d* 1935: *m* 19—, Bessie Burrow:—
Hardress Jocelyn (10635 Maumee-Western Rd, Swanton, Ohio 43558-9681, USA), *b* 1928; PhD; Neurophysiologist, Medical Coll of Ohio, Toledo, Ohio: *m* 1953, Gertrude Gearhart, and has issue living, Andrew Jocelyn (2318 Buckingham Rd, Ann Arbor, Michigan 48104-4912, USA), *b* 1960; MD; Physician: *m* 1985, Adreanne Chabler, and has issue living, Jonathan Andrew *b* 1998, Nicole Alyce *b* 1988, Leah Victoria *b* 1991.

Grandchildren of late Jocelyn Waller (ante):—
Issue of late Rev Alfred Jocelyn Waller, *b* 1870, *d* 1950: *m* 1903, Katherine Tarrence:—
Richard (9400 E Iliff Av, No 281, Denver, Colorado, 80231-3489, USA), *b* 1915: *m* 1949, Mildred Lucka, and has issue living, Sharon Rose, *b* 1951: *m* 1st, 19—, Charles Counts; 2ndly, 1998, Peter Day, of 939 Cerrito St, Albany, Calif 94706, USA.

Issue of late Harry Bernard Waller, *b* 1882, *d* 1971: *m* 1920, Anna Kruger Jorgensen, of Denmark, who *d* 1946:—
Evelyn May, *b* 1924: *m* 1949, Selwyn Barton Hoag, of 1350 Ridge Rd, Littleton, Colorado 80120, USA, and has issue living, Selwyn Barton, *b* 1950: *m* 1st, 1972, Claudia Lukas; 2ndly, 1978, Lee Lacey, and has issue living, Jason Henry *b* 1979, — Christopher Henry, *b* 1958, — Anthony Wayne, *b* 1960, — Eugenia Anne, *b* 1943: *m* 1st, 1965, Laurence V Monniger; 2ndly, 1981, Dennis Homrighausen, and has issue living (by 2nd *m*), Darren Warren *b* 1983, Amanda Ann *b* 1981, — Jocelyn Deane, *b* 1955: *m* 1981, John Parker Mertens, and has issue living, Charles Parker *b* 1983.

The 1st baronet, Sir Robert Waller (son of late Samuel Waller, of Newport, Tipperary) was MP for Dundalk 1761-80, and one of the Commissioners of the Revenue. Sir Robert, 2nd Baronet, was High Sheriff for King's co in 1806.

WALLER (UK) 1815, of Braywick Lodge, Berkshire (Extinct 1995)

Sir JOHN STANIER WALLER, 7th and last *Baronet*.

SISTER LIVING OF SEVENTH BARONET

Elizabeth Mary Louisa (Winchcombe, 37B Madeira Rd, Ventnor, I o Wight PO38 1QS), *b* 1923; *ed* Oxford High Sch, and St Hilda's Coll, Oxford (Exhibitioner in History, MA BLitt); Assist Lecturer, Medieval History, Liverpool Univ, 1949-53; Baghdad 1953-58; joined HM Diplo Ser; Regional Assist Information Officer for Women's Affairs, Beirut 1961-67, Women's Affairs Officer, FCO London 1967-78, subsequently (self-employed) Women's Affairs Consultant until 1993.

COLLATERAL BRANCH LIVING

Issue of late Richard Alured Waller, 2nd Lieut Roy Fusiliers, yst brother of 6th baronet, *b* 1884, *d* on active ser 1917: *m* 1912, Ethel Gertrude, who *d* 1978, da of late John Tippet Drake, of Plumstead, Kent:—

Margaret Patience (The Cottage, Crawley Down, Sussex), *b* 1917: a State Registered Nurse (ret).

WALSHAM (UK) 1831, of Knill Court, Herefordshire
(Name pronounced "Walsam")

Rest under liberty

Sir TIMOTHY JOHN WALSHAM, 5th *Baronet*; *b* 26 April 1939; *s* his father, *Rear Adm Sir* JOHN SCARLETT WARREN, CB, OBE, 1992; *ed* Sherborne.

Arms – Quarterly: 1st and 4th per pale azure and gules, a grffin segreant wings elevated or, supporting on a tilting spear a banner flowing to the dexter argent, charged with a cross couped sable, *Garbett*; 2nd and 3rd, sable, on a cross voided or, five crosslets patée-fitchée of the last, *Walsham*. Crest – A demi-eagle with two heads displayed sable, having suspended from the neck, by a gold chain, an escutcheon argent, and thereon a Saracen's head erased at the neck proper, round the temples a wreath argent and azure.
Residence – Dromquinna Manor, Blackwater Bridge PO, nr Kenmare, co Kerry.

SISTERS LIVING

Susan Elizabeth, *b* 1941: *m* 1st, 1963, Christopher James Harbour; 2ndly, 1988, Charles Michael Robertson, of Dromquinna Manor, nr Kenmare, co Kerry, and has issue living (by 1st *m*), Mark Christopher Bannerman, *b* 1964, — Benedict David Walsham, *b* 1967: *m* 1996, Georgina Ella Smith, and has issue living, Tiger Jackson *b* 1997, — Matthew Alexander Walsham, *b* 1969; has issue living, (by Lisa Pendlebury) Jodie Kai *b* 1998, — Caroline Lucy Scarlett, *b* 1965: *m* 1997, Dennis Brown, and has issue living, Daisy *b* 1998. ── Jane Scarlett (Ower Farm, Ower Lane, Upham, Southampton SO32 1HN), *b* 1942: *m* 1963, Cdr David Colin Nairne, RN, who *d* 1998, and has issue living, Charles David Scarlett, *b* 1965, — Alexander John Dalmahoy, *b* 1970, — Sarah Catriona, *b* 1964: *m* 1990, John Alexander Santos, and has issue living, Alexander James *b* 1995, Anouska Beatriz *b* 1992.

AUNT LIVING (*daughter of 3rd baronet*)

Gundreda Brydget Coytmore, *b* 1909: *m* 1931, Chichester Kennedy Crookshank, and has issue living, John Kennedy (Ivy House, Westbourne, nr Chichester, W Sussex), *b* 1932; *ed* Repton, and RMA, Sandhurst; Capt late 5th Royal Inniskilling Dragoon Gds: *m* 1963, Phyllida Anne, yr da of Capt Ernest Charles Mylne, of Godmanstone Manor, Dorchester, and has issue living, Charles James Chichester *b* 1966, Antonia Scarlett *b* 1969: *m* 1998, Michael Guy Jenkinson, of Kilmester Farm, Lechlade, — Peter Scarlett, *b* 1935; *ed* Sherbourne: *m* 1958, Susan, da of Thomas George Watwood, of Stafford, and has issue living, Richard Chichester *b* 1962, William Thomas *b* 1965.

WIDOW LIVING OF FOURTH BARONET

SHEILA CHRISTINA (*Lady Walsham*), only da of late Cdr Bertrand Bannerman, DSO, RN (*see* Bannerman, Bt, colls): *m* 1936, Rear Adm Sir John Scarlett Warren Walsham, 4th Bt, CB, OBE, who *d* 1992. *Residence* – 19 Beckford Close, Tisbury, Wilts.

COLLATERAL BRANCH LIVING

Issue of late Percy Romilly Walsham, 2nd son of 2nd baronet, *b* 1871, *d* 1933: *m* 1899, Charlotte
Cunningham Scott, who *d* 1945, da of William Wykeham Myers, MB:—
PERCY ROBERT STEWART *b* 6 April 1904; *ed* —: *m* 1937, Tamara, who *d* 1981, da of — Ellis, of —, and has issue living,
Gerald Percy Robert, *b* —1939; *ed* : *m* 1984, Evelyn, da of —Niebes, of —, — Diana Charlotte, *b* 1938: *m* 1959, SCM/Sgt
Harley R. Linley, USAF (ret), and has issue living, Paul R— *b* 1961, Charlotte Diana *b* 1960.

The name of this family is supposed to be derived either from Walsham le Willows in Suffolk, or Walsham St Mary in
Norfolk, in both of which counties, as in Cambridgeshire, the Walshams were of note, and often of knightly rank, from
the end of the 11th to the beginning of the 18th century. The Walshams of Knill represent a branch that settled in
Radnorshire about 400 years ago, through the marriage of John Walsham with Mary, granddaughter and heiress of Sir
Jenkin Harvey of Llanvair, Knight. From this marriage lineally descended John Walsham, who *m* Barbara, granddaughter
and heiress of John Knill, of Knill Court, MP for Radnor, *temp* Mary I, and was the direct ancestor of the present
baronet. The 1st baronet received his baronetcy as being the eldest co-heir and representative of Gen Sir Thomas
Morgan, Bt, whose title created 1660, became extinct on the death of Sir John Morgan, 4th Bt in 1767. Sir John
Walsham, KCMG, 2nd Bt, was Envoy Extraor and Min Plen to China 1885-92 and to Roumania 1892-3.

WARD (UK) 1911, of Wellington, New Zealand

By courage and faith

Sir JOSEPH JAMES LAFFEY WARD, 4th *Baronet*; *b* 11 Nov 1946; *s*
his father, *Sir* JOSEPH GEORGE DAVIDSON, LLM, 1970: *m* 1968,
Robyn Allison, da of William Maitland Martin, of Rotorua, NZ,
and has issue.

Arms – Azure, a cross moline argent between four keys wards upwards or.
Crest – A demi-griffin azure in front of two keys in saltire wards upwards or.
Residence – 3 Regal Place, Milford, Auckland, NZ.

SON LIVING

JOSEPH JAMES MARTIN, *b* 20 Feb 1971.

DAUGHTER LIVING

Theresa Jane, *b* 1972.

BROTHERS LIVING

Roderic Anthony (35 Coates Park Rd, Cobbitty, NSW 2570, Australia), *b* 23
April 1948: *m* 1993, Faye Mary Morrisson. —— Michael John (RD1, Wallis
Rd, Ruawai, NZ), *b* 1954: *m* 1977, Alamein Sharlene Connelly, and has issue
living, Christopher Davidson *b* 1979, — Felicity Te Puawai, *b* 1980, — Joan
Marie Ngaroma, *b* 1985.

SISTERS LIVING

Angela Mary (Cambria Cottage,31 Vauxhall Rd, Devonport, Auckland, NZ), *b*
1945. —— Felicity Elizabeth Elinor Joan, *b* 1951: *m* 1979, Dr Graeme Warren Kidd, of 243 Bleakhouse Rd, Howick, NZ,
and has issue living, Guy George Joseph, *b* 1983, — Cecille Mary, *b* 1981. —— Catherine Josephine Mina (c/o Arts
Training Centre, 130 Flinder St, Victoria, Melbourne 3000, Australia), *b* 1963.

UNCLE LIVING (*Son of 2nd baronet*)

John Rannie (47 Webb St, Christchurch, NZ), *b* (twin) 1924; is Lt Roy New Zealand Naval VR; 1939-45 War: *m* 1948,
Adrienne Lascelles, da of Herbert Hill, OBE, JP, of Christchurch, and has issue living, Jeremy John (6 Mortimer
Terrace, Wellington, NZ), *b* 1957: *m* 1985, Anne Susan Lockhart, and has issue living, Oscar Joseph *b* 1989, Barnaby
John Lockhart *b* 1992, — Rupert Rannie (289 Prinsensracht, Amsterdam, The Netherlands), *b* 1964: *m* 1994, Willemina
Eilander, and has issue living, Theresa Eleanor Elisabeth *b* 1997, — Caroline Diana, *b* 1950: *m* 1970, Daniel Frederick
von Dadelszen, of Hinerangi, RD2, Waipukurau, NZ, and has issue living, Samuel John *b* 1973, Victoria Mary *b* 1975,
Lucinda Gretchen *b* 1977, — Jennifer Ann *b* 1952: *m* 1973, Julian Simon Cowper Payton, of 64 Cole St, Masterton, NZ,
and has issue living, Joseph Simon *b* 1979, Toby James *b* 1982, Anna Caroline *b* 1977.

AUNT LIVING (*Daughter of 2nd baronet*)

Theresa Dorothea, *b* 1916: *m* 1941, John Swaine Corry, and has issue living, David Herbert Cyril, *b* 1949, — Robert
John, *b* 1953, — Angela Susan, *b* 1942: *m* 1965, Iain Anderson Ridge, of 145 London Rd, Sevenoaks, and has issue living,
Angus James Anderson *b* 1966, — Rosemary Ann, *b* 1946. *Residence* – Lawn Bungalow, Bitchett Green, Sevenoaks.

COLLATERAL BRANCHES LIVING

Issue of late Cyril James Ward, 2nd son of 2nd baronet, *b* 1913, *d* 1984: *m* 1939, Janet Graham (10 Queen's Av, Christchurch, NZ) da of late Dr John Stevenson, of Fendalton, Christchurch:—
Joanna Theresa (*Lady Clifford*), *b* 1940: *m* 1968, Sir Roger Joseph Clifford, 7th Bt, and has issue (*see* Clifford, Bt).
—— Celia Mary Louise, *b* 1950: *m* 1983, Richard John Craig, of PO Box 80, Te Horo, NZ, and has issue living, Holly Louise, *b* 1984, — Hannah Rose, *b* 1988.

Issue of late Gladstone William Ward, 3rd son of 1st baronet, *b* 1891, *d* 1965: *m* 1920, Sophia Pole-medis, who *d* 1959, of Jerusalem:—
Myrcine, *b* 1921: *m* 1942, Dr Peter Mowbray Tripp, of 22 Clissold St, Christchurch, NZ, and has issue living, David Mowbray Ward, *b* 1949: *m* 1973, Martha McQuilkin, and has issue living, Peter James *b* 1977, Sophie Catherine *b* 1976, — John Peter, *b* 1950: *m* 1975, Amanda Moore, and has issue living, Celia Jane *b* 1980, Jessica *b* 1982, — Penelope Mary, *b* 1943: *m* 1974, Phillip Klap, and has issue living, Nicola Sophia *b* 1975, Annabelle Marie-Therese *b* 1976, — Anthia Susan, *b* 1947: *m* 1969, Richard Rollo Warburton, and *d* 1993, leaving issue, Richard John *b* 1976, Tessa Myrcine *b* 1970, Anna *b* 1972. —— Eileen Dorothea, *b* 1922: *m* 1943, Patrick Sinclair Hunter, solicitor, of Ardmore, 9 Vicarage Hill, Farnham, Surrey, and has issue living, Michael Sinclair Ward, *b* 1947: *m* 1970, Carol Rosemary Shorter, and has issue living, Piers Charles Sinclair *b* 1974, Charles Patrick Sinclair *b* 1977, Victoria Lucinda *b* 1972, — Patricia Ann (*Lady Spicer*), *b* 1943: *m* 1967, Sir (William) Michael Hardy Spicer, MP, of Cropthorne Manor, nr Pershore, Worcs WR10 3LT, and has issue living, Edward Sinclair Hardy *b* 1969, Antonia Hardy *b* 1971, Annabel Jane Hardy *b* 1974.

Issue of late Awarua Patrick Joseph George Ward, yst son of 1st baronet, *b* 1901, *d* 1961: *m* 1930, Marjorie, who *d* 19—, only da of O. M. McCormack, of Detroit, Michigan, USA:—
Patricia Marjorie, *b* 1933: *m* 1955, Duncan Cameron Bryan, who *d* 19—, and has issue living, Sheryl Cameron, *b* 1956, — Jennifer Ward, *b* 1958, — Denise *b* 1961.

The 1st baronet, the Rt Hon Sir Joseph George Ward, GCMG, VD, PC (son of William Thomas Ward, merchant), was Prime Min of New Zealand 1906-12 and 1928-30.

WARD (UK) 1914, of Wilbraham Place, Chelsea (Extinct 1973)

Sir MELVILLE WILLIS WARD, 3rd and last *Baronet*.

WIDOW LIVING OF THIRD BARONET

MARGARET MARY (*Lady Ward*), da of late Anthony Davis, of New York, USA, and widow of Capt Ralph Risley, USN: *m* 1965, as his 3rd wife, Cdr Sir Melvill Willis Ward, DSC, RN, 3rd Bt, who *d* 1973, when the title became ext.

WARD (UK) 1929, of Blyth, co Northumberland (Extinct 1956)

Sir (ALBERT) LAMBERT WARD, CVO, DSO, TD, 1st and last *Baronet*.

DAUGHTER LIVING OF FIRST BARONET

Diana Josephine (*Lady Spearman*), *b* 1921: *m* 1951, as his 2nd wife, Sir Alexander Cadwallader Mainwaring Spearman (*see* Spearman, Bt, colls), who *d* 1982. *Residences* – The Old Rectory, Sarratt, Herts; Fealer, Blairgowrie, Perthshire; 22 Queen Anne's Gate, SW1.

WARDLAW (NS) 1631, of Pitreavie, Fifeshire

Domestic virtue strengthens families

Sir HENRY JOHN WARDLAW, 21st *Baronet*; *b* 30 Nov 1930; *s* his father, *Sir* HENRY, 1983, but his name does not appear on the Official Roll of the Baronetage; *ed* Melbourne Univ (MB, BS): *m* 1962, Julie-Ann, da of late Edward Patrick Kirwan, and has issue.

Arms – Quarterly: 1st and 4th, azure, three mascles or, *Wardlaw*; 2nd and 3rd, azure, three water bougets or, *Valance*. Crest – An estoile or.
Residence – 82 Vincent St, Sandringham, Victoria 3191, Australia.

SONS LIVING

(HENRY) JUSTIN, *b* 10 Aug 1963: *m* 1988, Rachel Jane, yst da of James Kennedy Pitney. —— Edward Patrick, *b* 1964. —— Simon John, *b* 1965. —— Anthony James, *b* 1968. —— Adrian Stewart, *b* 1971.

DAUGHTERS LIVING

Janet Montgomerie, *b* 1969. —— Marie Ellen, *b* 1977.

BROTHERS LIVING

Robert Murdoch (4 Connemarra St, Bexley, NSW), *b* 1940: *m* 1971, Dale Edith, da of Joseph Fetherston, and has issue lving, Dominic, *b* 1972. —— Andrew David Montgomerie; *b* 1941; *ed* Melbourne Univ (LLB): *m* 1965, Elizabeth, da of Dennis Leary, and has issue living, David, *b* 1965, — Matthew, *b* 1966, — Michael, *b* 1969, — Timothy, *b* 1964, Louise, *b* 1971. —— Gregory Wylie (15 Millicent Av, Buleen, Vic, Aust), *b* 1943: *m* 19—, and has issue living, Cameron, *b* 1970, — Alastair, *b* 1973.

SISTER LIVING

Cynthia Mary, *b* 1931; (BA, DipEd): *m* 19—, — of St Andrew's, Vic, Aust, and has issue living, Jeremy, *b* 19—, — Melanie, *b* 19—, — Abigail, *b* 19—.

COLLATERAL BRANCHES LIVING

Granddaughters of late John Walter Wardlaw (infra):—
Issue of late James Walter Wardlaw, *b* 1921, *d* 1983: *m* 1951, Carina Guenthner:—
Jane Katherine, *b* 1958: *m* 1976, Ralph Duek, of Olds, Alberta, and has issue living, Jason Brent, *b* 1981, — Lori Anne, *b* 1977, — Cheryl Lynn, *b* 1979. —— Judy Carina, *b* 1961: *m* 1982, Kenneth Randall, of Edmonton, Alberta.

Grandchildren of late Thomas Davidson Wardlaw, son of late John Wardlaw, brother of 18th baronet:—
Issue of late John Walter Wardlaw, *b* 1882, *d* 1944: *m* 1914, Iva, da of late W. W. Brigham:—
Mary Macallum, *b* 1914: *m* 1938, Safford E. Thorp, and has had issue, Walter Wakeman, *b* 1944, *d* 1979: *m* 1967, Cynthia Anne Szegda (57 Lorenzo St, Norwich, Conn, USA), and had issue living, Walter Allen *b* 1970, Dawn Marie *b* 1968, Kristy Louise *b* 1939: *m* 1st, 1956, Cofer Lee Gray, of Ledyard, Conn, USA; 2ndly, 1983, Earl Ewers, of Milner's Mobile Home Est, Lot 20, Lynchburg, Virginia, USA, and has had issue, Safford Emory *b* 1964, Bonnie *b* 1957, *d* 1966, Ramona Lee *b* 1958: *m* 1983, Donald Jeay, of Rt 3, Box 95-A, Dillwyn, Virg, USA (and has issue), — Lorna Elizabeth, *b* 1946: *m* 1965, Lee William Coleman, of 5072C Polaris St, Eielson AFB, Alaska, USA, and has issue living, Tina Marie *b* 1966, Leah J. *b* 1969. —— Margaret Brigham, *b* 1918: *m* 1949, James Gethyn Jones, of 71 Lawrence Av West, Toronto 12, Canada, and has issue living, Richard Gethyn, *b* 1952: *m* 1981, Maureen Grierson, of Vancouver, BC, — Elizabeth Ellen, *b* 1958. —— Elizabeth Davidson (56 Jedburgh Rd, Toronto, Canada), *b* 1926.

Issue of late James Macallum Wardlaw, *b* 1884, *d* 1967: *m* 1923, Mary, who *d* 1953, da of late Robert Law:—
Thomas Davidson (72 Main St, Waterford, Ont, Canada), *b* 1924: *m* 1950, Grace Smith, and has issue living, David Macallum (316 Eunice Drive, Kingston, Ont, Canada), *b* 1952: *m* 1st, 1978 (*m diss* 1984), Jennifer Leigh, da of Wilbur Garvie, of Oaville, Ont, Canada; 2ndly, 1985, Margaret Ann, da of late Irvin Andrew Bartee, and has issue living (by 2nd *m*), Andrew Thomas *b* 1989, Alison Marie *b* 1987, and has also legally adopted his stepda, Sarah Lynn WARDLAW *b* 1980, — Robert Duncan (317 Roywood Crescent, Newmarket, Ont, Canada), *b* 1954: *m* 1982, Rita C., da of William G. More, of Ottawa, Ont, and has issue living, James More *b* 1983, Daniel Robert MORE *b* 1989, — Craig Davidson (2681 Jerseyville Rd, Jerseyville, Ont, L0R 1R0, Canada), *b* 1956: *m* 1979, Flora Margaret, da of late Duncan Hector Allan Simpson, and has issue living, Duncan Ian Macleod *b* 1992, Liethan Davidson *b* 1996. — Jonathan Stewart, *b* 1959: *m* 1988, Beth Yvonne, da of Rev John William Houstoun, of Aurora, Ontario, and has issue living, Mackenzie Jonathan *b* 1995, Rebecca Jillian *b* 1992. —— Robert Law (9 Oriole Drive, Gloucester, Ont, Canada K1J 7E8), *b* 1927; BASc, MEng, PEng: *m* 1954, Felicia Jane, da of late Frank Hallett Milsum, and has issue living, Stephen James, *b* 1957: *m* 1995, Margaret Jane, da of late Norman Wallace, of Carnarvon, Ontario, Canada, — Michael John, *b* 1960, — Anne Margaret, *b* 1958: *m* 1988, Eric Steven Teutsch, of Nepean, Ont, Canada, and has issue living, Jeffrey Stephen *b* 1989, Alexander Robert *b* 1992, Laura Jane *b* 1994, — Patricia Mary, *b* 1962: *m* 1985, Peter Hermann Laurich, of Nepean, Ont, Canada, and has issue living, Jason Robert *b* 1989, Andrew Anthony *b* 1990, Bruce Patrick *b* 1993, — Laura Kathleen, *b* 1963: *m* 1993, Allan Gregory Osborne, of Nepean, Ont, Canada, and has issue living, Charles Isaac *b* 1997, Shannon Rose *b* 1996. —— Janet Melville (20 Suffolk St, W, Guelph, Ont, Canada), *b* 1924.

Sir Henry Wardlaw, 1st Bt, was Chamberlain to Anne of Denmark, when Queen Consort of Scotland. He acquired Pitreavie 1606, which was erected into a Barony 1627. His baronetcy was with remainder to heirs male whatsoever, with presumably a grant of 16,000 acres in Nova Scotia, called the Barony of Wardlaw.

WARING (UK) 1935, of St Bartholomew's, City of London

WHATEVER YOU UNDERTAKE DO WELL

Sir (ALFRED) HOLBURT WARING, 3rd *Baronet; b* 2 Aug 1933; *s* his father, *Sir* (ALFRED) HAROLD, 1981; *ed* Rossall: *m* 1958, Anita, da of late Valentin Medinilla, of Madrid, Spain, and has issue.

Arms – Argent on a bend engrailed azure betwen two Rods of Aesculapius proper three crescents. **Crest** – A demi-wolf resting the sinister paw on a Rod of Aesculapius proper.
Residence – Earl's Croft, 30 Russell Rd, Moor Park, Northwood, Middx.

SON LIVING

MICHAEL HOLBURT, *b* 3 Jan 1964.

DAUGHTERS LIVING

Margaret Rose, *b* 1961. —— Susan Caroline, *b* 1967.

SISTERS LIVING

(Winifred) Anne, *b* 1931: *m* 1954, Michael Scott Mark, of The White House, Easingwold, nr York YO6 3AA, and has issue living, Jonathan Scott, *b* 1956, — Christopher Edward, *b* 1959. —— (Joan Catherine) Cassandra, *b* 1937: *m* 1962 (*m diss* 19—), John Barry William Holderness, of Les Varvots, St Lawrence, Jersey, and has issue living, Corinne Louisa Cassandra, *b* 1969, — Marina Isabelle Cassandra, *b* 1974.

The 1st baronet, Sir Holburt Jacob Waring, CBE, MS, FRCS (son of late Isaac Waring, of Southport, Lancashire), was sometime Dean of Faculty of Medicine, London Univ, Vice-Chancellor, London Univ, Gov of Imperial Coll of Science and Technology 1930-47, and Pres Roy Coll of Surgeons 1932-35.

WARMINGTON (UK) 1908, of Pembridge Square, Royal Borough of Kensington

NON MIHI SED OMNIBUS

Not for myself, but for all

Sir DAVID MARSHALL WARMINGTON, 5th *Baronet; b* 14 Feb 1944; *s* his half-brother, *Sir* (MARSHALL DENHAM) MALCOLM, 1996; *ed* Charterhouse, and Madrid Univ: *m* 1st, 1966 (*m diss* 1980), Susan Mary, da of Very Rev Clifford Thomas Chapman, Dean of Exeter; 2ndly, 1981, Mrs Eileeen Verdin, da of Frank W. Johnston, of Edinburgh, and has issue by 1st *m*.

Arms – Or, a lion rampant sable, charged on the shoulder with two fleurs-de-lis palewise of the first, holding between the paws a full-bottomed wig proper. **Crest** – An owl or, holding in the beak a penna and ink horn sable.
Residences – 139 Norfolk House, Highlands Heath, SW15 3TZ; Finca Montanchez, Alhaurin Elgrande, 29012 Malaga, Spain. *Club* – MCC.

SONS LIVING (By 1st marriage)

RUPERT MARSHALL, *b* 17 June 1969; *ed* Charterhouse, and Exeter Univ. —— Guy Denham, *b* 1972; *ed* Charterhouse, and Exeter Univ.

BROTHER LIVING

Anthony Marshall, *b* 1946; *ed* Charterhouse; late 1st Queen's Dragoon Gds: *m* 1973 (*m diss* 1987), Carolyn Patricia, who *d* 1993, eldest da of late John A. Hayes Simonds, and has issue living, Oliver Marshall Simonds, *b* 1974; *ed* Charterhouse, and Southampton Univ, — Katherine Louise, *b* 1977. *Residences* – 19 Bloom Park Rd, SW6; Brookside, Swan St, Kingsclere, Newbury, Berks RG15 8PL. *Club* – MCC.

HALF-SISTER LIVING

(Margaret) Anne, *b* 1936; *ed* Open Univ (BA): *m* 1962, Cdr Colin Alan (Charles) Bricknell, RN, and has issue living, Martin Charles Marshall, *b* 1963; *ed* Christ's Hosp, and Southampton Univ; BM, MMedSci, MRCGP, MFOM, DRCOG; Maj RAMC: *m* 1987, Kathryn Margaret, da of late Kurt Felbaum, and has issue living, Jessica Anne *b* 1990, Georgina Elizabeth *b* 1992, — Julian John (23 Winterbrook Rd, SE24 9HZ), *b* 1965; *ed* Christ's Hosp: *m* 1993, Julie, da of Thomas Edward Kellett, and has issue living, a son *b* 1999, Isabella Mollie *b* 1995, — Peter Marshall, *b* 1969; *ed* Hurstpierpoint; MA Cantab; MIEE, CEng. *Residence* – 71a High St, Hurstpierpoint, W Sussex BN6 9RE.

AUNT LIVING (daughter of 2nd baronet)

Elisabeth Barbara Marshall, *b* 1909: *m* 1st, 1933, Ian Somerled Macdonald, who *d* 1958; 2ndly, 1961, John Perfect, who *d* 1979, and has issue living (by 1st *m*), John Marshall (Flat 1, Tillyard House, 70-72 St George St, Norwich NR3 1AB), *b* 1937; *ed* Marlborough; MIEE, CEng, — Euan Ross (Suffolk House, Chiswick Mall, W4 2PR), *b* 1940; *ed* Marlborough, and Trin Coll, Camb: *m* 1965, Jacqueline Anne Gatacre, da of Graham Fortescue Evelyn-Wright, and has issue living, Iain Graham *b* 1966, Russell Ross *b* 1969, James Curtis *b* (twin) 1969, Dougal Evelyn *b* 1974, — Elisabeth Margaret (Raasay, Rockvale Rd, Armidale, NSW, Australia), *b* 1935; *ed* New England Univ, NSW (MA), — Sheila Joy, *b* 1942: *m* 1st, 1967 (*m diss* 1978), Richard Spencer Vaughan de Horsey; 2ndly, 1982, Antony Taylor Mitchell, of Byway, Ousden, Newmarket, Suffolk, and has issue living (by 1st *m*), Michael William John *b* 1971; *ed* King's Sch, Ely, and Liverpool Univ, Catherine Mary *b* 1968: *m* 1991, Adrian Terence Adams (and has issue living, Thomas Oliver *b* 1995). *Residence* – 18 Cryspen Court, Garland St, Bury St Edmunds, Suffolk.

MOTHER LIVING OF FOURTH BARONET

Mollie, eldest da of late Capt Malcolm Alfred Kennard, RN, of Bampton, N Devon, by his wife Favoretta Walterina (da of Walter Herbert Ingram) (who *m* 2ndly, 1952, Capt Howard John Kennard, RN): *m* 1st, 1933 (*m diss* 1941), as his 1st wife, Sir Marshall George Clitheroe Warmington, 3rd Bt, who *d* 1995; 2ndly, 1946, Edward Edgar George Somerset, who *d* 1985. *Residence* – Castle Grove, Bampton, Tiverton, Devon.

COLLATERAL BRANCH LIVING

　　　　Issue of late Herbert Andrew Cromartie Warmington, 2nd son of 1st baronet, *b* 1874, *d* 1952: *m* 1st, 1904 (*m diss* 1926), Elsie, who *d* 1956, da of late John Stuart, of Stonehurst, Ardingly, Sussex; 2ndly, 1938, Helena, da of late Albert de Mersey:—
(By 1st *m*) Joan Pamela Stuart WARMINGTON, *b* 1906; has resumed her maiden name: *m* 1st, 1926, Cmdr Nigel Bellairs Deare, RN; 2ndly, 1934 (*m diss* 1953), Dr Vincenzo Bottari. *Residence* –

　　The 1st baronet, Sir (Cornelius) Marshall, KC, sat as MP for W Div of Monmouthshire (*L*) 1885-95, and Sir (Marshall) Denham Warmington, 2nd Bt, was a Registrar in Bankruptcy, High Court of Justice.

WARNER (UK) 1910, of Brettenham, Suffolk

I hope

Sir (EDWARD COURTENAY) HENRY WARNER, 3rd *Baronet*; *b* 3 Aug 1922; *s* his father, *Col Sir* EDWARD COURTENAY THOMAS, DSO, MC, 1955; *ed* Eton, and Ch Ch, Oxford; sometime Lieut Scots Guards; European War 1944-45 in France (wounded): *m* 1949, Jocelyn Mary, da of Com Sir Thomas Lubbock Beevor, 6th Bt, RN, and has issue.

　　Arms – Per bend argent and gules two-bendlets between six roses all counterchanged. **Crest** – A Saracen's head affrontée couped at the shoulders proper, vested gules, on the head a cap checky argent and of the second, in front thereof three roses fessewise of the third.
　　Residence – The Grove, Great Baddow, Essex. *Club* – Guards'.

SONS LIVING

PHILIP COURTENAY THOMAS (The Grange, Marden, Devizes, Wilts), *b* 3 April 1951; *ed* Eton: *m* 1982, Penelope Anne, yr da of late John Lack Elmer, and has issue living, Charles, *b* 30 Sept 1989, — Alexandra, *b* 1985, — Katharine Jocelyn, *b* 1987, — Eleanor, *b* 1992, — Isabella, *b* 1995. ━━ Richard Edward Lubbock (Oakways, Tilford Rd, Hindhead, Surrey GU26 6RH), *b* 1952: *ed* Eton: *m* 1st, 1976 (*m diss* 1992), Claire Jennifer Furlonger; 2ndly, 1998, Mrs Amanda Gabrielle Vlasto, only da of James Samuel Lewis, of Guildford, Surrey, and has issue living (by 1st *m*), Peter Edward Courtenay, *b* 1983; *ed* Eton, — Lucy Claire, *b* 1979, — Sarah Louise, *b* 1981. ━━ Robert Henry (Perrotts Hill Farm, N Leigh, Witney, Oxon), *b* 1957: *ed* Eton: *m* 1983, Sophie Anne Rosalie, da of Timothy Davis, of Steeple Aston, Oxon, and has issue living, Henry, *b* 19—, — George, *b* 19—, — John Robert, *b* 1994, — Rosalie, *b* 19—.

SISTERS LIVING

Anne Philippa (*Hon Mrs Henry E. Boscawen*), *b* 1927: *m* 1951, Hon Henry Edward Boscawen, Lieut RE (*see* V Falmouth). *Residence* – Garden House, High Beeches Lane, Handcross, Sussex. ━━ Leucha Daphne Mary, *b* 1929: *m* 1962, Mark Gerald Edward North Buxton, of Coffyns, Spreyton, Crediton, Devon (*see* Buxton, Bt, colls).

COLLATERAL BRANCH LIVING

　　　　Issue of late Capt Thomas Seymour Marius Warner, 3rd son of 1st Baronet, *b* 1903, *d* 1965: *m* 1st, 1926 (*m diss* 1929), Mrs Dorothy Russell, da of William Durran, of Caithness; 2ndly, 1929 (*m diss* 1938), Mrs Edith Dorothy Morrison, da of late Robert Bold, of Liverpool; 3rdly, 1938, Louise Cameron (Ely Cottage, Wharf Lane, Henley-on-Thames), da of late Edward M. Roberts:—
(By 3rd *m*) Courtenay Forbes (12/46 Lowndes Sq, SW1), *b* 1939; *ed* Eton; late 2nd Lt Scots Gds: *m* 1st, 1969 (*m diss* 1974), Veronica, da of Lt-Col W. M. W. Cooper, of Medlands Farm House, Hurstbourne Tarrant, Andover; 2ndly, 1974,

Venetia Elizabeth, da of Maj Richard Atkinson-Turner, of Worlington, Suffolk, and has issue living (by 2nd *m*), Harry Richard Courtenay *b* 1975.

The 1st baronet, Col Sir (Thomas) Courtenay (Theydon) Warner, CB, was Lord-Lieut of Suffolk, and sat as MP for N Div of Somerset (*L*) 1892-95, and for Lichfield Div of Staffs 1896-1923. The 2nd baronet, Col Sir Edward Courtenay Thomas Warner, DSO, MC, was High Sheriff of Suffolk 1947-8, and Lieut-Col Comdg Scots Guards and Regtl Dist 1932-4.

WARREN (I) 1784, of Warren's Court, co Cork

Not for me, but for God and the king

Sir (BRIAN) CHARLES PENNEFATHER WARREN, 9th *Baronet; b* 4 June 1923; *s* his father, *Col Sir* THOMAS RICHARD PENNEFATHER, CBE, 1961; *ed* Wellington Coll; 1939-45 War as Lieut Irish Guards *m* 1st, 1976 (*m diss* 1983), Nicola Louise, el da of Capt Edward de Lérisson Cazenove, of Great Dalby, Leics (*see* Kennedy, Bt); 2ndly, 1996, Rosemary, da of Bingley Day, OBE, of Hovingham, Yorks.

Arms – Argent, a fesse checky or and azure, between three talbots passant proper. Crest – A lion rampant holding a crozier proper. *Residence* – The Wilderness, Castle Oliver, Kilmallock, co Limerick. *Club* – Guards'.

SISTERS LIVING AND DECEASED

Patricia Bene Pennefather, *b* 1908: *m* 1st, 1934, William Sharman Bull, RAF, who was *ka* 1940; 2ndly, 1945, Col Frederick Wynford Dewhurst, RM, and has issue living, (by 1st *m*) Victoria *b* 1939: *m* 1st, 1957 (*m diss* 1981), Maj Robert Darwall, MC, RM, who *d* 19—; 2ndly, 1981, Col Beverley John Austin, Royal Signals (ret), of Lamerton Mill, Tavistock, Devon PL19 8RJ and has issue living, (by 1st *m*) William Robert Thomas *b* 1961: *m* 1998, Valerie Choiseul, Antonia Mary *b* 1958: *m* 1981, Top D. Tuckett (and has issue living, Philip *b* 1984, James *b* 1987, Emma Mary *b* 1982), — (by 2nd *m*) Charles Frederick (Ellanore House, W Wittering, W Sussex PO20 8AN), *b* 1946, — Sarah Elizabeth, *b* 1948: *m* 19—, Edward Spencer Coryton, of Tinnel Farmhouse, Landulph, Saltash, Cornwall. *Residence* – The Red House, Clonway, Yelverton, Devon. ——— Eileen Lavinia Pennefather (Biddy), *b* 1910; *d* 1993: *m* 1st, 1930, Group Capt Joseph Herbert Arthur Landon, DSO, OBE, RAF, who *d* 1935; 2ndly, 1950, George Joseph Spiers, who *d* 19—.

COLLATERAL BRANCHES LIVING

Issue of late Lt-Col William Robert Vaughton Warren, OBE, MC, RASC, brother of 8th baronet, *b* 1889, *d* 1981: *m* 1st, 1914 (*m diss* 1926), Marjorie May, only child of Harold Briggs, of Broadford, Chobham, Surrey; 2ndly, 1926, Violet Elsie, who *d* 1963, da of Lt-Col John Wallis Gill, JP, of Fairfield, St German's, Cornwall:—
(By 1st *m*) †MICHAEL BLACKLEY (La Basse Ruol, Puget-Ville, Var, France), *b* 12 Nov 1918: *m* 1941, Marie Noelle, who *d* 1997, el da of Ernest Marcel Laffaille, OBE, hon Capt French Navy, and *d* 1999, leaving issue, Danielle Mary, *b* 1943: *m* 1967, Jean Pierre d'Adda, of 63 Av Pasteur, La Valette, Var, France, and has issue living, Sebastian Marie *b* 1973, Catherine Marie *b* 1970: *m* 1997, Eric Blanchard, of Les Fleurs, Ave François Fabie, 83160 La Valette, France (and has issue living, Mathieu *b* 1996). ——— Bridget Macree, *b* 1922: *m* 1st, 1944 (*m diss* 19—), F/O Frank Walter Ladbrook; 2ndly, 19—, Ernest William Beale, who *d* 1994, of 32 Knapton Lane, Acomb, York, and has issue living (by 1st *m*), Sara Virginia, *b* 1945: *m* 1974, David Walter Hayward, and has issue living, Peter David *b* 1978, Robin William *b* 1982, — Philippa Mary, *b* 1953: *m* 1972, John David Mead, and has issue living, Christopher John *b* 1974, Thomas William *b* 1980, — (by 2nd *m*) Andrew William, *b* 1958: *m* 1984, April Michelle Mitchell, and has issue living, Martin Andrew *b* 1987, Richard *b* 1991.

Descendants, if any, of late Capt Charles Duncan Warren, RN (*b* 1797), 4th son of late Thomas Warren, MP (infra).

Descendants, if any, of late Augustus Warren (*b* 1798), 5th son of late Thomas Warren, MP (infra).

Descendants, if any, of late William Warren (*b* 1805), 8th son of late Thomas Warren, MP (infra).

Branch from 9th son of 3rd son of 1st baronet

Granddaughter of late Very Rev Thomas Brisbane Warren, MA, Dean of Cork, el son of late Brisbane Warren, 9th son of late Thomas Warren, MP, 3rd son of 1st baronet:—
Issue of late Brisbane Charles Somerville Warren, *b* 1887, *d* 1979: *m* 1922, Janey Neill (Joan), who *d* 1986, da of late T. F. M. Cartwright, of Petteridge, Brenchley, Kent:
Elizabeth Joan Mary (Flat 2, 31 Clifton Cres, Folkestone, Kent CT20 2EN), *b* 1929.

Grandson of late Philip Somerville Warren, LRCP, LRCS, yr son of late Brisbane Warren (ante):—
Issue of late Denis Patrick SOMERVILLE WARREN, *b* 1901; *d* 1974: *m* 1946, Valerie Antonia Lloyd, da of late Frederick Lloyd Harper:—
Phillip Digby Somerville (Well Cottage, Cliffe Rd, Seaford, Sussex), *b* 1948; *ed* Columbia's Sch, St Albans: *m* 1980, Violette Khajenouri, and has issue living, Antonia Nooshin, *b* 1981, — Natasha Soussan, *b* 1982.

Branch from 5th son of 1st baronet

Grandson of late Robert Warren (*b* 1870), (infra):—
Issue of late Augustus John Warren, *b* 1909, *d* 1969: *m* 1949, Irene Joyce (The Cottage, Dunmanway, co Cork), da of late James Edwards Atkins, JP, of Brook Park, Dunmanway, co Cork:—
Rev Robert (14 Springfield Drive, Dooradoyle, Limerick), *b* 1954; *ed* St Columba's, and Trin Coll, Dublin; ordained Priest 1979; Curate St Mary's Cathedral, Limerick, Rector, Adare, Co Limerick, 1981.

Granddaughter of late Robert Warren (*b* 1826), el son of late Rev Robert Warren (*b* 1794), el son of late Rev Robert Warren (*d* 1830), 5th son of 1st baronet:—
Issue of late Robert Warren, *b* 1870, *d* 1947: *m* 1904, Maria Frances Lumley, da of late William Lumley Perrier, of Maryborough, Douglas, co Cork:—
Gladys Irene, *b* 1908.

Descendants, if any, of late Edward Richard Lauder Warren, *b* 1888, elder son of late Edward Albert Warren, 3rd son of late Maj-Gen Richard Warren, 2nd son of late Rev Robert Warren (*b* 1794) (ante).

Grandchildren of late Lieut-Col Percy Bliss Warren, 6th son of late Maj-Gen Richard Warren, 2nd son of late Rev Robert Warren (*b* 1794) (ante):—
Issue of late Wallis Langdon Warren, *b* 1900, *d* 1974: *m* 1934, Barbara, who *d* 1990, da of Harold Henry Durell Christian:—
Robert Nicholas Christian (Willowcroft, Thicket Grove, Newlands Drive, Maidenhead), *b* 1945: *m* 1976, Judith Catherine Harvey, and has issue living, David Nicholas Joseph, *b* 1985, — Victoria Catherine, *b* 1978, — Rebecca Louise, *b* 1981, — Christina Annette Daisy, *b* 1989. —— Shirley Margaret Christian, *b* 1936: *m* 1958, Jacovas Ioannou James Koukoularides, of 261 Brownhill Rd, SE6, and has issue living, Panos John, *b* 1966, — Janet Sophia, *b* 1958: *m* 19—, Steven Nelsey, and has issue living, Nicholas *b* 19—, Michael *b* 19—, — Daphne Barbara, *b* 1963. ——Jennifer Mary Christian, *b* 1940: *m* 1963, Keith Dallas Brown, of 6 Bridgenorth Rd, PO Greendale, Harare, Zimbabwe, and has issue living, Mark Dallas, *b* 1966: *m* 1993, Alison Fiona, da of Michael John Henry Beckett, of Choma, Zambia, and has issue living, Sacha Keith Beckett *b* 1998, — Anton Dallas, *b* 1970, — Sherrill Anne, *b* 1968: *m* 1998, Hugh Taggart, son of Michael Taggart, of Enterprise, Zimbabwe. ——Jocelyne Anne Christian, *b* 1942: *m* 1969, Michael Edward Younghusband, of PO Box 6130, Westgate 1734, Transvaal, S Africa, and has issue living, Sharon Leigh, *b* 1971: *m* 1996, Mark Holden, — Tracey Anne, *b* 1972.

Grandchildren of late Maj Geoffrey Martin Warren, 3rd son of late Lt-Col Percy Bliss Warren (ante):—
Issue of late Brian Richard Warren, *b* 1939, *d* 1987: *m* 1965, Angela Jean, who *m* 2ndly, 1989, Ronald Toye, of Hill Farm House, Butts Bank, Broadwas-on-Teme, nr Worcester, da of late Arthur L. Yarranton, of Eardiston, Worcs:—
Oliver Martin (9 Fort Royal Hill, Worcester), *b* 1968: *m* 1998, Tiffany Hobbs. —— Emily Claire, *b* 1966: *m* 1992, Dean Benbow, of 21 Mill St, Kington, Herefs, and has issue living, Chloe, *b* 1995, — Molly, *b* 1997. —— Lucy Maud, *b* 1970: *m* 1994, Jean-Claude Raes, of Le Malan, L'Albenc, France, and has issue living, Alice, *b* 1996, — Zoe *b* 1998.

Branch from 7th son of 1st baronet

Grandsons of late Vivian Brudenell Warren, 8th and yst son of Maj-Gen Augustus Edmund Warren (infra):—
Issue of late Charles Vivian Brudenell, *b* 1907, *d* 1975: *m* 1st, 1945, Maeve, who *d* 1965, da of late John Davis, of Ballina, Ireland; 2ndly, 1972, Jaqueta Maeve, who *d* 1979, da of Sir Arnold Henry Moore Lunn:—
(By 1st *m*) Robert Augustus Michael Mary (65 London Rd, Baldock, Herts), *b* 1948: *m* 1977, Jacqueline Olive Dawn Baynes, and has issue living, Dominic Charles Augustus Warren, *b* 1979, — Guy Andrew Francis Warren, *b* 1980. —— Patrick Martin Vivian Mary (7 St Ann's Crescent, SW18 2ND), *b* 1951: *m* 1974, Frances Ann, da of Frederick Lloyd, and has issue living, Luke Lloyd, *b* 1975, — Duncan Charles, *b* 1980, — Nathan Alexander, *b* 1982, — Camille Elizabeth, *b* 1976, — Saskia Anne, *b* 1982.

Granddaughters of Maj-Gen Augustus Edmund Warren, 2nd son of late Richard Benson Warren, 7th son of 1st baronet:—
Issue of late Dudley Edward Warren, *b* 1875, *d* 1949: *m* 1913, Gundreda, da of late Col Duncan Spiller:—
Adèle Valerie, *b* 1928.

Issue of Vivian Brudenell Warren, *b* 1877, *d* 1973: *m* 1900, Lilie Barrington, who *d* 1937, da of Capt C. A. G. Heysham, RN:—
Vivienne Ellen, *b* 1912: *m* 1943, George Frederick Alston Shilling, who *d* 1978. *Residence* – 13 Upper Wimpole St, W1.

Branch from 8th son of 1st baronet

Grandson of late Rt Hon Robert Richard Warren, LLD son of late Capt Henry Warren, 8th son of 1st baronet:—
Issue of late Henry Charles Jackson Warren, *b* 1852, *d* 1937: *m* 1877, Florence, who *d* 1944, da of late Lieut-Col Hon Robert French Handcock, 8th son of 2nd Baron Castlemaine:—
Desmond Cecil Robert, *b* 1895: *m* 1929, Violet Arabella, da of Dr F. O. Lasbrey, and has issue living, Donal, *b* 1930, — Jennifer Edyth Helen, *b* 1932, — Juliet Alice Louise, *b* 1938. *Residence* – Cherry Hill, Ballybrack, co Dublin.

This family descends from Wallis Warren who purchased in 1688 Kilbarry, co Cork, which later was renamed Warren's Court. His grandson, Sir Robert Warren, 1st Bt, was High Sheriff of co Cork 1752. Major Sir Augustus Riversdale Warren, 5th Bt, served in Crimean War and in Indian Mutiny, and was High Sheriff for co Cork in 1867. Col Sir Thomas Richard Pennefather Warren, CBE, late RASC, was Ch Constable of Bucks 1928.

WATERLOW (UK) 1873, of London

Sir CHRISTOPHER RUPERT WATERLOW, 5th *Baronet*, son of late (Peter) Rupert Waterlow, only son of 4th Bt; *b* 12 Aug 1959; *s* his grandfather, *Sir* PHILIP ALEXANDER, 1973; *ed* Stonyhurst; Metropolitan Police Civil Staff: *m* 1986, Sally-Ann, only da of Maurice Bitten, of Abbey Wood, SE2.

Arms – Azure, a demi-eagle displayed, erased or, in the beak a cross-crosslet fitchee argent, on a chief of the last three wolves' heads erased sable. **Crest** – Upon a mount vert an oak tree in front thereof a plough, both proper. *Residence* – 26 Barfield Rd, Bickley, Kent.

STEPMOTHER LIVING

Ruth Margaret (*Lady Reilly*), yst da of late Edmund Cude, of Ashbrittle, Church Vale, N2: *m* 1st, 1946, Frank Davies, who *d* 1959; 2ndly, 1962, (Peter) Rupert Waterlow, who *d* 1969; 3rdly, 1969, Sir Arthur Lionel Pugh Norrington, who *d* 1982, of Grenville Manor, Haddenham, Bucks; 4thly, 1987, Sir (D'Arcy) Patrick Reilly, GCMG, OBE, of 75 Warrington Crescent, W9.

WIDOW LIVING OF FOURTH BARONET

GWENDOLINE FLORENCE ELIZABETH (*Dowager Lady Waterlow*), yr da of late Léon Balanché, and formerly wife of Baden Roberts Murch: *m* 1972, as his 3rd wife, Sir Philip Alexander Waterlow, 4th Bt, who *d* 1973.

LABOR OMNIA VINCIT

Work conquers everything

COLLATERAL BRANCHES LIVING

Issue of late Anthony Edgar Russell Waterlow, 3rd son of 3rd baronet, *b* 1914, *d* 1946: *m* 1940, Barbara Winifred, da of late Ronald Davy, of Limber Harbrough, Lincolnshire:—
NICHOLAS ANTHONY RONALD (58 Willoughby St, Kirribilli, Sydney 2061, NSW, Aust), *b* 30 Aug 1941; *ed* Harrow: *m* 1965, Rosemary, who *d* 1998, da of W. J. O'Brien, of Sydney, and has issue living, Antony William Nicholas *b* 1967, — Luke Frederick Ronald, *b* 1969, — Chloe Diana, *b* 1972.

Grandchildren of late George Sydney Waterlow, 4th son of 1st baronet:—
Issue of late Sir Sydney Philip Perigal Waterlow, KCMG, CBE, *b* 1878, *d* 1944: *m* 1st, 1902 (*m diss* 1912), Alice Isabella, who *d* 1953, da of the Right Hon Sir Frederick Pollock, 3rd Bt (*cr* 1866): 2ndly, 1913, Helen Margery, who *d* 1973, da of Gustav Eckhard, of Didsbury, Manchester:—
(By 2nd *m*) John Conrad, CMG, *b* 1916; *ed* Eton, and Trin Coll, Camb (BChir, MD, ScD; FRS); formerly Prof of Human Nutrition, London Sch of Hygiene and Tropical Med, Univ of London; FRCP; CMG 1970; FRS 1982: *m* 1939, Angela, da of late G. Wynter Gray, and has issue living, Oliver Sydney, *b* 1943, — Richard John, *b* 1945, — Sarah Jean, *b* 1941. *Residence* – Oare, Marlborough, Wilts. —— Charlotte Mary, MBE, *b* 1915; sometime an Administrative Officer, Foreign Office; Sch Teacher and Author; MBE (Civil) 1950. *Residence* – 12 Newcombe Court, Victoria Rd, Cirencester, Glos GL7 1EN.

Issue of late David Sydney Waterlow, 7th son of 1st baronet, *b* 1857, *d* 1924: *m* 1883, Edith Emma, who *d* 1932, da of late Frederick Maitland, of 18 Primrose Hill Rd, NW:—
Rosalind Maitland, *b* 1911: *m* 1936, Sheriton Clements Swan, and has issue living, David, *b* 1940, — Nicholas Clements (Brook House, Stocksfield, Northumberland) *b* 1944: *m* 1970, Susan, da of F. Wells, of Berwick-on-Tweed, and has issue living, Catharine Victoria *b* 1970, Diana Rachel *b* 1972, — Lesley Jean, *b* 1942: *m* 1964, Richard James Hamments, of Gypsy, Sandhills Meadow, Shepperton, Middx TW17 9HY. *Residence* – Milestone Cottage, Wall, Hexham, Northumberland.

Sir Sydney Hedley Waterlow, KCVO, 1st Bt, Founder and Chm of Improved Industrial Dwellings Co, Ltd, Lord Mayor of London 1872-73; MP for Maidstone 1874-80 and Gravesend 1880-85, gave Waterlow Park, Highgate to LCC in 1889. The 2nd baronet, Sir Philip Hickson Waterlow, was Chm of Waterlow and Sons, Ltd.

WATERLOW (UK) 1930, of Harrow Weald, Middlesex

I conquer through death

Sir (JAMES) GERARD WATERLOW, 4th *Baronet*; *b* 3 Sept 1939; *s* his father, *Sir* THOMAS GORDON, CBE, 1982; *ed* Marlborough, and Trin Coll, Camb: *m* 1965, Diana Suzanne, yr da of Sir William Thomas Skyrme, KCVO (*see* B Lyle of Westbourne, 1995 Edn), and has issue.

Arms – Argent, a lion rampant within a bordure nebuly azure, on a chief sable two shin-bones saltirewise, the dexter surmounted by the sinister or. Crest – A demi-lion guardant azure, in the mouth a shin-bone in bend, and holding between the paws a human skull both or.
Residence – Rushall Lodge, Pewsey, Wilts SN9 6EN.

SON LIVING

THOMAS JAMES, *b* 20 March 1970.

DAUGHTER LIVING

Amanda Jane, *b* 1968: *m* 1991, Jason Patrick Howard, eldest son of Hon Patrick Greville Howard (*see* E Suffolk and Berkshire).

BROTHERS LIVING

Simon Gordon (208 Lewisburg Av, Franklin, Nashville, Tennessee, USA), *b* 1941; *ed* Marlborough, and Trin Coll Camb (MA): *m* 1971, Jane, da of late Wing Cdr Cameron Underhill, RCAF, and has issue living, Caroline Elizabeth, *b* 1973.
—— John William (81 Streathbourne Rd, SW17), *b* 1945; *ed* Marlborough: *m* 1972, Camilla Dudley, da of late Wing Cdr Dudley Farmer, DFC, of Rowleys, Frieth, Henley, Oxon, and has issue living, Rufus Dudley Robinson, *b* 1976, — Alec Gordon Brownrigg, *b* 1980.

Sir William Alfred Waterlow, KBE, 1st Bt, who was Man Dir of Waterlow Bros & Layton, Chm of Waterlow & Sons Ltd, and Lord Mayor of London 1929-30, was grandson of Alfred James Waterlow, el brother of Sir Sydney Hedley Waterlow, 1st Bt (*cr* 1873).

WATSON (UK) 1866, of Henrietta Street, Cavendish Square, St Marylebone, co Middlesex

Sufferings are lessons

Sir JAMES ANDREW WATSON, 5th *Baronet*; *b* 30 Dec 1937; *s* his father, *Sir* THOMAS AUBREY, 1941; *ed* Eton; Bar Inner Temple 1966; Recorder 1989: *m* 1965, Christabel Mary, el da of late Maj Kenneth Ralph Malcolm Carlisle, Rifle Brigade, of 18 York House, W8 (*see* B Aberconway, 1990 Edn), and has issue.

Arms – Azure, on a fesse dancetté between three crescents argent, as many martlets sable. Crest – A gryphon's head erased azure, ducally crowned or, between two branches of palm proper.
Residence – Talton House, Newbold on Stour, Stratford on Avon, Warwicks.

SONS LIVING

ROLAND VICTOR, *b* 4 March 1966. —— Alexander Bruce, *b* 1969.

DAUGHTER LIVING

Olivia Mary, *b* 1972.

COLLATERAL BRANCH LIVING

Issue of late John Rushworth Watson, yr son of 3rd baronet, *b* 1913, *d* 1984: *m* 1963, Amy Diana (who *m* 3rdly, 19—, Philip John Warburton-Lee, of Broad Oaks, Whitchurch, Shrops), eldest da of late Maj Harold Petit Rushton, TD, JP, of Phepson Manor, Worcs, and formerly wife of Maj Peter Wesley Dean:—
Camilla Mary (38 Lancaster Rd, W11 1QR), *b* 1967.

The 1st baronet, a distinguished Physician in London, was President of the Royal College of Physicians (London), the first representative of the Royal College of Physicians in Medical Council, and a Physician-in-Ordinary to HM Queen Victoria, and the 4th baronet, Sir Thomas Aubrey, Lieut Life Guards, *d* on active ser 1941.

INGLEFIELD-WATSON (UK) 1895, of Earnock, Hamilton, Lanarkshire

It has flourished beyond expectation

Lt-Col Sir JOHN FORBES INGLEFIELD-WATSON, 5th *Baronet*; *b* 16 May 1926; *s* his father, *Capt Sir* DERRICK WILLIAM, 1987; *ed* Eton; Lt-Col RE (ret); Football Assoc Staff Referee Instructor since 1978.

Arms – Per pale argent and or, on a mount vert an oak tree proper, the whole surmounted by two bars sable. Crest – The stump of an oak tree with a branch sprouting from either side, each grasped by a hand issuing from a cloud all proper.
Residence – The Ross, Hamilton, Lanarkshire ML3 7UF.

SISTER LIVING

Sheila Margrett (14 Murrayfield Gdns, Edinburgh EH12 6DF), *b* 1931: *m* 1958, Dugald Graham-Campbell, yr of Shirvan, who *d* 1967, and has issue living, Robert John, *b* 1964: *m* 1992, Henrietta, only child of George Robert Heneage, and has issue living, William Dugald *b* 1996, Emily Marguerite *b* 1997, — Sarah Alexandra *b* 1960.

WIDOW LIVING OF FOURTH BARONET

THERESE (TERRY) (*Lady Inglefield-Watson*), only da of late Prof Charles Bodon, of Budapest: *m* 1946, as his 2nd wife, Capt Sir Derrick William Inglefield-Watson, 4th Bt, TD, who *d* 1987. *Residence* – Ringshill House, Wouldham, nr Rochester, Kent ME1 3RB.

COLLATERAL BRANCHES LIVING

Grandchildren of late Thomas William Watson, WS, 3rd son of 1st baronet:—
Issue of late Capt Leslie Dundas Watson, *b* 1894, *d* 1975: *m* 1923, Enid Margaret, who *d* 1990, da of late Col George Hay Montgomery Conran:—
SIMON CONRAN HAMILTON (51 Clapham Manor St, SW4 6DT), *b* 11 Aug 1939; *ed* Harrow: *m* 1971, Madeleine Stiles, who *d* 1998, el da of late Wagner Mahlon Dickerson, of New York City. —— Gillian Faye Lucy, *b* 1928, *d* 1990.

Grandson of late Thomas William Watson, WS:—
Issue of late Somerled Hamilton Watson, *b* 1899, *d* 1938: *m* 1925, Elma Mary, who *d* 1983, only da of late William Walker, of High Canons, Shenley, Herts:—
Julian Frank Somerled, *b* 1931; *ed* Harrow, and RAC Cirencester. *Residence* – Baythorne Park, nr Halstead, Essex CO9 4AG. *Clubs* – Carlton, Lansdowne, Cavalry and Guards'.

Sir John Watson, 1st Bt, of Earnock, was second son of John Watson, of Bathville, Linlithgow, by his first wife. The 3rd baronet, Sir John, Lieut 16th Lancers, was *ka* 1918. Sir Derrick William Inglefield-Watson, 4th Bt, assumed by deed poll 1945 his christian name of Inglefield as an additional surname for himself and his issue.

MILNE-WATSON (UK) 1937, of Ashley, Longbredy, co Dorset

I owe all to God and country

Sir ANDREW MICHAEL MILNE-WATSON, 4th *Baronet*; *b* 10 Nov 1944; *s* his father, *Sir* MICHAEL, CBE, 1999; *ed* Eton; Proprietor ADR Associates Ltd since 1993; Liveryman Grocers' Co: *m* 1st, 1970 (*m diss* 1981), Beverley Jane Gabrielle, el da of Philip Cotton, of Majorca; 2ndly, 1983, Mrs Gisella Stafford, da of Hans Tisdall, of 105 Cheyne Walk, SW10, and has issue.

Arms – Argent, on a mount vert, an oak tree proper fructed or, over all a chevron azure charged with two mullets gold. Crest – A demi-griffin sable, gorged with an antique crown and charged on the body with two mullets palewise or.
Residences – The Stables, Oakfeld, Mortimer, Berks; 22 Musgrave Crescent, SW6 4QE.

SONS LIVING (By 1st marriage)

DAVID ALASTAIR, *b* 24 Aug 1971.

(By 2nd marriage)

Oliver, *b* 1985.

DAUGHTER LIVING (*By 1st marriage*)

Emma Victoria, *b* 1974.

AUNT LIVING (*Daughter of 1st baronet*)

Gabriel, *b* 1901: *m* 1929, Christian William Laurence Peel Reed, who *d* 1984, (E Peel, colls), and has issue living, Laurence Cecil (Hookhams Lurgashall, Petworth, W Sussex GU28 9SW), *b* 1930; *ed* Eton, and Worcester Coll, Oxford (MA): *m* 1956, Georgina, da of Thomas St John Alston, of Petworth, and has issue living, Nicholas William *b* 1958, Charles Christian Thomas *b* 1959, Andrew Laurence, *b* 1962, — Martin David (Standgates, Kirdford, Billingshurst, Sussex RH14 0LH), *b* 1932; *ed* Eton: *m* 1957, Shirley, da of late Charles C. Naumann, of Rudgwick, Sussex, — Denys Christian (Well Court, Corfe Castle, Wareham, Dorset BH20 5HD), *b* 1935; *ed* Eton: *m* 1st, 1959 (*m diss* 1972), Tessa Caroline, da of Stephen Cannon; 2ndly, 1973 (*m diss* 1998), Angela Frances Croft; 3rdly, 19—, Patricia Margaret Haldane, and has issue living (by 1st *m*), Christopher Stephen *b* 1961, Jeremy Matthew *b* 1962 — (by 2nd *m*), James Christian *b* 1975.

The 1st baronet, Sir David Milne-Watson (son of late David Watson, of Edinburgh) was Gov and Managing Director of Gas Light & Coke Co, Vice-Pres of Federation of British Industries, and Hon Col The Rangers, King's Roy Rifle Corps.

HARVIE-WATT (UK) 1945, of Bathgate, co Linlithgow

Sir JAMES HARVIE-WATT, 2nd *Baronet*; *b* 25 Aug 1940; *s* his father, *Sir* GEORGE STEVEN, TD, QC, 1989; *ed* Eton, and Ch Ch Oxford (MA); FCA; Chartered Accountant; Exec Brit Electric Traction Co Ltd 1970-78; Man Dir Wembley Stadium Ltd 1973-78; Dir of Penna Holdings plc since 1995, US Smaller Cos Investment Trust plc, since 1998, and other Cos; Member Exec Cttee of London Tourist Board 1977-80; Member The Sports Council 1980-88 (Vice-Chm 1985-88); Chm Crystal Palace National Sports Centre 1984-88; late Lt 1st Bn London Scottish Regt (TA): *m* 1966, Roseline Gladys Virginia, da of late Baron Louis de Chollet, of Le Guintzet, Fribourg, Switzerland, and has issue.

Arms – Quarterly: per fess wavy; 1st, per pale ermine and azure upon a mound in base vert, a tower proper masoned, sable roof gules, between two oak trees, also proper fructed or; 2nd, argent fretty sable, a grenade azure inflamed of nine flames, seven or and two gules; 3rd, barry wavy argent and azure, a portcullis gules; 4th, barry wavy gules and or, a dexter hand proper issuing from a manche fessways sable. Crest – A lion's gamb issuing from the torse argent, armed gules, grasping a writing quill paleways or, feathered sable.

Residence – 15 Somerset Sq, W14 8EE. *Clubs* – White's, Pratt's, Sunningdale, Queen's (Dir 1987-, Vice-Chm 1987-90, Chm 1990-93).

SON LIVING

MARK LOUIS, *b* 19 Aug 1969; *ed* Eton, and Yale Univ: *m* 1996, Miranda Mary, da of Martin Charles Neale Thompson (*see* B Middleton, colls).

DAUGHTER LIVING

Isabelle Frances, *b* 1967; *ed* St Mary's, Ascot, and Edinburgh Univ: *m* 1995, Nobile Carlo Amadeo Giovanni Maria dei Marchesi Clavarino, and has issue living, Elena Roseline, *b* 1997.

BROTHER LIVING

Euan (333 East 56th St, New York City, NY, USA; Yarborough Cottage, Earlsferry, Fife KY9 1AD), *b* 1942; *ed* Eton; late 2nd Lt 1st Bn London Scottish Regt (TA); *m* 1967 (*m diss* 1979), Olivia Mason, da of William Mason Smith, of New York City, USA, and has issue living, Katrina, *b* 1968; *ed* Wycombe Abbey, Georgetown Univ, and George Washington Univ: *m* 1994, Marc A. Faerber, of 2402 4th Av North, Seattle, Washington 98109, USA, son of Frederick W. Faerber III, of Newport, RI, and of Mrs Danielle A. Champion, of Manotick, Ont, and has issue living, Jackson *b* 1998, Alexis (a da) *b* 1995, — Jennifer (2149 Boyer Av E, Seattle, Washington 98112, USA), *b* 1969; *ed* Benenden, and Claremont McKenna Univ.

SISTER LIVING

Rachel, *b* 1944; *ed* Sherborne Sch for Girls, and Perugia and Edinburgh (MA) Univs: *m* 1970, Iain Gordon Fraser, WS, of 20 Lynedoch Place, Edinburgh EH3 7PY, and has issue living, Duncan, *b* 1972; *ed* Glenalmond, and St Andrews Univ, — Olivia, *b* 1974; *ed* Sherborne Girls' Sch, and Newcastle Univ.

WIDOW LIVING OF FIRST BARONET

JANE ELIZABETH (BETTIE) (*Bettie, Lady Harvie-Watt*), only da of late Paymaster-Capt Archibald Taylor, OBE, RN: *m* 1932, Sir George Steven Harvie-Watt, 1st Bt, TD, QC, who *d* 1989. *Residence* – Sea Tangle, Earlsferry, Fife, KY9 1AD.

The 1st baronet, Sir George Steven Harvie-Watt (son of James McDougal Watt of Armadale) was Parl Priv Sec to the Prime Minister (Rt Hon Winston Churchill, MP) 1941-45.

DON-WAUCHOPE (NS) 1667, of Newton
(Name pronounced "Wauchup", "ch" pronounced as in "Loch")

Sir ROGER HAMILTON DON-WAUCHOPE, 11th *Baronet*; *b* 16 Oct 1938; *s* his father, *Sir* PATRICK GEORGE, 1989; *ed* Hilton Coll, Natal, Durban and Pietermaritzburg Univ; a Chartered Accountant (S Africa); with Deloitte Pim Goldby: *m* 1963, Sallee, yr da of Lt-Col Harold Mill-Colman, OBE, ED, AMICE, of Durban, and has issue.

Arms – Quarterly, 1st and 4th azure, a crescent between two mullets in chief and a garb in base or (*Wauchope of Edmonstone*), 2nd, vert, on a fess argent three mascles sable (*Don of Newton Don*); 3rd, or a cross engrailed sable accompanied by an escutcheon gules in dexter chief and in sinister base a cinquefoil azure (*Rait of Edmonstone*); over all the Badge of a Baronet of Nova Scotia on an inescutcheon surmounted of an imperial crown. **Crests** – Dexter, a garb or charged of a crescent vert (*Wauchope of Edmonstone*); *sinister*, a fruit of pomegranate vert slit and seeded or (*Don of Newton Don*).
Residence – Newton, 53 Montrose Drive, Pietermaritzburg 3201, Natal, S Africa.

SONS LIVING

ANDREW CRAIG, *b* 18 May 1966; *ed* Hilton Coll, and Univ of Witwatersrand (MB, BCh): *m* 1990, Louise Sylvia, da of John Crawford Johnstone-Dougall, of Durban. —— John Hamilton, *b* 1969; *ed* Hilton Coll, and Pietermaritzburg Univ (BCom).

DAUGHTER LIVING

Georgina Anne, *b* 1970.

BROTHER LIVING

Malcolm John (P/BAG X23, Winterton 3340, Natal, S Africa), *b* 1939; *ed* Kearsney Coll, Botha's Hill, Natal: *m* 1968, Rea Marion, da of Phillip Montague Adams, of Doonside, South Coast, Natal, and has issue living, Keith John, *b* 1970, — Iain John, *b* 1975, — Jane Alice, *b* 1972, — Helen Louise, *b* 1977.

MOTHER LIVING

Ismay Lilian Ursula, da of late Sidney Richard Hodges, of Edendale, S Africa: *m* 1st, 1936 (*m diss* 1947), Sir Patrick George Don-Wauchope, 10th Bt, who *d* 1989; 2ndly, 19—, G. W. Shipman. *Address* – 16 Elgarth, St Patrick's Rd, Pietermaritzburg 3209, Natal, S Africa.

COLLATERAL BRANCHES LIVING

　　　Grandchildren of late Rev David Maitland Wauchope, son of late Rev David Wauchope, uncle of 8th baronet:—
　　Issue of late Andrew Maxey Wauchope, *b* 1890, *d* 1987: *m* 1918, Mary Veronica Fisher, who *d* 1986:—

Michael Andrew Anthony (Brookfield House, Dallington, E Sussex TN21 9NH), *b* 1925; *ed* Douai; late Lieut The Black Watch: *m* 1st, 1955, Margaret Mary Eleanor Victoria, who *d* 1994, yst da of I. S. Thomas, of Dublin; 2ndly, 1996, G. S. R. de Wet (*née* Carter), of Natal, SA, and has issue living, (by 1st *m*) Piers Andrew Charles, *b* 1956; *ed* Worth; Barrister; Kt of Sov Mil Order of Malta, — Francis Alasdair, *b* 1959; late Maj Gren Guards: *m* 1987, Jessica, da of Lt-Gen Sir Peter Hudson, KCB, CBE, DL, of Little Orchard, Frilsham, Newbury, Berks, and has issue living, Alasdair William *b* 1992, Peter Robert *b* 1995, Lydia Anne *b* 1997, — Matthew Michael, *b* 1960; *ed* Douai; Kt of Sov Mil Order of Malta: *m* 1988, Elveira Ramos de Deus, and has issue living, Alice Margaret *b* 1990, Isabel Ellen *b* 1996, — James Jonathon, *b* 1962; *ed* Winchester; LLB: *m* 1993, Helen, da of Dr W. Spiegel, and has issue living, George Arthur *b* 1996, Robert John *b* 1999, Elizabeth Margaret *b* 1994. ——— Deirdre Veronica WAUCHOPE (3 Lime Kiln Close, Rip Croft, Southwell, Portland, Dorset DT5 2JL), *b* 1921; has resumed her maiden surname: *m* 1964 (*m diss* 1975), Alan Henry Augustus Emery.

Issue of late Oswald Stewart Wauchope, *b* 1897, *d* 1956: *m* 1914, Dorothy Lettice White:—
†James David, *b* 1924: *m* 1950, Maria Sophia Zanucolli, who *d* 19—, of Florence, and *d* 1999. ——— Estella Olive (72 Old Wyche Rd, Malvern, Worcs), *b* 1916: *m* 1943, Dr Michael West, who *d* 1946, and has issue living, Annie Jean, *b* 1922: *m* 1st, 1943 (*m diss* 1953), Leon Zuckerman; 2ndly, 1958, Zbigniew Ernest Jaworski, of Ira Privada de la Luz, No 1, 62450 Col. Chapultepec, Cuernavaca, Mexico, and has issue living.

Sir Alexander Don of Newton Don, Berwickshire, was *cr* a Bt with remainder to heirs male of his body. Sir William Henry Don, 7th Bt, sold Newton Don for £85,000 and became an actor. On his death in 1862 he was *s* by his kinsman, Sir John Don-Wauchope (who resumed the surname of Don), son of Lt-Col John Wauchope, of Edmonstone, Midlothian, great-great-grandson of Patrick Don (who *m* Anne, sister and in her issue heir of Andrew Wauchope of Edmonstone), 3rd son of 1st Bt.

OGILVY-WEDDERBURN (UK) 1803, of Balindean, Perthshire

Sir ANDREW JOHN ALEXANDER OGILVY-WEDDERBURN, 7th *Baronet*, *b* 4 Aug 1952; *s* his father *Cdr* Sir (JOHN) PETER, 1977; *ed* Gordonstoun: *m* 1984, Gillian Meade, yr da of Richard Boyle Adderley, OBE, of Shepherds Hill, Pickering, N Yorks, and has had issue.

𝕬rms – Not yet matriculated for present line of baronets.
Residence – Silvie, Alyth, Blairgowrie, Perthshire PH11 8NA.

SONS LIVING AND DECEASED

PETER ROBERT ALEXANDER, *b* 20 April 1987. ——— Geordie Richard Andrew, *b* (twin) 1987. ——— †Sam, *b* 1990; *d* 1992.

DAUGHTER LIVING

Katherine Emma, *b* 1985.

SISTERS LIVING

Henrietta Katharine, *b* 1947: *m* 1972, Sebastian P. Thewes, of Strathgarry House, Killiecrankie, Pitlochry, Perthshire PH16 5LJ, and has issue living, Robert John Peter, *b* 1974, — James Andrew, *b* 1976, — Arabella Katharine, *b* 1979, — Jemima Caroline, *b* 1981. ——— Jean Aileen, *b* 1948: *m* 1983, Sam Henry Chesterton, of Buen Vino, Los Marines 21293, Prov de Huelva, Spain, yr son of Sir Oliver Sidney Chesterton, MC, and has issue living, Peter-Patrick Santiago (Jago) *b* 1984, — Charles Ernest Alfonso, *b* 1988, — Grania Laura, *b* 1986. ——— Elizabeth Helen, *b* 1950.

AUNTS LIVING (*Daughters of 5th baronet*)

Elspeth Mary, *b* 1913. ——— Katharine Andrea *b* 1915; is a JP: *m* 1940, George Macfarlan Sisson, OBE, and has issue living, John Edward *b* 1943: *m* 1981, Dr Judy Pino, of California, — David George (Providence House, Blackford, Wedmore, Somerset BS28 4NA), *b* 1945: *m* 1st, 1970 (*m diss* 1993), Gillian, el da of Dr Dennis Barnes, of Mayfield, Botchergate, Carlisle; 2ndly, 1993, Deirdre Sally Angela, only da of Colin Page, of 10 Eascote Rd, Aylesbury, and has issue living (by 1st *m*), Katharine Rachel *b* 1971, Rosemary Ann *b* 1973, Suzannah Clare *b* 1975, (by 2nd *m*) Charles David Page *b* 1995, — Alexander William, *b* 1949: *m* 1973 (*m diss* 19—), Penelope, 2nd da of Cdr Harold Turner, of The Old Rectory, Tacolneston, Norwich, and has issue living, William George *b* 1976, Alice Mary *b* 1978, Emily Rose *b* 1981, — Julia Andrea (Conifers, West End Rd, Box End, Kempston, Bedford MK43 8RU), *b* 1952: *m* 1972 (*m diss* 1987), Timothy Dallas Cairns. *Residence* – Planetrees, Wall, Hexham, Northumberland NE46 4EQ.

WIDOW LIVING OF SIXTH BARONET

ELIZABETH KATHARINE (*Dowager Lady Ogilvy-Wedderburn*) (Wester Strathgarry, Killiecrankie, Pitlochry, Perthshire PH16 5LJ), da of late John A. Cox: *m* 1946, Cdr Sir (John) Peter Ogilvy-Wedderburn, 6th Bt, who *d* 1977.

COLLATERAL BRANCHES LIVING

Grandchildren of late Thomas Wedderburn-Ogilvy, son of late Major John Andrew Wedderburn-Ogilvy, 4th son of Peter Wedderburn Ogilvy, 2nd son of James Wedderburn Colvile (infra):—
Issue of late Donald Stephen Wedderburn-Ogilvy, Sub-Lieut RNVR, *b* 1900, *ka* 1941: *m* 1st, 1924, Mona Alys Eustace, who *d* 1925; 2ndly 1929, Myra Carolyn Henrietta (Joy), who *d* 1990, da of late Lieut-Col Henry Montague Eustace, DSO:—
(By 1st *m*) Caryl Eustace (Pucklepeggies, 21 South Glassford St, Milngavie, Glasgow), *b* 1925; ARIBA: *m* 1953, Katharine Mary, da of William Steele, of Dundee, and has issue living, Niall, *b* 1955: *m* 1977, Elaine Isobel Margaret, el da John Coutts Meekison, and has issue living, Sarah Victoria *b* 1983, — Penelope, *b* 1959, — Verity, *b* 1965. —— (By 2nd *m*) Peter (Oak House, Froxfield, Petersfield, Hants), *b* 1931; Lt-Cdr RN (ret): *m* 1959, Philippa Sabine Burt, daughter of late Col F. A. Woods, of Winchester House, St Leonards, Sussex, and has issue living, Finella Sabine Clare, *b* 1962, — Helen Augusta Sophia, *b* 1964: *m* 1992, Angus James Lawson, of Wilby House, Wilby, Northants, son of Capt John Lawson, of Newton Ferrers, Devon, and has issue living, Max Peter Fergusson *b* 1996, Jasper Oliver Henry *b* 1998, — Andrea Henrietta Louise, *b* 1968. —— Alys (Denton Lodge, Shute End, Wokingham, Berks), *b* 1930: *m* 1961, John Curtis Wernher Eustace, CIE, who *d* 1972, and has issue living, Catherine Helena, *b* 1962, — Cassandra Mary, *b* 1963, — Margaret Alison, *b* (twin) 1963, — Emily Anne, *b* 1967.

Grandchildren of late Major James Andrew Colvile Wedderburn-Maxwell, son of late Andrew Wedderburn-Maxwell, son of late James Wedderburn, son of James Wedderburn Colvile, 3rd son of 5th baronet, who was el son of 4th baronet of 1st creation:—
Issue of late Brig John Wedderburn-Maxwell, DSO, MC, *b* 1894, *d* 1990: *m* 1922, Hon Ann Madeline Cunliffe, who *d* 1986, da of 1st Baron Cunliffe:—
Keir, *b* 1924: *m* 1st, 1951, Ann, eldest da of Jan Brink, of Johannesburg; 2ndly, 1962, Janet, da of Oliver Hodgkin, of Rivonia, Johannesburg, and and issue living, (by 1st *m*) John, *b* 1952: *m* 1973, Barbara, only da of G.G. Bruwer, of 3 Stevenson Rd, Malindela, Bulawayo, and has issue living, James *b* 1978, a son *b* 1984, — Philip, *b* 1954: *m* 1978, Lynda Hopkins, — (by 2nd *m*) Andrew, *b* 1963, — Adrian Keir, *b* 1965, — Eloise, *b* 1967. —— John Anthony (Brewers Farm, West Tisted, Alresford, Hants SO24 OHQ), *b* 1941: *m* 1969, Priscilla Aileen Ann, da of Maj H.C. Mooney, of 37 Windermere Rd, Pietermaritzburg, Natal, S Africa, and has issue living, Andrew Franklyn, *b* 1975, — Matthew Charles, *b* 1981, — Claire Louise, *b* 1971. —— Gillian, *b* 1928; LRAM 19—; is an Asso of Guildhall Sch of Music: *m* 1954, Robert Beaumont Shepheard, son of late Percy Beaumont Shepheard, of Ewell, Surrey, and has issue living, Simon Beaumont, *b* 1957, — Janet Robina, *b* 1955, — Anne Catherine, *b* 1963, — Emma Gillian, *b* 1964. —— Robina, *b* 1932: *m* 1960, Douglas John Turner, of Huntsman's Cottage, Whistley Green, Hurst, Reading, and has issue living, Amanda Jane, *b* 1961.

Grandchildren of late Maj James Andrew Colvile Wedderburn-Maxwell (ante):—
Issue of late Henry Godfrey Wedderburn-Maxwell, MBE, *b* 1897, *d* 1970: *m* 1948, Breda O'Connor:—
Andrew Patrick, *b* 1949. —— Harry, *b* 1958. —— Dorothy, *b* 1952.

Grandchildren of late Harry George Wedderburn, 2nd son of Andrew Wedderburn-Maxwell (ante):—
Issue of late Charles Carmichael Wedderburn, *b* 1882, *d* 1951: *m* 1918, Jessie Mary, who *d* 1955, only da of late Walter Edwin Fairlie, of Bishopstone, Northwood:—
Michael Charles Fairlie, *b* 1924: *m* 1955, Mary Catherine, da of Sidney George Esbester, of Duffield, Derbyshire, and has issue living, John Michael Champion, *b* 1957, — Katherine Jane, *b* 1958, — Claire Mary, *b* 1962. *Residence* – Short Hoo, Hasketon, Woodbridge, Suffolk. *Address* – c/o American Overseas Petroleum Co, PO Box 693, Tripoli, Libya.

Issue of late Lt-Col Harry Francis Keir Wedderburn, *b* 1899, *ka* 1943: *m* 1929, Mary Sharp, who *d* 1996, da of Lt-Col Henry Alexander Bethune (*see* Bethune, Bt, colls, 1995 Edn):—
Andrew Harry Bethune WEDDERBURN-BETHUNE (Mountquhanie, Cupar, Fife) *b* 1933; assumed 1959, the additional surname of Bethune after his patronymic; Capt The Black Watch (ret): *m* 1960, Mary Felicity Lovat Frazer, and has issue living, (Alexander) Guy, *b* 1965: *m* 1992, Lucy A., yst da of D. S. Rhodes, of Blairgowrie, Perthshire, and has issue living, Jamie Alexander *b* 1996, Laura Rose *b* 1993, Anna Jasmine *b* (twin) 1993, — Patrick Keir, *b* 1967: *m* 1999, Louise, yr da of Danny McLennan, of Crail, — Andrew Michael Stewart, *b* 1969, — Charles Dominic, *b* 1973, — Gabrielle Mary, *b* 1962: *m* 1996, Maj Greville A. C. Ramsay, KOSB, yst son of late Alan Ramsay, of Bowland, Galashiels, and has issue living, Hugh *b* 1999, — Frances Catriona, *b* 1964: *m* 1991, Richard G. Thurlow, son of Arthur Thurlow, of Godalming, Surrey, and has issue living, Sebastian *b* 1998, Lydia *b* 1994. —— Penelope Mary Bethune, *b* 1930: *m* 1949, John Piggott, and has issue living, John Wedderburn, *b* 1950: *m* 1976, Lynette, da of William Newstead, of Mareham-le-Fen, Lincs, and has had issue, James William *b* 1980, *d* 1999, Laura Elizabeth *b* 1983, — Robin Andrew Keir Wedderburn, *b* 1957: *m* 1984, Helen Mary, da of Anthony French, of Brentford, Essex, and has issue living, Emily Charlotte Mary *b* 1988, Eleanor Alice Mary *b* 1991. *Residence* – New Holm, 10 Auskendyke Rd, Weston Hills, Spalding, Lincs.

Granddaughter of late Capt Charles Francis Webster-Wedderburn, 2nd son of Sir James Webster-Wedderburn, grandson of Robert Wedderburn, 2nd son of 4th baronet (of 1st creation):—
Issue of late Arthur Augustus Helyar Webster-Wedderburn, *b* 1853; *d* 1919: *m* 1st, 1888, Katharine Elspeth Maude, who *d* 1907, da of late Henry Charles Hamilton, CSI (Hamilton, Bt, *cr* 1646, colls); 2ndly, 1913, Henrietta Caroline Bradley, who *d* 1946, da of late Thomas Henry Haddan, BCL Bar-at-law, and Fellow of Exeter Coll, Oxford:—
(By 1st *m*) Dorothy Hamilton, *b* 1901: *m* 1st, 1921, Capt Richard P. Hewetson, formerly RFA; 2ndly, 1934, Maj-Gen Allan Cholmondeley Arnold, CIE, CBE, MC, late Roy Fusiliers, who *d* 1962, and has issue living, (by 1st *m*) Richard Tatton Wedderburn, *b* 1924; formerly Pilot Officer RAF.

Grandson of late Lieut-Col John Walter Wedderburn, son of late John Wedderburn, *b* 1798, son of late John Wedderburn, son of late Thomas Wedderburn, 3rd son of 4th baronet (of 1st creation):—
Issue of late Charles David St Clair Wedderburn, OBE, *b* 1864, *d* 1931: *m* 1898, Louisa Mary, who *d* 1931, da of late Major J. E. Whaite:—
David Walter, *b* 1899; is Major RE: *m* 1925, Elizabeth, who *d* 1950, da of J. Robertson, of Perth, and has issue living, Patricia Helen Marjorie, *b* 1927: *m* 1950, Colin Henry du Plessis, and has issue living, Robin St Clair *b* 1951, Richard Geoffrey *b* 1952, — Averil Elizabeth Vernon *b* 1932.

Granddaughters of late Alexander Dundas Ogilvy Wedderburn,CBE, KC, son of late James Alexander Wedderburn, son of late John Wedderburn, *b* 1798 (ante):—
Issue of late Alexander Henry Melvill Wedderburn, CBE, *b* 1892, *d* 1968: *m* 1921, Cynthia Margaret, who *d* 1986, da of late Cecil Lubbock (*see* B Avebury, colls):—
Catherine Clarissa (The Chantry, Gt Barford, Bedford MK44 3JH), *b* 1925: *m* 1955, James Francis Robinson, TD, JP, DL, who *d* 1980, and has issue living, Adam James Nicholas, *b* 1959: *m* 1990, Katherine Adelaide Harben, and has issue living, Adelaide Harriet *b* 1991, Rebecca Harben *b* 1996, — David Thomas, *b* 1962: *m* 1996, Debra Jane, da of Anthony Ross, of 31 Woodgate Way, Belbroughton, Bromsgrove, Worcs, and has issue living, Thomas Isaac *b* 1995, Oliver *b* 1996, — Harriet Clarissa, *b* 1957: *m* 1985, Richard Piers Bacon, of 2 Waveney House, 30 Ormonde Gate, SW3 4HA, son of Edward George Hedley Bacon. —— Elizabeth Jane, *b* 1926; *m* 1949, Nicolas Ralph Dolignon Furse, son of Maj Sir Ralph Dolignon Furse, KCMG, DSO, and has issue living, Mark Nicolas Ralph Dolignon, *b* 1957: *m* 1981, Heather Campbell, and has issue living, Samuel Robert *b* 1982, Thomas Henry *b* 1992, Alice Jane *b* 1984, — Vanessa Jane Dolignon, *b* 1950: *m* 1987, Dr Robert S. Jackson, — Miranda Jill Dolignon, *b* 1951: *m* 1976, Carl Johnson, and has issue living, Jack Nicolas Drummond *b* 1981, Tess Jane Dolignon *b* 1986, — Corinna Margaret Dolignon, *b* 1954. —— Olivia Joan (Little White House, Church Lane, Longworth, Oxon OX13 5DX), *b* 1934: *m* 1st, 1957 (*m diss* 1972), Richard Weston Herbert; 2ndly, 1985, as his 3rd wife, Rodney Archibald Douglas-Pennant, who *d* 1993 (*see* B Penrhyn, colls), and has issue living (by 1st *m*), Catherine Alexandra, *b* 1963: *m* 1988, Richard J. Spencer, of 6505 Machodoc Court, Falls Church, Virginia 22043, USA, son of Geoffrey Spencer, of Lectoure, France, and has issue living, Henry Frederick *b* 1993, India Jane *b* 1998.

Grandchildren of late Alexander Henry Melvill Wedderburn, CBE (ante):—
Issue of late Major David Michael Alexander Wedderburn, *b* 1922, *d* 1960: *m* 1946, Marigold Diana Sneyd, MA (who *m* 2ndly, 1960, Maj Harold Warren Freeman-Attwood, of West Flexford, Wanborough, Guildford), da of late Edward Philips, OBE, of Alsop-en-le-Dale, Derbys:—
Robert David Alexander, MA, GRSM, *b* 1948: *m* 1985, Hazel Eloisa, ARCM, da of late Rev John Humphrey Ifor-Jones, of Uppingham, Leics, and has issue living, Alister Humphrey, *b* 1987, — Susannah Kate, *b* 1990. *Residence* – 13 Rothesay Av, Richmond, Surrey TW10 5EB. —— Henry Edward Alexander (*Club* Cavalry and Guards'), *b* 1954; Lt Gren Gds: *m* 1984, Sarah Juliet, da of Anthony John Round, of Layer Marney, Essex, and has issue living, Polly Alexandra Round, *b* 1986, — Louisa Catherine Round, *b* 1990. —— Sarah Catherine, *b* 1952; *ed* Somerville Coll, Oxford (MA): *m* 1979, Ian Caughlin, and has issue living, Edward David, *b* 1980, — Hannah Delia, *b* 1982.

Sir John Wedderburn of Blackness, co Forfar, an advocate and Clerk of Bills, was *cr* a baronet of Nova Scotia with remainder to his heirs male for ever. On the death of Sir John, 3rd Bt in 1723, he was *s* by Sir Alexander, 4th Bt, nephew of 1st Bt. Sir John, 5th Bt, having embraced the cause of the Stuarts, served as a volunteer at the battle of Culloden, where he was taken prisoner. He was executed on Kennington Common, 1746, and his estate forfeited. His descendants, however, continued to assume the title until Sir David (7th Bt but for the attainder) PMG for Scotland, was *cr* a Baronet of UK 1803 with special remainder to the heirs male of the 4th Bt of the original creation. The 4th Bt, Sir William Wedderburn, MP for Banffshire (*L*) 1893-1903, was *s* in 1918 by his kinsman Sir John Andrew Wedderburn-Ogilvy (who assumed the surname of Ogilvy-Wedderburn 1918), 3rd in descent from James Wedderburn-Colville, yst son of 5th Bt (of first creation). His grandfather Peter Wedderburn *m* 1811, Anna, da and heir of James Ogilvy of Ruthven, co Forfar, and assumed the surname of Wedderburn-Ogilvy on the death of his father-in-law 1826.

WEDGWOOD (UK) 1942, of Etruria, co Stafford

Sir (HUGO) MARTIN WEDGWOOD, 3rd *Baronet*; *b* 27 Dec 1933; *s* his father, *Sir* JOHN HAMILTON, TD, 1989; *ed* Eton, and Trin Coll, Oxford (BA); Mem of Stock Exchange 1973-91, partner of Laurence, Prust & Co 1973-84, Dir of Smith New Court International Ltd 1986-91: *m* 1963, Alexandra Mary Gordon, authoress and architectural archivist at Palace of Westminster, elder da of late Judge Alfred Alexander Gordon Clark, of Berry's Croft, Westhumble, Dorking, Surrey (Lawrence, Bt *cr* 1867), and has issue.

ᴀʀᴍꜱ Gules, four mullets in cross and a canton argent. ᴄʀᴇꜱᴛ – On a ducal coronet, a lion passant argent.
Residence – Pixham Mill, Pixham Lane, Dorking, Surrey.

SON LIVING

I split asunder obstacles   RALPH NICHOLAS, 10 Dec 1964; *ed* Westminster, Magdalen Coll, Oxford (BA), King's Coll, London (MPhil), and Cornell Univ, USA; Assist Prof Dept of Linguistics and Philosophy, Massachusetts Inst of Technology.

DAUGHTERS LIVING

Julia Mary, *b* 1966; *ed* St Theresa's, Effingham, and Sts Hilda and Bede Coll, Durham (BA): *m* 1995, Nicholas Dominic Bernard Johnson, only son of Bernard Johnson, of Woodbridge, Suffolk, and has issue living, Daniel Lawrence, *b* 1997. —— Frances Veronica Mary, *b* 1969; *ed* Sutton High Sch, Christ's Coll, Cambridge (BA), and Univ Coll, London: *m* 1997, Gareth M. Edwards, son of John Edwards, of Bristol, and has issue living, Joseph Josiah Emrys, *b* 1998.

BROTHERS LIVING

(John) Julian, *b* 1936; *ed* Stowe: *m* 1961, Sheila Mary, eldest da of late George Robert Meade, of London, and has issue living, (John) Adam, *b* 1962, — Rupert Julian, *b* 1964, — Felix Hawkshaw, *b* 1966. —— Oliver Ralph, *b* 1940; *ed* Eton.

SISTER LIVING

(Germaine) Olivia, *b* 1944: *m* 1965, David Louis Posner, who *d* 1985, son of Louis S. Posner, of New York, and has issue living, Piers Oliver, *b* 1966, — Dominic Tobias, *b* 1968.

WIDOW LIVING OF SECOND BARONET

PAMELA (*Pamela, Lady Wedgwood*), da of Herbert Wynn Reeves, of London, and widow of (Algernon) James Riccarton Tudor-Craig, FSA; PhD, FSA, author and art historian: *m* 1982, as his 2nd wife, Sir John Hamilton Wedgwood, 2nd Bt, TD, who *d* 1989. *Residence* – 9 St Anne's Crescent, Lewes, E Sussex BN7 1SB.

The 1st baronet, Brig-Gen Sir Ralph Lewis Wedgwood, CB, CMG, TD, was Ch Gen Manager of LNER 1923-39, and Chm of Railway Executive 1939-41. His el brother Josiah Clement was *cr* Baron Wedgwood 1942. Their father, Clement Francis Wedgwood, Master Potter, of Barlaston, Staffs, was great-grandson of Josiah Wedgwood, FRS, of Etruria, Staffs (*d* 1795), creator of the pottery which bears his name.

WELBY (UK) 1801, of Denton Manor, Lincolnshire

Per ignem per gladium

By fire, by sword

Sir (RICHARD) BRUNO GREGORY WELBY, 7th *Baronet*; *b* 11 March 1928; *s* his father, *Sir* OLIVER CHARLES EARLE, TD, 1977; *ed* Eton and Ch Ch Oxford (BA): *m* 1952, Jane Biddulph, youngest da of late Ralph Hodder-Williams, MC, and has issue.

𝕬rms – Sable, a fesse between three fleurs-de-lis argent. 𝕮rest – A cubit arm in armour issuing in bend sinister from clouds, holding a sword pommel and hilt or over flames of fire issuant from a wreath proper.
Seat – Denton Manor, Grantham, Lincs. *Residence* – 20 St Mary Abbot's Terrace, W14

SONS LIVING

CHARLES WILLIAM HODDER (Stroxton House, Grantham, Lincs), *b* 6 May 1953; *ed* Eton and RAC Cirencester; FRICS: *m* 1978, Suzanna Fiona, only da of the late Maj Ian Stuart-Routledge, of Harston Hall, Grantham, Lincs, and has issue living, Venetia Victoria, *b* 1981, — Zinnia Louisa, *b* 1985, — Isadora Barbara Pia, *b* 1993. —— Dominic John Earle, *b* 1960: *m* 1982, Camilla Janet, yr da of Christopher Gerald Pole-Carew, of Shute Barton, Devon (*see* Pole, Bt, *cr* 1628, colls), and has issue living, Hector George, *b* 1993, — Maria Elizabeth, *b* 1987, — Octavia Lind, *b* 1990. —— Richard Henry Gregory, *b* 1970.

DAUGHTER LIVING

Miranda Lind, *b* 1955: *m* 1st, 1977 (*m diss* 1989), Gavin Laird-Craig; 2ndly, 1991, as his 2nd wife, Col Hugh Earle Welby-Everard, MBE, late RA (infra), and has issue living (by 1st *m*), Oliver John Gregory, *b* 1985, — Emma le Flay, *b* 1981.

COLLATERAL BRANCHES LIVING

Grandchildren of late Edward Everard Earle WELBY-EVERARD, eldest son of late Edward Montague Earle Welby, 4th son of 3rd baronet:—
Issue of late Capt Philip Herbert Earle Welby-Everard, OBE, DSC, RN (ret), *b* 1902, *d* 1985: *m* 1928, Lilla Anna Florence Maree Castell, JP (Owl's House, Frieston, Caythorpe, Grantham, Lincs), da of Magnus Spence, of Springfontein, Fig Tree, Zimbabwe:—
†Glynne Earle, *b* 1935: *m* 1963, Jan Plaisette, who *d* 1973, da of late Milton Lee Stroud, of Texas, USA, and *d* 1990, leaving issue, Ariel Edward Earle, *b* 1970, — Amanda Gay, *b* 1971, — Ariadne Melissa, *b* 1972. —— Roger Earle (Owl's

House, Frieston, Caythorpe, Grantham, Lincs), *b* 1942; *ed* Eton; Lt RN (ret): *m* 1966, Isabel Anne, da of late Maj Lloyd Bucknall, and has issue living, Julian Richard Earle, *b* 1967, — Patrick Jonathan Earle, *b* 1969, — Anna Christabel, *b* 1974. —— Susan, *b* 1931: *m* 1959, George William Durrant, who *d* 1995, of Tintern, Long St, Sherborne, Dorset, and has issue living, Henry, *b* 1960, — Lucinda, *b* 1963: *m* 1987, Peter Stockley, and has issue living, Timothy Charles George *b* 1993, Laura Amber Maree *b* 1990, — Georgina, *b* 1965: *m* 1992, Miles Bodimeade, and has issue living, Holly Jo *b* 1995.

Issue of late Maj-Gen Sir Christopher Earle Welby-Everard, KBE, CB, *b* 1909, *d* 1996: *m* 1938, Sybil Juliet Wake, who *d* 1994, da of late Guy Shorrock, of Sandford Orleigh, Newton Abbot, S Devon (*see* Wake, Bt, colls, 1909 Edn):—
Peter Rodney Earle (Army & Navy Club), *b* 1942; *ed* Charterhouse; late Lieut The Royal Anglian Regt (ret 1969): *m* 1972, Jennifer Frances, twin da of Lt-Col Samuel Terence Cracroft Parsons-Smith, of Pill Heath Cottage, Andover, Hants, and has issue living, Christopher Nicholas Earle, *b* 1976, — Peter George Earle, *b* 1982, — Patricia Christabel, *b* 1974. —— Hugh Earle, MBE (Church Farm Cottage, Hurstbourne Tarrant, Andover, Hants), *b* 1944; *ed* Charterhouse; Col late RA; MBE (Mil) 1984: *m* 1st, 1970, Virginia Gresley, who *d* 1989, as the result of an accident, elder da of late Maj-Gen John Edward Longworth Morris, CB, CBE, DSO, of Garden House, Burley, Hants; 2ndly, 1991, Mrs Miranda Lind Laird-Craig, only da of Sir (Richard) Bruno Gregory Welby, 7th Bt, and has issue living (by 1st *m*), Guy John Earle, *b* 1979, — Louisa Gresley Wake, *b* 1975.

Granddaughter of late Henry Earle Welby, eldest son of late Rt Rev Thomas Earle Welby, DD, 2nd son of 2nd baronet:—
Issue of late Hugh Earle Welby, *b* 1867, *d* 1952: *m* 1908, Evelyn Borradaile, MBE, who *d* 1972, da of Adam Bell, formerly Rhodesian Civil Ser:—
Gwynyth Mary, *b* 1910: *m* 1937, Arthur Wyatt Aust, who *d* 1975, and has issue living, John Charles Wyatt, *b* 1942; Maj Rhodesian Army: *m* 1969, Pamela Drusilla Phillips, of Essexvale, Zimbabwe, and has issue living, Patrick Welby, *b* 1975, Caroline Joyce *b* 1970, Cherith Mary *b* 1972, — Elizabeth Mary, *b* 1940: *m* 1966, Brian Tozer, of Harare, Zimbabwe, and has issue living, Ian Richard *b* 1968, Nigel Stewart *b* 1970, Timothy Charles *b* 1975.

Grandchildren of late Arthur Thomas Earle Welby (infra):—
Issue of late Charles Earle Welby, *b* 1901, *d* 1975: *m* 1926, Lydia Elizabeth, who *d* 1984, da of Harry L. Hunt, of Madison, Wisconsin, USA:—
Arthur Earle (58 Oak Ridge Lane, Barrington, Ill 60010, USA), *b* 1927: *m* 1947, Giuliana, da of Alfredo Bruni, of Pisa, Italy, and has issue living, Allan Earle, *b* 1958: *m* 1984, Sandra Capriotti, of Kanakee, Illinois, and has issue living, Adam Earle *b* 1988, Adriana Eda *b* 1990, — Steven Earle, *b* 1961, — Janet Rose, *b* 1955: *m* 1979, Dennis Joseph Sullivan, and has issue living, Dennis Arthur *b* 1985, Charles Orlando *b* 1990. —— Charles Earle, Jr (1357 Oxford Way, Upland, Ca 91786, USA), *b* 1935: *m* 1955, Doris Annen, of Madison, Wisc, and has issue living, Charles Earle, III, *b* 1959: *m* 1984, Laura Helen Wood, of Claremont, Calif, and has issue living, Bradley Charles *b* 1992, Megan Neville *b* 1988, Michele Doris *b* 1989, — Peter Thomas Earle, *b* 1962, — Susan Kaye, *b* 1958: *m* 1982, William Scott Jones, of Zephyr Cove, Nevada, and has issue living, William Scott *b* 1986, Peter Charles *b* 1993, Margaret Ashley *b* 1983, — Joanne Marie, *b* 1960: *m* 1988, Ricardo Aguilar, of Ontario, California, and has issue living, Steven Manuel *b* 1989, Joseph Ricardo *b* 1992, Samuel Earle *b* 1994. —— Mary Elizabeth, *b* 1931: *m* 1954, Bruce W. Ringey, of 1204 Airfield Lane, Midland, Michigan 48642, USA, and has issue living, David Bruce, *b* 1967: *m* 1997, Melissa Manhart, — Lynn Marie, *b* 1954: *m* 1977, Philip J Baker III, and has issue living, Andrew *b* 1979, Patrick *b* 1981, Laura *b* 1985, Erin *b* 1988, Sarah *b* 1993, — Catherine Ann: *m* 1977, Mark Willbur, and has issue living, Matthew Paul *b* 1980, Kimberly *b* 1982, Travis *b* 1988, — Karen Elizabeth, *b* 1960: *m* 1985, Roger Brandi, — Diane Lea, *b* 1963: *m* 1990, Paul Swoboda.

Granddaughters of late Rt Rev Thomas Earle Welby, DD (ante):—
Issue of late Arthur Thomas Earle Welby, *b* 1855, *d* 1908: *m* 1st, 1874, Phœbe, who *d* 1895, da of Capt de Cew; 2ndly, 1898, Maria, da of J. F. Mitchell:—
(By 2nd *m*) Muriel: *m* 1921, Major Harold Godfrey St George Morgan, who *d* 1929, late RMA.

Issue of late Frederick Earle Welby, FRCSE, *b* 1858, *d* 1900: *m* 1883, Janet Anne, who *d* 1935, da of late F. Henderson, of Wick, NB:—
Edith Jessie: *m* 1st, 1920, William Adams, who *d* 19—; 2ndly, 19—. *Residence* –

Grandchildren of late Rev Arthur Earle Welby, 3rd son of 2nd baronet:—
Issue of late William Macdonald Earle Welby, *b* 1845, *d* 1885: *m* 2ndly, 1878, Jessie, da of Frederick Lucas, of Grahamstown, S Africa:—
Spencer Earle, *b* 1879. —— Glynne Earle, *b* 1881. —— Isabel Florence. —— May.

Issue of late Richard Earle Welby, *b* 1854, *d* 1932: *m* 1st, 1886, Mary Isabelle, who *d* 1892, da of late Thomas Paget, of Forton Lodge, near Lancaster; 2ndly, 1899, Alice Frances Blackburne, 3rd da of late Lieut-Col Cyril Blackburne Tew, and widow of late Vice-Adm Frederick Charles Bryan Robinson (Crofton, Bt, *cr* 1801, colls); 3rdly, 1918, Helen Mary, who *d* 1973, da of late Capt Creagh Scott:—
(By 3rd *m*) Glynne Richard Earle, *b* 1921; *ed* Camb Univ (BA 1948, MA 1957); Sqdn Ldr RAF (ret); ACIS: *m* 1st, 1945, Hilarie Elizabeth, who *d* 1957, da of H. Cecil Rowse, of St Austell, Cornwall; 2ndly, 1958, Margaret Mary, yr da of late Pius C. Brodrick, of Bolton, Lancs, and has issue living, (by 2nd *m*) Richard Edmund Charles, *b* 1961, — (by 1st *m*) Elizabeth Anne, *b* 1947, — Rosalyne Mary, *b* 1950, — Penelope Jane, *b* 1954, — (by 2nd *m*) Elizabeth Mary, *b* 1959.

The Welbys are an ancient Lincolnshire family. The first known member was Rannulf de Welleby, mil tenant of Wydo de Credun in Welby, near Grantham 1086. Sir John de Wellebi, son of Roger, gave land there to Vallis Dei Abbey in the reign of Stephen. The "Liber Niger Scaccarii," *temp* Hen II, records that Johannes de Wellebi held, in Welby, near Grantham, under Mauricius de Crun, a knight's fee and a half, "de antiquo feodo" enfeoffed before 1135. Many of them have successively sat in Parliament since 9 Henry V. The first who served as Sheriff of Lincolnshire was Roger de Welby in the 20 Richard II. The 1st, 2nd and 3rd baronets successively represented Grantham in Parliament, and the 3rd baronet assumed the additional surname of Gregory. Sir William, 4th baronet, also sat as MP for Grantham (*C*)

1857-68 and for Lincolnshire S 1868-84, and assumed by Roy licence 1876 the additional surname of Gregory. The 5th Baronet was MP for Newark Div of Notts (C) 1900-1906.

WELCH (UK) 1957, of Chard, co Somerset

Sir JOHN READER WELCH, 2nd *Baronet*; *b* 26 July 1933; *s* his father, *Sir* (GEORGE JAMES) CULLUM, OBE, MC, 1980; *ed* Marlborough, and Hertford Coll, Oxford (MA); late Roy Corps of Signals; admitted a Solicitor 1960; ptnr Bell Brodrick & Gray 1961-71, Wedlake Bell 1972-96; Ward Clerk of Walbrook Ward (City of London) 1961-74; Registrar of Archdeaconry of London 1964-99; Liveryman of Worshipful Company of Haberdashers 1955 (Court of Assistants 1973, Master 1990); Freeman of Worshipful Company of Parish Clerks 1954 (Master 1967); Chm of Cttee of Management, Lond Homes for the Elderly 1981-90; Mem of Ct of Common Council (City of Lond) 1975-86 and Chm of Planning and Communications Cttee 1981, 1982; Chm of John Fairfax (UK) Ltd 1977-90; Pres Grand Charity of Freemasons 1985-95, City Livery Club 1986; Chm Walbrook Ward Club 1978; CStJ; FRSA: *m* 1962, Margaret Kerry, da of Kenneth Douglass, of Killara, NSW, and has issue.

𝕬rms – Or on a fesse gules between six martlets azure two lions passant respectant of the first. 𝕮rest – An heraldic antelope's head erased or armed gules gorged with a collar composed of six pierced mullets azure chained also gules.
Residence – 28 Rivermead Court, Ranelagh Gdns, SW6 3RU. *Clubs* – City Livery; Hurlingham.

SON LIVING

JAMES DOUGLASS CULLUM, *b* 10 Nov 1973.

DAUGHTERS LIVING

Margaret Trudy Cullum, *b* 1965: *m* 1992, Anthony Richard Loveys Jervoise, of Rowden Manor Farm, Sampford Courtenay, Okehampton, Devon EX 20 2SJ, yr son of John Loveys Jervoise, of Herriard Park, Hants, and has issue living, Elizabeth Antonia, *b* 1995, — Cecily Jane, *b* 1996. —— Jane Olive Comrie Cullum, *b* (twin) 1965: *m* 1992, David Ross Waller, elder son of John Waller, of Alderley Edge, Cheshire.

SISTER LIVING

Rosemary Avril (6 Dunleary Court, Westcote Rd, Reading, Berks RG3 2DJ), *b* 1927: *m* 1st, 1952 (*m diss* 1963), John Osmond; 2ndly, 1963, Leighton Griffith Jones, who *d* 1983.

The 1st baronet, Sir Cullum Welch, was Lord Mayor of London 1956-57.

WELDON (I) 1723, of Dunmore, co Carlow

Sir ANTHONY WILLIAM WELDON, 9th *Baronet*; *b* 11 May 1947; *s* his father, *Sir* THOMAS BRIAN, 1979; *ed* Sherbourne; late Lt Irish Gds; Gen Ser Medal S Arabia: *m* 1980, Amanda, da of Maj Geoffrey Edward Ford North, MC (*see* B Walsingham, colls), and formerly wife of Anthony John Wigan, and has issue.

Arms – Argent, a cinquefoil pierced gules, on a chief of the second a demi-lion issuant of the first. Crests – 1st, a demi-lion rampant argent guttée de sang; 2nd, the bust of Queen Elizabeth I (granted by Queen Elizabeth I as a special mark of favour).
Residence – Easton Manor, Easton Royal, Pewsey, Wilts. *Club* – White's.

DAUGHTERS LIVING

Alice Louise Iona *b* 1981. —— Oonagh Leone Isobel, *b* 1983.

SISTER LIVING

Well done

Tara Louise Winifred, *b* 1943: *m* 1967, Alan Christopher Elliot, of The Old Rectory, Chilton Foliat, Hungerford, Berks, and has issue living, Dominic Ian Christopher, *b* 1975, — Sacha Louise, *b* 1968, — Larissa Mary, *b* 1970, — Natalya Isobel, *b* 1978.

WIDOW LIVING OF EIGHTH BARONET

MARIE ISOBEL (*Dowager Countess Cathcart*) (Moor Hatches, W Amesbury, Salisbury, Wilts), da of late Hon William Joseph French (*see* B de Freyne, colls): *m* 1st, 1942, Sir Thomas Brian Weldon, 8th baronet, who *d* 1979; 2ndly, 1984, as his 2nd wife, Maj Gen 6th Earl Cathcart, CB, DSO, MC, who *d* 1999.

COLLATERAL BRANCHES LIVING

Issue of late Sqdn-Ldr Terence Gordon Mackworth de Weltden Weldon, yst son of 6th baronet, *b* 1909, *d* 1970: *m* 1st, 1941 (*m diss* 1946), Suzanne Marie, da of Percy Hopkinson, of Sea Barn, Kingston Gorse, Sussex; 2ndly, 1946 (*m diss* 1969), Simonne Mireille, da of late Armand Philippon, of Aix-en-Provence, France:—
(By 2nd *m*) Oonagh Serena Elizabeth (Les Hortensias 15, 753 Route de La Colle, 06270 Villeneuve Loubet, France) *b* 1947; has issue living, Sarah Ilitch WELDON, *b* 1984.

Grandchildren of late Lt-Col Henry Walter Weldon, DSO (infra):—
Issue of late Brig Hamilton Edward Crosdill Weldon, CBE, RA, *b* 1910, *d* 1985: *m* 1st, 1935 (*m diss* 1946), Margaret Helen Katharine, da of Maj Frederic Passy, of Blachford, Cornwood, Devon; 2ndly, 1948, Elwyne Priscilla (3 Burnt Hill Rd, Wrecclesham, Surrey), da of Harold Richards Chaldecott, OBE, of Chantry, Leyburn, Yorks:—
(By 1st *m*) Wendy Juliet, *b* 1937: *m* 1960, Capt Ian Fothergill Grant, RN, and has issue living, Jonathan James Fothergill, *b* 1962, — Andrew William Edward Fothergill, *b* 1963: *m* 1989, Katrina Louise, da of Henry Evill, of London, — Amanda Katherine Lindley, *b* 1968. —— (By 2nd *m*) KEVIN NICHOLAS (2/93A Jubilee Rd, Khandallah, Wellington, NZ), *b* 19 April 1951: *m* 1973, Catherine Irène Angèle Main, of Fontenay le Comte, France, and has issue living, Alexander Nicholas, *b* 1977. —— Mark Henry de Weltden, *b* 1953; Lt-Col RA: *m* 1980, Catherine M., yr da of late Lt-Col D. J. P. Weld, of Manor Farm, Apethorpe, Northants, and has issue living, John, *b* 1981, — Lucinda Katie, *b* 1983. —— Andrea Sari Victoria (53 Green Lane, Farnham, Surrey GU9 8QE), *b* 1948: *m* 1st, 1974 (*m diss* 1983), Richard Amyas Evetts; 2ndly, 1998, Michael John Smith, and has issue living (by 1st *m*), Benjamin George, *b* 1976, — Thomas Edward, *b* 1979.

Issue of late Lieut-Col Henry Walter Weldon, DSO, 5th son of 5th baronet, *b* 1878, *d* 1925: *m* 1909, Helen Louise Victoria, who *d* 1965, da of late Sir Edward Porter Cowan, of Craig-a-vad, co Down:—
Aurea Elizabeth (Southwood House, Southwood, Baltonsborough, Glastonbury, Som), *b* 1915: *m* 1942, Capt Humphrey John James Stuart, RA (B Norton), who *d* 1969, and has issue living, Julian de Weltden, *b* 1947.

Granddaughter of late Col Thomas Weldon, CIE, 5th son of 4th baronet:—
Issue of late Walter Ivan Weldon, *b* 1871, *d* 1934: *m* 1899, Edith Lucy, who *d* 1956, da of Clifton Whiting, formerly of Ashtead Grange, Surrey:—
Violet Iva, *b* 1900. *Residence* – Sentosa, 34 Summerdown Rd, Eastbourne BN20 8DR.

Grandsons of late Walter Langford Weldon (infra):—
Issue of late Lt-Col Francis William Charles Weldon, MVO, MBE, MC, *b* 1913, *d* 1993: *m* 1946, Diana Geraldine, who *d* 1999, da of Stephen Anderson, of Straloch, by Blairgowrie, Perthshire:—
George Francis Daryl (64 Erpingham Rd, SW15 1BG), *b* 1946; *ed* Wellington Coll, Keble Coll, Oxford, and Carnegie-Mellon Univ, USA: *m* 1981 (*m diss* 1997), Jane Margaret, elder da of Maurice William George Knapman, of Orchard Close, Stoke Gabriel, Devon, and has issue living, Claire Elizabeth, *b* 1984, — Sarah Jane, *b* 1987. —— David Walter, *b* 1949; *ed* Wellington Coll: *m* 1975, Tessa Herron, and has issue living, Emilio, *b* 1982, — Sophie, *b* 1976.

Grandson of late Col Francis Weldon, 6th son of 4th baronet:—
Issue (by 2nd *m*) of late Walter Langford Weldon, *b* 1872, *d* 1922: *m* 1st, 1904, Emma Anne, who *d* 1905, da of late John Henry Tod, of 10 Courtfield Gdns, SW; 2ndly, 1910, Muriel Stewart, who *d* 1966 (having *m* 2ndly,

1924, Lt-Col William Weldon Herring-Cooper, CBE, DSO, who *d* 1953), da of William Richardson, formerly of 11 Harley House, Regent's Park, NW.
Patrick Langford Daryl MC, *b* 1917; *ed* Wellington Coll, and Trin Coll, Camb; Maj (ret) RA; 1939-45 War with 2nd Bn Wilts Regt, Korea 1951 (despatches, MC): *m* 1955, Pamela Jane, da of Col L. B. Grant, of Burnt House, Benenden, Kent, and has issue living, Thomas Daryl (84 Brackenbury Rd, W6 0BD), *b* 1963; *ed* Westminster Sch, and St John's Coll, Camb, — Guy Patrick (2 Burgh St, N1 8HF), *b* 1967; *ed* Westminster Sch, and Durham Univ: *m* 1998, Sarah Katharine, da of late Dr Peter le Huray, — Anna Grant, *b* 1958: *m* 1987, Andrew William Gadsden Reed, of Church House, Church St, Byfield, Northants NN11 6XN, son of Gp Capt William Reed, of Eydon, Northants, and has issue living, Charles William Weldon *b* 1994, Louisa Charlotte Weldon *b* 1991, — (Sarah) Kate, *b* 1960: *m* 1984, Andrew James Durham Wilkinson, of 48 Woodstock Rd, W4, son of late Geoffrey Wilkinson, and has issue living, Lucy Natasha *b* 1988, Amelia Grace *b* 1990, Matilda Rose *b* 1994. *Residence* – 18 Westbourne Park Rd, W2 5PH.

Grandsons of late Lt-Col Ernest Steuart Weldon, CBE, DSO, yr son of Col Francis Weldon (ante):—
Issue of late Maj Arthur Reginald Weldon, RA, *b* 1918; *d* 1982: *m* 1945, Dorothy Ann (Beanlands Park, Irthington, Carlisle), only child of William Monkhouse Pratchitt, of Crosby-on-Eden, Cumberland:—
Steuart William Pratchitt (The Drift, Upper Farringdon, nr Alton, Hants GU34 3EA), *b* 1947; *ed* Wellington: *m* 1984, Carola Helen Victoria, elder da of John Hugh Loch, of The Market House, Aldbourne, Wilts (*see* M Hertford, colls, 1968 Edn), and has issue living, Helen Ann Freda, *b* 1986. ⸺ Robert Arthur de Weltden, *b* 1950; *ed* Wellington: *m* 1993, Clare Frances, yr da of Richard Killingworth Hedges, of Charlton House, Shaftesbury, Dorset, and has issue living, James, *b* 1996.

Granddaughter of late Rev Lewen Burton Weldon, DD, 7th son of 4th baronet:—
Issue of late Lieut-Col Kenneth Charles Weldon, DSO, *b* 1877, *d* 1958: *m* 1906, Elizabeth Constance Jane, who *d* 1960, only da of late Major William Croker, Roy Inniskilling Fusiliers, of Byblox, Doneraile, co Cork:—
Clemence Jane (28 Leamington Rd, Charminster, Bournemouth, Hants), *b* 1915.

The patent of the 1st baronet, Sir Thomas Burdett, was conferred with remainder to the male issue of his sister Anne, wife of Walter Weldon. Col Sir Anthony A. Weldon, CVO, DSO, 6th Bt, a JP for Queen's co and co Kildare, was State Steward and Chamberlain to Lord-Lieut of Ireland and Lieut of co Kildare; *d* 1917 from the effects of shell shock.

WELLS (UK) 1944, of Felmersham, co Bedford

Qui patitur vincit
He who endures patiently conquers

Sir CHRISTOPHER CHARLES WELLS, 3rd *Baronet*; *b* 12 Aug 1936; *s* his father, *Lt-Col Sir* CHARLES MALTBY, TD, 1996; *ed* McGill and Toronto (MD) Univs: *m* 1st, 1960 (*m diss* 1983), Elizabeth Florence Vaughan, da of Isaac Foulkes Griffiths, of Outremont, Quebec; 2ndly, 1985, Lynda Anne, da of Robert MacDonnell Cormack, of Toronto, and has issue by 1st and 2nd *m*.

𝔄rms – Gules between two pallets a garb or bound with a ribbon azure buckled of the second pendant therefrom a hunting horn sable stringed of the third between two fountains. 𝔈rest – A demi bear sable muzzled gules the sinister paw resting on a portcullis chained or.
Residence – 1268 Seaforth Crescent, RR Number 3, Lakefield, Ontario, Canada K0L 2H0.

SONS LIVING (by 1st marriage)

MICHAEL CHRISTOPHER GRUFFYDD, *b* 24 Oct 1966; *ed* Carlton Univ, Ont. ⸺ Geoffrey Charles Vaughan, *b* 1970; *ed* Trent Univ, and Sir Wilfrid Laurier Univ.

(by 2nd marriage)

Andrew Christopher Brennan, *b* 1983.

DAUGHTERS LIVING (by 1st marriage)

Felicity Elizabeth Boulton, *b* 1964. ⸺ Megan Sarah Kenrick, *b* 1969.

BROTHER LIVING

Anthony Richard (55 Glengrove Av W, Toronto, Ont, Canada M4R 1N8), *b* 1947; *ed* Toronto Univ: *m* 1st, 1969 (*m diss* 1974), Frances Jane, da of Brig Gerard Boycott, of Berwick, Vic, Australia; 2ndly, 1976, Judith, da of Rev Arthur Hamilton, of Toronto; 3rdly, 1985, Heather Ann, da of Paul Johnston, of Toronto, and has issue living (by 1st *m*), Matthew Kenrick, *b* 1970, — (by 2nd *m*), Charles Hamilton, *b* 1978, — (by 3rd *m*), Katharine Dee, *b* 1994, — Sydney Molly, *b* (twin)1994.

UNCLES LIVING AND DECEASED (sons of 1st baronet)

David Franey, MC, *b* 1913; *ed* Bedford Sch, and RMA Woolwich; Maj (ret) RA; 1939-45 War (MC): *m* 1948, Patricia Mary, da of Rev Reginald Henry Goode, R of Houghton Conquest, Bedford, and has had issue, Thomas Franey (Riverside House, The High Rd, Felmersham, Bedford MK43 7HN), *b* 1951; *ed* Shiplake Coll, and Shuttleworth Coll, Bedford: *m* 1977, Jane Alison, da of E. G. Hussey, of Thame, Oxon, and has issue living, Jeremy Franey *b* 1981, Nicholas Franey *b* 1986, Lucy Sarah *b* 1983, — Priscilla Jane, *b* 1949: *d* as the result of a motor accident 1969. *Residence* – 43 Day's Lane, Biddenham, Bedford MK40 4AE. —— †George Crichton, *b* 1914; *ed* Bedford Sch, and Pembroke Coll, Camb (MB and BCh 1939); MRCP Lond 1946, FRCP 1959; Maj RAMC; 1939-45 War: *m* 1951, Margaret Caroline, who *d* 1998, da of late Dr Lewis Campbell Bruce. —— Oliver John, OBE, *b* 1922; *ed* Uppingham; W/Cmdr (ret) RAF; 1939-45 War; DL Beds 1964, High Sheriff 1970; OBE (Civil) 1990: *m* 1949, Felicity Anne, da of Brig Maurice Edward Mascall, DSO, OBE, and has issue living, Michael Mascall (28 Laurier Rd, Highgate, NW5 1SG), *b* 1951; *ed* Uppingham, and Oriel Coll, Oxford, — Paul Richard (Chellington House, Bridge End, Carlton, Beds), *b* 1958, — Joanna Felicity, *b* 1953: *m* 19—, Tom Robinson, of Stapleford Hall, 59 Bar Lane, Stapleford, Cambs. *Residence* – Ickwell Grange, Biggleswade, Beds. *Club* – RAF.

AUNTS LIVING (*daughters of 1st baronet*)

Sydney Mary, *b* 1917: *m* 1938, Cmdr George Edward Pollington Milburn, RN, and has issue living, Edward Barnaby Pollington (The Old Vicarage, Sibton, Saxmundham, Suffolk), *b* 1944, — Philippa, *b* 1939: *m* 19—, Owen Lawrence-Jones, of 10 Market Hill, Maldon, Chelmsford, Essex, — Georgina, *b* 1940: *m* 19—, Jonathan Harrison, of Castle Farm House, Odell, Beds. *Residence* – Garden House, Sibton, Saxmundham, Suffolk. —— Sarah Josephine, *b* (twin) 1922; 1939-45 War in WRNS: *m* 1947, Michael Oliver John Gibson, MD, FRCP, and has issue living, James Michael (Frome Vauchurch Cottage, Frome Vauchurch, Dorchester DT2 0DY), *b* 1950; *ed* Winchester, — Timothy Wells (30 Blandford Rd, W4 1DX), *b* 1952; *ed* Winchester. *Residence* – The Garden House, Piddlehinton, Dorset DT2 7TE.

COLLATERAL BRANCH LIVING

Issue of late Lt-Cdr Christopher Hayward Wells, RN, 2nd son of 1st baronet, *b* 1909, *ka* 1940: *m* 1937, Christina Hilary (who *m* 2ndly, 1949, Sir James Holmes Henry, 2nd Bt, CMG, MC, TD, who *d* 1997), da of late Sir Hugh Oliver Holmes, KBE, CMG, MC, QC:—
John Hayward (Old Rectory, Shelton, Kimbolton, Cambs; Royal Thames Yacht Club), *b* 1938; *ed* Harrow, and Pembroke Coll, Camb; JP Beds 1971, High Sheriff 1989, DL 1992: *m* 1965, Heather Donriel, da of John Gordon Christie Kelly, MC, of Cape Town, and has issue living, Christopher Hayward, *b* 1966; *ed* Harrow, and RAC Cirencester, — Richard Michael, *b* 1967; *ed* Harrow, and Durham Univ, — Peter John, *b* 1970; *ed* Harrow, and Nottingham Univ.

The 1st baronet, Sir (Sydney) Richard Wells (son of late Charles Wells, of Bedford), was Chancellor of Primrose League 1946-8, and sat as MP for Bedford Div of Bedfordshire (*U*) 1922-45.

WERNHER (UK) 1905, of Luton Hoo, Luton, Bedfordshire (Extinct 1973)

Sir HAROLD AUGUSTUS WERNHER, GCVO, TD, 3rd and last *Baronet*.

DAUGHTERS LIVING OF THIRD BARONET

Georgina (*Lady Kennard*) (13 Burton Court, Franklin's Row, SW3; Ardhuncart Lodge, Alford, Aberdeen), *b* 1919: *m* 1st, 1944, Lt-Col Harold Pedro Joseph Phillips, FRGS, who *d* 1980; 2ndly, 1992, as his 4th wife, Lt-Col Sir George Arnold Ford Kennard, 3rd Bt, and has had issue (by 1st *m*), †Nicholas Harold, *b* 1947; *ed* Eton, London Univ, and Lausanne Univ: *m* 1975, Maria Lucia (Luton Hoo, Luton, Beds), da of late Count Paul Czernin von und zu Chudenitz, of Austria, and *d* 1991, leaving issue, Edward Paul Nicholas *b* 1981, Charlotte Sonia Maria *b* 1976, — Alexandra Anastasia (*Duchess of Abercorn*), *b* 1946; a Gov Harrow Sch since 1986: *m* 1966, 5th Duke of Abercorn, KG, — Fiona Mercedes, *b* 1951: *m* 1971, James Comyn Amherst Burnett of Leys (*see* B Amherst of Hackney, colls), — Marita Georgina, *b* 1954; co-founder of The Mime Centre: *m* 1982, Randall Stafford Crawley, who was *k* in an air crash 1988 in Italy, yr son of late Aidan Merivale Crawley, MBE, of Oak Cottage, Farthinghoe, Northants (*see* Crawley-Boevey, Bt, colls, 1968 Edn), and has issue living, Aidan Harold Winston *b* 1983, Galen Randall George *b* (*posthumous*) 1988, Cosima Georgina *b* 1985, — Natalia Ayesha (*Duchess of Westminster*), *b* 1959: *m* 1978, 6th Duke of Westminster. —— Myra Alice (*Lady Butter*), CVO, *b* 1925; CVO 1992: *m* 1946, Maj Sir David Henry Butter, KCVO, MC, JP, Scots Gds, and has issue living, Charles Harold Alexander (12 Pelham Crescent, SW7), *b* 1960, — Sandra Elizabeth Zia, *b* 1948: *m* 1983, William D. Morrison, of 34 Norland Sq, W11 4PQ, yr son of Maxey N. Morrison, of Swarthmore, Penn, USA, and has issue living, Charles Nicholas *b* 1985, Sophie Natasha *b* 1987, — Marilyn Davina (*Countess of Dalhousie*), *b* 1950: *m* 1973, 17th Earl of Dalhousie, of Brechin Castle, Brechin, Angus DD9 6SH, — Rohays Georgina (*Princess Alexander Galitzine*), *b* 1952: *m* 1988, Prince Alexander Peter Galitzine, of 109 Abingdon Rd, W8 6QU, elder son of late Prince George Galitzine, of Eaton Sq, SW1, and has issue living, Sasha Alice Natalia *b* 1989, Nadezhda Georgina *b* 1990, — Georgina Marguerite, *b* 1956: *m* 1982, Peter Pejacsevich, of 12 Norland Sq, W11 4PX, son of Count Mark Pejacsevich, of 33 Victoria Rd, W8, and has issue living, Alexander Geza Marcus *b* 1988, Anastasia Lilla Sophie *b* 1992. *Residence* – Cluniemore, Pitlochry, Perthshire PH16 5NE.

DAUGHTER LIVING OF SECOND BARONET

Anna Alexandra (50 Langbourne Mansions, Langbourne Av, N6 6PT), *b* 1924.

PRESCOTT-WESTCAR (GB) 1794, of Theobalds Park, Hertfordshire (Extinct 1959)

Sir WILLIAM VILLIERS LEONARD PRESCOTT-WESTCAR, DSO, 7th and last *Baronet*.

DAUGHTER LIVING OF SEVENTH BARONET

Jellis, *b* 1926: *m* 19—, William Cameron.

WIDOW LIVING OF FIFTH BARONET

Elizabeth Hughes, da of William Melcer, of California, USA, and widow of Arthur Grier Fell: *m* 2ndly, 1932, Sir George Lionel Lawson Prescott, 5th Bt, who *d* 1942; 3rdly, 1953 (*m diss* 1957), Capt Peregrine Fellowes, Irish Guards, who *d* 1972.

WHEELER (UK) 1920, of Woodhouse Eaves, co Leicester

Sir JOHN HIERON WHEELER, 3rd *Baronet*; *b* 22 July 1905; *s* his brother, *Sir* ARTHUR (FREDERICK PULLMAN), 1964; *ed* Charterhouse: *m* 1929, Gwendolen Alice, da of late Alfred Ernest Oram, of Kirby Muxloe, nr Leicester, and has issue.

Arms – Sable, a chevron between in chief two talbots heads erased and in base an eagle displayed or. **Crest** – A talbot's head erased sable, eared and charged on the neck with a catherine wheel or.
Residence – 39 Morland Av, Stoneygate, Leicester LE2 2PF.

SONS LIVING

JOHN FREDERICK (Round Hill, Aldeburgh, Suffolk), *b* 3 May 1933; *ed* Bedales and Lond Sch of Printing: *m* 1963, Barbara Mary, da of late Raymond Flint, of Stoneygate, Leicester, and has issue living, John Radford, *b* 1965, — Andrew Charles, *b* 1969, — Jane Louise, *b* 1964. —— Benjamin (Benscliffe Haye Cottage, Newtown Linford, Leics), *b* 1935: *m* 1962, Brenda Ellen, da of late Arthur Goodman, of Syston, Leics, and has issue living, Miles John, *b* 1962, — Edward James, *b* 1964, — Matthew Benjamin, *b* 1966, — Rebecca Mary, *b* 1972.

WIDOW LIVING OF SECOND BARONET

Alice Webster (*Alice, Lady Wheeler*) (E12, Marine Gate, Marine Parade, Brighton 7, BN2 5TQ), da of late George Heath Stones: *m* 1938, Sir Arthur (Frederick Pullman) Wheeler, 2nd Bt, who *d* 1964.

The 1st baronet, Sir Arthur Wheeler (son of late Benjamin Wheeler, of Northampton) was High Sheriff of Leicestershire 1922.

Wheeler Cuffe, see Cuffe.

WHELER (E) 1660, of City of Westminster, co London

Sir EDWARD WOODFORD WHELER, 14th *Baronet*; *b* 13 June 1920; *s* his father, *Sir* TREVOR WOOD, 1986; *ed* Radley; Capt Roy Sussex Regt 1941-47, attached Indian Army 1942-45; Overseas Audit Dept 1948-58, Kenya 1958-70: *m* 1945, Molly Ashworth, da of late Thomas Lever, late Gold Coast Civil Ser, and has issue.

Arms – Or a chevron between three leopards' faces sable. **Crest** – On a ducal coronet or, an eagle displayed gules.
Residence – 34 Carantoc Way, Newquay, Cornwall.

SON LIVING

TREVOR WOODFORD (83 Middle Park, Inverurie, Aberdeenshire), *b* 11 April 1946; *ed* St Edmund's, Canterbury: *m* 1974, Rosalie Margaret, da of late Ronald Thomas Stunt, and has issue living, Edward William, *b* 14 June 1976, — Andrew Robert, *b* 1978.

DAUGHTER LIVING

Dinah Margaret, *b* 1947: *m* 1st, 1968 (*m diss* 1983), Clive Richard Knight; 2ndly, 1987, Bernard Teasdale Tomlinson, and has issue living, (by 1st *m*) Anthony Clive Wheler, *b* 1968, — Simon Mark, *b* 1972. *Residence* – 32 St Carantoc Way, Crantock, nr Newquay, Cornwall TR8 5SB.

SISTERS LIVING AND DECEASED

Up to the mark

Audrey Idris, *b* 1916: *m* 1940, Maj John Humphrey Wightwick, late Suffolk Regt, who *d* 1970, and *d* 1996, having had issue, Christopher Kenneth Wheler, *b* 1940: *m* 1st, 1966 (*m diss* 1975), Sarah Gordon Macdonald; 2ndly, 1978, Sheila Gay (who *m* 2ndly, 1996, Cmdr Henry Stern, RN, of 5 Horton Rd, Kings Lynn, Norfolk PE30 4XU), only da of late Paul Morton-George, and *d* 1994, leaving issue (by 1st *m*), Kathryn Jennifer *b* 1969, (by 2nd *m*) Jennifer Audrey Margaret Idris *b* 1989, — Simon John Patrick Wheler (Flat 3-3a Surf Motel, Maer Lane, Bude, Cornwall EX23 8NG), *b* 1949: *m* 1973 (*m diss* 19—), Annee Alfsen, of Oslo, Norway, and has issue living, Christian John *b* 1974, — Nigel Martin Humphrey Wheler (11 Drover's Way, Woodley, Reading W2 2YY), *b* 1951: *m* 1981 (*m diss* 1995), Susan Irene Gambie, and has issue living, Simon John *b* 1978, — Vanessa Ann Margaret Wheler, *b* 1947: *m* 1970, John Bray Needham, of 20 Legion Court, Green Lane, Morden, Surrey, and has issue living, Gavin Timothy John *b* 1971, Edward Richard *b* 1974: *m* 1998, Kelly Ward, Timothy David *b* 1979. —— Diana Edmée (43 Elizabeth Court, Milmans St, SW10 0DA), *b* 1918: *m* 1941, Lt-Col Leslie Francis Gordon Pritchard, MBE, TD, who *d* 1977, and has issue living, Caroline Jane CASS (Flat 6, 25 Earl's Court Sq, SW5 9DA), *b* 1943: *m* 1966 (*m diss* 19—), Dean Edward Fischer, and has issue living, Tara Jane FISCHER *b* 1970, Tasmin La Cloche *b* 1971: *m* 1995, Rupert Montagu Norman (*see* B Vivian, colls) (and has issue living, Callum Collett Dean *b* 1998), — Susan Letitia, *b* 1947: *m* 1972, Roderic Gordon Hill, of 19 Scarsdale Villas, W8 6PT, and has issue living, Caspar Giles *b* 1974, Chloe Louise *b* 1977, — Anne Charlotte, *b* 1948: *m* 1973, Todd Combs Civardi, of 14 Lynette Av, SW4 9HD, and has issue living, Jake Giles *b* 1976, Sophie Lorelei *b* 1979, Amber Eloise Rose *b* 1986, — Rachel Sarah, *b* 1955: *m* 1978, Henry Mark Wyndham, of The Old Rectory, Southease, Lewes, E Sussex, and has issue (*see* B Egremont).

COLLATERAL BRANCHES LIVING

Grandchildren of late Lt-Col Francis Henry Wheler, 2nd son of 10th baronet:—
Issue of late Capt Trevor Wheler, *b* 1888, *d* 1967: *m* 1935, Enid, who *d* 1983, da of late H. R. Stokes;—
Glynne Henry Trevor, *b* 1941. —— Jane Frances Trevor, *b* 1938: *m* 1962, Kenneth Ross Thompson, of Ardmore, Gundagai, NSW 2722, Australia, and has issue living, John Kenneth Glynne, *b* 1967: *m* 1995, Michelle Margaret Cook, — Susan Jane, *b* 1963: *m* 1992, Brett Donald McAllister, and has issue living, Angus Donald *b* 1995, Julia Jane *b* 1998, — Jennifer Anne Frances, *b* 1965.

Granddaughters of late Aubrey Stuart Wheler, only son of late Col Charles Stuart Wheler, 3rd son of 10th baronet:—
Issue of late Stephen Jameson Wheler, *b* 1907, *d* 1967: *m* 1950, Annette, who *d* 1968, da of Frank Eden Smith:—
Amanda WHELER (The Summerhouse, Lodge Lane, Keymer, W Sussex BN6 8NA), *b* 1952; continues to use her maiden name: *m* 1996, Robert Brindley Kenhard. —— Jacqueline, *b* 1956: *m* 1987, Christopher French, of 714 NW 2nd Av, Delray Beach, Florida 33444, USA, and has issue living, William Stephen Holmes, *b* 1995.

The 1st baronet, Sir William, was MP for Queensborough *temp* Charles II, and his wife was Laundress to the Royal Family. The 2nd baronet, Col Sir Charles, his cousin, who succeeded by a special limitation, was Governor of the Leeward Islands, MP for Cambridge University in the Long Parliament, and one of the gentlemen entrusted to carry the plate of that University to Charles II. The 9th baronet, Lieut-Col Sir Trevor, served throughout the Peninsular War, including Waterloo; and the 10th baronet, Lieut-Gen Sir Francis, CB, served in Bundlecund 1821-2, in Afghanistan 1839-40, in the Punjab 1848-9, and in Indian Mutiny 1858-9. His son, Lt-Col Sir Trevor Wheler, 11th Bt, was *b* 1828 in Lucknow, where all the wives were assembled for safety during the Indian Mutiny, while his father was on active ser.

WHICHCOTE (E) 1660, of The Inner Temple, London (Dormant or Extinct 1949)

Sir HUGH CHRISTOPHER WHICHCOTE, 10th and last *Baronet*.

DAUGHTERS LIVING OF TENTH BARONET

Isolda Sophia, *b* 1910. —— Diana Juliane, *b* 1911.

WHITAKER (UK) 1936, of Babworth, Nottinghamshire

Sir JOHN JAMES INGHAM WHITAKER, 4th *Baronet*; *b* 23 Oct 1952; *s* his father, *Sir* JAMES HERBERT INGHAM, OBE, 1999; *ed* Eton, and Bristol Univ (BSc), FCA, AMIEE: *m* 1981, Elizabeth Jane Ravenscroft, da of L. J. R. Starke, of New Zealand, and has issue.

Hope and faith

Arms – Per pale argent and azure a chevron embattled between three mascles counterchanged. **Crest** – A horse passant argent, gorged with a collar gemel, and resting the dexter foreleg on a mascle azure.
Seats – Babworth Hall, Retford, Notts DN22 8EP; Auchnafree, Dunkeld, Perthshire.

SON LIVING

HARRY JAMES INGHAM, *b* 16 March 1984.

DAUGHTERS LIVING

Lucy Harriet Ravenscroft, *b* 1982. —— Alix Catherine Hepburn, *b* 1987. —— Eleanor Mary Harvie, *b* 1989.

SISTER LIVING

Shervie Ann Lander, *b* 1950: *m* 1971, David William James Price, of Harrington Hall, Spilsby, Lincs, and has issue living, William James Emlyn, *b* 1973, — Hesther Jane Lander, *b* 1971.

UNCLES LIVING (*sons of 2nd baronet*)

Rev David Arthur Edward (Wits End, Hereford Rd, Weobley, Herefordshire), *b* 1927; *ed* Eton, and New Coll, Oxford; formerly Lt Coldm Gds; is a Clerk in Holy Orders: *m* 1956, Susan Mary, da of the Rev Canon Richard Hamilton Babington, of St Mary-le-Tower, Vicarage, Ipswich, and has issue living, Robert John, *b* 1957, — *Rev* Michael Benjamin, *b* 1960, — Jonathan *b* 1972, — Caroline Lucy, *b* 1959, — Iona Ruth, *b* 1963. —— Benjamin Charles George (16 Adamson Rd, NW3), *b* 1934; *ed* Eton and New Coll, Oxford; Bar Inner Temple 1959; formerly 2nd Lt Coldm Gds; author of *The Police* 1964, *Crime and Society* 1967, editor of *A Radical Future* 1967; *Participation and Poverty* 1968, *Parks for People* 1971, *The Foundations* 1974, *Police in Society* 1979, *A Bridge of People* 1983, *The Global Connection* 1987; UN report on Genocide 1985; editor of *The Fourth World* 1972 and of *Minorities: a question of human rights* 1984; Lieut, Order of Merit (Portugal) 1993; PPS to Min of Overseas Development 1966 and to Min of Housing and Local Govt 1966-67 and Parl Sec, Min of Overseas Development 1969-70; MP for Hampstead (*L*) 1966-70; Exec Dir of Minority Rights Groups 1971-88; Exec Dir of Gulbenkian Foundation (UK) 1988-99; UK Member, UN Human Rights Sub-Commission 1975-88: *m* 1964, Janet Alison, da of Alan Stewart, of Beeston, and has issue living, Daniel Peter Alan, *b* 1966, — Rasaq Andrew Ian, *b* 1972, — Quincy Rachel Suzy, *b* 1968.

The 1st baronet, Col Sir Albert Edward Whitaker, CBE, TD, (son of late Joseph Whitaker, of Hesley Hall, Notts), was a JP and DL for Notts (High Sheriff 1921) and Lord High Steward of E Retford. The 2nd baronet, Maj-Gen Sir John Albert Charles Whitaker, CB, CBE, late Coldstream Guards, was High Sheriff of Nottingham 1950, and Lord High Steward of E Retford 1952-57. He commanded Coldstream Guards 1937-39, and was Director of Mil Training 1942-45.

WHITE (UK) 1802, of Wallingwells, Nottinghamshire

Sir NICHOLAS PETER ARCHIBALD WHITE, 6th *Baronet*, eldest son of late Capt Richard Taylor White, DSO, RN, 2nd son of 4th baronet; *b* 2 March 1939; *s* his uncle, *Sir* THOMAS ASTLEY WOOLLASTON, 1996; *ed* Eton: *m* 1970, Susan Irene, da of George William Baron Pollock, of Blackrock, co Dublin, and has issue.

𝕬rms – Gules, a chevron vaire between three lions rampant or. Crest – Out of a ducal coronet argent, a demi-eagle displayed sable.
Residence – The Stables, Canon Lane, Wateringbury, Kent.

SONS LIVING

CHRISTOPHER DAVID NICHOLAS, *b* 20 July 1972; *ed* Harrow. —— Simon Richard William, *b* 1974; *ed* Harrow.

DAUGHTER LIVING

Annabelle Victoria Jocelyn, *b* 1976.

BROTHERS LIVING

Robert Leslie, *b* 1945; *ed* Eton: *m* 1989, Hong Chen, da of Ren Qing Chen, of Beijing, China. *Residence* – 73 Clevedon House, Cressingham Grove, Sutton, Surrey SM1 4DR. —— Richard Mark, TD, *b* (twin) 1945; *ed* Eton; Lt-Col: *m* 1988, Catherine Anne Isobel, only da of late Judge Karl Roy Barrington Brandon, of Fairwater, Chew Stoke, Som, and has issue living, Richard Karl Sebastian Woollaston, *b* 1991, —— Rosanna Catherine Elisabeth Oriana, *b* 1990. *Residence* – 65 Ponsonby Place, SW1.

SISTERS LIVING

Victoria Rosamond (*Dowager Lady Sebright*), *b* 1937: *m* 1st, 1965 (*m diss* 1983), David Ashton Ashton-Bostock; 2ndly, 1984, Sir Hugo Giles Edmund Sebright, 14th Bt, who *d* 1985, and has issue living (by 1st *m*), (Henrietta) Sophia, *b* 1967: *m* 1990, Dominic Bertram Charles Tayler, son of Michael Tayler, of The Old Parsonage, Aust, nr Bristol, and has issue living, Alexander Charles Bostock *b* 1994, Natasha Victoria Patricia *b* 1996, Isabella Francesca Olivia *b* 1999. *Address* – RP3, Clarensac 30870, France. —— Jocelyn Henrietta, *b* 1943: *m* 1966, Michael Christopher Mallock, and has issue living, James Rawlyn, *b* 1972; *ed* Bryanston, and De Montfort Univ, —— Sarah Penelope, *b* 1970: *m* 1992, Lieut James Edward Buck, RN (Broad Oak, Sherfield English Rd, Landford, Salisbury, Wilts SP5 2BD), eldest son of W. A. Buck, of Stramshall, Uttoxeter, Staffs, and has issue living, Nicholas James *b* 1997, Alexander Christopher *b* 1999. *Residence* – Manor Lodge, Bringhurst, Market Harborough, Leics.

DAUGHTER LIVING OF FIFTH BARONET

Bridget Juliet, *b* 1936: *m* 1962, Lt-Cdr Charles David Orr Ewing, RN, and has issue (*see* Orr Ewing, Bt, colls, *cr* 1886). *Residence* – Torhousemuir, Wigtown, Wigtownshire.

WIDOW LIVING OF FIFTH BARONET

DAPHNE MARGARET (*Dowager Lady White*), da of late Lt-Col Francis Remi Imbert Athill, CMG, OBE, DL, of Brinkburn High House, Longframlington, Northumberland: *m* 1935, Sir Thomas Astley Woollaston White, 5th Bt, who *d* 1996. *Residence* – Ha Hill, Wigtown, Wigtownshire.

COLLATERAL BRANCHES LIVING

Issue of late Capt Archibald John Ramsay White, CBE, DSC, RN, yst son of 4th Bt, *b* 1910, *d* 1991: *m* 1949, Marguerite Elise (Lavender Cottage, Evenlode, Moreton in Marsh, Glos GL56 0NN), only da of late Sir Ernest Nathaniel Bennett, JP, MP, of Cwmllecoedlog, Montgomery:—
Thomas Charles Ramsay, *b* 1952; Maj 9th/12th R Lancers (ret): *m* 1981, Mary, yr da of Edward Ross-Hime, of Orchard Cottage, 12 Chapel Street, East Malling, Maidstone, Kent, and has issue living, Charles Thomas Ramsay, *b* 1988, — Elizabeth Susannah, *b* 1983, — Clare Marguerite, *b* 1986. —— John Woollaston (Warneford House, Oxford St, Moreton in Marsh, Glos GL56 0LA), *b* 1958: *m* 1991, Susanna, elder da of John Burgess, of Burgate House, Loxhill, Godalming, Surrey. —— Caroline Marguerite, *b* 1950. —— Sarah Elizabeth, *b* 1960.

Grandchildren of late John White (infra):—
Issue of late George Towry White, *b* 1889, *d* 1973: *m* 1922, Evangeline, who *d* 1981, da of late John Arthur, of Feilding, NZ:—
John Woollaston (74 Broadway, Waitara, NZ), *b* 1923. —— Louis Arthur Taylor, *b* 1928: *m* 1957, Gladys Daphne, only da of John Stokes, farmer, of Kinohaku, NZ, and has issue living, Stanley George, *b* 1958, — Norman John, *b* 1959: *m* 1979, Sheryle, da of P. L. Duxfield, of Ongarue, NZ, and has issue living, Jered Colin *b* 1980, Jackie Anna *b* 1983, Camilla Amy-Anne *b* 1986, — Jeffrey Taylor, *b* 1964, — Jocelyn Amy Anne, *b* 1961, — Miriam Una, *b* 1962: *m* 1985, Robert Skinner, and has issue living, Sherilyn Rose *b* 1986, Jasmine Marie *b* 1988, Karley Anne *b* 1989, — Patricia Gladys (twin), *b* 1964, — Eva Marie, *b* 1966: *m* 1993, Alexander George Yeo, of Gowan Valley, RD3, Murchison, NZ, and has issue living, Natasha Ruby *b* 1993. —— Marion Penelope, *b* 1926.

Granddaughter of late Rev Taylor White, 2nd son of 1st baronet:—
Issue of late John White, b 1839, d 1911: m 1876, his cousin, Louisa Caroline, who d 1915, da of late George Towry White, Bar-at-law:—
Joyce Alice Finderne, b 1897. Residence – 64 Ambleside Av, Telscombe Cliffs, nr Newhaven, Sussex.

(In special remainder)

Descendants (if any) of the late Lieut-Col Taylor White, brother of 1st baronet.

Sir Thomas Woollaston White, 1st baronet, who was created with remainder to his father's issue male, was 7th in descent from Thomas White, of Tuxford Manor, Notts, who m Anne Cecil, sister of the famous William, Lord Burghley.

WHITE (UK) 1904, of Cotham House, Bristol

Sir GEORGE STANLEY JAMES WHITE, 4th Baronet; b 4 Nov 1948; s his father, Sir GEORGE STANLEY MIDELTON, 1983; ed Harrow; JP, FSA: m 1st, 1974 (m diss 1979), Susan Elizabeth, da of late John Langmaid Ford; 2ndly, 1979, Elizabeth Jane, da of late Sir (William) Reginald Verdon-Smith, and formerly wife of Robert George Clinton, and has issue living by both m.

Arms – Barry wavy of six argent and azure, over all a lymphad sable, on a chief of the second two roses of the first. Crest – Upon a mount vert a beacon fired proper, pendent therefrom a sail azure charged with a rose as in the arms.

SON LIVING (By 2nd marriage)

GEORGE PHILIP JAMES, b 1987.

DAUGHTERS LIVING (By 1st marriage)

Caroline Morwenna, b 1978.

(By 2nd marriage)

Kate Elizabeth, b 1983.

SISTER LIVING

Daphne Eleanor, b 1945: m 1969, Jonathan Wheeler, of 19 Glebe Place, SW3, and has issue living, Robert Frederick William George, b 1972; ed Harrow, and Bristol Univ.

WIDOW LIVING OF THIRD BARONET

DIANE ELEANOR ABDY (Diane, Lady White), da of late Bernard Abdy Collins, CIE, of Deccan House, Aldeburgh: m 1939, Sir George Stanley Midelton White, 3rd Bt, who d 1983. Residence – Acton House, Park Street, Iron Acton, nr Bristol.

The 1st baronet, Sir George White, head of the firm of George White and Co, of Bristol, was one of the pioneers of Electric Street Traction (being the first to introduce it into London, Dublin, Bristol, Middlesbrough, etc), and established the first manufactory of aeroplanes in England and introduced "Bristol" biplanes and monoplanes.

WHITE (UK) 1922, of Salle Park, Norfolk

Go forward not back

Sir JOHN WOOLMER WHITE, 4th *Baronet*; *b* 4 Feb 1947; *ed* Cheltenham Coll; *s* his father, *Sir* HEADLEY DYMOKE, 1971; *ed* Cheltenham, and RAC Cirencester: *m* 1987, Joan, da of late T. D. Borland, of Flemington, W Linton, Peebleshire, and has issue.

Arms – Quarterly, 1st and 4th, argent, a fesse chequy gules and or, over all a bend engrailed azure, an arrow point downwards of the field, *White*; 2nd and 3rd, azure, a lion rampant between four estoiles or, *Dymock*. Crest – A boar's head erased proper, pierced through the mouth with an arrow or.
Residence – Salle Park, Reepham, Norwich, Norfolk NR10 4SG.

SON LIVING

KYLE DYMOKE WILFRID, *b* 16 March 1988.

SISTERS LIVING

Morna, *b* 1944. —— Isabelle Sarah, *b* 1948.

UNCLE LIVING (*Son of 2nd baronet*)

Sir Lynton Stuart, MBE, TD, *b* 1916; *ed* Harrow, and Trin Coll, Camb (MA); DL of Hants; Member of Hants CC 1970, Vice-Chm 1976, Chm 1977-85; 2nd Lieut TA 1939; 1939-45 War in Far East (despatches, MBE); Hon Lt-Col RA, TA 1946; TARO 1948-71; MBE (Mil) 1943, Kt Bach 1985: *m* 1945, Phyllis Marie Rochfort, da of late Sir Newnham Arthur Worley, KBE, and has issue living, Anthony Douglas, *b* 1946, — Richard Lynton, *b* 1953, — Robert Newnham Stuart, *b* 1956: *m* 1989, Jennifer Elizabeth Anne, da of Rev Barry Hughes-Gibbs, of Pretoria, S Africa, — Philip Dymoke (Chidden Farmhouse, Hambledon, Hants), *b* 1958: *m* 1984, Fiona Elizabeth, da of James Lunn, of West Meon, Hants, and has issue living, Alexander Stuart Dymoke *b* 1988, Emelia Louise *b* 1990, Annabel Madeleine *b* 1994, — Katharine Anne Rochfort, *b* 1949: *m* 1976, Christopher John Wernham, of Sydney, Aust. *Residence* – Oxenbourne House, East Meon, nr Petersfield, Hants GU32 1QL.

AUNTS LIVING (*Daughters of 2nd baronet*)

Marguerite Isabelle (*Lady Martell*) (2 Marcuse Fields, Bosham, Chichester, W Sussex PO18 8NA), *b* 1920: *m* 1941 (*m diss* 1983), Vice Adm Sir Hugh Colenso Martell, KBE, CB, who *d* 1999, and has issue living, Richard James, *b* 1942: *m* 1966 (*m diss* 1991), Theresa Hannah Wickins, and has issue living, Jonathan James *b* 1969, Jeremy Paul *b* 1971, Emma Jane *b* 1979, — Stuart (Flat 26, Neville's Court, Dollis Hill Lane, NW2), *b* 1943: *m* 1st, 1968 (*m diss* 1976), Penelope Gay, da of late Christopher Hunt: *m* 2ndly, 1978, Carol, only da of Lt-Col R. H. N. Simonds, of Aldwick Bay, W Sussex (Hickman, Bt, colls), and has issue living, (by 1st *m*), Benjamin Stuart *b* 1969, Christopher Hugh Stuart *b* 1973, — Charles, *b* 1946: *m* 1968, Monica, da of Martin Gillman, of Gloucester, and has issue living, Charles Edward *b* 1971, Elizabeth *b* 1969, — Timothy Hugh, *b* 1952: *m* 1973, Elizabeth Grazyna, da of Frank Szostak, and has issue living, Marcus Timothy *b* 1977, John Robert *b* 1981, — Michael Gordon *b* (twin) 1952: *m* 1981, Fiona Jane, da of W. C. Dack, of Worthing, and has issue living, William Michael *b* 1986, Natalie Fiona *b* 1981, — Sarah Jessica, *b* 1957. —— Hélène Pauline *b* 1924; MA: *m* 1954, Lt-Col William Neville Cairns, King's Dragoon Gds (ret), who *d* 1973, and has issue living, Jeremy Dymoke Russell, *b* 1955: *m* 1984, Teresa Jane, da of Gene L. Lewis, of Rocky Mount, N Carolina, USA, — Patrick Neville, *b* 1957. *Residence* – Alderton House, New Ross, co Wexford.

Sir Woolmer White, 1st baronet, was son of late Maj Timothy White, of Salle Park, Norfolk.

WHITE (UK) 1937, of Boulge Hall, co Suffolk

Not for self but for others

Sir CHRISTOPHER ROBERT MEADOWS WHITE, 3rd *Baronet*; *b* 26 Aug 1940; *s* his father, *Sir* (ERIC) RICHARD MEADOWS, 1972; *ed* Bradfield Coll: *m* 1st, 1962 (*m diss* 1968), Anne Marie Ghislaine, yr da of late Maj Tom Brown, OBE, MC; 2ndly, 1968 (*m diss* 1972), Dinah Mary Sutton; 3rdly, 1976, Ingrid Carolyn, el da of Eric Jowett, of Gt Baddow, Essex.

Arms – Gules, a chevron nebuly between three boars' heads couped, two flaunches argent each charged with a cross patée of the field. Crest – In front of a demi tower gules, issuant therefrom, a boar's head argent, tusked and maned or, charged on the neck with a cross patée also gules, three crosses patée also argent.
Address – c/o Mrs Steinschaden-Silver, Pinkney Court, nr Malmesbury, Wilts SN16 0PD.

The 1st baronet, Sir Robert Eaton White, VD (son of late Robert Holmes White, of Boulge Hall, Suffolk), was a JP and DL for Suffolk, and Chm of E Suffolk Quarter Sessions, and Co Council, and served during European War 1914-17 as Lieut-Col Comdg 14th Batn Suffolk Regt (TF).

White (Jervis-White-Jervis), see Jervis.

DALRYMPLE-WHITE (UK) 1926, of High Mark, co Wigtown

Virtus · sibi · munus

Virtue is worth

Sir HENRY ARTHUR DALRYMPLE DALRYMPLE-WHITE, DFC, 2nd *Baronet*; *b* 5 Nov 1917; *s* his father, *Lieut-Col Sir* GODFREY DALRYMPLE, 1954; *ed* Eton, Magdalene Coll, Camb and London Univ; formerly Wing-Com RAF Vol Reserve; European War 1939-45 (DFC and Bar): *m* 1948 (*m diss* 1956), Mary, da of Capt Robert Thomas, and has issue.

Arms – Quarterly, 1st and 4th, vert a naval crown or between three roses argent, barbed and seeded proper, in centre chief an escutcheon argent charged with a representation of the gold medal presented to Adm Sir John Chambers White for his services in Egypt in the year 1801, pendant from a riband tenné, *White*; 2nd and 3rd, or, on a saltire azure between two water bougets in pale sable nine lozenges of the field, *Dalrymple*. Crest – 1st issuant from a coronet composed of four roses set upon a rim or a lion's head argent, *White*; 2nd, in front of a rock proper water bouget sable, *Dalrymple*.
Address – Fairseat Foundation, PO Box 670, Village Market, Nairobi, Kenya.

SON LIVING

JAN HEW, (7 Jonas Drive, Wadhurst, E Sussex TN5 6RJ) *b* 26 Nov 1950; *ed* Stowe.
Sir Godfrey Dalrymple Dalrymple-White, 1st Bt (son of Gen Sir Henry Dalrymple White, KCB, who commanded 6th Inniskilling Dragoons throughout Crimean War), was Lieut-Col Grenadier Guards, served in S Africa 1900-02 and in European War 1914-18. He assumed by deed poll 1926, the additional surname of Dalrymple, and sat as MP for Southport Div of Lancashire (C) 1910-18, and for Southport 1918-23 and 1924-31.

WHITEHEAD (UK) 1889, of Highfield House, Catford Bridge, Kent.

By pluck and work

Sir ROWLAND JOHN RATHBONE WHITEHEAD, 5th *Baronet*; *b* 24 June 1930; *s* his father *Major Sir* PHILIP HENRY RATHBONE, 1953; *ed* Radley, and Trin Hall, Camb (BA 1953); late 2nd Lieut RA; Trustee of Rowland Hill Fund since 1961 (Chm since 1982), The Standing Council of the Baronetage since 1972 (Chm Exec Cttee 1984-87), Founder and Trustee of The Baronets' Trust since 1984 (Chm 1984-87), Trustee, Kelmscott House Trust since 1972, The Royal Aero Club Trust since 1998, Brogdale Horticultural Trust since 1993, and Appleby School Whitehead Trust since 1960, Pres Inst of Translation and Interpreting since 1996; Church-warden of St Mary Abchurch, City of London since 1997; Freeman of City of Lond and Liveryman of the Fruiterers' Co: *m* 1954, Marie-Louise, da of late Arnold Christian Gausel, of Stavanger, Norway, and has issue.

Arms – Per pale azure and sable, on a fesse invected and plain cottised or between three fleurs-de-lis of the last, a fasces erect between two eagles' heads erased proper. Crest – An eagle, wings expanded proper, each wing charged with a fasces erect or, supporting with the dexter claw an escutcheon of the arms.
Residences – Walnut Tree Cottage, Fyfield, Lechlade, Glos GL7 3LT; Sutton House, Chiswick Mall, W4 2PR. *Club* – Arts.

SON LIVING

PHILIP HENRY RATHBONE, *b* 13 Oct 1957; *ed* Eton, and Bristol Univ; late Welsh Guards: *m* 1987, Emma Charlotte, da of Capt Alexander Michael Darley Milne Home, RN (ret) (*see* E Minto, colls, 1970 Edn), of Sydney, Australia, and has issue living, Orlando James Rathbone, *b* 8 Oct 1994. *Residence* – 8 Herbert Crescent, SW1X 0EZ. *Clubs* – Cavalry and Guards', Special Forces.

DAUGHTER LIVING

Philippa Martha Gausel (*Hon Mrs Frederick C. A. Hamilton*), *b* 1955: *m* 1st, 1976 (*m diss* 1988), Brian James Douglas Collins (*see* E Morton); 2ndly, 1991, as his 2nd wife, Frederick Carmichael Arthur, Master of Belhaven, son of 13th Lord Belhaven and Stenton, and has issue, (by 1st *m*) (*see* E Morton), — (by 2nd *m*) (*see* L Belhaven and Stenton). *Address* – c/o Coutts & Co Ltd, 15 Lombard St, EC3.

COLLATERAL BRANCHES LIVING

Issue of late Dr Peter James Palmer Whitehead, PhD, yr (twin) son of 4th baronet, *b* 1930, *d* 1992: *m* 1st, 1953 (*m diss* 1960), Monica, who *d* 1969, only da of James O'Dwyer, of Tipperary; 2ndly, 1967, Greta Maureen Caecelia (Sud-de-Villiage, 65670 Monleon Magnoac, Hautes Pyrenées, France), da of late Capt Frederick John Ransom, of Greenwich:—
(By Mrs Mavis Argwings-Kodhek (*née* Tate), who *d* 1968, of Armagh, and Kenya) Paul James (51 Lydalls Rd, Didcot, Oxon), *b* 1961: *m* 1993, Anne-Marie Mulcahy, and has issue living, Thomas Harrison, *b* 1991. ——— Amanda Oonagh, *b* 1960: *m* 1987, Paul Lloyd Griffiths, of 22 Tavistock Av, Didcot, Berks, and has issue living, William Kai, *b* 1987, — Luke Aidan, *b* 1989. ——— (By 2nd *m*) †Peter Rathbone Palmer, *b* 1970, *d* 1998. ——— Victoria-Augusta Gordon Rathbone, *b* 1968.

Issue of late Lt-Col Gilbert Rathbone Whitehead, TD, yr son of 3rd baronet, *b* 1910, *d* 1968: *m* 1934, Adeline Joy, MA, only child of late Sydney F. Rumball, of St Leonards-on-Sea:—
Gilia Fleur (11 Fyfield Rd, Oxford), *b* 1936; MA Oxon, BSc London: *m* 1960 (*m diss* 1990), Martin Oliver Slocock, and has issue living, Oliver Rowland Benjamin, *b* 1964, — Thomas Gilbert, *b* 1969, — Eleanor Sophia *b* (twin), 1964: *m* 1997, Angus Edward Bailey, and has issue living, Honor Catherine Jeni *b* 1999. ——— Celia Lynette, *b* 1939: *m* 1970, Edward Raphael Rowe, of 23 Portsmouth Av, Thames Ditton, Surrey KT7 0RU, and has issue living, Russell Stephen, *b* 1978, — Anthea Rosalind, *b* 1976. ——— Anthea Margaret Joy, *b* 1943; MA Edinburgh: *m* 1972, John Valentine Hutchinson, of 2 The Green North, Warborough, Oxon.

Grandchildren of late Lt-Col Wilfred James Whitehead, DSO, 4th son of 1st baronet:—
Issue of late John Chase Whitehead, MBE, *b* 1913, *d* 1956: *m* 1941, Lorna Davey, who *d* 1974, da of Walter Rupert Belk:—
Carolyn, *b* 1946: *m* 1967, Patrick Geoghegan Smyth, BA, and has issue living, Dominic, *b* 1970, — Siobhan, *b* 1972, — Bridget, *b* 1974. ——— Saffron Ann, *b* 1948; BSc, PhD: *m* 1st, 1974 (*m diss* 1977), Christopher Robert Butler, BSc, PhD; 2ndly, 1978, John Kenneth Davies, BSc, of 265 Burntwood Lane, SW17 0AW, and has issue living (by 2nd *m*), Thomas John, *b* 1978, — Daniel Lloyd, *b* 1980, — Lewis Robert, *b* 1983. ——— Nicola Jane (265 The Parkway, Iver Heath, Bucks SL0 0RJ), *b* 1956; BSc, PhD, ARCS, DIC, CBiol, MIBiol. has issue (by Ian Stuart Thomas Fisher), Benjamin Alexander, *b* 1991, — Rebecca Emily, *b* 1990.

The 1st baronet, Sir James, was Lord Mayor of London 1888-9, and sat as MP for Leicester (*L*) 1892-4; his Baronetcy was conferred upon him "in recognition of highly valuable services during an eventful Mayoralty," in the course of which he was instrumental in settling the great Dock Strike. The 3rd baronet, Sir Rowland Edward, KC, sat as MP for Essex, S-E Div (*L*) 1906-10. Sir Philip Henry Rathbone Whitehead, 4th Bt, was Major Oxfordshire and Bucks LI, a Gov of Appleby Gram Sch, and a Trustee of Rowland Hill Benevolent Fund.

HUNTINGTON-WHITELEY (UK) 1918, of Grimley, Worcester

Sir HUGO BALDWIN HUNTINGTON-WHITELEY, 3rd *Baronet*; *b* 31 March 1924; *s* his father *Capt Sir* (HERBERT) MAURICE, RN, 1975; *ed* Eton; FCA; a DL of Worcs; High Sheriff 1971; 1939-45 War with RN (despatches); Prime Warden of Goldsmiths' Co 1989: *m* 1959, Jean Marie Ramsay, JP, DStJ, da of late Arthur Francis Ramsay Bock, and has two das.

Arms – 1st and 4th, per fesse dancette sable and gules in chief a pale or, thereon three bars of the second, in base a fleur-de-lis argent, *Whiteley;* 2nd and 3rd or, on a pale between two roses in fesse gules, barbed and seeded proper, a lion rampant between two water bougets of the first, *Huntington.* **Crests** – 1st, a stag's head couped argent, attired or, holding in the mouth a bell gold, *Whiteley;* 2nd, upon a mount vert a lion's head couped at the neck or, gorged with a collar vair between two roses gules, barbed, leaved and stalked proper, *Huntington*
Residences – Ripple Hall, Tewkesbury, Glos GL20 6EY; Balleure, 71240 Etrigny, France. **Club** – Brooks's.

DAUGHTERS LIVING

Sophie Elizabeth *b* 1964: *m* 1988, Dr Steven Michael Zdatny, eldest son of W. J. Zdatny, of Florida, USA, and has issue living, Samuel Oliver, *b* 1993, — Isabelle, *b* 1990. ——— Charlotte Anne, *b* 1965: *m* 1993, Andrew Philip McAuliffe, ACA, and has issue living, Jasper James, *b* 1996, — Matilda Kate, *b* 1994, — Daisy Sarah, *b* 1997.

BROTHER LIVING

(JOHN) MILES, VRD (6 Matheson Rd, W14 8SW), *b* 18 July 1929; *ed* Eton, and Trin Coll, Camb; Lt-Cdr RNR; VRD and two clasps: *m* 1960, HIIIH Countess Victoria Adelheid Clementine Luise, da of HIIIH late Count Friedrich Wolfgang zu Castell-Rüdenhausen (ROYAL FAMILY), and has issue living, Leopold Maurice, *b* 1965, — (Alice) Louise Esther Margot, *b* 1961: *m* 1985, (Charles) Percy Sewell (*see* Williams-Wynn, Bt, 1990 Edn), and has issue living, Henry Alexander *b* 1988, Benjamin Leopold *b* 1990, — Beatrice Irene Helen Victoria, *b* 1962: *m* 1995, Andrew William Grant, FRICS, son of late Francis Denis Grant, of Bransford Manor, Worcs, and has issue living, a son *b* 1999.

COLLATERAL BRANCH LIVING

Issue of late Eric Arthur Huntington-Whiteley, yr son of 1st baronet, *b* 1903, *d* 1972: *m* 1st, 1929 (*m diss* 1938), Enid Etta Cohn, who *d* 1983; 2ndly, 1938, Evelyn Mary, who *d* 1978, da of late Henry Munt, and formerly wife of Denis Clarke:—

(By 1st *m*) Nigel Charles (Highway, Cansiron Lane, Ashurst Wood, East Grinstead, W Sussex RH19 3SD), *b* 1931; *ed* Radley: *m* 1956, Gillian Margaret, da of late Jacob Franks, MRCS, LRCP, and has issue living, Charles Andrew (West Quither Farm, Milton Abbot, Tavistock, Devon PL19 0PZ), *b* 1957; FRICS: *m* 1981, Fiona Yvonne, da of Alan Jackson, of Somerton, Som, and has issue living, Toby Charles *b* 1989, Rosie Alice *b* 1987, Florence Amelia *b* 1992, — James Alexander, *b* 1963: *m* 1996, Magdalen L. C., elder da of Martin Evans, of London W11, and has issue living, William Joseph *b* 1997, — Kate Elizabeth, *b* 1959: *m* 1984, Peter Charles Lowry de Montfort, elder son of Charles Henry Cliffe de Montfort, of Skibbereen, co Cork, and has issue living, Guy Alexander *b* 1987, Charles Nicholas *b* 1989, Sean Thomas *b* 1994. —— Philip Cecil (Llangattock House, Penpergwm, Abergavenny, Gwent), *b* 1933; *ed* Radley: *m* 1968, Susan Laird, da of late Maj-Gen George Warren Richards, CB, CBE, DSO, MC, and has issue living, George Adam, *b* 1971, — Camilla Mary, *b* 1970.

The 1st baronet, Sir Herbert James Huntington-Whiteley (son of late George Whiteley, of Woodlands, Blackburn, and brother of 1st Baron Marchamley), was a JP for Lancs and Worcs (High Sheriff 1913), MP for Ashton-under-Lyne (*C*) 1895-1906, and for Mid, or Droitwich Div of Worcestershire 1916-18, and assumed by Roy licence 1918, for himself and issue, the additional surname and arms of Huntington. His wife, Florence Kate, who *d* 1948, was el da of William Balle Huntington, JP, DL, of Woodlands, Darwen, Lancs. The 2nd baronet, Sir Maurice, was a naval officer who served in both World Wars and was wounded at Jutland 1916. He was High Sheriff of Worcs 1968. He *m* 1919, Lady (Pamela) Margaret Baldwin, who *d* 1976, 3rd da of 1st Earl Baldwin of Bewdley.

WHITMORE (UK) 1954, of Orsett, co Essex

Sir JOHN HENRY DOUGLAS WHITMORE, 2nd *Baronet*; *b* 16 Oct 1937; *s* his father, *Col Sir* FRANCIS HENRY DOUGLAS CHARLTON, KCB, CMG, DSO, TD, TED, 1962; *ed* Eton; Sports Psychologist and currently Dep Dir of Centre for International Peacebuilding: *m* 1st, 1962 (*m diss* 1969), Ella Gunilla, el da of Sven A. Hansson, of Danderyd, Sweden; 2ndly, 1977, Diana Elaine, el da of Fred A. Becchetti, of California, USA, and has issue living by 1st and 2nd *m*.

Arms – Quarterly: 1st and 4th, vert, fretty or: 2nd and 3rd, vert, fretty and a canton or charged with a cinquefoil azure pierced of the second. **Crest** – 1st, a falcon sitting on the stump of a tree with a branch springing from the dexter side all proper; 2nd, an arm couped at the elbow erect and habited or, turned up azure, holding in the hand, proper a cinquefoil of the second pierced of the first, slipped vert, all within two wings expanded gold.
Residence – Southfield, Leigh, nr Tonbridge, Kent TN11 8PJ. *Club* – British Racing Drivers.

SON LIVING (*By 2nd marriage*)

JASON, *b* 26 Jan 1983.

DAUGHTER LIVING (*By 1st marriage*)

Tina, *b* 1966.

SISTER LIVING

Anne Catherine, *b* 1933: *m* 1966, Daniel Jose Emilio O'Connell (Presidente Roca 150, Adrogué, FCGR, Buenos Aires, Argentina), and has issue living, Lucy Elizabeth, *b* 1967, — Patricia Elena, *b* 1969, — Anna Elisa, *b* 1970.

MOTHER LIVING

Ellis Christense (*Ellis, Lady Whitmore*) (a DStJ), el da of Knud Christian Johnsen, of Bergen, Norway: *m* 1931, as his second wife, Col Sir Francis Henry Douglas Charlton Whitmore, KCB, CMG, DSO, TD, TED, 1st Bt, who *d* 1962.

Sir William Whitmore of London (descended from Whitmores of Claverley, Salop) purchased the estate of Apley, Salop and *d* 1648. His son, Sir Thomas Whitmore, was created a Bt 1641. This title became ext on the death of the 2nd Bt in 1699. The present baronet descends from Richard Whitmore of Lower Slaughter, Glos, brother of 1st Bt (*cr* 1641). Capt Thomas Charles Douglas Whitmore of Orsett Hall, Essex, father of 1st Bt (*cr* 1954), sold Apley in 1867.

WIGAN (UK) 1898, of Clare Lawn, Mortlake, Surrey, and Purland Chase, Ross, Herefordshire

Sir MICHAEL IAIN WIGAN, 6th *Baronet*; *b* 3 Oct 1951; *s* his father, *Capt Sir* ALAN LEWIS, 1996; *ed* Eton, and Exeter Coll, Oxford; *m* 1st, 1984 (*m diss* 1985), Frances, da of late Fl Lt Angus Barr Faucett, and of Mrs Anthony Reid, of Balnakilly, Kirkmichael, Perthshire; 2ndly, 1989, Julia Teresa, eldest da of John de Courcy Ling, CBE, of Lamb House, Bladon, Woodstock, Oxon, and has issue by 2nd *m*.

𝕬rms – Vair, on a pile or a mount in base vert, thereon a mountain ash tree proper. 𝕮rest – On a mount vert a mountain ash tree surmounted by a rainbow, all proper.
Residence – Borrobol, Kinbrace, Sutherland KW11 6UB.

SONS LIVING (*By 2nd marriage*)

FERGUS ADAM, *b* 30 April 1990. —— Thomas Iain, *b* 1993, — Finnbarr Frederick, *b* 1997.

DAUGHTER LIVING (*By 2nd marriage*)

Lilias Margaret, *b* 1992.

THE SIXTH BARONET ALSO HAS ISSUE (*By Lady Alexandra Hay, da of Diana Denyse, Countess of Erroll*)

Ivar Francis Grey de Miremont WIGAN, *b* 1979.

SISTER LIVING

Await the day

Rebecca, *b* 1953: *m* 1st, 1976 (*m diss* 1978), John Dominic Spearman (*see* Spearman, Bt, colls); 2ndly, 1980 (*m diss* 1986), James Alwyne Compton (*see* M Northampton, colls); 3rdly, 1991, Nicolas Pascal Camu (*see* Crossley, Bt, colls), and has issue (by 2nd *m*) (*see* M Northampton, colls), — (by 3rd *m*) (*see* Crossley, Bt, colls). *Residence* – 65 Finlay St, SW6.

WIDOW LIVING OF FIFTH BARONET

ROBINA (*Robina, Lady Wigan*), da of Lt-Col Sir Iain Colquhoun of Luss, 7th Bt, KT, DSO: *m* 1950, Capt Sir Alan Lewis Wigan, 5th Bt, who *d* 1996. *Residence* – Badingham House, Badingham, Woodbridge, Suffolk IP13 8JP.

COLLATERAL BRANCH LIVING

Grandchildren of late Denis Grey Wigan, 3rd son of 2nd baronet:—
Issue of late Maj Adair Michael Charles Wigan, Coldstream Gds Reserve of Officers, *b* 1916, *d* 1993: *m* 1939, Dawn (West Blagdon, Cranborne, Dorset), da of Charles Wilfred Gordon, of Boveridge Park, Cranborne, Salisbury:—
James Adair (Biddlesgate Farm, Cranborne, Dorset BH21 5RS; *Club* – White's), *b* 1950: *m* 1977 (*m diss* 1991), Rose Cecilia, elder da of John Johnston Kirkpatrick, FLAS, FRICS, of Horn Park, Beaminster, Dorset (*see* Loder, Bt, colls), and has issue living, Harry Edward, *b* 1986, — Thomas Adair, *b* 1986, — Emma Charlotte, *b* 1983. —— Dominic Richard Ludlow (Rose Cottage, Martin, Fordingbridge, Hants), *b* 1951: *m* 1989, Julia, only da of late Richard Russell, of Newnham Manor, Daventry, Northants, and has issue living, Anna Jessie, *b* 1991, — Nesta Megan, *b* 1995. —— Lola Dawn, *b* 1940. —— Camilla Rose, *b* 1944.

The 1st baronet, Sir Frederick Wigan, son of late John Alfred Wigan, of Clare House near Maidstone, a Director of North London Railway, and High Sheriff of cos London and Surrey 1894, *d* March 1907, and his son, Sir Frederick William, 2nd baronet, *d* in April of same year. Sir Alan Lewis, 5th baronet, was Capt KRRC (Reserve of Officers), served 1939-45 War (wounded, prisoner), and Dir Charrington & Co (Brewers).

WIGGIN (UK) 1892, of Metchley Grange, Harborne, Staffordshire

Sir CHARLES RUPERT JOHN WIGGIN, 5th *Baronet*; *b* 2 July 1949; *s* his father, *Sir* JOHN HENRY, MC, 1992; *ed* Eton; Maj Gren Guards: *m* 1979, Mrs Mary Burnett-Hitchcock, only da of Brig Samuel Craven Chambers, CBE, and has issue.

Arms – Gules, three mullets of six points argent, on a chief invected or two spurs sable. **Crest** – Over a fleur-de-lis sable, a spur or between two wings erect proper, each charged with a fleur-de-lis of the first.
Address – c/o Child & Co, 1 Fleet St, EC4Y 1BD.

SON LIVING

RICHARD EDWARD JOHN, *b* 1 July 1980.

DAUGHTER LIVING

Cecilia Charlotte, *b* 1984.

BROTHER LIVING

Benjamin Henry Edward, *b* 1951; *ed* Eton, and McGill Univ, Montreal.

HALF-BROTHERS LIVING

Daniel Mark, *b* 1964; *ed* Eton: *m* 1996, Simone Colleen, yr da of Malcolm Hooper, of Cornwall, and has issue living, Edward John James, *b* 1997. — Alice Charlotte Rose, *b* 1999. —— Jeremy James, *b* 1966; *ed* Milton Abbey.

WIDOW LIVING OF FOURTH BARONET

SARAH (*Sarah, Lady Wiggin*), da of Brig Stewart Arthur Forster, late Coldm Gds: *m* 1963, as his 2nd wife, Sir John Henry Wiggin, 4th Bt, MC, who *d* 1992. *Residence* – Honington Hall, Shipston-on-Stour, Warwickshire.

COLLATERAL BRANCHES LIVING

　　　　Grandchildren of late Alfred Harold Wiggin, 4th son of 1st baronet:—
　　Issue of late Col Sir William Henry Wiggin, KCB, DSO, TD, DL, JP, *b* 1888, *d* 1951: *m* 1935, Elizabeth Ethelston (Betty), who *d* 1959, da of late J. Danvers Power, MVO:—
Sir Alfred William (Jerry), TD, MP (The Court, Axbridge, Som; *Clubs* – Beefsteak, Pratt's, and R Yacht Squadron), *b* 1937; *ed* Eton, and Trin Coll, Camb; Maj The R Yeo (ret 1978); Hon Col "A" Sqdn (Warwickshire & Worcs Yeo), The Royal Mercian & Lancastrian Yeo, TA 1992; MP for Weston-super-Mare (*C*) 1969-97: *m* 1st, 1964 (*m diss* 1982), Rosemary Janet, only da of David L. D. Orr, of Keithley, Sandhills, Wormley, Surrey; 2ndly, 1991, Mrs Morella C. M. Bulmer (*née* Kearton), formerly wife of James Esmond Bulmer, of Poston, Herefords, and has issue living (by 1st *m*), William David, *b* 1966: *m* 1999, Camilla J., yst da of Donald Chilvers, of Brightwell Baldwin, Oxon, — Thomas Henry, *b* 1969, — Audrey Mary *b* 1974. —— Henry Walter (*Club* – Brooks's), *b* 1939; *ed* Eton, and Trin Coll, Camb (MA); Solicitor 1965: *m* 1st, 1962 (*m diss* 1978), Hon Julia Redmond Vaughan-Morgan, da of Baron Reigate (Life Baron): *m* 2ndly, 1978 (*m diss* 1985), Robin Margaret, da of A. Campbell B. Linwood, of Wanganui, NZ, and formerly wife of David Erskine Tolhurst; 3rdly, 1986 (*m diss* 1997), Mrs Diana Anstey, da of late Adm Sir Robin Leonard Francis Durnford-Slater, KCB, and formerly wife of Simon Anstey, of Toronto, Canada; 4thly, 1998, Pam J. Webster, of Anguilla, BWI, and has issue living, (by 1st *m*), Lucy Redmond, *b* 1965: *m* 1990, Joel Patrick Ford, of 7413 Drexelbrook Drive, Chesterfield, Va 23832, USA, son of Roy B. Ford, of San Antonio, Texas, — Caroline Julia, *b* 1970, — (by 2nd *m*), Jonathan Henry, *b* 1978.

　　　　Issue of late Lt-Col Richard Arthur Wiggin, TD, *b* 1903, *d* 1977: *m* 1952, Joan Mary, who *d* 1979, only da of late Smith Whitehead, of The Croft, Nelson:—
Margaret Joan, *b* 1954: *m* 1979, Christopher John Heath, 7 Bloomfield Terr, SW1W 8PG, and has issue living, William Henry Christopher, *b* 1983.

　　　　Grandchildren of late Lt-Col Peter Milner Wiggin (infra):—
　　Issue of late George David Henry Wiggin, *b* 1934, *d* 1990: *m* 1958, Jennifer (who was raised to the rank of a Viscount's da 1995, having *m* 2ndly, 1993, Charles Arthur Smith-Bingham), da of late Capt Ian Stanley Akers-Douglas (see V Chilston, colls):—
David Peter, *b* 1960; *ed* Harrow; Lieut The Royal Hussars: *m* 1991, Susan Emma, yst (twin) da of Maj Robert Philip Burrowes, of Dorrington Priory, nr Lincoln, and has issue living, George Robert, *b* 1994, — Nicholas Peter, *b* 1996. —— James George, *b* 1968; *ed* Eton; 2nd Lieut The Royal Hussars. —— Davina Jane, *b* 1962: *m* 1986, Michael Gatehouse, yr son of Capt Richard Gatehouse, DSC, RN (ret), of Easton Farm House, Newbury, Berks, and has issue living, James Richard, *b* 1987, — Sophie Charlotte, *b* 1989, — a da, *b* 1994.

　　　　Grandchildren of late Brig-Gen Edgar Askin Wiggin, DSO, 5th son of 1st baronet:—
　　Issue of late Lt-Col Peter Milner Wiggin, *b* 1907, *d* 1994: *m* 1933, Margaret Frances (Chapel Cottage, Plaistow Green, Headley, Newbury, Berks), da of late Capt Noel Christian Livingstone-Learmonth, of Cleveland House, 19 St James's Sq, SW:—
Michael Peter (Downton Hall, Ludlow, Shropshire), *b* 1937; *ed* Eton; late Lieut 11th Hussars: *m* 1962, Victoria Zara, da of late Malcolm Vaughan, of Old Westfield Farm House, Moreton Morrell, Warwicks, and has issue living, Mark David, *b*

1963; *ed* Eton: *m* 1991, Philippa A., da of David Burrows, of Tetbury, Glos, and has issue living, Max David Boughton *b* 1998, Tara Daisy *b* 1994, Camilla Victoria *b* 1995, — Rupert Michael, *b* 1969; *ed* Wellington, — Miranda Zara, *b* 1965: *m* 1990, Graham J. Walsh, of 456 Taconic Rd, Greenwich, Conn 06831, USA, son of Walter Walsh, of Barrow-in-Furness, Cumbria, and has issue living, Luke Walter *b* 1992, Zara Patricia *b* (twin) 1992, — Kate Victoria, *b* 1972: *m* 1998, Oliver James Spark, yst son of Peter Spark, of Chillesford, Suffolk. —— Sara Margaret (*Viscountess Allenby*), *b* 1942: *m* 1965, 3rd Viscount Allenby, and has issue (see that title).

The 1st baronet, Sir Henry Samuel, sat as MP for E Staffordshire (*L*) 1880-85, and for Staffordshire, Handworth Div (LU) 1885-92. Sir Henry Arthur, 2nd baronet, was High Sheriff of Staffs 1896, and Col Sir Charles Richard, 3rd baronet, was High Sheriff of Warwicks 1942.

WIGRAM (UK) 1805, of Walthamstow, Essex

Sweet is the love of one's country

Rev Canon Sir CLIFFORD WOOLMORE WIGRAM, 7th *Baronet*, son of late Robert Ainger Wigram, son of late Rev Woolmore Wigram, 5th son of Money Wigram, 2nd son of 1st baronet; *b* 24 Jan 1911; *s* his uncle, *Sir* EDGAR THOMAS AINGER, 1935; *ed* Winchester, and Trin Coll, Camb (BA 1932, MA 1936); formerly V of Marston St Lawrence, with Warkworth and Thenford, near Banbury; Non-Residentiary Canon of Peterborough Cathedral 1973-83 since when Canon Emeritus: *m* 1948, Christobel Joan, who *d* 1983, da of late William Winter Goode, of Curry Rivel, Somerset, and widow of Eric Llewellyn Marriott, CIE.

𝕬rms – Argent, on a pale gules three escallops or; over all a chevron engrailed counterchanged, and on the chief waves of the sea, thereon a ship representing an English vessel of war of the 16th century, with four masts, sails furled proper, colors flying gules. 𝕮rest – On a mount vert, a hand in armour in fesse couped at the wrist proper charged with an escallop holding a fleur-de-lis erect or. 𝕾upporters – On either side an eagle with wings elevated argent, collared gules and charged on the breast with a shamrock vert.
Residence – Flat 8, Emden House, Barton Lane, Headington, Oxford OX3 9JU.

BROTHER LIVING

EDWARD ROBERT WOOLMORE (1 Skipster Hagg Cottage, Sinnington, York YO62 6SP), *b* 19 July 1913: *ed* Winchester, and Trin Coll, Camb (BA 1934), sometime Major Indian Army; formerly a Master at Westminster Sch: *m* 1944, Viva Ann, who *d* 1997, da of late Douglas Bailey, of Laughton Lodge, nr Lewes, Sussex, and has issue living, Ann Catherine, *b* 1945: *m* 1973, Fredrik Procopé, and has issue living, Robert Hjalmar *b* 1974, Christopher Cresswell *b* 1976, Harry Michael *b* 1977.

COLLATERAL BRANCHES LIVING

Branch from 2nd son of 1st Baronet:—

Grandchildren of late Arthur Woolmore Wigram (infra):—
Issue of late Peter Woolmore Wigram, *b* 1913, *d* 1998: *m* 1st, 1936 (*m diss* 1953), Ellen Brenda, da of late William Hill, of Rockferry, Cheshire; 2ndly, 1953, Sylvia Mary (Red Lodge, 22 Chiltern Hills Rd, Beaconsfield, Bucks), da of late Rev John Smithson Barstow, of Woolsthorpe, by Belvoir:—
(By 2nd *m*) John Woolmore (11 Doneraile St, SW6 6EL), *b* 1957: *m* 1996, Sally J., only da of late Tom Winnington, of Abingdon, Oxon, and has issue living, James Woolmore, *b* 1997, — Harry Woolmore, *b* 1999. —— Caroline Judith, *b* 1955. —— Sylvia Clare, *b* 1963.

Granddaughter of late Rev Woolmore Wigram, 5th son of late Money Wigram (*b* 1790), 2nd son of 1st baronet:—
Issue of late Arthur Woolmore Wigram, *b* 1875, *d* 1946: *m* 1911, Avis Marion, who *d* 1972, da of late Hartley Hartley-Smith, of Upwey, Dorset:—
Daphne Marion Woolmore *b* 1919.

Grandson of late Robert Wigram, 6th son of late Money Wigram (*b* 1790) (ante):—
Issue of late Robert Wigram, *b* 1874, *d* 1932: *m* 1st, 1920, Adela Mabel, who *d* 1923, da of Richard Reid, of Bramcote, Weybridge; 2ndly, 1925, Winifred Maria, who *d* 1987, da of late Capt Phipps, 24th Regt:—
(By 2nd *m*) Francis John, *b* 1926; *ed* Eton. *Residence* – Cotters Barn, Penn, Bucks.

Branch from 5th son of 1st Baronet:—

Grandchildren of late Capt Ronald Scott Jervoise Wigram, DSO, RN, son of Henry James Wigram (infra):—
Issue of late Maj Henry Frederick James Wigram, DCLI, *b* 1916, *d* (Dec) 1984: *m* 1938, (Helen) Enid, who *d* (Oct) 1984, da of F. Clyde Smith, of Netherclay House, Bishop's Hull, Somerset:—
Roger Charles Kinglake (15 Redwood Drive, Bradley, Huddersfield, W Yorks HD2 1PW), *b* 1940; *ed* Wellington Coll; Capt Light Inf (ret): *m* 1965 (*m diss* 1982), Wendy Joan, who *d* 1985, eldest da of late Brig Philip Herbert Richardson, DSO, OBE, of The Manor House, Merriott, Som; 2ndly, 1983, Christine, da of late James Kenneth Pratt, and has issue living (by 1st *m*), Giselle Rose, *b* 1966, — Susanna Nicola, *b* 1968. —— James Somerset (Rockall, 3 Rendells Meadow, Bovey Tracey, Devon TQ13 8QW), *b* 1950; *ed* Nautical Coll, Pangbourne: *m* 1974, Susan Jane, only da of Bryan Braithwaite-Exley, of Pant Head, Austwick, Yorks, and has issue living, Thomas Peter James, *b* 1978, — William Henry James, *b* 1981, — Tessa Vera Joyce, *b* 1988. —— Sally Kinglake, *b* 1939: *m* 1st, 1972 (*m diss* 1982), William Arthur Rose, who *d* 1987; 2ndly, 1989, Anthony Robin Atton, of 581 Doyle Rd, RR #3, Victoria, BC, Canada V8X 3X1, and has issue living (by 1st *m*), Alan Kindred, *b* 1972. —— (Janet) Gail, *b* 1953: *m* 1975, Timothy Wallace Kyle, Lt RN (ret), of Zirlden, 51 Broomleaf Rd, Farnham, Surrey GU9 8DQ, and has issue living, Robert Henry Remington, *b* 1986, — Laura Rachel, *b* 1977, — Thea Helen, *b* 1981.

Granddaughter of late Henry James Wigram, el son of James Richard Wigram, el son of Rt Hon Sir James Wigram, 5th son of 1st baronet:—
Issue of late Major Cyril Charles Wigram, *b* 1882, *d* 1952: *m* 1st, 1912 (*m diss* 1917), Mabel Adams; 2ndly, 1918 (*m diss* 1928), Olivia Marie, who *d* 1970, da of late Maj-Gen W. Truman, of Winterbourne, Bonchurch, I of Wight; 3rdly, 1929, Mrs Dorothy Scott, who *d* 1938; 4thly, 1946, Elizabeth, who *d* 1970, da of late Dr F. E. Sondern, of New York, and widow of J. W. New:—
(By 2nd *m*) Isolde Marianne, *b* 1919. *Residence* – Greathed Manor, Lingfield, Surrey RH7 6PA.

Branch from 6th son of 1st Baronet:—

Grandchildren of late Charles Knox Wigram (infra):—
Issue of late Maj James Robert Knox Wigram, *b* 1915, *d* 1984: *m* 1942, Beatrice Elizabeth, who *d* 1984, da of late Rev W. A. Sandford, of Dunstable, Beds:—
Brian Arthur Knox (1 Chevin Bank, Hazlewood Rd, Duffield, Derby DE6 4AA), *b* 1947; *ed* Wellington: *m* 1982, Glynnis Anne, da of Maurice Owens, of Kilburn, Derbyshire. —— Michele Anne, *b* 1946; BA (Hons) Reading.

Grandchildren of late William Arthur Wigram, grandson of Octavius Wigram, 6th son of 1st baronet:—
Issue of late Charles Knox Wigram, *b* 1889, *d* 1966: *m* 1st, 1914, Gladys Mary (who *d* 1955, (*m diss* 1931)), da of late Rev Robert Edward Baynes (Preb of Combe); 2ndly, 1931, Margaret Esther, who *d* 1974, da of late Capt Henry Valentine Simpson, CMG, RN (ret):—
(By 1st *m*) Valentine Knox (c/o Barclays Bank, Horsham, Sussex), *b* 1920; *ed* Haileybury; late Cpl RAF; ARICS. —— (By 2nd *m*) Susan Alice Ann, *b* 1932; *ed* London Univ (BA): *m* 1965, Colin Scorer, of 11 Stuart Grove, Teddington, Middx TW11 8RR, and has an adopted son and an adopted da, Andrew Michael, *b* 1968, — Jane Sarah, *b* 1971. —— Jennifer Jane (3022 Linda Vista, Alameda, CA 94502, USA), *b* 1935: *m* 1967, Allen Griswold, who *d* 1998.

Grandchildren (by 2nd *m*) of late Charles Knox Wigram (ante):—
Issue of late Patrick Knox Wigram, *b* 1937, *d* 1992: *m* 1964, Susan Mary Fyers (Peterport, Lavender Rd, Maybury, Woking, Surrey), da of Col A.R.F. Martin, of Camberley, Surrey:—
Charles Robert Knox, *b* 1968. —— Sandra Jane Fyers, *b* 1965. —— Julia Margaret Fyers, 1967.

Branch from 8th son of 1st Baronet:—

Grandchildren of late Gerrard Andrewes Wigram, 2nd son of Rt Rev Joseph Cotton Wigram, DD, Bishop of Rochester, 8th son of 1st baronet:—
Issue of late Rev Gerrard Edmund Wigram, *b* 1877, *d* 1947: *m* 1902, Maria Ismèna, who *d* 1944, 2nd da of late William Townson-Mayne:—
Francis Gerrard Mayne, *b* 1905; formerly Regional Officer, Coal Utilization Council, and an Asso Member of Institute of Fuel: *m* 1934, Helen Frances, who *d* 1990, younger da of late Dr Sidney Worthington, of Warwick, and has issue living, Gerrard Charles (Lenana, 25 Duckitt Av, Constantia 7800, S Africa), *b* 1936; FCA, and a CA, S Africa: *m* 1965, Joan Patricia, da of late James Lang, of Nairobi, and has issue living, Keith Gerrard *b* 1969, Zena Patricia Jean *b* 1966, Eileen Frances *b* 1972, — Nigel Francis (8 Heseldon Av, Rondesboch, Cape Town, S Africa), *b* 1939; CCS, BCom, MBA, PhD: *m* 1974, Lynette Monique, da of Dr Leon Stern, of Kenilworth, Cape Town, and has issue living, Andrew David *b* 1976, — Deborah Helen, *b* 1938: *m* 1961, Capt Richard Hugh Farnfield, RN, of The Rydings, Park Rd, Forest Row, Sussex RH18 5BX, and has issue living, Anthony Gilbert *b* 1963, Andrew Richard *b* 1970: *m* 1999, Tracey Amanda, da of Brian Freeman, of Perth, Western Australia, Timothy Francis *b* 1971: *m* 1993, Belinda Alice Irene, da of Oliver Preston Benn (*see* Benn, *cr* 1914, colls), Helen Rosemary *b* 1965: *m* 1993, Mark Jeremy Moore-Gillon, MA, PhD, son of J. A. Moore-Gillon, of Surbiton (and has issue living, Charles William *b* 1996, James Robert *b* 1998, Katherine Lucy *b* 1997). *Residence* – 132 Bridgewater Manor, Somerset West 7130, Cape Province, S Africa. —— Marion Rochford (Quarndon Hill, 78 The Common, Quarndon, Derbys DE6 4JY), *b* 1909: *m* 1930, William Hadden Richardson, who *d* 1968, and has issue living, James Hadden (Fern Hill, Quarndon, Derbys), *b* 1937: *m* 1961, Susan Mary, only da of J. H. K. Thomson, of Derby, and has issue living, Nicholas Hadden *b* 1963: *m* 1991, Lynn Clements (and has issue living, Katherine Jane *b* 1992, Susannah Mary *b* 1994), Timothy James Keith *b* 1970, Wendy Diana *b* 1965, — Judith Mary (Flat 4B, The Lillies, Windley, Derbys DE6 2LQ), *b* 1934: *m* 1963, John Swain Yeomans, and has issue living, Philip Hadden *b* 1964: *m* 1990, Louise Dale (and has issue living, Bethany Angela *b* 1991, Charlotte Rowena *b* 1993).

Branch from 11th son of 1st Baronet:—

Grandchildren of late Rev Edmund Francis Edward Wigram, son of late Rev Frederic Edward Wigram, el son of late Edward Wigram, 11th son of 1st baronet:—
Issue of late Rev Oswald Thomas Edward Wigram, b 1905, d 1990: m 1935, Margaret (Scotleigh Lodge, 76 Old Exeter St, Chudleigh, Devon TQ13 OJX), da of late R.N. Barnes, of Sutton Coldfield:—
Robert Edmund (93 Investigator St, Red Hill, ACT, Australia), b 1936: m 1963, Patricia, da of L.C. Collisson, of Liverpool, NSW, and has issue living, Simon Andrew, b 1967: m 1987, Caroline Threlfall, — Christopher Anthony, b 1977, — Frances Elizabeth, b 1964, — Louise Annette, b 1966: m 1987, Anthony Fryer, and has issue living, Amy Louise b 1994, Ashley-Jane b 1997. ——Paul Frederic (PO Box 10, Limuru, Kenya), b 1937; ed Marlborough, and Pembroke Coll, Camb (MA): m 1963, Christian Virginia, (da of Maj H.A.R. Bucknall, MC, and has issue living, Thomas Paul Henry, b 1964, — Lucy Helen Gabrielle, b 1966, — Bronwen Serena Christian, b 1971. ——Rev Andrew Oswald (The Vicarage, 2 Dobbin Close, Cropwell Bishop, Nottingham NG12 3GR), b 1939; ed Marlborough; BD London: m 1964, Catharine, da of late Rev Canon Geoffrey Rogers, of 37 Bradford Park, Foxhill, Combe Down, Bath, and has issue iving, John Michael, b 1967: m 1989, Rachel, da of Rev Guy Chapman, and has issue living, David James b 1991, Peter Jonathan b 1996, Hannah Catharine b 1992, — Susanna Dora, b 1966: m 1998, Stener Richard Vogt, of Vendla 55C, 1315 Nesøya, Norway, — Margaret Jane Majala, b 1970. ——Francis Aidan (Riggles Farm, Upottery, Honiton, Devon), b 1949; ed Marlborough, and Seale Hayne Agric Coll: m 1973 (m diss 1995), Christine Susan, da of late T.E. Abbey, of Tilney, Sellicks Green, Taunton, and has issue living, Timothy Francis, b 1974, — Richard James, b 1976, — Nicholas Mark, b 1977. ——Rev Ruth Margaret (The Vicarage, St Paul's Drive, Brompton-on-Swale, Richmond, N Yorks DL10 7HQ), b 1941; ed St Michael's, Limpsfield, and Salisbury Training Coll.

Issue of late Lieut Aidan Frederic Wigram, RNVR, b 1907, k on air operations 1941: m 1938, Marjorie Joyce, who d 1963, da of late Lt-Col E. R. I. Chitty, Indian Army:—
Aidan David (High Timbers, Hartley Rd, Cranbrook, Kent, TN17 3QX), b 1938; ed Marlborough, and Univ of Wales (BSc): m 1968, Jeniffer Ann, da of E. N. Firmager, of Godstone, Surrey, and has issue living, Lesley Rosalind, b 1969.

Issue of late Edmund Hugh Lewis Wigram, MB, BCh, b 1911, d 1945: m 1938, Kathleen Maud (who d 1998, having m 2ndly, 1948 (m diss 1968)), Christopher Henry Kaye, BM, BCh (Wigram Bt, colls), yr da of late L. C. S. Hallam, of Port Arthur, Canada:—
Peter Hallam (PO Box 1557, Banff, Alberta, Canada T0L 0C0), b 1939: m 19— (m diss 19—), Michelle —. ——Edmund William (Boghouse, Blagdon, Seaton Burn, Newcastle-upon-Tyne NE13 6DB), b 1942: m 1965, Diana Frances, da of Anthony Douglas Bell, MB, BS, of Sanday Is, via Kirkwall, Orkney, and has issue living, Anthony Christopher b 1966, — Clare Frances b 1969.

Grandchildren of late Rev Beresford Edward Wigram, 2nd son of late Rev Frederic Edward Wigram (ante):—
Issue of late Rev Marcus Walter Wigram, b 1917, d 1989: m 1941, Christina Cantrell (19 Capel Court, Prestbury, Glos GL52 3EL):—
Ann Margaret Joyce (10 Cairncross St, St Ives, Cornwall), b 1942: m 1964 (m diss 1998), Derek William Blandford, and has issue living, Andrew Paul, b 1966, — Ian Keith, b 1969, — Kieron John, b 1971. ——Carol Frances Violet WIGRAM (1B Cross St, Old Town, Swindon, Wilts SW1 3JT), b 1946; resumed her maiden name: m 1976 (m diss 1994), Peter Guilderoy Croskin, and has issue living, Jonathan Guilderoy, b 1978. ——Sarah Christina Agnes, b 1949: m 1970, Humphrey David Lane, of Huckstones, Cottons Lane, Ashton-under-Hill, Evesham, Worcs, and has issue living, Bridget Anna, b 1972, — Corinne Victoria, b 1974, — Kathryn Alice, b 1978. ——Jane Eleanor Bridget, b 1954: m 1st, 1971 (m diss 1986), Mark Christian Eckersley; 2ndly, 1988, Kenneth William Augustus Robeson, of 288 Woodend Rd, Frampton Cotterell, Glos BS17 2JE, and has issue living (by 1st m), Naomi Jane, b 1974, — Samantha Claire, b 1979.

Grandchildren of late Rev Frederic Edward Wigram (ante):—
Issue of late Rev Harold Frederic Edward Wigram, b 1873, d 1946: m 1913, Gladys Christine, who d 1985 (aged 100), da of Sir Howard Warburton Elphinstone, 3rd Bt:—
Andrew Harold (17 Albury Rd, Newcastle-upon-Tyne, NE2 3PE), b 1919; ed Wellington Coll, and Trin Hall, Camb (BA); Maj RA (ret): m 1953, Alice Jefferson Trewhitt, who d 1989. ——Alexander Robert, b 1925; ed Wellington Coll, and Brasenose Coll, Oxford (MA): m 1958, Virginia Claire, da of late Group Capt Philip Patrick Strachan Rickard, OBE, and has issue living, Kester Jonathan, b 1959; ed Univ of Canterbury, NZ (BE Chem); C Eng, I Chem E: m 1983 (m diss 1989), Lynn, da of James Davidson, and has issue living, Elliot Simon b 1984, — Nicholas Simon, b 1960, — Luke, b 1977, — Sarah Christine, b 1963, — Aroha Kirsty, b 1975. Address – Le Bons Bay, Rural Delivery, Akaroa, Banks Peninsula, NZ. ——Gladys Veronica (The Old Vicarage, Moulsford, nr Wallingford, Oxon OX10 9JB), b 1916: m 1st, 1938, Lt William George Player Brigstocke, RNVR (ka 1940); 2ndly, 1943, Reginald Charles Grisedale Fennell, who d 1994, and has issue living (by 2nd m), Robert John (Kilve House, 315 Andover Rd, Newbury, Berks RG15 0WY), b 1944; ARICS (1970); ed Oundle: m 1975, Phoebe Joscelyn, da of Gordon Wilfred Langley-Smith, of 19 Kenilworth Av, Gloucester, and has issue living, Thomas Edward b 1979, Anthea Sarah b 1977, Megan b 1986, — William Richard Kenneth (22 Place Farm Way, Monks Risborough, Bucks HP17 9JH), b 1952; ARICS (1977); ed Oundle, and Birmingham Univ (BSc): m 1979, Sylvia Mary, da of Wilfred Fletcher, and has issue living, Margaret Ann b 1983. ——Rose Eleanor, b 1923: m 1954, Richard Edward Barry, of 37 Bennells Av, Tankerton, Whistable, Kent CT5 2HL, and has issue living, John Andrew, b 1958: m 1982 (m diss 1998), Marion, da of late Julian Warwick, and has issue living, Alistair James b 1988, Elaine Christine b 1990, — Sylvia May, b 1956; BA: m 1976, Kim Marsh, of 127 Dene Rd, Wylam, Northumberland NE41 8EZ, and has issue living, Philip Robert b 1977.

Issue of late Loftus Edward Wigram, MB, b 1877, d 1963: m 1912, Constance Emma Letitia, who d 1970, da of late Rev William Gilbert Edwards, Surrogate of Oxford, and Hon Canon, formerly R of Great Haseley, Wallingford, Oxon, and Rural Dean of Cuddesdon:—
Gerald Frederic (Little Water Park, Furze, Chittlehampton, Umberleigh, Devon EX37 0RL), b 1016; ed Marlborough; formerly Capt King's African Rifles: m 1948, Anne Christal, who d 1981, da of late Brig-Gen Hon Lesley James Probyn Butler, CMG, DSO (see B Dunboyne, colls), and has issue living, Carolyn Lesley, b 1950: m 1986, John Eastman Perry, and has issue living, Mark Andrew b 1987, Ben Jack b 1988, — Marylee Anne, b 1952: m 1997, Maj K. P. Mark Ravnkilde, Royal Scots Dragoon Gds, — Bridget Margaret, b 1954: m 1982, Jonathan Patrick Simmons, and has issue living, Michael Anthony b 1987, Anne Julia b 1985. ——Lettice Margaret, b 1920; ed Oxford Univ (BA 1942); formerly Section Officer WAAF: m 1951, Maj Edward Arthur Hadow, late RE, of 2 Highlands Park, Chudleigh, Devon TQ13 0JZ (M Anglesey, colls), and has issue living, John Wigram, b 1959: m 1988, Susan Frances, yr da of F.W. Naylor, of Totnes, Devon, and has issue living, George Louis b 1992, Patrick William b 1994, Angus John b 1997, — Robert Edward, b 1968, — Rosemary Maude, b 1953: m 1st, 1974 (m diss 1988), David Ericson; 2ndly, 1989, Graham John White, and has issue living, (by 1st m) Daniel Dov b 1985, (by 2nd m) Rebecca Hadow b 1991, — Juliet Letitia, b 1955: m 1979, Graham

Paul Herbert, and has issue living, Mark Graham *b* 1985, Emma Letitia *b* 1983, Rosanna Bethan *b* 1987, — Celia Catherine, *b* 1957: *m* 1984, Ian Cranston Shields, and has issue living, Joe *b* 1988, Kerry Mohira *b* 1985.

Granddaughter of late Rev Beresford Edward Wigram (ante):—
Issue of late Capt Winstone Beresford Wigram, *b* 1908, *d* 1988: *m* 1942, Adelaide Joyce (Dair), who *d* 1966, elder da of Rev William Aldworth Ferguson, DD:—
Erica Joyce, *b* 1943; BA Bristol: *m* 1970, Maj Ian Ferguson Sharp, RAOC, and has issue living, Jasper Henry Ferguson, *b* 1971, — Daniel William, *b* 1973. *Address* – PO Box 14748, Nairobi, Kenya.

Granddaughters of late Loftus Edward Wigram MB (ante):—
Issue of late Michael Wigram, MRCS, LRCP, *b* 1919, *d* 1973: *m* 1945, Margaret Edith Ann (Crickerton, Buckfastleigh, S Devon), da of late W. E. Watson-Baker, of Toddington, Beds:—
Laurette (Wateroak, Ludgores Lane, Danbury, Chelmsford, Essex), *b* 1946: *m* 1971, Brian Guest, who *d* 1998, and has issue living, William Michael, *b* 1974, — Josephine Briony, *b* 1972. —— Sarah Margaret, *b* 1949: *m* 1973 (*m diss* 19—), Timothy Veise, of Rectortown, Virginia, USA, and has issue living, Katherine Anne Bovington, *b* 1975, — Emily Sarah, *b* 1978. —— Jennifer Rose, *b* 1953: *m* 1974, Robert Lawson-Peebles, PhD.

Branch from 14th and yst son of 1st Baronet:—

Grandson of late Herbert Wigram, 2nd son of Rev William Pitt Wigram (infra):—
Issue of late Rt Hon Sir Clive (*Baron Wigram*) GCB, GCVO, CSI, PC *cr Baron Wigram* 1935 (see that title).

Grandchildren of late Roland Lewis Wigram, elder son of late Lewis Wigram (infra):—
Issue of late Derek Roland Wigram, *b* 1908, *d* 1996: *m* 1944, Catharine Mary, who *d* 1997, da of late Very Rev William Ralph Inge, KCVO, DD:—
Richard Inge (Woodlynch, Branksomewood Rd, Fleet, Hants GU13 8JS), *b* 1944; *ed* Marlborough, and Royal Coll of Art (MDes); Senior Ptnr Wigram Tivendale Associates: *m* 1971, Angela Patricia, who *d* 1995, da of Capt M. D. Rahilly, RN, of 2 Great Orchard, Upper Westwood, Bradford on Avon, and has issue living, David Roland, *b* 1976, — Helen Marguerite, *b* 1974. —— Janet Catharine Inge, *b* 1948: *m* 1975, Nicholas Charles Miller, MA, MSc, of The Old Schoolhouse, The Common, Swordeston, Norwich NR14 8EB, and has issue living, Lydia Catharine, *b* 1980, — Emily Joy, *b* 1984.

Issue of late Mervyn Roland Wigram, *b* 1916, *d* 1994: *m* 1947, Beryl Margaret (27 Glasshouse Lane, Kenilworth, Warwicks CV8 2AH), yr da of Howard Morriss, of Gladeside, Letchworth:—
Christopher Edward Mervyn (28 The Drive, Sevenoaks, Kent TN13 3AE), *b* 1954; *ed* Monkton Combe Sch: *m* 1982, Susanne Ruth, da of Paul Johannes Schnabel, of Grossbottwar, Germany, and has issue living, Michael Luke, *b* 1986, — Jessica Jade, *b* 1983, — Stephanie Rachel, *b* 1989. —— Rowena Margaret, *b* 1949: *m* 1978, Francisco Muñoz Ramirez, of Federico Garcia Lorca 4, 18198-Cajar, Granada, Spain. —— Diana Catharine, *b* 1956: *m* 1991, Paul Francis McGuire, and has issue living, Kate Danielle *b* 1996, Naomi Roe *b* 1999.

Granddaughter of late Lewis Wigram, yst son of Rev William Pitt Wigram, 14th and yst son of 1st baronet:—
Issue of late Oswald Lewis Wigram, *b* 1878, *d* 1960: *m* 1914, Lucy Clare Elaine, who *d* 1962, da of the Rev Thomas Wilkinson Stephenson, V of Addingham, Penrith, and Hon Canon of Carlisle:—
Margaret Elaine, *b* 1921. *Residence* – Holme Lea, Armathwaite, Carlisle.

Grandchildren of late Oswald Lewis Wigram (ante):—
Issue of late Maj Michael Lewis Wigram, RA, *b* 1918; *d* 1983: *m* 1950, Dorothea Mary, who *d* 1964, el da of late Yorke Wood, of The Braye, Georgeham, N Devon:—
Anthony Lewis (18 Spencer Gate, St Albans, Herts), *b* 1953; *ed* St Lawrence Coll, Ramsgate: *m* 1976, Jennifer Hilary, da of Albert Thom, of 43 The Grove, Brookmans Park, Herts, and has issue living, Robert Alexander Lewis, *b* 1981, — Michael Anthony Yorke, *b* 1983, — David Arthur Kennedy, *b* 1986. —— Mary Elaine, *b* 1951: *m* 1977, Anthony Laurence Tucker, of 50 Woodcote Rd, Caversham, Reading RG4 7BB, and has issue living, John Michael, *b* 1982, — Mark Andrew Laurence, *b* 1987, — Sarah Frances, *b* 1979.

The 1st baronet, Sir Robert Wigram, successively MP for Fowey and co Wexford, obtained eminence as a merchant; he died 1830, having had twenty-three children. The 2nd baronet, MP for Fowey, in 1832 changed, by Roy licence, his surname to FitzWygram. Lieut-Gen Sir Frederick FitzWygram, 4th Bt, sat as MP for Hampshire S. (C) 1884-5, and for Hampshire S, or Fareham, Div 1885-1900, and Major Sir Frederick Loftus Francis FitzWygram, MC, 5th Bt, was taken prisoner and twice wounded during European War 1914-19 (despatches, prisoner when severely wounded; *d* from effects of captivity).

BAKER WILBRAHAM (GB) 1776, of Loventor, co Devon
(Name pronounced "Baker Wilbrum")

Rest in the haven

Sir RICHARD BAKER WILBRAHAM, 8th *Baronet*; *b* 5 Feb 1934; *s* his father, *Sir* RANDLE JOHN, 1980; *ed* Harrow; Lt Welsh Guards 1952-54; High Sheriff Cheshire 1991, DL 1992; Dir of J. Henry Schroder Wagg & Co Ltd 1969-89, a Trustee of Grosvenor Estate 1981-99, a Gov of Harrow Sch 1982-92, Dir Christie Hosp NHS Trust 1990-96; Chm Bibby Line Group Ltd 1992-97, Dep Chm Brixton Estate plc since 1994 (Dir since 1985), Dir Majedie Investments plc since 1989; Govr Nuffield Hospitals since 1990; a Church Commissioner since 1994; Renter Bailiff, Worshipful Co of Weavers 1993-94 and Upper Bailiff 1994-95; Trustee, Dyson Perrins Museum of Worcester Porcelain 1993-99; Govr The Manchester Metropolitan Univ since 1998; Govr The King's Sch, Macclesfield since 1986; Member of Gen Council of King Edward's Hospital Fund for London 1986-98: *m* 1962, Anne Christine Peto, da of late Charles Peto Bennett, OBE, of La Haute, Fliquet, Jersey, and has issue.

𝕬rms – Quarterly, 1st and 4th argent, three bends wavy azure, *Wilbraham*; 2nd and 3rd, per pale argent and, or on a saltire nebuly sable five escallops of the first, on a chief of the third a lion passant of the second, *Baker*. 𝕮rests – 1st, a wolf's head erased argent, *Wilbraham*; 2nd, a dexter arm embowed, vested azure, charged with three annulets interlaced or, cuffed argent, holding in the hand proper an arrow of the last, *Baker*.

Residence – Rode Hall, Scholar Green, Cheshire ST7 3QP.

SON LIVING

RANDLE, *b* 28 May 1963, *ed* Harrow: *m* 1997, Amanda, eldest da of Robert Glossop, of Dogmersfield, Hants.

DAUGHTERS LIVING

Sibella Caroline, *b* 1965: *m* 1994, Timothy Makower, and has issue (*see* V Chetwynd, colls). —— Charlotte Cecilia Anne, *b* 1968. —— Alice Maria Elisabeth, *b* 1971.

SISTER LIVING

Letitia Ann, *b* 1931: *m* 1960, Timothy George Kirkbride, of Little Hill Farm, Buckland St Mary, nr Chard, Som TA20 3SS, and has issue living, George Edward, *b* 1967, — Harriet Ann, *b* 1964: *m* 1993, Anthony Leonard Clinton Bloomer (*see* B Vivian, colls), and has issue (see that title).

The 5th baronet, Sir George Barrington Baker, assumed by Royal licence 1900 the additional surname of Wilbraham, having *m* Katharine Frances, who *d* 1945, da and heir of Gen Sir Richard Wilbraham, KCB, of Rode Hall, nephew of 1st Baron Skelmersdale. The 6th baronet, Sir Philip Wilbraham Baker Wilbraham, KBE, DCL, was Sec, National Assembly of Church of England 1920-39, First Church Estates Commr 1939-54, Chancellor of Dioceses of Chester, York, Truro, Chelmsford and Durham, and Vicar-Gen of Province of York 1915-34, and of Province of Canterbury (and Dean of the Arches) 1934-55.

WILKINSON (UK) 1941, of Brook, Witley, co Surrey

Sir (DAVID) GRAHAM BROOK WILKINSON, 3rd *Baronet*; *b* 18 May 1947; *s* his father, *Sir* (LEONARD) DAVID, DSC, 1972; *ed* Millfield, and Ch Ch, Oxford; CStJ: *m* 1st, 1977 (*m diss* 1996), Sandra Caroline, da of Dr Richard Rossdale; 2ndly, 1998, Mrs Hilary Jane Griggs, da of late William H. C. Bailey, CBE, and has issue by 1st *m*.

Arms – Quarterly, argent and vair sable and or, a cross gules, in the 1st and 4th quarters a lion rampant of the fourth on a chief also of the fourth three mullets of the third. Crest – Issuant from a chaplet of roses argent barbed and seeded proper a demi-unicorn or.
Clubs – Royal Yacht Sqdn, White's.

DAUGHTERS LIVING (*By 1st marriage*)

Louise Caroline Sylvia, *b* 1979. ——— Tara Katherine Juliet, *b* 1982.

SISTER LIVING

Sylvia Davinia Gay, *b* 1948: *m* 1978, Peter Martin Gort Beaufort Grimaldi, FRCS, 16th Marquis Grimaldi, of Tyne Hall, Bembridge, IoW PO35 5NH (only son of Philip R. B. Grimaldi, 15th Marquis, who *d* 1983), and has issue living, Alicia Anne Davinia, *b* 1979, — Carina Rose Anne, *b* 1981, — Sophia Anne Camilla, *b* 1987.

AUNT LIVING (*Daughter of 1st baronet*)

Eileen, *b* 1916: *m* 1941, John MacNaughton Sidey, DSO, who *d* 1990, son of late John Sidey, and has issue living, Ian MacNaughton (69 Windrow Lane, New Canaan, CT 06840, USA), *b* 1947: *m* 1970, Christina Willing Ashdown, and has issue living, James MacNaughton *b* 1975, Guy Xavier *b* 1979. *Residence* – 50 Ledge Rd, #237, Darien, CT 06820, USA.

MOTHER LIVING

Sylvia Ruby Eva Anne (*Sylvia, Lady Wilkinson*), only da of late Prof Bosley Alan Rex Gater, of Grahamstown, S Africa; DStJ: *m* 1946 (*m diss* 1967), Sir (Leonard) David Wilkinson, DSC, 2nd Bt, who *d* 1972.
Sir George Henry Wilkinson, KCVO, 1st Bt, was Lord Mayor of London 1940-41.

WILLIAMS (GB) 1798, of Bodelwyddan, Flintshire

Strong and crafty

Sir LAWRENCE HUGH WILLIAMS, 9th *Baronet*; *b* 25 Aug 1929; *s* his half-brother, *Sir* FRANCIS JOHN WATKIN, 1995; *ed* RNC Dartmouth; Capt RM (ret); High Sheriff Anglesey 1970: *m* 1952, Sara Margaret Helen, 3rd da of Sir Harry Platt, 1st Bt, MD, MS, FRCS, and has issue.

Arms – Argent, two foxes counter-salient in saltire the sinister surmounted of the dexter gules, a crescent for difference.
Residence – Parciau, Marianglas, Anglesey LL73 8PH.

DAUGHTERS LIVING

Emma Louise (*Hon Mrs Charles A. A. Harbord-Hamond*), *b* 1961; BA, ACII: *m* 1st, 1988 (*m diss* 1998), Radcliffe Percy Royds; 2ndly, 1999, Hon Charles Anthony Assheton Harbord-Hamond, eldest son of 11th Baron Suffield, MC, and has issue living (by 1st *m*), Harry Lawrence Percy, *b* 1991, — Jack Michael William, *b* 1992, — Mollie Isabella Rose, *b* 1995. *Residence* – 4 Lysias Rd, SW12 8BP.
——— Antonia Margaret, *b* 1963: *m* 1998, Antonin Leif Peter Markutza.

HALF-SISTER LIVING

Violet Kathleen Mary, *b* 1902: *m* 1926, Thomas Arthur Pearson, late Lieut-Cdr RNVR, who *d* 1974, and has issue living, David Arthur (Banastre Cottage, Parkgate, South Wirral, Ches L64 4RW), *b* 1931: *m* 1st, 1960 (*m diss* 1977), Carolyn Frances, el da of F. H. Minoprio, of Hessle Well House, Heswall, Merseyside; 2ndly, 1981, Gillian Mary, da of G. Buckley, of Badgers, Paddock Dr, Parkgate, South Wirral, Ches, and has issue living (by 1st *m*), Charles David *b* 1961:

m 1989, Zoë Louise Hancox (and has issue living, Benjamin Michael *b* 1996, Oliver David *b* 1999), Joanna Mary *b* 1963: *m* 1996, Timothy Squice-Sanders (and has issue living, Annabel Mary *b* 1998), Lucy Alexandra *b* 1968, — Thomas Martin, *b* 1933. *Residence* – Meadow Croft, Cae Mair, Beaumaris, Anglesey.

DAUGHTERS LIVING OF EIGHTH BARONET

Jennifer Frances Ann, *b* 1933; Freeman City of Chester 1994: *m* 1st, 1954 (*m diss* 1975), Lt-Col Ivan Wise Lynch, Royal Green Jackets; 2ndly, 1979, Maj Basil Hugh Philips Heaton, MBE, of Rhûal, Mold, Flintshire CH7 5DB, and has issue living (by 1st *m*), Francis William Adrian, *b* 1957: *m* 1982 (*m diss* 1994), Julia Mary Battram, and has issue living, James Lawrence Francis *b* 1983, Nicholas John Richard *b* 1985, — William John Ivan (11 Wycombe Place, SW18), *b* 1965: *m* 1990, Charlotte Claire, da of John Michael Howard, of Cramond House, Pirbright, Woking, Surrey, and has issue living, Alexander William Maximillian *b* 1992, Charles William Oscar *b* 1994, Frederick William Francis *b* 1996, Theodore William Edward *b* 1999, — and a da, Amanda-Jayne Charlotte, *b* 1961: *m* 1994, Thomas Sebastian Spark, of 27 Fawcett St, SW10, and has issue living, Stanley Ivan *b* 1998. —— Tessa Gillian Rosamond, MBE (Plas Llanddyfnan, Talwrn, Llangefni, Anglesey LL77 7TH), *b* 1935; High Sheriff Gwynedd 1990: *m* 1958 (*m diss* 1995), Michael John Stewart Preece, and has issue living, James Francis Stewart (The Gatehouse, Chelford, Cheshire SK11 9AH), *b* 1964: *m* 1990, Annabelle Katherine, eldest da of John Hartley Beckett, of Belton, Whitchurch, Shropshire, and has issue living, Barnaby James Francis *b* 1997, Daisy Angela Tessa *b* 1993, Katherine Angharad *b* 1995, — Hugh Michael Stewart, *b* 1969, — and two das, Emily Margaret, *b* 1961: *m* 1993, Christopher Starkie Foden, of 108 Ramsden Rd, SW12 8RB, and has issue living, Harrison Francis Starkey *b* 1996, Madeline Tessa *b* 1993, — Rosamond Alice, *b* 1963: *m* 1990, Robert James Woolf, of Rose Cottage, Great Shelford, Cambridge CB2 5EH, and has issue living, Sophie Antonia *b* 1995. —— Antonia Kathleen Brenda, *b* 1939: *m* 1st, 1960 (*m diss* 1974), Timothy Roy Henry Kimber, eldest son of Sir Charles Dixon Kimber, 3rd Bt; 2ndly, 1974 (*m diss* 1982), Timothy George Emanuel, and has issue living (by 1st *m*) (see Kimber, Bt), — (by 2nd *m*) Harry Sebastian, *b* 1975. —— Victoria Elizabeth Alice, *b* 1944: *m* 1965, Andrew Walter Loraine Paterson, of Church Stile, Town End, Radnage, Bucks, and has issue living, Harry Adrian Loraine, *b* 1968, — Douglas Watkin Loraine, *b* 1972, — Lucinda Mona Alice, *b* 1966: *m* 1990, James Frederick Foster, and has issue living, Sophie Jessie *b* 1997, — Jessie Brenda Antonia, *b* 1970: *m* 1997, Duncan James Sillence.

DAUGHTER LIVING OF SEVENTH BARONET

Laurelie Meriol Winifrida (*Lady Laurie*), *b* 1939: *m* 1968, Sir Robert Bayley Emilius Laurie, 7th Bt, and has issue (*see* Laurie, Bt).

DAUGHTER LIVING OF FIFTH BARONET

Freda Violet, *b* 1913: *m* 1st, 1937 (*m diss* 1950), Sydney Walton Hinde, who *d* 1967; 2ndly, 1959, William Vere Hodgson, of Surrey, and has had issue (by 1st *m*), Richard Courtney Buckley (Madilla Farm, Centenary, Zimbabwe), *b* 1939: *m* 1st, 1961 (*m diss* 1977), Sally Makins; 2ndly, 1978, Jeanette Kramburger, and has issue living (by 1st *m*), Stephen Ross *b* 1962: *m* 1994, Noirin Fitzpatrick (and has issue living, Sinead *b* 1997), Craig Sydney *b* 1964: *m* 1989, Amanda Dalkin (and has issue living, Darren *b* 1991, Tamsan *b* 1993), Felicity Anne *b* 1967: *m* 1992, Glen Mirams (and has issue living, Shelby *b* 1993, Kelsey *b* 1996), (by 2nd *m*) Glen Richard *b* 1979, Douglas Patrick *b* 1981, Patrick Christopher *b* 1985, — Deirdre Penelope Anne, *b* 1938: *m* 1958, Basil Birkbeck Wakefield, of Piedmont, P/Bag 915, Bindura, Zimbabwe, and was killed by terrorists 1979, leaving issue, Dean Roger *b* 1960: *m* 1985, Alexandra Westwood (and has issue living, Jason *b* 1986, Tara *b* 1988), Clive Basil *b* 1964: *m* 1989, Heather Genet (and has issue living, Kendal *b* 1991, Carlton *b* 1993), Richard Owen *b* 1967, Darryl William *b* (twin) 1967: *m* 1987 (*m diss* 1989), Amanda Moeller (and has issue living, Warren *b* 1988), Deborah Odile *b* 1959: *m* 1981, Graham Taylor (and has issue living, Grant *b* 1981, Brendan *b* 1986, Keegan *b* 1989), — Patricia Rosamund *b* 1941: *m* 1961, Patrick David Hyde Smith, of 25 Belfast Rd, Emerald Hill, Zimbabwe, and has issue living, Vaughn Christopher *b* 1962: *m* 1989, Sandra Egeland (and has issue living, Ryan Patrick *b* 1992, Craig *b* 1996), Brent Richard *b* 1964: *m* 1994, Joanna Banks, Natasha Jane *b* 1967, Samantha *b* 1971, — Caroline Bryer, *b* 1946: *m* 1st, 1970, Emmanuel Riez, who *d* 1971; 2ndly, 1981 (*m diss* 1992), William Rooke, and has issue living (by 2nd *m*), Amber Zuleika *b* 1987. *Residence* – Box 1914, Gaborone, Botswana.

WIDOW LIVING OF EIGHTH BARONET

BRENDA BERYL, JP (*Brenda, Lady Williams*), da of Sir (Joseph) John Jarvis, MP, 1st Bt: *m* 1932, Wing/Cdr Sir Francis John Watkin Williams, 8th Bt, QC, who *d* 1995. *Residence* – Llys, Middle Lane, Denbigh.

COLLATERAL BRANCHES LIVING

Issue of late Hugh Richard Grenville Williams, only son of 6th baronet, *b* 1927, *dvp* 1952: *m* 1948, Jacqueline Ferney, da of John Davison, of Livingstone, Zambia:—
Jennifer Mary, *b* 1949: *m* 1st, 19—, E...... Stead; 2ndly, 19—, John Manning. —— Melanie Jane, *b* 1950: *m* 19—, J...... Krienke. —— Richardyne Megan, *b* 1952: *m* 19—, D...... Van Emmenis.

Granddaughter of late Major Charles Henry Bennett Williams, 5th son of 3rd baronet:—
Issue of late Col Evelyn Hugh Watkin Williams, DSO, *b* 1884, *d* 1934: *m* 1910, Florence, da of late G. A. Brett, of Ryde, Isle of Wight:—
Gwenllian Elizabeth Anne, *b* 1911: *m* 1st, 1935, Lieut Christopher Ryle Wood, RN, who assumed by deed poll 1936, the surname of Williams in lieu of his patronymic, and by Roy licence 1936, the arms of Williams; 2ndly, 1948, Campbell Sherston Smith, who assumed by deed poll 1949 the surname of Williams in lieu of his patronymic, and by Roy licence 1949 the arms of Williams, and has issue living, (by 1st *m*) Jane, *b* 1936, — Prudence, *b* 1938: *m* 1960, David Turnbull, and has issue living, Christopher Neil *b* 1962, Catherine Fiona *b* 1965.

Sir John Williams, 1st Bt, High Sheriff, Flintshire 1794-5, was grandson of John Williams, Ch Justice of Brecon, Glamorgan, and Radnor, son of John Williams, Welsh Judge, 2nd son of Sir William Williams, 1st Bt (cr 1688) (see Williams-Wynn, Bt). Sir John Williams, 2nd Bt, assumed in 1842 the additional surname of Hay, but died in 1859 without male issue.

WILLIAMS (UK) 1866, of Tregullow, Cornwall

Sir DONALD MARK WILLIAMS, 10th *Baronet*; *b* 7 Nov 1954; *s* his father, *Sir* ROBERT ERNEST, 1976; *ed* W Buckland Sch: *m* 1982, Denise, only da of Royston H. Cory, of Kashmir, Raleigh Hill, Bideford, Devon, and has had issue (Matthew, *b* and *d* 1985).

𝕬rms – Vair, three crescents or. 𝕮rest – A demi-eagle azure, wings elevated sable, each charged with four bezants.
Residences – Upcott House, Barnstaple, N Devon; Kamsack, Saskatchewan, Canada.

DAUGHTER LIVING

Hannah Louise, *b* 1987.

BROTHER LIVING

BARTON MATTHEW, *b* 21 Nov 1956.

SISTER LIVING

Phyllis June, *b* 1949.

AUNT LIVING

Never despair

Leila June, *b* 1926: *m* 1st, 1952 (*m diss* 1972), Norman E. Hambley; 2ndly, 1972, Adam Casson, (141 Creighton Cres, Penticton, BC, Canada), and has issue living (by 1st *m*), Kenneth Charles Claude, *b* 1953, — Thomas Keith, *b* 1957, — Kim Lee Ann, *b* 1959.

DAUGHTERS LIVING OF SEVENTH BARONET

Eva Kathleen Victoria Daisy, *b* 1900: *m* 1935, Lt-Cdr Christopher Ernest Inman Gibbs, RNR (ret), who *d* 1947, and has issue living. —— Winifred, *b* 1901.

GREAT-AUNTS LIVING

Beatrice Lavinia *b* 1902. —— Matilda Maude, *b* 1909: *m* 1942, Robert McFadyen and has issue living, Diane Beatrice, *b* 1942.

GRANDMOTHER LIVING

Theresa Gertrude, da of R. Greafer: *m* 1922, Ernest Claude Williams, who *d* 1933. *Address* – c/o Rivercrest Lodge, Fort Saskatchewan, Alberta T0B 1P0, Canada.

WIDOW LIVING OF NINTH BARONET

RUTH MARGARET (*Ruth, Lady Williams*) (Upcott House, Barnstaple, N Devon, and Kamsack, Saskatchewan, Canada), da of Charles Edwin Butcher, of Hudson Bay: *m* 1948, Sir Robert Ernest Williams, 9th Bt, who *d* 1976.

COLLATERAL BRANCHES LIVING

Granddaughter of late Rev Leonard Alfred Williams, 4th son of 2nd baronet:—
Issue of late Lieut-Com David Cameron Williams, RN, *b* 1898, *d* 1931: *m* 1929, Violet Mary (who *d* 1998, having *m* 2ndly, 1946, Humphrey Douglas Tyringham, who *d* 1986), da of late Rev Arthur Townshend Boscawen (*see* V Falmouth, colls):—
Susan Mary, *b* 1931: *m* 1954, Maj John Michael Halford, RM (ret), and has issue living, John Wallis Williams, *b* 1955; *ed* Stanbridge Earls, — Peter David (The Cottage, Philpotts Lane, Hildenborough, Kent TN11 8PB), *b* 1957; *ed* Wellington Coll: *m* 1985, Caroline Smith, and has issue living, Edward David *b* 1988, Lucy Alexandra *b* 1991, — Julia Karenza, *b*

1961: *m* 1988, Michael Peter Mansergh, of Midwood, West Walberton Lane, Walberton, nr Arundel, Sussex BN18 0QS, and has issue living, Annabel Karenza *b* 1990, Philippa Louise *b* 1991. *Residence* – 31 Knowle Rd, Knowle, Budleigh Salterton, Devon EX9 6AR.

Grandson of late Victor George Williams, 7th son of 2nd baronet:—
Issue of late Frederick Martyn Charles Williams, *b* 1898, *d* 1961: *m* 1935, Maud Ann (112 Kingston Row, Winnipeg, Manitoba, R2M O59), da of late Dennis Bawif, of Winnipeg, Canada:—
Martyn Dennis Victor (8-9 Ipswich Cres, Willodale, Toronto, Canada), *b* 1936; *ed* Toronto Univ (BSc Eng): *m* 1968, Beth Diane, el da of E. John Koch, of Kitchener, Ont, and has issue living, Robin Lynn, *b* 1972, — Michael David, *b* 1978, — Sandra Diana, *b* 1975, — Karen Patricia, *b* 1978 (twin).

Grandchildren of late Bertram Leopold Williams (infra):—
Issue of late William Bertram Williams, *b* 1906, *d* 1960: *m* 1932, Agnes, who *d* 1968, da of John Allen, of Vancouver, BC:—
Judith Patricia, *b* 1934: *m* 1954, William Demuth McLean, of 4537 Portland St, Burnaby, BC, V5J 2P1, Canada, and has issue living, Douglas William, *b* 1958: has issue (by Patricia Kensington), Alicia Lareina *b* 1991, — Kay Elizabeth, *b* 1956: *m* 1983, Gordon Gray, and has issue living, Kristin Patricia *b* 1985, Andrea Barbara *b* 1987, — Lynn Marion, *b* 1960: *m* 1990, Paul Kirkpatrick, and has issue living, Michael William *b* 1992. —— Barbara Anne, *b* 1939: *m* 1959, Douglas Norman Tartaglio, and has issue living, Norman William, *b* 1962; has issue living, Ryan Wayne *b* 1982, — Neil Joseph, *b* 1964: *m* 1987, Mary Kathleen, da of Walter MacNeill, — Joanne Denise, *b* 1967: *m* 1993, Peter Bukacell.

Issue of late Claude Martin Williams, *b* 1911, *d* 1977: *m* 1944, Hannah Louisa, da of late Capt William Massey, of Courtown Harbour, Gorey, co Wexford:—
Bertram Douglas (20571 49 A Av, Langley, BC, V3A 5Z4), *b* 1945; Journeyman Diesel Engineer; VV Coll (JD Eng): *m* 19—, Wanda Charlotte, only da of Capt Trim, of Nanimo, BC, and has issue living, Brianne Kathleen, *b* 1979, — Colleen Kate, *b* 1981, — Leaerin Elizabeth, *b* 1982. —— William Claude (2640 Moss Av, Prince George, BC V2L 5J3), *b* 1947; BSF (BC Univ): *m* 19—, Leslie Gaye, da of Norman Steward of 4752 60 B St, Delta, BC, and has issue living, Matthew Stewart, *b* 1980, — Andrew James, *b* 1982.

Issue of late Bertram Leopold Williams, 7th son of 2nd baronet, *b* 1878, *d* 1962: *m* 1st, 1906 (*m diss*), Vera Mary, only da of Arthur Venables, JP, of Wooburn Ranche, near Vernon, British Columbia; 2ndly, 1926, Amy Muriel Douglas, yst da of late Douglas Fourdrinier, of Teddington, Middlesex:—
(By 1st *m*) Peter Robert (RR1 Big Maple, Sechelt, BC, Canada V05 380), *b* 1913.

Granddaughter of late Lieut-Col Richard Michael Williams, 2nd son of 1st baronet:—
Issue of late Capt William Phillpotts Williams, *b* 1860, *d* 1916: *m* 1901, Edith Bonella, da of the Rev James Harvey Simpson, formerly R of St Mark's, Bexhill, and Preb of Chichester:—
Elizabeth Georgiana Phillpotts, *b* 1904.

The 1st baronet, Sir William, was High Sheriff of Cornwall 1851; and the 2nd baronet, Sir Frederick Martin, sat as MP for Truro (*C*) 1865-78. The 6th baronet, Sir Burton Robert, Lieut Devonshire Regt, was *ka* 1917.

WILLIAMS (UK) 1909, of Castell Deudraeth, and Borthwen, co Merioneth

No good but God

Sir (MICHAEL) OSMOND WILLIAMS, MC, 2nd *Baronet*, son of late Capt Osmond Trahaern Deudraeth Williams, DSO, el son of 1st baronet; *b* 22 April 1914; *s* his grandfather, *Sir* (ARTHUR) OSMOND, 1927; *ed* Eton, and Freiburg Univ; Maj late R Scots Greys; a JP (1960) for Merionethshire; 1939-45 War in Middle East, Italy and N-W Europe (MC, 1944 Chevalier of Orders of Leopold II of Belgium with Palm, Belgian Croix de Guerre with Palm): *m* 1947, Benita Mary, da of late G. Henry Booker, of 3 Chesterfield House, W1, and has issue.

Arms – Argent, a chevron between in chief two mullets pierced and in base a buck trippant sable. Crest – A griffin segreant sable, holding between the fore claws a buck's head cabossed gold.
Residence – Borthwen, Minffordd, Penrhyndeudraeth, Gwynedd. *Club* – Travellers'.

DAUGHTERS LIVING

Sarah Theresa Ceridwen, *b* 1948: *m* 1981, Leo Kruidbos, otherwise Kay, of 179 Ière Rue Mont Suisse, St Sauveur des Monts, Quebec J0R 1R2, Canada, —— Julia Mary Myfanwy, *b* 1952: *m* 1982, Richard Shaun O'Conor, of 31 Clarendon Rd, W11 4JB.
The 1st baronet, Sir (Arthur) Osmond Williams, was Lord-Lieut of Merionethshire, 1909-27, and MP for Merionethshire (*L*) Oct 1900 to Jan 1910.

WILLIAMS (UK) 1915, of Bridehead, co Dorset

Nil Solidum

Sir (ROBERT) PHILIP NATHANIEL WILLIAMS, 4th *Baronet*; *b* 3 May 1950; *s* his father, *Sir* DAVID PHILIP, 1970; *ed* Marlborough, and St Andrew's Univ: *m* 1979, Catherine Margaret Godwin, da of Rev Canon Cosmo Gabriel Rivers Pouncey, of Church Walk, Littlebredy, Dorchester, Dorset, and has issue.

Arms – Argent, a greyhound between three Cornish choughs sable, beaked and membered purpure; on a bordure engrailed gules four crosses formée or between as many besants. **Crest** – A dexter arm couped, the sleeve barry of four sable and argent, charged with a cross formée per fesse counterchanged between four besants, the hand proper grasping a branch of oak vert, fructed or.
Seat – Bridehead, Littlebredy, Dorchester, Dorset DT2 9JA.

SON LIVING

DAVID ROBERT MARK, *b* 31 Oct 1980.

DAUGHTERS LIVING

Sarah Catherine Anne, *b* 1982. —— Margaret Jane Louise, *b* 1984. —— Clare Elizabeth Philippa, *b* 1987.

BROTHER LIVING

(David) Michael Ralph, *b* 1955; *ed* Marlborough, and Durham Univ: *m* 1992, Charlotte P.E., only da of Capt Malcolm Syms, of Mile Path House, Woking, Surrey, and has issue living, James Mark Edward, *b* 1995, —— Emily Honor *b* 1997.

HALF-SISTER LIVING

(Mary) Venetia Honor, *b* 1939: *m* 1964, John Copson Peake, of Corscombe Court, Dorchester, Dorset.

SISTER LIVING

(Elizabeth Margaret) Ruth, *b* 1951: *m* 1975, Michael Widén, of Batsford House, St Mary Bourne, nr Andover, Hants, and has issue living, William David Alexander, *b* 1978.

AUNT LIVING (*Daughter of 2nd baronet*)

Juliet Dorothea Chassereau *b* 1933: *m* 1956, John Douglas Young Hickman, and has issue living, (Philip) Douglas, *b* 1956: *m* 1981, Pamela Mary Hunter, and has issue living, Angela Lindsay *b* 1986, Connie Marie *b* 1988, Jennifer Lee *b* 1990, —— Stephen James, *b* 1958: *m* 1988, Catherine Jean King, and has an adopted son, Alexander James *b* 1991, —— Charles Nicholas, *b* 1960: *m* 1987, Gay Giselle Augustin Drescher, and has issue living, Katherine Ashley *b* 1990.

WIDOW LIVING OF THIRD BARONET

ELIZABETH MARY GARNEYS (*Elizabeth, Lady Williams*) (Stable House, Moigne Coombe, Owermoigne, Dorchester, Dorset DT2 8JA); a DL of Dorset; High Sheriff of Dorset 1979; da of William Ralph Garneys Bond (Meysey-Thompson, Bt): *m* 1948, as his 2nd wife, Sir David Philip Williams, 3rd Bt, who *d* 1970.

COLLATERAL BRANCH LIVING

Issue of late Robert Mark Edgar Williams, 2nd son of 2nd baronet, *b* 1913, *d* 1969: *m* 1942, Juliet Susan Harriet (5 Winters Lane, Portesham, Dorchester, Dorset), da of Cdr Kenneth Berkeley Mackenzie Churchill, RN:—
Robert Norrie (77 Bearcroft, Weobley, Hereford HR4 8TD), *b* 1943; *ed* Radley: *m* 1971, Nesta Rosemary, da of Stewart Bell, CBE, of Stretton, Broadway, Llandrindod Wells, and has issue living, Andrew John Mark, *b* 1975, —— Ann Margaret, *b* 1973: *m* 1997, Malcolm David Binns, and has issue living, Hannah Mary *b* 1997. —— John Philip Mackenzie (5951 Cormorant Court, Richmond, BC, Canada), *b* 1947; *ed* Radley: *m* 1978, Louise Beverly, da of David Douglas, of Vancouver, Canada, and has issue living, Jonathan Mark, *b* 1988, —— Hayley Michelle *b* 1992. —— Marcia Jane, *b* 1945: *m* 1st, 1977 (*m diss* 1979) Christopher Maples; 2ndly, 1983, Robert Machin, of Grey Cottage, Askerswell, Dorset, and has issue living (by 2nd *m*), Luke Robert, *b* 1983, —— Mark George, *b* 1984, —— Sarah Ann, *b* (twin) 1984.

The 1st baronet, Col Sir Robert Williams, VD, TD (el son of late Robert Williams, of Bridehead, Dorchester), was MP for W Div of Dorset (*C*) 1895-1922, and sometime Hon Col 4th Batn Dorsetshire Regt. The second baronet, Sir Philip Francis Cunningham Williams, was High Sheriff of Dorset 1949.

WILLIAMS (UK) 1953, of Cilgeraint, co Caernarvon

Sir ROBIN PHILIP WILLIAMS, 2nd *Baronet*; *b* 27 May 1928; *s* his father, Sir HERBERT GERAINT, MP, 1954; *ed* Eton, and St John's Coll, Camb (MA); Bar Middle Temple 1954; an Insurance Broker; Member of Lloyd's; 2nd Lt (ret) RA; Vice-Chm, Fedn of Univ Conservative and Unionist Assos 1951-52, and acting Chm 1952; Chm of Bow Group 1954, and of Anti-Common Market League 1969-84; a Borough Councillor of Haringay 1968-74; Hon Sec Campaign for an Independent Britain since 1989; Lt RA 1947: *m* 1955, Wendy Adele Marguerite, only da of late Felix Joseph Alexander, of Hong Kong, and has issue.
Residence – 1 Broadlands Close, Highgate, N6 4AF.

SONS LIVING

ANTHONY GERAINT, *b* 22 Dec 1958: *m* 1990, Rachel J., elder da of Norman Jennings, of Fenny Drayton, Warwicks. *Residence* – 6 Willow Bridge Rd, N1 2LB. —— Stephen Robin Alexander, *b* 1962.

The 1st baronet, Sir Herbert Geraint Williams (son of late Thomas Williams, LLD, of Hooton, Cheshire), was MP for Reading (*U*) 1924-29, for S Div of Croydon, 1932-45, and for E Div of Croydon 1950-54, and Parliamentary Sec to Board of Trade 1928-9.

DUDLEY-WILLIAMS (UK) 1964, of City and Co of the City of Exeter

Sir ALASTAIR EDGCUMBE JAMES DUDLEY-WILLIAMS, 2nd *Baronet*; *b* 26 Nov 1943; *s* his father, Sir ROLF DUDLEY, 1987; *ed* Nautical Coll, Pangbourne: *m* 1972, Diana Elizabeth Jane, twin da of Robert Henry Clare Duncan, of The Wall House, High St, Haslemere, Surrey, and has issue.

Arms – Gules a chevron engrailed plain cotised between in chief two cranes respectant proper, and in base a triangular castle of three towers or. **Crest** – In front of a castle as in the arms, a wild cat rampant guardant proper.
Address – c/o The Old Manse, S Petherton, Som TA13 5DB.

DAUGHTERS LIVING

Marina Elizabeth Catherine, *b* 1974. —— Lorna Caroline Rachel, *b* 1977. —— Eleanor Patricia Rosemary, *b* 1979.

BROTHER LIVING

MALCOLM PHILIP EDGCUMBE (Down Farm, Cruwys Morchard, Tiverton, Devon EX16 8NA), *b* 10 Aug 1947; *ed* Nautical Coll Pangbourne: *m* 1973, Caroline Anne Colina, twin da of Robert Henry Clare Duncan, of The Wall House, High St, Haslemere, Surrey (ante), and has issue living, Nicholas Mark Edgcumbe, *b* 1975, — Patrick Guy Edgcumbe, *b* 1978, — Clare Helen Colina, *b* 1982.

WIDOW LIVING OF FIRST BARONET

MARGARET HELEN (*Helen, Lady Dudley-Williams*), eldest da of late Frederick Eaton Robinson, OBE, AMICE, AMIMechE, of Enfield, Middx: *m* 1940, Sir Rolf Dudley Dudley-Williams, 1st Bt, who *d* 1987. *Residence* – The Old Manse, S Petherton, Somerset TA13 5DB.

RHYS WILLIAMS (UK) 1918, of Miskin, Parish of Llantrisant, co Glamorgan

Sir (ARTHUR) GARETH LUDOVIC EMRYS RHYS WILLIAMS, 3rd *Baronet*; *b* 9 Nov 1961; *s* his father, *Sir* BRANDON MEREDITH, MP, 1988; *ed* Eton, Durham Univ, and INSEAD: *m* 1996, Harriet, da of Maj Tom Codner, of Glos.

Arms – Per chevron argent and gules, in chief two cocks of the second and in base as many chevronels of the first. **Crest** – Between two fleur-de-lis argent, a goat's head couped sable, with curved horns.
Residence – 9 Matheson Rd, W14. *Club* – Garrick.

SISTERS LIVING

Elinor Caroline, *b* 1964. —— Miranda Pamela Cariadwen, *b* 1968.

AUNTS LIVING (*daughters of 1st baronet*)

Susan Eleanor (*Lady Glyn*), *b* 1923; Bar Inner Temple 1950; late Junior Com ATS: *m* 1946, Capt Sir Anthony Geoffrey Leo Simon Glyn, 2nd Bt (*cr* 1927), who *d* 1998. *Residence* – Marina Baie des Anges, Ducal Apt U-03, 06270 Villeneuve-Loubet, Alpes Maritimes, France. —— (Marion) Elspeth, *b* 1937: *m* 1981, George Chowdharay-Best, MA (Oxon). *Residence* – 27 Walpole St, SW3.

WIDOW LIVING OF SECOND BARONET

CAROLINE SUSAN (*Caroline, Lady Rhys Williams*), eldest da of late Ludovic Anthony Foster, of Greatham Manor, Pulborough, Sussex: *m* 1961, Sir Brandon Meredith Rhys Williams, 2nd Bt, MP, who *d* 1988. *Residence* – 52 Limerston St, SW10 0HH.

Col Sir Rhys Rhys Williams, DSO, QC, 1st baronet (son of late Gwilym Williams, a Judge of County Courts, of Miskin Manor, Glamorgan), Parl Sec to Min of Transport 1919, Recorder of Cardiff 1922-30, Chm of Quarter Sessions, Glamorgan, and MP for N Oxon (*L*) 1918 and for Banbury 1918-22. He assumed by deed poll 1938 the additional surname of Rhys. Sir Brandon Rhys Williams, 2nd Bt, was MP for S Kensington (*C*) March 1968 to Feb 1974, and for Kensington 1974-88, and MEP for London South East 1973-84.

Williams-Bulkeley, see Bulkeley.

Williams-Wynn, see Wynn.

WILLIAMSON (E) 1642, of East Markham, Nottinghamshire

Sir NICHOLAS (FREDERICK HEDWORTH) WILLIAMSON, 11th *Baronet*, son of late Major William Hedworth Williamson, grandson of 8th baronet; *b* 26 Oct 1937; *s* his uncle, *Sir* CHARLES HEDWORTH, 1946; *ed* Eton; late 4th/7th Roy Dragoon Guards.

Arms – Or, a chevron gules between three trefoils slipped sable. **Crest** – Out of a mural crown gules, a wyvern's head or.
Residence – Abbey Croft, Mortimer, Reading.

COLLATERAL BRANCH LIVING

Granddaughter of late Capt Cecil Hedworth J. C. L. G. Williamson, only son of late Robert Hudleston Williamson, 3rd son of 6th baronet:—
Issue of late Brig Hudleston Noel Hedworth Williamson, DSO, MC, *b* 1886, *d* 1971: *m* 1st, 1923 (*m diss* 1926), Helen Marjorie, da of Arthur Lord; 2ndly, 1926, Leila Isabel, who *d* 1983, only da of Lt-Col Robert William Peter Lodwick, of Lisheen, Camberley:—
(By 2nd *m*) Mary (*Lady Nicholas C. Gordon Lennox*), *b* 1934; an Extra Lady-in-Waiting to HRH Princess Alexandra, the Hon Lady Ogilvy, since 1990: *m* 1958, Lord Nicholas Charles Gordon Lennox, KCMG, KCVO (*see* D Richmond and Gordon).

Sir Thomas, the 1st baronet, suffered greatly for his loyalty in the civil wars, and paid £3,400 to the sequestrators for his estate. Sir Hedworth, the 7th baronet, was MP for the northern division of Durham (*L*) 1832-7, and High Sheriff of that county.

WILLINK (UK) 1957, of Dingle Bank, City of Liverpool

Sir CHARLES WILLIAM WILLINK, 2nd *Baronet*, *b* 10 Sept 1929; *s* his father *The Rt Hon Sir* HENRY URMSTON, MC, QC, 1973; *ed* Eton, and Trin Coll, Camb (MA, PhD); Housemaster, Eton Coll 1964-77: *m* 1954, Elizabeth, el da of Humfrey Andrewes, of North Grove, Highgate, N6, and has issue.

𝔄rms – Azure, three acorns on one stem slipped or. ℭrest – Issuant from a wreath of oak leaves or, a dexter cubit arm bendwise grasping in the hand a chaplet of laurel proper.
Residence – 22 North Grove, Highgate, N6 4SL.

SON LIVING

EDWARD DANIEL, *b* 18 Feb 1957.

DAUGHTER LIVING

Penelope Jane, *b* 1959: *m* 1987, Simon John Lawrence Linnett, only son of late Prof John Linnett, of Brookside, Cambridge, and has issue living, John Lawrence Humfrey, *b* 1991, — Henry Simon Albert, *b* 1993.

BROTHER LIVING

Stephen Henry (7 Clifton St, Plymouth PL4 9QA), *b* 1932; *ed* Eton, and Trin Coll, Oxford: *m* 1970, Mary Louise, da of Ernest R. Royston, of 52 Carslake Rd, SW, and has issue living, Henry Augustine, *b* 1971, — Annabella Mary Victoria, *b* 1975.

SISTERS LIVING

Rachel Frances: *m* 1947, Michael Kinchin Smith, son of Francis J. Kinchin Smith, of Emperor's Gate, SW7, and has issue living, Christopher Henry, *b* 1950: *m* 1974, Susan Valerie, yr da of William G. Adams, of W Wickham, Kent, and has issue living, Holly Rebecca *b* 1983, Katherine Alice *b* 1988, — *Rev* John Michael (The Rectory, Mursley, Milton Keynes, Bucks MK17 0RT), *b* 1952: *m* 1981 Caroline Anne, yr da of G. Francis Harris, of Copdock, Suffolk, and has issue living, Joseph Francis *b* 1983, Samuel John *b* 1988, David Luke *b* 1990, Eleanor Mary *b* 1985, — David Francis *b* 1954: *m* 1976 Rosalind Jane, yr da of Dr Frank Holden, of Bessacarr, Yorks, — Robert Mark, *b* 1960, — Lavinia Mary, *b* 1948: *m* 1975, John Cunningham, son of William Henry Cunningham, of Minchinhampton, Glos, and has issue living, Anna Clare *b* 1980, Ruth Elizabeth *b* 1983, Helen Mary *b* 1984, — Juliet Clare, *b* 1957: *m* 1985, Rev Malcolm James Hancock, of King Charles Vicarage, 5D Frant Rd, Tunbridge Wells, Kent TN2 5SB, son of Isaac Hancock, of Newark, and has issue living, James Timothy Michael *b* 1989, Benjamin Andrew *b* 1991. *Residence* – Pitts Orchard, Cumberford, Bloxham, Banbury, Oxon OX15 4QG. —— Elisabeth Mary, *m* 1951, Frank Erskine Bell, son of late Sir Ernest Albert Seymour Bell, CIE, and has issue living, Nicholas John, *b* 1953, — Catharine Elisabeth, *b* 1955: *m* 1986, Timothy Cutting, son of George Cutting, of Cambo, Northumberland, and has issue living, Daniel Christopher Frank *b* 1993, Amber *b* 1997. *Residence* – Stables Barn, Trimnells, Colerne, Wilts SN14 8FP.

The Rt Hon Sir Henry Urmston Willink, MC, QC, son of William Edward Willink, FRIBA, of Liverpool, was MP for N Croydon (C) 1940-48, Min of Health 1943-45, Master of Magdalene Coll, Camb 1948-66, and Vice-Chancellor of Camb Univ, 1953-55, and Chancellor of Norwich and St Edmundsbury and Ipswich Dioceses 1948-55, and Dean of Arches 1955-70.

WILLS (UK) 1904, of Hazelwood, Stoke Bishop, Westbury-on-Trym, Gloucestershire, and Clapton-in-Gordano, Somerset

Sir (DAVID) SETON WILLS, 5th *Baronet*; *b* 29 Dec 1939, only son of late Maj George Seton Wills, Roy Wilts Yeo, yr son of Sir Ernest Salter Wills, 3rd Bt; *s* his uncle, *Lt-Col Sir* (ERNEST) EDWARD DE WINTON, 1983; *ed* Eton; FRICS; *m* 1968, Gillian, twin da of Albert Percival Eastoe, of Windmill Cottage, Aldbourne, Wilts, and has issue.

Arms – Gules, three suns in splendour fessewise, between two griffins passant or. Crest – Issuant from an annulet or, a demi-griffin gules, charged with a sun in splendour, and holding in the dexter claw a battle-axe also or.
Residence – Eastridge House, Ramsbury, nr Marlborough, Wilts SN8 2HJ.

SON LIVING

JAMES SETON, *b* 24 Nov 1970.

DAUGHTERS LIVING

Sarah Elizabeth, *b* 1969: *m* 1994, Dominic E. Pearson, son of Edward J. Pearson, of Barbican, EC2, and has issue living, Thomas Edward, *b* 1995, — Lucy Annabel, *b* 1997. —— Victoria Lucy, *b* 1975. —— Alice Louise, *b* 1980.

DAUGHTERS LIVING OF FOURTH BARONET (*By 1st marriage*)

Venetia Dawn, *b* 1927: *m* 1st, 1948 (*m diss* 1962), as his 2nd wife, Charles Robert Cecil Weld Forester (*see* B Forester); 2ndly, 1962, Alan Cripps Nind Hopkins, of Chalet Topaze, Anzere, Valais, Switzerland, and has issue living (by 1st *m*) (*see* B Forester), — (by 2nd *m*) Mark Edward Wills *b* 1963, — Peter Alan Wills (twin) *b* 1963. —— Edwina Sylvia, *b* 1933: *m* 1st, 1952 (*m diss* 1961), Viscount Savernake (later 8th Marquess of Ailesbury); 2ndly, 1963, Maj Christopher Leslie Leo Bonn, late Welsh Gds, of La Maison du Coin, St Ouen, Jersey, CI, and has issue living (by 1st *m*) (*see* M Ailesbury), — (by 2nd *m*) Philip Edward Leo, *b* 1964, — Camilla Georgina Alexandra, *b* 1965, — Melanie Marina Roselle, *b* 1974.

MOTHER LIVING

Lilah Mary, yst da of late Capt Percy Richard Hare (*see* E Listowel, colls): *m* 1st, 1935 (*m diss* 1946), Maj George Seton Wills (ante), who *d* 1979; 2ndly, 1946, as his 2nd wife, Col Nigel Victor Stopford Sackville, who *d* 1972 (*see* E Courtown, colls). *Residence* – The Weirs, Chilton Foliat, Hungerford, Berks.

COLLATERAL BRANCH LIVING

Issue of late Capt Arnold Stancomb Wills, yst son of 1st baronet, *b* 1877, *d* 1961: *m* 1905, Hilda Carolin, who *d* 1965, da of late Edward Lyon, of London, and New York:—
John Lycett, *b* 1910; is Maj (ret) Life Gds: *m* 1936, Hon Jean Constance Buller-Fullerton-Elphinstone, da of 16th Lord Elphinstone, and has had issue, †Andrew Arnold Lyon, *b* 1937; Capt (ret) Life Gds: *m* 1961, Hon Elizabeth Anne Cecil (Middleton House, Longparish, Andover, Hants), da of 2nd Baron Rockley, and *d* 1998, leaving issue, Richard Arnold *b* 1962: *m* 1988, Netta, elder da of Lt-Col Trevor Morris, of Butlers, Donhead St Mary, Shaftesbury, Dorset (and has issue living, Edward *b* 1994, Anna *b* 1990, Charlotte *b* 1991), Alexander John *b* 1967: *m* 1992 (*m diss* 1994), Wendy A., elder da of Robin H. Leach, of Ugley Park, Ugley Green, Essex, Tessa Elizabeth *b* 1963: *m* 1993, Richard E. M. Affleck, son of Michael Affleck, of Park Farm, N Moreton, Oxon, — Susan Griselda Ann Lyon, *b* 1940: *m* 1960, Capt Charles Peregrine Albemarle Bertie, late Scots Gds (*see* E Lindsey and Abingdon, colls). *Residence* – Allanbay Park, Binfield, Berks.

The 1st baronet, Sir Edward Payson Wills, KCB (son of late Henry Overton Wills JP, of Bristol), was a Director of the Imperial Tobacco Co (Limited), and a Gov of Bristol Gen Hospital. The 2nd baronet, Sir Edward Chaning Wills (also a Director of the Imperial Tobacco Co, Limited), was High Sheriff of Devon 1915. The 3rd baronet, Sir Ernest Salter Wills, was Lord Lieut of Wilts 1930-42, and a Director of Imperial Tobacco Co.

WILLS (UK) 1923, of Blagdon, co Somerset

Sir DAVID JAMES VERNON WILLS, 5th *Baronet*; *b* 2 Jan 1955; *s* his father, *Sir* JOHN VERNON, KCVO, TD, 1998: *m* 1999, Mrs Paula Burke.

Arms – Gules, a sun in splendour between two gryphons passant in pale or. Crest – Issuant from an annulet or, a demi-gryphon gules, holding in the dexter claw a battle-axe gold.
Residence – Vale Cottage, Blagdon, Bristol BS18 6RQ.

BROTHERS LIVING

ANTHONY JOHN VERNON (Kinlochruel House, Colintraive, Argyll PA22 3AH), *b* 10 Dec 1956: *m* 1983, Katherine A., 3rd da of Thomas Wilks, of Laggan, Bowmore, Isle of Islay. —— Rupert Charles Vernon (22 Perryn Rd, W3 7NA), *b* 1959: *m* 1989, Kathryn A., 2nd da of late Gordon Board Matthews, and of Mrs W. Clarke Graham, of Binixica, Menorca. —— Julian Robert Vernon (Lodge Farmhouse, Langford, Bristol BS18 7BW), *b* 1963: *m* 1989, Fiona E. K., eldest da of T. R. Thom, of The Forge, Lower Langford, Bristol.

AUNT LIVING (*daughter of 2nd baronet*)

Jean Mary Vernon, *b* 1925: *m* 1948, Richard Hill of Harptree Court, East Harptree, Somerset (Harford, Bt), and has issue living, Charles Peter Loraine, *b* 1954: *m* 1980, Linda Elizabeth Anne, da of Alan Beresford Gordon, of Little Tumnerscourt, Godalming, Surrey, and has issue living, Matthew *b* 1989, Katie *b* 1983, Emily *b* 1986, — Angela Mary Loraine, *b* 1949, — Caryll Loraine, *b* 1951, — Sarah Loraine, *b* 1957.

For our altars and our hearths

WIDOW LIVING OF FOURTH BARONET

DIANA VERONICA CECIL (JANE) (*Lady Wills*) only da of Douglas R. M. Baker, of Winsford, Somerset: *m* 1953, Sir John Vernon Wills, 4th Bt, who *d* 1998. *Residence* – Langford Court, Langford, Bristol BS18 7DA.

The 1st baronet, Sir George Alfred Wills, was Pres of Imperial Tobacco Co of Great Britain and Ireland (Limited), and his son, Sir George Vernon Proctor Wills, 2nd Bt, was a Director of the same Company. The 3rd baronet, Sir George Peter Vernon, Lt Coldm Gds, was *ka* 1945.

WILLSHIRE (UK) 1841 (Extinct 1947)

Sir GERARD ARTHUR MAXWELL WILLSHIRE, 3rd and last *Baronet*.

DAUGHTER LIVING OF THIRD BARONET

Patricia Frederica, *b* 1925: *m* 1st, 1943 (*m diss* 1949) Greville Pollard Baylis, Lt Irish Guards; 2ndly, 1949, George Breary Girardet, and has issue living, (by 1st *m*) Greville Mark Willshire, *b* 1944, — (by 2nd *m*) Guy Maxwell, *b* 1953, — Gail Beatriz Willshire, *b* 1952.

WILMOT (GB) 1759, of Chaddesden, Derbyshire

Sir HENRY ROBERT WILMOT, 9th *Baronet*, *b* 10 April 1967; *s* his father, *Capt Sir* ROBERT ARTHUR, 1974; *ed* Eton: *m* 1995, Susan C., elder da of John Malvern, of Roehampton, London, and has issue.

𝕬rms – Sable, on a fesse or, between three eagles' heads couped argent as many escallops gules, a canton vaire ermine and gules. 𝕮rest – An eagle's head couped argent gorged with a mural coronet sable, in the beak an escallop gules.
Residence – Beck House, Great Broughton, Stokesley, N Yorks TS39 7EZ.

SON LIVING

OLIVER CHARLES, *b* 12 July 1999.

BROTHER DECEASED

†Charles Sacheverel, *b* 1969; *d* 1993.

SISTER LIVING

Zoë Meriel, *b* 1971.

AUNT LIVING (*Daughter of 7th baronet*)

Pamela Ann (*Baroness Norrie*) (Chapel-on-the-Water, Ramsbury, Wilts SN8 2QE), *b* 1937: *m* 1st, 1959 (*m diss* 1967), Capt William James Stockton, late R Scots Greys; 2ndly, 1967 (*m diss* 1982), Antony Paul McCaffry; 3rdly, 1997, as his 2nd wife, 2nd Baron Norrie, and has issue living, (by 1st *m*) Adela Louise, *b* 1961, — Henrietta Maria Caroline, *b* 1963, — (by 2nd *m*) Sophie Claire, *b* 1968.

MOTHER LIVING

Juliet Elvira WILMOT (The Garden Lodge, Chittoe, Chippenham, Wilts SN15 2EW), elder da of late Capt Michael Neville Tufnell, CVO, DSC, RN, of Curdridge Grange, Botley, Hants; has resumed her former married surname: *m* 1st, 1965 (*m diss* 1974), Capt Sir Robert Arthur Wilmot, 8th Bt, Scots Gds, who *d* 1974; 2ndly, 1976 (*m diss* 1980), Richard James Stanes.

COLLATERAL BRANCHES LIVING

Grandchildren of late Capt Sacheverel Darwin Wilmot (infra):—
Issue of late Maj Martyn Sacheverel Wilmot, RA, *b* 1914, *d* 1997: *m* 1948, Mona Elizabeth, who *d* 1996, yr da of late Stanley David Milnes Horner, of Farnham, Surrey:—
Brian Sacheverel (127 Rosehill Rd, Ipswich, Suffolk IP3 8ET), *b* 25 March 1949; *ed* Rugby: *m* 1979, Beatrice, 3rd da of late Dr Ormonde George Pickard, CBE, of Little Dingle, Dunwich, Saxmundham, Suffolk, and has issue living, Thomas Sacheverel, *b* 29 Sept 1980, — Lucy Eleanor, *b* 1982. —— Robin Wollett (Foxlair, Fifehead St Quintin, Sturminster Newton, Dorset DT10 2AP), *b* 1950; *ed* Rugby. —— Anabel Sarah, *b* 1960; has issue living (by Ewan Barker), Jade Matthew WILMOT, *b* 1991, — Caio Dominic WILMOT, *b* 1994.

Grandson of the Rev Darwin Wilmot, son of late Edward Woollett Wilmot 5th son of 3rd baronet:—
Issue of late Capt Sacheverel Darwin Wilmot, RA, *b* 1885, *d* 1918: *m* 1912, Annie Dudley, who *d* 1960, da of late Maj Gen Strover, RA:—
Gordon Darwin, *b* 1918; *ed* Rugby; Major (ret) Roy Scots Fusiliers: *m* 1941, Margaret Virginia, who *d* 1994, 3rd da of late Robert Murray Thorburn, of Peebles and has issue living, Patrick Gordon, *b* 1954; *ed* Rugby: *m* 1996, Susan Jane, da of Dr Brian Latham, of Hove, Sussex, and has issue living, Emma Francesca Margot *b* 1998, — Virginia Ann, *b* 1942: *m* 1965, Jeremy Adrian Hill, of Peyton Hall, Bures, Suffolk, and has issue living, Edward Justin *b* 1969, Tristram Darwin *b* 1970, Marcus Jeremy *b* 1977, — Felicity Joyce, *b* 1944: *m* 1964, Anthony Peter Ziegler, of Titcombs, Burford, Oxon, and has issue living, Thomas Pippin *b* 1965, Martyn Nicholas *b* 1967. *Residence* – 6 Witney St, Burford, Oxon OX18 4SN.

Grandchildren of late Edmund Wilmot, 7th son of 3rd baronet:—
Issue of late Rev Francis Edmund William Wilmot, *b* 1849, *d* 1911: *m* 1878, Katharine, who *d* 1939, da of late Col Thomas Coningsby Norbury Norbury, CB, of Sherridge, near Malvern (V Guillamore):—
Katharine Joyce, *b* 1888: *m* 1930, Henry Sutcliffe Crook, who *d* 1945, and has issue living, Faith Marygold, *b* 1931.

Issue of late Capt Edmund Mead Wilmot, *b* 1860, *d* 1935: *m* 1885, Agatha Georgiana, who *d* 1931, da of Francis J. Jessopp:—
Francis Hurt, *b* 1894: *m* 1935, Dorothy Fownes, el da of Harry W. Keith, MD, of Enderby, British Columbia, and has issue living, Penelope, *b* 19-. *Residence* – Vancouver, British Columbia.

The family of Wilmot settled at Sutton-upon-Soar, in Nottinghamshire, soon after the Conquest, and removed from thence into Derbyshire about the year 1539. The 1st baronet, Sir Edward Wilmot, an eminent Physician, was Physician-General to the Army, and Physician in Ordinary to George II. Col Sir Henry Wilmot, KCB, VC, 5th Bt, sat as MP for Derbyshire, S (*C*) 1869-85. The 6th baronet, Sir Ralph Henry Sacheverel Wilmot Capt Coldstream Guards, *d* of wounds received on active service 1918 and the 7th baronet, Maj Sir Arthur Ralph Wilmot, *d* (result of an accident whilst on active ser in Middle East) 1942. Capt Sir Robert Arthur Wilmot, 8th baronet, Scots Gds, was Equerry to HRH the Duke of Gloucester 1963-65.

WILMOT (GB) 1772, of Osmaston, Derbyshire (Extinct 1931)

Sir ROBERT RODNEY WILMOT, 6th and last *Baronet.*

DAUGHTER LIVING OF SIXTH BARONET (*By 2nd marriage*)

Kathleen Eleanor, *b* 1893: *m* 1921, Arthur Charles Melville Pym, who *d* 1956, and has issue living, Robert Marcus *b* 1922. *Residence* –

EARDLEY-WILMOT (UK) 1821, of Berkswell Hall, Warwickshire

Sir MICHAEL JOHN ASSHETON EARDLEY-WILMOT, 6th *Baronet*; *b* 13 Jan 1941; *s* his father, *Cmdr Sir* JOHN ASSHETON, LVO, DSC, RN, 1995; *ed* Clifton: *m* 1st, 1971 (*m diss* 1985), Wendy, yr da of Anthony John Wolstenholme; 2ndly, 1987, Diana Margaret, da of Robert Graham Wallis, and has issue by 1st and 2nd *m.*

Arms – Quarterly, 1st, sable, a fesse or, between three eagles' heads couped argent, in the beak of each an escallop gules, *Wilmot*; 2nd, argent, on a chevron azure, three garbs or; a canton gules charged with a fret or, *Eardley*; 3rd, azure, a fesse engrailed or, between three maidens' heads proper, crined or, *Marow*; 4th, quarterly, argent and sable, a bend gules, charged with three mullets of the first. **Crests** – 1st, an eagle's head couped argent, in his beak an escallop gules; 2nd, a buck courant gules, attired and unguled or.
Residence – 26 Arundel Gdns, Holland Park, W11 2LB.

SONS LIVING (*By 1st marriage*)

BENJAMIN JOHN, *b* 24 Jan 1974; *ed* Bedales. —— Guy Assheton, *b* 1979; *ed* Bedales.

DAUGHTERS LIVING (*By 1st marriage*)

Holly Joanna, *b* 1976.

(*by 2nd marriage*)

Poppy Clementine, *b* 1987.

SISTER LIVING

Patricia Enid, *b* 1944: *m* 1966, Andrew McMeekan, late RN, and has issue living, Emily Charlotte, *b* 1974, — Isabel Heloise, *b* 1978. *Residence* – 41 Margravine Gdns, W6.

UNCLE LIVING (*brother of 5th baronet*)

Michael, *b* 1924: *m* 1956, Sylvia, da of Arthur Irish, of Sydney, NSW. *Residence* – Villa 3, 195 Albany St, Point Frederick, NSW 2259, Australia.

AUNT LIVING (*sister of 5th baronet*)

Rosemary (*Hon Mrs Basil E. Feilding*), *b* 1920: *m* 1939, Capt the Hon Basil Egerton Feilding, Coldm Gds, who *d* 1970, and has issue (*see* E Denbigh, colls). *Residence* – The Park Cottage, Monks Kirby, Rugby CV23 0RB.

WIDOW LIVING OF FIFTH BARONET

DIANA ELIZABETH (*Dowager Lady Eardley-Wilmot*), yr da of late Cmdr Aubrey Moore, RN: *m* 1939, Cmdr Sir John Assheton Eardley-Wilmot, 5th Bt, LVO, DSC, RN, who *d* 1995. *Residence* – 41 Margravine Gdns, W6.

COLLATERAL BRANCHES LIVING

Grandson of late Col Irton Eardley-Wilmot, yst son of Maj-Gen Frederick Marow Eardley-Wilmot, 2nd son of 1st baronet:—
Issue of late Capt Vere Levinge Eardley-Wilmot, *b* 1886, *d* 1965: *m* 1915, Mary Cecil, who *d* 1968, da of late H. Moffatt of Toronto:—
Hugh Irton (RR No 1, Norland, Ont), *b* 1925; *ed* McGill Univ (BSc).

Grandchildren of late Francis Eardley-Wilmot, 3rd son of late Rev Edward Revell Eardley-Wilmot, 3rd son of 1st baronet:—
Issue of late Rev Hubert Valentine Eardley-Wilmot, *b* 1878, *d* 1963: *m* 1908, Muriel Ivy, who *d* 1966, da of late William Lovett, of Norwich:—
Paul Revell (Woodland View, Cookham Rise, Berks), *b* 1917; *ed* St Paul's Sch: *m* 1953, Joan Violet, da of H. J. W. Shepherd, of High Wycombe, and has issue living, David Revell, *b* 1954, — Susan Mary, *b* 1957: *m* 1978, Peter William Rushton, of Clare Cottage, 40 Hale Rd, Farnham, Surrey GU9 9QH, and has issue living, Oliver William *b* 1983, Morgan David *b* 1988, Theodore Alexander *b* 1992.

Issue of late Rev Canon Charles Revell Eardley-Wilmot, *b* 1880, *d* 1962: *m* 1914, Rose Meredyth, who *d* 1954, da of C. H. Bowen, of Sherbrooke, Province of Quebec, Canada:—
Robert Lloyd (3 Lisa St, Apt 1502, Brampton, Ontario L6T 4A2, Canada), *b* 1921; 1941-45 War as Sgt RCAF, attached RAF: *m* 1949, Joyce Ethel, da of Delbert Dagles, of Three Rivers, Quebec, Canada, and has issue living, David Robert, *b* 1952. —— Barbara Rose (33 Cedar Crescent, Whitehorse, Yukon, Canada Y7A 4PZ), *b* 1915; 1943-45 War as Nursing Sister RCAF attached RAF: *m* 1st, 1942, John Franklin Carr, Leading Aircraftman RCAF, who was *ka* 1942; 2ndly, 1947, Geoffrey Constable, who *d* 1997, and has issue living (by 2nd *m*), Peter Geoffrey, *b* 1961, — Catherine Judith, *b* 1950, — Janet Meredyth, *b* 1953, — Susan Emily, *b* 1956. —— Cecilia Torlesse, *b* 1917; 1942-45 War as Private Canadian Women's Army Corps: *m* 1946, Eliol Albert Leyden, who *d* 1995, and has issue living, Richard Harold, *b* 1950 *d* 1996, — Michael Peyton, *b* 1952, — Andrew Charles, *b* 1954, — Sylvia Dawn, *b* 1947, — Elizabeth Rose, *b* 1957. —— Sylvia Revell, *b* 1926: *m* 1948, Allan Adolphus Saunders, of RR2 Petitcodiac, New Brunswick, Canada E0A 2H0, and has issue living, Nancy Peyton, *b* 1951, — Sylvia Lee, *b* 1953.

Issue of late Ernest Lancelot Eardley-Wilmot, *b* 1888; *d* 1975: *m* 1919, Margaret, da of late L. Hanlon, of Whangarei, NZ.
Philip (2 Snell's Beach Rd, Snell's Beach, Warkwork, NZ), *b* 1920; 1939-45 War as Flight Sgt, RNZAF: *m* 1948, Joan Hazel, da of G. R. Fox, of Auckland, NZ, and has issue living, Ronald Ernest (9 Carolyn Court, Frankston, Victoria 3199, Australia), *b* 1953: *m* 1972 (*m diss* 1991), Gaylene Mildon, of Mt Wellington, Auckland, and has issue living, Matthew Ronald *b* 1973, Jamie *b* 1975, Nicholas *b* 1977, Lance *b* 1981, — Kay, *b* 1951: *m* 1972, William James Chapman, of Roslyn, Dunedin, NZ, and has issue living, Kirsten *b* 1974, Melanie *b* 1977. —— Eileen, *b* 1922: *m* 1943, Richard Quentin Taylor, and has issue living, Peter Raymond, *b* 1945, — Lynne Carol, *b* 1946.

Granddaughter of late Robert Eardley-Wilmot, MB, 5th son of Rev Edward Revell Eardley-Wilmot (ante):—
Issue of late Lieut-Col Theodore Eardley-Wilmot, DSO, *b* 1879, *ka* 1918: *m* 1908, Mildred Clare, who *d* 1956, el da of late W. F. Reynolds, of Woodland Grange, near Leamington:—
Mildred Joan (*Baroness Cross of Chelsea*), *b* 1912: *m* 1st, 1939, Thomas Walton Davies, who *d* 1948; 2ndly, 1952, Baron Cross of Chelsea (Life Baron), who *d* 1989, and has issue living (by 1st *m*), Charles *b* 1943, — Caroline, *b* 1941, — Sophia, *b* 1946: *m* 1969, Henning Rasmussen, — (by 2nd *m*) (*see* B Cross of Chelsea). *Residence* – The Bridge House, Leintwardine, Craven Arms, Salop.

Grandson of late Maj Henry Eardley-Wilmot, 6th and yst son of Rev Edward Revell Eardley-Wilmot (ante):—
Issue of late Lambert Eardley-Wilmot, OBE, Fl Lt RAF, *b* 1894, *d* 1987: *m* 1930, Angela Clare Gertrude, who *d* 1955, 2nd da of late Col Arthur Hare Vincent, of Summerhill House, Castle Connell, co Limerick:—
Charles Vincent Burgoyne (Fir Tree House, Lower Morton, Thornbury, Bristol, Avon BS12 1LF), *b* 1932: *m* 1961, Sheila, only da of late George Frederick Broomfield, of Thornbury, Glos, and has issue living, Jane Clare, *b* 1962: *m* 1984, Geoffrey J. Sprackman, and has issue living, Ben Charles *b* 1991, Katie-Jane *b* 1988, — Sarah Elizabeth, *b* 1963: *m* 1990, Jeremy Northcott, of Hazel Cottage, St Tudy, Bodmin, Cornwall, and has issue living, Emma Claire *b* 1993.

Grandchildren of late Gerald Stuart Eardley-Wilmot, son of late Stuart Eardley-Wilmot (infra):—
Issue of late Stuart Jeffery Eardley-Wilmot, *b* 1907, *d* 1986: *m* 1933, Mary, who *d* 1994, da of W. Y. Fleming, of Bexhill-on-Sea:—
Brian (15 Fernglen Rd S, St Heliers, Auckland, NZ), *b* 1939: *m* 1st, 1960 (*m diss* 1972), Margaret Robyn, da of A. Doust; 2ndly, 1980, Maureen Jean, da of George Huddlestone, of Cambridge, and has had issue (by 1st *m*), †Stuart Allen, *b* 1961 *d* 1998, — Kathryn Anne, *b* 1966. —— Gillian Mary (5007 Alicante Way, Oceanside, California, USA), *b* 1935: *m* 1957, William H. Cook, who *d* 1998, and has issue living, Victoria Mary, *b* 1961. —— Valerie, *b* 1946: *m* 1st, 1968 (*m diss* 1978), L. K. Eitzen; 2ndly, 1981, R. P. Haley, of 70463 Nick Thomas Rd, Rainier, Oregon 97048, USA.

Grandson of late Augustus Hillier Eardley-Wilmot, 6th son of 1st baronet:—
Issue of late Stuart Eardley-Wilmot, *b* 1847, *d* 1932: *m* 1875, Rosa Cornelia, who *d* 1924, da of William Johnstone, of Launceston, Tasmania:—

Parry, *b* 1888: *m* 1912, Amy, da of Percy Reynolds, of Hobartville, Richmond, NSW, and has issue living, a son, *b* 19—.

This family has common ancestry with the Wilmots, baronets of Osmaston (ext), and Wilmots, baronets of Chaddesden. John Eardley-Wilmot, father of 1st baronet, assumed by Roy Licence 1812 the additional surname of Eardley, as great-grandson of Elizabeth, sole heiress of Edward Eardley of Eardley, Staffs. The 1st baronet, Sir John Eardley-Wilmot, FRS, was sometime MP for North Warwickshire, and Gov of Van Diemen's Land 1843-7, and the 2nd baronet sat as MP for Warwickshire S (*C*) 1874-85, and was Recorder of Warwick 1852-7, and Judge of Bristol County Court 1854-63, and of Marylebone County Court 1863-71.

WILSON (UK) 1874, of Eshton Hall, co York

Loyal in everything

Brig Sir MATHEW JOHN ANTHONY WILSON, OBE, MC, 6th *Baronet*, son (by 1st *m*) of late Anthony Thomas Wilson, 2nd son of 4th Bt; *b* 2 Oct 1935; *s* his uncle, *Sir* (MATHEW) MARTIN, 1991; *ed* Trin Coll Sch, Ontario; formerly Exec Dir of the Wilderness Foundation (UK), and Vice-Pres of International Wilderness Leadership Foundation; Pres and Chief Exec Offr Dolphin Voyaging Inc 1995; author; Brig King's Own Yorkshire LI (ret); MC 1972, MBE (Mil) 1971 and OBE (Mil) 1979: *m* 1962, Janet Mary, elder da of late Edward Worsfold Mowll, JP, of Coldblow, Walmer, Kent, and has issue.

꽃rms – Sable, a wolf rampant or, gorged with a collar gemel of the field between four mullets of six points, three in chief and one in base of the second. Crest – A demi-wolf or, gorged with a collar gemel sable, and resting the sinister paw on an escutcheon of the last, charged with a mullet as in the arms. Seconꝺ jꝼotto – Res non verba (*Facts not words*).
Address – RR1, Box 293, Woodstock, VT 05091, USA. *Club* – Explorers'.

SON LIVING

(MATHEW) EDWARD AMCOTTS, *b* 13 Oct 1966; *ed* The King's Sch, Canterbury, and King's Coll, London Univ; Capt LI (despatches 1993); Vice-Pres Communications, Earthwatch Inst, Boston, USA: *m* 1995, his 2nd cousin, Imogen Nancy, yr da of Richard Thomas Wilson (infra), and has issue living, Matthew Titus Henry, *b* 20 June 1998. *Residence* – 461 Huron Av, Cambridge, MA 02138, USA.

DAUGHTER LIVING

Victoria Mary, *b* 1968; *ed* The King's Sch, Canterbury, and New Hall, Camb; Solicitor: *m* 1998, Edward S. W. Roskill, son of Nicholas Roskill, of Camberwell, SE5.

COLLATERAL BRANCHES LIVING

Issue of late Peter Cecil Wilson, CBE, 3rd son of 4th Bt, *b* 1913, *d* 1984: *m* 1935 (*m diss* 1947), Grace Helen, da of late Arthur Ranken:—
(Richard) Thomas (Petrovsky, Tereulok 5, Flat 44, 103031, Moscow), *b* 1937: *m* 1964 (*m diss* 1974), Judith, da of Ford Jenkins, of Lowestoft, and has issue living, Alice Thomasina, *b* 1966, — Imogen Nancy, *b* 1967: *m* 1995, her 2nd cousin, (Mathew) Edward Amcotts Wilson, son of Brig Sir Mathew John Anthony Wilson, 6th Bt, OBE, MC (ante). —— (Edward) Philip (24 Highbury Place, N5 1QP), *b* 1940: *m* 1970, Lady Alexandra Patricia Gwendoline Jellicoe, da of 2nd Earl Jellicoe, and has issue living, Anthony Benedict, *b* 1980, — Patrick Peter, *b* 1984.

Granddaughters of late Com Alec Thomas Lee Wilson (infra):—
Issue of late Lt-Col James Thomas Amcotts Wilson, *b* 1916, *d* 1992: *m* 1947, Judy Featherstone (Manor Farm, Wraxall, nr Dorchester, Dorset), da of late Maj Pierre Elliot Inchbald, MC (*see* Bingham, Bt, 1985 Edn):—
Carol Ann, *b* 1948: *m* 1972, David John Hugh Parry, of Broomhill, Rampisham, Dorchester, Dorset, son of late Alan Wheeler Parry, of Stoneleigh, Beaconsfield Rd, Liverpool, and has issue living, James Alan David, *b* 1976, — Benjamin Alec, *b* 1979. —— Pamela Gay, *b* 1951: *m* 1974, Edward Trevor Gwyn Lewis, of 77 Lexham Gdns, W8, son of late Rev Gwyn Lewis, and has issue living, Frances Leone, *b* 1975, — Kim Olivia, *b* 1979, — Tamsin Gwynne, *b* (twin) 1979. —— Vianna Jane, *b* 1959: *m* 1988, John Michael Dene, of Manor Farm, Wraxall, Dorchester, Dorset, son of late Lt-Col John Anthony Dene, of Kilteelagh Stud, Dromineer, Nenagh, co Tipperary, and has issue living, Polly Alexandra, *b* 1990.

Issue of late Com Alec Thomas Lee Wilson, 3rd son of 3rd baronet, *b* 1883, *d* 1956: *m* 1913, Margaret (a DStJ), who *d* 1966, da of late Leopold Hirsch, of 10 Kensington Palace Gdns, W:—
Francis Amcotts (Garth House, Llangammarch Wells, Powys; Army and Navy Club), *b* 1922; 1939-45 War as Sub-Lt RNVR: *m* 1968, Mrs Katherine Mary Scott, da of late Robert Charles Bruce, MC (*see* E Elgin, colls), and has an adopted son and da, Robert Mathew, *b* 1970, — Jane Mary, *b* 1972.

Sir Mathew Wilson, 1st baronet, sat as MP for Clitheroe (*L*) 1847-52, for N Div of W Riding of Yorks 1874-85, and for

Skipton Div of N part of W Riding of Yorks 1885-6. The 4th baronet, Lieut-Col Sir Mathew Richard Henry Wilson, CSI, DSO, 10th Hussars, served in S Africa 1899-1902 and sat as MP for S-W Div of Bethnal Green (*C*) 1914-22.

WILSON (UK) 1906, of Airdrie, New Monkland, co Lanark

Sir JAMES WILLIAM DOUGLAS WILSON, 5th *Baronet*; *b* 8 Oct 1960; *s* his father, *Capt Sir* THOMAS DOUGLAS, MC, 1984; *ed* Marlborough, and London Univ (BA): *m* 1985, Julia Margaret Louise, da of Joseph Charles Francis Mutty, of Mulberry Hall, Melbourn, nr Royston, Herts, and has issue.

Arms – Argent, a lion rampant between three mullets sable, on a chief vert a crescent of the first between two mullets pierced or. Crest – A demi-lion sable, charged on the body with a crescent argent between two mullets pierced or, all in pale.
Residence – Lillingstone Lovell Manor, Buckingham, MK18 5BQ.

SONS LIVING

THOMAS EDWARD DOUGLAS, *b* 15 April 1990. —— Harry William Patrick, *b* 1995.

DAUGHTERS LIVING

Jessica Sarah, *b* 1988. —— Katrina Elizabeth, *b* 1992.

SISTERS LIVING

Sarah Ann, *b* 1950: *m* 1976, Michael J. Fleming, of Ye Olde Malting House, Greens Norton, Towcester, Northants NN12 8BE, and has issue living, Simon James, *b* 1982. —— Susan Mary, *b* 1954: *m* 1978, Robert James Nield, of 5 Belle Vue Rd, Exmouth, Devon, and has issue living, Timothy James, *b* 1979, — Michael Jonathon, *b* 1980, — Emilia Mary, *b* 1984. —— Margaret Rose, *b* 1957: *m* 1983, Jonathan Kendal James Gurney, of Mount Mill, Stratford Rd, Wicken MK19 6DG, elder son of Brian Gurney, of Handley Park, Towcester, and has issue living, Joseph Brian Thomas, *b* 1985, — Olivia Kate, *b* 1987.

AUNT LIVING (*Sister of 4th baronet*)

Aileen (16 Bramble Close, Oaklands Park, Redhill, Surrey), *b* 1915: *m* 1939, Roger Benjamin Constant, who *d* 1986, and has issue living, Roger Clive, *b* 1945; *ed* Sherborne, — Stella, *b* 1943.

DAUGHTER LIVING OF THIRD BARONET

Daphne Margaret, *b* 1922: *m* 1945, Thomas Morton Macdonald, of Coanwood Jordans, Bucks, and has had issue, Ian James, *b* 1946; *ed* Stowe, — Neil Stuart, *b* 1947; *ed* Oakham, — Alastair, *b* and *d* 1950.

WIDOW LIVING OF FOURTH BARONET

PAMELA AILEEN (*Pamela, Lady Wilson*), da of Sir (Griffin Wyndham) Edward Hanmer, 7th Bt: *m* 1947, Capt Sir Thomas Douglas Wilson, 4th Bt, who *d* 1984. *Residence* – Lillingstone Lovell Manor, Buckingham, MK18 5BQ.

COLLATERAL BRANCH LIVING

Issue of late Maj John Wilson, Lanarkshire Yeo, only son of 2nd baronet, *b* 1911, *ka* 1942: *m* 1936, Zoe Jane (who *m* 2ndly, 1943, Guy C. Turner, AFC, who *d* 1993, of Keepers Cottage, Nuneham Park, Nuneham Courtnay, Oxford), 2nd da of George Orr, of Kilduff House, East Lothian:—
Sarah Jane, *b* 1937: *m* 1959, Michael Claud Ogilvie-Thomson, WS, and has issue living, David John, *b* 1961, — Sheelagh Jane, *b* 1960: *m* 1986, John Hugh Hay, of 10 St Catherine's Place, Edinburgh 9, and has issue living, Alexander Michael Edward *b* 1995, Zoe Margaret Thomson *b* 1988, Romilly Jane Wilson *b* 1991. *Residence* – Keepers Cottage, Nuneham Park, Nuneham Courtenay, Oxford.

The 1st baronet, Sir John, was Chm of Wilsons and Clyde Coal Co (Limited), and sat as MP for Falkirk Dist (LU and L) 1895 to 1905.

WILSON (UK) 1920, of Carbeth, Killearn, co Stirling

Sir DAVID WILSON, 3rd *Baronet*; *b* 30 Oct 1928; *s* his father, *Sir*
JOHN MITCHELL HARVEY, KCVO, 1975; *ed* Deerfield Acad, Mass,
Harrow, and Oriel Coll, Oxford (MA); Bar Lincoln's Inn 1954;
solicitor 1962: *m* 1955, Eva Margareta, el da of Tore Lindell, of
Malmo, Sweden, and has issue.

Arms – (as recorded at Lyon Office)—Argent, a chevron gules between two
mullets in chief, and in base a trefoil slipped vert. **Crest** – A demi-lion
rampant gules, armed and langued azure.
Seat – Carbeth, Killearn, by Glasgow. *Residence* – Tandem House, Queen's
Drive, Oxshott, Surrey KT22 0PH. *Clubs* – Lond Arts, Roy Southern Yacht,
Hamble.

SONS LIVING

THOMAS DAVID (The Lodge, 41 Wandle Rd, SW17 7DL), *b* 6 Jan 1959; *ed*
Harrow: *m* 1984, Valerie, elder da of Vivian David Davies Stogdale, of Monks
Farm, Shotover, Oxon, and has issue living, Fergus, *b* 24 April 1987, —
Oscar, *b* 1989. —— Andrew (Mulberry Cottage, 4 Fairway, Merrow, nr
Guildford, Surrey GU1 2XG), *b* 16 Dec 1959: *m* 1984, Penelope May, 2nd da
of Brig William Turner, of The Holt, Woolton Hill, Newbury, Berks.

DAUGHTER LIVING

Annika, *b* 1961: *m* 1984, Dr David Malcolm Ratcliffe, of 63 Winchester Rd,
Walton-on-Thames, Surrey KT12 2RH, son of M. Ratcliffe, of 440 Ombersley
Rd, Worcester, and has issue living, Camilla, *b* 1992, — Tegaela, *b* 1995.

Always watchful

BROTHERS LIVING

John Richards (Heron's Court, Killearn, Stirlingshire), *b* 1930: *m* 1969, H. Jane, da of Maj Gilbert B. Rahr, of Huntbourne
Farm, Tenterden, Kent. —— Andrew George (Little Carbeth, Killearn, by Glasgow), *b* 1933: *m* 1967, Anne-Marie Tekla,
yr da of Tore Lindell, of Malmo, Sweden.

The 1st baronet, Sir David Wilson, was Convener (sometime Vice-Convener) of Stirlingshire, and a Member of Board of
Agriculture for Scotland's Advisory Committee. The 2nd baronet, Sir John Mitchell Harvey Wilson, KCVO, was Keeper
of The Royal Philatelic Collection 1938-69, and Pres Royal Philatelic Soc 1934-40.

Windham, see Bowyer-Smith.

WINNINGTON (GB) 1755, of Stanford Court, Worcestershire

Sir FRANCIS SALWEY WILLIAM WINNINGTON, 6th *Baronet*, son of late Francis
Salwey Winnington, el son of 5th baronet, *b* 24 June 1907; *s* his grandfather,
Sir FRANCIS SALWEY, 1931; Lieut Welsh Guards; European War 1939-40
(prisoner); is patron of three livings: *m* 1944, Anne Beryl Jane, only da of
late Capt Lawrence Drury-Lowe, Scots Guards, and has issue.

Arms – Quarterly; 1st and 4th, argent, an orle between eight martlets sable, *Winnington*;
2nd and 3rd, sable, a saltire engrailed or, *Salwey*. **Crest** – A Saracen's head full-faced,
couped at the shoulders proper, wreathed about the temples argent and sable.

DAUGHTER LIVING

Charmian Anne, *b* 1945.

Gratâ sume manu
*Take with a grateful
hand*

BROTHER DECEASED

Thomas Foley Churchill, MBE, *b* 16 Aug 1910; *ed* Eton, and Balliol Coll, Oxford; Col
Grenadier Guards; MBE (Mil) 1948: *m* 1944, Lady Betty Marjorie Anson (182 Rivermead
Court, Ranelagh Gdns, SW6 3SG), da of 4th Earl of Lichfield, and *d* 1999, leaving issue, ANTHONY EDWARD (20
Baskerville Rd, SW18 3RW), *b* 13 May 1948: *m* 1978, Karyn, da of Francis Hubbs Kettles, and Mrs Alan Dayton, of Palm

Beach, Florida, USA and has issue living, Edward Alan *b* 15 Nov 1987, Victoria Elizabeth *b* 1981, Sophia Rose *b* 1985, — Henry Thomas, *b* 1961, — Sarah Rose, LVO (*Viscountess Campden*), *b* 1951; formerly Lady in Waiting to HRH The Princess of Wales; LVO 1996: *m* 1972, Anthony Baptist, Viscount Campden, el son of 5th Earl of Gainsborough, — Emma Elizabeth, *b* 1956: *m* 1981, Christopher J. Milne, of 67 Hendham Rd, SW17, and has issue living, Rupert John *b* 1986, Isabella Katherine *b* 1984, Lucinda Alice *b* 1991.

COLLATERAL BRANCHES LIVING

Granddaughters of late Capt John Taylor Winnington, son of late Capt John Taylor Winnington, 2nd son of 3rd baronet:—
Issue of late Lieut-Col John Francis Sartorius Winnington, DSO, Worcestershire Regt, *b* 1876, *d* of wounds received in action 1918: *m* 1910, Joyce Mary, who *d* 1970, da of David Marriage, of Chorley, Lancs:—
Susanne, *b* 1913: *m* 1st, 1936 (*m diss* 19—), Russell Cowell; 2ndly, 1950, John Duerdin, of Affcot Manor, Church Stretton, Salop, and has issue living (by 2nd *m*), John Patrick, *b* 1952: *m* 1986, Judy Mary Trow, of Little Stretton, and has issue living, Emma Mary *b* 1988, Sophie Elizabeth *b* 1989, — Joanna Elizabeth, *b* 1950: *m* 1st 1978 (*m diss* 1992), R. Wise; 2ndly, 1996, Andrew Crofts, OBE, of Dursley, Glos, and has issue living (by 1st *m*) George John *b* 1988, Suzanna Frances *b* 1986, — Frances June, *b* 1951: *m* 1973, Graham Bowcher, of Portland, Dorset, and has issue living, Sian Monique *b* 1977, Ceri Anne *b* 1980. —— Patricia Rose, *b* 1917: *m* 1949, Robin Darell Unwin, OBE, who *d* 1991, of Longdon Hall, Tewkesbury, Glos, and has issue living, Carol John *b* 1951, — Guy Darell, *b* 1952: *m* 1984, Patricia Ann, da of Alan Derek Boydell, of Winchcombe, Glos, and has issue living, William Francis *b* 1988, Sally Victoria *b* 1986, Elizabeth Laura Dorothy *b* 1990, — Barry James, *b* 1956: *m* 1984, Susan Louise, da of George Dennis Gilbert, of Redmarley, Glos, and has issue living, Louise Rose *b* 1987, Rosanna Helen *b* 1989, Phoebe Grace *b* 1993.

Grandchildren of late Ven Edward Henry Winnington-Ingram, eldest son of Rev Edward Winnington-Ingram (*b* 1814), 2nd son of Rev Edward Winnington-Ingram (*b* 1785), 2nd son of 2nd baronet:—
Issue of late Rev Preb Edward Francis Winnington-Ingram, *b* 1883, *d* 1963: *m* 1924, Gladys Winifred, who *d* 1995, da of John Armstrong, of Tenbury, Worcs:—
(Edward) John (Old Manor Farm, Cottisford, Brackley, Northants NN13 5SW), *b* 1926; *ed* Shrewsbury, and Keble Coll, Oxford (BA): *m* 1st, 1953, Shirley Yvoire, el da of Gerald Lamotte; 2ndly, 1973, Mrs Elizabeth Linda Few Brown, da of Geoffrey Milling, of Brading, Isle of Wight, and formerly wife of Peter Few Brown, and has issue living, (by 1st *m*) Edward Nicholas, *b* 1957, — Gerald Francis, *b* 1960: *m* 1987, Rebecca Susan, da of Terence Cocks, of Geneva, Switzerland, and has issue living, Lucy Margaret *b* 1990. —— Gladys Ann, *b* 1929: *m* 1952, Lt-Cdr Francis Nigel Oldfield Bartlett, RN (Eaton Cottage, Eaton Hill, Baslow, Bakewell, Derbys), and has issue living, Charles Nicholas Oldfield, *b* 1954, — Sarah Frances, *b* 1955, — Rachel Victoria, *b* 1957, — Joanna Elizabeth, *b* 1959.

Grandchildren of late Francis Herbert Winnington-Ingram, 2nd son of Rev Edward Winnington-Ingram (*b* 1814) (ante):—
Issue of late Charles William Edward Winnington-Ingram, *b* 1881, *d* 1958: *m* 1902, Maud Esther (Aylmer, Ont), da of Richard R. Jones, of Copenhagen, Ont:—
†(Francis) Herbert, *b* 1906: *m* 1930, Ruth Agnes, who *d* 1990, da of Newton Newell, of Aylmer, Ont, and *d* 1994, leaving issue, †Gerald Newell, *b* 1935: *m* 1957, Lillian Tremblay, who *d* 1972, and *d* 1984, leaving issue, James Brian (102 Charles St, Bracebridge, Ont P1L 1M1) *b* 1959, Douglas Michael *b* 1964, Phyllis Anne *b* 1958, Angela Marie *b* 1969, — Charles Edward, *b* 1938: *m* Dorothy, da of —, and has issue living, one son, — Philip Herbert, *b* 1943: *m* Bea, da of —. —— †Arthur Foley, *b* 1908: *m* 1928, Ruby Louisa, who *d* 1987, da of Edward Herries, of Luton, Ont, and *d* 1988, leaving issue, Donald Foley (RR6, Aylmer, Ont N5H 2R5), *b* 1935: *m* 1957, Dawn Marlyn Hussar, da of the Rev Garnet Hussar Aylmer, and has issue living, Allan Foley *b* 1968, Cheryl Lynn *b* 1962: *m* 1982, Geo Mallia (and has issue living, Brian Foley *b* 1988, Lynn Marie *b* 1992). —— †(Charles) Alexander, *b* 1912: *m* 1939, Doris Marjorie Buck, who *d* 19—, and *d* 19—, leaving issue, Alexander Grant (20 Talavere Crescent, London, Ont N5V 1K8), *b* 1940: *m* 1966, Carolyn Fuchsia Johnston, and has issue living, Sherri Lynn *b* 1966, and two das, — David Gary (30 Diane Crescent, Lambeth, Ont N0L 1S0), *b* 1943: *m* 1965, Mary Ilene McClure, and has issue living, David, Deborah. —— Cecil Harold (150 Grey St, Dundalk, Ontario, Canada, N0C 1B0), *b* 1918: *m* 1947, Patricia Howse Green, and has issue living, William Edward (Nairn Center, Ontario, Canada P0M 2L0), *b* 1948: *m* 1971, Cecile Noelle Ringuette, and has issue living, Jason Edward *b* 1973, Gregory Lee *b* 1974 (has issue living, Gavin Lee *b* 1995), Neil Edward *b* 1978, — Brian Charles, *b* 1959: *m* 1986, Cheryl Ann Lortie, and has issue living, Michael Blaine *b* 1986, Kerri Louise, *b* 1989, Kimberly Anne *b* 1992, — Frank Berton, *b* (twin) 1959: *m* 1st, 1981, Janice Shelton; 2ndly, 1995, Christine Jane Cooper, and has issue living, (by 1st *m*) Jeffrey Michael *b* 1986, Amanda Megan *b* 1983, (by 2nd *m*) Jayna Lorraine *b* 1997, — Beth Arlene, *b* 1952: *m* 1971, Gavin Whitney, and has issue living, Christopher *b* 1975, Tammy *b* 1977 (has issue living, Jacob *b* 1998), — Beverley Irene, *b* 1953: *m* 1st, 19—, Randy Banish; 2ndly, 1999, Michael Black, and has issue living (by 1st *m*), Terry *b* 1976, Angela *b* 1975. —— Gerald (96 York St, Aylmer, Ontario N5H 2X7, Canada), *b* 1926: *m* 1947, Edna Arletta Johnson, and has issue living, Judith Susanne, *b* 1949: *m* — Jones, and has issue living, Jennifer, — Janet Marie, *b* 1951. —— Vera Louise, *b* 1903: *m* 1928, Kenneth McGregor Hatch, who *d* 1964, and has issue living, Kenneth Herbert (49 Connaught Av, Willowdale, Ont M2M 1G9), *b* 1931: *m* 1953, Pamela Dianne House, and has issue living, Steven Kenneth *b* 1955: *m* 19—, Kati Mary McClung (and has issue living, Kenneth Robert *b* 1982, Gregory Steven *b* 1984), Peter Donald *b* 1957: *m* 19—, Wendy Elizabeth Vaughan (and has issue living, Kevin Donald *b* 1989), Thomas Alan *b* 1966: *m* 19—, Debbie Lyn Hardie, Nancy Laura *b* (twin) 1957: *m* 19—, Stuart William Jackson (and has issue living, Jason Blair *b* 1988), Wendy Vivian *b* 1962: *m* 1987, Edward Evan Etchells (and has issue living, Timothy Evan *b* 1994, Matthew Donald *b* 1997), — Donna Lucille, *b* 1928: *m* 1949, Clayton Vickers McKechnie, of 25 Helen Av, Thornhill, Ont L4J 1S6, and has issue living, Stewart Douglas *b* 1952: *m* 1st, 1972, Kathleen Haskey; 2ndly, 1993, Coreen Annette Karges (and has issue living, (by 1st *m*) Christopher Stewart *b* 1974, Erin *b* 1979), Dean Charles *b* 1958: *m* 1982, Andrea Dawn Gambell (and has issue living, Michael James *b* 1981, Scott William *b* 1985), Janice Louise *b* 1953: *m* 1st, 1971, Edward Adrian Vanherk; 2ndly, 1994, William Ronald Warnica (and has issue living (by 1st *m*), Pamela Jenifer *b* 1971: *m* 1997, Kevin Poste, Adranna Donna *b* 1982). —— Helen Patricia, *b* 1914: *m* 1938, James Arthur Ferris, who *d* 1989, and has issue living, Charles David, *b* 1942: *m* 19—, Richard Hartney, of Vancouver, BC (and has issue living, Kirk Russell *b* 19—, Kody James Ferris *b* 19—), Danielle Jacqueline *b* 1973, — Heather Anne, *b* 1956: *m* 1980, Rolf Larsen, of Sudbury, Ont. —— Marjorie, *b* 1920: *m* 1946, John M. Hale, of RR2, Aylmer, Ont N5H 2R2, and has issue living, John, *b* 19—: *m* Johanna, da of —, and has issue living, Jonathon, Jennifer, — Barbara, *b* 19—: *m* Wayne Stafford, and has issue living, Adam, Jorden. —— Audrey Lucille, *b* 1921: *m* 1948, William Ozarko, of 632 Lime Ridge Rd, RR3 Hamilton, Ont, and has had issue, John, *b* 19—, *d* 19—, — William, *b* 19—, — Catherine *b* 19—. —— Pauline, *b* 1928: *m* 1948, Edward Golibaski, of 390 St Pauls Av, Brantford, Ont N3R 1U5, and has issue living, Paul, *b* 19—, — Linda, *b* 19—.

Issue of late Herbert Arthur Winnington-Ingram, b 1881, d 1941: m 1912, Anna, who d 1924, da of Angus D. Grant, of Edmonton, Canada:—

†Herbert Grant, b 1914: m 1941, Florence Beatrice Lea, and d 1995, leaving issue, Donald Grant (6092 Oakland Rd, Halifax, Nova Scotia B3H 1N8, Canada), b 1947: m 1977, Ethel Langille, of Pugwash, Nova Scotia, and has issue living, Daniel Grant b 1979, Megan Elizabeth b 1981, Emily Hope b (twin) 1981, — Robert Craig, b 1953: m 1987, Hélène Dobrowolsky, of Whitehouse, Yukon, and has issue living, Joelle Xenia Aunalea b 1988, — Lea Gordon, b 1946: m 1978, Lovie Mohammed, of Toronto. —— †Charles Gordon (66 Glenhaven Crescent, St Albert, Alberta T8N 1A5, Canada), b 1918: m 1st, 1944, Marion Winkler (decd); 2ndly, Joan Youngand, and d 1990, leaving issue (by 1st m), Robert Gordon, b 1943: m 1st, 19— (m diss 19—), Jane Bennett; 2ndly, 19—, Sharon Mills, and has issue living, (by 1st m) Robert Paul b 1966, Jill b 1969, (by 2nd m) Graham Gordon b 1978, Mathew James b 1981, Laura Sharon b 1982, — James Hugh, b 1948: m 1968 (m diss 19—), Joan Smith, — Donna Marion, b 1946: m 19—, Gerard Lemieux, of 10217-132 St, Edmonton, Alberta T5N 1Y8, Canada and has issue living, André Gerard b 1971, Alène Margaret b 1973, Collette Marie b 1977. —— Marion Elizabeth, b 1920: m 1945, William Niven Duff, of 14515-84 Av, Edmonton, Alberta T5R 3X1, Canada, and has issue living, William Neil, b 1948: m 1st, 1969 (m diss 1971), Christine Judy Melmoth; 2ndly, 1973, Joanne Margaret Fedorow; 3rdly, 19—, Marlene Anne Hilker, and has issue living (by 1st m), Shae Nancy Marion b 1967, (by 2nd m), William Michael Scott b 1977, Brindy Veronica b 1981, — David Duff, b 1954: m 1976, Elizabeth Maria, da of John Van Lier, of Edmonton, and has issue living, Erin Nicole b 1985, Rebecca Anne b 1990, — Nancy Marion, b 1947: m 1969, Derek David Nash, and has issue living, Katharine Elizabeth b 1976, Margaret Lindsey b 1979. —— Anna, b 1924: m 1947, Raymond Benjamin Hager, of Box 376, Alberta Beach, Alberta T0E 0A0, Canada, and has issue living, Richard Raymond, b 1949: m 1982, Lesley Jane Etty, of Edmonton, — Douglas Gordon, b 1951: m Melanie Lissa Jahrig, of Ontario, and has issue living, Natalie Bree b 1985, — Donald Benjamin, b 1957: m Dolores Freda Patterson, of Alberta Beach, and has issue living, Jarret Benjamin b 1986, Jamie Donald b 1988, — Laura Lillian b 1954: m 1977, Darryl Bruce Smith, of Edmonton, and has issue living, Joel Jeffrey b 1982, Jess Cole b 1981.

Issue of late Gerald John Gordon Winnington-Ingram, b 1889, d 1945: m 1922, Florence Mabel Byron, who d 1985:—

Florence Maxine (2119 Oak Bay Av, # 307, Victoria, BC V8R 1E8, Canada), b 1923: m 1945, Alexander Harold Clark, and has issue living, David Gerald, b 1946: m 1970, Linda Jeffery, of Devon, and has issue living, Scott Jeffery b 1973, Cindi Jennifer b 1975: m 1997, Kris Allan Lee, — Randall Gregory, b 1957: m 1988, Debora Ann Degryse, of Winnipeg, Man, and has issue living, Carly Anne b 1992, — Kathleen Laura, b 1948: m 1969, Robert Kenneth Chalmers, of Winnipeg, and has issue living, Laura Susan b 1969: m 1993, Cornelius Vandertop (and has issue living, Devonny Kathrine b 1994), Barbara Ruth, b 1973: m 1998, Kevin Franklin Bill. —— Kathleen Hazel (Box 583, Fort Qu'Appelle, Saskatchewan, Canada S0G 1S0), b 1931: m 1956, Rev Gordon Samuel Jardine, and has issue living, Edwin James, b 1961, — Arthur John, b 1964, — Bonnie Jean, b 1959: m 1984, Hugh Mclellan, and has issue living, Stephen Patrick b 1985, Kathleen Joan b 1987, — Donna Jean, b 1965, — Naomi Kathleen, b 1972.

Grandson of late Rev Edward Winnington-Ingram (b 1814) (ante):—
Issue of late George Frederick Winnington-Ingram, b 1859, d 1929: m 1901, Mary Beatrice, who d 1957, da of late John Burridge, of Charminster, Bournemouth:—
John Felix, b 1909.

Grandsons of late Rev Alfred Winnington-Ingram (infra):—
Issue of late Cecil Winnington-Ingram, MBE, b 1914, d 1990: m 1954, Maude (14 Main Rd, Biddenham, Bedford MK40 4BB), yr da of late James Bartlett Lee, of Portsmouth:—
Charles Pepys, b 1955. —— (Francis) Christopher, b 1957.

Grandson of late Rev Edward Winnington-Ingram (b 1814) (ante):—
Issue of late Rev Alfred Winnington-Ingram, b 1861, d 1929: m 1906, Julia Margaret, who d 1958, da of late William Augeraud:—
Richard Sullivan, b 1919; Maj (ret) RE; 1939-45 War (despatches): m 1952, Isobel Margaret, only da of late Robin McCrae, of Kabete, Kenya, and has issue living, Rev David Robert (The Rectory, Offwell, Honiton, Devon EX14 9SB), b 1959: m 1990, Carol Jarvis, and has issue living, Jonathan Richard b 1992, Christopher Edward b 1995, — Peter Richard (4 Home Farm Cottages, Malshanger, Basingstoke, Hants RG23 7ET), b 1960: m 1989, Mrs Sarah L. J. Addie, yst da of late Archie Weir, of Edinburgh, and has issue living, Archie b 1993, Kitty Rose b 1992, Lara Louisa b 1997, — Julia Caroline, b 1954: m 1982, Peter Derek Gregson, of 15 Harling Bank, Kirkby Lonsdale, Carnforth, Lancs LA6 2DJ, 2nd son of W. D. H. Gregson, of 15 Barnton Avenue, Edinburgh, and has issue living, Heather Mary b 1986, Sheila Rosalind b 1988, — Mary Cynthia, b 1956: m 1985, Dr Edward Mark Hundert, of 3875 East Av, Rochester, NY 14618, USA, son of Irwin Hundert, of East Brunswick, New Jersey, USA, and has issue living, Carol Grace b 1991, Laura Kristina b 1996, Anna Faith b (twin) 1996. Address – Supuko, 36 Barnton Av, Edinburgh EH4 6JL.

Grandchildren of late Gerald Constantine Winnington-Ingram, son of late Rev Edward Winnington-Ingram (ante):—
Issue of late Eric Alfred Winnington-Ingram, b 1902, d 1986: m 1930, Jean Emma Caroline, who d 1998, da of F. G. Hopkins, of Haddon Hill, Christchurch, Hants:—
Mariamne Jean, b 1933: m 1968, Roderick MacBeath, of The Pines, Deanland Rd, Balcombe, W Sussex RH17 6LX. —— Iris Hawthorne, b 1935: m 1964, John Awberry Field, of Yewtrees Farm, Balcombe, W Sussex, and has issue living, Fiona Clare, b 1967, — Alison Joyce, b 1969.

This family were lords of the manor of Winnington temp Edward I, and continued to reside there till the beginning of the eighteenth century. The 4th baronet was MP for Bewdley (L) 1832-46 and 1857-68. The present baronet is descended from Sir Francis Winnington, Knt, of Stanford Court, who was appointed in 1678 Solicitor-General to Charles II, a post which he resigned, that he might act consistently with his conscience, by supporting the Exclusion Bill. Sir Francis Salwey Winnington, 5th Bt, was High Sheriff of Worcestershire 1894.

WISEMAN (E) 1628, of Canfield Hall, Essex

Sir JOHN WILLIAM WISEMAN, 11th *Baronet*; *b* 16 March 1957; *s* his father, *Sir* WILLIAM GEORGE EDEN, CB, 1962; *ed* Millfield, and Hartford Univ Conn USA: *m* 1980, Nancy Ann, da of Casimer Zyla, of New Britain, Conn, USA, and has issue.

ᴬrms – Sable, a chevron ermine between three cronels argent. Crest – A tower or, port open argent, out of the top a demi-Moor issuant armed proper, in his right hand a dart argent, barbed or plumed or, in his left a Roman target of the last. *Residence* – USA.

Sapit qui Deo sapit

He is wise who is wise through God

DAUGHTERS LIVING

Elizabeth, *b* 1983. —— Patricia Alison, *b* 1986.

HALF-SISTERS LIVING

Rosemary, *b* 1916: *m* 1936, Lt-Col Frederick R. Hulton, RA (ret), and has issue living, Frederick William (Rambridge Cottage, Weyhill, Andover, Hants SP11 0QG), *b* 1938: *m* 1973, Ruth Parsons, and has issue living, Mark *b* 1975, Dominic *b* (twin) 1975, — Peter Richard, *b* 1941: *m* 1969, Dorinda Stewart, and has issue living, Anna Sky *b* 1979, — Thomas Michael, *b* 1943: *m* 19—, Susan Oldman, and has issue living, Claire *b* 1973, Kathleen *b* 1975, — Rosemary Jane, *b* 1949: *m* 1970, Christopher Eliot, and has issue living, James *b* 1975, David *b* 1978, Peter *b* 1984. *Residence* – Firles, 14 Chyngton Rd, Seaford, Sussex BN25 4HH. —— Sheila (Box 359, Mamaroneck, NY 10343, USA), *b* 1928; is a Journalist.

WIDOW LIVING OF TENTH BARONET

JOAN MARY (*Joan, Lady Wiseman*), da of late Arthur Phelps, of Woodridge, Harrow, and formerly wife of Lawrence E. Lesueur: *m* 1944, as his 3rd wife, Sir William George Eden Wiseman, CB, 10th baronet, who *d* 1962.

COLLATERAL BRANCHES LIVING

Grandchildren of late Thomas Edward Wiseman (*b* 1851) (infra):—
Issue of late Thomas Edward Wiseman, *b* 1878, *d* 1959: *m* 1916, Annie, who *d* 1970, da of George William Allen:—
THOMAS ALAN, *b* 8 July 1921; *ed* Gravesend County Sch; formerly Admin Officer for Forest Products Ltd; late Staff Sergeant RAOC: *m* 1946, Hildemarie, who *d* 1991, da of Gustav Domnik, of Allenstein, E Prussia, Germany. *Residence* – 14 Havisham Rd, Chalk, Gravesend, Kent DA12 4UN.

Issue of late Frank Eldred Wiseman, *b* 1880, *d* 1938: *m* 1923, Lily Amy, who *d* 1957, da of Harry Lewis Little-wood, of Gravesend, Kent:—
†Wallis Littlewood, *b* 1924: *m* 1st, 1951, Brenda Doris, who *d* 1990, da of late Arthur Allanson, of Walmer, Port Elizabeth, S Africa; 2ndly, 1991, Margaret-Ann (PO Box 5689, Walmer 6070, Port Elizabeth, S Africa), da of late Malcolm Edward Rittenhouse, of Osgood, Indiana, USA, and *d* 1993, leaving issue (by 1st *m*), Jonathan Charles (11 Huilboom St, Randpark, Johannesburg, S Africa), *b* 1953: *m* 1980, Rita Hilda, da of L. A. Williams, of Port Elizabeth, and has issue living, Lauren Ann *b* 1983, Nicola Jane *b* 1986, — Richard Christopher, *b* 1954: *m* 1986, Dawn Lorraine, da of Patrick Hart, of Springs, S Africa, and has issue living, Christopher Phillip *b* 1987, — Barry James (19 Pamela Crescent, Walmer Downs, Port Elizabeth, S Africa), *b* 1956: *m* 1979, Brigitte, da of Hans Bülbring, of Port Elizabeth, S Africa, and has issue living, Jarrod *b* 1984, Paul Mark *b* 1986, — Margaret Alexandra, *b* 1960: *m* 1985, Peter Wilson Newton, of 19 Barrydale Rd, Miramar, Port Elizabeth, S Africa, son of Michael Newton, of Nairobi, Kenya, and has issue living, Matthew Michael *b* 1987, Bailey Louise *b* 1985.

Issue of late Frederick William Wiseman, *b* 1885, *d* 1954: *m* 1914, Charlotte Hepshibah Ward, who *d* 1966:—
John Henry Ware (75 Lucas St, North Rockhampton, Queensland 4701, Australia), *b* 1924; 1939-45 War with R Australian Artillery in New Guinea, Bouganville and New Britain (wounded): *m* 1962, Delma Margaret, da of Douglas James Lung, of Bundaburg, Queensland. —— Marie Eleanor (14 Ryrie St, N Ryde, Sydney, NSW), *b* 1919: *m* 1941, Capt Stanley Thornton Shaw, RAA, who *d* 1956, and has issue living, John Alexander, *b* 1943, — Philip Thornton, *b* 1945, — Laurence Edward, *b* 1946.

Grandson of late Edward Thomas Wiseman, son of late Thomas Wiseman (*b* 1778), son of late Thomas Wiseman (*b* 1760), 2nd son of 6th baronet:—
Issue of late Thomas Edward Wiseman, *b* 1851, *d* 1918: *m* 1877, Ellen Justinia, da of George Ware:—
Louis Gerald, *b* 1881: *m* 19—, Agnes, da of —, and has issue living, Edward Thomas, *b* 19—, — Louis George, *b* 19—, — Teresa, *b* 19—, — Audrey, *b* 19—.

Granddaughter of late Edwin Wycliffe Wiseman (infra):—
Issue of late Edwin Leonard Wiseman, *b* 1897, *d* 1964: *m* 1921, Winifred May (27 Davis Av, Northfleet, Kent), da of Edward William Bassant:—
Mary, *b* 1933.

Granddaughter of late William Henry Wiseman, son of late Charles Pierce Wiseman, son of late
Thomas Wiseman (*b* 1778) (ante):—
    Issue of late Edwin Wycliffe Wiseman, *b* 1864, *d* 1954: *m* 1st, 1893, Rosa, who *d* 1926, da of Leonard Leonard;
    2ndly, 1928, Alice Maud Mary, who *d* 1966, da of Horace Plant:—
(By 2nd *m*) Alice Rosa, *b* 1930. *Residence* – 47 Pelham Rd South, Gravesend.

Grandchildren of late Pierce Wiseman, son of Charles Pierce Wiseman (ante):—
    Issue of late Thomas Charles Wiseman, *b* 1873, *d* 1940: *m* 1896, Eliza, da of Charles Carpenter:—
Albert Victor, *b* 1915; is a Police Officer; formerly Flying Officer RAF: *m* 1941, Nicola, da of Leonard Foreman, and has
issue living, Jonathan Thomas Charles, *b* 1946, — Simon Pierce, *b* 1949, — Elizabeth Victoria, *b* 1942. —— Gertrude
Minnie, *b* 1903, *m* 1936, Thomas Jarvis, who *d* 1976, and has issue living, Michael (Glenview House, Leith Park Rd,
Gravesend), *b* 1942: *m* 1972, Brenda Shaftoe, and has issue living, Alton James *b* 1976, Julia Simone *b* 1975, — Trevor
(The Hollies, Byworth, Petworth, W Sussex), *b* 1946: *m* 19-, Patricia English, and has issue living, Charles Alexander *b*
1977.

Granddaughter of late Thomas Charles Wiseman (ante):—
    Issue of late William Henry Wiseman, *b* 1910, *d* 1979: *m* 1937, Winifred, who *d* 1988, da of William Charles
    Ambrose Knight:—
Susan Marjorie, *b* 1940: *m* 1977, Ian Crowe, of 12A West End Grove, Farnham, Surrey GU9 7EG.

Grandson of late Charles John Wiseman (*b* 1862) (infra):
    Issue of late Charles John Wiseman, *b* 1904, *d* 1990: *m* 1937, Jessie (17 Holburne Gdns, Kidbrooke, SE3), da of
    James Arthur Laming:—
David John (East Dulwich), *b* 1939; BEd Hons; Lieut The Parachute Regt TAVR: *m* 1st, 1964 (*m diss* 1968), Susan Anne,
da of Charles William Tait; 2ndly, 1977, Ann, da of Dr Henry James Walls.

Grandchildren of late Thomas Palmer Wiseman, son of late Edmund Wiseman, son of late Thomas
Wiseman (*b* 1760) (ante):—
    Issue of late Charles John Wiseman, *b* 1862, *d* 1936: *m* 1890, Lillie Jane, da of William Oakley:—
†John Robert, *b* 1908, *d* 1999: *m* 1931, Ethel, da of Joseph Thomas Beecham. —— Annie Elizabeth, *b* 1896: *m* 1918,
Zacharia William Coles, and has issue living, Nancy Joan, *b* 1921: *m* 1944, Edward Henry Willard, of The Cock, Church
St, Staines, Middx, and has issue living, Paul William, *b* 1946. —— Grace Mary, *b* 1900: *m* 1923, Walter Jefferies, and
has issue living, Ronald Walter, *b* 1925, — Dennis Gordon, *b* 1927: *m* 19-, and has issue living, Beverley *b* 1952.
—— Violet Mary, *b* 1903: *m* 1930, Frank Tranter, and has issue living, Jean Alma, *b* 1931.

Grandchildren of late Charles John Wiseman (*b* 1862) (ante):—
    Issue of late Thomas Charles Wiseman, *b* 1897, *d* 1928: *m* 1919:—
Ronald Henry, *b* 1924; NW Europe 1944-45: *m* 1943, and has issue living, Dawn, *b* 19-. —— Constance Queenie, *b* 1921:
m 1940. —— Betty Thomasina, *b* 1928: *m* 1946.

Granddaughter of late Charles John Wiseman (*b* 1862) (ante):—
    Issue of late Alfred John Wiseman, *b* 1906, *d* 1979: *m* 1st, 1931 (*m diss* 1946), Rose Knight; 2ndly, 1946, Enid
    May Hurford (3 Pound Cres, Fetcham, Surrey):—
(By 2nd *m*) Linda, *b* 1949: *m* 1970, Michael Ramsay, of Athelney, 25 Scalwell Park, Seaton, S Devon.

Sir John Wiseman, great grandfather of 1st baronet, was one of the Auditors of the Exchequer, *temp* Henry VIII, was
knighted at Battle of the Spurs, and purchased Canfield Park, in Essex, *temp* Edward VI. The 1st baronet, Sir William
Wiseman, was High Sheriff of Essex 1638-9. The 2nd baronet, Sir William, was High Sheriff of Essex 1659-60. The 5th
baronet, Sir William, was Lieut-Col Coldstream Guards. The 7th baronet, Sir William Saltonstall, was Capt RN. The 8th
baronet, Sir William Saltonstall, KCB, was Rear-Adm. The 9th baronet, Sir William, was Capt RN, and served in New
Zealand War 1864-5, and Niger Expedition 1869. The 10th baronet, Lt-Col Sir William George Eden, CB, was Ch of
British Intelligence Ser in USA 1917-18, and Chm of New York Cttee of Dollar Exports Board 1951-62.

WOLSELEY (E) 1628, of Wolseley, Staffordshire

Man is as a wolf towards his fellow man

Sir CHARLES GARNET RICHARD MARK WOLSELEY, 11th *Baronet*, son of late Capt Stephen Garnet Hubert Francis Wolseley, RA, el son of 10th baronet; *b* 16 June 1944; *s* his grandfather, *Sir* EDRIC CHARLES JOSEPH, 1954; *ed* Ampleforth; FRICS; Partner Smiths Gore until 1987: *m* 1st, 1968 (*m diss* 1984), Anita Maria, el da of late Hugo J. Fried; 2ndly, 1984, Mrs Imogene E. Brown (*née* May), of Dayton, Ohio, USA, and has issue (by 1st *m*).

Arms – Argent, a talbot passant gules. Crest – Out of a ducal coronet or, a wolf's head erased proper.
Seat – Wolseley Park, Rugeley, Staffs WS15 2TU.

SON LIVING (*By 1st marriage*)

STEPHEN GARNET HUGO CHARLES, *b* 2 May 1980.

DAUGHTERS LIVING (*By 1st marriage*)

Annabelle Clare Maria, *b* 1969. ——— Emily Lavinia, *b* 1972. ——— Lucy Margaret, *b* 1977.

SISTER LIVING

Mary Patricia Anne, *b* 1942: *m* 1973, Steuart Martin Moor, TD, FRICS, of Park Side, 4 Cliff Rd, Stamford, Lincs PE9 1AB, and has issue living, Theresa Mary Geraldine, *b* 1974, — Sonya Mary Elizabeth, *b* 1976, — Caroline Stephanie Elaine, *b* 1978.

UNCLES LIVING AND DECEASED (*Sons of 10th baronet*)

Basil Charles Daniel Rudolph, *b* 1921; *ed* Ampleforth; 1939-45 War as Flight-Lt RAF: *m* 1950, Ruth Key, da of late Lt-Col William Tom Carter, OBE, of Offham, Kent, and has issue living, Anne Teresa Margaret, *b* 1951: *m* 1980, Robert Hext-Fremlin, of Southborough, Kent, and has issue living, Shelley Naomi *b* 1980, — Susanna Elizabeth Mary, *b* 1952, — Sarah Angela Clare, *b* 1954: *m* 1983, Michael George Alexander McCurrach, of Fleet, Hants, — Joanna Ruth *b* 1958. *Residence* – Moor Oak, Dymock, Glos. ——— George John Carlos, *b* 1925; *ed* Ampleforth, Cate's Sch, Santa Barbara, Calif, and British Columbia Univ; 1943-47 War with RAF; with BAe 1960-88 (ret). *Residence* – Rosamunda, Fulwell Rd, Finmere, Buckingham MK18 4AS. ——— †Richard Edric Vincent, *b* 1928; *ed* Ampleforth, and New Brunswick Univ; sometime in Rifle Bde, and RCN: *m* 1950 (*m diss* 1969, re-*m* 1971) Alice Baltazzi, who *d* 1987, da of late Amos Tuck French, and *d* 1991, leaving issue, Stephen Richard Dulany, *b* 1954: *m* 1993, Kathleen Frances O'Ahern, — Christopher Michael Garnet, *b* 1956: *m* 1989, Cheryl M. McCormick, — Carlotta Andrea Tuck WOLSELEY-LAHCHIOUACH (313 Old Main Rd, PO Box 74, N Falmouth, Mass 02556, USA), *b* 1951: *m* 1972 (*m diss* 1982), Abdelhadi Lahchiouach, of Essaioura, Morocco, — Heather Maria Warner, *b* 1957; resumed her maiden name of WOLSELEY 1983: *m* 1975 (*m diss* 1981), James De Mello, of N Falmouth, Mass, and has issue living, Tara Maria French *b* 1976; and further issue, Brianna Maria Lindo *b* 1993.

AUNTS LIVING (*Daughters of 10th baronet*)

Frances Mary Mona Clare (Casa's Cortijo, 139, Sotogrande (Cadiz), Spain), *b* 1920; late WRNS: *m* 1953, Bernhard Wilmsen, who *d* 1983, having assumed by deed poll 1954, the additional surname of Wolseley before his patronymic, and has issue living, Anthony Edric Charles (Villa Gosen, Sotogrande (Cadiz), Spain), *b* 1955; *ed* St Christopher's Sch, Letchworth, Univ of Wales, and Univ of Granada, Spain. ——— Agnes Mary Ann Hilda, *b* 1923. *Residence* – Rosamunda, Fulwell Rd, Finmere, Buckingham MK18 4AS.

MOTHER LIVING

PAMELA VIOLETTE (*Pamela, Lady Wolseley*), da of late Capt F. Barry, of Old Court, Whitchurch, Ross-on-Wye; granted 1955 the style, title, place, and precedence as if her late husband had survived and succeeded to the title: *m* 1942, Capt Stephen Garnet Hubert Francis Wolseley, RA (ante), *d* of wounds received in action 1944. *Residence* – The Cottage, Wolseley Bridge, Stafford, Staffs ST17 0XR.

COLLATERAL BRANCHES LIVING

Grandchildren of late William Ralph Joseph Wolseley, (infra):—
Issue of late Robert William Hargreaves Wolseley, *b* 1924, *d* 1998: *m* 1965, Beryl Marjorie (Dodhill Firs, Nailsbourne, Taunton, Som), da of F. G. Harvey, of Norman Chapel, Aston Magna, Glos:—
Alistair Robert Hargreaves, *b* 1969. ——— Heather Frances, *b* 1967

Issue of late William Ralph Joseph Wolseley, TD, JP, yr son of 9th baronet, *b* 1887, *d* 1977: *m* 1923, Ruth Gertrude, who *d* 1962, yst da of late Lt-Col Robert Halstead Hargreaves, JP, DL, of Knightley Grange, Staffordshire, and Barnside, Lancs:—
Veronica Ruth Teresa Rose, *b* 1928.

Granddaughter of late William Augustus Wolseley, MD, son of late William Bertie Wolseley, son of late Capt Henry Wolseley, 4th son of 6th baronet:—
Issue (by 2nd *m*) of late William Augustus (Daniel) Wolseley, *b* 1847, *d* 1929: *m* 1st, 1891, Harriet, who *d* 1894, da of Fraser Luckie; 2ndly, 1895, Lilian Laura, who *d* 1941, da of late Horatio Bethune Leggatt, of Worth, Sussex:—
Lilian Patricia Dysart (Flat 6, Chester Mansions, 151/153, Oakhill Rd, SW15), *b* 1908: *m* 1933 (*m diss* 1948), Alexander Mervyn Archdale, and has issue living, Dominic Edward Wolseley, *b* 1937; *ed* St Paul's Sch, and Downing Coll, Camb (MA); late RAF: *m* 1st, 1959 (*m diss* 1974), Ruth Selby, da of Charles Johnston, late US Foreign Ser; 2ndly, 1976, Donna, da of Albert Leroy Baird, of Sun City, Arizona, USA, — Anthony Quintin Wolseley, *b* 1940; *ed* Saltus Gram Sch, Bermuda.

Grandchildren of late William Wykeham Frederick Bourne, 2nd son of late Rev John Frederick Bourne, by his wife Eliza Jane, 4th da of late William Bertie Wolseley (ante):—
Issue of late James Robert Wykeham Bourne, ARICS, *b* 1885, *d* 1971: *m* 1926, Mabel, who *d* 1974, da of late William Robert Reigate:—
Norah Ann Wykeham (19 Bloomsbury Pl, Brighton, E Sussex BN2 1DB), *b* 1932: *m* 1966, Colin James Outram Monro, who *d* 1983, and has issue living, John Seton, *b* 1968: *m* 1999, Ilham, da of Gen A. Aqary, of Rabat, Morocco, — Fiona Eleanor Wykeham, *b* 1967: *m* 1989, Anthony Nathan Greenstein, and has issue living, Daniel James Sheridan *b* 1989, Thomas John *b* 1997, Eleanor Rebecca Ann *b* 1991.

Issue of late Sybil Katherine Bourne, *b* 1887, *d* 1976: *m* 1915, Maj Vernon Milner Montague-Smith, late W Yorks Regt, who *d* 1951:—
Patrick Wykeham *b* 1920; *ed* Mercers' Sch; Assist Editor of *Debrett* 1946-62, Editor 1962-80, Consultant Editor 1980-86; NW Europe 1944-45 as Sgt RASC: *m* 1974, Annabelle Christina Calvert (5 Debden Close, off Duke's Ave, Kingston upon Thames, Surrey KT2 5JD), da of late Noel Newton, MA, of 65 Abbotsbury Close, Kensington, W14, and *d* 1986.

Issue of late Kathleen Bourne, *b* 1898, *d* 1992: *m* 1917, Paul Francis Wheler Bush, who *d* 1961:—
Pauline Carol Wheler LANCASTER (Galloway, Waterley Bottom, N Nibley, Glos GL11 6EF), *b* 1920; assumed surname of Lancaster by deed poll 19—: *m* 1942 (*m diss* 19—), Cyril Thomas James, and has issue living, Michael Thomas, *b* 1944: *m* 1997, Dominique Smith, — Robert Steven, *b* 1948; late L/Cpl RE: *m* 19—, — , and has issue living, a son *b* 19—, — Kathleen Mary (Lloegr-fach, Llangadog, Llandovery, Dyfed SA19 6HR), *b* 1943: *m* 1st, 1967, Cdr David Heron Jennings, RN (ret), who *d* 1988; 2ndly, 19—, David Watkins, who *d* 1994, and has issue living (by 1st *m*), Sarah *b* 1968: *m* 1990, Stephen Smith.

Descendants of late Richard Wolseley (2nd brother of 5th baronet), who was *cr* a Baronet 1745:—
See Wolseley, Bt, *cr* 1745.

This ancient Staffordshire family is descended from Siward, Lord of Wisele, fourth in descent from whom was Robert, Lord of Wolseley, *temp* 1281. Ralph, sixth in descent from Robert, was Fourth Baron of the Exchequer *temp* Edward IV. Sir Robert, 1st baronet, was a Col in Charles I's army, and suffered sequestration. Sir Charles, 2nd baronet, represented Stafford in the Parliaments of Charles I and II, and was a member of Cromwell's House of Lords. Sir William, 6th baronet, was a Gentleman of the Privy Chamber to George III.

WOLSELEY (I) 1745, of Mount Wolseley, co Carlow

HOMO HOMINI LUPUS

Man is as a wolf towards his fellow man

Sir JAMES DOUGLAS WOLSELEY, 13th *Baronet* (but his name does not, at the time of going to press, appear on the official Roll of Baronets), son of late James Douglas Wolseley, son of late Douglas St John Wolseley, only son of late Robert Warren St John Wolseley, el son of late Rev Robert Warren Wolseley, yr son of late Maj Robert Benjamin Wolseley, 6th son of late Rev William Wolseley, 3rd son of 1st baronet; *b* 17 Sept 1937; *s* his kinsman, Sir GARNET, 1991; *ed* Texas Christian Univ (BBA): *m* 1st, 1965 (*m diss* 1971), Patricia Lynn, da of William R. Hunter, of Mount Shasta, California, USA; 2ndly, 1984, Mary Anne, da of Thomas G, Brown, of Hilo, USA.

Arms – Argent, a talbot passant gules, a crescent for difference. Crest – Out of a ducal coronet, a wolf's head proper.
Residence – 4317 Clay Av, Fort Worth, Texas 76109-5220, USA.

SISTERS LIVING OF TWELFTH BARONET

Rubina Bingham, *b* 1909; *m* 1st, 1946, Walter Leonard Openshaw, who *d* 1951; 2ndly, 1952, Frank Whitby, who *d* 1960. *Residence* – 47 Telegraph Rd, Heswall, Cheshire. —— Lalla, *b* 1914.

MOTHER LIVING

Olive, da of Carroll Walter Wofford: *m* 1935, James Douglas Wolseley, who *d* 1960. *Residence* – 4242 Bryant Irvin Rd #226, Fort Worth, Texas 76109, USA.

WIDOW LIVING OF TWELFTH BARONET

LILLIAN MARY (*Dowager Lady Wolseley*), da of late William Bertram Ellison, of Love Lane, Wallasey, Cheshire: *m* 1950, Sir Garnet Wolseley, 12th Bt, who *d* (Oct) 1991 *Residence* – 73 Dorothy St, Brantford, Ontario N3S 1H1, Canada.

COLLATERAL BRANCHES LIVING

Granddaughter of late William Robert Wolseley, 2nd son of Richard John Wolseley, yr son of John Wolseley, MD, 4th son of late Rev William Wolseley, 3rd son of 1st baronet:—
Issue of late Noel Cecil Wolseley, *b* 1889, *d* 1969 (naturalized as American citizen 1920): *m* 1913, Mae Evelyn, who *d* 1965, da of John J. O'Connell:—
Eileen Rita, *b* 1916; Dir Nursing Ser, Concord Hosp, Concord, New Hampshire, USA.

Granddaughters of late Francis Ernest Wolseley, 3rd son of late Richard John Wolseley (ante):—
Issue of late Francis Richard Wolseley, *b* 1875, *d* 1934: *m* 1906, Elizabeth Ellen, who *d* 1966, da of late John Abbott Shippey:—
Kathleen Frances Hilda, *b* 1908: *m* 1938, Hugh Wynn Jones, and has issue living, Kathleen Margaret, *b* 1939. —— Jacqueline Eulalie Patricia, *b* 1911: *m* 1932, John Lewis Jones, and has issue living, Jane Eulalie, *b* 1942, — Anne Jessie Alexandra, *b* 1947.

Grandchildren of late Rev Robert Warren Wolseley, yr son of late Maj Robert Benjamin Wolseley, 6th son of late Rev William Wolseley (ante):—
Issue of late Garnet Ruskin Wolseley, *b* 1884, *d* 1967: *m* 1937, Joan Alys, who *d* 1943, da of Sir Walter John Trevelyan, 8th Bt:—
JOHN WALTER (Nettlecombe, Williton, Som; 4/25 Dalgety St, St Kilda, Melbourne, Vic 3182, Australia), *b* 21 April 1938; *ed* Westminster: *m* 1964 (*m diss* 1978), Patricia Ann Newland, and has issue living, William, *b* 1967, — Thomas, *b* 1970. —— Jane Alys Trevelyan, *b* 1939; assumed surname of Trevelyan 1976: *m* 1963 (*m diss* 1976), Nicolas Alexander, architect, and *d* 1993, leaving issue, Julius Diccon, *b* 1968, — Tamsyn Trevelyan, *b* 1966. —— Jennifer Ann Ruskin, *b* 1941: *m* 1979, Baron Roman Heinrich Gamotha, of Castello 4967, I-30122, Venice, Italy, and *d* 1983, leaving issue, Tatiana Romana, *b* 1982.

The 1st baronet, MP for Carlow, was brother of Sir William, 5th baronet, *cr* 1628. Sir Capel, 9th Bt, was Vice-Consul at Archangel 1900-1909, and served during European War 1914-18 in Gallipoli, Egypt, and Palestine, also with Army of Occupation in Albania and N Russia 1919.

WOMBWELL (GB) 1778, of Wombwell, Yorkshire
(Name pronounced "Woomwell")

Sir GEORGE PHILIP FREDERICK WOMBWELL, 7th Baronet; *b* 21 May 1949; *s* his father, *Maj Sir* (FREDERICK) PHILIP ALFRED WILLIAM, MBE, 1977; *ed* Repton: *m* 1974, (Hermione) Jane, el da of Thomas S. Wrightson, of Ulshaw Grange, Middleham, Leyburn, Yorks, and has issue.

ᗩrms – Gules, a bend between six unicorns' heads couped argent. ℭrest – A unicorn's head couped argent.
Residence – Newburgh Priory, Coxwold, York YO6 4AS.

SON LIVING

STEPHEN PHILIP HENRY, *b* 12 May 1977.

DAUGHTER LIVING

Sarah Georgina, *b* 1980.

SISTER LIVING

Hazel Maureen, *b* 1947; assumed the surname of WILLIAMSON by deed poll 1977.

COLLATERAL BRANCH LIVING

Grandson of late Arthur Charles Wombwell, only son of Charles Orby Wombwell, 4th son of 2nd baronet:—
Issue of late Major Claude Ronald Wombwell, Seaforth Highlanders, *b* 1900, *d* 1959: *m* 1936, Eva Mabel, who *d* 1988, da of late Lieut-Col Gerald Hugh Charles Madden (Macpherson-Grant, Bt):—
Gerald Arthur (40 Quarrendon St, SW6), *b* 1937; *ed* Wellington Coll: *m* 1968, Elizabeth Ann, da of John Victor Gent, of Thika, Kenya, and has issue living, Richard Brian, *b* 1973, — Camilla Susan, *b* 1970.

The 1st baronet, Sir George Wombwell, was Chairman of the East India Company, and MP for Huntingdonshire 1774-80. The 4th baronet, Sir George, served in the Crimean War, and was in the Charge at Balaclava. The 5th baronet, Sir Henry Herbert Wombwell, was Capt Roy Horse Guards.

WOMERSLEY (UK) 1945, of Grimsby, co Lincoln

Sir PETER JOHN WALTER WOMERSLEY, 2nd *Baronet*, son of late Capt John Walter Womersley, Lincolnshire Regt, yr son of 1st baronet; *b* 10 Nov 1941; *s* his grandfather, *Rt Hon Sir* WALTER JAMES, 1961; late Lt King's Own R Border Regt: *m* 1968, Janet Margaret, da of Alistair Grant, of Drayton, Norwich, and has issue.
Residence – Broomfields, 23 Goring Rd, Steyning, W Sussex, BN44 3GF.

SONS LIVING

JOHN GAVIN GRANT, *b* 7 Dec 1971. —— Matthew Alastair Peter, *b* 1973.

DAUGHTERS LIVING

Margaret Frances, *b* 1969. —— Helen Kathryn, *b* 1974.

AUNT LIVING (*Daughter of 1st baronet*)

Dorothy, *b* 1911: *m* 1934, Cyril Howard Moseley, and has issue living, Walter Howard, *b* 1941, — Lavinia Anne, *b* 1938, — Philippa Clare, *b* 1944.

MOTHER LIVING

Betty, da of Cyril Williams, of Elstead, Surrey: *m* 1st, 1941, Capt John Walter Womersley, Lincolnshire Regt (ante), *ka* Italy 1944; 2ndly, 1948, Gordon Shuttlewood, who *d* 1980.

The 1st baronet, the Rt Hon Sir Walter James Womersley (son of late William Womersley, of Bradford), was MP for Grimsby (C) 1924-45, and Min of Pensions 1939-45.

WOOD (UK) 1897, of The Hermitage, Chester-le-Street, co Durham (Extinct 1946)

Sir IAN LINDSAY WOOD, 3rd and last *Baronet*.

SISTER LIVING OF THIRD BARONET

Heather Lindsay, *b* 1908: *m* 1932, Gilbert Keith Dunning, who *d* 1967, and has issue living, Michael Lindsay, *b* 1941. *Residence* – Keeper's Cottage, Fontmell Parva, Blandford, Dorset.

WOOD (UK) 1918, of Hengrave, Suffolk (Extinct 1974)

Sir JOHN ARTHUR HAIGH WOOD, DSC, MC, 2nd and last *Baronet*.

DAUGHTER LIVING OF SECOND BARONET

Shirley Cartaret, *b* 1922: *m* 1st, 1946 (*m diss* 1964), Sqdn Ldr Ivon Arthur Frederic Donnelly; 2ndly, 1972, John Hyde Villiers, who *d* 1980, of Fort Saumarez, L'Eree, Guernsey GY7 9LR, CI, and has had issue (by 1st *m*), Miles Saumarez (Little Halnaker, nr Chichester, W Sussex PO18 0NF), *b* 1949: *m* 1981, Caroline McKay, — Marcia Anne Lavinia (resumed her maiden name of DONNELLY), *b* 1948: *m* 1967 (*m diss* 19—), Jean Gabriel Mitterand, and *d* 1984, leaving issue living, Edward *b* 1968, — Claire Leonie, *b* 1953: *m* 1st, 1975 (*m diss* 1978), Craig Francis, of Nassau; 2ndly, 1978, Richard Berlin, of 261 Hart St, Beverley Farms, MA 01915, USA, and has issue living (by 2nd *m*), Eleanor *b* 1980, Dana *b* 1981, Carina Alexandra *b* 1985.

COLLATERAL BRANCH LIVING

Issue of late Maj Edmund Walter Hanbury Wood, JP, 2nd son of 1st baronet, *b* 1898, *d* 1947: *m* 1920, Margaret, who *d* 1977, only child of late George Coles Walton:—
Rhona Gertrude Jean (6 Douro Place, W8), *b* 1921: *m* 1948 (*m diss* 1962), Jeremy Norman Peyton-Jones, who *d* 1984 (*see* B Ebury, colls, 1980 Edn), and has issue living, Julia Caroline, *b* 1952, — Lucinda Margaret, *b* 1954: *m* 1987, R. John Guy, elder son of Edgar Guy, of Raynes Park, London.

HILL-WOOD (UK) 1921, of Moorfield, Glossop, co Derby

Every good thing is the gift of God

Sir DAVID BASIL HILL-WOOD, 3rd *Baronet*; *b* 12 Nov 1926; *s* his father, *Sir* BASIL SAMUEL HILL, 1954; *ed* Eton: *m* 1970, Jennifer Anne McKenzie Stratmann (assumed that surname by deed poll 1960), da of late Peter McKenzie Strang, and has issue.

Arms – Quarterly, 1st and 4th sable, on a bend between two roses argent, barbed and seeded or, three fleurs-de-lis gules, *Wood*; 2nd and 3rd per chevron argent and vert, in chief two acorns leaved and slipped, and in base a cross-bow bent all counterchanged, *Hill*. Crests – 1st, within a crown palisado or a tree proper, *Wood*; 2nd, on a mount vert a bugle horn stringed gules, *Hill*.
Residences – Dacre Farm, Farley Hill, Reading, Berks; 58 Cathcart Rd, SW10.

SONS LIVING

SAMUEL THOMAS, *b* 24 Aug 1971. —— Edward Charles, *b* 1974.

DAUGHTER LIVING

Emma Victoria, *b* 1972.

SISTER LIVING

Anne Katherine, *b* 1928.

COLLATERAL BRANCHES LIVING

Issue of late Maj Denis John Charles Hill Hill-Wood, MC, 3rd son of 1st baronet, *b* 1906; *d* 1982: *m* 1932, Mary Cecilia Martin, who *d* 1997, da of late Capt Everard Martin Smith, of Codicote Lodge, Herts:—

Peter Denis (13 Smith's Terr, SW3), *b* 1936; *ed* Eton; 2nd Lt Coldm Gds: *m* 1971, Sarah, da of Albert O'Beirne Andrews, and has issue living, Julian Peter, *b* 1974, — Charles Denis, *b* 1976, — Sarah Frances, *b* 1972. ——— Angela Mary, *b* 1933: *m* 1956, Mark Eric Smith, of Ballacurn, Ballaugh, IoM, and has issue living, Matthew Eric, *b* 1960: *m* 1989 (*m diss* 1992), Hon Melanie Frances Broughton, yr da of 3rd Baron Fairhaven, and has issue living, Shamus Oliver Eric *b* 1990, — Luke Eric, *b* 1968: *m* 1998, Victoria Jan, da of Ian Jarritt, of Ballasalla, IoM, — Amanda Mary, *b* 1957: *m* 1984, Matthew Frewer, of Los Angeles, USA, and has issue living, Scout Lillian *b* 1996, — Lucinda Rachael, *b* 1958. ——— Rachael Vivien, *b* 1940: *m* 1972, Anthony Wood, who *d* 1989, of 31 Surrey Lane, SW11, and has issue living, Cheska Mary, *b* 1974, — Selina Rachael, *b* 1976.

Issue of late Lt-Col Charles Kerrison Hill Hill-Wood, yst son of 1st baronet, *b* 1907, *d* (21 Sept) 1988: *m* 1936, Cecilia Katharine, who *d* (16 June) 1988, 3rd da of late Capt Everard Reginald Martin Smith, of Codicote Lodge, Herts:—

Michael Kerrison (Hill Cot, Branch Rd, Ainley Top, Huddersfield, W Yorks), *b* 1946; *ed* Milton Abbey: *m* 1st, 1970 (*m diss* 1991), Patricia Guy, of Stainland, Yorks; 2ndly, 1991, Patricia Ann Caldon, of Biggleswade, Beds, and has issue living (by 1st *m*), Steven Guy, *b* 1977, — Susan Michelle, *b* 1974. ——— Ian Charles (The Bury, Barton-le-Cley, Beds), *b* 1947; *ed* Milton Abbey. ——— Georgina Sarah, *b* 1940: *m* 1962, Richard Basil Holt, of Hessett House, Beyton, Suffolk, and of 3 Caroline Place Mews, W2, and has issue living, Nicholas James, *b* 1965: *m* 1994, Kathryn M., da of John Power, of Wendens Ambo, Essex, and of Mrs James Waymouth, of Eastbourne, Sussex, and has issue living, Jessica *b* 1996, Jemima Mary *b* 1998, — Camilla Katherine, *b* 1967: *m* 1999, Dr Matthew Wootton, son of Dr Alan Wootton, of Uley, Glos, — Susanna Rachael, *b* 1969: *m* 1998, Bernard D. G. Barton, only son of John Barton, of Tonbridge, Kent, — Caroline Lucinda, *b* 1972. ——— Diana Susan, *b* 1943: *m* 1st, 1966 (*m diss* 1971), Lestock Harold George Livingstone-Learmonth; 2ndly, 1975, Ian Phillips, of 18 Campion Rd, Putney, SW15, and has issue living (by 1st *m*), Lestock Alexander Iain, *b* 1969, — (by 2nd *m*) Alastair Patrick Markham, *b* 1980, — Simon Richard Markham, *b* 1982.

The 1st baronet, Sir Samuel Hill Hill-Wood, only son of late Samuel Wood, of Moorfield, Derbyshire (whose el brother, John Hill Wood, was father of Sir John Wood, 1st Bt (*see* Wood, Bt, *cr* 1918)) assumed by Roy licence 1912 the additional surname of Hill, his grandmother having been Alice, da of John Hill, of Liverpool. He sat as MP for High Peak Div of Derbyshire (C) 1910-29.

PAGE WOOD (UK) 1837, of Hatherley House, Gloucestershire

DEFEND

Sir ANTHONY JOHN PAGE WOOD, 8th *Baronet*; *b* 6 Feb 1951; *s* his father, Sir DAVID JOHN HATHERLEY PAGE WOOD, 1955; *ed* Harrow.

Arms – Quarterly, argent and or, the mace of the Lord Mayor of London in pale, between an oak-tree on a mount vert fructed proper in the 1st and 4th quarters and in the 2nd and 3rd, a bull's head erased sable, charged on the neck with a bezant. **Crest** – Out of a mural crown argent, a demi-wild man, wreathed about the temples with oak fructed, in the dexter hand an oak-tree eradicated and fructed, and in the sinister a club, all proper.
Residence – 77 Dovehouse St, SW3.

SISTER LIVING

Rosemary Anne, *b* 1948: *m* 1977 (*m diss* 1995), Hugh Macdonald Teacher (*see* Macnaghten, Bt, colls, 1995 Edn), and has issue living, James Henry MacDonald, *b* 1979; *ed* Eton, and Aberdeen Univ. *Residence* – George Cottage, Gifford, E Lothian.

WIDOW LIVING OF SEVENTH BARONET

EVELYN HAZEL ROSEMARY (*Lady Page Wood*), da of late Capt George Ernest Bellville, of Fermyn Woods Hall, Brigstock, Northants; assumed by deed poll 1956 the additional surname of Page: *m* 1947, Sir David John Hatherley Page Wood, 7th baronet, who *d* (Nov) 1955. *Residence* – The Old Cottage, Wolverton, Basingstoke, Hants.

COLLATERAL BRANCHES LIVING

Issue of late Capt Matthew Page Wood, 2nd son of 6th baronet, *b* 1924, *d* 1999; assumed by deed poll 1955 the additional surname of Page before his patronymic: *m* 1947, Betsann (31 Halsey St, SW3), da of late Lieut-Col Francis Christison Darby Tothill (*see* E Bandon):—

Belinda Jane, *b* 1952: *m* 1st, 1973 (*m diss* 1977), Richard John Crowder (*see* B Mowbray); 2ndly, 1985, Charles Frederick Rutford Hoste, and has issue living (by 2nd *m*), James Matthew William Rutford, *b* 1986. ——— Miranda Elizabeth, *b* 1962: *m* 1993, William B. Kendall, of 32 Cloudesley St, N1 0HX, son of Graham Kendall, of Millow Hall, Biggleswade, Beds, and has issue living, Emily Lucy Page, *b* 1994, — Sophia Elizabeth Page, *b* 1996.

Grandson of late FM Sir (Henry) Evelyn Wood, VC, GCB, GCMG, LLD, 5th son of 2nd baronet:—
Issue of late Col Evelyn FitzGerald Michell Wood, CB, DSO, OBE, *b* 1869, *d* 1943: *m* 1st, 1893, Lilian, who *d* 1910, da of late Charles Edward Hutton, of 63 Porchester Terrace, W; 2ndly, 1915, Alla, who *d* 1950, da of R. Morton, and widow of Hatherley Page Wood, son of late Charles Page Wood, 2nd son of 2nd baronet:—
(By 2nd *m*) MATTHEW WAKEFIELD DRURY EVELYN (The Orchard, Bishopsteignton, Teignmouth, Devon), *b* 9 July 1917; *ed* Brighton Coll; Lt-Col (ret) RE, late Essex Regt: *m* 1st, 1939, Marjorie, who *d* 1963, da of late Henry Thomas Longmire, of Liverpool; 2ndly, 1967, Mrs Phyllis Margaret Chavasse Whateley (infra), and has issue living, (by 1st *m*) Mark William Evelyn (Holly Lodge, Sparrowhawk Close, Ewshot, Farnham, Surrey GU10 5TJ), *b* 1 Aug 1940: *m* 1962, Mary June, da of George Percy Miller, of Brightlingsea, and has issue living, Martin Evelyn *b* 14 Jan 1963, Michelle Leslie Evelyn *b* 1965.

Grandchildren (by 1st *m*) of late Lt-Col Arthur Herbert Wood (*infra*):—
Issue of late Evelyn (Ronald) Wood, *b* 1903, *d* 1976: *m* 1st, 1932 (*m diss* 1943), Maeve Audrey, da of late Arthur Theobald Wolfe, and widow of Emile Jacot; 2ndly, 1943, Kamal Jehangir, who *d* 1976, da of Jehangir Fardunji Dastur, of Bombay:—
(By 1st *m*) Diarmuid Evelyn (Leachin House, Tarbert, Isle of Harris, Outer Hebrides HS3 3AH), *b* 1933; *ed* Gordonstoun: *m* 1st, 1960, Beverly, BSc, who *d* 1976, da of William Richard Pearce, of La Oratava, Tenerife; 2ndly, 1977, Linda Rosemary, BA, DipEd, da of Leonard Pierpoint Petty, of Merry Meadow, Winters Lane, Redhill, Wrington, Avon, and has issue living (by 1st *m*), Damian Evelyn, *b* 1962: *m* 1991, Clare Natalie, BA, da of Richard Dallas Harington, of Hill Farm, Felsham, Suffolk, and has issue living, Benedict Damian Evelyn *b* 1993, Barnaby Jonathan Evelyn *b* 1996, — Thalia Evelyn, *b* 1965, — (by 2nd *m*), Duncan Fitzgerald Evelyn, *b* 1981, — Eleanor Maeve Evelyn, *b* 1984. —— (By 2nd *m*) Ananda Evelyn, *b* 1947: *m* 19—, Meena Dyal, of Bombay. —— Leela Aditi, *b* 1946: *m* 19—, Nick Dirks, of Santa Monica, USA, and has issue living, Sandhya Elina, *b* 1978.

Grandchildren of late FM Sir (Henry) Evelyn Wood, VC, GCB, GCMG, LLD (*ante*):—
Issue of late Lt-Col Arthur Herbert Wood, *b* 1877, *d* 1940: *m* 1st, 1900, Ethel Mary, who *d* 1923, da of late Andrew Duncan, Bar-at-law, of 71 Gloucester Place, W; 2ndly, 1923, Andrina Hunter, who *d* 1985, da of John Fernie, of Aberfeldy, Perthshire:—
(By 2nd *m*) Victor Arthur Evelyn, *b* 1927; *ed* Tonbridge; a Chartered Surveyor: *m* 1st, 1951, Olwen Mary, who *d* 1960, only da of Thomas Davies, of Studley, Warwicks; 2ndly, 1963, Matilde Francesca Rosanna, da of Girolamo Zucchelli, of Brione, Riva del Garda, Italy, and has issue living, (by 1st *m*) David Arthur Evelyn, *b* 1954, — Vaughan Thomas Evelyn, *b* 1959, — Bernice Margaret Andrina, *b* 1952, — (by 2nd *m*) Victor Vincent, *b* 1966, — Antonia Marcella Matilde *b* 1964. —— Marcella Mary, *b* 1931; *ed* New Hall Boreham, Chelmsford and London Univ (BA DipEd); Canoness Registrar of Holy Sepulchre; Headmistress of New Hall Sch, Chelmsford since 1963.

Grandchildren of late George Orme Western Wood (*infra*):—
Issue of late Ernest Cresswell Gaden Western Wood, MBE, *b* 1906, *d* 1984: *m* 1938, Mary Tudor (Moonie, 35 Douro Rd, Wellington Point, Queensland 4160, Australia), da of James Winnel Hill, of Goorarooman, Thallon, Queensland:—
Richard Orme Western (Moonie, 35 Douro Rd, Wellington Point, Queensland 4160, Australia), *b* 1942; *ed* Queensland Univ (BEng): *m* 1968, Jennifer Lynne, da of N.W.S. Johns, of Clayfield, Brisbane, and has issue living, Matthew Gaden Western, *b* 1969, — Gregory Orme Western, *b* 1971, — Simon James Western, *b* 1975. —— Bruce James Western (Moonie, 35 Douro Rd, Wellington Point, Queensland 4160, Australia), *b* 1951; *ed* Queensland Univ (BEng): *m* 1977, Yolande Marie-Louise, da of late Pierre Le Manach, of Morlaix, France, and has had issue, Nina Marie Western, *b* 1978, — Adeline Marie Western, *b* and *d* 1981, — Sophie Yolande Western, *b* 1981, — Nicole Alexandrina Western, *b* 1985, — Stephanie Adeline Western, *b* 1987. —— Nina Helen Western, *b* 1939. —— Rosamond Mary Western, *b* 1944; *ed* Queensland univ (Dip Speech Therapy): *m* 1972, John Franklin Verity Haselwood, and has issue living, Richard Franklin, *b* 1974, — Douglas Holmes, *b* 1976, — Louise Mary, *b* 1975.

Grandchildren of late Western Wood, *b* 1830; 3rd son of 1st baronet:—
Issue of late George Orme Western Wood, *b* 1868, *d* 1926: *m* 1904, Helen Portia, who *d* 1963, da of Adam Davidson, of Darling Downs, Queensland:—
Bernard Page Western, *b* 1908; 1939-45 War as Lt RANVR: *m* 1951, Phyllis May, da of William Henry Andrew, of 48 Shakespeare St, Mackay, Qld. *Residence* – 57 Gregory St, Mackay, Qld. —— Evelyn Hatherley Davidson, *b* 1911: *m* 1937, Ena Myer, and has issue living, Ian Hatherley Western, *b* 1942: *m* 19—, June Margaret Huch, da of Huch Redcliffe, and has issue living, Cameron Hatherley *b* 1966, Scott Norman *b* 1969, Rowena Maree *b* 1971, — David Orme Western,*b* 1946; *ed* Qld Univ (MB, BS). —— Helen Constance Western, *b* 1905: *m* 1949, Stanley Gordon. *Residence* – 29 Herries Street, Toowoomba, Queensland. —— Waveney Patricia Western, *b* 1914: *m* 1943, Capt Robert Gladstone Deacon, Australian Forces, and has issue living, Helen Page, *b* 1945.

The 1st baronet, Sir Matthew Wood, born 1767, was the son of a serge manufacturer, of Tiverton and at eleven years of age worked in his father's factory. At fourteen he was apprenticed to Mr Newton, druggist, at Exeter. After serving seven years, he became a traveller in the drug trade, and subsequently established himself in London as a chemist. He afterwards became a hop-merchant, and was chosen Alderman, served as a Sheriff, and in the year of the Peace, 1815, was elected Lord Mayor of London, to which office he was re-elected the following year. He also sat as MP for London (*L*) 1816-43. During his mayoralty he was bold and fearless. On one occasion, after a lawless mob had shot a man on Snow Hill, and were approaching the Exchange, he, with only seven others, rushed through that building, and held the rioters in check, while he arrested several of the ringleaders. He took an active part in the cause of Queen Caroline: he accompanied her through Calais and Dover, on her journey to London in 1820, and placed his house in South Audley Street at her disposal. His fortune was, after much litigation, augmented on the death of Jemmy Wood, the banker, of Gloucester, to the extent of £250,000. Among these possessions was the estate of Hatherley Court, in Gloucestershire, a fine old ivy-mantled mansion, and from its name his second son, William Page, who was Lord High Chancellor 1868-72, selected his title. Sir John Stuart Page Wood, 6th Bt, who was Com (ret) RN, *d* April 1955, and his son Sir David John Hatherley Page Wood, 7th Bt, *d* Nov 1955.

WORLEY (UK) 1928, of Ockshott, co Surrey (Extinct 1937)

Sir ARTHUR WORLEY, CBE, 1st and last *Baronet*.

DAUGHTER LIVING OF FIRST BARONET

Stella, *b* 1918: *m* 1940, Raymond Ades, TD, JP, MA, who *d* 1993, and has issue living, Timothy Raymond (94 North Rd, N6), *b* 1941; MA: *m* 1966, Josephine Dawn Tylden-Pattenson, MA, Prof of Art History, and has issue living, Thomas Joseph Edmund *b* 1971; M Phil; composer, Henry Arthur Raymond *b* 1973; MA, Robert Paul Timothy *b* 1981, — Anthony Edmond, *b* 1947; BSc, PhD, MSc: *m* 1995, Dr Diana Mary Gibb, MB ChB, Dip Obs, FRCPCH, MD, MSc, and has issue living, Eva Rose *b* 1995, — Susan Jane, *b* 1943; MA, — Rosemary Sally (3 Pottery St, SE16), *b* 1951; MA. *Residence* – 37 Princes Dr, Oxshott, Surrey KT22 0UL.

WORSLEY (UK) 1838, of Hovingham, Yorkshire

Do good to as many persons as possible

Sir (WILLIAM) MARCUS JOHN WORSLEY, 5th *Baronet*; *b* 6 April 1925; *s* his father, *Col Sir* WILLIAM ARTHINGTON, 1973; *ed* Eton, and New Coll, Oxford; a JP, DL and High Sheriff (1982) for N Yorks, HM Lord Lieut 1987-99; PPS to Min of Health 1960-61, to Min without Portfolio 1962-64, and to Lord Pres of Council 1970-72; Chm Nat Trust Properties Cttee 1980-90, Dep Chm Nat Trust 1986-92; Pres of Roy Forestry Soc of Eng, Wales and N Ire 1980-82; 1939-45 War in India and W Africa with Green Howards; MP for Keighley (*C*) 1959-64, and for Chelsea (*C*) 1966-74; Second Church Estates Commr 1970-74: *m* 1955, Hon Bridget Assheton, da of 1st Baron Clitheroe, and has issue.

Arms – Argent, a chief gules. Crest – A wyvern vert.
Seat – Hovingham Hall, York. *Club* – Boodle's.

SONS LIVING

WILLIAM RALPH (Wool Knoll, Hovingham, York. *Club* – White's), *b* 12 Sept 1956; *ed* Harrow, and RAC; late Lt QOY (TAVR), FRICS: *m* 1987, Marie-Noëlle, yr da of Bernard H. Dreesmann, of Mas de la Madone, Miramar, Alpes Maritimes, France, and has issue living, Marcus William Bernard, *b* 2 Nov 1995, — Isabella Claire, *b* 1988, — Francesca Sylvia, *b* 1992. —— Giles Arthington, *b* 1961: *m* 1996, Joanna Beaufort, da of Peter John Pitman, of Pewsey, Wilts (*see* B Luke, 1980 Edn), and has issue living, Alice Beaufort, *b* 1998. —— Peter Marcus, *b* 1963.

DAUGHTER LIVING

Sarah Marianne, *b* 1958: *m* 1984, Martin Stephen Robert Elwes, of Holywell House, Shellingford, nr Farringdon, Oxon SN7 7PU, elder son of late Capt Robert (Robin) Valentine Gervase Elwes, and Mrs J.H. Taylor, and has issue living, James Robert, *b* 1986, — Hugo Marcus, *b* 1991, — Sophie Bridget, *b* 1988.

BROTHERS LIVING

George Oliver, TD (Midgley House, Heslington, York, YO10 5DX. *Club* – Boodle's), *b* 1927; *ed* Eton, and Trin Coll, Oxford (MA): *m* 1966, Penelope Suzanne Fleetwood, da of late Lt-Col Christopher Herbert Fleetwood Fuller, TD (*see* Fuller, Bt, colls), and has had issue, David Christopher, *b* 1969, — †Richard Oliver Arthington, *b* 1972; *ed* Uppingham, and RMA Sandhurst; Lieut RAC (The Light Dragoons); *k* in a motor accident in Germany 1996, — Georgina Joyce, *b* 1967, — Anne Penelope, *b* 1974. —— John Arthington (RR2 Uxbridge, Ont, Canada), *b* 1928; *ed* Eton, and Trin Coll, Oxford; Pres Morgan Trust Co of Canada: *m* 1954, Hon Carolyn Wynard Hardinge, da of 4th Viscount Hardinge, and has issue living, Henry John, *b* 1958, — Jonathan Hugh, *b* 1960, — Dickon Carol, *b* 1966, — Willa Victoria, *b* 1955, — Katharine Margot, *b* 1968.

SISTER LIVING

Katharine Lucy Mary, GCVO (*HRH the Duchess of Kent*), *b* 1933; Col-in-Ch Prince of Wales's Own Regt of Yorks, Dep Col-in-Ch Royal Dragoon Guards and The Royal Logistic Corps; Patron Kent Co Playing Fields Assocn, and Scope; Pres Macmillan Cancer Relief, and Royal Northern Coll of Music; GCVO 1977: *m* 8 June 1961, HRH Prince Edward George Nicholas Paul Patrick, KG, GCMG, GCVO, 2nd Duke of Kent (*see* ROYAL FAMILY). *Residence* – Kensington Palace, W8.

COLLATERAL BRANCH LIVING

Issue of late Capt Edward Marcus Worsley, yr son of 3rd baronet, *b* 1891, *d* 1971: *m* 1941, Joyce

Marian (Cawton Hall, Cawton, York YO62 4LW), da of late Stanley Graham Beer, of Northernhay, Bickley, Kent:—
Thomas Edward (35D Gibson Sq, N1 0RB), *b* 1947; *ed* Eton: *m* 1989, Sheila Christie, and has issue living, Nicholas Richard, *b* 1990, — Charles Robert, *b* 1993. —— Susan Marian, *b* 1942: *m* 1989, Christopher Edwin Oliver, of 46 Woodville Rd, Richmond, Surrey TW10 7QN, only son of late E. J. C. Oliver. —— Angela Joyce, *b* 1950: *m* 1973, Ian Michael Downing Strickland-Skailes, of Harston Hall, Grantham, Lincs NG32 1PS, and has issue living, Robin Edward, *b* 1977, — Lucinda Isabel, *b* 1979. —— Diana Rosalind, *b* 1953.

This family is a senior branch of the Worsleys of Worsley, Lancs. Another branch, formerly baronets of Appuldurcombe, Isle of Wight, whose title became extinct on the death of the 9th baronet in 1825, is now represented by the Earl of Yarborough.

Worsley-Taylor, see Taylor.

Worthington-Evans, see Evans.

WRAXALL (UK) 1813, of Wraxall, Somersetshire

Sir CHARLES FREDERICK LASCELLES WRAXALL, 9th *Baronet*; *b* 17 Sept 1961; *s* his father, *Sir* MORVILLE WILLIAM LASCELLES, 1978; *ed* Archbishop Tenison's Gram Sch, Croydon; a Civil Servant 1978-80; Assist Accountant British Steel Corp 1981-87, Morgan Stanley Int since 1987: *m* 1983, Lesley Linda, da of late William Albert Allan, of Ashford, Kent, and has issue.

Arms – Lozengy erminois and azure, on a chevron gules three estoiles of eight points or. **Crest** – A buck's head cabossed and erased gules, charged on the breast with two lozenges in fesse, and between the attires an estoile or.

SON LIVING

WILLIAM NATHANIEL LASCELLES, *b* 3 April 1987; *ed* Norton Knatchbull Grammar Sch.

DAUGHTER LIVING

Lucy Rosemary Lascelles, *b* 1992.

BROTHER LIVING

Peter Edward Lascelles, *b* 1967.

SISTER LIVING

Sylvia Laura, *b* 1957: *m* 19—, Andrew John Lack, of Northampton, and has issue living, Matthew Peter, *b* 1982, — Natalie Sarah, *b* 1983.

AUNT LIVING (Daughter of 7th baronet)

Gwendolyn Aileen, *b* 1927: *m* 1945, John Hunter, CEng, FIMechE, AFRAeS, FInstPet of Stirling, who *d* 1987, and has issue living, Kenneth Charles John (Firwood, 15 Hamfield Cl, Oxted, Surrey) *b* 1951; BSc Hons (Warwick): *m* 1976, Gillian Margaret Sutton, of Billericay, Essex, and has issue living, Martin Robert *b* 1981, Simon Richard *b* 1985, Alicia Jennifer *b* 1988, — Keith Philip (1 Tower Gdns, Bearsted, Kent), *b* 1957; BSc Hons (London Univ): *m* 1983, Louise Bernadette Maria Baede, of Amsterdam, Holland, and has issue living, Nicholas John *b* 1988, Christopher Marinus *b* 1990, Alexander Keith *b* 1993, Sebastian Nicholas *b* 1996. *Residence* – 110 Devonshire Way, Shirley, Croydon, Surrey.

WIDOW LIVING OF EIGHTH BARONET

IRMGARD WILHELMINA MARIA (*Dowager Lady Wraxall*), da of late Alois Larry Schnidrig, of Zunftacker Rain 13a, Pratteln, Switzerland: *m* 1956, Sir Morville William Lascelles Wraxall, 8th baronet, who *d* 1978.

The 1st baronet, Sir Nathaniel William Wraxall, was in the Civil Service of the East India Company. The 3rd baronet, Sir Frederick, was sometime Assistant-Commissary in the Turkish Contingent and was author of several works. Sir Morville William, 6th baronet, enlisted in the Commissariat and Transport Corps, served in Nile Expedition 1884-5, and subsequently joined, in 1891, the Egyptian Coast Guard Administration.

WREY (E) 1628, of Trebitch, Cornwall

The good time will come

Sir (GEORGE RICHARD) BOURCHIER WREY, 15th *Baronet*; *b* 2 Oct 1948; *s* his father, *Sir* (CASTEL RICHARD) BOURCHIER, 1991; *ed* Eton: *m* 1981, Lady Caroline Janet Lindesay-Bethune, only da of 15th Earl of Lindsey, and has issue.

Arms – Sable, a fesse between three pole-axes argent, helved gules. (Quarterings: Bourchier, Plantagenet, de Bohun, etc).
Residence – Hollamoor Farm, Tawstock, Barnstaple, N Devon EX31 3NY.

SONS LIVING

HARRY DAVID BOURCHIER, *b* 3 Oct 1984; *ed* Eton. —— Humphrey George Bourchier, *b* 1991.

DAUGHTER LIVING

Rachel Pearl, *b* 1987.

BROTHER LIVING

(Edward) Sherard Bourchier, *b* 1961; *ed* Milton Abbey: *m* 1992, Hon Catherine Margaret Baring, yst da of 5th Baron Northbrook, and has issue living, Tallulah Kitty, *b* 1996. *Residence* – East Stratton House, E Stratton, Winchester, Hants SO21 3DU.

AUNT LIVING (Sister of 14th baronet)

Diana Joan (*Hon Mrs William Rollo*), *b* 19—: *m* 1st, 1932 (*m diss* 1946), Jocelyn Abel Smith, who *d* 1966; 2ndly, 1946, as his 2nd wife, Hon William Hereward Charles Rollo, MC, who *d* 1962 (*see* L Rollo), and has issue living (by 1st *m*), John William (Hickory House Farm, PO Box 1420, Middleburg, Virginia 20118, USA), *b* 1933: *m* 1st, 1957, Ruth, da of late Sir John Huggins, GCMG, MC; 2ndly, 1965 (*m diss* 1974), Christine, only da of Keith Taylor, of Adelaide; 3rdly, 1975, Mary Chichester Mills, — (Bertram) Robin, *b* 1938: *m* 1st, 1961 (*m diss* 1976), Anne, yst da of Walter Kidman, of Eringa, Unley Park, Adelaide, S Aust; 2ndly, 1978 (*m diss* 1991), Kathleen Eugenie, da of George Cecil Houghton Cowell, of Elms Farm, Ashley, Newmarket, and widow of Robert Bibby Collie; 3rdly, 1993, Diana Marjorie Fielder, da of Patrick Forsell, and has issue living (by 1st *m*), William Walter *b* 1964, Rachel Muriel *b* 1969, (by 3rd *m*) Thomas Patrick *b* 1993. *Residence* – Barleythorpe, Oakham, Rutland LE15 7EQ.

DAUGHTER LIVING OF TWELFTH BARONET

Barbara Marion Celia (*Lady Strachan*): *m* 1st, 1925, Robert Darley Whelan, Flying Officer RAF, who *d* 1927; 2ndly, 1929, Sir Andrew Henry Strachan, CBE, who *d* 1976, and has issue living (by 2nd *m*), Richard Neville, *b* 1930, — Judith Meriel, *b* 1936.

WIDOW LIVING OF FOURTEENTH BARONET

SYBIL MABEL ALICE (*Sybil, Lady Wrey*), older da of Dr George Lubke, of Durban, S Africa. *m* 1940, Sir (Castel Richard) Bourchier Wrey, 14th Bt, who *d* 1991. *Residence* – 511 Currie Rd, Durban, S Africa; Les Bellevue de Mougins, Val de Mougins, S France.

COLLATERAL BRANCHES LIVING

Grandsons of late Edward Castell Wrey, 7th son of 10th baronet:—
Issue of late Maj Christopher Bourchier Wrey, TD, *b* 1906, *d* 1976: *m* 1932 (*m diss* 1947), Ruth, only da of late Sir Harold Bowden, GBE, 2nd Bt:—

Timothy Christopher Bourchier (Certitude, Auroville 605 101, India), *b* 1937; *ed* Blundells: *m* 1964, Susan, el da of late William Brewer, of Troymark House, Johannesburg, S Africa, and has issue living, Marcus Valerian Bourchier, *b* 1969: *m* 1998, Charlotte Emma Idenden, da of late John David Swatland, — Camilla Melusine, *b* 1966. ——— Benjamin Harold Bourchier (8 Somerset Sq, Addison Rd, W14 8EE), *b* 1940: *m* 1970, Mrs Anne Christine Aubrey Cherry, da of late Col Christopher Bushnell Stephenson, and formerly wife of Roger Cherry, of Sydney, Australia, and has issue living, Tanya Serena, *b* 1971.

Grandsons of late Maj Reginald Charles Wrey, 8th son of 10th baronet:—
Issue of late Capt Denys Charles Bourchier Wrey, TD, *b* 1913, *d* 1991: *m* 1942, Katherine Frances Theodora (Peggy), who *d* 1996, da of late Rev William Francis Eliot (*see* Devitt, Bt, *cr* 1916, 1964 Edn):—
Charles Bourchier (Breach House, Compton Basset, Calne, Wilts), *b* 1949; *ed* Eton: *m* 1982, Catriona Anne, el da of Ian Wilson, and has issue living, Thomas Alexander Bourchier, *b* 1983, — Edward Charles Bourchier, *b* 1986, — Maximillian George Bourchier, *b* 1989. ——— Mark Eliot Bourchier (The Quag, Midhurst, W Sussex GU29 0JH), *b* 1955; *ed* Harrow: *m* 1985, Loveday Elizabeth, yr da of Maj Simon Bolitho, of Trengwainton, Penzance, Cornwall, and has issue living, Alexander Mark Bourchier, *b* 1986, — Simon Sherard Bourchier, *b* 1992, — Charlotte Loveday, *b* 1989.

Granddaughters of late George Edward Bourchier Wrey, only son of late George Bourchier Wrey, son of late Edward Bourchier Wrey, 2nd son of late Rev Bourchier William Wrey, yr son of 6th baronet:—
Issue of late Cdr Edward Charles Wrey, OBE, RN, *b* 1889, *d* 1972: *m* 1914, Grace Elsie, who *d* 1940, da of late James C. Rimer, of Kelvin Grove, Newlands, Cape, S Africa:—
Elizabeth Anne, *b* 1917: *m* 1946, William Welch Flexner, who *d* 1998, of 9 Paultons St, SW3 5DP. ——— Marie Jean, *b* 1919: *m* 1st, 1940, David Cecil Patrick Hastings, who was *ka* Burma 1943, son of late Sir Patrick Hastings, KC; 2ndly, 1949, Michael Dowden, who *d* 1972, and has issue living, (by 1st *m*) Judith Maryanne, *b* 1941: *m* 1963, Colin Etienne Dickinson, of The Old Vicarage, Coaley, Dursley, Glos GL11 5EB, and has issue living, Anthony David Richard *b* 1965, Charlotte Lucy *b* (twin) 1965, Sophie Louise *b* 1971, — (by 2nd *m*) Edward David Michael (11 Bath Rd, Bradford-on-Avon, Wilts BA15 1SN), *b* 1950: *m* 1970 (*m diss* 1985), Sarah Anne Sherwin, and has issue living, Benjamin Thomas Edward *b* 1978, Emma Mary *b* 1973, Matilda Jane *b* 1975.

Granddaughter of late Rev John Wrey, yr son of late Rev Bourchier William Wrey (ante):—
Issue of late Rev Arthur Bourchier Wrey, *b* 1831, *d* 1918: *m* 1st, 1859, Helen, who *d* 1878, da of the Rev Thomas Phillpotts, Canon of Truro; 2ndly, 1881, Claudine Maud, who *d* 1904, da of late Charles Twining, KC, formerly of Halifax, NS:—
(By 1st *m*) Mary Claudine: *m* 1st, 1913, Capt Humphrey Richard Locke Lawrence, Indian Army, *ka* 1915; 2ndly, 1928, Heathcote Dicken Statham, CBE, MusD, who *d* 1973, and has issue living (by 2nd *m*), Michael Heathcote Wrey, *b* 1929.

The family of Wrey is of considerable antiquity in Devonshire. Sir Chichester, the 3rd baronet, a faithful adherent to the royal cause, became in 1652 possessed, by marriage, of Tawstock, where the family formerly resided. His wife, Anne was 3rd da and co-heir of Edward Bourchier, Earl of Bath, and a co-heir to Barony of Fitzwarine (*cr* 1295). After the Restoration he was successively Colonel of the Duke of York's Regiment, Governor of Sheerness, and MP for Lostwithiel. Sir Bourchier, the 4th baronet, served under the Duke of Monmouth, and after the Restoration commanded a regiment of horse.

CORY-WRIGHT (UK) 1903, of Caen Wood Towers, Highgate, St Pancras, co London, and Hornsey, Middlesex

Sir RICHARD MICHAEL CORY-WRIGHT, 4th *Baronet*, *b* 17 Jan 1944; *s* his grandfather, *Maj Sir* GEOFFREY, 1969; *ed* Eton, and Birmingham Univ; late Lt Leics and Derbys Yeo; Patron of one living: *m* 1st, 1976 (*m diss* 1994), Veronica Mary, only da of James Harold Lucas Bolton, of Church Farm, Morningthorpe, Norwich; 2ndly, 1998, Mrs Helga Wright, of Dorchester-on-Thames, Oxon, and has issue by 1st *m*.

𝕬rms – Or, a fesse company counter-compony azure and argent between in chief two eagles' heads erased, and in base a unicorn passant reguardant of the second. 𝕮rest – Upon a mount proper between two caltraps or a unicorn passant reguardant argent, armed, crined, and unguled, also or.
Residence – 21 Trenchard Close, Wallingford, Oxon OX10 9BB.

SONS LIVING (*By 1st marriage*)

ROLAND ANTHONY, *b* 11 March 1979. ——— Jonathan James, *b* 1981. ——— Felix Michael, *b* 1986.

SISTER LIVING

Juliet Susan, *b* 1942: *m* 1977, John Frederick Webster, of Beech Grove Farm House, Hethersett, Norwich, and has issue living, Robert John Julian, *b* 1983, — Charlotte Josephine, *b* 1981.

DUM VIVIMUS VIVAMUS

UNCLES LIVING (Sons of 3rd baronet)

David Arthur, *b* 1925; *ed* Eton; Capt Scots Guards; 1939-45 War: *m* 1st, 1949 (*m diss* 1985), Lady Jane Katherine Douglas, da of 11th Marquess of Queensberry; 2ndly, 1985, Mrs Joy Elizabeth Jefferson, who *d* 1996, only da of late Albert Edward Dursley, of Hanham, Bristol, and has issue living, (by 1st *m*) Anthony Jonathan, *b* 1950: *m* 1988, Susana M., only da of Alfonso Torrents dels Prats, of Geneva, and London SW5, and has issue living, James Alfonso *b* 1994, Emma Mercedes *b* 1992, — Simon, *b* 1952, — Christopher James, *b* 1965. *Residence* – Quoin Cottage, Biddestone, Chippenham, Wilts SN14 7DQ. —— Mark Richard Geoffrey, *b* 1930; late 2nd Lieut 10th Roy Hussars: *m* 1956, Tania, da of late John Culcheth Holcroft (*see* Holcroft, Bt), of Northbrook, Bentley, Hants, and has issue living, Charles Alexander (Burnham Market, Kings Lynn, Norfolk), *b* 1958: *m* 1988, Dorothy McNaughton, da of Samuel Watson, of Penwortham, Lancs, and has issue living, Ella Doone *b* 1991, Poppy Maud *b* 1993, — Harry William Mark, *b* 1963. *Residence* – Tilhill House, Tilford, Surrey. *Clubs* – Brooks's, Pratt's.

COLLATERAL BRANCHES LIVING

Issue of late Ronald Cory-Wright, MC, 2nd son of 2nd baronet, *b* 1893, *d* 1932: *m* 1917, Geraldyn Mary, who *d* 1976, da of late Maj Henry Charles Windsor Villiers-Stuart, of Dromana, co Waterford (*see* M Bute):—
Francis Newman (Oakridge, Little Gaddesden, Berkhamsted, Herts), *b* 1925; *ed* Eton, and Merton Coll, Oxford (BA 1949, MA 1954): late Lt 15th/19th King's Roy Hussars; European War 1945 (wounded).

Issue of late Lt-Cdr Alan Cory-Wright, DSC, RN, 3rd son of 2nd baronet, *b* 1896, *d* 1964: *m* 1923, Leila Yda Cyrillia, who *d* 1982, da of Arthur Lobb, of Hatters Croft, Sawbridgeworth, Herts:—
Godfrey William (Hatfield Park, Takeley, Essex), *b* 1928; *ed* Harrow: *m* 1958, Nicole Emma, da of E. Vermeiren, of Brussels, and has issue living, Alan William (Auchessan, Crianlarich, Perthshire FK20 8QS), *b* 1965: *m* 1989, Nicki, 2nd da of Rt Rev John Richardson, Bishop of Bedford, and has issue living, Hamish Bean William *b* 1991, Jack *b* 1993, — Elizabeth Yda, *b* 1961: *m* 1989, Christopher Edward Mannion, of Ploughdens, Bush End, Bishop's Stortford, Herts CM22 6NG, and has issue living, Zachariah Ernest Gustave (Pingu) *b* 1993, Sassi Edward Paris (a da) *b* 1990, Araminta Tanzy Ophelia *b* 1992.

Issue of late Douglas Cory-Wright, CBE, 4th and yst son of 2nd baronet, *b* 1901, *d* 1987: *m* 1924, Margaret Vivien Sarina, who *d* 1987, da of Rudolph Levy, of Birkdale, Lancs:—
June (*June, Lady Horlick*), *b* 1926: *m* 1948, Sir John James Macdonald Horlick, 5th Bt, who *d* 1995, and has issue (*see* Horlick, Bt). —— (Olive) Marigold, MB BS, *b* 1929: *m* 1954, David Richard Michael Curling, who *d* 1993, of The Rosary, Coleshill, Bucks (*see* Curtis, Bt, 1945 Edn), and has had issue, Richard Michael, *b* 1958, — Rosanna Virginia, *b* 1960: *m* 1990, Nicholas Guy Charles della Casa, and presumed murdered (with her husband) in N Iraq 1991, — Davina Cordelia, *b* 1964. —— Cleone Anne, *b* 1935: *m* 1956: John Sedgwood Thellusson Wood (*see* E Kimberley, colls, 1990 Edn), of Lois Weedon House, Weedon Lois, nr Towcester, Northants, and has issue living, Nicholas John Wedgwood, *b* 1961, — Amelia Jane, *b* 1959, — Rebecca Anne, *b* 1964, — Anna, *b* 1969.

Grandchildren of late Dudley Cory-Wright, yr son of 1st baronet—
Issue of late Esmond Godfrey Cory-Wright, *b* 1908, *d* 1989: *m* 1st, 1931 (*m diss* 1942), Amanda, who *d* 1981, da of E. P. Menhinick, of Treguddick, Gresham Gardens, Golders Green, NW11; 2ndly, 1949, Pepita Jane Grey, who *d* 1995, da of Harry William Grey Bell:—
(By 1st *m*) Edward James Dudley (Briar Cottage, 26 Broadmark Lane, Rustington, W Sussex BN16 2HL), *b* 1932; *ed* Merton Coll, Oxford: *m* 1955, Jean Olive, da of George Young, of St Albans, Herts, and has issue living, James Edward (6 Westbourne St, Hove, E Sussex), *b* 1956; *ed* Univ of E Anglia (BA), PGCE: *m* 1st, 1978 (*m diss* 1993), Susan Laura, da of Sydney Bricknell, of Sutton Grove, Shrewsbury; 2ndly, 1995, Jill Williams, and has issue living, (by 2nd *m*) Max James *b* 1996, — Nicholas John, *b* 1964: *m* 1991, Ana, da of Rodolfo Sanchez, of Madrid, and has issue living, Alexandra Delia *b* 1995, — Juliet Amanda, *b* 1959: *m* 1984, Philip Fielder, of Church House, Timsbury, Hants, and has issue living, Mark Edward *b* 1988, Charles John *b* 1995, Victoria Frances *b* 1986. —— Amanda Menhinick, *b* 1933.

The 1st baronet, Sir Cory Francis Cory-Wright, was Chm of Wm Cory and Son (Limited), and assumed by Roy licence 1903, the additional surname of Cory. The 2nd baronet, Sir Arthur Cory-Wright, was High Sheriff for Herts 1921. The 3rd baronet, Maj Sir Geoffrey Cory-Wright, *m* 1915, Felicity, who *d* 1978, 2nd da of late Sir Herbert Beerbohm Tree, the actor-manager. His eldest son, Capt Anthony John Julian Cory-Wright, RA, *b* 1916, was *ka* 1944, at St Mauvieu, Normandy, having *m* 1940, Susan Esterel (who *d* 1993, having *m* 2ndly, 1949, Lt-Col Jocelyn Eustace Gurney, DSO, MC, of Tacolneston Hall, Norfolk, who *d* 1973), eldest da of late Capt Robert Hamond Arthur Elwes, of Congham House, Norfolk. His only son is Sir Richard Michael Cory-Wright, 4th and present baronet.

WRIGHTSON (UK) 1900, of Neasham Hall, co Durham

Sir CHARLES MARK GARMONDSWAY WRIGHTSON, 4th *Baronet*; *b* 18 Feb 1951; *s* his father, *Col Sir* JOHN GARMONDSWAY, TD, 1983; *ed* Eton and Queens' Coll, Camb: *m* 1975, Stella Virginia, da of late George Dean, MPS, of Garden Cottage, Middleton Tyas, N Yorks, and has issue.

Arms – Or, a fesse invected checky azure and argent between two eagles' heads erased in chief sable, and a saltire couped in base gules. Crest – In front of a saltire gules, a unicorn salient or.
Seat – Neasham Hall, near Darlington. *Residence* – 39 Westbourne Park Rd, W2

SONS LIVING

BARNABY THOMAS GARMONDSWAY, *b* 5 Aug 1979. —— James George, *b* 1982. —— William John, *b* 1985.

SISTERS LIVING

Veritas omnia vincit
Truth conquers all things

Penelope Linda, *b* 1940. —— Juliet Diana, *b* 1943. —— Elizabeth Ann, *b* 1946: *m* 1978, Laurent Tisné, of La Roche Abilen, St Georges du Bois, Maine et Loire, France, and has issue living, Martin, *b* 1979, — Louis, *b* 1981.

COLLATERAL BRANCHES LIVING

Issue of late Lt-Col Peter Wrightson, OBE, *b* 1914, *d* 1995: *m* 1946, Pamela (Manfield Grange, Manfield, nr Darlington DL2 2RE), da of late Lt-Col Sir Murrough John Wilson, KBE:—
Simon Murrough (Manfield Grange, Manfield, nr Darlington DL2 2RE), *b* 1954: *m* 1975, Elisabeth Yvonne, da of Hubert Marcel Michelin, of Le Gressigny, 63870 Orcines, France, and has issue living, Richard Charles Peter, *b* 1985, — Emma Mary Rose, *b* 1982. —— Joanna Mary, *b* 1947: *m* 1st, 1969 (*m diss* 19—), Peter Jonathan Howard; 2ndly, 1995, Arthur Goodwin, who *d* 1995, and has issue living, (by 1st *m*) Benjamin Simon, *b* 1975, — James Edward Peter, *b* 1979, — Penelope Sarah, *b* 1971, — Alison Rebecca, *b* 1972. —— Susan Jennifer, *b* 1948: *m* 1970, Montague William Style, of 27 rue des Romains, 68480 Bettlach, Alsace, France, and has issue (*see* Style, Bt, colls). *Residence* – Manfield Grange, Manfield, nr Darlington.

Issue of late Cdr Rodney Wrightson, RN, 3rd son of 2nd baronet, *b* 1916, *d* 1992: *m* 1st, 1940, Florence Jean, who *d* 1944, elder da of late James Dunn Dunn, of Ferniecraig, Skelmorlie, Ayrshire; 2ndly, 1947, Janet Elizabeth (22 West St, Wilton, Wilts SP2 0DF), eldest da of late Brig Raymond Henry Arnold Davison Love, RA, of Overcroft, Mayford, Surrey, and formerly wife of Brig William Branfoot Wilson, OBE:—
(By 1st *m*) Jeremy Rodney (29 Lynn Close, Leigh Sinton, Malvern, Worcs WR13 5DU), *b* 1941; *ed* Eton: *m* 1970, Lindsay, da of Dr John Milroy Glen Parker, of 9 The Mount, Malton, Yorks, and has issue living, Rufus Guy, *b* 1975, — Christopher John, *b* 1985, — Amy Jean, *b* 1974. —— (By 2nd *m*) Lucinda, *b* 1948: *m* 1st, 1969, Jonathan Philip Hudson; 2ndly, 1985, John Riddell White Abbott, of Mas de Juston, Serviers, 30700 Uzes, France, only son of late John Nesbitt White Abbott, MBE, TD, and has issue living (by 1st *m*), Henry Andrew, *b* 1972, — Emily Alice, *b* 1974.

Issue of late Wilfrid Ingram Wrightson, yst son of 1st baronet, *b* 1876, *d* 1949: *m* 1913, Victoria, who *d* 1966, da of late F. C. Winby, of 47 Portland Place, W:—
Ann Winby, *b* 1917: *m* 1952, Robert le Rougetel White, BArch, ARIBA, LRAM, who *d* 1979. *Residence* – Cross Gates, Lorton, Cockermouth, Cumbria CA13 9UL.

The 1st baronet, Sir Thomas, was Chm of Head, Wrightson and Co (Limited), bridge builders, of Stockton, and sat as MP for Stockton-on-Tees (*C*) 1892-95, and for E Div of St Pancras July 1899 to Jan 1906.

Wrixon-Becher, see Becher.

Wykeham (Twisleton-Wykeham-Fiennes), see Fiennes.

WILLIAMS-WYNN (E) 1688, of Gray's Inn, co Middlesex

Sir (DAVID) WATKIN WILLIAMS-WYNN, 11th *Baronet*; *b* 18 Feb 1940; *s* his father, *Lt-Col Sir* (OWEN) WATKIN, CBE, 1988; *ed* Eton; late Maj 1st Royal Dragoons; OC Ches Yeo Sqdn, QOY 1971-77; Master Sir W. W. Wynn's Hounds 1971-77, Master Flint and Denbigh Hounds 1978-90, Master of own hounds (Sir W. W. Wynn's) 1991-98; DL Clwyd 1966; High Sheriff Clwyd 1990: *m* 1st, 1968 (*m diss* 1981), (Harriet) Veryan Elspeth, da of late Gen Sir Norman Hastings Tailyour, KCB, DSO; 2ndly, 1983 (*m diss* 1998), Mrs Victoria Jane Dillon, da of late Lt-Col Ian Dudley De Ath, DSO, MBE, and formerly wife of Lt-Col R. E. Dillon, RM, and has issue by 1st and 2nd *m.*

Arms – Quarterly: 1st and 4th vert, three eagles displayed in fesse wings inverted or, *Wynn*; 2nd and 3rd gules, argent, two foxes counter-salient in saltire the sinister surmounted of the dexter gules, *Williams.* Crest – An eagle displayed or. *Residence* – Plas-yn-Cefn, St Asaph, Clwyd LL17 0EY. *Clubs* – Cavalry and Guards', and Pratts.

Eryr Eryrod Eryri

The Eagle of the Eagles of Snowdon

SONS LIVING *(By 1st marriage)*

CHARLES EDWARD WATKIN, *b* 1970. —— Robert Euan Watkin, *b* 1977.

(by 2nd marriage)

Nicholas Watkin, *b* 1988. —— Harry Watkin, *b* (twin) 1988.

DAUGHTERS LIVING *(by 1st marriage)*

Alexandra June, *b* 1972. —— Lucinda Jean, *b* (twin) 1972.

AUNTS LIVING *(daughters of 9th baronet)*

Joyce, *b* 1906: *m* 1929, Duncan Robertson, who *d* 1987, son of late Sir Henry Beyer Robertson, and has had issue, Sheila Ann, *b* 1929: *m* 1st, 1953 (*m diss* 1975), Henry Saxon Tate (*see* Tate, Bt); 2ndly, 1976, Humphrey Sandford, of The Isle, Shrewsbury, Shropshire, and *d* 1987, leaving issue (by 1st *m*) (*see* Tate, Bt), —— Jean Margaret, *b* 1932: *m* 1956, Capt Peter Miles de Wend Greenwell, of Tregeiriog, nr Llangollen, Clwyd LL20 7HU, and has had issue, Rupert Peter *b* 1959; *ed* Milton Abbey, James Robertson *b* 1963; *ed* Eton; murdered in Zimbabwe 1982, Duncan Charles de Wend *b* 1966; *ed* King's Sch, Bruton, —— Bridget Jennifer (*Baroness de Clifford*), *b* 1935: *m* 1959, 27th Baron de Clifford, of Riggledown, Pennymoor, Tiverton, Devon EX16 8LR. *Residence* – ……. —— Margaret (*Hon Mrs Peter Hotham*), *b* 1911: *m* 1934, Maj Hon Peter Hotham, late King's Own Yorkshire LI (*see* B Hotham), who *d* 1991. *Residence* – Plas Newydd, Glascoed, Abergele, N Wales.

WIDOW LIVING OF TENTH BARONET

GABRIELLE HADEN (*Dowager Lady Williams-Wynn*), da of late Herbert Alexander Caffin, of Hazlemere, Surrey, and formerly wife of Wing Cdr W. R. A. Matheson: *m* 1968, as his 2nd wife, Lt-Col Sir (Owen) Watkin Williams-Wynn, 10th Bt, CBE, who *d* 1988. *Residence* – Eryl, Llangedwyn, Oswestry, Shropshire.

COLLATERAL BRANCHES LIVING

Grandchildren of late Major Frederick Rowland Williams-Wynn, CB, son of late Charles Watkin Williams-Wynn (infra):—

Issue of late Col John Francis Williams-Wynne, CBE, DSO, *b* 1980, *d* 1998; assumed by deed poll 1940 the surname of Williams-Wynne in lieu of his patronymic: *m* 1938, Margaret Gwendoline Heyward, who *d* 1991, da of late Rev George Eliott Roper:—

William Robert Charles WILLIAMS-WYNNE (Peniarth, Tywyn, Gwynedd), *b* 1947; FRICS 1972; JP 1972: *m* 1975, Hon Veronica Frances Buxton, da of Baron Buxton of Alsa (Life Baron), and has issue living, Chloë Frances, *b* 1978, —— Leonora Mary, *b* 1980, — Rose Margaret, *b* 1981. —— Virginia (Oryx House, PO Box 456, Mina al Fahal, CP 116, Sultanate of Oman), *b* 1941: renounced her former christian names of Merion Beatrice by deed poll 1908. *m* 1st, 1964, Maj Peter Thomas Anthony Davies (who assumed the surname Abbot-Davies by deed poll 1969), who *d* 1979; 2ndly, 1980, HH Sayyid Faher bin Taimur Alsaid, who *d* 1996, and has issue living (by 1st *m*), Orion Jonathan, *b* 1965, — Hardwin, *b* 1968, — (by 2nd *m*), Latifah, *b* 1981. —— Jane Margaret (*Countess of Home*), *b* 1949: *m* 1972, 15th Earl of Home, CVO, CBE, of The Hirsel, Coldstream, Berwickshire, and has issue (*see* E Home).

Granddaughter of late Charles Watkin Williams-Wynn, son of late Rt Hon Charles Watkin Williams-Wynn, 2nd son of 4th baronet:—

Issue of late Major Frederick Rowland Williams-Wynn, CB, *b* 1865, *d* 1940: *m* 1907, Beatrice Kathleen, who *d* 1913, el da of late Major Francis Cooper, RFA, of Markree Castle, Collooney, Ireland:—

Annora Beatrice, *b* 1911: *m* 1st, 1935 (*m diss* 1945), Lt-Col David Sacheverell Curtis, Roy Fus (*see* Curtis, Bt, colls); 2ndly, 1945, Charles George Gordon Wainman, who *d* 1988, and has issue living (by 1st *m*) (*see* Curtis, Bt, colls), — (by 2nd *m*) Annora Mary, *b* 1946: *m* 1970, Evangelos Koemtzopoulos, of Athens, Greece, and has had issue, Nicholas *b* 1974, Mark *b* 1979, Laura *b* 1971, *d* 1978, Marina *b* 1981. *Residence* – The Tower House, Hinton St George, Som, TA17 8SS.

Descendants of late John Williams (great-grandson of John Williams, 2nd son of 1st baronet), who was *cr* a *Baronet* 1798.
See Williams, Bt, *cr* 1798.

This family descends from Cadrod Hardd, or the Handsome, a Welsh chieftain, who was Lord of Talybolion in the Isle of Anglesey about the year 1100. The 1st baronet, Sir William Williams, MP for Chester in three Parliaments, was Speaker of the House of Commons 1679-85. In 36 Car II he was tried for libel, in causing to be printed the information of Thomas Dangerfield, and although he pleaded the law and custom of Parliament, he was fined £10,000. After the Revolution, this judgement was declared illegal and against the freedom of Parliament. The 3rd baronet, Sir Watkin Williams, succeeded to the estate of Wynnstay (formerly Watstay) in 1718 under the will of Sir John Wynn, 5th Bt of Gwydir (ext), who had acquired that estate through his wife, and assumed the additional surname of Wynn. The 6th baronet sat as MP for Denbighshire (*C*) 1841-85. The 7th baronet, Col Sir Herbert Lloyd Watkin Williams-Wynn, CB, was Hon Col Yeo, Lord-Lieut of Montgomeryshire, and a County Councillor for Denbighshire. He sat as MP for Denbighshire (*C*) May to Nov 1885. The 9th baronet, Col Sir Robert William Herbert Watkin Williams-Wynn, KCB, DSO, TD, was Lord-Lieut of Denbighshire 1928-51, and served in S Africa 1900-02, and European War 1914-18. The 10th baronet, Lt-Col Sir Watkin Williams-Wynn, CBE, was High Sheriff and Lord-Lieut of Denbighshire, and Lord-Lieut of Clwyd; served 1939-45 War (taken prisoner by Japanese and forced to work for three and a half years on the infamous Siam and Burma Rlwy); Master of Flint and Denbigh Hounds, Joint Master of Sir Watkin Williams-Wynn's Hounds (his yr son, Robert, was killed in N Ireland while serving with the 14th/20th King's Hus, 1972).

WYVILL (E) 1611, of Constable Burton, Yorkshire (Dormant 1774)

COLLATERAL BRANCHES LIVING

Granddaughter living of late William Edward Wyvill, probably *de jure* 15th Bt:—
Issue of late Newlon D'Arcy Wyvill, probably *de jure* 17th Bt, *b* 1895, *d* 1971: *m* 1920, Helen Lamar, da of Henry Laboin Wood:—
Willie Juanita, *b* 1923: *m* 1st, 1952 (*m diss* 1953), Walter Daniel Scheuch; 2ndly, Donald Douglas Lamond.

Grandson of late Maj Marmaduke Ibbetson Wyvill, Rifle Bde, only son of Marmaduke D'Arcy Wyvill of Constable Burton Hall and Denton Park, Yorks, el son of Marmaduke Wyvill (*d* 1896), third in descent from Edward Wyvill, 2nd son of D'Arcy Wyvill (*infra*), 2nd son of 4th baronet:—
Issue of late Marmaduke Frederic Wyvill, *b* 1912, *d* 1953: *m* 1st, 19— (*m diss* 19—), Cissy Scott; 2ndly, 1943 (*m diss* 1946), May, da of Henry Holland Bennet; 3rdly, 1947, Mrs Mary Jones, who *d* 1968, da of late Frederick Pope:—
(By 2nd *m*) Marmaduke Charles Asty (Constable Burton Hall, Leyburn, N Yorks; Brooks's Club), *b* 1945; *ed* Stowe and Roy Agric Coll, Cirencester; ARICS; Lord of Manor of Constable Burton, Leyburn, Yorks, and patron of three livings; High Sheriff of N Yorks 1986-87: *m* 1972, Margaret Ann, el da of Maj Sydney Hardcastle, RA, of Hutchins Farm, Etchingham, Sussex, and has issue living, Marmaduke D'Arcy William, *b* 1975, — Edward Paul Anthony, *b* 1977, — Frederick Charles Penrose, *b* 1983, — Katherine Marye Laura, *b* 1981.

This Baronetcy has remained dormant since the death in 1774 of Sir Marmaduke Asty Wyvill, 7th Bt. According to GEC's "Complete Baronetage", his probable heir was Marmaduke Wyvill of Anne Arundel co, Maryland, son and heir of William, who emigrated to Frederick Co, Maryland, el son of Darcy, 2nd son of 4th Bt. Marmaduke left two sons by his 1st wife, Harriet Rateby (*m* 1764) and two sons by his 2nd wife, Susanna Burgess (*m* 1775). His el son, Darcy (probably *de jure* 9th Bt) had one son Robert (probably *de jure* 10th Bt) who *dsp* about 1800. His 2nd son, Marmaduke (probably *de jure* 11th Bt) *dsp* male 1808. The succession presumably reverted to his half-brother, Walter of Calvert co, Maryland (el son of Marmaduke by his 2nd wife, and probably *de jure* 12th Bt). His son, Edward Hale (probably *de jure* 13th Bt), *b* 1812, *d c* 1894, was *s* by his son, Walter Davis (probably *de jure* 14th Bt), *b* 1834, *d* 1898. This is as far as GEC takes the line, but recent research has established that he was *s* by his only son, William Edward (probably *de jure* 15th Bt), *b* 1859, *d* 1911, who was *s* by his el son Carlisle Osborne (probably *de jure* 16th Bt), *b* 1894, *d* 1941, who was *s* by his brother Newlon D'Arcy (probably *de jure* 17th Bt), *b* 1895, *d* 1971.

YARROW (UK) 1916, of Homestead, Hindhead, Frensham, co Surrey

Be just and fear not

Sir ERIC GRANT YARROW, MBE, 3rd *Baronet*, b 23 April 1920; s his father, *Sir* HAROLD EDGAR, GBE, 1962; *ed* Marlborough and Glasgow Univ; a DL of Renfrewshire; Managing Dir Yarrow and Co Ltd 1958-67, Chm 1962-85, Pres 1985-87; Chm Yarrow (Shipbuilders) Ltd 1962-79; Memb Lloyd's Register of Shipping, Scottish Comm 1956-87, General Comm 1960-89; Hon Vice-Pres Roy Instn of Naval Architects since 1972; Memb of Council of Institute of Directors 1983-90; Chm of Clydesdale Bank 1985-91; Pres Burma Star Assoc, Scottish Area since 1990; FRSE; Burma 1942-45, as Maj RE; MBE (Mil) 1946; OStJ: *m* 1st, 1951, Rosemary Ann, who *d* 1957, yr da of late H. T. Young, of Roehampton, SW15; 2ndly, 1959 (*m diss* 1975), Annette Elizabeth Françoise, only da of late A. J. E. Steven, of Ardgay, Ross-shire; 3rdly, 1982, Caroline Rosa Joan, da of late R. F. Masters, of Piddinghoe, Sussex, and formerly wife of Philip Botting, of Allington Farm, Offham, and has had issue by 1st and 2nd *m*.

Arms – Azure, in base on the sea proper, an ancient three-masted ship, sailing to the sinister argent, in chief two swallows volant of the last, each holding in the beak a harebell slipped also proper. **Crest** – Above clouds proper a swallow volant argent, holding in the beak a yarrow flower slipped also proper.

Residence – Cloak, Kilmacolm, Renfrewshire, PA13 4SD. *Club* – Army and Navy.

GRANDSONS LIVING

Issue of late Richard Grant Yarrow, eldest son of Sir Eric Grant Yarrow, 3rd Bt, MBE, b 1953, d 1987: *m* 1982, Sheila Elizabeth (Craigmore Lodge, Nethy Bridge, Inverness-shire PH25 3ED), elder da of Ronald William Paul Allison, CVO, commentator, of 14 Arlington Place, King Alfred Terrace, Winchester:—
ROSS WILLIAM GRANT, b 14 Jan 1985. —— Thomas Christopher, b 1987.

SONS LIVING (*By 2nd marriage*)

Norman Murray b 1960: *m* 1988, Carol Jane, elder da of Nicholas Hawkins, of Noble Tree House, Hildenborough, Kent, and has issue living, Richard Eric, b 1994, — Katie Diana, b 1990, — Lucy Carol, b 1992. —— Peter Harold b (twin) 1960: *m* 1998, Mrs Sara J. Galbraith, yst da of late Peter Parry, of Furneux Pelham, Herts. —— David Eric, b 1966.

SISTERS LIVING

Eleanor Audrey (Balauchen Lodge, Milngavie, Glasgow G62 8EJ), b 1907: *m* 1934, Maj Harry Duncanson Boyd, MBE, TD, RA, who *d* 1964, and has issue living, Eleanor Margaret, b 1937: *m* 1959, Peter Murray Bruce Hutt (Strathisla, Box 33, PO Hillcrest 3650, Natal), el son of Sir (Alexander McDonald) Bruce Hutt, KBE, CMG, and has issue living, Colin Murray Bruce b 1960, Nigel Duncan b 1964: *m* 1994, Fiona Cameron, Nichola Margaret b 1966: *m* 1992, James Baker, — Eda Daphne, b 1940: *m* 1963, Christopher Roche Enslin, of 5 Bothwell Close, Tokai 7945, nr Cape Town, S Africa, and has issue living, Michael Roche b 1967: *m* 1997, Tracy Rouse, Ian Boyd b 1970: *m* 1988, Katya Gagg, Camilla Fiona b 1964: *m* 1987, Brent Grimbeeil, — Sylvia Audrey, b 1944: *m* 1st, 1967 (*m diss* 1983), Alexander Baird Fergus Morton; 2ndly, 1983, David Charles Alan Norris, of Graghvar, Milngavie, Glasgow G62 8EJ, and has issue living (by 1st *m*), Peter Fergus b 1970, Anita Audrey b 1973. —— Beryl Winifred Ethne (Netherblane, Blanefield, Glasgow, G62 8EJ), b 1910: *m* 1st, 1932, Charles Wood Scott, who *d* 1960; 2ndly, 1969, Graeme Hardie, BEM, who *d* 1973, and has had issue (by 1st *m*), Grahame Charles Wood, b 1933: *m* 1962, Jean Isabel Mary Manners (10 Mosspark Av, Milngavie, Glasgow G62 8NL), and *d* 1981, leaving issue, Alan Charles Wood b 1966, Fiona Anne b 1963, Lorna Jean Ethne b 1965: *m* 1991, Nicholas Iain Hudson (and has issue living, Michael Grahame b 1997, Claire Eleanor b 1995), — Avril Eleanor Yarrow, b 1936: *m* 1959, James Alistair Spence Meighan, of Fernbrae, Moor Rd, Strathblane, Stirlingshire G63 9EY, and has issue living, Andrew Alistair Spence b 1963, Marjorie Eleanor Spence b 1961: *m* 1984, Ranald Morton White (and has issue living, Sarah Jane b 1987, Alice Jennifer b 1990), Avril Gillian Spence b 1966.

HALF-SISTER LIVING

Angela Mary Rosalynde, b 1937: *m* 1961, David Clive Griffiths, who *d* 1997, of Wyfold Grange, Wyfold, Reading, Berks, and has issue living, David William Yarrow, b 1969, — Rosemary Kate, b 1962, — Amanda Mary, b 1964.

COLLATERAL BRANCH LIVING

Issue of late Norman Alfred Yarrow, 2nd son of 1st baronet, b 1891, d 1955: *m* 1915, Ada Hope (who *d* 1990, having *m* 2ndly, 1959, as his third wife, Sir Eric Stuart Taylor, OBE, MD, MRCP, 2nd Bt, who *d* 1977), da of Forrest Bertram Leeder, MRCS, LRCP, of Victoria, BC:—
Cynthia Hope (638 Transit Rd, Vict, BC, Canada V85 4Z5), b 1921: *m* 1st, 1944 (*m diss* 1954), Lieut Clifton Thomas Williams Hyslop, Roy Canadian Naval Vol Reserve; 2ndly, 1955 (*m diss* 19——), William F. Pinckard, and has issue living, (by 1st *m*) John David Allan, b 1946, — Andrew Peter, b 1951, — Gillian Cynthia, b 1949, — (by 2nd *m*) Christopher

William Norman, *b* 1958, — Jonathan Mark, *b* 1960. —— Daphne Veryan, *b* 1924: *m* 1952, Lt Cdr Howard Victor Clark, RCN, of 2440 Chiltern Place, Victoria, BC, Canada V8R 3S8, and has issue living, Susan Veryan, *b* 1954, — Stephanie Jane, *b* 1958.

The 1st baronet, Sir Alfred Fernandez Yarrow (an engineer and shipbuilder), was Chm of Yarrow and Co, Ltd, shipbuilders, of Scotstoun, Glasgow, until 1922.

YOUNG (GB) 1769, of North Dean, Buckinghamshire

Sir WILLIAM NEIL YOUNG, 10th *Baronet*, son of late Capt William Elliot Young, RAMC, only son of 9th baronet; *b* 22 Jan 1941; *s* his grandfather, *Sir* (CHARLES) ALBAN, KCMG, MVO, 1944; *ed* Wellington Coll, and RMA Sandhurst; Capt 16th/5th The Queen's R Lancers (ret); Dir Barclays Private Bank Ltd: *m* 1965 Christine Veronica, only da of late Robert Boland Morley, and has issue.
Residence – Penchrise Peel, Hawick, Roxburghshire.

SON LIVING

WILLIAM LAWRENCE ELLIOT, *b* 26 May 1970; *ed* Eton, and Edin Univ (MA).

DAUGHTER LIVING

Catherine Clare, *b* 1967; *ed* Downe House, and Somerville Coll, Oxford (BA): *m* 1993, Hugh E. Powell, son of Sir Charles Powell, KCMG, and has issue living, Joshua, *b* 1996, — Nathaniel *b* 1997.

COLLATERAL BRANCHES LIVING

Grandsons of late Rev Henry Savill Young, son of Rev Henry Tufnell Young, 2nd son of 3rd Bt:—
Issue of late Rev Henry Brook Young, *b* 1869, *d* 1937: *m* 1920, Emmie, who *d* 1934, da of Henry Everitt, of Exning:—
William Brook Charles, *b* 1922; Sq-Ldr RAF (ret); a Civil Airline Pilot; Queen's Commendation for Valuable Ser in the Air: *m* 1949, Alma Evelyn, da of F. C. Harvey, of Reading, and has issue living, Paul Anthony Brook, *b* 1950: *m* 1st, 1975 Barbara Inkley; 2ndly, 1993, Lyn White, — Christopher Charles Brook, *b* 1953: *m* 1975, Mary Patricia Walls, — Amanda Jane Brook, *b* 1956: *m* 1st, 1975, Delwyn Dowse; 2ndly, 1982, Randal Dobbs. *Residence* – No 2 Chugg's Orchard, Cloutman's Lane, Croyde, Braunton, Devon.

Issue of late Major George Edward Savill Young, Irish Guards, *b* 1884, *d* of wounds received in action 1917: *m* 1914, Alison Jane, who *d* 1957, da of Rev Frederick John Poole, of Bishop Monkton, Ripon:—
Henry Lawrence Savill, DSO, *b* 1915; *ed* Harrow; Brig (ret) late Irish Gds; 1939-45 War (despatches, DSO); DSO 1944: *m* 1939, Noreen de Vere, da of late Thomas Brabazon Ponsonby (*see* E Bessborough, colls), and has issue living, (George Trevor) Savill (37 Lessar Av, Clapham, SW4 9HW), *b* 1941: *ed* Harrow, and Trin Coll, Dublin; late Lt Irish Gds: *m* 1983, Marion Sonia, da of Jean Paul Koch, of Rome, and has issue living, Sophie Georgiana *b* 1984, — Verona, *b* 1943: *m* 1976, Colin Lionel Angus Fraser-Mackenzie, of Cedar House, Pilton, Somerset, and has issue living, Richard Savill Thomas *b* 1981, Peter Alexander Francis *b* 1983. *Residence* – The End House, Pilton, Somerset.

Grandchildren of late Lieut-Col Hugh Greville Young, DSO, RHA (ante):—
Issue of late Hugh Findlay Young, *b* 1919, *d* 1987: *m* 19—, Angela Elaine, da of late R. G. M. Whigham:—
James Greville (Hampshire House, Hampshire Gdns, Coleford, Glos), *b* 1957: *m* 1990, Samantha, da of Lawrence Edward Sillett, of Hill Park, Stag Hill, Yorkley, Glos, and has issue living, Cecilia Angela, *b* 1990, — Matilda Judith Alice, *b* 1992. —— Giles Hugh Findlay, *b* 1964. —— Piers Jonathan, *b* 1965: *m* 19—, Julia Marie, da of Sidney Charles Barnfield, of Tewkesbury, Glos. —— Mary Rose Frederica (Oak House, The Folly, Parkend, Lydney, Glos), *b* 1958.

Granddaughter of late George Augustus Young, 4th son of 3rd baronet:—
Issue of late Harold Lawrence Young, *b* 1866, *d* 1909: *m* 1894, Beatrix Kinsey (who *m* 2ndly, 1911, George Gully), da of late William Kinsey Hayward:—
Dorothy, *b* 1903: *m* 1928, Walter Adam, MB. *Residence* – Johannesburg, S Africa.

The 1st baronet, Sir William Young (son of late William Young, MD), was Lieut-Governor of Dominica. Sir William Young, FRS, 2nd baronet, was Governor of Tobago. Sir William Norris, 5th baronet, was killed at the battle of the Alma, 1854; and his brother, Sir George John, 6th baronet, died before Sebastopol the same year. Sir (Charles) Alban, KCMG, MVO, 9th baronet, was Envoy Extraor and Min Plen and Consul-Gen to Guatemala 1913-19, and to Yugoslavia 1919-25.

YOUNG (UK) 1813, of Formosa Place, Berkshire

Rt Hon Sir GEORGE SAMUEL KNATCHBULL YOUNG, 6th *Baronet*; *b* 16 July 1941; *s* his father, *Sir* GEORGE PEREGRINE, CMG, 1960; *ed* Eton, and Ch Ch, Oxford (Open Exhibitioner); Fellow Univ of Surrey; a Member Lambeth Borough Council 1968-71, and GLC 1970-73; Economist, Nat Economic Development Office 1967-68; Research Fellow, Univ of Surrey 1968-69; Economic Adviser, PO Corpn 1969-74; Opposition Whip 1976-79, Chm Acton House Assocn 1972-79; Under Sec of State DHSS 1979-81, Under Sec of State for the Environment 1981-86; Comptroller HM Household, and Min for Housing, Dept of Environment 1990-92, Min for Housing and Inner Cities 1992-94, Financial Sec to the Treasury 1994-95, Sec of State for Transport 1995-97; PC 1993; author of "Tourism, Blessing or Blight?"; MP for Ealing Acton (*C*) 1974-97; *m* 1964, Aurelia, el da of Oscar Nemon, of Boars Hill, Oxford, and has issue.

Arms – Per fesse sable and argent: in chief two lions rampant-guardant, and in base an anchor erect with a cable, all counterchanged. **Crest** – A demi-unicorn couped ermine, armed, maned, and hoofed or, gorged with a naval crown azure supporting an anchor erect sable.
Address – c/o House of Commons, SW1A 0AA.

SONS LIVING

GEORGE HORATIO (Flat 4, 27 Elsham Rd, W14 8HB) *b* 11 Oct 1966; *ed* Windsor Coll of Further Educn, and Ch Ch, Oxford. —— Hugo Patrick, *b* 1970.

DAUGHTERS LIVING

Sophia Angelica, *b* 1965: *m* 1996, David D. Butler, of 96A Elmbourne Rd, SW17 8JH, yst son of Ian Butler, of Kingston-upon-Thames, Surrey, and has issue living, Leo Samuel Randolph, *b* 1997, — Alexander Sterling, *b* 1999. —— Camilla Mary, *b* 1975.

BROTHER LIVING

Charles Evory (62 Old Rd, Oxford OX3 7LL), *b* 1943; *ed* Eton, and Ch Ch, Oxford (Open Exhibitioner): *m* 1973, Wiltrud, da of H. J. Frömbling, and has issue living, Emily Lucinde, *b* 1974, — Juliet, *b* 1975.

SISTER LIVING

Helen Mary, *b* 1947: *m* 1st, 1969 (*m diss* 1986), Digby Robert William Norton; 2ndly, 1988, Dr Tom Winnifrith, of 69 Gloucester Rd, Malmesbury, Wilts, 2nd son of Sir John Winnifrith, KCB, and has issue living (by 1st *m*), Thomas Alan Hughe, *b* 1975, — Joanna Elisabeth, *b* 1972, — Felicity Margaret, *b* 1979.

AUNT LIVING (*Daughter of 4th baronet*)

Virginia Jacomyn (*Lady Hutton*), *b* 1911: *m* 1936, Sir Noel Kilpatrick Hutton, GCB, QC, who *d* 1984, and has issue living, William Noel, *b* 1937; MA, MB, Camb; BChir; FRCP (London); inventor: *m* 1960, Doris Mary Nesfield, and has issue living, Timothy Noel *b* 1963, Duncan Neil *b* 1964, Rupert MacIntyre *b* 1971, Virginia Rozanne *b* 1961, Julia Mary *b* 1967, — Charles Edward Ilbert (31 Av Henri Mas, Roujan 34320, France), *b* 1943: *m* 1967, Alison Victoria Featherstone, yr da of John Harvey, and has issue living, Samuel Barnaby *b* 1968, William Gabriel *b* 1970, Pegotty Alice *b* 1974, — Melissa Grace, *b* 1939: *m* 1963, James Perot, of 316 Maple Av, Doylestown, PA 18901-4412, USA, and has issue living, James Blair *b* 1965, Noelle Melissa, *b* 1963, Szerina Alice *b* 1968, — Dorothea Eacy, *b* 1948. *Residence* – 33 St John Street, Oxford OX1 2LH.

COLLATERAL BRANCHES LIVING

Issue of late Courtenay Trevelyan Young, yr son of 4th baronet, *b* 1914, *d* 1974: *m* 1942, June Brinley (Browne's Lodge, ?? West St, Reigate, Surrey RH2 9BS), da of G. Brinley Richards:—
Frederick Courtenay, *b* 1948: *m* 1971 (*m diss* 19—), Heather Brunskell, and has issue living, Daniel Justin, *b* 1972, — Jude Aaron, *b* 1976, — Gudrun Rachael, *b* 1974, — Rhiannon Brislee, *b* 1983. —— Jessica Catherine, *b* 1950: *m* 1976, Paul Staddon, of 7 Chepstow Rd, W2 5BP, and has issue living, Anthony David, *b* 1988.

Issue of late Geoffrey Winthrop Young, 2nd son of 3rd baronet, *b* 1876, *d* 1958: *m* 1918, Eleanor, who *d* 1994, da of William Cecil Slingsby, formerly of Heversham, Westmorland:—
Jocelin Slingsby Winthrop, OBE (Gräfin Hildegard Str 9, 78354 Sipplingen, Germany; Alpine Club), *b* 1919; Founder and Headmaster of Anavryta Sch, Athens 1948-59, and Tutor to Crown Prince of Greece 1948-58; is a Com of Order of St George and St Constantine of Greece; 1939-45 War as Lt RNVR; OBE (Civil) 1960: *m* 1st, 1951 (*m diss* 1973), Countess

Ghislaine, who *d* 1987, da of late Count Gustaf De la Gardie, of Malmö, Sweden; 2ndly, 1974, Countess Sibylle, DPhil, da of late Alexander, Count von der Schulenburg, of Duisburg, and has issue living (by 1st *m*), Mark Gustav (Holbein Str 16, 88212 Ravensburg, Germany), *b* 1952, — Geoffrey Hubert, *b* 1960; PhD; Prof of German, Univ of Waterloo, Ontario, Canada, — Sophie, *b* 1954: *m* 1985, Roger Weidlich, of Gräfin Hildegard Str, 9, 78354 Sipplingen, Germany, and has issue living, Amelie Ebba Ghislaine *b* 1989. —— Marcia Eacy Winthrop, *b* 1925: *m* 1948, Peter Newbolt, of Green Banks, Cley, Norfolk, and has had issue, Thomas Winthrop, *b* 1951, — Harry Triffitt, *b* 1953, *d* 1978, — Barnaby Charles Slingsby, *b* 1955, — Catherine Eacy, *b* 1956.

Issue of late Rt Hon Sir Edward Hilton Young, GBE, DSO, DSC, PC, yst son of 3rd baronet, who was *cr Baron Kennet* 1935 (*see* that title).

Grandchildren of late Sir (William) Mackworth Young, KCSI, 3rd son of 2nd baronet:—
Issue of late Gerard Mackworth Mackworth-Young, CIE, *b* 1884, *d* 1965; assumed by deed poll 1947, the additional surname of Mackworth: *m* 1916, Natalie Lelia Margaret, who *d* 1981, da of late Rt Hon Sir Walter Francis Hely-Hutchinson, GCMG (*see* E Donoughmore, colls):—
Sir Robin (Robert Christopher Mackworth) MACKWORTH-YOUNG, GCVO (c/o Barclays Bank plc, 61 Cheap St, Sherborne, Dorset DT9 3BB; *Club* – Roxburghe), *b* 1920: *ed* Eton, and King's Coll, Camb (MA); in HM's Foreign Ser 1948-55; appointed Dep Librarian, Windsor Castle 1955, and Librarian, Windsor Castle, and Assist Keeper of the Queen's Archives 1958; 1939-45 War as Sqdn-Ldr RAFVR; assumed by deed poll 1947 the additional surname of Mackworth; MVO (4th class) 1961, CVO 1968, KCVO 1975, GCVO 1985: *m* 1953, Helen Editha Rosemarie, da of W. C. R. Aue, of Menton, France, and has issue living, Charles Gerard (18 The Chase, Clapham, SW4; *Club* – Travellers'), *b* 1954: *ed* Eton and Magdalene Coll (Camb) (MA); MRCP 1980; MD 1987, FRCP 1995: *m* 1983, Lady Iona Sina Lindsay, yr da of 29th Earl of Crawford and Balcarres, KT, and has issue living, Robin Gerard Lindsay *b* 1994, Rose Bettina Natalie *b* 1987, Constance Ruth Sina *b* 1990. —— †Gerard William MACKWORTH-YOUNG, *b* 1926: *m* 1949, Lady Evelyn Leslie (Fisherton Mill, Fisherton de la Mere, Warminster, Wilts BA12 0PZ), da of 20th Earl of Rothes, and *d* 1984, leaving issue, Angela Clare (11 Ursula St, SW11 3DW), *b* 1951, — Susan Charlotte (5625 Beach Drive SW, Seattle, WA 98136, USA), *b* 1953: *m* 1987 (*m diss* 1996), Andrew Tribolini, son of late A. L. Tribolini, of Milwaukee, Wisconsin, — Lucinda Jane, *b* 1957: *m* 1st, 1981 (*m diss* 1984), Charles J. Lumsden; 2ndly, 1986, Oliver Matthew Sells, QC, of 5 Paper Bldgs, Temple, EC4 7HB, son of late Sir David Perronet Sells, of Tadlow House, Royston, Herts, and has issue living (by 2nd *m*), Hugo William *b* 1988, Rosanna Mary *b* 1991, — Tessa Natalie, *b* 1959: *m* 1986, Michael G. Hardingham, of 12 Genoa Av, SW15 6DY, yst son of Maj M. L. Hardingham, of Haslemere, Surrey, and has issue living, Robin Matthew *b* 1990, Luke Charles *b* 1993, Clara Louise *b* 1992. —— Honor Margaret Mackworth (2 Old Parsonage Court, Otterbourne, Winchester, Hants), *b* 1917: *m* 1938, Maj Archibald Douglas George Braithwaite, RA (ret) (Forestier-Walker, Bt, *cr* 1835, colls), who *d* 1990, and has issue living, Richard William (Tayvallich, Argyll), *b* 1944: *m* 1st, 1970 (*m diss* 1975), Claire Patricia, da of A. H. Sangster, of Kilmarnock, Ayrshire; 2ndly, 1981, Belinda Anne, da of D. F. Sheerman, of Truro, and has issue living, (by 2nd *m*) Iain Dudley *b* 1986, Shuna Anne *b* (twin) 1986, — Gerard Nicholas, *b* 1954, — Janis Mary *b* 1942: *m* 1973, James Mattinson, of Keswick, Cumbria, and has issue living, Hamish Edward *b* 1973, Sarah Jane *b* 1976, — Sarah Helen, *b* 1948. —— Lucia May Mackworth, *b* 1931: *m* 1966, Paul Mayersberg, of 5 Lowndes Court, Lowndes Sq, SW1, and has issue living, Zoltan Alexander, *b* 1969, — Natasha Catherine, *b* 1966.

Issue of late Maj Sir Hubert Winthrop Young, KCMG, DSO, *b* 1885, *d* 1950: *m* 1924, Margaret Rose Mary, who *d* 1981, da of late Col Frank Romilly Reynolds, RE:—
†Nicholas, *b* 1924; *ed* Eton, and Trin Coll, Camb: *m* 1969, Antonia Rosetta (7 Hamilton Terr, NW8 9RE), el da of late Brig Nigel Dugdale, CBE, 17th/21st Lancers (*see* Cunard, Bt, colls, 1995 Edn), and *d* 1992, leaving issue, Thomas Daniel Noah, *b* 1972, — Zoë Alexandra, *b* 1970. —— Martin Francis (Finca La Magdalena Baja, Apartado 13, 29400 Ronda, Malaga, Spain), *b* 1927; *ed* Eton, and King's Coll, Camb (MA); HM's Foreign Ser, 1948-63: *m* 1988, Catherine Carlotta, only da of late John Marshall, of Jacksonville, Florida. —— †Simon Bainbridge, *b* 1928: *m* 1954, Diana Tyndale (Martins, Whitehill, Bradford-upon-Avon), only da of late Oswald Lewis, and *d* 1984, leaving issue, James Hubert, *b* 1955, — †Mark *b* 1957, *d* 1987, — Stephen, *b* 1959: *m* 1991, Margaret, da of Peter McBride, of Donegal, and has issue living, Caoimhe *b* 1993, Fionnuala *b* 1994, — Emma, *b* 1961: *m* 1991, Stephen Lewis-Dale, yr son of Douglas Lewis-Dale, of Cheshire.

Issue of late Sir Mark Aitchison Young, GCMG, *b* 1886, *d* 1974: *m* 1919, Josephine Mary, who *d* 1977; a CStJ; da of late Walter C. Price:—
Sir Brian Walter Mark (Hill End, Woodhill Av, Gerrards Cross, Bucks), *b* 1922; *ed* Eton, and King's Coll, Camb (MA), Hon D Litt (Heriot Watt Univ) 1980; 1939-45 War as Lt RNVR; Headmaster of Charterhouse 1952-64; Dir of Nuffield Foundation 1964-70; Dir Gen of IBA 1970-82; Chm Christian Aid 1983-90; Memb Arts Council 1983-88; Knt 1976: *m* 1947, Fiona Marjorie, who *d* 1997, only da of late Allan Winslow Stewart, 16th Chief of Appin, and has issue living, Timothy Mark Stewart, *b* 1951; *ed* Eton, and Magdalene Coll, Camb (BA): *m* 1990, Alison M., yr da of late Geoffrey Keightley, of Wellingborough, Northants, and has issue living, Dugald Robert *b* 1992, Rowland Mark Keightley *b* 1993, — Joanna Margaret, *b* 1949; BA Durham: *m* 1974, Maj-Gen Peter Grant Peterkin, OBE, Queen's Own Highlanders, of Grange Hall, Forres, Moray, and has issue living, James Mark *b* 1977, Alexandra Mary *b* 1975, — Deborah Jane, *b* 1953: *m* 1979, Geoffrey Robert Francois Hudson (E Mar and Kellie, colls, 1963 Edn), of 26 Bolton Av, Windsor, Berks, and has issue living, Thomas Geoffrey Mark *b* 1980, Charlotte Jane *b* 1983, Sophie Emma *b* 1988. —— Denis Egerton, *b* 1926; *ed* Winchester, and King's Coll, Camb (MA); Housemaster and Head of History Dept, Strathallan Sch, Perthshire, 1952-79; Antique dealer since 1979; 1939-45 War in RNVR: *m* 1957, Judith Mary, el da of late Dr E. R. Matthews, of Nettleton, Wilts, and has issue living, Matthew Egerton, *b* 1959, — Walter Samuel Egerton *b* 1965, — Emma Faith, *b* 1960, — Cecilia Frances, *b* 1962: *m* 1982, Paul John Thompson, of London, and has issue living, Matthew Harry William, *b* 1983. —— Janet Cecilia Josephine (22 Norman Rd, Hout Bay 7806, S Africa), *b* 1930; MB BS London; LRCP MRCS 1955: *m* 1973, Dr R. Jerome Owens, who *d* 1995.

Grandson of late Henry Cathcart Arthur Young (infra):—
Issue of late Lieut-Com Malcolm Henry Cathcart Young, RN, *b* 1903, *ka* 1940: *m* 1930, Gwenda (who *d* 1953, having *m* 2ndly, 1946, the Rev A. Alan W. Gray), only da of late Wiliam Bromley Taylor:—
Christopher Malcolm (5 Belmont, Bath BA1 5DZ), *b* 1936; *ed* Dragon Sch, Oxford, Geelong Gram Sch, Victoria, Australia, and Magdalene Coll, Camb: *m* 1960, Mary, da of late Ralph Lindsay, of Hurstmonceux, and has issue living, Richard Malcolm, *b* 1966: *m* 1998, Emma-Jane Whitwham, — Caroline Mary, *b* 1962, — Victoria Jane, *b* 1964: *m* 1990, Robert Adams, and has issue living, Francis *b* 1992, Michael *b* 1994, Imogen *b* 1995.

Granddaughter of late Henry Young, HEICS (infra):—

Issue of late Henry Cathcart Arthur Young, b 1850, d 1940: m 1902, Florence, who d 1968, yst da of late Alfred Eccles, FRCS:—
Katharine Elizabeth (8 Campden House, 29 Sheffield Terr, W8 7NE), b 1908; 1939-45 War with VAD.

Grandchildren of late Horace Edward Broughton Young, 2nd son of late Henry Young, HEICS, 3rd son of 1st baronet:—
Issue of late Henry Herbert Young, b 1895, d 1988: m (Feb 1920), Margaret Caroline Britania, da of late Capt James Somerville Murray, of Wentworth Fall, NSW:—
Andrew Broughton (Comrie, Garra, NSW 2866), b (Dec) 1920: m 1956, Julia Gray, da of Geoffrey Gray Cambridge, of Sydney, NSW, and has issue living, Nicholas Garth Broughton, b 1957, — Vanessa Frances Caroline, b 1960. —— Arnold Somerville (Box 74, Molong, NSW 2866), b 1923: m 1956, Erica Joy, da of Joseph Little, of Perth, W Aust, and has issue living, Michael Robert, b 1957, — Graeme Arnold, b 1964, — Gillian Brita, b 1958, — Susan Margaret (now known as Rowena Margaret), b 1960. —— Horace Anthony, b 1925: m 1946, Margaret Jean, da of M. Bryce, of Brisbane, Qld, and has issue living, Malcolm Herbert, b 1948: m 1st, 1970 (m diss 1980), Dorothy Madeleine Stephenson; 2ndly, 1982, Marcelle Kathleen Robinson, and has issue living, (by 1st m) Sarah-Jean Dorothy b 1970, (by 2nd m) Henry Malcolm Macarthur b 1986, Phoebe Alice Macarthur b 1991, — James Forbes, b 1952, — Angus Anthony, b 1957: m 1978, Hilary Ruth Venton, and has issue living, Timothy Robert b 1980, Andrew Lloyd b 1982, Helen Brita b 1985, — Lisa Margaret, b 1954: m 1980, Darryl Maxwell-Yeo. —— Robert Alexander (PO Box 30, Buninyong, Vic 3357), b 1927: m 1956, Rosemary, da of Thomas Mostyn Jasper, of Hamilton, Vic, and has issue living, Justin Mark, b 1960, — Martyn Andrew, b (twin) 1960, — Lesley Philippa, b 1958; has issue living, Katrina Sarah b 1972. —— Janet Elizabeth, b 1931: m 1952, Dr John Saxton, of 465 Galston Rd, Dural, NSW 2158, son of Dr William Saxton, of Brisbane, Qld, and has issue living, Jeremy John, b 1956, — William Bevan, b 1963, — Julie Belinda, b 1953, — Fiona Jane, b 1958, — Georgina Margaret, b 1961.

Grandchildren of late Charles Ernest Young, 3rd son of late Henry Young, HEICS (ante):—
Issue of late Capt Henry Shedden Baring Young, MC, RA, b 1894, d 1976: m 1st, 1929, Eva Theodora, who d 1940, da of T. C. Maltby, of The Oaks, Tauranga, NZ, 2ndly, 1953, Janet Mary, who d 1994, only da of late Rev J. Milton Thompson, of Tonbridge, Kent:—
(By 1st m) James Ernest Baring (370 Upper Rosemount Rd, Nambour, Queensland 4560, Australia), b 1933: m 1st, 1959 (m diss 1975), Annette Florence, da of Kenneth Lane, of St Ives, NSW; 2ndly, 1976, Cheryl Beverley, da of — Price, and has issue living (by 1st m), Timothy James Baring, b 1960, — Michael Henry Baring, b 1962, — David Kenneth Baring, b 1969, — Anthony William Baring b 1971. —— Dorothy Joan Baring, b 1930; ed Sydney Univ (BSc) and London Univ (MSc): m 1957, John Lionel Wheeler, PhD, of 34 Irvines Rd, Bonville, NSW 2441, and has issue living, Rev Philip John Henry, b 1961; BEng, BTh: m 1985, Jillian Margaret Collins, MB, BS, and has issue living, Samuel Murray b 1991, Luke Jonathan b 1993, Madeline Naomi b 1996, — Ian Charles Andrew, b 1963: m 1986, Diane Topham, BA, and has issue living, Matthew Geoffrey b 1987, Daniel Scott b 1989, Michelle Alison b 1990, — Rosemary Helen, b 1959; BA: m 1982, Chaplain Andrew John Sempell, BA, BTh, JP (NSW), RAAChD, of Royal Mil Coll, Duntroon, ACT 2600, and has issue living, Katherine Alexandra Margaret b 1994. —— (By 2nd m), Stephen Henry Baring, b 1954: m 1st, 1976 (m diss 1989), Grace Marianne, da of Stewart Dinnen, of Launceston, Tasm; 2ndly, 1992, Nicola Helen, da of William Main, of Turramurra, NSW, and has issue living (by 1st m), Rachel Grace Marie b 1981, Clare Ruth Mary b 1983. —— Angela Mary Katherine, b 1957: m 1988, Dr Mark Oliver Diesendorf, of PO Box 48, O'Connor, ACT, Australia, and has issue living, Joseph James, b 1993.

Issue of late Charles Arthur Noel Young, AM, b 1899, d 1992: m 1923, Margery Bisdee Maynard, da of late Dr Maynard Pain, of Sydney and Cain:—
Charles Edward Christopher (Moore Park Rd, Bundaberg, Qld 4670), b 1926: m 1st, 1949, Margaret Florence, who d 1976, da of W. Guilford, of Killara, Sydney, NSW; 2ndly, 1986, Mrs Beverley Gaze, who d 1998, da of late Roger Edwards, of Leamington Spa, and his late wife Margaret Alison (see Macara, Bt, colls, 1980 Edn), and has issue living, (by 1st m) Christopher Roderick (4 Edzell Place, Carindale, Brisbane, Qld), b 1950; ed Brisbane Anglican Gram Sch, and Univ of Queensland (B Comm, B App Sc (Applied Chem), Cert Sugar Chem); ARACI, FCIS; Company Sec of Bundaberg Sugar Co: m 1973, Jennifer Ann, da of J. Mackrill, of Bundaberg, Qld, and has issue living, Benjamin Roderick b 1982, Bianca Margaret b 1979, — Timothy Charles (15 Bronte Place, Eight Mile Plains, Brisbane, Qld), b 1952; ed Brisbane Anglican Gram Sch, and Univ of Qld (B Bus); AASA: m 1979, Leonie, da of R. McDowell, of Bundaberg, Qld, and has issue living, Erin Nancy b 1983, Vanessa Megan b 1985, — Rev Gregory Mark, b 1955; ed Brisbane Anglican Gram Sch: m 1983, Michelle Suzanne, da of A. Baster, of Perth, W. Aust, and has issue living, Adam Christopher b 1991, Hayley Claire b 1985, Alyce Nicole b 1988, — Nicholas William, b 1961; ed N Bund High Sch: m 1991, Wendy Lee, da of late R. W. Basmin, of Penshurst, Sydney, and has issue living, Harrison Ronald b 1998. —— Margery Marian (Box 181 PO, Moss Vale, NSW 2577, Australia), b 1924; ed Abbotsleigh Sch; SRN: m 1949 (m diss 1976), Norman Bruce Berry, and has issue living, Andrew Bruce (30 Shadforth St, Mosman, Sydney, NSW 2088, Australia), b 1950; ed Sydney Univ and Adelaide Univ; MB, BS, FRACP; State Dir, Emergency Neonatal Transport; Head, Dept of Neonatology, Royal Alexandra Hosp for Children, Sydney, — Simon Mark (Box 1, Bowral, NSW 1976), b 1956; ed ANU (BEc): m 1982, Sue, da of D. Imric, — Hugh Jonathan (Montage, 62 Albany St, Crowsnest, NSW), b 1962: m 1992, Jennifer Green, — Susan Marian, b 1952; ed Macquarie Univ (BA): m 1984, William Alexander Ryan, and has issue living, Alexander Cheyne b 1985, Phoebe Imogen Alice b 1987, Clare Margery Francis b 1989, — Philippa Jane, b 1954; ed Scegg Sch; SRN: m 1979, David William Learmonth Palmer, of 8 Downes Place, Hughes, Canberra, ACT, and has issue living, Angus Norman Learmonth b 1980, Simon David b 1982, Olivia Jane b 1984. —— Elizabeth Wendy, b 1927: m 1957, Neil James Yorkston, FRACP, FRC Psych, of 59 Blackwell, Darlington, co Durham DL3 8QT, and has issue living, Ian Charles (1 Deerness Hts, Brandon, co Durham DH7 8TQ), b 1960: m 1985, Valerie Dunford, of Edmonton, Alberta, — Catherine Judith, b 1958; ed Blackheath High Sch, Univ of Brit Columbia (BA): m 1985 John Christopher Allinson, of 31 Kingsmead Rd, SW2 3HV, son of James Allinson, of Bradford, and has issue living, Simon James b 1992, Emma Charlotte b 1988, — Ruth Elizabeth, b 1959; ed Blackheath High Sch, London Univ (BSc), — Ann Margery, b 1965; ed Blackheath High Sch, Univ of Brit Columbia. —— Lois Margaret, b 1929; ed Macquarie Univ; SRN: m 1957, Arthur Frederick Pennington, MB, BS, of 119 Kissing Point Rd, Dundas, NSW 2117, and has issue living, Jennifer Grace b 1989, Melanie Denis b 1991, — Martin Frederick, b 1961: m 1984, Heath, da of Brian Richards, of Adelaide, S Aust, and has issue living, Huon Frederick b 1994, Elise Patricia b 1988, Myanna Ellen b 1991, — Judith Charis, b 1960: m 1989, Malcolm Rundle, of Boronia Park, Melbourne, and has issue living, Julia Helen b 1993, — Mary Priscilla, b 1964: m 1986, Rev Richard Lane, and has issue living, Sebastian Arthur b 1992, Emily Cassandra b 1991, — Fiona Margaret, b 1974. —— Catherine Anne, b 1930. —— Philippa Lucia Charis, b 1937: m 1963, Donald Campbell Thorn, FRAIA, of Perth, W Aust, and has issue living, Christopher Ian, b 1964; ed Melbourne Univ (BCom): m 1990, Rosalind Heather Mills, and has issue living, Benjamin Lawrence b 1993, — Samuel Douglas, b 1967; ed Melbourne Univ (BEng): m 1990, Jane, da of Brian Willis, of Hawthorn, and has issue living, Maxwell David b 1992, Harrison Campbell b 1993, — Bronwen Margery, b 1965; ed Melbourne Univ (MB BS), FRACGP: m 1993, Robert Graham Wilson, of S Perth, W Aust, — Sarah Penelope Joan, b 1972; ed Monash Univ. —— Helen Rosalind (618 Windermere Av, Toronto, Ont M6S 3L8, Canada), b 1939; ed Univ of Toronto (BA, MA): m 1959 (m diss 19—), John Henry Northcote Deck, MD, FRCP (C), and has issue living, Wilbert John Northcote, b 1960; ed Upper

Canada Coll, and McGill Univ (BSc, MB): *m* 1986, Carmen Leger, and has issue living, Max Antonio *b* 1991, Zoe Lise *b* 1987, Anouk *b* 1989, Emma *b* 1993. — Philip Charles, *b* 1962; *ed* Univ of Toronto (BA), — Roger Norman, *b* 1964; *ed* Upper Canada Coll, and Univ of Toronto (B Com), — Kathleen Margery, *b* 1963; *ed* Univ of Toronto (BA) and Univ of Ottawa (B Soc Sc), — Rachel Frances, *b* 1971, — Jennifer Luci Maynard *b* 1973. —— Adrienne Penelope, *b* 1943: *m* 1976, Wilfred Galbraith, of Medway, Barolin Pony Stud, Moss Vale, NSW 2577, Australia, and has issue living, Thomas Charles *b* 1977, James Wilfred *b* 1978, Barnaby Donald *b* 1984, Annabel Christiana *b* 1980, Charina Bisdee *b* 1982. —— Carolyn Bronwen (7 Pickford Av, Eastwood, Sydney, NSW), *b* 1945: *m* 1974 (*m diss* 19—), Keith Wolfson, son of Hymie Wolfson, of Johannesburg, and has issue living, Robin Lawrence, *b* 1978, Asher David, *b* 1981, Chloe Samantha, *b* 1977.

Issue of late Ernest Stafford Young, *b* 1903, *d* 1996: *m* 1946, Lilian Olive, JP (13 Karranga Av, Killara, Sydney, NSW 2071), da of late C. E. Mumford, of Cremorne, Sydney, NSW:—
David Hilton (23 Greenhill Crescent, St Ives, NSW 2075), *b* 1947; *ed* Sydney Univ (BEc): *m* 1st, 1972 (*m diss* 1982), Katherine Beatrice, da of Dr E. L. A. Rod, of Gordon, Sydney; 2ndly, 1998, Sharon Michelle Watts, of Cape Town, S Africa, and has issue living, (by 1st *m*) Jeremy Andrew, *b* 1973; *ed* Qld Univ of Technology, — Virginia Bronwyn, *b* 1976; *ed* Sydney Univ, — Amanda Penelope, *b* 1977; *ed* Sydney Univ of Technology. —— Lesley Ann, *b* 1949; *ed* Sydney Univ (BA, Dip Ed): *m* 1972, Rodney Elkington Allen, MB, BS, of 55 Kensington Rd, Bolwarra, NSW 2320, and has issue living, Matthew James Elkington, *b* 1974, — Benjamin Mark Elkington, *b* 1976, — Andrew Stephen Elkington, *b* 1979. —— Rosemary Frances, *b* 1953.

Issue of late Geoffrey Lawrence Young, *b* 1910, *d* 1993: *m* 1935, Irene, OAM, BSc, (33 Denman Parade, Normanhurst, NSW) da of P. W. Petter, of Swallowcliffe, Yeovil, Somerset:—
Peter Lawrence (4 Narelle Av, Pymble, NSW 2073), *b* 1935; FCILA, FCPA: *m* 1961, Jennifer Mary, da of J. M. Clift, and has issue living, Michael Lawrence *b* 1968; *ed* Sydney Univ (BE, BSc), — Judith Anne *b* 1971. —— Geoffrey Branscombe, *b* 1942. —— Susan Irene, *b* 1938; BA 1961: *m* 1966 (*m diss* 1977), William Werden Wilson, and has issue living, John Werden, *b* 1968, — Anthea, *b* 1969. —— Kathleen Patricia, *b* 1940; BSc 1961: *m* 1969, Stuart Braga, MA, M Ed Admin, FACE, of 52 Seaview St, Ashfield, NSW 2131, and has issue living, David Hugh, *b* 1970, — Christopher Stuart, *b* 1972, Andrew Geoffrey, *b* 1975. —— Jocelyn Olivia, *b* 1946: *m* 1969, Wayne Mackenzie, of 12a Felton Rd, Carlingford, NSW, and has issue living, Malcolm Geoffrey, *b* 1972, — Barbara Lorraine, *b* 1970.

Sir Samuel Young, 1st baronet, was the el son of Sir George Young, of Formosa Place, Berks, Adm of the White who served at Quebec 1759, Havana 1762, and Pondicherry 1778. Sir George Young, 3rd baronet, was a Charity Commr 1882-99, Third Charity Commr 1899-1900, 2nd Charity Commr 1900-03, and Ch Charity Commr 1903-06. Sir George Young, MVO, 4th baronet, was in Diplo Ser 1896-1914, Professor of Portuguese and Examiner in Ottoman Law in Univ of London 1919-23, and Professor of Political Science, American Univs 1929-30. Sir George Peregrine Young, CMG, 5th baronet, was Head of W Depart, Foreign Office 1950-51, HM's Min in Rome 1951-3, Assist Sec Cabinet Office 1953-5, Head of News Depart, Foreign Office 1955-56, and HBM's Min in Paris 1956-60. He *m* 1939, Elisabeth, who *d* 1957, da of Sir Hughe Montgomery Knatchbull-Hugessen, KCMG (B Brabourne, colls).

YOUNG (UK) 1821, of Bailieborough Castle, co Cavan

Sir JOHN KENYON ROE YOUNG, 6th *Baronet*, *b* 23 April 1947; *s* his father, *Sir* JOHN WILLIAM ROE, 1981; *ed* Hurncourt Sch, Christchurch, Hants: *m* 1977, Frances Elise, only da of W. R. Thompson, and has issue.

Arms – Argent, three piles sable, each charged with a trefoil, slipped or; on a chief of the second three annulets of the third. **Crest** – A demi-lion rampant gules, charged on the shoulder with a trefoil slipped or, and holding in the dexter paw a sprig of three maple leaves, all proper.
Residence – Bolingey, 159 Chatham Rd, Maidstone, Kent ME14 2ND.

SON LIVING

RICHARD CHRISTOPHER ROE, *b* 14 June 1983.

DAUGHTER LIVING

Tamara Elizabeth Eve, *b* 1986.

SISTER LIVING

Eve Maureen Aldous, *b* 1949: *m* 1976 (*m diss* 1989), — Robertson.

UNCLES LIVING (*Sons of 4th baronet*)

Patrick Elliott, *b* 1917: *m* 1946, Sadie Reid, only da of Laurence Beattie, of Prestwick, Ayrshire, and has issue living, Christopher Brian Harrington, *b* 1965, — Patricia, *b* 1947, — Veronica Anne, *b* 1949, — Nancy Gay, *b* 1952. —— Michael Cyril Harrington (39 Grove Rd, Wamberal, NSW), *b* 1928: *m* 1955, Anita Patricia, who *d* 1994, only da of C. H. Duff, of Hong Kong, and has issue living, Peter Charles Harrington, *b* 1956, — Anthony Michael, *b* 1961, — Gail Louraine, *b* 1960.

The 1st baronet, Sir William, was a Director of the East India Company; and the 2nd baronet, Sir John (Gov of New S Wales 1860-67, and Gov-Gen of Canada 1868-72), was raised to the Peerage in 1870 as Baron Lisgar, but dying without issue, his peerage became extinct, and the baronetcy devolved upon his nephew, Sir William Muston Need, 3rd baronet.

YOUNG (UK) 1945, of Partick, co City of Glasgow

Sir STEPHEN STEWART TEMPLETON YOUNG, 3rd *Baronet*; *b* 24 May 1947; *s* his father, *Sir* ALASTAIR SPENCER TEMPLETON, DL, 1963; *ed* Rugby, Trin Coll, Oxford and Edinburgh Univ; Advocate (Scotland); Sheriff of Glasgow and Strathkelvin March-June 1984, since when Sheriff of North Strathclyde at Greenock: *m* 1974, Viola Margaret, da of Prof Patrick Horace Nowell-Smith (B Vernon, colls) and has issue.

ᚨrms – Argent, on three piles issuant from a chief sable, charged with three lymphads under full sail of the 1st flagged gules, as many annulets of the 3rd. ᚱrest – A lymphad or, under full sail, its sail charged of the arms, having a pennon gules with the badge of Scotland viz azure, a saltire argent, in the hoist.
Residence – Glen Rowan, Shore Rd, Cove, Dunbartons, G84 0NU.

SONS LIVING

CHARLES ALASTAIR STEPHEN, *b* 21 July 1979. —— Alexander David, *b* 1982.

SISTER LIVING

Clare Elizabeth, *b* 1953: *m* 1975, Stephen John Beaty, of 35 Chestnut Rd, SE27 9EZ, and has issue living, Thomas Alastair Stephen, *b* 1977, — Corinne Elizabeth, *b* 1979, — Josepha Isobel, *b* 1981.

UNCLE DECEASED (*son of 1st baronet*)

†Patrick Templeton, *b* 1925; *ed* Rugby; ARIBA: *m* 1950, Jenny Loxton (3F Lansdowne Rd, W11 3AL), only da of Sir Walter Eric Bassett, KBE, MC, of Melbourne, Australia, and *d* 1992, leaving issue, Roger Spencer Masson, *b* 1954; *ed* Radley: *m* 1979, Margaret Alice Wilhelmina —, — Jane Templeton, *b* 1952: has issue living, Gemma Lucy, *b* 1983.

AUNT LIVING (*Daughter of 1st baronet*)

Barbara Mary, *b* 1916: *m* 1939, William Echlin Hollington Grayburn, who *d* 1988, and has had issue, Jon Alastair, *b* 1943, *d* 1978: *m* 1970, Valerie Irlam, and had issue, William Alastair George *b* 1973, — Lesley Mary, *b* 1949. *Residence* – 12 Lee Rd, Aldeburgh, Suffolk.

The 1st baronet, Sir Arthur Stewart Leslie Young (son of late Daniel Henderson Lusk Young, of Glasgow), was Parliamentary Private Sec to Under-Sec of State for Scotland 1937-39, and to Sec of State for Scotland 1939-42, a Lord Commr of The Treasury 1942-44, and Vice-Chamberlain of HM's Household 1944-45; sat as MP for Partick Div of Glasgow (*U*) 1935-50.

YOUNGER (UK) 1911, of Auchen Castle, Kirkpatrick-Juxta, co Dumfries

Quite ready

Sir JOHN WILLIAM YOUNGER, CBE, 3rd *Baronet*; *b* 18 Nov 1920; *s* his father, *Sir* WILLIAM ROBERT, 1973; *ed* Canford and RMC Sandhurst; Maj-Gen late Coldm Gds; Dir Management and Support Intelligence 1973-76 since when C in C of St John Ambulance; 1939-45 War in Middle East (prisoner, MBE); Commr-in-Chief, St John Ambulance 1980-85; MBE (Mil) 1945, CBE (Mil) 1969; KStJ 1980: *m* 1st, 1948 (*m diss* 1952), Mrs Stella Jane Dodd, da of Rev John George Lister; 2ndly, 1953, Marcella Granito, Princess Pignatelli di Belmonte, who *d* 1989, da of late Prof Avv Roberto Scheggi; 3rdly, 1991, Mrs Anne Henrietta Maria St Paul Seely, who *d* 1996, only da of Horace George St Paul Butler, and formerly wife of (i) James Dugdale Burridge, and (ii) Timothy Ward Seely (*see* Seely, Bt, colls), and has issue (by 1st *m*).

ᴁrms – Or, on a bend azure, between two martlets sable, three roses argent, barbed and seeded vert, on a chief gules, a crescent between two mullets of the first. ᴄrest – A dexter hand holding a lance in bend proper.
Residence – 4 Wilbraham Mansions, 10 Wilbraham Place, SW1X 9AA. *Club* – Boodle's, Berks Golf.

SON LIVING (*By 1st marriage*)

JULIAN WILLIAM RICHARD, *b* 10 Feb 1950; *ed* Eton, and Grinnell Univ, USA: *m* 1981, Deborah Ann Wood, and has issue living, Andrew William, *b* 14 Jan 1986. *Residence* – 11811 Henley Lane, Los Angeles, CA 90077-1368, NY 10803, USA.

DAUGHTER LIVING (*By 1st marriage*)

Joanna Jane, *b* 1951: *m* 1972, Timothy John Binnington, of Thakeham Place, Thakeham, nr Pulborough, W Sussex, and has issue living, Nicholas William David, *b* 1977, — Kate Louise Frances, *b* 1975.

SISTER LIVING

Margaret Elizabeth, *b* 1916: *m* 1937, John Howard Moller, late Queen's Own Cameron Highlanders, who *d* 1983, and has issue living, Christopher Pierre William Howard, *b* 1943; *ed* Charterhouse: *m* 1973, Susan Maria Scougal Burdette, da of Alban Millar Ross-Smith, of Heyshott, Sussex, and has issue living, Cassandra Maria *b* 1975, Tara Elizabeth *b* 1976, — Caroline Victoria Margaret, *b* 1939, — Maxine Faith Alexandra, *b* 1940: *m* 1966 (*m diss* 1978), Rory B. M. Nicholas. *Residence* – 4 Cherrimans Orchard, Liphook Rd, Haslemere, Surrey GU27 1NP. —— Diana Joan, *b* 1919: *m* 1st, 1940 (*m diss* 1947), Hon William Francis Brinsley Le Poer Trench (later 8th Earl of Clancarty), who *d* 1995; 2ndly, 1947, Dr H. Wentworth Eldredge, Prof of Sociology, Dartmouth Coll, NH, and has issue living (by 2nd *m*), James Wentworth (6161 Fieldcrest Drive, Frederick, Maryland 21701, USA), *b* 1950, — Alan Wentworth (RR2, Box 2093, Salem, New York 12865, USA), *b* 1953. *Residence* – 6161 Fieldcrest Drive, Frederick, Maryland 21701, USA.

The 1st baronet, Sir William Younger (son of late William Younger, of Auchen Castle, Moffat), was MP for S Kesteven or Stamford Division of Lincolnshire (*L*) 1895-1906, and for Peebles and Selkirk Jan to Nov 1910.

YOUNGER (UK) 1964, of Fountainbridge, co and City of Edinburgh (extinct 1992)

Sir WILLIAM McEWAN YOUNGER, DSO, DL, 1st and last *Baronet*.

DAUGHTER LIVING OF FIRST BARONET (*By 1st marriage*)

Caroline Ruth, *b* 1946: *m* 1968, Barney Platts-Mills, of 52 Novello St, SW6, 4th son of John Faithful Fortescue Platts-Mills, QC, and has issue living, Jake, *b* 19—, — Arthur, *b* 19—, — Eleanor, *b* 19—.

WIDOW LIVING OF FIRST BARONET

JUNE PECK (*Lady Younger*): *m* 1983, as his 2nd wife, Sir William McEwan Younger, DSO, DL, 1st baronet, who *d* 1992. *Residence* – 29 Moray Place, Edinburgh EH3 6DA.

PEERAGES THAT HAVE BECOME
EXTINCT, DORMANT, ABEYANT, OR DISCLAIMED

Since 1950. For Extinctions in the years 1900-50 see 1958 and earlier editions.

Peerages junior in rank will be found under the senior titles.

The family surname appears in italics (between parentheses) immediately after the title

    * Peerage of United Kingdom || Peerage of Scotland
    † Peerage of Great Britain   § Peerage of Ireland
    ‡ Peerage of England

HEREDITARY PEERAGES EXTINCT, DORMANT or ABEYANT

* ADAMS, Baron (*Adams*) Cr 1949 Ext 1960
* ADRIAN, Baron (*Adrian*) Cr 1955 Ext 1995
* AIREDALE, Baron (*Kitson*) Cr 1907 Ext 1996
* AILWYN, Baron (*Fellowes*) Cr 1921 Ext 1988
* ALEXANDER OF HILLSBOROUGH, Earl
   (*Alexander*) Cr 1963; also *V. Alexander of
   Hillsborough 1950, and *B. Weston-super-Mare,
   1963 Ext 1965
* ALNESS, Baron (*Munro*) Cr 1934 Ext 1955
* AMHERST, Earl (*Amherst*) Cr 1826; also *V
   Holmesdale, and †B Amherst Ext 1993
* AMMON, Baron (*Ammon*) Cr 1944 Ext 1960
* AMORY, Viscount (*Heathcoat-Amory*) Cr 1960
   Ext 1981
* AMULREE, Baron (*Mackenzie*) Cr 1929 Ext 1983
* ANCASTER, Earl (*Heathcote-Drummond-*
   Willoughby) Cr 1892; also † Baron Aveland 1856
   Ext 1983
* ARCHIBALD, Baron (*Archibald*) Cr 1949 Ext 1996
* ARMSTRONG, Baron (*Watson-Armstrong*) Cr 1903
   Ext 1987
* ATHLONE, Earl of (*Cambridge*) Cr 1917; also V.
   Trematon 1917 Ext 1957
‡ AUDLEY, Barony of (*Souter*) Cr 1312-13 Abeyant
   1997.
* AVON, Earl (*Eden*) Cr 1961; also *V Eden 1961 Ext
   1985.
* BADELEY, Baron (*Badeley*) Cr 1949 Ext 1951
§ BANDON, Earl of (*Bernard*) Cr 1800; also §V.
   Bernard 1809. §B. Bandon 1793; §V. Bandon 1795
   Ext 1979
* BARNBY, Baron (*Willey*) Cr 1922 Ext 1982
§ BARRINGTON, Viscount (*Barrington*) Cr 1720; also
   *B Shute 1880 Dormant or Ext 1990
* BEAUCHAMP, Earl (*Lygon*) Cr 1815; also *V. Elmley
   1815; *B. Beauchamp of Powyke 1806 Ext 1979
* BENNETT OF EDGBASTON, Baron (*Bennett*)
   Cr 1953 Ext 1957
‡ BERNERS, Baron (*Williams*) Cr 1455 Abey 1992.
* BERTIE OF THAME, Viscount (*Bertie*) Cr 1918; also
   *B. Bertie of Thame 1915 Ext 1954
* BERWICK, Baron (*Noel-Hill*) Cr 1784 Ext 1953
* BESSBOROUGH, Earl (*Ponsonby*) Cr 1937 Ext 1993
* BEVERIDGE, Baron (*Beveridge*) Cr 1946 Ext 1963
* BILSLAND, Baron (*Bilsland*) Cr 1950 Ext 1970
* BIRKENHEAD, Earl (*Smith*) Cr 1922; also *V
   Furneaux 1922, V Birkenhead 1921, and B
   Birkenhead 1919 ext 1985
* BLACKFORD, Baron (*Mason*) Cr 1935 Ext 1988
* BOLSOVER, Baron (*Cavendish-Bentinck*) Cr 1880
   Ext 1977
‡ BOTETOURT, Baron (*Somerset*) Cr 1305. Abey 1984
‡ BOTREAUX, Baron (*Hastings*) Cr 1368. Abey 1960
* BOYD-ORR, Baron (*Orr*) Cr 1949 Ext 1971
* BRACKEN, Viscount (*Bracken*) Cr 1952 Ext 1958
* BRAINTREE, Baron (*Crittall*) Cr 1948 Ext 1961
* BRAND, Baron (*Brand*) Cr 1946 Ext 1963
|| BREADALBANE AND HOLLAND, Earl (*Campbell*)
   Cr 1677; also V of Tay and Paintland, and L
   Glenorchy, Benederaloch, Ormelie and Weick
   Dormant 1995
* BRECON, Baron (*Lewis*) Cr 1958 Ext 1976
* BRUCE OF MELBOURNE, Viscount (*Bruce*)
   Cr 1947 Ext 1967
‡ CALTHORPE, Baron (*Gough-Calthorpe*) Cr 1796
   Ext 1997.
* CAMBRIDGE, Marquess of (*Cambridge*) Cr 1917;
   also *E. of Eltham 1917; *V. Northallerton 1917
   Ext 1981
* CAMPION, Baron (*Campion*) Cr 1950 Ext 1958
* CARISBROOKE, Marquess of (*Mountbatten*)
   Cr 1917; also V. Launceston, E. of Berkhamsted
   1917 Ext 1960
* CECIL OF CHELWOOD, Viscount (*Gascoyne-Cecil*)

   Cr 1923 Ext 1958
* CHAPLIN, Viscount (*Chaplin*) Cr 1916 Ext 1981
* CHARNWOOD, Baron (*Benson*) Cr 1911 Ext 1955
* CHERWELL, Viscount (*Lindemann*) Cr 1956; also B.
   Cherwell 1941 Ext 1957
‡ CHESTERFIELD and †STANHOPE, Earl of
   (*Stanhope*) Cr 1628 and 1718, also ‡B. Stanhope of
   Shelford 1616 Ext 1967
* CHEYLESMORE, Baron (*Eaton*) Cr 1887 Ext 1974
* CILCENNIN, Viscount (*Thomas*) Cr 1956 Ext 1960
§ CLARINA, Baron (*Massey*) Cr 1800 Ext 1952
§ CLIFDEN, Viscount (*Agar-Robartes*) Cr 1781. Also
   §Baron Clifden 1776, and *Baron Robartes 1869
   Ext 1974
‡ COBHAM, Baron (*Alexander*) Cr 1312-13. Abey 1951
* COHEN OF BIRKENHEAD, Baron (*Cohen*)
   Cr 1956 Ext 1977
* CONESFORD, Baron (*Strauss*) Cr 1955 Ext 1974
‡ CONYERS, Baron (*Pelham*) Cr 1509. Abey 1948
* COOPER OF CULROSS, Baron (*Cooper*) Cr 1954
   Ext 1955
* COURTAULD-THOMSON, Baron (*Courtauld-*
   Thomson) Cr 1944 Ext 1954
* COURTHOPE, Baron (*Courthope*) Cr 1945 Ext 1955
* COZENS-HARDY, Baron (*Cozens-Hardy*) Cr 1914
   Ext 1975
* CROOKSHANK, Viscount (*Crookshank*) Cr 1956
   Ext 1961
* CUNNINGHAM OF HYNDHOPE, Viscount
   (*Cunningham*) Cr 1945 Ext 1963
* DARYNGTON, Baron (*Pease*) Cr 1923 Ext 1994
* DORCHESTER, Baron (*Carleton*) Cr 1899 Ext 1963
* DOUGLAS OF BARLOCH, Baron (*Douglas*) Cr 1950
   Ext 1980
* DOUGLAS OF KIRTLESIDE, Baron (*Douglas*)
   Cr 1948 Ext 1965
* DOUGLAS OF BARLOCH, Baron (*Douglas*) Cr 1950
   Ext 1980
* DOVERCOURT, Baron (*Holmes*) Cr 1954 Ext 1961
* DRUMALBYN, Baron (*Macpherson*) Cr 1963
   Ext 1987
* DUFFERIN AND AVA, Marquess (*Hamilton-Temple-*
   Blackwood) Cr 1888; also * E of Dufferin 1871, E of
   Ava 1888, V Clandeboye 1871, and B Clandeboye
   1850 Ext 1988
* DUGAN OF VICTORIA, Baron (*Dugan*) Cr 1949
   Ext 1951
* EBBISHAM, Baron (*Blades*) Cr 1928 Ext 1991
* EGERTON OF TATTON, Baron (*Egerton*) Cr 1859
   Ext 1958
* ELIBANK, Viscount (*Murray*) Cr 1911 Ext 1962
* ENNISDALE, Baron (*Lyons*) Cr 1939 Ext 1963
* ERSKINE OF RERRICK, Baron (*Erskine*) Cr 1964
   Ext 1995
* ESSENDON, Baron (*Lewis*) Cr 1932 Ext 1978
* EVANS, Baron (*Evans*) Cr 1957 Ext 1963
* EVERSHED, Baron (*Evershed*) Cr 1956 Ext 1966
|| FALCONER OF HALKERTON, Lord (*Keith*)
   Cr 1646 Dormant 1966
* FAIRHAVEN, Baron (*Broughton*) Cr 1929 Ext 1966
* FARRER, Baron (*Farrer*) Cr 1893 Ext 1964
‡ FAUCONBERG, Baron (*Pelham*) Cr 1283 Abey
   1948
* FEVERSHAM, Earl of (*Duncombe*) Cr 1868; also *V.
   Helmsley 1868 Ext 1963
§ FINGALL, Earl of (*Plunkett*) Cr 1628; also §Baron
   Killeen 1449; * Baron Fingall 1831 Ext 1984
* FITZ ALAN OF DERWENT, Viscount (*Fitzalan-*
   Howard) Cr 1921 Ext 1962
† FITZWILLIAM, Earl (*Wentworth-Fitzwilliam*)
   Cr 1746; also §E. Fitzwilliam 1716; V Milton 1716;
   †Lord Fitzwilliam 1742; †B of Milton 1742; §B
   Fitzwilliam 1620 Ext 1979
* FLECK, Baron (*Fleck*) Cr 1961 Ext 1968

* FORSTER OF HARRABY, Baron (*Forster*) Cr 1959 Ext 1972
‡ FRASER OF NORTH CAPE, Baron (*Fraser*) Cr 1946 Ext 1981
* FRASER OF ALLANDER, Baron (*Fraser*) Cr 1964, disclaimed 1966 Ext 1987
* FURNESS, Viscount (*Furness*) Cr 1918 Ext 1995
‡ FURNIVALL, Baron (*Dent*) Cr 1295 Abeyant 1968
* GLENAVY, Baron (*Campbell*) Cr 1921 Ext 1984
* GLENTANAR, Baron (*Coats*) Cr 1916 Ext 1971
* GLYN, Baron (*Glyn*) Cr 1953 Ext 1960
* GODBER, Baron (*Godber*) Cr 1956 Ext 1976
* GREENE, Baron (*Greene*) Cr 1941 Ext 1952
* GREVILLE, Baron (*Greville*) Cr 1869 Ext 1987
‡ GREY DE RUTHYN, Baron (*Butler-Bowdon*) Cr 1324 Abey 1963
§ GUILLAMORE, Viscount (*O'Grady*) Cr 1831; also §B. O'Grady 1831 Ext 1955
* HAILES, Baron (*Buchan-Hepburn*) Cr 1957 Ext 1974
* HAILEY, Baron (*Hailey*) Cr 1936 Ext 1969
* HARCOURT, Viscount (*Harcourt*) Cr 1917; also *B. Nuneham 1917 Ext 1979
‡ HASTINGS, Baron (*Hastings*) Cr 1461 Abey 1960
§ HEADLEY, Baron (*Allanson-Winn*) Cr 1797 Ext 1994
* HENDERSON, Baron (*Henderson*) Cr 1945 Ext 1984
* HENEAGE, Baron (*Heneage*) Cr 1896 Ext 1967
* HEWART, Viscount (*Hewart*) Cr 1940; also *B. Hewart 1922 Ext 1964
* HEYWORTH, Baron (*Heyworth*) Cr 1955 Ext 1974
* HILLINGDON, Baron (*Mills*) Cr 1886 Ext 1982
* HOLDEN, Baron (*Holden*) Cr 1908 Ext 1951
* HORDER, Baron (*Horder*) Cr 1938 Ext 1997
* HORE-BELISHA, Baron (*Hore-Belisha*) Cr 1954 Ext 1957
* HUDSON, Viscount (*Hudson*) Cr 1952 Ext 1963
* HUNGARTON, Baron (*Crawford*) Cr 1951 Ext 1966
* HYNDLEY, Viscount (*Hindley*) Cr 1948 Ext 1963
* ILKESTON, Baron (*Foster*) Cr 1910 Ext 1952
* INMAN, Baron (*Inman*) Cr 1946 Ext 1979
* INVERCHAPEL, Baron (*Kerr Clark Kerr*) Cr 1946 Ext 1951
* INVERCLYDE, Baron (*Burns*) Cr 1897 Ext 1957
* ISMAY, Baron (*Ismay*) Cr 1947 Ext 1965
* JACKSON, Baron (*Jackson*) Cr 1945 Ext 1954
* JESSEL, Baron (*Jessel*) Cr 1924 Ext 1990
* JOWITT, Earl (*Jowitt*) Cr 1951; also *B. Jowitt 1945, and *V. Jowitt 1947 Ext 1957
*§KENMARE, Earl of (*Browne*) Cr 1801; also §B. Castlerosse and V. Kenmare 1798, §V. Castlerosse 1801, and *B. Kenmare 1856 Ext 1952
§ KILLEEN, Baron (*Plunkett*) Crca 1449 Ext 1984
* KILMUIR, Earl of (*Fyfe*) Cr 1962; also *B. Fyfe of Dornock 1962, and *V. Kilmuir 1954 Ext 1967
‖ KINNAIRD, Lord (*Kinnaird*) Cr 1682; also *Baron Kinnaird Ext or Dormant 1997
* KINTORE, Baron (*Keith*) Cr 1838 Ext 1966
* LAMBURY, Baron (*Lord*) Cr 1962 Ext 1967
* LAMINGTON, Baron (*Cochrane-Baillie*) Cr 1880 Ext 1951
§ LANESBOROUGH, Earl of (*Butler*) Cr 1756; also § Newtown Butler 1715 Ext 1998
* LAWSON, Baron (*Lawson*) Cr 1950 Ext 1965
‡ LEEDS, Duke of (*Osborne*) Cr 1694; also ‡B. Osborne and ‡V. Latimer, 1673, ‡E. of Danby 1674, ‡M. of Carmarthen 1689 Ext 1964
§ LEITRIM, Earl of (*Clements*) Cr 1795; also B. Leitrim 1783, V. Leitrim 1793, and *B. Clements 1831 Ext 1952
* LLEWELLIN, Baron (*Llewellin*) Cr 1945 Ext 1957
* LLOYD, Baron (*Lloyd*) Cr 1925 Ext 1985
* LOCH, Baron (*Loch*) Cr 1895 Ext 1991
* LURGAN, Baron (*Brownlow*) Cr 1839 Ext 1991
* LYLE OF WESTBOURNE, Baron (*Lyle*) Cr 1945 Ext 1976
* MABANE, Baron (*Mabane*) Cr 1962 Ext 1969
* McCORQUODALE OF NEWTON, Baron (*McCorquodale*) Cr 1955 Ext 1971
* McENTEE, Baron (*McEntee*) Cr 1951 Ext 1953
* MAENAN, Baron (*Taylor*) Cr 1948 Ext 1951
* MAGHERAMORNE, Baron (*McGarel-Hogg*) Cr 1887 Ext 1957
* MANVERS, Earl (*Pierrepont*) Cr 1806; also †B. Pierrepont and V. Newark 1796 Ext 1955
* MARLEY, Baron (*Aman*) Cr 1930 Ext 1990
* MATHERS, Baron (*Mathers*) Cr 1952 Ext 1956
* MAUGHAM, Viscount (*Maugham*) Cr 1939; also *B. Maugham 1935. Ext 1981
* MERRIMAN, Baron (*Merriman*) Cr 1941 Ext 1962
* MICHELHAM, Baron (*Stern*) Cr 1905 Ext 1984
* MIDLETON, Earl (*Brodrick*) Cr 1920; also *V. Dunsford 1920. Ext 1979
* MONCKTON, Baron (*Monckton*) Cr 1887 Ext 1971

* MONSELL, Viscount (*Eyres Monsell*) Cr 1935 Ext 1993
* MORRISON, Baron (*Morrison*) Cr 1945 Ext 1997
§ MOUNTMORRES, Viscount (*de Montmorency*) Cr 1763 Ext 1951
* MUIRSHIEL, Viscount (*Maclay*) Cr 1963 Ext 1992
† NEWCASTLE, Duke of (*Pelham-Clinton*) Cr 1756 Ext 1988
* NORMAN, Baron (*Norman*) Cr 1944 Ext 1950
* NORMANBROOK, Baron (*Brook*) Cr 1963 Ext 1967
‡ NORTH, Baron (*North*) Cr 1554. Abey 1942
* NUFFIELD, Viscount (*Morris*) Cr 1938; also *B. Nuffield 1934. Ext 1963
* NUGENT, Baron (*Nugent*) Cr 1960 Ext 1973
* ORMATHWAITE, Baron (*Walsh*) Cr 1868 Ext 1984
§ ORMONDE, Marquess of (*Butler*) Cr 1825; also § Viscount Thurles 1541, and * Baron Ormonde 1821 Ext 1997
§ ORMONDE, Earl of (*Butler*) Cr 1538, and Ossory (*Butler*) Cr 1527 Dormant 1997
* PENTLAND, Baron (*Sinclair*) Cr 1909 Ext 1984
* PERCY OF NEWCASTLE, Baron (*Percy*) Cr 1953 Ext 1958
* PERRY, Baron (*Perry*) Cr 1938 Ext 1956
* PETHICK-LAWRENCE, Baron (*Pethick-Lawrence*) Cr 1945 Ext 1961
* PORTAL OF HUNGERFORD, Viscount (*Portal*) Cr 1946 Ext 1971
* PORTAL OF HUNGERFORD, Baroness (*Portal*) Cr 1945 Ext 1990
† PORTLAND, Duke of (*Cavendish-Bentinck*) Cr 1716; also †Marquess of Titchfield 1716 Ext 1990
‡ POULETT, Earl (*Poulett*) Cr 1706; also ‡V. Hinton and ‡B. Poulett of Hinton St George (may be dormant) Ext 1973
* QUIBELL, Baron (*Quibell*) Cr 1945 Ext 1962
* QUICKSWOOD, Baron (*Gascoyne-Cecil*) Cr 1941 Ext 1956
* RADCLIFFE, Viscount (*Radcliffe*) Cr 1962 Ext 1977
§ RADSTOCK, Baron (*Waldegrave*) Cr 1800 Ext 1953
* RAMSDEN, Baron (*Ramsden*) Cr 1945 Ext 1955
* RANK, Baron (*Rank*) Cr 1957 Ext 1972
* RHONDDA, Viscount (*Thomas*) Cr 1918; also B. Rhondda 1918 Ext 1958
* ROBERTS, Countess (*Roberts*) Cr 1901; also *V. St Pierre 1901. Ext 1955
* ROBINS, Baron (*Robins*) Cr 1958 Ext 1962
* ROBINSON, Baron (*Robinson*) Cr 1947 Ext 1952
* ROMILLY, Baron (*Romilly*) Cr 1866 Ext 1983
* RUFFSIDE, Viscount (*Brown*) Cr 1951 Ext 1958
* RUSHOLME, Baron (*Palmer*) Cr 1945 Ext 1977
* ST AUDRIES, Baron (*Fuller-Acland-Hood*) Cr 1911 Ext 1971
* ST JUST, Baron (*Grenfell*) Cr 1935 Ext 1984
* ST LEONARDS, Baron (*Sugden*) Cr 1852 Ext 1985
* SALTER, Baron (*Salter*) Cr 1953 Ext 1975
* SCHUSTER, Baron (*Schuster*) Cr 1944 Ext 1956
* SEATON, Baron (*Colborne-Vivian*) Cr 1839 Ext 1955
§ SEFTON, Earl of (*Molyneux*) Cr 1771; also V. Molyneux, and B. Sefton 1831 Ext 1972
† SHERBORNE, Baron (*Dutton*) Cr 1784 Ext 1985
* SHERWOOD, Baron (*Seely*) Cr 1941 Ext 1970
* SIMONDS, Viscount (*Simonds*) Cr 1954; also *B. Simonds (Life Baron, Law Lord) 1944, * Baron 1952 Ext 1971
* SONDES, Earl (*Milles-Lade*) Cr 1880; also *V Throwley 1880, and ‡B Sondes Ext 1996
* SOUTHBOROUGH, Baron (*Hopwood*) Cr 1917 Ext 1992
‡ STAMFORD, Earl of (*Grey*) Cr 1628 Ext 1976; also ‡B. Grey of Groby 1603
‡ STANLEY, Baron (*Hastings*) Cr 1456. Abey 1960
* STANMORE, Baron (*Hamilton-Gordon*) Cr 1893 Ext 1957
* STRACHIE, Baron (*Strachey*) Cr 1911 Ext 1973
† STRANGE, Earl (*Stewart-Murray*) Cr 1786; also †B. Murray of Stanley 1786 and *B. Glenlyon 1821 Ext 1957
* TALBOT DE MALAHIDE, Baron (*Talbot*) Cr 1856 Ext 1973
§ TEIGNMOUTH, Baron (*Shore*) Cr 1797 Ext 1981
§ TEMPLETOWN, Viscount (*Upton*) Cr 1806; also §B. Templetown 1776 Ext 1981
* TEMPLEWOOD, Viscount (*Hoare*) Cr 1944 Ext 1959
* TONYPANDY, Viscount (*Thomas*) Cr 1983 Ext 1997
* TOVEY, Baron (*Tovey*) Cr 1946 Ext 1971
* TREDEGAR, Baron (*Morgan*) Cr 1859 Ext 1962

* TRENT, Baron (*Boot*) Cr 1929 Ext 1956
* TURNOUR, Baron (*Turnour*) Cr 1952 Ext 1962
* UVEDALE OF NORTH END, Baron (*Woodall*) Cr 1946 Ext 1974
* VANSITTART, Baron (*Vansittart*) Cr 1941 Ext 1957
* WAKEFIELD OF KENDAL, Baron (*Wakefield*) Cr 1963 Ext 1983
* WALERAN, Baron (*Walrond*) Cr 1905 Ext 1966
* WATKINSON, Viscount (*Watkinson*) Cr 1964 Ext 1995
* WAVELL, Earl (*Wavell*) Cr 1947; also V. Wavell 1943, and V. Keren 1947 Ext 1954
* WEBB-JOHNSON, Baron (*Webb-Johnson*) Cr 1945 Ext 1958
* WEEKS, Baron (*Weeks*) Cr 1956 Ext 1960

* WHITBURGH, Baron (*Borthwick*) Cr 1912 Ext 1967
§ WICKLOW, Earl of (*Forward-Howard*) Cr 1793; also §V. Wicklow, 1785, §B. Clonmore 1776 Ext 1978
* WILLIAMS, Baron (*Williams*) Cr 1948 Ext 1966
* WILLINGDON, Marquess of (*Freeman-Thomas*) Cr 1936; also *B. Willingdon 1910; * V. Willingdon 1924; *V. Ratendon 1931; *E. of Willingdon 1931 Ext 1979
* WILMOT OF SELMESTON, Baron (*Wilmot*) Cr 1950 Ext 1964
* WINDSOR, Duke of (*Windsor*) Cr 1927 Ext 1972
* WINSTER, Baron (*Fletcher*) Cr 1942 Ext 1961
* WYFOLD, Baron (*Hermon-Hodge*) Cr 1919 Ext 1999
* YPRES, Earl of (*French*) Cr 1922 Ext 1988

LIFE PEERAGES EXTINCT

ADEANE, Baron (*Adeane*) Cr 1972 Ext 1984
AIREY OF ABINGDON, Baroness (*Airey*) Cr 1979 Ext 1992
ALEXANDER OF POTTERHILL, Baron (*Alexander*) Cr 1974 Ext 1993
ALLAN OF KILMAHEW, Baron (*Allan*) Cr 1973 Ext 1979
ALLEN OF FALLOWFIELD (*Allen*) Cr 1974 Ext 1985
ALPORT, Baron (*Alport*) Cr 1961 Ext 1998
AMERY OF LUSTLEIGH (*Amery*) Cr 1992 Ext 1996
ARDWICK, Baron (*Beavan*) Cr 1970 Ext 1994
ARMSTRONG OF SANDERSTEAD, Baron (*Armstrong*) Cr 1975 Ext 1980
ARWYN, Baron (*Arwyn*) Cr 1964 Ext 1978
ASHBY, Baron (*Ashby*) Cr 1973 Ext 1992
ASHDOWN, Baron (*Silverstone*) Cr 1974 Ext 1977
ASQUITH OF BISHOPSTONE, Baron (*Asquith*) Cr 1951 (Law Lord) Ext 1954
ASQUITH OF YARNBURY, Baroness (*Bonham Carter*) Cr 1964 Ext 1969
AYLESTONE, Baron (*Bowden*) Cr 1967 Ext 1994
BACON, Baroness (*Bacon*) Cr 1970 Ext 1993
BAKER, Baron (*Baker*) Cr 1977 Ext 1985
BALERNO, Baron (*Buchanan-Smith*) Cr 1963 Ext 1984
BALOGH, Baron (*Balogh*) Cr 1968 Ext 1985
BALLANTRAE, Baron (*Fergusson*) Cr 1972 Ext 1980
BANCROFT, Baron (*Bancroft*) Cr 1982 Ext 1996
BANKS, Baron (*Banks*) Cr 1974 Ext 1997
BANNERMAN OF KILDONAN, Baron (*Bannerman*) Cr 1967 Ext 1969
BARNETSON, Baron (*Barnetson*) Cr 1975 Ext 1981
BEECHING, Baron (*Beeching*) Cr 1965 Ext 1985
BELOFF, Baron (*Beloff*) Cr 1981 Ext 1999
BENSON, Baron (*Benson*) Cr 1981 Ext 1995
BERNSTEIN, Baron (*Bernstein*) Cr 1969 Ext 1993
BESWICK, Baron (*Beswick*) Cr 1964 Ext 1987
BIRK, Baroness (*Birk*) Cr 1967 Ext 1996
BISHOPSTON, Baron (*Bishop*) Cr 1981 Ext 1984
BLACK, Baron (*Black*) Cr 1968 Ext 1984
BLACKETT, Baron (*Blackett*) Cr 1969 Ext 1974
BLANCH, Baron (*Blanch*) Cr 1983 Ext 1994
BLYTON, Baron (*Blyton*) Cr 1964 Ext 1987
BONHAM-CARTER, Baron (*Bonham-Carter*) Cr 1986 Ext 1994
BOOTHBY, Baron (*Boothby*) Cr 1958 Ext 1986
BOSSOM, Baron (*Bossom*) Cr 1960 Ext 1965
BOTTOMLEY, Baron (*Bottomley*) Cr 1984 Ext 1995
BOURNE, Baron (*Bourne*) Cr 1964 Ext 1982
BOWLES, Baron (*Bowles*) Cr 1964 Ext 1970
BOYD-CARPENTER, Baron (*Boyd-Carpenter*) Cr 1972 Ext 1998
BOYLE OF HANDSWORTH, Baron (*Boyle*) Cr 1970 Ext 1981
BRADWELL, Baron (*Driberg*) Cr 1975 Ext 1976
BRANDON OF OAKBROOK, Baron (*Brandon*) Cr 1981 (Law Lord), Ext 1999
BRAYLEY, Baron (*Brayley*) Cr 1973 Ext 1977
BRIMELOW, Baron (*Brimelow*) Cr 1976 Ext 1995
BRITTEN, Baron (*Britten*) Cr 1976 Ext 1976
BROCK, Baron (*Brock*) Cr 1965 Ext 1980
BROCKWAY, Baron (*Brockway*) Cr 1964 Ext 1988
BROOKE OF CUMNOR, Baron (*Brooke*) Cr 1966 Ext 1984
BROWNE, Baron (*Brown*) Cr 1964 Ext 1985
BROXBOURNE, Baron (*Walker-Smith*) Cr 1983 Ext 1992
BRUCE-GARDYNE, Baron (*Bruce-Gardyne*) Cr 1983 Ext 1990
BUCKTON, Baron (*Storey*) Cr 1966 Ext 1978
BURNTWOOD, Baron (*Snow*) Cr 1970 Ext 1982
BURTON OF COVENTRY, Baroness (*Burton*) Cr 1962 Ext 1991

BUTLER OF SAFFRON WALDEN, Baron (*Butler*) Cr 1965 Ext 1982
BYERS, Baron (*Byers*) Cr 1964 Ext 1984
CACCIA, Baron (*Caccia*) Cr 1965 Ext 1990
CAMERON OF BALHOUSIE, Baron (*Cameron*) Cr 1983 Ext 1985
CAMPBELL OF ESKAN, Baron (*Campbell*) Cr 1966 Ext 1994
CARADON, Baron (*Foot*) Cr 1964 Ext 1990
CARRON, Baron (*Carron*) Cr 1967 Ext 1969
CASEY, Baron (*Casey*) Cr 1960 Ext 1976
CASTLE, Baron (*Castle*) Cr 1974 Ext 1979
CAYZER, Baron (*Cayzer*) Cr 1981 Ext 1999
CHAMPION, Baron (*Champion*) Cr 1962 Ext 1985
CHELMER, Baron (*Edwards*) Cr 1963 Ext 1997
CHESHIRE, Baron (*Cheshire*) Cr 1991 Ext 1992
CHUTER-EDE, Baron (*Chuter-Ede*) Cr 1965 Ext 1965
CLARK, Baron (*Clark*) Cr 1969 Ext 1983
COHEN, Baron (*Cohen*) Cr 1951 (Law Lord), Ext 1973
COHEN OF BRIGHTON, Baron (*Cohen*) Cr 1965 Ext 1966
COLE, Baron (*Cole*) Cr 1965 Ext 1979
COLLISON, Baron (*Collison*) Cr 1964 Ext 1995
COLNBROOKE, Baron (*Atkins*) Cr 1987 ext 1996
CONSTANTINE, Baron (*Constantine*) Cr 1969 Ext 1971
COOPER OF STOCKTON HEATH, Baron (*Cooper*) Cr 1966 Ext 1988
COUTANCHE, Baron (*Coutanche*) Cr 1961 Ext 1973
CRAIGTON, Baron (*Browne*) Cr 1959 Ext 1993
CRAWSHAW OF AINTREE, Baron (*Crawshaw*) Cr 1985 Ext 1986
CROSS OF CHELSEA, Baron (*Cross*) Cr 1971 (Law Lord), Ext 1989
CROWTHER, Baron (*Crowther*) Cr 1968 Ext 1972
CROWTHER-HUNT, Baron (*Crowther-Hunt*) Cr 1973 Ext 1987
CUDLIPP, Baron (*Cudlipp*) Cr 1974 Ext 1998
DAINTON, Baron (*Dainton*) Cr 1986 Ext 1997
DALTON, Baron (*Dalton*) Cr 1960 Ext 1962
DARLINGTON OF HILLSBOROUGH, Baron (*Darling*) Cr 1974 Ext 1985
DAVIES OF LEEK, Baron (*Davies*) Cr 1970 Ext 1985
DAVIES OF PENRHYS, Baron (*Davies*) Cr 1974 Ext 1992
DEAN OF BESWICK, Baron (*Dean*) Cr 1983 Ext 1999
DELACOURT-SMITH, Baron (*Delacourt-Smith*) Cr 1967 Ext 1972
DELFONT, Baron (*Delfont*) Cr 1976 Ext 1994
DENNING, Baron (*Denning*) Cr 1957 (Law Lord), Ext 1999
DEVLIN, Baron (*Devlin*) Cr 1961 (Law Lord), Ext 1992
DIPLOCK, Baron (*Diplock*) Cr 1968 (Law Lord), Ext 1985
DONALDSON OF KINGSBRIDGE, Baron (*Donaldson*) Cr 1967 Ext 1998
DONNET OF BALGAY, Baron (*Donnet*) Cr 1978 Ext 1985
DONOVAN, Baron (*Donovan*) Cr 1963 (Law Lord), Ext 1971
DOUGLASS OF CLEVELAND, Baron (*Douglass*) Cr 1967 Ext 1978
DUNCAN SANDYS, Baron (*Duncan-Sandys*) Cr 1974 Ext 1987
EDMUND-DAVIES, Baron (*Edmund-Davies*) Cr 1974 (Law Lord), Ext 1992
ELLIOT OF HARWOOD, Baroness (*Elliot*) Cr 1958 Ext 1994
ELWORTHY, Baron (*Elworthy*) Cr 1971 Ext 1993

EMMET OF AMBERLEY, Baroness, (*Emmet*)
Cr 1964   Ext 1980
ENERGLYN, Baron (*Energlyn*) Cr 1968 Ext 1985
ENNALS, Baron (*Ennals*) Cr 1983 Ext 1995
EVANS OF CLAUGHTON, Baron (*Evans*) Cr 1978
Ext 1992
EVANS OF HUNGERSHALL, Baron (*Evans*)
Cr 1967   Ext 1982
EWART-BIGGS, Baroness (*O'Sullivan*) Cr 1981
Ext 1992
FAITHFULL, Baroness (*Faithfull*) Cr 1975 Ext 1996
FAULKNER OF DOWNPATRICK, Baron (*Faulkner*)
Cr 1977   Ext 1977
FEATHER, Baron (*Feather*) Cr 1974 Ext 1976
FERRIER, Baron (*Noel-Paton*) Cr 1958 Ext 1992
FIELDHOUSE, Baron (*Fieldhouse*) Cr 1990
Ext 1992
FINSBERG, Baron (*Finsberg*) Cr 1992 Ext 1996
FISHER OF CAMDEN, Baron (*Fisher*) Cr 1974
Ext 1979
FISHER OF LAMBETH, Baron (*Fisher*) Cr 1961
Ext 1972
FISKE, Baron (*Fiske*) Cr 1967 Ext 1975
FLETCHER, Baron (*Fletcher*) Cr 1970 Ext 1990.
FLOREY, Baron (*Florey*) Cr 1965 Ext 1968
FRANCIS-WILLIAMS, Baron (*Williams*) Cr 1962
Ext 1970
FRANKS, Baron (*Franks*) Cr 1962 Ext 1992
FRASER OF KILMORACK, Baron (*Fraser*) Cr 1974
Ext 1996
FRASER OF LONSDALE, Baron (*Fraser*) Cr 1958
Ext 1974
FRASER OF TULLYBELTON, Baron (*Fraser*)
Cr 1974 (Law Lord), Ext 1989
FULTON, Baron (*Fulton*) Cr 1966 Cr 1986 Ext 1974
GAITSKELL, Baroness (*Gaitskell*) Cr 1963
Ext 1989
GALPERN, Baron (*Galpern*) Cr 1979 Ext 1993
GARDINER, Baron (*Gardiner*) Cr 1963 Ext 1990
GARNER, Baron (*Garner*) Cr 1969 Ext 1983
GARNSWORTHY, Baron (*Garnsworthy*) Cr 1967
Ext 1974
GEDDES OF EPSOM, Baron (*Geddes*) Cr 1958
Ext 1983
GEORGE-BROWN, Baron (*George-Brown*) Cr 1970
Ext 1985
GILLMORE OF THAMESFIELD, Baron (*Gillmore*)
Cr 1996 Ext 1999
GLENKINGLAS, Baron (*Noble*) Cr 1974 Ext 1984
GODBER OF WILLINGTON, Baron (*Godber*)
Cr 1979   Ext 1980
GODDARD, Baron (*Goddard*) Cr 1944 (Law Lord),
Ext 1971
GOODMAN, Baron (*Goodman*) Cr 1965 Ext 1995
GOOLD, Baron (*Goold*) Cr 1987 Ext 1997
GORDON-WALKER, Baron (*Gordon-Walker*)
Cr 1974   Ext 1980
GORE-BOOTH, Baron (*Gore-Booth*) Cr 1969
Ext 1984
GORONWY-ROBERTS, Baron (*Roberts*) Cr 1974
Ext 1981
GRADE, Baron (*Grade*) Cr 1976 Ext 1998
GRANVILLE OF EYE, Baron (*Granville*) Cr 1967
Ext 1998
GRANVILLE-WEST, Baron (*West*) Cr 1958 Ext 1984
GREENWOOD OF ROSSENDALE, Baron
(*Greenwood*) Cr 1970 Ext 1982
GUEST, Baron (*Guest*) Cr 1961 (Law Lord),
Ext 1984
HAIRE OF WHITEABBEY, Baron (*Haire*) Cr 1965
Ext 1966
HALE, Baron (*Hale*) Cr 1972 Ext 1985
HAMNETT, Baron (*Hamnett*) Cr 1970 Ext 1980
HART OF SOUTH LANARK, Baroness (*Hart*)
Cr 1987   Ext 1991
HARVEY OF PRESTBURY, Baron (*Harvey*) Cr 1971
Ext 1994
HARVINGTON, Baron (*Grant-Ferris*) Cr 1974
Ext 1997
HATCH OF LUSBY, Baron (*Hatch*) Cr 1978
Ext 1992
HAVERS, Baron (*Havers*) Cr 1987 Ext 1992
HELSBY, Baron (*Helsby*) Cr 1968 Ext 1978
HEWLETT, Baron (*Hewlett*) Cr 1972 Ext 1979
HEYCOCK, Baron (*Heycock*) Cr 1967 Ext 1990
HILL OF LUTON, Baron (*Hill*) Cr 1963 Ext 1989
HILL OF WIVENHOE, Baron (*Hill*) Cr 1967
Ext 1969
HILTON OF UPTON, Baron (*Hilton*) Cr 1965
Ext 1977
HINTON OF BANKSIDE, Baron (*Hinton*) Cr 1965
Ext 1983
HIRSHFIELD, Baron (*Hirshfield*) Cr 1967 Ext 1993
HOBSON, Baron (*Hobson*) Cr 1963 Ext 1966
HODSON, Baron (*Hodson*) Cr 1960 (Law Lord),
Ext 1984
HOLFORD, Baron (*Holford*) Cr 1965 Ext 1975

HOME OF THE HIRSEL, Baron (*Douglas-Home*)
(Earl of Home, disclaimed) Cr 1974 Ext 1995
HORNSBY-SMITH, Baroness (*Hornsby-Smith*)
Cr 1974   Ext 1985
HORSBRUGH, Baroness (*Horsbrugh*) Cr 1959
Ext 1969
HOUGHTON OF SOWERBY, Baron (*Houghton*)
Cr 1974   Ext 1996
HOWARD OF HENDERSKELFE, Baron (*Howard*)
Cr 1983   Ext 1985
HOWELL, Baron (*Howell*) Cr 1992 Ext 1998
HOY, Baron (*Hoy*) Cr 1970 Ext 1976
HUNT OF FAWLEY, Baron (*Hunt*) Cr 1973
Ext 1987
HUNT, Baron (*Hunt*) Cr 1966 Ext 1998
HUNTER OF NEWINGTON, Baron (*Hunter*)
Cr 1978   Ext 1994
HURD, Baron (*Hurd*) Cr 1964 Ext 1966
ILFORD, Baron (*Hutchinson*) Cr 1962 Ext 1974
IRVING OF DARTFORD, Baron (*Irving*) Cr 1979
Ext 1989
JACKSON OF BURNLEY, Baron (*Jackson*) Cr 1967
Ext 1970
JACKSON OF LODSWORTH, Baroness, (*Jackson*)
Cr 1976   Ext 1981
JACOBSON, Baron (*Jacobson*) Cr 1975 Ext 1988
JACQUES, Baron (*Jacques*) Cr 1968 Ext 1995
JAMES OF RUSHOLME, Baron (*James*) Cr 1959
Ext 1992
JANNER, Baron (*Janner*) Cr 1970 Ext 1982
JAY, Baron (*Jay*) Cr 1987 Ext 1996
JENKINS, Baron (*Jenkins*) Cr 1959 (Law Lord)
Ext 1969
JOSEPH, Baron (*Joseph*) Cr 1987 Ext 1994
KABERRY OF ADEL, Baron (*Kaberry*) Cr 1983
Ext 1991
KADOORIE, Baron (*Kadoorie*) Cr 1981 Ext 1993
KAGAN, Baron (*Kagan*) Cr 1976 Ext 1995
KAHN, Baron (*Kahn*) Cr 1965 Ext 1989
KALDOR, Baron (*Kaldor*) Cr 1974 Ext 1986
KEARTON, Baron (*Kearton*) Cr 1970 (Law Lord),
Ext 1992
KEITH OF AVONHOLM, Baron (*Keith*) Cr 1953
(Law Lord), Ext 1964
KILBRANDON, Baron (*Shaw*) Cr 1971 Ext 1989
KILMANY, Baron (*Anstruther-Gray*) Cr 1966
Ext 1985
KING-HALL, Baron (*King-Hall*) Cr 1966 Ext 1966
KINGS NORTON, Baron (*Roxbee Cox*) Cr 1965
Ext 1997
KISSIN, Baron (*Kissin*) Cr 1974 Ext 1997
LANE-FOX, Baroness (*Lane-Fox*) Cr 1981 Ext 1988
LEATHERLAND, Baron (*Leatherland*) Cr 1964
Ext 1992
LEE OF ASHERIDGE, Baroness (*Bevan*) Cr 1970
Ext 1988
LEE OF NEWTON, Baron (*Lee*) Cr 1974 Ext 1984
LEONARD, Baron (*Leonard*) Cr 1978 Ext 1983
LESTOR OF ECCLES, Baroness (*Lestor*) Cr 1997
Ext 1998
LEVER, Baron (*Lever*) Cr 1975 Ext 1977
LEVER OF MANCHESTER, Baron (*Lever*) Cr 1979
Ext 1995
LEWIN, Baron (*Lewin*) Cr 1982 Ext 1999
LINDGREN, Baron (*Lindgren*) Cr 1961 Ext 1971
LLEWELYN-DAVIES, Baron (*Llewelyn Davies*)
Cr 1963   Ext 1981
LLEWELYN-DAVIES OF HASTOE, Baroness
(*Llewelyn-Davies*) Cr 1967 Ext 1997
LLOYD OF HAMPSTEAD, Baron (*Lloyd*) Cr 1965
Ext 1993
LOWRY, Baron (*Lowry*) Cr 1979 (Law Lord),
Ext 1999
LYONS OF BRIGHTON, Baron (*Lyons*) Cr 1974
Ext 1978
McALPINE OF MOFFAT, Baron (*McAlpine*)
Cr 1980   Ext 1990
MACDERMOTT, Baron (*MacDermott*) Cr 1947
Ext 1979
McFADZEAN, Baron (*McFadzean*) Cr 1966 Ext 1996
McFADZEAN OF KELVINSIDE, Baron (*McFadzean*)
Cr 1980   Ext 1992
McGREGOR OF DURRIS, Baron (*McGregor*)
Cr 1978   Ext 1997
MACLEAN, Baron (*Maclean*) Cr 1971 Ext 1990
McLEAVY, Baron (*McLeavy*) Cr 1967 Ext 1976
MacLEOD OF FUINARY, Baron (*MacLeod*) Cr 1967
Ext 1991
MACMILLAN, Baron (*Macmillan*) Cr 1930 (Law
Lord) Ext 1952
MAELOR, Baron (*Jones*) Cr 1966 Ext 1984
MAIS, Baron (*Mais*) Cr 1967 Ext 1993
MARPLES, Baron (*Marples*) Cr 1974 Ext 1978
MARSHALL OF GORING, Baron (*Marshall*)
Cr 1985   Ext 1996
MARSHALL OF LEEDS, Baron (*Marshall*) Cr 1980
Ext 1990

MATTHEWS, Baron (*Matthews*) Cr 1980 Ext 1995
MAUDE OF STRATFORD-UPON-AVON, Baron
(*Maude*) Cr 1983 Ext 1993
MAYBRAY-KING, Baron (*Maybray-King*) Cr 1971
Ext 1986
MAYHEW, Baron (*Mayhew*) Cr 1981 Ext 1997
MELLISH, Baron (*Mellish*) Cr 1985 Ext 1998
MENUHIN, Baron (*Menuhin*) Cr 1993 Ext 1999
MILES, Baron (*Miles*) Cr 1979 Ext 1991
MITCHISON, Baron (*Mitshison*) Cr 1964 Ext 1970
MOLSON, Baron (*Molson*) Cr 1961 Ext 1991
MONSLOW, Baron (*Monslow*) Cr 1966 Ext 1966
MORRIS OF BORTH-Y-GEST, Baron (*Morris*)
Cr 1960 (Law Lord), Ext 1979
MORRIS OF GRASMERE, Baron (*Morris*) Cr 1967
Ext 1990
MORRISON OF LAMBETH, Baron (*Morrison*)
Cr 1959 Ext 1965
MORTON OF HENRYTON, Baron (*Morton*) Cr 1947
(Law Lord) Ext 1973
MORTON OF SHUNA, Baron (*Morton*) Cr 1985
ext 1995
MOYLE, Baron (*Moyle*) Cr 1966 Ext 1974
MULLEY, Baron (*Mulley*) Cr 1984 Ext 1995
MURRAY OF GRAVESEND, Baron (*Murray*)
Cr 1976 Ext 1980
MURRAY OF NEWHAVEN, Baron (*Murray*)
Cr 1964 Ext 1993
NOEL-BAKER, Baron (*Noel-Baker*) Cr 1977
Ext 1982
NORMAND, Baron (*Normand*) Cr 1947 (Law Lord)
Ext 1962
NORTHCHURCH, Baroness (*Davidson*) Cr 1963
Ext 1985
NUGENT OF GUILDFORD, Baron (*Nugent*)
Cr 1966 Ext 1994
OAKSHOTT, Baron (*Oakshott*) Cr 1964 Ext 1975
O'BRIEN OF LOTHBURY, Baron (*O'Brien*) Cr 1973
Ext 1995
OLIVIER, Baron (*Olivier*) Cr 1970 Ext 1989
O'NEILL OF THE MAINE, Baron (*O'Neill*) Cr 1970
Ext 1990
PANNELL, Baron (*Pannell*) Cr 1974 Ext 1980
PARGITER, Baron (*Pargiter*) Cr 1966 Ext 1982
PARKER OF WADDINGTON, Baron (*Parker*)
Cr 1958 (Law Lord) Ext 1972
PEARCE, Baron (*Pearce*) Cr 1962 (Law Lord)
Ext 1990
PEARSON, Baron (*Pearson*) Cr 1965 (Law Lord),
Ext 1980
PEART, Baron (*Peart*) Cr 1976 Ext 1988
PEDDIE, Baron (*Peddie*) Cr 1961 Ext 1978
PENNEY, Baron (*Penney*) Cr 1967 Ext 1991
PHILLIPS, Baroness (*Phillips*) Cr 1964 Ext 1992
PHILLIPS OF ELLESMERE, Baron (*Phillips*)
Cr 1994 Ext 1999
PILKINGTON, Baron (*Pilkington*) Cr 1968 Ext 1983
PITT OF HAMPSTEAD, Baron (*Pitt*) Cr 1975
Ext 1994
PLANT, Baron (*Plant*) Cr 1978 Ext 1986
PLATT, Baron (*Platt*) Cr 1967 Ext 1978
PLUMMER, Baron (*Plummer*) Cr 1965 Ext 1972
PLURENDEN, Baron (*Sternberg*) Cr 1975 Ext 1978
POPPLEWELL, Baron (*Popplewell*) Cr 1966
Ext 1977
PORRITT, Baron (*Porritt*) Cr 1973 Ext 1994
PORTER, Baron (*Porter*) Cr 1938 (Law Lord)
Ext 1956
PRITCHARD, Baron (*Pritchard*) Cr 1975 Ext 1995
RAMSEY OF CANTERBURY, Baron (*Ramsey*)
Cr 1974 Ext 1988
RAVENSDALE OF KEDLESTON, Baroness (*Curzon*)
Cr 1958 Ext 1966
RAYNER, Baron (*Rayner*) Cr 1983 Ext 1998
REDCLIFFE-MAUD, Baron (*Redcliffe-Maud*)
Cr 1967 Ext 1982
REDMAYNE, Baron (*Redmayne*) Cr 1966 Ext 1983
REID, Baron (*Reid*) Cr 1948 (Law Lord) Ext 1975
REIGATE, Baron (*Vaughan-Morgan*) Cr 1970
Ext 1995
REILLY, Baron (*Reilly*) Cr 1978 Ext 1990
RHODES, Baron (*Rhodes*) Cr 1964 Ext 1987
RHYL, Baron (*Birch*) Cr 1970 Ext 1981
RIDLEY OF LIDDESDALE, Baron (*Ridley*) Cr 1992
Ext 1993
RIPPON OF HEXHAM, Baron (*Rippon*) Cr 1987
Ext 1997
RITCHIE-CALDER, Baron (*Calder*) Cr 1966
Ext 1982
ROBBINS, Baron (*Robbins*) Cr 1959 Ext 1984
ROBERTHALL, Baron (*Hall*) Cr 1969 Ext 1988
ROBSON OF KIDDINGTON, Baroness (*Robson*)
Cr 1974 Ext 1999
ROCHE, Baron (*Roche*) Cr 1935 (Law Lord)
Ext 1956
ROSENHEIM, Baron (*Rosenheim*) Cr 1970 Ext 1972
ROSKILL, Baron (*Roskill*) Cr 1980 (Law Lord),

Ext 1996
ROWLEY, Baron (*Henderson*) Cr 1966 Ext 1968
ROYLE, Baron (*Royle*) Cr 1964 Ext 1975
RUNCORN, Baron (*Vosper*) Cr 1964 Ext 1968
RUSSELL OF KILOWEN, Baron (*Russell*) Cr 1975
Ext 1986
SAINSBURY, Baron (*Sainsbury*) Cr 1962 Ext 1998
SAINT BRIDES, Baron (*James*) Cr 1977 Ext 1989
SALMON, Baron (*Salmon*) Cr 1972 (Law Lord)
Ext 1991
SAMUEL OF WYCH CROSS, Baron (*Samuel*)
Cr 1972 Ext 1988
SCHON, Baron (*Schon*) Cr 1976 Ext 1995
SEEAR, Baroness (*Seear*) Cr 1971 Ext 1997
SEEBOHM, Baron (*Seebohm*) Cr 1972 Ext 1990
SEGAL, Baron (*Segal*) Cr 1964 Ext 1985
SELWYN-LLOYD, Baron (*Lloyd*) Cr 1976 Ext 1978
SHACKLETON, Baron (*Shackleton*) Cr 1958
Ext 1994
SHARP OF GRIMSDYKE, Baron (*Sharp*) Cr 1989
Ext 1994
SHINWELL, Baron (*Shinwell*) Cr 1970 Ext 1986
SIEFF, Baron (*Sieff*) Cr 1966 Ext 1972
SILKIN OF DULWICH, Baron (*Silkin*) Cr 1985
Ext 1988
SIMEY, Baron (*Simey*) Cr 1965 Ext 1969
SIMONDS, Baron (*see* HEREDITARY PEERAGES)
SKRIMSHIRE OF QUARTER, Baroness,
(*Skrimshire*) Cr 1979 Ext 1979
SLATER, Baron (*Slater*) Cr 1970 Ext 1977
SMITH, Baron (*Smith*) Cr 1978 Ext 1998
SNOW, Baron (*Snow*) Cr 1964 Ext 1980
SOAMES, Baron (*Soames*) Cr 1978 Ext 1987
SOMERVELL OF HARROW, Baron (*Somervell*)
Cr 1954 (Law Lord) Ext 1960
SOPER, Baron (*Soper*) Cr 1965 Ext 1998
SORENSEN, Baron (*Sorensen*) Cr 1964 Ext 1971
SPENCER-CHURCHILL, Baroness, (*Spencer-*
Churchill) Cr 1965 Ext 1977
STEDMAN, Baroness (*Stedman*) Cr 1974 Ext 1996
STEWART OF ALVECHURCH, Baroness (*Stewart*)
Cr 1974 Ext 1984
STEWART OF FULHAM, Baron (*Stewart*) Cr 1979
Ext 1990
STOCKS, Baroness, (*Stocks*) Cr 1966 Ext 1975
STONE, Baron (*Stone*) Cr 1976 Ext 1986
STONHAM, Baron (*Collins*) Cr 1958 Ext 1971
STOPFORD OF FALLOWFIELD, Baron (*Stopford*)
Cr 1958 Ext 1961
STOW HILL, Baron (*Soskice*) Cr 1966 Ext 1979
SUMMERSKILL, Baroness, (*Summerskill*) Cr 1961
Ext 1980
SWANBOROUGH, Baroness, (*Isaacs*) Cr 1958
Ext 1971
SWANN, Baron (*Swann*) Cr 1981 Ext 1990
TANGLEY, Baron (*Herbert*) Cr 1963 Ext 1973
TAYLOR, Baron (*Taylor*) Cr 1958 Ext 1988
TAYLOR OF GOSFORTH, Baron (*Taylor*) Cr 1992
Ext 1997
TAYLOR OF HADFIELD, Baron (*Taylor*) Cr 1983
Ext 1995
TAYLOR OF MANSFIELD, Baron (*Taylor*) Cr 1966
Ext 1991
TAYSIDE, Baron (*Urquhart*) Cr 1967 Ext 1975
THOMAS, Baron (*Thomas*) Cr 1971 Ext 1980
THORNEYCROFT, Baron (*Thorneycroft*) Cr 1967
Ext 1994
TODD, Baron (*Todd*) Cr 1962 Ext 1997
TRAFFORD, Baron (*Trafford*) Cr 1987 Ext 1989
TRANMIRE, Baron (*Turton*) Cr 1974 Ext 1994
TREVELYAN, Baron (*Trevelyan*) Cr 1968 Ext 1985
TUCKER, Baron (*Tucker*) Cr 1950 Ext 1975
TWEEDSMUIR OF BELHELVIE, Baroness,
(*Thomson*) Cr 1970 Ext 1978
TWINING, Baron (*Twining*) Cr 1958 Ext 1967
UNDERHILL, Baron (*Underhill*) Cr 1979 Ext 1993
UPJOHN, Baron (*Upjohn*) Cr 1963 (Law Lord)
Ext 1971
VAIZEY, Baron (*Vaizey*) Cr 1976 Ext 1984
VICKERS, Baroness (*Vickers*) Cr 1974 Ext 1994
WADE, Baron (*Wade*) Cr 1964 Ext 1988
WALSTON, Baron (*Walston*) Cr 1961 Ext 1991
WALL, Baron (*Wall*) Cr 1976 Ext 1980
WALLACE OF CAMPSIE, Baron (*Wallace*) Cr 1974
Ext 1997
WATKINS, Baron (*Watkins*) Cr 1972 Ext 1983
WELLS-PESTELL, Baron (*Wells-Pestell*) Cr 1965
Ext 1991
WHITE OF HULL, Baron (*White*) Cr 1991 Ext 1995
WIDGERY, Baron (*Widgery*) Cr 1971 Ext 1981
WIGG, Baron (*Wigg*) Cr 1967 Ext 1983
WILLIAMS OF BARNBURGH, Baron (*Williams*)
Cr 1961 Ext 1967
WILLIAMSON, Baron (*Williamson*) Cr 1962
Ext 1983
WILLS, Baron (*Willis*) Cr 1963 Ext 1992
WILSON OF HIGH WRAY, Baron (*Wilson*) Cr 1976

Ext 1980
WILSON OF LANGSIDE, Baron (*Wilson*)   Cr 1969
    Ext 1997
WILSON OF RADCLIFFE, Baron (*Wilson*)   Cr 1974
    Ext 1983
WILSON OF RIEVAULX, Baron (*Wilson*)   Cr 1983
    Ext 1995
WINSTANLEY, Baron (*Winstanley*)   Cr 1975
    Ext 1993
WINTERBOTTOM, Baron (*Winterbottom*)   Cr 1965
    Ext 1992
WOLFENDEN, Baron (*Wolfenden*)   Cr 1974   Ext 1985
WOOLLEY, Baron (*Woolley*)   Cr 1967   Ext 1986
WOOTTON OF ABINGER, Baroness (*Wootton*)
    Cr 1958   Ext 1988
WRIGHT, Baron (*Wright*)   Cr 1932 (Law Lord)
    Ext 1964
WRIGHT OF ASHTON UNDER LYNE, Baron
    (*Wright*)   Cr 1968   Ext 1974
WYATT OF WEEFORD, Baron (*Wyatt*)   Cr 1987
    Ext 1997
WYNNE-JONES, Baron (*Wynne-Jones*)   Cr 1964
    Ext 1982
ZUCKERMAN, Baron (*Zuckerman*)   Cr 1971
    Ext 1993

PEERAGES DISCLAIMED
Under the terms of the Peerage Act, 1963

* ALTRINCHAM, Barony of (*Grigg*)
    Cr 1945   Disclaimed 1963
* CAMROSE, Viscountcy of (*Berry*)   Cr 1941, and
    *Baron Camrose Disclaimed 1995
* DURHAM, Earldom of (*Lambton*)   Cr Baron
    Durham 1828, Viscount Lambton and Earl of
    Durham 1833   Disclaimed 1970
* HAILSHAM, Viscountcy of (*Hogg*)   Cr Baron
    Hailsham 1928, and Viscount Hailsham
    1929   Disclaimed 1963
* MERTHYR, Barony of (*Lewis*)   Cr 1911   Disclaimed
    1977
* REITH, Barony of (*Reith*)   Cr 1940   Disclaimed
    1972
* SANDERSON OF AYOT, Barony of (*Sanderson*)
    Cr 1960   Disclaimed 1971
‖ SELKIRK, Earldom of (*Douglas-Hamilton*)   Cr Lord
    Daer and Shortcleuch 1646, and Earl of Selkirk
    1646   Disclaimed 1994
* SILKIN, Barony of (*Silkin*)   Cr 1950   Disclaimed
    1972
* STANSGATE, Viscountcy of (*Benn*)
    Cr 1942   Disclaimed 1963

BARONETCIES THAT HAVE BECOME EXTINCT OR DORMANT

Since 1950. For Extinctions in the years 1900-50 see 1958 and earlier editions.

‡ Baronets of England (1611-1707)
† Baronets of Great Britain (1707-1800)
‖ Baronets of Nova Scotia (or Scotland) (1625-1707)
* Baronets of United Kingdom (1801 onwards)
§ Baronets of Ireland (1619-1800).

* ADAIR Cr 1838 Ext 1988
* ALISON Cr 1852 Ext 1970
* ANDERSON Cr 1920 Ext 1963
* ASTLEY Cr 1821 Ext 1994
* AYLWEN Cr 1949 Ext 1967
* BAKER Cr 1802 Ext 1959
* BANNER, HARMOOD- Cr 1924 Ext 1990
* BARBOUR Cr 1943 Ext 1951
* BARLOW, MONTAGUE- Cr 1924 Ext 1951
* BARRATT, LAYLAND- Cr 1908 Ext 1968
* BARWICK Cr 1912 Ext 1979
* BASS, Cr 1882 Ext. 1952
* BEAUCHAMP Cr 1911 Ext 1976
* BEAUCHAMP Cr 1918 Ext 1983
* BEIT Cr 1924 Ext 1994
* BELL Cr 1909 Ext 1955
* BELL, MORRISON- Cr 1923 Ext 1956
* BENN Cr 1920 Ext 1992
* BENYON Cr 1958 Ext 1959
‖ BETHUNE Cr 1683 Ext 1997
* BIGGE, SELBY- Cr 1919 Ext 1973
* BILSLAND (*Baron Bilsland*) Cr 1907 Ext 1970
* BLADES (*Baron Ebbisham*) Cr 1922 Ext 1991
* BLAIR Cr 1945 Ext 1962
† BLAKE Cr 1772 Ext 1975
* BOLTON Cr 1927 Ext 1982
* BOOT Cr 1916 Ext 1956
* BOULTON Cr 1905 Ext 1996
* BOWMAN Cr 1961 Ext 1990
‡ †BROUGHTON, ROUSE- Cr 1641 and 1791 Ext 1963
‡ BOYNTON Cr 1618 Ext 1966
* BRAITHWAITE Cr 1954 Ext 1958
* BROCKLEHURST Cr 1903 Ext 1982
§ BROWNE (*Earl of Kenmare*) Cr 1622 Ext 1952
* BULLOCK Cr 1954 Ext 1966
‡ BURDETT Cr 1619 Ext or Dormant 1951
‖ BURNETT Cr 1626 Dormant 1959
* BURNS (*Baron Inverclyde*) Cr 1889 Ext 1957
† BURRARD Cr 1769 Ext 1965
* BUTCHER Cr 1960 Ext 1966
* BYASS Cr 1926 Ext 1976
* CAIN Cr 1920 Ext 1969
* CAINE Cr 1937 Ext 1971
* CAIRD Cr 1928 Ext 1954
‡ CALTHORPE, GOUTH- (*Baron Calthorpe*) Cr 1728 Ext 1997
* CAMERON Cr 1893 Ext 1968
* CAMPBELL (*Baron Glenavy*) Cr 1916 Ext 1984
* CAMPBELL Cr 1939 Ext 1954
‖ CAMPBELL, HOME-PURVES-HUME- Cr 1665 Ext 1960
* CARGILL Cr 1920 Ext 1954
* CAYZER (*Baron Cayzer*) Cr 1921 Ext 1999
* CHAMPNEYS, DALRYMPLE- Cr 1910 Ext 1980
* CHAMBERLAIN Cr 1828 Ext 1980
* CHARLES Cr 1928 Ext 1975
* CHILD Cr 1868 Ext 1958
* CHUBB Cr 1919 Ext 1957
* CHURCH Cr 1901 Ext 1979
* CHUTE Cr 1952 Ext 1956
* CLARK Cr 1883 Ext 1979
* COATS, GLEN- Cr 1894 Ext 1954
* COHEN Cr 1905 Ext 1968
* COLMAN Cr 1952 Ext 1966
* COOPER Cr 1905 Ext 1961
‡ COPE Cr 1611 Ext or Dormant 1972
‡ COPE Cr 1918 Ext 1966
* CORBET Cr 1808 Ext 1996
† CORNEWALL Cr 1764 Ext 1962
* CORNWALL Cr 1918 Ext 1962
* COURTHOPE (*Baron Courthope*) Cr 1925 Ext 1955
* COWAN Cr 1921 Ext 1956
* CRAIK Cr 1926 Ext 1955

* CROSS Cr 1912 Ext 1963
* CROSS Cr 1941 Ext 1968
* CUNARD Cr 1859 Ext 1989
* CUNNINGHAM (*Viscount Cunningham of Hyndhope*) Cr 1942 Ext 1963
* CUNNINGHAM Cr 1963 Ext 1976
† CURTIS Cr 1794 Ext 1954
* DALRYMPLE Cr 1887 Ext 1971
* DALRYMPLE, ELPHINSTONE- Cr 1828 Dormant 1956
* DAVID Cr 1911 Ext 1964
* DAWSON Cr 1929 Ext 1974
* de CAPELL BROOKE Cr 1803 Ext 1968
* DE CRESPIGNY, CHAMPION- Cr 1805 Ext 1952
* DEELEY, MALLABY- Cr 1922 Ext 1963
* DENYS Cr 1813 Ext 1960
‡ DERING Cr 1527 Ext 1975
* DILLON Cr 1801 Ext 1982
* DIMSDALE Cr 1902 Ext 1978
‡ DIXIE Cr 1660 Ext 1975
* DOMVILLE, POE- Cr 1912 Ext 1959
* DOMVILLE Cr 1814 Ext 1981
† DOUGLAS Cr 1786 Ext 1969
* DOUGLAS Cr 1831 Ext 1986
* DOYLE Cr 1828 Ext 1987
* DRUMMOND, WILLIAMS- Cr 1828 Ext 1976
* DUFF Cr 1911 Ext 1980
* DUFF Cr 1952 Ext 1952
* DUNCAN Cr 1905 Ext 1964
* DUNCAN Cr 1957 Ext 1974
* DUNDAS Cr 1821 Ext 1981
* DUNDAS Cr 1898 Ext 1970
* DUNN Cr 1917 Ext 1971
* DUNN Cr 1921 Ext 1976
* DUNNELL Cr 1922 Ext 1960
* EDWARDS Cr 1921 Ext 1999
* ELLERMAN Cr 1905 Ext 1973
* ELLIS Cr 1932 Ext 1956
* ERSKINE (*Baron Erskine of Rerrick*) Cr 1961 Ext 1995
* EVANS Cr 1902 Ext 1970
* EVANS Cr 1963 Ext 1983
* EVANS, WORTHINGTON- Cr 1916 Ext 1971
* FARRER (*Baron Farrer*) Cr 1883 Ext 1964
* FINDLAY Cr 1925 Ext 1979
* FLANNERY Cr 1904 Ext 1959
* FLAVELLE Cr 1917 Ext 1985
* FOSTER Cr 1838 Ext 1960
* FOX Cr 1924 Ext 1959
* FRASER Cr 1806 Ext 1979
* FRASER Cr 1921 Ext 1992
* FRASER (*Baron Fraser of Allander*) Cr 1961 Ext 1987
* FREAKE Cr 1882 Ext 1951
* FRY Cr 1894 Ext 1987
* FRY Cr 1929 Ext 1960
* GAMMANS Cr 1956 Ext 1957
* GIBSON Cr 1926 Ext 1997
* GLYN (*Baron Glyn*) Cr 1934 Ext 1960
§ GODFREY Cr 1785 Ext 1971
* GOLDNEY Cr 1880 Ext 1974
* D'AVIGDOR-GOLDSMID Cr 1934 Ext 1987
‖ GORDON Cr 1631 Dormant 1950
‖ GRACE Cr 1795 Ext 1977
† GRAEME, HAMOND- Cr 1783 Ext 1969
* GRANT, MACPHERSON- Cr 1838 Ext 1983
* GRAY, ANSTRUTHER- (*Baron Kilmany*) Cr 1956 Ext 1985
* GREEN Cr 1901 Ext 1959
* GREGORY Cr 1931 Ext 1952
‡ GRESLEY Cr 1611 Ext 1976
‖ GRIERSON Cr 1685 Ext 1987
* GUNTER Cr 1901 Ext 1980
* HAMILTON Cr 1937 Ext 1992

* HAMPSON Cr 1642 Ext 1969
‡ HANSEN Cr 1921 Ext 1958
* HANSON Cr 1887 Ext 1996
* HARMAN, STAFFORD-KING- Cr 1914 Ext 1987
* HARMSWORTH Cr 1918 Ext 1980
* HARRIS Cr 1953 Ext 1996
* HART Cr 1893 Ext 1970
* HAWKEY Cr 1945 Ext 1975
* HAY Cr 1635 Dormant 1966
‖ HEADLAM Cr 1935 Ext 1964
* HILLS Cr 1939. Ext 1955
* HINDLEY (*Viscount Hyndley*) Cr 1927 Ext 1963
* HOARE (*Viscount Templewood*) Cr 1899 Ext 1959
* HOARE Cr 1962 Ext 1986
* HERMON-HODGE (*Baron Wyfold*) Cr 1902
  Ext 1999
* HOLDEN Cr 1909 Ext 1965
* HOLLAND Cr 1917 Ext 1997
* HOLLINS Cr 1907 Ext 1963
* HOLT Cr 1916 Ext 1968
* HOOD (formerly BATEMAN) Cr 1806 Ext 1991
* HOOD (later FULLER-ACLAND-HOOD) Cr 1809
  Ext 1990
* HOOPER Cr 1962 Ext 1987
* HOPE Cr 1932 Ext 1993
* HORDER (*Baron Horder*) Cr 1923 Ext 1997
* HORNBY Cr 1899 Ext 1971
* HOULDSWORTH Cr 1956 Ext 1990
* HUGHES Cr 1942 Ext 1958
* HULTON Cr 1905 Ext 1993
* HUNTER, HUGHES- Cr 1906 Ext 1951
* HUTCHISON Cr 1928 Ext 1972
* JAFFREY Cr 1931 Ext 1953
* JAMES Cr 1823 Ext 1979
* JARDINE Cr 1919 Ext 1965
* JARVIS Cr 1922 Ext 1965
* JENNER Cr 1868 Ext 1954
* JESSEL (*Baron Jessel*) Cr 1917 Ext 1990
* JOHNSON, WEBB- (*Baron Webb-Johnson*)
  Cr 1945 Ext 1958
* JONES Cr 1917 Ext 1952
* JONES, PROBYN- Cr 1926 Ext 1951
* JONES, PRYCE- Cr 1918 Ext 1963
* KERR Cr 1957 Ext 1974
† KING, DUCKWORTH- Cr 1792 Ext 1972
* KITSON (*Baron Airedale*) Cr 1886 Ext 1996
* LAMBART Cr 1911 Ext 1986
* LANE Cr 1913 Ext 1972
* LANGMAN Cr 1906 Ext 1985
* LAURIE Cr 1942 Ext 1954
* LAWSON Cr 1831 Ext 1959
* LAWSON Cr 1905 Ext 1973
* LEE Cr 1941 Ext 1967
‡ LEICESTER Cr 1671 Ext 1968
* LENNARD Cr 1880 Ext 1980
‖ LESLIE Cr 1625 Dormant 1967
* LETT Cr 1941 Ext 1964
* LEVY Cr 1913 Ext 1996
* LEWIS (*Baron Essendon*) Cr 1918 Ext 1978
* ORR-LEWIS Cr 1920 Ext 1980
* LLEWELLYN Cr 1959 Ext 1994
* LOCOCK Cr 1857 Ext 1965
* LORAINE Cr 1664 Ext 1961
* LYLE (*Baron Lyle of Westbourne*) Cr 1932
  Ext 1976
* LYON (*Baron Ennisdale*) Cr 1937 Ext 1963
* McCULLAGH Cr 1935 Ext 1974
* MADGE Cr 1919 Ext 1962
* MAGNAY 1844 Ext 1960
* MAITLAND, RAMSAY-STEEL- Cr 1917 Ext 1965
* MAPPIN Cr 1886 Ext 1975
* MASON (*Baron Blackford*) Cr 1918 Ext 1988
* MATHIAS Cr 1917 Ext 1991
‖ MAXWELL, STIRLING- Cr 1682 Dormant 1956
* MELVIN Cr 1933 Ext 1952
* METCALFE Cr 1802 Ext 1979
* MIDDLEBROOK Cr 1930 Ext 1971
* MIDDLEMORE Cr 1919 Ext 1987
‡ MIDDLETON Cr 1662 Ext 1999
† MILDMAY, ST JOHN- Cr 1772 Dormant 1955
* MILLER, NORIE- Cr 1936 Ext 1973
* MILLS (*Baron Hillingdon*) Cr 1868 Ext 1982
* MITCHELL Cr 1945 Ext 1983
‡ MOLYNEUX (*Earl of Sefton*) Cr 1611 Ext 1972
* MONSON Cr 1905 Ext 1969
* MOORE Cr 1923 Ext 1971
* MOORE Cr 1956 Ext 1971
† MORGAN (*Baron Tredegar*) Cr 1792 Ext 1962
* MORGAN, VAUGHAN- (*Baron Reigate*) Cr 1960
  Ext 1995
* MORRIS (*Viscount Nuffield*) Cr 1929 Ext 1963
* MOWAT Cr 1932 Ext 1968

* MURPHY Cr 1912 Ext 1963
* NEVILLE Cr 1927 Ext 1994
* NEWNES Cr 1895 Ext 1955
* NICHOLSON Cr 1859 Ext 1986
‖ NICOLSON Cr 1629 Dormant 1961
* NUGENT Cr 1961 Ext 1962
* NUGENT (*Baron Nugent of Guildford*) Cr 1960
  Ext 1994
* NUSSEY Cr 1909 Ext 1971
* OCHTERLONY Cr 1823 Ext 1964
‡ OSBORNE (*Duke of Leeds*) Cr 1620 Ext 1964
§ PAUL Cr 1794 Ext 1961
* PAUL Cr 1821 Ext 1972
* PEARSON Cr 1916 Ext 1982
* PECHELL Cr 1797 Ext 1984
* PERKS Cr 1908 Ext 1979
† PEYTON Cr 1776 Ext 1962
* PHILIPPS, FOLEY- Cr 1887 Ext 1962
* PLATT Cr 1958 Ext 1998
* POOLEY Cr 1953 Ext 1966
* PORTER Cr 1889 Ext 1974
* POYNTER Cr 1902 Ext 1968
* PRICE Cr 1953 Ext 1963
* PRYSE, SAUNDERS- Cr 1866 Ext 1962
‖ RAMSAY Cr 1666 Ext 1986
* RAMSDEN Cr 1938 Ext 1955
* RANKIN Cr 1937 Ext 1960
* REES Cr 1919 Ext 1970
† RICH Cr 1791 Dormant 1983
* RICHARDSON Cr 1929 Ext 1981
* RIPLEY Cr 1897 Ext 1954
* RITCHIE Cr 1918 Ext 1991
* ROLL Cr 1921 Ext 1998
* ROSE Cr 1935 Ext 1976
* ROSS Cr 1919 Ext 1958
* ROWLAND Cr 1950 Ext 1970
‡ ROWLEY Cr 1786 Dormant 1997
* SAMMAN Cr 1921 Ext 1960
* SASSOON Cr 1909 Ext 1961
* SAVORY Cr 1890 Ext 1961
* SCARISBRICK Cr 1855 Ext 1909
* SCHUSTER Cr 1906 Ext 1996
* SCOTT Cr 1821 Ext 1962
* SCOTT, CONSTABLE-MAXWELL- Cr 1932
  Ext 1954
† SHORE (*Baron Teignmouth*) Cr 1792 Ext 1981
* SIMPSON Cr 1935 Ext 1981
§ SMITH, CUSACK- Cr 1799 Ext 1970
* SMITH (*Earl of Birkenhead*) Cr 1918 Ext 1985
* SMITH Cr 1920 Ext 1961
* SNADDEN Cr 1955 Ext 1959
* SPEARS Cr 1953 Ext 1974
* STANHOPE, SCUDAMORE- (*Earl of Chesterfield*)
  Cr 1807 Ext 1952
‡ STAPLETON Cr 1679 Ext 1995
* STEPHEN Cr 1891 Ext 1987
* STERN (*Baron Michelham*) Cr 1905 Ext 1984
* STEWART Cr 1881 Ext 1951
* STEWART Cr 1920 Ext 1979
* STEWART Cr 1937 Ext 1999
* STOCKENSTROM Cr 1840 Ext 1957
* STURDEE Cr 1916 Ext 1970
‡ SWINBURNE Cr 1660 Ext 1967
* TANGYE Cr 1912 Ext 1969
* TAYLOR Cr 1963 Ext 1972
* TAYLOR, WORSLEY- Cr 1917 Ext 1958
‡ THROCKMORTON Cr 1642 Ext 1994
‡ TWYSDEN Cr 1611 Ext 1970
† THOMAS Cr 1766 Ext 1972
* THOMSON Cr 1938 Ext 1953
‡ TICHBORNE, DOUGHTY- Cr 1621 Ext 1968
* VERNER Cr 1846. Ext 1975
* WALROND (*Baron Waleran*) Cr 1876 Ext 1966
* WALLER Cr 1815 Ext 1995
* WALSH (*Baron Ormathwaite*) Cr 1804 Ext 1984
§ WALSH, JOHNSON- Cr 1775 Ext 1953
* WARD Cr 1914 Ext 1973
* WARD Cr 1929 Ext 1956
* WATSON Cr 1912 Ext 1983
* WATSON Cr 1918 Ext 1959
* WEIGALL Cr 1938 Ext 1952
* WELLS Cr 1948 Ext 1966
† WESTCAR, PRESCOTT- Cr 1794 Ext 1959
* WILLIAMS Cr 1955 Ext 1958
* WILLIAMS Cr 1935 Ext 1959
* WILLIAMS, HUME- Cr 1922 Ext 1980
‡ WILSON MARYON- Cr 1661 Ext 1978
* WINGATE Cr 1920 Ext 1978
‡ WINN (*Baron Headley*) Cr 1660 Ext 1994
† WINN (*Baron Headley*) Cr 1776 Ext 1994
* WOOD Cr 1918 Ext 1974
* YOUNGER Cr 1964 Ext 1992